DK ILLUSTRATED OXFORD DICTIONARY

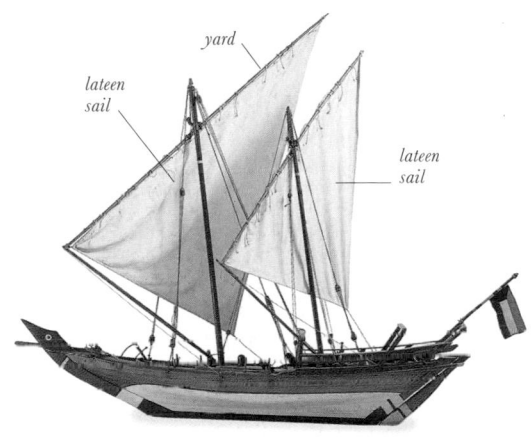

yard

lateen sail

lateen sail

DHOW

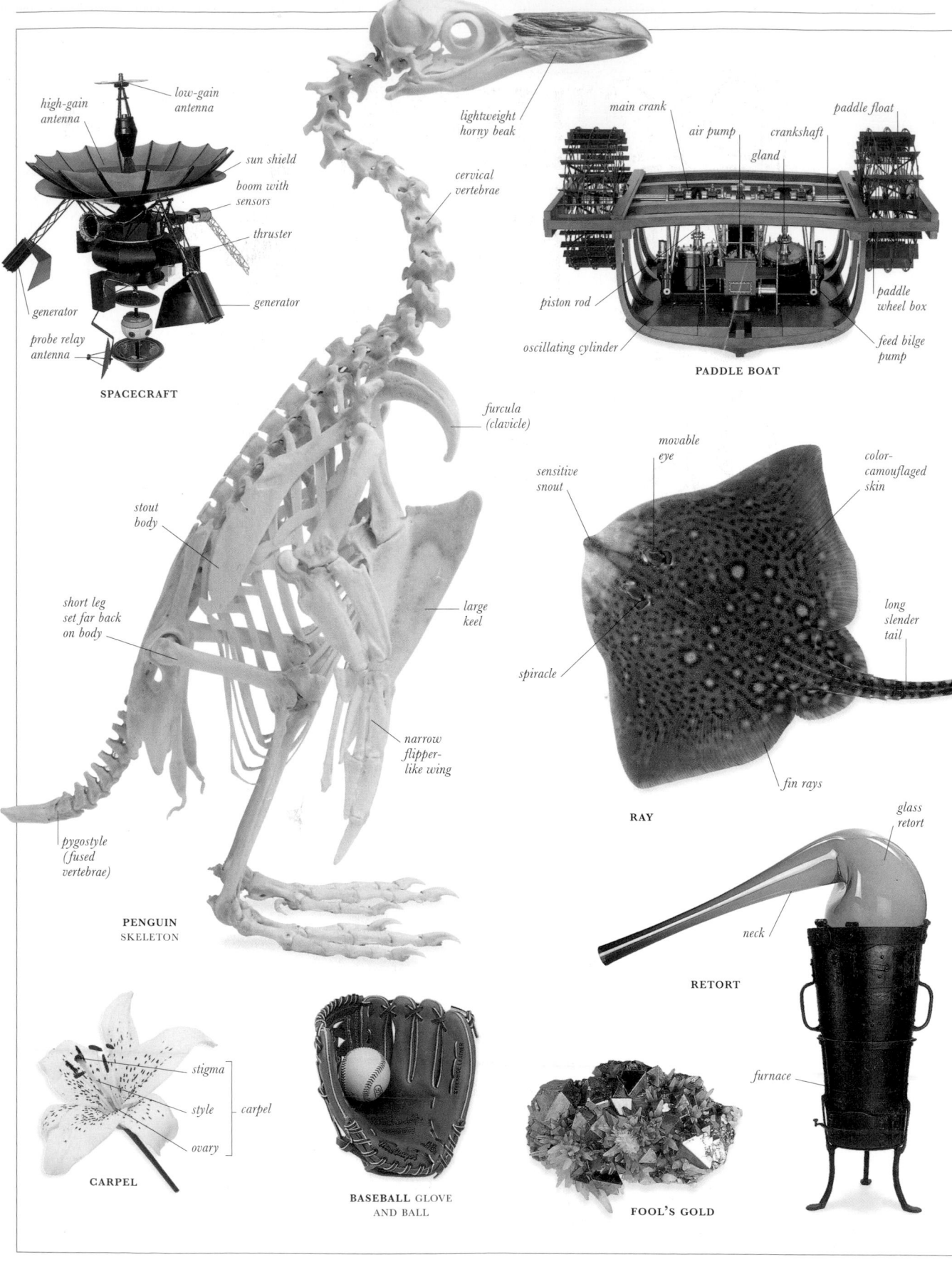

SPACECRAFT

high-gain antenna

low-gain antenna

sun shield

boom with sensors

thruster

generator

generator

probe relay antenna

lightweight horny beak

cervical vertebrae

PADDLE BOAT

main crank

air pump

crankshaft

gland

paddle float

piston rod

oscillating cylinder

paddle wheel box

feed bilge pump

furcula (clavicle)

stout body

short leg set far back on body

large keel

narrow flipper-like wing

pygostyle (fused vertebrae)

PENGUIN SKELETON

RAY

movable eye

sensitive snout

color-camouflaged skin

spiracle

long slender tail

fin rays

RETORT

glass retort

neck

furnace

CARPEL

stigma

style

ovary

carpel

BASEBALL GLOVE AND BALL

FOOL'S GOLD

DK ILLUSTRATED
OXFORD
DICTIONARY

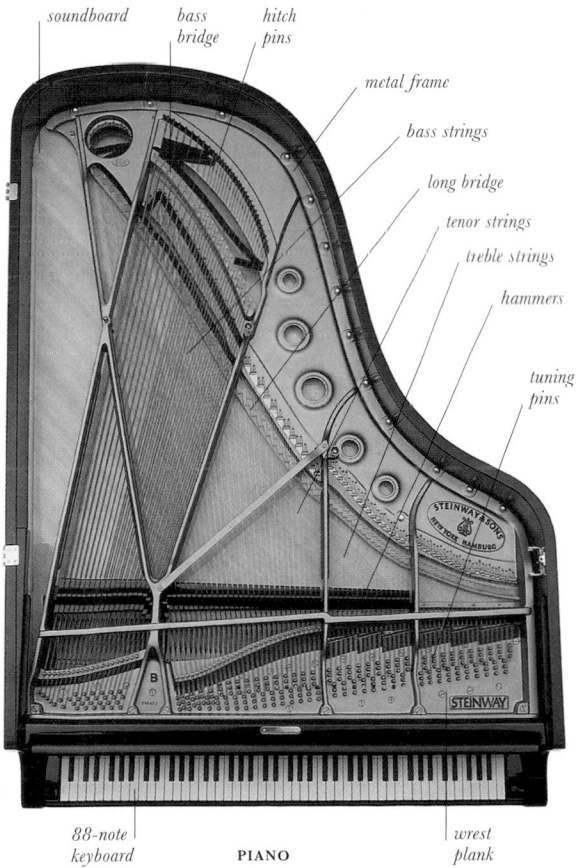

soundboard bass bridge hitch pins

metal frame

bass strings

long bridge

tenor strings

treble strings

hammers

tuning pins

88-note keyboard

PIANO

wrest plank

DORLING KINDERSLEY
London • New York • Munich
Melbourne • Delhi

OXFORD UNIVERSITY PRESS
Oxford • New York

LONDON NEW YORK MUNICH MELBOURNE DELHI
and
OXFORD UNIVERSITY PRESS, INC.

First American Edition, 1998
00 01 02 03 04 05 10 9 8 7 6 5 4 3 2 1

Published in the United States by
DK Publishing, Inc.
375 Hudson Street
New York, New York 10014

This revised edition first published in the United States and Great Britain in 2003
Lexicographic text copyright © 1998, 2003 Oxford University Press, adapted from
The Oxford Dictionary and Thesaurus, American Edition (1996), with updating and additions.

Images copyright © 1998, 2003 Dorling Kindersley Limited, London
Non-lexicographic text copyright © 1998, 2003 Dorling Kindersley Limited, London
Layout and design copyright © 1998, 2003 Dorling Kindersley Limited, London

Library of Congress Cataloging-in-Publication Data
DK Oxford Illustrated American Dictionary
p.   cm.
ISBN 0-7894-9359-4
1. English language–Dictionaries.   2. English language–United States–Dictionaries.
3. Americanisms.   I. DK Publishing, Inc.

PE1628.D58   2000
423–dc21   00-027458

2   4   6   8   10   9   7   5   3   1

Color reproduction by Colourpath, London, England
Printed and bound in Germany by Mohndruck GmbH, Gütersloh

———————— OXFORD UNIVERSITY PRESS, INC. ————————
198 Madison Avenue, New York, NY 10016
OXFORD NEW YORK ATHENS AUCKLAND BANGKOK BOGOTA MUMBAI BUENOS AIRES KOLKATA CAPE TOWN DAR ES SALAAM
DELHI FLORENCE HONG KONG ISTANBUL KARACHI KUALA LUMPUR CHENNAI MADRID MELBOURNE MEXICO CITY
NAIROBI PARIS SINGAPORE TAIPEI TOKYO TORONTO and associated companies in BERLIN IBADAN

Oxford is a registered trademark of Oxford University Press

Visit us on the World Wide Web at www.oup-usa.org

———————— DK PUBLISHING, INC. ————————
375 Hudson Street, New York, NY 10014
LONDON NEW YORK DELHI JOHANNESBURG MUNICH PARIS SYDNEY

See our complete product line at
www.dk.com

NOTE ON PROPRIETARY STATUS
This dictionary includes some words that have, or are asserted to have, proprietary status as trademarks or otherwise.
Their inclusion does not imply that they have acquired for legal purposes a nonproprietary or general significance,
nor any other judgment concerning their legal status. In cases where the editorial staff has some evidence that
a word has proprietary status, this is indicated in the entry for that word by the word Trademark or propr. (proprietary)
but no judgment concerning the legal status of such words is made or implied hereby.

CONTENTS

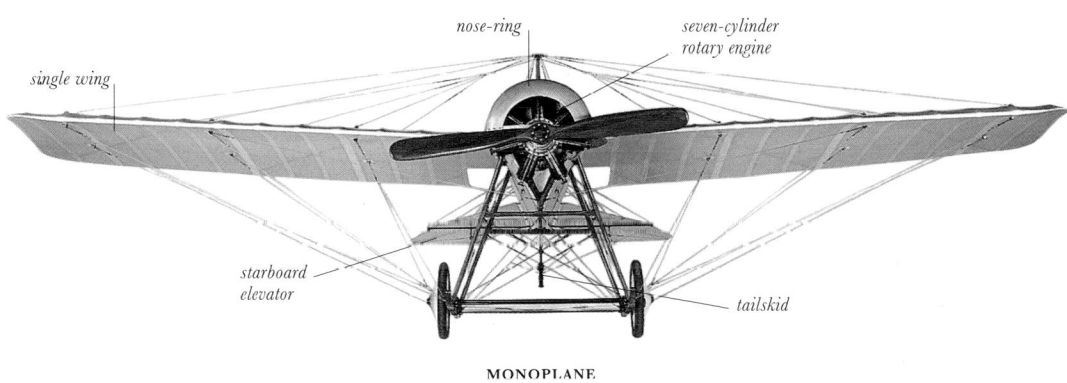

nose-ring

seven-cylinder
rotary engine

single wing

starboard
elevator

tailskid

MONOPLANE

STAFF AND CONTRIBUTORS

FOREWORD

WHEN THE OPPORTUNITY AROSE for DK Publishing to collaborate with Oxford University Press on an illustrated dictionary, it seemed like a perfect marriage of talents. The harnessing of the complementary strengths of the two houses generated the possibility of creating a new landmark in this area of publishing. I believe that this has been realized. The double branding of Oxford, the most renowned name in the world for the English language, and DK, recognized as a quality imprint on illustrated home reference, offers the reader not only care, expertise, and high production values but also a volume that reaches beyond the traditional confines of a language-only dictionary.

This is no mere dictionary with pictures. The rationale behind the choice of illustrations has been as rigorous as for word selection. To have added pictures whose value was simply decorative would not have afforded any benefits beyond the coffee table. The selection of images has been governed by their usefulness, their accuracy, their capacity to bring the unfamiliar to life, their potential for expanding a definition, for shedding light on the obscure, or illuminating those dark corners where the reach of verbal description is challenged. Illustration panels have been created to provide a wide range of themes with additional information: the wordfields of annotation placed around images expand the reader's vocabulary; cutaway diagrams and cross sections deepen understanding and add detail to a variety of subjects; galleries of images demonstrate the diversity between objects or types defined by a single word.

These benefits are genuinely substantial, and the fact that the dictionary itself is a handsome object to have and to hold is an additional bonus. We are proud to be associated with it.

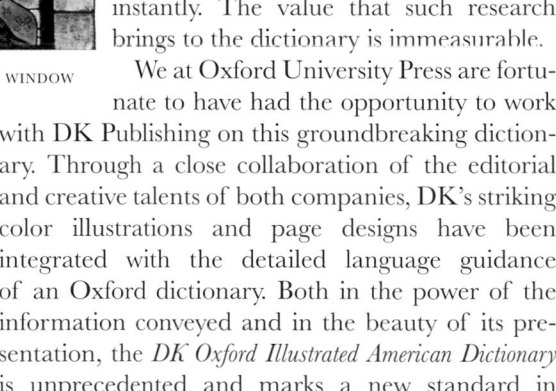

STAINED-GLASS WINDOW

THE TEXT OF THE *DK Oxford Illustrated American Dictionary* was specially compiled for this edition by Oxford's US Dictionaries Program. While this is a dictionary of American English, it is in keeping with the renowned lexicographic traditions of Oxford University Press. Oxford's unrivaled language research, including the North American Reading Program (NARP), constantly monitors growth and change in English, providing masses of evidence to Oxford's lexicographers. Using computerized search-and-analysis tools developed originally for the 20-volume *Oxford English Dictionary*, our American lexicographers can explore the 40 million words of citation text collected by NARP and consult many other English language databases. The result is a more sharply refined picture of the language of today, elucidating complex aspects of meaning, grammar, and usage.

As in every Oxford book, this dictionary reflects the scholarly guidance of our academic advisors, as well as the experience of special consultants in many fields. And with the Internet and the World Wide Web, Oxford lexicographers are now able to be in daily contact with expert sources worldwide, receiving answers to queries almost instantly. The value that such research brings to the dictionary is immeasurable.

We at Oxford University Press are fortunate to have had the opportunity to work with DK Publishing on this groundbreaking dictionary. Through a close collaboration of the editorial and creative talents of both companies, DK's striking color illustrations and page designs have been integrated with the detailed language guidance of an Oxford dictionary. Both in the power of the information conveyed and in the beauty of its presentation, the *DK Oxford Illustrated American Dictionary* is unprecedented and marks a new standard in American dictionaries.

CHRISTOPHER DAVIS
PUBLISHER, DK PUBLISHING

FRANK ABATE
EDITOR IN CHIEF, US DICTIONARIES,
OXFORD UNIVERSITY PRESS, INC.

HOW TO USE THE DICTIONARY

THE FOLLOWING PAGES (8–14) illustrate and explain all the features and conventions that are used throughout this dictionary – from the structure and content of individual word entries to a complete list of abbreviations. The ILLUSTRATED DICTIONARY itself appears on pages 15–970,

and is followed by a comprehensive selection of ready-reference material (pages 971–1007). With the exception of feature panels (see opposite), all illustrations appear in alphabetical order, and can be found below or adjacent to the precise definition to which they are relevant.

NEW LETTER SECTION
Each alphabetical section of the dictionary begins on a new page, and is introduced by a large capital letter to make it easier to find.

ALPHABETICAL ORDER
Words are listed in "letter by letter" alphabetical order, with spaces and punctuation disregarded.

QUICK-REFERENCE GUIDE TO WORD ENTRIES

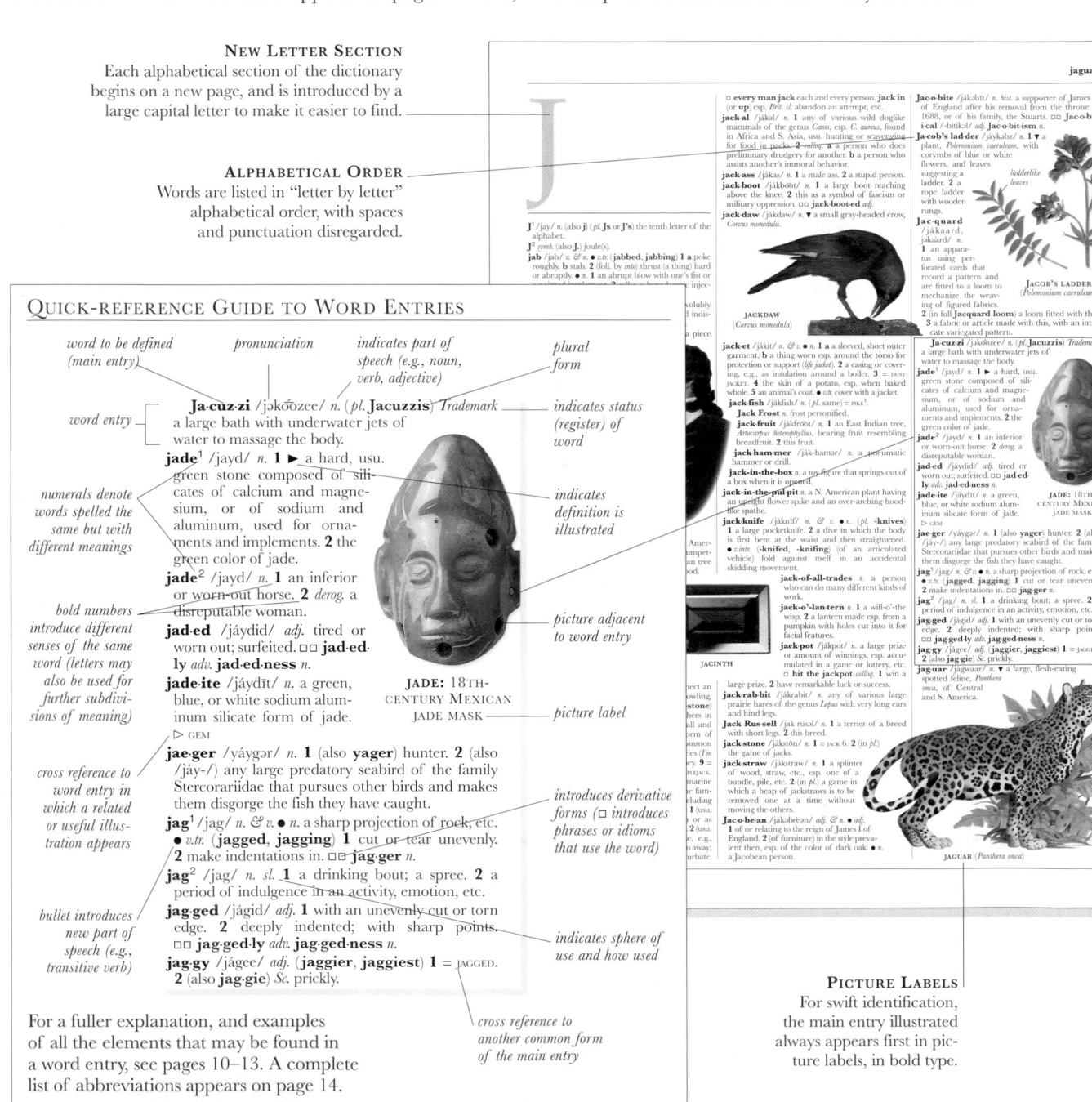

word to be defined (main entry)

pronunciation

indicates part of speech (e.g., noun, verb, adjective)

plural form

word entry

indicates status (register) of word

Ja·cuz·zi /jəkōozee/ n. (pl. **Jacuzzis**) Trademark a large bath with underwater jets of water to massage the body.

jade[1] /jayd/ n. 1 ▶ a hard, usu. green stone composed of silicates of calcium and magnesium, or of sodium and aluminum, used for ornaments and implements. 2 the green color of jade.

numerals denote words spelled the same but with different meanings

indicates definition is illustrated

jade[2] /jayd/ n. 1 an inferior or worn-out horse. 2 derog. a disreputable woman.

jad·ed /jáydid/ adj. tired or worn out; surfeited. □□ **jad·ed·ly** adv. **jad·ed·ness** n.

bold numbers introduce different senses of the same word (letters may also be used for further subdivisions of meaning)

jade·ite /jáydīt/ n. a green, blue, or white sodium aluminum silicate form of jade.
▷ GEM

JADE: 18TH-CENTURY MEXICAN JADE MASK

picture adjacent to word entry

picture label

jae·ger /yáygər/ n. 1 (also **yager**) hunter. 2 (also /jáy-/) any large predatory seabird of the family Stercorariidae that pursues other birds and makes them disgorge the fish they have caught.

cross reference to word entry in which a related or useful illustration appears

jag[1] /jag/ n. & v. • n. a sharp projection of rock, etc. • v.tr. (**jagged**, **jagging**) 1 cut or tear unevenly. 2 make indentations in. □□ **jag·ger** n.

jag[2] /jag/ n. sl. 1 a drinking bout; a spree. 2 a period of indulgence in an activity, emotion, etc.

introduces derivative forms (□ introduces phrases or idioms that use the word)

jag·ged /jágid/ adj. 1 with an unevenly cut or torn edge. 2 deeply indented; with sharp points. □□ **jag·ged·ly** adv. **jag·ged·ness** n.

bullet introduces new part of speech (e.g., transitive verb)

indicates sphere of use and how used

jag·gy /jágee/ adj. (**jaggier, jaggiest**) 1 = JAGGED. 2 (also **jag·gie**) Sc. prickly.

cross reference to another common form of the main entry

For a fuller explanation, and examples of all the elements that may be found in a word entry, see pages 10–13. A complete list of abbreviations appears on page 14.

Right-hand sample dictionary column

jaguar

J[1] /jay/ n. (also **j**) (pl. **Js** or **J's**) the tenth letter of the alphabet.

J[2] symb. (also **J**,) joule(s).

jab /jab/ v. & n. • v.tr. (**jabbed, jabbing**) 1 a poke roughly. b stab. 2 (foll. by into) thrust (a thing) hard or abruptly. • n. 1 an abrupt blow with one's fist or...

□ **every man jack** each and every person. **jack in** (or **up**) esp. Brit. sl. abandon an attempt, etc.

jack·al /jákəl/ n. 1 any of various usu. doglike mammals of the genus Canis, esp. C. aureus, found in Africa and S. Asia, usu. hunting or scavenging for food in packs. 2 colloq. a a person who does preliminary drudgery for another. b a person who assists another's immoral behavior.

jack·ass /jákas/ n. 1 a male ass. 2 stupid person.

jack·boot /jákbōot/ n. 1 a large boot reaching above the knee. 2 this as a symbol of fascism or military oppression. □□ **jack·boot·ed** adj.

jack·daw /jákdaw/ n. ▼ a small gray-headed crow, Corvus monedula.

JACKDAW
(Corvus monedula)

jack·et /jákit/ n. 1 a a sleeved, short outer garment. b a thing worn esp. around the torso for protection or support (life jacket). 2 a casing or covering, e.g., as insulation around a boiler. 3 = DUST JACKET. 4 the skin of a potato, esp. when baked whole. 5 an animal's coat. • v.tr. cover with a jacket.

jack·fish /jákfish/ n. (pl. same) = PIKE[1].

Jack Frost n. frost personified.

jack·fruit /jákfrōot/ n. 1 an East Indian tree, Artocarpus heterophyllus, bearing fruit resembling breadfruit. 2 this fruit.

jack·ham·mer /ják-hamər/ n. a pneumatic hammer or drill.

jack-in-the-box n. a toy figure that springs out of a box when it is opened.

jack-in-the-pul·pit n. a N. American plant having an upright flower spike and an over-arching hood-like spathe.

jack·knife /jáknīf/ n. & v. • n. (pl. **-knives**) 1 a large pocketknife. 2 a dive in which the body is first bent at the waist and then straightened. • v.intr. (**-knifed, -knifing**) (of an articulated vehicle) fold against itself in an accidental skidding movement.

jack-o'-lan·tern n. 1 a will-o'-the-wisp. 2 a lantern made esp. from a pumpkin with holes cut into it for facial features.

jack·pot /jákpot/ n. a large prize or amount of winnings, esp. accumulated in a game or lottery, etc. □ **hit the jackpot** colloq. 1 win a large prize. 2 have remarkable luck or success.

jack·rab·bit /jákrabit/ n. any of various large prairie hares of the genus Lepus with very long ears and hind legs.

Jack Russell /jak rúsəl/ n. a terrier of a breed with short legs. 2 this breed.

jack·stone /jákstōn/ n. 1 = JACK 6. 2 (in pl.) the game of jacks.

jack·straw /jákstraw/ n. 1 a splinter of wood, straw, etc., esp. one of a bundle, pile, etc. 2 (in pl.) a game in which a heap of jackstraws is to be removed one at a time without moving the others.

Jac·o·be·an /jákəbéeən/ adj. & n. • adj. 1 of or relating to the reign of James I of England. 2 (of furniture) in the style prevalent then, esp. of the color of dark oak. • n. a Jacobean person.

Jac·o·bite /jákəbīt/ n. hist. a supporter of James II of England after his removal from the throne in 1688, or of his family, the Stuarts. □□ **Jac·o·bit·i·cal** /-bítikəl/ adj. **Jac·o·bit·ism** n.

Ja·cob's lad·der /jáykəbz/ n. 1 ▼ a plant, Polemonium caeruleum, with corymbs of blue or white flowers, and leaves suggesting a ladder. 2 a rope ladder with wooden rungs.

ladderlike leaves

JACOB'S LADDER
(Polemonium caeruleum)

2 (in full **Jacquard loom**) a loom fitted with this. 3 a fabric or article made with this, with an intricate variegated pattern.

Jac·quard /jákaard, jəkaárd/ n. 1 an apparatus using perforated cards that record a pattern and are fitted to a loom to mechanize the weaving of figured fabrics.

Ja·cuz·zi /jəkōozee/ n. (pl. **Jacuzzis**) Trademark a large bath with underwater jets of water to massage the body.

jade[1] /jayd/ n. 1 ▶ a hard, usu. green stone composed of silicates of calcium and magnesium, or of sodium and aluminum, used for ornaments and implements. 2 the green color of jade.

jade[2] /jayd/ n. 1 an inferior or worn-out horse. 2 derog. a disreputable woman.

JADE: 18TH-CENTURY MEXICAN JADE MASK

jad·ed /jáydid/ adj. tired or worn out; surfeited. □□ **jad·ed·ness** n.

jade·ite /jáydīt/ n. a green, blue, or white sodium aluminum silicate form of jade.

jae·ger /yáygər/ n. 1 (also **yager**) hunter. 2 (also /jáy-/) any large predatory seabird of the family Stercorariidae that pursues other birds and makes them disgorge the fish they have caught.
▷ GEM

jag[1] /jag/ n. & v. • n. a sharp projection of rock, etc. • v.tr. (**jagged, jagging**) 1 cut or tear unevenly. 2 make indentations in. □□ **jag·ger** n.

jag[2] /jag/ n. sl. 1 a drinking bout; a spree. 2 a period of indulgence in an activity, emotion, etc.

jag·ged /jágid/ adj. 1 with an unevenly cut or torn edge. 2 deeply indented; with sharp points. □□ **jag·ged·ness** n.

jag·gy /jágee/ adj. (**jaggier, jaggiest**) 1 = JAGGED. 2 (also **jag·gie**) Sc. prickly.

jag·uar /jágwaar/ n. ▼ a large, flesh-eating spotted feline, Panthera onca, of Central and S. America.

JAGUAR (Panthera onca)

JACINTH

PICTURE LABELS
For swift identification, the main entry illustrated always appears first in picture labels, in bold type.

FEATURE PANELS

Feature panels give more detailed explanations of words, and often employ larger illustrations or a series of illustrations to aid understanding. Associated vocabulary may be introduced in the picture annotation. Feature panels appear on the same double-page spread as the word defined; picture symbols (e.g., ▲) indicate the direction in which to look.

GUIDE WORDS
The left-hand page heading identifies the first word entry to appear in full on that page; the right-hand heading identifies the last entry to appear.

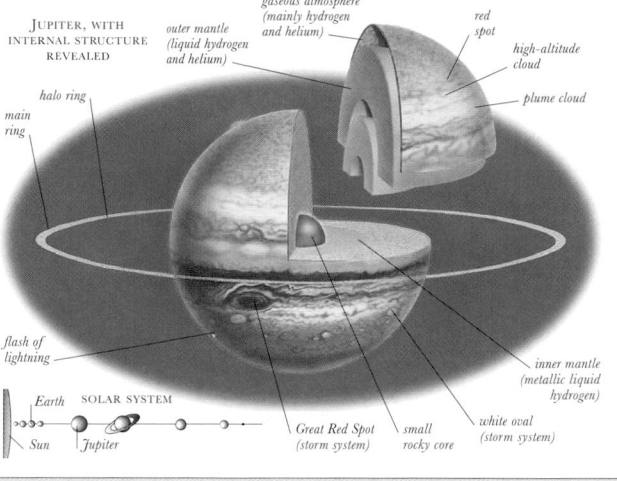

JUPITER

Jupiter is the largest, most massive planet in the solar system. Its rapid rate of rotation in 9 hours 55 minutes causes the clouds in its atmosphere to form dark, low-altitude "belts" and bright, high-altitude "zones" – both with huge storm systems – which encircle the planet parallel with the equator. Jupiter has two faint rings and is orbited by 16 known moons, of which Ganymede, Callisto, Io, and Europa (the Galileans) are the largest.

jaguarundi

jazz

JALAPEÑO PEPPER

JAPAN: JAPANNED AND LACQUERED ANTIQUE SCREEN

JASPER: RED JASPER

JAY: EURASIAN JAY
(*Garrulus glandarius*)

JASMINE: YELLOW JASMINE
(*Jasminum humile*)

433

THUMB TABS
Alphabetical sections are easily located by using the thumb tabs positioned at the side of each page.

J

SEPARATE ENTRIES
Compounds are given their own entry, rather than being grouped under one general heading (e.g., **Japanese beetle** appears separately, rather than under **Japanese**).

SYLLABIFICATION
Syllabification of main entries and derivatives aids pronunciation and hyphenation.

PICTURE LOCATION
Pictures usually appear adjacent to or below their text entry, for ease of reference.

KEY TO SYMBOLS

● Introduces a new part of speech (e.g., noun, verb, adjective)

□ Introduces a section containing phrases and idioms

□□ Introduces derivatives of the main entry (see page 10)

¶ Introduces a usage note (see page 11)

▷ Refers to a main entry where a relevant illustration can be found

► Indicates that a definition is illustrated, and in which direction to look

STRUCTURE OF ENTRIES

These two pages contain examples from the dictionary, illustrating all elements found in word entries. Annotation identifies the typographic style and location of each part, and explains the editorial approach where appropriate. Proper names listed in the dictionary include major cultural, historical, and political entities, ethnic groups, and languages. More detailed information on forms and labels appears on pages 12–13, and a list of abbreviations on page 14. Grammar and style are discussed further on pages 1002–1007 of the REFERENCE SECTION.

MAIN ENTRIES

DIFFERENT FORMS

main entry printed in bold type with syllabification indicated by dots

different forms of the main entry are given for different parts of speech

variant spelling (where applicable)

car·ol /kárəl/ *n. & v.* ● *n.* a joyous song, esp. a Christmas hymn. ● *v.* (**caroled, caroling;** esp. *Brit.* **carolled, carolling**) **1** *intr.* sing carols, esp. outdoors at Christmas. **2** *tr. & intr.* sing joyfully. □□ **car·ol·er** *n.* (also esp. *Brit.* **caroller**).

symbol introduces derivative forms of the main entry

fiz·zle /fizəl/ *v. & n.* ● *v.intr.* make a feeble hissing sound. ● *n.* such a sound. □ **fizzle out** end feebly (*the party fizzled out at 10 o'clock*).

symbol introduces phrasal verbs (as here) or idioms

foreign entry printed in bold italic type

pronunciation guide (with stress indicated)

je ne sais quoi /zhə nə say kwaa/ *n.* an indefinable something.

compounds appear as main entries

zoom lens *n.* a lens allowing a camera to zoom by varying the focal length. ▷ CAMCORDER

DIVISION OF ENTRIES INTO DIFFERENT SENSES

different senses are numbered, and ordered by currency or comparative significance

letters are used to indicate closely related subdivisions within a sense

bull[1] /bool/ *n. & adj.* ● *n.* **1 a** an uncastrated male bovine animal. **b** a male of the whale, elephant, and other large animals. **2** (**the Bull**) the zodiacal sign or constellation Taurus. ▷ TAURUS. **3** *Stock Exch.* a person who buys shares hoping to sell them at a higher price later (cf. BEAR[3]). ● *adj.* like that of a bull (*bull neck*).
bull[2] /bool/ *n.* a papal edict.

superior numerals are used to denote separate entries for words spelled the same but with different meanings or origins

spelling change applicable to a specific sense

LABELING

PARTS OF SPEECH (E.G., VERB, NOUN, ADJECTIVE)

grammatical form in common use

labels indicate intransitive and transitive subdivisions of a verb

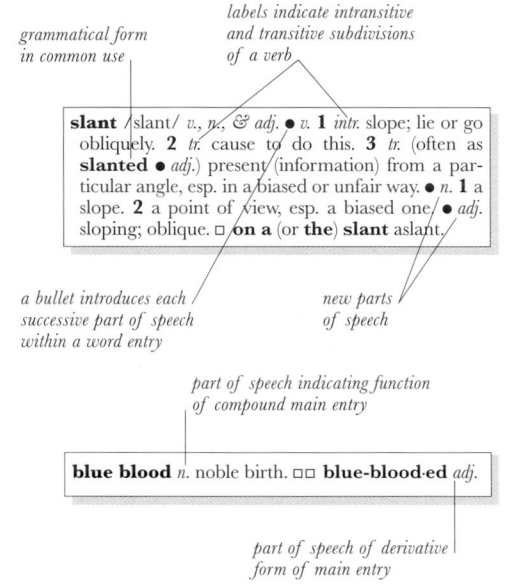

slant /slant/ *v., n., & adj.* ● *v.* **1** *intr.* slope; lie or go obliquely. **2** *tr.* cause to do this. **3** *tr.* (often as **slanted** ● *adj.*) present (information) from a particular angle, esp. in a biased or unfair way. ● *n.* **1** a slope. **2** a point of view, esp. a biased one. ● *adj.* sloping; oblique. □ **on a** (or **the**) **slant** aslant.

a bullet introduces each successive part of speech within a word entry

new parts of speech

part of speech indicating function of compound main entry

blue blood *n.* noble birth. □□ **blue-blood·ed** *adj.*

part of speech of derivative form of main entry

USAGE ADVICE WITHIN WORD ENTRIES

grammatical information

information in parentheses indicates subject area(s)

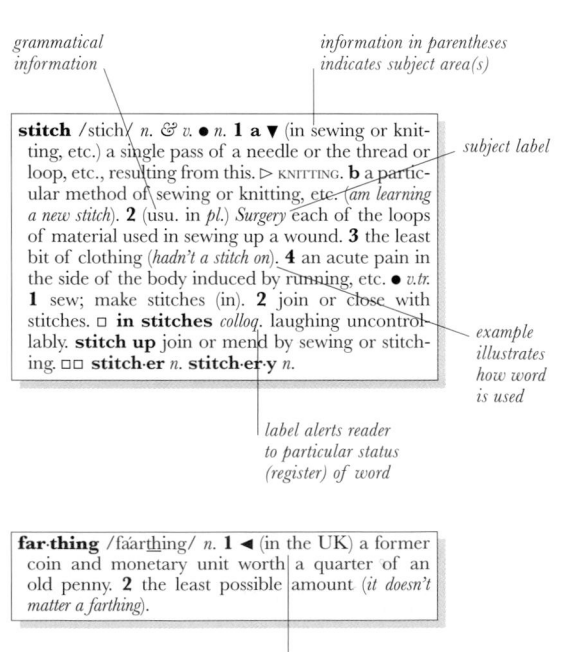

stitch /stich/ *n. & v.* ● *n.* **1 a** ▼ (in sewing or knitting, etc.) a single pass of a needle or the thread or loop, etc., resulting from this. ▷ KNITTING. **b** a particular method of sewing or knitting, etc. (*am learning a new stitch*). **2** (usu. in *pl.*) *Surgery* each of the loops of material used in sewing up a wound. **3** the least bit of clothing (*hadn't a stitch on*). **4** an acute pain in the side of the body induced by running, etc. ● *v.tr.* **1** sew; make stitches (in). **2** join or close with stitches. □ **in stitches** *colloq.* laughing uncontrollably. **stitch up** join or mend by sewing or stitching. □□ **stitch·er** *n.* **stitch·er·y** *n.*

subject label

example illustrates how word is used

label alerts reader to particular status (register) of word

far·thing /fáarthing/ *n.* **1** ◄ (in the UK) a former coin and monetary unit worth a quarter of an old penny. **2** the least possible amount (*it doesn't matter a farthing*).

comment in parentheses specifies country associated with the defined institution

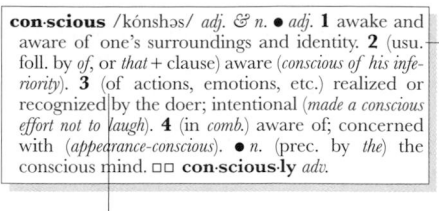

con·scious /kónshəs/ *adj. & n.* ● *adj.* **1** awake and aware of one's surroundings and identity. **2** (usu. foll. by *of*, or *that* + clause) aware (*conscious of his inferiority*). **3** (of actions, emotions, etc.) realized or recognized by the doer; intentional (*made a conscious effort not to laugh*). **4** (in *comb.*) aware of; concerned with (*appearance-conscious*). ● *n.* (prec. by *the*) the conscious mind. □□ **con·scious·ly** *adv.*

specifies formula for grammatical construction

indicates limited use of word in this sense

a·ghast /əgást/ *adj.* (usu. *predic.*; often foll. by *at*) filled with dismay, shock, or consternation.

adjective usually used predicatively

folk /fōk/ *n.* (*pl.* **folk** or **folks**) **1** (treated as *pl.*) people in general or of a specified class (*few folks about*; *townsfolk*). **2** (in *pl.*) (usu. **folks**) one's parents or relatives. **3** (treated as *sing.*) a people. **4** (treated as *sing.*) *colloq.* traditional music, esp. a style featuring acoustic guitar. **5** (*attrib.*) of popular origin; traditional (*folk art*).

noun used attributively in this sense

Usage notes

Usage notes (preceded by the symbol ¶) are placed at the end of a word entry, before phrases and derivatives. These usage notes offer additional information, such as symbols, abbreviations, and language guidance. Further notes on grammar and style appear on pages 1002–1007 of the REFERENCE SECTION.

in·fin·i·ty /infinitee/ *n.* (*pl.* **-ies**) **1** the state of being infinite. **2** an infinite number or extent. **3** infinite distance. **4** *Math.* infinite quantity. ¶ Symb.: ∞

usage note showing symbol used to represent main entry

can·de·la /kandeélə, -délə/ *n.* the SI unit of luminous intensity. ¶ Abbr.: **cd**.

usage note giving abbreviation used to denote main entry

ac·tu·al /ákcho͞oəl/ *adj.* (usu. *attrib.*) **1** existing in fact; real (often as distinct from ideal). **2** existing now. ¶ Redundant use, as in *tell me the actual facts*, is *disp.*, but common.

usage note offering language guidance

Cross references

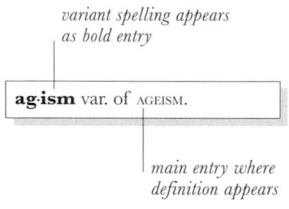

variant spelling appears as bold entry

ag·ism var. of AGEISM.

main entry where definition appears

square-rigged *adj.* ▼ with the principal sails at right angles to the length of the ship and extended by horizontal yards slung to the mast by the middle (opp. *fore-and-aft rigged* (see FORE AND AFT).

antonym given for comparison

indicates further information is to be found at main entry named

phos·phor /fósfər/ *n.* **1** = PHOSPHORUS. **2** a synthetic fluorescent or phosphorescent substance esp. used in cathode-ray tubes.

small capitals used to indicate main entry appearing elsewhere

calves *pl.* of CALF[1], CALF[2].

irregular forms appear as cross-referenced bold entries, when they are three or more entries away from main entry

trod·den *past part.* of TREAD.

Pictures

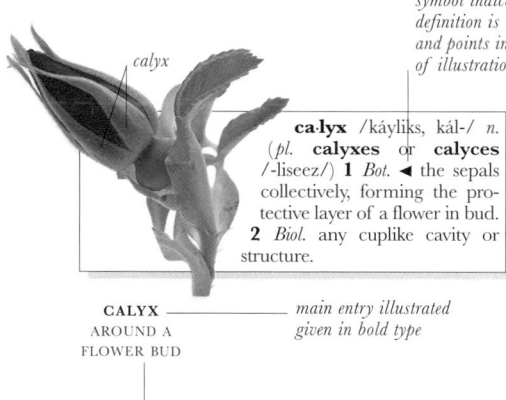

symbol indicates that definition is illustrated, and points in direction of illustration

calyx

ca·lyx /káyliks, kál-/ *n.* (*pl.* **calyxes** or **calyces** /-liseez/) **1** *Bot.* ◄ the sepals collectively, forming the protective layer of a flower in bud. **2** *Biol.* any cuplike cavity or structure.

CALYX AROUND A FLOWER BUD

main entry illustrated given in bold type

illustration label

fish·er /fishər/ *n.* **1** any animal that catches fish, esp. the marten, *Martes pennanti*, valued for its fur. ▷ MUSTELID. **2** *archaic* a fisherman.

symbol indicates main entry where relevant illustration appears

PRONUNCIATION

Pronunciations are given for all main entries, as well as for any inflected forms or derivatives whose pronunciation differs markedly from that of the main entry. The pronunciation is shown between diagonal slashes, usually just after the word itself, using the symbols shown below. For words of two or more syllables, the syllable(s) pronounced with greater stress are marked with a stress mark (´) over the appropriate vowel symbol. An apostrophe (') is occasionally used to show a slight break between sounds, as

in /bát'l/ for **battle** and /kand'l/ for **candle**. More than one acceptable pronunciation may be given, as in the entry for **news** /nōōz, nyōōz/. If variant pronunciations differ only in part, then only the syllable or syllables affected are given, as in the entry for **bedroom** /bédrōōm, -rŏŏm/ and **forest** /fáwrist, fór-/. The same applies to pronunciations of derivative forms that differ only in part, as in the main entry for **complete** /kəmpléet/, with its derivative **completion** /-pléeshən/.

The symbols used to represent sounds in pronunciations are as follows:

a *as in* cat	ee *as in* meet	j *as in* jam	ö *as in* voyeur	th *as in* this
aa *as in* calm	eer *as in* beer	k *as in* king	ŏŏ *as in* wood	u *as in* cup
aar *as in* bar	ə *as in* ago, soda, pollen,	kh *as in* loch	ōō *as in* food	v *as in* van
air *as in* hair	civil, lemon, suppose	l *as in* leg	ow *as in* cow	w *as in* will
aw *as in* law	ər *as in* her	m *as in* man	oy *as in* boy	y *as in* yes
awr *as in* born	f *as in* fat	n *as in* not	p *as in* pen	z *as in* zebra
ay *as in* say	g *as in* get	N *as in* en route	r *as in* red	zh *as in* vision
b *as in* bat	h *as in* hat	(nasalized *n*)	s *as in* sit	
ch *as in* chin	i *as in* pin	ng *as in* sing, finger	sh *as in* shop	
d *as in* day	ī *as in* pie	o *as in* top	t *as in* top, butter	
e *as in* bed	īr *as in* fire	ō *as in* most	th *as in* thin	

LABELS

These are used to clarify the particular context in which a word or phrase is normally used. They appear in italic type, often in abbreviated form (an alphabetical list of all abbreviations is given on page 14).

SUBJECT
Some subject labels are used to indicate the particular relevance of a term or subject with which it is associated, e.g., *Mus.* (music). They are not used when this is sufficiently clear from the definition itself.

GEOGRAPHICAL
The geographical label *Brit.* (British) indicates that the use of a word or phrase is found chiefly in British English (and often in other Commonwealth countries) but not in American English. Other geographical labels, such as *Austral.* (Australian) and *Canad.* (Canadian) show that use is generally restricted to the area named.

REGISTER (E.G., FORMAL, SLANG, DISPUTED)
● *formal, colloq., sl.*
Words and phrases more common in formal (esp. written English) are labeled *formal.* Those more common in informal spoken English are labeled *colloq.* (colloquial) or, especially if very informal or restricted to a particular social group, *sl.* (slang).

● *coarse sl., offens.*
Two categories of deprecated usage are indicated by special markings: *coarse sl.* (coarse slang) indicates a word that, although widely found, is still unacceptable to many people; *offens.* (offensive) indicates a use that is regarded as offensive by members of a particular religious, ethnic, or other group. While certain words regarded as offensive have not been included in the dictionary, others are followed by a usage note denoting their taboo status.

● *disp.*
Where usage is disputed or controversial, *disp.* (disputed) alerts the user to a danger or difficulty; further information may be given in a usage note at the end of the entry (see page 11).

STYLE
● *literary, poet.*
Words or phrases found mainly in literature are indicated by *literary,* whereas *poet.* (poetical) indicates that use is confined generally to poetry or other contexts with romantic connotations.

● *joc., derog.*
Where use is intended to be humorous, the label *joc.* (jocular) is given; *derog.* (derogatory) denotes the intentionally disparaging use of the word or phrase.

CURRENCY
● *archaic, hist.*
For words that have lost currency except perhaps in special contexts such as legal or religious use, *archaic* is given; *hist.* (historical) denotes a word or use that is confined to historical reference, normally because the thing referred to is no longer in everyday use.

STATUS
● *propr., Trademark*
The labels *propr.* (*proprietary*) and *Trademark* indicate a term that has the status of a trademark (see the Note on Proprietary Status on page 4).

FORMS

In general, different forms of nouns, verbs, adjectives, and adverbs are given when the form is irregular (as described below) or when, though regular, it causes difficulty (as with forms such as **budgeted**, **coos**, and **taxis**).

PLURALS OF NOUNS

For nouns that form their plural regularly by adding -s (or -es when they end in -s, -x, -z, -sh, or soft -ch), the plural form is not shown. Other plural forms are given, notably for:

- nouns ending in -i or -o (e.g., **alibi**, **gazebo**).
- nouns ending in Latinate forms such as -a and -um (e.g., **amphora**, **ileum**).
- nouns ending in the suffix -y (e.g,. **colloquy**).
- nouns with more than one plural form (e.g., **fish**, **aquarium**).
- nouns with plurals showing a change in the stem (e.g., **foot**).
- nouns with a plural form unchanged from the singular form (e.g., **sheep**).
- nouns ending in -ful (e.g., **handful**).

FORMS OF VERBS

The following forms are regarded as regular:

- third person singular present forms adding -s to the stem (or -es to stems ending in -s, -x, -z, -sh, or soft -ch).
- past tenses and past participles dropping a final silent e and adding -ed to the stem (e.g., **changed**, **danced**).
- present participles dropping a final silent e and adding -ing to the stem (e.g., **changing**, **dancing**).

Other forms are given, notably for:

- verbs that change form by doubling a consonant (e.g., **bat**, **batted**, **batting**). Where practice differs in British usage, this is noted (e.g., at **cavil**).
- verbs with strong and irregular forms showing a change in the stem (e.g., **go**, **went**, **gone**).
- verbs ending in -y that change form by substituting -i for -y (e.g., **try**, **tries**, **tried**).

COMPARATIVE AND SUPERLATIVE OF ADJECTIVES

For the following regular forms, changes in form are not given:

- Words of one syllable adding -er and -est (e.g., **greater**, **greatest**).
- Words of one syllable dropping a final silent e and adding -er and -est (e.g., **braver**, **bravest**).

Other forms are given, notably for:

- Those adjectives that double a final consonant (e.g., **hot**, **hotter**, **hottest**).
- Two-syllable words that have comparative and superlative forms in -er and -est (of which very many are words ending in -y, e.g., **happy**, **happier**, **happiest**), and their negative forms (e.g., **unhappy**, **unhappier**, **unhappiest**).

Specification of the above forms indicates only that they are available; it is usually also possible to form comparatives with *more* and superlatives with *most* (e.g., *more happy*, *most unhappy*).

ADJECTIVES IN -ABLE

These are given as derivative forms when there is sufficient evidence of their currency, and as headwords when further definition is called for. In general they are formed as follows:

- Verbs drop silent final -e except after soft c and g (e.g., **movable**, **peaceable**, **manageable**).
- Verbs of more than one syllable ending in -y (preceded by a consonant or qu) change y to i (e.g., **enviable**).

A final consonant is often doubled as in a normal form change (e.g., **conferrable**, **regrettable**).

PREFIXES, SUFFIXES, AND COMBINING FORMS

A selection of these is given in the main body of the text; prefixes are given in the form **ex-**, **re-**, etc., and suffixes in the form **-able**, **-ably**, etc.

For a usage note on combining forms see the entry COMBINING FORM in the dictionary itself.

ABBREVIATIONS

Most abbreviations appear in italics. Abbreviations in general use (such as *etc.*) are explained in the dictionary itself.

abbr.	abbreviation
absol.	absolute
adj.	adjective
adv.	adverb
Aeron.	Aeronautics
Amer.	American
Anat.	Anatomy
Anglo-Ind.	Anglo-Indian
Anthropol.	Anthropology
Antiq.	Antiquities; Antiquity
Archaeol.	Archaeology
Archit.	Architecture
assim.	assimilated
Astrol.	Astrology
Astron.	Astronomy
attrib.	attributive(ly)
attrib.adj.	attributive adjective
Austral.	Australian
aux.	auxiliary
Bibl.	Biblical
Biochem.	Biochemistry
Biol.	Biology
Bot.	Botany
Brit.	British
Canad.	Canadian
Chem.	Chemistry; chemical
Cinematog.	Cinematography
collect.	collective
colloq.	colloquial
comb.	combination; combining
compar.	comparative
compl.	complement
conj.	conjunction
contr.	contraction
derog.	derogatory
dial.	dialect
disp.	disputed
Eccl.	Ecclesiastical
Ecol.	Ecology
Econ.	Economics
Electr.	Electricity
ellipt.	elliptical(ly)
emphat.	emphatic
Engin.	Engineering
esp.	especially
euphem.	euphemistically
fem.	feminine

foll.	followed
Geog.	Geography
Geol.	Geology
Geom.	Geometry
Gk.	Greek
Gram.	Grammar
Hist.	History
hist.	with historical reference
imper.	imperative
infin.	infinitive
int.	interjection
interrog.	interrogative
interrog.adv.	interrogative adverb
interrog.pron.	interrogative pronoun
intr.	intransitive
Ir.	Irish
iron.	ironically
joc.	jocular
masc.	masculine
Math.	Mathematics
Mech.	Mechanics
Med.	Medicine
Meteorol.	Meteorology
Mil.	Military
Mineral.	Mineralogy
Mus.	Music
Mythol.	Mythology
n.	noun
N. Amer.	North American
Naut.	Nautical
neg.	negative
neut.	neuter
n.pl.	noun plural
NZ	New Zealand
offens.	offensive
opp.	opposite; (as) opposed (to)
orig.	originally
Parl.	Parliament; parliamentary
part.	participle
past part.	past participle
Pharm.	Pharmacy; Pharmacology
Philol.	Philology
Philos.	Philosophy
Phonet.	Phonetics
Photog.	Photography
phr.	phrase
phrs.	phrases
Physiol.	Physiology

pl.	plural
poet.	poetical
Polit.	Politics
poss.	possessive
prec.	preceded
predic.	predicate; predicative(ly)
predic.adj.	predicative adjective
prep.	preposition
pres. part.	present participle
pron.	pronoun
pronunc.	pronunciation
propr.	proprietary
Psychol.	Psychology
RC Ch.	Roman Catholic Church
refl.	reflexive
rel.adv.	relative adverb
Relig.	Religion
rel.pron.	relative pronoun
Rhet.	Rhetoric
Rom.	Roman
S.Afr.	South African
Sc.	Scottish
Sci.	Science
sing.	singular
Stock Exch.	Stock Exchange
superl.	superlative
symb.	symbol
Telev.	Television
Theatr.	Theater; Theatrical
Theol.	Theology
tr.	transitive
US	American; United States
usu.	usually
v.	verb
var.	variant(s)
v.aux	auxiliary verb
v.intr.	intransitive verb
v.refl.	reflexive verb
v.tr.	transitive verb
W.Ind.	West Indian
Zool.	Zoology

THE ILLUSTRATED
DICTIONARY

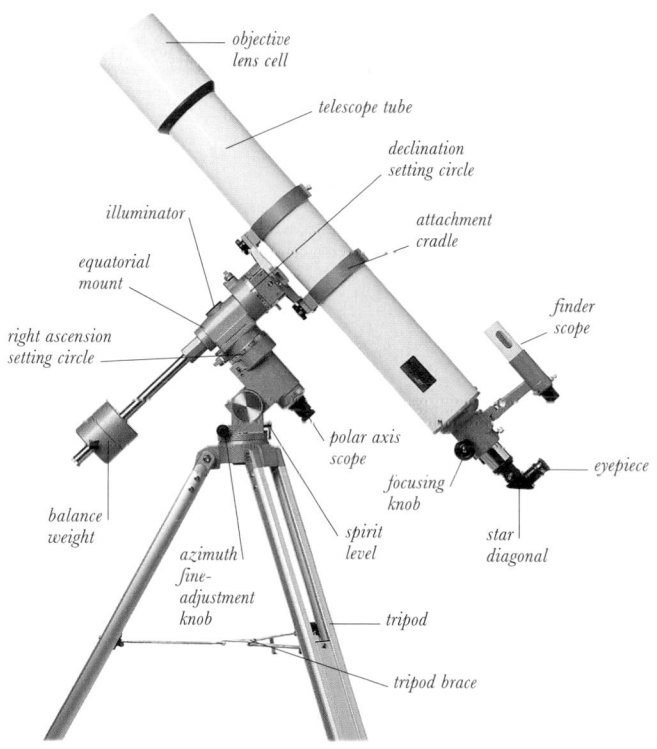

objective
lens cell

telescope tube

declination
setting circle

illuminator

attachment
cradle

equatorial
mount

finder
scope

right ascension
setting circle

polar axis
scope

eyepiece

focusing
knob

balance
weight

spirit
level

star
diagonal

azimuth
fine-
adjustment
knob

tripod

tripod brace

TELESCOPE

A

A[1] /ay/ *n.* (also **a**) (*pl.* **As** or **A's**) **1** the first letter of the alphabet. **2** *Mus.* the sixth note of the diatonic scale of C major. ▷ NOTATION. **3** the first hypothetical person or example. **4** the highest class or category (of academic grades, etc.). **5** (usu. **a**) *Algebra* the first known quantity. **6** a human blood type of the ABO system. □ **from A to B** from one place to another. **from A to Z** over the entire range; completely.

A[2] /ay/ *abbr.* (also **A.**) **1** ampere(s). **2** answer. **3** Associate of. **4** atomic (energy, etc.).

a[1] /ə, ay/ *adj.* (also **an** before a vowel) (called the indefinite article) **1** (as an unemphatic substitute) one; some; any. **2** one like (*a Judas*). **3** one single (*not a thing in sight*). **4** the same (*all of a size*). **5** in, to, or for each (*twice a year*).

a[2] /ə/ *prep.* (usu. as *prefix*) **1** to; toward (*ashore*). **2** (with verb in pres. part. or infin.) in the process of; in a specified state (*a-hunting*). **3** on (*afire*).

Å *abbr.* ångström(s).

a- /ay, a/ *prefix* not; without (*amoral*; *apetalous*).

-a /ə/ *suffix colloq.* **1** of (*kinda*; *coupla*). **2** have (*mighta*; *coulda*). **3** to (*oughta*).

A1 /áy wún/ *n.* & *adj.* ● *n. Naut.* a first-class vessel. ● *adj. colloq.* excellent; first-class.

AA *abbr.* **1** Alcoholics Anonymous. **2** Associate of Arts. **3** *Mil.* antiaircraft.

AAA *abbr.* **1** American Automobile Association. **2** Amateur Athletic Association. **3** antiaircraft artillery.

aard·vark /áardvaark/ *n.* a nocturnal mammal of southern Africa, *Orycteropus afer*, with a tubular snout and a long tongue, that feeds on termites. ▷ MAMMAL

aard·wolf /áardwo͝olf/ *n.* (*pl.* **aardwolves** /-wo͝olvz/) an African mammal, *Proteles cristatus*, of the hyena family, with gray fur and black stripes, that feeds on insects.

Aar·on's rod /áirən, ár-/ *n.* any of several tall plants, esp. mullein.

AAU *abbr.* Amateur Athletic Union.

AB[1] /áybeè/ *n.* a human blood type of the ABO system.

AB[2] *abbr.* Bachelor of Arts.

ab /ab/ *n.* (usu. **abs**) *colloq.* an abdominal muscle.

a·ba /əbaá, aábə/ *n.* (also **abba**, **abaya** /əbáy-yə, əbíyə/) a sleeveless outer garment worn by Arabs.

a·back /əbák/ *adv.* **1** *archaic* backward; behind. □ **take aback** surprise; disconcert (*I was greatly taken aback by the news*). **2** *Naut.* (of a sail) pressed against the mast by a head wind.

ab·a·cus /ábəkəs, əbákəs/ *n.* (*pl.* **abacuses**) **1** ▼ an oblong frame with rows of wires or grooves along which beads are slid, used for calculating. **2** *Archit.* the flat slab of a capital, supporting the architrave.

ABACUS

a·baft /əbáft/ *adv.* & *prep. Naut.* ● *adv.* in the stern half of a ship. ● *prep.* nearer the stern than; aft of.

ab·a·lo·ne /ábəlónee/ *n.* ► any mollusk of the genus *Haliotis*, with a shallow ear-shaped shell having respiratory holes, and lined with mother-of-pearl.

ABALONE SHELL (INTERIOR)

a·ban·don /əbándən/ *v.* & *n.* ● *v.tr.* **1** give up completely or before completion (*abandoned hope*; *abandoned the game*). **2** forsake or desert (a person or a post of responsibility). **b** leave or desert (a motor vehicle, ship, etc.). **3 a** give up to another's control or mercy. **b** *refl.* yield oneself completely to a passion or impulse. ● *n.* lack of inhibition or restraint. □□ **a·ban·don·ment** *n.*

a·ban·doned /əbándənd/ *adj.* **1 a** (of a person or animal) deserted; forsaken (*an abandoned child*). **b** (of a building, vehicle, etc.) left empty or unused (*an abandoned car*). **2** (of a person or behavior) unrestrained; profligate.

a·base /əbáys/ *v.tr.* & *refl.* humiliate or degrade. □□ **a·base·ment** *n.*

a·bash /əbásh/ *v.tr.* (usu. as **abashed** *adj.*) embarrass; disconcert. □□ **a·bash·ment** *n.*

a·bate /əbáyt/ *v.* **1** *tr.* & *intr.* make or become less strong, severe, etc. **2** *tr. Law* **a** quash (a writ or action). **b** put an end to (a nuisance). □□ **a·bate·ment** *n.*

ab·at·toir /ábətwaar/ *n.* a slaughterhouse.

ab·ax·i·al /abákseeəl/ *adj. Bot.* facing away from the stem of a plant, esp. of the lower surface of a leaf (cf. ADAXIAL).

ab·ba·cy /ábəsee/ *n.* (*pl.* **-ies**) the office, jurisdiction, or period of office of an abbot or abbess.

ab·ba·tial /əbáyshəl/ *adj.* of an abbey, abbot, or abbess.

ab·bé /əbáy, ábay/ *n.* (in France) an abbot; a man entitled to wear ecclesiastical dress.

ab·bess /ábis/ *n.* a woman who is the head of certain communities of nuns.

ab·bey /ábee/ *n.* (*pl.* **-eys**) **1** ▼ the building(s) occupied by a community of monks or nuns. ▷ CHURCH. **2** the community itself.

ab·bot /ábət/ *n.* a man who is the head of an abbey of monks. □□ **ab·bot·ship** *n.*

ab·bre·vi·ate /əbréevee-ayt/ *v.tr.* shorten (a word, etc.).

ab·bre·vi·a·tion /əbréevee-áyshən/ *n.* **1** an abbre-viated form, esp. a shortened form of a word or phrase. **2** the process or result of abbreviating.

ABC[1] /áybeeseé/ *n.* **1** the alphabet. **2** the rudiments of any subject. **3** an alphabetical guide.

ABC[2] *abbr.* American Broadcasting Company.

ab·di·cate /ábdikayt/ *v.tr.* give up or renounce (a throne, duty, etc.). □□ **ab·di·ca·tion** /-káyshən/ *n.*

ab·do·men /ábdəmən, abdó-/ *n.* **1** the part of the body containing the stomach, bowels, reproductive organs, etc. **2** *Zool.* the hind part of an insect, crustacean, spider, etc. ▷ INSECT, SPIDER. □□ **ab·dom·i·nal** /abdómīnəl/ *adj.*

ab·duct /əbdúkt/ *v.tr.* carry off or kidnap (a person) illegally by force or deception. □□ **ab·duc·tion** /-dúkshən/ *n.* **ab·duc·tor** *n.*

a·beam /əbeém/ *adv.* on a line at right angles to a ship's or an aircraft's length.

a·bed /əbéd/ *adv. archaic* in bed.

a·bele /əbéel, áybəl/ *n.* the white poplar, *Populus alba*.

A·be·na·ki /abənaákee/ *n.* (also **Ab·na·ki** /abnaákee/) **1 a** a N. American people native to northern New England and adjoining parts of Quebec. **b** a member of this people. **2** either of the two languages of this people.

Ab·er·deen An·gus /ábərdeen ánggəs/ *n.* ▼ an animal of a Scottish breed of hornless black beef cattle.

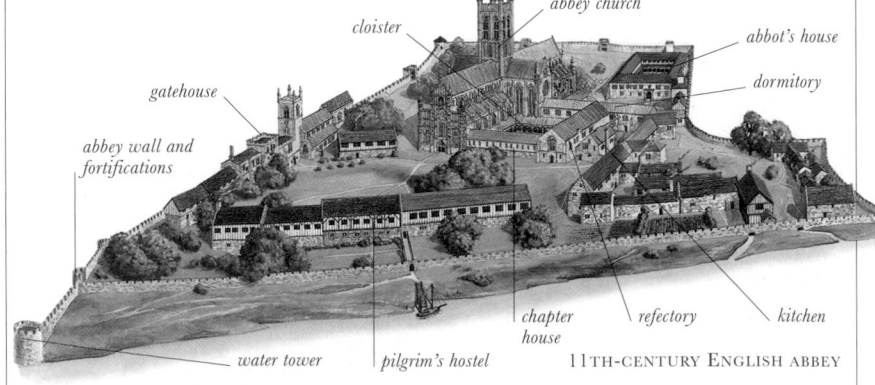

ABERDEEN ANGUS

ab·er·rant /əbérənt, ábə-/ *adj.* **1** esp. *Biol.* diverging from the normal type. **2** departing from an accepted standard. □□ **ab·er·rance** /-rəns/ *n.* **ab·er·ran·cy** *n.*

ab·er·ra·tion /ábəráyshən/ *n.* **1** a departure from what is normal or accepted or regarded as right.

ABBEY

The layout of buildings within an abbey complex often follows a common pattern. Essential to the pattern is the abbey church, with a cloister adjacent to it. Flanking the cloister on the remaining three sides are buildings housing a refectory and kitchens, a dormitory, and a chapter house. Other buildings in the abbey complex might include an abbot's house and a hostel for visiting pilgrims.

cloister
abbey church
abbot's house
gatehouse
dormitory
abbey wall and fortifications
chapter house
refectory
kitchen
water tower
pilgrim's hostel
11TH-CENTURY ENGLISH ABBEY

2 a moral or mental lapse. 3 *Biol.* deviation from a normal type. 4 *Optics* the failure of rays to converge at one focus because of a defect in a lens or mirror.

a·bet /əbét/ *v.tr.* (**abetted**, **abetting**) (usu. in **aid and abet**) encourage or assist (an offender or offense). □□ **a·bet·ment** *n.*

a·bet·tor /əbétər/ *n.* (also **a·bet·ter**) one who abets.

a·bey·ance /əbáyəns/ *n.* (usu. prec. by *in*) temporary disuse or suspension.

ab·hor /əbháwr/ *v.tr.* (**abhorred**, **abhorring**) detest; regard with disgust and hatred. □□ **ab·hor·rer** *n.*

ab·hor·rence /əbháwrəns, -hór-/ *n.* 1 disgust; detestation. 2 a detested thing.

ab·hor·rent /əbháwrənt, -hór-/ *adj.* (often foll. by *to*) (of conduct, etc.) inspiring disgust; repugnant; hateful; detestable.

a·bide /əbíd/ *v.* (*past* **abode** /əbṓd/ or **abided**) 1 *tr.* (usu. in *neg.* or *interrog.*) tolerate; endure (*can't abide him*). 2 *intr.* (foll. by *by*) a act in accordance with (*abide by the rules*). b remain faithful to (a promise). 3 *intr. archaic* dwell. □□ **a·bid·ance** *n.*

a·bid·ing /əbíding/ *adj.* enduring; permanent (*an abiding sense of loss*). □□ **a·bid·ing·ly** *adv.*

a·bil·i·ty /əbílitee/ *n.* (*pl.* **-ies**) 1 (often foll. by *to* + infin.) capacity or power. 2 cleverness; talent; mental power (*a person of great ability; has many abilities*).

-ability /əbílitee/ *suffix* forming nouns of quality from, or corresponding to, adjectives in *-able* (*capability; vulnerability*).

ab in·i·ti·o /áb inísheeō/ *adv.* from the beginning.

a·bi·o·gen·e·sis /áybīōjénisis/ *n.* 1 the formation of living organisms from inanimate substances. 2 the supposed spontaneous generation of living organisms. □□ **a·bi·o·gen·ic** /-jénik/ *adj.*

ab·ject /ábjekt, abjékt/ *adj.* 1 miserable; wretched. 2 degraded; self-abasing; humble. 3 despicable. □□ **ab·ject·ly** *adv.* **ab·ject·ness** *n.*

ab·jec·tion /əbjékshən/ *n.* a state of misery or degradation.

ab·jure /əbjŏŏr/ *v.tr.* renounce under oath (an opinion, cause, claim, etc.). □□ **ab·ju·ra·tion** /-ráyshən/ *n.*

ab·la·tion /abláyshən/ *n.* 1 the surgical removal of body tissue. 2 *Geol.* the wasting or erosion of a glacier, iceberg, or rock by melting, evaporation, or the action of water. 3 *Astronaut.* the evaporation or melting of part of the outer surface of a spacecraft through heating by friction with the atmosphere. □□ **ab·late** *v.tr.*

ab·la·tive /áblətiv/ *n.* & *adj. Gram.* ● *n.* the case (esp. in Latin) of nouns and pronouns (and words in grammatical agreement with them) indicating an agent, instrument, or location. ● *adj.* of or in the ablative.

ab·laut /áblowt/ *n.* a change of vowel in related words or forms, esp. in Indo-European languages, arising from differences of accent and stress in the parent language, e.g., in *sing, sang, sung.*

a·blaze /əbláyz/ *predic.adj.* & *adv.* 1 on fire. 2 (often foll. by *with*) glittering; glowing; radiant.

a·ble /áybəl/ *adj.* (**abler**, **ablest**) 1 (often foll. by *to* + infin.) having the capacity or power (*was not able to come*). 2 having great ability; clever; skillful.

-able /əbəl/ *suffix* forming adjectives meaning: 1 that may or must be (*forgivable; payable*). 2 that can be made the subject of (*dutiable*). 3 that is relevant to or in accordance with (*fashionable; seasonable*). 4 (with active sense, in earlier word formations) that may (*comfortable; suitable*).

a·ble-bod·ied *adj.* fit; healthy.

a·bled /áybəld/ *adj.* having a full range of physical and mental abilities; able-bodied. □ **differently abled** *euphem.* disabled.

a·ble·ism /áybəlizəm/ *n.* (also **a·blism**, **a·ble·bod·ied·ism**) discrimination in favor of the able-bodied.

a·bloom /əblŏŏm/ *predic.adj.* blooming; in flower.

ab·lu·tion /əblŏŏshən/ *n.* (usu. in *pl.*) 1 the ceremonial washing of parts of the body or sacred vessels, etc. 2 *colloq.* the ordinary washing of the body. □□ **ab·lu·tion·ar·y** *adj.*

a·bly /áyblee/ *adv.* capably; cleverly; competently.

-ably /əblee/ *suffix* forming adverbs corresponding to adjectives in *-able.*

ABM *abbr.* antiballistic missile.

ab·ne·gate /ábnigayt/ *v.tr.* 1 give up or deny oneself (a pleasure, etc.). 2 renounce or reject (a right or belief). □□ **ab·ne·ga·tor** *n.*

ab·ne·ga·tion /ábnigáyshən/ *n.* 1 the rejection of a doctrine. 2 = SELF-ABNEGATION.

ab·nor·mal /abnáwrməl/ *adj.* deviating from what is normal or usual; exceptional. □□ **ab·nor·mal·ly** *adv.*

ab·nor·mal·i·ty /ábnawrmálitee/ *n.* (*pl.* **-ies**) 1 an abnormal quality, occurrence, etc. 2 the state of being abnormal.

ab·nor·mi·ty /abnáwrmitee/ *n.* (*pl.* **-ies**) an abnormality or irregularity.

a·board /əbáwrd/ *adv.* & *prep.* on or into (a ship, aircraft, train, etc.).

a·bode[1] /əbṓd/ *n.* a dwelling; one's home.

a·bode[2] *past* of ABIDE.

a·bol·ish /əbólish/ *v.tr.* put an end to (esp. a custom or institution). □□ **a·bol·ish·ment** *n.*

ab·o·li·tion /ábəlíshən/ *n.* the act or process of abolishing or being abolished.

ab·o·li·tion·ist /ábəlíshənist/ *n.* one who favors the abolition of a practice or institution, esp. of capital punishment or slavery. □□ **ab·o·li·tion·ism** *n.*

ab·o·ma·sum /ábəmáysəm/ *n.* (*pl.* **abomasa** /-sə/) the fourth stomach of a ruminant. ▷ RUMINANT

A-bomb /áybom/ *n.* = ATOM BOMB.

a·bom·i·na·ble /əbóminəbəl/ *adj.* 1 detestable; loathsome. 2 *colloq.* very bad or unpleasant (*abominable weather*). □□ **a·bom·i·na·bly** *adv.*

a·bom·i·na·ble snow·man *n.* a humanoid or bear-like animal said to exist in the Himalayas; a yeti.

a·bom·i·nate /əbóminayt/ *v.tr.* detest; loathe.

a·bom·i·na·tion /əbóminávshən/ *n.* 1 loathing. 2 an odious habit or act. 3 an object of disgust.

ab·o·ral /abáwrəl/ *adj.* away from or opposite the mouth.

ab·o·rig·i·nal /ábəríjinəl/ *adj.* & *n.* ● *adj.* 1 inhabiting or existing in a land from the earliest times or before the arrival of colonists. 2 (**Aboriginal**) of the Australian Aborigines. ● *n.* 1 an aboriginal inhabitant. 2 (**Aboriginal**) an aboriginal inhabitant of Australia.

ab·o·rig·i·ne /ábəríjinee/ *n.* (usu. in *pl.*) 1 an aboriginal inhabitant. 2 (**Aborigine**) an aboriginal inhabitant of Australia. 3 an aboriginal plant or animal.

a·bort /əbáwrt/ *v.* 1 *intr.* a (of a woman) undergo abortion; miscarry. b (of a fetus) suffer abortion. 2 *tr.* a effect the abortion of (a fetus). b effect abortion in (a mother). 3 a *tr.* cause to end fruitlessly or prematurely. b *intr.* end unsuccessfully or prematurely. 4 a *tr.* abandon or terminate (a space flight or other technical project) before its completion. b *intr.* terminate such an undertaking.

a·bor·ti·fa·cient /əbáwrtifáyshənt/ *adj.* & *n.* ● *adj.* effecting abortion. ● *n.* a drug or other agent that effects abortion.

a·bor·tion /əbáwrshən/ *n.* 1 the expulsion of a fetus (naturally or esp. by medical induction) from the womb before it is able to survive independently, esp. in the first 28 weeks of a human pregnancy. 2 a stunted or deformed creature or thing.

a·bor·tion·ist /əbáwrshənist/ *n.* a person who carries out abortions, esp. illegally.

a·bor·tive /əbáwrtiv/ *adj.* 1 fruitless; unsuccessful; unfinished. 2 resulting in abortion. □□ **a·bor·tive·ly** *adv.*

ABO system /áybee-ṓ/ *n.* a system of four types (A, AB, B, and O) by which human blood may be classified, based on the presence or absence of certain inherited antigens.

a·bound /əbównd/ *v.intr.* 1 be plentiful. 2 (foll. by *in*) be rich.

a·bout /əbówt/ *prep.* & *adv.* ● *prep.* 1 a on the subject of; in connection with (*a book about birds*). b relating to (*something funny about this*). c in relation to (*symmetry about a plane*). d so as to affect (*can do nothing about it*). 2 at a time near to (*come about four*). 3 a in; around; surrounding (*wandered about the town; a scarf about her neck*). b all around from a center (*look about you*). 4 at points throughout (*toys lying about the house*). 5 at a point or points near to (*fighting going on about us*). ● *adv.* 1 a approximately. b *colloq.* used to indicate understatement (*just about had enough*). 2 here and there; at points nearby (*a lot of flu about*). 3 all around; in every direction (*look about*). 4 on the move; in action (*out and about*). 5 in partial rotation or alteration from a given position (*the wrong way about*). 6 in rotation or succession (*turn and turn about*). 7 *Naut.* on or to the opposite tack (*put about*). □ **be about to** be on the point of (doing something).

a·bout-face /əbówtfáys/ *n.*, *v.*, & *int.* ● *n.* 1 a turn made so as to face the opposite direction. 2 a change of opinion or policy, etc. ● *v.intr.* make an about-face. ● *int. Mil.* a command to make an about-face.

a·bove /əbúv/ *prep.*, *adv.*, *adj.*, & *n.* ● *prep.* 1 over; on the top of; higher than. 2 more than (*above average*). 3 higher in rank, position, importance, etc., than. 4 a too great or good for (*is not above cheating*). b beyond the reach of; not affected by (*above my understanding*). ● *adv.* 1 at or to a higher point; overhead (*the floor above; the clouds above*). 2 upstairs (*lives above*). 3 (of a text reference) further back on a page or in a book (*as noted above*). 4 in addition (*over and above*). 5 *rhet.* in heaven (*Lord above!*). ● *adj.* mentioned earlier; preceding (*the above argument*). ● *n.* (prec. by *the*) what is mentioned above (*the above shows*). □ **above all** most of all; more than anything else. **above one's head** see HEAD. **above oneself** conceited; arrogant.

a·bove·board /əbúvbawrd/ *adj.* & *adv.* fair or fairly; open or openly.

a·bove·ground /əbúvgrownd/ 1 alive. 2 not secret or underground.

ab o·vo /ab ṓvō/ *adv.* from the very beginning.

ab·ra·ca·dab·ra /ábrəkədábrə/ *n.* 1 a supposedly magic word used by magicians in performing a trick. 2 a spell or charm. 3 jargon or gibberish.

a·brade /əbráyd/ *v.tr.* scrape or wear away by rubbing. □□ **a·brad·er** *n.*

a·bra·sion /əbráyzhən/ *n.* 1 scraping or wearing away. 2 a damaged area resulting from this.

a·bra·sive /əbráysiv/ *adj.* & *n.* ● *adj.* 1 a tending to rub or abrade. b capable of polishing by rubbing. 2 harsh in manner. ● *n.* an abrasive substance.

ab·re·act /ábreeákt/ *v.tr. Psychol.* release (an emotion) by abreaction.

ab·re·ac·tion /ábreeákshən/ *n. Psychol.* the free expression and consequent release of a previously repressed emotion. □□ **ab·re·ac·tive** *adj.*

a·breast /əbrést/ *adv.* 1 side by side and facing the same way. 2 a (often foll. by *with*) up to date. b (foll. by *of*) well-informed (*abreast of all the changes*).

a·bridge /əbríj/ *v.tr.* shorten (a book, movie, etc.). □□ **abridgable** or **a·bridge·a·ble** *adj.* **a·bridg·er** *n.*

a·bridg·ment /əbríjmənt/ *n.* (also **a·bridge·ment**) 1 shortened version, esp. of a book. 2 the process of producing this.

a·broad /əbráwd/ *adv.* 1 in or to a foreign country or countries. 2 over a wide area; in different directions (*scatter abroad*). 3 in circulation (*there is a rumor abroad*). □ **from abroad** from another country.

ab·ro·gate /ábrəgayt/ *v.tr.* repeal or abolish (a law or custom). □□ **ab·ro·ga·tion** /-gáyshən/ *n.*

ab·rupt /əbrúpt/ *adj.* 1 sudden and unexpected; hasty (*his abrupt departure*). 2 (of speech, manner, etc.) lacking continuity; curt. 3 steep; precipitous. □□ **ab·rupt·ly** *adv.* **ab·rupt·ness** *n.*

ABS *abbr.* antilock brake (or braking) system.

A

A

ABSCESS

An abscess is a sac of pus formed from destroyed tissue cells. The destroyed cells are the result of a localized infection and are composed of leucocytes and microorganisms, such as bacteria. A pyogenic membrane, or lining, contains the pus.

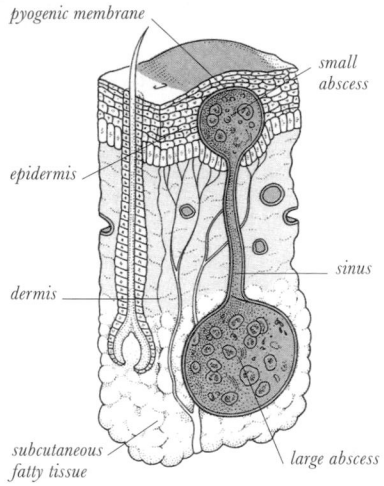

pyogenic membrane

small abscess

epidermis

sinus

dermis

subcutaneous fatty tissue

large abscess

CROSS SECTION OF HUMAN SKIN SHOWING
A COLLAR-AND-STUD (DOUBLE) ABSCESS

ab·scess /ábses/ n. ▲ a swollen area accumulating pus within a body tissue. □□ **ab·scessed** adj.

ab·scis·ic ac·id /ábsízik/ n. a plant hormone which promotes leaf detachment and bud dormancy and inhibits germination.

ab·scis·sa /əbsísə/ n. (pl. **abscissae** /-ee/ or **ab·scissas**) Math. (in a system of coordinates) the shortest distance from a point to the vertical or y-axis (cf. ORDINATE).

ab·scis·sion /əbsízhən/ n. the act or an instance of cutting off.

ab·scond /əbskónd/ v.intr. depart hurriedly, esp. unlawfully. □□ **ab·scond·er** n.

ab·seil /áapzīl, ábsayl/ esp. Brit. = RAPPEL.

ab·sence /ábsəns/ n. **1** the state of being away from a place or person. **2** the time or duration of being away. **3** (foll. by of) the nonexistence or lack of. □ **absence of mind** inattentiveness.

ab·sent adj. & v. ● adj. /ábsənt/ **1** not present. **2** not existing. **3** inattentive. ● v.refl. /absént/ **1** stay away. **2** withdraw. □□ **ab·sent·ly** adv. (in sense 3 of adj.).

ab·sen·tee /ábsəntéé/ n. a person not present, esp. one who is absent from work or school.

ab·sen·tee bal·lot n. a ballot, usu. returned by mail, for a voter who cannot be present at the polls.

ab·sen·tee·ism /ábsəntééizəm/ n. the practice of absenting oneself from work or school, etc., esp. frequently or illicitly.

ab·sen·tee land·lord n. a landlord who rents out a property while living elsewhere.

ab·sent·mind·ed /ábsəntmíndid/ adj. habitually forgetful or inattentive. □□ **ab·sent·mind·ed·ly** adv. **ab·sent·mind·ed·ness** n.

ab·sinthe /ábsinth/ n. (also **ab·sinth**) a green aniseed flavored liqueur based on wormwood.

ab·so·lute /ábsəlōōt/ adj. & n. ● adj. **1** complete; utter (an absolute fool). **2** unconditional; unlimited (absolute authority). **3** ruling arbitrarily or with unrestricted power (an absolute monarch). **4** (of a standard or other concept) universally valid; not relative or comparative. **5** Gram. **a** (of a construction) syntactically independent of the rest of the sentence, as in dinner being over, we left the table. **b** (of an

adjective or transitive verb) used or usable without an expressed noun or object (e.g., the deaf; guns kill). **6** (of a legal decree, etc.) final. ● n. Philos. a value, standard, etc., which is objective and universally valid. □□ **ab·so·lute·ness** n.

ab·so·lute·ly /ábsəlōōtlee/ adv. **1** completely; utterly (absolutely marvelous; he absolutely denies it). **2** (foll. by neg.) (no or none) at all (absolutely no chance). **3** Gram. in an absolute way, esp. (of a verb) without a stated object. **4** colloq. (used in reply) quite so; yes.

ab·so·lute pitch n. Mus. **1** the ability to recognize the pitch of a note or produce any given note. **2** a fixed standard of pitch defined by the rate of vibration.

ab·so·lute ze·ro n. a theoretical lowest possible temperature, calculated as –273.15˚C (or 0˚K).

ab·so·lu·tion /ábsəlōōshən/ n. **1** a formal release from guilt, obligation, or punishment. **2** an ecclesiastical declaration of forgiveness of sins.

ab·so·lut·ism /ábsəlōōtizəm/ n. the acceptance of or belief in absolute principles in political, philosophical, ethical, or theological matters. □□ **ab·so·lut·ist** n. & adj.

ab·solve /əbzólv, -sólv/ v.tr. (often foll. by from, of) set or pronounce free from blame or obligation, etc. **2** pardon or give absolution for (a sin, etc.).

ab·sorb /əbsáwrb, -záwrb/ v.tr. **1** include or incorporate as part of itself or oneself. **2** take in; suck up (liquid, heat, knowledge, etc.). **3** reduce the effect or intensity of; deal easily with (an impact, sound, difficulty, etc.). **4** consume (income, time, resources, etc.). **5** engross the attention of. □□ **ab·sorb·a·ble** adj. **ab·sorb·er** n. **ab·sorb·ing** adj.

ab·sorbed /əbsáwrbd, -záwrbd/ adj. intensely engaged or interested. □□ **ab·sorb·ed·ly** /-bidlee/ adv.

ab·sorb·ent /əbsáwrbənt, -záwr-/ adj. & n. ● adj. having a tendency to absorb (esp. liquids). ● n. an absorbent substance. □□ **ab·sorb·en·cy** /-bənsee/ n.

ab·sorp·tion /əbsáwrpshən, -záwrp-/ n. **1** the process or action of absorbing or being absorbed. **2** mental engrossment. □□ **ab·sorp·tive** adj.

ab·stain /əbstáyn/ v.intr. **1 a** (usu. foll. by from) refrain from indulging in (abstained from candy). **b** refrain from drinking alcohol. **2** formally decline to use one's vote. □□ **ab·stain·er** n.

ab·ste·mi·ous /əbsteémeeəs/ adj. moderate, esp. in eating and drinking. □□ **ab·ste·mi·ous·ly** adv. **ab·ste·mi·ous·ness** n.

ab·sten·tion /əbsténshən/ n. the act of abstaining from voting.

ab·sti·nence /ábstinəns/ n. the act of abstaining, esp. from food, alcohol, or sexual relations.

ab·sti·nent /ábstinənt/ adj. practicing abstinence.

ab·stract adj., v., & n. ● adj. /ábstrakt/ **1 a** to do with or existing in thought rather than matter, or in theory rather than practice. **b** (of a word, esp. a noun) denoting a quality or condition or intangible thing rather than a concrete object. **2** ▶ (of art) achieving its effect by grouping shapes and colors in satisfying patterns rather than by the recognizable representation of physical reality. ● v. /əbstrákt/ **1** tr. (often foll. by from) take out of; extract; remove. **2** tr. summarize (an article, book, etc.). **3** tr. & refl. (often foll. by from) disengage (a person's attention, etc.); distract. **4** tr. (foll. by from) consider abstractly or separately from something else. ● n. /ábstrakt/ **1** a summary or statement of the contents of a book, etc. **2** an abstract work of art. □ **in the abstract** in theory rather than in practice. □□ **ab·stract·ly** adv. **ab·stract·or** n. (in sense 2 of v.).

ab·stract·ed /əbstráktid/ adj. inattentive; preoccupied. □□ **ab·stract·ed·ly** adv.

ab·stract ex·pres·sion·ism n. a development of abstract art aiming at subjective emotional expression.

ab·strac·tion /əbstrákshən/ n. **1** the act or an instance of abstracting or taking away. **2** an abstract or visionary idea. **3** abstract qualities (esp. in art). **4** absentmindedness.

ab·struse /əbstrōōs/ adj. hard to understand. □□ **ab·struse·ly** adv. **ab·struse·ness** n.

ab·surd /əbsárd/ adj. wildly unreasonable, illogical, or ludicrous. □□ **ab·surd·ly** adv. **ab·surd·ness** n.

ab·surd·i·ty /əbsárditee/ n. (pl. **-ies**) **1** wild inappropriateness or incongruity. **2** an absurd act or statement.

a·bun·dance /əbúndəns/ n. **1** a very great quantity, usu. considered to be more than enough. **2** wealth; affluence.

a·bun·dant /əbúndənt/ adj. **1** existing or available in large quantities; plentiful. **2** (foll. by in) having an abundance of. □□ **a·bun·dant·ly** adv.

a·buse v. & n. ● v.tr. /əbyōōz/ **1** use to bad effect or for a bad purpose. **2** insult verbally. **3** maltreat; assault (esp. sexually). ● n. /əbyōōs/ **1** improper use (the abuse of power). **2** insulting language (a torrent of abuse). **3** unjust or corrupt practice. **4** maltreatment (child abuse). □□ **a·bus·er** /əbyōōzər/ n.

a·bu·sive /əbyōōsiv/ adj. **1** using insulting language. **2** (of language) insulting. **3** given to physical abuse. □□ **a·bu·sive·ly** adv. **a·bu·sive·ness** n.

a·but /əbút/ v. (**abutted**, **abutting**) **1** intr. (foll. by on) (of countries, etc.) adjoin (another). **2** intr. (foll. by on) (of part of a building) touch or lean on (another) with a projecting end or point. **3** tr. abut on.

a·but·ment /əbútmənt/ n. the lateral supporting structure of a bridge, arch, etc. ▷ ARCH

a·bys·mal /əbízməl/ adj. **1** colloq. extremely bad (abysmal weather). **2** profound; utter (abysmal ignorance). □□ **a·bys·mal·ly** adv.

a·byss /əbís/ n. **1** a deep or seemingly bottomless chasm. **2** an immeasurable depth (abyss of despair).

a·byss·al /əbísəl/ adj. at or of the ocean depths or floor.

AC abbr. **1** (also **ac**) alternating current. **2** air conditioning.

Ac symb. Chem. the element actinium.

a/c abbr. account.

a·ca·cia /əkáyshə/ n. **1** ◀ any tree of the genus Acacia, with yellow or white flowers. **2** (also **false acacia**) the locust tree, Robinia pseudoacacia.

ACACIA: SILVER WATTLE
(Acacia dealbata)

ac·a·deme /ákədeem/ n. **1** the world of learning. **2** universities collectively. □ **groves of Academe** a university environment.

ac·a·de·mi·a /ákədeémeeə/ n. the academic world; scholastic life.

ac·a·dem·ic /ákədémik/ adj. & n. ● adj. **1 a** scholarly; to do with learning. **b** of or relating to a scholarly institution (academic dress). **2** abstract; not of practical relevance. **3** Art conventional; overly formal. ● n. a teacher or scholar in a university or college. □□ **ac·a·dem·i·cal·ly** adv.

ac·a·de·mi·cian /ákədəmíshən, əkádə-/ n. **1** a member of an Academy. **2** = ACADEMIC.

ac·a·dem·i·cism /ákədémisizəm/ n. (also **a·cad·e·mism** /əkádəmizəm/) academic principles or their application in art.

ac·a·dem·ic year n. the customary period of instruction in schools, colleges, and universities.

a·cad·e·my /əkádəmee/ n. (pl. **-ies**) **1** a place of study or training in a special field (military academy; academy of dance). **2** (usu. **Academy**) a society or institution of distinguished scholars, artists, scientists, etc. (Royal Academy). **3** a secondary school, esp. one that is private. **4** the community of scholars; academe.

Ac·a·de·my a·ward n. an award given by the Academy of Motion Picture Arts and Sciences for achievement in the film industry; an Oscar.

A·ca·di·an /əkáydeeən/ n. & adj. ● n. **1** a native or inhabitant of Acadia in Nova Scotia, esp. a French-

ABSTRACT

Although the term *abstract* can be attributed to art throughout its history, it is applied specifically to an artistic style that began among avant-garde movements in Europe and the US in the early 20th century. Such movements rejected recognizable styles of representation and instead chose either to reduce subjects to simplified forms, as exemplified by the sculpture of Brancusi and Henry Moore, or to create works without a physical subject in the real world, as evident in paintings by Kandinsky and by Mondrian after 1917.

Composition in Red, Blue, Yellow and Black (1929), PIET MONDRIAN

TIMELINE

| 1500 | 1550 | 1600 | 1650 | 1700 | 1750 | 1800 | 1850 | 1900 | 1950 | 200 |

speaking one. **2** a descendant of French-speaking Nova Scotian immigrants in Louisiana. ● *adj.* of or relating to Acadians.

a·can·thus /əkánthəs/ *n.* **1** any herbaceous plant of the genus *Acanthus*, with spiny leaves. **2** *Archit.* ▼ a conventionalized representation of an acanthus leaf.

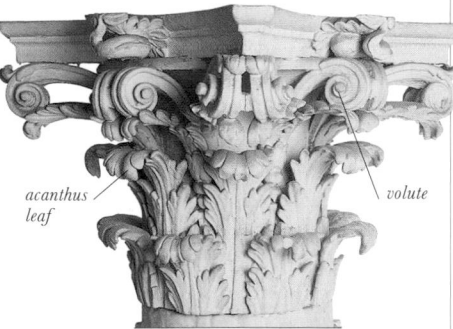

ACANTHUS: CORINTHIAN CAPITAL WITH ACANTHUS-LEAF DECORATION

acanthus leaf — volute

a cap·pel·la /a̋ə kəpélə/ *adj. & adv.* (also **al·la cap·pel·la** /álə/) *Mus.* (of choral music) unaccompanied.

ac·a·rid /ákərid/ *n.* any small arachnid of the order Acarina.

a·car·pous /aykáarpəs/ *adj. Bot.* (of a plant, etc.) without fruit or that does not produce fruit.

ac·cede /akseéd/ *v.intr.* (often foll. by *to*) **1** assent or agree. **2** take office, esp. become monarch. **3** formally subscribe to a treaty or other agreement.

ac·cel·er·an·do /əksélərándō, aachéləraán-/ *adv. & adj. Mus.* with a gradual increase of speed.

ac·cel·er·ate /əksélərayt/ *v.* **1** *intr.* **a** (of a moving body) increase speed. **b** (of a process) happen more quickly. **2** *tr.* **a** cause to increase speed. **b** cause to happen more quickly.

ac·cel·er·a·tion /əkséləráyshən/ *n.* **1** the process or act of accelerating. **2** (of a vehicle, etc.) the capacity to gain speed (*the car has good acceleration*).

ac·cel·er·a·tive /əkséləraytiv, -ərətiv/ *adj.* tending to increase speed.

ac·cel·er·a·tor /əkséləraytər/ *n.* **1** a device for increasing speed, esp. the pedal that controls the speed of a vehicle's engine. **2** *Physics* an apparatus for imparting high speeds to charged particles. **3** *Chem.* a substance that speeds up a chemical reaction.

ac·cel·er·om·e·ter /əksélərómitər/ *n.* an instrument for measuring acceleration.

ac·cent *n. & v.* ● *n.* /áksent/ **1** a mode of pronunciation, esp. one associated with a particular region or group. **2** prominence given to a syllable by stress or pitch. **3** a mark on a letter or word to indicate pitch, stress, or the quality of a vowel. **4** emphasis (*an accent on comfort*). **5** *Mus.* emphasis on a particular note or chord. ● *v.tr.* also /aksént/ **1** pronounce with an accent; emphasize. **2** write or print accents on (words, etc.). **3** *Mus.* play with an accent. □□ **ac·cen·tu·al** /aksénchōōəl/ *adj.*

ac·cen·tu·ate /aksénchōōayt/ *v.tr.* emphasize; make prominent. □□ **ac·cen·tu·a·tion** /-áyshən/ *n.*

ac·cept /aksépt/ *v.tr.* **1** (also *absol.*) consent to receive (a thing offered). **2** (also *absol.*) give an affirmative answer to. **3** regard favorably (*her mother-in-law never accepted her*). **4 a** receive (an opinion, explanation, etc.) as valid. **b** be prepared to subscribe to (a belief, philosophy, etc.). **5** receive as suitable (*the hotel accepts traveler's checks*). **6** tolerate; submit to (*accepted the umpire's decision*). □□ **ac·cept·er** *n.*

ac·cept·a·ble /akséptəbəl/ *adj.* **1 a** worthy of being accepted. **b** pleasing; welcome. **2** adequate; satisfactory. **3** tolerable (*an acceptable risk*). □□ **ac·cept·a·bil·i·ty** /-bílitee/ *n.* **ac·cept·a·ble·ness** *n.* **ac·cept·a·bly** *adv.*

ac·cept·ance /akséptəns/ *n.* **1** willingness to receive or accept. **2** an affirmative answer to an invitation or proposal. **3 a** approval; belief (*found wide acceptance*). **b** willingness or ability to tolerate.

ac·cept·ant /akséptənt/ *adj.* (foll. by *of*) willingly accepting.

ac·cep·ta·tion /ákseptáyshən/ *n.* a particular sense, or the generally recognized meaning, of a word or phrase.

ac·cep·tor /akséptər/ *n.* **1** *Commerce* a person who accepts a bill. **2** *Physics* an atom or molecule able to receive an extra electron, esp. an impurity in a semiconductor. **3** *Chem.* a molecule or ion, etc., to which electrons are donated in the formation of a bond. **4** *Electr.* a circuit able to accept a given frequency.

ac·cess /ákses/ *n. & v.* ● *n.* **1** a way of approaching or reaching or entering (*a building with rear access*). **2 a** (often foll. by *to*) the right or opportunity to reach or use or visit; admittance (*has access to secret files*). **b** accessibility. **3** (often foll. by *of*) an attack or outburst (*an access of anger*). ● *v.tr. Computing* gain access to (data, a file, etc.).

ac·ces·si·ble /aksésibəl/ *adj.* (often foll. by *to*) **1** that can readily be reached, entered, or used. **2** (of a person) readily available (esp. to subordinates). **3** (in a form) easy to understand. □□ **ac·ces·si·bil·i·ty** /-bílitee/ *n.* **ac·ces·si·bly** *adv.*

ac·ces·sion /akséshən/ *n. & v.* ● *n.* **1** entering upon an office (esp. the throne) or a condition (as adulthood). **2** (often foll. by *to*) a thing added (e.g., a book to a library). **3** assent; the formal acceptance of a treaty, etc. ● *v.tr.* record the addition of (a new item) to a library or museum.

ac·ces·so·rize /aksésərīz/ *v.tr.* provide (clothing, etc.) with accessories.

ac·ces·so·ry /aksésəree/ *n. & adj.* (also **ac·ces·sa·ry**) ● *n.* (*pl.* **-ies**) **1** an additional or extra thing. **2** (usu. in *pl.*) **a** a small attachment or fitting. **b** a small item of (esp. a woman's) dress (e.g., shoes, gloves, etc.). **3** (often foll. by *to*) a person who helps in or knows the details of an (esp. illegal) act, without taking part in it. ● *adj.* additional; aiding in a minor way; dispensable. □□ **ac·ces·so·ri·al** /áksesáwreeəl/ *adj.*

ac·cess time *n. Computing* the time taken to retrieve data from storage.

ac·ciac·ca·tu·ra /əchaákətŏŏrə/ *n. Mus.* a grace note performed as quickly as possible before an essential note of a melody.

A

A

ac·ci·dence /áksidəns/ *n.* the part of grammar that deals with the variable parts or inflections of words.

ac·ci·dent /áksidənt/ *n.* **1** an event that is without apparent cause, or is unexpected. **2** an unfortunate event, esp. one causing physical harm or damage, brought about unintentionally. **3** occurrence of things by chance; the working of fortune (*accident accounts for much in life*). □ **by accident** unintentionally.

ac·ci·den·tal /áksidént'l/ *adj. & n.* ● *adj.* **1** happening by chance or unexpectedly. **2** not essential to a conception. ● *n.* **1** *Mus.* a sign indicating a departure from the key signature by raising or lowering a note. ▷ NOTATION. **2** something not essential to a conception. □□ **ac·ci·den·tal·ly** *adv.*

ac·ci·dent-prone *adj.* (of a person) subject to frequent accidents.

ac·ci·die /áksidee/ var of ACEDIA.

ac·claim /əkláym/ *v. & n.* ● *v.tr.* **1** praise publicly. **2** (foll. by compl.) hail as (*was acclaimed the winner*). ● *n.* **1** applause; public praise. **2** a shout of acclaim.

ac·cla·ma·tion /ákləmáyshən/ *n.* **1** loud and eager assent. **2** (usu. in *pl.*) shouting in a person's honor. **3** the act or process of acclaiming.

ac·cli·mate /áklimayt, əklímít/ *v.tr.* acclimatize.

ac·cli·ma·tion /ákləmáyshən/ *n.* acclimatization.

ac·cli·ma·tize /əklímətíz/ *v.* **1** *tr.* accustom to a new climate or to new conditions. **2** *intr.* become acclimatized. □□ **ac·cli·ma·ti·za·tion** /-tizáyshən/ *n.*

ac·cliv·i·ty /əklívitee/ *n.* (*pl.* **-ies**) an upward slope. □□ **ac·cliv·i·tous** *adj.*

ac·co·lade /ákəláyd/ *n.* an acknowledgment of merit.

ac·com·mo·date /əkómədayt/ *v.tr.* **1** provide lodging or room for. **2** adapt; harmonize; reconcile. **3** do a service or favor to.

ac·com·mo·dat·ing /əkómədayting/ *adj.* obliging; compliant. □□ **ac·com·mo·dat·ing·ly** *adv.*

ac·com·mo·da·tion /əkómədáyshən/ *n.* **1** (in *pl.*) lodgings; a place to live. **2 a** an adjustment or adaptation to suit a special or different purpose. **b** a convenient arrangement; a settlement or compromise.

ac·com·mo·da·tion lad·der *n.* a ladder up the side of a ship for access to or from a small boat.

ac·com·pa·ni·ment /əkúmpəniment/ *n.* **1** *Mus.* an instrumental part supporting a solo instrument, voice, or group. **2** an accompanying thing.

ac·com·pa·nist /əkúmpənist/ *n.* (also **ac·com·pa·ny·ist** /-nee-ist/) a person who provides a musical accompaniment.

ac·com·pa·ny /əkúmpənee/ *v.tr.* (**-ies, -ied**) **1** go with; escort. **2** (usu. in *passive*; foll. by *with, by*) be done or found with; supplement. **3** *Mus.* support with accompaniment.

ac·com·plice /əkómplis, əkúm-/ *n.* a partner or helper, esp. in a crime.

ac·com·plish /əkómplish/ *v.tr.* perform; complete; succeed in doing.

ac·com·plished /əkómplisht/ *adj.* clever; skilled; well trained or educated.

ac·com·plish·ment /əkómplishmənt/ *n.* **1** the fulfillment or completion (of a task, etc.). **2** an acquired skill, esp. a social one. **3** a thing done or achieved.

ac·cord /əkáwrd/ *v. & n.* ● *v.* **1** *intr.* (often foll. by *with*) (esp. of a thing) be in harmony; be consistent. **2** *tr.* **a** grant (permission, a request, etc.). **b** give (a welcome, etc.). ● *n.* **1** agreement; consent. **2** harmonious correspondence in pitch, tone, color, etc. □ **of one's own accord** on one's own initiative; voluntarily. **with one accord** unanimously.

ac·cord·ance /əkáwrd'ns/ *n.* harmony; agreement. □ **in accordance with** in a manner corresponding to (*we acted in accordance with your wishes*).

ac·cord·ant /əkáwrd'nt/ *adj.* (often foll. by *with*) in tune; agreeing.

ac·cord·ing /əkáwrding/ *adv.* (foll. by *to*) **1** as stated by or in (*according to my sister*). **2** in a manner corresponding to; in proportion to (*he lives according to his principles*).

ac·cord·ing·ly /əkáwrdinglee/ *adv.* **1** as suggested or required by the (stated) circumstances. **2** consequently; therefore.

ac·cor·di·on /əkáwrdeeən/ *n.* ▼ a portable musical instrument with reeds blown by bellows and played by means of keys and buttons. □□ **ac·cor·di·on·ist** *n.*

keyboard   carrying straps

bellows

sound grill   bass and chord buttons

ACCORDION: 20TH-CENTURY
ITALIAN ACCORDION

ac·cost /əkáwst, əkóst/ *v.tr.* approach and address (a person), esp. boldly.

ac·couche·ment /ákōoshmón/ *n.* **1** childbirth. **2** the period of childbirth.

ac·count /əkównt/ *n. & v.* ● *n.* **1** a narration or description. **2 a** an arrangement or facility at a bank, etc., for commercial or financial transactions, esp. for depositing and withdrawing money. **b** an arrangement at a store for buying goods on credit. **3 a** (often in *pl.*) a record or statement of money, goods, or services received or expended, with the balance. **b** (in *pl.*) the practice of accounting (*is good at accounts*). ● *v.tr.* (foll. by *to be* or compl.) consider; regard as (*account him wise; account him to be guilty*). □ **account for 1** serve as or provide an explanation or reason for (*that accounts for their misbehavior*). **2 a** give a reckoning of or answer for (money, etc., entrusted). **b** answer for (one's conduct). **3** succeed in killing, destroying, or defeating. **4** make up a specified amount or proportion of (*rent accounts for 50 percent of expenditures*). **by all accounts** in everyone's opinion. **call to account** require an explanation from (a person). **give a good** (or **bad**) **account of oneself** make a favorable (or unfavorable) impression. **keep account of** keep a record of; follow closely. **leave out of account** fail or decline to consider. **of no account** unimportant. **of some account** important. **on account 1** (of goods or services) to be paid for later. **2** (of money) in part payment. **on account of** because of. **on no account** under no circumstances; certainly not. **on one's own account** for one's own purposes; at one's own risk. **take account of** (or **take into account**) consider along with other factors (*took their age into account*). **turn to good account** turn to one's advantage.

ac·count·a·ble /əkówntəbəl/ *adj.* responsible; required to account for one's conduct (*accountable for one's actions*). □□ **ac·count·a·bil·i·ty** /-bílitee/ *n.* **ac·count·a·bly** *adv.*

ac·count·an·cy /əkównt'nsee/ *n.* the profession or duties of an accountant.

ac·count·ant /əkównt'nt/ *n.* a professional keeper or inspector of accounts.

ac·count·ing /əkównting/ *n.* the process of or skill in keeping accounts.

ac·cou·ter /əkōotər/ *v.tr.* (also **ac·cou·ter**) (usu. as **accoutred** *adj.*) attire, equip.

ac·cou·tre·ment /əkōotrəmənt, -tərmənt/ *n.* (also **ac·cou·ter·ment** /-tərmənt/) (usu. in *pl.*) **1** equipment; trappings. **2** *Mil.* a soldier's outfit other than weapons and garments.

ac·cred·it /əkrédit/ *v.tr.* (**accredited, accrediting**) **1** (foll. by *to*) attribute (a saying, etc.) to (a person). **2** (foll. by *with*) credit (a person) with (a saying, etc.). **3** (usu. foll. by *to* or *at*) send (an ambassador, etc.) with credentials. □□ **ac·cred·i·ta·tion** /-táyshən/ *n.*

ac·cred·it·ed /əkréditid/ *adj.* (of a person or organization) officially recognized.

ac·crete /əkréet/ *v.* **1** *intr.* grow together or into one. **2** *intr.* (often foll. by *to*) form around or on, as around a nucleus. **3** *tr.* attract (such additions).

ac·cre·tion /əkréeshən/ *n.* **1** growth by organic enlargement. **2 a** the growing of separate things into one. **b** the product of such growing. **3** extraneous matter added to anything. □□ **ac·cre·tive** *adj.*

ac·crue /əkrōo/ *v.intr.* (**accrues, accrued, accruing**) (often foll. by *to*) come as a natural increase or advantage, esp. financial. □□ **ac·cru·al** *n.* **ac·crued** *adj.*

ac·cul·tur·ate /əkúlchərayt/ *v.* **1** *intr.* adapt to or adopt a different culture. **2** *tr.* cause to do this. □□ **ac·cul·tur·a·tion** /-ráyshən/ *n.* **ac·cul·tur·a·tive** /-rətiv/ *adj.*

ac·cu·mu·late /əkyōomyəlayt/ *v.* **1** *tr.* **a** acquire an increasing number or quantity of. **b** produce or acquire (a resulting whole) in this way. **2** *intr.* grow numerous or considerable; form an increasing mass or quantity.

ac·cu·mu·la·tion /əkyōomyəláyshən/ *n.* **1** the act or process of accumulating or being accumulated. **2** an accumulated mass. **3** the growth of capital by continued interest.

ac·cu·mu·la·tive /əkyōomyəlaytiv, -lətiv/ *adj.* **1** arising from accumulation; cumulative (*accumulative evidence*). **2** arranged so as to accumulate. **3** acquisitive; given to hoarding.

ac·cu·mu·la·tor /əkyōomyəlaytər/ *n.* a person who accumulates things.

ac·cu·ra·cy /ákyərəsee/ *n.* exactness or precision, esp. arising from careful effort.

ac·cu·rate /ákyərət/ *adj.* **1** careful; precise; lacking errors. **2** conforming exactly with a qualitative standard. □□ **ac·cu·rate·ly** *adv.*

ac·curs·ed /əkársid, əkárst/ *adj.* (*archaic* **accurst** /əkúrst/) **1** being under a curse; ill-fated. **2** *colloq.* detestable; annoying.

ac·cu·sal /əkyōozəl/ *n.* accusation.

ac·cu·sa·tion /ákyəzáyshən/ *n.* **1** the act or process of accusing or being accused. **2** a statement charging a person with an offense or crime.

ac·cu·sa·tive /əkyōozətiv/ *n. & adj. Gram.* ● *n.* the case of nouns, pronouns, and adjectives expressing the object of an action or the goal of motion. ● *adj.* of or in this case.

ac·cu·sa·to·ri·al /əkyōozətáwreeəl/ *adj. Law* (of proceedings) involving accusation by a prosecutor and a verdict reached by an impartial judge or jury.

ac·cu·sa·to·ry /əkyōozətawree/ *adj.* of or implying accusation.

ac·cuse /əkyōoz/ *v.tr.* **1** (foll. by *of*) charge (a person, etc.) with a fault or crime; indict (*accused them of murder*). **2** lay the blame on. □□ **ac·cus·er** *n.* **ac·cus·ing·ly** *adv.*

ac·cus·tom /əkústəm/ *v.tr. & refl.* (foll. by *to*) make (a person or thing or oneself) used to (*the army accustomed him to discipline*).

ac·cus·tomed /əkústəmd/ *adj.* **1** (foll. by *to*) used to. **2** customary.

ACE: PLAYING
CARD ACES

AC/DC *adj.* **1** alternating current/
direct current. ▷ ALTERNATING CUR-
RENT, CIRCUIT **2** *colloq.* bisexual.

ace /ays/ *n. & adj.* ● *n.* **1** ◄ a playing card, domino, etc., with a single
spot and generally having the value
"one" or in card games the highest
value in each suit. **2 a** a person who
excels in some activity. **b** *Mil.* a pilot
who has shot down many enemy
aircraft. **3** (in tennis) a service too
good for the opponent to touch.
4 *Golf* a hole in one. ● *adj. sl.* excellent. □ **within
an ace of** on the verge of.

a·cel·lu·lar /aysélyoolər/ *adj. Biol.* **1** having no
cells; not consisting of cells. **2** (esp. of protozoa)
consisting of one cell only; unicellular.

a·ceph·a·lous /əséfələs, əkéf-/ *adj.* **1** headless.
2 *Zool.* ◄ having no part of the body
specially organized as a head.

a·cer·bic /əsérbik/ *adj.* **1** astrin-
gently sour. **2** bitter in
speech, manner, or
temper. □□ **a·cer·bi·
cal·ly** *adv.* **a·cer·bi·ty**
n. (*pl.* **-ies**).

ac·e·tab·u·lum /ásitábyoo-
ləm/ *n.* (*pl.* **acetabulums**
or **acetabula** /-lə/) *Zool.*
1 the socket for the head
of the thighbone, or of
the leg in insects. **2** a cup-
shaped sucker of various
organisms, including tapeworms and cuttlefish.

ACEPHALOUS ORGANISM
(STARFISH)

a·cet·a·min·o·phen /əseetəmínəfən/ *n.* a crystalline substance, $C_8H_9NO_2$, that is used medically to
reduce fever and relieve pain.

ac·e·tate /ásitayt/ *n.* **1** a salt or ester of acetic acid,
esp. the cellulose ester used to make textiles,
phonograph records, etc. **2** a fabric made from
cellulose acetate.

a·ce·tic /əséetik/ *adj.* of or like vinegar.

a·ce·tic ac·id *n.* the clear liquid acid that gives vinegar its characteristic taste.

ac·e·tone /ásitōn/ *n.* a colorless, volatile liquid
ketone valuable as a solvent of organic compounds,
esp. paints, varnishes, etc. Also called **propanone**.

a·ce·tous /ásitəs, əsée-/ *adj.* **1** having the qualities
of vinegar. **2** producing vinegar. **3** sour.

a·ce·tyl /ásitil, -tīl/ *n. Chem.* the univalent radical of
acetic acid.

ACID RAIN

The clouds that produce acid rain are
formed when polluting gases, such as
sulfur dioxide and nitrogen oxide,
combine with oxygen and moisture
in the air. The resultant
precipitation – acid rain –
is a dilute mixture
of sulfuric acid
and nitric acid.
Acid rain causes
damage to forests,
and hastens the
erosion of many
ancient buildings
and sculptures.

FORMATION
OF ACID RAIN

polluted cloud

*acidic
rainfall*

*nitrogen oxide from
industry emissions*

*sulfur dioxide
from the burning
of fossil fuels*

*nitrogen
oxide emissions
from vehicles*

a·ce·tyl·cho·line /ásitilkóleen, ásitīl-/ *n.* a compound
serving to transmit impulses from nerve fibers.

a·cet·y·lene /əsétileen/ *n.* a colorless hydrocarbon
gas, burning with a bright flame, used esp. in
welding. ▷ UNSATURATED

a·ce·tyl·sal·i·cyl·ic ac·id /ásitīlsálisílik/ *n.* = ASPIRIN.

A·chae·an /əkéeən/ *adj. & n.* ● *adj.* **1** of or relating
to Achaea in ancient Greece. **2** *literary* Greek. ● *n.*
1 an inhabitant of Achaea. **2** *literary* a Greek.

ache /ayk/ *n. & v.* ● *n.* **1** a continuous or prolonged
dull pain. **2** mental distress. ● *v.intr.* **1** suffer from or
be the source of an ache (*I ached all over; my left leg
ached*). **2** (foll. by *to* + infin.) desire greatly. □□ **ach·
ing·ly** *adv.*

a·chene /əkéen/ *n. Bot.* a small, dry, one-seeded
fruit that does not open to liberate the seed (e.g., a
strawberry pip).

A·cheu·li·an /əshóolien/ *adj. & n.* (also **Acheulean**)
● *adj.* of the Paleolithic period in Europe, etc.,
following the Abbevillian and preceding the Mous-
terian. ● *n.* the culture of this period.

a·chieve /əchéev/ *v.tr.* **1 a** reach or attain by effort
(*achieved victory*). **b** acquire; gain; earn (*achieved notoriety*). **2** accomplish or carry out (a feat or task).

3 *absol.* be successful; attain a desired level of performance. □□ **a·chiev·a·ble** *adj.* **a·chiev·er** *n.*

a·chieve·ment /əchéevmənt/ *n.* **1** something
achieved; an instance of achieving. **2** the act of
achieving.

A·chil·les heel /əkíleez/ *n.* a person's weak or
vulnerable point.

A·chil·les ten·don /əkíleez/
n. ► the tendon connecting
the heel with the calf
muscles. ▷ MUSCULATURE

ach·ro·mat /ákrōmat/ *n.* a
lens made achromatic by
correction.

ach·ro·mat·ic /ákrōmátik/
adj. Optics **1** that transmits
light without separating
it into constituent colors
(*achromatic lens*). **2** without
color (*achromatic fringe*).
□□ **ach·ro·mat·i·cal·ly** *adv.*
a·chro·ma·tism /əkrṓ-
mətizəm/ *n.*

ach·y /áykee/ *adj.* (**achier**,
achiest) full of or
suffering from aches.

ac·id /ásid/ *n. &
adj.* ● *n.* **1** *Chem.* ◄
any of a class of
substances that liberate hydrogen ions in water, are
usu. sour and corrosive, turn litmus red, and have a
pH of less than 7. ▷ ACID RAIN, PH. **2** (in general use)
any sour substance. **3** *sl.* the drug LSD. ● *adj.*
1 sharp-tasting; sour. **2** biting; sharp (*an acid wit*).
3 *Chem.* having the essential properties of an acid.
4 (of a color) intense; bright. □□ **a·cid·ic** /əsídik/
adj. **a·cid·i·ty** /əsídimitree/ *n.* **a·cid·ly** *adv.*

ac·id·head /ásidhed/ *n. sl.* a user of the drug LSD.

a·cid·i·fy /əsídifī/ *v.tr. & intr.* (**-ies, -ied**) make or
become acid. □□ **a·cid·i·fi·ca·tion** /-fikáyshən/ *n.*

a·cid·i·ty /əsíditee/ *n.* (*pl.* **-ies**) an acid quality or
state, esp. an excessively acid condition of the
stomach.

ac·id jazz *n.* a kind of dance music incorporating
elements of jazz, funk, soul, and hip hop.

ac·i·do·sis /ásidósis/ *n.* an overacid condition of
the body fluids or tissues.

ac·id rain *n.* ▲ acid formed in the atmosphere,
esp. from industrial waste gases, and falling with
rain.

ac·id test *n.* **1** a severe or conclusive test. **2** a test in
which acid is used to test for gold, etc.

a·cid·u·lous /əsídyooləs/ *adj.* somewhat acid.

calf

*Achilles
tendon*

heel

ACHILLES
TENDON

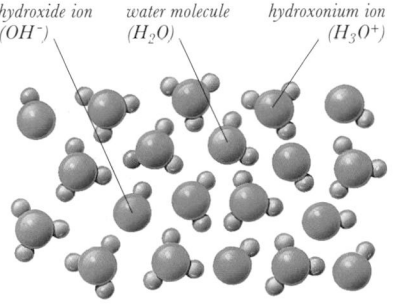

ACID

In chemistry, an acid is a water-soluble
substance capable of donating protons
(hydrogen ions, H^+) when dissolved in
water. The protons attach to water molecules
(H_2O) to produce hydroxonium ions (H_3O^+).

In neutral water, there are equal numbers
of hydroxonium ions and hydroxide ions
(OH^-), but in an acid solution there are
more hydroxonium ions. The greater
their concentration, the stronger the acid.

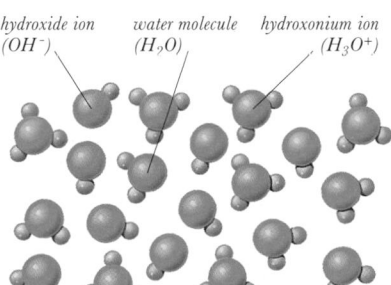

*hydroxide ion
(OH^-)*   *water molecule
(H_2O)*   *hydroxonium ion
(H_3O^+)*

*hydroxide ion
(OH^-)*   *water molecule
(H_2O)*   *hydroxonium ion
(H_3O^+)*

MOLECULES AND IONS
IN NEUTRAL WATER

MOLECULES AND IONS
IN AN ACIDIC SOLUTION

A

ac·i·nus /ásinəs/ n. (pl. **acini** /-nī/) **1** any of the small elements that make up a compound fruit of the blackberry, raspberry, etc. **2** the seed of a grape or berry. **3** *Anat.* **a** any multicellular gland with saclike secreting ducts. **b** the terminus of a duct in such a gland.

ack-ack /ákák/ adj. & n. colloq. ● adj. antiaircraft. ● n. an antiaircraft gun.

ackee var. of ACKEE.

ac·knowl·edge /əknólij/ v.tr. **1 a** recognize; accept. **b** (often foll. by *to be* + compl.) recognize as. **c** (often foll. by *that* + clause or *to* + infin.) admit that something is so. **2** confirm the receipt of. **3 a** show that one has noticed. **b** express appreciation of (a service, etc.). □□ **ac·knowl·edge·a·ble** adj.

ac·knowl·edg·ment /əknólijmənt/ n. (also **ac·knowl·edge·ment**) **1** the act or an instance of acknowledging. **2 a** a thing given or done in return for a service, etc. **b** a letter confirming receipt of something. **3** (usu. in pl.) an author's statement of indebtedness to others.

ACLU abbr. American Civil Liberties Union.

ac·me /ákmee/ n. the highest point or period; the peak of perfection.

ac·ne /áknee/ n. a skin condition characterized by red pimples. □□ **ac·ned** adj.

ac·o·lyte /ákəlīt/ n. **1** a person assisting a priest. **2** an assistant; a beginner.

ac·o·nite /ákənīt/ n. **1 a** any poisonous plant of the genus *Aconitum*. **b** the drug obtained from this. Also called **aconitine**. **2** (in full **winter aconite**) any ranunculaceous plant of the genus *Eranthis*, with yellow flowers.

a·con·i·tine /əkóniteen/ n. *Pharm.* a poisonous alkaloid obtained from the aconite plant.

a·corn /áykorn/ n. the fruit of the oak, a smooth nut in a rough cuplike base. ▷ OAK

a·cot·y·le·don /əkótileéd'n/ n. a plant with no distinct seed leaves. □□ **a·cot·y·le·don·ous** adj.

a·cous·tic /əko͞ostik/ adj. & n. ● adj. **1** relating to sound or hearing. **2** ▼ (of a musical instrument or recording) not having electrical amplification. **3** (of building materials) used for soundproofing. ● n. **1** (usu. in pl.) the properties or qualities (esp. of a room or hall) in transmitting sound. **2** (in pl.; usu. treated as sing.) the science of sound. □□ **a·cous·ti·cal** adj. **a·cous·ti·cal·ly** adv.

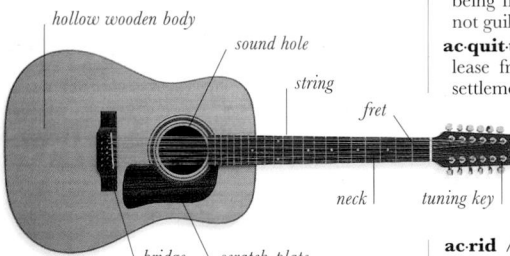

hollow wooden body

sound hole

string

fret

neck *tuning key*

bridge *scratch-plate*

ACOUSTIC GUITAR

a·cous·tic cou·pler n. *Computing* a modem that converts digital signals into audible signals and vice versa.

ac·ous·ti·cian /ákoostíshən/ n. an expert in acoustics.

ac·quaint /əkwáynt/ v.tr. & refl. (usu. foll. by *with*) make (a person or oneself) familiar with. □ **be acquainted with** have personal knowledge of.

ac·quaint·ance /əkwáyntəns/ n. **1** (usu. foll. by *with*) slight knowledge. **2** the fact of being acquainted. **3** a person one knows slightly. □ **make a person's acquaintance** first meet another person. □□ **ac·quaint·ance·ship** n.

ac·qui·esce /ákwee-és/ v.intr. **1** agree, esp. tacitly. **2** (foll. by *in*) accept (an arrangement, etc.). □□ **ac·qui·es·cence** n. **ac·qui·es·cent** adj.

ac·quire /əkwír/ v.tr. **1** gain by and for oneself; obtain. **2** come into possession of. □□ **ac·quir·a·ble** adj.

ac·quired char·ac·ter·is·tic n. *Biol.* a characteristic caused by the environment, not inherited.

ac·quired im·mune de·fi·cien·cy syn·drome n. *Med.* see AIDS.

ac·quired taste n. **1** a liking gained by experience. **2** the object of such a liking.

ac·quire·ment /əkwírmənt/ n. **1** something acquired, esp. a mental attainment. **2** the act or an instance of acquiring.

ac·qui·si·tion /ákwizishən/ n. **1** something acquired, esp. if regarded as useful. **2** the act or an instance of acquiring.

ac·quis·i·tive /əkwízitiv/ adj. eager to acquire things. □□ **ac·quis·i·tive·ly** adv. **ac·quis·i·tive·ness** n.

ac·quit /əkwít/ v. (**acquitted, acquitting**) **1** tr. (often foll. by *of*) declare (a person) not guilty. **2** refl. **a** conduct oneself in a specified way (*we acquitted ourselves well*). **b** (foll. by *of*) discharge (a duty or responsibility).

ac·quit·tal /əkwít'l/ n. **1** the process of freeing or being freed from a charge, esp. by a judgment of not guilty. **2** performance of a duty.

ac·quit·tance /əkwít'ns/ n. **1** payment of or release from a debt. **2** a written receipt attesting settlement of a debt.

a·cre /áykər/ n. **1** a measure of land, 4,840 sq. yds., 4,047 sq. m. **2** (in pl.) a large area. □□ **a·cred** adj. (also in comb.).

a·cre·age /áykərij, áykrij/ n. **1** a number of acres. **2** an extent of land.

ac·rid /ákrid/ adj. (**acrider, acridest**) **1** bitterly pungent; irritating; corrosive. **2** bitter in temper or manner. □□ **a·crid·i·ty** /-ríditee/ n. **ac·rid·ly** adv.

ac·ri·mo·ni·ous /ákrimóneeəs/ adj. bitter in manner or temper. □□ **ac·ri·mo·ni·ous·ly** adv.

ac·ri·mo·ny /ákrimónee/ n. (pl. **-ies**) bitterness of temper or manner; ill feeling.

ac·ro·bat /ákrəbat/ n. a performer of spectacular gymnastic feats. □□ **ac·ro·bat·ic** /-bátik/ adj. **ac·ro·bat·i·cal·ly** adv.

ac·ro·bat·ics /ákrəbátiks/ n.pl. **1** acrobatic feats. **2** (as sing.) the art of performing these. **3** a skill requiring ingenuity (*mental acrobatics*).

ac·ro·gen /ákrəjən/ n. *Bot.* any nonflowering plant having a perennial stem with the growing point at its apex, e.g., a fern or moss. □□ **a·crog·e·nous** /əkrójinəs/ adj.

ac·ro·meg·a·ly /ákrəmégəlee/ n. *Med.* the abnormal growth of the hands, feet, and face, caused by excessive activity of the pituitary gland. □□ **ac·ro·meg·al·ic** /-migálik/ adj.

ac·ro·nym /ákrənim/ n. a word, usu. pronounced as such, formed from the initial letters of other words (e.g., *laser, NATO*).

a·crop·e·tal /əkrópit'l/ adj. *Bot.* developing from below upwards. □□ **a·crop·e·tal·ly** adv.

ac·ro·pho·bi·a /ákrəfóbeeə/ n. *Psychol.* an abnormal dread of heights. □□ **ac·ro·pho·bic** /-fóbik/ adj.

a·crop·o·lis /əkrópəlis/ n. ▲ a citadel of an ancient Greek city.

a·cross /əkráws, əkrós/ prep. & adv. ● prep. **1** to or on the other side of (*lives across the river*). **2** from one side to another side of (*a bridge across the river*). **3** at or forming an angle (esp. a right angle) with (*deep cuts across his legs*). ● adv. **1** to or on the other side (*ran across*). **2** from one side to another (*a blanket stretched across*). **3** forming a cross (*with cuts across*). **4** (of a crossword clue or answer) read horizontally. □ **across the board** applying to all.

a·cros·tic /əkráwstik, əkrós-/ n. **1** a poem in which certain letters in each line form a word or words. **2** a word puzzle constructed in this way.

a·cryl·ic /əkrílik/ adj. & n. ● adj. **1** made with a synthetic polymer derived from acrylic acid. **2** *Chem.* of or derived from acrylic acid. ● n. an acrylic fiber.

a·cryl·ic ac·id n. a pungent liquid organic acid.

ACT abbr. American College Test.

act /akt/ n. & v. ● n. **1** something done; an action. **2** the process of doing something (*caught in the act*). **3 a** a piece of entertainment. **b** the performer(s) of this. **4** a pretense (*it was all an act*). **5** a main division of a play or opera. **6 a** a written ordinance of a legislative body. **b** a document attesting a legal transaction. **7** (often in pl.) the recorded decisions or proceedings of a committee, etc. **8** (**Acts**) (in full **Acts of the Apostles**) the New Testament book relating the growth of the early Church. ● v. **1** intr. behave. **2** intr. perform actions or functions; take action (*act as referee; we must act quickly*). **3** intr. (also foll. by *on*) exert energy or influence (*alcohol acts on the brain*). **4** intr. **a** perform a part in a play, movie, etc. **b** pretend. **5** tr. **a** perform the part of (*acts the fool*). **b** perform (a play, etc.). **c** portray (an incident) by actions. **d** feign. □ **act for** be the representative of. **act out 1** translate (ideas, etc.) into action. **2** *Psychol.* represent (one's subconscious desires, etc.) in action. **act up** colloq. misbehave; give trouble. **get one's act together** sl. become properly organized. **get in on the act** sl. become a participant (esp. for profit). **put on an act** colloq. carry out a pretense.

act·ing /ákting/ n. & attrib. adj. ● n. **1** the art or occupation of performing parts in plays, movies, etc. **2** in senses of ACT v. ● attrib.adj. serving temporarily or on behalf of another or others (*acting manager; Acting President*).

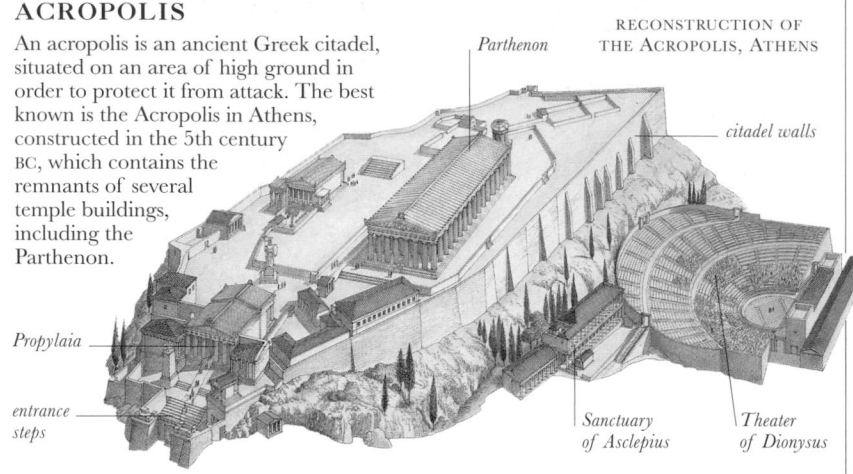

ACROPOLIS

An acropolis is an ancient Greek citadel, situated on an area of high ground in order to protect it from attack. The best known is the Acropolis in Athens, constructed in the 5th century BC, which contains the remnants of several temple buildings, including the Parthenon.

RECONSTRUCTION OF THE ACROPOLIS, ATHENS

Parthenon

citadel walls

Propylaia

entrance steps

Sanctuary of Asclepius

Theater of Dionysus

ac·ti·nide /áktinīd/ *n. Chem.* any of the series of 15 radioactive elements having increasing atomic numbers from actinium to lawrencium.

ac·tin·ism /áktinizəm/ *n.* the property of short-wave radiation that produces chemical changes, as in photography. □□ **ac·tin·ic** /aktínik/ *adj.*

ac·tin·i·um /aktíneeəm/ *n. Chem.* a radioactive metallic element of the actinide series, occurring naturally in pitchblende. ¶ Symb.: **Ac.**

ac·ti·nom·e·ter /áktinómitər/ *n.* an instrument for measuring the intensity of radiation, esp. ultraviolet radiation.

ac·tin·o·mor·phic /áktinəmáwrfik/ *adj. Biol.* radially symmetrical.

ac·tion /ákshən/ *n. & v.* ● *n.* **1** the fact or process of doing or acting (*demanded action; put ideas into action*). **2** forcefulness or energy as a characteristic (*a woman of action*). **3** the exertion of energy or influence (*the action of acid on metal*). **4** something done; a deed or act (*not aware of his own actions*). **5 a** a series of events represented in a story, play, etc. **b** *sl.* exciting activity (*arrived late and missed the action; want some action*). **6 a** armed conflict; fighting (*killed in action*). **b** an occurrence of this, esp. a minor military engagement. **7 a** the way in which a machine, instrument, etc., works (*explain the action of an air pump*). **b** the mechanism that makes a machine, instrument, etc. (e.g., a musical instrument, a gun, etc.), work. **c** the mode or style of movement of an animal or human (usu. described in some way) (*a runner with good action*). **8** a legal process; a lawsuit (*bring an action*). **9** (in *imper.*) a word of command to begin, esp. used by a film director, etc. ● *v.tr.* bring a legal action against. □ **out of action** not working. **take action** begin to act (esp. energetically in protest).

ac·tion·a·ble /ákshənəbəl/ *adj.* giving cause for legal action.

act·ion-packed *adj.* full of action or excitement.

ac·tion paint·ing *n.* ► an aspect of abstract expressionism with paint applied by the artist's random or spontaneous gestures.

ac·ti·vate /áktivayt/ *v.tr.* **1** make active; bring into action. **2** *Chem.* cause reaction in; excite (a substance, molecules, etc.). **3** *Physics* make radioactive. □□ **ac·ti·va·tion** /-váyshən/ *n.* **ac·ti·va·tor** *n.*

ac·ti·vat·ed car·bon *n.* carbon, esp. charcoal, treated to increase its adsorptive power.

ac·tive /áktiv/ *adj. & n.* ● *adj.* **1 a** consisting in or marked by action; energetic; diligent (*leads an active life*). **b** able to move about or accomplish practical tasks. **2** working. **3** originating action; not merely passive (*active support*). **4** radioactive. **5** *Gram.* designating the voice that attributes the action of a verb to the person or thing from which it logically proceeds (e.g., of the verbs in *guns kill; we saw him*). ● *n. Gram.* the active form or voice of a verb. □□ **ac·tive·ly** *adv.* **ac·tive·ness** *n.*

ac·tive car·bon *n.* = ACTIVATED CARBON.

ac·tive serv·ice *n.* service in the armed forces during a war.

ac·tiv·ism /áktivizəm/ *n.* a policy of vigorous action in a cause, esp. in politics. □□ **ac·tiv·ist** *n.*

ac·tiv·i·ty /aktívitee/ *n.* (*pl.* **-ies**) **1 a** the condition of being active or moving about. **b** the exertion of energy. **2** (often in *pl.*) a particular occupation or pursuit (*outdoor activities*). **3** = RADIOACTIVITY.

act of God *n.* the operation of uncontrollable natural forces.

ac·tor /áktər/ *n.* **1** the performer of a part in a play, movie, etc. **2** a person whose profession is performing such parts.

ac·tress /áktris/ *n.* a female actor.

ac·tu·al /ákchōoəl/ *adj.* (usu. *attrib.*) **1** existing in fact; real (often as distinct from ideal). **2** existing now. ¶ Redundant use, as in *tell me the actual facts*, is *disp.*, but common. □□ **ac·tu·al·ize** *v.tr.* **ac·tu·al·i·za·tion** /-lizáyshən/ *n.*

ac·tu·al·i·ty /ákchōo-álitee/ *n.* (*pl.* **-ies**) **1** reality. **2** (in *pl.*) existing conditions.

ac·tu·al·ly /ákchōoəlee/ *adv.* **1** as a fact; really

ACTION PAINTING

A method of painting that originated in the US during the 1940s, action painting is associated with a wider artistic movement called abstract expressionism. Artists producing action paintings intended their works to be a record of the act of painting itself, to the exclusion of all other subject matter.

The paintings are often extremely vibrant, conveying the spontaneity and impulsiveness of their creation. This is best exemplified in the work of Jackson Pollock, whose paintings clearly show the energetic gestures of the artist, who splashed, dripped, flicked, and threw paint onto the canvas.

Convergence (1952), JACKSON POLLOCK

TIMELINE
1500 1550 1600 1650 1700 1750 1800 1850 1900 1950 2000

(*I asked for ten, but actually got nine*). **2** as a matter of fact; even (strange as it may seem) (*he actually refused!*). **3** at present; for the time being.

ac·tu·ar·y /ákchōoeree/ *n.* (*pl.* **-ies**) an expert in statistics, esp. one who calculates insurance risks. □□ **ac·tu·ar·i·al** /-chōoáireeəl/ *adj.* **ac·tu·ar·i·al·ly** *adv.*

ac·tu·ate /ákchōo-ayt/ *v.tr.* **1** communicate motion to (a machine, etc.). **2** cause the operation of (an electrical device, etc.). **3** cause (a person) to act. □□ **ac·tu·a·tion** /-áyshən/ *n.* **ac·tu·a·tor** *n.*

a·cu·i·ty /əkyōoitee/ *n.* sharpness; acuteness (of a needle, understanding).

a·cu·le·ate /əkyōoleeət, -ayt/ *adj.* **1** *Zool.* having a sting. **2** *Bot.* prickly. **3** pointed; incisive.

a·cu·men /ákyəmən, əkyōo-/ *n.* keen insight or discernment; penetration.

a·cu·mi·nate /əkyōominət, -nayt/ *adj. Biol.* tapering to a point.

ac·u·pres·sure /ákyəpreshər/ *n.* a form of therapy in which symptoms are relieved by applying pressure with the fingers to specific points on the body.

ac·u·punc·ture /ákyəpungkchər/ *n.* a method (orig. Chinese) of treating various conditions by pricking the skin or tissues with needles. □□ **ac·u·punc·tur·ist** *n.*

a·cut·ance /əkyōot'ns/ *n.* sharpness of a photographic or printed image; a measure of this.

a·cute /əkyōot/ *adj. & n.* ● *adj.* (**acuter**, **acutest**) **1 a** (of senses, etc.) keen; penetrating. **b** (of pain) intense; severe; sharp or stabbing rather than dull, aching, or throbbing. **2** shrewd; perceptive (*an acute critic*). **3** (of a disease) coming sharply to a crisis; severe. **4** (of a difficulty or controversy) critical; serious. **5 a** (of an angle) less than 90°. ▷ TRIANGLE. **b** sharp; pointed. **6** (of a sound) shrill. ● *n.* = ACUTE ACCENT. □□ **a·cute·ly** *adv.* **a·cute·ness** *n.*

a·cute ac·cent *n.* a mark (´) placed over letters in some languages to show quality, vowel length, pronunciation (e.g., *maté*), etc.

ac·yl /ásil/ *n. Chem.* the univalent radical of an organic acid.

AD *abbr.* (of a date) of the Christian era. ¶ Strictly, AD should precede a date (e.g., AD 410), but uses such as *the tenth century AD* are well established.

ad /ad/ *n. colloq.* an advertisement.

ad·age /ádij/ *n.* a traditional maxim; a proverb.

a·da·gio /ədaázheeō/ *adv., adj., & n. Mus.* ● *adv. & adj.* in slow time. ● *n.* (*pl.* **-os**) an adagio movement or passage.

Ad·am /ádəm/ *n.* the first man, in the biblical and Koranic traditions. □ **not know a person from Adam** be unable to recognize the person in question.

ad·a·mant /ádəmənt/ *adj. & n.* ● *adj.* stubbornly resolute; resistant to persuasion. ● *n. archaic* diamond or other hard substance. □□ **ad·a·mance** *n.* **ad·a·man·tine** /-mántīn/ *adj.* **ad·a·mant·ly** *adv.*

Ad·am's ap·ple *n.* ▼ a projection of the thyroid cartilage of the larynx.

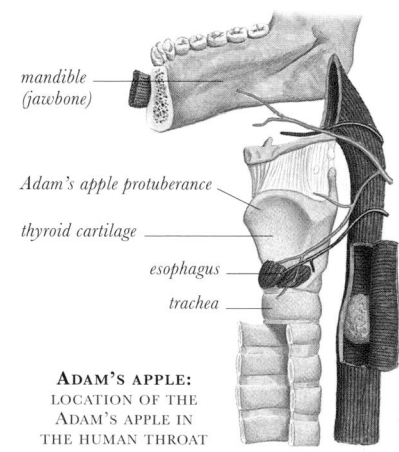

mandible (jawbone)

Adam's apple protuberance

thyroid cartilage

esophagus

trachea

ADAM'S APPLE: LOCATION OF THE ADAM'S APPLE IN THE HUMAN THROAT

A

a·dapt /ədápt/ v. **1** tr. **a** (foll. by to) fit; adjust (one thing to another). **b** (foll. by to, for) make suitable for a purpose. **c** alter or modify (esp. a text). **2** intr. & refl. (usu. foll. by to) become adjusted to new conditions. □□ **a·dap·tive** adj.

a·dapt·a·ble /ədáptəbəl/ adj. **1** able to adapt oneself to new conditions. **2** that can be adapted. □□ **a·dapt·a·bil·i·ty** /-bílitee/ n. **a·dapt·a·bly** adv.

ad·ap·ta·tion /ádaptáyshən/ n. **1** the act or process of adapting or being adapted. **2** a thing that has been adapted.

a·dapt·er /ədáptər/ n. (also **a·dap·tor**) **1** a device for making equipment compatible. **2** a person who adapts.

ad·ax·i·al /adákseeəl/ adj. Bot. facing toward the stem of a plant, esp. of the upper side of a leaf (cf. ABAXIAL).

ADD abbr. attention deficit disorder.

add /ad/ v.tr. **1** join (one thing to another) as an increase or supplement. **2** put together (numbers) to find their combined value. **3** say in addition. □ **add in** include. **add to** increase (this adds to our difficulties). **add-on** something added to an existing object or quantity. **add up 1** find the total of. **2** (foll. by to) amount to (adds up to a disaster). **3** colloq. make sense. □□ **add·ed** adj.

ad·den·dum /ədéndəm/ n. (pl. **addenda** /-də/) a thing (usu. something omitted) to be added, esp. (in pl.) as additional matter at the end of a book.

ad·der /ádər/ n. **1** any of various small venomous snakes, esp. the common European viper, *Vipera berus*. **2** any of various small N. American snakes similar to the viper.

ad·dict v. & n. ● v.tr. & refl. /ədíkt/ (usu. foll. by to) devote or apply habitually or compulsively; make addicted. ● n. /ádikt/ **1** a person addicted to a substance or a habit (drug addict). **2** colloq. an enthusiastic devotee of a pastime (movie addict).

ad·dict·ed /ədíktid/ adj. (usu. foll. by to) **1** dependent on; unable to do without (addicted to heroin; addicted to smoking). **2** devoted (addicted to football).

ad·dic·tion /ədíkshən/ n. the fact or process of being addicted.

ad·dic·tive /ədíktiv/ adj. (of a drug, habit, etc.) causing addiction.

ad·di·tion /ədíshən/ n. **1** the act or process of adding or being added. **2** a person or thing added (a useful addition to the team). □ **in addition** moreover; furthermore; as well.

ad·di·tion·al /ədíshənəl/ adj. added; extra; supplementary. □□ **ad·di·tion·al·ly** adv.

ad·di·tive /áditiv/ n. a thing added (food additive).

ad·dle /ád'l/ v. & adj. ● v. **1** tr. muddle; confuse. **2** intr. (of an egg) become addled. ● adj. muddled; unsound.

ad·dled /ád'ld/ adj. **1** (of an egg) rotten, producing no chick. **2** muddled.

ad·dress /ədrés/ n. & v. ● n. **1** (also /ádres/) **a** the place where a person lives or an organization is situated. **b** particulars of this, esp. for postal purposes. **c** Computing the location of an item of stored information. **2** a discourse delivered to an audience. **3** skill; dexterity; readiness. **4** (in pl.) a courteous approach; courtship (pay one's addresses to). ● v.tr. **1** write directions for delivery (esp. the name and postal location of the intended recipient) on (an envelope, package, etc.). **2** direct in speech or writing (remarks, a protest, etc.). **3** speak or write to, esp. formally (addressed the audience; asked me how to address the ambassador). **4** direct one's attention to. **5** Golf take aim at or prepare to hit (the ball). □ **address oneself to 1** speak or write to. **2** attend to.

ad·dress·ee /ádresée/ n. the person to whom something is addressed.

ad·duce /ədóos, ədyóos/ v.tr. cite as an instance or as proof or evidence. □□ **ad·duc·i·ble** adj.

ad·e·nine /ád'neen, -in/ n. a purine derivative found in all living tissue as a component base of DNA or RNA. ▷ DNA

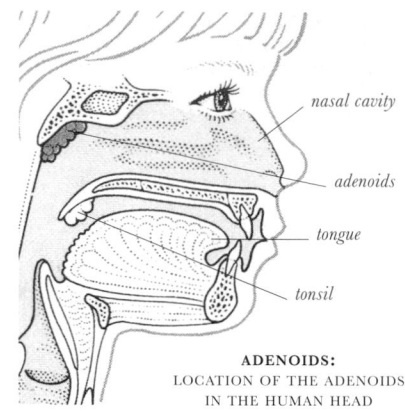

nasal cavity

adenoids

tongue

tonsil

ADENOIDS:
LOCATION OF THE ADENOIDS
IN THE HUMAN HEAD

ad·e·noids /ád'noydz/ n.pl. Med. ▲ a mass of enlarged lymphatic tissue between the back of the nose and the throat, often hindering speaking and breathing in the young. □□ **ad·e·noi·dal** /-nóyd'l/ adj.

ad·e·no·ma /ád'nómə/ n. (pl. **adenomas** or **adenomata** /-mətə/) a glandlike benign tumor.

a·den·o·sine /ədénəseen/ n. a nucleoside of adenine and ribose present in all living tissue in a combined form (see ADP, AMP, ATP).

a·dept adj. & n. ● adj. /ədépt/ (foll. by at, in) thoroughly proficient. ● n. /ádept/ a skilled performer; an expert. □□ **a·dept·ly** adv. **a·dept·ness** n.

ad·e·quate /ádikwət/ adj. **1** sufficient; satisfactory. **2** (foll. by to) proportionate. **3** barely sufficient. □□ **ad·e·qua·cy** n. **ad·e·quate·ly** adv.

ad fin. /ad fin/ abbr. at or near the end.

ADHD abbr. attention deficit hyperactivity disorder.

ad·here /ədheér/ v.intr. **1** (usu. foll. by to) (of a substance) stick fast to a surface, another substance, etc. **2** (foll. by to) behave according to; follow in detail (adhered to our plan). **3** (foll. by to) give support or allegiance.

ad·her·ent /ədheérənt, -hér-/ n. & adj. ● n. **1** a supporter of a party, person, etc. **2** a devotee of an activity. ● adj. **1** (foll. by to) faithfully observing a rule, etc. **2** (often foll. by to) (of a substance) sticking fast. □□ **ad·her·ence** /-rəns/ n.

ad·he·sion /ədheézhən/ n. **1** the act or process of adhering. **2** the capacity of a substance to stick fast. **3** Med. an unnatural union of surfaces due to inflammation. **4** the maintenance of contact between the wheels of a vehicle and the road. **5** the giving of support or allegiance. ¶ More common in physical senses (e.g., the glue has good adhesion), with adherence used in abstract senses (e.g., adherence to principles).

ad·he·sive /ədheésiv, -ziv/ adj. & n. ● adj. enabling surfaces or substances to adhere to one another. ● n. an adhesive substance, esp. one used to stick other substances together. □□ **ad·he·sive·ly** adv.

ad·hib·it /ədhíbit/ v.tr. (**adhibited, adhibiting**) **1** affix. **2** apply or administer (a remedy). □□ **ad·hi·bi·tion** /ádhibíshən/ n.

ad hoc /ád hók/ adv. & adj. for a particular (usu. exclusive) purpose (an ad hoc appointment).

ad hom·i·nem /ad hóminem, hó-/ adv. & adj. **1** relating to or associated with a particular person. **2** (of an argument) appealing to the emotions and not to reason.

ad·i·a·bat·ic /ádeeəbátik, áydī-/ adj. & n. Physics ● adj. **1** impassable to heat. **2** occurring without heat entering or leaving the system. ● n. a curve or formula for adiabatic phenomena. □□ **ad·i·a·bat·i·cal·ly** adv.

ad·i·an·tum /ádeeántəm/ n. **1** any fern of the genus *Adiantum*, e.g. maidenhair. **2** (in general use) a spleenwort.

a·dieu /ədyóo, ədóo/ int. & n. ● int. good-bye. ● n. (pl. **adieus** or **adieux** /ədyóoz, ədóoz/) a goodbye.

ad in·fi·ni·tum /ad ínfinítəm/ adv. without limit; for ever.

ad in·te·rim /ad íntərim/ adv. & adj. for the meantime.

ad·i·os /áadee-ós, ádee-/ int. good-bye.

ad·i·po·cere /ádipōséer/ n. a grayish fatty or soapy substance generated in dead bodies subjected to moisture.

ad·i·pose /ádipōs/ adj. of or characterized by fat. ▷ BREAST, FAT. □□ **ad·i·pos·i·ty** /-pósitee/ n.

ad·it /ádit/ n. a horizontal entrance or passage in a mine.

ad·ja·cent /əjáysənt/ adj. (often foll. by to) lying near or adjoining. □□ **ad·ja·cen·cy** /-sənsee/ n.

ad·jec·tive /ájiktiv/ n. a word or phrase naming an attribute, added to or grammatically related to a noun to modify it or describe it. □□ **ad·jec·ti·val** /ájiktívəl/ adj. **ad·jec·ti·val·ly** adv.

ad·join /əjóyn/ v.tr. (often as **adjoining** adj.) be next to and joined with.

ad·journ /əjórn/ v. **1** tr. **a** put off; postpone. **b** break off (a meeting, discussion, etc.) with the intention of resuming later. **2** intr. (of persons at a meeting): **a** break off proceedings and disperse. **b** (foll. by to) transfer the meeting to another place.

ad·journ·ment /əjórnmənt/ n. adjourning or being adjourned.

ad·judge /əjúj/ v.tr. **1** adjudicate (a matter). **2** (often foll. by that + clause, or to + infin.) pronounce judicially. **3** (foll. by to) award judicially.

ad·ju·di·cate /əjōōdikayt/ v. **1** intr. act as judge in a competition, court, tribunal, etc. **2** tr. decide judicially regarding (a claim, etc.). □□ **ad·ju·di·ca·tion** /-dikáyshən/ n. **ad·ju·di·ca·tive** adj. **ad·ju·di·ca·tor** n.

ad·junct /ájungkt/ n. **1** (foll. by to, of) a subordinate or incidental thing. **2** an assistant; a subordinate person, esp. one with temporary appointment only. □□ **ad·junc·tive** /əjúngktiv/ adj.

ad·jure /əjŏŏr/ v.tr. (usu. foll. by to + infin.) charge or request (a person) solemnly or earnestly, esp. under oath. □□ **ad·ju·ra·tion** /ájŏŏráyshən/ n.

ad·just /əjúst/ v. **1** tr. **a** arrange; put in the correct order or position. **b** regulate, esp. by a small amount. **2** tr. (usu. foll. by to) make suitable. **3** tr. harmonize (discrepancies). **4** tr. assess (loss or damages). **5** intr. (usu. foll. by to) make oneself suited to; become familiar with. □□ **ad·just·a·ble** adj. **ad·just·a·bil·i·ty** /əjústəbílitee/ n. **ad·just·er** n. **ad·just·ment** n.

ad·ju·tant /ájət'nt/ n. **1 a** Mil. an officer who assists superior officers by communicating orders, conducting correspondence, etc. **b** an assistant. **2** a giant Indian stork.

Ad·ju·tant Gen·er·al n. a high-ranking Army or National Guard administrative officer.

ad·ju·vant /ájəvənt/ adj. & n. ● adj. helpful; auxiliary. ● n. an adjuvant person or thing.

ad lib /ád lib/ v., adj., adv., & n. ● v.intr. (**ad libbed, ad libbing**) speak or perform without preparation; improvise. ● adj. improvised. ● adv. as one pleases; to any desired extent. ● n. something spoken or played extempore.

ad li·bi·tum /ad líbitəm/ adv. = AD LIB adv.

ad li·tem /ad lítem/ adj. (of a guardian, etc.) appointed for a lawsuit.

ad·man /ádman/ n. (pl. **admen**) colloq. a person who produces advertisements commercially.

ad·meas·ure /admézhər/ v.tr. apportion; assign in due shares. □□ **ad·meas·ure·ment** n.

ad·min /ádmin/ n. Brit. colloq. administration.

ad·min·is·ter /ədmínistər/ v. **1** tr. attend to the running of (business affairs, etc.). **2** tr. **a** be responsible for the implementation of (the law, punishment, etc.). **b** Eccl. perform the rites of (a sacrament). **c** (usu. foll. by to) direct the taking of (an oath). **3** tr. **a** provide; apply (a remedy). **b** give; deliver (a rebuke). **4** intr. act as administrator. □□ **ad·min·is·tra·ble** adj.

ad·min·is·trate /ədmínistrayt/ *v.tr. & intr.* administer (esp. business affairs).

ad·min·is·tra·tion /ədmínistráyshən/ *n.* **1** management of a business. **2** the management of public affairs. **3** the government in power. **4 a** a President's period of office. **b** a President's advisers, cabinet officials, and their subordinates. **5** *Law* the management of another person's estate. **6** (foll. by *of*) **a** the administering of justice, an oath, etc. **b** application of remedies.

ad·min·is·tra·tive /ədmínistráytiv, -trətiv/ *adj.* concerning or relating to the management of affairs. □□ **ad·min·is·tra·tive·ly** *adv.*

ad·min·is·tra·tor /ədmínistraytər/ *n.* (*fem.* **ad·min·i·stra·trix** /ədmínistrátriks/) **1** a person who administers a business or public affairs. **2** a person capable of organizing. **3** *Law* a person appointed to manage the estate of a person who has died intestate.

ad·mi·ra·ble /ádmərəbəl/ *adj.* **1** deserving admiration. **2** excellent. □□ **ad·mi·ra·bly** *adv.*

ad·mi·ral /ádmərəl/ *n.* **1 a** the commander in chief of a country's navy. **b** a naval officer of high rank, the commander of a fleet or squadron. **2** ◄ any of various butterflies (*red admiral*).

ADMIRAL
BUTTERFLIES

INDIAN RED
ADMIRAL
(*Vanessa indica*)

BLUE ADMIRAL
(*Vanessa canace*)

Ad·mi·ral·ty /ádmərəltee/ *n.* (*pl.* **-ies**) **1** (*hist.* except in titles) (in the UK) the department administering the Royal Navy. **2** (**admiralty**) *Law* trial and decision of maritime questions and offenses.

ad·mi·ra·tion /ádmiráyshən/ *n.* **1** pleased contemplation. **2** respect; warm approval. **3** an object of this (*was the admiration of the whole town*).

ad·mire /ədmír/ *v.tr.* **1** regard with approval, respect, or satisfaction. **2** express one's admiration of.

ad·mir·er /ədmírər/ *n.* **1** a woman's suitor. **2** a person who admires esp. a fan of a famous person.

ad·mir·ing /ədmíring/ *adj.* showing or feeling admiration. □□ **ad·mir·ing·ly** *adv.*

ad·mis·si·ble /ədmísibəl/ *adj.* **1** (of an idea or plan) worth accepting or considering. **2** *Law* allowable as evidence. **3** (foll. by *to*) capable of being admitted. □□ **ad·mis·si·bil·i·ty** /-bílitee/ *n.*

ad·mis·sion /ədmíshən/ *n.* **1** an acknowledgment (*admission of error*). **2 a** the right of entering. **b** a charge for this (*admission is $5*). **3** a person admitted to a hospital.

ad·mit /ədmít/ *v.* (**admitted, admitting**) **1** *tr.* **a** (often foll. by *to be*, or *that* + clause) acknowledge; recognize as true. **b** accept as valid. **2** *intr.* (foll. by *to*) acknowledge responsibility (for a deed, fault, etc.). **3** *tr.* **a** allow (a person) entrance or access. **b** allow (a person) to be a member of (a group, etc.) or to share in (a privilege, etc.). **c** (of a hospital, etc.) bring in (a person) for inpatient treatment. **4** *tr.* (of an enclosed space) have room for. **5** *intr.* (foll. by *of*) allow as possible.

ad·mit·tance /ədmít'ns/ *n.* the right of admitting (*no admittance except on business*).

ad·mit·ted·ly /ədmítidlee/ *adv.* as an acknowledged fact.

ad·mix /admíks/ *v.* **1** *tr. & intr.* (foll. by *with*) mingle. **2** *tr.* add as an ingredient.

ad·mix·ture /admíkschər/ *n.* **1** a thing added. **2** the act of adding this.

ad·mon·ish /ədmónish/ *v.tr.* **1** reprove. **2** (foll. by *to* + infin., or *that* + clause) urge. **3** give earnest advice to. **4** (foll. by *of*) warn. □□ **ad·mon·ish·ment** *n.* **ad·mo·ni·tion** /ádməníshən/ *n.* **ad·mon·i·to·ry** *adj.*

ad nau·se·am /ad náwzeeəm/ *adv.* to an excessive or disgusting degree.

ad·nom·i·nal /adnóminəl/ *adj.* *Gram.* attached to a noun.

a·do /ədóo/ *n.* (*pl.* **ados**) fuss; busy activity; trouble; difficulty. □ **without more** (or **further**) **ado** immediately.

a·do·be /ədóbee/ *n.* **1** a sun-dried brick of clay and straw. **2** the clay used for making such bricks.

ad·o·les·cent /ádəlésənt/ *adj. & n.* ● *adj.* between childhood and adulthood. ● *n.* an adolescent person. □□ **ad·o·les·cence** /-səns/ *n.*

A·don·is /ədónis, ədó-/ *n.* a handsome young man.

a·dopt /ədópt/ *v.tr.* **1** take (a person) into a relationship, esp. another's child as one's own. **2** choose to follow (a course of action, etc.). **3** take over (a name, idea, etc.). **4** accept; formally approve (a report, etc.). □□ **a·dop·tion** /-dópshən/ *n.*

a·dop·tive /ədóptiv/ *adj.* due to adoption (*adoptive son; adoptive father*).

a·dor·a·ble /ədáwrəbəl/ *adj.* **1** deserving adoration. **2** *colloq.* delightful; charming. □□ **a·dor·a·bly** *adv.*

a·dore /ədáwr/ *v.tr.* **1** regard with honor and deep affection. **2** worship as divine. **3** *colloq.* like very much. □□ **ad·o·ra·tion** /ádəráyshən/ *n.* **a·dor·er** *n.* **a·dor·ing** *adj.* **a·dor·ing·ly** *adv.*

a·dorn /ədáwrn/ *v.tr.* **1** add beauty or luster to; be an ornament to. **2** furnish with ornaments; decorate. □□ **a·dorn·ment** *n.*

ad rem /ad rém/ *adv. & adj.* to the point; to the purpose.

ad·re·nal /ədréenəl/ *adj. & n.* ● *adj.* **1** at or near the kidneys. ▷ KIDNEY. **2** of the adrenal glands. ● *n.* (in full **adrenal gland**) ▼ either of two ductless glands above the kidneys, secreting adrenaline. ▷ ENDOCRINE

adrenal gland inferior vena cava

adrenal gland

aorta

kidney

renal artery

renal vein

ADRENAL GLANDS

a·dren·a·line /ədrénəlin/ *n.* = EPINEPHRINE.

a·drift /ədríft/ *adv. & predic.adj.* **1** drifting. **2** at the mercy of circumstances.

a·droit /ədróyt/ *adj.* dexterous; skillful. □□ **a·droit·ly** *adv.* **a·droit·ness** *n.*

ADSL *abbr.* asymmetric digital subscriber line, a technology for transmitting digital information over standard telephone lines which allows high-speed transmission of signals from the telephone network to an individual subscriber.

ad·sorb /adsáwrb, -záwrb/ *v.tr.* (usu. of a solid) hold (molecules of a gas or liquid or solute) to its surface, causing a thin film to form. □□ **ad·sorb·a·ble** *adj.* **ad·sorb·ent** *adj. & n.* **ad·sorp·tion** *n.* (also **ad·sorb·tion**).

ad·u·late /ájəlayt/ *v.tr.* flatter obsequiously. □□ **ad·u·la·tion** /-láyshən/ *n.* **ad·u·la·to·ry** *adj.*

a·dult /ədúlt, ádult/ *adj. & n.* ● *adj.* **1** mature; grown-up. **2 a** of or for adults (*adult education*). **b** *euphem.* sexually explicit (*adult films*). ● *n.* **1** an adult person. **2** *Law* a person who has reached the age of majority. □□ **a·dult·hood** *n.*

a·dul·ter·ant /ədúltərənt/ *adj. & n.* ● *adj.* used in adulterating. ● *n.* an adulterant substance.

a·dul·ter·ate /ədúltərayt/ *v.tr.* debase (esp. foods) by adding other substances. □□ **a·dul·ter·a·tion** /-ráyshən/ *n.* **a·dul·ter·a·tor** *n.*

a·dul·ter·er /ədúltərər/ *n.* (*fem.* **adulteress** /-təris/) a person who commits adultery.

a·dul·ter·ine /ədúltərīn, -reen/ *adj.* **1** illegal; unlicensed. **2** spurious. **3** born of adultery.

a·dul·ter·ous /ədúltərəs/ *adj.* of or involved in adultery.

a·dul·ter·y /ədúltəree/ *n.* voluntary sexual intercourse between a married person and a person other than his or her spouse.

ad·um·brate /ádumbrayt/ *v.tr.* **1** indicate faintly. **2** represent in outline. **3** foreshadow; typify. **4** overshadow. □□ **ad·um·bra·tion** /-bráyshən/ *n.*

ad va·lo·rem /ád vəláwrəm/ *adv. & adj.* (of taxes) in proportion to the estimated value of the goods concerned.

ad·vance /ədváns/ *v., n., & adj.* ● *v.* **1** *tr. & intr.* move or put forward. **2** *intr.* make progress. **3** *tr.* **a** pay (money) before it is due. **b** lend (money). **4** *tr.* give active support to; promote (a person, cause, or plan). **5** *tr.* put forward (a claim or suggestion). **6** *tr.* cause (an event) to occur at an earlier date. **7** *tr.* raise (a price). **8** *intr.* rise (in price). **9** *tr.* (as **advanced** *adj.*) **a** far on in progress. **b** ahead of the times (*advanced ideas*). ● *n.* **1** an act of going forward. **2** progress. **3** a payment made before the due time. **4** a loan. **5** (esp. in *pl.*; often foll. by *to*) an amorous approach. **6** a rise in price. ● *attrib.adj.* done or supplied beforehand (*advance warning*). □ **advance on** approach threateningly. **in advance** ahead in place or time.

ad·vance di·rec·tive *n.* a living will that gives power of attorney to a surrogate decision-maker when the testator is no longer able to communicate wishes regarding medical treatment.

ad·vance·ment /ədvánsmənt/ *n.* the promotion of a person, cause, or plan.

ad·van·tage /ədvántij/ *n. & v.* ● *n.* **1** a beneficial feature; a favorable circumstance. **2** benefit; profit (*to your advantage*). **3** (often foll. by *over*) a better position. **4** (in tennis) the next point won after deuce. ● *v.tr.* **1** be beneficial or favorable to. **2** further; promote. □ **take advantage of 1** make good use of (a favorable circumstance). **2** exploit (a person), esp. unfairly. **3** *euphem.* seduce. **to advantage** in a way which exhibits the merits (*seen to advantage*). □□ **ad·van·ta·geous** /ádvəntáyjəs/ *adj.* **ad·van·ta·geous·ly** *adv.*

ad·vec·tion /ədvékshən/ *n.* **1** *Meteorol.* transfer of heat by the horizontal flow of air. **2** horizontal flow of air or water. □□ **ad·vec·tive** *adj.*

Ad·vent /ádvent/ *n.* **1** the season before Christmas, incl. the four preceding Sundays. **2** the coming or second coming of Christ. **3** (**advent**) the arrival of an important person or thing.

Ad·vent cal·en·dar *n.* a calendar for Advent, usu. of cardboard with flaps to open for each day revealing a picture or scene.

Ad·vent·ist /ádventist/ *n.* a member of a Christian sect that believes in the imminent second coming of Christ. □□ **Ad·vent·ism** *n.*

ad·ven·ti·tious /ádventíshəs/ *adj.* **1** accidental; casual. **2** added from outside. **3** *Biol.* formed accidentally or under unusual conditions. ▷ BULB. □□ **ad·ven·ti·tious·ly** *adv.*

Ad·vent Sun·day *n.* the first Sunday in Advent.

A

ad·ven·ture /ədvénchər/ *n. & v.* ● *n.* **1** an unusual and exciting experience. **2** a daring enterprise. **3** enterprise (*the spirit of adventure*). **4** a commercial speculation. ● *v.intr.* **1** (often foll. by *into, upon*) dare to go. **2** (foll. by *on, upon*) dare to undertake. **3** engage in adventure. □□ **ad·ven·ture·some** *adj.*

ad·ven·tur·er /ədvénchərər/ *n.* (*fem.* **adventuress** /-chəris/) **1** a person who seeks adventure, esp. for personal gain or enjoyment. **2** a financial speculator.

ad·ven·tur·ism /ədvénchərizəm/ *n.* a tendency to take risks, esp. in foreign policy. □□ **ad·ven·tur·ist** *n.*

ad·ven·tur·ous /ədvénchərəs/ *adj.* **1** rash; venturesome; enterprising. **2** characterized by adventures. □□ **ad·ven·tur·ous·ly** *adv.* **ad·ven·tur·ous·ness** *n.*

ad·verb /ádvərb/ *n.* a word or phrase that modifies or qualifies another word or a group of words, expressing a relation of place, time, manner, degree, etc. (e.g., *gently, quite, then, there*). □□ **ad·ver·bi·al** /ədvérbeeəl/ *adj.*

ad·ver·sar·i·al /ádvərsáireeəl/ *adj.* **1** involving conflict. **2** opposed; hostile.

ad·ver·sar·y /ádvərseree/ *n.* (*pl.* **-ies**) **1** an enemy. **2** an opponent in a sport.

ad·ver·sa·tive /ədvérsətiv/ *adj.* (of words, etc.) expressing opposition or antithesis. □□ **ad·ver·sa·tive·ly** *adv.*

ad·verse /advórs, ád-/ *adj.* (often foll. by *to*) **1** contrary; hostile. **2** harmful. □□ **ad·verse·ly** *adv.*

ad·ver·si·ty /ədvérsitee/ *n.* (*pl.* **-ies**) **1** adverse fortune. **2** a misfortune.

ad·vert /ədvórt/ *v.intr.* (foll. by *to*) *literary* refer in speaking or writing.

ad·ver·tise /ádvərtīz/ (also **ad·ver·tize**) *v.* **1** *tr.* draw attention to or describe favorably (goods or services) in a public medium to promote sales. **2** *tr.* make generally or publicly known. **3** *intr.* (foll. by *for*) seek by public notice. □□ **ad·ver·tis·er** *n.*

ad·ver·tise·ment /ádvərtīzmənt, ədvértis-, -tiz-/ *n.* **1** a public notice or announcement, esp. one advertising goods or services. **2** the act or process of advertising.

ad·vice /ədvís/ *n.* **1** words offered as a recommendation about future action. **2** information given. **3** formal notice of a transaction.

ad·vis·a·ble /ədvízəbəl/ *adj.* **1** to be recommended. **2** expedient. □□ **ad·vis·a·bil·i·ty** /-bílitee/ *n.*

ad·vise /ədvíz/ *v.* **1** *tr.* (also *absol.*) give advice to. **2** *tr.* recommend (*they advise caution*). **3** *tr.* inform; notify. **4** *intr.* (foll. by *with*) consult.

ad·vised /ədvízd/ *adj.* deliberate; considered. □□ **ad·vis·ed·ly** /-zidlee/ *adv.*

ad·vis·er /ədvízər/ *n.* (also **ad·vis·or**) a person who advises, esp. one appointed to do so.

ad·vi·so·ry /ədvízəree/ *adj.* **1** giving advice; constituted to give advice (*an advisory body*). **2** consisting in giving advice.

ad·vo·caat /ádvəkaat/ *n.* a liqueur of eggs, sugar, and brandy.

ad·vo·ca·cy /ádvəkəsee/ *n.* **1** (usu. foll. by *of*) verbal support or argument for a cause, policy, etc. **2** the function of an advocate.

ad·vo·cate *n. & v.* ● *n.* /ádvəkət/ **1** (foll. by *of*) a person who supports or speaks in favor. **2** a person who pleads for another. **3** a professional pleader in a court of justice. ● *v.tr.* /ádvəkayt/ **1** recommend or support by argument (a cause, policy, etc.). **2** plead for; defend. □□ **ad·vo·cate·ship** *n.*

ad·voc·a·to·ry /advókətawree, ádvəkə-, ádvəkaytəree/ *adj.*

ad·y·tum /áditəm/ *n.* (*pl.* **adyta** /-tə/) the innermost part of an ancient temple.

adze /adz/ *n. & v.* (also **adz**) ● *n.* an axelike tool for cutting away the surface of wood. ● *v.tr.* dress or cut with an adze.

ad·zu·ki /ədzóokee/ *n.* **1** an annual leguminous plant, *Vigna angularis*, native to China and Japan. **2** ▶ the small, round, dark red edible bean of this plant.

ADZUKI BEANS
(*Vigna angularis*)

ae·dile /éedīl/ *n.* either of a pair of Roman magistrates who administered public works, maintenance of roads, public games, the grain supply, etc. □□ **ae·dile·ship** *n.*

ae·gis /éejis/ *n.* □ **under the aegis of** under the auspices of.

ae·o·li·an harp /eeṓleean/ *n.* a stringed instrument or toy that produces musical sounds when the wind passes through it.

Ae·o·li·an mode /eeṓleeən/ *n. Mus.* the mode represented by the natural diatonic scale A–A.

ae·on var. of EON.

aer·ate /áirayt/ *v.tr.* **1** expose to the mechanical or chemical action of the air. **2** *Brit.* = CARBONATE. □□ **aer·a·tion** /-ráyshən/ *n.* **aer·a·tor** *n.*

aer·en·chy·ma /aréngkəmə/ *n. Bot.* a soft plant tissue containing air spaces, found esp. in many aquatic plants.

aer·i·al /áireeəl/ *n. & adj.* ● *n.* = ANTENNA 2. ● *adj.* **1** by or from or involving aircraft (*aerial photography*). **2 a** existing, moving, or happening in the air. **b** of or in the atmosphere; atmospheric. □□ **aer·i·al·ly** *adv.*

aer·i·al·ist /áireeəlist/ *n.* a high-wire or trapeze artist.

aer·ie /áiree, áree/ *n.* (also **eyrie**) **1** a nest of a bird of prey, esp. an eagle, built high up. **2** a house, etc., perched high up.

aer·i·form /áirifawrm/ *adj.* **1** of the form of air; gaseous. **2** unsubstantial; unreal.

aero- /áirō/ *comb. form* **1** air. **2** aircraft.

aer·o·bat·ics /áirəbátiks/ *n.pl.* **1** feats of expert and usu. spectacular flying and maneuvering of aircraft. **2** (as *sing.*) a performance of these.

aer·obe /áirōb/ *n.* a microorganism usu. growing in the presence of oxygen, or needing oxygen for growth.

aer·o·bic /airṓbik/ *adj.* **1** existing or active only in the presence of oxygen. **2** of or relating to aerobes. **3** of or relating to aerobics.

aer·o·bics /airṓbiks/ *n.pl.* vigorous exercises designed to increase the body's heart rate and oxygen intake.

aer·o·bi·ol·o·gy /áirōbīóləjee/ *n.* the study of airborne microorganisms, pollen, spores, etc., esp. as agents of infection.

aer·o·dy·nam·ics /áirōdīnámiks/ *n.pl.* (usu. treated as *sing.*) the study of the interaction between the air and solid bodies moving through it. □□ **aer·o·dy·nam·ic** *adj.* **aer·o·dy·nam·i·cal·ly** *adv.* **aer·o·dy·nam·i·cist** /-misist/ *n.*

aer·o·em·bo·lism /áirōémbəlizəm/ *n.* a condition caused by the sudden lowering of air pressure and formation of bubbles in the blood. Also called **caisson disease**, **decompression sickness**, **the bends** (see BEND[1] *n.* 4).

aer·o·gram /áirəgram/ *n.* (also **aer·o·gramme**) an airmail letter in the form of a single sheet that is folded and sealed.

aer·o·lite /áirəlīt/ *n.* a stony meteorite.

aer·ol·o·gy /airóləjee/ *n.* the study of the upper levels of the atmosphere. □□ **aer·o·log·i·cal** /áirəlójikəl/ *adj.*

aer·o·nau·tics /áirənáwtiks/ *n.pl.* (usu. treated as *sing.*) the science or practice of motion or travel in the air. □□ **aer·o·nau·tic** *adj.* **aer·o·nau·ti·cal** *adj.*

aer·on·o·my /airónəmee/ *n.* the science, esp. the physics and chemistry, of the upper atmosphere.

aer·o·plane esp. *Brit.* var. of AIRPLANE.

aer·o·sol /áirəsawl, -sol/ *n.* **1 a** a container used to hold a substance packed under pressure with a device for releasing it as a fine spray. **b** the releasing device. **c** the substance contained in an aerosol. **2** a system of colloidal particles dispersed in a gas (e.g., fog or smoke).

aer·o·space /áirōspays/ *n.* **1** the Earth's atmosphere and outer space. **2** the technology of aviation in this region.

aer·o·train /áirōtrayn/ *n.* an experimental train that is supported on an air cushion and guided by a track.

Aes·cu·la·pi·an /éskyəláypeeən/ *adj.* of or relating to medicine or physicians.

aes·thete /és-theet/ *n.* (also **es·thete**) a person who has or professes to have a special appreciation of beauty.

aes·thet·ic /es-thétik/ *adj. & n.* (also **es·thet·ic**) ● *adj.* **1** concerned with beauty or the appreciation of beauty. **2** having such appreciation. **3** in accordance with good taste. ● *n.* **1** (in *pl.*) the philosophy of the beautiful. **2** a set of principles of good taste and the appreciation of beauty. □□ **aes·thet·i·cal·ly** *adv.* **aes·thet·i·cism** /-tisizəm/ *n.*

aest·i·val esp. *Brit.* var. of ESTIVAL.

aest·i·vate esp. *Brit.* var. of ESTIVATE.

aet·i·ol·o·gy esp. *Brit.* var. of ETIOLOGY.

AF *abbr.* **1** Air Force. **2** audio frequency.

a·far /əfáar/ *adv.* at or to a distance. □ **from afar** from a distance.

AFB *abbr.* Air Force Base.

AFC *abbr.* American Football Conference.

af·fa·ble /áfəbəl/ *adj.* approachable and friendly. □□ **af·fa·bil·i·ty** /-bílitee/ *n.* **af·fa·bly** *adv.*

af·fair /əfáir/ *n.* **1** a concern; a business (*that is my affair*). **2** a celebrated or notorious happening or sequence of events. **3** = LOVE AFFAIR. **4** (in *pl.*) **a** ordinary pursuits of life. **b** business dealings. **c** public matters (*current affairs*).

af·fect[1] /əfékt/ *v.tr.* **1** produce an effect on. **2** touch the feelings of (*affected me deeply*). ¶ Often confused with *effect*, which as a verb means 'bring about; accomplish.'

af·fect[2] /əfékt/ *v.tr.* **1** pretend to feel (*affected indifference*). **2** (foll. by *to* + infin.) pretend. **3** assume the manner of (*affect the freethinker*). **4** make a show of liking (*she affects fancy hats*).

af·fect[3] /áfekt/ *n. Psychol.* a feeling, emotion, or desire, esp. as leading to action.

af·fec·ta·tion /áfektáyshən/ *n.* **1** an assumed or contrived manner of behavior, esp. in order to impress. **2** (foll. by *of*) a studied display. **3** pretense.

af·fect·ed /əféktid/ *adj.* **1** in senses of AFFECT[1], AFFECT[2]. **2** artificially assumed; pretended (*an affected air of innocence*). **3** (of a person) full of affectation. □□ **af·fect·ed·ly** *adv.*

af·fec·tion /əfékshən/ *n.* (often foll. by *for, toward*) goodwill; fond feeling.

af·fec·tion·ate /əfékshənət/ *adj.* loving; tender. □□ **af·fec·tion·ate·ly** *adv.*

af·fec·tive /əféktiv/ *adj.* concerning the affections; emotional. □□ **af·fec·tiv·i·ty** /áfektívitee/ *n.*

af·fen·pin·scher /áfənpinshər/ *n.* **1** a dog of a small breed resembling the griffon. **2** this breed.

af·fi·ance /əffīəns/ *v.tr.* (usu. in *passive*) *literary* promise solemnly to give (a person) in marriage.

af·fi·da·vit /áfidáyvit/ *n.* a written statement confirmed under oath, for use as evidence in court.

af·fil·i·ate *v. & n.* ● *v.* /əfíleeayt/ **1** *tr.* (usu. in *passive*; foll. by *to, with*) attach or connect (a person or society) with a larger organization. **2** *tr.* (of an institution) adopt (persons as members, societies as branches, etc.). **3** *intr.* **a** (foll. by *to*) associate oneself with a society. **b** (foll. by *with*) associate oneself with a political party. ● *n.* /əfíleeət, -leeayt/ an affiliated person or organization.

af·fil·i·a·tion /əfíleeáyshən/ *n.* the act or process of affiliating or being affiliated.

af·fined /əfīnd/ *adj.* related; connected.

af·fin·i·ty /əfínitee/ *n.* (*pl.* **-ies**) **1** a natural attraction to a person or thing. **2** relationship, esp. by marriage. **3** resemblance in structure between animals, plants, or languages. **4** a similarity of character suggesting a relationship. **5** *Chem.* the tendency of certain substances to combine with others.

af·firm /əfə́rm/ v. **1** tr. assert strongly; state as a fact. **2** intr. **a** Law make an affirmation. **b** make a formal declaration.

af·fir·ma·tion /áfərmáyshən/ n. **1** the act or process of affirming or being affirmed. **2** Law a solemn declaration by a person who conscientiously declines to take an oath.

af·firm·a·tive /əfə́rmətiv/ adj. & n. ● adj. **1** asserting that a thing is so. **2** (of a vote) expressing approval. ● n. **1** an affirmative statement, reply, or word. **2** (prec. by the) a positive or affirming position. □ **in the affirmative** so as to accept or agree to a proposal; yes (the answer was in the affirmative). □□ **af·firm·a·tive·ly** adv.

af·firm·a·tive ac·tion n. action favoring those who often suffer from discrimination.

af·fix v. & n. ● v.tr. /əfíks/ **1** (usu. foll. by to, on) attach; fasten. **2** add in writing. **3** impress (a seal or stamp). ● n. /áfiks/ **1** an appendage; an addition. **2** Gram. an addition placed at the beginning (prefix) or end (suffix) of a root, stem, or word to modify its meaning. □□ **af·fix·a·tion** /áfiksáyshən/ n.

af·fla·tus /əfláytəs/ n. a divine creative impulse.

af·flict /əflíkt/ v.tr. inflict suffering on. □ **afflicted with** suffering from.

af·flic·tion /əflíkshən/ n. **1** physical or mental distress. **2** a cause of this.

af·flu·ence /áflŏŏəns/ n. an abundant supply of money, etc.; wealth.

af·flu·ent /áflŏŏənt/ adj. **1** wealthy; rich. **2** abundant. □□ **af·flu·ent·ly** adv.

af·flux /áfluks/ n. a flow toward a point; an influx.

af·ford /əfáwrd/ v.tr. **1** (prec. by can or be able to) **a** have enough money, means, time, etc., for; be able to spare (can afford $50; can we afford to buy a new television?). **b** be in a position to do something (can't afford to let him think so). **2** provide (affords a view of the sea). □□ **af·ford·a·ble** adj. **af·ford·a·bil·i·ty** n.

af·for·est /əfáwrist, əfór-/ v.tr. **1** convert into forest. **2** plant with trees. □□ **af·for·est·a·tion** /-stáyshən/ n.

af·fran·chise /əfránchīz/ v.tr. release from servitude or an obligation.

af·fray /əfráy/ n. a breach of the peace by fighting or rioting in public.

af·fri·cate /áfrikət/ n. Phonet. a combination of a stop, or plosive, with an immediately following fricative or spirant, e.g., ch.

af·front /əfrúnt/ n. & v. ● n. an open insult (feel it an affront). ● v.tr. **1** insult openly. **2** offend the modesty or self-respect of.

Af·ghan /áfgan/ n. & adj. ● n. **1 a** a native or inhabitant of Afghanistan. **b** a person of Afghan descent. **2** the official language of Afghanistan. **3** Brit. (in full **Afghan coat**) a kind of sheepskin coat with the skin outside and usu. with a shaggy border. ● adj. of or relating to Afghanistan or its people or language.

Af·ghan hound n. ▼ a tall hunting dog with long silky hair. ▷ DOG

AFGHAN HOUND

a·fi·ci·o·na·do /əfisheeənáadō, əfisee-/ n. (pl. **-os**) a devotee of a sport or pastime.

a·field /əféeld/ adv. away from home; to or at a distance (esp. **far afield**).

a·fire /əfír/ adv. & predic.adj. **1** on fire. **2** intensely roused or excited.

a·flame /əfláym/ adv. & predic.adj. **1** in flames. **2** = AFIRE 2.

a·float /əflṓt/ adv. & predic.adj. **1** floating in water or air. **2** at sea; on board ship. **3** out of debt or difficulty. **4** in general circulation; current.

a·foot /əfŏŏt/ adv. & predic.adj. in operation; progressing.

a·fore /əfáwr/ prep. & adv. archaic & dial. before; previously; in front (of).

afore- /əfáwr/ comb. form before; previously (aforementioned; aforesaid).

a·fore·thought /əfáwrthawt/ adj. premeditated (following a noun: malice aforethought).

a for·ti·o·ri /áa fawrtiáwrī/ adv. & adj. with a yet stronger reason (than a conclusion already accepted); more conclusively.

a·foul /əfówl/ adv. □ **run afoul of** come into conflict with.

a·fraid /əfráyd/ predic.adj. **1** (often foll. by of, or that or lest + clause) frightened. **2** (foll. by to + infin.) reluctant for fear of the consequences (afraid to go in). □ **be afraid** (foll. by that + clause) colloq. admit or declare with regret (I'm afraid there's none left).

a·fresh /əfrésh/ adv. anew; with a fresh beginning.

Af·ri·can /áfrikən/ n. & adj. ● n. **1** a native of Africa (esp. a black person). **2** a person of African descent. ● adj. of or relating to Africa.

Af·ri·ca·na /áfrikáanə/ n.pl. things connected with Africa.

Af·ri·can-A·mer·i·can n. & adj. ● n. an American citizen of African origin or descent, esp. a black American. ● adj. of or relating to American blacks or their culture.

Af·ri·can vi·o·let n. ▶ a small E. African plant of the genus Saintpaulia, with velvety leaves and blue, purple, or pink flowers, esp. S. ionantha.

Af·ri·kaans /áfrikáans/ n. the language of the Afrikaner people developed from Cape Dutch, an official language of the Republic of South Africa.

Af·ri·ka·ner /áfrikáanər/ n. an Afrikaans-speaking white person in S. Africa, esp. one of Dutch descent.

Af·ro /áfrō/ adj. & n. ● adj. (of a hairstyle) full and bushy, as naturally grown originally by blacks. ● n. (pl. **-os**) an Afro hairstyle.

Afro- /áfrō/ comb. form African (Afro-Asian).

Af·ro-A·mer·i·can /áfrōəmérikən/ adj. & n. = AFRICAN-AMERICAN.

af·ror·mo·si·a /áfrawrmṓzeeə, -zhə/ n. **1** an African tree, Pericopsis elata, yielding a hard wood resembling teak. **2** this wood.

aft /aft/ adv. Naut. & Aeron. at or toward the stern or tail.

af·ter /áftər/ prep., conj., adv., & adj. ● prep. **1 a** following in time; later than (after midnight). **b** in specifying time (a quarter after eight). **2** in view of (after your behavior tonight what do you expect?). **3** in spite of (after all my efforts I'm no better off). **4** behind (shut the door after you). **5** in pursuit or quest of (run after them). **6** about; concerning (asked after her). **7** in allusion to (named him William after his uncle). **8** in imitation of (a painting after Rubens). **9** next in importance to (the best book on the subject after mine). **10** according to (after a fashion). ● conj. in or at a time later than that when (left after we arrived). ● adv. **1** later in time (soon after). **2** behind in place (followed on after). ● adj. **1** later; following (in after years). **2** Naut. nearer the stern (after mast). □ **after all 1** in spite of all that has happened or has been said, etc. (after all, what does it

AFRICAN VIOLET
(Saintpaulia 'Bright Eyes')

matter?). **2** in spite of one's exertions, expectations, etc. (they tried for an hour and failed after all; so you have come after all!).

af·ter·birth /áftərbərth/ n. Med. the placenta and fetal membranes discharged from the womb after childbirth.

af·ter·burn·er /áftərbərnər/ n. an auxiliary burner in a jet engine to increase thrust.

af·ter·care /áftərkair, -ker/ n. care of a patient after a stay in hospital or of a person on release from prison.

af·ter·damp /áftərdamp/ n. choking gas left after an explosion of firedamp in a mine.

af·ter·ef·fect /áftərəfékt/ n. an effect that follows after an interval or after the primary action of something.

af·ter·glow /áftərglō/ n. a light or radiance remaining after its source has disappeared or been removed.

af·ter·im·age /áftərímij/ n. an image retained by a sense organ, esp. the eye, and producing a sensation after the cessation of the stimulus.

af·ter·life /áftərlīf/ n. **1** life after death. **2** life at a later time.

af·ter·mar·ket /áftərmaarkit/ n. **1** a market in spare parts and components. **2** Stock Exch. a market in shares after their original issue.

af·ter·math /áftərmath/ n. consequences; aftereffects (the aftermath of war).

af·ter·most /áftərmōst/ adj. **1** last. **2** Naut. farthest aft.

af·ter·noon /áftərnṓn/ n. **1** the time from noon or lunchtime to evening (this afternoon; during the afternoon). **2** this time spent in a particular way (had a lazy afternoon).

af·ter·pains /áftərpaynz/ n.pl. pains caused by contraction of the womb after childbirth.

af·ter·shave /áftərshayv/ n. an astringent lotion for use after shaving.

af·ter·shock /áftərshok/ n. a lesser shock following the main shock of an earthquake.

af·ter·taste /áftərtáyst/ n. a taste remaining after eating or drinking.

af·ter·tax /áftərtáks/ adj. (of income) after the deduction of taxes.

af·ter·thought /áftərthawt/ n. an item or thing that is thought of or added later.

af·ter·ward /áftərwórd/ adv. (also **af·ter·wards**) later; subsequently.

af·ter·word /áftərwərd/ n. concluding remarks in a book.

Ag symb. Chem. the element silver.

a·ga /áagə/ n. (in Muslim countries) a commander; a chief.

a·gain /əgén/ adv. **1** another time; once more. **2** as in a previous position or condition (back again; healthy again). **3** in addition (as much again). **4** further; besides (again, what about the children?). **5** on the other hand (I might, and again I might not). □ **again and again** repeatedly.

a·gainst /əgénst/ prep. **1** in opposition to (fight against the invaders; arson is against the law). **2** into collision or in contact with (ran against a rock; lean against the wall; up against a problem). **3** to the disadvantage of (his age is against him). **4** in contrast to (against a dark background; 99 as against 102 yesterday). **5** in anticipation of or preparation for (protected against the cold; against a rainy day). **6** as a compensating factor to (income against expenditure). **7** in return for (issued against a later payment).

A·ga Khan n. the spiritual leader of the Ismaili Muslims.

a·gam·ic /əgámik/ adj. characterized by the absence of sexual reproduction.

ag·a·mo·gen·e·sis /əgámōjénisis, ágəmō-/ n. Biol. asexual reproduction. □□ **ag·a·mo·ge·net·ic** /-jinétik/ adj.

A

ag·a·pan·thus /ágəpánthəs/ *n.* any African plant of the genus *Agapanthus*, esp. the ornamental African lily, with blue or white flowers.

a·gape[1] /əgáyp/ *adv. & predic.adj.* gaping; open-mouthed, esp. with wonder.

a·ga·pe[2] /əgáapay, ágə-/ *n.* **1** a Christian feast in token of fellowship, esp. one held by early Christians in commemoration of the Last Supper. **2** love for one's fellow humans, esp. as distinct from erotic love.

a·gar /áygaar/ *n.* a gelatinous substance obtained from any of various kinds of red seaweed and used in food, microbiological media, etc.

a·ga·ric /ágərik, əgár-/ *n.* ◀ any fungus of the family Agaricaceae, with cap and stalk, including the common edible mushroom. ▷ MUSHROOM, TOADSTOOL

AGARIC: SHAGGY PARASOL (*Macrolepiota rhacodes*)

ag·ate /ágət/ *n.* **1** ▶ any of several varieties of hard usu. streaked chalcedony. **2** a colored toy marble resembling this.

a·gave /əgáavee, əgáy-/ *n.* any plant of the genus *Agave*, with rosettes of narrow spiny leaves and tall inflorescences, e.g., the aloe.

a·gaze /əgáyz/ *adv.* gazing.

age /ayj/ *n. & v.* ● *n.* **1 a** the length of time that a person or thing has existed. **b** a particular point in or part of one's life, often as a qualification (*old age; voting age*). **2 a** *colloq.* (often in *pl.*) a long time (*took an age to answer; have been waiting for ages*). **b** a distinct period of the past (*golden age; Middle Ages*). **c** *Geol.* a period of time. **d** a generation. **3** the latter part of life; old age (*the infirmity of age*). ● *v.* (*pres. part.* **aging**, **ageing**) **1** *intr.* show signs of advancing age (*has aged a lot recently*). **2** *intr.* grow old. **3** *intr.* mature. **4** *tr.* cause or allow to age. ● **come of age** reach adult status. **of age** old enough; of adult status.

aged *adj.* **1** /ayjd/ **a** of the age of (*aged ten*). **b** that has been subjected to aging. **2** /áyjid/ having lived long; old.

age·ism /áyjizəm/ *n.* (also **ag·ism**) prejudice or discrimination on the grounds of age. □□ **age·ist** *adj. & n.* (also **ag·ist**).

age·less /áyjlis/ *adj.* **1** never growing or appearing old or outmoded. **2** eternal; timeless.

age·long /áyjlong/ *adj.* lasting for a very long time.

a·gen·cy /áyjənsee/ *n.* (*pl.* **-ies**) **1 a** the business or establishment of an agent (*employment agency*). **b** the function of an agent. **2 a** active operation; action. **b** intervening action (*fertilized by the agency of insects*). **c** action personified (*an invisible agency*). **3** a specialized department, as of a government.

a·gen·da /əjéndə/ *n.* **1** (*pl.* **agendas**) a list of items of business to be considered at a meeting. **2** a series of things to be done. **3** an ideology or underlying motivation.

a·gent /áyjənt/ *n.* **1 a** a person who acts for another in business, politics, etc. (*insurance agent*). **b** a spy. **2 a** a person or thing that exerts power or produces an effect. **b** the cause of a natural force or effect on matter (*oxidizing agent*).

A·gent Or·ange *n.* a dioxin-containing herbicide used as a defoliant by the US during the Vietnam War; so-called from the orange stripe on storage drums.

a·gent pro·vo·ca·teur /áazhon prəvókətŏr/ *n.* (*pl.* **agents provocateurs** *pronunc.* same) a person employed to detect suspected offenders by tempting them to overt self-incriminating action.

age of con·sent *n.* the age at which consent to sexual intercourse is valid by law.

age-old *adj.* having existed for a very long time.

ag·glom·er·ate *v., n., & adj.* ● *v.tr. & intr.* /əglómərayt/

1 collect into a mass. **2** accumulate in a disorderly way. ● *n.* /əglómərət/ a mass or collection of things. ● *adj.* /əglómərət/ collected into a mass. □□ **ag·glom·er·a·tion** /-ráyshən/ *n.* **ag·glom·er·a·tive** /əglómərətiv, -raytiv/ *adj.*

ag·glu·ti·nate /əgloot'nayt/ *v.* **1** *tr.* unite as with glue. **2** *tr. & intr. Biol.* cause or undergo adhesion (of bacteria, erythrocytes, etc.). □□ **ag·glu·ti·na·tion** /-náyshən/ *n.* **ag·glu·ti·na·tive** /əglóot'nətiv, -aytiv/ *adj.*

ag·glu·ti·nin /əgloot'nin/ *n. Biol.* a substance or antibody causing agglutination.

ag·gran·dize /əgrándīz/ *v.tr.* **1** increase the power, rank, or wealth of. **2** cause to appear greater than is the case. □□ **ag·gran·dize·ment** /-dizmənt/ *n.*

ag·gra·vate /ágrəvayt/ *v.tr.* **1** increase the seriousness of (an illness, offense, etc.). **2** *disp.* annoy; exasperate (a person). □□ **ag·gra·va·tion** /-váyshən/ *n.*

ag·gre·gate *n., adj., & v.* ● *n.* /ágrigət/ **1** a collection of, or the total of, disparate elements. **2** pieces of crushed stone, gravel, etc., used in making concrete. **3 a** *Geol.* ▶ a mass of minerals formed into solid rock. **b** a mass of particles. ● *adj.* /ágrigət/ **1** (of disparate elements) collected into one mass. **2** constituted by the collection of many units into one body. ● *v.* /ágrigayt/ *tr. & intr.* collect together; combine into one mass. □ **in the aggregate** as a whole. □□ **ag·gre·ga·tion** /-gáyshən/ *n.* **ag·gre·ga·tive** /-gáytiv/ *adj.*

AGATE: POLISHED SLICE

ag·gres·sion /əgréshən/ *n.* **1** the act or practice of attacking without provocation, esp. beginning a fight or war. **2** an unprovoked attack. **3** forcefulness; self-assertiveness. **4** *Psychol.* hostile or destructive tendency or behavior.

ag·gres·sive /əgrésiv/ *adj.* **1** of a person: **a** given to aggression. **b** forceful. **2** (of an act) offensive; hostile. **3** of aggression. □□ **ag·gres·sive·ly** *adv.* **ag·gres·sive·ness** *n.*

ag·gres·sor /əgrésər/ *n.* a person who attacks without provocation.

ag·grieved /əgréevd/ *adj.* having a grievance. □□ **ag·griev·ed·ly** /-vidlee/ *adv.*

ag·gro /ágrō/ *n. Brit. sl.* **1** aggressive troublemaking. **2** trouble; difficulty.

a·ghast /əgást/ *adj.* (usu. *predic.*; often foll. by *at*) filled with dismay, shock, or consternation.

ag·ile /ájəl, ájīl/ *adj.* nimble; active. □□ **ag·ile·ly** *adv.* **a·gil·i·ty** /əjílitee/ *n.*

ag·ing /áyjing/ *n.* (also **age·ing**) **1** growing old. **2** giving the appearance of advancing age. **3** a change of properties occurring in some metals after heat treatment or cold working.

ag·ism var. of AGEISM.

ag·i·tate /ájitayt/ *v.* **1** *tr.* disturb or excite (a person or feelings). **2** *intr.* (often foll. by *for, against*) stir up interest or concern, esp. publicly (*agitated for tax reform*). **3** *tr.* shake or move, esp. briskly. □□ **ag·i·tat·ed·ly** *adv.*

ag·i·ta·tion /ájitáyshən/ *n.* **1** the act or process of agitating or being agitated. **2** mental anxiety.

a·gi·ta·to /ájitáatō/ *adv. & adj. Mus.* in an agitated manner.

ag·i·ta·tor /ájitaytər/ *n.* **1** a person who agitates, esp. publicly for a cause, etc. **2** an apparatus for shaking or mixing liquid, etc.

ag·it·prop /ájitprop/ *n.* the dissemination of Communist political propaganda, esp. in plays, movies, books, etc.

a·glow /əglố/ *adv. & adj.* ● *adv.* glowingly. ● *predic. adj.* glowing.

ag·ma /ágmə/ *n.* **1** the sound represented by the

pronunciation /ng/. **2** a symbol (ŋ) used for this sound.

ag·nail /ágnayl/ = HANGNAIL.

ag·nate /ágnayt/ *adj. & n.* ● *adj.* **1** descended esp. by male line from the same male ancestor (cf. COGNATE). **2** descended from the same forefather; of the same clan or nation. **3** of the same nature; akin. ● *n.* one who is descended, esp. by male line, from the same male ancestor. □□ **ag·nat·ic** /-nátik/ *adj.* **ag·na·tion** /-náyshən/ *n.*

ag·no·sia /agnṓzhə/ *n. Med.* the loss of the ability to interpret sensations.

ag·nos·tic /agnóstik/ *n. & adj.* ● *n.* a person who believes that nothing is known, or can be known, of the existence or nature of God, or of anything beyond material phenomena. ● *adj.* of or relating to agnostics. □□ **ag·nos·ti·cism** *n.*

Ag·nus De·i /ágnəs dáyee, deé-ī, áanyŏōs/ *n.* **1** a figure of a lamb bearing a cross or flag, as an emblem of Christ. **2** the prayer in the Mass beginning with the words "Lamb of God."

a·go /əgố/ *adv.* earlier; before the present (*ten years ago; long ago*).

a·gog /əgóg/ *adv. & adj.* ● *adv.* eagerly; expectantly. ● *predic.adj.* eager; expectant.

à go·go /əgőgō/ *adv.* in abundance (*whiskey à gogo*).

a·gon·ic /əgónik/ *adj.* having or forming no angle. □ **agonic line** a line passing through the two poles, along which a magnetic needle points directly north or south.

ag·o·nis·tic /ágənístik/ *adj.* polemical; combative. □□ **ag·o·nis·ti·cal·ly** *adv.*

AGGREGATE: ROCK

mica   *quartz*   *feldspar*

ag·o·nize /ágənīz/ *v.* **1** *intr.* (often foll. by *over*) undergo (esp. mental) anguish; suffer agony. **2** *tr.* (as **agonized** *adj.*) expressing agony (*an agonized look*). □□ **ag·o·niz·ing·ly** *adv.*

ag·o·ny /ágənee/ *n.* (*pl.* **-ies**) **1** extreme mental or physical suffering. **2** a severe struggle.

ag·o·ny aunt *Brit. colloq.* a person (esp. a woman) who answers letters in an agony column.

ag·o·ny col·umn *colloq.* **1** *Brit.* a column in a newspaper or magazine offering personal advice to readers who write in. **2** = *personal column.*

ag·o·ra·phobe /ágərəfŏb/ *n.* a person who suffers from agoraphobia.

ag·o·ra·pho·bi·a /ágərəfŏbeeə/ *n. Psychol.* an abnormal fear of open spaces or public places. □□ **ag·o·ra·pho·bic** *adj. & n.*

a·grar·i·an /əgráireeən/ *adj. & n.* ● *adj.* **1** of or relating to the land or its cultivation. **2** relating to the ownership of land. ● *n.* a person who advocates a redistribution of land ownership.

a·gree /əgreé/ *v.* (**agrees**, **agreed**, **agreeing**) **1** *intr.* hold a similar opinion (*I agree with you about that; they agreed that it would rain*). **2** *intr.* (often foll. by *to*, or *to* + infin.) consent (*agreed to the arrangement; agreed to go*). **3** *intr.* (often foll. by *with*) **a** become or be in harmony. **b** suit; be good for (*caviar didn't agree with him*). **c** *Gram.* have the same number, gender, case, or person as. **4** *intr.* (foll. by *on*) decide by mutual consent (*agreed on a compromise*). □ **agree to differ** leave a difference of opinion, etc., unresolved. **be agreed** have reached the same opinion.

a·gree·a·ble /əgreéəbəl/ *adj.* **1** (often foll. by *to*) pleasing. **2** (of a person) willing to agree (*was agreeable to going*). **3** (foll. by *to*) conformable; consonant with. □□ **a·gree·a·ble·ness** *n.* **a·gree·a·bly** *adv.*

a·gree·ment /əgreémənt/ *n.* **1** the act of agreeing; the holding of the same opinion. **2** mutual understanding. **3** an arrangement between parties as to a course of action, etc. **4** *Gram.* having the same number, gender, case, or person. **5** mutual conformity of things; harmony.

A

ag·ri·busi·ness /ágribiznis/ *n.* **1** agriculture conducted on strictly commercial principles, esp. using advanced technology. **2** an organization engaged in this. □□ **ag·ri·busi·ness·man** *n.* (*pl.* **-men**; *fem.* **agribusinesswoman**, *pl.* **-women**).

ag·ri·cul·ture /ágrikulchər/ *n.* the science or practice of cultivating the soil, raising crops, and rearing animals. □□ **ag·ri·cul·tur·al** /-kúlchərəl/ *adj.* **ag·ri·cul·tur·al·ist** *n.* **ag·ri·cul·tur·al·ly** *adv.* **ag·ri·cul·tur·ist** *n.*

ag·ri·mo·ny /ágrimōnee/ *n.* (*pl.* **-ies**) ◄ any perennial plant of the genus *Agrimonia*, esp. *A. eupatoria* with small yellow flowers.

agro- /ágrō/ *comb. form* agricultural (*agrochemical*; *agro-ecological*).

ag·ro·chem·i·cal /ágrōkémikəl/ *n.* a chemical used in agriculture.

a·gron·o·my /əgrónəmee/ *n.* the science of soil management and crop production. □□ **ag·ro·nom·ic** /ágrənómik/ *adj.* **a·gron·o·mist** /-grón-/ *n.*

a·ground /əgrównd/ *predic.adj. & adv.* (of a ship) on or on to the bottom of shallow water (*be aground*; *run aground*).

a·gue /áygyōo/ *n.* **1** *hist.* a malarial fever, with cold, hot, and sweating stages. **2** a shivering fit. □□ **a·gued** *adj.* **a·gu·ish** *adj.*

AH *abbr.* in the year of the Hegira (AD 622); of the Muslim era.

ah /aa/ *int.* expressing surprise, pleasure, realization, resignation, etc.

a·ha /aaháá, əháá/ *int.* expressing surprise, triumph, mockery, irony, etc.

a·head /əhéd/ *adv.* **1** further forward in space or time. **2** in the lead; further advanced (*ahead on points*). **3** in the line of one's forward motion (*road construction ahead*). **4** straight forward.

a·hem /əhém/ *int.* used to attract attention, gain time, or express disapproval.

a·him·sa /əhímsaa/ *n.* (in the Hindu, Buddhist, and Jainist tradition) respect for all living things and avoidance of violence toward others.

a·his·tor·i·cal /ayhistórikəl/ *adj.* lacking historical perspective or context.

a·hoy /əhóy/ *int. Naut.* a call used in hailing.

AI *abbr.* **1** artificial insemination. **2** artificial intelligence.

AID *abbr.* Agency for International Development.

aid /ayd/ *n. & v.* ● *n.* **1** help. **2** financial or material help, esp. given by one country to another. **3** a person or thing that helps. ● *v.tr.* **1** (often foll. by *to* + infin.) help. **2** promote or encourage (*sleep will aid recovery*).

aide /ayd/ *n.* **1** an aide-de-camp. **2** an assistant.

aide-de-camp /áyd-də-kámp/ *n.* (*pl.* **aides-de-camp** *pronunc.* same) an officer acting as a confidential assistant to a senior officer.

aide-mé·moire /áydmemwáar/ *n.* (*pl.* **aides-mémoire** *pronunc.* same) **1** an aid to the memory. **2** a book or document meant to aid the memory.

AIDS /aydz/ *n.* acquired immune deficiency syndrome, a fatal disorder caused by a virus transmitted in the blood and other bodily fluids, marked by severe loss of resistance to infection.

ai·grette /áygret, aygrét/ *n.* **1** a tuft of feathers or hair, esp. the plume of an egret. **2** a spray of gems or similar ornament.

ai·guille /áygweél/ *n.* a sharp piece of rock.

ai·guil·lette /áygwilét/ *n.* a tagged braid or cord hanging from the shoulder on the breast of some uniforms.

ai·ki·do /íkeedō/ *n.* a Japanese form of self-defense making use of the attacker's own movements without causing injury.

ail /ayl/ *v.* **1** *tr. archaic* trouble or afflict (*what ails him?*). **2** *intr.* be ill.

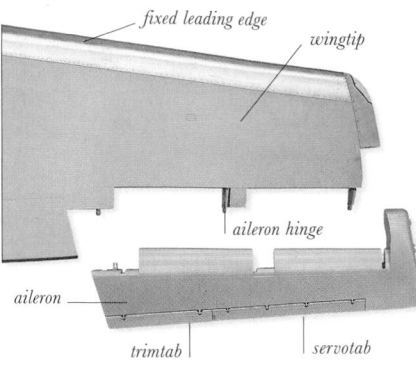

AILERON: AIRPLANE WINGTIP
WITH AILERON DETACHED

fixed leading edge · wingtip · aileron hinge · aileron · trimtab · servotab

ai·ler·on /áyləron/ *n.* ▲ a hinged surface in the trailing edge of an airplane wing, used to control lateral balance and initiate banking for turns, etc. ▷ WING

ail·ing /áyling/ *adj.* **1** ill, esp. chronically. **2** in poor condition.

ail·ment /áylmənt/ *n.* an illness, esp. a minor or chronic one.

aim /aym/ *v. & n.* ● *v.* **1** *intr.* intend or try (*aim at winning*; *aim to win*). **2** *tr.* direct or point (a weapon, remark, etc.). **3** *intr.* take aim. **4** *intr.* (foll. by *at, for*) seek to attain or achieve. ● *n.* **1** a purpose; a design; an object aimed at. **2** the directing of a weapon, missile, etc., at an object. □ **take aim** direct a weapon, etc., at an object.

aim·less /áymlis/ *adj.* without purpose. □□ **aim·less·ly** *adv.* **aim·less·ness** *n.*

ain't /aynt/ *contr. colloq.* **1** am not; are not; is not (*she ain't nice*). **2** has not; have not (*we ain't seen him*).

air /air/ *n. & v.* ● *n.* **1** an invisible gaseous substance surrounding the Earth, a mixture mainly of oxygen and nitrogen. **2 a** the free space in the atmosphere (*in the open air*). **b** the atmosphere as a place where aircraft operate. **3 a** a distinctive characteristic (*an air of absurdity*). **b** one's manner, esp. a confident one (*with a triumphant air*). **c** (esp. in *pl.*) an affected manner; pretentiousness (*gave himself airs*). **4** *Mus.* a melody. **5** a breeze or light wind. ● *v.tr.* **1** esp. *Brit.* warm (washed laundry) to dry, esp. at a fire or in a heated closet. **2** expose (a room, etc.) to the open air; ventilate. **3** express publicly (an opinion, grievance, etc.). **4** broadcast, esp. a radio or television

program. □ **in the air** (of opinions, feelings, etc.) prevalent; gaining currency. **on** (or **off**) **the air** (or not in) the process of broadcasting. **up in the air** (of projects, etc.) uncertain; not decided. **walk on air** feel elated.

air bag *n.* ▼ a safety device that fills with nitrogen on impact to protect occupants of a vehicle in a collision.

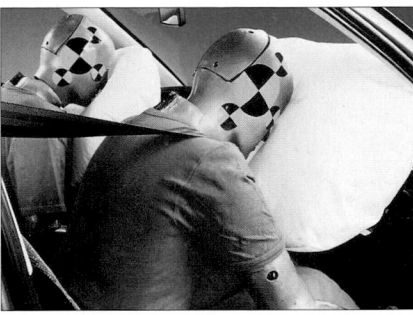

AIR BAG: CAR IMPACT TEST WITH INFLATABLE AIR BAGS

air ball *n. Basketball* a shot which misses the basket and backboard entirely.

air base /áir bays/ *n.* a base for the operation of military aircraft.

air blad·der *n.* a bladder or sac filled with air in fish or some plants.

air·borne /áirbawrn/ *adj.* **1** transported by air. **2** (of aircraft) in the air after taking off.

air brake *n.* **1** a brake worked by air pressure. **2** a movable flap or spoiler on an aircraft to reduce speed.

air·brush /áirbrush/ *n. & v.* ● *n.* ▼ an artist's device for spraying paint by means of compressed air. ● *v.tr.* paint with an airbrush.

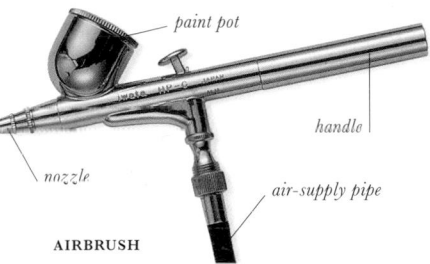

paint pot · handle · nozzle · air-supply pipe

AIRBRUSH

air-con·di·tion·ing *n.* ▼ a system for regulating the humidity, ventilation, and temperature in a building. □□ **air-con·di·tioned** *adj.* **air con·di·tion·er** *n.*

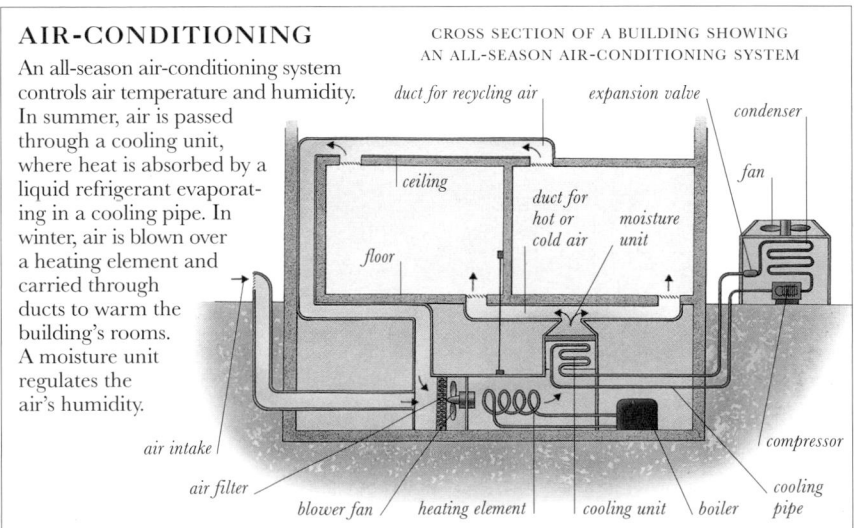

AIR-CONDITIONING

An all-season air-conditioning system controls air temperature and humidity. In summer, air is passed through a cooling unit, where heat is absorbed by a liquid refrigerant evaporating in a cooling pipe. In winter, air is blown over a heating element and carried through ducts to warm the building's rooms. A moisture unit regulates the air's humidity.

CROSS SECTION OF A BUILDING SHOWING
AN ALL-SEASON AIR-CONDITIONING SYSTEM

duct for recycling air · expansion valve · condenser · ceiling · duct for hot or cold air · moisture unit · fan · floor · air intake · air filter · blower fan · heating element · cooling unit · boiler · compressor · cooling pipe

AIRCRAFT

Airplanes, helicopters, and microlights use aerodynamics to overcome gravity. An upward force, known as lift, is achieved by creating more air pressure beneath the wings (or rotary blades) than above them. The degree of lift depends on the surface area of the wings or blades, and the speed of airflow across them. These factors can be varied by increasing or decreasing engine power and by adjusting wing dynamics. Hot-air balloons and airships become airborne using light gas or heated air within a balloon envelope. Gliders must be towed or winched into the air, but, once airborne, their light, aerodynamic construction prolongs descent.

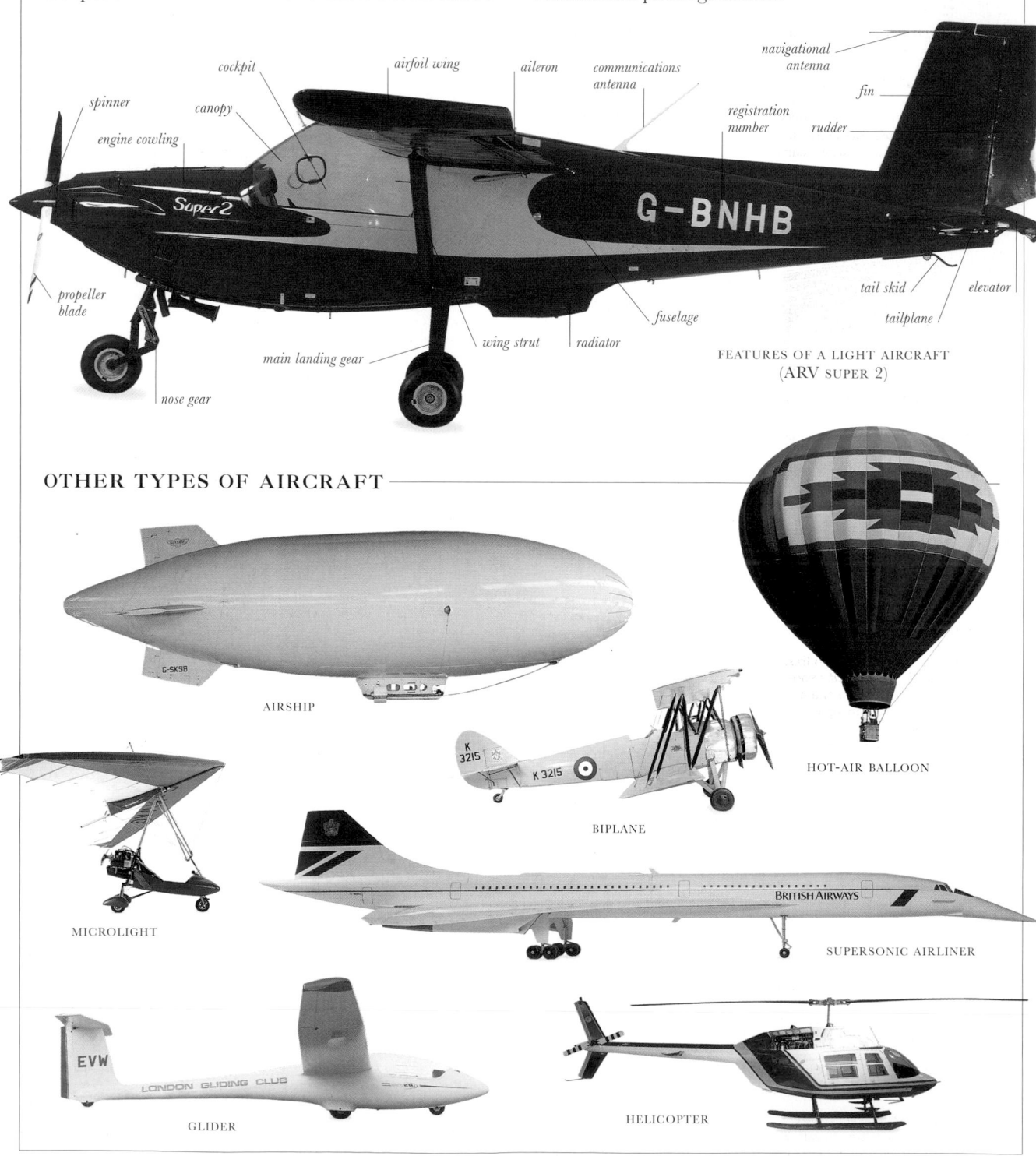

spinner
cockpit
airfoil wing
aileron
communications antenna
navigational antenna
fin
canopy
registration number
rudder
engine cowling
G-BNHB
propeller blade
tail skid
elevator
fuselage
tailplane
main landing gear
wing strut
radiator
nose gear

FEATURES OF A LIGHT AIRCRAFT
(ARV SUPER 2)

OTHER TYPES OF AIRCRAFT

AIRSHIP

HOT-AIR BALLOON

BIPLANE

MICROLIGHT

SUPERSONIC AIRLINER

GLIDER

HELICOPTER

air cor·ri·dor *n.* = CORRIDOR 3.

air·craft /áirkraft/ *n.* (*pl.* same) ◄ a machine capable of flight, esp. an airplane or helicopter.

air·craft car·ri·er *n.* a warship that carries and serves as a base for airplanes.

air·crew /áirkrōō/ *n.* **1** the crew manning an aircraft. **2** (*pl.* **aircrew**) a member of such a crew.

air cush·ion *n.* **1** an inflatable cushion. **2** the layer of air supporting a hovercraft or similar vehicle.

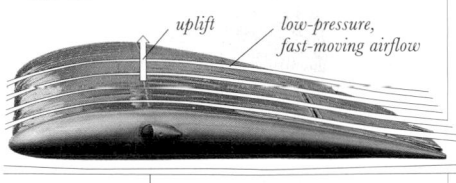

Aire·dale /áirdayl/ *n.* ◄ a large terrier of a rough-coated breed. ▷ DOG

air·fare /áirfair/ *n.* the price of a passenger ticket for travel by aircraft.

air·field /áirfeeld/ *n.* an area of land where aircraft take off and land, are maintained, etc.

air·foil /áirfoyl/ *n.* ▼ a structure with curved surfaces (e.g., a wing, fin, or horizontal stabilizer) designed to give lift in flight. ▷ AIRCRAFT, INDY CAR

AIREDALE

uplift   *low-pressure, fast-moving airflow*

high-pressure, slower-moving airflow

AIRFOIL: AIRPLANE WING

air force *n.* a branch of the armed forces concerned with fighting or defense in the air.

air·frame /áirfraym/ *n.* the body of an aircraft as distinct from its engine(s).

air·freight /áirfrayt/ *n. & v.* ● *n.* cargo carried by an aircraft. ● *v.tr.* transport by air.

air·glow /áirglō/ *n.* radiation from the upper atmosphere, detectable at night.

air gun *n.* ▶ a gun using compressed air to propel pellets.

air·head /áirhed/ *n.* **1** *Mil.* a forward base for aircraft in enemy territory. **2** *sl.* a silly or stupid person.

air·ing /áiring/ *n.* **1** exposure to fresh air, esp. for exercise. **2** esp. *Brit.* exposure (of laundry, etc.) to warm air. **3** public expression of an opinion, etc. **4** a broadcast.

air lane *n.* a path or course regularly used by aircraft.

air·less /áirlis/ *adj.* **1** stuffy. **2** without wind or breeze. □□ **air·less·ness** *n.*

air·lift /áirlift/ *n. & v.* ● *n.* the transport of troops, supplies, or passengers by air, esp. in a blockade or other emergency. ● *v.tr.* transport in this way.

air·line /áirlīn/ *n.* an organization providing a regular public service of air transport on one or more routes.

air·lin·er /áirlīnər/ *n.* a passenger aircraft, esp. a large one. ▷ AIRCRAFT

air·lock /áirlok/ *n.* **1** a stoppage of the flow in a pump or pipe, caused by an air bubble. **2** a compartment with controlled pressure and parallel sets of doors, to permit movement between areas at different pressures.

air·mail /áirmayl/ *n. & v.* ● *n.* **1** a system of transporting mail by air. **2** mail carried by air. ● *v.tr.* send by airmail.

air·man /áirmən/ *n.* (*pl.* **-men**) **1** a pilot or member of the crew of an aircraft. **2** a member of the USAF or RAF below commissioned rank.

---

air mat·tress *n.* an inflatable mattress.

air·mo·bile /áirmōbeel, -beel, -bīl/ *adj.* (of troops) that can be moved about by air.

air·plane /áirplayn/ *n.* a powered heavier-than-air flying vehicle with fixed wings. ▷ AIRCRAFT, FIGHTER

air plant *n.* ▶ a plant growing naturally without soil, esp. an epiphyte.

air·play /áirplay/ *n.* broadcasting (of recorded music).

air pock·et *n.* an apparent downdraft in the air causing an aircraft to drop suddenly.

air·port /áirpawrt/ *n.* a complex of runways and buildings for the takeoff, landing, and maintenance of civil aircraft, with facilities for passengers.

air pow·er *n.* the ability to defend and attack by means of aircraft, missiles, etc.

air raid *n.* an attack by aircraft.

air ri·fle *n.* a rifle using compressed air to propel pellets.

air sac *n.* an extension of the lungs in birds or the tracheae in insects. ▷ SONGBIRD

air·ship /áirship/ *n.* a power-driven aircraft that is lighter than air. ▷ AIRCRAFT

air·sick /áirsik/ *adj.* affected with nausea due to travel in an aircraft. □□ **air·sick·ness** *n.*

air·space /áirspays/ *n.* the air available to aircraft to fly in, esp. the part subject to the jurisdiction of a particular country.

air·speed /áirspeed/ *n.* the speed of an aircraft relative to the air through which it is moving.

air·strip /áirstrip/ *n.* a strip of ground suitable for the takeoff and landing of aircraft but usu. without other facilities.

air·tight /áirtīt/ *adj.* **1** not allowing air to pass through. **2** having no visible or apparent weaknesses (*an airtight alibi*).

air·time /áirtīm/ *n.* time allotted for a broadcast.

air-traf·fic con·trol·ler *n.* an airport official who controls air traffic by giving radio instructions to pilots.

air·waves /airwayvz/ *n.pl. colloq.* radio waves used in broadcasting.

air·way /áirway/ *n.* **1 a** a recognized route followed by aircraft. **b** (often in *pl.*) = AIRLINE. **2** *Med.* the passage through which air passes into the lungs.

air·wom·an /áirwŏŏmən/ *n.* (*pl.* **-women**) **1** a woman pilot or member of the crew of an aircraft. **2** a member of the USAF or WRAF below commissioned rank.

air·wor·thy /áirwərthee/ *adj.* (of an aircraft) fit to fly.

air·y /áiree/ *adj.* (**airier, airiest**) **1** well ventilated; breezy. **2** flippant; superficial. **3 a** light as air. **b** graceful; delicate. **4** insubstantial; ethereal; immaterial. □□ **air·i·ly** *adv.* **air·i·ness** *n.*

aisle /īl/ *n.* **1** part of a church parallel to the nave, choir, or transept. **2** a passage between rows of pews, seats, etc. **3** a passageway. □□ **aisled** *adj.*

aitch /aych/ *n.* the name of the letter H.

aitch·bone /áychbōn/ *n.* **1** the buttock or rump bone. **2** a cut of beef lying over this.

a·jar /əjáar/ *adv. & predic.adj.* (of a door) slightly open.

AK *abbr.* Alaska (in official postal use).

a.k.a. *abbr.* also known as.

AK-47 *n.* a type of assault rifle originally manufactured in the Soviet Union.

AIR PLANT
(*Tillandsia caput-medusae*)

AKC *abbr.* American Kennel Club.

a·kee /əkée/ *n.* (also **ac·kee**) **1** a tropical tree, *Blighia sapida.* **2** its fruit.

a·ke·la /əkéelə, aakáylə/ *n.* the adult leader of a group of Cub Scouts.

a·kim·bo /əkímbō/ *adv.* (of the arms) with hands on the hips and elbows turned outwards.

a·kin /əkín/ *predic.adj.* **1** related by blood. **2** of similar or kindred character.

ak·va·vit var. of AQUAVIT.

AL *abbr.* Alabama (in official postal use).

Al *symb. Chem.* the element aluminum.

Ala. *abbr.* Alabama.

à la /áa laa/ *prep.* after the manner of (*à la russe*).

al·a·bas·ter /áləbastər/ *n. & adj.* ● *n.* a translucent usu. white form of gypsum, often carved into ornaments. ● *adj.* **1** of alabaster. **2** like alabaster in whiteness or smoothness.

à la carte /áa laa káart/ *adv. & adj.* ordered as separately priced item(s) from a menu, not as part of a set meal.

a·lack /əlák/ *int.* (also **a·lack-a-day** /əlákəday/) *archaic* an expression of regret or surprise.

a·lac·ri·ty /əlákritee/ *n.* briskness or cheerful readiness.

A·lad·din's cave /əlád·nz/ *n.* a place of great riches.

A·lad·din's lamp *n.* a talisman enabling its holder to gratify any wish.

à la mode /áa laa mŏd/ *adv. & adj.* **1** in fashion; fashionable. **2 a** served with ice cream. **b** (of beef) braised in wine.

a·lar /áylər/ *adj.* **1** relating to wings. **2** winglike or wing-shaped. **3** axillary.

a·larm /əláarm/ *n. & v.* ● *n.* **1** a warning of danger, etc. **2 a** a warning sound or device. **b** = ALARM CLOCK. **3** frightened expectation of danger or difficulty. ● *v.tr.* **1** frighten or disturb. **2** arouse to a sense of danger.

a·larm clock *n.* a clock with a device that can be made to sound at a time set in advance. ▷ CLOCK

a·larm·ing /əláarming/ *adj.* disturbing; frightening. □□ **a·larm·ing·ly** *adv.*

a·larm·ist /əláarmist/ *n. & adj.* ● *n.* a person given to spreading needless alarm. ● *adj.* creating needless alarm. □□ **a·larm·ism** *n.*

a·lar·um /əláarəm/ *n. archaic* = ALARM. □ **alarums and excursions** confused noise and activity.

Alas. *abbr.* Alaska.

a·las /əlás/ *int.* an expression of grief, pity, or concern.

a·late /áylayt/ *adj.* having wings or winglike appendages.

alb /alb/ *n.* a usu. white vestment reaching to the feet, worn by some Christian priests at church ceremonies.

al·ba·core /álbəkawr/ *n.* **1** a long-finned tuna, *Thunnus alalunga.* **2** any of various other related fish.

Al·ba·ni·an /albáyneən, awl-/ *n. & adj.* ● *n.* **1 a** a native or inhabitant of Albania in SE Europe. **b** a person of Albanian descent. **2** the language of Albania. ● *adj.* of or relating to Albania or its people or language.

al·ba·tross /álbətraws, -tros/ *n.* **1 a** ◄ any long-winged stout-bodied bird of the family Diomedeidae, inhabiting the Pacific Ocean. ▷ SEABIRD. **b** a source of frustration or guilt; an encumbrance. **2** *Golf* DOUBLE EAGLE.

AIR GUN: REFLEXED AIR PISTOL

cocking lever and barrel

piston

trigger

hand grip   *pellets*

ALBATROSS:
WANDERING
ALBATROSS
(*Diomedea exulans*)

A

al·be·do /albéedō/ *n.* (*pl.* **-os**) the proportion of light or radiation reflected by a surface, esp. of a planet or moon.

al·be·it /áwlbéeit/ *conj. formal* though (*he tried, albeit without success*).

al·bes·cent /albésənt/ *adj.* growing or shading into white.

al·bi·no /albínō/ *n.* (*pl.* **-os**) ◄ a person or animal having a congenital absence of pigment in the skin and hair (which are white), and the eyes (which are usu. pink). □□ **al·bi·nism** /álbinizəm/ *n.*

Al·bi·on /álbeeən/ *n. literary* (also **perfidious Albion**) Britain or England.

al·bum /álbəm/ *n.* **1** a blank book for the insertion of photographs, stamps, etc. **2 a** a long-playing phonograph, audio cassette, or compact disc recording. **b** a set of these.

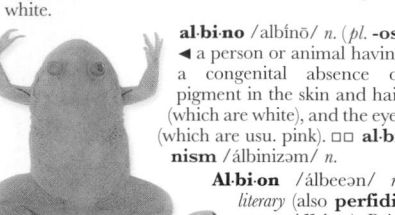

ALBINO AFRICAN CLAWED TOAD (*Xenopus laevis*)

al·bu·men /albyoŏmin/ *n.* **1** egg white. ▷ EGG. **2** *Bot.* the substance found between the skin and embryo of many seeds, usu. the edible part; = ENDOSPERM.

al·bu·min /albyoŏmin/ *n.* any of a class of water-soluble proteins found in egg white, milk, blood, etc. □□ **al·bu·mi·nous** *adj.*

al·bu·mi·nu·ri·a /albyoŏminoŏreeə, -nyoŏr-/ *n.* the presence of albumin in the urine, usu. as a symptom of kidney disease.

al·che·my /álkəmee/ *n.* (*pl.* **-ies**) **1** the medieval forerunner of chemistry, esp. seeking to turn base metals into gold or silver. **2** a miraculous transformation or the means of achieving this. □□ **al·chem·i·cal** /-kémikəl/ *adj.* **al·che·mist** *n.*

al·co·hol /álkəhawl, -hol-/ *n.* **1** (in full **ethyl alcohol**) a colorless volatile flammable liquid forming the intoxicating element in wine, beer, liquor, etc., and also used as a solvent, as fuel, etc. Also called **ethanol**. **2** any liquor containing this. **3** *Chem.* any of a large class of organic compounds that contain one or more hydroxyl groups attached to carbon atoms.

al·co·hol·ic /álkəháwlik, -hól-/ *adj. & n.* ● *adj.* of, relating to, containing, or caused by alcohol. ● *n.* a person suffering from alcoholism.

al·co·hol·ism /álkəhawlízəm, -ho-/ *n.* **1** an addiction to the consumption of alcoholic liquor. **2** the diseased condition resulting from this.

al·co·hol·om·e·ter /álkəhawlómitər, -ho-/ *n.* an instrument for measuring alcoholic concentration in a liquid. □□ **al·co·hol·om·e·try** *n.*

al·cove /álkōv/ *n.* a recess, esp. in the wall of a room or of a garden.

al·de·hyde /áldihīd/ *n. Chem.* any of a class of compounds formed by the oxidation of alcohols. □□ **al·de·hy·dic** /áldihīdik/ *adj.*

al den·te /aal déntay, al déntee/ *adj.* (of pasta, etc.) cooked so as to be still firm when bitten.

al·der /áwldər/ *n.* any tree of the genus *Alnus*, related to the birch, with catkins and toothed leaves.

al·der·man /áwldərmən/ *n.* (*pl.* **-men**; *fem.* **alderwoman**, *pl.* **-women**) an elected municipal official serving on the governing council of a city. □□ **al·der·man·ic** /-mánik/ *adj.*

ale /ayl/ *n.* **1** beer. **2** a similar beverage with a more pronounced, often bitter taste.

a·le·a·tor·ic /áyleeətáwrik, -tór-/ *adj.* depending on the throw of a dice or on chance. **2** *Mus & Art* involving random choice by a performer or artist; improvisational.

a·le·a·to·ry /áyleeətawree/ *adj.* = ALEATORIC.

ale·house /áylhows/ *n.* a tavern.

a·lem·bic /əlémbik/ *n. hist.* ► an apparatus formerly used in distilling.

a·leph /áálif/ *n.* the first letter of the Hebrew alphabet.

a·lert /əlért/ *adj., n., & v.* ● *adj.* **1** watchful or vigilant; ready to take action. **2** quick (esp. of mental faculties); attentive. ● *n.* a warning call or alarm. ● *v.tr.* (often foll. by *to*) make alert; warn (*were alerted to the danger*). □ **on the alert** on the lookout against danger or attack. □□ **a·lert·ly** *adv.* **a·lert·ness** *n.*

Al·eut /aleeoŏt, əlóŏt/ *n.* **1 a** a N. American people native to the Aleutian Islands and the western Alaskan Peninsula. **b** a member of this people. **2** the language of this people. □□ **A·leu·tian** *adj.*

Al·ex·an·der tech·nique *n.* a system designed to promote well-being through the control of posture.

Al·ex·an·dri·an /áligzándreeən/ *adj.* **1** of or characteristic of Alexandria in Egypt. **2** belonging to or akin to the schools of literature and philosophy of Alexandria.

al·ex·an·drine /áligzándrin, -dreen/ *adj. & n.* ● *adj.* (of a line of verse) having six iambic feet. ● *n.* an alexandrine line.

al·ex·an·drite /áligzándrīt/ *n. Mineral.* ► a green variety of chrysoberyl.

a·lex·i·a /əlékseeə/ *n.* the inability to see words or to read, caused by a condition of the brain.

al·fal·fa /alfálfə/ *n.* a leguminous plant, *Medicago sativa*, with cloverlike leaves and flowers used for fodder.

al·fres·co /alfréskō/ *adv. & adj.* in the open air (*we dined alfresco; an alfresco lunch*).

al·ga /álgə/ *n.* (*pl.* **algae** /áljee/ also **algas**) (usu. in *pl.*) ▼ a nonflowering stemless water plant, esp. seaweed and phytoplankton. □□ **al·gal** *adj.*

al·ge·bra /áljibrə/ *n.* **1** the branch of mathematics that uses letters to represent numbers and quantities in formulae and equations. **2** a system of this based on given axioms (*linear algebra; the algebra of logic*). □□ **al·ge·bra·ic** /áljibráyik/ *adj.* **al·ge·bra·i·cal·ly** *adv.*

-algia /áljə/ *comb. form Med.* denoting pain in a part specified by the first element (*neuralgia*). □□ **-algic** *comb. form* forming adjectives.

al·gi·cide /áljisīd/ *n.* a preparation for destroying algae.

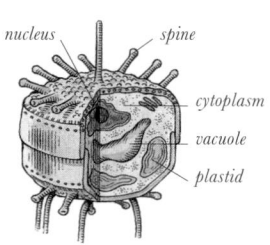

alembic head

condensing vapors

vaporizing liquid

distilled liquid

cucurbit

ALEMBIC

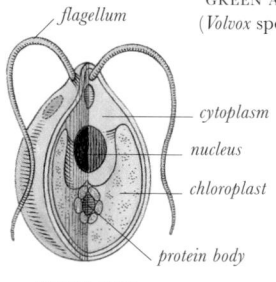

ALEXANDRITE

al·gid /áljid/ *adj. Med.* cold; chilly. □□ **al·gid·i·ty** /aljíditee/ *n.*

al·gi·nate /áljinayt/ *n.* a salt or ester of alginic acid.

al·gin·ic ac·id /aljínik/ *n.* an insoluble carbohydrate found (chiefly as salts) in many brown seaweeds.

Al·gol /álgawl, -gol/ *n.* a high-level computer programming language.

al·go·lag·ni·a /álgəlágneeə/ *n.* sexual pleasure derived from inflicting pain on oneself or others; masochism or sadism. □□ **al·go·lag·nic** *adj. & n.*

Al·gon·qui·an /álgóngkweeən/ *n.* any of the languages or dialects used by the Algonquin peoples.

Al·gon·quin /algóngkwən/ *n.* **1** a N. American people native to the Ottawa River valley and the northern St. Lawrence River valley. **2** a member of this people.

al·go·rithm /álgərithəm/ *n. Math.* a process or set of rules used for calculation or problem-solving, esp. with a computer. □□ **al·go·rith·mic** /álgərithmik/ *adj.*

a·li·as /áyleeəs/ *adv. & n.* ● *adv.* also known as. ● *n.* a false name.

al·i·bi /álibī/ *n.* (*pl.* **alibis**) **1** a claim, or the evidence supporting it, that when an alleged act took place, one was elsewhere. **2** an excuse of any kind.

al·i·dade /álidayd/ *n. Surveying & Astron.* an instrument for determining directions or measuring angles.

al·ien /áyleeən/ *adj. & n.* ● *adj.* **1 a** (often foll. by *to*) unfamiliar; not in accordance; unfriendly; hostile; repugnant (*army discipline was alien to him; struck an alien note*). **b** different or separated. **2** from a foreign country. **3** of or relating to beings supposedly from other worlds. **4** *Bot.* (of a plant) introduced from elsewhere and naturalized in its new home. ● *n.* **1** a foreigner, esp. one who is not a naturalized citizen of the country where he or she is living. **2** a being supposedly from another world. **3** *Bot.* an alien plant. □□ **al·ien·ness** *n.*

al·ien·a·ble /áyleeənəbəl/ *adj. Law* able to be transferred to new ownership. □□ **al·ien·a·bil·i·ty** /-bílitee/ *n.*

al·ien·age /áyleeənij/ *n.* the state of being an alien.

al·ien·ate /áyleeənayt/ *v.tr.* **1 a** cause (a person) to become unfriendly or hostile. **b** (often foll. by *from*) cause (a person) to feel estranged from (friends, society, etc.). **2** transfer ownership of (property) to another person, etc.

ALGA

There are over 20,000 species of these organisms, ranging from microscopic, single-celled diatoms to giant seaweeds. Most algae live in water, and nearly all are autotrophic, producing their own food through photosynthesis as plants do.

EXAMPLES OF ALGAE

colony of cells
daughter colony
gelatinous sheath

GREEN ALGA (*Volvox* species)

nucleus
spine
cytoplasm
vacuole
plastid

flagellum
cytoplasm
nucleus
chloroplast
protein body

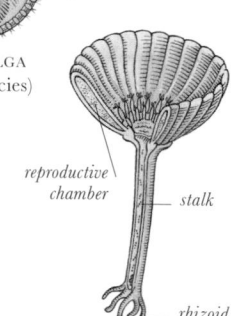

reproductive chamber
stalk
rhizoid

DIATOM (*Thalassiosira* species)

GREEN ALGA (*Chlamydomonas* species)

GREEN ALGA (*Acetabularia* species)

al·ien·a·tion /áyleeənáyshən/ *n.* **1** the act or result of alienating. **2** (*Theatr.* **alienation effect**) a theatrical effect whereby an audience remains objective, not identifying with the characters or action of a play.

a·light[1] /əlít/ *v.intr.* **1** esp. *Brit.* **a** descend from a vehicle. **b** dismount from a horse. **2** come to earth from the air. **3** (foll. by *on*) find by chance; notice.

a·light[2] /əlít/ *predic.adj.* **1** on fire; burning. **2** lighted up; excited.

a·lign /əlín/ *v.tr.* **1** put in a straight line or bring into line (*three books were neatly aligned on the shelf*). **2** (usu. foll. by *with*) bring (oneself, etc.) into alliance with (a cause, policy, political party, etc.). □□ **a·lign·ment** *n.*

a·like /əlík/ *adj. & adv.* ● *adj.* (usu. *predic.*) similar; like one another; indistinguishable. ● *adv.* in a similar way or manner (*all were treated alike*).

al·i·ment /áliment/ *n. formal* **1** food. **2** support or mental sustenance. □□ **al·i·men·tal** /áliméntˈl/ *adj.*

al·i·men·ta·ry /áliméntəree/ *adj.* of, relating to, or providing nourishment.

al·i·men·ta·ry ca·nal *n. Anat.* the passage along which food is passed from the mouth to the anus during digestion. ▷ DIGESTION

al·i·men·ta·tion /álimentáyshən/ *n.* **1** nourishment. **2** maintenance; support.

al·i·mo·ny /álimōnee/ *n.* the money payable by a man to his wife or former wife or by a woman to her husband or former husband after they are separated or divorced.

A-line /áylīn/ *adj.* (of a garment) having a narrow waist or shoulders and somewhat flared skirt.

al·i·phat·ic /álifátik/ *adj. Chem.* of, denoting, or relating to organic compounds in which carbon atoms form open chains, not aromatic rings.

al·i·quot /álikwot/ *adj. & n.* ● *adj.* (of a part or portion) contained by the whole an integral or whole number of times. ● *n.* **1** an aliquot part; an integral factor. **2** a known fraction of a whole.

A-list *n.* a real or imaginary list of the most celebrated or sought after individuals, esp. in show business.

a·live /əlív/ *adj.* (usu. *predic.*) **1** (of a person, animal, plant, etc.) living. **2 a** (of a thing) continuing; in operation or action (*kept his interest alive*). **b** provoking interest (*the topic is still very much alive*). **3** lively; active. **4** charged with an electric current; connected to a source of electricity. **5** (foll. by *to*) alert or responsive to. **6** (foll. by *with*) **a** swarming or teeming with. **b** full of. □ **alive and kicking** *colloq.* very active; lively. **alive and well** still alive. □□ **a·live·ness** *n.*

al·ka·hest /álkəhest/ *n.* (also **al·ca·hest**) the universal solvent sought by alchemists.

al·ka·li /álkəlī/ *n.* (*pl.* **alkalis**) **1 a** ▲ any of a class of substances that liberate hydroxide ions in water, usu. form caustic or corrosive solutions, turn litmus blue, and have a pH of more than 7, e.g., sodium hydroxide. ▷ PH. **b** any other substance with similar but weaker properties, e.g., sodium carbonate. **2** *Chem.* any substance that reacts with or neutralizes hydrogen ions.

al·ka·line /álkəlīn/ *adj.* of, relating to, or having the nature of an alkali. □□ **al·ka·lin·i·ty** /álkəlinitee/ *n.*

al·ka·loid /álkəloyd/ *n.* any of a series of nitrogenous organic compounds of plant origin, many of which are used as drugs, e.g., morphine, quinine.

al·ka·lo·sis /álkəlósis/ *n. Med.* an excessive alkaline condition of the body fluids or tissues.

al·kane /álkayn/ *n. Chem.* ▶ any of a series of saturated aliphatic hydrocarbons having the general formula C_nH_{2n+2}, including methane, ethane, and propane.

al·kene /álkeen/ *n. Chem.* ▶ any of a series of unsaturated aliphatic hydrocarbons containing a double bond and having the general formula C_nH_{2n}.

al·kyd /álkid/ *n.* any of the group of synthetic resins derived from various alcohols and acids.

ALKALI

An alkali is a water-soluble substance capable of accepting protons (hydrogen ions). When an alkali is added to water, it accepts protons (H^+), from some of the hydronium ions (H_3O^+) and water molecules (H_2O) present, forming more water molecules and hydroxide ions (OH^-). The greater the number of hydroxide ions in the solution, the stronger is its alkalinity and the higher its pH value.

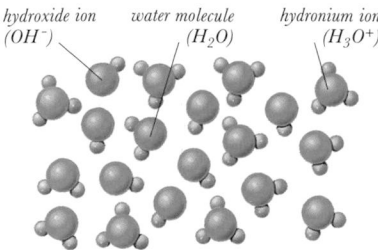

hydroxide ion (OH⁻)   *water molecule (H₂O)*   *hydronium ion (H₃O⁺)*

MOLECULES AND IONS IN NEUTRAL WATER

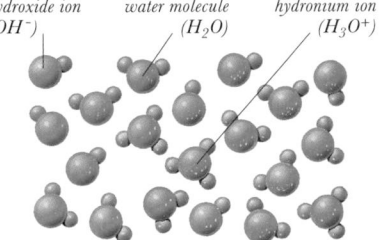

hydroxide ion (OH⁻)   *water molecule (H₂O)*   *hydronium ion (H₃O⁺)*

MOLECULES AND IONS IN ALKALINE SOLUTION

---

al·kyl /álkil/ *n. Chem.* any radical derived from an alkane by the removal of a hydrogen atom.

al·kyl·ate /álkilayt/ *v.tr. Chem.* introduce an alkyl radical into (a compound).

al·kyne /álkīn/ *n. Chem.* ▼ any of a series of unsaturated aliphatic hydrocarbons containing a triple bond and having the general formula C_nH_{2n-2}.

all /awl/ *adj., n., & adv.* ● *adj.* **1 a** the whole amount, quantity, or extent of (*waited all day; all his life; we all know why*). **b** (with *pl.*) the entire number of (*all the others left; all ten men*). **2** any whatever (*beyond all doubt*). **3** greatest possible (*with all speed*). ● *n.* **1 a** all the persons or things concerned (*all were present*). **b** everything (*that is all*). **2** (foll. by *of*) **a** the whole of (*take all of it*). **b** every one of (*all of us*). **c** *colloq.* as much as (*all of six feet tall*). **d** *colloq.* in a state of (*all of a dither*). **3** one's whole strength or resources (prec. by *my, your*, etc.). **4** (in games) on both sides (*the score was two all*). ¶ Widely used with *of* in sense 2a, b, esp. when followed by a pronoun or by a noun implying a number of persons or things, as in *all of the children are here*. However, use with mass nouns (as in *all of the bread*) is often avoided. ● *adv.* **1 a** entirely (*dressed all in black; all around the room*). **b** as an intensifier (*a book all about ships; stop all this grumbling*). **2** (foll. by *the* + compar.) **a** to that extent (*if they go, all the better*). **b** in the full degree to be expected (*that makes it all the worse*). □ **all along** all the time (*he was joking all along*). **all and sundry** everyone. **all but** very nearly (*it was all but impossible*). **all for** *colloq.* strongly in favor of. **all in** *colloq.* exhausted. **all in all** everything considered. **all manner of** many different kinds of. **all one** (or **the same**) a matter of indifference (*it's all one to me*). **all over 1** completely finished. **2** in or on all parts of (esp. the body) (*went hot and cold all over*). **3** *colloq.* typically (*that is you all over*). **all the same** nevertheless; in spite of this (*he was innocent but was punished all the same*). **all set** *colloq.* ready to start. **all there** *colloq.* mentally alert. **all together** all at once; all in one place or in a group (*they came all together*) (cf. ALTOGETHER). **all told** in all. **all very well** *colloq.* an expression used to imply skepticism about a favorable or consoling remark. **all the way** the whole distance; completely. **at all** (with *neg.* or *interrog.*) to any extent (*did not swim at all; did you like it at all?*). **in all** in total number.

al·la bre·ve /álə brév, áalaa brévay/ *n. Mus.* a time signature indicating 2 half-note beats in a bar.

al·la cap·pel·la var. of A CAPPELLA.

Al·lah /álə, áalaa/ *n.* the name of God in Islam.

all-A·mer·i·can *adj.* **1** representing the whole of (or only) America or the US. **2** truly American (*all-American boy*). **3** *Sports* recognized as one of the best in a particular sport.

all-a·round *adv.* **1** in all respects (*a good performance all around*). **2** for each person (*he bought drinks all around*). **3** (*attrib.*) (of a person) versatile.

ALKANE, ALKENE, ALKYNE

Alkanes, alkenes, and alkynes are all hydrocarbons (compounds made of hydrogen and carbon only). The three differ in the types of bonds between their atoms. Alkanes have only single covalent bonds, which are formed by two carbon atoms sharing a pair of electrons. Alkenes have one or more double bonds between carbon atoms, whereby two pairs of electrons are shared. Alkynes have one or more triple bonds, with the carbon atoms sharing three pairs of electrons.

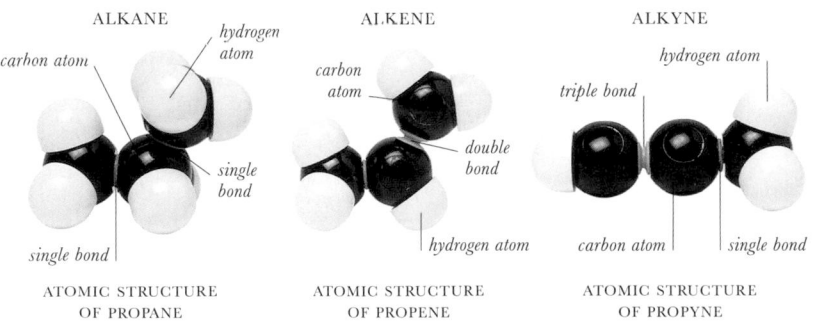

ALKANE — *carbon atom, hydrogen atom, single bond*

ATOMIC STRUCTURE OF PROPANE

ALKENE — *carbon atom, double bond, hydrogen atom*

ATOMIC STRUCTURE OF PROPENE

ALKYNE — *hydrogen atom, triple bond, carbon atom, single bond*

ATOMIC STRUCTURE OF PROPYNE

A

ALLEGORY

This complex allegorical painting is based on classical mythology, and warns of dangers and deceit disguised in false love. Venus, the goddess of love, is seducing Cupid with a kiss while reaching to steal the arrow from his quiver. Behind the central figures are Fraud, depicted as an empty mask, and Pleasure, portrayed as a young girl offering honey, but possessing the hind quarters of a serpent. Time is pictured reaching to expose Fraud, and in the shadows the distraught figure of Jealousy pulls at her hair.

Fraud　*Time*　*Jealousy*　*Folly*　*Cupid*　*Pleasure*　*Venus*

An Allegory (Venus, Cupid, Folly, and Time)
(1540–45), AGNOLO BRONZINO

---

al·lay /əláy/ *v.tr.* **1** diminish (fear, suspicion, etc.). **2** relieve or alleviate (pain, hunger, etc.).

all clear *n.* a signal that danger or difficulty is over.

al·le·ga·tion /áligáyshən/ *n.* **1** an assertion, esp. an unproved one. **2** the act or an instance of alleging.

al·lege /əléj/ *v.tr.* **1** declare to be the case, esp. without proof. **2** advance as an argument or excuse. □□ **al·leged** *adj.*

al·leg·ed·ly /əléjidlee/ *adv.* as is alleged or said to be the case.

al·le·giance /əléejəns/ *n.* **1** loyalty (to a person or cause, etc.). **2** the duty of a subject to his or her sovereign or government.

al·le·gor·i·cal /áligáwrikəl, -gór-/ *adj.* consisting of or relating to allegory; by means of allegory. □□ **al·le·gor·i·cal·ly** *adv.*

al·le·go·rize /áligərīz/ *v.tr.* treat as or by means of an allegory. □□ **al·le·go·ri·za·tion** /-rizáyshən/ *n.*

al·le·go·ry /áligawree/ *n.* (*pl.* **-ies**) **1** ▲ a story, picture, etc., in which the meaning is represented symbolically. **2** the use of such symbols. **3** a symbol.

al·le·gret·to /áligrétō/ *adv., adj., & n. Mus.* ● *adv. & adj.* in a fairly brisk tempo. ● *n.* (*pl.* **-os**) an allegretto passage or movement.

al·le·gro /əléggrō, əláy-/ *adv., adj., & n. Mus.* ● *adv. & adj.* in a brisk tempo. ● *n.* (*pl.* **-os**) an allegro passage or movement.

al·lele /əléel/ *n.* one of the (usu. two) alternative forms of a gene. □□ **al·lel·ic** /əléelik/ *adj.*

al·le·lu·ia /álilóōyə/ *int. & n.* (also **al·le·lu·ya, hallelujah** /hál-/) ● *int.* God be praised. ● *n.* **1** praise to God. **2** a song of praise to God. **3** *RC Ch.* the part of the mass including this.

Al·len screw /álən/ *n.* a screw with a hexagonal socket in the head.

Al·len wrench /álən/ *n.* ◄ a hexagonal wrench designed to fit into and turn an Allen screw.

al·ler·gen /álərjən/ *n.* any substance that causes an allergic reaction. □□ **al·ler·gen·ic** /-jénik/ *adj.*

al·ler·gic /əlórjik/ *adj.* **1** (foll. by *to*) **a** having an allergy to. **b** *colloq.* having a strong dislike for (a person or thing). **2** caused by or relating to an allergy.

ALLEN WRENCHES

al·ler·gy /álərjee/ *n.* (*pl.* **-ies**) **1** *Med.* a condition of reacting adversely to certain substances. **2** *colloq.* an antipathy or dislike. □□ **al·ler·gist** *n.*

al·le·vi·ate /əléeveeayt/ *v.tr.* lessen or make less severe (pain, suffering, etc.). □□ **al·le·vi·a·tion** /-áyshən/ *n.*

alley /álee/ *n.* (*pl.* **-eys**) **1** (also **al·ley·way**) **a** a narrow street. **b** a narrow passageway between or behind buildings. **2** a path in a park or garden. **3** an enclosure for bowling, etc.

All Fools' Day *n.* esp. *Brit.* April 1.

al·lia·ce·ous /álee-áyshəs/ **1** relating to the genus *Allium.* **2** tasting or smelling like onion or garlic

al·lied /əlíd, álīd/ *adj.* **1** united or associated in an alliance. **2** connected or related (*studied medicine and allied subjects*).

al·li·ga·tor /áligaytər/ *n.* **1** ▼ a large reptile of the crocodile family native to the Americas and China, with a head broader and shorter than that of the crocodile. ▷ CROCODILE. **2** (in general use) any of several large members of the crocodile family. **3** the skin of such an animal or material resembling it.

rounded snout　*protruding eyes*

ALLIGATOR: AMERICAN ALLIGATOR
(*Alligator mississippiensis*)

cone-shaped teeth

short leg

al·li·ga·tor clip *n.* a clip with teeth for gripping.

al·li·ga·tor pear *n.* an avocado.

all-im·por·tant *adj.* crucial; vitally important.

al·lit·er·ate /əlítərayt/ *v.* **1** *intr.* **a** contain alliteration. **b** use alliteration in speech or writing. **2** *tr.* **a** construct (a phrase, etc.) with alliteration. **b** speak or pronounce with alliteration. □□ **al·lit·er·a·tive** /əlítəraytiv, -rətiv/ *adj.*

al·lit·er·a·tion /əlítəráyshən/ *n.* the occurrence of the same letter or sound at the beginning of adjacent or closely connected words (e.g., *calm, cool, and collected*).

al·li·um /áleeəm/ *n.* ► any plant of the genus *Allium,* usu. bulbous and strong smelling, e.g., onion and garlic.

allo- /álō, əló/ *comb. form* other (*allophone*; *allogamy*).

al·lo·cate /áləkayt/ *v.tr.* (usu. foll. by *to*) assign, apportion, or devote to (a purpose, person, or place). □□ **al·lo·ca·ble** /-kəbəl/ *adj.* **al·lo·ca·tion** /-káyshən/ *n.*

al·lo·cu·tion /áləkyōōshən/ *n.* formal or hortatory speech or manner of address.

al·log·a·my /əlógəmee/ *n. Bot.* cross-fertilization in plants.

al·lo·morph /áləmawrf/ *n. Linguistics* any of two or more alternative forms of a morpheme. □□ **al·lo·mor·phic** *adj.*

al·lo·path /əlópəth/ *n.* one who practices allopathy.

al·lop·a·thy /əlópəthee/ *n.* the treatment of disease with drugs or other agents having opposite effects to the symptoms (cf. HOMEOPATHY). □□ **al·lo·path·ic** /áləpáthik/ *adj.*

al·lo·phone /áləfōn/ *n. Linguistics* any of the variant sounds forming a single phoneme. □□ **al·lo·phon·ic** /-fónik/ *adj.*

al·lot /əlót/ *v.tr.* (**allotted, allotting**) **1** give or apportion to (a person) as a share or task; distribute officially to (*they allotted us each a pair of boots; the men were allotted duties*). **2** (foll. by *to*) give or distribute officially (*a sum was allotted to each charity*).

al·lot·ment /əlótmənt/ *n.* **1** a share allotted. **2** the action of allotting.

al·lo·trope /álətrōp/ *n.* ► any of two or more different physical forms in which an element can exist.

al·lot·tee /əloteé/ *n.* a person to whom something is allotted.

all out *adj.* involving all one's strength; at full speed (also (with hyphen) *attrib.: an all-out effort*).

al·low /əlów/ *v.* **1** *tr.* permit (*smoking is not allowed; we allowed them to speak*). **2** *tr.* give or provide; permit (a person) to have (a limited quantity or sum) (*we were allowed $500 a year*). **3** *tr.* provide or set aside for a purpose; add or deduct in consideration of something (*allow 10% for inflation*). **4** *tr.* **a** admit; concede (*he allowed that it was so*). **b** be of the opinion. **5** *refl.* permit oneself; indulge oneself in (conduct) (*allowed herself to be persuaded*). **6** *intr.* (foll. by *of*) admit of. **7** *intr.* (foll. by *for*) take into consideration; make addition or deduction corresponding to (*allowing for waste*). □□ **al·low·a·ble** *adj.*

al·low·ance /əlówəns/ *n. & v.* ● *n.* **1** an amount or sum allowed to a person, esp. regularly. **2** an amount allowed in reckoning. **3** a deduction or discount. **4** (foll. by *of*) tolerance of. ● *v.tr.* **1** make an allowance to (a person). **2** supply in limited quantities. □ **make allowances** (often foll. by *for*) **1** take into consideration (mitigating circumstances) (*made allowances for his demented state*). **2** look with tolerance upon; make excuses for (a person, bad behavior, etc.).

al·low·ed·ly /əlówidlee/ *adv.* as is generally allowed or acknowledged.

al·loy /áloy, əlóy/ *n. & v.* ● *n.* **1** a mixture of two or more chemical elements, at least one of which is a metal. **2** an inferior metal mixed esp. with gold or silver. ● *v.tr.* **1** mix (metals). **2** debase (a pure substance) by admixture.

all-pur·pose *adj.* suitable for many uses.

all right *adj., adv., & int.* ● *adj.* (*predic.*) satisfactory; safe and sound. ● *adv.* satisfactorily (*it worked out all right*). ● *int.* **1** expressing consent or assent to a proposal or order. **2** as an intensifier (*that's the one all right*).

ALLOTROPE

An element such as carbon has several allotropic forms. In each case, the carbon atoms link up differently to produce distinct forms, with very different properties. Shown here are two allotropes of carbon: diamond and graphite. The pyramidal configuration of atoms in a diamond produces a very strong structure, whereas graphite is composed of layers of carbon atoms, with only weak bonds between the layers.

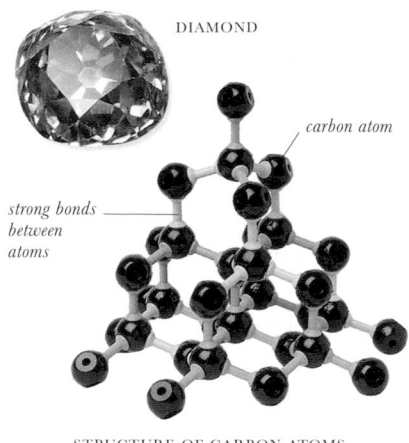

DIAMOND

carbon atom

strong bonds between atoms

STRUCTURE OF CARBON ATOMS
IN A DIAMOND

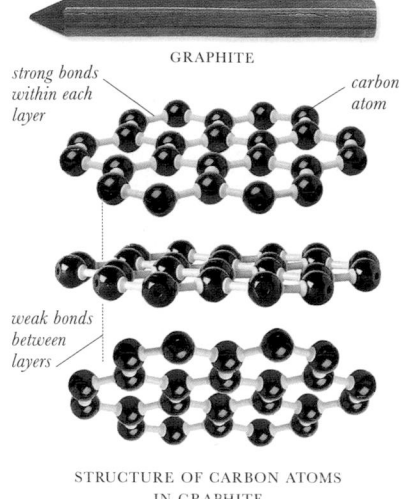

GRAPHITE

strong bonds within each layer

carbon atom

weak bonds between layers

STRUCTURE OF CARBON ATOMS
IN GRAPHITE

all-right *attrib.adj. colloq.* fine; acceptable (*an all-right guy*).

All Saints' Day *n.* Nov. 1.

All Souls' Day *n.* Nov. 2.

all·spice /áwlspīs/ *n.* **1** ► the aromatic spice obtained from the ground berry of the pimento plant, *Pimenta dioica*. ▷ SPICE. **2** the berry of this. **3** any of various other aromatic shrubs.

ground spice

allspice berries

ALLSPICE
(*Pimenta dioica*)

all-time *adj.* (of a record, etc.) hitherto unsurpassed.

al·lude /əlŏŏd/ *v.intr.* (foll. by *to*) **1** refer, esp. indirectly, covertly, or briefly, to. **2** mention.

al·lure /əlŏŏr/ *v. & n.* ● *v.tr.* attract, charm, or fascinate. ● *n.* attractiveness; personal charm; fascination. □□ **al·lure·ment** *n.* **al·lur·ing** *adj.*

al·lu·sion /əlŏŏzhən/ *n.* a reference, esp. a passing, covert, or indirect one. ¶ Often confused with *illusion*.

al·lu·sive /əlŏŏsiv/ *adj.* **1** (often foll. by *to*) containing an allusion. **2** containing many allusions. □□ **al·lu·sive·ly** *adv.*

al·lu·vi·al /əlŏŏveeəl/ *adj.* of or relating to alluvium.

al·lu·vi·on /əlŏŏveeən/ *n.* **1** the wash of the sea against the shore, or of a river against its banks. **2 a** a large overflow of water. **b** matter deposited by this, esp. alluvium. **3** the formation of new land by the movement of the sea or of a river.

al·lu·vi·um /əlŏŏveeəm/ *n.* (*pl.* **alluviums** or **alluvia** /-ə/) a deposit of usu. fine fertile soil left during a time of flood, esp. in a river valley or delta. ▷ ERODE, SEDIMENT

al·ly /álī/ *n. & v.* ● *n.* (*pl.* **-ies**) **1** a government formally cooperating or united with another for a special purpose, esp. by a treaty. **2** a person or organization that cooperates with or helps another. ● *v.tr.* also /əlí/ (**-ies, -ied**) (often foll. by *with*) combine or unite in alliance.

al·ma ma·ter /áalmə máatər, álmə máytər/ *n.* (also **Al·ma Ma·ter**) **1** the university, school, or college one attends or attended. **2** the official anthem or song of a university, school, or college.

al·ma·nac /áwlmənak, ál-/ *n.* an annual calendar of months and days, usu. with astronomical data and other information.

al·might·y /áwlmītee/ *adj. & adv.* ● *adj.* **1** having complete power; omnipotent. **2 (the Almighty)** God. **3** *sl.* very great (*an almighty crash*). ● *adv. sl.* extremely; very much.

al·mond /áamənd, ám-/ *n.* **1** the oval nutlike seed (kernel) of the fruit from the tree *Prunus dulcis*, of which there are sweet and bitter varieties. ▷ NUT. **2** the tree itself, of the rose family and related to the peach and plum.

al·most /áwlmōst/ *adv.* all but; very nearly.

alms /aamz/ *n.pl. hist.* the charitable donation of money or food to the poor.

alms·house /áamz-hows/ *n.* esp. *Brit. hist.* a house founded by charity for the poor.

al·oe /álō/ *n.* **1** any plant of the genus *Aloe*, usu. having toothed fleshy leaves. ▷ XEROPHYTE. **2** (in *pl.*) (in full **bitter aloes**) a strong laxative obtained from the bitter juice of various species of aloe. **3** (also **A·mer·i·can al·oe**) an agave native to Central America. **4** (also **aloe vera**) a species of aloe whose leaves yield an emollient juice.

a·loft /əláwft, əlóft/ *predic.adj. & adv.* **1** high up; overhead. **2** upwards.

a·log·i·cal /áylójikəl/ *adj.* **1** not logical. **2** opposed to logic.

a·lo·ha /əlōhaa, aa-/ *int.* a Hawaiian salutation at meeting or parting.

a·lone /əlōn/ *predic.adj. & adv.* **1 a** without others present (*he wanted to be alone; the tree stood alone*). **b** without others' help (*succeeded alone*). **c** lonely and isolated (*felt alone*). **2** (often foll. by *in*) standing by oneself in an opinion, quality, etc. (*was alone in thinking this*). **3** only; exclusively (*you alone can help me*). □ **go it alone** act by oneself without assistance. □□ **a·lone·ness** *n.*

a·long /əláwng, əlóng/ *prep. & adv.* ● *prep.* **1** from one end to the other end of (*a handkerchief with lace along the edge*). **2** on or through any part of the length of (*was walking along the road*). **3** beside or through the length of (*shelves stood along the wall*). ● *adv.* **1** onward; into a more advanced state (*come along; getting along nicely*). **2** at or to a particular place; arriving (*I'll be along soon*). **3** in company with a person, esp. oneself (*bring a book along*). **4** beside or through part or the whole length of a thing. □ **along with** together with; alongside or simultaneously with.

a·long·shore /əláwngsháwr, əlóng-/ *adv.* along or by the shore.

a·long·side /əláwngsíd, əlóng-/ *adv. & prep.* ● *adv.* at or to the side (of a ship, pier, etc.). ● *prep.* close to the side of; next to. □ **alongside of** side by side with.

a·loof /əlŏŏf/ *adj. & adv.* ● *adj.* distant; unsympathetic. ● *adv.* away; apart (*he kept aloof from his colleagues*). □□ **a·loof·ly** *adv.* **a·loof·ness** *n.*

al·o·pe·ci·a /áləpéesheeə/ *n. Med.* the loss (complete or partial) of hair from areas of the body where it normally grows; baldness.

a·loud /əlówd/ *adv.* **1** audibly; not silently or in a whisper. **2** *archaic* loudly.

a·low /əlō/ *adv. & predic.adj. Naut.* in or into the lower part of a ship.

alp /alp/ *n.* **1** a high mountain. **2** (**the Alps**) the high range of mountains in Switzerland and adjoining countries. **3** (in Switzerland) pastureland on a mountainside.

al·pac·a /alpákə/ *n.* **1** ▼ a S. American mammal, *Lama pacos*, related to the llama, with long shaggy hair. **2** the wool from the animal. **3** a fabric made from the wool, with or without other fibers.

ALPACA
(*Lama pacos*)

al·pen·horn /álpənhawrn/ *n.* a long wooden horn used by Alpine herdsmen to call their cattle.

al·pen·stock /álpənstok/ *n.* a long iron-tipped staff used in hiking and mountain climbing.

al·pha /álfə/ *n.* **1** the first letter of the Greek alphabet (A, α). **2** a beginning; something that is primary or first. **3** *Brit.* a first-class mark, given for a piece of work or on an examination. **4** *Astron.* the chief star in a constellation. □ **alpha and omega** the beginning and the end; the most important features.

al·pha·bet /álfəbet/ *n.* **1** the set of letters used in writing a language. **2** a set of symbols or signs representing letters.

al·pha·bet·i·cal /álfəbétikəl/ *adj.* (also **al·pha·bet·ic** /-bétik/) **1** of or relating to an alphabet. **2** in the order of the letters of the alphabet. □□ **al·pha·bet·i·cal·ly** *adv.*

al·pha·bet·ize /álfəbətīz/ *v.tr.* arrange (words, names, etc.) in alphabetical order. □□ **al·pha·bet·i·za·tion** /-izáyshən/ *n.*

al·pha·nu·mer·ic /álfənŏŏmérik, -nyŏŏ-/ *adj.* containing both alphabetical and numerical symbols.

al·pha par·ti·cle (or **ray**) *n.* a helium nucleus emitted by a radioactive substance, orig. regarded as a ray. ▷ RADIOACTIVITY

al·pine /álpīn/ *adj. & n.* ● *adj.* **1 a** of or relating to high mountains. **b** growing or found on high mountains. **2** (**Alpine**) of or relating to the Alps. ● *n.* a plant native or suited to a high mountain habitat.

Al·pin·ist /álpinist/ *n.* (also **alpinist**) a climber of high mountains, esp. the Alps.

al·read·y /áwlrédee/ *adv.* **1** before the time in question (*I knew that already*). **2** as early or as soon as this (*already at the age of six*).

al·right /áwlrít/ *adj., adv., & int. disp.* = ALL RIGHT.

Al·sa·tian /alsáyshən/ *n.* a native of Alsace, a region of E. France.

al·so /áwlsō/ *adv.* in addition; likewise; besides.

al·so-ran *n.* **1** a horse or dog, etc., not among the winners in a race. **2** an undistinguished person.

Alta. *abbr.* Alberta.

al·tar /áwltər/ *n.* **1** a table or flat-topped block, often of stone, for sacrifice or offering to a deity. **2 ▶** a raised surface or table at which a Christian service, esp. the Eucharist, is celebrated. ▷ CATHEDRAL, CHURCH

al·tar·piece /áwltərpees/ *n.* a piece of art, esp. a painting, set above an altar.

alt·az·i·muth /altáziməth/ *n.* a telescope or other instrument mounted so as to allow both vertical and horizontal movement, esp. one used for measuring the altitude and azimuth of celestial bodies.

al·ter /áwltər/ *v.* **1** *tr. & intr.* make or become different; change. **2** *tr.* castrate or spay. □□ **al·ter·a·ble** *adj.* **al·ter·a·tion** /-ráyshən/ *n.*

al·ter·a·tive /áwltəráytiv, -rətiv/ *adj.* tending to alter.

al·ter·cate /áwltərkayt/ *v.intr.* (often foll. by *with*) dispute hotly; wrangle. □□ **al·ter·ca·tion** /-káyshən/ *n.*

al·ter e·go /áwltər éegō, égō/ *n.* (*pl.* **alter egos**) **1** an intimate and trusted friend. **2** a person's secondary or alternative personality.

al·ter·nate *v., adj., & n.* ● *v.* /áwltərnayt, ál-/ **1** *intr.* (often foll. by *with*) (of two things) succeed each other by turns (*elation alternated with depression*). **2** *intr.* (foll. by *between*) change repeatedly (between two conditions) (*the patient alternated between hot and cold fevers*). **3** *tr.* (often foll. by *with*) cause (two things) to succeed each other by turns (*the band alternated fast and slow tunes*). ● *adj.* /áwltərnət, ál-/ **1** (with noun in *pl.*) every other (*comes on alternate days*). **2** (of things of two kinds) each following and succeeded by one of the other kind (*alternate joy and misery*). **3** (of a sequence, etc.) consisting of alternate things. **4** = ALTERNATIVE. ● *n.* /áwltərnət, ál-/ something or someone that is an alternative; a deputy or substitute. □□ **al·ter·nate·ly** *adv.*

al·ter·nate an·gles *n.pl.* two angles, not adjoining one another, that are formed on opposite sides of a line that intersects two other lines.

al·ter·nat·ing cur·rent *n.* **▶** an electric current that reverses its direction at regular intervals.

al·ter·na·tion /áwltərnáyshən, ál-/ *n.* the action or result of alternating.

al·ter·na·tive /awltərnətiv, al-/ *adj. & n.* ● *adj.* **1** (of one or more things) available or usable instead of another (*an alternative route*). ¶ Use with reference to more than two options (e.g., *many alternative methods*) is common and acceptable. **2** (of two things) mutually exclusive. **3** of or relating to practices that offer a substitute for conventional ones (*alternative theater*). ● *n.* any of two or more possibilities. □□ **al·ter·na·tive·ly** *adv.*

al·ter·na·tor /áwltərnaytər, ál-/ *n.* a generator that produces an alternating current.

alt·horn /ált-hawrn/ *n. Mus.* an instrument of the saxhorn family, esp. the alto or tenor saxhorn in E flat.

al·though /awlthṓ/ *conj.* = THOUGH *conj.* 1–3.

al·tim·e·ter /altímitər, áltimeetər/ *n.* an instrument for showing height above sea or ground level, esp. one fitted in an aircraft. ▷ INSTRUMENT PANEL

ALTAR IN 19TH-CENTURY CATHOLIC CHURCH, IRELAND

al·ti·tude /áltitōōd, -tyōōd/ *n.* the height of an object in relation to a given point, esp. sea level or the horizon. □□ **al·ti·tu·di·nal** /-tōōdin'l, -tyōō-/ *adj.*

al·to /áltō/ *n.* (*pl.* **-os**) **1** = CONTRALTO. **2** = COUNTERTENOR. **3** (*attrib.*) denoting the member of a family of instruments pitched next below a soprano of its type.

al·to·cu·mu·lus /áltōkyṓōmyələs/ *n.* (*pl.* **alto-cumuli** /-lī/) *Meteorol.* a cloud formation at medium altitude consisting of rounded masses with a level base. ▷ CLOUD

al·to·geth·er /áwltəgéthər/ *adv.* **1** totally; completely (*you are altogether wrong*). **2** on the whole (*altogether it had been a good day*). **3** in total. ¶ Note that *all together* is used to mean "all at once" or "all in one place," as in *there are six bedrooms all together*. □ **in the altogether** *colloq.* naked.

al·to-re·lie·vo /áltōrileévō/ *n.* (also **al·to·ri·lie·vo** /áltōrilyáyvō/) (*pl.* **-os**) *Sculpture* **1** a form of relief in which the sculptured shapes stand out from the background to at least half their actual depth. **2** a sculpture characterized by this.

al·to·stra·tus /áltōstráytəs, -strátəs/ *n.* (*pl.* **altostrati** /-tī/) a continuous and uniformly flat cloud formation at medium altitude. ▷ CLOUD

al·tru·ism /áltrōōizəm/ *n.* **1** regard for others as a principle of action. **2** unselfishness; concern for other people. □□ **al·tru·ist** *n.* **al·tru·is·tic** /-ístik/ *adj.* **al·tru·is·ti·cal·ly** *adv.*

a·lum /áləm/ *n.* a double sulfate of aluminum and potassium.

a·lu·mi·na /əlōōminə/ *n.* the compound aluminum oxide occurring naturally as corundum and emery.

a·lu·mi·nize /əlōōminīz/ *v.tr.* coat with aluminum. □□ **a·lu·mi·ni·za·tion** /-izáyshən/ *n.*

a·lu·mi·num /əlōōminəm/ *n.* (*Brit.* **aluminium** /ályəmíneeəm/) a silvery light and malleable metallic element resistant to tarnishing by air. ▷ ORE. ¶ Symb.: **Al**.

a·lum·nus /əlúmnəs/ *n.* (*pl.* **alumni** /-nī/; *fem.* **alumna**, *pl.* **alumnae** /-nee, nī/) a former pupil or student of a particular school, college, or university.

al·ve·o·lar /alvéeələr/ *adj. Phonet.* (of a consonant) pronounced with the tip of the tongue in contact with the ridge of the upper teeth, e.g., *n, s, t.*

al·ve·o·lus /alvéeələs/ *n.* (*pl.* **alveoli** /-lī/) **1** a small cavity, pit, or hollow. **2** any of the many tiny air sacs of the lungs which allow for rapid gaseous exchange. ▷ LUNG. **3** the bony socket for the root of a tooth. □□ **al·ve·o·late** *adj.*

al·ways /áwlwayz/ *adv.* **1** at all times; on all occasions (*they are always late*). **2** whatever the circumstances (*I can always sleep on the floor*). **3** repeatedly; often (*they are always complaining*). **4** for ever; for all time (*I am with you always*).

a·lys·sum /álisəm/ *n.* any plant of the genus *Alyssum*, widely cultivated and usu. having yellow or white flowers.

Alz·hei·mer's dis·ease /áalts-hīmərz, álts-, áwlts-, áwlz-/ *n.* a serious disorder of the brain manifesting itself in premature senility.

AM *abbr.* **1** amplitude modulation. **2** Master of Arts.

Am *symb. Chem.* the element americium.

am *1st person sing. present* of BE.

a.m. *abbr.* (also **A.M.** or **AM**) between midnight and noon.

AMA *abbr.* American Medical Association.

a·mal·gam /əmálgəm/ *n.* **1** a mixture or blend. **2** an alloy of mercury with one or more other metals, used esp. in dentistry.

a·mal·ga·mate /əmálgəmayt/ *v.* **1** *tr. & intr.* combine or unite to form one structure, organization, etc. **2** *intr.* (of metals) alloy with mercury. □□ **a·mal·ga·ma·tion** /-máyshən/ *n.*

a·man·u·en·sis /əmányōō-énsis/ *n.* (*pl.* **amanu-enses** /-seez/) **1** a person who writes from dictation or copies manuscripts. **2** a literary assistant.

am·a·ret·ti /aməretee/ *n.* Italian almond-flavored biscuits.

am·a·ret·to /amərétō/ *n.* an almond-flavored liqueur.

am·a·ryl·lis /ámərílis/ *n.* **1** *Amaryllis belladonna*, a

ALTERNATING CURRENT

An alternating current is produced by a type of generator known as an alternator. In the alternator, a wire is coiled around an armature situated between opposing poles of a magnet. When the armature is rotated by an external power source, the magnet induces current in the wire that can be conducted for use in an electrical appliance, such as a light. With each half turn of the armature, the current changes direction.

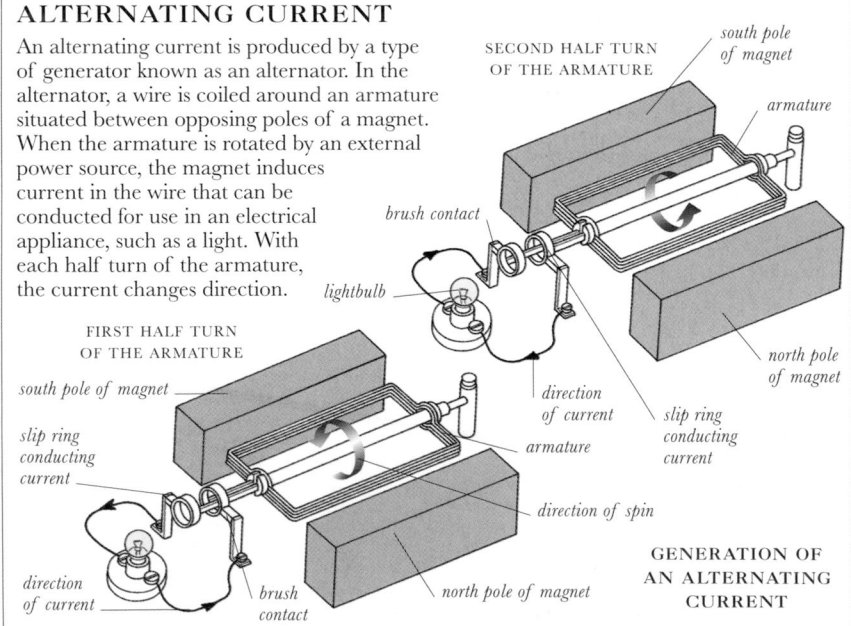

SECOND HALF TURN OF THE ARMATURE

south pole of magnet

armature

brush contact

lightbulb

north pole of magnet

FIRST HALF TURN OF THE ARMATURE

south pole of magnet

slip ring conducting current

armature

direction of current

slip ring conducting current

direction of spin

direction of current

brush contact

north pole of magnet

GENERATION OF AN ALTERNATING CURRENT

A

bulbous lilylike plant native to S. Africa with white, pink, or red flowers.

a·mass /əmás/ *v.tr.* **1** gather or heap together. **2** accumulate (esp. riches). □□ **a·mass·er** *n.* **a·mass·ment** *n.*

am·a·teur /áməchŏŏr, -chər, -tər, -tэ́r/ *n. & adj.* ● *n.* **1 a** a person who engages in a pursuit as a pastime rather than as a profession. **b** *derog.* a person who does something unskillfully. **2** (foll. by *of*) a person who is fond of (a thing). ● *adj.* for or done by amateurs; unskillful (*amateur athletics; did an amateur job*). □□ **am·a·teur·ism** *n.*

am·a·teur·ish /áməchŏŏr, -chərish, tər-, -tэ́r-/ *adj.* characteristic of an amateur, esp. unskillful or inexperienced. □□ **am·a·teur·ish·ly** *adv.* **am·a·teur·ish·ness** *n.*

am·a·to·ry /ámətawree/ *adj.* of or relating to sexual love or desire.

am·au·ro·sis /ámərṓsis/ *n.* the partial or total loss of sight, from disease of the optic nerve, retina, spinal cord, or brain. □□ **am·au·rot·ic** /-rótik/ *adj.*

a·maze /əmáyz/ *v.tr.* (often foll. by *at,* or *that* + clause, or *to* + infin.) surprise greatly. □□ **a·maze·ment** *n.* **a·maz·ing** *adj.* **a·maz·ing·ly** *adv.* **a·maz·ing·ness** *n.*

Am·a·zon /áməzon, -zən/ *n.* **1** ▼ a member of a mythical race of female warriors. **2** (**amazon**) a very tall or athletic woman. □□ **Am·a·zo·ni·an** /-zṓneeən/ *adj.*

AMAZON WARRIOR BEING SLAIN BY
THE ANCIENT GREEK HERO ACHILLES

am·bas·sa·dor /ambásədər, -dawr/ *n.* **1** an accredited diplomat sent by a nation on a mission to, or as its permanent representative in, a foreign country. **2** a representative or promoter of a specified thing (*an ambassador of peace*). □□ **am·bas·sa·do·ri·al** /-dáwreeəl/ *adj.* **am·bas·sa·dor·ship** *n.*

am·bas·sa·dress /ambásədris/ *n.* **1** a female ambassador. **2** an ambassador's wife.

am·ber /ámbər/ *n. & adj.* ● *n.* **1 a** ▶ a yellowish translucent fossilized resin deriving from extinct trees and used in jewelry. ▷ GEM. **b** the honey-yellow color of this. **2** a yellow traffic signal meaning caution, showing between red for "stop" and green for "go." ● *adj.* made of or colored like amber.

am·ber·gris /ámbərgris, -grees/ *n.* a strong-smelling waxlike secretion of the intestine of the sperm whale, used in perfume manufacture.

am·bi·ance var. of AMBIENCE.

am·bi·dex·trous /ámbidékstrəs/ *adj.* able to use the right and left hands equally well. □□ **am·bi·dex·ter·i·ty** /-stéritee/ *n.* **am·bi·dex·trous·ly** *adv.* **am·bi·dex·trous·ness** *n.*

am·bi·ence /ámbeeəns, aаnbeeáаns/ *n.* (also **am·bi·ance**) the surroundings or atmosphere of a place.

am·bi·ent /ámbeeənt/ *adj.* surrounding.

am·bi·gu·i·ty /ámbigyŏŏitee/ *n.* (*pl.* **-ies**) **1** double meaning. **2** an expression able to be interpreted in more than one way (e.g., *fighting dogs should be avoided*).

am·big·u·ous /ambígyŏŏəs/ *adj.* having an obscure or double meaning. □□ **am·big·u·ous·ly** *adv.* **am·big·u·ous·ness** *n.*

am·bit /ámbit/ *n.* the scope, extent, or bounds of something.

am·bi·tion /ambíshən/ *n.* **1** the determination to achieve success or distinction, usu. in a chosen field. **2** the object of this determination.

am·bi·tious /ambíshəs/ *adj.* **1** full of ambition. **2** showing ambition (*an ambitious attempt*). □□ **am·bi·tious·ly** *adv.* **am·bi·tious·ness** *n.*

am·biv·a·lence /ambívələns/ *n.* **1** the coexistence in one person's mind of opposing feelings, esp. love and hate, in a single context. **2** uncertainty over a course of action or decision. □□ **am·biv·a·lent** *adj.* **am·biv·a·lent·ly** *adv.*

am·bi·vert /ámbivert/ *n. Psychol.* a person who fluctuates between being an introvert and an extrovert. □□ **am·bi·ver·sion** /-vérzhən/ *n.*

am·ble /ámbəl/ *v. & n.* ● *v.intr.* **1** move at an easy pace. **2** (of a horse, etc.) move by lifting the two feet on one side together. **3** ride an ambling horse; ride at an easy pace. ● *n.* an easy pace; the gait of an ambling horse.

am·bro·sia /ambrṓzhə/ *n.* **1** (in Greek and Roman mythology) the food of the gods. **2** anything very pleasing to taste or smell. □□ **am·bro·sial** *adj.* **am·bro·sian** *adj.*

am·bu·lance /ámbyələns/ *n.* **1** a vehicle for conveying the sick or injured to and from a hospital. **2** *hist.* a mobile hospital following an army.

am·bu·lance-chas·er *n. derog.,* chiefly *N. Amer.* a lawyer who specializes in bringing cases seeking damages for personal injury.

am·bu·lant /ámbyələnt/ *adj. Med.* **1** (of a patient) able to walk about; not confined to bed. **2** (of treatment) not confining a patient to bed.

am·bu·la·to·ry /ámbyələtawree/ *adj. & n.* ● *adj.* **1** = AMBULANT. **2** of or adapted for walking. ● *n.* (*pl.* **-ies**) a place for walking, esp. in a monastery.

am·bush /ámbŏŏsh/ *n. & v.* ● *n.* **1** a surprise attack by persons (e.g., troops) in a concealed position. **2 a** the concealment of troops, etc., to make such an attack. **b** the place where they are concealed. ● *v.tr.* attack by means of an ambush.

a·me·ba var. of AMOEBA.

a·meer var. of EMIR.

a·mel·io·rate /əméelyərayt/ *v.tr. & intr.* make or become better; improve. □□ **a·mel·io·ra·tion** /-ráyshən/ *n.* **a·mel·io·ra·tive** *adj.* **a·mel·io·ra·tor** *n.*

a·men /áamén, áy-/ *int. & n.* ● *int.* **1** uttered at the end of a prayer or hymn, etc., meaning "so be it." **2** (foll. by *to*) expressing agreement or assent (*amen to that*). ● *n.* an utterance of "amen" (sense 1).

a·me·na·ble /əméenəbəl, əmén-/ *adj.* **1** responsive; tractable. **2** (often foll. by *to*) responsible to law. **3** (foll. by *to*) (of a thing) subject or liable. □□ **a·me·na·bil·i·ty** /-bílitee/ *n.* **a·me·na·bly** *adv.*

a·mend /əménd/ *v.tr.* **1** make minor improvements in (a text or a written proposal). **2** correct an error or errors in (a document). ¶ Often confused with *emend,* a more technical word used in the context of textual correction. □□ **a·mend·a·ble** *adj.* **a·mend·er** *n.*

a·mend·ment /əméndmənt/ *n.* **1** a minor change in a document (esp. a legal or statutory one). **2** an article added to the US Constitution.

a·mends /əméndz/ *n.* □ **make amends** (often foll. by *for*) compensate (for).

a·men·i·ty /əménitee, əmée-/ *n.* (*pl.* **-ies**) **1** (usu. in

pl.) a pleasant or useful feature. **2** pleasantness (of a place, person, etc.).

a·men·or·rhe·a /aymēnəréeə/ *n. Med.* an abnormal absence of menstruation.

a·men·tia /əménshə/ *n. Med.* severe congenital mental deficiency.

Am·er·a·sian /áməráyzhən/ *n.* a person of American and Asian descent.

a·merce /əmэ́rs/ *v.tr.* **1** *Law* punish by fine. **2** punish arbitrarily. □□ **a·merce·ment** *n.* **a·mer·ci·a·ble** /-seeəbəl/ *adj.*

A·mer·i·can /əmérikən/ *adj. & n.* ● *adj.* **1** of, relating to, or characteristic of the United States or its inhabitants. **2** (usu. in *comb.*) of or relating to the continents of America (*Latin-American*). ● *n.* **1** a native or citizen of the United States. **2** (usu. in *comb.*) a native or inhabitant of the continents of America (*North Americans*). **3** (also **A·mer·i·can Eng·lish**) the English language as it is used in the United States.

A·mer·i·ca·na /əmérikánə, -káanə, -káynə/ *n.pl.* things connected with America, esp. with the United States.

A·mer·i·can dream *n.* the traditional social ideals of the American people, such as equality, democracy, and material prosperity.

A·mer·i·can In·di·an *n.* a member of the aboriginal peoples of America or their descendants.

A·mer·i·can·ism /əmérikənizəm/ *n.* **1 a** a word or phrase peculiar to or originating from the United States. **b** a thing or feature characteristic of or peculiar to the United States. **2** attachment to or sympathy for the United States.

A·mer·i·can·ize /əmérikənīz/ *v.* **1** *tr.* **a** make American in character. **b** naturalize as an American. **2** *intr.* become American in character. □□ **A·mer·i·can·i·za·tion** /-nizáyshən/ *n.*

A·mer·i·can Le·gion *n.* an association of US ex-servicemen formed in 1919.

am·er·i·ci·um /ámərísheeəm/ *n. Chem.* an artificial radioactive metallic element. ¶ Symb.: **Am.**

Am·er·in·di·an /áмərindeeən/ *adj. & n.* (also **Am·er·ind** /áмərind/) = AMERICAN INDIAN. □□ **Am·er·in·dic** /-rindik/ *adj.*

am·e·thyst /ámithist/ *n.* a precious stone of a violet or purple variety of quartz. ▷ GEM, QUARTZ. □□ **am·e·thys·tine** /-thísteen/ *adj.*

a·mi·a·ble /áymeeəbəl/ *adj.* friendly and pleasant; likable. □□ **a·mi·a·bil·i·ty** /-bílitee/ *n.* **a·mi·a·bly** *adv.*

am·i·ca·ble /ámikəbəl/ *adj.* showing a friendly spirit. □□ **am·i·ca·bly** *adv.*

am·ice /ámis/ *n.* a white linen cloth worn on the neck and shoulders by a priest celebrating the Eucharist.

a·mid /əmíd/ *prep.* (also **a·midst** /əmídst/) **1** in the middle of. **2** in the course of.

am·ide /áymīd, ám-/ *n. Chem.* a compound formed from ammonia by replacement of one or more hydrogen atoms by a metal or an acyl radical.

a·mid·ships /əmídships/ *adv.* (also **a·mid·ship**) in or into the middle of a ship.

a·midst var. of AMID.

a·mi·go /əméegō/ *n.* (*pl.* **-os**) a friend, esp. in Spanish-speaking areas.

a·mine /əméen, ámeen/ *n. Chem.* a compound formed from ammonia by replacement of one or more hydrogen atoms by an organic radical or radicals.

a·mi·no /əméenō/ *n.* (*attrib.*) *Chem.* of the monovalent group $-NH_2$.

a·mi·no ac·id /əméenō/ *n. Biochem.* any of a group of organic compounds containing both the carboxyl and amino groups, forming the basic constituents of proteins.

a·mir var. of EMIR.

A·mish /áamish, ám-/ *adj. & n.* ● *adj.* belonging to a strict Mennonite sect in the US. ● *n.* a follower of this sect.

AMBER ORNAMENT IN THE
SHAPE OF A PANDA

A

a·miss /əmís/ *predic.adj. & adv.* ● *predic.adj.* wrong (*something was amiss*). ● *adv.* wrong (*everything went amiss*). □ **take amiss** be offended by.

am·i·trip·ty·line /ámitríptileen/ *n. Pharm.* an antidepressant drug that has a mild tranquilizing action.

am·i·ty /ámitee/ *n.* friendship; friendly relations.

am·me·ter /ám-meetər/ *n.* an instrument for measuring electric current in amperes. ▷ INDUCTION

am·mo /ámō/ *n. colloq.* ammunition.

am·mo·nia /əmṓnyə/ *n.* **1** a colorless gas with a characteristic pungent smell. **2** (in general use) a solution of ammonia gas in water.

am·mo·ni·a·cal /ámənī́əkəl/ *adj.* of or containing ammonia or sal ammoniac.

am·mo·ni·at·ed /əmṓneeaytid/ *adj.* combined or treated with ammonia.

am·mo·nite /ámənīt/ *n.* ◄ any extinct cephalopod mollusk of the order Ammonoidea, with a flat coiled spiral shell found as a fossil. ▷ FOSSIL

am·mo·ni·um /əmṓneeəm/ *n.* the univalent ion NH_4^+, formed from ammonia.

AMMONITE FOSSIL

am·mu·ni·tion /ámyəníshən/ *n.* **1** a supply of projectiles (esp. bullets, shells, and grenades). **2** points used or usable to advantage in an argument.

am·ne·sia /amnéezhə/ *n.* a partial or total loss of memory. □□ **am·ne·si·ac** /-zeeak, -zheeak/ *n.* **am·ne·sic** *adj. & n.*

am·nes·ty /ámnistee/ *n. & v.* ● *n.* (*pl.* **-ies**) a general pardon, esp. for political offenses. ● *v.tr.* (**-ies, -ied**) grant an amnesty to.

Am·nes·ty In·ter·na·tion·al *n.* an international organization in support of human rights, esp. for prisoners of conscience.

am·ni·o·cen·te·sis /ámneeōsentéesis/ *n.* (*pl.* **amniocenteses** /-seez/) *Med.* the sampling of amniotic fluid to determine certain abnormalities in an embryo.

am·ni·on /ámneeən/ *n.* (*pl.* **amnia** /-neeə/) *Zool. & Physiol.* the innermost membrane that encloses the embryo of a reptile, bird, or mammal. ▷ EGG

□□ **am·ni·ot·ic** /ámneeótik/ *adj.* ▷ FETUS

a·moe·ba /əméebə/ *n.* (also **a·me·ba**) (*pl.* **amoebas** or **amoebae** /-bee/) ◄ any usu. aquatic protozoan of the genus *Amoeba,* esp. *A. proteus,* capable of changing shape. ▷ PSEUDOPODIUM. □□ **a·moe·bic** *adj.* **a·moe·boid** *adj.*

a·mok /əmúk, əmók/ *adv.* (also **a·muck** /əmúk/) □ **run amok** run about wildly in an uncontrollable violent rage.

AMOEBA
(*Amoeba* species)

a·mong /əmúng/ *prep.* (also esp. *Brit.* **a·mongst** /əmúngst/) **1** surrounded by; in the company of. **2** in the number of (*among us were those who disagreed*). **3** in the class or category of (*is among the richest men alive*). **4** between; shared by (*had $5 among us; divide it among you*). **5** with one another; by the reciprocal action of (*talked among themselves*).

a·mor·al /áymáwrəl, -mór-/ *adj.* **1** not concerned with morality (cf. IMMORAL). **2** having no moral principles. □□ **a·mor·al·ism** *n.* **a·mor·al·ist** *n.* **a·mo·ral·i·ty** /-rálitee/ *n.*

am·o·rist /ámərist/ *n.* a person who professes or writes of (esp. sexual) love.

a·mo·ro·so /ámərṓsō/ *adv. & adj. Mus.* in a loving or tender manner.

am·o·rous /ámərəs/ *adj.* **1** showing, feeling, or

inclined to sexual love. **2** of or relating to sexual love. □□ **am·o·rous·ly** *adv.* **am·o·rous·ness** *n.*

a·mor·phous /əmáwrfəs/ *adj.* **1** shapeless. **2** vague; ill-organized. **3** *Mineral. & Chem.* having neither definite form nor structure. □□ **a·mor·phous·ly** *adv.* **a·mor·phous·ness** *n.*

am·or·tize /ámərtīz, əmáwr-/ *v.tr. Commerce* **1** gradually extinguish (a debt) by money regularly put aside. **2** gradually write off the initial cost of (assets). □□ **am·or·ti·za·tion** /-tizáyshən/ *n.*

a·mount /əmównt/ *n. & v.* ● *n.* a quantity, esp. the total of a thing or things in number, size, value, extent, etc. (*a large amount of money*). ● *v.intr.* (foll. by *to*) **1** be equivalent to in number, size, significance, etc. (*amounted to $100*). **2** (of a person) become (*might one day amount to something*). □ **any amount of** a great deal of. **no amount of** not even the greatest possible amount of.

a·mour /əmṓr/ *n.* a love affair, esp. a secret one.

a·mour pro·pre /áamṓrr práwprə/ *n.* self-respect.

AMP *abbr.* adenosine monophosphate.

amp[1] /amp/ *n. Electr.* an ampere.

amp[2] /amp/ *n. colloq.* an amplifier.

am·per·age /ámpərij/ *n. Electr.* the strength of an electric current in amperes.

am·pere /ámpeer/ *n. Electr.* the SI base unit of electric current.

am·per·sand /ámpərsand/ *n.* the sign & (= *and*).

am·phet·a·mine /amfétəmeen, -min/ *n.* a synthetic drug used esp. as a stimulant.

amphi- /ámfee/ *comb. form* **1** both. **2** of both kinds. **3** on both sides. **4** around.

am·phib·i·an /amfíbeeən/ *adj. & n.* ● *adj.* **1** living both on land and in water. **2** *Zool.* of or relating to the class Amphibia. **3** (of a vehicle) able to operate on land and water. ● *n.* **1** *Zool.* ▲ any vertebrate of the class Amphibia, with a life history of an aquatic gill-breathing larval stage followed by a terrestrial lung-breathing adult stage, including frogs, toads, newts, and salamanders. **2** (in general use) a creature living on land and in water. **3** an amphibian vehicle.

am·phib·i·ous /amfíbeeəs/ *adj.* **1** living on land and in water. **2** relating to or suited for land and water. **3** *Mil.* **a** (of a military operation) involving forces landed from the sea. **b** (of forces) trained for such operations. □□ **am·phib·i·ous·ly** *adv.*

am·phi·bol·o·gy /ámfibóləjee/ *n.* (*pl.* **-ies**) **1** a quibble. **2** an ambiguous wording.

am·phi·ro·style /ámfiprəstīl, amfiprṓ-/ *n. & adj.*

AMPHIBIAN

Beginning life as larvae or tadpoles, amphibians go through a metamorphosis as they grow into their adult state. All but the caecilians grow legs, and most develop lungs, which supersede gills for oxygen intake. Many amphibians are also able to absorb oxygen through their skin. The three main divisions of the Amphibia class are shown here.

URODELA
(newts, salamanders)
▷ NEWT, SALAMANDER

ANURA
(frogs, toads)
▷ FROG, TOAD

APODA
(caecilians)

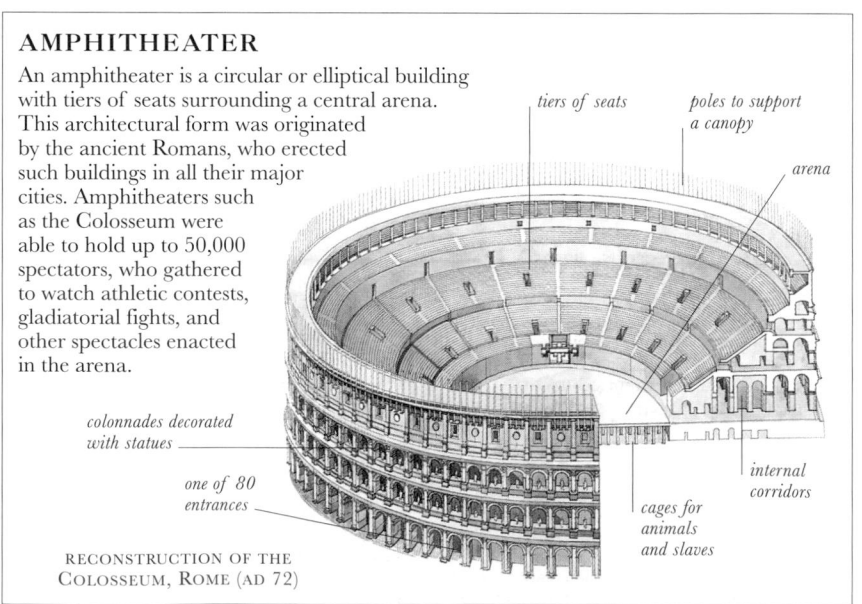

AMPHITHEATER

An amphitheater is a circular or elliptical building with tiers of seats surrounding a central arena. This architectural form was originated by the ancient Romans, who erected such buildings in all their major cities. Amphitheaters such as the Colosseum were able to hold up to 50,000 spectators, who gathered to watch athletic contests, gladiatorial fights, and other spectacles enacted in the arena.

tiers of seats

poles to support a canopy

arena

colonnades decorated with statues

one of 80 entrances

internal corridors

cages for animals and slaves

RECONSTRUCTION OF THE
COLOSSEUM, ROME (AD 72)

● *n.* a classical building with a portico at each end. ● *adj.* of or in this style.

am·phi·the·a·ter /ámfitheeətər/ *n.* **1** ▼ a round, usu. unroofed building with tiers of seats surrounding a central space. **2** a semicircular gallery in a theater. **3** a large circular hollow. **4** the scene of a contest.

am·pho·ra /ámfərə/ *n.* (*pl.* **amphorae** /-ree/ or **amphoras**) ▶ a Greek or Roman vessel with two handles and a narrow neck.

am·pi·cil·lin /ámpisilin/ *n. Pharm.* a semisynthetic penicillin used esp. in treating infections of the urinary and respiratory tracts.

am·ple /ámpəl/ *adj.* (**ampler, amplest**) **1 a** plentiful; abundant; extensive. **b** *euphem.* (esp. of a person) large; stout. **2** enough or more than enough. □□ **am·ple·ness** *n.* **am·ply** *adv.*

am·pli·fi·er /ámplifïər/ *n.* an electronic device for increasing the strength of electrical signals, esp. for conversion into sound in radio, etc., equipment.

am·pli·fy /ámplifï/ *v.* (**-ies, -ied**) **1** *tr.* increase the volume or strength of (sound, electrical signals, etc.). **2** *tr.* add detail to (a story, etc.). □□ **am·pli·fi·ca·tion** /-fikáyshən/ *n.*

am·pli·tude /ámplitōod, -tyōod/ *n.* **1** *Physics* the maximum extent of a vibration from the position of equilibrium. **2** *Electr.* the maximum departure of the value of an alternating current or wave from the average value.

am·pli·tude mod·u·la·tion *n. Electr.* **1** the modulation of a wave by variation of its amplitude. **2** the system using such modulation.

am·poule /ámpyōol, -pōol/ *n.* (also **am·pule** or **am·pul**) a small capsule in which measured quantities of liquids or solids, esp. for injecting, are sealed ready for use.

am·pul·la /ampōolə/ *n.* (*pl.* **ampullae** /-ee/) a Roman globular flask with two handles.

am·pu·tate /ámpyətayt/ *v.tr.* cut off by surgical operation (a part of the body, esp. a limb). □□ **am·pu·ta·tion** /-táyshən/ *n.* **am·pu·ta·tor** *n.*

am·pu·tee /ámpyətée/ *n.* a person who has lost a limb, etc., by amputation.

am·trac /ámtrak/ *n.* (also **am·track**) an amphibious tracked vehicle used for landing assault troops on a shore.

Am·trak /ámtrak/ *n. Trademark US* passenger railroad system.

amu *abbr.* atomic mass unit.

a·muck var. of AMOK.

am·u·let /ámyəlit/ *n.* an ornament worn as a charm against evil.

a·muse /əmyōoz/ *v.* **1** *tr.* cause (a person) to laugh or smile. **2** *tr. & refl.* (often foll. by *with, by*) interest or occupy; keep (a person) entertained. □□ **a·mus·ing** *adj.* **a·mus·ing·ly** *adv.*

a·muse·ment /əmyōozmənt/ *n.* **1** something that amuses, esp. a pleasant diversion, game, or pastime. **2** the state of being amused. **3** *Brit.* a mechanical device (e.g., a merry-go-round) for entertainment at a fairground, etc.

a·muse·ment park *n.* a park with rides such as a merry-go-round, Ferris wheel, roller coaster, etc.

am·yl /ámil/ *n.* (used *attrib.*) *Chem.* the monovalent group C_5H_{11}-, derived from pentane. Also called **pentyl.**

am·yl·ase /ámilays, -layz/ *n. Biochem.* any of several enzymes that convert starch and glycogen into simple sugars.

am·yl ni·trite /ámil nítrīt/ *n.* a synthetic liquid that is used in medicine to expand blood vessels and is sometimes inhaled for its stimulatory effects.

a·my·o·troph·ic lat·er·al scle·ro·sis /aymīə-trófik, -tró-/ *n.* an incurable degenerative disease of the nervous system marked by increasing muscle weakness and eventual paralysis. Also called **Lou Gehrig's disease.**

an /an, ən/ *adj.* the form of the indefinite article (see A[1]) used before words beginning with a vowel sound (*an egg; an hour*). ¶ Now less often used before aspirated words beginning with *h* and stressed on a syllable other than the first (so *a hotel,* not *an hotel*).

an- /ən, an/ *prefix* not; without (*anarchy*) (cf. A-).

-ana /ánə, áanə, áynə/ *suffix* forming plural nouns meaning "things associated with" (*Victoriana; Americana*).

An·a·bap·tism /ánəbáptizəm/ *n.* the doctrine that baptism should only be administered to believing adults. □□ **An·a·bap·tist** *n.*

an·a·bol·ic /ánəbólik/ *adj. Biochem.* of or relating to anabolism.

an·a·bol·ic ste·roid *n.* any of a group of synthetic steroid hormones used to increase muscle size.

a·nab·o·lism /ənábəlizəm/ *n. Biochem.* the synthesis of complex molecules in living organisms from simpler ones together with the storage of energy; constructive metabolism (opp. CATABOLISM).

an·a·branch /ánəbranch/ *n.* a stream that leaves a river and reenters it lower down.

a·nach·ro·nism /ənákrənizəm/ *n.* **1 a** the attribution of a custom, event, etc., to the wrong period. **b** a thing attributed in this way. **2** an old-fashioned or out-of-date person or thing. □□ **a·nach·ro·nis·tic** /-nístik/ *adj.* **a·nach·ro·nis·ti·cal·ly** *adv.*

an·a·co·lu·thon /ánəkəlōothon/ *n.* (*pl.* **anacolutha** /-thə/) a sentence or construction that lacks grammatical sequence (e.g., *while in the garden the door banged shut*). □□ **an·a·co·lu·thic** *adj.*

an·a·con·da /ánəkóndə/ *n.* ▶ a large nonpoisonous snake living mainly in water or in trees that kills its prey by constriction. ▷ SNAKE

an·a·cru·sis /ánəkrōosis/ *n.* (*pl.* **anacruses** /-seez/) **1** (in poetry) an unstressed syllable at the beginning of a verse. **2** *Mus.* an unstressed note or notes before the first bar line.

an·aer·obe /ánərōb, anáirōb/ *n.* an organism that grows without air, or requires oxygen-free conditions to live. □□ **an·aer·o·bic** *adj.*

an·a·glyph /ánəglif/ *n.* **1** *Photog.* a composite stereoscopic photograph printed in superimposed complementary colors. **2** an embossed object cut in low relief. □□ **an·a·glyph·ic** /-glífik/ *adj.*

an·a·gram /ánəgram/ *n.* a word or phrase formed by transposing the letters of another word or phrase. □□ **an·a·gram·mat·ic** /-mátik/ *adj.* **an·a·gram·mat·i·cal** *adj.* **an·a·gram·ma·tize** /-grám-ətīz/ *v.tr.*

a·nal /áynəl/ *adj.* **1** relating to or situated near the anus. **2** = ANAL RETENTIVE. □□ **a·nal·ly** *adv.*

an·a·lects /ánəlekts/ *n.pl.* (also **an·a·lec·ta** /ánəléktə/) a collection of short literary extracts.

an·a·lep·tic /ánəléptik/ *adj. & n.* ● *adj.* restorative. ● *n.* a restorative medicine or drug.

an·al·ge·si·a /ánəljéezeeə, -séeə/ *n.* the absence or relief of pain.

an·al·ge·sic /ánəljéezik, -sik/ *adj. & n.* ● *adj.* relieving pain. ● *n.* an analgesic drug.

an·a·log /ánəlog/ *n.* **1** an analogous or parallel thing. **2** (*attrib.*) (of a computer or electronic process) using physical variables, e.g., voltage, weight, or length, to represent numbers (cf. DIGITAL). ▷ DIGITIZE, RECORD

a·nal·o·gize /ənáləjīz/ *v.* **1** *tr.* represent or explain by analogy. **2** *intr.* use analogy.

a·nal·o·gous /ənáləgəs/ *adj.* (usu. foll. by *to*) partially similar or parallel; showing analogy. □□ **a·nal·o·gous·ly** *adv.*

an·a·logue var. of ANALOG.

a·nal·o·gy /ənáləjee/ *n.* (*pl.* **-ies**) **1** (usu. foll. by *to, with, between*) correspondence or partial similarity. **2** *Biol.* the resemblance of function between organs essentially different. **3** = ANALOG 1. □□ **an·a·log·i·cal** /ánəlójikəl/ *adj.* **an·a·log·i·cal·ly** *adv.*

a·nal re·ten·tive *adj.* (of a person) excessively orderly and fussy (supposedly owing to aspects of toilet training in infancy).

a·nal·y·sand /ənálisand/ *n.* a person undergoing psychoanalysis.

a·nal·y·sis /ənálisis/ *n.* (*pl.* **analyses** /-seez/) **1 a** a detailed examination of elements or structure. **b** a statement of the result of this. **2** *Chem.* the determination of the constituent parts of a mixture or compound. **3** psychoanalysis. □ **in the final analysis** after all due consideration; in the end.

an·a·lyst /ánəlist/ *n.* **1** a person skilled in (esp. chemical) analysis. **2** a psychoanalyst.

an·a·lyt·ic /ánəlítik/ *adj.* of or relating to analysis.

an·a·lyt·i·cal /ánəlítikəl/ *adj.* using analytic methods. □□ **an·a·lyt·i·cal·ly** *adv.*

an·a·lyt·i·cal ge·om·e·try *n.* geometry using coordinates.

an·a·lyze /ánəlīz/ *v.tr.* **1** examine in detail the constitution or structure of. **2** *Chem.* ascertain the constituents of (a sample of a mixture or compound). **3** find or show the essence or structure of (a book, music, etc.). **4** psychoanalyze. □□ **an·a·lyz·a·ble** *adj.* **an·a·lyz·er** *n.*

an·am·ne·sis /ánəmnéesis/ *n.* (*pl.* **anamneses** /-seez/) recollection (esp. of a supposed previous existence).

an·a·pest /ánəpest/ *n. Prosody* a foot consisting of two short or unstressed syllables followed by one long or stressed syllable. □□ **an·a·pes·tic** /-péstik/ *adj.*

a·naph·o·ra /ənáfərə/ *n.* **1** *Rhet.* the repetition of a word or phrase at the beginning of successive clauses. **2** *Gram.* the use of a word referring to or replacing a word used earlier in a sentence, to avoid repetition (e.g., *do* in *I like it and so do they*). □□ **an·a·phor·ic** /ánəfórik/ *adj.*

an·aph·ro·dis·i·ac /anáfrədéezeeak, -díz-/ *adj. & n.* ● *adj.* tending to reduce sexual desire. ● *n.* an anaphrodisiac drug.

an·a·phy·lax·is /ánəfiláksis/ *n.* (*pl.* **anaphylaxes** /-seez/) *Med.* hypersensitivity of tissues to a dose of antigen, as a reaction against a previous dose. □□ **an·a·phy·lac·tic** /-láktik/ *adj.*

an·ap·tyx·is /ánəptíksis/ *n.* (*pl.* **anaptyxes** /-seez/) *Phonet.* the insertion of a vowel between two consonants to aid pronunciation (as in *went that-away*). □□ **an·ap·tyc·tic** /-tiktik/ *adj.*

an·ar·chism /ánərkizəm/ *n.* the doctrine that all government should be abolished.

an·ar·chist /ánərkist/ *n.* an advocate of anarchism or of political disorder. □□ **an·ar·chis·tic** *adj.*

an·ar·chy /ánərkee/ *n.* **1** disorder, esp. political or social. **2** lack of government in a society. □□ **an·ar·chic** /ənáarkik/ *adj.* **an·ar·chi·cal** *adj.* **an·ar·chi·cal·ly** *adv.*

A·na·sa·zi /onəsáazee/ *n.* **1 a** a prehistoric N. American people native to the southwestern US. **b** a member of this people. **2** the language of this people.

an·a·stig·mat /ənástigmat/ *n.* a lens or system of lenses made free from astigmatism by correction.

an·a·stig·mat·ic /ánəstigmátik/ *adj.* free from astigmatism.

AMPHORA:
8TH-CENTURY BC
GREEK AMPHORA

ANACONDA
(*Eunectes murinus*)

A

A

a·nas·to·mose /ənástəmōz, -mōs/ *v.intr.* link by anastomosis.

a·nas·to·mo·sis /ənástəmósis/ *n.* (*pl.* **anastomoses** /-seez/) a cross-connection of arteries, branches, rivers, etc.

a·nas·tro·phe /ənástrəfee/ *n. Rhet.* the inversion of the usual order of words or clauses.

a·nath·e·ma /ənáthəmə/ *n.* (*pl.* **anathemas**) **1** a detested thing or person (*is anathema to me*). **2 a** an ecclesiastical curse, excommunicating a person or denouncing a doctrine. **b** a cursed thing or person. **c** a strong curse.

a·nath·e·ma·tize /ənáthəmətīz/ *v.tr. & intr.* curse.

an·a·tom·i·cal /ánətómikəl/ *adj.* **1** of or relating to anatomy. **2** structural. □□ **an·a·tom·i·cal·ly** *adv.*

a·nat·o·mist /ənátəmist/ *n.* a person skilled in anatomy.

a·nat·o·mize /ənátəmīz/ *v.tr.* **1** examine in detail. **2** dissect.

a·nat·o·my /ənátəmee/ *n.* (*pl.* **-ies**) **1** the science of the bodily structure of animals and plants. **2** this structure. **3** *colloq.* a human body. **4** analysis.

a·nat·ta (also **a·nat·to**) var. of ANNATTO.

ANC *abbr.* African National Congress.

an·ces·tor /ánsestər/ *n.* (*fem.* **ancestress** /-stris/) **1** any (esp. remote) person from whom one is descended. **2** an early type of animal or plant from which others have evolved. **3** an early prototype (*ancestor of the computer*).

an·ces·tral /anséstrəl/ *adj.* belonging to or inherited from one's ancestors.

an·ces·try /ánsestree/ *n.* (*pl.* **-ies**) one's (esp. remote) family descent.

an·chor /ángkər/ *n. & v.* ● *n.* **1** a heavy metal weight used to moor a ship to the seafloor or a balloon to the ground. ▷ MAN-OF-WAR, SHIP. **2** (in full **anchorman, anchorperson, anchorwoman**) **a** a person who plays a vital part, as the end member of a tug-of-war team, the last member of a relay team, etc. **b** a news broadcaster who introduces segments and reads the main portion of the news. ● *v.* **1** *tr.* secure (a ship or balloon) by means of an anchor. **2** *tr.* fix firmly. **3** *intr.* be moored by means of an anchor. □ **cast** (or **come to**) **anchor** let the anchor down. **weigh anchor** take the anchor up.

an·chor·age /ángkərij/ *n.* a place where a ship may be anchored.

an·cho·rite /ángkərīt/ *n.* (*fem.* **anchoress** /-ris/) **1** a hermit; a religious recluse. **2** a person of secluded habits. □□ **an·cho·ret·ic** /-rétik/ *adj.* **an·cho·rit·ic** /-rítik/ *adj.*

an·chor·man /ángkərmən/ *n.* (*pl.* **-men**) = ANCHOR *n.* 2.

an·cho·vy /ánchōvee/ *n.* (*pl.* **-ies**) any of various small silvery fish of the herring family usu. preserved in salt and oil and having a strong taste.

an·chu·sa /ankyōōzə, anchōōzə/ *n.* any plant of the genus *Anchusa*.

an·chy·lose var. of ANKYLOSE.

an·chy·lo·sis var. of ANKYLOSIS.

an·cien ré·gime /onsyán rezhéem/ *n.* (*pl.* **anciens régimes** *pronunc.* same) **1** the political and social system in France before the Revolution of 1789. **2** any superseded regime.

an·cient /áynshənt/ *adj. & n.* ● *adj.* **1** of long ago. **2** having existed long. ● *n.* **1** *archaic* an old man. **2** (*pl.*) the people of ancient times, esp. the Greeks and Romans. □□ **an·cient·ness** *n.*

an·cient his·to·ry *n.* **1** the history of the ancient civilizations of the Mediterranean area and the Near East before the fall of the Western Roman Empire in 476. **2** something already long familiar.

an·cient·ly /áynshəntlee/ *adv.* long ago.

an·cil·lar·y /ánsəleree/ *adj. & n.* ● *adj.* **1** providing essential support to a central service or industry, esp. the medical service. **2** (often foll. by *to*) subordinate. ● *n.* (*pl.* **-ies**) **1** an ancillary worker. **2** something which is ancillary.

and /and, ənd/ *conj.* **1 a** connecting words, clauses, or sentences, that are to be taken jointly (*cakes and pastries; buy and sell*). **b** implying progression (*better and better*). **c** implying causation (*do that and I'll hit you*). **d** implying great duration (*he cried and cried*). **e** implying a great number (*miles and miles*). **f** implying addition (*two and two are four*). **g** implying variety (*there are books and books*). **2** *colloq.* to (*try and open it*). **3** in relation to (*Britain and the US*).

an·dan·te /aandáantay, andántē/ *adv., adj., & n. Mus.* ● *adv. & adj.* in a moderately slow tempo. ● *n.* an andante passage or movement.

an·dan·ti·no /áandaantéenō, ándan-/ *adv., adj., & n. Mus.* ● *adv. & adj.* somewhat quicker (orig. slower) than andante. ● *n.* (*pl.* **-os**) an andantino passage or movement.

and·i·ron /ándīrn/ *n.* a metal stand (usu. one of a pair) for supporting burning wood in a fireplace; a firedog.

an·dro·gen /ándrəjən/ *n.* a male sex hormone or other substance capable of developing and maintaining certain male sexual characteristics. □□ **an·dro·gen·ic** /-jénik/ *adj.*

an·drog·y·nous /andrójinəs/ *adj.* **1** hermaphroditic. **2** not clearly male or female; exhibiting the appearance or attributes of both sexes. **3** *Bot.* with stamens and pistils in the same flower or inflorescence.

an·drog·y·ny /andrójinee/ *n.* hermaphroditism.

an·droid /ándroyd/ *n.* a robot with a human form or appearance.

an·ec·dote /ánikdōt/ *n.* a short account (or painting, etc.) of an entertaining or interesting incident. □□ **an·ec·do·tal** /-dót'l/ *adj.* **an·ec·do·tal·ist** /-dót'list/ *n.*

an·e·cho·ic /ánikóik/ *adj.* free from echo.

a·ne·mi·a /ənéemeeə/ *n.* a deficiency in the blood, usu. of red cells or their hemoglobin, resulting in pallor and weariness.

a·ne·mic /ənéemik/ *adj.* **1** relating to or suffering from anemia. **2** pale; lacking in vitality.

a·nem·o·graph /ənéməgraf/ *n.* an instrument for recording on paper the direction and force of the wind. □□ **a·nem·o·graph·ic** /-gráfik/ *adj.*

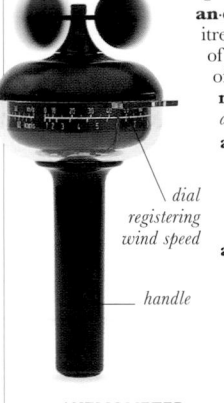

rotating cups

dial registering wind speed

handle

ANEMOMETER

an·e·mom·e·ter /ánimómitər/ *n.* ◄ an instrument for measuring the force of the wind.

an·e·mom·e·try /ánimómitree/ *n.* the measurement of the force, direction, etc., of the wind. □□ **an·e·mo·met·ric** /-məmétrik/ *adj.*

a·nem·o·ne /ənémənee/ *n.* any plant of the genus *Anemone*, akin to the buttercup, with flowers of various vivid colors.

an·er·oid /ánəroyd/ *adj. & n.* ● *adj.* (of a barometer) that measures air pressure by its action on the elastic lid of an evacuated box, not by the height of a column of fluid. ● *n.* an aneroid barometer.

an·es·the·sia /ánis-théezhə/ *n.* the absence of sensation, esp. artificially induced insensitivity to pain usu. achieved by the administration of gases or the injection of drugs. □□ **an·es·the·si·ol·o·gy** /-zeeóləjee/ *n.*

an·es·thet·ic /ánis-thétik/ *adj. & n.* ● *n.* a substance that produces insensibility to pain, etc. ● *adj.* producing partial or complete insensibility to pain, etc.

an·es·the·tist /ənés-thətist/ *n.* a specialist in the administration of anesthetics.

an·es·the·tize /ənés-thətīz/ *v.tr.* **1** administer an

anesthetic to. **2** deprive of physical or mental sensation. □□ **an·es·the·ti·za·tion** /-tizáyshən/ *n.*

an·eu·rysm /ányərizəm/ *n.* (also **an·eu·rism**) an excessive localized enlargement of an artery.

a·new /ənōō, ənyōō/ *adv.* **1** again. **2** in a different way.

an·gel /áynjəl/ *n.* **1 a** an attendant or messenger of God. **b** a representation of this in human form with wings. **c** an attendant spirit (*guardian angel*). **2 a** a very virtuous person. **b** an obliging person. **3** *sl.* a financial backer of an enterprise, esp. in the theater. **4** an unexplained radar echo.

an·gel dust *n. sl.* the hallucinogenic drug phencyclidine hydrochloride.

an·gel·fish /áynjəlfish/ *n.* ◄ any of various fish, esp. *Pterophyllum scalare*, with large dorsal and ventral fins.

an·gel food cake *n.* a very light sponge cake.

an·gel·ic /anjélik/ *adj.* **1** like or relating to angels. **2** having characteristics attributed to angels, esp. beauty and innocence. □□ **an·gel·i·cal·ly** *adv.*

an·gel·i·ca /anjélikə/ *n.* **1** an aromatic umbelliferous plant, *Angelica archangelica*, used in cooking and medicine. **2** candied stalks.

an·ge·lus /ánjiləs/ *n.* **1** a Roman Catholic devotion said at morning, noon, and sunset. **2** a bell rung to announce this.

an·ger /ánggər/ *n. & v.* ● *n.* extreme displeasure. ● *v.tr.* make angry.

an·gi·na /anjínə, ánjənə/ *n.* **1** an attack of intense constricting pain often causing suffocation. **2** in full **angina pectoris** /péktəris/) pain in the chest brought on by exertion, owing to an inadequate blood supply to the heart.

dorsal fin

ANGELFISH: DEEP ANGELFISH (*Pterophyllum altum*)

ventral fin

anal fin

an·gi·o·gram /ánjeeəgram/ *n.* an X ray taken by angiography.

an·gi·og·ra·phy /ánjeeáagrəfee/ *n.* the visualization by X ray of blood vessels following injection with a substance that is radiopaque.

an·gi·o·plas·ty /ánjeeōplastee/ *n.* a surgical operation to repair or unblock a blood vessel, esp. a coronary artery.

an·gi·o·sperm /ánjeeəspərm/ *n.* ► any plant producing flowers and reproducing by seeds enclosed within a carpel.

An·gle /ánggəl/ *n.* (usu. in *pl.*) a member of a tribe from Schleswig, Germany, that settled in eastern Britain in the 5th c. □□ **An·gli·an** *adj.*

an·gle[1] /ánggəl/ *n. & v.* ● *n.* **1 a** the space between two meeting lines or surfaces. **b** the inclination of two lines or surfaces to each other. **2 a** a corner. **b** a sharp projection. **3 a** the direction from which a photograph, etc., is taken. **b** the aspect from which a matter is considered. **c** an approach, technique, etc. ● *v.* **1** *tr. & intr.* move or place obliquely; point in a particular direction. **2** *tr.* present (information) in a biased way.

an·gle[2] /ánggəl/ *v.intr.* **1** (often foll. by *for*) fish with hook and line. **2** (foll. by *for*) seek an objective by devious or calculated means (*angled for a pay raise*).

an·gle brack·ets *n.pl.* brackets in the form < > (see BRACKET *n.* 3).

an·gled /ánggəld/ *adj.* **1** placed at an angle to something else. **2** presented to suit a particular point of view. **3** having an angle.

an·gler /ángglər/ *n.* a person who fishes with a hook and line.

ANGIOSPERM

The angiosperms, or flowering plants, number at least 250,000 species and form the largest division in the plant world. Unlike other seed plants, such as conifers, they produce seeds inside protective ovaries, which later ripen to form fruits. There are over 250 families of angiosperms, divided into two unequal groups. The dicotyledons, which make up the largest group, all have two seed leaves or cotyledons. They include a huge variety of herbaceous plants, shrubs, and all broad-leaved trees. The monocotyledons have a single seed leaf. They are mainly herbaceous, and include only a few treelike forms, such as palms.

EXAMPLES OF DICOTYLEDON FAMILIES

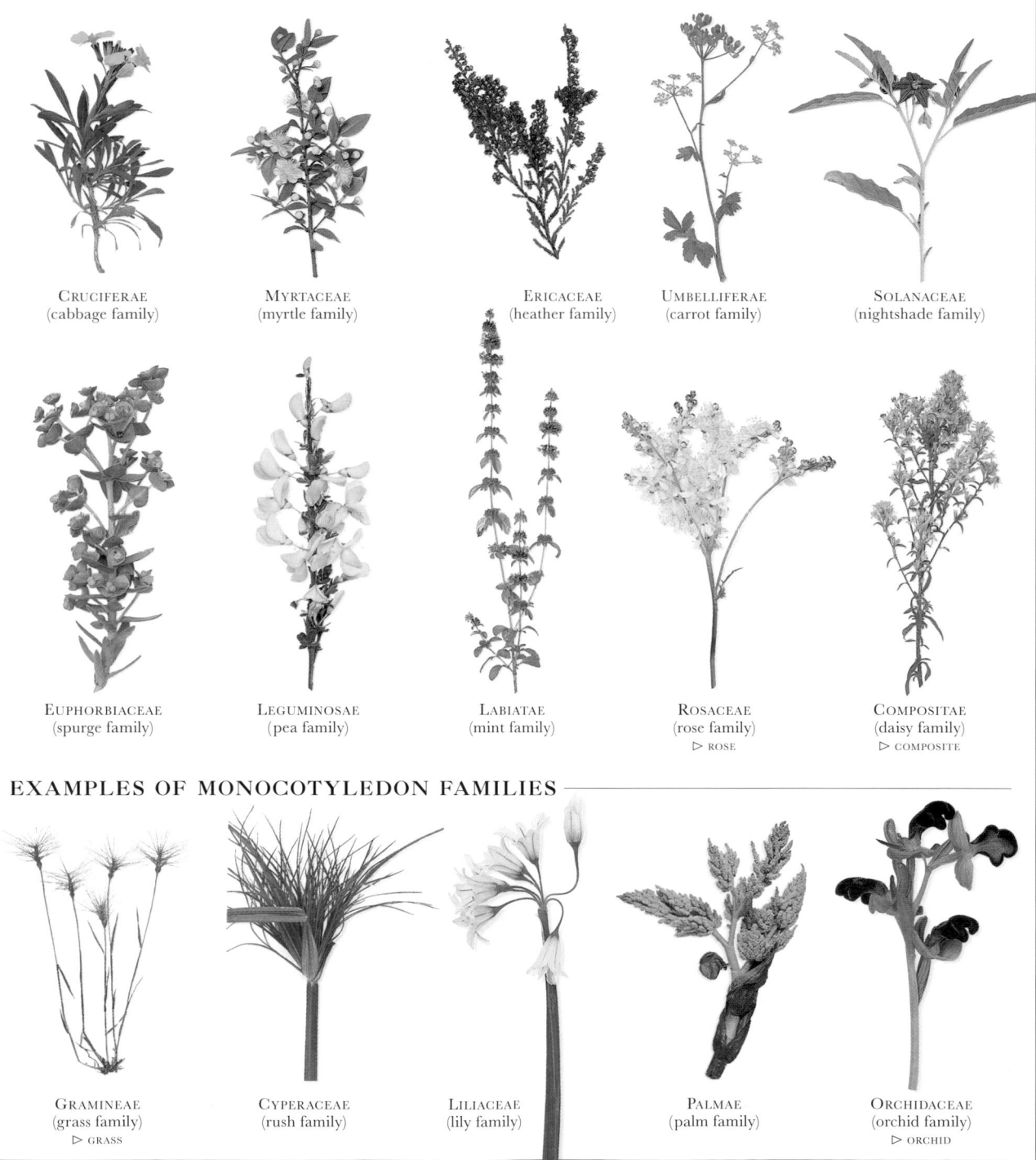

CRUCIFERAE
(cabbage family)

MYRTACEAE
(myrtle family)

ERICACEAE
(heather family)

UMBELLIFERAE
(carrot family)

SOLANACEAE
(nightshade family)

EUPHORBIACEAE
(spurge family)

LEGUMINOSAE
(pea family)

LABIATAE
(mint family)

ROSACEAE
(rose family)
▷ ROSE

COMPOSITAE
(daisy family)
▷ COMPOSITE

EXAMPLES OF MONOCOTYLEDON FAMILIES

GRAMINEAE
(grass family)
▷ GRASS

CYPERACEAE
(rush family)

LILIACEAE
(lily family)

PALMAE
(palm family)

ORCHIDACEAE
(orchid family)
▷ ORCHID

A

an·gler·fish /ángglərfish/ *n.* any of various fishes that prey upon small fish, attracting them by filaments arising from the dorsal fin. Also called **frogfish**.

An·gli·can /ángglikən/ *adj. & n.* • *adj.* of or relating to the Church of England or any Church in communion with it. • *n.* a member of an Anglican Church. □□ **An·gli·can·ism** *n.*

An·gli·cism /ángglisizəm/ *n.* **1** a peculiarly English word or custom. **2** Englishness. **3** preference for what is English.

An·gli·cize /ángglisīz/ *v.tr.* make English in form or character.

An·glo /ángglō/ *n.* (*pl.* **-os**) **1** a person of British or northern European origin. **2** a white, English-speaking person not of Hispanic descent.

Anglo- /ángglō/ *comb. form* **1** English (*Anglo-Catholic*). **2** of English origin (*an Anglo-American*). **3** English or British and (*an Anglo-American agreement*).

An·glo-Cath·o·lic /ángglōkáthəlik, -káthlik/ *adj. & n.* • *adj.* of a High Church Anglican group that emphasizes its Roman Catholic tradition. • *n.* a member of this group.

An·glo·cen·tric /ángglōséntrik/ *adj.* considered in terms of England.

An·glo-French /ángglōfrénch/ *adj. & n.* • *adj.* **1** English (or British) and French. **2** of Anglo-French. • *n.* the French language as retained and separately developed in England after the Norman Conquest.

An·glo-In·di·an /ángglō-índeeən/ *adj. & n.* • *adj.* **1** of or relating to England and India. **2 a** of British descent or birth but living or having lived long in India. **b** of mixed British and Indian parentage. **3** (of a word) adopted into English from an Indian language. • *n.* an Anglo-Indian person.

An·glo-Lat·in /ángglōlát'n/ *adj. & n.* • *adj.* of Latin as used in medieval England. • *n.* this form of Latin.

An·glo·ma·ni·a /ángglōmáyneeə/ *n.* excessive admiration of English customs.

An·glo-Nor·man /ángglōnáwrmən/ *adj. & n.* • *adj.* **1** English and Norman. **2** of the Normans in England after the Norman Conquest. **3** of the dialect of French used by them. • *n.* the Anglo-Norman dialect.

An·glo·phile /ánggləfīl/ *n. & adj.* (also **An·glo·phil** /-fil/) • *n.* a person who is fond of or greatly admires England or the English. • *adj.* being an Anglophile.

An·glo·phobe /ánggləfōb/ *n. & adj.* • *n.* a person who greatly hates or fears England or the English. • *adj.* being an Anglophobe.

An·glo·pho·bi·a /ánggləfóbeeə/ *n.* intense hatred or fear of England or the English.

an·glo·phone /ánggləfōn/ *adj. & n.* • *adj.* English-speaking. • *n.* an English-speaking person.

An·glo-Sax·on /ángglō-sáksən/ *adj. & n.* • *adj.* **1** of the English Saxons (as distinct from the Old Saxons of the European continent, and from the Angles) before the Norman Conquest. **2** of the Old English people as a whole before the Norman Conquest. **3** of English descent. • *n.* **1** an Anglo-Saxon person. **2** the Old English language. **3** *colloq.* plain (esp. crude) English.

an·go·ra /anggáwrə/ *n.* **1** a fabric made from the hair of the angora goat or rabbit. **2** ▶ a long-haired variety of cat, goat, or rabbit. ▷ CAT

ANGORA GOAT

an·go·ra wool *n.* a mixture of sheep's wool and angora rabbit hair.

an·gos·tu·ra /ánggəstŏŏrə, -styŏŏrə/ *n.* (in full **angostura bark**) an aromatic bitter bark used as a flavoring, and formerly as a tonic and to reduce fever.

an·gry /ánggree/ *adj.* (**angrier**, **angriest**) **1** feeling or showing anger. **2** (of a sore, etc.) inflamed; painful. **3** suggesting anger (*an angry sky*). □□ **an·gri·ly** *adv.*

angst /aangkst/ *n.* **1** anxiety. **2** a feeling of guilt or remorse.

ang·strom /ángstrəm/ *n.* (also **ångström** /áwng-ström/) a unit of length equal to 10^{-10} meter.

an·guish /ánggwish/ *n.* severe misery or suffering.

an·guished /ánggwisht/ *adj.* suffering or expressing anguish.

an·gu·lar /ánggyələr/ *adj.* **1 a** having angles or sharp corners. **b** (of a person) having sharp features. **c** awkward in manner. **2** forming an angle. **3** measured by angle. □□ **an·gu·lar·i·ty** /-láritee/ *n.* **an·gu·lar·ly** *adv.*

an·hy·drous /anhídrəs/ *adj.* *Chem.* without water, esp. water of crystallization.

an·i·line /ánillin, -līn/ *n.* a colorless oily liquid, used in the manufacture of dyes, drugs, and plastics.

an·i·line dye *n.* **1** any of numerous dyes made from aniline. **2** any synthetic dye.

an·i·ma /ánimə/ *n.* *Psychol.* **1** the inner personality (opp. PERSONA). **2** Jung's term for the feminine part of a man's personality (opp. ANIMUS).

an·i·mad·vert /ánimadvért/ *v.intr.* (foll. by *on*) criticize; censure (conduct, a fault, etc.). □□ **an·i·mad·ver·sion** /-vérzhən/ *n.*

an·i·mal /ánimə/ *n. & adj.* • *n.* **1** a living organism which feeds on organic matter, usu. one with specialized sense organs and a nervous system. **2** such an organism other than human beings. **3** a brutish or uncivilized person. **4** *colloq.* a person or thing of any kind (*no such animal*). • *adj.* **1** characteristic of animals. **2** of animals as distinct from vegetables (*animal charcoal*). **3** characteristic of the physical needs of animals; carnal; sensual.

an·i·mal·ism /ániməlizəm/ *n.* **1** the nature and activity of animals. **2** the belief that humans are not superior to other animals. **3** sensuality.

an·i·mal·i·ty /ánimálitee/ *n.* **1** the animal world. **2** the nature of animals.

an·i·mal rights *n.pl.* the natural right of animals to live free from human exploitation.

an·i·mate *adj. & v.* • *adj.* /ánimət/ **1** having life. **2** lively. • *v.tr.* /ánimayt/ **1** enliven; make lively. **2** give life to. **3** inspire; actuate. **4** encourage. **5** produce using animation.

an·i·mat·ed /ánimaytid/ *adj.* **1** lively; vigorous. **2** having life. **3** (of a movie, etc.) using techniques of animation. □□ **an·i·mat·ed·ly** *adv.* **an·i·ma·tor** *n.* (in sense 3).

an·i·ma·tion /ánimáyshən/ *n.* **1** vivacity; ardor. **2** the state of being alive. **3** *Cinematog.* the technique of filming successive drawings or positions of puppets, etc., to create an illusion of movement when the film is shown as a sequence.

an·i·mism /ánimizəm/ *n.* the attribution of a living soul to plants, inanimate objects, and natural phenomena. □□ **an·i·mist** *n.* **an·i·mis·tic** /-místik/ *adj.*

an·i·mos·i·ty /ánimósitee/ *n.* (*pl.* **-ies**) a spirit or feeling of strong hostility.

an·i·mus /ániməs/ *n.* **1** a display of animosity. **2** ill feeling. **3** a motivating spirit or feeling. **4** *Psychol.* Jung's term for the masculine part of a woman's personality (opp. ANIMA).

an·go·ra wool — *see above*

an·i·on /áníən/ *n.* a negatively charged ion; an ion that is attracted to the anode in electrolysis (opp. CATION).

an·i·on·ic /áníónik/ *adj.* **1** of an anion or anions. **2** having an active anion.

an·ise /ánis/ *n.* an umbelliferous plant, *Pimpinella anisum*, having aromatic seeds (see ANISEED).

an·i·seed /ániseed/ *n.* ▶ the seed of the anise, used to flavor liqueurs and candy.

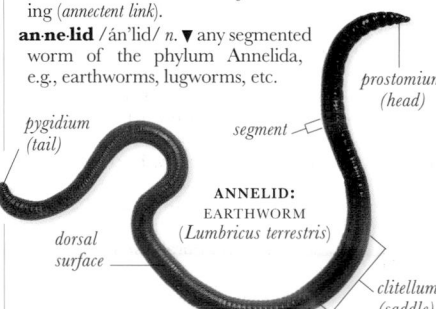

ground aniseed

whole aniseed

ANISEED
(*Pimpinella anisum*)

ankh /angk/ *n.* a device consisting of a looped bar with a shorter crossbar, used in ancient Egypt as a symbol of life.

an·kle /ángkəl/ *n.* **1** ◀ the joint connecting the foot with the leg. ▷ JOINT. **2** the part of the leg between this and the calf.

an·klet /ángklit/ *n.* an ornament or fetter worn around the ankle.

an·ky·lose /ángkilōs/ *v.tr. & intr.* (also **an·chy·lose**) (of bones or a joint) stiffen or unite by ankylosis.

an·ky·lo·sis /ángkilósis/ *n.* (also **an·chy·lo·sis**) **1** the abnormal stiffening and immobility of a joint by fusion of the bones. **2** such fusion. □□ **an·ky·lot·ic** /-lótik/ *adj.*

an·nal /ánəl/ *n.* **1** the annals of one year. **2** a record of one item in a chronicle.

an·nal·ist /ánəlist/ *n.* a writer of annals. □□ **an·nal·is·tic** /-lístik/ *adj.*

an·nals /ánəlz/ *n.pl.* **1** a narrative of events year by year. **2** historical records.

an·nat·to /ənátō/ *n.* (also **an·at·ta** /-tə/, **a·nat·to**) an orangish red dye from the pulp of a tropical fruit, used for coloring foods.

an·neal /ənéel/ *v. & n.* • *v.tr.* **1** heat (metal or glass) and allow it to cool slowly, esp. to toughen it. **2** toughen. • *n.* treatment by annealing. □□ **an·neal·er** *n.*

an·nec·tent /ənéktənt/ *adj. Biol.* connecting (*annectent link*).

an·ne·lid /án'lid/ *n.* ▼ any segmented worm of the phylum Annelida, e.g., earthworms, lugworms, etc.

prostomium (head)

pygidium (tail)

segment

ANNELID:
EARTHWORM
(*Lumbricus terrestris*)

dorsal surface

clitellum (saddle)

an·nex *v. & n.* /anéks, áneks / • *v.tr.* **1** add as a subordinate part. **2** incorporate (territory of another) into one's own. **3** add as a condition. **4** *colloq.* take without right. • *n.* (*Brit.* also **annexe** /áneks, ániks/) **1** a separate or added building. **2** an addition to a document. □□ **an·nex·a·tion** /-sáyshən/ *n.*

an·ni·hi·late /ən-íəlayt/ *v.tr.* **1** completely destroy. **2** defeat utterly; make insignificant or powerless. □□ **an·ni·hi·la·tor** *n.*

an·ni·hi·la·tion /əníəláyshən/ *n.* the act or process of annihilating.

ANKLE JOINT IN THE HUMAN FOOT

tibia

fibula

ligament

ankle joint

talus

tarsal

metatarsal

calcaneus

cuboid

an·ni·ver·sa·ry /ániivársəree/ n. (pl. **-ies**) **1** the date on which an event took place in a previous year. **2** the celebration of this.

An·no Dom·i·ni /ánō dóminī, -nee/ adv. in the year of our Lord; in the year of the Christian era.

an·no·tate /ánōtayt/ v.tr. add explanatory notes to (a book, document, etc.). □□ **an·no·tat·a·ble** adj. **an·no·ta·tion** /-táyshən/ n. **an·no·ta·tor** n.

an·nounce /ənówns/ v. **1** tr. (often foll. by that) make publicly known. **2** tr. make known the arrival or imminence of (a guest, dinner, etc.). **3** be a sign of.

an·nounce·ment /ənównsmənt/ n. **1** the action of announcing; something announced. **2** an official communication or statement. **3** an advertisement.

an·nounc·er /ənównsər/ n. a person who announces, esp. introducing programs or describing sports events in broadcasting.

an·noy /ənóy/ v.tr. **1** cause slight anger or mental distress to. **2** (in passive) be somewhat angry. **3** harass repeatedly. □□ **an·noy·er** n. **an·noy·ing** adj.

an·noy·ance /ənóyəns/ n. **1** irritation; vexation. **2** something that annoys.

an·nu·al /ányōōəl/ adj. & n. ● adj. **1** reckoned by the year. **2** occurring every year. **3** living or lasting for one year. ● n. **1** a book, etc., published once a year. **2** a plant that lives only for a year or less. □□ **an·nu·al·ly** adv.

an·nu·al·ized /ányōōəlīzd/ adj. (of rates of interest, inflation, etc.) calculated on an annual basis, as a projection from figures obtained for a shorter period.

an·nual ring n. a ring in the cross section of a plant, esp. a tree, produced by one year's growth.

an·nu·i·tant /ənóoit'nt, ənyóo-/ n. a person who holds or receives an annuity.

an·nu·i·ty /ənóoitee, ənyóo-/ n. (pl. **-ies**) **1** a yearly grant or allowance. **2** an investment of money entitling the investor to a series of equal annual sums.

an·nul /ənúl/ v.tr. (**annulled, annulling**) **1** declare (a marriage, etc.) invalid. **2** cancel; abolish. □□ **an·nul·ment** n.

an·nu·lar /ányələr/ adj. ring shaped; forming a ring. □□ **an·nu·lar·ly** adv.

an·nu·late /ányəlot, -layt/ adj. having rings; marked with or formed of rings. □□ **an·nu·la·tion** /-láyshən/ n.

an·nu·let /ányəlit/ n. **1** Archit. a small fillet or band encircling a column. **2** a small ring.

an·nu·lus /ányələs/ n. (pl. **annuli** /-lī/) esp. Math. & Biol. a ring.

an·nun·ci·ate /ənúnseeayt/ v.tr. **1** proclaim. **2** indicate as coming or ready.

an·nun·ci·a·tion /ənúnseeáyshən/ n. **1** (**Annunciation**) **a** the announcing of the Incarnation, related in Luke 1:26–38. **b** the festival commemorating this on March 25. **2 a** the act or process of announcing. **b** an announcement.

an·nun·ci·a·tor /ənúnseeaytər/ n. **1** a device giving an audible or visible indication of which of several electrical circuits has been activated, of the position of a train, etc. **2** an announcer.

an·nus mi·ra·bi·lis /ánəs mirábilis/ n. a remarkable or auspicious year.

an·ode /ánōd/ n. Electr. **1** the positively charged electrode by which electrons leave an electric device. **2** the negatively charged electrode of a device supplying current, e.g., a primary cell. □□ **an·od·al** adj. **an·od·ic** /ənódik/ adj.

an·ode ray n. a beam of particles emitted from the anode of a high vacuum tube.

an·o·dize /ánədīz/ v.tr. coat (a metal, esp. aluminum) with a protective oxide layer by electrolysis. □□ **an·o·diz·er** n.

an·o·dyne /ánədīn/ adj. **1** able to relieve pain. **2** mentally soothing.

an·o·e·sis /ánō-éesis/ n. Psychol. consciousness with sensation but without thought. □□ **an·o·et·ic** /-étik/ adj.

a·noint /ənóynt/ v.tr. **1** apply oil or ointment to, esp. as a religious ceremony (e.g., at baptism). **2** (usu. foll. by with) smear; rub. □□ **a·noint·er** n.

a·nom·a·lous /ənómələs/ adj. having an irregular or deviant feature; abnormal. □□ **a·nom·a·lous·ly** adv. **a·nom·a·lous·ness** n.

a·nom·a·ly /ənóməlee/ n. (pl. **-ies**) **1** an anomalous circumstance or thing; an irregularity. **2** irregularity of motion, behavior, etc.

an·o·mie /ánəmee/ n. (also **an·o·my**) lack of the usual social or ethical standards in an individual or group. □□ **a·nom·ic** /ənómik/ adj.

a·non /ənón/ adv. archaic or literary soon; shortly (will say more of this anon).

anon. /ənón/ abbr. anonymous; an anonymous author.

a·no·nym /ánənim/ n. **1** an anonymous person or publication. **2** a pseudonym.

a·non·y·mous /ənóniməs/ adj. **1** of unknown name. **2** of unknown or undeclared source or authorship. **3** without character; featureless; impersonal. □□ **an·o·nym·i·ty** /ánənímitee/ n. **a·non·y·mous·ly** adv.

a·noph·e·les /ənófileez/ n. any of various mosquitoes of the genus Anopheles, many of which are carriers of the malarial parasite.

an·o·rak /ánərak/ n. a waterproof jacket of cloth or synthetic material, usu. with a hood, of a kind orig. used in polar regions; a parka.

an·o·rec·tic var. of ANOREXIC.

an·o·rex·i·a /ánərékseeə/ n. **1** a lack or loss of appetite for food. **2** (in full **anorexia ner·vo·sa** /nərvósə/) a psychological illness characterized by an obsessive desire to lose weight by refusing to eat.

an·o·rex·ic /ánəréksik/ adj. & n. (also **an·o·rec·tic** /-réktik/) ● adj. **1** characterized by a lack of appetite, esp. in anorexia nervosa. **2** colloq. extremely thin. ● n. a person with anorexia.

an·os·mi·a /anózmeeə/ n. the loss of the sense of smell. □□ **an·os·mic** adj.

an·oth·er /ənúthər/ adj. & pron. ● adj. **1** an additional (have another piece of cake). **2** a person comparable to (another Lincoln). **3** a different (quite another matter). **4** some or any other (will not do another person's work). ● pron. **1** an additional one (have another). **2** a different one (take this book away and bring me another). **3** some or any other one (I love another). □ **such another** another of the same sort.

an·ov·u·lant /anóvyələnt/ n. & adj. Pharm. ● n. a drug preventing ovulation. ● adj. preventing ovulation.

an·swer /ánsər/ n. & v. ● n. **1** something said or done in reaction to a question, statement, or circumstance. **2** the solution to a problem. ● v. **1** tr. make an answer to (answer me; answer my question). **2** intr. (often foll. by to) make an answer. **3** tr. respond to the summons or signal of (answer the door; answer the telephone). **4** tr. be satisfactory for (a purpose or need). **5** intr. **a** (foll. by for, to) be responsible (you will answer to me for your conduct). **b** (foll. by for) vouch (for a person, conduct, etc.). **6** intr. (foll. by to) correspond, esp. to a description. **7** intr. be satisfactory or successful. □ **answer back** answer a rebuke, etc., impudently. **answer to the name of** be called.

an·swer·a·ble /ánsərəbəl/ adj. **1** (usu. foll. by to, for) responsible (answerable to them for any accident). **2** that can be answered.

an·swer·ing ma·chine n. a tape recorder which supplies a recorded answer to a telephone call and usu. records incoming messages.

an·swer·ing serv·ice n. a business that receives and answers telephone calls for its clients.

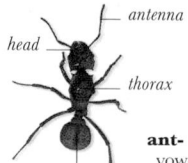

ANT

ant /ant/ n. ◄ any small insect of a widely distributed hymenopterous family, living in complex social colonies, and proverbial for industry. □ **have ants in one's pants** colloq. be fidgety; be restless.

ant- /ant/ assim. form of ANTI- before a vowel or h (Antarctic).

ant·ac·id /antásid/ n. & adj. ● n. a substance that prevents or corrects acidity, esp. in the stomach. ● adj. having these properties.

an·tag·o·nism /antágənizəm/ n. active opposition or hostility.

an·tag·o·nist /antágənist/ n. **1** an opponent or adversary. **2** Biol. a substance, muscle, or organ that partially or completely opposes the action of another. □□ **an·tag·o·nis·tic** adj. **an·tag·o·nis·ti·cal·ly** adv.

an·tag·o·nize /antágənīz/ v.tr. **1** evoke hostility or opposition in. **2** (of one force, etc.) counteract or tend to neutralize (another).

ant·al·ka·li /antálkəlī/ n. (pl. **antalkalis**) any substance that counteracts an alkali.

Ant·arc·tic /antáarktik/ adj. & n. ● adj. of the south polar regions. ● n. this region.

Ant·arc·tic Cir·cle n. ◄ the parallel of latitude 66° 32′ S., forming an imaginary line around this region.

Antarctic Circle   Antarctic regions

ANTARCTIC CIRCLE

an·te /ántee/ n. & v. ● n. **1** a stake put up by a player in poker, etc., before receiving cards. **2** an amount to be paid in advance. ● v.tr. (**antes, anted**) **1** put up as an ante. **2 a** bet; stake. **b** (foll. by up) pay.

ante- /ántee/ prefix forming nouns and adjectives meaning "before; preceding" (anteroom; antenatal).

ant·eat·er /ánteetər/ n. ▼ any of various mammals feeding on ants and termites.

ANTEATER: GIANT ANTEATER
(Myrmecophaga tridactyla)

an·te·bel·lum /ánteebéləm/ adj. occurring or existing before a particular war, esp. the US Civil War.

an·te·ced·ent /ántiséed'nt/ n. & adj. ● n **1** a preceding thing or circumstance. **2** Gram. a word, phrase, etc., to which another word (esp. a relative pronoun) refers. **3** (in pl.) past history, esp. of a person. ● adj. **1** (often foll. by to) previous. **2** presumptive; a priori. □□ **an·te·ced·ence** /-d'ns/ n. **an·te·ced·ent·ly** adv.

an·te·cham·ber /ánteechaymbər/ n. a small room leading to a main one.

an·te·date /ántidáyt/ v. & n. ● v.tr. **1** occur at a date earlier than. **2** assign an earlier date to (a document, event, etc.). ● n. a date earlier than the actual one.

an·te·di·lu·vi·an /ánteedilóoveeən/ adj. **1** of or belonging to the time before the Biblical flood. **2** colloq. very old or out of date.

an·te·lope /ántilōp/ n. (pl. same or **antelopes**) **1** any of various deerlike ruminants of the family

A

Bovidae, esp. abundant in Africa and typically tall, slender, graceful, and swift-moving with upward-pointing horns. **2** leather made from the skin of any of these.

an·te·na·tal /ánteenáyt'l/ *adj.* **1** existing or occurring before birth; prenatal. **2** relating to the period of pregnancy.

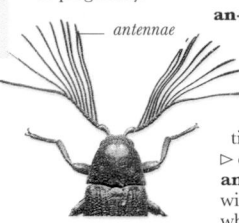

ANTENNAE
OF A BEETLE

an·ten·na /anténə/ *n.* **1** (*pl.* **antennae** /-ee/) *Zool.* ◄ one of a pair of mobile appendages on the heads of insects, crustaceans, etc., sensitive to touch and taste. ▷ CRUSTACEAN, HOUSEFLY. **2** (*pl.* **antennas**) a metal rod, wire, or other structure by which signals are transmitted or received as part of a radio or television transmission or receiving system. □□ **an·ten·nal** *adj.* (in sense 1). **an·ten·na·ry** *adj.* (in sense 1).

an·te·nup·tial /ánteenúpshəl/ *adj.* = PRENUPTIAL.

an·te·pe·nul·ti·mate /ánteepinúltimət/ *adj.* last but two.

an·te·ri·or /antéereeər/ *adj.* **1** nearer the front. **2** (often foll. by *to*) earlier; prior. □□ **an·te·ri·or·i·ty** /-reeáwritee/ *n.* **an·te·ri·or·ly** *adv.*

an·te·room /ánteeroōm, -roŏm/ *n.* a small room leading to a main one.

ant·heap /ánt-heep/ *n.* = ANTHILL.

ant·he·li·on /ant-héeleeən, anthée-/ *n.* (*pl.* **anthelia** /-liə/) a luminous halo projected on a cloud or fog bank opposite to the Sun.

ant·hel·min·tic /ánt-helmíntik, ánthel-/ (also **ant·hel·min·thic** /-thik/) *n.* any drug or agent used to destroy parasitic worms, e.g., tapeworms, roundworms, and flukes.

an·them /ánthəm/ *n.* **1** an elaborate choral composition usu. based on a passage of scripture. **2** a solemn hymn of praise, etc., esp. = NATIONAL ANTHEM.

an·ther /ánthər/ *n. Bot.* ► the apical portion of a stamen containing pollen. ▷ FLOWER. □□ **an·ther·al** *adj.*

ant·hill /ánt-hil/ *n.* **1** a moundlike nest built by ants or termites. **2** a community teeming with people.

an·thol·o·gize /anthóləjīz/ *v.tr. & intr.* compile or include in an anthology.

an·thol·o·gy /anthóləjee/ *n.* (*pl.* **-ies**) a published collection of passages from literature, songs, reproductions of paintings, etc. □□ **an·thol·o·gist** *n.*

an·tho·zo·an /ánthəzóən/ *n. & adj.*
● *n.* any of the sessile marine coelenterates of the class Anthozoa, including sea anemones and corals. ▷ CNIDARIAN. ● *adj.* of or relating to this class.

an·thra·cene /ánthraseen/ *n.* a colorless crystalline aromatic hydrocarbon obtained by the distillation of crude oils and used in the manufacture of chemicals.

an·thra·cite /ánthrasīt/ *n.* coal of a hard variety burning with little flame and smoke. ▷ COAL. □□ **an·thra·cit·ic** /-sítik/ *adj.*

an·thrax /ánthraks/ *n.* a disease of sheep and cattle transmissible to humans.

anthropo- /ánthrəpō/ *comb. form* human; humankind.

an·thro·po·cen·tric /ánthrəpōséntrik/ *adj.* regarding humankind as the center of existence. □□ **an·thro·po·cen·trism** *n.*

an·thro·po·gen·e·sis /ánthrəpōjénisis/ *n.* the study of the origin of humans.

an·thro·po·gen·ic /ánthrəpōjénik/ *adj.* produced or caused by human beings.

an·thro·poid /ánthrəpoyd/ *adj. & n.* ● *adj.* **1** human in form. ▷ PRIMATE. **2** *colloq.* (of a person) apelike. ● *n.* a being that is human in form only.

an·thro·pol·o·gy /ánthrəpóləjee/ *n.* **1** the study of humankind. **2** the study of the structure and evolution of human beings as animals. □□ **an·thro·po·log·i·cal** /-pəlójikəl/ *adj.* **an·thro·pol·o·gist** *n.*

an·thro·pom·e·try /ánthrəpómitree/ *n.* the scientific study of the measurements of the human body. □□ **an·thro·po·met·ric** /-pəmétrik/ *adj.*

an·thro·po·mor·phic /ánthrəpəmáwrfik/ *adj.* of or characterized by anthropomorphism. □□ **an·thro·po·mor·phi·cal·ly** *adv.*

an·thro·po·mor·phism /ánthrəpəmáwrfizəm/ *n.* the attribution of a human form or personality to a god, animal, or thing. □□ **an·thro·po·mor·phize** *v.tr.*

an·thro·po·mor·phous /ánthrəpəmáwrfəs/ *adj.* human in form.

an·thro·poph·a·gy /ánthrəpófəjee/ *n.* cannibalism. □□ **an·thro·poph·a·gous** *adj.*

an·ti /ántee, -tī/ *prep. & n.* ● *prep.* (also *absol.*) opposed to (*is anti everything*). ● *n.* (*pl.* **antis**) a person opposed to a particular policy, etc.

anti- /ántee/ *prefix* (also **ant-** before a vowel or *h*) forming nouns and adjectives meaning: **1** opposed to; against (*antivivisectionism*). **2** preventing (*antiscorbutic*). **3** the opposite of (*anticlimax*). **4** rival (*antipope*). **5** unlike the conventional form (*antihero*). **6** *Physics* the antiparticle of a specified particle (*antiproton*).

an·ti·a·bor·tion /ánteeəbáwrshən, ántī-/ *adj.* opposing abortion. □□ **an·ti·a·bor·tion·ist** *n.*

an·ti·air·craft /ánteeáirkraft, ántī-/ *adj.* (of a gun, missile, etc.) used to attack enemy aircraft.

an·ti·bal·lis·tic mis·sile /ánteebəlístik, ántī-/ *n.* a missile designed for intercepting and destroying a ballistic missile while in flight.

an·ti·bi·o·sis /ánteebīósis, ántī-/ *n.* an antagonistic association between two organisms (esp. microorganisms), in which one is adversely affected (cf. SYMBIOSIS).

an·ti·bi·ot·ic /ántibīótik, ántī-/ *n. Pharm.* any of various substances (e.g., penicillin) produced by microorganisms or made synthetically, that can inhibit or destroy susceptible microorganisms.

an·ti·bod·y /ántibodee/ *n.* (*pl.* **-ies**) any of various blood proteins produced in response to and then counteracting antigens.

an·tic /ántik/ *n.* **1** (usu. in *pl.*) absurd or foolish behavior. **2** an absurd or silly action.

An·ti·christ /ánteekrīst, ántī-/ *n.* **1** an archenemy of Christ. **2** a postulated personal opponent of Christ expected by some denominations of the Christian church to appear before the end of the world.

an·tic·i·pate /antísipayt/ *v.tr.* **1** deal with or use before the proper time. **2** *disp.* expect (*did not anticipate any difficulty*). **3** forestall (a person or thing). **4** look forward to. □□ **an·tic·i·pa·tive** *adj.* **an·tic·i·pa·tor** *n.* **an·tic·i·pa·to·ry** *adj.*

an·tic·i·pa·tion /antísipáyshən/ *n.* the act or process of anticipating.

an·ti·cler·i·cal /ánteeklérikəl, ántī-/ *adj. & n.* ● *adj.* opposed to the influence of the clergy, esp. in politics. ● *n.* an anticlerical person. □□ **an·ti·cler·i·cal·ism** *n.*

an·ti·cli·max /ánteeklímaks, ántī-/ *n.* a disappointingly trivial conclusion to something significant. □□ **an·ti·cli·mac·tic** /-máktik/ *adj.*

an·ti·cline /ántiklīn/ *n. Geol.* ► a ridge or fold of stratified rock in which the strata slope down from the crest. □□ **an·ti·cli·nal** *adj.*

ANTICLINE: SECTION OF THE
EARTH'S CRUST SHOWING
THE STRUCTURE OF AN ANTICLINE

an·ti·clock·wise /ánteeklókwīz, ántī-/ *adv. & adj. Brit.* = COUNTERCLOCKWISE.

an·ti·co·ag·u·lant /ánteekō-ágyələnt, ántī-/ *n.* any drug or agent that retards or inhibits coagulation, esp. of the blood.

an·ti·con·vul·sant /ánteekənvúlsənt, ántī-/ *n.* any drug or agent that prevents or reduces the severity of convulsions, esp. as in epilepsy.

an·ti·cy·clone /ánteesíklōn, ántī-/ *n.* a system of winds rotating outwards from an area of high barometric pressure. □□ **an·ti·cy·clon·ic** /-klónik/ *adj.*

an·ti·de·pres·sant /ánteediprésənt, ántī-/ *n.* any drug or agent that alleviates depression.

an·ti·dote /ántidōt/ *n.* **1** a medicine, etc., taken or given to counteract poison. **2** anything that counteracts something unpleasant or evil. □□ **an·ti·dot·al** *adj.*

an·ti·freeze /ántifreez, ántee-/ *n.* a substance (usu. ethylene glycol) added to water to lower its freezing point, esp. in the radiator of a motor vehicle.

an·ti·gen /ántijən/ *n.* a foreign substance (e.g., toxin) that causes the body to produce antibodies. □□ **an·ti·gen·ic** /-jénik/ *adj.*

an·ti·grav·i·ty /ánteegrávitee, ántī-/ *n. Physics* a hypothetical force opposing gravity.

an·ti·he·ro /ánteeheerō, ántī-/ *n.* (*pl.* **-oes**) a central character in a story or drama who noticeably lacks conventional heroic attributes.

an·ti·his·ta·mine /ánteehístəmin, -meen, ántī-/ *n.* a substance that counteracts the effects of histamine, used esp. in the treatment of allergies.

an·ti·in·flam·ma·to·ry /anteeinflámətōree, ántī-/ *adj. & n.* ● *adj.* reducing inflammation. ● *n.* (*pl.* **-ies**) an anti-inflammatory medication.

an·ti·knock /ánteenók, ántī-/ *n.* a substance added to motor fuel to prevent premature combustion.

an·ti·lock /ánteelók, ántī-/ *attrib. adj.* (of brakes) designed so as to prevent locking and skidding when applied suddenly.

an·ti·log·a·rithm /ánteeláwgərithəm, -lóg-, ántī-/ *n.* the number to which a logarithm belongs (*100 is the common antilogarithm of 2*).

an·til·o·gy /antíləjee/ *n.* (*pl.* **-ies**) a contradiction in terms.

an·ti·ma·cas·sar /ánteeməkásər/ *n.* a covering put over furniture, esp. over the back of a chair as protection or as an ornament.

an·ti·mat·ter /ánteematər, ántī-/ *n. Physics* matter composed solely of antiparticles.

an·ti·mo·ny /ántimōnee/ *n. Chem.* a brittle silvery white metallic element used esp. in alloys. ¶ Symb.: **Sb**. □□ **an·ti·mo·ni·al** /-móneeəl/ *adj.* **an·ti·mo·nic** *adj.* **an·ti·mo·ni·ous** /-móneeəs/ *adj.*

an·ti·node /ánteenōd, ántī-/ *n. Physics* the position of maximum displacement in a standing wave system.

an·ti·no·mi·an /ántinómeeən/ *adj.* of or relating to the view that Christians are released from the obligation of observing the moral law. □□ **an·ti·no·mi·an·ism** *n.*

an·tin·o·my /antínəmee/ *n.* (*pl.* **-ies**) **1** a contradiction between two beliefs or conclusions that are in themselves reasonable; a paradox. **2** a conflict between two laws or authorities.

an·ti·nov·el /ánteenovəl, ántī-/ *n.* a novel in which the conventions of the form are studiously avoided.

an·ti·nu·cle·ar /ánteenoōkleeər, -nyoō-, ántī-/ *adj.*

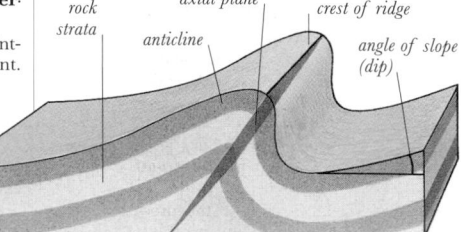

opposed to the development of nuclear weapons or nuclear power.

an·ti·ox·i·dant /ántee-óksid'nt, ántī-/ *n.* an agent that inhibits oxidation, esp. used to reduce deterioration of products stored in air.

an·ti·par·ti·cle /ánteepaartikəl, ántī-/ *n. Physics* an elementary particle having the same mass as a given particle but opposite electric or magnetic properties.

an·ti·pas·to /ánteepáastō/ *n.* (*pl.* **-os** or **antipasti** /-tee/) an hors d'oeuvre, esp. in an Italian meal.

an·ti·pa·thet·ic /ántipəthétik/ *adj.* (usu. foll. by *to*) having a strong aversion or natural opposition. □□ **an·ti·pa·thet·i·cal·ly** *adv.*

an·tip·a·thy /antípəthee/ *n.* (*pl.* **-ies**) a strong aversion or dislike.

an·ti·per·son·nel /ánteepərsənél, ántī-/ *adj.* (of a bomb, mine, etc.) designed to kill or injure people rather than to damage buildings or equipment.

an·ti·per·spi·rant /ánteepərspirənt, ántī-/ *n. & adj.* ● *n.* a substance applied to the skin to prevent perspiration. ● *adj.* that acts as an antiperspirant.

an·ti·phon /ántifon/ *n.* **1** a hymn or psalm, the parts of which are sung or recited alternately by two groups. **2** a versicle or phrase from this.

an·tiph·o·nal /antífənəl/ *adj. & n.* ● *adj.* **1** sung or recited alternately by two groups. **2** responsive; answering. ● *n.* a collection of antiphons. □□ **an·tiph·o·nal·ly** *adv.*

an·tiph·o·ny /antífənee/ *n.* (*pl.* **-ies**) **1** antiphonal singing or chanting. **2** a response or echo.

an·ti·pode /ántipōd/ *n.* (usu. foll. by *of, to*) the exact opposite.

an·tip·o·des /antípədeez/ *n.pl.* **1 a** (also **Antipodes**) a place diametrically opposite another, esp. Australasia as the region on the opposite side of the Earth from Europe. **b** places diametrically opposite each other. **2** (usu. foll. by *of, to*) the exact opposite. □□ **an·tip·o·dal** *adj.* **an·tip·o·de·an** /-déeən/ *adj. & n.*

an·ti·pope /ántipōp, ántī-/ *n.* a person set up as pope in opposition to one (held by others to be) canonically chosen.

an·ti·pro·ton /ánteeprôton, ántī/ *n. Physics* the negatively charged antiparticle of a proton.

an·ti·py·ret·ic /ánteepīrétik, ántī-/ *adj.* preventing or reducing fever.

an·ti·quar·i·an /ántikwáireeən/ *adj. & n.* ● *adj.* **1** of or dealing in antiques or rare books. **2** of the study of antiquities. ● *n.* an antiquary. □□ **an·ti·quar·i·an·ism** *n.*

an·ti·quar·y /ántikweree/ *n.* (*pl.* **-ies**) a student or collector of antiques or antiquities.

an·ti·quat·ed /ántikwaytid/ *adj.* old-fashioned; out of date.

an·tique /anteék/ *n. & adj.* ● *n.* an object of considerable age, esp. an item of furniture or the decorative arts having a high value. ● *adj.* **1** of or existing from an early date. **2** old-fashioned; archaic. **3** of ancient times.

an·tiq·ui·ty /antíkwitee/ *n.* (*pl.* **-ies**) **1** ancient times, esp. the period before the Middle Ages. **2** great age (*a city of great antiquity*). **3** (usu. in *pl.*) physical remains or relics from ancient times, esp. buildings and works of art. **4** (in *pl.*) customs, events, etc., of ancient times.

an·ti·rac·ism /ánteeráysizəm, ántī-/ *n.* the policy or practice of opposing racism and promoting racial tolerance. □□ **an·ti·rac·ist** *n. & adj.*

an·tir·rhi·num /ántirínəm/ *n.* any plant of the genus *Antirrhinum*, esp. the snapdragon. ▷ SNAPDRAGON

an·ti·scor·bu·tic /ánteeskawrbyốōtik, ántī-/ *adj.* preventing or curing scurvy.

an·ti·Sem·ite /ántisémīt, ántī-/ *n.* a person hostile to or prejudiced against Jews. □□ **an·ti·Se·mit·ic** /-simítik/ *adj.* **an·ti·sem·i·tism** /-sémi·tizəm/ *n.*

an·ti·sep·sis /ántisépsis/ *n.* the process of using antiseptics to eliminate undesirable microorgan-

isms such as bacteria, viruses, and fungi that cause disease.

an·ti·sep·tic /ántiséptik/ *adj. & n.* ● *adj.* **1** counteracting sepsis, esp. by preventing the growth of disease-causing microorganisms. **2** free from contamination. **3** lacking character. ● *n.* an antiseptic agent. □□ **an·ti·sep·ti·cal·ly** *adv.*

an·ti·se·rum /ántiseerəm/ *n.* (*pl.* **antisera** /-rə/) a blood serum containing antibodies against specific antigens, injected to treat specific diseases.

an·ti·so·cial /ánteesôshəl, ántī-/ *adj.* **1** contrary to normal social instincts or practices. **2** not sociable. **3** opposed to the existing social order.

an·ti·stat·ic /ánteestátik, ántī-/ *adj.* that counteracts the effects of static electricity.

an·tith·e·sis /antíthisis/ *n.* (*pl.* **antitheses** /-seez/) **1** (foll. by *of, to*) the direct opposite. **2** (usu. foll. by *of, between*) contrast or opposition between two things.

an·ti·thet·i·cal /ántithétikəl/ *adj.* (also **an·ti·thet·ic**) **1** contrasted; opposite. **2** connected with, containing, or using antithesis. □□ **an·ti·thet·i·cal·ly** *adv.*

an·ti·tox·in /ánteetóksin/ *n.* an antibody that counteracts a toxin. □□ **an·ti·tox·ic** *adj.*

an·ti·trades /ántitráydz/ *n.pl.* winds that blow in the opposite direction to (and usu. above) a trade wind.

an·ti·trust /ánteetrúst, ántī-/ *adj.* (of a law, etc.) opposed to or controlling trusts or other monopolies.

an·ti·type /ánteetīp/ *n.* **1** that which is represented by a type or symbol. **2** a person or thing of the opposite type. □□ **an·ti·typ·i·cal** /-típikəl/ *adj.*

an·ti·vi·ral /ánteevírəl, ántī-/ *adj.* effective against viruses.

an·ti·viv·i·sec·tion·ism /ánteevívisékshənizəm, ántī-/ *n.* opposition to vivisection. □□ **an·ti·viv·i·sec·tion·ist** *n.*

ant·ler /ántlər/ *n.* **1** each of the branched horns of a stag or other (usu. male) deer. ▷ DEER. **2** a branch of this. □□ **ant·lered** *adj.*

ant li·on *n.* ▼ any of various dragonflylike insects, the larvae of which dig pits in which to trap ants and other insects for food.

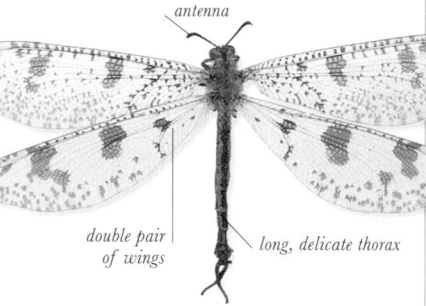

antenna

double pair of wings

long, delicate thorax

ANT LION (*Palpares libelluloides*)

an·to·no·ma·sia /ántənəmáyzhə/ *n.* **1** the substitution of an epithet or title, etc., for a proper name (e.g., *the Maid of Orleans* for Joan of Arc). **2** the use of a proper name to express a general idea (e.g., a *Scrooge* for a miser).

an·to·nym /ántənim/ *n.* a word opposite in meaning to another in the same language (e.g., *bad* and *good*) (opp. SYNONYM). □□ **an·ton·y·mous** /antóniməs/ *adj.*

an·trum /ántrəm/ *n.* (*pl.* **antra** /-trə/) *Anat.* a natural chamber or cavity in the body, esp. in a bone. □□ **an·tral** *adj.*

ants·y /ántsee/ *adj. colloq.* irritated; impatient; fidgety; restless.

an·u·ran /ənōōrən, ənyōōr-/ *n. & adj.* ● *n.* any tailless amphibian of the order Anura, including frogs and toads. ▷ FROG, TOAD. ● *adj.* of or relating to this order.

a·nus /áynəs/ *n. Anat.* the excretory opening at the end of the alimentary canal. ▷ INTESTINE

an·vil /ánvil/ *n.* **1** a block (usu. of iron) with a flat top, concave sides, and often a pointed end, on which metals are worked in forging. **2** *Anat.* a bone of the ear; the incus.

anx·i·e·ty /angzíətee/ *n.* (*pl.* **-ies**) **1** the state of being anxious. **2** concern about an imminent danger, difficulty, etc. **3** (foll. by *for*, or *to* + infin.) anxious desire.

anx·ious /ángkshəs/ *adj.* **1** uneasy in the mind. **2** causing or marked by anxiety (*an anxious moment*). **3** (foll. by *for*, or *to* + infin.) earnestly or uneasily wanting (*anxious to please*). □□ **anx·ious·ly** *adv.* **anx·ious·ness** *n.*

an·y /énee/ *adj., pron., & adv.* ● *adj.* **1** (with *interrog., neg.,* or *conditional* expressed or implied) **a** one, no matter which, of several (*cannot find any answer*). **b** some, no matter how much or many or of what sort (*if any books arrive; have you any sugar?*). **2** a minimal amount of (*hardly any difference*). **3** whichever is chosen (*any fool knows that*). **4 a** a significant (*did not stay for any length of time*). **b** a very large (*has any amount of money*). ● *pron.* **1** any one (*did not know any of them*). **2** any number (*are any of them yours?*). **3** any amount (*is there any left?*). ● *adv.* (usu. with *neg.* or *interrog.*) at all (*is that any good?*).

an·y·bod·y /éneebudee, -bodee/ *n. & pron.* **1 a** a person, no matter who. **b** a person of any kind. **c** whatever person is chosen. **2** a person of importance.

an·y·how /éneehow/ *adv.* **1** anyway. **2** in a disorderly manner or state.

an·y·more /eneemáwr/ *adv.* to any further extent (*don't like you anymore*).

an·y·one /éneewun/ *pron.* anybody. ¶ Written as two words to imply a numerical sense, as in *any one of us can do it.*

an·y·place /éneeplays/ *adv.* anywhere.

an·y·thing /éneething/ *pron.* **1** a thing, no matter which. **2** a thing of any kind. **3** whatever thing is chosen. □ **anything but** not at all (*was anything but honest*).

an·y·time /éneetīm/ *adv. colloq.* at any time.

an·y·way /éneeway/ *adv.* (also *dial.* **anyways** /éneewayz/) **1** in any way or manner. **2** in any case. **3** to resume (*anyway, as I was saying*).

an·y·where /éneehwair, -wair/ *adv. & pron.* ● *adv.* in or to any place. ● *pron.* any place (*anywhere will do*).

an·y·wise /éneewīz/ *adv.* in any manner.

An·zac /ánzak/ *n.* **1** a soldier in the Australian and New Zealand Army Corps (1914–18). **2** any person from Australia or New Zealand.

An·zus /ánzəs/ *n.* (also **ANZUS**) Australia, New Zealand, and the US, as an alliance for the Pacific area.

A-OK *abbr. colloq.* excellent; in good order.

a·o·rist /áyərist/ *n. & adj. Gram.* ● *n.* an unqualified past tense of a verb, without reference to duration or completion. ● *adj.* of or designating this tense. □□ **a·o·ris·tic** *adj.*

a·or·ta /ayáwrtə/ *n.* (*pl.* **aortas**) the main artery, giving rise to the arterial network through which oxygenated blood is supplied to the body from the heart. ▷ CARDIOVASCULAR, HEART. □□ **a·or·tic** *adj.*

a·pace /əpáys/ *adv. literary* swiftly; quickly.

A·pach·e /əpáchee/ *n.* **1** a member of a N. American Indian tribe of the southwestern US. **2** (*apache* /əpásh/) a violent street ruffian, orig. in Paris.

a·part /əpaárt/ *adv.* **1** separately; not together (*stand apart from the crowd*). **2** into pieces (*came apart in my hands*). **3 a** to or on one side. **b** out of consideration (*placed after noun: joking apart*). **4** to or at a distance. □ **apart from** excepting; not considering.

a·part·heid /əpaárt-hayt, -hīt/ *n.* (esp. as formerly in S. Africa) a policy or system of segregation or discrimination on grounds of race.

A

a·part·ment /əpáartmənt/ n. **1** a set of rooms, usu. on one floor, used as a residence. **2** (in pl.) a suite of rooms, usu. rented.

a·part·ment build·ing n. (also **a·part·ment house**) a building containing a number of separate apartments.

ap·a·thet·ic /ápəthétik/ adj. having no emotion. □□ **ap·a·thet·i·cal·ly** adv.

ap·a·thy /ápəthee/ n. (often foll. by toward) lack of interest or feeling.

a·pa·to·sau·rus /əpátəsáwrəs/ n. ▼ a large plant-eating dinosaur of the genus Apatosaurus, with a long tail and trunklike legs. Formerly known as BRONTOSAURUS.

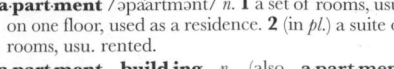

APATOSAURUS

ape /ayp/ n. & v. ● n. **1** any of the various primates of the family Pongidae, characterized by the absence of a tail. **2** (in general use) any monkey. **3 a** an imitator. **b** an apelike person. ● v.tr. imitate; mimic. □ **go ape** sl. **1** become crazy. **2** be emotional or enthusiatic.

ape-man n. (pl. **-men**) any of various apelike primates held to be forerunners of present-day human beings.

a·per·çu /aapersv/ n. **1** a summary or survey. **2** an insight.

a·per·i·ent /əpéereeənt/ adj. & n. ● adj. laxative. ● n. a laxative medicine.

a·pe·ri·od·ic /áypeereeeódik/ adj. not periodic; irregular.

a·pe·ri·tif /əpéritéef/ n. an alcoholic drink taken before a meal to stimulate the appetite.

ap·er·ture /ápərchər/ n. **1** an opening; a gap. **2** ▼ a space through which light passes in an optical or photographic instrument.

A·pex /áypeks/ n. (also **APEX**) (often attrib.) a system of reduced fares for scheduled airline flights when paid for before a certain period in advance of departure.

a·pex /áypeks/ n. (pl. **apexes** or **apices** /áypiseez/) **1** the highest point. **2** a climax. **3** the vertex of a triangle or cone. **4** a tip or pointed end.

a·phaer·e·sis /əférisis/ n. (also **a·pher·e·sis**) (pl. **aphaereses, aphereses** /-seez/) the omission of a letter or syllable at the beginning of a word as a

morphological development (e.g., in the derivation of adder from naddre).

a·pha·sia /əfáyzhə/ n. Med. the loss of ability to understand or express speech, owing to brain damage. □□ **a·pha·sic** /-zik/ adj. & n.

a·phe·li·on /əféeleeən, ap-héeleeən/ n. (pl. **aphelia** /-leeə/) the point in a body's orbit where it is furthest from the Sun (opp. PERIHELION).

aph·e·sis /áfisis/ n. (pl. **apheses** /-seez) the gradual loss of an unstressed vowel at the beginning of a word (e.g., of e from esquire to form squire). □□ **a·phet·ic** /əfétik/ adj. **a·phet·i·cal·ly** adv.

a·phid /áyfid, áfid/ n. any small homopterous insect which feeds by sucking sap from leaves, stems, or roots of plants; a plant louse. ▷ HEMIPTERA

a·phis /áyfis, áfis/ n. (pl. **aphides** /áyfideez/) an aphid, esp. of the genus Aphis, including the greenfly.

aph·o·rism /áfərizəm/ n. **1** a short pithy maxim. **2** a brief statement of a principle. □□ **aph·o·ris·tic** adj.

aph·ro·dis·i·ac /áfrədéezeeak, -díz-/ adj. & n. ● adj. that arouses sexual desire. ● n. an aphrodisiac drug.

a·pi·ar·y /áypee-eree/ n. (pl. **-ies**) a place where bees are kept. ▷ BEEHIVE. □□ **a·pi·a·rist** n.

a·pi·cal /áypikəl, áp-/ adj. of, at, or forming an apex. □□ **a·pi·cal·ly** adv.

a·pi·ces pl. of APEX.

a·pi·cul·ture /áypikulchər/ n. beekeeping. □□ **a·pi·cul·tur·al** /-kúlchərəl/ adj. **a·pi·cul·tur·ist** n.

a·piece /əpées/ adv. for each one (had five dollars apiece).

ap·ish /áypish/ adj. **1** of or like an ape. **2** silly. □□ **ap·ish·ly** adv. **ap·ish·ness** n.

a·plen·ty /əpléntee/ adv. in plenty.

a·plomb /əplóm, əplúm/ n. assurance; self-confidence.

ap·ne·a /ápneeə, apnéeə/ n. Med. a temporary cessation of breathing.

APO abbr. US Army post office.

apo- /ápə/ prefix **1** away from (apogee). **2** separate (apocarpous).

a·poc·a·lypse /əpókəlips/ n. **1** (**the Apocalypse**) Revelation, the last book of the New Testament, recounting a divine revelation to St. John. **2** a revelation. **3** a grand or violent event resembling those described in the Apocalypse.

a·poc·a·lyp·tic /əpókəlíptik/ adj. **1** of or resembling the Apocalypse. **2** revelatory.

a·po·co·pe /əpókəpee/ n. the omission of a letter or letters at the end of a word as a morphological development (e.g., in the derivation of curio from curiosity).

A·poc·ry·pha /əpókrifə/ n.pl. **1** the books included in the Septuagint and Vulgate versions of the Old Testament but not in the Hebrew Bible. ¶ Modern Bibles sometimes include them in the Old Testament or as an appendix, and sometimes omit them. **2** (**apocrypha**) writings not considered genuine.

a·poc·ry·phal /əpókrifəl/ adj. **1** of doubtful authenticity. **2** invented; mythical (an apocryphal story). **3** of or belonging to the Apocrypha.

a·pod·o·sis /əpódəsis/ n. (pl. **apodoses** /-seez/) the main (consequent) clause of a conditional sentence (e.g., I would agree in if you asked me I would agree).

ap·o·gee /ápəjee/ n. **1** the point in a celestial body's orbit where it is farthest from the Earth (opp. PERIGEE). **2** the most distant or highest point.

a·po·lit·i·cal /áypəlítikəl/ adj. not interested in or concerned with politics.

a·pol·o·get·ic /əpóləjétik/ adj. & n. ● adj. **1** regretfully acknowledging an offense. **2** diffident. **3** of

reasoned defense. ● n. (usu. in pl.) a reasoned defense. □□ **a·pol·o·get·i·cal·ly** adv.

ap·o·lo·gi·a /ápəlójeeə/ n. a formal defense of one's opinions or conduct.

a·pol·o·gist /əpóləjist/ n. a person who defends something by argument.

a·pol·o·gize /əpóləjīz/ v.intr. (often foll. by for) make an apology.

ap·o·logue /ápəlawg, -log/ n. a moral fable.

a·pol·o·gy /əpóləjee/ n. (pl. **-ies**) **1** a regretful acknowledgment of an offense. **2** an assurance that no offense was intended. **3** an explanation or defense. **4** (foll. by for) a poor specimen of (this apology for a letter).

ap·o·plec·tic /ápəpléktik/ adj. **1** of or liable to apoplexy. **2** colloq. enraged.

ap·o·plex·y /ápəpleksee/ n. a sudden loss of consciousness, voluntary movement, and sensation caused by blockage or rupture of a brain artery; a stroke.

a·pos·ta·sy /əpóstəsee/ n. (pl. **-ies**) **1** renunciation of a belief or faith. **2** abandonment of principles or of a party. **3** an instance of apostasy.

a·pos·tate /əpóstayt/ n. & adj. ● n. a person who renounces a former belief, adherence, etc. ● adj. engaged in apostasy.

a·pos·ta·tize /əpóstətīz/ v.intr. renounce a former belief, adherence, etc.

a pos·te·ri·o·ri /áy posteéree-áwree, -áwrī/ adj. & adv. ● adj. (of reasoning) inductive; empirical; proceeding from effects to causes. ● adv. inductively; empirically; from effects to causes (opp. A PRIORI).

a·pos·tle /əpósəl/ n. **1** (**Apostle**) **a** any of the chosen twelve first sent out to preach the Christian Gospel. **b** the first successful Christian missionary in a country or to a people. **2** a leader or outstanding figure, esp. of a reform movement (apostle of temperance). **3** a messenger or representative.

a·pos·to·late /əpóstələt, -layt/ n. **1** the position or authority of an Apostle. **2** leadership in reform.

ap·os·tol·ic /ápəstólik/ adj. **1** of or relating to the Apostles. **2** of the Pope regarded as the successor of St. Peter. **3** of the character of an Apostle.

ap·os·tol·ic suc·ces·sion n. the uninterrupted transmission of spiritual authority from the Apostles through successive popes and bishops.

a·pos·tro·phe[1] /əpóstrəfee/ n. a punctuation mark used to indicate: **1** the omission of letters or numbers (e.g., can't; he's). **2** the possessive case (e.g., Harry's book).

a·pos·tro·phe[2] /əpóstrəfee/ n. an exclamatory passage in a speech or poem, addressed to a person. □□ **a·pos·tro·phize** v.tr. & intr.

a·poth·e·car·ies' mea·sure n. (also **a·poth·e·car·ies' weight**) units of weight and liquid volume formerly used in pharmacy.

a·poth·e·car·y /əpóthəkeree/ n. (pl. **-ies**) archaic a pharmacist licensed to dispense medicines.

ap·o·thegm /ápəthem/ n. a terse saying or maxim; an aphorism. □□ **ap·o·theg·mat·ic** /-thegmátik/ adj.

ap·o·them /ápəthem/ n. Geom. a line from the center of a regular polygon at right angles to any of its sides.

a·poth·e·o·sis /əpóthee-ósis/ n. (pl. **apotheoses** /-seez/) **1** elevation to divine status; deification. **2** a glorification of a thing (apotheosis of the dance).

a·poth·e·o·size /əpótheeəsīz/ v.tr. **1** make divine; deify. **2** idealize; glorify.

ap·o·tro·pa·ic /ápətrōpáyik/ adj. supposedly having the power to avert an evil influence or bad luck.

ap·pall /əpáwl/ v.tr. (also **ap·pal**) (**appalled, appalling**) **1** greatly dismay. **2** (as **appalling** adj.) colloq. shocking; unpleasant; bad. □□ **ap·pall·ing·ly** adv.

Ap·pa·loo·sa /ápəlóōsə/ n. a horse of a N. American breed having dark spots on a light background.

ap·pa·rat·chik /áapəraátchik/ n. (pl. **apparatchiks** or Russ. **apparatchiki** /-kee/) **1 a** a

---

APERTURE

Behind a camera lens, an aperture can be altered to let differing amounts of light fall onto the photographic film. A wide aperture, indicated by a low f-number, lets in the most light, but reduces the depth of field (the range of the image that is in focus). Conversely, a small aperture, indicated by a higher f-number, lets in little light but allows the greatest depth of field.

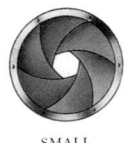

| WIDE APERTURE (f/2.8) | MEDIUM APERTURE (f/8) | SMALL APERTURE (f/16) |

member of the administrative system of a Communist party. **b** a Communist agent or spy. **2 a** any member of a political party who blindly executes policy; a zealous functionary. **b** an official of a public or private organization.

ap·pa·rat·us /ápərátəs, -ráytəs/ *n.* **1** the equipment needed for a particular purpose or function, esp. scientific or technical. **2** a political or other complex organization. **3** *Anat.* the organs used to perform a particular process. **4** (in full **apparatus criticus**) a collection of variants and annotations accompanying a printed text and usu. appearing below it.

ap·par·el /əpárəl/ *n.* **1** clothing; dress. **2** embroidered ornamentation on some ecclesiastical vestments.

ap·par·ent /əpárənt/ *adj.* **1** readily visible or perceivable. **2** seeming. □□ **ap·par·ent·ly** *adv.*

ap·pa·ri·tion /ápəríshən/ *n.* a sudden or dramatic appearance, esp. of a ghost or phantom; a visible ghost.

ap·peal /əpéel/ *v. & n.* ● *v.* **1** *intr.* make an earnest or formal request; plead (*appealed for calm; appealed to us not to leave*). **2** *intr.* (usu. foll. by *to*) be attractive or of interest; be pleasing. **3** *intr.* (foll. by *to*) resort to or cite for support. **4** *Law* **a** *intr.* (often foll. by *to*) apply (to a higher court) for a reconsideration of the decision of a lower court. **b** *tr.* refer to a higher court to review (a case). **c** *intr.* (foll. by *against*) apply to a higher court to reconsider (a verdict or sentence). **5** *intr. Sports* call on an umpire or referee to reverse a decision. ● *n.* **1** the act or an instance of appealing. **2** a formal or urgent request for public support, esp. financial, for a cause. **3** *Law* the referral of a case to a higher court. **4** attractiveness; appealing quality (*sex appeal*).

ap·peal·a·ble /əpéeləbəl/ *adj. Law* (of a case) that can be referred to a higher court for review.

ap·peal·ing /əpéeling/ *adj.* attractive; likable. □□ **ap·peal·ing·ly** *adv.*

ap·pear /əpéer/ *v.intr.* **1** become or be visible. **2** be evident (*a new problem then appeared*). **3** seem; have the appearance of being (*appeared unwell; you appear to be right*). **4** present oneself publicly or formally, esp. on stage or as the accused or counsel in a court of law. **5** be published (*it appeared in the papers; a new edition will appear*).

ap·pear·ance /əpéerəns/ *n.* **1** the act or an instance of appearing. **2** an outward form as perceived (whether correctly or not), esp. visually (*neaten up one's appearance; gives the appearance of trying hard*). **3** a semblance. □ **keep up appearances** maintain an impression or pretense of virtue, affluence, etc. **make** (or **put in**) **an appearance** be present, esp. briefly. **to all appearances** as far as can be seen; apparently.

ap·pease /əpéez/ *v.tr.* **1** make calm or quiet, esp. conciliate (a potential aggressor) by making concessions. **2** satisfy (an appetite, scruples). □□ **ap·pease·ment** *n.* **ap·peas·er** *n.*

ap·pel·lant /əpélənt/ *n. Law* a person who appeals to a higher court.

ap·pel·late /əpélət/ *adj. Law* (esp. of a court) concerned with appeals.

ap·pel·la·tion /ápəláyshən/ *n. formal* a name or title; nomenclature.

ap·pel·la·tive /əpélətiv/ *adj.* **1** naming. **2** *Gram.* (of a noun) that designates a class; common.

ap·pend /əpénd/ *v.tr.* attach, affix, add, esp. to a written document, etc.

ap·pend·age /əpéndij/ *n.* **1** something attached; an addition. **2** *Zool.* a limb or other projecting part of a body.

ap·pend·ant /əpéndənt/ *adj. & n.* ● *adj.* (usu. foll. by *to*) attached in a subordinate capacity. ● *n.* an appendant person or thing.

ap·pen·dec·to·my /ápəndéktəmee/ *n.* (also **ap·pen·di·cec·to·my** /-diséktəmee/) (*pl.* **-ies**) the surgical removal of the appendix.

ap·pen·di·ci·tis /əpéndisítis/ *n.* inflammation of the appendix.

ap·pen·dix /əpéndiks/ *n.* (*pl.* **appendices** /-diseez/; **appendixes**) **1** (in full **vermiform appendix**) *Anat.* ▼ a small outgrowth of tissue forming a tube-shaped sac attached to the lower end of the large intestine. ▷ INTESTINE. **2** subsidiary matter at the end of a book or document.

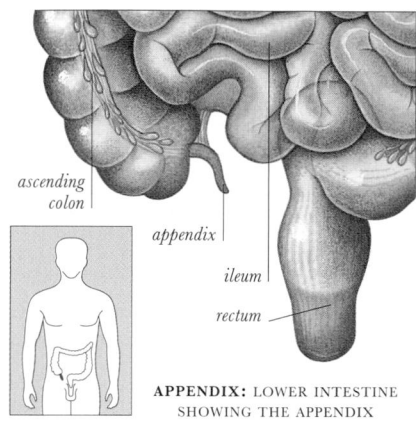

ascending colon

appendix

ileum

rectum

APPENDIX: LOWER INTESTINE SHOWING THE APPENDIX

ap·per·ceive /ápərséev/ *v.tr.* **1** be conscious of perceiving. **2** *Psychol.* compare (a perception) to previously held ideas so as to extract meaning from it. □□ **ap·per·cep·tion** /-sépshən/ *n.* **ap·per·cep·tive** *adj.*

ap·per·tain /ápərtáyn/ *v.intr.* (foll. by *to*) **1** relate. **2** belong as a possession or right. **3** be appropriate.

ap·pe·tence /ápitəns/ *n.* (also **ap·pe·ten·cy** /-tənsee/) (foll. by *for*) longing or desire.

ap·pe·tite /ápitīt/ *n.* **1** a natural desire to satisfy bodily needs, esp. for food or sexual activity. **2** (usu. foll. by *for*) an inclination or desire. □□ **ap·pe·ti·tive** /ápitītiv/ *adj.*

ap·pe·tiz·er /ápitīzər/ *n.* a small amount to stimulate an appetite.

ap·pe·tiz·ing /ápitīzing/ *adj.* stimulating an appetite. □□ **ap·pe·tiz·ing·ly** *adv.*

ap·plaud /əpláwd/ *v.* **1** *intr.* express strong approval or praise, esp. by clapping. **2** *tr.* express approval of (a person or action).

ap·plause /əpláwz/ *n.* **1** an expression of approbation, esp. from an audience, etc., by clapping. **2** emphatic approval.

ap·ple /ápəl/ *n.* **1** the fruit of a tree of the genus *Malus*, rounded in form and with a crisp flesh. ▷ FRUIT, SEED. **2** the tree bearing this. □ **apple of one's eye** a cherished person or thing. **upset the applecart** spoil careful plans.

ap·ple·jack /ápəljak/ *n.* an alcoholic beverage made by distilling or freezing fermented apple cider.

ap·ple-pie or·der *n.* perfect order; extreme neatness.

ap·plet /áplət/ *n. Computing* a small application running within a larger program.

ap·pli·ance /əplíəns/ *n.* a device or piece of equipment used for a specific task, esp. a household device for washing, drying, cooking, etc.

ap·pli·ca·ble /áplikəbəl, əplíkə-/ *adj.* **1** that may be applied. **2** having reference; appropriate. □□ **ap·pli·ca·bil·i·ty** *n.*

ap·pli·cant /áplikənt/ *n.* a person who applies for something, esp. a job.

ap·pli·ca·tion /áplikáyshən/ *n.* **1** the act of applying. **2** a formal request for employment, membership, etc. **3 a** relevance. **b** the use to which something can or should be put. **4** sustained effort; diligence.

ap·pli·ca·tor /áplikaytər/ *n.* a device for applying a substance to a surface.

ap·plied /əplíd/ *adj.* (of a subject of study) put to practical use as opposed to being theoretical (cf. PURE *adj.* 10).

ap·plied math·e·mat·ics *n.* see MATHEMATICS.

ap·pli·qué /áplikáy/ *n., adj., & v.* ● *n.* ▶ ornamental work in which fabric is cut out and attached to the surface of another fabric to form pictures or patterns. ● *adj.* executed in appliqué. ● *v.tr.* (**appliqués**, **appliquéd**, **appliquéing**) decorate with appliqué; make using appliqué technique.

APPLIQUÉ DETAIL ON 19TH-CENTURY AMERICAN QUILT

ap·ply /əplí/ *v.* (**-ies**, **-ied**) **1** *intr.* make a formal request for something to be done, given, etc. (*apply for a job*). **2** *intr.* have relevance (*does not apply in this case*). **3** *tr.* **a** make use of as relevant or suitable (*apply the rules*). **b** operate (*apply the hand brake*). **4** *tr.* **a** put or spread on (*applied the ointment to the cut*). **b** administer (*applied common sense to the problem*). **5** *refl.* devote oneself (*applied myself to the task*).

ap·pog·gia·tu·ra /əpójətoorə/ *n. Mus.* a grace note performed before an essential note of a melody and normally taking half or less than half its time value.

ap·point /əpóynt/ *v.tr.* **1** assign a post to (*appoint him governor*). **2** fix; decide on (a time, place, etc.) (*8:30 was the appointed time*). **3** (as **appointed** *adj.*) equipped; furnished (*a badly appointed hotel*). □□ **ap·point·ee** /-tée/ *n.* **ap·poin·tive** *adj.*

ap·point·ment /əpóyntmənt/ *n.* **1** an arrangement to meet at a specific time and place. **2 a** a post available for applicants, or recently filled (*took up the appointment on Monday*). **b** a person appointed. **3** (usu. in *pl.*) **a** furniture; fittings. **b** equipment.

ap·por·tion /əpáwrshən/ *v.tr.* share out; assign as a share. □□ **ap·por·tion·ment** *n.*

ap·po·site /ápəzit/ *adj.* (often foll. by *to*) **1** apt; well chosen. **2** well expressed. □□ **ap·po·site·ly** *adv.* **ap·po·site·ness** *n.*

ap·po·si·tion /ápəzíshən/ *n.* **1** placing side by side; juxtaposition. **2** *Gram.* the placing of a word next to another, esp. the addition of one noun to another, in order to qualify or explain the first (e.g., *William the Conqueror*). □□ **ap·po·si·tion·al** *adj.*

ap·prais·al /əpráyzəl/ *n.* the act or an instance of appraising.

ap·praise /əpráyz/ *v.tr.* **1** estimate the quality of (*appraised her skills*). **2** set a price on; value. □□ **ap·prais·er** *n.* **ap·prais·ive** *adj.*

ap·pre·ci·a·ble /əpréeshəbəl/ *adj.* large enough to be noticed; significant; considerable (*appreciable progress has been made*). □□ **ap·pre·ci·a·bly** *adv.*

ap·pre·ci·ate /əpréesheeáyt/ *v.* **1** *tr.* **a** esteem highly; value. **b** be grateful for (*we appreciate your sympathy*). **c** be sensitive to (*appreciate the nuances*). **2** *tr.* (often foll. by *that* + clause) understand; recognize. **3 a** *intr.* (of property, etc.) rise in value. **b** *tr.* raise in value. □□ **ap·pre·ci·a·tive** /-shətiv, -shee-áytiv/ *adj.* **ap·pre·ci·a·tive·ly** *adv.* **ap·pre·ci·a·tor** *n.*

ap·pre·ci·a·tion /əpréeshee-áyshən/ *n.* **1** favorable recognition. **2** an estimation; sensitive understanding (*a quick appreciation of the problem*). **3** an increase in value.

ap·pre·hend /áprihénd/ *v.tr.* **1** understand; perceive (*apprehend your meaning*). **2** seize; arrest (*apprehended the criminal*).

ap·pre·hen·si·ble /áprihénsibəl/ *adj.* capable of being apprehended by the senses or the intellect (*an apprehensible change in her expression*).

ap·pre·hen·sion /áprihénshən/ *n.* **1** uneasiness; dread. **2** understanding; perception. **3** arrest; capture. **4** an idea; a conception.

ap·pre·hen·sive /áprihénsiv/ *adj.* uneasily fearful; dreading. □□ **ap·pre·hen·sive·ly** *adv.* **ap·pre·hen·sive·ness** *n.*

A

ap·pren·tice /əpréntis/ *n. & v.* ● *n.* **1** a person who is learning a trade by being employed in it for an agreed period at low wages. **2** a beginner; a novice. ● *v.tr.* engage as an apprentice. □□ **ap·pren·tice·ship** *n.*

ap·prise /əpríz/ *v.tr.* inform. □ **be apprised of** be aware of.

ap·proach /əprốch/ *v. & n.* ● *v.* **1** *tr.* come near or nearer to (a place or time). **2** *intr.* come near or nearer in space or time. **3** *tr.* make a tentative proposal to. **4** *tr.* **a** be similar in character, quality, etc., to. **b** approximate to. **5** *tr.* attempt to influence or bribe. **6** *tr.* set about, tackle (a task, etc.). **7** *intr. Golf* play an approach shot. ● *n.* **1** an act or means of approaching. **2** an approximation. **3** a way of dealing with a person or thing (*needs a new approach*). **4** (usu. in *pl.*) a sexual advance. **5** *Golf* a stroke from the fairway to the green. **6** *Aeron.* the final descent of a flight before landing.

ap·proach·a·ble /əprốch-əbəl/ *adj.* **1** friendly; easy to talk to. **2** able to be approached. □□ **ap·proach·a·bil·i·ty** /-bíiiteé/ *n.*

ap·pro·ba·tion /áprəbáyshən/ *n.* approval; consent. □□ **ap·pro·ba·to·ry** /əprốbətawree/ *adj.*

ap·pro·pri·ate *adj. & v.* ● *adj.* /əprốpreeət/ **1** suitable or proper. **2** belonging or particular to. ● *v.tr.* /əprốpreeayt/ **1** take possession of. **2** devote (money, etc.) to special purposes. □□ **ap·pro·pri·ate·ly** *adv.* **ap·pro·pri·ate·ness** *n.* **ap·pro·pri·a·tor** *n.*

ap·pro·pri·a·tion /əprōpreeáyshən/ *n.* **1** an act or instance of appropriating. **2** something appropriated, as money officially set aside for a specific use.

ap·prov·al /əprōōvəl/ *n.* **1** the act of approving. **2** consent; a favorable opinion. □ **on approval** (of goods supplied) to be returned if not satisfactory.

ap·prove /əprōōv/ *v.* **1** *tr.* confirm; sanction (*approved her application*). **2** *intr.* give or have a favorable opinion. **3** *tr.* commend. □ **approve of** pronounce or consider good or satisfactory; commend. □□ **ap·prov·ing·ly** *adv.*

approx. *abbr.* **1** approximate. **2** approximately.

ap·prox·i·mate *adj. & v.* ● *adj.* /əprốksimət/ fairly correct or accurate; near to the actual. ● *v.tr. & intr.* /əprốksimayt/ bring or come near (esp. in quality, number, etc.), but not exactly. □□ **ap·prox·i·mate·ly** /-mətlee/ *adv.* **ap·prox·i·ma·tion** /-máyshən/ *n.*

ap·pur·te·nance /əpórt'nəns/ *n.* (usu. in *pl.*) a belonging; an appendage.

APR *abbr.* annual or annualized percentage rate.

Apr. *abbr.* April.

a·prax·i·a /əprákseeə/ *n. Med.* inability to perform particular activities as a result of brain damage.

a·près-ski /áprayskéé, áapray-/ *n. & adj.* ● *n.* the evening, esp. its social activities, following a day's skiing. ● *attrib.adj.* (of clothes, drinks, etc.) appropriate to social activities following skiing.

ap·ri·cot /áprikot, áypri-/ *n. & adj.* ● *n.* **1 a** a juicy soft fruit, smaller than a peach, of an orange-yellow color. **b** the tree, *Prunus armeniaca*, bearing it. **2** the ripe fruit's orange-yellow color. ● *adj.* orange-yellow.

A·pril /áypril/ *n.* the fourth month of the year.

April fool *n.* a person successfully tricked on April 1.

April Fool's (or **Fools'**) **Day** *n.* April 1.

a pri·o·ri /áa pree-áwree, áy prī-áwrī/ *adj. & adv.* ● *adj.* **1** (of reasoning) deductive; proceeding from causes to effects (opp. A POSTERIORI). **2** (of concepts, knowledge, etc.) logically independent of experience (opp. EMPIRICAL). **3** not submitted to critical investigation. ● *adv.* **1** in an a priori manner. **2** as far as one knows. □□ **a·pri·o·rism** /aypríériizəm/ *n.*

a·pron /áyprən/ *n.* **1** a garment covering and protecting the front of a person's clothes. **2** *Theatr.* the part of a stage in front of the curtain. **3** the paved area of an airfield used for maneuvering or loading aircraft. **4** an endless conveyor belt. □□ **a·proned** *adj.* **a·pron·ful** *n.* (*pl.* **-fuls**)

a·pron strings *n.pl.* □ **tied to a person's apron strings** dominated by or dependent on that person (usu. a woman).

ap·ro·pos /áprəpố/ *adj., adv., & prep.* ● *adj.* to the point; appropriate. ● *adv.* **1** appropriately. **2** by the way; incidentally. ● *prep.* (foll. by *of*) in respect to; concerning.

apse /aps/ *n.* **1** ◄ a large semicircular or polygonal recess, esp. at the eastern end of a church. ▷ BASILICA. **2** = APSIS. □□ **ap·si·dal** /ápsid'l/ *adj.*

ap·sis /ápsis/ *n.* (*pl.* **apsides** /-sideez/) either of two points in the orbit of a planet or satellite that are nearest to or farthest from the body around which it moves. □□ **ap·si·dal** /ápsid'l/ *adj.*

apt /apt/ *adj.* **1** appropriate. **2** (foll. by *to* + infin.) having a tendency. **3** clever; quick to learn (*an apt pupil*). □□ **apt·ly** *adv.* **apt·ness** *n.*

ap·ter·yx /áptəriks/ *n.* = KIWI 1.

ap·ti·tude /áptitōōd, -tyōōd/ *n.* **1** a natural talent (*an aptitude for drawing*). **2** ability or suitability.

aq·ua /ákwə, áakwə/ *n.* the color aquamarine.

aq·ua·cul·ture /ákwəkulchər, áakwə-/ *n.* (also **aq·ui·cul·ture**) the rearing of aquatic plants or animals. □□ **aq·ua·cul·tur·al** *adj.* **aq·ua·cul·tur·ist** *n.*

Aq·ua-Lung /ákwəlung, áakwə-/ *n. Trademark* ▼ a portable breathing apparatus for divers, consisting of cylinders of compressed air strapped on the back, feeding air through a mask or mouthpiece. ▷ SCUBA DIVING

row of apsidal chapels

nave

APSE:
PLAN OF AMIENS CATHEDRAL, FRANCE, SHOWING THE APSE

mouthpiece to inflate buoyancy jacket

mouthpiece and demand valve

cylinder stop valve

main air cylinder

buoyancy jacket

compass

air, time, and depth display

AQUA-LUNG™

emergency air cylinder

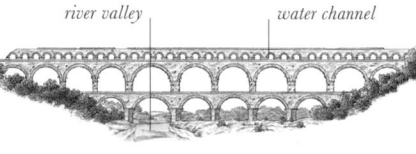

aq·ua·ma·rine /ákwəməréén, áakwə-/ *n.* **1** ▶ a light bluish green beryl. ▷ GEM. **2** its color.

aq·ua·naut /ákwənawt, áakwə-/ *n.* an underwater swimmer or explorer.

aq·ua·plane /ákwəplayn, áakwə-/ *n. & v.* ● *n.* a board for riding on water, pulled by a speedboat. ● *v.intr.* ride on an aquaplane.

AQUAMARINE

a·quar·i·um /əkwáireeəm/ *n.* (*pl.* **aquariums** or **aquaria** /-reeə/) ► an artificial environment designed for keeping live aquatic plants and animals.

A·quar·i·us /əkwáireeəs/ *n.* **1** ▼ a constellation, traditionally regarded as portraying the figure of a water carrier. **2 a** the eleventh sign of the zodiac (the Water Carrier). ▷ ZODIAC. **b** a person born when the Sun is in this sign. □□ **A·quar·i·an** *adj. & n.*

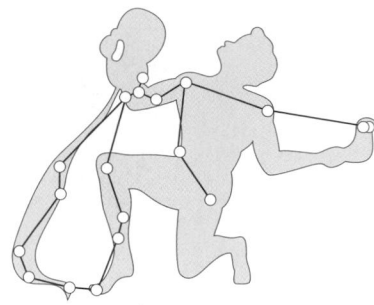

AQUARIUS:
FIGURE OF A WATER CARRIER FORMED FROM THE STARS OF AQUARIUS

a·quat·ic /əkwátik, əkwótik/ *adj. & n.* ● *adj.* **1** growing or living in or near water. **2** (of a sport) played in or on water. ● *n.* **1** an aquatic plant or animal. **2** (in *pl.*) aquatic sports.

aq·ua·tint /ákwətint, áakwə-/ *n.* **1** a print resembling a watercolor, produced from a copper plate etched with nitric acid. **2** the process of producing this.

aq·ua·vit /áakwəveet, ákwə-/ *n.* (also **ak·va·vit** /áakvə-/) *n.* an alcoholic liquor made from potatoes, etc., and usu. flavored with caraway seeds.

aq·ua vi·tae /áakwə víttee, vée-/ *n.* a strong alcoholic liquor, esp. brandy.

aq·ue·duct /ákwidukt/ *n.* ▼ an artificial channel for conveying water, esp. in the form of a bridge supported by tall columns across a valley.

river valley   *water channel*

AQUEDUCT BUILT BY THE ANCIENT ROMANS

a·que·ous /áykweeəs, ák-/ *adj.* **1** of, containing, or like water. **2** *Geol.* produced by water (*aqueous rocks*).

a·que·ous hu·mor *n. Anat.* the clear fluid in the eye between the lens and the cornea. ▷ EYE

aq·ui·fer /ákwifər/ *n. Geol.* a layer of rock or soil able to hold or transmit much water. ▷ ARTESIAN WELL

aq·ui·le·gi·a /ákwileéejə/ *n.* any (often blue-flowered) plant of the genus *Aquilegia*.

aq·ui·line /ákwilīn/ *adj.* **1** like an eagle. **2** (of a nose) curved like an eagle's beak.

AR *abbr.* Arkansas (in official postal use).

Ar *symb. Chem.* the element argon.

Ar·ab /árəb/ *n. & adj.* ● *n.* **1** a member of a Semitic people inhabiting originally Saudi Arabia and the neighboring countries, now the Middle East generally. **2** = ARABIAN 2. ● *adj.* of Arabia or the Arabs (esp. with ethnic reference).

ar·a·besque /árəbésk/ *n.* **1** *Ballet* a posture with one leg extended horizontally backward, torso extended forward, and arms outstretched. ▷ GYMNASTICS. **2** a design of intertwined leaves, scrolls, etc. **3** *Mus.* a florid melodic section or composition. **4** an elaborate, florid or intricate design.

A·ra·bi·an /əráybeeən/ *adj. & n.* ● *adj.* of

A

AQUARIUM

Fishkeeping was common in Roman times but was refined into a hobby in Japan and China. An aquarium's features are usually chosen to imitate the natural habitat of the fish on display. Four types of fish are kept in home aquariums: tropical freshwater species, tropical marine species, coldwater freshwater species, and coldwater marine species.

power filter
reef rock
vagabond butterfly fish
malu anemone
coral sand
power head for oxygenation
glass-sided tank
squirrelfish
crushed coral

"CORAL-REEF" MARINE AQUARIUM

---

or relating to Arabia. ● n. **1** a native of Arabia. ¶ Now less common than *Arab* in this sense. **2** a horse of a breed orig. native to Arabia. ▷ HORSE

A·ra·bi·an cam·el n. a domesticated camel, *Camelus dromedarius*, native to the deserts of N. Africa and the Near East, with one hump. Also called **drome·dary**. ▷ CAMEL

Ar·a·bic /árəbik/ n. & adj. ● n. the Semitic language of the Arabs. ● adj. of or relating to Arabia (esp. with reference to language or literature).

Ar·a·bic nu·mer·al n. any of the numerals 0, 1, 2, 3, 4, 5, 6, 7, 8, and 9 (cf. ROMAN NUMERAL).

Ar·ab·ist /árəbist/ n. **1** a student of Arabic civilization, language, etc. **2** an advocate of Arabic interests, etc.

ar·a·ble /árəbəl/ adj. **1** (of land) suitable for crop production. **2** (of crops) that can be grown on arable land.

Ar·a·by /árəbee/ n. poet. Arabia.

a·rach·nid /əráknid/ n. ▼ any arthropod of the class Arachnida, having four pairs of walking legs and simple eyes, e.g., scorpions, spiders, mites, and ticks. □□ **a·rach·ni·dan** adj. & n.

a·rach·noid /əráknoyd/ n. Anat. (in full **arachnoid membrane**) one of the three membranes (see MENINX) that surround the brain and spinal cord of vertebrates.

a·rach·no·pho·bi·a /əráknəfóbeeə/ n. an abnormal fear of spiders. □□ **a·rach·no·phobe** /əráknəfōb/ n.

Ar·a·ma·ic /árəmáyik/ n. & adj. ● n. a branch of the Semitic family of languages, esp. the language of Syria used as a lingua franca in the Near East. ● adj. of or in Aramaic.

A·rap·a·ho /ərápəhō/ n. **1 a** a N. American people native to the central plains of Canada and the US. **b** a member of this people. **2** the language of this people.

a·ra·tion·al /áyráshənəl/ adj. that does not purport to be rational.

ar·au·car·i·a /árawkáireeə/ n. any evergreen conifer of the genus *Araucaria*.

ar·bi·ter /áarbitər/ n. **1 a** an arbitrator in a dispute. **b** a judge; an authority (*arbiter of taste*). **2** (often foll. by *of*) a person who has entire control of something.

ar·bi·trage /áarbitraazh, -trij/ n. the buying and selling of stocks or bills of exchange to take advantage of varying prices in different markets.

ar·bi·tra·geur /áarbitraazhŏr/ n. (also **ar·bi·trag·er** /áarbitraazhər/) a person who engages in arbitrage.

ar·bi·tral /áarbitrəl/ adj. concerning arbitration.

ar·bit·ra·ment /áarbitrəmənt/ n. **1** the deciding of a dispute by an arbiter. **2** an authoritative decision made by an arbiter.

ar·bi·trar·y /áarbitreree/ adj. **1** based on or derived from uninformed opinion or random choice; capricious. **2** despotic. □□ **ar·bi·trar·i·ly** adv. **ar·bi·trar·i·ness** n.

ar·bi·trate /áarbitrayt/ v.tr. & intr. decide by arbitration.

ar·bi·tra·tion /áarbitráyshən/ n. the settlement of a dispute by an arbitrator.

ar·bi·tra·tor /áarbitraytər/ n. a person appointed to settle a dispute; an arbiter.

ar·bor[1] /áarbər/ n. **1** an axle or spindle on which something revolves. **2** a device holding a tool in a lathe, etc.

ar·bor[2] /áarbər/ n. a shady alcove with the sides and roof formed by trees or climbing plants; a bower. □□ **ar·bored** adj.

ar·bo·ra·ceous /áarbəráyshəs/ adj. **1** treelike. **2** wooded.

Ar·bor Day /áarbər/ n. a day dedicated annually to tree planting in the US, Australia, and other countries.

ar·bo·re·al /aarbáwreeəl/ adj. of, living in, or connected with trees.

ar·bo·res·cent /áarbərésənt/ adj. treelike in growth or general appearance. □□ **ar·bo·res·cence** n.

ar·bo·re·tum /áarbəreetəm/ n. (pl. **arboretums** or **arboreta** /-tə/) a botanical garden devoted to trees, shrubs, etc.

ar·bor·i·cul·ture /áarbərikúlchər, aarbáwri-/ n. the cultivation of trees and shrubs. □□ **ar·bor·i·cul·tur·al** adj. **ar·bor·i·cul·tur·ist** n.

ar·bor·i·za·tion /áarbərizáyshən/ n. a treelike arrangement, esp. in anatomy.

ar·bor·vi·tae /áarbərvítee/ n. ▶ any of the evergreen conifers of the genus *Thuja*, native to N. Asia and N. America, usu. of pyramidal shape.

arc /aark/ n. & v. ● n. **1** part of the circumference of a circle or any other curve. **2** *Electr.* a luminous discharge between two electrodes. ● v.intr. (**arced** /aarkt/; **arcing** /áarking/) form an arc.

ar·cade /aarkáyd/ n. **1** a passage with an arched roof. **2** any covered walk, esp. with shops along one or both sides. **3** *Archit.* a series of arches supporting or set along a wall. ▷ NORMAN, ROMANESQUE. **4** an entertainment establishment with coin-operated games, etc. □□ **ar·cad·ed** adj.

Ar·ca·di·an /aarkáydeeən/ n. & adj. ● n. an idealized peasant or country dweller, esp. in poetry. ● adj. simple and poetically rural. □□ **Ar·ca·di·an·ism** n.

Ar·ca·dy /áarkədee/ n. poet. an ideal rustic paradise.

ar·cane /aarkáyn/ adj. mysterious; secret; understood by few. □□ **ar·cane·ly** adv.

ar·ca·num /aarkáynəm/ n. (pl. **arcana** /-nə/) (usu. in pl.) a mystery; a profound secret.

ARACHNID

Ranging from tiny mites and ticks to giant bird-eating spiders, arachnids constitute a principal division of the phylum Arthropoda, with at least 70,000 species. Arachnids have two main body parts (the cephalothorax and abdomen), clearly distinguishing them from insects, which have three. Arachnids generally have eight legs, and most live on land. Spiders and scorpions are carnivorous, while mites ingest fluid from plants, animals, or dead remains.

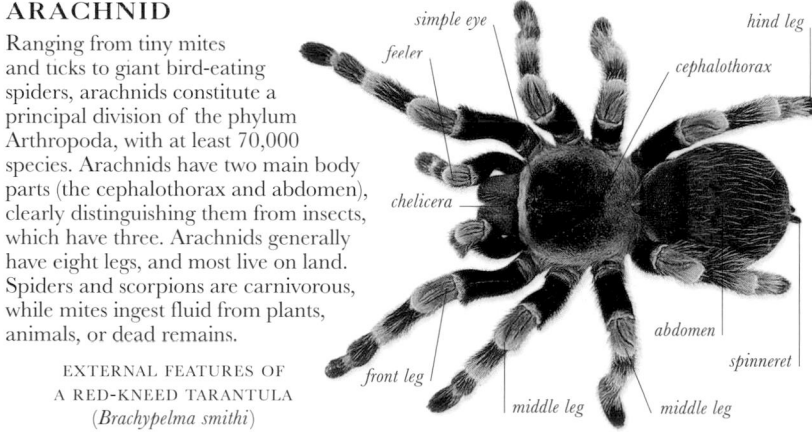

simple eye
feeler
hind leg
cephalothorax
chelicera
front leg
abdomen
spinneret
middle leg
middle leg

EXTERNAL FEATURES OF A RED-KNEED TARANTULA (*Brachypelma smithi*)

MAIN ARACHNID ORDERS

ARANEAE (spiders) ▷ SPIDER

SCORPIONES (scorpions) ▷ SCORPION

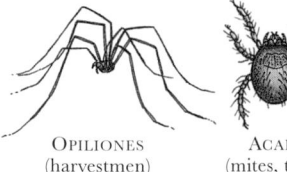
OPILIONES (harvestmen)

ACARI (mites, ticks)

ARBORVITAE: EASTERN WHITE CEDAR (*Thuja occidentalis*)

A

ARCH

The curve of an arch displaces weight from above, directing it to the spring line, where it is then supported vertically by abutments or pillars. In a classical arch, such as the basket type, the curve is formed from a series of interlocking blocks (voussoirs), with the central stone referred to as the keystone. A reinforcing piece of stonework, known as the impost, is situated at the spring line. The first curved arches were built by the Etruscans, but as architectural styles have varied in different locations and eras, so too has the form of the arch.

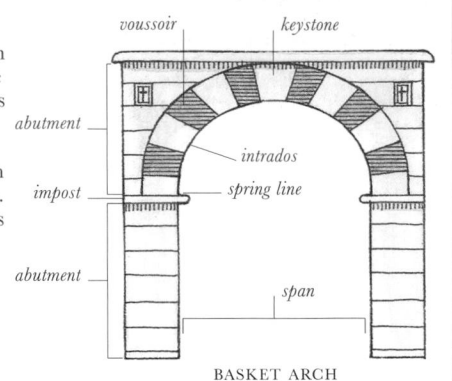

BASKET ARCH

OTHER TYPES OF ARCH

CALIPHAL   NASRID   TREFOIL   LANCET   TUDOR

arch[1] /aarch/ *n. & v.* ● *n.* **1** ▲ a curved structure as an opening or a support for a bridge, roof, floor, etc. **2** any arch-shaped curve, as on the inner side of the foot, the eyebrows, etc. ● *v.* **1** *tr.* provide with or form into an arch. **2** *intr.* form an arch.

arch[2] /aarch/ *adj.* self-consciously or affectedly playful or teasing. □□ **arch·ly** *adv.* **arch·ness** *n.*

arch- /aarch/ *comb. form* **1** chief; superior (*archbishop*; *archduke*). **2** preeminent of its kind (esp. in unfavorable senses) (*archenemy*).

ar·chae·ol·o·gy /áarkee-ólǝjee/ *n.* (also **ar·che·ol·o·gy**) the study of human history and prehistory through the excavation of sites and the analysis of physical remains. □□ **ar·chae·o·log·i·cal** *adj.* **ar·chae·ol·o·gist** *n.*

ar·chae·op·ter·yx /áarkee-óptǝriks/ *n.* the oldest known fossil bird, *Archaeopteryx lithographica*, with teeth, feathers, and a reptilian tail.

ar·cha·ic /aarkáyik/ *adj.* **1 a** antiquated. **b** (of a word, etc.) no longer in ordinary use, though retained for special purposes. **2** primitive. □□ **ar·cha·i·cal·ly** *adv.*

ar·cha·ism /áarkeeizǝm, -kay-/ *n.* **1** the retention or imitation of the obsolete, esp. in language or art. **2** an archaic word. □□ **ar·cha·is·tic** *adj.*

ar·cha·ize /áarkeeīz, -kay-/ *v.* **1** *intr.* imitate the archaic. **2** *tr.* make (a work of art, literature, etc.) imitate the archaic.

arch·an·gel /áarkaynjǝl/ *n.* **1** an angel of the highest rank. **2** a member of the eighth order of the nine ranks of heavenly beings.

arch·bish·op /áarchbíshǝp/ *n.* the chief bishop of a province.

arch·bish·op·ric /áarchbíshǝprik/ *n.* the office or diocese of an archbishop.

arch·dea·con /áarchdéekǝn/ *n.* a cleric in various churches ranking below a bishop.

arch·di·o·cese /áarchdíǝsis, -sees, -seez/ *n.* the diocese of an archbishop. □□ **arch·di·oc·e·san** /áarchdīósisǝn/ *adj.*

arch·duke /áarchdŏŏk, -dyŏŏk/ *n.* (*fem.* **arch·duchess** /-dúchis/) *hist.* the chief duke (esp. of Austria). □□ **arch·du·cal** *adj.* **arch·duch·y** /-dúchee/ *n.* (*pl.* **-ies**).

Ar·che·an /aarkéeǝn/ *adj. & n.* ● *adj.* of or relating to the earlier part of the Precambrian era. ● *n.* this time.

archenemy /áarchénǝmee/ *n.* (*pl.* **-ies**) **1** a chief enemy. **2** the Devil.

ar·che·ol·o·gy var. of ARCHAEOLOGY.

arch·er /áarchǝr/ *n.* **1** a person who shoots with a bow and arrows. **2** (**the Archer**) the zodiacal sign or constellation Sagittarius.

ar·cher·fish /áarchǝfish/ *n.* an Asian and Australasian freshwater fish that knocks insect prey off vegetation by shooting water from its mouth.

ar·cher·y /áarchǝree/ *n.* ▼ shooting with a bow and arrows, esp. as a sport.

ar·che·type /áarkitīp/ *n.* **1** an original model. **2** a typical specimen. **3** a recurrent symbol or motif in literature, art, etc. □□ **ar·che·typ·al** *adj.* **ar·che·typ·i·cal** /-típikǝl/ *adj.*

ar·chi·di·ac·o·nal /áarkidīákǝnǝl/ *adj.* of or relating to an archdeacon. □□ **ar·chi·di·ac·o·nate** /-nǝt, -nayt/ *n.*

ar·chi·e·pis·co·pal /áarkee-ipískǝpǝl/ *adj.* of or relating to an archbishop. □□ **ar·chi·e·pis·co·pate** /-pǝt, -payt/ *n.*

Ar·chi·me·de·an /áarkiméedeeǝn/ *adj.* of or associated with the Greek mathematician Archimedes.

Ar·chi·me·de·an screw *n.* a device of ancient origin for raising water by means of a spiral inside a tube.

ar·chi·pel·a·go /áarkipélǝgō/ *n.* (*pl.* **-os** or **-oes**) a group of islands.

ar·chi·tect /áarkitekt/ *n.* **1** a designer who prepares plans for buildings, ships, etc., and supervises their construction. **2** (foll. by *of*) a person who brings about a specified thing (*the architect of the tax reform bill*).

ar·chi·tec·ton·ic /áarkitektónik/ *adj. & n.* ● *adj.* **1** of architecture. **2** of the systematization of knowledge. ● *n.* (in *pl.*; usu. treated as *sing.*) **1** the scientific study of architecture. **2** the study of the systematization of knowledge.

ar·chi·tec·ture /áarkitekchǝr/ *n.* **1** the art or science of designing and constructing buildings. **2** the style of a building as regards design and construction. **3** buildings or other structures collectively. □□ **ar·chi·tec·tur·al** /-tékchǝrǝl/ *adj.* **ar·chi·tec·tur·al·ly** *adv.*

ar·chi·trave /áarkitrayv/ *n.* **1** (in classical architecture) a main beam resting across the tops of columns. ▷ COLUMN, ENTABLATURE. **2** the molded frame around a doorway or window.

ar·chive /áarkīv/ *n. & v.* ● *n.* (usu. in *pl.*) **1** a collection of esp. public or corporate documents or records. **2** the place where these are kept. ● *v.tr.* **1** place or store in an archive. **2** *Computing* transfer (data) to a less frequently used file or less easily accessible medium. □□ **ar·chi·val** /aarkívǝl/ *adj.*

ar·chi·vist /áarkivist, áarkī-/ *n.* a person who maintains archives.

ar·chi·volt /áarkivōlt/ *n.* **1** a band of moldings around the lower curve of an arch. **2** the lower curve itself from impost to impost of the columns.

arch·lute /áarchlŏŏt/ *n.* a bass lute with an extended neck and unstopped bass strings.

arch·way /áarchway/ *n.* **1** a vaulted passage. **2** an arched entrance.

arc lamp *n.* (also **arc light**) a light source using an electric arc.

Arc·tic /áarktik, áartik/ *adj. & n.* ● *adj.* **1** of the north polar regions. **2** (**arctic**) *colloq.* (esp. of weather) very cold. ● *n.* the Arctic regions.

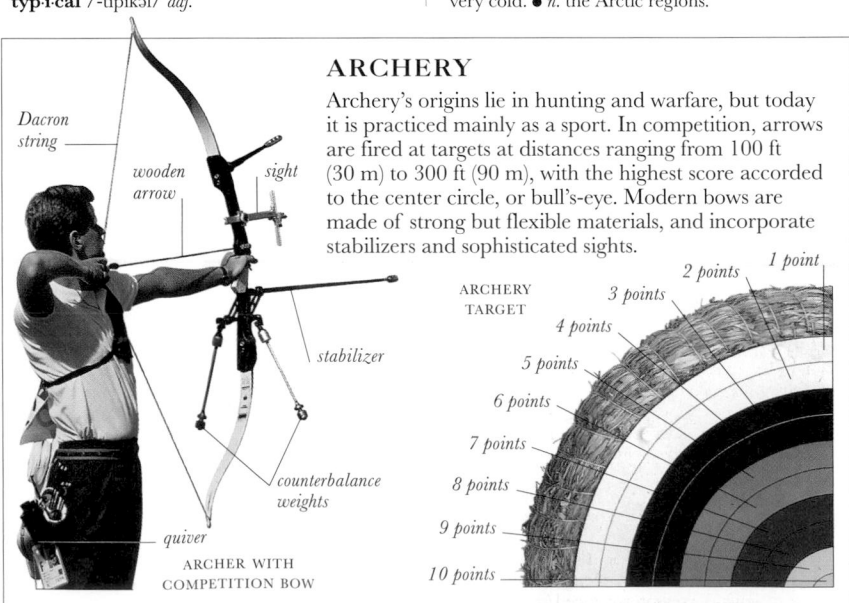

ARCHERY

Archery's origins lie in hunting and warfare, but today it is practiced mainly as a sport. In competition, arrows are fired at targets at distances ranging from 100 ft (30 m) to 300 ft (90 m), with the highest score accorded to the center circle, or bull's-eye. Modern bows are made of strong but flexible materials, and incorporate stabilizers and sophisticated sights.

Dacron string

wooden arrow

sight

stabilizer

counterbalance weights

quiver

ARCHER WITH COMPETITION BOW

ARCHERY TARGET

2 points   1 point
3 points
4 points
5 points
6 points
7 points
8 points
9 points
10 points

Arc·tic Cir·cle *n.* ▶ the parallel of latitude 66° 33' N., forming an imaginary line around this region.

ar·cu·ate /áarkyōōət, -ayt/ *adj.* shaped like a bow; curved. ▷ DELTA

arc weld·ing *n.* a method of using an electric arc to melt metals to be welded.

ar·dent /áard'nt/ *adj.* eager; zealous; fervent; passionate. □□ **ar·den·cy** /-d'nsee/ *n.* **ar·dent·ly** *adv.*

ar·dor /áardər/ *n.* zeal; burning enthusiasm; passion.

ar·du·ous /áarjōōəs/ *adj.* **1** (of a task, etc.) hard to achieve or overcome; laborious. **2** (of an action, etc.) strenuous. □□ **ar·du·ous·ly** *adv.* **ar·du·ous·ness** *n.*

are[1] *2nd sing. present* & *1st, 2nd, 3rd pl. present* of BE.

are[2] /aar/ *n.* a metric unit of measure, equal to 100 square meters.

ar·e·a /áireeə/ *n.* **1** the extent or measure of a surface (*over a large area*). **2** a region or tract (*the southern area*). **3** a space allocated for a specific purpose (*dining area*). **4** the scope or range of an activity or study. **5** = AREAWAY. □□ **ar·e·al** *adj.*

ar·e·a code *n.* a three-digit number that identifies one of the telephone service regions into which the US, Canada, etc., are divided and which is dialed when calling from one area to another.

ar·e·a·way /áireeaway/ *n.* a space in front of the basement of a building.

a·re·ca /əréékə, árikə/ *n.* any tropical palm of the genus *Areca*, native to Asia.

a·re·ca nut *n.* the astringent seed of a species of areca, *A. catechu.*

a·re·na /əréénə/ *n.* **1** the central part of an amphitheater, etc., where contests take place. ▷ AMPHITHEATER. **2** a scene of conflict; a sphere of action or discussion.

ar·e·na·ceous /árináyshəs/ *adj.* **1** (of rocks) containing sand; having a sandy texture. **2** sandlike. **3** (of plants) growing in sand.

aren't /aarnt, áarənt/ *contr.* **1** are not. **2** (in *interrog*) am not (*aren't I coming too?*).

a·re·o·la /əréeələ/ *n.* (*pl.* **areolae** /-lee/) *Anat.* a circular pigmented area, esp. that surrounding a nipple. ▷ BREAST. □□ **a·re·o·lar** *adj.*

a·rête /əráyt/ *n.* a sharp mountain ridge. ▷ GLACIER.

ar·gent /áarjənt/ *n.* & *adj. Heraldry* silver; silvery white.

ar·gen·tif·er·ous /áarjəntífərəs/ *adj.* containing natural deposits of silver.

Ar·gen·tine /áarjənteen, -tīn/ *adj.* & *n.* (also **Ar·gen·tin·i·an** /-tíneeən/) ● *adj.* of or relating to Argentina. ● *n.* **1** a native or citizen of Argentina. **2** a person of Argentine descent. **3** (**the Argentine**) Argentina.

ar·gil /áarjil/ *n.* clay, esp. that used in pottery. □□ **ar·gil·la·ceous** /-jiláyshəs/ *adj.*

ar·gon /áargon/ *n. Chem.* an inert gaseous element of the noble gas group. ¶ Symb.: **Ar**.

ar·go·sy /áargəsee/ *n.* (*pl.* **-ies**) *poet.* **1** a large merchant ship, orig. esp. from Ragusa (now Dubrovnik) or Venice. **2** an opulent or abundant supply.

ar·got /áargō, -gət/ *n.* the jargon of a group or class.

ar·gu·a·ble /áargyōōəbəl/ *adj.* open to dispute. □□ **ar·gu·a·bly** *adv.*

ar·gue /áargyōō/ *v.* (**argues, argued, arguing**) **1** *intr.* (often foll. by *with, about,* etc.) exchange views or opinions, especially heatedly or contentiously. **2** *tr.* & *intr.* (often foll. by *that* + clause) maintain by reasoning. **3** *intr.* (foll. by *for, against*) reason (*argued against joining*). **4** *tr.* treat by reasoning (*argue the point*). □□ **ar·gu·er** *n.*

ar·gu·ment /áargyəmənt/ *n.* **1** an exchange of views, esp. a contentious or prolonged one. **2** (often foll. by *for, against*) a reason advanced (*an argument for*

abolition). **3** a summary of the line of reasoning of a book.

ar·gu·men·ta·tion /áargyəmentáyshən/ *n.* **1** methodical reasoning. **2** debate.

ar·gu·men·ta·tive /áargyəméntətiv/ *adj.* **1** fond of arguing; quarrelsome. **2** using methodical reasoning. □□ **ar·gu·men·ta·tive·ly** *adv.* **ar·gu·men·ta·tive·ness** *n.*

Ar·gus /áargəs/ *n.* a watchful guardian.

Ar·gus-eyed *adj.* vigilant.

a·ri·a /áareeə/ *n. Mus.* a long accompanied song for solo voice in an opera.

Ar·i·an /áireeən/ *n.* & *adj.* ● *n.* an adherent of the doctrine of Arius of Alexandria (4th c.), who denied the divinity of Christ. ● *adj.* of or concerning this doctrine. □□ **Ar·i·an·ism** *n.*

ar·id /árid/ *adj.* **1 a** (of ground, climate, etc.) dry. **b** too dry to support vegetation. **2** uninteresting. □□ **a·rid·i·ty** /əríditee/ *n.* **ar·id·ly** *adv.* **ar·id·ness** *n.*

Ar·ies /áireez/ *n.* (*pl.* same) **1** ◀ a constellation, traditionally regarded as portraying the figure of a ram. **2 a** the first sign of the zodiac (the Ram). ▷ ZODIAC. **b** a person born when the Sun is in this sign. □□ **Ar·i·an** /áireeən/ *adj.* & *n.*

a·right /ərít/ *adv.* rightly.

ARIES: FIGURE OF A RAM FORMED FROM THE STARS OF ARIES

ar·il /áril/ *n. Bot.* an extra seed covering, e.g., around a yew seed. □□ **ar·il·late** *adj.*

a·rise /əríz/ *v.intr.* (*past* **arose** /ərōz/; *past part.* **arisen** /ərizən/) **1** originate. **2** (usu. foll. by *from, out of*) result (*accidents can arise from carelessness*). **3** come to one's notice; emerge (*the question of payment arose*). **4** rise.

ar·is·toc·ra·cy /áristókrəsee/ *n.* (*pl.* **-ies**) **1** the highest class in society; the nobility. **2 a** government by a privileged group. **b** a nation governed in this way.

a·ris·to·crat /ərístəkrat, áris-/ *n.* a member of the aristocracy.

a·ris·to·crat·ic /ərístəkrátik/ *adj.* **1** of or relating to the aristocracy. **2 a** distinguished in manners or bearing. **b** grand; stylish. □□ **a·ris·to·crat·i·cal·ly** *adv.*

Ar·is·to·te·lian /áristətéeleeən, əris-/ *n.* & *adj.* ● *n.* a disciple or student of the Greek philosopher Aristotle. ● *adj.* of or concerning Aristotle.

a·rith·me·tic *n.* & *adj.* ● *n.* /əríthmətik/ **1** the science of numbers. **2** the use of numbers; computation. ● *adj.* /árithmétik/ (also **a·rith·met·i·cal** /-métikəl/) of or concerning arithmetic. □□ **a·rith·me·ti·cian** /əríthmətíshən/ *n.*

a·rith·me·tic mean *n.* an average calculated by adding quantities and dividing the total by the number of quantities.

a·rith·me·tic pro·gres·sion *n.* **1** an increase or decrease by a constant quantity (e.g., 1, 2, 3, 4, etc., 9, 7, 5, 3, etc.). **2** a sequence of numbers showing this.

Ariz. *abbr.* Arizona.

Ark. *abbr.* Arkansas.

ark /aark/ *n.* **1** = NOAH'S ARK 1. **2** *archaic* a chest or box. **3** a refuge.

aril (mace)

ARIL: NUTMEG SEED WITH AND WITHOUT ARIL

uncovered seed

ARK OF THE COVENANT IN AN 18TH-CENTURY DUTCH SYNAGOGUE

shields protecting the Torah scrolls

Ark of the Cov·enant *n.* ▶ a chest or box containing the tablets of the Ten Commandments.

arm[1] /aarm/ *n.* **1** each of the upper limbs of the human body from the shoulder to the hand. **2 a** the forelimb of an animal. **b** the flexible limb of an invertebrate animal (e.g., an octopus). ▷ OCTOPUS. **3 a** the sleeve of a garment. **b** the side part of a chair, etc., used to support a sitter's arm. **c** a thing resembling an arm in branching from a main stem (*an arm of the sea*). **4** a control; a means of reaching. **5** a division of a larger group (*the pacifist arm of the movement*). □ **an arm and a leg** a large sum of money. **arm in arm** (of two or more persons) with arms linked. **at arm's length 1** as far as an arm can reach. **2** far enough to avoid undue familiarity. **in arms** (of a baby) too young to walk. **under one's arm** between the arm and the body. **with open arms** cordially. □□ **arm·ful** *n.* (*pl.* **-fuls**). **arm·less** *adj.*

arm[2] /aarm/ *n.* & *v.* *n.* **1** (usu. in *pl.*) **a** a weapon. **b** = FIREARM. **2** (in *pl.*) the military profession. **3** a branch of the military (e.g., infantry, cavalry, artillery). **4** (in *pl.*) heraldic devices (*coat of arms*). ● *v.tr.* & *refl.* **1** supply with weapons. **2** supply with tools or other requisites or advantages (*armed with the truth*). **3** make (a bomb, etc.) able to explode. □ **in arms** armed. **lay down one's arms** cease fighting. **take up arms** begin fighting. **under arms** ready for war or battle. **up in arms** (usu. foll. by *against, about*) actively rebelling. □□ **arm·less** *adj.*

ar·ma·da /aarmáadə/ *n.* a fleet of warships, esp. that sent by Spain against England in 1588.

ar·ma·dil·lo /áarmədílō/ *n.* (*pl.* **-os**) ▼ a nocturnal insect-eating mammal of the family Dasypodidae, native to Central and S. America, with large claws for digging and a body covered in bony plates. ▷ EDENTATE

protective bony plates

ARMADILLO: NINE-BANDED ARMADILLO (*Dasypus novemcinctus*)

armored tail

Ar·ma·ged·don /áarmagéd'n/ *n.* **1** (in the New Testament) the last battle between good and evil before the Day of Judgment. **2** a bloody battle or struggle on a huge scale.

ar·ma·ment /áarməmənt/ *n.* **1** (often in *pl.*) military weapons and equipment, esp. guns on a warship. **2** the process of equipping for war.

ar·ma·men·tar·i·um /áarməmentáireeəm/ *n.* (*pl.* **armamentaria** /-reeə/) **1** a set of medical equip-

A

ment or drugs. **2** the resources available to a person engaged in a task.

ar·ma·ture /áarməchŏŏr/ *n.* **1** the rotating coil or coils of a generator or electric motor. ▷ ALTERNATING CURRENT. **2** a piece of soft iron placed in contact with the poles of a horseshoe magnet to preserve its power. Also called **keeper**. **3** *Biol.* the protective covering of an animal or plant. **4** a metal framework on which a sculpture is molded.

arm·band /áarmband/ *n.* a band worn around the upper arm to hold up a shirtsleeve or as a form of identification, etc.

arm can·dy *n. colloq.* a sexually attractive companion accompanying a person at social events.

arm·chair /áarmcháir/ *n.* **1** a comfortable chair with side supports for the arms. **2** (*attrib.*) theoretical rather than active (*an armchair critic*).

Ar·me·ni·an /aarméeneeən/ *n. & adj.* ● *n.* **1 a** a native of Armenia, an ancient kingdom corresponding to an area in modern Armenia, Turkey, and Iran. **b** a person of Armenian descent. **2** the language of Armenia. ● *adj.* of or relating to Armenia, its language, or the Christian Church established there *c.*300.

arm·hole /áarmhōl/ *n.* each of two holes in a garment through which the arms are put.

ar·mi·ger /áarmijər/ *n.* a person entitled to heraldic arms. □□ **ar·mig·er·ous** /-míjərəs/ *adj.*

ar·mil·lar·y sphere *n. hist.* a representation of the celestial globe constructed from metal rings and showing the celestial equator, the celestial tropics, etc.

Ar·min·i·an /aarmíneeən/ *adj. & n.* ● *adj.* relating to the doctrine of Arminius, a Dutch Protestant theologian (d. 1609), who opposed the views of Calvin, esp. on predestination. ● *n.* an adherent of this doctrine. □□ **Ar·min·i·an·ism** *n.*

ar·mi·stice /áarmistis/ *n.* a stopping of hostilities by agreement of the opposing sides; a truce.

Ar·mi·stice Day *n.* former name of Veteran's Day, the anniversary of the World War I armistice of Nov. 11, 1918.

arm·let /áarmlit/ *n.* a band worn around the arm.

ar·moire /aarmwáar/ *n.* a tall, upright, often ornate cupboard or wardrobe.

ar·mor *n.* /áarmər/ *n. & v.* ● *n.* **1** ▶ a defensive covering, usu. of metal, formerly worn to protect the body in fighting. ▷ SAMURAI. **2 a** (in full **armor plate**) a protective metal covering for an armed vehicle, ship, etc. **b** armored fighting vehicles collectively. **3** a protective covering or shell on certain animals and plants. ● *v.tr.* (usu. as **armored** *adj.*) provide with a protective covering, and often with guns (*armored car*).

ar·mor·er /áarmərər/ *n.* **1** a maker or repairer of arms or armor. **2** an official in charge of a ship's or a regiment's arms.

ar·mor·y[1] /áarməree/ *n.* (*pl.* **-ies**) **1** a place where arms are kept. **2** an array of weapons, defensive resources, etc.

ar·mor·y[2] /áarməree/ *n.* (*pl.* **-ies**) heraldry. □□ **ar·mo·ri·al** /aarmóreeəl/ *adj.*

arm·pit /áarmpit/ *n.* the hollow under the arm at the shoulder.

arm·rest /áarmrest/ *n.* = ARM[1] 3b.

arm-twist·ing *n. colloq.* (persuasion by) the use of physical force or moral pressure.

arm wres·tling *n.* a trial of strength in which each party tries to force the other's arm down onto a table on which their elbows rest.

ar·my /áarmee/ *n.* (*pl.* **-ies**) **1** an organized force armed for fighting on land. **2** (*prec. by the*) the military profession. **3** (often foll. by *of*) a very large number (*an army of helpers*). **4** an organized body regarded as working for a particular cause.

ar·ni·ca /áarnikə/ *n.* **1** a plant of the genus *Arnica*, having yellow daisy-like flower heads. **2** a medicine prepared from this, used for bruises, etc.

a·ro·ma /ərómə/ *n.* a fragrance; a distinctive and pleasing smell, often of food.

a·ro·ma·ther·a·py /ərómothérəpee/ *n.* the use of plant extracts and essential oils in massage. □□ **a·ro·ma·ther·a·peu·tic** /-pyŏŏtik/ *adj.* **a·ro·ma·ther·a·pist** *n.*

ar·o·mat·ic /árəmátik/ *adj. & n.* ● *adj.* **1** fragrant. **2** *Chem.* of organic compounds having an unsaturated ring, esp. a benzene ring. ● *n.* an aromatic substance. □□ **ar·o·mat·i·cal·ly** *adv.* **ar·o·ma·tic·i·ty** /árəmətísitee/ *n.*

a·ro·ma·tize /ərómətīz/ *v.tr. Chem.* convert (a compound) into an aromatic structure. □□ **a·ro·ma·ti·za·tion** /-tizáyshən/ *n.*

a·rose *past of* ARISE.

a·round /ərównd/ *adv. & prep.* ● *adv.* **1** on every side; on all sides. **2** in various places; here and there (*fool around*; *shop around*). **3** *colloq.* **a** in existence; available. **b** near at hand. **4** approximately. **5** with circular motion. **6** with return to the starting point or an earlier state. **7 a** with rotation, or change to an opposite position. **b** with change to an opposite opinion, etc. **8** to, at, or affecting all or many points of an area or the members of a company, etc. **9** in every direction from a center or within a radius. **10** by a circuitous way. **11 a** to a person's house, etc. **b** to a more prominent or convenient position. **12** measuring (a specified distance) in girth. ● *prep.* **1** on or along the circuit of. **2** on every side of; enveloping. **3** here and there; in or near (*chairs around the room*). **4** (of amount, time, etc.) about; at a time near to (*come around four o'clock*). **5** so as to encircle or enclose. **6** at or to points on the circumference of. **7** with successive visits to. **8** in various directions from or with regard to. **9** having as an axis of revolution or as a central point. **10 a** so as to double or pass in a curved course. **b** having passed in this way (*be around the corner*). **c** in the position that would result from this. **11** so as to come close from various sides but not into contact. **12** at various places in or around. □ **around the bend** see BEND[1]. **have been around** *colloq.* be widely experienced.

a·rouse /ərówz/ *v.tr.* **1** induce (esp. a feeling, emotion, etc.). **2** awake from sleep. **3** stir into activity. **4** stimulate sexually. □□ **a·rous·a·ble** *adj.* **a·rous·al** *n.*

ar·peg·gi·o /aarpéjeeō/ *n.* (*pl.* **-os**) *Mus.* the notes of a chord played in succession, either ascending or descending.

ar·que·bus var. of HARQUEBUS.

arr. *abbr.* **1** *Mus.* arranged by. **2** arrives.

ar·rack /árək/ *n.* (also **ar·ak** /árək/) an alcoholic liquor, esp. distilled from rice or various palms.

ar·raign /əráyn/ *v.tr.* **1** indict before a court; formally accuse. **2** find fault with; call into question (an action or statement). □□ **ar·raign·ment** *n.*

ar·range /əráynj/ *v.* **1** *tr.* put into the required order. **2** *tr.* plan or provide for. **3** *intr.* take measures; make plans; give instructions. **4** *intr.* come to an agreement. **5** *tr. Mus.* adapt (a composition) for performance with instruments or voices other than

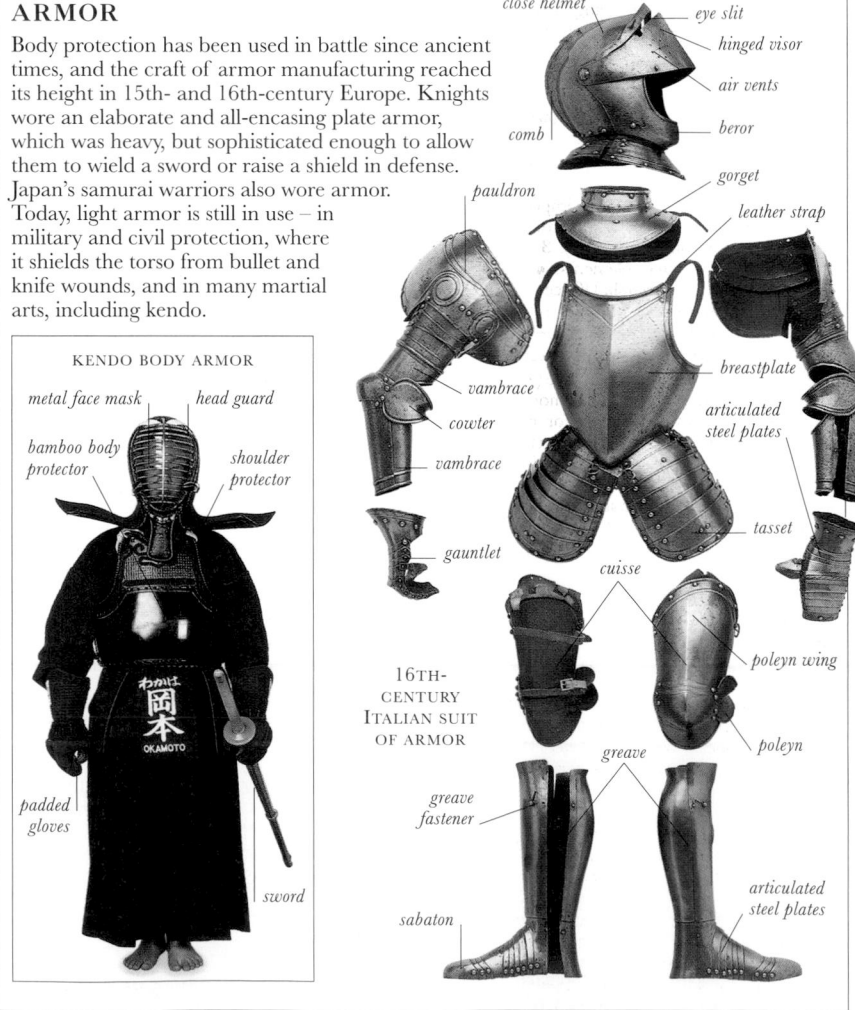

ARMOR

Body protection has been used in battle since ancient times, and the craft of armor manufacturing reached its height in 15th- and 16th-century Europe. Knights wore an elaborate and all-encasing plate armor, which was heavy, but sophisticated enough to allow them to wield a sword or raise a shield in defense. Japan's samurai warriors also wore armor. Today, light armor is still in use – in military and civil protection, where it shields the torso from bullet and knife wounds, and in many martial arts, including kendo.

KENDO BODY ARMOR

metal face mask
head guard
bamboo body protector
shoulder protector
padded gloves
sword

close helmet
eye slit
hinged visor
air vents
beror
comb
gorget
pauldron
leather strap
vambrace
cowter
breastplate
articulated steel plates
vambrace
tasset
gauntlet
cuisse
poleyn wing
poleyn
16TH-CENTURY ITALIAN SUIT OF ARMOR
greave
greave fastener
sabaton
articulated steel plates

ART DECO

The term *art deco* originates from an exhibition of decorative and industrial design held in Paris in 1925. Owing something to art nouveau, but with a greater emphasis on geometry than on organic forms, it became the most fashionable style of the 1920s and 1930s. With high regard to fine workmanship and materials, the style affected jewelry and furniture as well as interior design and architecture. William van Alen's Chrysler Building epitomizes art deco style, from the overall structure to interior detailing, such as the elevator doors shown here.

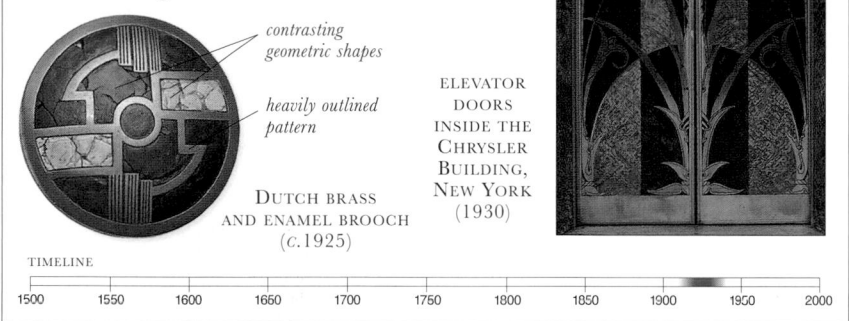

contrasting geometric shapes

heavily outlined pattern

DUTCH BRASS AND ENAMEL BROOCH (*c.*1925)

ELEVATOR DOORS INSIDE THE CHRYSLER BUILDING, NEW YORK (1930)

TIMELINE

| 1500 | 1550 | 1600 | 1650 | 1700 | 1750 | 1800 | 1850 | 1900 | 1950 | 2000 |

---

those originally specified. □□ **ar·range·a·ble** *adj.* **ar·rang·er** *n.* (esp. in sense 5).

ar·range·ment /əráynjmənt/ *n.* **1** the act or process of arranging or being arranged. **2** the manner in which a thing is arranged. **3** something arranged. **4** (in *pl.*) plans; preparations (*make your own arrangements*). **5** *Mus.* a composition arranged for performance by different instruments or voices.

ar·rant /árənt/ *attrib.adj.* utter (*arrant nonsense*). □□ **ar·rant·ly** *adv.*

ar·ras /árəs/ *n. hist.* a rich tapestry, often hung on the walls of a room.

ar·ray /əráy/ *n. & v.* ● *n.* **1** an imposing or well-ordered series or display. **2** an ordered arrangement, esp. of troops (*battle array*). **3** *Computing* an ordered set of related elements. ● *v.tr.* **1** deck; adorn. **2** set in order; marshal (forces).

ar·rears /əreerz/ *n.pl.* an amount still outstanding or uncompleted. □ **in arrears** (or **arrear**) behindhand, esp. in payment. □□ **ar·rear·age** *n.*

ar·rest /ərést/ *v. & n.* ● *v.tr.* **1 a** seize (a person) and take into custody, esp. by legal authority. **b** seize (a ship) by legal authority. **2** stop or check (esp. a process or moving thing). **3** attract (a person's attention). ● *n.* **1** the act of arresting or being arrested. **2** a stoppage or check (*cardiac arrest*). □□ **ar·rest·a·ble** *adj.* **ar·rest·ing·ly** *adv.*

ar·rhyth·mi·a /ayríthmeeə/ *n. Med.* a condition in which the heart beats with an irregular or abnormal rhythm.

ar·ri·val /ərívəl/ *n.* **1** the act of arriving. **2** a person or thing that has arrived.

ar·rive /ərív/ *v.intr.* (often foll. by *at, in*) **1** reach a destination; come to the end of a journey or a specified part of a journey. **2** (foll. by *at*) reach (a conclusion, decision, etc.). **3** *colloq.* establish one's reputation or position. **4** *colloq.* (of a child) be born. **5** (of a time) come (*her birthday arrived at last*).

ar·ri·ve·der·ci /aréevədárchee/ *int.* goodbye until we meet again.

ar·ri·viste /áreevéest/ *n.* an ambitious or ruthlessly self-seeking person. □□ **ar·ri·vism** *n.*

ar·ro·gant /árəgənt/ *adj.* aggressively assertive or presumptuous. □□ **ar·ro·gance** *n.* **ar·ro·gant·ly** *adv.*

ar·ro·gate /árəgayt/ *v.tr.* **1** (often foll. by *to oneself*) claim (power, responsibility, etc.) without justification. **2** (often foll. by *to*) attribute unjustly (to a person). □□ **ar·ro·ga·tion** /-gáyshən/ *n.*

ar·row /árō/ *n.* **1** a sharp pointed wooden or metal stick shot from a bow as a weapon. ▷ ARCHERY. **2** a drawn or printed, etc., representation of an arrow indicating a direction. □□ **ar·row·y** *adj.*

ar·row·head /árōhed/ *n.* **1** the pointed end of an arrow. **2** a decorative device resembling an arrowhead.

ar·row·root /árōrŏŏt, -rŏŏt/ *n.* a plant of the family Marantaceae from which a starch is prepared and used for nutritional and medicinal purposes.

ar·roy·o /əróyō/ *n.* (*pl.* **-os**) **1** a brook or stream, esp. in an arid region. **2** a gully.

arse esp. *Brit.* var. of ASS[2].

ar·se·nal /áarsənəl/ *n.* **1** a store of weapons. **2** a government establishment for the storage and manufacture of weapons and ammunition. **3** resources regarded collectively.

ar·se·nic /áarsənik/ *n.* **1** a nonscientific name for arsenic trioxide, a highly poisonous substance used in weed killers, rat poison, etc. **2** *Chem.* a brittle semimetallic element, used in semiconductors and alloys. ¶ Symb.: **As**. □□ **ar·se·ni·ous** /aarséeniəs/ *adj.*

ar·sen·i·cal /aarsénikəl/ *adj. & n.* ● *adj.* of or containing arsenic. ● *n.* a drug containing arsenic.

ar·son /áarsən/ *n.* the act of maliciously setting fire to property. □□ **ar·son·ist** *n.*

art /aart/ *n.* **1 a** human creative skill or its application. **b** work exhibiting this. **2 a** (in *pl.*; prec. by *the*) the various branches of creative activity, e.g., painting, music, writing, considered collectively. **b** any one of these branches. **3** creative activity, esp. painting and drawing, resulting in visual representation. **4** human skill as opposed to the work of nature. **5** (often foll. by *of*) a skill, aptitude, or knack (*the art of writing clearly*). **6** (in *pl.*; usu. prec. by *the*) those branches of learning (esp. languages, literature, and history) associated with creative skill as opposed to scientific, technical, or vocational skills.

art dec·o /dékō/ *n.* ◀ the predominant decorative art style of the period 1910–30, characterized by precise and boldly delineated geometric motifs, shapes, and strong colors.

ar·te·ri·al /aarteereeəl/ *adj.* **1** of or relating to an artery (*arterial blood*). **2** (esp. of a road) main, important, esp. linking large cities or towns.

ar·te·ri·al·ize /aarteereeəliz/ *v.tr.* **1** convert venous into arterial (blood) by reoxygenation esp. in the lungs. **2** provide with an arterial system. □□ **ar·te·ri·al·i·za·tion** *n.*

ar·te·ri·ole /aarteereeōl/ *n.* a small branch of an artery leading into capillaries.

ar·te·ri·o·scle·ro·sis /aarteereeōsklərósis/ *n.* the loss of elasticity and thickening of the walls of the arteries, esp. in old age. □□ **ar·te·ri·o·scle·rot·ic** /-rótik/ *adj.*

ar·ter·y /áartəree/ *n.* (*pl.* **-ies**) **1** ▼ any of the muscular-walled tubes forming part of the blood circulation system of the body (cf. VEIN). ▷ CARDIOVASCULAR. **2** a main road or railroad line. □□ **ar·te·ri·tis** /-rítis/ *n.*

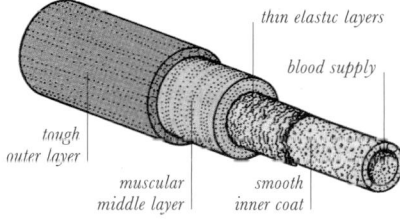

thin elastic layers

blood supply

tough outer layer

muscular middle layer

smooth inner coat

ARTERY: CUTAWAY SECTION OF A HUMAN ARTERY

ar·te·sian well /aarteézhən/ *n.* ▼ a well bored so that natural pressure produces a constant supply of water.

ARTESIAN WELL

An artesian well makes use of hydrostatic pressure to raise water to the Earth's surface. Such a well may be bored into an aquifer (a saturated stratum of rock or earth) that is sandwiched between layers of impermeable rock. Provided the water table is higher than ground level at the wellhead, water will naturally rise to the surface.

SECTION OF THE EARTH REVEALING AN AQUIFER AND AN ARTESIAN WELL

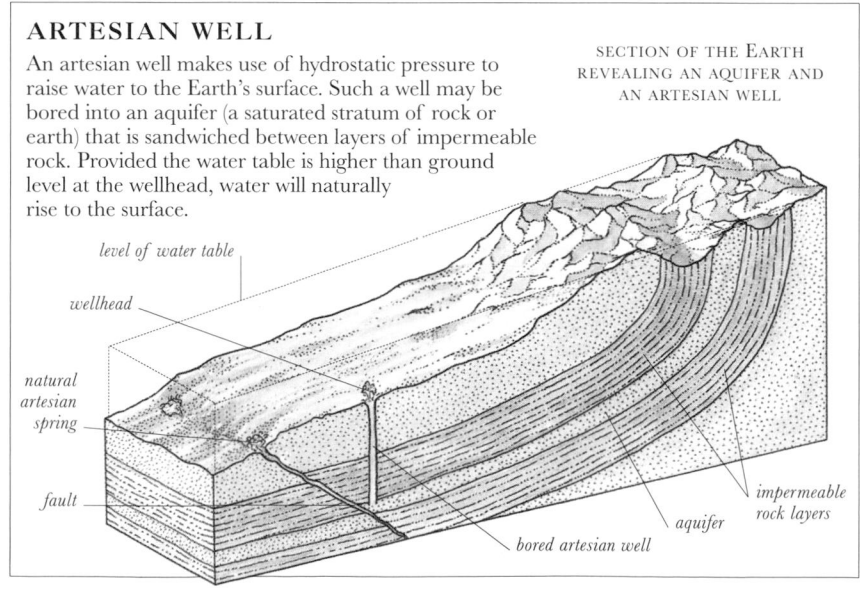

level of water table

wellhead

natural artesian spring

fault

bored artesian well

aquifer

impermeable rock layers

A

ARTHROPOD

Arthropods are the largest invertebrate group, with more than one million known species existing on land and in water. All have jointed bodies protected by a tough, waterproof exoskeleton, which is shed several times as they grow into their adult state. The main groups of arthropods are shown here.

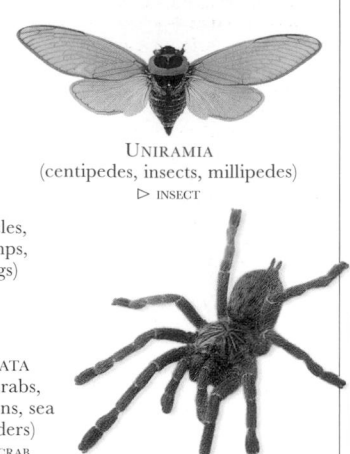

UNIRAMIA
(centipedes, insects, millipedes)
▷ INSECT

CRUSTACEA (barnacles, crabs, lobsters, shrimps, water fleas, sow bugs)
▷ CRAB, CRUSTACEAN

CHELICERATA (horseshoe crabs, mites, scorpions, sea spiders, spiders)
▷ ARACHNID, CRAB, SCORPION, SPIDER

art·ful /áartfŏŏl/ *adj.* **1** (of a person or action) crafty; deceitful. **2** skillful; clever. □□ **art·ful·ly** *adv.* **art·ful·ness** *n.*

ar·thri·tis /aarthrítis/ *n.* inflammation of a joint. □□ **ar·thrit·ic** /-thrítik/ *adj. & n.*

ar·thro·pod /áarthrəpod/ *n. Zool.* ▲ any invertebrate animal of the phylum Arthropoda, with a segmented body, jointed limbs, and an external skeleton.

ar·thro·scope /áarthrəskŏp/ *n.* an endoscope for viewing the interior of a joint, as the knee. □□ **ar·thro·scop·ic** *adj.* **ar·thros·co·py** *n.*

Ar·thu·ri·an /aarthŏŏreeən/ *adj.* relating to or associated with King Arthur, the legendary British ruler, or his court.

ar·ti·choke /áartichŏk/ *n.* **1** a European plant, *Cynara scolymus*, allied to the thistle. **2** (in full **globe artichoke**) the flower head of the artichoke, the bracts of which have edible bases. ▷ GLOBE ARTICHOKE, VEGETABLE. **3** = Jerusalem artichoke.

ar·ti·cle /áartikəl/ *n. & v.* ● *n.* **1** (often in *pl.*) an item or commodity, usu. not further distinguished (*a collection of odd articles*). **2** a nonfictional essay, esp. one included with others in a newspaper, magazine, journal, etc. **3 a** a particular part (*an article of faith*). **b** a separate clause or portion of any document (*articles of apprenticeship*). **4** *Gram.* the definite or indefinite article. ● *v.tr.* bind by articles of apprenticeship.

ar·tic·u·lar /aartíkyələr/ *adj.* of or relating to the joints.

ar·tic·u·late *adj. & v.* ● *adj.* /aartíkyələt/ **1** able to speak fluently and coherently. **2** (of sound or speech) having clearly distinguishable parts. **3** having joints. ● *v.* /aartíkyəlayt/ **1** *tr.* **a** pronounce (words, syllables, etc.) clearly and distinctly. **b** express (an idea, etc.) coherently. **2** *intr.* speak distinctly (*was quite unable to articulate*). **3** *tr.* (usu. in *passive*) connect by joints. **4** *tr.* mark with apparent joints. **5** *intr.* (often foll. by *with*) form a joint. □□ **ar·tic·u·la·cy** *n.* **ar·tic·u·late·ly** *adv.* **ar·tic·u·late·ness** *n.* **ar·tic·u·la·tor** *n.*

ar·tic·u·la·tion /aartíkyəláyshən/ *n.* **1 a** the act of speaking. **b** articulate utterance; speech. **2 a** the act or a mode of jointing. **b** a joint.

ar·ti·fact /áartifakt/ *n.* **1** a product of human art and workmanship. **2** *Archaeol.* a product of prehistoric or aboriginal workmanship as distinguished from a similar object naturally produced. □□ **ar·ti·fac·tu·al** /-fákchŏŏəl/ *adj.*

ar·ti·fice /áartifis/ *n.* **1** cunning. **2** an instance of this.

ar·tif·i·cer /aartífisər/ *n.* **1** an inventor. **2** a craftsman.

ar·ti·fi·cial /áartifishəl/ *adj.* **1** produced by human art or effort rather than originating naturally (*an artificial lake*). **2** not real; imitation; fake (*artificial flowers*). **3** affected; insincere (*an artificial smile*). □□ **ar·ti·fi·ci·al·i·ty** /-sheeálitee/ *n.* **ar·ti·fi·cial·ly** *adv.*

ar·ti·fi·cial in·sem·i·na·tion *n.* the injection of semen into the vagina or uterus other than by sexual intercourse.

ar·ti·fi·cial in·tel·li·gence *n.* the application of computers to areas normally regarded as requiring human intelligence.

ar·ti·fi·cial kid·ney *n.* an apparatus that performs the functions of the human kidney (outside the body), when one or both organs are damaged. ▷ DIALYSIS

ar·ti·fi·cial res·pi·ra·tion *n.* the restoration or initiation of breathing by manual or mechanical or mouth-to-mouth methods.

ar·til·ler·y /aartílaree/ *n.* (*pl.* **-ies**) **1** large-caliber guns used in warfare on land. **2** a branch of the armed forces that uses these. □□ **ar·til·ler·ist** *n.*

ar·til·ler·y·man /aartílareeman/ *n.* (*pl.* **-men**) a member of the artillery.

ar·ti·o·dac·tyl /aarteeōdáktil/ *adj. & n.* ● *adj.* ▶ of or relating to the order Artiodactyla of ungulate mammals with two main toes on each foot, including camels, pigs, and ruminants. ▷ UNGULATE. ● *n.* an animal of this order.

ar·ti·san /áartizən, -sən/ *n.* a skilled, esp. manual, worker or craftsman.

art·ist /áartist/ *n.* **1** a painter. **2** a person who practices any of the arts. **3** a professional performer, esp. a singer or dancer. **4** *colloq.* a practicer of a specified activity (*con artist*). □□ **art·ist·ry** *n.*

ARTIODACTYL: TWO-TOED CAMEL HOOF

ar·tis·tic /aartístik/ *adj.* **1** having natural skill in art. **2** made or done with art. **3** of art or artists. □□ **ar·tis·ti·cal·ly** *adv.*

art·less /áartlis/ *adj.* **1** guileless. **2** not displaying art. □□ **art·less·ly** *adv.*

art nou·veau /áart nŏŏvố/ *n.* ▼ an art style of the late 19th century characterized by flowing lines and natural organic forms.

arts and crafts *n.pl.* decorative design and handcrafts.

art·sy-craft·sy /ártsee-kráftsee/ *adj.* quaintly artistic; (of furniture, etc.) seeking stylistic effect rather than usefulness or comfort.

art·work /áartwərk/ *n.* the illustrations in a printed work.

art·y /áartee/ *adj.* (**artier, artiest**) *colloq.* pretentiously artistic. □□ **art·i·ness** *n.*

ar·um /áirəm/ *n.* any plant of the genus *Arum*, usu. stemless.

ar·um lil·y *n.* = CALLA.

Ar·y·an /áireeən/ *n. & adj.* ● *n.* **1** a member of the peoples speaking any of the languages of the Indo-European (esp. Indo-Iranian) family. **2** the parent language of this family. **3** *improperly* (in Nazi ideology) a Caucasian not of Jewish descent. ● *adj.* of or relating to Aryan or the Aryans.

AS *abbr.* **1** Anglo-Saxon. **2** American Samoa (in official postal use).

As *symb. Chem.* the element arsenic.

as[1] /az, *unstressed* əz/ *adv., conj., & pron.* ● *adv. & conj.* (*adv.* as antecedent in main sentence; *conj.* in relative

ART NOUVEAU

Popular throughout Europe and influential in the US, the style of art nouveau is characterized by the use of extended, flowing lines based on organic forms such as plants, waves, and the human body. Taking its name from a Parisian shop of the time, art nouveau was most prevalent in the fields of decorative art and architecture. One of its leading exponents was the French architect Hector Guimard. He is best known for his elaborate entrances to the metro stations in Paris, which are characterized by shell-shaped canopies made of glass and wrought iron.

ENTRANCE TO THE PARIS METRO (*c.*1900), HECTOR GUIMARD

TIMELINE

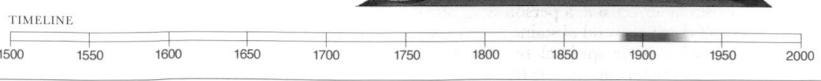

| 1500 | 1550 | 1600 | 1650 | 1700 | 1750 | 1800 | 1850 | 1900 | 1950 | 2000 |

clause expressed or implied) . . . to the extent to which . . . is or does, etc. (*I am as tall as he; am as tall as he is; am not so tall as he; colloq.*) am as tall as him; as many as six; as recently as last week). ● *conj.* (with relative clause expressed or implied) **1** (with antecedent *so*) expressing result or purpose (*came early so as to meet us*). **2** (with antecedent adverb omitted) having concessive force (*good as it is* = although it is good). **3** (without antecedent adverb) **a** in the manner in which (*do as you like*). **b** in the capacity or form of (*I speak as your friend; as a matter of fact*). **c** during or at the time that (*came up as I was speaking; fell just as I reached the door*). **d** for the reason that (*as you are here, we can talk*). ● *rel.pron.* (with verb of relative clause expressed or implied) **1** that; who; which (*I had the same trouble as you; he is a writer, as is his wife; such countries as France*). **2** (with sentence as antecedent) a fact that (*he lost, as you know*). □ **as and when** to the extent and at the time that (*I'll do it as and when I want to*). **as for** with regard to (*as for you, I think you are wrong*). **as from** esp. *Brit.* = *as of* 1. **as if** (or **though**) as would be the case if (*acts as if she were in charge; looks as though we've won*). **as it is** in the existing circumstances. **as it were** in a way; to a certain extent (*he is, as it were, infatuated*). **as long as** LONG[1]. **as much** see MUCH. **as of 1** on and after (a specified date). **2** as at (a specified time). **as per** see PER. **as regards** see REGARD. **as soon as** see SOON. **as such** see SUCH. **as though** see *as if*. **as to** with respect to (*as to you, I think you are wrong*). **as well** see WELL[1]. **as yet** until now or a particular time in the past (usu. with *neg*: *have received no news as yet*).

as² /as/ *n.* (*pl.* **asses**) a Roman copper coin.

a.s.a.p. *abbr.* (also **ASAP**) as soon as possible.

as·bes·tos /asbéstəs, az-/ *n.* a fibrous silicate mineral that is not flammable. □□ **as·bes·tine** /-tin/ *adj.*

as·bes·to·sis /ásbestṓsis, áz-/ *n.* a lung disease resulting from the inhalation of asbestos particles.

as·cend /əsénd/ *v.* **1** *intr.* move upward. **2** *intr.* slope upward. **3** *tr.* climb. **4** *intr.* rise in rank or status. **5** *intr.* (of sound) rise in pitch. □ **ascend the throne** become king or queen.

as·cen·dan·cy /əséndənsee/ *n.* (also **as·cen·den·cy**) (often foll. by *over*) a superior position.

as·cen·dant /əséndənt/ *adj. & n.* ● *adj.* **1** rising. **2** *Astron.* rising toward the zenith. **3** *Astrol.* just above the eastern horizon. **4** predominant. ● *n. Astrol.* the point of the Sun's apparent path that is ascendant at a given time. □ **in the ascendant 1** supreme or dominating. **2** rising; gaining power or authority.

as·cend·er /əséndər/ *n.* **1 a** a part of a letter that extends above the main part (as in *b* and *d*). **b** a letter having this. **2** a person or thing that ascends.

as·cen·sion /əsénshən/ *n.* **1** the act or an instance of ascending. **2** (**Ascension**) the ascent of Christ into heaven on the fortieth day after the Resurrection. □□ **as·cen·sion·al** *adj.*

As·cen·sion Day *n.* the Thursday 40 days after Easter on which Christ's ascension is celebrated.

as·cent /əsént/ *n.* **1** the act or an instance of ascending. **2 a** an upward movement or rise. **b** advancement or progress (*the ascent of mammals*). **3** a way by which one may ascend; an upward slope (*a steep ascent*).

as·cer·tain /ásərtáyn/ *v.tr.* **1** find out as a definite fact. **2** get to know. □□ **as·cer·tain·a·ble** *adj.* **as·cer·tain·ment** *n.*

as·ce·sis /əséesis/ *n.* the practice of self-discipline.

as·cet·ic /əsétik/ *n. & adj.* ● *n.* a person who practices severe self-discipline and abstains from pleasure, esp. for religious or spiritual reasons. ● *adj.* relating to or characteristic of ascetics or asceti-

cism; abstaining from pleasure. □□ **as·cet·i·cal·ly** *adv.* **as·cet·i·cism** /-tisizəm/ *n.*

ASCII /áskee/ *abbr. Computing* American Standard Code for Information Interchange.

as·ci·tes /əsíteez/ *n.* (*pl.* same) *Med.* the accumulation of fluid in the abdominal cavity, causing swelling.

a·scor·bic ac·id /əskáwrbik/ *n.* a vitamin found in citrus fruits and green vegetables, a deficiency of which results in scurvy. Also called **vitamin C**.

as·cot /áskot, -kət/ *n.* a scarf-like item of neckwear with broad ends worn looped to lie flat one over the other against the chest.

as·cribe /əskríb/ *v.tr.* (usu. foll. by *to*) **1** attribute or impute (*ascribes his well-being to a sound constitution*). **2** (usu. *be ascribed to*) attribute a text, quotation, or work of art to (a person or period). □□ **a·scrib·a·ble** *adj.*

as·crip·tion /əskrípshən/ *n.* **1** the act or an instance of ascribing. **2** a preacher's words ascribing praise to God at the end of a sermon.

ASEAN /áseeən/ *abbr.* Association of South East Asian Nations.

a·sep·sis /aysépsis/ *n.* the absence of harmful bacteria, viruses, or other microorganisms.

a·sep·tic /ayséptik/ *adj.* free from contamination caused by harmful bacteria, viruses, or other microorganisms.

a·sex·u·al /ayséksho͞ol/ *adj. Biol.* **1** without sex or sexual organs. **2** (of reproduction) not involving the fusion of gametes. □□ **a·sex·u·al·i·ty** /-sho͞oálitee/ *n.* **a·sex·u·al·ly** *adv.*

ash¹ /ash/ *n.* **1** (often in *pl.*) the powdery residue left after the burning of any substance. **2** (*pl.*) the remains of the human body after cremation.

ash² /ash/ *n.* **1** ◄ any tree of the genus *Fraxinus*, with silvery-gray bark and hard wood. **2** its wood. ▷ WOOD

a·shamed /əsháymd/ *adj.* (usu. *predic.*) **1** (often foll. by *of* (= with regard to) or *to* + infin.) embarrassed by shame (*ashamed of having lied; ashamed to be seen with him*). **2** (foll. by *to* + infin.) hesitant, reluctant (*ashamed to admit that I was wrong*). □□ **a·sham·ed·ly** /-midlee/ *adv.*

ash blond *n.* (also **ash blonde**) **1** a very pale blond color. **2** a person with hair of this color.

ash can /áshkan/ *n.* a container for household trash.

ash·en¹ /áshən/ *adj.* **1** of or resembling ashes. **2** ash colored; gray or pale.

ash·en² /áshən/ *adj.* **1** of or relating to the ash tree. **2** *archaic* made of ash wood.

Ash·ke·naz·i /áashkənáazee/ *n.* (*pl.* **Ashkenazim** /-zim/) a Jew of eastern European ancestry (cf. SEPHARDI). □□ **Ash·ke·naz·ic** *adj.*

ash·lar /áshlər/ *n.* **1** a large square-cut stone used in building. **2** masonry made of ashlars.

ash·lar·ing /áshləring/ *n.* **1** ashlar masonry. **2** the short upright boarding in a garret which cuts off the acute angle between the roof and the floor.

a·shore /əsháwr/ *adv.* toward or on the shore (*sailed ashore; stayed ashore*).

ash·ram /áashrəm/ *n. Ind.* a place of religious retreat for Hindus; a hermitage.

ash·tray /áshtray/ *n.* a small receptacle for cigarette ashes, butts, etc.

Ash Wednes·day *n.* the first day of Lent (from the custom of marking the foreheads of penitents with ashes on that day).

ash·y /áshee/ *adj.* (**ashier**, **ashiest**) **1** = ASHEN. **2** covered with ashes.

A·sian /áyzhən, -shən/ *n. & adj.* ● *n.* **1** a native of Asia. **2** a person of Asian descent. ● *adj.* of or relating to Asia or its people, customs, or languages.

A·si·at·ic /áyzheeátik, -shee-, -zee-/ *n. & adj.* ● *n. offens.* an Asian. ● *adj.* Asian.

A-side /áy-síd/ *n.* the side of a phonograph record regarded as the main one.

a·side /əsíd/ *adv. & n.* ● *adv.* **1** to or on one side. **2** out of consideration (*joking aside*). ● *n.* **1** words spoken in a play for the audience to hear, but supposed not to be heard by the other characters. **2** an incidental remark. □ **aside from** apart from. **set aside 1** put to one side. **2** keep for future use. **3** reject. **4** annul. **5** remove (land) from agricultural production. **take aside** engage (a person) esp. in a private conversation.

as·i·nine /ásinīn/ *adj.* stupid.

ask /ask/ *v.* **1** *tr.* call for an answer to or about. **2** *tr.* seek to obtain from another person. **3** *tr.* (usu. foll. by *out* or *over*, or *to* (a function, etc.)) invite. **4** *intr.* (foll. by *for*) seek to obtain, meet, or be directed to. □ **ask after** inquire about (esp. a person). **ask for it** *sl.* invite trouble. **for the asking** for nothing. **if you ask me** *colloq.* in my opinion. □□ **ask·er** *n.*

a·skance /əskáns/ *adv.* sideways or squinting. □ **look askance at** regard with suspicion or disapproval.

a·ska·ri /askáaree/ *n.* (*pl.* same or **askaris**) an East African soldier or policeman.

a·skew /əsky͞oo/ *adv. & predic.adj.* ● *adv.* obliquely; awry. ● *predic.adj.* oblique; awry.

ask·ing price *n.* the price of an object set by the seller.

a·slant /əslánt/ *adv. & prep.* ● *adv.* at a slant. ● *prep.* obliquely across.

a·sleep /əsléep/ *predic.adj. & adv.* **1 a** in or into a state of sleep (*he fell asleep*). **b** inactive; inattentive (*the nation is asleep*). **2** (of a limb, etc.) numb. **3** *euphem.* dead.

ASM *abbr.* air-to-surface missile.

a·so·cial /aysṓshəl/ *adj.* not social; antisocial.

asp /asp/ *n.* **1** a small viper, *Vipera aspis*, native to southern Europe, resembling the adder. **2** a small venomous snake, *Naja haje*, native to northern Africa and Arabia.

as·par·a·gus /əspárəgəs/ *n.* **1** any plant of the genus *Asparagus*. **2** ◄ one species of this, *A. officinalis*, with edible young shoots and leaves.

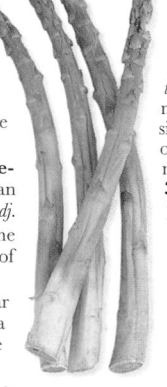

ASPARAGUS
(*Asparagus
officinalis*)

as·par·tame /əspáartaym/ *n.* a very sweet, low-calorie substance used as a sweetener instead of sugar or saccharin.

as·pect /áspekt/ *n.* **1 a** a particular component or feature of a matter (*only one aspect of the problem*). **b** a particular way in which a matter may be considered. **2 a** a facial expression; a look (*a cheerful aspect*). **b** the appearance of a person or thing, esp. as presented to the mind of the viewer (*has a frightening aspect*). **3** the side of a building or location facing a particular direction (*southern aspect*).

as·pect ra·tio *n.* **1** *Aeron.* the ratio of the span to the mean chord of an airfoil. **2** *Telev.* the ratio of picture width to height.

as·pen /áspən/ *n.* a poplar tree, *Populus tremula*, with tremulous leaves.

As·per·ger's syn·drome /áspərjəz sindrōm/ *n. Psychol.* a mild autistic disorder characterized by awkwardness in social interaction, pedantry in speech, and preoccupation with very narrow interests.

as·per·i·ty /əspérətee/ *n.* (*pl.* **-ies**) **1** harshness of temper or tone. **2** roughness.

as·per·sion /əspérzhən/ *n.* □ **cast aspersions on** attack the reputation of.

as·phalt /ásfalt/ *n. & v.* ● *n.* **1** a dark bituminous pitch occurring naturally or made from petroleum. **2** a mixture of this with sand, gravel, etc., for surfacing roads, etc. ● *v.tr.* surface with asphalt. □□ **as·phal·tic** /-fáltik/ *adj.*

ASH: EUROPEAN ASH
(*Fraxinus excelsior*)

*pinnate
leaf*

seed pods

ASPHODEL (*Asphodelus aestivus*)

as·pho·del /ásfədel/ *n.* **1** ◀ any plant of the genus *Asphodelus*, of the lily family. **2** *poet.* an immortal flower growing in Elysium.

as·phyx·i·a /asfíkseeə/ *n.* a lack of oxygen in the blood, causing unconsciousness or death; suffocation. ▫▫ **as·phyx·i·ant** *adj.* & *n.*

as·phyx·i·ate /asfíkseeayt/ *v.tr.* cause (a person) to have asphyxia; suffocate; smother. ▫▫ **as·phyx·i·a·tion** /-áyshən/ *n.*

as·pic /áspik/ *n.* a savory meat jelly used as a garnish.

as·pi·dis·tra /áspidístrə/ *n.* a foliage plant of the genus *Aspidistra*, with broad tapering leaves, often grown as a houseplant.

as·pir·ant /áspirənt, əspírənt/ *adj.* & *n.* ● *adj.* aspiring. ● *n.* a person who aspires.

as·pi·rate /áspirət/ *adj.*, *n.*, & *v. Phonet.* ● *adj.* **1** pronounced with an exhalation of breath. **2** blended with the sound of *h*. ● *n.* **1** a consonant pronounced in this way. **2** the sound of *h*. ● *v.* also /áspiráyt/ **1 a** *tr.* pronounce with a breath. **b** *intr.* make the sound of *h*. **2** *tr.* draw (fluid) by suction from a vessel or cavity.

as·pi·ra·tion /áspiráyshən/ *n.* **1** an ambition. **2** the act of drawing breath. **3** the action of aspirating.

as·pi·ra·tor /áspiraytər/ *n.* an apparatus for aspirating fluid.

as·pire /əspír/ *v.intr.* have ambition.

as·pi·rin /ásprin/ *n.* (*pl.* same or **aspirins**) **1** a white powder, acetylsalicylic acid, used to relieve pain and reduce fever. **2** a tablet of this.

ass[1] /as/ *n.* **1 a** either of two kinds of four-legged long-eared mammals of the horse genus *Equus*, *E. africanus* of Africa and *E. hemionus* of Asia. **b** (in general use) a donkey. **2** a stupid person.

ass[2] /as/ *n.* & *v.* (*Brit.* **arse** /aars/) *coarse sl.* ● *n.* the buttocks. ● *v.intr.* (usu. foll. by *about, around*) play the fool. ¶ Usually considered a taboo word.

as·sa·gai var. of ASSEGAI.

as·sa·i /así/ *adv. Mus.* very (*adagio assai*).

as·sail /əsáyl/ *v.tr.* **1** make a concerted attack on. **2** make a resolute start on (a task). **3** make a constant verbal attack on. ▫▫ **as·sail·a·ble** *adj.*

as·sail·ant /əsáylənt/ *n.* a person who attacks another physically or verbally.

as·sas·sin /əsásin/ *n.* a killer, esp. of a political or religious leader.

as·sas·si·nate /əsásinayt/ *v.tr.* kill for political or religious motives. ▫▫ **as·sas·si·na·tion** /-náyshən/ *n.* **as·sas·si·na·tor** *n.*

as·sault /əsáwlt/ *n.* & *v.* ● *n.* **1** a violent attack. **2 a** *Law* an act that threatens physical harm to a person. **b** *euphem.* an act of rape. **3** (*attrib.*) relating to an assault (*assault troops*). **4** a vigorous start made to a lengthy task. **5** a final rush on a fortified place. ● *v.tr.* **1** make an assault on. **2** *euphem.* rape. ▫▫ **as·sault·er** *n.* **as·saul·tive** *adj.*

as·say /əsáy, ásay/ *n.* & *v.* ● *n.* **1** the testing of a metal or ore to determine its ingredients and quality. **2** *Chem.*, etc., the determination of the content or strength of a substance. ● *v.* **1** *tr.* make an assay of (a metal or ore). **2** *tr. Chem.* etc. perform a concentration on (a substance). **3** *tr.* show (content) on being assayed. **4** *intr.* make an assay. ▫▫ **as·say·er** *n.*

as·say of·fice *n.* an establishment which assays and registers prospecters' claims, gold sales, etc.

ass·back·wards *adv.* & *adj. N. Amer. colloq.* ● *adv.* in a manner contrary to what is usual, expected, or logical. ● *adj.* contrary to what is usual, expected, or logical.

as·se·gai /ásigī/ *n.* (also **as·sa·gai** /ásəgī/) ▶ a slender iron-tipped spear of hard wood, used by southern African peoples.

ASSEGAI

as·sem·blage /əsémblij/ *n.* **1** the act of bringing or coming together. **2** a collection of things or gathering of people.

as·sem·ble /əsémbəl/ *v.* **1** *tr.* & *intr.* gather together; collect. **2** *tr.* arrange in order. **3** *tr.* esp. *Mech.* fit together the parts of.

as·sem·bler /əsémblər/ *n.* **1** a person who assembles a machine or its parts. **2** *Computing* **a** a program for converting instructions written in low-level symbolic code into machine code. **b** the low-level symbolic code itself.

as·sem·bly /əsémblee/ *n.* (*pl.* **-ies**) **1** the act of gathering together. **2 a** a group of persons gathered together, esp. as a deliberative or legislative body. **b** a gathering of the entire membership of a school. **3** the assembling of a machine or structure or its parts. **4** *Mil.* a call to assemble, given by drum or bugle.

as·sem·bly lan·guage *n. Computing* the low-level symbolic code converted by an assembler.

as·sem·bly line *n.* machinery arranged in stages by which a product is progressively assembled.

as·sent /əsént/ *v.* & *n.* ● *v.intr.* (usu. foll. by *to*) **1** express agreement (*assented to my view*). **2** consent (*assented to my request*). ● *n.* **1** mental acceptance or agreement (*a nod of assent*). **2** consent or sanction, esp. official.

as·sert /əsə́rt/ *v.* **1** *tr.* state clearly. **2** *refl.* insist on one's rights. **3** *tr.* vindicate a claim to.

as·ser·tion /əsə́rshən/ *n.* **1** a forthright statement. **2** the act of asserting. **3** (also **self-assertion**) insistence on the recognition of one's rights.

as·ser·tive /əsə́rtiv/ *adj.* **1** tending to assert oneself; forthright; positive. **2** dogmatic. ▫▫ **as·ser·tive·ly** *adv.* **as·ser·tive·ness** *n.*

as·sess /əsés/ *v.tr.* **1 a** estimate the size or quality of. **b** estimate the value of (a property) for taxation. **2 a** fix the amount of (a tax, etc.) and impose it on a person or community. **b** fine or tax (a person, community, etc.) at a specific amount. ▫▫ **as·sess·a·ble** *adj.* **as·sess·ment** *n.*

as·ses·sor /əsésər/ *n.* **1** a person who assesses taxes or estimates the value of property for taxation purposes. **2** a person called upon to advise a judge, committee of inquiry, etc., on technical questions.

as·set /áset/ *n.* **1 a** a useful or valuable quality. **b** a person or thing possessing such a quality. **2** (usu. in *pl.*) property and possessions, regarded as having value in meeting debts, commitments, etc.

as·set strip·ping *n.* the practice of taking over a company and selling off its assets to make a profit.

as·sev·er·ate /əsévərayt/ *v.tr.* declare solemnly. ▫▫ **as·sev·er·a·tion** /-ráyshən/ *n.*

ass·hole /ás-hōl/ *n.* **1** the anus. **2** *offens.* a term of contempt for a person.

as·si·du·i·ty /ásidōō̆itee, -dyōō-/ *n.* (*pl.* **-ies**) constant or close attention to what one is doing.

as·sid·u·ous /əsíjōōəs/ *adj.* persevering; hardworking. ▫▫ **as·sid·u·ous·ly** *adv.* **as·sid·u·ous·ness** *n.*

as·sign /əsín/ *v.* & *n.* ● *v.tr.* **1 a** allot as a share or responsibility. **b** appoint to a position, task, etc. **2** fix (a time, place, etc.) for a specific purpose. **3** (foll. by *to*) ascribe to (a reason, date, etc.). **4** (foll. by *to*) transfer formally to. ● *n.* a person to whom property or rights are legally transferred. ▫▫ **as·sign·a·ble** *adj.*

as·sig·na·tion /ásignáyshən/ *n.* **1 a** an appointment to meet. **b** a secret appointment, esp. between illicit lovers. **2** the act of assigning.

as·sign·ee /ásīnée/ *n.* **1** a person appointed to act for another. **2** an assign.

as·sign·ment /əsínmənt/ *n.* **1** something assigned, esp. a task allotted to a person. **2** the act of assigning. **3 a** a legal transfer. **b** the document effecting this.

as·sim·i·late /əsímilayt/ *v.* **1** *tr.* **a** absorb (food, etc.) into the body. **b** absorb (information, etc.) into the mind. **c** absorb (people) into a larger group. **2** *tr.* cause to resemble. ▫▫ **as·sim·i·la·ble** /əsímələbəl/ *adj.* **as·sim·i·la·tion** /-láyshən/ *n.* **as·sim·i·la·tive** *adj.* **as·sim·i·la·tor** *n.* **as·sim·i·la·to·ry** /-lətáwree/ *adj.*

As·sin·i·boin /əsinəboyn/ *n.* **1 a** a N. American people native to northeastern Montana and adjoining parts of Canada. **b** a member of this people. **2** the language of this people.

as·sist /əsíst/ *v.* & *n.* ● *v.* **1** *tr.* help (a person, process, etc.). **2** *intr.* attend or be present. ● *n. Sports* a player's action of helping a teammate to put out a runner (as in baseball) or score (as in basketball). ▫▫ **as·sis·tance** *n.*

as·sis·tant /əsístənt/ *n.* **1** a helper. **2** (often *attrib.*) a person who assists.

as·so·ci·a·ble /əsṓshəbəl/ *adj.* (usu. foll. by *with*) capable of being connected in thought. ▫▫ **as·so·ci·a·bil·i·ty** *n.*

as·so·ci·ate *v.*, *n.*, & *adj.* ● *v.* /əsṓsheeayt, -see-/ **1** *tr.* connect in the mind. **2** *tr.* join or combine. **3** *refl.* make oneself a partner; declare oneself in agreement. **4** *intr.* combine for a common purpose. **5** *intr.* meet frequently or have dealings. ● *n.* /əsṓsheeət, -see-/ **1** a business partner or colleague. **2** a friend or companion. **3** a subordinate member of a body, institute, etc. ● *adj.* /əsṓshiət, əsṓsee-/ **1** joined in companionship, function, or dignity. **2** allied; in the same group or category. **3** of less than full status. ▫▫ **as·so·ci·ate·ship** *n.*

as·so·ci·a·tion /əsṓseeáyshən/ *n.* **1** a group of people organized for a joint purpose. **2** the act or an instance of associating. **3** fellowship; human contact or cooperation. **4** a mental connection between ideas. ▫▫ **as·so·ci·a·tion·al** *adj.*

as·so·ci·a·tive /əsṓsheeətiv, -see-/ *adj.* **1** of or involving association. **2** *Math.* & *Computing* involving the condition that a group of quantities connected by operators (see OPERATOR 4) gives the same result whatever their grouping, as long as their order remains the same, e.g., $(a \times b) \times c = a \times (b \times c)$.

as·so·nance /ásənəns/ *n.* the resemblance of sound between two syllables in nearby words, arising from the rhyming of two or more accented vowels, but not consonants, or the use of identical consonants with different vowels.

as·sort /əsáwrt/ *v.* **1** *tr.* classify in groups. **2** *intr.* suit; harmonize with.

as·sort·ed /əsáwrtid/ *adj.* **1** of various kinds put together; miscellaneous. **2** sorted into groups. **3** matched (*ill-assorted*; *poorly assorted*).

as·sort·ment /əsáwrtmənt/ *n.* a mixed collection.

as·suage /əswáyj/ *v.tr.* **1** soothe (a person, pain, etc.). **2** appease or relieve (an appetite or desire). ▫▫ **as·suage·ment** *n.*

as·sume /əsṓōm/ *v.tr.* **1** accept as being true, without proof, for the purpose of argument or action. **2** pretend (ignorance, etc.). **3** undertake (an office or duty). **4** take or put on oneself or itself (an aspect, attribute, etc.). **5** arrogate, usurp, or seize (credit, power, etc.).

as·sumed /əsṓōmd/ *adj.* **1** false; adopted (*went under an assumed name*). **2** supposed; accepted (*assumed income*).

as·sum·ing /əsṓōming/ *adj.* (of a person) taking too much for granted; arrogant; presumptuous.

as·sump·tion /əsúmpshən/ *n.* **1** the act or an instance of assuming. **2 a** the act or an instance of accepting without proof. **b** a thing assumed in this way. **3** arrogance. **4** (**Assumption**) the reception of the Virgin Mary bodily into heaven, according to Roman Catholic and Orthodox Christian belief.

as·sur·ance /əshŏŏrəns/ *n.* **1** a positive declaration that a thing is true. **2** a solemn promise or guarantee. **3** esp. *Brit.* insurance. **4** certainty. **5 a** self-confidence. **b** impudence.

as·sure /əshŏŏr/ *v.tr.* **1 a** make (a person) sure; convince (*assured him of my sincerity*). **b** tell (a person) confidently (*assured him the bus went to Baltimore*). **2 a** make certain of; ensure the happening, etc., of (*will assure her success*). **b** make safe (against overthrow, etc.). **3** *Brit.* insure. **4** (as **assured** *adj.*) **a** guaranteed.

ASTEROID

Asteroids are small bodies, composed of rock and iron, that did not aggregate to form planets when the solar system was born. They orbit the Sun, most of them traveling in a belt between Mars and Jupiter. Jupiter's gravitational pull can send asteroids into erratic orbits, causing them to collide with planets and other asteroids.

ASTEROID BELT
ORBITING THE SUN

Sun

asteroid belt

Earth

Jupiter

Venus

Mars

A

b self-confident. □ **rest assured** remain confident. □□ **as·sur·er** *n.*

as·sur·ed·ly /əshŏŏridlee/ *adv.* certainly.

as·sur·ed·ness /əshŏŏridnis/ *n.* certainty; (self-) assurance.

AST *abbr.* Atlantic Standard Time.

as·ta·tine /ástəteen, -tin/ *n. Chem.* a radioactive element, the heaviest of the halogens, which occurs naturally. ¶ Symb.: **At**.

as·ter /ástər/ *n.* a plant of the genus *Aster*, with bright daisylike flowers.

as·ter·isk /ástərisk/ *n. & v.* ● *n.* a symbol (*) used in printing and writing to mark words, etc., for reference, to stand for omitted matter, etc. ● *v.tr.* mark with an asterisk.

as·ter·ism /ástərizəm/ *n.* **1** a cluster of stars. **2** a group of three asterisks (* *) calling attention to following text.

a·stern /əstərn/ *adv. Naut. & Aeron.* **1** aft; away to the rear. **2** backward.

as·ter·oid /ástəroyd/ *n.* **1** ▲ any of the small celestial bodies revolving around the Sun. **2** *Zool.* a starfish. ▷ ECHINODERM, STARFISH. □□ **as·ter·oi·dal** /ástəróyd'l/ *adj.*

as·the·ni·a /asthéeneeə/ *n. Med.* loss of strength.

as·then·ic /asthénik/ *adj.* **1** of a lean or long-limbed build; ectomorphic. **2** *Med.* of or characterized by asthenia.

asth·ma /ázmə, ás-/ *n.* a respiratory disease, often with paroxysms of difficult breathing.

asth·mat·ic /azmátik, as-/ *adj. & n.* ● *adj.* relating to or suffering from asthma. ● *n.* a person suffering from asthma. □□ **asth·mat·i·cal·ly** *adv.*

a·stig·ma·tism /əstígmətizəm/ *n.* a defect in the eye or in a lens resulting in distorted images, as light rays are prevented from meeting at a common focus. □□ **a·stig·mat·ic** /ástigmátik/ *adj.*

a·stir /əstər/ *predic.adj. & adv.* **1** in motion. **2** awake and out of bed (*astir early; already astir*). **3** excited.

as·ton·ish /əstónish/ *v.tr.* amaze; surprise greatly. □□ **as·ton·ish·ing** *adj.* **as·ton·ish·ing·ly** *adv.* **as·ton·ish·ment** *n.*

as·tound /əstównd/ *v.tr.* shock with alarm or surprise; amaze. □□ **as·tound·ing** *adj.* **as·tound·ing·ly** *adv.*

as·tra·khan /ástrəkan/ *n.* the dark curly fleece of young karakul lambs from central Asia.

as·tral /ástrəl/ *adj.* **1** of or connected with the stars. **2** consisting of stars.

a·stray /əstráy/ *adv. & predic.adj.* **1** in or into error or sin (esp. **lead astray**). **2** out of the right way. □ **go astray** be lost or misled.

a·stride /əstríd/ *adv. & prep.* ● *adv.* **1** with a leg on each side. **2** with legs apart. ● *prep.* with a leg on each side of.

as·trin·gent /əstrínjənt/ *adj. & n.* ● *adj.* **1** causing the contraction of body tissues. **2** checking bleeding. **3** severe; austere. ● *n.* an astringent substance or drug. □□ **as·trin·gen·cy** /-jənsee/ *n.* **as·trin·gent·ly** *adv.*

astro- /ástrō/ *comb. form* **1** relating to the stars. **2** relating to outer space.

as·tro·chem·is·try /ástrōkémistree/ *n.* the study of molecules and radicals in interstellar space.

as·tro·dome /ástrədōm/ *n.* a domed window in an aircraft for astronomical observations.

as·tro·hatch /ástrəhach/ *n.* = ASTRODOME.

as·tro·labe /ástrəlayb/ *n.* ▶ an instrument, usu. consisting of a disk and pointer, formerly used to make astronomical measurements, esp. of the altitudes of celestial bodies, and as an aid in navigation.

as·trol·o·gy /əstróləjee/ *n.* the study of the movements and relative positions of celestial bodies interpreted as an influence on human affairs. ▷ ZODIAC. □□ **as·trol·o·ger** *n.* **as·tro·log·i·cal** /ástrəlójikəl/ *adj.* **as·trol·o·gist** *n.*

as·tro·naut /ástrənawt/ *n.* a person who is trained to travel in a spacecraft. □□ **as·tro·nau·ti·cal** /-náwtikəl/ *adj.*

as·tro·nau·tics /ástrənáwtiks/ *n.* the science of space travel.

as·tro·nom·i·cal /ástrənómikəl/ *adj.* (also **as·tro·nom·ic**) **1** of or relating to astronomy. **2** extremely large; too large to contemplate. □□ **as·tro·nom·i·cal·ly** *adv.*

as·tro·nom·i·cal u·nit *n.* a unit of measurement in astronomy equal to the mean distance from the center of the Earth to the center of the Sun.

as·tron·o·my /əstrónəmee/ *n.* the scientific study of celestial bodies and other matter beyond Earth's atmosphere. □□ **as·tron·o·mer** *n.*

as·tro·phys·ics /ástrōfíziks/ *n.* a branch of astronomy concerned with the physics of celestial bodies. □□ **as·tro·phys·i·cal** *adj.* **as·tro·phys·i·cist** /-zisist/ *n.*

As·tro·turf /ástrōtərf/ *n. propr.* an artificial grass surface, esp. for sports fields.

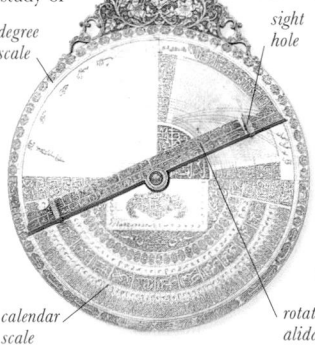

sight hole

degree scale

calendar scale

rotating alidade

ASTROLABE: 18TH-CENTURY PERSIAN ASTROLABE

as·tute /əstŏŏt, əstyŏŏt/ *adj.* **1** shrewd. **2** crafty. □□ **as·tute·ly** *adv.* **as·tute·ness** *n.*

a·sun·der /əsúndər/ *adv. literary* apart.

a·sy·lum /əsíləm/ *n.* **1** sanctuary; protection (*seek asylum*). **2** *hist.* any of various kinds of institution offering shelter to distressed individuals, esp. the mentally ill.

a·sym·me·try /aysímitree/ *n.* lack of symmetry. □□ **a·sym·met·ric** /-métrik/ *adj.* **a·sym·met·ri·cal** *adj.* **a·sym·met·ri·cal·ly** /-métrikəlee/ *adv.*

a·symp·to·mat·ic /áysimptəmátik/ *adj.* producing or showing no symptoms.

a·syn·chro·nous /aysíngkrənəs/ *adj.* not synchronous. □□ **a·syn·chro·nous·ly** *adv.*

a·syn·de·ton /əsínditən/ *n.* (*pl.* **asyndeta** /-tə/) the omission of a conjunction. □□ **as·yn·det·ic** /ásindétik/ *adj.*

At *symb. Chem.* the element astatine.

at /at, *unstressed* ət/ *prep.* **1** expressing position, exact or approximate (*wait at the corner; is at school; at a distance*). **2** expressing a point in time (*see you at three; went at dawn*). **3** expressing a point in a scale or range (*at boiling point; at his best*). **4** expressing engagement or concern in a state or activity (*at work; at odds*). **5** expressing a value or rate (*sell at $10 each*). **6 a** with or with reference to; in terms of (*at a disadvantage; annoyed at losing; good at soccer; sick at heart; at short notice*). **b** by means of (*drank it at a gulp*). **7** expressing: **a** motion toward (*went at them*). **b** aim toward or pursuit of (*aim at the target; guess at the truth; laughed at us; has been at the milk again*). □ **at that** moreover (*found one, and a good one at that*).

at·a·rac·tic /átəráktik/ *adj. & n.* (also **at·a·rax·ic** /-ráksik/) ● *adj.* calming. ● *n.* a tranquilizing drug.

at·a·rax·y /átəraksee/ *n.* (also **at·a·rax·i·a** /-rákseeə/) calmness or tranquility; imperturbability.

at·a·vism /átəvizəm/ *n.* **1** a resemblance to remote ancestors rather than to parents in plants or animals. **2** reversion to an earlier type. □□ **at·a·vis·tic** *adj.* **at·a·vis·ti·cal·ly** *adv.*

a·tax·i·a /ətáskseeə/ *n. Med.* the loss of full control of bodily movements. □□ **a·tax·ic** *adj.*

ATC *abbr.* **1** air traffic control. **2** Air Training Corps.

ate *past of* EAT.

at·el·ier /átəlyáy/ *n.* a workshop or studio, esp. of an artist or designer.

a tem·po /aa témpō/ *adv. Mus.* in the previous tempo.

a·the·ism /áytheeizəm/ *n.* the theory or belief that God does not exist. □□ **a·the·ist** *n.* **a·the·is·tic** *adj.* **a·the·is·ti·cal** *adj.*

a·the·mat·ic /áytheemátik/ *adj.* **1** *Mus.* not based on the use of themes. **2** *Gram.* (of a verb form) having a suffix attached to the stem without a connecting (thematic) vowel.

ath·e·nae·um /áthinéeəm/ *n.* (also **ath·e·ne·um**) **1** an institution for literary or scientific study. **2** a library.

ath·er·o·scle·ro·sis /áthərōsklərṓsis/ *n.* a form of arteriosclerosis characterized by the degeneration of the arteries because of a buildup of fatty deposits. □□ **ath·er·o·scle·rot·ic** /-rótik/ *adj.*

a·thirst /əthúrst/ *predic.adj. poet.* **1** (usu. foll. by *for*) eager (*athirst for knowledge*). **2** thirsty.

ath·lete /áthleet/ *n.* **1** a skilled performer in sports and physical activities, esp. *Brit.* in track and field events. **2** a person with natural athletic ability.

ath·lete's foot *n.* a fungal foot condition affecting esp. the skin between the toes.

ath·let·ic /athlétik/ *adj.* **1** of or relating to athletes or athletics (*an athletic competition*). **2** muscular or physically powerful. □□ **ath·let·i·cal·ly** *adv.* **ath·let·i·cism** /-tizəm/ *n.*

A

ATMOSPHERE

The Earth's atmosphere is about 430 miles (700 km) deep and is divided into five main layers according to the way the temperature changes with height. The lowest layer, the troposphere, contains over 75 percent of all the gas in the atmosphere, as well as vast quantities of water. Air movement in this layer produces the Earth's weather. Above the troposphere are the stratosphere, mesosphere, thermosphere, and exosphere. The ozone layer lies within the stratosphere, providing protection from the Sun's harmful ultraviolet rays. Some radio signals travel great distances by bouncing off the ionosphere, a layer that is made up of electrically charged (ionized) gas particles.

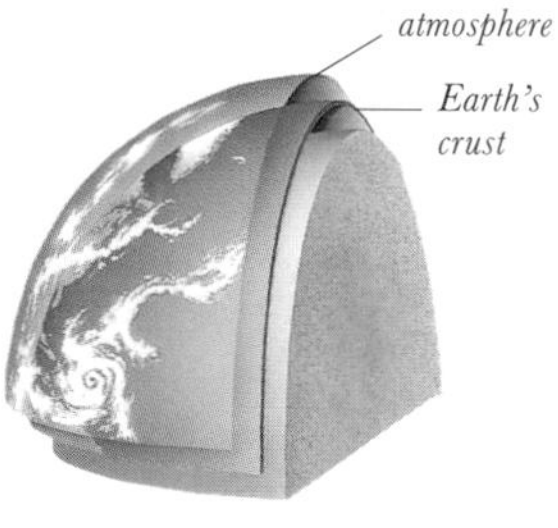

exosphere

satellite

high-level aurora

meteor

thermosphere

low-level aurora

ionosphere

radio waves

mesosphere

stratosphere

troposphere

atmosphere

Earth's crust

SECTION OF THE EARTH SHOWING THE RELATIVE THICKNESS OF ITS ATMOSPHERE

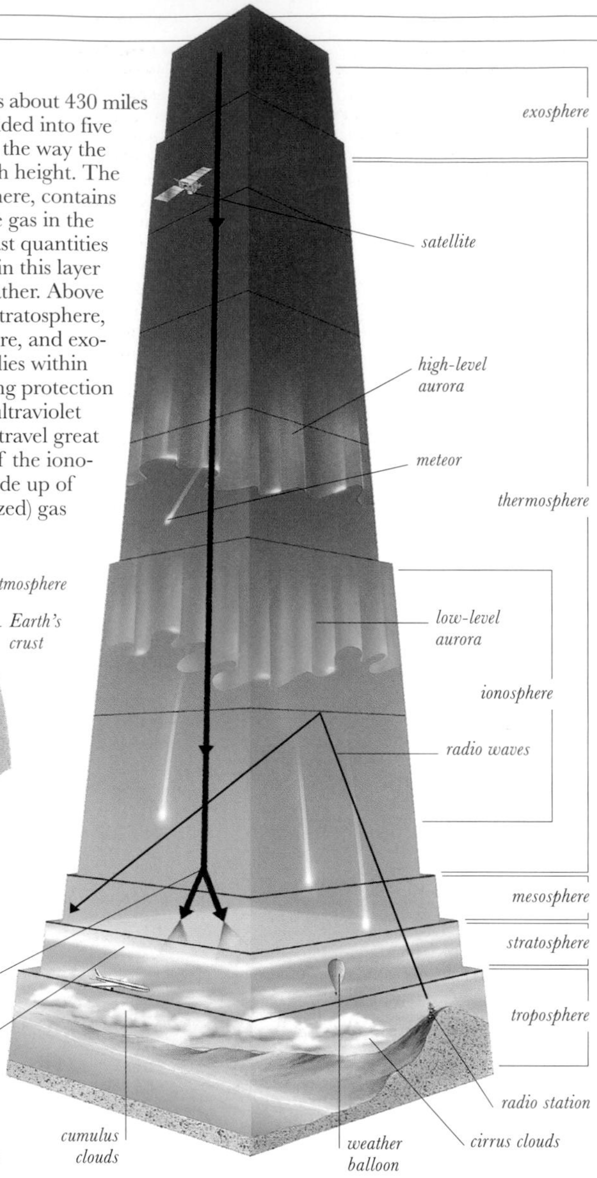

ultraviolet rays

ozone layer

DIVISIONS OF THE EARTH'S ATMOSPHERE

cumulus clouds

weather balloon

radio station

cirrus clouds

---

at·om bomb *n.* a bomb involving the release of energy by nuclear fission.

a·tom·ic /ǝtómik/ *adj.* **1** concerned with or using atomic energy or atomic bombs. **2** of or relating to an atom or atoms. □□ **a·tom·i·cal·ly** *adv.*

a·tom·ic bomb *n.* = ATOM BOMB.

a·tom·ic clock *n.* ▼ a clock in which the time scale is regulated by the vibrations of an atomic or molecular system, such as cesium.

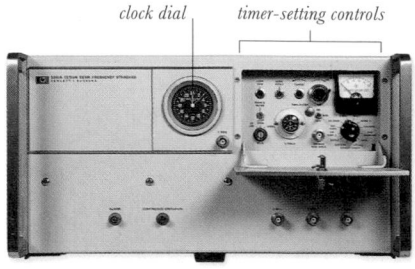

clock dial   *timer-setting controls*

ATOMIC CLOCK

a·tom·ic en·er·gy *n.* nuclear energy. ▷ NUCLEAR POWER

at·o·mic·i·ty /átǝmísitee/ *n.* **1** the number of atoms in the molecules of an element. **2** the state or fact of being composed of atoms.

a·tom·ic mass *n.* the mass of an atom measured in atomic mass units.

a·tom·ic mass u·nit *n.* a unit of mass used to express atomic and molecular weight.

a·tom·ic num·ber *n.* the number of protons in the nucleus of an atom, which is characteristic of a chemical element and determines its place in the periodic table.

a·tom·ic par·ti·cle *n.* any one of the particles of which an atom is constituted.

a·tom·ic phys·ics *n.* the branch of physics concerned with the structure of the atom and the characteristics of the elementary particles of which it is composed.

a·tom·ic pow·er *n.* nuclear power. ▷ NUCLEAR POWER

a·tom·ic struc·ture *n.* the structure of an atom as being a central positively charged nucleus surrounded by negatively charged orbiting electrons.

a·tom·ic the·o·ry *n.* **1** the concept of an atom as being composed of elementary particles. **2** the theory that all matter is made up of small indivisible particles called atoms.

a·tom·ic weight *n.* the ratio of the average mass of

---

ath·let·ics /athlétiks/ *n.pl.* (usu. treated as *sing.*) **1 a** physical exercises, esp. *Brit.* track and field events. ▷ TRACK. **b** the practice of these. **2** physical sports and games of any kind.

a·thwart /ǝthwáwrt/ *adv. & prep.* ● *adv.* **1** across from side to side (usu. obliquely). **2** perversely or in opposition. ● *prep.* **1** from side to side of. **2** in opposition to.

a·tilt /ǝtílt/ *adv.* tilted and nearly falling.

At·lan·tic /ǝtlántik/ *n. & adj.* ● *n.* the ocean between Europe and Africa to the east, and North and South America to the west. ▷ OCEAN. ● *adj.* of the Atlantic.

At·lan·tic time *n.* the standard time used in the most eastern parts of Canada and in parts of the Caribbean.

at·las /átlǝs/ *n.* a book of maps or charts.

ATM *abbr.* automatic teller machine.

at·man /áatmǝn/ *n. Hinduism* **1** the real self. **2** the supreme spiritual principle.

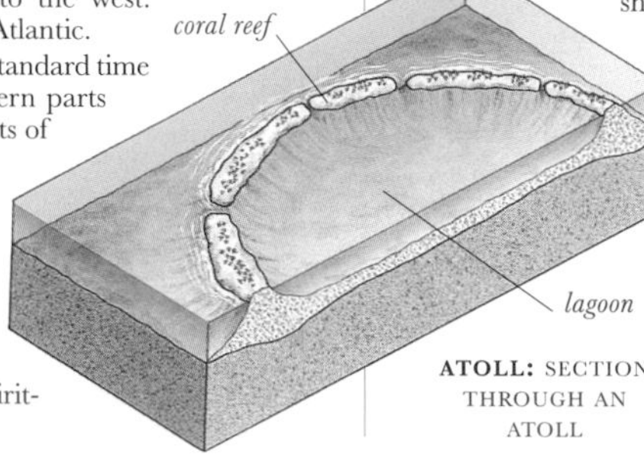

at·mos·phere /átmǝsfeer/ *n.* **1 a** ▲ the envelope of gases surrounding the Earth, any other planet, or any substance. **b** the air in any particular place. **2** the pervading tone or mood of a place or situation. **3** *Physics* a unit of pressure equal to mean atmospheric pressure at sea level. □□ **at·mos·pher·ic** /-férik, -féer-/ *adj.* **at·mos·pher·i·cal·ly** *adv.*

at·mos·pher·ics /átmǝsfériks, -féer-/ *n.pl.* **1** electrical disturbance in the atmosphere. **2** interference with telecommunications caused by this.

at·oll /átawl, átol, áy-/ *n.* ◀ a ring-shaped coral reef enclosing a lagoon.

at·om /átǝm/ *n.* **1 a** ▶ the smallest particle of a chemical element that can take part in a chemical reaction. ▷ NUCLEUS. **b** this particle as a source of nuclear energy (*the power of the atom*). ▷ NUCLEAR FISSION, NUCLEAR FUSION. **2** (usu. with *neg.*) the least portion of a thing or quality (*not an atom of pity*).

coral reef

lagoon

ATOLL: SECTION THROUGH AN ATOLL

ATOM

Inside an atom is a nucleus composed of protons and neutrons. The nucleus is orbited by electrons, traveling so fast that they seem to form a solid shell. The atom of carbon-12 shown is so named because its nucleus has six protons and six neutrons. Electrons surround its nucleus in two separate layers.

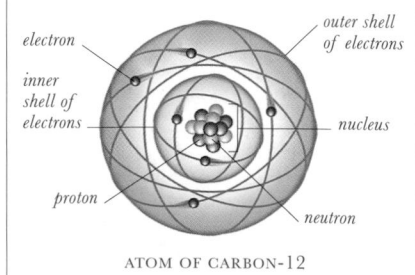

electron

inner shell of electrons

proton

outer shell of electrons

nucleus

neutron

ATOM OF CARBON-12

one atom of an element to one twelfth of the mass of an atom of carbon-12. Also called **relative atomic mass**.

at·om·ism /átəmizəm/ *n. Philos.* **1** the theory that all matter consists of tiny individual particles. **2** *Psychol.* the theory that mental states are made up of elementary units. □□ **at·om·ist** *n.* **at·om·is·tic** /-místik/ *adj.*

at·om·ize /átəmíz/ *v.tr.* reduce to atoms or fine particles. □□ **at·om·i·za·tion** *n.*

at·om·iz·er /átəmīzər/ *n.* an instrument for emitting liquids as a fine spray.

at·om·y /átəmee/ *n.* (*pl.* **-ies**) *archaic* **1** a skeleton. **2** an emaciated body.

a·ton·al /áytōn'l/ *adj. Mus.* not written in any key or mode. □□ **a·to·nal·i·ty** /-nálitee/ *n.*

a·tone /ətón/ *v.intr.* (usu. foll. by *for*) make amends.

a·tone·ment /ətónmənt/ *n.* **1** expiation; reparation for a wrong or injury. **2** the reconciliation of God and humans. **3** (**the Atonement**) the expiation by Christ of humankind's sin.

a·ton·ic /ətónik/ *adj.* **1** without accent or stress. **2** *Med.* lacking bodily tone. □□ **at·o·ny** /átənee/ *n.*

a·top /ətóp/ *adv. & prep.* ● *adv.* on the top. ● *prep.* on the top of.

ATP *abbr.* adenosine triphosphate.

at·ra·bil·i·ous /átrəbílyəs/ *adj.* melancholy; ill-tempered.

a·tri·um /áytreeəm/ *n.* (*pl.* **atriums** or **atria** /-treeə/) **1 a** the central court of an ancient Roman house. **b** ▶ a central court rising through several stories with galleries and rooms opening off at each level. **c** (in a modern house) a central hall or courtyard with rooms opening off it. **2** *Anat.* a cavity in the body, esp. one of the two upper cavities of the heart, receiving blood from the veins. ▷ HEART. □□ **a·tri·al** *adj.*

a·tro·cious /ətróshəs/ *adj.* **1** very bad or unpleasant (*atrocious weather*). **2** extremely savage or wicked (*atrocious cruelty*). □□ **a·tro·cious·ly** *adv.*

a·troc·i·ty /ətrósitee/ *n.* (*pl.* **-ies**) **1** an extremely evil or cruel act. **2** extreme wickedness.

at·ro·phy /átrəfee/ *v. & n.* ● *v.* (**-ies, -ied**) **1** *intr.* waste away through undernourishment or lack of use. **2** *tr.* cause to atrophy. ● *n.* the process of atrophying.

at·ro·pine /átrəpeen, -pin/ *n.* a poisonous alkaloid found in deadly nightshade, used in medicine to treat renal and biliary colic, etc.

at·tach /ətách/ *v.* **1** *tr.* fasten; affix; join. **2** *tr.* (in *passive*; foll. by *to*) be very fond of or devoted to (*am deeply attached to her*). **3** *tr.* attribute; assign (some function, quality, or characteristic) (*attaches great importance to it*). **4 a** *tr.* include (*attach no conditions to the agreement*). **b** *intr.* (foll. by *to*) be an attribute or characteristic (*great prestige attaches to the job*). **5** *refl.* join; take part (*climbers attached themselves to the expedition*). **6** *tr.* appoint for special or temporary duties. **7** *tr. Law* seize (a person or property) by legal authority. □□ **at·tach·a·ble** *adj.*

at·ta·ché /atasháy/ *n.* a person appointed to an ambassador's staff (*military attaché; press attaché*).

at·ta·ché case *n.* a small flat rectangular case for carrying documents, etc.

at·tached /ətácht/ *adj.* **1** fixed; connected; enclosed. **2** (of a person) involved in a long-term relationship, esp. engagement or marriage.

at·tach·ment /ətáchmənt/ *n.* **1** a thing attached or to be attached. **2** affection; devotion. **3** a means of attaching. **4** the act of attaching. **5** legal seizure.

at·tack /əták/ *v. & n.* ● *v.* **1** *tr.* act against with force. **2** *tr.* seek to hurt or defeat. **3** *tr.* criticize adversely. **4** *tr.* act harmfully upon (*a virus attacking the nervous system*). **5** *tr.* vigorously apply oneself to (*attacked his meal with gusto*). **6** *intr.* make an attack. **7** *intr.* be in a mode of attack. ● *n.* **1** the act of attacking. **2** an offensive operation. **3** *Mus.* the action of beginning a piece, passage, etc. **4** gusto; vigor. **5** a sudden occurrence of an illness. **6** a player or players seeking to score goals, etc.; offensive players. □□ **at·tack·er** *n.*

at·tain /ətáyn/ *v.* **1** *tr.* reach (a goal, etc.). **2** *tr.* accomplish (an aim, distinction, etc.). **3** *intr.* (foll. by *to*) arrive at by conscious development. □□ **at·tain·a·ble** *adj.* **at·tain·a·bil·i·ty** *n.*

at·tain·der /ətáyndər/ *n. hist.* the forfeiture of land and civil rights suffered as a consequence of a sentence of death for treason or felony. □ **act** (or **bill**) **of attainder** an item of legislation inflicting attainder without judicial process.

at·tain·ment /ətáynmənt/ *n.* **1** something achieved. **2** the act of attaining.

at·taint /ətáynt/ *v.tr.* **1** *hist.* subject to attainder. **2 a** (of disease, etc.) strike; affect. **b** *archaic* taint.

at·tar /átaar/ *n.* (also **ot·to** /ótō/) a fragrant essential oil, esp. from rose petals.

at·tempt /ətémpt/ *v. & n.* ● *v.tr.* seek to achieve or master (a task, action, etc.). ● *n.* an endeavor (*an attempt to succeed*).

at·tend /əténd/ *v.* **1** *tr.* **a** be present at (*attended the meeting*). **b** go regularly to (*attends the local school*). **2** *intr.* **a** be present (*many members failed to attend*). **b** be present in a serving capacity. **3** *a. tr.* escort (*the king was attended by soldiers*). **b** *intr.* (foll. by *on*) wait on. **4** *intr.* **a** apply one's mind (*attend to what I am saying*). **b** (foll. by *to*) deal with (*shall attend to the matter myself*). **5** *tr.* follow as a result from (*the error was attended by serious consequences*). □□ **at·tend·er** *n.*

at·tend·ance /əténdəns/ *n.* **1** the act of attending. **2** the number of people present (*a high attendance*).

at·tend·ant /əténdənt/ *n. & adj.* ● *n.* a person employed to wait on others. ● *adj.* **1** accompanying. **2** waiting on.

at·tend·ee /áténdeé/ *n.* a person who attends (a meeting, etc.).

at·ten·tion /əténshən/ *n. & int.* ● *n.* **1** the act or faculty of applying one's mind (*attract his attention*). **2** a consideration (*give attention to the problem*). **3** (in *pl.*) **a** ceremonious politeness (*he paid his attentions to her*). **b** wooing (*he was the subject of her attentions*). **4** *Mil.* an erect attitude of readiness (*stand at attention*). ● *int.* (in full **stand to attention!**) *Mil.* an order to assume an attitude of attention.

at·ten·tion def·i·cit hy·per·ac·tiv·i·ty dis·or·der *n.* (also **attention deficit disorder**) a behavioral disorder occurring primarily in children, including such symptoms as poor concentration, hyperactivity, and learning difficulties. ¶ Abbr.: **ADHD**.

at·ten·tive /əténtiv/ *adj.* **1** paying attention. **2** assiduously polite. **3** heedful. □□ **at·ten·tive·ly** *adv.* **at·ten·tive·ness** *n.*

at·ten·u·ate *v. & adj.* ● *v.tr.* /ətényōoayt/ **1** make thin. **2** reduce in force, value, or virulence. ● *adj.* /ətényōoət/ **1** slender. **2** tapering gradually. **3** rarefied. □□ **at·ten·u·at·ed** *adj.* **at·ten·u·a·tion** /-áyshən/ *n.* **at·ten·u·a·tor** *n.*

at·test /ətést/ *v.* **1** *tr.* certify the validity of. **2** *intr.* (foll. by *to*) bear witness to. □□ **at·test·a·ble** *adj.* **at·tes·tor** *n.*

ATRIUM IN A 19TH-CENTURY AUSTRALIAN SHOPPING ARCADE

At·tic /átik/ *adj.* of or relating to ancient Athens or Attica, or the form of Greek spoken there.

at·tic /átik/ *n.* **1** the uppermost story in a house, usu. under the roof. **2** a room in the attic area.

at·tire /ətír/ *v. & n. formal* ● *v.tr.* dress, esp. in fine clothes or formal wear. ● *n.* clothes, esp. fine or formal.

at·ti·tude /átitōod, -tyōod/ *n.* **1 a** a settled opinion. **b** behavior reflecting this. **2 a** a bodily posture. **b** a pose adopted for dramatic effect. □□ **at·ti·tu·di·nal** /-tōod'nəl, -tyōod-/ *adj.*

at·ti·tu·di·nize /átitōod'nīz, -tyōod-/ *v.intr.* **1** practice or adopt attitudes, esp. for effect. **2** speak, write, or behave affectedly.

at·tor·ney /ətórnee/ *n.* (*pl.* **-eys**) **1** a person appointed to act for another in business or legal matters. **2** a qualified lawyer, esp. one representing a client in a court of law. □□ **at·tor·ney·ship** *n.*

at·tor·ney gen·er·al *n.* the chief legal officer in the US, England, and other countries.

at·tract /ətrákt/ *v.tr.* **1** (also *absol.*) draw to oneself or itself. **2** be attractive to. **3** (of a magnet, etc.) exert a pull on (an object). □□ **at·tract·a·ble** *adj.* **at·trac·tor** *n.*

at·tract·ant /ətráktənt/ *n. & adj.* ● *n.* a substance which attracts (esp. insects). ● *adj.* attracting.

at·trac·tion /ətrákshən/ *n.* **1 a** the power of attracting (*the attraction of foreign travel*). **b** a person or thing that attracts by arousing interest (*the fair is a big attraction*). **2** *Physics* the force by which bodies attract or approach each other (opp. REPULSION).

at·trac·tive /ətráktiv/ *adj.* **1** attracting or capable of attracting (*an attractive proposition*). **2** aesthetically pleasing. □□ **at·trac·tive·ly** *adv.* **at·trac·tive·ness** *n.*

at·trib·ute *v. & n.* ● *v.tr.* /ətríbyōot/ (foll. by *to*) **1** regard as belonging or appropriate (*a poem attributed to Shakespeare*). **2** ascribe; regard as the effect of a stated cause (*the delays were attributed to the heavy traffic*). ● *n.* /átribyōot/ **1 a** a quality ascribed to a person or thing. **b** a characteristic quality. **2 a** material object recognized as appropriate to a person, office, or status. □□ **at·trib·ut·a·ble** /ətríbyōotəbəl/ *adj.* **at·tri·bu·tion** /-byōoshən/ *n.*

at·trib·u·tive /ətríbyətiv/ *adj. Gram* (of an adjective or noun) preceding the word described and expressing an attribute, as *old* in *the old dog* and *expiration* in *expiration date* (opp. PREDICATIVE). □□ **at·trib·u·tive·ly** *adv.*

at·tri·tion /ətríshən/ *n.* **1** the act or process of gradually wearing out, esp. by friction. **2** abrasion. □□ **at·tri·tion·al** *adj.*

at·tune /ətōōn, ətyōōn/ *v.tr.* **1** adjust (a person or thing) to a situation. **2** bring (an orchestra, instrument, etc.) into musical accord.

atty. *abbr.* attorney.

Atty. Gen. *abbr.* Attorney General.

ATV *abbr.* all-terrain vehicle.

a·typ·i·cal /áytípikəl/ *adj.* not conforming to a type. □□ **a·typ·i·cal·ly** *adv.*

Au *symb. Chem.* the element gold.

au·bade /ōbáad/ *n.* a poem or piece of music appropriate to the dawn or early morning.

au·burn /áwbərn/ *adj.* reddish brown (usu. of a person's hair).

AUC *abbr.* (of a date) from the foundation of the city (of Rome) (Latin *ab urbe condita*).

auc·tion /áwkshən/ *n. & v.* ● *n.* a sale of goods in which articles are sold to the highest bidder. ● *v.tr.* sell at auction.

auc·tion bridge *n.* a form of bridge in which players bid for the right to name trumps.

auc·tion·eer /áwkshəneér/ *n.* a person who conducts auctions professionally, by calling for bids and declaring goods sold. □□ **auc·tion·eer·ing** *n.*

au·da·cious /awdáyshəs/ *adj.* **1** daring; bold. **2** impudent. □□ **au·da·cious·ly** *adv.* **au·da·cious·ness** *n.* **au·dac·i·ty** /awdásitee/ *n.*

au·di·ble /áwdibəl/ *adj.* capable of being heard. □□ **au·di·bil·i·ty** *n.* **au·di·bly** *adv.*

A

AUDITORIUM

Myriad seating variations have been devised to allow an audience to fully appreciate a performance in a theater or concert hall. Most make use of tiered seating, angled to give spectators an unobstructed view of the stage. In the auditorium shown here, balconies and seating behind the stage are included to maximize audience capacity.

rear seating　*movable tier*　*balcony*

tiered seating　*stage-side seating*

CUTAWAY MODEL OF A THEATER AUDITORIUM　*stage*　*orchestra*

---

au·di·ence /áwdeeəns/ *n.* **1 a** the assembled listeners or spectators at an event. **b** the people addressed by a movie, play, etc. **2** a formal interview with a person in authority.

au·dile /áwdīl/ *adj.* of or referring to the sense of hearing.

au·di·o /áwdeeō/ *n.* (usu. *attrib.*) sound or the reproduction of sound.

audio- /áwdeeō/ *comb. form* hearing or sound.

au·di·o·cas·sette /áwdeeōkəsét/ *n.* an audiotape enclosed within a cassette.

au·di·o fre·quen·cy *n.* a frequency capable of being perceived by the human ear.

au·di·ol·o·gy /áwdeeóləjee/ *n.* the science of hearing. □□ **au·di·ol·o·gist** *n.*

au·di·om·e·ter /áwdeeómitər/ *n.* an instrument for testing hearing.

au·di·o·phile /áwdeeōfīl/ *n.* a high-fidelity sound enthusiast.

au·di·o·tape /áwdeeōtayp/ *n.* **1 a** magnetic tape on which sound can be recorded. **b** a length of this. **2** a sound recording on tape.

au·di·o·vis·u·al /áwdeeōvízhyōōəl/ *adj.* using both sight and sound.

au·dit /áwdit/ *n. & v.* ● *n.* an official examination of accounts. ● *v.tr.* (**audited, auditing**) **1** conduct an audit of. **2** attend (a class) informally, without working for a grade or credit.

au·di·tion /awdíshən/ *n. & v.* ● *n.* an interview for a performer, consisting of a practical demonstration of suitability. ● *v.* **1** *tr.* interview (a candidate) at an audition. **2** *intr.* be interviewed at an audition.

au·di·tive /áwditiv/ *adj.* concerned with hearing.

au·di·tor /áwditər/ *n.* **1** a person who audits accounts. **2** a person who audits a class. **3** a listener. □□ **au·di·to·ri·al** /-táwreeəl/ *adj.*

au·di·to·ri·um /áwditáwreeəm/ *n.* (*pl.* **auditoriums** or **auditoria** /-reeə/) ▲ the part of a theater, etc., in which the audience sits. ▷ AMPHITHEATER, THEATER

au·di·to·ry /áwditawree/ *adj.* **1** concerned with hearing. **2** received by the ear.

au fait /ō fáy/ *predic.adj.* (usu. foll. by *with*) having current knowledge (*au fait with the arrangements*).

Aug. *abbr.* August.

Au·ge·an /awjéeən/ *adj.* **1** filthy. **2** extremely difficult and unpleasant.

au·ger /áwgər/ *n.* a tool resembling a large corkscrew, for boring holes. ▷ COMBINE HARVESTER

aught /awt/ *n.* (also **ought**) *archaic* (usu. implying *neg.*) anything at all.

aug·ment /awgmént/ *v.tr. & intr.* increase. □□ **aug·ment·er** *n.*

aug·men·ta·tion /áwgmentáyshən/ *n.* **1** enlargement; growth; increase. **2** *Mus.* the lengthening of the time values of notes in melodic parts.

aug·men·ta·tive /awgméntətiv/ *adj.* having the property of increasing.

au grat·in /ō grátán/ *adj. Cookery* cooked with a crisp brown crust, usu. of breadcrumbs or melted cheese.

au·gur /áwgər/ *v. & n.* ● *v.* **1** *intr.* (of an event, circumstance, etc.) suggest a specified outcome (usu. **augur well** or **ill**). **2** *tr.* **a** foresee; predict. **b** portend. ● *n.* an ancient Roman religious official who observed natural signs, esp. the behavior of birds, interpreting these as an indication of divine approval or disapproval of a proposed action. □□ **au·gu·ral** *adj.*

au·gu·ry /áwgyəree/ *n.* (*pl.* **-ies**) **1** an omen. **2** the interpretation of omens.

Au·gust /áwgəst/ *n.* the eighth month of the year.

au·gust /awgúst/ *adj.* inspiring reverence. □□ **au·gust·ly** *adv.* **au·gust·ness** *n.*

Au·gus·tan /awgústən/ *adj. & n.* ● *adj.* **1** connected with the reign of the Roman emperor Augustus, esp. as an outstanding period of Latin literature. **2** (of a nation's literature) refined and classical in style (as the literature of the 17th–18th century in England). ● *n.* a writer of the Augustan age of any literature.

Au·gus·tin·i·an /áwgəstíneeən/ *adj. & n.* ● *adj.* **1** of or relating to St. Augustine or his doctrines. **2** belonging to a religious order observing a rule derived from St. Augustine's writings. ● *n.* one of the order of Augustinian friars.

auk /awk/ *n.* ▶ any sea diving bird of the family Alcidae, with heavy body, short wings, and black and white plumage, e.g., the puffin. ▷ SEABIRD

AUK:
LITTLE AUK
(*Alle alle*)

---

auld lang syne /áwld lang zīn, sín/ *n.* **1** times long past. □ **for auld lang syne** for old times' sake.

au na·tu·rel /ő nachərél/ *predic.adj. & adv.* **1** uncooked; (cooked) in the most natural or simplest way. **2** naked.

aunt /ant, aant/ *n.* **1** the sister of one's father or mother. **2** an uncle's wife. **3** *colloq.* an unrelated woman friend of a child or children.

aunt·ie /ántee, aántee/ *n.* (also **aunt·y**) (*pl.* **-ies**) *colloq.* = AUNT.

au pair /ō páir/ *n.* a young foreign person, esp. a woman, helping with housework, etc., in exchange for room, board, and pocket money.

au·ra /áwrə/ *n.* (*pl.* **aurae** /-ree/ or **auras**) **1** the distinctive atmosphere diffused by or attending a person, place, etc. **2** (in mystic or spiritualistic use) a supposed subtle emanation, surrounding the body of a living creature. **3** a subtle emanation or aroma from flowers, etc. **4** *Med.* premonitory symptom(s) in epilepsy, etc.

au·ral[1] /áwrəl/ *adj.* of or relating to or received by the ear. □□ **au·ral·ly** *adv.*

au·ral[2] /áwrəl/ *adj.* of, relating to, or resembling an aura; atmospheric.

au·re·ate /áwreeət/ *adj.* **1** golden, gold colored. **2** resplendent.

au·re·ole /áwreeōl/ *n.* (also **au·re·o·la** /awréeələ/) **1** a halo or circle of light. **2** a corona around the Sun or Moon.

au re·voir /ő rəvwáar/ *int. & n.* good-bye (until we meet again).

au·ri·cle /áwrikəl/ *n. Anat.* **1 a** a small muscular pouch on the surface of each atrium of the heart. **b** the atrium itself. **2** the external ear of animals. ▷ EAR

au·ric·u·la /awríkyələ/ *n.* a primrose, *Primula auricula*, with leaves shaped like bears' ears.

au·ric·u·lar /awríkyələr/ *adj.* **1** of or relating to the ear or hearing. **2** of or relating to the auricle of the heart. **3** shaped like an auricle.

au·ric·u·late /awríkyələt, -layt/ *adj.* having one or more auricles or ear-shaped appendages.

au·rif·er·ous /awrífərəs/ *adj.* naturally bearing gold.

au·rochs /áwroks, őwroks/ *n.* (*pl.* same) an extinct wild ox, *Bos primigenius*, ancestor of domestic cattle.

au·ro·ra /awráwrə/ *n.* (*pl.* **auroras** or **aurorae** /-ree/) **1 ▼** a luminous electrical atmospheric phenomenon, usu. of streamers of light in the sky above the northern or southern magnetic pole. ▷ ATMOSPHERE. **2** *poet.* the dawn. □□ **au·ro·ral** *adj.*

au·ro·ra aus·tra·lis /awstráylis/ *n.* a southern occurrence of aurora.

au·ro·ra bo·re·al·is /báwree-ális/ *n.* a northern occurrence of aurora.

AURORA

The aurora borealis (northern lights) and their equivalent in the southern hemisphere, the aurora australis, are colorful lights, seen in the sky near the polar regions. The lights are caused by charged particles carried from the Sun by the solar wind. As they enter the Earth's atmosphere, they create an incandescent light display.

AURORA BOREALIS

aus·cul·ta·tion /áwskəltáyshən/ *n.* the act of listening to sounds from the heart, lungs, etc., as a part of medical diagnosis. □□ **aus·cul·ta·to·ry** /-kúltətawree/ *adj.*

aus·pice /áwspis/ *n.* **1** (in *pl.*) patronage (esp. **under the auspices of**). **2** a forecast.

aus·pi·cious /awspíshəs/ *adj.* **1** of good omen; favorable. **2** prosperous. □□ **aus·pi·cious·ly** *adv.* **aus·pi·cious·ness** *n.*

Aus·sie /áwsee, -zee/ *n. & adj.* (also **Os·sie, Oz·zie**) *colloq.* ● *n.* an Australian. ● *adj.* Australian.

aus·tere /awstéer/ *adj.* (**austerer, austerest**) **1** severely simple. **2** morally strict. **3** harsh; stern. □□ **aus·tere·ly** *adv.*

aus·ter·i·ty /awstéritee/ *n.* (*pl.* **-ies**) **1** sternness; moral severity. **2** severe simplicity. **3** (esp. in *pl.*) an austere practice.

aus·tral /áwstrəl/ *adj.* southern.

Aus·tral·a·sian /áwstrəláyzhən, -shən/ *adj.* of or relating to Australasia, a region consisting of Australia and islands of the SW Pacific.

Aus·tral·ian /awstráylyən/ *n. & adj.* ● *n.* **1** a native or inhabitant of Australia. **2** a person of Australian descent. ● *adj.* of or relating to Australia. □□ **Aus·tral·ian·ism** *n.*

Aus·tral·i·an·a /awstráyleeánə, -áanə/ *n. pl.* objects relating to or characteristic of Australia.

Aus·tra·lo·pith·e·cus /ostrəlōpíthəkoos/ *n.* a genus of fossil primates with both ape-like and human characteristics, found in Pliocene and Lower Pleistocene deposits in Africa. ▷ HOMINID

Austro- /áwstrō/ *comb. form* Austrian; Austrian and (*Austro-Hungarian*).

au·tar·chy /áwtaarkee/ *n.* (*pl.* **-ies**) **1** absolute sovereignty. **2** despotism. **3** an autarchic country or society. □□ **au·tar·chic** /-táarkik/ *adj.* **au·tar·chi·cal** *adj.*

au·tar·ky /áwtaarkee/ *n.* (*pl.* **-ies**) **1** self-sufficiency, esp. as an economic system. **2** a government, etc., run according to such a system. □□ **au·tar·kic** /-táarkik/ *adj.* **au·tar·kist** *n.*

au·teur /awtór/ *n.* a film director regarded as the author of his or her films.

au·then·tic /awthéntik/ *adj.* **1** of undisputed origin; genuine. **2** reliable or trustworthy. **3** *Mus.* (of a mode) containing notes between the final and an octave higher. □□ **au·then·ti·cal·ly** *adv.* **au·then·tic·i·ty** /áwthentísitee/ *n.*

au·then·ti·cate /awthéntikayt/ *v.tr.* **1** establish the truth or genuineness of. **2** validate. □□ **au·then·ti·ca·tion** /-káyshən/ *n.* **au·then·ti·ca·tor** *n.*

au·thor /áwthər/ *n. & v.* ● *n.* (*fem.* **authoress** /áwthris, áwthrés/) **1** a writer, esp. of books. **2** the originator of an event, a condition, etc. (*the author of all my woes*). ● *v.tr.* be the author of. □□ **au·tho·ri·al** /awtháwriəl/ *adj.* **au·thor·ship** *n.*

au·thor·i·tar·i·an /ətháwritáireeən, əthór-/ *adj.* **1** favoring, encouraging, or enforcing strict obedience to authority, as opposed to individual freedom. **2** tyrannical or domineering. □□ **au·thor·i·tar·i·an·ism** *n.*

au·thor·i·ta·tive /ətháwritáytiv, əthór-/ *adj.* **1** being recognized as true or dependable. **2** (of a person, behavior, etc.) commanding or self-confident. **3** official; supported by authority (*an authoritative document*). **4** having or claiming influence through recognized knowledge or expertise. □□ **au·thor·i·ta·tive·ly** *adv.* **au·thor·i·ta·tive·ness** *n.*

au·thor·i·ty /ətháwritee, əthór-/ *n.* (*pl.* **-ies**) **1 a** the power or right to enforce obedience. **b** (often foll. by *for,* or *to* + infin.) delegated power. **2** (esp. in *pl.*) a person or body having authority, esp. political or administrative. **3 a** an influence exerted on opinion because of recognized knowledge or expertise. **b** such an influence expressed in a book, quotation, etc. (*an authority on vintage cars*). **c** an expert in a subject.

au·thor·ize /áwthərīz/ *v.tr.* **1** sanction. **2** (foll. by *to* + infin.) **a** give authority. **b** commission (a person or body) (*authorized to trade*). □□ **au·thor·i·za·tion** /-rizáyshən/ *n.*

Au·thor·ized Ver·sion *n.* an English translation of the Bible made in 1611. Also called **King James Version**.

au·tism /áwtizəm/ *n.* a mental condition, usu. present from childhood, characterized by complete self-absorption and a reduced ability to respond to or communicate with the outside world. □□ **au·tis·tic** /awtístik/ *adj.*

au·to /áwtō/ *n.* (*pl.* **-os**) *colloq.* an automobile.

auto- /áwtō/ *comb. form* (usu. **aut-** before a vowel) **1** self (*autism*). **2** one's own (*autobiography*). **3** by oneself or spontaneous (*autosuggestion*). **4** by itself or automatic (*automobile*).

au·to·bahn /áwtōbaan/ *n.* a German, Austrian, or Swiss highway.

au·to·bi·og·ra·phy /áwtōbīógrəfee/ *n.* (*pl.* **-ies**) **1** a personal account of one's own life. **2** this as a process or literary form. □□ **au·to·bi·og·ra·pher** *n.* **au·to·bi·o·graph·ic** /-bíəgráfik/ *adj.* **au·to·bi·o·graph·i·cal** *adj.*

au·to·ceph·a·lous /áwtōséfələs/ *adj.* **1** (esp. of an Eastern church) appointing its own head. **2** (of a bishop, church, etc.) independent.

au·toch·thon /awtókthən/ *n.* (*pl.* **autochthons** or **autochthones** /-thəneez/) (in *pl.*) the original or earliest known inhabitants of a country; aboriginals. □□ **au·toch·tho·nous** *adj.*

au·to·clave /áwtōklayv/ *n.* **1** a strong vessel used for chemical reactions at high pressures and temperatures. **2** a sterilizer using high pressure steam.

au·toc·ra·cy /awtókrəsee/ *n.* (*pl.* **-ies**) **1** absolute government by one person. **2** the power exercised by such a person. **3** an autocratic country or society.

au·to·crat /áwtōkrat/ *n.* **1** an absolute ruler. **2** a dictatorial person. □□ **au·to·crat·ic** /-krátik/ *adj.* **au·to·crat·i·cal·ly** *adv.*

au·to·cross /áwtōkraws, -kros/ *n.* automobile racing on a challenging course that usu. includes twisting turns and obstacles.

au·to-da-fé /áwtōdaafáy/ *n.* (*pl.* **autos-da-fé** /áwtōz-/) **1** a sentence of punishment by the Spanish Inquisition. **2** the execution of such a sentence, esp. the burning of a heretic.

au·to·di·dact /áwtōdīdakt, -dákt/ *n.* a self-taught person. □□ **au·to·di·dac·tic** /-dáktik/ *adj.*

au·to·e·ro·tism /áwtō-érətizəm/ *n.* (also **au·to·e·rot·i·cism** /-irótisizəm/) *Psychol.* sexual excitement generated by stimulating one's own body; masturbation. □□ **au·to·e·rot·ic** /-irótik/ *adj.*

au·to·fo·cus /áwtōfokəs/ *n.* a device for focusing a camera, etc., automatically.

au·tog·a·my /awtógəmee/ *n. Bot.* self-fertilization in plants. □□ **au·tog·a·mous** *adj.*

au·tog·e·nous /awtójinəs/ *adj.* self-produced.

au·tog·e·nous weld·ing *n.* a process of joining metal by melting the edges together without adding material.

au·to·gi·ro /áwtōjírō/ *n.* (also **au·to·gy·ro**) (*pl.* **-os**) an early form of helicopter with freely rotating horizontal vanes and a propeller.

au·to·graft /áwtōgraft/ *n. Surgery* a graft of tissue from one point to another of the same person's body.

au·to·graph /áwtəgraf/ *n. & v.* ● *n.* **1 a** a signature, esp. that of a celebrity. **b** handwriting. **2** a manuscript in an author's handwriting. **3** a document signed by its author. ● *v.tr.* **1** sign (a photograph etc.). **2** write (a letter, etc.) by hand. □□ **au·to·graph·ic** /-təgráfik/ *adj.*

au·to·gy·ro var. of AUTOGIRO.

Au·to·harp /áwtōhaarp/ *n. Trademark* a kind of zither with a mechanical device to allow the playing of chords.

au·to·im·mune /áwtōimyóōn/ *adj. Med.* (of a disease) caused by antibodies produced against substances naturally present in the body. □□ **au·to·im·mu·ni·ty** *n.*

au·to·in·tox·i·ca·tion /áwtōintóksikáyshən/ *n. Med.* poisoning by a toxin formed within the body itself.

au·tol·y·sis /awtólisis/ *n.* the destruction of cells by their own enzymes. □□ **au·to·lyt·ic** /áwtəlítik/ *adj.*

Au·to·mat /áwtəmat/ *n. Trademark* a cafeteria containing coin-operated machines dispensing food and drink.

au·to·mate /áwtəmayt/ *v.tr.* convert to or operate by automation (*the ticket office has been automated*).

au·to·mat·ed tel·ler ma·chine *n. colloq.* cash machine; automatic teller machine.

au·to·mat·ic /áwtəmátik/ *adj. & n.* ● *adj.* **1** (of a device or its function) working by itself, without direct human intervention. **2 a** done spontaneously; without conscious thought or intention (*an automatic reaction*). **b** necessary and inevitable (*an automatic penalty*). **3** *Psychol.* performed unconsciously or subconsciously. **4** (of a firearm) that continues firing until the ammunition is exhausted or the pressure on the trigger is released. **5** (of a motor vehicle or its transmission) using gears that change automatically according to speed and acceleration. ● *n.* **1** an automatic device, esp. a gun or transmission. **2** *colloq.* a vehicle with automatic transmission. □□ **au·to·mat·i·cal·ly** *adv.* **au·to·ma·tic·i·ty** /áwtəmətísitee/ *n.*

au·to·mat·ic tel·ler ma·chine *n.* ▼ electronic machine that allows customers to insert a card, punch in an identification number, and then perform banking transactions, such as depositing or withdrawing funds, etc.

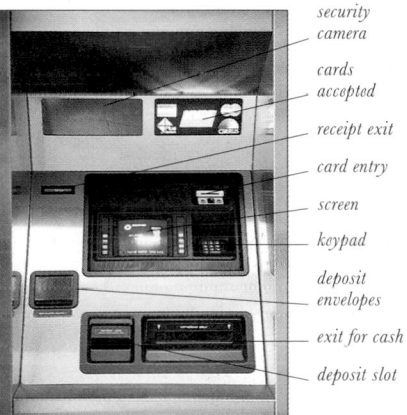

security camera
cards accepted
receipt exit
card entry
screen
keypad
deposit envelopes
exit for cash
deposit slot

AUTOMATIC TELLER MACHINE

au·to·mat·ic pi·lot *n.* a device for keeping an aircraft on a set course.

au·to·ma·tion /áwtəmáyshən/ *n.* **1** the use of automatic equipment to save labor. **2** the automatic control of the manufacture of a product through its successive stages.

au·tom·a·tism /awtómətizəm/ *n.* **1** *Psychol.* the performance of actions unconsciously or subconsciously. **2** involuntary action. **3** unthinking routine.

au·tom·a·tize /awtómətīz/ *v.tr.* **1** make (a process, system, etc.) automatic. **2** subject (a business, enterprise, etc.) to automation. □□ **au·tom·a·ti·za·tion** *n.*

au·tom·a·ton /awtómətən, -ton/ *n.* (*pl.* **automata** /-tə/ or **automatons**) **1** a piece of mechanism with concealed motive power. **2** a person who behaves mechanically or leads a routine, monotonous life.

au·to·mo·bile /áwtəməbeel/ *n.* a motor vehicle for road use with an enclosed passenger compartment; a car. ▷ CAR

au·to·mo·tive /áwtəmótiv/ *adj.* concerned with motor vehicles.

au·to·nom·ic /áwtənómik/ *adj.* esp. *Physiol.* functioning involuntarily.

A

AUTONOMIC NERVOUS SYSTEM

The autonomic nervous system comprises those nerves of the peripheral nervous system that transmit nerve impulses to the glands and visceral organs. It controls involuntary functions, such as heart rate, sweating, and digestion, and is itself divided into the sympathetic and parasympathetic systems. The sympathetic system works in response to stress, increasing heart rate and blood pressure; the parasympathetic system counteracts these effects, decreasing heart rate and blood pressure, as well as stimulating the digestive system.

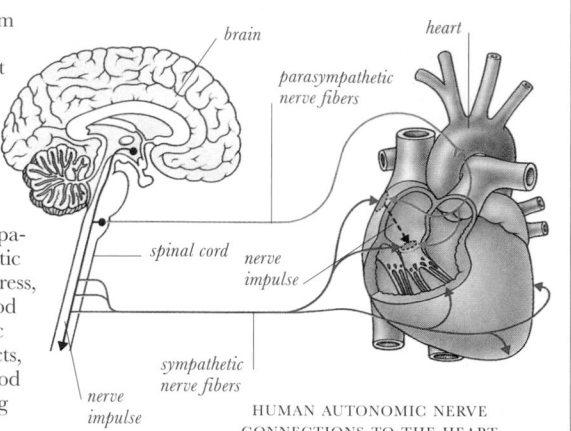

brain

heart

parasympathetic nerve fibers

spinal cord

nerve impulse

sympathetic nerve fibers

nerve impulse

HUMAN AUTONOMIC NERVE CONNECTIONS TO THE HEART

---

au·to·nom·ic nerv·ous sys·tem *n.* ▲ the part of the nervous system responsible for control of the bodily functions not consciously directed, e.g., heartbeat. ▷ PERIPHERAL NERVOUS SYSTEM

au·ton·o·mous /awtónəməs/ *adj.* **1** having self-government. **2** acting independently or having the freedom to do so. □□ **au·ton·o·mous·ly** *adv.*

au·ton·o·my /awtónəmee/ *n.* (*pl.* **-ies**) **1** the right of self-government. **2** personal freedom. **3** freedom of the will. **4** a self-governing community. □□ **au·ton·o·mist** *n.*

au·to·pi·lot /áwtōpīlət/ *n.* an automatic pilot.

au·top·sy /áwtopsee/ *n.* (*pl.* **-ies**) **1** a postmortem examination. **2** any critical analysis.

au·to·ra·di·o·graph /áwtōráydeeəgraf/ *n.* a photograph of an object, produced by radiation from radioactive material in the object. □□ **au·to·ra·di·o·graph·ic** *adj.* **au·to·ra·di·og·ra·phy** /áwtōráydi-ógrəfee/ *n.*

au·to·save *n. & v.* ● *n.* a software facility that automatically saves a computer user's work at regular intervals. ● *v.tr.* save (keyed work) automatically.

au·to·sug·ges·tion /áwtōsəgjéschən/ *n.* a hypnotic or subconscious suggestion made by a person to himself or herself and affecting behavior.

au·to·tel·ic /áwtōtélik/ *adj.* having or being a purpose in itself.

au·tot·o·my /awtótəmee/ *n. Zool.* the casting off of a part of the body when threatened, e.g., the tail of a lizard.

au·to·tox·in /áwtōtóksin/ *n.* a poisonous substance originating within an organism. □□ **au·to·tox·ic** *adj.*

au·to·trans·form·er /áwtōtransfáwrmər/ *n.* an electrical transformer that has a single coil winding, part of which is common to both primary and secondary circuits.

au·to·type /áwtətīp/ *n.* **1** a facsimile. **2 a** a photographic printing process for monochrome reproduction. **b** a print made by this process.

au·tox·i·da·tion /awtóksidáyshən/ *n. Chem.* oxidation by exposure to air at room temperature.

au·tumn /áwtəm/ *n.* **1** the third season of the year, when crops and fruits are gathered, and leaves fall. Also called **fall**. ▷ SEASON. **2** *Astron.* the period from the autumnal equinox to the winter solstice.

au·tum·nal /awtúmnəl/ *adj.* **1** of, characteristic of, or appropriate to autumn (*autumnal colors*). **2** occurring in autumn (*autumnal equinox*).

au·tum·nal e·qui·nox *n.* the equinox that occurs on or about Sept. 22.

au·tumn cro·cus *n.* any plant of the genus *Colchicum*, esp. meadow saffron.

aux·il·ia·ry /awgzílyəree/ *adj. & n.* ● *adj.* **1** (of a person or thing) that gives help. **2** (of services or equipment) subsidiary; additional. ● *n.* (*pl.* **-ies**) **1** an auxiliary person or thing. **2** (in *pl.*) *Mil.* auxiliary troops.

aux·il·ia·ry verb *n. Gram.* one used in forming tenses, moods, and voices of other verbs.

aux·in /áwksin/ *n.* a plant hormone that regulates growth.

AV *abbr.* **1** audiovisual (teaching aids, etc.). **2** Authorized Version (of the Bible).

a·vail /əváyl/ *v. & n.* ● *v.* **1** *tr.* help; benefit. **2** *refl.* (foll. by *of*) profit by; take advantage of. **3** *intr.* **a** provide help. **b** be of use, value, or profit. ● *n.* (usu. in *neg.* or *interrog.* phrases) use; profit (*to no avail*; *without avail*; *of what avail?*).

a·vail·a·ble /əváyləbəl/ *adj.* (often foll. by *to, for*) **1** capable of being used; at one's disposal. **2** within one's reach. **3** (of a person) **a** free. **b** able to be contacted. □□ **a·vail·a·bil·i·ty** *n.* **a·vail·a·ble·ness** *n.* **a·vail·a·bly** *adv.*

av·a·lanche /ávəlanch/ *n.* **1** a mass of snow and ice tumbling rapidly down a mountain. **2** a sudden arrival of anything in large quantities (*faced with an avalanche of work*).

a·vant-garde /avón-gaárd/ *n. & adj.* ● *n.* pioneers or innovators. ● *adj.* (of ideas, etc.) new; progressive. □□ **a·vant-gard·ism** *n.* **a·vant-gard·ist** *n.*

av·a·rice /ávəris/ *n.* extreme greed for money or gain; cupidity. □□ **av·a·ri·cious** /-ríshəs/ *adj.* **av·a·ri·cious·ly** *adv.* **av·a·ri·cious·ness** /-ríshəsnis/ *n.*

a·vast /əvást/ *int. Naut.* stop; cease.

av·a·tar /ávətaar/ *n.* **1** (in Hindu mythology) the descent of a deity or released soul to Earth in bodily form. **2** incarnation. **3** a manifestation or phase.

a·vaunt /əváwnt, əvaánt/ *int. archaic* begone.

Ave. *abbr.* Avenue.

a·ve /áavay/ *int.* **1** welcome. **2** farewell.

a·venge /əvénj/ *v.tr.* **1** inflict retribution on behalf of. **2** take vengeance for (an injury). □ **be avenged** avenge oneself. □□ **a·veng·er** *n.*

av·ens /ávənz/ *n.* any of various plants of the genus *Geum*.

av·e·nue /ávənōō, -nyōō/ *n.* **1** ▶ a broad road or street, often with trees at regular intervals along its sides. **2** a way of dealing with something.

AVENUE:
VIA APPIA, ITALY

a·ver /əvér/ *v.tr.* (**averred**, **averring**) *formal* assert; affirm.

av·er·age /ávərij, ávrij/ *n., adj., & v.* ● *n.* **1 a** the usual amount, extent, or rate. **b** the ordinary standard. **2** an amount obtained by dividing the total of given amounts by the number of amounts in the set. ● *adj.* **1 a** usual; typical. **b** mediocre. **2** estimated by average. ● *v.tr.* **1** amount on average to. **2** do on average. **3 a** estimate the average of. **b** estimate the general standard of. □ **average out** result in an average. **average out at** result in an average of. **on** (or **on an**) **average** as an average rate or estimate. □□ **av·er·age·ly** *adv.*

a·ver·ment /əvérmənt/ *n.* an affirmation, esp. *Law* one with an offer of proof.

a·verse /əvérs/ *predic.adj.* (usu. foll. by *to*; also foll. by *from*) opposed; disinclined (*not averse to helping*). ¶ Construction with *to* is now more common.

a·ver·sion /əvérzhən, -shən/ *n.* **1** (usu. foll. by *to, from, for*) a dislike or unwillingness. **2** an object of dislike (*my pet aversion*).

a·ver·sion ther·a·py *n.* therapy designed to make a subject averse to an existing habit.

a·vert /əvért/ *v.tr.* (often foll. by *from*) **1** turn away (one's eyes or thoughts). **2** prevent (an undesirable occurrence). □□ **a·vert·a·ble** *adj.* **a·vert·i·ble** *adj.*

A·ves·ta /əvéstə/ *n.* (usu. prec. by *the*) the sacred writings of Zoroastrianism.

A·ves·tan /əvéstən/ *adj. & n.* ● *adj.* of or relating to

AVIARY

Many birds can be housed in an outdoor aviary for at least part of the year in temperate climates. The birds are essentially confined to two sections: the flight and the shelter. The flight is an area partially open to the elements, where the birds have a certain amount of freedom to fly. The shelter is protected from the elements; here birds are fed and encouraged to roost. A third section, the safety porch, allows the keeper to enter the aviary without birds escaping.

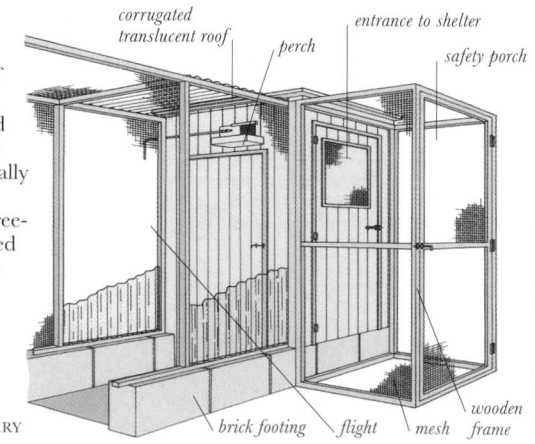

corrugated translucent roof

perch

entrance to shelter

safety porch

brick footing   flight   mesh   wooden frame

TYPICAL DESIGN OF AN AVIARY

the Avesta. ● *n.* the ancient Iranian language of the Avesta.

a·vi·an /áyveeən/ *adj.* of or relating to birds.

a·vi·ar·y /áyvee-eree/ *n.* (*pl.* **-ies**) ▼ a large enclosure or building for keeping birds.

a·vi·ate /áyveeayt/ *v.* **1** *intr.* fly in an airplane. **2** *tr.* pilot (an airplane).

a·vi·a·tion /áyveeáyshən/ *n.* **1** the skill or practice of operating aircraft. **2** aircraft manufacture.

a·vi·a·tor /áyveeaytər/ *n.* (*fem.* **a·vi·a·trix** /áyvee-áytriks/) a person who pilots an aircraft.

a·vi·cul·ture /áyvikulchər/ *n.* the rearing and keeping of birds. □□ **a·vi·cul·tur·ist** /-kúlchərist/ *n.*

av·id /ávid/ *adj.* eager; greedy. □□ **a·vid·i·ty** /əvíditee/ *n.* **av·id·ly** *adv.*

a·vi·fau·na /áyvifawnə/ *n.* birds of a region or country collectively.

a·vi·on·ics /áyveeóniks/ *n.pl.* (treated as *sing.*) electronics as applied to aviation.

a·vi·ta·min·o·sis /ayvītəminósis/ *n. Med.* a condition resulting from a deficiency of one or more vitamins in the diet.

av·o·ca·do /ávəkáádō, aávə-/ *n.* (*pl.* **-os**) **1** (also **avocado pear**) ◄ a pear-shaped fruit with a smooth oily edible flesh and a large stone. **2** the tropical evergreen tree, *Persea americana*, native to Central America, bearing this fruit. Also called **alligator pear**. **3** the light green color of the flesh of this fruit.

AVOCADO
(*Persea americana*)

av·o·ca·tion /ávōkáyshən/ *n.* **1** a minor occupation. **2** *colloq.* a vocation or calling.

av·o·cet /ávəset/ *n.* ◄ any wading bird of the genus *Recurvirostra* with long legs and a long slender upward-curved bill and usu. black and white plumage.
▷ WADING BIRD

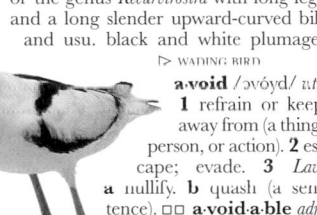

a·void /əvóyd/ *v.tr.* **1** refrain or keep away from (a thing, person, or action). **2** escape; evade. **3** *Law* **a** nullify. **b** quash (a sentence). □□ **a·void·a·ble** *adj.* **a·void·a·bly** *adv.* **a·void·ance** *n.* **a·void·er** *n.*

av·oir·du·pois /ávərdə-póyz/ *n.* (in full **avoirdupois weight**) a system of weights based on a pound of 16 ounces or 7,000 grains.

AVOCET:
PIED AVOCET
(*Recurvirostra avosetta*)

a·vouch /əvówch/ *v.tr.* & *intr.* guarantee; affirm; confess. □□ **a·vouch·ment** *n.*

a·vow /əvów/ *v.tr.* **1** admit. **2** *refl.* admit that one is (*avowed himself the author*). □□ **a·vow·al** *n.* **a·vow·ed·ly** /əvówidlee/ *adv.*

a·vul·sion /əvúlshən/ *n.* **1** a tearing away. **2** *Law* a sudden removal of land by a flood, etc., to another person's property.

a·vun·cu·lar /əvúngkyələr/ *adj.* like or of an uncle; kind and friendly.

AWACS /áywaks/ *n.* a long-range radar system for detecting enemy aircraft.

a·wait /əwáyt/ *v.tr.* **1** wait for. **2** (of an event or thing) be in store for.

a·wake /əwáyk/ *v.* & *adj.* ● *v.* (*past* **awoke** /əwṓk/; *past part.* **awoken** /əwṓkən/) **1** *intr.* **a** cease to sleep. **b** become active. **2** *intr.* (foll. by *to*) become aware of. **3** *tr.* rouse from sleep. ● *predic.adj.* **1 a** not asleep. **b** vigilant. **2** (foll. by *to*) aware of.

a·wak·en /əwáykən/ *v.* **1** *tr.* & *intr.* = AWAKE *v.* **2** *tr.* (often foll. by *to*) make aware.

a·ward /əwáwrd/ *v.* & *n.* ● *v.tr.* **1** give or order to be given as a payment, compensation, or prize (*awarded her a scholarship; was awarded damages*). **2** grant; assign. ● *n.* **1** a payment, compensation, or prize awarded. **2** a judicial decision. □□ **a·ward·er** *n.*

a·ware /əwáir/ *predic.adj.* **1** (often foll. by *of*, or *that* + clause) conscious; not ignorant; having knowledge. **2** well-informed. ¶ Also found in *attrib.* use in sense 2, as in *a very aware person*; this is *disp.* □□ **a·ware·ness** *n.*

a·wash /əwósh, əwáwsh/ *predic.adj.* **1** level with the surface of water, so that it just washes over. **2** carried or washed by the waves; flooded or as if flooded.

a·way /əwáy/ *adv., adj.,* & *n.* ● *adv.* **1** to or at a distance from the place, person, or thing in question (*go away; give away; they are away*). **2** toward or into nonexistence (*sounds die away; explain it away*). **3** constantly; persistently. **4** without delay. ● *adj. Sports* played at an opponent's field, etc. ● *n. Sports* an away game or win. □ **away with** (as *imper.*) take away; let us be rid of.

awe /aw/ *n.* & *v.* ● *n.* reverential fear or wonder. ● *v.tr.* inspire with awe.

a·wea·ry /əwéeree/ *predic.adj. poet.* (often foll. by *of*) weary.

a·weigh /əwáy/ *predic.adj. Naut.* (of an anchor) clear of the sea or river bed.

awe-in·spir·ing *adj.* causing awe or wonder; amazing; magnificent. □□ **awe-inspiringly** *adv.*

awe·some /áwsəm/ *adj.* **1** inspiring awe. **2** *sl.* excellent. □□ **awe·some·ly** *adv.* **awe·some·ness** *n.*

awe·strick·en /áwstrikən/ *adj.* (also **awe·struck** /-struk/) struck or affected by awe.

aw·ful /áwfŏŏl/ *adj.* **1** *colloq.* **a** unpleasant (*awful weather*). **b** poor in quality; very bad (*has awful writing*). **c** (*attrib.*) excessive; remarkably large (*an awful lot of money*). **2** *poet.* inspiring awe. □□ **aw·ful·ness** *n.*

aw·ful·ly /áwfəlee, -flee/ *adv.* **1** *colloq.* in an unpleasant or horrible way. **2** *colloq.* very.

a·while /əhwíl, əwíl/ *adv.* for a short time.

awk·ward /áwkwərd/ *adj.* **1** ill-adapted for use; causing difficulty in use. **2** clumsy or bungling. **3 a** embarrassed (*felt awkward about it*). **b** embarrassing (*an awkward situation*). □□ **awk·ward·ly** *adv.* **awk·ward·ness** *n.*

awk·ward age *n.* adolescence.

awl /awl/ *n.* a small pointed tool used for piercing holes, esp. in leather.

awn /awn/ *n.* ▼ a stiff bristle growing from the grain sheath of grasses. □□ **awned** *adj.*

awn

seed
sheath

awn·ing /áwning/ *n.* a sheet of canvas or similar material stretched on a frame and used to shade a window, doorway, or other area from the sun or rain.

a·woke *past* of AWAKE.

a·wo·ken *past part.* of AWAKE.

AWOL /áywawl/ *abbr.* absent without leave.

a·wry /ərí/ *adv.* & *adj.* ● *adv.* **1** crookedly or askew. **2** improperly or amiss. ● *predic.adj.* crooked; deviant or unsound (*his theory is awry*). □ **go awry** go wrong.

ax /aks/ *n.* & *v.* (also **axe**) ● *n.* **1** a chopping tool, usu. with a steel edge at a right angle to a wooden handle. **2** the drastic cutting of staff, etc. ● *v.tr.* (**axing**) **1** use an ax. **2** cut (esp. costs or services) drastically. **3** remove or dismiss. □ **an ax to grind** a private or selfish purpose to serve.

AWN: EAR OF
WHEAT WITH
AWNED SHEATHS

AXIS

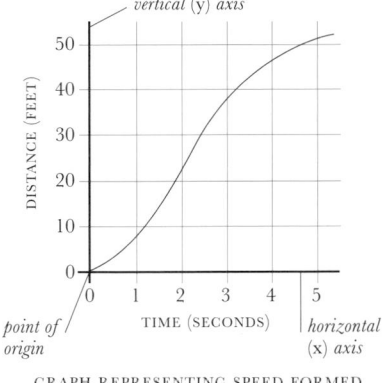

Axes provide the framework to visualize an equation. Speed, for example, is an equation of distance divided by time. If distance is shown on the *y* axis and time on the *x* axis, a line representing speed can be plotted on the grid they form.

vertical (*y*) *axis*

DISTANCE (FEET)

50
40
30
20
10
0

0   1   2   3   4   5

TIME (SECONDS)

point of origin

horizontal (*x*) *axis*

GRAPH REPRESENTING SPEED FORMED WITHIN THE AXES OF DISTANCE AND TIME

ax·el /áksəl/ *n.* a jumping movement in figure skating, similar to a loop (see LOOP *n.* 7) but from one foot to the other.

ax·es *pl.* of AXIS.

ax·i·al /ákseeəl/ *adj.* **1** forming or belonging to an axis. **2** around or along an axis (*axial rotation; axial symmetry*). □□ **ax·i·al·ly** *adv.*

ax·il /áksil/ *n.* ◄ the upper angle between a leaf and the stem it springs from, or between a branch and the trunk.

ax·il·la /aksílə/ *n.* (*pl.* **axillae** /-ee/) **1** *Anat.* the armpit. **2** an axil.

ax·il·lar·y /áksiléree/ *adj.* **1** *Anat.* of or relating to the armpit. **2** *Bot.* in or growing from the axil.

axillary bud

ax·i·om /ákseeəm/ *n.* **1** an established or widely accepted principle. **2** esp. *Geom.* a self-evident truth.

stem   *axil*

AXIL BETWEEN A
LEAF AND STEM

ax·i·o·mat·ic /ákseeəmátik/ *adj.* **1** self-evident. **2** relating to or containing axioms. □□ **ax·i·o·mat·i·cal·ly** *adv.*

ax·is /áksis/ *n.* (*pl.* **axes** /-seez/) **1 a** an imaginary line about which a body rotates or about which a plane figure is conceived as generating a solid. **b** a line that divides a regular figure symmetrically. **2** *Math.* ▲ a fixed reference line for the measurement of coordinates, etc. **3 a** an agreement or alliance between two or more countries forming a center for an eventual larger grouping of nations sharing an ideal or objective. **b** (**the Axis**) the alliance of Germany and Italy formed before and during World War II, later extended to include Japan and other countries; these countries as a group.

ax·le /áksəl/ *n.* a rod or spindle on which a wheel or group of wheels is fixed. ▼

ax·o·lotl /áksəlot'l/ *n.* ▼ an aquatic newtlike salamander, *Ambystoma mexicanum*, from Mexico which in natural conditions retains its larval form but is able to breed.

AXOLOTL
(*Ambystoma mexicanum*)

AXON

An axon is a sinuous extension of a nerve cell body that conveys impulses to targets such as muscles, glands, and other nerve cells. Axons range from an inch to six feet or more in length and are protected by cells that form a myelin sheath around them. Intermittent gaps in the sheath are referred to as the nodes of Ranvier.

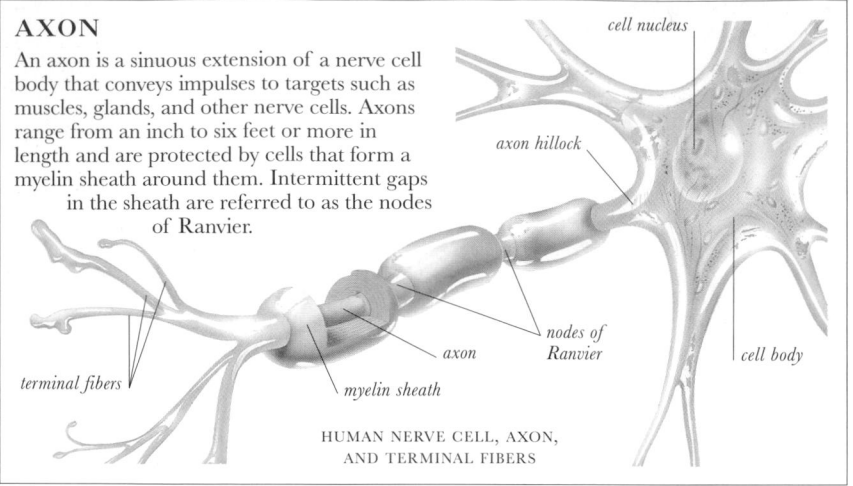

HUMAN NERVE CELL, AXON, AND TERMINAL FIBERS

ax·on /ákson/ *n. Anat. & Zool.* ▲ a long threadlike part of a nerve cell, conducting impulses from the cell body. ▷ NERVOUS SYSTEM

a·yah /íə/ *n.* a native nurse or maidservant, esp. in India and other former British overseas territories.

a·ya·tol·lah /íətólə/ *n.* a Shiite religious leader in Iran.

ay var. of AYE[1].

aye[1] /ī/ *adv. & n.* (also **ay**) ● *adv.* **1** *archaic* or *dial.* yes. **2** (in voting) I assent. **3** (as **aye aye**) *Naut.* a response accepting an order. ● *n.* an affirmative answer, esp. in voting.

aye[2] /ay/ *adv.* (also **ay**) *archaic* ever; always.

aye-aye /í-í/ *n.* ▼ an arboreal nocturnal lemur, *Daubentonia madagascariensis*, native to Madagascar.

AYE-AYE
(*Daubentonia madagascariensis*)

Ayles·bur·y /áylzbəree/ *n.* **1** a bird of a breed of large white domestic ducks. **2** this breed.

Ayr·shire /áirshər, -sheer/ *n.* **1** one of a mainly white breed of dairy cattle. **2** this breed.

AZ *abbr.* Arizona (in official postal use).

a·zal·ea /əzáylyə/ *n.* any of various flowering deciduous shrubs of the genus *Rhododendron*, with large pink, purple, white, or yellow flowers (originally classified as the genus *Azalea*).

a·ze·o·trope /əzéeətrōp, áyzee-/ *n. Chem.* a mixture of liquids in which the boiling point remains constant during distillation at a given pressure, without change in composition.

az·i·muth /áziməth/ *n.* **1** the angular distance from a north or south point of the horizon to the intersection with the horizon of a vertical circle passing through a given celestial body. **2** the horizontal angle or direction of a compass bearing.

a·zi·muth·al pro·jec·tion /ázimúthəl/ *n.* ▼ a map projection in which a region of the Earth is projected on to a plane tangential to the surface, usually at the pole or equator.

az·ine /ázeen, áy-/ *n. Chem.* any organic compound with two or more nitrogen atoms in a six-atom ring.

a·zo·ic /ayzṓik/ *adj.* **1** having no trace of life. **2** *Geol.* (of an age, etc.) having left no organic remains.

AZT *n. Trademark* azidothymidine, a drug used against the AIDS virus.

Az·tec /áztek/ *n. & adj.* ● *n.* **1** a member of the native people dominant in Mexico before the Spanish conquest of the 16th century. **2** the language of the Aztecs. ● *adj.* of the Aztecs or their language.

az·ure /ázhər/ *n. & adj.* ● *n.* **1** a deep sky-blue color. **2** *poet.* the clear sky. ● *adj.* of the color azure.

az·y·gous /ayzígəs/ *adj. & n. Anat.* ● *adj.* (of any organic structure) single; not existing in pairs. ● *n.* an organic structure occurring singly.

AZIMUTHAL PROJECTION

An azimuthal projection shows half of the Earth at once. It is produced as though a light were shone through the globe from its center. The grid of longitudinal and latitudinal lines on the globe's surface is projected onto the flat plane of the map. The best use of an azimuthal projection is to show the true direction between two points on the Earth.

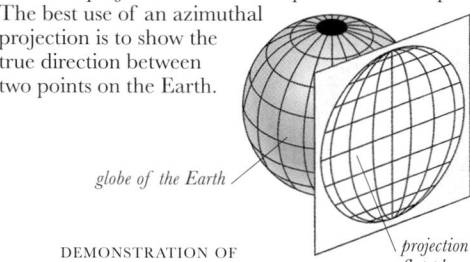

DEMONSTRATION OF
AZIMUTHAL PROJECTION

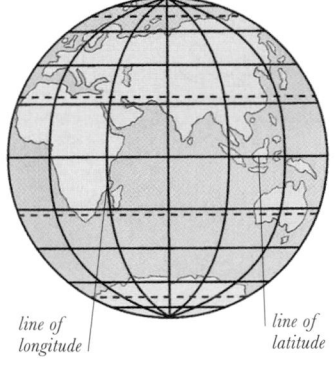

AZIMUTHAL MAP

B

B[1] /bee/ *n.* (also **b**) (*pl.* **Bs** or **B's**) **1** the second letter of the alphabet. **2** *Mus.* the seventh note of the diatonic scale of C major. ▷ NOTATION. **3** the second hypothetical person or example. **4** the second highest class or category. **5** *Algebra* (usu. **b**) the second known quantity. **6** a human blood type of the ABO system.

B[2] *symb. Chem.* the element boron.

B[3] *abbr.* (also **B.**) **1** Bachelor. **2** bel(s). **3** *Chess* bishop. **4** black (pencil lead). **5** *Baseball* base; baseman.

b. *abbr.* born.

BA *abbr.* Bachelor of Arts.

Ba *symb. Chem.* the element barium.

baa /baa/ *v.intr.* (**baas, baaed** or **baa'd**) (esp. of a sheep) bleat.

ba·ba /baábaa/ *n.* (in full **baba au rhum** /ō rúm/) a small rich sponge cake, usu. soaked in rum syrup.

Bab·bitt[1] /bábit/ *n.* (also **babbitt**) (in full **Babbitt metal**) any of a group of soft alloys of tin, antimony, copper, and usu. lead, used for lining bearings, etc., to diminish friction. □□ **bab·bler** *n.*

Bab·bitt[2] /bábit/ *n.* a materialistic, complacent businessman (for the title character in a 1922 Sinclair Lewis novel). □□ **Bab·bitt·ry** *n.*

bab·ble /bábəl/ *v. & n.* ● *v.* **1** *intr.* **a** talk in an incoherent manner. **b** chatter excessively. **c** (of a stream, etc.) murmur. **2** *tr.* divulge through chatter. ● *n.* **1 a** incoherent speech. **b** idle or childish talk. **2** the murmur of voices, water, etc. □□ **bab·bler** *n.*

babe /bayb/ *n.* **1** *literary* a baby. **2** an innocent or helpless person (*babes in the woods*). **3** *sometimes derog. sl.* a young woman (often as a form of address).

ba·bel /báybəl, báb-/ *n.* **1** a confused noise, esp. of voices. **2** a noisy assembly. **3** a scene of confusion.

Ba·bis /bábis/ *n.* a member of a Persian eclectic sect founded in 1844 whose doctrine includes Muslim, Christian, Jewish, and Zoroastrian elements. □□ **Bab·ism** *n.*

ba·boon /babóon/ *n.* ◀ any of various large Old World monkeys of the genera *Papio* and *Mandrillus*, having a long snout, large teeth, and callosities on the buttocks.

ba·bush·ka /bəbóoshkə/ *n.* **1** a headscarf tied under the chin. **2** an elderly or grandmotherly Russian woman.

ba·by /báybee/ *n. & v.* ● *n.* (*pl.* **-ies**) **1** a very young child or infant. **2** an unduly childish person. **3** the youngest member of a family, team, etc. **4** (often *attrib.*) **a** a young or newly born animal. **b** a thing that is small of its kind (*baby rose*). **5** *sl.* a young woman; sweetheart (often as a form of address). **6** one's own responsibility, invention, etc., regarded in a personal way. ● *v.tr.* (**-ies, -ied**) **1** treat like a baby. **2** pamper. □□ **ba·by·hood** *n.* **ba·by·ish** *adj.* **ba·by·ish·ly** *adv.*

ba·by boom *n. colloq.* a temporary marked increase in the birthrate. □ **baby boomer** *n.* a person born during a baby boom, esp. after World War II.

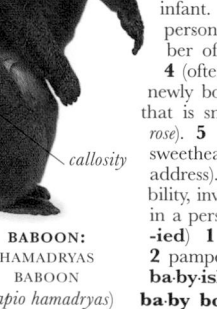

BABOON:
HAMADRYAS
BABOON
(*Papio hamadryas*)

cheek pouch

callosity

ba·by car·riage *n.* a four-wheeled carriage for a baby, pushed by a person on foot.

ba·by grand *n.* the smallest size of grand piano.

ba·by-sit *v.intr.* (**-sitting**; *past and past part.* **-sat**) look after a child while the parents are out. □□ **ba·by·sit·ter** *n.*

ba·by talk *n.* childish talk used by or to young children.

Ba·car·di /bəkáardee/ *n.* (*pl.* **Bacardis**) *Trademark* a West Indian rum produced orig. in Cuba.

bac·ca·lau·re·ate /bákəláwreeət/ *n.* **1** the college or university degree of bachelor. **2** an examination intended to qualify successful candidates for higher education.

bac·ca·rat /baakəraá, bá-/ *n.* a gambling card game played against the dealer.

bac·cate /bákayt/ *adj. Bot.* **1** bearing berries. **2** or like a berry.

bac·cha·nal /bakənál, bákənəl/ *n. & adj.* ● *n.* **1** a wild and drunken revelry. **2** a drunken reveler. **3** a priest, worshiper, or follower of Bacchus, the Greek or Roman god of wine. ● *adj.* **1** of or like Bacchus or his rites. **2** riotous; roistering.

Bac·cha·na·li·a /bákənáylyə/ *n.pl.* **1** the Roman festival of Bacchus. **2** (**bacchanalia**) a drunken revelry. □□ **Bac·cha·na·li·an** *adj. & n.*

bac·chant /bəkánt, -kaánt, bákənt/ *n. & adj.* ● *n.* (*pl.* **bacchants** or **bacchantes** /bəkánteez/; *fem.* **bacchante** /bəkántee, -kaánt-/) **1** a priest, worshiper, or follower of Bacchus. **2** a drunken reveler. ● *adj.* **1** of or like Bacchus or his rites. **2** riotous; roistering. □□ **bac·chan·tic** *adj.*

bach·e·lor /báchələr, báchlər/ *n.* **1** an unmarried man. **2** a man or woman who has taken the degree of Bachelor of Arts or Science, etc. □□ **bach·e·lor·hood** *n.*

bac·il·lar·y /básəleree, bəsíləree/ *adj.* relating to or caused by bacilli.

ba·cil·li·form /bəsílifawrm/ *adj.* rod-shaped.

ba·cil·lus /bəsíləs/ *n.* (*pl.* **bacilli** /-lī/) **1** any rod-shaped bacterium. ▷ BACTERIUM. **2** (usu. in *pl.*) any pathogenic bacterium.

back /bak/ *n., adv., v., & adj.* ● *n.* **1 a** the rear surface of the human body from the shoulders to the hips. **b** the corresponding upper surface of an animal's body. **c** the spine (*fell and broke his back*). **2 a** any surface regarded as corresponding to the human back, e.g., of the head or hand, or of a chair. **b** the part of a garment that covers the back. **3 a** the less important part of something functional, e.g., of a knife or a piece of paper (*write it on the back*). **b** the part normally away from the spectator or the direction of motion or attention, e.g., of a car, house, or room (*stood at the back*). **4 a** a defensive player in some games. **b** this position. ● *adv.* **1** to the rear; away from what is considered to be the front (*go back a little; ran off without looking back*). **2 a** in or into an earlier position or condition (*came back late; ran back to the car; put it back on the shelf*). **b** in return (*pay back*). **3** in or into the past (*back in June, three years back*). **4** at a distance (*stand back from the road*). **5** in check (*hold him back*). **6** (foll. by *of*) behind (*in the back of the house*). ● *v.* **1** *tr.* **a** help with moral or financial support. **b** bet on the success of (a horse, etc.). **2** *tr. & intr.* move, or cause (a vehicle, etc.) to move, backward. **3** *tr.* **a** put or serve as a back, background, or support to. **b** *Mus.* accompany. **4** *tr.* lie at the back of (*a beach backed by steep cliffs*). **5** *intr.* (of the wind) move around to a counterclockwise direction. ● *adj.* **1** situated behind (*back teeth; back entrance*). **2** of or relating to the past (*back pay; back issue*). **3** reversed (*back flow*). □ **at the back of one's mind** remembered but not consciously thought of. **back and forth** to and fro. **back down** withdraw one's claim; concede defeat in an argument, etc. **back off 1** draw back; retreat. **2** abandon one's intention, stand, etc.

back on to have its back adjacent to (*the house backs on to a field*). **back out** (often foll. by *of*) withdraw from a commitment. **back up 1** give support to. **2** *Computing* make a spare copy of (data, a disk, etc.). **3** (of running water) accumulate behind an obstruction. **4** reverse (a vehicle) into a desired position. **5** form a line of vehicles, etc. **get** (or **put**) **a person's back up** annoy or anger a person. **get off a person's back** stop troubling a person. **go back on** fail to honor (a promise or commitment). **know like the back of one's hand** be entirely familiar with. **on the back burner** see BURNER. **put one's back into** approach (a task, etc.) with vigor. **turn one's back on 1** abandon. **2** ignore. **with one's back to** (or **up against**) **the wall** in a desperate situation; hard-pressed. □□ **back·er** *n.* (in sense 1 of *v.*). **back·less** *adj.*

back·ache /bákayk/ *n.* a (usu. prolonged) pain in one's back.

back·bite /bákbīt/ *v.tr.* slander; speak badly of. □□ **back·bit·er** *n.*

back·board /bákbawrd/ *n.* **1** a board placed at the back of anything. **2** *Basketball* the board behind the basket.

back·bone /bákbōn/ *n.* **1** the spine. **2** the main support of a structure. **3** firmness of character.

back·break·ing /bákbrayking/ *adj.* (esp. of manual work) extremely hard.

back·coun·try /bák-kuntree/ *n.* an area away from settled districts.

back·cross /bák-kraws/ *v. & n. Biol.* ● *v.tr.* cross a hybrid with one of its parents. ● *n.* an instance or the product of this.

back·date /bákdayt/ *v.tr.* put an earlier date on (an agreement, etc.) than the actual one.

back door *n.* **1** the door at the back of a building. **2** a secret means of gaining an objective.

back·door /bákdáwr/ *adj.* clandestine; underhand (*backdoor deal*).

back·drop /bákdrop/ *n.* **1** *Theatr.* a painted cloth at the back of the stage as a main part of the scenery. **2** the background to a situation.

back·fill /bákfil/ *v.tr. & intr.* refill an excavated hole with the material dug out of it.

back·fire /bákfīr/ *v. & n.* ● *v.intr.* **1** undergo a mistimed explosion in the cylinder or exhaust of an internal-combustion engine. **2** (of a plan, etc.) have the opposite effect to what was intended. ● *n.* an instance of backfiring.

back-for·ma·tion *n.* **1** the formation of a word from its seeming derivative (e.g., *laze* from *lazy*). **2** a word formed in this way.

back·gam·mon /bákgámən/ *n.* a game for two played on a board with pieces moved according to throws of the dice.

back·ground /bákgrownd/ *n.* **1** part of a scene, picture, or description that serves as a setting to the chief figures or objects and foreground. **2** an inconspicuous position (*kept in the background*). **3** a person's education, knowledge, or social circumstances. **4** explanatory information.

back·hand /bák-hand/ *n. Tennis*, etc. **1** ◀ a stroke played with the back of the hand turned toward the opponent. **2** (*attrib.*) of or made with a backhand (*backhand volley*).

back·hand·ed /bák-hándid/ *adj.* **1** (of a blow, etc.) delivered with the back of the hand, or in a direction opposite to the usual one. **2** indirect; ambiguous (*a backhanded compliment*). **3** = BACKHAND.

back·hand·er /bák-hándər/ *n.* **1 a** a backhand stroke. **b** a backhanded blow. **2** *colloq.* an indirect attack.

back·hoe *n.* a mechanical excavator which draws towards itself a bucket attached to a hinged boom.

BACKHAND
TENNIS STROKE

B

back·ing /báking/ *n.* **1 a** support. **b** a body of supporters. **c** material used to form a back or support. **2** musical accompaniment.

back·lash /báklash/ *n.* **1** a marked adverse reaction. **2 a** a sudden recoil or reaction between parts of a mechanism. **b** excessive play between such parts.

back·list /báklist/ *n.* a publisher's list of books published before the current season and still in print.

back·lit /báklit/ *adj.* (esp. in photography) illuminated from behind.

back·log /báklawg, -log/ *n.* accumulation of uncompleted work, etc.

back·most /bákmōst/ *adj.* furthest back.

back num·ber *n.* **1** an issue of a periodical earlier than the current one. **2** *sl.* an out-of-date person or thing.

back·pack /bákpak/ *n. & v.* ● *n.* a bag slung by straps from both shoulders and resting on the back. ● *v.intr.* travel with a backpack. □□ **back·pack·er** *n.*

back·ped·al /bákped'l/ *v.* (**-pedaled**, **-pedaling**) **1** pedal backward on a bicycle, etc. **2** reverse one's previous action or opinion.

back·rest /bákrest/ *n.* a support for the back.

back·scratch·er /bákskrachər/ *n.* **1** a rod terminating in a clawed hand for scratching one's own back. **2** a person who performs mutual services with another for gain.

back·seat /báksēet/ *n.* **1** a seat in the rear. **2** an inferior position or status.

back·seat driv·er *n.* a person who is eager to advise without responsibility (orig. of a passenger in a car, etc.).

back·sheesh var. of BAKSHEESH.

back·side /báksīd/ *n. colloq.* the buttocks.

back·sight /báksīt/ *n.* the sight of a rifle, etc., that is nearer the stock.

back·slap·ping /bákslaping/ *adj.* vigorously hearty.

back·slash /bákslash/ *n.* a reverse slash (\).

back·slide /bákslīd/ *v.intr.* (*past* **-slid** /-slid/; *past part.* **-slid** or **-slidden** /-slid'n/) relapse into bad ways or error. □□ **back·slid·er** *n.*

back·space /bákspays/ *v.intr.* move a typewriter carriage or computer cursor back one or more spaces.

back·spin /bákspin/ *n.* a backward spin imparted to a ball causing it to fly off at an angle on hitting a surface.

back·stab·bing *n. & adj.* ● *n.* criticizing someone while pretending to be friendly. ● *adj.* behaving in such a way.

back·stage /bákstáyj/ *adv. & adj.* ● *adv.* **1** *Theatr.* out of view of the audience. **2** not known to the public. ● *adj.* that is backstage; concealed.

back·stairs /bákstairz/ *n.pl.* **1** stairs at the back of a building. **2** (also **back·stair**) (*attrib.*) denoting underhand or clandestine activity.

back·stitch /bákstich/ *n. & v.* ● *n.* a stitch bringing the thread back to the preceding stitch. ▷ STITCH. ● *v.tr.* & *intr.* sew using backstitch.

back·stop /bákstaap/ *n.* **1** *Baseball* a fence or screen positioned behind home plate. **2** something that provides support or reinforcement.

back street *n.* a street away from the main streets.

back-street *adj.* denoting illicit activity (*a back-street drug deal*).

back·stroke /bákstrōk/ *n.* a swimming stroke performed on the back with the arms lifted alternately out of the water in a backward circular motion and the legs extended in a kicking action.

back talk *n. colloq.* the practice of replying rudely or impudently.

back to back *adv.* **1** with backs adjacent and opposite each other (*we stood back to back*). **2** consecutively.

back-to-back *adj.* **1** consecutive. **2** esp. *Brit.* (of houses) with a party wall at the rear.

back to front *adv.* **1** with the back at the front and the front at the back. **2** in disorder.

back-to-na·ture *adj.* (usu. *attrib.*) applied to a movement or enthusiast for the reversion to a simpler way of life.

back·track /báktrak/ *v.intr.* **1** retrace one's steps. **2** reverse one's previous action or opinion.

back·up /bákup/ *n.* **1** moral or technical support (*called for extra backup*). **2** a reserve. **3** *Computing* (often *attrib.*) **a** the procedure for making security copies of data (*backup facilities*). **b** the copy itself (*made a backup*). **4** a line of vehicles, etc.

back·up light *n.* a white light at the rear of a vehicle operated when the vehicle is in reverse gear.

back·veld /bákvelt/ *n. S.Afr.* remote country districts, esp. those strongly conservative. □□ **back·veld·er** *n.*

back·ward /bákwərd/ *adv. & adj.* ● *adv.* (also **back·wards**) **1** away from one's front (*lean backward*). **2 a** with the back foremost (*walk backward*). **b** in reverse of the usual way (*count backward*). **3 a** into a worse state (*new policies are taking us backward*). **b** into the past (*looked backward over the years*). **c** back toward the starting point (*rolled backward*). ● *adj.* **1** directed to the rear or starting point (*a backward look*). **2** reversed. **3** mentally retarded or slow. **4** reluctant; shy; unassertive. □ **backward and forward** to and fro. **bend** (or **fall** or **lean**) **over backward** (often foll. by *to* + infin.) *colloq.* make every effort. **know backward and forward** be entirely familiar with. □□ **back·ward·ness** *n.*

back·wash /bákwosh, -wawsh/ *n.* **1 a** a receding waves created by the motion of a ship, etc. **b** a backward current of air created by a moving aircraft. **2** repercussions.

back·wa·ter /bákwawtər, -wotər/ *n.* **1** a place or condition remote from the center of activity or thought. **2** stagnant water.

back·woods /bákwŏŏdz/ *n.pl.* **1** uncleared forest land. **2** any remote or sparsely inhabited region.

back·woods·man /bákwŏŏdzmən/ *n.* (*pl.* **-men**) **1** an inhabitant of backwoods. **2** an uncouth person.

back·yard /bakyaárd/ *n.* a yard at the back of a house, etc. □ **in one's own backyard** *colloq.* near at hand.

ba·cla·va var. of BAKLAVA.

ba·con /báykən/ *n.* cured meat from the back or sides of a pig. □ **bring home the bacon** *colloq.* **1** succeed in one's undertaking. **2** supply material provision or support.

Ba·co·ni·an /baykốneeən/ *adj. & n.* ● *adj.* of or relating to the English philosopher Sir Francis Bacon (d. 1626), or to his inductive method of reasoning and philosophy. ● *n.* **1** a supporter of the view that Bacon was the author of Shakespeare's plays. **2** a follower of Bacon.

bac·te·ri·a *pl.* see BACTERIUM.

bac·te·ri·cide /bakteérisīd/ *n.* a substance capable of destroying bacteria. □□ **bac·te·ri·cid·al** /-risíd'l/ *adj.*

bac·te·ri·ol·o·gy /bákteereeóləjee/ *n.* the study of bacteria. □□ **bac·te·ri·o·log·i·cal** /-reeəlójikəl/ *adj.* **bacteriologist** /-lójist/ *n.*

bac·te·ri·o·lyt·ic /bakteéreeəlítik/ *adj.* capable of rupturing bacteria.

bac·te·ri·o·phage /bakteéreeəfayj/ *n.* a virus parasitic on a bacterium.

bac·te·ri·o·sta·sis /bakteéreeōstáysis/ *n.* the inhibition of the growth of bacteria without destroying them. □□ **bac·te·ri·o·stat·ic** /-státik/ *adj.*

bac·te·ri·um /bakteéreeəm/ *n.* (*pl.* **bacteria** /-reeə/) ◂ a member of a large group of unicellular micro-organisms lacking organelles and an organized nucleus, some of which can cause disease. □□ **bac·te·ri·al** *adj.*

plasma membrane
ribosome
flagellum

BACTERIUM:
SECTION THROUGH
A BACTERIUM

Bac·tri·an cam·el /báktreeən/ *n.* a camel, *Camelus bactrianus*, native to central Asia, with two humps. ▷ CAMEL

bad /bad/ *adj., n., & adv.* ● *adj.* (**worse** /wərs/; **worst** /wərst/) **1** inferior; inadequate; defective (*bad work; a bad driver; bad light*). **2 a** unpleasant (*bad weather; bad news*). **b** unfortunate (*bad business*). **3** harmful (*is bad for you*). **4 a** (of food) decayed. **b** polluted (*bad air*). **5** ill; injured (*am feeling bad today; a bad leg*). **6** *colloq.* regretful; ashamed (*feels bad about it*). **7** (of an unwelcome thing) serious; severe (*a bad mistake*). **8 a** morally unsound or offensive (*a bad man; bad language*). **b** disobedient; badly behaved (*a bad child*). **9** not valid (*a bad check*). **10** (**badder**, **baddest**) *sl.* good; excellent. ● *n.* **1 a** ill fortune (*take the bad with the good*). **b** ruin; a degenerate condition (*go to the bad*). **2** the debit side of an account (*$500 to the bad*). **3** (as *pl.*; prec. by *the*) bad people. ● *adv. colloq.* badly (*took it bad*). □ **in a bad way** ill; in trouble (*looked in a bad way*). **too bad** *colloq.* (of circumstances, etc.) regrettable but now beyond retrieval. □□ **bad·ness** *n.*

bad blood *n.* ill feeling.

bad break *n. colloq.* **1** a piece of bad luck. **2** a mistake or blunder.

bad breath *n.* unpleasant-smelling breath.

bad debt *n.* a debt that is not recoverable.

bad·die /bádee/ *n.* (also **bad·dy**) (*pl.* **-ies**) *colloq.* a villain.

bade see BID.

bad faith *n.* intent to deceive.

badge /baj/ *n.* **1** a distinctive emblem worn as a mark of office, membership, achievement, licensed employment, etc. **2** any feature or sign which reveals a characteristic condition or quality.

badg·er /bájər/ *n. & v.* ● *n.* ▾ an omnivorous gray-coated nocturnal mammal of the family Mustelidae with a white stripe flanked by black stripes on its head, which lives in sets. ▷ VERTEBRATE. ● *v.tr.* pester; harass; tease.

BADGER
(*Meles meles*)

bad·i·nage /bád'naázh/ *n.* humorous or playful ridicule.

bad job *n. Brit. colloq.* an unfortunate state of affairs.

bad·lands /bádlandz/ *n.pl.* extensive uncultivable eroded tracts in arid areas.

bad lot *n.* a person of bad character.

bad·ly /bádlee/ *adv.* (**worse** /wərs/; **worst** /wərst/) **1** in a bad manner (*it works badly*). **2** *colloq.* very much (*wants it badly*). **3** severely (*he was badly defeated*).

bad man·nered *adj.* having bad manners; rude.

bad·min·ton /bádmint'n/ *n.* ▲ a game played with rackets in which a shuttlecock is volleyed back and forth across a net.

bad-mouth *v.tr.* subject to malicious gossip or criticism.

bad news *n. colloq.* an unpleasant or troublesome person or thing.

bad-tem·pered /bádtémpərd/ *adj.* having a bad temper; irritable; easily annoyed.

Bae·de·ker /báydikər/ *n.* any of various travel guidebooks published by the firm founded by the German Karl *Baedeker* (d. 1859).

baf·fle /báfəl/ *v. & n.* ● *v.tr.* **1** confuse or perplex. **2 a** frustrate or hinder (plans, etc.). **b** restrain or regulate the progress of (fluid, etc.). ● *n.* (also **baf·fle-board**, **baf·fle-plate**) a device used to restrain the flow of fluid, gas, etc., or to limit the

BADMINTON

Often an indoor sport, played on a court with a high net, badminton singles is played by two opponents and doubles by teams of two people. The object of the game is to hit the shuttlecock to the floor on the opposite side of the net, so that the shot cannot be returned. Only the serving player can score a point from a rally.

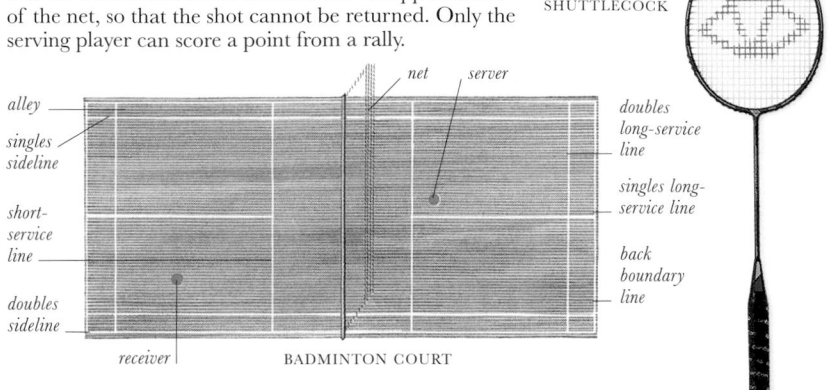

BADMINTON RACKET

SHUTTLECOCK

net   *server*

alley

singles sideline

short-service line

doubles sideline

doubles long-service line

singles long-service line

back boundary line

receiver | BADMINTON COURT

---

emission of sound, light, etc. □□ **baf·fle·ment** *n.* **baf·fling** *adj.* **baf·fling·ly** *adv.*

bag /bag/ *n. & v.* ● *n.* **1** a receptacle of flexible material with an opening at the top. **2 a** (usu. in *pl.*) a piece of luggage (*put the bags in the trunk*). **b** a woman's handbag. **3** (in *pl.*; usu. foll. by *of*) *colloq.* a large amount; plenty (*bags of money*). **4** (in *pl.*) *Brit. colloq.* trousers. **5** *sl. derog.* a woman, esp. regarded as unattractive or unpleasant. **6** an amount of game shot or allowed. **7** (usu. in *pl.*) baggy folds of skin under the eyes. **8** *sl.* a person's particular interest or preoccupation (*his bag is baroque music*). ● *v.* (**bagged**, **bagging**) **1** *tr.* put in a bag. **2** *tr. a colloq.* secure; get hold of (*bagged the best seat*). **b** *colloq.* steal. **c** shoot (game). **3 a** *intr.* hang loosely; bulge. **b** *tr.* cause to do this. □ **bag and baggage** with all one's belongings. **bag** (or **whole bag**) **of tricks** *colloq.* a set of ingenious plans or resources. **in the bag** *colloq.* achieved; as good as secured. □□ **bag·ful** *n.* (*pl.* **-fuls**).

ba·gasse /bəgás/ *n.* the dry pulpy residue left after the extraction of juice from sugar cane, usable as fuel or to make paper, etc.

bag·a·telle /bágətél/ *n.* **1** a game in which small balls are struck into numbered holes on a board, with pins as obstructions. **2** a mere trifle. **3** *Mus.* a short piece of music, esp. for the piano.

ba·gel /báygəl/ *n.* a hard bread roll in the shape of a ring.

bag·gage /bágij/ *n.* **1** everyday belongings packed up in suitcases, etc., for traveling; luggage. **2** the portable equipment of an army. **3** *derog.* a girl or woman. □ **baggage car** a car on a passenger train used for luggage, etc.

bag·gy /bágee/ *adj.* (**baggier**, **baggiest**) **1** hanging in loose folds. **2** puffed out. □□ **bag·gi·ness** *n.*

bag la·dy *n.* (*pl.* **-ies**) a homeless woman who carries her possessions around in shopping bags.

bag·man /bágmən/ *n.* (*pl.* **-men**) *sl.* an agent who collects or distributes illicitly gained money.

bag·nio /báanyō/ *n.* (*pl.* **-os**) **1** a brothel. **2** *hist.* a prison in the Orient.

bag·pipe /bágpīp/ *n.* (usu. in *pl.*) ◄ a musical instrument consisting of a windbag which is squeezed by the player's arm to force air into reeded pipes.

drone

bag

mouthpiece

chanter

BAGPIPE: MID-19TH-CENTURY FRENCH SHEEPSKIN BINIOU

---

ba·guette /bagét/ *n.* a long narrow French loaf.

bah /baa/ *int.* an expression of contempt or disbelief.

Ba·ha·'i /bəhaá-ee, -hí/ *n.* (*pl.* **Baha'is**) a member of a monotheistic religion founded in 1863 as a branch of Babism (an offshoot of Islam), emphasizing religious unity and world peace. □□ **Ba·ha·'ism** *n.*

Ba·ha·mi·an /bəháymeeən, -háa-/ *n. & adj.* ● *n.* **1** a native or inhabitant of the Bahamas in the W. Indies. **2** a person of Bahamian descent. ● *adj.* of or relating to the Bahamas.

Ba·ha·sa In·do·ne·sia /baaháasə indənéezhə/ *n.* the official language of Indonesia.

bail[1] /bayl/ *n. & v.* ● *n.* **1** money, etc., required as security for the temporary release of a prisoner pending trial. **2** a person or persons giving such security. ● *v.tr.* (usu. foll. by *out*) **1** release or secure the release of (a prisoner) on payment of bail. **2** release from a difficulty; come to the rescue of. □ **forfeit** (or *colloq.* **jump**) **bail** fail to appear for trial after being released on bail. **go** (or **stand**) **bail** (often foll. by *for*) act as surety (for an accused person).

bail[2] /bayl/ *n.* ● *n.* **1** the bar on a typewriter holding the paper against the platen. **2** *Cricket* either of the two crosspieces bridging the stumps. ▷ CRICKET. **3** an arched usu. wire handle, as of a pail. **4** a bar separating horses in an open stable.

bail[3] /bayl/ *v.tr.* **1** (usu. foll. by *out*) scoop water out of (a boat, etc.). **2** scoop (water, etc.) out. □ **bail out** (of a pilot, etc.) make an emergency parachute descent from an aircraft.

bail·ee /baylée/ *n. Law* a person or party to whom goods are committed for a purpose, e.g., custody or repair, without transfer of ownership.

bai·ley /báylee/ *n.* (*pl.* **-eys**) **1** the outer wall of a castle. **2** ▼ a court enclosed by it. ▷ CASTLE.

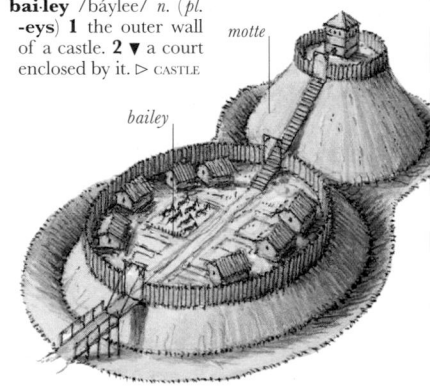

motte

bailey

BAILEY: NORMAN MOTTE AND BAILEY CASTLE

Bai·ley bridge /báylee/ *n.* a temporary bridge of lattice steel designed for rapid assembly from prefabricated standard parts, used esp. in military operations.

bail·iff /báylif/ *n.* **1** an official in a court of law who keeps order, looks after prisoners, etc. **2** *Brit.* the agent or steward of a landlord.

bai·li·wick /báyliwik/ *n.* **1** *Law* the district or jurisdiction of a bailiff. **2** *joc.* a person's sphere of operations or particular area of interest.

bail·ment /báylmənt/ *n.* the act of delivering goods, etc., for a (usu. specified) purpose.

bail·or /báylər/ *n. Law* a person or party that entrusts goods to a bailee.

bail·out /báylowt/ *n.* a rescue from a dire situation (*a financial bailout for an ailing company*).

bails·man /báylzmən/ *n.* (*pl.* **-men**) a person who provides bail for another.

bain-ma·rie /báNmaréé/ *n.* (*pl.* **bains-marie** *pronunc.* same) a cooking utensil consisting of a vessel of hot water in which a receptacle can be slowly and gently heated.

bairn /bairn/ *n. Sc. & No. of Engl.* a child.

bait /bayt/ *n. & v.* ● *n.* **1** food used to entice a prey. **2** an allurement; something intended to tempt or entice. ● *v.tr.* **1 a** harass or annoy (a person). **b** torment (a chained animal). **2** put bait on (a hook, trap, etc.) to entice a prey.

baize /bayz/ *n.* a coarse usu. green woolen material resembling felt as a covering or lining, esp. on the tops of billiard and card tables. ▷ POOL

bake /bayk/ *v. & n.* ● *v.* **1 a** *tr.* cook (food) by dry heat in an oven or on a hot surface, without direct exposure to a flame. **b** *intr.* undergo the process of being baked. **2** *intr. colloq.* **a** (usu. as **be baking**) (of weather, etc.) be very hot. **b** (of a person) become hot. **3 a** *tr.* harden (clay, etc.) by heat. **b** *intr.* (of clay, etc.) be hardened by heat. ● *n.* **1** the act or an instance of baking. **2** a batch of baking. **3** a social gathering at which baked food is eaten.

baked A·las·ka /əláaskə/ *n.* sponge cake and ice cream with a meringue covering, baked in an oven.

baked beans *n.pl.* baked white beans usu. cooked with salt pork and brown sugar or molasses.

bake·house /báyk-hows/ *n.* = BAKERY.

Ba·ke·lite /báykəlīt, báyk-līt/ *n. Trademark* ► any of various thermosetting resins or plastics made from formaldehyde and phenol and used for cables, buttons, plates, etc. ▷ COSTUME JEWELRY

bak·er /báykər/ *n.* a person who bakes and sells bread, cakes, etc, esp. professionally.

BAKELITE SPEAKER (1937)

bak·er's doz·en *n.* thirteen (so called from the former bakers' custom of adding an extra loaf to a dozen sold; the exact reason for this is unclear).

bak·er·y /báykəree/ *n.* (*pl.* **-ies**) a place where bread and cakes are made or sold.

bak·ing pow·der *n.* a mixture of sodium bicarbonate, cream of tartar, etc., used instead of yeast in baking.

bak·ing so·da *n.* sodium bicarbonate.

bak·la·va /báakləvaa/ *n.* (also **ba·cla·va**) a rich dessert of flaky pastry, honey, and nuts, originating in Turkey.

bak·sheesh /báksheesh/ *n.* (also **back·sheesh**) (in some eastern countries) a small sum of money given as a gratuity or as alms.

bal·a·cla·va /báləkláavə/ *n.* (in full **balaclava helmet**) a tight woolen garment covering the whole head and neck except for the eyes, nostrils, and mouth.

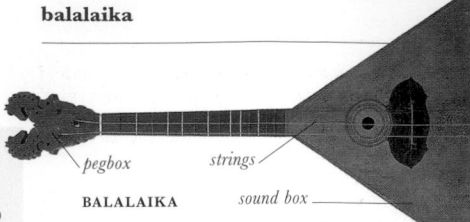

BALALAIKA

pegbox   *strings*   *sound box*

B

bal·a·lai·ka /bálǝlíkǝ/ *n.* ▲ a guitar-like musical instrument having a triangular body and 2–4 strings, popular in Russia and other Slav countries. ▷ STRINGED

bal·ance /bálǝns/ *n. & v.* ● *n.* **1** an apparatus for weighing. **2 a** a counteracting weight or force. **b** (in full **balance wheel**) the regulating device in a clock, etc. **3 a** an even distribution of weight or amount. **b** stability of body or mind (*regained his balance*). **4** a preponderating weight or amount (*the balance of opinion*). **5 a** an agreement between or the difference between credits and debits in an account. **b** the difference between an amount due and an amount paid (*will pay the balance next week*). **c** an amount left over; the rest. **6 a** *Art* harmony of design and proportion. **b** *Mus.* the relative volume of various sources of sound (*bad balance between violins and trumpets*). **7** (**the Balance**) the zodiacal sign or constellation Libra. ▷ LIBRA. ● *v.* **1** *tr.* (foll. by *with*, *against*) offset or compare (one thing) with another (*must balance the advantages with the disadvantages*). **2** *tr.* counteract, equal, or neutralize the weight or importance of. **3 a** *tr.* bring into or keep in equilibrium (*balanced a book on her head*). **b** *intr.* be in equilibrium (*balanced on one leg*). **4** *tr.* (usu. as **balanced** *adj.*) establish equal or appropriate proportions of elements in (*a balanced diet*). **5** *tr.* weigh (arguments, etc.) against each other. **6 a** *tr.* compare debits and credits of (an account). **b** *intr.* (of an account) have credits and debits equal. □ **in the balance** uncertain; at a critical stage. **on balance** all things considered. **strike a balance** choose a moderate course or compromise. □□ **bal·anc·er** *n.*

bal·ance of pay·ments *n.* the difference in value between payments into and out of a country.

bal·ance of pow·er *n.* **1** a situation in which the chief nations of the world have roughly equal power. **2** the power held by a small group or larger groups of equal strength.

bal·ance of trade *n.* the difference in value between imports and exports.

bal·ance sheet *n.* a statement giving the balance of an account.

ba·la·ta /bǝlótǝ/ *n.* **1** any of several latex-yielding trees of Central America, esp. *Manilkara bidentata*. **2** the dried sap of this used as a substitute for gutta-percha.

bal·brig·gan /balbrígǝn/ *n.* a knitted cotton fabric used for underwear, etc.

bal·co·ny /bálkǝnee/ *n.* (*pl.* **-ies**) **1** a platform on the outside of a building, with access from an upper floor window or door. **2 a** a tier of seats in a gallery in a theater, etc. **b** the upstairs seats in a movie theater, etc. □□ **bal·co·nied** *adj.*

bald /bawld/ *adj.* **1** with the scalp wholly or partly lacking hair. **2** not covered by the usual hair, feathers, leaves, etc. **3** *colloq.* with the surface worn away (*a bald tire*). **4 a** blunt; unelaborated (*a bald statement*). **b** undisguised (*the bald effrontery*). □□ **bald·ing** *adj.* (in senses 1–3). **bald·ly** *adv.* (in sense 4). **bald·ness** *n.*

bal·da·chin /báwldǝkin/ *n.* (also **bal·da·chi·no** /-kéenō/, **baldaquin**) a ceremonial canopy over an altar, throne, etc.

bald ea·gle *n.* a white-headed eagle (*Haliaeetus leucocephalus*), used as the emblem of the United States. ▷ EAGLE

bal·der·dash /báwldǝrdash/ *n.* senseless talk or writing; nonsense.

bald·head /báwldhed/ *n.* a person with a bald head.

bal·dric /báwldrik/ *n. hist.* a belt for a sword, bugle,

etc., hung from the shoulder across the body to the opposite hip.

bale[1] /bayl/ *n. & v.* ● *n.* **1** a bundle of merchandise or hay, etc., tightly wrapped and bound with cords or hoops. **2** the quantity in a bale as a measure, esp. 500 lb. of cotton. ● *v.tr.* make up into bales.

bale[2] /bayl/ *n. archaic or poet.* evil; destruction; woe; pain; misery.

ba·leen whale /bǝléen/ *n.* ▼ any of various whales of the suborder Mysticeti, having plates of whalebone in the mouth for straining plankton from the water. ▷ FILTER FEEDING, WHALE

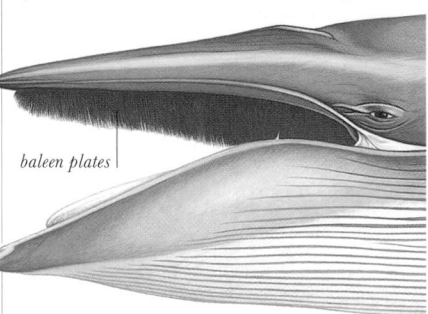

baleen plates

BALEEN WHALE: BLUE WHALE
(*Balaenoptera musculus*)

bale·ful /báylfŏŏl/ *adj.* **1** gloomy; menacing. **2** harmful; malignant; destructive. □□ **bale·ful·ly** *adv.*

bal·er /báylǝr/ *n.* a machine for making bales of hay, straw, metal, etc.

Ba·li·nese /báǝlineéz/ *n. & adj.* ● *n.* (*pl.* same) **1** a native of Bali, an island in Indonesia. **2** the language of Bali. ● *adj.* of or relating to Bali or its people or language.

balk /bawk/ *v. & n.* ● *v.* **1** *intr.* **a** refuse to go on. **b** (often foll. by *at*) hesitate. **2** *tr.* **a** thwart; hinder. **b** disappoint. **3** *tr.* **a** let slip (a chance, etc.). **b** ignore; shirk. ● *n.* **1** a stumbling block. **2** a roughly-squared timber beam. **3** *Baseball* an illegal action made by a pitcher.

Bal·kan /báwlkǝn/ *adj. & n.* ● *adj.* **1** of or relating to the region of SE Europe bounded by the Adriatic, the Aegean, and the Black Sea. **2** of or relating to its peoples or countries. ● *n.* (**the Balkans**) the Balkan countries.

balk·y /báwkee/ *adj.* (**-ier**, **-iest**) reluctant; perverse. □□ **balk·i·ness** *n.*

ball[1] /bawl/ *n. & v.* ● *n.* **1** a solid or hollow sphere, esp. for use in a game. **2 a** a ball-shaped object (*ball of wool*). **b** a rounded part of the body (*ball of the foot*). **3** a solid nonexplosive missile for a cannon, etc. **4** a single delivery of a ball in cricket, etc., or passing of a ball in soccer. **5** *Baseball* a pitched ball that is not swung at by the batter and that does not pass through the strike zone. **6** (in *pl.*) *coarse sl.* **a** the testicles. **b** courage. ¶ Sense 6 is usually considered a taboo use. ● *v.* **1** *tr.* squeeze or wind into a ball. **2** *intr.* form into a ball or balls. **3** *tr. & intr. coarse sl.* have sexual intercourse. □ **the ball is in your**, etc., **court** you, etc., must be next to act. **on the ball** *colloq.* alert. **play ball 1** start or continue a ballgame. **2** *colloq.* cooperate. **start**, etc., **the ball rolling** set an activity in motion.

ball[2] /bawl/ *n.* **1** a formal social gathering for dancing. **2** *sl.* an enjoyable time (esp. *have a ball*).

bal·lad /bálǝd/ *n.* **1** a poem or song narrating a popular story. **2** a slow sentimental or romantic song.

bal·lade /bǝláad/ *n.* **1** a poem of one or more triplets of stanzas with a repeated refrain and an envoy. **2** *Mus.* a short lyrical piece, esp. for piano.

bal·lad·eer /bálǝdéer/ *n.* a singer or composer of ballads.

bal·lad·ry /bálǝdree/ *n.* ballad poetry.

ball-and-sock·et joint *n. Anat.* a joint in which a

rounded end lies in a concave cup or socket, allowing freedom of movement. ▷ JOINT

bal·last /bálǝst/ *n. & v.* ● *n.* **1** any heavy material placed in a ship or the basket of a balloon, etc., to secure stability. **2** coarse stone, etc., used to form the bed of a railroad track or road. ● *v.tr.* **1** provide with ballast. **2** afford stability or weight to.

ball bear·ing *n.* **1** ► a bearing in which the two halves are separated by a ring of small metal balls which reduce friction. **2** one of these balls.

BALL BEARING

ball·boy /báwlboy/ *n.* (*fem.* **ballgirl** /-gǝrl/) a boy or girl who retrieves balls that go out of play during a game.

ball cock *n.* a floating ball on a hinged arm, whose movement up and down controls the water level in a cistern, etc.

bal·le·ri·na /bálǝreénǝ/ *n.* a female ballet dancer.

bal·let /baláy, bálay/ *n.* **1 a** a dramatic or representational style of dancing and mime, using set steps and techniques and usu. (esp. in classical ballet) accompanied by music. **b** a particular piece or performance of ballet. **c** the music for this. **2** a company performing ballet. □□ **bal·let·ic** /balétik/ *adj.*

bal·let·o·mane /balétǝmayn/ *n.* a devotee of ballet.

ball game *n.* **1** any game played with a ball, esp. a game of baseball. **2** *colloq.* a particular affair or concern (*a whole new ball game*).

bal·lis·ta /bǝlístǝ/ *n.* (*pl.* **ballistae** /-stee/) a catapult used in ancient warfare for hurling large stones, etc.

bal·lis·tic /bǝlístik/ *adj.* **1** of or relating to projectiles. **2** moving under the force of gravity only. □ **go ballistic** *colloq.* become furious.

bal·lis·tic mis·sile *n.* ► a missile which is initially powered and guided but falls under gravity on its target.

bal·lis·tics /bǝlístiks/ *n.pl.* (usu. treated as *sing.*) the science of projectiles and firearms.

bal·locks var. of BOLLOCKS.

bal·loon /bǝlóon/ *n. & v.* ● *n.* **1** a small inflatable rubber pouch with a neck, used as a child's toy or as decoration. **2** a large bag inflatable with hot air or gas to make it rise in the air, often carrying a basket for passengers. ▷ HOT-AIR BALLOON. **3** a balloon shape enclosing the words or thoughts of characters in a comic strip. **4** a large globular drinking glass. ● *v.* **1** *intr. & tr.* swell out or cause to swell out like a balloon. **2** *intr.* travel by balloon. □ **when the balloon goes up** *colloq.* when the action or trouble starts. □□ **bal·loon·ist** *n.*

bal·lot /bálǝt/ *n. & v.* ● *n.* **1** a process of voting. **2** the total of votes recorded in a ballot. **3** the drawing of lots. **4** a paper or ticket, etc., used in voting. ● *v.* (**balloted**, **balloting**) **1** *intr.* (usu. foll. by *for*) **a** hold a ballot; give a vote. **b** draw lots for precedence, etc. **2** *tr.* take a ballot of (*the union balloted its members*).

bal·lot box *n.* a sealed box into which voters put completed ballot papers.

ball·park /báwlpaark/ *n.* **1** a baseball field. **2** (*attrib.*) *colloq.* approximate; rough (*a ballpark figure*). □ **in the (right) ballpark** *colloq.* close to one's objective; approximately correct.

nose cone
whistle

BALLISTIC MISSILE: WORLD WAR I MESSAGE ROCKET

rocket body

stabilizing fin

ball·point /báwlpoint/ *n.* (in full **ball·point pen**) a pen with a tiny ball as its writing point.

ball·room /báwlrōom, -rŏom/ *n.* a large room or hall for dancing.

ball·room danc·ing *n.* formal social dancing as a recreation.

bal·ly·hoo /báleehōō/ *n.* **1** a loud noise or fuss; a confused state or commotion. **2** extravagant or sensational publicity.

balm /baam/ *n.* **1** an aromatic ointment for anointing, soothing, or healing. **2** a fragrant and medicinal exudation from certain trees and plants. **3** a healing or soothing influence or consolation. **4** ▶ any aromatic herb, esp. one of the genus *Melissa*. **5** a pleasant perfume or fragrance.

balm·y /báamee/ *adj.* (**balmier, balmiest**) **1** mild and fragrant; soothing. **2** yielding balm. **3** *sl.* stupid; crazy; foolish.

bal·ne·ol·o·gy /bálneeóləjee/ *n.* the scientific study of bathing and medicinal springs. □□ **bal·ne·o·log·i·cal** /-neeəlójikəl/ *adj.* **bal·ne·ol·o·gist** *n.*

ba·lo·ney /bəlónee/ *n.* (also **bo·lo·ney**) (*pl.* **-eys**) *sl.* **1** humbug; nonsense. **2** = BOLOGNA.

bal·sa /báwlsə/ *n.* **1** (in full **balsa wood**) a type of tough lightweight wood used for making models, etc. **2** the tropical American tree, *Ochroma lagopus*, from which it comes.

bal·sam /báwlsəm/ *n.* **1** an aromatic resinous exudation obtained from various trees and shrubs and used as a base for certain fragrances and medical preparations. **2** an ointment, esp. one composed of a substance dissolved in oil or turpentine. **3** any of various trees or shrubs which yield balsam. **4** any of several flowering plants of the genus *Impatiens*. **5** a healing or soothing agency. □□ **balsamic** /-sámik/ *adj.*

bal·sam fir *n.* a N. American tree (*Abies balsamea*) which yields balsam.

bal·sam pop·lar *n.* any of various N. American poplars, esp. *Populus balsamifera*, yielding balsam.

Bal·tic /báwltik/ *n. & adj.* **1** (**the Baltic**) **a** an almost landlocked sea of NE Europe. **b** the nations bordering this sea. **2** an Indo-European branch of languages comprising Old Prussian, Lithuanian, and Latvian. ● *adj.* of or relating to the Baltic or the Baltic branch of languages.

bal·us·ter /báləstər/ *n.* each of a series of often ornamental short posts or pillars supporting a rail or coping, etc. ▷ WROUGHT IRON. ¶ Often confused with *banister*.

bal·us·trade /báləstráyd/ *n.* a railing supported by balusters.

bam·bi·no /bambéenō/ *n.* (*pl.* **bambini** /-nee/) *colloq.* a young child.

bam·boo /bambōo/ *n.* **1** ▼ a mainly tropical giant woody grass of the subfamily Bambusidae. **2** its hollow jointed stem, used as a stick or to make furniture, etc.

bam·boo·zle /bambōozəl/ *v.tr. colloq.* cheat; hoax; mystify. □□ **bam·boo·zle·ment** *n.* **bam·boo·zler** *n.*

ban /ban/ *v. & n.* ● *v.tr.* (**banned, banning**) forbid; prohibit (an action, etc), esp. formally; refuse admittance to (a person). ● *n.* **1** a formal or authoritative prohibition (*a ban on smoking*). **2** a tacit prohibition by public opinion. **3** *hist.* a sentence of outlawry. **4** *archaic* a curse or execration.

BAMBOO: BLACK BAMBOO
(*Phyllostachys nigra*)

BALM:
LEMON BALM
(*Melissa officinalis*)

ba·nal /bənál, báynəl, bənaál/ *adj.* trite; feeble; commonplace. □□ **banality** /-nálitee/ *n.* (*pl.* **-ies**).

ba·nan·a /bənánə/ *n.* **1** a long curved fruit with soft pulpy flesh and yellow skin when ripe, growing in clusters. ▷ BERRY. **2** (in full **banana tree**) the tropical and subtropical treelike plant, *Musa sapientum*, bearing this. □ **go bananas** *sl.* become crazy or angry.

ba·nan·a re·pub·lic *n. derog.* a small nation, esp. in Central America, dependent on one crop or the influx of foreign capital.

ba·nan·a skin *n.* **1** the skin of a banana. **2** a cause of upset or humiliation; a blunder.

ba·nan·a split *n.* a dessert made with split bananas, ice cream, sauce, whipped cream, etc.

ba·nau·sic /bənáwsik/ *adj.* usu. *derog.* **1 a** uncultivated. **b** materialistic. **2** utilitarian.

banc /bangk/ *n.* a judge's seat in court. □ **in banc** *Law* sitting as a full court.

band¹ /band/ *n. & v.* ● *n.* **1** a flat, thin strip or loop of material put around something, esp. to hold it together or decorate it (*headband; rubber band*). **2 a** a strip of material forming part of a garment (*hatband; waistband*). **b** a stripe of a different color or material in or on an object. **3 a** a range of frequencies or wavelengths in a spectrum (esp. of radio frequencies). **b** a range of values within a series. **4** a plain or simple ring, esp. without a gem. **5** *Mech.* a belt connecting wheels or pulleys. **6** (in *pl.*) a collar having two hanging strips, worn by some lawyers, ministers, and academics in formal dress. **7** *archaic* a thing that restrains, binds, connects, or unites; a bond. ● *v.tr.* **1** put a band on. **2 a** mark with stripes. **b** (as **banded** *adj.*) *Bot. & Zool.* marked with colored bands or stripes.

band² /band/ *n. & v.* ● *n.* **1** an organized group of people having a common object, esp. of a criminal nature (*band of cutthroats*). **2 a** a group of musicians, esp. playing wind intruments and percussion (*brass band; military band*). **b** a group of musicians playing jazz, pop, or dance music (*rock band*). **c** *colloq.* an orchestra. **3** a herd or flock. ● *v.tr. & intr.* form into a group for a purpose (*band together for mutual protection*).

band·age /bándij/ *n. & v.* ● *n.* **1** a strip of material for binding up a wound, etc. **2** a piece of material used as a blindfold. ● *v.tr.* bind (a wound, etc.) with a bandage.

Band-Aid /bándayd/ *n.* **1** *Trademark* an adhesive bandage with a gauze pad in the center for covering minor wounds. **2** (**band-aid**) a stopgap solution.

ban·dan·na /bandánə/ *n.* a large handkerchief or neckerchief, usu. of silk or cotton, and often having a colorful pattern.

b. & b. *abbr.* (also **B. & B.**) bed and breakfast.

band·box /bándboks/ *n.* a usu. circular cardboard box for carrying hats. □ **out of a bandbox** extremely neat.

ban·deau /bandó/ *n.* (*pl.* **bandeaux** /-dōz/) **1** a narrow band worn around the head. **2** a narrow covering for the breasts.

ban·de·ril·la /bándərée·ə, -rílyə/ *n.* a decorated dart thrust into a bull's neck or shoulders during a bullfight.

ban·de·role /bándərōl/ *n.* (also **banderol**) **1 a** a long narrow flag with a cleft end, flown at a masthead. **b** an ornamental streamer on a knight's lance. **2 a** a ribbonlike scroll. **b** a stone band resembling a banderole, bearing an inscription.

ban·di·coot /bándikōōt/ *n.* **1** ▶ any of the insect- and plant-eating marsupials of the family Peramelidae. **2** (in full **bandicoot rat**) *Ind.* a destructive rat, *Bandicota benegalensis*.

BANDICOOT:
RABBIT-EARED
BANDICOOT
(*Macrotis lagotis*)

BANDOLIER:
WORLD WAR I
BRITISH BANDOLIER

buckle

waist-belt loop

ammunition pouch

ban·dit /bándit/ *n.* (*pl.* **bandits** or **banditti** /-dítee/) **1** a robber or murderer, esp. a member of a band. **2** an outlaw. □□ **ban·dit·ry** *n.*

band·mas·ter /bándmastər/ *n.* the conductor of a band.

ban·do·lier /bándəléer/ *n.* (also **ban·do·leer**) ▶ a shoulder belt with loops or pockets for cartridges.

band saw *n.* a mechanical saw with a blade formed by an endless toothed band.

bands·man /bándzmən/ *n.* (*pl.* **-men**) a player in a band.

band·stand /bándstand/ *n.* a covered outdoor platform for a band to play on.

band·wag·on /bándwagən/ *n.* a wagon used for carrying a band in a parade, etc. □ **climb** (or **jump**) **on the bandwagon** join a party, cause, or group that seems likely to succeed.

band·width /bándwidth, -with/ *n.* the range of frequencies within a given band (see BAND¹ *n.* 3a).

ban·dy¹ /bándee/ *adj.* (**bandier, bandiest**) **1** (of the legs) curved so as to be wide apart at the knees. **2** (also **ban·dy-leg·ged** /-légəd, -legd/) (of a person) having bandy legs.

ban·dy² /bándee/ *v.tr.* (**-ies, -ied**) **1** (often foll. by *about*) **a** pass (a story, rumor, etc.) to and fro. **b** throw or pass (a ball, etc.) to and fro. **2** (often foll. by *about*) discuss disparagingly (*bandied his name about*). **3** (often foll. by *with*) exchange (blows, insults, etc.) (*don't bandy words with me*).

bane /bayn/ *n.* the cause of ruin or trouble (esp. *the bane of one's life*). □□ **bane·ful** *adj.*

bang /bang/ *n., v., & adv.* ● *n.* **1 a** a loud short sound. **b** an explosion. **c** the report of a gun. **2 a** a sharp blow. **b** the sound of this. **3** a fringe of hair cut straight across the forehead. ● *v.* **1** *tr.* strike or shut noisily (*banged on the table*). **2** *tr. & intr.* make or cause to make the sound of a blow or an explosion. **3** *tr.* cut (hair) in bangs. ● *adv.* with a bang or sudden impact. □ **go bang 1** (of a door, etc.) shut noisily. **2** explode. **3** *colloq.* be suddenly destroyed (*bang went their chances*). **go with a bang** go successfully.

ban·gle /bánggəl/ *n.* a rigid ornamental band worn around the arm.

bang-up *adj. sl.* first-class; excellent (esp. *bang-up job*).

ban·ish /bánish/ *v.tr.* **1** formally expel. **2** dismiss from one's presence or mind. □□ **ban·ish·ment** *n.*

ban·is·ter /bánistər/ *n.* (also **ban·nis·ter**) **1** the uprights and handrail at the side of a staircase. ▷ NEWEL. **2** an upright supporting a handrail. Often confused with *baluster*.

ban·jo /bánjō/ *n.* (*pl.* **-os** or **-oes**) a stringed musical instrument with a neck and head like a guitar and an open-backed body consisting of parchment stretched over a metal hoop.

bank¹ /bangk/ *n. & v.* ● *n.* **1 a** the sloping edge of land

B

by a river. **b** the area of ground alongside a river (*had a picnic on the bank*). **2** a raised shelf of ground; a slope. **3** an elevation in the sea or a river bed. **4** the artificial slope of a road, etc., enabling vehicles to maintain speed around a curve. **5** a mass of cloud, fog, snow, etc. ● *v.* **1** *tr. & intr.* (often foll. by *up*) heap or rise into banks. **2** *tr.* heap up (a fire) tightly so that it burns slowly. **3** *a intr.* (of a vehicle or aircraft or its occupant) travel with one side higher than the other in rounding a curve. **b** *tr.* cause (a vehicle or aircraft) to do this.

bank² /bangk/ *n. & v.* ● *n.* **1 a** a financial establishment which uses money deposited by customers for investment, pays it out when required, makes loans at interest, etc. **b** a building in which this business takes place. **2** = PIGGY BANK. **3 a** the money or tokens held by the banker in some gambling games. **b** the banker in such games. **4** a place for storing anything for future use (*data bank*). ● *v.* **1** *tr.* deposit in a bank. **2** *intr.* engage in business as a banker. **3** *intr.* (often foll. by *at, with*) keep money (at a bank). □ **bank on** rely on (*I'm banking on your help*).

bank³ /bangk/ *n.* **1** a row of similar objects, esp. of keys, lights, or switches. **2** a tier of oars.

bank·a·ble /bángkəbəl/ *adj.* **1** acceptable at a bank. **2** reliable (*a bankable reputation*). **3** certain to bring profit; good for the box office.

bank balance *n.* the amount of money held in a bank account.

bank·card /bángk-kard/ *n.* a bank-issued credit card or automatic teller machine card.

bank·er¹ /bángkər/ *n.* **1** a person who manages or owns a bank. **2** a keeper of the bank or dealer in some gambling games.

bank·er² /bángkər/ *n.* **1** a fishing boat off Newfoundland. **2** a Newfoundland fisherman.

bank·ing /bángking/ *n.* the business transactions of a bank.

bank·note /bángknōt/ *n.* ▼ a banker's promissory note payable to the bearer on demand, and serving as money.

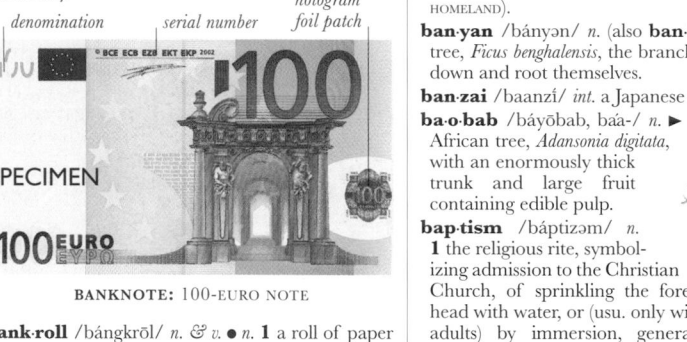

BANKNOTE: 100-EURO NOTE

bank·roll /bángkrōl/ *n. & v.* ● *n.* **1** a roll of paper currency. **2** funds. ● *v.tr. colloq.* support financially.

bank·rupt /bángkrupt/ *adj., n., & v.* ● *adj.* **1** insolvent; declared in law unable to pay debts. **2** undergoing the legal process resulting from this. ● *n.* **1** an insolvent person whose estate is administered and disposed of for the benefit of the creditors. **2** an insolvent debtor. ● *v.tr.* make bankrupt. □□ **bank·rupt·cy** /-ruptsee/ *n.* (*pl.* **-ies**).

bank·sia /bángkseeə/ *n.* any evergreen flowering shrub of the genus *Banksia*, native to Australia.

bank statement *n.* a printed statement of transactions and balance issued periodically to the holder of a bank account.

ban·ner /bánər/ *n.* **1 a** a large rectangular sign bearing a slogan or design and usu. carried on two side poles or a crossbar in a demonstration or procession. **b** a long strip of cloth, etc., bearing a slogan. **2** a flag on a pole used as the standard of a king, knight, etc. **3** (*attrib.*) excellent; outstanding (*a banner year in sales*).

ban·ner·et /bánəret/ *n.* **1** a small banner. **2** (also /-rit/) *hist.* a knight who commanded his own troops in battle under his own banner. **3** *hist.* a knighthood given on the battlefield for courage.

ban·nis·ter var. of BANISTER.

banns /banz/ *n.pl.* a notice read out, esp. on three successive Sundays in a parish church, announcing an intended marriage and giving the opportunity for objections.

ban·quet /bángkwit/ *n. & v.* ● *n.* **1** an elaborate feast. **2** a dinner for many people followed by speeches. ● *v.* (**banqueted, banqueting**) **1** *intr.* hold a banquet. **2** *tr.* entertain with a banquet.

ban·quette /bangkét/ *n.* an upholstered bench along a wall.

ban·shee /bánshee, -sheé/ *n.* a female spirit whose wailing warns of a death in a house.

ban·tam /bántəm/ *n.* **1** ► any of several small breeds of domestic fowl, of which the male is very aggressive. **2** a small but aggressive person.

ban·tam·weight /bántəmwayt/ *n.* **1** a weight in certain sports intermediate between flyweight and featherweight. **2** a sportsman of this weight.

ban·ter /bántər/ *n. & v.* ● *n.* good-humored teasing. ● *v.* **1** *tr.* ridicule in a good-humored way. **2** *intr.* talk teasingly.

Ban·tu /bántōō/ *n. & adj.* ● *n.* (*pl.* same or **Bantus**) **1** often *offens.* **a** a large group of Negroid peoples of central and southern Africa. **b** a member of any of these peoples. **2** the group of languages spoken by them. ● *adj.* of or relating to these peoples or languages.

Ban·tu·stan /bántōōstan/ *n. S.Afr. hist.* often *offens.* any of several partially self-governing areas formerly reserved for black South Africans (see also HOMELAND).

ban·yan /bányən/ *n.* (also **ban·ian**) an Indian fig tree, *Ficus benghalensis*, the branches of which hang down and root themselves.

ban·zai /baanzí/ *int.* a Japanese battle cry.

ba·o·bab /báyōbab, baá-/ *n.* ► an African tree, *Adansonia digitata*, with an enormously thick trunk and large fruit containing edible pulp.

bap·tism /báptizəm/ *n.* **1** the religious rite, symbolizing admission to the Christian Church, of sprinkling the forehead with water, or (usu. only with adults) by immersion, generally accompanied by name giving. **2** the act of baptizing or being baptized. □□ **baptismal** /-tízməl/ *adj.*

bap·tism of fire *n.* **1** initiation into battle. **2** a painful new undertaking or experience.

bap·tist /báptist/ *n.* **1** a person who baptizes, esp. John the Baptist. **2** (**Baptist**) a member of a Protestant Christian denomination advocating baptism by total immersion, esp. of adults.

bap·tis·ter·y /báptistree/ *n.* (also **bap·tis·try**) (*pl.* **-ies**) **1 a** the part of a church used for baptism. **b** *hist.* a building next to a church, used for baptism. **2** (in a Baptist chapel) a sunken receptacle used for total immersion.

bap·tize /báptíz/ *v.tr.* **1** (also *absol.*) administer baptism to. **2** give a name or nickname to; christen.

bar¹ /baar/ *n., v., & prep.* ● *n.* **1** a long rod or piece of rigid wood, metal, etc. **2** a something resembling a bar (*bar of soap*; *candy bar*). **b** the heating element of an electric heater. **c** = CROSSBAR. **d** *Mil.* a metal or cloth strip worn as part of an officer's insignia. **e** a sandbank or shoal as at the mouth of a harbor or an estuary. **3 a** a barrier of any shape.

BANTAM:
PEKIN BANTAM
COCK

BAOBAB
(*Adansonia
digitata*)

b a restriction (*a bar to promotion*). **4 a** a counter in a restaurant, etc., across which alcohol or refreshments are served. **b** a room in which alcohol is served and customers may sit and drink. **c** an establishment selling alcoholic drinks to be consumed on the premises. **d** a small store or stall serving refreshments (*snack bar*). **5** an enclosure in which a defendant stands in a court of law. **6** *Mus.* **a** any of the sections of usu. equal time value into which a musical composition is divided by vertical lines across the staff. **b** (*in full* **bar line**) a vertical line used to mark divisions between bars. ▷ NOTATION. **7** (**the Bar**) *Law* **a** lawyers collectively. **b** the profession of lawyers. ● *v.tr.* (**barred, barring**) **1 a** fasten with a bar or bars. **b** (usu. foll. by *in, out*) shut or keep in or out. **2** obstruct (*bar his progress*). **3** (usu. foll. by *from*) exclude (*bar them from attending*). **4** mark with stripes. ● *prep.* except (*all were there bar a few*). □ **bar none** with no exceptions. **be called to the Bar** be admitted as a lawyer or barrister. **behind bars** in prison.

bar² /baar/ *n. esp. Meteorol.* a unit of pressure, 10^5 newtons per square meter, approx. one atmosphere.

bar·a·the·a /bárətheéə/ *n.* a fine woolen cloth, sometimes mixed with silk or cotton, used esp. for coats, suits, etc.

barb /baarb/ *n. & v.* ● *n.* **1** ► a secondary, backward facing projection from an arrow, fishhook, etc. ▷ FLUKE. **2** a deliberately hurtful remark. **3** a beardlike filament at the mouth of some fish. ● *v.tr.* **1** provide (an arrow, etc.) with a barb or barbs. **2** (as **barbed** *adj.*) (of a remark, etc.) deliberately hurtful.

barb

Bar·ba·di·an /baarbáydeeən/ *n. & adj.* ● *n.* **1** a native or inhabitant of Barbados in the W. Indies. **2** a person of Barbadian descent. ● *adj.* of or relating to Barbados or its people.

BARBS ON
AN ARROW-
HEAD

bar·bar·i·an /baarbáireeən/ *n. & adj.* ● *n.* **1** an uncultured or brutish person; a lout. **2** a member of a primitive community or tribe. ● *adj.* **1** rough and uncultured. **2** uncivilized.

bar·bar·ic /-bárik/ *adj.* **1** brutal; cruel (*flogging is a barbaric punishment*). **2** rough and uncultured; unrestrained. **3** of or like barbarians and their art or taste; primitive. □□ **bar·bar·i·cal·ly** *adv.*

bar·ba·rism /báarbərizəm/ *n.* **1 a** the absence of culture and civilized standards; ignorance and rudeness. **b** an example of this. **2** a word or expression not considered correct; a solecism. **3** anything considered to be in bad taste.

bar·bar·i·ty /baarbáritee/ *n.* (*pl.* **-ies**) **1** savage cruelty. **2** an example of this.

bar·ba·rize /báarbərīz/ *v.tr. & intr.* make or become barbarous. □□ **bar·ba·ri·za·tion** *n.*

bar·ba·rous /báarbərəs/ *adj.* **1** uncivilized. **2** cruel. **3** coarse and unrefined. □□ **bar·ba·rous·ly** *adv.* **bar·ba·rous·ness** *n.*

Bar·ba·ry ape /báarbəree/ *n.* a macaque, *Macaca sylvanus*, of N. Africa and Gibraltar.

bar·be·cue /báarbikyōō/ *n. & v.* ● *n.* **1 a** a meal cooked on an open fire out of doors, esp. meat grilled on a metal appliance. **b** a party at which such a meal is cooked. **2 a** the metal appliance used for the preparation of a barbecue. **b** a fireplace, usu. of brick, containing such an appliance. ● *v.tr.* (**barbecues, barbecued, barbecuing**) cook (esp. meat) on a barbecue.

bar·be·cue sauce *n.* a highly seasoned sauce, usu. containing chilies, in which meat, etc., may be cooked.

barbed wire *n.* wire bearing sharp pointed spikes close together and used in fencing, or in warfare as an obstruction.

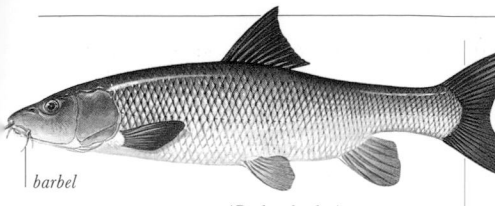

BARBEL (*Barbus barbus*)

barbel

bar·bel /báarbəl/ *n.* **1 ▲** any large European fresh-water fish of the genus *Barbus*, with fleshy filaments hanging from its mouth. **2** such a filament.

bar·bell /báarbel/ *n.* **▼** an iron bar with a series of weighted disks at each end, used for weightlifting exercises.

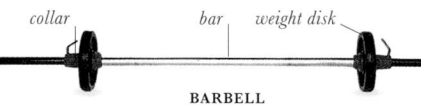

collar   *bar*   *weight disk*

BARBELL

bar·ber /báarbər/ *n.* a men's hairdresser.

bar·ber pole *n.* a spirally painted striped red and white pole hung outside barbers' shops as a business sign.

bar·ber·ry /báarberee/ *n.* (*pl.* **-ies**) **1** any shrub of the genus *Berberis*, with spiny shoots, yellow flowers, and ovoid red berries. **2** its berry.

bar·ber·shop /báarbərshop/ *n.* **1** a barber's place of business. **2** (often *attrib.*) a popular style of close harmony singing for four male voices (*barbershop quartet*).

bar·bi·can /báarbikən/ *n.* the outer defense of a city, castle, etc., esp. a double tower above a gate or drawbridge.

bar·bi·tal /báarbitawl, -tal/ *n.* a sedative drug.

bar·bi·tu·rate /baarbítchərət, -rayt/ *n.* any deriva-tive of barbituric acid used in the preparation of sedative and sleep-inducing drugs.

bar·bi·tu·ric ac·id /báarbitoorik, -tyoor-/ *n. Chem.* an organic acid from which various sedatives are derived.

bar·bule /báarbyool/ *n.* a minute filament project-ing from the barb of a feather.

barb·wire /báarbwīr/ *n.* = BARBED WIRE.

Bar·ca·Loung·er /báarkəlownjər/ *n. US propr.* a type of deeply padded reclining chair.

bar·ca·role /báarkərōl/ *n.* (also **bar·ca·rolle**) **1** a song sung by Venetian gondoliers. **2** music in imi-tation of this.

bar chart *n.* a chart using bars to represent quantity.

BAR CODE

bar code *n.* **◄** a ma-chine-readable code in the form of a pat-tern of stripes print-ed on and identifying a commodity.

bard¹ /baard/ *n.* **1** *hist.* a Celtic minstrel. **2** *poet.* a poet, esp. one treating heroic themes. **3 the Bard** (or **the Bard of Avon**) Shakespeare. □□ **bard·ic** *adj.*

bard² /baard/ *n. & v.* ● *n.* a strip of fat placed on meat or game before roasting. ● *v.tr.* cover (meat, etc.) with bards.

bare /bair/ *adj. & v.* ● *adj.* **1** (esp. of part of the body) unclothed or uncovered (*with bare head*). **2** without appropriate covering or contents: **a** (of a tree) leafless. **b** empty (*bare rooms; the cupboard was bare*). **c** (of a floor) uncarpeted. **3 a** undisguised (*the bare truth*). **b** unadorned (*bare facts*). **4** (*attrib.*) **a** scanty (*a bare majority*). **b** mere (*bare necessities*). ● *v.tr.* **1** uncover (*bared his teeth*). **2** reveal (*bared his soul*). □ **bare of** without. **with one's bare hands** with-out using tools or weapons. □□ **bare·ness** *n.* **bare·back** /báirbak/ *adj. & adv.* on an unsaddled horse, donkey, etc.

bare bones *n.pl.* the minimum essential facts, ingredients, etc.

bare·faced /báirfáyst/ *adj.* undisguised; impudent (*barefaced lie*). □□ **bare·fac·ed·ly** /-fáysidlee/ *adv.*

bare·foot /báirfoot/ *adj. & adv.* (also **bare·foot·ed** /-footid/) with nothing on the feet.

bare·ly /báirlee/ *adv.* **1** only just; scarcely (*barely escaped*). **2** scantily (*barely furnished*).

barf /baarf/ *v. & n. sl.* ● *v.intr.* vomit or retch. ● *n.* vomit.

bar·fly /báarflī/ *n.* (*pl.* **-flies**) *colloq.* a person who frequents bars.

bar·gain /báargin/ *n. & v.* ● *n.* **1 a** an agreement on the terms of a transaction or sale. **b** this seen from the buyer's viewpoint (*a bad bargain*). **2** something acquired or offered cheaply. ● *v.intr.* (often foll. by *with, for*) discuss the terms of a trans-action. □ **bargain for** (or *colloq.* **on**) (usu. with *neg.* actual or implied) expect (*didn't bargain for bad weather*). **bargain on** rely on. **in** (or **into**) **the bargain** in addition to what was expected. □□ **bar·gain·er** *n.*

bar·gain base·ment *n.* (also *attrib.*) the basement of a store where bargains are displayed.

barge /baarj/ *n. & v.* ● *n.* **1** a long flat-bottomed boat for carrying freight on canals, etc. **2** a long ornamental boat used for pleasure or ceremony. **3** a boat used by the chief officers of a warship. ● *v.intr.* **1** (often foll. by *around*) lurch or rush clumsily about. **2** (foll. by *in, into*) **a** interrupt rudely (*barged in while we were kissing*). **b** collide with (*barged into her*).

barge·board /báarjbawrd/ *n.* a board (often orna-mental) fixed to the gable end of a roof to hide the ends of the roof timbers.

barge·pole /báarjpōl/ *n.* a long pole used for punt-ing barges, etc.

bar·ist·a /baréestə/ *n.* a person who serves in a coffee bar.

bar·ite /báirīt, bár-/ *n.* **◄** a mineral form of barium sulfate.

bar·i·tone /bárritōn/ *n.* **1 a** the second-lowest adult male singing voice. **b** a singer with this voice. **2** an instrument that is second-lowest in pitch in its family.

bar·i·um /báireeəm, bár-/ *n. Chem.* a white reactive soft metal-lic element. ¶ Symb.: **Ba**.

BARITE

bar·i·um meal *n.* a preparation containing barium sulphate, opaque to X-rays, which is swallowed so that the stomach or intestines can be studied radio-logically.

bark¹ /baark/ *n. & v.* ● *n.* **1** the sharp explosive cry of a dog, fox, etc. **2** a sound resembling this. ● *v.* **1** *intr.* give a bark. **2** *tr. & intr.* speak or utter sharply or brusquely. □ **bark up the wrong tree** be on the wrong track.

bark² /baark/ *n. & v.* ● *n.* the tough protective outer sheath of the trunks, branches, and twigs of trees or woody shrubs. ▷ WOOD. ● *v.tr.* graze or scrape (one's shin, etc.).

bar·keep·er /báarkeepər/ *n.* (also **bar·keep**) a person who owns or serves drinks in a bar.

bark·en·tine /báarkənteen/ *n.* (also **barquentine**, **barquantine**) a sailing ship with the foremast square-rigged and the remaining (usu. two) masts fore-and-aft rigged.

bark·er /báarkər/ *n.* a tout at an auction, sideshow, etc., who calls out to passers-by as advertising.

bar·ley /báarlee/ *n.* **1** any of various hardy awned cereals of the genus *Hordeum* widely used as food and in malt liquors and spirits such as whiskey. **2** the grain produced from this (cf. PEARL BARLEY). ▷ GRAIN

bar·ley·corn /báarleekawrn/ *n.* **1** the grain of bar-ley. **2** a former unit of measure (about a third of an inch) based on the length of a grain of barley.

bar·ley wa·ter *n.* a drink made from water and a boiled barley mixture.

barm /baarm/ *n.* the froth on fermenting malt liquor.

bar·maid /báarmayd/ *n.* a woman serving drinks in a bar, restaurant, etc.

bar mitz·vah /baar mítsvə/ *n.* **1** the religious initi-ation ceremony of a Jewish boy who has reached the age of 13. **2** the boy undergoing this ceremony.

barn¹ /baarn/ *n.* **1** a large farm building for storing grain, housing livestock, etc. **2** *derog.* a large plain or unattractive building. **3** a large shed for storing road or railroad vehicles.

barn² /baarn/ *n. Physics* a unit of area, 10^{-24} square centimeters, used esp. in particle physics. ¶ Symb.: **b**.

bar·na·cle /báarnəkəl/ *n.* **1 ▼** any of various small marine crustaceans of the class Cirripedia which in adult form cling to rocks, ships' hulls, etc. ▷ CRUSTACEAN. **2** a tenacious attendant or follower who cannot easily be shaken off. □□ **bar·na·cled** *adj.*

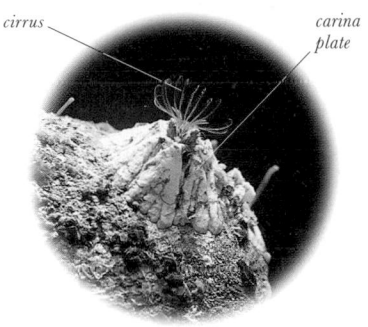

cirrus   *carina plate*

BARNACLE (*Balanus* species)

bar·na·cle goose *n.* a goose with a white face and black neck, breeding in arctic tundra.

barn dance *n.* **1** an informal social gathering for country dancing, orig. in a barn. **2** a dance for a number of couples forming a line or circle, with couples moving along it in turn.

barn owl *n.* a kind of owl, *Tyto alba*, frequenting barns. ▷ OWL.

barn·storm /báarnstawrm/ *v.intr.* **1** tour rural districts giving theatrical performances (formerly often in barns). **2** make a rapid tour, esp. for polit-ical meetings. □□ **barn·storm·er** *n.*

barn·yard /báarnyaard/ *n.* the area around a barn.

bar·o·graph /bárəgraf/ *n.* a barometer equipped to record its readings.

ba·rom·e·ter /bərómitər/ *n.* **1 ▶** an instrument for meas-uring atmospheric pres-sure, esp. in forecasting the weather and determ-ining altitude. **2** any-thing which reflects changes in circum-stances, etc. □□ **bar·o·met·ric** /bárəmétrik/ *adj.* **bar·o·met·ri·cal** /bárəmétrikəl/ *adj.*

pressure scale

pointer

BAROMETER: ANEROID BAROMETER

bar·on /bárən/ *n.* **1** a member of the lowest order of a nobility. **2** a powerful or influential person (*sugar baron*). **3** *hist.* a person who held lands or property from the sovereign or a powerful overlord. □□ **ba·ro·ni·al** /bəróneeəl/ *adj.*

bar·on·age /bárənij/ *n.* **1** barons or nobles collec-tively. **2** an annotated list of barons or peers.

B

B

BAROQUE

The baroque style emerged in Rome during the 17th century, rising from the growing confidence of the Roman Catholic Church. Originally it was developed to appeal to the increasing number of new members of the congregation and to lure others away from the more austere Protestantism. Characterized by religious subjects, this ornate and theatrical style traveled across Italy, into other parts of Europe, and to the American colonies, as the influence of Catholicism spread internationally. The style was adopted by many of the architects, sculptors, and painters of the period.

Ecstasy of Teresa (1646),
GIANLORENZO BERNINI

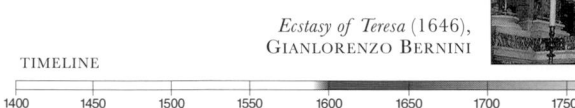

TIMELINE
| 1400 | 1450 | 1500 | 1550 | 1600 | 1650 | 1700 | 1750 | 1800 | 1850 | 1900 |

bar·on·ess /bárənis/ *n.* **1** a woman holding the rank of baron. **2** the wife or widow of a baron.

bar·on·et /bárənit, -nét/ *n.* a member of the lowest hereditary titled British order. □□ **bar·on·et·cy** /bárənitsee, -nét-/ *n.* (*pl.* **-ies**)

bar·o·ny /bárənee/ *n.* (*pl.* **-ies**) the domain, rank, or tenure of a baron.

ba·roque /bərók/ *adj. & n.* • *adj.* **1** ▲ highly ornate and extravagant in style, esp. of European art, etc., of the 17th and 18th c. **2** of or relating to this period. • *n.* **1** the baroque style. **2** baroque art collectively.

ba·rouche /bəroosh/ *n.* a horse-drawn carriage with four wheels and a collapsible hood over the rear half, used esp. in the 19th c.

barque /baark/ *n.* (also **bark**) **1** a sailing ship with the rear mast fore-and-aft rigged and the remaining (usu. two) masts square-rigged. **2** *poet.* any boat.

bar·rack /bárək/ *n.* (usu. in *pl.*, often treated as *sing.*) **1** a building or complex used to house soldiers. **2** any building used to accommodate large numbers of people. **3** a large building of a bleak or plain appearance.

bar·ra·cou·ta /bárəkōotə/ *n.* (*pl.* same or **barracoutas**) a long slender fish, *Thyrsites atun*, usu. found in southern oceans.

bar·ra·cu·da /bárəkōodə/ *n.* (*pl.* same or **barracudas**) ▼ a large and voracious tropical marine fish of the family Sphyraenidae.

BARRACUDA: GREAT BARRACUDA
(*Sphyraena barracuda*)

bar·rage /bəráazh/ *n.* **1** a concentrated artillery bombardment over a wide area. **2** a rapid succession of questions or criticisms. **3** /báarij/ an artificial barrier, esp. in a river.

bar·rage bal·loon *n.* a large anchored balloon, often with netting suspended from it, used as a defense against low-flying aircraft.

bar·ra·mun·di /baramōondee/ *n.* a large, chiefly freshwater fish of Australia and SE Asia.

barre /baar/ *n.* a horizontal bar at waist level used in dance exercises.

bar·ré /baaráy/ *n. Mus.* a method of playing a chord on the guitar, etc., with a finger laid across the strings at a particular fret, raising their pitch.

bar·rel /bárəl/ *n. & v.* • *n.* **1** a cylindrical container usu. bulging out in the middle, traditionally made of wooden staves with metal hoops around them. **2** the contents of this. **3** a measure of capacity, usu. varying from 30 to 40 gallons. **4** a cylindrical tube forming part of an object such as a gun. ▷ BLUNDERBUSS, CANNON. • *v.tr.* (**barreled, barreling** or **barrelled, barrelling**) put into a barrel or barrels. □ **over a barrel** *colloq.* in a helpless position; at a person's mercy.

bar·rel-chest·ed *adj.* having a large rounded chest.

bar·rel or·gan *n.* a mechanical musical instrument in which a rotating pin-studded cylinder acts on a series of pipe valves, strings, or metal tongues.

bar·rel vault *n. Archit.* a vault forming a half-cylinder.

bar·ren /bárən/ *adj.* **1** (**barrener, barrenest**) **1** unable to bear young, fruit, etc. **2** meager; unprofitable. **3** dull; unstimulating. **4** (foll. by *of*) lacking in (*barren of wit*). □□ **bar·ren·ly** *adv.* **bar·ren·ness** *n.*

bar·rette /bərét/ *n.* a typically bar-shaped clip or ornament for the hair.

bar·ri·cade /bárikáyd/ *n. & v.* • *n.* a barrier, esp. one improvised across a street, etc. • *v.tr.* block or defend with a barricade.

bar·ri·er /báreeər/ *n.* **1** a fence or other obstacle that bars advance or access. **2** an obstacle or circumstance that keeps people or things apart (*class barriers; a language barrier*).

bar·ri·er reef *n.* a coral reef separated from the shore by a broad deep channel.

bar·ring /báaring/ *prep.* except; not including.

bar·ri·o /báareeō, bár-/ *n.* (*pl.* **-os**) **1** (in Spanish-speaking countries) a division or district of a city or town. **2** (in the US) the Spanish-speaking quarter or neighborhood of a town or city.

bar·ris·ter /báristər/ *n.* (in full **barrister-at-law**) **1** *Brit.* a person called to the Bar and entitled to practice as an advocate in the higher courts. **2** a lawyer.

bar·room /báaroom, -room/ *n.* an establishment specializing in serving alcoholic drinks.

bar·row[1] /báro/ *n.* **1** a metal frame with two wheels used for transporting luggage, etc. **2** = WHEEL BARROW.

bar·row[2] /báro/ *n. Archaeol.* ▼ an ancient grave mound or tumulus.

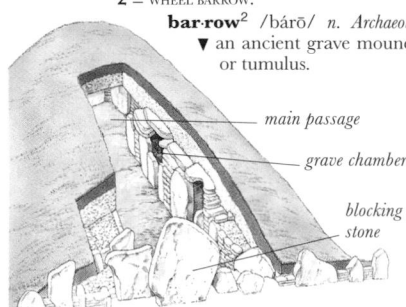

main passage

grave chamber

blocking stone

BARROW: SECTION THROUGH NEOLITHIC
LONG BARROW (*c.* 2500 BC)

Bart. /baart/ *abbr.* Baronet.

bar·tend·er /báartendər/ *n.* a person serving behind the bar of a tavern, bar, etc.

bar·ter /báartər/ *v. & n.* • *v.* **1** *tr.* exchange (goods or services) without using money. **2** *intr.* make such an exchange. • *n.* trade by exchange of goods.

bar·y·on /báreeon/ *n. Physics* an elementary particle that is of equal mass to or greater mass than a proton. □□ **bar·y·on·ic** /-ónik/ *adj.*

bar·y·sphere /bárisfeer/ *n.* the dense interior of the Earth, including the mantle and core, enclosed by the lithosphere.

ba·sal /báysəl, -zəl/ *adj.* **1** of, at, or forming a base. **2** fundamental.

ba·sal me·tab·o·lism *n.* the chemical processes occurring in an organism at complete rest.

ba·salt /bəsáwlt, báysawlt/ *n.* **1** ▶ a dark basic volcanic rock whose strata sometimes form columns. ▷ ROCK CYCLE. **2** a kind of black stoneware resembling basalt. □□ **ba·sal·tic** /-sáwltik/ *adj.*

base[1] /bays/ *n. & v.* • *n.* **1 a** a part that supports from beneath or serves as a foundation. **b** a notional structure on which something depends (*power base*). **2** a principle or starting point. **3** esp. *Mil.* a place from which activity is directed. **4 a** a main or important ingredient. **b** a substance, e.g., water, in combination with which pigment forms paint, etc. **5** a substance used as a foundation for makeup. **6** *Chem.* a substance capable of combining with an acid to form a salt and water and usu. producing hydroxide ions when dissolved in water. **7** *Math.* a number in terms of which other numbers or logarithms are expressed (see RADIX). **8** *Baseball,* etc. one of the four stations that must be reached in turn to score a run. ▷ BASEBALL. • *v.tr.* **1** (usu. foll. by *on, upon*) establish (*a theory based on speculation*). **2** (foll. by *at, in,* etc.) station (*troops were based in Malta*).

base[2] /bays/ *adj.* **1** cowardly; despicable. **2** menial. **3** alloyed (*base coin*). **4** (of a metal) low in value. □□ **base·ly** *adv.* **base·ness** *n.*

base·ball /báysbawl/ *n.* **1** ▶ a game played with two teams of nine, a bat and ball, and a circuit of four bases that must be completed to score. ▷ HOME PLATE. **2** the ball used in this game.

base·board /báysbawrd/ *n.* a narrow board, etc., along the bottom of the wall of a room.

base·head *n. slang* a person who habitually takes either of the drugs freebase or crack.

base hit *n. Baseball* a fair ball that enables the batter to get on base without benefit of an opponent's error and without forcing out another player already on base.

base jump *n.* ▶ a parachute jump from a fixed point, e.g. a high building or promontory.

base·less /báyslis/ *adj.* unfounded; groundless. □□ **base·less·ly** *adv.* **base·less·ness** *n.*

base·line /báyslīn/ *n.* **1** a line used as a base or starting point. **2** (in tennis, basketball, etc.) the line marking each end of a court. ▷ TENNIS. **3** *Baseball* either of the lines leading from home plate and determining the boundaries of fair territory.

BASE JUMP FROM A CLIFF

base·man /báysmən/ *n.* (*pl.* **-men**) *Baseball* a fielder stationed near a base.

base·ment /báysmənt/ *n.* the lowest floor of a building, usu. at least partly below ground level.

base on balls *n. Baseball* advancement to first base by a player who has been pitched four balls while at bat.

bash /bash/ *v. & n.* • *v.* **1** *tr.* **a** a strike bluntly or heavily. **b** (often foll. by *up*) *colloq.* attack or criticize violently. **c** (often foll. by *down, in,* etc.) damage or break by striking forcibly. **2** *intr.* (foll. by *into*) collide with. • *n.* a heavy blow.

bash·ful /báshfŏŏl/ *adj.* **1** shy; self-conscious. **2** sheepish. □□ **bash·ful·ly** *adv.* **bash·ful·ness** *n.*

BASIC /báysik/ *n.* a computer programming language using familiar English words and designed for beginners.

ba·sic /báysik/ *adj. & n.* ● *adj.* **1** forming or serving as a base. **2** fundamental. **3 a** simplest or lowest in level (*basic requirements*). **b** vulgar (*basic humor*). **4** *Chem.* having the properties of or containing a base. ● *n.* (usu. in *pl.*) the fundamental facts or principles.

ba·si·cal·ly *adv.* **1** fundamentally. **2** (qualifying a clause) in fact; actually.

ba·sid·i·um /bəsídeeəm/ *n.* (*pl.* **basidia** /-deeə/) a microscopic spore-bearing structure produced by certain fungi.

bas·il /bázəl, báyzəl/ *n.* an aromatic herb of the genus *Ocimum*, esp. *O. basilicum* (in full **sweet basil**), whose leaves are used as a flavoring in cooking. ▷ HERB

bas·i·lar /básilər/ *adj.* of or at the base (esp. of the skull).

ba·sil·i·ca /bəsílikə/ *n.* **1 ▼** an ancient Roman public hall with an apse and colonnades. **2** a similar building used as a Christian church. **3** a church having special privileges from the Pope. □□ **ba·sil·i·can** *adj.*

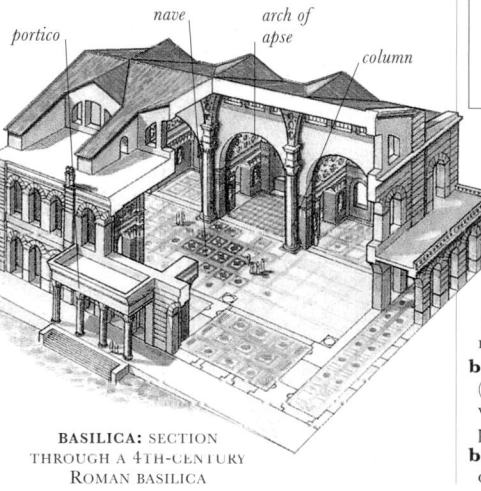

portico   *nave*   *arch of apse*   *column*

BASILICA: SECTION THROUGH A 4TH-CENTURY ROMAN BASILICA

BASKETBALL

Basketball is a fast-moving sport in which players move the ball across the court by dribbling and passing. The aim of the game is to take possession of the ball, and then to score points by throwing it into the defending team's basket.

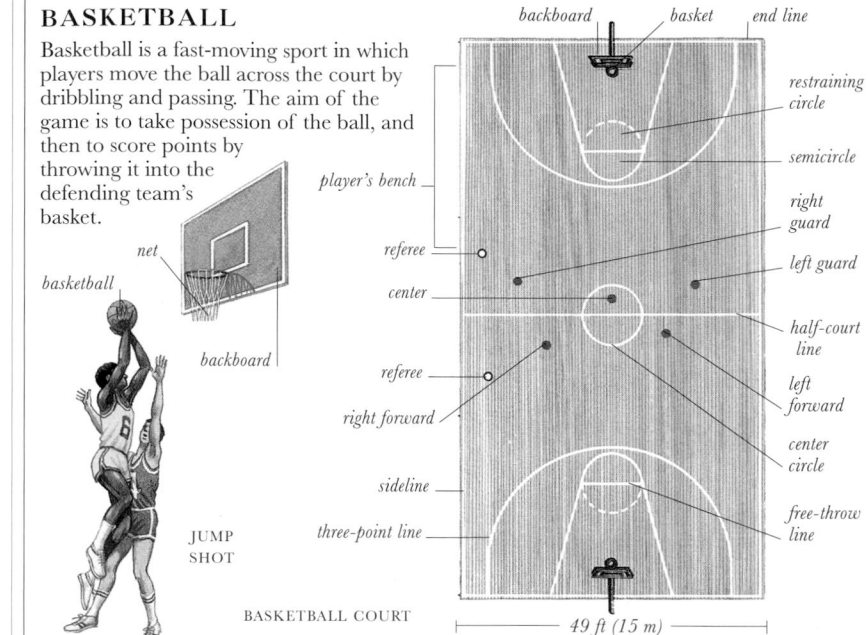

backboard   *basket*   *end line*
restraining circle
semicircle
player's bench   *right guard*
net   *left guard*
referee
basketball   *center*   *half-court line*
backboard   *left forward*
referee   *center circle*
right forward   *free-throw line*
sideline
three-point line

JUMP SHOT

BASKETBALL COURT

49 ft (15 m)

bas·i·lisk /básilisk, báz-/ *n.* **1** a mythical reptile with a lethal breath and look. **2 ►** any small American lizard of the genus *Basiliscus*, with a crest from its back to its tail.

ba·sin /báysən/ *n.* **1** a wide, shallow, open container, esp. a fixed one for holding water. **2** a hollow, rounded depression. **3** any sheltered area of water where boats can moor safely. **4** a round valley. **5** an area drained by rivers and tributaries. □□ **ba·sin·ful** *n.* (*pl.* **-fuls**).

ba·sip·e·tal /baysípit'l/ *adj. Bot.* (of each new part produced) developing nearer the base than the previous one did. □□ **ba·sip·e·tal·ly** *adv.*

ba·sis /báysis/ *n.* (*pl.* **bases** /-seez/) **1** the foundation or support of esp. an idea or argument.

BASILISK (*Basiliscus plumifrons*)

2 the determining principle (*on a purely friendly basis*).

bask /bask/ *v.intr.* **1** sit or lie back lazily in warmth and light. **2** (foll. by *in*) derive great pleasure (from) (*basking in glory*).

bas·ket /báskit/ *n.* **1** a container made of interwoven cane, etc. **2** a container resembling this. **3** the amount held by a basket. **4** the goal in basketball, or a goal scored. ▷ BASKET-BALL. □□ **bas·ket·ful** *n.* (*pl.* **-fuls**).

bas·ket·ball /báskitbawl/ *n.* **1 ▲** a game between two teams, usu. of five, in which points are scored by making the ball drop through hooped nets fixed high up at each end of the court. **2** the ball used in this game.

basket case *n.* **1** *offens.* a person who has had all four limbs amputated. **2** a person who cannot function because of tension, stress, etc.

bas·ket·ry /báskitree/ *n.* **1** the art of making baskets. **2** baskets collectively.

basket weave *n.* a weave resembling that of a basket.

bas·ket·work /báskitwərk/ *n.* **1** material woven in the style of a basket. **2** the art of making this.

bas·ma·ti /baasmaátee/ *n.* (in full **basmati rice**) a long-grained aromatic kind of Indian rice.

bas mitz·vah /bas mítsvə/ *n.* (also **bat mitz·vah**) **1** the religious initiation ceremony of a Jewish girl who has reached the age of 12 or 13. **2** the girl undergoing this ceremony.

Basque /bask/ *n.* **1** a member of a people of the Western Pyrenees. **2** the language of this people.

basque /bask/ *n.* a close-fitting bodice extending from the shoulders to the waist and often with a short continuation below waist level.

bas-re·lief /baa-rileéf, bás-/ *n.* (also **low relief**) sculpture or carving in which the figures project slightly from the background.

bass[1] /bays/ *n. & adj.* ● *n.* **1 a** the lowest adult male singing voice. **b** a singer with this voice. **c** a part written for it. **2** the lowest part in harmonized music. **3 a** an instrument that is the lowest in pitch

BASEBALL

Baseball is played by two teams of nine players who take turns batting and fielding. The batter stands at home plate and attempts to hit a pitched ball. The outcome determines if the batter is "out" or able to reach a base, or if a player on base can advance to the next base. A run is scored when a player completes the circuit of four bases.

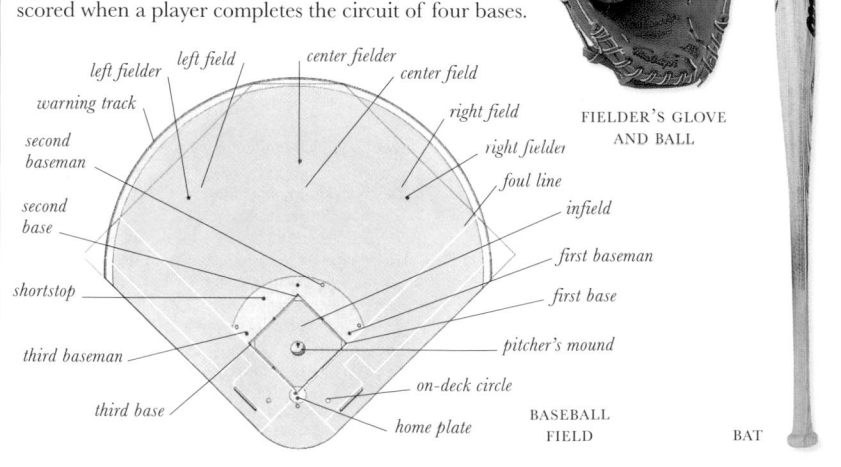

left fielder   *left field*   *center fielder*   *center field*
warning track   *right field*
second baseman   *right fielder*
second base   *foul line*
infield
shortstop   *first baseman*
first base
third baseman   *pitcher's mound*
on-deck circle
third base
home plate

FIELDER'S GLOVE AND BALL

BASEBALL FIELD

BAT

B

B

in its family. **b** its player. **4** *colloq.* a bass guitar or double bass. **5** the low-frequency output of a radio, CD player, etc., corresponding to the bass in music. ● *adj.* **1** lowest in musical pitch. **2** deep-sounding. □□ **bass·ist** *n.* (in sense 3b).

bass² /bas/ *n.* (*pl.* same or **basses**) ▼ any of various edible fishes including the common European perch and several N. American marine and freshwater fishes, esp. *Morone saxatilis* and *Micropterus salmoides*.

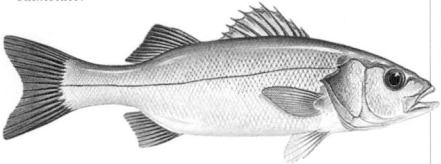

BASS: EUROPEAN SEA BASS (*Dicentrarchus labrax*)

bass³ /bas/ *n.* = BAST.

bass clef *n.* a clef placing F below middle C on the second highest line of the staff. ▷ NOTATION

bas·set /básit/ *n.* (in full **basset hound**) a sturdy hunting dog of a breed with a long body, short legs, and big ears.

bas·set horn /básit hawrn/ *n.* an alto horn in F, with a dark tone.

bas·si·net /básinét/ *n.* a child's wicker cradle, usu. with a hood.

bas·so /báso, baá-/ *n.* (*pl.* **-os** or **bassi** /-see/) a singer with a bass voice.

bas·soon /bəsoon/ *n.* ▼ a bass instrument of the oboe family. ▷ ORCHESTRA, WOODWIND. □□ **bas·soon·ist** *n.*

BASSOON

double reed
mouthpiece
bell
crook
right-hand rest
left thumb keys
right thumb keys

bas·so pro·fun·do /báso prōfoŏondō, baá-/ *n.* a bass singer with an exceptionally low range.

bas·so-re·lie·vo /báso-riléevō/ *n.* (also **basso-rilievo** /báso-reelyáyvō/) (*pl.* **-os**) = BAS-RELIEF.

bass·wood /báswoŏod/ *n.* **1** the American linden, *Tilia americana.* **2** the wood of this tree.

bast /bast/ *n.* the inner bark of linden, or other flexible fibrous bark, used as fiber in matting, etc.

bas·tard /bástərd/ *n. & adj.* ● *n.* **1** a person born of parents not married to each other. **2** *sl.* **a** an unpleasant or despicable person. **b** a person of a specified kind (*poor bastard*). **3** *sl.* a difficult or awkward thing. ● *adj.* **1** illegitimate. **2** (of things): **a** unauthorized; counterfeit. **b** hybrid. □□ **bas·tar·dy** *n.* (in sense 1 of *n.*).

bas·tard·ize /bástərdiz/ *v.tr.* **1** declare (a person) illegitimate. **2** corrupt; debase. □□ **bas·tard·i·za·tion** *n.*

baste¹ /bayst/ *v.tr.* moisten (meat) with gravy or melted fat during cooking.

baste² /bayst/ *v.tr.* stitch loosely together in preparation for sewing; tack.

baste³ /bayst/ *v.tr.* beat soundly; thrash.

bas·tille /bastéel/ *n. hist.* a fortress or prison.

bas·ti·na·do /bástináydō, -naá-/ *n.* punishment by beating with a stick on the soles of the feet.

bas·tion /báschən, -teeən/ *n.* **1** a projecting part of a fortification built at an angle of, or against the line of, a wall. **2** a thing regarded as protecting (*bastion of freedom*).

BAT

Bats form the second largest order of mammals, with almost 1,000 species, which are divided into two groups. Fruit-eating megabats find food by sight and smell, while mainly insect-eating microbats locate their prey using sound waves in a process known as echolocation.

forelimb
patagium (wing membrane)
digit
thumb
tragus (echolocator)

EXTERNAL FEATURES OF A GREATER HORSESHOE BAT
(*Rhinolophus ferrumequinum*)

EXAMPLES OF OTHER BATS

COMMON VAMPIRE BAT (*Desmodus rotundus*)   PROBOSCIS BAT (*Rhynchonycteris naso*)   FRANQUET'S FRUITBAT (*Epomops franqueti*)   NOCTULE BAT (*Nyctalus noctula*)   FUNNEL-EARED BAT (*Natalus tumidirostris*)

---

bat¹ /bat/ *n. & v.* ● *n.* **1** an implement with a handle and a flat or curved surface, used for hitting balls in games. ▷ CRICKET **2** *Cricket* a turn at using this. **3** a batsman described in some way (*an excellent bat*). **4** (usu. in *pl.*) an object like a table tennis paddle used to guide aircraft when taxiing. ● *v.* (**batted, batting**) **1** *tr.* hit with or as with a bat. **2** *intr.* take a turn at using a bat. □ **bat around 1** *sl.* drift or putter aimlessly. **2** discuss (an idea or proposal). **3** *Baseball* have each player in a lineup bat in the course of a single inning. **right off the bat** immediately.

bat² /bat/ *n.* ▲ any mouselike nocturnal mammal of the order Chiroptera, capable of flight by means of membranous wings extending from its forelimbs. □ **have bats in the belfry** be eccentric or crazy. **like a bat out of hell** very fast.

bat³ /bat/ *v.tr.* (**batted, batting**) □ **not** (or **never**) **bat an eye** *colloq.* show no reaction.

batch /bach/ *n. & v.* ● *n.* **1** a number of things or persons forming a group. **2** an installment (*sent off the latest batch*). **3** the loaves produced at one baking. **4** (*attrib.*) using or dealt with in batches, not as a continuous flow (*batch production*). **5** *Computing* a group of records processed as a single unit. ● *v.tr.* arrange or deal with in batches.

bate /bayt/ *v.* **1** *tr.* moderate; restrain. **2** *tr.* diminish; deduct. **3** *intr.* diminish; abate.

ba·teau /bató/ *n.* (*pl.* **bateaux** /-tōz/) a light riverboat, esp. of the flat-bottomed kind used in Canada and the southern US.

bat·ed /báytid/ *adj.* □ **with bated breath** very anxiously.

bath /bath/ *n. & v.* ● *n.* (*pl.* **baths** /bathz, baths/) **1 a** = BATHTUB. **b** a bathtub with its contents (*your bath is ready*). **2** the act or process of immersing the body for washing or therapy (*take a bath*). **3 a** a vessel containing liquid in which something is immersed, e.g., a film for developing. **b** this with its contents. ● *v. Brit.* **1** *tr.* wash (esp. a person) in a bath. **2** *intr.* take a bath. □ **take a bath** *sl.* suffer a large financial loss.

bathe /bayth/ *v. & n.* ● *v.* **1** *intr.* immerse oneself in water, esp. to wash oneself or (*Brit.*) to swim. **2** *tr.* **a** wash (esp. a person) in a bath. **b** treat with liquid for cleansing or medicinal purposes. **3** *tr.* (of sunlight, etc.) envelop. ● *n. Brit.* an immersion in liquid, esp. to swim. □□ **bath·er** *n.*

bath·house /báth-hows/ *n.* a building with baths for public use.

ba·thing suit (also *Brit.* **ba·thing cos·tume**) *n.* a garment worn for swimming.

---

bath·o·lith /báthəlith/ *n.* a dome of igneous rock extending inwards to an unknown depth.

ba·thom·e·ter /bəthómitər/ *n.* an instrument used to measure the depth of water.

ba·thos /báythaws, -thos/ *n.* **1** an unintentional lapse in mood from the sublime to the absurd or trivial. **2** a commonplace or ridiculous feature offsetting an otherwise sublime situation. □□ **ba·thet·ic** /bəthétik/ *adj.* **ba·thot·ic** /bəthótik/ *adj.*

bath·robe /báthrōb/ *n.* a loose robe, often of toweling, worn before and after taking a bath.

bath·room /báthroŏom, -room/ *n.* **1** a room containing a toilet. **2** a room containing a bath and usu. other washing facilities.

bath salts *n.pl.* soluble salts used for softening or scenting bathwater.

bath·tub /báthtəb/ *n.* a container for liquid, usu. water, used for immersing and washing the body.

bath·y·scaphe /báthiskaf/ *n.* ▼ a manned vessel for deep-sea diving.

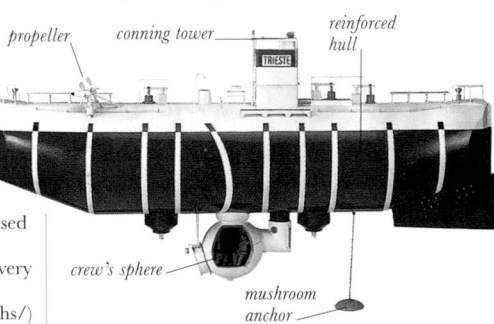

propeller   *conning tower*   *reinforced hull*   *crew's sphere*   *mushroom anchor*

BATHYSCAPHE: MID-20TH-CENTURY BATHYSCAPHE

bath·y·sphere /báthisfeer/ *n.* a spherical vessel for deep-sea observation.

ba·tik /bətéek, bátik/ *n.* a method (orig. used in Indonesia) of producing colored designs on textiles by applying wax to the parts to be left uncolored.

ba·tiste /batéest/ *n. & adj.* ● *n.* a fine linen or cotton cloth. ● *adj.* made of batiste.

bat mitz·vah /bat mítsvə/ var. of BAS MITZVAH.

ba·ton /bətón, ba-, bát'n/ *n.* **1** a thin stick used by a conductor to direct an orchestra, etc. **2** *Sports* a short stick or tube carried and passed on in a relay race. **3** a long stick carried and twirled by a drum major. **4** a staff of office or authority, esp. (*Brit.*) a field marshal's.

ba·tra·chi·an /bətráykeeən/ *n. & adj.* ● *n.* a frog or toad. ● *adj.* of or relating to frogs or toads. ▷ FROG, TOAD

bats /bats/ *predic.adj. sl.* crazy.

bats·man /bátsmən/ *n.* (*pl.* **-men**) a person who bats or is batting, esp. in cricket. ▷ CRICKET. □□ **bats·man·ship** *n.*

bat·tal·ion /bətályən/ *n.* **1** a large body of men ready for battle, esp. an infantry unit forming part of a brigade. **2** a large group of people pursuing a common aim or sharing a major undertaking.

bat·ten[1] /bát'n/ *n. & v.* ● *n.* a long flat strip of squared lumber or metal, esp. used to hold something in place or as a fastening against a wall, etc. ● *v.tr.* strengthen or fasten with battens. □ **batten down the hatches 1** *Naut.* secure a ship's tarpaulins. **2** prepare for a difficulty or crisis.

bat·ten[2] /bát'n/ *v.intr.* (foll. by *on*) thrive or prosper at another's expense.

bat·ter[1] /bátər/ *v.* **1 a** *tr.* strike repeatedly with hard blows. **b** *intr.* (often foll. by *against, at,* etc.) pound heavily and insistently. **2** *tr.* (often in *passive*) handle roughly, esp. over a long period. □□ **bat·ter·er** *n.*

bat·ter[2] /bátər/ *n.* a fluid mixture of flour, egg, and milk or water, used in cooking, esp. for cakes, etc., and for coating food before frying.

bat·ter[3] /bátər/ *n. Sports* a player batting, esp. in baseball. ▷ HOME PLATE

bat·ter[4] /bátər/ *n. & v.* ● *n.* **1** a wall, etc., with a sloping face. **2** a receding slope. ● *v.intr.* have a receding slope.

bat·tered /bátərd/ *adj.* coated in batter and deep-fried.

bat·ter·ing ram *n. hist.* a heavy beam, orig. with an end in the form of a carved ram's head, used in breaching fortifications.

bat·ter·y /bátəree/ *n.* (*pl.* **-ies**) **1** ▼ a usu. portable container of a cell or cells carrying an electric charge, as a source of current. **2** (often *attrib.*) esp. *Brit.* a series of cages for the intensive breeding and rearing of poultry or cattle. **3** a set of similar units of equipment, esp. connected. **4** a series of tests, esp. psychological. **5 a** a fortified emplacement for heavy guns. **b** an artillery unit of guns, soldiers, and vehicles. **6** *Law* an act inflicting unlawful personal violence on another (see ASSAULT). **7** *Baseball* the pitcher and the catcher.

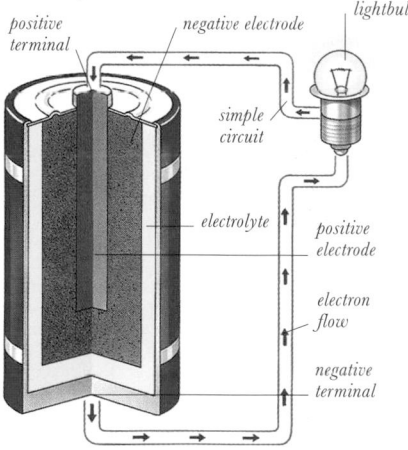

BATTERY: DEMONSTRATION OF A DRY-CELL BATTERY AS A SOURCE OF CURRENT

bat·ting /báting/ *n.* **1** the action of hitting with a bat. **2** cotton wadding prepared in sheets for use in quilts, etc.

bat·ting or·der *n. Sports* the order in which batters or batsmen take their turns.

bat·tle /bát'l/ *n. & v.* ● *n.* **1** a prolonged fight, esp. between large organized armed forces. **2** a contest (*a battle of wits*). ● *v.* **1** *intr.* fight persistently (*battled against the elements*). **2** *tr.* fight (one's way, etc.). □□ **bat·tler** *n.*

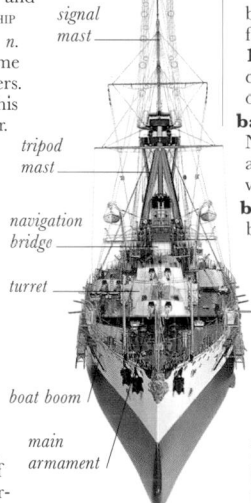

BATTLE-AX

bat·tle-ax *n.* **1** ◀ a large ax used in ancient warfare. **2** *colloq.* a formidable or domineering older woman.

bat·tle cruis·er *n.* a heavily armed ship faster and more lightly armored than a battleship.

bat·tle cry *n.* a cry or slogan of participants in a battle or contest.

bat·tle·dore /bát'ldawr/ *n. hist.* **1 a** (in full **battledore and shuttlecock**) a game similar to badminton played with a shuttlecock and rackets. **b** the racket used in this. **2** a kind of wooden utensil like a paddle, formerly used in washing, baking, etc.

bat·tle fa·tigue *n.* = COMBAT FATIGUE.

bat·tle·field /bát'lfeeld/ *n.* (also **bat·tle·ground** /-grownd/) the piece of ground on which a battle is or was fought.

bat·tle·ment /bát'l-mənt/ *n.* (usu. in *pl.*) **1** a parapet with recesses along the top of a wall, as part of a fortification. **2** a section of roof enclosed by this. □□ **bat·tle·ment·ed** *adj.*

bat·tle roy·al *n.* (*pl.* **battles royal**) **1** a battle in which several combatants or all available forces engage; a free fight. **2** a heated argument.

bat·tle·ship /bát'lship/ *n.* ▶ a warship with the heaviest armor and the largest guns. ▷ WARSHIP

bat·tue /batóō, -tyóō/ *n.* **1 a** the driving of game toward hunters by beaters. **b** a hunt arranged in this way. **2** wholesale slaughter.

bat·ty /bátee/ *adj.* (**battier, battiest**) *sl.* crazy. □□ **bat·ti·ly** *adv.* **bat·ti·ness** *n.*

bat·wing /bátwing/ *attrib.adj.* (esp. of a sleeve) shaped like the wing of a bat.

bat·wom·an /bátwoŏ-mən/ *n.* (*pl.* **-women**) *Brit.* a female attendant serving an officer in the women's services.

bau·ble /báwbəl/ *n.* **1** a showy trinket or toy of little value. **2** a baton formerly used as an emblem by jesters.

baud /bawd/ *n.* (*pl.* same or **bauds**) *Computing,* etc. **1** a unit used to express the speed of electronic code signals, corresponding to one information unit per second. **2** (loosely) a unit of data transmission speed of one bit per second.

Bau·haus /bówhows/ *n.* **1** a German school of architectural design (1919–33). **2** its principles, based on functionalism and development of existing skills.

baulk *Brit.* var. of BALK.

baux·ite /báwksīt/ *n.* ▶ a clay-like mineral containing varying proportions of alumina, the chief ore of aluminum. ▷ ORE. □□ **baux·i·tic** /-sítik/ *adj.*

bawd /bawd/ *n.* a woman who runs a brothel.

bawd·y /báwdee/ *adj.* (**bawdier, bawdiest**) (esp. humorously) indecent; raunchy. □□ **bawd·i·ly** *adv.* **bawd·i·ness** *n.*

bawd·y house *n.* a brothel.

signal mast — **tripod mast** — **navigation bridge** — **turret** — **boat boom** — **main armament**

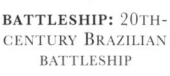

BATTLESHIP: 20TH-CENTURY BRAZILIAN BATTLESHIP

BAUXITE

bawl /bawl/ *v.* **1** *tr.* speak or call out noisily. **2** *intr.* weep loudly. □ **bawl out** *colloq.* reprimand angrily.

bay[1] /bay/ *n.* **1** a broad inlet of the sea where the land curves inwards. **2** a recess in a mountain range.

bay[2] /bay/ *n.* **1** (in full **bay laurel**) ▶ a laurel, *Laurus nobilis,* having deep green leaves and purple berries. ▷ HERB. **2** (in *pl.*) a wreath made of bay leaves, for a victor or poet.

BAY LAUREL: SWEET BAY (*Laurus nobilis*)

bay[3] /bay/ *n.* **1** a space created by a window line projecting outwards from a wall. **2** a recess. **3** a compartment (*bomb bay*). **4** an area specially allocated (*loading bay*).

bay[4] /bay/ *adj. & n.* ● *adj.* (esp. of a horse) dark reddish brown. ● *n.* ◀ a bay horse with a black mane and tail.

BAY: CLEVELAND BAY

bay[5] /bay/ *v. & n.* ● *v.* **1** *intr.* (esp. of a large dog) bark or howl loudly and plaintively. **2** *tr.* bay at. ● *n.* the sound of baying, esp. in chorus from hounds in close pursuit. □ **at bay 1** cornered; apparently unable to escape. **2** in a desperate situation. **hold** (or **keep**) **at bay** hold off (a pursuer).

bay·ber·ry /báyberee/ *n.* (*pl.* **-ies**) any of various N. American plants of the genus *Myrica,* having aromatic leaves and bearing berries covered in a wax coating.

bay leaf *n.* the aromatic (usu. dried) leaf of the bay tree, used in cooking.

bay·o·net /báyənét/ *n. & v.* ● *n.* **1** ▶ a stabbing blade attachable to the muzzle of a rifle. **2** an electrical or other fitting engaged by being pushed into a socket and twisted. ● *v.tr.* (**bayoneted, bayoneting**) stab with a bayonet.

bay·ou /bí-ōō/ *n.* a marshy offshoot of a river, etc., in the southern US.

bay rum *n.* a perfume, esp. for the hair, distilled orig. from bayberry leaves in rum.

Bay State *n.* Massachusetts.

bay win·dow *n.* a window built into a bay.

ba·zaar /bəzáar/ *n.* **1** a market in an Eastern or Middle Eastern country. **2** a fund-raising sale of goods, esp. for charity.

ba·zoo·ka /bəzóōkə/ *n.* a tubular short-range rocket launcher used against tanks.

BB *abbr.* a shot pellet about .18 inch in diameter, for use in a BB gun or air gun.

b-ball *n. N. Amer. colloq.* basketball.

BBC *abbr.* British Broadcasting Corporation.

BC *abbr.* **1** (of a date) before Christ. **2** British Columbia.

BCE *abbr.* (of a date) before the Common Era.

BCG *abbr.* Bacillus Calmette-Guérin, an anti-tuberculosis vaccine.

BD *abbr.* Bachelor of Divinity.

bdel·li·um /déleeəm/ *n.* **1** any of various trees, esp. of the genus *Commiphora,* yielding resin. **2** this fragrant resin used in perfumes.

BE *abbr.* **1** Bachelor of Education. **2** Bachelor of Engineering.

Be *symb. Chem.* the element beryllium.

be /bee/ *v. & v.aux.* (*sing. present* **am** /am, əm/; **are** /aar, ər/; **is** /iz/; *pl. present* **are**; *1st and 3rd sing. past*

BAYONET: SOCKET BAYONET

was /wuz, woz, wəz/; *2nd sing. past and pl. past* **were** /wər/; *present subj.* **be**; *past subj.* **were**; *pres. part.* **being**; *past part.* **been** /bin/ ● *v.intr.* **1** (often *prec. by there*) exist; live (*there is a house on the corner*). **2 a** take place (*dinner is at eight*). **b** occupy a position in space (*he is in the garden*). **3** remain; continue (*let it be*). **4** linking subject and predicate, expressing: **a** identity (*today is Thursday*). **b** condition (*he is ill today*). **c** state or quality (*he is very kind*). **d** opinion (*I am against hanging*). **e** total (*two and two are four*). **f** cost or significance (*it is $5 to enter*). ● *v.aux.* **1** with a past participle to form the passive mood (*it was done*). **2** with a present participle to form continuous tenses (*we are coming*). **3** with an infinitive to express duty or commitment, intention, possibility, destiny, or hypothesis (*he is to come at four*; *if I were to die*). □ **be about** occupy oneself with (*is about his business*). **be off** *colloq.* go away; leave. **be that as it may** see MAY. **-to-be** of the future (in *comb.*: *bride-to-be*).

beach /beech/ *n. & v.* ● *n.* a pebbly or sandy shore. ▷ LONGSHORE DRIFT. ● *v.tr.* run or haul up (a boat, etc.) on to a beach.

beach ball *n.* a large inflated ball for games on the beach.

beach·comb·er /beechkōmər/ *n.* **1** a vagrant who lives by searching beaches for articles of value. **2** a long wave rolling in from the sea.

beach·head /beech-hed/ *n. Mil.* a fortified position established on a beach by landing forces.

bea·con /beekən/ *n.* **1** a fire or light set up in a high or prominent position as a warning, etc. **2** a visible guiding point or device (e.g., a lighthouse). **3** a radio transmitter whose signal helps fix the position of a ship or aircraft.

bead /beed/ *n. & v.* ● *n.* **1 a** a small usu. rounded and perforated piece of glass, stone, etc., for threading with others. **b** (in *pl.*) a string of beads; a rosary. **2** a drop of liquid. **3** a small knob in the foresight of a gun. **4** the inner edge of a pneumatic tire. ● *v.* **1** *tr.* furnish or decorate with beads. **2** *tr.* string together. **3** *intr.* form or grow into beads. □ **draw a bead on** take aim at. □□ **bead·ed** *adj.*

bead·ing /beeding/ *n.* **1** decoration in the form of or resembling a row of beads, esp. looped edging. **2** the inner edge of a pneumatic tire. ▷ TIRE

beads·man /beedzmən/ *n.* (*pl.* **-men**) *Brit. hist.* **1** a pensioner provided for by a benefactor in return for prayers. **2** an inmate of an almshouse.

bead·y /beedee/ *adj.* (**beadier**, **beadiest**) **1** (of the eyes) small, round, and bright. **2** covered with beads or drops. □□ **bead·i·ly** *adv.* **bead·i·ness** *n.*

bead·y-eyed *adj.* with beady eyes.

bea·gle /beegəl/ *n.* ▶ a small hound of a breed with a short coat, orig. used for hunting hares. ▷ DOG

beak /beek/ *n.* **1 a** ▼ a bird's horny projecting jaws; a bill. **b** the similar projecting jaw of other animals, e.g., a turtle. **2** *sl.* a hooked nose. **3** *Naut. hist.* the projection at the prow of a warship. □□ **beaked** *adj.* **beak·y** *adj.*

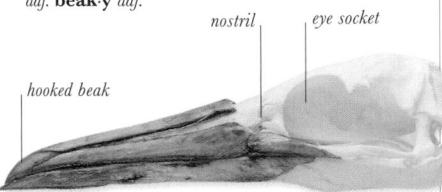

BEAGLE

nostril · eye socket · hooked beak

BEAK AND SKULL OF A GANNET
(*Sula bassana*)

beak·er /beekər/ *n.* **1** a tall drinking vessel, usu. of plastic and tumbler-shaped. **2** a lipped cylindrical glass vessel for scientific experiments. **3** *archaic* or *literary* a large drinking vessel with a wide mouth.

BEAR

There are seven species of bear, all of which belong to the mammalian order Carnivora. Despite this, only the polar bear is wholly carnivorous, feeding on seals and fish. Other bears eat plant material when meat is not available. Bears have poor eyesight and rely on hearing and an acute sense of smell to locate their food. With the exception of the polar bear, bears are forest animals. Those living in warmer areas are active throughout the year, while those in cooler regions hibernate in dens during the winter.

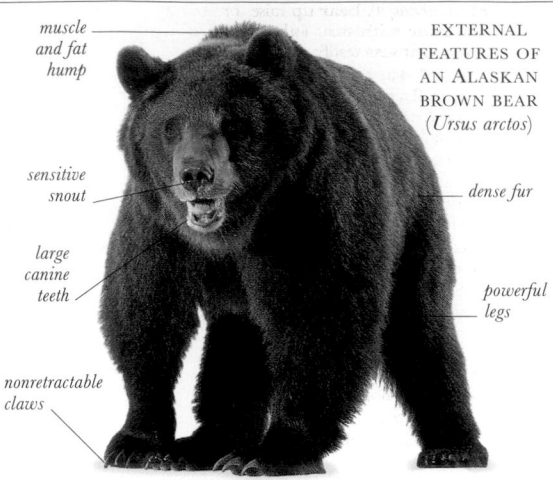

muscle and fat hump

sensitive snout

large canine teeth

nonretractable claws

EXTERNAL FEATURES OF AN ALASKAN BROWN BEAR (*Ursus arctos*)

dense fur

powerful legs

EXAMPLES OF OTHER BEARS

ASIAN BLACK BEAR (*Selenarctos thibetanus*)

POLAR BEAR (*Ursus maritimus*)

SPECTACLED BEAR (*Tremarctos ornatus*)

SLOTH BEAR (*Melursus ursinus*)

be-all and end-all *n. colloq.* (often foll. by *of*) the whole being or essence.

beam /beem/ *n. & v.* ● *n.* **1** a long sturdy piece of squared timber or metal spanning an opening or room, usu. to support the structure above. ▷ QUEEN POST, ROOF. **2 a** a ray or shaft of light. **b** a directional flow of particles or radiation. **3** a bright look or smile. **4 a** a series of radio or radar signals as a guide to a ship or aircraft. **b** the course indicated by this (*off beam*). **5** the crossbar of a balance. **6 a** a ship's breadth at its widest point. **b** the width of a person's hips (esp. *broad in the beam*). **7** (in *pl.*) the horizontal cross-timbers of a ship supporting the deck and joining the sides. **8** the side of a ship (*land on the port beam*). **9** the chief timber of a plow. **10** the main stem of a stag's antlers. ● *v.* **1** *tr.* emit or direct (light, radio waves, etc.). **2** *intr.* **a** shine. **b** look or smile radiantly. □ **off** (or **off the**) **beam** *colloq.* mistaken. **on the beam** *colloq.* on the right track. **on one's beam-ends** near the end of one's resources.

beam·y /beemee/ *adj.* (of a ship) broad-beamed.

bean /been/ *n. & v.* ● *n.* **1 a** any kind of leguminous plant with edible seeds in long pods. ▷ VEGETABLE. **b** one of these seeds. **2** a similar seed of coffee and other plants. **3** *sl.* the head. **4** (in *pl.*; with *neg.*) *sl.* anything at all (*doesn't know beans about it*). ● *v.tr. sl.* hit on the head. □ **full of beans** *colloq.* **1** lively; in high spirits. **2** mistaken. **spill the beans** see SPILL.

bean·bag /beenbag/ *n.* **1** a small bag filled with dried beans and used esp. in children's games. **2** (in full **bean·bag chair**) a large cushion filled usu. with polystyrene beads and used as a seat.

bean curd *n.* a soft cheeselike cake or paste made from soybeans, used esp. in Asian cooking.

bean·er·y /beenəree/ *n.* (*pl.* **-ies**) *sl.* a cheap restaurant.

bean·ie /beenee/ *n.* a small close-fitting cap worn on the back of the head.

bean·pole /beenpōl/ *n.* **1** a stick for supporting bean plants. **2** *colloq.* a tall thin person.

bean sprout *n.* a sprout of a bean seed, esp. of the mung bean, used as food.

bean·stalk /beenstawk/ *n.* the stem of a bean plant.

bear[1] /bair/ *v.* (*past* **bore** /bor/; *past part.* **borne**, **born** /bawrn/) ¶ In the passive *born* is used with reference to birth (e.g., *was born in July*), except for *borne by* foll. by the name of the mother (e.g., *was borne by Sarah*). **1** *tr.* carry, bring, or take (*bear gifts*). **2** *tr.* show; be marked by; have as an attribute or characteristic (*bear marks of violence*; *bears no relation to the case*). **3** *tr.* **a** produce; yield (fruit, etc.). **b** give birth to (*has borne a son*; *was born last week*). **4** *tr.* **a** sustain (a weight, responsibility, cost, etc.). **b** stand; endure (an ordeal, difficulty, etc.). **5** *tr.* (usu. with *neg.* or *interrog.*) **a** tolerate; put up with (*can't bear him*; *how can you bear it?*). **b** admit of; be fit for (*does not bear thinking about*). **6** *tr.* carry in thought or memory (*bear a grudge*). **7** *intr.* veer in a given direction (*bear left*). □ **bear down** exert downward pressure. **bear down on** approach rapidly or purposefully. **bear fruit** have results. **bear hard on** oppress. **bear in mind** take into account having remembered. **bear on** (or **upon**) be relevant to. **bear out** support or confirm (an account or the person giving it). **bear up** raise one's spirits; not despair. **bear with** treat forbearingly; tolerate patiently. **bear witness** testify.

bear² /bair/ *n.* **1** ◄ any large heavy mammal of the family Ursidae. **2** a rough, unmannerly, or uncouth person. **3** *Stock Exch.* a person who sells shares hoping to buy them back later at a lower price. **4** = TEDDY.

bear·a·ble /báirəbəl/ *adj.* that may be endured or tolerated.

bear·bait·ing /báirbayting/ *n. hist.* an entertainment involving setting dogs to attack a captive bear.

beard /beerd/ *n. & v.* ● *n.* **1** hair growing on the chin and lower cheeks. **2** a similar tuft or part on an animal (esp. a goat). ● *v.tr.* oppose openly; defy. □□ **beard·ed** *adj.* **beard·less** *adj.*

bear·er /báirər/ *n.* **1** a person or thing that bears, carries, or brings. **2** a carrier of equipment on an expedition, etc. **3** a person who presents a check or other order to pay money. **4** (*attrib.*) payable to the possessor (*bearer stock*).

bear·gar·den /báirgaard'n/ *n.* a rowdy or noisy scene.

bear hug *n.* a tight embrace.

bear·ing /báiring/ *n.* **1** a person's bodily attitude or outward behavior. **2** (foll. by *on*, *upon*) relation or relevance to (*his comments have no bearing on the subject*). **3** endurability (*beyond bearing*). **4** a part of a machine that supports a rotating or other moving part. **5** direction or position relative to a fixed point. **6** (in *pl.*) **a** one's position relative to one's surroundings. **b** awareness of this (*get one's bearings; lose one's bearings*).

bear·ish /báirish/ *adj.* **1** like a bear, esp. in temper. **2** *Stock Exch.* causing or associated with a fall in prices.

bear mar·ket *n. Stock Exch.* a market with falling prices.

Béar·naise sauce /báirnáyz/ *n.* a rich sauce thickened with egg yolks and flavored with tarragon.

bear·skin /báirskin/ *n.* **1** the skin of a bear. **2** ► a tall furry hat worn ceremonially by some regiments.

beast /beest/ *n.* **1** an animal other than a human being, esp. a wild quadruped. **2 a** a brutal person. **b** *colloq.* an objectionable or unpleasant person or thing. **3** (prec. by *the*) a human being's brutish or uncivilized characteristics (*saw the beast in him*).

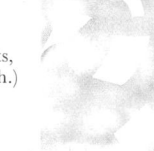

BEARSKIN
OF A BRITISH
GRENADIER GUARD

beast·ie /beestee/ *n.* a small animal.

beast·ly /beestlee/ *adj. & adv.* ● *adj.* (**beastlier**, **beastliest**) **1** *colloq.* objectionable; unpleasant. **2** like a beast; brutal. ● *adv. Brit. colloq.* very; extremely. □□ **beast·li·ness** *n.*

beast of bur·den *n.* an animal used for carrying loads.

beast of prey *n.* an animal that hunts animals for food.

beat /beet/ *v., n., & adj.* ● *v.* (*past* **beat**; *past part.* **beaten** /beet'n/) **1** *tr.* **a** strike (a person or animal) persistently. **b** strike (a thing) repeatedly, e.g., to remove dust from (a carpet, etc.), or to sound (a drum, etc.). **2** *intr.* (foll. by *against, at, on,* etc.) **a** pound or knock repeatedly (*beat at the door*). **b** = *beat down* 3. **3** *tr.* **a** overcome; surpass. **b** complete an activity before (another person, etc.). **c** be too hard for. **4** *tr.* (often foll. by *up*) stir (eggs, etc.) vigorously into a frothy mixture. **5** *tr.* (often foll. by *out*) shape (metal, etc.) by blows. **6** *intr.* (of the heart, a drum, etc.) pulsate rhythmically. **7** *tr.* (often foll. by *out*) **a** indicate (a tempo or rhythm) by gestures, tapping, etc. **b** sound (a signal, etc.) by striking a drum or other means (*beat a tattoo*). **8 a** *intr.* (of a bird's wings) move up and down. **b** *tr.* cause (wings) to move in this way. **9** *tr.* make (a path, etc.) by trampling. **10** *tr.* strike (bushes, etc.) to rouse game. ● *n.* **1 a** a main accent or rhythmic unit in music or verse (*three beats to the bar*). **b** the indication of rhythm by a conductor's movements (*watch the beat*). **c** the tempo or rhythm of a piece of music as indicated by the repeated fall of the main beat. **d** (in popular music) a strong rhythm. **e** (*attrib.*) characterized by a strong rhythm (*beat music*). **2 a** a stroke or blow. **b** a measured sequence of strokes (*the beat of the waves on the rocks*). **c** a throbbing movement or sound (*the beat of his heart*). **3 a** a route or area allocated to a police officer, etc. **b** a person's habitual round. ● *predic.adj. sl.* exhausted; tired out. □ **beat about** (often foll. by *for*) search (for an excuse, etc.). **beat around (or about) the bush** discuss a matter without coming to the point. **beat the clock** complete a task within a stated time. **beat down 1 a** bargain with (a seller) to lower the price. **b** cause a seller to lower (the price). **2** strike (a resisting object) until it falls (*beat the door down*). **3** (of the sun, rain, etc.) radiate heat or fall continuously and vigorously. **beat in** crush. **beat it** *sl.* go away. **beat off** drive back (an attack, etc.)

beat a retreat withdraw; abandon an undertaking. **beat time** indicate or follow a musical tempo with a baton or other means. **beat a person to it** arrive or achieve something before another person. **beat up** give a beating to, esp. with punches and kicks. □□ **beat·a·ble** *adj.* **beat·ing** *n.*

beat·en /beet'n/ *adj.* **1** outwitted; defeated. **2** exhausted; dejected. **3** (of gold or any other metal) shaped by a hammer. **4** (of a path, etc.) well-trodden; much used. □ **off the beaten track** (or **path**) **1** in or into an isolated place. **2** unusual.

beat·er /beetər/ *n.* **1** a person employed to rouse game for shooting. **2** an implement used for beating (esp. a carpet or eggs). ▷ DRUM, PERCUSSION. **3** a person who beats metal.

beat gen·er·a·tion *n.* the members of a movement of young people esp. in the 1950s who rejected conventional society in their dress, habits, and beliefs.

be·a·tif·ic /beeətifik/ *adj.* **1** *colloq.* blissful (*a beatific smile*). **2 a** of or relating to blessedness. **b** making blessed.

be·a·tif·i·ca·tion /beeátifikáyshən/ *n. RC Ch.* the act of formally declaring a dead person "blessed."

be·at·i·fy /beeátifī/ *v.tr.* (**-ies**, **-ied**) **1** *RC Ch.* announce the beatification of. **2** make happy.

be·at·i·tude /beeátitōod, -tyōod/ *n.* **1** blessedness. **2** (in *pl.*) the declarations of blessedness in Matt. 5:3–11. **3** a title given to patriarchs in the Orthodox Church.

beat·nik /beetnik/ *n.* a member of the beat generation.

beat-up *adj. colloq.* in a state of disrepair.

beau /bō/ *n.* (*pl.* **beaux** or **beaus** /bōz, bō/) **1** an admirer; a boyfriend. **2** a dandy.

Beau·fort scale /bófərt/ *n.* ▼ a scale of wind speed ranging from 0 (calm) to 12 (hurricane).

beau geste /bō zhést/ *n.* (*pl.* **beaux gestes** *pronunc.* same) a generous or gracious act.

beau id·e·al /bó īdeéəl/ *n.* (*pl.* **beau ideals** /bó īdeéəlz/) the highest type of excellence or beauty.

Beau·jo·lais /bózhəlay/ *n.* a red or white burgundy wine from the Beaujolais district of France.

beau monde /bō mónd, máwⁿd/ *n.* fashionable society.

beaut /byōot/ *n. sl.* an excellent or beautiful person or thing.

beau·te·ous /byōoteeəs/ *adj. poet.* beautiful.

beau·ti·cian /byōotishən/ *n.* **1** a person who gives beauty treatment. **2** a person who runs or owns a beauty salon.

B

BEAUFORT SCALE

Based on observation of wind effects on sailing vessels and waves, the Beaufort scale was devised in 1806 as a method of gauging wind force at sea. Later adapted for use on land, this scale continues to be utilized by some weather stations.

FORCE 0
CALM
(less than
1 knot,
0.62 m.p.h.)

FORCE 1
LIGHT AIR
(1–3 knots,
0.62–4
m.p.h.)

FORCE 2
LIGHT
BREEZE
(4–6 knots,
4–7 m.p.h.)

FORCE 3
GENTLE
BREEZE
(7–10 knots,
8–12 m.p.h.)

FORCE 4
MODERATE
BREEZE
(11–16 knots,
12.5–18.5
m.p.h.)

FORCE 5
FRESH
BREEZE
(17–21 knots,
19–24 m.p.h.)

FORCE 6
STRONG
BREEZE
(22–27 knots,
25–31 m.p.h.)

FORCE 7
MODERATE
GALE
(28–33 knots,
32–39 m.p.h.)

FORCE 8
FRESH GALE
(34–40 knots,
39–46 m.p.h.)

FORCE 9
STRONG
GALE
(41–47 knots,
46–54 m.p.h.)

FORCE 10
WHOLE GALE
(48–55 knots,
55–63
m.p.h.)

FORCE 11
STORM
(56–63 knots,
64–72.5
m.p.h.)

FORCE 12
HURRICANE
(equal to or
more than
64 knots,
73 m.p.h.)

B

beau·ti·ful /byóotifŏol/ *adj.* **1** delighting the aesthetic senses (*a beautiful voice*). **2** pleasant; enjoyable (*had a beautiful time*). **3** excellent (*a beautiful specimen*). □□ **beau·ti·ful·ly** *adv.*

beau·ti·fy /byóotifī/ *v.tr.* (**-ies, -ied**) make beautiful; adorn. □□ **beau·ti·fi·ca·tion** /-fikáyshən/ *n.*

beau·ty /byóotee/ *n.* (*pl.* **-ies**) **1 a** a combination of qualities that pleases the aesthetic senses. **b** a combination of qualities that pleases the intellect or moral sense. **2** *colloq.* **a** an excellent specimen (*what a beauty!*). **b** an attractive feature; an advantage (*that's the beauty of it!*). **3** a beautiful woman.

beau·ty par·lor *n.* (also **beauty salon, beauty shop**) an establishment in which manicure, make-up, etc., are offered to women.

beau·ty queen *n.* the woman judged most beautiful in a competition.

beau·ty sleep *n.* sleep before midnight, supposed to be health-giving.

beau·ty spot *n.* **1** a place known for its beauty. **2** a small natural or artificial mark such as a mole on the face, considered to enhance another feature.

beaux *pl.* of BEAU.

beaux arts /bōz áar/ *n.pl.* **1** fine arts. **2** (*attrib.*) relating to the rules and conventions of the École des Beaux-Arts in Paris (later called Académie des Beaux Arts).

bea·ver[1] /béevər/ *n.* (*pl.* same or **beavers**) **1** ▼ any large amphibious broad-tailed rodent of the genus *Castor*, native to N. America, Europe, and Asia, and able to cut down trees and build dams. ▷ RODENT. **2** its soft light-brown fur. **3** a hat of this.

BEAVER: AMERICAN BEAVER
(*Castor canadensis*)

bea·ver[2] /béevər/ *n. hist.* the lower face-guard of a helmet.

Bea·ver·board /béevərbawrd/ *n. Trademark* a kind of fiberboard.

be·bop /béebop/ *n.* a type of jazz originating in the 1940s and characterized by complex harmony and rhythms. □□ **bebopper** *n.*

be·calm /bikáam/ *v.tr.* (usu. in *passive*) deprive (a sailing ship) of wind.

be·came *past of* BECOME.

be·cause /bikáwz, -kúz/ *conj.* for the reason that; since. □ **because of** on account of; by reason of.

bé·cha·mel /béshəmel/ *n.* a kind of thick white sauce.

beck /bek/ *n.* □ **at a person's beck and call** having constantly to obey a person's orders.

beck·et /békit/ *n. Naut.* a contrivance such as a hook, bracket, or rope loop, for securing loose ropes, tackle, or spars.

beck·on /békən/ *v.* **1** *tr.* **a** attract the attention of; summon by gesture. **b** entice. **2** *intr.* (usu. foll. by *to*) make a signal to attract a person's attention; summon a person by doing this.

be·cloud /biklówd/ *v.tr.* **1** obscure (*becloud the argument*). **2** cover with clouds.

be·come /bikúm/ *v.* (*past* **became** /bikáym/; *past part.* **become**) **1** *intr.* (foll. by *compl.*) begin to be (*became president; will become famous*). **2** *tr.* **a** look well on; suit (*blue becomes him*). **b** befit (*it ill becomes you to complain*). **3** *intr.* (as **becoming** *adj.*) **a** a flattering appearance. **b** suitable; decorous. □ **become of** happen to. □□ **be·com·ing·ly** *adv.*

B.Ed. *abbr.* Bachelor of Education.

bed /bed/ *n. & v.* ● *n.* **1 a** a piece of furniture used for sleeping on. **b** a mattress, with or without coverings. **2** any place used by a person or animal for sleep or rest. **3 a** a garden plot. **b** a place where other things may be grown (*osier bed*). **4** the use of a bed: **a** *colloq.* for sexual intercourse. **b** for rest. **5** something flat, forming a support or base as in: **a** the bottom of the sea or a river. **b** the foundations of a road or railroad. **6** a stratum, such as a layer of oysters, etc. ● *v.* (**bedded, bedding**) **1** *tr. & intr.* (usu. foll. by *down*) put or go to bed. **2** *tr. colloq.* have sexual intercourse with. **3** *tr.* (usu. foll. by *out*) plant in a garden bed. **4** *tr.* cover up or fix firmly in something. **5 a** *tr.* arrange as a layer. **b** *intr.* be or form a layer. □ **go to bed 1** retire for the night. **2** have sexual intercourse. **3** (of a newspaper) go to press. **make the bed** arrange the bed for use. **put to bed 1** cause to go to bed. **2** make (a newspaper) ready for press. **take to one's bed** stay in bed because of illness.

be·dab·ble /bidábəl/ *v.tr.* stain or splash with dirty liquid, blood, etc.

bed and break·fast *n.* **1** one night's lodging and breakfast. **2** an establishment that provides this.

be·daub /bidáwb/ *v.tr.* smear or daub with paint, etc.; decorate gaudily.

be·daz·zle /bidázəl/ *v.tr.* **1** dazzle. **2** confuse (a person).

bed·bug /bédbug/ *n.* either of two flat, wingless, evil-smelling insects of the genus *Cimex*, infesting beds and houses and sucking blood.

bed·cham·ber /bédchaymbər/ *n. archaic* a bedroom.

bed·clothes /bédklōthz, -klōz/ *n.pl.* coverings for a bed, such as sheets, blankets, etc.

bed·da·ble /bédəbəl/ *adj. colloq.* sexually attractive; able to be seduced.

bed·der /bédər/ *n.* **1** a plant suitable for a garden bed. **2** a bedmaker.

bed·ding /béding/ *n.* **1** a mattress and bedclothes. **2** litter for cattle, horses, etc. **3** a bottom layer. **4** *Geol.* the stratification of rocks.

bed·ding plant *n.* = BEDDER 1.

be·deck /bidék/ *v.tr.* adorn.

be·dev·il /bidévəl/ *v.tr.* (**bedeviled, bedeviling**) **1** plague; afflict. **2** confound; confuse. **3** possess as if with a devil.

be·dew /bidóo, -dyóo/ *v.tr.* **1** cover or sprinkle with dew or drops of water. **2** *poet.* sprinkle with tears.

bed·fel·low /bédfelō/ *n.* **1** a person who shares a bed. **2** an associate.

be·dight /bidít/ *adj. archaic* arrayed; adorned.

BEE

All bees bear a stinger, and have hairy bodies and a narrow waist between the thorax and abdomen. They are usually solitary creatures, but some species, such as the honeybee, live in complex social colonies. Important pollinators, they disperse pollen as they collect nectar and are essential to the reproductive process of many flowers.

compound eye · *wing* · *waist* · *antenna* · *stinger* · *tube-like mouthpart* · *thorax* · *claw* · *jointed leg* · *abdomen*

EXTERNAL FEATURES OF A HONEYBEE
(*Apis mellifera*)

EXAMPLES OF OTHER BEES

MOUNTAIN BUMBLEBEE
(*Bombus monticola*)

ORCHID BEE
(*Euglossa assarophora*)

ASIAN CARPENTER BEE
(*Xylocopa laticeps*)

PARASITIC BEE
(*Aglae caerulea*)

be·dim /bidím/ *v.tr.* (**bedimmed, bedimming**) *poet.* make (the eyes, mind, etc.) dim.

be·di·zen /bidízən, -dízən/ *v.tr. poet.* deck out gaudily.

bed·jack·et /bédjakit/ *n.* a jacket worn when sitting up in bed.

bed·lam /bédləm/ *n.* a scene of uproar and confusion.

bed lin·en *n.* sheets and pillowcases.

Bed·ling·ton ter·ri·er /bédlingtən/ *n.* **1** a terrier of a breed with narrow head, long legs, and curly gray hair. **2** this breed.

bed·mak·er /bédmaykər/ *n.* **1** a person who makes beds. **2** *Brit.* a person employed to clean students' rooms in a college.

Bed·ou·in /bédŏoin/ *n. & adj.* (also **Bed·u·in**) ● *n.* (*pl.* same) a nomadic Arab of the desert. ● *adj.* of or relating to the Bedouin.

bed·pan /bédpan/ *n.* a receptacle used by a bedridden patient for urine and feces.

bed·plate /bédplayt/ *n.* a metal plate forming the base of a machine, etc.

bed·post /bédpōst/ *n.* any of the four upright supports of a bedstead.

be·drag·gle /bidrágəl/ *v.tr.* **1** (often as **bedraggled** *adj.*) wet (a dress, etc.) by trailing it, or so that it hangs limp. **2** (as **bedraggled** *adj.*) untidy; disheveled.

bed rest *n.* confinement of an invalid to bed.

bed·rid·den /bédrid'n/ *adj.* confined to bed by infirmity.

bed·rock /bédrok/ *n.* solid rock underlying alluvial deposits, etc. ▷ GAS FIELD, SOIL.

bed·roll /bédrōl/ *n.* portable bedding rolled into a bundle.

bed·room /bédrŏom, -rŏom/ *n.* **1** a room for sleeping in. **2** (*attrib.*) of or referring to sexual relations (*bedroom comedy*).

bed·side /bédsīd/ *n.* **1** the space beside, esp. a patient's bed. **2** (*attrib.*) of or relating to the side of a bed (*bedside lamp*).

bed·side man·ner *n.* (of a doctor) an approach or attitude to a patient.

bed·sit·ter /bédsitər/ *n.* (also **bed·sit**) *Brit. colloq.* = BEDSITTING ROOM.

bed·sock /bédsok/ *n.* each of a pair of thick socks worn in bed.

bed·sore /bédsawr/ *n.* a sore developed by an invalid because of pressure caused by lying in bed.

bed·spread /bédspred/ *n.* a cloth used to cover a bed when not in use.

bed·stead /bédsted/ *n.* the framework of a bed.

bed·straw /bédstraw/ *n.* **1** any herbaceous plant of the genus *Galium*, once used as straw for bedding. **2** (in full **Our Lady's bedstraw**) a bedstraw, *G. verum*, with yellow flowers.

bed·time /bédtīm/ *n.* **1** the usual time for going to bed. **2** (*attrib.*) of or relating to bedtime (*bedtime story*).

Bed·u·in var. of BEDOUIN.

bed·wet·ting /bédweting/ *n.* involuntary urination during the night.

bee /bee/ *n.* **1** ◀ any four-winged insect of the superfamily Apoidea which collects nectar and pollen, produces wax and honey, and lives in large communities. ▷ HYMENOPTERAN, INSECT. **2** ◀ any insect of a similar type. **3** (usu. **busy bee**) a busy person. **4** a meeting for communal work or amusement (*spelling bee*). □ **a bee in one's bonnet** an obsession.

bee·bread /bébred/ *n.* honey or pollen used as food by bees.

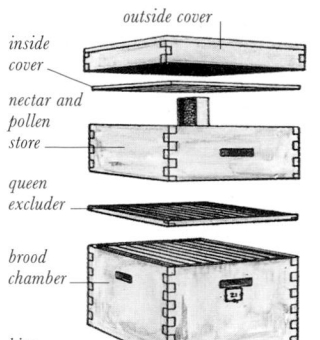

beechmast (fruit)

BEECH: COMMON BEECH (*Fagus sylvatica*)

beech /beech/ *n.* **1** (also **beech tree**) ◀ any large forest tree of the genus *Fagus*, having smooth gray bark and glossy leaves. **2** (also **beech·wood**) its wood.

bee·eat·er *n.* ▶ any brightly plumaged insect-eating bird of the family Meropidae with a long slender curved bill.

beef /beef/ *n. & v.*

● *n.* **1** the flesh of the ox, bull, or cow for eating. ▷ CUT. **2** *colloq.* well-developed male muscle. **3** (*pl.* **beeves** /beevz/ or **beefs**) a cow, bull, or ox fattened for beef; its carcass. **4** (*pl.* **beefs**) *sl.* a complaint; a protest. ● *v.intr. sl.* complain. □ **beef up** *sl.* strengthen; reinforce.

beef·burg·er /béefbərgər/ *n.* = HAMBURGER.

beef·cake /béefkayk/ *n. sl.* well-developed male muscles, esp. when photographed and displayed for admiration.

beef·eat·er /béefeetər/ *n.* a warder in the Tower of London.

beef·steak /béefstáyk/ *n.* a thick slice of lean beef, esp. from the rump.

beef·y /béefee/ *adj.* (**beefier, beefiest**) **1** like beef. **2** solid; muscular. □□ **beef·i·ly** *adv.* **beef·i·ness** *n.*

bee·hive /béehīv/ *n.* **1** ▶ an artificial habitation for bees. ▷ BEE. **2** a busy place. **3** anything resembling a wicker beehive in being domed.

bee·keep·ing /békēping/ *n.* the occupation of keeping bees. □□ **bee·keep·er** *n.*

bee·line /béelīn/ *n.* a straight line between two places. □ **make a bee·line for** hurry directly to.

BEE-EATER: CARMINE BEE-EATER (*Merops nubicus*)

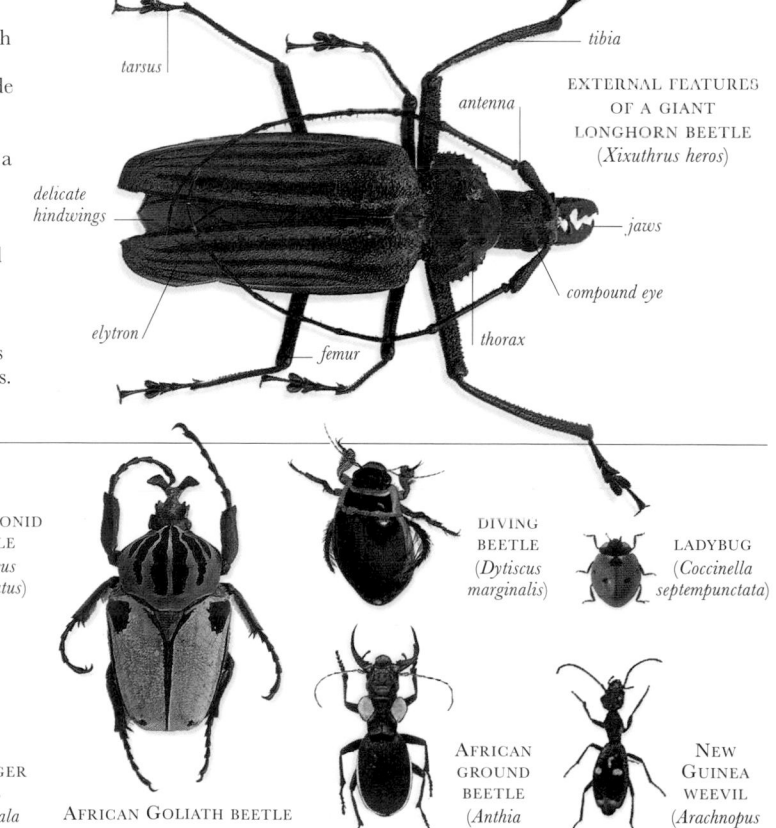

outside cover
inside cover
nectar and pollen store
queen excluder
brood chamber
hive entrance
base

BEEHIVE: EXPLODED VIEW OF A LANGSTROTH BEEHIVE

Be·el·ze·bub /bee-élzibub/ *n.* the Devil.

been *past part.* of BE.

beep /beep/ *n. & v.* ● *n.* **1** the sound of an automobile horn. **2** any similar short high-pitched noise. ● *v.intr.* emit a beep.

beep·er /bépər/ *n.* an electronic device that receives signals and emits a beep to page the person carrying it.

beer /beer/ *n.* **1** an alcoholic drink made from yeast-fermented malt, etc., flavored with hops. **2** any of several other fermented drinks, e.g., ginger beer.

beer gar·den *n.* an outdoor bar where beer is sold.

beest·ings /béestingz/ *n.pl.* (also treated as *sing.*) the first milk (esp. of a cow) after giving birth.

bees·wax /béezwaks/ *n. & v.* ● *n.* **1** the wax secreted by bees to make honeycombs. **2** this wax refined and used to polish wood. ● *v.tr.* polish (furniture, etc.) with beeswax.

bees·wing /béezwing/ *n.* a filmy second crust on old port.

beet /beet/ *n.* any plant of the genus *Beta*, with an edible root (see BEETROOT, SUGAR BEET).

bee·tle[1] /bét'l/ *n.* **1** ▼ any insect of the order Coleoptera, with modified front wings forming hard protective cases closing over the back wings. **2** *colloq.* any similar insect. **3** *sl.* a type of compact rounded Volkswagen car.

B

BEETLE

Beetles make up by far the largest order of insects, with more than 375,000 species currently identified. They are found in almost all land habitats and feed on a wide range of food, from carrion, pollen, and plant sap to rotting wood. As adults, beetles have heavily armored bodies and hardened elytra, or forewings, which form a protective cover over the more delicate hindwings. Beetle larvae have softer bodies and are usually protected by remaining hidden inside their foodstores. Some beetles are important pests of crops or of stored food, but in nature beetles play a useful role in recycling the nutrients in dead remains. Some beetle larvae – particularly those of wood-eating species – live for more than 10 years before becoming adult. The adults themselves typically live for only a few weeks or months.

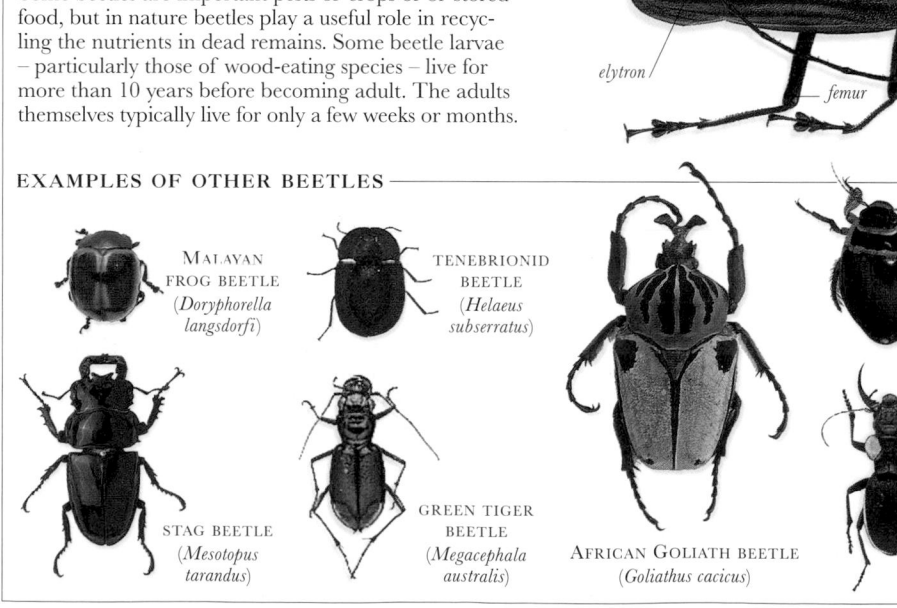

tarsus
tibia
antenna
delicate hindwings
jaws
compound eye
thorax
femur
elytron

EXTERNAL FEATURES OF A GIANT LONGHORN BEETLE (*Xixuthrus heros*)

EXAMPLES OF OTHER BEETLES

MALAYAN FROG BEETLE (*Doryphorella langsdorfi*)

TENEBRIONID BEETLE (*Helaeus subserratus*)

DIVING BEETLE (*Dytiscus marginalis*)

LADYBUG (*Coccinella septempunctata*)

STAG BEETLE (*Mesotopus tarandus*)

GREEN TIGER BEETLE (*Megacephala australis*)

AFRICAN GOLIATH BEETLE (*Goliathus cacicus*)

AFRICAN GROUND BEETLE (*Anthia thoracica*)

NEW GUINEA WEEVIL (*Arachnopus gazella*)

bee·tle[2] /béet'l/ *adj.* & *v.* • *adj.* (esp. of the eyebrows) projecting; shaggy; scowling. • *v.intr.* (usu. as **beetling** *adj.*) (of brows, cliffs, etc.) project; overhang threateningly.

bee·tle[3] /béet'l/ *n.* & *v.* • *n.* **1** a tool with a heavy head and a handle, used for ramming, crushing, driving wedges, etc. **2** a machine used for heightening the luster of cloth by pressure from rollers. • *v.tr.* **1** ram, crush, drive, etc., with a beetle. **2** finish (cloth) with a beetle.

bee·tle-browed *adj.* with shaggy, projecting, or scowling eyebrows.

beet·root /béetroot, -oot/ *n.* esp. *Brit.* **1** a beet, *Beta vulgaris*, with an edible spherical dark red root. **2** this root used as a vegetable.

beeves *pl.* of BEEF.

be·fall /bifáwl/ *v.* (*past* **befell** /bifél/; *past part.* **befallen** /bifáwlən/) *poet.* **1** *intr.* happen (*so it befell*). **2** *tr.* happen to (a person, etc.) (*what has befallen her?*).

be·fit /bifít/ *v.tr.* (**befitted, befitting**) **1** be fitted or appropriate for; suit. **2** be incumbent on. ▫▫ **be·fit·ting** *adj.*

be·fog /bifawg, -fóg/ *v.tr.* (**befogged, befogging**) **1** confuse; obscure. **2** envelop in fog.

be·fool /bifóol/ *v.tr.* make a fool of; delude.

be·fore /bifáwr/ *conj., prep.,* & *adv.* • *conj.* **1** earlier than the time when (*crawled before he walked*). **2** rather than that (*would starve before he stole*). • *prep.* **1 a** in front of (*before her in the queue*). **b** ahead of (*crossed the line before him*). **c** under the impulse of (*recoil before the attack*). **d** awaiting (*the future before them*). **2** earlier than; preceding (*Lent comes before Easter*). **3** rather than (*death before dishonor*). **4 a** in the presence of (*appear before the judge*). **b** for the attention of (*a plan put before the committee*). • *adv.* **1 a** earlier than the time in question; already (*heard it before*). **b** in the past (*happened long before*). **2** ahead (*go before*). **3** on the front (*hit before and behind*). ▫ **before time** see TIME.

Be·fore Christ *adv.* (of a date) reckoned backward from the birth of Christ.

be·fore·hand /bifáwrhand/ *adv.* in anticipation; in advance (*had prepared the meal beforehand*).

be·foul /bifówl/ *v.tr. poet.* **1** make foul or dirty. **2** degrade; defile.

be·friend /bifrénd/ *v.tr.* act as a friend to; help.

be·fud·dle /bifúd'l/ *v.tr.* **1** make drunk. **2** confuse. ▫▫ **be·fud·dle·ment** *n.*

beg /beg/ *v.* (**begged, begging**) **1 a** *intr.* (usu. foll. by *for*) ask for (esp. food, money, etc.) (*begged for alms*). **b** *tr.* ask for (food, money, etc.) as a gift. **c** *intr.* live by begging. **2** *tr.* & *intr.* (usu. foll. by *for*, or *to* + infin.) ask earnestly or humbly. **3** *tr.* ask formally for (*I beg your pardon*). **4** *intr.* (of a dog, etc.) sit up with the front paws raised expectantly. **5** *tr.* take or ask leave (to do something) (*I beg to differ; beg to enclose*). ▫ **beg off** decline to take part in or attend. **beg the question 1** assume the truth of an argument or proposition to be proved. **2** *disp.* pose the question. **3** *colloq.* evade a difficulty. **go begging** (of a chance or a thing) not be taken; be unwanted.

be·gan *past* of BEGIN.

be·gat *archaic past* of BEGET.

be·get /bigét/ *v.tr.* (**begetting**; *past* **begot** /bigót/; *archaic* **begat** /bigát/; *past part.* **begotten** /bigót'n/) *literary* **1** (usu. of a father, sometimes of a father and mother) procreate. **2** give rise to; cause (*beget strife*). ▫▫ **be·get·ter** *n.*

beg·gar /bégər/ *n.* & *v.* • *n.* **1** a person who begs, esp. one who lives by begging. **2** a poor person. **3** *colloq.* a person; a fellow (*poor beggar*). • *v.tr.* **1** reduce to poverty. **2** exhaust the resources of (*it beggars description*).

beg·gar·ly /bégərlee/ *adj.* **1** poverty-stricken; needy. **2** intellectually poor. **3** mean; sordid. **4** ungenerous.

beg·gar·y /bégəree/ *n.* extreme poverty.

be·gin /bigín/ *v.* (**beginning**; *past* **began** /bigán/; *past part.* **begun** /bigún/) **1** *tr.* perform the first part of; start (*begin work; begin crying; begin to understand*). **2** *intr.* come into being; arise: **a** in time (*the season began last week*). **b** in space (*your jurisdiction begins beyond the river*). **3** *tr.* (usu. foll. by *to* + infin.) start at a certain time (*then began to feel ill*). **4** *intr.* be begun (*the meeting will begin at 7*). **5** *intr.* **a** start speaking (*"No," he began*). **b** be the first to do something (*who wants to begin?*). **6** *intr. colloq.* (usu. with *neg.*) show any attempt or likelihood (*can't begin to compete*).

be·gin·ner /bigínər/ *n.* a person just beginning to learn a skill, etc.

be·gin·ning /bigíning/ *n.* **1** the time or place at which anything begins. **2** a source or origin. **3** the first part.

be·gone /bigáwn, -gón/ *int. poet.* go away at once!

be·go·nia /bigónyə/ *n.* any plant of the genus *Begonia*, with brightly colored sepals and no petals.

be·got *past* of BEGET.

be·got·ten *past part.* of BEGET.

be·grime /bigrím/ *v.tr.* make grimy.

be·grudge /bigrúj/ *v.tr.* **1** resent; be dissatisfied at. **2** envy (a person) the possession of. ▫▫ **be·grudg·ing·ly** *adv.*

be·guile /bigíl/ *v.tr.* **1** charm; amuse. **2** divert attention pleasantly from (work, etc.). **3** (often foll. by *of, out of*, or *into* + verbal noun) delude; cheat (*beguiled him into paying*). ▫▫ **be·guil·ing** *adj.* **be·guil·ing·ly** *adv.*

be·guine /bigéen/ *n.* **1** a popular dance of W. Indian origin. **2** its rhythm.

be·gun *past part.* of BEGIN.

be·half /biháf/ *n.* ▫ **on** (also **in**) **behalf of** (or **on a person's behalf**) **1** in the interests of (a person, principle, etc.). **2** as representative of (*acting on behalf of my client*).

be·have /biháyv/ *v.* **1** *intr.* **a** act or react (in a specified way) (*behaved well*). **b** conduct oneself properly. **2** *refl.* show good manners (*behaved herself*).

be·hav·ior /biháyvyər/ *n.* (*Brit.* **behaviour**) **1 a** the way one conducts oneself; manners. **b** the treatment of others; moral conduct. **2** the way in which a machine, chemical substance, etc., acts or works. ▫▫ **be·hav·ior·al** *adj.* (*Brit.* **behavioural**)

be·hav·ior·al sci·ence *n.* the scientific study of human and animal behavior (see BEHAVIORISM).

be·hav·ior·ism /biháyvyərizəm/ *n.* (*Brit.* **behaviourism**) *Psychol.* the theory that human behavior is determined by conditioning rather than by thoughts or feelings, and that psychological disorders are best treated by altering behavior patterns. ▫▫ **be·hav·ior·ist** *n.* **be·hav·ior·is·tic** /-rístik/ *adj.*

be·head /bihéd/ *v.tr.* cut off the head of (a person).

be·held *past* and *past part.* of BEHOLD.

be·he·moth /bihéeməth, béeə-/ *n.* an enormous creature or thing.

be·hest /bihést/ *n. literary* a command; an entreaty (*went at his behest*).

be·hind /bihínd/ *prep., adv.,* & *n.* • *prep.* **1 a** in, toward, or to the rear of. **b** on the farther side of (*behind the bush*). **c** hidden by (*something behind that remark*). **2 a** in the past in relation to (*trouble is behind me now*). **b** late in relation to (*behind schedule*). **3** inferior to; weaker than (*behind the others in math*). **4 a** in support of (*she's right behind us*). **b** responsible for; giving rise to (*the person behind the project; the reasons behind his resignation*). **5** in the tracks of; following. • *adv.* **1 a** in or to or toward the rear; farther back (*the street behind*). **b** on the farther side (*a high wall with a field behind*). **2** remaining after the departure of most others (*stay behind*). **3** (usu. foll. by *with*) **a** in arrears (*behind with the rent*). **b** late in accomplishing a task, etc. (*working too slowly and getting behind*). **4** in a weak position; backward (*behind in Latin*). **5** following (*his dog running behind*). • *n. colloq.* the buttocks. ▫ **behind the scenes** see SCENE. **behind the times** old-fashioned. **come from behind** win after being behind in scoring.

be·hind·hand /bihíndhand/ *adv.* & *predic.adj.* (usu. foll. by *with, in*) late (in discharging a duty, paying a debt, etc.).

be·hind-the-scenes *adj.* secret, using secret information (*a behind-the-scenes investigation*).

be·hold /bihóld/ *v.tr.* (*past* & *past part.* **beheld** /bihéld/) *literary* (esp. in *imper.*) see; observe. ▫▫ **be·hold·er** *n.*

be·hold·en /bihóldən/ *predic.adj.* (usu. foll. by *to*) under obligation.

be·hoof /bihóof/ *n. archaic* (prec. by *to, for, on*; foll. by *of*) benefit; advantage.

be·hoove /bihóov/ *v.tr.* (*Brit.* **behove** /-hóv/) (prec. by *it* as subject; foll. by *to* + infin.) **1** be incumbent on. **2** (usu. with *neg.*) befit (*ill behooves him to protest*).

beige /bayzh/ *n.* & *adj.* • *n.* a pale sandy fawn color. • *adj.* of this color.

be·ing /béeing/ *n.* **1** existence. **2** the nature or essence (of a person, etc.) (*his whole being revolted*). **3** a human being. **4** anything that exists or is imagined.

be·jew·eled /bijóoəld/ *adj.* adorned with jewels.

bel /bel/ *n.* a unit used in the comparison of power levels in electrical communication or intensities of sound, corresponding to an intensity ratio of 10 to 1 (cf. DECIBEL).

be·la·bor /biláybər/ *v.tr.* **1 a** thrash; beat. **b** attack verbally. **2** argue or elaborate (a subject) in excessive detail.

be·lat·ed /biláytid/ *adj.* coming late. ▫▫ **be·lat·ed·ly** *adv.* **be·lat·ed·ness** *n.*

be·lay /biláy/ *v.* & *n.* • *v.* **1** *tr.* fix (a running rope) around a cleat, pin, rock, etc., to secure it. ▷ ROCK-CLIMBING. **2** *tr.* & *intr.* (usu. in *imper.*) *Naut. sl.* stop; enough! (esp. *belay there!*). • *n.* **1** an act of belaying. **2** a spike of rock, etc., used for belaying.

bel can·to /bel kántō, káan-/ *n.* **1** a lyrical style of operatic singing using a full rich broad tone. **2** (*attrib.*) characterized by this type of singing.

belch /belch/ *v.* & *n.* • *v.* **1** *intr.* emit wind noisily from the stomach through the mouth. **2** *tr.* (of a chimney, volcano, gun, etc.) send (smoke, etc.) out or up. • *n.* an act of belching.

bel·dam /béldəm, -dam/ *n.* (also **bel·dame**) *archaic* **1** an old woman; a hag. **2** a virago.

be·lea·guer /biléegər/ *v.tr.* **1** besiege. **2** vex; harass.

bel es·prit /bél espree/ *n.* (*pl. beaux esprits* /bóz espree/) a witty person.

bel·fry /bélfree/ *n.* (*pl.* **-ies**) **1** a bell tower or steeple housing bells. **2** a space for hanging bells in a church tower. ▷ CHURCH. ▫ **have bats in the belfry** see BAT[2].

Bel·gian /béljən/ *n.* & *adj.* • *n.* **1** a native or inhabitant of Belgium in W. Europe. **2** a person of Belgian descent. • *adj.* of or relating to Belgium.

be·lie /bilí/ *v.tr.* (**belying**) **1** give a false notion of (*its appearance belies its age*). **2 a** fail to fulfill (a promise, etc.). **b** fail to justify (a hope, etc.).

be·lief /biléef/ *n.* **1 a** a person's religion; religious conviction (*has no belief*). **b** a firm opinion (*my belief is that he did it*). **c** an acceptance (of a fact, statement, etc.) (*belief in the afterlife*). **2** (usu. foll. by *in*) trust or confidence. ▫ **beyond belief** incredible.

be·lieve /biléev/ *v.* **1** *tr.* accept as true or as conveying the truth (*I believe it; don't believe him*). **2** *tr.* think; suppose (*I believe it's raining*). **3** *intr.* (foll. by *in*) **a** have faith in the existence of (*believes in God*). **b** have confidence in (*believes in alternative medicine*). **c** have trust in the advisability of (*believes in telling the truth*). **4** *intr.* have faith. ▫▫ **be·liev·a·ble** *adj.* **be·liev·a·bil·i·ty** /-léevəbílitee/ *n.*

be·liev·er /biléevər/ *n.* **1** an adherent of a specified religion. **2** a person who believes (*a great believer in exercise*).

be·lit·tle /bilít'l/ *v.tr.* **1** disparage; depreciate. **2** make small; dwarf.

bell /bel/ *n.* & *v.* • *n.* **1** a hollow object in the shape of a deep upturned cup, made to sound a clear musical note when struck (either externally or by means of a clapper inside). **2 a** a sound or stroke of a bell. **b** (prec. by a numeral) *Naut.* the time as indicated every half hour of a watch by the striking of the ship's bell one to eight times. **3** anything that sounds like or functions as a bell. **4 a** any bell-shaped part, e.g., of a musical instrument. ▷ BRASS.

b the corolla of a flower when bell-shaped. **5** (in *pl.*) *Mus.* a set of cylindrical metal tubes of different lengths are struck with a hammer. ● *v.tr.* provide with a bell or bells. □ **ring a bell** *colloq.* revive a distant recollection.

bel·la·don·na /bélədónə/ *n.* **1** deadly nightshade. **2** *Med.* a drug prepared from this.

bell-bot·tom *n.* **1** a marked flare below the knee (of a pants leg). **2** (in *pl.*) pants with bell-bottoms. □□ **bell-bot·tomed** *adj.*

bell·boy /bélboy/ *n. Brit.* = BELLHOP.

bell bu·oy *n.* a buoy equipped with a warning bell rung by the motion of the sea.

bell curve *n. Statistics* ▶ a graph of a normal distribution, with a large rounded peak which tapers away at each end.

belle /bel/ *n.* **1** a beautiful woman. **2** a woman recognized as the most beautiful or most charming (*the belle of the ball*).

BELL CURVE

belle é·poque /bél epúk/ *n.* the period of settled and comfortable life preceding the First World War.

belles let·tres /bel-létrə/ *n.pl.* (also treated as *sing.*) writings or studies of a literary nature, esp. essays and criticisms. □□ **belletrist** /bel-létrist/ *n. & adj.*

bell·hop /bélhop/ *n.* a person who carries luggage, runs errands, etc., in a hotel or club.

bel·li·cose /bélikōs/ *adj.* eager to fight; warlike. □□ **bellicosity** /-kósitee/ *n.*

bel·lig·er·ent /bilíjərənt/ *adj. & n.* ● *adj.* **1** engaged in war or conflict. **2** given to constant fighting; pugnacious. ● *n.* a nation or person engaged in war or conflict. □□ **bel·lig·er·ence** *n.* (also **bel·lig·er·en·cy**) **bel·lig·er·ent·ly** *adv.*

bell jar *n.* a bell-shaped glass cover or container for use in a laboratory.

bell·man /bélmən/ *n.* (*pl.* **-men**) *hist.* a town crier.

bell met·al *n.* an alloy of copper and tin for making bells (the tin content being greater than in bronze).

bel·low /bélō/ *v. & n.* ● *v.* **1** *intr.* **a** emit a deep loud roar. **b** cry or shout with pain. **2** *tr.* utter loudly and usu. angrily. ● *n.* a bellowing sound.

bel·lows /bélōz/ *n.pl.* (also treated as *sing.*) **1** a device with an air bag that emits a stream of air when squeezed, esp. (in full **pair of bellows**) a kind with two handles used for blowing air onto a fire. ▷ ACCORDION. **2** ▼ an expandable component, e.g., joining the lens to the body of a camera.

single-lens reflex camera   *bellows*   *lens*

mount

BELLOWS: CAMERA AND STANDARD BELLOWS ON A MOUNT

bell pep·per *n.* a sweet pepper of the genus *Capsicum*, with a bell shape.

bell·pull /bélpŏŏl/ *n.* a cord or handle which rings a bell when pulled.

bells and whis·tles *n.pl. colloq.* attractive but unnecessary additional features.

bell·weth·er /bélwethər/ *n.* **1** the leading sheep of a flock, with a bell on its neck. **2** a ringleader.

bel·ly /bélee/ *n.* (*pl.* **-ies**) **1** the part of the human body below the chest, containing the stomach and bowels. **2** the stomach, esp. representing the body's

need for food. ▷ DIGESTION. **3** the front of the body from the waist to the groin. **4** the underside of a four-legged animal. **5 a** a cavity or bulging part of anything. **b** the surface of an instrument of the violin family, across which the strings are placed. □ **go belly up** *colloq.* fail financially. □□ **bel·ly·ful** *n.* (*pl.* **-fuls**).

bel·ly·ache /béleeayk/ *n. & v.* ● *n. colloq.* a stomach pain. ● *v.intr. sl.* complain noisily or persistently. □□ **bel·ly·ach·er** *n.*

bel·ly·band /béleeband/ *n.* a band placed around a horse's belly, holding the shafts of a cart, etc.

bel·ly but·ton *n. colloq.* the navel.

bel·ly dance *n.* a Middle Eastern dance performed by a woman, involving voluptuous movements of the belly. □□ **bel·ly danc·er** *n.* **bel·ly danc·ing** *n.*

bel·ly·flop /béleeflop/ *n. & v.* ● *n.* a dive in which the body lands with the belly flat on the water. ● *v.intr.* perform this dive.

bel·ly laugh *n.* a loud unrestrained laugh.

be·long /bilawng, -lóng/ *v.intr.* **1** (foll. by *to*) **a** be the property of. **b** be rightly assigned to as a duty, right, part, member, characteristic, etc. **c** be a member of (a club, etc.). **2** have the right qualities to be a member of a particular group (*he's nice but just doesn't belong*). **3** (foll. by *in, under*) be rightly placed or classified. **b** fit a particular environment.

be·long·ings /biláwngingz, -lóng-/ *n.pl.* one's movable possessions or luggage.

Be·lo·rus·sian /bélōrúshən/ *n. & adj.* (also **Bye·lo·rus·sian** /byélō-/) ● *n.* **1** a native of Belorussia, now officially the Republic of Belarus. **2** the East Slavonic language of Belorussia. ● *adj.* of or relating to Belorussia or its people or language.

be·lov·ed /bilúvid, -lúvd/ *adj. & n.* ● *adj.* much loved. ● *n.* a much loved person.

be·low /bilō/ *prep. & adv.* ● *prep.* **1** lower in position (down a slope, etc.) than. **2** at or to a greater depth than (*below 500 feet*). **3** lower or less than in amount or degree (*below freezing*). **4** lower in position or importance than. **5** unworthy of. ● *adv.* **1** at or to a lower point or level. **2 a** downstairs (*lives below*). **b** downstream. **3** (of a text reference) further forward in a book (*as noted below*). **4** on the lower side (*looks similar above and below*).

belt /belt/ *n. & v.* ● *n.* **1** a strip of leather or other material worn around the waist or across the chest. **2** a belt worn as a sign of rank or achievement. **3 a** a circular band used as a driving medium in machinery. **b** a conveyor belt. **c** a flexible strip carrying machine gun cartridges. **4** a strip of color or texture, etc., differing from that on each side. **5** a distinct region or extent (*cotton belt*). **6** *sl.* a heavy blow. ● *v.* **1** *tr.* put a belt around. **2** *tr.* (often foll. by *on*) fasten with a belt. **3** *tr.* **a** beat with a belt. **b** *sl.* hit hard. **4** *intr. sl.* rush (usu. with compl.: *belted along; belted home*). □ **below the belt** unfair or unfairly. **belt out** *sl.* sing or utter loudly and forcibly. **belt up** *colloq.* **1** put on a seat belt. **2** *Brit. sl.* be quiet. **tighten one's belt** live more frugally. **under one's belt 1** (of food) eaten. **2** securely acquired (*has a degree under her belt*). □□ **belt·er** *n.* (esp. in sense of *belt out*).

belt·way /béltway/ *n.* **1** a highway skirting a metropolitan region. **2** (**the Beltway**) the highway skirting Washington DC.

be·lu·ga /bəlóogə/ *n.* **1 a** a large kind of sturgeon, *Huso huso*. **b** caviar obtained from it. **2** ▶ a white whale. ▷ WHALE

bel·ve·dere /bélvideer/ *n.* a summerhouse or open-sided gallery, usu. at rooftop level.

be·ly·ing *pres. part.* of BELIE.

BEM *abbr.* British Empire Medal.

be·moan /bimón/ *v.tr.* express regret or sorrow over; lament.

be·muse /bimyóoz/ *v.tr.* bewilder (a person). □□ **be·musedly** /-zidlee/ *adv.* **be·muse·ment** *n.*

bench /bench/ *n.* **1** a long seat of wood or stone. **2** a worktable, e.g., for a carpenter or mechanic. **3** (prec. by *the*) **a** the office of judge or magistrate. **b** a judge's seat in a court of law. **c** a court of law. **d** judges and magistrates collectively. **4** *Sports* an area to the side of a field with seating where coaches and players not taking part can watch the game. □ **on the bench 1** appointed a judge or magistrate. **2** *Sports* acting as substitute or reserve.

bench·mark /bénchmaark/ *n.* **1** a surveyor's mark cut in a wall, etc., used for reference in measuring altitudes. **2** a standard or point of reference.

bench press *n.* an exercise in which one lies on a bench with feet on the floor and raises a weight with both arms.

bench test *n. & v.* esp. *Computing* ● *n.* a test made by benchmarking. ● *v.tr.* (**bench-test**) run a series of tests on (a computer, etc.) before its use.

bend[1] /bend/ *v. & n.* ● *v.* (*past* **bent**; *past part.* **bent** exc. in **bended knee**) **1 a** *tr.* force or adapt into a curve or angle. **b** *intr.* (of an object) be altered in this way. **2** *intr.* move in a curved course (*the road bends to the left*). **3** *intr. & tr.* (often foll. by *down, over*, etc.) incline or cause to incline from the vertical. **4** *tr.* interpret or modify (a rule). **5** *tr. & refl.* (foll. by *to, on*) direct or devote (oneself or one's attention, energies, etc.). **6** *tr.* turn (one's steps or eyes) in a new direction. **7** *tr.* (in *passive;* foll. by *on*) be determined (*was bent on selling*). **8 a** *intr.* stoop or submit (*bent before his master*). **b** *tr.* force to submit. ● *n.* **1** a curve in a road, stream, etc. **2** a departure from a straight course. **3** a bent part of anything. **4** (in *pl.;* prec. by *the*) *colloq.* sickness due to too rapid decompression underwater. □ **around the bend** *colloq.* insane. **bend over backward** see BACKWARD. □□ **bend·a·ble** *adj.* **bend·y** *adj.* (**bendier, bendiest**)

bend[2] /bend/ *n.* **1** *Naut.* any of various knots for tying ropes. ▷ KNOT. **2** *Heraldry* **a** a diagonal stripe from top left to bottom right of a shield. **b** (**bend sinister**) a diagonal stripe from top right to bottom left, as a sign of bastardy.

bend·er /béndər/ *n. sl.* a wild drinking spree.

be·neath /binéeth/ *prep. & adv.* ● *prep.* **1** too demeaning for (*beneath him to reply*). **2** below; under. ● *adv.* underneath.

Ben·e·dic·tine /bénidiktin/ *n.* a monk or nun of an order following the rule of St. Benedict.

ben·e·dic·tion /bénidíkshən/ *n.* **1** the utterance of a blessing. **2** the state of being blessed.

ben·e·dic·to·ry /bénidiktəree/ *adj.* of or expressing benediction.

Ben·e·dic·tus /bénidiktəs/ *n.* **1** the section of the Latin Mass beginning *Benedictus qui venit in nomine Domini* (Blessed is he who comes in the name of the Lord). **2** a canticle beginning *Benedictus Dominus Deus* (Blessed be the Lord God) from Luke 1:68–79.

ben·e·fac·tion /bénifákshən/ *n.* **1** a donation or gift. **2** an act of giving or doing good.

ben·e·fac·tor /bénifaktər/ *n.* (*fem.* **benefactress** /-tris/) a person who gives support (esp. financial) to a person or cause.

ben·e·fice /bénifis/ *n.* **1** an income from a church office. **2** the property attached to a church office. □□ **ben·e·ficed** *adj.*

be·nef·i·cent /binéfisənt/ *adj.* doing good; actively kind. □□ **be·nef·i·cence** /-səns/ *n.* **be·nef·i·cent·ly** *adv.*

BELUGA (*Delphinapterus leucas*)

B

B

ben·e·fi·cial /bénifíshəl/ *adj.* advantageous; having benefits. □□ **ben·e·fi·cial·ly** *adv.*

ben·e·fi·ci·ar·y /bénifíshee-e-ree, -fishə-ree/ *n.* (*pl.* **-ies**) **1** a person who receives benefits under a will, etc. **2** a holder of a benefice.

ben·e·fit /bénifit/ *n. & v.* ● *n.* **1** a favorable or helpful factor or circumstance; advantage; profit. **2** (often in *pl.*) payment made under insurance, etc. **3** a public performance or game of which the proceeds go to a particular charitable cause. ● *v.* (**benefited**, **benefiting**; also **benefitted**, **benefitting**) **1** *tr.* bring advantage to. **2** *intr.* (often foll. by *from*, *by*) receive an advantage or gain. □ **the benefit of the doubt** a concession that a person is innocent, correct, etc., although doubt exists.

be·nev·o·lent /binévələnt/ *adj.* **1** wishing to do good; actively helpful. **2** charitable (*benevolent fund*). □□ **be·nev·o·lence** /-ləns/ *n.* **be·nev·o·lent·ly** *adv.*

Ben·ga·li /benggáwlee, -gáalee/ *n. & adj.* ● *n.* **1** a native of Bengal, a former Indian province. **2** the language of this people. ● *adj.* of or relating to Bengal or its people or language.

be·night·ed /binítid/ *adj.* **1** intellectually or morally ignorant. **2** overtaken by darkness.

be·nign /binín/ *adj.* **1** gentle; kindly. **2** salutary. **3** (of the climate, etc.) mild. **4** *Med.* not malignant. □□ **be·nign·ly** *adv.*

be·nig·nant /binígnənt/ *adj.* **1** kindly, esp. to inferiors. **2** salutary; beneficial. **3** *Med.* = BENIGN 4.

bent[1] /bent/ *past* and *past part.* of BEND[1] *v. adj. & n.* ● *adj.* **1** curved or having an angle. **2** (foll. by *on*) determined to do or have. ● *n.* **1** an inclination or bias. **2** (foll. by *for*) a talent (*a bent for mimicry*).

bent[2] /bent/ *n.* **1 a** any stiff grass of the genus *Agrostis*. **b** any of various grasslike reeds, rushes, or sedges. **2** a stiff stalk of a grass.

ben·thos /bénthos/ *n.* the flora and fauna found at the bottom of a sea or lake. □□ **ben·thic** /-thik/ *adj.*

ben·to /béntō/ *n.* **1** a lacquered or decorated wooden Japanese lunch box. **2** a Japanese-style packed lunch, consisting of such items as rice, vegetables, and sashimi.

ben·ton·ite /béntənīt/ *n.* a kind of absorbent clay used esp. as a filler.

bent·wood /béntwŏod/ *n.* wood that is artificially shaped for use in making furniture.

Ben·ze·drine /bénzidreen/ *n. Trademark* amphetamine.

ben·zene /bénzeen/ *n.* a colorless carcinogenic volatile liquid found in coal tar, etc. □□ **ben·ze·noid** /-zənoyd/ *adj.*

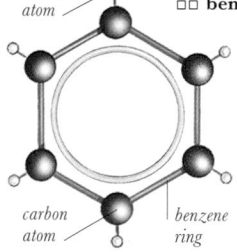

BENZENE RING IN A BENZENE MOLECULE

hydrogen atom   *carbon atom*   *benzene ring*

ben·zene ring *n.* ◄ the hexagonal unsaturated ring of six carbon atoms in the benzene molecule.

ben·zine /bénzeen/ *n.* (also **ben·zin** /-zin/) a mixture of liquid hydrocarbons obtained from petroleum.

ben·zo·in /bénzōin/ *n.* a fragrant gum resin obtained from various E. Asian trees of the genus *Styrax*, and used in the manufacture of perfumes and incense.

ben·zol /bénzawl, -zol/ *n.* (also **ben·zole** /-zōl/) benzene, esp. unrefined and used as a fuel.

be·queath /bikwéeth, -kwéeth/ *v.tr.* **1** leave to a person by a will. **2** hand down to posterity.

be·quest /bikwést/ *n.* **1** the act or an instance of bequeathing. **2** a thing bequeathed.

be·rate /biráyt/ *v.tr.* scold; rebuke.

ber·ber·ine /bárbəreen/ *n.* a bitter yellow alkaloid compound, obtained from barberry and other plants.

ber·ber·is /bárbəris/ *n.* = BARBERRY.

be·reave /biréev/ *v.tr.* (esp. as **bereaved** *adj.*) (foll. by *of*) deprive of a relation, etc., esp. by death. □□ **be·reave·ment** *n.*

be·reft /biréft/ *adj.* (foll. by *of*) deprived (*bereft of hope*).

be·ret /bəráy/ *n.* ◄ a round flattish visorless cap of felt or cloth.

BERET

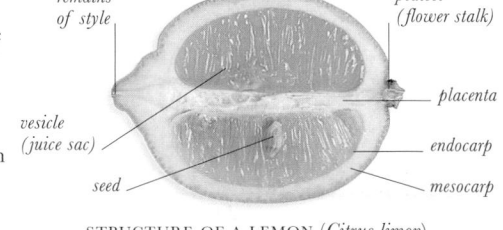

berg /bərg/ *n.* = ICEBERG.

ber·ga·mot[1] /bárgəmot/ *n.* **1** ► an aromatic herb, esp. *Mentha citrata*. **2** an oily perfume extracted from the rind of the fruit of the citrus tree *Citrus bergamia*. **3** the tree itself.

ber·i·ber·i /béreebéree/ *n.* a disease causing inflammation of the nerves due to a deficiency of vitamin B_1.

ber·ke·li·um /bərkéeleeəm, bárkleeəm/ *n. Chem.* a transuranic radioactive metallic element. ¶ Symb.: **Bk**.

berm /bərm/ *n.* a narrow path or grass strip beside a road, canal, etc.

Ber·mu·da onion /bərmyŏoda/ *n.* a large yellow-skinned onion with a mild flavor.

BERGAMOT
(*Mentha citrata*)

Ber·mu·da shorts /bərmyŏodə/ *n.pl.* (also **Ber·mu·das**) shorts reaching almost to the knees.

ber·ry /béree/ *n.* (*pl.* **-ies**) **1** any small roundish juicy fruit without a stone. ▷ FRUIT. **2** *Bot.* ▼ a fruit with its seeds enclosed in a pulp (e.g., a banana). **3** any of various kernels or seeds (e.g., coffee bean).

ber·serk /bərsárk, -zárk/ *adj.* (esp. in **go berserk**) wild; in a violent rage.

berth /bərth/ *n. & v.* ● *n.* **1** a fixed bunk on a ship, train, etc., for sleeping in. **2** a ship's place at a wharf. **3** adequate sea room. **4** *colloq.* a situation or appointment. **5** the proper place for anything. ● *v.* **1** *tr.* moor (a ship) in its berth. **2** *tr.* provide a sleeping place for. **3** *intr.* (of a ship) come to its mooring place. □ **give a wide berth to** stay away from.

ber·yl /béril/ *n.* **1** ► a kind of transparent precious stone, esp. pale green, blue, or yellow. **2** a mineral species which includes this, emerald, and aquamarine.

be·ryl·li·um /bəríleeəm/ *n. Chem.* a hard white

prismatic beryl crystal

rock groundmass

BERYL

metallic element used in the manufacture of light corrosion-resistant alloys. ¶ Symb.: **Be**.

be·seech /biséech/ *v.tr.* (*past* and *past part.* **besought** /-sáwt/ or **beseeched**) **1** (foll. by *for*, or to + infin.) entreat. **2** ask earnestly for. □□ **be·seech·ing** *adj.*

be·set /bisét/ *v.tr.* (**besetting**; *past* and *past part.* **beset**) **1** harass persistently (*beset by worries*). **2** hem in (a person, etc.).

be·side /bisíd/ *prep.* **1** at the side of. **2** compared with. **3** irrelevant to (*beside the point*). **4** = BESIDES. □ **beside oneself** overcome with worry, etc.

be·sides /bisídz/ *prep. & adv.* ● *prep.* in addition to. ● *adv.* also; as well; moreover.

be·siege /biséej/ *v.tr.* **1** lay siege to. **2** harass. □□ **be·sieg·er** *n.*

be·smirch /bismórch/ *v.tr.* **1** soil; discolor. **2** dishonor; sully the reputation or name of.

be·som /béezəm/ *n.* ► a broom made of twigs tied round a stick.

be·sot·ted /bisótid/ *adj.* **1** intoxicated. **2** confused. **3** infatuated.

be·sought *past* and *past part.* of BESEECH.

be·spat·ter /bispátər/ *v.tr.* **1** spatter (an object) all over. **2** spatter (liquid, etc.). **3** overwhelm with abuse, etc.

be·speak /bispéek/ *v.tr.* (*past* **bespoke** /-spók/; *past part.* **bespoken** /-spókən/ or as *adj.* **bespoke**) **1** engage in advance. **2** order (goods). **3** be evidence of (*bespeaks a kind heart*).

be·spec·ta·cled /bispéktəkəld/ *adj.* wearing eyeglasses.

be·spoke *past* and *past part.* of BESPEAK.

be·spo·ken *past part.* of BESPEAK.

BESOM

best /best/ *adj., adv., n., & v.* ● *adj.* (*superl.* of GOOD) of the most excellent or outstanding or desirable kind (*my best work; the best thing to do would be to confess*). ● *adv.* (*superl.* of WELL[1].) **1** in the best manner (*does it best*). **2** to the greatest degree (*like it best*). **3** most usefully (*is best ignored*). ● *n.* **1** that which is best (*the best is yet to come*). **2** the chief merit or advantage; the best aspect or side; a person's best performance, achievement, etc. (*brings out the best in him; gave their best to the task*). **3** (foll. by *of*) a winning majority of a certain number of games, etc., played) (*the best of five*). ● *v.tr. colloq.* defeat, outwit, outbid,

---

BERRY

Berries are produced by a wide range of flowering plants. Although many are cultivated for human consumption, their soft, succulent flesh originally evolved to attract animals and thereby aid seed dispersal. When an animal eats a berry, the fruit's flesh is digested, but the seeds pass through its body unharmed.

remains of style   *pedicel (flower stalk)*   *placenta*   *endocarp*   *mesocarp*   *vesicle (juice sac)*   *seed*

STRUCTURE OF A LEMON (*Citrus limon*)

EXAMPLES OF OTHER BERRIES

CAPE GOOSE-BERRY
(*Physalis peruviana*)

BANANA
(*Musa nana*)

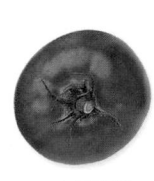

TOMATO
(*Lycopersicum esculentum*)

CACAO
(*Theobroma cacao*)

CHARENTAIS MELON
(*Cucumis melo*)

etc. □ **as best one can** as well as possible under the circumstances. **at best** on the most optimistic view. **be for** (or **all for**) **the best** be desirable in the end. **the best part of** most of. **do one's best** do all one can. **get the best of** defeat; outwit. **had best** would find it wisest to. **to the best of one's ability, knowledge**, etc., as far as one can do, know, etc.

bes·tial /béschəl, bées-/ *adj.* **1** brutish; cruel; savage. **2** sexually depraved; lustful. **3** of or like a beast. □□ **bes·tial·ize** *v.tr.* **bes·tial·ly** *adv.*

bes·ti·al·i·ty /béscheeálitee, bées-/ *n.* (*pl.* **-ies**) **1** bestial behavior or an instance of this. **2** sexual intercourse between a person and an animal.

bes·ti·ar·y /béschee-eree, bées-/ *n.* (*pl.* **-ies**) a moralizing medieval treatise on real and imaginary beasts.

be·stir /bistə́r/ *v.refl.* (**bestirred, bestirring**) exert or rouse (oneself).

best man *n.* the bridegroom's chief attendant at a wedding.

be·stow /bistṓ/ *v.tr.* **1** (foll. by *on, upon*) confer (a gift, right, etc.). **2** deposit. □□ **be·stow·al** *n.*

be·strew /bistrṓō/ *v.tr.* (*past part.* **bestrewed** or **bestrewn** /-strṓōn/) **1** (foll. by *with*) cover or partly cover (a surface). **2** scatter (things) about. **3** lie scattered over.

be·stride /bistríd/ *v.tr.* (*past* **bestrode** /-strṓd/; *past part.* **bestridden** /-stríd'n/) **1** sit astride on. **2** stand astride over.

best sell·er *n.* a book or other item that has sold in large numbers.

bet /bet/ *v.* & *n.* ● *v.* (**betting**; *past* and *past part.* **bet** or **betted**) **1** *intr.* (foll. by *on* or *against* with ref. to the outcome) risk a sum of money, etc., against another's on the basis of the outcome of an unpredictable event. **2** *tr.* risk (an amount) on such an outcome (*bet $10 on a horse*). **3** *tr.* risk a sum of money against (a person). **4** *tr. colloq.* feel sure (*bet they've forgotten it*). ● *n.* **1** the act of betting (*make a bet*). **2** the money, etc., staked (*put a bet on*). **3** *colloq.* an opinion (*my bet is that he won't come*). **4** *colloq.* a choice or course of action (*she's our best bet*). □ **you bet** *colloq.* you may be sure.

be·ta /báytə, bee-/ *n.* **1** the second letter of the Greek alphabet (Β, β). **2** the second member of a series.

be·ta-block·er *n. Pharm.* a drug that prevents the stimulation of increased cardiac action, used to reduce high blood pressure.

be·take /bitáyk/ *v.refl.* (*past* **betook** /bitŏŏk/; *past part.* **betaken** /bitáykən/) (foll. by *to*) go to (a place or person).

be·ta par·ti·cle *n.* (also **be·ta ray**) a fast-moving electron emitted by radioactive decay of substances (orig. regarded as rays). ▷ RADIOACTIVITY

be·ta·tron /báytətron, bée-/ *n. Physics* an apparatus for accelerating electrons in a circular path by magnetic induction.

be·tel /béet'l/ *n.* the leaf of the Asian evergreen climbing plant *Piper betle*, chewed in parts of Asia with the areca nut.

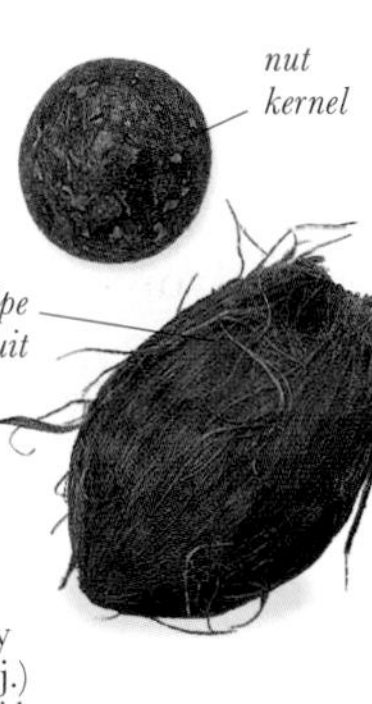
nut
kernel
half-ripe
fruit

BETEL NUT
(*Areca catechu*)

be·tel nut *n.* ▶ the areca nut.

bête noire /bet nwaár/ *n.* (*pl.* **bêtes noires** *pronunc.* same) a person or thing one particularly dislikes or fears; a bugbear.

be·tide /bitíd/ *v. poet.* (only in infin. and 3rd sing. subj.) **1** *tr.* happen to (*woe betide him*). **2** *intr.* happen (*whate'er may betide*).

be·to·ken /bitṓkən/ *v.tr.* **1** be a sign of; indicate. **2** augur.

bet·o·ny /bét'nee/ *n.* **1** ▶ a purple-flowered plant, *Stachys officinalis*. **2** any of various similar plants.

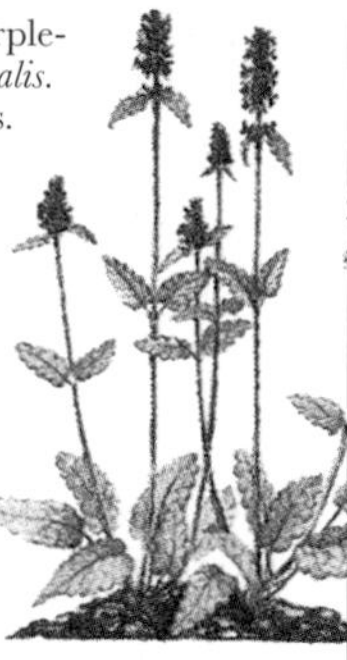

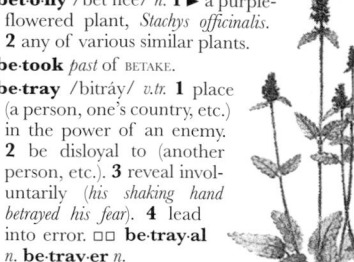

BETONY
(*Stachys officinalis*)

be·took *past* of BETAKE.

be·tray /bitráy/ *v.tr.* **1** place (a person, one's country, etc.) in the power of an enemy. **2** be disloyal to (another person, etc.). **3** reveal involuntarily (*his shaking hand betrayed his fear*). **4** lead into error. □□ **be·tray·al** *n.* **be·tray·er** *n.*

be·troth /bitrṓth, -tráwth/ *v.tr.* (usu. as **betrothed** *adj.*) bind with a promise to marry. □□ **be·troth·al** *n.*

bet·ter[1] /bétər/ *adj., adv., n.,* & *v.* ● *adj.* (*compar.* of GOOD). **1** of a more excellent or outstanding or desirable kind (*a better product; it would be better to go home*). **2** partly or fully recovered from illness (*feeling better*). ● *adv.* (*compar.* of WELL[1]). **1** in a better manner (*she sings better*). **2** to a greater degree (*like it better*). **3** more usefully or advantageously (*is better forgotten*). ● *n.* **1** that which is better (*the better of the two*). **2** (usu. in *pl.*; prec. by *my*, etc.) one's superior in ability or rank (*take notice of your betters*). ● *v.* **1** *tr.* improve on; surpass. **2** *tr.* make better; improve. **3** ● *refl.* improve one's position, etc. **4** *intr.* become better; improve. □ **the better part of** most of. **get the better of** defeat; outwit; win an advantage over. **go one better 1** outbid, etc., by one. **2** outdo another person. **had better** would find it wiser to. □□ **bet·ter·ment** *n.*

bet·ter[2] var. of BETTOR.

bet·ter half *n. colloq.* one's wife or husband.

bet·ting /béting/ *n.* **1** gambling by risking money on an unpredictable outcome. **2** the odds offered in this.

bet·tor /bétər/ *n.* (also **bet·ter**) a person who bets.

be·tween /bitwéen/ *prep.* & *adv.* ● *prep.* **1 a** at or to a point in the area or interval bounded by two or more other points in space, time, etc. (*broke down between Boston and Providence; we must meet between now and Friday*). **b** along the extent of such an interval (*there are five shops between here and the main road; works best between five and six; the numbers between 10 and 20*). **2** separating, physically or conceptually (*the distance between here and the Moon; the difference between right and wrong*). **3 a** by combining the resources of (*between us we could afford it*). **b** as the joint resources of (*$5 between them*). **c** by joint or reciprocal action (*an agreement between us*). **4** to and from (*runs between New York and Philadelphia*). **5** taking one and rejecting the other of (*decide between eating here and going out*). ● *adv.* (also **in between**) at a point or in the area bounded by two or more other points in space, time, sequence, etc. (*not fat or thin but in between*).

be·twixt /bitwíkst/ *prep.* & *adv. archaic* between. □ **betwixt and between** *colloq.* neither one thing nor the other.

bev·el /bévəl/ *n.* & *v.* ● *n.* **1** a slope from the horizontal or vertical in carpentry and stonework. **2** (in full **bevel square**) a tool for marking angles in carpentry and stonework. ● *v.* (**beveled, beveling** or **bevelled, bevelling**) **1** *tr.* reduce (a square edge) to a sloping edge. **2** *intr.* slope at an angle; slant.

bev·el gear *n.* a gear working another gear at an angle to it by means of beveled wheels.

bev·er·age /bévərij, bévrij/ *n.* a drink.

bev·y /bévee/ *n.* (*pl.* **-ies**) **1** a flock of quails or larks. **2** a company or group (orig. of women).

be·wail /biwáyl/ *v.tr.* **1** greatly regret or lament. **2** wail over; mourn for.

be·ware /biwáir/ *v.* (only in *imper.* or *infin.*) **1** *intr.* (often foll. by *of*, or *that, lest*, etc. + clause) be cautious; take heed (*beware of the dog; told us to beware; beware that you don't fall*). **2** *tr.* be cautious of (*beware the Ides of March*).

be·wil·der /biwíldər/ *v.tr.* utterly perplex or confuse. □□ **be·wil·dered·ly** *adv.* **be·wil·der·ing** *adj.* **be·wil·der·ment** *n.*

be·witch /biwích/ *v.tr.* **1** enchant; greatly delight. **2** cast a spell on. □□ **be·witch·ing** *adj.* **be·witch·ing·ly** *adv.*

be·yond /biyónd/ *prep., adv.,* & *n.* ● *prep.* **1** at or to the farther side of (*beyond the river*). **2** outside the scope, range, or understanding of (*beyond repair; beyond a joke; it is beyond me*). **3** more than. ● *adv.* **1** at or to the farther side. **2** farther on. ● *n.* (prec. by *the*) the unknown after death.

B

bez·el /bézəl/ *n.* **1** ▶ the sloped edge of a chisel. **2** the oblique faces of a cut gem. **3** a groove holding a watch crystal or gem.

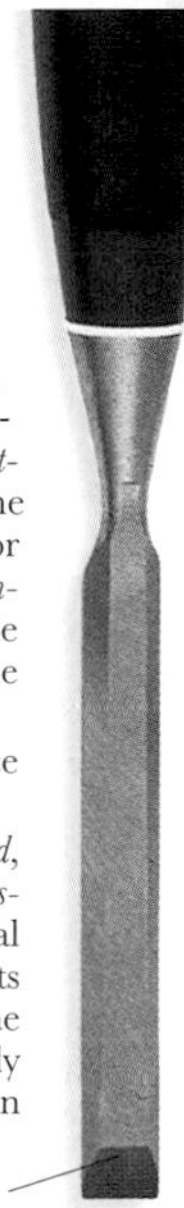
bezel

BEZEL OF A CHISEL

be·zique /bəzéek/ *n.* a trick-taking card game for two, played with a double pack of 64 cards.

Bi *symb. Chem.* the element bismuth.

bi- /bī/ *comb. form* (often **bin-** before a vowel) forming nouns and adjectives meaning: **1** having two; a thing having two (*bilateral; biplane*). **2 a** occurring twice in every one or once in every two (*biweekly*). **b** lasting for two (*biennial*). **3** doubly; in two ways (*biconcave*). **4** *Chem.* a substance having a double proportion of the acid, etc., indicated by the simple word (*bicarbonate*).

bi·an·nu·al /bī-ányōōəl/ *adj.* occurring twice a year (cf. BIENNIAL). □□ **bi·an·nu·al·ly** *adv.*

bi·as /bíəs/ *n.* & *v.* ● *n.* **1** (often foll. by *toward, against*) a predisposition or prejudice. **2** *Statistics* a systematic distortion of a statistical result due to a factor not allowed for in its derivation. **3** an edge cut obliquely across the weave of a fabric. ▷ WEFT. **4** *Electr.* a steady voltage, magnetic field, etc., applied to an electronic system or device. ● *v.tr.* (**biased, biasing**; **biassed, biassing**) **1** (esp. as **biased** *adj.*) influence (usu. unfairly); prejudice. **2** give a bias to. □ **on the bias** obliquely; diagonally.

bi·ath·lon /bī-áthlon, -lən/ *n. Sports* an athletic contest in skiing and shooting or in cycling and running. □□ **bi·ath·lete** *n.*

bib[1] /bib/ *n.* **1** a piece of cloth or plastic fastened round a child's neck to keep the clothes clean while eating. **2** the top front part of an apron, overalls, etc.

Bi·ble /bíbəl/ *n.* **1 a** the Christian scriptures consisting of the Old and New Testaments. **b** the Jewish scriptures. **c** (**bible**) any copy of these (*three bibles on the table*). **d** a particular edition of the Bible (*New English Bible*). **2** (**bible**) *colloq.* any authoritative book (*the woodworker's bible*). **3** the scriptures of any religion.

Bi·ble belt *n.* the area of the southern and central US where fundamentalist Protestant beliefs prevail.

Bi·ble-thump·ing *n. sl.* aggressive fundamentalist preaching. □□ **Bi·ble-thump·er** *n.*

bib·li·cal /bíblikəl/ *adj.* **1** of, concerning, or contained in the Bible. **2** resembling the language of the Authorized Version of the Bible. □□ **bib·li·cal·ly** *adv.*

biblio- /bíbleeō/ *comb. form* denoting a book or books.

bib·li·og·ra·phy /bíbleeógrəfee/ *n.* (*pl.* **-ies**) **1 a** a list of the books referred to in a scholarly work. **b** a list of the books of a specific author or publisher, or on a specific subject, etc. **2 a** the history or description of books, including authors, editions, etc. **b** any book containing such information. □□ **bib·li·og·ra·pher** *n.* **bib·li·o·graph·ic** /-leeəgráfik/ *adj.* **bib·li·o·graph·i·cal** *adj.*

bib·li·o·phile /bíbleeəfīl/ *n.* a person who collects or is fond of books.

bib·u·lous /bíbyələs/ *adj.* given to drinking alcoholic beverages.

bi·cam·er·al /bīkámərəl/ *adj.* (of a parliament or legislative body) having two chambers.

bi·car·bo·nate /bīkaárbənit/ *n.* **1** *Chem.* any acid salt of carbonic acid. **2** (in full **bicarbonate of soda**) sodium bicarbonate used as an antacid or in baking powder.

B

bi·cen·ten·ar·y /bísenténəree, bīséntəneree/ *n. & adj.* esp. *Brit.* = BICENTENNIAL.

bi·cen·ten·ni·al /bísenténeeəl/ *n. & adj.* ● *n.* **1** a two-hundredth anniversary. **2** a celebration of this. ● *adj.* **1** lasting two hundred years or occurring every two hundred years. **2** of or concerning a bicentennial.

bi·ceps /bíseps/ *n.* (*pl.* same) ▼ a muscle having two heads or attachments at one end, esp. the muscle that bends the elbow. ▷ MUSCULATURE

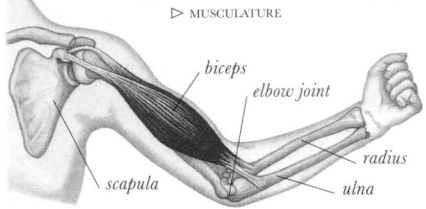

biceps

elbow joint

radius

ulna

scapula

BICEPS: HUMAN ARM SHOWING THE BICEPS

bi·chon frise /béeshoɴ freez/ *n.* a breed of toy dog with a fine, curly, white coat.

bick·er /bíkər/ *v.intr.* quarrel pettily; wrangle.

bi·cus·pid /bíkúspid/ *adj. & n.* ● *adj.* having two cusps or points. ● *n.* **1** the premolar tooth in humans. **2** a tooth with two cusps.

bi·cy·cle /bísikəl, -síkəl/ *n. & v.* ● *n.* ▶ a vehicle of two wheels held in a frame one behind the other, propelled by pedals and steered with handlebars attached to the front wheel. ▷ DERAILLEUR. ● *v.intr.* ride a bicycle. □□ **bi·cy·clist** /-klist/ *n.*

bid /bid/ *v. & n.* ● *v.* (**bidding**; *past* **bid**, *archaic* **bade** /bayd, bad/; *past part.* **bid**, *archaic* **bidden** /bíd'n/) **1** *tr. & intr.* (*past* and *past part.* **bid**) (often foll. by *for, against*) **a** offer (a certain price) (*did not bid for the vase; bid against the dealer; bid $20*). **b** offer to do work, etc., for a stated price. **2** *tr. archaic* or *literary* **a** command (*bid the soldiers to shoot*). **b** invite (*bade her to start*). **3** *tr. archaic* or *literary* utter (greeting or farewell) to (*I bade him welcome*). **4** (*past* and *past part.* **bid**) *Cards* **a** *intr.* state before play how many tricks one intends to make. **b** *tr.* state (one's intended number of tricks). ● *n.* **1 a** an offer (of a price) (*a bid of $5*). **b** an offer (to do work, supply goods, etc.) at a stated price; a tender. **2** *Cards* a statement of the number of tricks a player proposes to make. **3** an attempt (*a bid for power*). □ **bid fair to** seem likely to. **make a bid for** try to gain (*made a bid for freedom*). □□ **bid·der** *n.*

bid·den *archaic past part.* of BID.

bid·ding /bíding/ *n.* **1** the offers at an auction. **2** *Cards* the act of making a bid or bids. **3** a command, request, or invitation.

bid·dy /bídee/ *n.* (*pl.* **-ies**) *sl. derog.* a woman (esp. *old biddy*).

bide /bīd/ *v.tr.* □ **bide one's time** await one's best opportunity.

bi·det /beedáy/ *n.* a low oval basinlike bathroom fixture used esp. for washing the genital area.

Bie·der·mei·er /béedərmīər/ *attrib.adj.* **1** (of styles, furnishings, etc.) characteristic of the period 1815–48 in Germany. **2** *derog.* conventional; bourgeois.

bi·en·ni·al /bī-éneeəl/ *adj. & n.* ● *adj.* **1** lasting two years. **2** recurring every two years (cf. BIANNUAL). ● *n.* **1** *Bot.* a plant that takes two years to grow from seed to fruition and die. **2** an event celebrated or taking place every two years.

bi·en·ni·um /bī-éneeəm/ *n.* (*pl.* **bienniums** or **biennia** /-neeə/) a period of two years.

bier /beer/ *n.* a movable frame on which a coffin or a corpse is placed.

bi·fo·cal /bífókəl/ *adj. & n.* ● *adj.* having two focuses, esp. of a lens with a part for distant vision and a part for near vision. ● *n.* (in *pl.*) bifocal eyeglasses.

bi·fur·cate /bífərkayt/ *v. & adj.* ● *v.tr. & intr.* divide into two branches; fork. ● *adj.* forked; branched.

bi·fur·ca·tion /bífərkáyshən/ *n.* **1 a** a division into two branches. **b** either or both of such branches. **2** the point of such a division.

BICYCLE

The bicycle converts the energy of the cyclist into propulsion: pressure exerted on levers – the pedals – is transferred through the gear system to turn the wheels. The modern bicycle dates from the introduction of pneumatic tires and gears at the end of the 19th century. A wide variety of types is now available, from general purpose bicycles to more specialized machines for off-road cycling and racing.

FEATURES OF A MOUNTAIN BICYCLE

saddle — seat bolt — handlebars — headset — top tube — brake cable — brake block — cantilever brake arm — reflector — cog — spoke — front derailleur — wheel rim — tire tread — water bottle holder — rear derailleur cage — toe clip — chain — pedal — front fork — quick-release hub clamp

EXAMPLES OF OTHER BICYCLES

RACING BICYCLE   RECUMBENT BICYCLE   SPEED-TRIAL BICYCLE

---

big /big/ *adj. & adv.* ● *adj.* (**bigger**, **biggest**) **1 a** of considerable size, amount, intensity, etc. (*a big mistake; a big helping*). **b** of a large or the largest size (*big toe; big drum*). **2** important; significant; outstanding (*my big chance*). **3 a** grown up (*a big boy now*). **b** elder (*big sister*). **4** *colloq.* **a** boastful (*big words*). **b** often *iron.* generous (*big of him*). **c** ambitious (*big ideas*). **d** popular (*when disco was big*). **5** (usu. foll. by *with*) advanced in pregnancy; fecund (*big with child; big with consequences*). ● *adv. colloq.* in a big manner, esp.: **1** effectively (*went over big*). **2** boastfully (*talk big*). **3** ambitiously (*think big*). □ **in a big way 1** on a large scale. **2** *colloq.* with great enthusiasm, display, etc. **talk big** boast. □□ **big·gish** *adj.* **big·ness** *n.*

big air *n.* a high jump in sports such as skateboarding and snowboarding.

big·a·my /bígəmee/ *n.* (*pl.* **-ies**) the crime of marrying when one is lawfully married to another person. □□ **big·a·mist** *n.* **big·a·mous** *adj.*

Big Ap·ple *n. sl.* New York City.

big band *n.* a large jazz or swing orchestra.

big bang the·o·ry *n.* ▼ the theory that the universe began with the explosion of dense matter.

BIG BANG THEORY

Many astronomers subscribe to the big bang theory, which proposes that space, time, and matter were created by a huge explosion between 10 and 20 billion years ago. At first the universe was a hot, dense fireball of particles and radiation. In theory, it continues to expand, with galaxies rushing away from one another.

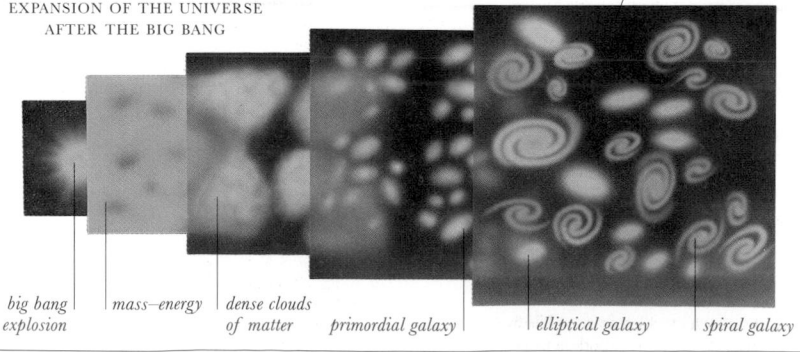

EXPANSION OF THE UNIVERSE AFTER THE BIG BANG

present-day universe

big bang explosion — mass—energy — dense clouds of matter — primordial galaxy — elliptical galaxy — spiral galaxy

Big Broth·er *n.* an all-powerful supposedly benevolent dictator (as in Orwell's *1984*).

big busi·ness *n.* large-scale financial dealings and the businesses involved in them.

big deal! *int. sl. iron.* I am not impressed.

Big Dip·per *n.* a constellation of seven bright stars in Ursa Major in the shape of a dipper. ▷ URSA MAJOR

big end *n.* ▼ (in a motor vehicle) the end of the connecting rod that encircles the crankpin. ▷ INTERNAL-COMBUSTION ENGINE

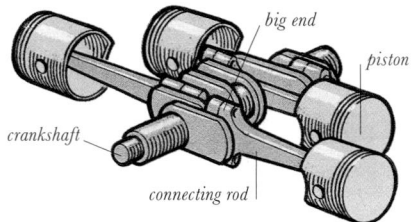

BIG END IN A FLAT FOUR CYLINDER ARRANGEMENT

Big·foot *n.* = SASQUATCH.

big game *n.* large animals hunted for sport.

big gun *n. sl.* = BIGWIG.

big·head /bíghed/ *n. colloq.* a conceited person. □□ **big·head·ed** *adj.*

big·heart·ed /bighártid/ *adj.* generous.

big·horn /bíghawrn/ *n.* (in full **bighorn sheep**) an American sheep, *Ovis canadensis*, esp. native to the Rocky Mountains.

big house *n. sl.* a prison.

bight /bīt/ *n.* **1** a curve or recess in a coastline, river, etc. **2** a loop of rope.

big·mouth /bígmowth/ *n. colloq.* a boastful or talkative person; a gossipmonger.

big·ot /bígət/ *n.* an obstinate and intolerant believer in a religion, political theory, etc. □□ **big·ot·ry** *n.*

big·ot·ed /bígətid/ *adj.* unreasonably prejudiced and intolerant.

big top *n.* the main tent in a circus.

big wheel *n.* **1** a Ferris wheel. **2** *sl.* = BIGWIG.

big·wig /bígwig/ *n. colloq.* an important person.

bi·jou /beezhóo/ *attrib.adj.* small and elegant.

bike /bīk/ *n. & v. ● n. colloq.* a bicycle or motorcycle. ● *v.intr.* ride a bicycle or motorcycle.

bik·er /bíkər/ *n.* a cyclist, esp. a motorcyclist.

bi·ki·ni /bikéenee/ *n.* a two-piece swimsuit for women.

bi·ki·ni briefs *n.pl.* women's or men's scanty briefs.

bi·lat·er·al /bílátərəl/ *adj.* **1** of, on, or with two sides. **2** affecting or between two parties, countries, etc. (*bilateral negotiations*). □□ **bi·lat·er·al·ly** *adv.*

bi·lat·er·al sym·me·try *n.* ► symmetry about a plane.

bil·ber·ry /bílberee/ *n.* (*pl.* **-ies**) **1** ◄ a hardy dwarf shrub, *Vaccinium myrtillus*, of N. Europe, growing on heaths and mountains, and having dark blue berries. **2** the berry of this species.

Bil·dungs·ro·man /bíld-oongzrōmaan/ *n.* a novel dealing with someone's formative years or spiritual education.

BILBERRY
(*Vaccinium myrtillus*)

bile /bīl/ *n.* **1** a bitter greenish brown alkaline fluid which aids digestion and is secreted by the liver and stored in the gallbladder. **2** peevish anger.

bile duct *n.* the duct which conveys bile from the liver and the gall bladder to the duodenum. ▷ GALL BLADDER

bilge /bilj/ *n.* **1 a** the almost flat part of a ship's bottom, inside or out. ▷ SHIP. **b** (in full **bilgewater**) filthy water that collects inside the bilge. **2** *sl.* nonsense.

bil·har·zi·a /bilhaártseeə/ *n.* **1** a tropical flatworm of the genus *Schistosoma* (formerly *Bilharzia*) which is parasitic in blood vessels in the human pelvic region. Also called **schistosome**. **2** the chronic tropical disease produced by its presence. Also called BILHARZIASIS, SCHISTOSOMIASIS.

bil·i·ary /bílee-eree/ *adj.* of the bile.

bi·lin·gual /bílínggwəl/ *adj. & n. ● adj.* **1** able to speak two languages. **2** spoken or written in two languages. **● n.** a bilingual person. □□ **bi·lin·gual·ism** *n.*

bil·ious /bílyəs/ *adj.* **1** affected by a disorder of the bile. **2** bad-tempered. □□ **bil·ious·ness** *n.*

bilk /bilk/ *v.tr. sl.* **1** cheat. **2** give the slip to. **3** avoid paying (a creditor or debt).

bill¹ /bil/ *n. & v. ● n.* **1 a** a statement of charges for goods supplied or services rendered. **b** the amount owed (*ran up a bill of $300*). **2** a draft of a proposed law. **3 a** a poster; a placard. **b** = HANDBILL. **4 a** a printed list, esp. a theater program. **b** the entertainment itself (*top of the bill*). **5** a piece of paper money (*ten-dollar bill*). **● v.tr.** **1** put in the program; announce. **2** (foll. by *as*) advertize. **3** send a note of charges to (*billed him for the books*). □□ **bill·a·ble** *adj.*

bill² /bil/ *n. & v. ● n.* **1** the beak of a bird. ▷ DUCK. **2** the muzzle of a platypus. **3** a narrow promontory. **● v.intr.** (of doves, etc.) stroke a bill with a bill. □ **bill and coo** exchange caresses. □□ **billed** *adj.* (usu. in *comb.*).

bill³ /bil/ *n.* = BILLHOOK.

bill·board /bílbawrd/ *n.* a large outdoor board for advertisements, etc.

bil·let¹ /bílit/ *n. & v. ● n.* **1 a** a place where troops, etc., are lodged. **b** a written order requiring a householder to lodge the bearer. **2** *colloq.* a situation; a job. **● v.tr.** (**billeted, billeting**) **1** (usu. foll. by *on, in, at*) quarter (soldiers, etc.). **2** (of a householder) provide (a soldier, etc.) with board and lodging.

bil·let² /bílit/ *n.* **1** a thick piece of firewood. **2** a small metal bar.

bil·let-doux /bílaydóo/ *n.* (*pl.* **billets-doux** /-dóoz/) often *joc.* a love letter.

bill·fold /bílfōld/ *n.* a wallet for keeping paper money.

bill·hook /bílhŏok/ *n.* a sickle-shaped tool with a sharp inner edge, used for pruning, lopping, etc.

bil·liards /bílyərdz/ *n.* **1** any of several games played on an oblong cloth-covered table, esp. one with three balls struck with cues into pockets around the edge of the table. **2** (**billiard**) (in *comb.*) used in billiards (*billiard ball*).

bil·lion /bílyən/ *n. & adj. ● n.* (*pl.* same or (in sense 3) **billions**) (in *sing.* prec. by *a* or *one*) **1** a thousand million (1,000,000,000 or 10^9). **2** *Brit.* a million million (1,000,000,000,000 or 10^{12}). **3** (in *pl.*) *colloq.* a very large number (*billions of years*). **● adj.** that amount to a billion. □□ **bil·lionth** *adj. & n.*

bil·lion·aire /bílyənáir/ *n.* a person possessing over a billion dollars, pounds, etc.

bill of ex·change *n. Econ.* a written order to pay a sum of money on a given date to the drawer or to a named payee.

bill of fare *n.* a menu.

bill of goods *n.* **1** a shipment of merchandise, often for resale. **2** *colloq.* an article that is misrepresented, fraudulent, etc. (*at first it seemed a bargain, but we were being sold a bill of goods*).

bill of health *n. Naut.* a certificate regarding infectious disease on a ship or in a port at the time of sailing. **2** (**clean bill of health**) **a** such a certificate stating that there is no disease. **b** a declaration that a person or thing examined has been found to be free of illness or in good condition.

bill of lad·ing *n. Naut.* **1** a detailed list of a ship's cargo. **2** = WAYBILL.

Bill of Rights *n.* **1** *Law* (in the US) the original constitutional amendments of 1791. **2** *Law* the English constitutional settlement of 1689. **3** a statement of the rights of a class of people.

bill of sale *n. Econ.* a certificate of transfer of personal property, esp. as a security against debt.

bil·lon /bílən/ *n.* an alloy of gold or silver with a predominating admixture of a base metal.

bil·low /bílō/ *n. & v. ● n.* **1** a wave. **2** a soft upward-curving flow. **3** any large soft mass. **● v.intr.** move in billows. □□ **bil·low·y** *adj.*

bill·post·er /bílpōstər/ *n.* (also **bill·stick·er** /-stik-ər/) a person who pastes up advertisements. □□ **bill·post·ing** *n.*

bil·ly goat /bíligōt/ *n.* (also **bil·ly** (*pl.* **-ies**)) a male goat.

bi·ma·nal /bímənəl/ *adj.* (also **bimanous** /-nəs/) having two hands.

bim·bo /bímbō/ *n.* (*pl.* **-os** or **-oes**) *sl.* usu. *derog.* **1** a foolish person. **2** an empty-headed woman, esp. an attractive one.

bi·me·tal·lic /bímitálik/ *adj.* made of two metals.

bi·mil·le·nar·y /bímíləneree, -miléneree/ *adj. & n.* (also **bimillenial** /-léneeəl/) **● adj.** of or relating to a two thousandth anniversary. **● n.** (*pl.* **-ies**) a bimillenary year or festival.

bi·month·ly /bímúnthlee/ *adj., adv., & n. ● adj.* occurring twice a month or every two months. **● adv.** twice a month or every two months. **● n.** (*pl.* **-ies**) a bimonthly periodical. ¶ Often avoided, because of the ambiguity of meaning, in favor of *every two months* and *twice a month.*

bin /bin/ *n. & v. ● n.* a large receptacle for storage or for depositing trash, garbage, etc. **● v.tr.** (**binned, binning**) *colloq.* store or put in a bin.

bin- /bin, bīn/ *prefix* var. of BI- before a vowel.

bi·na·ry /bíneree/ *adj. & n. ● adj.* **1 a** dual. **b** of or involving pairs. **2** of the arithmetical system using 2 as a base. **● n.** (*pl.* **-ies**) **1** something having two parts. **2** a binary number. **3** a binary star.

bi·na·ry code *n. Computing* a coding system using the binary digits 0 and 1.

bi·na·ry com·pound *n. Chem.* a compound having two elements or radicals.

bi·na·ry num·ber *n.* (also **binary digit**) one of two digits (usu. 0 or 1) in a binary system of notation.

bi·na·ry star *n.* ▼ a system of two stars orbiting each other.

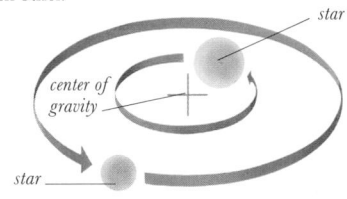

BINARY STAR

bi·na·ry sys·tem *n.* a system in which information can be expressed by combinations of the digits 0 and 1.

bi·na·ry tree *n.* a data structure in which a record is branched to the left when greater and to the right when less than the previous record.

bi·nate /bínayt/ *adj. Bot.* **1** growing in pairs. **2** composed of two equal parts.

bind /bīnd/ *v. & n. ● v.* (*past* and *past part.* **bound** /bownd/) (see also BOUNDEN). **1** *tr.* (often foll. by *to, on, together*) tie or fasten tightly. **2** *tr.* **a** restrain; put in bonds. **b** (as **-bound** *adj.*) constricted; obstructed (*snowbound*). **3** *tr.* esp. *Cookery* cause (ingredients) to cohere. **4** *tr.* fasten or hold together as a single mass. **5** *tr.* compel; impose a duty on. **6** *tr.* **a** edge with braid, etc. **b** fasten (the pages of a book) in a cover. **z7** *tr.* constipate. **8** *tr.* (in *passive*) be required by an

B

obligation or duty (*am bound to answer*). **9** *tr.* (often foll. by *up*) **a** put a bandage or other covering around. **b** fix together with something put around (*bound her hair*). **8** *n. colloq.* a nuisance; a restriction. □ **be bound up with** be closely associated with. **bind over** *Law* order (a person) to do something, esp. keep the peace. **I'll be bound** a statement of assurance, or guaranteeing the truth of something.

bind·er /bíndər/ *n.* **1** a cover for sheets of paper, for a book, etc. **2** a substance that acts cohesively. **3** a reaping machine that binds grain into sheaves. **4** a bookbinder. **5** a temporary agreement providing insurance coverage until a policy is issued.

bind·er·y /bíndəree/ *n.* (*pl.* **-ies**) a workshop or factory for binding books.

bind·ing /bínding/ *n. & adj.* ● *n.* something that binds, esp. the covers, glue, etc., of a book. ● *adj.* (often foll. by *on*) obligatory.

bind·weed /bíndweed/ *n.* **1** convolvulus. **2** any of various species of climbing plants such as honeysuckle.

bine /bīn/ *n.* **1** the twisting stem of a climbing plant, esp. the hop. **2** a flexible shoot.

binge /binj/ *n. & v. sl.* ● *n.* a period of uncontrolled eating, drinking, etc. ● *v.intr.* indulge in uncontrolled eating, drinking, etc. □□ **bing·er** *n.*

bin·go /bínggō/ *n. & int.* ● *n.* a game for any number of players, each having a card of squares with numbers which are marked off as numbers are randomly drawn by a caller. ● *int.* expressing sudden surprise, satisfaction, etc.

bin·na·cle /bínəkəl/ *n.* a built-in housing for a ship's compass.

bin·oc·u·lar /bínókyələr/ *adj.* adapted for or using both eyes.

bin·oc·u·lars /bínókyələrz/ *n.pl.* ▼ an optical instrument with a lens for each eye, for viewing distant objects.

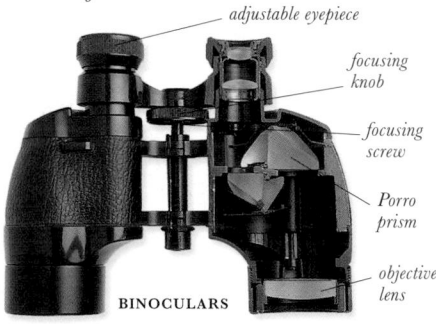

adjustable eyepiece
focusing knob
focusing screw
Porro prism
objective lens

BINOCULARS

bi·no·mi·al /bīnómeeəl/ *n. & adj.* ● *n.* **1** an algebraic expression of the sum or the difference of two terms. **2** a two-part name, esp. in taxonomy. ● *adj.* consisting of two terms.

bi·o /bí-ō/ *n. & adj.* ● *n.* **1** biology. **2** (*pl.* **bios**) biography. ● *adj.* biological.

bio- /bí-ō/ *comb. form* **1** life (*biography*). **2** biological (*biomathematics*). **3** of living beings (*biophysics*).

bi·o·ac·tive /bí-ōáktiv/ *adj.* (of foods, cosmetic compounds, etc.) having an effect on or interacting with living tissue. □□ **bi·o·ac·tiv·i·ty**

bi·o·chem·is·try /bí-ōkémistree/ *n.* the study of the chemical and physicochemical processes of living organisms. □□ **bi·o·chem·i·cal** *adj.* **bi·o·chem·ist** *n.*

bi·o·de·grad·a·ble /bí-ōdigráydəbəl/ *adj.* capable of being decomposed by bacteria or other living organisms. □□ **bi·o·de·grad·a·bil·i·ty** *n.* **bi·o·deg·ra·da·tion** /bí-ōdégrədáyshən/ *n.*

bi·o·di·ver·si·ty /bí-ōdivársitee/ *n.* diversity of plant and animal life.

bi·o·en·gi·neer·ing /bí-ō-énjinéering/ *n.* **1** the application of engineering techniques to biological processes. **2** the use of artificial tissues, organs, or organ components to replace damaged or absent parts of the body. □□ **bi·o·en·gi·neer** *n. & v.*

bi·o·eth·ics /bí-ō-éthiks/ *n.pl.* (treated as *sing.*) the ethics of medical and biological research.

bi·o·feed·back /bí-ōféedbak/ *n.* the technique of using the feedback of a normally automatic bodily response to a stimulus in order to acquire voluntary control of that response.

bi·o·fla·vo·noid /bíōflávənoyd/ *n.* any of a group of compounds occurring mainly in fruit, sometimes regarded as vitamins.

bi·o·gas /bí-ōgas/ *n.* gaseous fuel, esp. methane, produced by fermentation of organic matter.

bi·o·gen·e·sis /bí-ōjénisis/ *n.* **1** the synthesis of substances by living organisms. **2** the hypothesis that a living organism arises only from another similar living organism. □□ **bi·o·ge·net·ic** /-jinétik/ *adj.*

bi·o·gen·ic /bí-ōjénik/ *adj.* produced by living organisms.

bi·og·ra·phy /bīógrəfee/ *n.* (*pl.* **-ies**) **1 a** a written account of a person's life. **b** such writing as a branch of literature. **2** the course of a living being's life. □□ **bi·og·ra·pher** *n.* **bi·o·graph·i·cal** *adj.*

bi·o·haz·ard /bí-ōházərd/ *n.* a risk to human health or the environment arising from biological work, esp. with microorganisms.

bi·o·log·i·cal /bíəlójikəl/ *adj.* **1** of or relating to biology or living organisms. **2** related genetically, not by marriage, adoption, etc. □□ **bi·o·log·i·cal·ly** *adv.*

bi·o·log·i·cal clock *n.* an innate mechanism controlling the rhythmic physiological activities of an organism.

bi·o·log·i·cal war·fare *n.* warfare involving the use of toxins or microorganisms.

bi·ol·o·gy /bīóləjee/ *n.* **1** the study of living organisms. **2** the plants and animals of a particular area. □□ **bi·ol·o·gist** *n.*

bi·o·lu·mi·nes·cence /bí-ō-lóominésəns/ *n.* the emission of light by living organisms such as the firefly and glowworm. □□ **bi·o·lu·mi·nes·cent** *adj.*

bi·o·mass /bí-ōmas/ *n.* the total quantity or weight of organisms in a given area or volume.

bi·ome /bí-ōm/ *n.* a large naturally occurring community of flora and fauna adapted to the particular conditions in which they occur, e.g., tundra.

bi·o·me·chan·ics /bí-ōmikániks/ *n.* the study of the mechanical laws relating to the movement or structure of living organisms.

bi·om·e·try /bīómitree/ *n.* (also **bi·o·met·rics** /bí-əmétriks/) the application of statistical analysis to biological data. □□ **bi·o·met·ric** /bí-əmétrik/ *adj.*

bi·o·morph /bí-ōmawrf/ *n.* a decorative form based on a living organism. □□ **bi·o·mor·phic** /-əmáwrfik/ *adj.*

bi·on·ic /bīónik/ *adj.* **1** having artificial body parts or the superhuman powers resulting from these. **2** relating to bionics.

bi·on·ics /bīóniks/ *n.pl.* (treated as *sing.*) the study of mechanical systems that function like living organisms or parts of living organisms.

bi·o·nom·ics /bíənómiks/ *n.pl.* (treated as *sing.*) the study of the mode of life of organisms in their natural habitat and their adaptations to their surroundings; ecology. □□ **bi·o·nom·ic** *adj.*

bi·o·phys·ics /bí-ōfiziks/ *n.* the science of the application of the laws of physics to biological phenomena. □□ **bi·o·phys·i·cal** *adj.* **bi·o·phys·i·cist** *n.*

bi·o·pic /bí-ōpik/ *n. colloq.* a biographical movie.

bi·op·sy /bíopsee/ *n.* (*pl.* **-ies**) the examination of tissue removed from a living body to discover the presence, cause, or extent of a disease.

bi·o·rhythm /bí-ōrithəm/ *n.* any of the recurring cycles of biological processes thought to affect a person's emotional, intellectual, and physical activity.

bi·o·sphere /bí-ōsfeer/ *n.* the regions of the Earth's crust and atmosphere occupied by living organisms.

bi·o·syn·the·sis /bí-ōsínthisis/ *n.* the production of organic molecules by living organisms. □□ **bi·o·syn·thet·ic** *adj.*

bi·o·ta /bī-ótə/ *n.* the animal and plant life of a region.

bi·o·tech·nol·o·gy /bí-ōteknóləjee/ *n.* the exploitation of biological processes for industrial and other purposes, esp. genetic manipulation of microorganisms.

bi·o·ter·ror·ism /bíōtérəizəm/ *n.* the use of infectious agents or other harmful biological or biochemical substances as weapons of terrorism.

bi·ot·ic /bīótik/ *adj.* **1** relating to life or to living things. **2** of biological origin.

bi·o·tin /bíətin/ *n.* a vitamin of the B complex, found in egg yolk, liver, and yeast, and involved in the metabolism of carbohydrates, fats, and proteins. Also called **vitamin H.**

bi·par·ti·san /bīpáartizən, -sən/ *adj.* of or involving two parties. □□ **bi·par·ti·san·ship** *n.*

bi·par·tite /bīpáartīt/ *adj.* **1** consisting of two parts. **2** shared by or involving two parties.

bi·ped /bíped/ *n. & adj.* ● *n.* a two-footed animal. ● *adj.* two-footed. □□ **bi·ped·al** *adj.*

bi·plane /bíplayn/ *n.* ▼ a type of airplane having two sets of wings, one above the other. ▷ AIRCRAFT

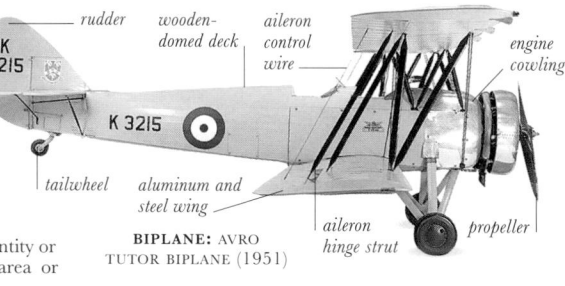

rudder   *wooden-domed deck*   *aileron control wire*   *engine cowling*

tailwheel   *aluminum and steel wing*   *aileron hinge strut*   *propeller*

BIPLANE: AVRO TUTOR BIPLANE (1951)

bi·po·lar /bīpólər/ *adj.* having two poles or extremities. □□ **bi·po·lar·i·ty** /-láritee/ *n.*

birch /bərch/ *n. & v.* ● *n.* **1** ◄ any tree of the genus *Betula*, bearing catkins, and found predominantly in northern temperate regions. **2** (in full **birchwood**) the hard fine-grained pale wood of these trees. **3** (in full **birch rod**) a bundle of birch twigs used for flogging. ● *v.tr.* beat with a birch (in sense 3).

catkin

BIRCH: PAPER BIRCH (*Betula papyrifera*)

birch bark *n.* **1** the bark of *Betula papyrifera* used to make canoes. **2** such a canoe.

bird /bərd/ *n.* **1** ▶ a feathered vertebrate with a beak, two wings, and two feet, egg-laying and usu. able to fly. **2** a game bird. **3** *colloq.* a person (*a wily old bird*). □ **a bird in the hand** something secured or certain. **birds of a feather** people of like character. **for** (or **strictly for**) **the birds** *colloq.* trivial; uninteresting.

bird·brain /bárdbrayn/ *n. colloq.* a stupid or flighty person. □□ **bird·brained** *adj.*

bird·cage /bárdkayj/ *n.* **1** a cage for birds usu. made of wire or cane. **2** an object of a similar design.

bird call *n.* **1** a bird's natural call. **2** an instrument imitating this.

bird dog *n. N. Amer.* **1** a gun dog trained to retrieve birds. **2** *colloq.* a talent scout in the field of sport.

bird·er /bárdər/ *n.* a bird-watcher. □□ **bird·ing** *n.*

bird·ie /bárdee/ *n. & v.* ● *n.* **1** *colloq.* a little bird. **2** *Golf* a score of one stroke less than par at any hole. ● *v.tr.* (**birdies, birdied, birdying**) *Golf* play (a hole) in a birdie.

BIRD

There are over 9,000 species of birds, and they live in a wide range of environments, from deserts to the open ocean. Birds are the only animals that have feathers, which they use for flight, insulation, camouflage, and for attracting mates. Flying birds have lightweight skeletons with air-filled bones, but in many diving and flightless species the bones are solid. Birds lack teeth but instead rely on a muscular gizzard to grind up what they eat, using their beak or feet to collect or catch food. Birds lay hard-shelled eggs. In almost all species, the eggs are incubated by the parents.

EXTERNAL FEATURES OF A
BLACK-HEADED STARLING
(*Sturnus pagodarum*)

upper mandible · *crown* · *nape* · *lower mandible* · *nostril* · *lesser wing coverts* · *median wing coverts* · *greater wing coverts* · *secondary flight feathers (secondary remiges)* · *primary flight feathers (primary remiges)* · *breast* · *flank* · *under-tail coverts* · *tail feathers (rectrices)* · *tarsometatarsus* · *claw* · *toe*

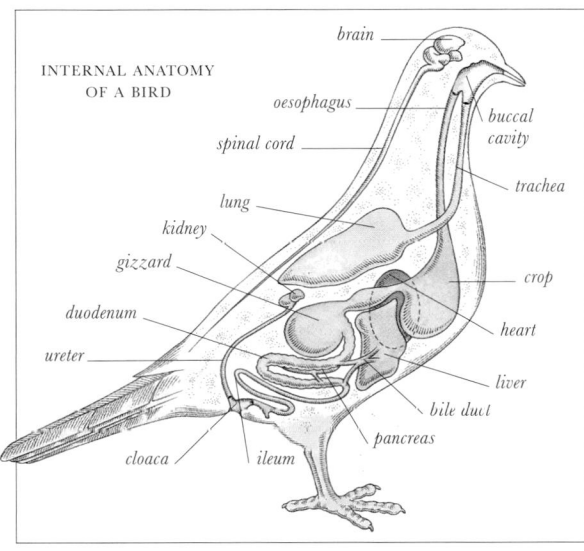

INTERNAL ANATOMY
OF A BIRD

brain · *oesophagus* · *spinal cord* · *buccal cavity* · *trachea* · *lung* · *kidney* · *gizzard* · *crop* · *duodenum* · *heart* · *ureter* · *liver* · *bile duct* · *cloaca* · *ileum* · *pancreas*

MAIN BIRD ORDERS

STRUTHIONIFORMES
(ostriches)

SPHENISCIFORMES
(penguins)
▷ PENGUIN

CICONIIFORMES
(herons, ibises, storks)

ANSERIFORMES
(waterfowl)
▷ WATERFOWL

FALCONIFORMES
(birds of prey)
▷ RAPTOR

GALLIFORMES
(game birds)

CHARADRIIFORMES
(auks, gulls, terns, waders)
▷ SEABIRD, WADING BIRD

COLUMBIFORMES
(pigeons)

PSITTACIFORMES
(parrots)
▷ PARROT

CUCULIFORMES
(cuckoos, turacos)

STRIGIFORMES
(owls)
▷ OWL

APODIFORMES
(hummingbirds, swifts)

CORACIIFORMES
(bee-eaters, hoopoes, kingfishers)

PICIFORMES
(barbets, toucans, woodpeckers)

PASSERIFORMES
(passerines)
▷ PASSERINE

bird·lime /bə́rdlīm/ *n.* sticky material painted on twigs to trap small birds.

bird of par·a·dise *n.* any bird of the family Paradiseidae, the males having very beautiful brilliantly colored plumage.

bird of prey *n.* a bird that hunts animals for food. ▷ RAPTOR

bird·seed /bə́rdseed/ *n.* seed or a blend of seed for feeding caged or wild birds.

bird's-eye view *n.* a general view from above.

bird·song /bə́rdsawng, -song/ *n.* the musical cry of a bird or birds.

bird-watch·er *n.* a person who observes birds in their natural surroundings. ▫▫ **bird-watch·ing** *n.*

bi·ret·ta /birétə/ *n.* a square cap with three flat projections on top, worn by clergymen.

bi·ri·a·ni var. of BIRYANI.

Bi·ro /bī́rō/ *n.* (*pl.* **-os**) *Brit. Trademark* a kind of ballpoint pen.

birth /bərth/ *n.* & *v.* ● *n.* **1** the emergence of an infant or other young from the body of its mother. **2** *rhet.* the beginning of something (*the birth of socialism*). **3 a** origin; descent; ancestry (*of noble birth*). **b** noble birth; inherited position. ● *v.tr. colloq.* **1** give birth to. **2** assist (a woman) to give birth. ▫ **give birth** bear a child, etc. **give birth to 1** produce (young) from the womb. **2** cause to begin.

birth cer·tif·i·cate *n.* an official document identifying a person by name, place and date of birth.

birth con·trol *n.* the control of the number of children one conceives.

birth·day /bə́rthday/ *n.* **1** the day on which a person, etc., was born. **2** the anniversary of this. ▫ **in one's birthday suit** *joc.* naked.

birth de·fect *n.* a physical, mental, or biochemical abnormality present at birth.

birth·mark /bə́rthmaark/ *n.* an unusual brown or red mark on a person's body at or from birth.

birth·place /bə́rthplays/ *n.* the place where a person was born.

birth rate *n.* the number of live births per thousand of population per year.

birth·right /bə́rthrīt/ *n.* a right of possession or privilege one has from birth.

birth sign *n. Astrol.* the zodiacal sign through which the sun is passing when a person is born. ▷ ZODIAC

birth·stone /bə́rthstōn/ *n.* a gemstone popularly associated with the month of one's birth.

bi·ry·a·ni /bíree-áanee/ *n.* (also **biriani**) an Indian dish made with highly seasoned rice, and meat or fish, etc.

bis·cuit /bískit/ *n.* & *adj.* ● *n.* **1** a small bread or cake leavened with baking soda or baking powder. **2** *Brit.* **a** = COOKIE. **b** = CRACKER. **3** fired unglazed pottery. **4** a light brown color. ● *adj.* light brown.

bi·sect /bīsékt/ *v.tr.* divide into two (equal) parts. ▫▫ **bi·sec·tion** /-sékshən/ *n.*

bi·sex·u·al /bīsékshōōəl/ *adj.* & *n.* ● *adj.* **1** sexually attracted to persons of both sexes. **2** *Biol.* having characteristics of both sexes. **3** of or concerning both sexes. ● *n.* a bisexual person. ▫▫ **bi·sex·u·al·i·ty** /-sékshoo-álitee, -séksyoo-álitee/ *n.*

bish·op /bíshəp/ *n.* **1** a senior member of the Christian clergy empowered to confer holy orders. **2** a chess piece with the top sometimes shaped like a miter. ▷ CHESS

bish·op·ric /bíshəprik/ *n.* **1** the office of a bishop. **2** a diocese.

bis·muth /bízməth/ *n. Chem.* **1** ► a brittle reddish-tinged metallic element, occurring naturally and used in alloys. ¶ Symb.: **Bi**. **2** any compound of this element used medicinally.

bi·son /bī́sən/ *n.* (*pl.* same) either of two wild humpbacked shaggy-haired oxen of the genus *Bison*, native to N. America (*B. bison*) or Europe (*B. bonasus*).

bisque¹ /bisk/ *n.* a rich shellfish soup.

BISMUTH

bisque² /bisk/ *n. Tennis*, *Croquet*, & *Golf* an advantage of scoring one free point, or taking an extra turn or stroke.

bisque³ /bisk/ *n.* = BISCUIT 3.

bi·sta·ble /bīstáybəl/ *adj.* (of an electrical circuit, etc.) having two stable states.

bis·ter /bístər/ *n.* & *adj.* ● *n.* **1** a brownish pigment made from the soot of burned wood. **2** the brownish color of this. ● *adj.* of this color.

bis·tro /béestrō, bís-/ *n.* (*pl.* **-os**) a small restaurant.

bit¹ /bit/ *n.* **1** a small piece or quantity (*a bit of cheese*). **2** (prec. by *a*) **a** a fair amount (*sold quite a bit*). **b** *colloq.* somewhat (*am a bit tired*). **c** (foll. by *of*) *colloq.* rather (*a bit of an idiot*). **3** a short time or distance (*wait a bit*; *move up a bit*). **4** *sl.* an amount equal to 12 ½ cents (esp. in the phrase *two bits*). ▫ **bit by bit** gradually. **do one's bit** *colloq.* make a useful contribution to an effort or cause. **not a bit** not at all. **to bits** into pieces.

bit² *past* of BITE.

bit³ /bit/ *n.* **1** a metal mouthpiece on a bridle, used to control a horse. ▷ BRIDLE. **2** a tool or piece for boring or drilling. ▷ DRILL. **3** the cutting or gripping part of a plane, pliers, etc. ▫ **take the bit between one's teeth 1** take decisive personal action. **2** escape from control.

bit⁴ /bit/ *n. Computing* a unit of information expressed as a choice between two possibilities; a 0 or 1 in binary notation.

bitch /bich/ *n.* & *v.* ● *n.* **1** a female dog or other canine animal. **2** *sl. offens.* a spiteful woman. **3** *sl.* a very unpleasant or difficult thing. ● *v.intr. colloq.* **1** (often foll. by *about*) speak scathingly. **2** complain.

bitch·y /bíchee/ *adj.* (**bitchier**, **bitchiest**) *sl.* spiteful; bad-tempered. ▫▫ **bitch·i·ness** *n.*

bite /bīt/ *v.* & *n.* ● *v.* (*past* **bit** /bit/; *past part.* **bitten** /bít'n/) **1** *tr.* cut or puncture using the teeth. **2** *tr.* (often foll. by *off*, etc.) detach with the teeth. **3** *tr.* (of an insect, snake, etc.) wound with a sting, fangs, etc. **4** *intr.* (of a wheel, screw, etc.) grip; penetrate. **5** *intr.* accept bait. **6** *intr.* have a (desired) adverse effect. **7** *tr.* (in *passive*) **a** take in; swindle. **b** (foll. by *by*, *with*, etc.) be infected by (enthusiasm, etc.). **8** *tr.* (as **bitten** *adj.*) cause a smarting pain to (*frostbitten*). **9** *intr.* (foll. by *at*) snap at. ● *n.* **1** an act of biting. **2** a wound or sore made by biting. **3 a** a mouthful of food. **b** a snack or light meal. **4** the taking of bait by a fish. **5** pungency. **6** incisiveness; sharpness. ▫ **bite back** restrain (one's speech, etc.) by or as if by biting the lips. ▫ **bite the bullet** *sl.* behave bravely or stoically. **bite the dust** *sl.* **1** die. **2** fail; break down. **bite the hand that feeds one** hurt a benefactor. **bite a person's head off** *colloq.* respond fiercely or angrily. **bite off more than one can chew** take on a commitment one cannot fulfill. ▫▫ **bit·er** *n.*

bit·ing /bī́ting/ *adj.* **1** stinging; intensely cold (*a biting wind*). **2** sharp; effective (*biting sarcasm*). ▫▫ **bit·ing·ly** *adv.*

bit·map /bítmap/ *n.* a representation in which each item corresponds to one or more bits of information, especially the information used to control the display of a computer screen.

bit part *n.* a minor part in a play or a movie.

bits and pieces *n.pl.* an assortment of small items.

bit·stream /bítsreem/ *n. Electronics* a stream of data in binary form.

bit·ten *past part.* of BITE.

bit·ter /bítər/ *adj.* & *n.* ● *adj.* **1** having a sharp pungent taste; not sweet. **2 a** caused by or showing mental pain or resentment (*bitter memories*; *bitter rejoinder*). **b** painful or difficult to accept (*bitter disappointment*). **3 a** harsh; virulent (*bitter animosity*). **b** piercingly cold. ● *n.* **1** *Brit.* beer strongly flavored with hops and having a bitter taste. **2** (in *pl.*) liquor with a bitter flavor used as an additive in cocktails. ▫ **to the bitter end** to the very end in spite of difficulties. ▫▫ **bit·ter·ly** *adv.* **bit·ter·ness** *n.*

bit·tern /bítərn/ *n.* any of a group of wading birds of the heron family.

bit·ter pill *n.* something unpleasant that has to be accepted.

bit·ter·sweet /bítərswēt/ *adj.* **1** sweet with a bitter aftertaste. **2** arousing pleasure tinged with pain or sorrow.

bit·ty /bítee/ *adj. colloq.* tiny (esp. in phrs. **little bitty**, **itty-bitty**).

bi·tu·men /bītōōmin, -tyōō-, bi-/ *n.* **1** any of various tarlike mixtures of hydrocarbons derived from petroleum and used for road surfacing and roofing. **2** *Austral. colloq.* an asphalt road.

bi·tu·mi·nous /bītōōminəs, -tyōō-, bi-/ *adj.* of, relating to, or containing bitumen.

bi·tu·mi·nous coal *n.* a form of coal burning with a smoky flame. ▷ COAL

bi·valve /bī́valv/ *n.* & *adj.* ● *n.* ► any of a group of aquatic mollusks of the class Bivalvia, with laterally compressed bodies enclosed within two hinged shells, e.g., oysters, clams, etc. ● *adj.* **1** with a hinged double shell. **2** *Biol.* having two valves, e.g., of a peapod.

biv·ou·ac /bívōō-ak, bívwak/ *n.* & *v.* ● *n.* a temporary open encampment without tents. ● *v.intr.* (**bivouacked**, **bivouacking**) camp in a bivouac, esp. overnight.

bi·week·ly /bīwéeklee/ *adv.*, *adj.*, & *n.* ● *adv.* **1** every two weeks. **2** twice a week. ● *adj.* produced or occurring biweekly. ● *n.* (*pl.* **-ies**) a biweekly periodical. ¶ See the note at *bimonthly*.

bi·year·ly /bīyéerlee/ *adv.* & *adj.* ● *adv.* **1** every two years. **2** twice a year. ● *adj.* produced or occurring biyearly. ¶ See the note at *bimonthly*.

biz /biz/ *n. colloq.* business.

bi·zarre /bizáar/ *adj.* strange; eccentric; grotesque. ▫▫ **bi·zarre·ly** *adv.*

bi·zar·ro /bizáarō/ *adj. colloq.*, chiefly *N.Amer.* bizarre.

Bk *symb. Chem.* the element berkelium.

bk. *abbr.* book.

bl. *abbr.* **1** barrel. **2** black.

blab /blab/ *v.* & *n.* ● *v.* (**blabbed**, **blabbing**) **1** *intr.* **a** talk foolishly or indiscreetly. **b** reveal secrets. **2** *tr.* reveal (a secret, etc.) by indiscreet talk. ● *n.* a person who blabs.

blab·ber /blábər/ *n.* & *v.* ● *n.* (also **blab·ber·mouth** /blábərmowth/) a person who blabs. ● *v.intr.* (often foll. by *on*) talk foolishly or inconsequentially, esp. at length.

black /blak/ *adj.*, *n.*, & *v.* ● *adj.* **1** very dark; having no color from the absorption of all or nearly all incident light (like coal or soot). **2** completely dark from the absence of a source of light (*black night*). **3 a** of the human group having dark-colored skin. **b** of or relating to black people (*black rights*). **4** (of the sky, a cloud, etc.) dusky; heavily overcast. **5** angry; threatening (*a black look*). **6** implying disgrace or condemnation (*in his black books*). **7** sinister; deadly (*black-hearted*). **8** depressed; sullen (*a black mood*). **9** portending trouble or difficulty (*things looked black*). **10** (of hands, clothes, etc.) dirty; soiled. **11** (of humor or its representation) macabre (*black comedy*). **12** (of coffee or tea) without milk. **13** dark in color as distinguished from a lighter variety (*black bear*). ● *n.* **1** a black color or pigment. **2** black clothes or material (*dressed in black*). **3 a** (in a game or sport) a black piece, ball, etc. **b** the player using such pieces. **4** the credit side of an account (*in the black*). **5** a member of a dark-skinned race. ● *v.tr.* **1** make black (*blacked his face*). **2** polish with blacking. ▫ **black out 1 a** effect a blackout on. **b** undergo a blackout. **2** obscure windows, etc., or extinguish all lights for protection, esp. against an air attack. ▫▫ **black·ish** *adj.* **black·ly** *adv.* **black·ness** *n.*

black and blue *adj.* discolored by bruises.

black and white *n.* & *adj.* ● *n.* writing or print (*down in black and white*). ● *adj.* **1** (of film, etc.) not in color. **2** consisting of extremes only; oversimplified (*interpreted the problem in black and white terms*).

black art *n.* (prec. by *the*) = BLACK MAGIC.

black·ball /blákbawl/ *v.tr.* **1** reject (a candidate) in

BIVALVE

Bivalves are mollusks whose shells consist of two hinged valves that protect the soft body; when faced with danger the two halves are pulled together by a powerful abductor muscle. Found in marine and freshwater habitats, mollusks are typically unable to extend far out of their shells, and live either embedded in sand or mud or fastened to rocks. A few, such as scallops, can open and close their valves to propel themselves away from danger. Most bivalves have large gills that are used for both breathing and filter-feeding.

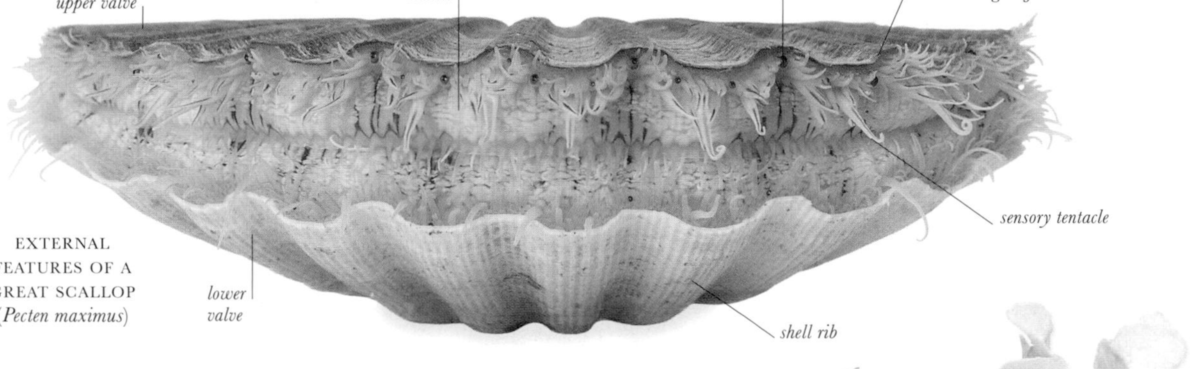

upper valve *mantle* *ocellus* *ventral margin of shell*

sensory tentacle

EXTERNAL FEATURES OF A GREAT SCALLOP (*Pecten maximus*)

lower valve

shell rib

EXAMPLES OF OTHER BIVALVES

NEW ZEALAND MUSSEL (*Mytilacea* species)

SWAN MUSSEL (*Anodonta cygnea*)

ZEBRA MUSSEL (*Dreissena polymorpha*)

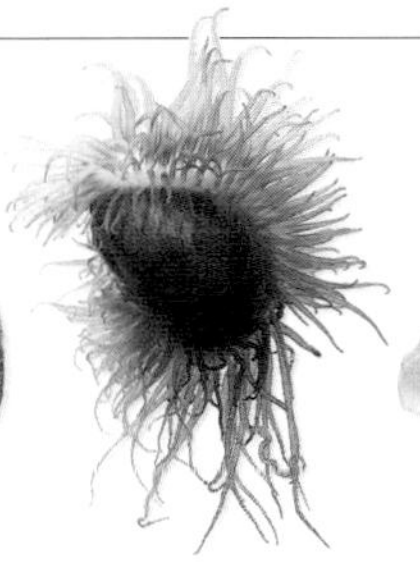

GAPING FILE SHELL (*Lima hians*)

SPINY SAND COCKLE (*Acanthoiardia echinata*)

COCKSCOMB OYSTER (*Lopha cristagalli*)

THORNY OYSTER (*Spondylus* species)

NOBLE PEN SHELL (*Pinna nobilis*)

FLUTED GIANT CLAM (*Tridacna squamosa*)

---

a ballot (orig. by voting with a black ball). **2** exclude; ostracize.

black belt *n.* **1** a black belt worn by an expert in judo, karate, etc. **2** a person qualified to wear this.

black·ber·ry /blákberee/ *n.* (*pl.* **-ies**) **1** a climbing thorny rosaceous shrub, *Rubus fruticosus*, bearing white or pink flowers and purplish-black berries. **2** the edible berry of this plant. ▷ FRUIT

black·bird /blákbərd/ *n.* **1** a common Eurasian thrush, *Turdus merula*, the male of which is black with an orange beak. **2** any of various birds, esp. a grackle, with black plumage.

black·board /blákbawrd/ *n.* a board with a smooth usu. dark surface for writing on with chalk.

black·bod·y /blákbáadē/ *n. Physics* a hypothetical perfect absorber and radiator of energy, with no reflecting power.

black box *n.* **1** a flight recorder in an aircraft. **2** any complex piece of equipment with contents which are mysterious to the user.

black·cap /blák-kap/ *n.* any of various black-crowned birds, esp. the chickadee, *Parus atricapillus*, and the Old World warbler, *Sylvia atricapilla*.

black·cur·rant /blák-kárənt, -kúr-/ *n.* **1** a widely cultivated shrub, *Ribes nigrum*, bearing flowers in racemes. **2** the small dark edible berry of this plant.

Black Death *n.* (usu. prec. by *the*) a widespread epidemic of bubonic plague in Europe in the 14th c.

black dia·monds *n.pl.* coal.

black e·con·o·my *n.* unofficial economic activity.

black·en /blákən/ *v.* **1** *tr. & intr.* make or become black or dark. **2** *tr.* speak evil of; defame (*blacken someone's character*).

black Eng·lish *n.* the form of English spoken by many African-Americans, esp. as an urban dialect of the US.

black eye *n.* bruised skin around the eye resulting from a blow.

black-eyed Su·san *n.* any of several flowers, esp. of the genus *Rudbeckia*, with yellow colored petals and a dark center.

black·fly /blákflī/ *n.* (*pl.* **-flies**) **1** any of various small biting flies of the family Simuliidae. **2** any of various thrips or aphids, esp. *Aphis fabae*, infesting plants.

Black·foot /blákfŏŏt/ *n.* **1 a** a N. American people native to Montana and adjoining parts of Canada. **b** a member of this people. **2** the language of this people.

black for·est cake *n.* a chocolate cake with layers of morello cherries or cherry jam and whipped cream and topped with chocolate icing, orig. from S. Germany.

black·guard /blágaard, -ərd/ *n.* a villain; a scoundrel.

black·head /blák-hed/ *n.* a black-topped pimple on the skin.

black hole *n.* **1** ▶ a region of space possessing a strong gravitational field from which matter and radiation cannot escape. **2** a place of confinement for punishment.

black ice *n.* thin hard transparent ice, esp. on a road surface.

black·ing /bláking/ *n.* any black paste or polish, esp for shoes.

black·jack /blákjak/ *n.* **1** a card game in which players try to acquire cards with a face value totaling 21 and no more. **2** a flexible, usu. lead-filled bludgeon. **3** a pirate's black flag. **4** a tar-coated leather vessel for beer, ale, etc.

BLACK HOLE

If the mass of the collapsed core of a supernova exceeds the mass of our Sun by three times, it continues to collapse, forming a black hole. Invisible because its gravity is so dense that light cannot escape, a black hole can be detected if gas from a companion star is drawn toward it.

quasar *black hole* *event horizon*

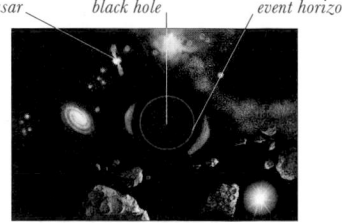

ARTIST'S IMPRESSION OF A BLACK HOLE

B

black light n. Physics the invisible ultraviolet or infrared radiations of the electromagnetic spectrum.

black·list /bláklist/ n. & v. • n. a list of persons under suspicion, in disfavor, etc. • v.tr. put the name of (a person) on a blacklist.

black lung n. a chronic lung disease caused by the inhalation of coal dust.

black mag·ic n. magic involving invocation of evil spirits.

black·mail /blákmayl/ n. & v. • n. **1 a** an extortion of payment in return for not disclosing a secret, etc. **b** any payment extorted in this way. **c** the use of threats or moral pressure. • v.tr. **1** extort or try to extort money, etc., from (a person) by blackmail. **2** threaten; coerce. □□ **black·mail·er** n.

black mark n. a mark of discredit.

black mar·ket n. an illicit traffic in officially controlled or scarce commodities. □□ **black mar·ke·teer** n.

black med·ic n. ◀ a leguminous plant, Medicago lupulina, with black pods.

Black Mus·lim n. a member of an exclusively African-American Islamic sect proposing a separate African-American community.

Black Na·tion·al·ism n. advocacy of civil rights and separatism for African-Americans and occas. blacks in other countries.

black·out /blákowt/ n. **1** a temporary or complete loss of vision, consciousness, or memory. **2** a loss of power, radio reception, etc. **3** a compulsory period of darkness as a precaution against air raids. **4** a temporary suppression of the release of information, esp. from police or government sources. **5** a sudden darkening of a theater stage.

Black Pan·ther n. one of a group of extremist activists for African-American civil rights.

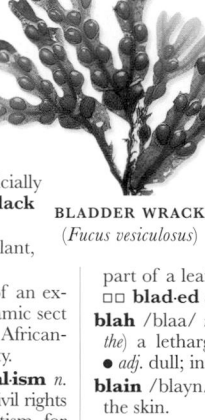

BLACK MEDIC
(Medicago lupulina)

black pep·per n. pepper made by grinding the whole dried berry, including the husk, of the pepper plant.

Black Pow·er n. a movement in support of rights and political power for blacks in various Western countries.

black rasp·ber·ry n. **1** a N. American shrub, Rubus occidentalis. **2** the edible fruit of this shrub.

black sheep n. colloq. a disreputable member of a family, etc.; a misfit.

black·shirt /blákshərt/ n. a member of a fascist organization.

black·smith /bláksmith/ n. **1** a smith who works in iron. **2** a smith who shoes horses.

black tea n. tea that is fully fermented before drying.

black·thorn /blákthawrn/ n. **1** a thorny rosaceous shrub, Prunus spinosa, bearing white flowers before small blue-black fruits. Also called **sloe**. **2** a cudgel or walking stick made from its wood.

black tie n. **1** a black bow tie worn with a dinner jacket. **2** colloq. formal evening dress.

black·top /bláktop/ n. a type of surfacing material for roads.

black·wa·ter fe·ver /blákwawtər/ n. a complication of malaria in which blood cells are rapidly destroyed, resulting in dark urine.

black wid·ow n. ▶ a venomous spider, Latrodectus mactans, of which the female has an hourglass-shaped red mark on her abdomen. ▷ SPIDER

BLACK WIDOW
(Latrodectus mactans)

blad·der /bládər/ n. **1 a** any of various membranous sacs in some animals, containing urine (**urinary bladder**), bile (**gallbladder**), or air (**swim bladder**). ▷ FISH, GALL BLADDER, URINARY SYSTEM. **b** this or part of it or a similar object prepared for various uses. **2** an inflated pericarp or vesicle in various plants. **3** anything inflated and hollow.

blad·der wrack /bládərak/ n. ◀ a common brown seaweed, Fucus vesiculosus, with fronds containing air bladders which give buoyancy.

BLADDER WRACK
(Fucus vesiculosus)

blade /blayd/ n. **1 a** the flat part of a knife, chisel, etc., that forms the cutting edge. **b** a flat piece of metal with a sharp edge or edges used in a razor. **2** ▶ the flattened functional part of an oar, spade, propeller, skate, snowplow, etc. **3 a** the flat, narrow leaf of grass and cereals. **b** Bot. the broad thin part of a leaf. **4** (in full **bladebone**) a flat bone. □□ **blad·ed** adj. (also in comb.).

blade

blah /blaa/ n. & adj. colloq. • n. (in pl.) (prec. by the) a lethargic, dissatisfied feeling of malaise. • adj. dull; insipid.

blain /blayn/ n. an inflamed swelling or sore on the skin.

blame /blaym/ v. & n. • v.tr. **1** assign fault or responsibility to. **2** (foll. by on) assign the responsibility for (an error or wrong) to a person, etc. (blamed his death on a poor diet). • n. **1** responsibility for a bad result (shared the blame equally). **2** the act of blaming or attributing responsibility (she got all the blame). □ **be to blame** (often foll. by for) be responsible; deserve censure (she is not to blame for the accident).

blame·ful /bláymfŏŏl/ adj. deserving blame; guilty. □□ **blame·ful·ly** adv.

blame·less /bláymlis/ adj. innocent; free from blame. □□ **blame·less·ly** adv.

blame·wor·thy /bláymwərthee/ adj. deserving blame. □□ **blame·wor·thi·ness** n.

blanch /blanch/ v. **1** tr. make white or pale by extracting color. **2** intr. & tr. grow or make pale from shock, fear, etc. **3** tr. Cookery **a** peel (almonds, etc.) by scalding. **b** immerse (vegetables or meat) briefly in boiling water. **4** tr. whiten (a plant) by depriving it of light.

blanc·mange /bləmáanj/ n. a sweet opaque gelatinous dessert made with flavored cornstarch and milk.

bland /bland/ adj. **1 a** mild; not irritating. **b** tasteless; unstimulating; insipid. **2** gentle in manner; smooth. □□ **bland·ly** adv. **bland·ness** n.

bland·ish /blándish/ v.tr. flatter; coax; cajole.

bland·ish·ment /blándishmənt/ n. (usu. in pl.) flattery; cajolery.

blank /blangk/ adj., n., & v. • adj. **1 a** (of paper) not written or printed on. **b** (of a document) with spaces left for a signature or details. **2 a** empty (a blank space). **b** unrelieved; plain; undecorated (a blank wall). **3 a** having or showing no interest or expression (a blank face). **b** void of incident or result. **c** puzzled; nonplussed. **d** having (temporarily) no knowledge (my mind went blank). **4** (with neg. import) complete; downright (blank despair). **5** euphem. used in place of an adjective regarded as coarse or abusive. • n. **1 a** a space left to be filled in a document. **b** a document having blank spaces to be filled. **2** (in full **blank cartridge**) a cartridge containing gunpowder but no bullet. **3** an empty space or period of time. **4 a** a dash written instead of a word or letter. **b** euphem. used

in place of a noun regarded as coarse. • v.tr. (usu. foll. by off, out) screen; obscure (clouds blanked out the sun). □ **draw a blank** elicit no response; fail. □□ **blank·ly** adv. **blank·ness** n.

blank check n. **1** a check with the amount left for the payee to fill in. **2** colloq. unlimited freedom of action (cf. CARTE BLANCHE).

blan·ket /blángkit/ n., adj., & v. • n. **1** a large piece of woolen or other material used esp. as a bed covering or to wrap up a person or an animal for warmth. **2** (usu. foll. by of) a thick mass or layer that covers something (blanket of fog; blanket of silence). • attrib.adj. covering all cases or classes; inclusive (blanket condemnation; blanket agreement). • v.tr. (**blanketed, blanketing**) **1** cover with or as if with a blanket (snow blanketed the land). **2** stifle (blanketed all discussion).

blan·ket stitch n. a stitch used to neaten the edges of a blanket or other material. ▷ STITCH

blank·e·ty /blángkətee/ adj. & n. (also **blanky** /blángkee/) colloq. = BLANK adj. 5 & n. 4b.

blank verse n. unrhymed verse.

blan·quette /bloŋkét/ n. Cookery a dish consisting of white meat, e.g., veal, in a white sauce.

blare /blair/ v. & n. • v. **1** tr. & intr. sound or utter loudly. **2** intr. make the sound of a trumpet. • n. a loud sound resembling that of a trumpet.

blar·ney /bláarnee/ n. **1** cajoling talk; flattery. **2** nonsense.

blas·é /blaazáy/ adj. **1** unimpressed or indifferent because of over-familiarity. **2** tired of pleasure; surfeited.

blas·pheme /blasféém, blásfeem/ v. **1** intr. talk profanely, making use of religious names, etc. **2** tr. talk profanely about; revile. □□ **blas·phem·er** n.

blas·phe·my /blásfəmee/ n. (pl. **-ies**) **1** profane talk. **2** an instance of this. □□ **blas·phe·mous** adj. **blas·phe·mous·ly** adv.

blast /blast/ n. & v. • n. **1** a strong gust of air. **2 a** a destructive wave of highly compressed air spreading outwards from an explosion. **b** such an explosion. **3** the single loud note of a wind instrument, car horn, etc. **4** colloq. a severe reprimand. **5** a strong current of air used in smelting, etc. • v. **1** tr. blow up (rocks, etc.) with explosives. **2** tr. **a** wither, shrivel, or blight (a plant, animal, limb, etc.) (blasted oak). **b** ruin (blasted her hopes). **c** strike with divine anger. **3** intr. & tr. make or cause to make a loud noise (blasted away on his trumpet). **4** tr. colloq. reprimand severely. **5** colloq. **a** tr. shoot; shoot at. **b** intr. shoot. □ **at full blast** colloq. working at maximum speed, force, etc. **blast off** (of a rocket, etc.) take off from a launching site.

BLADE
ON A
PADDLE

-blast /blast/ comb. form Biol. an embryonic cell (cf. -CYTE).

blast·ed /blástid/ attrib.adj. damned; annoying (that blasted dog!).

blast fur·nace n. ▲ a smelting furnace into which compressed hot air is driven.

blast·off /blástawf/ n. **1** the launching of a rocket, etc. **2** the initial thrust for this.

blas·tu·la /bláschələ/ n. (pl. **blastulas** or **blastulae** /-lee/) Biol. an animal embryo at an early stage of development when it is a hollow ball of cells.

bla·tant /bláyt'nt/ adj. **1** flagrant; unashamed (blatant attempt to steal). **2** offensively noisy or obtrusive. □□ **bla·tan·cy** /-t'nsee/ n. **bla·tant·ly** adv.

blath·er /bláthər/ n. & v. (also **bleth·er** /bléthər/) • n. foolish chatter. • v.intr. chatter foolishly.

blath·er·skite /bláthərskīt/ (also **bleth·er·skate** /bléthərskayt/) n. **1** a person who blathers. **2** = BLATHER n.

blaze[1] /blayz/ n. & v. • n. **1** a bright flame or fire. **2 a** a bright glaring light. **b** a full light (a blaze of publicity). **3** a violent outburst (of passion, etc.). **4 a** a glow of color (roses were a blaze of scarlet). **b** a bright display (a blaze of glory). • v.intr. **1** burn with a bright flame. **2** be brilliantly lit. **3** be consumed with anger, excitement, etc. **4 a** show bright colors

B

BLAST FURNACE

During the iron smelting process, coke burned in a blast furnace reacts with oxygen in the air to release carbon monoxide. This combines with iron oxide in the iron ore to produce both carbon dioxide and molten iron. Limestone acts as a flux, helping to separate impurities from the iron by turning them into molten slag.

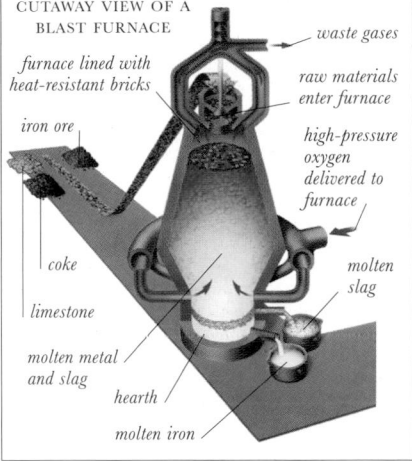

CUTAWAY VIEW OF A BLAST FURNACE

waste gases

furnace lined with heat-resistant bricks

raw materials enter furnace

iron ore

high-pressure oxygen delivered to furnace

coke

molten slag

limestone

molten metal and slag

hearth

molten iron

(*blazing with jewels*) **h** emit light (*stars blazing*). □ **blaze away** (often foll. by *at*) **1** fire continuously with rifles, etc. **2** work enthusiastically. **blaze up 1** burst into flame. **2** burst out in anger. **like blazes** *sl.* **1** with great energy. **2** very fast. □□ **blaz·ing** *adj.* **blaz·ing·ly** *adv.*

blaze[2] /blayz/ *n. & v.* ● *n.* **1** a white mark on an animal's face. **2** a mark made on a tree by slashing the bark. ● *v.tr.* mark (a tree or a path) by slashing bark. □ **blaze a trail 1** mark out a path or route. **2** be the first to do, invent, or study something; pioneer.

blaze[3] /blayz/ *v.tr.* proclaim as with a trumpet. □ **blaze abroad** spread (news) about.

blaz·er /bláyzər/ *n.* **1** a man's or woman's sports jacket not worn with matching trousers. **2** a colored summer jacket worn by schoolchildren, sportsmen, etc., as part of a uniform.

bla·zon /bláyzən/ *v.tr. & n.* ● *v.tr.* **1** proclaim (esp. *blazon abroad*). **2** *Heraldry* **a** describe or paint (arms). **b** inscribe or paint (an object) with arms, names, etc. ● *n. Heraldry* a correct description of armorial bearings, etc.

bla·zon·ry /bláyzənree/ *n. Heraldry* **1 a** the art of describing or painting heraldic devices or armorial bearings. **b** such devices or bearings. **2** brightly colored display.

bleach /bleech/ *v. & n.* ● *v.tr. & intr.* whiten by exposure to sunlight or by a chemical process. ● *n.* **1** a bleaching substance. **2** the process of bleaching.

bleach·er /bleechər/ *n.* **1 a** a person who bleaches. **b** a vessel or chemical used in bleaching. **2** (usu. in *pl.*) a bench seat at a sports field or arena, esp. one in an outdoor uncovered stand usu. arranged in tiers and very cheap.

bleak /bleek/ *adj.* **1** bare; exposed; windswept. **2** unpromising; dreary (*bleak prospects*). □□ **bleak·ly** *adv.* **bleak·ness** *n.*

blear /bleer/ *adj. & v.* ● *adj.* **1** (of the eyes or the mind) dim; dull; filmy. **2** indistinct. ● *v.tr.* make dim or obscure; blur.

blear·y /bleeree/ *adj.* (**blearier**, **bleariest**) **1** (of

the eyes) dim, as from sleep or fatigue. **2** indistinct; blurred. □□ **blear·i·ly** *adv.*

blear·y-eyed *adj.* having bleary eyes.

bleat /bleet/ *v. & n.* ● *v.* **1** *intr.* (of a sheep, goat, or calf) make a weak, wavering cry. **2** *intr. & tr.* (often foll. by *out*) speak or say feebly, foolishly, or plaintively. ● *n.* **1** the sound made by a sheep, goat, etc. **2** a weak, plaintive, or foolish cry.

bleb /bleb/ *n.* **1** esp. *Med.* a small blister on the skin. **2** a small bubble in glass or on water.

bleed /bleed/ *v. & n.* ● *v.* (*past* and *past part.* **bled** /bled/) **1** *intr.* emit blood. **2** *tr.* draw blood from surgically. **3** *tr.* extort money from. **4** *intr.* (often foll. by *for*) suffer wounds or violent death (*bled for the Revolution*). **5** *intr.* **a** (of a plant) emit sap. **b** (of dye) come out in water. **6** *tr.* **a** allow (fluid or gas) to escape from a closed system through a valve, etc. **b** treat (such a system) in this way. **7** *intr. Printing* (of a printed area) to the cut edge of a page. ● *n.* an act of bleeding (cf. NOSEBLEED). □ **one's heart bleeds** usu. *iron.* one is very sorrowful.

bleed·er /bleedər/ *n. colloq.* a hemophiliac.

bleed·ing heart *n.* **1** *colloq.* a dangerously or foolishly soft-hearted person. **2** any of various plants, esp. *Dicentra spectabilis*, having heart-shaped crimson flowers hanging from an arched stem.

bleep /bleep/ *n. & v.* ● *n.* an intermittent high-pitched sound made electronically. ● *v.* **1** *intr. & tr.* make or cause to make such a sound, esp. as a signal. **2** *tr.* alert or summon by a bleep or bleeps.

blem·ish /blémish/ *n. & v.* ● *n.* a physical or moral defect; a stain; a flaw (*not a blemish on his character*). ● *v.tr.* spoil the beauty or perfection of (*spots blemished her complexion*).

blench /blench/ *v.intr.* flinch; quail.

blend /blend/ *v. & n.* ● *v.* **1** *tr.* **a** mix together to produce a desired flavor, etc. **b** produce by this method (*blended whiskey*). **2** *intr.* form a harmonious compound; become one. **3 a** *tr. & intr.* (often foll. by *with*) mingle or be mingled (*blends well with the locals*). **b** *tr.* (often foll. by *in, with*) mix thoroughly. **4** *intr.* (esp. of colors): **a** pass imperceptibly into each other. **b** go well together; harmonize. ● *n.* **1 a** a mixture, esp. of various sorts of a substance. **b** a combination (of different abstract or personal qualities). **2** a portmanteau word.

blende /blend/ *n.* any of various metal sulfides used as ores, esp. zinc sulfide.

blend·er /bléndər/ *n.* **1** a mixing machine used in food preparation for liquefying, chopping, or puréeing. **2 a** a thing that blends. **b** a person who blends.

blen·ny /blénee/ *n.* (*pl.* **-ies**) ◄ any of a family of small spiny-finned marine fish, esp. of the genus *Blennius*, having scaleless skins.

blent /blent *poet./ past* and *past part.* of BLEND.

BLENNY: BUTTERFLY BLENNY (*Blennius ocellaris*)

bleph·a·ri·tis /bléfərítis/ *n.* inflammation of the eyelids.

bless /bles/ *v.tr.* (*past* and *past part.* **blessed**, *poet.* **blest** /blest/) **1** pronounce words, esp. in a religious rite, asking for divine favor. **2 a** consecrate. **b** sanctify by the sign of the cross. **3** call (God) holy; adore. **4** attribute one's good fortune to (an auspicious time, one's fate, etc.); thank (*bless the day I met her*). **5** (usu. in *passive*; often foll. by *with*) make happy or successful (*they were truly blessed*). □ **(God) bless me** (or **my soul**) an exclamation of surprise, pleasure, indignation, etc. **(God) bless you! 1** an exclamation of endearment, gratitude, etc. **2** an exclamation made to a person who has just sneezed. **I'm** (or **well I'm**) **blessed** an exclamation of surprise, etc.

bless·ed /blésid, blest/ *adj.* (also *poet.* **blest**) **1 a** consecrated (*Blessed Sacrament*). **b** revered. **2** /blest/ (usu. foll. by *with*) often *iron.* fortunate (in

the possession of) (*blessed with children*). **3** *euphem.* cursed; damned (*blessed nuisance!*). **4 a** in paradise. **b** *RC Ch.* a title given to a dead person as an acknowledgment of his or her holy life. **5** bringing happiness; blissful (*blessed ignorance*). □□ **bless·ed·ly** *adv.*

bless·ed·ness /blésidnis/ *n.* **1** happiness. **2** the enjoyment of divine favor.

bless·ing /blésing/ *n.* **1** the act of declaring, seeking, or bestowing favor (*sought God's blessing; mother gave them her blessing*). **2** grace said before or after a meal. **3** a gift of God, nature, etc.; a thing one is glad of (*what a blessing he brought it!*).

blest /blest *poet./* var. of BLESSED.

bleth·er var. of BLATHER.

blew *past* of BLOW[1].

blew·its /bloooits/ *n.* ◄ any fungus of the genus *Tricholoma*, with edible lilac-stemmed mushrooms. ▷ MUSHROOM

BLEWITS (*Tricholoma* species)

blight /blīt/ *n. & v.* ● *n.* **1** any plant disease caused by mildews, rusts, smuts, fungi, or insects. ▷ FUNGUS. **2** any insect or parasite causing such a disease. **3** any obscure force which is harmful. **4** an unsightly or neglected urban area. ● *v.tr.* **1** affect with blight. **2** harm; destroy.

blimp /blimp/ *n.* **1 a** a small nonrigid airship. **b** a barrage balloon. **2** *derog. sl.* a fat person. □□ **blimp·ish** *adj.*

blind /blīnd/ *adj., v., n., & adv.* ● *adj.* **1** lacking the power of sight. **2 a** without foresight, discernment, intellectual perception, or adequate information. **b** (often foll. by *to*) unwilling or unable to appreciate (a factor, circumstance, etc.) (*blind to argument*). **3** not governed by purpose or reason (*blind forces*). **4** reckless (*blind hitting*). **5 a** concealed (*blind ditch*). **b** (of a door, window, etc.) walled up. **c** closed at one end. **6** *Aeron.* (of flying) without direct observation, using instruments only. ● *v.* **1** *tr.* deprive of sight (*blinded by tears*). **2** *tr.* (often foll. by *to*) rob of judgment; deceive (*blinded them to the danger*). ● *n.* **1** a screen for a window (*Venetian blind*). **2** something designed or used to hide the truth. **3** any obstruction to sight or light. ● *adv.* blindly (*fly blind*). □ **turn a** (or **one's**) **blind eye to** pretend not to notice. □□ **blind·ly** *adv.* **blind·ness** *n.*

blind al·ley *n.* **1** a cul-de-sac. **2** a course of action leading nowhere.

blind date *n.* **1** a social engagement between two people who have not previously met. **2** either of the couple on a blind date.

blind·er /blīndər/ *n. colloq.* (in *pl.*) ► either of a pair of screens or flaps attached to a horse's bridle to prevent it from seeing sideways.

bridle

blind·fold /blīndfōld/ *v., n., adj., & adv.* ● *v.tr.* deprive (a person) of sight by covering the eyes, esp. with a tied cloth. ● *n.* a bandage or cloth used to blindfold. ● *adj. & adv.* **1** with eyes bandaged. **2** without care or circumspection (*went into it blindfold*).

blinder

collar

BLINDER

blind·ing /blīnding/ *n.* **1** the process of covering a newly made road, etc., with grit to fill cracks. **2** such grit.

blind man's buff *n.* a game in which a blindfold player tries to catch others while being pushed about by them.

blind·side /blīndsīd/ *v.tr.* **1** strike or attack unexpectedly from one's blind side. **2** spring a disagreeable surprise upon.

B

blind spot *n.* **1** *Anat.* the point of entry of the optic nerve on the retina, insensitive to light. **2** an area in which a person lacks understanding or impartiality.

bling-bling *n.* *US colloq.* expensive, ostentatious clothing and jewelry, or the wearing of them.

bli·ni /blínee/ *n.* (also **bli·nis**) pancakes made from buckwheat flour.

blink /blingk/ *v. & n.* ● *v.* **1** *intr.* shut and open the eyes quickly. **2** *intr.* (often foll. by *at*) look with eyes opening and shutting. **3** *tr.* (often foll. by *back*) prevent (tears) by blinking. **4** *tr. &* (foll. by *at*) *intr.* ignore. **5** *intr.* shine with an intermittent light. **6** *tr.* blink with (eyes). ● *n.* **1** an act of blinking. **2** a momentary gleam or glimpse. □ **on the blink** *sl.* out of order, esp. intermittently.

blink·er /blíngkər/ *n. & v.* ● *n.* **1** a device that blinks. **2** = BLINDER. ● *v.tr.* **1** obscure with blinders. **2** (as **blinkered** *adj.*) having narrow views.

blip /blip/ *n. & v.* ● *n.* **1** a quick popping sound, as of dripping water or an electronic device. **2** a small image of an object on a radar screen. **3** a minor deviation or error. ● *v.intr.* (**blipped, blipping**) make a blip.

blip·vert /blípvət/ *n.* a television advert of a few seconds' duration.

bliss /blis/ *n.* **1 a** a perfect joy or happiness. **b** enjoyment; gladness. **2** a state of blessedness. □□ **bliss·ful** *adj.* **bliss·ful·ly** *adv.* **bliss·ful·ness** *n.*

blis·ter /blístər/ *n. & v.* ● *n.* **1** a small bubble on the skin filled with serum and caused by burning, etc. **2** a similar swelling on any other surface. ● *v.* **1** *tr.* raise a blister on. **2** *intr.* come up in a blister or blisters. **3** *tr.* attack sharply (*blistered them with his criticisms*).

blis·ter pack *n.* a bubble pack.

blithe /blīth/ *adj.* **1** *poet.* gay; joyous. **2** careless; casual (*with blithe indifference*). □□ **blithe·ly** *adv.* **blithe·ness** *n.* **blithesome** *adj.*

blith·er·ing /blíthəring/ *attrib.adj.* *colloq.* **1** senselessly talkative. **2** utter; hopeless (*blithering idiot*).

B.Litt. *abbr.* Bachelor of Letters.

blitz /blits/ *n. & v.* *colloq.* ● *n.* **1 a** an intensive or sudden (esp. aerial) attack. **b** an energetic intensive attack (*must have a blitz on this room*). **2** (**the Blitz**) the German air raids on London in 1940 during World War II. **3** *Football* a charge of the passer by the defensive linebackers just after the ball is snapped. ● *v.tr.* attack, damage, or destroy by a blitz.

blitz·krieg /blítskreeg/ *n.* an intense military campaign intended to bring about a swift victory.

bliz·zard /blízərd/ *n.* a severe snowstorm with high winds.

bloat /blōt/ *v.* **1** *tr. & intr.* inflate; swell (*bloated with gas*). **2** *tr.* (as **bloated** *adj.*) **a** swollen. **b** puffed up with pride or wealth (*bloated plutocrat*). **3** *tr.* cure (a herring) by salting and smoking lightly.

bloat·er /blōtər/ *n.* a herring cured by bloating.

blob /blob/ *n.* **1** a small roundish mass; a drop of matter. **2** a drop of liquid. **3** a spot of color.

bloc /blok/ *n.* a combination of governments, groups, etc., sharing a common purpose.

block /blok/ *n., v., & adj.* ● *n.* **1** a solid hewn or unhewn piece of hard material (*block of ice*). **2** a flat-topped base for chopping, hammering on, etc., or for mounting a horse from. **3** a compact mass of buildings bounded by (usu. four) streets. **4** an obstruction. **5** a pulley or system of pulleys mounted in a case. **6** (in *pl.*) any of a set of solid cubes used as a child's toy. **7** *Printing* a piece of wood or metal engraved for printing on paper or fabric. **8** *sl.* the head (*knock his block off*). **9 a** the area between streets in a town or suburb. **b** the length of such an area (*lives three blocks away*). **10** a large quantity of things treated as a unit, esp. shares, seats in a theater, etc. **11** *Track & Field* = STARTING BLOCK. ● *v.tr.* **1 a** (often foll. by *up, off*) obstruct (a passage, etc.) (*you are blocking my view*). **b** put obstacles in the way of (progress, etc.). **2** restrict the use or conversion of (currency or any other asset). **3** *Sports* stop or impede. ● *attrib.adj.* treating (many similar things) as one unit (*block booking*). □ **block in 1** sketch roughly; plan. **2** confine. **block out 1 a** shut out (light, noise, etc.). **b** exclude from memory, as being too painful. **2** sketch roughly; plan. **block up 1** shut (a person, etc.) in. **2** fill in with bricks, etc. **put the blocks on** prevent from proceeding. □□ **block·er** *n.*

block·ade /blokáyd/ *n. & v.* ● *n.* **1** the surrounding or blocking of a place, esp. a port, by an enemy to prevent entry and exit of supplies, etc. **2** anything that prevents access or progress. ● *v.tr.* **1** subject to a blockade. **2** obstruct (a passage, etc.). □ **run a blockade** enter or leave a blockaded port by evading the blockading force. □□ **block·ad·er** *n.*

block·ade-run·ner *n.* a vessel which runs or attempts to run into a blockaded port.

block·age /blókij/ *n.* **1** an obstruction. **2** a blocked state.

block and tack·le *n.* ◀ a system of pulleys and ropes, esp. for lifting.

block·bust·er /blókbustər/ *n.* *sl.* **1** something of great power or size, esp. an epic or extremely popular movie or a book. **2** a huge aerial bomb.

block·head /blókhed/ *n.* a stupid person. □□ **block·head·ed** *adj.*

block·house /blókhows/ *n.* **1** a reinforced concrete shelter used as an observation point, etc. **2** *hist.* a one-story timber building with loopholes, used as a fort. **3** a house made of squared logs.

block·ish /blókish/ *adj.* **1** resembling a block. **2** excessively dull; stupid; obtuse. **3** clumsy; rude; roughly hewn. □□ **block·ish·ly** *adv.* **block·ish·ness** *n.*

blond /blond/ *adj. & n.* ● *adj.* **1** (of hair) light-colored; fair. **2** (of the complexion, esp. as an indication of race) light-colored. ● *n.* a person with fair hair and skin. □□ **blond·ish** *adj.* **blond·ness** *n.*

blonde /blond/ *adj. & n.* ● *adj.* (of a woman or a woman's hair) blond. ● *n.* a blond-haired woman.

blood /blud/ *n. & v.* ● *n.* **1 ▲** a liquid, usually red and circulating in the arteries and veins of vertebrates, that carries oxygen to and carbon dioxide from the tissues of the body. **2** a corresponding fluid in invertebrates. **3** bloodshed, esp. killing. **4** passion; temperament. **5** race; parentage (*of the same blood*). ● *v.tr.* initiate (a person) by experience. □ **in one's blood** inherent in one's character. **make a person's blood boil** infuriate. **make a person's blood run cold** horrify. **new** (or **fresh**) **blood** new members admitted to a group, esp. as an invigorating force.

blood bank *n.* a place where supplies of blood or plasma for transfusion are stored.

blood bath *n.* a massacre.

blood broth·er *n.* a brother by birth or by the ceremonial mingling of blood.

blood count *n.* **1** the counting of the number of corpuscles in a specific amount of blood. **2** the number itself.

blood·cur·dling /blúdkərdling/ *adj.* horrifying.

blood do·nor *n.* a person who gives blood for transfusion.

blood·ed /blúdid/ *adj.* **1** (of horses, etc.) of good pedigree. **2** (in *comb.*) having blood or a disposition of a specified kind (*cold-blooded; red-blooded*).

blood feud *n.* a feud between families involving killing or injury.

BLOOD

Nutrients and hormones are transported around the body in blood. Its constituent fluid is plasma, in which blood cells are suspended. White blood cells (neutrophils and lymphocytes) guard against infection, red blood cells (erythrocytes) transport oxygen, and platelets help the blood to clot.

CROSS SECTION OF A BLOOD VESSEL

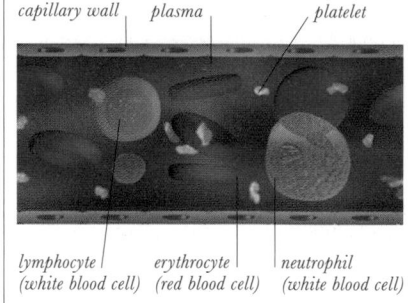

capillary wall *plasma* *platelet*

lymphocyte (white blood cell) *erythrocyte (red blood cell)* *neutrophil (white blood cell)*

blood group *n.* any one of the various types of human blood determining compatibility in transfusion.

blood·hound /blúdhownd/ *n.* **1 ▶** a large hound of a breed used in tracking and having a very keen sense of smell. **2** this breed.

blood·less /blúdlis/ *adj.* **1** without blood. **2** unemotional. **3** pale. **4** without bloodshed (*a bloodless coup*). **5** feeble. □□ **blood·less·ly** *adv.* **blood·less·ness** *n.*

blood·let·ting /blúdleting/ *n.* **1** the surgical removal of some of a patient's blood. **2** bloodshed.

blood·line /blúdlīn/ *n.* a line of descent; pedigree; descent.

BLOODHOUND

blood·mobile /blúdmōbéel/ *n.* a van, truck, or bus equipped and staffed to take blood from donors.

blood mon·ey *n.* **1** money paid to the next of kin of a person who has been killed. **2** money paid to a hired murderer. **3** money paid for information about a murder.

blood or·ange *n.* an orange with red or red-streaked pulp.

blood poi·son·ing *n.* a diseased state caused by the presence of microorganisms in the blood.

blood pres·sure *n.* the pressure of the blood in the circulatory system, often measured for diagnosis since it is closely related to the force and rate of the heartbeat and the diameter and elasticity of the arterial walls. ▷ SPHYGMOMANOMETER

blood re·la·tion *n.* (also **blood relative**) a relative by blood, not by marriage or adoption.

blood·shed /blúdshed/ *n.* **1** the spilling of blood. **2** slaughter.

blood·shot /blúdshot/ *adj.* (of an eyeball) inflamed; tinged with blood.

blood sport *n.* sport involving the wounding or killing of animals, esp. hunting.

blood·stain /blúdstayn/ *n.* a discoloration caused by blood.

blood·stained /blúdstaynd/ *adj.* **1** stained with blood. **2** guilty of bloodshed.

blood·stock /blúdstok/ *n.* thoroughbred horses.

blood·stone /blúdstōn/ *n.* a type of green chalcedony spotted or streaked with red, often used as a gemstone.

Illustration labels (BLOCK AND TACKLE): eye, shoulder, shell, sail maker's whipping, cheek, shank

BLOCK AND TACKLE

blood·stream /blúdstreem/ *n.* blood in circulation.

blood·suck·er /blúdsukər/ *n.* **1** an animal or insect that sucks blood, esp. a leech. **2** an extortioner. □□ **blood·suck·ing** *adj.*

blood sug·ar *n.* the amount of glucose in the blood.

blood test *n.* a scientific examination of blood, esp. for diagnosis.

blood·thirst·y /blúdthərstee/ *adj.* (**bloodthirst-ier, bloodthirstiest**) eager for bloodshed. □□ **blood·thirst·i·ly** *adv.* **blood·thirst·i·ness** *n.*

blood type *n.* see BLOOD GROUP.

blood ves·sel *n.* a vein, artery, or capillary carrying blood. ▷ BLOOD, CARDIOVASCULAR

blood·y /blúdee/ *adj., adv., & v.* ● *adj.* (**bloodier, bloodiest**) **1 a** of or like blood. **b** running or smeared with blood. **2 a** involving bloodshed (*bloody battle*). **b** sanguinary; cruel (*bloody butcher*). **3** esp. *Brit. coarse sl.* expressing annoyance or antipathy, or as an intensive (*a bloody shame*). **4** red. ● *adv.* esp. *Brit. coarse sl.* as an intensive (*I'll bloody thump him*). ● *v.tr.* (**-ies, -ied**) make bloody; stain with blood. □□ **blood·i·ly** *adv.* **blood·i·ness** *n.*

Blood·y Mar·y *n.* a drink composed of vodka and tomato juice.

bloom[1] /bloom/ *n. & v.* ● *n.* **1 a** a flower, esp. one cultivated for its beauty. **b** the state of flowering (*in bloom*). **2** a state of perfection or loveliness (*in full bloom*). **3 a** (of the complexion) a flush; a glow. **b** a delicate powdery surface deposit on plums, leaves, etc., indicating freshness. **c** a cloudiness on a shiny surface. **4** an overgrowth of algae, plankton, etc. ● *v.* **1** *intr.* be in flower. **2** *intr.* a come into, or remain in, full beauty. **b** be in a healthy, vigorous state. **3** *intr.* become overgrown with algae, plankton, etc. (esp. of a lake or stream). **4** *tr. Photog.* coat (a lens) so as to reduce reflection from its surface. □ **take the bloom off** make stale.

bloom[2] /bloom/ *n. & v.* ● *n.* a mass of puddled iron hammered or squeezed into a thick bar. ● *v.tr.* make into bloom.

bloom·er /bloomər/ *n.* a plant or person that blooms (in a specified way) (*early autumn bloomer; late bloomer*).

bloo·mers /bloomərz/ *n.pl.* **1** women's loose almost knee-length underpants. **2** *colloq.* any women's underpants. **3** *hist.* women's loose trousers, gathered at the knee or (orig.) the ankle.

bloom·er·y /bloomaree/ *n.* (*pl.* **-ies**) a factory that makes puddled iron into blooms.

bloom·ing /blooming/ *adj.* flourishing; healthy.

Blooms·bur·y /bloomzbaree, -bree/ *n. & adj.* ● *n.* (in full **Bloomsbury Group**) a group of writers, artists, and philosophers living in or associated with Bloomsbury in London in the early 20th c. ● *adj.* **1** associated with or similar to the Bloomsbury Group. **2** intellectual; highbrow.

bloop·er /bloopər/ *n. colloq.* an embarrassing error.

blos·som /blósəm/ *n. & v.* ● *n.* **1** ▶ a flower or a mass of flowers, esp. of a fruit tree. **2** the state or time of flowering. **3** a promising stage (*the blossom of youth*). ● *v.intr.* **1** open into flower. **2** mature; thrive. □□ **blos·som·y** *adj.*

blot /blot/ *n. & v.* ● *n.* **1** a stain of ink, etc. **2** a disgraceful act or quality. **3** any disfigurement or blemish. ● *v.* (**blotted, blotting**) **1 a** *tr.* spot or stain, esp. with ink. **b** *intr.* (of a pen, etc.) make blots. **2** *tr.* **a** use blotting paper, etc., to absorb excess liquid, esp. ink, from. **b** (of blotting paper, etc.) soak up (esp. ink). **3** *tr.* disgrace (*blotted his reputation*). □ **blot out 1** obliterate; obscure. **2** destroy.

blotch /bloch/ *n. & v.* ● *n.* **1** a discolored or inflamed patch on the skin. **2** an irregular patch of ink or color. ● *v.tr.* cover with blotches. □□ **blotch·y** *adj.* (**blotch·i·er, blotch·i·est**).

blot·ter /blótər/ *n.* a sheet or sheets of blotting paper, usu. inserted into a frame.

blot·ting pa·per *n.* unsized absorbent paper used for soaking up excess ink.

blot·to /blótō/ *adj. sl.* very drunk, esp. unconscious from drinking.

blouse /blows, blowz/ *n. & v.* ● *n.* **1** a woman's upper garment, usu. buttoned and collared. **2** the upper part of a military uniform. ● *v.tr.* make (a shirt, etc.) fall loosely like a blouse.

blous·on /blówson, bloozon/ *n.* a short blouse-shaped jacket.

blow[1] /blō/ *v. & n.* ● *v.* (*past* **blew** /blōo/; *past part.* **blown** /blōn/) **1 a** *intr.* (of the wind or impersonally) move along; act as an air current (*it was blowing hard*). **b** be driven by an air current (*paper blew along*). **c** *tr.* drive with an air current (*blew the door open*). **2 a** *tr.* send out (esp. air) by breathing (*blew cigarette smoke*). **b** *intr.* send a directed air current from the mouth. **3** *tr. & intr.* sound or be sounded by blowing (*the whistle blew*). **4** *tr.* **a** direct an air current at (*blew the embers*). **b** (foll. by *off, away,* etc.) clear of by means of an air current. **5** *tr.* clear (the nose) of mucus by blowing. **6** *intr.* puff; pant. **7** *sl.* **a** *tr.* depart suddenly from (*blew the town yesterday*). **b** *intr.* depart suddenly. **8** *tr.* shatter or send flying by an explosion (*blew them to smithereens*). **9** *tr.* make or shape (glass or a bubble) by blowing air in. **10** *tr. & intr.* melt from overloading (*the fuse has blown*). **11** *intr.* (of a whale) eject air and water through a blowhole. **12** *tr.* break into (a safe, etc.) with explosives. **13** *tr. sl.* **a** spend recklessly (*blew $20 on a meal*). **b** bungle (an opportunity, etc.) (*he's blown his chances*). **c** reveal (a secret, etc.). **14** *tr.* (of flies) deposit eggs in. ● *n.* **1 a** an act of blowing (e.g., one's nose). **b** *colloq.* a turn or spell of playing jazz (on any instrument). **2 a** a gust of air. **b** exposure to fresh air. □ **be blowed if one will** *sl.* be unwilling to. **blow hot and cold** *colloq.* vacillate. **blow in 1** break inward by an explosion. **2** *colloq.* arrive unexpectedly. **blow a person's mind** *sl.* cause a person to have drug-induced hallucinations or a similar experience. **blow off 1** escape or allow (steam, etc.) to escape forcibly. **2** *sl.* renege on (an obligation) (*I decided to blow off studying so I could go to the party*). **blow out 1 a** extinguish by blowing. **b** send outwards by an explosion. **2** (of a tire) burst. **3** (of a fuse, etc.) melt. **blow over** fade away without serious consequences. **blow one's own trumpet** praise oneself. **blow one's top** (or **stack**) *colloq.* explode in rage. **blow up 1 a** shatter or destroy by an explosion. **b** erupt. **2** *colloq.* rebuke strongly. **3** inflate (a tire, etc.). **4** *colloq.* **a** enlarge (a photograph). **b** exaggerate. **5** *colloq.* arise. **6** *colloq.* lose one's temper. □□ **blow·y** *adj.* (**blow·i·er, blow·i·est**).

blow[2] /blō/ *n.* **1** a hard stroke with a hand or weapon. **2** a sudden shock or misfortune. □ **come to blows** end up fighting.

blow[3] /blō/ *v. & n. archaic* ● *v.intr.* (*past* **blew** /blōo/; *past part.* **blown** /blōn/) burst into or be in flower. ● *n.* blossoming; bloom (*in full blow*).

blow-by-blow *attrib.adj.* (of a description, etc.) giving all the details in sequence.

blow-dry *v.tr.* arrange (the hair) while drying it with a hand-held dryer. □□ **blow-dry·er** *n.*

blow·er /blóər/ *n.* **1** in senses of BLOW[1] *v.* **2** a device for creating a current of air.

blow·fish /blófish/ *n.* any of several kinds of fish able to inflate their bodies when frightened, etc.

blow·fly /blóflī/ *n.* (*pl.* **-flies**) a meat fly; a bluebottle. ▷ BLUEBOTTLE

blow·gun /blógun/ *n.* a tube used esp. by primitive peoples for propelling darts by blowing.

blow·hard /blóhaard/ *n. & adj. colloq.* ● *n.* a boastful person. ● *adj.* boastful; blustering.

BLOWHOLE OF A BOWHEAD WHALE (OVERHEAD VIEW)

blowhole

blow·hole /blóhōl/ *n.* **1** ▲ the nostril of a whale, on the top of its head. ▷ CETACEAN. **2** a hole (esp. in ice) for breathing or fishing through. **3** a vent for smoke, etc., in a tunnel.

blown *past part.* of BLOW.

blow·out /blô-owt/ *n. colloq.* **1** a burst tire. **2** a melted fuse. **3** a huge meal. **4** a large party. **5** *Sports* victory by a wide margin.

blow·pipe /blópīp/ *n.* **1** = BLOWGUN. **2** a tube used to intensify the heat of a flame by blowing air or other gas through it at high pressure. **3** a tube used in glass blowing.

blow·torch /blótawrch/ *n.* a portable device with a very hot flame used for burning off paint, soldering, etc.

blow-up *n.* **1** *colloq.* an enlargement (of a photograph, etc.). **2** an explosion.

blowz·y /blówzee/ *adj.* (**blowzier, blowziest**) **1** coarse-looking; red-faced. **2** disheveled.

BLT *abbr.* (*pl.* **BLT's** or **BLTs**) a bacon, lettuce, and tomato sandwich.

blub·ber[1] /blúbər/ *n. & v.* ● *n.* ▼ whale fat. ● *v.* **1** *intr.* sob loudly. **2** *tr.* sob out (words). □□ **blub·ber·er** *n.* **blub·ber·y** *adj.*

blood vessel　　　　　*skin*

blubber

muscle

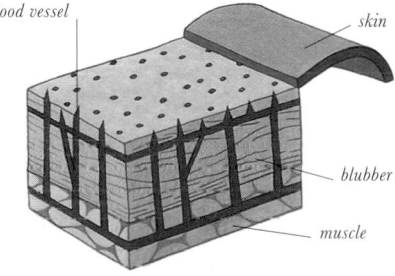

BLUBBER: SECTION THROUGH WHALE BLUBBER

blub·ber[2] /blúbər/ *adj.* (of the lips) swollen; protruding.

blu·chers /blookərz/ *n.pl. hist.* strong leather half boots or high shoes.

bludg·eon /blújən/ *n. & v.* ● *n.* a club with a heavy end. ● *v.tr.* **1** beat with a bludgeon. **2** coerce.

blue /bloo/ *adj., n., & v.* ● *adj.* (**bluer, bluest**) **1** having a color like that of a clear sky. **2** sad; gloomy (*feel blue*). **3** pornographic (*a blue film*). **4** with bluish skin through cold, anger, etc. ● *n.* **1** a blue color or pigment. **2** blue clothes or material (*dressed in blue*). **3** (usu. **Blue**) **a** a soldier in the Union army in the US Civil War. **b** the Union army. **4** (prec. by *the*) the clear sky. ● *v.tr.* (**blues, blued, bluing** or **blue·ing**) make blue. □ **once in a blue moon** very rarely. **out of the blue** unexpectedly.

blue ba·by *n.* a baby with a blue complexion from lack of oxygen in the blood due to a congenital defect of the heart or major vessels.

BLUEBELL (*Hyacinthoides nonscripta*)

blue·bell /bloobel/ *n.* ◄ a liliaceous plant, *Hyacinthoides nonscripta*, with clusters of bell-shaped blue flowers on a stem arising from a rhizome.

BLOSSOM OF A CRAB APPLE (*Malus* × *lemoinei*)

B

blue·ber·ry /blóoberee/ n. (pl. **-ies**) **1** any of several plants of the genus *Vaccinium*, with an edible fruit. **2** the small blue-black fruit of these plants.

blue·bird /blóobərd/ n. any of various N. American songbirds of the thrush family, esp. of the genus *Sialia*, with distinctive blue plumage usu. on the back or head.

blue blood n. noble birth. □□ **blue-blood·ed** adj.

blue book n. **1** a listing of socially prominent people. **2** (**Blue Book**) a reference book listing the prices of used cars. **3** (**Blue Book**) a report issued by the government.

blue·bot·tle /blóobot'l/ n. ▼ a large buzzing fly, *Calliphora vomitoria*, with a metallic blue body.

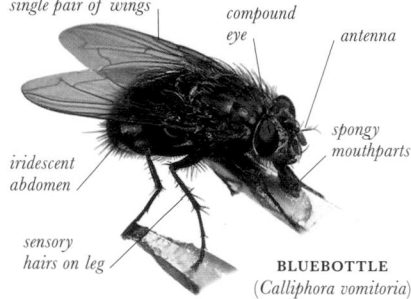

single pair of wings
compound eye
antenna
spongy mouthparts
iridescent abdomen
sensory hairs on leg

BLUEBOTTLE
(*Calliphora vomitoria*)

blue cheese n. cheese produced with veins of blue mold, e.g., Stilton and Danish Blue. ▷ CHEESE

blue-chip attrib. adj. (of stock) of reliable investment, though less secure than gilt-edged stock.

blue-col·lar attrib. adj of workers who wear work clothes or specialized protective clothing, as miners, mechanics, etc.

blue crab n. an edible bluish-green crab, *Callinectes sapidus*, of the Atlantic and Gulf coasts.

blue·fish /blóofish/ n. a voracious marine fish, *Pomatomus saltatrix*, inhabiting tropical and temperate waters and popular as a game fish.

blue·grass /blóogras/ n. **1** any of several bluish-green grasses, esp. Kentucky bluegrass, *Poa pratensis*. **2** a kind of unamplified country music characterized by virtuosic playing of banjos, guitars, etc.

blue-green al·ga = CYANOBACTERIUM.

blue·gum /blóogum/ n. ◀ any tree of the genus *Eucalyptus*, esp. *E. regnans* with blue-green aromatic leaves.

blue·jack·et /blóojakit/ n. a sailor in the navy.

blue jay n. a crested jay, *Cyanocitta cristata*, common to N. America, with a blue back and head and a gray breast.

blue jeans n.pl. pants made of blue denim.

blue mold n. a bluish fungus growing on food and other organic matter.

BLUEGUM
(*Eucalyptus globulus*)

blue-pen·cil v.tr. (**-penciled**, **-penciling**; also **-pencilled**, **-pencilling**) censor (a movie, etc.).

blue·print /blóoprint/ n. **1** a photographic print of the final stage of engineering, esp. plans in white on a blue background. **2** a detailed plan, esp. in the early stages of a project or idea.

blue ri·band n. & adj. • n. (also **blue ribbon**) a ribbon of blue silk given to the winner of a competition or as a mark of great distinction. • adj. (**blue-ribbon**) N. Amer. of the highest quality; first-class.

blues /blóoz/ n.pl. **1** (prec. by *the*) a bout of depression. **2** (prec. by *the*; often treated as *sing.*) melancholic music of African-American folk origin, often in a twelve-bar sequence. □□ **blues·y** adj. (in sense 2).

blue·stock·ing /blóostoking/ n. usu. *derog.* an intellectual or literary woman.

blue tit n. ▶ a common European tit, *Parus caeruleus*, with a distinct blue crest on a black and white head.

blue whale n. a rorqual, *Balaenoptera musculus*, the largest known living mammal. ▷ WHALE

BLUE TIT
(*Parus caeruleus*)

bluff[1] /bluf/ v. & n. • v. **1** intr. make a pretense of strength or confidence to gain an advantage. **2** tr. mislead by bluffing. • n. an act of bluffing. □ **call a person's bluff** challenge a person thought to be bluffing.

bluff[2] /bluf/ adj. & n. • adj. **1** (of a cliff, or a ship's bows) having a vertical or steep broad front. **2** (of a person or manner) blunt; frank; hearty. • n. a steep cliff or headland. □□ **bluff·ly** adv. (in sense 2 of adj.). **bluff·ness** n. (in sense 2 of adj.).

blu·ing /blóoing/ n. (also **blueing**) blue powder used to whiten laundry.

blu·ish /blóoish/ adj. (also **blue·ish**) somewhat blue. □□ **blu·ish·ness** n.

blun·der /blúndər/ n. & v. • n. a clumsy or foolish mistake. • v. **1** intr. make a blunder. **2** tr. deal incompetently with. **3** intr. move about clumsily. □□ **blun·der·er** n. **blun·der·ing·ly** adv.

blun·der·buss /blúndərbus/ n. hist. ▼ a short large-bored gun firing balls or slugs.

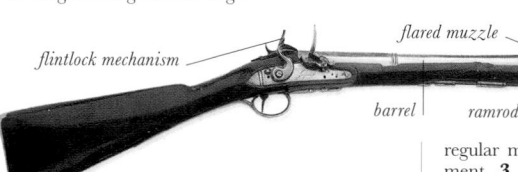

flintlock mechanism
flared muzzle
barrel
ramrod

BLUNDERBUSS: 18TH-CENTURY
FLINTLOCK BLUNDERBUSS

blunge /blunj/ v.tr. (in ceramics, etc.) mix (clay, etc.) with water. □□ **blung·er** n.

blunt /blunt/ adj. & v. • adj. **1** (of a knife, pencil, etc.) lacking sharpness; having a worn-down edge or point. **2** (of a person or manner) direct; uncompromising; outspoken. • v.tr. make blunt or less sharp. □□ **blunt·ly** adv. (in sense 2 of adj.). **blunt·ness** n.

blur /blər/ v. & n. • v. (**blurred**, **blurring**) **1** tr. & intr. make or become unclear or less distinct. **2** tr. smear; partially efface. **3** tr. make (one's memory, perception, etc.) dim or less clear. • n. something that appears or sounds indistinct or unclear. □□ **blur·ry** adj. (**blur·ri·er**, **blur·ri·est**).

blurb /blərb/ n. a (usu. eulogistic) description of a book, esp. printed on its jacket, as promotion by its publishers.

blurt /blərt/ v.tr. (usu. foll. by *out*) utter abruptly, thoughtlessly, or tactlessly.

blush /blush/ v. & n. • v. **1 a** develop a pink tinge in the face from embarrassment or shame. **b** (of the face) redden in this way. **2** feel embarrassed or ashamed. • n. **1** the act of blushing. **2** a pink tinge.

blush·er /blúshər/ n. a cosmetic used to give a usu. reddish or pinkish color to the face. ▷ MAKEUP

blus·ter /blústər/ v. & n. • v.intr. **1** behave pompously and boisterously; utter empty threats. **2** (of the wind, etc.) blow fiercely. • n. **1** noisily self-assertive talk. **2** empty threats. □□ **blus·ter·er** n. **blus·ter·y** adj.

blvd. abbr. boulevard.

BM abbr. **1** Bachelor of Medicine. **2** Bachelor of Music. **3** British Museum. **4** bowel movement.

B mov·ie n. a supporting movie in a theater's program.

B.Mus. abbr. Bachelor of Music.

BMX /bee-eméks/ n. **1** organized bicycle racing on a dirt track, esp. for youngsters. **2** a kind of bicycle used for this.

Bn. abbr. Battalion.

BO abbr. colloq. body odor.

bo·a /bóə/ n. **1** any large nonpoisonous snake from tropical America, esp. of the genus *Boa*, which kills its prey by crushing and suffocating it in its coils. **2** any snake which is similar in appearance, such as Old World pythons. **3** a long scarf made of feathers or fur.

bo·a con·stric·tor n. ▼ a large snake, *Boa constrictor*, native to tropical America and the West Indies, which crushes its prey. ▷ SNAKE

prey

BOA CONSTRICTOR
(*Boa constrictor*)

boar /bawr/ n. **1** (in full **wild boar**) the tusked wild pig, *Sus scrofa*, from which domestic pigs are descended. **2** an uncastrated male pig. **3** its flesh. **4** a male guinea pig, etc.

board /bawrd/ n. & v. • n. **1 a** a flat thin piece of sawn lumber, usu. long and narrow. **b** a piece of material resembling this, made from compressed fibers. **c** a thin slab of wood or a similar substance, often with a covering, used for any of various purposes (*chessboard; ironing board*). **d** thick stiff cardboard used in bookbinding. **2** the provision of regular meals, usu. with accommodation, for payment. **3** the directors of a company; any other specially constituted administrative body. **4** (in *pl.*) the stage of a theater (cf. *tread the boards*). • v. **1** tr. a go on board (a ship, etc.). **b** force one's way on board (a ship, etc.) in attack. **2 a** intr. receive meals or meals and lodging, for payment. **b** tr. provide with regular meals **3** tr. (usu. foll. by *up*) cover with boards; seal. □ **go by the board** be neglected, omitted, or discarded. **on board** on or on to a ship, etc.

board·er /báwrdər/ n. **1** a person who boards (see BOARD v. 2a), esp. a pupil at a boarding school. **2** a person who boards a ship, esp. an enemy.

board game n. a game played on a board.

board·ing·house /báwrdinghows/ n. an establishment providing board and lodging.

board·ing school /báwrding skóol/ n. a school where pupils reside during the school term.

board·room /báwrdrōom, -rŏom/ n. a room in which a board of directors, etc., meets regularly.

board·sail·ing /báwrdsayling/ n. = WINDSURFING. □□ **board·sail·or** n.

board·walk /báwrdwawk/ n. **1** a wooden walkway across sand, marsh, etc. **2** a promenade, esp. of wooden planks, along a beach.

boast /bōst/ v. & n. • v. **1** intr. declare one's achievements, possessions, or abilities with indulgent pride and satisfaction. **2** tr. own or have as something praiseworthy, etc. (*boasts magnificent views*). • n. **1** an act of boasting. **2** something one is proud of. □□ **boast·er** n. **boast·ing·ly** adv.

boast·ful /bóstfŏol/ adj. given to or characterized by boasting. □□ **boast·ful·ly** adv. **boast·ful·ness** n.

boat /bōt/ n. & v. • n. **1** ▶ a small vessel propelled on water by an engine, oars, or sails. **2** (in general use) a ship of any size. **3** a boat-shaped jug used for holding sauce, etc. • v.intr. travel in a boat, esp. for pleasure. □ **in the same boat** sharing the same adverse circumstances.

BOAT

The term "boat" is generally applied to small, light, single-decked craft that travel on inland and coastal waters. The power source and design are determined by the roles they fulfill. Rudimentary vessels, such as the log boat canoe, have been used since ancient times to transport people and goods, and craft like these still play an important role in many parts of the world for both transportation and fishing. However, many boats today are used exclusively for leisure and sport. Powerboats are designed mainly for racing, while dinghies and yachts are used for competitive sailing and cruising. Other craft are built for more specific practical functions. Lifeboats, for example, are used to rescue other vessels in distress and are designed to be rugged, buoyant, and maneuverable.

EXAMPLES OF BOATS

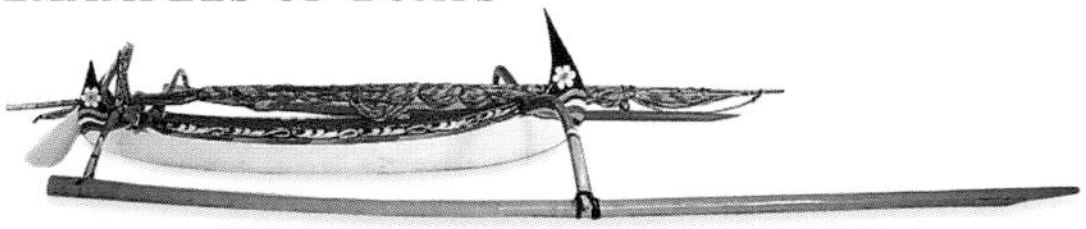

JUKUNG

SAMPAN

LOG BOAT

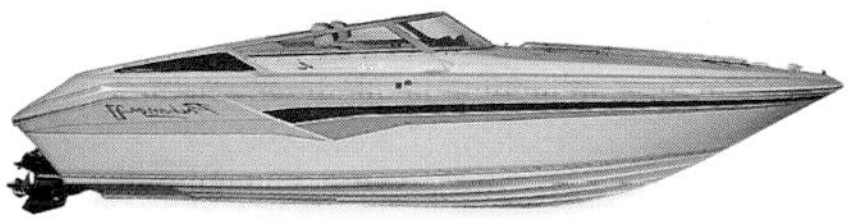

POWERBOAT

DINGHY

SAILING YACHT

MOTOR YACHT

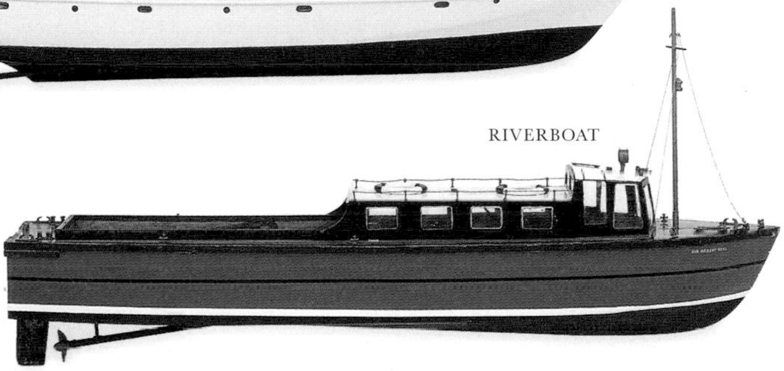

RIVERBOAT

LIFEBOAT

---

boat·house /bốt-hows/ *n.* a shed at the edge of a river, lake, etc., for housing boats.

boat·ing /bốting/ *n.* rowing or sailing in boats as a sport or form of recreation.

boat·load /bốtlōd/ *n.* **1** enough to fill a boat. **2** *colloq.* a large number of people.

boat·man /bốtmən/ *n.* (*pl.* **-men**) a person who hires out boats or provides transport by boat.

boat peo·ple *n.pl.* refugees who have left a country by sea.

boat·swain /bốs'n/ *n.* (also **bo'sun, bo·sun, bo's'n**) a ship's officer in charge of equipment and the crew.

bob[1] /bob/ *v. & n.* ● *v.intr.* (**bobbed, bobbing**) **1** move quickly up and down. **2** (usu. foll. by *back, up*) **a** bounce buoyantly. **b** emerge suddenly; become active again. **3** curtsy. **4** (foll. by *for*) try to catch with the mouth alone (an apple, etc., floating or hanging). ● *n.* **1** a jerking or bouncing movement, esp. upward. **2** a curtsy.

bob[2] /bob/ *n. & v.* ● *n.* **1** a short hairstyle for women and children. **2** a weight on a pendulum, plumb line, or kite tail. **3** = BOBSLED. **4** a horse's docked tail. ● *v.* (**bobbed, bobbing**) **1** *tr.* cut (a woman's or child's hair) so that it hangs clear of the shoulders. **2** *intr.* ride on a bobsled.

BOBBIN:
COTTON
SPOOL

bob·bin /bốbin/ *n.* **1** ◀ a cylinder or cone holding thread, etc. **2** a spool or reel.

bob·ble /bốbəl/ *n. & v.* ● *n.* **1** a small woolly or tufted ball as a decoration or trimming. **2** a fumble, esp. of a baseball or football. ● *v.tr.* to fumble or juggle (a ball).

bob·by pin /bốbeepin/ *n.* a flat, closed hairpin.

bob·by socks *n.pl.* (also **bob·by sox**) short socks reaching just above the ankle.

bob·cat /bốbkat/ *n.* ▼ a small N. American lynx, *Lynx rufus*, with a spotted reddish brown coat and a short tail.

BOBCAT (*Lynx rufus*)   *thick side-whiskers*

bob·sled /bốbsled/ (also *Brit.* **bobsleigh** /bốbslay/) *n.* ▼ a mechanically steered and braked sled used for racing down a steep ice-covered run. □□ **bob·sled·ding** (also *Brit.* **bob·sleigh·ing**) *n.*

BOBSLED: TWO-MAN BOBSLED

bob·stay /bốbstay/ *n.* the chain or rope holding down a ship's bowsprit.

bob·white /bốbhwít, bốbwít/ *n.* an American quail of the genus *Colinus*.

Boche /bosh, bawsh/ *n. sl. derog.* (prec. by *the*) Germans, esp. German soldiers, collectively.

bock /bok/ *n.* a strong dark German beer.

bod /bod/ *n.* a person's physique.

bo·da·cious /bōdáyshəs/ *adj. sl.* **1** remarkable; excellent. **2** bold; audacious.

bode /bōd/ *v.tr.* **1** portend; promise. **2** foresee; foretell (evil). □ **bode well** (or **ill**) show good (or bad) signs for the future.

BODY

The human body consists of a number of interacting systems. The skeleton forms a rigid framework, to which muscles are attached, facilitating movement initiated by the nervous system, which is responsible for the body's reaction to stimuli. Hormones, produced by the endocrine system, control many functions, including growth and developmental changes like puberty. The cardiovascular system circulates blood around the body, delivering oxygen and nutrients and collecting carbon dioxide and waste, while the respiratory system exchanges carbon dioxide for inhaled oxygen. The lymphatic system fights infection. The digestive system derives energy and nutrients for growth and repair from food, and, with the urinary system, eliminates waste; the urinary system also helps to regulate chemicals in the body. The reproductive system is concerned with producing offspring.

SYSTEMS OF THE HUMAN BODY

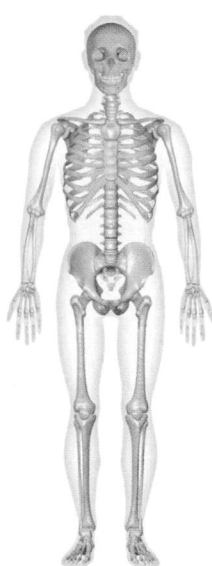

SKELETON

▷ SKELETON

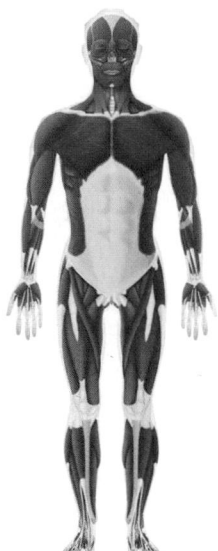

MUSCULAR SYSTEM

▷ MUSCULATURE

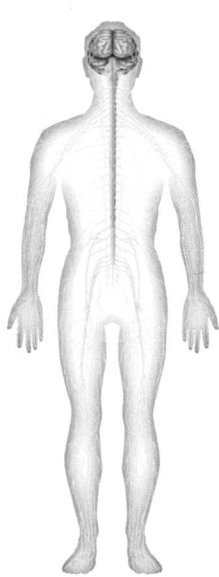

NERVOUS SYSTEM

▷ AUTONOMIC NERVOUS SYSTEM, NERVOUS SYSTEM, PERIPHERAL NERVOUS SYSTEM

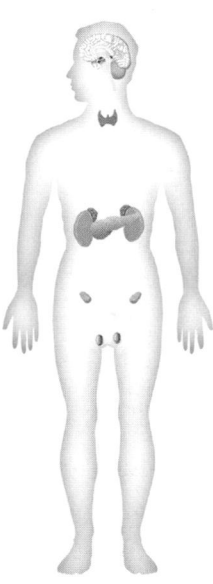

ENDOCRINE SYSTEM

▷ ENDOCRINE

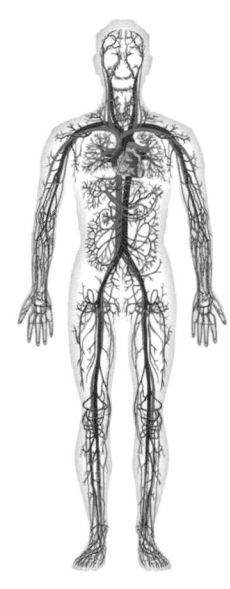

CARDIOVASCULAR SYSTEM

▷ CARDIOVASCULAR

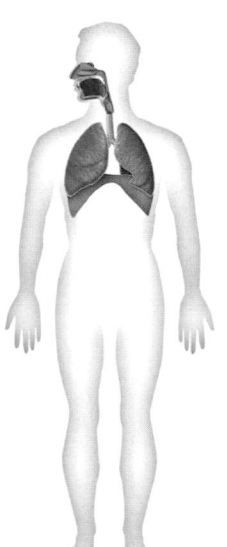

RESPIRATORY SYSTEM

▷ RESPIRATION

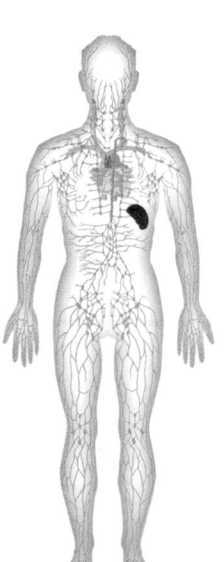

LYMPHATIC SYSTEM

▷ LYMPHATIC SYSTEM

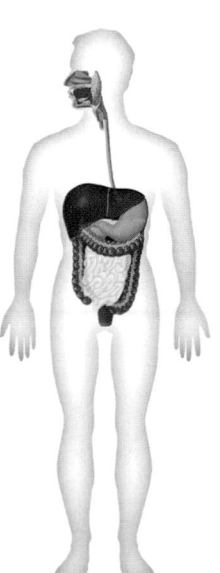

DIGESTIVE SYSTEM

▷ DIGESTION

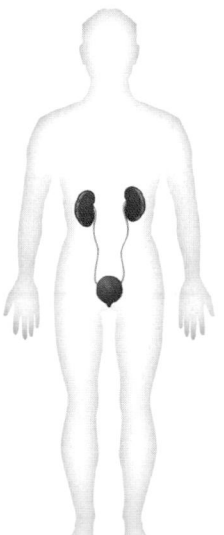

URINARY SYSTEM

▷ URINARY SYSTEM

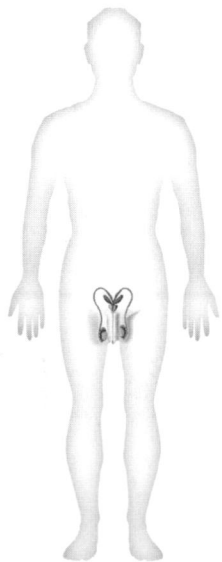

REPRODUCTIVE ORGANS

▷ REPRODUCTIVE ORGANS

bo·de·ga /bōdáygə/ *n.* **1** a grocery store in a Spanish-speaking neighborhood. **2** a wineshop.

bo·dhi·satt·va /bṓdisútvə/ *n.* in Mahayana Buddhism, one who is able to reach nirvana but delays doing so through compassion for suffering beings.

bod·ice /bódis/ *n.* **1** the part of a woman's dress above the waist. **2** a woman's vest, esp. a laced vest worn as an outer garment.

bod·i·less /bódeelis/ *adj.* **1** lacking a body. **2** insubstantial.

bod·i·ly /bód'lee/ *adj. & adv.* ● *adj.* of or concerning the body. ● *adv.* **1** as a whole (*threw them bodily*). **2** as a person.

bod·kin /bódkin/ *n.* **1** a blunt thick needle with a large eye. **2** a long pin for fastening hair.

bod·y /bódee/ *n. & v.* ● *n.* (*pl.* **-ies**) **1** ◄ the physical structure, including the bones, flesh, and organs, of a person or an animal. **2** the trunk apart from the head and the limbs. **3 a** the main or central part of a thing (*body of the car*). **b** the majority (*body of opinion*). **4 a** a group of persons regarded collectively (*governing body*). **b** (usu. foll. by *of*) a collection (*body of facts*). **5** a quantity (*body of water*). **6** a piece of matter (*heavenly body*). **7** *colloq.* a person. **8** a substantial quality of flavor, tone, etc. ● *v.tr.* (**-ies**, **-ied**) (usu. foll. by *forth*) give body or substance to. □□ **-bodied** *adj.* (in *comb.*) (*able-bodied*).

bod·y·build·ing /bódeebilding/ *n.* the practice of strengthening the body, esp. enlarging the muscles, by exercise.

bod·y·check /bódeechek/ *v.tr. Sports* obstruct or impede another player with one's own body.

bod·y clock *n.* a person's biological clock.

bod·y dou·ble *n.* a stand-in for a film actor during stunt or nude scenes.

bod·y·guard /bódeegaard/ *n.* a person or group of persons escorting and protecting another person.

bod·y lan·guage *n.* the process of communicating through conscious or unconscious gestures and poses.

bod·y mass in·dex *n.* (abbrev.: **BMI**) an approximate measure of whether someone is over- or underweight, calculated by dividing their weight in kilograms by the square of their height in meters.

bod·y o·dor *n.* the smell of the human body, esp. when unpleasant.

bod·y pol·i·tic *n.* the nation or government as a corporate body.

bod·y shop *n.* a workshop where repairs to the bodies of vehicles are carried out.

bod·y stock·ing *n.* a woman's undergarment which covers the torso.

bod·y·suit /bódeesōot/ *n.* a close-fitting one-piece stretch garment for women.

bod·y·surf /bódeesərf/ *v.intr.* surf without using a board.

bod·y·work /bódeewərk/ *n.* the outer shell of a vehicle.

Boer /bōr, bawr/ *n.* a South African of Dutch descent.

boeuf bour·gui·gnon /bə́rf báwginyoɴ/ *n.* a dish consisting of beef stewed in red wine.

bog /bog, bawg/ *n. & v.* ● *n.* **1** ▲ wet spongy ground. **2** a stretch of such ground. ● *v.tr.* (**bogged**, **bogging**) (foll. by *down*; usu. in *passive*) impede (*bogged down by difficulties*). □□ **bog·gy** *adj.* (**boggier**, **boggiest**). **bog·gi·ness** *n.*

bo·gey[1] /bṓgee/ *n.* (*pl.* **-eys**) *Golf* a score of one stroke more than par at any hole.

bo·gey[2] /bṓgee/ *n.* (also **bo·gy**) (*pl.* **-eys** or **-ies**) **1** an evil or mischievous spirit. **2** an awkward thing or circumstance.

bo·gey·man /bŏ̄geeman, bṓgee-, bŏ̄ogee-/ *n.* (also **bo·gy·man**, **boog·ey·man**, **boog·ie·man**) (*pl.* **-men**) a person (real or imaginary) causing fear or difficulty.

bog·gle /bógəl/ *v.intr. colloq.* **1** be startled or baffled (esp. *the mind boggles*). **2** (usu. foll. by *about, at*) hesitate; demur.

BOG

Bogs form where plants invade lakes and pools, and where waterlogged conditions prevent them from decomposing once they have died. As a result, plant remains build up to form peat. Once the peat has begun to accumulate, the plants that grow on its surface – such as *Sphagnum* mosses – steadily add to it as they die. In blanket bogs, the peat forms connected pockets. In raised bogs, it forms a large dome that can be over 0.5 mile (1 km) across.

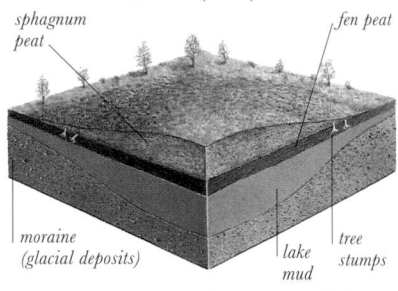

SECTION THROUGH A RAISED BOG

---

bo·gus /bṓgəs/ *adj.* sham; spurious.

bo·gy var. of BOGEY[2].

bo·gy·man var. of BOGEYMAN.

Bo·he·mi·an /bōhéemeeən/ *n. & adj.* ● *n.* **1** a native of Bohemia, a former kingdom in central Europe corresponding to part of the modern Czech Republic; Czech. **2** (also **bohemian**) a socially unconventional person. ● *adj.* **1** of or characteristic of Bohemia or its people. **2** socially unconventional.

boil[1] /boyl/ *v. & n.* ● *v.* **1** *intr.* **a** (of a liquid) start to bubble up and turn into vapor; reach a temperature at which this happens. **b** (of a vessel) contain boiling liquid (*the kettle is boiling*). **2 a** *tr.* bring (a liquid or vessel) to a temperature at which it boils. **b** *tr.* cook (food) by boiling. **c** *intr.* (of food) be cooked by boiling. **d** *tr.* subject to the heat of boiling water, e.g., to clean. **3** *intr.* **a** (of the sea, etc.) undulate or seethe like boiling water. **b** (of a person or feelings) be greatly agitated, esp. by anger. **c** *colloq.* (of a person or the weather) be very hot. ● *n.* the act or process of boiling; boiling point (*at a boil*). □ **boil down 1** reduce volume by boiling. **2** reduce to essentials. **3** (foll. by *to*) basically. **boil over 1** spill over in boiling. **2** lose one's temper.

boil[2] /boyl/ *n.* an inflamed pus-filled swelling caused by infection of a hair follicle, etc.

boil·er /bóylər/ *n.* **1** a fuel-burning apparatus for heating a hot water supply. **2** a tank for heating water to steam under pressure. ▷ STEAM ENGINE. **3** a fowl, etc., suitable for cooking only by boiling.

boil·er·plate /bóylərplayt/ *n.* **1** rolled steel plates for making boilers. **2** chiefly *N. Amer.* stereotyped or clichéd writing. **3** standardized pieces of text for use as clauses in contracts or as part of a computer program.

boil·ing /bóyling/ *adj.* (also **boil·ing hot**) *colloq.* very hot.

boil·ing point /bóyling poynt/ *n.* the temperature at which a liquid starts to boil.

bois·ter·ous /bóystərəs/ *adj.* **1** (of a person) rough; noisily exuberant. **2** (of the weather, etc.) stormy. □□ **bois·ter·ous·ly** *adv.* **bois·ter·ous·ness** *n.*

bok choy /bok chóy/ *n.* a Chinese vegetable resembling cabbage.

bo·las /bṓləs/ *n.* (as *sing.* or *pl.*) (esp. in S. America) a missile consisting of a number of balls connected by strong cord, which when thrown entangles the limbs of the quarry. ▷ GAUCHO

---

bold /bōld/ *adj.* **1** confidently assertive; adventurous. **2** impudent. **3** vivid; distinct (*bold colors*). **4** *Printing* (in full **boldface** or **-faced**) printed in a thick black typeface. □□ **bold·ly** *adv.* **bold·ness** *n.*

bole /bōl/ *n.* the stem or trunk of a tree.

bo·le·ro /bōláirō, bə-/ *n.* (*pl.* **-os**) **1** a Spanish dance or music in simple triple time. **2** a woman's short open jacket.

boll /bōl/ *n.* a rounded capsule containing seeds, esp. flax or cotton.

bol·lard /bólərd/ *n.* a short post on a wharf or ship for securing a rope.

boll wee·vil *n.* a small American or Mexican weevil, *Anthonomus grandis*, whose larvae destroy cotton bolls.

Bol·ly·wood /bóleewŏ̄od/ *n. colloq.* the Indian popular film industry, based in Bombay.

bo·lo·gna /bəlṓnee, -nyə/ *n.* a large smoked sausage made of beef, veal, pork, and other meats, and sold ready for eating.

bo·lo·ney var. of BALONEY.

Bol·she·vik /bólshəvik, ból-/ *n.* **1** *hist.* a member of the radical faction of the Russian Social Democratic party, which became the Communist party in 1918. **2** a Russian communist. **3** (in general use) any revolutionary socialist. □□ **Bol·she·vism** *n.*

Bol·shie /bólshee/ *n. sl.* a Bolshevik.

bol·ster[1] /bólstər/ *n. & v.* ● *n.* **1** a long thick pillow. **2** a pad or support, esp. in a machine. ● *v.tr.* (usu. foll. by *up*) **1** reinforce (*bolstered our morale*). **2** prop up. □□ **bol·ster·er** *n.*

bolt[1] /bōlt/ *n., v., & adv.* ● *n.* **1** a sliding bar and socket used to fasten a door, etc. **2** a large usu. metal pin with a head, used to hold things together. **3** a discharge of lightning. **4** a sudden escape for freedom. **5** an arrow for shooting from a crossbow. **6** a roll of fabric (orig. as a measure). ● *v.* **1** *tr.* fasten or lock with a bolt. **2** *tr.* (foll. by *in, out*) keep from leaving or entering by bolting a door. **3** *tr.* fasten together with bolts. **4** *intr.* dash suddenly away. **5** *tr.* gulp down (food) unchewed. **6** *intr.* (of a plant) run to seed. ● *adv.* (usu. in **bolt upright**) rigidly; stiffly. □ **a bolt from the blue** a complete surprise. □□ **bolt·er** *n.* (in sense 4 of *v.*).

bolt[2] /bōlt/ *v.tr.* sift (flour, etc.).

bomb /bom/ *n. & v.* ● *n.* **1 a** ◄ a container with explosive gas, etc., designed to explode on impact or by means of a mechanism, lit fuse, etc. **b** an ordinary object fitted with an explosive device (*letter bomb*). **2** (prec. by *the*) the atomic or hydrogen bomb. **3** *colloq.* a failure (esp. a theatrical one). ● *v.* **1** *tr.* drop bombs on. **2** *tr.* (foll. by *out*) drive out by using bombs. **3** *intr.* throw bombs. **4** *intr. sl.* fail badly. **5** *intr. colloq.* go very quickly.

bom·bard /bombáard/ *v.tr.* **1** attack with heavy guns or bombs. **2** (often foll. by *with*) subject to persistent questioning, etc. **3** *Physics* direct a stream of high-speed particles at (a substance). □□ **bom·bard·ment** *n.*

BOMB: GERMAN WORLD WAR II INCENDIARY DEVICES

bom·bar·dier /bómbərdéer/ *n.* **1** a member of a bomber crew responsible for sighting and releasing bombs. **2** *Brit.* a non-commissioned officer in the artillery.

bom·bast /bómbast/ *n.* pompous or extravagant language. □□ **bom·bas·tic** /-bástik/ *adj.* **bom·bas·ti·cal·ly** *adv.*

Bom·bay duck /bómbay dúk/ *n.* a dried fish, esp. bummalo, usu. eaten in Indian cuisine with curried dishes.

bombe /boɴb/ *n. Cookery* a dome-shaped dish or confection, freq. frozen.

B

B

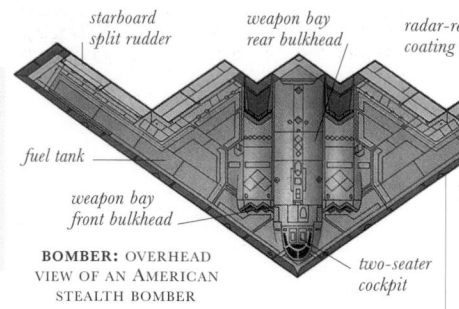

starboard split rudder • weapon bay rear bulkhead • radar-resistant coating • fuel tank • weapon bay front bulkhead • two-seater cockpit

BOMBER: OVERHEAD VIEW OF AN AMERICAN STEALTH BOMBER

bomb·er /bómər/ *n.* **1** ▲ an aircraft equipped to carry and drop bombs. ▷ FIGHTER. **2** a person using bombs, esp. illegally.

bomb·er jack·et *n.* a short esp. leather jacket tightly gathered at the waist and cuffs.

bomb·proof /bómpr̄oof/ *adj.* strong enough to resist the effects of blast from a bomb.

bomb·shell /bómshel/ *n.* **1** an overwhelming surprise or disappointment. **2** an artillery bomb. **3** *sl.* a very attractive woman (*blonde bombshell*).

bo·na fide /bónə fīd, fidee, bónə/ *adj. & adv.* ● *adj.* genuine; sincere. ● *adv.* genuinely; sincerely.

bo·na fides /bónaa féedes, fīdeez, bónə, (*esp.* for 2) bónə fīdz/ *n.* **1** esp. *Law* an honest intention; sincerity. **2** (as *pl.*) *colloq.* documentary evidence of acceptability.

bo·nan·za /bənánzə/ *n.* **1** a source of wealth or prosperity. **2** a large output (esp. of a mine). **3 a** prosperity; good luck. **b** a run of good luck.

bon·bon /bónbon/ *n.* a piece of candy, esp. with a chocolate or fondant coating.

bond /bond/ *n. & v.* ● *n.* **1 a** a thing that ties another down or together. **b** (usu. in *pl.*) a thing restraining bodily freedom (*broke his bonds*). **2** (often in *pl.*) **a** a uniting force (*sisterly bond*). **b** a restraint; a responsibility (*bonds of duty*). **3** a binding engagement (*his word is his bond*). **4** *Commerce* a debenture. **5** adhesiveness. **6** *Law* a deed by which a person is bound to make payment to another. ● *v.* **1** *tr.* **a** lay (bricks) overlapping. **b** bind together (resin with fibers, etc.). **2** *intr.* adhere; hold together. **3** *tr.* connect with a bond. **4** *tr.* place (goods) in bond. **5 a** *intr.* become emotionally attached. **b** *tr.* link by an emotional or psychological bond. □ **in bond** (of goods) stored until the importer pays the duty owing.

bond·age /bóndij/ *n.* **1** slavery. **2** subjection to constraint, obligation, etc. **3** sadomasochistic prac-

tices, including the use of physical restraints or mental enslavement.

bond·ed /bóndid/ *adj.* (of goods) placed in bond.

bond pa·per *n.* high-quality writing paper.

bonds·man /bóndzmən/ *n.* (*pl.* **-men**) **1** a slave. **2** a person in thrall to another.

bone /bōn/ *n. & v.* ● *n.* **1 ▼** any of the pieces of hard tissue making up the skeleton in vertebrates. ▷ SKELETON. **2** (in *pl.*) **a** the skeleton, esp. as remains after death. **b** the body, esp. as a seat of intuitive feeling (*felt it in my bones*). **3 a** the material of which bones consist. **b** a similar substance such as ivory. **4** a thing made of bone. **5** (in *pl.*) the essential part of a thing (*the bare bones*). **6** (in *pl.*) **a** dice. **b** flat bone or wood clappers held between the fingers and used as a simple rhythm instrument. **7** a strip of stiffening in a corset, etc. ● *v.tr.* **1** take out the bones from (meat or fish). **2** stiffen (a garment) with bone, etc. □ **bone up** (often foll. by *on*) *colloq.* study (a subject) intensively. **close to** (or **near**) **the bone 1** tactless to the point of offensiveness. **2** destitute; hard up. **have a bone to pick** (usu. foll. by *with*) have a cause for dispute (with another person). **make no bones about 1** admit or allow without fuss. **2** not hesitate or scruple. □□ **bone·less** *adj.*

bone chi·na *n.* fine china made of clay mixed with the ash from bones.

bone-dry *adj.* quite dry.

bone·head /bónhed/ *n. sl.* a stupid person. □□ **bone·head·ed** *adj.*

bone·meal /bónmeel/ *n.* crushed or ground bones used esp. as a fertilizer.

bone of con·ten·tion *n.* a source or ground of dispute.

bon·er /bónər/ *n. sl.* a stupid mistake.

bone·set·ter /bónsetər/ *n.* a person who sets broken or dislocated bones, esp. without being a qualified physician.

bon·fire /bónfīr/ *n.* a large open-air fire.

bong /bong, bawng/ *n.* a water pipe for smoking marijuana or the like.

bon·go /bónggō/ *n.* (*pl.* **-os** or **-oes**) either of a pair of small connected drums usu. held between the knees and played with the fingers.

bon·ho·mie /bónomee/ *n.* good-natured friendliness. □□ **bon·ho·mous** *adj.*

bo·ni·to /bənéétō/ *n.* (*pl.* **-os**) any of several fish similar to the tuna and striped like mackerel.

bonk /bongk/ *v. & n.* ● *v.* **1** *tr.* hit resoundingly. **2** *intr.* bang; bump. ● *n.* an instance of bonking (*a bonk on the head*).

bon·kers /bóngkərz/ *adj. sl.* crazy.

bon mot /bawn mō/ *n.* (*pl.* **bons mots** *pronunc.* same or /-mōz/) a witty saying.

bon·net /bónit/ *n.* **1 a** a woman's or child's hat tied under the chin and usu. with a brim framing the face. **b** a soft round brimless hat like a beret worn by men and boys in Scotland. **c** *colloq.* any hat. **2** *Brit.* a hinged cover over the engine of a motor vehicle; a hood. **3** the ceremonial feathered headdress of a Native American.

bon·sai /bónsī, -zī/ *n.* (*pl.* same) **1** the art of cultivating ornamental artificially dwarfed varieties of trees and shrubs. **2 ▶** a tree or shrub grown by this method.

bon·spiel /bónspeel/ *n.* a curling match (usu. between two clubs).

bo·nus /bónəs/ *n.* **1** an unsought or unexpected extra benefit. **2 a** a gratuity to employees beyond their normal pay. **b** an extra dividend or issue paid to shareholders.

bon vi·vant /báwn veeváaN/ *n.* (*pl.* **bon vivants** or **bons vivants** *pronunc.* same) a person indulging in good living.

bon vo·yage /báwn vwaayaázh/ *int.* an expression of good wishes to a departing traveler.

bon·y /bónee/ *adj.* (**bonier, boniest**) **1** (of a person) thin with prominent bones. **2** having many bones. **3** of or like bone. **4** (of a fish) having bones rather than cartilage. ▷ FISH. □□ **bon·i·ness** *n.*

bonze /bonz/ *n.* a Japanese or Chinese Buddhist monk.

boo /b̄oo/ *int., n., & v.* ● *int.* **1** an expression of disapproval or contempt. **2** a sound, made esp. to a child, intended to surprise. ● *n.* an utterance of *boo*, esp. as an expression of disapproval to a performer, etc. ● *v.* (**boos, booed**) **1** *intr.* utter a boo or boos. **2** *tr.* jeer at (a performer, etc.) by booing.

boob[1] /b̄oob/ *n.* a simpleton.

boob[2] /b̄oob/ *n. sl.* a woman's breast.

boob tube *n. sl.* (usu. prec. by *the*) television; one's television set.

boo·boo /b̄oob̄oo/ *n. sl.* **1** a mistake. **2** (esp. by or to a child) a minor injury.

boo·by /b̄oobee/ *n.* (*pl.* **-ies**) **1** a stupid person. **2** a small gannet of the genus *Sula*.

boo·by hatch *n. sl.* a mental hospital.

boo·by prize *n.* a prize given to the least successful competitor in a contest.

boo·by trap *n. & v.* ● *n.* **1** a trap intended as a practical joke, e.g., an object placed on top of a door ajar. **2** *Mil.* an apparently harmless explosive device intended to kill or injure anyone touching it. ● *v.tr.* (**booby-trap**) (**-trapped, -trapping**) place a booby trap or traps in or on.

boo·dle /b̄ood'l/ *n. sl.* money, esp. when gained or used dishonestly.

boog·ey·man var. of BOGEYMAN.

boog·ie /b̄oogee/ *v. & n.* ● *v.intr.* (**boogies, boogied, boogying**) *sl.* **1** dance to rock music. **2** leave, esp. quickly. ● *n.* **1** = BOOGIE-WOOGIE. **2** *sl.* a dance to rock music.

boog·ie·man var. of BOGEYMAN.

boog·ie-woog·ie /b̄oogeew̄oogee, b̄oogeew̄oogee/ *n.* a style of playing blues or jazz on the piano, marked by a persistent bass rhythm.

book /b̄ook/ *n. & v.* ● *n.* **1 a ▲** a written or printed work consisting of pages fixed together along one side and bound in covers. **b** a literary composition intended for publication (*is working on her book*). **2** a bound set of blank sheets for writing on or keeping records in. **3** a set of tickets, stamps, matches, checks, samples of cloth, etc., bound up together. **4** (in *pl.*) a set of records or accounts. **5** a main division of a literary work, or of the Bible. **6** a libretto, script of a play, etc. **7** *colloq.* a magazine. **8** a telephone directory. **9** a record of bets made and money paid out at a racetrack by a bookmaker. ● *v.* **1** *tr.* **a** engage (a seat, etc.) in advance; make a reservation for. **b** engage (a guest, etc.) for some occasion. **2** *tr.* **a** take the personal details of (esp. a criminal offender). **b** enter in a book or list. **3** *tr.* issue an airline, bus, etc., ticket to. **4** *intr.* make a reservation (*no need to book*). □ **bring to book** call to account. **go by the book** proceed according to the rules. **the good Book** the Bible. **in a person's bad** (or **good**) **books** in disfavor (or favor) with a person. **in my book** in my opinion. **make book** take bets and pay out winnings on a race, game, etc. **one for the books** an event worthy of being recorded. **on the books** contained in a list of members, etc. **take a leaf out of a person's book** imitate a person. **throw the book at** *colloq.* punish to the utmost. □□ **book·ing** *n.*

book·bind·er /b̄ookbīndər/ *n.* a person who binds books professionally. □□ **book·bind·ing** *n.*

BONE

Each layer of a bone is composed of specialized cells, protein fibers, and minerals. The medullary cavity contains bone marrow and is enclosed in a spongy cancellous layer. This is surrounded by hard cortical bone (made up of osteons), with an outer covering of periostium. This combination of layers makes bones strong and light.

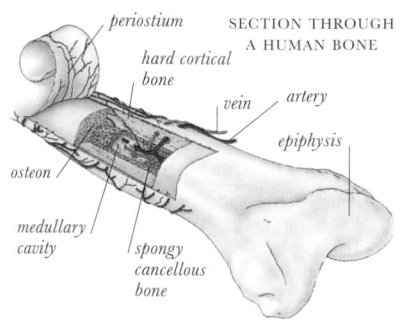

SECTION THROUGH A HUMAN BONE

periostium • hard cortical bone • vein • artery • epiphysis • osteon • medullary cavity • spongy cancellous bone

BONSAI: ENGLISH OAK (*Quercus robur*)

BOOK

The first books were written on papyrus by the ancient Egyptians. Religious scribes copied manuscripts by hand until book production was revolutionized by Johannes Gutenburg in 1455. He created a press with re-usable metal type, enabling the production of multiple copies. Books are now created using computers, and printing and binding are mechanized.

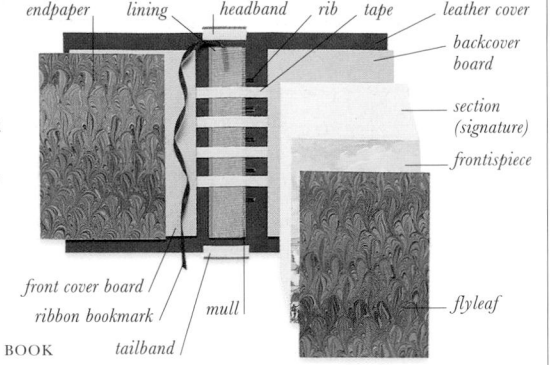

PARTS OF A LEATHER-BOUND BOOK

endpaper · lining · headband · rib · tape · leather cover · backcover board · section (signature) · frontispiece · front cover board · ribbon bookmark · mull · tailband · flyleaf

book·case /bŏŏk-kays/ n. a set of shelves for books in the form of a cabinet.

booked adj. (also **booked up**) with all places reserved.

book·end /bŏŏkend/ n. a usu. ornamental prop used to keep a row of books upright.

book·ie /bŏŏkee/ n. colloq. = BOOKMAKER.

book·ing /bŏŏking/ n. the act or an instance of booking or reserving a seat, a room in a hotel, etc.; a reservation (see BOOK v. 1).

book·ish /bŏŏkish/ adj. **1** studious; fond of reading. **2** acquiring knowledge from books. **3** (of language, etc.) literary. □□ **book·ish·ly** adv. **book·ish·ness** n.

book·keep·er /bŏŏk-keepər/ n. a person who keeps accounts for a business, etc. □□ **book·keep·ing** n.

book learn·ing n. theory, as opposed to practical knowledge.

book·let /bŏŏklit/ n. a small book, usu. with paper covers.

book·mak·er /bŏŏkmaykər/ n. a person who takes bets, calculates odds, and pays out winnings. □□ **book·mak·ing** n.

book·man /bŏŏkmən/ n. (pl. **-men**) a literary person, esp. one involved in the business of books.

book·mark /bŏŏkmaark/ n. a strip of card, etc., used to mark one's place in a book.

book·plate /bŏŏkplayt/ n. a decorative label stuck in the front of a book bearing the owner's name.

book·sell·er /bŏŏkselər/ n. a dealer in books.

book·shop /bŏŏkshop/ n. esp. Brit. = BOOKSTORE.

book·store /bŏŏkstawr/ n. a store where books are sold.

book val·ue n. the value of a commodity as entered in a book of accounts (opp. market value).

book·work /bŏŏkwərk/ n. the study of books (as opposed to practical work).

book·worm /bŏŏkwərm/ n. **1** colloq. a person devoted to reading. **2** the larva of a moth or beetle which feeds on the paper and glue used in books.

Bool·e·an /bŏŏleeən/ adj. denoting a system of algebraic notation to represent logical propositions.

Bool·e·an log·ic n. the use of the logical operators 'and,' 'or,' and 'not' in retrieving information from a computer database.

boom[1] /bŏŏm/ n. & v. ● n. a deep resonant sound. ● v.intr. make or speak with a boom.

boom[2] /bŏŏm/ n. & v. ● n. a period of prosperity or sudden activity in commerce. ● v.intr. be suddenly prosperous or successful.

boom[3] /bŏŏm/ n. **1** Naut. a pivoted spar to which the foot of a sail is attached, allowing the angle of the sail to be changed. ▷ DINGHY, SAILBOAT. **2** a long pole over a movie or television stage set, carrying microphones, cameras, etc. **3** a floating barrier across the mouth of a harbor or river.

boom box n. sl. a portable radio, often with a cassette and/or CD player.

boo·mer·ang /bŏŏmərang/ n. & v. ● n. a curved flat missile used by Australian Aboriginals to kill prey, and often able to return to the thrower. ● v.intr. **1** act as a boomerang. **2** (of a plan or action) backfire.

boom town n. a town undergoing sudden growth due to a boom.

boon[1] /bŏŏn/ n. an advantage; a blessing.

boon[2] /bŏŏn/ adj. intimate; favorite (usu. boon companion).

boon·docks /bŏŏndoks/ n.pl. sl. rough, remote, or isolated country.

boon·dog·gle /bŏŏndogəl, -daw-/ n. **1** work or activity that is wasteful or pointless but gives the appearance of having value. **2** a public project of questionable merit that typically involves political patronage and graft.

boon·ies /bŏŏneez/ n.pl. (prec. by the) sl. = BOONDOCKS.

boor /bŏŏr/ n. a rude, clumsy person. □□ **boor·ish** adj. **boor·ish·ly** adv. **boor·ish·ness** n.

boost /bŏŏst/ v. & n. ● v.tr. **1 a** promote (a person, scheme, commodity, etc.) by praise or advertizing; increase or assist (boosted his spirits; boost sales). **b** push from below (boosted me up into the tree). **2 a** raise the voltage of (an electric circuit, etc.). **b** amplify (a radio signal). ● n. an act, process, or result of boosting; a push

boost·er /bŏŏstər/ n. **1** a device for increasing electrical power or voltage. **2** an auxiliary engine or rocket used to give initial acceleration. ▷ SPACECRAFT. **3** Med. a dose of an immunizing agent increasing or renewing the effect of an earlier one.

boost·er ca·bles n.pl. = JUMPER CABLES.

boot[1] /bŏŏt/ n. & v. ● n. **1** an outer covering for the foot, reaching above the ankle. **2** colloq. a firm kick. **3** (prec. by the) colloq. dismissal (gave them the boot). **4** Mil. a navy or marine recruit. **5** (also **Denver Boot**) a device for immobilizing an illegally parked car. ● v.tr. **1** kick, esp. hard. **2** (often foll. by out) dismiss (a person) forcefully. **3** (usu. foll. by up) put (a computer) in a state of readiness (cf. BOOTSTRAP 2). □□ **boot·ed** adj.

boot[2] /bŏŏt/ n. □ **to boot** as well; to the good.

boot·black /bŏŏtblak/ n. a person who polishes boots and shoes.

boot camp n. Mil. a camp for training navy or marine recruits.

boot-cut adj. (of trousers) flared very slightly below the knee, so as to be worn comfortably over boots.

boot·ee /bŏŏtee/ n. (also **boot·ie**) **1** a soft shoe worn by a baby. **2** a woman's short boot.

booth /bŏŏth/ n. (pl. **booths** /bŏŏthz, bŏŏths/) **1** a small temporary roofed structure used esp. for the sale or display of goods at a market, fair, etc. **2** a compartment for various purposes, e.g., telephoning or voting. **3** a set of a table and benches in a restaurant or bar.

boot·ie var. of BOOTEE.

boot·lace /bŏŏtlays/ n. a cord or leather thong for lacing boots.

boot·leg /bŏŏtleg/ adj., v., & n. ● adj. (esp. of liquor) smuggled; illicitly sold. ● v.tr. (**-legged, -legging**) make, distribute, or smuggle (illicit goods, esp. alcohol, computer software, etc.). ● n. **1** illicitly made or sold liquor. **2** an illicitly made recording. □□ **boot·leg·ger** n.

boot·less /bŏŏtlis/ adj. unavailing; useless.

boot·lick·er /bŏŏtlikər/ n. colloq. a person who behaves obsequiously.

boot·strap /bŏŏtstrap/ n. **1** a loop at the back of a boot used to pull it on. **2** Computing a technique of loading a program into a computer by means of a few initial instructions which enable the introduction of the rest of the program from an input device.

boo·ty /bŏŏtee/ n. **1** plunder gained esp. in war or by piracy. **2** colloq. something gained or won.

booze /bŏŏz/ n. & v. colloq. ● n. **1** alcohol, esp. hard liquor. **2** the drinking of this (on the booze). ● v.intr. drink alcohol, esp. excessively or habitually.

booz·er /bŏŏzər/ n. colloq. a person who drinks alcohol, esp. to excess.

booz·y /bŏŏzee/ adj. (**boozier, booziest**) colloq. intoxicated; addicted to drink. □□ **booz·i·ly** adv. **booz·i·ness** n.

bop[1] /bop/ n. = BEBOP.

bop[2] /bop/ v. & n. colloq. ● v.tr. (**bopped, bopping**) hit; punch lightly. ● n. a light blow or hit.

bo·ra /báwrə/ n. a strong cold dry NE wind blowing in the upper Adriatic.

bo·rac·ic /bərásik/ adj. of borax; containing boron.

bor·age /báwrij, bór-/ n. ◀ any plant of the genus Borago, esp. Borago officinalis, native to Europe, with bright blue flowers and leaves used as flavoring. ▷ HERB

BORAGE
(Borago officinalis)

bo·rate /báwrayt/ n. a salt or ester of boric acid.

bo·rax /báwraks/ n. ▶ **1** the mineral salt sodium borate. **2** the purified form of this salt, used in making glass and china, and as an antiseptic.

BORAX

Bor·deaux /bawdó/ n. a wine from Bordeaux, a district of SW France.

bor·del·lo /bawrdélō/ n. (pl. **-os**) a brothel.

bor·der /báwrdər/ n. & v. ● n. **1** the edge or boundary of anything, or the part near it. **2 a** the line separating two political or geographical areas, esp. countries. **b** the district on each side of this. **3** a distinct edging around anything, esp. for strength or decoration. **4** a long narrow bed of flowers or shrubs. ● v. **1** be a border to. **2** provide with a border. **3** intr. (usu. foll. by on, upon) **a** adjoin; come close to being. **b** approximate; resemble.

Bor·der col·lie n. a common working sheepdog of British origin.

bord·er·er /báwrdərər/ n. a person who lives near a border.

bord·er·land /báwrdərland/ n. **1** the district near a border. **2** an intermediate condition between two extremes. **3** an area for debate.

bord·er·line /báwrdərlīn/ n. & adj. ● n. **1** the line dividing two (often extreme) conditions. **2** a line marking a boundary. ● adj. **1** on the borderline. **2** verging on an extreme condition; only just acceptable.

Bord·er ter·ri·er n. a small terrier of a breed with rough hair.

B

B

bore[1] /bawr/ *v. & n.* ● *v.* **1** *tr.* make a hole in, esp. with a revolving tool. **2** *tr.* hollow out (a tube, etc.). **3** *tr.* make (a hole) by boring or excavation. **4** *intr.* drill a well, mine, etc. ● *n.* **1** the hollow of a firearm barrel or of a cylinder in an internal-combustion engine. **2** the caliber of this. **3** = BOREHOLE.

bore[2] /bawr/ *n. & v.* ● *n.* a tiresome or dull person or thing. ● *v.tr.* weary by tedious talk or dullness. □□ **bore·dom** *n.*

bore[3] /bawr/ *n.* a high tidal wave rushing up a narrow estuary.

bore[4] *past* of BEAR[1].

bo·re·al /báwreeəl/ *adj.* of the north or northern regions.

bore·hole /báwrhōl/ *n.* a deep narrow hole, esp. one made in the earth to find water, oil, etc.

bor·er /báwrər/ *n.* **1** any of several worms, mollusks, insects, or insect larvae which bore into wood, other plant material, or rock. **2** a tool for boring.

bo·ric /báwrik/ *adj.* of or containing boron.

bo·ric ac·id *n.* an acid derived from borax, used as a mild antiseptic and in the manufacture of heat-resistant glass and enamels.

bor·ing /báwring/ *adj.* that makes one bored; dull. □□ **bor·ing·ly** *adv.* **bor·ing·ness** *n.*

bor·lot·ti bean /bawlótee been/ *n.* a type of kidney bean with a pink speckled skin that turns brown when cooked.

born /bawrn/ *adj.* **1** existing as a result of birth. **2 a** being such or likely to become such by natural ability or quality (*a born leader*). **b** (usu. foll. by *to* + infin.) having a specified destiny (*born lucky*). **3** (in *comb.*) of a certain status by birth (*French-born*). □ **in all one's born days** *colloq.* in one's life so far. **not born yesterday** *colloq.* not stupid; shrewd.

born-a·gain *attrib.adj.* converted (esp. to fundamentalist Christianity).

borne /bawrn/ **1** *past part.* of BEAR[1]. **2** (in *comb.*) carried or transported by (*airborne*).

bo·ron /báwron/ *n. Chem.* a nonmetallic brown amorphous element extracted from borax and boric acid and mainly used for hardening steel. ¶ Symb.: **B**.

bo·ro·si·li·cate /báwrósílikit, -kayt/ *n.* any of many substances containing boron, silicon, and oxygen generally used in glazes and enamels and in the production of glass.

bor·ough /bárō, búrō/ *n.* **1** an incorporated municipality in certain states. **2** each of five political divisions of New York City. **3** (in Alaska) a county equivalent.

bor·row /bórō, báwrō/ *v.* **1 a** *tr.* acquire temporarily with the promise or intention of returning. **b** *intr.* obtain money in this way. **2** *tr.* use (an idea, etc.) originated by another. □□ **bor·row·er** *n.* **bor·row·ing** *n.*

bor·rowed time *n.* an unexpected extension.

borscht /bawrsht/ *n.* (also **borsch** /bawrsh, bawrshch/) a highly seasoned Russian or Polish soup of esp. beets and cabbage and served with sour cream.

bort /bawrt/ *n.* (also **boart**) **1** an inferior or malformed diamond, used for cutting. **2** fragments of diamonds used in cutting or abrasion.

bor·zoi /báwrzoy/ *n.* ▼ a large Russian wolfhound of a breed with a narrow head and silky, usu. white, coat.

BORZOI

bosh /bosh/ *n. & int. sl.* nonsense; foolish talk.

bosk·y /bóskee/ *adj.* (**boskier, boskiest**) wooded; bushy.

bo's'n var. of BOATSWAIN.

bos·om /bŏŏzəm/ *n.* **1 a** a person's breast or chest, esp. a woman's. **b** *colloq.* each of a woman's breasts. **c** the enclosure formed by a person's breast and arms. **2** an emotional center.

bos·om friend *n.* a very close or intimate friend.

bos·om·y /bŏŏzəmee/ *adj.* (of a woman) having large breasts.

bo·son /bózon/ *n. Physics* a subatomic particle, such as a photon, which has a spin of zero or a whole number.

boss[1] /baws, bos/ *n. & v.* ● *n.* **1** a person in charge. **2** a person who controls or dominates a political organization. ● *v.tr.* **1** (usu. foll. by *around*) give constant peremptory orders to. **2** be the master or manager of. □□ **boss·y** *adj.* (**boss·i·er, boss·i·est**) *colloq.* **boss·i·ly** *adv.* **boss·i·ness** *n.*

boss[2] /baws, bos/ *n.* **1** a round knob or other protuberance, esp. in ornamental work. ▷ SHIELD. **2** *Archit.* ► a piece of ornamental carving, etc., covering the point where the ribs in a vault or ceiling cross.

bos·sa no·va /bósə nóvə, báwsə/ *n.* **1** a dance like the samba, originating in Brazil. **2** a piece of music for this or in its rhythm.

bo·sun (also **bo'sun**) var. of BOATSWAIN.

bot /bot/ *n.* (also **bott**) the larva of a botfly.

bot·a·ny /bót'nee/ *n.* **1** the study of plants. **2** the plant life of a particular area or time. □□ **bo·tan·ic** /bətánik/ *adj.* **bo·tan·i·cal** *adj.* **bo·tan·i·cal·ly** *adv.* **bot·a·nist** /bót'nist/ *n.*

botch /boch/ *v. & n.* ● *v.tr.* **1** bungle. **2** repair clumsily. ● *n.* bungled or spoiled work (*made a botch of it*).

bot·fly /bótflī/ *n.* (*pl.* **-flies**) any dipterous fly of the genus *Oestrus*, with a stout hairy body.

both /bōth/ *adj., pron., & adv.* ● *adj. & pron.* the two; not only one (*both boys; the boys are both here*). ¶ Widely used with *of*, esp. when followed by a pronoun (e.g., *both of us*) or a noun implying separate rather than collective consideration, e.g., *both of the boys* suggests *each boy* rather than the two together. ● *adv.* with equal truth in two cases (*both the boy and his sister are here*).

both·er /bóthər/ *v., n., & int.* ● *v.* **1** *tr.* **a** worry; disturb. **b** *refl.* be concerned. **2** *intr.* **a** (often foll. by *to* + infin.) worry or trouble oneself (*don't bother about that*). **b** (foll. by *with*) be concerned. ● *n.* **1 a** a person or thing that causes worry. **b** a minor nuisance. **2** trouble; fuss. ● *int.* expressing annoyance or impatience. □ **cannot be bothered** will not make the effort needed.

both·er·a·tion /bótheráyshən/ *n. & int. colloq.* = BOTHER *n., int.*

both·er·some /bóthərsəm/ *adj.* troublesome.

Bo·tox /bótoks/ *n. Trademark* a drug prepared from botulin, used medically to treat certain muscular conditions and cosmetically to remove wrinkles by temporarily paralyzing facial muscles.

bo tree /bótree/ *n.* ► the Indian fig tree, *Ficus religiosa*, regarded as sacred by Buddhists.

bott var. of BOT.

bot·tle /bót'l/ *n. & v.* ● *n.* **1** a container, usu. of glass or plastic and with a narrow neck, for storing liquid. **2** the amount that will fill a bottle. **3** a container used in feeding a baby (esp. formula or milk). **4** = HOT-WATER BOTTLE. ● *v.tr.* **1** put into bottles or jars. **2** (foll. by *up*) **a** conceal or restrain for a time

BOSS COVERING
RIBS IN A CEILING

BO TREE
(*Ficus religiosa*)

(esp. a feeling). **b** keep (an enemy force, etc.) contained or entrapped. □ **hit the bottle** *sl.* drink heavily. **on the bottle** *sl.* drinking (alcohol) heavily.

bot·tle-brush /bót'lbrush/ *n.* **1** a cylindrical brush for cleaning inside bottles. **2** any of various plants with a flower of this shape.

bot·tle-feed *v.tr.* (*past* and *past part.* **-fed**) feed (a baby) with milk, formula, etc., by means of a bottle.

bot·tle·neck /bót'lnek/ *n.* **1** a point at which the flow of traffic, production, etc., is constricted. **2** a narrow place causing constriction.

bot·tle-nosed dol·phin /bót'l-nōzd/ *n.* a dolphin, *Tursiops truncatus*, with a bottle-shaped snout. ▷ DOLPHIN

bot·tom /bótəm/ *n., adj., & v.* ● *n.* **1 a** the lowest point or part (*bottom of the stairs*). **b** the part on which a thing rests (*bottom of a frying pan*). **c** the underneath part (*scraped the bottom of the car*). **d** the farthest or innermost part (*bottom of the yard*). **2** *colloq.* **a** the buttocks. **b** the seat of a chair, etc. **3 a** the less important or successful end of a class, etc. (*at the bottom of the list of requirements*). **b** a person occupying this place (*he's always the bottom of the class*). **c** *Baseball* the second half of an inning. **4** the ground under the water of a lake, etc. (*swam until she touched the bottom*). **5** the basis (*he's at the bottom of it*). **6** the essential character. **7** staying power; endurance. ● *adj.* **1** lowest (*bottom button*). **2** last (*got the bottom score*). ● *v.* **1** *tr.* put a bottom on (a chair, pot, etc.). **2** *intr.* (of a ship) reach or touch the bottom. **3** *tr.* work out. **4** *tr.* (usu. foll. by *on*) base (an argument, etc.) (*reasoning bottomed on logic*). **5** *tr.* touch the bottom or lowest point of. □ **at bottom** basically; essentially. **bet one's bottom dollar** *sl.* stake everything. **bottom falls out** collapse occurs. **bottom out** reach the lowest level. **bottoms up!** a call to drain one's glass. **get to the bottom of** fully investigate and explain. □□ **bot·tom·most** /bótəm-mōst/ *adj.*

bot·tom feed·er *n.* **1** any marine creature that lives on the seabed and feeds by scavenging. **2** *N. Amer. colloq.* a member of a group of very low social status who survives by whatever means possible.

bot·tom·less /bótəmlis/ *adj.* **1** without a bottom. **2** (of a supply, etc.) inexhaustible.

bot·tom line *n. colloq.* the underlying or ultimate truth; the ultimate, esp. financial, criterion.

bot·u·lism /bóchəlizəm/ *n.* poisoning caused by a toxin produced by the bacillus *Clostridium botulinum* growing in spoiled food.

bou·clé /bŏŏkláy/ *n.* **1** a looped or curled yarn (esp. wool). **2** a fabric made of this.

bou·doir /bŏŏdwaar/ *n.* a woman's private room or bedroom.

bouf·fant /bŏŏfáant/ *adj.* (of a dress, hair, etc.) puffed out.

bou·gain·vil·le·a /bóŏgənvílyə, -véeə/ *n.* (also **bou·gain·vil·la·ea**) any tropical widely cultivated plant of the genus *Bougainvillaea*, with large colored bracts.

bough /bow/ *n.* a branch of a tree.

bought *past* and *past part.* of BUY.

bou·gie /bŏŏzhee/ *n.* **1** *Med.* a thin flexible surgical instrument for exploring, dilating, etc., the passages of the body. **2** a wax candle.

bouil·la·baisse /bŏŏlyəbés, bŏŏyəbáys/ *n. Cookery* a rich, spicy fish stew, orig. from Provence.

bouil·lon /bŏŏlyən, -yon, bŏŏyón/ *n.* a clear soup; broth.

boul·der /bóldər/ *n.* a large stone worn smooth by erosion.

boul·der clay *n. Geol.* a mixture of boulders, etc., formed by deposition from massive bodies of melting ice, to give distinctive glacial formations.

B

boule¹ /bool/ *n.* (also **boules** *pronunc.* same) ► a French form of lawn bowling, played on rough ground with usu. metal balls.

bou·le² /bóolee/ *n.* a legislative body of an ancient Greek city or of modern Greece.

boule³ var. of BUHL.

boules var. of BOULE¹.

boul·e·vard /bóoləvaard/ *n.* **1** a broad tree-lined avenue. **2** a broad main road.

boulle var. of BUHL.

boult var. of BOLT².

bounce /bowns/ *v. & n.* ● *v.* **1 a** *intr.* (of a ball, etc.) rebound. **b** *tr.* cause to rebound. **c** *tr. & intr.* bounce repeatedly. **2** *intr. sl.* (of a check) be returned by a bank when there are insufficient funds to meet it. **3** *intr.* **a** (foll. by *about, up*) (of a person, dog, etc.) jump or spring energetically. **b** (foll. by *in, out*, etc.) rush angrily, enthusiastically, etc. (*bounced out in a temper*). ● *n.* **1 a** a rebound. **b** the power of rebounding. **2** *colloq.* **a** self-confidence (*has a lot of bounce*). **b** liveliness. □ **bounce back** regain one's good health, spirits, etc. □□ **bounc·y** *adj.* (**bounc·i·er, bounc·i·est**). **bounc·i·ly** *adv.* **bounc·i·ness** *n.*

bounc·er /bównsər/ *n. sl.* a person employed to eject troublemakers from a nightclub, etc.

bounc·ing /bównsing/ *adj.* **1** (esp. of a baby) big and healthy. **2** boisterous.

bound¹ /bownd/ *v. & n.* ● *v.intr.* **1 a** spring; leap (*bounded out of bed*). **b** move with leaping strides (*the dog bounded across the lawn*). **2** (of a ball, etc.) recoil; bounce. ● *n.* **1** a leap. **2** a bounce. □ **by leaps and bounds** see LEAP.

bound² /bownd/ *n. & v.* ● *n.* (usu. in *pl.*) **1** a restriction (*beyond the bounds of possibility*). **2** a boundary. ● *v.tr.* **1** (esp. in *passive*; foll. by *by*) limit (*views bounded by prejudice*). **2** be the boundary of. □ **out of bounds 1** outside designated limits, a restricted area, etc. **2** beyond what is acceptable.

bound³ /bownd/ *adj.* **1** (usu. foll. by *for*) ready to start or having started (*bound for stardom*). **2** (in *comb.*) moving in a specified direction (*northbound*).

bound⁴ /bownd/ *past* and *past part.* of BIND. □ **bound to** certain to (*he's bound to come*).

bound·a·ry /bówndəree, -dree/ *n.* (*pl.* **-ies**) a line marking the limits of an area, territory, etc.

bound·en du·ty /bówndən/ *n.* solemn responsibility.

bound·less /bówndlis/ *adj.* unlimited; immense (*boundless enthusiasm*). □□ **bound·less·ly** *adv.* **bound·less·ness** *n.*

boun·te·ous /bównteeəs/ *adj. poet.* = BOUNTIFUL¹. □□ **boun·te·ous·ly** *adv.* **boun·te·ous·ness** *n.*

boun·ti·ful /bówntifool/ *adj.* **1** generous; liberal. **2** ample. □□ **boun·ti·ful·ly** *adv.*

boun·ty /bówntee/ *n.* (*pl.* **-ies**) **1** liberality. **2** a gift or reward, made usu. by a government.

boun·ty hunt·er *n.* a person who pursues a criminal or seeks an achievement for the sake of the reward.

bou·quet /bookáy, bō-/ *n.* **1** a bunch of flowers esp. for carrying at a wedding, or other ceremony. **2** the scent of wine, etc. **3** a favorable comment; a compliment.

bour·bon /bárbən/ *n.* whiskey distilled from corn and rye.

bour·don /bóordən/ *n. Mus.* **1** a low-pitched stop in an organ, etc. **2** the lowest bell in a peal of bells. **3** the drone pipe of a bagpipe.

bour·geois /boorzhwáa/ *adj. & n.* often *derog.* ● *adj.* **1 a** conventionally middle class. **b** unimaginative. **c** selfishly materialistic. **2** upholding the interests of the capitalist class. ● *n.* (*pl.* same) a bourgeois person. □□ **bour·geoi·sie** *n.*

bourn¹ /bawrn, bōorn/ *n.* (also **bourne**) a small stream.

bourn² /bawrn, bōorn/ *n.* (also **bourne**) *archaic* **1** a goal; a destination. **2** a limit.

bour·rée /booráy/ *n.* **1** a lively French dance like a gavotte. **2** the music for this dance.

bourse /boors/ *n.* **1** a stock exchange, esp. on the European continent. **2** a money market.

bou·stro·phe·don /boostrəfeéd'n, bów-/ *adj. & adv.* (of written words) from right to left and from left to right in alternate lines.

bout /bowt/ *n.* (often foll. by *of*) **1 a** a limited period (of intensive work or exercise). **b** a drinking session. **c** a period or spell (of illness) (*a bout of flu*). **2 a** a wrestling or boxing match. **b** a trial or contest of strength.

bou·tique /bootéek/ *n.* a small shop or department of a store, esp. one selling fashionable clothes or accessories.

bou·ton·niere /bootəneér, -tənyáir/ *n.* (also **bou·tonnière**) a flower or spray of flowers worn in a buttonhole.

bou·zou·ki /boozóokee/ *n.* a Greek form of mandolin.

bo·vate /bóvayt/ *n. hist.* a measure of land, as much as one ox could plow in a year, varying from 10 to 18 acres.

bo·vine /bóvīn, -veen/ *adj.* **1** of or relating to cattle. **2** stupid. □□ **bo·vine·ly** *adv.*

bow¹ /bō/ *n. & v.* ● *n.* **1 a** a slipknot with a double loop. **b** a ribbon, shoelace, etc., tied with this. **c** a decoration in the form of a bow. **2** a device for shooting arrows with a taut string joining the ends of a curved piece of wood, etc. ▷ ARCHERY. **3** a rod with horsehair stretched along its length, used for playing the violin, cello, etc. ▷ STRINGED. **4** a shallow curve or bend. ● *v.tr.* (also *absol.*) use a bow on (a violin, etc.).

bow² /bow/ *v. & n.* ● *v.* **1** *intr.* incline the head or trunk, in acknowledgment of applause, etc. **2** *intr.* submit (*bowed to the inevitable*). **3** *tr.* cause to incline or submit (*bowed his head; bowed his will to hers*). **4** *tr.* (foll. by *in, out*) usher or escort obsequiously. ● *n.* an inclining of the head or body. □ **bow down 1** bend or kneel in submission or reverence. **2** (usu. in *passive*) crush (*was bowed down by care*). **bow out 1** make one's exit (esp. formally). **2** retreat; withdraw; retire gracefully. **take a bow** acknowledge applause.

bow³ /bow/ *n. Naut.* the forward end of a boat or ship. ▷ MAN-OF-WAR. □ **on the bow** within 45° of the point directly ahead. **a shot across the bows** a warning.

bowd·ler·ize /bówdlərīz/ *v.tr.* expurgate (a book, etc.). □□ **bowd·ler·ism** *n.* **bowd·ler·i·za·tion** /-rizáyshən/ *n.*

bow·el /bówəl/ *n.* **1** the intestine. **2** (in *pl.*) the depths (*the bowels of the earth*).

bow·el move·ment *n.* **1** discharge from the bowels. **2** the feces discharged.

bow·er¹ /bówər/ *n. & v.* ● *n.* **1** a secluded place enclosed by foliage; an arbor. **2** *poet.* a boudoir. ● *v.tr. poet.* embower.

bow·er² /bówər/ *n.* (in full **bower anchor**) either of two anchors carried at a ship's bow.

bow·er·bird /bówərbərd/ *n.* any of various birds of the Ptilonorhynchidae family, native to Australia and New Guinea, the males of which construct elaborate bowers of feathers, grasses, shells, etc., during courtship.

bow·er·y /bówəree, bówree/ *n.* (also **Bowery**) (*pl.* **-ies**) a district known as a neighborhood of drunks and derelicts.

bow·head /bóhed/ *n.* an Arctic whale, *Balaena mysticetus.*

bow·ie /bóoee, bó-/ *n.* (in full **bowie knife**) a long knife with a blade double-edged at the point.

bowl¹ /bōl/ *n.* **1 a** a usu. round deep basin used for food or liquid. **b** the quantity a bowl holds. **c** the contents of a bowl. **2 a** any deep-sided container shaped like a bowl (*toilet bowl*). **b** the bowl-shaped part of a tobacco pipe, spoon, balance, etc. **3** a bowl-shaped region or building, esp. an amphitheater (*Hollywood Bowl*). **4** *Sports* a post-season football game between invited teams or as a championship. □□ **bowl·ful** *n.* (*pl.* **-fuls**).

bowl² /bōl/ *n. & v.* ● *n.* **1 a** a wooden or hard rubber ball, slightly asymmetrical, used in the game of bowls. **b** a wooden ball or disk used in playing skittles. **2** esp. *Brit.* (in *pl.*; usu. treated as *sing.*) lawn bowling. **3** a spell or turn of bowling in cricket. ● *v.* **1 a** roll (a hoop, etc.) along the ground. **b** *intr.* play bowls or skittles. **2** *intr.* (often foll. by *along*) go along rapidly, esp. on wheels (*the cart bowled along the road*). **3** *tr.* (also *absol.*) *Cricket*, etc. **a** deliver (a ball, etc.). **b** (often foll. by *out*) dismiss (a batsman) by knocking down the wicket with a ball. □ **bowl over 1** knock down. **2** *colloq.* **a** impress greatly. **b** overwhelm.

bow·legs /bólegz/ *n.pl.* legs that curve outward at the knee. □□ **bow·leg·ged** /bólegid/ *adj.*

bowl·er¹ /bólər/ *n.* **1** a player at bowls or bowling. **2** *Cricket*, etc., a member of the fielding side who bowls or is bowling. ▷ CRICKET

bowl·er² /bólər/ *n.* (in full **bowler hat**) a man's hard felt hat with a round dome-shaped crown. ▷ HAT

bow·line /bólin/ *n. Naut.* ▼ a knot for forming a nonslipping loop at the end of a rope. ▷ KNOT

BOWLINE

bowl·ing /bóling/ *n.* the games of tenpins, skittles, or bowls as a sport or recreation.

bowl·ing al·ley *n.* **1** a long enclosure for skittles or tenpin bowling. **2** a building containing these.

bowl·ing ball *n.* a hard ball with holes drilled in it for gripping, used in tenpin bowling.

bowl·ing green *n.* a lawn used for playing bowls.

bow·man¹ /bómən/ *n.* (*pl.* **-men**) an archer.

bow·man² /bówmən/ *n.* (*pl.* **-men**) the rower nearest the bow of esp. a racing boat.

bow saw *n. Carpentry* a narrow saw stretched like a bowstring on a light frame.

bow·shot /bóshot/ *n.* the distance to which a bow can send an arrow.

bow·sprit /bówsprit/ *n. Naut.* ▼ a spar running out from a ship's bow to which the forestays are fastened. ▷ SAILBOAT, SHIP

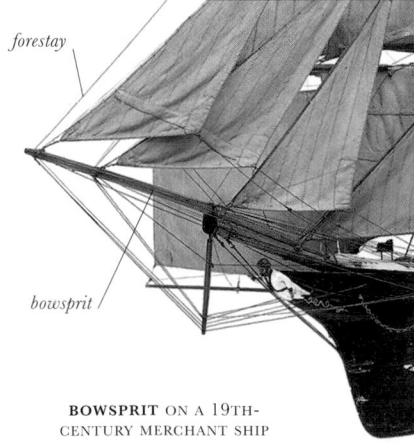

forestay

bowsprit

BOWSPRIT ON A 19TH-CENTURY MERCHANT SHIP

BOULE: SET OF BALLS FOR PLAYING BOULE

B

bow·string /bṓstring/ *n.* the string of an archer's bow. ▷ ARCHERY

bow tie *n.* a necktie in the form of a bow (see BOW[1] *n.* 1a).

bow-wow /bów-wów/ *int. & n.* ● *int.* an imitation of a dog's bark. ● *n.* **1** *colloq.* a dog. **2** a dog's bark.

bow·yer /bṓ-yər/ *n.* a maker or seller of archers' bows.

box[1] /boks/ *n. & v.* ● *n.* **1** a container, usu. with flat sides and of firm material, esp. for holding solids. **2** the amount that will fill a box. **3** a separate compartment, e.g., in a theater. **4** an enclosure or receptacle for a special purpose (*cash box*). **5** a facility for receiving replies to an advertizement. **6** (prec. by *the*) *colloq.* television (*what's on the box?*). **7** a space or area of print on a page, enclosed by a border. **8** a protective casing for a piece of mechanism. **9** (prec. by *the*) *Soccer colloq.* the penalty area. **10** *Baseball* one of several areas occupied by the batter, catcher, pitcher, and first and third base coaches. **11** a coachman's seat. ● *v.tr.* **1** put in or provide with a box. **2** (foll. by *in, up*) confine. □□ **box·ful** *n.* (*pl.* **-fuls**). **box·like** *adj.*

box[2] /boks/ *v.* **1 a** *tr.* fight (an opponent) at boxing. **b** *intr.* practice boxing. **2** slap (esp. a person's ears).

box[3] /boks/ *n.* **1 a** any small evergreen tree or shrub of the genus *Buxus*, esp. *B. sempervirens*, often used in hedging. ▷ TOPIARY. **b** any of various trees in Australasia, esp. those of several species of *Eucalyptus*. **2** = BOXWOOD.

box cam·er·a *n.* ▼ a simple box-shaped hand camera.

film winder   *eyepiece*   *lens*

BOX CAMERA: EARLY 20TH-CENTURY MODEL

box·car /bókskaar/ *n.* an enclosed railroad freight car, usu. with sliding doors on the sides.

box el·der *n.* the American ash-leaved maple, *Acer negundo*.

Box·er /bóksər/ *n. hist.* a member of a fiercely nationalist Chinese secret society that flourished in the 19th c.

box·er /bóksər/ *n.* **1** a person who practices boxing, esp. for sport. **2** ▶ a medium-sized dog of a breed with a smooth brown coat and puglike face.

box·er shorts *n.pl.* men's underwear similar to shorts.

box·ing /bóksing/ *n.* the practice of fighting with the fists, esp. in padded gloves as a sport.

box·ing glove *n.* each of a pair of heavily padded gloves used in boxing.

BOXER

box kite *n.* a kite in the form of a long box open at each end.

box lunch *n.* a lunch packed in a box.

box of·fice *n.* **1** an office for booking seats and buying tickets at a theater, movie theater, etc. **2** the commercial aspect of the arts and entertainment (often *attrib.: a box-office failure*).

box pleat *n.* a pleat consisting of two parallel creases forming a raised band.

box score *n. Sports* printed information about a game in which players for both teams are listed with statistics about their performances.

box seat *n.* a seat in a box enclosure, as at a theater, sports arena, etc.

box spring *n.* each of a set of vertical springs housed in a frame, e.g., in a mattress.

box·wood /bókswŏŏd/ *n.* **1** the wood of the box used esp. by engravers for the fineness of its grain and for its hardness. **2** = BOX[3] 1.

box·y /bóksee/ *adj.* (**boxier**, **boxiest**) (of a room or space) very cramped.

boy /boy/ *n. & int.* ● *n.* **1** a male child or youth. **2** a young man. **3** a male servant, attendant, etc. **4** (**the boys**) *colloq.* a group of men mixing socially. ● *int.* expressing pleasure, surprise, etc. □□ **boy·hood** *n.* **boy·ish** *adj.* **boy·ish·ly** *adv.* **boy·ish·ness** *n.*

bo·yar /bō-yaár/ *n. hist.* a member of the old aristocracy in Russia.

boy·cott /bóy-kot/ *v. & n.* ● *v.tr.* **1** combine in refusing relations with (a person, group, country, etc.). **2** refuse to handle (goods). ● *n.* such a refusal.

boy·friend /bóyfrend/ *n.* a person's regular male companion or lover.

Boyle's law /boylz/ *n.* the law that the pressure of a given mass of gas is inversely proportional to its volume at a constant temperature.

boy scout *n.* **1** (also **Boy Scout**) a member of an organization of boys, esp. the Boy Scouts of America, that promotes character, outdoor activities, community service, etc. **2** a boy or man who demonstrates the qualities associated with a Boy Scout.

boy·sen·ber·ry /bóyzənberee/ *n.* (*pl.* **-ies**) **1** a hybrid of several species of bramble. **2** the large red edible fruit of this plant.

bo·zo /bṓzō/ *n.* (*pl.* **-os**) *sl.* a stupid or obnoxious person.

BP *abbr.* **1** boiling point. **2** blood pressure. **3** before the present (era).

B.Phil. *abbr.* Bachelor of Philosophy.

bps *abbr.* (also **BPS**) *Computing* bits per second.

Br *symb. Chem.* the element bromine.

bra /braa/ *n.* (*pl.* **bras**) *colloq.* = BRASSIERE.

brace /brays/ *n. & v.* ● *n.* **1 a** a device that clamps or fastens tightly. **b** a strengthening piece of iron or lumber in building. ▷ QUEEN POST. **2** (in *pl.*) *Brit.* = SUSPENDER 1. **3** (in *pl.*) a wire device for straightening the teeth. **4** (*pl.* same) a pair. **5** a rope attached to the yard of a ship for trimming the sail. ▷ SHIP. **6 a** a connecting mark { or } used in printing. **b** *Mus.* a similar mark connecting staves to be performed at the same time. ● *v.tr.* **1** fasten tightly; give strength to. **2** make steady by supporting. **3** (esp. as **bracing** *adj.*) invigorate; refresh. **4** (often *refl.*) prepare for a difficulty, shock, etc. □□ **brac·ing·ly** *adv.*

brace and bit *n.* a revolving tool with a D-shaped central handle for boring. ▷ DRILL.

brace·let /bráyslit/ *n.* **1** an ornamental band, hoop, or chain worn on the wrist or arm. **2** *sl.* a handcuff.

bracer /bráysər/ *n. colloq.* a tonic, esp. an alcoholic drink.

bra·cer·o /brəseeáirō/ *n.* a Mexican laborer allowed into the United States for a limited time as a seasonal agricultural worker.

bra·chi·al /bráykeeəl, brák-/ *adj.* **1** of or relating to the arm (*brachial artery*). **2** like an arm.

bra·chi·ate /bráykeeit, -ayt, brák-/ *v. & adj.* ● *v.intr.* (of certain apes and monkeys) move by using the arms to swing from branch to branch. ● *adj. Biol.* **1** having arms. **2** having paired branches on alternate sides. □□ **bra·chi·a·tion** /-áyshən/ *n.* **bra·chi·a·tor** *n.*

bra·chi·o·pod /bráykeeəpod, brák-/ *n.* ▶ any marine invertebrate of the phylum Brachiopoda (esp. a fossil one) having a bivalved chalky shell and a ciliated feeding arm.

BRACHIOPOD SHELL

BRACHIOSAURUS (*Brachiosaurus* species)

bra·chi·o·sau·rus /bráykeeəsáwrəs, brák-/ *n.* ◀ any huge plant-eating dinosaur of the genus *Brachiosaurus* with forelegs longer than its hind legs.

brach·y·ce·phal·ic /brákeesifálik/ *adj.* having a broad short head. □□ **brach·y·ceph·a·lous** /-séfələs/ *adj.*

bra·chyl·o·gy /brəkílojee/ *n.* (*pl.* **-ies**) **1** conciseness of expression. **2** an instance of this.

brack·en /brákən/ *n.* **1** any large coarse fern, esp. *Pteridium aquilinum*, abundant in tropical and temperate areas. **2** a mass of such ferns.

brack·et /brákit/ *n. & v.* ● *n.* **1** a support attached to and projecting from a vertical surface. **2** a shelf fixed with such a support to a wall. **3** each of a pair of marks ( ) (**round brackets** or **parentheses**), [ ] (**square brackets**) or < > (**angle brackets**) used to enclose words or figures. **4** a group classified as containing similar elements or falling between given limits (*income bracket*). ● *v.tr.* (**bracketed**, **bracketing**) **1 a** combine (names, etc.) within brackets. **b** imply a connection or equality between. **2 a** enclose in brackets as parenthetic or spurious. **b** *Math.* enclose in brackets as having specific relations to what precedes or follows.

brack·ish /brákish/ *adj.* (of water, etc.) slightly salty.

bract /brakt/ *n.* a modified leaf, with a flower or an inflorescence in its axil. ▷ POINSETTIA.

brad /brad/ *n.* a thin flat nail with a head in the form of a slight enlargement at the top.

brad·awl /brádawl/ *n.* ▶ a small tool with a pointed end for boring holes by hand.

brad·y·car·di·a /brádikaárdeeə/ *n. Med.* abnormally slow heart action.

brag /brag/ *v. & n.* ● *v.* (**bragged**, **bragging**) **1** *intr.* talk boastfully. **2** *tr.* boast about. ● *n.* **1** a card game like poker. **2** a boastful statement; boastful talk.

brag·ga·do·ci·o /brágədósheeō/ *n.* empty boasting; a boastful manner of speech and behavior.

brag·gart /brágərt/ *n. & adj.* ● *n.* a person given to bragging. ● *adj.* boastful.

Brah·ma /braámə/ *n.* **1** the Hindu Creator. **2** the supreme divine reality in Hindu belief.

Brah·man[1] /braámən/ *n.* (also **brahman**) (*pl.* **-mans**) a member of the highest Hindu caste, whose members are traditionally eligible for the priesthood.

Brah·man[2] /bráymən, braámən/ *n.* (also **brahman**) any of various breeds of Indian cattle, esp. a US breed of humped, heat-resistant, grayish cattle.

brah·ma·put·ra /braáməpŏŏtrə/ *n.* **1** any bird of a large Asian breed of domestic fowl. **2** this breed.

Brah·min /braámin/ *n.* **1** = BRAHMAN. **2** (esp. in New England) a socially or culturally superior person.

braid /brayd/ *n. & v.* ● *n.* **1** a woven band used for edging or trimming. **2** a length of hair, straw, etc. in three or more interlaced strands. ● *v.tr.* **1** weave or intertwine (hair or thread). **2** trim or decorate with braid.

braid·ing /bráyding/ *n.* **1** various types of braid collectively. **2** braided work.

Braille /brayl/ *n. & v.* ● *n.* a system of writing and printing for the blind, in which characters are represented by patterns of raised dots. ● *v.tr.* print or transcribe in Braille.

BRADAWL

BRAIN

The brain, together with the spinal cord, constitutes the central nervous system. It is responsible for monitoring and regulating unconscious and voluntary actions and reactions in the body. It is also the intellectual center that allows thought, learning, memory, and creativity.

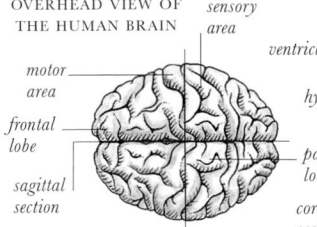

OVERHEAD VIEW OF
THE HUMAN BRAIN

sensory area
motor area
frontal lobe
sagittal section
ventricle
hypothalamus
parietal lobe
coronal section

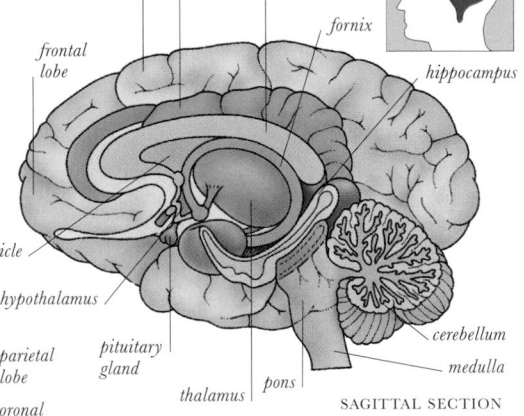

cerebrum   *cingulate gyrus*   *corpus callosum*   *fornix*
frontal lobe
hippocampus
pituitary gland
thalamus   *pons*
cerebellum
medulla

SAGITTAL SECTION
OF THE HUMAN BRAIN

B

brain /brayn/ *n. & v.* ● *n.* **1** ▲ an organ of soft nervous tissue contained in the skull of vertebrates, functioning as the coordinating center of sensation and of intellectual and nervous activity. ▷ HEAD, NERVOUS SYSTEM. **2** (in *pl.*) the substance of the brain, esp. as food. **3 a** a person's intellectual capacity (*has a weak brain*). **b** (often in *pl.*) intelligence; high intellectual capacity (*has a brain; has brains*). **c** *colloq.* a clever person. **4** (in *pl.*; prec. by *the*) *colloq.* **a** the cleverest person in a group. **b** a person who originates a complex plan or idea (*the brains behind the robbery*). **5** an electronic device with functions comparable to those of a brain. ● *v.tr.* **1** dash out the brains of. **2** strike hard on the head. □ **on the brain** *colloq.* obsessively in one's thoughts.

brain-dead *adj.* suffering from brain death.

brain death *n.* irreversible brain damage causing the end of independent respiration, regarded as indicative of death.

brain drain *n. colloq.* the loss of skilled personnel by emigration.

brain·i·ac /bráyneeak/ *n. N. Amer. colloq.* a very intelligent person.

brain·pan /bráynpan/ *n. colloq.* the skull.

brain·pow·er /bráynpowr/ *n.* mental ability or intelligence.

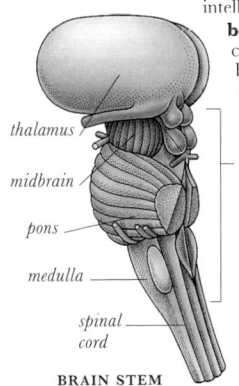

thalamus
midbrain
pons
medulla
spinal cord

BRAIN STEM

brain stem *n.* ◄ the central trunk of the brain, upon which the cerebrum and cerebellum are set, and which continues downward to form the spinal cord. ▷ BRAIN, HEAD

brain·storm /bráyn-stawrm/ *n. & v.* ● *n.* **1** a violent or excited outburst often as a result of a sudden mental disturbance. **2** *colloq.* mental confusion. **3** a sudden bright idea. **4** a concerted intellectual treatment of a problem by discussing spontaneous ideas about it. ● *v.intr.* discuss ideas spontaneously and openly. □□ **brain·storm·ing** *n.* (in sense 4).

brain·teas·er /bráyntēzər/ *n.* (also **brain·twist·er** /-twistər/) *colloq.* a puzzle or problem.

brain trust *n.* a group of experts, official or unofficial, who advise on policy and strategy.

brain·wash /bráynwosh, -wawsh/ *v.tr.* subject (a person) to a prolonged process by which ideas at variance with those already held are implanted in the mind. □□ **brain·wash·ing** *n.*

brain wave *n.* **1** (usu. in *pl.*) an electrical impulse in the brain. **2** *colloq.* = BRAINSTORM[3].

brain·y /bráynee/ *adj.* (**brainier, brainiest**) intellectually clever or active.

braise /brayz/ *v.tr.* fry lightly and then stew slowly with a little liquid in a closed container.

brake[1] /brayk/ *n. & v.* ● *n.* **1** (often in *pl.*) ▼ a device for checking the motion of a mechanism, esp. a wheel or vehicle, or for keeping it at rest. **2** anything that has the effect of hindering or impeding something (*put a brake on their enthusiasm*). ● *v.* **1** *intr.* apply a brake. **2** *tr.* retard or stop with a brake.

brake[2] /brayk/ *n. Brit.* a large station wagon.

brake[3] /brayk/ *n. & v.* ● *n.* **1** a toothed instrument used for crushing flax and hemp. **2** (in full **brake harrow**) a heavy kind of harrow for breaking up large lumps of earth. ● *v.tr.* crush (flax or hemp) by beating it.

brake[4] /brayk/ *n.* **1** a thicket. **2** brushwood.

brake[5] *archaic past of* BREAK[1].

brake drum *n.* a cylinder attached to a wheel on which the brake shoe presses to brake. ▷ BRAKE

brake flu·id *n.* fluid used in a hydraulic brake system.

brake horse·pow·er *n.* the power of an engine reckoned in terms of the force needed to brake it.

brake lin·ing *n.* a strip of material which increases the friction of the brake shoe. ▷ BRAKE

brake·man /bráykmən/ *n.* (*pl.* **-men**) a railroad worker responsible for maintenance on a journey.

brake shoe *n.* a long curved block which presses on the brake drum to brake. ▷ BRAKE

bram·ble /brámbəl/ *n.* **1** any of various thorny shrubs bearing fleshy red or black berries, esp. (*Brit.*) the blackberry bush, *Rubus fructicosus.* **2** any of various other rosaceous shrubs with similar foliage, esp. the dog rose (*Rosa canina*). □□ **bram·bly** *adj.*

bram·bling /brámbling/ *n.* the speckled finch, *Fringilla montifringilla,* native to northern Eurasia, the male having a distinctive red breast.

bran /bran/ *n.* grain husks separated from the flour.

branch /branch/ *n. & v.* ● *n.* **1** a limb extending from a tree or bough. **2** a lateral extension or subdivision, esp. of a river, or railroad. **3** a conceptual subdivision of a family, knowledge, etc. **4** a local division or office, etc., of a large business, library, etc. ● *v.intr.* (often foll. by *off*) **1** diverge from the main part. **2** divide into branches. **3** (of a tree) bear or send out branches. □ **branch out** extend one's field of interest. □□ **branched** *adj.* **branch·let** *n.*

bran·chi·a /brángkeeə/ *n.pl.* (also **bran·chi·ae** /-kee-ee/) gills. □□ **bran·chi·al** *adj.* **bran·chi·ate** /-eeit, -eeayt/ *adj.*

brand /brand/ *n. & v.* ● *n.* **1 a** a particular make of goods. **b** an identifying trademark, label, etc. **2** (often foll. by *of*) a special or characteristic kind (*brand of humor*). **3** an identifying mark burned on livestock or (formerly) prisoners, etc., with a hot iron. **4** an iron used for this. **5** a piece of burning, smoldering, or charred wood. **6** a stigma; a mark of disgrace. **7** *poet.* a torch. ● *v.tr.* **1** mark with a hot iron. **2** stigmatize; mark with disgrace (*was branded for life*). **3** impress unforgettably on one's mind **4** assign a trademark or label to.

brand·ish /brándish/ *v.tr.* wave as a threat or in display.

brand·ling /brándling/ *n.* a red earthworm, *Eisenia foetida,* with rings of a brighter color, which is often found in manure and used as bait.

brand-name *attrib.adj.* having an identifying trademark, label, etc., esp. one that is well known.

brand-new *adj.* completely new.

bran·dy /brándee/ *n.* (*pl.* **-ies**) a strong alcoholic spirit distilled from wine or fermented fruit juice.

brant /brant/ *n.* a small migratory goose, *Branta bernicla.*

brash[1] /brash/ *adj.* **1** vulgarly or overly self-assertive. **2** hasty; rash. **3** impudent. □□ **brash·ly** *adv.* **brash·ness** *n.*

brash[2] /brash/ *n.* **1** loose broken rock or ice. **2** clippings from hedges, shrubs, etc.

BRAKE

Brakes are essential to vehicle safety. Illustrated below are the main types of car brake. The disc brake is used on the front wheels of a car: when the foot brake is applied, hydraulic pressure forces pads inside the wheel to press against the disc, slowing the wheel. Drum brakes are often used for a car's rear or parking brakes: curved shoes inside the metal drum push outward against the drum when the brake is applied.

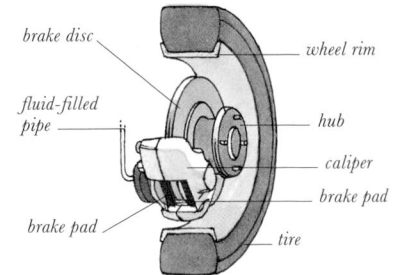

brake disc
fluid-filled pipe
brake pad
wheel rim
hub
caliper
brake pad
tire

SECTION THROUGH A BRAKE DISC

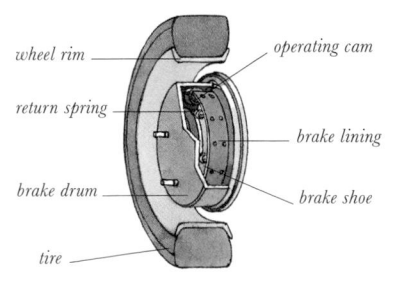

wheel rim
return spring
brake drum
tire
operating cam
brake lining
brake shoe

SECTION THROUGH A BRAKE DRUM

BRASS

Brass instruments derive from shells, horns, and branches used to make music in ancient times. Modern versions such as the trumpet were first constructed from brass – a malleable and relatively cheap metal. Although they are now made from a variety of materials, the name has remained. In modern instruments, notes are produced by two methods: adjusting the tension of the lips on the cup- or funnel-shaped mouthpiece, or altering the length of the tube through which air passes. The length of air passing through the tube is altered using piston valves or sliding sections – the longer the column of air produced, the lower the pitch.

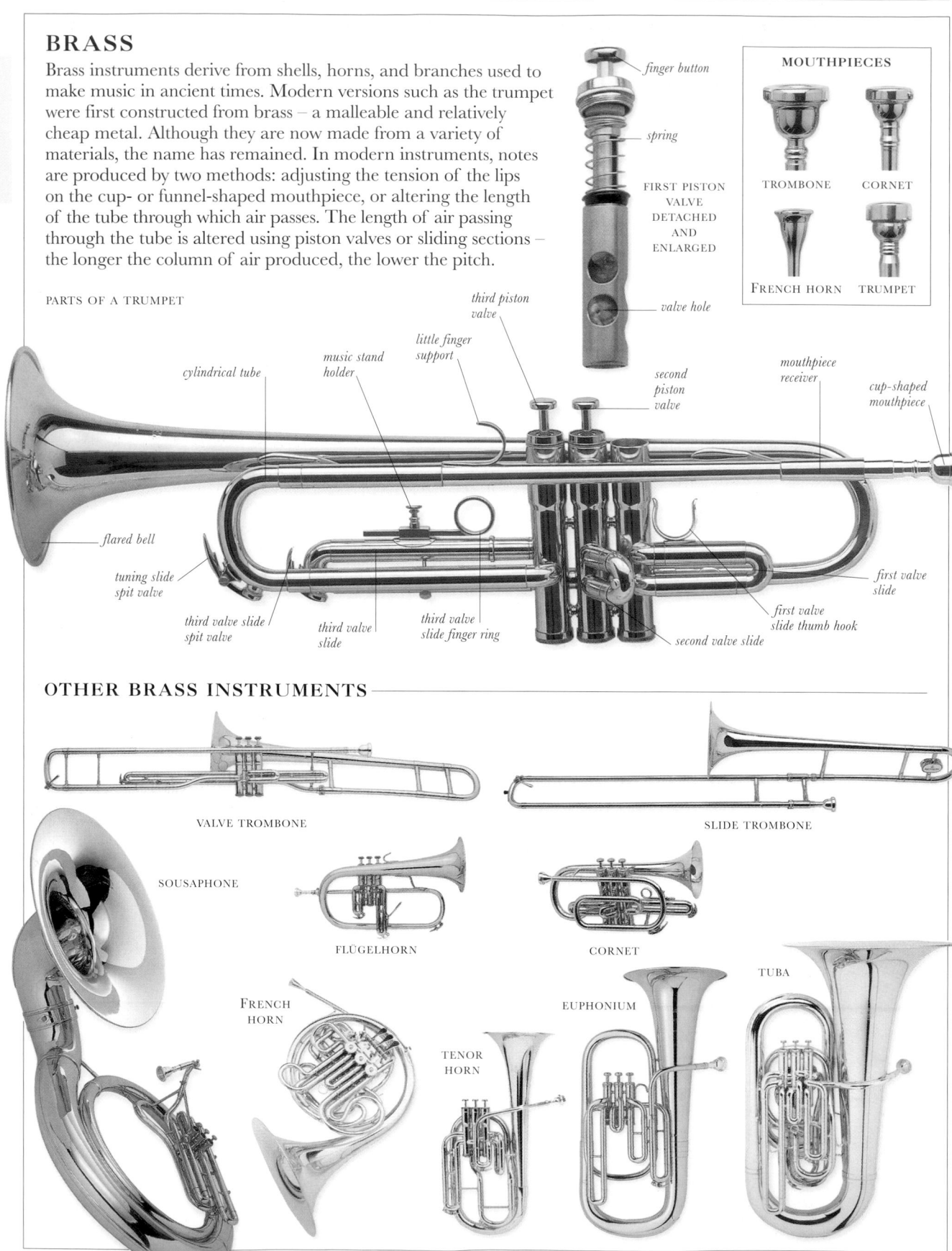

finger button

spring

FIRST PISTON VALVE DETACHED AND ENLARGED

valve hole

MOUTHPIECES

TROMBONE

CORNET

FRENCH HORN

TRUMPET

PARTS OF A TRUMPET

third piston valve

little finger support

music stand holder

cylindrical tube

second piston valve

mouthpiece receiver

cup-shaped mouthpiece

flared bell

tuning slide spit valve

third valve slide spit valve

third valve slide

third valve slide finger ring

second valve slide

first valve slide thumb hook

first valve slide

OTHER BRASS INSTRUMENTS

VALVE TROMBONE

SLIDE TROMBONE

SOUSAPHONE

FLÜGELHORN

CORNET

TUBA

FRENCH HORN

EUPHONIUM

TENOR HORN

B

brass /bras/ *n.* & *adj.* ● *n.* **1** a yellow alloy of copper and zinc. **2 a** a decorated piece of brass. **b** brass objects collectively. **3** *Mus.* ◂ brass wind instruments. ▷ ORCHESTRA. **4** (in full **top brass**) *colloq.* persons in authority or of high rank. **5** *colloq.* effrontery (*then had the brass to demand money*). ● *adj.* made of brass.

bras·sard /brəsaárd, brásaard/ *n.* a band worn on the sleeve.

brass band *n.* a group of musicians playing brass instruments, sometimes also with percussion.

bras·se·rie /brásəree/ *n.* a restaurant, orig. one serving beer with food.

bras·si·ca /brásikə/ *n.* any cruciferous plant of the genus *Brassica*, having tap roots and erect branched stems, including cabbage, rutabaga, broccoli, brussels sprout, mustard, rape, cauliflower, kohlrabi, kale, and turnip.

bras·sie /brásee/ *n.* (also **brassy**) (*pl.* **-ies**) a wooden-headed golf club with a brass sole.

bras·siere /brəzeér/ *n.* an undergarment worn by women to support the breasts. ▷ CORSELETTE

brass knuck·les *n.pl.* a metal guard worn over the knuckles in fighting, esp. to increase the effect of the blows.

brass ring *n. sl.* an opportunity for wealth or success; a rich prize.

brass tacks *n.pl. sl.* actual details; real business (*get down to brass tacks*).

brass·y[1] /brásee/ *adj.* (**brassier**, **brassiest**) **1** impudent. **2** pretentious; showy. **3** loud and blaring. **4** of or like brass. □□ **brassily** *adv.* **brassiness** *n.*

bras·sy[2] var. of BRASSIE.

brat /brat/ *n.* usu. *derog.* a child, esp. a badly-behaved one. □□ **brat·ty** *adj.*

brat·tice /brátis/ *n.* a wooden partition or shaft lining in a mine.

brat·wurst /brátwərst, -vŏŏrst/ *n.* a type of small pork sausage.

bra·va·do /brəvaádō/ *n.* a bold manner or a show of boldness.

brave /brayv/ *adj.*, *n.*, & *v.* ● *adj.* **1** able or ready to face and endure danger or pain. **2** splendid (*make a brave show*). ● *n.* a Native American warrior. ● *v.tr.* defy; encounter bravely. □□ **brave·ly** *adv.*

brav·er·y /bráyvəree/ *n.* **1** brave conduct. **2** a brave nature.

bra·vo[1] /braávō/ *int.* & *n.* ● *int.* expressing approval of a performer, etc. ● *n.* (*pl.* **-os**) a cry of bravo.

bra·vo[2] /braávō/ *n.* (*pl.* **-oes** or **-os**) a hired thug or killer.

bra·vu·ra /brəvŏŏrə, -vyŏŏrə/ *n.* (often *attrib.*) **1** a brilliant or ambitious action or display. **2 a** a style of music requiring exceptional ability. **b** a passage of this kind. **3** bravado.

brawl /brawl/ *n.* & *v.* ● *n.* a noisy quarrel or fight. ● *v.intr.* quarrel noisily or roughly. □□ **brawl·er** *n.*

brawn /brawn/ *n.* **1** muscular strength. **2** muscle; lean flesh.

brawn·y /bráwnee/ *adj.* (**brawnier**, **brawniest**) muscular; strong.

bray[1] /bray/ *n.* & *v.* ● *n.* **1** the cry of a donkey. **2** a sound like this cry. ● *v.* **1** *intr.* make a braying sound. **2** *tr.* utter harshly.

bray[2] /bray/ *v.tr.* pound or crush to small pieces, esp. with a pestle and mortar.

braze[1] /brayz/ *v.tr.* solder with a nonferrous at a high temperature.

braze[2] /brayz/ *v.tr.* **1 a** make of brass. **b** cover or ornament with brass. **2** make hard like brass.

bra·zen /bráyzən/ *adj.* & *v.* ● *adj.* **1** (also **bra·zen-faced**) flagrant and shameless; insolent. **2** made of brass. **3** of or like brass. ● *v.tr.* (foll. by *out*) face or undergo defiantly. □ **brazen it out** be defiantly unrepentant. □□ **bra·zen·ly** *adv.* **bra·zen·ness** *n.*

bra·zier[1] /bráyzhər/ *n.* a portable heater consisting of a pan or stand for holding lighted coals.

bra·zier[2] /bráyzhər/ *n.* a worker in brass.

Bra·zil /brəzíl/ *n.* **1** a tall tree, *Bertholletia excelsa*, forming large forests in S. America. **2** (in full **Brazil nut**) a large three-sided nut with an edible kernel from this tree. ▷ NUT

bra·zil·wood /brəzílwŏŏd/ *n.* a hard red wood from any tropical tree of the genus *Caesalpinia*, that yields dyes.

breach /breech/ *n.* & *v.* ● *n.* **1** (often foll. by *of*) the breaking of a law, contract, etc. **2 a** a breaking of relations. **b** a quarrel. **3 a** a broken state. **b** a gap. ● *v.tr.* **1** break through; make a gap in. **2** break (a law, contract, etc.). □ **step into the breach** give help in a crisis, esp. by replacing someone.

breach of prom·ise *n.* the breaking of a promise, esp. a promise to marry.

breach of the peace *n.* a violation of the public peace by any disturbance or riot, etc.

bread /bred/ *n.* & *v.* ● *n.* **1** baked dough made of flour usu. leavened with yeast and moistened. **2 a** necessary food. **b** (also **daily bread**) one's livelihood. **3** *sl.* money. ● *v.tr.* coat with breadcrumbs for cooking. □ **know which side one's bread is buttered on** know where one's advantage lies.

bread and but·ter *n.* **1** bread spread with butter. **2 a** one's livelihood. **b** routine work to ensure an income.

bread bas·ket *n.* **1** a basket for bread. **2** *sl.* the stomach.

bread·board /brédbawrd/ *n.* **1** a board for cutting bread on. **2** a board for making an experimental model of an electric circuit.

bread·crumb /brédkrum/ *n.* **1** a small fragment of bread. **2** (in *pl.*) bread crumbled for use in cooking.

bread·fruit /brédfrōōt/ *n.* **1** a tropical evergreen tree, *Artocarpus altilis*, bearing edible usu. seedless fruit. **2** ▸ the fruit of this tree which when roasted becomes soft like new bread.

BREADFRUIT
(*Artocarpus altilis*)

bread·line /brédlīn/ *n.* a line of people waiting to receive free food.

breadth /bredth/ *n.* **1** the distance or measurement from side to side of a thing. **2** a piece (of cloth, etc.) of standard or full breadth. **3** extent; distance; room. **4** (usu. foll. by *of*) freedom from prejudice or intolerance (esp. *breadth of mind* or *view*).

bread·win·ner /brédwinər/ *n.* a person who earns the money to support a family.

break[1] /brayk/ *v.* & *n.* ● *v.* (*past* **broke** /brōk/ or *archaic* **brake** /brayk/; *past part.* **broken** /brṓkən/ or *archaic* **broke**) **1** *tr.* & *intr.* **a** separate into pieces under a blow or strain. **b** make or become inoperative (*the toaster has broken*). **c** break a bone in or dislocate (part of the body). **d** break the skin of (the head). **2 a** *tr.* cause an interruption in (*broke our journey; broke the silence*). **b** *intr.* have an interval between periods of work (*we broke for coffee*). **3** *tr.* fail to keep (a law, promise, etc.). **4 a** *tr.* & *intr.* make or become subdued or weakened; yield or cause to yield (*broke his spirit; he broke under the strain*). **b** *tr.* weaken the effect of (a fall, blow, etc.). **c** *tr.* tame or discipline (an animal); accustom (a horse) to saddle and bridle, etc. **d** *tr.* defeat; destroy (*broke the enemy's power*). **e** *tr.* defeat the object of (a strike). **5** *tr.* surpass (a record). **6** *intr.* (foll. by *with*) cease association with (another person, etc.). **7** *tr.* **a** be no longer subject to (a habit). **b** (foll. by *of*) cause (a person) to be free of a habit (*broke them of their addiction*). **8** *tr.* & *intr.* reveal or be revealed (*broke the news; the story broke on Friday*). **9** *intr.* **a** (of the weather) change suddenly. **b** (of waves) curl over and dissolve into foam. **c** (of the day) dawn. **d** (of clouds) move apart. **e** (of a storm) begin violently. **10** *tr. Electr.* disconnect (a circuit). **11** *intr.* **a** (of the voice) change with emotion. **b** (of a boy's voice) change in register, etc., at puberty. **12** *tr.* **a** (often foll. by *up*) divide (a set, etc.) into parts, e.g., by selling to different buyers. **b** change (a bill, etc.) for coins or smaller denominations. **13** *tr.* ruin financially (see also BROKE *predic. adj.*). **14** *tr.* penetrate (e.g., a safe) by force. **15** *tr.* decipher (a code). **16** *tr.* make (a path, etc.) by separating obstacles. **17** *intr.* burst forth (*the sun broke through the clouds*). **18** *Mil.* **a** *intr.* (of troops) disperse in confusion. **b** *tr.* make a rupture in (ranks). **19 a** *intr.* (usu. foll. by *free*, *loose*, *out*, etc.) escape from constraint by a sudden effort. **b** *tr.* escape or emerge from (prison, cover, etc.). **20** *tr. Tennis*, etc. win a game against (an opponent's service). **21** *intr. Boxing*, etc. (of two fighters) come out of a clinch. **22** *tr. Mil.* demote (an officer). **23** *intr.* esp. *Stock Exch.* (of prices) fall sharply. **24** *intr.* (of a thrown or bowled ball) change direction abruptly. **25** *intr. Billiards*, etc. disperse the balls at the beginning of a game. ● *n.* **1 a** an act or instance of breaking. **b** a point where something is broken; a gap. **2** an interval; an interruption; a pause in work. **3** a sudden dash. **4** *colloq.* **a** a piece of good luck; a fair chance. **b** (also **bad break**) an unfortunate remark or action; a blunder. **5** a change in direction of a thrown or bowled ball. **6** *Billiards*, etc. **a** a series of points scored during one turn. **b** the opening shot that disperses the balls. **7** *Mus.* (in jazz, etc.) a short unaccompanied passage for a soloist. **8** *Electr.* a discontinuity in a circuit. □ **break away** make or become free or separate (see also BREAKAWAY). **break the back of 1** do the hardest or greatest part of. **2** overburden (a person). **break down 1 a** fail in mechanical action; cease to function. **b** (of human relationships, etc.) collapse. **c** fail in (esp. mental) health. **d** be overcome by emotion. **2 a** demolish. **b** suppress (resistance). **c** force (a person) to yield under pressure. **3** analyze into components (see also BREAKDOWN). **break even** emerge from a transaction, etc., with neither profit nor loss. **break the ice 1** begin to overcome formality or shyness. **2** make a start. **break in 1** enter premises by force. **2** interrupt. **3 a** accustom to a habit, etc. **b** wear until comfortable. **c** = BREAK. 4c. **break into 1** enter forcibly or violently. **2 a** suddenly begin; burst forth with (a song, laughter, etc.). **b** suddenly change one's pace for (a faster one) (*broke into a gallop*). **3** interrupt. **break a leg** *Theatr.* phrase to wish a performer good luck. **break new ground** innovate; start on something new. **break off 1** detach by breaking. **2** bring to an end. **3** cease talking, etc. **break open** open forcibly. **break out 1** escape by force. **2** begin suddenly (*then violence broke out*). **3** (foll. by *in*) become covered in (a rash, etc.). **4** exclaim. **5 a** open up (a receptacle) and remove its contents. **b** remove (articles) from a place of storage. **break step** get out of step. **break up 1** break into small pieces. **2** disperse. **3 a** terminate a relationship; disband. **b** cause to do this. **4 a** upset or be upset. **b** excite or be excited. **c** convulse or be convulsed (see also BREAKUP). **break wind** release gas from the anus. □□ **break·a·ble** *adj.* & *n.*

break[2] /brayk/ *n.* **1** a carriage frame without a body, for breaking in young horses. **2** = BRAKE[2].

breakable /bráykəbəl/ *adj.* & *n.* ● *adj.* that may or is apt to be broken easily. ● *n.* (esp. in *pl.*) a breakable thing.

break·age /bráykij/ *n.* **1 a** a broken thing. **b** damage caused by breaking. **2** an act or instance of breaking.

break·a·way /bráykəway/ *n.* **1** the act or an instance of breaking away or seceding. **2** (*attrib.*) that breaks away or has broken away.

break danc·ing *n.* an energetic style of street-dancing, developed by African-Americans.

break·down /bráykdown/ *n.* **1 a** a mechanical failure. **b** a loss of (esp. mental) health and strength. **2 a** a collapse or disintegration (*breakdown of communication*). **b** physical or chemical decomposition. **3** a detailed analysis (of statistics, etc.).

break·er /bráykər/ *n.* **1** a person or thing that breaks something. **2** a person who breaks in a horse. **3** a heavy wave that breaks.

break·fast /brékfəst/ *n.* & *v.* ● *n.* the first meal of the day. ● *v.intr.* have breakfast.

B

B

break-in *n.* an illegal forced entry into premises.

break·ing and en·ter·ing *n.* the illegal entering of a building with intent to commit a felony.

break·ing point *n.* the point of greatest strain, at which a thing breaks or a person gives way.

break·neck /bráyknek/ *attrib.adj.* (of speed) dangerously fast.

break of day *n.* dawn.

break·out /bráykowt/ *n.* a forcible escape.

break point *n.* **1** a place or time at which an interruption or change is made. **2** *Computing* (usu. **breakpoint**) a place in a computer program where the sequence of instructions is interrupted, esp. by another program. **3** *Tennis* a point which would win the game for the player(s) receiving service (*three break points*). **4** = BREAKING POINT.

break·through /bráykthrōo/ *n.* **1** a major advance or discovery. **2** an act of breaking through an obstacle, etc.

break·up /bráykup/ *n.* **1** disintegration; collapse. **2** dispersal.

break·wa·ter /bráykwawtər, -wotər/ *n.* a barrier built out into the sea to break the force of waves.

bream[1] /breem/ *n.* (*pl.* same) **1** ▼ a yellowish arch-backed European freshwater fish, *Abramis brama*. **2** (in full **sea bream**) **a** a similarly shaped marine fish of the family Sparidae, of the NE Atlantic. **b** an Atlantic porgy, *Archosargus rhomboidalis*.

bream[2] /breem/ *v.tr. Naut. hist.* clean (a ship's bottom) by burning and scraping.

breast /brest/ *n. & v.* ● *n.* **1 a** ▲ either of two milk-secreting organs on the upper front of a woman's body. **b** the corresponding part of a man's body. **2 a** the chest. **b** the corresponding part of an animal. **3** the part of a garment that covers the breast. ● *v.tr.* **1** face; meet in full opposition (*breast the wind*). **2** contend with (*prepared to breast the difficulties of the journey*). **3** reach the top of (a hill). □ **make a clean breast of** confess fully. □□ **breast·ed** *adj.* (also in *comb.*).

BREAM:
BRONZE BREAM
(*Abramis brama*)

breast·bone /bréstbōn/ *n.* a thin flat vertical bone and cartilage in the chest connecting the ribs. ▷ STERNUM

breast-feed *v.tr.* (*past* and *past part.* **-fed**) feed (a baby) from the breast.

breast·plate /bréstplayt/ *n.* ▶ a piece of armor covering the breast. ▷ ARMOR, ROUNDHEAD

breast·stroke /bréststrōk/ *n.* a stroke made while swimming face down by extending arms forward and sweeping them back in unison.

breast·sum·mer /brésəmər, -umər/ *n. Archit.* a beam across a broad opening, sustaining a superstructure.

breast·work /bréstwərk/ *n.* a low temporary defense or parapet.

strap to attach backplate

lance-rest

strap to attach metal-plate skirt

BREASTPLATE:
16TH-CENTURY ITALIAN
BREASTPLATE

breath /breth/ *n.* **1 a** the air taken into or expelled from the lungs. **b** one respiration of air. **c** an exhalation of air that can be seen, smelled, or heard (*bad breath*). **2 a** a slight movement of air. **b** a whiff of perfume, etc. **3** a whisper; a murmur. **4** the power of breathing; life (*is there breath in him?*). □ **below** (or **under**) **one's breath** in a whisper. **breath of fresh air 1** a small amount of or a brief time in the fresh air. **2** a refreshing change. **catch one's breath 1** cease breathing momentarily in surprise, etc. **2** rest after exercise to restore normal breathing. **draw breath** breathe; live. **hold one's breath 1** cease breathing temporarily. **2** *colloq.* wait in eager anticipation. **in the same breath** (esp. of saying two contradictory things) within a short time. **out of breath** gasping for air. **take a person's breath away** astound; surprise; awe; delight. **waste one's breath** talk or give advice without effect.

Breath·a·lyz·er /bréthəlìzər/ *n.* (also *Brit.* **Breathalyser**) *Trademark* an instrument for measuring the amount of alcohol in the breath of a driver. □□ **breath·a·lyze** *v.tr.*

breathe /breeth/ *v.* **1** *intr.* take air into and expel it from the lungs. **2** *intr.* be or seem alive (*is she breathing?*). **3** *tr.* **a** utter; say, esp. quietly (*breathed her forgiveness*). **b** express; display (*breathed defiance*). **4** *intr.* take a breath; pause. **5** *tr.* send out or take in (as if) with breathed air (*breathed enthusiasm into them; breathed whiskey*). **6** *intr.* (of wine, fabric, etc.) be exposed to fresh air. □ **breathe down a person's neck** follow or check up on a person, esp. menacingly. **breathe new life into** revitalize; refresh. **breathe one's last** die. **not breathe a word** keep silent. **not breathe a word of** keep secret.

breath·er /bréethər/ *n. colloq.* a brief pause for rest.

breath·ing /bréething/ *n.* **1** the process of taking air into and expelling it from the lungs. **2** *Phonet.* a sign in Greek indicating that an initial vowel is aspirated (**rough breathing**) or not aspirated (**smooth breathing**).

breath·less /bréthlis/ *adj.* **1** panting, out of breath. **2** (as if) holding the breath because of excitement, suspense, etc. (*a state of breathless expectancy*). **3** unstirred by wind; still. □□ **breath·less·ly** *adv.* **breath·less·ness** *n.*

breath·tak·ing /bréthtayking/ *adj.* remarkably beautiful; awe-inspiring (*a breathtaking view*). □□ **breath·tak·ing·ly** *adv.*

breath test *n.* a test of a person's alcohol consumption, using a Breathalyzer.

breath·y /bréthee/ *adj.* (**breathier**, **breathiest**) (of a singing voice, etc.) containing the sound of breathing. □□ **breath·i·ly** *adv.* **breath·i·ness** *n.*

brec·ci·a /brécheeə/ *n. & v.* ● *n.* ▶ a rock of angular stones, etc., cemented by finer material. ● *v.tr.* form into breccia. □□ **brecciate** /-eeayt/ *v.tr.* **brec·ci·a·tion** *n.*

bred /bred/ *past* and *past part.* of BREED.

breech /breech/ *n.* **1** the part of a cannon behind the bore. **2** the back part of a rifle or gun barrel.

BRECCIA

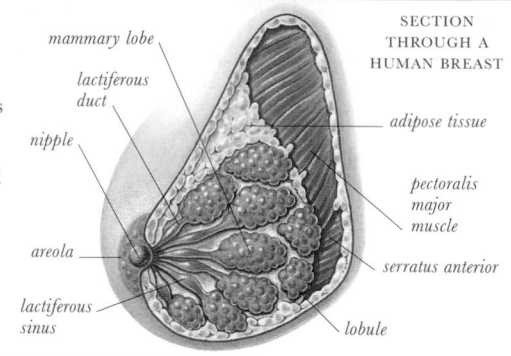

BREAST

Breasts are organs of fleshy tissue that overlie the pectoralis major muscles. The female breast contains 15–20 lobes of milk-producing glands, supported by ligaments. During pregnancy, under hormonal influence, these glands enlarge and prepare to secrete milk (lactate) to feed the suckling infant. Milk gathers in the lactiferous sinuses and is released through the ducts when the nipple is sucked.

mammary lobe

lactiferous duct

nipple

areola

lactiferous sinus

SECTION THROUGH A HUMAN BREAST

adipose tissue

pectoralis major muscle

serratus anterior

lobule

breech birth *n.* (also **breech delivery**) the delivery of a baby with the buttocks or feet foremost.

breech·block /bréechblok/ *n.* a metal block that closes the breech aperture in a gun.

breech·es /brichiz/ *n.pl.* (also **pair of breeches**) *sing.* short trousers, esp. fastened below the knee.

breech·load·er /bréechlōdər/ *n.* a gun loaded at the breech, not through the muzzle. □□ **breech-loading** *adj.*

breed /breed/ *v. & n.* ● *v.* (*past* and *past part.* **bred** /bred/) **1** *tr. & intr.* bear; generate (offspring). **2** *tr. & intr.* propagate or cause to propagate; raise (livestock). **3** *tr.* **a** yield; result in (*war breeds famine*). **b** spread (*discontent bred by rumor*). **4** *intr.* arise; spread (*disease breeds in poor sanitation*). **5** *tr.* bring up; train (*Hollywood breeds stars*). **6** *tr. Physics* create (fissile material) by nuclear reaction. ● *n.* **1** a stock of animals or plants within a species, having a similar appearance, and usu. developed by deliberate selection. **2** a race; a lineage. **3** a sort; a kind. □□ **breed·er** *n.*

breed·er re·ac·tor *n.* a nuclear reactor that can create more fissile material than it consumes.

breed·ing /bréeding/ *n.* **1** the process of developing or propagating (animals, plants, etc.). **2** generation; childbearing. **3** the result of training or education; behavior. **4** good manners (*has no breeding*).

breeze[1] /breez/ *n. & v.* ● *n.* **1** a gentle wind. **2** *Meteorol.* a wind of 4–31 m.p.h. and between force 2 and force 6 on the Beaufort scale. ▷ BEAUFORT SCALE. **3** a wind blowing from land at night or sea during the day. **4** *colloq.* an easy task. ● *v.intr.* (foll. by *in*, *out*, *along*, etc.) *colloq.* come or go in a casual manner.

breeze[2] /breez/ *n.* small cinders.

breez·y /bréezee/ *adj.* (**breezier**, **breeziest**) **1 a** windswept. **b** pleasantly windy. **2** *colloq.* lively; jovial. **3** *colloq.* careless (*breezy indifference*). □□ **breez·i·ly** *adv.* **breez·i·ness** *n.*

Bren /bren/ *n.* (in full **Bren gun**) a lightweight quick-firing machine gun.

breth·ren see BROTHER.

Bre·ton /brétən, brətáwn/ *n. & adj.* ● *n.* **1** a native of Brittany. **2** the Celtic language of Brittany. ● *adj.* of or relating to Brittany or its people or language.

breve /brev, breev/ *n.* **1** *Mus.* a note having the time value of two whole notes. ▷ NOTATION. **2** a written or printed mark (˘) indicating a short or unstressed vowel.

bre·vet /brəvét, brévit/ *n.* (often *attrib.*) a document conferring a privilege from a government, esp. a rank in the army, without the appropriate pay (*was promoted by brevet*; *brevet major*).

bre·vi·a·ry /bréevee-eree, brév-/ *n.* (*pl.* **-ies**) *RC Ch.* a book containing the service for each day.

brev·i·ty /brévitee/ *n.* **1** conciseness. **2** shortness (of time, etc.) (*the brevity of happiness*).

brew /brōo/ *v. & n.* ● *v.* **1** *tr.* **a** make (beer, etc.) by infusion, boiling, and fermentation. **b** make (tea, coffee, etc.) by infusion or (punch, etc.) by mixture. **2** *intr.* undergo either of these

BRICK

Strong, durable, and inexpensive, bricks have been made since ancient times, and are usually cast in standard sizes and shapes to simplify their laying. Styles of brickwork are typical of a particular region and era. The English bond was used in early brickwork of late medieval times, while the Flemish bond was popular during the early 17th century. The stretcher bond is often favored for modern buildings.

TYPES OF BRICKWORK

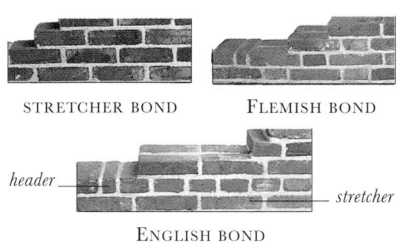

STRETCHER BOND   FLEMISH BOND

header   stretcher

ENGLISH BOND

processes (*the tea is brewing*). **3** *intr.* (of trouble, a storm, etc.) gather force; threaten. **4** *tr.* bring about; concoct. ● *n.* **1** an amount (of beer, etc.) brewed at one time (*this year's brew*). **2** what is brewed (*a strong brew*). **3** the process of brewing. □□ **brew·er** *n.*

brew·er·y /brōōəree, brōōree/ *n.* (*pl.* **-ies**) a place where beer, etc., is brewed commercially.

brew·ski /brōōskee/ *n. N. Amer. colloq.* a beer.

bri·ar var. of BRIER[1] and BRIER[2].

bribe /brīb/ *v. & n.* ● *v.tr.* (often foll. by *to* + infin.) persuade to act improperly in one's favor by a gift of money, services, etc. ● *n.* money or services offered in the process of bribing. □□ **brib·er·y** *n.*

bric-à-brac /bríkəbrak/ *n.* (also **bric-a-brac**, **bric·a·brac**) miscellaneous ornaments, furniture, etc., of no great value.

brick /brik/ *n., v., & adj.* ● *n.* **1 a** ▲ a small block of fired or sun-dried clay, used in building. ▷ HOUSE. **b** the material used to make these. **c** a similar block of concrete, etc. **2** a brick-shaped solid object (*a brick of ice cream*). **3** *sl.* a generous or loyal person. ● *v.tr.* (foll. by *in, up, over*) close or block with brickwork. ● *adj.* **1** built of brick (*brick wall*). **2** of a dull red color.

brick·bat /bríkbat/ *n.* **1** a piece of brick, esp. when used as a missile. **2** an uncomplimentary remark.

BRIDGE

Bridges vary in construction according to the gap they must span and their projected load. A cantilever bridge is ideal for supporting heavy loads, although an arch bridge is preferable where terrain prevents erection of pier supports. A suspension bridge may span widths of more than 4,000 feet (1.2 km).

EXAMPLES OF BRIDGES

roadway   *arch*

ARCH BRIDGE

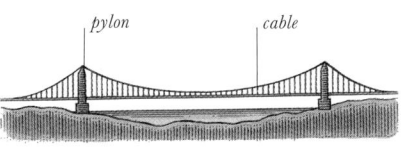
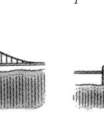
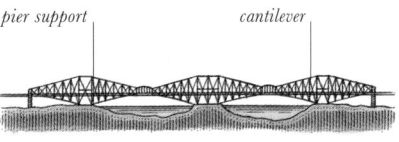

pylon   *cable*   *pier support*   *cantilever*

SUSPENSION BRIDGE   CANTILEVER BRIDGE

brick·lay·er /bríklayər/ *n.* a worker who builds with bricks. □□ **brick·lay·ing** *n.*

brick·work /bríkwərk/ *n.* **1** building in brick. **2** a wall, etc., made of brick. ▷ BRICK

brid·al /bríd'l/ *adj.* of or concerning a bride or a wedding.

bride /brīd/ *n.* a woman on her wedding day and for some time before and after the wedding.

bride·groom /brídgrōōm, -grŏŏm/ *n.* a man on his wedding day and for some time before and after the wedding.

brides·maid /brídzmayd/ *n.* a girl or woman attending a bride on her wedding day.

bridge[1] /brij/ *n. & v.* ● *n.* **1 a** ▼ a structure carrying a road, path, railroad, etc., across a stream, ravine, road, railroad, etc. **b** anything providing a connection between different things. **2** the superstructure on a ship from which the officers direct operations. **3** the upper bony part of the nose. **4** *Mus.* an upright piece of wood on a violin, etc., over which the strings are stretched. ▷ ACOUSTIC, STRINGED. **5** = BRIDGEWORK. ● *v.tr.* **1 a** be a bridge over (*a fallen tree bridges the stream*). **b** make a bridge over. **2** span as if with a bridge (*bridged their differences with understanding*).

bridge[2] /brij/ *n.* a card game derived from whist.

bridge·head /brijhed/ *n. Mil.* a fortified position held on the enemy's side of a river or other obstacle.

bridge·work /bríjwərk/ *n. Dentistry* a dental structure used to cover a gap, joined to the teeth on either side.

bri·dle /bríd'l/ *n. & v.* ● *n.* ► the headgear used to control a horse, consisting of leather straps and a metal bit. ▷ HARNESS. ● *v.* **1** *tr.* put a bridle on (a horse, etc.). **2** *tr.* bring under control. **3** *intr.* (often foll. by *at* or *up at*) express offense, etc., esp. by throwing up the head and drawing in the chin.

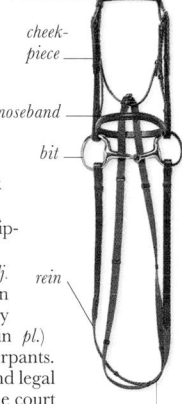

head piece
browband
cheek-piece
noseband
bit
rein

BRIDLE:
SNAFFLE
BRIDLE

bri·dle path *n.* a rough path or road suitable for horseback riding.

Brie /bree/ *n.* a kind of soft ripened cheese. ▷ CHEESE

brief /breef/ *adj., n., & v.* ● *adj.* **1** of short duration. **2** concise in expression. **3** brusque. **4** scanty (*wearing a brief skirt*). ● *n.* **1** (in *pl.*) women's or men's brief underpants. **2** *Law* a summary of the facts and legal points of a case drawn up for the court or counsel. **3** instructions given for a task, etc. **4** *RC Ch.* a letter from the Pope on a matter of discipline. ● *v.tr.* instruct (an employee, etc.) in preparation for a task (*briefed him for the interview*) (cf. DEBRIEF). □ **hold a brief for** argue in favor of. **in brief** in short. □□ **brief·ing** *n.* **brief·ly** *adv.* **brief·ness** *n.*

brief·case /breefkays/ *n.* a flat rectangular case for carrying documents, etc.

bri·er[1] /bríər/ *n.* (also **bri·ar**) any prickly bush, esp. of a wild rose.

bri·er[2] /bríər/ *n.* (also **bri·ar**) **1** a white heath, *Erica arborea*, native to southern Europe. **2** a tobacco pipe made from its root.

brig /brig/ *n.* **1** a two-masted square-rigged ship with an additional lower fore-and-aft sail on the gaff and a boom to the mainmast. **2** a prison, esp. in the navy.

Brig. *abbr.* Brigadier.

bri·gade /brigáyd/ *n.* **1** *Mil.* **a** a subdivision of an army. **b** an infantry unit consisting usu. of three battalions and forming part of a division. **c** a corresponding armored unit. **2** an organized or uniformed band of workers (*fire brigade*). **3** *colloq.* any group of people with a characteristic in common (*the couldn't-care-less brigade*).

brig·a·dier /brígədeer/ *n. Mil.* **1** *Brit.* an officer commanding a brigade. **2 a** *Brit.* a staff officer of similar standing, above a colonel and below a major general. **b** the titular rank granted to such an officer.

brig·a·dier gen·er·al *n.* an officer ranking between colonel and major general.

brig·and /brígənd/ *n.* a member of a robber band living by pillage and ransom. □□ **brig·and·age** *n.* **brig·and·ry** *n.*

brig·an·tine /brígənteen/ *n.* a two-masted sailing ship with a square-rigged foremast and a fore-and-aft rigged mainmast.

bright /brīt/ *adj. & adv.* ● *adj.* **1** emitting or reflecting much light; shining. **2** (of color) intense. **3** clever (*a bright idea; a bright child*). **4** cheerful. ● *adv.* esp. *poet.* brightly (*the moon shone bright*). □□ **bright·ish** *adj.* **bright·ly** *adv.* **bright·ness** *n.*

bright·en /brít'n/ *v.tr. & intr.* (often foll. by *up*) make or become brighter.

bright eyed *adj.* **1** having bright eyes. **2** alert; eager. □ **bright-eyed and bushy-tailed** *colloq.* alert and energetic.

Bright's dis·ease /bríts/ *n.* inflammation of the kidney from any of various causes; nephritis.

brill /bril/ *n.* a European flatfish, *Scophthalmus rhombus*, resembling a turbot.

bril·liance /brílyəns/ *n.* (also **bril·lian·cy** /-ənsee/) **1** great brightness; radiant quality. **2** outstanding talent or intelligence.

bril·lian·cy var. of BRILLIANCE.

bril·liant /brílyənt/ *adj. & n.* ● *adj.* **1** very bright; sparkling. **2** outstandingly talented or intelligent. ● *n.* a diamond of the finest cut with many facets. ▷ DIAMOND, GEM. □□ **bril·liant·ly** *adv.*

bril·lian·tine /brílyənteen/ *n.* an oily liquid ointment for making the hair glossy.

brim /brim/ *n. & v.* ● *n.* **1** the edge or lip of a cup, etc., or of a hollow. **2** the projecting edge of a hat. ▷ HAT. ● *v.tr. & intr.* (**brimmed**, **brimming**) fill or be full to the brim. □ **brim over** overflow. □□ **brimmed** *adj.* (usu. in *comb.*).

brim·ful /brímfŏŏl/ *adj.* (also **brim·full**) (often foll. by *of*) filled to the brim.

brim·stone /brímstōn/ *n.* **1** the element sulfur. **2** a butterfly, *Gonepteryx rhamni*, or moth, *Opisthograptis luteolata*, having yellow wings.

brin·dled /bríndʹld/ *adj.* (also **brin·dle**) brownish or tawny with streaks of other color(s) (esp. of domestic animals).

brine /brīn/ *n.* **1** water saturated or strongly impregnated with salt. **2** sea water.

bring /bring/ *v.tr.* (*past and past part.* **brought** /brawt/) **1 a** come conveying esp. by carrying or leading. **b** come with. **2** cause to come (*what brings you here?*). **3** result in (*war brings misery*). **4** produce as

B

B

income. **5 a** prefer (a charge). **b** initiate (legal action). **6** cause to become or to reach a particular state (*brought them to their senses*). **7** adduce (evidence, an argument, etc.). □ **bring about 1** cause to happen. **2** turn (a ship) around. **bring around 1** restore to consciousness. **2** persuade. **bring back** call to mind. **bring down 1** cause to fall. **2** lower (a price). **3** *sl.* make unhappy or less happy. **4** *colloq.* damage the reputation of; demean. **bring forth** produce. **bring forward 1** move to an earlier time. **2** transfer from the previous page or account. **3** draw attention to. **bring home to** cause to realize fully (*brought home to me that I was wrong*). **bring the house down** receive rapturous applause. **bring in 1** introduce (legislation, a custom, etc.). **2** yield as income or profit. **bring into play** activate. **bring low** overcome. **bring off** achieve successfully. **bring on 1** cause to happen or appear. **2** accelerate the progress of. **bring out 1** make evident. **2** publish. **bring through** aid (a person) through adversity. **bring to 1** restore to consciousness (*brought him to*). **2** check the motion of. **bring to bear** (usu. foll. by *on*) direct and concentrate (forces). **bring to light** reveal. **bring to mind** recall. **bring to pass** cause to happen. **bring up 1** rear (a child). **2** vomit. **3** call attention to. **4** (*absol.*) stop suddenly. **bring upon oneself** be responsible for (something one suffers). □□ **bring·er** *n.*

brink /bringk/ *n.* **1** the extreme edge of land before a precipice, etc. **2** the furthest point before something dangerous or exciting is discovered. □ **on the brink of** about to experience or suffer; in imminent danger of.

brink·man·ship /bríngkmənship/ *n.* the art or policy of pursuing a dangerous course to the brink of catastrophe before desisting, esp. in politics.

brin·y /brínee/ *adj.* (**brinier, briniest**) of brine or the sea; salty. □□ **brin·i·ness** *n.*

bri·o /brée-ó/ *n.* dash; vivacity.

bri·oche /bree-ósh, bree-ōsh, -osh/ *n.* a small rounded sweet roll made with a light yeast dough.

bri·quette /brikét/ *n.* (also **bri·quet**) a block of compressed coal dust or charcoal used as fuel.

brisk /brisk/ *adj.* & *v.* ● *adj.* **1** quick; lively (*a brisk pace*). **2** enlivening; fresh (*a brisk wind*). ● *v.tr.* & *intr.* (often foll. by *up*) make or grow brisk. □□ **brisk·ly** *adv.* **brisk·ness** *n.*

bris·ket /brískit/ *n.* an animal's breast, esp. as a cut of meat.

bris·ling /brízling, brís-/ *n.* (*pl.* same or **brislings**) a small herring or sprat.

bris·tle /brísəl/ *n.* & *v.* ● *n.* **1** a short stiff hair, esp. one of those on an animal's back. **2** this, or an artificial substitute, used in clumps to make a brush. ● *v.* **1 a** *intr.* (of the hair) stand upright. **b** *tr.* make (the hair) do this. **2** *intr.* show irritation or defensiveness. **3** *intr.* (usu. foll. by *with*) be abundant (in). □□ **bristly** /brislee/ *adj.* (**bristlier, bristliest**).

Bris·tol board /bríst'l/ *n.* a kind of fine smooth pasteboard for drawing on.

Brit /brit/ *n. colloq.* a British person.

Bri·tan·ni·a /britányə/ *n.* the personification of Britain, esp. as a helmeted woman with shield and trident.

Bri·tan·ni·a metal a silvery alloy of tin, antimony, and copper.

Bri·tan·nic /británik/ *adj.* (esp. in **His** (or **Her**) **Britannic Majesty**) of Britain.

Brit·i·cism /brítisizəm/ *n.* (also **Brit·ish·ism** /-tishizəm/) an idiom used in Britain but not in other English-speaking countries.

Brit·ish /brítish/ *adj.* & *n.* ● *adj.* **1** of or relating to Great Britain or the United Kingdom, or to its people or language. **2** of the British Common-

wealth or (formerly) the British Empire (*British subject*). ● *n.* **1** (prec. by *the*; treated as *pl.*) the British people. **2** = BRITISH ENGLISH.

Brit·ish Eng·lish *n.* English as used in Great Britain, as distinct from that used elsewhere.

Brit·ish·er /brítishər/ *n.* a British subject.

Brit·ish·ism var. of BRITICISM.

Brit·on /brít'n/ *n.* **1** one of the people of S. Britain before the Roman conquest. **2** a native or inhabitant of Great Britain or (formerly) of the British Empire.

brit·tle /brít'l/ *adj.* & *n.* ● *adj.* **1** hard and fragile; apt to break. **2** frail, weak, unstable. ● *n.* a brittle confection made from nuts and hardened melted sugar.

brit·tle-bone disease = OSTEOPOROSIS. □□ **brit·tle·ness** *n.*

brit·tle star *n.* ◄ an echinoderm of the class Ophiuroidea, with long brittle arms radiating from a small central body. ▷ ECHINODERM

BRITTLE STAR:
BLACK BRITTLE
STAR
(*Ophiocomina nigra*)

broach /brōch/ *v.* & *n.* ● *v.tr.* **1** raise (a subject) for discussion. **2** pierce (a cask) to draw liquor, etc. **3** open and start using contents of (a box, bale, bottle, etc.). ● *n.* **1** a bit for boring. **2** a roasting spit.

broad /brawd/ *adj.* & *n.* ● *adj.* **1** large in extent from one side to the other; wide. **2** in breadth (*2 yards broad*). **3** extensive (*broad acres*). **4** full and clear (*broad daylight*). **5** explicit; unmistakable (*broad hint*). **6** general (*a broad inquiry*). **7** principal (*the broad facts*). **8** tolerant; liberal (*take a broad view*). **9** somewhat coarse (*broad humor*). **10** (of speech) markedly regional (*broad Brooklyn accent*). ● *n.* **1** the broad part of something (*broad of the back*). **2** *sl.* a woman. □□ **broad·ness** *n.*

broad bean *n.* **1** a kind of bean, *Vicia faba*, with pods containing large edible flat seeds. **2** one of these seeds. ▷ SEED

broad·cast /bráwdkast/ *v., n., adj.,* & *adv.* ● *v.* (*past* **broadcast** or **broadcasted**; *past part.* **broadcast**) **1** *tr.* **a** transmit by radio or television. **b** disseminate (information) widely. **2** *intr.* undertake or take part in a radio or television transmission. **3** *tr.* scatter (seed, etc.) over a large area. ● *n.* a radio or television program or transmission. ● *adj.* **1** transmitted by radio or television. **2** widely disseminated. ● *adv.* over a large area. □□ **broad·cast·er** *n.* **broad·cast·ing** *n.*

broad·cloth /bráwdklawth, -kloth/ *n.* a fine cloth of wool, cotton, or silk.

broad·en /bráwdən/ *v.tr.* & *intr.* make or become broader.

broad·loom /bráwdloom/ *adj.* (esp. of carpet) woven in broad widths.

broad·ly /bráwdlee/ *adv.* widely (*grinned broadly*). □ **broadly speaking** disregarding minor exceptions.

broad-mind·ed *adj.* tolerant or liberal in one's views. □□ **broad-mind·ed·ly** *adv.* **broad-mind·ed·ness** *n.*

broad·sheet /bráwdsheet/ *n.* a large sheet of paper printed on one side only, esp. with information.

broad·side /bráwdsīd/ *n.* **1** the firing of all guns from one side of a ship. **2** a vigorous verbal onslaught. □ **broadside on** sideways on.

broad spec·trum *adj.* (of a drug) effective against a large variety of microorganisms.

broad·sword /bráwdsawrd/ *n.* a sword with a broad blade, for cutting rather than thrusting. ▷ SWORD

broad·tail /bráwdtayl/ *n.* **1** the karakul sheep. **2** the fleece or wool from its lamb.

broad·way /bráwdway/ *n.* **1** a large open or main road. **2** (as **Broad·way**) a principal thoroughfare in New York City, noted for its theaters, and the center of U.S. commercial theater production.

bro·cade /brōkáyd/ *n.* ► a rich fabric with a silky finish woven with a raised pattern, and often with gold or silver thread.

broc·co·li /brókəlee/ *n.* a vegetable related to cabbage with a loose cluster of greenish flower buds.

bro·chette /brōshét/ *n.* a skewer on which chunks of meat are cooked, esp. over an open fire.

bro·chure /brōshŏŏr/ *n.* a pamphlet or leaflet, esp. one giving descriptive information

BROCADE:
18TH-CENTURY
BROCADE DRESS

brock·et /brókit/ *n.* any small deer of the genus *Mazama*, native to Central and S. America, having short straight antlers.

brogue[1] /brōg/ *n.* **1** a strong outdoor shoe with perforated bands. **2** a rough shoe of untanned leather.

brogue[2] /brōg/ *n.* a marked accent, esp. Irish.

broil[1] /broyl/ *v.* **1** *tr.* cook (meat) on a rack or a grill. **2** *tr. & intr.* make or become very hot, esp. from the sun.

broil[2] /broyl/ *n.* a brawl; a tumult.

broil·er /bróylər/ *n.* **1** a young chicken raised for broiling or roasting. **2 a** a device or oven setting on a stove for radiating heat downward. **b** a grill, griddle, etc., for broiling.

broke /brōk/ *past* of BREAK. ● *predic. adj. colloq.* having no money. □ **go for broke** *sl.* risk everything in a strenuous effort.

bro·ken /brókən/ *past part.* of BREAK. ● *adj.* **1** that has been broken. **2** (of a person) reduced to despair. **3** spoken falteringly and with many mistakes (*broken English*). **4** interrupted. **5** uneven. □□ **bro·ken·ly** *adv.* **bro·ken·ness** *n.*

bro·ken-down *adj.* **1** worn out. **2** out of order.

bro·ken-heart·ed /brókənháartid/ *adj.* overwhelmed with sorrow.

bro·ken home *n.* a family in which the parents are divorced or separated.

bro·ker /brókər/ *n.* **1** an agent who buys and sells for others. **2** a member of the stock exchange dealing in stocks and bonds.

bro·ker·age /brókərij/ *n.* **1** a broker's fee or commission. **2** a broker's business.

bro·ker·ing /brókəring/ *n.* the trade or business of a broker.

brome /brōm/ *n.* (also **brome·grass**) any oatlike grass of the genus *Bromus*, having slender stems with flowering spikes.

bro·me·li·ad /brōmée·lee·ead/ *n.* ► any plant of the family Bromeliaceae (esp. of the genus *Bromelia*), native to the New World, having short stems with rosettes of stiff leaves, e.g., pineapple. ▷ EPIPHYTE

bro·mic /brómik/ *adj. Chem.* of or containing bromine.

bro·mic ac·id *n.* a strong acid used as an oxidizing agent.

BROMELIAD
(*Bromelia balansae*)

bro·mide /brómīd/ *n.* **1** *Chem.* any binary compound of bromine. **2** *Pharm.* a preparation of usu. potassium bromide, used as a sedative. **3** a trite remark.

bro·mine /brómeen/ *n. Chem.* a liquid element with a choking irritating smell, used in the manufacture of chemicals for photography and medicine. ¶ Symb.: **Br**.

bron·chi *pl.* of BRONCHUS.

bron·chi·al /brónkeeəl/ *adj.* of or relating to the bronchi or bronchioles.

bron·chi·al tube *n.* a bronchus or any tube branching from it. ▷ LUNG

bron·chi·ole /bróngkeeōl/ *n.* ▶ any of the minute divisions of a bronchus. ▷ LUNG

bron·chi·tis /brongkítis/ *n.* inflammation of the mucous membrane in the bronchial tubes. □□ **bron·chit·ic** /-kítik/ *adj. & n.*

broncho- /brónkō/ *comb. form* bronchi.

bron·cho·cele /brónkəseel/ *n.* a goiter.

bron·cho·pneu·mo·nia /brónkōnoōmṓnyə, -nyoō-/ *n.* inflammation of the lungs, arising in the bronchi or bronchioles.

bron·cho·scope /brónkəskōp/ *n.* a usu. fiber-optic instrument for inspecting the bronchi. □□ **bron·chos·co·py** /-kóskəpee/ *n.*

bron·chus /brónkəs/ *n.* (*pl.* **bronchi** /-kī/) any of the major air passages of the lungs. ▷ BRONCHIOLE, LUNG

bron·co /brónkō/ *n.* (*pl.* **-os**) a wild or half-tamed horse of western N. America.

broncobuster /brónkōbustər/ *n.* a person who breaks wild horses.

bron·to·sau·rus /bróntəsáwrəs/ *n.* (also **bron·to·saur** /bróntəsawr/) a large plant-eating dinosaur of the genus *Brontosaurus*, with a long tail and trunklike legs. Now more correctly APATOSAURUS.

Bronx cheer /brongks/ *n. colloq.* = RASPBERRY 3 a.

bronze /bronz/ *n. & adj.* ● *n.* **1** an alloy of copper with up to one third tin. **2** its brownish color. **3** ▶ a thing made of bronze, esp. as a work of art. ● *adj.* made of or colored like bronze.

Bronze Age *n.* the period when weapons and tools were usu. made of bronze.

bronz·er /brónzər/ *n.* a cosmetic liquid or powder applied to the skin to give it color or shine, typically to give the appearance of a suntan.

brooch /brōch, broōch/ *n.* an ornament fastened to clothing with a hinged pin.

brood /broōd/ *n. & v.* ● *n.* **1** the young of an animal (esp. a bird) produced at one hatching or birth. **2** *colloq.* the children in a family. **3** a group of related things. **4** bee or wasp larvae. **5** (*attrib.*) kept for breeding (*brood mare*). ● *v.* **1** *intr.* (often foll. by *on, over,* etc.) worry or ponder (esp. resentfully). **2 a** *intr.* sit as a hen on eggs to hatch them. **b** *tr.* sit on (eggs) to hatch them. **3** *intr.* (usu. foll. by *over*) (of silence, a storm, etc.) hang or hover closely. □□ **brood·ing·ly** *adv.*

brood·er /broōdər/ *n.* **1** a heated house for chicks, piglets, etc. **2** a person who broods.

brook¹ /broōk/ *n.* a small stream. □□ **brooklet** /-lət/ *n.*

brook² /broōk/ *v.tr.* (usu. with *neg.*) *formal* tolerate.

brook trout *n.* the speckled trout (*Salvelinus fontinalis*), a game fish of N. America.

broom /broōm, broom/ *n.* **1** a long-handled brush of bristles, twigs, etc., for sweeping. **2** any of various shrubs, esp. *Cytisus scoparius,* bearing bright yellow flowers.

broom·stick /broōmstik, broom-/ *n.* the handle of a broom, esp. as allegedly ridden on through the air by witches.

Bros. *abbr.* Brothers (esp. in the name of a business).

broth /brawth, broth/ *n. Cookery* **1** a thin soup of

BRONCHIOLE:
HUMAN
BRONCHIOLE

(diagram labels: tertiary bronchus, trachea, secondary bronchus, primary bronchus, bronchiole)

BRONZE DECORATION
FROM CELTIC CHARIOT
(*c.*100 BC–AD 100)

---

meat or fish stock. **2** unclarified meat, fish or vegetable stock.

broth·el /bróthəl/ *n.* a house, etc., where prostitution takes place.

broth·er /brúthər/ *n.* **1** a man or boy in relation to other sons and daughters of his parents. **2 a** a close male friend or associate. **b** a male fellow member of a labor union, etc. **3** (*pl.* also **brethren** /bréthrin/) **a** a member of a male religious order. **b** a fellow member of a religion, etc. **4** a fellow human being. □□ **broth·er·less** *adj.* **broth·er·ly** *adj. & adv.* **broth·er·li·ness** *n.*

broth·er·hood /brúthərhoōd/ *n.* **1 a** the relationship between brothers. **b** brotherly friendliness. **2 a** an association or community of people linked by a common interest, etc. **b** its members collectively. **3** a labor union. **4** community of feeling between all human beings.

broth·er-in-law *n.* (*pl.* **brothers-in-law**) **1** the brother of one's wife or husband. **2** the husband of one's sister. **3** the husband of one's sister-in-law.

brough·am /broōəm, broōm, brōəm/ *n. hist.* a horse-drawn closed carriage with a driver perched outside in front.

brought *past* and *past part.* of BRING.

brou·ha·ha /broōhaahaa/ *n.* commotion.

brow /brow/ *n.* **1** the forehead. **2** (usu. in *pl.*) an eyebrow. **3** the summit of a hill or pass. **4** the edge of a cliff, etc. □□ **-browed** *adj.*

brow·beat /brówbeet/ *v.tr.* (*past* **-beat**; *past part.* **-beaten**) intimidate with stern looks and words. □□ **brow·beat·er** *n.*

brown /brown/ *adj., n., & v.* ● *adj.* **1** having the color as of dark wood or rich soil. **2** dark-skinned or suntanned. **3** (of bread) made from a dark flour. ● *n.* **1** a brown color or pigment. **2** brown clothes or material (*dressed in brown*). ● *v.tr. & intr.* make or become brown. □□ **brown·ish** *adj.* **brown·ness** *n.* **brown·y** *adj.*

brown bag·ging *n.* **1** taking one's lunch to work, etc., in a brown paper bag. **2** taking one's own wine etc., into a restaurant that is not licensed to serve alcohol.

brown bear *n.* a large N. American brown bear, *Ursus arctos.* ▷ BEAR

brown dwarf *n. Astron.* a celestial object intermediate in size between a giant planet and a small star.

brown·field /brównfeeld/ *adj.* (of an urban site) having had previous development on it. Compare with GREENFIELD.

Brown·i·an mo·tion /brówniən/ *n.* (also **Brown·i·an move·ment**) *Physics* the erratic random movement of microscopic particles in a liquid, gas, etc., as a result of continuous bombardment from molecules of the surrounding medium.

Brown·ie /brównee/ *n.* **1** a member of the junior branch of the Girl Scouts. **2** (**brownie**) *Cookery* a small square of rich, usu. chocolate, cake with nuts. **3** (**brownie**) a benevolent elf said to do household work secretly.

Brown·ie point *n. colloq.* a notional credit for something done to win favor.

brown·nose /brównnōz/ *v.intr. coarse sl.* ingratiate oneself; be servile. □□ **brown·nos·er** *n.*

brown·out /brównowt/ *n.* a period during which electrical voltage is reduced to avoid a blackout, resulting in lowered illumination.

brown owl *n.* any of various owls, esp. the tawny owl.

brown rice *n.* unpolished rice with only the husk of the grain removed.

Brown shirt *n.* a Nazi; a member of a fascist organization.

brown·stone /brównstōn/ *n.* **1** a kind of reddish brown sandstone used for building. **2** a building faced with this.

brown sug·ar *n.* unrefined or partially refined sugar.

browse /browz/ *v. & n.* ● *v.* **1** *intr. & tr.* read or survey desultorily. **2** *intr.* (often foll. by *on*) feed (on leaves, etc.). **3** *tr.* crop and eat. **4** *intr. & tr. Computing* etc. read or survey (data files, etc.), esp. via a network. ● *n.* **1** young shoots, etc., as fodder for cattle. **2** an act of browsing. □□ **brows·er** *n.*

bru·cel·lo·sis /broōsəlṓsis/ *n.* a disease caused by bacteria of the genus *Brucella,* affecting esp. cattle and causing undulent fever in humans.

bruise /broōz/ *n. & v.* ● *n.* **1** an injury appearing as an area of discolored skin on a human or animal body, caused by impact. **2** an area of damage on a fruit, etc. ● *v.* **1** *tr.* inflict a bruise on. **2** *intr.* be susceptible to bruising. **3** *tr.* crush or pound.

bruis·er /broōzər/ *n. colloq.* a large tough-looking person.

bruit /broōt/ *v.tr.* (often foll. by *abroad, about*) spread (a report or rumor).

brume /broōm/ *n.* mist; fog.

brunch /brunch/ *n.* a late-morning meal eaten as the first meal of the day.

bru·nette /broōnét/ *n. & adj.* (also *masc.* **bru·net**) ● *n.* a woman with dark hair. ● *adj.* (of a woman) having dark hair.

brunt /brunt/ *n.* the chief impact of an attack, task, etc. (esp. *bear the brunt of*).

bru·schet·ta /broōskétə/ *n.* toasted Italian bread drenched in olive oil.

brush /brush/ *n. & v.* ● *n.* **1** an implement with bristles, hair, wire, etc., set into a block or projecting from the end of a handle, for any of various purposes, esp. cleaning or scrubbing, painting, arranging the hair, etc. ▷ CALLIGRAPHY. **2** the application of a brush; brushing. **3 a** (usu. foll. by *with*) a short esp. unpleasant encounter (*a brush with the law*). **b** a skirmish. **4 a** the bushy tail of a fox. **b** a brushlike tuft. **5** *Electr.* a piece of carbon or metal serving as an electrical contact. **6 a** undergrowth; small trees and shrubs. **b** such wood cut or broken. **c** land covered with brush. ● *v.* **1 a** a sweep or scrub or put in order with a brush. **b** treat (a surface) with a brush so as to change its nature or appearance. **2** *tr.* **a** remove (dust, etc.) with a brush. **b** apply (a liquid preparation) to a surface with a brush. **3** *tr. & intr.* graze or touch in passing. **4** *intr.* perform a brushing action or motion. □ **brush aside** dismiss curtly or lightly. **brush off** rebuff; dismiss abruptly. **brush over** paint lightly. **brush up** (often foll. by *on*) revive one's former knowledge of (a subject). □□ **brush·less** *n.* **brush·y** *adj.*

brush-off *n.* a rebuff.

brush·wood /brúshwoōd/ *n.* **1** cut or broken twigs, etc. **2** undergrowth.

brush·work /brúshwərk/ *n.* **1** manipulation of the brush in painting. **2** a painter's style in this.

brusque /brusk/ *adj.* abrupt or offhand in manner or speech. □□ **brusque·ly** *adv.* **brusque·ness** *n.*

Brus·sels lace /brúsəlz/ *n.* an elaborate needlepoint or pillow lace.

brus·sels sprout /brúsəlz/ *n.* **1** a vegetable related to cabbage with small compact cabbagelike buds borne close together along a tall single stem. **2** any of these buds used as a vegetable.

brut /broōt/ *adj.* (of wine) very dry; unsweetened.

bru·tal /broōt'l/ *adj.* **1** savagely cruel. **2** harsh; merciless. □□ **brutality** /-tálitee/ *n.* (*pl.* **-ies**). **bru·tal·ly** *adv.*

bru·tal·ism /broōt'lizəm/ *n.* **1** brutality. **2** a heavy plain style of architecture, etc. □□ **bru·tal·ist** *n. & adj.*

bru·tal·ize /broōt'līz/ *v.tr.* **1** make brutal. **2** treat brutally. □□ **brutalization** /-lizáyshən/ *n.*

B

B

brute /broŏt/ *n. & adj.* ● *n.* **1 a** a brutal person or animal. **b** *colloq.* an unpleasant person. **2** an animal as opposed to a human being. ● *adj.* **1** not possessing the capacity to reason. **2 a** cruel. **b** stupid; sensual. **3** unthinking; merely physical (*brute force*; *brute matter*). □□ **brut·ish** *adj.* **brut·ish·ness** *n.*

bry·ol·o·gy /brī-óləjee/ *n.* the study of bryophytes. □□ **bry·o·log·i·cal** /brīəlójikəl/ *adj.* **bry·ol·o·gist** *n.*

bry·o·ny /brīənee/ *n.* (*pl.* **-ies**) any climbing plant of the genus *Bryonia*, esp. *B. dioica*, bearing greenish white flowers and red berries.

bry·o·phyte /brīəfīt/ *n.* ▶ any plant of the phylum Bryophyta, including mosses and liverworts.

bry·o·zo·an /brīəzṓən/ *n. & adj.* ● *n.* any aquatic invertebrate animal of the phylum Bryozoa, forming colonies attached to rocks, seaweeds, etc. ● *adj.* of or relating to the phylum Bryozoa.

Bry·thon·ic /brithónik/ *n. & adj.* ● *n.* the language of the Celts of southern Britain and Brittany. ● *adj.* of or relating to this people or their language.

BS *abbr.* **1** Bachelor of Science. **2** Bachelor of Surgery.

B.Sc. *abbr.* Bachelor of Science.

B-side /beésīd/ *n.* the side of a phonograph record regarded as less important.

B2B *abbr.* business-to-business, denoting trade conducted via the Internet between businesses.

BTU *abbr.* (also **B.t.u.**) British thermal unit(s).

bub /bub/ *n. colloq.* a boy or a man, often used as a form of address.

bub·ble /búbəl/ *n. & v.* ● *n.* **1 a** a thin sphere of liquid enclosing air, etc. **b** an air-filled cavity in a liquid or a solidified liquid such as glass or amber. **2** the sound or appearance of boiling. **3** a semicylindrical or domed cavity. ● *v.intr.* **1** rise in or send up bubbles. **2** make the sound of boiling. □ **bubble over** (often foll. by *with*) be exuberant with laughter, excitement, anger, etc.

bub·ble bath *n.* **1** a preparation for adding to bath water to make it foam. **2** a bath with this added.

bub·ble gum *n.* chewing gum that can be blown into bubbles.

bub·ble mem·o·ry *n. Computing* a type of memory which stores data as a pattern of magnetized regions in a thin layer of magnetic material.

bub·ble wrap *n.* a clear plastic wrap with air bubbles in it.

bub·bly /búblee/ *adj. & n.* ● *adj.* (**bubblier, bubbliest**) **1** having or resembling bubbles. **2** exuberant. ● *n. colloq.* champagne.

bu·bo /byoŏbō, boŏ-/ *n.* (*pl.* **-oes**) a swollen inflamed lymph node in the armpit or groin.

bu·bon·ic plague /byoŏbónik, boŏ-/ *n.* a contagious bacterial disease characterized by fever, delirium, and the formation of buboes.

buc·cal /búkəl/ *adj.* **1** of or relating to the cheek. **2** of or in the mouth.

buc·ca·neer /búkəneér/ *n.* **1** a pirate. **2** an unscrupulous adventurer. □□ **buc·ca·neer·ing** *n. & adj.*

buc·ci·na·tor /búksinaytər/ *n.* a flat thin cheek muscle.

buck[1] /buk/ *n. & v.* ● *n.* **1** the male of various animals, esp. the deer, hare, or rabbit. **2** (*attrib.*) **a** *sl.* male (*buck antelope*). **b** *Mil.* of the lowest rank (*buck private*). ● *v.* **1** *intr.* (of a horse) jump upwards with back arched and feet drawn together. **2** *tr.* **a** (usu. foll. by *off*) throw (a rider or burden) in this way. **b** oppose; resist. **3** *tr. & intr.* (usu. foll. by *up*) *colloq.* make or become more cheerful.

buck[2] /buk/ *n. sl.* a dollar. □ **a fast buck** easy money.

buck[3] /buk/ *n. sl.* an article placed as a reminder before a player whose turn it is to deal at poker. □ **pass the buck** *colloq.* shift responsibility (to another).

buck[4] /buk/ *n.* **1** a sawhorse. **2** a vaulting horse.

buck[5] /buk/ *n.* the body of a cart.

BRYOPHYTE

Bryophytes – liverworts and mosses – are simple low-growing plants, anchored to the ground or to tree bark by tiny filamentous rhizoids. They lack vascular tissue and an outer waterproof cuticle, and so thrive best in moist habitats. Most mosses form cushionlike clumps, while liverworts are either leafy or flat and encrusting.

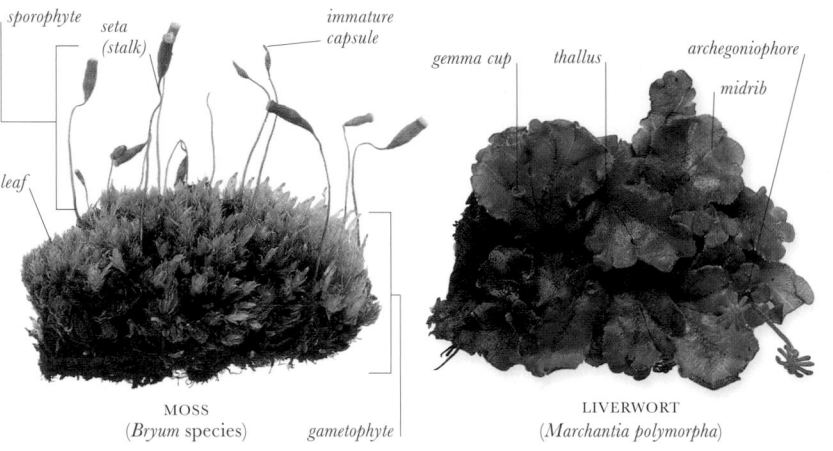

sporophyte
seta (stalk)
immature capsule
leaf
MOSS (*Bryum* species)
gametophyte

gemma cup
thallus
archegoniophore
midrib
LIVERWORT (*Marchantia polymorpha*)

buck·board /búkbawrd/ *n.* a horse-drawn vehicle with the body formed by a plank fixed to the axles.

buck·et /búkit/ *n. & v.* ● *n.* **1 a** a roughly cylindrical open container, used for carrying, catching, or holding water, etc. **b** the amount contained in this (*need three buckets to fill the tub*). **2** (in *pl.*) large quantities of liquid, esp. rain or tears (*wept buckets*). **3** a compartment on the outer edge of a waterwheel. **4** the scoop of a dredger or a grain elevator. ● *v.intr.* (**bucketed, bucketing**) (often foll. by *down*) (of liquid, esp. rain) pour heavily. □□ **buck·et·ful** *n.* (*pl.* **-fuls**)

buck·et seat *n.* a seat with a rounded back to fit one person, esp. in a car.

buck·eye /búkī/ *n.* **1** any shrub of the genus *Aesculus* of the horse chestnut family, with large sticky buds and showy red or white flowers. **2** the shiny brown nutlike seed of this plant.

buck·horn /búkhawrn/ *n.* horn of a buck as a material for knife handles, etc.

buck·hound /búkhownd/ *n.* a small kind of staghound.

buck·le /búkəl/ *n. & v.* ● *n.* **1** a flat frame with a hinged pin, used for joining the ends of a belt, strap, etc. **2** a similarly shaped ornament. ● *v.* **1** *tr.* (often foll. by *up, on*, etc.) fasten with a buckle. **2** *tr. & intr.* give way or cause to give way under longitudinal pressure. □ **buckle down** make a determined effort. **buckle to** (or **down to**) prepare for; set about (work, etc.). **buckle to** get to work; make a vigorous start.

buck·ler /búklər/ *n. hist.* a small round shield held by a handle.

buck·o /búkō/ *n. & adj. sl.* ● *n.* (*pl.* **-oes**) a swaggering or domineering fellow. ● *adj.* blustering; swaggering; bullying.

buck·ram /búkrəm/ *n.* a coarse linen or other cloth stiffened with gum or paste, and used as interfacing or in bookbinding.

buck·saw /búksaw/ *n.* a two-handed saw set in an H-shaped frame and used for sawing wood.

buck·shot /búkshot/ *n.* large-sized lead shot.

buck·skin /búkskin/ *n.* **1 a** the skin of a buck. **b** leather made from a buck's skin. **2** a thick smooth cloth.

buck·thorn /búkthawrn/ *n.* any thorny shrub of the genus *Rhamnus*, esp. *R. cathartica* with berries formerly used as a cathartic.

buck·tooth /búktoŏth/ *n.* (*pl.* **-teeth**) an upper tooth that projects.

buck·wheat /búkhweet, -weet/ *n.* any cereal plant of the genus *Fagopyrum*, esp. *F. esculentum* with seeds used for fodder and for flour.

bu·col·ic /byoŏkólik/ *adj.* of or concerning shepherds, the pastoral life, etc.; rural.

bud[1] /bud/ *n. & v.* ● *n.* **1 a** an immature knoblike shoot from which a stem, leaf, or flower develops. ▷ CALYX. **b** a flower or leaf that is not fully open. **2** *Biol.* an asexual outgrowth from a parent organism that separates to form a new individual. ● *v.* (**budded, budding**) **1** *intr. Bot. & Zool.* form a bud. **2** *intr.* begin to develop (*a budding violinist*). **3** *tr. Hort.* graft a bud (of a plant) on to another plant. □ **in bud** having newly formed buds.

bud[2] /bud/ *n. colloq.* (as a form of address) = BUDDY.

Bud·dha /boŏdə, boŏdə/ *n.* **1** a title given to successive teachers of Buddhism, esp. to its founder, Gautama. **2** a statue or picture of the Buddha.

Bud·dhism /boŏdizəm, boŏd-/ *n.* a widespread Asian religion or philosophy, founded by Gautama Buddha in India in the 5th c. BC, which teaches that elimination of the self and earthly desires is the highest goal. □□ **Bud·dhist** *n. & adj.*

bud·dle·ia /búdleeə/ *n.* any shrub of the genus *Buddleia*, with fragrant flowers attractive to butterflies.

bud·dy /búdee/ *n. & v. colloq.* ● *n.* (*pl.* **-ies**) (often as a form of address) a close friend or companion. ● *v.intr.* (**-ies, -ied**) (often foll. by *up*) become friendly.

budge /buj/ *v.* (usu. with *neg.*) **1** *intr.* **a** make the slightest movement. **b** change one's opinion. **2** *tr.* cause or compel to budge (*nothing will budge him*).

budg·er·i·gar /bújəreegaar/ *n.* a small parrot, *Melopsittacus undulatus*, native to Australia, and often kept as a cage bird.

budg·et /bújit/ *n. & v.* ● *n.* **1** the amount of money needed or available (*a budget of $200*). **2 a** the usu. annual estimate of national revenue and expenditure. **b** an estimate or plan of expenditure in relation to income for a business, etc. **c** a private person's or family's similar estimate. **3** (*attrib.*) inexpensive. ● *v.tr. & intr.* (**budgeted, budgeting**) (often foll. by *for*) allow or arrange for in a budget (*have budgeted for a new car*). □ **on a budget** avoiding expense; cheap. □□ **budg·et·ar·y** *adj.*

budg·ie /bújee/ *n. colloq.* = BUDGERIGAR.

buff /buf/ *adj., n., & v.* ● *adj.* of a yellowish beige color. ● *n.* **1** a yellowish beige color. **2** *colloq.* an enthusiast (*railroad buff*). **3** *colloq.* the human skin unclothed. **4 a** a velvety dull yellow ox leather. **b** (*attrib.*) made of this. ● *v.tr.* **1** polish (metal, fingernails, etc.). **2** make (leather) velvety like buff, by removing the surface. □ **in the buff** *colloq.* naked.

buf·fa·lo /búfəlō/ *n. & v.* ● *n.* (*pl.* same or **-oes**) **1** a N. American bison, *Bison bison.* **2** either of two species of ox, *Synceros caffer*, native to Africa, or *Bubalus arnee*, native to Asia with heavy backswept horns. ● *v.tr.* (**-oes, -oed**) *sl.* overawe; outwit.

Buf·fa·lo wings *n. pl.* fried chicken wings coated in a hot, spicy sauce and served with blue cheese dressing.

buff·er /búfər/ *n. & v.* ● *n.* **1 a** a device that protects against or reduces the effect of an impact. **b** such a device (usu. one of a pair) on the front and rear of a railroad vehicle or at the end of a track. ▷ TENDER. **2** *Biochem.* a substance that maintains the hydrogen ion concentration of a solution when an acid or alkali is added. **3** *Computing* a temporary memory area or queue for data to aid its transfer between devices or programs operating at different speeds, etc. ● *v.tr.* **1** act as a buffer to. **2** *Biochem.* treat with a buffer.

buff·er state *n.* a small nation situated between two larger ones potentially hostile to one another and regarded as reducing the likelihood of open hostilities.

buff·er zone *n.* **1** a neutral area between two warring groups. **2** any area separating those in conflict.

buf·fet[1] /bōōfáy, bə-/ *n.* a meal consisting of several dishes set out from which guests serve themselves (*buffet lunch*).

buf·fet[2] /búfit/ *v. & n.* ● *v.* (**buffeted, buffeting**) **1** *tr.* **a** strike or knock repeatedly (*wind buffeted the trees*). **b** strike with the hand or fist. **2** *tr.* (of fate, etc.) treat badly; plague (*buffeted by misfortune*). **3 a** *intr.* struggle; fight one's way (through difficulties, etc.). **b** *tr.* contend with (waves, etc.). ● *n.* **1** a blow, esp. of the hand. **2** a shock.

buf·fet·ing /búfiting/ *n.* **1** a beating; repeated blows. **2** *Aeron.* an irregular oscillation, caused by air eddies, of any part of an aircraft.

buf·fle·head /búflhed/ *n.* a duck, *Bucephala albeola*, native to N. America, with a head that appears overlarge.

buf·fo /bōōfō/ *n. & adj.* ● *n.* (*pl.* **-os**) a comic actor, esp. in Italian opera. ● *adj.* comic; burlesque.

buf·foon /bəfōōn/ *n.* **1** a jester; a mocker. **2** a stupid person. □□ **buf·foon·er·y** *n.* **buf·foon·ish** *adj.*

bug /bug/ *n. & v.* ● *n.* **1 a** any of various hemipterous insects with oval flattened bodies and mouthparts modified for piercing and sucking. **b** *colloq.* any small insect. **2** *sl.* a microorganism, esp. a bacterium, or a disease caused by it. **3** a concealed microphone. **4** *sl.* an error in a computer program or system, etc. **5** *sl.* **a** an obsession, enthusiasm, etc. **b** an enthusiast. ● *v.* (**bugged, bugging**) **1** *tr.* conceal a microphone in. **2** *tr. sl.* annoy; bother. **3** *intr.* (often foll. by *out*) *sl.* leave quickly.

bug·a·boo /búgəbōō/ *n.* a bogey (see BOGEY[2]) or bugbear.

bug·bear /búgbair/ *n.* **1** a cause of annoyance or anger. **2** an object of baseless fear.

bug-eyed *adj.* with bulging eyes.

bug·ger /búgər/ *n., v., & int.* ● *n.* **1** a person who commits buggery. ● *v.tr.* **1** *coarse sl.* as an exclamation of annoyance (*bugger the thing!*). **2** commit buggery with. ● *int. coarse sl.* expressing annoyance.

bug·ger·y /búgəree/ *n.* = BESTIALITY 2.

bug·gy /búgee/ *n.* (*pl.* **-ies**) **1** a light, horse-drawn vehicle for one or two people. **2** a small, sturdy

motor vehicle (*beach buggy; dune buggy*). **3** a baby carriage.

bu·gle[1] /byōōgəl/ *n.* (also **bu·gle horn**) a brass instrument like a small trumpet, used esp. for military signals. □□ **bu·gler** /byōōglər/ *n.*

bu·gle[2] /byōōgəl/ *n.* a blue-flowered mat-forming European plant, *Ajuga reptans.*

bu·gle[3] /byōōgəl/ *n.* a tube-shaped bead sewn on a dress, etc., for ornament.

bu·gloss /byōōglaws, -glos/ *n.* any of various bristly plants related to borage, esp. of the genus *Anchusa*, with bright blue tubular flowers.

buhl /bōōl/ *n.* (also **boule**, **boulle**) **1** pieces of brass, tortoiseshell, etc., cut to make a pattern and used as decorative inlays esp. on furniture. **2** work inlaid with buhl. **3** (*attrib.*) inlaid with buhl.

build /bild/ *v. & n.* ● *v.tr.* (*past* and *past. part.* **built** /bilt/) **1 a** construct (a house, vehicle, fire, road, model, etc.) by putting parts or material together. **b** commission, finance, and oversee the building of (*the board has built two new schools*). **2 a** (often foll. by *up*) establish, develop, make, or accumulate gradually (*built the business up from scratch*). **b** (often foll. by *on*) base (hopes, theories, etc.) (*ideas built on a false foundation*). **3** (as **built** *adj.*) having a specified build (*sturdily built; brick-built*). ● *n.* **1** the proportions of the body (*a slim build*). **2** a style of construction. □ **build in** incorporate as part of a structure. **build up 1** increase in size or strength. **2** praise; boost. **3** gradually become established. **built on sand** unstable.

build·er /bíldər/ *n.* **1** a contractor for building houses, etc. **2** a person engaged as a construction worker, etc., on a building site.

build·ing /bílding/ *n.* **1** a permanent fixed structure forming an enclosure and providing protection from the elements, etc. (e.g. a house, school, factory, or stable) **2** the constructing of such structures.

build·up /bíldəp/ *n.* **1** a favorable description in advance. **2** a gradual approach to a climax or maximum.

built *past* and *past part.* of BUILD.

built-in *adj.* **1** forming an integral part of a structure. **2** forming an integral part of a person's character (*built-in integrity*).

built-up *adj.* **1** (of a locality) densely covered by houses, etc. **2** increased in height, etc., by the addition of parts. **3** composed of separately prepared parts.

bulb /bulb/ *n.* **1 a** ◄ an underground fleshy-leaved storage organ of some plants (e.g., lily, onion) sending roots downward and leaves upward. **b** a plant grown from this, e.g. a daffodil. **2** = LIGHTBULB. **3** any object or part shaped like a bulb.

bul·bous /búlbəs/ *adj.* **1** shaped like a bulb; fat or bulging. **2** having a bulb or bulbs. **3** (of a plant) growing from a bulb.

bul·bul /bōōlbōōl/ *n.* **1** any songbird of the family Pycnonotidae, of dull plumage with contrasting bright patches. **2** a singer or poet.

bul·gar var. of BULGUR.

Bul·gar·i·an /bulgáireeən/ *n. & adj.* ● *n.* **1 a** a native or inhabitant of Bulgaria. **b** a person of Bulgarian descent. **2** the language of Bulgaria. ● *adj.* of or relating to Bulgaria or its people or language.

bulge /bulj/ *n. & v.* ● *n.* **1 a** a convex part of an otherwise flat or flatter surface. **b** an irregular swelling; a lump. **2** *colloq.* a temporary increase in quantity or number (*baby bulge*). **3** *Mil.* a salient. ● *v.* **1** *intr.* swell outwards. **2** *intr.* be full or

new foliage leaf

shoot

apical bud

protective leaf scale

fleshy scale leaf

stem

adventitious root

BULB: CROSS SECTION OF AN AMARYLLIS BULB (*Hippeastrum* species)

replete. **3** *tr.* swell (a bag, etc.) by stuffing. □□ **bulg·y** *adj.*

bul·gur /búlgər/ *n.* (also **bul·gar**, **bul·ghur**) whole wheat that has been partially boiled then dried.

bu·lim·a·rex·i·a /bōōlímərékseeə, -léemə-, byōō-/ *n.* = BULIMIA 2. □□ **bu·lim·a·rex·ic** *adj. & n.*

bu·lim·i·a /bōōléemeeə, -li-, byōō-/ *n. Med.* **1** insatiable overeating. **2** (in full **bulimia nervosa**) an emotional disorder in which bouts of extreme overeating are followed by depression and self-induced vomiting, purging, or fasting. □□ **bu·lim·ic** *adj. & n.*

bulk /bulk/ *n. & v.* ● *n.* **1 a** size; magnitude (esp. large). **b** a large mass. **c** a large quantity. **2** a large shape, body, or person (*jacket barely covered his bulk*). **3** (usu. prec. by *the*; treated as *pl.*) the greater part or number (*the bulk of the applicants are women*). **4** roughage. ● *v.* **1** *intr.* seem in respect to size or importance (*bulks large in his reckoning*). **2** *tr.* (often foll. by *out*) make (a book, a textile yarn, etc.) seem thicker by suitable treatment (*bulked it with irrelevant stories*). □ **in bulk** in large quantities.

bulk·head /búlk-hed/ *n.* **1** an upright partition separating the compartments in a ship, aircraft, vehicle, etc. ▷ SUBMARINE. **2** an embankment or retaining wall, esp. along a water front.

bulk·y /búlkee/ *adj.* (**bulkier**, **bulkiest**) **1** taking up much space; large. **2** awkwardly large; unwieldy. □□ **bulk·i·ly** *adv.* **bulk·i·ness** *n.*

bull[1] /bōōl/ *n. & adj.* ● *n.* **1 a** an uncastrated male bovine animal. **b** a male of the whale, elephant, and other large animals. **2** (**the Bull**) the zodiacal sign or constellation Taurus. ▷ TAURUS. **3** *Stock Exch.* a person who buys shares hoping to sell them at a higher price later (cf. BEAR[3]). ● *adj.* like that of a bull (*bull neck*).

bull[2] /bōōl/ *n.* a papal edict.

bull[3] /bōōl/ *n.* **1** (also **Irish bull**) an expression containing a contradiction in terms or implying ludicrous inconsistency. **2** *sl.* **a** unnecessary routine tasks or discipline. **b** nonsense. **c** trivial or insincere talk or writing.

bul·lace /bōōlis/ *n.* a thorny European shrub, *Prunus insitita*, bearing globular yellow or purple-black fruits, of which the damson plum is the cultivated form.

bull·dog /bōōl-dawg, -dog/ *n.* ► a dog of a sturdy breed with a large head and smooth hair.

BULLDOG

bull·doze /bōōldōz/ *v.tr.* **1** clear with a bulldozer. **2** *colloq.* **a** intimidate. **b** make (one's way) forcibly.

bull·doz·er /bōōldōzər/ *n.* ▼ a powerful tractor with a broad curved vertical blade at the front for clearing ground.

driver's cab

hydraulic system

steel bucket

cog

tread

blade

crawler tracks

BULLDOZER

B

bul·let /boŏolit/ *n.* **1** ▶ a small round or cylindrical missile with a pointed end, fired from a rifle, revolver, etc. **2** *Printing* a round black dot used as a marker (●).

bullet

cartridge

BULLET

bul·le·tin /boŏolitin/ *n.* **1** a short official statement of news. **2** a regular periodical issued by an organization or society.

bul·le·tin board *n.* **1** a board for posting notices, information, etc. **2** *Computing* a public computer file serving the function of a bulletin board.

bul·let·proof /boŏolitprōōf/ *adj.* (of a material) designed to resist the penetration of bullets.

bull·fight /boŏolfīt/ *n.* a sport of baiting and (usu.) killing bulls as a public spectacle. □□ **bull·fight·er** *n.* **bull·fight·ing** *n.*

bull·finch /boŏolfinch/ *n.* a European finch, *Pyrrhula pyrrhula*, with a short stout beak and bright plumage.

bull·frog /boŏolfrawg, -frog/ *n.* ▶ a large frog, *Rana catesbiana*, native to eastern N. America, with a deep croak.

bull·head /boŏolhed/ *n.* any of various marine fishes with large flattened heads.

bull·head·ed /boŏolhédid/ *adj.* obstinate; impetuous; blundering. □□ **bull·head·ed·ly** *adv.* **bull·head·ed·ness** *n.*

BULLFROG
(Rana catesbiana)

bull·horn /boŏolhawrn/ *n.* an electronic device for amplifying the sound of the voice so it can be heard at a distance.

bul·lion /boŏolyən/ *n.* a metal (esp. gold or silver) in bulk before coining, or valued by weight.

bull·ish /boŏolish/ *adj.* **1** like a bull, esp. in size or temper. **2 a** *Stock Exch.* causing or associated with a rise in prices. **b** optimistic. □□ **bull·ish·ly** *adv.* **bull·ish·ness** *n.*

bull mar·ket *n.* *Stock Exch.* a market with shares rising in price.

bul·lock /boŏolək/ *n.* a castrated bull.

bull pen *n.* (also **bull·pen**) **1** *Baseball* **a** an area in which relief pitchers warm up during a game. **b** the relief pitchers on a team. **2** a large holding cell for prisoners awaiting court appearances. **3** *colloq.* an open, unpartitioned area for several workers.

bull·ring /boŏolring/ *n.* an arena for bullfights.

bull ses·sion *n.* an informal group discussion.

bull's-eye *n.* **1 a** the center of a target. **b** a shot that hits this. **2** a large hard peppermint-flavored candy. **3** a hemisphere or thick disk of glass in a ship's deck or side to admit light. **4** a small circular window. **5 a** a hemispherical lens. **b** a lantern fitted with this. **6** a boss of glass at the center of a blown glass sheet.

bull·shit /boŏolshit/ *n. & v. coarse sl.* ● *n.* **1** (often as *int.*) nonsense. **2** trivial or insincere talk or writing. ● *v.intr.* (**-shitted, -shitting**) talk nonsense; bluff. □□ **bull·shit·ter** *n.*

bull ter·ri·er *n.* a short-haired dog of a breed that is a cross between a bulldog and a terrier.

bul·ly[1] /boŏolee/ *n. & v.* ● *n.* (*pl.* **-ies**) a person who uses strength or power to coerce others by fear. ● *v.tr.* (**-ies, -ied**) **1** persecute by force or threats. **2** (foll. by *into* + verbal noun) pressure (a person) to do something (*bullied him into agreeing*).

bul·ly[2] /boŏolee/ *adj. & int. colloq.* ● *adj.* very good. ● *int.* (foll. by *for*) expressing admiration or approval, or *iron.* (*bully for them!*).

bul·ly[3] /boŏolee/ *n. & v.* (in full **bully off**) ● *n.* (*pl.* **-ies**) the start of play in field hockey in which two opponents strike each other's sticks or the ground three times and then go for the ball. ● *v.intr.* (**-ies, -ied**) start play in this way.

bul·ly[4] /boŏolee/ *n.* (in full **bully beef**) corned beef.

bul·ly·boy /boŏoleeboy/ *n.* a hired thug.

bul·ly·rag /boŏoleerag/ *v.tr.* (also **ballyrag** /bál-/)

(**-ragged, -ragging**) *sl.* play tricks on; intimidate; harass.

bul·rush /boŏolrush/ *n.* **1** a rushlike water plant, *Scirpus lacustris*, used for weaving. **2** *Bibl.* a papyrus plant.

bul·wark /boŏolwərk/ *n.* **1** a defensive wall, esp. of earth; a breakwater. **2** a person, principle, etc., that acts as a defense. **3** (usu. in *pl.*) a ship's side above deck.

bum /bum/ *n., v., & adj. sl.* ● *n.* a habitual loafer or tramp; a lazy dissolute person. ● *v.* (**bummed, bumming**) **1** *intr.* (often foll. by *about, around*) loaf or wander around. **2** *tr.* cadge. ● *attrib.adj.* **1** of poor quality. **2** not entirely functional (*bum ankle*).

bum·ble /búmbəl/ *v.intr.* **1** (foll. by *on*) speak in a rambling way. **2** (often as **bumbling** *adj.*) move or act ineptly. **3** make a buzz or hum. □□ **bum·bler** *n.*

bum·ble·bee /búmbəlbee/ *n.* any large humming bee of the genus *Bombus*. ▷ BEE

bum·boat /búmbōt/ *n.* any small boat selling provisions, etc., to ships.

bum·ma·lo /búməlō/ *n.* (*pl.* same) a small fish, *Harpodon nehereus*, of S. Asian coasts, dried and used as food (see BOMBAY DUCK).

bum·mer /búmər/ *n. sl.* **1** a bum; a loafer. **2** an unpleasant occurrence.

bump /bump/ *n., v., & adv.* ● *n.* **1** a dull-sounding blow or collision. **2** a swelling or dent caused by this. **3** an uneven patch on a road, field, etc. **4** *Phrenol.* any of various prominences on the skull thought to indicate different mental faculties. ● *v.* **1 a** *tr.* hit or come against with a bump. **b** *intr.* (of two objects) collide. **2** *intr.* (foll. by *against, into*) hit with a bump; collide with. **3** *tr.* (often foll. by *against, on*) hurt or damage by striking (*bumped my head on the ceiling*). **4** *intr.* (usu. foll. by *along*) move with much jolting (*bumped along the road*). **5** *tr.* displace, esp. by seniority. ● *adv.* with a bump; suddenly; violently. □ **bump into** *colloq.* meet by chance. **bump off** *sl.* murder. **bump up** *colloq.* increase (prices, etc.).

bump·er /búmpər/ *n.* **1** a horizontal bar fixed across the front or back of a vehicle to reduce damage in a collision or as a trim. ▷ CAR. **2** (usu. *attrib.*) an unusually large or fine example (*a bumper crop*). **3** a brimful glass of wine, etc.

bump·er car *n.* each of a number of small electrically driven cars in an enclosure at an amusement park, driven around and bumped into each other.

bump·er stick·er *n.* a strip of paper backed with adhesive that may be affixed to an automobile bumper, usu. bearing a joke, political slogan, tourism advertisement, etc.

bump·kin /búmpkin/ *n.* a rustic or socially inept person.

bump·tious /búmpshəs/ *adj.* offensively self-assertive or conceited. □□ **bump·tious·ly** *adv.* **bump·tious·ness** *n.*

bump·y /búmpee/ *adj.* (**bumpier, bumpiest**) **1** having many bumps (*a bumpy road*). **2** affected by bumps (*a bumpy ride*). □□ **bump·i·ly** *adv.* **bump·i·ness** *n.*

bum rap *n.* imprisonment on a false charge.

bum's rush *n.* forcible ejection.

bum steer *n.* false information.

bun /bun/ *n.* **1** a small often sweet bread roll, often with dried fruit. **2** hair worn in the shape of a bun. **3** (in *pl.*) *sl.* the buttocks. □ **have a bun in the oven** *sl.* be pregnant.

bunch /bunch/ *n. & v.* ● *n.* **1** a cluster of things growing or fastened together (*bunch of grapes; bunch of keys*). **2** a collection; a set (*best of the bunch*). **3** *colloq.* a group; a gang. ● *v.* **1** *tr.* make into a bunch; gather into close folds. **2** *intr.* form into a group or crowd. □□ **bunch·y** *adj.*

bun·co /búngkō/ *n. & v.* (also **bunko**) *sl.* ● *n.* (*pl.*

-os) a swindle, esp. by card sharping or a confidence trick. ● *v.tr.* (**-oes, -oed**) swindle; cheat.

bun·combe var. of BUNKUM.

Bun·des·rat /boŏondəsraat/ *n.* the Upper House of Parliament in Germany or in Austria.

Bun·des·tag /boŏondəstaag/ *n.* the Lower House of Parliament in Germany.

bun·dle /búndəl/ *n. & v.* ● *n.* **1** a collection of things tied or fastened together. **2** a set of nerve fibers, etc., banded together. **3** *sl.* a large amount of money. ● *v.* **1** *tr.* **a** (usu. foll. by *up*) tie in or make into a bundle (*bundled up my exercise things*). **b** sell (a product) together with another one in a single transaction. **2** *tr.* (usu. foll. by *into*) throw or push, esp. quickly or confusedly (*bundled the papers into the drawer*). **3** *tr.* (usu. foll. by *out, off, away*, etc.) send away hurriedly or unceremoniously (*bundled them off the premises*). □ **bundle up** dress warmly or cumbersomely.

bung /bung/ *n. & v.* ● *n.* a stopper for closing a hole in a container. ● *v.tr.* stop with a bung. □ **bunged up** closed; blocked.

bun·ga·low /búnggəlō/ *n.* a one-storied house.

bun·gee /búnjee/ *n.* (in full **bungee cord**) elasticized cord or rope.

bun·gee jump·ing *n.* the sport of jumping from a height while secured by a bungee from the ankles or a harness.

bun·gle /búnggəl/ *v. & n.* ● *v.* **1** *tr.* mismanage or fail at (a task). **2** *intr.* work badly or clumsily. ● *n.* a bungled attempt; bungled work. □□ **bun·gler** *n.*

bun·ion /búnyən/ *n.* a swelling on the foot, esp. at the first joint of the big toe.

bunk[1] /bungk/ *n. & v.* ● *n.* a shelflike bed against a wall. ● *v.intr.* **1** sleep in a bunk. **2** occupy sleeping quarters.

bunk[2] /bungk/ *n. sl.* = BUNKUM.

bunk bed *n.* each of two or more beds one above the other, forming a unit.

bun·ker /búngkər/ *n. & v.* ● *n.* **1** a large container or compartment for storing fuel. **2** a reinforced underground shelter. **3** a hollow filled with sand, used as an obstacle in a golf course. ▷ FAIRWAY, GOLF. ● *v.tr.* **1** fill the fuel bunkers of (a ship, etc.). **2** (usu. in *passive*) trap in a bunker (in sense 3).

bunk·house /búngk-hows/ *n.* a house where workers, etc., are lodged.

bun·kum /búngkəm/ *n.* (also **bun·combe**) nonsense; humbug.

bun·ny /búnee/ *n.* (*pl.* **-ies**) a child's name for a rabbit.

Bun·sen burn·er /búnsən/ *n.* ◀ a small adjustable gas burner used in scientific work as a source of intense heat.

chimney

air valve

gas supply

BUNSEN BURNER

bunt[1] /bunt/ *n.* the baggy center of a fishing net, sail, etc.

bunt[2] /bunt/ *n.* a disease of wheat caused by the fungus *Tilletia caries*.

bunt·ing[1] /búnting/ *n.* any of numerous seed-eating birds of the family Emberizidae, related to the finches.

bunt·ing[2] /búnting/ *n.* **1** flags and other decorations. **2** a loosely woven fabric used for these.

bunt·ing[3] /búnting/ *n.* a baby's hooded sleeping bag made of soft fabric.

bu·oy /boŏo-ee, boy/ *n. & v.* ● *n.* **1** ▶ an anchored float serving as a navigation mark or to show reefs, etc. **2** a lifebuoy. ● *v.tr.* **1** (usu. foll. by *up*) **a** keep afloat. **b** sustain the courage or spirits of (a person, etc.); uplift; encourage. **2** (often foll. by *out*) mark with a buoy or buoys.

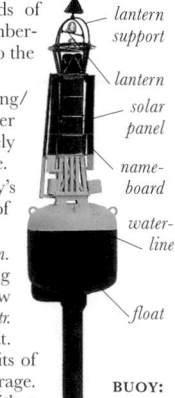

top-mark

lantern support

lantern

solar panel

name-board

water-line

float

BUOY: PILLAR MARK

buoy·an·cy /bóyənsee/ *n.* **1** the capacity to be or remain buoyant. **2** resilience. **3** cheerfulness.

buoy·ant /bóyənt/ *adj.* **1 a** able or apt to keep afloat or rise to the top of a liquid or gas. **b** (of a liquid or gas) able to keep something afloat. **2** light-hearted. □□ **buoy·ant·ly** *adv.*

bur /bər/ *n.* var. of BURR.

bur·ble /bárbəl/ *v.* & *n.* ● *v.intr.* **1** speak ramblingly. **2** make a murmuring noise. ● *n.* **1** a murmuring noise. **2** rambling speech.

bur·bot /bárbət/ *n.* ▼ an eellike, bearded freshwater fish, *Lota lota*.

barbel

BURBOT (*Lota lota*)

bur·den /bárdən/ *n.* & *v.* ● *n.* **1** a load. **2** an oppressive duty, obligation, expense, emotion, etc. **3** the bearing of loads (*beast of burden*). **4** a ship's carrying capacity. **5 a** the refrain of a song. **b** the chief theme of a speech, book, poem, etc. ● *v.tr.* load with a burden; oppress. □□ **bur·den·some** *adj.*

bur·den of proof *n.* the obligation to prove one's case.

bur·dock /bárdok/ *n.* ► any plant of the genus *Arctium*, with prickly flowers and docklike leaves.

bu·reau /byŏŏrō/ *n.* (*pl.* **bureaus** or **bureaux** /-rōz/) **1** a chest of drawers. **2** an office or department for transacting specific business.

BURDOCK (*Arctium lappa*)

bu·reauc·ra·cy /byŏŏrókrəsee/ *n.* (*pl.* **-ies**) **1** government by central administration. **2** the officials of such a government. **3** conduct typical of such officials.

bu·reau·crat /byŏŏrəkrat/ *n.* **1** an official in a bureaucracy. **2** an inflexible or insensitive administrator. □□ **bu·reau·crat·ic** /-krátik/ *adj.* **bu·reau·crat·i·cal·ly** *adv.*

bu·reauc·ra·tize /byŏŏrókrətīz/ *v.tr.* govern by or transform into a bureaucratic system. □□ **bu·reauc·ra·ti·za·tion** /-tizáyshən/ *n.*

bu·reau de change /byŏŏrō də shaánzh/ *n.* a place where one can exchange foreign money.

bu·rette /byŏŏrét/ *n.* (also **bu·ret**) a graduated glass tube with a stopcock for measuring small volumes of liquid in chemical analysis.

burg /bərg/ *n.* a town or city.

bur·gee /bərjée/ *n.* a triangular or swallow-tailed flag bearing the colors or emblem of a yacht club.

bur·geon /bárjən/ *v.intr. literary* **1** begin to grow rapidly; flourish. **2** put forth young shoots; bud.

burg·er /bárgər/ *n.* **1** *colloq.* a hamburger. **2** (in *comb.*) a certain kind of hamburger or variation of it (*beefburger; veggieburger*).

bur·gess /bárjis/ *n. hist.* a borough magistrate or legislator in colonial Maryland or Virginia.

burgh·er /bárgər/ *n.* a citizen of a town on the European continent.

bur·glar /bárglər/ *n.* a person who commits burglary.

bur·glar·ize /bárglərīz/ *v.* **1** *tr.* commit burglary against (a building or person). **2** *intr.* commit burglary.

bur·gla·ry /bárgləree/ *n.* (*pl.* **-ies**) **1** entry into a building illegally with intent to commit theft, do bodily harm, or do damage. **2** an instance of this.

bur·gle /bárgəl/ *v.tr.* & *intr.* = BURGLARIZE.

bur·gun·dy /bárgəndee/ *n.* (*pl.* **-ies**) **1 a** the wine (usu. red) of Burgundy in E. France. **b** a similar wine from another place. **2** the dark red color of Burgundy wine.

bur·i·al /béreeəl/ *n.* **1 a** the burying of a dead body. **b** a funeral. **2** *Archaeol.* a grave or its remains.

bur·i·al ground *n.* a cemetery.

bu·rin /byŏŏrin, bár-/ *n.* **1** a steel tool for engraving on copper or wood. **2** *Archaeol.* a flint tool with a chisel point.

burka /bárkə/ *n.* a long enveloping garment worn in public by Muslim women.

Bur·kitt's lym·pho·ma /bárkits/ *n. Med.* a malignant tumor of the lymphatic system, esp. affecting children of Central Africa.

burl /bərl/ *n.* **1** a knot or lump in wool or cloth. **2** a rounded knotty growth on a tree.

bur·lap /bárlap/ *n.* **1** coarse canvas esp. of jute used for sacking, etc. ▷ UPHOLSTERY. **2** a similar lighter material for use in dressmaking or furnishing. ▷ PADDING

bur·lesque /bərlésk/ *n., adj.,* & *v.* ● *n.* **1 a** comic imitation, parody. **b** a performance or work of this kind. **c** bombast; mock-seriousness. **2** a variety show, often including striptease. ● *adj.* of or in the nature of burlesque. ● *v.tr.* (**burlesques, burlesqued, burlesquing**) make or give a burlesque of.

bur·ly /bárlee/ *adj.* (**burlier, burliest**) of stout sturdy build; big and strong.

Bur·mese /bárméez/ *n.* & *adj.* ● *n.* (*pl.* same) **1 a** a native or inhabitant of Burma (also called **Myanmar**) in SE Asia. **b** a person of Burmese descent. **2 a** a member of the largest ethnic group of Burma. **3** the language of this group. **4** (in full **Burmese cat**) ► a breed of short-coated domestic cat. ● *adj.* of or relating to Burma or its people or language.

BURMESE CAT

burn /bərn/ *v.* & *n.* ● *v.* (*past and past part.* **burned** or **burnt**) **1** *tr.* & *intr.* be or cause to be consumed or destroyed by fire. **2** *intr.* **a** blaze or glow with fire. **b** be in the state characteristic of fire. **3** *tr.* & *intr.* be or cause to be injured or damaged by fire or great heat or by radiation. **4** *tr.* & *intr.* use or be used as a source of heat, light, or other energy. **5** *tr.* & *intr.* char in cooking (*burned the vegetables; the vegetables are burning*). **6** *tr.* produce (a hole, a mark, etc.) by fire or heat. **7** *tr.* **a** subject (clay, chalk, etc.) to heat for a purpose. **b** harden (bricks) by fire. **c** make (lime or charcoal) by heat. **8** *tr.* color, tan, or parch with heat or light. **9** *tr.* & *intr.* put or be put to death by fire or electrocution. **10** *tr.* **a** cauterize; brand. **b** (foll. by *in*) imprint by burning. **11** *tr.* & *intr.* make or be hot; give or feel a sensation or pain of or like heat. **12** *tr.* & *intr.* (often foll. by *with*) make or be passionate; feel or cause to feel great emotion (*burn with shame*). **13** *intr.* (foll. by *into*) (of acid, etc.) gradually penetrate (into) causing disintegration. ● *n.* **1** a mark or injury caused by burning. **2** the ignition of a rocket engine in flight, giving extra thrust. **3** a forest area cleared by burning. □ **burn one's bridges** commit oneself irrevocably. **burn the candle at both ends** exhaust one's resources by undertaking too much. **burn down 1 a** destroy (a building) by burning. **b** (of a building) be destroyed by fire. **2** burn less vigorously as fuel fails. **burn one's fingers** suffer for meddling or rashness. **burn a hole in one's pocket** (of money) be quickly spent. **burn low** (of fire) be nearly out. **burn the midnight oil** read or work late into the night. **burn out 1** be reduced to nothing by burning. **2** fail or cause to fail by burning. **3** (usu. *refl.*) suffer physical or emotional exhaustion. **4** consume the contents of by burning. **burn up 1** get rid of by fire. **2** begin to blaze. **3** *sl.* be or make furious.

burned-out *adj.* physically or emotionally exhausted.

burn·er /bárnər/ *n.* the part of a gas stove, lamp, etc., that emits and shapes the flame. ▷ HOT-AIR BALLOON. □ **on the back** (or **front**) **burner** *colloq.* receiving little (or much) attention.

bur·net /bárnét, bárnit/ *n.* **1** any plant of the genus *Sanguisorba*, with pink or red flowers. **2** any of several moths of the family Zygaenidae, with crimson spots. ▷ MOTH

burn·ing /bárning/ *adj.* **1** ardent; intense (*burning desire*). **2** hotly discussed; exciting; vital, urgent (*burning question*). **3** flagrant (*burning shame*). □□ **burn·ing·ly** *adv.*

bur·nish /bárnish/ *v.tr.* polish by rubbing. □□ **bur·nish·er** *n.*

bur·noose /bərnŏŏs/ *n.* (also **bur·nous**) an Arab or Moorish hooded cloak.

burn·out /bárnowt/ *n.* **1** physical or emotional exhaustion. **2** depression; disillusionment.

burnt /bərnt/ *past* and *past part.* of BURN.

burnt of·fer·ing *n.* **1** an offering burned on an altar as a sacrifice. **2** *joc.* overcooked food.

bur oak *n.* a N. American oak, *Quercus macrocarpa*, with large fringed acorn cups.

burp /bərp/ *v.* & *n. colloq.* ● *v.* **1** *intr.* belch. **2** *tr.* make (a baby) belch. ● *n.* a belch.

burr /bər/ *n.* & *v.* ● *n.* **1 a** a whirring sound. **b** a rough sounding of the letter *r*. **2 a** a rough edge left on cut or punched metal or paper. **b** a surgeon's or dentist's small drill. **3 a** a prickly clinging seed-case or flowerhead. **b** any plant producing these. ● *v.* **1** *tr.* pronounce with a burr. **2** *intr.* make a whirring sound.

bur·ri·to /bəréetō/ *n.* (*pl.* **-os**) a tortilla rolled around a meat or bean filling.

bur·ro /bárō, bŏŏrō, búrō/ *n.* (*pl.* **-os**) a small donkey used as a pack animal.

bur·row /bárō, búrō/ *n.* & *v.* ● *n.* ▼ a hole or tunnel dug by a small animal as a dwelling. ● *v.* **1** *intr.* make a burrow. **2** *tr.* make (a hole, etc.) by digging. **3** *intr.* hide oneself. **4** *intr.* (foll. by *into*) investigate; search. □□ **bur·row·er** *n.*

fortress   *nest*   *mole*   *food supply*   *hunting tunnels*

BURROW: CROSS SECTION OF A MOLE BURROW

bur·sa /bársə/ *n.* (*pl.* **bursae** /-see/ or **bursas**) *Anat.* a fluid-filled sac or saclike cavity to lessen friction. □□ **bur·sal** *adj.*

bur·sar /bársər/ *n.* a treasurer, esp. the person in charge of the funds and other property of a college.

bur·sa·ry /bársəree/ *n.* (*pl.* **-ies**) the post or room of a bursar.

bur·si·tis /bərsítis/ *n.* inflammation of a bursa.

burst /bərst/ *v.* & *n.* ● *v.* (*past* and *past part.* **burst**) **1 a** *intr.* break suddenly and violently apart by expansion of contents or internal pressure. **b** *tr.* cause to do this. **c** *tr.* send (a container, etc.) violently apart. **2 a** *tr.* open forcibly. **b** *intr.* come open or be opened forcibly. **3 a** *intr.* (usu. foll. by *in, out*) make one's way suddenly or by force. **b** *tr.* break away from or through (*the river burst its banks*). **4** *tr.* & *intr.* fill or be full to overflowing. **5** *intr.* appear or

B

B

come suddenly (*burst into flame*; *sun burst out*). **6** *intr.* (foll. by *into*) suddenly begin to shed or utter (esp. *burst into tears* or *laughter* or *song*). **7** *intr.* be as if about to burst because of effort, excitement, etc. **8** *tr.* suffer bursting of (*burst a blood vessel*). **9** *tr.* separate (continuous stationery) into single sheets. ● *n.* **1** the act of or an instance of bursting; a split. **2** a sudden issuing forth (*burst of flame*). **3** a sudden outbreak (*burst of applause*). **4 a** a short sudden effort; a spurt. **b** a gallop. **5** an explosion. □ **burst out 1** suddenly begin (*burst out laughing*). **2** exclaim.

bur·y /béree/ *v.tr.* (**-ies**, **-ied**) **1** place (a dead body) in the earth, in a tomb, or in the sea. **2** lose by death (*has buried three husbands*). **3 a** put under ground (*bury alive*). **b** hide in the earth. **c** cover up; submerge. **4 a** put out of sight (*buried his face in his hands*). **b** consign to obscurity (*the idea was buried*). **c** put away; forget. **4** involve deeply (*buried himself in his work*). □ **bury the hatchet** cease to quarrel.

bus /bus/ *n. & v.* ● *n.* (*pl.* **buses** or **busses**) **1** a large passenger vehicle, esp. one serving the public on a fixed route. **2** *colloq.* an automobile, airplane, etc. **3** *Computing* a defined set of conductors carrying data and control signals within a computer. ▷ COMPUTER. ● *v.* (**buses** or **busses**, **bused** or **bussed**, **busing** or **bussing**) **1** *intr.* go by bus. **2** *tr.* transport by bus.

bus·bar /búsbaar/ *n. Electr.* a system of conductors in a generating or receiving station on which power is concentrated for distribution.

bus·boy /búsboy/ *n.* an assistant to a restaurant waiter who performs such chores as filling water glasses and removing dirty dishes.

bus·by /búzbee/ *n.* (*pl.* **-ies**) a tall fur hat worn by some military, esp. British, units.

bush /boosh/ *n.* **1** a shrub or clump of shrubs. **2** a thing resembling this. **3** a wild uncultivated area (*the Australian bush*).

bush baby *n.* (*pl.* **-ies**) ► a small African tree-climbing lemur; a galago. ▷ PROSIMIAN

bushed /boosht/ *adj. colloq.* tired out.

bush·el /booshəl/ *n.* a measure of capacity for grain, fruit, etc. (64 pints; *Brit.* 8 gallons, or 36.4 liters).

bush·fire /booshfir/ *n.* a fire in a forest or in scrub often spreading widely.

bu·shi·do /boosheedo/ *n.* the code of honor and morals of the Japanese samurai.

BUSH BABY: LESSER BUSH BABY (*Galago senegalensis*)

bush·ing /booshing/ *n.* **1** a metal lining for a round hole enclosing a revolving shaft, etc. **2** a sleeve proving electrical insulation.

bush·man /booshmən/ *n.* (*pl.* **-men**) **1** a person who lives or travels in the Australian bush. **2** (**Bushman**) **a** a member of an aboriginal people in S. Africa. **b** the language of this people.

bush·whack /boosh-hwak, -wak/ *v.* **1** *intr.* **a** clear woods and bush country. **b** live or travel in bush country. **2** *tr.* ambush.

bush·whack·er /boosh-hwakər, -wakər/ *n.* **1 a** a person who clears woods and bush country. **b** a person who lives or travels in bush country. **2** a guerrilla fighter (orig. in the American Civil War).

bush·y /booshee/ *adj.* (**bushier**, **bushiest**) **1** growing thickly like a bush. **2** having many bushes. **3** covered with bush. □□ **bush·i·ness** *n.*

busi·ness /bíznis/ *n.* **1** one's regular occupation, profession, or trade. **2** a thing that is one's concern. **3 a** a task or duty. **b** a reason for coming (*what is your business?*). **4** serious activity (*get down to business*). **5** *derog.* a matter (*sick of the whole business*). **6** a thing or series of things to be dealt with (*the business of the day*). **7** buying and selling; trade; dealings, esp. of a commercial nature (*good stroke of business*). **8** a commercial firm. **9** *Theatr.* action on stage. **10** a

difficult matter (*what a business*). □ **has no business to** has no right to. **in business 1** trading. **2** able to begin operations. **in the business of 1** engaged in. **2** intending to (*we are not in the business of surrendering*). **like nobody's business** *colloq.* extraordinarily. **mind one's own business** not meddle. **on business** with a definite purpose, esp. one relating to one's regular occupation.

busi·ness card *n.* a card printed with one's name and professional details.

busi·ness·like /bíznislīk/ *adj.* efficient; practical.

busi·ness·man /bíznismən/ *n.* (*pl.* **-men**; *fem.* **businesswoman**, *pl.* **-women**) a man or woman engaged in trade or commerce, esp. at a senior level.

busi·ness per·son *n.* a businessman or business-woman.

busk /busk/ *v.intr.* perform for voluntary donations. □□ **busk·er** *n.*

bus·man /búsmən/ *n.* (*pl.* **-men**) the driver of a bus.

bus·man's hol·i·day *n.* leisure time spent in an activity similar to one's regular work.

buss /bus/ *n. & v. colloq.* ● *n.* a kiss. ● *v.tr.* kiss.

bus sta·tion *n.* a center where buses depart and arrive.

bus stop *n.* **1** a regular stopping place for a bus. **2** a sign marking this.

bust[1] /bust/ *n.* **1 a** the human chest, esp. that of a woman; the bosom. **b** the circumference of the body at bust level (*a 36-inch bust*). **2** a sculpture of a person's head, shoulders, and chest.

bust[2] /bust/ *v., n., & adj. colloq.* ● *v.* (*past* and *past part.* **busted** or **bust**) **1** *tr. & intr.* burst; break. **2** *tr.* reduce (a soldier, etc.) to a lower rank; dismiss. **3** *tr.* **a** raid; search. **b** arrest. ● *n.* **1** a sudden failure; a bankruptcy. **2 a** a police raid. **b** an arrest. ● *adj.* (also **bust·ed**) **1** broken; burst; collapsed. **2** bankrupt. **3** arrested. □ **bust up 1** bring or come to collapse; explode. **2** (of a couple) separate. **go bust** become bankrupt; fail.

bus·tard /bústərd/ *n.* any large terrestrial bird of the family Otididae, with long neck, long legs, and stout tapering body.

bust·er /bústər/ *n.* **1** *sl.* buddy; fellow (used esp. as a disrespectful form of address). **2** a violent gale.

bus·tier /boostyáy, bústeeay/ *n.* a strapless close-fitting bodice.

bus·tle[1] /búsəl/ *v. & n.* ● *v.* **1** *intr.* (often foll. by *about*) **a** work, etc., showily, energetically, and officiously. **b** hasten. **2** *tr.* make (a person) hurry or work hard (*bustled him into his overcoat*). **3** *intr.* (as **bustling** *adj.*) *colloq.* full of activity. ● *n.* excited activity; a fuss.

bus·tle[2] /búsəl/ *n. hist.* ► a pad or frame worn under a skirt and puffing it out behind.

bust·y /bústee/ *adj.* (**bustier**, **bustiest**) (of a woman) having a prominent bust.

bus·y /bízee/ *adj., & v.* ● *adj.* (**busier**, **busiest**) **1** (often foll. by *in, with, at,* or pres. part.) occupied or engaged in work, etc., with the attention concentrated. **2** full of activity or detail; fussy (*a busy evening; a picture busy with detail*). **3** employed continuously; unresting. **4** meddlesome; prying. **5** (of a telephone line) in use. ● *v.tr.* (**-ies**, **-ied**) (often *refl.*) keep busy; occupy. □□ **busily** /bízilee/ *adv.*

bus·y·bod·y /bízeebodee, -budee/ *n.* (*pl.* **-ies**) a meddlesome person.

bus·y sig·nal *n.* an intermittent buzzing sound indicating that a telephone line is in use.

BUSTLE ON A 19TH-CENTURY DRESS

but /but, bət/ *conj., prep., adv., pron., & n.* ● *conj.* **1 a** nevertheless; however (*tried hard but did not succeed*). **b** on the other hand; on the contrary (*I am old but you are young*). **2** (prec. by *can*, etc.; in *neg.* or *interrog.*) except; other than; otherwise than (*cannot choose but do it*; *what could we do but run?*). **3** without the result that (*it never rains but it pours*). **4** prefixing an interruption to the speaker's train of thought (*the weather is ideal – but is that a cloud on the horizon?*). ● *prep.* except; apart from; other than (*everyone went but me*). ● *adv.* **1** only; no more than; only just (*we can but try*; *is but a child*; *had but arrived*). **2** introducing emphatic repetition; definitely (*wanted to see nobody, but nobody*). ● *rel.pron.* who not; that not (*there is not a man but feels pity*). ● *n.* an objection (*ifs and buts*). □ **but for** without the help or hindrance, etc., of (*but for you I'd be rich by now*). **but one** (or **two**, etc.) excluding one (or two, etc.) from the number (*next door but one*; *last but one*). **but then** (or **yet**) however; on the other hand (*I won, but then the others were beginners*).

bu·tane /byóotayn/ *n. Chem.* a gaseous hydrocarbon of the alkane series used in liquefied form as fuel.

butch /booch/ *adj.* masculine; tough-looking.

butch·er /boochər/ *n. & v.* ● *n.* **1 a** a person whose trade is dealing in meat. **b** a person who slaughters animals for food. **2** a person who kills indiscriminately or brutally. ● *v.tr.* **1** slaughter or cut up (an animal) for food. **2** kill wantonly or cruelly. **3** ruin through incompetence.

butch·er·y /boochəree/ *n.* (*pl.* **-ies**) **1** needless or cruel slaughter. **2** the butcher's trade. **3** a slaughterhouse.

but·ler /bútlər/ *n.* the principal manservant of a household.

butt[1] /but/ *v. & n.* ● *v.* **1** *tr. & intr.* push with the head or horns. **2 a** *intr.* (usu. foll. by *against, upon*) touch with one end flat; meet end to end; abut. **b** *tr.* (usu. foll. by *against*) place (lumber, etc.) with the end flat against a wall, etc. ● *n.* **1** a push with the head. **2** a join of two edges. □ **butt in** interrupt; meddle. **butt out 1** stop interrupting. **2** stop doing something.

butt[2] /but/ *n.* **1** (often foll. by *of*) an object (of ridicule, etc.) (*the butt of his jokes*). **2 a** a mound behind a target. **b** (in *pl.*) a shooting range. **c** a target.

butt[3] /but/ *n.* **1** (also **butt end**) the thicker end, esp. of a tool or a weapon (*gun butt*). ▷ MACHINE GUN. **2 a** the stub of a cigar or a cigarette. **b** (also **butt end**) a remnant. **3** *sl.* the buttocks.

butt[4] /but/ *n.* a cask, esp. as a measure of wine or ale.

butte /byoot/ *n.* a high, isolated, steep-sided hill. ▷ ERODE

but·ter /bútər/ *n. & v.* ● *n.* **1** a fatty substance made by churning cream and used as a spread or in cooking. **2** a substance of a similar consistency or appearance (*peanut butter*). ● *v.tr.* spread, cook, or serve with butter (*butter the bread; buttered rum*). □ **butter up** *colloq.* flatter excessively.

but·ter-and-eggs *n.* any of several plants having two shades of yellow in the flower, e.g., toadflax.

but·ter·ball /bútərbawl/ *n. sl.* a fat person or animal.

but·ter bean *n.* **1** the flat, dried, white lima bean. **2** a yellow-podded bean.

but·ter cream *n.* (also **but·ter ic·ing**) a mixture of butter, confectioner's sugar, etc., used as a filling or a topping for a cake.

but·ter·cup /bútərkup/ *n.* any common yellow-flowered plant of the genus *Ranunculus*.

but·ter·fat /bútərfat/ *n.* the essential fats of pure butter.

but·ter·fin·gers /bútərfinggərz/ *n. colloq.* a clumsy person prone to drop things.

but·ter·fly /bútərflī/ *n.* (*pl.* **-flies**) **1** ► any diurnal insect of the order Lepidoptera, with four usu. brightly colored wings held erect when at rest. ▷ METAMORPHOSIS. **2** a showy or frivolous person. **3** (in *pl.*) *colloq.* a nervous sensation felt in the stomach.

BUTTERFLY

Butterflies and moths form a single order of about 200,000 species, but it is sometimes difficult to distinguish between the two. Butterflies can usually be identified by their bright colors and clubbed antennae. They fly during the daytime, and the base of the hindwing is expanded and strengthened to support the forewing in flight. When resting, butterflies fold their wings upright over their backs. Butterflies feed by sucking liquids through a long proboscis. All species undergo complete metamorphosis, developing as a larva (caterpillar) before emerging from a chrysalis as an adult butterfly.

front leg
clubbed antenna
compound eye
head
middle leg
proboscis
thorax
pupal case
femur
tibia
hind leg
abdomen
costal margin
forewing
vein
hindwing
apex
outer margin
wing folded upright
spur

EXTERNAL FEATURES OF A SWALLOWTAIL BUTTERFLY (*Papilio* species)

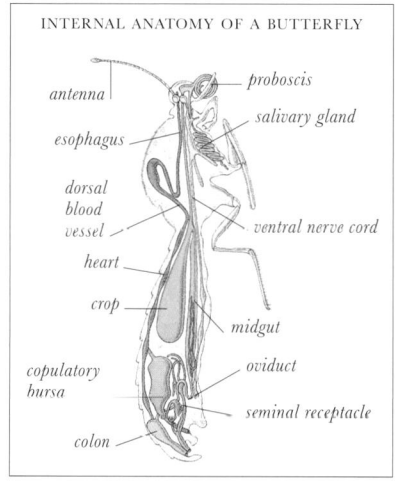

INTERNAL ANATOMY OF A BUTTERFLY

antenna
proboscis
esophagus
salivary gland
dorsal blood vessel
heart
ventral nerve cord
crop
midgut
copulatory bursa
oviduct
seminal receptacle
colon

EXAMPLES OF OTHER BUTTERFLIES

| SWALLOWTAILS AND BIRDWINGS | SKIPPERS | WHITES AND RELATIVES | BLUES AND COPPERS | NYMPHALIDS |

CAIRNS BIRDWING (*Ornithoptera priamus*)

SILVER-SPOTTED SKIPPER (*Epargyreus clarus*)

LARGE WHITE (*Pieris brassicae*)

ADONIS BLUE (*Lysandra bellargus*)

CAMBERWELL BEAUTY (*Nymphalis antiopa*)

TIGER SWALLOWTAIL (*Papilio glaucus*)

REGENT SKIPPER (*Euschemon rafflesia*)

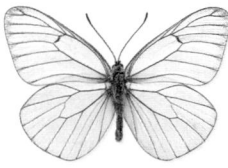

BLACK-VEINED WHITE (*Aporia crataegi*)

GREEN-UNDERSIDE BLUE (*Glaucopsyche alexis*)

BLUE MORPHO (*Morpho menelaus*)

APOLLO (*Parnassius apollo*)

GUAVA SKIPPER (*Phocides polybius*)

CLEOPATRA (*Gonepteryx cleopatra*)

LARGE COPPER (*Lycaena dispar*)

MONARCH BUTTERFLY (*Danaus plexippus*)

but·ter·fly net *n.* a fine net on a ring attached to a pole, used for catching butterflies.

but·ter·fly stroke *n.* a stroke in swimming, with both arms raised out of the water and lifted forward together.

but·ter knife *n.* (*pl.* **knives**) a blunt knife used for cutting butter at table.

but·ter·milk /bútərmilk/ *n.* a slightly acid liquid left after churning butter.

but·ter·nut /bútərnut/ *n.* **1** a N. American tree, *Juglans cinerea.* **2** the oily nut of this tree.

but·ter·scotch /bútərskoch/ *n.* **1** a brittle candy made from butter, brown sugar, etc. **2** this flavor in dessert toppings, puddings, etc.

but·ter·y[1] /bútəree/ *n.* (*pl.* **-ies**) a pantry.

but·ter·y[2] /bútəree/ *adj.* like, containing, or spread with butter. □□ **but·ter·i·ness** *n.*

butt·in·sky /butínskee/ *n. N. Amer. colloq.* an interfering person.

but·tock /bútək/ *n.* (usu. in *pl.*) **1** each of two fleshy protuberances on the lower rear part of the human trunk. **2** the corresponding part of an animal.

but·ton /bút'n/ *n. & v.* ● *n.* **1** a small disk or knob sewn on to a garment, either to fasten it by being pushed through a buttonhole, or as an ornament or badge. **2** a knob on a piece of equipment which is pressed to operate it. **3 a** a small round object (*chocolate buttons*). **b** (*attrib.*) anything resembling a button (*button nose*). **4 a** a bud. **b** a button mushroom. **5** *Fencing* a terminal knob on a foil making it harmless. ● *v.* **1** *tr. & intr.* = BUTTON UP 1. **2** *tr.* supply with buttons. □ **buttoned up** *colloq.* **1** formal and inhibited in manner. **2** silent. **button one's lip** *sl.* remain silent. **button up 1** fasten with buttons. **2** *colloq.* complete satisfactorily. **3** *colloq.* become silent. **on the button** *sl.* precisely. □□ **but·toned** *adj.* **but·ton·less** *adj.*

but·ton·hole /bút'nhōl/ *n. & v.* ● *n.* a slit made in a garment to receive a button for fastening. ● *v.tr. colloq.* accost and detain (a reluctant listener).

but·tress /bútris/ *n. & v.* ● *n.* **1** a projecting support built against a wall. ▷ CATHEDRAL. **2** a source of help or encouragement. ● *v.tr.* (often foll. by *up*) **1** support with a buttress. **2** support by argument, etc.

bu·tyl /byóot'l/ *n. Chem.* the univalent alkyl radical C_4H_9.

bux·om /búksəm/ *adj.* (esp. of a woman) plump and healthy-looking; busty.

buy /bī/ *v. & n.* ● *v.* (**buys, buying**; *past* and *past part.* **bought** /bawt/) **1** *tr.* a obtain in exchange for money, etc. **b** (usu. in *neg.*) serve to obtain (*money can't buy happiness*). **2** *tr.* **a** procure (the loyalty, etc.) of a person by bribery, promises, etc. **b** win over (a person) in this way. **3** *tr.* get by sacrifice, great effort, etc. (*dearly bought*). **4** *tr. sl.* accept; believe in; approve of. **5** *absol.* be a buyer for a store, etc. (*buys for Macy's*). ● *n. colloq.* a purchase (*a good buy*). □ **buy the farm** die. **buy in 1** buy a supply of. **2** withdraw (an item) at auction because of failure to reach the reserve price. **buy into 1** obtain a share in (an enterprise) by payment. **2** *colloq.* support, embrace (an idea, etc.). **buy it** (usu. in *past*) *sl.* be killed. **buy off** get rid of (a claim, a claimant, a blackmailer) by payment. **buy oneself out** obtain one's release (esp. from the armed services) by payment. **buy out** pay (a person) to give up an ownership, etc. **buy time** delay an event, conclusion, etc., temporarily. **buy up 1** buy as much as possible of. **2** absorb (another business, etc.) by purchase.

buy·er /bīər/ *n.* **1** a person employed to select and purchase stock for a large store, etc. **2** a purchaser.

buyer's market *n.* (also **buyers' market**) an economic position in which goods are plentiful and cheap and buyers have the advantage.

buy·out /bíowt/ *n.* the purchase of a controlling share in a company, etc.

buzz /buz/ *n. & v.* ● *n.* **1** the hum of a bee, etc. **2** the sound of a buzzer. **3 a** a confused low sound as of people talking; a murmur. **b** a stir (*a buzz of*

excitement). **c** *colloq.* a rumor. **4** *sl.* a telephone call. **5** *sl.* a thrill; a euphoric sensation. ● *v.* **1** *intr.* make a humming sound. **2 a** *tr. & intr.* signal or signal to with a buzzer. **b** *tr. sl.* telephone. **3** *intr.* **a** (often foll. by *about*) move or hover busily. **b** (of a place) have an air of excitement or purposeful activity. **4** *tr. Aeron. colloq.* fly fast and very close to (another aircraft, the ground, etc.). □ **buzz off** *sl.* go or hurry away.

buz·zard /búzərd/ *n.* **1** a turkey vulture. **2** a European hawk, esp. of the genus *Butea*, with broad wings well adapted for soaring.

buzz cut *n.* a very short haircut in which the hair is clipped close to the head with a razor.

buzz·er /búzər/ *n.* **1** an electrical device that makes a buzzing noise. **2** a whistle or siren.

buzz saw *n.* a circular saw.

buzz·word /búzwərd/ *n. sl.* **1** a fashionable piece of jargon. **2** a catchword; a slogan.

by /bī/ *prep., adv., & n.* ● *prep.* **1** near; beside (*stand by the door; sit by me*). **2** through the agency, means, instrumentality, or causation of (*bought by a millionaire; a poem by Frost; went by bus; succeeded by persisting; divide four by two*). **3** not later than (*by next week*). **4 a** *past*; beyond (*drove by the zoo*). **b** passing through; via (*went by Paris*). **5** in the circumstances of (*by day*). **6** to the extent of (*missed by a foot*). **7** according to; using as a standard or unit (*judge by appearances; paid by the hour*). **8** with the succession of (*worse by the minute*). **9** concerning; in respect of (*did our duty by them*). **10** used in mild oaths (orig. = as surely as one believes in) (*by God*). **11** placed between specified lengths in two directions (*three feet by two*). **12** avoiding; ignoring (*passed us by*). **13** inclining to (*north by northwest*). ● *adv.* **1** near (*sat by, watching*). **2** aside; in reserve (*put $5 by*). **3** past (*marched by*). ● *n.* (*pl.* **byes**) = BYE. □ **by and by** before long; eventually. **by and large** on the whole; everything considered. **by the by** (or **bye**) incidentally; parenthetically. **by oneself 1 a** unaided. **b** without prompting. **2** alone.

by- /bī/ *prefix* (also **bye-**) subordinate; incidental; secondary (*by-effect; byroad*).

bye[1] /bī/ *n.* **1** the status of an unpaired competitor in a sport, who proceeds to the next round as if having won. **2** *Golf* one or more holes remaining unplayed after the match has been decided. □ **by the bye** = *by the by.*

bye[2] /bī/ *int. colloq.* = GOOD-BYE.

bye- *prefix* var. of BY-.

bye-bye[1] /bíbí, bəbí/ *int. colloq.* = GOOD-BYE.

bye-bye[2] /bíbí/ *n.* (also **bye-byes** /-bíz/) (a child's word for) sleep.

bye·law *n.* var. of BYLAW.

by-e·lec·tion /bí-ilekshən/ *n. Brit.* the election of an MP in a single constituency to fill a vacancy arising during a government's term of office.

by-form /bífawrm/ *n.* a collateral form of a word, etc.

by·gone /bígawn, -gon/ *adj. & n.* ● *adj.* past; antiquated (*bygone years*). ● *n.* (in *pl.*) past offenses (*let bygones be bygones*).

by·law /bílaw/ *n.* (also **bye·law**) a regulation made by an organization for its members.

by·line /bílīn/ *n.* **1** a line in a newspaper, etc., naming the writer of an article. **2** a secondary line of work.

by·name /bínaym/ *n.* a sobriquet; a nickname.

by·pass /bípas/ *n. & v.* ● *n.* **1** a road passing around a town or its center. **2 a** a secondary channel or pipe, etc., to allow a flow when the main one is closed or blocked. **b** an alternative passage for the circulation of blood during a surgical operation on the heart. ● *v.tr.* **1** avoid; go around. **2** provide with a bypass.

by·path /bípath/ *n.* **1** a secluded path. **2** a minor or obscure branch of a subject.

by·play /bíplay/ *n.* a secondary action or sequence of events, esp. in a play.

by-prod·uct /bíprodəkt/ *n.* **1** an incidental product of the manufacture of something else. **2** a secondary result.

by·road /bírōd/ *n.* a minor road.

By·ron·ic /bīrónik/ *adj.* **1** characteristic of Lord Byron, English poet d. 1824, or his romantic poetry. **2** (of a man) handsomely dark, mysterious, or moody.

by·stand·er /bístandər/ *n.* a person who stands by but does not take part.

byte /bīt/ *n. Computing* a group of eight binary digits, often used to represent one character.

by·way /bíway/ *n.* a small seldom-traveled road.

by·word /bíwərd/ *n.* **1** a person or thing cited as a notable example (*is a byword for luxury*). **2** a familiar saying; a proverb.

Byz·an·tine /bízənteen, -tīn, bizántin/ *adj. & n.* ● *adj.* **1** of Byzantium or the E. Roman Empire. **2** (of a political situation, etc.): **a** extremely complicated. **b** inflexible. **c** carried on by underhand methods. **3** *Archit. & Painting* ▼ of a highly decorated style developed in the Eastern Empire. ● *n.* a citizen of Byzantium or the E. Roman Empire.

BYZANTINE

Following the division of the Roman Empire in AD 395, the Eastern section sited its capital in Byzantium (now Istanbul). Architects fused Roman and Oriental styles, constructing buildings from brick and concrete, faced with marble. External walls were ornamented with decorative brickwork and internal walls with intricate mosaics. A large central dome was often surrounded by smaller domes.

CUTAWAY VIEW OF A 6TH-CENTURY BYZANTINE CHURCH (HAGIA SOPHIA, ISTANBUL, TURKEY), NOW A MOSQUE

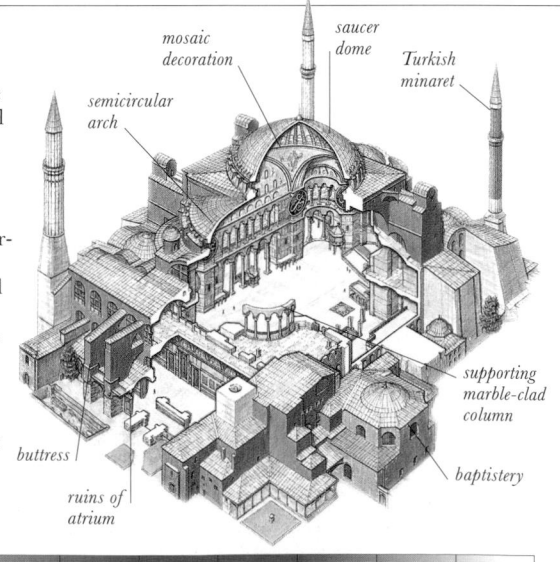

mosaic decoration
saucer dome
Turkish minaret
semicircular arch
supporting marble-clad column
buttress
baptistery
ruins of atrium

TIMELINE

| 400 | 500 | 600 | 700 | 800 | 900 | 1000 | 1100 | 1200 | 1300 | 1400 |

B

C[1] /see/ *n.* (also **c**) (*pl.* **Cs** or **C's**) **1** the third letter of the alphabet. **2** *Mus.* the first note of the diatonic scale of C major. ▷ NOTATION. **3** the third hypothetical person or example. **4** the third highest class or category. **5** *Algebra* (usu. **c**) the third known quantity. **6** (as a Roman numeral) 100. **7** (**c**) the speed of light in a vacuum. **8** (also ©) copyright.

C[2] *symb. Chem.* the element carbon.

C[3] *abbr.* (also **C.**) **1** Cape. **2** Celsius; centigrade. **3** Coulomb(s); capacitance.

c. *abbr.* **1** century; centuries. **2** chapter. **3** cent(s). **4** cold. **5** cubic. **6** *Baseball* catcher. **7** centi-. **8** circa; about.

CA *abbr.* **1** California (in official postal use). **2** *Sc. & Can.* chartered accountant.

Ca *symb. Chem.* the element calcium.

ca. *abbr.* circa, about.

CAA *abbr.* Civil Aeronautics Administration.

CAB *abbr.* Civil Aeronautics Board.

cab /kab/ *n.* **1** a taxi. **2** the driver's compartment in a truck, train, crane, etc.

ca·bal /kəbál/ *n.* **1** a secret intrigue. **2** a political clique or faction.

cab·a·la /kábələ, kəbaálə/ *n.* (also **cab·ba·la**, **kab·bala**) **1** the Jewish mystical tradition. **2** mystic interpretation; any esoteric doctrine or occult lore. □□ **cab·a·lism** *n.* **cab·a·list** *n.* **cab·a·lis·tic** *adj.*

ca·ba·na /kəbánə, -báanyə/ *n.* a shelter, bathhouse, etc., at a beach or swimming pool.

cab·a·ret /kabəráy/ *n.* **1** an entertainment in a nightclub or restaurant while guests eat or drink at tables. **2** such a nightclub, etc.

cab·bage /kábij/ *n.* **1 a** any of several cultivated varieties of *Brassica oleracea*, with thick green or purple leaves forming a round heart or head. **b** this head usu. eaten as a vegetable. ▷ VEGETABLE. **2** *Brit. colloq. derog.* a person who is inactive or lacks interest. □□ **cab·bag·y** *adj.*

cab·bage white *n.* ▼ a butterfly, *Pieris brassicae*, whose caterpillars feed on cabbage leaves.

CABBAGE WHITE
(*Pieris brassicae*)

cab·ba·la var. of CABALA.

cab·by /kábee/ *n.* (also **cab·bie**) (*pl.* **-ies**) *colloq.* a cabdriver.

cab·driv·er /kábdrīvər/ *n.* the driver of a cab.

ca·ber /káybər/ *n.* a roughly trimmed tree trunk used in the Scottish Highland sport of tossing the caber.

Ca·ber·net Sau·vi·gnon /kabərnay sóvinyon/ *n.* a variety of black wine grape originally from the Bordeaux area of France.

cab·in /kábin/ *n. & v.* ● *n.* **1** a small shelter or house. ▷ LOG CABIN. **2** a room or compartment in an aircraft or ship for passengers or crew. ▷ WING. **3** a driver's cab. ● *v.tr.* (**cabined**, **cabining**) confine in a small place; cramp.

cab·in cruis·er *n.* a large motorboat with living accommodation.

cab·i·net /kábinit/ *n.* **1 a** ▼ a cupboard or case with drawers, shelves, etc., for storing or displaying articles. **b** a piece of furniture housing a radio or television set, etc. **2** (**Cabinet**) the committee of senior advisers responsible for counseling the head of state on government policy.

open shelf   *projecting shelf*   *glazed display cupboard*

closed cupboard

CABINET: 19TH-CENTURY ENGLISH MAHOGANY CABINET

cab·i·net·mak·er /kábinitmáykər/ *n.* a skilled joiner.

cab·i·net·ry /kábnitree/ *n.* finished woodwork, esp. of professional quality.

cab·in fe·ver *n.* a state of restlessness and irritability from having been confined or in a remote location for an extended period.

ca·ble /káybəl/ *n. & v.* ● *n.* **1** a thick rope of wire or hemp. **2** an encased group of insulated wires for transmitting electricity or electrical signals. **3** a cablegram. **4** *Naut.* **a** the chain of an anchor. **b** (in full **ca·ble length**) a measure of 720 feet (US Navy) or 608 feet (Brit. Navy). **5** (in full **cable-stitch**) a knitted stitch resembling twisted rope. ▷ KNITTING. ● *v.* **1 a** *tr.* transmit (a message) by cablegram. **b** *tr.* inform (a person) by cablegram. **c** *intr.* send a cablegram. **2** *tr.* furnish or fasten with a cable or cables.

ca·ble car *n.* **1** a small cabin (often one of a series) suspended on an endless cable and drawn up and down a mountainside, etc., by an engine at one end. **2** a vehicle drawn along a cable railway.

ca·ble-read·y *adj.* (of a TV, VCR, etc.) designed for direct connection to a coaxial cable TV system.

ca·ble tel·e·vi·sion *n.* a broadcasting system with signals transmitted by cable to subscribers' sets.

ca·ble·way /káybəlwáy/ *n.* a transporting system with a usu. elevated cable.

cab·man /kábmən/ *n.* (*pl.* **-men**) a cabdriver.

cab·o·chon /kábəshon/ *n.* ▶ a gem polished but not faceted. ▷ GEM

CABOCHON: SODALITE CABOCHON

ca·boo·dle /kəbood'l/ *n.* □ **the whole** (**kit and**) **caboodle** *sl.* the whole lot (of persons or things).

ca·boose /kəboos/ *n.* **1** a car on a freight train for workers, often the final car. **2** esp. *Brit.* a kitchen on a ship's deck.

cab·ri·ole /kábreeōl/ *n.* a kind of curved leg characteristic of Queen Anne and Chippendale furniture.

cab·ri·o·let /kábreeōláy/ *n.* **1** a light, two-wheeled carriage with a hood, drawn by one horse. **2** an automobile with a folding top.

ca·ca·o /kəkáa-ō, -káyō/ *n.* (*pl.* **-os**) **1** a seed pod from which cocoa and chocolate are made. ▷ BERRY. **2** a small, widely cultivated evergreen tree, *Theobroma cacao*, bearing these.

cache /kash/ *n. & v.* ● *n.* **1** a hiding place for treasure, provisions, ammunition, etc. **2** what is hidden in a cache. ● *v.tr.* put in a cache.

ca·chet /kasháy/ *n.* **1** a distinguishing mark or seal. **2** prestige. **3** *Med.* a flat capsule enclosing a dose of unpleasant-tasting medicine.

ca·cique /kəseék/ *n.* **1** a native tribal chief of the West Indies or Mexico. **2** a political boss in Spain or Latin America.

cack-hand·ed /kák-hándid/ *adj. Brit. colloq.* **1** awkward; clumsy. **2** left-handed. □□ **cack-hand·ed·ly** *adv.* **cack-hand·ed·ness** *n.*

cack·le /kákəl/ *n. & v.* ● *n.* **1** a clucking sound as of a hen or a goose. **2** a loud, silly laugh. **3** noisy inconsequential talk. ● *v.* **1** *intr.* emit a cackle. **2** *intr.* talk noisily and inconsequentially. **3** *tr.* utter or express with a cackle.

ca·cog·ra·phy /kəkógrəfee/ *n.* **1** bad handwriting. **2** bad spelling. □□ **ca·cog·ra·pher** *n.* **caco·graph·ic** /kákəgráfik/ *adj.* **cac·o·graph·i·cal** *adj.*

ca·col·o·gy /kəkóləjee/ *n.* **1** bad choice of words. **2** bad pronunciation.

ca·coph·o·ny /kəkófənee/ *n.* (*pl.* **-ies**) **1** a harsh discordant mixture of sound. **2** dissonance; discord. □□ **ca·coph·o·nous** *adj.*

cac·tus /káktəs/ *n.* (*pl.* **cacti** /-tī/ or **cactuses**) ▶ any succulent plant of the family Cactaceae, with a thick fleshy stem and usu. spines but no leaves. ▷ SUCCULENT, XEROPHYTE. □□ **cac·ta·ceous** /-táyshəs/ *adj.*

areole   *radial spines*

CACTUS: SPINY CACTUS (*Oreocereus intertexta*)

CAD /kad/ *abbr.* computer-aided design.

cad /kad/ *n.* a person (esp. a man) who behaves dishonorably. □□ **cad·dish** *adj.* **cad·dish·ly** *adv.* **cad·dish·ness** *n.*

ca·das·tral /kədástrəl/ *adj.* of or showing the extent, value, and ownership, of land for taxation.

ca·dav·er /kədávər/ *n.* esp. *Med.* a corpse. □□ **ca·dav·er·ic** /-dávərik/ *adj.*

ca·dav·er·ous /kədávərəs/ *adj.* **1** corpselike. **2** deathly pale.

cad·die /kádee/ *n. & v.* (also **cad·dy**) ● *n.* (*pl.* **-ies**) a person who assists a golfer during a match, by carrying clubs, etc. ● *v.intr.* (**caddies**, **caddied**, **caddying**) act as caddie.

cad·dis fly /kádisflī/ *n.* (*pl.* **flies**) any small, hairy-winged nocturnal insect of the order Trichoptera, living near water. ▷ LARVA

cad·dish see CAD.

cad·dis·worm /kádiswərm/ *n.* (also **cad·dis**) a larva of the caddis fly, living in water and making protective cylindrical cases of sticks, leaves, etc.

C

cad·dy[1] /kádee/ *n.* (*pl.* **-ies**) a small container, esp. a box for holding tea.

cad·dy[2] var. of CADDIE.

ca·dence /káyd'ns/ *n.* **1** a fall in pitch of the voice, esp. at the end of a phrase or sentence. **2** intonation; tonal inflection. **3** *Mus.* the close of a musical phrase. **4** rhythm; the measure or beat of sound or movement. □□ **ca·denced** *adj.*

ca·den·tial /kədénshəl/ *adj.* of a cadence or cadenza.

ca·den·za /kədénzə/ *n. Mus.* a virtuosic passage for a solo instrument or voice, usu. near the close of a movement of a concerto, sometimes improvised.

ca·det /kədét/ *n.* **1** a young trainee in the armed services or police force. **2** a business trainee. **3** a younger son. □□ **ca·det·ship** *n.*

cadge /kaj/ *v.* **1** *tr.* get or seek by begging. **2** *intr.* beg. □□ **cadg·er** *n.*

cad·mi·um /kádmeeəm/ *n.* a soft, bluish-white metallic element occurring naturally with zinc ores, and used in the manufacture of solders and in electroplating. ¶ Symb.: **Cd**.

ca·dre /kádree, ka-ádray/ *n.* **1** a basic unit, esp. of servicemen, forming a nucleus for expansion when necessary. **2 a** a group of activists in a communist or any revolutionary party. **b** a member of such a group.

ca·du·ce·us /kədо̄́oseeəs, -shəs, -dyо̄́o-/ *n.* (*pl.* **ca·ducei** /-see-ī/) an ancient Greek or Roman herald's wand, esp. as carried by the messenger god Hermes or Mercury.

cae·cil·ian /səsíleeən/ *n.* any burrowing wormlike amphibian of the order Gymnophiona, having poorly developed eyes and no limbs. ▷ AMPHIBIAN

cae·cum *Brit.* var. of CECUM. ▷ COLON

Cae·no·zo·ic var. of CENOZOIC.

Cae·sar /séezər/ *n.* **1** the title of the Roman emperors, esp. from Augustus to Hadrian. **2** an autocrat. □□ **Cae·sar·e·an, Cae·sar·i·an** /-záireeən/ *adj.*

Cae·sar·e·an (also **Cae·sar·i·an**) var. of CESAREAN.

cae·su·ra /sizhо̄́orə, -zо̄́orə/ *n.* (*pl.* **caesuras** or **caesurae** /-zhо̄́oree, -zо̄́oree/) *Prosody* a pause near the middle of a line. □□ **cae·su·ral** *adj.*

CAF *abbr.* cost and freight.

ca·fé /kafáy/ *n.* (also **ca·fe**) **1** a small coffeehouse; a simple restaurant. **2** a bar.

ca·fé au lait /kafáy ō láy/ *n.* **1** coffee with milk. **2** the color of this.

caf·e·te·ri·a /káfitéereeə/ *n.* a restaurant in which customers collect their meals on trays at a counter and usu. pay before sitting down to eat.

caf·feine /káfeen, kaféen/ *n.* an alkaloid drug with stimulant action, found in tea and coffee beans.

caf·tan /káftan/ *n.* (also **kaftan**) **1** a long, usu. belted tunic worn in countries of the Near East. **2 a** a long, loose dress. **b** a loose shirt or top.

cage /kayj/ *n. & v.* ● *n.* **1** a structure of bars or wires, esp. for confining animals or birds. **2** any similar open framework, as an enclosed platform for passengers in a freight elevator, etc. ● *v.tr.* place or keep in a cage.

cag·ey /káyjee/ *adj.* (also **cag·y**) (**cagier, cagiest**) *colloq.* cautious and uncommunicative; wary. □□ **cag·i·ly** *adv.* **cag·i·ness** *n.* (also **cag·ey·ness**).

ca·hoots /kəhо̄́ots/ *n.pl.* □ **in cahoots** (often foll. by *with*) *sl.* in collusion.

CAI *abbr.* computer-assisted (or -aided) instruction.

cai·man /káymən/ *n.* (also **cay·man**) ▼ any of various S. American alligatorlike reptilians, esp. of the genus *Caiman*.

CAIMAN: JUVENILE SPECTACLED CAIMAN
(*Caiman crocodilus*)

Cain /kayn/ *n.* □ **raise Cain** *colloq.* make a disturbance; create trouble.

caique /kīeék/ *n.* **1** a light rowing boat used on the Bosporus. **2** a small eastern Mediterranean sailing ship.

cairn /kairn/ *n.* **1** a mound of rough stones as a monument or landmark. **2** (in full **cairn terrier**) ▼ a small terrier of a breed with short legs, a longish body, and a shaggy coat.

CAIRN TERRIER

cairn·gorm /káirngawrm/ *n.* a yellow or wine-colored semiprecious form of quartz.

cais·son /káyson, -sən/ *n.* **1** a watertight chamber in which underwater construction work can be done. **2** a floating vessel used as a floodgate in docks. **3** an ammunition chest or wagon.

ca·jole /kəjо̄l/ *v.tr.* (often foll. by *into, out of*) persuade by flattery, deceit, etc. □□ **ca·jole·ment** *n.* **ca·jol·er** *n.* **ca·jol·er·y** *n.*

cake /kayk/ *n. & v.* ● *n.* **1 a** a mixture of flour, butter, eggs, sugar, etc., baked in the oven. **b** a quantity of this baked in a flat round or ornamental shape and often iced and decorated. **2** other food in a flat round shape (*fish cake*). **3** a flattish compact mass (*a cake of soap*). ● *v.* **1** *tr. & intr.* form into a compact mass. **2** *tr.* (usu. foll. by *with*) cover (with a hard or sticky mass) (*boots caked with mud*). □ **have one's cake and eat it too** *colloq.* enjoy both of two mutually exclusive alternatives. **a piece of cake** *colloq.* something easily achieved.

cake·walk /káykwawk/ *n.* **1** a dance developed from a black American contest in graceful walking with a cake as a prize. **2** *colloq.* an easy task.

CAL *abbr.* computer-assisted learning.

Cal *abbr.* large calorie(s).

Cal. *abbr.* California.

cal *abbr.* small calorie(s).

cal·a·bash /kálabash/ *n.* **1 a** an evergreen tree, *Crescentia cujete*, native to tropical America, bearing fruit in the form of large gourds. **b** a gourd from this tree. **2** the shell of this or a similar gourd used as a vessel, etc.

cal·a·boose /kálabо̄os/ *n. sl.* a prison.

cal·a·ma·ri /kaalamáaree, ka-/ *n.* (*pl.* **-ies**) any cephalopod mollusk with a long, tapering, penlike horny internal shell, esp. a squid of the genus *Loligo*.

cal·a·mine /kálamīn/ *n.* **1** a pink powder consisting of zinc carbonate and ferric oxide used as a lotion or ointment. **2** a zinc mineral, zinc carbonate.

ca·lam·i·ty /kəlámitee/ *n.* (*pl.* **-ies**) **1** a disaster, a great misfortune. **2 a** adversity. **b** deep distress. □□ **ca·lam·i·tous** *adj.* **ca·lam·i·tous·ly** *adv.*

calc- /kalk/ *comb. form* lime or calcium.

cal·ca·ne·us /kalkáyneeəs/ *n.* (also **cal·ca·ne·um** /-neeəm/) (*pl.* **calcanei** /-nee-ī/ or **calcanea** /-neeə/) the bone forming the heel.

cal·car·e·ous /kalkáireeəs/ *adj.* (also **cal·car·i·ous**) of or containing calcium carbonate; chalky.

cal·ce·o·lar·i·a /kálseeəláireeə/ *n. Bot.* any plant of the genus *Calceolaria*, native to S. America, with slipper-shaped flowers.

cal·cif·er·ol /kalsífərōl, -rol/ *n.* one of the D vitamins, routinely added to dairy products, essential for the deposition of calcium in bones. Also called **ergocalciferol**, **vitamin D₂**.

cal·cif·er·ous /kalsífərəs/ *adj.* yielding calcium salts, esp. calcium carbonate.

cal·ci·fy /kálsifī/ *v.tr. & intr.* (**-ies, -ied**) **1** harden or become hardened by deposition of calcium salts; petrify. **2** convert or be converted to calcium carbonate. □□ **cal·cif·ic** /-sifik/ *adj.* **cal·ci·fi·ca·tion** *n.*

cal·cine /kálsīn, -sin/ *v.* **1** *tr.* **a** reduce, oxidize, or desiccate by strong heat. **b** burn to ashes; consume by fire; roast. **c** reduce to calcium oxide by roasting or burning. **2** *tr.* consume or purify as if by fire. **3** *intr.* undergo any of these. □□ **cal·ci·na·tion** /-sináyshən/ *n.*

cal·cite /kálsīt/ *n.* ▼ natural crystalline calcium carbonate. ▷ MATRIX

CALCITE CRYSTALS

cal·ci·um /kálseeəm/ *n.* a soft, gray metallic element of the alkaline earth group occurring naturally in limestone, marble, chalk, etc., that is important in industry and essential for normal growth in living organisms. ¶ Symb.: **Ca**.

cal·ci·um car·bon·ate /kálseeəm káarbənayt/ *n.* a white, insoluble solid occurring naturally as chalk, limestone, marble, and calcite, and used in the manufacture of lime and cement.

calc-spar /kálkspaar/ *n.* = CALCITE.

cal·cu·la·ble /kálkyələbəl/ *adj.* able to be calculated or estimated. □□ **cal·cu·la·bil·i·ty** *n.* **cal·cu·la·bly** *adv.*

cal·cu·late /kálkyəlayt/ *v.* **1** *tr.* ascertain or determine beforehand, esp. by mathematics or by reckoning. **2** *tr.* plan deliberately. **3** *intr.* (foll. by *on, upon*) rely on; make an essential part of one's reckoning. **4** *tr. dial.* suppose; believe. □□ **cal·cu·la·tive** /-lətiv/ *adj.*

cal·cu·lat·ed /kálkyəlaytid/ *adj.* **1** (of an action) done with awareness of the likely consequences. **2** (foll. by *to* + infin.) designed or suitable; intended. □□ **cal·cu·lat·ed·ly** *adv.*

cal·cu·lat·ing /kálkyəlayting/ *adj.* (of a person) shrewd; scheming. □□ **cal·cu·lat·ing·ly** *adv.*

cal·cu·la·tion /kálkyəláyshən/ *n.* **1** the act or process of calculating. **2** a result got by calculating. **3** a reckoning or forecast.

cal·cu·la·tor /kálkyəlaytər/ *n.* **1** a device (esp. a small electronic one) used for making mathematical calculations. **2** a person or thing that calculates.

cal·cu·lus /kálkyələs/ *n.* (*pl.* **calculi** /-lī/ or **calculuses**) **1** *Math.* **a** a particular method of calculation or reasoning (*calculus of probabilities*). **b** the infinitesimal calculi of integration or differentiation (see INTEGRAL CALCULUS, DIFFERENTIAL CALCULUS). **2** *Med.* a stone or concretion of minerals formed within the body. □□ **cal·cu·lous** *adj.* (in sense 2).

cal·de·ra /kaldáirə/ *n.* a large volcanic depression. ▷ VOLCANO

cal·dron var. of CAULDRON.

Cal·e·do·ni·an /kálidōneeən/ *adj. & n.* ● *adj.* **1** of or relating to Scotland. **2** *Geol.* of a mountain-forming period in Europe in the Paleozoic era. ● *n.* a Scotsman.

cal·e·fa·cient /kálifáyshənt/ *n. & adj. Med.* ● *n.* a substance producing or causing a sensation of warmth. ● *adj.* of this substance.

cal·en·dar /kálindər/ *n. & v.* ● *n.* **1** a system by which the beginning, length, and subdivisions of the year are fixed. **2** a chart or series of pages showing the days, weeks, and months of a particular year, or giving special seasonal information. **3** a timetable or program of appointments, special events, etc. ● *v.tr.* register or enter in a calendar or timetable, etc. □□ **ca·len·dric** /-léndrik/ *adj.* **ca·len·dri·cal** *adj.*

cal·en·der /kálindər/ *n. & v.* ● *n.* a machine in which cloth, paper, etc., is pressed by rollers to glaze or smooth it. ● *v.tr.* press in a calender.

cal·ends /kálendz/ *n.pl.* (also **kalends**) the first of the month in the ancient Roman calendar.

ca·len·du·la /kəlénjələ/ *n.* ◀ any plant of the genus *Calendula*, with large yellow or orange flowers.

calf[1] /kaf/ *n.* (*pl.* **calves** /kavz/) **1** a young bovine animal, used esp. of domestic cattle. **2** the young of other animals, e.g., elephant, deer, and whale. □□ **calf·hood** *n.* **calf·ish** *adj.* **calf·like** *adj.*

calf[2] /kaf/ *n.* (*pl.* **calves** /kavz/) the fleshy hind part of the human leg below the knee. □□ **-calved** /kavd/ *adj.* (in *comb.*).

CALENDULA
(*Calendula officinalis*)

calf·skin /káfskin/ *n.* calf leather.

cal·i·ber /kálibər/ *n.* (*Brit.* **calibre**) **1 a** the internal diameter of a gun or tube. **b** the diameter of a bullet or shell. **2** strength or quality of character; ability; importance (*we need someone of your caliber*). □□ **cal·i·bered** *adj.*

cal·i·brate /kálibrayt/ *v.tr.* **1** mark (a gauge) with a standard scale of readings. **2** correlate the readings of (an instrument) with a standard. **3** determine the caliber of (a gun). **4** determine the correct capacity or value of. □□ **cal·i·bra·tion** /-bráyshən/ *n.* **cal·i·bra·tor** *n.*

cal·i·bre *Brit.* var. of CALIBER.

cal·i·che /kəléechee/ *n.* a mineral deposit of gravel, sand, and nitrates, esp. found in Chile and Peru.

cal·i·co /kálikō/ *n. & adj.* ● *n.* (*pl.* **-oes** or **-os**) **1** a printed cotton fabric. **2** *Brit.* a cotton cloth, esp. plain white or unbleached. ● *adj.* **1** made of calico. **2** multicolored; piebald.

Calif. *abbr.* California.

cal·i·for·ni·um /kálifáwrneeəm/ *n. Chem.* a transuranic radioactive metallic element produced artificially from curium. ¶ Symb.: **Cf**.

cal·i·per /kálipər/ *n. & v.* ● *n.* **1** (in *pl.*) (also **cal·i·per com·pass·es**) compasses with bowed legs for measuring the diameter of convex bodies, or with out-turned points for measuring internal dimensions. **2** (in full **caliper splint**) a metal splint to support the leg. ● *v.tr.* measure with calipers.

ca·liph /káylif, kál-/ *n.* esp. *hist.* the chief Muslim civil and religious ruler, regarded as the successor of Muhammad. □□ **cal·iph·ate** *n.*

cal·is·then·ics /kálisthéniks/ *n.pl.* (also esp. *Brit.* **cal·lis·then·ics**) gymnastic exercises to achieve bodily fitness and grace of movement. □□ **cal·is·then·ic** *adj.*

calk var. of CAULK.

call /kawl/ *v. & n.* ● *v.* **1 a** (often foll. by *out*) cry; shout; speak loudly. **b** (of a bird or animal) emit its characteristic note or cry. **2** *tr.* communicate or converse with by telephone or radio. **3** *tr.* **a** bring to one's presence by calling; summon (*will you call the children?*). **b** arrange for (a person or thing) to come or be present (*called a taxi*). **4** *intr.* (often foll. by *at, on*) pay a brief visit (*called at the house; come and call on me*). **5** *tr.* **a** order to take place; fix a time for (*called a meeting*). **b** direct to happen; announce (*call a halt*). **6 a** *intr.* require one's attention (*duty calls*). **b** *tr.* urge; invite; nominate (*call to run for office*). **7** *tr.* name; describe as (*call her Jennifer*). **8** *tr.* consider; regard or estimate as (*I call that silly*). **9** *tr.* rouse from sleep (*call me at 8*). **10** *intr.* guess the outcome of tossing a coin, etc. **11** *intr.* (foll. by *for*) order; require; demand (*called for silence*). **12** *intr.* (foll. by *on, upon*) invoke; appeal to; request or require (*called on us to be quiet*). **13** *tr. Cards* specify (a suit or contract) in bidding. ● *n.* **1** a shout or cry; an act of calling. **2 a** the characteristic cry of a bird or animal. **b** an imitation of this. **c** an instru-

ment for imitating it. **3** a brief visit (*paid them a call*). **4 a** an act of telephoning. **b** a telephone conversation. **5 a** an invitation or summons to appear or be present. **b** an appeal or invitation (from a specific source or discerned by a person's conscience, etc.) to follow a certain profession, set of principles, etc. **6** (foll. by *for*, or *to* + infin.) a duty, need, or occasion (*no call for violence*). **7** (foll. by *for, on*) a demand (*not much call for it these days; a call on one's time*). **8** a signal on a bugle, etc.; a signaling whistle. **9** *Stock Exch.* an option of buying stock at a fixed price at a given date. **10** *Cards* **a** a player's right or turn to make a bid. **b** a bid made. □ **call away** divert; distract. **call down 1** invoke. **2** reprimand. **call forth** elicit. **call in 1** withdraw from circulation. **2** seek the advice or services of. **call in** (or **into**) **question** dispute; doubt the validity of. **call into play** give scope for; make use of. **call a person names** abuse a person verbally. **call off 1** cancel (an arrangement, etc.). **2** order (an attacker or pursuer) to desist. **call of nature** a need to urinate or defecate. **call out 1** summon (troops, etc.) to action. **2** order (workers) to strike. **call the shots** (or **tune**) be in control; take the initiative. **call to mind** recollect; cause one to remember. **call to order 1** request to be orderly. **2** declare (a meeting) open. **call up 1** reach by telephone. **2** imagine; recollect. **3** summon, esp. to serve on active military duty. **on call 1** (of a doctor, etc.) available if required but not formally on duty. **2** (of money lent) repayable on demand. **within call** near enough to be summoned by calling.

cal·la /kálə/ *n.* (in full **calla lily**) a tall, lilylike plant, *Zantedeschia aethiopica*, with white spathe and spadix.

call·boy /káwlboy/ *n.* **1** a theater attendant who summons actors when needed on stage. **2** a bellhop. **3** (also **call boy**) a male prostitute who accepts appointments by telephone.

call·er /káwlər/ *n.* a person who calls, esp. one who pays a visit or makes a telephone call.

call girl *n.* a female prostitute who accepts appointments by telephone.

cal·lig·ra·phy /kəlígrəfee/ *n.* **1** ▼ handwriting, esp. when fine or pleasing. **2** the art of handwriting. □□ **cal·lig·ra·pher** *n.* **cal·li·graph·ic** /káligráfik/ *adj.* **cal·lig·ra·phist** *n.*

call·ing /káwling/ *n.* **1** a profession or occupation. **2** an inwardly felt call or summons; a vocation.

call·ing card /káwling kaard/ *n.* **1** a card with a person's name, etc., sent or left in lieu of a formal visit. **2** evidence of someone's presence; an identifying mark, etc., left behind (by someone). **3** a card used to charge a telephone call to a number other than that from which the call is placed.

cal·li·per *Brit.* var. of CALIPER.

cal·lis·then·ics esp. *Brit.* var. of CALISTHENICS.

cal·los·i·ty /kəlósitee/ *n.* (*pl.* **-ies**) a hard, thick area of skin usu. occurring in parts of the body subject to pressure or friction.

cal·lous /káləs/ *adj.* **1** unfeeling; insensitive. **2** (of skin) hardened or hard. □□ **cal·lous·ly** *adv.* (in sense 1). **cal·lous·ness** *n.*

C

CALLIGRAPHY

Over the past 2,000 years the alphabet has been written in a wide range of scripts. Some are formal and have been used as an expression of authority. Cursive (joined) forms, meanwhile, are quickly written for everyday transactions. Today's calligraphers can also select the tool most appropriate to their choice of script – either traditional, such as a quill, or modern, like a dip pen. Each letter is then formed by a recommended sequence of strokes, as shown here.

WRITING TOOLS

BROAD SABLE BRUSH

POINTED SABLE BRUSH

CALLIGRAPHIC FOUNTAIN PEN

DIP PEN

FIBER-TIPPED PEN

QUILL

sweeping curved stroke

FORMATION OF THE LETTER D IN ROTUNDA CAPITALS

dip pen

hairline tail   *space-filling device*   *direction of stroke*

EXAMPLES OF CALLIGRAPHIC SCRIPTS

EARLY GOTHIC   ITALIC   TEXTURA PRESCISUS

C

cal·low /kálō/ *adj.* inexperienced; immature. □□ **cal·low·ly** *adv.* **cal·low·ness** *n.*

cal·lus /káləs/ *n.* **1** a hard, thick area of skin or tissue. **2** a hard tissue formed around bone ends after a fracture. **3** *Bot.* a new protective tissue formed over a wound.

calm /kaam/ *adj., n., & v.* ● *adj.* **1** tranquil; quiet; windless (*a calm sea; a calm night*). **2** (of a person or disposition) settled; not agitated (*remained calm throughout the ordeal*). **3** self-assured; confident (*his calm assumption that we would wait*). ● *n.* **1** a state of being calm; stillness; serenity. **2** a period without wind or storm. ● *v.tr. & intr.* (often foll. by *down*) make or become calm. □□ **calm·ly** *adv.* **calm·ness** *n.*

calm·a·tive /káamətiv, kálm-/ *adj. & n. Med.* ● *adj.* tending to calm or sedate. ● *n.* a calmative drug, etc.

cal·o·mel /káləmel/ *n.* a compound of mercury, esp. when used medicinally as a cathartic.

ca·lor·ic /kəláwrik, -lór-/ *adj.* of heat or calories.

cal·o·rie /káləree/ *n.* (also **cal·o·ry**) (*pl.* **-ies**) a unit of quantity of heat: **1** (in full **small calorie**) the amount needed to raise the temperature of 1 gram of water through 1°C. ¶ Abbr.: **cal. 2** (in full **large calorie**) the amount needed to raise the temperature of 1 kilogram of water through 1°C, often used to measure the energy value of foods. ¶ Abbr.: **Cal.**

cal·o·rif·ic /kálərífik/ *adj.* producing heat. □□ **cal·o·rif·i·cal·ly** *adv.*

cal·o·rim·e·ter /kálərímitər/ *n.* any of various instruments for measuring quantity of heat, esp. to find calorific values. □□ **cal·o·ri·met·ric** /-métrik/ *adj.* **cal·o·rim·e·try** *n.*

cal·o·ry var. of CALORIE.

cal·trop /káltrəp/ *n.* (also **cal·trap**) **1** *hist.* a four-spiked iron ball thrown on the ground to impede cavalry horses. **2** any creeping plant of the genus *Tribulus*, with woody carpels usu. having hard spines.

cal·u·met /kályəmét/ *n.* ◄ a Native American ceremonial peace pipe.

hollow v.tr. **ca·lum·ni·ate** /kəlúmneeayt/ *wooden* **ca·lum·ni·ate** *v.tr.* slander. □□ **ca·lum·ni·a·tion** /-neeáyshən/ *n.* **ca·lum·ni·a·tor** *n.* **ca·lum·ni·a·to·ry** /-ətáwree/ *adj.*

reed

eagle feathers

cal·um·ny /káləmnee/ *n. & v.* ● *n.* (*pl.* **-ies**) **1** slander; malicious representation. **2** an instance of this. ● *v.tr.* (**-ies, -ied**) slander. □□ **ca·lum·ni·ous** /-lúmneeəs/ *adj.*

cal·va·dos /kálvədōs/ *n.* (also **Cal·va·dos**) an apple brandy.

Cal·va·ry /kálvəree/ *n.* the place where Christ was crucified.

calve /kav/ *v.* **1** *intr.* give birth to a calf. **2** *tr.* (esp. in *passive*) give birth to (a calf).

mouthpiece

CALUMET

calves *pl.* of CALF[1], CALF[2].

Cal·vin·ism /kálvinizəm/ *n.* the theology of the French theologian J. Calvin (d. 1564) or his followers, in which predestination and justification by faith are important elements. □□ **Cal·vin·ist** *n.* **Cal·vin·is·tic** *adj.* **Cal·vin·is·ti·cal** *adj.*

ca·lyp·so /kəlípsō/ *n.* (*pl.* **-os**) a W. Indian song in African rhythm, improvised on a topical theme.

calyx

ca·lyx /káyliks, kál-/ *n.* (*pl.* **calyxes** or **calyces** /-liseez/) **1** *Bot.* ◄ the sepals collectively, forming the protective layer of a flower in bud. **2** *Biol.* any cuplike cavity or structure.

CALYX AROUND A FLOWER BUD

CAMCORDER

There are two main parts to a camcorder – a camera and a video recorder. The basic functions are usually automatic so that when the power is switched on, the camcorder can record. The recording can be played back using the viewfinder as a monitor, while the sound can be checked with headphones.

eyecup
magnifying lens
miniature TV screen
tape
pinch wheel
capstan
angled recording drum
charge-coupled device image sensor
zoom lens
optical filter

MECHANISM OF A CAMCORDER

---

cal·zo·ne /kalzṓnee/ *n.* a type of pizza that is folded in half before cooking to contain a filling.

cam /kam/ *n.* a projection on a rotating part in machinery, shaped to impart reciprocal or variable motion to the part in contact with it.

ca·ma·ra·de·rie /káaməraádəree/ *n.* mutual trust and sociability among friends.

cam·ber /kámbər/ *n. & v.* ● *n.* **1** the slightly convex or arched shape of the surface of a ship's deck, aircraft wing, etc. **2** the slight sideways inclination of the front wheel of a motor vehicle. ● *v.* **1** *intr.* (of a surface) have a camber. **2** *tr.* give a camber to; build with a camber.

cam·bi·um /kámbeeəm/ *n.* (*pl.* **cambiums** or **cambia** /-beeə/) *Bot.* a cellular plant tissue responsible for the increase in girth of stems and roots. ▷ STEM, WOOD. □□ **cam·bi·al** *adj.*

Cam·bo·di·an /kambṓdeeən/ *n. & adj.* ● *n.* **1 a** a native or national of Cambodia (Kampuchea) in SE Asia. **b** a person of Cambodian descent. **2** the language of Cambodia. ● *adj.* of or relating to Cambodia or its people or language. Also called **Kampuchean**.

Cam·bri·an /kámbreeən/ *adj. & n.* ● *adj.* **1** Welsh. **2** *Geol.* of or relating to the first period in the Paleozoic era, marked by the occurrence of many forms of invertebrate life (including trilobites and brachiopods). ● *n.* this period or system.

cam·bric /kámbrik/ *n.* a fine white fabric.

cam·cord·er /kámkawrdər/ *n.* ▲ a combined video camera and sound recorder.

came past of COME.

cam·el /káməl/ *n.* **1 ▼** either of two kinds of large, cud-chewing mammals having slender, cushion-footed legs and one hump (**Arabian camel**, *Camelus dromedarius*) or two humps (**Bactrian camel**, *Camelus bactrianus*). **2** a fawn color. **3** an apparatus for providing additional buoyancy to ships, etc.; a pontoon.

cam·el (or **camel's**) **hair** *n.* **1** the hair of a camel. **2 a** a fine, soft hair used in artists' brushes. **b** a fabric made of this.

cam·el·eer /kaméleer/ *n.* a camel driver.

ca·mel·lia /kəméelyə/ *n.* ▶ any evergreen shrub of the genus *Camellia*, native to E. Asia, with shiny leaves and showy flowers.

cam·el·o·pard /kəméləpaard/ *n. archaic* a giraffe.

ca·mel·ry /káməlree/ *n.* (*pl.* **-ies**) troops mounted on camels.

CAMELLIA (*Camellia* 'Dreamboat')

Cam·em·bert /káməmbair/ *n.* a kind of soft, creamy cheese, usu. with a strong flavor. ▷ CHEESE

CAMEL

There are two species of camel: the Arabian and the Bactrian. Both get nourishment from desert plants and store it as fat in their humps. When food is scarce, the fat in their humps is used up and they shrink. Arabian camels can lose up to one-third of their body fluid; they can, however, drink about 20 gallons of water (100 liters) at one time.

BACTRIAN CAMEL (*Camelus bactrianus*)

ARABIAN CAMEL (*Camelus dromedarius*)

cam·e·o /kámeeō/ *n.* (*pl.* **-os**) **1 a** ▶ a small piece of onyx or other hard stone carved in relief with a background of a different color. **b** a similar relief design using other materials. **2 a** a short descriptive literary sketch or acted scene. **b** a small character part in a play or film, usu. played by a distinguished actor.

CAMEO
CARVED IN
SARDONYX

cam·er·a /kámrə, kámərə/ *n.* **1** ▶ an apparatus consisting of a lightproof box to hold light-sensitive film, a lens, and a shutter mechanism, either for taking still photographs or for motion-picture film. **2** *Telev.* a piece of equipment that forms an optical image and converts it into electrical impulses for transmission or storage. □ **in camera 1** *Law* in a judge's private room. **2** privately; not in public.

cam·er·a·man /kámrəmən/ *n.* (*pl.* **-men**) a person who operates a camera professionally, esp. in film-making or television.

cam·er·a ob·scu·ra /obskyŏŏrə/ *n.* ▼ an internally darkened box with an aperture for projecting the image of an external object on a screen inside it.

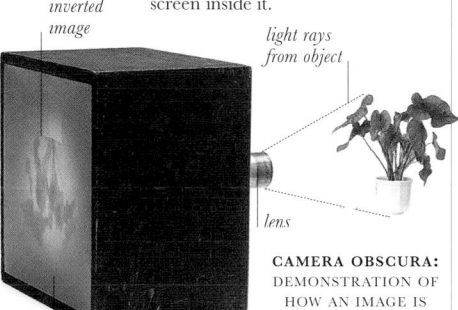

inverted image

light rays from object

lens

screen

CAMERA OBSCURA:
DEMONSTRATION OF
HOW AN IMAGE IS
PROJECTED

cam·er·a-read·y *adj. Printing* (of copy) in a form suitable for immediate photographic reproduction.

cam·i·knick·ers /kámənikərz/ *n.pl. Brit.* a one-piece close-fitting undergarment formerly worn by women.

cam·i·sole /kámisōl/ *n.* an upper-body undergarment, often embroidered.

cam·o·mile var. of CHAMOMILE.

cam·ou·flage /káməflaazh/ *n. & v.* ● *n.* **1 a** the disguising, by the military, of people, vehicles, aircraft, ships, and installations by painting them or covering them to make them blend with their surroundings. ▷ COMBAT DRESS. **b** such a disguise. **2** ▶ the natural coloring of an animal that enables it to blend in with its surroundings. **3** a misleading or evasive precaution or expedient. ● *v.tr.* hide or disguise by means of camouflage.

camp[1] /kamp/ *n. & v.* ● *n.* **1** a place where troops are lodged or trained. **2** temporary overnight lodging in tents, etc., in the open. **3 a** temporary accommodation of various kinds, usu. consisting of huts or tents, for detainees, homeless persons, and other emergency use. **b** a complex of buildings for vacation accommodation. **4** the adherents of a particular party or doctrine regarded collectively (*the Republican camp was jubilant*). **5** *S. Afr.* a portion of veld fenced off for pasture on farms. ● *v.intr.* **1** set up or spend time in a camp (in senses 1 and 2 of *n.*). **2** (often foll. by *out*) lodge in temporary quarters or in the open. □□ **camp·ing** *n.*

camp[2] /kamp/ *adj., n., & v. colloq.* ● *adj.* **1** done in

butterfly's head

wing

CAMOUFLAGE: LEAF
BUTTERFLY AT REST

CAMERA

All cameras have the same basic design – a lightproof container with a lens opposite a light-sensitive surface. The 35 mm SLR (single-lens reflex) is the most popular format for still photography. This is because it allows both photographer and lens to see the subject framed in exactly the same way. Light from the subject enters the lens, reflects off a mirror, and travels through the pentaprism to the rear eyepiece. Pressing the shutter release flips the mirror out of the way, then operates the shutter to expose the film. Most digital cameras have a viewing screen for instant feedback.

program selector

viewing screen

menu selector

BACK VIEW OF A DIGITAL CAMERA

rear eyepiece

pentaprism

frame counter

angled mirror

iris diaphragm

light path

shutter speed dial

shutter release

film spool

film

focal plane shutter

internal lens elements

lens housing

front lens element

CUTAWAY VIEW OF A 35 MM SLR CAMERA

an exaggerated way for effect. **2** affected; effeminate. ● *n.* a camp manner or style. ● *v.intr. & tr.* behave or do in a camp way. □ **camp it up** over-act; behave affectedly. □□ **camp·y** *adj.* (**campier, campiest**). **camp·i·ly** *adv.* **camp·i·ness** *n.*

cam·paign /kampáyn/ *n. & v.* ● *n.* **1** an organized course of action for a particular purpose, esp. to arouse public interest (e.g., before a political election). **2 a** a series of military operations in a definite area or to achieve a particular objective. **b** military service in the field (*on campaign*). ● *v.intr.* conduct or take part in a campaign. □□ **cam·paign·er** *n.*

cam·pa·ni·le /kámpənéelee, -néel/ *n.* a bell tower (usu. freestanding), esp. in Italy.

cam·pa·nol·o·gy /kámpənóləjee/ *n.* **1** the study of bells. **2** the art or practice of bell ringing. □□ **cam·pa·nol·o·ger** *n.* **cam·pa·no·log·i·cal** /-nəlójikəl/ *adj.* **cam·pa·nol·o·gist** *n.*

cam·pan·u·la /kampányələ/ *n.* any plant of the genus *Campanula*, with bell-shaped usu. blue, purple, or white flowers.

camp·er /kámpər/ *n.* **1** a person who camps out or lives temporarily in a tent, hut, etc., esp. for recreation. **2** a large motor vehicle with accommodation for camping out.

cam·pe·si·no /kámpəzéenō/ *n.* (in Spanish-speaking countries) a peasant farmer.

camp·fire /kámpfīr/ *n.* an open-air fire in a camp, etc.

camp fol·low·er *n.* **1** a civilian worker in a military camp. **2** a disciple or adherent.

cam·phor /kámfər/ *n.* a white, translucent, crystalline volatile substance with aromatic smell and bitter taste, used to make celluloid and in medicine. □□ **cam·phor·ic** /-fórik/ *adj.*

cam·pi·on /kámpeeən/ *n.* **1** any plant of the genus *Silene*, with usu. pink or white notched flowers. **2** any of several similar cultivated plants of the genus *Lychnis*.

camp·site /kámpsīt/ *n.* a place suitable for camping; a site used by campers.

cam·pus /kámpəs/ *n.* (*pl.* **campuses**) **1** the grounds of a university or college. **2** a college or university, esp. as a teaching institution.

cam·shaft /kámshaft/ *n.* a shaft with one or more cams attached to it.

Can. *abbr.* Canada; Canadian.

can[1] /kan, kən/ *v.aux.* (*3rd sing. present* **can**; *past* **could** /kŏŏd/) (foll. by infin. without *to*, or *absol.*; present and past only in use) **1 a** be able to; know how to (*I can run fast; can he?; can you speak German?*). **b** be potentially capable of (*you can do it if you try*). **2** be permitted to (*can we go to the party?*).

can[2] /kan/ *n. & v.* ● *n.* **1** a metal vessel for liquid. **2** a metal container in which food or drink is hermetically sealed to enable storage over long periods. **3** (prec. by *the*) *sl.* **a** prison (*sent to the can*). **b** *sl.* toilet. **4** *sl.* the buttocks. ● *v.tr.* (**canned, canning**) **1** put or preserve in a can. **2** record on film or tape for future use. □ **in the can** *colloq.* completed; ready (*orig.* of filmed or recorded material). □□ **can·ner** *n.*

Can·a·da goose *n.* a wild goose, *Branta canadensis*, with a brownish-gray body and white cheeks and breast.

ca·nal /kənál/ *n.* **1** an artificial waterway for inland navigation or irrigation. **2** any of various tubular ducts in a plant or animal, for carrying food, liquid, or air.

ca·nal boat *n.* a long, narrow boat for use on canals.

ca·nal·ize /kánəlīz/ *v.tr.* **1** make a canal through. **2** convert (a river) into a canal. **3** provide with canals. **4** give the desired direction or purpose to. □□ **ca·nal·i·za·tion** *n.*

can·a·pé /kánəpay, -pee/ *n.* a small piece of bread or pastry with a savory food on top, often served as an hors d'oeuvre.

ca·nard /kənáard/ *n.* an unfounded rumor or story.

ca·nar·y /kənáiree/ *n.* (*pl.* **-ies**) **1** any of various small finches of the genus *Serinus*, esp. *S. canaria*, a songbird native to the Canary Islands, with mainly yellow plumage. **2** *hist.* a sweet wine from the Canary Islands.

ca·nar·y yel·low bright yellow.

ca·nas·ta /kənástə/ *n.* **1** a card game using two packs and resembling rummy, the aim being to collect sets (or melds) of cards. **2** a set of seven cards in this game.

can·can /kánkan/ *n.* a lively stage dance with high kicking, performed by women in ruffled skirts and petticoats.

can·cel /kánsəl/ *v.* (**canceled, canceling**; esp. *Brit.* **cancelled, cancelling**) **1** *tr.* **a** withdraw or revoke (a previous arrangement). **b** discontinue (an arrangement in progress). **2** *tr.* obliterate or delete (writing, etc.). **3** *tr.* mark or pierce (a ticket, stamp, etc.) to invalidate it. **4** *tr.* annul; make void; abolish. **5** (often foll. by *out*) **a** *tr.* (of one factor or circumstance) neutralize or counterbalance (another). **b** *intr.* (of two factors or circumstances) neutralize each other. **6** *tr. Math.* strike out (an equal factor) on each side of an equation or from the numerator and denominator of a fraction. □□ **can·cel·er** *n.*

can·cel·la·tion /kánsəláyshən/ *n.* (also **can·cel·a·tion**) **1** the act of canceling or being canceled. **2** something that has been canceled, esp. a reservation.

can·cel·lous /kánsiləs/ *adj.* (of a bone) with pores. ▷ BONE

can·cer /kánsər/ *n.* **1 a** any malignant growth or tumor from an abnormal and uncontrolled division of body cells. **b** a disease caused by this. **2** an evil influence or corruption spreading uncontrollably. **3** (**Cancer**) **a** ◄ a constellation, traditionally regarded as contained in the figure of a crab. **b** the fourth sign of the zodiac (the Crab). ▷ ZODIAC. **c** a person born when the sun is in this sign. □ **Tropic of Cancer** see TROPIC. □□ **Can·cer·i·an** /-séreeən/ *n. & adj.* (in sense 3). **can·cer·ous** *adj.*

CANCER:
FIGURE OF A CRAB FORMED FROM THE STARS OF CANCER

can·cer stick *n. sl.* a cigarette.

can·croid /kángkroyd/ *adj. & n.* ● *adj.* **1** crablike. **2** resembling cancer. ● *n.* a disease resembling cancer.

can·de·la /kandeélə, -délə/ *n.* the SI unit of luminous intensity. ¶ Abbr.: **cd.**

can·de·la·brum /kánd'laábrəm/ *n.* (also **can·de·la·bra** /-brə/) (*pl.* **candelabra, candelabrums, candelabras**) a large branched candlestick or lamp holder.

can·des·cent /kandésənt/ *adj.* glowing with or as with white heat. □□ **can·des·cence** *n.*

can·did /kándid/ *adj.* **1** frank; not hiding one's thoughts. **2** (of a photograph) taken informally, usu. without the subject's knowledge. □□ **can·did·ly** *adv.* **can·did·ness** *n.*

can·di·da /kándidə/ *n.* any yeastlike parasitic fungus of the genus *Candida*, esp. *C. albicans* causing thrush.

can·di·date /kándidət, -dayt/ *n.* **1** a person who seeks or is nominated for an office, award, etc. **2** a person or thing likely to gain some distinction or position. **3** a person entered for an examination. □□ **can·di·da·cy** /-dəsee/ *n.* **can·di·da·ture** /-dəchər/ *n. Brit.*

can·dle /kánd'l/ *n.* **1** a cylinder or block of wax or tallow with a central wick, for giving light when burning. **2** = CANDLEPOWER. □ **cannot hold a**

candle to cannot be compared with; is much inferior to. **not worth the candle** not justifying the cost or trouble.

can·dle·light /kánd'l-līt/ *n.* light provided by candles. □□ **can·dle·lit** *adj.*

Can·dle·mas /kánd'ləməs/ *n.* a feast with blessing of candles (Feb. 2), commemorating the Purification of the Virgin Mary and the presentation of Christ in the Temple.

can·dle·pow·er /kánd'lpowr/ *n.* a unit of luminous intensity.

can·dle·stick /kánd'lstik/ *n.* a holder for one or more candles.

can·dle·wick /kánd'lwik/ *n.* **1** a thick soft cotton yarn. **2** material made from this, usu. with a tufted pattern.

can·dor /kándər/ *n.* (*Brit.* **candour**) candid behavior or action; frankness.

C. & W. *abbr.* country-and-western.

can·dy /kándee/ *n. & v.* ● *n.* (*pl.* **-ies**) **1** a sweet confection, usu. containing sugar, chocolate, etc. **2** (in full **sugar candy**) sugar crystallized by repeated boiling and slow evaporation. ● *v.tr.* (**-ies, -ied**) (usu. as **candied** *adj.*) preserve by coating and impregnating with a sugar syrup (*candied fruit*).

can·dy-strip·er *n.* a hospital volunteer, esp. a teenager, who wears a brightly striped uniform.

can·dy·tuft /kándeetuft/ *n.* any of various plants of the genus *Iberis*, native to W. Europe, with white, pink, or purple flowers in tufts.

cane /kayn/ *n. & v.* ● *n.* **1 a** the hollow jointed stem of giant reeds or grasses (*bamboo cane*). **b** the solid stem of slender palms (*malacca cane*). **2** = SUGAR CANE. **3** a raspberry cane. **4** material of cane used for wickerwork, etc. **5 a** a cane used as a walking stick or a support for a plant or an instrument of punishment. **b** any slender walking stick. ● *v.tr.* **1** beat with a cane. **2** weave cane into (a chair, etc.). □□ **can·er** *n.* (in sense 2 of *v.*). **can·ing** *n.*

cane sug·ar *n.* sugar obtained from sugar cane.

ca·nine /káynīn/ *adj. & n.* ● *adj.* **1** of or resembling a dog or dogs. **2** of or belonging to the family Canidae, including dogs, wolves, foxes, etc. ● *n.* **1** a dog. **2** (in full **canine tooth**) ► a pointed tooth situated between the incisors and premolars. ▷ DENTITION, TOOTH

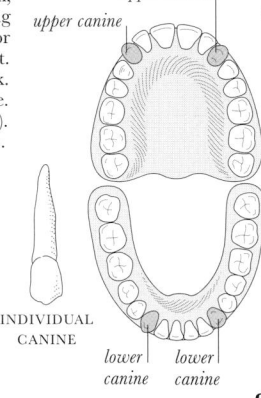

upper canine

upper canine

INDIVIDUAL CANINE

lower canine

lower canine

CANINE TOOTH

PLAN OF HUMAN DENTITION

can·is·ter /kánistər/ *n.* **1** a small container, usu. of metal and cylindrical, for storing sugar, etc. **2 a** cylinder of shot, tear gas, etc., that explodes on impact. **b** such cylinders collectively.

can·ker /kángkər/ *n. & v.* ● *n.* **1 a** a destructive fungus disease of trees and plants. **b** an open wound in the stem of a tree or plant. **2** *Zool.* an ulcerous ear disease of animals, esp. cats and dogs. **3** *Med.* an ulceration, esp. of the lips. **4** a corrupting influence. ● *v.tr.* **1** consume with canker. **2** corrupt. **3** (as **cankered** *adj.*) soured; malignant; crabbed. □□ **can·ker·ous** *adj.*

can·ker·worm /kángkərwərm/ *n.* any caterpillar of various wingless moths that consume the buds and leaves of shade and fruit trees in N. America.

can·na /kánə/ *n.* any tropical plant of the genus *Canna* with bright flowers and ornamental leaves.

can·na·bis /kánəbis/ *n.* **1** any hemp plant of the genus *Cannabis*, esp. Indian hemp. **2** a preparation of parts of this used as an intoxicant or hallucinogen.

canned /kand/ *adj.* **1** prerecorded (*canned laughter; canned music*). **2** supplied in a can (*canned beer*). **3** *sl.* drunk.

can·nel /kánəl/ *n.* (in full **cannel coal**) a bituminous coal burning with a bright flame.

can·nel·lo·ni /kánəlónee/ *n.pl.* tubes or rolls of pasta stuffed with meat or a vegetable mixture.

can·ner·y /kánəree/ *n.* (*pl.* **-ies**) a factory where food is canned.

can·ni·bal /kánibəl/ *n. & adj.* ● *n.* **1** a person who eats human flesh. **2** an animal that feeds on flesh of its own species. ● *adj.* of or like a cannibal. □□ **can·ni·bal·ism** *n.* **can·ni·bal·is·tic** *adj.* **can·ni·bal·is·ti·cal·ly** *adv.*

can·ni·bal·ize /kánibəlīz/ *v.tr.* use (a machine, etc.) as a source of spare parts for others. □□ **can·ni·bal·i·za·tion** *n.*

can·non /kánon/ *n. & v.* **1** *hist.* (*pl.* same) ▼ a large, heavy gun installed on a carriage or mounting. **2** an automatic aircraft gun firing shells. **3** *Billiards Brit.* CAROM. ● *v.intr. Brit.* (usu. foll. by *against, into*) collide heavily or obliquely.

can·non·ade /kánənáyd/ *n. & v.* ● *n.* a period of continuous heavy gunfire. ● *v.tr.* bombard with a cannonade.

can·non·ball /kánənbawl/ *n. & v.* ● *n.* **1** a large, usu. metal ball fired by a cannon. **2** *Tennis* a very rapid serve. **3** a very fast vehicle, etc., esp. an express train. ● *v.intr.* travel with great force, momentum, and speed.

can·non fod·der *n.* soldiers regarded merely as material to be expended in war.

can·not /kánot, kanót/ *v.aux.* can not.

CANNON

Until the mid-19th century, cannon were muzzle-loading. When preparing to fire, the gunners would ram gunpowder and a cannon ball down the bore of the barrel from the muzzle. When ready to fire, a lighted portfire was applied to the vent. Such cannon were superseded by more efficient breech-loading weapons.

portfire

vent

gunner's seat

muzzle

barrel

trunnion

gunner's seat

ring for attachment of limber (ammunition carriage)

carriage

breech

wheel

19TH-CENTURY BRITISH MUZZLE-LOADING CANNON

can·nu·la /kányələ/ *n.* (*pl.* **cannulas** or **cannulae** /-lee/) *Surgery* a small tube for inserting into the body to allow fluid to enter or escape.

can·ny /kánee/ *adj.* (**cannier, canniest**) **1 a** shrewd; worldly-wise. **b** thrifty. **c** circumspect. **2** sly; dryly humorous. □□ **can·ni·ly** *adv.* **can·ni·ness** *n.*

ca·noe /kənóo/ *n. & v.* ● *n.* ▼ a small, narrow boat with pointed ends usu. propelled by paddling. ▷ OUTRIGGER. ● *v.intr.* (**canoes, canoed, canoeing**) travel in a canoe. □□ **ca·noe·ist** *n.*

CANOE AND PADDLE

can of worms *n. colloq.* unwanted complications (*let's not open a can of worms*)

canola oil /kənólə/ *n.* cooking oil derived from the seed of a variety of the rape plant.

can·on /kánən/ *n.* **1 a** a general law, rule, principle, or criterion. **b** a church decree or law. **2** (*fem.* **canoness**) **a** a member of a cathedral chapter. **b** a member of certain Roman Catholic orders. **3 a** a collection or list of sacred books, etc., accepted as genuine. **b** the recognized genuine works of a particular author; a list of these. **4** *Eccl.* the part of the Mass containing the words of consecration. **5** *Mus.* a piece with different parts taking up the same theme successively.

ca·non·ic /kənónik/ *adj.* = CANONICAL *adj.*

ca·non·i·cal /kənónikəl/ *adj. & n.* ● *adj.* **1 a** according to canon law. **b** included in the canon of Scripture. **2** authoritative; standard; accepted. **3** of a cathedral chapter or a member of it. **4** *Mus.* in canon form. ● *n.* (in *pl.*) the canonical dress of the clergy. □□ **ca·non·i·cal·ly** *adv.*

can·on·ize /kánənīz/ *v.tr.* **1 a** declare officially to be a saint, usu. with ceremony. **b** regard as a saint. **2** admit to the canon of Scripture. **3** sanction by church authority. □□ **can·on·i·za·tion** *n.*

can·on law *n.* ecclesiastical law.

can·on·ry /kánənree/ *n.* (*pl.* **-ies**) the office or benefice of a canon.

ca·noo·dle /kənóod'l/ *v.intr. colloq.* kiss and cuddle amorously.

can o·pen·er *n.* a device for opening cans (in sense 2 of *n.*). ▷ UTENSIL

can·o·py /kánəpee/ *n.* (*pl.* **-ies**) **1 a** a covering hung or held up over a throne, bed, person, etc. **b** the sky. **c** an overhanging shelter. **2** *Archit.* a rooflike projection over a niche, etc. **3** the uppermost layers of foliage, etc., in a forest. ▷ RAIN FOREST. **4 a** the expanding part of a parachute. **b** the cover of an aircraft's cockpit. ▷ AIRCRAFT

canst /kanst/ *archaic 2nd person sing.* of CAN[1].

cant[1] /kant/ *n. & v.* ● *n.* **1** insincere pious or moral talk. **2** ephemeral or fashionable catchwords. **3** language peculiar to a class, profession, sect, etc.; jargon. ● *v.intr.* use cant.

cant[2] /kant/ *n. & v.* ● *n.* **1 a** a slanting surface, e.g., of a bank. **b** a bevel of a crystal, etc. **2** an oblique push or movement that upsets or partly upsets something. **3** a tilted position; tilt. ● *v.* **1** *tr.* push or pitch out of level; tilt. **2** *intr.* take or lie in a slanting position. **3** *tr.* impart a bevel to.

can't /kant/ *contr.* can not.

Cantab. /kántab/ *abbr.* Cantabrigian; of Cambridge University or Harvard University.

can·ta·bi·le /kantaábilay/ *adv., adj., & n. Mus.* ● *adv. & adj.* in a smooth singing style. ● *n.* a cantabile passage or movement.

Can·ta·brig·i·an /kántəbríjeeən/ *adj. & n.* ● *adj.* of Cambridge (England or Massachusetts), or Cambridge University or Harvard University. ● *n.*

1 a student of Cambridge University or Harvard University. **2** a native of Cambridge (England or Massachusetts).

can·ta·loupe /kánt'lōp/ *n.* ▶ a small, round ribbed variety of melon with orange flesh.

can·tan·ker·ous /kantángkərəs/ *adj.* bad-tempered; quarrelsome. □□ **can·tan·ker·ous·ly** *adv.* **can·tan·ker·ous·ness** *n.*

can·ta·ta /kəntaátə/ *n. Mus.* a short narrative or descriptive composition with vocal solos and usu. chorus and orchestral accompaniment.

can·teen /kantéen/ *n.* **1 a** a restaurant for employees in an office or factory, etc. **b** a store selling provisions or liquor in a barracks or camp. **2** *Brit.* a case or box of cutlery. **3** a soldier's or camper's water flask or set of eating or drinking utensils.

can·ter /kántər/ *n. & v.* ● *n.* a gentle gallop. ● *v.* **1** *intr.* (of a horse or its rider) go at a canter. **2** *tr.* make (a horse) canter.

can·ter·bur·y /kántərberee/ *n.* (*pl.* **-ies**) a piece of furniture with partitions for holding music, etc.

Can·ter·bur·y bell /kántərbaree/ *n.* a cultivated campanula with large flowers.

can·thar·i·des /kanthárideez/ *n.pl.* a preparation made from dried bodies of a beetle *Lytta vesicatoria*, causing blistering of the skin and formerly used in medicine and as an aphrodisiac. Also called **Spanish fly**.

can·thus /kánthəs/ *n.* (*pl.* **canthi** /-thī/) the outer or inner corner of the eye, where the upper and lower lids meet.

can·ti·cle /kántikəl/ *n.* a usu. nonmetrical hymn, chant, or poem, typically with a biblical text, forming a regular part of a church service.

can·ti·le·na /kánt'léenə/ *n. Mus.* a simple or sustained melody.

can·ti·le·ver /kánt'leevər, -evər/ *n. & v.* ● *n.* **1** a long bracket or beam, etc., projecting from a wall to support a balcony, etc. **2** a beam or girder fixed at only one end. ▷ BRIDGE. ● *v.intr.* **1** project as a cantilever. **2** be supported by cantilevers.

can·ti·na /kantéenə/ *n.* esp. *SW US* a tavern, bar, etc.

can·to /kántō/ *n.* (*pl.* **-os**) a division of a long poem.

can·ton *n. & v.* ● *n.* **1** /kántən/ **a** a subdivision of a country. **b** a state of the Swiss confederation. **2** /kántən/ *Heraldry* a square division, less than a quarter, in the upper (usu. dexter) corner of a shield. ● *v.tr.* **1** /kántən, -tón/ *Brit.* put (troops) into quarters. **2** /kántón/ divide into cantons. □□ **can·ton·al** /kánt'nəl, kántónəl/ *adj.*

Can·ton·ese /kántəneéz/ *adj. & n.* ● *adj.* of Canton or the Cantonese dialect of Chinese. ● *n.* (*pl.* same) **1** a native of Canton. **2** the dialect of Chinese spoken in SE China and Hong Kong.

can·ton·ment /kantónmənt, -tón-/ *n.* **1** quarters assigned to troops. **2** a permanent military station in India.

can·tor /kántər/ *n.* **1** the leader of the singing in church; a precentor. **2** the precentor in a synagogue.

can·to·ri·al /kantáwreeəl/ *adj.* **1** of or relating to the cantor. **2** of the north side of the choir in a church (cf. DECANAL).

Ca·nuck /kənúk/ *n. & adj. sl.* often *derog.* ● *n.* **1** a Canadian, esp. a French Canadian. **2** a Canadian horse or pony. ● *adj.* Canadian, esp. French Canadian.

can·vas /kánvəs/ *n. & v.* ● *n.* **1 a** a strong coarse kind of cloth made from hemp or flax or other coarse yarn and used for sails and tents, etc., and as a surface for oil painting. **b** a piece of this. **2** a painting on canvas, esp. in oils. **3** an open kind of canvas used as a basis for tapestry and embroidery. **4** *sl.* the floor of a boxing or wrestling ring. ● *v.tr.*

CANTALOUPE
MELON

(**canvased, canvasing**; esp. *Brit.* **canvassed, canvassing**) cover with canvas. □ **under canvas 1** in a tent or tents. **2** with sails spread.

can·vas·back /kánvəsbak/ *n.* a wild duck, *Aythya valisineria*, of N. America, with back feathers the color of unbleached canvas.

can·vass /kánvəs/ *v. & n.* ● *v.* **1 a** *intr.* solicit votes. **b** *tr.* solicit votes from (electors in a constituency). **2** *tr.* **a** ascertain opinions of. **b** seek business from. **c** discuss thoroughly. **3** *tr. Brit.* propose (an idea or plan, etc.). ● *n.* the process of or an instance of canvassing, esp. of electors. □□ **can·vass·er** *n.*

can·yon /kányən/ *n.* a deep gorge, often with a stream or river. ▷ ERODE

caou·tchouc /kówchook/ *n.* raw rubber.

CAP *abbr.* Civil Air Patrol.

cap /kap/ *n. & v.* ● *n.* **1 a** a covering for the head, often of soft fabric and with a visor. **b** a head covering worn in a particular profession (*nurse's cap*). **c** esp. *Brit.* a cap awarded as a sign of membership of a sports team. **d** an academic mortarboard or soft hat. **2 a** a cover like a cap in shape or position (*kneecap, toecap*). **b** a device to seal a bottle or protect the point of a pen, lens of a camera, etc. **3** = MOBCAP. **4** = PERCUSSION CAP. **5** = CROWN *n.* 9b. ● *v.tr.* (**capped, capping**) **1 a** put a cap on. **b** cover the top or end of. **c** set a limit to (expenditure, etc.). **2** esp. *Brit.* award a sports cap to. **3 a** lie on top of; form the cap of. **b** surpass; excel. **c** improve on (a story, quotation, etc.), esp. by producing a better or more apposite one. □ **cap in hand** humbly. **set one's cap for** try to attract as a suitor. □□ **cap·ful** *n.* (*pl.* **-fuls**). **cap·ping** *n.*

cap. *abbr.* **1** capital. **2** capital letter. **3** chapter.

ca·pa·bil·i·ty /káypəbílitee/ *n.* (*pl.* **-ies**) **1** (often foll. by *of, for, to*) ability; power; the condition of being capable. **2** an undeveloped or unused faculty.

ca·pa·ble /káypəbəl/ *adj.* **1** competent; able; gifted. **2** (foll. by *of*) **a** having the ability or fitness or necessary quality for. **b** susceptible or admitting of (explanation or improvement, etc.). □□ **ca·pa·bly** *adv.*

ca·pa·cious /kəpáyshəs/ *adj.* roomy; able to hold much. □□ **ca·pa·cious·ly** *adv.* **ca·pa·cious·ness** *n.*

ca·pac·i·tance /kəpásit'ns/ *n. Electr.* **1** the ability of a system to store an electric charge. **2** the ratio of the change in an electric charge in a system to the corresponding change in its electric potential. ¶ Symb.: **C**.

ca·pac·i·tate /kəpásitayt/ *v.tr.* **1** (usu. foll. by *for*, or *to* + infin.) render capable. **2** make legally competent.

ca·pac·i·tor /kəpásitər/ *n. Electr.* ▼ a device of one or more pairs of conductors separated by insulators used to store an electric charge. ▷ RADIO

ca·pac·i·ty /kəpásitee/ *n.* (*pl.* **-ies**) **1 a** the power to contain, receive, experience, or produce (*capacity for heat, pain*, etc.). **b** the maximum amount that can be produced or contained, etc. **c** the volume, e.g., of the cylinders in an internal-combustion engine. **d** (*attrib.*) fully occupying the available space, resources etc. (with *a capacity audience*). **2 a** a mental power. **b** a faculty or talent. **3** a position or function (*in a civil ca-*

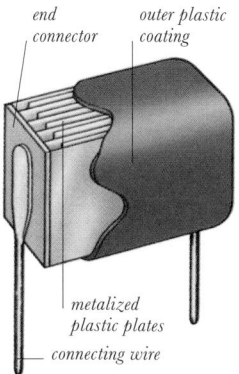

end connector   *outer plastic coating*

metalized plastic plates

connecting wire

CAPACITOR: CUTAWAY VIEW OF A METALIZED-FILM CAPACITOR

C

123

C

pacity; *in my capacity as a critic*). **4** legal competence. **5** *Electr.* capacitance. □ **to capacity** fully; using all resources (*working to capacity*). □□ **ca·pac·i·ta·tive** /-táytiv/ *adj.* (also **ca·pac·i·tive**) (in sense 5).

ca·par·i·son /kəpárisən/ *n.* **1** (usu. in *pl.*) a horse's trappings. ▷ JOUST. **2** equipment; finery.

cape¹ /kayp/ *n.* **1** a sleeveless cloak. **2** a short, sleeveless cloak as a fixed or detachable part of a longer cloak or coat.

cape² /kayp/ *n.* **1** a headland or promontory. **2** (**the Cape**) **a** the Cape of Good Hope. **b** the S. African province containing it. **c** Cape Cod, Massachusetts.

cap·e·lin /kápəlin, káplin/ *n.* (also **cap·lin** /káplin/) a small smeltlike fish, *Mallotus villosus*, of the N. Atlantic, used as food and as bait for catching cod, etc.

ca·pel·li·ni /kapəléenee/ *n.* pasta in the form of very thin strands. ▷ PASTA

ca·per¹ /káypər/ *v. & n.* ● *v.intr.* jump or run about playfully. ● *n.* **1** a playful jump or leap. **2 a** a fantastic proceeding; a prank. **b** *sl.* any activity or occupation. □ **cut a caper** (or **capers**) act friskily.

ca·per² /káypər/ *n.* **1** ◀ a bramblelike S. European shrub, *Capparis spinosa*. **2** (in *pl.*) its flower buds cooked and pickled for use as flavoring, esp. for a savory sauce.

cap·er·cail·lie /kápərkáylee/ *n.* (also **cap·er·cail·zie** /-káylzee/) a large European grouse, *Tetrao urogallus*. ▷ DISPLAY

cap·il·lar·i·ty /kápiláritee/ *n.* = CAPILLARY ACTION.

cap·il·lar·y /kápəleree/ *adj. & n.* ● *adj.* **1** of or like a hair. **2** (of a tube) of hairlike internal diameter. **3** of one of the delicate ramified blood vessels intervening between arteries and veins. ▷ CARDIOVASCULAR. ● *n.* (*pl.* **-ies**) **1** a capillary tube. ▷ CAPILLARY ACTION. **2** a capillary blood vessel.

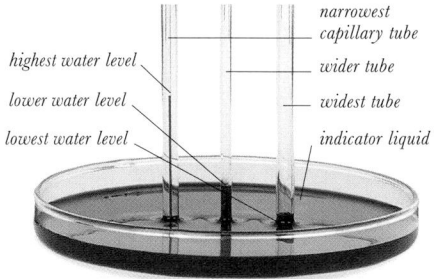

CAPER (*Capparis spinosa*)

flower bud

cap·il·lar·y ac·tion *n.* ▼ the tendency of a liquid in a capillary tube or absorbent material to rise and fall as a result of surface tension. Also called **capillarity**. ▷ TRANSPIRE

narrowest capillary tube
highest water level
wider tube
lower water level
widest tube
lowest water level
indicator liquid

CAPILLARY ACTION: DEMONSTRATION OF LIQUID RISING IN CAPILLARY TUBES

cap·i·tal¹ /kápit'l/ *n., adj., & int.* ● *n.* **1** the most important town or city of a country, state, or region, usu. its seat of government and administrative center. **2 a** the money or other assets with which a company starts in business. **b** accumulated wealth, esp. as used in further production. **c** money invested or lent at interest. **3** capitalists generally. **4** a capital letter. ● *adj.* **1 a** principal; most important; leading. **b** *colloq.* excellent; first-rate. **2 a** involving or punishable by death (*capital punishment*; *a capital offense*). **b** (of an error, etc.) vitally harmful; fatal. **3** (of letters of the alphabet) large in size and of the form used to

begin sentences and names, etc. ● *int.* expressing approval or satisfaction. □ **make capital out of** use to one's advantage. **with a capital —** emphatically such (*art with a capital A*). □□ **cap·i·tal·ly** *adv.*

cap·i·tal² /kápit'l/ *n. Archit.* ► the head or cornice of a pillar or column. ▷ ENTABLATURE

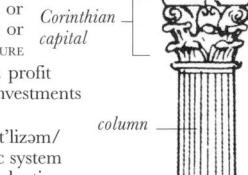

Corinthian capital
column
CAPITAL

cap·i·tal gain *n.* a profit from the sale of investments or property.

cap·i·tal·ism /kápit'lizəm/ *n.* **1 a** an economic system in which the production and distribution of goods depend on invested private capital and profit making. **b** the possession of capital or wealth. **2** *Polit.* the dominance of private owners of capital and production for profit.

cap·i·tal·ist /kápit'list/ *n. & adj.* ● *n.* **1** a person using or possessing capital; a rich person. **2** an advocate of capitalism. ● *adj.* of or favoring capitalism. □□ **cap·i·tal·is·tic** *adj.* **cap·i·tal·is·ti·cal·ly** *adv.*

cap·i·tal·ize /kápit'līz/ *v.* **1** *tr.* **a** convert into or provide with capital. **b** calculate or realize the present value of an income. **c** reckon (the value of an asset) by setting future benefits against the cost of maintenance. **2** *tr.* **a** write (a letter of the alphabet) as a capital. **b** begin (a word) with a capital letter. **3** *intr.* (foll. by *on*) use to one's advantage; profit from. □□ **cap·i·tal·i·za·tion** *n.*

cap·i·ta·tion /kápitáyshən/ *n.* **1** a tax or fee at a set rate per person. **2** the levying of such a tax or fee.

Cap·i·tol /kápit'l/ *n.* **1** the building in Washington, D.C., in which the U.S. Congress meets. **2** (as **cap·i·tol**) a building in which a state legislature meets.

ca·pit·u·late /kəpíchəlayt/ *v.intr.* surrender, esp. on stated conditions. □□ **ca·pit·u·la·tor** *n.*

ca·pit·u·la·tion /kəpíchəláyshən/ *n.* **1** the act of capitulating; surrender. **2** a statement of the main divisions of a subject. **3** an agreement or set of conditions.

cap·lin var. of CAPELIN.

cap'n /káp'm/ *n. sl.* captain.

ca·po /káypō/ *n.* (in full **capotasto** /-tástō/) (*pl.* **capos** or **capotastos**) *Mus.* ▼ a device secured across the neck of a fretted instrument to raise equally the tuning of all strings by the required amount.

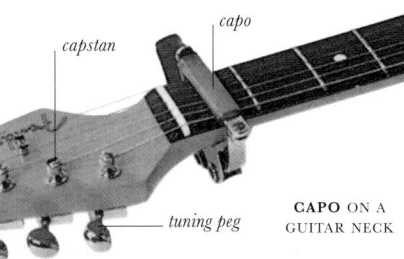

capo
capstan
CAPO ON A GUITAR NECK
tuning peg

ca·po·ei·ra /kapōéérə/ *n.* a system of physical discipline and movement featuring elements from dance and the martial arts, originating among Brazilian slaves.

ca·pon /káypon, -pən/ *n.* a domestic cock castrated and fattened for eating. □□ **ca·pon·ize** *v.tr.*

ca·pote /kəpót, kapó/ *n. hist.* a long cloak with a hood, formerly worn by soldiers and travelers, etc.

cap·puc·ci·no /kápōōchéenō/ *n.* (*pl.* **-os**) espresso coffee with milk made frothy with pressurized steam.

ca·pric·ci·o /kəpréécheeō/ *n.* (*pl.* **-os**) **1** a lively and usu. short musical composition. **2** a painting, etc., representing a fantasy or a mixture of real and imaginary features.

ca·price /kəprées/ *n.* **1 a** an unaccountable or

whimsical change of mind or conduct. **b** a tendency to this. **2** a work of lively fancy in painting, drawing, or music; a capriccio.

ca·pri·cious /kəpríshəs, -prée-/ *adj.* **1** guided by or given to caprice. **2** irregular; unpredictable. □□ **ca·pri·cious·ly** *adv.* **ca·pri·cious·ness** *n.*

Cap·ri·corn /káprikawrn/ *n.* (also **Cap·ri·cor·nus** /-káwrnəs/) **1** *Astron.* ► a constellation (the Goat) said to represent a goat with a fish's tail. **2** *Astrol.* **a** the tenth sign of the zodiac, which the Sun enters at the winter solstice (about Dec 21). ▷ ZODIAC. **b** a person born when the sun is in this sign. □□ **Cap·ri·corn·i·an** *n. & adj.*

CAPRICORN: FIGURE OF A GOAT FORMED FROM THE STARS OF CAPRICORNUS

cap·rine /káprīn, -rin/ *adj.* of or like a goat.

cap·ri·ole /kápreeōl/ *n. & v.* ● *n.* **1** a leap or caper. **2** a trained horse's high leap and kick without advancing. ● *v.* **1** *intr.* (of a horse or its rider) perform a capriole. **2** *tr.* make (a horse) capriole.

ca·pris /kəpréez/ *n.pl.* (also **ca·pri pants**) women's close-fitting tapered trousers that end above the ankle.

caps. *abbr.* capital letters.

cap·si·cum /kápsikəm/ *n.* **1** any plant of the genus *Capsicum*, having edible capsular fruits containing many seeds, esp. *C. annuum* yielding chili and sweet peppers. **2** the fruit of any of these plants.

cap·sid¹ /kápsid/ *n.* any bug of the family Capsidae, esp. one that feeds on plants.

cap·sid² /kápsid/ *n.* the protein coat or shell of a virus.

cap·size /kápsīz, -síz/ *v.* **1** *tr.* upset or overturn (a boat). **2** *intr.* be capsized.

cap·stan /kápstən/ *n.* **1** ► a thick revolving cylinder with a vertical axis, for winding an anchor cable or a halyard, etc. ▷ SHIP. **2** a motor-driven revolving spindle on a tape recorder, that guides the tape past the head.

drumhead
bar
hole
barrel
whelp
tapered spindle (axis)
spigot
pin
CAPSTAN

cap·stone /kápstōn/ *n.* **1** a copestone. **2** a crowning achievement.

cap·sule /kápsəl/ *n.* **1** a small gelatinous case enclosing a dose of medicine and swallowed with it. ▷ MEDICINE. **2** a detachable compartment of a spacecraft or nose cone of a rocket. ▷ SPACECRAFT. **3** an enclosing membrane in the body. **4 a** a dry fruit that releases its seeds when ripe. ▷ FRUIT. **b** the spore-producing part of mosses and liverworts. **5** *Biol.* an enveloping layer surrounding certain bacteria. **6** (*attrib.*) concise; highly condensed (*a capsule history of jazz*). □□ **cap·su·lar** *adj.* **cap·su·late** *adj.*

cap·su·lize /kápsəlīz, -syōō-/ *v.tr.* put (information, etc.) in compact form.

Capt. *abbr.* Captain.

cap·tain /káptin/ *n. & v.* ● *n.* **1 a** a chief or leader. **b** the leader of a team, esp. in sports. **c** a powerful or influential person (*captain of industry*). **2 a** the person in command of a merchant or passenger ship. **b** the pilot of a civil aircraft. **3 a** an army or air force officer next above lieutenant. **b** a navy officer in command of a warship; one ranking below commodore or rear admiral and above commander. **c** a police officer in charge of a precinct, ranking below chief. **4** a supervisor of waiters or bellboys. **5 a** a great soldier or strategist. **b** an experienced commander. ● *v.tr.* be captain of; lead. □□ **cap·tain·cy** *n.* (*pl.* **-ies**). **cap·tain·ship** *n.*

CAR

The first internal-combustion cars were built by Karl Benz and Gottlieb Daimler in 1885. The early cars ran on only one or two cylinders. By 1908 Henry Ford began mass-producing four-cylinder cars, and about 15,000,000 of his Model-T cars were sold by 1928. Today's cars are built for greater efficiency, safety, comfort, and style. Many modern engines consume less fuel because of computerized ignition systems, fuel injectors, and multivalve cylinder heads. Exhaust pollution is reduced by catalytic converters; plastic and fiberglass bumpers, steel frames, safety-glass windshields, and airbags improve safety. Coil-spring suspension, pneumatic tires, adjustable padded seats, and other add-ons, like air-conditioning, enhance passenger comfort.

C

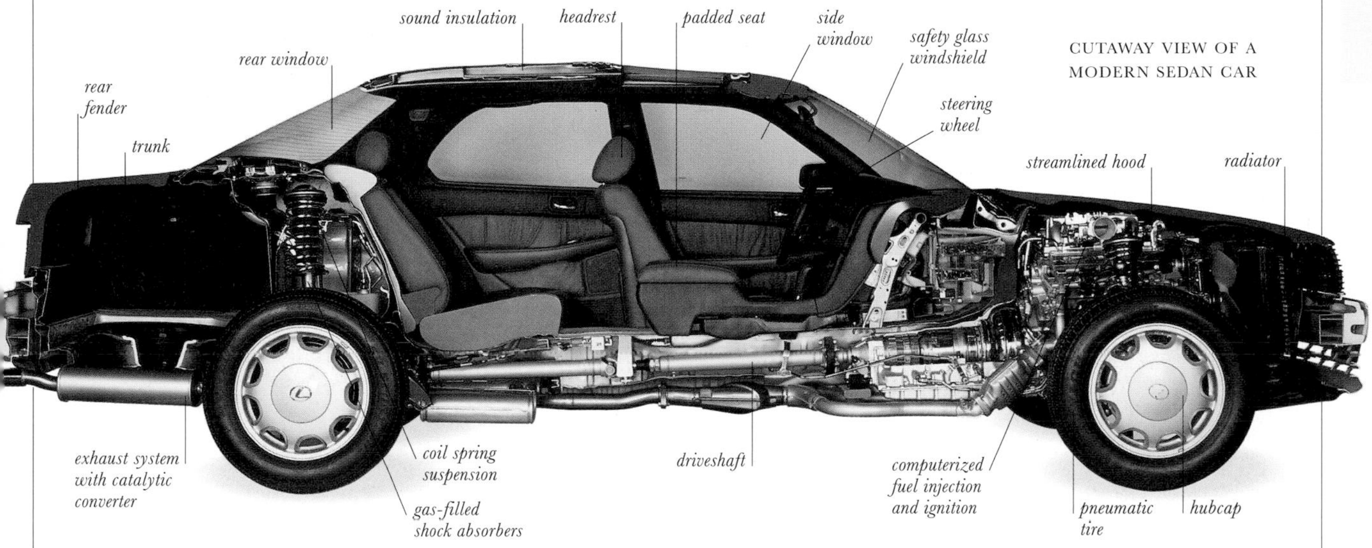

CUTAWAY VIEW OF A MODERN SEDAN CAR

rear fender · trunk · rear window · sound insulation · headrest · padded seat · side window · safety glass windshield · steering wheel · streamlined hood · radiator

exhaust system with catalytic converter · coil spring suspension · gas-filled shock absorbers · driveshaft · computerized fuel injection and ignition · pneumatic tire · hubcap

MAIN TYPES OF CAR

STATION WAGON   HATCHBACK   FAMILY SEDAN   MINIVAN

SPORT UTILITY VEHICLE   SPORTS CAR   CONVERTIBLE CAR   CUSTOMIZED CAR

cap·tion /kápshən/ n. & v. ● n. **1** a title or brief explanation appended to an illustration, cartoon, etc. **2** wording appearing on a motion-picture or television screen as part of a movie or broadcast. **3** the heading of a chapter or article, etc. **4** *Law* a certificate attached to or written on a document. ● v.tr. provide with a caption.

cap·tious /kápshəs/ adj. given to finding fault or raising petty objections. □□ **cap·tious·ly** adv. **cap·tious·ness** n.

cap·ti·vate /káptivayt/ v.tr. **1** overwhelm with charm or affection. **2** fascinate. □□ **cap·ti·vat·ing** adj. **cap·ti·vat·ing·ly** adv. **cap·ti·va·tion** /-váyshən/ n.

cap·tive /káptiv/ n. & adj. ● n. a person or animal that has been taken prisoner or confined. ● adj. **1 a** taken prisoner. **b** kept in confinement or under restraint. **2 a** unable to escape. **b** in a position of having to comply. **3** of or like a prisoner (*captive state*).

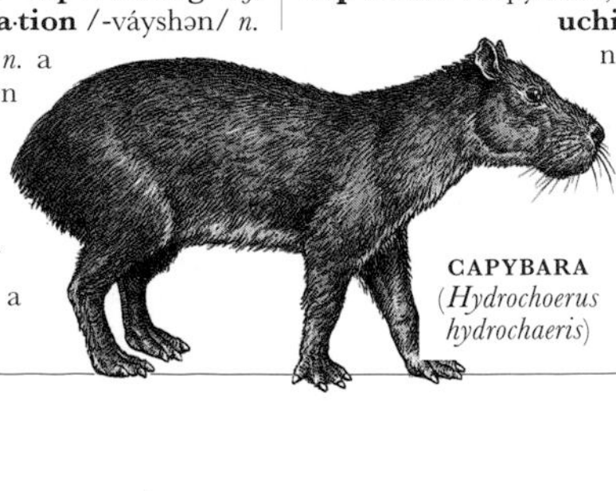

cap·tiv·i·ty /kaptívitee/ n. (pl. **-ies**) the condition or circumstances of being a captive.

cap·tor /káptər, -tawr/ n. a person who captures.

cap·ture /kápchər/ v. & n. ● v.tr. **1 a** take prisoner; seize as a prize. **b** obtain by force or trickery. **2** portray in permanent form (*could not capture the likeness*). **3** *Physics* absorb (a subatomic particle). **4** (in board games) make a move that secures the removal of (an opposing piece) from the board. **5** cause (data) to be stored in a computer. ● n. **1** the act of capturing. **2** a thing or person captured. □□ **cap·tur·er** n.

cap·u·chin /kápyəchin, -shin, kəpyoo-/ n. **1** (**Cap·uchin**) a Franciscan friar of the new rule of 1529. **2** any monkey of the genus *Cebus* of S. America, with cowl-like head hair.

cap·y·ba·ra /kápə-báárə/ n. ◄ a very large semi-aquatic rodent, *Hydrochoerus hydrochaeris*, native to S. America.

CAPYBARA (*Hydrochoerus hydrochaeris*)

car /kaar/ n. **1** ▲ a road vehicle with an enclosed passenger compartment, powered by an internal-combustion engine; an automobile. **2** a vehicle that runs on rails, esp. a railroad car or a streetcar. **3** a railroad car of a specified type (*dining car*). **4** the passenger compartment of an elevator, cable railway, balloon, etc. **5** *poet.* a wheeled vehicle; a chariot. □ **car coat** n. a short coat designed esp. for car drivers. □□ **car·ful** n. (pl. **-fuls**).

car·a·bi·ner /karəbeenər/ n. ▶ a coupling with safety closure, used by mountaineers. ▷ ROCK CLIMBING

car·a·bi·nie·re /káaraabeenyére, kárəbinyáiree/ n. (pl. **carabinieri** *pronunc.* same) an Italian gendarme.

car·a·cal /kárəkal/ n. a lynx, *Felis caracal*, native to N. Africa and SW Asia.

car·a·cole /kárəkōl/ n. & v. ● n. a horse's half turn to the right or left. ● v. **1** *intr.* (of a horse or its rider) perform a caracole. **2** *tr.* make (a horse) caracole.

CARABINER: SNAP CARABINER

C

car·a·cul var. of KARAKUL.

ca·rafe /kəráf/ n. a glass container for water or wine, esp. at a table or bedside.

ca·ram·bo·la /kárəmbốlə/ n. **1** a small tree, *Averrhoa carambola*, native to SE Asia, bearing golden-yellow ribbed fruit. **2** this fruit. (Also called **starfruit**.)

car·a·mel /kárəmel, -məl, kaárməl/ n. **1 a** a sugar or syrup heated until it turns brown, then used as a flavoring or to color spirits, etc. **b** a kind of soft toffee made with sugar, butter, etc., melted and further heated. **2** the light-brown color of caramel.

car·a·mel·ize /kárəməlīz, kaármə-/ v. **1 a** tr. convert (sugar or syrup) into caramel. **b** intr. (of sugar or syrup) be converted into caramel. **2** tr. coat or cook (food) with caramelized sugar or syrup. □□ **car·a·mel·i·za·tion** /-lizáyshən/ n.

car·a·pace /kárəpays/ n. ◄ the hard upper shell of a turtle or a crustacean. ▷ CRUSTACEAN

car·at /kárət/ n. **1** a unit of weight for precious stones, now equivalent to 200 milligrams. **2** Brit. var. of KARAT.

CARAPACE: STARRED TORTOISE WITH A RIDGED CARAPACE

car·a·van /kárəvan/ n. & v. ● n. **1 a** a covered or enclosed wagon or truck; van. **b** Brit. a vehicle equipped for living in and usu. towed by a motor vehicle or a horse; trailer. **2** a company of merchants or pilgrims, etc., traveling together, esp. across a desert in Asia or N. Africa. **3** a covered cart or carriage. ● v.intr. (**caravaned**, **caravaning** or **caravanned**, **caravanning**) travel or live in a caravan. □□ **car·a·van·ner** n.

car·a·van·sa·ry /kárəvánsəree, -rī/ n. (also **car·a·van·se·rai**) a Near Eastern inn with a central court where caravans (see CARAVAN 2) may rest.

car·a·way /kárəway/ n. an umbelliferous plant, *Carum carvi*, bearing clusters of tiny white flowers.

car·a·way seed n. the fruit of the caraway plant used as flavoring and as a source of oil. ▷ SPICE

carb /kaarb/ n. colloq. a carburetor.

car·bide /kaárbīd/ n. Chem. a binary compound of carbon.

car·bine /kaárbeen, -bīn/ n. ▼ a lightweight firearm, usu. a rifle, orig. for cavalry use.

carrying handle　*front sight*　*slip ring*　*barrel*　*plastic hand-guard*　*bayonet lug*　*trigger guard*　*magazine*

CARBINE: US COLT COMMANDO 5.56 MM CARBINE

carbo- /kaárbō/ comb. form carbon (*carbohydrate*; *carbolic*; *carboxyl*).

car·bo·hy·drate /kaárbəhídrayt, -bō-/ n. Biochem. any of a large group of energy-producing organic compounds containing carbon, hydrogen, and oxygen, e.g., starch, glucose, and other sugars.

car·bol·ic /kaarbólik/ n. (in full **carbolic acid**) phenol, esp. when used as a disinfectant.

car bomb n. a terrorist bomb concealed in or under a parked car.

car·bon /kaárbən/ n. **1** a nonmetallic element occurring naturally as diamond, graphite, and charcoal, and in all organic compounds. ▷ ALLOTROPE, CARBON CYCLE. ¶ Symb.: **C. 2 a** = CARBON COPY. **b** = CARBON PAPER. **3** a rod of carbon in an arc lamp.

carbon 14 n. a long-lived radioactive carbon

CARBON CYCLE

Carbon is an essential element in the bodies of all living things. Present in gases in the atmosphere, it nourishes green plants and bacteria. Some of this carbon is absorbed when animals eat plants. It returns to the atmosphere as carbon dioxide when living things respire, defecate, or die and decay.

carbon dioxide in the atmosphere

carbon dioxide released by plants

carbon dioxide absorbed by plants

carbon dioxide exhaled by animals

carbon in animal dung

carbon in plants eaten by animals

decay of plants and animals releases carbon

carbon dioxide released by worms, fungi, and bacteria

isotope of mass 14, used in radiocarbon dating, and as a tracer in biochemistry.

car·bo·na·ceous /kaárbənáyshəs/ adj. **1** consisting of or containing carbon. **2** of or like coal or charcoal.

car·bo·na·do /kaárbənáydō/ n. (pl. **-os**) a dark opaque or impure kind of diamond used as an abrasive, for drills, etc.

car·bo·na·ra /karbənáarə/ adj. denoting a pasta sauce made with bacon or ham, egg, and cream.

car·bo·nate /kaárbənayt/ n. & v. ● n. Chem. a salt of carbonic acid. ● v.tr. **1** impregnate with carbon dioxide; aerate. **2** convert into a carbonate. □□ **car·bo·na·tion** /-náyshən/ n.

car·bon cop·y n. **1** a copy made with carbon paper. **2** a person or thing identical or similar to another (*is a carbon copy of his father*).

car·bon cy·cle n. Biol. ▲ the cycle in which carbon compounds are interconverted, usu. by living organisms.

car·bon dat·ing n. the determination of the age of an organic object from the ratio of isotopes, which changes as carbon 14 decays.

car·bon di·ox·ide n. a colorless, odorless gas occurring naturally in the atmosphere and formed by respiration. ▷ CARBON CYCLE. ¶ Chem. formula: CO_2.

car·bon·ic /kaarbónik/ adj. Chem. containing carbon.

carbonic acid n. a very weak acid formed from carbon dioxide dissolved in water.

car·bon·if·er·ous /kaárbənífərəs/ adj. & n. ● adj. **1** producing coal. **2** (**Carboniferous**) Geol. of or relating to the fifth period in the Paleozoic era, with evidence of the first reptiles and extensive coal-forming swamp forests. ● n. (**Carboniferous**) Geol. this period or system.

car·bon·ize /kaárbənīz/ v.tr. **1** convert into carbon by heating. **2** reduce to charcoal or coke. **3** coat with carbon. □□ **car·bon·i·za·tion** /-nizáyshən/ n.

car·bon mon·ox·ide n. a colorless, odorless toxic gas formed by the incomplete burning of carbon. ¶ Chem. formula: CO.

car·bon pa·per n. a thin carbon-coated paper used between two sheets of paper when writing to make a copy onto the bottom sheet.

car·bo·run·dum /kaárbərúndəm/ n. a compound of carbon and silicon used esp. as an abrasive.

car·box·yl /kaarbóksil/ n. Chem. the univalent acid radical (-COOH), present in most organic acids. □□ **car·box·yl·ic** /-boksílik/ adj.

car·boy /kaárboy/ n. a large bottle often protected by a frame, used for containing liquids.

car·bun·cle /kaárbungkəl/ n. **1** a severe abscess in the skin. **2** a bright red gem. □□ **car·bun·cu·lar** /-búngkyələr/ adj.

car·bu·ra·tion /kaárbəráyshən, -byə-/ n. the process of charging air with a spray of liquid hydrocarbon fuel, esp. in an internal-combustion engine.

car·bu·ret /kaárbəráyt, -rét, -byə-/ v.tr. (**carbureted**, **carbureting**; esp. Brit. **carburetted**, **carburetting**) combine (a gas, etc.) with carbon.

car·bu·re·tor /kaárbəráytter, -byə-/ n. (also **car·bu·ra·tor**, esp. Brit. **carburettor**, **carburetter**) ▼ an apparatus for carburation of fuel and air in an internal-combustion engine.

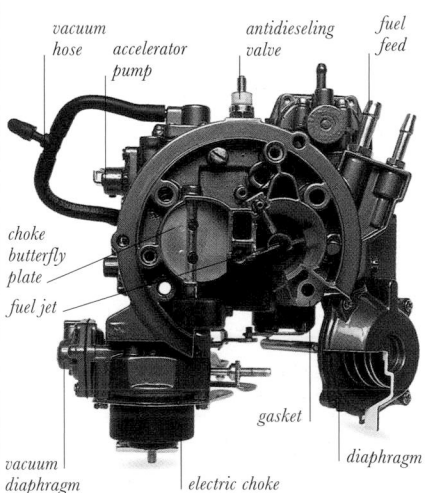

vacuum hose　*accelerator pump*　*antidieseling valve*　*fuel feed*　*choke butterfly plate*　*fuel jet*　*gasket*　*vacuum diaphragm*　*electric choke*　*diaphragm*

CARBURETOR OF A GAS-DRIVEN ENGINE

car·ca·jou /kaárkəjōō, -kəzhōō/ n. = WOLVERINE.

car·cass /kaárkəs/ n. (also Brit. **carcase**) **1** the dead body of an animal, esp. for cutting up as meat. **2** the bones of a cooked bird. **3** derog. the human body, living or dead. **4** the skeleton, framework of a building, ship, etc. **5** worthless remains.

car·cin·o·gen /kaarsínəjən, kaársinəjən/ *n.* any substance that produces cancer.

car·cin·o·gen·e·sis /kaársinəjénisis/ *n.* the production of cancer.

car·cin·o·gen·ic /kaársinəjénik/ *adj.* producing cancer. □□ **car·ci·no·ge·nic·i·ty** /-nísitee/ *n.*

car·ci·no·ma /kaársinómə/ *n.* (*pl.* **carcinomas** or **carcinomata** /-mətə/) a cancer, esp. one arising in epithelial tissue. □□ **car·ci·no·ma·tous** *adj.*

Card. *abbr.* Cardinal.

card[1] /kaard/ *n. & v.* ● *n.* **1** thick, stiff paper or thin pasteboard. **2 a** a flat piece of this, esp. for writing or printing on. **b** = POSTCARD. **c** a card used to send greetings, issue an invitation, etc. (*birthday card*). **d** = CALLING CARD. **e** = BUSINESS CARD. **f** a ticket of admission or membership. **3 a** = PLAYING CARD. **b** a similar card in a set designed for board games, etc. **c** (in *pl.*) card playing; a card game. **4 a** a program of events at boxing matches, races, etc. **b** a scorecard. **c** a list of holes on a golf course, on which a player's scores are entered. **5** *colloq.* a person, esp. an odd or amusing one. **6** a small rectangular piece of plastic issued by a bank, retail establishment, etc., with personal (often machine-readable) data on it, chiefly to obtain cash or credit (*credit card*; *do you have a card?*). ● *v.tr.* **1** fix to a card. **2** write on a card, esp. for indexing. **3** ask for proof of age, as at a bar. □ **ask for** (or **get**) **one's cards** *Brit.* ask (or be told) to leave one's employment. **in the cards** possible or likely. **put** (or **lay**) **one's cards on the table** reveal one's resources, intentions, etc.

card[2] /kaard/ *n. & v.* ● *n.* a toothed instrument, wire brush, etc., for raising a nap on cloth or for disentangling fibers before spinning. ● *v.tr.* brush, comb, cleanse, or scratch with a card. □□ **card·er** *n.*

car·da·mom /kaárdəməm/ *n.* (also **car·da·mum**) **1** an aromatic SE Asian plant, *Elettaria cardamomum.* **2** ◄ the seed capsules of this used as a spice. ▷ SPICE

CARDAMOM SEED CAPSULES
(*Elettaria cardamomum*)

card·board /kaárdbawrd/ *n. & adj.* ● *n.* pasteboard or stiff paper, esp. for making cards or boxes. ● *adj.* **1** made of cardboard. **2** flimsy; insubstantial.

card-car·ry·ing *adj.* being a registered member of an organization, esp. a political party or labor union.

card game *n.* a game in which playing cards are used.

car·di·ac /kaárdeeak/ *adj. & n.* ● *adj.* of or relating to the heart. ▷ HEART. ● *n.* a person with heart disease.

car·di·gan /kaárdigən/ *n.* a knitted sweater fastening down the front, usu. with long sleeves.

car·di·nal /kaárd'nəl/ *n. & adj.* ● *n.* **1** (as a title **Cardinal**) a leading dignitary of the RC Church, one of the college electing the Pope. **2** any small American songbird of the genus *Richmondena*, the males of which have scarlet plumage. ● *adj.* **1** chief; fundamental; on which something hinges. **2** of deep scarlet (like a cardinal's cassock). □□ **car·di·nal·ate** /-nəlayt/ *n.* (in sense 1 of *n.*). **car·di·nal·ly** *adv.* **car·di·nal·ship** *n.* (in sense 1 of *n.*).

car·di·nal num·ber *n.* a number denoting quantity (one, two, three, etc.), as opposed to ordinal numbers (first, second, third, etc.).

car·di·nal point *n.* each of the four main points of the compass (N., S., E., W.). ▷ COMPASS

cardio- /kaárdeeō/ *comb. form* heart (*cardiogram*; *cardiology*).

car·di·o·gram /kaárdeeəgram/ *n.* a record of muscle activity within the heart, made by a cardiograph.

car·di·o·graph /kaárdeeəgraf/ *n.* an instrument for recording heart muscle activity. □□ **car·di·og·ra·pher** /-deeógrəfər/ *n.* **car·di·og·ra·phy** *n.*

car·di·ol·o·gy /kaárdeeóləjee/ *n.* the branch of

CARDIOVASCULAR

The human cardiovascular (circulatory) system consists of the heart, the blood vessels, and, within them, the blood. Oxygenated blood is pumped out of the heart through arteries, transporting nutrients and oxygen through the capillaries to all cells in the body. It also removes waste products excreted from these cells. Blood also contains specialized cells that protect against infection or blood loss as a result of injury. Once deoxygenated, blood is returned to the heart through the veins. The entire circuit is completed in about one minute.

temporal artery
superficial temporal vein
common carotid artery
internal jugular vein
aortic arch
subclavian vein
superior vena cava
pulmonary artery
pulmonary vein
heart
brachial vein
brachial artery
inferior vena cava
descending aorta
renal artery
renal vein
common iliac vein
common iliac artery
ulnar vein
great saphenous vein
femoral vein
popliteal vein
knee veins
anterior tibial artery
anterior tibial vein
posterior tibial vein
dorsal metatarsal arteries and veins

hepatic portal vein
branch of superior mesenteric artery
radial artery
ulnar artery
femoral artery
knee arteries
popliteal artery
posterior tibial artery
peroneal artery
dorsal digital veins and arteries

KEY TO BLOOD VESSELS
ARTERY
VEIN
CAPILLARY

HUMAN CARDIOVASCULAR SYSTEM

medicine concerned with diseases and abnormalities of the heart. □□ **car·di·ol·o·gist** *n.*

car·di·o·pul·mo·nar·y re·sus·ci·ta·tion /kardeeō-poolməneree/ *n.* emergency medical procedures for restoring normal heartbeat and breathing to victims of heart failure, drowning, etc. ¶ Abbr.: **CPR**.

car·di·o·vas·cu·lar /kaárdeeōváskyələr/ *adj.* ▲ of or relating to the heart and blood vessels. ▷ BLOOD, HEART

car·doon /kaardóōn/ *n.* a thistlelike plant, *Cynara cardunculus,* allied to the globe artichoke, with leaves used as a vegetable.

card·phone /kaárdfōn/ *n. Brit.* a public telephone operated by the insertion of a prepaid plastic machine-readable card instead of money.

card·sharp /kaárdsharp/ *n.* (also **card·sharp·er**) a swindler at card games.

card ta·ble *n.* a table for card playing, esp. folding.

care /kair/ *n. & v.* ● *n.* **1** worry; anxiety. **2** an occasion for this. **3** serious attention; heed; caution (*assembled with care*; *handle with care*). **4** protection; charge. **5** a thing to be done or seen to. ● *v.intr.* **1** (usu. foll. by *about, for, whether*) feel concern or interest. **2** (usu. foll. by *for, about*) feel liking, affection, regard, or deference (*don't care for jazz*; *she cares for him a great deal*). **3** (foll. by *to* + infin.) wish or be willing (*do not care to be seen with him*; *would you care to try them?*). □ **care for** provide for; look after. **care of** at the address of (*sent it care of his sister*). **for all one cares** *colloq.* denoting uninterest or unconcern (*I could be dying for all you care*). **have a care** take care; be careful. **I** (etc.) **couldn't** (freq. **could**) **care less** *colloq.* an expression of complete indifference. **take care 1** be careful. **2** (foll. by *to* + infin.) not fail nor neglect. **take care of 1** look after; keep safe. **2** deal with. **3** dispose of.

C

C

CARNIVORE

Mammals of the order Carnivora are predominantly flesh eaters and share features that reflect a hunting lifestyle. Powerful, agile limbs make them swift, while forward-facing eyes assist in judging distance accurately. All have strong canine teeth for cutting. Many also have specialized premolars and molars (carnassials) that operate like shears to slice through meat. One exception is the giant panda, which is almost entirely herbivorous, although most other members of the order Carnivora will supplement their diets with vegetation when necessary. In some systems of classification, pinnipeds are considered as members of the Carnivora.

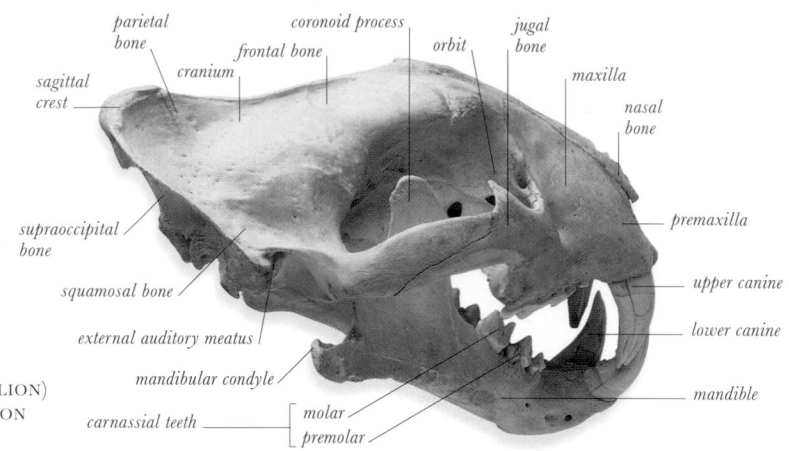

SKULL OF A CARNIVOROUS MAMMAL (LION)
SHOWING CHARACTERISTIC DENTITION

FAMILIES OF THE ORDER CARNIVORA

PROCYONIDAE
(raccoons, red pandas)

URSIDAE
(bears) ▷ BEAR

HYAENIDAE
(aardwolves, hyenas)

FELIDAE
(cats, cheetahs, lions) ▷ CAT

VIVERRIDAE
(civets, genets, mongooses)

MUSTELIDAE
(badgers, skunks, weasels) ▷ MUSTELID

CANIDAE
(dogs, foxes, wolves) ▷ DOG

ca·reen /kəréen/ v. **1** tr. turn (a ship) on one side for cleaning, caulking, or repair. **2 a** intr. tilt; lean over. **b** tr. cause to do this. **3** intr. swerve about; career. ¶ Sense 3 is infl. by career (v.). □□ **ca·reen·age** n.

ca·reer /kəréer/ n. & v. ● n. **1 a** one's advancement through life, esp. in a profession. **b** the progress through history of a group or institution. **2 a** profession or occupation, esp. as offering advancement. **3** (attrib.) **a** pursuing or wishing to pursue a career (career woman). **b** working permanently in a specified profession (career diplomat). ● v.intr. **1** move or swerve about wildly. **2** go swiftly.

ca·reer·ist /kəréerist/ n. a person predominantly concerned with personal advancement.

care·free /káirfree/ adj. free from anxiety or responsibility; lighthearted. □□ **care·free·ness** n.

care·ful /káirfŏŏl/ adj. **1** painstaking; thorough. **2** cautious. **3** done with care and attention. **4** (usu. foll. by that + clause, or to + infin.) taking care; not neglecting. **5** (foll. by for, of) concerned for; taking care of. □□ **care·ful·ly** adv. **care·ful·ness** n.

care·giv·er /káirgivər/ n. a person who provides care for children, the sick, the elderly, etc.

care la·bel n. a label attached to clothing, with instructions for washing, etc.

care·less /káirlis/ adj. **1** not taking care nor paying attention. **2** unthinking; insensitive. **3** done without care; inaccurate. **4** lighthearted. **5** (foll. by of) not concerned about; taking no heed of. **6** effortless; casual. □□ **care·less·ly** adv. **care·less·ness** n.

car·er /káirər/ n. Brit. a person who cares for a sick or elderly person.

ca·ress /kərés/ v. & n. ● v.tr. **1** touch or stroke gently or lovingly; kiss. **2** treat fondly or kindly. ● n. a loving or gentle touch or kiss.

car·et /kárət/ n. a mark (^) indicating a proposed insertion in printing or writing.

care·tak·er /káirtaykər/ n. **1 a** a person employed to look after something, esp. a house in the owner's absence. **b** Brit. a janitor. **2** (attrib.) exercising temporary authority (caretaker government).

care·worn /káirwawrn/ adj. showing the effects of prolonged worry.

car·fare /káarfair/ n. a passenger's fare to travel by public transport (orig. streetcar).

car·go /káargō/ n. (pl. **-oes** or **-os**) **1 a** goods carried on a ship or aircraft. **b** a load of such goods. **2 a** goods carried in a motor vehicle. **b** a load of such goods.

car·hop /káarhop/ n. colloq. a waiter at a drive-in restaurant.

Car·ib /kárib/ n. & adj. ● n. **1** an aboriginal inhabitant of the southern W. Indies or the adjacent coasts. **2** the language of this people. ● adj. of or relating to this people.

Car·ib·be·an /káribéeən, kəríbeeən/ n. & adj. ● n. the part of the Atlantic between the southern W. Indies and Central America. ● adj. **1** of or relating to this region. **2** of the Caribs or their language or culture.

car·i·bou /káribŏŏ/ n. (pl. same) a N. American reindeer.

car·i·ca·ture /kárikəchər, -chŏŏr/ n. & v. ● n. **1** a usu. comic representation of a person by exaggeration of characteristic traits, in a picture, writing, or mime. **2** a ridiculously poor or absurd imitation or version. ● v.tr. make or give a caricature of. □□ **car·i·ca·tur·al** /-chŏŏrəl/ adj. **car·i·ca·tur·ist** n.

car·ies /káireez/ n. (pl. same) decay and crumbling of a tooth or bone.

car·il·lon /kárilon, -lən/ n. **1** a set of bells sounded either from a keyboard or mechanically. **2** a tune played on bells. **3** an organ stop imitating a peal of bells.

ca·ri·na /kəréenə/ n. (pl. **carinas** or **carinae** /-nee/) Biol. a keel-shaped structure, esp. the ridge of a bird's breastbone. □□ **ca·ri·nal** adj.

car·i·nate /kárinayt/ adj. (of a bird) having a keeled breastbone.

car·ing /káiring/ adj. **1** compassionate. **2** involving the care of the sick, elderly, or disabled.

car·i·o·ca /káreeókə/ n. **1 a** a Brazilian dance like the samba. **b** the music for this. **2** a native of Rio de Janeiro.

car·i·o·gen·ic /káreeōjénik/ adj. causing caries.

car·i·ole /káreeōl/ *n.* **1** a small open carriage for one. **2** a covered light cart. **3** a Canadian sleigh.

car·i·ous /káireeəs/ *adj.* (of bones or teeth) decayed.

car·jack·ing /kárjaking/ *n.* theft of an automobile whose driver is forced to leave the vehicle or is kept captive while the thief drives. □□ **car·jack** *v.tr.* **car·jack·er** *n.*

car·load /káarlōd/ *n.* **1** a quantity that can be carried in a car. **2** the minimum quantity of goods for which a lower rate is charged for transport.

Car·lo·vin·gi·an var. of CAROLINGIAN.

Car·mel·ite /káarmilīt/ *n. & adj.* ● *n.* **1** a friar of the Order of Our Lady of Mount Carmel, following a rule of extreme asceticism. **2** a nun of a similar order. ● *adj.* of or relating to the Carmelites.

car·min·a·tive /kaarmínətiv, káarminaytiv/ *adj. & n.* ● *adj.* relieving flatulence. ● *n.* a carminative drug.

car·mine /káarmin, -mīn/ *adj. & n.* ● *adj.* of a vivid crimson color. ● *n.* this color.

car·nage /káarnij/ *n.* great slaughter, esp. of human beings in battle.

car·nal /káarnəl/ *adj.* **1** of the body or flesh; worldly. **2** sensual; sexual. □□ **car·nal·i·ty** /-áalitee/ *n.* **car·nal·ize** *v.tr.* **car·nal·ly** *adv.*

carnal knowl·edge *n. Law* sexual intercourse.

car·na·tion[1] /kaarnáyshən/ *n.* **1** any of several cultivated varieties of clove-scented pink, with variously colored showy flowers (see also CLOVE[1] 2). **2** this flower.

car·na·tion[2] /kaarnáyshən/ *n. & adj.* ● *n.* a rosy pink color. ● *adj.* of this color.

car·nau·ba /kaarnówbə, -náwbə, -nō̄ōbə/ *n.* **1** a fan palm, *Copernicia cerifera*, native to NE Brazil. **2** (in full **carnauba wax**) the yellowish leaf wax of this tree used as a polish, etc.

different colored bands

car·nel·ian /kaarneélyən/ *n.* (also **cornelian** /kawr-/) ◄ a dull red or reddish-white variety of chalcedony. ▷ GEM

car·net /kaarnáy/ *n.* a customs permit to take a motor vehicle across a frontier for a limited period.

car·ni·val /káarnivəl/ *n.* **1 a** the festivities usual during the period before Lent in Roman Catholic countries. **b** any festivities, esp. those occurring at a regular date. **2** merrymaking; revelry. **3** a traveling fair or circus.

CARNELIAN

car·ni·vore /káarnivawr/ *n.* **1 a** ◄ any mammal of the order Carnivora, including cats, dogs, and bears, with powerful jaws and teeth adapted for stabbing, tearing, and eating flesh. **b** any other flesh-eating mammal. **2** any flesh-eating plant.

car·niv·o·rous /kaarnívərəs/ *adj.* **1** (of an animal) feeding on flesh. **2** (of a plant) digesting trapped insects or other animal substances. **3** of or relating to the order Carnivora. □□ **car·niv·o·rous·ly** *adv.* **car·niv·o·rous·ness** *n.*

car·ob /kárəb/ *n.* **1** an evergreen tree, *Ceratonia siliqua*, native to the Mediterranean, bearing edible pods. **2** its bean-shaped edible seed pod sometimes used as a substitute for chocolate.

car·ol /kárəl/ *n. & v.* ● *n.* a joyous song, esp. a Christmas hymn. ● *v.* (**caroled, caroling**; esp. *Brit.* **carolled, carolling**) **1** *intr.* sing carols, esp. outdoors at Christmas. **2** *tr. & intr.* sing joyfully. □□ **car·ol·er** *n.* (also esp. *Brit.* **caroller**).

Car·o·lin·gi·an /károlínjən, -jeeən/ *adj. & n.* (also **Car·o·lo·vin·gi·an** /káarɔlɔvínjeeən/) ● *adj.* of or relating to the second Frankish dynasty, founded by

Charlemagne (d. 814). ● *n.* a member of the Carolingian dynasty.

car·om /kárəm/ *n. & v. Billiards* ● *n.* the hitting of two balls by the one ball on one shot. ● *v.intr.* **1** make a carom. **2** (usu. foll. by *off*) strike and rebound.

car·o·tene /kárəteen/ *n.* any of several orange-colored plant pigments found in carrots, tomatoes, etc., acting as a source of vitamin A.

ca·rot·id /kərótid/ *n. & adj.* **1** each of the two main arteries carrying blood to the head and neck. ▷ CARDIOVASCULAR. ● *adj.* of or relating to either of these arteries.

ca·rouse /kərówz/ *v. & n.* ● *v.intr.* **1** have a noisy or lively drinking party. **2** drink heavily. ● *n.* a noisy or lively drinking party. □□ **ca·rous·al** *n.* **ca·rous·er** *n.*

car·ou·sel /kárəsél, -zél/ *n.* (also **car·rou·sel**) **1** a merry-go-round. **2** a rotating delivery or conveyor system, esp. for passengers' luggage at an airport.

carp[1] /kaarp/ *n.* (*pl.* same) ▼ any freshwater fish of the family Cyprinidae, esp. *Cyprinus carpio*, often bred for use as food.

CARP: COMMON CARP
(*Cyprinus carpio*)

carp[2] /kaarp/ *v.intr.* (usu. foll. by *at*) find fault; complain pettily. □□ **carp·er** *n.*

car·pal /káarpəl/ *adj. & n.* ● *adj.* of or relating to the bones in the wrist. ● *n.* any of the bones forming the wrist. ▷ HAND, SKELETON.

carpal tun·nel syn·drome *n.* a painful condition of the hand and fingers caused by compression of a major nerve where it passes over the carpal bones.

car·pel /káarpəl/ *n. Bot.* ► the female reproductive organ of a flower, consisting of a stigma, style, and ovary. □□ **car·pel·lar·y** *adj.*

stigma

carpel — style

ovary

CARPEL: LILY FLOWER SHOWING THE CARPEL

car·pen·ter /káarpintər/ *n. & v.* ● *n.* a person skilled in woodwork, esp. of a structural kind (cf. JOINER). ● *v.* **1** *intr.* do carpentry. **2** *tr.* make by means of carpentry.

carpenter ant *n.* any large ant of the genus *Camponotus*, boring into wood to nest.

car·pen·try /káarpintree/ *n.* **1** the work or occupation of a carpenter. **2** work constructed by a carpenter.

car·pet /káarpit/ *n. & v.* ● *n.* **1 a** thick fabric for covering a floor or stairs. **b** a piece of this fabric. **2** an expanse or layer resembling a carpet in being smooth, soft, bright, or thick (*carpet of snow*). ● *v.tr.* **1** cover with or as with a carpet. **2** *colloq.* reprimand; reprove. □ **on the carpet 1** *colloq.* being

reprimanded. **2** under consideration. **sweep under the carpet** conceal (a problem or difficulty) in the hope that it will be forgotten.

car·pet·bag /káarpitbag/ *n.* a traveling bag of a kind orig. made of carpetlike material.

car·pet·bag·ger /káarpitbagər/ *n.* **1** a political candidate in an area where the candidate has no local connections (orig. a Northerner in the South after the Civil War). **2** an unscrupulous opportunist, esp. an outsider.

car·pet·ing /káarpiting/ *n.* **1** material for carpets. **2** carpets collectively.

carpet sweep·er *n.* a household implement with a revolving brush or brushes for sweeping carpets.

car phone *n.* a cellular telephone for use in an automobile.

car·pool /káarpool/ *n. & v.* ● *n.* (also **car pool**) **1** an arrangement by which a group of commuters travel to and from their destination in a single vehicle, often with the members taking turns as driver. **2** the commuters taking part in such an arrangement (*there are four people in our carpool*). ● *v.intr.* (also **car·pool**) participate in or organize a carpool.

car·port /káarpawrt/ *n.* a shelter with a roof and open sides for a car, usu. beside a house.

car·pus /káarpəs/ *n.* (*pl.* **carpi** /-pī/) the small bones between the forelimb and metacarpus in terrestrial vertebrates, forming the wrist in humans.

car·ra·geen /kárəgeen/ *n.* (also **car·ra·gheen**) an edible red seaweed, *Chondrus crispus*, of the N. hemisphere.

car·rel /kárəl/ *n.* **1** a small cubicle for a reader in a library. **2** *hist.* a small enclosure or study in a cloister.

car·riage /kárij/ *n.* **1** a wheeled vehicle, esp. one with four wheels and pulled by horses. **2** *Brit.* a railroad passenger coach. **3** *Brit.* **a** the conveying of goods. **b** the cost of this (*carriage paid*). **4** the part of a machine (e.g., a typewriter) that carries other parts into the required position. **5** a gun carriage. **6** a manner of carrying oneself; one's bearing or deportment.

car·riage·way /kárijway/ *n. Brit.* the part of a road intended for vehicles; highway.

car·ri·er /káreeər/ *n.* **1** a person or thing that carries. **2** a person or company undertaking to convey goods or passengers for payment. **3** a part of a bicycle, etc., for carrying luggage or a passenger. **4** an insurance company. **5** a person or animal that may transmit a disease or a hereditary characteristic without suffering from or displaying it. **6** = AIRCRAFT CARRIER. **7** a substance used to support or convey a pigment, a catalyst, radioactive material, etc. **8** *Physics* a mobile electron or hole that carries a charge in a semiconductor.

car·ri·er pig·eon *n.* a pigeon trained to carry messages tied to its neck or leg.

car·ri·on /káreeən/ *n.* **1** dead putrefying flesh. **2** something vile or filthy.

car·rot /kárət/ *n.* **1 a** an umbelliferous plant, *Daucus carota*, with a tapering orange-colored root. **b** this root as a vegetable. ▷ VEGETABLE. **2** a means of enticement or persuasion. **3** (in *pl.*) *sl.* a red-haired person. □□ **car·rot·y** *adj.*

car·rou·sel var. of CAROUSEL.

car·ry /káree/ *v. & n.* ● *v.* (**-ies, -ied**) **1** *tr.* support or hold up, esp. while moving. **2** *tr.* convey with one from one place to another. **3** *tr.* have on one's person (*carry a watch*). **4** *tr.* conduct or transmit (*pipe carries water; wire carries electric current*). **5** *tr.* take (a process, etc.) to a specified point (*carry into effect; carry a joke too far*). **6** *tr.* (foll. by *to*) continue or prolong (*carry modesty to excess*). **7** *tr.* involve; imply; have as a feature or consequence (*carries a two-year guarantee; principles carry consequences*). **8** *tr.* (in reckoning) transfer (a figure) to a column of higher value. **9** *tr.* hold in a specified way (*carry oneself erect*). **10** *tr.* **a** (of a newspaper or magazine) publish; include in its contents, esp. regularly. **b** (of a radio or television station) broadcast, esp. regularly. **11** *tr.* (of a retailing outlet) keep a regular stock of (particular goods for sale) (*have stopped carrying that brand*). **12** *intr.* **a** (of sound, esp. a voice) be audible at a distance. **b** (of a missile) travel; penetrate. **13** *tr.* (of a gun, etc.) propel to a specified distance. **14** *tr.* **a** win victory or acceptance for (a proposal, etc.). **b** win acceptance from (*carried the audience with them*). **c** win; capture (a prize, a fortress, etc.). **d** gain (a state or district) in an election. **e** *Golf* cause the ball to pass beyond (a bunker, etc.). **15** *tr.* **a** endure the weight of; support (*columns carry the dome*). **b** be the chief cause of the effectiveness of; be the driving force in (*you carry the sales department*). **16** *tr.* be pregnant with (*is carrying twins*). **17** *tr.* **a** (of a motive, money, etc.) cause or enable (a person) to go to a specified place. **b** (of a journey) bring (a person) to a specified point. ● *n.* (*pl.* **-ies**) **1** an act of carrying. **2** *Golf* the distance a ball travels before reaching the ground. **3** a portage between rivers, etc. **4** the range of a gun, etc. □ **carry all before one** succeed; overcome all opposition. **carry away 1** remove. **2** inspire; affect emotionally or spiritually. **3** deprive of self-control (*got carried away*). **carry back** take (a person) back in thought to a past time. **carry the can** *Brit. colloq.* bear the responsibility or blame. **carry conviction** be convincing. **carry the day** be victorious or successful. **carry forward** transfer to a new page or account. **carry it off** (or **carry it off well**) do well under difficulties. **carry off 1** take away, esp. by force. **2** win (a prize). **3** (esp. of a disease) kill. **4** render acceptable or passable. **carry on 1** continue (*carry on eating*; *carry on, don't mind me*). **2** engage in (a conversation or a business). **3** *colloq.* behave strangely or excitedly. **4** (often foll. by *with*) *Brit. colloq.* flirt or have a love affair. **5** advance (a process) by a stage. **carry out** put (ideas, instructions, etc.) into practice. **carry over 1** = *carry forward*. **2** postpone (work, etc.). **carry through 1** complete successfully. **2** bring safely out of difficulties. **carry weight** be influential or important. **carry with one** bear in mind.

car·ry·all /káreeawl/ *n.* a large bag or case.

car·ry·ing-on (or **car·ry·ings-on**) *n. sl.* **1** a state of excitement or fuss. **2** a questionable piece of behavior. **3** a flirtation or love affair.

car·ry·out /káreeowt/ *n.* & *adj.* ● *n.* **1** food prepared and packaged for consumption elsewhere than the place of sale. **2** an establishment that sells such food. ● *adj.* of or designating such foods.

car·ry·o·ver /káreeōvər/ *n.* something carried over.

car·sick /kaársik/ *adj.* affected with nausea caused by the motion of a car. □□ **car·sick·ness** *n.*

cart /kaart/ *n.* & *v.* ● *n.* **1** a strong vehicle with two or four wheels for carrying loads, usu. drawn by a horse. **2** a light vehicle for pulling by hand. **3** a light vehicle with two wheels for driving in, drawn by a single horse. ● *v.tr.* **1** convey in or as in a cart. **2** *sl.* carry (esp. a cumbersome thing) with difficulty or over a long distance (*carted it all the way home*). □ **cart off** remove, esp. by force. **put the cart before the horse 1** reverse the proper order or procedure. **2** take an effect for a cause. □□ **cart·er** *n.* **cart·ful** *n.* (*pl.* **-fuls**).

cart·age /kaártij/ *n.* the price paid for carting.

carte blanche /kaárt blónsh, blánch/ *n.* full discretionary power given to a person.

car·tel /kaartél/ *n.* **1** an informal association of manufacturers or suppliers to maintain prices at a high level, and control production, marketing arrangements, etc. **2** a political combination between parties. □□ **car·tel·ize** /kaártəlīz/ *v.tr.* & *intr.*

Car·te·sian /kaartée<u>zh</u>ən/ *adj.* & *n.* ● *adj.* of or relating to R. Descartes, 17th-c. French philosopher and mathematician. ● *n.* a follower of Descartes. □□ **Car·te·sian·ism** *n.*

Car·te·sian co·or·di·nates *n.pl.* a system for locating a point by reference to its distance from two or three axes intersecting at right angles.

Car·thu·sian /kaarthóo<u>zh</u>ən/ *n.* & *adj.* ● *n.* a monk of a contemplative order founded by St. Bruno in 1084. ● *adj.* of or relating to this order.

car·ti·lage /kaártʼlij/ *n.* gristle; a firm flexible connective tissue forming the infant skeleton, which is mainly replaced by bone in adulthood. ▷ EAR. □□ **car·ti·lag·i·nous** /-lájinəs/ *adj.*

car·ti·la·gi·nous fish /kaártʼlájinəs/ *n.* ▼ a fish of the class Selachii, including sharks and rays, with a skeleton of cartilage. ▷ ELASMOBRANCH, FISH, SHARK

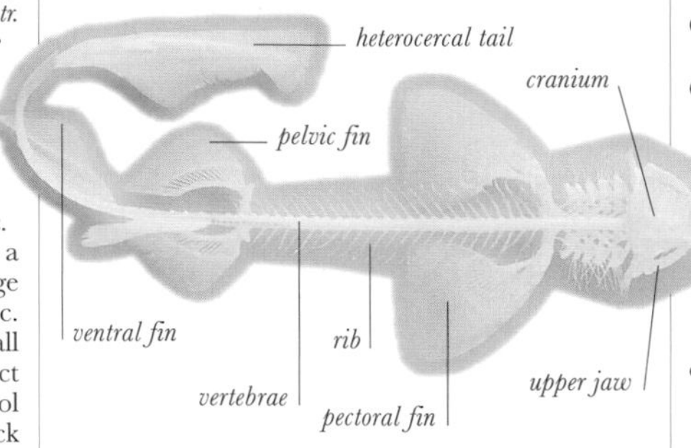
heterocercal tail
cranium
pelvic fin
ventral fin
rib
upper jaw
vertebrae
pectoral fin

CARTILAGINOUS FISH: DOGFISH SKELETON COMPOSED ENTIRELY OF CARTILAGE

cart·load /kaártlōd/ *n.* **1** an amount filling a cart. **2** esp. *Brit.* a large quantity of anything.

car·tog·ra·phy /kaartógrəfee/ *n.* the science or practice of map drawing. □□ **car·tog·ra·pher** *n.* **car·to·graph·ic** /-təgráfik/ *adj.* **car·to·graph·i·cal** *adj.*

car·ton /kaártʼn/ *n.* a light box or container, esp. one made of cardboard.

car·toon /kaartóon/ *n.* & *v.* ● *n.* **1** a humorous drawing in a newspaper, magazine, etc., esp. as a topical comment. **2** a sequence of drawings, often with speech indicated, telling a story; comic strip. **3** a filmed sequence of drawings using the technique of animation. **4** a full-size drawing as an artist's preliminary design for a painting, tapestry, mosaic, etc. ● *v.* **1** *tr.* draw a cartoon of. **2** *intr.* draw cartoons. □□ **car·toon·ist** *n.*

car·touche /kaartóosh/ *n.* **1** *Archit.* a scroll-like ornament. **2** *Archaeol.* an oval ring enclosing Egyptian hieroglyphs, usu. representing the name and title of a king.

car·tridge /kaártrij/ *n.* **1** a case containing a charge of propelling explosive for firearms or blasting, with a bullet or shot if for small arms. ▷ SHOTGUN. **2** a spool of film, magnetic tape, etc., in a sealed container ready for insertion. **3** a component carrying the stylus on the pickup head of a record player. **4** an ink container for insertion in a pen.

cart·wheel /kaárt-hweel, -weel/ *n.* **1** the (usu. spoked) wheel of a cart. **2** a circular sideways handspring with the arms and legs extended.

carve /kaarv/ *v.* **1** *tr.* produce or shape (a statue, representation in relief, etc.) by cutting into a hard material (*carved a figure out of rock*; *carved it in wood*). **2** *tr.* **a** cut patterns, designs, letters, etc., in (hard material). **b** (foll. by *into*) form a pattern, design, etc., from (*carved it into a bust*). **c** (foll. by *with*) cover or decorate (material) with figures or designs cut in it. **3** *tr.* (*absol.*) cut (meat, etc.) into slices for eating. □ **carve out 1** take from a larger whole. **2** establish (a career, etc.) purposefully (*carved out a name for themselves*). **carve up** divide into several pieces; subdivide (territory, etc.).

car·vel-built /kaárvəl-/ *adj.* (of a boat) made with planks flush, not overlapping (cf. CLINKER-BUILT).

Car·ver /kaárvər/ *n.* (in full **Carver chair**) a chair with arms, a rush seat, and a back having horizontal and vertical spindles.

car·ver /kaárvər/ *n.* **1** a person who carves. **2 a** a carving knife. **b** (in *pl.*) a knife and fork for carving. **3** *Brit.* the principal chair, with arms, in a set of dining chairs, intended for the person who carves. ¶ To be distinguished (in sense 3) from *Carver*.

carv·er·y /kaárvəree/ *n.* (*pl.* **-ies**) esp. *Brit.* a buffet or restaurant with cuts of meat displayed, and carved as required, in front of customers.

carv·ing /kaárving/ *n.* a carved object, esp. as a work of art.

car·y·at·id /káreeátid/ *n.* (*pl.* **caryatids** or **caryatides** /-deez/) *Archit.* a pillar in the form of a draped female figure, supporting an entablature.

car·y·op·sis /káreeópsis/ *n.* (*pl.* **caryopses** /-seez/) *Bot.* a dry, one-seeded indehiscent fruit, as in wheat and corn.

Cas·a·no·va /kásənóvə/ *n.* a man notorious for seducing women.

Cas·bah /kázbaa, kaáz-/ *n.* (also **Kasbah**) **1** the citadel of a N. African city. **2** an Arab quarter near this.

cas·cade /kaskáyd/ *n.* & *v.* ● *n.* **1** a small waterfall, esp. forming one in a series or part of a large broken waterfall. **2** a succession of electrical devices or stages in a process. **3** a quantity of material, etc., draped in descending folds. ● *v.intr.* fall in or like a cascade.

case[1] /kays/ *n.* **1** an instance of something occurring. **2** a state of affairs, hypothetical or actual. **3 a** an instance of a person receiving professional guidance, e.g., from a doctor or social worker. **b** this person or the circumstances involved. **4** a matter under official investigation, esp. by the police. **5** *Law* a cause or suit for trial. **6 a** the sum of the arguments on one side, esp. in a lawsuit (*that is our case*). **b** a set of arguments, esp. in relation to persuasiveness (*have a good case*). **c** a valid set of arguments (*have no case*). **7** *Gram.* **a** the relation of a word to other words in a sentence. **b** a form of a noun, adjective, or pronoun expressing this. **8** the position or circumstances in which one is. □ **as the case may be** according to the situation. **in any case** whatever the truth is; whatever may happen. **in case 1** in the event that; if. **2** lest; in provision against a stated or implied possibility (*take an umbrella in case it rains*; *took it in case*). **in case of** in the event of. **in the case of** as regards. **in no case** under no circumstances. **in that case** if that is true; should that happen. **is** (or **is not**) **the case** is (or is not) so.

case[2] /kays/ *n.* & *v.* ● *n.* **1** a container or covering serving to enclose or contain. **2** a container with its contents. **3** the outer protective covering of a watch, book, seed vessel, sausage, etc. **4** *Brit.* an item of luggage, esp. a suitcase. **5** *Printing* a partitioned receptacle for type. **6** a glass box for showing specimens, curiosities, etc. ● *v.tr.* **1** enclose in a case. **2** (foll. by *with*) surround. **3** *sl.* reconnoiter (a house, etc.), esp. with a view to robbery.

case·book /káysbook/ *n.* a book containing a record of legal or medical cases.

case·bound /káysbownd/ *adj.* (of a book) in a hard cover.

case-hard·en *v.tr.* **1** harden the surface of, esp. give a steel surface to (iron) by carbonizing. **2** make callous.

case his·to·ry *n.* information about a person for use in professional treatment, e.g., by a doctor.

ca·sein /káyseen, káyseein/ *n.* the main protein in milk, esp. in coagulated form as in cheese.

case law *n.* the law as established by the outcome of former cases.

case·load /káyslōd/ *n.* the cases with which a lawyer, doctor, etc., is concerned at one time.

case·ment /káysmənt/ *n.* **1** ► a window or part of a window hinged vertically to open like a door. ▷ WINDOW. **2** *poet.* a window.

case-sen·si·tive *adj. Computing* distinguishing upper- and lower-case letters.

case stud·y 1 an attempt to understand a person, institution, etc., from collected information. **2** a record of such an attempt. **3** the use of a particular instance as an examplar of principles.

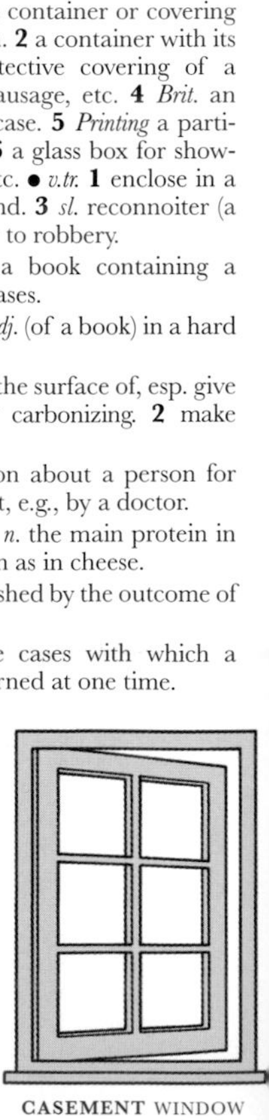

CASEMENT WINDOW

case·work /káyswərk/ *n.* social work concerned with individuals, esp. involving understanding of the client's family and background. □□ **case·work·er** *n.*

cash /kash/ *n. & v.* ● *n.* **1** money in coins or bills, as distinct from checks or orders. **2** (also **cash down**) money paid as full payment at the time of purchase, as distinct from credit. **3** *colloq.* wealth. ● *v.tr.* give or obtain cash for (a note, check, etc.). □ **cash in 1** obtain cash for. **2** *colloq.* (usu. foll. by *on*) profit (from); take advantage (of). **3** (in full **cash in one's chips**) *colloq.* die. **cash up** *Brit.* count and check cash takings at the end of a day's trading. □□ **cash·a·ble** *adj.* **cash·less** *adj.*

cash and car·ry *n.* **1** a system in which goods are paid for in cash and taken away by the purchaser. **2** a store where this system operates.

cash·book /kashbŏŏk/ *n.* a book in which receipts and payments of cash are recorded.

cash cow *n.* a business, product, etc., generating steady profits usu. used to fund other enterprises.

cash crop *n.* a crop produced for sale, not for use as food, etc.

cash·ew /káshŏŏ, kashŏŏ/ *n.* **1** a bushy evergreen tree, *Anacardium occidentale*, native to Central and S. America, bearing kidney-shaped nuts attached to fleshy fruits. **2** (in full **cashew nut**) the edible nut of this tree.

cash flow *n.* the movement of money into and out of a business, as a measure of profitability, or as affecting liquidity.

cash·ier[1] /kasheér/ *n.* a person dealing with cash transactions in a store, bank, etc.

cash·ier[2] /kasheér/ *v.tr.* dismiss from service, esp. from the armed forces with disgrace.

cash·mere /kázhmeer, kásh-/ *n.* **1** a fine soft wool, esp. that of a Kashmir goat. **2** a material made from this.

cash reg·is·ter *n.* a machine in a store, etc., with a drawer for money, recording the amount of each sale, totaling receipts, etc.

cas·ing /káysing/ *n.* **1** a protective or enclosing cover or shell. **2** the material for this.

ca·si·no /kəseénō/ *n.* (*pl.* **-os**) a public room or building for gambling.

ca·si·ta /kəseétə/ *n.* *N. Amer.* a small house or wooden cabin.

cask /kask/ *n.* **1** a large barrellike container made of wood, metal, or plastic, esp. one for alcoholic liquor. **2** its contents. **3** its capacity.

cas·ket /káskit/ *n.* **1 a** a coffin, esp. a rectangular one. **b** a small wooden box for cremated ashes. **2** a small, often ornamental box or chest for jewels, letters, etc.

Cas·san·dra /kəsándrə/ *n.* a prophet of disaster, esp. one who is disregarded.

cas·sa·va /kəsaávə/ *n.* **1 a** any plant of the genus *Manihot*, esp. the cultivated varieties *M. esculenta* (**bitter cassava**) and *M. dulcis* (**sweet cassava**), having starchy tuberous roots. **b** the roots themselves. **2** a starch or flour obtained from these roots. Also called **tapioca**, **manioc**.

cas·se·role /kásərōl/ *n. & v.* ● *n.* **1** a covered dish, usu. of earthenware or glass, in which food is cooked, esp. slowly in the oven. **2** food cooked in a casserole. ● *v.tr.* cook in a casserole.

cas·sette /kəsét, ka-/ *n.* a sealed case containing a length of tape, ribbon, etc., ready for insertion in a machine, esp.: **1** a length of magnetic tape wound on to spools, ready for insertion in a tape recorder. **2** a length of photographic film, ready for insertion in a camera.

cas·sia /káshə/ *n.* **1 ◄** any tree of the genus *Cassia*, bearing leaves from which senna is extracted. ▷ SENNA. **2** the cinnamonlike bark of this tree used as a spice.

cas·sis /kaseés/ *n.* a syrupy usu. alcoholic blackcurrant flavoring for drinks, etc.

cas·sock /kásək/ *n.* a long, close-fitting, usu. black or red garment worn by clergy, members of choirs, etc. □□ **cas·socked** *adj.*

cas·sou·let /kasŏŏláy/ *n.* a stew of meat and beans.

cas·so·war·y /kásəwairee/ *n.* (*pl.* **-ies**) any large flightless Australasian bird of the genus *Casuarius*, with a heavy body and a bony crest on its forehead.

stalk

leaflet

stipule

CASSIA LEAF
(*Cassia senna*)

cast /kast/ *v. & n.* ● *v.* (*past* and *past part.* **cast**) **1** *tr.* throw, esp. deliberately or forcefully. **2** *tr.* **a** direct or cause to fall (one's eyes, a glance, light, a shadow, a spell, etc.). **b** express (doubts, aspersions, etc.). **3** *tr.* throw out (a fishing line) into the water. **4** *tr.* let down (an anchor, etc.). **5** *tr.* **a** throw off; get rid of. **b** shed (skin, etc.), esp. in the process of growth. **c** (of a horse) lose (a shoe). **6** *tr.* record, register, or give (a vote). **7** *tr.* **a** shape (molten metal or plastic material) in a mold. **b** make (a product) in this way. **8** *tr. Printing* make (type). **9** *tr.* (usu. foll. by *as*) assign (an actor) to play a particular character. **b** allocate roles in (a play, motion picture, etc.). **10** *tr.* (foll. by *in*, *into*) arrange or formulate (facts, etc.) in a specified form. **11** *tr. & intr.* reckon; add up; calculate (accounts or figures). **12** *tr.* calculate and record details of (a horoscope). ● *n.* **1 a** the throwing of a missile, etc. **b** the distance reached by this. **2 a** a throw or a number thrown at dice. **3** a throw of a net, fishing line, etc. **4** *Fishing* **a** that which is cast, esp. the line with hook and fly. **b** a place for casting

(*a good cast*). **5 a** an object of metal, clay, etc., made in a mold. **b** a molded mass of solidified material, esp. plaster protecting a broken limb. **6** the actors taking part in a play, motion picture, etc. **7** form, type, or quality (*cast of features*; *cast of mind*). **8** a tinge or shade of color. **9 a** (in full **cast in the eye**) a slight squint. **b** a twist or inclination. **10 a** a mass of earth excreted by a worm. **b** a mass of indigestible food thrown up by a hawk, owl, etc. **11** the form into which any work is thrown or arranged. □ **cast about** (or **around**) make an extensive search (actually or mentally) (*cast about for a solution*). **cast adrift** leave to drift. **cast aside** give up using; abandon. **cast away 1** reject. **2** (in *passive*) be shipwrecked (cf. CASTAWAY). **cast down** depress; deject (cf. DOWNCAST). **cast loose** detach; detach oneself. **cast lots** see LOT. **cast off 1** abandon. **2** *Knitting* ▼ take the stitches off the needle by looping each over the next to finish the edge. **3** *Naut.* **a** set a ship free from a mooring, etc. **b** loosen and throw off (rope, etc.). **4** *Printing* estimate the space that will be taken in print by manuscript copy. **cast on** *Knitting* make the first row of loops on the needle. **cast out** expel. **cast up 1** (of the sea) deposit on the shore. **2** add up (figures, etc.).

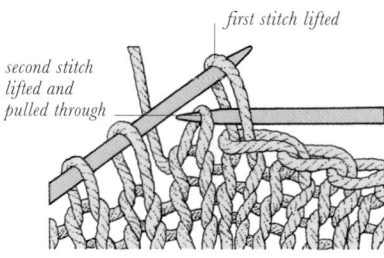

first stitch lifted

second stitch lifted and pulled through

CAST OFF

cas·ta·net /kástənét/ *n.* (usu. in *pl.*) ▼ a small concave piece of hardwood, ivory, etc., in pairs held in the hands and clicked together by the fingers as a rhythmic accompaniment, esp. by Spanish dancers. ▷ ORCHESTRA, PERCUSSION

cast·a·way /kástəway/ *n. & adj.* ● *n.* a shipwrecked person. ● *adj.* **1** shipwrecked. **2** cast aside; rejected.

caste /kast/ *n.* **1** any of the Hindu hereditary classes, distinguished by relative degrees of purity or pollution, whose members are socially equal with one another and often follow the same occupations. **2** a more or less exclusive social class. **3** a system of such classes. **4** the position it confers. **5** *Zool.* a form of social insect having a particular function. □ **lose caste** descend in the social order.

CASTANETS

cas·tel·lan /kástələn/ *n. hist.* the governor of a castle.

cas·tel·lat·ed /kástəlaytid/ *adj.* **1** having battlements. **2** castlelike. □□ **cas·tel·la·tion** /-láyshən/ *n.*

cast·er /kástər/ *n.* **1** (also *Brit.* **castor**) **a** small swiveled wheel (often one of a set) fixed to a leg (or the underside) of a piece of furniture. **2** a small container with holes in the top for sprinkling the contents. **3** a person who casts. **4** a machine for casting type.

cas·ti·gate /kástigayt/ *v.tr.* rebuke or punish severely. □□ **cas·ti·ga·tion** /-gáyshən/ *n.* **cas·ti·ga·tor** *n.* **cas·ti·ga·to·ry** /-gətáwree/ *adj.*

Cas·til·ian /kəstílyən/ *n. & adj.* ● *n.* **1** a native of Castile in Spain. **2** the language of Castile, standard spoken and literary Spanish. ● *adj.* of or relating to Castile.

cast·ing /kásting/ *n.* an object made by casting, esp. of molten metal.

cast i·ron *n.* a hard alloy of iron, carbon, and silicon cast in a mold. □□ **cast-i·ron** *adj.* **1** made of cast iron. **2** hard; unchallengeable; unchangeable.

cas·tle /kásəl/ *n. & v.* ● *n.* **1 a ◄** a large fortified building or group of buildings; a stronghold. ▷ KEEP.

CASTLE

The first castles appeared in Europe in the 9th century and were little more than earth and timber strongholds. They evolved with no standard shape or structure, except for tall walls and keeps, often constructed on a natural high point. Castles lost their military importance at the end of the 15th century as societies became more stable.

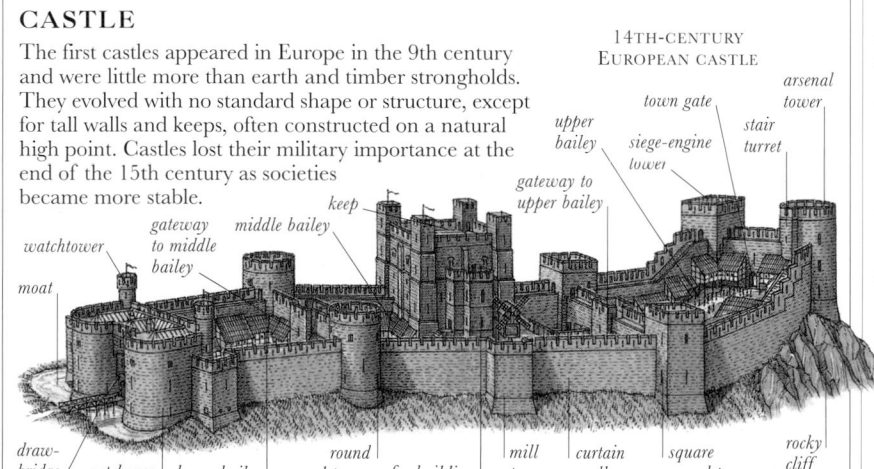

14TH-CENTURY
EUROPEAN CASTLE

arsenal tower

town gate

upper bailey

stair turret

siege-engine tower

gateway to upper bailey

keep

gateway to middle bailey

middle bailey

watchtower

moat

draw-bridge

gatehouse

lower bailey

round mural tower

forebuilding

mill tower

curtain wall

square mural tower

rocky cliff

C

CAT

Cats were domesticated by the ancient Egyptians more than 8,000 years ago, yet it was only in the late 19th century that the first pedigree breeds were developed. Now at least 300 breeds and varieties are recognized, although they vary relatively little in appearance. Differing head shapes are one of the main distinguishing characteristics, as is length of hair. The coat-length feature is, perhaps, the most straightforward method of categorizing pedigree and nonpedigree cats. Shorthair breeds outnumber longhair ones.

C

pupil

whiskers

nose leather

chest

ribcage

front paw

body

hips

thigh

tail

heel

hind foot

rear paw

EXTERNAL FEATURES OF A CHOCOLATE TORTOISESHELL BURMESE SHORTHAIR

EXAMPLES OF CAT BREEDS

PEDIGREE LONGHAIR CATS

CHOCOLATE POINT LONGHAIR

RED PERSIAN LONGHAIR

BROWN CLASSIC TABBY

LILAC ANGORA

PEDIGREE SHORTHAIR CATS

BLUE EXOTIC

FOREIGN LILAC ORIENTAL SHORTHAIR

CREAM POINT COLOR POINTED BRITISH SHORTHAIR

USUAL ABYSSINIAN

CINNAMON SILVER CORNISH REX

NONPEDIGREE CATS

TORTOISESHELL AND WHITE SHORTHAIR

BLUE LONGHAIR

RED CLASSIC TABBY MANX

RED AND WHITE JAPANESE BOBTAIL

BROWN AND WHITE SPHYNX

SEAL POINT SIAMESE

BROWN SPOTTED SHORTHAIR

BLUE-CREAM SHORTHAIR

b a formerly fortified mansion. **2** *Chess* = ROOK². ● *v. Chess* **1** *intr.* make a special move (once only in a game on each side) in which the king is moved two squares along the back rank and the nearer rook is moved to the square passed over by the king. **2** *tr.* move (the king) by castling. □ **castles in the air** (or **in Spain**) a visionary unattainable scheme; a daydream. □□ **cas·tled** *adj.*

cast·off /kástawf/ *n.* a cast-off thing, esp. a garment.

cast-off /kástawf/ *adj.* abandoned; discarded.

cas·tor¹ *Brit.* var. of CASTER 1 & 2.

cas·tor² /kástər/ *n.* **1** an oily substance secreted by beavers, used in medicine and perfumes. **2** a beaver.

cas·tor oil /kástər/ *n.* **1** an oil from the seeds of a plant, *Ricinus communis*, used as a purgative and lubricant. **2** (in full **castor-oil plant**) this plant.

cas·trate /kástrayt/ *v.tr.* **1** remove the testicles of; geld. **2** deprive of vigor. □□ **cas·tra·tion** /-tráyshən/ *n.* **cas·tra·tor** *n.*

cas·tra·to /kastráátō/ *n.* (*pl.* **castrati** /-tee/) *hist.* a male singer castrated in boyhood so as to retain a soprano or alto voice.

cas·u·al /kázhōōəl/ *adj. & n.* ● *adj.* **1** accidental; due to chance. **2** not regular nor permanent; temporary; occasional (*casual work; a casual affair*). **3 a** unconcerned; uninterested (*was very casual about it*). **b** made or done without great care or thought (*a casual remark*). **c** acting carelessly or unmethodically. **4** (of clothes) informal. ● *n.* **1** a casual worker. **2** (usu. in *pl.*) casual clothes or shoes. □□ **cas·u·al·ly** *adv.* **cas·u·al·ness** *n.*

cas·u·al·ty /kázhōōəltee/ *n.* (*pl.* **-ies**) **1** a person killed or injured in a war or accident. **2** a thing lost or destroyed. **3** (in full **casualty department**) *Brit.* a hospital emergency room.

ca·su·a·ri·na /kázhōōərēnə/ *n.* any tree of the genus *Casuarina*, native to Australia and SE Asia, resembling gigantic horsetails.

cas·u·ist /kázhōōist/ *n.* **1** a person, esp. a theologian, who resolves problems of conscience, duty, etc., often with clever but false reasoning. **2** a sophist or quibbler. □□ **cas·u·is·tic** *adj.* **cas·u·is·ti·cal** *adj.* **cas·u·is·ti·cal·ly** *adv.* **cas·u·ist·ry** /kázhōōəstree/ *n.*

CAT /kat/ *abbr.* **1** *Med.* computerized axial tomography. **2** clear-air turbulence.

cat /kat/ *n. & v.* **1** ◄ a small, soft-furred, four-legged domesticated animal, *Felis catus* or *F. domestica*. **2** any wild animal of the genus *Felis*, e.g., a lion, tiger, or leopard. **3** a catlike animal of any other species (*civet cat*). **4** *colloq.* a malicious or spiteful woman. **5** *sl.* a jazz enthusiast. **6** *Naut.* = CATHEAD. **7** = CAT-O'-NINE-TAILS. ● *v.tr.* (also *absol.*) (**catted**, **catting**) *Naut.* raise (an anchor) from the surface of the water to the cathead. □ **let the cat out of the bag** reveal a secret, esp. involuntarily. **rain cats and dogs** *colloq.* rain very hard.

cata- /kátə/ *prefix* (usu. **cat-** before a vowel or *h*) **1** down; downward (*catadromous*). **2** wrongly; badly (*catachresis*).

ca·tab·o·lism /kətábəlizəm/ *n. Biochem.* the breakdown of complex molecules in living organisms to form simpler ones with the release of energy; destructive metabolism (opp. ANABOLISM). □□ **cat·a·bol·ic** /kátəbólik/ *adj.*

cat·a·chre·sis /kátəkréesis/ *n.* (*pl.* **catachreses** /-seez/) an incorrect use of words. □□ **cat·a·chres·tic** /-kréstik/ *adj.*

cat·a·cla·sis /kátəkláysis/ *n.* (*pl.* **cataclases** /-seez/) *Geol.* the natural process of fracture, shearing, or breaking up of rocks. □□ **cat·a·clas·tic** /-klástik/ *adj.*

cat·a·clysm /kátəklizəm/ *n.* **1 a** a violent, esp. social or political, upheaval or disaster. **b** a great change. **2** a great flood or deluge. □□ **cat·a·clys·mal** /-klízməl/ *adj.* **cat·a·clys·mic** *adj.* **cat·a·clys·mi·cal·ly** *adv.*

cat·a·comb /kátəkōm/ *n.* (often in *pl.*) **1** an underground cemetery, esp. a Roman subterranean gallery with recesses for tombs. **2** a similar underground construction; a cellar.

ca·tad·ro·mous /kətádrəməs/ *adj.* (of a fish, e.g., the eel) that swims down rivers to the sea to spawn.

cat·a·falque /kátəfawk, -fawlk/ *n.* a decorated wooden framework for supporting the coffin of a distinguished person during a funeral or while lying in state.

Cat·a·lan /kát'lan/ *n. & adj.* ● *n.* **1** a native of Catalonia in Spain. **2** the language of Catalonia. ● *adj.* of or relating to Catalonia or its people or language.

cat·a·lase /kát'lays, -layz/ *n. Biochem.* an enzyme that catalyzes the reduction of hydrogen peroxide.

cat·a·lep·sy /kát'lepsee/ *n.* a state of trance or seizure with loss of sensation and consciousness accompanied by rigidity of the body. □□ **cat·a·lep·tic** /-léptik/ *adj. & n.*

cat·a·log /kát'lawg, -log/ *n. & v.* (also **cat·a·logue**) ● *n.* **1** a list of items (e.g., articles for sale, books held by a library), usu. in alphabetical or other systematic order and often with a description of each. **2** an extensive list (*a catalog of crimes*). **3** a listing of a university's courses, etc. ● *v.tr.* (**catalogs, cataloged, cataloging**; **catalogues, catalogued, cataloguing**) **1** make a catalog of. **2** enter in a catalog. □□ **cat·a·log·er** *n.* (also **cat·a·logu·er**).

cat·al·pa /kətálpə/ *n.* any tree of the genus *Catalpa*, with heart-shaped leaves, trumpet-shaped flowers, and long pods.

cat·a·lyse *Brit.* var. of CATALYZE.

cat·al·y·sis /kətálisis/ *n.* (*pl.* **catalyses** /-seez/) *Chem. & Biochem.* the acceleration of a chemical or biochemical reaction by a catalyst.

cat·a·lyst /kát'list/ *n.* **1** *Chem.* a substance that, without itself undergoing any permanent chemical change, increases the rate of a reaction. **2** a person or thing that precipitates a change.

cat·a·lyt·ic /kát'litik/ *adj. Chem.* relating to or involving catalysis.

cat·a·lyt·ic con·vert·er *n.* ▼ a device incorporated in the exhaust system of a motor vehicle, with a catalyst for converting pollutant gases into harmless products. ▷ CAR

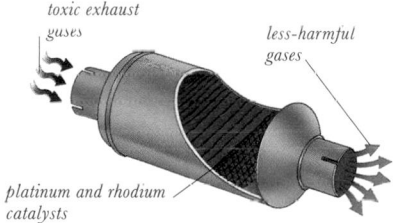

toxic exhaust gases

less-harmful gases

platinum and rhodium catalysts

CATALYTIC CONVERTER: CUTAWAY VIEW

cat·a·lyze /kát'līz/ *v.tr.* (*Brit.* **catalyse**) *Chem.* produce (a reaction) by catalysis.

cat·a·ma·ran /kát'mərán/ *n.* **1** a boat with twin hulls in parallel. ▷ POWERBOAT. **2** a raft of yoked logs or boats.

cat·a·mite /kát'mīt/ *n.* the passive partner in sodomy.

cat·a·moun·tain /kát'mowntin/ *n.* (also **cat-a-moun·tain, cat·a·mount**) **1** a lynx, leopard, puma, or other wild cat. **2** *Brit.* a wild quarrelsome person.

cat·a·nan·che /kát'nángkee/ *n.* any composite plant of the genus *Catanache*, with blue or yellow flowers.

cat-and-mouse *adj.* of or similar to behavior like that of a cat toying with a mouse, in which the prey is uncertain of when the predator will strike.

cat·a·plex·y /kát'plekseee/ *n.* sudden temporary paralysis due to fright, etc. □□ **cat·a·plec·tic** /-pléktik/ *adj.*

cat·a·pult /kát'pult, -pŏōlt/ *n. & v.* ● *n.* **1** a mechanical device for launching a glider, an aircraft from the deck of a ship, etc. **2** *hist.* ► a military machine worked by a lever and ropes for hurling large stones, etc. **3** *Brit.* = SLINGSHOT. ● *v.* **1** *tr.* **a** hurl from or launch with a catapult. **b** fling forcibly. **2** *intr.* leap or be hurled forcibly.

cat·a·ract /kátərakt/ *n.* **1 a** a large waterfall or cascade. **b** a downpour; a rush of water. **2** *Med.* a condition in which the lens of the eye becomes progressively opaque resulting in blurred vision.

ca·tarrh /kətáar/ *n.* **1** inflammation of the mucous membrane of the nose, air passages, etc. **2** a watery discharge in the nose or throat due to this. □□ **ca·tarrh·al** *adj.*

ca·tas·tro·phe /kətástrəfee/ *n.* **1** a great and usu. sudden disaster. **2** a disastrous end; ruin. **3** an event producing a subversion of the order of things. □□ **cat·a·stroph·ic** /kátəstrófik/ *adj.* **cat·a·stroph·i·cal·ly** /kátəstrófikəlee/ *adv.*

ca·tas·tro·phism /kətástrəfizəm/ *n. Geol.* the theory that changes in the Earth's crust have occurred in sudden violent and unusual events. □□ **ca·tas·tro·phist** *n.*

cat·a·to·ni·a /kátətōneeə/ *n.* **1** schizophrenia with intervals of catalepsy and sometimes violence. **2** catalepsy. □□ **cat·a·ton·ic** /-tónik/ *adj. & n.*

Ca·taw·ba /kətáwbə/ *n.* **1** a variety of grape. **2** a white wine made from it.

cat·boat /kátbōt/ *n.* a sailboat with a single mast placed well forward and carrying only one sail.

cat bur·glar *n.* a burglar who enters by climbing to an upper story.

cat·call /kátkawl/ *n. & v.* ● *n.* a shrill whistle of disapproval made at sporting events, stage performances, meetings, etc. ● *v.* **1** *intr.* make a catcall. **2** *tr.* make a catcall at.

catch /kach/ *v. & n.* ● *v.* (*past* and *past part.* **caught** /kawt/) **1** *tr.* **a** lay hold of so as to restrain or prevent from escaping; capture in a trap, in one's hands, etc. **b** (also **catch hold of**) get into one's hands so as to retain, operate, etc. (*caught hold of the handle*). **2** *tr.* detect or surprise (a person, esp. in a wrongful or embarrassing act) (*caught me in the act; caught him smoking*). **3** *tr.* intercept and hold (a moving thing) in the hands, etc. (*catch the ball; a bowl to catch the drips*). **4** *tr.* **a** contract (a disease) by infection or contagion. **b** acquire (a quality or feeling) from another's example (*caught her enthusiasm*). **5** *tr.* **a** reach in time and board (a train, bus, etc.). **b** be in time to see, etc. (a person or thing about to leave or finish) (*if you hurry you'll catch them; caught the end of the performance*). **6** *tr.* **a** apprehend with the senses or the mind (esp. a thing occurring quickly or briefly) (*didn't catch what he said*). **b** (of an artist, etc.) reproduce faithfully. **7 a** *intr.* become fixed or entangled; be checked (*the bolt began to catch*). **b** *tr.* cause to do this (*caught her sleeve on a nail*). **c** (often foll. by *on*) hit; deal a blow to (*caught him on the nose; caught his elbow on the table*). **8** *tr.* draw the attention of; captivate (*caught his eye*). **9** *intr.* begin to burn. **10** *tr.* (often foll. by *up*) reach or overtake (a person, etc., ahead). **11** *tr.* check suddenly (*caught his breath*). **12** *tr.* (foll. by *at*) grasp or try to grasp. ● *n.* **1 a** an act of catching. **b** *Baseball* a chance or act of catching the ball. **2 a** an amount of a thing caught, esp. of fish. **b** a thing or person caught or worth catching, esp. in marriage. **3 a** a question, trick, etc., intended to deceive, incriminate, etc. **b** an

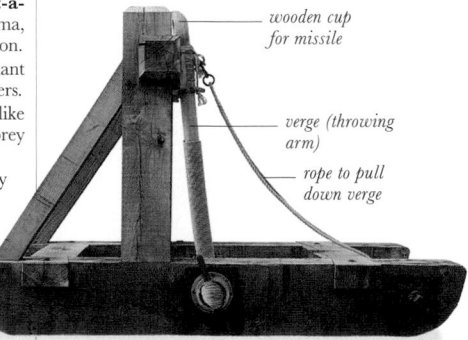

wooden cup for missile

verge (throwing arm)

rope to pull down verge

CATAPULT: REPLICA OF A 15TH-CENTURY MILITARY CATAPULT

C

C

unexpected or hidden difficulty or disadvantage. **4** a device for fastening a door or window, etc. **5** *Mus.* a round, esp. with words arranged to produce a humorous effect. □ **catch one's death** see DEATH. **catch fire** see FIRE. **catch it** *sl.* be punished or in trouble. **catch on** *colloq.* **1** (of a practice, fashion, etc.) become popular. **2** (of a person) understand what is meant. **catch out** *Brit.* **1** detect in a mistake, etc. **2** take unawares; cause to be bewildered or confused. **catch the sun 1** be in a sunny position. **2** *Brit.* become sunburned. **catch up 1 a** (often foll. by *with*) reach a person, etc., ahead (*he caught up with us*). **b** (often foll. by *with, on*) make up arrears (of work, etc.) (*must catch up with my correspondence*). **2** snatch or pick up hurriedly. **3** (often in *passive*) **a** involve; entangle (*caught up in suspicious dealings*). **b** fasten up (*hair caught up in a ribbon*). □□ **catch·a·ble** *adj.*

catch·all /káchawl/ *n.* (often *attrib.*) **1** something designed to be all-inclusive. **2** a container for odds and ends.

catch-as-catch-can *n.* **1** a style of wrestling with few holds barred. **2** using any method available.

catch·er /káchər/ *n.* **1** a person or thing that catches. **2** *Baseball* a fielder positioned behind home plate. ▷ HOME PLATE

catch·fly /káchflī/ *n.* (*pl.* **-ies**) any plant of the genus *Silene* or *Lychnis* with a sticky stem.

catch·ing /káching/ *adj.* **1 a** (of a disease) infectious. **b** (of a practice, habit, etc.) likely to be imitated. **2** attractive; captivating.

catch·line /káchlīn/ *n. Printing* a short line of type, esp. at the head of copy or as a running headline.

catch·ment /káchmənt/ *n.* **1** the collection of rainfall. **2** an opening or basin for storm water, etc.

catch·ment ar·e·a *n.* **1** the area from which rainfall flows into a river, etc. **2** the area served by a school, hospital, etc.

catch·pen·ny /káchpenee/ *adj.* intended merely to sell quickly; superficially attractive.

catch·phrase /káchfrayz/ *n.* a phrase in frequent use.

catch-22 /káchtwenteetóō/ *n.* (often *attrib.*) *colloq.* a

circumstance that presents a dilemma because of mutually conflicting or dependent conditions.

catch·up var. of KETCHUP.

catch·weight /káchwayt/ *adj. & n.* ● *adj.* unrestricted as regards weight. ● *n.* unrestricted weight, as a weight category in sports.

catch·word /káchwərd/ *n.* **1** a word or phrase in common (often temporary) use; a topical slogan. **2** a word so placed as to draw attention.

catch·y /káchee/ *adj.* (**catchier, catchiest**) (of a tune) easy to remember; attractive. □□ **catch·i·ly** *adv.* **catch·i·ness** *n.*

cat·e·chism /kátikizəm/ *n.* **1 a** a summary of the principles of a religion in the form of questions and answers. **b** a book containing this. **2** a series of questions put to anyone. □□ **cat·e·chis·mal** /-kízməl/ *adj.*

cat·e·chist /kátikist/ *n.* a religious teacher, esp. one using a catechism.

cat·e·chize /kátikīz/ *v.tr.* **1** instruct by means of question and answer, esp. from a catechism. **2** put questions to; examine. □□ **cat·e·chiz·er** *n.*

cat·e·chu /kátichōō/ *n.* (also **ca·chou** /káshōō/) gambier or similar vegetable extract, containing tannin.

cat·e·chu·men /kátikyōōmən/ *n.* a Christian convert under instruction before baptism.

cat·e·gor·i·cal /kátigáwrikəl, -gór-/ *adj.* (also **cat·e·gor·ic**) unconditional; absolute; explicit; direct (*a categorical refusal*). □□ **cat·e·gor·i·cal·ly** *adv.*

cat·e·go·rize /kátigərīz/ *v.tr.* place in a category or categories. □□ **cat·e·go·ri·za·tion** *n.*

cat·e·go·ry /kátigawree, -goree/ *n.* (*pl.* **-ies**) a class or division. □□ **cat·e·go·ri·al** /-gáwreeəl/ *adj.*

cat·e·nar·y /kát'neree, kətéenaree/ *n. & adj.* ● *n.* (*pl.* **-ies**) a curve formed by a uniform chain hanging freely from two points not in the same vertical line. ● *adj.* of or resembling such a curve.

cat·e·nate /kát'nayt/ *v.tr.* connect like links of a chain. □□ **cat·e·na·tion** /-náyshən/ *n.*

ca·ter /káytər/ *v.* **1 a** *intr.* (often foll. by *for*) provide food. **b** *tr.* provide food and service (*cater a party*). **2** *intr.* (foll. by *for, to*) provide what is desired

or needed by. **3** *intr.* (foll. by *to*) pander to (esp. low tastes).

cat·er·cor·nered /kátərkáwrnərd/ *adj. & adv.* (also **cat·er·cor·ner, cat·ty·cor·nered** /kátee-/, **kitty-corner** /kítee-/) ● *adj.* placed or situated diagonally. ● *adv.* diagonally.

ca·ter·er /káytərər/ *n.* a person who supplies food for social events, esp. professionally.

ca·ter·ing /káytəring/ *n.* the profession or work of a caterer.

cat·er·pil·lar /kátərpilər/ *n.* **1 a** ◄ the larva of a butterfly or moth. **b** (in general use) any similar larva of various insects. ▷ METAMORPHOSIS. **2** (**Caterpillar**) **a** (in full **Caterpillar track** *or* **tread**) *Trademark* ▼ a continuous belt of linked pieces passing around the wheels of a tractor, etc., for travel on rough ground. ▷ SNOWMOBILE. **b** a vehicle equipped with these tracks, e.g., a tractor or a tank.

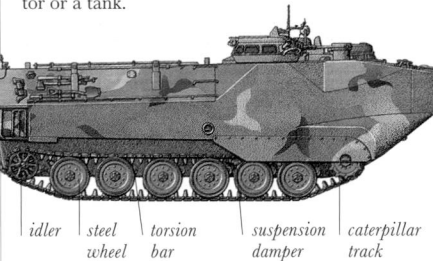

mouthpart

spiracle

segment

suckerlike proleg

exoskeleton

claspers

CATERPILLAR OF A CITRUS
SWALLOWTAIL BUTTERFLY
(*Papilio demodocus*)

idler | *steel wheel* | *torsion bar* | *suspension damper* | *caterpillar track*

CATERPILLAR TRACK ON AN
AMPHIBIOUS TRACTOR

CATHEDRAL

As Christianity began to spread some 1,000 years ago, larger churches were needed. New building techniques of the time allowed for the construction of the first cathedrals. These had thinner walls, with taller windows that led the eye heavenward and flooded the building with light. As Christian places of worship, many cathedrals, whatever their style, were built in the shape of a cross, with chapels in the arms (transepts), and the altar lying to the east to face the rising sun.

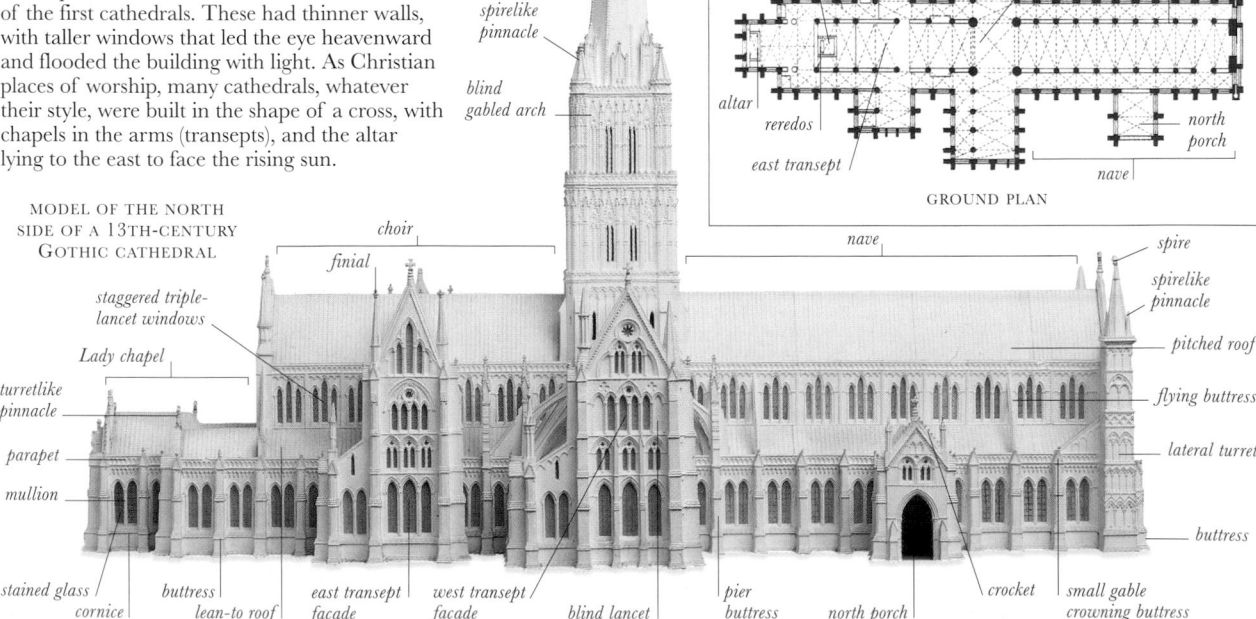

sacristy

high altar　　*west transept arcade*　　*west front*

altar

reredos

east transept

north porch

nave

GROUND PLAN

spire

spirelike pinnacle

blind gabled arch

MODEL OF THE NORTH
SIDE OF A 13TH-CENTURY
GOTHIC CATHEDRAL

choir

finial

nave

spire

spirelike pinnacle

staggered triple-lancet windows

Lady chapel

pitched roof

flying buttress

turretlike pinnacle

lateral turret

parapet

mullion

buttress

stained glass | *buttress* | *east transept façade* | *west transept façade* | *blind lancet* | *pier buttress* | *north porch* | *crocket* | *small gable crowning buttress*

cornice | *lean-to roof*

cat·er·waul /kátərwawl/ v. & n. ● v.intr. make the shrill howl of a cat. ● n. a caterwauling noise.

cat·fish /kátfish/ n. ▼ any of various esp. freshwater fish, usu. having whiskerlike barbels around the mouth.

CATFISH: BLUE CATFISH
(*Ictalurus furcatus*)   *barbel*

cat·gut /kátgut/ n. a material used for the strings of musical instruments and surgical sutures, made of the twisted intestines of the sheep, horse, or ass (but not the cat).

Cath. abbr. **1** cathedral. **2** Catholic.

ca·thar·sis /kətháarsis/ n. (pl. **catharses** /-seez/) **1** an emotional release in drama or art. **2** Psychol. the process of freeing repressed emotion by association with the cause, and elimination by abreaction. **3** Med. purgation.

ca·thar·tic /kətháartik/ adj. & n. ● adj. **1** effecting catharsis. **2** purgative. ● n. a cathartic drug. □□ **ca·thar·ti·cal·ly** adv.

Ca·thay /katháy/ n. archaic or poet. the country China.

cat·head /kát-hed/ n. Naut. a horizontal beam from each side of a ship's bow for raising and carrying the anchor.

ca·the·dral /kəthéedrəl/ n. ◄ the principal church of a diocese, containing the bishop's throne.

Cath·er·ine wheel /káthrin/ n. a firework in the form of a flat coil that spins when fixed and lit.

cath·e·ter /káthitər/ n. Med. a tube for insertion into a body cavity for introducing or removing fluid.

cath·e·ter·ize /káthitərīz/ v.tr. Med. insert a catheter into.

cath·e·tom·e·ter /káthitómitər/ n. a telescope mounted on a graduated scale along which it can slide, used for accurate measurement of small vertical distances.

cath·ode /káthōd/ n. Electr. **1** the negatively charged electrode by which electrons enter or leave a system. **2** the positively charged electrode of a device supplying current, e.g., a battery (opp. ANODE). □□ **cath·o·dal** adj. **cath·o·dic** /kəthódik/ adj.

cath·ode ray n. a beam of electrons emitted from the cathode of a high-vacuum tube.

cath·ode-ray tube n. a high-vacuum tube in which cathode rays produce a luminous image on a fluorescent screen. ▷ TELEVISION. ¶ Abbr.: **CRT**.

cath·o·lic /káthəlik, káthlik/ adj. & n. ● adj. **1** of interest or use to all; universal. **2** all-embracing; of wide sympathies or interests (has catholic tastes). **3** (**Catholic**) **a** of the Roman Catholic religion. **b** including all Christians. **c** including all of the Western Church. ● n. (**Catholic**) a Roman Catholic. □□ **ca·thol·i·cal·ly** /kəthóliklee/ adv. **Ca·thol·i·cism** /kəthólisizəm/ n. **cath·o·lic·i·ty** /káthəlísitee/ n. **ca·thol·ic·ly** adv.

ca·thol·i·cize /kəthólisīz/ v.tr. & intr. **1** make or become catholic. **2** (**Catholicize**) make or become a Roman Catholic.

cat·i·on /kátīən/ n. a positively charged ion; an ion that is attracted to the cathode in electrolysis (opp. ANION).

cat·i·on·ic /kátīónik/ adj. **1** of a cation or cations. **2** having an active cation.

cat·kin /kátkin/ n. a spike of usu. downy or silky male or female flowers hanging from a willow, hazel, etc.

cat·like /kátlīk/ adj. **1** like a cat. **2** stealthy.

cat·nap /kátnap/ n. & v. ● n. a short sleep. ● v.intr. (**-napped**, **-napping**) have a catnap.

cat·nip /kátnip/ n. a white-flowered plant, *Nepeta cataria*, having a pungent smell attractive to cats.

cat-o'-nine-tails n. hist. ► a rope whip with nine knotted lashes for flogging sailors, soldiers, or criminals.

CAT scan /kat/ n. an X-ray image made using computerized axial tomography. □□ **CAT scan·ner** n.

cat's cra·dle n. a child's game in which a loop of string is held between the fingers and patterns are formed.

cat's-eye n. a precious stone of Sri Lanka and Malabar.

cat's-paw n. **1** a person used as a tool by another. **2** a slight breeze rippling the surface of the water.

cat·sup /kátsəp, kéchəp, kách-/ var. of KETCHUP.

cat·tail /kát-tayl/ n. ► any tall, reedlike marsh plant of the genus *Typha*, esp. *T. latifola*, with long, flat leaves and brown, velvety flower spikes. (Also called **bulrush** and **reed mace**.)

cat·ter·y /kátəree/ n. (pl. **-ies**) a place where cats are boarded or bred.

cat·tish /kátish/ adj. = CATTY. □□ **cat·tish·ly** adv. **cat·tish·ness** n.

cat·tle /kát'l/ n.pl. **1** bison, buffalo, yaks, or domesticated bovine animals, esp. of the genus *Bos*. ▷ RUMINANT. **2** archaic livestock.

cat·tle·man /kát'lmən/ n. (pl. **-men**) a person who breeds or rears cattle.

cat·tley·a /kátleeə/ n. any epiphytic orchid of the genus *Cattleya*, with handsome violet, pink, or yellow flowers.

cat·ty /kátee/ adj. (**cattier**, **cattiest**) **1** sly; spiteful; deliberately hurtful in speech. **2** catlike. □□ **cat·ti·ly** adv. **cat·ti·ness** n.

cat·ty-cor·nered var. of CATERCORNERED.

CATV abbr. community antenna television.

cat·walk /kátwawk/ n. **1** a narrow footway along a bridge, above a theater stage, etc. **2** a narrow platform or gangway used in fashion shows, etc.

Cau·ca·sian /kawkáyzhən/ adj. & n. ● adj. **1** of or relating to the white or light-skinned division of mankind. **2** of or relating to the Caucasus. ● n. a Caucasian person.

Cau·ca·soid /káwkəsoyd/ adj. of or relating to the Caucasian division of mankind.

cau·cus /káwkəs/ n. **1 a** a meeting of the members of a political party, esp. in a legislature or convention, to decide policy. **b** a bloc of such members. **c** this system as a political force. **2** often derog. (esp. in the UK) **a** a usu. secret meeting of a group within a larger organization or party. **b** such a group.

cau·dal /káwd'l/ adj. **1** of or like a tail. ▷ FISH. **2** of the posterior part of the body. □□ **cau·dal·ly** adv.

cau·date /káwdayt/ adj. having a tail.

cau·dil·lo /kawdeélyō, -deéyō, kowtheélyō, -theéyō/ n. (pl. **-os**) (in Spanish-speaking countries) a military or political leader.

caught past and past part. of CATCH.

caul /kawl/ n. **1** the inner membrane enclosing a fetus. **2** part of this occasionally found on a child's head at birth, thought to bring good luck.

caul·dron /káwldrən/ n. (also **cal·dron**) a large, deep, bowl-shaped vessel for boiling over an open fire; an ornamental vessel resembling this.

cau·li·flow·er /káwliflowr, kól-/ n. **1** a variety of cabbage with a large immature flower head of small usu. creamy-white flower buds. **2** the flower head eaten as a vegetable. ▷ VEGETABLE

cau·li·flow·er ear n. an ear deformed by repeated blows, esp. in boxing.

caulk /kawk/ v.tr. (also **calk**) **1** stop up (the seams of a boat, etc.) with oakum, etc., and waterproofing material, or by driving plate junctions together. **2** make (esp. a boat) watertight by this method. □□ **caulk·er** n.

caus·al /káwzəl/ adj. **1** of, forming, or expressing a

cause or causes. **2** relating to, or of the nature of, cause and effect. □□ **caus·al·ly** adv.

cau·sal·i·ty /kawzálitee/ n. **1** the relation of cause and effect. **2** the principle that everything has a cause.

cau·sa·tion /kawzáyshən/ n. **1** the act of causing or producing an effect. **2** = CAUSALITY.

caus·a·tive /káwzətiv/ adj. **1** acting as cause. **2** (foll. by of) producing; having as effect. **3** Gram. expressing cause. □□ **caus·a·tive·ly** adv.

cause /kawz/ n. & v. ● n. **1 a** that which produces an effect, or gives rise to an action, phenomenon, or condition. **b** a person or thing that occasions something. **c** a reason or motive; a ground that may be held to justify something (no cause for complaint). **2** a reason adjudged adequate (show cause). **3** a principle, belief, or purpose that is advocated or supported (faithful to the cause). **4 a** a matter to be settled at law. **b** an individual's case offered at law (plead a cause). **5** the side taken by any party in a dispute. ● v.tr. **1** be the cause of; produce; make happen (caused a commotion). **2** (foll. by to + infin.) induce (caused me to smile; caused it to be done). □ **in the cause of** to maintain, defend, or support (in the cause of justice). **make common cause with** join the side of. □□ **caus·a·ble** adj. **cause·less** adj. **caus·er** n.

'cause /kawz, kuz/ conj. & adv. colloq. = BECAUSE.

cause cé·lè·bre /káwz selébr/ n. (pl. **causes célèbres** pronunc. same) a trial or case that attracts much attention.

cau·se·rie /kōzrée, kōzə-/ n. (pl. **causeries** pronunc. same) an informal article or talk, esp. on a literary subject.

cause·way /káwzway/ n. **1** a raised road or track across low or wet ground or a stretch of water. **2** a raised path by a road.

caus·tic /káwstik/ adj. & n. ● adj. **1** that burns or corrodes organic tissue. **2** sarcastic; biting. **3** Chem. strongly alkaline. **4** Physics formed by the intersection of reflected or refracted parallel rays from a curved surface. ● n. a caustic substance. **2** Physics a caustic surface or curve. □□ **caus·ti·cal·ly** adv. **caus·tic·i·ty** /-tisitee/ n.

cau·ter·ize /káwtərīz/ v.tr. Med. burn or coagulate (tissue) with a heated instrument or caustic substance, esp. to stop bleeding. □□ **cau·ter·i·za·tion** n.

cau·ter·y /káwtəree/ n. (pl. **-ies**) Med. **1** an instrument or caustic for cauterizing. **2** the operation of cauterizing.

cau·tion /káwshən/ n. & v. ● n. **1** attention to safety; prudence; carefulness. **2 a** esp. Brit. a warning, esp. a formal one in law. **b** a formal warning and reprimand. **3** colloq. an amusing or surprising person or thing. ● v.tr. **1** (often foll. by against, or to + infin.) warn or admonish. **2** esp. Brit. issue a caution to.

cau·tion·ar·y /káwshəneree/ adj. that gives or serves as a warning (a cautionary tale).

cau·tious /káwshəs/ adj. careful; prudent; attentive to safety. □□ **cau·tious·ly** adv. **cau·tious·ness** n.

cav·al·cade /kávəlkáyd/ n. a procession or formal company of riders, motor vehicles, etc.

cav·a·lier /kávəleér/ n. & adj. ● n. **1** hist. (**Cavalier**) a supporter of Charles I in the English Civil War. **2** a courtly gentleman, esp. as a lady's escort. **3** archaic a horseman. ● adj. offhand; supercilious; blasé. □□ **cav·a·lier·ly** adv.

CAT-O'-NINE-TAILS

CATTAIL
(*Typha latifolia*)

C

C

CAVE

Most caves occur in limestone because this type of rock is soluble in rainwater. Acidic rain seeps in, dissolving calcite out of the sedimentary rock and gradually producing hollows. As rain continues to drip in, it leaves behind tiny calcite sediments. These deposits accumulate to form stalactites and stalagmites, and columns where the two meet.

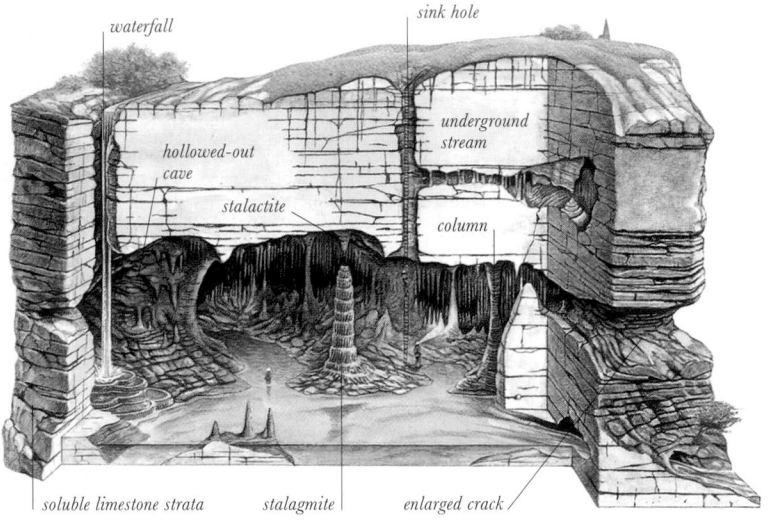

CROSS SECTION THROUGH A LIMESTONE CAVE

Labels: waterfall · sink hole · hollowed-out cave · underground stream · stalactite · column · soluble limestone strata · stalagmite · enlarged crack

cav·al·ry /kávəlree/ *n.* (*pl.* **-ies**) (usu. treated as *pl.*) soldiers on horseback or in armored vehicles.

cav·al·ry·man /kávəlrimən/ *n.* (*pl.* **-men**) a soldier of a cavalry regiment.

cavalry twill *n.* a strong fabric in a double twill, used for clothing.

cav·a·ti·na /kávətéénə/ *n.* **1** a short simple song. **2** a similar piece of instrumental music, usu. slow and emotional.

cave /kayv/ *n. & v.* ● *n.* ▲ a large hollow in the side of a cliff, hill, etc., or underground. ● *v.intr.* explore caves, esp. interconnecting or underground. □ **cave in 1 a** (of a wall, earth over a hollow, etc.) subside; collapse. **b** cause (a wall, earth, etc.) to do this. **2** yield or submit under pressure; give up. □□ **cave·like** *adj.* **cav·er** *n.*

ca·ve·at /kávee-aat, káa-, -at/ *n.* **1** a warning or proviso. **2** *Law* a process in court to suspend proceedings.

ca·ve·at emp·tor /émptawr/ *n.* the principle that the buyer alone is responsible if dissatisfied.

cave bear *n.* a large extinct bear, *Ursus spelaeus*, of the Pleistocene epoch, whose bones have been found in caves throughout Europe.

cave-in *n.* a collapse, submission, etc.

cave dwell·er *n.* **1** = CAVEMAN. **2** *sl.* a person who lives in an apartment building in a big city.

cave·man /káyvman/ *n.* (*pl.* **-men**) **1** (*fem.* **cave-woman**, *pl.* **-women**) a prehistoric human living in a cave. **2** a primitive or crude person, esp. a man who behaves roughly toward women.

cav·ern /kávərn/ *n.* **1** a cave, esp. a large or dark one. **2** a dark, cavelike place, e.g., a room. □□ **cav·ern·ous** *adj.* **cav·ern·ous·ly** *adv.*

cav·i·ar /kávee-aár/ *n.* (also **cav·i·are**) the pickled roe of sturgeon or other large fish, eaten as a delicacy.

cav·il /kávil/ *v. & n.* ● *v.intr.* (**caviled, caviling**; esp. *Brit.* **cavilled, cavilling**) (usu. foll. by *at, about*) make petty objections; carp. ● *n.* a trivial objection. □□ **cav·il·er** *n.*

cav·ing /káyving/ *n.* exploring caves as a sport or pastime.

cav·i·ta·tion /kávitáyshən/ *n.* **1** the formation of a cavity in a structure. **2** the formation of bubbles, or of a vacuum, in a liquid.

cav·i·ty /kávitee/ *n.* (*pl.* **-ies**) **1** a hollow within a solid body. **2** a decayed part of a tooth.

cav·i·ty wall *n.* a wall formed from two thicknesses of masonry with a space between them.

ca·vort /kəváwrt/ *v.intr. sl.* caper excitedly; gambol; prance.

ca·vy /káyvee/ *n.* (*pl.* **-ies**) any small rodent of the family Caviidae, native to S. America and having a sturdy body and vestigial tail, including guinea pigs.

caw /kaw/ *n. & v.* ● *n.* the harsh cry of a rook, crow, etc. ● *v.intr.* utter this cry.

cay /kee, kay/ *n.* a low insular bank or reef of coral, sand, etc. (cf. KEY²).

cay·enne /kī-én, kay-/ *n.* (in full **cayenne pepper**) a pungent red powder obtained from various plants of the genus *Capsicum* and used for seasoning. ▷ CHILI, SPICE

cay·man var. of CAIMAN.

Ca·yu·ga /kayōogə, kī-/ *n.* **1 a** a N. American people native to New York. **b** a member of this people. **2** the language of this people.

CB *abbr.* **1** citizens' band. **2** *Mil.* construction battalion.

Cb *symb. Chem.* the element columbium.

CBC *abbr.* **1** Canadian Broadcasting Corporation. **2** complete blood count.

CBE *abbr.* Commander of the Order of the British Empire.

CBI *abbr.* computer-based instruction.

CBS *abbr.* Columbia Broadcasting System.

CC *abbr.* **1** city council. **2** county clerk. **3** circuit court.

cc *abbr.* (also **c.c.**) **1** cubic centimeter(s). **2** (carbon) copy; copies.

CCTV *abbr.* closed-circuit television.

CCU *abbr.* **1** cardiac care unit. **2** coronary care unit. **3** critical care unit.

CD *abbr.* **1** compact disc. **2** certificate of deposit. **3** congressional district. **4** civil defense. **5** diplomatic corps (*corps diplomatique*).

Cd *symb. Chem.* the element cadmium.

cd *abbr.* candela(s).

CDC *abbr.* Centers for Disease Control (and Prevention).

Cdr. *abbr. Mil.* commander.

Cdre. *abbr.* commodore.

CD-ROM /séedeeróm/ *abbr.* compact disc read-only memory, a medium for data storage and distribution.

CDT *abbr.* central daylight time.

CE *abbr.* **1** Church of England. **2** civil engineer. **3** (with dates) Common Era.

Ce *symb. Chem.* the element cerium.

ce·a·no·thus /séeənóthəs/ *n.* any shrub of the genus *Ceanothus*, with small blue or white flowers.

cease /sees/ *v. & n.* ● *v.tr. & intr.* stop; bring or come to an end (*ceased breathing*). ● *n.* (in **without cease**) unendingly. □ **cease fire** *Mil.* stop firing.

cease-fire *n.* **1** the order to stop firing. **2** a period of truce; a suspension of hostilities.

cease·less /séeslis/ *adj.* without end; not ceasing. □□ **cease·less·ly** *adv.*

ce·ci·tis /sikítis/ *n.* inflammation of the cecum.

ce·cro·pi·a moth /sikrốpeeə/ *n.* a large N. American silk moth with boldly marked reddish-brown wings.

ce·cum /séekəm/ *n.* (*Brit.* **caecum**) (*pl.* **-ca** /-kə/) a blind-ended pouch at the junction of the small and large intestines. ▷ COLON. □□ **ce·cal** *adj.*

ce·dar /séedər/ *n.* **1** ▼ any spreading evergreen conifer of the genus *Cedrus*, bearing tufts of small needles and cones of papery scales. **2** any of various similar conifers yielding timber. **3** = CEDARWOOD.

CEDAR: CEDAR OF LEBANON (*Cedrus libani*)

Labels: needlelike leaf · barrel-shaped cone

ce·dar·wood /séedərwŏŏd/ *n.* the fragrant durable wood of any cedar tree.

cede /seed/ *v.tr.* give up one's rights to or possession of; yield.

ce·dil·la /sidílə/ *n.* **1** a mark written under the letter *c*, esp. in French, to show that it is sibilant (as in *façade*). **2** a similar mark under *s* in Turkish and other Eastern languages.

cei·lidh /káylee/ *n. orig. Ir. & Sc.* an informal gathering for conversation, music, dancing, songs, and stories.

ceil·ing /séeling/ *n.* **1 a** the upper interior surface of a room or other similar compartment. **b** the material forming this. **2** an upper limit on prices, wages, performance, etc. **3** *Aeron.* the maximum altitude a given aircraft can reach. **4** *Naut.* the inside planking of a ship's bottom and sides.

cel·a·don /sélədon/ *n. & adj.* ● *n.* **1** a willow-green color. **2** a gray-green glaze used on some pottery. **3** Chinese pottery glazed in this way. ● *adj.* of a gray-green color.

cel·an·dine /séləndīn, -deen/ *n.* either of two yellow-flowered plants, the greater celandine, *Chelidonium majus*, and the lesser celandine, *Ranunculus ficaria*.

-cele /seel/ *comb. form* (also **-coele**) *Med.* swelling; hernia (*gastrocele*).

ce·leb /siléb/ *n. colloq.* a celebrity; a star.

cel·e·brant /sélibrənt/ *n.* a person who performs a rite, esp. a priest at the Eucharist.

cel·e·brate /sélibrayt/ *v.* **1** *tr.* mark (a festival or special event) with festivities, etc. **2** *tr.* perform publicly and duly (a religious ceremony, etc.). **3 a** *tr.* officiate at (the Eucharist). **b** *intr.* officiate, esp. at the Eucharist. **4** *intr.* engage in festivities, usu. after a special event, etc. **5** *tr.* (esp. as **celebrated** *adj.*)

honor publicly; make widely known. □□ **cel·e·bra·tion** /-bráyshən/ *n*. **cel·e·bra·tor** *n*. **cel·e·bra·to·ry** /-brətáwree, səlébrətáwree/ *adj*.

ce·leb·ri·ty /silébritee/ *n*. (*pl*. **-ies**) **1** a well-known person. **2** fame.

ce·ler·i·ac /siléereeak, silér-/ *n*. ◄ a variety of celery with a swollen turniplike stem base used as a vegetable.

ce·ler·i·ty /siléritee/ *n. archaic* or *literary* swiftness (esp. of a living creature).

cel·er·y /séləree/ *n*. an umbelliferous plant, *Apium graveolens*, with closely packed succulent leafstalks used as a vegetable.

ce·les·ta /siléstə/ *n. Mus.* a small keyboard instrument resembling a glockenspiel, with hammers striking steel plates suspended over wooden resonators, giving an ethereal bell-like sound.

ce·leste /silést/ *n. Mus.* **1** an organ and harmonium stop with a soft tremulous tone. **2** = CELESTA.

ce·les·tial /siléschəl/ *adj.* **1** heavenly; divinely good or beautiful; sublime. **2** of the sky; of the part of the sky commonly observed in astronomy, etc. □□ **ce·les·tial·ly** *adv.*

CELERIAC
(*Apium graveolens*)

ce·les·tial e·qua·tor *n.* the great circle of the sky in the plane perpendicular to the Earth's axis. ▷ CELESTIAL SPHERE

ce·les·tial sphere *n.* ▼ an imaginary sphere of which the observer is the center and in which celestial objects are represented as lying. ▷ ZODIAC

CELL

The cell is the basic structural unit of every living thing, and most plants and animals are composed of millions of them. Cells work in unison to perform the tasks needed to keep an organism alive. They vary in shape according to function: a human red blood cell is disk-shaped, while a nerve cell is threadlike and may be a yard long. Unlike animal cells, plant cells can produce their own food through photosynthesis.

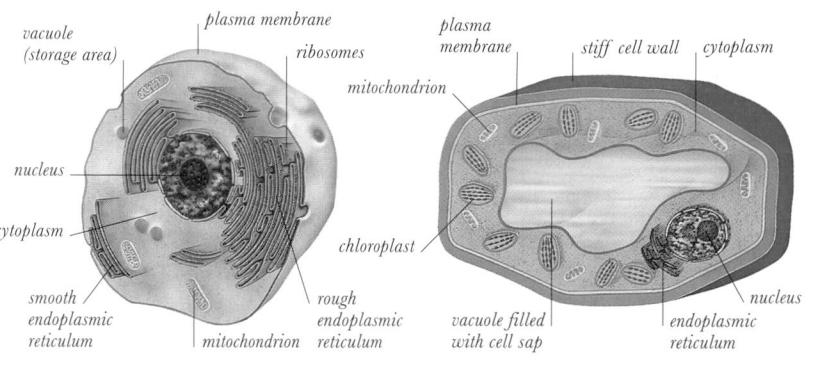

CROSS SECTION OF AN ANIMAL CELL   CROSS SECTION OF A PLANT CELL

ce·li·ac /séeleeak/ *adj.* (esp. *Brit.* **coeliac**) of or affecting the belly.

cel·i·bate /sélibət/ *adj. & n.* ● *adj.* **1** committed to abstention from sexual relations and from marriage, esp. for religious reasons. **2** abstaining from sexual relations. ● *n.* a celibate person. □□ **cel·i·ba·cy** /-bəsee/ *n.*

cell /sel/ *n.* **1** a small room, esp. in a prison or monastery. **2** a small compartment, e.g., in a honeycomb. **3** a small group as a nucleus of political activity, esp. of a subversive kind. **4** *Biol.* **a** ▲ the structural and functional usu. microscopic unit of an organism, consisting of cytoplasm and a nucleus enclosed in a membrane. ▷ ALGA. **b** an enclosed cavity in an organism, etc. **5** *Electr.* a vessel for containing electrodes within an electrolyte for current generation or electrolysis. ▷ BATTERY. □□ **celled** *adj.* (also in *comb.*).

cel·lar /sélər/ *n. & v.* ● *n.* **1** a room below ground level in a house, used for storage, etc. **2** a stock of wine in a cellar (*has a good cellar*). ● *v.tr.* store or put in a cellar.

cel·lar·age /séləriy/ *n.* **1** cellar accommodation. **2** the charge for the use of a cellar or storehouse.

cel·lar·et /sélərét/ *n.* a case, cabinet, etc., for holding wine bottles in a dining room.

cel·lo /chélō/ *n.* (*pl.* **-os**) ▼ a bass instrument of the violin family, held upright on the floor between the legs of the seated player. ▷ ORCHESTRA, STRINGED. □□ **cel·list** *n.*

CELESTIAL SPHERE

For the Earth-based observer, the positions of celestial bodies, such as the Sun, Moon, stars, and planets, can be described by locating them on an imaginary sphere – the celestial sphere – that is centered on the Earth and which rotates around the Earth once a day. The north and south poles of the celestial sphere lie directly above those of the Earth, at the points where the Earth's axis of rotation intersects the sphere. The celestial equator marks a projection of the Earth's equator onto the sphere, while the ecliptic marks the path of the Sun across the sky as the Earth orbits the Sun.

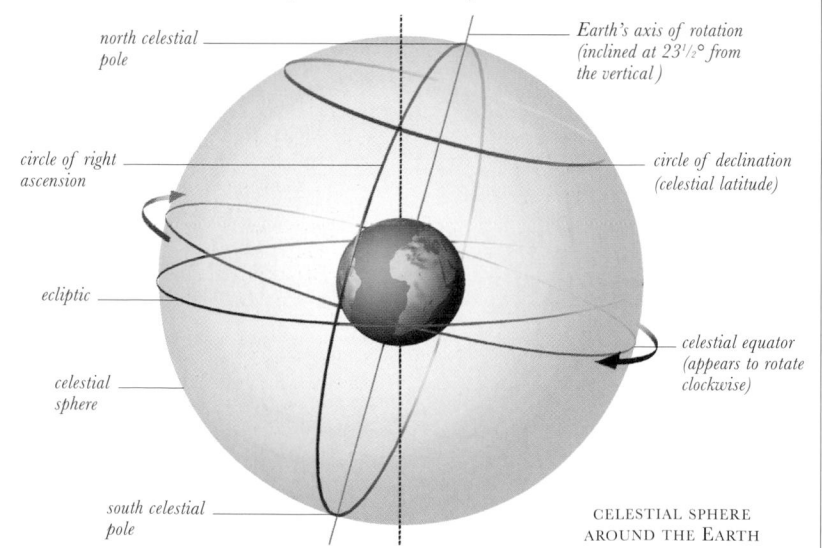

CELESTIAL SPHERE
AROUND THE EARTH

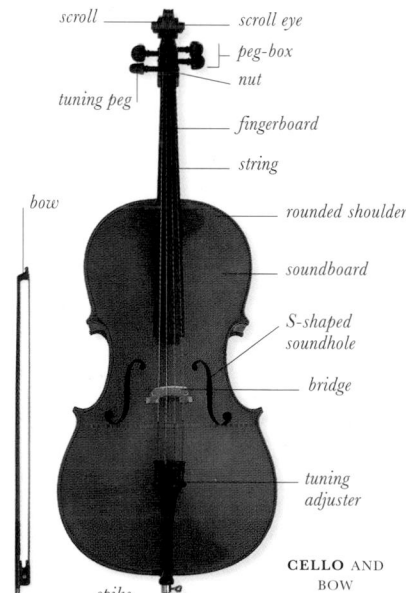

CELLO AND
BOW

cel·lo·phane /séləfayn/ *n. formerly propr.* a thin transparent wrapping material that is made from viscose.

cell·phone /sélfōn/ *n.* a small, portable radiotelephone having access to a cellular telephone system.

C

cel·lu·lar /sélyələr/ *adj.* **1** of or having small compartments or cavities. **2** of open texture; porous. **3** *Physiol.* of or consisting of cells. □□ **cel·lu·lar·i·ty** /-láritee/ *n.*

cel·lu·lar tel·e·phone (or **phone**) *n.* a system of mobile radiotelephone transmission with an area divided into "cells" each served by its own small transmitter.

cel·lule /sélyōōl/ *n. Biol.* a small cell or cavity.

cel·lu·lite /sélyəlīt/ *n.* a lumpy form of fat, esp. on the hips and thighs of women, causing puckering of the skin.

cel·lu·loid /sélyəloyd/ *n.* **1** a transparent flammable plastic made from camphor and cellulose nitrate. **2** motion-picture film.

cel·lu·lose /sélyəlōs, -lōz/ *n.* **1** *Biochem.* a carbohydrate forming the main constituent of plant cell walls, used in the production of textile fibers. ▷ CELL. **2** (in general use) a paint or lacquer consisting of esp. cellulose acetate or nitrate in solution. □□ **cel·lu·lo·sic** /-lōsik/ *adj.*

Cel·si·us /sélseeəs/ *adj.* of or denoting a temperature on the Celsius scale.

Cel·si·us scale *n.* a scale of temperature on which water freezes at 0° and boils at 100° under standard conditions.

Celt /kelt, selt/ *n.* (also **Kelt**) a member of a group of W. European peoples, including the pre-Roman inhabitants of Britain and Gaul and their descendants, esp. in Ireland, Wales, Scotland, Cornwall, Brittany, and the Isle of Man.

celt /kelt/ *n. Archaeol.* a stone or metal prehistoric implement with a chisel edge.

Celt·ic /kéltik, séltik/ *adj. & n.* ● *adj.* of or relating to the Celts. ● *n.* a group of languages spoken by Celtic peoples, including Gaelic, Welsh, Cornish, and Breton. □□ **Celt·i·cism** /-tisizəm/ *n.*

Celt·ic cross *n.* ◀ a Latin cross with a circle around the center.

cem·ba·lo /chémbəlō/ *n.* (*pl.* **-os**) a harpsichord.

ce·ment /simént/ *n. & v.* ● *n.* **1** a powdery substance made by calcining lime and clay, mixed with water to form mortar or used in concrete (see also PORTLAND CEMENT). **2** any similar substance that hardens and fastens on setting. **3** a uniting factor or principle. **4** a substance for filling cavities in teeth. **5** (also **cementum**) *Anat.* a thin layer of bony material that fixes teeth to the jaw. ● *v.tr.* **1** a unite with or as with cement. **b** establish or strengthen (a friendship, etc.). **2** apply cement to. **3** line or cover with cement. □□ **ce·men·ta·tion** *n.* **ce·ment·er** *n.*

CELTIC CROSS

cem·e·ter·y /sémiteree/ *n.* (*pl.* **-ies**) a burial ground, esp. one not in a churchyard.

ce·no·bite /séenəbīt/ *n.* (esp. *Brit.* **coenobite**) a member of a monastic community. □□ **ce·no·bit·ic** /-bítik/ *adj.*

ce·no·taph /sénətaf/ *n.* a tomblike monument, esp. a war memorial, to a person whose body is elsewhere.

Ce·no·zo·ic /séenəzóik, sén-/ (also **Cai·no·zo·ic** /kínə-/, **Caenozoic** /séenə-/) *adj. & n. Geol.* ● *adj.* of, denoting, or relating to the most recent era of geological time, which began 70,000,000 years ago, marked by the evolution and development of mammals, birds, and flowers. ● *n.* this era (cf. MESOZOIC, PALEOZOIC).

cen·ser /sénsər/ *n.* ▶ a vessel in which incense is burned, esp. during a religious procession or ceremony.

gilded chains

vessel for incense

CENSER

cen·sor /sénsər/ *n. & v.* ● *n.* **1** an official authorized to examine printed matter, movies, news, etc., before public release, and to suppress any parts on the grounds of obscenity, a threat to security, etc. **2** *Rom. Hist.* either of two annual magistrates responsible for holding censuses and empowered to supervise public morals. ● *v.tr.* **1** act as a censor of. **2** make deletions or changes in. ¶ As a verb, often confused with *censure.* □□ **cen·so·ri·al** /-sáwreeəl/ *adj.* **cen·sor·ship** *n.*

cen·so·ri·ous /sensáwreeəs/ *adj.* severely critical; faultfinding; quick or eager to criticize. □□ **cen·so·ri·ous·ly** *adv.* **cen·so·ri·ous·ness** *n.*

cen·sure /sénshər/ *v. & n.* ● *v.tr.* criticize harshly; reprove. ● *n.* harsh criticism; expression of disapproval. □□ **cen·sur·a·ble** *adj.*

cen·sus /sénsəs/ *n.* (*pl.* **censuses**) the official count of a population or of a class of things, often with various statistics noted.

cent /sent/ *n.* **1** a a monetary unit valued at one-hundredth of a dollar or other metric unit. **b** a coin of this value. **2** *colloq.* a very small sum of money. **3** see PERCENT.

cent. *abbr.* century.

cen·taur /séntawr/ *n.* ▶ a creature in Greek mythology with the head, arms, and torso of a man and the body and legs of a horse.

CENTAUR

cen·ta·vo /sentaávō/ *n.* a small coin of Spain, Portugal, and some Latin American countries, worth one-hundredth of the standard unit.

cen·te·nar·i·an /séntináireeən/ *n. & adj.* ● *n.* a person a hundred or more years old. ● *adj.* a hundred or more years old.

cen·ten·ar·y /senténəree, séntəneree/ *n. & adj.* ● *n.* (*pl.* **-ies**) = CENTENNIAL *n.* ● *adj.* **1** of or relating to a centenary. **2** occurring every hundred years.

cen·ten·ni·al /senténeeəl/ *adj. & n.* ● *adj.* **1** lasting for a hundred years. **2** occurring every hundred years. ● *n.* **1** a hundredth anniversary. **2** a celebration of this.

cen·ter /séntər/ *n. & v.* (*Brit.* **centre**) ● *n.* **1** the middle point, esp. of a line, circle, or sphere, equidistant from the ends or from any point on the circumference or surface. **2** a pivot or axis of rotation. **3 a** a place or group of buildings forming a central point in a district, city, etc., or a main area for an activity (*shopping center; town center*). **b** (with preceding word) a piece or set of equipment for a number of connected functions (*music center*). **4** a point of concentration or dispersion; a nucleus or source. **5** a political party or group holding moderate opinions. **6** the filling in a candy, etc. **7** *Sports* **a** the middle player in a line or group in many games. ▷ RUGBY. **b** a kick or hit from the side to the center of the playing area. **8** (*attrib.*) of or at the center. ● *v.* **1** *intr.* (foll. by *in, on; disp.* by *around*) have as its main center. **2** *tr.* place in the center. **3** *tr.* mark with a center. **4** *tr.* (foll. by *in*, etc.) concentrate. **5** *tr. Sports* kick or hit (the ball) from the side to the center of the playing area. □□ **cen·tered** *adj.* (often in *comb.*). **cen·ter·most** *adj.* **cen·tric** *adj.* **cen·tri·cal** *adj.* **cen·tric·i·ty** /-trísitee/ *n.*

cen·ter·board /séntərbawrd/ (*Brit.* **centre·board**) *n.* a retractable keel, as for a small sailboat. ▷ DINGHY.

cen·ter·fold /séntərfōld/ (*Brit.* **centre·fold**) *n.* a printed and usu. illustrated sheet folded to form the center spread of a magazine, etc.

cen·ter·ing /séntəring/ *n.* a temporary frame used to support an arch, dome, etc., while under construction.

cen·ter of grav·i·ty *n.* the point at which the weight of a body may be considered to act.

centi- /séntee/ *comb. form* **1** one-hundredth, esp. of a unit in the metric system (*centigram; centiliter*). **2** hundred. ¶ Abbr.: **c.**

cen·ti·grade /séntigrayd/ *adj.* **1** = CELSIUS. **2** having a scale of a hundred degrees. ¶ In sense 1 *Celsius* is usually preferred in technical use.

cen·ti·gram /séntigram/ *n.* (also *Brit.* **centi·gramme**) a metric unit of mass, equal to one-hundredth of a gram.

cen·ti·li·ter /séntileetər/ *n.* (*Brit.* **centilitre**) a metric unit of capacity, equal to one-hundredth of a liter.

cen·time /sontéem/ *n.* **1** (until the introduction of the euro in 2002) a monetary unit valued at one-hundredth of a franc. **2** a coin of this value.

cen·ti·me·ter /séntimeetər/ *n.* (*Brit.* **centimetre**) a metric unit of length, equal to one-hundredth of a meter.

cen·ti·pede /séntipeed/ *n.* ▶ any arthropod of the class Chilopoda, with a wormlike body of many segments each with a pair of legs.

antenna

one pair of legs per body segment

cen·tral /séntrəl/ *adj.* **1** of, at, or forming the center. **2** from the center. **3** chief; essential; most important. □□ **cen·tral·i·ty** /-trálitee/ *n.* **cen·tral·ly** *adv.*

Cen·tral A·mer·i·ca *n.* the isthmus joining N. and S. America, usually comprising the countries from Guatemala and Belize south to Panama.

CENTIPEDE
(*Lithobius* species)

cen·tral·ism /séntrəlizəm/ *n.* a system that centralizes (esp. an administration). □□ **cen·tral·ist** *n. & adj.*

cen·tral·ize /séntrəlīz/ *v.* **1** *tr. & intr.* bring or come to a center. **2** *tr.* **a** concentrate (administration) at a single center. **b** subject (a government) to this system. □□ **cen·tral·i·za·tion** *n.*

cen·tral nerv·ous sys·tem *n. Anat.* the complex of nerve tissues that controls the activities of the body, in vertebrates the brain and spinal cord. ▷ NERVOUS SYSTEM

cen·tral proc·es·sor *n.* (also **cen·tral proc·ess·ing u·nit**) the principal operating part of a computer. ▷ PCB

cen·tre *Brit.* var. of CENTER.

cen·tre·board *Brit.* var. of CENTERBOARD.

cen·tre·fold *Brit.* var. of CENTERFOLD.

-centric /séntrik/ *comb. form* forming adjectives with the sense 'having a (specified) center' (*eccentric*).

cen·trif·u·gal /sentrífyəgəl, -trífə-/ *adj.* moving or tending to move from a center (cf. CENTRIPETAL). □□ **cen·trif·u·gal·ly** *adv.*

cen·trif·u·gal force *n.* an apparent force that acts outward on a body moving about a center.

cen·tri·fuge /séntrifōoj/ *n. & v.* ● *n.* ▶ a machine with a rapidly rotating device designed to separate liquids from solids or other liquids (e.g., cream from milk). ● *v.tr.* **1** subject to the action of a centrifuge. **2** separate by centrifuge. □□ **cen·trif·u·ga·tion** /-fyəgáyshən, -fə-/ *n.*

direction of rotation

arm   *guard*

swinging tube

sediment

spindle

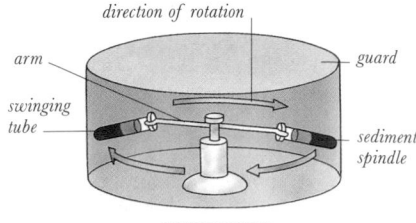

CENTRIFUGE

cen·trip·e·tal /sentrípit'l/ *adj.* moving or tending to move toward a center (cf. CENTRIFUGAL). □□ **cen·trip·e·tal·ly** *adv.*

cen·trip·e·tal force *n.* the force acting on a body causing it to move about a center.

cen·trist /séntrist/ *n. Polit.* often *derog.* a person who holds moderate views. □□ **cen·trism** *n.*

cen·tu·ple /séntəpəl, séntyə-/ *n., adj.,* & *v.* ● *n.* a hundredfold amount. ● *adj.* increased a hundredfold. ● *v.tr.* multiply by a hundred; increase a hundredfold.

cen·tu·ri·on /sentyōōreeən, -tyŏŏr-/ *n.* the commander of a century in the ancient Roman army.

cen·tu·ry /sénchəree/ *n.* (*pl.* **-ies**) **1 a** a period of one hundred years. **b** any of the centuries calculated from the birth of Christ (*twentieth century* = 1901–2000; *fifth century* BC = 500–401 BC). ¶ In modern use often calculated as, e.g., 1900–1999. **2 a** a score, etc., of a hundred in a sporting event, esp. a hundred runs by one batsman in cricket. **b** a group of a hundred things. **3 a** a company in the ancient Roman army, orig. of 100 men. **b** an ancient Roman political division for voting.

cen·tu·ry plant *n.* a plant, *Agave americana*, flowering once in many years and yielding sap from which tequila is distilled: also called **American aloe**.

CEO *abbr.* chief executive officer.

cepe /sep/ *n.* ◄ an edible mushroom, *Boletus edulis*, with a stout stalk and brown smooth cap.

-cephalic /sifálik/ *comb. form* = -CEPHALOUS.

ceph·a·lo·pod /séfələpod/ *n.* ▼ any mollusk of the class Cephalopoda, having a distinct tentacled head, e.g., octopus, squid, and cuttlefish.

ceph·a·lo·tho·rax /séfəlōtháwraks/ *n.* (*pl.* **-thoraxes** or **-thoraces** /-tháwrəseez/) *Anat.* the fused head and thorax of a spider, crab, or other arthropod.

-cephalous /séfələs/ *comb. form* -headed (*brachycephalous*).

Ce·pheid /séefeeid, séf-/ *n.* (in full **Cepheid variable**) *Astron.* any of a class of variable stars with a regular cycle of brightness that can be used to measure distances.

CEPE
(Boletus edulis)

CERAMIC

Fashioned from clay or other nonmetallic minerals, ceramics were originally baked until hard in an open oven but are now fired in a kiln or furnace. Widely used as decorative articles, they also have a more functional purpose: for building house walls, insulating cables, and mending broken teeth. New ceramics are being developed for car and aircraft engines. More durable than traditional ceramics, they can be as strong as steel and are capable of withstanding extremely high temperatures.

EXAMPLES OF CERAMICS

PORCELAIN

BRICK

GLAZED CLAY BEADS

CEMENT

GLASS

ce·ram·ic /sirámik/ *adj.* & *n.* ● *adj.* **1** made of (esp.) clay and permanently hardened by heat (*a ceramic bowl*). **2** of or relating to ceramics (*the ceramic arts*). ● *n.* **1** ▲ a ceramic article or product. **2** a substance, esp. clay, used to make ceramic articles.

ce·ram·ics /sirámiks/ *n.pl.* **1** ceramic products collectively (*exhibition of ceramics*). **2** (usu. treated as *sing.*) the art of making ceramic articles.

ce·ram·ist /sirámist, sérə-/ *n.* a person who makes ceramics.

cere /seer/ *n.* a waxy fleshy covering at the base of the upper beak in some birds.

ce·re·al /séereeəl/ *n.* & *adj.* ● *n.* **1** (usu. in *pl.*) **a** any kind of grain used for food. ▷ GRAIN. **b** any grass producing this, e.g., wheat, corn, rye, etc. **2** a breakfast food made from a cereal and requiring no cooking. ● *adj.* of edible grain or products of it.

ce·re·bel·lum /séribéləm/ *n.* (*pl.* **cerebellums** or **cerebella** /-lə/) the part of the brain at the back of the skull in vertebrates, which coordinates and regulates muscular activity. ▷ BRAIN, SPINAL CORD. □□ **cer·e·bel·lar** *adj.*

ce·re·bral /séribrəl, sərée-/ *adj.* **1** of the brain. **2** intellectual rather than emotional. □□ **ce·re·bral·ly** *adv.*

ce·re·bral hem·i·sphere *n.* each of the two halves of the vertebrate cerebrum. ▷ BRAIN

ce·re·bral pal·sy *n. Med.* spastic paralysis from brain damage before or at birth, with jerky or uncontrolled movements.

cer·e·bra·tion /séribráyshən/ *n.* working of the brain. □□ **cer·e·brate** /-brayt/ *v.intr.*

cerebro- /séribrō, sərée-/ *comb. form* brain (*cerebrospinal*).

ce·re·bro·spi·nal /séribrōspínəl, sərée-/ *adj.* of the brain and spine.

ce·re·bro·vas·cu·lar /séribrōváskyələr, sərée-/ *adj.* of the brain and its blood vessels. ▷ BRAIN

ce·re·brum /séribrəm, sərée-/ *n.* (*pl.* **cerebrums** or **cerebra** /-brə/) the principal part of the brain in vertebrates, located in the front area of the skull, which integrates complex sensory and neural functions. ▷ BRAIN, SPINAL CORD

cere·cloth /séerklawth, -kloth/ *n. hist.* waxed cloth used as a waterproof covering or (esp.) as a shroud.

cer·e·mo·ni·al /sérimóneeəl/ *adj.* & *n.* ● *adj.* **1** with or concerning ritual or ceremony. **2** formal (*a ceremonial bow*). ● *n.* **1** a system of rites, etc., to be used esp. at a formal or religious occasion. **2** the formalities or behavior proper to any occasion (*the ceremonial of a presidential appearance*). □□ **cer·e·mo·ni·al·ism** *n.* **cer·e·mo·ni·al·ist** *n.* **cer·e·mo·ni·al·ly** *adv.*

cer·e·mo·ni·ous /sérimóneeəs/ *adj.* **1** excessively polite; punctilious. **2** having or showing a fondness for ritualistic observance or formality. □□ **cer·e·mo·ni·ous·ly** *adv.* **cer·e·mo·ni·ous·ness** *n.*

cer·e·mo·ny /sérimōnee/ *n.* (*pl.* **-ies**) **1** a formal religious or public occasion, esp. celebrating a particular event or anniversary. **2** formalities, esp. of an empty or ritualistic kind (*ceremony of exchanging compliments*). **3** excessively polite behavior (*bowed low with great ceremony*). □ **stand on ceremony** insist on the observance of formalities. **without ceremony** informally.

ce·rise /sərées, -réez/ *adj.* & *n.* ● *adj.* of a light, clear red. ● *n.* this color.

ce·ri·um /séereeəm/ *n. Chem.* a silvery metallic element of the lanthanide series occurring naturally in various minerals and used in the manufacture of lighter flints. ¶ Symb.: **Ce**.

cer·met /sórmet/ *n.* a heat resistant material made of ceramic and sintered metal.

CERN /sərn/ *abbr.* European Organization for Nuclear Research.

cero- /séerō/ *comb. form* wax (cf. CEROGRAPHY).

ce·rog·ra·phy /seerógrəfee/ *n.* the technique of engraving or designing on or with wax.

cert. /sərt/ *abbr.* **1** a certificate. **2** certified.

CEPHALOPOD

Compared to most other invertebrates, cephalopods are fast-moving and intelligent animals. To swim at speed, they use a form of jet propulsion in which water is expelled backward through a funnel-shaped siphon.

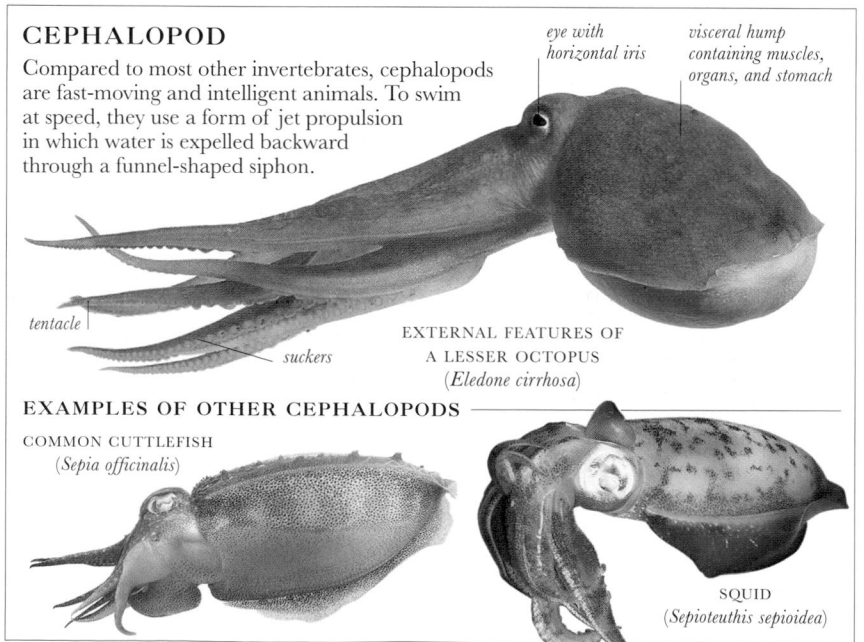

eye with horizontal iris

visceral hump containing muscles, organs, and stomach

tentacle

suckers

EXTERNAL FEATURES OF A LESSER OCTOPUS
(Eledone cirrhosa)

EXAMPLES OF OTHER CEPHALOPODS

COMMON CUTTLEFISH
(Sepia officinalis)

SQUID
(Sepioteuthis sepioidea)

C

CETACEAN

The order Cetacea comprises whales, porpoises, and dolphins. Like all other mammals, cetaceans breathe air, but they are adapted to a life spent entirely in water. They breathe through a blowhole, which can be closed on diving, and have flippers instead of front limbs. Their hind limbs have been lost over the course of time.

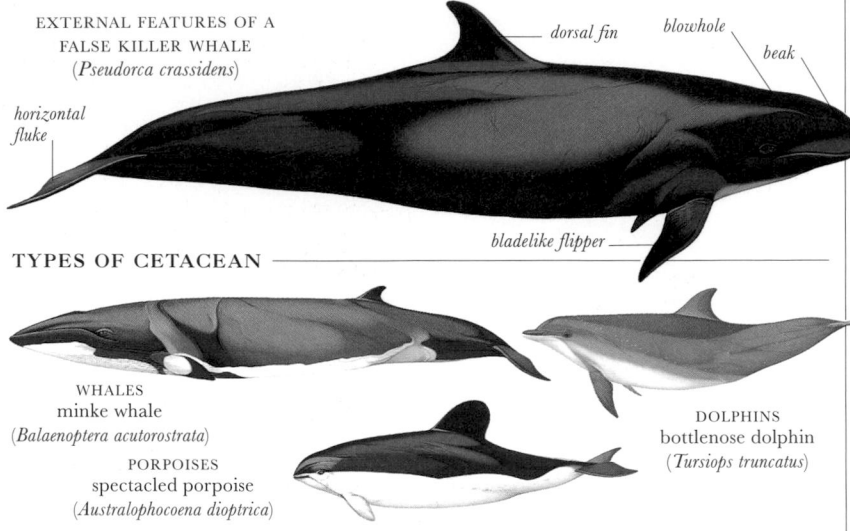

EXTERNAL FEATURES OF A FALSE KILLER WHALE
(*Pseudorca crassidens*)

dorsal fin　　*blowhole*

beak

horizontal fluke

bladelike flipper

TYPES OF CETACEAN

WHALES
minke whale
(*Balaenoptera acutorostrata*)

PORPOISES
spectacled porpoise
(*Australophocoena dioptrica*)

DOLPHINS
bottlenose dolphin
(*Tursiops truncatus*)

---

cer·tain /sárt'n/ *adj. & pron.* ● *adj.* **1 a** (often foll. by *of*, or *that* + clause) confident; convinced (*certain that I put it here*). **b** (often foll. by *that* + clause) indisputable; known for sure (*it is certain that he is guilty*). **2** (often foll. by *to* + infin.) **a** that may be relied on to happen (*it is certain to rain*). **b** destined (*certain to become a star*). **3** definite; unfailing; reliable (*a certain indication of the coming storm; his touch is certain*). **4** (of a person, place, etc.) that might be specified, but is not (*a certain lady; of a certain age*). **5** some though not much (*a certain reluctance*). **6** (of a person, place, etc.) existing, though probably unknown to the reader or hearer (*a certain John Smith*). ● *pron.* (as *pl.*) some but not all (*certain of them were wounded*). □ **for certain** without doubt. **make certain** = *make sure* (see SURE).

cer·tain·ly /sárt'nlee/ *adv.* **1** undoubtedly; definitely. **2** confidently. **3** (in affirmative answer to a question or command) yes; by all means.

cer·tain·ty /sárt'ntee/ *n.* (*pl.* **-ies**) **1 a** an undoubted fact. **b** a certain prospect (*his return is a certainty*). **2** (often foll. by *of*, or *that* + clause) an absolute conviction (*has a certainty of his own worth*). **3** (often foll. by *to* + infin.) a thing or person that may be relied on (*a certainty to win the Derby*). □ **for a certainty** beyond the possibility of doubt.

cer·ti·fi·a·ble /sártifiabəl/ *adj.* **1** able or needing to be certified. **2** *colloq.* insane.

cer·tif·i·cate *n. & v.* ● *n.* /sərtifikət/ a formal document attesting a fact, esp. birth, marriage, death, a medical condition, a level of achievement, a fulfillment of requirements, ownership of shares, etc. ● *v.tr.* /sərtifikayt/ (esp. as **certificated** *adj.*) provide with or license or attest by a certificate. □□ **cer·tif·i·ca·tion** /sártifikáyshən/ *n.*

cer·tif·i·cate of de·pos·it *n.* a certificate issued by a bank to a depositor, stating the amount of money on deposit, usu. at a specified rate of interest and for a specified time period.

cer·ti·fied check *n.* a check the validity of which is guaranteed by a bank.

cer·ti·fied pub·lic ac·count·ant *n.* a member of an officially accredited professional body of accountants.

cer·ti·fy /sártifī/ *v.tr.* (**-ies**, **-ied**) **1** make a formal statement of; attest; attest to (*certified that he had witnessed the crime*). **2** declare by certificate (that a person is qualified or competent) (*certified as a trained bookkeeper*). **3** officially declare insane (*he should be certified*).

cer·ti·o·ra·ri /sársheeəráiree, -raírī/ *n. Law* a writ from a higher court requesting the records of a case tried in a lower court.

cer·ti·tude /sártitood, -tyood/ *n.* a feeling of absolute certainty or conviction.

ce·ru·le·an /sərooleeən/ *adj. & n. literary* ● *adj.* deep blue like a clear sky. ● *n.* this color.

ce·ru·men /səroomen/ *n.* the yellow waxy substance in the outer ear. □□ **ce·ru·mi·nous** *adj.*

cer·ve·lat /sárvəlaa, -lat/ *n.* a kind of smoked pork or beef sausage.

cer·vi·cal /sárvikəl/ *adj. Anat.* **1** of or relating to the neck (*cervical vertebrae*). ▷ VERTEBRA. **2** of or relating to the cervix.

cer·vi·cal screen·ing *n.* examination of a large number of apparently healthy women for cervical cancer.

cer·vi·cal smear *n.* a specimen of cellular material taken from the neck of the womb for detection of cancer.

cer·vine /sárvīn/ *adj.* of or like a deer.

cer·vix /sárviks/ *n.* (*pl.* **cervices** /-viseez/ or **cervixes**) *Anat.* **1** the neck. **2** any necklike structure, esp. the neck of the womb. ▷ REPRODUCTIVE ORGANS

Ce·sar·e·an /sizáireeən/ *adj. & n.* (also **Ce·sar·i·an, Cae·sar·e·an, Cae·sar·i·an**) ● *adj.* (of a birth) effected by Cesarean section. ● *n.* a Cesarean section.

Ce·sar·e·an sec·tion *n.* (also **C-section**) an operation for delivering a child by cutting through the wall of the abdomen (*Julius Caesar supposedly having been born this way*).

ce·sar·e·vitch /sizáirivich, -zaár-/ *n. hist.* the eldest son of the emperor of Russia.

ce·si·um /séezeeəm/ *n.* (*Brit.* **caesium**) a soft, silver-white element of the alkali metal group, occurring naturally in a number of minerals, and used in photoelectric cells. ¶ Symb.: **Cs**.

ce·si·um clock *n.* an atomic clock that uses cesium.

ces·sa·tion /sesáyshən/ *n.* **1** a ceasing (*cessation of the truce*). **2** a pause (*resumed fighting after the cessation*).

ces·sion /séshən/ *n.* **1** (often foll. by *of*) the ceding or giving up (of rights, property, and esp. of territory by a nation). **2** the territory, etc., so ceded.

ces·sion·ar·y /séshəneree/ *n.* (*pl.* **-ies**) *Law* an assignee.

cess·pit /séspit/ *n.* a pit for the disposal of refuse. **2** = CESSPOOL.

cess·pool /séspool/ *n.* **1** an underground container for the temporary storage of liquid waste or sewage. **2** a center of corruption, depravity, etc.

ces·tode /séstōd/ *n.* (also **ces·toid** /séstoyd/) any flatworm of the class Cestoda, including tapeworms.

ce·ta·ce·an /sitáyshən/ *n. & adj.* ● *n.* ◀ any marine mammal of the order Cetacea with streamlined hairless body and dorsal blowhole for breathing, including whales, dolphins, and porpoises. ▷ DOLPHIN, PORPOISE, WHALE. ● *adj.* of cetaceans. □□ **ce·ta·ceous** /-táyshəs/ *adj.*

ce·tane /séetayn/ *n. Chem.* a colorless liquid hydrocarbon of the alkane series used in standardizing ratings of diesel fuel.

ce·tane num·ber *n.* a measure of the ignition properties of diesel fuel.

Cey·lon moss /silón, say-/ *n.* a red seaweed, *Gracilaria lichenoides*, from E. India.

Cf *symb. Chem.* the element californium.

cf. *abbr.* compare.

c.f. *abbr.* **1** carried forward. **2** *Baseball* center fielder.

CFA *abbr.* chartered financial analyst.

CFC *abbr. Chem.* chlorofluorocarbon, any of various usu. gaseous compounds of carbon, hydrogen, chlorine, and fluorine, used in refrigerants, aerosol propellants, etc., and thought to be harmful to the ozone layer in the Earth's atmosphere.

cfm *abbr.* cubic feet per minute.

cfs *abbr.* cubic feet per second.

cg *abbr.* centigram(s).

cgs *abbr.* centimeter-gram-second.

ch. *abbr.* **1** church. **2** chapter. **3** *Chess* check.

c.h. *abbr.* (also **C.H.**) **1** clearing house. **2** courthouse.

cha var. of CHAR[3].

Cha·blis /shablée, sháblee/ *n.* (*pl.* same /-leez/) a type of dry white wine.

cha-cha /cháachaa/ (also **cha-cha-cha** /cháa-chaacháa/) *n. & v.* ● *n.* **1** a ballroom dance with a Latin-American rhythm. **2** music for or in the rhythm of a cha-cha. ● *v.intr.* (**cha-chas, cha-chaed** /-chaad/, **cha-chaing** /-chaa-ing/) dance the cha-cha.

cha·conne /shakáwn, -kón/ *n. Mus.* **1** a musical form consisting of variations on a ground bass. **2** *hist.* a dance performed to this music.

chad·or /chaadáwr/ *n.* (also **chad·ar, chud·dar**) a large piece of cloth worn in some countries by Muslim women, wrapped around the body to leave only the face exposed.

chafe /chayf/ *v. & n.* ● *v.* **1** *tr. & intr.* make or become sore or damaged by rubbing. **2** *tr.* rub (esp. the skin to restore warmth or sensation). **3** *tr. & intr.* make or become annoyed; fret (*was chafed by the delay*). ● *n.* **1 a** an act of chafing. **b** a sore resulting from this. **2** a state of annoyance.

chaf·er /cháyfər/ *n.* any of various large, slow-moving beetles of the family Scarabaeidae, esp. the cockchafer.

chaff /chaf/ *n. & v.* ● *n.* **1** the husks of grain or other seed separated by winnowing or threshing. **2** chopped hay and straw used as fodder. **3** light-hearted joking; banter. **4** worthless things; rubbish. ● *v.tr.* **1** tease; banter. **2** chop (straw, etc.). □ **separate the wheat from the chaff** distinguish good from bad. □□ **chaff·y** *adj.*

chaf·fer /cháfər/ *v. & n.* ● *v.intr.* haggle; bargain. ● *n.* bargaining; haggling. □□ **chaf·fer·er** *n.*

chaf·finch /cháfinch/ *n.* a common European finch, *Fringilla coelebs*, the male of which has a blue-gray head with pinkish cheeks.

chaf·ing dish /cháyfing/ *n.* **1** a cooking pot with an outer pan of hot water, used for keeping food warm. **2** a dish with an alcohol lamp, etc., for cooking at table.

Cha·gas' dis·ease /sháagəs/ *n.* (also **Chagas's disease**) a kind of sleeping sickness caused by a protozoan transmitted by bloodsucking bugs.

cha·grin /shəgrín/ *n. & v.* ● *n.* acute vexation or mortification. ● *v.tr.* affect with chagrin.

chain /chayn/ *n. & v.* ● *n.* **1 a** a connected flexible series of esp. metal links as decoration or for a practical purpose. **b** something resembling this (*formed a human chain*). **2** (in *pl.*) **a** fetters used to confine prisoners. **b** any restraining force. **3** a sequence, series, or set (*chain of events; mountain chain*). **4** a group of associated hotels, shops, newspapers, etc. **5** esp. *Brit.* a badge of office in the form of a chain worn around the neck (*mayoral chain*). **6** a measure of length (66 or 100 ft.). **7** *Chem.* a group of (esp. carbon) atoms bonded in sequence in a molecule. ● *v.tr.* **1** (often foll. by *up*) secure or confine with a chain. **2** confine or restrict (a person) (*is chained to the office*).

chain gang *n.* a team of convicts chained together and forced to work in the open air.

chain let·ter *n.* one of a sequence of letters the recipient of which is requested to send copies to a specific number of other people.

chain mail *n.* ▼ armor made of interlaced rings. ▷ JOUST, VIKING

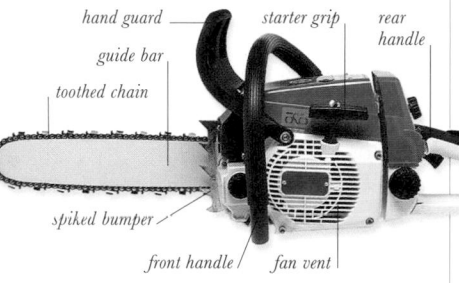

metal rings

CHAIN MAIL:
ORIENTAL
CHAIN MAIL
SHIRT

chain re·ac·tion *n.* **1** *Physics* a self-sustaining nuclear reaction, esp. one in which a neutron from a fission reaction initiates a series of these reactions. **2** *Chem.* a self-sustaining molecular reaction in which intermediate products initiate further reactions. **3** a series of events, each caused by the previous one.

chain saw *n.* ▼ a motor-driven saw with teeth on an endless chain. ▷ SAW

hand guard   *starter grip*   *rear handle*

guide bar

toothed chain

spiked bumper

front handle   *fan vent*

CHAIN SAW

chain-smok·er *n.* a person who smokes continually, esp. one who lights a cigarette, etc., from the stub of the last one smoked.

chain·wheel /cháynwheel, -weel/ *n.* a wheel transmitting power by a chain fitted to its edges; a sprocket.

chair /chair/ *n. & v.* ● *n.* **1** a separate seat for one person, of various forms, usu. having a back and four legs. **2 a** a professorship (*offered the chair in physics*). **b** a seat of authority, esp. on a board of directors. **3 a** a chairperson. **b** the seat or office of

a chairperson (*will you take the chair?; I'm in the chair*). **4** = ELECTRIC CHAIR. **5** *hist.* = sedan chair. ● *v.tr.* **1** act as chairperson of or preside over (a meeting). **2** *Brit.* carry (a person) aloft in a chair or in a sitting position, in triumph. **3** install in a chair, esp. as a position of authority. □ **take a chair** sit down.

chair·borne /cháirbawrn/ *adj.* **1** (of an administrator) not active. **2** (of military personnel) assigned to a desk job rather than field duty.

chair·la·dy /cháirlaydee/ *n.* (*pl.* **-ies**) = chairwoman (see CHAIRMAN).

chair·lift /cháirlift/ *n.* a series of chairs on an endless cable for carrying passengers up and down a mountain, etc.

chair·man /cháirmən/ *n.* (*pl.* **-men**; *fem.* **chairwoman**, *pl.* **-women**) **1** a person chosen to preside over a meeting. **2** the permanent president of a committee, a board of directors, (*Brit.*) a firm, etc. **3** the master of ceremonies at an entertainment, etc. **4** *hist.* either of two sedan bearers. □□ **chair·man·ship** *n.*

chair·per·son /cháirpərsən/ *n.* a chairman or chairwoman (used as a neutral alternative).

chaise /shayz/ *n.* **1** esp. *hist.* a horse-drawn carriage for one or two persons, esp. one with an open top and two wheels. **2** = POST CHAISE.

chaise longue /sháyz lóng, shéz/ *n.* a reclining chair with a lengthened seat forming a leg rest.

cha·la·za /kəláyzə/ *n.* (*pl.* **chalazae** /-zee/ or **chalazas**) each of two twisted membranous strips joining the yolk to the ends of an egg.

chal·ced·o·ny /kalséd·nee/ *n.* a type of quartz occurring in several different forms, e.g., onyx, agate, tiger's eye, etc. ▷ MINERAL. □□ **chal·ce·don·ic** /kálsidónik/ *adj.*

Chal·de·an /kaldéeən/ *n. & adj.* ● *n.* **1 a** a native of ancient Chaldea or Babylonia. **b** the language of the Chaldeans. **2** an astrologer. **3** a member of the Uniat (formerly Nestorian) sect in Iran, etc. ● *adj.* **1** of or relating to ancient Chaldea or its people or language. **2** of or relating to astrology. **3** of or relating to the Uniat sect.

Chal·dee /kaldée/ *n.* **1** the language of the Chaldeans. **2** a native of ancient Chaldea. **3** the Aramaic language as used in Old Testament books.

cha·let /shaláy, shálay/ *n.* **1** a small suburban house or bungalow, esp. with an overhanging roof. **2** a small, usu. wooden hut or house at a ski resort, beach, etc. **3** ▶ a Swiss hut or wooden cottage with overhanging eaves.

CHALET: TRADITIONAL
WOODEN SWISS CHALET

chal·ice /chális/ *n.* **1** a wine cup used in the Communion service. **2** *literary* a goblet.

chalk /chawk/ *n. & v.* ● *n.* **1 a** a white, soft, earthy limestone (calcium carbonate) formed from the skeletal remains of sea creatures. **2 a** a similar substance (calcium sulfate), sometimes colored, used for writing or drawing. **b** a piece of this (*a box of chalk*). **3** a series of strata consisting mainly of chalk. ● *v.tr.* **1** rub, mark, draw, or write with chalk. **2** (foll. by *up*) **a** write or record with chalk. **b** register (a success, etc.). **c** *Brit.* charge (to an account). □ **as different as chalk and** (or **from**) **cheese** *Brit.* fundamentally different. **by a long chalk** *Brit.* by far (from the use of chalk to mark the score in games). **chalk out** sketch or plan a thing to be accomplished.

chalk·board /cháwkbawrd/ *n.* = BLACKBOARD.

chalk stripe *n.* a pattern of thin white stripes on a dark background.

chalk·y /cháwkee/ *adj.* (**chalkier**, **chalkiest**)

1 a abounding in chalk. **b** white as chalk. **2** like or containing chalk stones. □□ **chalk·i·ness** *n.*

chal·lenge /chálinj/ *n. & v.* ● *n.* **1 a** a summons to take part in a contest or a trial of strength, etc., esp. to a duel. **b** a summons to prove or justify something. **2** a demanding or difficult task (*rose to the challenge of the new job*). **3** an act of disputing or denying a statement, claim, etc. **4** *Law* an objection made to a jury member. **5** a call to respond, esp. a sentry's call for a password, etc. **6** an invitation to a sporting contest, esp. one issued to a reigning champion. ● *v.tr.* **1** (often foll. by *to* + infin.) **a** invite to take part in a contest, game, debate, duel, etc. **b** invite to prove or justify something. **2** dispute; deny (*I challenge that remark*). **3 a** stretch; stimulate (*challenges him to produce his best*). **b** (as **challenging** *adj.*) demanding; stimulatingly difficult. **4** (of a sentry) call to respond. **5** claim (attention, etc.). **6** *Law* object to (a jury member, evidence, etc.). □□ **chal·lenge·a·ble** *adj.* **chal·leng·er** *n.*

chal·lis /shálee/ *n.* a lightweight, soft clothing fabric.

cha·lyb·e·ate /kəlíbeeət/ *adj.* (of mineral water, etc.) impregnated with iron salts.

cham·ber /cháymbər/ *n.* **1 a** a hall used by a legislative or judicial body. **b** the body that meets in it. **c** any of the houses of a legislature (*the House chamber*). **2** (in *pl.*) a judge's room used for hearing cases not needing to be taken in court. **3** *poet.* or *archaic* a room, esp. a bedroom. **4** *Mus.* (*attrib.*) of or for a small group of instruments (*chamber orchestra; chamber music*). **5** an enclosed space in machinery, etc. (esp. the part of a gun bore that contains the charge). **6 a** a cavity in a plant or in the body of an animal. **b** a compartment in a structure.

cham·bered /cháymbərd/ *adj.* (of a tomb) containing a burial chamber.

cham·ber·lain /cháymbərlin/ *n.* an officer managing the household of a sovereign or a great noble. □□ **cham·ber·lain·ship** *n.*

cham·ber·maid /cháymbərmayd/ *n.* **1** a housemaid at a hotel, etc. **2** a housemaid.

cham·ber mu·sic *n.* instrumental music played by a small ensemble.

cham·ber of com·merce *n.* an association to promote local commercial interests.

cham·ber pot *n.* a receptacle for urine, etc., used in a bedroom.

Cham·ber·tin /shoxbertán/ *n.* a high-quality, dry, red wine.

cham·bray /shámbray/ *n.* a cotton, silk, or linen gingham cloth with a white weft and a colored warp.

cha·me·le·on /kəméel·yən/ *n.* **1** ▶ any of a family of small lizards having grasping tails, long tongues, protruding eyes, and the power of changing color. ▷ LIZARD. **2** a variable or inconstant person. □□ **cha·me·le·on·ic** /-leeónik/ *adj.*

cham·fer /chámfər/ *v. & n.* ● *v.tr.* bevel symmetrically (a right-angled edge or corner). ● *n.* a beveled surface at an edge or corner.

protruding eye

spines

opposable toes

laterally flattened body

prehensile tail

CHAMELEON:
MADAGASCAN CHAMELEON
(*Chamaeleo ousteleti*)

C

C

cham·ois /shámee/ n. (pl. same /-eez/) **1** ▶ an agile goat antelope, *Rupicapra rupicapra*, native to the mountains of Europe and Asia. **2** (in full **chamois leather**) **a** a soft pliable leather from sheep, goats, deer, etc. **b** a piece of this for polishing, etc.

cham·o·mile /kámǝmīl, -meel/ n. (also **cam·o·mile**) any aromatic plant of the genus *Anthemis* or *Matricaria*, with daisylike flowers. ▷ HERB

CHAMOIS
(*Rupicapra rupicapra*)

champ[1] /champ/ v. & n. ● v. **1** tr. & intr. munch or chew noisily. **2** tr. (of a horse, etc.) work (the bit) noisily between the teeth. **3** intr. fret with impatience (*is champing to be away*). ● n. a chewing noise or motion. □ **champ at the bit** be restlessly impatient.

champ[2] /champ/ n. sl. a champion.

cham·pagne /shampáyn/ n. **1 a** a white sparkling wine from Champagne in France. **b** a similar wine from elsewhere. ¶ Use in sense b is strictly incorrect. **2** a pale cream or straw color.

cham·per·ty /chámpǝrtee/ n. (pl. **-ies**) *Law* an illegal agreement in which a person not naturally interested in a lawsuit finances it with a view to sharing the disputed property. □□ **cham·per·tous** adj.

cham·pi·on /chámpeeǝn/ n. & v. ● n. **1** (often attrib.) a person (esp. in a sport or game), an animal, plant, etc., that has defeated or surpassed all rivals in a competition, etc. **2 a** a person who fights or argues for a cause or on behalf of another person. **b** hist. a knight, etc., who fought in single combat on behalf of a king, etc. ● v.tr. support the cause of; defend; argue in favor of.

cham·pi·on·ship /chámpeeǝnship/ n. **1** (often in pl.) a contest for the position of champion in a sport, etc. **2** the position of champion over all rivals. **3** the advocacy or defense (of a cause, etc.).

champ·le·vé /shónlǝváy/ n. & adj. ● n. a type of enamelwork in which hollows made in a metal surface are filled with colored enamels. ● adj. of or relating to champlevé (cf. CLOISONNÉ).

chance /chans/ n., adj., & v. ● n. **1 a** a possibility (*just a chance we will catch the train*). **b** (often in pl.) probability (*the chances are against it*). **2 a** risk (*have to take a chance*). **3 a** an undesigned occurrence (*just a chance that they met*). **b** the absence of design or discoverable cause (*here merely because of chance*). **4** an opportunity (*didn't have a chance to speak to him*). **5** the way things happen; fortune; luck (*we'll just leave it to chance*). **6** (often **Chance**) the course of events regarded as a power; fate (*blind Chance rules the universe*). ● adj. fortuitous; accidental (*a chance meeting*). ● v. **1** tr. colloq. risk (*we'll chance it and go*). **2** intr. (often foll. by *that* + clause, or *to* + infin.) happen without intention (*it chanced that I found it; I chanced to find it*). □ **by any chance** as it happens; perhaps. **by chance** without design; unintentionally. **chance one's arm** Brit. make an attempt though unlikely to succeed. **chance on** (or **upon**) happen to find, meet, etc. **the off chance** the slight possibility. **on the chance** (often foll. by *of*, or *that* + clause) in view of the possibility. **stand a chance** have a prospect of success, etc. **take a chance** (or **chances**) behave riskily; risk failure. **take a** (or **one's**) **chance on** (or **with**) consent to take the consequences of; trust to luck.

chan·cel /chánsǝl/ n. the part of a church near the altar, usu. enclosed by a screen or separated from the nave by steps.

chan·cel·ler·y /chánsǝlǝree, chánslǝ-/ n. (pl. **-ies**) **1 a** the position, office, staff, department, etc., of a chancellor. **b** the official residence of a chancellor. **2** an office attached to an embassy or consulate.

chan·cel·lor /chánsǝlǝr, chánslǝr/ n. **1** a government official of various kinds; the head of the government in some European countries, e.g., Germany. **2 a** the chief administrator at certain universities. **b** Brit. the non-resident honorary head of a university. **3** a bishop's law officer. □□ **chan·cel·lor·ship** n.

chan·cer·y /chánsǝree/ n. (pl. **-ies**) **1** (**Chancery**) Brit. Law the Lord Chancellor's court, a division of the High Court of Justice. **2** an office attached to an embassy or consulate. □ **in chancery** sl. (of a boxer or wrestler) with the head held under the opponent's arm and being pummeled.

chan·cre /shángkǝr/ n. a painless ulcer developing in venereal disease, etc.

chan·croid /shángkroyd/ n. ulceration of lymph nodes in the groin, from venereal disease.

chanc·y /chánsee/ adj. (**chancier, chanciest**) subject to chance; uncertain; risky. □□ **chanc·i·ly** adv. **chanc·i·ness** n.

chan·de·lier /shándǝleér/ n. an ornamental branched hanging support for several candles or electric lightbulbs.

chan·dler /chándlǝr/ n. a dealer in candles, oil, soap, paint, groceries, etc.

chan·dler·y /chándlǝree/ n. **1** the warehouse or store of a chandler. **2** the goods sold by a chandler.

change /chaynj/ n. & v. ● n. **1 a** the act or an instance of making or becoming different. **b** an alteration or modification (*the change in her expression*). **2 a** money given in exchange for money in larger units or a different currency. **b** money returned as the balance of that given in payment. **c** = SMALL CHANGE. **3** a new experience; variety (*fancied a change; for a change*). **4 a** the substitution of one thing for another; an exchange (*change of scene*). **b** a set of clothes, etc., put on in place of another. **5** (in full **change of life**) colloq. the menopause. **6** (usu. in pl.) the different orders in which a peal of bells can be rung. ● v. **1** tr. & intr. undergo, show, or subject to change; make or become different (*the toupee changed his appearance; changed from an introvert into an extrovert*). **2** tr. **a** take or use another instead of; go from one to another (*change one's socks; changed his doctor; changed trains*). **b** (usu. foll. by *for*) give up or get rid of in exchange (*changed the car for a van*). **3** tr. **a** give or get change in smaller denominations for (*can you change a ten-dollar bill?*). **b** (foll. by *for*) exchange (a sum of money) for (*changed his dollars for pounds*). **4** tr. & intr. put fresh clothes or coverings on (*changed the baby as he was wet; changed into something loose*). **5** tr. (often foll. by *with*) give and receive; exchange (*changed places with him; we changed places*). **6** intr. change trains, etc. (*changed at Grand Central Station*). □ **change color** blanch or flush. **change gear** engage a different gear in a vehicle. **change hands 1** pass to a different owner. **2** substitute one hand for another. **change one's mind** adopt a different opinion or plan. **change of heart** a conversion to a different view. **change over** change from one system or situation to another; effect a changeover. **change step** begin to keep step with the opposite leg when marching, etc. **change the subject** begin talking of something different, esp. to avoid embarrassment. **change one's tune 1** voice a different opinion from that expressed previously. **2** change one's style of language or manner, esp. from an insolent to a respectful tone. □□ **change·ful** adj. **chang·er** n.

change·a·ble /cháynjǝbǝl/ adj. **1** irregular; inconstant. **2** that can change or be changed. □□ **change·a·bil·i·ty** n. **change·a·ble·ness** n. **change·a·bly** adv.

change·less /cháynjlis/ adj. unchanging. □□ **change·less·ly** adv. **change·less·ness** n.

change·ling /cháynjling/ n. a child believed to be substituted for another by stealth, esp. an elf child left by fairies.

change·o·ver /cháynjōvǝr/ n. a change from one system or situation to another.

chan·nel /chánǝl/ n. & v. ● n. **1 a** a length of water wider than a strait, joining two larger areas, esp. seas. **b** (**the Channel**) the English Channel between Britain and France. **2** a medium of communication; an agency for conveying information (*through the usual channels*). **3** Broadcasting **a** a band of frequencies used in radio and television transmission, esp. as used by a particular station. **b** a service or station using this. **4** the course in which anything moves; a direction. **5 a** a natural or artificial hollow bed of water. **b** the navigable part of a waterway. **6** a tubular passage for liquid. **7** Electronics a lengthwise strip on recording tape, etc. **8** a groove or a flute, esp. in a column. ● v.tr. (**channeled, channeling**; esp. Brit. **channelled, channelling**) **1** guide; direct (*channeled them through customs*). **2** form channels in; groove.

chan·nel·ize /chánǝlīz/ v.tr. convey in, or as if in, a channel; guide.

chant /chant/ n. & v. ● n. **1 a** a spoken singsong phrase, esp. one performed in unison by a crowd, etc. **b** a repetitious singsong way of speaking. **2** Mus. **a** a short musical passage in two or more phrases used for singing unmetrical words, e.g., psalms, canticles. **b** the psalm or canticle so sung. **c** a song, esp. monotonous or repetitive. ● v.tr. & intr. **1** talk or repeat monotonously (*a crowd chanting slogans*). **2** sing or intone (a psalm, etc.).

chant·er /chántǝr/ n. Mus. the melody pipe, with finger holes, of a bagpipe. ▷ BAGPIPE

chan·te·relle /chántǝrél/ n. ◀ an edible fungus, *Cantharellus cibarius*, with a yellow, funnel-shaped cap and smelling of apricots.

chan·teuse /shaantőz/ n. a female singer of popular songs.

chant·ey /shántee, chán-/ n. (also **chant·y, shanty**) (pl. **chanteys, -ies**) (in full **sea chantey**) a song with alternating solo and chorus, of a kind orig. sung by sailors while hauling ropes, etc.

CHANTERELLE:
COMMON
CHANTERELLE
(*Cantharellus cibarius*)

Chan·til·ly /shantílee, shón-teeyée/ n. **1** a delicate kind of bobbin lace. **2** sweetened or flavored whipped cream.

chan·try /chántree/ n. (pl. **-ies**) **1** an endowment for a priest or priests to celebrate Masses for the founder's soul. **2** the priests, chapel, altar, etc., endowed.

chant·y var. of CHANTEY.

Cha·nuk·kah var. of HANUKKAH.

cha·os /káyos/ n. **1** utter confusion. **2** the formless matter supposed to have existed before the creation of the universe. □□ **cha·ot·ic** /kayótik/ adj. **cha·ot·i·cal·ly** adv.

cha·os the·o·ry n. the branch of science concerned with the behavior of complex systems in which tiny changes can have major effects, and which therefore seem unpredictable.

chap[1] /chap/ v. & n. ● v. (**chapped, chapping**) **1** intr. (esp. of the skin; also of dry ground, etc.) crack in fissures, esp. because of exposure and dryness. **2** tr. (of the wind, cold, etc.) cause to chap. ● n. (usu. in pl.) **1** a crack in the skin. **2** an open seam.

chap[2] /chap/ n. esp. Brit. colloq. a man; a boy; a fellow.

chap. abbr. chapter.

chap·ar·ral /shápǝrál, cháp-/ n. dense, tangled brushwood; undergrowth.

cha·pa·ti /chǝpáatee/ n. (also **cha·pat·ti**) (pl. **-is**) a flat thin cake of unleavened whole-wheat bread.

chape /chayp/ n. the back piece of a buckle attaching it to a strap, etc.

chap·el /chápǝl/ n. **1 a** a place for private Christian worship in a large church or esp. a cathedral, with its own altar and dedication. ▷ CATHEDRAL. **b** a place of Christian worship attached to a private house or institution. **2** a building or room in which funeral services are held. **3** Brit. **a** a place of worship for certain Protestant denominations. **4** an Anglican church subordinate to a parish church. **5** the members or branch of a printers' union.

chap·er·on /shápərōn/ *n. & v.* (also **chap·er·one**) ● *n.* **1** a person, esp. an older woman, who ensures propriety by accompanying a young unmarried woman on social occasions. **2** a person who takes charge of esp. young people in public. ● *v.tr.* act as a chaperon to. □□ **chap·er·on·age** /shápərōnij/ *n.*

chap·lain /cháplin/ *n.* a member of the clergy attached to a private chapel, institution, ship, regiment, etc. □□ **chap·lain·cy** *n.* (*pl.* **-ies**)

chap·let /cháplit/ *n.* **1** a garland or circlet for the head. **2** a string of 55 beads (one-third of the rosary number) for counting prayers, or as a necklace. **3** a bead molding. □□ **chap·let·ed** *adj.*

chaps /chaps/ *n.pl.* ▼ a cowboy's leather leggings worn over the trousers as protection for the front of the legs.

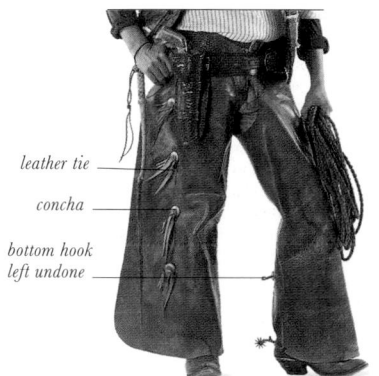

leather tie

concha

*bottom hook
left undone*

CHAPS: TEXAN BATWING CHAPS

chap·ter /cháptər/ *n.* **1** a main division of a book. **2** a period of time (in a person's life, a nation's history, etc.). **3** a series or sequence (*a chapter of misfortunes*). **4 a** the canons of a cathedral or other religious community or knightly order. **b** a meeting of these. **5** *Brit.* an Act of Parliament numbered as part of a session's proceedings. **6** a local branch of a society. □ **chapter and verse** an exact reference or authority.

chap·ter house *n.* a building used for the meetings of a chapter. ▷ MONASTERY

char¹ /chaar/ *v.tr. & intr.* (**charred**, **charring**) **1** make or become black by burning, scorch. **2** burn or be burned to charcoal.

char² /chaar/ *n. & v. Brit. colloq.* ● *n.* = CHARWOMAN. ● *v.intr.* (**charred**, **charring**) work as a charwoman.

char³ /chaar/ *n.* (also **cha** /chaa/) *Brit. sl.* tea.

char⁴ /chaar/ *n.* (also **charr**) (*pl.* same) ▼ any small troutlike fish of the genus *Salvelinus*.

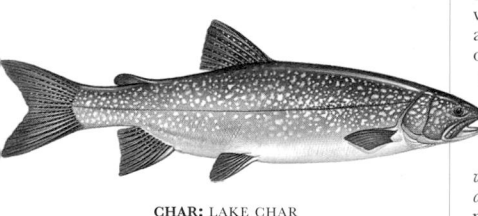

CHAR: LAKE CHAR
(*Salvelinus namaycush*)

char·a·banc /shárəbang/ *n. Brit. hist.* ▼ an early form of tour bus.

CHARABANC: 1926 MODEL

char·ac·ter /káriktər/ *n. & v.* ● *n.* **1** the collective qualities or characteristics, esp. mental and moral, that distinguish a person or thing. **2 a** moral strength (*has a weak character*). **b** reputation, esp. good reputation. **3 a** a person in a novel, play, etc. **b** a part played by an actor; a role. **4** *colloq.* a person, esp. an eccentric or outstanding individual (*he's a real character*). **5 a** a printed or written letter, symbol, or distinctive mark (*Chinese characters*). **b** *Computing* any of a group of symbols representing a letter, etc. **6** a written description of a person's qualities; a testimonial. **7** a characteristic (esp. of a biological species). ● *v.tr. archaic* inscribe; describe. □ **in** (or **out of**) **character** consistent (or inconsistent) with a person's character. □□ **char·ac·ter·ful** *adj.* **char·ac·ter·ful·ly** *adv.* **char·ac·ter·less** *adj.*

char·ac·ter as·sas·si·na·tion *n.* a malicious attempt to harm or destroy a person's good reputation.

char·ac·ter·is·tic /káriktərístik/ *adj. & n.* ● *adj.* typical; distinctive (*with characteristic expertise*). ● *n.* **1** a characteristic feature or quality. **2** *Math.* the whole number or integral part of a logarithm. □□ **char·ac·ter·is·ti·cal·ly** *adv.*

char·ac·ter·ize /káriktərīz/ *v.tr.* **1 a** describe the character of. **b** (foll. by *as*) describe as. **2** be characteristic of. **3** impart character to. □□ **char·ac·ter·i·za·tion** *n.*

cha·rade /shəráyd/ *n.* **1 a** (usu. in *pl.*, treated as *sing.*) a game of guessing a word from a written or acted clue given for each syllable and for the whole. **b** one such clue. **2** an absurd pretense.

char·coal /cháarkōl/ *n.* **1 a** an amorphous form of carbon consisting of a porous black residue from partially burned wood, bones, etc. **b** ◄ a piece of this used for drawing. **2** a drawing in charcoal. **3** (in full **charcoal gray**) a dark gray color.

chard /chaard/ *n.* (in full **Swiss chard**) a kind of beet, *Beta vulgaris cicla*, with edible broad, white leafstalks and green leaves. ▷ VEGETABLE

CHARCOAL
STICK AND MARK

Char·don·nay /sháard'náy/ *n.* **1** a variety of white grape used for making champagne and other wines. **2** the vine on which this grape grows. **3** a wine made from Chardonnay grapes.

charge /chaarj/ *v. & n.* ● *v.* **1** *tr.* **a** ask (an amount) as a price (*charges $5 a ticket*). **b** ask (a person) for an amount as a price (*you forgot to charge me*). **2** *tr.* **a** (foll. by *to, up to*) debit the cost of to (a person or account) (*charge it to my account; charge it up to me*). **b** debit (a person or an account) (*bought a new car and charged the company*). **3** *tr.* **a** (often foll. by *with*) accuse (of an offense) (*charged him with theft*). **b** (foll. by *that* + clause) make an accusation that. **4** *tr.* (foll. by *to* + infin.) instruct or urge. **5** (foll. by *with*) **a** *tr.* entrust with. **b** *refl.* undertake. **6 a** *intr.* make a rushing attack; rush headlong. **b** *tr.* make a rushing attack on; throw oneself against. **7** *tr.* (often foll. by *up*) **a** give an electric charge to (a body). **b** store energy in (a battery). **8** *tr.* (often foll. by *with*) load or fill (a vessel, gun, etc.) to the full or proper extent. **9** *tr.* (usu. as **charged** *adj.*) **a** (foll. by *with*) saturated with (*air charged with vapor*). **b** (usu. foll. by *with*) pervaded (with strong feelings, etc.) (*atmosphere charged with emotion; a charged atmosphere*). ● *n.* **1 a** a price asked for goods or services. **b** a financial liability or commitment. **2** an accusation, esp. against a prisoner brought to trial. **3 a** a task, duty, or commission. **b** care; custody; responsible possession. **c** a person or thing entrusted; a minister's congregation. **4 a** an impetuous rush or attack, esp. in a battle. **b** the signal for this. **5** the appropriate amount of material to be put into a receptacle, mechanism, etc., at one time, esp. of explosive for a gun. **6 a** a property of matter that is a consequence of the interaction between its constituent particles and exists in a positive or negative form, causing electrical phenomena. **b** the quantity of this carried by a body. **c** energy stored chemically for conversion into electricity. ▷ BATTERY. **d** the process of charging a battery. **7** an exhortation; directions; orders. **8** a burden or load. **9** *Heraldry* a device; a bearing. □ **free of charge** gratis. **give a person in charge** *Brit.* hand a person over to the police. **in charge** having command. **return to the charge** begin again, esp. in argument. **take charge** (often foll. by *of*) assume control or direction. □□ **charge·a·ble** *adj.*

charge ac·count *n.* a credit account at a store, etc.

charge card *n.* a credit card for which the account must be paid in full when a statement is issued.

char·gé d'af·faires /shaarzháy dafáir/ *n.* (also **chargé**) (*pl.* **chargés** *pronunc.* same) **1** an ambassador's deputy. **2** an envoy to a minor country.

charg·er¹ /cháarjər/ *n.* **1 a** a cavalry horse. **b** *poet.* any horse. **2** an apparatus for charging a battery.

charg·er² /cháarjər/ *n.* a large, flat dish; a platter.

char·grill /cháargril/ *v.tr.* broil (food, typically meat or fish) quickly at a very high heat.

char·i·ot /cháreeət/ *n. & v.* ● *n.* **1** *hist.* **a** ▼ a two-wheeled vehicle drawn by horses, used in ancient warfare and racing. **b** a four-wheeled carriage with back seats only. **2** *poet.* a stately or triumphal vehicle. ● *v.tr. literary* convey in or as in a chariot.

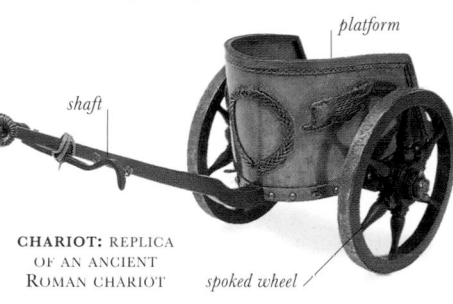

platform

shaft

spoked wheel

CHARIOT: REPLICA
OF AN ANCIENT
ROMAN CHARIOT

char·i·ot·eer /cháreeəteer/ *n.* a chariot driver.

cha·ris·ma /kərízmə/ *n.* (*pl.* **charismata** /-mətə/) the ability to inspire followers with devotion and enthusiasm.

char·is·mat·ic /kárizmátik/ *adj.* **1** having charisma; inspiring enthusiasm. **2** (of Christian worship) characterized by spontaneity, ecstatic utterances, etc. □□ **char·is·mat·i·cal·ly** *adv.*

char·is·mat·ic move·ment *n.* a Christian movement emphasizing ecstatic religious experience and gifts of healing, speaking in tongues, etc.

char·i·ta·ble /cháritəbəl/ *adj.* **1** generous in giving to those in need. **2** of, relating to, or connected with a charity or charities. **3** apt to judge favorably of persons, acts, and motives. □□ **char·i·ta·ble·ness** *n.* **char·i·ta·bly** *adv.*

char·i·ty /cháritee/ *n.* (*pl.* **-ies**) **1 a** a giving voluntarily to those in need; almsgiving. **b** the help, esp. money, so given. **2** an institution or organization for helping those in need. **3 a** a kindness; benevolence. **b** tolerance in judging others. **c** love of one's fellow men.

cha·ri·va·ri /shívəree/ *n.* (also **shivaree**) **1** a serenade of banging saucepans, etc., to a newly married couple. **2** a medley of sounds; a hubbub.

char·la·dy /cháarlaydee/ *n.* (*pl.* **-ies**) = CHARWOMAN.

char·la·tan /sháarlətən/ *n.* a person falsely claiming a special knowledge or skill. □□ **char·la·tan·ism** *n.* **char·la·tan·ry** *n.*

Charles·ton /cháarlstən/ *n. & v.* ● *n.* a lively American dance of the 1920s with side kicks from the knee. ● *v.intr.* dance the Charleston.

char·ley horse /cháarlee/ *n. sl.* stiffness or cramp in an arm or leg.

char·lock /cháarlok/ *n.* a wild mustard, *Sinapis arvensis*, with yellow flowers.

char·lotte /sháarlət/ *n.* a dessert made of stewed fruit with a casing or layers or covering of bread, sponge cake, cookies, or breadcrumbs (*apple charlotte*).

charm /chaarm/ *n. & v.* ● *n.* **1 a** the power or quality of giving delight or arousing admiration. **b** fascination; attractiveness. **c** (usu. in *pl.*) an attractive or enticing quality. **2** a trinket on a bracelet, etc. **3 a** an

C

C

CHÂTEAU

During the 15th century, French society became less turbulent, allowing noblemen to design homes more for comfort and display than fortification. They converted, or had built, châteaus with large windows and luxurious state rooms. Defensive features, such as moats, were often maintained, but these served only as decoration.

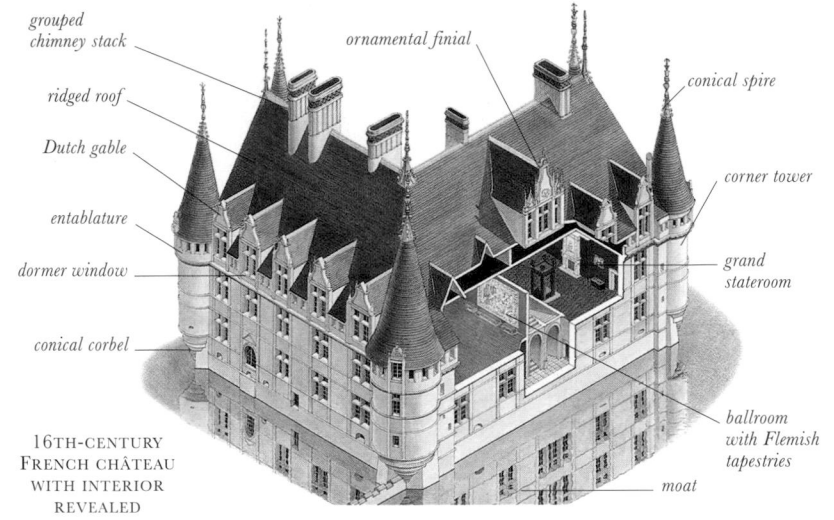

grouped chimney stack

ridged roof

Dutch gable

entablature

dormer window

conical corbel

ornamental finial

conical spire

corner tower

grand stateroom

ballroom with Flemish tapestries

moat

16TH-CENTURY FRENCH CHÂTEAU WITH INTERIOR REVEALED

object, act, or word(s) supposedly having occult or magic power; a spell. **b** a thing worn to avert evil, etc.; an amulet. **4** *Physics* a property of matter manifested by some elementary particles. ● *v.tr.* **1** delight; captivate (*charmed by the performance*). **2** influence or protect as if by magic (*leads a charmed life*). **3 a** gain by charm (*charmed agreement out of him*). **b** influence by charm (*charmed her into consenting*). **4** cast a spell on; bewitch. □ **like a charm** perfectly; wonderfully (*worked like a charm; fits like a charm*). □□ **charm·er** *n.*

charm·ing /chaárming/ *adj.* **1** delightful; attractive; pleasing. **2** (often as *int.*) *iron.* expressing displeasure or disapproval. □□ **charm·ing·ly** *adv.*

charm·less /chaármlis/ *adj.* lacking charm; unattractive. □□ **charm·less·ly** *adv.* **charm·less·ness** *n.*

char·nel house /chaárnəlhows/ *n.* a house or vault in which dead bodies or bones are piled.

char·poy /chaárpoy/ *n. Ind.* a light bedstead.

charr var. of CHAR⁴.

chart /chaart/ *n. & v.* ● *n.* **1** a geographical map or plan, esp. for navigation by sea or air. **2** a sheet of information in the form of a table, graph, or diagram. **3** (usu. in *pl.*) *colloq.* a listing of the currently most popular music recordings. ● *v.tr.* make a chart of; map.

chart·bust·er /chaártbustər/ *n. colloq.* a best-selling popular song, recording, etc.

char·ter /chaártər/ *n. & v.* ● *n.* **1 a** a written grant of rights, by the sovereign or legislature, esp. the creation of a borough, company, university, etc. **b** a written constitution or description of an organization's functions, etc. **2** a contract to hire an aircraft, ship, etc., for a special purpose. ● *v.tr.* **1** grant a charter to. **2** hire (an aircraft, ship, etc.). □□ **char·ter·er** *n.*

char·ter mem·ber *n.* an original member of a society, corporation, etc.

Chart·ism /chaártizəm/ *n. hist.* the principles of the UK Parliamentary reform movement of 1837–48. □□ **Chart·ist** *n.*

char·treuse /shaartrőőz, -trőős/ *n.* **1** (**Chartreuse**) a pale green or yellow liqueur of brandy and aromatic herbs, etc. **2** the pale yellow or pale green color of this.

char·wom·an /chaárwoŏmən/ *n.* (*pl.* **-women**) a woman employed as a cleaner in houses or offices.

char·y /cháiree/ *adj.* (**charier**, **chariest**) **1** cautious; wary (*chary of employing such people*). **2** sparing; ungenerous (*chary of giving praise*). **3** shy. □□ **char·i·ly** *adv.* **char·i·ness** *n.*

Cha·ryb·dis see SCYLLA AND CHARYBDIS.

chase¹ /chays/ *v. & n.* ● *v.* **1** *tr.* pursue in order to catch. **2** *tr.* (foll. by *from, out of, to*, etc.) drive. **3** *intr.* **a** (foll. by *after*) hurry in pursuit of (a person). **b** (foll. by *around*, etc.) *colloq.* act or move about hurriedly. **4** *tr. Brit.* (usu. foll. by *up*) *colloq.* pursue (overdue work, payment, etc., or the person responsible for it). **5** *tr. colloq.* **a** try to attain. **b** court persistently and openly. ● *n.* **1** pursuit. **2** *Brit.* unenclosed hunting land. **3** (prec. by *the*) hunting, esp. as a sport. **4** = STEEPLECHASE.

chase² /chays/ *v.tr.* emboss or engrave (metal).

chase³ /chays/ *n.* **1** the part of a gun enclosing the bore. **2** a trench or groove cut to receive a pipe, etc.

chas·er /cháysər/ *n.* **1** a person or thing that chases. **2** a horse for steeplechasing. **3** *colloq.* a drink taken after another of a different kind.

chasm /kázəm/ *n.* **1** a deep fissure or opening in the earth, rock, etc. **2** a wide difference of feeling, interests, etc.; a gulf. **3** *archaic* a hiatus.

chas·sé /shasáy/ *n. & v.* ● *n.* a gliding step in dancing. ● *v.intr.* (**chasséd**, **chasséing**) make this step.

chas·sis /shásee, chás-/ *n.* (*pl.* same /-siz/) **1** the base frame of a motor vehicle, carriage, etc. **2** a frame to carry radio, etc., components.

chaste /chayst/ *adj.* **1** abstaining from extramarital, or from all, sexual intercourse. **2** (of behavior, speech, etc.) pure; virtuous; decent. □□ **chaste·ly** *adv.* **chaste·ness** *n.*

chas·ten /cháysən/ *v.tr.* **1** (esp. as **chastening**, **chastened** *adjs.*) subdue; restrain (*a chastening experience; chastened by his failure*). **2** discipline; punish. **3** moderate. □□ **chas·ten·er** *n.*

chas·tise /chastíz, chástīz/ *v.tr.* **1** rebuke or reprimand severely. **2** punish, esp. by beating. □□ **chas·tise·ment** *n.* **chas·tis·er** *n.*

chas·ti·ty /chástitee/ *n.* **1** being chaste. **2** sexual abstinence; virginity. **3** simplicity of style or taste.

chas·ti·ty belt *n. hist.* a garment designed to prevent a woman from having sexual intercourse.

chas·u·ble /cházəbəl, cházyə-, chás-/ *n.* a loose, sleeveless, often ornate outer vestment worn by a priest celebrating Mass or the Eucharist. ▷ VESTMENT

chat /chat/ *v. & n.* ● *v.intr.* (**chatted**, **chatting**) talk in a light familiar way. ● *n.* **1** informal conversation or talk. **2** an instance of this. □ **chat up** *Brit. colloq.* chat to, esp. flirtatiously or with an ulterior motive.

châ·teau /shatố/ *n.* (*pl.* **châteaus** or **châteaux** /-tōz/) ◀ a large French country house or castle, often giving its name to wine made in its neighborhood.

cha·teau·bri·and /shatôbree-ón/ *n.* a thick fillet of beef steak usu. served with a béarnaise sauce.

chat·e·laine /shát'layn/ *n.* the mistress of a large house.

chat room *n.* an area on the Internet where users can communicate.

chat·tel /chát'l/ *n.* (usu. in *pl.*) a moveable possession; any possession or piece of property other than real estate or a freehold. □ **goods and chattels** personal possessions.

chat·ter /chátər/ *v. & n.* ● *v.intr.* **1** talk quickly, incessantly, trivially, or indiscreetly. **2** (of a bird) emit short, quick notes. **3** (of the teeth) click repeatedly together (usu. from cold). ● *n.* chattering talk or sounds. □□ **chat·ter·er** *n.* **chat·ter·y** *adj.*

chat·ter·box /chátərboks/ *n.* a talkative person.

chat·ty /chátee/ *adj.* (**chattier**, **chattiest**) **1** fond of chatting; talkative. **2** resembling chat; informal and lively (*a chatty letter*). □□ **chat·ti·ly** *adv.* **chat·ti·ness** *n.*

Chau·ce·ri·an /chawseéreeən/ *adj. & n.* ● *adj.* of or relating to the English poet Chaucer (d. 1400) or his style. ● *n.* a student of Chaucer.

chaud·froid /shōfrwaá/ *n.* a dish of cold cooked meat or fish in jelly or sauce.

chauf·feur /shốfər, -főr/ *n. & v.* ● *n.* (*fem.* **chauffeuse** /-főz/) a person employed to drive a private or rented automobile or limousine. ● *v.tr.* drive (a car or a person) as a chauffeur.

chau·tau·qua /shətáwkwə, chə-/ *n.* (also **Chautau·qua**) a cultural and educational program of lectures, performances, etc., usu. held outdoors in the summer.

chau·vin·ism /shốvinizəm/ *n.* **1** exaggerated or aggressive patriotism. **2** excessive or prejudiced support or loyalty for one's cause or group or sex (*male chauvinism*).

chau·vin·ist /shốvinist/ *n.* **1** a person exhibiting chauvinism. **2** (in full **male chauvinist**) a man showing excessive loyalty to men and prejudice against women. □□ **chau·vin·is·tic** /-nístik/ *adj.* **chau·vin·is·ti·cal·ly** /-nístikəlee/ *adv.*

Ch.E. *abbr.* chemical engineer.

cheap /cheep/ *adj. & adv.* ● *adj.* **1** low in price; worth more than its cost (*a cheap vacation; cheap labor*). **2** charging low prices; offering good value (*a cheap restaurant*). **3** of poor quality; inferior (*cheap housing*). **4 a** costing little effort or acquired by discreditable means and hence of little worth (*cheap popularity; a cheap joke*). **b** contemptible; despicable (*a cheap criminal*). ● *adv.* cheaply (*got it cheap*). □ **feel cheap** feel ashamed or contemptible. **on the cheap** cheaply. □□ **cheap·ish** *adj.* **cheap·ly** *adv.* **cheap·ness** *n.*

cheap·en /cheépən/ *v.tr. & intr.* make or become cheap or cheaper; depreciate; degrade.

cheap·skate /cheépskayt/ *n. colloq.* a stingy person.

cheat /cheet/ *v. & n.* ● *v.* **1** *tr.* **a** (often foll. by *into, out of*) deceive or trick (*cheated into parting with his savings*). **b** (foll. by *of*) deprive of (*cheated of a chance to reply*). **2** *intr.* gain unfair advantage by deception or breaking rules, esp. in a game or examination. **3** *tr.* avoid (something undesirable) by luck or skill (*cheated the bad weather*). **4** *tr. archaic* divert attention from; beguile (time, tedium, etc.). ● *n.* **1** a person who cheats. **2** a trick, fraud, or deception. **3** an act of cheating. □ **cheat on** *colloq.* be sexually unfaithful to. □□ **cheat·ing·ly** *adv.*

cheat·er /cheétər/ *n.* **1** a person who cheats. **2** (in *pl.*) *sl.* eyeglasses.

check¹ /chek/ *v., n., & int.* ● *v.* **1** *tr.* (also *absol.*) **a** examine the accuracy, quality, or condition of. **b** (often foll. by *that* + clause) make sure; verify; establish to one's satisfaction (*checked the train times*).

2 *tr.* **a** stop or slow the motion of; curb; restrain (*progress was checked by bad weather*). **b** *colloq.* find fault with. **3** *tr. Chess* move a piece into a position that directly threatens (the opposing king). **4** *intr.* agree or correspond when compared. **5** *tr.* mark with a check mark, etc. **6** *tr.* deposit (luggage, etc.) for storage or dispatch. **7** *intr.* (of hounds) pause to ensure or regain scent. ● *n.* **1** a means or act of testing or ensuring accuracy, quality, satisfactory condition, etc. **2 a** a stopping or slowing of motion; a restraint on action. **b** a rebuff or rebuke. **c** a person or thing that restrains. **3** *Chess* (also as *int.*) **a** the exposure of a king to direct attack from an opposing piece. **b** an announcement of this by the attacking player. **4** a bill in a restaurant. **5** a token of identification for left luggage, etc. **6** *Cards* a counter used in various games, esp. a poker chip. **7** a temporary loss of the scent in hunting. **8** a flaw in lumber. **9** = CHECK MARK. ● *int.* expressing assent or agreement. □ **check in 1** arrive or register at a hotel, airport, etc. **2** record the arrival of. **check into** register one's arrival at (a hotel, etc.). **check off** mark on a list, etc., as having been examined or dealt with. **check on** examine carefully or in detail; ascertain the truth about; keep a watch on (a person, work done, etc.). **check out 1** (often foll. by *of*) leave a hotel, etc., with due formalities. **2** *colloq.* investigate; examine for authenticity or suitability. **check over** examine for errors; verify. **check through** inspect or examine exhaustively; verify successive items of. **check up** ascertain; verify; make sure. **check up on** = *check on.* **in check** under control; restrained. □□ **check·a·ble** *adj.*

check² /chek/ *n.* **1** a pattern of small squares. **2** fabric having this pattern.

check³ /chek/ *n.* (*Brit.* **cheque**) **1** a written order to a bank to pay the stated sum from the drawer's account. **2** the printed form on which such an order is written.

check·book /chékbŏŏk/ *n.* a book of blank checks with a register for recording checks written.

checked /chekt/ *adj.* having a pattern of small squares.

check·er¹ /chékər/ *n.* **1** a person or thing that verifies or examines, esp. in a factory, etc. **2** a cashier in a supermarket, etc.

check·er² /chékər/ *n. & v.* (*Brit.* **chequer**) ● *n.* **1** (often in *pl.*) a pattern of squares often alternately colored. **2 a** (in *pl.*) a game for two played with 12 pieces each on a checkerboard. **b** each of the usu. red or black disk-shaped playing pieces in a game of checkers. ● *v.tr.* **1** mark with checkers. **2** variegate; break the uniformity of. **3** (as **checkered** *adj.*) with varied fortunes (*a checkered career*).

check·er·ber·ry /chékərberee/ *n.* (*pl.* **-ies**) **1** a wintergreen, *Gaultheria procumbens.* **2** the fruit of this plant.

check·er·board /chékərbawrd/ *n.* **1** a checkered board, identical to a chessboard, used in the game of checkers. **2** a pattern or design resembling it.

check·ing ac·count /chéking/ *n.* an account at a bank against which checks can be drawn by the account depositor.

check·list /chéklist/ *n.* a list for reference and verification.

check mark *n.* a mark (✓) to denote correctness, check items, etc.

check·mate /chékmayt/ *n. & v.* ● *n.* **1** (also as *int.*) *Chess* a check from which a king cannot escape. **b** an announcement of this. **2** a final defeat or deadlock. ● *v.tr.* **1** *Chess* put into checkmate. **2** defeat; frustrate.

check·out /chékowt/ *n.* **1** an act of checking out. **2** a point at which goods are paid for in a supermarket, etc.

check·point /chékpoynt/ *n.* a place, esp. a barrier or manned entrance, where documents, vehicles, etc., are inspected.

check·rein /chékrayn/ *n.* a rein attaching one horse's rein to another's bit, or preventing a horse from lowering its head.

CHEESE

Cheese is made by curdling milk or cream with rennet or lactic acid. The solid curds are then removed, drained, and put into molds; sometimes a bacterial culture is added. The nature of the finished product is greatly influenced by the duration of the ripening period, during which the characteristic flavor and texture develop, and also by the type of milk or cream used – whether whole or skim; whether cow's milk, goat's milk, etc. Blue-veined cheeses derive their color from a particular mold.

C

EXAMPLES OF HARD CHEESES

JARLSBERG   PARMESAN   GRUYÈRE   EMMENTAL   TRADITIONAL CHEDDAR   DOUBLE GLOUCESTER

EXAMPLES OF SOFT CHEESES

MONTEREY JACK   BRIE   LIVAROT   WISCONSIN BRICK   CAMEMBERT

EXAMPLES OF BLUE CHEESES

ROQUEFORT   STILTON   DANISH BLUE   GORGONZOLA   BRESSE BLEU

GOAT OR SHEEP CHEESES

FETA   BUCHERON   BUCHETTE D'ANJOU   CROTTIN DE CHAVIGNOL   PYRENEES

check·room /chékrŏŏm, -rŏŏm/ *n.* **1** a cloakroom in a hotel or theater. **2** an office for left luggage, etc.

check·up /chékup/ *n.* a thorough (esp. medical) examination.

ched·dar /chédər/ *n.* (in full **cheddar cheese**) a kind of firm smooth cheese orig. made in Cheddar in southern England. ▷ CHEESE

cheek /cheek/ *n. & v.* ● *n.* **1 a** the side of the face below the eye. **b** the side wall of the mouth. **2** esp. *Brit.* impertinence; cool confidence (*had the cheek to ask for more*). **3** *sl.* either buttock. **4 a** either of the side posts of a door, etc. **b** either of the sidepieces of various parts of machines arranged in lateral pairs. ● *v.tr.* speak impertinently to. □ **cheek by jowl** close together; intimate. **turn the other cheek** accept attack, etc., meekly; refuse to retaliate.

cheek·bone /cheekbōn/ *n.* the bone below the eye.

cheek·y /cheekee/ *adj.* (**cheekier, cheekiest**) impertinent; impudent. □□ **cheek·i·ly** *adv.* **cheek·i·ness** *n.*

cheep /cheep/ *n. & v.* ● *n.* the weak shrill cry of a young bird. ● *v.intr.* make such a cry.

cheer /cheer/ *n. & v.* ● *n.* **1** a shout of encouragement or applause. **2** mood; disposition (*full of good cheer*). **3** cheerfulness; joy. **4** (in *pl.*; as *int.*) *colloq.* **a** expressing good wishes on parting. **b** expressing good wishes before drinking. **c** expressing gratitude. ● *v.* **1** *tr.* **a** applaud with shouts. **b** (usu. foll. by *on*) urge or encourage with shouts. **2** *intr.* shout for joy. **3** *tr.* gladden; comfort. □ **cheer up** make or become less depressed.

cheer·ful /cheerfŏŏl/ *adj.* **1** in good spirits; noticeably happy (*a cheerful disposition*). **2** bright; pleasant (*a cheerful room*). **3** willing; not reluctant. □□ **cheer·ful·ly** *adv.* **cheer·ful·ness** *n.*

cheer·i·o /cheereeő/ *int. Brit. colloq.* expressing good wishes on parting or before drinking.

cheer·lead·er /cheerleedər/ *n.* a person who leads cheers of applause, etc., esp. at a sports event.

cheer·less /cheerlis/ *adj.* gloomy; dreary; miserable. □□ **cheer·less·ly** *adv.* **cheer·less·ness** *n.*

cheer·y /cheeree/ *adj.* (**cheerier, cheeriest**) lively; in good spirits; genial; cheering. □□ **cheer·i·ly** *adv.* **cheer·i·ness** *n.*

cheese¹ /cheez/ *n.* **1 a** ▲ a food made from the pressed curds of milk. **b** a complete cake of this with rind. **2** *Brit.* a conserve having the consistency of soft cheese (*lemon cheese*).

C

cheese² /cheez/ *v.tr. Brit. sl.* (as **cheesed** *adj.*) (often foll. by *off*) bored; fed up. □ **cheese it 1** look out. **2** run away.

cheese³ /cheez/ *n.* (also **big cheese**) *sl.* an important person.

cheese·board /cheezbawrd/ *n.* **1** a board from which cheese is served. **2** a selection of cheeses.

cheese·burg·er /cheezbərgər/ *n.* a hamburger with cheese on it.

cheese·cake /cheezkayk/ *n.* **1** a rich dessert cake made with cream cheese, etc. **2** *sl.* the portrayal of women in a sexually attractive manner.

cheese·cloth /cheezklawth, -kloth/ *n.* thin loosely woven cloth, used orig. for wrapping cheese.

cheese·mon·ger /cheezmunggər, -monggər/ *n. Brit.* a dealer in cheese, butter, etc.

cheese·par·ing /cheezpairing/ *adj. & n.* ● *adj.* stingy. ● *n.* stinginess.

chees·y /cheezee/ *adj.* (**cheesier, cheesiest**) **1** like cheese in taste, smell, appearance, etc. **2** *sl.* inferior; cheap and nasty. □□ **chees·i·ness** *n.*

chee·tah /cheetə/ *n.* a swift-running feline, *Acinonyx jubatus*, with a leopardlike spotted coat.

chef /shef/ *n.* a cook, esp. the chief cook in a restaurant, etc.

chef d'oeu·vre /shaydővrə/ *n.* (*pl.* **chefs d'oeuvre** *pronunc.* same) a masterpiece.

cheiro- *comb. form* var. of CHIRO-.

che·la¹ /keelə/ *n.* (*pl.* **chelae** /-lee/) a prehensile claw of crabs, lobsters, scorpions, etc.

che·la² /cháylə/ *n.* **1** (in esoteric Buddhism) a novice qualifying for initiation. **2** a disciple; a pupil.

che·late /keelayt/ *n. & adj.* ● *n. Chem.* a usu. organometallic compound containing a bonded ring of atoms including a metal atom. ● *adj.* **1** *Chem.* of a chelate. **2** *Zool. & Anat.* of or having chelae.

che·lo·ni·an /kilőneeən/ *n. & adj.* ● *n.* ▼ any reptile of the order Chelonia, including turtles, terrapins, and tortoises, having a shell of bony plates covered with horny scales. ● *adj.* of or relating to this order.

chem. *abbr.* **1** chemical. **2** chemist. **3** chemistry.

chemi- *comb. form* var. of CHEMO-.

chem·i·cal /kémikəl/ *adj. & n.* ● *adj.* of, made by, or employing chemistry or chemicals. ● *n.* a substance obtained or used in chemistry. □□ **chem·i·cal·ly** *adv.*

chem·i·cal en·gi·neer·ing *n.* the design, manufacture, and operation of industrial chemical plants.

chem·i·cal war·fare *n.* warfare using poison gas and other chemicals.

chemico- /kémikō/ *comb. form* chemical; chemical and (*chemico-physical*).

chem·i·lum·i·nes·cence /kémilőőminésəns/ *n.* the emission of light during a chemical reaction. □□ **chem·i·lu·mi·nes·cent** /-nésənt/ *adj.*

chem·in de fer /shəmáɴ də fáir/ *n.* a form of baccarat.

che·mise /shəmeéz/ *n. hist.* a woman's loose-fitting undergarment or dress hanging straight from the shoulders.

chem·i·sorp·tion /kémisáwrpshən/ *n.* adsorption by chemical bonding.

chem·ist /kémist/ *n.* **1** a person practicing or trained in chemistry. **2** *Brit.* **a** a dealer in medicinal drugs, usu. also selling other medical goods and toiletries. **b** an authorized dispenser of medicines.

chem·is·try /kémistree/ *n.* (*pl.* **-ies**) **1** the study of the elements and the compounds they form and the reactions they undergo. **2** any complex (esp. emotional) change or process (*the chemistry of fear*). **3** *colloq.* a person's personality or temperament.

chemo- /kéemō/ *comb. form* (also **chemi-** /kémee/) chemical.

che·mo·syn·the·sis /kéemōsínthisis/ *n.* the synthesis of organic compounds by energy derived from chemical reactions.

che·mo·ther·a·py /kéemōthérəpee/ *n.* the treatment of disease, esp. cancer, by use of chemical substances. □□ **che·mo·ther·a·pist** *n.*

chem·ur·gy /kémərjee, kimór-/ *n.* the chemical and industrial use of organic raw materials. □□ **chem·ur·gic** /-órjik/ *adj.*

che·nille /shənéel/ *n.* **1** a tufty, velvety cord or yarn, used in trimming furniture, etc. **2** fabric made from this.

cheong·sam /chawngsám/ *n.* a Chinese woman's garment with a high neck and slit skirt.

cheque *Brit.* var. of CHECK³.

chequ·er *Brit.* var. of CHECKER².

cher·ish /chérish/ *v.tr.* **1** protect or tend (a child, etc.) lovingly. **2** hold dear; cling to (hopes, feelings, etc.).

cher·no·zem /chérnəzem, chírnəzyáwm/ *n.* a fertile, black soil rich in humus, found in temperate regions, esp. southern Russia.

Cher·o·kee /chérəkee/ *n. & adj.* ● *n.* **1 a** a N. American people formerly inhabiting much of the southern US. **b** an individual of this people. **2** the language of this people. ● *adj.* of or relating to the Cherokees or their language.

che·root /shərőőt/ *n.* a cigar with both ends open.

cher·ry /chéree/ *n. & adj.* ● *n.* (*pl.* **-ies**) **1 a** a small, soft, round stone fruit. **b** ◄ any of several trees of the genus *Prunus* bearing this or grown for its ornamental flowers. **2** (in full **cherry wood**) the wood of a cherry. ▷ WOOD. **3** *coarse sl.* **a** hymen. **b** virginity. ● *adj.* of a light red color.

cher·ry bran·dy *n.* a dark-red liqueur of brandy in which cherries have been steeped.

cher·ry lau·rel *n. Brit.* a small evergreen tree, *Prunus laurocerasus*, with white flowers and cherrylike fruits.

cher·ry pick·er *n. colloq.* a crane for raising and lowering people.

cher·ry plum *n.* **1** a tree, *Prunus cerasifera*, native to southwestern Asia, with solitary white flowers and red fruits. **2** the fruit of this tree.

cher·ry to·ma·to *n.* a miniature tomato. ▷ TOMATO

cher·so·nese /kársəneez, -nees/ *n.* a peninsula, esp. the Thracian peninsula west of the Hellespont.

chert /chərt/ *n.* a flintlike form of quartz composed of chalcedony. □□ **chert·y** *adj.*

cher·ub /chérəb/ *n.* **1** (*pl.* **cherubim** /-bim/) an angelic being of the second order of the celestial hierarchy. **2** (*pl.* usu. **cherubs**) **a** a representation of a winged child or the head of a winged child. **b** a beautiful or innocent child. □□ **che·ru·bic** /chirőőbik/ *adj.* **che·ru·bi·cal·ly** /chirőőbikəlee/ *adv.*

cher·vil /chárvil/ *n.* ► an umbelliferous plant, *Anthriscus cerefolium*, with small white flowers, used as an herb for flavoring.

Chesh·ire /chéshər/ *n.* (in full **Cheshire cheese**) a kind of firm crumbly cheese, orig. made in Cheshire. □ **like a Cheshire cat** with a broad fixed grin.

chess /ches/ *n.* ▲ a game for two with 16 pieces each, played on a chessboard.

chess·board /chésbawrd/ *n.* a checkered board of 64 squares on which chess and checkers are played. ▷ CHESS

chess·man /chésman, -mən/ *n.* (*pl.* **-men**) a piece used in playing chess. ▷ CHESS

chest /chest/ *n.* **1** a large strong box, esp. for storage or transport, e.g., of blankets, tea, etc. **2 a** the part of a human or animal body enclosed by the ribs. **b** the front surface of the body from neck to waist. **3** a small cabinet for medicines, etc. **4 a** the treasury or financial resources of an institution. **b** the money available from it. □ **get a thing off one's chest** *colloq.* disclose a fact, secret, etc., to relieve one's anxiety about it; say what is on one's mind. **play (one's cards, a thing,** etc.) **close to one's chest** *colloq.* be cautious or secretive about; give nothing away; keep quiet. □□ **-chested** *adj.* (in comb.).

ches·ter·field /chéstərfeeld/ *n.* **1** a sofa with arms and back of the same height and curved outward at the top. **2** (also **Ches·ter·field**) a plain overcoat usu. with a velvet collar.

lanceolate leaf

cherry fruit

CHERRY:
TIBETAN CHERRY
(*Prunus serrula*)

CHERVIL
(*Anthriscus cerefolium*)

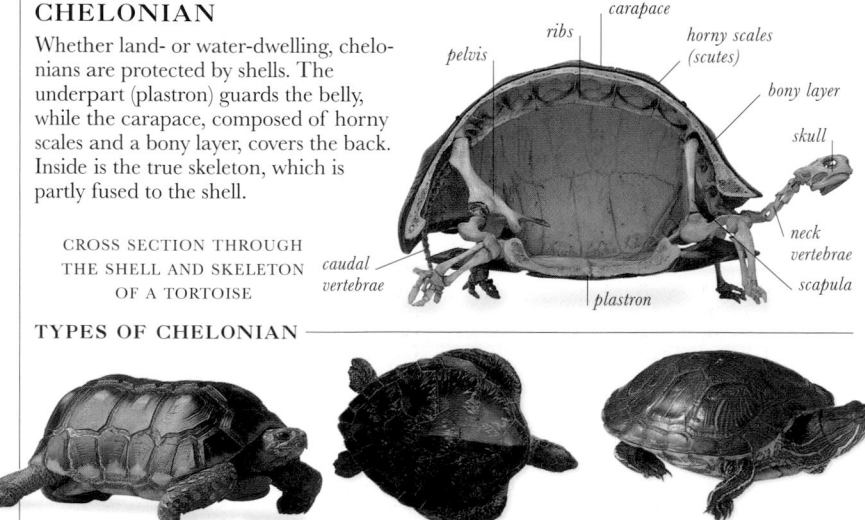

CHELONIAN

Whether land- or water-dwelling, chelonians are protected by shells. The underpart (plastron) guards the belly, while the carapace, composed of horny scales and a bony layer, covers the back. Inside is the true skeleton, which is partly fused to the shell.

carapace
ribs
pelvis
horny scales (scutes)
bony layer
skull
neck vertebrae
scapula
plastron
caudal vertebrae

CROSS SECTION THROUGH THE SHELL AND SKELETON OF A TORTOISE

TYPES OF CHELONIAN

TORTOISES
red-footed tortoise
(*Geochelone carbonaria*)

TURTLES
green turtle
(*Chelonia mydas*)

TERRAPINS
red-eared slider terrapin
(*Pseudemys cripta*)

CHESS

Devised some 1,400 years ago in India or China, chess is an imitation of warfare, with the sole object being to capture the opponent's king. The game is played on a board of 64 squares, with each of the two players having 16 chessmen. These represent different ranks and offices, and each is moved according to a predetermined pattern.

knight   bishop   queen   king   bishop   knight

rook (castle)

row of 8 pawns

square

rook (castle)

16 black chessmen

chessboard

16 white chessmen

CHESSBOARD AND CHESSMEN

---

chest·nut /chésnut/ *n. & adj.* ● *n.* **1 a** a glossy, hard, brown edible nut. ▷ NUT. **b** ▶ the tree *Castanea sativa*, bearing flowers in catkins and nuts enclosed in a spiny fruit. **2** any other tree of the genus *Castanea*, esp. the American chestnut *C. dentata*. **3** ‒ HORSE CHESTNUT. **4** (in full **chestnut wood**) the heavy wood of any chestnut tree. **5** a horse of a reddish-brown or yellowish-brown color. **6** *colloq.* a stale joke or anecdote. **7** a small hard patch on a horse's leg. **8** a reddish-brown color. ● *adj.* of the color chestnut.

chest of draw·ers *n.* a piece of furniture consisting of a set of drawers in a frame.

chest·y /chéstee/ *adj.* (**chestier**, **chestiest**) **1** *colloq.* having a large chest or prominent breasts. **2** *sl.* arrogant. **3** *Brit. colloq.* inclined to or symptomatic of chest disease. □□ **chest·i·ly** *adv.* **chest·i·ness** *n.*

Chet·nik /chétnik/ *n. hist.* a member of a guerrilla force in the Balkans, esp. during World Wars I and II.

che·val glass /shəválglas/ *n.* a tall mirror swung on an upright frame.

chev·a·lier /shévəleér/ *n.* **1 a** a member of certain orders of knighthood, and of modern French orders, as the Legion of Honor. **b** *archaic* or *hist.* a knight. **2** *Brit. hist.* the title of James and Charles Stuart, pretenders to the British throne.

che·vet /shəváy/ *n.* the apsidal end of a church, sometimes with an attached group of apses.

chè·vre /shévrə/ *n.* a variety of goat cheese.

chev·ron /shévrən/ *n.* **1** ▶ a badge in a V shape on the sleeve of a uniform indicating rank or length of service. **2** *Heraldry & Archit.* a bent bar of an inverted V shape. **3** any V-shaped line or stripe.

coarse-toothed leaf margins

green fruit husk

ripe nuts

CHESTNUT: SWEET CHESTNUT (*Castanea sativa*)

chevron

CHEVRON ON A NAPOLEONIC CORPORAL'S UNIFORM

---

chev·ro·tain /shévrətayn/ *n.* (also **chev·ro·tin** /-tin/) any small deerlike animal of the family Tragulidae, native to Africa and SE Asia, having small tusks. Also called **mouse deer.**

chev·y var. of CHIVVY.

chew /choō/ *v. & n.* ● *v.tr.* (also *absol.*) work (food, etc.) between the teeth; crush or indent with the teeth. ● *n.* **1** an act of chewing. **2** something for chewing, esp. a chewy candy. □ **chew the cud** reflect; ruminate. **chew the fat** (or **rag**) *sl.* **1** chat. **2** grumble. **chew on 1** work continuously between the teeth (*chewed on a piece of string*). **2** think about; meditate on. **chew out** *colloq.* reprimand. **chew over 1** discuss; talk over. **2** think about; meditate on. □□ **chew·a·ble** *adj.* **chew·er** *n.*

chew·ing gum *n.* flavored gum, esp. chicle, for chewing.

chew·y /choōee/ *adj.* (**chewier**, **chewiest**) **1** needing much chewing. **2** suitable for chewing. □□ **chew·i·ness** *n.*

Chey·enne /shīán, -én/ *n. & adj.* ● *n.* **1 a** a N. American people formerly living between the Missouri and Arkansas rivers. **b** a member of this people. **2** the language of this people. ● *adj.* of or relating to the Cheyenne or their language.

chez /shay/ *prep.* at the house or home of.

chi /kī/ *n.* the twenty-second letter of the Greek alphabet (X, χ).

Chi·an·ti /keeáantee, keeán-/ *n.* (*pl.* **Chiantis**) a dry, red Italian wine.

chi·a·ro·scu·ro /keeáárəskoōrō/ *n.* **1** the treatment of light and shade in drawing and painting. **2** the use of contrast in literature, etc. **3** (*attrib.*) half-revealed.

chi·as·ma /kīázmə/ *n.* (*pl.* **chiasmata** /-mətə/) *Biol.* the point at which paired chromosomes remain in contact after crossing over during meiosis.

chic /sheek/ *adj. & n.* ● *adj.* (**chicer**, **chicest**) stylish; elegant (in dress or appearance). ● *n.* stylishness; elegance. □□ **chic·ly** *adv.*

chi·cane /shikáyn/ *n. & v.* ● *n.* **1** chicanery. **2** an artificial barrier or obstacle on an automobile racecourse. **3** *Bridge* a hand without trumps, or without

---

cards of one suit. ● *v. archaic* **1** *intr.* use chicanery. **2** *tr.* (usu. foll. by *into, out of,* etc.) cheat (a person).

chi·can·er·y /shikáynəree/ *n.* (*pl.* **-ies**) **1** clever but misleading talk; a false argument. **2** trickery; deception.

Chi·ca·no /chikáanō/ *n.* (*pl.* **-os**; *fem.* **Chicana**, *pl.* **-as**) an American of Mexican origin.

chi·chi /sheéshee/ *adj. & n.* ● *adj.* **1** (of a thing) frilly; showy. **2** (of a person or behavior) fussy; affected. ● *n.* **1** overrefinement; pretentiousness; fussiness. **2** a frilly, showy, or pretentious object.

chick /chik/ *n.* **1** a young bird, esp. one newly hatched. **2** *sl.* a young woman.

chick·a·dee /chíkədee/ *n.* ◀ any of various small birds of the titmouse family, esp. *Parus atricapillus* with a distinctive black crown and throat.

Chick·a·saw /chíkəsaw/ *n.* **1 a** a N. American people native to Mississippi and Alabama. **b** a member of this people. **2** the language of this people.

chick·en /chíkin/ *n., adj., & v.* ● *n.* (*pl.* same or **chickens**) **1** a common breed of domestic fowl. **2 a** a domestic fowl prepared as food. **b** its flesh. **3** *colloq.* a pastime testing courage, usu. recklessly. ● *adj. colloq.* cowardly. ● *v.intr.* (foll. by *out*) *colloq.* withdraw from or fail in some activity through fear or lack of nerve.

chick·en feed *n.* **1** food for poultry. **2** *colloq.* an unimportant amount, esp. of money.

chick·en·heart·ed /chíkinhaartəd/ *adj.* easily frightened; lacking nerve or courage.

chick·en pox *n.* an infectious disease, esp. of children, with a rash of small blisters. (Also called **varicella**).

chick·en wire *n.* a light wire netting with a hexagonal mesh.

chick·pea /chíkpee/ *n.* **1** a leguminous plant, *Cicer arietnum*, with short, swollen pods containing yellow, beaked seeds. **2** ◀ this seed used as a vegetable.

chick·weed /chíkweed/ *n.* any of numerous small plants, esp. *Stellaria media*, a garden weed with slender stems and tiny white flowers.

chic·le /chíkəl/ *n.* the milky juice of the sapodilla tree, used in the manufacture of chewing gum.

chic·o·ry /chíkəree/ *n.* (*pl.* **-ies**) **1** a blue-flowered plant, *Cichorium intybus*, cultivated for its salad leaves and its root. **2** its root, roasted and ground for use with or instead of coffee. **3** = ENDIVE.

chide /chīd/ *v.tr. & intr.* (*past* **chided** or **chid** /chid/; *past part.* **chided** or **chid** or **chidden** /chíd'n/) *archaic* or *literary* scold; rebuke. □□ **chid·er** *n.* **chid·ing·ly** *adv.*

chief /cheef/ *n. & adj.* ● *n.* **1 a** a leader or ruler. **b** the head of a tribe, clan, etc. **2** the head of a department; the highest official. **3** *Heraldry* the upper third of a shield. ● *adj.* (usu. *attrib.*) **1** first in position, importance, influence, etc. (*chief engineer*). **2** prominent; leading. □ **in chief** supreme (*commander in chief*). □□ **chief·dom** *n.*

chief ex·ec·u·tive of·fi·cer *n.* the highest ranking executive in a corporation, organization, etc. ¶ Abbr.: **CEO.**

chief jus·tice *n.* **1** the presiding judge in a court having several judges. **2** (**Chief Justice of the United States**) the presiding judge of the US Supreme Court.

CHICKADEE: BLACK-CAPPED CHICKADEE (*Parus atricapillus*)

CHICKPEA SEEDS (*Cicer arietinum*)

C

C

chief·ly /cheéflee/ *adv.* above all; mainly but not exclusively.

chief of staff *n.* the senior staff officer of a service or command.

chief·tain /cheéftən/ *n.* (*fem.* **chieftainess** /-tən-is/) the leader of a tribe, clan, etc. □□ **chief·tain·cy** /-tənsee/ *n.* (*pl.* **-ies**). **chief·tain·ship** *n.*

chiff·chaff /chifchaf/ *n.* a small European bird, *Phylloscopus collybita*, of the warbler family.

chif·fon /shifón, shifon/ *n. & adj.* ● *n.* a light, diaphanous fabric of silk, nylon, etc. ● *adj.* **1** made of chiffon. **2** (of a pie filling, dessert, etc.) light-textured.

chif·fo·nier /shifəneér/ *n.* **1** a tall chest of drawers. **2** a movable low cupboard with a sideboard top.

chig·ger /chígər/ *n.* **1** = CHIGOE. **2** any harvest mite of the genus *Leptotrombidium*, with parasitic larvae.

chig·non /sheényon, sheenyón/ *n.* a coil or knot of hair worn at the back of the head.

chig·oe /chígō/ *n.* a tropical flea, *Tunga penetrans*, the females of which burrow beneath the skin causing painful sores. Also called **chigger**.

chi·hua·hua /chiwáawə/ *n.* ▼ a very small dog of a smooth-haired, large-eyed breed originating in Mexico.

CHIHUAHUA: LONGHAIRED CHIHUAHUA

chil·blain /chílblayn/ *n.* a painful, itchy swelling of the skin, usu. on a hand, foot, etc., caused by exposure to cold and by poor circulation. □□ **chil·blained** *adj.*

child /chīld/ *n.* (*pl.* **children** /chíldrən/) **1 a** a young human being below the age of puberty. **b** an unborn or newborn human being. **2** one's son or daughter (at any age). **3** (foll. by *of*) a descendant, follower, adherent, or product of (*children of Israel*; *child of God*; *child of nature*). **4** a childish person. □□ **child·less** *adj.* **child·less·ness** *n.*

child a·buse *n.* maltreatment of a child, esp. by physical violence or sexual molestation.

child·bear·ing /chíldbairing/ *n.* the act of giving birth to a child or children.

child·bed /chíldbed/ *n. archaic* = CHILDBIRTH.

child·birth /chíldbərth/ *n.* the act of giving birth to a child.

child care *n.* the care of children, esp. by someone other than a parent, as at a day-care center, etc.

child·hood /chíldhŏŏd/ *n.* the state or period of being a child.

child·ish /chíldish/ *adj.* **1** of, like, or proper to a child. **2** immature, silly. □□ **child·ish·ly** *adv.* **child·ish·ness** *n.*

child·like /chíldlīk/ *adj.* having the good qualities of a child as innocence, frankness, etc.

child·mind·er /chíldmīndər/ *n. Brit.* a person who looks after children for payment; baby-sitter.

child·proof /chíldprŏŏf/ *adj.* that cannot be damaged nor operated by a child.

chil·dren *pl.* of CHILD.

child's play *n.* an easy task.

Chil·e·an /chíleeən, chiláyən/ *n. & adj.* ● *n.* **1** a native or national of Chile in S. America. **2** a person of Chilean descent. ● *adj.* of or relating to Chile.

Chil·e pine /chilee, cheélay/ *n.* a monkey puzzle tree.

Chil·e salt·pe·ter /chilee/ *n.* (also **Chil·e ni·ter**) naturally occurring sodium nitrate.

chil·i /chílee/ *n.* (*pl.* **-ies**) ▲ a small, hot-tasting dried red pod of a capsicum, *Capsicum frutescens*, used as seasoning and in curry powder, cayenne pepper, etc. ▷ SPICE

chil·i·ad /kíleead/ *n.* **1** a thousand. **2** a thousand years.

chil·i·asm /kíleeazəm/ *n.* the doctrine of or belief in Christ's prophesied reign of 1,000 years on earth (SEE MILLENNIUM).

chil·i·ast /kíleeast/ *n.* a believer in chiliasm. □□ **chil·i·as·tic** /-ástik/ *adj.*

chil·i con car·ne /kon káarnee/ *n.* a stew of chili-flavored ground meat and usu. beans.

chil·i pow·der *n.* a powder made of dried chilies, garlic, herbs, spices, etc., used as a seasoning.

chill /chil/ *n., v., & adj.* ● *n.* **1 a** an unpleasant cold sensation; lowered body temperature. **b** a feverish cold (*catch a chill*). **2** unpleasant coldness (of air, water, etc.). **3** a depressing influence (*cast a chill over*). **b** a feeling of fear or dread accompanied by coldness. **4** coldness of manner. ● *v.* **1** *tr. & intr.* make or become cold. **2** *tr.* depress; dispirit. **3** *tr.* cool (food or drink); preserve by cooling. **4** *intr. sl.* = chill out. **5** *tr.* harden (molten metal) by contact with cold material. ● *adj.* = CHILLY. □ **chill**

out become calm or less agitated. **take the chill off** warm slightly. □□ **chill·er** *n.* **chill·ing·ly** *adv.* **chill·ness** *n.*

chill·y /chílee/ *adj.* (**chillier, chilliest**) **1** (of the weather or an object) somewhat cold. **2** (of a person or animal) feeling somewhat cold; sensitive to the cold. **3** unfriendly; unemotional. □□ **chill·i·ness** *n.*

chi·mae·ra var. of CHIMERA.

chime /chīm/ *n. & v.* ● *n.* **1 a** a set of attuned bells. **b** the series of sounds given by this. **c** (usu. in *pl.*) a set of attuned bells as a door bell. **2** agreement; correspondence; harmony. ● *v.* **1 a** *intr.* (of bells) ring. **b** *tr.* sound (a bell or chime) by striking. **2** *tr.* show (the hour) by chiming. **3** *intr.* (usu. foll. by *together, with*) be in agreement; harmonize. □ **chime in 1** interject a remark. **2** join in harmoniously. **3** (foll. by *with*) agree with. □□ **chim·er** *n.*

chi·me·ra /kīmeérə, kee-/ (also **chi·mae·ra**) *n.* **1** ◄ (in Greek mythology) a fire-breathing female monster with a lion's head, a goat's body, and a serpent's tail. **2** a fantastic or grotesque product of the imagination; a bogey. **3** any fabulous beast with parts taken from various animals. **4** *Biol.* **a** an organism containing genetically different tissues, formed by grafting, mutation, etc. **b** a nucleic acid formed by laboratory manipulation. □□ **chi·mer·ic** /-mérik/ *adj.* **chi·mer·i·cal** *adj.* **chi·mer·i·cal·ly** *adv.*

CHIMERA

chim·ney /chímnee/ *n.* (*pl.* **-eys**) **1** a vertical channel conducting smoke or combustion gases, etc., up and away from a fire, furnace, etc. **2** the part of this

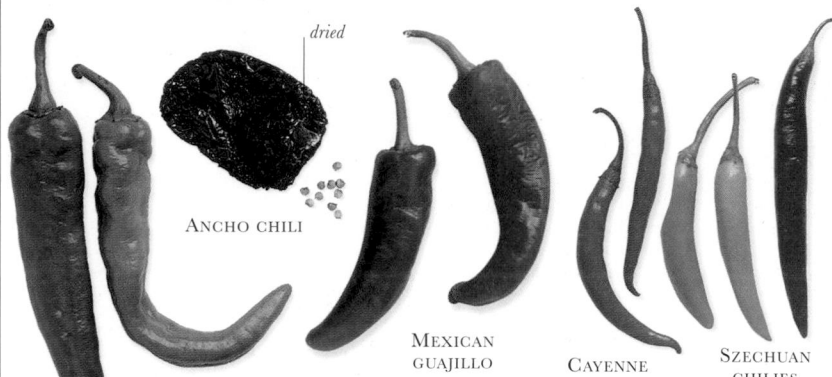

CHILI

Often purchased in their dried form, chilies are also available as immature or ripe fruits, in colors ranging from orange to purplish black. Dozens of varieties are grown commercially in the tropics and subtropics. For the cook, chilis add a wide range of flavors to savory dishes; in general, the smaller the fruit, the hotter the taste.

EXAMPLES OF CHILIES

dried

ANCHO CHILI

MEXICAN GUAJILLO CHILIES

CAYENNE PEPPERS

SZECHUAN CHILIES

ANAHEIM CHILIES

dried

fresh

dried

CASCABEL CHILIES   BUTTER CHILIES   BIRD'S-EYE CHILIES   SERRANO CHILIES

that projects above a roof. **3** a glass tube protecting the flame of a lamp. **4** a narrow vertical crack in a rock face, often used by mountaineers to ascend.

chim·ney·piece /chímneepees/ *n. esp. Brit.* an ornamental structure around an open fireplace; a mantelpiece.

chim·ney sweep *n.* a person whose job is removing soot from inside chimneys.

chimp /chimp/ *n. colloq.* = CHIMPANZEE.

chim·pan·zee /chímpanzée, chimpánzee/ *n.* a small African anthropoid ape, *Pan troglodytes.* ▷ PRIMATE

chin /chin/ *n.* the front of the lower jaw. □ **chin up** *colloq.* cheer up. **keep one's chin up** *colloq.* remain cheerful, esp. in adversity. **take on the chin 1** suffer a severe blow from (a misfortune, etc.). **2** endure courageously. □□ **-chinned** *adj.* (in comb.).

chi·na /chína/ *n. & adj.* ● *n.* **1** a kind of fine white or translucent ceramic ware, porcelain, etc. **2** things made from ceramic, esp. household tableware. **3** *Brit. rhyming sl.* one's 'mate,' i.e., husband or wife (short for *china plate*). ● *adj.* made of china.

chi·na clay *n.* kaolin.

Chi·na·graph /chínagraf/ *n. Trademark* a waxy colored pencil used to write on china, glass, etc.

Chi·na·man /chínaman/ *n.* (*pl.* **-men**) *archaic* or *derog.* (now usu. *offens.*) a native of China.

Chi·na·town /chínatown/ *n.* a district of any non-Chinese city in which the population is predominantly Chinese.

chinch /chinch/ *n.* (in full **chinch bug**) **1** a small insect, *Blissus leucopterus,* that destroys the shoots of grasses and grains. **2** a bedbug.

CHINCHILLA
(*Chinchilla laniger*)

chin·chil·la /chinchílla/ *n.* **1 a** ◄ any small rodent of the genus *Chinchilla,* native to S. America, having soft, silver-gray fur and a bushy tail. **b** its highly valued fur. **2** a breed of cat or rabbit.

chin-chin /chínchín/ *int. Brit. colloq.* a toast; a greeting or farewell.

Chin·dit /chíndit/ *n. hist.* a member of the Allied forces behind the Japanese lines in Burma (now Myanmar) in 1943–45.

chine /chīn/ *n. & v.* ● *n.* **1 a** a backbone, esp. of an animal. **b** a joint of meat containing all or part of this. **2** a ridge or arête. ● *v.tr.* cut (meat) across or along the backbone.

Chi·nese /chíneéz/ *adj. & n.* ● *adj.* **1** of or relating to China. **2** of Chinese descent. ● *n.* **1** the Chinese language. **2** (*pl.* same) **a** a native or national of China. **b** a person of Chinese descent.

Chi·nese cab·bage *n.* a lettucelike cabbage, *Brassica chinensis.*

Chi·nese lan·tern *n.* **1** a collapsible paper lantern. **2** a solanaceous plant, *Physalis alkekengi,* bearing white flowers and globular orange fruits enclosed in an orange-red, papery calyx.

Chink /chingk/ *n. sl. offens.* a Chinese person. □□ **Chink·y** *adj.*

chink[1] /chingk/ *n.* **1** an unintended crack that admits light or allows an attack; a flaw. **2** a narrow opening; a slit.

chink[2] /chingk/ *v. & n.* ● *v.* **1** *intr.* make a slight ringing sound, as of glasses or coins striking together. **2** *tr.* cause to make this sound. ● *n.* this sound.

chin·less /chínlis/ *adj. colloq.* weak or feeble in character.

chi·no /cheéno/ *n.* (*pl.* **-os**) **1** a cotton twill fabric, usu. khaki-colored. **2** (in *pl.*) a garment, esp. trousers, made from this.

Chino- /chíno/ *comb. form* = SINO-.

---

chi·noi·se·rie /sheenwáazaree/ *n.* **1** the imitation of Chinese motifs and techniques in painting and in decorating furniture. **2** an object or objects in this style.

Chi·nook /shanŏŏk, cha-/ *n.* **1 a** a N. American people native to the northwestern coast of the US. **b** a member of this people. **2** the language of this people and other nearby peoples. **3** (**chinook**) **a** a warm, dry wind that blows east of the Rocky Mountains. **b** a warm, wet southerly wind west of the Rocky Mountains. □□ **Chi·nook·an** *adj.*

chintz /chints/ *n. & adj.* ● *n.* a printed, multicolored cotton fabric with a glazed finish. ● *adj.* made from or upholstered with this fabric.

chintz·y /chíntsee/ *adj.* (**chintzier, chintziest**) **1** like chintz. **2** gaudy; cheap. **3** characteristic of the decor associated with chintz soft furnishings. □□ **chintz·i·ly** *adv.* **chintz·i·ness** *n.*

chin-up *n.* an exercise in which the chin is raised up to the level of an overhead horizontal bar that one grasps.

chi·o·no·dox·a /kíanadóksa/ *n.* ◄ any liliaceous plant of the genus *Chionodoxa,* having early-blooming blue flowers.

chip /chip/ *n. & v.* ● *n.* **1** a small piece removed by or in the course of chopping, cutting, or breaking, esp. from hard material such as wood or stone. **2** the place where such a chip has been made. **3 a** = POTATO CHIP. **b** (usu. in *pl.*) a strip of potato, deep fried (*fish and chips*). **4** a counter used in some gambling games to represent money. **5** *Electronics* = MICROCHIP. **6** *Brit.* **a** a thin strip of wood, straw, etc., used for weaving hats, baskets, etc. **b** a basket made from these. **7** *Soccer,* etc., & *Golf* a short shot, kick, or pass with the ball describing an arc. ● *v.* (**chipped, chipping**) **1** *tr.* (often foll. by *off, away*) cut or break (a piece) from a hard material. **2** *intr.* (foll. by *at, away at*) cut pieces off (a hard material) to alter its shape, break it up, etc. **3** *intr.* (of stone, china, etc.) be susceptible to being chipped; be apt to break at the edge (*will chip easily*). **4** *tr.* (also *absol.*) *Soccer,* etc., & *Golf* strike or kick (the ball) with a chip (cf. sense 7 of *n.*). **5** *tr.* (usu. as **chipped** *adj.*) cut into chips. □ **chip in** *colloq.* **1** interrupt or contribute abruptly to a conversation (*chipped in with a reminiscence*). **2** contribute (money or resources). **a chip off the old block** a child who resembles a parent, esp. in character. **a chip on one's shoulder** *colloq.* a disposition or inclination to feel resentful or aggrieved. **have had one's chips** *Brit. colloq.* be unable to avoid defeat, punishment, etc. **in the chips** *sl.* moneyed; affluent. **when the chips are down** *colloq.* in times of discouragement or disappointment.

chip·board /chípbawrd/ *n.* a rigid sheet or panel made from compressed wood chips and resin.

chip·munk /chípmungk/ *n.* ▶ any ground squirrel of the genus *Tamias* or *Eutamias,* having alternate light and dark stripes running down the body. ▷ RODENT

Chip·pen·dale /chípandayl/ *adj.* **1** (of furniture) designed or made by the English cabinetmaker Thomas Chippendale (d. 1779). **2** in the ornately elegant style of Chippendale's furniture.

chip·per /chípar/ *adj. colloq.* **1** cheerful. **2** smartly dressed.

Chip·pe·wa /chípawaw, -wa, -waa, -way/ *n.* = OJIBWA.

chip·ping /chíping/ *n. Brit.* **1** a small fragment of stone, wood, etc. **2** (in *pl.*) these used as a surface for roads, roofs, etc.

chip·py[1] /chípee/ *adj.* (**chippier, chippiest**) marked by belligerence or aggression, esp. in the play of ice hockey.

CHISEL

Chisels have specific functions. A bolster chisel is suitable for cutting masonry, lifting floorboards, or prying off tiles. The bevel-edge chisel is used for chipping out strips of wood, while the wood-cutting chisel is best for fashioning wooden joints.

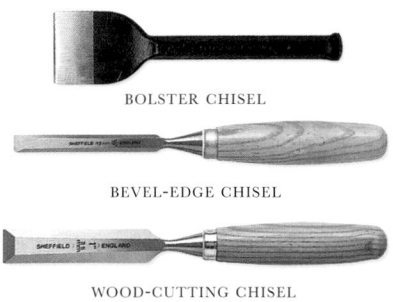

BOLSTER CHISEL

BEVEL-EDGE CHISEL

WOOD-CUTTING CHISEL

C

chip·py[2] /chípee/ *n.* (also **chip·pie**) (*pl.* **-ies**) **1** *derog.* a promiscuous female; a prostitute. **2** *Brit. colloq.* a fish-and-chip store.

chip shot = CHIP sense 7 of *n.*

chi·ral /kíral/ *adj. Chem.* (of a crystal, etc.) not superimposable on its mirror image. □□ **chi·ral·i·ty** /-rálitee/ *n.*

chiro- /kíro/ (also **cheiro-**) *comb. form* of the hand.

chi·rog·ra·phy /kírógrafee/ *n.* handwriting; calligraphy.

chi·ro·man·cy /kíromansee/ *n.* palmistry.

chi·rop·o·dy /kirópadee/ = PODIATRY. □□ **chi·rop·o·dist** *n.*

chi·ro·prac·tic /kírapráktik/ *n.* the diagnosis and manipulative treatment of mechanical disorders of the joints, esp. of the spinal column. □□ **chi·ro·prac·tor** *n.*

chi·rop·ter·an /kíróptaran/ *n.* any member of the order Chiroptera, with membraned limbs serving as wings, including bats and flying foxes. ▷ BAT. □□ **chi·rop·ter·ous** *adj.*

chirp /charp/ *v. & n.* ● *v.* **1** *intr.* (usu. of small birds, grasshoppers, etc.) utter a short, sharp, high-pitched note. **2** *tr. & intr.* (esp. of a child) speak or utter in a lively or jolly way. ● *n.* a chirping sound. □□ **chirp·er** *n.*

chirp·y /chárpee/ *adj. colloq.* (**chirpier, chirpiest**) cheerful; lively. □□ **chirp·i·ly** *adv.* **chirp·i·ness** *n.*

chirr /char/ *v. & n.* (also **churr**) ● *v.intr.* (esp. of insects) make a prolonged low trilling sound. ● *n.* this sound.

chir·rup /chírap/ *v. & n.* ● *v.intr.* (**chirruped, chirruping**) (esp. of small birds) chirp, esp. repeatedly; twitter. ● *n.* a chirruping sound. □□ **chir·rup·y** *adj.*

chis·el /chízal/ *n. & v.* ● *n.* ▲ a hand tool with a squared, beveled blade for shaping wood, stone, or metal. ▷ BEZEL. ● *v.* **1** *tr.* (**chiseled, chiseling;** esp. *Brit.* **chiselled, chiselling**) cut or shape with a chisel. **2** *tr.* (as **chiseled** *adj.*) (of facial features) clear-cut; fine. **3** *tr. & intr. sl.* cheat; swindle. □□ **chis·el·er** *n.*

chi-square test *n.* a method of comparing observed and theoretical values in statistics.

chit[1] /chit/ *n.* **1** *derog.* or *joc.* a young, small, or frail girl or woman (esp. a chit of a girl). **2** a young child.

chit[2] /chit/ *n.* **1** a note of requisition; a note of a sum owed, esp. for food or drink. **2** esp. *Brit.* a note or memorandum.

chit·chat /chítchat/ *n. & v. colloq.* ● *n.* light conversation; gossip. ● *v.intr.* (**-chatted, -chatting**) talk informally; gossip.

CHIONODOXA
(*Chionodoxa luciliae*)

CHIPMUNK: EASTERN CHIPMUNK
(*Tamias striatus*)

C

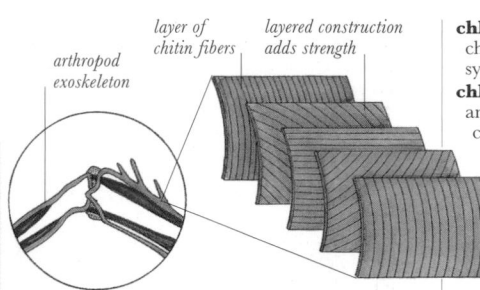

CHITIN: CROSS SECTION OF AN ARTHROPOD EXOSKELETON, WITH DETAIL OF CHITIN LAYERS

arthropod exoskeleton

layer of chitin fibers

layered construction adds strength

chi·tin /kít'n/ *n. Chem.* ▲ a polysaccharide forming the major constituent in the exoskeleton of arthropods and in the cell walls of fungi. ▷ EXOSKELETON. □□ **chi·tin·ous** *adj.*

chi·ton /kít'n, -ton/ *n.* **1** a long, woolen tunic worn by ancient Greeks. **2** any marine mollusk of the class Amphineura, having a shell of overlapping plates.

chit·ter·lings /chítlinz/ *n.* (also **chit·lings, chit·lins**) the small intestines of pigs, etc., esp. as cooked for food.

chiv·al·rous /shívəlrəs/ *adj.* **1** (usu. of a male) gallant; honorable; courteous. **2** involving or showing chivalry. □□ **chiv·al·rous·ly** *adv.*

chiv·al·ry /shívəlree/ *n.* **1** the medieval knightly system with its religious, moral, and social code. **2** the combination of qualities expected of an ideal knight, esp. courage, honor, courtesy, justice, and readiness to help the weak. **3** a man's courteous behavior, esp. toward women. □□ **chiv·al·ric** *adj.*

chive /chīv/ *n.* ► a small alliaceous plant, *Allium schoenoprasum*, having purple-pink flowers and dense tufts of long tubular leaves, which are used as an herb.

chiv·vy /chívee/ *v.tr.* (**-ies, -ied**) (also **chiv·y, chev·y** /chévee/) harass; nag; pursue.

chla·myd·i·a /kləmídeeə/ *n.* (*pl.* **chla·mydiae** /-dee-ee/) any parasitic bacterium of the genus *Chlamydia*, some of which cause diseases such as trachoma, psittacosis, and nonspecific urethritis.

chlor- var. of CHLORO-.

chlo·ride /kláwrīd/ *n. Chem.* any compound of chlorine with another element or group.

chlo·ri·nate /kláwrinayt/ *v.tr.* **1** impregnate or treat with chlorine. **2** *Chem.* cause to react or combine with chlorine. □□ **chlo·ri·na·tor** *n.*

chlo·ri·na·tion /kláwrináyshən/ *n.* **1** the treatment of water with chlorine to disinfect it. **2** *Chem.* a reaction in which chlorine is introduced into a compound.

chlo·rine /kláwreen/ *n. Chem.* a poisonous, greenish-yellow gaseous element of the halogen group occurring naturally in salt, seawater, rock salt, etc., and used for purifying water, bleaching, and the manufacture of many organic chemicals. ¶ Symb.: **Cl.**

chloro- /kláwrō/ *comb. form* (also **chlor-** esp. before a vowel) **1** *Bot. & Mineral.* green. **2** *Chem.* chlorine.

chlo·ro·fluor·o·car·bon *n.* see CFC.

chlo·ro·form /kláwrəfawrm/ *n. & v.* ● *n.* a colorless, volatile, sweet-smelling liquid used as a solvent and formerly used as a general anesthetic. ¶ Chem. formula: $CHCl_3$. ● *v.tr.* render (a person) unconscious with this.

chlo·ro·phyll /kláwrəfil/ *n.* the green pigment found in most plants, responsible for light absorption to provide energy for photosynthesis. □□ **chlo·ro·phyl·lous** /-filəs/ *adj.*

CHIVE
(*Allium schoenoprasum*)

chlo·ro·plast /kláwrōplast/ *n.* a plastid containing chlorophyll, found in plant cells undergoing photosynthesis. ▷ CELL

chlo·ro·sis /klərṓsis/ *n.* **1** *hist.* a severe form of anemia from iron deficiency esp. in young women, causing a greenish complexion (cf. GREENSICK). **2** *Bot.* a reduction or loss of the normal green coloration of plants. □□ **chlo·rot·ic** /-rótik/ *adj.*

choc /chok/ *n. & adj. Brit. colloq.* chocolate.

chock /chok/ *n., v., & adv.* ● *n.* a block or wedge of wood to check motion, esp. of a cask or a wheel. ● *v.tr.* **1** fit or make fast with chocks. **2** (usu. foll. by *up*) *Brit.* cram full. ● *adv.* as closely or tightly as possible.

chock·a·block /chókəblók/ *adj. & adv.* crammed close together; crammed full (*a street chockablock with cars*).

chock-full *adj. & adv.* = CHOCKABLOCK (*chock-full of rubbish*).

choc·o·late /cháwkələt, cháwklət, chók-/ *n. & adj.* ● *n.* **1 a** a food preparation in the form of a paste or solid block made from roasted and ground cacao seeds, usually sweetened. **b** a candy made of or coated with this. **c** a drink made with chocolate. **2** a deep brown color. ● *adj.* **1** made from or of chocolate. **2** chocolate-colored. □□ **choc·o·lat·y** *adj.* (also **choc·o·lat·ey**)

Choc·taw /chóktaw/ *n.* (*pl.* same or **Choctaws**) **1 a** a N. American people orig. from Alabama. **b** an individual of this people. **c** the language of this people. **2** (in skating) a step from one edge of a skate to the other edge of the other skate in the opposite direction.

choice /choys/ *n. & adj.* ● *n.* **1 a** the act or an instance of choosing. **b** a thing or person chosen (*not a good choice*). **2** a range from which to choose. **3** (usu. foll. by *of*) the élite; the best. **4** the power or opportunity to choose (*what choice have I?*). ● *adj.* of superior quality; carefully chosen. □□ **choice·ly** *adv.* **choice·ness** *n.*

choir /kwīr/ *n.* **1** a regular group of singers, esp. taking part in church services. **2** the part of a cathedral or large church between the altar and the nave, used by the choir and clergy. ▷ CATHEDRAL, CHURCH. **3** a company of singers, birds, angels, etc. (*a heavenly choir*). **4** *Mus.* a group of instruments of one family playing together.

choir·boy /kwīrboy/ *n.* (*fem.* **choirgirl**) a child who sings in a church or cathedral choir.

choir loft *n.* a church gallery in which the choir is situated.

choke[1] /chōk/ *v. & n.* ● *v.* **1** *tr.* hinder or impede the breathing of (a person or animal), esp. by constricting the windpipe or (of gas, smoke, etc.) by being unbreathable. **2** *intr.* suffer a hindrance or stoppage of breath. **3** *tr. & intr.* make or become speechless from emotion. **4** *tr.* retard the growth of or kill (esp. plants) by the deprivation of light, air, nourishment, etc. **5** *tr.* (often foll. by *back*) suppress (feelings) with difficulty. **6** *tr.* block or clog (a passage, tube, etc.). **7** *tr.* enrich the fuel mixture in (an internal-combustion engine) by reducing the intake of air. ● *n.* **1** the valve in the carburetor of an internal-combustion engine that controls the intake of air, esp. to enrich the fuel mixture. ▷ CARBURETOR. **2** *Electr.* an inductance coil used to smooth the variations of an alternating current or to alter its phase. □ **choke down** swallow with difficulty. **choke up 1** become overly anxious or emotionally affected (*got all choked up over that sad movie*). **2** block (a channel, etc.).

choke[2] /chōk/ *n.* the center part of an artichoke.

choke·ber·ry /chṓkberee/ *n.* (*pl.* **-ies**) *Bot.* **1** any rosaceous shrub of the genus *Aronia*. **2** its scarlet berrylike fruit.

choke chain (or **col·lar**) *n.* a chain looped around a dog's neck to exert control by pressure on its windpipe when the dog pulls.

choke·cher·ry /chṓkcheree/ *n.* (*pl.* **-cherries**) an astringent N. American cherry, *Prunus virginiana*.

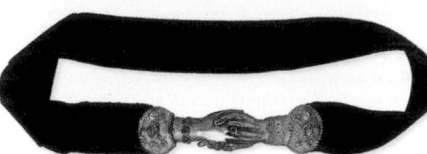

CHOKER: 18TH-CENTURY FABRIC CHOKER WITH ORNAMENTAL CLASP

chok·er /chṓkər/ *n.* **1** ▲ a close-fitting necklace or ornamental neckband. **2** a clerical or other high collar.

chole- /kṓlee/ *comb. form* (also **chol-** esp. before a vowel) *Med. & Chem.* bile.

cho·le·cal·cif·er·ol /kṓlikalsífərawl, -rol/ *n.* one of the D vitamins, produced by the action of sunlight on a cholesterol derivative widely distributed in the skin, a deficiency of which results in rickets in children and osteomalacia in adults. Also called **vitamin D₃**.

chol·er /kólər/ *n.* **1** *hist.* one of the four humors, bile. **2** *poet.* or *archaic* anger; irascibility.

chol·er·a /kólərə/ *n. Med.* an infectious and often fatal disease of the small intestine caused by the bacterium *Vibrio cholerae*, resulting in severe vomiting and diarrhea. □□ **chol·e·ra·ic** /-ráyik/ *adj.*

chol·er·ic /kólərik, kəlérik/ *adj.* irascible; angry. □□ **chol·er·i·cal·ly** *adv.*

cho·les·ter·ol /kəléstərawl, -rōl/ *n. Biochem.* a sterol found in most body tissues, including the blood, where high concentrations promote arteriosclerosis.

cho·li·am·bus /kṓleeámbəs/ *n. Prosody* a line of iambic meter with the last foot being a spondee or trochee. □□ **cho·li·am·bic** /-ámbik/ *adj.*

chomp /chomp/ *v.tr.* = CHAMP[1].

choo-choo /chóōchōō/ *n. colloq.* (esp. as a child's word) a railroad train or locomotive, esp. a steam engine.

choose /chōōz/ *v.* (*past* **chose** /chōz/; *past part.* **chosen** /chṓzən/) **1** *tr.* select out of a greater number. **2** *intr.* (usu. foll. by *between, from*) take or select one or another. **3** *tr.* (usu. foll. by *to* + infin.) decide; be determined (*chose to stay behind*). **4** *tr.* (foll. by *complement*) select as (*was chosen king*). **5** *tr. Theol.* (esp. as **chosen** *adj.*) destine to be saved (*God's chosen people*). □ **nothing** (or **little**) **to choose between them** they are equivalent. □□ **choos·er** *n.*

choos·y /chṓōzee/ *adj.* (**choosier, choosiest**) *colloq.* fastidious. □□ **choos·i·ly** *adv.* **choos·i·ness** *n.*

chop[1] /chop/ *v. & n.* ● *v.tr.* (**chopped, chopping**) **1** (usu. foll. by *off, down*, etc.) cut or fell by a blow, usu. with an axe. **2** (often foll. by *up*) cut (esp. meat or vegetables) into small pieces. **3** strike (esp. a ball) with a short heavy edgewise blow. **4** *colloq.* dispense with; shorten or curtail. ● *n.* **1** a cutting blow, esp. with an axe. **2** a thick slice of meat (esp. pork or lamb) usu. including a rib. ▷ CUT. **3** a short, sharp, edgewise stroke or blow in tennis, karate, boxing, etc. **4** the broken motion of water, usu. owing to the action of the wind against the tide. **5** (prec. by *the*) *Brit. sl.* **a** dismissal from employment. **b** the action of killing or being killed. □ **chop logic** argue pedantically; engage in choplogic.

chop[2] /chop/ *n.* (usu. in *pl.*) the jaw of an animal, etc.

chop[3] /chop/ *v.intr.* (**chopped, chopping**) □ **chop and change** *Brit.* vacillate; change direction frequently.

chop-chop /chópchóp/ *adv. & int.* (pidgin English) quickly; quick.

chop·log·ic /chóplojik/ *n. & adj.* ● *n.* overly pedantic or complicated argument. ● *adj.* (also **chop·log·i·cal**) engaging in or exhibiting such.

chop·per /chópər/ *n.* **1** a person or thing that chops. **2** a butcher's cleaver. **3** *colloq.* a helicopter. **4** *colloq.* a type of bicycle or motorcycle with high handlebars. **5** (in *pl.*) *sl.* teeth.

chop·py /chópee/ *adj.* (**choppier, choppiest**) (of the sea, the weather, etc.) fairly rough. □□ **chop·pi·ly** *adv.* **chop·pi·ness** *n.*

chop shop *n. colloq.* a garage in which stolen cars are dismantled so that the parts can be sold separately.

chop·stick /chópstik/ *n.* each of a pair of small thin sticks of wood or ivory, etc., held both in one hand as eating utensils by the Chinese, Japanese, etc. ▷ WOK

chop su·ey /chopsóo-ee/ *n.* (*pl.* **-eys**) a Chinese-style dish of meat stewed and fried with bean sprouts, bamboo shoots, onions, and served with rice.

cho·ral /káwrəl/ *adj.* of, for, or sung by a choir or chorus. □□ **cho·ral·ly** *adv.*

cho·rale /kərál, -ráal/ *n.* (also **cho·ral**) **1** a stately and simple hymn tune; a harmonized version of this. **2** a choir or choral society.

chord[1] /kawrd/ *n. Mus.* a group of (usu. three or more) notes sounded together, as a basis of harmony. □□ **chord·al** *adj.*

chord[2] /kawrd/ *n.* **1** *Math.* & *Aeron.*, etc. ◄ a straight line joining the ends of an arc, the wings of an airplane, etc. **2** *Anat.* = CORD. □ **strike a chord 1** recall something to a person's memory. **2** elicit sympathy. **touch the right chord** appeal skillfully to the emotions. □□ **chord·al** *adj.*

chor·date /káwrdayt/ *n. & adj.* ● *n.* any animal of the phylum Chordata, possessing a notochord at some stage during its development. ● *adj.* of or relating to the chordates.

chore /chawr/ *n.* a tedious or routine task, esp. domestic.

cho·re·a /kawrée-ə/ *n. Med.* a disorder characterized by jerky involuntary movements affecting esp. the shoulders, hips, and face.

cho·re·o·graph /káwreeəgraf/ *v.tr.* compose the choreography for (a ballet, etc.). □□ **cho·re·og·ra·pher** /-reeógrəfər/

cho·re·og·ra·phy /káwreeógrəfee/ *n.* **1** the design or arrangement of a ballet or other staged dance. **2** the sequence of steps and movements in dance. **3** the written notation for this. □□ **cho·re·o·graph·ic** /-reeəgráfik/ *adj.* **cho·re·o·graph·i·cal·ly** *adv.*

cho·ri·am·bus /káwreeámbəs/ *n.* (*pl.* **choriambi** /-bī/) *Prosody* a metrical foot consisting of two short (unstressed) syllables between two long (stressed) ones. □□ **cho·ri·am·bic** *adj.*

cho·rine /káwreen/ *n.* a chorus girl.

cho·ri·on /káwreeon/ *n.* the outermost membrane surrounding an embryo of a reptile, bird, or mammal. □□ **cho·ri·on·ic** /-reeónik/ *adj.*

cho·ris·ter /káwristər, kór-/ *n.* **1** a member of a choir, esp. a choirboy. **2** the leader of a church choir.

cho·ri·zo /choréezō/ *n.* a spicy Spanish pork sausage.

cho·roid /káwroyd/ *adj. & n.* ● *adj.* like a chorion in shape or vascularity. ● *n.* (in full **choroid coat** or **membrane**) a layer of the eyeball between the retina and the sclera. ▷ EYE

chor·tle /cháwrt'l/ *v. & n.* ● *v.intr. colloq.* chuckle gleefully. ● *n.* a gleeful chuckle.

cho·rus /káwrəs/ *n. & v.* ● *n.* (*pl.* **choruses**) **1** a group of singers (esp. a large one); a choir. **2** a piece of music composed for a choir. **3** the refrain or the main part of a popular song, in which a chorus participates. **4** any simultaneous utterance by many persons, etc. **5** a group of singers and dancers performing in concert in a musical comedy, opera, etc. **6** *Gk Antiq.* **a** in Greek tragedy, a group of performers who comment together in voice and movement on the main action. **b** an utterance of the chorus. **7** esp. in Elizabethan drama, a character who speaks the prologue and other linking parts

of the play. **8** the part spoken by this character. ● *v.tr. & intr.* (*of a group*) speak or utter simultaneously. □ **in chorus** (uttered) together; in unison.

cho·rus girl *n.* a young woman who sings or dances in the chorus of a musical comedy, etc.

chose *past* of CHOOSE.

cho·sen *past part.* of CHOOSE.

chough /chuf/ *n.* ► a European corvine bird of the genus *Pyrrhocorax*, with a glossy, blue-black plumage and red legs.

choux pastry /shoo/ *n.* (also **chou**) very light pastry enriched with eggs.

chow /chow/ *n.* **1** *sl.* food. **2** *offens.* a Chinese. **3** (in full **chow chow**) **a** a dog of a Chinese breed with long hair and bluish-black tongue. **b** this breed.

chow-chow /chówchow/ *n.* **1** a Chinese preserve of ginger, orange-peel, etc., in syrup. **2** a mixed vegetable pickle.

chow·der /chówdər/ *n.* a rich soup or stew usu. containing fresh fish, clams, or corn with potatoes, onions, etc.

chow mein /chów máyn/ *n.* a Chinese-style dish of fried noodles with shredded meat or shrimp, etc., and vegetables.

Chr. *abbr.* Chronicles (Old Testament).

chres·to·ma·thy /krestóməthee/ *n.* (*pl.* **-ies**) a selection of passages used esp. to help in learning a language.

chrism /krízəm/ *n.* a consecrated oil or unguent used esp. for anointing in Roman Catholic, Anglican, and Orthodox Christian rites.

chris·om /krízəm/ *n.* **1** = CHRISM. **2** (in full **chrisom cloth**) *hist.* a white robe put on a child at baptism, and used as its shroud if it died within the month.

Christ /krīst/ *n. & int.* ● *n.* **1** the title, also now treated as a name, given to Jesus of Nazareth, believed by Christians to have fulfilled the Old Testament prophecies of a coming Messiah. **2** the Messiah as prophesied in the Old Testament. ● *int. sl.* expressing surprise, anger, etc. □□ **Christ·hood** *n.* **Christ·like** *adj.* **Christ·ly** *adj.*

Chris·ta·del·phi·an /krístədélfeeən/ *n. & adj.* ● *n.* a member of a Christian sect rejecting the doctrine of the Trinity and expecting a second coming of Christ on Earth. ● *adj.* of or adhering to this sect and its beliefs.

chris·ten /krísən/ *v.tr.* **1** give a Christian name to at baptism as a sign of admission to a Christian church. **2** give a name to anything, esp. formally or with a ceremony. **3** *colloq.* use for the first time. □□ **chris·ten·er** *n.* **chris·ten·ing** *n.*

Chris·ten·dom /krísəndəm/ *n.* Christians worldwide, regarded as a collective body.

Chris·tian /krís·chən/ *adj. & n.* ● *adj.* **1** of Christ's teachings or religion. **2** believing in or following the religion based on the teachings of Jesus Christ. **3** showing the qualities associated with Christ's teachings. **4** *colloq.* (of a person) kind; fair; decent. ● *n.* **1 a** a person who has received Christian baptism. **b** an adherent of Christ's teachings. **2** a person exhibiting Christian qualities. □□ **Chris·tian·ize** *v.tr. & intr.* **Chris·tian·i·za·tion** *n.* **Chris·tian·ly** *adv.*

Chris·tian e·ra *n.* the era calculated from the traditional date of Christ's birth.

Chris·ti·an·i·ty /krischeeánitee/ *n.* **1** the Christian religion; its beliefs and practices. **2** being a Christian; Christian quality or character. **3** = CHRISTENDOM.

Chris·tian name *n.* a forename, esp. as given at baptism.

Chris·tian Sci·ence *n.* a Christian sect believing in the power of healing by prayer alone. □□ **Chris·tian Sci·en·tist** *n.*

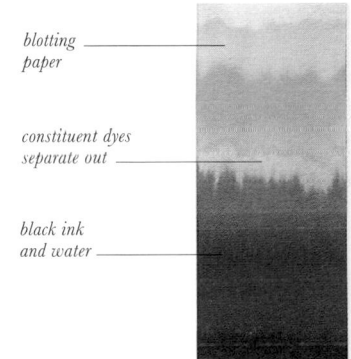

CHOUGH:
ALPINE CHOUGH
(*Pyrrhocorax graculus*)

chris·tie /krístee/ *n.* (also **chris·ty**) (*pl.* **-ies**) *Skiing* a sudden turn in which the skis are kept parallel, used for changing direction fast or stopping short.

Christ·mas /krísməs/ *n.* (*pl.* **Christmases**) **1** (also **Christ·mas Day**) the annual festival of Christ's birth, celebrated on Dec. 25. **2** the season in which this occurs; the time immediately before and after Dec. 25. □□ **Christ·mas·sy** *adj.*

Christ·mas rose a white-flowered, winter-blooming evergreen, *Helleborus niger*.

Christo- /krístō/ *comb. form* Christ.

chro·ma /krómə/ *n.* purity or intensity of color.

chro·mat·ic /krōmátik/ *adj.* **1** of or produced by color; in (esp. bright) colors. **2** *Mus.* **a** of or having notes not belonging to a diatonic scale. **b** (of a scale) ascending or descending by semitones. □□ **chro·mat·i·cal·ly** *adv.* **chro·mat·i·cism** /-tisizəm/ *n.*

chro·ma·tic·i·ty /krómətísitee/ *n.* the quality of color regarded independently of brightness.

chro·ma·tid /krómətid/ *n.* either of two threadlike strands into which a chromosome divides longitudinally during cell division. ▷ CHROMOSOME, MEIOSIS

chro·ma·tin /krómətin/ *n.* the material in a cell nucleus that stains with basic dyes and consists of protein, RNA, and DNA, of which eukaryotic chromosomes are composed.

chromato- /krómətō/ *comb. form* (also **chromo-** /krómō/) color (*chromatopsia*).

chro·ma·tog·ra·phy /krómətógrəfee/ *n. Chem.* ▼ the separation of the components of a mixture by slow passage through or over a material which adsorbs them differently. □□ **chromat·o·graph** /-mátəgraf/ *n.* **chro·mat·o·graph·ic** *adj.*

blotting paper

constituent dyes separate out

black ink and water

CHROMATOGRAPHY: DEMONSTRATION OF SEPARATION OF BLACK INK ON BLOTTING PAPER

chro·ma·top·si·a /krómətópseeə/ *n. Med.* abnormally colored vision.

chrome /krōm/ *n.* **1** chromium, esp. as plating. **2** (in full **chrome yellow**) a yellow pigment obtained from lead chromate.

chro·mic /krómik/ *adj. Chem.* of or containing trivalent chromium.

chro·mite /krómīt/ *n.* **1** *Mineral.* ► a black mineral of chromium and iron oxides, which is the principal ore of chromium. **2** *Chem.* a salt of bivalent chromium.

chro·mi·um /krómeeəm/ *n. Chem.* a hard, white metallic transition element, occurring naturally as chromite and used as a shiny decorative electroplated coating. ¶ Symb.: **Cr.**

chromite crystals

serpentinite groundmass

CHROMITE

C

chromo-¹ /krṓmō/ *comb. form Chem.* chromium.

chromo-² *comb. form* var. of CHROMATO-.

chro·mo·lith·o·graph /krṓmōlíthəgraf/ *n. & v.* ● *n.* a colored picture printed by lithography. ● *v.tr.* print or produce by this process. □□ **chro·mo·li·thog·ra·pher** /-lithógrəfər/ *n.* **chro·mo·lith·o·graph·ic** *adj.* **chro·mo·li·thog·ra·phy** /-lithógrəfee/ *n.*

chro·mo·some /krṓməsōm/ *n. Biochem.* ◀ one of the threadlike structures, usu. found in the cell nucleus, that carry the genetic information in the form of genes. ▷ GENE, MEIOSIS, MITOSIS. □□ **chro·mo·so·mal** *adj.*

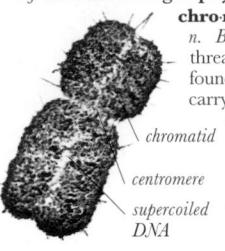

CHROMOSOME: HUMAN CHROMOSOME SEEN THROUGH A MICROSCOPE

chromatid

centromere

supercoiled DNA

chro·mo·some map *n.* a plan showing the relative positions of genes along the length of a chromosome.

chro·mo·sphere /krṓməsfeer/ *n.* a gaseous layer of the Sun's atmosphere between the photosphere and the corona. □□ **chro·mo·spher·ic** /-sféerik, -sfér-/ *adj.*

Chron. *abbr.* Chronicles (Old Testament).

chron·ic /krónik/ *adj.* **1** persisting for a long time (usu. of an illness or a personal or social problem). **2** having a chronic complaint. **3** *colloq. disp.* habitual; inveterate (*a chronic liar*). **4** *Brit. colloq.* very bad; intense; severe. □□ **chron·i·cal·ly** *adv.* **chron·ic·i·ty** /krónísitee/ *n.*

chron·i·cle /krónikəl/ *n. & v.* ● *n.* **1** a register of events in order of their occurrence. **2** a narrative; a full account. **3** (**Chronicles**) the name of two of the historical books of the Old Testament or Hebrew bible. ● *v.tr.* record (events) in the order of their occurrence. □□ **chron·i·cler** *n.*

chrono- /krónō/ *comb. form* time.

chron·o·graph /krónəgraf, krṓnə-/ *n.* **1** an instrument for recording time with extreme accuracy. **2** a stopwatch. □□ **chron·o·graph·ic** *adj.*

chron·o·log·i·cal /krónəlójikəl/ *adj.* **1** (of a number of events) arranged or regarded in the order of their occurrence. **2** of or relating to chronology. □□ **chron·o·log·i·cal·ly** *adv.*

chro·nol·o·gy /krənóləjee/ *n.* (*pl.* **-ies**) **1** the study of historical records to establish the dates of past events. **2 a** the arrangement of events, dates, etc., in the order of their occurrence. **b** a table or document displaying this. □□ **chro·nol·o·gist** *n.* **chro·nol·o·gize** *v.tr.*

chro·nom·e·ter /krənómitər/ *n.* a time-measuring instrument, esp. one keeping accurate time at all temperatures and used in navigation.

chro·nom·e·try /krənómitree/ *n.* the science of accurate time measurement. □□ **chron·o·met·ric** /krónəmétrik/ *adj.* **chron·o·met·ri·cal** *adj.* **chron·o·met·ri·cal·ly** *adv.*

chrys·a·lis /krísəlis/ *n.* (also **chrysalid**) (*pl.* **chrysalides** /krisálideez/ or **chrysalises**) **1 a** ◀ a quiescent pupa of a butterfly or moth. ▷ METAMORPHOSIS. **b** the hard outer case enclosing it. **2** a preparatory or transitional state.

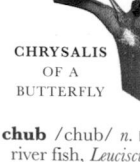

CHRYSALIS OF A BUTTERFLY

chrysalis

girdle

silken pad

chrys·an·the·mum /krisánthəməm/ *n.* any composite plant of the genus *Chrysanthemum*, having brightly colored flowers.

chrys·o·ber·yl /krísəbéril/ *n.* a yellowish-green gem consisting of a beryllium salt.

chthon·ic /thónik/ *adj.* (also **chtho·ni·an** /thóneeən/) of, relating to, or inhabiting the underworld.

chub /chub/ *n.* ▶ a thick-bodied, coarse-fleshed river fish, *Leuciscus cephalus*.

chub·by /chúbee/ *adj.* (**chubbier**, **chubbiest**) plump and rounded (esp. of a person or a part of the body). □□ **chub·bi·ly** *adv.* **chub·bi·ness** *n.*

chuck¹ /chuk/ *v. & n.* ● *v.tr.* **1** *colloq.* fling or throw carelessly or with indifference. **2** *colloq.* give up; reject; abandon; jilt (*chucked my job*; *chucked her boyfriend*). **3** touch playfully, esp. under the chin. ● *n.* a playful touch under the chin. □ **chuck it** *sl.* stop; desist. **chuck out** *colloq.* **1** expel (a person) from a gathering, etc. **2** get rid of; discard.

chuck² /chuk/ *n. & v.* ● *n.* **1** a cut of beef between the neck and the ribs. **2** ▶ a device for holding a workpiece in a lathe or a tool in a drill. ▷ DRILL. ● *v.tr.* fix (wood, a tool, etc.) to a chuck.

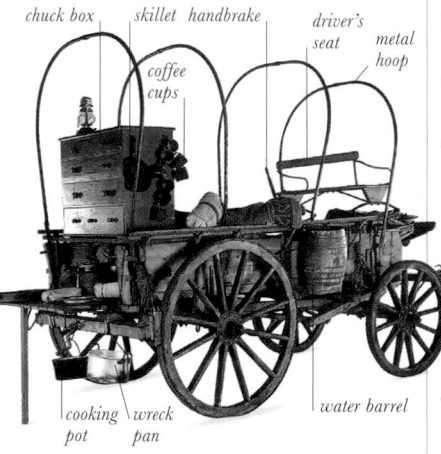

chuck

CHUCK ON A POWER DRILL

chuck·le /chúkəl/ *v. & n.* ● *v.intr.* laugh quietly or inwardly. ● *n.* a quiet or suppressed laugh. □□ **chuck·ler** *n.*

chuck·le·head /chúkəlhed/ *n. colloq.* a stupid person. □□ **chuck·le·head·ed** *adj.*

chuck wag·on *n.* ▼ a wagon for storing food and preparing meals on a ranch, etc.

coffee cups

chuck box skillet handbrake driver's seat metal hoop

cooking pot wreck pan water barrel

CHUCK WAGON: 19TH-CENTURY CHUCK WAGON

chud·dar var. of CHADOR.

chuff /chuf/ *v.intr.* (of a steam engine, etc.) work with a regular sharp puffing sound.

chuffed /chuft/ *adj. Brit. sl.* delighted.

chug /chug/ *v. & n.* ● *v.intr.* (**chugged**, **chugging**) **1** emit a regular muffled explosive sound, as of an engine running slowly. **2** move with this sound. ● *n.* a chugging sound.

chu·kar /chukáar/ *n.* a red-legged partridge, *Alectoris chukar*, native to India.

chuk·ker /chúkər/ *n.* (also **chuk·ka**) each of the periods of play into which a game of polo is divided.

chum /chum/ *n. & v.* ● *n. colloq.* (esp. among schoolchildren) a close friend. ● *v.intr.* (often foll. by *with*) *Brit.* share rooms. □ **chum up** (often foll. by *with*) become a close friend (of). □□ **chum·my** *adj.* (**chum·mi·er**, **chum·mi·est**). **chum·mi·ly** *adv.* **chum·mi·ness** *n.*

chump /chump/ *n.* **1** *colloq.* a foolish person. **2** *Brit.* the thick end, esp. of a loin of lamb or mutton (*chump chop*). **3** a short thick block of wood. **4** *Brit. sl.* the head. □ **off one's chump** *Brit. sl.* crazy.

CHUB (*Leuciscus cephalus*)

chun·der /chúndər/ *v.intr. & n. Austral. sl.* vomit.

chunk /chungk/ *n.* **1** a thick, solid slice or piece of something firm or hard. **2** a substantial amount or piece.

chunk·y /chúngkee/ *adj.* (**chunkier**, **chunkiest**) **1** containing or consisting of chunks. **2** short and thick; small and sturdy. **3** (of clothes) made of a thick material. □□ **chunk·i·ness** *n.*

Chun·nel /chúnəl/ *n. colloq.* a tunnel under the English Channel linking England and France.

chun·ter /chúntər/ *v.intr. Brit. colloq.* mutter; grumble.

church /chərch/ *n. & v.* ● *n.* **1** ▶ a building for public (usu. Christian) worship. **2** a meeting for public worship in such a building (*go to church*; *met after church*). **3** (**Church**) the body of all Christians. **4** (**Church**) the clergy or clerical profession (*went into the Church*). **5** (**Church**) an organized Christian group or society of any time, country, or distinct principles of worship (*the Baptist Church*; *Church of England*). **6** institutionalized religion as a political or social force (*church and state*). ● *v.tr.* bring to church for a service of thanksgiving.

church·go·er /chərchgōər/ *n.* a person who goes to church, esp. on a regular basis. □□ **church·go·ing** *n. & adj.*

church·man /chərchmən/ *n.* (*pl.* **-men**) **1** a member of the clergy or of a church. **2** a supporter of the church.

Church of England *n.* the English Church, recognized by the British government and having the British sovereign as its head.

church·ward·en /chərchwáwrd'n/ *n.* **1** *Anglican Ch.* either of two elected lay representatives of a parish, assisting with routine administration. **2** *Brit.* a long-stemmed clay pipe.

church·wom·an /chərchwŏŏmən/ *n.* (*pl.* **-women**) **1** a woman member of the clergy or of a church. **2** a woman supporter of the Church.

church·y /chərchee/ *adj.* **1** obtrusively or intolerantly devoted to the Church or opposed to religious dissent. **2** like a church. □□ **church·i·ness** *n.*

church·yard /chərchyaard/ *n.* the enclosed ground around a church, esp. as used for burials.

churl /chərl/ *n.* **1** an ill-bred person. **2** *archaic* a peasant; a person of low birth. **3** *archaic* a surly or mean person.

churl·ish /chərlish/ *adj.* surly; mean. □□ **churl·ish·ly** *adv.* **churl·ish·ness** *n.*

churn /chərn/ *n. & v.* ● *n.* **1** ▶ a machine for making butter by agitating milk or cream. **2** *Brit.* a large milk can. ● *v.* **1** *tr.* agitate (milk or cream) in a churn. **2** *tr.* produce (butter) in this way. **3** *tr.* (usu. foll. by *up*) cause distress to; upset; agitate. **4** *intr.* (of a liquid) see the foam violently (*the churning sea*). **5** *tr.* agitate or move (liquid) vigorously, causing it to foam. □ **churn out** produce routinely or mechanically, esp. in large quantities.

lid clasp glass peephole

crank handle

barrel

drainage hole

CHURN: 18TH-CENTURY END-OVER-END CHURN

churr var. of CHIRR.

chute¹ /shōōt/ *n.* **1** a sloping channel or slide, with or without water, for conveying things to a lower level. **2** a slide into a swimming pool. **3** a cataract or cascade of water; a steep descent in a riverbed producing a swift current.

chute² /shōōt/ *n. colloq.* parachute. □□ **chut·ist** *n.*

chut·ney /chútnee/ *n.* (*pl.* **-eys**) a pungent orig. Indian condiment made of fruits or vegetables, vinegar, spices, sugar, etc.

CHURCH

The earliest churches were constructed in the Mediterranean region during the Roman Empire. They were small, with space only for an altar and a limited congregation. As Christianity spread, larger churches with separate areas for the clergy and congregation were built, often in the cruciform (cross-shaped) plan with a central tower.

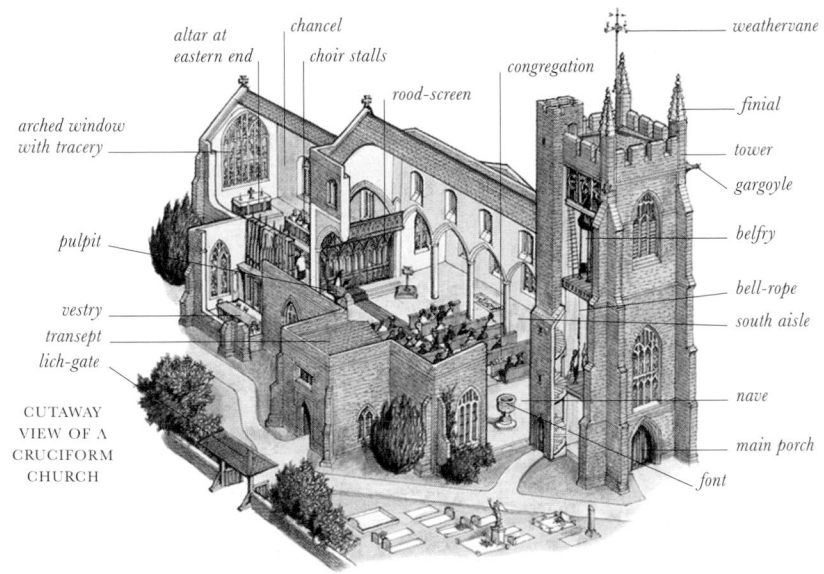

altar at eastern end · chancel · choir stalls · rood-screen · congregation · weathervane · finial · tower · gargoyle · belfry · bell-rope · south aisle · nave · main porch · font · arched window with tracery · pulpit · vestry · transept · lich-gate

CUTAWAY VIEW OF A CRUCIFORM CHURCH

EXAMPLES OF CHURCHES

11TH-CENTURY BYZANTINE CHURCH (GREECE)

13TH-CENTURY CATHEDRAL (IRELAND)

16TH-CENTURY CHURCH (ITALY)

17TH-CENTURY CHURCH (PORTUGAL)

17TH-CENTURY RUSSIAN ORTHODOX CHURCH (RUSSIAN FEDERATION)

18TH-CENTURY. MISSION CHURCH (MEXICO)

19TH-CENTURY CHAPEL (N. AMERICA)

19TH-CENTURY EPISCOPAL CHURCH (N. AMERICA)

---

chutz·pah /khŏŏtspə/ *n.* (also **chutzpa**) *sl.* shameless audacity; gall.

chyme /chīm/ *n. Physiol.* the fluid which passes from the stomach to the small intestine, consisting of gastric juices and partly digested food.

CI *abbr.* Channel Islands.

Ci *abbr.* curie(s).

CIA *abbr.* Central Intelligence Agency.

cia·o /chow/ *int. colloq.* **1** good-bye. **2** hello.

ci·bo·ri·um /sibáwreeəm/ *n.* (*pl.* **ciboria** /-reeə/) a vessel with an arched cover used to hold the Eucharist.

ci·ca·da /sikáydə, -kaádə/ *n.* (also **ci·ca·la** /sikaálə/) (*pl.* **cicadas** or **cicadae** /-dee/) any transparent-winged large insect of the family Cicadidae, the males of which make a loud, rhythmic, chirping sound. ▷ HEMIPTERA

cic·a·trix /síkətriks, sikáy-/ *n.* (also **cic·a·trice** /síkətris/) (*pl.* **cicatrices** /-tríseez/) **1** a scar. **2** *Bot.* a mark on a stem, etc., left when a leaf or other part becomes detached.

cic·a·trize /síkətrīz/ *v.* **1** *tr.* heal (a wound) by scar formation. **2** *intr.* (of a wound) heal by scar formation. □□ **cic·a·tri·za·tion** *n.*

cic·e·ly /sísəlee/ *n.* (*pl.* **-ies**) any of various umbelliferous plants, esp. sweet cicely (*Myrrhis odorata*).

cic·e·ro·ne /chíchərónee, sísə-/ *n.* (*pl.* **ciceroni** *pronunc.* same) a guide who gives information about antiquities, places of interest, etc., to sightseers.

cich·lid /síklid/ *n.* ▼ any tropical freshwater fish of the family Cichlidae, esp. the kinds kept in aquariums.

CICHLID: AFRICAN BUTTERFLY CICHLID (*Anomalachromis thomasi*)

CID *abbr.* (in the UK) Criminal Investigation Department.

-cide /sīd/ *suffix* forming nouns meaning: **1** a person or substance that kills (*regicide*; *insecticide*). **2** the killing of (*infanticide*; *suicide*).

ci·der /sídər/ *n.* **1** *US* a usu. unfermented drink made from crushed apples. **2** *Brit.* (also **cy·der**) an alcoholic drink made from fermented apple juice.

ci·de·vant /seédəvón/ *adj. & adv.* that has been (with person's earlier name or status); former.

c.i.f. *abbr.* cost, insurance, freight (as being included in a price).

cig /sig/ *n. colloq.* cigarette; cigar.

ci·gar /sigaár/ *n.* a cylinder of tobacco rolled in tobacco leaves for smoking.

cig·a·rette /sígərét/ *n.* (also **cig·a·ret**) **1** a thin cylinder of finely cut tobacco rolled in paper for smoking. **2** a similar cylinder containing a narcotic or medicated substance.

cig·a·ril·lo /sigərílō/ *n.* (*pl.* **-os**) a small cigar.

cig·gy /sígee/ *n.* (*pl.* **-ies**) *colloq.* cigarette.

cil·i·um /síleeəm/ *n.* (*pl.* **cilia** /-leeə/) **1** a short, minute, hairlike vibrating structure on the surface of some cells, causing currents in the surrounding fluid. **2** an eyelash. ▷ EYE. □□ **cil·i·ate** /-ayt, -ət/ *adj.* **cil·i·at·ed** *adj.* **cil·i·a·tion** *n.*

C. in C. *abbr.* commander in chief.

cinch /sinch/ *n. & v.* ● *n.* **1** *colloq.* **a** a sure thing; a certainty. **b** an easy task. **2** a firm hold. **3** a girth for a saddle or pack. ● *v.tr.* **1 a** tighten as with a cinch (*cinched at the waist with a belt*). **b** secure a grip on. **2** *sl.* make certain of. **3** put a cinch (sense 3) on.

cin·cho·na /singkónə/ *n.* **1 a** any evergreen tree or shrub of the genus *Cinchona*, native to S. America. **b** the bark of this tree, containing quinine. **2** any

C

drug from this bark formerly used as a tonic and to stimulate the appetite. □□ **cin·cho·nic** /-kónik/ *adj.* **cin·cho·nine** /síngkəneen/ *n.*

cinc·ture /síngkchər/ *n.* **1** *literary* a girdle, belt, or border. **2** *Archit.* a ring at either end of a column shaft.

cin·der /síndər/ *n.* **1** the residue of coal or wood, etc., that has stopped giving off flames but still has combustible matter in it. **2** *slag.* **3** (in *pl.*) ashes. □ **burned to a cinder** made useless by burning. □□ **cin·der·y** *adj.*

cin·der block *n.* a concrete building block, usu. made from cinders mixed with sand and cement.

Cin·der·el·la /síndərélə/ *n.* **1** a person or thing of unrecognized or disregarded merit or beauty. **2** a neglected or despised member of a group.

cine- /síni/ *comb. form* pertaining to film or movies (*cinephotography*).

cin·e·aste /síneeast/ *n.* (also **cin·e·ast**) **1** a person who makes films, esp. professionally. **2** a movie lover.

cin·e·ma /sínəmə/ *n.* **1 a** films collectively. **b** the production of films as an art or industry; cinematography. **2** *Brit.* a theater where motion pictures are shown.

cin·e·ma·theque /sínəmətek/ *n.* **1** a film library or archive. **2** a small movie theater.

cin·e·mat·ic /sínəmátik/ *adj.* **1** having the qualities characteristic of the cinema. **2** of or relating to motion pictures. □□ **cin·e·mat·i·cal·ly** *adv.*

cin·e·mat·o·graph /sínəmátəgraf/ (also **kin·e·mat·o·graph** /kín-/) *n.* a movie camera.

cin·e·ma·tog·ra·phy /sínəmətógrəfee/ *n.* the art of making motion pictures. □□ **cin·e·ma·tog·ra·pher** *n.* **cin·e·mat·o·graph·ic** /-mátəgráfik/ *adj.* **cin·e·mat·o·graph·i·cal·ly** *adv.*

ci·ne·ma ve·ri·té /séenemáa véreetáy/ *n. Cinematog.* **1** the art or process of making realistic (esp. documentary) films that avoid artificiality and artistic effect. **2** such films collectively.

cineplex /sínipleks/ *n.* a multiplex cinema.

cin·e·ra·ri·a /sínəráireeə/ *n.* any of several varieties of the composite plant, *Cineraria cruentus,* having bright flowers and ash-colored down on its leaves.

cin·e·rar·y /sínəreree/ *adj.* of ashes.

cin·na·bar /sínəbaar/ *n.* **1** ◄ a bright red mineral form of mercuric sulfide from which mercury is obtained. ▷ ORE. **2** vermilion.

CINNABAR

cin·na·mon /sínəmən/ *n.* **1** an aromatic spice from the peeled, dried, and rolled bark of a SE Asian tree. ▷ SPICE. **2** any tree of the genus *Cinnamomum,* esp. *C. zeylanicum* yielding the spice. **3** yellowish-brown.

cinque·foil /síngkfoyl/ *n.* **1** any plant of the genus *Potentilla,* with compound leaves of five leaflets. **2** *Archit.* a five-cusped ornament in a circle or arch.

ci·on var. of SCION 1.

ci·pher /sífər/ *n. & v.* (*Brit.* **cipher** or **cypher**) ● *n.* **1 a** a secret or disguised way of writing. **b** a thing written in this way. **c** the key to it. **2** the arithmetical symbol (0) denoting no amount but used to occupy a vacant place in decimal, etc., numeration (as in 12.05). **3** a person or thing of no importance. **4** the interlaced initials of a person or company, etc.; a monogram. ● *v.* **1** *tr.* put into secret writing; encipher. **2 a** *tr.* (usu. foll. by *out*) work out by arithmetic; calculate. **b** *intr. archaic* do arithmetic.

cir. *abbr.* (also **circ.**) **1** circle. **2** circuit. **3** circular. **4** circulation. **5** circumference.

cir·ca /sárkə/ *prep.* (preceding a date) about.

cir·ca·di·an /sərkáydeeən/ *adj. Physiol.* occurring or recurring about once per day.

Cir·ce /sársee/ *n.* a dangerously attractive enchantress.

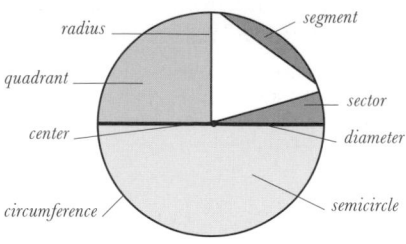

radius

segment

quadrant

sector

center

diameter

circumference

semicircle

CIRCLE AND ASSOCIATED PARTS

cir·cle /sárkəl/ *n. & v.* ● *n.* **1 a** ▲ a round plane figure whose circumference is everywhere equidistant from its center. **b** the line enclosing a circle. **2** a roundish enclosure or structure. **3** a ring. **4** a curved upper tier of seats in a theater, etc. **5** a circular route. **6** *Archaeol.* a group of (usu. large embedded) stones arranged in a circle. **7** persons grouped around a center of interest. **8** a set or class or restricted group (*literary circles*). **9** a period or cycle (*the circle of the year*). **10** (in full **vicious circle**) **a** an unbroken sequence of reciprocal cause and effect. **b** the fallacy of proving a proposition from another which depends on the first for its own proof. ● *v.* **1** *intr.* (often foll. by *around, about*) move in a circle. **2** *tr.* revolve around. **b** form a circle around. □ **circle back** move in a wide loop toward the starting point. **come full circle** return to the starting point. **go around in circles** make no progress despite effort. **run around in circles** *colloq.* be fussily busy with little result. □□ **cir·cler** *n.*

cir·clet /sárklit/ *n.* **1** a small circle. **2** a circular band, esp. of gold or jeweled, etc., as an ornament.

cir·cuit /sárkit/ *n.* **1 a** a line or course enclosing an area; the distance around; the circumference. **b** the area enclosed. **2** *Electr.* **a** ▼ the path of a current. **b** the apparatus through which a current passes. **3 a** the journey of a judge in a particular district to hold courts. **b** this district. **c** the lawyers following a circuit. **4** a chain of theaters, etc., under a single management. **5** *Brit.* an automobile racing track. **6 a** a sequence of sporting events (*the US tennis circuit*). **b** a sequence of athletic exercises. **7** a roundabout journey. **8 a** a group of local Methodist churches forming a minor administrative unit. **b** the journey of an itinerant minister within this.

cir·cuit board *n. Electronics* a board of nonconductive material on which integrated circuits, printed circuits, etc., are mounted or etched. ▷ TELEPHONE, VIDEO CASSETTE RECORDER

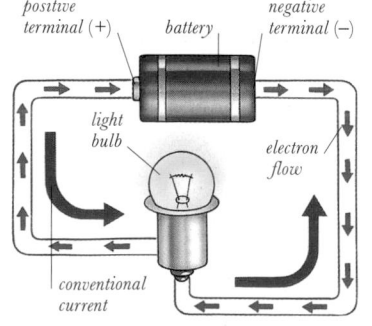

CIRCUIT

Electricity flows in an unbroken path around a circuit from a power source's negative terminal to its positive one. The contrary was once believed: circuit theory is still based on this "conventional current."

positive
terminal (+)

battery

negative
terminal (−)

light
bulb

electron
flow

conventional
current

SIMPLE CIRCUIT SHOWING CURRENT

cir·cuit break·er *n.* an automatic device for stopping the flow of current in an electrical circuit.

cir·cu·i·tous /sərkyóo-itəs/ *adj.* **1** indirect (and usu. long). **2** going a long way around. □□ **cir·cu·i·tous·ly** *adv.* **cir·cu·i·tous·ness** *n.*

cir·cuit·ry /sárkitree/ *n.* (*pl.* **-ies**) **1** a system of electric circuits. **2** the equipment forming this.

cir·cu·lar /sárkyələr/ *adj. & n.* ● *adj.* **1 a** having the form of a circle. **b** moving or taking place along a circle; indirect; circuitous (*circular route*). **2** *Logic* (of reasoning) depending on a vicious circle. **3** (of a letter or advertisement, etc.) printed for distribution to a large number of people. ● *n.* a circular letter, leaflet, etc. □□ **cir·cu·lar·i·ty** /-láritee/ *n.* **cir·cu·lar·ly** *adv.*

cir·cu·lar·ize /sárkyələrīz/ *v.tr.* **1** distribute circulars to. **2** seek opinions of (people) by means of a questionnaire. □□ **cir·cu·lar·i·za·tion** *n.*

cir·cu·lar saw *n.* a power saw with a rapidly rotating toothed disk. ▷ SAW

cir·cu·late /sárkyəlayt/ *v.* **1** *intr.* go around from one place or person, etc., to the next and so on; be in circulation. **2** *tr.* **a** cause to go around; put into circulation. **b** give currency to (a report, etc.). **c** circularize. **3** *intr.* be actively sociable at a party, gathering, etc. □□ **cir·cu·la·tive** *adj.* **cir·cu·la·tor** *n.*

cir·cu·la·tion /sárkyəláyshən/ *n.* **1 a** a movement to and fro, or from and back to a starting point, esp. of a fluid in a confined area or circuit. **b** the movement of blood from and to the heart. **c** a similar movement of sap, etc. **2 a** the transmission or distribution (of news or information or books, etc.). **b** the number of copies sold, esp. of journals and newspapers. **3 a** currency, coin, etc. **b** the movement or exchange of this in a country, etc. □ **in** (or **out of**) **circulation** participating (or not participating) in activities, etc.

cir·cu·la·to·ry /sárkyələtawree/ *adj.* of or relating to the circulation of blood or sap.

circum. *abbr.* circumference.

cir·cum·cise /sárkəmsīz/ *v.tr.* **1** cut off the foreskin, as a Jewish or Muslim rite or a surgical operation. **2** cut off the clitoris (and sometimes the labia), usu. as a religious rite.

cir·cum·ci·sion /sárkəmsízhən/ *n.* **1** the act or rite of circumcising or being circumcised. **2** (**Circumcision**) *Eccl.* the feast of the Circumcision of Christ, Jan. 1.

cir·cum·fer·ence /sərkúmfərəns/ *n.* **1** the enclosing boundary, esp. of a circle or other figure enclosed by a curve. ▷ CIRCLE. **2** the distance around. □□ **cir·cum·fer·en·tial** /-fərénshəl/ *adj.* **cir·cum·fer·en·tial·ly** *adv.*

cir·cum·flex /sárkəmfleks/ *n. & adj.* ● *n.* (in full **circumflex accent**) a mark (^) placed over a vowel in some languages to indicate a contraction, length, or a special quality. ● *adj. Anat.* curved, bending around something else (*circumflex nerve*).

cir·cum·lo·cu·tion /sárkəmlōkyóoshən/ *n.* **1 a** a roundabout expression. **b** evasive talk. **2** the use of many words where fewer would do; verbosity. □□ **cir·cum·lo·cu·tion·al** *adj.* **cir·cum·lo·cu·tion·ar·y** *adj.* **cir·cum·lo·cu·tion·ist** *n.* **cir·cum·loc·u·to·ry** /-lókyətáwree/ *adj.*

cir·cum·nav·i·gate /sárkəmnávigayt/ *v.tr.* sail around (esp. the world). □□ **cir·cum·nav·i·ga·tion** /-gáyshən/ *n.* **cir·cum·nav·i·ga·tor** *n.*

cir·cum·po·lar /sárkəmpólər/ *adj.* **1** *Geog.* around or near one of the Earth's poles. **2** *Astron.* (of a star or motion, etc.) above the horizon at all times in a given latitude.

cir·cum·scribe /sárkəmskrīb/ *v.tr.* **1** (of a line, etc.) enclose or outline. **2** lay down the limits of; confine; restrict. **3** *Geom.* draw (a figure) around another, touching it at points but not cutting it (cf. INSCRIBE). □□ **cir·cum·scrib·a·ble** *adj.* **cir·cum·scrib·er** *n.* **cir·cum·scrip·tion** /-skrípshən/ *n.*

cir·cum·spect /sárkəmspekt/ *adj.* wary; cautious; taking everything into account. □□ **cir·cum·spec·tion** /-spékshən/ *n.* **cir·cum·spect·ly** *adv.*

cir·cum·stance /sórkəmstans/ *n.* **1 a** a fact, occurrence, or condition, esp. (in *pl.*) the time, place, manner, cause, occasion, etc., or surroundings of an act or event. **b** (in *pl.*) the external conditions that affect or might affect an action. **2** (often foll. by *that* + clause) an incident, occurrence, or fact, as needing consideration. **3** (in *pl.*) one's state of financial or material welfare. **4** ceremony; fuss. □ **in** (or **under**) **the** (or **these**) **circumstances** the state of affairs being what it is. **in** (or **under**) **no circumstances** not at all; never. □□ **cir·cum·stanced** *adj.*

cir·cum·stan·tial /sórkəmstánshəl/ *adj.* **1** given in full detail (*a circumstantial account*). **2** (of evidence, a legal case, etc.) tending to establish a conclusion by inference from known facts hard to explain otherwise. **3 a** depending on circumstances. **b** adventitious; incidental. □□ **cir·cum·stan·ti·al·i·ty** /-sheeálitee/ *n.* **cir·cum·stan·ti·al·ly** *adv.*

cir·cum·vent /sórkəmvént/ *v.tr.* **1 a** evade (a difficulty); find a way around. **b** baffle; outwit. **2** entrap (an enemy) by surrounding. □□ **cir·cum·ven·tion** /-vénshən/ *n.*

cir·cus /sórkəs/ *n.* (*pl.* **circuses**) **1** a traveling show of performing animals, acrobats, clowns, etc. **2** *colloq.* **a** a scene of lively action; a disturbance. **b** a group of people in a common activity, esp. sports. **3** *Brit.* an open space in a town or city, where several streets converge (*Piccadilly Circus*). **4** a circular hollow surrounded by hills. **5** *Rom. Antiq.* a rounded or oval arena with tiers of seats, for equestrian and other sports and games.

ci·ré /siráy/ *n. & adj.* ● *n.* a fabric with a smooth shiny surface obtained esp. by waxing and heating. ● *adj.* having such a surface.

cire per·due /seér perdóō, -dyóō/ = LOST WAX.

cirque /sərk/ *n.* **1** *Geol.* ▼ a deep, bowl-shaped hollow at the head of a valley or on a mountainside. **2** *poet.* **a** a ring. **b** an amphitheater or arena.

cir·rho·sis /sirósis/ *n.* a chronic disease of the liver marked by the degeneration of cells and the thickening of surrounding tissues, as a result of alcoholism, hepatitis, etc. □□ **cir·rhot·ic** /sirótik/ *adj.*

cir·ri·ped /síriped/ *n.* (also **cir·ri·pede** /síripeed/) any marine crustacean of the class Cirripedia, having a valved shell and usu. sessile when adult, e.g., a barnacle.

cirro- /síro/ *comb. form* cirrus (cloud). ▷ CLOUD

cir·rus /sírəs/ *n.* (*pl.* **cirri** /-rī/) **1** *Meteorol.* a form of white wispy cloud, esp. at high altitude. ▷ CLOUD. **2** *Bot.* a tendril. **3** *Zool.* a long, slender appendage or filament. ▷ BARNACLE. □□ **cir·rose** *adj.* **cir·rous** *adj.*

cis·al·pine /sisálpīn/ *adj.* on the southern side of the Alps.

cis·at·lan·tic /sísətlántik/ *adj.* (from the speaker's point of view) on this side of the Atlantic.

cis·co /siskó/ *n.* (*pl.* **-oes**) any of various freshwater whitefish of the genus *Coregonus*, native to N. America.

cis·lu·nar /sislóōnər/ *adj.* between the Earth and the Moon.

cist /sist, kist/ *n.* (also **kist** /kist/) *Archaeol.* a coffin or burial chamber made from stone or a hollowed tree.

CIRQUE

As snow accumulates in shallow mountain hollows, it compresses into ice. The soil is loosened by frost wedging and abrasion, and the hollow deepens to form a cirque.

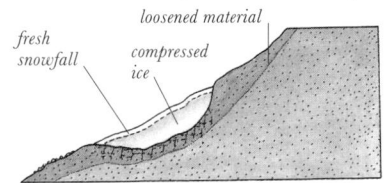

fresh snowfall
loosened material
compressed ice

CROSS SECTION THROUGH A CIRQUE

CITRUS FRUIT

Cultivated for at least 2,000 years in subtropical climates, citrus fruits are valued chiefly for their edible fruit, peel, and juice. They provide vital flavorings in food and drink and are a rich source of vitamin C.

Cosmetics, scents, and aromatherapy also rely on essential oils yielded by their peel, leaves, and shoots, while soaps are made from the seed oils. Colds, coughs, and sore throats can all be soothed by citrus juices.

EXAMPLES OF CITRUS FRUITS

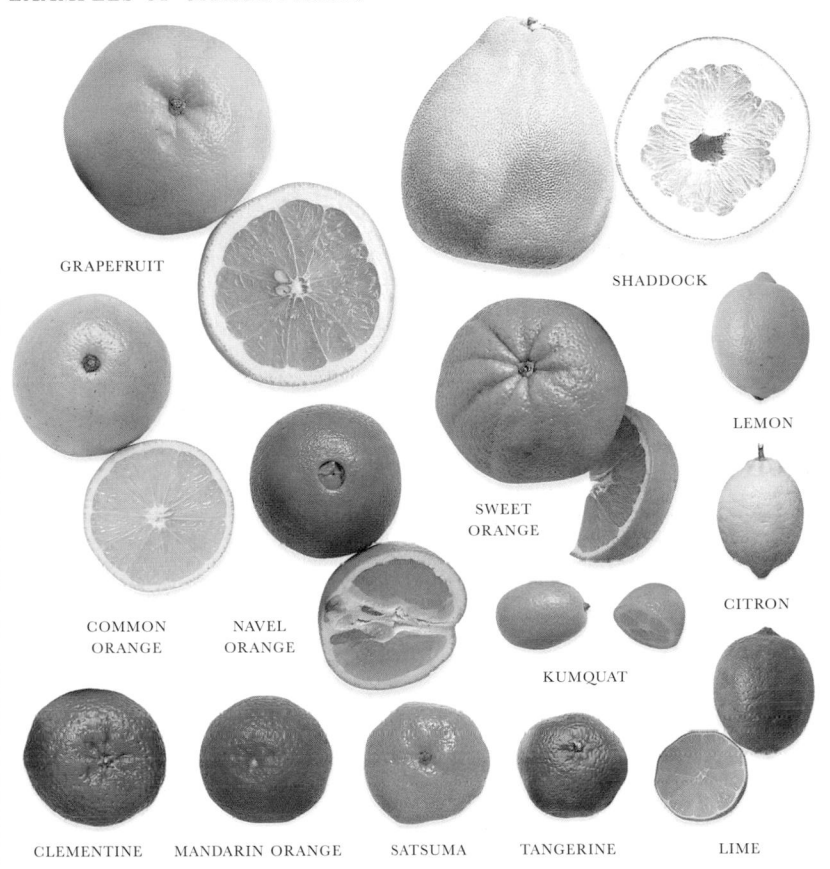

GRAPEFRUIT • SHADDOCK • LEMON • SWEET ORANGE • CITRON • COMMON ORANGE • NAVEL ORANGE • KUMQUAT • CLEMENTINE • MANDARIN ORANGE • SATSUMA • TANGERINE • LIME

C

Cis·ter·cian /sistórshən/ *n. & adj.* ● *n.* a monk or nun of an order founded in 1098 as a stricter branch of the Benedictines. ● *adj.* of the Cistercians.

cis·tern /sistərn/ *n.* **1** a tank or container for storing water, etc. **2** an underground reservoir for rainwater.

cis·tus /sistəs/ *n.* any shrub of the genus *Cistus*, with large white or red flowers. Also called **rockrose**.

cit. *abbr.* **1** citation. **2** cited. **3** citizen.

cit·a·del /sítəd'l, -del/ *n.* **1** a fortress, usu. on high ground protecting or dominating a city. ▷ ACROPOLIS. **2** a meeting hall of the Salvation Army.

ci·ta·tion /sītáyshən/ *n.* **1** the citing of a book or other source; a passage cited. **2** a mention in an official dispatch. **3** a note accompanying an award, describing the reasons for it.

cite /sīt/ *v.tr.* **1** adduce as an instance. **2** quote (a passage, book, or author) in support of an argument, etc. **3** mention in an official dispatch. **4** summon to appear in a court of law. □□ **cit·a·ble** *adj.*

cit·i·fied /sítifīd/ *adj.* (also **cit·y·fied**) usu. *derog.* citylike or urban in appearance or behavior.

cit·i·zen /sítizən/ *n.* **1** a member of a nation or commonwealth, either native or naturalized. **2** (usu. foll. by *of*) an inhabitant of a city. **3** a civilian. □□ **cit·i·zen·hood** *n.* **cit·i·zen·ry** *n.*

cit·i·zen's ar·rest *n.* an arrest by an ordinary person without a warrant, allowable in certain cases.

cit·i·zens band *n.* a system of local intercommunication by individuals on special radio frequencies.

cit·i·zen·ship /sítizənship/ *n.* **1** the state of being a citizen. **2** the character of a person, regarding his or her behaviour as a member of society (*a youth group that promoted good citizenship*).

cit·ric /sítrik/ *adj.* derived from citrus fruit. □□ **cit·rate** *n.*

cit·ric ac·id *n.* a sharp-tasting, water-soluble organic acid found in the juice of lemons and other sour fruits.

cit·rin /sítrin/ *n.* a group of substances occurring mainly in citrus fruits and black currants, and formerly thought to be a vitamin.

cit·rine /sítreen, sitréen/ *adj. & n.* ● *adj.* lemon-colored. ● *n.* a transparent yellow variety of quartz.

cit·ron /sítrən/ *n.* **1** a shrubby tree, *Citrus medica*, bearing large lemonlike fruits with thick fragrant peel. **2** this fruit. ▷ CITRUS FRUIT

cit·ron·el·la /sítrənélə/ *n.* **1** any fragrant grass of the genus *Cymbopogon*, native to S. Asia. **2** the scented oil from these, used in insect repellent, and in perfume and soap manufacture.

cit·rus /sítrəs/ *n.* **1** any tree of the genus *Citrus*, including citron, lemon, lime, orange, and grapefruit. **2** (in full **citrus fruit**) ▲ a fruit from such a tree. □□ **cit·rous** *adj.*

cit·tern /sítərn/ *n. hist.* a wire-stringed, lutelike instrument usu. played with a plectrum.

cit·y /sítee/ *n.* (*pl.* **-ies**) **1 a** a large town. **b** *US* a state-chartered municipal corporation occupying a definite area. **c** *Brit.* (strictly) a town created a city by charter and containing a cathedral. **2** (**the City**) **a** the major center of a region. **b** the part of London governed by the Lord Mayor and the Corporation. **c** the business part of this. **d** *Brit.* commercial circles; high finance. □□ **cit·y·ward** *adj. & adv.* **cit·y·wards** *adv.*

cit·y·fied var. of CITIFIED.

cit·y hall *n.* municipal offices or officers.

cit·y·scape /síteeskayp/ *n.* **1** a view of a city (actual or depicted). **2** city scenery.

cit·y slick·er *n.* usu. *derog.* **1** a smart and sophisticated city dweller. **2** a plausible rogue as found in cities.

cit·y-state *n.* esp. *hist.* a city that with its surrounding territory forms an independent state.

civ·et /sívit/ *n.* **1** (in full **civet cat**) any catlike animal of the mongoose family, esp. *Civettictis civetta* of Central Africa, having well-developed anal scent glands. **2** a strong musky perfume obtained from the secretions of these scent glands.

civ·ic /sívik/ *adj.* **1** of a city; municipal. **2** of or proper to citizens (*civic virtues*). **3** of citizenship; civil. □□ **civ·i·cal·ly** *adv.*

civ·ic cen·ter *n.* **1** *Brit.* the area where municipal offices and other public buildings are situated; the buildings themselves. **2** a municipal building with space for conventions, sports events, etc., and other public facilities, often publicly supported.

civ·ics /síviks/ *n.pl.* (usu. treated as *sing.*) the study of the rights and duties of citizenship.

civ·il /sívəl/ *adj.* **1** of or belonging to citizens. **2** of ordinary citizens and their concerns, as distinct from military or naval or ecclesiastical matters. **3** polite; obliging; not rude. **4** *Law* relating to civil law (see below), not criminal or political matters (*civil court; civil lawyer*). **5** (of the length of a day, year, etc.) fixed by custom or law, not natural or astronomical. **6** occurring within a community or among fellow citizens; internal (*civil unrest*). □□ **civ·il·ly** *adv.*

civ·il de·fense *n.* the organization and training of civilians for the protection of lives and property during and after attacks in wartime, natural disasters, emergencies, etc.

civ·il dis·o·be·di·ence *n.* the refusal to comply with certain laws or to pay taxes, etc., as a peaceful form of political protest.

civ·il en·gi·neer *n.* an engineer who designs or maintains roads, bridges, dams, etc. □□ **civ·il en·gi·neer·ing** *n.*

civ·il·ian /sivílyən/ *n. & adj.* ● *n.* a person not in the armed services or the police force. ● *adj.* of or for civilians.

ci·vil·ian·ize /sivílyənīz/ *v.tr.* make civilian in character or function. □□ **ci·vil·ian·i·za·tion** *n.*

ci·vil·i·ty /sivílitee/ *n.* (*pl.* **-ies**) **1** politeness. **2** an act of politeness.

civ·i·li·za·tion /sívilizáyshən/ *n.* **1** an advanced stage or system of social development. **2** those peoples of the world regarded as having this. **3** a people or nation (esp. of the past) regarded as an element of social evolution (*ancient civilizations; the Inca civilization*). **4** making or becoming civilized.

civ·i·lize /sívilīz/ *v.tr.* **1** bring out of a barbarous or primitive stage of society. **2** enlighten; refine and educate. □□ **civ·i·liz·a·ble** *adj.* **civ·i·liz·er** *n.*

civ·il law *n.* **1** law concerning private rights (opp. CRIMINAL LAW). **2** *hist.* Roman or nonecclesiastical law.

civ·il lib·er·tar·i·an *n.* an advocate of increased civil liberty.

civ·il lib·er·ty *n.* (often in *pl.*) freedom of action and speech subject to the law.

civ·il rights *n.pl.* the rights of citizens to political and social freedom and equality.

civ·il serv·ant *n.* a member of the civil service.

civ·il serv·ice *n.* the permanent professional branches of governmental administration, excluding military and judicial branches and elected politicians.

civ·il war *n.* a war between citizens of the same country.

civ·vies /síveez/ *n.pl. sl.* civilian clothes.

Civ·vy Street /sívee/ *n. Brit. sl.* civilian life.

CJ *abbr.* Chief Justice.

Cl *symb. Chem.* the element chlorine.

cl *abbr.* **1** centiliter(s). **2** class.

clack /klak/ *v. & n.* ● *v.intr.* **1** make a sharp sound as of boards struck together. **2** chatter, esp. loudly. ● *n.* **1** a clacking sound. **2** clacking talk. □□ **clack·er** *n.*

clad[1] /klad/ *adj.* **1** clothed. **2** provided with cladding.

clad[2] /klad/ *v.tr.* (**cladding**; *past* and *past part.* **cladded** or **clad**) provide with cladding.

clad·ding /kláding/ *n.* a covering or coating on a structure or material, etc.

clade /klayd/ *n. Biol.* a group of organisms evolved from a common ancestor.

cla·dis·tics /kládístiks/ *n.pl.* (usu. treated as *sing.*) *Biol.* a method of classification of animals and plants on the basis of shared characteristics, which are assumed to indicate common ancestry. □□ **clad·ism** /kládizəm/ *n.*

claim /klaym/ *v. & n.* ● *v.tr.* **1 a** (often foll. by *that* + clause) demand as one's due or property. **b** (usu. *absol.*) submit a request for payment under an insurance policy. **2 a** represent oneself as having or achieving (*claim victory*). **b** (foll. by *to* + infin.) profess (*claimed to be the owner*). **c** assert; contend (*claim that one knows*). **3** have as a consequence (*the fire claimed many victims*). **4** (of a thing) deserve (one's attention, etc.). ● *n.* **1 a** a demand or request for something considered one's due (*lay claim to; put in a claim*). **b** an application for compensation under the terms of an insurance policy. **2** (foll. by *to, on*) a right or title to a thing (*his only claim to fame; have many claims on my time*). **3** a contention or assertion. **4** a thing claimed. **5** *Mining* a piece of land allotted or taken. □□ **claim·a·ble** *adj.* **claim·er** *n.*

claim·ant /kláymənt/ *n.* a person making a claim, esp. in a lawsuit or for a government benefit.

clair·voy·ance /klairvóyəns/ *n.* **1** the supposed faculty of perceiving things or events in the future or beyond normal sensory contact. **2** exceptional insight.

clair·voy·ant /klairvóyənt/ *n. & adj.* ● *n.* a person having clairvoyance. ● *adj.* having clairvoyance. □□ **clair·voy·ant·ly** *adv.*

clam /klam/ *n. & v.* ● *n.* **1** ▼ any bivalve mollusk, esp. the edible N. American hard or round clam (*Mercenaria mercenaria*) or the soft or long clam (*Mya arenaria*). ▷ BIVALVE. **2** *colloq.* a shy or withdrawn person. ● *v.intr.* (**clammed, clamming**) **1** dig for clams. **2** (foll. by *up*) *colloq.* refuse to talk.

CLAM: SOFT-SHELL CLAM (*Mya arenaria*)

clam·bake /klámbayk/ *n.* a picnic at the seashore typically featuring clams, lobsters, and ears of corn steamed over hot stones beneath a layer of seaweed.

clam·ber /klámbər/ *v. & n.* ● *v.intr.* climb with hands and feet, esp. with difficulty or laboriously. ● *n.* a difficult climb.

clam·dig·gers /klámdigəz/ *n.* close-fitting calf-length trousers for women.

clam·my /klámee/ *adj.* (**clammier, clammiest**) **1** unpleasantly damp and sticky or slimy. **2** (of weather) cold and damp. □□ **clam·mi·ly** *adv.* **clam·mi·ness** *n.*

clam·or /klámər/ *n. & v.* (*Brit.* **clamour**) ● *n.* **1** loud or vehement shouting or noise. **2** a protest or complaint; an appeal or demand. ● *v.* **1** *intr.* make a clamor. **2** *tr.* utter with a clamor. □□ **clam·or·ous** *adj.* **clam·or·ous·ly** *adv.* **clam·or·ous·ness** *n.*

clamp /klamp/ *n. & v.* ● *n.* a device, esp. a brace or band of iron, etc., for strengthening other materials or holding things together. ● *v.tr.* **1** strengthen or fasten with a clamp. **2** place or hold firmly. **3** immobilize (an illegally parked car) by fixing a clamp to one of its wheels. □ **clamp down 1** (often foll. by *on*) be rigid in enforcing a rule, etc. **2** (foll. by *on*) try to suppress.

clamp·down /klámpdown/ *n.* severe restriction or suppression.

clan /klan/ *n.* **1** a group of people with a common ancestor, esp. in the Scottish Highlands. **2** a large family as a social group. **3** a group with a strong common interest.

clan·des·tine /klandéstin/ *adj.* surreptitious; secret. □□ **clan·des·tine·ly** *adv.*

clang /klang/ *n. & v.* ● *n.* a loud, resonant, metallic sound as of a bell or hammer, etc. ● *v.* **1** *intr.* make a clang. **2** *tr.* cause to clang.

clang·er /klángər/ *n. Brit. sl.* a mistake or blunder. □ **drop a clanger** commit a conspicuous indiscretion.

clang·or /klánggər/ *n.* (*Brit.* **clangour**) **1** a prolonged or repeated clanging noise. **2** an uproar or commotion. □□ **clang·or·ous** *adj.* **clang·or·ous·ly** *adv.*

clank /klangk/ *n. & v.* ● *n.* a sound as of heavy pieces of metal meeting or a chain rattling. ● *v.* **1** *intr.* make a clanking sound. **2** *tr.* cause to clank. □□ **clank·ing·ly** *adv.*

clan·nish /klánish/ *adj.* usu. *derog.* **1** (of a family or group) tending to hold together. **2** of or like a clan. □□ **clan·nish·ly** *adv.* **clan·nish·ness** *n.*

clan·ship /klánship/ *n.* **1** a patriarchal system of clans. **2** loyalty to one's clan.

clans·man /klánzmən/ *n.* (*pl.* **-men**; *fem.* **clanswoman**, *pl.* **-women**) a member or fellow member of a clan.

clap[1] /klap/ *v. & n.* ● *v.* (**clapped, clapping**) **1 a** *intr.* strike the palms of one's hands together as a signal or repeatedly as applause. **b** *tr.* strike (the hands) together in this way. **2** *tr.* **a** *Brit.* applaud or show one's approval of (esp. a person) in this way. **b** slap with the palm of the hand as a sign of approval or encouragement. **3** *tr.* (of a bird) flap (its wings) audibly. **4** *tr.* put or place quickly or with determination (*clapped him in prison; clap a tax on whiskey*). ● *n.* **1** the act of clapping, esp. as applause. **2** an explosive sound, esp. of thunder. **3** a slap; a pat. □ **clap eyes on** *colloq.* see.

clap[2] /klap/ *n. coarse sl.* venereal disease, esp. gonorrhea.

clap·board /klábərd, kláp·bawrd/ *n. & v.* ● *n.* **1** each of a series of horizontal boards with edges overlapping to keep out the rain, etc., used as a siding esp. of houses. **2** = CLAPPERBOARD. ● *v.tr.* fit or supply with clapboards (in sense 1 of *n.*).

clap·per /klápər/ *n.* the tongue or striker of a bell. □ **like the clappers** *Brit. sl.* very fast or hard.

clap·per·board /klápərbawrd/ *n. Cinematog.* a device of hinged boards struck together to synchronize the starting of picture and sound machinery in filming.

clap·trap /kláptrap/ *n.* **1** insincere or pretentious talk; nonsense. **2** language used or feelings expressed only to gain applause.

claque /klak/ *n.* a group of people hired to applaud in a theater, etc.

cla·queur /klakőr/ *n.* a member of a claque.

clar·et /klárət/ *n. & adj.* ● *n.* **1** red wine, esp. from

Bordeaux. **2 a** deep purplish-red. ● *adj.* claret-colored.

clar·i·fy /klárifī/ *v.* (**-ies, -ied**) **1** *tr.* & *intr.* make or become clearer. **2** *tr.* **a** free (liquid, butter, etc.) from impurities. **b** make transparent. **c** purify. □□ **clar·i·fi·ca·tion** *n.* **clar·i·fi·er** *n.*

mouthpiece

barrel joint

head joint

keys for left hand

middle joint

keys for right hand

cork sealing ring

bell

flared end

CLARINET:
B-FLAT
CLARINET

clar·i·net /klárinét/ *n.* **1 a** ◄ a woodwind instrument with a single-reed mouthpiece, a cylindrical tube with a flared end, holes, and keys. ▷ OR-CHESTRA, WOODWIND. **b** its player. **2** an organ stop with a quality resembling a clarinet. □□ **clar·i·net·ist** *n.* (also **clar·i·net·tist**).

clar·i·on /kláreeən/ *n.* & *adj.* ● *n.* **1** a clear, rousing sound. **2** *hist.* a shrill, narrow-tubed war trumpet. **3** an organ stop with the quality of a clarion. ● *adj.* clear and loud.

clar·i·ty /kláritee/ *n.* the state or quality of being clear, esp. of sound or expression.

clark·i·a /kláarkeeə/ *n.* any plant of the genus *Clarkia*, with showy white, pink, or purple flowers.

clar·y /kláiree/ *n.* (*pl.* **-ies**) any of various aromatic herbs belonging to the genus *Salvia*.

clash /klash/ *n.* & *v.* ● *n.* **1 a** a loud, jarring sound as of metal objects being struck together. **b** a collision, esp. with force. **2 a** a conflict or disagreement. **b** a discord of colors, etc. ● *v.* **1 a** *intr.* make a clashing sound. **b** *tr.* cause to clash. **2** *intr.* collide; coincide awkwardly. **3** *intr.* (often foll. by *with*) **a** come into conflict or be at variance. **b** (of colors) be discordant. □□ **clash·er** *n.*

clasp /klasp/ *n.* & *v.* ● *n.* **1 a** a device with interlocking parts for fastening. **b** a buckle or brooch. **c** a metal fastening on a book cover. **2 a** an embrace; a person's reach. **b** a grasp or handshake. **3** a bar of silver on a medal ribbon with the name of the battle, etc., at which the wearer was present. ● *v.* **1** *tr.* fasten with or as with a clasp. **2** *tr.* **a** grasp; hold closely. **b** embrace, encircle. **3** *intr.* fasten a clasp. □ **clasp hands** shake hands with fervor or affection. **clasp one's hands** interlace one's fingers. □□ **clasp·er** *n.*

clasp·er /kláspər/ *n.* (in *pl.*) the appendages of some male fish and insects used to hold the female in copulation.

class /klas/ *n.* & *v.* ● *n.* **1** any set of persons or things grouped together, or graded or differentiated from others esp. by quality (*first class*; *economy class*). **2 a** a division or order of society (*upper class*; *professional classes*). **b** a caste system; a system of social classes. **c** (**the classes**) *archaic* the rich or educated. **3** *colloq.* distinction or high quality in appearance, behavior, etc.; stylishness. **4 a** a group of students taught together. **b** the occasion when they meet. **c** their course of instruction. **5** all the college or school students of the same standing or graduating in a given year (*the class of 1990*). **6** (in conscripted armies) all the recruits born in a given year (*the 1950 class*). **7** *Brit.* a division of candidates according to merit in an examination. **8** *Biol.* a grouping of organisms, the next major rank below a division or phylum. ● *v.tr.* assign to a class or category. □ **in a class of** (or **on**) **its** (or **one's**) **own** unequaled. **no class** *colloq.* a lack of quality or distinction, esp. in behavior.

class ac·tion *n. Law,* chiefly *N. Amer.* a law suit filed or defended by an individual acting on behalf of a group.

class-con·scious *adj.* aware of and reacting to social divisions or one's place in a system of social class. □□ **class-con·scious·ness** *n.*

clas·sic /klásik/ *adj.* & *n.* ● *adj.* **1 a** of the first class; of acknowledged excellence. **b** remarkably typical; outstandingly important (*a classic case*). **c** having enduring worth; timeless. **2 a** of ancient Greek and Latin literature, art, or culture. **b** (of style in art, music, etc.) simple, harmonious, well-proportioned; in accordance with established forms (cf. ROMANTIC). **3** having literary or historic associations (*classic ground*). **4** (of clothes) made in a simple elegant style not much affected by changes in fashion. ● *n.* **1** a classic writer, artist, work, or example. **2 a** an ancient Greek or Latin writer. **b** (in *pl.*) the study of ancient Greek and Latin literature and history. **c** *archaic* a scholar of ancient Greek and Latin. **3 a** a follower of classic models (cf. ROMANTIC). **4** a garment in classic style.

clas·si·cal /klásikəl/ *adj.* **1 a** of ancient Greek or Latin literature or art. **b** (of language) having the form used by the ancient standard authors (*classical Latin*; *classical Hebrew*). **c** based on the study of ancient Greek and Latin (*a classical education*). **d** learned in classical studies. **2 a** (of music) serious or conventional; following traditional principles and intended to be of permanent rather than ephemeral value (cf. POPULAR, LIGHT). **b** of the period *c.*1750–1800

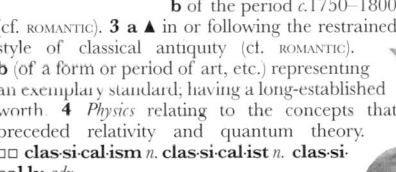

CLASSICAL SCULPTURE:
The Three Graces (1813),
ANTONIO CANOVA

(cf. ROMANTIC). **3 a** ▲ in or following the restrained style of classical antiquity (cf. ROMANTIC). **b** (of a form or period of art, etc.) representing an exemplary standard; having a long-established worth. **4** *Physics* relating to the concepts that preceded relativity and quantum theory. □□ **clas·si·cal·ism** *n.* **clas·si·cal·ist** *n.* **clas·si·cal·ly** *adv.*

clas·si·cism /klásisizəm/ *n.* **1** the following of a classic style. **2** classical scholarship. **b** the advocacy of a classical education. **3** an ancient Greek or Latin idiom. □□ **clas·si·cist** *n.*

clas·si·cize /klásisīz/ *v.* **1** *tr.* make classic. **2** *intr.* imitate a classical style.

clas·si·fied /klásifīd/ *adj.* **1** arranged in classes or categories. **2** (of information, etc.) designated as officially secret. **3** *Brit.* (of a road) assigned to a category according to its importance. **4** (of newspaper advertisements) arranged in columns according to various categories.

clas·si·fy /klásifī/ *v.tr.* (**-ies, -ied**) **1 a** arrange in classes or categories. **b** assign (a thing) to a class or category. **2** designate as officially secret or not for general disclosure. □□ **clas·si·fi·a·ble** *adj.* **clas·si·fi·ca·tion** *n.* **clas·si·fi·ca·to·ry** /klásifikətáwree, kləsífi-, klásifikáytəree/ *adj.* **clas·si·fi·er** *n.*

class·less /kláslis/ *adj.* making or showing no distinction of classes (*classless society*; *classless accent*). □□ **class·less·ness** *n.*

class·mate /klásmayt/ *n.* a fellow member of a class, esp. at school.

class·room /klásroom, -room/ *n.* a room in which a class of students is taught, esp. in a school.

class war *n.* conflict between social classes.

class·y /klásee/ *adj.* (**classier, classiest**) *colloq.* superior; stylish. □□ **class·i·ly** *adv.* **class·i·ness** *n.*

clat·ter /klátər/ *n.* & *v.* ● *n.* **1** a rattling sound as of many hard objects struck together. **2** noisy talk. ● *v.*

1 *intr.* **a** make a clatter. **b** fall or move, etc., with a clatter. **2** *tr.* cause (plates, etc.) to clatter.

clau·di·ca·tion /kláwdikáyshən/ *n. Med.* a cramping pain, esp. in the leg, caused by arterial obstruction; limping.

clause /klawz/ *n.* **1** *Gram.* a distinct part of a sentence, including a subject and predicate. **2** a single statement in a treaty, law, bill, or contract. □□ **claus·al** *adj.*

claus·tral /kláwstrəl/ *adj.* **1** of or associated with the cloister; monastic. **2** narrow-minded.

claus·tro·pho·bi·a /kláwstrəfṓbeeə/ *n.* an abnormal fear of confined places. □□ **claus·tro·phobe** /-rəfōb/ *n.*

claus·tro·pho·bic /kláwstrəfṓbik/ *adj.* **1** suffering from claustrophobia. **2** inducing claustrophobia. □□ **claus·tro·pho·bi·cal·ly** *adv.*

cla·vate /kláyvayt/ *adj. Bot.* club-shaped.

clave[1] /klayv/ *n. Mus.* a hardwood stick used in pairs to make a hollow sound when struck together.

clave[2] *past* of CLEAVE[2].

clav·i·chord /klávikawrd/ *n.* a small keyboard instrument with a very soft tone.

clav·i·cle /klávikəl/ *n.* ▼ the collarbone. □□ **cla·vic·u·lar** /kləvíkyələr/ *adj.* ▷ SKELETON

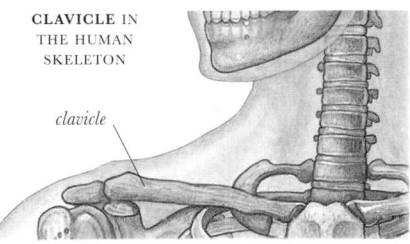

CLAVICLE IN THE HUMAN SKELETON

clavicle

cla·vier /kləveér, kláveeər, kláyveeər/ *n. Mus.* **1** any keyboard instrument. **2** its keyboard.

clav·i·form /klávifawrm/ *adj.* club-shaped.

claw /klaw/ *n.* & *v.* ● *n.* **1 a** ◄ a pointed horny nail on an animal's or bird's foot. ▷ BIRD. **b** a foot armed with claws. **2** the pincers of a shellfish. **3 a** device for grappling, holding, etc. ● *v.* **1** *tr.* & *intr.* scratch, maul, or pull (a person or thing) with claws. **2** *intr.* (often foll. by *at*) grasp, clutch, or scrabble at as with claws. □ **claw back** regain laboriously or gradually. □□ **clawed** *adj.* (also in *comb.*). **claw·er** *n.* **claw·less** *adj.*

phalanx

claw

claw

CLAW: SKELETON OF A SNOWY OWL'S CLAWS

claw ham·mer *n.* a hammer with one side of the head forked for extracting nails.

clay /klay/ *n.* **1** a stiff, sticky earth, used for making bricks, pottery, ceramics, etc. **2** *poet.* the substance of the human body. **3** (in full **clay pipe**) a tobacco pipe made of clay. □□ **clay·ey** *adj.* **clay·ish** *adj.* **clay·like** *adj.*

clay·more /kláymawr/ *n.* **1** *hist.* **a** ▼ a Scottish two-edged broadsword. **b** a broadsword, often with a single edge, having a hilt with a basketwork design. **2** a type of antipersonnel mine.

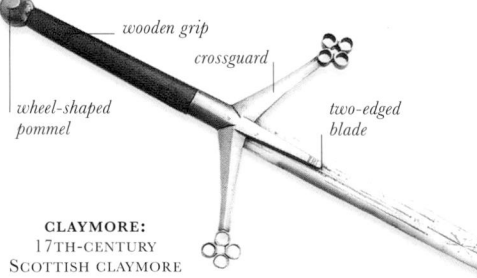

wooden grip

crossguard

wheel-shaped pommel

two-edged blade

CLAYMORE:
17TH-CENTURY
SCOTTISH CLAYMORE

C

C

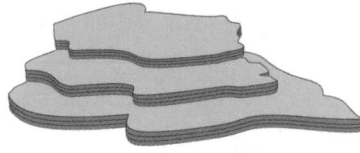

CLEAVAGE

When crystals break, some have a tendency to split along well-defined cleavage lines – planes of weakness between layers of atoms. In flaky cleavage, the crystals flake apart on one plane only, whereas a two-way break lies in two directions. Rhombic breaks and block breaks cleave on three planes, but the latter does so at right angles.

TYPES OF CLEAVAGE

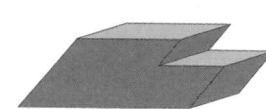

FLAKY CLEAVAGE

TWO-WAY BREAK   BLOCK BREAK   RHOMBIC BREAK

clay pig·eon *n.* a breakable disk thrown up from a trap as a target for shooting.

-cle /kəl/ *suffix* forming (orig. diminutive) nouns (*article*; *particle*).

clean /kleen/ *adj.*, *adv.*, *v.*, & *n.* ● *adj.* **1** (often foll. by *of*) free from dirt or contaminating matter; unsoiled. **2** clear; unused or unpolluted; preserving what is regarded as the original state (*clean air*; *clean page*). **3** free from obscenity or indecency. **4 a** attentive to personal hygiene and cleanliness. **b** (of animals) house-trained. **5** complete; clear-cut; unobstructed; even. **6 a** (of a ship, aircraft, or car) streamlined; smooth. **b** well-formed; slender and shapely (*clean-limbed*; *the car has clean lines*). **7** adroit; skillful (*clean fielding*). **8** (of a nuclear weapon) producing relatively little fallout. **9 a** free from ceremonial defilement or from disease. **b** (of food) not prohibited. **10 a** free from any record of a crime, offense, etc. (*a clean driving record*). **b** *colloq.* (of an alcoholic or drug addict) not possessing or using alcohol or drugs. **c** *sl.* not carrying a weapon or incriminating material; free from suspicion. **11** (of a taste, smell, etc.) sharp; fresh; distinctive. ● *adv.* **1** completely; outright; simply (*cut clean through*; *clean forgot*). **2** in a clean manner. ● *v.* **1** *tr.* (also foll. by *of*) & *intr.* make or become clean. **2** *tr.* eat all the food on (one's plate). **3** *tr. Cookery* remove the innards of (fish or fowl). **4** *intr.* make oneself clean. ● *n.* esp. *Brit.* the act or process of cleaning or being cleaned (*give it a clean*). □ **clean out 1** clean or clear thoroughly. **2** *sl.* empty or deprive (esp. of money). **clean up 1 a** clear (a mess) away. **b** (also *absol.*) make (things) neat. **c** make (oneself) clean. **2** restore order or morality to. **3** *sl.* **a** acquire as gain or profit. **b** make a gain or profit. **come clean** *colloq.* own up; confess everything. **make a clean breast of** see BREAST. **make a clean sweep of** see SWEEP. □□ **clean·a·ble** *adj.* **clean·ish** *adj.* **clean·ness** *n.*

clean-cut *adj.* **1** sharply outlined. **2** neatly groomed.

clean·er /kleenər/ *n.* **1** a person employed to clean the interior of a building. **2** (usu. in *pl.*) a commercial establishment for cleaning clothes. **3** a device or substance for cleaning. □ **take to the cleaners** *sl.* **1** defraud or rob (a person) of all his or her money. **2** criticize severely.

clean-liv·ing *adj.* of upright character.

clean·ly[1] /kleenlee/ *adv.* **1** in a clean way. **2** efficiently; without difficulty.

clean·ly[2] /klenlee/ *adj.* (**cleanlier, cleanliest**) habitually clean; with clean habits. □□ **clean·li·ly** *adv.* **clean·li·ness** *n.*

cleanse /klenz/ *v.tr.* **1** usu. *formal* make clean. **2** (often foll. by *of*) purify from sin or guilt.

cleans·er /klenzər/ *n.* **1** one that cleanses. **2** an agent, as a lotion or an abrasive powder, used for cleansing.

clean-shav·en *adj.* without beard, whiskers, mustache.

clean slate *n.* freedom from commitments or imputations; the removal of these from one's record.

clean·up /kleenup/ *n.* **1** an act of cleaning up. **2** *sl.* a huge profit. **3** *Baseball* the fourth position in the batting order.

clear /kleer/ *adj.*, *adv.*, & *v.* ● *adj.* **1** free from dirt or contamination. **2** (of weather, the sky, etc.) not dull or cloudy. **3 a** transparent. **b** lustrous; shining. **c** (of the complexion) fresh and unblemished. **4** (of soup) not containing solid ingredients. **5 a** distinct; easily perceived by the senses. **b** unambiguous; easily understood (*make oneself clear*). **c** manifest; not confused nor doubtful (*clear evidence*). **6** that discerns or is able to discern readily and accurately (*clear thinking*; *clear-sighted*). **7** (usu. foll. by *about*, *on*, or *that* + clause) confident; convinced; certain. **8** (of a conscience) free from guilt. **9** (of a road, etc.) unobstructed; open. **10 a** net; without deduction (*a clear $1,000*). **b** complete (*three clear days*). **11** (often foll. by *of*) free; unhampered; unencumbered by debt, commitments, etc. **12** (foll. by *of*) not obstructed by. ● *adv.* **1** clearly (*speak loud and clear*). **2** completely (*he got clear away*). **3** apart; out of contact (*keep clear*; *stand clear of the doors*). **4** (foll. by *to*) all the way. ● *v.* **1** *tr.* & *intr.* make or become clear. **2 a** *tr.* (often foll. by *of*) free from prohibition or obstruction. **b** *tr.* & *intr.* make or become empty or unobstructed. **c** *tr.* free (land) for cultivation or building by cutting down trees, etc. **d** *tr.* cause people to leave (a room, etc.). **3** *tr.* (often foll. by *of*) show or declare (a person) to be innocent (*cleared them of complicity*). **4** *tr.* approve (a person) for special duty, access to information, etc. **5** *tr.* pass over or by safely or without touching, esp. by jumping. **6** *tr.* make (an amount of money) as a net gain or to balance expenses. **7** *tr.* pass (a check) through a clearinghouse. **8** *tr.* pass through (a customs office, etc.). **9** *tr.* remove (an obstruction, an unwanted object, etc.). **10** *tr.* (also *absol.*) *Sports* send (the ball, puck, etc.) out of one's defensive zone. **11** *intr.* (often foll. by *away*, *up*) (of physical phenomena) disappear; gradually diminish (*mist cleared by lunchtime*). **12** *tr.* (often foll. by *off*) discharge (a debt). □ **clear the air 1** make the air less sultry. **2** disperse an atmosphere of suspicion, tension, etc. **clear away 1** remove completely. **2** remove the remains of a meal from the table. **clear the decks** prepare for action, esp. fighting. **clear off 1** get rid of. **2** *colloq.* go away. **clear out 1** empty. **2** remove. **3** *colloq.* go away. **clear one's throat** cough slightly to make one's voice clear. **clear up 1** tidy up. **2** solve (a mystery, etc.); remove (a difficulty, etc.). **3** (of weather) become fine. **clear the way 1** remove obstacles. **2** stand aside. **clear a thing with** get approval or authorization for a thing from (a person). **in the clear** free from suspicion or difficulty. **out of a clear (blue) sky** as a complete surprise. □□ **clear·a·ble** *adj.* **clear·er** *n.* **clear·ly** *adv.* **clear·ness** *n.*

clear·ance /kleerəns/ *n.* **1** the removal of obstructions, etc., esp. removal of buildings, persons, etc.,

so as to clear land. **2** clear space allowed for the passing of two objects or two parts in machinery, etc. **3** special authorization or permission (esp. for an aircraft to take off or land, or for access to information, etc.). **4 a** the clearing of a person, ship, etc., by customs. **b** a certificate showing this. **5** the clearing of checks.

clear-cut *adj.* **1** sharply defined. **2** obvious.

clear·ing /kleering/ *n.* **1** in senses of CLEAR *v.* **2** an area in a forest cleared for cultivation.

clear·ing·house /kleeringhows/ *n.* **1** a bankers' establishment where checks and bills from member banks are exchanged, so that only the balances need be paid in cash. **2** an agency for collecting and distributing information, etc.

clear·sto·ry var. of CLERESTORY.

clear·way /kleerway/ *n. Brit.* a main road (other than a freeway) on which vehicles are not normally permitted to stop.

cleat /kleet/ *n.* **1** a piece of metal, wood, etc., bolted on for fastening ropes to, or to strengthen woodwork, etc. **2** a projecting piece on a spar, gangway, athletic shoe, etc., to give footing or prevent slipping. **3** a wedge.

cleav·age /kleevij/ *n.* **1** the hollow between a woman's breasts, esp. as exposed by a low-cut garment. **2** a division or splitting. **3 ◄** the splitting of rocks, crystals, etc., in a preferred direction.

cleave[1] /kleev/ *v.* (*past* **cleaved** or **cleft** /kleft/ or **clove** /klōv/; *past part.* **cleaved** or **cleft** or **cloven** /klóvən/) *literary* **1 a** *tr.* chop or break apart; split, esp. along the grain or the line of cleavage. **b** *intr.* come apart in this way. **2** *tr.* make one's way through (air or water). □□ **cleav·a·ble** *adj.*

cleave[2] /kleev/ *v.intr.* (*past* **cleaved** or **clove** /klōv/ or **clave** /klayv/) (foll. by *to*) *literary* stick fast; adhere.

cleav·er /kleevər/ *n.* a tool for cleaving, esp. a heavy chopping tool used by butchers.

cleav·ers /kleevərz/ *n.* (also **cliv·ers** /klivərz/) (treated as *sing.* or *pl.*) a plant, *Galium aparine*, having hooked bristles on its stem that catch on clothes, etc.

clef /klef/ *n. Mus.* any of several symbols placed at the beginning of a staff, indicating the pitch of the notes written on it. ▷ NOTATION

cleft[1] /kleft/ *adj.* split; partly divided.

cleft[2] /kleft/ *n.* a split or fissure; a space or division made by cleaving.

cleft pal·ate *n.* a congenital split in the lip or the roof of the mouth.

clem·a·tis /klemətis, kləmátis/ *n.* **◄** any erect or climbing plant of the genus *Clematis*, bearing white, pink, or purple flowers and feathery seeds, e.g., old man's beard.

clem·ent /klemənt/ *adj.* **1** mild (*clement weather*). **2** merciful. □□ **clem·en·cy** /-mənsee/ *n.*

clem·en·tine /klemənteen, -teen/ *n.* a small citrus fruit, thought to be a hybrid between a tangerine and a sweet orange. ▷ CITRUS FRUIT

CLEMATIS
(*Clematis* 'Carnaby')

clench /klench/ *v.* & *n.* ● *v.tr.* **1** close (the teeth or fingers) tightly. **2** grasp firmly. **3** = CLINCH *v.* 4. ● *n.* **1** a clenching action. **2** a clenched state.

clere·sto·ry /kleerstawree/ *n.* (also **clear·sto·ry**) (*pl.* **-ies**) **1 ►** an upper row of windows in a cathedral or large church, above the level of the aisle roofs. ▷ FAÇADE **2** a raised section of the roof of a railroad car, with windows or ventilators.

clerestory

aisle roof

CLERESTORY OF A GOTHIC CATHEDRAL

cler·gy /klə́rjee/ n. (pl. **-ies**) (usu. treated as pl.) **1** (usu. prec. by *the*) the body of all persons ordained for religious duties. **2** a number of such persons (*ten clergy were present*).

cler·gy·man /klə́rjeemən/ n. (pl. **-men**; fem. **cler·gywoman**, pl. **-women**) a member of the clergy.

cler·ic /klérik/ n. a member of the clergy.

cler·i·cal /klérikəl/ adj. **1** of the clergy or clergymen. **2** of or done by a clerk or clerks. □□ **cler·i·cal·ism** n. **cler·i·cal·ist** n. **cler·i·cal·ly** adv.

cler·i·cal er·ror n. an error made in copying or writing out.

cler·i·hew /klérihyōō/ n. a short comic or nonsensical verse, usu. in two rhyming couplets with lines of unequal length and referring to a famous person.

clerk /klərk/ n. & v. ● n. **1** a person employed in an office, bank, etc., to keep records, accounts, etc. **2** a secretary, agent, or record keeper of a municipality (*town clerk*), court, etc. **3** a lay officer of a church (*parish clerk*), college chapel, etc. **4** *Brit.* a senior official in Parliament. **5** a person who works at the sales counter of a store, at a hotel desk, etc. **6** *archaic* a clergyman. ● v.intr. work as a clerk. □□ **clerk·dom** n. **clerk·ess** n. **clerk·ly** adj. **clerk·ship** n.

clev·er /klévər/ adj. (**cleverer**, **cleverest**) **1 a** skillful; talented; quick to understand and learn. **b** showing good sense or wisdom; wise. **2** adroit; dextrous. **3** (of the doer or the thing done) ingenious; cunning. □□ **clev·er·ly** adv. **clev·er·ness** n.

clev·is /klévis/ n. **1** a U-shaped piece of metal at the end of a beam for attaching tackle, etc. **2** a connection in which a bolt holds one part that fits between the forked ends of another.

clew /klōō/ n. & v. ● n. **1** *Naut.* **a** ◀ a lower or after corner of a sail **b** a set of small cords suspending a hammock. **2** *archaic* **a** a ball of thread or yarn, esp. with reference to the legend of Theseus and the labyrinth. **b** *Brit.* = CLUE. ● v.tr. *Naut.* **1** (foll. by *up*) draw the lower ends of (a sail) to the upper yard or the mast ready for furling. **2** (foll. by *down*) let down (a sail) by the clews in unfurling.

CLEW OF A DINGHY SAIL

boom

clew / top block

cli·an·thus /kleeánthəs/ n. any leguminous plant of the genus *Clianthus*, native to Australia and New Zealand, bearing drooping clusters of red pealike flowers.

cli·ché /kleesháy/ n. (also **cli·che**) **1** a hackneyed phrase or opinion. **2** *Brit.* a metal casting of a stereotype or electrotype.

cli·chéd /kleesháyd/ adj. hackneyed; full of clichés.

click /klik/ n. & v. ● n. **1** a slight, sharp sound, as of a switch being operated. **2** a sharp nonvocal suction, used as a speech sound in some languages. **3** a catch in machinery acting with a slight, sharp sound. **4** (of a horse) an action causing a hind foot to touch the shoe of a forefoot. ● v. **1 a** intr. make a click. **b** tr. cause (one's tongue, heels, etc.) to click. **2** intr. colloq. **a** become clear or understandable (often prec. by *it* as subject: *when I saw them it all clicked*). **b** be successful; secure one's object. **c** (foll. by *with*) become friendly, esp. with a person of the opposite sex. **d** come to an agreement. □□ **click·er** n.

click bee·tle n. any of a family of beetles (Elateridae) that make a click in recovering from being overturned.

cli·ent /klī́ənt/ n. **1** a person using the services of a lawyer, architect, social worker, or other professional person. **2** a customer. □□ **cli·ent·ship** n.

cli·en·tele /klī́əntél, kléeon-/ n. **1** clients collectively. **2** customers, esp. of a store or restaurant. **3** the patrons of a theater, etc.

cli·ent-serv·er attrib.adj. *Computing* relating to a computer system in which a central server provides data to a number of networked workstations.

cliff /klif/ n. a steep rock face, as at the edge of the sea. □□ **cliff·like** adj. **cliff·y** adj.

cliff-hang·er n. a story, etc., with a strong element of suspense; a suspenseful ending to an episode of a serial. □□ **cliff-hang·ing** adj.

cli·mac·ter·ic /klīmáktərik, klímaktérik/ n. & adj. ● n. **1** *Med.* the period of life when fertility and sexual activity are in decline. **2** a supposed critical period in life (esp. occurring at intervals of seven years). ● adj. **1** *Med.* occurring at the climacteric. **2** constituting a crisis; critical.

cli·mac·tic /klīmáktik/ adj. of or forming a climax. □□ **cli·mac·ti·cal·ly** adv.

cli·mate /klī́mit/ n. **1** the prevailing weather conditions of an area. **2** a region with particular weather conditions. **3** the prevailing trend of opinion or public feeling. □□ **cli·mat·ic** /-mátik/ adj. **cli·mat·i·cal** adj. **cli·mat·i·cal·ly** adv.

cli·ma·tol·o·gy /klī́mətóləjee/ n. the scientific study of climate. □□ **cli·ma·to·log·i·cal** /-təlójikəl/ adj. **cli·ma·tol·o·gist** n.

cli·max /klī́maks/ n. & v. ● n. **1** the event or point of greatest intensity or interest; a culmination or apex. **2** a sexual orgasm. **3** *Rhet.* **a** a series arranged in order of increasing importance, etc. **b** the last term in such a series. **4** *Ecol.* a state of equilibrium reached by a plant community. ● v.tr. & intr. colloq. bring or come to a climax.

climb /klīm/ v. & n. ● v. **1** tr. & intr. (often foll. by *up*) ascend; mount; go or come up, esp. by using one's hands. **2** intr. (of a plant) grow up a wall, tree, trellis, etc., by clinging with tendrils or by twining. **3** intr. make progress from one's own efforts, esp. in social rank, intellectual or moral strength, etc. **4** intr. (of an aircraft, the Sun, etc.) go upward. **5** intr. slope upward. ● n. **1** an ascent by climbing. **2 a** a place, esp. a hill, climbed or to be climbed. **b** a recognized route up a mountain, etc. □ **climb down 1** descend with the help of one's hands. **2** withdraw from a stance taken up in argument, negotiation, etc. □□ **climb·a·ble** adj.

climb·er /klī́mər/ n. **1** a mountaineer. **2** a climbing plant. **3** a person with strong social, etc., aspirations.

clime /klīm/ n. literary **1** a region. **2** a climate.

clinch /klinch/ v. & n. ● v. **1** tr. confirm or settle (an argument, bargain, etc.) conclusively. **2** intr. *Boxing & Wrestling* (of participants) become too closely engaged. **3** intr. colloq. embrace. **4** tr. secure (a nail or rivet) by driving the point sideways when through. **5** tr. *Naut.* fasten (a rope) with a particular half hitch. ● n. **1 a** a clinching action. **b** a clinched state. **2** colloq. an (esp. amorous) embrace. **3** *Boxing & Wrestling* an action or state in which participants become too closely engaged.

clinch·er /klínchər/ n. colloq. a remark or argument that settles a matter conclusively.

clinch·er-built var. of CLINKER-BUILT.

cline /klīn/ n. *Biol.* the graded sequence of differences within a species, etc. □□ **clin·al** adj.

cling /kling/ v.intr. (*past* and *past part.* **clung** /klung/) **1** (foll. by *to*) adhere, stick, or hold on (by means of stickiness, suction, grasping, or embracing). **2** (foll. by *to*) remain persistently or stubbornly faithful (to a friend, habit, idea, etc.). **3** maintain one's grasp; keep hold; resist separation. □ **cling together** remain in one body or in contact. □□ **cling·ing·ly** adv.

cling·y /klíngee/ adj. (**clingier**, **clingiest**) liable to cling. □□ **cling·i·ness** n.

clin·ic /klínik/ n. **1** a private or specialized hospital. **2** a place or occasion for giving specialist medical treatment or advice (*eye clinic; fertility clinic*). **3** a gathering at a hospital bedside for the teaching of medicine or surgery. **4** a conference or short course on a particular subject (*golf clinic*). □□ **cli·ni·cian** /kliníshən/ n.

clin·i·cal /klínikəl/ adj. **1** *Med.* **a** of or for the treatment of patients. **b** taught or learned at the hospital bedside. **2** dispassionate; coldly detached. □□ **clin·i·cal·ly** adv.

clink[1] /klingk/ n. & v. ● n. a sharp ringing sound. ● v. **1** intr. make a clink. **2** tr. cause (glasses, etc.) to clink.

clink[2] /klingk/ n. (often prec. by *in*) sl. prison.

clink·er /klíngkər/ n. **1** a mass of slag or lava. **2** a stony residue from burned coal.

clink·er-built /klíngkərbilt/ adj. (also **clinch·er-built** /klínchərbilt/) ▼ (of a boat) having external planks overlapping downward and secured with clinched copper nails.

overlapping planks   *rope fender*

CLINKER-BUILT DINGHY

cli·nom·e·ter /klīnómitər/ n. *Surveying* an instrument for measuring slopes.

clip[1] /klip/ n. & v. ● n. **1** a device for holding things together or for attachment to an object as a marker, esp. a paper clip or a device worked by a spring. **2** a piece of jewelry fastened by a clip. **3** a set of attached cartridges for a firearm. ● v.tr. (**clipped, clipping**) **1** fix with a clip. **2** grip tightly.

clip[2] /klip/ v. & n. ● v.tr. (**clipped, clipping**) **1** cut with shears or scissors, esp. cut short or trim (hair, wool, etc.). **2** trim or remove the hair or wool of (a person or animal). **3** colloq. hit smartly. **4 a** curtail; diminish; cut short. **b** omit (a letter, etc.) from a word; omit letters or syllables of (words pronounced). **5** *Brit.* remove a small piece of (a ticket) to show that it has been used. **6** cut (an extract) from a newspaper, etc. **7** sl. swindle; rob. ● n. **1** an act of clipping, esp. shearing or haircutting. **2** colloq. a smart blow, esp. with the hand. **3** a short sequence from a motion picture. **4** colloq. speed, esp. rapid. □ **clip a person's wings** prevent a person from pursuing ambitions or acting effectively. □□ **clip·pa·ble** adj.

clip art n. pre-drawn pictures and symbols provided with word-processing software and drawing packages.

clip·board /klípbawrd/ n. a small board with a spring clip for holding papers, etc., and providing support for writing.

clip-clop /klípklóp/ n. & v. ● n. a sound such as the beat of a horse's hooves. ● v.intr. (**-clopped, -clopping**) make such a sound.

clip joint n. sl. a club, etc., charging exorbitant prices.

clip·per /klípər/ n. **1** (usu. in pl.) any of various instruments for clipping hair, fingernails, hedges, etc. **2** a fast sailing ship, esp. one with raking bows and masts. **3** a fast horse.

clip·ping /klíping/ n. a piece clipped or cut from something, esp. from a newspaper.

clique /kleek, klik/ n. a small exclusive group of people. □□ **cli·quey** adj. (**cliquier, cliquiest**). **cli·quish** adj. **cli·quish·ness** n. **cli·quism** n.

clit·o·ris /klítəris, klī́-/ n. a small erectile part of the female genitals at the upper end of the vulva. ▷ REPRODUCTIVE ORGANS. □□ **clit·o·ral** adj.

cliv·ers var. of CLEAVERS.

clo·a·ca /klō-áykə/ n. (pl. **cloacae** /-áysee/) **1** the genital and excretory cavity at the end of the intestinal canal in birds, reptiles, etc. ▷ BIRD. **2** a sewer. □□ **clo·a·cal** adj.

cloak /klōk/ n. & v. ● n. **1** an outdoor overgarment, usu. sleeveless, hanging loosely from the shoulders. **2** a covering (*cloak of snow*). **3** *Brit.* (in pl.) = CLOAKROOM. ● v.tr. **1** cover with a cloak. **2** conceal;

C

disguise. □ **under the cloak of** using as a pretext or for concealment.

cloak-and-dag·ger *adj.* involving intrigue and espionage.

cloak·room /klókrŏŏm, -rŏŏm/ *n.* **1** a room where outdoor clothes or luggage may be left by visitors, clients, etc. **2** *Brit. euphem.* a toilet.

clob·ber[1] /klóbər/ *v.tr. sl.* **1** hit repeatedly; beat up. **2** defeat. **3** criticize severely.

clob·ber[2] /klóbər/ *n. Brit. sl.* clothing or personal belongings.

CLOCHE: INDIVIDUAL
CLOCHE COVERING A
LETTUCE PLANT

cloche /klōsh/ *n.* **1** ◄ a small translucent cover for protecting or forcing outdoor plants. **2** (in full **cloche hat**) a woman's close-fitting, bell-shaped hat.

clock /klok/ *n. & v.* ● *n.* **1** ► an instrument for measuring time, driven mechanically or electrically and indicating hours, minutes, etc., by hands on a dial or by displayed figures. **2 a** any measuring device resembling a clock. **b** *colloq.* a speedometer, taximeter, or stopwatch. **3** time taken as an element in competitive sports, etc. (*ran against the clock*). **4** *Brit. sl.* a person's face. **5** *Brit.* a downy seed head, esp. that of a dandelion. ● *v.tr.* **1** *colloq.* **a** (often foll. by *up*) attain or register (a stated time, distance, or speed, esp. in a race). **b** time (a race) with a stopwatch. **2** *sl.* hit, esp. on the head. □ **around the clock** all day and (usu.) night. **clock in** (or **on**) register one's arrival at work, esp. by means of an automatic recording clock. **clock off** (or **out**) register one's departure similarly.

clock·wise /klókwīz/ *adj. & adv.* in a curve corresponding in direction to the movement of the hands of a clock.

clock·work /klókwərk/ *n.* **1** ▼ a mechanism like that of a mechanical clock, with a spring and gears. **2** (*attrib.*) **a** driven by clockwork. **b** regular; mechanical. □ **like clockwork** smoothly; regularly; automatically.

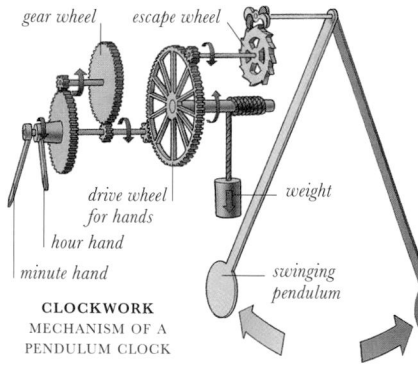

gear wheel   *escape wheel*

drive wheel for hands

hour hand

minute hand

weight

swinging pendulum

CLOCKWORK
MECHANISM OF A
PENDULUM CLOCK

clod /klod/ *n.* **1** a lump of earth, clay, etc. **2** *sl.* a silly or foolish person. □□ **clod·dy** *adj.*

clod·dish /klódish/ *adj.* loutish; foolish; clumsy. □□ **clod·dish·ly** *adv.* **clod·dish·ness** *n.*

clod·hop·per /klódhopər/ *n.* **1** (usu. in *pl.*) *colloq.* a large heavy shoe. **2** = CLOD 2.

clod·hop·ping /klódhoping/ *adj.* = CLODDISH.

clog /klawg, klog/ *n. & v.* ● *n.* **1** a shoe with a thick wooden sole. **2** *archaic* an encumbrance or impediment. ● *v.* (**clogged**, **clogging**) **1** (often foll. by *up*) **a** *tr.* obstruct, esp. by accumulation of glutinous matter. **b** *intr.* become obstructed. **2** *tr.* impede; hamper. **3** *tr. & intr.* (often foll. by *up*) fill with glutinous or choking matter.

clog·gy /klawgee, klógee/ *adj.* (**cloggier**, **cloggiest**) **1** lumpy; knotty. **2** sticky.

cloi·son·né /klóyzənáy, klwáa-/ *n. & adj.* ● *n.* **1** an

CLOCK

Mechanical clocks were invented in the 13th century. Worked by a falling weight and a swinging spindle, they frequently had to be corrected with a sundial. Greater accuracy was first achieved with the introduction of the mainspring, followed by the pendulum, and then the spiral balance wheel. Electricity and atomic power have since revolutionized the accuracy of timekeeping.

EXAMPLES OF CLOCKS

CARRIAGE CLOCK

CUCKOO CLOCK

WATER CLOCK

DIGITAL ALARM CLOCK

MECHANICAL ALARM CLOCK

GRANDFATHER CLOCK

---

enamel finish produced by forming areas of different colors separated by strips of wire placed edgeways on a metal backing. **2** this process. ● *adj.* (of enamel) made by this process.

clois·ter /klóystər/ *n. & v.* ● *n.* **1** a covered walk, often with a wall on one side and a colonnade open to a quadrangle on the other, esp. in a convent, monastery, college, or cathedral. ▷ MONASTERY. **2** monastic life or seclusion. **3** a convent or monastery. ● *v.tr.* seclude or shut up usu. in a convent or monastery. ▷ MONASTERY. □□ **clois·tral** *adj.*

clois·tered /klóystərd/ *adj.* **1** secluded; sheltered. **2** monastic.

clomp var. of CLUMP *v.* 2.

clone /klōn/ *n. & v.* ● *n.* **1 a** a group of organisms produced asexually from one stock or ancestor. **b** one such organism. **2** a person or thing regarded as identical with another. ● *v.tr.* propagate as a clone. □□ **clon·al** *adj.*

clonk /klonk, klawngk/ *n. & v.* ● *n.* an abrupt heavy sound of impact. ● *v.* **1** *intr.* make such a sound. **2** *tr. colloq.* hit.

clon·us /klṓnəs/ *n. Physiol.* a spasm with alternate muscular contractions and relaxations.

clop /klop/ *n. & v.* ● *n.* the sound made by a horse's hooves. ● *v.intr.* (**clopped**, **clopping**) make this sound.

close[1] /klōs/ *adj., adv., & n.* ● *adj.* **1** (often foll. by *to*) situated at only a short distance or interval. **2 a** having a strong or immediate relation or connection (*close friend*; *close relative*). **b** in intimate friendship or association (*were very close*). **c** corresponding almost exactly (*close resemblance*). **d** fitting tightly (*close cap*). **e** (of hair, etc.) short; near the surface. **3** in or almost in contact (*close combat*; *close proximity*). **4** dense; compact; with no or only slight intervals (*close texture*; *close writing*; *close formation*). **5** in which competitors are almost equal (*close contest*). **6** leaving no gaps or weaknesses; rigorous (*close reasoning*). **7** concentrated; searching (*close examination*; *close attention*). **8** (of air, etc.) stuffy or humid. **9 a** closed; shut. **b** shut up; under secure confinement. **10** limited or restricted to certain persons, etc. (*close corporation*; *close scholarship*). **11 a** hidden; secret; covered. **b** secretive. **12** (of a danger, etc.) directly threatening; narrowly avoided (*that was close*). **13** niggardly. **14** (of a vowel) pronounced with a relatively narrow opening of the mouth. ● *adv.* **1** (often foll. by *by, to*) at only a short distance or interval (*they live close by*; *close to the church*). **2** closely; in a close manner (*shut close*). ● *n.* **1** an enclosed space. **2** *Brit.* a street closed at one end. **3** *Brit.* the precinct of a cathedral. **4** *Brit.* a school playing field or playground. □ **at close quarters** very close together. **close to the wind** see SAIL. □□ **close·ly** *adv.* **close·ness** *n.* **clos·ish** *adj.*

close[2] /klōz/ *v. & n.* ● *v.* **1 a** *tr.* shut (a lid, box, door, room, house, etc.). **b** *intr.* become shut (*the door closed slowly*). **c** *tr.* block up. **2 a** *tr. & intr.* bring or come to an end. **b** *intr.* finish speaking (*closed with an expression of thanks*). **c** *tr.* settle (a bargain, etc.). **3 a** *intr.* end the day's business. **b** *tr.* end the day's business at (a store, office, etc.). **4** *tr. & intr.* bring or come closer or into contact (*close ranks*). **5** *tr.* make (an electric circuit, etc.) continuous. **6** *intr.* (often foll. by *with*) come within striking distance; grapple. **7** *intr.* (foll. by *on*) (of a hand, box, etc.) grasp or entrap. ● *n.* **1** a conclusion; an end. **2** *Mus.* a cadence. □ **close down 1** (of a store, factory, etc.) discontinue business, esp. permanently. **2** *Brit.* (of a broadcasting station) end transmissions, esp. until the next day. **close one's eyes 1** (foll. by *to*) pay no attention. **2** die. **close in 1** enclose. **2** come nearer. **3** (of days) get successively shorter with the approach of the winter solstice. **close off** prevent access to by blocking or sealing the entrance. **close out** discontinue; terminate; dispose of (a business). **close up 1** (often foll. by *to*) move closer. **2** shut, esp. temporarily. **3** block up. **4** (of an aperture) grow smaller. □□ **clos·a·ble** *adj.* **clos·er** *n.*

closed /klōzd/ *adj.* **1** not giving access; shut. **2** (of a store, etc.) having ceased business temporarily. **3** (of a society, system, etc.) self-contained; not communicating with others. **4** (of a sport, etc.) restricted to specified competitors, etc.

closed-cap·tioned *adj.* (of a television program) broadcast with captions visible only to viewers with a decoding device attached to their television set.

closed-cir·cuit *adj.* (of television) transmitted by wires to a restricted set of receivers.

closed syl·la·ble *n.* a syllable ending in a consonant.

close-fist·ed /klṓsfistid/ *adj.* niggardly.

close-fit·ting *adj.* (of a garment) fitting close to the body.

close-knit *adj.* tightly bound or interlocked; closely united in friendship.

close-mouthed /klṓsmówt͟hd/ *adj.* reticent.

close shave *n. colloq.* a narrow escape.

clos·et /klózit/ *n. & v.* • *n.* **1** a small or private room. **2** a cupboard or recess. **3** (*attrib.*) secret; covert (*closet homosexual*). • *v.tr.* (**closeted, closeting**) shut away, esp. in private conference or study. □ **come out of the closet** stop hiding something about oneself, esp. one's homosexuality.

close-up *n.* **1** a photograph, etc., taken at close range and showing the subject on a large scale. **2** an intimate description.

clos·ing time *n.* the time at which a bar, store, etc., ends business.

clo·sure /klṓz͟hər/ *n.* **1** the act or process of closing. **2** a closed condition. **3** something that closes or seals, e.g., a cap or tie.

clot /klot/ *n. & v.* • *n.* **1 a** ▼ a thick mass of coagulated liquid, esp. of blood exposed to air. **b** a mass of material stuck together. **2** *Brit. colloq.* a silly or foolish person. • *v.tr. & intr.* (**clotted, clotting**) form into clots.

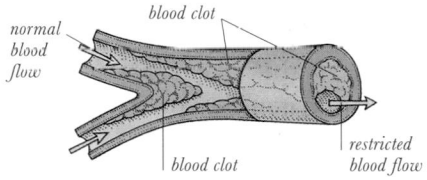

normal blood flow   *blood clot*   *blood clot*   *restricted blood flow*

CLOT: BLOOD CLOTS IN A HUMAN VEIN

cloth /klawth, kloth/ *n.* (*pl.* **cloths** /kloths, klot͟hz/) **1** woven or felted material. **2** a piece of this. **3** a piece of cloth for a particular purpose; a tablecloth, dishcloth, etc. **4** woolen woven fabric as used for clothes. **5 a** profession or status, esp. of the clergy, as shown by clothes (*respect due to his cloth*). **b** (prec. by *the*) the clergy.

cloth-eared *colloq.* somewhat deaf.

clothe /klōt͟h/ *v.tr.* (*past* and *past part.* **clothed** or *formal* **clad**) **1** put clothes on; provide with clothes. **2** cover as with clothes or a cloth.

clothes /klōz, klōt͟hz/ *n.pl.* **1** garments worn to cover the body and limbs. **2** bedclothes.

clothes·horse /klṓz-hawrs, klṓt͟hz-/ *n.* **1** a frame for airing washed clothes. **2** *colloq.* an affectedly fashionable person.

clothes·line /klṓzlīn, klṓt͟hz-/ *n.* a rope or wire, etc., on which washed clothes are hung to dry.

clothes·pin /klṓzpin, klṓt͟hz-/ *n.* a clip or forked device for securing clothes to a clothesline.

cloth·ier /klṓt͟heeər/ *n.* a seller of clothes.

cloth·ing /klṓt͟hing/ *n.* clothes collectively.

clo·ture /klṓchər/ *n. & v.* • *n.* the legislative procedure for ending debate and taking a vote. • *v.tr.* apply cloture to.

cloud /klowd/ *n. & v.* • *n.* **1** ▲ a visible mass of condensed watery vapor floating in the atmosphere high above the general level of the ground. **2** a mass of smoke or dust. **3** (foll. by *of*) a great number of insects, birds, etc., moving together. **4 a** a state of gloom, trouble, or suspicion. **b** a frowning or depressed look (*a cloud on his brow*). **5 a** local dimness or a vague patch of color in or on a liquid or a transparent body. **6** an insubstantial or fleeting thing. **7** obscurity. • *v.* **1** *tr.* cover or darken with clouds or gloom or trouble. **2** *intr.*

CLOUD

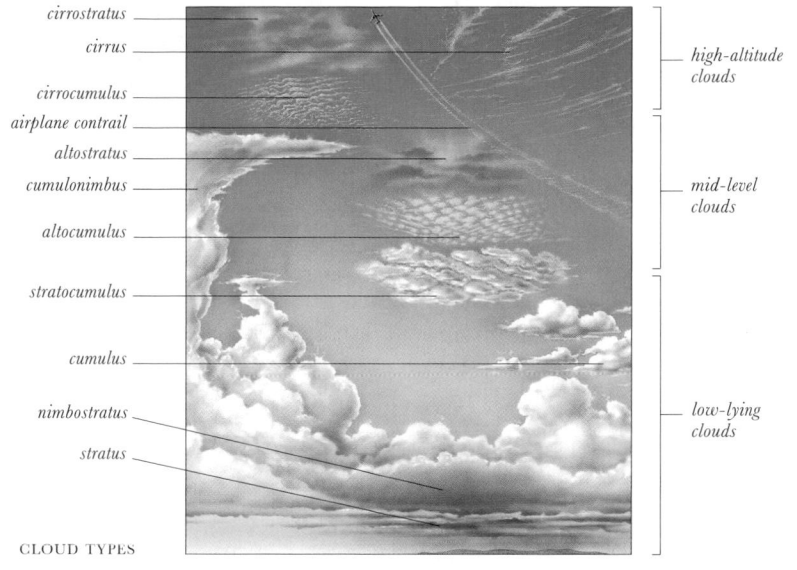

With the advent of aviation in the early 20th century, clouds were classified into ten main types, according to height and appearance. High-altitude clouds are wispy and thin and composed of tiny ice crystals, with their bases 16,000–39,000 ft (5–12 km) above ground. Sheet- or lumplike, mid-level clouds, at 6,500–16,000 ft (2–5 km), presage rain or snow. Low-lying clouds, below 6,500 ft (2 km), are moundlike, or form sheets. Cloud bases can, however, be affected by location, season, or time of day.

cirrostratus — *cirrus* — *cirrocumulus* — *airplane contrail* — *altostratus* — *cumulonimbus* — *altocumulus* — *stratocumulus* — *cumulus* — *nimbostratus* — *stratus*

} *high-altitude clouds*

} *mid-level clouds*

} *low-lying clouds*

CLOUD TYPES

(often foll. by *over, up*) become overcast or gloomy. **3** *tr.* make unclear. **4** *tr.* variegate with vague patches of color. □ **in the clouds 1** unreal; imaginary; mystical. **2** (of a person) abstracted; inattentive. **on cloud nine** *colloq.* extremely happy. **under a cloud** out of favor; discredited; under suspicion. **with one's head in the clouds** daydreaming; unrealistic. □□ **cloud·less** *adj.* **cloud·less·ly** *adv.* **cloud·let** *n.*

cloud·ber·ry /klówdberee/ *n.* (*pl.* **-ies**) a small mountain bramble, *Rubus chamaemorus*, with a white flower and an orange-colored fruit.

cloud·burst /klówdbərst/ *n.* a sudden violent rainstorm.

cloud-cuck·oo-land /klowdkŏŏkŏŏland, -kŏŏkŏŏ-/ *n.* a fanciful or ideal place.

cloud·scape /klówdskayp/ *n.* **1** a picturesque grouping of clouds. **2** a picture or view of clouds.

cloud·y /klówdee/ *adj.* (**cloudier, cloudiest**) **1 a** (of the sky) covered with clouds; overcast. **b** (of weather) characterized by clouds. **2** not transparent; unclear. □□ **cloud·i·ly** *adv.* **cloud·i·ness** *n.*

clout /klowt/ *n. & v.* • *n.* **1** a heavy blow. **2** *colloq.* influence; power of effective action esp. in politics or business. **3** a nail with a large, flat head. • *v.tr.* hit hard.

clove[1] /klōv/ *n.* **1 a** a dried flower bud of a tropical plant, *Eugenia aromatica*, used as a pungent aromatic spice. **b** this plant. **2** (in full **clove gillyflower** or **clove pink**) a clove-scented pink, *Dianthus caryophyllus*, the original of the carnation and other double pinks.

clove[2] /klōv/ *n.* any of the small bulbs making up a compound bulb of garlic, shallot, etc.

clove[3] *past* of CLEAVE.

clove hitch *n.* ► a knot by which a rope is secured by passing it twice around a spar or rope that it crosses at right angles. ▷ KNOT

CLOVE HITCH

clo·ven /klóv'n/ *adj.* split; partly divided.

clo·ven hoof *n.* (also **clo·ven foot**) the divided hoof of ruminant quadrupeds (e.g., oxen, sheep, goats); also ascribed to the god Pan, and so to the Devil. □ **show the cloven hoof** reveal one's evil nature. □□ **clo·ven-foot·ed** /-fŏŏtid/ *adj.* **clo·ven-hoofed** /-hŏŏft/ *adj.*

clo·ver /klṓvər/ *n.* any leguminous fodder plant of the genus *Trifolium*, having dense flower heads and leaves each consisting of usu. three leaflets. □ **in clover** in ease and luxury.

clo·ver·leaf /klṓvərleef/ *n.* a junction of roads intersecting at different levels with connecting sections forming a pattern resembling a four-leaf clover.

clown /klown/ *n. & v.* • *n.* **1** a comic entertainer, esp. in a pantomime or circus, usu. with traditional costume and makeup. **2** a silly, foolish, or playful person. • *v.* **1** *intr.* (often foll. by *about, around*) behave like a clown; act foolishly or playfully. **2** *tr.* perform (a part, an action, etc.) like a clown. □□ **clown·er·y** *n.* **clown·ish** *adj.* **clown·ish·ly** *adv.* **clown·ish·ness** *n.*

cloy /kloy/ *v.tr.* (usu. foll. by *with*) satiate or sicken with an excess of sweetness, richness, etc. □□ **cloy·ing·ly** *adv.*

cloze /klōz/ *n.* the exercise of supplying a word that has been omitted from a passage as a test of readability or comprehension (usu. *attrib.: cloze test*).

CLU *abbr.* chartered life underwriter.

club /klub/ *n. & v.* • *n.* **1** a heavy stick with a thick end, used as a weapon, etc. **2** a stick used in a game, esp. a stick with a head used in golf. **3 a** a playing card of a suit denoted by a black trefoil. **b** (in *pl.*) this suit. **4** an association of persons united by a common interest, usu. meeting periodically for a shared activity (*tennis club; yacht club*). **5 a** an organization or premises offering members social amenities, meals, and temporary residence, etc. **b** a nightclub. **6** an organization offering subscribers certain benefits (*book club*). **7** a group of persons, nations, etc., having something in common. **8** = CLUBHOUSE.

C

● *v.* **clubbed, clubbing**) **1** *tr.* beat with or as with a club. **2** *intr.* (foll. by *together, with*) combine for joint action, esp. making up a sum of money for a purpose. □ **in the club** *Brit. sl.* pregnant. □□ **club·ber** *n.*

club·ba·ble /klúbəbəl/ *adj.* sociable; fit for membership of a club. □□ **club·ba·bil·i·ty** /-bílitee/ *n.* **club·ba·ble·ness** *n.*

club·by /klúbee/ *adj.* (**clubbier, clubbiest**) sociable; friendly.

club·foot /klúbfŏŏt/ *n.* a congenitally deformed foot. □□ **club·foot·ed** *adj.*

club·house /klúbhows/ *n.* the premises used by a club, esp. a golf club.

club·man /klúbmən, -man/ *n.* (*pl.* **-men**; *fem.* **-woman**, *pl.* **-women**) a member of one or more social clubs.

club·moss /klúbmaws, -mos/ *n.* ◄ any pteridophyte of the family Lycopodiaceae, bearing upright spikes of spore cases.

CLUBMOSS
(*Lycopodium* species)

club·root /klúbroot/ *n.* a disease of cabbages, etc., caused by the fungus *Plasmodiophora brassicae*, which causes swelling at the base of the stem.

club sand·wich *n.* a sandwich with two layers of filling between three slices of toast or bread.

club so·da *n.* = SODA *n.* 2.

cluck /kluk/ *n. & v.* ● *n.* **1** a guttural cry like that of a hen. **2** *sl.* a silly or foolish person (*dumb cluck*). ● *v.intr.* emit a cluck or clucks.

clue /klōō/ *n. & v.* ● *n.* **1** a fact or idea that serves as a guide, or suggests a line of inquiry, in a problem or investigation. **2** a piece of evidence, etc., in the detection of a crime. **3** a verbal formula serving as a hint as to what is to be inserted in a crossword. **4 a** the thread of a story. **b** a train of thought. ● *v.tr.* (**clues, clued, clueing** or **cluing**) provide a clue to. □ **clue in** (or *Brit.* **up**) *sl.* inform. **not have a clue** *colloq.* be ignorant or incompetent.

clue·less /klōōlis/ *adj. colloq.* ignorant; stupid. □□ **clue·less·ly** *adv.* **clue·less·ness** *n.*

clump /klump/ *n. & v.* ● *n.* **1** (foll. by *of*) a cluster of plants, esp. trees or shrubs. **2** an agglutinated mass of blood cells, etc. **3** a thick extra sole on a boot or shoe. ● *v.* **1 a** *intr.* form a clump. **b** *tr.* heap or plant together. **2** *intr.* (also **clomp** /klomp/) walk with heavy tread. **3** *tr. colloq.* hit. □□ **clump·y** *adj.* (**clump·i·er, clump·i·est**).

clum·sy /klúmzee/ *adj.* (**clumsier, clumsiest**) **1** awkward in movement or shape; ungainly. **2** difficult to handle or use. **3** tactless. □□ **clum·si·ly** *adv.* **clum·si·ness** *n.*

clung *past* and *past part.* of CLING.

clunk /klungk/ *n. & v.* ● *n.* a dull sound as of thick pieces of metal meeting. ● *v.intr.* make such a sound.

clus·ter /klústər/ *n. & v.* ● *n.* **1** a close group or bunch of similar things growing together. **2** a close group or swarm of people, animals, faint stars, gems, etc. **3** a group of successive consonants or vowels. ● *v.* **1** *tr.* bring into a cluster or clusters. **2** *intr.* be or come into a cluster or clusters. **3** *intr.* (foll. by *around*) gather; congregate.

clus·ter bomb *n.* an antipersonnel bomb spraying pellets on impact.

clus·tered /klústərd/ *adj.* **1** growing in or brought into a cluster. **2** *Archit.* (of pillars, columns, or shafts) several close together, or disposed around or half detached from a pier.

clus·ter pine *n.* a Mediterranean pine, *Pinus pinaster*, with clustered cones.

clutch[1] /kluch/ *v. & n.* ● *v.* **1** *tr.* seize eagerly; grasp tightly. **2** *intr.* (foll. by *at*) snatch suddenly. ● *n.* **1 a** a tight grasp. **b** (foll. by *at*) grasping. **2** (in *pl.*) grasping hands, esp. as representing a cruel or relentless grasp or control. **3 a** ► (in a motor vehicle) a device for connecting and disconnecting the engine to the transmission. **b** the pedal operating this. ▷ GEARBOX. **c** an arrangement for connecting or disconnecting working parts of a machine. **4** a critical situation in a game, etc. (*always comes through in the clutch*).

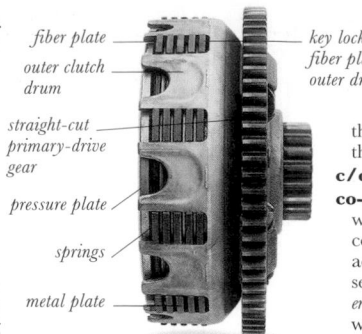

CLUTCH: MULTIPLATE CLUTCH OF A MOTORCYCLE ENGINE

fiber plate
outer clutch drum
straight-cut primary-drive gear
pressure plate
springs
metal plate
key locks fiber plate to outer drum

clutch[2] /kluch/ *n.* **1** a set of eggs for hatching. **2** a brood of chickens.

clutch bag *n.* (also **clutch purse**) a slim, flat handbag without handles.

clut·ter /klútər/ *n. & v.* ● *n.* **1** a crowded and untidy collection of things. **2** an untidy state. ● *v.tr.* (often foll. by *up, with*) crowd untidily; fill with clutter.

Clydes·dale /klídzdayl/ *n.* **1** a horse of a heavy powerful breed, used as draft horses. **2** this breed.

Cm *symb. Chem.* the element curium.

cm *abbr.* centimeter(s).

Cmdr. *abbr.* commander.

Cmdre. *abbr.* commodore.

cni·dar·i·an /nidáireeən/ *n.* ▼ an aquatic invertebrate animal of the phylum Cnidaria (formerly Coelenterata), typically having a simple tube-shaped or cup-shaped body and tentacles with stinging hairs and including jellyfish, corals, and sea anemones.

cnr. *abbr.* corner.

CNS *abbr.* central nervous system.

CO *abbr.* **1** Colorado (in official postal use). **2** commanding officer. **3** conscientious objector. **4** carbon monoxide.

Co *symb. Chem.* the element cobalt.

Co. *abbr.* **1** company. **2** county. □ **and Co.** /kō/ *Brit. colloq.* and the rest of them; and similar things.

c/o *abbr.* care of.

co- /kō/ *prefix* **1** added to: **a** nouns, with the sense 'joint, mutual, common' (*coauthor; coequality*). **b** adjectives and adverbs, with the sense 'jointly, mutually' (*cobelligerent; coequal; coequally*). **c** verbs, with the sense 'together with another or others' (*cooperate; coauthor*). **2** *Math.* **a** of the complement of an angle (*cosine*). **b** the complement of (*coset*).

coach /kōch/ *n. & v.* ● *n.* **1** a passenger bus, usu. comfortably equipped for longer journeys. **2** a railroad car. ▷ LOCOMOTIVE. **3** a horse-drawn carriage, usu. closed. **4 a** an instructor or trainer in sport. **b** a private tutor. **5** economy-class seating in an aircraft. **6** *Austral.* a docile cow or bullock used as a decoy to attract wild cattle. ● *v.* **1** *tr.* **a** train or teach (a pupil, sports team, etc.) as a coach. **b** give hints to; prime with facts. **2** *intr.* travel by stagecoach (*in the old coaching days*).

coach·house *n.* an outbuilding for carriages.

coach·man /kōchmən/ *n.* (*pl.* **-men**) the driver of a horse-drawn carriage.

coach·work /kōchwərk/ *n.* the bodywork of a road or rail vehicle.

co·ad·ju·tor /kō-ájətər, kōəjōo-/ *n.* an assistant, esp. an assistant bishop.

co·ag·u·lant /kō-ágyələnt/ *n.* a substance that produces coagulation.

co·ag·u·late /kō-ágyəlayt/ *v.tr. & intr.* **1** change from a fluid to a solid or semisolid state. **2** clot; curdle. **3** set; solidify. □□ **co·ag·u·la·ble** *adj.* **co·ag·u·la·tive** /-láytiv, -lətiv/ *adj.* **co·ag·u·la·tor** *n.*

co·ag·u·la·tion /kō-agyəláyshən/ *n.* the process by which a liquid changes to a semisolid mass.

CNIDARIAN

Cnidarians have two different body forms. A polyp, such as a sea anemone, has a tube-shaped body, attached at one end to a solid object. Medusas, such as the jellyfish, move by contracting their cup-shaped bodies. Both feed by using stinging tentacles to draw food into a gastrovascular cavity.

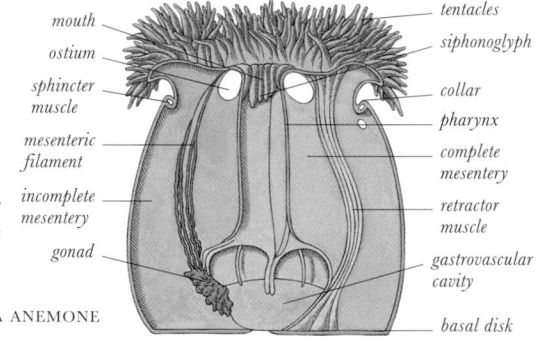

mouth
ostium
sphincter muscle
mesenteric filament
incomplete mesentery
gonad
tentacles
siphonoglyph
collar
pharynx
complete mesentery
retractor muscle
gastrovascular cavity
basal disk

INTERNAL ANATOMY OF A SEA ANEMONE

EXAMPLES OF CNIDARIANS

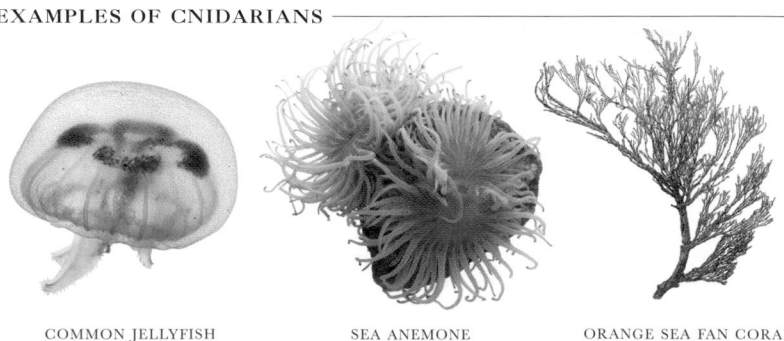

COMMON JELLYFISH
(*Aurelia aurita*)

SEA ANEMONE
(*Condylactis* species)

ORANGE SEA FAN CORAL
(*Gorgonia* species)

COAL: DIFFERENT STAGES IN
THE FORMATION OF COAL

layer of woody plants

compacted layer of peat

lignite (30% carbon content)

bituminous coal (60% carbon content)

anthracite (over 90% carbon content)

coal /kōl/ *n. & v.* ● *n.* **1 ▲ a** a hard black or blackish rock, mainly carbonized plant matter, found in underground seams and used as a fuel and in the manufacture of gas, tar, etc. ▷ SEDIMENT. **2** a red-hot piece of coal, wood, etc., in a fire. ● *v.* **1** *intr.* take in a supply of coal. **2** *tr.* put coal into (an engine, fire, etc.). □ **coals to Newcastle** something brought or sent to a place where it is already plentiful. **haul** (or **call**) **over the coals** reprimand. □□ **coal·y** *adj.*

co·a·lesce /kṓəlés/ *v.intr.* **1** come together and form one whole. **2** combine in a coalition. □□ **co·a·les·cence** *n.* **co·a·les·cent** *adj.*

coal·face /kṓlfays/ *n.* an exposed surface of coal in a mine.

coal·field /kṓlfeeld/ *n.* an extensive area with strata containing coal.

coal·hole /kṓlhōl/ *n.* a hole, as from a sidewalk, leading to a coal bin.

co·a·li·tion /kṓəlíshən/ *n.* **1** *Polit.* a temporary alliance for combined action, esp. of distinct parties forming a government, or of nations. **2** fusion into one whole. □□ **co·a·li·tion·ist** *n.*

coal·man /kṓlmən/ *n.* (*pl.* **-men**) a person who carries or delivers coal.

coal tar *n.* a thick, black, oily liquid distilled from coal and used as a source of benzene.

coam·ing /kṓming/ *n.* a raised border around the hatches, etc., of a ship to keep out water.

coarse /kawrs/ *adj.* **1 a** rough or loose in texture or grain; made of large particles. **b** (of a person's features) rough or large. **2** lacking refinement or delicacy; crude; obscene (*coarse humor*). **3** rude; uncivil. **4** inferior; common. □□ **coarse·ly** *adv.* **coarse·ness** *n.* **coars·ish** *adj.*

coars·en /káwrsən/ *v.tr. & intr.* make or become coarse.

coast /kōst/ *n. & v.* ● *n.* **1 a** the border of the land near the sea; the seashore. **b** (**the Coast**) the Pacific coast of the US. **2 a** a run, usu. downhill, on a bicycle without pedaling or in a motor vehicle without using the engine. **b** a toboggan slide or slope. ● *v.intr.* **1** ride or move, usu. downhill, without use of power; freewheel. **2** make progress without much effort. **3** slide down a hill on a toboggan or other sled. □ **the coast is clear** there is no danger of being observed or caught. □□ **coast·al** *adj.*

coast·er /kṓstər/ *n.* **1** a ship that travels along the coast from port to port. **2** a small tray or mat for a bottle or glass.

Coast Guard /kṓst gaard/ *n.* the U.S. military service that protects coastal waters, aids shipping and pleasure craft, and enforces maritime laws.

coast·line /kṓstlīn/ *n.* ▶ the line of the seashore, esp. with regard to its shape (*a rugged coastline*).

coast-to-coast *adj., adv.* across an island or continent.

coat /kōt/ *n. & v.* ● *n.* **1** an outer garment with sleeves and often extending below the hips; an overcoat or jacket. **2 a** an animal's fur, hair, etc. **b** *Physiol.* a structure, esp. a membrane, enclosing or lining an organ. **c** a skin, rind, or husk. **d** a layer of a bulb, etc. **3 a** a layer or covering. **b** a covering of paint, etc., laid on a surface at one time. ● *v.tr.* **1** (usu. foll. by *with, in*) **a** apply a coat of paint, etc., to; provide with a layer or covering. **b** (as **coated** *adj.*) covered with. **2** (of paint, etc.) form a covering to. □□ **coat·ed** *adj.* (also in *comb.*).

coat·dress /kṓtdres/ *n.* a woman's tailored dress resembling a coat.

coat hang·er *n.* see HANGER[2].

co·a·ti /kṓ-áatee/ *n.* (*pl.* **coatis**) any raccoonlike, flesh-eating mammal of the genus *Nasua*, with a long, flexible snout and a long, usu. ringed tail.

co·a·ti·mun·di /kṓ-aateemúndee/ *n.* (*pl.* **coatimundis**) = COATI.

coat·ing /kṓting/ *n.* a thin layer or covering of paint, etc.

coat ar·mor *n.* coats of arms.

coat of arms *n.* the heraldic bearings or shield of a person, family, or corporation.

coat of mail *n.* a jacket covered with mail or composed of mail. ▷ CHAIN MAIL

coat·tail /kṓttayl/ *n.* **1** the back flap of a man's jacket or coat. **2** (in *pl.*) **a** the back skirts of a dress coat, cutaway, etc. **b** *Polit.* (of a party candidate) popularity such as to attract votes for other party candidates.

co·au·thor /kṓ-áwthər/ *n. & v.* ● *n.* a joint author. ● *v.tr.* be a joint author of.

coax /kōks/ *v.tr.* **1** (usu. foll. by *into*, or *to* + infin.) persuade (a person) gradually or by flattery. **2** (foll. by *out of*) obtain (a thing from a person) by coaxing. **3** manipulate (a thing) carefully or slowly. □□ **coax·er** *n.* **coax·ing·ly** *adv.*

co·ax·i·al /kṓ-ákseeəl/ *adj.* **1** having a common axis. **2** *Electr.* (of a cable or line) transmitting by means of two concentric conductors separated by an insulator. □□ **co·ax·i·al·ly** *adv.*

C

COASTLINE

Coastlines evolve mainly by erosion and deposition. Depositional coasts are built up by rivers dropping sediment in deltas, or by waves transporting sand and small rocks (a process that includes longshore drift). Coasts are referred to as "drowned" when land sinks or sea levels rise.

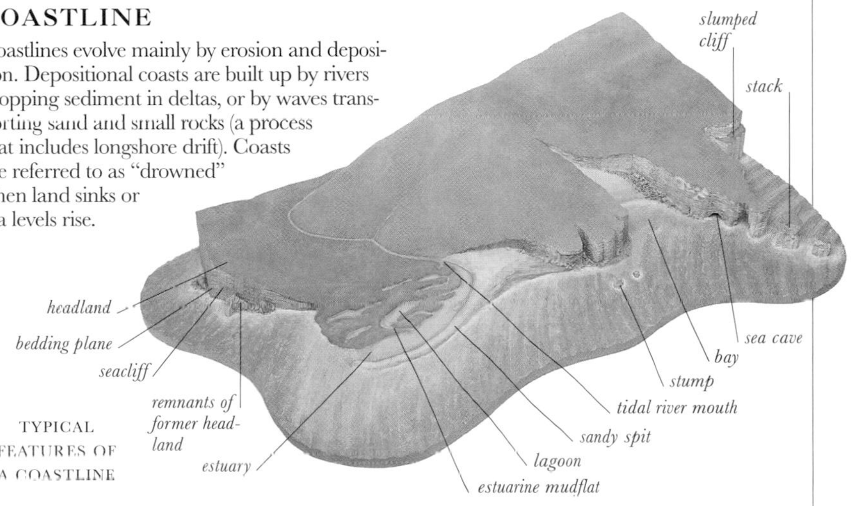

slumped cliff

stack

sea cave

bay

stump

tidal river mouth

sandy spit

lagoon

estuarine mudflat

estuary

remnants of former headland

seacliff

bedding plane

headland

TYPICAL FEATURES OF A COASTLINE

MAIN TYPES OF COASTLINE

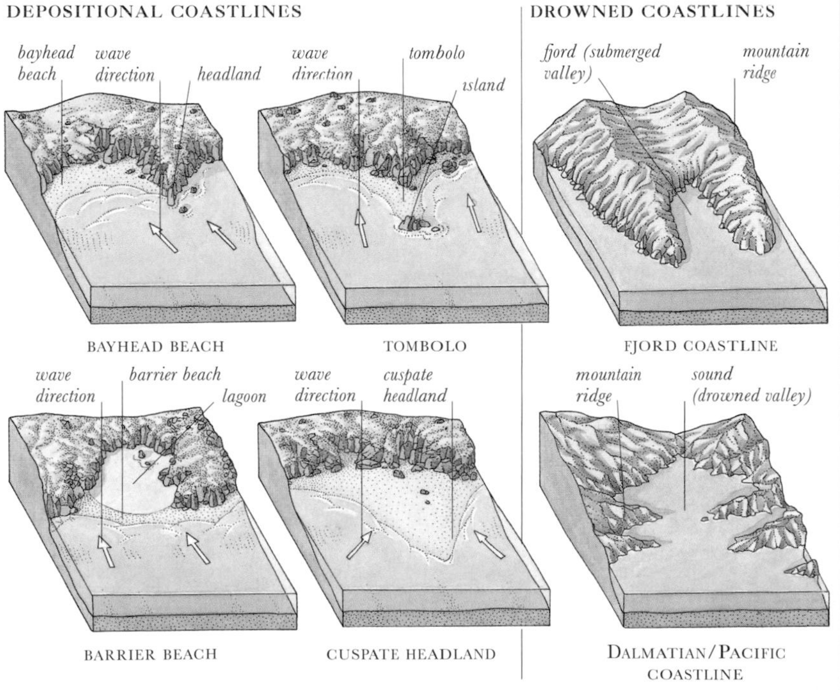

DEPOSITIONAL COASTLINES

bayhead beach   *wave direction*   *headland*

BAYHEAD BEACH

wave direction   *tombolo*   *island*

TOMBOLO

wave direction   *barrier beach*   *lagoon*

BARRIER BEACH

wave direction   *cuspate headland*

CUSPATE HEADLAND

DROWNED COASTLINES

fjord (submerged valley)   *mountain ridge*

FJORD COASTLINE

mountain ridge   *sound (drowned valley)*

DALMATIAN/PACIFIC COASTLINE

C

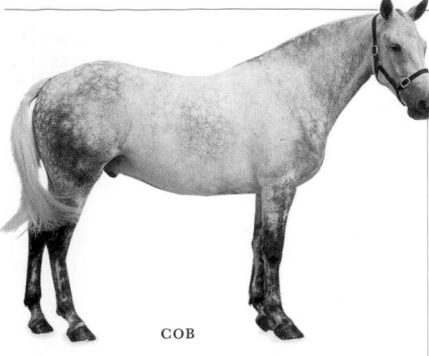

COB

cob /kob/ *n.* **1** = CORN COB. **2** ▲ a sturdy riding or driving horse with short legs. **3** a male swan. **4** *Brit.* a roundish lump, loaf of bread, etc.

co·balt /kṓbawlt/ *n. Chem.* a silvery-white, magnetic metallic element occurring naturally as a mineral in combination with sulfur and arsenic, and used in many alloys. ¶ Symb.: **Co**. □□ **co·bal·tic** /kōbáwltik/ *adj.* **co·bal·tous** /kōbáwltəs/ *adj.*

co·balt blue *n.* **1** a pigment containing a cobalt salt. **2** the deep-blue color of this.

cob·ber /kóbər/ *n. Austral. & NZ colloq.* a companion or friend.

cob·ble¹ /kóbəl/ *n. & v.* ● *n.* (in full **cobblestone**) a small rounded stone of a size used for paving. ● *v.tr.* pave with cobbles.

cob·ble² /kóbəl/ *v.tr.* **1** mend or patch up (esp. shoes). **2** (often foll. by *together*) join or assemble roughly.

cob·bler /kóblər/ *n.* **1** a person who mends shoes, esp. professionally. **2** an iced drink of wine, etc., sugar, and lemon (*sherry cobbler*). **3** a fruit pie with a rich, thick biscuit crust, usu. only on the top.

COBOL /kṓbawl/ *n. Computing* a programming language designed for use in commerce.

co·bra /kṓbrə/ *n.* ► any venomous snake of the genus *Naja*, native to Africa and Asia, with a neck dilated like a hood when excited. ▷ SNAKE

cob·web /kóbweb/ *n.* **1 a** a fine network of threads spun by a spider from a liquid secreted by it, used to trap insects, etc. **b** the thread of this. **2** anything compared with a cobweb, esp. in flimsiness of texture. **3** a trap or insidious entanglement. **4** (in *pl.*) a state of languishing; fustiness. □□ **cob·webbed** *adj.* **cob·web·by** *adj.*

co·ca /kṓkə/ *n.* **1** a S. American shrub, *Erythroxylum coca*. **2** its dried leaves, chewed as a stimulant.

Co·ca-Co·la /kṓkəkṓlə/ *n. Trademark* a carbonated soft drink flavored with extract of cola nuts.

co·caine /kōkáyn/ *n.* a drug derived from coca or prepared synthetically, used as a local anesthetic and as a stimulant.

coc·cus /kókəs/ *n.* (*pl.* **cocci** /kóksī, kókī/) any spherical or roughly spherical bacterium. □□ **coc·cal** *adj.* **coc·coid** *adj.*

coc·cyx /kóksiks/ *n.* (*pl.* **coccyges** /-sijeez/ or **coccyxes**) ► the small triangular bone at the base of the spinal column in humans and some apes, representing a vestigial tail. ▷ SPINE. □□ **coc·cyg·e·al** /koksíjeeəl/ *adj.*

spinal column

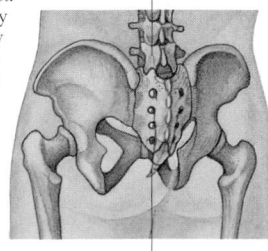

coccyx

COCCYX: HUMAN LOWER TORSO (BACK VIEW) SHOWING THE COCCYX

coch·i·neal /kóchineél/ *n.* **1** a scarlet dye used esp. for coloring food. ▷ DYE. **2** the dried bodies of the female of the Mexican insect, *Dactylopius coccus*, yielding this.

coch·le·a /kókleeə/ *n.* (*pl.* **cochleas** or **cochleae** /-lee-ee/) the spiral cavity of the internal ear. ▷ INNER EAR. □□ **coch·le·ar** *adj.*

cock¹ /kok/ *n. & v.* ● *n.* **1** a male bird, esp. of a domestic fowl. **2** *coarse sl.* the penis. **3** *Brit. sl.* (usu. **old cock** as a form of address) a friend; a fellow. **4 a** a firing lever in a gun which can be raised to be released by the trigger. ▷ GUN. **b** the cocked position of this (*at full cock*). **5** a tap or valve controlling flow. ¶ In sense 2 usually considered a taboo word. ● *v.tr.* **1** raise or make upright or erect. **2** turn or move (the eye or ear) attentively or knowingly. **3** set aslant, or turn up the brim of (a hat). **4** raise the cock of (a gun). □ **at half cock** only partly ready. **knock into a cocked hat** defeat utterly.

cock² /kok/ *n.* a small pile of hay, straw, etc., with vertical sides and a rounded top.

cockade

cock·ade /kokáyd/ *n.* ◄ a rosette, etc., worn in a hat as a badge of office or party, or as part of a livery. ▷ REDCOAT. □□ **cock·ad·ed** *adj.*

cock-a-leek·ie /kókəleékee/ *n.* (also **cock·y-leek·y** /-kókee-/) a soup traditionally made in Scotland with boiled chicken and leeks.

cock·a·lo·rum /kókəláwrəm/ *n. colloq.* a self-important little person.

cock-and-bull sto·ry *n.* an absurd or incredible account.

cock·a·tiel /kókəteél/ *n.* (also **cock·a·teel**) *Austral.* a small, delicately colored crested parrot, *Nymphicus hollandicus*.

COCKADE ON A 19TH-CENTURY FRENCH OFFICER'S CZAPSKA

cock·a·too /kókətoo/ *n.* any of several parrots of the family Cacatuinae, having powerful beaks and erectile crests. ▷ PARROT

cock·a·trice /kókətris, -trīs/ *n.* **1** = BASILISK 1. **2** *Heraldry* a fabulous animal, a cock with a serpent's tail.

cock·boat /kókbōt/ *n.* a small boat, esp. one used as a ship's tender.

cock·chaf·er /kókchayfər/ *n.* a large nocturnal beetle, *Melolontha melolontha*, which feeds on leaves and whose larva feeds on the roots of crops, etc. ▷ COLEOPTERON

cock·er /kókər/ *n.* (in full **cocker spaniel**) a small spaniel of a breed with a silky coat.

cock·er·el /kókrəl/ *n.* a young cock.

cock·eyed /kókíd/ *adj. colloq.* **1** crooked; askew; not level. **2** (of a scheme, etc.) absurd; not practical. **3** drunk. **4** squinting.

cock·fight /kókfīt/ *n.* a fight between cocks as sport. □□ **cock·fight·ing** *n.*

cock·le¹ /kókəl/ *n.* **1 a** any edible mollusk of the genus *Cardium*, having a chubby, ribbed bivalve shell. ▷ SHELL. **2** (in full **cockleshell**) its shell. **b** (in full **cockleshell**) a small shallow boat. □ **warm the cockles of one's heart** make one contented; be satisfying.

cock·le² /kókəl/ *v. & n.* ● *v.* **1** *intr.* pucker; wrinkle. **2** *tr.* cause to cockle. ● *n.* a pucker or wrinkle in paper, glass, etc.

cock·ney /kóknee/ *n. & adj.* ● *n.* (*pl.* **-eys**) **1** a native of East London, esp. one born within hearing of Bow Bells (of the Bow church in London's East End district). **2** the dialect or accent typical of this area. ● *adj.* of or characteristic of cockneys or their dialect or accent. □□ **cock·ney·ism** *n.*

cock·pit /kókpit/ *n.* **1** a compartment for the pilot (or the pilot and crew) of an aircraft or spacecraft. ▷ FIGHTER. **2** a similar compartment for the driver in a racing car. ▷ DRAGSTER. **3** a space for the helmsman in some small yachts.

cock·roach /kókrōch/ *n.* ▼ any of various flat brown insects, esp. *Blatta orientalis* and *Periplaneta americana*, infesting kitchens, bathrooms, etc.

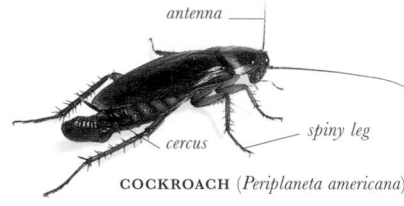

antenna

cercus   spiny leg

COCKROACH (*Periplaneta americana*)

cocks·comb /kókskōm/ *n.* ▼ the crest or comb of a cock.

cock·sure /kókshoŏr/ *adj.* **1** presumptuously or arrogantly confident. **2** (foll. by *of*, *about*) absolutely sure. □□ **cock·sure·ly** *adv.* **cock·sure·ness** *n.*

cock·tail /kóktayl/ *n.* **1** a usu. alcoholic drink made by mixing various spirits, fruit juices, etc. **2** a dish of mixed ingredients (*fruit cocktail*; *shellfish cocktail*). **3** any hybrid mixture.

cock·y /kókee/ *adj.* (**cockier, cockiest**) **1** conceited; arrogant. **2** saucy; impudent. □□ **cock·i·ly** *adv.* **cock·i·ness** *n.*

cockscomb

COCKSCOMB

cock·y-leek·y var. of COCK-A-LEEKIE.

co·co /kṓkō/ *n.* (*pl.* **cocos**) a tall tropical palm tree, *Cocos nucifera*, bearing coconuts.

co·coa /kṓkō/ *n.* **1** a powder made from crushed cacao seeds, often with other ingredients. **2** a hot drink made from this.

co·coa but·ter *n.* a fatty substance obtained from cocoa beans and used for candy, cosmetics, etc.

co·co-de-mer /kṓkōdəmáir/ *n.* a tall palm tree, *Lodoicea maldivica*, of the Seychelles.

co·co·nut /kṓkənut/ *n.* (also **co·coa·nut**) **1 a** a large ovate brown seed of the coco, with a hard shell and edible white fleshy lining enclosing a milky juice. **b** = COCO. **c** the edible white fleshy lining of a coconut. **2** *sl.* the human head.

co·coon /kəkoon/ *n. & v.* ● *n.* **1 a** a silky case spun by many insect larvae for protection as pupae. ▷ METAMORPHOSIS, SILKWORM. **b** a similar structure made by other animals. **2** a protective covering, esp. to prevent corrosion of metal equipment. ● *v.* **1** *tr. & intr.* wrap in or form a cocoon. **2** *tr.* spray with a protective coating.

co·cotte /kəkót, kawkáwt/ *n.* **1** a small fireproof dish for cooking and serving an individual portion of food. **2** a deep cooking pot with a tight-fitting lid and handles.

COD *abbr.* **1 a** cash on delivery. **b** collect on delivery. **2** Concise Oxford Dictionary.

cod¹ /kod/ *n.* (*pl.* same) any large marine fish of the family Gadidae, used as food, esp. *Gadus morhua*.

cod² /kod/ *n. & v. Brit. sl.* ● *n.* **1** a parody. **2** a hoax. **3** (*attrib.*) = MOCK. *adj.* ● *v.* (**codded, codding**) **1 a** *intr.* perform a hoax. **b** *tr.* play a trick on; fool. **2** *tr.* parody.

cod³ /kod/ *n. Brit. sl.* nonsense.

co·da /kṓdə/ *n.* **1** *Mus.* the concluding passage of a piece or movement, usu. forming an addition to the basic structure. **2** *Ballet* the concluding section of a dance. **3** a concluding event or series of events.

cod·dle /kód'l/ *v.tr.* **1 a** treat as an invalid; protect attentively. **b** *Brit.* (foll. by *up*) strengthen by feeding. **2** cook (an egg) in water below boiling point. □□ **cod·dler** *n.*

code /kōd/ *n. & v.* ● *n.* **1** a system of words, letters, figures, or symbols, used to represent others for secrecy or brevity. **2** a system of prearranged signals, esp. used to ensure secrecy in transmitting messages. **3** *Computing* a piece of program text. **4 a** a system of laws, etc. so arranged as to avoid inconsistency and overlapping. **b** a set of rules on any subject. **5 a** the prevailing morality of a society or class (*code of honor*). **b** a person's standard of moral behavior. ● *v.tr.* put (a message, program, etc.) into code. □□ **cod·er** *n.*

code·book /kṓdbŏŏk/ *n.* a list of symbols, etc., used in a code.

co·deine /kṓdeen/ *n.* an alkaloid derived from morphine and used to relieve pain.

co·de·pend·en·cy /kṓdipéndənsee/ *n.* addiction to a supportive role in a relationship. □□ **co·de·pend·ent** /-dənt/ *adj. & n.*

co·de·ter·mi·na·tion /kṓditə́rminááyshən/ *n.* co-operation between management and workers in decision making.

co·dex /kṓdeks/ *n.* (*pl.* **co·dices** /kṓdiseez, kód-/) **1** ▶ an ancient manuscript text in book form. **2** a collection of pharmaceutical descriptions of drugs, etc.

cod·fish /kódfish/ *n.* = COD[1].

codg·er /kójər/ *n.* (usu. in **old codger**) *colloq.* a person, esp. an old or strange one.

co·di·ces *pl.* of CODEX.

cod·i·cil /kódisil/ *n.* an addition explaining, modifying, or revoking a will or part of one. □□ **cod·i·cil·la·ry** /kódisílər-ee/ *adj.*

cod·i·fy /kódifī, kód-/ *v.tr.* (**-ies, -ied**) arrange (laws, etc.) systematically into a code. □□ **cod·i·fi·ca·tion** /-fikáy-shən/ *n.* **cod·i·fi·er** *n.*

cod·ling /kódling/ *n.* *Brit.* (also **cod·lin**) **1** any of several varieties of cooking apple, having a long tapering shape. **2** a small moth, *Carpocapsa pomonella*, the larva of which feeds on apples.

cod-liv·er oil *n.* an oil pressed from the fresh liver of cod, which is rich in vitamins D and A.

cod·piece /kódpees/ *n.* *hist.* an appendage like a small bag or flap at the front of a man's breeches.

co·driv·er /kṓdrī́vər/ *n.* a person who shares the driving of a vehicle with another.

co·ed /kṓ-ed, -éd/ *n. & adj. colloq.* ● *n.* **1** a coeducational system or institution. **2** a female student at a coeducational institution. ● *adj.* coeducational.

co·ed·u·ca·tion /kṓejōōkáyshən/ *n.* the education of pupils of both sexes together. □□ **co·ed·u·ca·tion·al** *adj.*

co·ef·fi·cient /kṓifíshənt/ *n.* **1** *Math.* a quantity placed before and multiplying an algebraic expression (e.g., 4 in $4x^y$). **2** *Physics* a multiplier or factor that measures some property (*coefficient of expansion*).

coe·la·canth /séeləkanth/ *n.* ▼ a large bony marine fish, *Latimeria chalumnae*, formerly thought to be extinct, having a trilobed tail fin and fleshy pectoral fins.

COELACANTH
(*Latimeria chalumnae*)

-coele *comb. form* var. of -CELE.

coe·len·ter·ate /seeléntərayt, -tərit/ = CNIDARIAN.

coel·i·ac esp. *Brit.* var. of CELIAC.

coen·o·bite esp. *Brit.* var. of CENOBITE.

co·en·zyme /kō-énzīm/ *n.* *Biochem.* a nonproteinaceous compound that assists in the action of an enzyme.

co·e·qual /kō-éekwəl/ *adj. & n.* *archaic* or *literary* ● *adj.* equal with one another. ● *n.* an equal. □□ **co·e·qual·i·ty** /kṓ-eekwólitee/ *n.* **co·e·qual·ly** *adv.*

co·erce /kō-ə́rs/ *v.tr.* (often foll. by *into*) persuade or restrain (an unwilling person) by force (*coerced you into signing*). □□ **co·er·ci·ble** *adj.*

co·er·cion /kō-ə́rzhən, -shən/ *n.* **1** the act or process of coercing. **2** government by force. □□ **co·er·cive** /-siv/ *adj.* **co·er·cive·ly** *adv.* **co·er·cive·ness** *n.*

Coeur d'Alene /kə́rd'láyn/ *n.* **1 a** a N. American people native to northern Idaho. **b** a member of this people. **2** the language of this people.

co·e·val /kō-éevəl/ *adj. & n.* ● *adj.* **1** having the same age or date of origin. **2** living or existing at the same epoch. **3** having the same duration. ● *n.* a coeval person; a contemporary. □□ **co·e·val·i·ty** /-válitcc/ *n.* **co·e·val·ly** *adv.*

co·ex·ist /kṓigzíst/ *v.intr.* (often foll. by *with*) **1** exist together (in time or place). **2** (esp. of nations) exist in mutual tolerance though professing different ideologies, etc. □□ **co·ex·ist·ence** *n.* **co·ex·ist·ent** *adj.*

co·ex·ten·sive /kṓiksténsiv/ *adj.* extending over the same space or time.

coffee /káwfee, kófee/ *n.* **1 a** a drink made from the roasted and ground beanlike seeds of a tropical shrub. **b** a cup of this. **2 a** any shrub of the genus *Coffea*, yielding berries containing one or more seeds. **b** its seeds. **3** a pale brown color, as of coffee mixed with milk.

coffee break *n.* a short rest from work during which refreshments are usually taken.

coffee cake *n.* a type of cake or sweetened bread, often served with coffee.

coffee·house /káwfeehows, kóf-/ *n.* a place serving coffee and other refreshments, and often providing informal entertainment.

coffee table *n.* a small low table.

coffer /káwfər, kóf-/ *n.* **1** a box, esp. a large strongbox for valuables. **2** (in *pl.*) a treasury or store of funds. **3** ▼ a sunken panel in a ceiling, etc. □□ **coffered** *adj.*

carved mason's tools • coffer

COFFER: SQUARE COFFER SET IN A VAULTED CEILING

coffer·dam /káwfərdam, kóf-/ *n.* a watertight enclosure pumped dry to permit work below the waterline on building bridges, etc., or for repairing a ship.

coffin /káwfin, kóf-/ *n. & v.* ● *n.* **1** a long, narrow, usu. wooden box in which a corpse is buried or cremated. **2** the part of a horse's hoof below the coronet. ● *v.tr.* (**coffined, coffining**) put in a coffin.

cog /kawg, kog/ *n.* **1** ▶ each of a series of projections on the edge of a wheel or bar transferring motion by engaging with another series. ▷ BULLDOZER. **2** an unimportant member of an organization, etc. □□ **cogged** *adj.*

co·gent /kṓjənt/ *adj.* (of arguments, reasons, etc.) convincing; compelling. □□ **co·gen·cy** /-jənsee/ *n.* **co·gent·ly** *adv.*

cog·i·ta·ble /kójitəbəl/ *adj.* able to be grasped by the mind; conceivable.

cog·i·tate /kójitayt/ *v.tr. & intr.* ponder; meditate. □□ **cog·i·ta·tion** /-táyshən/ *n.* **cog·i·ta·tive** *adj.* **cog·i·ta·tor** *n.*

co·gnac /káwnyak, kón-/ *n.* a high-quality brandy, properly that distilled in Cognac in W. France.

cog·nate /kógnayt/ *adj. & n.* ● *adj.* **1** related to or descended from a common ancestor (cf. AGNATE). **2** *Philol.* (of a word) having the same linguistic family or derivation (as another); representing the same original word or root (e.g., English *father*, German *Vater*, Latin *pater*). ● *n.* **1** a relative. **2** a cognate word. □□ **cog·nate·ly** *adv.* **cog·nate·ness** *n.*

cognate object *n.* *Gram.* an object that is related in origin and sense to the verb governing it (as in *live a good life*).

cog·ni·tion /kogníshən/ *n.* **1** *Philos.* knowing, perceiving, or conceiving as an act or faculty distinct from emotion and volition. **2** a result of this; a perception, sensation, notion, or intuition. □□ **cog·ni·tion·al** *adj.* **cog·ni·tive** /kógnitiv/ *adj.*

cognitive therapy *n.* a type of psychotherapy in which negative patterns of thought about the self and the world are challenged.

cog·ni·za·ble /kógnizəbəl, kón-, kogní-/ *adj.* **1** perceptible; recognizable; clearly identifiable. **2** within the jurisdiction of a court.

cog·ni·zance /kógnizəns/ *n.* **1** knowledge or awareness; perception; notice. **2** the sphere of one's observation or concern. **3** *Law* the right of a court to deal with a matter. **4** *Heraldry* a distinctive device or mark. □ **have cognizance of** know, esp. officially. **take cognizance of** attend to; take account of.

cog·ni·zant /kógnizənt/ *adj.* (foll. by *of*) having knowledge or being aware of.

cog·no·men /kognṓmen/ *n.* **1** a nickname. **2** an ancient Roman's personal name or epithet.

co·gno·scen·te /kónyəshéntee, kógnə-/ *n.* (*pl.* **cognoscenti** *pronunc.* same) (usu. in *pl.*) a connoisseur.

cog rail·way *n.* = RACK RAILWAY.

cog·wheel /kóghweel, -weel/ *n.* a wheel with cogs.

co·hab·it /kōhábit/ *v.intr.* (**cohabited, cohabiting**) live together, esp. as husband and wife without being married to one another. □□ **co·hab·i·tant** *n.* **co·hab·i·ta·tion** *n.* **co·hab·i·tee** /-téé/ *n.* **co·hab·i·ter** *n.*

co·here /kōheér/ *v.intr.* **1** (of parts or a whole) stick together; remain united. **2** (of reasoning, etc.) be logical or consistent.

co·her·ent /kōheérənt, -hér-/ *adj.* **1** (of a person) able to speak intelligibly and articulately. **2** (of speech, an argument, etc.) logical and consistent;

CODEX: DETAIL FROM *CODEX VATICANUS 3256*

C

sloping-tooth cog

pinion wheel

crown wheel

cog

COGS ON A WOODEN BEVEL-TYPE GEAR

easily followed. **3** cohering; sticking together. **4** *Physics* (of waves) having a constant phase relationship. □□ **co·her·ence** /-rəns/ *n.* **co·her·en·cy** *n.* **co·her·ent·ly** *adv.*

co·he·sion /kōhééżhən/ *n.* **1 a** the act or condition of sticking together. **b** a tendency to cohere. **2** *Chem.* the force with which molecules cohere. □□ **co·he·sive** /-héésiv/ *adj.* **co·he·sive·ly** /-héé-sivlee/ *adv.* **co·he·sive·ness** /-héésivnis/ *n.*

co·ho /kố hō/ *n.* (also **co·hoe**) (*pl.* same or **-os** or **-oes**) a silver salmon, *Oncorhynchus kisutch*, of the N. Pacific.

co·hort /kố hawrt/ *n.* **1** an ancient Roman military unit, equal to one-tenth of a legion. **2** a band of warriors. **3 a** persons banded or grouped together, esp. in a common cause. **b** a group of persons with a common statistical characteristic. **4** a companion or colleague.

coif /koyf/ *n. hist.* **1** a close-fitting cap, esp. as worn by nuns under a veil. **2** a protective metal skullcap worn under armor. **3** = COIFFURE.

coif·feur /kwaaför/ *n.* (*fem.* **coiffeuse** /-főz/) a hairdresser.

coif·fure /kwaafyőör/ *n. & v.* ● *n.* (also **coif**) the way hair is arranged; a hairstyle. ● *v.tr.* to provide with a coiffure.

coign of van·tage /koyn/ *n.* a favorable position for observation or action.

coil[1] /koyl/ *n. & v.* ● *n.* **1** anything arranged in a joined sequence of concentric circles. **2** a length of rope, a spring, etc., arranged in this way. **3** a single turn of something coiled, e.g., a snake. **4** a lock of hair twisted and coiled. **5** an intrauterine contraceptive device in the form of a coil. **6** *Electr.* a device consisting of a coiled wire for converting low voltage to high voltage, esp. for transmission to the spark plugs of an internal-combustion engine. ▷ MAGLEV. ● *v.* **1** *tr.* arrange in a series of concentric loops or rings. **2** *tr. & intr.* twist or be twisted into a circular or spiral shape. **3** *intr.* move sinuously.

coil[2] /koyl/ *n.* □ **this mortal coil** the difficulties of earthly life (with ref. to Shakesp. *Hamlet* III. i. 67).

coin /koyn/ *n. & v.* ● *n.* **1** a piece of flat, usu. round metal stamped and issued by authority as money. **2** (*collect.*) metal money. ● *v.tr.* **1** make (coins) by stamping. **2** make (metal) into coins. **3** invent or devise (esp. a new word or phrase). □ **coin money** make much money quickly. **to coin a phrase** *iron.* introducing a banal remark or cliché. □□ **coin·er** *n.*

coin·age /kóynij/ *n.* **1** the act or process of coining. **2 a** coins collectively. **b** a system or type of coins in use (*decimal coinage; bronze coinage*). **3** an invention, esp. of a new word or phrase.

co·in·cide /kố insíd/ *v.intr.* **1** occur at or during the same time. **2** occupy the same portion of space. **3** (often foll. by *with*) be in agreement; have the same view.

co·in·ci·dence /kō-insidəns/ *n.* **1 a** occurring or being together. **b** an instance of this. **2** a remarkable concurrence of events or circumstances without apparent causal connection. **3** *Physics* the presence of ionizing particles, etc., in two or more detectors simultaneously, or of two or more signals simultaneously in a circuit.

co·in·ci·dent /kō-insidənt/ *adj.* **1** occurring together in space or time. **2** (foll. by *with*) in agreement; harmonious. □□ **co·in·ci·dent·ly** *adv.*

co·in·ci·den·tal /kō-insidént'l/ *adj.* **1** in the nature of or resulting from a coincidence. **2** happening or existing at the same time. □□ **co·in·ci·den·tal·ly** *adv.*

Coin·treau /kwáantrō/ *n.* Trademark a colorless orange-flavored liqueur.

coir /kóyər/ *n.* ▶ fiber from the outer husk of the coconut, used for ropes, matting, etc. ▷ ROPE

coir

COIR FIBER ON A COCONUT HUSK

co·i·tion /kō-íshən/ *n. Med.* = COITUS.

co·i·tus /kố-itəs, kō-éé-/ *n. Med.* sexual intercourse. □□ **co·i·tal** *adj.*

co·i·tus in·ter·rup·tus /íntərúptəs/ *n.* sexual intercourse in which the penis is withdrawn before ejaculation.

Coke /kōk/ *n. Trademark* Coca-Cola.

coke[1] /kōk/ *n. & v.* ● *n.* **1** a solid substance left after the gases have been extracted from coal. ▷ BLAST FURNACE. **2** a residue left after the incomplete combustion of gasoline, etc. ● *v.tr.* convert (coal) into coke.

coke[2] /kōk/ *n. sl.* cocaine.

Col. *abbr.* **1** colonel. **2** Colossians (New Testament).

col /kol/ *n.* **1** a depression in the summit line of a chain of mountains, generally affording a pass from one slope to another. **2** *Meteorol.* a low-pressure region between anticyclones.

col. *abbr.* column.

COLA /kốlə/ *abbr.* **1** cost-of-living adjustment. **2** cost-of-living allowance.

co·la /kốlə/ *n.* (also **kola**) **1** any small tree of the genus *Cola*, native to W. Africa, bearing seeds containing caffeine. **2** a carbonated drink usu. flavored with these seeds.

col·an·der /kúləndər, kól-/ *n.* a perforated vessel used to strain off liquid in cookery. ▷ UTENSIL

co·lat·i·tude /kōlátitōod, -tyōod/ *n. Astron.* the complement of the latitude, the difference between it and 90°.

col·chi·cine /kólchiseen, kốl-, kólkee-/ *n.* a yellow alkaloid obtained from colchicum, used in the treatment of gout.

col·chi·cum /kólchikəm, kólkee-/ *n.* **1** ◀ any liliaceous plant of the genus *Colchicum*, esp. meadow saffron. **2** its dried corm or seed. Also called **autumn crocus**.

COLCHICUM: MEADOW SAFFRON (*Colchicum autumnale*)

cold /kōld/ *adj., n., & adv.* ● *adj.* **1** of or at a low or relatively low temperature, esp. when compared with the human body. **2** not heated; cooled after being heated. **3** (of a person) feeling cold. **4** lacking ardor, friendliness, or affection; undemonstrative; apathetic. **5** depressing; uninteresting (*cold facts*). **6 a** dead. **b** *colloq.* unconscious. **7** *colloq.* at one's mercy (*had me cold*). **8** sexually frigid. **9** (of soil) slow to absorb heat. **10** (of a scent in hunting) having become weak. **11** (in children's games) far from finding or guessing what is sought. **12** without preparation or rehearsal. ● *n.* **1 a** the prevalence of a low temperature, esp. in the atmosphere. **b** cold weather; a cold environment (*went out into the cold*). **2** an infection in which the mucous membrane of the nose and throat becomes inflamed, causing running at the nose, sneezing, sore throat, etc. ● *adv.* completely; entirely (*was stopped cold midsentence*). □ **catch a cold 1** become infected with a cold. **2** esp. *Brit.* encounter trouble or difficulties. **cold call** sell goods or services by making unsolicited calls on prospective customers by telephone or in person. **in cold blood** without feeling or passion; deliberately; ruthlessly. **out in the cold** ignored; neglected. **throw** (or **pour**) **cold water on** be discouraging or depreciatory about. □□ **cold·ish** *adj.* **cold·ly** *adv.* **cold·ness** *n.*

cold-blood·ed /kốldblúdid/ *adj.* **1** (of fish, etc.) having a body temperature varying with that of the environment. **2 a** callous; deliberately cruel. **b** without excitement or sensibility, dispassionate. □□ **cold-blood·ed·ly** *adv.* **cold-blood·ed·ness** *n.*

cold cath·ode *n.* a cathode that emits electrons without being heated.

cold chis·el *n.* a chisel suitable for cutting metal.

cold cream *n.* ointment for cleansing and softening the skin.

cold cuts *n.pl.* slices of cold cooked meats.

cold feet *n.pl. colloq.* loss of nerve or confidence.

cold frame *n.* ▶ an unheated frame with a glass top for growing small plants.

glass top   *heat-retaining wooden frame*

cold front *n.* the forward edge of an advancing mass of cold air.

cold fu·sion *n.* hypothetical nuclear fusion at room temperature esp. as a possible energy source.

COLD FRAME

cold-heart·ed /kốldháártid/ *adj.* lacking affection or warmth; unfriendly. □□ **cold-heart·ed·ly** *adv.* **cold-heart·ed·ness** *n.*

cold shoul·der *n. & v.* ● *n.* a show of intentional unfriendliness. ● *v.tr.* (**cold-shoulder**) be deliberately unfriendly to.

cold sore *n.* inflammation and blisters in and around the mouth, caused by a virus infection.

cold stor·age *n.* **1** storage in a refrigerator or other cold place for preservation. **2** a state in which something (esp. an idea) is put aside temporarily.

cold sweat *n.* a state of sweating induced by fear or illness.

cold tur·key *n. sl.* **1** a series of blunt statements or behavior. **2** abrupt withdrawal from addictive drugs; the symptoms of this.

cold war *n.* a state of hostility between nations without actual fighting.

cole /kōl/ *n.* (usu. in *comb.*) **1** cabbage. **2** = RAPE[2].

co·le·op·ter·on /kốleeóptərən/ *n.* ▼ any insect of the order Coleoptera, with front wings modified into sheaths to protect the hind wings, e.g., a beetle or weevil. ▷ BEETLE. □□ **co·le·op·ter·an** *adj.* **co·le·op·ter·ist** *n.* **co·le·op·ter·ous** *adj.*

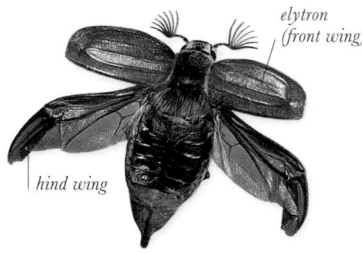

elytron (front wing)

hind wing

COLEOPTERON: COCKCHAFER (*Melolontha melolontha*)

cole·seed /kốlseed/ *n.* = COLE 2.

cole·slaw /kốlslaw/ *n.* a dressed salad of sliced raw cabbage, carrot, onion, etc.

co·le·us /kốleeəs/ *n.* any plant of the genus *Coleus*, having variegated colored leaves.

col·ic /kólik/ *n.* a severe spasmodic abdominal pain. □□ **col·ick·y** *adj.*

col·i·se·um /kólisééəm/ *n.* (also **col·os·se·um**) a large stadium or amphitheater.

co·li·tis /kəlítis/ *n.* inflammation of the lining of the colon.

coll. *abbr.* **1** collect. **2** collection. **3** collateral. **4** college.

col·lab·o·rate /kəlábərayt/ *v.intr.* (often foll. by *with*) **1** work jointly, esp. in a literary or artistic production. **2** cooperate traitorously with an enemy. □□ **col·lab·o·ra·tion** /-ráyshən/ *n.* **col·lab·o·ra·tion·ist** *n. & adj.* **col·lab·o·ra·tive** /-ráytiv, -rətiv/ *adj.* **col·lab·o·ra·tor** *n.*

col·lage /kəláazh/ *n.* **1** a form of art in which various materials (e.g., photographs, pieces of paper, matchsticks) are arranged and glued to a backing. **2 ▶** a work of art done in this way. **3** a collection of unrelated things. □□ **col·lag·ist** *n.*

col·la·gen /kóləjən/ *n.* a protein found in animal connective tissue that yields gelatin on boiling.

col·lapse /kəláps/ *n. & v.* ● *n.* **1** the tumbling down or falling in of a structure; folding up; giving way. **2** a sudden failure of a plan, undertaking, etc. **3** a physical or mental breakdown. ● *v.* **1 a** *intr.* undergo or experience a collapse. **b** *tr.* cause to collapse. **2** *intr. colloq.* lie or sit down and relax, esp. after prolonged effort (*collapsed into a chair*). **3 a** *intr.* (of furniture, etc.) be foldable into a small space. **b** *tr.* fold (furniture) in this way. □□ **col·laps·i·ble** *adj.* **col·laps·i·bil·i·ty** /-səbílitee/ *n.*

col·lar /kólər/ *n. & v.* ● *n.* **1** the part of a shirt, dress, coat, etc., that goes around the neck, either upright or turned over. **2** a band of linen, lace, etc., completing the upper part of a costume. **3** a band of leather or other material put around an animal's (esp. a dog's) neck. **4** a restraining or connecting band, ring, or pipe in machinery. **5 ▶** a colored marking resembling a collar around the neck of a bird or animal. ● *v.tr.* **1** seize (a person) by the collar or neck. **2** capture; apprehend. **3** *colloq.* accost. **4** *sl.* take, esp. illicitly. □□ **col·lared** *adj.* (also in *comb.*). **col·lar·less** *adj.*

col·lar·bone /kólərbōn/ *n.* either of two bones joining the breastbone and the shoulder blades; the clavicle. ▷ CLAVICLE

col·late /kəláyt, kolayt, kó-/ *v.tr.* **1** analyze and compare (texts, statements, etc.) to identify points of agreement and difference. **2** arrange (pages) in proper sequence. **3** assemble (information) from different sources. □□ **col·la·tor** *n.*

col·lat·er·al /kəlátərəl/ *n. & adj.* ● *n.* **1** security pledged as a guarantee for repayment of a loan. **2 a** person having the same descent as another but by a different line. ● *adj.* **1** descended from the same stock but by a different line. **2** side by side; parallel. **3 a** additional but subordinate. **b** contributory. **c** connected but aside from the main subject, course, etc. □□ **col·lat·er·al·i·ty** /-rálitee/ *n.* **col·lat·er·al·ly** *adv.*

col·la·tion /kəláyshən, ko-/ *n.* **1** the act or an instance of collating. **2** a light informal meal.

col·league /kóleeg/ *n.* a fellow official or worker, esp. in a profession or business.

col·lect¹ /kəlékt/ *v., adj., & adv.* ● *v.* **1** *tr. & intr.* bring or come together; assemble; accumulate. **2** *tr.* systematically seek and acquire (books, stamps, etc.), esp. as a continuing hobby. **3 a** *tr.* obtain (taxes, contributions, etc.) from a number of people. **b** *intr. colloq.* receive money. **4** *tr.* call for; fetch (*went to collect the laundry*). **5 a** *refl.* regain control of oneself esp. after a shock. **b** *tr.* concentrate (one's energies, thoughts, etc.). **c** *tr.* (as **collected** *adj.*) calm and cool; not perturbed nor distracted. **6** *tr.* infer; gather; conclude. ● *adj. & adv.* to be paid for by the receiver (of a telephone call, parcel, etc.). □□ **col·lect·a·ble** *adj.* **col·lect·ed·ly** *adv.*

col·lect² /kólekt, -ikt/ *n.* a short prayer of the Anglican and Roman Catholic churches, esp. one assigned to a particular day or season.

COLLAGE: COILED, WOVEN, AND CUT PAPER BAS-RELIEF COLLAGE

woven paper

coiled paper

cut paper

corrugated paper

COLLAR ON A BLUE RING-NECKED PARAKEET

collar

col·lect·i·ble /kəléktibəl/ *adj. & n.* ● *adj.* worth collecting. ● *n.* an item sought by collectors.

col·lec·tion /kəlékshən/ *n.* **1** the act or process of collecting or being collected. **2** a group of things collected together (e.g., works of art, literary items, or specimens), esp. systematically. **3** (foll. by *of*) an accumulation; a mass or pile (*a collection of dust*). **4 a** the collecting of money, esp. in church or for a charitable cause. **b** the amount collected. **5** the regular removal of mail, esp. from a public mailbox, for dispatch.

col·lec·tive /kəléktiv/ *adj. & n.* ● *adj.* **1** formed by or constituting a collection. **2** taken as a whole; aggregate (*our collective opinion*). **3** of or from several or many individuals; common. ● *n.* **1 a** any cooperative enterprise. **b** its members. **2** = COLLECTIVE NOUN. □□ **col·lec·tive·ly** *adv.* **col·lec·tive·ness** *n.* **col·lec·tiv·i·ty** /kóléktívitee/ *n.*

col·lec·tive bar·gain·ing *n.* negotiation of wages, salaries, etc., by an organized body of employees.

col·lec·tive noun *n. Gram.* a noun that is grammatically singular and denotes a collection or number of individuals (e.g., *assembly, family, troop*).

col·lec·tiv·ism /kəléktivizəm/ *n.* the theory and practice of the collective ownership of land and the means of production. □□ **col·lec·tiv·ist** *n.* **col·lec·tiv·is·tic** /-vístik/ *adj.*

col·lec·tiv·ize /kəléktivīz/ *v.tr.* organize on the basis of collective ownership. □□ **col·lec·ti·vi·za·tion** *n.*

col·lec·tor /kəléktər/ *n.* **1** a person who collects, esp. things of interest as a hobby. **2** a person who collects money, etc., due (*tax collector; ticket collector*). **3** *Electronics* the region in a transistor that absorbs carriers of a charge.

col·lec·tor's i·tem *n.* (also **col·lec·tor's piece**) a valuable object, esp. one of interest to collectors.

col·leen /koleén/ *n. Ir.* a girl.

col·lege /kólij/ *n.* **1** an establishment for further or higher education, sometimes part of a university. **2** an establishment for specialized professional education (*business college; college of music; naval college*). **3** *Brit.* the buildings or premises of a college (*lived in college*). **4** the students and teachers in a college. **5** *Brit.* a public school. **6** an organized body of persons with shared functions and privileges (*electoral college*). □□ **col·le·gial** /kəléejəl/ *adj.*

col·le·gian /kəléejən/ *n.* a member of a college.

col·le·giate /kəléejət/ *adj.* constituted as or belonging to a college; corporate. □□ **col·le·giate·ly** *adv.*

col·lide /kəlíd/ *v.intr.* (often foll. by *with*) **1** come into abrupt or violent impact. **2** be in conflict.

col·lie /kólee/ *n.* **1** a sheepdog orig. of a Scottish breed, with a long pointed nose and usu. dense, long hair. ▷ DOG. **2** this breed.

col·lier /kólyər/ *n.* **1** a coal miner. **2** a coal-carrying ship.

col·lier·y /kólyəree/ *n.* (*pl.* **-ies**) a coal mine and its associated buildings. ▷ MINE

col·li·gate /kóligayt/ *v.tr.* bring into connection (esp. isolated facts by a generalization). □□ **col·li·ga·tion** /-gáyshən/ *n.*

col·lin·e·ar /kəlíneeər/ *adj. Geom.* (of points) lying in the same straight line. □□ **col·lin·e·ar·i·ty** /-neeáiritee/ *n.* **col·lin·e·ar·ly** *adv.*

col·lins /kólinz/ *n.* (also **Col·lins**) an iced drink made of gin or whiskey, etc., with soda water, lemon or lime juice, and sugar.

col·li·sion /kəlízhən/ *n.* **1** a violent impact of a moving body, esp. a vehicle or ship, with another or with a fixed object. **2** the clashing of opposed interests or considerations. □□ **col·li·sion·al** *adj.*

col·li·sion course *n.* a course or action that is bound to cause a collision or conflict.

col·lo·cate /kóləkayt/ *v.tr.* **1** place together or side by side. **2** arrange; set in a particular place. **3** (often foll. by *with*) *Linguistics* juxtapose (a word, etc.) with another. □□ **col·lo·ca·tion** /-káyshən/ *n.*

col·loid /kóloyd/ *n.* **1** *Chem.* **a ◀** a substance consisting of ultramicroscopic particles. **b** a mixture of such a substance uniformly dispersed through a second substance, esp. to form a viscous solution. **2** *Med.* a substance of a homogeneous gelatinous consistency. □□ **col·loi·dal** /kəlóyd'l/ *adj.*

COLLOID: HAIR GEL COMPOSED OF SOLID FAT PARTICLES SUSPENDED IN WATER

col·lop /kóləp/ *n.* a slice, esp. of meat or bacon; an escalope.

col·lo·qui·al /kəlṓkweeəl/ *adj.* belonging to or proper to ordinary or familiar conversation, not formal or literary. □□ **col·lo·qui·al·ly** *adv.*

col·lo·qui·al·ism /kəlṓkweeəlizəm/ *n.* **1** a colloquial word or phrase. **2** the use of colloquialisms.

col·lo·qui·um /kəlṓkweeəm/ *n.* (*pl.* **colloquiums** or **colloquia** /-kweeə/) an academic conference or seminar.

col·lo·quy /kóləkwee/ *n.* (*pl.* **-quies**) **1** the act of conversing. **2** a conversation. **3** *Eccl.* a gathering for discussion of theological questions.

col·lo·type /kólətīp/ *n. Printing* **1** a thin sheet of gelatin exposed to light, treated with reagents, and used to make high quality prints by lithography. **2** a print made by this process.

col·lude /kəlṓod/ *v.intr.* come to an understanding or conspire together, esp. for a fraudulent purpose. □□ **col·lud·er** *n.*

col·lu·sion /kəlṓozhən/ *n.* **1** a secret understanding, esp. for a fraudulent purpose. **2** *Law* such an understanding between ostensible opponents in a lawsuit. □□ **col·lu·sive** /-lṓosiv/ *adj.* **col·lu·sive·ly** *adv.*

col·ly·ri·um /kəléereeəm/ *n.* (*pl.* **collyria** /-reeə/ or **collyriums**) a medicated eyewash.

col·ly·wob·bles /kóleewobəlz/ *n.pl. colloq.* **1** a rumbling or pain in the stomach. **2** a feeling of strong apprehension.

Colo. *abbr.* Colorado.

col·o·bus /kóləbəs/ *n.* ◀ any leaf-eating monkey of the genus *Colobus*, native to Africa, having shortened or absent thumbs.

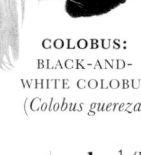

COLOBUS: BLACK-AND-WHITE COLOBUS (*Colobus guereza*)

co·logne /kəlṓn/ *n.* (in full **cologne water**) eau de cologne or a similar scented toilet water, made of essential oils and alcohol.

co·lon¹ /kṓlən/ *n.* a punctuation mark (:), used esp. to introduce a quotation or a list of items or to separate clauses when the second expands or illustrates the first; also between numbers in a statement of proportion (as in 10:1) and in biblical references (as in Exodus 3:2).

C

C

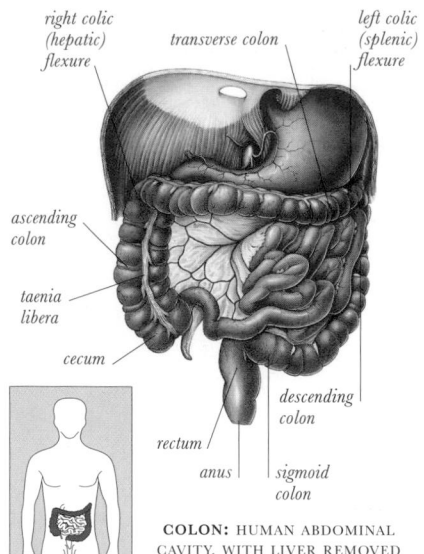

COLON: HUMAN ABDOMINAL CAVITY, WITH LIVER REMOVED TO SHOW THE COLON

COLOR

For the artist, there are three primary colors – yellow, blue, and red. Derived from these three are the secondary colors – green, orange, and violet. Their composition is shown in this double color wheel. For example, blue mixed with its adjacent yellow produces secondary green. Similarly, blue and its neighboring red combine to make violet. The wheel also illustrates complementary colors. These lie opposite each other, like violet and yellow. Laid side by side, they heighten and intensify each other.

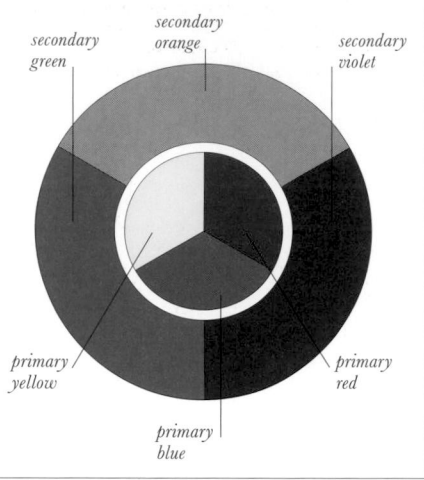

DOUBLE COLOR WHEEL SHOWING PRIMARY, SECONDARY, AND COMPLEMENTARY COLORS

co·lon² /kôlən/ *n. Anat.* ▲ the lower and greater part of the large intestine, from the cecum to the rectum. ▷ DIGESTION. □□ **co·lon·ic** /kəlónik/ *adj.*

colo·nel /kôrnəl/ *n.* **1** an army, air force, or marine officer, immediately below a brigadier general in rank. **2** = LIEUTENANT COLONEL. □□ **colo·nel·cy** *n.* (*pl.* **-ies**).

co·lo·ni·al /kəlôneeəl/ *adj. & n.* ● *adj.* **1** of, relating to, or characteristic of a colony or colonies. **2** (esp. of architecture or furniture) built or designed in, or in a style characteristic of, the period of the British colonies in America before independence. ● *n.* **1** a native or inhabitant of a colony. **2** a house built in colonial style. □□ **co·lo·ni·al·ly** *adv.*

co·lo·ni·al·ism /kəlôneeəlizəm/ *n.* **1** a policy of acquiring or maintaining colonies. **2** *derog.* this policy regarded as the esp. economic exploitation of weak or backward peoples by a larger power. □□ **co·lo·ni·al·ist** *n.*

col·o·nist /kólənist/ *n.* a settler in or inhabitant of a colony.

col·o·nize /kólənīz/ *v.* **1** *tr.* **a** establish a colony or colonies in (a country or area). **b** settle as colonists. **2** *intr.* establish or join a colony. **3** *tr. Biol.* (of plants and animals) become established (in an area). □□ **col·o·ni·za·tion** *n.* **col·o·niz·er** *n.*

col·on·nade /kólənáyd/ *n.* ▼ a row of columns, esp. supporting an entablature or roof. ▷ AMPHITHEATER, ROMANESQUE. □□ **col·on·nad·ed** *adj.*

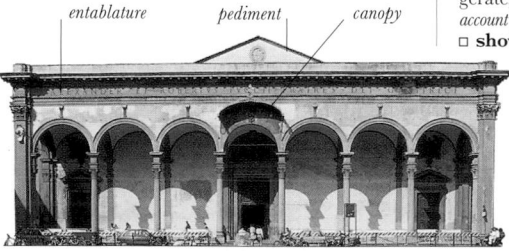

COLONNADE OF A 15TH-CENTURY RENAISSANCE CHURCH

col·o·ny /kólənee/ *n.* (*pl.* **-ies**) **1 a** a group of settlers in a new country fully or partly subject to the mother country. **b** the settlement or its territory. **2 a** a people of one nationality or race or occupation in a city, esp. if living more or less in isolation or in a special quarter. **b** a separate or segregated group (*nudist colony*). **3** *Biol.* a collection of animals, plants, etc., connected, in contact, or living close together. ▷ ALGA

col·o·phon /kólofon, -fən/ *n.* **1** ▶ a publisher's device or imprint, esp. on the title page. **2** a tailpiece in a manuscript or book, often ornamental, giving the writer's or printer's name, the date, etc.

col·o·pho·ny /kəlófənee/ *n.* = ROSIN.

col·or /kúlər/ *n. & v.* ● *n.* (*Brit.* **colour**) **1 a** the sensation produced on the eye by rays of light when resolved as by a prism, selective reflection, etc., into different wavelengths. **b** ▲ perception of color; a system of colors. **2** one, or any mixture, of the constituents into which light can be separated as in a spectrum or rainbow, sometimes including (loosely) black and white. **3** a coloring substance, esp. paint. **4** the use of all colors, not only black and white, as in photography and television. **5 a** pigmentation of the skin, esp. when dark. **b** this as a ground for prejudice or discrimination. **6** ruddiness of complexion (*a healthy color*). **7** (in *pl.*) appearance or aspect (*see things in their true colors*). **8** (in *pl.*) **a** *Brit.* a colored ribbon or uniform, etc., worn to signify membership of a school, club, team, etc. **b** the flag of a regiment or ship. **c** a national flag. **9** quality, mood, or variety in music, literature, speech, etc.; distinctive character or timbre. **10** a pretext (*under color of*). ● *v.* **1** *tr.* apply color to, esp. by painting or dyeing or with colored pens or pencils. **2** *tr.* influence (*an attitude colored by experience*). **3** *tr.* **a** misrepresent, exaggerate, esp. with spurious detail (*a highly colored account*). **b** disguise. **4** *intr.* take on color; blush. □ **show one's true colors.** reveal one's true character or intentions. **under false colors** falsely; deceitfully. **with flying colors** see FLYING.

col·or·a·ble /kúlərəbəl/ *adj.* **1** specious; plausible. **2** counterfeit. □□ **col·or·a·bly** *adv.*

Col·o·ra·do po·ta·to bee·tle /kólərádō, -ráadō/ *n.* ▶ a yellow and black striped beetle, *Leptinotarsa decemlineata*, the larva of which is highly destructive to the potato plant.

col·or·ant /kúlərənt/ *n.* a coloring substance.

col·or·a·tion /kúləráyshən/ *n.* **1** coloring; a scheme or method of applying color. **2** the natural (esp. variegated) color of living things or animals.

col·o·ra·tu·ra /kúlərətŏorə, -tyŏor-/ *n.* **1** elaborate ornamentation of a

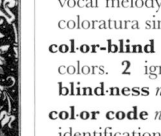

COLOPHON FROM AN EARLY FRENCH BOOK

vocal melody. **2** a singer (esp. a soprano) skilled in coloratura singing.

col·or-blind *adj.* **1** unable to distinguish certain colors. **2** ignoring racial prejudice. □□ **col·or-blind·ness** *n.*

col·or code *n.* use of colors as a standard means of identification.

col·ored /kúlərd/ *adj. & n.* ● *adj.* **1** having color(s). **2** (also **Colored**) **a** often *offens.* wholly or partly of nonwhite descent. **b** *S.Afr.* of mixed white and nonwhite descent. ● *n.* (also **Colored**) **1** a colored person. **2** *S.Afr.* a person of mixed descent speaking Afrikaans or English as the mother tongue.

col·or·fast /kúlərfast/ *adj.* dyed in colors that will not fade nor be washed out. □□ **col·or·fast·ness** *n.*

col·or·ful /kúlərfŏol/ *adj.* **1** having much or varied color; bright. **2** full of interest; vivid; lively. □□ **col·or·ful·ly** *adv.* **color·ful·ness** *n.*

col·or·if·ic /kúlərífik/ *adj.* **1** producing color. **2** highly colored.

col·or·im·e·ter /kúlərímitər/ *n.* an instrument for measuring the intensity of color. □□ **col·or·i·met·ric** /-métrik/ *adj.* **color·im·e·try** *n.*

col·or·ing /kúləring/ *n.* **1** the process of or skill in using color(s). **2** the style in which a thing is colored, or in which an artist uses color. **3** facial complexion.

col·or·ist /kúlərist/ *n.* a person who uses color, esp. in art.

col·or·ize /kúlərīz/ *v.tr.* (**colorized, colorizing**) add color to (orig. black-and-white movie film) using computer technology.

col·or·less /kúlərlis/ *adj.* **1** without color. **2** lacking character or interest. **3** dull or pale in hue. **4** neutral; impartial; indifferent. □□ **col·or·less·ly** *adv.*

col·or scheme *n.* an arrangement or planned combination of colors, esp. in interior design.

co·los·sal /kəlósəl/ *adj.* **1** of immense size; huge; gigantic. **2** *colloq.* remarkable; splendid. □□ **co·los·sal·ly** *adv.*

co·los·sus /kəlósəs/ *n.* (*pl.* **colossi** /-sī/ or **colossuses**) **1** a statue much bigger than life size. **2** a gigantic person, animal, building, etc. **3** an imperial power personified.

co·los·to·my /kəlóstəmee/ *n.* (*pl.* **-ies**) *Surgery* an operation on the colon to make an opening in the abdominal wall to provide an artificial anus.

co·los·trum /kəlóstrəm/ *n.* the first secretion from the mammary glands occurring after giving birth.

col·pos·co·py /kolpóskəpee/ *n.* (*pl.* **-ies**) examination of the vagina and the neck of the womb. □□ **col·po·scope** /kólpəskōp/ *n.*

COLORADO POTATO BEETLES (*Leptinotarsa decemlineata*)

colt /kōlt/ *n.* a young, uncastrated male horse, usu. less than four years old. □□ **colt·hood** *n.* **colt·ish** *adj.* **colt·ish·ly** *adv.* **colt·ish·ness** *n.*

col·ter /kṓltər/ *n.* a vertical cutting blade fixed in front of a plowshare.

colts·foot /kṓltsfŏŏt/ *n.* (*pl.* **coltsfoots**) a wild composite plant, *Tussilago farfara*, with large leaves and yellow flowers.

col·u·brine /kóləbrīn, kólyə-/ *adj.* **1** snakelike. **2** of the subfamily Colubrinae of nonpoisonous snakes.

col·um·bine /kóləmbīn/ *n.* ◀ any plant of the genus *Aquilegia*, esp. *A. canadensis*, having purple-blue flowers.

COLUMBINE
(*Aquilegia vulgaris*)

col·um·bi·um /kəlúmbiəm/ *n. Chem.* = NIOBIUM.

col·umn /kóləm/ *n.* **1** *Archit.* ▼ an upright cylindrical pillar often slightly tapering and usu. supporting an entablature or arch. ▷ FAÇADE. **2** a structure or part shaped like a column. **3** a vertical cylindrical mass of liquid or vapor. **4 a** a vertical division of a page, chart, etc., containing a sequence of figures or words. **b** the figures or words themselves. **5** a part of a newspaper regularly devoted to a particular subject. **6** *Mil.* an arrangement of troops in successive lines, with a narrow front. □□ **co·lum·nar** /kəlúmnər/ *adj.* **col·umned** *adj.*

col·um·nist /kóləmnist, -mist/ *n.* a journalist contributing regularly to a newspaper.

col·za /kólzə, kōl-/ *n.* = RAPE[2].

co·ma /kṓmə/ *n.* (*pl.* **comas**) a prolonged deep unconsciousness.

Co·man·che /kəmánchee/ *n.* **1 a** a N. American people native to the western plains. **b** a member of this people. **2** the language of this people.

com·a·tose /kṓmətōs, kóm-/ *adj.* **1** in a coma. **2** drowsy.

comb /kōm/ *n. & v.* ● *n.* **1** a toothed strip of rigid material for tidying and arranging the hair. **2** a part of a machine having a similar design or purpose. **3** the red, fleshy crest of a fowl, esp. a cock. ▷ COCKSCOMB. **4** a honeycomb. ● *v.tr.* **1** arrange or tidy (the hair) by drawing a comb through. **2** curry (a horse). **3** dress (wool or flax) with a comb. **4** search (a place) thoroughly. □□ **combed** *adj.*

com·bat *n. & v.* ● *n.* /kómbat, kúm-/ **1** a fight; an armed encounter or conflict; fighting; battle. **2** a struggle, contest, or dispute. ● *v.* /kəmbát, kómbat/ (**combated, combating**) **1** *intr.* engage in combat. **2** *tr.* oppose; strive against.

com·bat·ant /kəmbát'nt, kómbət'nt/ *n. & adj.* ● *n.* a person engaged in fighting. ● *adj.* fighting.

com·bat dress *n.* ▼ a soldier's uniform worn for combat and field training, usu. of olive-green, camouflage, or khaki fabric.

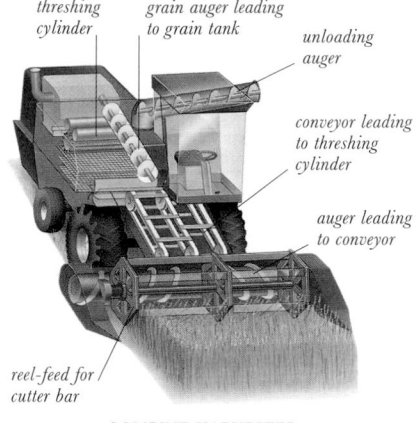

hood   camouflage fabric
shoulder strap   drawstring
patch pocket   Velcro® fastening
foul-weather cuff

COMBAT DRESS: US ARMY URBAN-PATTERN CAMOUFLAGE JACKET

com·bat fa·tigue *n.* a mental disorder caused by stress in wartime combat.

com·bat·ive /kəmbátiv/ *adj.* ready or eager to fight; pugnacious. □□ **com·bat·ive·ly** *adv.* **com·bat·ive·ness** *n.*

com·bat trou·sers *n.* loose trousers with large patch pockets on each leg, typically made of hard-wearing cotton.

comb·er /kṓmər/ *n.* **1** a machine for combing cotton or wool. **2** a long curling wave; a breaker.

com·bi·na·tion /kómbináyshən/ *n.* **1** the act or an instance of combining; the process of being combined. **2** a combined state (*in combination with*). **3** a combined set of things or people. **4** a sequence of numbers or letters used to open a combination lock. □□ **com·bi·na·tion·al** *adj.* **com·bi·na·tive** /kómbináytiv, kəmbínə-/ *adj.* **com·bi·na·to·ri·al** /kómbinətáwreeəl, kəmbínə-/ *adj.* **com·bin·a·to·ry** /kəmbínətawree/ *adj.*

com·bi·na·tion lock *n.* a lock that can be opened only by rotating a dial or set of dials through a specific sequence of movements.

com·bine *v. & n.* ● *v.* /kəmbín/ **1** *tr. & intr.* join together; unite for a common purpose. **2** *tr.* possess (qualities usually distinct) together (*combines charm and authority*). **3 a** *intr.* coalesce in one substance. **b** *tr.* cause to do this. **c** *intr.* form a chemical compound. **4** /kómbīn/ *tr.* harvest (crops, etc.) by means of a combine harvester. ● *n.* /kómbīn/ a combination of esp. commercial interests to control prices, etc.

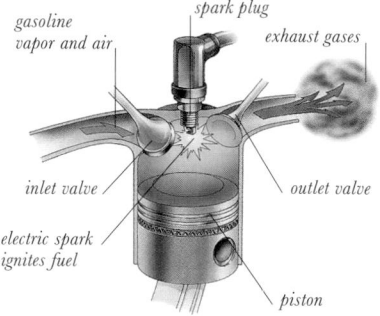

threshing cylinder   grain auger leading to grain tank   unloading auger
conveyor leading to threshing cylinder
auger leading to conveyor
reel-feed for cutter bar

COMBINE HARVESTER

com·bine har·ves·ter /kómbīn/ *n.* ▲ a mobile machine that reaps and threshes in one operation.

com·bin·ing form *n. Gram.* a linguistic element used in combination with another element to form a word (e.g., *Anglo-* = English, *bio-* = life, *graphy* = writing). In this dictionary, *combining form* is used of an element that contributes to the particular sense of words (as with both elements of *biography*), as distinct from a prefix or suffix that adjusts the sense of or determines the function.

com·bo /kómbō/ *n.* (*pl.* **-os**) *sl.* a small jazz or dance band.

comb-o·ver *n.* a strip of hair combed over a bald patch on a man's head in an attempt to conceal it.

com·bust /kəmbúst/ *v.tr.* subject to combustion.

com·bus·ti·ble /kəmbústibəl/ *adj. & n.* ● *adj.* **1** capable of or used for burning. **2** excitable; easily irritated. ● *n.* a combustible substance.

com·bus·tion /kəmbúschən/ *n.* **1** burning; consumption by fire. **2** *Chem.* the development of light and heat from the chemical combination of a substance with oxygen. □□ **com·bus·tive** /-bústiv/ *adj.*

com·bus·tion cham·ber *n.* ▼ a space in which combustion takes place, e.g., of gases in a boiler-furnace or fuel in an internal-combustion engine. ▷ INTERNAL-COMBUSTION ENGINE

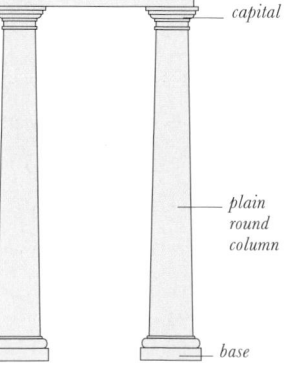

spark plug
gasoline vapor and air   exhaust gases
inlet valve   outlet valve
electric spark ignites fuel   piston

COMBUSTION CHAMBER OF AN INTERNAL-COMBUSTION ENGINE

Comdr. *abbr.* commander.

come /kum/ *v.intr.* (*past* **came** /kaym/; *past part.* **come**) **1** move, be brought toward, or reach a place thought of as near or familiar to the speaker or hearer (*come and see me; the books have come*). **2** reach or be brought to a specified situation or result (*you'll come to no harm; have come to believe it; came into prominence*). **3** extend to a specified point (*the road comes within a mile of us*). **4** traverse or accomplish (with compl.: *have come a long way*). **5** get to be in a certain condition (*how did you come to break your leg?*). **6** take or occupy a specified position (*it comes on the*

COLUMN

The ancient Egyptians and Greeks first incorporated columns into architectural designs. There were three orders, Doric, Ionic, and Corinthian, each with clearly defined conventions governing proportion and appearance. Roman and Renaissance architects imitated these and devised two others: Composite and Tuscan.

TYPES OF COLUMN

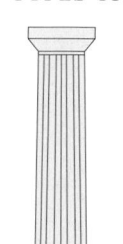 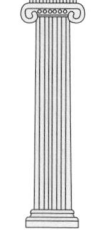  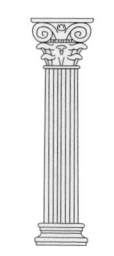

cornice
frieze
architrave
capital

plain round column

base

DORIC   IONIC   CORINTHIAN   COMPOSITE   TUSCAN (AND ENTABLATURE) *third page*). **7** become perceptible or known (*the church came into sight; it will come to me*). **8** be available (*comes in three sizes*). **9** become (with compl.: *come loose*). **10** (foll. by *of*) **a** be descended from (*comes of a rich family*). **b** be the result of (*that comes of complaining*). **11** *colloq.* play the part of; behave like (with compl.: *don't come the bully with me*). **12** *sl.* have a sexual orgasm. **13** (in *subj.*) *colloq.* when a specified time is reached (*come next month*). **14** (as *int.*) expressing caution or reserve (*come now, it cannot be that bad*). □ **as ... as they come** typically or supremely so (*is as tough as they come*). **come about** happen; take place. **come across 1 a** be effective or understood. **b** appear or sound in a specified way. **2** (foll. by *with*) *sl.* hand over what is wanted. **3** meet or find by chance (*came across an old jacket*). **come again** *colloq.* **1** make a further effort. **2** (as *imper.*) what did you say? **come along 1** make progress; move forward. **2** (as *imper.*) hurry up. **come and go 1** pass to and fro; be transitory. **2** pay brief visits. **come apart** fall or break into pieces; disintegrate. **come around 1** pay an informal visit. **2** recover consciousness. **3** be converted to another person's opinion. **4** (of a date or regular occurrence) recur; be imminent again. **come at 1** reach; discover; get access to. **2** attack (*came at me with a knife*). **come away 1** become detached or broken off (*came away in my hands*). **2** (foll. by *with*) be left with a feeling, impression, etc. **come back 1** return. **2** recur to one's memory. **3** become popular again. **4** reply; retort. **come before** be dealt with by (a judge, etc.). **come between 1** interfere with the relationship of. **2** separate; prevent contact between. **come by 1** pass; go past. **2** call on a visit (*come by tomorrow*). **3** acquire (*came by a new bicycle*). **come clean** see CLEAN. **come down 1** come to a place or position regarded as lower. **2** lose position or wealth. **3** be handed down by tradition or inheritance. **4** be reduced; show a downward trend (*prices are coming down*). **5** (foll. by *against, in favor of, on the side of*) reach a decision or recommendation (*the report came down against change*). **6** (foll. by *to*) signify basically; be dependent on (a factor). **7** (foll. by *on*) criticize harshly; punish. **8** (foll. by *with*) begin to suffer from (a disease). **come for 1** come to collect or receive. **2** attack (*came for me with a hammer*). **come forward 1** advance. **2** offer oneself for a task, post, etc. **come in 1** enter a house or room. **2** take a specified position in a race, etc. (*came in third*). **3** become fashionable or seasonable. **4 a** have a useful role or function. **b** (with compl.) prove to be (*came in very handy*). **c** have a part to play (*where do I come in?*). **5** be received (*news has just come in*). **6** begin speaking, esp. in radio transmission. **7** be elected; come to power. **8** (foll. by *for*) receive; be the object of (*came in for much criticism*). **9** (foll. by *on*) join (an enterprise, etc.). **10** (of a tide) turn to high tide. **11** (of a train, ship, or aircraft) approach its destination. **come into 1** see senses 2, 7 of *v.* **2** receive, esp. as heir. **come near** see NEAR. **come of age** see AGE. **come off 1** *colloq.* (of an action) succeed; be accomplished. **2** (with compl.) fare; turn out (*came off badly*). **3** be detached or detachable (from). **4** fall (from). **5** be reduced or subtracted from (*$5 came off the price*). **come off it** (as *imper.*) *colloq.* an expression of disbelief or refusal to accept another's opinion, behavior, etc. **come on 1** continue to come. **2** (foll. by *to*) make sexual advances. **3** make progress; thrive (*is really coming on*). **4** appear on the stage, field of play, etc. **5** be heard or seen on television, on the telephone, etc. **6** arise to be discussed. **7** (as *imper.*) expressing encouragement. **8** = *come upon*. **come out 1** emerge; become known (*it came out that he had left*). **2** appear or be published (*comes out every Saturday*). **3 a** declare oneself; make a decision (*came out in favor of joining*). **b** openly declare that one is a homosexual. **4 a** be satisfactorily visible in a photograph, etc., or present in a specified way (*he came out badly*). **b** (of a photograph) be produced satisfactorily (*only three have come out*). **5** attain a specified result in an examination, etc. **6** (of a stain, etc.) be removed. **7** make one's début in society. **8** (foll. by *in*) be covered with (*came out in spots*). **9** (of a problem) be solved. **10** (foll. by *with*) declare openly; disclose. **come over 1** come from some distance or nearer to the speaker (*came over from Paris; come over here*). **2** (of a feeling, etc.) overtake or affect (a person). **come through 1** be successful; survive. **2** be received by telephone. **3** survive or overcome (a difficulty) (*came through the ordeal*). **come to 1** recover consciousness. **2** *Naut.* bring a vessel to a stop. **3** reach in total; amount to. **4** *refl.* recover consciousness. **5** have as a destiny; reach (*what is the world coming to?*). **come to light** see LIGHT[1]. **come to nothing** have no useful result in the end; fail. **come to pass** occur. **come to rest** cease moving. **come to one's senses** see SENSE. **come to that** *colloq.* in fact; if that is the case. **come under 1** be classified as or among. **2** be subject to (influence or authority). **come up 1** come to a place or position regarded as higher. **2** attain wealth or position. **3** (of an issue, problem, etc.) arise; be mentioned or discussed. **4** (often foll. by *to*) **a** approach a person, esp. to talk. **b** (foll. by *to, on*) approach a specified time, etc. (*is coming up to eight o'clock*). **5** (foll. by *to*) match (a standard, etc.). **6** (foll. by *with*) produce (an idea, etc.), esp. in response to a challenge. **7** (of a plant, etc.) spring up out of the ground. **8** become brighter (e.g., with polishing). **come up against** be faced with. **come upon 1** meet or find by chance. **2** attack by surprise. **come what may** no matter what happens. **have it coming to one** *colloq.* be about to get one's deserts. **how come?** *colloq.* how did that happen? **if it comes to that** in that case. **to come** future; in the future (*the year to come*).

come·back /kúmbak/ *n.* **1** a return to a previous (esp. successful) state. **2** *sl.* a retaliation.

co·me·di·an /kəméedeeən/ *n.* **1** a humorous entertainer. **2** an actor in comedy. **3** *sl.* an amusing person.

co·me·di·enne /kəméedee-én/ *n.* a female comedian.

com·e·dist /kómidist/ *n.* a writer of comedies.

come·down /kúmdown/ *n.* **1** a loss of status; decline. **2** a disappointment.

com·e·dy /kómidee/ *n.* (*pl.* **-ies**) **1 a** a play, film, etc., of an amusing character, usu. with a happy ending. **b** the genre consisting of works of this kind (cf. TRAGEDY). **2** an amusing incident or series of incidents in everyday life. **3** humor, esp. in a work of art. □□ **co·me·dic** /kəméedik/ *adj.*

com·e·dy of man·ners *n.* satirical portrayal of social behavior, esp. of the upper classes.

come·ly /kúmlee/ *adj.* (**comelier**, **comeliest**) pleasant to look at. □□ **come·li·ness** /kúmleenis/ *n.*

come-on *n. sl.* a lure or enticement.

com·er /kúmər/ *n.* **1** a person who comes, esp. as an applicant, participant, etc. (*offered the job to the first comer*). **2** *colloq.* a person likely to be a success.

co·mes·ti·ble /kəméstibəl/ *n.* (usu. in *pl.*) *formal* or *joc.* food.

com·et /kómit/ *n.* ▼ a hazy object usu. with a nucleus of ice and dust surrounded by gas and with a tail pointing away from the Sun, moving in an eccentric orbit around the Sun. □□ **com·et·ar·y** *adj.*

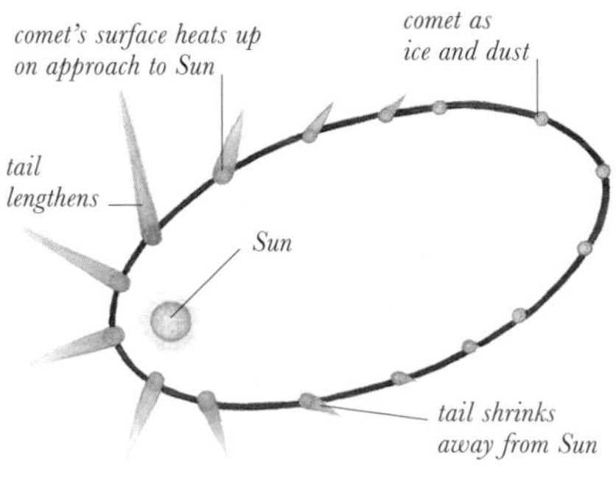
comet's surface heats up on approach to Sun
comet as ice and dust
tail lengthens
Sun
tail shrinks away from Sun

COMET: ORBIT OF A PERIODIC COMET IN THE INNER SOLAR SYSTEM

come·up·pance /kumúpəns/ *n. colloq.* one's deserved fate (*got his comeuppance*).

com·fort /kúmfərt/ *n.* & *v.* ● *n.* **1** consolation; relief in affliction. **2 a** a state of physical well-being (*live in comfort*). **b** (usu. in *pl.*) things that make life easy or pleasant. **3** a cause of satisfaction (*a comfort to me that you are here*). **4** a person who consoles or helps one (*he's a comfort to her in her old age*). ● *v.tr.* **1** soothe in grief; console. **2** make comfortable (*comforted by the warmth of the fire*). □□ **com·fort·ing** *adj.* **com·fort·ing·ly** *adv.* **com·fort·less** *adj.*

com·fort·a·ble /kúmftəbəl, -fərtəbəl/ *adj.* **1 a** such as give comfort or ease (*a comfortable pair of shoes*). **b** (of a person) relaxing to be with; congenial. **2** free from discomfort; at ease. **3** *colloq.* having an adequate standard of living. **4** having an easy conscience (*did not feel comfortable about refusing him*). **5** with a wide margin (*a comfortable win*). □□ **com·fort·a·ble·ness** *n.* **com·fort·a·bly** *adv.*

com·fort·er /kúmfərtər/ *n.* **1** a person who comforts. **2** a warm quilt.

com·frey /kúmfree/ *n.* (*pl.* **-eys**) ► any of various plants of the genus *Symphytum*, esp. *S. officinale*, having large, hairy leaves and clusters of usu. white or purple bell-shaped flowers.

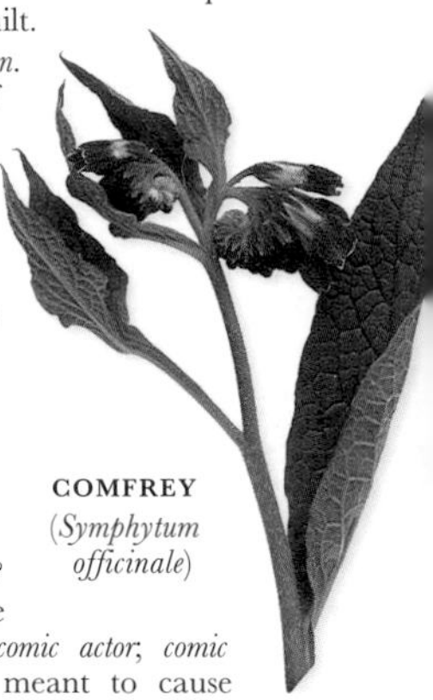

COMFREY (*Symphytum officinale*)

com·fy /kúmfee/ *adj.* (**comfier**, **comfiest**) *colloq.* comfortable. □□ **com·fi·ly** *adv.* **com·fi·ness** *n.*

com·ic /kómik/ *adj.* & *n.* ● *adj.* **1** of, or in the style of, comedy (*a comic actor; comic opera*). **2** causing or meant to cause laughter; funny. ● *n.* **1** a professional comedian. **2** (*pl.*) section or page of a newspaper featuring several comic strips.

com·i·cal /kómikəl/ *adj.* funny; causing laughter. □□ **com·i·cal·i·ty** /-kálitee/ *n.* **com·i·cal·ly** *adv.*

com·ic book *n.* a magazine in the form of comic strips.

com·ic op·er·a *n.* **1** an opera with much spoken dialogue, usu. with humorous treatment. **2** this genre.

com·ic strip *n.* a horizontal series of drawings in a comic book, newspaper, etc., telling a story.

com·ing /kúming/ *adj.* & *n.* ● *attrib.adj.* **1** approaching; next (*in the coming week*). **2** of potential importance (*a coming man*). ● *n.* arrival; approach.

com·i·ty /kómitee/ *n.* (*pl.* **-ies**) **1** civility; considerate behavior toward others. **2 a** an association of nations, etc., for mutual benefit. **b** (in full **comity of nations**) the mutual recognition by nations of the laws and customs of others.

com·ma /kómə/ *n.* **1** a punctuation mark (,) indicating a pause between parts of a sentence, or dividing items in a list, string of figures, etc. **2** *Mus.* a definite minute interval or difference of pitch.

com·mand /kəmánd/ *v.* & *n.* ● *v.tr.* **1** (also *absol.*; often foll. by *to* + infin., or *that* + clause) give formal order or instructions to (*commands us to obey; commands that it be done*). **2** (also *absol.*) have authority over. **3 a** (often *refl.*) restrain; master. **b** gain the use of; have at one's disposal (skill, resources, etc.). **4** deserve and get (sympathy, respect, etc.). **5** *Mil.* dominate (a strategic position) from a superior height; look down over. ● *n.* **1** an order; an instruction. **2** mastery; control (*a good command of languages*). **3** the exercise or tenure of authority, esp. naval or military (*has command of this ship*). **4** *Mil.* **a** a body of troops, etc. (*Artillery Command*). **b** a district under a commander (*Western Command*). **5** *Computing* **a** an instruction causing a computer to perform one of its basic functions. **b** a signal initiating such an operation. □ **in command of** commanding. **under command of** commanded by.

com·man·dant /kómǝndánt, -dánt/ *n.* a commanding officer. □□ **com·man·dant·ship** *n.*

com·man·deer /kómǝndéer/ *v.tr.* **1** seize (men or goods) for military purposes. **2** take possession of without authority.

com·mand·er /kǝmándǝr/ *n.* a person who commands, esp. a naval officer next in rank below captain. □□ **com·mand·er·ship** *n.*

com·mand·er-in-chief *n.* (*pl.* **commanders in chief**) the supreme commander, esp. of a nation's forces.

com·mand·ing /kǝmánding/ *adj.* **1** dignified; exalted; impressive. **2** (of a hill, etc.) giving a wide view. **3** (of an advantage, a position, etc.) controlling; superior. □□ **com·mand·ing·ly** *adv.*

com·mand·ment /kǝmándmǝnt/ *n.* a divine command.

com·mand mod·ule *n.* the control compartment in a spacecraft.

com·man·do /kǝmándō/ *n.* (*pl.* **-os**) *Mil.* **1 a** a unit of amphibious shock troops. **b** a member of such a unit. **2 a** a party of men called out for military service. **b** a body of troops.

com·mand per·for·mance *n.* a theatrical or film performance given at the request of a head of state or sovereign.

com·me·di·a dell'ar·te /kǝmedeeyǝ del áarte/ *n.* an Italian kind of improvised comedy popular in the 16th–18th centuries, based on stock characters.

com·mem·o·rate /kǝmémǝrayt/ *v.tr.* **1** celebrate in speech or writing. **2 a** preserve in memory by some celebration. **b** (of a plaque, etc.) be a memorial of. □□ **com·mem·o·ra·tion** /kǝmémǝráyshǝn/ *n.* **com·mem·o·ra·tive** /-ráytiv, -rǝtiv/ *adj.* **com·mem·o·ra·tor** *n.*

com·mence /kǝméns/ *v.tr & intr. formal* begin.

com·mence·ment /kǝménsmǝnt/ *n. formal* **1** a beginning. **2** a ceremony of degree conferment.

com·mend /kǝménd/ *v.tr.* **1** (often foll. by *to*) entrust; commit (*commends his soul to God*). **2** praise.

com·mend·a·ble /kǝméndǝbǝl/ *adj.* praiseworthy. □□ **com·mend·a·bly** *adv.*

com·men·da·tion /kómendáyshǝn/ *n.* **1** an act of commending or recommending. **2** praise.

com·men·da·to·ry /kǝméndǝtawree/ *adj.* commending; recommending.

com·men·sal /kǝménsǝl/ *adj. & n. Biol.* ● *adj.* of, relating to, or exhibiting commensalism. ● *n.* a commensal organism. □□ **com·men·sal·i·ty** /kómǝnsálitee/ *n.* **com·men·sal·ly** *adv.*

com·men·sal·ism /kǝménsǝlizǝm/ *n. Biol.* ▲ an association between two organisms in which one benefits and the other derives no benefit or harm.

com·men·su·ra·ble /kǝménsǝrǝbǝl, -shǝrǝ-/ *adj.* **1** measurable by the same standard. **2** (foll. by *to*) proportionate to. **3** *Math.* (of numbers) in a ratio equal to the ratio of integers. □□ **com·men·su·ra·bil·i·ty** *n.* **com·men·su·ra·bly** *adv.*

com·men·su·rate /kǝménsǝrǝt, -shǝrǝt/ *adj.* **1** (usu. foll. by *with*) having the same size, duration, etc. **2** (often foll. by *to, with*) proportionate. □□ **com·men·su·rate·ly** *adv.*

com·ment /kóment/ *n. & v.* ● *n.* **1 a** a remark, esp. critical (*passed a comment on her hat*). **b** commenting; criticism (*his behavior aroused much comment*). **2** an explanatory note (e.g., on a written text). ● *v.tr.* **1** (often foll. by *on, upon,* or *that* + clause) make (esp. critical) remarks (*commented on her choice of friends*). **2** (often foll. by *on, upon*) write explanatory notes. □ **no comment** *colloq.* I decline to answer your question. □□ **com·ment·er** *n.*

com·men·tar·y /kómǝntǝree/ *n.* (*pl.* **-ies**) **1** a set of explanatory or critical notes on a text, etc. **2** a descriptive spoken account (esp. on radio or television) of an event as it happens.

com·men·tate /kómǝntayt/ *v.intr. disp.* act as a commentator.

com·men·ta·tor /kómǝntaytǝr/ *n.* **1** a person who provides a commentary on an event, etc. **2** the

COMMENSALISM

Meaning *eating at the same table*, commensalism is a partnership between two species in which food is often involved. Usually, only one partner benefits, while the other is unaffected. Remoras live commensally with sharks. The remora fastens itself to the shark as a means of free transportation, and detaches itself temporarily to feed.

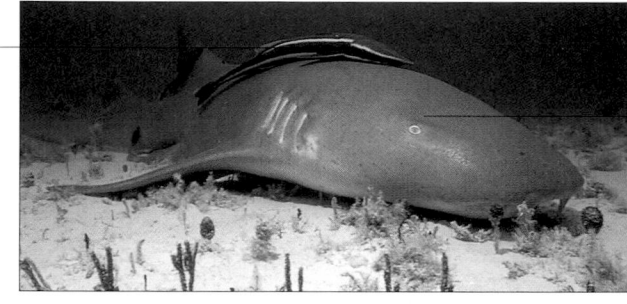

remora

nurse shark

COMMENSALISM BETWEEN A NURSE SHARK AND A REMORA

writer of a commentary. **3** a person who writes or speaks on current events.

com·merce /kómǝrs/ *n.* financial transactions, esp. the buying and selling of merchandise, on a large scale.

com·mer·cial /kǝmárshǝl/ *adj. & n.* ● *adj.* **1** of, engaged in, or concerned with, commerce. **2** having profit as a primary aim rather than artistic, etc., value; philistine. ● *n.* a television or radio advertisement. □□ **com·mer·ci·al·i·ty** /-sheéálitee/ *n.* **com·mer·cial·ly** *adv.*

com·mer·cial·ism /kǝmárshǝlizǝm/ *n.* **1** the principles and practice of commerce. **2** (esp. excessive) emphasis on financial profit as a measure of worth.

com·mer·cial·ize /kǝmárshǝlīz/ *v.tr.* **1** exploit or spoil for gaining profit. **2** make commercial. □□ **com·mer·cial·i·za·tion** *n.*

com·mie /kómee/ *n. sl. derog.* (also **Com·mie**) a Communist.

com·mi·na·tion /kómináyshǝn/ *n.* the threatening of divine vengeance.

com·mi·na·to·ry /kǝmínǝtawree, kómínǝ-/ *adj.* threatening.

com·min·gle /kǝmínggǝl/ *v.tr. & intr. literary* mingle together.

com·mi·nute /kómǝnōōt, -nyōōt/ *v.tr.* **1** reduce to small fragments. **2** divide (property) into small portions. □□ **com·mi·nu·tion** /-nōōshǝn, -nyōō-/ *n.*

com·mis·er·ate /kǝmízǝrayt/ *v. intr.* (usu. foll. by *with*) express or feel pity. □□ **com·mis·er·a·tion** /-ráyshǝn/ *n.* **com·mis·er·a·tive** /-ráytiv/ *adj.*

com·mis·sar·i·at /kómisáireeǝt/ *n.* esp. *Mil.* **1** a department for the supply of food, etc. **2** the food supplied.

com·mis·sar·y /kómiseree/ *n.* (*pl.* **-ies**) **1** *Mil.* **a** a store for the supply of food, etc., to soldiers. **b** an officer responsible for the supply of food, etc., to soldiers. **2 a** a restaurant in a movie studio, etc. **b** the food supplied. **3** a deputy or delegate. □□ **com·mis·sar·i·al** *adj.* **com·mis·sar·y·ship** *n.*

com·mis·sion /kǝmíshǝn/ *n. & v.* ● *n.* **1 a** the authority to perform a task or certain duties. **b** a person or group entrusted esp. by a government with such authority. **c** an instruction or duty given to such a group or person (*their commission was to simplify the procedure*). **2** an order for something, esp. a work of art, to be produced specially. **3** *Mil.* **a** a warrant conferring the rank of officer in the army, navy, marines, or air force. **b** the rank so conferred. **4 a** the authority to act as agent for a company, etc., in trade. **b** a percentage paid to the agent from the business obtained (*his wages are low, but he gets 20 percent commission*). **5** the act of committing (a crime, sin, etc.). **6** the office or department of a commis-sioner. ● *v.tr.* **1** authorize or empower by a commission. **2** give (an artist, etc.) a commission for a piece of work. **b** order (a work) to be written. **3** *Naut.* **a** give (an officer) the command of a ship. **b** prepare (a ship) for active service. **4** bring (a machine, equipment, etc.) into operation. □ **in commission** (of a warship, etc.) manned, armed, and ready for service. **out of commission** (esp. of a ship) not in service; not in working order.

com·mis·sion·er /kǝmíshǝnǝr/ *n.* **1** a person appointed by a commission to perform a specific task. **2** a person appointed as a member of a government commission. **3** a representative of the supreme authority in a district, department, etc.

com·mis·sure /kómishōōr/ *n.* ◄ a junction, joint, or seam, as between bones or the line where the lips meet.

commissure

COMMISSURE

com·mit /kǝmít/ *v.tr.* (**committed, committing**) **1** (usu. foll. by *to*) entrust or consign for **a** safe keeping (*I commit him to your care*). **b** treatment, usu. destruction (*committed the book to the flames*). **c** official custody as a criminal or as insane (*you could be committed for such behavior*). **2** perpetrate, do (esp. a crime, sin, or blunder). **3** pledge, involve, or bind (esp. oneself) to a certain course or policy. **4** (as **committed** *adj.*) (often foll. by *to*) **a** morally dedicated or politically aligned (*a committed Christian; committed to the cause*). **b** obliged (to take certain action). □ **commit to memory** memorize. □□ **com·mit·ta·ble** *adj.* **com·mit·ter** *n.*

com·mit·ment /kǝmítmǝnt/ *n.* **1** an engagement or obligation that restricts freedom of action. **2** the process or an instance of committing oneself.

com·mit·tal /kǝmít'l/ *n.* **1** the act of committing a person to an institution, esp. prison or a psychiatric hospital. **2** the burial of a dead body.

com·mit·tee /kǝmitee/ *n.* **1** a body of persons appointed for a specific function by, and usu. out of, a larger body. **2** such a body appointed by a legislature, etc., to consider the details of proposed legislation.

com·mode /kǝmód/ *n.* **1** a chest of drawers. **2 a** = TOILET 1. **b** (also **night commode**) a bedside table with a cupboard containing a chamber pot.

com·mo·di·ous /kǝmódeeǝs/ *adj.* roomy and comfortable. □□ **com·mo·di·ous·ly** *adv.* **com·mo·di·ous·ness** *n.*

com·mod·i·ty /kǝmóditee/ *n.* (*pl.* **-ies**) **1** *Commerce* an article or raw material that can be bought and sold. **2** a useful thing.

com·mo·dore /kómǝdawr/ *n.* **1** a naval officer above a captain and below a rear admiral. **2** the commander of a squadron or other division of a fleet. **3** the president of a yacht club.

C

C

com·mon /kómən/ *adj. & n.* ● *adj.* (**commoner, commonest**) **1 a** occurring often (*a common mistake*). **b** ordinary; of ordinary qualities; without special rank or position (*no common mind; common soldier; the common people*). **2 a** shared by, coming from, or done by, more than one (*common knowledge; by common consent*). **b** belonging to, open to, or affecting, the whole community (*common land*). **3** *derog.* low-class; inferior (*a common little man*). **4** of the most familiar type (*common cold*). **5** *Math.* belonging to two or more quantities (*common factor*). **6** *Gram.* (of gender) referring to individuals of either sex (e.g., *teacher*). **7** *Mus.* having two or four beats, esp. four quarter notes, in a bar. ● *n.* a piece of open public land, esp. in a village or town. □ **in common 1** in joint use; shared. **2** of joint interest (*have little in common*). **in common with** in the same way as. □□ **com·mon·ly** *adv.* **com·mon·ness** *n.*

com·mon·al·i·ty /kómənálitee/ *n.* (*pl.* **-ies**) **1** the sharing of an attribute. **2** a common occurrence. **3** = COMMONALTY.

com·mon·al·ty /kómənəltee/ *n.* (*pl.* **-ies**) **1** the common people. **2** the general body (esp. of mankind). **3** a corporate body.

com·mon de·nom·i·na·tor *n.* **1** a common multiple of the denominators of several fractions. **2** a common feature of members of a group.

com·mon·er /kómənər/ *n.* one of the common people, as opposed to the aristocracy.

Com·mon E·ra *n.* the Christian era.

common ground *n.* a point or argument accepted by both sides in a dispute.

common law *n.* law derived from custom and judicial precedent (cf. CASE LAW, STATUTE LAW).

Com·mon Mar·ket *n.* the European Economic Community.

common noun *n.* (also **common name**) *Gram.* a name denoting a class of objects or a concept as opposed to a particular individual (e.g., *boy, chocolate*).

com·mon·place /kómənplays/ *adj. & n.* ● *adj.* lacking originality; trite. ● *n.* **1 a** an everyday saying; a platitude. **b** an ordinary topic of conversation. **2** anything usual or trite. □□ **com·mon·place·ness** *n.*

com·mons /kómənz/ *n.pl.* **1** *US* a dining hall at a university, etc. **2** *New Eng.* a central public park or ground in a town, etc. **3** the common people.

com·mon sense *n.* sound practical sense, esp. in everyday matters.

com·mon·sen·si·cal /kómənsénsikəl/ *adj.* possessing or marked by common sense.

com·mon stock *n.* ordinary shares of stock in a corporation (cf. PREFERRED STOCK).

com·mon·wealth /kómənwelth/ *n.* **1** an independent state or community, esp. a democratic republic. **2** (**the Commonwealth**) **a** (in full **the British Commonwealth of Nations**) an international association consisting of the UK together with nations that were previously part of the British Empire. **b** the republican period of government in Britain 1649–60. **c** a part of the title of Puerto Rico and some of the states of the US.

com·mo·tion /kəmṓshən/ *n.* **1** a confused and noisy disturbance. **2** loud and confusing noise.

com·mu·nal /kəmyōonəl, kómyə-/ *adj.* **1** relating to or benefiting a community; for common use (*communal baths*). **2** between different esp. ethnic or religious communities (*communal violence*). □□ **com·mu·nal·i·ty** /-nálitee/ *n.* **com·mu·nal·ly** *adv.*

com·mu·nal·ism /kəmyōonəlizəm, kómyənə-/ *n.* **1** a principle of political organization based on federated communes. **2** the principle of communal ownership, etc.

com·mu·nal·ize /kəmyōonəlīz, kómyənə-/ *v.tr.* make communal. □□ **com·mu·nal·i·za·tion** *n.*

com·mu·nard /kómyənaard/ *n.* a member of a commune.

com·mune[1] /kómyōon/ *n.* **1 a** a group of people sharing living accommodation, goods, etc. **b** a communal settlement esp. for the pursuit of shared interests. **2 a** the smallest French territorial division for administrative purposes. **b** a similar division elsewhere.

com·mune[2] /kəmyōon/ *v.intr.* **1** (usu. foll. by *with*) speak intimately **2** feel in close touch (with nature, etc.) (*communed with the hills*).

com·mu·ni·ca·ble /kəmyōonikəbəl/ *adj.* (esp. of a disease) able to be passed on. □□ **com·mu·ni·ca·bil·i·ty** *n.* **com·mu·ni·ca·bly** *adv.*

com·mu·ni·cant /kəmyōonikənt/ *n.* **1** a person who receives Holy Communion. **2** a person who imparts information.

com·mu·ni·cate /kəmyōonikayt/ *v.* **1** *tr.* **a** transmit or pass on by speaking or writing. **b** transmit (heat, motion, etc.). **c** pass on (an infectious illness). **d** impart (feelings, etc.) nonverbally. **2** *intr.* (often foll. by *with*) succeed in conveying information, evoking understanding, etc. (*she communicates well*). **3** *intr.* (often foll. by *with*) relate socially. **4** *intr.* (often foll. by *with*) (of a room, etc.) have a common door (*my room communicates with yours*). □□ **com·mu·ni·ca·tor** *n.* **com·mu·ni·ca·to·ry** /-nikətáwree/ *adj.*

com·mu·ni·ca·tion /kəmyōonikáyshən/ *n.* **1 a** the act of imparting, esp. news. **b** an instance of this. **c** the information, etc., communicated. **2** a means of connecting different places. **3** social intercourse. **4** (in *pl.*) the practice of transmitting information.

com·mu·ni·ca·tive /kəmyōonikáytiv, -kətiv/ *adj.* **1** open; talkative; informative. **2** ready to communicate. □□ **com·mu·ni·ca·tive·ly** *adv.*

com·mun·ion /kəmyōonyən/ *n.* **1** a sharing, esp. of thoughts, etc.; fellowship. **2** participation; a sharing in common (*communion of interests*). **3** (**Communion, Holy Communion**) **a** the Eucharist. **b** participation in the Communion service. **4** a body or group within the Christian faith (*the Methodist communion*).

com·mu·ni·qué /kəmyōonikáy/ *n.* an official communication, esp. a news report.

com·mu·nism /kómyənizəm/ *n.* **1** a political theory advocating a society in which all property is publicly owned and each person is paid and works according to his or her needs and abilities. **2** (usu. **Communism**) **a** the communistic form of society established in the former USSR and elsewhere. **b** any movement or political doctrine advocating communism, esp. Marxism. **3** = COMMUNALISM.

com·mu·nist /kómyənist/ *n. & adj.* ● *n.* **1** a person advocating or practicing communism. **2** (**Communist**) a member of a Communist party. ● *adj.* of or relating to communism (*a communist play*). □□ **com·mu·nis·tic** /-nístik/ *adj.*

com·mu·ni·tar·i·an /kəmyōonitáireeən/ *n. & adj.* ● *n.* a member of a communistic community. ● *adj.* of or relating to such a community.

com·mu·ni·ty /kəmyōonitee/ *n.* (*pl.* **-ies**) **1** all the people living in a specific locality. **2** a body of people having a religion, a profession, etc., in common (*the immigrant community*). **3** fellowship; similarity (*community of intellect*). **4** a monastic, socialistic, etc., body practicing common ownership. **5** joint ownership or liability (*community of goods*). **6** (prec. by *the*) the public.

com·mu·ni·ty cen·ter *n.* a place providing social, etc., facilities for a neighborhood.

com·mu·ni·ty col·lege *n.* a college offering courses to a local community or region.

com·mu·ni·ty serv·ice *n.* unpaid work performed in service to the community, esp. as part of a criminal sentence.

com·mut·a·ble /kəmyōotəbəl/ *adj.* **1** convertible into money; exchangeable. **2** *Law* (of a punishment) able to be commuted. **3** within commuting distance. □□ **com·mut·a·bil·i·ty** *n.*

com·mu·tate /kómyətayt/ *v.tr. Electr.* **1** regulate the direction of (an alternating current), esp. to make it a direct current. **2** reverse the direction (of an electric current).

com·mu·ta·tion /kómyətáyshən/ *n.* **1** the act or process of commuting or being commuted (in legal and exchange senses). **2** *Electr.* the act or process of commutating or being commutated. **3** *Math.* the reversal of the order of two quantities.

com·mu·ta·tive /kəmyōotətiv/ *adj.* **1** relating to or involving substitution. **2** *Math.* unchanged in result by the interchange of the order of quantities.

com·mu·ta·tor /kómyətaytər/ *n. Electr.* a device for reversing electric current.

com·mute /kəmyōot/ *v.* **1** *intr.* travel to and from one's daily work, usu. in a city, esp. by car or train. **2** *tr. Law* (usu. foll. by *to*) change (a judicial sentence, etc.) to another less severe. **3** *tr.* (often foll. by *into, for*) change (one kind of payment) for another. **4** *tr.* **a** exchange; interchange. **b** change (to another thing).

com·mut·er /kəmyōotər/ *n.* a person who travels some distance to work, usu. in a city, esp. by car or train.

comp /komp/ *n. colloq.* compensation.

com·pact[1] *adj., v., & n.* ● *adj.* /kəmpákt, kóm-/ **1** closely or neatly packed together. **2** (of a piece of equipment, a room, etc.) well-fitted and practical though small. **3** (of style, etc.) condensed. **4** (esp. of the human body) small but well-proportioned. ● *v.tr.* /kəmpákt/ **1** join or press firmly together. **2** condense. ● *n.* /kómpakt/ **1** a small, flat case for face powder, a mirror, etc. **2** a medium-sized automobile. □□ **com·pac·tion** /-pákshən/ *n.* **com·pact·ly** *adv.* **com·pact·ness** *n.* **com·pac·tor** *n.*

com·pact[2] /kómpakt/ *n.* an agreement or contract between two or more parties.

com·pact disc /kómpakt/ *n.* ▼ a disk on which information or sound is recorded digitally and reproduced by reflection of laser light.

COMPACT DISC

Launched in 1982, compact discs (CDs) store sound as a sequence of millions of tiny pits and spaces, which capture the sound wave as a series of digital codes. As the disc spins, the CD player uses a laser beam to read the sequence and recreates the original waveform from the digital codes. Once amplified, this waveform drives a loudspeaker, reproducing the sound.

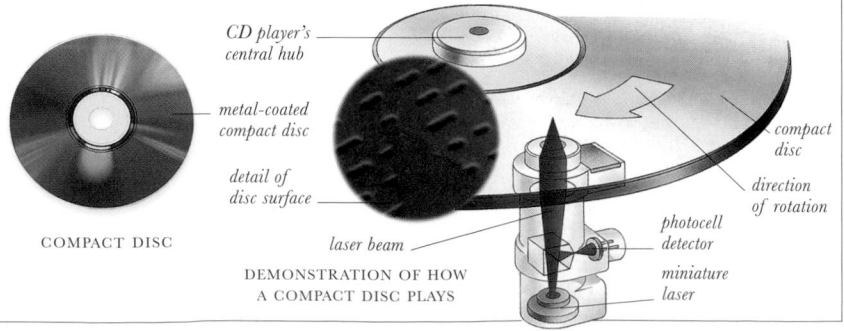

CD player's central hub

metal-coated compact disc

detail of disc surface

COMPACT DISC

laser beam

compact disc

direction of rotation

photocell detector

miniature laser

DEMONSTRATION OF HOW
A COMPACT DISC PLAYS

com·pan·ion[1] /kəmpányən/ *n.* **1 a** (often foll. by *in, of*) a person who accompanies, associates with, or shares with, another. **b** a person employed to live with and assist another. **2** a handbook or reference book. **3** a thing that matches another. **4** (**Companion**) a member of the lowest grade of some orders of knighthood (*Companion of the Bath*).

com·pan·ion[2] /kəmpányən/ *n. Naut.* **1** a raised frame on a quarterdeck used for lighting the cabins, etc., below. **2** = COMPANIONWAY.

com·pan·ion·a·ble /kəmpányənəbəl/ *adj.* agreeable as a companion; sociable. □□ **com·pan·ion·a·ble·ness** *n.* **com·pan·ion·a·bly** *adv.*

com·pan·ion·ate /kəmpányənit/ *adj.* **1** well-suited; (of clothes) matching. **2** of or like a companion.

com·pan·ion·ship /kəmpányənship/ *n.* good fellowship; friendship.

com·pan·ion·way /kəmpányənway/ *n. Naut.* a staircase to a ship's cabin.

com·pa·ny /kúmpənee/ *n.* (*pl.* **-ies**) **1 a** a number of people assembled. **b** guests or a guest (*am expecting company*). **2** companionship, esp. of a specific kind (*enjoys low company; do not care for his company*). **3 a** a commercial business. **b** (usu. **Co.**) the partner or partners not named in the title of a firm (*Smith and Co.*). **4** a troupe of actors or entertainers. **5** *Mil.* a subdivision of an infantry battalion. **6** a ship's crew. □ **in company** not alone. **in company with** together with. **keep company** (often foll. by *with*) associate habitually. **keep a person company** accompany a person; be sociable. **part company** (often foll. by *with*) cease to associate.

com·pa·ra·ble /kómpərəbəl/ *adj.* **1** (often foll. by *with*) able to be compared. **2** (often foll. by *to*) fit to be compared; worth comparing. ¶ Use with *to* and *with* corresponds to the senses at *compare; to* is more common. □□ **com·pa·ra·bil·i·ty** *n.* **com·pa·ra·ble·ness** *n.* **com·pa·ra·bly** *adv.*

com·par·a·tive /kəmpárətiv/ *adj. & n.* ● *adj.* **1** perceptible by comparison; relative (*in comparative comfort*). **2** estimated by comparison (*the comparative merits of the two ideas*). **3** of or involving comparison (*a comparative study*). **4** *Gram.* (of an adjective or adverb) expressing a higher degree of a quality, but not the highest possible (e.g., *braver, more fiercely*) (cf. POSITIVE, SUPERLATIVE). ● *n. Gram.* **1** the comparative expression or form of a word. **2** a word in the comparative. □□ **com·par·a·tive·ly** *adv.*

com·pare /kəmpáir/ *v. & n.* ● *v.* **1** *tr.* (usu. foll. by *to*) express similarities in; liken (*compared the landscape to a painting*). **2** *tr.* (often foll. by *to, with*) estimate the similarity or dissimilarity of (*compared radio with television; that lacks quality compared to this*). ¶ In current use *to* and *with* are generally interchangeable, but *with* often implies a greater element of formal analysis, as in *compared my account with yours*. **3** *intr.* (often foll. by *with*) bear comparison (*compares favorably with the rest*). ● *n. literary* comparison (*beyond compare*). □ **compare notes** exchange ideas or opinions.

com·par·i·son /kəmpárisən/ *n.* **1** the act or an instance of comparing. **2** a simile or semantic illustration. **3** capacity for being likened; similarity (*there's no comparison*). **4** (in full **degrees of comparison**) *Gram.* the positive, comparative, and superlative forms of adjectives and adverbs. □ **bear** (or **stand**) **comparison** (often foll. by *with*) be able to be compared favorably. **beyond comparison 1** totally different in quality. **2** greatly superior; excellent. **in comparison with** compared to.

com·part·ment /kəmpaartmənt/ *n.* **1** a space within a larger space, separated from the rest by partitions. **2** *Naut.* a watertight division of a ship. □□ **com·part·men·ta·tion** /-mentáyshən/ *n.*

com·part·men·tal /kómpaartmént'l/ *adj.* consisting of or relating to compartments or a compartment. □□ **com·part·men·tal·ly** *adv.*

com·part·men·tal·ize /kómpaartmént'līz, kómpaart-/ *v.tr.* divide into compartments or categories. □□ **com·part·men·tal·i·za·tion** *n.*

com·pass /kúmpəs, kóm-/ *n. & v.* ● *n.* **1** (in full **magnetic compass**) ► an instrument showing the direction of magnetic north and bearings from it. **2** (often *pl.*) an instrument for taking measurements and describing circles, with two arms connected at one end by a movable joint. **3** circumference or boundary. **4** area, extent; scope; range. ● *v.tr. literary* **1** hem in. **2** grasp mentally. □□ **com·pass·a·ble** *adj.*

com·pass card *n.* a circular rotating card showing the 32 principal bearings, forming the indicator of a magnetic compass.

com·pas·sion /kəmpáshən/ *n.* pity inclining one to help or be merciful.

com·pas·sion·ate /kəmpáshənət/ *adj.* sympathetic; pitying. □□ **com·pas·sion·ate·ly** *adv.*

com·pat·i·ble /kəmpátəbəl/ *adj.* **1** (often foll. by *with*) **a** able to coexist; well-suited; mutually tolerant. **b** consistent (*their views are not compatible with their actions*). **2** (of equipment, etc.) capable of being used in combination. □□ **com·pat·i·bil·i·ty** *n.* **com·pat·i·bly** *adv.*

com·pa·tri·ot /kəmpáytreeət, -ot/ *n.* a fellow countryman. □□ **com·pa·tri·ot·ic** /-reeótik/ *adj.*

com·peer /kómpeer, -péer/ *n.* **1** an equal; a peer. **2** a comrade.

com·pel /kəmpél/ *v.tr.* (**compelled, compelling**) **1** (usu. foll. by *to* + infin.) force, constrain. **2** bring about (an action) by force (*compel submission*). **3** (as **compelling** *adj.*) rousing strong interest, attention, conviction, or admiration. □□ **com·pel·la·ble** *adj.* **com·pel·ling·ly** *adv.*

com·pen·di·ous /kəmpéndeeəs/ *adj.* (esp. of a book, etc.) comprehensive but fairly brief. □□ **com·pen·di·ous·ly** *adv.* **com·pen·di·ous·ness** *n.*

com·pen·di·um /kəmpéndeeəm/ *n.* (*pl.* **compendiums** or **compendia** /-deeə/) **1 a** a summary or abstract of a larger work. **b** an abridgment. **3** a collection of games in a box.

com·pen·sate /kómpənsayt/ *v.* **1** *tr.* (often foll. by *for*) recompense (a person) (*compensated him for his loss*). **2** *intr.* (usu. foll. by *for*) make amends (*compensated for the insult*). **3** *tr.* counterbalance. **4** *intr. Psychol.* offset a disability or frustration by development in another direction. □□ **com·pen·sa·tive** /kəmpénsətiv, kómpənsáytiv/ *adj.* **com·pen·sa·tor** *n.* **com·pen·sa·to·ry** /-pénsətáwree/ *adj.*

com·pen·sa·tion /kómpənsáyshən/ *n.* **1 a** the act of compensating. **b** the process of being compensated. **2** something, esp. money, given as a recompense. **3** a salary or wages. □□ **com·pen·sa·tion·al** *adj.*

com·pete /kəmpéet/ *v.intr.* **1** (often foll. by *with, against* a person, *for* a thing) strive for superiority or supremacy (*competed with his brother; compete for the victory*). **2** (often foll. by *in*) take part (in a contest, etc.) (*competed in the hurdles*).

com·pe·tence /kómpit'ns/ *n.* (also **com·pe·ten·cy** /kómpitənsee/) **1** (often foll. by *for*, or *to* + infin.) ability; the state of being competent. **2** an income large enough to live on, usu. unearned. **3** *Law* the legal capacity (of a court, a magistrate, etc.) to deal with a matter.

com·pe·tent /kómpit'nt/ *adj.* **1 a** (usu. foll. by *to* + infin. or *for*) properly qualified or skilled (*not competent to drive*); adequately capable. **2** *Law* (of a judge, court, or witness) legally qualified or qualifying. □□ **com·pe·tent·ly** *adv.*

com·pe·ti·tion /kómpətíshən/ *n.* **1** (often foll. by *for*) competing, esp. in an examination, in trade, etc. **2** an event or contest in which people compete. **3 a** the people competing against a person. **b** the opposition they represent.

com·pet·i·tive /kəmpétitiv/ *adj.* **1** involving, offered for, or by competition (*competitive contest*). **2** (of prices, etc.) low enough to compare well with those of rival traders. **3** (of a person) having a strong urge to win. □□ **com·pet·i·tive·ly** *adv.* **com·pet·i·tive·ness** *n.*

com·pet·i·tor /kəmpétitər/ *n.* **1** a person who competes. **2** a rival, esp. in business or commerce.

com·pi·la·tion /kómpiláyshən/ *n.* **1 a** the act of compiling. **b** the process of being compiled. **2** something compiled, esp. a book, etc., composed of separate articles, stories, etc.

com·pile /kəmpíl/ *v.tr.* **1 a** collect (material) into a list, volume, etc. **b** make up (a volume, etc.) from such material. **2** accumulate (a large number of) (*compiled a score of 160*). **3** *Computing* produce (a machine-coded form of a high-level program).

com·pil·er /kəmpílər/ *n.* **1** *Computing* a program for translating a high-level programming language into machine code. **2** a person who compiles.

com·pla·cent /kəmpláysənt/ *adj.* **1** smugly self-satisfied. **2** calmly content. ¶ Often confused with *complaisant*. □□ **com·pla·cence** *n.* **com·pla·cen·cy** /kəmpláysənsee/ *n.* **com·pla·cent·ly** *adv.*

com·plain /kəmpláyn/ *v.intr.* **1** (often foll. by *about, at,* or *that* + clause) express dissatisfaction (*complained at the state of the room; is always complaining*). **2** (foll. by *of*) **a** announce that one is suffering from (an ailment) (*complained of a headache*). **b** state a grievance concerning (*complained of the delay*). **3** make a mournful sound; groan, creak under a strain. □□ **com·plain·er** *n.* **com·plain·ing·ly** *adv.*

com·plain·ant /kəmpláynənt/ *n. Law* a plaintiff in certain lawsuits.

com·plaint /kəmpláynt/ *n.* **1** an act of complaining. **2** a grievance. **3** an ailment or illness. **4** *Law* the plaintiff's case in a civil action.

com·plai·sant /kəmpláysənt/ *adj.* **1** politely deferential. **2** willing to please; acquiescent. Often confused with *complacent*. □□ **com·plai·sance** /-səns/ *n.*

com·pleat *archaic* var. of COMPLETE.

com·ple·ment *n. & v.* ● *n.* /kómplimənt/ **1 a** something that completes. **b** one of two things that go together. **2** (often **full complement**) the full number needed to man a ship, etc. **3** *Gram.* a word or phrase added to a verb to complete the predicate of a sentence. **4** *Biochem.* a group of proteins in the blood capable of lysing bacteria, etc. **5** *Math.* any element not belonging to a specified set or class. **6** *Geom.* ▲ the amount by which an angle is less than 90°. ● *v.tr.* /kómpliment/ **1** complete; round out or off. **2** form a complement to (*the scarf complements her dress*). □□ **com·ple·men·tal** /-mént'l/ *adj.*

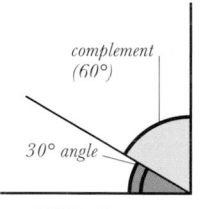

COMPLEMENT
OF A 30° ANGLE

com·ple·men·tar·i·ty /kómplimentáritee/ *n.* (*pl.* **-ies**) **1** a complementary relationship or situation. **2** *Physics* the concept that a single model may not be adequate to explain atomic systems in different experimental conditions.

com·ple·men·ta·ry /kómpliméntəree/ *adj.* **1** completing; forming a complement. **2** (of two or more things) complementing each other. □□ **com·ple·men·ta·ri·ly** /-táirəlee/ *adv.* **com·ple·men·ta·ri·ness** *n.*

com·ple·men·ta·ry an·gle *n.* either of two angles making up 90°.

com·ple·men·ta·ry col·or *n.* a color that combined with a given color makes white or black.

Illustration (compass):

degree notation

magnetic needle points north

cardinal point (west)

pivot

COMPASS

complement (60°)

30° angle

com·ple·men·ta·ry med·i·cine *n.* alternative medicine.

com·plete /kəmpléet/ *adj. & v.* ● *adj.* **1** having all its parts; entire (*the set is complete*). **2** finished (*my task is complete*). **3** of the maximum extent or degree (*a complete surprise; a complete stranger*). **4** (also **com·pleat** after Walton's *Compleat Angler*) *joc.* accomplished (*the complete horseman*). ● *v.tr.* **1** finish. **2 a** make whole or perfect. **b** make up the amount of (*completes the quota*). **3** fill in the answers to (a questionnaire, etc.). **4** (usu. *absol.*) *Law* conclude a sale of property. □ **complete with** having (as an important accessory) (*comes complete with instructions*). □□ **com·plete·ly** *adv.* **com·plete·ness** *n.* **com·ple·tion** /-pléeshən/ *n.*

com·plex *n. & adj.* ● *n.* /kómpleks/ **1** a building, a series of rooms, a network, etc. made up of related parts. **2** *Psychol.* a related group of usu. repressed feelings or thoughts which cause abnormal behavior or mental states (*inferiority complex; Oedipus complex*). **3** (in general use) a pre-occupation or obsession (*has a complex about punctuality*). **4** *Chem.* a compound in which molecules or ions form coordinate bonds to a metal atom or ion. ● *adj.* /kəmpléks, kómpleks/ **1** consisting of related parts; composite. **2** complicated (*a complex problem*). **3** *Math.* containing real and imaginary parts (cf. IMAGINARY). □□ **com·plex·i·ty** /-pléksitee/ *n.* (*pl.* **-ies**). **com·plex·ly** *adv.*

com·plex·ion /kəmplékshən/ *n.* **1** the natural color, texture, and appearance, of the skin, esp. of the face. **2** an aspect; a character (*puts a different complexion on the matter*). □□ **com·plex·ioned** *adj.* (also in *comb.*)

com·plex sen·tence *n.* a sentence containing a subordinate clause or clauses.

com·pli·ance /kəmplíəns/ *n.* **1** the act or an instance of complying. **2** *Mech.* **a** the capacity to yield under an applied force. **b** the degree of such yielding. **3** unworthy acquiescence. □ **in compliance with** according to (a wish, command, etc.).

com·pli·ant /kəmplíənt/ *adj.* yielding; obedient. □□ **com·pli·ant·ly** *adv.*

com·pli·cate /kómplikayt/ *v.tr. & intr.* **1** (often foll. by *with*) make or become difficult, confused, or complex. **2** (as **complicated** *adj.*) complex; intricate. □□ **com·pli·cat·ed·ly** *adv.* **com·pli·cat·ed·ness** *n.*

com·pli·ca·tion /kómplikáyshn/ *n.* **1 a** an involved or confused condition or state. **b** a complicating circumstance; a difficulty. **2** *Med.* a secondary disease or condition aggravating a previous one.

com·plic·i·ty /kəmplísitee/ *n.* partnership in a crime or wrongdoing.

com·pli·ment *n. & v.* ● *n.* /kómplimənt/ **1 a** a spoken or written expression of praise. **b** an act or circumstance implying praise (*their success was a compliment to their efforts*). **2** (in *pl.*) **a** formal greetings, esp. as a written accompaniment to a gift, etc. (*with the compliments of the management*). **b** praise (*my compliments to the cook*). ● *v.tr.* /kómplimént/ **1** (often foll. by *on*) congratulate; praise. **2** (often foll. by *with*) present as a mark of courtesy (*complimented her with his attention*). □ **pay a compliment to** praise. **return the compliment 1** give a compliment in return for another. **2** retaliate or recompense in kind.

com·pli·men·ta·ry /kómpliméntəree/ *adj.* **1** expressing a compliment; praising. **2** (of a ticket for a play, etc.) given free of charge.

com·pline /kómplin, -plīn/ (also **com·plin**) *n. Eccl.* **1** the last of the canonical hours of prayer. **2** the service taking place during this.

com·ply /kəmplí/ *v.intr.* (**-ies**, **-ied**) (often foll. by *with*) act in accordance (with a wish, command, etc.).

com·po·nent /kəmpónənt/ *n. & adj.* ● *n.* **1** a part of a larger whole, esp. part of a motor vehicle. **2** *Math.* one of two or more vectors equivalent to a given vector. ● *adj.* being part of a larger whole (*assembled the component parts*). □□ **com·po·nen·tial** /kómpənénshəl/ *adj.*

com·port /kəmpáwrt/ *v.refl. literary* conduct oneself; behave. □□ **com·port·ment** *n.*

com·pos var. of COMPOS MENTIS.

com·pose /kəmpóz/ *v.* **1 a** *tr.* construct or create (a work of art, esp. literature or music). **b** *intr.* compose music (*gave up composing in 1917*). **2** *tr.* constitute; make up (*six tribes which composed the German nation*). Preferred to *comprise* in this sense. **3** *tr.* order; arrange (*composed the group for the photographer*). **4** *tr.* **a** (often *refl.*) calm; settle (*compose your expression; composed himself to wait*). **b** (as **com·posed** *adj.*) settled. **5** *tr.* settle (a dispute, etc.). **6** *tr. Printing* **a** ◀ set up (type) to form words and blocks of words. **b** set up (a manuscript, etc.) in type. □ **composed of** made up of; consisting of. □□ **com·pos·ed·ly** /-zidlee/ *adv.*

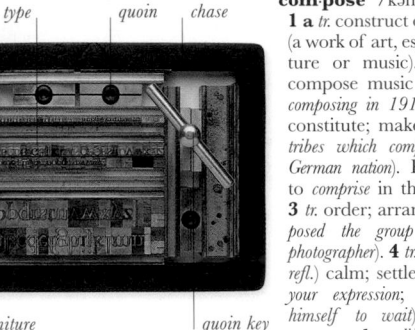
COMPOSE: TYPE COMPOSED IN A PRINTER'S FORM

block of type *quoin* *chase*

furniture *quoin key*

com·pos·er /kəmpózər/ *n.* a person who composes (esp. music).

com·pos·ite /kəmpózit/ *adj., n., & v.* ● *adj.* **1** made up of various parts; blended. **2** (esp. of a synthetic building material) made up of recognizable constituents. **3** *Archit.* of the fifth classical order of architecture, consisting of elements of the Ionic and Corinthian orders. ▷ COLUMN. **4** *Bot.* of the plant family Compositae. ● *n.* **1** a thing made up of several parts or elements. **2** a synthetic building material. **3** a reconstructed picture of a person (esp. one sought by the police) made by combining images of separate facial features. **4** *Bot.* ◀ any plant of the family Compositae, having a head of many small flowers forming one bloom, e.g., the daisy. **5** *Polit.* a resolution composed of two or more related resolutions. ● *v.tr. Polit.* amalgamate (two or more similar resolutions). □□ **com·pos·ite·ly** *adv.* **com·pos·ite·ness** *n.*

COMPOSITE: WALL DAISY (*Erigeron karvinskianus*)

disk florets (small flowers in a head)

ray floret

com·po·si·tion /kómpəzíshən/ *n.* **1 a** the act of putting together; formation or construction. **b** something so composed; a mixture. **c** the constitution of such a mixture; the nature of its ingredients. **2 a** a literary or musical work. **b** the act or art of producing such a work. **c** an essay, esp. written by a schoolchild. **d** an artistic arrangement (of parts of a picture, subjects for a photograph, etc.). **3** mental constitution; character (*jealousy is not in his composition*). **4** (often *attrib.*) a compound artificial substance. **5** *Printing* the setting-up of type. **6** *Gram.* the formation of words into a compound word. **7** *Law* a compromise, esp. a legal agreement to pay a sum in lieu of a larger sum, or other obligation (*made a composition with his creditors*). **b** a sum paid in this way. **8** *Math.* the combination of functions in a series. □□ **com·po·si·tion·al** *adj.* **com·po·si·tion·al·ly** *adv.*

com·pos·i·tor /kəmpózitər/ *n. Printing* a person who sets up type for printing.

com·pos men·tis /kómpəs méntis/ *adj.* (also **com·pos**) having control of one's mind; sane.

com·post /kómpōst/ *n. & v.* ● *n.* **1 a** mixed manure, esp. of organic origin. **b** a loam soil or other medium with added compost, used for growing plants. **2** a mixture of ingredients (*a rich compost of lies and innuendo*). ● *v.tr.* **1** treat (soil) with compost. **2** make (manure, vegetable matter, etc.) into compost.

com·post heap (or **pile**) *n.* a layered structure of garden refuse, etc., which decays to become compost.

com·po·sure /kəmpózhər/ *n.* a tranquil manner; calmness.

com·pote /kómpōt/ *n.* fruit preserved or cooked in syrup.

com·pound[1] *n., adj., & v.* ● *n.* /kómpownd/ **1** a mixture of two or more things, qualities, etc. **2** (also **com·pound word**) a word made up of two or more existing words. **3** *Chem.* a substance formed from two or more elements chemically united in fixed proportions. ● *adj.* /kómpownd/ **1 a** made up of several ingredients. **b** consisting of several parts. **2** combined; collective. **3** *Zool.* consisting of individual organisms. **4** *Biol.* consisting of several or many parts. ● *v.* /kəmpównd/ **1** *tr.* mix or combine (ingredients, ideas, motives, etc.) (*grief compounded with fear*). **2** *tr.* increase or complicate (difficulties, etc.) (*anxiety compounded by discomfort*). **3** *tr.* make up or concoct (a composite whole). **4** (also *absol.*) settle (a debt, dispute, etc.) by concession or special arrangement. **5** *tr. Law* **a** condone (a liability or offense) in exchange for money, etc. **b** forbear from prosecuting (a felony) from private motives. **6** *intr.* (usu. foll. by *with*, *for*) *Law* come to terms with a person, for forgoing a claim, etc., for an offense. **7** *tr.* combine (words or elements) into a word. □□ **com·pound·a·ble** /-pówndəbəl/ *adj.*

com·pound[2] /kómpownd/ *n.* **1** a large open enclosure for housing workers, etc., esp. miners in S. Africa. **2** an enclosure, esp. in India, China, etc., in which a factory or a house stands. **3** a large enclosed space in a prison or prison camp. **4** = POUND[3].

com·pound eye *n.* ▼ an eye consisting of numerous visual units, as found in insects and crustaceans. ▷ INSECT

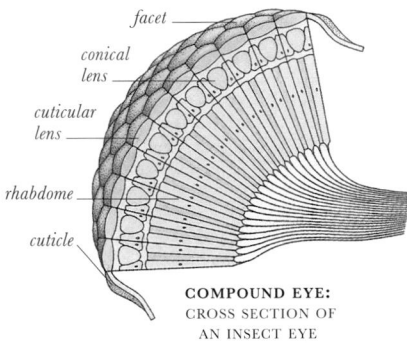
COMPOUND EYE: CROSS SECTION OF AN INSECT EYE

facet
conical lens
cuticular lens
rhabdome
cuticle

com·pound frac·ture *n.* a fracture complicated by a skin wound.

com·pound in·ter·est *n.* interest payable on capital and its accumulated interest (cf. SIMPLE INTEREST).

com·pound in·ter·val *n. Mus.* an interval exceeding one octave.

com·pound leaf *n.* ▶ a leaf consisting of several or many leaflets.

com·pound sen·tence *n.* a sentence with more than one main, independent clause.

com·pre·hend /kómprihénd/ *v.tr.* **1** grasp mentally; understand (*a person or thing*). **2** include; take in.

COMPOUND LEAF OF A ROWAN TREE

leaflet

COMPUTER

Developed in the Second World War (1939–45), computers are currently composed of four basic parts: an input unit, such as a keyboard that feeds data into the computer; a central processing unit (CPU) that performs the computer's tasks; an output unit, such as a monitor that displays the results; and a memory unit for storing information and instructions.

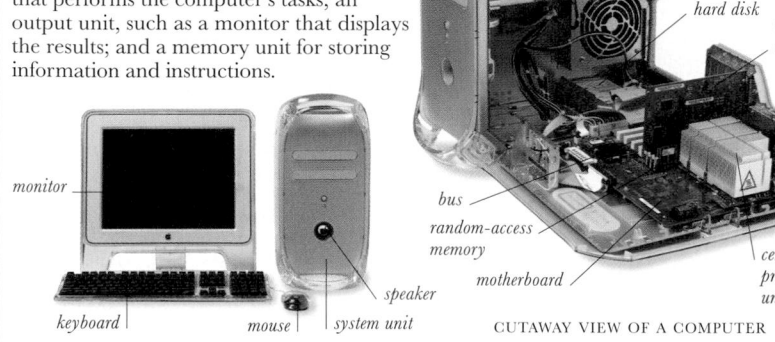

CUTAWAY VIEW OF A COMPUTER

---

com·pre·hen·si·ble /kómprihénsibəl/ *adj.* **1** that can be understood; intelligible. **2** that can be included or contained. □□ **com·pre·hen·si·bil·i·ty** /-bílitee/ *n.* **com·pre·hen·si·bly** *adv.*

com·pre·hen·sion /kómprihénshən/ *n.* **1** the act or capability of understanding, esp. writing or speech. **2** inclusion.

com·pre·hen·sive /kómprihénsiv/ *adj.* **1** complete; including all or nearly all elements, aspects, etc. (*a comprehensive grasp of the subject*). **2** of or relating to understanding (*the comprehensive faculty*). **3** (of motor-vehicle insurance) providing complete protection. □□ **com·pre·hen·sive·ly** *adv.* **com·pre·hen·sive·ness** *n.*

com·press *v. & n.* ● *v.tr.* /kəmprés/ **1** squeeze together. **2** bring into a smaller space or shorter extent. ● *n.* /kómpres/ a pad pressed on to part of the body to relieve inflammation, stop bleeding, etc. □□ **com·press·i·ble** /kəmprésəbəl/ *adj.* **com·press·i·bil·i·ty** *n.* **com·pres·sive** /kəmprésiv/ *adj.*

com·pres·sion /kəmpréshən/ *n.* **1** the act of compressing or being compressed. **2** the reduction in volume (causing an increase in pressure) of the fuel mixture in an internal-combustion engine before ignition.

com·pres·sor /kəmprésər/ *n.* an instrument or device for compressing, esp. a machine used for increasing the pressure of air or other gases. ▷ AIR-CONDITIONING

com·prise /kəmpríz/ *v.tr.* **1** include; comprehend. **2** consist of; be composed of (*the book comprises 350 pages*). **3** *disp.* make up, compose. □□ **com·pris·a·ble** *adj.*

com·pro·mise /kómprəmīz/ *n. & v.* ● *n.* **1** the settlement of a dispute by mutual concession. **2** (often foll. by *between*) an intermediate state between conflicting opinions, actions, etc., reached by mutual concession. ● *v.* **1** *intr.* settle a dispute by mutual concession. **2** *tr.* bring into disrepute or danger esp. by indiscretion or folly. □□ **com·pro·mis·er** *n.* **com·pro·mis·ing·ly** *adv.*

comp·trol·ler /kəntrólər/ *n.* a controller (used in the title of some financial officers) (*comptroller and auditor general*).

com·pul·sion /kəmpúlshən/ *n.* **1** a constraint; an obligation. **2** *Psychol.* an irresistible urge to a form of behavior, esp. against one's conscious wishes. □ **under compulsion** because one is compelled.

com·pul·sive /kəmpúlsiv/ *adj.* **1** compelling. **2** resulting or acting from, or as if from, compulsion (*a compulsive gambler*). **3** *Psychol.* resulting or acting from compulsion against one's conscious wishes. **4** irresistible (*compulsive viewing*). □□ **com·pul·sive·ly** *adv.* **com·pul·sive·ness** *n.*

com·pul·so·ry /kəmpúlsəree/ *adj.* **1** required by law or a rule. **2** essential; necessary. □□ **com·pul·so·ri·ly** *adv.* **com·pul·so·ri·ness** *n.*

com·punc·tion /kəmpúngkshən/ *n.* (usu. with *neg.*) **1** the pricking of the conscience. **2** a slight regret; a scruple.

com·pu·ta·tion /kompyóotáyshən/ *n.* **1** the act or an instance of reckoning; calculation. **2** the use of a computer. **3** a result obtained by calculation. □□ **com·pu·ta·tion·al** *adj.* **com·pu·ta·tion·al·ly** *adv.*

com·pute /kəmpyóot/ *v.* **1** *tr.* (often foll. by *that* + clause) reckon or calculate (a number, an amount, etc.). **2** *intr.* make a reckoning, esp. using a computer. □□ **com·pu·ta·bil·i·ty** /-təbílitee/ *n.* **com·put·a·ble** *adj.*

com·put·er /kəmpyóotər/ *n.* **1** ▲ a usu. electronic device for storing and processing data (usu. in binary form), according to instructions given to it in a variable program. **2** a person who computes or makes calculations.

com·put·er·ize /kəmpyóotərīz/ *v.tr.* **1** equip with a computer; install a computer in. **2** store, perform, or produce by computer. □□ **com·put·er·i·za·tion** *n.*

com·put·er-lit·er·ate *adj.* able to use computers; familiar with the operation of computers.

com·put·er sci·ence *n.* the study of the principles and use of computers.

com·put·er vi·rus *n.* a hidden code within a computer program intended to corrupt a system or destroy data stored in it.

com·rade /kómrad, -rid/ *n.* **1** (also **com·rade in arms**) **a** a coworker, friend, or companion. **b** a fellow soldier, etc. **2** *Polit.* a fellow socialist or communist. □□ **com·rade·ly** *adj.* **com·rade·ship** *n.*

con[1] /kon/ *n. & v. sl.* ● *n.* a confidence trick. ● *v.tr.* (**conned, conning**) swindle; deceive (*conned him into thinking he had won*).

con[2] /kon/ *n., prep., & adv.* ● *n.* (usu. in *pl.*) a reason against. ● *prep. & adv.* against (cf. PRO[2]).

con[3] /kon/ *n. sl.* a convict.

con bri·o /kón brée-ō, káwn/ *adv. Mus.* with vigor.

con·cat·e·nate /konkát'nayt/ *v. & adj.* ● *v.tr.* link together (a chain of events, things, etc.). ● *adj.* joined; linked. □□ **con·cat·e·na·tion** /-náyshən/ *n.*

con·cave /kónkáyv/ *adj.* having an outline or surface curved like the interior of a circle or sphere (cf. CONVEX). □□ **con·cave·ly** *adv.* **con·cav·i·ty** /-kávitee/ *n.*

con·ceal /kənséel/ *v.tr.* **1** (often foll. by *from*) keep secret (*concealed her motive from him*). **2** not allow to be seen; hide. □□ **con·ceal·er** *n.* **con·ceal·ment** *n.*

con·cede /kənséed/ *v.tr.* **1 a** (often foll. by *that*

+ clause) admit (a defeat, etc.) to be true (*conceded that his work was inadequate*). **b** admit defeat in. **2** (often foll. by *to*) grant or surrender (a right, points in a game, etc.). **3** *Sports* allow an opponent to score (a goal, etc.) or to win (a match), etc. □□ **con·ced·er** *n.*

con·ceit /kənséet/ *n.* **1** personal vanity; pride. **2** *literary* **a** a far-fetched comparison. **b** a fanciful notion.

con·ceit·ed /kənséetid/ *adj.* vain; proud. □□ **con·ceit·ed·ly** *adv.* **con·ceit·ed·ness** *n.*

con·ceiv·a·ble /kənséevəbəl/ *adj.* capable of being grasped or imagined; understandable. □□ **con·ceiv·a·bil·i·ty** /-bílitee/ *n.* **con·ceiv·a·bly** *adv.*

con·ceive /kənséev/ *v.* **1** *intr.* become pregnant. **2** *tr.* become pregnant with (a child). **3** *tr.* (often foll. by *that* + clause) **a** imagine; fancy; think. **b** (usu. in *passive*) formulate; express (a belief, a plan, etc.). □ **conceive of** form in the mind; imagine.

con·cen·trate /kónsəntrayt/ *v.* ● *v.* **1** *intr.* (often foll. by *on, upon*) focus one's attention or mental ability. **2** *tr.* bring together (troops, power, attention, etc.) to one point. **3** *tr.* increase the strength of (a liquid, etc.) by removing water or any other diluting agent. **4** *tr.* (as **concentrated** *adj.*) (of hate, etc.) intense; strong. ● *n.* **1** a concentrated substance. **2** a concentrated form of esp. food. □□ **con·cen·trat·ed·ly** *adv.* **con·cen·tra·tive** /-tráytiv, -séntrə-/ *adj.* **con·cen·tra·tor** *n.*

con·cen·tra·tion /kónsəntráyshən/ *n.* **1 a** the act or power of concentrating (*needs to develop concentration*). **b** an instance of this (*interrupted my concentration*). **2** something concentrated. **3** something brought together; a gathering. **4** the weight of substance in a given weight or volume of material.

con·cen·tra·tion camp *n.* a camp for the detention of political prisoners, etc., esp. in Nazi Germany.

con·cen·tric /kənséntrik/ *adj.* (often foll. by *with*) ▶ (esp. of circles) having a common center (cf. ECCENTRIC). □□ **con·cen·tri·cal·ly** *adv.* **con·cen·tric·i·ty** /kónsentrísitee/ *n.*

CONCENTRIC CIRCLES

common center

con·cept /kónsept/ *n.* **1** a general notion; an abstract idea (*the concept of evolution*). **2** *colloq.* an idea or invention to help sell or publicize a commodity (*a new concept in swimwear*). **3** *Philos.* an idea or mental picture of a group or class of objects formed by combining all their aspects.

con·cep·tion /kənsépshən/ *n.* **1 a** the act or an instance of conceiving; the process of being conceived. **b** the faculty of conceiving in the mind; apprehension; imagination. **2** an idea or plan, esp. as being new or daring (*the whole conception showed originality*). □□ **con·cep·tion·al** *adj.* **con·cep·tive** /kənséptiv/ *adj.*

con·cep·tu·al /kənsépchōoəl/ *adj.* of mental conceptions or concepts. □□ **con·cep·tu·al·ly** *adv.*

con·cep·tu·al·ize /kənsépchōoəlīz/ *v.tr.* form a concept or idea of. □□ **con·cep·tu·al·i·za·tion** *n.*

con·cern /kənsórn/ *v. & n.* ● *v.tr.* **1** be relevant or important to (*this concerns you*). **b** relate to; be about. **2** (usu. *refl.*; often foll. by *with, in, about,* or *to* + infin.) interest or involve oneself. **3** worry; cause anxiety to. ● *n.* **1 a** anxiety; worry (*felt a deep concern*). **b** solicitous regard; care; consideration. **2 a** a matter of interest or importance to one (*no concern of mine*). **b** (usu. in *pl.*) affairs; private business. **3** a business; a firm. **4** *colloq.* a complicated or awkward thing (*have lost the whole concern*). □ **have a concern in** have an interest or share in. **have no concern with** have nothing to do with. **to whom it may concern** to those who have a proper interest in the matter (as an address to the reader of a testimonial, reference, etc.).

con·cerned /kənsórnd/ *adj.* **1** involved; interested (*the people concerned; concerned with proving his innocence*). **2** (often foll. by *that, about, at, for,* or *to* + infin.)

C

C

troubled; anxious (*concerned about her*; *concerned to hear that*). □ **as** (or **so**) **far as I am concerned** as regards my interests. **be concerned** (often foll. by *in*) take part. **I am not concerned** it is not my business. □□ **con·cern·ed·ly** /-sórnidlee/ *adv.* **con·cern·ed·ness** /-sórnidnis/ *n.*

con·cern·ing /kənsórning/ *prep.* about; regarding.

con·cert *n. & v.* ● *n.* /kónsərt/ **1 a** a musical performance of usu. several separate compositions. **b** a comedy, etc., performance in a large hall. **2** agreement, harmony. **3** a combination of voices or sounds. ● *v.tr.* /kənsórt/ arrange (by mutual agreement or coordination). □ **in concert 1** (often foll. by *with*) acting jointly and accordantly. **2** (*predic.*) (of a musician) in a performance.

con·cert·ed /kənsórtid/ *adj.* **1** jointly arranged or planned (*a concerted effort*). **2** *Mus.* arranged in parts for voices or instruments.

con·cert grand *n.* the largest size of grand piano, used for concerts. ▷ PIANO

con·cer·ti·na /kónsərteénə/ *n. & v.* ● *n.* ► a musical instrument held in the hands and stretched and squeezed like bellows, having reeds and a set of buttons at each end to control the valves. ● *v.tr. & intr.* (**concertinas**, **concertinaed** /-nəd/, **concertina-ing**) compress or collapse in folds like those of a concertina (*the car concertinaed into the bridge*).

valve buttons | *bellows*
CONCERTINA

con·cert·mas·ter /kónsərtmástər/ *n.* the leading first-violin player in some orchestras.

con·cer·to /kəncháirtō/ *n.* (*pl.* **concerti** /-tee/ or **-os**) *Mus.* a composition for a solo instrument or instruments accompanied by an orchestra.

concert pitch *n.* **1** *Mus.* the internationally agreed pitch whereby the A above middle C = 440 Hz. **2** a state of unusual readiness, efficiency, and keenness (for action, etc.).

con·ces·sion /kənséshən/ *n.* **1 a** the act or an instance of conceding. **b** a thing conceded. **2** a reduction in price for a certain category of person. **3 a** the right to use land or other property. **b** the right to sell goods, esp. in a particular territory. **c** the land or property used or given. □□ **con·ces·sion·ar·y** *adj.* (also **con·ces·sion·al**).

con·ces·sion·aire /kənseshənáir/ *n.* (also **con·ces·sion·er**) the holder of a concession or grant.

con·ces·sive /kənsésiv/ *adj.* **1** of or tending to concession. **2** *Gram.* **a** (of a preposition or conjunction) introducing a phrase or clause which might be expected to preclude the action of the main clause, but does not (e.g., *in spite of*, *although*). **b** (of a phrase or clause) introduced by a concessive preposition or conjunction.

conch /kongk, konch/ *n.* (*pl.* **conchs** /kongks/ or **conches** /kónchiz/) **1 a** ◀ a thick, heavy spiral shell, occasionally bearing long projections, of various marine gastropod mollusks of the family Strombidae. ▷ SHELL. **b** any of these gastropods. **2** *Archit.* the domed roof of a semicircular apse.

con·chol·o·gy /kongkóləjee/ *n.* *Zool.* the scientific study of shells. □□ **con·cho·log·i·cal** /-kəlójikəl/ *adj.* **con·chol·o·gist** *n.*

con·cierge /konseeáirzh, káwnsyáirzh/ *n.* **1** a hotel worker who arranges tours, transportation, etc., for guests. **2** (esp. in France) a doorkeeper or porter for an apartment building, etc.

con·cil·i·ar /kənsíleeər/ *adj.* of or concerning a council.

CONCH:
ROOSTER TAIL CONCH
(*Strombus gallus*)

con·cil·i·ate /kənsíleeayt/ *v.tr.* **1** make calm and amenable; pacify. **2** gain (esteem or goodwill). □□ **con·cil·i·a·tion** /kənsilee-áyshən/ *n.* **con·cil·i·a·tive** /-síleeətiv, -áytiv/ *adj.* **con·cil·i·a·tor** *n.* **con·cil·i·a·to·ry** /-síleeətáwree/ *adj.* **con·cil·i·a·to·ri·ness** *n.*

con·cise /kənsís/ *adj.* (of speech, writing, style, or a person) brief but comprehensive in expression. □□ **con·cise·ly** *adv.* **con·cise·ness** *n.* **con·ci·sion** /kənsízhən/ *n.*

con·clave /kónklayv, kóng-/ *n.* **1** a private meeting. **2** *RC Ch.* **a** the assembly of cardinals for the election of a pope. **b** the meeting place for a conclave.

con·clude /kənklood/ *v.* **1** *tr. & intr.* bring or come to an end. **2** *tr.* (often foll. by *from*, or *that* + clause) infer (from given premises). **3** *tr.* settle; arrange (a treaty, etc.). **4** *intr.* decide.

con·clu·sion /kənkloozhən/ *n.* **1** a final result; a termination. **2** a judgment reached by reasoning. **3** a summing-up. **4** a settling; an arrangement (*the conclusion of peace*). **5** *Logic* a proposition that is reached from given premises. □ **in conclusion** lastly; to conclude. **try conclusions with** engage in a trial of skill, etc., with.

con·clu·sive /kənkloosiv/ *adj.* decisive; convincing. □□ **con·clu·sive·ly** *adv.* **con·clu·sive·ness** *n.*

con·coct /kənkókt/ *v.tr.* **1** make by mixing ingredients. **2** invent (a story, a lie, etc.). □□ **con·coct·er** *n.* **con·coc·tion** /-kókshən/ *n.* **con·coct·or** *n.*

con·com·i·tant /kənkómit'nt/ *adj. & n.* ● *adj.* going together; associated (*concomitant circumstances*). ● *n.* an accompanying thing. □□ **con·com·i·tance** /kənkómit'ns/ *n.* **con·com·i·tan·cy** *n.* **con·com·i·tant·ly** *adv.*

con·cord /kónkawrd, kóng-/ *n.* **1** agreement or harmony between people or things. **2** a treaty. **3** *Mus.* a chord that is pleasing or satisfactory in itself. **4** *Gram.* agreement between words in gender, number, etc.

con·cord·ance /kənkáwrd'ns/ *n.* **1** agreement. **2** an alphabetical list of the important words used in a book or by an author.

con·cord·ant /kənkáwrd'nt/ *adj.* **1** (often foll. by *with*) agreeing; harmonious. **2** *Mus.* in harmony. □□ **con·cord·ant·ly** *adv.*

con·cor·dat /kənkáwrdat/ *n.* an agreement, esp. between the Roman Catholic Church and a nation.

con·course /kónkawrs/ *n.* **1** a crowd. **2** a coming together; a gathering (*a concourse of ideas*). **3** an open central area in a large public building.

con·crete /kónkreet, kóng-, konkréet, kong-/ *adj., n., & v.* ● *adj.* **1 a** existing in a material form; real. **b** specific; definite (*concrete evidence*; *a concrete proposal*). **2** *Gram.* (of a noun) denoting a material object. ● *n.* (often *attrib.*) ▼ a composition of gravel, sand, cement, and water, used for building. ▷ HOUSE. ● *v.* **1** *tr.* **a** cover with concrete. **b** embed in concrete. **2** /konkréet, kong-/ **a** *tr. & intr.* form into

coarse concrete | *medium-coarse concrete* | *fine-texture concrete*

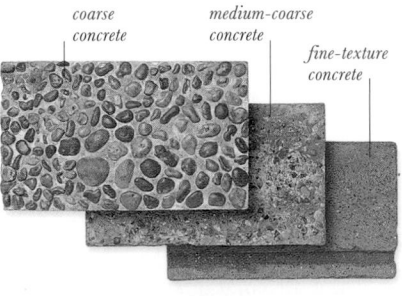

CONCRETE: THREE GRADES OF CONCRETE

a mass; solidify. **b** *tr.* make concrete instead of abstract. □□ **con·crete·ly** *adv.* **con·crete·ness** *n.*

con·crete jun·gle *n.* an urban area with a high density of large modern buildings.

con·cre·tion /kənkréeshən/ *n.* **1 a** a hard, solid concreted mass. **b** the forming of this by coalescence. **2** *Med.* a stony mass formed within the body. **3** *Geol.* a small, round mass of rock particles embedded in limestone or clay. □□ **con·cre·tion·ar·y** *adj.*

con·cre·tize /kónkritīz/ *v.tr.* make concrete instead of abstract. □□ **con·cret·i·za·tion** *n.*

con·cu·bi·nage /konkyoobinij/ *n.* **1** the cohabitation of a man and woman not married to each other. **2** the state of being or having a concubine.

con·cu·bine /kóngkyəbīn/ *n.* **1** a woman who lives with a man as his wife. **2** (among polygamous peoples) a secondary wife.

con·cu·pis·cence /konkyoopisəns/ *n.* *formal* sexual desire. □□ **con·cu·pis·cent** /-sənt/ *adj.*

con·cur /kənkór/ *v.intr.* (**concurred, concurring**) **1** happen together; coincide. **2** (often foll. by *with*) **a** agree in opinion. **b** express agreement.

con·cur·rent /kənkórənt, -kúr-/ *adj.* **1** (often foll. by *with*) **a** existing or in operation at the same time (*served two concurrent sentences*). **b** existing or acting together. **2** *Geom.* (of three or more lines) meeting at or tending toward one point. **3** agreeing; harmonious. □□ **con·cur·rence** /-rəns/ *n.* **con·cur·rent·ly** *adv.*

con·cuss /kənkús/ *v.tr.* subject to concussion.

con·cus·sion /kənkúshən/ *n.* **1** *Med.* temporary unconsciousness or incapacity due to injury to the head. **2** violent shaking; shock.

con·demn /kəndém/ *v.tr.* **1** express utter disapproval of; censure. **2 a** find guilty; convict. **b** (usu. foll. by *to*) sentence to (a punishment, esp. death). **c** bring about the conviction of (*his looks condemn him*). **3** pronounce (a building, etc.) unfit for use or habitation. **4** (usu. foll. by *to*) doom or assign (to something unwelcome or painful) (*condemned to spending hours at the kitchen sink*). **5 a** declare (smuggled goods, property, etc.) to be forfeited. **b** pronounce incurable. □□ **con·dem·na·ble** /-démnəbəl/ *adj.* **con·dem·na·tion** /kóndemnáyshən/ *n.* **con·dem·na·to·ry** /-démnətáwree/ *adj.*

con·den·sate /kəndénsayt, kóndən-/ *n.* a substance produced by condensation.

con·den·sa·tion /kóndensáyshən/ *n.* **1** the act of condensing. **2** any condensed material (esp. water on a cold surface). **3** an abridgment. **4** *Chem.* the combination of molecules with the elimination of water or other small molecules. ▷ MATTER

con·dense /kəndéns/ *v.* **1** *tr.* make denser or more concentrated. **2** *tr.* express in fewer words; make concise. **3** *tr. & intr.* reduce or be reduced from a gas or vapor to a liquid or solid. □□ **con·den·sa·ble** *adj.*

con·densed milk *n.* milk thickened by evaporation and sweetened.

con·dens·er /kəndénsər/ *n.* **1** an apparatus or vessel for condensing vapor. ▷ DISTILL, REFRIGERATOR. **2** *Electr.* = CAPACITOR. **3** a lens or system of lenses for concentrating light. **4** a person or thing that condenses.

con·de·scend /kóndisénd/ *v.intr.* **1** (usu. foll. by *to* + infin.) be gracious enough (to do a thing) esp. while showing one's sense of dignity or superiority (*condescended to attend the meeting*). **2** (foll. by *to*) behave as if one is on equal terms with (an inferior), while maintaining an attitude of superiority. **3** (as **condescending** *adj.*) patronizing; kind to inferiors. □□ **con·de·scend·ing·ly** *adv.* **con·de·scen·sion** /kóndisénshən/ *n.*

con·dign /kəndín/ *adj.* (of a punishment, etc.) severe and well-deserved. □□ **con·dign·ly** *adv.*

con·di·ment /kóndimənt/ *n.* a seasoning or relish for food.

con·di·tion /kəndíshən/ *n. & v.* ● *n.* **1** a stipulation; something upon the fulfillment of which something else depends. **2 a** the state of being or fitness of a person or thing (*arrived in bad condition*). **b** an ailment or abnormality (*a heart condition*). **3** (in *pl.*) circumstances, esp. those affecting the functioning or existence of something (*working conditions are good*). **4** *Gram.* a clause expressing a condition. **5** a requirement that a student must pass an examination, etc., within a stated time to receive credit for a course. **b** the grade indicating this. ● *v.tr.* **1 a** bring into a good or desired state or condition. **b** make fit (esp. dogs or horses). **2** teach or accustom to adopt certain habits, etc. (*conditioned by society*). **3** govern; determine. **4 a** impose conditions on. **b** be essential to. **5** test the condition of (textiles, etc.). **6** subject (a student) to a condition. □ **in** (or **out of**) **condition** in good (or bad) condition. **in no condition to** certainly not fit to. **on condition that** with the stipulation that.

con·di·tion·al /kəndíshənəl/ *adj. & n.* ● *adj.* **1** (often foll. by *on*) dependent; not absolute; containing a condition or stipulation (*a conditional offer*). **2** *Gram.* (of a clause, mood, etc.) expressing a condition. ● *n. Gram.* **1** a conditional clause, etc. **2** the conditional mood. □□ **con·di·tion·al·i·ty** /-nálitee/ *n.* **con·di·tion·al·ly** *adv.*

con·di·tion·er /kəndíshənər/ *n.* an agent that brings something into good condition, esp. a substance applied to the hair.

con·do /kóndō/ *n.* (*pl.* **-os**) *colloq.* a condominium.

con·dole /kəndốl/ *v.intr.* (foll. by *with*) express sympathy with a person over a loss, grief, etc. ¶ Often confused with *console.* □□ **con·do·la·to·ry** /kəndốlətawree/ *adj.*

con·do·lence /kəndốləns/ *n.* (often in *pl.*) an expression of sympathy (*sent my condolences*).

con·dom /kóndom/ *n.* a rubber sheath worn on the penis during sexual intercourse as a contraceptive or to prevent infection.

con·do·min·i·um /kóndəmíneeəm/ *n.* **1** a building or complex containing apartments that are individually owned. **2** the joint control of a nation's affairs by other nations.

con·done /kəndốn/ *v.tr.* **1** forgive or overlook (an offense or wrongdoing). **2** approve or sanction, usu. reluctantly. **3** (of an action) atone for (an offense); make up for. □□ **con·do·na·tion** /kóndənáyshən/ *n.* **con·don·er** *n.*

con·dor /kóndawr/ *n.* **1** (in full **Andean condor**) ▼ a large vulture, *Vultur gryphus*, of S. America, having black plumage with a white neck ruff. **2** (in full **California condor**) a small vulture, *Gymnogyps californianus*, of California.

CONDOR:
ANDEAN
CONDOR
(*Vultur gryphus*)

con·duce /kəndoos, -dyoos/ *v.intr.* (foll. by *to*) contribute to (a result).

con·du·cive /kəndoosiv, -dyoo-/ *adj.* (often foll. by *to*) contributing or helping (toward something).

con·duct *n. & v.* ● *n.* /kóndukt/ **1** behavior (esp. in its moral aspect). **2** the action or manner of directing or managing (business, war, etc.). **3** *Art* mode of treatment; execution. **4** leading; guidance. ● *v.* /kəndúkt/ **1** *tr.* lead or guide (a person). **2** *tr.* direct or manage (business, etc.). **3** *tr.* (also *absol.*) be the conductor of (an orchestra, etc.). **4** *tr. Physics* transmit (heat, electricity, etc.) by conduction. **5** *refl.* behave. □□ **con·duct·i·ble** /kəndúktibəl/ *adj.* **con·duct·i·bil·i·ty** *n.*

con·duc·tion /kəndúkshən/ *n.* **1** the transmission of heat or electricity through a substance. **2** the

transmission of impulses along nerves. **3** the conducting of liquid through a pipe, etc.

con·duc·tive /kəndúktiv/ *adj.* having the property of conducting (esp. heat, electricity, etc.). □□ **con·duc·tive·ly** *adv.*

con·duc·tiv·i·ty /kónduktívitee/ *n.* the conducting power of a specified material.

con·duc·tor /kəndúktər/ *n.* **1** a person who directs the performance of an orchestra or choir, etc. **2** (*fem.* **conductress** /-tris-/) **a** an official in charge of a train. **b** a person who collects fares in a bus, etc. **3** *Physics* **a** a thing that conducts or transmits heat or electricity, esp. regarded in terms of its capacity to do this (*a poor conductor*). **b** = LIGHTNING ROD. **4** a guide or leader. **5** a manager or director. □□ **con·duc·tor·ship** *n.*

con·duit /kóndōoit, -dyōoit, -dit/ *n.* **1** a channel or pipe for conveying liquids. **2 a** a tube or trough for protecting insulated electric wires. **b** a length or stretch of this.

con·dyle /kóndil, -d'l/ *n. Anat.* ▼ a rounded process at the end of some bones, forming an articulation with another bone. ▷ SKELETON. □□ **con·dy·lar** *adj.* **con·dy·loid** *adj.*

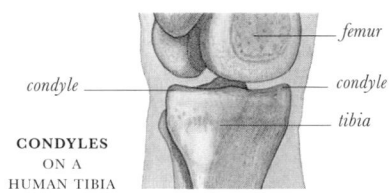

femur
condyle — — *condyle*
— *tibia*

CONDYLES
ON A
HUMAN TIBIA

cone /kōn/ *n.* **1** ▶ a solid figure with a circular (or other curved) plane base, tapering to a point. **2** a thing of a similar shape, solid or hollow, e.g., as used to mark off areas of roads. **3** the dry fruit of a conifer. ▷ CONIFER. **4** a cone-shaped wafer for holding ice cream. **5** any of the minute cone-shaped structures in the retina. **6** a conical mountain esp. of volcanic origin. **7** (in full **cone shell**) any marine gastropod mollusk of the family Conidae. **8** *Pottery* a ceramic pyramid, melting at a known temperature, used to indicate the temperature of a kiln.

circular plane base

CONE

Con·es·to·ga /kónəstốgə/ *n.* **1** a N. American people native to the northeastern US. **2** a member of this people.

co·ney /kốnee/ *n.* (also **co·ny**) (*pl.* **-eys** or **-ies**) **1 a** a rabbit. **b** its fur. **2** *Bibl.* a hyrax.

con·fab /kónfab/ *n. & v. colloq.* ● *n.* a conversation; a chat. ● *v.intr.* (**confabbed, confabbing**) = CONFABULATE.

con·fab·u·late /kənfábyəlayt/ *v.intr.* **1** converse; chat. **2** *Psychol.* fabricate imaginary experiences as compensation for the loss of memory. □□ **con·fab·u·la·tion** /-láyshən/ *n.* **con·fab·u·la·to·ry** /-lətáwree/ *adj.*

con·fec·tion /kənfékshən/ *n.* **1** a dish or delicacy made with sweet ingredients. **2** mixing; compounding. **3** a fashionable or elaborate article of women's dress.

con·fec·tion·er /kənfékshənər/ *n.* a maker or retailer of confectionery.

con·fec·tion·ers' su·gar *n.* very fine powdered sugar.

con·fec·tion·er·y /kənfékshəneree/ *n.* candy and other confections.

con·fed·er·a·cy /kənfédərəsee/ *n.* (*pl.* **-ies**) **1** a league or alliance, esp. of confederate nations. **2** a league for an unlawful or evil purpose; a conspiracy. **3** the condition or fact of being confederate; alliance; conspiracy. **4** (**the Confederacy**) = CONFEDERATE STATES OF AMERICA.

con·fed·er·ate *adj., n., & v.* ● *adj.* /kənfédərət/ esp. *Polit.* allied; joined by an agreement or treaty. ● *n.* /kənfédərət/ **1** an ally, esp. (in a bad sense) an accomplice. **2** (**Confederate**) a supporter of the Confederate States of America. ● *v.* /kənfédərayt/ (often foll. by *with*) **1** *tr.* bring (a person, state, or oneself) into alliance. **2** *intr.* come into alliance.

Con·fed·er·ate States of A·mer·i·ca *n.pl.* ▼ the eleven southern states that seceded from the US in 1860–61.

con·fed·er·a·tion /kənfédəráyshən/ *n.* **1** a union or alliance of nations, etc. **2** the act or an instance of confederating; the state of being confederated.

con·fer /kənfár/ *v.* (**conferred, conferring**) **1** *tr.* (often foll. by *on, upon*) grant or bestow (a title, degree, favor, etc.). **2** *intr.* (often foll. by *with*) consult. □□ **con·fer·ra·ble** *adj.*

con·fer·ence /kónfərəns, -frəns/ *n.* **1** consultation; discussion. **2** a meeting for discussion, esp. a regular one held by an association or organization. **3** an annual assembly of the Methodist Church. **4** an association in commerce, sport, etc. **5** the linking of several telephones, computer terminals, etc., so that each user may communicate with the others simultaneously. □ **in conference** engaged in discussion.

C

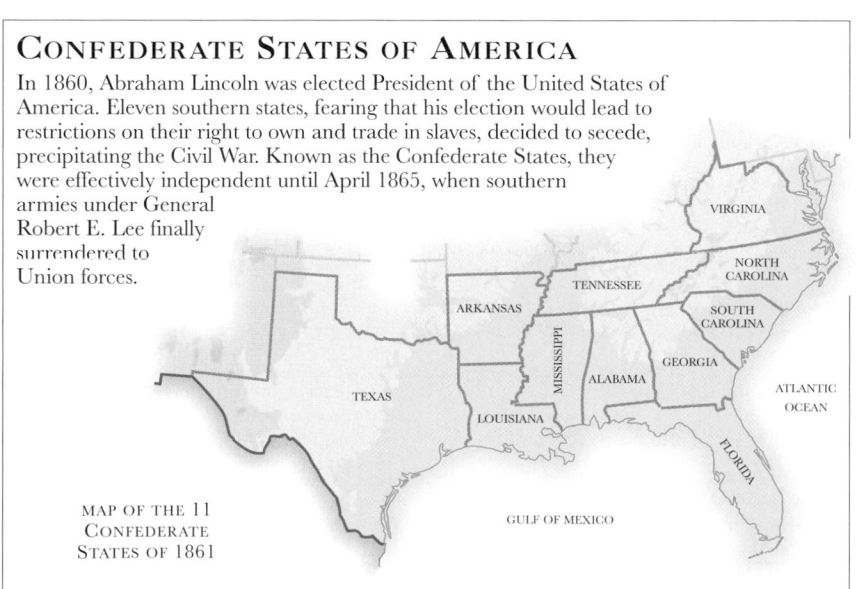

CONFEDERATE STATES OF AMERICA

In 1860, Abraham Lincoln was elected President of the United States of America. Eleven southern states, fearing that his election would lead to restrictions on their right to own and trade in slaves, decided to secede, precipitating the Civil War. Known as the Confederate States, they were effectively independent until April 1865, when southern armies under General Robert E. Lee finally surrendered to Union forces.

VIRGINIA
NORTH CAROLINA
TENNESSEE
ARKANSAS
SOUTH CAROLINA
MISSISSIPPI
GEORGIA
ALABAMA
ATLANTIC OCEAN
TEXAS
LOUISIANA
FLORIDA
GULF OF MEXICO

MAP OF THE 11
CONFEDERATE
STATES OF 1861

C

con·fer·ence call *n.* a telephone call in which three or more people are connected.

con·fer·ment /kənfə́rmənt/ *n.* **1** the conferring of a degree, honor, etc. **2** an instance of this.

con·fer·ral /kənfə́rəl/ *n.* = CONFERMENT.

con·fess /kənfés/ *v.* **1 a** *tr.* (also *absol.*) acknowledge or admit (a fault, wrongdoing, etc.). **b** *intr.* (foll. by *to*) admit to (*confessed to having lied*). **2** *tr.* admit reluctantly (*confessed it would be difficult*). **3 a** *tr.* (also *absol.*) declare (one's sins) to a priest. **b** *tr.* (of a priest) hear the confession of. **c** *refl.* declare one's sins to a priest.

con·fess·ed·ly /kənfésidlee/ *adv.* by one's own or general admission.

con·fes·sion /kənféshən/ *n.* **1 a** confessing or acknowledgment of a fault, wrongdoing, a sin to a priest, etc. **b** an instance of this. **c** a thing confessed. **2** (in full **confession of faith**) **a** a declaration of one's religious beliefs. **b** a statement of one's principles. ◻◻ **con·fes·sion·ar·y** *adj.*

con·fes·sion·al /kənféshənəl/ *n.* & *adj.* ● *n.* an enclosed stall in a church in which a priest hears confessions. ● *adj.* **1** of or relating to confession. **2** denominational.

con·fes·sor /kənfésər/ *n.* **1** a person who makes a confession. **2** a priest who hears confessions and gives spiritual counsel. **3** a person who avows a religion in the face of its suppression, but does not suffer martyrdom.

con·fet·ti /kənfétee/ *n.* small bits of colored paper thrown during celebrations, etc.

con·fi·dant /kónfidánt, -daánt/ *n.* (*fem.* **confidante** *pronunc.* same) a person trusted with knowledge of one's private affairs.

con·fide /kənfíd/ *v.* **1** *tr.* (usu. foll. by *to*) tell (a secret, etc.) in confidence. **2** *tr.* (foll. by *to*) entrust (an object of care, a task, etc.) to. **3** *intr.* (foll. by *in*) **a** have trust or confidence in. **b** talk confidentially to. ◻◻ **con·fid·ing·ly** *adv.*

con·fi·dence /kónfidəns/ *n.* **1** firm trust. **2 a** a feeling of reliance or certainty. **b** a sense of self-reliance; boldness. **3 a** something told confidentially. **b** the telling of private matters with mutual trust. ◻ **in confidence** as a secret. **in a person's confidence** trusted with a person's secrets. **take into one's confidence** confide in.

con·fi·dence game *n.* a swindle in which the victim is persuaded to trust the swindler.

con·fi·dence man *n.* (*pl.* **-men**) a man who robs by means of a confidence game.

con·fi·dent /kónfid'nt/ *adj.* **1** feeling or showing confidence; self-assured; bold. **2** (often foll. by *of*, or *that* + clause) assured; trusting. ◻◻ **con·fi·dent·ly** *adv.*

con·fi·den·tial /kónfidénshəl/ *adj.* **1** spoken or written in confidence. **2** entrusted with secrets (*a confidential secretary*). **3** confiding. ◻◻ **con·fi·den·ti·al·i·ty** /-sheeálitee/ *n.* **con·fi·den·tial·ly** *adv.*

con·fig·u·ra·tion /kənfigyəráyshən/ *n.* **1 a** an arrangement of parts or elements in a particular form or figure. **b** the form, shape, or figure resulting from such an arrangement. **2** *Astron.* & *Astrol.* the relative position of planets, etc. **3** *Psychol.* = GESTALT. **4** *Physics* the distribution of electrons among the energy levels of an atom, or of nucleons among the energy levels of a nucleus, as specified by quantum numbers. **5** *Chem.* the fixed three-dimensional relationship of the atoms in a molecule. **6** *Computing* **a** the interrelating or interconnecting of a computer system or elements of it so that it will accommodate a particular specification. **b** an instance of this. ◻◻ **con·fig·u·ra·tion·al** *adj.* **con·fig·ure** *v.tr.* (in senses 1, 2, 6).

con·fine *v.* & *n.* ● *v.tr.* /kənfín/ (often foll. by *in*, *to*, *within*) **1** keep or restrict (within certain limits, etc.). **2** hold captive; imprison. ● *n.* /kónfin/ (usu. in *pl.*) a limit or boundary (*within the confines of the town*). ◻ **be confined** be in childbirth.

con·fine·ment /kənfínmənt/ *n.* **1** the act or an instance of confining; the state of being confined. **2** the time of a woman's giving birth.

con·firm /kənfə́rm/ *v.tr.* **1** provide support for the truth or correctness of; make definitely valid (*confirmed my suspicions*; *confirmed his arrival time*). **2** ratify (a treaty, title, etc.); make formally valid. **3** (foll. by *in*) encourage (a person) in (an opinion, etc.). **4** establish more firmly (power, possession, etc.). **5** administer the religious rite of confirmation to. ◻◻ **con·firm·a·tive** *adj.* **con·firm·a·to·ry** *adj.*

con·fir·mand /kónfərmand/ *n. Eccl.* a person who is to be or has just been confirmed.

con·fir·ma·tion /kónfərmáyshən/ *n.* **1 a** the act or an instance of confirming; the state of being confirmed. **b** an instance of this. **2 a** a religious rite confirming a baptized person as a member of the Christian Church. **b** a ceremony of confirming persons of about this age in the Jewish faith.

con·firmed /kənfə́rmd/ *adj.* firmly settled in some habit or condition (*confirmed in her ways*; *a confirmed bachelor*).

con·fis·cate /kónfiskayt/ *v.tr.* **1** take or seize by authority. **2** appropriate to the public treasury (by way of a penalty). ◻◻ **con·fis·ca·ble** /kənfiskəbəl/ *adj.* **con·fis·ca·tion** /-káyshən/ *n.* **con·fis·ca·tor** *n.* **con·fis·ca·to·ry** /kənfiskətáwree/ *adj.*

con·fla·gra·tion /kónfləgráyshən/ *n.* a great and destructive fire.

con·flate /kənfláyt/ *v.tr.* blend or fuse together. ◻◻ **con·fla·tion** /-fláyshən/ *n.*

con·flict *n.* & *v.* ● *n.* /kónflikt/ **1 a** a state of opposition or hostilities. **b** a fight or struggle. **2** (often foll. by *of*) **a** the clashing of opposed principles, etc. **b** an instance of this. **3** *Psychol.* **a** the opposition of incompatible wishes or needs in a person. **b** an instance of this. **c** the distress resulting from this. ● *v.intr.* /kənflíkt/ **1** clash; be incompatible. **2** (often foll. by *with*) struggle or contend. **3** (as **conflicting** *adj.*) contradictory. ◻ **in conflict** conflicting. ◻◻ **con·flic·tion** /-flíkshən/ *n.* **con·flic·tu·al** /kənflíkchōōəl/ *adj.*

con·flu·ence /kónflōōəns/ *n.* **1** a place where two rivers meet. **2 a** a coming together. **b** a crowd of people.

con·flu·ent /kónflōōənt/ *adj.* & *n.* ● *adj.* flowing together; uniting. ● *n.* a stream joining another.

con·flux /kónfluks/ *n.* = CONFLUENCE.

con·form /kənfáwrm/ *v.* **1** *intr.* comply with rules or custom. **2** *intr.* & *tr.* (often foll. by *to*) be or make accordant or suitable. **3** *tr.* (often foll. by *to*) make similar. **4** *intr.* (foll. by *to*, *with*) comply with. ◻◻ **con·form·er** *n.*

con·form·a·ble /kənfáwrməbəl/ *adj.* **1** (often foll. by *to*) similar. **2** (often foll. by *with*) consistent. **3** (often foll. by *to*) adapted. **4** tractable. **5** *Geol.* (of strata in contact) lying in the same direction. ◻◻ **con·form·a·bil·i·ty** *n.* **con·form·a·bly** *adv.*

con·for·ma·tion /kónfawrmáyshən/ *n.* **1** the way in which a thing is formed. **2** (often foll. by *to*) adjustment in form or character; adaptation. **3** *Chem.* any spatial arrangement of atoms in a molecule from the rotation of part of the molecule about a single bond.

con·form·ist /kənfáwrmist/ *n.* & *adj.* ● *n.* a person who conforms to an established practice. ● *adj.* (of a person) conventional. ◻◻ **con·form·ism** *n.*

con·form·i·ty /kənfáwrmitee/ *n.* **1** (often foll. by *to*, *with*) action or behavior in accordance with established practice. **2** (often foll. by *to*, *with*) likeness; agreement.

con·found /kənfównd/ *v.* & *int.* ● *v.tr.* **1** throw into perplexity. **2** confuse (in one's mind). **3** *archaic* defeat; overthrow. ● *int.* expressing annoyance (*confound you!*).

con·found·ed /kənfówndid/ *adj. colloq.* damned (*a confounded nuisance!*). ◻◻ **con·found·ed·ly** *adv.*

con·frere /kónfrair/ *n.* (also **confrère**) a fellow member of a profession, scientific body, etc.

con·front /kənfrúnt/ *v.tr.* **1 a** face in hostility or defiance. **b** face up to and deal with (a problem, etc.). **2** (of a difficulty, etc.) present itself to. **3** (foll. by *with*) **a** bring (a person) face to face with (a circumstance). **b** set (a thing) face to face with (another) for comparison. **4** meet or stand facing. ◻◻ **con·fron·ta·tion** /kónfruntáyshən/ *n.* **con·fron·ta·tion·al** /kónfruntáyshənəl/ *adj.*

Con·fu·cian /kənfyóōshən/ *adj.* & *n.* ● *adj.* of or relating to Confucius, Chinese philosopher d. 479 BC, or his philosophy. ● *n.* a follower of Confucius. ◻◻ **Con·fu·cian·ism** *n.* **Con·fu·cian·ist** *n.*

con·fus·a·ble /kənfyóōzəbəl/ *adj.* that is able or liable to be confused. ◻◻ **con·fus·a·bil·i·ty** /-bílitee/ *n.*

con·fuse /kənfyóōz/ *v.tr.* **1 a** disconcert; perplex. **b** embarrass. **2** mistake (one for another). **3** make indistinct (*that point confuses the issue*). **4** (as **confused** *adj.*) **a** mentally decrepit. **b** puzzled; perplexed. **5** (often as **confused** *adj.*) throw into disorder (*a confused jumble of clothes*). ◻◻ **con·fus·ed·ly** /kənfyóōzidlee/ *adv.* **con·fus·ing** *adj.* **con·fus·ing·ly** *adv.*

con·fu·sion /kənfyóō<u>zh</u>ən/ *n.* **1 a** the act of confusing (*the confusion of fact and fiction*). **b** a misunderstanding (*confusions arise from a lack of communication*). **2 a** a confused state (*thrown into confusion*). **b** (foll. by *of*) a disorderly jumble (*a confusion of ideas*). **3 a** a civil commotion (*confusion broke out at the announcement*). **b** an instance of this.

con·fute /kənfyóōt/ *v.tr.* **1** prove (a person) to be in error. **2** prove (an argument) to be false. ◻◻ **con·fu·ta·tion** /kónfyootáyshən/ *n.*

con·ga /kónggə/ *n.* **1** a Latin American dance of African origin, usu. with several persons in a single line, one behind the other. **2** (also **conga drum**) ► a tall, narrow, low-toned drum beaten with the hands. ▷ PERCUSSION

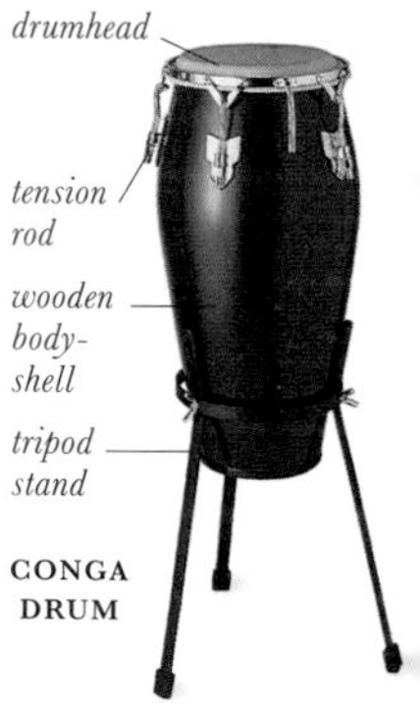
drumhead
tension rod
wooden body-shell
tripod stand
CONGA DRUM

con·geal /kənjéel/ *v.tr.* & *intr.* **1** make or become semisolid by cooling. **2** (of blood, etc.) coagulate. ◻◻ **con·geal·a·ble** *adj.* **con·geal·ment** *n.*

con·ge·la·tion /kónjiláyshən/ *n.* **1** the process of congealing. **2** a congealed state. **3** a congealed substance.

con·ge·ner /kónjənər/ *n.* a thing or person of the same kind or category as another (*the goldfinch is a congener of the canary*).

con·ge·ner·ic /kónjinérik/ *adj.* **1** of the same genus, kind, or race. **2** allied in nature or origin; akin. ◻◻ **con·gen·er·ous** /kənjénərəs/ *adj.*

con·gen·ial /kənjéenyəl/ *adj.* **1** (often foll. by *with*, *to*) (of a person, character, etc.) pleasant because akin to oneself in temperament or interests. **2** (often foll. by *to*) agreeable. ◻◻ **con·ge·ni·al·i·ty** /-jéeneeálitee/ *n.* **con·gen·ial·ly** *adv.*

con·gen·i·tal /kənjénitəl/ *adj.* **1** (esp. of a disease, defect, etc.) existing from birth. **2** that is (or as if) such from birth (*a congenital liar*). ◻◻ **con·gen·i·tal·ly** *adv.*

con·ger /kónggər/ *n.* (in full **conger eel**) any large marine eel of the family Congridae. ▷ EEL

con·ge·ries /kənjéereez, kónjə-/ *n.* (*pl.* same) a disorderly collection.

con·gest /kənjést/ *v.tr.* (esp. as **congested** *adj.*) affect with congestion. ◻◻ **con·ges·tive** *adj.*

con·ges·tion /kənjés-chən/ *n.* abnormal accumulation, crowding, or obstruction.

con·glom·er·ate *adj.*, *n.*, & *v.* ● *adj.* /kənglómərət/ **1** gathered into a rounded mass. **2** *Geol.* (of rock) made up of small stones held together. ● *n.* /kənglómərət/ **1** a number of things or parts forming a heterogeneous mass. **2** a group or corporation formed by the merging of separate and diverse firms. **3** *Geol.* conglomerate rock. ● *v.tr.* & *intr.* /kənglómərayt/ collect into a coherent mass. ◻◻ **con·glom·er·a·tion** /-ráyshən/ *n.*

Con·go·lese /kónggəleéz/ *adj. & n.* ● *adj.* of or relating to the Republic of the Congo in Central Africa, or the region surrounding the Zaire (formerly Congo) River. ● *n.* (*pl.* same) a native of either of these regions.

con·gou /kónggoo, -gō/ *n.* a variety of black China tea.

con·grats /kəngráts/ *n.pl. & int. colloq.* congratulations.

con·grat·u·late /kəngráchəlayt, -gráj-, kəng-/ *v.tr. & refl.* (often foll. by *on, upon*) **1** *tr.* express pleasure at the happiness or excellence of (a person) (*congratulated them on their success*). **2** *refl.* think oneself fortunate or clever. □□ **con·grat·u·la·to·ry** /-lə-táwree/ *adj.*

con·grat·u·la·tion /kəngráchəláyshən -gráj-, kəng-/ *n.* **1** congratulating. **2** (also as *int.*; usu. in *pl.*) an expression of this.

con·gre·gate /kónggrigayt/ *v.intr. & tr.* collect or gather into a crowd or mass.

con·gre·ga·tion /kónggrigáyshən/ *n.* **1** the process of congregating; collection into a crowd or mass. **2** a crowd or mass gathered together. **3 a** a body assembled for religious worship. **b** a body of persons regularly attending a particular church, etc. **c** *RC Ch.* a body of persons obeying a common religious rule. **d** *RC Ch.* any of several permanent committees of the Roman Catholic College of Cardinals.

con·gre·ga·tion·al /kónggrigáyshən-əl/ *adj.* **1** of a congregation. **2** (**Congregational**) of or adhering to Congregationalism.

Con·gre·ga·tion·al·ism /kónggrigáyshənəlizəm/ *n.* a system of ecclesiastical organization whereby individual churches are largely self-

governing. □□ **Con·gre·ga·tion·al·ist** *n.* **Con·gre·ga·tion·al·ize** *v.tr.*

con·gress /kónggris/ *n.* **1** a formal meeting of delegates for discussion. **2** (**Congress**) a national legislative body, esp. that of the US. **3** a society or organization. **4** meeting. □□ **con·gres·sion·al** /kəngréshən'l/ *adj.*

Con·gres·sion·al Med·al of Hon·or *n.* = MEDAL OF HONOR.

con·gress·man /kónggrismən/ *n.* (*pl.* **-men**; *fem.* **congresswoman**, *pl.* **-women**) a member of the US Congress, esp. of the US House of Representatives.

con·gru·ence /kónggrōōəns, kəngrōō-/ *n.* (also **con·gru·en·cy** /-ənsee/) **1** agreement; consistency. **2** *Geom.* the state of being congruent.

con·gru·ent /kónggrōōənt, kəngrōō-/ *adj.* **1** (often foll. by *with*) suitable; agreeing. **2** *Geom.* (of figures) coinciding exactly when superimposed. □□ **con·gru·ent·ly** *adv.*

con·gru·ous /kónggrōōəs/ *adj.* (often foll. by *with*) suitable; fitting. □□ **con·gru·i·ty** /-grōóitee/ *n.* **con·gru·ous·ly** *adv.*

con·ic /kónik/ *adj.* of a cone.

con·i·cal /kónikəl/ *adj.* cone-shaped. □□ **con·i·cal·ly** *adv.*

con·ic sec·tion *n.* ◄ a figure formed by the intersection of a cone and a plane.

co·ni·fer /kónifər, kó-/ *n.* ▼ any evergreen tree of a group usu. bearing cones, including pines, yews, cedars, and redwoods. ▷ GYMNOSPERM, SEED, TREE. □□ **con·if·er·ous** /kónifərəs/ *adj.*

con·jec·ture /kənjékchər/ *n. & v.* ● *n.* **1 a** the formation of an opinion on incomplete information; guessing. **b** an opinion or conclusion reached in

CONJUNCTION

A planet comes into conjunction with the Sun when it passes behind the Sun (superior conjunction), or between the Earth and the Sun (inferior conjunction). It then lies in the same direction (longitude) as the Sun, when viewed from the Earth. An inferior planet (one orbiting closer to the Sun than the Earth) alternately passes through both inferior and superior conjunction; a superior planet (one farther from the Sun than the Earth) can come only to superior conjunction.

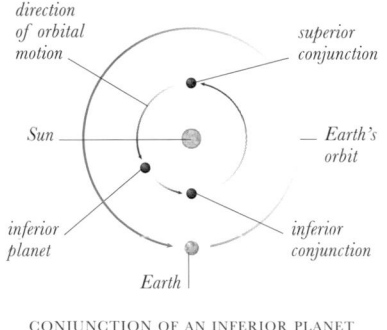

CONJUNCTION OF AN INFERIOR PLANET

this way. **2 a** (in textual criticism) the guessing of a reading not in the text. **b** a proposed reading. ● *v.* **1** *tr. & intr.* guess. **2** *tr.* (in textual criticism) propose (a reading). □□ **con·jec·tur·a·ble** *adj.* **con·jec·tur·al** /kənjékchərəl/ *adj.* **con·jec·tur·al·ly** *adv.*

con·join /kənjóyn/ *v.tr. & intr.* join; combine.

con·joint /kənjóynt/ *adj.* associated, conjoined. □□ **con·joint·ly** *adv.*

con·ju·gal /kónjəgəl/ *adj.* of marriage or the relation between husband and wife. □□ **con·ju·gal·i·ty** /-gálitee/ *n.* **con·ju·gal·ly** *adv.*

con·ju·gate *v., adj., & n.* ● *v.* /kónjəgayt/ **1** *tr. Gram.* give the different forms of (a verb). **2** *intr.* **a** unite sexually. **b** (of gametes) become fused. **3** *intr. Chem.* (of protein) combine with nonprotein. ● *adj.* /kónjəgət, -gayt/ **1** joined together, esp. as a pair. **2** *Gram.* derived from the same root. **3** *Biol.* fused. **4** *Chem.* (of an acid or base) related by loss or gain of an electron. **5** *Math.* joined in a reciprocal relation, esp. having the same real parts, and equal magnitudes but opposite signs of imaginary parts. ● *n.* /kónjəgət, -gayt/ a conjugate word or thing. □□ **con·ju·ga·tion** /kónjəgáyshən/ *n.* **con·ju·ga·tion·al** *adj.*

con·junct /kənjúngkt/ *adj.* joined together; combined.

con·junc·tion /kənjúngkshən/ *n.* **1 a** the action of joining; the condition of being joined. **b** an instance of this. **2** *Gram.* a word used to connect clauses or sentences or words in the same clause (e.g., *and, but, if*). **3 a** a combination (of events or circumstances). **b** a number of associated persons or things. **4** *Astron. & Astrol.* ▲ the alignment of two bodies in the solar system so that they have the same longitude as seen from the Earth. □ **in conjunction with** together with. □□ **con·junc·tion·al** *adj.*

con·junc·ti·va /kónjungktívə, kənjúngktivə-/ *n.* (*pl.* **conjunctivas** or **conjunctivae** /-vee/) *Anat.* the mucous membrane that covers the front of the eye and lines the inside of the eyelids. ▷ EYE. □□ **con·junc·ti·val** *adj.*

con·junc·tive /kənjúngktiv/ *adj.* **1** serving to join. **2** *Gram.* of the nature of a conjunction.

con·junc·ti·vi·tis /kənjúngktivítis/ *n.* inflammation of the conjunctiva.

con·junc·ture /kənjúngkchər/ *n.* a combination of events; a state of affairs.

circle
ellipse
parabola
hyperbola

CONIC SECTIONS

CONIFER

All 550 species in the order Coniferales bear cones for reproduction. In most, pollen-forming male cones and seed-forming female cones develop on the same tree, and cross-fertilization between them is necessary. In cool parts of the world, conifers form dense forests, and are commonly found on mountains. Most bear narrow evergreen leaves, capable of withstanding drying winds.

male cone produces pollen

female cone contains seeds

needle

ovuliferous scale

MALE AND FEMALE SCOTS PINE CONES (*Pinus sylvestris*)

immature cone

MAIN CONIFER FAMILIES

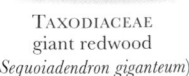

PINACEAE
Caucasian fir
(*Abies nordmanniana*)

ARAUCARIACEAE
monkey puzzle
(*Araucaria araucana*)

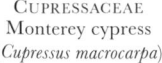

TAXODIACEAE
giant redwood
(*Sequoiadendron giganteum*)

TAXACEAE
California nutmeg
(*Torreya californica*)

CUPRESSACEAE
Monterey cypress
(*Cupressus macrocarpa*)

con·jun·to /konhŏŏntō/ *n.* (in Latin America or Hispanic communities) a small musical group or band.

con·jure /kónjər/ *v.* **1** *tr.* call upon (a spirit) to appear. **2** *tr.* (usu. foll. by *out of, away, to,* etc.) cause to appear or disappear as if by magic. **3** *intr.* perform marvels. **5** *tr.* /kənjŏŏr/ (often foll. by *to* + infin.) appeal solemnly to (a person). □ **conjure up 1** bring into existence or cause to appear as if by magic. **2** evoke.

con·jur·er /kónjərər, kún-/ *n.* (also **con·jur·or**) a person who conjures.

conk[1] /kongk/ *v.intr.* (usu. foll. by *out*) *colloq.* **1** (of a machine, etc.) break down. **2** (of a person) become exhausted and give up; faint; die.

conk[2] /kongk/ *v.tr. sl.* hit on the head, etc.

con·ker /kóngkər/ *n. Brit.* **1** ▶ the hard fruit of a horse chestnut. **2** (in *pl.*) *Brit.* a children's game played with conkers on strings, one hit against another to try to break it.

con man *n.* (*pl.* **men**) = CONFIDENCE MAN.

con mo·to /kón mótō, káwn/ *adv. Mus.* with movement.

Conn. *abbr.* Connecticut.

conn /kon/ *n. & v. Naut.* • *v.tr.* direct the steering of (a ship). • *n.* **1** the act of conning. **2** the responsibility or station of one who conns.

con·nect /kənékt/ *v.* **1 a** *tr.* (often foll. by *to, with*) join (one thing with another). **b** *tr.* join (two things) (*a track connected the two villages.* **c** *intr.* be joined or joinable (*the two parts do not connect*). **2** *tr.* (often foll. by *with*) associate mentally or practically (*did not connect the two ideas*). **3** *intr.* (foll. by *with*) (of a train, etc.) be synchronized at its destination with another train, etc., so that passengers can transfer. **4** *tr.* put into communication by telephone. **5 a** *tr.* (usu. in *passive*; foll. by *with*) unite or associate with others in relationships, etc. (*am connected with the royal family*). **b** *intr.* form a logical sequence; be meaningful. **6** *intr. colloq.* hit or strike effectively. □□ **con·nect·a·ble** *adj.* **con·nect·or** *n.*

con·nect·ed /kənéktid/ *adj.* **1** joined in sequence. **2** (of ideas, etc.) coherent. **3** related or associated. □□ **con·nect·ed·ly** *adv.* **con·nect·ed·ness** *n.*

con·nect·ing rod *n.* ▶ the rod between the piston and the crankshaft, etc., in an internal-combustion engine or between the wheels of a locomotive. ▷ INTERNAL-COMBUSTION ENGINE

con·nec·tion /kənékshən/ *n.* **1 a** the act of connecting; the state of being connected. **b** an instance of this. **2** the point at which two things are connected. **3 a** a link (*a radio formed the only connection*). **b** a telephone link (*got a bad connection*). **4** arrangement or opportunity for catching a connecting train, etc.; the train, etc., itself (*missed the connection*). **5** *Electr.* **a** the linking up of an electric current by contact. **b** a device for effecting this. **6** (often in *pl.*) a relative or associate, esp. one with influence (*has connections in the State Department*). **7** a relation of ideas; a context. **8** *sl.* **a** a transaction involving illegal drugs. **b** a supplier of narcotics. **9** a religious body, esp. Methodist. □ **in connection with** with reference to. **in this** (or **that**) **connection** with reference to this (or that). □□ **con·nec·tion·al** *adj.*

con·nec·tive /kənéktiv/ *adj. & n.* • *adj.* serving or tending to connect. • *n.* something that connects.

con·nec·tive tis·sue *n. Anat.* a fibrous tissue that supports, binds, or separates more specialized tissue. ▷ SKIN

conn·ing tow·er /kóning/ *n.* **1** the superstructure of a submarine which contains the periscope. ▷ SUBMARINE. **2** the armored pilothouse of a warship.

con·niv·ance /kənívəns/ *n.* **1** (often foll. by *at, in*) conniving (*connivance in the crime*). **2** tacit permission (*done with his connivance*).

con·nive /kənív/ *v.intr.* **1** (foll. by *at*) disregard or tacitly consent to (a wrongdoing). **2** (usu. foll. by *with*) conspire. □□ **con·niv·er** *n.*

con·nois·seur /kónəsör/ *n.* (often foll. by *of, in*) an expert judge in matters of taste. □□ **con·nois·seur·ship** *n.*

con·no·ta·tion /kónətáyshən/ *n.* **1** that which is implied by a word, etc., in addition to its literal or primary meaning. **2** the act of connoting or implying.

con·note /kənót/ *v.tr.* **1** (of a word, etc.) imply in addition to the literal or primary meaning. **2** (of a fact) imply as a consequence or condition. **3** mean; signify. □□ **con·no·ta·tive** /kónətaytiv, kənótətiv/ *adj.*

con·nu·bi·al /kənŏŏbeeəl, kənyŏŏ-/ *adj.* of or relating to marriage. □□ **con·nu·bi·al·i·ty** /-beeálitee/ *n.* **con·nu·bi·al·ly** *adv.*

con·quer /kóngkər/ *v.tr.* **1 a** overcome and control by military force. **b** *absol.* be victorious. **2** overcome (a habit, disability, etc.) by effort. **3** climb (a mountain) successfully. □□ **con·quer·a·ble** *adj.* **con·quer·or** *n.*

con·quest /kóngkwest/ *n.* **1** the act or an instance of conquering; the state of being conquered. **2 a** a conquered territory. **b** something won. **3** a person whose affection has been won. **4** (**the Conquest** or **Norman Conquest**) the conquest of England by William ("the Conqueror") of Normandy in 1066. □ **make a conquest of** win the affections of.

con·quis·ta·dor /konkwístədawr, kóngkéestə-/ *n.* (*pl.* **conquistadores** /-dáwrez/ or **conquistadors**) a conqueror, esp. one of the Spanish conquerors of Mexico and Peru in the 16th c.

con·san·guin·e·ous /kónsanggwíneeəs/ *adj.* descended from the same ancestor.

con·science /kónshəns/ *n.* **1** a moral sense of right and wrong. **2** an inner feeling as to the goodness or otherwise of one's behavior (*has a guilty conscience*). □ **for conscience** (or **conscience's**) **sake** to satisfy one's conscience. **in all conscience** by any reasonable standard. **on one's conscience** causing one feelings of guilt. □□ **con·science·less** *adj.*

con·science-strick·en *adj.* (also **conscience-struck**) made uneasy by a bad conscience.

con·sci·en·tious /kónshee-énshəs/ *adj.* (of a person or conduct) diligent and scrupulous. □□ **con·sci·en·tious·ly** *adv.* **con·sci·en·tious·ness** *n.*

con·sci·en·tious ob·jec·tor *n.* a person who for reasons of conscience objects to conforming to a requirement, esp. that of military service.

con·scious /kónshəs/ *adj. & n.* • *adj.* **1** awake and aware of one's surroundings and identity. **2** (usu. foll. by *of,* or *that* + clause) aware (*conscious of his inferiority*). **3** (of actions, emotions, etc.) realized or recognized by the doer; intentional (*made a conscious effort not to laugh*). **4** (in *comb.*) aware of; concerned with (*appearance-conscious*). • *n.* (prec. by *the*) the conscious mind. □□ **con·scious·ly** *adv.*

con·scious·ness /kónshəsnis/ *n.* **1** the state of being conscious (*lost consciousness*). **2 a** awareness; perception (*no consciousness of being ridiculed*). **b** (in *comb.*) awareness of (*class consciousness*). **3** the totality of a person's thoughts and feelings, or of a class of these (*moral consciousness*).

con·script *v. & n.* • *v.tr.* /kənskrípt/ enlist by conscription. • *n.* /kónskript/ a person enlisted by conscription.

con·scrip·tion /kənskrípshən/ *n.* compulsory enlistment for government service, esp. military service.

con·se·crate /kónsikrayt/ *v.tr.* **1** make or declare sacred. **2** (in Christian belief) make (bread and wine) into the body and blood of Christ. **3** (foll. by *to*) devote (one's life, etc.) to (a purpose). **4** ordain (esp. a bishop) to a sacred office. □□ **con·se·cra·tion** /-kráyshən/ *n.* **con·se·cra·tor** *n.* **con·se·cra·to·ry** /-krətawree/ *adj.*

con·sec·u·tive /kənsékyətiv/ *adj.* **1 a** following continuously. **b** in unbroken or logical order. **2** *Gram.* expressing consequence. □□ **con·sec·u·tive·ly** *adv.* **con·sec·u·tive·ness** *n.*

con·sen·sus /kənsénsəs/ *n.* (often foll. by *of*) **1 a** general agreement (of opinion, testimony, etc.). **b** an instance of this. **2** (*attrib.*) majority view; collective opinion (*consensus politics*). □□ **con·sen·su·al** /kənsénshŏŏəl/ *adj.* **con·sen·su·al·ly** *adv.*

con·sent /kənsént/ *v. & n.* • *v.intr.* (often foll. by *to*) give permission; agree. • *n.* voluntary agreement; permission; compliance.

con·sent·ing a·dult *n.* an adult who consents to something, esp. a sexual act.

con·se·quence /kónsikwens, -kwəns/ *n.* **1** the result or effect of an action or condition. **2 a** importance (*of no consequence*). **b** social distinction (*persons of consequence*). **3** (in *pl.*) a game in which a narrative is made up by the players, each ignorant of what has already been contributed. □ **in consequence** as a result. **take the consequences** accept the results of one's choice or action.

con·se·quent /kónsikwənt/ *adj. & n.* • *adj.* **1** (often foll. by *on, upon*) following as a result or consequence. **2** logically consistent. • *n.* **1** a thing that follows another. **2** *Logic* the second part of a conditional proposition, dependent on the antecedent.

con·se·quen·tial /kónsikwénshəl/ *adj.* **1** following as a result or consequence. **2** resulting indirectly (*consequential damage*). **3 a** significant. **b** (of a person) self-important. □□ **con·se·quen·ti·al·i·ty** /-shee-álitee/ *n.* **con·se·quen·tial·ly** *adv.*

con·se·quent·ly /kónsikwentlee/ *adv. & conj.* as a result; therefore.

con·serv·an·cy /kənsórvənsee/ *n.* (*pl.* **-ies**) **1** a body concerned with the preservation of natural resources (*Nature Conservancy*). **2** conservation; official preservation (of forests, etc.).

con·ser·va·tion /kónsərváyshən/ *n.* preservation, esp. of the natural environment. □ **conservation of energy** (or **mass** or **momentum**, etc.) *Physics* the principle that the total quantity of energy, etc., of any system not subject to external action remains constant. □□ **con·ser·va·tion·al** *adj.* **con·ser·va·tion·ist** *n.*

con·ser·va·tive /kənsórvətiv/ *adj. & n.* • *adj.* **1 a** averse to rapid change. **b** (of views, taste, etc.) avoiding extremes (*conservative in her dress*). **2** (of an estimate, etc.) purposely low; moderate. **3** (**Conservative**) of or characteristic of Conservatives or the British Conservative party. **4** tending to conserve. • *n.* **1** a conservative person. **2** (**Conservative**) a supporter or member of the British Conservative party. □□ **con·serv·a·tism** *n.* **con·serv·a·tive·ly** *adv.* **con·serv·a·tive·ness** *n.*

con·ser·va·toire /kənsórvətwaár/ *n.* a (usu. European) school of music or other arts.

con·ser·va·tor /kənsórvətər, kónsərvaytər/ *n.* a person who preserves something; an official custodian.

con·ser·va·to·ry /kənsórvətawree/ *n.* (*pl.* **-ies**) **1** ▶ a greenhouse for tender plants, esp. one attached to and communicating with a house. **2** = CONSERVATOIRE.

con·serve /kənsórv/ *v. & n.* • *v.tr.* **1** store up; keep from harm or damage, esp. for later use. **2** *Physics* maintain a quantity (of heat, etc.). **3** preserve (food,

---

conker

CONKER: HORSE CHESTNUT FRUIT (*Aesculus hippocastanum*)

spiny case

---

piston

connecting rod

crankpin

crankshaft

counterweight

CONNECTING ROD OF A FOUR-STROKE INTERNAL-COMBUSTION ENGINE

CONSERVATORY

esp. fruit), usu. with sugar. ● *n.* /also kónsərv/ **1** fruit, etc., preserved in sugar. **2** fresh fruit jam.

con·sid·er /kənsídər/ *v.tr.* (often *absol.*) **1** contemplate mentally, esp. in order to reach a conclusion. **2** examine the merits of (a candidate, claim, etc.). **3** give attention to. **4** take into account. **5** (foll. by *that* + clause) have the opinion. **6** (foll. by compl.) believe (*consider it to be genuine*). **7** (as **considered** *adj.*) formed after careful thought (*a considered opinion*). □ **all things considered** taking everything into account.

con·sid·er·a·ble /kənsídərəbəl/ *adj.* **1** enough in amount or extent to need consideration. **2** much; a lot of (*considerable pain*). **3** notable (*considerable achievement*). □□ **con·sid·er·a·bly** *adv.*

con·sid·er·ate /kənsídərət/ *adj.* thoughtful toward other people; careful not to cause hurt or inconvenience. □□ **con·sid·er·ate·ly** *adv.*

con·sid·er·a·tion /kənsídəráyshən/ *n.* **1** the act of considering; careful thought. **2** being considerate. **3** a fact or a thing taken into account. **4** compensation; a payment or reward. **5** *Law* (in a contractual agreement) anything given or promised or forborne by one party in exchange for the promise or undertaking of another. □ **in consideration of** in return for; on account of. **take into consideration** include as a factor, reason, etc. **under consideration** being considered.

con·sid·er·ing /kənsídəring/ *prep., conj., & adv.* ● *prep. & conj.* in view of; taking into consideration. ● *adv. colloq.* taking everything into account (*not so bad, considering*).

con·sign /kənsín/ *v.tr.* (often foll. by *to*) **1** deliver to a person's possession or trust. **2** commit decisively or permanently (*consigned it to the trash can*). **3** transmit or send (goods). □□ **con·sign·ee** /kónsīnée/ *n.* **con·sign·ment** *n.* **con·sign·or** *n.*

con·sist /kənsíst/ *v.intr.* **1** (foll. by *of*) be composed; have specified ingredients or elements. **2** (foll. by *in, of*) have its essential features as specified (*its beauty consists in the use of color*). **3** (usu. foll. by *with*) harmonize; be consistent.

con·sist·en·cy /kənsístənsee/ *n.* (*pl.* **-ies**) (also **con·sist·ence**) **1** the degree of density, esp. of thick liquids. **2** conformity with other or earlier attitudes, practice, etc. **3** the state or quality of holding or sticking together and retaining shape.

con·sist·ent /kənsístənt/ *adj.* (usu. foll. by *with*) **1** compatible or in harmony. **2** (of a person) constant to the same principles. □□ **con·sist·ent·ly** *adv.*

con·sis·to·ry /kənsístəree/ *n.* (*pl.* **-ies**) **1** *RC Ch.* the council of cardinals (with or without the pope). **2** (in full **consistory court**) (in the Church of England) a court presided over by a bishop, for the administration of ecclesiastical law in a diocese. **3** (in other churches) a local administrative body. □□ **con·sis·to·ri·al** /kónsistáwreeəl/ *adj.*

con·so·la·tion /kónsəláyshən/ *n.* **1** the act or an instance of consoling; the state of being consoled. **2** a consoling thing, person, or circumstance. □□ **con·sol·a·to·ry** /kənsólətawree, -sól-/ *adj.*

con·so·la·tion prize *n.* a prize given to a competitor who just fails to win a main prize.

con·sole[1] /kənsól/ *v.tr.* comfort, esp. in grief or disappointment. ¶ Often confused with *condole*. □□ **con·sol·a·ble** *adj.* **con·sol·er** *n.* **con·sol·ing·ly** *adv.*

con·sole[2] /kónsól/ *n.* **1** a panel or unit accommodating switches, controls, etc. **2** a cabinet for television, etc. **3** *Mus.* a cabinet with the keyboards, stops, pedals, etc., of an organ. **4** a bracket supporting a shelf, etc.

con·sol·i·date /kənsólidayt/ *v.* **1** *tr. & intr.* make or become strong or solid. **2** *tr.* strengthen (one's position, etc.). **3** *tr.* combine (territories, companies, debts, etc.) into one whole. □□ **con·sol·i·da·tion** /-dáyshən/ *n.* **con·sol·i·da·tor** *n.* **con·sol·i·da·to·ry** *adj.*

con·sols /kónsolz/ *n.pl.* British government securities without redemption date and with fixed annual interest.

CONSTELLATION

Astronomers divide the entire sky into 88 interlocking constellations, each with its own set boundaries. Within those boundaries, a pattern of stars, joined by imaginary lines, is visualized as representing an object or a human, animal, or mythological figure. Although constellations may appear to be grouped in the sky as viewed from the Earth, generally speaking they are in fact at varying distances from the Earth.

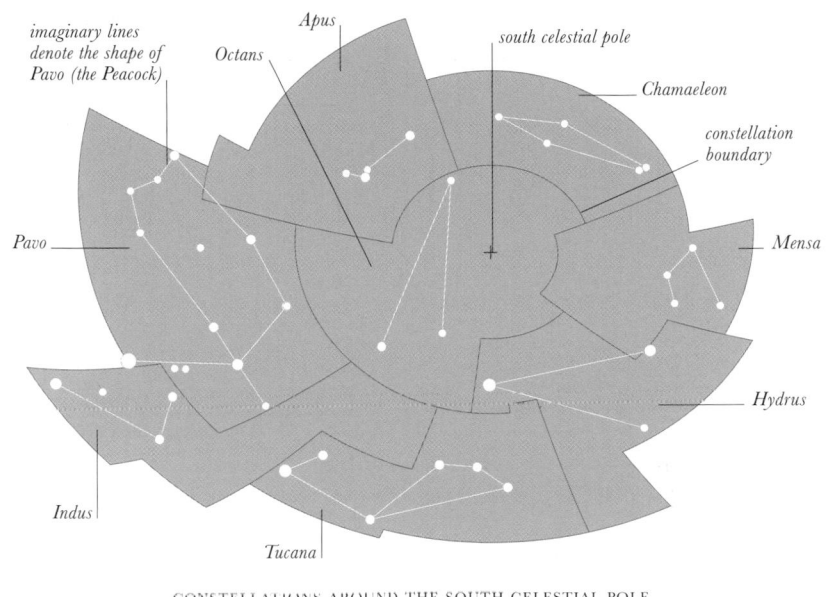

CONSTELLATIONS AROUND THE SOUTH CELESTIAL POLE

---

con·som·mé /kónsəmáy/ *n.* a clear soup made with meat stock.

con·so·nance /kónsənəns/ *n.* **1** agreement; harmony. **2** *Prosody* a recurrence of similar-sounding consonants. **3** *Mus.* a harmonious combination of notes; a harmonious interval.

con·so·nant /kónsənənt/ *n. & adj.* ● *n.* **1** a speech sound in which the breath is at least partly obstructed, and which to form a syllable must be combined with a vowel. **2** a letter or letters representing this. ● *adj.* (foll. by *with, to*) **1** consistent; in agreement or harmony. **2** similar in sound. **3** *Mus.* making a concord. □□ **con·so·nan·tal** /-nántʼl/ *adj.* **con·so·nant·ly** *adv.*

con·sort[1] *n. & v.* ● *n.* /kónsawrt/ **1** a wife or husband, esp. of royalty (*prince consort*). **2** a companion or associate. **3** a ship sailing with another. ● *v.* /kənsórt/ **1** *intr.* (usu. foll. by *with, together*) **a** keep company; associate. **b** harmonize. **2** *tr.* class or bring together.

con·sort[2] /kónsawrt/ *n. Mus.* a group of players or instruments, esp. playing early music (*recorder consort*).

con·sor·ti·um /kənsáwrsheeəm, -teeəm/ *n.* (*pl.* **consortia** /-sheeə, -teeə/ or **consortiums**) **1** an association, esp. of several business companies. **2** *Law* the right of association with a husband or wife (*loss of consortium*).

con·spe·cif·ic /kónspisifik/ *adj. Biol.* of the same species.

con·spec·tus /kənspéktəs/ *n.* **1** a general or comprehensive survey. **2** a summary or synopsis.

con·spic·u·ous /kənspíkyōōəs/ *adj.* **1** clearly visible; striking to the eye. **2** remarkable of its kind (*conspicuous extravagance*). □□ **con·spic·u·ous·ly** *adv.* **con·spic·u·ous·ness** *n.*

con·spir·a·cy /kənspírəsee/ *n.* (*pl.* **-ies**) **1** a secret plan to commit a crime or do harm; a plot. **2** the act of conspiring.

con·spir·a·cy of si·lence *n.* an agreement to say nothing.

con·spir·a·tor /kənspírətər/ *n.* a person who takes part in a conspiracy. □□ **con·spir·a·to·ri·al** /-táwreeəl/ *adj.* **con·spir·a·to·ri·al·ly** *adv.*

con·spire /kənspír/ *v.intr.* **1** combine secretly to plan and prepare an unlawful or harmful act. **2** (often foll. by *against*, or *to* + infin.) (of events or circumstances) seem to be working together, esp. disadvantageously.

con·sta·ble /kónstəbəl, kún-/ *n.* **1** esp. *Brit.* **a** a policeman or policewoman. **b** (also **police constable**) a police officer of the lowest rank. **2** the governor of a royal castle.

con·stab·u·lar·y /kənstábyələree/ *n. & adj.* ● *n.* **1** (*pl.* **-ies**) a police force. **2** armed police organized as a military unit. ● *attrib.adj.* of or concerning the police force.

con·stan·cy /kónstənsee/ *n.* **1** the quality of being unchanging and dependable; faithfulness. **2** firmness; endurance.

con·stant /kónstənt/ *adj. & n.* ● *adj.* **1** continuous (*constant attention*). **2** occurring frequently (*constant complaints*). **3** (often foll. by *to*) unchanging; faithful; dependable. ● *n.* **1** anything that does not vary. **2** *Math. & Physics* a quantity or number that remains the same. □□ **con·stant·ly** *adv.*

con·stel·la·tion /kónstəláyshən/ *n.* **1** ▲ a group of stars that form an imaginary pattern representing an object, animal, or person, as seen from the Earth. **2** ▲ one of the 88 areas into which the sky is divided by astronomers. **3** a group of associated persons, etc. □□ **con·stel·late** /kónstəlayt/ *v.tr.*

con·ster·nate /kónstərnayt/ *v.tr.* (usu. in *passive*) dismay; fill with anxiety.

con·ster·na·tion /kónstərnáyshən/ *n.* anxiety or dismay.

con·sti·pate /kónstipayt/ *v.tr.* (esp. as **constipated** *adj.*) affect with constipation.

con·sti·pa·tion /kónstipáyshən/ *n.* **1** difficulty in emptying the bowels. **2** a restricted state.

con·stit·u·en·cy /kənstíchōōənsee/ *n.* (*pl.* **-ies**) **1** a body of voters in a specified area who elect a representative member to a legislative body. **2** the area represented in this way. **3** a body of customers, supporters, etc.

con·stit·u·ent /kənstíchōōənt/ *adj. & n.* ● *adj.* **1** composing or helping to make up a whole. **2** able to make or change a (political, etc.) constitution (*constituent assembly*). **3** electing. ● *n.* **1** a member of a constituency. **2** a component part. **3** *Law* a person who appoints another as agent.

con·sti·tute /kónstitōōt, tyōōt/ *v.tr.* **1** be the components or essence of; make up; form. **2 a** be equivalent or tantamount to (*this constitutes a warning*). **b** formally establish (*constitute a precedent*). **3** give legal or constitutional form to.

con·sti·tu·tion /kónstitōóshən, -tyōō-/ *n.* **1** the act or method of constituting; composition. **2 a** the body of fundamental principles according to which a nation, state, or other organization is acknowledged to be governed. **b** (usu. written) record of this. **c** (**Constitution**) the US Constitution. **3** a person's physical state as regards health, strength, etc. **4** a person's psychological makeup.

con·sti·tu·tion·al /kónstitōóshənəl, -tyōō-/ *adj. & n.* ● *adj.* **1** of or consistent with a political constitution (*constitutional duties of office*). **2** inherent in the physical or mental constitution. ● *n.* a walk taken regularly to maintain or restore good health. □□ **con·sti·tu·tion·al·i·ty** /-nálitee/ *n.* **con·sti·tu·tion·al·ize** *v.tr.* **con·sti·tu·tion·al·ly** *adv.*

con·sti·tu·tive /kónstitōōtiv, -tyōō-/ *adj.* **1** able to form or appoint. **2** component. **3** essential. □□ **con·sti·tu·tive·ly** *adv.*

con·strain /kənstráyn/ *v.tr.* **1** compel. **2 a** confine forcibly; imprison. **b** restrict severely. **3** bring about by compulsion. **4** (as **constrained** *adj.*) forced; embarrassed (*a constrained manner*). □□ **con·strain·ed·ly** /-nidlee/ *adv.*

con·straint /kənstráynt/ *n.* **1** the act or result of constraining or being constrained; restriction of liberty. **2** something that constrains; a limitation on motion or action. **3** the restraint of natural feelings or their expression; a constrained manner.

con·strict /kənstríkt/ *v.tr.* **1** make narrow or tight; compress. **2** *Biol.* cause (organic tissue) to contract. □□ **con·stric·tion** /-strikshən/ *n.* **con·stric·tive** *adj.*

con·stric·tor /kənstríktər/ *n.* **1** any snake that kills by compressing. ▷ SNAKE. **2** *Anat.* any muscle that contracts an organ or part of the body.

con·struct *v. & n.* ● *v.tr.* /kənstrúkt/ **1** make by fitting parts together; build; form. **2** *Geom.* draw or delineate (*construct a triangle*). ● *n.* /kónstrukt/ **1** a thing constructed, esp. by the mind. **2** *Linguistics* a group of words forming a phrase. □□ **con·struc·tor** *n.*

con·struc·tion /kənstrúkshən/ *n.* **1** the act or a mode of constructing. **2** a thing constructed. **3** an interpretation or explanation. **4** *Gram.* an arrangement of words according to syntactical rules. □□ **con·struc·tion·al** *adj.* **con·struc·tion·al·ly** *adv.*

con·struc·tive /kənstrúktiv/ *adj.* **1 a** of construction; tending to construct. **b** tending to form a basis for ideas (*constructive criticism*). **2** helpful; positive (*a constructive approach*). **3** derived by inference (*constructive permission*). **4** belonging to the structure of a building. □□ **con·struc·tive·ly** *adv.* **con·struc·tive·ness** *n.*

con·strue /kənstrōō/ *v.tr.* (**construes, construed, construing**) **1** interpret. **2** (often foll. by *with*) combine (words) grammatically (*"rely" is construed with "on"*). **3** analyze the syntax of (a sentence). **4** translate word for word. □□ **con·stru·a·ble** *adj.* **construal** *n.*

con·sub·stan·tial /kónsəbstánshəl/ *adj. Theol.* of the same substance (esp. of the three persons of the Trinity). □□ **con·sub·stan·ti·al·i·ty** /-sheeálitee/ *n.*

con·sub·stan·ti·a·tion /kónsəbstánsheeáyshən/ *n. Theol.* the doctrine of the real substantial presence of the body and blood of Christ in and with the bread and wine in the Eucharist.

con·sul /kónsəl/ *n.* **1** an official appointed by a government to live in a foreign city and protect the

government's citizens and interests there. **2** *Roman Hist.* either of two annually elected chief magistrates in ancient Rome. □□ **con·su·lar** *adj.* **con·sul·ship** *n.*

con·su·late /kónsələt/ *n.* **1** the building officially used by a consul. **2** the office, position, or period of office of consul. **3** *Hist.* government by consuls. **4** *Hist.* the period of office of a consul.

con·sult /kənsúlt/ *v. & n.* **1** *tr.* seek information or advice from. **2** *intr.* (foll. by *with*) refer to a person for advice, etc. **3** *tr.* seek permission or approval from (a person) for a proposed action. **4** *tr.* take into account (feelings, interests, etc.). ● *n.* /kónsult/ = CONSULTATION 1, 2. □□ **con·sul·ta·tive** /-súltətiv/ *adj.*

con·sult·an·cy /kənsúltʼnsee/ *n.* (*pl.* **-ies**) the practice or position of a consultant.

con·sult·ant /kənsúltʼnt/ *n.* a person providing professional advice, etc., esp. for a fee.

con·sul·ta·tion /kónsəltáyshən/ *n.* **1** a meeting arranged to consult. **2** the act or an instance of consulting. **3** a conference.

con·sult·ing /kənsúlting/ *attrib. adj.* giving professional advice to others working in the same field or subject (*consulting physician*).

con·sum·a·ble /kənsōōməbəl/ *adj. & n.* ● *adj.* that can be consumed; intended for consumption. ● *n.* (usu. in *pl.*) a commodity that is eventually used up, worn out, or eaten.

con·sume /kənsōōm/ *v.tr.* **1** eat or drink. **2** completely destroy. **3** (often as **consumed** *adj.*) possess or entirely take up (foll. by *with*: *consumed with rage*). **4** use up. □□ **con·sum·ing·ly** *adv.*

con·sum·er /kənsōōmər/ *n.* **1** a person who consumes, esp. one who uses a product. **2** a purchaser of goods or services.

con·sum·er goods *n.pl.* goods put to use by consumers, not used in producing other goods.

con·sum·er·ism /kənsōōmərizəm/ *n.* the protection or promotion of consumers' interests in relation to the producer. □□ **con·sum·er·ist** *adj. & n.*

con·sum·mate *v. & adj.* ● *v.tr.* /kónsəmayt/ **1** complete; make perfect. **2** complete (a marriage) by sexual intercourse. ● *adj.* /kənsúmit, kónsəmit/ complete; perfect; fully skilled. □□ **con·sum·mate·ly** *adv.* **con·sum·ma·tor** *n.*

con·sum·ma·tion /kónsəmáyshən/ *n.* **1** completion, esp. of a marriage by sexual intercourse. **2** a desired end or goal; perfection.

con·sump·tion /kənsúmpshən/ *n.* **1** the act or an instance of consuming; the process of being consumed. **2** an amount consumed. **3** the purchase and use of goods, etc.

con·sump·tive /kənsúmptiv/ *adj. & n.* ● *adj.* **1** of or tending to consumption. **2** tending to or affected with pulmonary tuberculosis. ● *n.* a consumptive patient. □□ **con·sump·tive·ly** *adv.*

cont. *abbr.* **1** contents. **2** continued.

con·tact *n. & v.* ● *n.* /kóntakt/ **1** the state or condition of touching, meeting, or communicating. **2** a person who is or may be communicated with for information, assistance, etc. **3** *Electr.* **a** a connection for the passage of a current. ▷ ALTERNATING CURRENT, RHEOSTAT. **b** a device for providing this. **4** a person likely to carry a contagious disease through being associated with an infected person. **5** (usu. in *pl.*) *colloq.* a contact lens. ● *v.tr.* /kóntakt, kəntákt/ **1** get into communication with (a person). **2** begin correspondence or personal dealings with. □□ **con·tact·a·ble** *adj.*

con·tact lens *n.* a small lens placed on the eyeball to correct the vision.

con·tact sport *n.* a sport in which participants necessarily come into bodily contact with one another.

con·ta·gion /kəntáyjən/ *n.* **1 a** the communication of disease from one person to another by bodily contact. **b** a contagious disease. **2** a contagious or

harmful influence. **3** moral corruption, esp. when tending to be widespread.

con·ta·gious /kəntáyjəs/ *adj.* **1 a** (of a person) likely to transmit disease by contact. **b** (of a disease) transmitted in this way. **2** (of emotions, reactions, etc.) likely to affect others (*contagious enthusiasm*). □□ **con·ta·gious·ly** *adv.* **con·ta·gious·ness** *n.*

con·tain /kəntáyn/ *v.tr.* **1** hold or be capable of holding within itself; include; comprise. **2** (of measures) be equal to (*a gallon contains eight pints*). **3** prevent (an enemy, difficulty, etc.) from moving or extending. **4** control or restrain (feelings, etc.). **5** (of a number) be divisible by (a factor) without a remainder. □□ **con·tain·a·ble** *adj.*

con·tain·er /kəntáynər/ *n.* **1** a vessel, box, etc., for holding things. **2** a large boxlike receptacle for the transport of goods, esp. one readily transferable from one form of transport to another (also *attrib.*: *container cargo*).

container ship *n.* ▼ a ship designed to carry goods stored in containers.

bridge

containers stem

propeller

CONTAINER SHIP

con·tain·er·ize /kəntáynəriz/ *v.tr.* **1** pack in or transport by container. **2** adapt to transport by container. □□ **con·tain·er·i·za·tion** *n.*

con·tain·ment /kəntáynmənt/ *n.* the action or policy of preventing the expansion of a hostile country or influence.

con·tam·i·nate /kəntáminayt/ *v.tr.* **1** pollute, esp. with radioactivity. **2** infect; corrupt. □□ **con·tam·i·nant** /-minənt/ *n.* **con·tam·i·na·tion** /-náyshən/ *n.* **con·tam·i·na·tor** *n.*

con·temn /kəntém/ *v.tr. literary* despise; treat with disregard. □□ **con·temn·er** /-témər, -témnər/ *n.*

con·tem·plate /kóntəmplayt/ *v.* **1** *tr.* survey with the eyes or in the mind. **2** *tr.* regard (an event) as possible. **3** *tr.* intend (*we contemplate leaving tomorrow*). **4** *intr.* meditate. □□ **con·tem·pla·tion** /-pláyshən/ *n.* **con·tem·pla·tor** *n.*

con·tem·pla·tive /kəntémplətiv, kóntəmpláy-/ *adj. & n.* ● *adj.* of or given to (esp. religious) contemplation; meditative. ● *n.* a person devoted to religious contemplation. □□ **con·tem·pla·tive·ly** *adv.*

con·tem·po·ra·ne·ous /kəntémpəráyneeəs/ *adj.* (usu. foll. by *with*) **1** existing or occurring at the same time. **2** of the same period. □□ **con·tem·po·ra·ne·i·ty** /-pəranáyitee, -neé-/ *n.* **con·tem·po·ra·ne·ous·ly** *adv.* **con·tem·po·ra·ne·ous·ness** *n.*

con·tem·po·rar·y /kəntémpəreree/ *adj. & n.* ● *adj.* **1** living or occurring at the same time. **2** approximately equal in age. **3** following modern ideas or fashion in style or design. ● *n.* (*pl.* **-ies**) **1** a person or thing living or existing at the same time as another. **2** a person of roughly the same age as another. □□ **con·tem·po·rar·i·ly** /-rérilee/ *adv.* **con·tem·po·rar·i·ness** *n.*

con·tempt /kəntémpt/ *n.* **1** a feeling that a person or a thing is beneath consideration or worthless, or deserving scorn or extreme reproach. **2** the condition of being held in contempt. **3** (in full **contempt of court**) disobedience to or disrespect for a court of law and its officers. □ **beneath contempt** utterly despicable. **hold in contempt** despise.

con·tempt·i·ble /kəntémptibəl/ *adj.* deserving contempt; despicable. □□ **con·tempt·i·bil·i·ty** /-bilitee/ *n.* **con·tempt·i·bly** *adv.*

con·temp·tu·ous /kəntémpchōōəs/ *adj.* (often foll. by *of*) showing contempt; scornful. □□ **con·temp·tu·ous·ly** *adv.* **con·temp·tu·ous·ness** *n.*

con·tend /kənténd/ *v.* **1** *intr.* (usu. foll. by *with*)

CONTINENT

The land masses of the Earth are divisible into seven main areas of land, known as continents. The continents are constantly moving over the Earth's surface as the lithospheric plates in which they are embedded move over the more liquid asthenosphere. This movement is thought to be driven by thermal convection in the Earth's mantle.

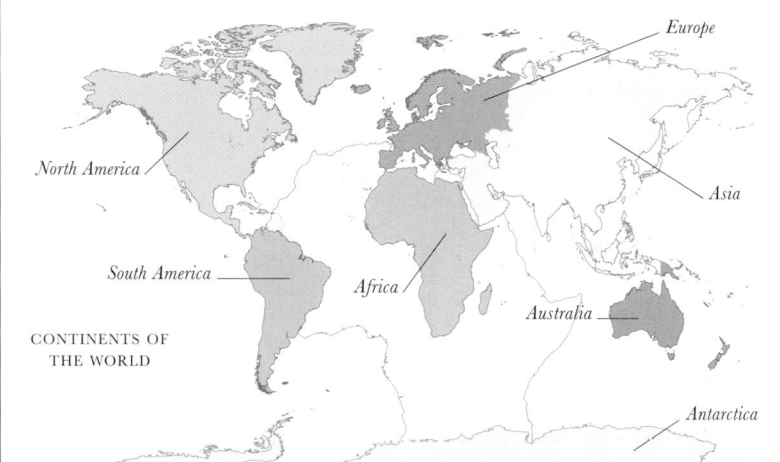

North America

Europe

Asia

South America

Africa

Australia

CONTINENTS OF THE WORLD

Antarctica

strive; fight. **2** *intr.* compete. **3** *tr.* (usu. foll. by *that* + clause) maintain. □□ **con·tend·er** *n.*

con·tent¹ /kəntént/ *adj., v., & n.* ● *predic.adj.* **1** satisfied; adequately happy. **2** (foll. by *to* + infin.) willing. ● *v.tr.* make content; satisfy. ● *n.* a contented state; satisfaction. □ **to one's heart's content** to the full extent of one's desires. □□ **con·tent·ment** *n.*

con·tent² /kóntent/ *n.* **1** (usu. in *pl.*) what is contained in something. **2** the amount of a constituent contained (*low sodium content*). **3** the substance dealt with (in a speech, etc.) as distinct from its form. **4** the capacity or volume of a thing.

con·tent·ed /kənténtid/ *adj.* (often foll. by *with*, or *to* + infin.) **1** happy, satisfied. **2** (foll. by *with*) willing to be content. □□ **con·tent·ed·ly** *adv.* **con·tent·ed·ness** *n.*

con·ten·tion /kənténshən/ *n.* **1** a dispute or argument; rivalry. **2** a point contended for in an argument (*it is my contention that you are wrong*). □□ **in contention** competing, esp. with a good chance of success.

con·ten·tious /kənténshəs/ *adj.* **1** argumentative; quarrelsome. **2** likely to cause an argument; disputed; controversial. □□ **con·ten·tious·ly** *adv.* **con·ten·tious·ness** *n.*

con·ter·mi·nous /kəntə́rminəs/ *adj.* (often foll. by *with*) **1** having a common boundary. **2** coextensive; coterminous. □□ **con·ter·mi·nous·ly** *adv.*

con·test *n. & v.* ● *n.* /kóntest/ **1** a competition. **2** a dispute; a controversy. ● *v.tr.* /kəntést, kóntest/ **1** challenge or dispute (a decision, etc.). **2** debate (a point, statement, etc.). **3** compete for (a prize, parliamentary seat, etc.); compete in (an election). □□ **con·test·a·ble** /kəntéstəbl/ *adj.* **con·test·er** /kəntéstər/ *n.*

con·test·ant /kəntéstənt/ *n.* a person who takes part in a contest or competition.

con·text /kóntekst/ *n.* **1** parts that immediately precede and follow a word or passage and clarify its meaning. **2** the circumstances relevant to something under consideration. □ **out of context** without the surrounding words or circumstances. □□ **con·tex·tu·al** /kəntéks-chooəl/ *adj.*

con·tex·tu·al·ize /kəntéks-chooəlīz/ *v.tr.* place in a context; study in context. □□ **con·tex·tu·al·i·za·tion** *n.* **con·tex·tu·al·ly** *adv.*

con·tig·u·ous /kəntígyooəs/ *adj.* (usu. foll. by *with*, *to*) touching, esp. along a line; in contact. □□ **con·ti·gu·i·ty** /kóntigyóoitee/ *n.* **con·tig·u·ous·ly** *adv.*

con·ti·nent¹ /kóntinənt/ *n.* **1** ▲ any of the main continuous expanses of land (Europe, Asia, Africa, N. and S. America, Australia, Antarctica). **2** continuous land; a mainland.

con·ti·nent² /kóntinənt/ *adj.* **1** able to control movements of the bowels and bladder. **2** exercising self-restraint, esp. sexually. □□ **con·ti·nence** /-nəns/ *n.* **con·ti·nent·ly** *adv.*

con·ti·nen·tal /kóntinéntl/ *adj. & n.* ● *adj.* of or characteristic of a continent. ● *n.* an inhabitant of mainland Europe. □□ **con·ti·nen·tal·ly** *adv.*

con·ti·nen·tal break·fast *n.* a light breakfast of coffee, rolls, etc.

con·ti·nen·tal drift *n. Geol.* the hypothesis that the continents are moving slowly over the surface of the Earth. ▷ PLATE TECTONICS

con·ti·nen·tal shelf *n.* ◀ an area of shallow seabed between the shore of a continent and the deeper ocean. ▷ SEABED

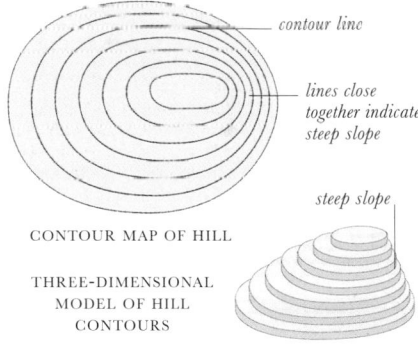

ocean

continental land mass

continental shelf

CONTINENTAL SHELF OFF SOUTH AMERICA

con·tin·gen·cy /kəntínjənsee/ *n.* (*pl.* **-ies**) **1** a future event or circumstance regarded as likely to occur, or as influencing present action. **2** something that is dependent on another uncertain event or occurrence. **3** uncertainty of occurrence. **4 a** one thing incident to another. **b** an incidental or unanticipated expense, etc.

con·tin·gent /kəntínjənt/ *adj. & n.* ● *adj.* **1** (usu. foll. by *on*, *upon*) dependent (on an uncertain event or circumstance). **2** associated. **3** (usu. foll. by *to*) incidental. **4 a** that may or may not occur. **b** fortuitous. **5** true only under existing or specified conditions. ● *n.* a body forming part of a larger group. □□ **con·tin·gent·ly** *adv.*

con·tin·u·al /kəntínyooəl/ *adj.* constantly or frequently recurring; always happening. □□ **con·tin·u·al·ly** *adv.*

con·tin·u·ance /kəntínyooəns/ *n.* **1** a state of continuing in existence or operation. **2** the duration of an event or action. **3** *Law* a postponement or adjournment.

con·tin·u·a·tion /kəntínyoo-áyshən/ *n.* **1** the act or an instance of continuing; the process of being continued. **2** a part that continues something else.

con·tin·ue /kəntínyoo/ *v.* (**continues, continued, continuing**) **1** *tr.* (often foll. by verbal noun, or *to* + infin.) maintain, not stop (an action, etc.). **2 a** *tr.* (also *absol.*) resume or prolong (a narrative, journey, etc.). **b** *intr.* recommence after a pause. **3** *tr.* be a sequel to. **4** *intr.* remain in existence or in a specified state (*the weather continued fine*). **5** *tr. Law* postpone or adjourn (proceedings). □□ **con·tin·u·a·ble** *adj.* **con·tin·u·er** *n.*

con·ti·nu·i·ty /kóntinóoitee, -nyóo-/ *n.* (*pl.* **-ies**) **1 a** the state of being continuous. **b** an unbroken succession. **c** a logical sequence. **2** the detailed scenario of a film or broadcast. **3** the linking of broadcast items.

con·tin·u·o /kəntínyoo-ō/ *n.* (*pl.* **-os**) *Mus.* an accompaniment providing a bass line, usu. played on a keyboard instrument.

con·tin·u·ous /kəntínyooəs/ *adj.* **1** unbroken; uninterrupted; connected throughout in space or time. **2** *Gram.* = PROGRESSIVE *adj.* 7. □□ **con·tin·u·ous·ly** *adv.* **con·tin·u·ous·ness** *n.*

con·tin·u·um /kəntínyooəm/ *n.* (*pl.* **continua** /-yooə/ or **continuums**) anything seen as having a continuous, not discrete, structure (*space-time continuum*).

con·tort /kəntáwrt/ *v.tr.* twist or force out of normal shape. □□ **con·tor·tion** /kəntáwrshən/ *n.*

con·tor·tion·ist /kəntáwrshənist/ *n.* an entertainer who adopts contorted postures.

con·tour /kóntoor/ *n. & v.* ● *n.* **1** an outline, esp. representing or bounding the shape or form of something. **2** the outline of a natural feature, e.g., a coast or mountain mass. **3** a line separating differently colored parts of a design. ● *v.tr.* **1** mark with contour lines. **2** carry (a road or railroad) around the side of a hill.

con·tour line *n.* a line on a map joining points of equal altitude. ▷ MAP

con·tour map *n.* ▼ a map marked with contour lines.

contour line

lines close together indicate steep slope

CONTOUR MAP OF HILL

steep slope

THREE-DIMENSIONAL MODEL OF HILL CONTOURS

CONTOUR MAP

con·tour plow·ing *n.* plowing along lines of constant altitude to minimize soil erosion.

contra- /kóntrə/ *comb. form* **1** against; opposite (*contradict*). **2** *Mus.* (of instruments, organ stops, etc.) pitched an octave below (*contrabassoon*).

con·tra·band /kóntrəband/ *n. & adj.* ● *n.* **1** goods that have been smuggled, or imported or exported illegally. **2** prohibited trade; smuggling. **3** (in full **contraband of war**) goods forbidden to be supplied by neutrals to belligerents. ● *adj.* **1** forbidden to be imported or exported (at all or without payment of duty). **2** concerning traffic in contraband (*contraband trade*). □□ **con·tra·band·ist** *n.*

con·tra·bass /kóntrəbays/ *n. Mus.* = DOUBLE BASS.

con·tra·cep·tion /kóntrəsépshən/ *n.* the intentional prevention of pregnancy; the use of contraceptives.

con·tra·cep·tive /kóntrəséptiv/ *adj. & n.* ● *adj.* preventing pregnancy. ● *n.* a contraceptive device or drug.

C

C

con·tract *n. & v.* ● *n.* /kóntrakt/ **1** a written or spoken agreement esp. one enforceable by law. **2** a document recording this. **3** marriage regarded as a binding commitment. **4** *Bridge*, etc., an undertaking to win the number of tricks bid. ● *v.* /kəntrákt, kóntrakt/ **1** *tr. & intr.* make or become smaller. **2 a** *intr.* (usu. foll. by *with*) make a contract. **b** *intr.* (usu. foll. by *for*, or *to* + infin.) enter formally into a business or legal arrangement. **c** *tr.* (often foll. by *out*) arrange (work) to be done by contract. **3** *tr.* catch or develop (a disease). **4** *tr.* form or develop (a friendship, habit, etc.). **5** *tr.* enter into (marriage). **6** *tr.* incur (a debt, etc.). **7** *tr.* shorten (a word) by combination or elision. **8** *tr.* draw (one's muscles, brow, etc.) together. □□ **con·trac·tive** /kəntráktiv/ *adj.*

con·tract·a·ble /kəntráktəbəl/ *adj.* (of a disease) that can be contracted.

con·tract bridge *n.* a form of bridge, in which only tricks bid and won count toward the game.

con·tract·i·ble /kəntráktibəl/ *adj.* that can be shrunk or drawn together.

con·trac·tile /kəntrákt'l, tīl/ *adj.* capable of or producing contraction. □□ **con·trac·til·i·ty** /kóntraktílitee/ *n.*

con·trac·tion /kəntrákshən/ *n.* **1** the act of contracting. **2** *Med.* (usu. in *pl.*) shortening of the uterine muscles during childbirth. **3** shrinking; diminution. **4 a** a shortening of a word by combination or elision. **b** a contracted word or group of words.

con·trac·tor /kóntraktər, kəntrák-/ *n.* a person who undertakes a contract, esp. to conduct building operations, etc.

con·trac·tu·al /kəntrákchooəl/ *adj.* of or in the nature of a contract. □□ **con·trac·tu·al·ly** *adv.*

con·tra·dict /kóntrədikt/ *v.tr.* **1** deny (a statement). **2** express the opposite of a statement made by (a person). **3** be in opposition to or in conflict with. □□ **con·tra·dic·tion** /kóntrədíkshən/ *n.* **con·tra·dic·tor** *n.*

con·tra·dic·to·ry /kóntrədíktəree/ *adj.* **1** expressing a denial or opposite statement. **2** (of statements, etc.) mutually opposed or inconsistent. **3** (of a person) inclined to contradict. **4** *Logic* (of two propositions) so related that one and only one must be true. □□ **con·tra·dic·to·ri·ly** *adv.*

con·tra·dis·tinc·tion /kóntrədistíngkshən/ *n.* a distinction made by contrasting.

con·trail /kóntráyl/ *n.* a condensation trail, esp. from an aircraft.

con·tra·in·di·cate /kóntrəíndikayt/ *v.tr. Med.* act as an indication against (the use of a particular substance or treatment). □□ **con·tra·in·di·ca·tion** /-káyshən/ *n.*

con·tral·to /kəntráltō/ *n.* (*pl.* **-os**) **1 a** the lowest female singing voice. **b** a singer with this voice. **2** a part written for contralto.

con·trap·tion /kəntrápshən/ *n.* often *derog.* or *joc.* a machine or device, esp. a strange or cumbersome one.

con·tra·pun·tal /kóntrəpúnt'l/ *adj. Mus.* of or in counterpoint. □□ **con·tra·pun·tal·ly** *adv.* **con·tra·pun·tist** *n.*

con·trar·i·wise /kəntráireewīz/ *adv.* **1** on the other hand. **2** in the opposite way. **3** perversely.

con·trar·y /kóntreree/ *adj., n., & adv.* ● *adj.* **1** (usu. foll. by *to*) opposed in nature or tendency. **2** /kəntráiree/ *colloq.* perverse; self-willed. **3** (of a wind) unfavorable. **4** mutually opposed. **5** opposite in position or direction. ● *n.* (*pl.* **-ies**) (prec. by *the*) the opposite. ● *adv.* (foll. by *to*) in opposition or contrast (*contrary to expectations it rained*). □ **on the contrary** intensifying a denial of what has just been implied or stated. **to the contrary** to the opposite effect. □□ **con·trar·i·ly** /-trérilee/ *adv.* **con·trar·i·ness** /-tréreenis/ *n.*

con·trast *n. & v.* ● *n.* /kóntrast/ **1 a** a juxtaposition or comparison showing striking differences. **b** a difference so revealed. **2** (often foll. by *to*) a thing or person having qualities noticeably different from

another. **3 a** ▼ the degree of difference between tones in a television picture or a photograph. **b** the change of apparent brightness or color of an object caused by the juxtaposition of other objects. ● *v.* /kəntrást, kóntrast/ (often foll. by *with*) **1** *tr.* distinguish or set together so as to reveal a contrast. **2** *intr.* have or show a contrast. □□ **con·trast·ing·ly** /-trást-/ *adv.* **con·tras·tive** /-trástiv/ *adj.*

HIGH CONTRAST

darker areas under umbrella

diffused even light

LOW CONTRAST

CONTRAST IN TONES EXHIBITED BY TWO PHOTOGRAPHS

con·trast·y /kontrástee, kón-/ *adj.* (of photographic prints, etc.) showing a high degree of contrast.

con·tra·vene /kóntrəvéen/ *v.tr.* **1** infringe (a law or code of conduct). **2** (of things) conflict with. □□ **con·tra·ven·er** *n.*

con·tra·ven·tion /kóntrəvénshən/ *n.* **1** infringement. **2** an instance of this. □ **in contravention of** violating (a law, etc.).

con·tre·temps /kóntrətón/ *n.* **1** an awkward or unfortunate occurrence. **2** an unexpected mishap.

con·trib·ute /kəntríbyōot/ *v.* (often foll. by *to*) **1** *tr.* give (money, an idea, help, etc.) toward a common purpose. **2** *intr.* help to bring about a result, etc. **3** *tr.* (also *absol.*) supply (an article, etc.) for publication with others in a journal, etc. □□ **con·trib·u·tive** *adj.* **con·trib·u·tor** /kəntríbyətər/ *n.*

con·tri·bu·tion /kóntribyōoshən/ *n.* **1** the act of contributing. **2** something contributed. **3** an article, etc., contributed to a publication.

con·trib·u·to·ry /kəntríbyətawree/ *adj.* **1** that contributes. **2** operated by means of contributions.

con·trib·u·to·ry neg·li·gence *n. Law* negligence on the part of the injured party through failure to take precautions against an accident.

con·trite /kəntrít, kóntrīt/ *adj.* **1** completely penitent. **2** feeling guilt. **3** (of an action) showing a contrite spirit. □□ **con·trite·ly** *adv.* **con·trite·ness** *n.* **con·tri·tion** /kəntríshən/ *n.*

con·triv·ance /kəntrívəns/ *n.* **1** something contrived, esp. a mechanical device or a plan. **2** an act of contriving, esp. deceitfully. **3** inventive capacity.

con·trive /kəntrív/ *v.tr.* **1** devise. **2** (often foll. by *to* + infin.) manage. □□ **con·triv·a·ble** *adj.* **con·triv·er** *n.*

con·trived /kəntrívd/ *adj.* planned so carefully as to seem unnatural; forced.

con·trol /kəntról/ *n. & v.* ● *n.* **1** command (*under the control of*). **2** the power of restraining, esp. self-restraint. **3** a means of restraint. **4** (usu. in *pl.*) a means of regulating prices, etc. **5** (usu. in *pl.*) switches and other devices by which a machine is controlled (also *attrib.*: *control panel*). **6 a** a place where something is controlled or verified. **b** a person or group that controls something. **7** (also *attrib.*: *control group*) a standard of comparison for checking the results of a survey or experiment. ● *v.tr.* (**controlled, controlling**) **1** have control or command of. **2** regulate. **3** restrain (*told him to control himself*). **4** serve as control to. **5** check; verify. □ **in control** (often foll. by *of*) directing an activity. **out**

of **control** no longer subject to containment, restraint, or guidance. **under control** being controlled. □□ **con·trol·la·bil·i·ty** *n.* **con·trol·la·ble** *adj.* **con·trol·la·bly** *adv.*

con·trol·ler /kəntrólər/ *n.* **1** a person or thing that controls. **2** a person in charge of expenditure. □□ **con·trol·ler·ship** *n.*

con·trol·ling in·ter·est *n.* a means of determining the policy of a business, etc., esp. by ownership of a majority of the stock.

con·trol tow·er *n.* ▼ a tall building at an airport, etc., from which air traffic is controlled.

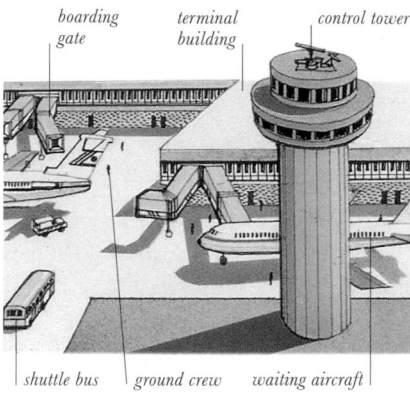

boarding gate   *terminal building*   *control tower*

shuttle bus   *ground crew*   *waiting aircraft*

CONTROL TOWER

con·tro·ver·sial /kóntrəvór shəl/ *adj.* **1** causing or subject to controversy. **2** of controversy. **3** given to controversy. □□ **con·tro·ver·sial·ism** *n.* **con·tro·ver·sial·ist** *n.* **con·tro·ver·sial·ly** *adv.*

con·tro·ver·sy /kóntrəvərsee/ *n.* (*pl.* **-ies**) a prolonged argument or dispute, esp. when conducted publicly.

con·tro·vert /kóntrəvərt/ *v.tr.* **1** dispute; deny. **2** argue about; discuss. □□ **con·tro·vert·i·ble** *adj.*

con·tu·ma·cious /kóntōōmáyshəs, -tyōō-/ *adj.* stubbornly or willfully disobedient. □□ **con·tu·ma·cious·ly** *adv.* **con·tu·ma·cy** /kóntōōməsee, -tyōō-/ *n.*

con·tu·me·li·ous /kóntōōmeéleeəs, -tyōō-/ *adj.* reproachful, insulting, or insolent. □□ **con·tu·me·li·ous·ly** *adv.*

con·tu·me·ly /kóntōōmələee, -tōomlee, -tōō, -tyōō/ *n.* **1** insolent or reproachful language or treatment. **2** disgrace.

con·tuse /kəntōóz, -tyōóz/ *v.tr.* bruise. □□ **con·tu·sion** /-zhən/ *n.*

co·nun·drum /kənúndrəm/ *n.* **1** a riddle, esp. one with a pun in its answer. **2** a puzzling question.

con·ur·ba·tion /kónərbáyshən/ *n.* an extended urban area, esp. one consisting of several towns and merging suburbs.

con·ure /kónyər/ *n.* ▼ any medium-sized parrot of the *Aratinga, Pyrrhura,* and related genera with mainly green plumage and a long gradated tail.

con·va·lesce /kónvəlés/ *v.intr.* recover one's health after illness.

con·va·les·cent /kónvəlésənt/ *adj. & n.* ● *adj.* **1** recovering from an illness. **2** of or for persons in convalescence. ● *n.* a convalescent person. □□ **con·va·les·cence** /-səns/ *n.*

CONURE: SUN CONURE (*Aratinga solstitialis*)

con·vec·tion /kənvékshən/ *n.* **1** transference of heat by upward movement of the heated and less dense medium. **2** *Meteorol.* the transfer of heat by the upward flow of hot air or downward flow of cold air. □□ **con·vec·tion·al** *adj.* **con·vec·tive** *adj.*

con·vec·tor /kənvéktər/ *n.* a heating appliance that circulates warm air by convection.

con·vene /kənvéen/ *v.* **1** *tr.* summon or arrange. **2** *intr.* assemble. **3** *tr.* summon (a person) before a tribunal. □□ **con·ven·a·ble** *adj.* **con·ven·er** *n.* **con·ve·nor** *n.*

con·ven·ience /kənvéenyəns/ *n. & v.* ● *n.* **1** the quality of being convenient; suitability. **2** *material* advantage (*for convenience*). **3** an advantage (*a great convenience*). **4** a useful thing. ● *v.* afford convenience to; suit; accommodate. □ **at one's convenience** at a time or place that suits one. **at one's earliest convenience** as soon as one can. **make a convenience of** take advantage of (a person) insensitively.

con·ven·ience store *n.* a store that stocks basic groceries, etc., usu. having extended opening hours.

con·ven·ient /kənvéenyənt/ *adj.* **1** (often foll. by *for, to*) **a** serving one's comfort or interests. **b** suitable. **c** free of trouble or difficulty. **2** available or occurring at a suitable time or place (*a convenient moment*). **3** well situated for some purpose. □□ **con·ven·ient·ly** *adv.*

con·vent /kónvent, -vənt/ *n.* **1** a religious community, esp. of nuns, under vows. **2** the premises occupied by this. **3** (in full **convent school**) a school attached to and run by a convent.

con·ven·tion /kənvénshən/ *n.* **1 a** general agreement, esp. agreement on social behavior, etc., by implicit consent of the majority. **b** a custom or customary practice. **2 a** a formal assembly for a common purpose. **b** an assembly of the delegates of a political party to select candidates for office. **3 a** a formal agreement. **b** an agreement between nations, esp. one less formal than a treaty. **4** *Cards* an accepted method of play (in leading, bidding, etc.) used to convey information to a partner. **5** the act of convening.

con·ven·tion·al /kənvénshənəl/ *adj.* **1** depending on or according to convention. **2** (of a person) attentive to social conventions. **3** usual. **4** not spontaneous nor sincere nor original. **5** (of weapons or power) nonnuclear. **6** *Art* following tradition rather than nature. □□ **con·ven·tion·al·ism** *n.* **con·ven·tion·al·ist** *n.* **con·ven·tion·al·i·ty** /-shənálitee/ *n.* (*pl.* **-ies**). **con·ven·tion·al·ize** *v.tr.* **con·ven·tion·al·ly** *adv.*

con·ven·tion·eer /kənvénshəneér/ *n.* a person attending a convention.

con·verge /kənvórj/ *v.intr.* **1** come together as if to meet or join. **2** (of lines) tend to meet at a point. **3** (foll. by *on, upon*) approach from different directions. **4** *Math.* (of a series) approximate in the sum of its terms toward a definite limit. □□ **con·ver·gence** /-jəns/ *n.* **con·ver·gen·cy** *n.* **con·ver·gent** /-jənt/ *adj.*

con·ver·sant /kənvórsənt, kónvərs-/ *adj.* (foll. by *with*) well experienced or acquainted with a subject or person, etc. □□ **con·ver·sance** /-vórsəns/ *n.* **con·ver·san·cy** *n.*

con·ver·sa·tion /kónvərsáyshən/ *n.* **1** the informal exchange of ideas by spoken words. **2** an instance of this.

con·ver·sa·tion·al /kónvərsáyshənəl/ *adj.* **1** of or in conversation. **2** fond of or good at conversation. **3** colloquial. □□ **con·ver·sa·tion·al·ly** *adv.*

con·ver·sa·tion·al·ist /kónvərsáyshənəlist/ *n.* one who is good at or fond of conversing.

con·verse[1] *v.intr.* /kənvórs/ (often foll. by *with*) engage in conversation. □□ **con·vers·er** /kənvórsər/ *n.*

con·verse[2] *adj. & n.* ● *adj.* /kənvórs, kónvərs/ opposite; contrary; reversed. ● *n.* /kónvərs/ **1** something that is opposite or contrary. **2** a statement formed from another statement by the transposition of certain words, e.g., *some philosophers are men* from *some men are philosophers*. **3** *Math.* a theorem whose

---

hypothesis and conclusion are the conclusion and hypothesis of another. □□ **con·verse·ly** *adv.*

con·ver·sion /kənvórzhən, -shən/ *n.* **1** the act or an instance of converting or the process of being converted, esp. in belief or religion. **2 a** an adaptation of a building for new purposes. **b** a converted building. **3** transposition; inversion. **4** *Theol.* the turning of sinners to God. **5** the transformation of fertile into fissile material in a nuclear reactor. **6** *Football* the scoring of an extra point or points after scoring a touchdown. **7** *Psychol.* the change of an unconscious conflict into a physical disorder or disease.

con·vert *v. & n.* ● *v.* /kənvórt/ **1** *tr.* (usu. foll. by *into*) change in form, character, or function. **2** *tr.* cause (a person) to change beliefs, etc. **3** *tr.* change (money, etc.) into others of a different kind. **4** *tr.* make structural alterations in (a building) to serve a new purpose. **5** *tr.* (also *absol.*) *Football* score an extra point or points after a touchdown. **6** *intr.* be converted or convertible (*the sofa converts into a bed*). **7** *tr.* *Logic* interchange the terms of (a proposition). ● *n.* /kónvərt/ (often foll. by *to*) a person who has been converted to a different belief, opinion, etc. □ **convert to one's own use** wrongfully make use of (another's property).

con·vert·er /kənvórtər/ *n.* (also **con·ver·tor**) **1** a person or thing that converts. **2** *Electr.* **a** an electrical apparatus for the interconversion of alternating current and direct current. **b** *Electronics* an apparatus for converting a signal from one frequency to another. **3** a reaction vessel used in making steel.

con·vert·i·ble /kənvórtibəl/ *adj. & n.* ● *adj.* **1** that may be converted. **2** (of currency, etc.) that may be converted into other forms, esp. into gold or US dollars. **3** (of a car) having a folding or detachable roof. **4** (of terms) synonymous. ● *n.* ▼ a car with a folding or detachable top. □□ **con·vert·i·bil·i·ty** *n.* **con·vert·i·bly** *adv.*

convertible top frame

fixed windshield

steel top cover

trunk lid

CONVERTIBLE:
CADILLAC ELDORADO, 1954

con·vex /kónveks, kənvéks/ *adj.* having an outline or surface curved like the exterior of a circle or sphere (cf. CONCAVE). □□ **con·vex·i·ty** /-véksitee/ *n.* **con·vex·ly** *adv.*

con·vey /kənváy/ *v.tr.* **1** transport or carry (goods, passengers, etc.). **2** communicate (an idea, meaning, etc.). **3** *Law* transfer the title to (property). **4** transmit (sound, smell, etc.). □□ **con·vey·a·ble** *adj.*

con·vey·ance /kənváyəns/ *n.* **1 a** the act or process of carrying. **b** the communication (of ideas, etc.). **c** transmission. **2** a means of transport; a vehicle. **3** *Law* **a** the transfer of property from one owner to another. **b** a document effecting this. □□ **con·vey·anc·er** *n.* (in sense 3). **con·vey·anc·ing** *n.* (in sense 3).

con·vey·or /kənváyər/ *n.* (also **con·vey·er**) a person or thing that conveys.

con·vey·or belt *n.* an endless moving belt for conveying articles or materials, esp. in a factory.

con·vict *v. & n.* ● *v.tr.* /kənvíkt/ **1** (often foll. by *of*) prove to be guilty (of a crime, etc.). **2** declare guilty by the verdict of a jury or the decision of a judge. ● *n.* /kónvikt/ **1** a person found guilty of a criminal offense. **2** a person serving a prison sentence.

con·vic·tion /kənvíkshən/ *n.* **1 a** the act or process of proving or finding guilty. **b** an instance of this

---

(*has two previous convictions*). **2 a** the action or resulting state of being convinced. **b** a firm belief or opinion. **c** an act of convincing.

con·vince /kənvíns/ *v.tr.* **1** (often foll. by *of*, or *that* + clause) persuade (a person) to believe or realize. **2** (as **convinced** *adj.*) firmly persuaded (*a convinced pacifist*). □□ **con·vinc·er** *n.* **con·vin·ci·ble** *adj.*

con·vinc·ing /kənvínsing/ *adj.* **1** able to or such as to convince. **2** substantial (*a convincing victory*). □□ **con·vinc·ing·ly** *adv.*

con·viv·i·al /kənvíveeəl/ *adj.* **1** sociable and lively. **2** festive (*a convivial atmosphere*). □□ **con·viv·i·al·i·ty** /-veeálitee/ *n.* **con·viv·i·al·ly** *adv.*

con·vo·ca·tion /kónvəkáyshən/ *n.* **1** the act of calling together. **2** a large formal gathering of people, esp. a formal ceremony at a university, as for giving awards. □□ **con·vo·ca·tion·al** *adj.*

con·voke /kənvók/ *v.tr. formal* call (people) together; summon to assemble.

con·vo·lut·ed /kónvəlóotid/ *adj.* **1** coiled; twisted. **2** complex; intricate. □□ **con·vo·lut·ed·ly** *adv.*

con·vo·lu·tion /kónvəlóoshən/ *n.* **1** coiling; twisting. **2** a coil or twist. **3** complexity. **4** a sinuous fold in the surface of the brain. ▷ BRAIN. □□ **con·vo·lu·tion·al** *adj.*

con·vol·vu·lus /kənvólvyələs/ *n.* ► any twining plant of the genus *Convolvulus*, with trumpet-shaped flowers, e.g., bindweed.

con·voy /kónvoy/ *n. & v.* ● *n.* **1** a group of ships traveling together or under escort. **2** a supply of provisions, etc., under escort. **3** a group of vehicles traveling on land together or under escort. **4** the act of traveling or moving in a group or under escort. ● *v.tr.* **1** (of a warship) escort (a merchant or passenger vessel). **2** escort, esp. with armed force.

CONVOLVULUS
(*Convolvulus arvensis*)

con·vul·sant /kənvúlsənt/ *adj. & n.* *Pharm.* ● *adj.* producing convulsions. ● *n.* a drug that may produce convulsions.

con·vulse /kənvúls/ *v.tr.* **1** (usu. in *passive*) affect with convulsions. **2** cause to laugh uncontrollably. **3** shake violently; agitate; disturb. □□ **con·vul·sive** *adj.* **con·vul·sive·ly** *adv.*

con·vul·sion /kənvúlshən/ *n.* **1** (usu. in *pl.*) violent irregular motion of a limb or limbs or the body caused by involuntary contraction of muscles, esp. as a disorder of infants. **2** a violent disturbance, esp. an earthquake. **3** violent social or political agitation. **4** (in *pl.*) uncontrollable laughter. □□ **con·vul·sion·ar·y** *adj.*

co·ny var. of CONEY.

coo /koo/ *n. & v.* ● *n.* a soft murmuring sound like that of a dove or pigeon. ● *v.* (**coos**, **cooed**) **1** *intr.* make the sound of a coo. **2** *intr. & tr.* talk or say in a soft or amorous voice. □□ **coo·ing·ly** *adv.*

cook /kook/ *v. & n.* ● *v.* **1** *tr.* prepare (food) by heating it. **2** *intr.* (of food) undergo cooking. **3** *tr. colloq.* falsify (accounts, etc.); alter to produce a desired result. **4** *tr. sl.* ruin; spoil. **5** *tr. & intr. colloq.* do or proceed successfully. **6** *intr.* (as **be cooking**) *colloq.* be happening or about to happen (*went to find out what was cooking*). ● *n.* a person who cooks. □ **cook a person's goose** ruin a person's chances. **cook up** *colloq.* invent or concoct (a story, excuse, etc.). □□ **cook·a·ble** *adj.*

cook·book /kookbook/ *n.* a book containing recipes and other information about cooking.

cook·er /kookər/ *n.* a container or device for cooking food.

cook·er·y /kookəree/ *n.* (*pl.* **-ies**) the art or practice of cooking.

C

C

COOKWARE

Pans and dishes are designed for particular methods of cooking, although many perform several functions. Saucepans and skillets are used on top of the stove, and are made from various metals, often with a nonstick coating. Casserole dishes and baking pans are used inside the oven, while cookware for microwaves must be nonmetallic.

EXAMPLES OF COOKWARE

SKILLET

OVENPROOF DISH

MICROWAVE-PROOF DISH

SAUCEPAN

TART PAN

CASSEROLE DISH

MUFFIN PAN

COOLING RACK

cook·ie /kŏókee/ *n.* (also **cooky**) (*pl.* **cookies**) a small sweet cake. □ **that's the way the cookie crumbles** *colloq.* that is how things turn out; that is the unalterable state of affairs.

cook·ie-cut·ter *adj.* made or done to an unchanging pattern; unvarying.

cook·ing /kŏoking/ *n.* **1** the art or process by which food is cooked. **2** (*attrib.*) suitable for or used in cooking (*cooking apple; cooking utensils*).

cook·out /kŏokowt/ *n.* a gathering with an open-air cooked meal; a barbecue.

cook·ware /kŏokwair/ *n.* ▲ utensils for cooking.

cook·y var. of COOKIE.

cool /kŏol/ *adj., n., & v.* ● *adj.* **1** of or at a fairly low temperature, fairly cold (*a cool day; a cool bath*). **2** suggesting or achieving coolness (*cool colors; cool clothes*). **3 a** (of a person) calm; unexcited. **b** (of an act) done without emotion. **4** lacking enthusiasm. **5** unfriendly; lacking cordiality (*got a cool reception*). **6** (of jazz playing) restrained; relaxed. **7** calmly audacious (*a cool customer*). **8** (prec. by *a*) *colloq.* not less than (*cost me a cool thousand*). **9** *sl.* excellent; marvelous. ● *n.* **1** coolness. **2** cool air; a cool place. **3** *sl.* calmness; composure (*keep one's cool; lose one's cool*). ● *v.* (often foll. by *down, off*) **1** *tr. & intr.* make or become cool. **2** *intr.* (of anger, emotions, etc.) lessen; become calmer. □ **cool one's heels** see HEEL[1]. **cool it** *sl.* relax, calm down. □□ **cool·ish** *adj.* **cool·ly** /kŏol-lee/ *adv.* **cool·ness** *n.*

coo·la·bah /kŏoləbaa/ *n.* (also **coolibah** /-libaa/) *Austral.* any of various gum trees, esp. *Eucalyptus microtheca.*

cool·ant /kŏolənt/ *n.* **1** a cooling agent, esp. fluid, to remove heat from an engine, nuclear reactor, etc. **2** a fluid used to lessen the friction of a cutting tool.

cool·er /kŏolər/ *n.* **1** a vessel in which a thing is cooled. **2 a** a refrigerated room. **b** an insulated container for keeping foods, drinks, etc., cold. **3** a long drink, esp. a spritzer. **4** *sl.* prison or a prison cell.

cool·head·ed /kŏolhéddid/ *adj.* not easily excited.

coo·li·bah var. of COOLABAH.

coo·lie /kŏolee/ *n.* *offens.* (also **cooly**) (*pl.* **-ies**) an unskilled native laborer in Asian countries.

coo·lie hat *n.* a broad conical hat as worn by coolies.

cool·ing-off pe·ri·od *n.* an interval to allow for a change of mind before commitment to action.

cool·ing tow·er *n.* a tall structure for cooling hot water before reuse, esp. in industry. ▷ POWER PLANT

coon /kŏon/ *n.* a raccoon.

coon's age *n. sl.* a long time.

coop /kŏop/ *n. & v.* ● *n.* **1** a cage placed over sitting or fattening fowls. **2** ▼ building for keeping chickens, etc. **3** a small place of confinement, esp. a prison. ● *v.tr.* **1** put or keep (a fowl) in a coop. **2** (often foll. by *up, in*) confine (a person) in a small space.

pop hole   *hinged door*

laying compartment

COOP FOR CHICKENS

co-op /kŏ-op/ *n. colloq.* **1** a cooperative business or enterprise. **2** = COOPERATIVE 4.

coop·er /kŏopər/ *n.* a maker or repairer of casks, barrels, etc.

co·op·er·ate /kō-ópərayt/ *v.intr.* (also **co-operate**) **1** (often foll. by *with*) work or act together; assist. **2** (of things) concur in producing an effect. □□ **co·op·er·ant** /-rənt/ *adj.* **co·op·er·a·tion** /-áyshən/ *n.* **co·op·er·a·tor** *n.*

co·op·er·a·tive /kō-ópərətiv, -ópra-/ *adj. & n.* (also **co-operative**) ● *adj.* **1** of or affording cooperation. **2** willing to cooperate. **3** *Econ.* (of a farm, shop, or other business) owned and run jointly by its members, with profits shared among them. **4** (of an apartment building) with individual units owned by their occupiers. ● *n.* a cooperative farm or society or business. □□ **co·op·er·a·tive·ly** *adv.* **co·op·er·a·tive·ness** *n.*

co-opt /kō-ópt, kŏ-opt/ *v.tr.* appoint to membership of a body by invitation of the existing members. □□ **co-optation** /-optáyshən/ *n.* **co-option** /-ópshən/ *n.* **co-optive** *adj.*

co·or·di·nate *v., adj., & n.* (also **co-ordinate**) ● *v.* /kō-áwrd'nayt/ **1** *tr.* bring (various parts, movements, etc.) into a proper or required relation. **2** *intr.* work or act together effectively. **3** *tr.* make coordinate; organize; classify. ● *adj.* /kō-áwrd'nət/ **1** equal in rank or importance. **2** in which the parts are coordinated; involving coordination. **3** *Gram.* (of parts of a compound sentence) equal in status. **4** *Chem.* denoting a type of covalent bond in which one atom provides both the shared electrons. ● *n.* /kō-áwrd'nət/ **1** *Math.* each of a system of magnitudes used to fix the position of a point, line, or plane. **2** a person or thing equal in rank or importance. **3** (in *pl.*) matching items of clothing. □□ **co·or·di·na·tion** /-d'náyshən/ *n.* **co·or·di·na·tive** *adj.* **co·or·di·na·tor** *n.*

coot /kŏot/ *n.* **1** ▼ any black aquatic bird of the genus *Fulica,* esp. *F. atra* with a white plate on the forehead. **2** *colloq.* a stupid person.

COOT (*Fulica atra*)

cootie /kŏotee/ *n. sl.* a body louse.

cop /kop/ *n. & v. sl.* ● *n.* a policeman. ● *v.tr.* (**copped, copping**) **1** catch or arrest (an offender). **2** take; seize. □ **cop out 1** withdraw; give up an attempt. **2** go back on a promise. **3** escape. **cop a plea** *sl.* = PLEA-BARGAIN.

cop·a·cet·ic /kŏpəsétik/ *adj. sl.* excellent; in good order.

co·pal /kŏpəl/ *n.* a resin from any of various tropical trees, used for varnish.

co·part·ner /kŏpáartnər/ *n.* a partner or associate, esp. when sharing equally. □□ **co·part·ner·ship** *n.*

cope[1] /kōp/ *v.intr.* **1** (foll. by *with*) deal effectively with a person or task. **2** deal with a situation or problem (*could no longer cope*).

cope[2] /kōp/ *n. & v.* ● *n. Eccl.* a long, cloaklike vestment worn by a priest or bishop. ● *v.tr.* cover with a cope or coping.

co·peck var. of KOPECK.

co·pe·pod /kŏpəpod/ *n.* any small aquatic crustacean of the class Copepoda, many of which form the minute components of plankton.

Co·per·ni·can sys·tem /kəpérnikən/ *n.* (also **Co·per·ni·can the·o·ry**) *Astron.* the theory that the planets (including the Earth) move around the Sun (cf. PTOLEMAIC SYSTEM).

cope·stone /kŏpstōn/ *n.* **1** ▶ a stone used in a coping. **2** a finishing touch.

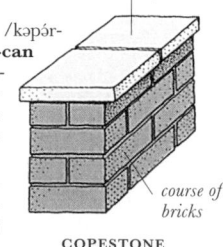

copestone

course of bricks

COPESTONE

cop·i·a·ble /kópeeəbəl/ *adj.* that can or may be copied.

cop·i·er /kópeeər/ *n.* a machine or person that copies (esp. documents).

co·pi·lot /kópílət/ *n.* a second pilot in an aircraft.

cop·ing /kóping/ *n.* the top (usu. sloping) course of masonry in a wall or parapet.

cop·ing saw /kóping/ *n.* a D-shaped saw for cutting curves in wood. ▷ SAW[1]

co·pi·ous /kópeeəs/ *adj.* **1** abundant; plentiful. **2** producing much. **3** providing much information. **4** profuse in speech. □□ **co·pi·ous·ly** *adv.* **co·pi·ous·ness** *n.*

co·pi·ta /kəpéetə/ *n.* **1** a tulip-shaped sherry glass. **2** a glass of sherry.

co·pol·y·mer /kõpólimər/ *n. Chem.* a polymer with units of more than one kind. □□ **co·pol·y·mer·ize** *v.tr. & intr.*

cop-out *n.* **1** a cowardly or feeble evasion. **2** an escape; a way of escape.

cop·per[1] /kópər/ *n., adj., & v.* ● *n.* **1** *Chem.* a malleable, red-brown metallic element occurring naturally and used esp. for electrical cables and apparatus. ▷ METAL. ¶ Symb.: **Cu**. **2** a bronze coin. ● *adj.* ▶ made of or colored like copper. ● *v.tr.* cover with copper.

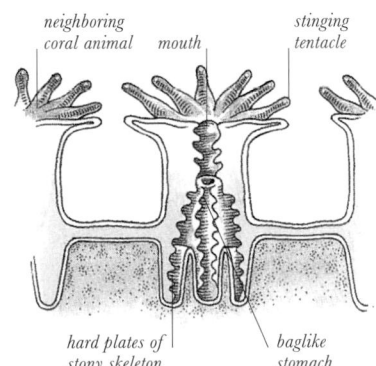

COPPER
DISTILLER'S JUG

cop·per[2] /kópər/ *n. sl.* a policeman.

cop·per beech *n.* a variety of beech with copper-colored leaves.

cop·per·head /kópərhed/ *n.* **1** ▼ a venomous viper, *Agkistrodon contortrix*, native to N. America. **2** a venomous cobra, *Denisonia superba*, native to Australia.

COPPERHEAD (*Agkistrodon contortrix*)

cop·per·plate /kópərplayt/ *n. & adj.* ● *n.* **1 a** a polished copper plate for engraving or etching. **b** a print made from this. **2** ▼ an ornate style of handwriting. ● *adj.* of or in copperplate writing.

Failings of others

COPPERPLATE: EXAMPLE OF ENGRAVED
COPPERPLATE HANDWRITING

cop·per·y /kópəree/ *adj.* of or like copper, esp. in color.

cop·pice /kópis/ *n. & v.* ● *n.* an area of undergrowth and small trees, grown for periodic cutting. ● *v.tr.* cut back (young trees) periodically to stimulate growth of shoots. □□ **cop·piced** *adj.*

co·pra /kóprə/ *n.* the dried kernels of the coconut.

co·pro·duc·tion /kóprədúkshən/ *n.* a production of a play, broadcast, etc., jointly by more than one company.

copse /kops/ *n.* **1** = COPPICE. **2** (in general use) a small forest.

copse·wood /kópswŏŏd/ *n.* undergrowth.

Copt /kopt/ *n.* **1** a native Egyptian in the Hellenistic and Roman periods. **2** a native Christian of the independent Egyptian Church.

cop·ter /kóptər/ *n. colloq.* a helicopter.

Cop·tic /kóptik/ *n. & adj.* ● *n.* the language of the Copts. ● *adj.* of or relating to the Copts.

cop·u·la /kópyələ/ *n.* (*pl.* **copulas** or **copulae** /-lee/) *Logic & Gram.* a connecting word, esp. a part of the verb *be* connecting a subject and predicate. □□ **cop·u·lar** *adj.*

cop·u·late /kópyəlayt/ *v.intr.* (often foll. by *with*) have sexual intercourse. □□ **cop·u·la·tion** /-láyshən/ *n.* **cop·u·la·to·ry** /-látəwree/ *adj.*

cop·y /kópee/ *n. & v.* (*pl.* **-ies**) **1** a thing made to imitate or be identical to another. **2** a single specimen of a publication or issue. **3 a** a matter to be printed. **b** material for a newspaper or magazine article (*scandals make good copy*). **c** the text of an advertisement. **4 a** a model to be copied. **b** a page written after a model (of penmanship). ● *v.* (**-ies, -ied**) **1** *tr.* make a copy of. **b** (often foll. by *out*) transcribe. **2** *intr.* make a copy, esp. clandestinely. **3** *tr.* (foll. by *to*) send a copy of (a letter) to a third party. **4** *tr.* do the same as; imitate.

cop·y·book /kópeebŏŏk/ *n.* **1** a book containing models of handwriting. **2** (*attrib.*) **a** a tritely conventional. **b** accurate, exemplary.

cop·y·cat /kópeekat/ *n. colloq.* a person who copies another, esp. closely.

cop·y·ed·it /kópee-édit/ *v.tr.* edit (copy) for printing.

cop·y ed·i·tor *n.* a person who edits copy for printing.

cop·y desk *n.* the desk at which copy is edited.

cop·y·ist /kópee-ist/ *n.* **1** a person who makes (esp. written) copies. **2** an imitator.

co·py·left /kópeeleft/ *n. Computing* an agreement allowing software to be used, modified, and distributed freely on condition that a notice to this effect is included with it.

cop·y·read·er /kópeereedər/ *n.* a person who reads and edits copy for a newspaper or book. □□ **copyread** *v.tr.*

cop·y·right /kópeerīt/ *n., adj., & v.* ● *n.* the exclusive legal right granted for a period to print, publish, perform, film, or record literary, artistic, or musical material. ● *adj.* (of such material) protected by copyright. ● *v.tr.* secure copyright for (material).

cop·y·writ·er /kópeerītər/ *n.* a person who writes or prepares copy (esp. of advertising material) for publication. □□ **cop·y·writ·ing** *n.*

coq au vin /kok ō ván/ *n.* a casserole of chicken pieces cooked in red wine.

co·quette /kōkét/ *n.* **1** a woman who flirts. **2** any crested hummingbird of the genus *Lophornis*. □□ **co·quet·ry** /kõkitree, kōkétree/ *n.* (*pl.* **-ies**). **co·quet·tish** *adj.* **co·quet·tish·ly** *adv.* **co·quet·tish·ness** *n.*

cor·a·cle /káwrəkəl, kór-/ *n. Brit.* a small boat of wickerwork covered with watertight material, used on Welsh and Irish lakes and rivers.

cor·al /káwrəl, kór-/ *n. & adj.* ● *n.* **1 a** a hard calcareous substance secreted by various marine polyps for support and habitation. **b** ▼ any of these usu. colonial organisms. ▷ CNIDARIAN. **2** the unimpregnated roe of a lobster or scallop. ● *adj.* **1** like coral, esp. in color; pinkish or reddish yellow. **2** made of coral.

neighboring coral animal   *mouth*   *stinging tentacle*

hard plates of stony skeleton   *baglike stomach*

CORAL: CROSS SECTION THROUGH A
CORAL ANIMAL

cor·al·line /káwrəlin, -līn, kór-/ *adj.* **1** coral red. **2** of or like coral.

cor·al·lite /káwrəlīt, kór-/ *n.* **1** the coral skeleton of a marine polyp. **2** fossil coral.

cor·al·loid /káwrəloyd, kór-/ *adj. & n.* ● *adj.* like or akin to coral. ● *n.* a coralloid organism.

cor·al reef *n.* one formed by the growth of coral. ▷ ATOLL.

cor·al snake *n.* any of various brightly colored poisonous snakes, esp. *Micrurus fulvius*, native to the southeastern US.

cor·bel /káwrbəl, -bel/ *n. & v. Archit.* ● *n.* **1** a projection of stone, timber, etc., jutting out from a wall to support a weight. ▷ CHATEAU. **2** a short timber laid longitudinally under a beam to help support it. ● *v.tr. & intr.* **corbeled**, **corbeling** (foll. by *out, off*) support or project on corbels.

cor·bie·steps /káwrbeesteps/ *n.pl.* the steplike projections on the sloping sides of a gable.

cord /kawrd/ *n. & v.* ● *n.* **1 a** a long, thin, flexible material made from several twisted strands. **b** a piece of this. **2** *Anat.* a body structure resembling a cord (*spinal cord*). **3 a** a ribbed fabric, esp. corduroy. **b** (in *pl.*) corduroy pants. **c** a cordlike rib on fabric. **4** *Electr.* a flexible insulated cable (*telephone cord*). **5** a measure of cut wood (usu. 128 cu.ft., 3.6 cubic meters). **6** a moral or emotional tie (*cords of affection*). ● *v.tr.* **1** fasten or bind with cord. **2** (as **corded** *adj.*) **a** (of cloth) ribbed. **b** provided with cords. **c** (of muscles) standing out like taut cords. □□ **cord·like** *adj.*

cor·date /káwrdayt/ *adj.* ◀ heart-shaped.

Cor·de·lier /káwrdəleér/ *n.* a Franciscan friar of the strict rule, wearing a knotted cord around the waist.

cor·dial /káwrjəl/ *adj. & n.* ● *adj.* **1** heartfelt; sincere. **2** warm; friendly. ● *n.* a liqueur. □□ **cor·dial·i·ty** /-jeeálitee/ *n.* **cor·dial·ly** *adv.*

cor·dil·le·ra /káwrd'lyáirə, kawrdílərə/ *n.* a system or group of usu. parallel mountain ranges together with intervening plateaus, etc., esp. of the Andes and in Central America and Mexico.

cor·dite /káwrdīt/ *n.* a smokeless explosive made from cellulose nitrate and nitroglycerine.

cord·less /káwrdlis/ *adj.* (of an electrical appliance, telephone, etc.) working without a connection to an electrical supply or central unit.

cor·don /káwrd'n/ *n. & v.* ● *n.* **1** a line or circle of police, soldiers, etc., esp. preventing access to or from an area. **2 a** an ornamental cord or braid. **b** the ribbon of a knightly order. **3** ▶ a fruit tree trained to grow as a single stem. ● *v.tr.* (often foll. by *off*) enclose or separate with a cordon of police, etc.

CORDON

cor·don bleu /káwrdawn blö/ *adj. & n. Cookery* ● *adj.* of the highest class. ● *n.* a cook of this class.

cor·don sa·ni·taire /kawrdáwn sáneetáir/ *n.* **1** a guarded line between infected and uninfected districts. **2** any measure designed to prevent communication or the spread of undesirable influences.

cor·du·roy /káwrdəroy/ *n.* **1** a thick cotton fabric with velvety ribs. **2** (in *pl.*) corduroy pants. □ **corduroy road** a road made of tree trunks.

cord·wood /káwrdwŏŏd/ *n.* wood that is or can easily be measured in cords.

CORDATE
LEAF

C

C

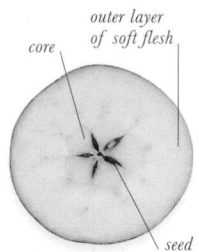

CORE: CROSS SECTION OF AN APPLE SHOWING THE CORE

core, *outer layer of soft flesh*, *seed*

core /kawr/ *n. & v.* ● *n.* **1** ◄ the horny central part of various fruits, containing the seeds. **2 a** the central or most important part of anything (also *attrib.: core curriculum*). **b** the central part, of different character from the surroundings. **3** the central region of the Earth. ▷ EARTH. **4** the central part of a nuclear reactor, containing the fissile material. ▷ NUCLEAR POWER. **5** magnetic structural unit in a computer, storing one bit of data (see BIT⁴). **6** the inner strand of an electric cable, rope, etc. **7** a piece of soft iron forming the center of an electromagnet or an induction coil. **8** an internal mold filling a space to be left hollow in a casting. **9** the central part cut out (esp. of rock, etc., in boring). **10** *Archaeol.* a piece of flint from which flakes or blades have been removed. ● *v.tr.* remove the core from. □□ **core·er** *n.*

core mem·o·ry *n. Computing* the memory of a computer consisting of many cores.

COREOPSIS
(*Coreopsis grandiflora* 'Early Sunrise')

co·re·op·sis /káwreeópsis/ *n.* ◄ any composite plant of the genus *Coreopsis*, having rayed usu. yellow flowers.

co·re·spond·ent /kṓ-rispóndənt/ *n.* a person cited in a divorce case as having committed adultery with the respondent.

cor·gi /káwrgee/ *n. (pl. cor·gis)* (in full **Welsh corgi**) **1** ▼ a dog of a short-legged breed with foxlike head. **2** this breed. ▷ DOG

CORGI: WELSH CORGI

co·ri·an·der /káwreeándər/ *n.* **1** a plant, *Coriandrum sativum*, with leaves used for flavoring and small, round, aromatic fruits. ▷ HERB. **2** (also **co·ri·an·der seed**) the dried fruit used for flavoring curries, etc. ▷ SPICE

Co·rin·thi·an /kəríntheeən/ *adj. & n.* ● *adj.* **1** of ancient Corinth in southern Greece. **2** *Archit.* ▼ of an order characterized by ornate decoration and flared capitals with acanthus leaves. ▷ COLUMN. ● *n.* a native of Corinth.

Co·ri·o·lis ef·fect /káwreeólis/ *n.* a hypothetical force used to explain rotating systems, such that the movement of air or water is directed clockwise in the northern hemisphere and counterclockwise in the southern hemisphere.

co·ri·um /káwreeəm/ *n. Anat.* the dermis.

cork /kawrk/ *n. & v.* ● *n.* **1** ► the buoyant light-brown bark of the cork oak. **2** a bottle stopper of cork or other material. **3** a float of cork used in fishing, etc. **4** *Bot.* a protective layer of dead cells immediately below the bark of woody plants. **5** (*attrib.*) made of cork. ● *v.tr.* (often foll. by *up*) **1** stop or confine. **2** restrain (feelings, etc.) **3** blacken with burned cork. □□ **cork·like** *adj.*

cork·age /káwrkij/ *n.* a charge made by a restaurant or hotel for serving wine, etc., when brought in by customers.

corked /kawrkt/ *adj.* **1** stopped with a cork. **2** (of wine) spoiled by a decayed cork. **3** blackened with burned cork.

cork·er /káwrkər/ *n. sl.* an excellent or astonishing person or thing.

cork·ing /káwrking/ *adj. sl.* strikingly large or splendid.

cork oak *n.* ► a S. European oak, *Quercus suber*.

cork·screw /káwrkskrōō/ *n. & v.* ● *n.* **1** a spirally twisted steel device for extracting corks from bottles. **2** (often *attrib.*) a thing with a spiral shape. ● *v.tr. & intr.* move spirally; twist.

cork·y /káwrkee/ *adj.* (**cork·ier, corkiest**) **1** corklike. **2** (of wine) corked.

CORK IN VARIOUS FORMS

untreated cork, *cork tile*, *cork stopper*

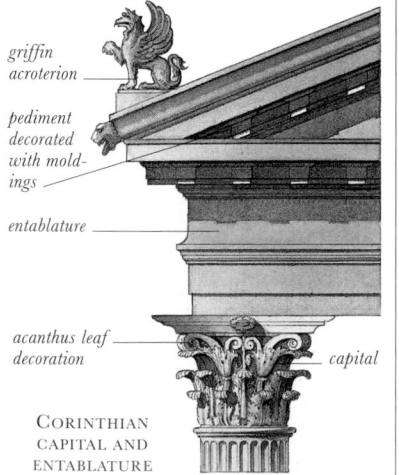

CORK OAK
(*Quercus suber*)

food storage tissue, *cormel (young corm)*

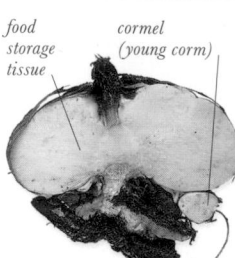

CORM: CROSS SECTION OF A GLADIOLUS CORM

corm /kawrm/ *n. Bot.* ◄ an underground swollen stem base of some plants, e.g., crocus.

cor·mo·rant /káwrmərənt, -mərənt/ *n.* any diving sea bird of the family Phalacrocoracidae, esp. *Phalacrocorax harrisi* having lustrous black plumage.

corn¹ /kawrn/ *n. & v.* ● *n.* **1 a** a tall-growing orig. N. American cereal plant, *Zea mays*, cultivated in many varieties, bearing kernels on a long ear (cob). **b** ► the cobs or kernels of this plant. ▷ GRAIN. **2** *colloq.* something corny or trite. ● *v.tr.* (as **corned** *adj.*) sprinkled or preserved with salt or brine (*corned beef*).

corn² /kawrn/ *n.* a small area of horny usu. tender skin esp. on the toes, extending into subcutaneous tissue.

corn·ball /kórnbawl/ *n. & adj.* ● *n.* an unsophisticated or mawkishly sentimental person. ● *adj.* = CORNY *adj.* 1.

corn bread *n.* bread made with cornmeal.

CORN
(*Zea mays*)

corn·cob /káwrnkaab/ *n.* the cylindrical center of the corn ear to which rows of grains (kernels) are attached.

corn·cob pipe *n.* a tobacco pipe made from a corncob.

corn·crake /káwrnkrayk/ *n.* a rail, *Crex crex*, inhabiting grassland and nesting on the ground.

corn dol·ly *n.* a symbolic or decorative figure made of plaited straw, corn husks, etc.

cor·ne·a /káwrneeə/ *n.* the transparent circular part of the front of the eyeball. ▷ EYE. □□ **cor·ne·al** *adj.*

corned beef *n.* **1** *Brit.* beef preserved in brine, chopped and pressed, and sold in tins. **2** *N. Amer.* beef brisket cured in brine and boiled, typically served cold.

cor·nel·ian var. of CARNELIAN.

cor·ner /káwrnər/ *n. & v.* ● *n.* **1** a place where converging sides or edges meet. **2** a projecting angle, esp. where two streets meet. **3** the internal space or recess formed by the meeting of two sides, esp. of a room. **4** a difficult position, esp. one from which there is no escape (*driven into a corner*). **5** a secluded or remote place. **6** a region or quarter, esp. a remote one (*from the four corners of the Earth*). **7** the action or result of buying or controlling the whole available stock of a commodity, thereby dominating the market. **8** *Boxing & Wrestling* **a** an angle of the ring, esp. one where a contestant rests between rounds. **b** a contestant's supporters offering assistance at the corner between rounds. **9** *Soccer* a free kick or hit from a corner of the field after the ball has been kicked over the goal line by a defending player. ● *v.* **1** *tr.* force (a person or animal) into a difficult or inescapable position. **2** *tr.* **a** establish a corner in (a commodity). **b** dominate (dealers or the market) in this way. **3** *intr.* (esp. of or in a vehicle) go around a corner. □ **just around the corner** *colloq.* very near; imminent.

cor·ner·stone /káwrnərstōn/ *n.* **1 a** a stone in a projecting angle of a wall. **b** a foundation stone. **2** an indispensable part or basis of something.

cor·ner·wise /káwrnərwīz/ *adv.* diagonally.

CORINTHIAN

Corinthian is a term applied to one of the three principal orders of classical architecture. Invented in Athens in the 5th century BC, Corinthian architecture was also widely used by the ancient Romans, and it borrowed some features from both the Doric and Ionian orders.

griffin acroterion

pediment decorated with moldings

entablature

flared capital

long slender column

cella entrance

acanthus leaf decoration

capital

FRONT ELEVATION OF A CORINTHIAN TEMPLE

CORINTHIAN CAPITAL AND ENTABLATURE

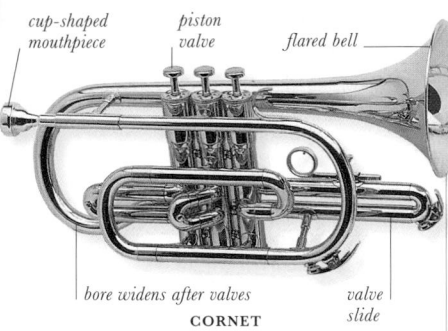

cup-shaped mouthpiece · piston valve · flared bell · bore widens after valves · valve slide

CORNET

cor·net /kawrnét/ *Mus.* **1 a** ▲ a brass instrument resembling a trumpet but shorter and wider. ▷ BRASS. **b** its player. **2** an organ stop with the quality of a cornet. □□ **cor·net·ist** or **cor·net·tist** *n.*

corn·field /káwrnfeeld/ *n.* a field in which corn is being grown.

corn·flake /káwrnflayk/ *n.* **1** (in *pl.*) a breakfast cereal of toasted flakes made from cornmeal. **2** a flake of this cereal.

corn·flow·er /káwrnflowər/ *n.* any plant of the genus *Centaurea*, growing among corn, esp. *C. cyanus*, with deep-blue flowers.

cor·nice /káwrnis/ *n.*
1 *Archit.* **a** ▶ an ornamental molding around the wall of a room just below the ceiling. **b** a horizontal molded projection crowning a building or structure. ▷ ENTABLATURE. **2** *Mountaineering* an overhanging mass of hardened snow at the edge of a precipice. □□ **cor·niced** *adj.*

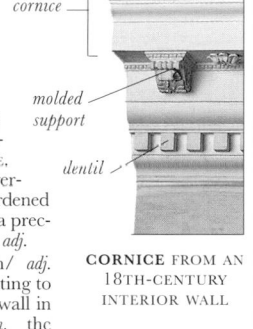

cornice · molded support · dentil

CORNICE FROM AN 18TH-CENTURY INTERIOR WALL

Cor·nish /káwrnish/ *adj. & n.* ● *adj.* of or relating to the county of Cornwall in SW England. ● *n.* the ancient Celtic language of Cornwall.

corn·meal /káwrnmeel/ *n.* meal ground from corn.

corn on the cob *n.* corn cooked and eaten from the cob.

corn·row /kórnrō/ *n. & v.* ● *n.* any of usu. several narrow plaits of hair braided close to the scalp. ● *v.tr.* plait (hair) in cornrows.

corn·starch /káwrnstaarch/ *n.* fine-ground flour made from corn.

cor·nu·co·pi·a /káwrnəkṓpeeə, -nyə-/ *n.* **1 a** a symbol of plenty consisting of a goat's horn overflowing with flowers, fruit, etc. **b** an ornamental vessel shaped like this. **2** an abundant supply. □□ **cor·nu·co·pi·an** *adj.*

corn·y /káwrnee/ *adj.* (**cornier, corniest**) **1** *colloq.* **a** trite. **b** feebly humorous. **c** sentimental. **d** old-fashioned; out of date. **2** of or abounding in corn. □□ **corn·i·ly** *adv.* **corn·i·ness** *n.*

co·rol·la /kərólə, -rṓ-/ *n. Bot.* a whorl or whorls of petals forming the inner envelope of a flower.

cor·ol·lar·y /káwrəleree, kór-/ *n. & adj.* ● *n.* (*pl.* **-ies**) **1 a** a proposition that follows from one already proved. **b** an immediate deduction. **2** (often foll. by *of*) a natural consequence or result. ● *adj.* **1** supplementary; associated. **2** (often foll. by *to*) forming a corollary.

co·ro·na¹ /kərṓnə/ *n.* (*pl.* **coronas** or **coronae** /-nee/) **1 a** a small circle of light around the Sun or Moon. ▷ SUN. **b** the rarefied gaseous envelope of the Sun, seen as an area of light around the Moon's disk during a total solar eclipse. **2** a circular chandelier hung from a roof. **3** *Anat.* a crown or crownlike structure. **4** *Bot.* ▶ a crownlike outgrowth from the inner side of a perianth.

5 *Archit.* a broad vertical face of a cornice, usu. of cons conductor at high potential. □□ **cor·o·nal** /kərónəl, káwrən'l, kór-/ *adj.*

co·ro·na² /kərónə/ *n.* a long cigar with straight sides.

cor·o·nar·y /káwrəneree, kór-/ *adj. & n.* ● *adj. Anat.* resembling or encircling like a crown. ● *n.* (*pl.* **-ies**) **1** = CORONARY THROMBOSIS. **2** a heart attack.

cor·o·nar·y throm·bo·sis *n.* a blockage of the blood flow caused by a blood clot in a coronary artery.

cor·o·na·tion /káwrənáyshən, kór-/ *n.* the ceremony of crowning a sovereign or a sovereign's consort.

cor·o·ner /káwrənər, kór-/ *n.* an officer of a county, district, or municipality, holding inquests on deaths thought to be violent or accidental. □□ **cor·o·ner·ship** *n.*

cor·o·net /káwrənit, -nét, kór-/ *n.* **1** a small crown. **2** a circlet of precious materials, esp. as a headdress. **3** a garland for the head. **4** the lowest part of a horse's pastern. **5** a ring of bone at the base of a deer's antler. □□ **cor·o·net·ed** *adj.*

Corp. *abbr.* **1** corporal. **2** corporation.

cor·po·ra *pl.* of CORPUS.

cor·po·ral¹ /káwrpərəl, káwrprəl/ *n.* **1** a noncommissioned army, air force, or marine officer ranking next below sergeant. **2** a freshwater fallfish, *Semotilis corporalis*.

cor·po·ral² /káwrpərəl, káwrprəl/ *adj.* of or relating to the human body (cf. CORPOREAL). □□ **cor·po·ral·ly** *adv.*

cor·po·ral·i·ty /káwrpərálitee/ *n.* (*pl.* **-ies**) **1** material existence. **2** a body.

cor·po·ral pun·ish·ment *n.* punishment inflicted on the body, esp. by beating.

cor·po·rate /káwrpərət, káwrprit/ *adj.* **1** forming a corporation (*corporate body*). **2** forming one body of many individuals. **3** of or belonging to a corporation or group (*corporate responsibility*). **4** corporative. □□ **cor·po·rate·ly** *adv.* **cor·po·rat·ism** *n.*

cor·po·rate raid·er *n.* a person who mounts an unwelcome takeover bid by buying up a company's shares on the stock market.

cor·po·ra·tion /káwrpəráyshən/ *n.* **1** a group of people authorized to act as an individual, esp. in business. **2** *joc.* a protruding stomach.

cor·po·ra·tive /káwrpərətiv, -ráytiv/ *adj.* **1** of a corporation. **2** governed by or organized in corporations. □□ **cor·po·ra·tiv·ism** *n*

cor·po·re·al /kawrpáwreeəl/ *adj.* **1** bodily, physical, material, esp. as distinct from spiritual (cf. CORPORAL²). **2** *Law* consisting of material objects. □□ **cor·po·re·al·i·ty** /-reeálitee/ *n.* **cor·po·re·al·ly** *adv.*

corps /kawr/ *n.* (*pl.* **corps** /kawrz/) **1** *Mil.* **a** a body of troops with special duties (*intelligence corps*; *Marine Corps*). **b** a main subdivision of an army in the field. **2** a body of people engaged in a special activity (*diplomatic corps*).

corps de bal·let /káwr də baláy/ *n.* the company of ensemble dancers in a ballet.

corps di·plo·ma·tique /káwrdíplɔmateék/ *n.* a diplomatic corps.

corpse /kawrps/ *n.* a dead (usu. human) body.

cor·pu·lent /káwrpyələnt/ *adj.* bulky in body; fat. □□ **cor·pu·lence** /-ləns/ *n.* **cor·pu·len·cy** *n.*

cor·pus /káwrpəs/ *n.* (*pl.* **corpora** /káwrpərə/ or **corpuses**) **1** a body or collection of writings, texts, spoken material, etc. **2** *Anat.* a structure of a special character in the animal body.

cor·pus·cle /káwrpusəl/ *n.* a minute body or cell in an organism, esp. (in *pl.*) the red or white cells in the blood of vertebrates. ▷ BLOOD. □□ **cor·pus·cu·lar** /kawrpúskyələr/ *adj.*

cor·pus de·lic·ti /káwrpəs diliktī/ *n. Law*

the facts and circumstances constituting a breach of a law.

cor·pus lu·te·um /káwrpəs lṓoteeəm/ *n.* (*pl.* **corpora lutea** /lṓotee-/) *Anat.* a body developed in the ovary after discharge of the ovum, remaining in existence only if pregnancy has begun. ▷ OVARY

cor·ral /kərál/ *n. & v.* ● *n.* **1** a pen for cattle, horses, etc. **2** an enclosure for capturing wild animals. ● *v.tr.* (**corralled, corralling**) **1** put or keep in a corral. **2** form (wagons) into a corral. **3** *colloq.* gather in; acquire.

cor·rect /kərékt/ *adj. & v.* ● *adj.* **1** true; right; accurate. **2** (of conduct, manners, etc.) proper; right. **3** in accordance with good standards of taste, etc. ● *v.tr.* **1** set right; amend (an error, omission, etc., or person). **2** mark the errors in (work). **3** substitute the right thing for (the wrong one). **4 a** admonish or rebuke (a person). **b** punish (a person or fault). **5** counteract (a harmful quality). **6** adjust (an instrument, etc.). □□ **cor·rect·ly** *adv.* **cor·rect·ness** *n.* **cor·rec·tor** *n.*

cor·rec·tion /kərékshən/ *n.* **1 a** the act or process of correcting. **b** an instance of this. **2** a thing substituted for what is wrong. **3** a program of incarceration, parole, probation, etc., for dealing with convicted offenders. □□ **cor·rec·tion·al** *adj.*

cor·rec·ti·tude /kəréktitood, -tyood/ *n.* correctness, esp. conscious correctness of conduct.

cor·rec·tive /kəréktiv/ *adj. & n.* ● *adj.* serving or tending to correct or counteract something undesired. ● *n.* a corrective measure or thing. □□ **cor·rec·tive·ly** *adv.*

cor·re·late /káwrəlayt, kór-/ *v. & n.* ● *v.* **1** *intr.* (foll. by *with*, *to*) have a mutual relation. **2** *tr.* (usu. foll. by *with*) bring into a mutual relation. ● *n.* each of two related or complementary things.

cor·re·la·tion /káwrəláyshən, kór-/ *n.* **1** a mutual relation between two or more things. **2 a** an interdependence of variable quantities. **b** a quantity measuring the extent of this. **3** the act of correlating. □□ **cor·re·la·tion·al** *adj.*

cor·rel·a·tive /kərélətiv/ *adj. & n.* ● *adj.* **1** (often foll. by *with*, *to*) having a mutual relation. **2** *Gram.* (of words) corresponding to each other and regularly used together (as *neither* and *nor*). ● *n.* a correlative word or thing. □□ **cor·rel·a·tive·ly** *adv.* **cor·rel·a·tiv·i·ty** /-tívitee/ *n.*

cor·re·spond /káwrispónd, kór-/ *v.intr.* **1 a** (usu. foll. by *to*) be analogous or similar. **b** (usu. foll. by *to*) agree in amount, position, etc. **c** (usu. foll. by *with*, *to*) be in harmony or agreement. **2** (usu. foll. by *with*) communicate by interchange of letters. □□ **cor·re·spond·ing·ly** *adv.*

cor·re·spond·ence /káwrispóndəns, kór-/ *n.* **1** (usu. foll. by *with*, *to*, *between*) agreement, similarity, or harmony. **2 a** a communication by letters. **b** letters sent or received.

cor·re·spond·ence course *n.* a course of study conducted by mail.

cor·re·spond·ent /káwrispóndənt, -kór-/ *n.* **1** a person who writes letters, esp. regularly. **2** a person employed to contribute material for a periodical or for broadcasting. **3** a person or firm having regular business relations with another, esp. in another country.

cor·ri·da /kawréedə, -thaa-/ *n.* **1** a bullfight. **2** bullfighting.

cor·ri·dor /káwridər, -dor, kór-/ *n.* **1** a passage from which doors lead into rooms. **2** a strip of the territory of one nation passing through that of another, esp. to the sea. **3** a route to which aircraft are restricted, esp. over a foreign country.

cor·ri·gen·dum /káwrijéndəm, kór-/ *n.* (*pl.* **corrigenda** /-də/) a thing to be corrected in a printed book.

cor·ri·gi·ble /káwrijibəl, kór-/ *adj.* **1** capable of being corrected. **2** (of a person) submissive; open to correction. □□ **cor·ri·gi·bly** *adv.*

cor·rob·o·rate /kəróbərayt/ *v.tr.* confirm or give support to (a statement or belief, or the person

corona · perianth

CORONA OF A DAFFODIL

C

C

holding it). □□ **cor·rob·o·ra·tion** /-ráyshən/ *n.* **cor·rob·o·ra·tive** /-rətiv, -ráytiv/ *adj.* **cor·rob·o·ra·tor** *n.* **cor·rob·o·ra·to·ry** /-rətáwree/ *adj.*

cor·rode /kərṓd/ *v.* **1 a** *tr.* wear away, esp. by chemical action. **b** *intr.* be worn away; decay. **2** *tr.* destroy gradually (*optimism corroded by recent misfortunes*). □□ **cor·rod·i·ble** *adj.*

cor·ro·sion /kərṓzhən/ *n.* **1** the process of corroding, esp. of a rusting metal. **2 a** damage caused by corroding. **b** a corroded area.

cor·ro·sive /kərṓsiv/ *adj. & n.* ● *adj.* tending to corrode or consume. ● *n.* a corrosive substance. □□ **cor·ro·sive·ly** *adv.* **cor·ro·sive·ness** *n.*

cor·ru·gate /káwrəgayt, kór-/ *v.* **1** *tr.* (esp. as **corrugated** *adj.*) form into alternate ridges and grooves, esp. to strengthen (*corrugated iron*; *corrugated cardboard*). **2** *tr. & intr.* contract into wrinkles or folds. □□ **cor·ru·ga·tion** /-gáyshən/ *n.*

cor·rupt /kərúpt/ *adj. & v.* ● *adj.* **1** morally depraved; wicked. **2** influenced by or using bribery or fraudulent activity. **3** (of a text, language, etc.) harmed (esp. made suspect or unreliable) by errors or alterations. **4** rotten. ● *v.* **1** *tr. & intr.* make or become corrupt or depraved. **2** *tr.* affect or harm by errors or alterations. **3** *tr.* infect; taint. □□ **cor·rupt·er** *n.* **cor·rupt·i·ble** *adj.* **cor·rupt·i·bil·i·ty** *n.* **cor·rup·tive** *adj.* **cor·rupt·ly** *adv.* **cor·rupt·ness** *n.*

cor·rup·tion /kərúpshən/ *n.* **1** moral deterioration, esp. widespread. **2** use of corrupt practices, esp. bribery or fraud. **3 a** irregular alteration (of a text, language, etc.) from its original state. **b** an irregularly altered form of a word. **4** decomposition, esp. of a corpse or other organic matter.

cor·sage /kawrsáazh/ *n.* **1** a small bouquet worn by a woman. **2** the bodice of a woman's dress.

cor·sair /káwrsair/ *n.* **1** a pirate ship. **2** a pirate.

cor·se·let /káwrsəlét/ *n.* (also **cor·se·lette**) ▶ a woman's foundation garment combining girdle and brassiere.

cor·set /káwrsit/ *n. & v.* ● *n.* **1** a closely fitting undergarment worn by women to support the abdomen. **2** a similar garment worn by men and women because of injury, weakness, or deformity. ● *v.tr.* **1** provide with a corset. **2** control closely. □□ **cor·set·ed** *adj.* **cor·se·try** *n.*

Cor·si·can /káwrsikən/ *adj. & n.* ● *adj.* of or relating to Corsica. ● *n.* **1** a native of Corsica. **2** the Italian dialect of Corsica.

cor·tege /kawrtéyzh/ *n.* (also **cortège**) **1** a procession, esp. for a funeral. **2** a train of attendants.

cor·tex /káwrteks/ *n.* (*pl.* **cortices** /-tiseez/ or **cortexes**) **1** *Anat.* the outer part of an organ, esp. of the brain (**cerebral cortex**) or kidneys (**renal cortex**). ▷ KIDNEY. **2** *Bot.* **a** an outer layer of tissue immediately below the epidermis. **b** bark. □□ **cor·ti·cal** /káwrtikəl/ *adj.*

cor·ti·cate /káwrtikayt/ *adj.* (also **cor·ti·cat·ed**) **1** having bark or rind. **2** barklike.

cor·ti·sone /káwrtisōn, -zōn/ *n. Biochem.* a steroid hormone used medicinally, esp. against inflammation and allergy.

co·run·dum /kərúndəm/ *n. Mineral.* ▶ extremely hard crystallized alumina, used esp. as an abrasive, and varieties of which are used for gemstones.

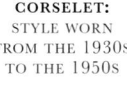

brassiere

elasticized underpanel

CORSELET:
STYLE WORN
FROM THE 1930S
TO THE 1950S

corset

CORUNDUM

cor·us·cate /káwrəskayt, kór-/ *v.intr.* **1** give off flashing light; sparkle. **2** be showy or brilliant. □□ **cor·us·ca·tion** /-káyshən/ *n.*

cor·vette /kawrvét/ *n. Naut.* a small naval escort vessel.

cor·vine /káwrvīn, -vin/ *adj.* of or akin to the raven or crow.

cor·ymb /káwrimb, -im, kór-/ *n. Bot.* a flat-topped cluster of flowers with the flower stalks proportionally longer lower down the stem. ▷ INFLORESCENCE. □□ **cor·ym·bose** *adj.*

cos[1] /kaws, kos/ *n.* a variety of lettuce with crisp narrow leaves forming a long, upright head.

cos[2] /kos, koz/ *abbr.* cosine.

cos[3] /kawz, koz/ *conj. & adv.* (also **'cos**) *colloq.* because.

Co·sa Nos·tra /kṓsə nṓstrə/ *n.* a US criminal organization resembling and related to the Mafia.

co·sec /kṓsek/ *abbr.* cosecant.

co·se·cant /kōsḗkant, -kənt/ *n. Math.* the ratio of the hypotenuse (in a right triangle) to the side opposite an acute angle; the reciprocal of sine.

cosh /kosh, kosáych/ *abbr. Math.* hyperbolic cosine.

co·sig·na·to·ry /kōsígnətáwree/ *n. & adj.* ● *n.* (*pl.* **-ies**) a person or nation signing (a treaty, etc.) jointly with others. ● *adj.* signing jointly.

co·sine /kṓsīn/ *n. Math.* the ratio of the side adjacent to an acute angle (in a right triangle) to the hypotenuse.

cos·met·ic /kozmétik/ *adj. & n.* ● *adj.* **1** intended to adorn or beautify the body, esp. the face. **2** intended to improve only appearances; superficially improving or beneficial (*a cosmetic change*). **3** (of surgery or a prosthetic device) imitating, restoring, or enhancing the normal appearance. ● *n.* a cosmetic preparation, esp. for the face. □□ **cos·met·i·cal·ly** *adv.*

cos·me·tol·o·gy /kosmətóləjee/ *n.* the art and technique of treating the skin, nails, and hair with cosmetic preparations. □□ **cosmetologist** *n.*

cos·mic /kózmik/ *adj.* **1** of the universe or cosmos. **2** of or for space travel. □□ **cos·mi·cal** *adj.* **cos·mi·cal·ly** *adv.*

cos·mic rays *n.pl.* radiations from space, etc., that reach the Earth from all directions.

cos·mog·o·ny /kozmógənee/ *n.* (*pl.* **-ies**) **1** the origin of the universe. **2** a theory about this. □□ **cos·mo·gon·ic** /-məgónik/ *adj.* **cos·mo·gon·i·cal** *adj.* **cos·mog·o·nist** /-móg-/ *n.*

cos·mog·ra·phy /kozmógrəfee/ *n.* (*pl.* **-ies**) a description or mapping of general features of the universe. □□ **cos·mog·ra·pher** *n.* **cos·mo·graph·ic** /-məgráfik/ *adj.* **cos·mo·graph·i·cal** *adj.*

cos·mol·o·gy /kozmóləjee/ *n.* the science or theory of the universe. □□ **cos·mo·log·i·cal** /-məlójikəl/ *adj.* **cos·mol·o·gist** *n.*

cos·mo·naut /kózmənawt/ *n.* a Russian astronaut.

cos·mo·pol·i·tan /kózmōpólit'n/ *adj. & n.* ● *adj.* **1 a** of or from or knowing many parts of the world. **b** consisting of people from many or all parts. **2** free from national limitations or prejudices. **3** *Ecol.* (of a plant, animal, etc.) widely distributed. ● *n.* **1** a cosmopolitan person. **2** *Ecol.* a widely distributed animal or plant. □□ **cos·mo·pol·i·tan·ism** *n.* **cos·mo·pol·i·tan·ize** *v.tr. & intr.*

cos·mos[1] /kózmōs, -məs, -mos/ *n.* **1** the universe, esp. as a well-ordered whole. **2 a** an ordered system of ideas, etc. **b** a sum total of experience.

cosmos[2] /kózməs, -mos, -mōs/ *n.* any composite plant of the genus *Cosmos*, bearing single dahlialike blossoms of various colors.

Cos·sack /kósak/ *n. & adj.* ● *n.* **1** a member of a people of southern Imperial Russia, Ukraine, and Siberia, orig. famous for their horsemanship and military skill. **2** a member

of a Cossack military unit. ● *adj.* of, relating to, or characteristic of the Cossacks.

cos·set /kósit/ *v.tr.* pamper.

cost /kawst/ *v. & n.* ● *v.* (*past* and *past part.* **cost**) **1** *tr.* be obtainable for (a sum of money); have as a price (*what does it cost?*; *it cost me $50*). **2** *tr.* involve as a loss or sacrifice (*it cost them much effort*; *it cost him his life*). **3** *tr.* (*past* and *past part.* **costed**) fix or estimate the cost or price of. **4** *colloq.* **a** *tr.* be costly to (*it'll cost you*). **b** *intr.* be costly. ● *n.* **1** what a thing costs; the price paid or to be paid. **2** a loss or sacrifice; an expenditure of time, effort, etc. **3** (in *pl.*) legal expenses. □ **at all costs** (or **at any cost**) no matter what the cost or risk may be. **at cost** at the initial cost; at cost price. **at the cost of** at the expense of losing or sacrificing. **cost a person dear** (or **dearly**) involve a person in a high cost or a heavy penalty. **to a person's cost** with loss or disadvantage to a person.

cos·tal /kóst'l, káwst'l/ *adj.* of the ribs.

co·star /kóstaar/ *n. & v.* ● *n.* a movie or stage star appearing with another or others of equal importance. ● *v.* (**-starred**, **-starring**) **1** *intr.* take part as a costar. **2** *tr.* (of a production) include as a costar.

cos·tate /kóstayt, káw-/ *adj.* ribbed; having ribs or ridges.

cost-ef·fec·tive *adj.* effective or productive in relation to its cost.

cos·tive /kóstiv/ *adj.* **1** constipated. **2** niggardly. □□ **cos·tive·ly** *adv.* **cos·tive·ness** *n.*

cost·ly /káwstlee/ *adj.* (**costlier**, **costliest**) **1** costing much; expensive. **2** of great value. □□ **cost·li·ness** *n.*

cost of liv·ing *n.* the level of prices, esp. of the basic necessities of life.

cos·tume /kóstoom, -tyoom/ *n. & v.* ● *n.* **1** a style of dress, esp. that of a particular place, time, or class. **2** a set of clothes. **3** clothing for a particular activity (*dancing costume*). **4** an actor's clothes for a part. **5** a woman's matching jacket and skirt. ● *v.tr.* provide with a costume.

cos·tume jew·el·ry *n.* ▶ inexpensive or imitation jewelry.

cos·tume play (or **piece** or **drama**) *n.* a drama in which the actors wear historical costume.

cos·tum·er /kóstoomər, -tyoo-/ *n.* a person who makes or deals in costumes, esp. for theatrical use.

cot[1] /kot/ *n.* **1** a small folding bed. **2** a hospital bed. **3** *Ind.* a light bedstead. **4** *Naut.* a kind of swinging bed hung from deck beams, formerly used by officers.

cot[2] /kot/ *n.* **1** a small shelter; a cote. **2** *poet.* a cottage.

cot[3] /kot/ *abbr. Math.* co-tangent.

metal chain

Bakelite heart

emblem of King George VI

COSTUME JEWELRY:
1930S BAKELITE™
NECKLACE

co·tan·gent /kōtánjənt/ *n. Math.* the ratio of the side adjacent to an acute angle (in a right triangle) to the opposite side.

cote /kōt/ *n.* a shelter, esp. for animals or birds; a shed or stall (*sheepcote*).

co·te·rie /kṓtəree/ *n.* **1** an exclusive group of people sharing interests. **2** a select circle in society.

co·ter·mi·nous /kōtə́rminəs/ *adj.* (often foll. by *with*) having the same boundaries or extent (in space, time, or meaning).

coth /koth/ *abbr. Math.* hyperbolic cotangent.

co·tid·al line /kōtíd'l/ *n.* a line on a map connecting points at which tidal levels (high or low tide) occur simultaneously.

COTONEASTER
(*Cotoneaster frigidus*)

co·to·ne·as·ter /kətṓneeástər/ *n.* ◀ any rosaceous shrub of the genus *Cotoneaster*, bearing usu. bright red berries.

cot·tage /kótij/ *n.* **1** a small, simple house, esp. in the country. **2** a dwelling forming part of a farm establishment, used by a worker. □□ **cot·tag·ey** *adj.*

cot·tage cheese *n.* soft white cheese made from curds of skimmed milk.

cot·tage in·dus·try *n.* a business activity partly or wholly carried on at home.

cot·tag·er /kótijər/ *n.* a person who lives in a cottage.

cot·ter /kótər/ *n.* **1** a bolt or wedge for securing parts of machinery, etc. **2** (in full **cotter pin**) a split pin that opens after passing through a hole.

cot·ton /kót'n/ *n. & v.* ● *n.* **1** ▶ a soft, white fibrous substance covering the seeds of certain plants. **2 a** (in full **cotton plant**) such a plant, esp. any of the genus *Gossypium*. **b** cotton plants cultivated as a crop for the fiber or the seeds. **3** thread or cloth made from the fiber. **4** (*attrib.*) made of cotton. ● *v.intr.* (foll. by *to*) be attracted by (a person). □ **cotton to** (or **on to**) *colloq.* **1** begin to be fond of or agreeable to. **2** begin to understand. □□ **cot·ton·y** *adj.*

remains of
fruit capsule

seed hairs
(cotton)

COTTON BOLL

cot·ton cake *n.* compressed cottonseed used as food for cattle.

cot·ton can·dy *n.* a fluffy mass of spun sugar, usu. served on a stick or a paper cone.

cotton gin *n.* a machine for separating cotton from its seeds.

cot·ton·mouth /kót'nmowth/ *n.* a venomous pit viper, *Agkistrodon piscivorus*, of swampy areas of the southeastern US, related to the coppermouth. Also called **water moccasin**.

cot·ton-pick·ing *adj. sl.* unpleasant; wretched.

cot·ton·tail /kót'ntayl/ *n.* any rabbit of the genus *Sylvilagus*, native to America, having a mainly white fluffy tail.

cot·ton·wood /kót'nwŏŏd/ *n.* **1** any of several poplars, native to N. America, having seeds covered in white cottony hairs. **2** any of several trees native to Australia, esp. a downy-leaved tree, *Bedfordia arborescens*.

true leaf

cot·y·le·don /kót'léed'n/ *n.* **1** ▶ an embryonic leaf in seed-bearing plants. **2** any succulent plant of the genus *Umbilicus*, e.g., pennywort. □□ **cot·y·le·don·ar·y** *adj.* **cot·y·le·don·ous** *adj.*

cotyledons

cou·cal /kŏŏkəl/ *n.* any ground-nesting bird of the genus *Centropus*, related to the cuckoos.

couch[1] /kowch/ *n. & v.* ● *n.* **1** an upholstered piece of furniture for several people; a sofa. **2** a long padded seat with a headrest at one end. ● *v.* **1** *tr.* (foll. by *in*) express in words of a specified kind (*couched in simple language*). **2** *tr.* lay on or as on a couch. **3** *intr.* **a** (of an animal) lie, esp. in its lair. **b** lie in ambush. **4** *tr.* lower

COTYLEDONS ON A DICOTYLEDONOUS SEEDLING

(a spear, etc.) to the position for attack. **5** *tr. Med.* treat (a cataract) by displacing the lens of the eye.

couch[2] /kowch, kŏŏch/ *n.* (in full **couch grass**) any of several grasses of the genus *Agropyron*, esp. *A. repens*, having long, creeping roots. ▷ GRASS

cou·chette /kŏŏshét/ *n.* **1** a railroad car with seats convertible into sleeping berths. **2** a berth in this.

couch po·ta·to *n. sl.* a person who likes lazing at home, esp. watching television.

cou·gar /kŏŏgər/ *n.* a puma.

cough /kawf, kof/ *v. & n.* ● *v.intr.* **1** expel air from the lungs with a sudden, sharp sound to remove an obstruction or congestion. **2** (of an engine, gun, etc.) make a similar sound. ● *n.* **1** an act of coughing. **2** a condition of the respiratory organs causing coughing. **3** a tendency to cough. □ **cough out 1** eject by coughing. **2** say with a cough. **cough up 1** = *cough out.* **2** *sl.* bring out or give (money or information) reluctantly. **3** *sl.* confess.

cough drop *n.* a medicated lozenge to relieve a cough.

cough med·i·cine *n.* (also **cough syrup**) a medicated liquid to relieve a cough.

could *past* of CAN[1].

couldn't /kŏŏd'nt/ *contr.* could not.

cou·lomb /kŏŏlom/ *n. Electr.* the SI unit of electric charge. ¶ Symb.: **C**.

coun·cil /kównsəl/ *n.* **1 a** an advisory, deliberative, or administrative body of people. **b** a meeting of such a body. **2 a** the elected local legislative body of a town, city, or county. **3** a body of persons chosen as advisers. **4** an ecclesiastical assembly.

coun·cil·man /kównsəlmən/ *n.* (*pl.* **-men**; *fem.* **councilwoman**, *pl.* **-women**) a member of a council.

coun·cil of war *n.* (*pl.* **councils of war**) **1** an assembly of officers called in a special emergency. **2** any meeting held to plan a response to an emergency.

coun·cil·or /kównsələr, -slər/ *n.* (also **coun·cil·lor**) an elected member of a council, esp. a local one. □□ **coun·cil·or·ship** *n.*

coun·sel /kównsəl/ *n. & v.* ● *n.* **1** advice, esp. formally given. **2** consultation, esp. to seek or give advice. **3** (*pl.* same) an attorney or other legal adviser; a body of these in a case. **4** a plan of action. ● *v.tr.* **1** (often foll. by *to* + infin.) advise (a person). **2 a** give advice to (a person) on personal problems, esp. professionally. **b** assist or guide (a person) in resolving personal difficulties. **3** (often foll. by *that*) recommend (a course of action). □□ **coun·sel·ing** /kównsəling, -sling/ *n.*

coun·se·lor /kównsələr, -slər/ *n.* **1** an adviser. **2** a person trained to give guidance on personal problems. **3** a senior officer in the diplomatic service. **4** (also **coun·se·lor-at-law** *pl.* **counselors-at-law**) a lawyer, esp. one who gives advice in law.

count[1] /kownt/ *v. & n.* ● *v.* **1** *tr.* determine the total number or amount of, esp. by assigning successive numbers. **2** *intr.* repeat numbers in ascending order. **3 a** *tr.* (often foll. by *in*) include in one's reckoning or plan (*you can count me in*; *fifteen people, counting the guide*). **b** *intr.* be included in a reckoning or plan. **4** *tr.* consider (a thing or a person) to be (lucky, etc.). **5** *intr.* (often foll. by *for*) have value; matter (*his opinion counts for a great deal*). ● *n.* **1 a** the act of counting (*after a count of fifty*). **b** the sum total of a reckoning (*pollen count*). **2** *Law* each charge in an indictment (*guilty on ten counts*). **3** a count of up to ten seconds by a referee when a boxer is knocked down. **4** *Polit.* the act of counting the votes after a general or local election. **5** one of several points under discussion. **6** the measure of the fineness of a yarn expressed as the weight of a given length or the length of a given weight. **7** *Physics* the number of ionizing particles detected by a counter. □ **count against** be reckoned to the disadvantage of. **count one's blessings** be grateful for what one has. **count one's chickens** be overoptimistic or hasty in anticipating good fortune. **count the cost**

consider the risks before taking action. **count the days** (or **hours**, etc.) be impatient. **count down** recite numbers backward to zero, esp. as part of a rocket-launching procedure. **count on** (or **upon**) depend on; rely on; expect confidently. **count out 1** count while taking from a stock. **2** complete a count of ten seconds over (a fallen boxer, etc.), indicating defeat. **3** (in children's games) select (a player) for dismissal or a special role by use of a counting rhyme, etc. **4** *colloq.* exclude from a plan or reckoning (*I'm too tired, count me out*). **count up** find the sum of. **down for the count 1** *Boxing* defeated by being unable to rise within ten seconds. **2 a** defeated or demoralized. **b** sound asleep. **keep count** take note of how many there have been, etc. **lose count** fail to take note of the number, etc. **not counting** excluding from the reckoning. **take the count** *Boxing* be defeated.

count[2] /kownt/ *n.* a noble of continental Europe corresponding in rank to a British earl. □□ **count·ship** *n.*

count·a·ble /kówntəbəl/ *adj.* **1** that can be counted. **2** *Gram.* (of a noun) that can form a plural or be used with the indefinite article (e.g., *book*, *kindness*).

count·down /kówntdown/ *n.* **1 a** the act of counting down, esp. at the launching of a rocket, etc. **b** the procedures carried out during this time. **2** the final moments before any significant event.

coun·te·nance /kówntinəns/ *n. & v.* ● *n.* **1 a** the face. **b** the facial expression. **2** composure. **3** moral support. ● *v.tr.* **1** give approval to (an act, etc.). **2** (often foll. by *in*) encourage (a person or a practice). □ **change countenance** alter one's expression as an effect of emotion. **keep one's countenance** maintain composure, esp. by refraining from laughter. **keep a person in countenance** support or encourage a person. **lose countenance** become embarrassed. **out of countenance** disconcerted.

coun·ter[1] /kówntər/ *n.* **1 a** a long, flat-topped fixture in a store, bank, etc., across which business is conducted. **b** a similar structure used for serving food, etc., in a cafeteria or bar. **2 a** a small disk used for keeping the score, etc., esp. in board games. **b** a token representing a coin. **c** something used in bargaining (*a counter in the struggle for power*). **3** an apparatus used for counting. **4** *Physics* an apparatus used for counting individual ionizing particles, etc. **5** a person or thing that counts. □ **over the counter a** (of stock) through a broker directly, not on an exchange **b** by ordinary retail purchase. **under the counter** (esp. of the sale of scarce goods) surreptitiously, esp. illegally.

coun·ter[2] /kówntər/ *v., adv., adj., & n.* ● *v.* **1** *tr.* **a** oppose; contradict (*countered our proposal with their own*). **b** meet by a countermove. **2** *intr.* **a** make a countermove. **b** make an opposing statement. **3** *intr. Boxing* give a return blow while parrying. ● *adv.* **1** in the opposite direction (*ran counter to the fox*). **2** contrary (*her action was counter to my wishes*). ● *adj.* **1** opposed; opposite. **2** duplicate; serving as a check. ● *n.* **1** a parry; a countermove. **2** something opposite or opposed. □ **counter to** (or **go**) **counter to** disobey (instructions, etc.). **go** (or **run**) **counter** run or ride against the direction taken by a quarry. **run counter to** act contrary to.

counter- /kówntər/ *comb. form* denoting: **1** retaliation, opposition, or rivalry (*counterthreat*; *countercheck*). **2** opposite direction (*countercurrent*). **3** correspondence, duplication, or substitution (*counterpart*; *countersign*).

coun·ter·act /kówntərákt/ *v.tr.* **1** hinder or oppose by contrary action. **2** neutralize. □□ **coun·ter·ac·tion** /-ákshən/ *n.* **coun·ter·ac·tive** *adj.*

coun·ter·at·tack *n. & v.* ● *n.* /kówntərətak/ an attack in reply to an attack by an enemy or opponent. ● *v.tr. & intr.* /kówntərəták/ attack in reply.

coun·ter·at·trac·tion /kówntərətrákshən/ *n.* **1** a rival attraction. **2** the attraction of a contrary tendency.

C

coun·ter·bal·ance *n. & v.* ● *n.* /kówntərbaləns/ **1** a weight balancing another. **2** an argument, force, etc., balancing another. ● *v.tr.* /kówntərbáləns/ act as a counterbalance to.

coun·ter·blast /kówntərblast/ *n.* (often foll. by *to*) an energetic or violent verbal or written reply to an argument, etc.

coun·ter·charge *n. & v.* ● *n.* /kówntərchaarj/ a charge or accusation in return for one received. ● *v.tr.* /kówntərcháarj/ make a countercharge against.

coun·ter·claim *n. & v.* ● *n.* /kówntərklaym/ **1** a claim made against another claim. **2** *Law* a claim made by a defendant in a suit against the plaintiff. ● *v.tr. & intr.* /kówntərkláym/ make a counterclaim (for).

coun·ter·clock·wise /kówntərklókwīz/ *adv. & adj.* ● *adv.* in a curve opposite in direction to the movement of the hands of a clock. ● *adj.* moving counterclockwise.

coun·ter·cul·ture /kówntərkulchər/ *n.* a way of life, etc., opposed to that usually considered normal.

coun·ter·es·pi·o·nage /kówntəréspeeə-naa**zh**, -nij/ *n.* action taken to frustrate enemy spying.

coun·ter·feit /kówntərfit/ *adj., n., & v.* ● *adj.* **1** not genuine. **2** (of a claimant, etc.) pretended. ● *n.* a forgery; an imitation. ● *v.tr.* **1 a** imitate fraudulently (a coin, handwriting, etc.); forge. **b** make an imitation of. **2** simulate (feelings, etc.) (*counterfeited interest*). **3** resemble closely. □□ **coun·ter·feit·er** *n.*

coun·ter·in·tel·li·gence /kówntərintélijəns/ *n.* = COUNTERESPIONAGE.

coun·ter·mand *v. & n.* ● *v.tr.* /kówntərmánd/ **1** *Mil.* **a** revoke (an order or command). **b** recall (forces, etc.) by a contrary order. **2** cancel an order for (goods, etc.). ● *n.* /kówntərmand/ an order revoking a previous one.

coun·ter·march *v. & n.* ● *v.intr. & tr.* /kówntər-máarch/ esp. *Mil.* march or cause to march in the opposite direction. ● *n.* /kówntərmaarch/ an act of countermarching.

coun·ter·meas·ure /kówntərme**zh**ər/ *n.* an action taken to counteract a danger, threat, etc.

coun·ter·move *n. & v.* ● *n.* /kówntərmoov/ a move or action in opposition to another. ● *v.intr.* /kówntərmoov/ make a countermove. □□ **coun·ter·move·ment** *n.*

coun·ter·of·fen·sive /kówntərəfénsiv/ *n. Mil.* an attack made from a defensive position.

coun·ter·pane /kówntərpayn/ *n.* a bedspread.

coun·ter·part /kówntərpaart/ *n.* **1 a** a person or thing extremely like another. **b** a natural complement or equivalent. **2** *Law* one of two copies of a legal document.

coun·ter·plot *n. & v.* ● *n.* /kówntərplot/ a plot intended to defeat another plot. ● *v.* /kówntərplót/ (**-plotted**, **-plotting**) **1** *intr.* make a counterplot. **2** *tr.* make a counterplot against.

coun·ter·point /kówntərpoynt/ *n. & v.* ● *n.* **1** *Mus.* **a** the art of writing or playing a melody or melodies in conjunction with another, according to fixed rules. **b** a melody played in conjunction with another. **2** a contrasting argument, plot, idea, etc., used to set off the main element. ● *v.tr.* **1** *Mus.* add counterpoint to. **2** set (an argument, plot, etc.) in contrast to (a main element).

coun·ter·poise *n. & v.* ● *n.* /kówntərpoyz/ **1** a force, etc., equivalent to another on the opposite side. **2** a state of equilibrium. **3** a counterbalancing weight. ● *v.tr.* /kówntərpóyz/ **1** counterbalance. **2** compensate. **3** bring into or keep in equilibrium.

coun·ter·pro·duc·tive /kówntərprədúktiv/ *adj.* having the opposite of the desired effect.

coun·ter·ref·or·ma·tion /kówntəréfərmáyshən/ *n.* **1** (**Counter-Reformation**) *hist.* the reform of the Roman Catholic Church in the 16th and 17th centuries that took place in response to the Protestant Reformation. **2** a reformation running counter to another.

coun·ter·rev·o·lu·tion /kówntərévəlóo̅shən/ *n.* a revolution opposing a former one or reversing its results. □□ **coun·ter·rev·o·lu·tion·ar·y** *adj. & n.* (*pl.* **-ies**).

coun·ter·sign /kówntərsīn/ *v. & n.* ● *v.tr.* **1** add a signature to (a document already signed by another). **2** ratify. ● *n.* **1** a watchword or password spoken to a person on guard. **2** a mark used for identification, etc. □□ **coun·ter·sig·na·ture** /-sígnəchər/ *n.*

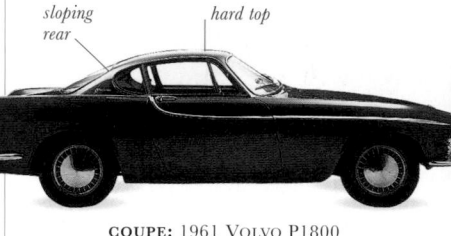

countersink drill bit

countersunk hole

COUNTERSINK

coun·ter·sink /kówntər-síngk/ *v.tr.* (*past* and *past part.* **-sunk**) **1** ◄ enlarge and bevel (the rim of a hole) so that a screw or bolt can be inserted flush with the surface. **2** sink (a screw, etc.) in such a hole.

coun·ter·stroke /kówntərstrōk/ *n.* a blow given in return for another.

coun·ter·ten·or /kówntərtenər/ *n. Mus.* **1 a** the highest adult male singing voice, above tenor. **b** a singer with this voice. **2** a part written for countertenor.

coun·ter·top /kówntərtop/ *n.* a horizontal, flat work surface, as in a kitchen.

coun·ter·vail /kówntərváyl/ *v.* **1** *tr.* counterbalance. **2** *tr. & intr.* (often foll. by *against*) oppose forcefully and usu. successfully.

coun·ter·weight /kówntərwayt/ *n.* a counterbalancing weight.

count·ess /kówntis/ *n.* **1** the wife or widow of a count or an earl. **2** a woman holding the rank of count or earl.

count·ing·house /kówntinghows/ *n.* a place where accounts are kept.

count·less /kówntlis/ *adj.* too many to be counted.

coun·tri·fied /kúntrifīd/ *adj.* (also **coun·try·fied**) often *derog.* rural or rustic, esp. of manners, appearance, etc.

coun·try /kúntree/ *n.* (*pl.* **-ies**) **1 a** the territory of a nation with its own government; a nation. **b** a territory possessing its own language, people, culture, etc. **2** (often *attrib.*) rural districts as opposed to towns and cities or the capital (*a cottage in the country*; *a country town*). **3** the land of a person's birth or citizenship; a fatherland. **4 a** a territory, esp. an area of interest or knowledge. **b** a region associated with a particular person, esp. a writer (*Faulkner country*). **5** a national population, esp. as voters (*the country won't stand for it*). □ **across country** not keeping to roads.

coun·try and west·ern *n.* rural or cowboy music originating in the US, and usu. accompanied by a guitar, etc.

coun·try club *n.* a golfing and social club, often in a rural setting.

coun·try·fied var. of COUNTRIFIED.

coun·try·man /kúntreemən/ *n.* (*pl.* **-men**; *fem.* **countrywoman**, *pl.* **-women**) **1** a person living in a rural area. **2 a** a person of one's own country or district. **b** (often in *comb.*) a person from a specified country or district (*north-countryman*).

coun·try mu·sic *n.* = COUNTRY AND WESTERN.

coun·try·side /kúntreesīd/ *n.* **1 a** a rural area. **b** rural areas in general. **2** the inhabitants of a rural area.

coun·ty /kówntee/ *n. & adj.* ● *n.* (*pl.* **-ies**) **1** *US* a political and administrative division of a state. **2** any of the territorial divisions of some countries, forming the chief unit of local administration.

coun·ty seat *n.* the administrative capital of a county.

coup /koo̅/ *n.* (*pl.* **coups** /koo̅z/) **1** a notable or successful stroke or move. **2** = COUP D'ÉTAT.

coup de grâce /koo̅ də gráas/ *n.* (*pl.* **coups de grâce** *pronunc.* same) a finishing stroke, esp. to kill a wounded animal or person.

coup d'état /koo̅ daytáa/ *n.* (*pl.* **coups d'état** *pronunc.* same) a violent or illegal seizure of power.

coupe /koo̅p/ *n.* (also **cou·pé** /koo̅páy/) ▼ a two-door car with a hard top.

sloping rear

hard top

COUPE: 1961 VOLVO P1800
TWO-PLUS-TWO COUPE

cou·ple /kúpəl/ *n. & v.* ● *n.* **1** (usu. foll. by *of*; often as *sing.*) **a** two (*a couple of girls*). **b** about two (*a couple of hours*). **2** (often as *sing.*) **a** a married, engaged, or similar pair. **b** a pair of partners in a dance, a game, etc. **c** a pair of rafters. **3** (*pl.* **couple**) a pair of hunting dogs. **4** (in *pl.*) a pair of joined collars used for holding hounds together. **5** *Mech.* a pair of equal and parallel forces acting in opposite directions, and tending to cause rotation about an axis perpendicular to the plane containing them. ● *v.* **1** *tr.* fasten or link together; connect (esp. railroad car). **2** *tr.* (often foll. by *together, with*) associate in thought or speech (*papers coupled their names*). **3** *intr.* copulate. **4** *tr. Physics* connect (oscillators) with a coupling.

cou·pler /kúplər/ *n.* **1** *Mus.* **a** a device in an organ for connecting two manuals, or a manual with pedals, so that they both sound when only one is played. **b** (also **octave coupler**) a similar device for connecting notes with their octaves above or below. **2** anything that connects two things, esp. a transformer used for connecting electric circuits.

cou·plet /kúplit/ *n. Prosody* two successive lines of verse, usu. rhyming and of the same length.

cou·pling /kúpling/ *n.* **1 a** a link connecting a railroad car, etc. ▷ TENDER. **b** a device for connecting parts of machinery. **2** *Physics* a connection between two systems, causing one to oscillate when the other does so. **3** *Mus.* **a** the arrangement of items on a phonograph record. **b** each such item. **4** (act of) sexual intercourse.

cou·pon /kóo̅pon, kyóo̅-/ *n.* **1** a form in a newspaper that may be filled in as an application for a purchase, information, etc. **2** a voucher for a discount on a purchase. **3 a** a detachable ticket entitling the holder to a ration of food, clothes, etc., esp. in wartime. **b** a similar ticket entitling the holder to payment, goods, services, etc.

cour·age /kórij, kúr-/ *n.* the ability to disregard fear; bravery. □ **courage of one's convictions** the courage to act on one's beliefs. **lose courage** become less brave. **pluck up** (or **take**) **courage** muster one's courage. **take one's courage in both hands** nerve oneself to a venture.

cou·ra·geous /kəráyjəs/ *adj.* brave; fearless. □□ **cou·ra·geous·ly** *adv.* **cou·ra·geous·ness** *n.*

cour·i·er /kóo̅reeər, kór-, kúr-/ *n.* **1** a person employed, usu. by a travel company, to guide and assist a group of tourists. **2** a special messenger.

course /kawrs/ *n. & v.* ● *n.* **1** a continuous onward movement or progression. **2 a** a line along which a person or thing moves; a direction taken (*has changed course*; *the course of the winding river*). **b** a correct or intended direction or line of movement. **c** the direction taken by a ship or aircraft. **3 a** the ground on which a race (or other sport involving extensive linear movement) takes place. **b** a series of fences, hurdles, or other obstacles to be crossed in a race, etc. **4 a** a series of lectures, lessons, etc., in a particular subject. **b** a book for such a course (*A Modern French Course*). **5** any of the successive parts of a meal. **6** *Med.* a sequence of medical treatment, etc. (*prescribed a course of antibiotics*). **7** a line of conduct. **8** *Archit.* a continuous horizontal layer of brick, stone, etc., in a building. **9** a channel in which water flows. **10** the pursuit of game (esp. hares) with hounds, esp. greyhounds, by sight rather than scent. **11** *Naut.* a sail on a square-rigged ship. ● *v.* **1** *intr.* (esp. of liquid) run, esp. fast (*blood coursed through his veins*). **2** *tr.* (also *absol.*) **a** use (hounds) to hunt. **b** pursue (hares, etc.) in hunting. □ **the course of nature** ordinary events or procedure. **in the course of** during. **in the course of time** as time goes by; eventually. **a matter of course** the natural or expected thing. **of course** naturally; as is or was to be expected; admittedly. **on** (or **off**) **course** following (or deviating from) the desired direction or goal. **run** (or **take**) **its course** (esp. of an illness) complete its natural development. □□ **cours·er** *n.* (in sense 2 of *v.*).

court /kawrt/ *n. & v.* ● *n.* **1** (in full **court of law**) **a** a judge or assembly of judges or other persons acting as a tribunal in civil and criminal cases. **b** = COURTROOM. **2 a** an enclosed quadrangular area for games, which may be open or covered (*tennis court*; *squash court*). **b** an area marked out for lawn tennis, etc. **3 a** a small enclosed street in a town, having a yard surrounded by houses, and adjoining a larger street. **b** the name of a large house, block of apartments, street, etc. (*Grosvenor Court*). **c** a subdivision of a building, usu. a large hall extending to the ceiling with galleries and staircases. **4 a** the establishment, retinue, and courtiers of a sovereign. **b** a sovereign and his or her councilors, constituting a ruling power. **c** a sovereign's residence. **d** an assembly held by a sovereign; a state reception. **5** attention paid to a person whose favor, love, or interest is sought (*paid court to her*). **6 a** the qualified members of a company or a corporation. **c** a meeting of a court. ● *v.tr.* **1 a** try to win the affection or favor of (a person). **b** pay amorous attention to (*courting couples*). **2** seek to win (applause, fame, etc.). **3** invite (misfortune) by one's actions (*you are courting disaster*). □ **go to court** take legal action. **in court** appearing as a party or an advocate in a court of law. **out of court 1** (of a plaintiff) not entitled to be heard. **2** before a hearing or judgment can take place. **3** not worthy of consideration (*that suggestion is out of court*).

court card *n. Brit.* = FACE CARD.

cour·te·ous /kárteeəs/ *adj.* polite, kind, or considerate. □□ **cour·te·ous·ly** *adv.* **cour·te·ous·ness** *n.*

cour·te·san /káwrtizán/ *n. literary* a prostitute, esp. one with wealthy or upper-class clients.

cour·te·sy /kártisee/ *n.* (*pl.* **-ies**) **1** courteous behavior. **2** a courteous act. □ **by courtesy** by favor, not by right. **by courtesy of** with the formal permission of (a person, etc.).

cour·te·sy light *n.* a light in a car that is switched on by opening a door.

court·house /káwrthows/ *n.* **1** a building in which a judicial court is held. **2** a building containing the administrative offices of a county.

cour·ti·er /káwrteeər/ *n.* a person who attends or frequents a sovereign's court.

court·ly /káwrtlee/ *adj.* (**courtlier, courtliest**) **1** polished or refined in manners. **2** obsequious. **3** punctilious. □□ **court·li·ness** *n.*

court-mar·tial /káwrt máarshəl/ *n. & v.* ● *n.* (*pl.* **courts-martial**) a judicial court for trying members of the armed services. ● *v.tr.* try by a court-martial.

court or·der *n.* a direction issued by a court or a judge, usu. requiring a person to do or not do something.

court re·port·er *n.* a stenographer who makes a verbatim record and transcription of the proceedings in a court of law.

court·room /káwrtroom, -room/ *n.* the place or room in which a court of law meets.

court·ship /káwrtship/ *n.* **1 a** courting with a view to marriage. **b** the courting behavior of male animals, birds, etc. **c** a period of courting. **2** an attempt, often protracted, to gain advantage by flattery, attention, etc.

court·yard /káwrtyaard/ *n.* an area enclosed by walls or buildings, often opening off a street.

cous·cous /kooskoos/ *n.*
▶ a type of N. African semolina in granules made from crushed durum wheat. **2** a spicy dish of this, usu. with meat or fruit added.

cous·in /kúzən/ *n.* **1** (also **first cousin, cous·in-ger·man,** *pl.* **cousins-german**) the child of one's uncle or aunt. **2** (usu. in *pl.*) applied to the people of kindred races or nations (*our British cousins*). □□ **cous·in·hood** *n.* **cous·in·ly** *adj.* **cous·in·ship** *n.*

COUSCOUS

cou·ture /kōotóor, -týr/ *n.* the design and manufacture of fashionable clothes; = HAUTE COUTURE.

cou·tu·ri·er /kōotóoree-ay, -eeər/ *n.* (*fem.* **couturière** /-reeáir/) a fashion designer or dressmaker.

co·va·lent /kōváylənt/ *adj. Chem.* ▼ of or designating chemical bonds formed by the sharing of electrons by two atoms in a molecule. □□ **co·va·lence** *n.* **co·va·len·cy** *n.* **co·va·lent·ly** *adv.*

co·va·lent bond *n. Chem.* a bond formed by sharing of electrons, usu. in pairs by two atoms in a molecule. ▷ ALKANE

cove /kōv/ *n. & v.* ● *n.* **1** a small, esp. sheltered, bay or creek. **2** a sheltered recess. **3** *Archit.* ▼ a concave arch or arched molding, esp. one formed by the junction of a wall with a ceiling. ● *v.tr. Archit.* **1** provide (a room, ceiling, etc.) with a cove. **2** slope (the sides of a fireplace) inward.

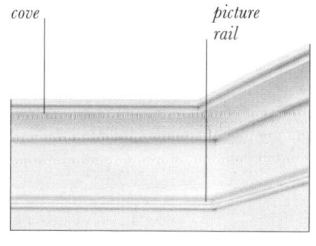

cove   *picture rail*

COVE

cov·en /kúvən/ *n.* an assembly of witches.

cov·e·nant /kúvənənt/ *n. & v.* ● *n.* **1** an agreement; a contract. **2** *Law* **a** a contract drawn up under a seal, esp. undertaking to make regular payments to a charity. **b** a clause of a covenant. **3** (**Covenant**) *Bibl.* the agreement between God and the Israelites (see ARK OF THE COVENANT). ● *v.tr. & intr.* agree, esp. by legal covenant. □□ **cov·e·nan·tal** /-nánt'l/ *adj.* **cov·e·nan·tor** *n.* **covenanter** *n.*

cov·er /kúvər/ *v. & n.* ● *v.tr.* **1 a** (often foll. by *with*) protect or conceal by means of a cloth, lid, etc. **b** prevent the perception or discovery of; conceal (*to cover my embarrassment*). **2 a** extend over; occupy the whole surface of (*covered in dirt*; *covered with writing*). **b** (often foll. by *with*) strew thickly or thoroughly (*covered the floor with straw*). **c** lie over; be a covering to (*the blanket scarcely covered him*). **3 a** protect; clothe. **b** (as **covered** *adj.*) wearing a hat; having a roof. **4** include; comprise; deal with (*the talk covered recent discoveries*). **5** travel (a specified distance) (*covered sixty miles*). **6** *Journalism* **a** report (events, a meeting, etc.). **b** investigate as a reporter. **7** be enough to defray (expenses, a bill, etc.). **8 a** *refl.* take precautionary measures so as to protect oneself (*had covered myself by saying I might be late*). **b** (*absol.*; foll. by *for*) deputize or stand in for (a colleague, etc.) (*will you cover for me?*). **9** *Mil.* **a** aim a gun, etc., at. **b** (of a fortress, guns, etc.) command (a territory). **c** stand behind (a person in the front rank). **d** protect (an exposed person, etc.) by being able to return fire. **10** (also

absol.) (in some card games) play a card higher than (one already played to the same trick). **11** (of a stallion, a bull, etc.) copulate with. ● *n.* **1** something that covers or protects, esp.: **a** a lid. **b** the binding of a book. **c** either board of this. **d** an envelope or the wrapping of a mailed package (*under separate cover*). **e** the outer case of a pneumatic tire. **f** (in *pl.*) bedclothes. **2** a hiding place; a shelter. **3** woods or undergrowth sheltering game or covering the ground (see COVERT *n.* 1). **4 a** a pretense; a screen (*under cover of humility*). **b** a spy's pretended identity or activity. **c** *Mil.* a supporting force protecting an advance party from attack. **5** a place setting at table, esp. in a restaurant. □ **break cover** (of game or a hunted person) leave a place of shelter, esp. vegetation. **cover in** provide with a roof, etc. **cover one's tracks** conceal evidence of what one has done. **cover up 1** completely cover or conceal. **2** conceal (circumstances, etc., esp. illicitly) (also *absol.*: *refused to cover up for them*). **from cover to cover** from beginning to end of a book, etc. **take cover** use a natural or prepared shelter against an attack.

cov·er·age /kúvərij/ *n.* **1** an area or an amount covered. **2** *Journalism* the amount of press, etc., publicity received by a particular story, person, etc. **3** a risk covered by an insurance policy. **4** an area reached by a particular broadcasting station or advertising medium.

cov·er·all /kúvərawl/ *n. & adj.* ● *n.* **1** something that covers entirely. **2** (usu. in *pl.*) a full-length protective outer garment often zipped up the front. ● *attrib.adj.* covering entirely (*a coverall term*).

cov·er charge *n.* an extra charge levied per head in a restaurant, nightclub, etc.

cov·er girl *n.* a female model whose picture appears on magazine covers, etc.

cov·er·ing /kúvəring/ *n.* something that covers, esp. a bedspread, blanket, etc., or clothing.

cov·er·ing let·ter *n.* = COVER LETTER.

cov·er·let /kúvərlit/ *n.* a bedspread.

cov·er let·ter *n.* (also **cov·er·ing let·ter**) an explanatory letter sent with an enclosure.

cov·er sto·ry *n.* a news story in a magazine, that is illustrated or advertised on the front cover.

COVALENT

Covalent compounds are made up of molecules whose atoms are held together by covalent bonds. For example, an ammonia molecule is made up of three hydrogen atoms and one nitrogen atom. Each covalent bond consists of two shared electrons – one from the nitrogen atom and one from a hydrogen atom.

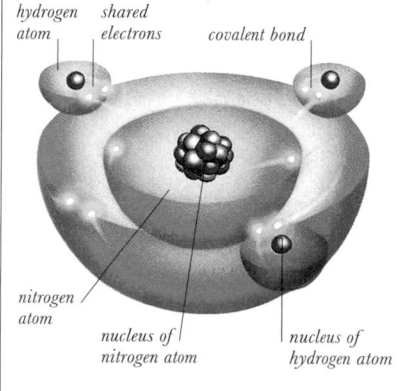

hydrogen atom   *shared electrons*   *covalent bond*

nitrogen atom

nucleus of nitrogen atom   *nucleus of hydrogen atom*

COVALENT BONDS IN AN AMMONIA MOLECULE (NH_3)

C

C

co·vert /kóvərt, kú-/ adj. & n. ● adj. secret or disguised (*a covert glance; covert operations*). ● n. 1 a shelter, esp. a thicket hiding game. 2 a feather covering the base of a bird's flight feather. ▷ BIRD, FEATHER. □□ **co·vert·ly** adv. **co·vert·ness** n.

cov·et /kúvit/ v.tr. desire greatly (esp. something belonging to another person). □□ **cov·et·a·ble** adj.

cov·et·ous /kúvitəs/ adj. (usu. foll. by *of*) 1 greatly desirous (esp. of another person's property). 2 grasping; avaricious. □□ **cov·et·ous·ly** adv. **cov·et·ous·ness** n.

cov·ey /kúvee/ n. (pl. **-eys**) 1 a brood of partridges. 2 a small party or group of people or things.

cov·ing n. = COVE n. 3.

cow[1] /kow/ n. 1 a fully grown female of any bovine animal, esp. used as a source of milk and beef. ▷ RUMINANT. 2 the female of other large animals, esp. the elephant, whale, and seal. 3 *sl. derog.* a woman, esp. a coarse or unpleasant one. □ **till the cows come home** *colloq.* an indefinitely long time.

cow[2] /kow/ v.tr. (usu. in *passive*) intimidate or dispirit (*cowed by ill-treatment*).

cow·ard /kówərd/ n. a person who is easily frightened or intimidated by danger or pain.

cow·ard·ice /kówərdis/ n. a lack of bravery.

cow·ard·ly /kówərdlee/ adj. 1 of or like a coward; lacking courage. 2 (of an action) done against one who cannot retaliate. □□ **cow·ard·li·ness** n.

cow·bell /kówbel/ n. 1 ◀ a bell worn around a cow's neck for easy location of the animal. 2 a similar bell used as a percussion instrument.

cow·boy /kówboy/ n. 1 (*fem.* **cow·girl**) a person who herds and tends cattle, esp. in the western US. 2 this as a conventional figure in American folklore, esp. in films. 3 *colloq.* an unscrupulous or reckless person in business.

COWBELL

cow·catch·er /kówkachər/ n. ◀ a peaked metal frame at the front of a locomotive for pushing aside obstacles on the line.

cow·er /kowər/ v.intr. 1 crouch or shrink back, esp. in fear; cringe. 2 stand or squat in a bent position.

cow·hand /kówhand/ n. = COWBOY 1.

cow·herd /kówhərd/ n. a person who tends cattle.

cow·hide /kówhīd/ n. 1 a a cow's hide. b leather made from this. 2 a leather whip made from cowhide.

cowcatcher

cowl /kowl/ n. 1 a the hood of a monk's habit. b a loose hood. c a monk's hooded habit. 2 the hood-shaped covering of a chimney or ventilating shaft. ▷ SHIP. 3 the removable cover of a vehicle or aircraft engine. ▷ AIRCRAFT, OUTBOARD. □□ **cowled** adj. (in sense 1).

COWCATCHER ON A 19TH-CENTURY NORTH AMERICAN LOCOMOTIVE

cow·lick /kówlik/ n. a projecting lock of hair.

cowl·ing /kówling/ n. = COWL 3.

cow·man /kówmən/ n. (pl. **-men**) 1 = COWHERD. 2 a cattle owner.

co·work·er /kó-wárkər/ n. a person who works in collaboration with another.

cow pars·ley n. a tall hedgerow plant, *Anthriscus sylvestris*, having lacelike umbels of flowers resembling Queen Anne's lace.

cow·pat /kówpat/ n. a flat, round piece of cow dung.

cow·pea /kówpee/ n. 1 a plant of the pea family, *Vigna unguiculata*, grown esp. in the southern US for forage and green manure. 2 its edible seed. Also called **black-eyed pea**.

columellar lip   *outer lip*

canal   *teeth*

COWRIE: GOLDEN COWRIE SHELL (*Cypraea aurantium*)

cow·poke /kówpōk/ n. = COWBOY 1.

cow·pox /kówpoks/ n. a disease of cows, of which the virus was formerly used in vaccination against smallpox.

cow·punch·er /kówpunchər/ n. = COWBOY 1.

cow·rie /kówree/ n. (also **cow·ry**) (pl. **-ies**) 1 any gastropod mollusk of the family Cypraeidae, having a smooth, glossy, and usu. brightly colored shell. 2 ◀ its shell, esp. used as money in parts of Africa and S. Asia. ▷ SHELL.

cow·shed /kówshed/ n. 1 a shed for cattle that are not at pasture. 2 a milking shed.

cow·slip /kówslip/ n. 1 ▶ a primula, *Primula veris*, with fragrant yellow flowers and growing in pastures. 2 a marsh marigold.

cox /koks/ n. & v. ● n. a coxswain, esp. of a racing boat. ● v. 1 *intr.* act as a cox (*coxed for Harvard*). 2 *tr.* act as cox for (*coxed the winning boat*).

cox·comb /kókskōm/ n. an ostentatiously conceited man; a dandy. □□ **cox·comb·ry** /-kōmree, -kəmree/ n. (pl. **-ies**).

cox·swain /kóksən, -swayn/ n. & v. ● n. a person who steers and directs the crew, esp. in a rowing boat.

COWSLIP (*Primula veris*)

● v. 1 *intr.* act as a coxswain. 2 *tr.* act as a coxswain of. □□ **cox·swain·ship** n.

coy /koy/ adj. (**coyer, coyest**) 1 archly or affectedly shy. 2 irritatingly reticent (*always coy about her age*). 3 (esp. of a girl) modest or shy. □□ **coy·ly** adv. **coy·ness** n.

coy·o·te /kīyótee, kíyót/ n. (pl. same or **coyotes**) a wolflike wild dog, *Canis latrans*, native to N. America.

coy·pu /kóypōō/ n. (pl. **coypus**) = NUTRIA 1.

co·zy /kózee/ adj., n., & v. ● adj. (**cozier, coziest**) 1 comfortable and warm. 2 *derog.* complacent; self-serving. 3 warm and friendly. ● n. (pl. **-ies**) a cover to keep something hot, esp. a teapot or a boiled egg. ● v.tr. (**-ies, -ied**) (often foll. by *along*) *colloq.* reassure, esp. deceptively. □ **cozy up to** *colloq.* 1 ingratiate oneself with. 2 snuggle up to. □□ **co·zi·ly** adv. **co·si·ness** n.

cp. abbr. compare.

CPA abbr. certified public accountant.

cpd abbr. compound.

CPI abbr. consumer price index.

Cpl. abbr. corporal.

CPR abbr. cardiopulmonary resuscitation.

cps abbr. (also **c.p.s.**) 1 *Computing* characters per second. 2 cycles per second.

Cpt. abbr. captain.

CPU abbr. *Computing* central processing unit.

Cr symb. *Chem.* the element chromium.

crab[1] /krab/ n. 1 a ▼ any of numerous ten-footed crustaceans having the first pair of legs modified as pincers. b the flesh of a crab, esp. *Cancer pagurus*, as food. 2 (**the Crab**) the

---

CRAB

Crabs live in many different aquatic habitats and – particularly in the Tropics – on dry land. All have a carapace, but there are two types of body shape. Brachyuran crabs, such as the edible crab (below), have broad bodies, with a small abdomen tucked beneath. Anomuran crabs are usually long-bodied, often with a soft, curled abdomen. Hermit crabs protect their abdomens by taking over the empty shells of mollusks.

dactylus

propodus

carpus

compound eye

EXTERNAL FEATURES OF AN EDIBLE CRAB (*Cancer pagurus*)

antenna

cheliped (pincer)

merus

second leg

third leg

fourth leg

fifth leg

abdomen   *carapace*

EXAMPLES OF CRABS

BRACHYURANS

enlarged pincer (male only)

eye on long stalk

FIDDLER CRAB (*Uca vocans*)

SHINY SPIDER CRAB (*Maja squinado*)

ANOMURANS

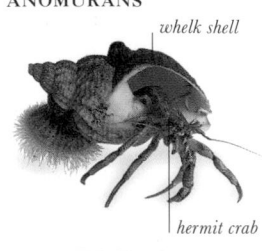

whelk shell

hermit crab

HERMIT CRAB (*Pagurus* species)

zodiacal sign or constellation Cancer. ▷ CANCER. **3** (in full **crab louse**) (often in *pl.*) a parasitic louse, *Phthirus pubis*, infesting hairy parts of the body. **4** a machine for hoisting heavy weights. □ **catch a crab** *Rowing* effect a faulty stroke in which the oar is jammed under water or misses the water altogether. □□ **crab·like** *adj.*

crab² /krab/ *n.* **1** (in full **crab-apple**) ▶ a small sour, apple-like fruit. **2** (in full **crab tree** or **crabapple tree**) any of several trees bearing this fruit. **3** a sour person.

CRABAPPLE
(*Malus* 'Crittenden')

crab³ /krab/ *v.* (**crabbed, crab-bing**) *colloq.* **1** *tr. & intr.* criticize adversely or captiously; grumble. **2** *tr.* act so as to spoil (*the mistake crabbed his chances*).

crabbed /krábid/ *adj.* **1** irritable or morose. **2** (of handwriting) ill-formed and hard to decipher. **3** perverse or cross-grained. **4** difficult to understand. □□ **crab·bed·ly** *adv.* **crab·bed·ness** *n.*

crab·by /krábee/ *adj.* (**crabbier, crabbiest**) = CRABBED 1,3. □□ **crab·bi·ly** *adv.* **crab·bi·ness** *n.*

crab·grass /krábgras/ *n.* a creeping grass infesting lawns.

crab·wise /krábwīz/ *adv. & attrib.adj.* (of movement) sideways or backward like a crab.

crack /krak/ *n., v., & adj.* ● *n.* **1 a** a sudden sharp or explosive noise (*the crack of a whip; a rifle crack*). **b** (in a voice) a sudden harshness or change in pitch. **2** a sharp blow (*a crack on the head*). **3 a** a narrow opening formed by a break (*entered through a crack in the wall*). **b** a partial fracture, with the parts still joined (*the teacup has a crack in it*). **c** a chink (*looked through the crack formed by the door; a crack of light*). **4** *colloq.* a mischievous or malicious remark or aside (*a nasty crack about my age*). **5** *colloq.* an attempt (*I'll have a crack at it*). **6** the exact moment (*at the crack of noon; the crack of dawn*). **7** *sl.* a potent hard crystalline form of cocaine broken into small pieces and inhaled or smoked for its stimulating effect. ● *v.* **1** *tr. & intr.* break without a complete separation of the parts (*cracked the window*). **2** *intr. & tr.* make or cause to make a sudden sharp or explosive sound. **3** *intr. & tr.* break or cause to break with a sudden, sharp sound. **4** *intr.* & *tr.* give way or cause to give way (under torture, etc.); yield. **5** *intr.* (of the voice, esp. of an adolescent boy or a person under strain) become dissonant; break. **6** *tr. colloq.* find a solution to (a problem, code, etc.). **7** *tr.* say (a joke, etc.). **8** *tr. colloq.* hit sharply or hard (*cracked her head on the ceiling*). **9** *tr. Chem.* decompose (heavy oils) by heat and pressure with or without a catalyst to produce lighter hydrocarbons (such as gasoline). **10** *tr.* break (wheat) into coarse pieces. ● *attrib.adj. colloq.* excellent; first-rate (*a crack shot*). □ **crack a bottle** open a bottle, esp. of wine, and drink it. **crack down on** *colloq.* take severe measures against. **crack up** *colloq.* **1** collapse under strain. **2** laugh. **3** repute (*not all it's cracked up to be*). **get cracking** *colloq.* begin promptly and vigorously. **have a crack at** *colloq.* attempt.

crack·brain /krákbrayn/ *n.* a crackpot. □□ **crack·brained** *adj.*

crack·down /krákdown/ *n. colloq.* severe measures (esp. against lawbreakers, etc.).

cracked /krakt/ *adj.* **1** having cracks. **2** (*predic.*) *sl.* crazy.

cracked wheat *n.* wheat that has been crushed into small pieces.

crack·er /krákər/ *n.* **1** a thin, dry biscuit often eaten with cheese. **2** a firework exploding with a sharp noise. **3** (usu. in *pl.*) an instrument for cracking (*nutcrackers*). **4** a paper cylinder both ends of which are pulled at Christmas, etc., making a sharp noise and releasing a small toy, etc. **5** *offens.* = POOR WHITE.

crack·er·bar·rel *adj.* (of philosophy, etc.) unsophisticated.

crack·er·jack /krákərjak/ *adj. sl.* exceptionally fine or expert.

crack·ers /krákərz/ *predic.adj. sl.* crazy.

crack·le /krákəl/ *v. & n.* ● *v.intr.* make a repeated slight cracking sound (*radio crackled; fire was crackling*). ● *n.* **1** such a sound. **2 a** paintwork, china, or glass decorated with a pattern of minute surface cracks. **b** the smooth surface of such paintwork, etc. □□ **crack·ly** *adj.*

crack·ling /krákling/ *n.* the crisp skin of roast pork.

crack·nel /kráknəl/ *n.* a light, crisp biscuit.

crack of doom *n.* a peal of thunder announcing the Day of Judgment.

crack·pot /krákpot/ *n. & adj. sl.* ● *n.* an eccentric or impractical person. ● *adj.* mad; unworkable (*a crackpot scheme*).

crack-up *n. colloq.* **1** a mental breakdown. **2** a car crash.

-cracy /krəsee/ *comb. form* denoting a particular form of government, rule, or influence (*aristocracy; bureaucracy*).

cra·dle /kráyd'l/ *n. & v.* ● *n.* **1 a** a child's bed, esp. one mounted on rockers. **b** a place in which a thing begins, esp. a civilization, etc., or is nurtured in its infancy (*cradle of democracy*). **2** a framework resembling a cradle, esp.: **a** that on which a ship, a boat, etc., rests during construction or repairs. **b** that on which a worker is suspended to work on a ceiling, a ship, the vertical side of a building, etc. **c** the part of a telephone on which the receiver rests when not in use. ● *v.tr.* **1** contain or shelter as if in a cradle (*cradled his head in her arms*). **2** place in a cradle. □ **from the cradle** from infancy. **from the cradle to the grave** from infancy till death.

cra·dle-rob·ber *n. sl.* a person amorously attached to a much younger person.

cra·dle·song /kráyd'lsong/ *n.* a lullaby.

craft /kraft/ *n. & v.* ● *n.* **1** skill, esp. in practical arts. **2 a** (esp. in *comb.*) a trade or an art (*statecraft; handicraft; priestcraft; the craft of pottery*). **b** the members of a craft. **3** (*pl.* **craft**) **a** a boat or vessel. **b** an aircraft or spacecraft. **4** cunning or deceit. **5** (**the Craft**) the brotherhood of Freemasons. ● *v.tr.* make in a skillful way (*he had crafted a poem; a well-crafted piece of work*).

crafts·man /kráftsmən/ *n.* (*pl.* **-men**; *fem.* **crafts·woman**, *pl.* **-women**) **1** a skilled worker, an artisan. **2** a person who practices a handicraft. □□ **crafts·man·ship** *n.*

craft·y /kráftee/ *adj.* (**craftier, craftiest**) cunning; artful; wily. □□ **craft·i·ly** *adv.* **craft·i·ness** *n.*

crag /krag/ *n.* a steep or rugged rock.

crag·gy /krágee/ *adj.* (**craggier, craggiest**) **1** (esp. of a person's face) rugged; rough-textured. **2** (of a landscape) having crags. □□ **crag·gi·ly** *adv.* **crag·gi·ness** *n.*

crake /krayk/ *n.* **1** any rail (see RAIL³), esp. a corncrake. **2** the cry of a corncrake.

cram /kram/ *v.* (**crammed, cramming**) **1** *tr.* **a** fill to bursting; stuff (*the room was crammed*). **b** (foll. by *in, into*) force (a thing) into (*cram the sandwiches into the bag*). **2** *tr. & intr.* prepare for an examination by intensive study. **3** *tr.* (often foll. by *with*) feed (poultry, etc.) to excess. **4** *tr. & intr. colloq.* eat greedily. □ **cram in** push in to bursting point (*crammed in another five minutes' work*).

cramp /kramp/ *n. & v.* ● *n.* **1 a** a painful involuntary contraction of a muscle or muscles from the cold, exertion, etc. **b** = WRITER'S CRAMP. **2** (also **cramp i·ron**) a metal bar with bent ends for holding masonry, etc., together. **3** a portable tool for holding two planks, etc., together; a clamp. **4** a restraint. ● *v.tr.* **1** affect with cramp. **2** confine narrowly. **3** restrict (energies, etc.). **4** (as **cramped** *adj.*) **a** (of handwriting) small and difficult to read. **b** (of a room, etc.) uncomfortably crowded; lacking space. **5** fasten with a cramp. □ **cramp a person's style** prevent a person from acting freely or naturally. **cramp up** confine narrowly.

cram·pon /krámpon/ *n.* (also **cram·poon** /-pŏŏn/) (usu. in *pl.*) **1** ▶ an iron plate with spikes fixed to a boot for walking on ice, climbing, etc. **2** a metal hook for lifting timber, rock, etc.; a grappling iron.

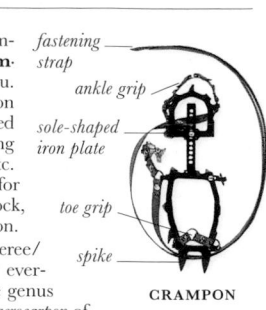
fastening strap
ankle grip
sole-shaped iron plate
toe grip
spike
CRAMPON

cran·ber·ry /kránberee/ *n.* (*pl.* **-ies**) **1** any evergreen shrub of the genus *Vaccinium*, esp. *V. macrocarpon* of America and *V. oxycoccos* of Europe, yielding small, red, acid berries. **2** a berry from this used in cooking.

crane /krayn/ *n. & v.* ● *n.* **1** a machine for moving heavy objects, usu. by suspending them from a projecting beam. **2** any tall wading bird of the family Gruidae, with long legs, long neck, and straight bill. **3** a moving platform supporting a television camera or movie camera. ● *v.tr.* **1** (also *absol.*) stretch out (one's neck) in order to see something. **2** *tr.* move (an object) by a crane.

crane fly /krayn flī/ *n.* (*pl.* **flies**) ▶ a large two-winged fly of the family Tipulidae, with very long legs.

cranes·bill /kráynzbil/ *n.* any of various plants of the genus *Geranium*.

cra·ni·al /kráyneeəl/ *adj.* of or relating to the skull.

cra·nio- /kráyneeō/ *comb. form* cranium.

cra·ni·ol·o·gy /kráyneeóləjee/ *n.* the scientific study of the shape and size of the human skull.

CRANE FLY: EUROPEAN CRANE FLY (*Ctenophora ornata*)

□□ **cra·ni·o·log·i·cal** /-neeəlójikəl/ *adj.* **cra·ni·ol·o·gist** *n.*

cra·ni·om·e·try /kráyneeómitree/ *n.* the scientific measurement of skulls. □□ **cra·ni·o·met·ric** /-neeəmétrik/ *adj.*

cra·ni·ot·o·my /kráyneeótəmee/ *n.* (*pl.* **-ies**) **1** surgical removal of a portion of the skull. **2** surgical perforation of the skull of a dead fetus to ease delivery.

cra·ni·um /kráyneeəm/ *n.* (*pl.* **craniums** or **crania** /-neeə/) **1** the skull. **2** the part of the skeleton that encloses the brain. ▷ SKELETON

crank¹ /krangk/ *n. & v.* ● *n.* **1** part of an axle or shaft bent at right angles for interconverting reciprocal and circular motion. **2** an elbow-shaped connection in bell hanging. ● *v.tr.* **1** cause to move by means of a crank. **2** bend into a crank shape. □ **crank up 1** start (a car engine) by turning a crank. **2** *sl.* increase (speed, etc.) by intensive effort.

crank² /krangk/ *n.* **1** an eccentric person. **2** a bad-tempered person. □□ **crank·y** /krángkee/ *adj.* (**crankier, crankiest**). **crank·i·ly** *adv.* **crank·i·ness** *n.*

crank·case /krángk-kays/ *n.* a case enclosing a crankshaft.

crank·pin /krángkpin/ *n.* a pin by which a connecting rod is attached to a crank. ▷ CRANKSHAFT

crank·shaft /krángkshaft/ *n.* ▼ a shaft driven by a crank (see CRANK¹ *n.* 1). ▷ INTERNAL-COMBUSTION ENGINE

crankshaft journal · *crankpin* · *balance weight* · *shaft*
CRANKSHAFT OF A CAR ENGINE

C

C

CRATER

Meteoric craters are formed by lumps of interplanetary rock striking a planet's surface. Debris is blasted in all directions, creating a circular crater, while rock compressed by the impact rebounds. Gradually, the meteoric crater partly fills in as debris slips from the wall and peak.

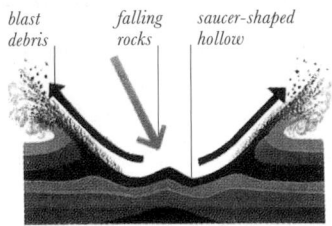

blast debris   falling rocks   saucer-shaped hollow

FORMATION OF A METEORIC CRATER

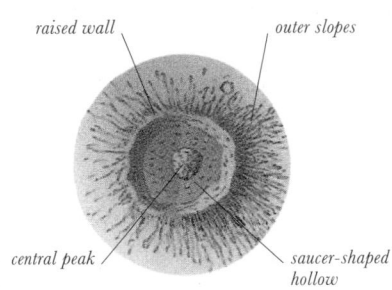

raised wall   outer slopes

central peak   saucer-shaped hollow

OVERHEAD VIEW OF A METEORIC CRATER

cran·ny /kránee/ n. (pl. **-ies**) a chink; a crevice. □□ **cran·nied** /-need/ adj.

crap /krap/ n. & v. coarse sl. ● n. **1** (often as int.) nonsense; rubbish. **2** feces. ● v.intr. (**crapped**, **crapping**) defecate. ¶ Usually considered a taboo word. □ **crap out 1** be unsuccessful. **2** withdraw from a game, etc. □□ **crap·py** /krápee/ adj. (**crappier, crappiest**)

crape /krayp/ n. **1** crepe, usu. of black silk or imitation silk, formerly used for mourning clothes. **2** a band of this formerly worn as a sign of mourning. □□ **crap·y** adj.

craps /kraps/ n.pl. a gambling game played with dice. □ **shoot craps** play craps.

crap·shoot /krápshoot/ n. sl. a venture marked by uncertainty and risk.

crap·u·lent /krápyələnt/ adj. **1** given to indulging in alcohol. **2** resulting from drunkenness. **3 a** drunk. **b** suffering from the effects of drunkenness. □□ **crap·u·lence** /-ləns/ n. **crap·u·lous** adj.

crash[1] /krash/ v., n., & adv. ● v. **1** intr. & tr. make or cause to make a loud smashing noise (the cymbals crashed). **2** tr. & intr. throw, drive, move, or fall with a loud smashing noise. **3** intr. & tr. **a** collide or cause (a vehicle) to collide violently with another vehicle, obstacle, etc. **b** fall or cause (an aircraft) to fall violently on to the land or the sea. **4** intr. (usu. foll. by into) collide violently (crashed into the window). **5** intr. undergo financial ruin. **6** tr. colloq. enter without permission (crashed the cocktail party). **7** intr. colloq. be heavily defeated (crashed to a 4–0 defeat). **8** intr. Computing (of a machine or system) fail suddenly. **9** intr. (often foll. by out) sl. sleep for a night, esp. in an improvised setting. ● n. **1 a** a loud and sudden smashing noise. **b** a breakage (esp. of china, etc.). **2 a** a violent collision, esp. of one vehicle with another or with an object. **b** the violent fall of an aircraft on to the land or sea. **3** ruin, esp. financial. **4** Computing a sudden failure which puts a system out of action. **5** (attrib.) done rapidly or urgently (a

crash course in first aid). ● adv. with a crash (the window went crash).

crash[2] /krash/ n. a coarse plain linen, cotton, etc., fabric.

crash-dive v. & n. ● v. **1** intr. **a** (of a submarine or its pilot) dive hastily and steeply in an emergency. **b** (of an aircraft or pilot) dive and crash. **2** tr. cause to crash-dive. ● n. such a dive.

crash hel·met n. a helmet worn to protect the head in a crash.

crash·ing /kráshing/ adj. colloq. overwhelming (a crashing bore).

crash-land v. **1** intr. (of an aircraft or its pilot) land hurriedly with a crash, usu. without lowering the undercarriage. **2** tr. cause (an aircraft) to crash-land. □□ **crash land·ing** n.

crass /kras/ adj. **1** grossly stupid. **2** gross (crass stupidity). □□ **cras·si·tude** n. **crass·ly** adv. **crass·ness** n.

-crat /krat/ comb. form a member or supporter of a particular form of government or rule (autocrat; democrat).

crate /krayt/ n. & v. ● n. **1** a large wickerwork basket or slatted wooden case, etc., for packing esp. fragile goods for transportation. **2** sl. an old airplane or other vehicle. ● v.tr. pack in a crate. □□ **crate·ful** n. (pl. **-fuls**).

cra·ter /kráytər/ n. & v. ● n. **1** the mouth of a volcano. ▷ VOLCANO. **2** a bowl-shaped cavity, esp. that made by an explosion. **3** Astron. ◀ a hollow with a raised rim on the surface of a planet or moon, caused by impact. ▷ MOON. ● v.tr. form a crater in. □□ **cra·ter·ous** adj.

cra·vat /krəvát/ n. a scarf worn by men inside an open-necked shirt. □□ **cra·vat·ted** adj.

crave /krayv/ v. **1** tr. **a** long for (craved affection). **b** beg for (craves a blessing). **2** intr. (foll. by for) long for; beg for (craved for comfort). □□ **crav·er** n.

cra·ven /kráyvən/ adj. & n. ● adj. (of a person, behavior, etc.) cowardly; abject. ● n. a cowardly person. □□ **cra·ven·ly** adv. **cra·ven·ness** n.

crav·ing /kráyving/ n. (usu. foll. by for) a strong desire or longing.

craw /kraw/ n. Zool. the crop of a bird or insect. □ **stick in one's craw** be unacceptable.

crawl /krawl/ v. & n. ● v.intr. **1** move slowly, esp. on hands and knees. **2** (of a snake, etc.) move slowly with the body close to the ground, etc. **3** walk or move slowly (the train crawled into the station). **4** (often foll. by to) colloq. behave obsequiously or ingratiatingly in the hope of advantage. **5** (often foll. by with) be covered or filled with crawling or moving things or people. **6** (esp. of the skin) feel a creepy sensation. **7** swim with a crawl stroke. ● n. **1** an act of crawling. **2** a slow rate of movement. **3** a high-speed swimming stroke with alternate overarm movements and rapid straight-legged kicks. □□ **crawl·y** adj. (in senses 5, 6 of v.).

crawl·er /kráwlər/ n. **1** (usu. in pl.) a baby's overall for crawling in. **2** anything that crawls, esp. an insect. **3** sl. a person who behaves obsequiously in the hope of advantage.

cray·fish /kráyfish/ n. (also **craw·dad** or **craw·fish**) (pl. same) **1** a small, lobsterlike freshwater crustacean. ▷ CRUSTACEAN. **2** a large marine spiny lobster.

cray·on /kráyon/ n. & v. ● n. **1** a stick or pencil of colored chalk, wax, etc., used for drawing. **2** a drawing made with this. ● v.tr. draw with crayons.

craze /krayz/ v. & n. ● v. **1** tr. (usu. as **crazed** adj.) make insane (crazed with grief). **2 a** tr. produce fine surface cracks on (pottery glaze, etc.). **b** intr. develop such cracks. ● n. **1 a** a usu. temporary enthusiasm (a craze for hula hoops). **b** the object of this. **2** an insane fancy or condition.

cra·zy /kráyzee/ adj. (**crazier, craziest**) **1** colloq. insane or mad; foolish. **2** colloq. (usu. foll. by about) extremely enthusiastic. **3** sl. exciting; unrestrained. **4** (attrib.) (of paving, etc.) made of irregular pieces

fitted together. □ **like crazy** colloq. = like mad (see MAD). □□ **cra·zi·ly** adv. **cra·zi·ness** n.

creak /kreek/ n. & v. ● n. a harsh scraping or squeaking sound. ● v.intr. **1** make a creak. **2 a** move with a creaking noise. **b** move stiffly and awkwardly. **c** show weakness under strain. □□ **creak·ing·ly** adv.

creak·y /kréekee/ adj. (**creakier, creakiest**) **1** liable to creak. **2 a** stiff or frail. **b** (of a practice, etc.) decrepit; outmoded. □□ **creak·i·ly** adv. **creak·i·ness** n.

cream /kreem/ n., v., & adj. ● n. **1 a** the fatty content of milk. **b** this eaten (often whipped) with a dessert, as a cake filling, etc. (strawberries and cream; cream cake). **2** the part of a liquid that gathers at the top. **3** (usu. prec. by the) the best or choicest part of something. **4** a creamlike preparation, esp. a cosmetic (hand cream). **5** a very pale yellow or off-white color. **6 a** a dish like or made with cream. **b** a soup or sauce containing milk or cream. **c** a full-bodied, mellow, sweet sherry. **d** a chocolate-covered usu. fruit-flavored fondant confection. ● v. **1** tr. (usu. foll. by off) **a** take the cream from (milk). **b** take the best or a specified part from. **2** tr. work (butter, etc.) to a creamy consistency. **3** tr. treat (the skin, etc.) with cosmetic cream. **4** tr. add cream to (coffee, etc.). **5** intr. (of milk or any other liquid) form a cream or scum. **6** tr. colloq. defeat soundly or by a wide margin (esp. in a sporting contest). ● adj. pale yellow; off-white.

cream cheese n. a soft, rich cheese made from unskimmed milk and cream.

cream·er /kréemər/ n. **1** a flat dish used for skimming the cream off milk. **2** a machine used for separating cream from milk. **3** a small pitcher for cream.

cream·er·y /kréeməree/ n. (pl. **-ies**) **1** a factory producing butter and cheese. **2** a dairy.

cream of tar·tar n. crystallized potassium hydrogen tartrate, used in medicine, baking powder, etc.

cream puff n. **1** a cake made of puff pastry filled with custard or whipped cream. **2** colloq. an ineffectual or effeminate person.

cream·y /kréemee/ adj. (**creamier, creamiest**) **1** like cream in consistency or color. **2** rich in cream. □□ **cream·i·ly** adv. **cream·i·ness** n.

crease /krees/ n. & v. ● n. **1 a** a line in paper, etc., caused by folding. **b** a fold or wrinkle. **2** an area near the goal in ice hockey or lacrosse into which the puck or the ball must precede the players. ● v. **1** tr. make creases in (material). **2** intr. become creased (linen creases badly).

cre·ate /kree-áyt/ v. **1** tr. **a** bring into existence (poverty creates resentment). **b** (of a person or persons) make or cause (create a diversion). **2** tr. originate (an actor creates a part). **3** tr. invest (a person) with a rank (created him a lord). □□ **cre·at·a·ble** adj.

cre·a·tion /kree-áyshən/ n. **1 a** the act of creating. **b** an instance of this. **2 a** (usu. **the Creation**) the creating of the universe regarded as an act of God. **b** (usu. **Creation**) everything so created; the universe. **3** a product of human intelligence, esp. of imaginative thought or artistic ability. **4 a** the act of investing with a title or rank. **b** an instance of this.

cre·a·tion·ism /kree-áyshənizəm/ n. Theol. a theory attributing all matter, biological species, etc., to separate acts of creation, rather than to evolution. □□ **cre·a·tion·ist** n.

cre·a·tive /kree-áytiv/ adj. **1** inventive and imaginative. **2** creating or able to create. □□ **cre·a·tive·ly** adv. **cre·a·tive·ness** n. **cre·a·tiv·i·ty** /-aytívitee, -ətiv-/ n.

cre·a·tor /kree-áytər/ n. **1** a person who creates. **2** (as **the Creator**) God.

crea·ture /kréechər/ n. **1 a** an animal, as distinct from a human being. **b** any living being (we are all God's creatures). **2** a person of a specified kind (poor creature). **3** a person owing status to and obsequiously subservient to another. **4** anything created. □□ **crea·ture·ly** adj.

crea·ture com·forts *n.pl.* material comforts such as good food, warmth, etc.

crea·ture of hab·it *n.* a person set in an unvarying routine.

crèche /kresh/ *n.* a representation of a Nativity scene.

cred·al see CREED.

cre·dence /kréed'ns/ *n.* **1** belief. **2** (in full **credence table**) a small table, shelf, or niche which holds the elements of the Eucharist before they are consecrated. □ **give credence to** believe.

cre·den·tial /kridénshəl/ *n.* (usu. in *pl.*) **1** evidence of a person's achievements or trustworthiness, usu. in the form of certificates, references, etc. **2** a letter or letters of introduction.

credenza /kridénzə/ *n.* a sideboard or cupboard.

cred·i·bil·i·ty /krédibílitee/ *n.* **1** the condition of being credible or believable. **2** reputation; status.

cred·i·bil·i·ty gap *n.* an apparent difference between what is said and what is true.

cred·i·ble /krédibəl/ *adj.* **1** (of a person or statement) believable or worthy of belief. **2** (of a threat, etc.) convincing. □□ **cred·i·bly** *adv.*

cred·it /krédit/ *n. & v.* ● *n.* **1** (usu. of a person) a source of honor, pride, etc. (*a credit to the school*). **2** the acknowledgment of merit (*must give her credit*). **3** a good reputation (*his credit stands high*). **4 a** a belief or trust (*I place credit in that*). **b** something believable or trustworthy (*that statement has credit*). **5 a** a person's financial standing; the sum of money at a person's disposal in a bank, etc. **b** the power to obtain goods, etc., before payment. **6** (usu. in *pl.*) an acknowledgment of a contributor's services to a film, etc. **7** a reputation for solvency and honesty in business. **8 a** (in bookkeeping) the acknowledgment of being paid by an entry on the credit side of an account. **b** the sum entered. **c** the credit side of an account. **9** a certification indicating that a student has completed a course. ● *v.tr.* **1** believe (*cannot credit it*). **2** (usu. foll. by *to, with*) **a** enter on the credit side of an account. **b** ascribe a good quality or achievement to (*he was credited with the improved sales*). □ **credit a person with** ascribe (a good quality) to a person. **do credit to a person** or **do a person credit** enhance the reputation of a person. **get credit for** be given credit for. **give a person credit for 1** enter (a sum) to a person's credit. **2** ascribe (a good quality) to a person. **give credit to** believe. **on credit** with an arrangement to pay later. **to one's credit** in one's praise or commendation.

cred·it·a·ble /kréditabəl/ *adj.* (often foll. by *to*) bringing credit or honor. □□ **cred·it·a·bil·i·ty** *n.* **cred·it·a·bly** *adv.*

cred·it card *n.* a card from a bank, etc., authorizing the obtaining of goods on credit.

cred·i·tor /kréditər/ *n.* **1** a person to whom a debt is owing (cf. DEBTOR). **2** a person or company that gives credit for money or goods.

cred·it un·ion *n.* a cooperative association that makes low-interest loans to its members.

cred·it·wor·thy /kréditwərthee/ *adj.* considered suitable to receive commercial credit. □□ **cred·it·wor·thi·ness** *n.*

cre·do /kréedō, kráy-/ *n.* (*pl.* **-os**) a statement of belief; a creed.

cred·u·lous /kréjələs/ *adj.* **1** too ready to believe; gullible. **2** (of behavior) showing such gullibility. □□ **cre·du·li·ty** /kridōōlitee, -dyōō-/ *n.* **cred·u·lous·ly** *adv.* **cred·u·lous·ness** *n.*

Cree /kree/ *n. & adj.* ● *n.* (*pl.* same or **Crees**) **1 a** a N. American people of E. and central Canada. **b** a member of this people. **2** the language of this people. ● *adj.* of or relating to the Crees or their language.

creed /kreed/ *n.* **1** a set of principles or opinions, esp. as a philosophy of life (*his creed is moderation in everything*). **2** (also **the Creed**) a brief formal summary of Christian belief. □□ **creed·al** /kréed'l/ *adj.* **cred·al** *adj.*

Creek /kreek/ *n.* **1 a** a confederacy of N. American peoples that formerly occupied much of Alabama and Georgia. **b** a member of these peoples. **2** the language used by these peoples.

creek /kreek, krik/ *n.* *Regional* a stream. □ **up shit creek** *coarse sl.* = *up the creek*. **up the creek** *sl.* in difficulties.

creel /kreel/ *n.* **1** ► a large wicker basket for fish. **2** an angler's fishing basket.

CREEL

creep /kreep/ *v. & n.* ● *v.intr.* (*past* and *past part.* **crept** /krept/) **1** move with the body prone and close to the ground. **2** (often foll. by *in, out, up*, etc.) come, go, or move slowly and stealthily or timidly. **3** enter slowly (into a person's affections, awareness, etc.) (*a feeling crept over her*). **4** *colloq.* act obsequiously in the hope of advancement. **5** (of a plant) grow along the ground or up a wall. **6** (as **creeping** *adj.*) developing slowly and steadily (*creeping inflation*). **7** (of the flesh) feel as if insects, etc., were creeping over it, as a result of fear, etc. **8** (of metals, etc.) undergo deformation. ● *n.* **1 a** the act of creeping. **b** an instance of this. **2** (in *pl.*; prec. by *the*) *colloq.* a feeling of revulsion or fear (*gives me the creeps*). **3** *sl.* an unpleasant person. **4** the gradual downward movement of disintegrated rock due to gravitational forces, etc. **5** (of metals, etc.) a gradual change of shape under stress. **6** a low arch under a railroad embankment, road, etc. □ **creep up on** approach (a person) stealthily or unnoticed.

creep·er /kréepər/ *n.* **1** *Bot.* ▼ any climbing or creeping plant. **2** any bird that climbs, esp. a tree creeper. **3** *sl.* a soft-soled shoe.

CREEPER: CREEPING JENNY
(*Lysimachia nummularia*)

creep·y /kréepee/ *adj.* (**creepier**, **creepiest**) **1** *colloq.* having or producing a creeping of the flesh (*a creepy movie*). **2** given to creeping. □□ **creep·i·ly** *adv.* **creep·i·ness** *n.*

creep·y-crawl·y /kréepeekráwlee/ *n. & adj.* *colloq.* ● *n.* (*pl.* **-ies**) an insect, worm, etc. ● *adj.* creeping and crawling.

cre·mate /kréemayt, krimáyt/ *v.tr.* consume (a corpse, etc.) by fire. □□ **cre·ma·tion** /krimáyshən/ *n.* **cre·ma·tor** *n.*

cre·ma·to·ri·um /kréemətáwreeəm/ *n.* (*pl.* **crematoriums** or **crematoria** /-reeə/) a place for cremating corpses in a furnace.

cre·ma·to·ry /kréemətawree, krém-/ *adj. & n.* ● *adj.* of or relating to cremation. ● *n.* (*pl.* **-ies**) = CREMATORIUM.

crème /krem/ *n.* **1** = CREAM *n.* 6a. **2** a name for various creamy liqueurs (*crème de cassis*).

crème brû·lée /krem brōōláy/ *n.* a dessert of custard topped with caramelized sugar.

crème de la crème /krem də laa krém/ *n.* the best part; the elite.

crème de menthe /krem də maánt, ménth, mínt/ *n.* a green, peppermint-flavored liqueur.

cren·el·ate /krénəlayt/ *v.tr.* ► provide (a castle tower, etc.) with battlements or loopholes. □□ **cren·el·a·tion** /-láyshən/ *n.*

crenelated parapet

CRENELATE:
SPANISH CASTLE TURRET
WITH CRENELATIONS

Cre·ole /krée-ōl/ *n. & adj.* ● *n.* **1 a** a descendant of European (esp. Spanish) settlers in the W. Indies or Central or S. America. **b** a white descendant of French settlers, esp. in Louisiana. **c** a person of mixed European and black descent. **2** a mother tongue formed from the contact of a European language (esp. English, French, or Portuguese) with another (esp. African) language. ● *adj.* **1** of or relating to a Creole or Creoles. **2** (usu. **creole**) of Creole origin or production (*creole cooking*).

cre·o·sote /kréeəsōt/ *n. & v.* ● *n.* **1** (in full **creosote oil**) a dark-brown oil distilled from coal tar, used as a wood preservative. **2** a colorless oily fluid distilled from wood tar, used as an antiseptic. ● *v.tr.* treat with creosote.

crepe /krayp/ *n.* (also **crêpe**) **1** a fine, often gauze-like fabric with a wrinkled surface. **2** a thin pancake, usu. with a savory or sweet filling. **3** (also **crepe rub·ber**) a very hard-wearing wrinkled sheet rubber used for the soles of shoes, etc. □□ **crep·ey** *adj.* **crep·y** *adj.*

crêpe paper *n.* thin crinkled paper.

crêpe suzette /sōōzét/ (also **crêpe Suzette**) a small dessert pancake flamed in alcohol at the table.

crep·i·tate /krépitayt/ *v.intr.* **1** make a crackling sound. **2** *Zool.* (of a beetle) eject pungent fluid with a sharp report. □□ **crep·i·tant** *adj.* **crep·i·ta·tion** /-táyshən/ *n.*

crept *past* and *past part.* of CREEP.

cre·pus·cu·lar /kripúskyələr/ *adj.* **1 a** of twilight. **b** dim. **2** *Zool.* appearing or active in twilight.

cre·scen·do /krishéndō/ *n., adv., adj., & v.* ● *n.* (*pl.* **-os** or **crescendi** /-dee/) **1** *Mus.* a passage gradually increasing in loudness. **2 a** a progress toward a climax (*a crescendo of emotions*). **b** *disp.* a climax (*reached a crescendo then died away*). ● *adv. & adj. Mus.* with a gradual increase in loudness. ● *v.intr.* (**-oes**, **-oed**) increase gradually in loudness or intensity.

cres·cent /krésənt/ *n.* **1** the curved sickle shape of the waxing or waning Moon. ▷ LUNAR MONTH. **2** anything of this shape. **3 a** the crescent-shaped emblem of Islam or Turkey. **b** (**the Crescent**) the world or power of Islam. □□ **cres·cen·tic** /kriséntik/ *adj.*

cress /kres/ *n.* any of various cruciferous plants usu. with pungent edible leaves.

crest /krest/ *n. & v.* ● *n.* **1 a** a comb or tuft on a bird's or animal's head. ▷ LIZARD. **b** something resembling this, esp. a plume of feathers on a helmet. **c** a helmet; the top of a helmet. **2** the top of a mountain, wave, etc. **3** *Heraldry* **a** a device above the shield and helmet of a coat of arms. **b** such a device reproduced on writing paper, etc. **4 a** a line along the top of the neck of some animals. **b** the hair growing from this; a mane. **5** *Anat.* a ridge along the surface of a bone. ● *v.* **1** *tr.* reach the crest of (a hill, wave, etc.). **2** *tr.* **a** provide with a crest. **b** serve as a crest to. **3** *intr.* (of a wave) form into a crest. □ **on the crest of a wave** at the most favorable moment in one's progress. □□ **crest·ed** *adj.* (also in *comb.*). **crest·less** *adj.*

crest·fal·len /kréstfawlən/ *adj.* **1** dejected. **2** with a fallen or drooping crest.

cre·ta·ceous /kritáyshəs/ *adj. & n.* ● *adj.* **1** of the nature of chalk. **2** (**Cretaceous**) *Geol.* of or relating to the last period of the Mesozoic era. ● *n. Geol.* this era or system.

cre·tin /kréetin/ *n.* **1** a person who is deformed and mentally retarded as the result of a thyroid deficiency. **2** *colloq.* a stupid person. □□ **cre·tin·ism** *n.* **cre·tin·ize** *v.tr.* **cre·tin·ous** *adj.*

cre·tonne /krétón, kréeton/ *n.* (often *attrib.*) a heavy cotton fabric with a usu. floral pattern printed on one or both sides, used for upholstery.

C

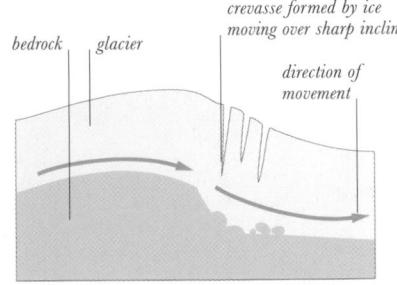

crevasse formed by ice moving over sharp incline

bedrock glacier

direction of movement

C

CREVASSE IN A DOWNWARD-MOVING GLACIER

cre·vasse /krəvás/ *n.* **1 ▲** a deep open crack, esp. in a glacier. ▷ GLACIER. **2** a breach in a river levee.

crev·ice /krévis/ *n.* a narrow opening or fissure in a rock, etc.

crew /kroō/ *n. & v.* ● *n.* (often treated as *pl.*) **1 a** a body of people manning a ship, aircraft, train, etc. **b** such a body as distinguished from the captain or officers. **c** a body of people working together. **2** *colloq.* a company of people (*a motley crew*). ● *v.* **1** *tr.* supply or act as a crew or member of a crew for. **2** *intr.* act as a crew or member of a crew.

crew cut *n.* a very short haircut.

crew·el /kroōəl/ *n.* a thin worsted yarn used for tapestry and embroidery.

crew·man /kroōmən/ *n.* (*pl.* **-men**) a member of a crew.

crew neck *n.* a close-fitting round neckline, esp. on a sweater.

crib /krib/ *n. & v.* ● *n.* **1 a** a child's bed with barred or latticed sides. **2** a barred rack for animal fodder. **3** *colloq.* **a** a translation of a text for the use of students. **b** plagiarized work, etc. **4** a small house or cottage. **5** a framework lining the shaft of a mine. **6** *colloq.* **a** cribbage. **b** a set of cards given to the dealer at cribbage by all the players. **7** heavy crossed timbers used in foundations in loose soil, etc. **8** *sl.* a brothel. ● *v.tr.* (also *absol.*) (**cribbed, cribbing**) **1** *colloq.* copy (another person's work) unfairly or without acknowledgment. **2** confine in a small space. **3** *colloq.* pilfer; steal. □□ **crib·ber** *n.*

crib·bage /kríbij/ *n.* a card game for two, three, or four players.

crib death *n.* = SUDDEN INFANT DEATH SYNDROME.

crick /krik/ *n. & v.* ● *n.* a sudden painful stiffness in the neck, etc. ● *v.tr.* produce a crick in.

crick·et[1] /críkit/ *n. & v.* ● *n.* ▼ a game played on a grass field with two teams of 11 players taking turns to bowl at a wicket defended by a batting player of the other team. ● *v.intr.* play cricket. □□ **crick·et·er** *n.*

crick·et[2] /críkit/ *n.* any of various grasshopperlike insects of the order Orthoptera. ▷ ORTHOPTERAN

cried *past* and *past part.* of CRY.

cri·er /kríər/ *n.* (also **cry·er**) **1** a person who cries. **2** an officer who makes public announcements in a court of justice.

crime /krīm/ *n.* **1 a** an offense punishable by law. **b** illegal acts as a whole (*resorted to crime*). **2** an evil act (*a crime against humanity*). **3** *colloq.* a shameful act (*a crime to tease them*).

crime of pas·sion *n.* a crime, esp. murder, committed in a fit of sexual jealousy.

crime wave *n.* a sudden increase in crime.

crim·i·nal /kríminəl/ *n. & adj.* ● *n.* a person who has committed a crime. ● *adj.* **1** of, involving, or concerning crime (*criminal records*). **2** having committed a crime. **3** *Law* relating to or expert in criminal law (*criminal code; criminal lawyer*). **4** *colloq.* scandalous; deplorable. □□ **crim·i·nal·i·ty** /-nálitee/ **crim·i·nal·ly** *adv.*

crim·i·nal law *n.* law concerned with punishment of offenders (opp. CIVIL LAW).

crim·i·nol·o·gy /kríminóləjee/ *n.* the scientific study of crime. □□ **crim·i·no·log·i·cal** /-nəlójikəl/ *adj.* **crim·i·nol·o·gist** *n.*

crimp /krimp/ *v. & n.* ● *v.tr.* **1** compress into small folds or ridges; frill. **2** corrugate. **3** make waves in (the hair) with a hot iron. ● *n.* a crimped thing or form. □ **put a crimp in** *sl.* thwart; interfere with. □□ **crimp·er** *n.* **crimp·y** *adj.* **crimp·i·ness** *n.*

crim·son /krímzən/ *adj., n., & v.* ● *adj.* of a rich, deep red inclining to purple. ● *n.* this color. ● *v.tr. & intr.* make or become crimson.

cringe /krinj/ *v. & n.* ● *v.intr.* **1** shrink back in fear; cower. **2** (often foll. by *to*) behave obsequiously. ● *n.* the act or an instance of cringing. □□ **cring·er** *n.*

crin·kle /kríngkəl/ *n. & v.* ● *n.* a wrinkle or crease in paper, cloth, etc. ● *v.* **1** *intr.* form crinkles. **2** *tr.* form crinkles in. □□ **crin·kly** *adj.*

crin·kle-cut *adj.* cut with wavy edges.

crin·o·line /krínəlin/ *n.* **1 ▶** a stiffened or hooped petticoat formerly worn to make a long skirt stand out. **2** a stiff fabric of horsehair, etc., used for linings, hats, etc.

crip·ple /krípəl/ *n. & v.* ● *n.* usu. *offens.* a person who is permanently lame. ● *v.tr.* **1** make a cripple of; lame. **2** disable; impair. **3** weaken or damage (an institution, enterprise, etc.) seriously (*crippled by the loss of funding*). □□ **crip·pler** *n.*

cri·sis /krísis/ *n.* (*pl.* **crises** /-seez/) **1 a** a decisive moment. **b** a time of danger or great difficulty. **2** the turning point, esp. of a disease.

crisp /krisp/ *adj., n., & v.* ● *adj.* **1** hard but brittle. **2 a** (of air) bracing. **b** (of a style or manner) lively; brisk and decisive. **c** (of features, etc.) neat and clear-cut. **d** (of paper) stiff and crackling. **e** (of hair) closely curling. ● *n.* a thing overdone in roasting, etc. (*burned to a crisp*). ● *v.tr. & intr.* **1** make or become crisp. **2** curl in short, stiff folds or waves. □□ **crisp·ly** *adv.* **crisp·ness** *n.*

crisp·bread /kríspbred/ *n.* **1** a thin, crisp cracker of crushed rye, etc. **2** these collectively (*a box of crispbread*).

crisp·er /kríspər/ *n.* a compartment in a refrigerator for storing fruit and vegetables.

crisp·y /kríspee/ *adj.* (**crispier, crispiest**) **1** crisp; brittle. **2** curly. **3** brisk. □□ **crisp·i·ness** *n.*

criss·cross /krískraws, -krós/ *n., adj., adv., & v.* ● *n.* **1** a pattern of crossing lines. **2** the crossing of lines or currents, etc. ● *adj.* crossing; in cross lines (*crisscross marking*). ● *adv.* crosswise; at cross purposes. ● *v.* **1** *intr.* **a** intersect repeatedly. **b** move crosswise. **2** *tr.* mark or make with a crisscross pattern.

cri·te·ri·on /krīteéreeən/ *n.* (*pl.* **criteria** /-reeə/ or **criterions**) a principle or standard that a thing is judged by. □□ **cri·te·ri·al** *adj.*

crit·ic /krítik/ *n.* **1** a person who censures. **2** a person who reviews literary, artistic, or musical works, etc. **3** a person engaged in textual criticism.

crit·i·cal /krítikəl/ *adj.* **1 a** making or involving adverse judgments. **b** expressing or involving criticism. **2** skillful at or engaged in criticism. **3** providing textual criticism (*a critical edition of Frost*). **4 a** of or at a crisis; involving risk or suspense (*in a critical condition*). **b** decisive; crucial (*at the critical moment*). **5 a** *Math. & Physics* marking transition from one state, etc., to another (*critical angle*). **b** *Physics* (of a nuclear reactor) maintaining a self-sustaining chain reaction. □□ **crit·i·cal·i·ty** /-kálitee/ *n.* (in sense 5). **crit·i·cal·ly** *adv.* **crit·i·cal·ness** *n.*

crit·i·cal list *n.* a list of those critically ill, esp. in a hospital.

CRINOLINE: MID-19TH-CENTURY CRINOLINE

waist tie

steel wires slotted through tapes

CRICKET

Originating in England in the 13th century, cricket is now an international sport, played over a fixed period (up to five days) or for a number of overs (one over is six balls, or pitches). Batsmen score runs by hitting the ball and then running between the wickets, or by hitting the ball to or over the boundary. A batsman is dismissed in several ways – by the bowler striking the wicket with the ball, for instance, or by the ball being caught.

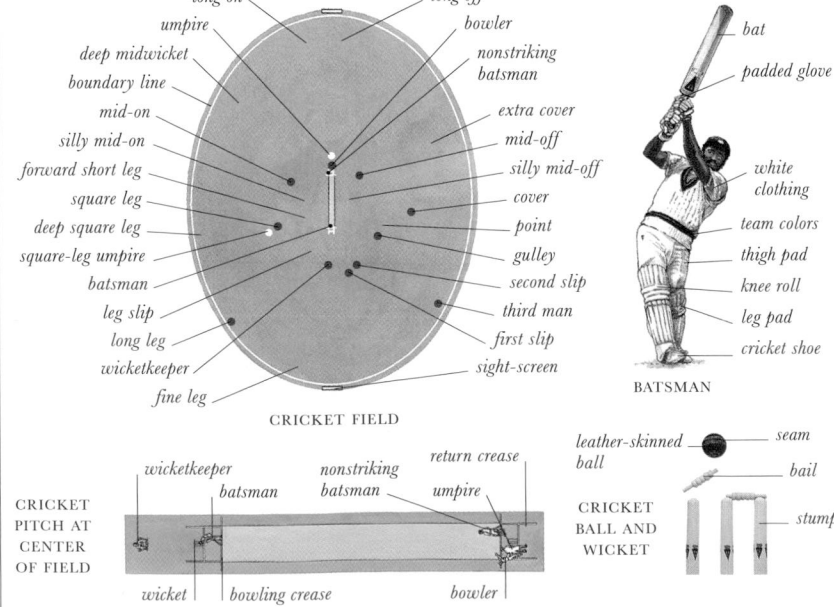

long on
umpire
deep midwicket
boundary line
mid-on
silly mid-on
forward short leg
square leg
deep square leg
square-leg umpire
batsman
leg slip
long leg
wicketkeeper
fine leg

long off
bowler
nonstriking batsman
extra cover
mid-off
silly mid-off
cover
point
gulley
second slip
third man
first slip
sight-screen

CRICKET FIELD

bat
padded glove
white clothing
team colors
thigh pad
knee roll
leg pad
cricket shoe

BATSMAN

CRICKET PITCH AT CENTER OF FIELD

wicketkeeper
batsman
nonstriking batsman
return crease
umpire
wicket
bowling crease
bowler

leather-skinned ball
seam
bail

CRICKET BALL AND WICKET

stump

CROCHET

The origins of crochet are difficult to trace, although the technique seems to have traveled extensively throughout the world. A length of yarn is formed into a looped fabric, using a hook, on which one stitch is worked at a time. Very fine yarns and the finest hooks form delicate open fabric. Thicker yarn on larger hooks is used for denser fabric. Flat pieces can be worked into tubular shapes or medallions.

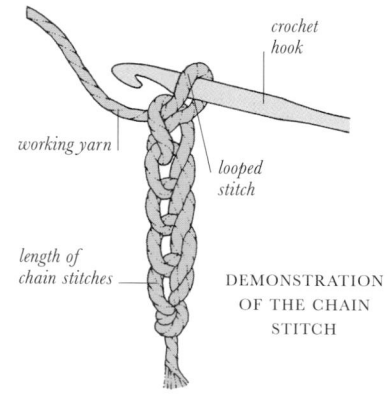

crochet hook

working yarn

looped stitch

length of chain stitches

DEMONSTRATION OF THE CHAIN STITCH

EXAMPLES OF STITCHES

BAR AND LATTICE

LOOP STITCH

PEACOCK STITCH

SPECKLE STITCH

PINEAPPLE STITCH

SPIRAL HEXAGON

---

crit·i·cal mass *n. Physics* the amount of fissile material needed to maintain a nuclear chain reaction.

crit·i·cism /krítisizəm/ *n.* **1 a** finding fault; censure. **b** a statement expressing this. **2 a** the work of a critic. **b** an article, essay, etc., expressing or containing an analytical evaluation of something.

crit·i·cize /krítisīz/ *v.tr.* (also *absol.*) **1** find fault with. **2** discuss critically. □□ **crit·i·ciz·a·ble** *adj.* **crit·i·ciz·er** *n.*

cri·tique /kriteék/ *n. & v.* ● *n.* a critical essay or analysis; an instance or the process of formal criticism. ● *v.tr.* (**critiques, critiqued, critiquing**) discuss critically.

crit·ter /krítər/ *n.* **1** *dial.* or *joc.* a creature. **2** *derog.* a person.

croak /krōk/ *n. & v.* ● *n.* **1** a deep, hoarse sound as of a frog. **2** a sound resembling this. ● *v.* **1 a** *intr.* utter a croak. **b** *tr.* utter with a croak or in a dismal manner. **2** *sl.* **a** *intr.* die. **b** *tr.* kill.

croak·y /krōkee/ *adj.* (**croakier, croakiest**) (of a voice) croaking; hoarse. □□ **croak·i·ly** *adv.* **croak·i·ness** *n.*

Cro·at /krō-at/ *n. & adj.* ● *n.* **1 a** a native of Croatia in the former Yugoslavia. **b** a person of Croatian descent. **2** the Slavonic dialect of the Croats (cf. SERBO-CROAT). ● *adj.* of or relating to the Croats or their dialect.

Cro·a·tian /krō-áyshən/ *n. & adj.* = CROAT.

croc /krok/ *n. colloq.* a crocodile.

cro·chet /krōsháy/ *n. & v.* ● *n.* **1** ▲ a handicraft in which yarn is made up into a patterned fabric by means of a hooked needle. **2** work made in this way. ● *v.* (**crocheted** /-sháyd/; **crocheting** /-sháying/) **1** *tr.* make by crocheting. **2** *intr.* do crochet. □□ **cro·chet·er** *n.*

cro·cid·o·lite /krōsídəlīt/ *n.* a fibrous blue or green silicate of iron and sodium; blue asbestos.

crock[1] /krok/ *n.* **1** an earthenware pot or jar. **2** a broken piece of earthenware.

crock[2] /krok/ *n. colloq.* nonsense; exaggeration (*his explanation is just a crock*).

crock·er·y /krókəree/ *n.* earthenware or china dishes, plates, etc.

crock·et /krókit/ *n. Archit.* a small carved ornament on the inclined side of a pinnacle, etc. ▷ CATHEDRAL

croc·o·dile /krókədīl/ *n.* **1** ▼ any large tropical amphibious reptile of the order Crocodilia, with long jaws. ▷ ALLIGATOR. **2** leather from its skin, used to make bags, shoes, etc. □□ **croc·o·dil·i·an** /-dileeən/ *adj.*

CROCODILE: NILE CROCODILE (*Crocodilus niloticus*)

croc·o·dile tears *n.pl.* insincere grief.

cro·cus /krōkəs/ *n.* (*pl.* **crocuses**) ► any dwarf plant of the genus *Crocus*, growing from a corm and having brilliant usu. yellow or purple flowers.

Croe·sus /kréesəs/ *n.* a person of great wealth.

croft /kráwft/ *n. & v. Brit.* ● *n.* **1** an enclosed piece of (usu. arable) land. **2** a small rented farm in Scotland or N. of England. ● *v.intr.* farm a croft.

croft·er /kráwftər/ *n. Brit.* a person who rents a small piece of land.

crois·sant /krwaasáaN, krəsánt/ *n.* a crescent-shaped roll made of rich yeast pastry.

Cro-Mag·non /krōmágnən, -mányən/ *adj. Anthropol.* of a tall, broad-faced European race of late Paleolithic times.

crom·lech /krómlekh, -lek/ *n.* **1** a dolmen; a megalithic tomb. **2** a circle of upright prehistoric stones.

crone /krōn/ *n.* **1** a withered old woman. **2** an old ewe.

cro·ny /krōnee/ *n.* (*pl.* **-ies**) a close friend or companion.

CROCUS (*Crocus versicolor*)

---

crook /krŏŏk/ *n. & v.* ● *n.* **1** ► the hooked staff of a shepherd or bishop. **2 a** a bend, curve, or hook. **b** anything hooked or curved. **3** *colloq.* **a** a rogue; a swindler. **b** a professional criminal. ● *v.tr. & intr.* bend; curve. □□ **crook·er·y** *n.*

crook·ed /krŏŏkid/ *adj.* (**crookeder, crookedest**) **1 a** not straight or level; bent. **b** deformed; bent with age. **2** *colloq.* not straightforward; dishonest. □□ **crook·ed·ly** *adv.* **crook·ed·ness** *n.*

croon /krōon/ *v. & n.* ● *v.tr. & intr.* hum or sing in a low subdued voice. ● *n.* such singing. □□ **croon·er** *n.*

crop /krop/ *n. & v.* ● *n.* **1 a** the produce of cultivated plants. **b** the season's yield of this (*a good crop*). **2 a** a group or an amount appearing at one time (*this year's crop of students*). **3** (in full **hunting crop**) the stock or handle of a whip. **4 a** a style of hair cut very short. **b** the cropping of hair. **5** *Zool.* **a** the pouch in a bird's gullet where food is prepared for digestion. ▷ BIRD. **b** a similar organ in other animals. **6** the entire tanned hide of an animal. **7** a piece cut off or out of something. ● *v.* (**cropped, cropping**) **1** *tr.* **a** cut off. **b** bite off (the tops of plants). **2** *tr.* cut (hair, cloth, edges of a book, etc.) short. **3** *tr.* gather or reap (produce). **4** *tr.* (foll. by *with*) sow or plant (land) with a crop. **5** *intr.* (of land) bear a crop. □ **crop out** *Geol.* appear at the surface. **crop up** **1** (of a subject, circumstance, etc.) appear or come to one's notice unexpectedly. **2** *Geol.* appear at the surface.

crop cir·cle *n.* a circular depression in a standing crop, often only visible from the air.

crop-dust·ing *n.* the sprinkling of powdered insecticide or fertilizer on crops, esp. from the air.

crop·per /krópər/ *n.* a crop-producing plant of specified quality (*a good cropper; a heavy cropper*). □ **come a cropper** *sl.* **1** fall heavily. **2** fail badly.

cro·quet /krōkáy/ *n. & v.* ● *n.* **1** ► a game played on a lawn, with wooden balls which are driven through a series of hoops with mallets. **2** the act of croqueting a ball. ● *v.tr.* (**croqueted** /-káyd/; **croqueting** /-káying/) drive away (one's opponent's ball in croquet) by placing one's own against it and striking one's own.

cro·quette /krōkét/ *n.* a fried, breaded roll or ball of mashed potato or ground meat, etc.

cro·sier /krōzhər/ *n.* (also **cro·zier**) **1** a hooked staff carried by a bishop as a symbol of pastoral office. **2** a crook.

cross /kraws, kros/ *n., v., & adj.* ● *n.* **1** an upright post with a transverse bar, as used in antiquity for crucifixion. **2 a** (**the Cross**) the cross on which Christ was crucified. **b** a representation of this as an emblem of Christianity. **c** = SIGN OF THE CROSS. **3** a staff surmounted by a cross and borne before an archbishop or in a religious procession. **4 a** a thing or mark shaped like a cross, esp. a figure made by two short intersecting lines (+ or x). **b** a monument in the form of a cross, esp. one in the center of a town or on a tomb. **5** a cross-shaped decoration indicating rank in some orders of knighthood or awarded for personal valor. **6 a** an intermixture of animal breeds or plant varieties. **b** an animal or plant resulting from this. **7** (foll. by *between*) a

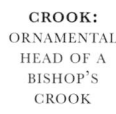

C

CROOK: ORNAMENTAL HEAD OF A BISHOP'S CROOK

handle made of ash

ball made of boxwood

CROQUET MALLET AND BALL

C

mixture of two things. **8 a** a crosswise movement. **b** *Soccer*, etc. a pass of the ball across the direction of play. **c** *Boxing* a blow with a crosswise movement of the fist. **9** a trial or affliction (*bear one's crosses*). ● *v.* **1** *tr.* (often foll. by *over*; also *absol.*) go across or to the other side of (a road, river, sea, etc.). **2 a** *intr.* intersect or be across one another (*the roads cross near the bridge*). **b** *tr.* cause to do this; place crosswise (*cross one's legs*). **3** *tr.* draw a line or lines across. **4** *tr.* (foll. by *off, out, through*) cancel or obliterate or remove from a list with lines drawn across. **5** *tr.* (often *refl.*) make the sign of the cross on or over. **6** *intr.* **a** pass in opposite or different directions. **b** (of letters between two correspondents) each be dispatched before receipt of the other. **c** (of telephone lines) become wrongly interconnected so that intrusive calls can be heard. **7** *tr.* **a** cause to interbreed. **b** cross-fertilize (plants). **8** *tr.* thwart or frustrate (*crossed in love*). **9** *tr. sl.* cheat. ● *adj.* **1** (often foll. by *with*) peevish; angry. **2** (usu. *attrib.*) transverse; reaching from side to side. **3** (usu. *attrib.*) intersecting. **4** (usu. *attrib.*) contrary; opposed; reciprocal. □ **at cross purposes** misunderstanding one another. **cross one's fingers** (or **keep one's fingers crossed**) **1** put one finger across another as a sign of hoping for good luck. **2** trust in good luck. **cross one's heart** make a solemn pledge, esp. by crossing one's front. **cross one's mind** (of a thought, etc.) occur to one, esp. transiently. **cross a person's palm** (usu. foll. by *with*) **1** pay a person for a favor. **2** bribe. **cross the path of 1** meet with (a person). **2** thwart. **cross swords** (often foll. by *with*) encounter in opposition; have an argument or dispute. **cross wires** (or **get one's wires crossed**) **1** become wrongly connected by telephone. **2** have a misunderstanding. □□ **cross·ly** *adv.* **cross·ness** *n.*

cross- /kraws, kros/ *comb. form* **1** denoting movement or position across something (*cross-channel*; *cross-country*). **2** denoting interaction (*cross-cultural*; *cross-fertilize*). **3 a** passing from side to side; transverse (*crossbar*; *crosscurrent*). **b** having a transverse part (*crossbow*). **4** describing the form or figure of a cross (*crossroads*).

cross·bar /kráwsbaar, krós-/ *n.* a horizontal bar, esp. held on a pivot or between two upright bars, etc., e.g., of a bicycle or of a football goal.

cross·bill /kráwsbil, krós-/ *n.* ◄ any stout finch of the genus *Loxia*, having a bill with crossed mandibles for use in opening pine cones.

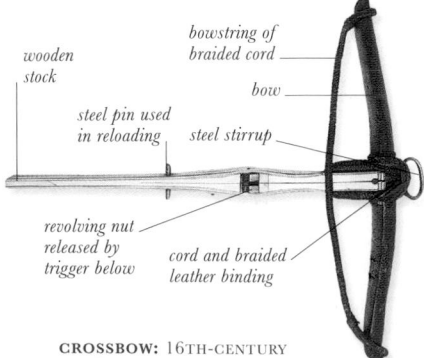

CROSSBILL: COMMON CROSSBILL (*Loxia curvirostra*)

cross·bones /kráwsbōnz, krós-/ *n.* a representation of two crossed leg or arm bones (see SKULL).

cross·bow /kráwsbō, krós-/ *n.* esp. *hist.* ▼ a bow fixed across a wooden stock, with a groove for an arrow and a mechanism for drawing and releasing the string. □□ **cross·bow·man** *n.* (pl. **-men**).

bowstring of braided cord

wooden stock

bow

steel pin used in reloading

steel stirrup

revolving nut released by trigger below

cord and braided leather binding

CROSSBOW: 16TH-CENTURY GERMAN CROSSBOW

CROSSBREED: LABRADOR RETRIEVER AND STANDARD POODLE (LABRADOODLE)

cross·breed *n. & v.* ● *n.* /kráwsbreed, krós-/ **1** a breed of animals or plants produced by crossing. **2** ▲ an individual animal or plant of a crossbreed. ● *v.tr.* /kráwsbréed, krós-/ (*past and past part.* **-bred**) produce by crossing.

cross-check *v. & n.* ● *v.tr.* /kráws-chék, krós-/ check by an alternative method, or by several methods. ● *n.* /kráws-chek, krós-/ an instance of cross-checking.

cross-coun·try /kráwskúntree, krós-/ *adj. & adv.* **1** across open country. **2** not keeping to main or direct roads.

cross·cut *adj. & n.* ● *adj.* /kráwskút, krós-/ cut across the main grain. ▷ SAW. ● *n.* /kráwskut, krós-/ a diagonal cut, path, etc.

cross-dress *v.intr.* wear clothing typically worn by members of the opposite sex.

crosse /kraws, kros/ *n.* a stick with a triangular net at the end for conveying the ball in lacrosse. ▷ LACROSSE.

cross-ex·am·ine /kráwsigzámin, krós-/ *v.tr.* examine (esp. a witness in a court of law) to check or extend testimony already given. □□ **cross-ex·am·i·na·tion** /-náyshən/ *n.* **cross-ex·am·in·er** *n.*

cross-eyed /kráwsíd, krós-/ *adj.* (as a disorder) having one or both eyes turned permanently inward toward the nose.

cross-fer·ti·lize /kráwsfért'līz, krós-/ *v.tr.* **1** fertilize (an animal or plant) from another. **2** help by the interchange of ideas, etc. □□ **cross-fer·ti·li·za·tion** /-fértəlīzáyshən/ *n.*

cross·fire /kráwsfīr, krós-/ *n.* (also **cross fire**) **1** firing in two crossing directions simultaneously. **2 a** an attack or criticism from several sources at once. **b** a lively or combative exchange of views, etc.

cross-grain /kráwsgrayn, krós-/ *n.* a grain in lumber, running across the regular grain.

cross-grained /kráwsgráynd, krós-/ *adj.* **1** (of lumber) having a cross-grain. **2** perverse; intractable.

cross·hair /kráws-hair, krós-/ *n.* a fine wire at the focus of an optical instrument, gun, sight, etc.

cross·hatch /kráws-hách, krós-/ *v. & n.* ● *v.tr.* shade with intersecting sets of parallel lines. ● *n.* ► a pattern made this way.

CROSSHATCH: DETAIL FROM A PENCIL DRAWING

cross·head /kráws-hed, krós-/*n.* a bar between the piston rod and connecting rod in a steam engine.

cross·ing /kráwsing, krós-/ *n.* **1** a place where things (esp. roads) cross. **2** a place at which one may cross a street, etc. **3** a journey across water (*had a smooth crossing*). **4** the intersection of a church nave and transepts. **5** *Biol.* mating.

cross-leg·ged /kráwslégid, -légd, krós-/ *adj.* with one leg crossed over the other.

cross-link /kráwslingk, krós-/ *n. Chem.* a bond between chains of atoms in a polymer, etc.

cross-match /kráwsmách, krós-/ *v.tr. Med.* test the compatibility of (a donor's and a recipient's blood). □□ **cross-matching** *n.* **crossmatch** *n.*

cross·o·ver /kráwsōvər, krós-/ *n. & adj.* ● *n.* a point or place of crossing from one side to the other. ● *adj.* having a crossover.

cross·piece /kráwspees, krós-/ *n.* a transverse beam or other component of a structure, etc.

cross-pol·li·nate /kráwspólinayt, krós-/ *v.tr.* pollinate (a plant) from another. □□ **cross-pol·li·na·tion** /-náyshən/ *n.*

cross-ques·tion /kráwskwés-chən, krós-/ *v.tr.* = CROSS-EXAMINE.

cross-re·fer /kráwsrifér, krós-/ *v.intr.* (**-referred, -referring**) refer from one part of a book, etc., to another.

cross-ref·er·ence /kráwsréfərəns, krós-/ *n. & v.* ● *n.* a reference from one part of a book, article, etc., to another. ● *v.tr.* provide with cross-references.

cross·road /kráwsrōd, krós-/ *n.* **1** (usu. in *pl.*) an intersection of two roads. **2** a road that crosses a main road or joins two main roads. □ **at the crossroads** at a critical point in one's life.

cross sec·tion /kráws-sékshən, krós-/ *n.* **1 a** a cutting of a solid at right angles to an axis. **b** a plane surface produced in this way. **c** a representation of this. **2** a representative sample. **3** *Physics* a quantity expressing the probability of interaction between particles. □□ **cross-sec·tion·al** *adj.*

cross-stitch /kráws-stich, krós-/ *n. & v.* ● *n.* **1** a stitch formed of two stitches crossing each other. **2** ► needlework done using this stitch. ● *v.intr. & tr.* work in cross-stitch.

CROSS-STITCH: EMBROIDERED CROSS-STITCH ON KNITTED FABRIC

cross·talk /kráws-tawk, krós-/ *n.* (also **cross talk**) unwanted transfer of signals between communication channels

cross·walk /kráwswawk, krós-/ *n.* a pedestrian crossing.

cross·voting /kráwsvóting, krós-/ *n.* voting for a party not one's own, or for more than one party.

cross·ways /kráwswayz, krós-/ *adv.* = CROSSWISE.

cross·wind /kráwswind, krós-/ *n.* a wind blowing across one's direction of travel.

cross·wise /kráwswīz, krós-/ *adj. & adv.* **1** in the form of a cross; intersecting. **2** transverse or transversely.

cross·word /kráwswərd, krós-/ *n.* (also **crossword puz·zle**) a puzzle of a grid of squares and blanks into which words crossing vertically and horizontally have to be filled from clues.

cros·ti·ni /krostéenee/ *n.* small pieces of toasted or fried bread served with a topping as a starter or canapé.

crotch /kroch/ *n.* a place where something forks, esp. the legs of the human body or a garment (cf. CRUTCH 3).

crotch·et·y /króchitee/ *adj.* peevish; irritable. □□ **crotch·et·i·ness** *n.*

cro·ton /krṓt'n/ *n.* **1** any of various small tropical trees or shrubs of the genus *Croton*, producing a capsule-like fruit. **2** ► any small tree or shrub of the genus *Codiaeum*, esp. *C. variegatum*, with colored ornamental leaves.

CROTON (*Codiaeum* 'Gold Star')

crouch /krowch/ *v. & n.* ● *v.intr.* lower the body with the limbs close to the chest; be in this position. ● *n.* an act of crouching; a crouching position.

croup[1] /kroop/ *n.* an inflammation of the larynx and trachea in children, with a hard cough. □□ **croup·y** *adj.*

croup[2] /kroop/ *n.* the rump or hindquarters esp. of a horse. ▷ HORSE

crou·pi·er /kroopeeər, -eeay/ *n.* **1** the person in charge of a gaming table, raking in and paying out money, etc. **2** the assistant chairperson at a public dinner, seated at the foot of the table.

crou·ton /krooton/ *n.* a small piece of fried or toasted bread served with soup or used as a garnish.

Crow /krō/ *n.* **1 a** a N. American people native to eastern Montana. **b** a member of this people. **2** the language of this people.

crow[1] /krō/ *n.* **1** ▶ any large, black bird of the genus *Corvus*, having a powerful black beak. **2** any similar bird of the family Corvidae. **3** *sl. derog.* a woman, esp. an old or ugly one. □ **as the crow flies** in a straight line. **eat crow** submit to humiliation.

CROW:
HOUSE CROW
(*Corvus splendens*)

crow[2] /krō/ *v. & n.* ● *n.intr.* **1** (*past* **crowed**) (of a cock) utter its characteristic loud cry. **2** (of a baby) utter happy cries. **3** (usu. foll. by *over*) express unrestrained gleeful satisfaction. ● *n.* **1** the cry of a cock. **2** a happy cry of a baby.

crow·bar /krōbaar/ *n.* ▶ an iron bar with a flattened end, used as a lever.

crowd /krowd/ *n. & v.* ● *n.* **1** a large number of people gathered together. **2** a mass of spectators; an audience. **3** *colloq.* a particular set of people. **4** (prec. by *the*) the mass or multitude of people. **5** a large number (of things). **6** actors representing a crowd. ● *v.* **1 a** *intr.* come together in a crowd **b** *tr.* cause to do this. **c** *intr.* force one's way. **2** *tr.* **a** (foll. by *into*) force or compress into a confined space. **b** (often foll. by *with*; usu. in *passive*) fill or make abundant with (*was crowded with tourists*). **3** *tr.* **a** come aggressively close to. **b** *colloq.* harass or pressure (a person). □ **crowd out** exclude by crowding. □□ **crowd·ed·ness** *n.*

crowd-pull·er *n. colloq.* an event or person that attracts a large audience.

flattened lever end

iron bar

clawed lever end

CROWBAR

crow·foot /krōfoot/ *n.* (*pl.* **crowfoots** for 1 & 2, **crowfeet** for 3 & 4) **1** any of various plants of the genus *Ranunculus*, esp. buttercup, often characterized by divided leaves that resemble a crow's foot. **2** any of various other plants whose leaves, etc., bear a similar resemblance. **3** *Mil.* a caltrop. **4** a three-legged antislip support for a motion-picture camera's tripod.

crown /krown/ *n. & v.* ● *n.* **1** a monarch's ornamental headdress. **2** (**the Crown**) **a** the monarch as head of state. **b** the power or authority residing in the monarchy. **3 a** a wreath worn on the head, esp. as an emblem of victory. **b** an award or distinction gained by a victory or achievement, esp. in sport. **4** a crown-shaped device or ornament. **5** the top part of a thing, esp. of the head or a hat. ▷ HAT. **6 a** the highest or central part of an arched or curved thing (*crown of the road*). **b** a thing that completes or forms the summit. **7** the part of a plant just above and below the ground. **8** the upper part of a cut gem above the girdle. **9 a** the part of a tooth projecting from the gum. ▷ TOOTH. **b** an artificial replacement or covering for this. **10** a former

size of paper, 504 x 384 mm. ● *v.tr.* **1** put a crown on (a person or a person's head). **2** invest (a person) with a royal crown or authority. **3** be a crown to; rest on the top of. **4 a** (often as **crowning** *adj.*) be or cause to be the consummation, reward, or finishing touch to (*the crowning glory*). **b** bring (efforts) to a happy issue. **5** fit a crown to (a tooth). **6** *sl.* hit on the head.

crown jew·els *n.pl.* the regalia and other jewelry worn by the sovereign on certain state occasions.

crown prince *n.* a male heir to a sovereign throne.

crown prin·cess *n.* **1** the wife of a crown prince. **2** a female heir to a sovereign throne.

crow's-foot *n.* (*pl.* **-feet**) **1** (usu. in *pl.*) a wrinkle at the outer corner of a person's eye. **2** *Mil.* a caltrop.

crow's nest *n.* a barrel or platform fixed at the masthead of a sailing vessel as a shelter for a lookout.

crow·steps /krōsteps/ *n.pl.* the steplike projections on the sloping sides of a gable.

cro·zier var. of CROSIER.

CRT *abbr.* cathode-ray tube.

cru·ces *pl.* of CRUX.

cru·cial /krooshəl/ *adj.* **1** decisive; critical. **2** *colloq. disp.* very important. **3** *sl.* excellent. □□ **cru·ci·al·i·ty** /-sheeálitee/ *n.* (*pl.* **-ies**) **cru·cial·ly** *adv.*

cru·ci·ble /kroosibəl/ *n.* **1** a melting pot for metals, etc. **2** a severe test or trial.

cru·ci·fer /kroosifər/ *n.* **1** one who carries a cross in an ecclesiastical procession. **2** a cruciferous plant.

cru·cif·er·ous /kroosifərəs/ *adj. Bot.* of the family Cruciferae, having flowers with four petals arranged in a cross.

cru·ci·fix /kroosifiks/ *n.* a model or image of a cross with a figure of Christ on it. ▷ ROSARY

cru·ci·fix·ion /kroosifikshən/ *n.* **1 a** crucifying or being crucified. **b** an instance of this. **2** (**Crucifixion**) **a** the crucifixion of Christ. **b** a representation of this.

cru·ci·form /kroosifawrm/ *adj.* cross-shaped.

cru·ci·fy /kroosifī/ *v.tr.* (**-ies, -ied**) **1** put to death by fastening to a cross. **2 a** cause extreme pain to. **b** persecute; torment. **c** *sl.* defeat thoroughly in an argument, match, etc.

crud /krud/ *n. sl.* **1 a** unwanted impurities, grease, etc. **b** something disgusting or undesirable **c** a corrosive deposit in a nuclear reactor. **2** an unpleasant person. **3** nonsense. □□ **crud·dy** *adj.* (**cruddier, cruddiest**).

crude /krood/ *adj. & n.* ● *adj.* **1 a** in the natural or raw state; not refined. **b** rough; unpolished; lacking finish. **2 a** (of an action or statement or manners) rude; blunt. **b** offensive; indecent (*a crude gesture*). **3 a** *Statistics* (of numerical totals) not adjusted or corrected. **b** rough (*a crude estimate*). ● *n.* natural mineral oil. □□ **crude·ly** *adv.* **crude·ness** *n.* **cru·di·ty** *n.*

cru·di·tés /rōoditáy/ *n.pl.* an hors d'oeuvre of mixed raw vegetables, often served with a sauce into which they are dipped.

cru·el /krooəl/ *adj.* (**crueler, cruelest**) **1** indifferent to or gratified by another's suffering. **2** causing pain or suffering, esp. deliberately. □□ **cru·el·ly** *adv.*

cru·el·ty /krooəltee/ *n.* (*pl.* **-ies**) **1** a cruel act or attitude; indifference to another's suffering. **2** a succession of cruel acts; a continued cruel attitude (*suffered much cruelty*). **3** *Law* physical or mental harm inflicted (whether or not intentional), esp. as a ground for divorce.

cru·el·ty-free *adj.* (of cosmetics, etc.)

produced without involving any cruelty to animals in the development or manufacturing process.

cru·et /krooit/ *n.* **1** a small container for oil or vinegar for use at the table. **2** (in full **cruet-stand**) a stand holding cruets. **3** *Eccl.* a small container for the wine and water in the celebration of the Eucharist.

cruise /krooz/ *v. & n.* ● *v.* **1** *intr.* make a journey by sea calling at a series of ports, esp. for pleasure. **2** *intr.* sail about without a precise destination. **3** *intr.* **a** (of a motor vehicle or aircraft) travel at a moderate or economical speed. **b** (of a vehicle or its driver) travel at random, esp. slowly. **4** *intr.* achieve an objective, win a race, etc., with ease. **5** *intr. & tr. sl.* walk or drive about (the streets, etc.) in search of a sexual (esp. homosexual) partner. ● *n.* a cruising voyage, esp. as a vacation.

cruise con·trol *n.* a device on a motor vehicle that maintains a constant speed and relieves the operator of the need to depress the accelerator.

cruise mis·sile *n.* a missile able to fly at low altitude and guide itself by reference to the features of the region it traverses.

cruis·er /koozor/ *n.* **1** a warship of high speed and medium armament. **2** = CABIN CRUISER. **3** a police patrol car.

cruis·er·weight /koozorwayt/ *n.* a weight class in professional boxing between light heavyweight and heavyweight.

cruis·ing speed *n.* a comfortable and economical speed for a motor vehicle, below its maximum speed.

crumb /krum/ *n. & v.* ● *n.* **1 a** a small fragment, esp. of bread. **b** a small particle (*a crumb of comfort*). **2** the soft inner part of a loaf of bread. **3** *sl.* an objectionable person. ● *v.tr.* **1** cover with breadcrumbs. **2** break into crumbs.

crum·ble /krumbəl/ *v. & n.* ● *v.* **1** *tr. & intr.* break or fall into fragments. **2** *intr.* (of power, a reputation, etc.) gradually disintegrate. ● *n.* a crumbly or crumbled substance.

crum·bly /krumblee/ *adj.* (**crumblier, crumbliest**) consisting of, or apt to fall into, crumbs or fragments. □□ **crum·bli·ness** *n.*

crumb·y /krumee/ *adj.* (**crumbier, crumbiest**) **1** like or covered in crumbs. **2** *colloq.* = CRUMMY.

crum·horn var. of KRUMMHORN.

crum·my /krumee/ *adj.* (**crummier, crummiest**) *colloq.* dirty; squalid; inferior; worthless. □□ **crum·mi·ness** *n.*

crum·pet /krumpit/ *n.* a soft, flat cake of a yeast mixture cooked on a griddle and eaten toasted and buttered.

crum·ple /krumpəl/ *v. & n.* ● *v.* **1** *tr. & intr.* (often foll. by *up*) a crush or become crushed into creases. **b** ruffle; wrinkle. **2** *intr.* (often foll. by *up*) collapse; give way. ● *n.* a crease or wrinkle. □□ **crum·ply** *adj.*

crunch /krunch/ *v. & n.* ● *v.* **1** *tr.* **a** crush noisily with the teeth. **b** grind (gravel, dry snow, etc.) under foot, wheels, etc. **2** *intr.* (often foll. by *up, through*) make a crunching sound in walking, moving, etc. ● *n.* **1** crunching; a crunching sound. **2** *colloq.* a decisive event or moment.

crunch·y /krunchee/ *adj.* (**crunchier, crunchiest**) hard and crispy. □□ **crunch·i·ly** *adv.* **crunch·i·ness** *n.*

crup·per /krupər/ *n.* **1** a strap buckled to the back of a saddle and looped under the horse's tail to hold the harness back. ▷ TROTTING. **2** the hindquarters of a horse.

cru·sade /kroosáyd/ *n. & v.* ● *n.* **1 a** ◀ any of several medieval military expeditions made by Europeans to recover the Holy Land from the Muslims. **b** a war instigated

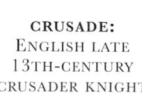

pennon

lance

mail glove

helm

mail coif

shield

surcoat

scabbard

CRUSADE:
ENGLISH LATE
13TH-CENTURY
CRUSADER KNIGHT

C

CRUSTACEAN

The subphylum Crustacea contains about 38,000 species and is one of the largest groups in the phylum Arthropoda. Crustaceans are named after the hard carapace, or "crust," that encloses their body. They vary greatly in size, but a typical species has compound eyes, antennae in pairs, and several pairs of jointed legs. They usually live in seawater, although a few, such as the sowbug, live on land.

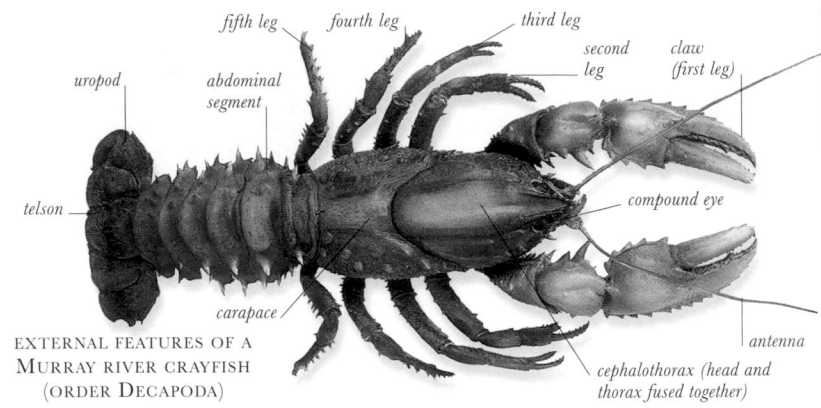

EXTERNAL FEATURES OF A
MURRAY RIVER CRAYFISH
(ORDER DECAPODA)

EXAMPLES OF OTHER CRUSTACEAN ORDERS

EUPHAUSIACEA
krill
(*Euphausia superba*)

THORACICA
barnacle

HARPACTICOIDA
freshwater copepod

ISOPODA
sowbug
(*Armadillidium vulgare*)

by the Roman Catholic Church for alleged religious ends. **2** a vigorous campaign in favor of a cause. ● *v.intr.* engage in a crusade. □□ **cru·sad·er** *n.*

crush /krush/ *v. & n.* ● *v.tr.* **1** compress with force or violence, so as to break, bruise, etc. **2** reduce to powder by pressure. **3** crease or crumple. **4** defeat or subdue completely (*crushed by my reply*). ● *n.* **1** an act of crushing. **2** a crowded mass of people. **3** a drink made from the juice of crushed fruit. **4** *colloq.* **a** (usu. foll. by *on*) an infatuation. **b** the object of an infatuation (*who's the latest crush?*). □□ **crush·a·ble** *adj.* **crush·er** *n.* **crush·ing** *adj.* (in sense 4 of *v.*). **crush·ing·ly** *adv.*

crust /krust/ *n. & v.* ● *n.* **1 a** the hard outer part of a loaf of bread. **b** a piece of this with some soft bread attached. **c** a hard, dry scrap of bread. **2** the pastry covering of a pie. **3** a hard casing of a softer thing. **4** *Geol.* the outer portion of the Earth. ▷ EARTH. **5 a** a coating or deposit on the surface of anything. **b** a hard, dry formation on the skin; a scab. **6** a deposit of tartar formed in bottles of old wine. **7** a superficial hardness of manner. ● *v.tr. & intr.* **1** cover or become covered with a crust. **2** form into a crust. □□ **crus·tal** *adj.* (in sense 4 of *n.*). □□ **crusted** *adj.*

crus·ta·cean /krustáyshən/ *n. & adj.* ● *n.* ▲ any arthropod of the class Crustacea, having a hard shell and usu. aquatic, e.g., the crab, lobster, and shrimp. ▷ CRAB. ● *adj.* of or relating to crustaceans. □□ **crus·ta·ceous** /-shəs/ *adj.*

crust·y /krústee/ *adj.* (**crustier**, **crustiest**) **1** having a crisp crust (*a crusty loaf*). **2** irritable; curt. **3** hard; crustlike. □□ **crust·i·ly** *adv.* **crust·i·ness** *n.*

crutch /kruch/ *n.* **1** a support for a lame person, usu. with a crosspiece at the top fitting under the armpit (*pair of crutches*). **2** any support or prop. **3** the crotch of the human body or garment.

crux /kruks/ *n.* (*pl.* **cruxes** or **cruces** /krṓoseez/) **1** the decisive point at issue. **2** a difficult matter; a puzzle.

cry /krī/ *v. & n.* ● *v.* (**cries**, **cried**) **1** *intr.* (often foll. by *out*) make a loud or shrill sound, esp. to express pain, grief, etc., or to appeal for help. **2 a** *intr.* shed tears; weep. **b** *tr.* shed (tears). **3** *tr.* (often foll. by *out*) say or exclaim loudly or excitedly. **4** *intr.* (of an animal, esp. a bird) make a loud call. ● *n.* (*pl.* **cries**) **1** a loud inarticulate utterance of grief, pain, fear, joy, etc. **2** a loud excited utterance of words. **3** an urgent appeal. **4** a spell of weeping. **5 a** public demand; a strong movement of opinion. **b** a watchword or rallying call. **6** the natural utterance of an animal. □ **cry down** disparage; belittle. **cry one's eyes** (or **heart**) **out** weep bitterly. **cry off** *colloq.* withdraw from a promise or undertaking. **cry out for** demand as a self-evident requirement or solution. **cry over spilled milk** see MILK. **cry up** praise; extol. **cry wolf** see WOLF. **a far cry 1** a long way. **2** a very different thing. **for crying out loud** *colloq.* an exclamation of surprise or annoyance. **in full cry** (of hounds) in keen pursuit.

cry·ba·by /krṓbaybee/ *n.* (*pl.* **-babies**) a person who sheds tears frequently.

cry·er var. of CRIER.

cry·ing /krṓ-ing/ *attrib.adj.* (of an injustice or other evil) flagrant; demanding redress (*a crying need*; *a crying shame*).

cryo- /krṓō/ *comb. form* (extreme) cold.

cry·o·gen·ics /krī̄ajéniks/ *n.* the branch of physics dealing with very low temperatures. □□ **cry·o·gen·ic** *adj.*

cry·o·sur·ger·y /krī̄ōsə́rjəree/ *n.* surgery using the local application of intense cold for anesthesia or therapy.

crypt /kript/ *n.* an underground room or vault, esp. one beneath a church, used usu. as a burial place.

cryp·tic /kríptik/ *adj.* **1 a** obscure in meaning. **b** (of a crossword clue, etc.) indicating the solution in a way that is not obvious. **c** secret; mysterious; enigmatic. **2** *Zool.* (of coloration, etc.) serving for concealment. □□ **cryp·ti·cal·ly** *adv.*

crypto- /kríptō/ *comb. form* concealed; secret (*cryptocommunist*).

cryp·to·gam /kríptəgám/ *n. Bot.* a plant that has no true flowers or seeds, e.g., ferns, mosses, algae, and fungi. □□ **cryp·to·gam·ic** *adj.* **cryp·tog·a·mous** /-tógəməs/ *adj.*

cryp·to·gram /kríptəgram/ *n.* a text written in code.

cryp·tog·ra·phy /kriptógrəfee/ *n.* the art of writing or solving codes. □□ **cryp·tog·ra·pher** *n.* **cryp·to·graph·ic** /-təgráfik/ *adj.* **cryp·to·graph·i·cal·ly** *adv.*

cryp·to·spo·rid·i·um /kriptōsporídeeəm/ *n.* a single-celled parasite found in the intestinal tract of many animals, where it sometimes causes disease.

crys·tal /kríst'l/ *n. & adj.* ● *n.* **1 a** a clear transparent mineral, esp. rock crystal. **b** a piece of this. **2** (in full **crystal glass**) **a** highly transparent glass; flint glass. **b** articles made of this. **3** the glass over a watch face. **4** *Electronics* a crystalline piece of semiconductor. **5** *Chem.* ▶ **a** an aggregation of molecules with a definite internal structure and the external form of a solid enclosed by symmetrically arranged plane faces. **b** a solid whose constituent particles are symmetrically arranged. ● *adj.* (usu. *attrib.*) made of, like, or clear as crystal. □ **crystal clear** unclouded; transparent.

crys·tal ball *n.* a glass globe used in crystal gazing.

crys·tal gaz·ing *n.* the process of concentrating one's gaze on a crystal ball supposedly in order to obtain a picture of future events, etc.

crys·tal·line /kríst'lin, -līn/ *adj.* **1** of, like, or clear as crystal. **2** *Chem. & Mineral.* having the structure and form of a crystal. □□ **crys·tal·lin·i·ty** /-línitee/ *n.*

crys·tal·lize /kríst'līz/ *v.* **1** *tr. & intr.* form or cause to form crystals. ▷ MATTER. **2** (often foll. by *out*) **a** *intr.* (of ideas or plans) become definite. **b** *tr.* make definite. **3** *tr. & intr.* coat or impregnate or become coated or impregnated with sugar (*crystallized fruit*). □□ **crys·tal·liz·a·ble** *adj.* **crys·tal·li·za·tion** *n.*

crys·tal·log·ra·phy /kríst'lógrəfee/ *n.* the science of crystal form and structure. ▷ CRYSTAL. □□ **crys·tal·log·ra·pher** *n.* **crys·tal·lo·graph·ic** /-ləgráfik/ *adj.*

Cs *symb. Chem.* the element cesium.

c/s *abbr.* cycles per second.

C-section *abbr.* of *Cesarean section.*

CST *abbr.* central standard time.

CT *abbr.* Connecticut (in official postal use).

Cu *symb. Chem.* the element copper.

cu. *abbr.* cubic.

cub /kub/ *n. & v.* ● *n.* **1** the young of a fox, lion, etc. **2** an ill-mannered young man. **3** (**Cub**) (in full **Cub Scout**) a member of the junior branch of the Boy Scouts. **4** (in full **cub reporter**) *colloq.* an inexperienced newspaper reporter. **5** an apprentice. ● *v.tr.* (**cubbed**, **cubbing**) (also *absol.*) give birth to (cubs).

Cu·ban /kyóōbən/ *adj. & n.* ● *adj.* of or relating to Cuba, an island republic in the Caribbean, or its people. ● *n.* a native or national of Cuba.

Cu·ban heel *n.* a moderately high straight-sided heel on a shoe or boot.

cub·by /kúbee/ *n.* (*pl.* **-ies**) (in full **cubbyhole**) **1** a very small room. **2** a snug space. **3** a boxlike compartment for storage, etc.

cube /kyōōb/ *n. & v.* ● *n.* **1** ▼ a solid contained by six equal squares. **2** a cube-shaped block. **3** *Math.* the product of a number multiplied by its square. ● *v.tr.* **1** find the cube of (a number). **2** cut (food for cooking, etc.) into small cubes. **3** tenderize (meat) by scoring it in a criss-cross pattern.

CUBE

CRYSTAL

Crystals grow in a variety of forms, known as habits. Well-formed crystals have external faces with parallel edges, each face having a parallel on the opposite side of the crystal. Crystals of this type conform to certain systems, related to their axes of symmetry, or imaginary lines, around which they may rotate and still show identical aspects.

reflections of light

striation lines

plane of intersection

crystals in random growth directions

FEATURES OF A TWIN ROCK CRYSTAL

EXAMPLES OF CRYSTAL HABITS

PRISMATIC   MASSIVE   RENIFORM

ACICULAR   DENDRITIC   BLADED

CRYSTAL SYSTEMS

three separate axes

CUBIC

sixfold/ threefold axis

HEXAGONAL/ TRIGONAL

fourfold and two twofold axes

TETRAGONAL

twofold axis

MONOCLINIC

three twofold axes

ORTHORHOMBIC

no axis

TRICLINIC

---

cube root *n.* the number which produces a given number when cubed.

cube steak *n.* a thin slice of steak that has been cubed.

cu·bic /kyōōbik/ *adj.* **1** cube-shaped. **2** of three dimensions. **3** involving the cube (and no higher power) of a number (*cubic equation*). **4** (*attrib.*) designating a unit of measure equal to the volume of a cube whose side is one of the linear unit specified

(*cubic meter*). **5** *Crystallog.* having three equal axes at right angles.

cu·bi·cal /kyōōbikəl/ *adj.* cubeshaped. □□ **cu·bi·cal·ly** *adv.*

cu·bic foot *n.* the volume of a cube whose edge is one foot.

cu·bi·cle /kyōōbikəl/ *n.* **1** a small partitioned space, screened for privacy. **2** a small, separate sleeping compartment.

cu·bi·form /kyōōbifawrm/ *adj.* cube-shaped.

cub·ism /kyōōbizəm/ *n.* ▼ a style and movement in art, esp. painting, in which objects are represented geometrically. □□ **cub·ist** *n. & adj.*

cu·boid /kyōōboyd/ *adj. & n.* ● *adj.* cube-shaped; like a cube. ● *n.* **1** *Geom.* a rectangular parallelepiped. **2** (in full **cuboid bone**) *Anat.* the outer bone of the tarsus. □□ **cu·boi·dal** /-bóyd'l/ *adj.*

cuck·old /kúkōld/ *n. & v.* ● *n.* the husband of an adulteress. ● *v.tr.* make a cuckold of. □□ **cuck·old·ry** *n.*

cuck·oo /kōōkōō/ *n. & adj.* ● *n.* ◄ any bird of the family Cuculidae, esp. *Cuculus canorus*, having a characteristic cry, and depositing its eggs in the nests of small birds. ● *predic. adj. sl.* crazy; foolish.

CUCKOO: COMMON CUCKOO (*Cuculus canorus*)

cuck·oo clock *n.* a clock that strikes the hour with a sound like a cuckoo's call, usu. with the emergence of a mechanical cuckoo. ▷ CLOCK

cuck·oo·pint /kōō-kōō-pīnt/ *n.* ► a wild arum, *Arum maculatum*, with arrow-shaped leaves and scarlet berries. Also called **lords-and-ladies**.

cu·cum·ber /kyōōkumbər/ *n.* **1** a long, green, fleshy fruit, used in salads. **2** the climbing plant, *Cucumis sativus*, yielding this fruit.

cud /kud/ *n.* half-digested food returned from the first stomach of ruminants to the mouth for further chewing.

cud·dle /kúd'l/ *v. & n.* ● *v.* **1** *tr.* hug; embrace; fondle. **2** *intr.* nestle together, as for affection or comfort; lie close and snug; kiss and fondle amorously. ● *n.* a prolonged and fond hug. □□ **cud·dle·some** *adj.*

spathe

berries

flower spike

CUCKOOPINT (*Arum maculatum*)

cud·dly /kúdlee/ *adj.* (**cuddlier, cuddliest**) tempting to cuddle; given to cuddling.

cudg·el /kújəl/ *n. & v.* ● *n.* a short, thick stick used as a weapon. ● *v.tr.* beat with a cudgel. □ **cudgel one's brains** think hard about a problem. **take up the cudgels** (often foll. by *for*) make a vigorous defense.

cud·weed /kúdweed/ *n.* any wild composite plant of the genus *Gnaphalium*, with scales and round flower heads, formerly given to cattle that had lost their cud.

cue[1] /kyōō/ *n. & v.* ● *n.* **1 a** the last words of an actor's speech serving as a signal to another actor to enter or speak. **b** a similar signal to a singer, etc. **2 a** a stimulus to perception, etc. **b** a signal for action. **c** a hint on how to behave in particular circumstances. **3** a facility for or an instance of cuing audio equipment (see sense 2 of *v.*). ● *v.tr.* (**cues, cued, cuing** or **cueing**) **1** give a cue to. **2** put (a piece of audio equipment esp. a record player or tape recorder) in readiness to play a particular part of the recorded material. □ **cue in 1** insert a cue for. **2** give information to. **on cue** at the correct moment. **take one's cue from** follow the example or advice of.

cue[2] /kyōō/ *n. & v. Billiards, etc.* ● *n.* a long, straight, tapering rod for striking the ball. ▷ SNOOKER. ● *v.* (**cues, cued, cuing** or **cueing**) **1** *tr.* strike (a ball) with a cue. **2** *intr.* use a cue. □□ **cue·ist** *n.*

cue ball *n. Billiards* the ball that is to be struck with the cue. ▷ SNOOKER

C

CUBISM

Cubism was a movement originated by Picasso and Braque. Partly inspired by the late paintings of Cézanne and also by African sculpture, cubists constructed paintings with multiple viewpoints, creating overlapping planes within the composition. This represented a significant break from the linear perspective that had prevailed since the Renaissance and revealed an aim to represent objects as perceived by the mind rather than the eye. Stressing reality without recourse to traditional forms of illusion, cubists after 1912 incorporated fragments of the "real world," such as newsprint, into their paintings.

Violin and Guitar (1913), PABLO PICASSO

TIMELINE

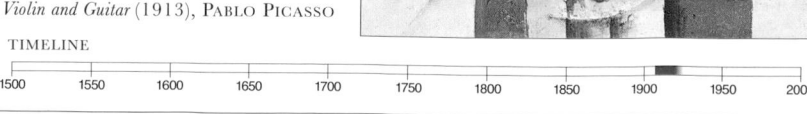

1500   1550   1600   1650   1700   1750   1800   1850   1900   1950   2000

C

cue card *n. colloq.* a card or board displaying a television script to a speaker as an aid to memory.

cuff[1] /kuf/ *n.* **1 a** the end part of a sleeve. **b** a separate band of linen worn around the wrist so as to appear under the sleeve. **c** the part of a glove covering the wrist. **2** a turned-up hem on pants. **3** (in *pl.*) *colloq.* handcuffs. □□ **cuffed** *adj.* (also in *comb.*).

cuff[2] /kuf/ *v. & n.* ● *v.tr.* strike with an open hand. ● *n.* such a blow.

cuff link *n.* a device of two joined studs, etc., to fasten the sides of a cuff together.

Cu·fic var. of KUFIC.

cui·rass /kwi-rás/ *n. hist.* ▼ a piece of armor consisting of breastplate and backplate fastened together. ▷ ARMOR

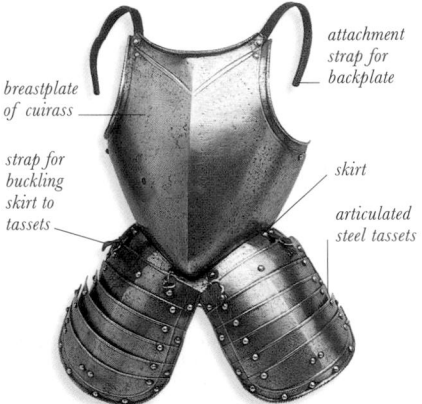

CUIRASS: 16TH-CENTURY ITALIAN CUIRASS
BREASTPLATE, SKIRT, AND TASSETS

breastplate of cuirass
strap for buckling skirt to tassets
attachment strap for backplate
skirt
articulated steel tassets

cui·sine /kwizéen/ *n.* a style or method of cooking, esp. of a particular country or establishment.

cul-de-sac /kúldəsak, kōōl-/ *n.* (*pl.* **culs-de-sac** *pronunc.* same) **1** a street or passage closed at one end. **2** a route or course leading nowhere; a position from which one cannot escape. **3** *Anat.* = DIVERTICULUM.

cu·li·nar·y /kyōōləneree, kúl-/ *adj.* of or for cooking or the kitchen. □□ **cu·li·nar·i·ly** *adv.*

cull /kul/ *v. & n.* ● *v.tr.* **1** select or gather (*knowledge culled from books*). **2** pick (flowers, fruit, etc.). **3** select (animals), esp. for killing. ● *n.* **1** an act of culling. **2** an animal or animals culled. □□ **cull·er** *n.*

cul·mi·nate /kúlminayt/ *v.* **1** *intr.* (usu. foll. by *in*) reach its highest or final point. **2** *tr.* bring to its highest or final point. **3** *intr. Astron.* be on the meridian. □□ **cul·mi·na·tion** /-náyshən/ *n.*

cu·lottes /kōōlóts, kyōō-/ *n.pl.* women's (usu. short) trousers cut to resemble a skirt.

cul·pa·ble /kúlpəbəl/ *adj.* deserving blame. □□ **cul·pa·bil·i·ty** *n.* **cul·pa·bly** *adv.*

cul·prit /kúlprit/ *n.* a person accused of or guilty of an offense.

cult /kult/ *n.* **1** a system of religious worship esp. as expressed in ritual. **2 a** devotion to a person or thing (*the cult of aestheticism*). **b** a popular fashion. **3** (*attrib.*) denoting a person or thing popularized in this way (*cult film; cult figure*). □□ **cul·tic** *adj.* **cult·ism** *n.* **cult·ist** *n.*

cul·ti·var /kúltivaar/ *n. Bot.* a plant variety produced by cultivation.

cul·ti·vate /kúltivayt/ *v.tr.* **1 a** prepare and use (soil, etc.) for crops or gardening. **b** break up (the ground) with a cultivator. **2 a** raise or produce (crops). **b** culture (bacteria, etc.). **3 a** (often as **cultivated** *adj.*) apply oneself to improving or developing (the mind, etc.). **b** pay attention to or nurture; ingratiate oneself with. □□ **cul·ti·va·ble** *adj.* **cul·ti·vat·a·ble** *adj.* **cul·ti·va·tion** *n.*

dead man's handle
horizontal handle adjuster
engine
clutch
accelerator
choke
lever for adjusting depth of cultivation
fold-away stand for stability
blades for turning soil
rear blades
transporter wheel for steering

CULTIVATOR: FRONT-ENGINED
GASOLINE-DRIVEN CULTIVATOR

cul·ti·va·tor /kúltivaytər/ *n.* **1** ▲ a mechanical implement for breaking up the ground and uprooting weeds. **2** a person or thing that cultivates.

cul·tur·al /kúlchərəl/ *adj.* of or relating to the cultivation of the mind or manners, esp. through artistic or intellectual activity. □□ **cul·tur·al·ly** *adv.*

cul·ture /kúlchər/ *n. & v.* ● *n.* **1 a** the arts and other manifestations of human intellectual achievement regarded collectively. **b** a refined understanding of this. **2** the customs, civilization, and achievements of a particular time or people (*studied Chinese culture*). **3** improvement by mental or physical training. **4 a** the cultivation of plants; the rearing of bees, etc. **b** the cultivation of the soil. **5** a quantity of microorganisms and the nutrient material supporting their growth. ● *v.tr.* maintain (bacteria, etc.) in conditions suitable for growth.

cul·tured /kúlchərd/ *adj.* having refined taste and manners and a good education.

cul·tured pearl *n.* a pearl formed by an oyster after the insertion of a foreign body into its shell.

cul·vert /kúlvərt/ *n.* an underground channel carrying water across a road, etc.

cum /kum/ *prep.* (usu. in *comb.*) with; combined with; also used as (*a bedroom-cum-study*).

cum·ber·some /kúmbərsəm/ *adj.* inconvenient in size, weight, or shape. □□ **cum·ber·some·ly** *adv.* **cum·ber·some·ness** *n.*

cum·in /kúmin, kōō-, kyōō-/ *n.* **1** ▼ an umbelliferous plant, *Cuminum cyminum*, bearing aromatic seeds. **2** these seeds used as flavoring. ▷ SPICE

cum·mer·bund /kúmərbund/ *n.* a waist sash.

cum·quat var. of KUMQUAT.

cu·mu·late *v. & adj.* ● *v.tr. & intr.* /kyōōmyəlayt/ accumulate; amass; combine. ● *adj.* /kyōōmyələt/ heaped up; massed. □□ **cu·mu·la·tion** /-láyshən/ *n.*

ripening seeds
lax stems

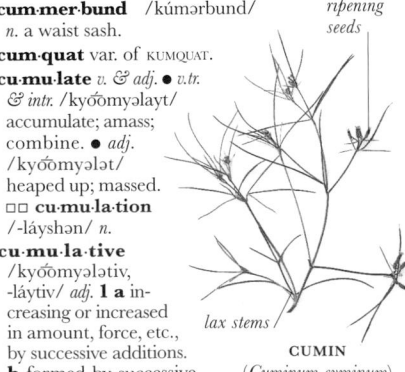

CUMIN
(*Cuminum cyminum*)

cu·mu·la·tive /kyōōmyələtiv, -láytiv/ *adj.* **1 a** increasing or increased in amount, force, etc., by successive additions. **b** formed by successive additions. **2** *Stock Exch.* (of shares) entitling holders to arrears of interest before any other distribution is made. □□ **cu·mu·la·tive·ly** *adv.* **cu·mu·la·tive·ness** *n.*

cu·mu·lo·nim·bus /kyōōmyəlōnímbəs/ *n.* cloud forming a towering mass with a flat base at fairly low altitude, as in thunderstorms. ▷ CLOUD

cu·mu·lus /kyōōmyələs/ *n.* (*pl.* **cumuli** /-lī/) a cloud formation consisting of rounded masses heaped on each other above a horizontal base. ▷ CLOUD, HURRICANE. □□ **cu·mu·lous** *adj.*

cumulo- /kyōōmyəlō/ *comb. form* cumulous (cloud). ▷ CLOUD, HURRICANE

cu·ne·i·form /kyōōnéeə-fawrm, kyōōneeə-, kyōōni-/ *adj. & n.* ● *adj.* **1** wedge-shaped. **2** ► of, relating to, or using the wedge-shaped writing in ancient Babylonian, etc., in-scriptions. ● *n.* cunei-form writing.

pictogram for beer
cuneiform wedge

CUNEIFORM: EXAMPLE
OF SUMERIAN
CUNEIFORM TEXT

cun·ni·lin·gus /kúni-linggəs/ *n.* (also **cun·ni·linc·tus** /-língktəs/) oral stimulation of the female genitals.

cun·ning /kúning/ *adj. & n.* ● *adj.* (**cunninger**, **cunningest**) **1 a** skilled in ingenuity or deceit. **b** selfishly clever or crafty. **2** ingenious (*a cunning device*). **3** attractive; quaint. ● *n.* **1** craftiness. **2** skill; ingenuity. □□ **cun·ning·ly** *adv.* **cun·ning·ness** *n.*

cunt /kunt/ *n. coarse sl.* **1** the female genitals. **2** *offens.* a stupid person. ¶ A highly taboo word.

cup /kup/ *n. & v.* ● *n.* **1** a small bowl-shaped container for drinking from. **2 a** its contents (*a cup of tea*). **b** = CUPFUL. **3** a cup-shaped thing. **4** flavored wine, cider, etc., usu. chilled. **5** an ornamental cup-shaped trophy. **6** one's fate or fortune (*a bitter cup*). **7** either of the two cup-shaped parts of a brassiere. **8** the chalice used or the wine taken at the Eucharist. ● *v.tr.* (**cupped**, **cupping**) **1** form (esp. one's hands) into the shape of a cup. **2** take or hold as in a cup. □ **one's cup of tea** *colloq.* what interests or suits one. **in one's cups** while drunk; drunk.

cup·board /kúbərd/ *n.* a recess or piece of furniture with a door and (usu.) shelves.

cup·cake /kúpkayk/ *n.* a small cake baked in a cup-shaped metal, foil, or paper container and often iced.

cup·ful /kúpfōōl/ *n.* (*pl.* **-fuls**) **1** the amount held by a cup, esp. a half-pint (8-ounce) measure in cookery. **2** a cup full of a substance. ¶ A *cupful* is a measure, and so *three cupfuls* is a quantity regarded in terms of a cup; *three cups full* denotes the actual cups, as in *three cups full of water*.

Cu·pid /kyōōpid/ *n.* **1** the Roman god of love represented as a naked winged boy with a bow and arrows. **2** (also **cupid**) a representation of Cupid.

cu·pid·i·ty /kyōōpíditee/ *n.* greed for gain.

cu·po·la /kyōōpələ/ *n.* **1 a** a rounded dome forming a roof or ceiling. **b** ▼ a small rounded dome adorning a roof. **2** a revolving dome protecting mounted guns. **3** (in full **cupola furnace**) a furnace for melting metals. □□ **cu·po·laed** /-ləd/ *adj.*

cupola
main dome

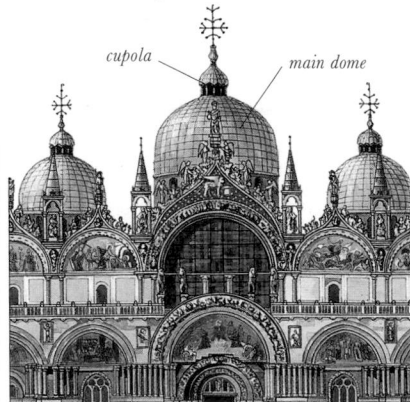

CUPOLA ON ST. MARK'S BASILICA,
VENICE, ITALY

cu·pre·ous /kŏprees, kyŏ-/ *adj.* of or like copper.

cu·pric /kŏprik, kyŏ-/ *adj.* of copper, esp. divalent copper. □□ **cu·prif·er·ous** /-prífərəs/ *adj.*

cu·pro·nick·el /kŏprōníkəl, kyŏ-/ *n.* an alloy of copper and nickel, esp. in the proportions 3:1 as used in "silver" coins.

cu·prous /kŏprəs, kyŏ-/ *adj.* of copper, esp. monovalent copper.

cur /kər/ *n.* **1** a worthless or snappy dog. **2** *colloq.* a contemptible person.

cur·a·ble /kyŏrəbəl/ *adj.* that can be cured. □□ **cur·a·bil·i·ty** *n.*

cu·ra·çao /kyŏrəsó, -sów/ *n.* (also **curaçoa** /-sóə/) (*pl.* **-os** or **curaçoas**) a liqueur of spirits flavored with the peel of bitter oranges.

cu·ra·cy /kyŏrəsee/ *n.* (*pl.* **-ies**) a curate's office or the tenure of it.

cu·ra·re /kyŏráaree, kŏ-/ *n.* a resinous bitter substance prepared from S. American plants of the genera *Strychnos* and *Chondodendron*, paralyzing the motor nerves.

cu·rate /kyŏrət/ *n.* a member of the clergy engaged as assistant to a parish priest.

cu·ra·tor /kyŏráytər, kyŏrə-/ *n.* a keeper or custodian of a museum or other collection. □□ **cu·ra·to·ri·al** /kyŏrətáwreeəl/ *adj.* **cu·ra·tor·ship** *n.*

curb /kərb/ *n. & v.* ● *n.* **1** a check or restraint. **2** a rim of concrete, stone, etc., along the side of a paved road. **3** ▶ a strap, etc., fastened to the bit and passing under a horse's lower jaw, used as a check. **4** an enclosing border or edging. ● *v.tr.* **1** restrain. **2** put a curb on (a horse).

curb·side /kárbsīd/ *n.* the side of a paved road or roadbed bordered by a curb.

curb·stone /kárbstōn/ *n.* each of a series of stones forming a curb.

curd /kərd/ *n.* **1** (often in *pl.*) a coagulated substance formed by the action of acids on milk, which may be made into cheese or eaten as food. **2** a fatty substance found between flakes of boiled salmon flesh. **3** the edible head of a cauliflower. □□ **curd·y** *adj.*

cur·dle /kárd'l/ *v.tr. & intr.* make into or become curds, (of milk) turn sour; congeal. □ **make one's blood curdle** fill one with horror. □□ **cur·dler** *n.*

cure /kyŏr/ *v. & n.* ● *v.* **1** *tr.* (often foll. by *of*) restore (a person or animal) to health (*was cured of pleurisy*). **2** *tr.* eliminate (a disease, evil, etc.). **3** *tr.* preserve (meat, fruit, tobacco, or skins) by salting, drying, etc. **4** *tr.* **a** vulcanize (rubber). **b** harden (concrete or plastic). **5** *intr.* effect a cure. **6** *intr.* undergo a process of curing. ● *n.* **1** restoration to health. **2** a thing that effects a cure. **3** a course of healing treatment. **4** **a** the office or function of a curate. **b** a parish or other sphere of spiritual ministration. **5** **a** the process of curing rubber or plastic. **b** (with qualifying adj.) the degree of this. □□ **cur·a·tive** /kyŏrativ/ *adj. & n.* **cur·er** *n.*

cu·ré /kyŏráy, kyŏray/ *n.* a parish priest in France, etc.

cure-all *n.* a panacea.

cu·rette /kyŏrét/ *n. & v.* ● *n.* a surgeon's small scraping instrument. ● *v.tr. & intr.* clean or scrape with a curette. □□ **cu·ret·tage** /kyŏritáazh/ *n.*

cur·few /kárfyŏ/ *n.* **1 a** a regulation requiring people to remain indoors between specified hours. **b** the hour designated as the beginning of such

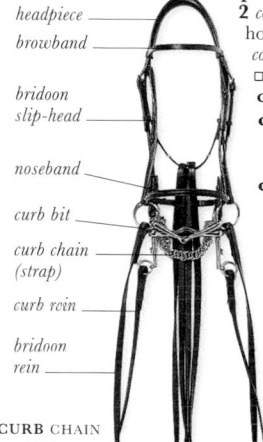

headpiece
browband
bridoon
slip-head
noseband
curb bit
curb chain
(strap)
curb rein
bridoon
rein

CURB CHAIN
AND BIT
OF A DOUBLE
BRIDLE

a restriction. **c** a daily signal indicating this. **2** the ringing of a bell at a fixed evening hour.

cu·ri·a /kyŏreeə/ *n.* (also **Curia**) (*pl.* **curiae**) the papal court; the government departments of the Vatican. □□ **cu·ri·al** *adj.*

cu·rie /kyŏree/ *n.* **1** a unit of radioactivity. ¶ Abbr.: **Ci. 2** a quantity of radioactive substance having this activity.

cu·ri·o /kyŏreeō/ *n.* (*pl.* **-os**) a rare or unusual object or person.

cu·ri·os·i·ty /kyŏreeósitee/ *n.* (*pl.* **-ies**) **1** inquisitiveness. **2** strangeness. **3** a strange, rare, or interesting object.

cu·ri·ous /kyŏreeəs/ *adj.* **1** inquisitive. **2** strange; surprising. □□ **cu·ri·ous·ly** *adv.* **cu·ri·ous·ness** *n.*

cu·ri·um /kyŏreeəm/ *n.* an artificially made transuranic radioactive metallic element. ¶ Symb.: **Cm.**

curl /kərl/ *v. & n.* ● *v.* **1** *tr.* (often foll. by *up*) bend or coil into a spiral. **2** *intr.* move in a spiral form. **3 a** *intr.* (of the upper lip) be raised slightly on one side in disapproval. **b** *tr.* cause (the lip) to do this. **4** *intr.* play curling. ● *n.* **1** a lock of curled hair. **2** anything spiral or curved inward. **3 a** a curling movement or act. **b** the state of being curled. **4** a disease of plants in which the leaves are curled up. □ **curl up 1** lie or sit with the knees drawn up. **2** *colloq.* writhe with embarrassment or horror. **make a person's hair curl** *colloq.* shock or horrify a person. □□ **curl·y** /kárlee/ *adj.* (**curlier**, **curliest**). **curl·i·ness** *n.*

curl·er /kárlər/ *n.* **1** a roller, etc., for curling the hair. **2** a player in the game of curling.

cur·lew /kárlōō, -lyōō/ *n.* ▶ any wading bird of the genus *Numenius* with a long, slender, down-curved bill. ▷ WADING BIRD

curl·i·cue /kárlikyōō/ *n.* a decorative curl or twist.

curl·ing /kárling/ *n.* **1** in senses of CURL *v.* **2** a game played on ice, in which large, round, flat stones are slid across the surface.

cur·mudg·eon /kərmújən/ *n.* a bad-tempered person. □□ **cur·mudg·eon·ly** *adj.*

cur·rant /kárənt, kúr-/ *n.* **1** a dried fruit of a small seedless variety of grape. **2** ▶ **a** any of various shrubs of the genus *Ribes* producing red, white, or black berries. **b** a berry of these shrubs.

cur·ren·cy /kárənsee, kúr-/ *n.* (*pl.* **-ies**) **1 a** the money in general use in a country. **b** any other commodity used as a medium of exchange. **2** the condition of being current (e.g., of words or ideas). **3** the time during which something is current.

cur·rent /kárənt, kúr-/ *adj. & n.* ● *adj.* **1** belonging to the present time; happening now (*current events; the current week*). **2** (of money, opinion, a rumor, a word, etc.) in general circulation or use. ● *n.* **1** a body of water, air, etc., moving esp. through a stiller surrounding body. **2 a** an ordered movement of electrically charged particles. ▷ ALTERNATING CURRENT. **b** a quantity representing the intensity of such movement. **3** (usu. foll. by *of*) a general tendency or course (of events, opinions, etc.).

cur·rent·ly /kárəntlee, kúr-/ *adv.* at the present time; now.

cur·ric·u·lum /kəríkyələm/ *n.* (*pl.* **curricula** /-lə/

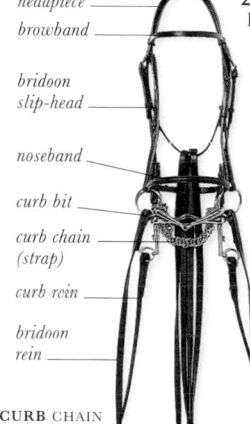

CURLEW: COMMON CURLEW
(*Numenius arquata*)

CURRANT:
BLACKCURRANT
(*Ribes nigrum*)

black berries

or **curriculums**) **1** the subjects that are studied or prescribed for study in a school. **2** any program of activities. □□ **cur·ric·u·lar** *adj.*

cur·ric·u·lum vi·tae /karíkyələm vítee, véetī/ *n.* (*pl.* **curricula vitae**) a brief account of one's education, qualifications, and previous occupations.

cur·ry[1] /káree, kúree/ *n. & v.* ● *n.* (*pl.* **-ies**) a dish of meat, vegetables, etc., cooked in a sauce of hot-tasting spices, usu. served with rice. ● *v.tr.* (**-ies**, **-ied**) prepare or flavor with a sauce of hot-tasting spices.

cur·ry[2] /káree, kúree/ *v.tr.* (**-ies**, **-ied**) **1** groom (a horse) with a currycomb. **2** treat (tanned leather) to improve its properties. **3** thrash. □ **curry favor** ingratiate oneself.

cur·ry·comb /káreekōm, kúree-/ *n. & v.* ● *n.* ▶ a handheld metal serrated device for grooming horses. ● *v.tr.* use a currycomb on.

cur·ry pow·der *n.* a preparation of spices for making curry.

curse /kərs/ *n. & v.* ● *n.* **1** a solemn utterance intended to invoke a supernatural power to inflict destruction or punishment on a person or thing. **2** the evil supposedly resulting from a curse. **3** a violent exclamation of anger; a profane oath. **4** a thing that causes evil or harm. **5** (prec. by *the*) *colloq.* menstruation. **6** a CURRYCOMB sentence of excommunication. ● *v.* **1** *tr.* **a** utter a curse against. **b** (in *imper.*) may God curse. **2** *tr.* (usu. in *passive*; foll. by *with*) afflict with (*cursed with blindness*). **3** *intr.* utter expletive curses; swear. **4** *tr.* excommunicate. □□ **curs·er** *n.*

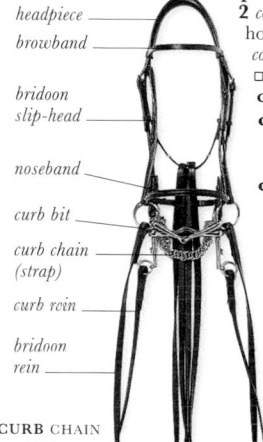

CURRYCOMB

curs·ed /kársid, kərst/ *adj.* damnable; abominable. □□ **curs·ed·ly** *adv.* **curs·ed·ness** *n.*

cur·sive /kársiv/ *adj. & n.* ● *adj.* (of writing) done with joined characters. ● *n.* cursive writing. □□ **cur·sive·ly** *adv.*

cur·sor /kársər/ *n.* **1** *Computing* a movable indicator on a monitor screen identifying a particular position in the display. **2** *Math.*, etc., a transparent slide engraved with a hairline and forming part of a slide rule.

cur·so·ry /kársəree/ *adj.* hasty, hurried. □□ **cur·so·ri·ly** *adv.* **cur·so·ri·ness** *n.*

curt /kərt/ *adj.* noticeably or rudely brief. □□ **curt·ly** *adv.* **curt·ness** *n.*

cur·tail /kərtáyl/ *v.tr.* cut short; reduce; terminate esp. prematurely (*curtailed his visit to Italy*). □□ **cur·tail·ment** *n.*

cur·tain /kártən/ *n. & v.* ● *n.* **1** a piece of cloth, etc., hung up as a screen, usu. movable sideways or upward, esp. at a window or between the stage and auditorium of a theater. ▷ THEATER. **2** *Theatr.* **a** the rise or fall of the stage curtain at the beginning or end of an act or scene. **b** = CURTAIN CALL. **3** a partition or cover. **4** (in *pl.*) *sl.* the end. ● *v.tr.* **1** furnish or cover with a curtain or curtains. **2** (foll. by *off*) shut off with a curtain or curtains.

cur·tain call *n. Theatr.* an audience's summons to performer(s) to take a bow after the fall of the curtain.

curt·sy /kártsee/ *n. & v.* (also **curt·sey**) ● *n.* (*pl.* **-ies** or **-eys**) a woman's or girl's formal greeting made by bending the knees and lowering the body. ● *v.intr.* (**-ies**, **-ied** or **-eys**, **-eyed**) make a curtsy.

cur·va·ceous /kərváyshəs/ *adj. colloq.* (esp. of a woman) having a shapely curved figure.

C

C

CUT

The way in which a butcher cuts a carcass of meat is dictated by the animal's anatomy and breed, consumer requirements, and religious custom. Regional climates and local ingredients, such as herbs, fruit, and vegetables, influence cooking methods and therefore demand cuts of a certain kind. Butchering techniques also vary widely from country to country, and so cuts of meat differ as well. Their names vary almost as much, with national and regional terminologies sometimes conflicting.

EXAMPLES OF CUTS OF MEAT

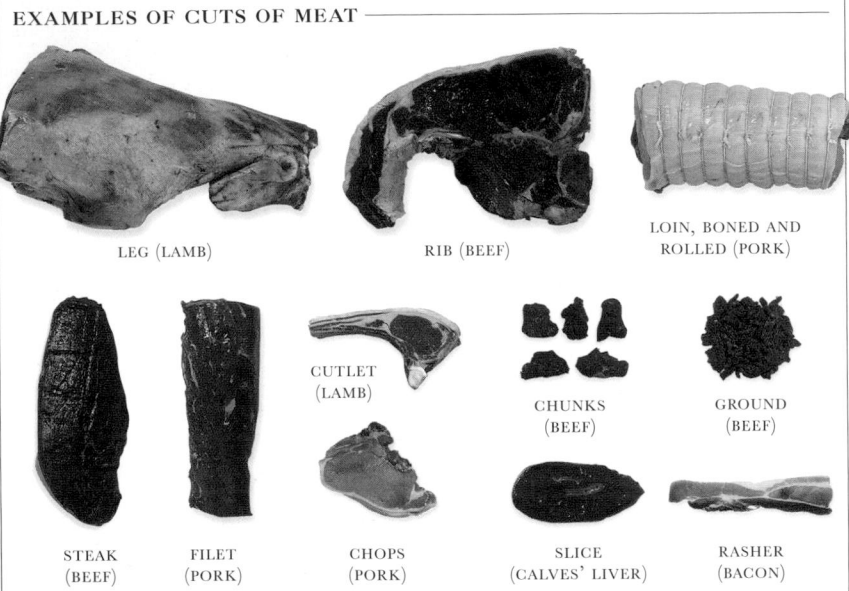

LEG (LAMB)

RIB (BEEF)

LOIN, BONED AND ROLLED (PORK)

CUTLET (LAMB)

CHUNKS (BEEF)

GROUND (BEEF)

STEAK (BEEF)

FILET (PORK)

CHOPS (PORK)

SLICE (CALVES' LIVER)

RASHER (BACON)

cur·va·ture /kárvəchər/ n. **1** the act or state of curving. **2** a curved form. **3** *Geom.* **a** the deviation of a curved surface from a plane. **b** the quantity expressing this.

curve /kərv/ n. & v. ● n. **1** a line or surface having along its length a regular deviation from being straight or flat. **2** a curved form or thing. **3** a curved line on a graph. **4** *Baseball* a ball caused to deviate by the pitcher's spin. ● v.tr. & intr. bend or shape so as to form a curve. □□ **curved** adj.

curve·ball /kárvbawl/ n. = CURVE n. 4.

cur·vet /kərvét/ n. & v. ● n. a horse's leap with the hind legs raised with a spring before the forelegs reach the ground. ● v.intr. (**curvetted, curvetting** or **curveted, curveting**) (of a horse or rider) make a curvet.

curvi- /kárvee/ comb. form curved.

cur·vi·lin·e·ar /kárvilíneeər/ adj. contained by or consisting of curved lines. □□ **cur·vi·lin·e·ar·ly** adv.

curv·y /kárvee/ adj. (**curvier, curviest**) **1** having many curves. **2** (of a woman's figure) shapely. □□ **curv·i·ness** n.

cush·ion /koฺoฺshən/ n. & v. ● n. **1** a bag stuffed with a mass of soft material for sitting or leaning on, etc. **2** a means of protection against shock. **3** the elastic lining of the sides of a billiard table, from which the ball rebounds. **4** a body of air supporting a hovercraft, etc. **5** the frog of a horse's hoof. ● v.tr. **1** provide or protect with a cushion or cushions. **2** provide with a defense; protect. **3** mitigate the adverse effects of. **4** quietly suppress. **5** place or bounce (the ball) against the cushion in billiards. ▷ POOL. □□ **cush·ion·y** adj.

cush·y /koฺoฺshee/ adj. (**cushier, cushiest**) colloq. **1** (a job, etc.) easy and pleasant. **2** (of a seat, surroundings, etc.) soft; comfortable. □□ **cush·i·ness** n.

cusp /kusp/ n. **1** an apex or peak. **2** the horn of a crescent moon, etc. **3** *Astrol.* the initial point of a house. **4** *Archit.* a projecting point between small arcs in Gothic tracery. **5** *Geom.* the point at which two curves meet. **6** *Bot.* a pointed end, esp. of a leaf. **7** a cone-shaped prominence on the surface of a tooth. **8** a pocket or fold in a valve of the heart. □□ **cus·pate** /kúspayt/ adj. **cusped** adj. **cus·pi·dal** /kúspid'l/ adj.

cus·pi·dor /kúspidawr/ n. a spittoon.

cuss /kus/ n. & v. colloq. ● n. **1** a curse. **2** usu. derog. a person; a creature. ● v.tr. & intr. curse.

cuss·ed /kúsid/ adj. colloq. awkward and stubborn. □□ **cuss·ed·ly** adv. **cuss·ed·ness** n.

cuss·word /kúswərd/ n. a swearword.

cus·tard /kústərd/ n. **1** a dish made with milk and eggs, usu. sweetened. **2** a sweet sauce made with milk and flavored cornstarch.

cus·to·di·an /kustódeeən/ n. a guardian or keeper, esp. of a public building, etc. □□ **cus·to·di·an·ship** n.

cus·to·dy /kústədee/ n. **1** guardianship; protective care. **2** imprisonment. □ **take into custody** arrest. □□ **cus·to·di·al** /kustódeeəl/ adj.

cus·tom /kústəm/ n. **1 a** the usual way of behaving or acting (a slave to custom). **b** a particular established way of behaving (our customs seem strange to foreigners). **2** *Law* established usage having the force of law. **3** esp. *Brit.* business patronage (lost a lot of custom). **4** (in pl.; also treated as sing.) **a** a duty levied on certain imported and exported goods. **b** the official department that administers this. **c** the area at a port, frontier, etc., where customs officials deal with incoming goods, etc.

cus·tom·ar·y /kústəmeree/ adj. & n. ● adj. **1** usual; in accordance with custom. **2** *Law* in accordance with custom. ● n. (pl. **-ies**) *Law* a book, etc., listing the customs and established practices of a community. □□ **cus·tom·ar·i·ly** adv. **cus·tom·ar·i·ness** n.

cus·tom-built adj. (also **cus·tom-made**) made to a customer's order.

cus·tom·er /kústəmər/ n. **1** a person who buys goods or services from a store or business. **2** a person one has to deal with (an awkward customer).

cus·tom·house /kústəmhows/ n. (also **cus·toms·house**) the office at a port or international border, etc., at which customs duties are levied.

cus·tom·ize /kústəmīz/ v.tr. make to order or modify according to individual requirements.

cus·tom-made see CUSTOM-BUILT.

cut /kut/ v. & n. ● v. (**cutting**; past and past part. **cut**) **1** tr. (also absol.) penetrate or wound with a sharp-edged instrument. **2** tr. & intr. (often foll. by into) divide or be divided with a knife, etc. **3** tr. **a** trim (hair, a hedge, etc.) by cutting. **b** detach (flowers, grain, etc.) by cutting. **c** reduce the length of (a book, movie, etc.). **4** tr. (foll. by loose, open, etc.) make loose, open, etc. by cutting. **5** tr. (esp. as **cutting** adj.) cause sharp physical or mental pain to (a cutting remark; a cutting wind). **6** tr. (often foll. by down) **a** reduce (wages, prices, time, etc.). **b** reduce or cease (services, etc.). **7** tr. **a** shape or fashion (a coat, gem, key, record, etc.) by cutting. **b** make (a path, tunnel, etc.) by removing material. **8** tr. perform; make (cut a caper; cut a sorry figure). **9** tr. (also absol.) cross; intersect (the line cuts the circle at two points). **10** intr. (foll. by across, through, etc.) traverse, esp. as a shorter way (cut across the grass). **11** tr. **a** ignore or refuse to recognize (a person). **b** renounce (a connection). **12** tr. deliberately fail to attend (a class, etc.). **13** Cards **a** tr. divide (a deck) into two parts. **b** intr. select a dealer, etc., by dividing the deck. **14** *Cinematog.* **a** tr. edit (a movie or tape). **b** intr. (often in imper.) stop filming or recording. **c** intr. (foll. by to) go quickly to (another shot). **15** tr. switch off (an engine, etc.). **16** tr. **a** hit (a ball) with a chopping motion. **b** Golf slice (the ball). **17** tr. dilute; adulterate. **18** intr. Cricket (of the ball) turn sharply on pitching. **19** intr. sl. run. **20** tr. castrate. ● n. **1** an act of cutting. **2** a division or wound made by cutting. **3** a stroke with a knife, sword, whip, etc. **4** a reduction (in prices, wages, etc.). **5** an excision of part of a play, movie, book, etc. **6** a wounding remark or act. **7** the way or style in which a garment, the hair, etc., is cut. **8 ◄** a piece of meat, etc., cut from a carcass. **9** colloq. commission; a share of profits. **10** *Tennis* , etc., a stroke made by cutting. **11** ignoring of or refusal to recognize a person. **12 a** an engraved block for printing. **b** a woodcut or other print. **13** a railroad cutting. **14** a new channel made for a river. □ **a cut above** colloq. noticeably superior to. **be cut out** (foll. by for, or to + infin.) be suited (was not cut out to be a teacher). **cut across 1** transcend or take no account of (normal limitations, etc.) (their concern cuts across normal rivalries). **2** see sense 10 of v. **cut and run** sl. run away. **cut and thrust 1** a lively interchange of argument, etc. **2** the use of both the edge and the point of a sword. **cut back 1** reduce (expenditure, etc.). **2** prune (a tree, etc.). **3** *Cinematog.* repeat part of a previous scene for dramatic effect. **cut both ways 1** serve both sides of an argument, etc. **2** (of an action) have both good and bad effects. **cut a corner** go across and not around it. **cut corners** do a task, etc., perfunctorily or incompletely, esp. to save time. **cut down 1 a** bring or throw down by cutting. **b** kill by means of a sword or disease. **2** see sense 6 of v. **3** reduce the length of (cut down the pants to make shorts). **4** (often foll. by on) reduce one's consumption (cut down on chocolate). **cut a person down to size** colloq. ruthlessly expose the limitations of a person's importance, ability, etc. **cut one's eyeteeth** (or **teeth**) attain worldly wisdom. **cut in 1** interrupt. **2** pull in too closely in front of another vehicle (esp. having overtaken it). **3** give a share of profits, etc. to (a person). **4** connect (a source of electricity). **5** join in a card game by taking the place of a player who cuts out. **6** interrupt a dancing couple to take over from one partner. **cut into 1** make a cut in. **2** interfere with and reduce (traveling cuts into my free time). **cut it fine** see FINE[1]. **cut it out** (usu. in imper.) sl. stop doing that (esp. quarreling). **cut loose 1** begin to act freely. **2** see sense 4 of v. **cut one's losses** (or **a loss**) abandon an unprofitable enterprise before losses become too great. **cut the mustard** sl. reach the

C

required standard. **cut no ice** *sl.* **1** have no influence or importance. **2** achieve little or nothing. **cut off 1** remove by cutting. **2 a** (often in *passive*) bring to an abrupt end or (esp. early) death. **b** intercept; interrupt; prevent from continuing (*cut off supplies*; *cut off the gas*). **c** disconnect (a person engaged in a telephone conversation) (*was suddenly cut off*). **3 a** prevent from traveling or venturing out (*cut off by the snow*). **b** (as **cut off** *adj.*) isolated; remote (*felt cut off in the country*). **4 a** disinherit (*was cut off without a penny*). **b** sever a relationship (*was cut off from the children*). **cut out 1** remove from the inside by cutting. **2** make by cutting from a larger whole. **3** omit; leave out. **4** *colloq.* stop doing or using (*cut out chocolate; let's cut out the arguing*). **5** cease or cause to cease functioning (*the engine cut out*). **6** outdo or supplant (a rival). **7** detach (an animal) from the herd. **8** *Cards* be excluded from a card game as a result of cutting the deck. **9** *colloq.* prepare; plan (*has his work cut out*). **cut short 1** interrupt; terminate prematurely (*cut short his visit*). **2** make shorter or more concise. **cut one's teeth on** acquire initial practice or experience from (something). **cut a tooth** first appear through the gum. **cut up 1** cut into pieces. **2** destroy utterly. **3** criticize severely. **4** behave in a comical or unruly manner. **have one's work cut out** see WORK.

cut-and-dried *adj.* (also **cut-and-dry**) **1** completely decided; prearranged; inflexible. **2** (of opinions, etc.) ready-made; lacking freshness or spontaneity; unimaginative.

cut and paste *v.tr.* (on a computer) move (an item) from one part of a text to another.

cu·ta·ne·ous /kyŏ̄táyneeəs/ *adj.* of the skin.

cut·a·way /kútəway/ *adj.* **1** (of a diagram, etc.) with some parts left out to reveal the interior. **2** (of a coat) with the front below the waist cut away.

cut·back /kútbak/ *n.* an instance or the act of cutting back, esp. a reduction in expenditure.

cute /kyŏ̄t/ *adj. colloq.* **1 a** attractive; quaint. **b** affectedly attractive. **2** clever; ingenious. □□ **cute·ly** *adv.* **cute·ness** *n.*

CUT-GLASS
TUMBLER

cut glass *n.* ◀ glass with patterns and designs cut on it.

cu·ti·cle /kyŏ̄ōtikəl/ *n.* **1 a** the dead skin at the base of a fingernail or toenail. ▷ NAIL. **b** the epidermis or other superficial skin. **2** *Bot.* a thin surface film on plants. □□ **cu·tic·u·lar** /-tíkyələr/ *adj.*

cu·tis /kyŏ̄ōtis/ *n. Anat.* the true skin or dermis, underlying the epidermis.

cut·lass /kútləs/ *n.* a ▼ short sword with a slightly curved blade, esp. of the type formerly used by sailors.

short blade — hand guard

sheath

CUTLASS: 17TH-CENTURY BRITISH
CUTLASS AND SHEATH

cut·ler /kútlər/ *n.* a person who makes or deals in knives and similar utensils.

cut·ler·y /kútləree/ *n.* knives, forks, and spoons for use at table.

cut·let /kútlit/ *n.* **1** a small piece of veal, etc., for frying. ▷ CUT. **2** a flat cake of ground meat or nuts and breadcrumbs, etc.

cut·line /kútlīn/ *n.* **1** a caption to an illustration. **2** the line in squash above which a served ball must strike the wall.

cut·off /kútawf/ *n.* **1** the point at which something is cut off. **2** a device for stopping a flow. **3** a shortcut. **4** (in *pl.*) shorts made from jeans, etc., whose legs have been cut off.

---

cut·out /kútowt/ *n.* **1** a figure cut out of paper, etc. **2** a device for automatic disconnection.

cut-out box *n.* = FUSE BOX.

cut rate *adj.* selling or sold at a reduced price.

cut·ter /kútər/ *n.* **1** a tailor, etc., who takes measurements and cuts cloth. **2** *Naut.* **a** a small, fast sailing ship. **b** a small boat carried by a large ship. **3** *Cricket* a ball turning sharply on pitching. **4** a light horse-drawn sleigh.

cut·throat /kút-thrōt/ *n. & adj.* ● *n.* **1** a murderer. **2** a species of trout, *Salmo clarki*, with a red mark under the jaw. ● *adj.* **1** (of competition) ruthless and intense. **2** (of a person) murderous. **3** (of a card game) three-handed.

cut·ting /kúting/ *n. & adj.* ● *n.* **1** a piece cut from a plant for propagation. **2** an excavated channel through high ground for a railroad or road. ● *adj.* see CUT *v.* 5. □□ **cut·ting·ly** *adv.*

cutting edge *n.* the forefront; the vanguard.

cut·tle /kútl/ *n.* **1** = CUTTLEFISH. **2** = CUTTLEBONE.

cut·tle·bone /kútlbon/ *n.* the internal shell of the cuttlefish.

cut·tle·fish /kútlfish/ *n.* any marine cephalopod mollusk of the genera *Sepia* and *Sepiola*, having ten arms and ejecting a black fluid when threatened or pursued. ▷ CEPHALOPOD

cut·wa·ter /kútwawtər, -woter/ *n.* **1** the forward edge of a ship's prow. **2** a wedge-shaped projection from a pier or bridge.

cut·worm /kútwərm/ *n.* any of various caterpillars that eat through the stems of young plants level with the ground.

c.v. *abbr.* curriculum vitae.

cwm /kŏōm/ *n. Geog.* a cirque.

cwt. *abbr.* hundredweight.

cy·an /síyan/ *n.* a greenish-blue color which is one of the primary colors, complementary to red. ▷ PRINTING

cy·a·nide /síənīd/ *n.* any of the highly poisonous salts or esters of hydrocyanic acid, esp. the potassium salt used in the extraction of gold and silver.

cy·a·no·bac·te·ri·um /síənŏbaktéereeəm, sīánō-/ *n.* any prokaryotic organism of the division Cyanobacteria, capable of photosynthesizing. Also called **blue-green alga.**

cy·a·no·co·bal·a·min /síənŏkōbáləmin, sīánō-/ *n.* a vitamin of the B complex, found in foods of animal origin such as liver, fish, and eggs. Also called **vitamin** B_{12}.

cy·a·no·gen /síənəjən/ *n. Chem.* a colorless, highly poisonous gas intermediate in the preparation of many fertilizers.

cy·a·no·sis /síənósis/ *n. Med.* a bluish discoloration of the skin due to the presence of oxygen-deficient blood. □□ **cy·a·not·ic** /-nótik/ *adj.*

cy·ber·net·ics /síbərnétiks/ *n.pl.* (usu. treated as *sing.*) the science of communications and automatic control systems in both machines and living things. □□ **cy·ber·net·ic** *adj.* **cy·ber·ne·ti·cian** /-nítishən/ *n.* **cy·ber·net·i·cist** /-tisist/ *n.*

cy·ber·space /síbərspays/ *n.* an environment in which information exchange by computer occurs.

cy·borg /síbawrg/ *n.* a fictional or hypothetical person whose physical abilities are extended beyond human limitations by mechanical elements built into the body.

cy·cad /síkad/ *n. Bot.* ▼ any of the palmlike plants of the order Cycadales (including fossil forms).

CYCAD:
SAGO PALM
(*Cycas revoluta*)

---

cy·cla·men /síkləmən, sík-/ *n.* **1** ▼ any plant of the genus *Cyclamen*, originating in Europe, having pink, red, or white flowers with reflexed petals. **2** the shade of color of the red or pink cyclamen flower.

CYCLAMEN
(*Cyclamen repandum*)

cy·cle /síkəl/ *n. & v.* ● *n.* **1 a** a recurrent round or period (of events, phenomena, etc.). **b** the time needed for one such round or period. **2 a** *Physics*, etc., a recurrent series of operations or states. **b** *Electr.* = HERTZ. **3** a series of songs, poems, etc., usu. on a single theme. **4** a bicycle, tricycle, or similar machine. ● *v.intr.* **1** ride a bicycle, etc. **2** move in cycles.

cy·clic /síklik, sík-/ *adj.* **1 a** recurring in cycles. **b** belonging to a chronological cycle. **2** *Chem.* with constituent atoms forming a ring. **3** of a cycle of songs, etc. **4** *Bot.* (of a flower) with its parts arranged in whorls. **5** *Math.* of a circle or cycle.

cy·cli·cal /síklikəl, sík-/ *adj.* = CYCLIC 1. □□ **cy·cli·cal·ly** *adv.*

cy·clist /síklist/ *n.* a rider of a bicycle.

cyclo- /síklo/ *comb. form* circle, cycle, or cyclic (*cyclometer*; *cyclorama*).

cy·cloid /síkloyd/ *n. Math.* a curve traced by a point on a circle when the circle is rolled along a straight line. □□ **cy·cloi·dal** /-klóyd'l/ *adj.*

cy·clom·e·ter /síklómitər/ *n.* **1** an instrument for measuring circular arcs. **2** an instrument for measuring the distance traversed by a bicycle, etc.

cy·clone /síklōn/ *n.* **1** a system of winds rotating inward to an area of low barometric pressure; a depression. ▷ DEPRESSION. **2** a violent hurricane of limited diameter. □□ **cy·clon·ic** /-klónik/ *adj.* **cy·clon·i·cal·ly** *adv.*

cy·clo·pe·di·a /síkləpéedeeə/ *n.* an encyclopedia. □□ **cy·clo·pe·dic** *adj.*

cy·clo·tron /síklətron/ *n. Physics* an apparatus in which charged atomic and subatomic particles are accelerated by an alternating electric field while following an outward spiral or circular path in a magnetic field.

cyg·net /sígnit/ *n.* a young swan.

cyl·in·der /sílindər/ *n.* **1 a** ◀ a uniform solid or hollow body with straight sides and a circular section. **b** a thing of this shape, e.g., a container for liquefied gas. **2** a cylinder-shaped part of various machines, esp. a piston chamber in an engine. ▷ INTERNAL-COMBUSTION ENGINE. **3** *Printing* a metal roller. ▷ PRINTING.

CYLINDER

cy·lin·dri·cal /silíndrikəl/ *adj.* **cy·lin·dri·cal·ly** *adv.*

cym·bal /símbəl/ *n.* ▶ a percussion instrument of indefinite pitch consisting of a brass or bronze plate struck with another or with a stick, etc., to make a ringing sound. ▷ DRUM SET, ORCHESTRA, PERCUSSION. □□ **cym·bal·ist** *n.*

leather handles

CYMBALS

cyn·ic /sínik/ *n. & adj.* ● *n.* **1** a person who has little faith in human sincerity and goodness. **2** (**Cynic**) one of a school of ancient Greek philosophers founded by Antisthenes, marked by ostentatious contempt for ease and pleasure. ● *adj.* **1** (**Cynic**) of the Cynics. **2** = CYNICAL. □□ **cyn·i·cism** /-nisizəm/ *n.*

cyn·i·cal /sínikəl/ *adj.* **1** incredulous of human sincerity and goodness. **2** disregarding normal standards. **3** sneering; mocking. □□ **cyn·i·cal·ly** *adv.*

cy·no·sure /sínəshŏŏr, sín-/ *n.* **1** a center of attraction or admiration. **2** a guiding star.

cy·pher var. of CIPHER.

cy·press /síprəs/ *n.* **1** ▶ any coniferous tree of the genus *Cupressus* or *Chamaecyparis*, with hard wood and dark foliage. ▷ CONIFER. **2** this, or branches from it, as a symbol of mourning.

Cyp·ri·ot /sípreeət/ *n. & adj.* (also **Cyp·ri·ote** /-ōt/) ● *n.* a native or national of Cyprus. ● *adj.* of Cyprus.

Cy·ril·lic /sirílik/ *adj. & n.* ● *adj.* denoting the alphabet used by the Slavonic peoples of the Orthodox Church; now used esp. for Russian and Bulgarian. ● *n.* this alphabet.

cyst /sist/ *n.* **1** *Med.* a sac formed in the body containing morbid matter, a parasitic larva, etc.

blunt leaves on branchlets

egg-shaped cones

CYPRESS:
ITALIAN CYPRESS
(*Cupressus sempervirens*)

2 *Biol.* **a** a hollow organ, bladder, etc., in an animal or plant, containing a liquid secretion. **b** a cell or cavity enclosing reproductive bodies, an embryo, parasite, microorganism, etc.

cys·te·ine /sístee-éen, -tee-in/ *n. Biochem.* a sulfur-containing amino acid, essential in the human diet and a constituent of many enzymes.

cys·tic /sístik/ *adj.* **1** of the urinary bladder. **2** of the gallbladder. **3** of the nature of like a cyst.

cys·tic fi·bro·sis *n. Med.* a hereditary disease affecting the exocrine glands and usu. resulting in respiratory infections.

cys·ti·tis /sistítis/ *n.* an inflammation of the urinary bladder, usu. accompanied by frequent painful urination.

cys·to- /sístō/ *comb. form* the urinary bladder (*cystoscope*; *cystotomy*).

cys·to·scope /sístəskōp/ *n.* an instrument inserted in the urethra for examining the urinary bladder. □□ **cys·to·scop·ic** /-skóp-ik/ *adj.* **cys·tos·co·py** /sistóskəpee/ *n.*

cys·tos·to·my /sistóstəmee/ *n.* (*pl.* **-ies**) a surgical incision into the urinary bladder.

-cyte /sīt/ *comb. form Biol.* a mature cell (*leukocyte*) (cf. -BLAST).

cyto- /sītō/ *comb. form Biol.* cells or a cell.

cy·to·ge·net·ics /sītōjinétiks/ *n.* the study of inheritance in relation to the structure and function of cells. □□ **cy·to·ge·net·ic** *adj.* **cy·to·ge·net·i·cal** *adj.*

cy·to·ge·net·i·cal·ly *adv.* **cy·to·ge·net·i·cist** /-nétisist/ *n.*

cy·tol·o·gy /sītóləjee/ *n.* the study of cells. □□ **cy·to·log·i·cal** /sītəlójikəl/ *adj.* **cy·tol·og·i·cal·ly** *adv.* **cy·tol·o·gist** *n.*

cy·to·plasm /sītəplazəm/ *n.* the protoplasmic content of a cell apart from its nucleus. ▷ CELL. □□ **cy·to·plas·mic** /-plázmik/ *adj.*

cy·to·sine /sītəseen/ *n.* one of the principal component bases of the nucleotides and the nucleic acids DNA and RNA, derived from pyrimidine. ▷ DNA

cy·to·tox·ic /sītətóksik/ *adj.* toxic to cells.

czar /zaar/ *n.* (also **tsar**) **1** *hist.* the title of the former emperor of Russia. **2** a person with great authority. □□ **czar·dom** *n.* **czar·ism** *n.* **czar·ist** *n.*

czar·e·vich /záarivich/ *n.* (also **tsarevich**) *hist.* the eldest son of an emperor of Russia.

cza·ri·na /zaaréenə/ *n.* (also **tsarina**) *hist.* the title of the former empress of Russia.

Czech /chek/ *n. & adj.* ● *n.* **1** a native or national of the Czech Republic, or Bohemia, or (*hist.*) Czechoslovakia. **2** the West Slavonic language of the Czech people. ● *adj.* of or relating to the Czechs or their language.

Czech·o·slo·vak /chékəslóvak, -vaak/ *n. & adj.* (also **Czech·o·slo·va·ki·an** /-sləváakeeən/) ● *n.* a native or national of Czechoslovakia, a former nation in central Europe including Bohemia, Moravia, and Slovakia. ● *adj.* of or relating to Czechoslovaks or the former nation Czechoslovakia.

C

D

D[1] /dee/ *n.* (also **d**) (*pl.* **ds** or **D's**) **1** the fourth letter of the alphabet. **2** *Mus.* the second note of the diatonic scale of C major. ▷ NOTATION. **3** (as a Roman numeral) 500. **4** = DEE. **5** the fourth highest class or category (of academic marks, etc.).

D[2] *symb. Chem.* the element deuterium.

d. *abbr.* **1** died. **2** departs. **3** delete. **4** daughter. **5** depth. **6** deci-.

'd *v. colloq.* (usu. after pronouns) had; would (*I'd; he'd*).

DA *abbr.* **1** district attorney. **2** *sl.* = DUCK'S ASS.

da *abbr.* deca-.

dab[1] /dab/ *v. & n.* ● *v.* (**dabbed**, **dabbing**) **1** *tr.* press (a surface) briefly with a cloth, etc., without rubbing. **2** *tr.* press (a sponge, etc.) lightly on a surface. **3** *tr.* (foll. by *on*) apply (a substance) by dabbing a surface. **4** *intr.* (usu. foll. by *at*) aim a feeble blow; tap. **5** *tr.* strike lightly; tap. ● *n.* **1** a brief application of a cloth, etc., to a surface without rubbing. **2** a small amount applied in this way (*a dab of paint*). **3** a light blow. □□ **dab·ber** *n.*

dab[2] /dab/ *n.* any flatfish of the genus *Limanda*.

dab·ble /dábəl/ *v.* **1** *intr.* (usu. foll. by *in*, *at*) take a superficial interest (in a subject or activity). **2** *intr.* move the feet, hands, etc., about in (usu. a small amount of) liquid. **3** *tr.* wet partly; stain; splash. □□ **dab·bler** *n.*

dab·chick /dábchik/ *n.* = LITTLE GREBE.

dace /days/ *n.* (*pl.* same) any small freshwater fish, esp. of the genus *Leuciscus*, related to the carp.

da·cha /dáachə/ *n.* a country house or cottage in Russia.

dachs·hund /daaks-hŏŏnt, daaksənt/ *n.* a dog of a short-legged, long-bodied breed.

da·coit /dəkóyt/ *n.* a member of a band of armed robbers in India or Burma (Myanmar).

dac·tyl /dáktil/ *n.* a metrical foot (---) consisting of one long syllable followed by two short. □□ **dac·tyl·ic** /daktilik/ *adj.*

dad /dad/ *n. colloq.* father.

Da·da /dáadaa/ *n.* an early 20th-c. international movement in art, literature, music, and film, repudiating conventions. □□ **Da·da·ism** /daadəizəm/ *n.* **Da·da·ist** *n. & adj.* **Da·da·is·tic** *adj.*

dad·dy /dádee/ *n.* (*pl.* **-ies**) *colloq.* **1** father. **2** (usu. foll. by *of*) the oldest or supreme example (*had a daddy of a headache*).

dad·dy long·legs *n.* a harvestman.

da·do /dáydō/ *n.* (*pl.* **-os**) **1** the lower part of the wall of a room when visually distinct from the upper part. **2** the plinth of a column. **3** the cube of a pedestal between the base and the cornice. ▷ PEDESTAL

dae·mon var. of DEMON 5.

dae·mon·ic var. of DEMONIC.

daf·fo·dil /dáfədil/ *n.* **1 a** a bulbous plant, *Narcissus pseudonarcissus*, with a yellow trumpet-shaped crown. **b** any of various other plants of the genus *Narcissus*. **c** a flower of any of these plants. **2** a pale-yellow color.

daf·fy /dáfee/ *adj.* (**daffier**, **daffiest**) *sl.* = DAFT. □□ **daf·fi·ly** *adv.* **daf·fi·ness** *n.*

daft /daft/ *adj. colloq.* **1** silly; foolish; crazy. **2** (foll. by *about*) fond of; infatuated with. □□ **daft·ly** *adv.* **daft·ness** *n.*

dag·ger /dágər/ *n.* **1** a short stabbing weapon with a pointed and edged blade. **2** *Printing* = OBELUS.
□ **at daggers drawn** in bitter enmity. **look daggers at** glare angrily at.

da·go /dáygō/ *n.* (*pl.* **-os** or **-oes**) *sl. offens.* a person of Italian, Spanish, or Portuguese ancestry.

da·guerre·o·type /dəgérətīp/ *n.* **1** ▶ a photograph taken by an early photographic process employing an iodine-sensitized silvered plate and mercury vapor. **2** this process.

dahl·ia /dályə, daál-, dáyl-/ *n.* any garden plant of the genus *Dahlia*, cultivated for its many-colored flowers.

Dáil /doyl/ *n.* (in full **Dáil Éireann** /áirən/) the lower house of parliament in the Republic of Ireland.

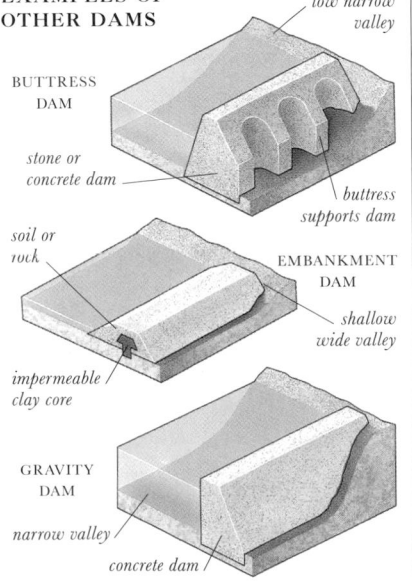

DAGUERREOTYPE

dai·ly /dáylee/ *adj., adv., & n.* ● *adj.* **1** done, produced, or occurring every day or every weekday. **2** constant; regular. ● *adv.* **1** every day; from day to day. **2** constantly. ● *n.* (*pl.* **-ies**) *colloq.* a daily newspaper.

dain·ty /dáyntee/ *adj. & n.* ● *adj.* (**daintier**, **daintiest**) **1** delicately pretty. **2** delicate. **3** (of food) choice. **4** fastidious. ● *n.* (*pl.* **-ies**) a choice delicacy. □□ **dain·ti·ly** *adv.* **dain·ti·ness** *n.*

dai·qui·ri /dákəree, dí-/ *n.* (*pl.* **daiquiris**) a cocktail of rum, lime juice, etc.

dair·y /dáiree/ *n.* (*pl.* **-ies**) **1** a building or room for the storage, processing, and distribution of milk and its products. **2** a store where milk and milk products are sold. **3** (*attrib.*) **a** of, containing, or concerning milk and its products (and sometimes eggs). **b** used for dairy products (*dairy cow*).

dair·y·maid /dáireemayd/ *n.* a woman employed in a dairy.

dair·y·man /dáireemən/ *n.* (*pl.* **-men**) **1** a person dealing in dairy products. **2** a person employed in a dairy.

da·is /dáyis, dí-/ *n.* a low platform, usu. at the upper end of a hall.

dai·sy /dáyzee/ *n.* (*pl.* **-ies**) **1 a** a small composite plant, *Bellis perennis*, bearing flowers each with a yellow disk and white rays. **b** any other plant with daisy-like flowers. **2** *sl.* a first-rate specimen of anything. □ **pushing up the daisies** *sl.* dead and buried.

D

dai·sy wheel *n.* a disk of spokes extending radially from a central hub, each terminating in a printing character, used as a printer in word processors and typewriters.

dal /daal/ *n.* (also **dhal**) **1** a kind of split pulse, a common foodstuff in India. **2** a dish made with this.

Da·lai la·ma /dáalī láamə/ *n.* the spiritual head of Tibetan Buddhism.

dale /dayl/ *n.* a valley, esp. a broad one.

dal·li·ance /dáleeəns, -yəns/ *n.* **1** a leisurely or frivolous passing of time. **2** an instance of lighthearted flirting.

dal·ly /dálee/ *v.intr.* (**-ies**, **-ied**) **1** delay; waste time, esp. frivolously. **2** (often foll. by *with*) play about; flirt; treat frivolously. □ **dally away** waste or fritter (one's time, life, etc.).

Dal·ma·tian /dalmáyshən/ *n.* a dog of a large, white, short-haired breed with dark spots.

dam[1] /dam/ *n. & v.* ● *n.* **1** ▼ a barrier constructed to hold back water and raise its level, forming a reservoir or preventing flooding. **2** a barrier constructed in a stream by a beaver. **3** anything functioning as a dam does. **4** a causeway. ● *v.tr.* (**dammed**, **damming**) **1** furnish or confine with a dam. **2** (often foll. by *up*) block up; obstruct.

dam[2] /dam/ *n.* the female parent of an animal, esp. a four-footed one.

DAM

A dam is a structure built to hold back water in order to prevent flooding, to store water for domestic and industrial use, and to provide hydroelectric power. Most dams are built across river valleys. The design of the dam depends on such factors as the size and shape of the valley and the type of rock and soil found there.

FEATURES OF AN ARCH DAM

reservoir

narrow valley

roadway

hydroelectric power station

discharged water

arched concrete wall

EXAMPLES OF OTHER DAMS

low narrow valley

BUTTRESS DAM

stone or concrete dam

buttress supports dam

soil or rock

EMBANKMENT DAM

shallow wide valley

impermeable clay core

GRAVITY DAM

narrow valley

concrete dam

D

dam·age /dámij/ *n.* & *v.* ● *n.* **1** harm or injury. **2** (in *pl.*) *Law* a sum of money claimed or awarded in compensation for a loss or an injury. **3** the loss of what is desirable. **4** (prec. by *the*) *sl.* cost (*what's the damage?*). ● *v.tr.* **1** inflict damage on. **2** (esp. as **damaging** *adj.*) detract from the reputation of (*a most damaging admission*). □□ **dam·ag·ing·ly** *adv.*

dam·a·scene /dáməséen/ *v.tr.* decorate (metal) by etching or inlaying, esp. with gold or silver.

dam·ask /dáməsk/ *n., adj.,* & *v.* ● *n.* **1 a** a figured woven fabric (esp. silk or linen) with a pattern visible on both sides. **b** twilled table linen with woven designs shown by the reflection of light. **2** a tablecloth made of this material. ● *adj.* **1** made of or resembling damask. **2** velvety pink or vivid red. ● *v.tr.* **1** weave with figured designs. **2** = DAMA-SCENE. **3** ornament.

dam·ask rose *n.* ◄ an old sweet-scented variety of rose, with very soft velvety petals, used to make attar.

dame /daym/ *n.* **1** (**Dame**) **a** (in the UK) the title given to a woman with the rank of Knight Commander or holder of the Grand Cross in the Orders of Chivalry. **b** a woman holding this title. **2** *sl.* a woman.

DAMASK ROSE
(*Rosa × damascena*)

damn /dam/ *v., n., adj.,* & *adv.* ● *v.tr.* **1** (often *absol.* or as *int.* of anger or annoyance, = *may God damn*) curse (a person or thing). **2** doom to hell; cause the damnation of. **3** condemn; censure (*a review damning the performance*). **4 a** (often as **damning** *adj.*) (of a circumstance, evidence, etc.) show or prove to be guilty. **b** be the ruin of. ● *n.* **1** an uttered curse. **2** *sl.* a negligible amount (*not worth a damn*). ● *adj.* & *adv. colloq.* = DAMNED. □ **damn with faint praise** commend so unenthusiastically as to imply disapproval. **I'll be damned if** *colloq.* I certainly do not, will not, etc. **not give a damn** see GIVE. **well I'll be damned** *colloq.* exclamation of surprise, dismay, etc. □□ **damn·ing·ly** *adv.*

dam·na·ble /dámnəbəl/ *adj.* hateful; annoying. □□ **dam·na·bly** *adv.*

dam·na·tion /damnáyshən/ *n.* & *int.* ● *n.* eternal punishment in hell. ● *int.* expressing anger.

damned /damd/ *adj.* & *adv. colloq.* ● *adj.* damnable. ● *adv.* extremely (*damned hot*). □ **do one's damned-est** do one's utmost.

damp /damp/ *adj., n.,* & *v.* ● *adj.* slightly wet. ● *n.* **1** diffused moisture in the air, on a surface, or in a solid. **2** dejection; discouragement. **3** = FIREDAMP. ● *v.tr.* **1** make damp; moisten. **2** (often foll. by *down*) **a** take the force out of (*damp one's enthusiasm*). **b** make spiritless. **c** make (a fire) burn less strongly by reducing the flow of air to it. **3** reduce or stop the vibration of (esp. the strings of a musical instrument). **4** quiet. □ **damp off** (of a plant) die from a fungus attack in damp conditions. □□ **damp·ly** *adv.* **damp·ness** *n.*

damp·en /dámpən/ *v.* **1** *v.tr.* & *intr.* make or become damp. **2** *tr.* make less forceful. □□ **damp·en·er** *n.*

damp·er /dámpər/ *n.* **1** a person or thing that discourages. **2** a device that reduces shock or noise. **3** a metal plate in a flue to control the draft. **4** *Mus.* ◄ a pad silencing a piano string. □ **put a damper on** take the enjoyment out of.

string —

damper —

DAMPER:
MODEL
SHOWING
A PIANO
DAMPER

key

dam·sel /dámzəl/ *n. archaic* or *literary* a young unmarried woman.

dam·sel·fly /dámzəlflī/ *n.* (*pl.* **-flies**) any of various insects of the order Odonata, like a dragonfly but with its wings folded over the body when resting.

dam·son /dámzən, -sən/ *n.* & *adj.* **1** (in full **dam·son plum**) **a** a small, dark-purple, plumlike fruit. **b** the small deciduous tree, *Prunus institia*, bearing this. **2** a dark-purple color. ● *adj.* damson-colored.

dan /daan, dan/ *n.* **1** any of twelve degrees of advanced proficiency in judo. **2** a person who has achieved any of these.

dance /dans/ *v.* & *n.* ● *v.* **1** *intr.* move rhythmically to music, alone or with a partner or in a set, usu. in fixed steps or sequences to music. **2** *intr.* skip or jump about; move in a lively way. **3** *tr.* **a** perform (a specified dance). **b** perform (a specified role) in a ballet, etc. **4** *intr.* move up and down (on water, in the field of vision, etc.). **5** *tr.* move (esp. a child) up and down. ● *n.* **1 a** a piece of dancing; a sequence of steps in dancing. **b** a special form of this. **2** a single round or turn of a dance. **3** a social gathering for dancing. **4** a piece of music for dancing to or in a dance rhythm. **5** a dancing or lively motion. □ **dance attendance on** follow or wait on (a person) obsequiously. **dance to a person's tune** accede obsequiously to a person's demands and wishes. □□ **dance·a·ble** *adj.* **danc·er** *n.*

dance·hall /dáns-hawl/ *n.* a public hall used for dancing.

d. and c. *abbr.* dilatation and curettage.

dan·de·li·on /dánd'líən/ *n.* a composite plant, *Taraxacum officinale*, with jagged leaves and a large, bright-yellow flower on a hollow stalk.

dan·der /dándər/ *n. colloq.* temper; indignation. □ **get one's dander up** become angry.

dan·di·fy /dándifī/ *v.tr.* (**-ies**, **-ied**) cause to resemble a dandy.

dan·dle /dánd'l/ *v.tr.* **1** dance (a child) on one's knees or in one's arms. **2** pamper; pet.

dan·druff /dándruf/ *n.* **1** dead skin in small scales among the hair. **2** the condition of having this.

dan·dy /dándee/ *n.* & *adj.* ● *n.* (*pl.* **-ies**) **1** a man unduly devoted to style, smartness, and fashion in dress and appearance. **2** *colloq.* an excellent thing. ● *adj.* (**dandier**, **dandiest**) *colloq.* very good of its kind; splendid. □□ **dan·dy·ish** *adj.* **dan·dy·ism** *n.*

Dane /dayn/ *n.* **1** a native or national of Denmark. **2** *hist.* a Viking invader of England in the 9th–11th c.

dan·ger /dáynjər/ *n.* **1** liability or exposure to harm. **2** a thing that causes or is likely to cause harm. **3** the status of a railroad signal directing a halt or caution. □ **in danger of** likely to incur or to suffer from.

dan·ger·ous /dáynjərəs/ *adj.* involving or causing danger. □□ **dan·ger·ous·ly** *adv.* **dan·ger·ous·ness** *n.*

dan·gle /dánggəl/ *v.* **1** *intr.* be loosely suspended, so as to be able to sway to and fro. **2** *tr.* hold or carry loosely suspended. **3** *tr.* hold out (a hope, temptation, etc.) enticingly. □□ **dan·gler** *n.*

Dan·ish /dáynish/ *adj.* & *n.* ● *adj.* of Denmark or the Danes. ● *n.* **1** the Danish language. **2** (prec. by *the*; treated as *pl.*) the Danish people.

Dan·ish blue *n.* a soft, salty white cheese with blue veins. ▷ CHEESE

Dan·ish pas·try *n.* a cake of sweetened yeast pastry topped with icing, fruit, nuts, etc.

dank /dangk/ *adj.* disagreeably damp and cold. □□ **dank·ly** *adv.* **dank·ness** *n.*

daph·ne /dáfnee/ *n.* any flowering shrub of the genus *Daphne*.

DAMSELFLY:
BEAUTIFUL
DEMOISELLE
(*Agrion virgo*)

daph·ni·a /dáfneeə/ *n.* any freshwater branchiopod crustacean of the genus *Daphnia*, enclosed in a transparent carapace and with long antennae and prominent eyes.

dap·per /dápər/ *adj.* **1** neat and precise, esp. in dress or movement. **2** sprightly. □□ **dap·per·ly** *adv.* **dap·per·ness** *n.*

dap·ple /dápəl/ *v.* & *n.* ● *v.tr.* **1** mark with spots or rounded patches of color or shade. **2** *intr.* become marked in this way. ● *n.* **1** a dappled effect. **2** a dappled animal, esp. a horse.

dap·ple gray *n.* **1** (of an animal's coat) gray or white with darker spots. **2** ▼ a horse of this color.

DAPPLE GRAY:
ORLOV TROTTER

D.A.R. *abbr.* Daughters of the American Revolution.

dare /dair/ *v.* & *n.* ● *v.tr.* (*3rd sing. present* usu. **dare** before an expressed or implied infinitive without *to*) **1** (foll. by infin. with or without *to*) venture (to); have the courage or impudence (to) (*dare he do it?*; *if they dare to come*; *how dare you?*). **2** (usu. foll. by *to* + infin.) defy or challenge (a person) (*I dare you to get up*). ● *n.* **1** an act of daring. **2** a challenge, esp. to prove courage. □ **I daresay 1** (often foll. by *that* + clause) it is probable. **2** probably; I grant that much. □□ **dar·er** *n.*

dare·dev·il /dáirdevəl/ *n.* & *adj.* ● *n.* a recklessly daring person. ● *adj.* recklessly daring. □□ **dare·dev·il·ry** *n.* **dare·dev·il·try** *n.*

dar·ing /dáiring/ *n.* & *adj.* ● *n.* adventurous courage. ● *adj.* adventurous; bold; prepared to take risks. □□ **dar·ing·ly** *adv.*

Dar·jee·ling /daarjéeling/ *n.* a high-quality tea grown in northern India.

dark /daark/ *adj.* & *n.* ● *adj.* **1** with little or no light. **2** of a deep or somber color. **3** (of a person) with deep brown or black hair or skin. **4** gloomy; depressing; dismal (*dark thoughts*). **5** evil; sinister (*dark deeds*). **6** sullen; angry (*a dark mood*). **7** secret; mysterious (*keep it dark*). **8** ignorant; unenlightened. ● *n.* **1** absence of light. **2** nightfall (*don't go out after dark*). **3** a lack of knowledge. **4** a dark area or color, esp. in painting. □ **in the dark** lacking information. □□ **dark·ish** *adj.* **dark·ly** *adv.* **dark·ness** *n.*

Dark Ag·es *n. pl.* (also **Dark Age**) (prec. by *the*) **1** the period of European history preceding the Middle Ages, esp. the 5th–10th c. **2** any period of supposed unenlightenment.

dark·en /dáarkən/ *v.* **1** *tr.* make dark or darker. **2** *intr.* become dark or darker. □ **never darken a person's door** keep away permanently.

dark horse *n.* a little-known person who is unexpectedly successful.

dark·ling /dáarkling/ *adj.* & *adv. poet.* in the dark; the night.

dark·room /dáarkrōōm, -rŏŏm/ *n.* a room for photographic work, with normal light excluded.

dar·ling /dáarling/ *n.* & *adj.* ● *n.* **1** a beloved or lovable person or thing. **2** a favorite. **3** *colloq.* a pretty or endearing person or thing. ● *adj.* **1** beloved; lovable. **2** favorite. **3** *colloq.* charming or pretty.

darn[1] /daarn/ *v.* & *n.* ● *v.tr.* **1** mend by interweaving yarn across a hole with a needle. **2** embroider with a large running stitch. ● *n.* a darned area in material.

darn[2] /daarn/ *v.tr., int., adj., & adv. colloq.* = DAMN (in imprecatory senses).

darned /daarnd/ *adj. & adv. colloq.* = DAMNED.

dar·nel /daárnəl/ *n.* any of several grasses of the genus *Lolium*, growing as weeds among cereal crops.

DARPA /daárpə/ *US abbr.* Defense Advanced Research Projects Agency.

darn·ing /daárning/ *n.* **1** the action of a person who darns. **2** things to be darned.

dart /daart/ *n. & v.* ● *n.* **1** ▶ a small pointed missile used *flight* as a weapon or in a game. **2** (in *pl.*; usu. treated as *sing.*) an indoor game in which light feathered darts are thrown at a circular target to score points. **3** a sudden rapid movement. **4** *Zool.* a dartlike structure, such as an insect's sting. **5** a tapering tuck stitched in a garment. ● *v.* **1** *intr.* (often foll. by *out, in, past,* etc.) move or go suddenly or rapidly (*darted into the store*). **2** *tr.* throw (a missile). **3** *tr.* direct suddenly (a glance, etc.).

DARTS

dart·board /daártbawrd/ *n.* a circular board marked with numbered segments, used as a target in darts.

dart·er /daártər/ *n.* any of various small, quick-moving freshwater fish of the family Percidae, native to N. America.

Dar·win·i·an /daarwíneeən/ *adj. & n.* ● *adj.* of or relating to Darwin's theory of the evolution of species by the action of natural selection. ● *n.* an adherent of this theory. □□ **Dar·win·ism** /daárwinizəm/ *n.* **Dar·win·ist** *n.*

dash /dash/ *v. & n.* ● *v.* **1** *intr.* rush hastily or forcefully (*dashed up the stairs*). **2** *tr.* strike or fling with great force (*dashed it to the ground*). **3** *tr.* frustrate; daunt; dispirit (*dashed their hopes*). **4** *tr. colloq.* (esp. **dash it** or **dash it all**) = DAMN *v.* 1. ● *n.* **1** a rush or onset; a sudden advance (*made a dash for shelter*). **2** a horizontal stroke in writing or printing to mark a pause or break in sense or to represent omitted letters or words. **3** impetuous vigor or the capacity for this. **4** showy appearance or behavior. **5** a sprinting race. **6** the longer signal of the two used in Morse code (cf. DOT *n.* 3). **7** a slight admixture, esp. of a liquid. **8** = DASHBOARD. □ **dash down** (or **off**) write or finish hurriedly.

dash·board /dáshbawrd/ *n.* the surface below the windshield inside a motor vehicle or aircraft, containing instruments and controls. ▷ INSTRUMENT PANEL

dash·ing /dáshing/ *adj.* **1** spirited; lively. **2** stylish. □□ **dash·ing·ly** *adv.*

das·tard·ly /dástərdlee/ *adj.* cowardly; despicable.

DAT *abbr.* digital audiotape.

da·ta /dáytə, dátə, daá-/ *n.pl.* (also treated as *sing.*, although the singular form is strictly *datum*) **1** known facts or things used as a basis for inference or reckoning. **2** quantities or characters operated on by a computer, etc.

da·ta·base /dáytəbays, dátə-/ *n.* a structured set of data held in a computer.

da·ta·ble /dáytəbəl/ *adj.* (often foll. by *to*) capable of being dated (to a particular time).

da·ta cap·ture *n.* the action or process of entering data into a computer.

da·ta pro·cess·ing *n.* a series of operations on data, esp. by a computer. □□ **da·ta proc·es·sor** *n.*

date[1] /dayt/ *n. & v.* ● *n.* **1** a day of the month, esp. specified by a number. **2** a particular day or year, esp. when a given event occurred. **3** a statement (usu. giving the day, month, and year) in a document or inscription, etc., of the time of composition or publication. **4** the period to which a work of art, etc., belongs. **5** the time when an event happens or is to happen. **6** *colloq.* **a** an engagement or appointment, esp. with a person of the opposite sex. **b** a person with whom one has a social engagement. ● *v.* **1** *tr.* mark with a date. **2** *tr.* **a** assign a date to (an object, event, etc.). **b** assign a date to a particular time, period, etc. **3** *intr.* (often foll. by *from, back to,* etc.) have its origins at a particular time. **4** *intr.* be recognizable as from a past or specific period; become evidently out of date (*a design that does not date*). **5** *tr.* indicate or expose as being out of date (*that hat really dates you*). **6** *colloq.* **a** *tr.* make an arrangement with (a person) to meet socially. **b** *intr.* meet socially by agreement (*they are now dating regularly*). □ **to date** until now.

date[2] /dayt/ *n.* **1** a dark, oval, single-stoned fruit. **2** (in full **date palm**) the tall tree *Phoenix dactylifera*, native to W. Asia and N. Africa, bearing this fruit.

dat·ed /dáytid/ *adj.* **1** showing or having a date (*a dated letter*). **2** old-fashioned; out-of-date.

date·less /dáytlis/ *adj.* **1** having no date. **2** of immemorial age. **3** not likely to become out of date.

date·line /dáytlīn/ *n.* **1** (also **date line**; in full **international date line**) the line from north to south partly along the 180th meridian, to the east of which the date is a day earlier than it is to the west. **2** a line at the head of a dispatch or special article in a newspaper showing the date and place of writing.

date rape *n.* sexual assault involving two people who have met socially.

da·tive /dáytiv/ *n. & adj. Gram.* ● *n.* the case of nouns and pronouns (and words in grammatical agreement with them) indicating an indirect object or recipient. ● *adj.* of or in the dative. □□ **da·ti·val** /dáytívəl/ **da·tive·ly** *adv.*

da·tum /dáytəm, dátəm, daátəm/ *n.* (*pl.* **data**: see DATA). **1** a piece of information. **2** a thing known or granted; an assumption or premise from which inferences may be drawn. **3** a fixed starting point of a scale, etc.

da·tu·ra /dətóórə, -tyóórə/ *n.* any poisonous plant of the genus *Datura*, e.g., the thorn apple.

daub /dawb/ *v. & n.* ● *v.tr.* **1** spread (paint, plaster, or some other thick substance) crudely or roughly. **2** coat or smear (a surface) with paint, etc. **3** a (also *absol.*) paint crudely or unskillfully. **b** lay (colors) on crudely and clumsily. ● *n.* **1** paint or other substance daubed on a surface. **2** plaster, clay, etc., for coating a surface, esp. mixed with straw and applied to laths or wattles to form a wall. ▷ WATTLE AND DAUB. **3** a crude painting.

daube /dōb/ *n.* a stew of braised meat (usu. beef) with wine, etc.

daugh·ter /dáwtər/ *n.* **1** a girl or woman in relation to either or both of her parents. **2** a female descendant. **3** (foll. by *of*) a female member of a family, nation, etc. **4** (foll. by *of*) a woman who is regarded as the spiritual descendant of, or as spiritually attached to, a person or thing. **5** a product or attribute personified as a daughter in relation to its source. **6** *Physics* a nuclide formed by the radioactive decay of another. **7** *Biol.* a cell, etc., formed by the division, etc., of another. □□ **daugh·ter·ly** *adj.*

daugh·ter-in-law *n.* (*pl.* **daughters-in-law**) the wife of one's son.

daunt /dawnt/ *v.tr.* discourage; intimidate. □□ **daunt·ing** *adj.* **daunt·ing·ly** *adv.*

daunt·less /dáwntlis/ *adj.* intrepid; persevering.

dau·phin /dáwfin, dōfáN/ *n. hist.* the eldest son of the king of France.

dav·en·port /dávənpawrt/ *n.* a large, heavily upholstered sofa.

da·vit /dávit, dáyvit/ *n.* a small crane on board a ship, esp. one of a pair for suspending or lowering a lifeboat.

Da·vy /dáyvee/ *n.* (*pl.* **-ies**) (in full **Davy lamp**) ◀ a miner's safety lamp with the flame enclosed by wire gauze.

Da·vy Jones /jōnz/ *n. sl.* **1** (in full **Davy Jones's locker**) the bottom of the sea, esp. regarded as the grave of those drowned at sea. **2** the evil spirit of the sea.

daw·dle /dáwd'l/ *v. & n.* ● *v.* **1** *intr.* **a** walk slowly and idly. **b** delay; waste time. **2** *tr.* (foll. by *away*) waste (time). ● *n.* an act or instance of dawdling.

dawn /dawn/ *n. & v.* ● *n.* **1** daybreak. **2** the beginning of something. ● *v.intr.* **1** (of a day) begin; grow light. **2** begin to appear or develop. **3** (often foll. by *on, upon*) begin to become evident or understood (by a person). □□ **dawn·ing** *n.*

day /day/ *n.* **1** the time between sunrise and sunset. **2** a period of 24 hours as a unit of time. **3** daylight (*clear as day*). **4** the time in a day during which work is normally done (*an eight-hour day*). **5** **a** (also *pl.*) a period of the past or present (*the modern day; the old days*). **b** (prec. by *the*) the present time (*the issues of the day*). **6** the lifetime of a person or thing, esp. regarded as useful or productive (*have had my day; in my day things were different*). **7** a point of time (*will do it one day*). **8** **a** the date of a specific festival. **b** a day associated with a particular event or purpose (*graduation day; payday; Christmas Day*). **9** a particular date; a date agreed on. **10** a day's endeavor, or the period of an endeavor, esp. as bringing success (*win the day*). □ **all in a** (or **the**) **day's work** part of normal routine. **at the end of the day** in the final reckoning, when all is said and done. **call it a day** end a period of activity, esp. resting content that enough has been done. **day after day** without respite. **day and night** all the time. **day by day** gradually. **day in, day out** routinely; constantly. **from day one** *colloq.* originally. **not one's day** a day of successive misfortunes for a person. **one of these days** before very long. **one of those days** a day when things go badly. **that will be the day** *colloq.* that will never happen. **this day and age** the present time or period.

day·break /dáybrayk/ *n.* the first appearance of light in the morning.

day care *n.* the supervision of young children, the elderly, etc., during the day.

day·dream /dáydreem/ *n. & v.* ● *n.* a pleasant fantasy or reverie. ● *v.intr.* indulge in this.

Day-Glo /dáyglō/ *n. & adj.* ● *n. Trademark* a brand of fluorescent paint or other coloring. ● *adj.* colored with or like this.

day·light /dáylīt/ *n.* **1** the light of day. **2** dawn (*before daylight*). **3** **a** openness; publicity. **b** open knowledge. **4** a visible gap or interval. **5** (usu. in *pl.*) *sl.* one's life or consciousness (*beat the living daylights out of them*). □ **see daylight** begin to understand what was previously obscure.

day·light sav·ing *n.* the achieving of longer evening daylight, esp. in summer, by setting the time an hour ahead of the standard time.

day of reck·on·ing *n.* the time when something must be atoned for or avenged.

day·room /dáyrōōm/ *n.* a room, esp. a communal room for leisure in an institution, used during the day.

day·side /dáysīd/ *n.* **1** staff, esp. of a newspaper, who work during the day. **2** *Astron.* the side of a planet that faces the Sun.

day·time /dáytīm/ *n.* the part of the day when there is natural light.

day-to-day *adj.* mundane; routine.

day-trip *n.* a trip or excursion completed in one day.

daze /dayz/ *v. & n.* ● *v.tr.* stupefy; bewilder. ● *n.* a state of confusion or bewilderment (*in a daze*). □□ **daz·ed·ly** /-zidlee/ *adv.*

daz·zle /dázəl/ *v. & n.* ● *v.* **1** *tr.* blind temporarily or confuse the sight of by an excess of light. **2** *tr.*

D

DAVY LAMP

D

impress or overpower (a person) with knowledge, ability, or any brilliant display or prospect. • *n.* bright confusing light. □□ **daz·zle·ment** *n.* **daz·zler** *n.* **daz·zling** *adj.* **daz·zling·ly** *adv.*

dB *abbr.* decibel(s).

DC *abbr.* **1** (also **d.c.**) direct current. **2** District of Columbia.

DCL *abbr.* doctor of civil law.

DD *abbr.* doctor of divinity.

D day /déeday/ *n.* (also **D Day**) **1** the day (June 6, 1944) on which Allied forces invaded N. France. **2** the day on which an important operation is to begin or a change to take effect.

DDT *abbr.* dichlorodiphenyltrichloroethane, a colorless chlorinated hydrocarbon used as an insecticide.

de- /dee, di/ *prefix* **1** forming verbs and their derivatives: **a** down; away (*descend*). **b** completely (*declare*; *denude*). **2** added to verbs and their derivatives to form verbs and nouns implying removal or reversal (*decentralize*; *de-ice*).

DEA *abbr. US* Drug Enforcement Administration.

dea·con /déekən/ *n.* & *v.* • *n.* **1** (in Episcopal churches) a minister of the third order, below bishop and priest. **2** (in various, esp. Protestant, churches) a lay officer attending to a congregation's secular affairs. **3** (in the early Christian church) an appointed minister of charity. • *v.tr.* appoint or ordain as a deacon.

dea·con·ess /déekənés, déekənis/ *n.* a woman in the early Christian church and in some modern churches with functions analogous to a deacon's.

de·ac·ti·vate /deeáktivayt/ *v.tr.* make inactive or less reactive. □□ **de·ac·ti·va·tion** /-váyshən/ *n.*

dead /ded/ *adj.*, *adv.*, & *n.* • *adj.* **1** no longer alive. **2** *colloq.* extremely tired or unwell. **3** benumbed (*my fingers are dead*). **4** (foll. by *to*) insensitive to. **5** no longer effective or in use; extinct. **6** (of a match, of coal, etc.) no longer burning; extinguished. **7** inanimate. **8 a** lacking force or vigor. **b** (of sound) not resonant. **c** (of sparkling wine, etc.) no longer effervescent. **9 a** quiet; lacking activity (*the dead season*). **b** motionless; idle. **10 a** (of a microphone, telephone, etc.) not transmitting any sound. **b** (of a circuit, conductor, etc.) carrying or transmitting no current (*a dead battery*). **11** (of the ball in a game) out of play. **12** abrupt; complete (*come to a dead stop*; *a dead faint*; *in dead silence*). **13** without spiritual life. • *adv.* **1** absolutely; exactly; completely (*dead on target*; *dead level*; *dead tired*). **2** *colloq.* very; extremely (*dead easy*). • *n.* (prec. by *the*) **1** (treated as *pl.*) those who have died. **2** a time of silence or inactivity (*the dead of night*). □ **dead as the dodo** see DODO. **dead as a doornail** see DOORNAIL. **dead from the neck up** *colloq.* stupid. **dead in the water** unable to move or to function. **dead to the world** *colloq.* fast asleep; unconscious. **dead weight** see DEADWEIGHT. **wouldn't be seen dead in** (or **with**, etc.) *colloq.* shall have nothing to do with; shall refuse to wear, etc. □□ **dead·ness** *n.*

dead·beat /dédbeet/ *n.* & *adj.* • *n.* **1** *colloq.* a penniless person. **2** *sl.* a person constantly in debt. • *adj. Physics* (of an instrument) without recoil.

dead·bolt /dédbōlt/ *n.* a bolt engaged by turning a knob or key, rather than by spring action.

dead duck *n. sl.* **1** an unsuccessful or useless person or thing. **2** a person who is beyond help; one who is doomed.

dead·en /déd'n/ *v.* **1** *tr.* & *intr.* deprive of or lose vitality, force, brightness, sound, feeling, etc. **2** *tr.* (foll. by *to*) make insensitive.

dead end *n.* **1** a closed end of a road, passage, etc. **2** (often (with hyphen) *attrib.*) a situation offering no prospects of progress.

dead·eye /dédī/ *n.* **1** *Naut.* a circular wooden block with a groove around the circumference to take a lanyard, used singly or in pairs to tighten a shroud. **2** *colloq.* an expert marksman.

dead·head /dédhed/ *n.* & *v.* • *n.* **1** a useless person. **2** a passenger or member of an audience who has made use of a free ticket. • *v.* **1** *intr.* (of a commercial driver, etc.) complete a trip without paying passengers or freight. **2** *tr.* remove faded flower heads from (a plant).

dead heat *n.* **1** a race in which two or more competitors finish in a tie. **2** the result of such a race.

dead lan·guage *n.* a language no longer spoken.

dead let·ter *n.* **1** a law or practice no longer observed or recognized. **2** a letter that is undeliverable and unreturnable, esp. one with an incorrect address. □□ **dead-let·ter of·fice** *n.*

dead·line /dédlīn/ *n.* a time limit for the completion of an activity, etc.

dead·lock /dédlok/ *n.* & *v.* • *n.* **1** a situation, esp. one involving opposing parties, in which no progress can be made. **2** a type of lock requiring a key to open or close it. • *v.tr.* & *intr.* bring or come to a standstill.

dead·ly /dédlee/ *adj.* & *adv.* • *adj.* (**deadlier**, **deadliest**) **1 a** causing or able to cause fatal injury or serious damage. **b** poisonous (*deadly snake*). **2** intense; extreme (*deadly dullness*). **3** (of an aim, etc.) extremely accurate or effective. **4** death-like (*deadly faintness*). **5** *colloq.* dreary; dull. **6** implacable. • *adv.* **1** like death; as if dead (*deadly faint*). **2** extremely; intensely (*deadly serious*). □□ **dead·li·ness** *n.*

dead·ly night·shade *n.* ► a poisonous plant, *Atropa belladonna*, with drooping purple flowers and black cherry-like fruit. Also called **belladonna**

DEADLY NIGHTSHADE
(*Atropa belladonna*)

dead·ly sin *n.* a sin regarded as leading to damnation, esp. pride, covetousness, lust, gluttony, envy, anger, and sloth.

dead-on *adj.* exactly right.

dead·pan /dédpán/ *adj.* & *adv.* with a face or manner totally lacking expression or emotion.

dead reck·on·ing *n. Naut.* calculation of a ship's position from the log, compass, etc., when observations are impossible.

dead sol·diers *n.pl. colloq.* bottles (esp. of beer, liquor, etc.) after the contents have been drunk.

dead·weight /dédwáyt/ *n.* (also **dead weight**) **1 a** an inert mass. **b** a heavy burden. **2** a debt not covered by assets. **3** the total weight carried on a ship.

dead·wood /dédwŏŏd/ *n.* **1** dead trees or branches. **2** *colloq.* one or more useless people or things. **3** *Bowling* knocked-down pins that remain on the alley.

deaf /def/ *adj.* **1** wholly or partly without hearing (*deaf in one ear*). **2** (foll. by *to*) refusing to listen or comply. **3** insensitive to harmony, rhythm, etc. (*tone-deaf*). □ **deaf as a post** completely deaf. **fall on deaf ears** be ignored. **turn a deaf ear** (usu. foll. by *to*) be unresponsive. □□ **deaf·ness** *n.*

deaf·en /défən/ *v.tr.* **1** (often as **deafening** *adj.*) overpower with sound. **2** deprive of hearing by noise, esp. temporarily. □□ **deaf·en·ing·ly** *adv.*

deaf-mute *n.* a deaf and dumb person.

deal[1] /deel/ *v.* & *n.* • *v.* (*past* and *past part.* **dealt** /delt/) **1** *intr.* **a** (foll. by *with*) take measures concerning (a problem, person, etc.), esp. in order to put something right. **b** (foll. by *with*) do business with; associate with. **c** (foll. by *with*) discuss or treat (a subject). **d** (often foll. by *by*) behave in a specified way toward a person (*dealt honorably by them*). **2** *intr.* (foll. by *in*) to sell or be concerned with commercially (*deals in insurance*). **3** *tr.* (often foll. by *out*) distribute or apportion to several people, etc. **4** *tr.* (also *absol.*) distribute (cards) to players. **5** *tr.* cause to be received; administer (*deal a heavy blow*). **6** *tr.* assign as a share or deserts to a person (*life dealt them much happiness*). **7** *tr.* (foll. by *in*) *colloq.* include (a person) in an activity (*you can deal me in*). • *n.* **1** (usu. **a good** *or* **great deal**) *colloq.* **a** a large amount (*a good deal of trouble*). **b** to a considerable extent (*is a great deal better*). **2** *colloq.* a business arrangement; a transaction. **3** a specified form of treatment (*gave them a bad deal*; *got a fair deal*). **4 a** the distribution of cards by dealing. **b** a player's turn to do this (*it's my deal*). **c** the round of play following this. **d** a set of hands dealt to players. □ **it's a deal** *colloq.* expressing assent to an agreement.

deal[2] /deel/ *n.* **1** fir or pine timber. **2 a** a board of this timber. **b** such boards collectively.

deal·er /déelər/ *n.* **1** a person or business dealing in (esp. retail) goods (*contact your dealer*; *car dealer*). **2** the player dealing at cards. **3** a person who sells illegal drugs. □□ **deal·er·ship** *n.* (in sense 1).

deal·ings /déelingz/ *n.pl.* contacts or transactions. □ **have dealings with** associate with.

dealt *past* and *past part.* of DEAL[1].

dean /deen/ *n.* **1 a** a college or university official with disciplinary and advisory functions. **b** the head of a university faculty or department or of a medical school. **2** the head of the chapter of a cathedral or collegiate church. **3** = DOYEN.

dean·er·y /déenəree/ *n.* (*pl.* **-ies**) a dean's house or office.

dear /deer/ *adj.*, *n.*, *adv.*, & *int.* • *adj.* **1 a** beloved or much esteemed. **b** as a merely polite or ironic form (*my dear man*). **2** used as a formula of address, esp. at the beginning of letters (*Dear Sir*). **3** (often foll. by *to*) precious; much cherished. **4** (usu. in *superl.*) earnest (*my dearest wish*). **5 a** high-priced relative to its value. **b** having high prices. **c** (of money) available as a loan only at a high rate of interest. • *n.* (esp. as a form of address) dear person. • *adv.* at great cost (*buy cheap and sell dear*; *will pay dear*). • *int.* expressing surprise, dismay, pity, etc. (*dear me!*; *oh dear!*; *dear, dear!*). □ **for dear life** see LIFE. □□ **dear·ly** *adv.* (esp. in sense 3 of *adj.*).

dear·ie /déeree/ *n.* (esp. as a form of address) usu. *joc.* or *iron.* my dear. □ **dearie me!** *int.* expressing surprise, dismay, etc.

Dear John *n. colloq.* a letter terminating a personal relationship.

dearth /dərth/ *n.* scarcity or lack.

death /deth/ *n.* **1** the ending of life. **2** the event that terminates life. **3 a** the fact or process of being killed or killing (*stone to death*). **b** the fact or state of being dead (*eyes closed in death*; *their deaths caused rioting*). **4 a** the destruction or permanent cessation of something (*the death of our hopes*). **b** *colloq.* something terrible or appalling. **5** (usu. **Death**) a personification of death, usu. represented by a skeleton. **6** a lack of religious faith or spiritual life. □ **as sure as death** quite certain. **at death's door** close to death. **be in at the death 1** be present when an animal is killed, esp. in hunting. **2** witness the (esp. sudden) ending of an enterprise, etc. **be the death of 1** cause the death of. **2** be very harmful to. **catch one's death** *colloq.* catch a serious chill, etc. **do to death 1** kill. **2** overdo. **fate worse than death** *colloq.* a disastrous misfortune or experience. **like death warmed over** *sl.* very tired or ill. **put to death** kill or cause to be killed. **to death** to the utmost; extremely (*bored to death*). □□ **death·less** *adj.* **death·like** *adj.*

death·bed /déthbed/ *n.* a bed as the place where a person is dying or has died.

death·blow /déthblō/ *n.* **1** a blow or other action that causes death. **2** an event or circumstance that abruptly ends an activity, enterprise, etc.

death cap (or **cup**) *n.* a poisonous mushroom, *Amanita phalloides.*

death cell *n.* a prison cell for a person condemned to death.

death cer·tif·i·cate *n.* an official statement of the cause and date and place of a person's death.

death·ly /déthlee/ *adj.* & *adv.* • *adj.* (**deathlier**, **deathliest**) suggestive of death (*deathly silence*). • *adv.* in a deathly way (*deathly pale*).

death mask *n.* ▶ a cast taken of a dead person's face.

death me·tal *n.* a form of heavy metal music using lyrics preoccupied with death, suffering, and destruction.

death pen·al·ty *n.* punishment by being put to death.

death rate *n.* the number of deaths per thousand of population per year.

death row *n.* a prison block or section for prisoners sentenced to death.

death squad *n.* an armed paramilitary group, formed to kill political enemies, etc.

death tax *n.* a tax on property payable on the owner's death.

death toll *n.* the number of people killed in an accident, battle, etc.

death trap *n. colloq.* a dangerous building, vehicle, etc.

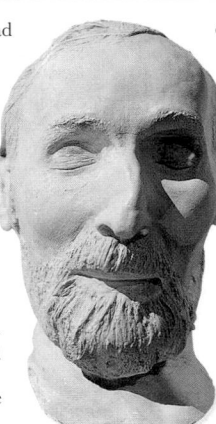

DEATH MASK OF HEINRICH HEINE (1797–1856), GERMAN POET AND WRITER

death war·rant *n.* **1** an order for the execution of a condemned person. **2** anything that causes the end of an established practice, etc.

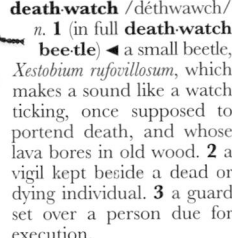

death·watch /déthwawch/ *n.* **1** (in full **death·watch bee·tle**) ◀ a small beetle, *Xestobium rufovillosum*, which makes a sound like a watch ticking, once supposed to portend death, and whose lava bores in old wood. **2** a vigil kept beside a dead or dying individual. **3** a guard set over a person due for execution.

DEATHWATCH BEETLE (*Xestobium rufovillosum*)

death wish *n. Psychol.* a desire (usu. unconscious) for the death of oneself or another.

deb /deb/ *n. colloq.* a debutante.

de·ba·cle /daybaakal, -bákel, da-/ *n.* (also **débâcle**) **1 a** an utter defeat or failure. **b** a sudden collapse or downfall. **2** a confused rush or rout.

de·bar /deebáar/ *v.tr.* (**debarred, debarring**) (foll. by *from*) exclude from admission or from a right; prohibit from an action (*was debarred from entering*).

de·bark[1] /dibáark/ *v.tr. & intr.* land from a ship.

de·bark[2] /déebáark/ *v.tr.* remove the bark from (a tree).

de·base /dibáys/ *v.tr.* **1** lower in quality, value, or character. **2** depreciate (coin) by alloying, etc. □□ **de·base·ment** *n.*

de·bat·a·ble /dibáytabal/ *adj.* **1** questionable; subject to dispute. **2** capable of being debated. □□ **de·bat·a·bly** *adv.*

de·bate /dibáyt/ *v. & n.* ● *v.* **1** *tr.* (also *absol.*) discuss or dispute about (an issue, proposal, etc.) esp. formally. **2 a** *tr.* consider; ponder (a matter). **b** *intr.* consider different sides of a question. ● *n.* **1** a formal discussion on a particular matter. **2** debating; discussion (*open to debate*). □□ **de·bat·er** *n.*

de·bauch /dibáwch/ *v. & n.* ● *v.tr.* **1** corrupt morally. **2** make intemperate or sensually indulgent. **3** deprave or debase (taste or judgment). **4** (as **debauched** *adj.*) dissolute. **5** seduce (a woman). ● *n.* **1** a bout of sensual indulgence. **2** debauchery.

deb·au·chee /díbawcheé, -sheé, déb-/ *n.* a person addicted to excessive sensual indulgence.

de·bauch·er·y /dibáwchəree/ *n.* excessive sensual indulgence.

de·ben·ture /dibénchər/ *n.* (in full **debenture bond**) a fixed-interest bond of a company, backed by general credit rather than specified assets.

de·bil·i·tate /dibílitayt/ *v.tr.* enfeeble; enervate. □□ **de·bil·i·ta·tion** /-táyshən/ *n.*

de·bil·i·ty /dibílitee/ *n.* feebleness, esp. of health.

deb·it /débit/ *n. & v.* ● *n.* **1** an entry in an account recording a sum owed. **2** the sum recorded. **3** the total of such sums. **4** the debit side of an account. ● *v.tr.* (**debited, debiting**) **1** (foll. by *against, to*) enter (an amount) on the debit side of an account (*debited $500 against me*). **2** (foll. by *with*) enter (a person) on the debit side of an account (*debited me with $500*).

deb·it card *n.* a card issued by a bank allowing the holder to transfer deposited funds electronically, as to make a purchase.

deb·o·nair /débənáir/ *adj.* **1** carefree; cheerful; self-assured. **2** having pleasant manners.

de·bouch /dibówch, -bo͞osh/ *v.intr.* **1** (of troops or a stream) issue from a ravine, wood, etc., into open ground. **2** (often foll. by *into*) (of a river, road, etc.) merge into a larger body or area.

de·brief /deebreéf/ *v.tr. colloq.* interrogate (a person) about a completed mission or undertaking. □□ **de·brief·ing** *n.*

de·bris /dəbreé, day-, débree/ *n.* scattered fragments, esp. of something wrecked or destroyed.

debt /det/ *n.* **1** something that is owed, esp. money. **2** a state of obligation to pay something owed (*in debt*). □ **in a person's debt** under an obligation to a person.

debt·or /détər/ *n.* a person who owes a debt, esp. money.

de·bug /deebúg/ *v.tr.* (**debugged, debugging**) **1** *colloq.* remove concealed listening devices from (a room, etc.). **2** *colloq.* identify and remove defects from (a computer program, etc.). **3** remove bugs from.

de·bunk /deebúngk/ *v.tr. colloq.* **1** show the good reputation of (a person, institution, etc.) to be spurious. **2** expose the falseness of (a claim, etc.). □□ **de·bunk·er** *n.*

de·but /dayboo͞o, dáybyo͞o/ *n.* (also **début**) **1** the first public appearance of a performer on stage, etc., or the opening performance of a show, etc. **2** the first appearance of a débutante in society.

deb·u·tante /débyətaant, dáybyo͞o-/ *n.* a (usu. wealthy) young woman making her social debut.

Dec. *abbr.* December.

deca- /dékə/ *comb. form* (also **dec-** before a vowel) **1** having ten. **2** tenfold. **3** ten (*decagram; decaliter*).

dec·ade /dékayd/ *n.* **1** a period of ten years. **2** a set, series, or group of ten.

dec·a·dence /dékəd'ns/ *n.* **1** moral or cultural deterioration. **2** decadent behavior; a state of decadence.

dec·a·dent /dékədənt/ *adj. & n.* ● *adj.* **1 a** in a state of moral or cultural deterioration; showing or characterized by decadence. **b** of a period of decadence. **2** self-indulgent. ● *n.* a decadent person. □□ **dec·a·dent·ly** *adv.*

de·caf·fein·ate /deekáfinayt/ *v.tr.* **1** remove caffeine from. **2** reduce the quantity of caffeine in (usu. coffee).

dec·a·gon /dékəgən/ *n.* ▼ a plane figure with ten sides and angles.

dec·a·he·dron /dékəheédrən/ *n.* ▼ a solid figure with ten faces.

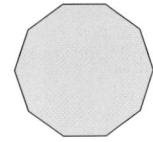

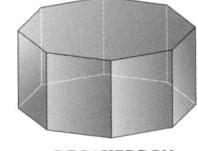

DECAGON   DECAHEDRON

de·cal /déekal/ *n.* = DECALCOMANIA 2.

de·cal·ci·fy /deekálsifī/ *v.tr.* (**-ies, -ied**) remove lime or calcareous matter from (a bone, tooth, etc.). □□ **de·cal·ci·fi·ca·tion** /-fikáyshən/ *n.*

de·cal·co·ma·ni·a /deekálkəmáyneeə/ *n.* **1** a process of transferring designs from specially prepared paper to the surface of glass, porcelain, etc. **2** a picture or design made by this process.

dec·a·li·ter /dékəleetər/ *n.* a metric unit of capacity, equal to 10 liters.

Dec·a·logue /dékəlawg, -log/ *n.* the Ten Commandments.

dec·a·me·ter /dékəmeetər/ *n.* a metric unit of length, equal to 10 meters.

de·camp /dikámp/ *v.intr.* **1** break up or leave a camp. **2** depart suddenly; abscond.

dec·a·nal /dékənəl, dikáy-/ *adj.* **1** of a dean or deanery. **2** of the south side of a choir, the side on which the dean sits (cf. CANTORIAL).

de·cant /dikánt/ *v.tr.* **1** gradually pour off (liquid) from one container to another, esp. without disturbing the sediment. **2** empty out; move as if by pouring.

de·cant·er /dikántər/ *n.* a stoppered glass container into which wine or brandy, etc., is decanted.

de·cap·i·tate /dikápitayt/ *v.tr.* **1** behead. **2** cut the head or end from. □□ **de·cap·i·ta·tion** /-táyshən/ *n.*

dec·a·pod /dékəpod/ *n.* **1** ▼ any crustacean of the chiefly marine order Decapoda, characterized by five pairs of walking legs, e.g., shrimps, crabs, and lobsters. **2** any of various mollusks of the class Cephalopoda, having ten tentacles, e.g., squids and cuttlefish.

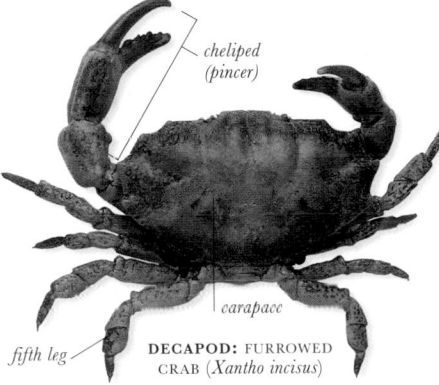

cheliped (pincer)

carapace

fifth leg

DECAPOD: FURROWED CRAB (*Xantho incisus*)

de·car·bon·ize /deekáarbənīz/ *v.tr.* remove carbon or carbonaceous deposits from (an internal-combustion engine, etc.).

dec·a·syl·la·ble /dékəsiləbəl/ *n.* a metrical line of ten syllables. □□ **dec·a·syl·la·bic** /-silábik/ *adj. & n.*

de·cath·lon /dikáthlon, -lən/ *n.* an athletic contest in which each competitor takes part in ten events. □□ **de·cath·lete** /-leet/ *n.*

de·cay /dikáy/ *v. & n.* ● *v.* **1 a** *intr.* rot; decompose. **b** *tr.* cause to rot or decompose. **2** *intr. & tr.* decline or cause to decline in quality, power, wealth, energy, beauty, etc. **3** *intr. Physics* **a** (usu. foll. by *to*) (of a substance, etc.) undergo change by radioactivity. **b** undergo a gradual decrease in magnitude of a physical quantity. ● *n.* **1** a rotten state; a process of wasting away. **2** decline in health, quality, etc. **3** *Physics* **a** change into another substance, etc. by radioactivity. **b** a decrease in the magnitude of a physical quantity, esp. the intensity of radiation or amplitude of oscillation. **4** decayed tissue.

de·cease /diseés/ *n. & v. formal* esp. *Law* ● *n.* death. ● *v.intr.* die.

de·ceased /diseést/ *adj. & n. formal* ● *adj.* dead. ● *n.* (usu. prec. by *the*) a person who has died, esp. recently.

de·ce·dent /diseéd'nt/ *n. Law* a deceased person.

de·ceit /diseét/ *n.* **1** the act or process of deceiving or misleading, esp. by concealing the truth. **2** a dishonest trick or stratagem. **3** willingness to deceive.

D

de·ceit·ful /diséetfŏŏl/ *adj.* **1** (of a person) using deceit. **2** (of an act, practice, etc.) intended to deceive. □□ **de·ceit·ful·ly** *adv.* **de·ceit·ful·ness** *n.*

de·ceive /diséev/ *v.* **1** *tr.* make (a person) believe what is false; mislead purposely. **2** *tr.* be unfaithful to, esp. sexually. **3** *intr.* use deceit. □ **be deceived** be mistaken or deluded. **deceive oneself** persist in a mistaken belief. □□ **de·ceiv·er** *n.*

de·cel·er·ate /deeséléràyt/ *v.* **1** *intr.* & *tr.* begin or cause to begin to reduce speed. **2** *tr.* make slower. □□ **de·cel·er·a·tion** /-ráyshən/ *n.*

De·cem·ber /disémbər/ *n.* the twelfth month of the year.

de·cen·cy /déesənsee/ *n.* (*pl.* **-ies**) **1** correct and tasteful standards of behavior as generally accepted. **2** conformity with current standards of behavior or propriety. **3** avoidance of obscenity. **4** (in *pl.*) the requirements of correct behavior.

de·cen·ni·al /disénéeəl/ *adj.* **1** lasting ten years. **2** recurring every ten years.

de·cent /déesənt/ *adj.* **1 a** conforming with current standards of behavior or propriety. **b** avoiding obscenity. **2** respectable. **3** acceptable; good enough. **4** kind; obliging; generous (*was decent enough to apologize*). □□ **de·cent·ly** *adv.*

de·cen·tral·ize /deeséntrəlìz/ *v.tr.* **1** transfer (powers, etc.) from a central to a local authority. **2** reorganize on the basis of greater local autonomy. □□ **de·cen·tral·ist** /-list/ *n.* & *adj.* **de·cen·tral·i·za·tion** *n.*

de·cep·tion /disépshən/ *n.* **1** the act or an instance of deceiving; the process of being deceived. **2** a thing that deceives.

de·cep·tive /diséptiv/ *adj.* apt to deceive; easily mistaken for something else or as having a different quality. □□ **de·cep·tive·ly** *adv.*

deci- /désee/ *comb. form* one-tenth (*deciliter; decimeter*).

dec·i·bel /désibel/ *n.* a unit (one-tenth of a bel) used in the comparison of two power levels relating to electrical signals or sound intensities. ¶ Abbr.: **dB**.

de·cide /disíd/ *v.* **1 a** *intr.* (often foll. by *on, about*) come to a resolution as a result of consideration. **b** *tr.* (usu. foll. by *to* + infin., or *that* + clause) have or reach as one's resolution about something (*decided to stay; decided that we should leave*). **2** *tr.* resolve or settle (a question, dispute, etc.). **3** *intr.* (usu. foll. by *between, for, against, in favor of,* or *that* + clause) give a judgment.

de·cid·ed /disídid/ *adj.* **1** (usu. *attrib.*) definite; unquestionable (*a decided difference*). **2** having clear opinions, resolute, not vacillating.

de·cid·ed·ly /disídidlee/ *adv.* undoubtedly; undeniably.

de·cid·er /disídər/ *n.* **1** a game, race, etc., to decide between competitors finishing equal in a previous contest. **2** any person or thing that decides.

de·cid·u·ous /disijŏŏəs/ *adj.* **1** ▼ (of a tree) shedding its leaves annually. ▷ TREE. **2** (of leaves, horns, teeth, etc.) shed periodically.

oak in winter

oak in full summer foliage

DECIDUOUS OAK IN WINTER AND SUMMER

dec·i·gram /désigram/ *n.* a metric unit of mass, equal to 0.1 gram.

dec·ile /désīl, -il/ *n. Statistics* any of the nine values of a random variable which divide a frequency distribution into ten groups, each containing one-tenth of the total population.

dec·i·li·ter /déseeleetər/ *n.* a metric unit of capacity, equal to 0.1 liter.

dec·i·mal /désiməl/ *adj.* & *n.* ● *adj.* **1** (of a system of numbers, weights, measures, etc.) based on the number ten, in which the smaller units are related to the principal units as powers of ten (units, tens, hundreds, thousands, etc.). **2** of tenths or ten; reckoning or proceeding by tens. ● *n.* a decimal fraction.

dec·i·mal·ize /désiməlīz/ *v.tr.* **1** express as a decimal. **2** convert to a decimal system. □□ **dec·i·mal·i·za·tion** *n.*

dec·i·mal point *n.* a period or dot placed before a numerator in a decimal fraction.

dec·i·mate /désimayt/ *v.tr.* **1** *disp.* destroy a large proportion of. ¶ Now the usual sense, although often deplored as an inappropriate use. **2** *orig. Mil.* kill or remove one in every ten of. □□ **dec·i·ma·tion** /-máyshən/ *n.*

dec·i·me·ter /désimeetər/ *n.* a metric unit of length, equal to 0.1 meter.

de·ci·pher /disífər/ *v.tr.* **1** convert (a text written in cipher) into an intelligible script or language. **2** determine the meaning of (anything obscure or unclear). □□ **de·ci·pher·a·ble** *adj.* **de·ci·pher·ment** *n.*

de·ci·sion /disízhən/ *n.* **1** the act or process of deciding. **2** a conclusion or resolution reached, esp. as to future action, after consideration (*have made my decision*). **3** (often foll. by *of*) **a** the settlement of a question. **b** a formal judgment. **4** a tendency to decide firmly; resoluteness.

de·ci·sive /disísiv/ *adj.* **1** that decides an issue; conclusive. **2** (of a person, esp. as a characteristic) able to decide quickly and effectively. □□ **de·ci·sive·ly** *adv.* **de·ci·sive·ness** *n.*

deck /dek/ *n.* & *v.* ● *n.* **1 a** a platform in a ship covering all or part of the hull's area at any level and serving as a floor. ▷ FERRY, HOVERCRAFT, SAILBOAT. **b** the accommodation on a particular deck of a ship. **2** anything compared to a ship's deck, e.g., the floor or compartment of a bus. **3** a component, usu. a flat horizontal surface, that carries a particular recording medium (such as a disk or tape) in sound-reproduction equipment. **4 a** a pack of cards. **b** *sl.* a packet of narcotics. **5** *sl.* the ground. **6 a** any floor or platform, esp. the floor of a pier or a platform for sunbathing. **b** a platformlike structure, usu. made of lumber and unroofed, attached to a house, etc. ● *v.tr.* **1** (often foll. by *out*) decorate; adorn. **2** furnish with or cover as a deck. □ **below deck** (or **decks**) in or into the space below the main deck. **on deck 1** in the open air on a ship's main deck. **2** ready for action, work, etc.

deck chair *n.* a folding chair of wood and canvas, of a kind used on deck on passenger ships.

-decker /dékər/ *comb. form* having a specified number of decks or layers (*double-decker*).

deck ten·nis *n.* a game in which a quoit of rope, rubber, etc., is tossed back and forth over a net.

deck·hand /dékhand/ *n.* a person employed in cleaning and odd jobs on a ship's deck.

deck·le /dékəl/ *n.* a device in a papermaking machine for limiting the size of the sheet.

deck·le edge *n.* the rough uncut edge formed by a deckle. □ **deck·le-edged** having a deckle edge.

de·claim /dikláym/ *v.* **1** *intr.* & *tr.* speak or utter rhetorically or affectedly. **2** *intr.* practice oratory or recitation. **3** *intr.* (foll. by *against*) protest forcefully. **4** *intr.* deliver an impassioned (rather than reasoned) speech. □□ **dec·la·ma·tion** /déklləmáyshən/ *n.* **de·clam·a·to·ry** /diklámmətawree/ *adj.*

dec·la·ra·tion /dékləráyshən/ *n.* **1** the act or process of declaring. **2 a** a formal, emphatic, or

deliberate statement or announcement. **b** a statement asserting or protecting a legal right. **3** a written public announcement of intentions, terms of an agreement, etc. **4** *Cricket* an act of declaring an innings closed. **5** *Cards* **a** the naming of trumps. **b** an announcement of a combination held. **6** *Law* **a** a plaintiff's statement of claim. **b** an affirmation made instead of taking an oath.

de·clar·a·tive *adj.* & *n.* ● *adj.* **1 a** of the nature of, or making, a declaration. **b** *Gram.* (of a sentence) that takes the form of a simple statement. **2** *Computing* designating high-level programming languages which can be used to solve problems without requiring the programmer to specify an exact procedure to be followed. ● *n.* **1** a declaratory statement or act. **2** *Gram.* a declarative sentence. □□ **de·clar·a·tive·ly** *adv.*

de·clare /dikláir/ *v.* **1** *tr.* announce openly or formally (*declare war; declare a dividend*). **2** *tr.* pronounce (a person or thing) to be something (*declared him to be an impostor; declared it invalid*). **3** *tr.* (usu. foll. by *that* + clause) assert emphatically; state explicitly. **4** *tr.* acknowledge possession of (dutiable goods, income, etc.). **5** *tr.* (as **declared** *adj.*) who admits to be such (*a declared atheist*). **6** *tr.* (also *absol.*) *Cricket* close (an innings) voluntarily before all the wickets have fallen. **7** *tr. Cards* **a** (also *absol.*) name (the trump suit). **b** announce that one holds (certain combinations of cards, etc.). **8** *tr.* (of things) make evident; prove (*your actions declare your honesty*). **9** *intr.* (foll. by *for, against*) take the side of one party or another. □ **declare oneself** reveal one's intentions or identity. **well, I declare** (or **I do declare**) an exclamation of incredulity, surprise, or vexation. □□ **de·clar·a·to·ry** /-klárətawree/ *adj.* **de·clar·er** *n*

de·clas·sé /dayklasáy/ *adj.* (*fem.* **declassée**) that has fallen in social status.

de·clas·si·fy /deeklássifì/ *v.tr.* (**-ies**, **-ied**) declare (information, etc.) to be no longer secret. □□ **de·clas·si·fi·ca·tion** /-fikáyshən/ *n.*

de·clen·sion /diklénshən/ *n.* **1** *Gram.* **a** the variation of the form of a noun, pronoun, or adjective, by which its grammatical case, number, and gender are identified. **b** the class in which a noun, etc., is put according to the exact form of this variation. **2** deterioration; declining. □□ **de·clen·sion·al** *adj.*

dec·li·na·tion /déklináyshən/ *n.* **1** a downward bend or turn. **2** *Astron.* the angular distance of a star, etc., north or south of the celestial equator. **3** *Physics* the angular deviation of a compass needle from true north. **4** a formal refusal. □□ **dec·li·na·tion·al** *adj.*

de·cline /diklín/ *v.* & *n.* ● *v.* **1** *intr.* deteriorate; lose strength or vigor; decrease. **2 a** *tr.* reply with formal courtesy that one will not accept (an invitation, honor, etc.). **b** *tr.* refuse, esp. formally and courteously (*declined to be made use of; declined doing anything*). **c** *tr.* turn away from (a challenge, battle, discussion, etc.). **d** *intr.* give or send a refusal. **3** *intr.* slope downward. **4** *intr.* bend down; droop. **5** *tr. Gram.* state the forms of (a noun, pronoun, or adjective) corresponding to cases, number, and gender. **6** *intr.* (of a day, life, etc.) draw to a close. **7** *intr.* decrease in price, etc. **8** *tr.* bend down. ● *n.* **1** gradual loss of vigor or excellence (*on the decline*). **2** decay; deterioration. **3** setting; the last part of the course (of the sun, of life, etc.). **4** a fall in price. □ **on the decline** in a declining state. □□ **de·clin·a·ble** *adj.* **de·clin·er** *n.*

de·cliv·i·ty /diklívitee/ *n.* (*pl.* **-ies**) a downward slope. □□ **de·cliv·i·tous** *adj.*

de·clutch /deeklúch/ *v.intr.* disengage the clutch of a motor vehicle.

de·coct /dikókt/ *v.tr.* extract the essence from by decoction.

de·coc·tion /dikókshən/ *n.* **1** a process of boiling down so as to extract some essence. **2** the extracted liquor resulting from this.

de·code /deekŏd/ *v.tr.* convert (a coded message) into intelligible language. □□ **de·cod·a·ble** *adj.*

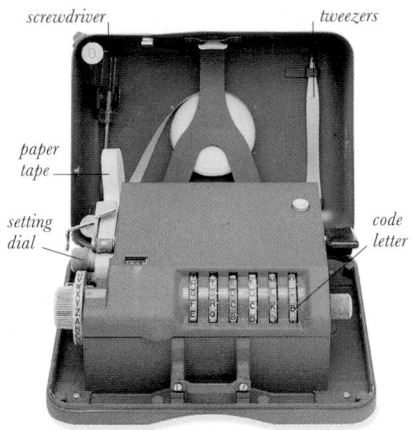

DECODER: WORLD WAR II
US CIPHER MACHINE

de·cod·er /deekṓdər/ *n.* **1** ▲ a person or thing that decodes. **2** an electronic device for analyzing signals and feeding separate amplifier channels.

de·col·late /dikólayt/ *v.tr. formal* **1** behead. **2** truncate. □□ **de·col·la·tion** /deekələ́yshən/ *n.*

dé·colle·tage /dáykawltaázh/ *n.* a low neckline of a woman's dress, etc.

dé·colle·té /daykawltáy/ *adj. & n.* ● *adj.* **1** (of a dress, etc.) having a low neckline. **2** (of a woman) wearing a dress with a low neckline. ● *n.* a low neckline.

de·col·o·nize /deekólənīz/ *v.tr.* (of a nation) withdraw from (a colony), leaving it independent. □□ **de·col·o·ni·za·tion** *n.*

de·com·mis·sion /deekəmíshən/ *v.tr.* **1** close down (a nuclear reactor, etc.). **2** take (a ship) out of service.

de·com·pose /deekəmpṓz/ *v.* **1** *intr.* decay; rot. **2** *tr.* separate into its elements or simpler constituents. **3** *intr.* disintegrate; break up. □□ **de·com·po·si·tion** /deekompəzíshən/ *n.*

de·com·press /deekəmprés/ *v.tr.* subject to decompression; relieve or reduce the compression on.

de·com·pres·sion /deekəmpréshən/ *n.* **1** release from compression. **2** a gradual reduction of air pressure on a person who has been subjected to high pressure (esp. underwater).

de·com·pres·sion cham·ber *n.* ▼ an enclosed space for subjecting a person to decompression.

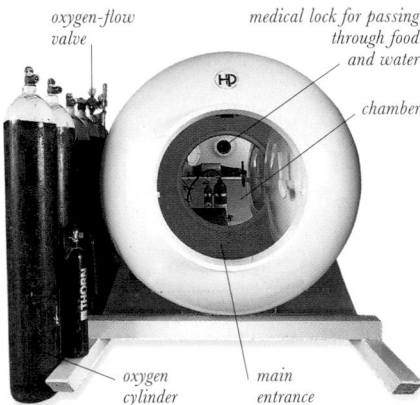

DECOMPRESSION CHAMBER

de·com·pres·sor /deekəmprésər/ *n.* a device for reducing pressure in the engine of a motor vehicle.

de·con·ges·tant /deekənjéstənt/ *adj. & n.* ● *adj.* that relieves (esp. nasal) congestion. ● *n.* a medicinal agent that relieves nasal congestion.

de·con·se·crate /deekónsikrayt/ *v.tr.* transfer (esp. a building) from sacred to secular use. □□ **de·con·se·cra·tion** /-kráyshən/ *n.*

de·con·struc·tion /deekənstrúkshən/ *n.* a method of critical analysis of philosophical and literary language. □□ **de·con·struct** *v.tr.* **de·con·struc·tion·ism** *n.* **de·con·struc·tion·ist** *adj. & n.* **de·con·struc·tive** *adj.*

de·con·tam·i·nate /deekəntámináyt/ *v.tr.* remove contamination from. □□ **de·con·tam·i·na·tion** /-náyshən/ *n.*

de·con·trol /deekəntrṓl/ *v. & n.* ● *v.tr.* (**decontrolled, decontrolling**) release (a commodity, etc.) from controls or restrictions, esp. those imposed by the government. ● *n.* the act of decontrolling.

de·cor /daykáwr, dáykawr/ *n.* (also **décor**) **1** the furnishing and decoration of a room, etc. **2** the decoration and scenery of a stage.

dec·o·rate /dékərayt/ *v.tr.* **1** provide with adornments. **2** provide (a room or building) with new paint, wallpaper, etc. **3** serve as an adornment to. **4** confer an award or distinction on.

dec·o·ra·tion /dékəráyshən/ *n.* **1** the process or art of decorating. **2** a thing that decorates or serves as an ornament. **3** a medal, etc., conferred as an honor. **4** (in *pl.*) flags, etc., put up on an occasion of public celebration.

Dec·o·ra·tion Day *n.* = Memorial Day.

dec·o·ra·tive /dékərətiv, dékrə-, -əray-/ *adj.* serving to decorate. □□ **dec·o·ra·tive·ly** *adv.* **dec·o·ra·tive·ness** *n.*

dec·o·ra·tor /dékəraytər/ *n.* a person who decorates, esp. one who paints or papers houses professionally.

de·co·rum /dikáwrəm/ *n.* **1 a** seemliness; propriety. **b** behavior required by politeness or decency. **2** a particular requirement of this kind. **3** etiquette. □□ **dec·o·rous** /dékərəs/ *adj.* **dec·o·rous·ly** *adv.*

de·cou·page /dáykoopaázh/ *n.* (also **découpage**) the decoration of surfaces with paper cutouts.

de·cou·ple /deekúpəl/ *v.tr.* **1** *Electr.* make the interaction between (oscillators, etc.) so weak that there is little transfer of energy between them. **2** separate; disengage; dissociate.

de·coy *n. & v.* ● *n.* /déekoy, dikóy/ **1** ▼ a person or thing used to lure an animal or person into a trap or danger. **2** a bait or enticement. ● *v.tr.* /dikóy/ (often foll. by *into, out of*) allure or entice, esp. by means of a decoy.

de·crease *v. & n.* ● *v.tr. & intr.* /dikreés/ make or become smaller or fewer. ● *n.* /déekrees/ **1** the act or an instance of decreasing. **2** the amount by which a thing decreases. □□ **de·creas·ing·ly** *adv.*

de·cree /dikreé/ *n. & v.* ● *n.* **1** an official order issued by a legal authority. **2** a judgment or decision of certain courts of law. ● *v.tr.* (**decrees, decreed, decreeing**) ordain by decree.

dec·re·ment /dékrimənt/ *n.* **1** *Physics* the ratio of the amplitudes in successive cycles of a damped oscillation. **2** the amount lost by diminution or waste. **3** the act of decreasing.

de·crep·it /dikrépit/ *adj.* weakened or worn out by age, infirmity or long use. □□ **de·crep·i·tude** *n.*

de·cres·cent /dikrésənt/ *adj.* (usu. of the Moon) waning; decreasing.

de·crim·i·nal·ize /deekríminəlīz/ *v.tr.* cease to treat as criminal. □□ **de·crim·i·nal·i·za·tion** *n.*

de·cry /dikrí/ *v.tr.* (**-ies, -ied**) disparage; belittle. □□ **de·cri·er** *n.*

de·crypt /deekrípt/ *v.tr.* decipher (a cryptogram). □□ **de·cryp·tion** /-krípshən/ *n.*

ded·i·cate /dédikayt/ *v.tr.* **1** (foll. by *to*) devote (esp. oneself) to a special task or purpose. **2** (foll. by *to*) address (a book, etc.) as a compliment to a friend, patron, etc. **3** (often foll. by *to*) devote (a building, etc.) to a deity or purpose. **4** (as **dedicated** *adj.*)

a (of a person) devoted to an aim or vocation. **b** (of equipment, esp. a computer) designed for a specific purpose. □□ **ded·i·ca·tee** /-kaytée/ *n.* **ded·i·ca·tive** *adj.* **ded·i·ca·tor** *n.* **ded·i·ca·to·ry** /-kətáwree/ *adj.*

ded·i·ca·tion /dédikáyshən/ *n.* **1** the act or an instance of dedicating; the quality or process of being dedicated. **2** the words with which a book, etc., is dedicated. **3** a dedicatory inscription.

de·duce /didoōs, -dyoōs/ *v.tr.* (often foll. by *from*) infer; draw as a logical conclusion. □□ **de·duc·i·ble** *adj.*

de·duct /didúkt/ *v.tr.* (often foll. by *from*) subtract, take away (an amount, portion, etc.).

de·duct·i·ble /didúktibəl/ *adj. & n.* ● *adj.* that may be deducted, esp. from tax to be paid or taxable income. ● *n.* part of an insurance claim to be paid by the insured.

de·duc·tion /didúkshən/ *n.* **1 a** the act of deducting. **b** an amount deducted. **2 a** the inferring of particular instances from a general law (cf. INDUCTION). **b** a conclusion deduced.

de·duc·tive /didúktiv/ *adj.* of or reasoning by deduction. □□ **de·duc·tive·ly** *adv.*

dee /dee/ *n.* **1** the letter D. **2** a thing shaped like this.

deed /deed/ *n. & v.* ● *n.* **1** a thing done intentionally or consciously. **2** a brave, skillful, or conspicuous act. **3** actual fact or performance (*kind in word and deed*). **4** *Law* a written or printed document often used for a legal transfer of ownership and bearing the disposer's signature. ● *v.tr.* convey or transfer by legal deed.

dee·jay /déejáy/ *n. sl.* a disk jockey.

deem /deem/ *v.tr. formal* regard; consider; judge.

de·em·pha·size /dee-émfəsīz/ *v.tr.* **1** remove emphasis from. **2** reduce emphasis on.

deep /deep/ *adj., n., & adv.* ● *adj.* **1 a** extending far down from the top (*deep hole*). **b** extending far in from the surface or edge (*deep border*). **2** (*predic.*) **a** extending to a specified depth (*water 6 feet deep; ankle-deep in mud*). **b** in a specified number of ranks one behind another (*soldiers drawn up six deep*). **3** situated far down or back (*hands deep in his pockets*). **4** coming or brought from far down or in (*deep sigh*). **5** low-pitched; full-toned; not shrill (*deep voice*). **6** intense; vivid; extreme (*deep disgrace*). **7** heartfelt; absorbing (*deep affection*). **8** (*predic.*) fully absorbed or overwhelmed (*deep in a book*). **9** profound; penetrating; not superficial (*deep thinker; deep insight*). **10** *Cricket* distant from the batsman (*deep mid-off*). **11** *Football, Soccer, etc.* distant from the front line of one's team. **12** *sl.* cunning or secretive (*a deep one*). ● *n.* **1** (prec. by *the*) *poet.* the sea. **2** a deep part of the sea. **3** an abyss, pit, or cavity. **4** (prec. by *the*) *Cricket* the position of a fielder distant from the batsman. **5** a deep state (*deep of the night*). **6** *poet.* a mysterious region of thought or feeling. ● *adv.* deeply; far down or in (*dig deep*). □ **go off the deep end** *colloq.* give way to anger or emotion. **in deep water** (or **waters**) in trouble or difficulty. □□ **deep·ly** *adv.* **deep·ness** *n.*

deep·en /déepən/ *v.tr. & intr.* make or become deep or deeper.

deep freeze *n.* **1** a refrigerator in which food can be quickly frozen and kept at a very low temperature. **2** a suspension of activity. □□ **deep-freeze** *v.tr.* (**-froze, frozen**).

deep-fry *v.tr.* (**-fries, -fried**) fry (food) in an amount of fat or oil sufficient to cover it.

deep-root·ed *adj.* (of convictions) firmly established.

deep sea *n.* the deeper parts of the ocean.

deep-seat·ed *adj.* (of emotion, disease, etc.) firmly established; profound.

Deep South *n.* (prec. by *the*) the region of the SE US, usu. including South Carolina, Georgia, Alabama, Mississippi, and Louisiana.

DECOY
DUCKS

D

D

DEER

Deer are ruminant, even-toed, hoofed mammals, found throughout Europe, Asia, and North and South America. With the exception of reindeer, only male deer bear antlers. During the breeding season, bucks use their antlers for fighting and establishing dominance. Most species are gregarious, living in herds with elaborate social organization.

RED DEER
(*Cervus elaphus*)

FALLOW DEER
(*Dama dama*)

REINDEER
(*Rangifer tarandus*)

MOOSE
(*Alces alces*)

deep space *n.* the regions of outer space beyond the solar system.

deep-vein throm·bo·sis *n.* thrombosis in a vein lying deep below the skin, esp. in the legs.

deer /deer/ *n.* (*pl.* same) ▲ any four-hoofed grazing animal of the family Cervidae, the males of which usu. have deciduous branching antlers.

deerfly /deerflī/ *n.* any bloodsucking fly of the genus *Chrysops*.

deer·stalk·er /deerstawkər/ *n.* **1** ▶ a soft cloth cap with peaks in front and behind and earflaps. **2** a person who stalks deer.

de·es·ca·late /dee-eskəlayt/ *v.tr.* reduce the level or intensity of. □□ **de·es·ca·la·tion** /-láyshən/ *n.*

de·face /difáys/ *v.tr.* **1** spoil the appearance of. **2** make illegible. □□ **de·face·a·ble** *adj.* **de·face·ment** *n.* **de·fac·er** *n.*

de fac·to /di fáktō, day/ *adv., adj., & n.* ● *adv.* in fact, whether by right or not. ● *adj.* that exists or is such in fact (*a de facto ruler*). ● *n.* (in full **de facto wife** or **husband**) a person living with another as if married.

de·fal·cate /deefálkayt, -fáwl-/ *v.intr. formal* misappropriate property in one's charge, esp. money. □□ **de·fal·ca·tor** *n.*

de·fame /difáym/ *v.tr.* attack the good reputation of. □□ **def·a·ma·tion** /défəmáyshən/ *n.* **de·fam·a·to·ry** /difámətawree/ *adj.*

de·fault /difáwlt/ *n. & v.* ● *n.* **1** failure to fulfill an obligation, esp. to appear, pay, or act in some way. **2** lack; absence. **3** a preselected option adopted by a computer program when no alternative is specified by the user or programmer. ● *v.* **1** *intr.* fail to fulfill an obligation. **2** *tr.* declare (a party) in default and give judgment against that party. □ **go by default 1** be ignored because of absence. **2** be absent. **in default of** because of the absence of. **win by default** win because an opponent fails to be present.

de·fault·er /difáwltər/ *n.* a person who defaults.

de·fea·si·ble /diféezibəl/ *adj.* **1** capable of annul-

DEERSTALKER

ment. **2** liable to forfeiture. □□ **de·fea·si·bil·i·ty** *n.* **de·fea·si·bly** *adv.*

de·feat /diféet/ *v. & n.* ● *v.tr.* **1** overcome in a battle or other contest. **2** frustrate; baffle. **3** reject (a motion, etc.) by voting. **4** *Law* annul. ● *n.* the act or process of defeating or being defeated.

de·feat·ism /diféetizəm/ *n.* **1** an excessive readiness to accept defeat. **2** conduct conducive to this. □□ **de·feat·ist** *n. & adj.*

def·e·cate /défikayt/ *v.intr.* discharge feces from the body. □□ **def·e·ca·tion** /-káyshən/ *n.*

de·fect *n. & v.* ● *n.* /deéfekt, difékt/ **1** lack of something essential; imperfection. **2** a shortcoming. **3** a blemish. **4** the amount by which a thing falls short. ● *v.intr.* /difékt/ abandon one's country or cause in favor of another. □□ **de·fec·tion** /difékshən/ *n.* **de·fec·tor** *n.*

de·fec·tive /diféktiv/ *adj. & n.* ● *adj.* **1** having a defect or defects; incomplete; faulty. **2** often *offens.* mentally subnormal. **3** (usu. foll. by *in*) lacking; deficient. **4** *Gram.* not having all the usual inflections. ● *n.* often *offens.* a mentally defective person. □□ **de·fec·tive·ly** *adv.* **de·fec·tive·ness** *n.*

de·fend /difénd/ *v.tr.* (also *absol.*) **1** (often foll. by *against, from*) resist an attack made on; protect. **2** uphold by argument. **3** conduct the case for (a defendant in a lawsuit). □□ **de·fend·er** *n.*

de·fend·ant /diféndənt, -ant/ *n.* a person, etc., sued or accused in a court of law.

de·fense /diféns/ *n.* **1** the act of defending from or resisting attack. **2 a** a means of resisting attack. **b** a thing that protects. **c** the military resources of a country. **3** (in *pl.*) fortifications. **4 a** justification; vindication. **b** a speech or piece of writing used to this end. **5 a** the defendant's case in a lawsuit. **b** the counsel for the defendant. **6** /deéfens/ **a** the action or role of defending one's goal, etc., against attack. **b** the players on a team who perform this role. □□ **de·fense·less** *adj.* **de·fense·less·ly** *adv.* **de·fense·less·ness** *n.*

de·fense mech·a·nism 1 the body's reaction against disease organisms. **2** a usu. unconscious mental process to avoid conscious conflict or anxiety.

de·fen·si·ble /difénsibəl/ *adj.* **1** supportable by argument. **2** that can be easily defended militarily. □□ **de·fen·si·bil·i·ty** *n.* **de·fen·si·bly** *adv.*

de·fen·sive /difénsiv/ *adj.* **1** done or intended for defense or to defend. **2** (of a person or attitude) concerned to challenge criticism. □ **on the defensive 1** expecting criticism. **2** in an attitude or position of defense. □□ **de·fen·sive·ly** *adv.* **de·fen·sive·ness** *n.*

de·fer[1] /difór/ *v.tr.* (**deferred, deferring**) **1** postpone. **2** postpone the conscription of (a person). □□ **de·fer·ment** *n.* **de·fer·ra·ble** *adj.* **de·fer·ral** *n.*

de·fer[2] /difór/ *v.intr.* (**deferred, deferring**) (foll. by *to*) yield or make concessions. □□ **de·fer·rer** *n.*

def·er·ence /défərəns, défrəns/ *n.* **1** courteous regard; respect. **2** compliance with the advice or wishes of another. □ **in deference to** out of respect for.

def·er·en·tial /défərénshəl/ *adj.* showing deference; respectful. □□ **def·er·en·tial·ly** *adv.*

de·fi·ance /diffəns/ *n.* **1** open disobedience; bold resistance. **2** a challenge to fight or maintain a cause, assertion, etc. □ **in defiance of** disregarding; in conflict with.

de·fi·ant /diffənt/ *adj.* **1** showing defiance. **2** openly disobedient. □□ **de·fi·ant·ly** *adv.*

de·fib·ril·la·tion /deéfibriláyshən/ *n. Med.* the stopping of the fibrillation of the heart. □□ **de·fib·ril·la·tor** /deefibriláytər/ *n.*

de·fi·cien·cy /difishənsee/ *n.* (*pl.* **-ies**) **1** the state or condition of being deficient. **2** (usu. foll. by *of*) a lack or shortage. **3** a thing lacking. **4** the amount by which a thing, esp. revenue, falls short.

de·fi·cient /difishənt/ *adj.* **1** (usu. foll. by *in*) incomplete; not having enough of a specified quality or ingredient. **2** insufficient in quantity, force, etc. **3** (in full **mentally deficient**) incapable of adequate social or intellectual behavior through imperfect mental development. □□ **de·fi·cient·ly** *adv.*

def·i·cit /défisit/ *n.* **1** the amount by which a thing (esp. a sum of money) is too small. **2** an excess of liabilities over assets (opp. SURPLUS).

de·file[1] /difíl/ *v.tr.* **1** make dirty; pollute. **2** corrupt. **3** desecrate. □□ **de·file·ment** *n.* **de·fil·er** *n.*

de·file[2] /difíl/ *n. & v.* ● *n.* also /deéfīl/ **1** a narrow way. **2** a gorge. ● *v.intr.* march in file.

de·fine /difín/ *v.tr.* **1** give the exact meaning of (a word, etc.). **2** describe or explain the scope of (*define one's position*). **3** make clear, esp. in outline (*well-defined image*). **4** mark out the limits of. **5** (of properties) make up the total character of. □□ **de·fin·a·ble** *adj.* **de·fin·er** *n.*

def·i·nite /définit/ *adj.* **1** having exact and discernible limits. **2** clear and distinct; not vague. ¶ See the note at *definitive*. □□ **def·i·nite·ness** *n.*

def·i·nite ar·ti·cle *n. Gram.* the word (*the* in English) preceding a noun and implying a specific or known instance (*the art of government*).

def·i·nite·ly /définitlee/ *adv. & int.* ● *adv.* **1** in a definite manner. **2** certainly; without doubt. ● *int. colloq.* yes, certainly.

def·i·ni·tion /définíshən/ *n.* **1 a** the act or process of defining. **b** a statement of the meaning of a word or the nature of a thing. **2 a** the degree of distinctness in outline of an object or image. **b** making or being distinct in outline.

de·fin·i·tive /difinitiv/ *adj.* **1** (of an answer, treaty, etc.) decisive; final. ¶ Often confused in this sense with *definite*, which does not have connotations of authority and conclusiveness: *a definite no* is a firm refusal, whereas *a definitive no* is an authoritative judgment or decision that something is not the case. **2** (of an edition of a book, etc.) most authoritative. □□ **de·fin·i·tive·ly** *adv.*

de·flate /diflâyt/ *v.* **1 a** *tr.* let air or gas out of. **b** *intr.* be emptied of air or gas. **2 a** *tr.* cause to lose confidence or conceit. **b** *intr.* lose confidence. **3** *Econ.*

a *tr.* subject (a currency or economy) to deflation. **b** *intr.* pursue a policy of deflation. **4** *tr.* reduce the importance of, depreciate. ▫▫ **de·fla·tor** *n.*

de·fla·tion /difláyshən/ *n.* **1** the act or process of deflating or being deflated. **2** *Econ.* reduction of the amount of money in circulation to increase its value as a measure against inflation. ▫▫ **de·fla·tion·ar·y** *adj.* **de·fla·tion·ist** *n.*

de·flect /diflékt/ *v.* **1** *tr. & intr.* bend or turn aside from a straight course or intended purpose. **2** (often foll. by *from*) **a** *tr.* cause to deviate. **b** *intr.* deviate. ▫▫ **de·flec·tion** /diflékshən/ *n.*

de·flec·tor /difléktər/ *n.* a thing that deflects, esp. a device for deflecting a flow of air, etc.

de·flow·er /diflówr/ *v.tr.* **1** deprive of virginity. **2** ravage; spoil. **3** strip of flowers.

de·fo·li·ate /deefṓleeayt/ *v.tr.* remove leaves from. ▫▫ **de·fo·li·ant** *n. & adj.* **de·fo·li·a·tion** /-áyshən/ *n.* **de·fo·li·a·tor** *n.*

de·for·est /deefáwrist, -fór-/ *v.tr.* clear of forests or trees. ▫▫ **de·for·est·a·tion** *n.*

de·form /difáwrm/ *v.* **1** *tr.* make ugly; deface. **2** *tr.* put out of shape. **3** *intr.* undergo deformation; be deformed. ▫▫ **de·form·a·ble** *adj.* **de·for·ma·tion** /déefawrmáyshən/ *n.*

de·formed /difáwrmd/ *adj.* (of a person or limb) misshapen.

de·form·i·ty /difáwrmitee/ *n.* (*pl.* **-ies**) **1** the state of being deformed; ugliness; disfigurement. **2** a malformation, esp. of body or limb.

de·fraud /difráwd/ *v.tr.* (often foll. by *of*) cheat by fraud. ▫▫ **de·fraud·er** *n.*

de·fray /difráy/ *v.tr.* provide money to pay (a cost). ▫▫ **de·fray·a·ble** *adj.* **de·fray·al** *n.* **de·fray·ment** *n.*

de·frock /deefrók/ *v.tr.* deprive (a person) of ecclesiastical status.

de·frost /difráwst, -fróst/ *v.* **1** *tr.* remove frost or ice from (a refrigerator, windshield of a motor vehicle, etc.). **2** *tr.* unfreeze (frozen food). **3** *intr.* become unfrozen. ▫▫ **de·frost·er** *n.*

deft /deft/ *adj.* neatly skillful or dexterous; adroit. ▫▫ **deft·ly** *adv.* **deft·ness** *n.*

de·funct /difúngkt/ *adj.* **1** no longer existing. **2** no longer used or in fashion. **3** dead or extinct.

de·fuse /deefyṓoz/ *v.tr.* **1** remove the fuse from (an explosive device). **2** reduce the tension or potential danger in (a crisis, difficulty, etc.).

de·fy /difí/ *v.tr.* (**-ies, -ied**) **1** resist openly; refuse to obey. **2** present insuperable obstacles to (*defies solution*). **3** (foll. by *to* + infin.) challenge (a person) to do or prove something.

de·gen·er·ate *adj., n., & v.* • *adj.* /dijénərət/ **1** having lost the qualities that are normal and desirable or proper to its kind. **2** *Biol.* having changed to a lower type. • *n.* /dijénərət/ a degenerate person or animal. • *v.intr.* /dijénərayt/ become degenerate. ▫▫ **de·gen·er·a·cy** *n.* **de·gen·er·ate·ly** *adv.* **de·gen·er·a·tion** /dijénəráyshən/ *n.*

de·gen·er·a·tive /dijénərətiv/ *adj.* **1** of or tending to degeneration. **2** (of disease) characterized by progressive often irreversible deterioration.

de·grade /digráyd/ *v.tr.* **1** reduce to a lower rank, esp. as a punishment. **2** bring into dishonor or contempt. **3** *Chem.* reduce to a simpler molecular structure. **4** *Physics* reduce (energy) to a less convertible form. ▫▫ **de·grad·a·ble** *adj.* **deg·ra·da·tion** /dégrədáyshən/ *n.* **deg·ra·da·tive** /-dáytiv/ *adj.*

de·grad·ing /digráyding/ *adj.* humiliating. ▫▫ **de·grad·ing·ly** *adv.*

de·grease /deégrées/ *v.tr.* remove unwanted grease or fat from.

de·gree /digrée/ *n.* **1** a stage in an ascending or descending scale or process. **2** a stage in intensity or amount (*in some degree*). **3** relative condition (*each is good in its degree*). **4** *Math.* a unit of measurement of angles. **5** *Physics* a unit in a scale of temperature, hardness, etc. **6** *Med.* an extent of burns on a scale characterized by the destruction of the skin. **7** an academic rank conferred usu. after examination or after completion of a course. **8** a grade of crime or criminality (*murder in the first degree*). **9** a step in direct genealogical descent. **10** social or official rank. ▫ **by degrees** a little at a time; gradually. **to a degree** *colloq.* considerably.

de·gree-day *n.* a unit of measurement equal to one degree of variation between a standard temperature and the mean temperature on a given day.

de·horn /deeháwrn/ *v.tr.* remove the horns from (an animal).

de·hu·man·ize /deehyṓomənīz/ *v.tr.* **1** deprive of human characteristics. **2** make impersonal or machinelike. ▫▫ **de·hu·man·i·za·tion** *n.*

de·hu·mid·i·fy /deéhyoomídifī/ *v.tr.* (**-ies, -ied**) reduce the degree of humidity of; remove moisture from (esp. air). ▫▫ **de·hu·mid·i·fi·ca·tion** /-fikáyshən/ *n.* **de·hu·mid·i·fi·er** *n.*

de·hy·drate /deéhīdráyt/ *v.* **1** *tr.* **a** remove water from (esp. foods for preservation). **b** make dry, esp. make (the body) deficient in water. **c** render lifeless or uninteresting. **2** *intr.* lose water. ▫▫ **de·hy·dra·tion** /-dráyshən/ *n.* **de·hy·dra·tor** *n.*

de·ice /deeís/ *v.tr.* **1** remove ice from. **2** prevent the formation of ice on. ▫▫ **de·ic·er** *n.*

de·i·cide /deé-isīd, dáy-/ *n.* **1** the killer of a god. **2** the killing of a god.

de·i·fy /deéifī, dáyee-/ *v.tr.* (**-ies, -ied**) **1** make a god of. **2** regard or worship as a god. ▫▫ **de·i·fi·ca·tion** /-fikáyshən/ *n.*

deign /dayn/ *v. intr.* (foll. by *to* + infin.) think fit; condescend.

de·in·sti·tu·tion·al·ize /deéinstitṓoshənəlīz, -tyṓo-/ *v.tr.* (usu. as **deinstitutionalized** *adj.*) remove from an institution or from the effects of institutional life. ▫▫ **de·in·sti·tu·tion·al·i·za·tion** *n.*

de·ism /deeizəm, day-/ *n.* belief in the existence of a supreme being arising from reason rather than revelation (cf. THEISM). ▫▫ **de·ist** *n.* **de·is·tic** *adj.* **de·is·ti·cal** *adj.*

de·i·ty /deéitee, dáy-/ *n.* (*pl.* **-ies**) **1** ► a god or goddess. **2** divine status, quality, or nature. **3** (**the Deity**) God.

DEITY: PAINTING DEPICTING THE HINDU DEITY GANESH

dé·jà vu /dáyzhaa vṓo/ *n.* **1** *Psychol.* an illusory feeling of having already experienced a present situation. **2** something tediously familiar.

de·ject /dijékt/ *v.tr.* (usu. as **dejected** *adj.*) make sad or dispirited; depress. ▫▫ **de·ject·ed·ly** *adv.* **de·jec·tion** /dijékshən/ *n.*

de ju·re /dee jṓoree, day jṓoray/ *adj. & adv.* • *adj.* rightful. • *adv.* rightfully; by right.

Delaware /déləwair/ *n.* **1 a** a N. American people native to the northeastern US. **b** a member of this people. **2** the language of this people. ¶ Also called **Lenape** or **Lenni Lenape**.

de·lay /diláy/ *v. & n.* • *v.* **1** *tr.* postpone; defer. **2** *tr.* make late (*was delayed by the traffic lights*). **3** *intr.* loiter; be late (*don't delay!*). • *n.* **1** the act or an instance of delaying; the process of being delayed. **2** time lost by inaction or the inability to proceed. **3** a hindrance. ▫▫ **de·lay·er** *n.*

de·lec·ta·ble /diléktəbəl/ *adj.* esp. *literary* delightful; pleasant. ▫▫ **de·lec·ta·bly** *adv.*

de·lec·ta·tion /deélektáyshən/ *n.* *literary* pleasure; enjoyment (*sang for his delectation*).

del·e·gate *n. & v.* • *n.* /déligət/ **1** an elected representative sent to a conference. **2** a member of a committee or deputation. • *v.tr.* /déligayt/ **1** (often foll. by *to*) **a** commit (authority, etc.) to an agent or deputy. **b** entrust (a task) to another person. **2** send or authorize (a person) as a representative. ▫▫ **del·e·ga·ble** /-gəbəl/ *adj.* **del·e·ga·tor** *n.*

del·e·ga·tion /déligáyshən/ *n.* **1** a body of delegates. **2** the act or process of delegating or being delegated.

de·lete /dileét/ *v.tr.* remove or obliterate (written or printed matter), esp. by striking out. ▫▫ **de·le·tion** /-leéshən/ *n.*

del·e·te·ri·ous /déliteéreeəs/ *adj.* harmful (to the mind or body). ▫▫ **del·e·te·ri·ous·ly** *adv.*

delft /delft/ *n.* (also **delft·ware** /délftwair/ ► glazed, usu. blue and white, earthenware, made in Delft in Holland.

DELFT: DELFTWARE TILE

del·i /délee/ *n.* (*pl.* **delis**) *colloq.* a delicatessen.

de·lib·er·ate *adj. & v.* • *adj.* /dilíbərət/ **1 a** intentional. **b** fully considered; not impulsive. **2** slow in deciding; cautious (*a ponderous and deliberate mind*). **3** (of movement, etc.) unhurried. • *v.* /dilíbərayt/ **1** *intr.* think carefully; take counsel (*the jury deliberated for an hour*). **2** *tr.* consider; discuss carefully. ▫▫ **de·lib·er·ate·ly** /dilíbərətlee/ *adv.* **de·lib·er·ate·ness** *n.*

de·lib·er·a·tion /dilíbəráyshən/ *n.* **1** careful consideration. **2** a debate; discussion. **3 a** caution and care. **b** (of movement) slowness or ponderousness.

de·lib·er·a·tive /dilíbərətiv, -ráytiv/ *adj.* of, or appointed for the purpose of, deliberation or debate (*a deliberative assembly*).

del·i·ca·cy /délikəsee/ *n.* (*pl.* **-ies**) **1** the quality of being delicate. **2** a choice or expensive food.

del·i·cate /délikət/ *adj.* **1 a** fine in texture or structure; soft, slender, or slight. **b** (of color) subtle or subdued. **c** subtle; hard to appreciate. **2** (of a person) easily injured; susceptible to illness. **3 a** requiring careful handling; tricky (*a delicate situation*). **b** (of an instrument) highly sensitive. **4** deft (*a delicate touch*). **5** (of a person) avoiding the immodest or offensive. **6** (esp. of actions) considerate. ▫▫ **del·i·cate·ly** *adv.* **del·i·cate·ness** *n.*

del·i·ca·tes·sen /délikətésən/ *n.* **1** a store selling cooked meats, cheeses, and unusual or foreign prepared foods. **2** (often *attrib.*) such foods collectively (*a delicatessen counter*).

de·li·cious /dilíshəs/ *adj.* **1** highly delightful and enjoyable to the taste or sense of smell. **2** (of a joke, etc.) very witty. ▫▫ **de·li·cious·ly** *adv.* **de·li·cious·ness** *n.*

de·light /dilít/ *v. & n.* • *v.* **1** *tr.* (often foll. by *with*, or *that* + clause, or *to* + infin.) please greatly. **2** *intr.* (often foll. by *in*, or *to* + infin.) take great pleasure; be highly pleased. • *n.* **1** great pleasure. **2** something giving pleasure. ▫▫ **de·light·ed** *adj.* **de·light·ed·ly** *adv.*

de·light·ful /dilítfŏol/ *adj.* causing delight; pleasant; charming. ▫▫ **de·light·ful·ly** *adv.* **de·light·ful·ness** *n.*

de·lim·it /dilímit/ *v.tr.* determine the limits or boundary of. ▫▫ **de·lim·i·ta·tion** /-táyshən/ *n.*

de·lin·e·ate /dilíneeayt/ *v.tr.* portray by drawing, etc., or in words. ▫▫ **de·lin·e·a·tion** /-áyshən/ *n.*

de·lin·quent /dilíngkwənt/ *n. & adj.* • *n.* an offender (*juvenile delinquent*). • *adj.* **1** guilty of a minor crime or a misdeed. **2** failing in one's duty. **3** in arrears. ▫▫ **de·lin·quen·cy** /dilíngkwənsee/ *n.* (*pl.* **-ies**) **de·lin·quent·ly** *adv.*

del·i·quesce /délikwés/ *v.intr.* **1** become liquid; melt. **2** *Chem.* dissolve in water absorbed from the air. ▫▫ **del·i·ques·cence** *n.* **del·i·ques·cent** *adj.*

de·lir·i·ous /dilíreeəs/ *adj.* **1** affected with delirium; temporarily or apparently mad; raving. **2** wildly excited; ecstatic. ▫▫ **de·lir·i·ous·ly** *adv.*

de·lir·i·um /dilíreeəm/ *n.* **1** an acutely disordered state of mind involving incoherent speech,

D

DELTA

As a river enters the sea it suddenly slows down. Its capacity for carrying sediment decreases, and it may drop part of its sediment load in a huge fan of alluvial deposits called a delta. Often the river splits up into many smaller branches called distributaries.

TYPES OF DELTA

BIRD'S-FOOT (MISSISSIPPI)

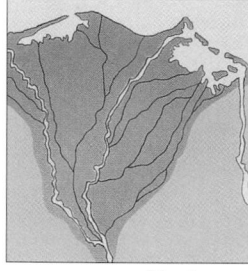

ARCUATE (NILE)

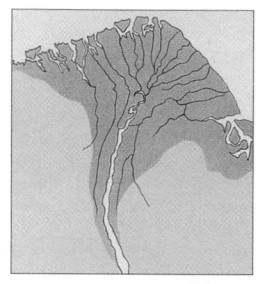

MODIFIED CUSPATE (NIGER)

hallucinations, and frenzied excitement. **2** great excitement; ecstasy.

de·lir·i·um tre·mens /tréemənz, -menz/ *n.* a psychosis of chronic alcoholism involving tremors and hallucinations.

de·liv·er /dilívər/ *v.tr.* **1 a** distribute (letters, packages, ordered goods, etc.) to the addressee or the purchaser. **b** (often foll. by *to*) hand over (*delivered the boy safely to his teacher*). **2** (often foll. by *from*) save, rescue, or set free (*delivered him from his enemies*). **3 a** give birth to (*delivered a girl*). **b** (in *passive*; often foll. by *of*) give birth (*was delivered of a child*). **c** assist at the birth of (*delivered six babies that week*). **d** assist in giving birth (*delivered the patient successfully*). **4** (often *refl.*) utter or recite (an opinion, a speech, etc.) (*delivered himself of the observation*; *delivered the sermon well*). **5** (often foll. by *up, over*) abandon; resign; hand over (*delivered his soul up to God*). **6** launch or aim (a blow, a ball, or an attack). **7** *colloq.* = deliver the goods. □ **deliver the goods** *colloq.* carry out one's part of an agreement. □□ **de·liv·er·a·ble** *adj.* **de·liv·er·er** *n.*

de·liv·er·ance /dilívərəns/ *n.* **1** the act or an instance of rescuing; the process of being rescued. **2** a rescue.

de·liv·er·y /dilívəree/ *n.* (*pl.* **-ies**) **1 a** the delivering of letters, etc. **b** something delivered. **2 a** the process of childbirth. **b** an act of this. **3** deliverance. **4 a** an act of throwing, as of a baseball. **b** the style of such an act (*a good delivery*). **5** the act of giving or surrendering (*delivery of the town to the enemy*). **6 a** the uttering of a speech, etc. **b** the manner or style of such a delivery. □ **take delivery of** receive (something purchased).

dell /del/ *n.* a small usu. wooded hollow or valley.

de·lo·cal·ize /deelókəlīz/ *v.tr.* **1 a** detach or remove (a thing) from its place. **b** not limit to a particular location. **2** (as **delocalized** *adj.*) *Chem.* (of electrons) shared among more than two atoms in a molecule. □□ **de·lo·cal·i·za·tion** *n.*

de·louse /deelóws/ *v.tr.* rid (a person or animal) of lice.

Del·phic /délfik/ *adj.* (also **Del·phi·an** /-feeən/) **1** (of an utterance, prophecy, etc.) obscure, ambiguous, or enigmatic. **2** of or concerning the ancient Greek oracle at Delphi.

del·phin·i·um /delfíneeəm/ *n.* any ranunculaceous garden plant of the genus *Delphinium*, with tall spikes of usu. blue flowers.

del·ta /déltə/ *n.* **1 ▲** a triangular tract of deposited earth, alluvium, etc., at the mouth of a river, formed by its diverging outlets. ▷ SEDIMENT. **2** the fourth letter of the Greek alphabet (Δ, δ). **3** *Astron.* the fourth star in a constellation. □□ **del·ta·ic** /deltáyik/ *adj.*

delta rhythm (or **wave**) low-frequency electrical activity of the brain during sleep.

delta wing *n.* ▶ the triangular swept-back wing of an aircraft. ▷ FIGHTER

del·toid /déltoyd/ *n.* (in full **deltoid muscle**) a thick triangular muscle covering the shoulder joint and used for raising the arm away from the body. ▷ MUSCULATURE

de·lude /dilóod/ *v.tr.* deceive or mislead.

del·uge /délyōōj, -yoozh/ *n. & v.* ● *n.* **1** a great flood. **2** (**the Deluge**) the biblical Flood (Gen. 6–8). **3** a great outpouring (of words, paper, etc.). **4** a heavy fall of rain. ● *v.tr.* **1** flood. **2** inundate with a great number or amount (*deluged with complaints*).

de·lu·sion /dilóozhən/ *n.* **1** a false belief or impression. **2** *Psychol.* this as a symptom or form of mental disorder. □□ **de·lu·sion·al** *adj.*

de·lu·sions of gran·deur *n.pl.* a false idea of oneself as being important, noble, famous, etc.

de·lu·sive /dilóosiv/ *adj.* deceptive or unreal. □□ **de·lu·sive·ly** *adv.* **de·lu·sive·ness** *n.*

de·luxe /də lúks, lóoks/ *adj.* **1** luxurious or sumptuous. **2** of a superior kind.

delve /delv/ *v.* **1** *intr.* (often foll. by *in, into*) **a** search energetically (*delved into his pocket*). **b** research (*delved into his family history*). **2** *tr. & intr. poet.* dig. □□ **delv·er** *n.*

de·mag·net·ize /deemágnitīz/ *v.tr.* remove the magnetic properties of. □□ **de·mag·net·i·za·tion** /-tizáyshən/ *n.* **de·mag·net·iz·er** *n.*

dem·a·gogue /déməgog, -gawg/ *n.* (also **-gog**) a political agitator appealing to the basest instincts of a mob. □□ **dem·a·gog·ic** /-gójik, -gógik, -gǒ-/ *adj.* **dem·a·gogu·er·y** /-gógəree, -gáwg-/ *n.* **dem·a·go·gy** /-gójee, -gáw-/ *n.*

de·mand /dimánd/ *n. & v.* ● *n.* **1** an insistent and peremptory request, made as of right. **2** *Econ.* the desire of purchasers or consumers for a commodity (*no demand for solid tires these days*). **3** an urgent claim (*care of her mother makes demands on her*). ● *v.tr.* **1** (often foll. by *of, from*, or *to* + infin., or *that* + clause) ask for (something) insistently and urgently, as of right. **2** require or need (*a task demanding skill*). **3** insist on being told (*demanded the truth*). **4** (as **demanding** *adj.*) making demands; requiring skill, effort, etc. (*a demanding job*). □ **in demand** sought after. **on demand** as soon as a demand is made (*a check payable on demand*). □□ **de·mand·ing·ly** *adv.*

de·man·toid /dimántoyd/ *n.* a lustrous green garnet.

de·mar·ca·tion /deemaarkáyshən/ *n.* the act of marking a boundary or limits. □□ **de·mar·cate** /dimáarkayt, deémaar-/ *v.tr.*

de·ma·te·ri·al·ize /deemətéereeəlīz/ *v.tr. & intr.* make or become nonmaterial or spiritual (esp. of psychic phenomena, etc.). □□ **de·ma·te·ri·al·i·za·tion** *n.*

de·mean /dimeén/ *v.tr.* (usu. *refl.*) lower the dignity of.

de·mean·or /dimeénər/ *n.* outward behavior or bearing.

de·ment·ed /diméntid/ *adj.* mad; crazy. □□ **de·ment·ed·ly** *adv.* **de·ment·ed·ness** *n.*

de·men·tia /diménshə/ *n. Med.* a chronic or persistent disorder of the mental processes, marked by memory disorders, personality changes, impaired reasoning, etc., due to brain disease or injury.

dem·e·ra·ra /déməráirə/ *n.* light-brown cane sugar coming orig. and chiefly from Demerara.

de·mer·it /dimérit/ *n.* **1** a quality or action deserving blame; a fault. **2** a mark given to an offender.

de·mesne /dimáyn, -meén/ *n.* **1 a** a sovereign's or nation's territory; a domain. **b** land attached to a mansion, etc. **c** landed property; an estate. **2** (usu. foll. by *of*) a region or sphere. **3** *Law hist.* possession (of real property) as one's own. □ **held in demesne** (of an estate) occupied by the owner, not by tenants.

dem·i- /démee/ *prefix* **1** half; half-size. **2** partially or imperfectly such (*demigod*).

dem·i·god /démeegod/ *n.* (*fem.* **-goddess** /-godis/) **1 a** a partly divine being. **b** the offspring of a god or goddess and a mortal. **2** *colloq.* a person of compelling beauty, powers, or personality.

dem·i·john /démeejon/ *n.* a bulbous, narrow-necked bottle holding from 3 to 10 gallons and usu. in a wicker cover. ▷ FERMENTATION

de·mil·i·ta·rize /deemílitərīz/ *v.tr.* remove a military organization or forces from (a frontier, a zone, etc.). □□ **de·mil·i·ta·ri·za·tion** *n.*

dem·i·monde /démeemond, -máwnd/ *n.* **1 a** *hist.* a class of women in 19th-c. France considered to be of doubtful social standing and morality. **b** a similar class of women in any society. **2** any group considered to be on the fringes of respectable society.

de·min·er·al·ize /deemínərəlīz/ *v.tr.* remove salts from (sea water, etc.). □□ **de·min·er·al·i·za·tion** *n.*

de·mise /dimíz/ *n. & v.* ● *n.* **1** death (*left a will on her demise*; *the demise of the agreement*). **2** *Law* conveyance or transfer (of property, a title, etc.) by demising. ● *v.tr. Law* **1** convey or grant (an estate) by will or lease. **2** transmit (a title, etc.) by death.

dem·i·urge /démeeyərj/ *n.* **1** the creator of the world in the works of the Greek philosopher Plato. **2** a heavenly being that controls the material world in the works of Gnostic philosophers.

dem·o /démō/ *n.* (*pl.* **-os**) *colloq.* = DEMONSTRATION 3.

de·mo·bi·lize /deemóbilīz/ *v.tr.* disband (troops). □□ **de·mo·bi·li·za·tion** *n.*

de·moc·ra·cy /dimókrəsee/ *n.* (*pl.* **-ies**) **1 a** a system of government by the whole population, usu. through elected representatives. **b** a nation so governed. **c** any organization governed on democratic principles. **2** a classless and tolerant form of society. **3** the principles of the Democratic party.

dem·o·crat /déməkrat/ *n.* **1** an advocate of democracy. **2** (**Democrat**) a member of the Democratic party.

dem·o·crat·ic /déməkrátik/ *adj.* **1** of, like, practicing, advocating, or constituting democracy or a democracy. **2** favoring social equality. □□ **dem·o·crat·i·cal·ly** *adv.*

Dem·o·crat·ic par·ty *n.* one of the two main US political parties, considered to support social reform and strong federal powers. (cf. REPUBLICAN PARTY)

de·moc·ra·tize /dimókrətīz/ *v.tr.* make (a nation, institution, etc.) democratic. □□ **de·moc·ra·ti·za·tion** *n.*

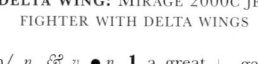

DELTA WING: MIRAGE 2000C JET FIGHTER WITH DELTA WINGS

de·mod·u·late /deemójəlayt/ *v.tr. Physics* extract (a modulating signal) from its carrier. □□ **de·mod·u·la·tion** /-láyshən/ *n.* **de·mod·u·la·tor** *n.*

de·mog·ra·phy /dimógrəfee/ *n.* the study of the statistics of births, deaths, disease, etc. □□ **de·mog·ra·pher** *n.* **dem·o·graph·ic** /déməgráfik/ *adj.* **dem·o·graph·i·cal·ly** *adv.*

de·mol·ish /dimólish/ *v.tr.* **1 a** pull down (a building). **b** completely destroy or break. **2** overthrow (an institution). **3** refute (an argument, theory, etc.). **4** *joc.* eat up completely and quickly. □□ **de·mol·ish·er** *n.* **dem·o·li·tion** /déməlíshən/ *n.*

de·mon /déemən/ *n.* **1 a** an evil spirit or devil, esp. one thought to possess a person. **b** the personification of evil passion. **2** a malignant supernatural being; the Devil. **3** (often *attrib.*) a forceful, fierce, or skillful performer (*a demon player*). **4** a cruel or destructive person. **5** (also **dae·mon**) **a** an inner or attendant spirit; a genius (*the demon of creativity*). **b** a supernatural being in ancient Greece. □ **a demon for work** *colloq.* a person who works strenuously.

de·mon·e·tize /deemónitīz, -mún-/ *v.tr.* withdraw (a coin, etc.) from use as money. □□ **de·mon·e·ti·za·tion** *n.*

de·mo·ni·ac /dimóneeak/ *adj. & n.* ● *adj.* **1** fiercely energetic or frenzied. **2 a** supposedly possessed by an evil spirit. **b** of or concerning such possession. **3** of or like demons. ● *n.* a person possessed by an evil spirit. □□ **de·mo·ni·a·cal** /déemənīəkəl/ *adj.* **de·mo·ni·a·cal·ly** *adv.*

de·mon·ic /dimónik/ *adj.* (also **dae·mon·ic**) **1** = DEMONIAC. **2** having or seeming to have supernatural genius or power.

de·mon·ism /déemənizəm/ *n.* belief in the power of demons.

de·mon·ize /déemənīz/ *v.tr.* **1** make into or like a demon. **2** represent as a demon.

de·mon·ol·a·try /déemənólətree/ *n.* the worship of demons.

de·mon·ol·o·gy /déemənóləjee/ *n.* the study of demons, etc. □□ **de·mon·ol·o·gist** *n.*

de·mon·stra·ble /dimónstrəbəl/ *adj.* capable of being shown or logically proved. □□ **de·mon·stra·bly** *adv.*

dem·on·strate /démənstrayt/ *v.* **1** *tr.* show evidence of (feelings, etc.). **2** *tr.* describe and explain (a scientific proposition, machine, etc.) by experiment, practical use, etc. **3** *tr.* **a** logically prove the truth of. **b** be proof of the existence of. **4** *intr.* take part in or organize a public demonstration. **5** *intr.* act as a demonstrator.

dem·on·stra·tion /démənstráyshən/ *n.* **1** (foll. by *of*) **a** the outward showing of feeling, etc. **b** an instance of this. **2 a** public meeting, march, etc., for a political or moral purpose. **3 a** the exhibiting or explaining of specimens or experiments as a method of esp. scientific teaching. **b** an instance of this. **4** proof provided by logic, argument, etc. **5** *Mil.* a show of military force. □□ **dem·on·stra·tion·al** *adj.*

de·mon·stra·tive /dimónstrətiv/ *adj. & n.* ● *adj.* **1** given to or marked by an open expression of feeling, esp. of affection. **2** (usu. foll. by *of*) logically conclusive; giving proof (*the work is demonstrative of their skill*). **3 a** serving to point out or exhibit. **b** involving esp. scientific demonstration (*demonstrative technique*). **4** *Gram.* (of an adjective or pronoun) indicating the person or thing referred to (e.g., *this, that, those*). ● *n. Gram.* a demonstrative adjective or pronoun. □□ **de·mon·stra·tive·ly** *adv.*

dem·on·stra·tor /démənstraytər/ *n.* **1** a person who takes part in a political demonstration, etc. **2** a person who demonstrates, esp. machines, equipment, etc., to prospective customers. **3** a person who teaches by demonstration, esp. in a laboratory, etc.

de·mor·al·ize /dimáwrəlīz, -mór-/ *v.tr.* destroy (a person's) morale; make hopeless. □□ **de·mor·al·i·za·tion** *n.* **de·mor·al·iz·ing** *adj.* **de·mor·al·iz·ing·ly** *adv.*

de·mote /dimót/ *v.tr.* reduce to a lower rank or class. □□ **de·mo·tion** /-móshən/ *n.*

de·mot·ic /dimótik/ *n. & adj.* ● *n.* **1** the popular colloquial form of a language. **2** a popular simplified form of ancient Egyptian writing (cf. HIERATIC). ● *adj.* **1** (esp. of language) popular, colloquial, or vulgar. **2** of or concerning the ancient Egyptian or modern Greek demotic.

de·mo·ti·vate /déemótivayt/ *v.tr.* (also *absol.*) cause to lose motivation; discourage. □□ **de·mo·ti·va·tion** /-váyshən/ *n.*

de·mul·cent /dimúlsənt/ *adj. & n.* ● *adj.* soothing. ● *n.* an agent that forms a protective film soothing irritation or inflammation in the mouth.

de·mur /dimár/ *v. & n.* ● *v.intr.* (**demurred, demurring**) **1** (often foll. by *to, at*) raise scruples or objections. **2** *Law* put in a demurrer. ● *n.* (also **de·mur·ral** /dimórəl/) (usu. in *neg.*) an objection (*agreed without demur*).

de·mure /dimyŏŏr/ *adj.* (**demurer, demurest**) **1** quiet and reserved; modest. **2** affectedly shy and quiet; coy. **3** decorous (*a demure high collar*). □□ **de·mure·ly** *adv.* **de·mure·ness** *n.*

de·mur·rage /dimórij, -múr-/ *n.* **1 a** a rate or amount payable to a shipowner by a charterer for failure to load or discharge a ship within the time agreed. **b** a similar charge on railroad cars, trucks, or goods. **2** such a detention or delay.

de·mur·rer /dimárər, -múr-/ *n. Law* an objection raised or exception taken.

de·my /deemí/ *n. Printing* a size of paper, 564 × 444 mm.

de·mys·ti·fy /deemístifī/ *v.tr.* (**-ies, -ied**) **1** clarify (obscure beliefs or subjects, etc.). **2** reduce or remove the irrationality in (a person). □□ **de·mys·ti·fi·ca·tion** /-fikáyshən/ *n.*

de·my·thol·o·gize /déemithóləjīz/ *v.tr.* **1** remove mythical elements from (a legend, famous person's life, etc.). **2** reinterpret what some consider to be the mythological elements in (the Bible).

den /den/ *n.* **1** a wild animal's lair. **2** a place of crime or vice (*den of iniquity; opium den*). **3** a small private room for pursuing a hobby, etc.

de·nar·i·us /dináireeəs/ *n.* (*pl.* **denarii** /-ree-ī/) ◀ an ancient Roman silver coin.

den·a·ry /dénəree, dée-/ *adj.* of ten; decimal.

den·a·ry scale *n.* a decimal scale.

de·na·tion·al·ize /deenáshənəlīz/ *v.tr.* **1** transfer (a nationalized industry or institution, etc.) from public to private ownership. **2 a** deprive (a nation) of its status or characteristics as a nation. **b** deprive (a person) of nationality or national characteristics. □□ **de·na·tion·al·i·za·tion** *n.*

de·nat·u·ral·ize /deenáchərəlīz/ *v.tr.* **1** change the nature or properties of; make unnatural. **2** deprive of the rights of citizenship. **3** = DENATURE *v.* 1 □□ **de·nat·u·ral·i·za·tion** *n.*

de·na·ture /deenáychər/ *v.tr.* **1** change the properties of (a protein, etc.) by heat, acidity, etc. **2** make (alcohol) unfit for drinking, esp. by the addition of another substance. □□ **de·na·tur·a·tion** /déenaychəráyshən/ *n.*

den·drite /déndrīt/ *n.* **1 a** a stone or mineral with natural treelike or mosslike markings. **b** such marks on stones or minerals. **2** *Chem.* a crystal with branching treelike growth. **3** *Zool. & Anat.* a branching process of a nerve cell conducting signals to a cell body.

den·drit·ic /dendritik/ *adj.* **1** of or like a dendrite. **2** treelike in shape or markings. □□ **den·drit·i·cal·ly** *adv.*

den·dro·chro·nol·o·gy /déndrōkrənóləjee/ *n.* **1** ▶ a system of dating using the annual growth rings of trees. **2** the study of these growth rings. □□ **den·dro·chron·o·log·i·cal** /-krónəlójikəl/ *adj.* **den·dro·chro·nol·o·gist** *n.*

den·drol·o·gy /dendróləjee/ *n.* the scientific study of trees. □□ **den·dro·log·i·cal** /-drəlójikəl/ *adj.* **den·drol·o·gist** *n.*

den·gue /dénggay, -gee/ *n.* an infectious viral disease of the tropics causing a fever and acute pains in the joints.

de·ni·a·ble /diníəbəl/ *adj.* that may be denied. □□ **de·ni·a·bil·i·ty** *n.*

de·ni·al /diníəl/ *n.* **1** the act or an instance of denying. **2** a refusal of a request or wish. **3** a statement that a thing is not true; a rejection (*denial of the accusation*). **4** a disavowal of a person as one's leader, etc. **5** = SELF-DENIAL.

de·nier /dényər, dənyáy, dəneér/ *n.* a unit of weight by which the fineness of silk, rayon, or nylon yarn is measured.

den·i·grate /dénigrayt/ *v.tr.* disparage the reputation of (a person). □□ **den·i·gra·tion** /-gráyshən/ *n.* **den·i·gra·tor** *n.* **den·i·gra·to·ry** /-grətáwree/ *adj.*

den·im /dénim/ *n.* **1** (often *attrib.*) a usu. blue, hardwearing, cotton twill fabric used for jeans, overalls, etc. (*a denim skirt*). **2** (in *pl.*) *colloq.* jeans, overalls, etc., made of this.

den·i·zen /dénizən/ *n.* **1** a foreigner admitted to certain rights in his or her adopted country. **2** a naturalized foreign word, animal, or plant. **3** (usu. foll. by *of*) an inhabitant or occupant.

de·nom·i·nate /dinóminayt/ *v.tr.* **1** give a name to. **2** call or describe (a person or thing) as.

de·nom·i·na·tion /dinómináyshən/ *n.* **1** a church or religious sect. **2** a class of units within a range or sequence of numbers, weights, money, etc. (*money of small denominations*). ▷ BANKNOTE. **3 a** a name or designation, esp. a characteristic or class name. **b** a class or kind having a specific name. **4** the rank of a playing card within a suit, or of a suit relative to others. □□ **de·nom·i·na·tion·al** *adj.*

de·nom·i·na·tor /dinóminaytər/ *n. Math.* the number below the line in a vulgar fraction; a divisor.

de·note /dinót/ *v.tr.* **1** be a sign of; indicate (*the arrow denotes direction*). **2** (usu. foll. by *that* + clause) mean; convey. **3** stand as a name for; signify. □□ **de·no·ta·tion** /déenōtáyshən/ *n.* **de·no·ta·tive** /déenōtáytiv, dinótətiv/ *adj.*

de·noue·ment /daynōōmōn/ *n.* (also **dénouement**) **1** the final unraveling of a plot or complicated situation. **2** the final scene in a play, novel, etc., in which the plot is resolved.

de·nounce /dinówns/ *v.tr.* **1** accuse publicly; condemn. **2** inform against. **3** give notice of the termination of (an armistice, treaty, etc.). □□ **de·nounce·ment** *n.* **de·nounc·er** *n.*

dense /dens/ *adj.* **1** closely compacted in substance; thick (*dense fog*). **2** crowded together (*the population is less dense on the outskirts*). **3** *colloq.* stupid. □□ **dense·ly** *adv.* **dense·ness** *n.*

den·si·ty /dénsitee/ *n.* (*pl.* **-ies**) **1** the degree of compactness of a substance. **2** *Physics* degree of

DENARIUS: SILVER DENARIUS OF JULIUS CAESAR, 44 BC

period of rapid growth   *period of slow growth*

DENDROCHRONOLOGY: CROSS SECTION THROUGH BISHOP PINE SHOWING GROWTH RINGS

D

D

consistency measured by the quantity of mass per unit volume. **3** the opacity of a photographic image. **4** a crowded state. **5** stupidity.

dent /dent/ *n. & v.* ● *n.* **1** a slight mark or hollow in a surface. **2** a noticeable effect (*lunch made a dent in our funds*). ● *v.tr.* **1** mark with a dent. **2** have (esp. an adverse) effect on (*the news dented our hopes*).

den·tal /déntl/ *adj.* **1** of the teeth; of or relating to dentistry. **2** *Phonet.* (of a consonant) produced with the tip of the tongue against the upper front teeth (as *th*) or the ridge of the teeth (as *n, s, t*).

dental floss *n.* a thread used to clean between the teeth.

den·tate /déntayt/ *adj. Bot. & Zool.* toothed; serrated.

den·ti·frice /déntifris/ *n.* a paste or powder for cleaning the teeth.

den·til /déntil/ *n. Archit.* ▼ each of a series of small rectangular blocks as a decoration under the molding of a cornice in classical architecture.

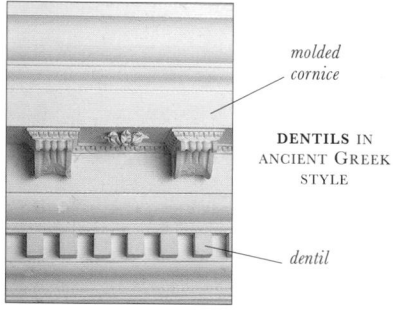

molded cornice

DENTILS IN ANCIENT GREEK STYLE

dentil

den·tin /dént'n/ *n.* (also **den·tine** /-teen/) a hard, dense, bony tissue forming the bulk of a tooth. ▷ TOOTH

den·tist /déntist/ *n.* a person who is qualified to treat the diseases and conditions that affect the mouth, jaws, teeth, etc. □□ **den·tis·try** *n.*

den·ti·tion /dentíshən/ *n.* **1** ▼ the type, number, and arrangement of teeth in a species, etc. **2** the cutting of teeth; teething.

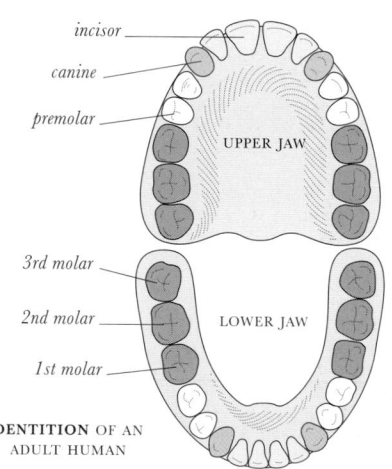

incisor
canine
premolar

UPPER JAW

3rd molar
2nd molar
1st molar

LOWER JAW

DENTITION OF AN ADULT HUMAN

den·ture /dénchər/ *n.* a removable artificial replacement for one or more teeth carried on a removable plate or frame.

de·nu·cle·ar·ize /deenóŏkleeərīz, -nyóŏ-/ *v.tr.* remove nuclear armaments from (a country, etc.). □□ **de·nu·cle·ar·i·za·tion** *n.*

de·nude /dinóŏd, -nyóŏd/ *v.tr.* **1** make naked or bare. **2** (foll. by *of*) **a** strip of clothing, a covering, etc. **b** deprive of a possession or attribute. □□ **de·nu·da·tion** /déenŏŏdáyshən, -nyŏŏ-, dényŏŏ-/ *n.*

de·nun·ci·a·tion /dinúnsee-áyshən, -shee-/ *n.* the act or an instance of denouncing. □□ **de·nun·ci·ate** /-seeayt/ *v.tr.* **de·nun·ci·a·to·ry** /-seeətawree/ *adj.*

de·ny /diní/ *v.tr.* (**-ies, -ied**) **1** declare untrue or nonexistent (*denied the charge; denied that it is so*). **2** repudiate or disclaim (*denied his faith; denied her signature*). **3** (often foll. by *to*) refuse (a person or thing, or something to a person) (*this was denied to me; denied him the satisfaction*). **4** refuse access to (a person sought) (*denied him his son*). □ **deny oneself** be abstinent. □□ **de·ni·er** *n.*

de·o·dor·ant /deeṓdərənt/ *n.* (often *attrib.*) a substance sprayed or rubbed on to the body or sprayed into the air to remove or conceal unpleasant smells (*a roll-on deodorant; has a deodorant effect*).

de·o·dor·ize /deeṓdərīz/ *v.tr.* remove or destroy the (usu. unpleasant) smell of. □□ **de·o·dor·i·za·tion** *n.* **de·o·dor·iz·er** *n.*

de·ox·y·gen·ate /deeóksijənayt/ *v.tr.* remove oxygen, esp. free oxygen, from. □□ **de·ox·y·gen·a·tion** /-náyshən/ *n.*

de·ox·y·ri·bo·nu·cle·ic ac·id /deeókseeríbōnŏŏkléeik, -kláyik, -nyŏŏ-/ *n.* see DNA.

dep. *abbr.* **1** departs. **2** deputy.

de·part /dipaárt/ *v.* **1** *intr.* **a** (usu. foll. by *from*) go away; leave (*the train departs from this platform*). **b** (usu. foll. by *for*) start; set out (*flights depart for New York every hour*). **2** *intr.* (usu. foll. by *from*) diverge; deviate (*departs from standard practice*). **3 a** *intr.* die. **b** *tr. formal* or *literary* leave by death (*departed this life*).

de·part·ed /dipaártid/ *n.* (prec. by *the*) *euphem.* a particular dead person or dead people (*we are here to mourn the departed*).

de·part·ment /dipaártmənt/ *n.* **1** a separate part of a complex whole, esp.: **a** a branch of municipal or federal administration (*State Department; Department of Agriculture*). **b** a branch of study and its administration at a university, school, etc. (*the physics department*). **c** a section of a large store (*hardware department*). **2** *colloq.* an area of special expertise. **3** an administrative district in France and other countries.

de·part·men·tal /deepaartmént'l/ *adj.* of or belonging to a department. □□ **de·part·men·tal·ize** *v.tr.* **de·part·men·tal·i·za·tion** *n.* **de·part·men·tal·ly** *adv.*

de·part·ment store *n.* a large retail establishment stocking many varieties of goods in different departments.

de·par·ture /dipaárchər/ *n.* **1** the act or an instance of departing. **2** (often foll. by *from*) a deviation (from the truth, a standard, etc.). **3** (often *attrib.*) the starting of a train, an aircraft, etc. (*the departure was late; departure lounge*). **4** a new course of action or thought (*driving a car is rather a departure for him*).

de·pend /dipénd/ *v.intr.* **1** (often foll. by *on, upon*) be controlled or determined by (*success depends on hard work; it depends how you tackle the problem*). **2** (foll. by *on, upon*) **a** be unable to do without (*depends on her mother*). **b** rely on (*I'm depending on you to come*). **3** (foll. by *on, upon*) be grammatically dependent on. □ **depend upon it!** you may be sure! **it** (or **it all** or **that**) **depends** expressing uncertainty or qualification in answering a question (*Will they come? It depends*).

de·pend·a·ble /dipéndəbəl/ *adj.* reliable. □□ **de·pend·a·bil·i·ty** *n.* **de·pend·a·bly** *adv.*

de·pend·ence /dipéndəns/ *n.* **1** the state of being dependent, esp. on financial or other support. **2** reliance; trust (*shows great dependence on his judgment*).

de·pend·en·cy /dipéndənsee/ *n.* (*pl.* **-ies**) **1** a country or province controlled by another. **2** anything subordinate or dependent.

de·pend·ent /dipéndənt/ *adj. & n.* ● *adj.* **1** (usu. foll. by *on*) depending, conditional, or subordinate. **2** unable to do without (esp. a drug). **3** maintained at another's cost. **4** *Math.* (of a variable) having a value determined by that of another variable. **5** *Gram.* (of a clause, phrase, or word) subordinate to a sentence or word. ● *n.* **1** a person who relies on another, esp. for financial support. **2** a servant. □□ **de·pend·ent·ly** *adv.*

de·per·son·al·ize /deepɔ́rsənəlīz/ *v.tr.* **1** make impersonal. **2** deprive of personality. □□ **de·per·son·al·i·za·tion** /deepɔ́rsənəlizáyshən/ *n.*

de·pict /dipíkt/ *v.tr.* **1** represent in a drawing or painting, etc. **2** portray in words; describe (*the play depicts him as vain and petty*). □□ **de·pic·tion** /-píkshən/ *n.*

de·pi·late /dépilayt/ *v.tr.* remove the hair from. □□ **dep·i·la·tion** /-láyshən/ *n.*

de·pil·a·to·ry /dipílətawree/ *adj. & n.* ● *adj.* that removes unwanted hair. ● *n.* (*pl.* **-ies**) a depilatory substance.

de·plete /dipléet/ *v.tr.* (esp. in *passive*) **1** reduce in numbers or quantity (*depleted forces*). **2** empty out; exhaust (*their energies were depleted*). □□ **de·ple·tion** /-pléeshən/ *n.*

de·plet·ed u·ra·ni·um *n.* uranium from which most of the fissile isotope U-235 has been removed.

de·plor·a·ble /diplawrəbəl/ *adj.* **1** exceedingly bad (*a deplorable meal*). **2** that can be deplored. □□ **de·plor·a·bly** *adv.*

de·plore /diplawr/ *v.tr.* **1** grieve over; regret. **2** be scandalized by; find exceedingly bad.

de·ploy /diplóy/ *v.* **1** *Mil.* **a** *tr.* cause (troops) to spread out from a column into a line. **b** *intr.* (of troops) spread out in this way. **2** *tr.* bring (arguments, forces, etc.) into effective action. □□ **de·ploy·ment** *n.*

de·po·lit·i·cize /deepəlítisīz/ *v.tr.* **1** make (a person, an organization, etc.) nonpolitical. **2** remove from political activity or influence. □□ **de·po·lit·i·ci·za·tion** *n.*

de·po·nent /dipṓnənt/ *adj. & n.* ● *adj. Gram.* (of a verb, esp. in Latin or Greek) passive or middle in form but active in meaning. ● *n.* **1** *Gram.* a deponent verb. **2** *Law* **a** a person making a deposition under oath. **b** a witness giving written testimony for use in court, etc.

de·pop·u·late /deepópyəlayt/ *v.* **1** *tr.* reduce the population of. **2** *intr.* decline in population. □□ **de·pop·u·la·tion** /-láyshən/ *n.*

de·port /dipáwrt/ *v.tr.* **1 a** remove (an immigrant or foreigner) forcibly to another country; banish. **b** exile (a native) to another country. **2** *refl.* conduct (oneself) or behave (in a specified manner) (*deported himself well*). □□ **de·por·ta·tion** /-táyshən/ *n.*

de·por·tee /deepawrtée/ *n.* a person who has been or is being deported.

de·port·ment /dipáwrtmənt/ *n.* bearing, demeanor, or manners, esp. of a cultivated kind.

de·pose /dipṓz/ *v.* **1** *tr.* remove from office, esp. dethrone. **2** *intr. Law* (usu. foll. by *to*, or *that* + clause) bear witness, esp. on oath in court.

de·pos·it /dipózit/ *n. & v.* ● *n.* **1 a** a sum of money placed in an account in a bank. **b** anything stored or entrusted for safekeeping, usu. in a bank. **2 a** a sum payable as a first installment on a time-payment purchase, or as a pledge for a contract. **b** a returnable sum payable on the short-term rental of a car, boat, etc. **3 a** a natural layer of sand, rock, coal, etc. **b** a layer of precipitated matter on a surface, e.g., on the inside of a kettle. ● *v.tr.* (**deposited, depositing**) **1 a** put or lay down in a (usu. specified) place (*deposited the book on the floor*). **b** (of water, wind, etc.) leave (matter, etc.) lying in a displaced position. **2 a** store or entrust for keeping. **b** pay (a sum of money) into a bank account, esp. a deposit account. **3** pay (a sum) as a first installment or as a pledge for a contract.

de·pos·i·tar·y /dipózitèree/ *n.* (*pl.* **-ies**) a person to whom something is entrusted.

dep·o·si·tion /dépəzíshən/ *n.* **1** the act or an instance of deposing, esp. a monarch. **2** *Law* **a** the process of giving sworn evidence; allegation. **b** an instance of this. **c** evidence given under oath. **3** the act or an instance of depositing. **4** (**the Deposition**) **a** the taking down of the body of Christ from the Cross. **b** a representation of this.

de·pos·i·to·ry /dipózitawree/ *n.* (*pl.* **-ies**) **1 a** a storehouse. **b** a store (of wisdom, knowledge, etc.). **2** = DEPOSITARY.

de·pot /deepō, depō/ *n.* **1** a storehouse. **2** *Mil.* a storehouse for equipment, etc. **3 a** a building for the servicing, parking, etc., of esp. buses, trains, or goods vehicles. **b** a railroad or bus station.

de·prave /dipráyv/ *v.tr.* pervert or corrupt, esp. morally. □□ **de·pra·va·tion** /déprəváyshən/ *n.* **de·praved** *adj.*

de·prav·i·ty /diprávitee/ *n.* (*pl.* **-ies**) **1** moral corruption; wickedness. **2** an instance of this; a wicked act.

dep·re·cate /déprikayt/ *v.tr.* **1** express disapproval of or a wish against; deplore (*deprecate hasty action*). ¶ Often confused with *depreciate.* **2** plead earnestly against. □□ **dep·re·cat·ing·ly** *adv.* **dep·re·ca·tion** /-káyshən/ *n.* **dep·re·ca·to·ry** /-kətawree/ *adj.*

de·pre·ci·ate /dipréesheeayt/ *v.* **1** *tr. & intr.* diminish in value (*the car has depreciated*). **2** *tr.* belittle (*they are always depreciating his taste*). **3** *tr.* reduce the purchasing power of (money). □□ **de·pre·ci·a·to·ry** /-sheeətáwree/ *adj.*

de·pre·ci·a·tion /dipreesheeáyshən/ *n.* **1** the amount of wear and tear (of a property, etc.) for which a reduction may be made in a valuation or a balance sheet. **2** *Econ.* a decrease in the value of a currency. **3** the act or an instance of depreciating; belittlement.

dep·re·da·tion /dépridáyshən/ *n.* (usu. in *pl.*) **1** ravaging or plundering. **2** an instance or instances of this.

de·press /diprés/ *v.tr.* **1** push or pull down; lower (*depressed the lever*). **2** make dispirited or dejected. **3** *Econ.* reduce the activity of (esp. trade). **4** (as **depressed** *adj.*) **a** dispirited or miserable. **b** *Psychol.* suffering from depression. □□ **de·press·ing** *adj.* **de·press·ing·ly** *adv.*

de·pres·sant /diprésənt/ *adj. & n.* ● *adj.* **1** that depresses. **2** *Med.* sedative. ● *n.* **1** *Med.* an agent, esp. a drug, that sedates. **2** an influence that depresses.

de·pres·sion /dipréshən/ *n.* **1 a** *Psychol.* a state of extreme dejection or morbidly excessive melancholy, often with physical symptoms. **b** a reduction in vitality, vigor, or spirits. **2 a** a long period of financial and industrial decline; a slump. **b** (**the Depression**) the depression of 1929–34. **3** *Meteorol.* ▼ a lowering of atmospheric pressure, esp. the center of a region of minimum pressure or the system of winds around it. ▷ WEATHER CHART. **4** a

DEPRESSION

Spiraling low-pressure areas, known as depressions or cyclones, often form in temperate latitudes where tropical and polar air masses meet. The cold air undercuts the warm air, and the fronts may merge to form an occluded front.

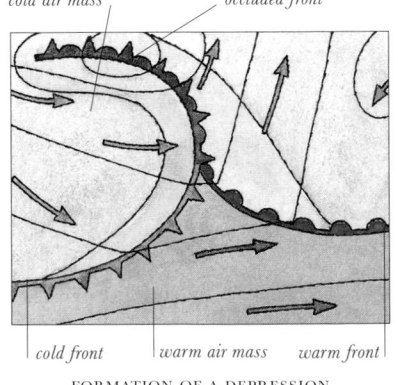

cold air mass   *occluded front*

cold front   *warm air mass*   *warm front*

FORMATION OF A DEPRESSION

---

sunken place or hollow on a surface. **5 a** a lowering or sinking (often foll. by *of*: *depression of freezing point*). **b** pressing down.

de·pres·sive /diprésiv/ *adj. & n.* ● *adj.* **1** tending to depress. **2** *Psychol.* involving or characterized by depression. ● *n. Psychol.* a person suffering or with a tendency to suffer from depression.

de·pres·sor /diprésər/ *n.* **1** *Anat.* **a** (in full **depressor muscle**) a muscle that causes the lowering of some part of the body. **b** a nerve that lowers blood pressure. **2** *Surgery* an instrument for pressing down an organ, etc.

de·pres·sur·ize /deepréshəriz/ *v.tr.* cause a drop in the pressure of the gas inside (a container), esp. to the ambient level. □□ **de·pres·sur·i·za·tion** *n.*

dep·ri·va·tion /déprivayshən/ *n.* **1** (usu. foll. by *of*) the act or an instance of depriving; the state of being deprived (*deprivation of liberty; suffered many deprivations*). **2 a** a deposition from esp. an ecclesiastical office. **b** an instance of this.

de·prive /dipriv/ *v.tr.* **1** (usu. foll. by *of*) strip, dispossess; debar from enjoying (*illness deprived him of success*). **2** (as **deprived** *adj.*) **a** (of a child, etc.) suffering from the effects of a poor or loveless home. **b** (of an area) with inadequate housing, facilities, employment, etc. □□ **de·priv·al** *n.*

Dept. *abbr.* Department.

depth /depth/ *n.* **1 a** deepness (*the depth is not great at the edge*). **b** the measurement from the top down, from the surface inward, or from the front to the back (*depth of the drawer is 12 inches*). **2** difficulty; abstruseness. **3 a** sagacity; wisdom. **b** intensity of emotion, etc. (*the poem has little depth*). **4** an intensity of color, darkness, etc. **5** (in *pl.*) **a** deep water, a deep place; an abyss. **b** a low, depressed state. **c** the lowest or inmost part (*the depths of the country*). **6** the middle (*in the depth of winter*). □ **in depth** comprehensively, thoroughly, or profoundly (cf. IN-DEPTH). **out of one's depth 1** in water over one's head. **2** engaged in a task or on a subject too difficult for one.

depth charge *n.* (also **depth bomb**) a bomb capable of exploding under water, esp. for dropping on a submerged submarine, etc.

dep·u·ta·tion /dépyōōtáyshən/ *n.* a group of people appointed to represent others.

de·pute *v.tr.* /dipyōōt/ (often foll. by *to*) **1** appoint as a deputy. **2** delegate (a task, authority, etc.) (*deputed the leadership to her*).

dep·u·tize /dépyətiz/ *v.intr.* (usu. foll. by *for*) act as a deputy or understudy.

dep·u·ty /dépyətee/ *n.* (*pl.* **-ies**) **1** a person appointed or delegated to act for another or others (also *attrib.*: *deputy sheriff*). **2** *Polit.* a parliamentary representative in certain countries, e.g., France. □ **by deputy** by proxy.

de·rac·in·ate /di-rásinayt/ *v.tr. literary* **1** tear up by the roots. **2** obliterate; expunge. □□ **de·rac·i·na·tion** /-náyshən/ *n.*

de·rail /diráyl/ *v.tr.* (usu. in *passive*) cause (a train, etc.) to leave the rails. □□ **de·rail·ment** *n.*

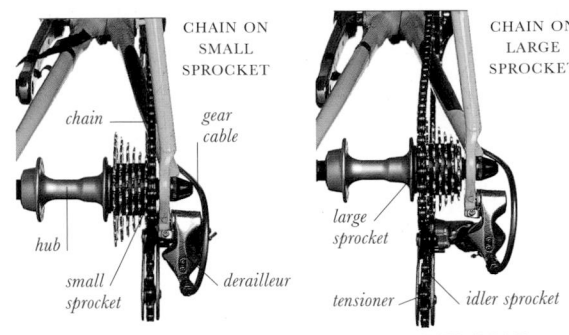

DERAILLEUR

Derailleur gears switch a bicycle chain between different-sized sprockets on the front and rear hubs, thereby permitting several gear ratios, or speeds. Adjusting a shift lever, usually mounted on the handlebars, pulls on the gear cable, which moves the derailleurs laterally, guiding the chain between the sprockets.

CHAIN ON SMALL SPROCKET   CHAIN ON LARGE SPROCKET

chain   *gear cable*

hub

small sprocket

large sprocket

derailleur

tensioner   *idler sprocket*

▷ BICYCLE

BICYCLE WHEEL HUB AND DERAILLEUR GEAR

---

de·rail·leur /dəráylər/ *n.* ▲ a gear-shifting mechanism on a bicycle that moves the chain from one sprocket to another.

de·range /diráynj/ *v.tr.* **1** throw into confusion; disorganize. **2** (esp. as **deranged** *adj.*) make insane (*deranged by the tragic events*). **3** disturb; interrupt. □□ **de·range·ment** *n.*

der·by /dárbee/ *n.* (*pl.* **-ies**) **1** any of several horse races that are run annually, esp. for three-year olds (*Kentucky Derby*). **2** a sporting contest, etc., esp. one open to all comers. **3** a bowler hat.

de·reg·u·late /dee-régyəlayt/ *v.tr.* remove regulations or restrictions from. □□ **de·reg·u·la·tion** /-láyshən/ *n.*

der·e·lict /dérilikt/ *adj. & n.* ● *adj.* **1** abandoned; ownerless (esp. of a ship at sea or an empty decrepit property). **2** (esp. of property) ruined; dilapidated. **3** negligent (of duty, etc.). ● *n.* **1** a person without a home, a job, or property. **2** abandoned property, esp. a ship.

der·e·lic·tion /dérilikshən/ *n.* **1** (usu. foll. by *of*) **a** neglect; failure to carry out one's obligations (*dereliction of duty*). **b** an instance of this. **2** the act or an instance of abandoning; the process of being abandoned. **3 a** the retreat of the sea exposing new land. **b** the land so exposed.

de·re·strict /deé-ristríkt/ *v.tr.* **1** remove restrictions from. **2** remove speed restrictions from (a road, area, etc.). □□ **de·re·stric·tion** /-tríkshən/ *n.*

de·ride /dirid/ *v.tr.* laugh scornfully at; mock. □□ **de·rid·er** *n.* **de·rid·ing·ly** *adv.*

de ri·gueur /də rigŕr/ *predic. adj.* required by custom or etiquette (*evening dress is de rigueur*).

de·ri·sion /dirizhən/ *n.* ridicule; mockery (*bring into derision*).

de·ri·sive /dirisiv/ *adj.* scoffing; ironical; scornful (*derisive cheers*). □□ **de·ri·sive·ly** *adv.* **de·ri·sive·ness** *n.*

de·ri·so·ry /dirisəree, zə-/ *adj.* **1** = DERISIVE. **2** so small or unimportant as to be ridiculous (*derisory offer*; *derisory costs*).

der·i·va·tion /dérivayshən/ *n.* **1** the act or an instance of deriving or obtaining from a source; the process of being derived. **2 a** the formation of a word from another word or from a root. **b** a derivative. **c** the tracing of the origin of a word. **d** a statement or account of this. **3** extraction; descent. **4** *Math.* a sequence of statements showing that a formula, theorem, etc., is a consequence of previously accepted statements. □□ **der·i·va·tion·al** *adj.*

de·riv·a·tive /dirivətiv/ *adj. & n.* ● *adj.* derived from another source; not original (*his music is derivative and uninteresting*). ● *n.* **1** something derived from another source, esp.: **a** a word derived from another or from a root (e.g., *quickly* from *quick*). **b** *Chem.* a chemical compound derived from another. **2** *Math.* a quantity measuring the rate of change of another. □□ **de·riv·a·tive·ly** *adv.*

de·rive /diriv/ *v.* **1** *tr.* (usu. foll. by *from*) get, obtain, or form (*derived satisfaction from work*). **2** *intr.* (foll. by *from*) arise from, originate in, be descended or obtained from (*happiness derives from many things*). **3** *tr.*

D

D

gather or deduce (*derived the information from the clues*). **4** *tr.* **a** trace the descent of (a person). **b** show the origin of (a thing). **5** *tr.* (usu. foll. by *from*) show or state the origin or formation of (a word, etc.) (*derived the word from Latin*). **6** *tr. Math.* obtain (a function) by differentiation. □□ **de·riv·a·ble** *adj.*

der·ma·ti·tis /dɔ́rmətítis/ *n.* inflammation of the skin.

der·ma·tol·o·gy /dɔ̀rmətólɔjee/ *n.* the study of skin disorders. □□ **der·ma·to·log·i·cal** /-təlójikəl/ *adj.* **der·ma·tol·o·gist** *n.*

der·mis /dɔ́rmis/ *n.* (also **der·ma** /dɔ́rmə/) **1** (in general use) the skin. **2** *Anat.* the true skin, the thick layer of living tissue below the epidermis. ▷ SKIN. □□ **der·mal** *adj.*

der·o·gate /dérəgayt/ *v.intr.* (foll. by *from*) *formal* **1 a** take away a part from; detract from (a merit, a right, etc.). **b** disparage. **2** deviate from (correct behavior, etc.).

der·o·ga·tion /dérəgáyshən/ *n.* **1** (foll. by *of*) a lessening or impairment of (a law, authority, etc.). **2** deterioration; debasement.

de·rog·a·to·ry /dirógətawree/ *adj.* (often foll. by *to*) involving disparagement or discredit; insulting; depreciatory (*made a derogatory remark*). □□ **de·rog·a·to·ri·ly** *adv.*

der·rick /dérik/ *n.* **1** a kind of crane for moving or lifting heavy weights, having a movable pivoted arm. **2** ▼ the framework over an oil well or similar excavation, holding the drilling machinery. ▷ OIL PLATFORM

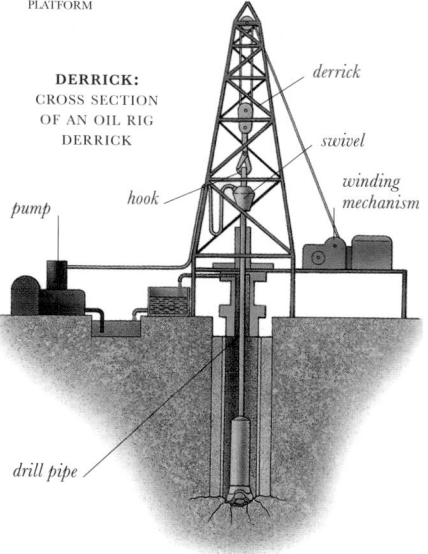

DERRICK:
CROSS SECTION
OF AN OIL RIG
DERRICK

pump   *hook*   *derrick*   *swivel*   *winding mechanism*

drill pipe

der·ri·ere /déreeáir/ *n. colloq. euphem.* (also **derrière**) the buttocks.

der·ring-do /déringdóo/ *n. literary joc.* heroic courage or action.

der·ris /déris/ *n.* **1** any woody, tropical climbing leguminous plant of the genus *Derris*, bearing leathery pods. **2** an insecticide made from the powdered root of some kinds of derris.

der·vish /dɔ́rvish/ *n.* a member of any of several Muslim fraternities vowed to poverty and austerity.

de·sal·i·nate /deesálinayt/ *v.tr.* remove salt from (esp. sea water). □□ **de·sal·i·na·tion** /-náyshən/ *n.*

de·scale /deeskáyl/ *v.tr.* remove the scale from.

des·cant *n. & v.* ● *n.* /déskant/ **1** *Mus.* an independent treble melody above a basic melody, esp. of a hymn tune. **2** *poet.* a melody; a song. ● *v.intr.* /diskánt/ **1** (foll. by *on, upon*) talk lengthily and prosily, esp. in praise of. **2** *Mus.* sing or play a descant.

des·cant re·cord·er *n.* the most common size of recorder, with a range of two octaves.

de·scend /disénd/ *v.* **1** *tr. & intr.* go or come down (*a hill, stairs, etc.*). **2** *intr.* (of a thing) sink; fall (*rain*

DESERT

A desert is an arid area of land where vegetation is scarce. It is also characterized by extremely high or low temperatures or by the evaporation of more water from the Earth's surface than is precipitated in the form of rain. Deserts cover about 33 percent of the Earth's land surface, and this proportion is increasing.

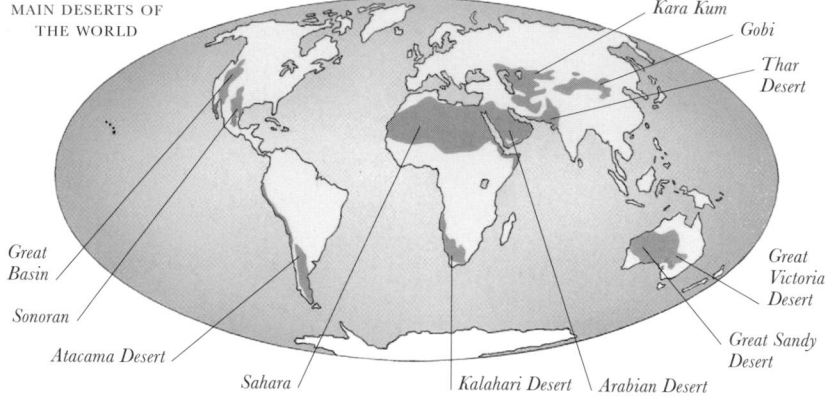

MAIN DESERTS OF THE WORLD

Kara Kum — *Gobi* — *Thar Desert* — *Great Basin* — *Sonoran* — *Atacama Desert* — *Sahara* — *Kalahari Desert* — *Arabian Desert* — *Great Sandy Desert* — *Great Victoria Desert*

descended heavily). **3** *intr.* slope downward; lie along a descending slope (*fields descended to the beach*). **4** *intr.* (usu. foll. by *on*) **a** make a sudden attack. **b** make an unexpected and usu. unwelcome visit. **5** *intr.* (usu. foll. by *from*, *to*) (of property, qualities, rights, etc.) be passed by inheritance. **6** *intr.* **a** sink in rank, quality, etc. **b** (foll. by *to*) degrade oneself morally to (an unworthy act) (*descend to violence*). **7** *intr. Mus.* (of sound) become lower in pitch. **8** *intr.* (usu. foll. by *to*) proceed (in discourse or writing): **a** in time (to a subsequent event, etc.). **b** from the general (to the particular) (*now let's descend to details*). **9** *tr.* go along (a river, etc.) to the sea, etc. □ **be descended from** have as an ancestor. □□ **de·scend·ent** *adj.*

de·scend·ant /diséndənt/ *n.* (often foll. by *of*) a person or thing descended from another (*a descendant of John Adams*).

de·scent /disént/ *n.* **1 a** the act of descending. **b** an instance of this. **c** a downward movement. **2 a** a way or path, etc., by which one may descend. **b** a downward slope. **3 a** being descended; lineage; family origin. **b** the transmission of qualities, property, privileges, etc., by inheritance. **4 a** a decline; a fall. **b** a lowering (of pitch, temperature, etc.). **5** a sudden violent attack.

de·scram·ble /deeskrámbəl/ *v.tr.* **1** convert or restore (a signal) to intelligible form. **2** counteract the effects of (a scrambling device). **3** recover an original signal from (a scrambled signal). □□ **de·scram·bler** *n.*

de·scribe /diskríb/ *v.tr.* **1 a** state the characteristics, appearance, etc., of, in spoken or written form (*described the landscape*). **b** (foll. by *as*) assert to be; call (*described him as a habitual liar*). **2 a** mark out or draw (esp. a geometrical figure). **b** move in (a specified way, esp. a curve) (*described a parabola through the air*). □□ **de·scrib·a·ble** *adj.* **de·scrib·er** *n.*

de·scrip·tion /diskrípshən/ *n.* **1 a** the act or an instance of describing; the process of being described. **b** a spoken or written representation (of a person, object, or event). **2** a sort, kind, or class (*no food of any description*). □ **answers** (or **fits**) **the description** has the qualities specified.

de·scrip·tive /diskríptiv/ *adj.* **1** serving or seeking to describe (*a descriptive writer*). **2** describing or classifying without expressing feelings or judging (*a purely descriptive account*). □□ **de·scrip·tive·ly** *adv.* **de·scrip·tive·ness** *n.*

de·scry /diskrí/ *v.tr.* (**-ies**, **-ied**) *literary* catch sight of; discern.

des·e·crate /désikrayt/ *v.tr.* **1** violate (a sacred place or thing) with violence, profanity, etc. **2** deprive (a

church, a sacred object, etc.) of sanctity; deconsecrate. □□ **des·e·cra·tion** /-kráyshən/ *n.* **des·e·cra·tor** *n.*

de·seed /deeséed/ *v.tr.* remove the seeds from (a plant, vegetable, etc.).

de·seg·re·gate /deeségrigayt/ *v.tr.* abolish racial segregation in (schools, etc.) or of (people, etc.). □□ **de·seg·re·ga·tion** /-gáyshən/ *n.*

de·se·lect /deesilékt/ *v.tr.* **1** dismiss (esp. a trainee); discharge; reject. **2** *Polit.* decline to select or retain as a constituency candidate in an election. □□ **de·se·lec·tion** /-lékshən/ *n.*

de·sen·si·tize /deesénsitīz/ *v.tr.* reduce or destroy the sensitivity of (photographic materials, an allergic person, etc.). □□ **de·sen·si·ti·za·tion** *n.* **de·sen·si·tiz·er** *n.*

de·sert[1] /dizɔ́rt/ *v.* **1** *tr.* abandon; give up; leave (*deserted the sinking ship*). **2** *tr.* forsake or abandon (a cause or a person, etc.). **3** *tr.* fail (*his presence of mind deserted him*). **4** *intr. Mil.* run away (esp. from military service). **5** *tr.* (as **deserted** *adj.*) empty; abandoned (*a deserted house*). □□ **de·sert·er** *n.* (in sense 4 of *v.*). **de·ser·tion** /-zɔ́rshən/ *n.*

des·ert[2] /dézərt/ *n. & adj.* ● *n.* ▲ a dry, barren, often sand-covered area of land; an uninteresting or barren subject, period, etc. (*a cultural desert*). ● *adj.* **1** uninhabited; desolate. **2** uncultivated; barren.

des·ert[3] /dizɔ́rt/ *n.* **1** (in *pl.*) **a** acts or qualities deserving reward or punishment. **b** such reward or punishment (*has gotten his just deserts*). **2** the fact of being worthy of reward or punishment; deservingness.

Des·ert boot *n. Trademark* a suede, etc., boot reaching to or extending just above the ankle. ▷ INFANTRYMAN

de·sert·i·fi·ca·tion /dizɔ̀rtifikáyshən/ *n.* the process of making or becoming a desert.

de·serve /dizɔ́rv/ *v.tr.* **1** (often foll. by *to* + infin.) show conduct or qualities worthy of (reward, punishment, etc.). **2** (as **deserved** *adj.*) rightfully merited or earned (*a deserved win*). □□ **de·serv·ed·ly** /-vidlee/ *adv.*

de·serv·ing /dizɔ́rving/ *adj.* meritorious. □ **deserving of** showing conduct or qualities worthy of (praise, blame, help, etc.). □□ **de·serv·ing·ly** *adv.*

de·sex·u·al·ize /deesékshŌŌəlīz/ *v.tr.* deprive of sexual character or of the distinctive qualities of a sex.

des·ha·bille var. of DISHABILLE.

des·ic·cant /désikənt/ *n. Chem.* a hygroscopic substance used as a drying agent.

des·ic·cate /désikayt/ *v.tr.* remove the moisture

from (esp. food for preservation). □□ **des·ic·ca·tion** /-káyshən/ *n.* **des·ic·ca·tive** *adj.*

des·ic·ca·tor /désikayt/ *n.* **1** an apparatus for desiccating. **2** *Chem.* ▼ an apparatus containing a drying agent to remove the moisture from specimens.

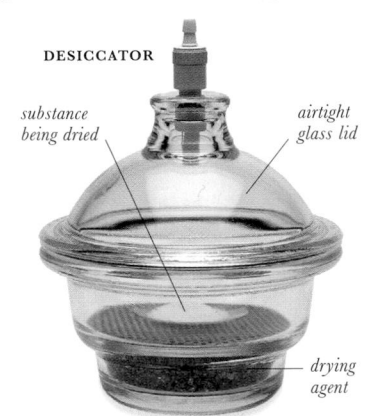

DESICCATOR

substance being dried

airtight glass lid

drying agent

de·sid·er·a·tum /disídəráytəm, -ráatəm/ *n.* (*pl.* **desiderata** /-tə/) something lacking but needed or desired.

de·sign /dizín/ *n. & v.* ● *n.* **1 a** a preliminary plan or sketch for making something. **b** the art of producing these. **2** a scheme of lines or shapes forming a pattern or decoration. **3** a plan, purpose, or intention. **4 a** the general arrangement or layout of a product. **b** an established version of a product (*our most popular designs*). ● *v.* **1** *tr.* produce a design for (a thing). **2** *tr.* intend, plan, or purpose (*designed to offend*). **3** *absol.* be a designer. □ **by design** on purpose. **have designs on** plan to harm or appropriate.

des·ig·nate *v. & adj.* ● *v.tr.* /dézignayt/ **1** (often foll. by *as*) appoint to an office or function (*designated him as postmaster general*). **2** specify (*at designated times*). **3** (often foll. by *as*) describe as; entitle; style. **4** serve as the name or distinctive mark of (*English uses French words to designate ballet steps*). ● *adj.* /dézignət/ (placed after noun) appointed to an office but not yet installed (*bishop designate*). □□ **des·ig·na·tor** *n.*

des·ig·nat·ed driv·er *n.* one member of a group who abstains from alcohol in order to drive the others safely.

des·ig·nat·ed hit·ter *n. Baseball* a batter in the lineup who hits for the pitcher. ¶ Abbr.: **DH**.

des·ig·na·tion /dézignáyshən/ *n.* **1** a name, description, or title. **2** the act or process of designating.

de·sign·ed·ly /dizínidlee/ *adv.* by design; on purpose.

de·sign·er /dizínər/ *n.* **1** a person who makes artistic designs or plans for construction, e.g., for clothing, theater sets. **2** (*attrib.*) (of clothing, etc.) bearing the name or label of a famous designer.

de·sign·er drug *n.* a synthetic analog, not itself illegal, of an illegal drug.

de·sign·ing /dizíning/ *adj.* crafty, artful, or scheming. □□ **de·sign·ing·ly** *adv.*

de·sir·a·ble /dizírəbəl/ *adj.* **1** worth having or wishing for (*it is desirable that nobody should smoke*). **2** arousing sexual desire. □□ **de·sir·a·bil·i·ty** *n.* **de·sir·a·ble·ness** *n.* **de·sir·a·bly** *adv.*

de·sire /dizír/ *n. & v.* ● *n.* **1 a** an unsatisfied longing or craving (*expressed a desire to rest*). **2** lust. **3** something desired (*her heart's desire*). ● *v.tr.* **1** (often foll. by *to* + infin., or *that* + clause) long for; crave. **2** request.

de·sir·ous /dizírəs/ *predic.adj.* **1** (usu. foll. by *of*) ambitious; desiring (*desirous of stardom*). **2** (usu. foll. by *to* + infin., or *that* + clause) hoping (*desirous to do the right thing*).

de·sist /dizíst/ *v.intr.* (often foll. by *from*) *literary* abstain; cease.

desk /desk/ *n.* **1** a piece of furniture with a flat or sloped surface for writing on, and often drawers. **2** a counter which separates the customer from the assistant. **3** a section of a newspaper office, etc., dealing with a specified topic (*the sports desk*). **4** *Mus.* a music stand in an orchestra regarded as a unit of two players.

desk·top /désktop/ *n.* **1 a** the working surface of a desk. **b** the working area for manipulating windows, icons, etc., in some computer software environments. **2** (*attrib.*) (esp. of a microcomputer) suitable for use at an ordinary desk.

desk·top pub·lish·ing *n.* the production of printed matter with a desktop computer and printer.

des·o·late *adj. & v.* ● *adj.* /désələt/ **1** left alone; solitary. **2** (of a building or place) uninhabited; neglected; barren; dreary; empty (*a desolate beach*). **3** forlorn; wretched (*was left desolate and weeping*). ● *v.tr.* /désəlayt/ **1** depopulate or devastate; lay waste to. **2** (esp. as **desolated** *adj.*) make forlorn (*desolated by grief*). □□ **des·o·late·ly** /-lətlee/ *adv.* **des·o·late·ness** *n.* **des·o·la·tion** /désəláyshən/ *n.*

de·spair /dispáir/ *n. & v.* ● *n.* the complete loss or absence of hope. ● *v.intr.* **1** (foll. by *of*) lose or be without hope. **2** (foll. by *of*) lose hope about (*his life is despaired of*). □ **be the despair of** be the cause of despair by badness or unapproachable excellence (*he's the despair of his parents*). □□ **de·spair·ing·ly** *adv.*

des·patch var. of DISPATCH.

des·per·a·do /déspəraadō/ *n.* (*pl.* **-oes** or **-os**) a desperate or reckless person, esp. a criminal.

des·per·ate /déspərət, -prit/ *adj.* **1** reckless from despair. **2 a** extremely dangerous or serious (*a desperate situation*). **b** staking all on a small chance (*a desperate remedy*). **3** very bad (*desperate poverty*). **4** (usu. foll. by *for*) needing or desiring very much (*desperate for recognition*). □□ **des·per·ate·ly** *adv.* **des·per·ate·ness** *n.* **des·per·a·tion** /-ráyshən/ *n.*

des·pi·ca·ble /déspikəbəl, dispík-/ *adj.* vile; contemptible, esp. morally. □□ **des·pi·ca·bly** *adv.*

de·spise /dispíz/ *v.tr.* look down on as inferior, worthless, or contemptible. □□ **de·spis·er** *n.*

de·spite /dispít/ *prep.* in spite of.

de·spoil /dispóyl/ *v.tr. literary* (often foll. by *of*) plunder; deprive. □□ **de·spoil·ment** *n.* **de·spo·li·a·tion** /dispóleeáyshən/ *n.*

de·spond /dispónd/ *v. & n.* ● *v.intr.* lose heart or hope; be dejected. ● *n. archaic* despondency.

de·spond·ent /dispóndənt/ *adj.* in low spirits; dejected. □□ **de·spond·ence** /-dəns/ *n.* **de·spond·en·cy** *n.* **de·spond·ent·ly** *adv.*

des·pot /déspət/ *n.* **1** an absolute ruler. **2** a tyrant. □□ **des·pot·ic** /-spótik/ *adj.* **des·pot·i·cal·ly** *adv.* **des·pot·ism** /déspətizəm/ *n.*

des·sert /dizárt/ *n.* the sweet course of a meal, served at or near the end.

des·sert·spoon /dizártspoon/ *n.* **1** a spoon used for dessert, smaller than a tablespoon and larger than a teaspoon. **2** the amount held by this. □□ **des·sert·spoon·ful** *n.* (*pl.* **-fuls**)

de·sta·bi·lize /deestáybiliz/ *v.tr.* **1** render unstable. **2** subvert (esp. a foreign government). □□ **de·sta·bi·li·za·tion** *n.*

des·ti·na·tion /déstináyshən/ *n.* a place to which a person or thing is going.

des·tine /déstin/ *v.tr.* (often foll. by *to, for,* or *to* + infin.) appoint; preordain; intend. □ **be destined to** be fated to.

des·ti·ny /déstinee/ *n.* (*pl.* **-ies**) **1 a** fate. **b** this regarded as a power. **2** what is destined to happen to a particular person, etc. (*it was their destiny*).

des·ti·tute /déstitoot, -tyoot/ *adj.* **1** without food, shelter, etc.; completely impoverished. **2** (usu. foll. by *of*) lacking. □□ **des·ti·tu·tion** /-tooshən, -tyoo-/ *n.*

de·stroy /distróy/ *v.tr.* **1** pull or break down. **2** end the existence of (*destroyed her confidence*). **3** kill (esp. a sick or savage animal). **4** make useless. **5** ruin

financially, professionally, or in reputation. **6** defeat (*destroyed the enemy*).

de·stroy·er /distróyər/ *n.* **1** a person or thing that destroys. **2** *Naut.* a fast warship with guns and torpedoes used to protect other ships.

de·struct /distrúkt/ *v. & n.* esp. *Astronaut.* ● *v.* **1** *tr.* destroy (one's own rocket, etc.) deliberately, esp. for safety reasons. **2** *intr.* be destroyed in this way. ● *n.* an act of destructing.

de·struc·ti·ble /distrúktibəl/ *adj.* able to be destroyed.

de·struc·tion /distrúkshən/ *n.* **1** the act or an instance of destroying; the process or being destroyed. **2** a cause of ruin (*greed was their destruction*).

de·struc·tive /distrúktiv/ *adj.* **1** (often foll. by *to, of*) destroying or tending to destroy (*a destructive child*). **2** negative in attitude or criticism. □□ **de·struc·tive·ly** *adv.* **de·struc·tive·ness** *n.*

des·ue·tude /déswitood, -tyood/ *n.* a state of disuse.

des·ul·to·ry /désəltawree, déz-/ *adj.* **1** going constantly from one subject to another, esp. in a half-hearted way. **2** disconnected; unmethodical; superficial. □□ **des·ul·to·ri·ly** *adv.* **des·ul·to·ri·ness** *n.*

de·tach /ditách/ *v.tr.* **1** (often foll. by *from*) unfasten or disengage and remove. **2** *Mil.* send (a ship, officer, etc.) on a separate mission. **3** (as **detached** *adj.*) **a** impartial; unemotional (*a detached viewpoint*). **b** (esp. of a house) not joined to another or others. □□ **de·tach·a·ble** *adj.* **de·tach·ed·ly** /ditáchidlee/ *adv.*

de·tach·ment /ditáchmənt/ *n.* **1 a** a state of aloofness or indifference. **b** disinterested independence of judgment. **2 a** the act or process of detaching or being detached. **b** an instance of this. **3** *Mil.* a separate group or unit used for a specific purpose.

de·tail /ditáyl, déetayl/ *n. & v.* ● *n.* **1 a** a small or subordinate particular. **b** such a particular, considered (ironically) to be unimportant (*the truth of the statement is just a detail*). **2 a** small items or particulars regarded collectively (*has an eye for detail*). **b** the treatment of them (*the detail was insufficient and unconvincing*). **3** (often in *pl.*) a number of particulars (*filled in the details*). **4 a** a minor decoration on a building, in a picture, etc. **b** a small part of a picture, etc., shown alone. **5** *Mil.* **a** the distribution of orders for the day. **b** a small detachment of soldiers, etc., for special duty. ● *v.tr.* **1** give particulars of. **2** relate circumstantially. **3** *Mil.* assign for special duty. **4** (as **detailed** *adj.*) **a** (of a picture, story, etc.) having many details. **b** itemized (*a detailed list*). □ **go into detail** give all the items or particulars. **in detail** minutely.

de·tain /ditáyn/ *v.tr.* **1** keep in confinement or under restraint. **2** delay. □□ **de·tain·ment** *n.*

de·tain·ee /déetaynée/ *n.* a person detained in custody.

de·tect /ditékt/ *v.tr.* **1 a** (often foll. by *in*) reveal the guilt of. **b** discover (a crime). **2** perceive the existence of (*detected a smell of burning*). **3** *Physics* use an instrument to observe (a signal, radiation, etc.). □□ **de·tect·a·ble** *adj.* **de·tec·tor** *n.*

de·tec·tion /ditékshən/ *n.* **1** the act or an instance of detecting; the process or an instance of being detected. **2** the work of a detective.

de·tec·tive /ditéktiv/ *n. & adj.* ● *n.* (often *attrib.*) a person, esp. a member of a police force, employed to investigate crime. ● *adj.* serving to detect.

dé·tente /daytónt/ *n.* an easing of strained relations, esp. between nations.

de·ten·tion /diténshən/ *n.* **1** detaining or being detained. **2 a** being kept in school after hours as a punishment. **b** an instance of this. **3** custody; confinement.

de·ter /ditór/ *v.tr.* (**deterred, deterring**) **1** (often foll. by *from*) discourage or prevent (a person) through fear or dislike of the consequences. **2** check or prevent (a thing, process, etc.).

de·ter·gent /ditórjənt/ *n. & adj.* ● *n.* a cleansing agent, esp. a synthetic substance (usu. other than soap) used with water as a means of removing dirt, etc. • *adj.* cleansing, esp. in the manner of a detergent.

de·te·ri·o·rate /diteéreeərayt/ *v.tr. & intr.* make or become bad or worse. □□ **de·te·ri·o·ra·tion** /-ráyshən/ *n.* **de·te·ri·o·ra·tive** *adj.*

de·ter·mi·nant /ditə́rminənt/ *adj. & n.* • *adj.* serving to determine or define. • *n.* **1** a determining factor, element, word, etc. **2** *Math.* a quantity obtained by the addition of products of the elements of a square matrix according to a given rule.

de·ter·mi·nate /ditə́rminət/ *adj.* **1** limited in time, space, or character. **2** of definite scope or nature. □□ **de·ter·mi·na·cy** /-nəsee/ *n.* **de·ter·mi·nate·ly** *adv.*

de·ter·mi·na·tion /ditərmináyshən/ *n.* **1** firmness of purpose; resoluteness. **2** the process of deciding, determining, or calculating. **3 a** the conclusion of a dispute by the decision of an arbitrator. **b** the decision reached.

de·ter·mine /ditə́rmin/ *v.* **1** *tr.* find out or establish precisely. **2** *tr.* decide or settle. **3** *tr.* be a decisive factor in regard to. **4** *intr. & tr.* make or cause (a person) to make a decision (*what determined you to do it?*). □ **be determined** be resolved (*was determined not to give up*). □□ **de·ter·mi·na·ble** *adj.*

de·ter·mined /ditə́rmind/ *adj.* **1** showing determination. **2** fixed in scope or character; settled; determinate. □□ **de·ter·mined·ly** *adv.* **de·ter·mined·ness** *n.*

de·ter·min·er /ditə́rminər/ *n.* **1** a person or thing that determines. **2** *Gram.* any of a class of words (e.g., *a, the, every*) that determine the kind of reference a noun or noun substitute has.

de·ter·min·ism /ditə́rminizəm/ *n. Philos.* the doctrine that all events, including human action, are determined by causes regarded as external to the will. □□ **de·ter·min·ist** *n.* **de·ter·min·is·tic** *adj.*

de·ter·rent /ditə́rənt, -túr-/ *adj. & n.* • *adj.* that deters. • *n.* a deterrent thing or factor. □□ **de·ter·rence** /-rəns/ *n.*

de·test /ditést/ *v.tr.* hate; loathe. □□ **de·tes·ta·tion** /déetestáyshən/ *n.*

de·test·a·ble /ditéstəbəl/ *adj.* intensely disliked; hateful. □□ **de·test·a·bly** *adv.*

de·throne /deethrṓn/ *v.tr.* **1** remove from the throne; depose. **2** remove from a position of authority. □□ **de·throne·ment** *n.*

det·o·nate /dét'nayt/ *v.intr. & tr.* explode with a loud noise. □□ **det·o·na·tion** /dét'náyshən/ *n.* **det·o·na·tive** *adj.*

det·o·na·tor /dét'naytər/ *n.* **1** a device for detonating an explosive. **2** a fog signal that detonates, e.g., as used on railroads.

de·tour /déetŏŏr, ditŏŏr/ *n. & v.* • *n.* a divergence from a direct or intended route. • *v.intr. & tr.* make or cause to make a detour.

de·tox·i·fy /deetóksifī/ *v.tr.* remove the poison from. □□ **de·tox·i·fi·ca·tion** /-fikáyshən/ *n.*

de·tract /ditrákt/ *v.tr.* (usu. foll. by *from*) take away (a part of something); reduce; diminish. □□ **de·trac·tion** /-trákshən/ *n.* **de·trac·tor** *n.*

det·ri·ment /détrimənt/ *n.* **1** harm; damage. **2** something causing this. □□ **det·ri·men·tal** /détrimént'l/ *adj.* **det·ri·men·tal·ly** *adv.*

de·tri·tus /ditrī́təs/ *n.* **1** matter produced by erosion. **2** debris. □□ **de·tri·tal** /ditrī́t'l/ *adj.*

deuce[1] /dōōs, dyōōs/ *n.* **1** the two on dice or playing cards. **2** (in tennis) the score of 40 all, at which two consecutive points are needed to win.

deuce[2] /dōōs, dyōōs/ *n.* the Devil, used esp. *colloq.* as an exclamation of surprise or annoyance (*who the deuce are you?*). □ **a** (or **the**) **deuce of a** very bad or remarkable (*a deuce of a problem; a deuce of a fellow*). **the deuce to pay** trouble to be expected.

de·us ex ma·chi·na /dáyəs eks máakinə, mák-/ *n.* an unexpected power or event saving a seemingly hopeless situation, esp. in a play or novel.

deu·ter·ag·o·nist /dŏŏtərágənist, dyŏŏ-/ *n.* the person second in importance to the protagonist in a drama.

deu·te·ri·um /dōōteéreeəm, dyōō-/ *n. Chem.* a stable isotope of hydrogen with a mass about double that of the usual isotope.

deu·ter·on /dŏŏtəron, dyŏŏ-/ *n. Physics* the nucleus of a deuterium atom, consisting of a proton and a neutron.

Deutsch·mark /dóych, dóychə/ *n.* (also **Deutsche·mark**) (until the introduction of the euro in 2002) the chief monetary unit of Germany.

de·val·ue /deeványōō/ *v.tr.* (**devalues, devalued, devaluing**) **1** reduce the value of. **2** *Econ.* reduce the value of (a currency) in relation to other currencies or to gold (opp. REVALUE). □□ **de·val·u·a·tion** *n.*

dev·as·tate /dévəstayt/ *v.tr.* **1** cause great destruction to. **2** (often in *passive*) overwhelm with shock or grief. □□ **dev·as·ta·tion** /-táyshən/ *n.* **dev·as·ta·tor** *n.*

dev·as·tat·ing /dévəstayting/ *adj.* **1** crushingly effective; overwhelming. **2** *colloq.* **a** incisive; savage (*devastating accuracy*). **b** extremely impressive or attractive. □□ **dev·as·tat·ing·ly** *adv.*

de·vel·op /divéləp/ *v.* (**developed, developing**) **1** *tr. & intr.* **a** make or become bigger or fuller or more elaborate or systematic. **b** bring or come to an active or visible state or to maturity. **2 a** *tr.* begin to suffer from (*developed a rattle*). **b** *intr.* come into existence (*a fault developed in the engine*). **3** *tr.* **a** construct on (land). **b** convert (land) to a new purpose. **4** *tr.* treat (photographic film, etc.) to make the image visible. □□ **de·vel·op·a·ble** /divéləpəbəl/ *adj.* **de·vel·op·er** *n.*

de·vel·op·ing coun·try *n.* a poor or undeveloped country that is becoming more advanced.

de·vel·op·ment /divéləpmənt/ *n.* **1** the act or an instance of developing; the process of being developed. **2 a** a stage of growth or advancement. **b** a thing that has developed (*the latest developments*). **3** a full-grown state. **4** the process of developing a photograph. **5** a developed area of land.

de·vel·op·men·tal /divéləpmént'l/ *adj.* **1** incidental to growth (*developmental diseases*). **2** evolutionary. □□ **de·vel·op·men·tal·ly** *adv.*

de·vi·ant /déeveeənt/ *adj. & n.* • *adj.* that deviates from the normal. • *n.* a deviant person or thing. □□ **de·vi·ance** /-veeəns/ *n.* **de·vi·an·cy** *n.*

de·vi·ate *v. & n.* • *v.intr.* /déeveeayt/ (often foll. by *from*) turn aside or diverge (from a course of action, truth, etc.); digress. • *n.* /déeveeət/ a deviant, esp. a sexual pervert. □□ **de·vi·a·tor** *n.* **de·vi·a·to·ry** /-veeətáwree/ *adj.*

de·vi·a·tion /déeveeáyshən/ *n.* **1 a** deviating; digressing. **b** an instance of this. **2** *Polit.* a departure from accepted (esp. Communist) party doctrine. **3** *Statistics* the amount by which a single measurement differs from the mean.

de·vice /divī́s/ *n.* **1 a** a thing made or adapted for a particular purpose. **b** an explosive contrivance. **2** a plan, scheme, or trick. **3 a** an emblematic or heraldic design. **b** a drawing or design. □ **leave a person to his** or **her own devices** leave a person to do as he or she wishes.

dev·il /dévəl/ *n. & v.* • *n.* **1** (usu. **the Devil**) (in Christian and Jewish belief) the supreme spirit of evil; Satan. **2 a** an evil spirit; a demon. **b** a personified evil force or attribute. **3 a** a wicked or cruel person. **b** a mischievously energetic, clever, or self-willed person. **4** *colloq.* a person; a fellow (*lucky devil*). **5** fighting spirit; mischievousness (*the devil is in him tonight*). **6** *colloq.* something awkward (*this door is a devil to open*). **7** (**the devil** or **the Devil**) *colloq.* used as an exclamation of surprise or annoyance (*who the devil are you?*). **8** a literary hack exploited by an employer. **9** = TASMANIAN DEVIL. **10** applied to various instruments and machines, esp. when used for destructive work. • *v.* (**deviled, deviling; devilled, devilling**) **1** *tr.* cook (food) with hot seasoning. **2** *tr.* harass; worry. □ **between the devil and the deep blue sea** in a dilemma. **a devil of** *colloq.* considerable, difficult, or remarkable. **devil take the hindmost** a motto of selfish competition. **the devil to pay** trouble to be expected. **go to the devil 1** be damned. **2** (in *imper.*) depart at once. **like the devil** with great energy. **play the devil with** cause severe damage to. **speak** (or **talk**) **of the devil** said when a person appears just after being mentioned. **the very devil** (*predic.*) *colloq.* a great difficulty or nuisance.

dev·il·ish /dévəlish/ *adj. & adv.* • *adj.* **1** of or like a devil; wicked. **2** mischievous. • *adv. colloq.* very; extremely. □□ **dev·il·ish·ly** *adv.* **dev·il·ish·ness** *n.*

dev·il-may-care *adj.* cheerful and reckless.

dev·il·ment /dévəlmənt/ *n.* mischief; wild spirits.

dev·il·ry /dévilree/ *n.* (also **dev·il·try** /-tree/) (*pl.* **-ies**) **1 a** reckless mischief. **b** an instance of this. **2 a** black magic. **b** the Devil and his works.

dev·il's ad·vo·cate *n.* a person who tests a proposition by arguing against it.

de·vi·ous /déeveeəs/ *adj.* **1** (of a person, etc.) not straightforward. **2** circuitous. **3** erring. □□ **de·vi·ous·ly** *adv.* **de·vi·ous·ness** *n.*

de·vise /divī́z/ *v. & n.* • *v.tr.* **1** plan or invent by careful thought. **2** *Law* leave (real estate) by will (cf. BEQUEATH). • *n.* **1** the act or an instance of devising. **2** *Law* a devising clause in a will. □□ **de·vis·a·ble** *adj.* **de·vi·see** /-zée/ *n.* (in sense 2 of *v.*). **de·vis·er** *n.* **de·vi·sor** *n.* (in sense 2 of *v.*).

de·vi·tal·ize /deevī́t'līz/ *v.tr.* take away strength and vigor from. □□ **de·vi·tal·i·za·tion** *n.*

de·void /divóyd/ *predic.adj.* (foll. by *of*) quite lacking or free from.

dev·o·lu·tion /déevəlóoshən/ *n.* **1** the delegation of power, esp. by central government to local or regional administration. **2 a** descent or passing on through a series of stages. **b** descent by natural or due succession from one to another of property or qualities. **3** the lapse of an unexercised right to an ultimate owner. □□ **dev·o·lu·tion·ar·y** *adj.* **dev·o·lu·tion·ist** *n.*

de·volve /divólv/ *v.* **1** (foll. by *on, upon*, etc.) **a** *tr.* pass (work or duties) to (a deputy, etc.). **b** *intr.* (of work or duties) pass to (a deputy, etc.). **2** *intr.* (foll. by *on, to, upon*) *Law* (of property, etc.) fall by succession to. □□ **de·volve·ment** *n.*

De·vo·ni·an /divṓneeən/ *adj. & n.* • *adj.* **1** of or relating to Devon in SW England. **2** *Geol.* of or relating to the fourth period of the Paleozoic era. • *n.* **1** this period or system. **2** a native of Devon.

de·vote /divṓt/ *v.tr. & refl.* (foll. by *to*) apply or give over to (a particular activity or purpose or person).

de·vot·ed /divṓtid/ *adj.* very loving or loyal. □□ **de·vot·ed·ly** *adv.* **de·vot·ed·ness** *n.*

dev·o·tee /dévətée, -táy/ *n.* **1** (usu. foll. by *of*) a zealous enthusiast or supporter. **2** a zealously pious person.

de·vo·tion /divṓshən/ *n.* **1** (usu. foll. by *to*) enthusiastic attachment or loyalty (to a person or cause); great love. **2 a** religious worship. **b** (in *pl.*) prayers. **c** devoutness; religious fervor. □□ **de·vo·tion·al** *adj.*

de·vour /divówr/ *v.tr.* **1** eat hungrily or greedily. **2** (of fire, etc.) engulf; destroy. **3** take in greedily with the eyes or ears. **4** absorb the attention of.

de·vout /divówt/ *adj.* **1** earnestly religious. **2** earnestly sincere (*devout hope*). □□ **de·vout·ly** *adv.* **de·vout·ness** *n.*

dew /dōō, dyōō/ *n. & v.* • *n.* **1** atmospheric vapor condensing in small drops on cool surfaces at night. **2** glistening moisture resembling this. **3** freshness; refreshing quality. • *v.tr.* wet with or as with dew. □□ **dew·y** /dŏŏ-ee, dyŏŏ-ee/ *adj.* (**dewier, dewiest**).

dew·ber·ry /dŏŏberee, dyŏŏ-/ *n.* (*pl.* **-ies**) **1** a bluish fruit like the blackberry. **2** the shrub, *Rubus caesius*, bearing this.

dew·claw /dŏŏklaw, dyŏŏ-/ *n.* **1** a rudimentary inner toe found on some dogs. **2** a false hoof on a deer, etc.

dew·drop /dŏŏdrop, dyŏŏ-/ *n.* a drop of dew.

Dew·ey sys·tem /dŏŏ-ee, dyŏŏ-ee/ *n.* a decimal system of library classification.

dew·fall /dŏŏfawl, dyŏŏ-/ *n.* **1** the time when dew begins to form. **2** the formation of dew.

dew·lap /dŏŏlap, dyŏŏ-/ *n.* **1** ◄ a loose fold of skin hanging from the throat of cattle, dogs, etc. **2** similar loose skin around the throat of an elderly person.

dew point *n.* the temperature at which dew forms.

dex·ter /dékstər/ *adj.* esp. *Heraldry* on or of the right-hand side (the observer's left) of a shield, etc.

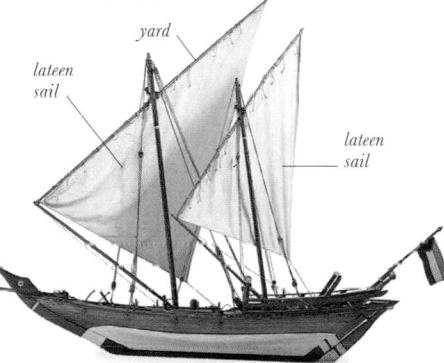

DEWLAP OF A HEREFORD BULL

dewlap

dex·ter·i·ty /dekstéritee/ *n.* **1** skill in handling. **2** manual or mental adroitness. **3** right-handedness.

dex·ter·ous /dékstrəs, -stərəs/ *adj.* (also **dex·trous** /-strəs/) having or showing dexterity. □□ **dex·ter·ous·ly** *adv.* **dex·ter·ous·ness** *n.*

dex·trose /dékstrōs/ *n. Chem.* a form of glucose.

dex·trous var. of DEXTEROUS.

DFC *abbr.* Distinguished Flying Cross.

DH *abbr. Baseball* designated hitter.

dhal var. of DAL.

dho·ti /dṓtee/ *n.* (*pl.* **dhotis**) the loincloth worn by male Hindus.

dhow /dow/ *n.* ▼ a lateen-rigged ship used esp. on the Arabian Sea.

yard

lateen sail

lateen sail

DHOW: PEARLING DHOW FROM KUWAIT

di- /dī/ *comb. form* **1** twice, two-, double. **2** *Chem.* containing two atoms, molecules, or groups of a specified kind (*dichromate*; *dioxide*).

dia. *abbr.* diameter.

dia- /dī́ə/ *prefix* (also **di-** before a vowel) **1** through (*diaphanous*). **2** apart (*diacritical*). **3** across (*diameter*).

di·a·be·tes /dī́əbeétis, -teez/ *n.* **1** any disorder of the metabolism with excessive thirst and the production of large amounts of urine. **2** (in full **diabetes mellitus**) the commonest form of diabetes in which sugar and starch are not properly metabolized.

di·a·bet·ic /dī́əbétik/ *adj. & n.* ● *adj.* **1** of or relating to or having diabetes. **2** for use by diabetics. ● *n.* a person suffering from diabetes.

di·a·ble·rie /dee-aáblôree, -áblə-/ *n.* **1** the devil's work; sorcery. **2** wild recklessness.

di·a·bol·ic /dī́əbólik/ *adj.* (also **di·a·bol·i·cal** /-bólikəl/) **1** of the Devil. **2** devilish; inhumanly cruel or wicked. **3** fiendishly clever or cunning or annoying. **4** *colloq.* disgracefully bad; outrageous. □□ **di·a·bol·i·cal·ly** *adv.*

di·a·bol·ism /dī́ábəlizəm/ *n.* **1 a** belief in or worship of the Devil. **b** sorcery. **2** devilish conduct or character.

di·a·chron·ic /dī́əkrónik/ *adj. Linguistics*, etc. concerned with the historical development of a subject (opp. SYNCHRONIC). □□ **di·a·chron·i·cal·ly** *adv.* **di·a·chron·ism** /dī́ákrənizəm/ *n.* **di·a·chron·ous** /dī́ákrənəs/ *adj.* **di·ach·ro·ny** /dī́ákrənee/ *n.*

di·a·co·nal /dī́ákənəl/ *adj.* of a deacon.

di·a·co·nate /dī́ákənayt, -nət/ *n.* **1 a** the office of deacon. **b** a person's time as deacon. **2** a body of deacons.

di·a·crit·ic /dī́əkrítik/ *n. & adj.* ● *n.* a sign used to indicate different sounds or values of a letter. ● *adj.* = DIACRITICAL.

di·a·crit·i·cal /dī́əkrítikəl/ *adj. & n.* ● *adj.* distinguishing; distinctive. ● *n.* (in full **diacritical mark** or **sign**) = DIACRITIC *n.*

di·a·dem /dī́ədəm/ *n. & v.* ● *n.* **1** a crown or headband worn as a sign of sovereignty. **2** a wreath of leaves or flowers worn around the head. **3** sovereignty. **4** a crowning distinction or glory. ● *v.tr.* (esp. as **diademed** *adj.*) adorn with or as with a diadem.

di·aer·e·sis /dī-érəsis/ *n.* (also **di·er·e·sis**) (*pl.* **-ses** /-seez/) a mark (as in *naïve*) over a vowel to indicate that it is sounded separately.

di·ag·nose /dī́əgnōs, -nōz/ *v.tr.* make a diagnosis of (a disease, a mechanical fault, etc.). □□ **di·ag·nos·a·ble** *adj.*

di·ag·no·sis /dī́əgnṓsis/ *n.* (*pl.* **diagnoses** /-seez/) **1 a** the identification of a disease by means of a patient's symptoms. **b** an instance or formal statement of this. **2 a** the identification of the cause of a mechanical fault, etc. **b** an instance of this. **3 a** the distinctive characterization in precise terms of a genus, species, etc. **b** an instance of this.

di·ag·nos·tic /dī́əgnóstik/ *adj. & n.* ● *adj.* of or assisting diagnosis. ● *n.* a symptom. □□ **di·ag·nos·ti·cal·ly** *adv.* **di·ag·nos·ti·cian** /-nostíshən/ *n.*

di·ag·nos·tics /dī́əgnóstiks/ *n.* **1** (treated as *pl.*) *Computing* mechanisms used to identify faults in hardware or software. **2** (treated as *sing.*) the science of diagnosing disease.

di·ag·o·nal /dī́ágənəl/ *adj. & n.* ● *adj.* **1** crossing a straight-sided figure from corner to corner. **2** slanting; oblique. ● *n.* a straight line joining two nonadjacent corners. □□ **di·ag·o·nal·ly** *adv.*

di·a·gram /dī́əgram/ *n. & v.* ● *n.* **1** a drawing showing the general scheme or outline of an object and its parts. **2** a graphic representation of the course or results of an action or process. ● *v.tr.* (**diagramed**, **diagraming** or **diagrammed**, **diagramming**) represent by means of a diagram.

di·a·gram·mat·ic /-grəmátik/ *adj.* **di·a·gram·mat·i·cal·ly** *adv.*

di·al /dī́əl/ *n. & v.* ● *n.* **1** the face of a clock or watch. **2** a plate with a scale for measuring weight, volume, etc., indicated by a pointer. **3** a movable disk on a telephone, with finger holes and numbers for making a connection. **4 a** a plate or disk, etc., on a radio or television set for selecting wavelength or channel. **b** a similar selecting device on other equipment. ● *v.* **1** *tr.* (also *absol.*) select (a telephone number) by means of a dial or set of buttons (*dialed 911*). **2** *tr.* measure, indicate, or regulate by means of a dial. □□ **di·al·er** *n.*

di·a·lect /dī́əlekt/ *n.* **1** a form of speech peculiar to a particular region. **2** a subordinate variety of a language with nonstandard vocabulary, pronunciation, or grammar. □□ **di·a·lec·tal** /-lékt'l/ *adj.* **di·a·lec·tol·o·gy** /-tóləjee/ *n.* **di·a·lec·tol·o·gist** /-tóləjist/ *n.*

di·a·lec·tic /dī́əléktik/ *n. & adj.* ● *n.* **1** (often in *pl.*) **a** the art of investigating the truth of opinions; the testing of truth by discussion. **b** logical disputation. **2** *Philos.* **a** inquiry into metaphysical contradictions and their solutions, esp. in the thought of Kant and Hegel. **b** the existence or action of opposing social forces, etc. ● *adj.* **1** of or relating to logical disputation. **2** fond of or skilled in logical disputation.

di·a·lec·ti·cal /dī́əléktikəl/ *adj.* of dialectic or dialectics. □□ **di·a·lec·ti·cal·ly** *adv.*

di·a·lec·ti·cian /dī́əlektíshən/ *n.* a person skilled in dialectic.

di·a·lec·tics /dī́əléktiks/ *n.* (treated as *sing.* or *pl.*) = DIALECTIC *n.*

di·a·logue /dī́əlawg, -log/ *n.* (also **di·a·log**) **1 a** conversation. **b** conversation in written form. **2 a** a discussion, esp. one between representatives of two groups. **b** a conversation; a talk (*long dialogues between the two main characters*).

di·al tone *n.* a sound indicating that a caller may start to dial.

di·al·y·sis /dī́álisis/ *n.* (*pl.* **dialyses** /-seez/) **1** *Chem.* ▼ the separation of particles in a liquid by differences in their ability to pass through a membrane into another liquid. **2** *Med.* ▼ the clinical purification of blood by this technique.

DIALYSIS

Dialysis is often used in cases of kidney failure to remove waste products from blood by diffusion through a semipermeable membrane. Smaller waste product molecules pass through the membrane into a solution, called dialysate, for disposal; larger molecules, such as those of red blood cells and proteins, are retained. In hemodialysis, blood from an artery passes through a coiled tube and back into a vein.

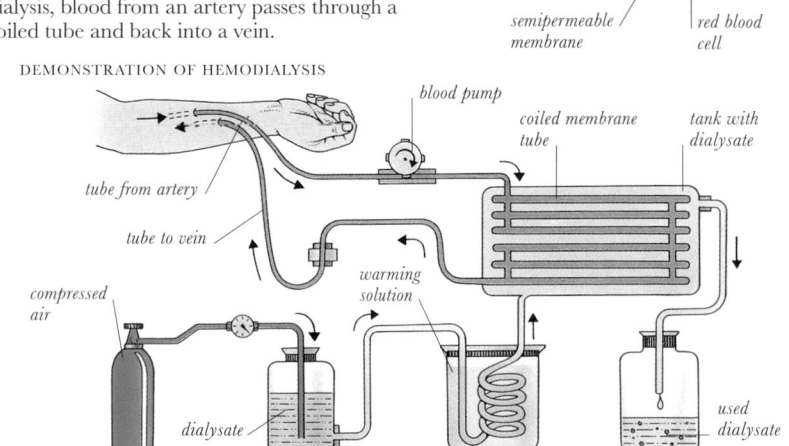

FILTERING ACTION OF A SEMIPERMEABLE MEMBRANE

dialysate

waste products

semipermeable membrane

red blood cell

DEMONSTRATION OF HEMODIALYSIS

blood pump

coiled membrane tube

tank with dialysate

tube from artery

tube to vein

warming solution

compressed air

dialysate

used dialysate

D

D

di·a·lyze /díəlīz/ *v.tr.* separate by means of dialysis.

di·a·man·té /deeəmontáy/ *adj. & n.* ● *adj.* decorated with powdered crystal or another sparkling substance. ● *n.* fabric or costume jewelry so decorated.

di·am·e·ter /dīámitər/ *n.* **1 a** ▶ a straight line passing from side to side through the center of a circle or sphere. **b** the length of this line. **2** a transverse measurement; width; thickness. **3** a unit of linear measurement of magnifying power (*a lens magnifying 2000 diameters*).

DIAMETER

di·a·met·ri·cal /dīəmétrikəl/ *adj.* (also **di·a·met·ric**) **1** of or along a diameter. **2** (of opposition, difference, etc.) complete. □□ **di·a·met·ri·cal·ly** *adv.*

di·a·mond /dímənd, díə-/ *n., adj., & v.* ● *n.* **1** ◀ a precious stone of pure crystallized carbon, the hardest naturally occurring substance. ▷ ALLOTROPE, GEM. **2** a rhombus. **3 a** a playing card of a suit denoted by a red rhombus. **b** (in *pl.*) this suit. **4** a glittering particle or point (of frost, etc.). **5** a tool with a small diamond for cutting glass. **6** *Baseball* **a** the space delimited by the bases. **b** the entire field. ▷ BASEBALL. ● *adj.* **1** made of or set with diamonds or a diamond. **2** rhombus-shaped. ● *v.tr.* adorn with or as with diamonds.

DIAMOND

di·a·mond·back /díməndbak, díə-/ *n.* **1** an edible freshwater terrapin, *Malaclemys terrapin*, native to N. America, with diamond-shaped markings on its shell. **2** any rattlesnake of the genus *Crotalus*, native to N. America, with diamond-shaped markings. ▷ SNAKE.

di·a·mor·phine /dīəmáwrfeen/ *n. technical* heroin.

di·an·thus /dīánthəs/ *n.* any flowering plant of the genus *Dianthus*, e.g., a carnation or pink.

di·a·pa·son /díəpáyzən, -sən/ *n. Mus.* **1** the compass of a voice or musical instrument. **2** a fixed standard of musical pitch. **3** (in full **open** or **stopped diapason**) either of two main organ stops extending through the organ's whole compass. **4 a** a combination of notes or parts in a harmonious whole. **b** a melodious succession of notes, esp. a grand swelling burst of harmony. **5** an entire compass, range, or scope.

di·a·per /dípər, díəpər/ *n. & v.* ● *n.* **1** a piece of toweling or other absorbent material wrapped around a baby to retain urine and feces. **2 a** a linen or cotton fabric with a small diamond pattern. **b** this pattern. **3** a similar ornamental design of diamonds, etc., for panels, walls, etc. ● *v.tr.* decorate with a diaper pattern.

di·aph·a·nous /dīáfənəs/ *adj.* (of fabric, etc.) light and delicate, and almost transparent.

di·a·phragm /díəfram/ *n.* **1** a muscular partition separating the thorax from the abdomen in mammals. ▷ RESPIRATION. **2** a partition in animal and plant tissues. **3** a disk pierced by one or more holes in optical and acoustic systems, etc. ▷ RECEIVER. **4** a device for varying the effective aperture of the lens in a camera, etc. **5** a thin contraceptive cap fitting over the cervix. **6** a thin sheet of material used as a partition, etc. □□ **di·a·phrag·mat·ic** /-fragmátik/ *adj.*

di·ar·chy /díaarkee/ *n.* (also **dy·ar·chy**) (*pl.* **-ies**) **1** government by two independent authorities (esp. in India 1921–37). **2** an instance of this.

di·a·rist /díərist/ *n.* a person who keeps a diary.

di·a·rize /díərīz/ *v.* **1** *intr.* keep a diary. **2** *tr.* enter in a diary.

di·ar·rhe·a /díəreeə/ *n.* a condition of excessively frequent and loose bowel movements. □□ **di·ar·rhe·al** *adj.*

di·a·ry /díəree/ *n.* (*pl.* **-ies**) **1** a daily record of events or thoughts. **2** a book for this or for noting future engagements.

Di·as·po·ra /dīáspərə/ *n.* **1** (prec. by *the*) **a** the dispersion of the Jews among the Gentiles mainly in the 8th–6th c. BC. **b** Jews dispersed in this way. **2** (also **diaspora**) **a** any group of people similarly dispersed. **b** their dispersion.

di·as·to·le /dīástəlee/ *n. Physiol.* the period between two contractions of the heart when the heart muscle relaxes and allows the chambers to fill with blood (cf. SYSTOLE). □□ **di·as·tol·ic** /díəstólik/ *adj.*

di·a·ther·man·cy /díəthórmənsee/ *n.* the quality of transmitting radiant heat. □□ **di·a·therm·ic** *adj.* **di·a·ther·mous** *adj.*

di·a·ther·my /díəthərmee/ *n.* the application of high-frequency electric currents to produce heat in the deeper tissues of the body.

di·a·tom /díətom/ *n.* ▼ a unicellular alga found as plankton and forming fossil deposits. □□ **di·a·to·ma·ceous** /-máyshəs/ *adj.*

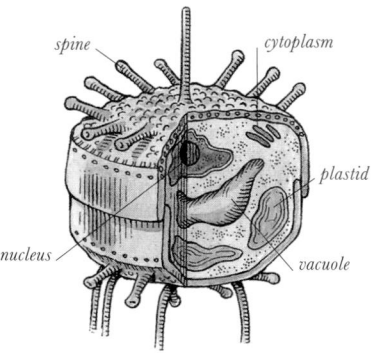

DIATOM (*Thalassiosira* species)

labels: spine, cytoplasm, plastid, nucleus, vacuole

di·a·tom·ic /díətómik/ *adj.* consisting of two atoms.

di·a·ton·ic /díətónik/ *adj. Mus.* **1** (of a scale, interval, etc.) involving only notes proper to the prevailing key without chromatic alteration. **2** (of a melody or harmony) constructed from such a scale.

di·a·tribe /díətrīb/ *n.* a forceful verbal attack.

di·az·e·pam /dīázipam/ *n.* a tranquilizing muscle-relaxant drug with anticonvulsant properties used to relieve anxiety, tension, etc.

dib·ble /díbəl/ *n. & v.* ● *n.* ▶ a hand tool for making holes in the ground for seeds or young plants. ● *v.* **1** *tr.* sow or plant with a dibble. **2** *tr.* prepare (soil) with a dibble. **3** *intr.* use a dibble.

DIBBLE

dibs /dibz/ *n.pl. sl.* rights; claim (*I have dibs on the last slice of pizza*).

dice /dīs/ *n. & v.* ● *n.pl.* **1 a** small cubes with faces bearing 1–6 spots used in games of chance. **b** (treated as *sing.*) one of these cubes (see DIE[2]). **2** a game played with one or more such cubes. **3** food cut into small cubes for cooking. ● *v.* **1 a** *intr.* play dice. **b** *intr.* take great risks; gamble (*dicing with death*). **c** *tr.* (foll. by *away*) gamble away. **2** *tr.* cut (food) into small cubes. **3** *tr.* mark with squares. □ **no dice** *sl.* no success or prospect of it.

dic·ey /dísee/ *adj.* (**dicier, diciest**) *sl.* risky; unreliable.

di·chot·o·my /dīkótəmee/ *n.* (*pl.* **-ies**) **1 a** a division into two, esp. a sharply defined one. **b** the result of such a division. **2** binary classification. **3** *Bot. & Zool.* repeated bifurcation. □□ **di·chot·o·mize** *v.* **di·chot·o·mous** *adj.*

di·chro·mat·ic /díkrōmátik/ *adj.* **1** two-colored. **2 a** (of animal species) having individuals that show different colorations. **b** having vision sensitive to only two of the three primary colors.

dick[1] /dik/ *n. coarse sl.* the penis. ¶ Usually considered a taboo word.

dick[2] /dik/ *n. sl.* a detective.

dick·ens /díkinz/ *n.* (usu. prec. by *how, what, why,* etc., *the*) *colloq.* (esp. in exclamations) deuce; the Devil (*what the dickens are you doing here?*).

Dick·en·si·an /dikénzeeən/ *adj. & n.* ● *adj.* **1** of or relating to Charles Dickens, Engl. novelist d. 1870, or his work. **2** resembling or reminiscent of the situations, poor social conditions, or comically repulsive characters described in Dickens's work. ● *n.* an admirer or student of Dickens or his work.

dick·er /díkər/ *v. & n.* ● *v.* **1 a** *intr.* bargain; haggle. **b** *tr.* barter; exchange. **2** *intr.* dither; hesitate. ● *n.* a deal; a barter.

dick·ey[1] /díkee/ *n.* (also **dick·y**) (*pl.* **-eys** or **-ies**) *colloq.* a false shirtfront.

dick·ey[2] /díkee/ *adj.* (**dickier, dickiest**) *sl.* unsound; likely to collapse or fail.

di·cot·y·le·don /díkot'leed'n/ *n.* any flowering plant having two cotyledons. ▷ ANGIOSPERM, COTYLEDON, FLOWER. □□ **di·cot·y·le·don·ous** *adj.*

dic·ta *pl.* of DICTUM.

Dic·ta·phone /díktəfōn/ *n. Trademark* a machine for recording and playing back dictated words.

dic·tate *v. & n.* ● *v.* /díktayt, diktáyt/ **1** *tr.* say or read aloud (words to be written down or recorded). **2 a** *tr.* prescribe or lay down authoritatively. **b** *intr.* give orders. ● *n.* /díktayt/ (usu. in *pl.*) an authoritative instruction (*dictates of conscience*).

dic·ta·tion /diktáyshən/ *n.* **1 a** the saying of words to be written down or recorded. **b** an instance of this. **c** the material that is dictated. **2 a** authoritative prescription. **b** an instance of this. **c** a command.

dic·ta·tor /díktaytər, diktáy-/ *n.* **1** a ruler with unrestricted authority. **2** a person with supreme authority in any sphere. **3** a domineering person. **4** a person who dictates for transcription.

dic·ta·to·ri·al /díktətáwreeəl/ *adj.* **1** of or like a dictator. **2** imperious; overbearing. □□ **dic·ta·to·ri·al·ly** *adv.*

dic·ta·tor·ship /diktáytərship/ *n.* **1** a nation ruled by a dictator. **2 a** the position, rule, or period of rule of a dictator. **b** rule by a dictator. **3** absolute authority in any sphere.

dic·tion /díkshən/ *n.* **1** the manner of enunciation in speaking or singing. **2** the choice of words or phrases.

dic·tion·ar·y /díkshəneree/ *n.* (*pl.* **-ies**) **1** a book that lists and explains the words of a language or gives equivalent words in another language. **2** a reference book on any subject, the items of which are arranged in alphabetical order.

dic·tum /díktəm/ *n.* (*pl.* **dicta** /-tə/ or **dictums**) **1** a formal utterance or pronouncement. **2** a saying or maxim.

dic·ty /díktee/ *adj. sl.* **1** conceited; snobbish. **2** elegant; stylish.

did *past of* DO[1].

di·dac·tic /dīdáktik/ *adj.* **1** meant to instruct. **2** (of a person) tediously pedantic. □□ **di·dac·ti·cal·ly** *adv.* **di·dac·ti·cism** /-tisizəm/ *n.*

did·dle /díd'l/ *v. colloq.* **1** *tr.* cheat; swindle. **2** *intr.* waste time.

did·dly /dídlee/ *n.* (also **did·dly squat**) *sl.* the slightest amount (*he hasn't done diddly to help us out*).

did·ger·i·doo /díjəreedó͞o/ *n.* (also **did·jer·i·doo**) ▶ an Australian Aboriginal musical wind instrument of long tubular shape.

DIDGERIDOO

did·n't /dídnt/ *contr.* did not.

die[1] /dī/ *v.* (**dies, died, dying** /dí-ing/) **1** *intr.* (often foll. by *of*) cease to live (*died of hunger*). **2** *intr.* **a** come to an end; fade away (*the project died within six months*). **b** cease to function (*the engine died*). **c** (of a flame) go out. **3** *intr.* (foll. by *on*) die or cease to function while in the presence or charge of (a person). **4** *intr.* (usu. foll. by *of, from, with*) be exhausted or tormented (*nearly died of boredom*). **5** *tr.* suffer (a specified death) (*died a natural death*). □ **be dying** (foll. by *for,* or *to* + infin.) wish for longingly or intently (*was dying for a drink; am dying to see you*). **die away** become weaker or fainter to the point of extinction. **die back** (of a plant) decay from the tip toward the root. **die down** become less loud or strong. **die hard** die reluctantly, not without a struggle (*old habits die hard*). **die off** die one after another. **die out** become extinct. **never say die** keep up courage, not give in.

die[2] /dī/ *n.* **1** *sing.* of DICE *n.* 1a. ¶ *Dice* is now standard in general use in this sense. **2** (*pl.* **dies**) **a** an engraved device for stamping a design on coins, medals, etc. **b** a device for stamping, cutting, or molding material into a particular shape. □ **as straight** (or **true**) **as a die 1** quite straight. **2** entirely honest or loyal. **the die is cast** an irrevocable step has been taken.

die cast·ing *n.* the process or product of casting from metal molds. □□ **die cast** *v.tr.* (*past* and *past part.* **cast**)

die-hard /díhaard/ *n. & adj.* ● *n.* a conservative or stubborn person. ● *adj.* stubborn; strongly devoted.

di·e·lec·tric /dí-iléktrik/ *adj. & n. Electr.* ● *adj.* insulating. ● *n.* an insulating medium or substance.

di·er·e·sis var. of DIAERESIS.

die·sel /déezəl/ *n.* **1** (in full **diesel engine**) an internal combustion engine in which the heat produced by the compression of air in the cylinder ignites the fuel. **2** a vehicle driven by a diesel engine. **3** fuel for a diesel engine.

di·et[1] /díət/ *n. & v.* ● *n.* **1** the kinds of food that a person or animal habitually eats. **2** a special course of food to which a person is restricted. **3** a regular occupation or series of activities to which one is restricted or which form one's main concern, usu. for a purpose (*a diet of light reading and fresh air*). ● *v.* (**dieted, dieting**) **1** *intr.* restrict oneself to small amounts or special kinds of food, esp. to control one's weight. **2** *tr.* restrict (a person or animal) to a special diet. □□ **di·et·er** *n.*

di·et[2] /díət/ *n.* **1** a legislative assembly in certain countries. **2** *hist.* a national or international conference, esp. of a federal government or confederation.

di·e·tar·y /díəteree/ *adj.* of or relating to a diet.

di·e·tet·ic /díətétik/ *adj.* of or relating to diet.

di·e·tet·ics /díətétiks/ *n.pl.* (usu. treated as *sing.*) the scientific study of diet and nutrition.

di·e·ti·tian /díətíshən/ *n.* (also **di·e·ti·cian**) an expert in dietetics.

dif·fer /dífər/ *v.intr.* **1** (often foll. by *from*) be unlike or distinguishable. **2** (often foll. by *with*) disagree.

dif·fer·ence /dífrəns/ *n.* **1** the state or condition of being different or unlike. **2** a point in which things differ. **3** a degree of unlikeness. **4 a** the quantity by which amounts differ; a deficit (*will have to make up the difference*). **b** the remainder left after subtraction. **5 a** a disagreement, quarrel, or dispute. **b** the grounds of disagreement (*put aside their differences*). **6** a notable change (*the difference in his behavior is remarkable*). □ **make a** (or **all the,** etc.) **difference** (often foll. by *to*) have a significant effect or influence. **make no difference** (often foll. by *to*) have no effect. **with a difference** having a new or unusual feature.

dif·fer·ent /dífrənt/ *adj.* **1** (often foll. by *from, to, than*) unlike; distinguishable in nature, form, or quality. ¶ *Different from* is generally regarded as the most acceptable collocation; *than* is established in use, esp. when followed by a clause, e.g., *I am a different person than I was a year ago.* **2** distinct; separate; not the same one. **3** *colloq.* unusual (*wanted to do something different*). **4** of various kinds; assorted; several; miscellaneous (*available in different colors*). □□ **dif·fer·ent·ly** *adv.* **dif·fer·ent·ness** *n.*

dif·fer·en·tial /dífərénshəl/ *adj. & n.* ● *adj.* **1 a** of, exhibiting, or depending on a difference. **b** varying according to circumstances. **2** *Math.* relating to infinitesimal differences. **3** constituting a specific difference; distinctive; relating to specific differences (*differential diagnosis*). **4** *Physics & Mech.* concerning the difference of two or more motions, pressures, etc. ● *n.* **1** a difference between individuals of the same kind. **2** a difference between rates of interest, etc. **3** *Math.* **a** an infinitesimal difference between successive values of a variable. **b** a function expressing this as a rate of change with respect to another variable. **4** (in full **differential gear**) a gear allowing a vehicle's driven wheels to revolve at different speeds in cornering. □□ **dif·fer·en·tial·ly** *adv.*

dif·fer·en·tial cal·cu·lus *n. Math.* a method of calculating rates of change, maximum or minimum values, etc. (cf. INTEGRAL).

dif·fer·en·tial e·qua·tion *n.* an equation involving derivatives of a function or functions.

dif·fer·en·ti·ate /dífərénsheeayt/ *v.* **1** *tr.* constitute a difference between or in. **2** *tr. & (often foll. by between) intr.* find differences (between); discriminate. **3** *tr. & intr.* make or become different in the process of development. **4** *tr. Math.* transform (a function) into its derivative. □□ **dif·fer·en·ti·a·tion** /-sheeáyshən/ *n.* **dif·fer·en·ti·a·tor** *n.*

dif·fi·cult /dífikult, -kəlt/ *adj.* **1 a** needing much effort or skill. **b** troublesome; perplexing. **2** (of a person): **a** not easy to please or satisfy. **b** uncooperative; troublesome. **3** characterized by hardships or problems (*a difficult period in his life*).

dif·fi·cul·ty /dífikultee, -kəl-/ *n.* (*pl.* **-ies**) **1** the state or condition of being difficult. **2 a** a difficult thing; a problem or hindrance. **b** (often in *pl.*) a cause of distress or hardship (*in financial difficulties*). □ **make difficulties** be intransigent or unaccommodating. **with difficulty** not easily.

dif·fi·dent /dífidənt/ *adj.* **1** shy; lacking self-confidence. **2** excessively reticent. □□ **dif·fi·dence** /-dəns/ *n.* **dif·fi·dent·ly** *adv.*

dif·fract /difrákt/ *v. Physics* undergo or cause diffraction.

dif·frac·tion /difrákshən/ *n. Physics* ▼ the process in which a beam of light or other system of waves is spread out as a result of passing through a narrow aperture or across an edge, often accompanied by interference between the waveforms produced.

dif·fuse *adj. & v.* ● *adj.* /difyoos/ **1** spread out; not concentrated. **2** not concise; long-winded; verbose.

● *v.tr. & intr.* /difyooz/ **1** disperse or be dispersed from a center. **2** spread or be spread widely. **3** *Physics* intermingle by diffusion. □□ **dif·fuse·ly** /difyooslee/ *adv.* **dif·fuse·ness** /difyoosnis/ *n.* **dif·fus·i·ble** /difyoozibəl/ *adj.* **dif·fu·sive** /difyoosiv/ *adj.*

dif·fus·er /difyoozər/ *n.* (also **dif·fu·sor**) **1** a person or thing that diffuses. **2** *Engin.* a duct for broadening an airflow and reducing its speed.

dif·fu·sion /difyoozhən/ *n.* **1** the act or an instance of diffusing; the process of being diffused. **2** *Physics & Chem.* ▼ the interpenetration of substances by the natural movement of their particles.

DIFFUSION OF POTASSIUM PERMANGANATE IN WATER

dig /dig/ *v. & n.* ● *v.* (**digging;** *past* and *past part.* **dug** /dug/) **1** *intr.* break up and remove or turn over soil, ground, etc. **2** *tr.* **a** break up and displace (the ground, etc.) in this way. **b** (foll. by *up*) break up the soil of (fallow land). **3** *tr.* make (a hole, grave, tunnel, etc.) by digging. **4** *tr.* (often foll. by *up, out*) **a** obtain or remove by digging. **b** find or discover after searching. **5** *tr.* (also *absol.*) excavate (an archaeological site). **6** *tr. sl.* like, appreciate, or understand. **7** *tr. & intr.* (foll. by *in, into*) thrust or poke into. **8** *intr.* make one's way by digging (*dug through the mountainside*). **9** *intr.* (usu. foll. by *into*) investigate or study closely; probe. ● *n.* **1** a piece of digging. **2** a thrust or poke (*a dig in the ribs*). **3** *colloq.* (often foll. by *at*) a pointed remark. **4** an archaeological excavation. **5** (in *pl.*) *colloq.* living quarters. □ **dig one's feet** (or **heels** or **toes**) **in** be obstinate. **dig in** *colloq.* begin eating. **dig oneself in 1** prepare a defensive trench or pit. **2** establish one's position.

D

DIFFRACTION

Diffraction is the bending or spreading out of waves, such as the water waves shown here in a ripple tank, as they pass the edge of a barrier. When waves pass through a small gap that consists of two edges, they spread out in concentric semicircles.

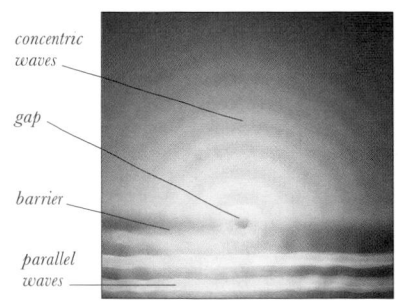

diffracted waves

barrier

parallel waves

DEMONSTRATION OF EDGE DIFFRACTION

concentric waves

gap

barrier

parallel waves

DEMONSTRATION OF DIFFRACTION THROUGH A SMALL GAP

D

DIGESTION

The digestive system is made up of a group of organs that break down food into particles that can be absorbed by the body, and eliminate waste products. In humans, the digestive tract begins at the mouth and includes the esophagus, stomach, small and large intestines, rectum, and anus. It is connected, via ducts, to salivary glands, the gall bladder, and the pancreas, which provide bile and enzymes to aid digestion, and to the liver, which helps to metabolize food products into a form that can be stored (e.g., fat and protein). Undigested food is solidified into feces in the large intestine, ready for excretion via the anus.

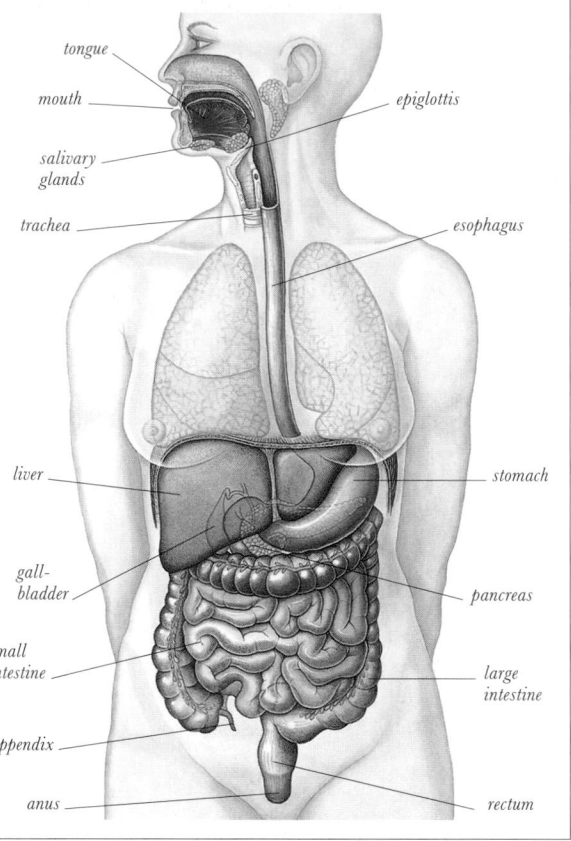

HUMAN DIGESTIVE SYSTEM

tongue · mouth · salivary glands · trachea · epiglottis · esophagus · liver · stomach · gall-bladder · pancreas · small intestine · large intestine · appendix · anus · rectum

dig·am·ma /dígámə/ *n.* the sixth letter (F, *F*) of the early Greek alphabet (prob. pronounced as the English *w*), later disused.

di·gas·tric /dīgástrik/ *adj. & n. Anat.* ● *adj.* (of a muscle) having two wide parts with a tendon between. ● *n.* the muscle that opens the jaw.

di·gest *v. & n.* ● *v.tr.* /dijést, dī-/ **1** assimilate (food) in the stomach and bowels. **2** understand and assimilate mentally. **3** *Chem.* treat (a substance) with heat, enzymes, or a solvent in order to decompose it, extract the essence, etc. **4 a** reduce to a systematic or convenient form; summarize. **b** think over; arrange in the mind. **5** bear without resistance; tolerate; endure. ● *n.* /díjest/ **1** a methodical summary, esp. of a body of laws. **2 a** a compendium or summary of information; a résumé. **b** a regular or occasional synopsis of current literature or news. □□ **di·gest·er** *n.* **di·gest·i·ble** *adj.* **di·gest·i·bil·i·ty** *n.*

di·ges·tion /díjés-chən, dī-/ *n.* **1** ▲ the process of digesting. **2** the capacity to digest food (*has a weak digestion*). **3** digesting a substance by means of heat, enzymes, or a solvent.

di·ges·tive /díjéstiv, dī-/ *adj. & n.* ● *adj.* **1** of or relating to digestion. **2** aiding or promoting digestion. ● *n.* a substance that aids digestion.

dig·ger /dígər/ *n.* **1** a person or machine that digs, esp. a mechanical excavator. **2** a miner. **3** *colloq.* Australian or New Zealander.

dight /dīt/ *adj. archaic* clothed; arrayed.

dig·it /díjit/ *n.* **1** any numeral from 0 to 9. **2** *Anat. & Zool.* a finger, thumb, or toe.

dig·it·al /díjit'l/ *adj.* **1** of or using a digit or digits. **2** (of a clock, watch, etc.) that gives a reading by means of displayed digits instead of hands. ▷ CLOCK. **3** (of a computer) operating on data represented as a series of usu. binary digits or in similar discrete form. **4 a** (of a recording) with sound information represented in digits for more reliable transmission.

▷ RECORD. **b** (of a recording medium) using this process. □□ **dig·it·al·ize** *v.tr.* **dig·it·al·ly** *adv.*

dig·it·al au·di·o tape *n.* magnetic tape on which sound is recorded digitally.

dig·it·al·in /díjitálin/ *n.* the pharmacologically active constituent(s) of the foxglove.

dig·it·al·is /díjitálĭs/ *n.* a drug prepared from the dried leaves of foxgloves and containing substances that stimulate the heart muscle.

dig·i·tize /díjitīz/ *v.tr.* ▼ convert (data, etc.) into digital form, esp. for a computer. □□ **dig·i·ti·za·tion** *n.*

dig·ni·fied /dígnifīd/ *adj.* having or expressing dignity.

dig·ni·fy /dígnifī/ *v.tr.* (**-ies, -ied**) **1** give dignity to. **2** ennoble; make worthy or illustrious. **3** give the form or appearance of dignity to (*dignified the house with the name of mansion*).

dig·ni·tar·y /dígniteree/ *n.* (*pl.* **-ies**) a person holding high rank or office.

dig·ni·ty /dígnitee/ *n.* (*pl.* **-ies**) **1** a composed and serious manner. **2** the state of being worthy of honor or respect. **3** worthiness; excellence (*the dignity of work*). **4** a high rank or position. **5** high regard or estimation. **6** self-respect. □ **beneath one's dignity** not worthy enough for one. **stand on one's dignity** insist on being treated with respect.

di·graph /dígraf/ *n.* a group of two letters representing one sound, as in *ph* and *ey*.

di·gress /dīgrés/ *v.intr.* depart from the main subject. □□ **di·gres·sion** /-gréshən/ *n.* **di·gres·sive** *adj.*

digs see DIG *n.* 5.

di·hed·ral /díhéedrəl/ *adj.* having or contained by two plane faces.

dike¹ /dīk/ *n. & v.* (also **dyke**) ● *n.* **1** a long wall or embankment built to prevent flooding, esp. from the sea. **2** a ditch. **3 a** a low wall, esp. of turf. **b** a causeway. **4** a barrier or obstacle; a defense. ● *v.tr.* provide or defend with a dike or dikes.

dike² var. of DYKE².

dik·tat /diktát/ *n.* a categorical statement or decree.

di·lap·i·dat·ed /dilápidaytid/ *adj.* in a state of disrepair or ruin.

di·lap·i·da·tion /dilápidáyshən/ *n.* **1 a** the process of dilapidating. **b** a state of disrepair. **2** (in *pl.*) repairs required at the end of a tenancy or lease.

dil·a·ta·tion /dilətáyshən, dī-/ *n.* **1** the widening or expansion of a hollow organ or cavity. **2** the process of dilating.

dil·a·ta·tion and cu·ret·tage *n.* an operation in which the cervix is expanded and the womb lining scraped off with a curette.

di·late /dīláyt, dílayt/ *v.* **1** *tr. & intr.* make or become wider or larger. **2** *intr.* (often foll. by *on, upon*) speak or write at length. □□ **di·la·tion** /-láyshən/ *n.*

dil·a·to·ry /dílətawree/ *adj.* given to or causing delay. □□ **dil·a·to·ri·ness** *n.*

dil·do /díldō/ *n.* (*pl.* **-os** or **-oes**) an object shaped like an erect penis and used for sexual stimulation.

di·lem·ma /dílémə/ *n.* **1** a situation in which a choice has to be made between two equally undesirable alternatives. **2** a state of indecision between two alternatives. **3** *disp.* a difficult situation. **4** an argument forcing an opponent to choose either of two unfavorable alternatives.

DIGITIZE

Digitizing involves converting a continuously varying signal, known as an analog signal, into one composed of discrete units, known as a digital signal. In the digitizing process, the analog waveform is measured many times every second, and each part of the measured wave is broken down into units. Each unit is given a binary number related to the height of the wave at that point.

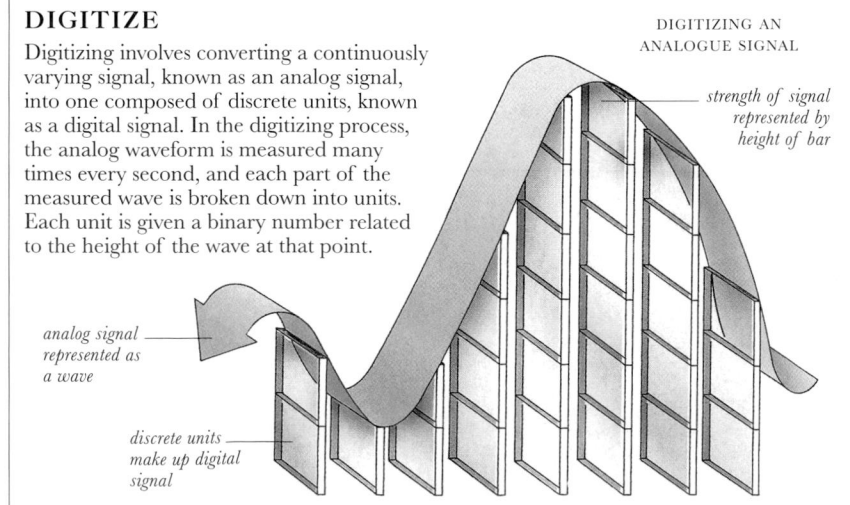

DIGITIZING AN ANALOGUE SIGNAL

strength of signal represented by height of bar

analog signal represented as a wave

discrete units make up digital signal

dil·et·tante /dílitaánt/ *n. & adj.* ● *n.* (*pl.* **dilettantes** or **dilettanti** /-tee/) **1** a person who studies a subject superficially. **2** a person who enjoys the arts. ● *adj.* trifling; not thorough; amateurish. □□ **dil·et·tant·ism** *n.*

dil·i·gence /dílijəns/ *n.* **1** careful and persistent application or effort. **2** industriousness.

dil·i·gent /dílijənt/ *adj.* **1** careful and steady in application to one's work or duties. **2** showing care and effort. □□ **dil·i·gent·ly** *adv.*

dill /dil/ *n.* **1** ◄ an umbelliferous herb, *Anethum graveolens*, with yellow flowers and aromatic seeds. **2** the leaves or seeds of this plant used for flavoring and medicinal purposes.

dil·ly /dílee/ *n.* (*pl.* **-ies**) *sl.* a remarkable or excellent person or thing.

dil·ly·dal·ly /díleedálee/ *v.intr.* (**-ies, -ied**) *colloq.* **1** dawdle; loiter. **2** vacillate.

di·lute /dilóot, dī-/ *v. & adj.* ● *v.tr.* **1** reduce the strength of (a fluid) by adding water or another solvent. **2** weaken or reduce the strength or forcefulness of. ● *adj.* also /dí-/ **1** diluted. **2** (of a color) washed out; low in saturation. **3** *Chem.* **a** (of a solution) having relatively low concentration of solute. **b** (of a substance) in solution (*dilute sulfuric acid*). □□ **di·lu·tion** /-lóoshən/ *n.*

dim /dim/ *adj. & v.* ● *adj.* (**dimmer, dimmest**) **1 a** only faintly luminous or visible; not bright. **b** obscure; ill-defined. **2** not clearly perceived or remembered. **3** *colloq.* stupid. **4** (of the eyes) not seeing clearly. ● *v.* (**dimmed, dimming**) **1** *tr. & intr.* make or become dim. **2** *tr.* switch (headlights) to low beam. □ **take a dim view of** *colloq.* **1** disapprove of. **2** feel gloomy about. □□ **dim·ly** *adv.* **dim·ness** *n.*

dime /dīm/ *n. US & Can.* **1** a ten-cent coin. **2** *colloq.* a small amount of money. □ **a dime a dozen** very cheap or commonplace. **turn on a dime** *colloq.* make a sharp turn in a vehicle.

di·men·sion /diménshən, dī-/ *n. & v.* ● *n.* **1** a measurable extent of any kind, as length, breadth, depth. **2** (in *pl.*) size; scope; extent. **3** an aspect or facet. ● *v.tr.* (usu. as **dimensioned** *adj.*) mark the dimensions on (a diagram, etc.). □□ **di·men·sion·al** *adj.* (also in *comb.*). **di·men·sion·less** *adj.*

di·mer /dímər/ *n. Chem.* a compound consisting of two identical molecules linked together (cf. MONOMER). □□ **di·mer·ic** /-mérik/ *adj.*

di·min·ish /dimínish/ *v.* **1** *tr. & intr.* make or become smaller or less. **2** *tr.* lessen the reputation of.

di·min·ished /dimínisht/ *adj.* **1** reduced; made smaller or less. **2** *Mus.* (of an interval) less by a semitone than the corresponding minor or perfect interval.

di·min·u·en·do /dimínyoo-éndō/ *adv. & n. Mus.* ● *adv.* with a gradual decrease in loudness. ● *n.* (*pl.* **-os**) a passage to be played in this way.

dim·i·nu·tion /dimínóoshən, -nyóo-/ *n.* **1 a** the act or an instance of diminishing. **b** the amount by which something diminishes. **2** *Mus.* the repetition of a passage in notes shorter than those originally used.

di·min·u·tive /dimínyətiv/ *adj. & n.* ● *adj.* **1** tiny. **2** *Gram.* (of a word or suffix) implying smallness, either actual or imputed in token of affection, scorn, etc. (e.g., *-let*, *-kins*). ● *n. Gram.* a diminutive word or suffix.

dim·mer /dímər/ *n.* **1** a device for varying the brightness of an electric light. **2** (in *pl.*) **a** small parking lights on a motor vehicle. **b** headlights on low beam.

di·mor·phic /dīmáwrfik/ *adj.* (also **di·mor·phous** /dīmáwrfəs/) *Biol., Chem., & Mineral.* exhibiting, or occurring in, two distinct forms. □□ **di·mor·phism** *n.*

dim·ple /dímpəl/ *n. & v.* ● *n.* a small hollow in the flesh, esp. in the cheeks or chin. ● *v.* **1** *intr.* produce or show dimples. **2** *tr.* produce dimples in (a cheek, etc.). □□ **dim·ply** *adj.*

dim sum /dim súm/ *n.* (also **dim sim** /sim/) a meal or course of savory Cantonese-style snacks.

dim·wit /dímwit/ *n. colloq.* a stupid person.

dim·wit·ted *adj. colloq.* stupid; unintelligent.

DIN /din/ *n.* any of a series of technical standards originating in Germany and used internationally, esp. to designate electrical connections, film speeds, and paper sizes.

din /din/ *n. & v.* ● *n.* a prolonged loud and distracting noise. ● *v.* (**dinned, dinning**) **1** *tr.* (foll. by *into*) instill (something to be learned) by constant repetition. **2** *intr.* make a din.

di·nar /dinaár, deénaar/ *n.* the chief monetary unit of the states of the former Yugoslavia and certain countries of the Middle East and N. Africa.

dine /dīn/ *v.* **1** *intr.* eat dinner. **2** *tr.* give dinner to. □ **dine out** dine away from home.

din·er /dínər/ *n.* **1** a person who dines, esp. in a restaurant. **2** a railroad dining car. **3** a small restaurant. **4** a small dining room.

di·nette /dīnét/ *n.* **1** a small room or part of a room used for eating meals. **2** (in full **dinette set**) table and chairs designed for such a room.

ding[1] /ding/ *v. & n.* ● *v.intr.* make a ringing sound. ● *n.* a ringing sound, as of a bell.

ding[2] /ding/ *v. & n.* ● *v.tr.* cause surface damage; dent. ● *n.* nick; minor surface damage; dent.

ding-a-ling /díngəling/ *n.* a foolish, flighty, or eccentric person.

ding·bat /díngbat/ *n. sl.* **1** a stupid or eccentric person. **2** *Printing* an ornamental sign in typography.

ding·dong /díngdawng, -dong/ *n., adj., & adv.* ● *n.* **1** the sound of alternate chimes. **2** *colloq.* an intense argument or fight. **3** *colloq.* a riotous party. ● *adj.* (of a contest, etc.) evenly matched and intensely waged; thoroughgoing. ● *adv.* with vigor and energy (*hammer away at it dingdong*).

din·ghy /díngee, dínggee/ *n.* (*pl.* **-ies**) **1** a small boat carried by a ship. **2** ▼ a small pleasure boat. **3** a small inflatable rubber boat (esp. for emergency use). ▷ BOAT

din·gle /dínggəl/ *n.* a deep, wooded valley or dell.

din·go /dínggō/ *n.* (*pl.* **-oes**) ▼ a wild Australian dog, *Canis dingo*.

DINGO
(*Canis dingo*)

din·gy /dínjee/ *adj.* (**dingier, dingiest**) dirty-looking; drab; dull-colored (*a dingy room*). □□ **din·gi·ness** *n.*

din·ing car *n.* a railroad car equipped as a restaurant.

din·ing room *n.* a room in which meals are eaten.

dink·um /dínkəm/ *adj. & n. Austral. & NZ colloq.* ● *adj.* genuine; right. ● *n.* work; toil.

dink·y /dínkee/ *adj.* (**dinkier, dinkiest**) *colloq.* **1** trifling; insignificant. **2** *Brit.* (esp. of a thing) neat and attractive; small; dainty.

D

DILL
(*Anethum graveolens*)

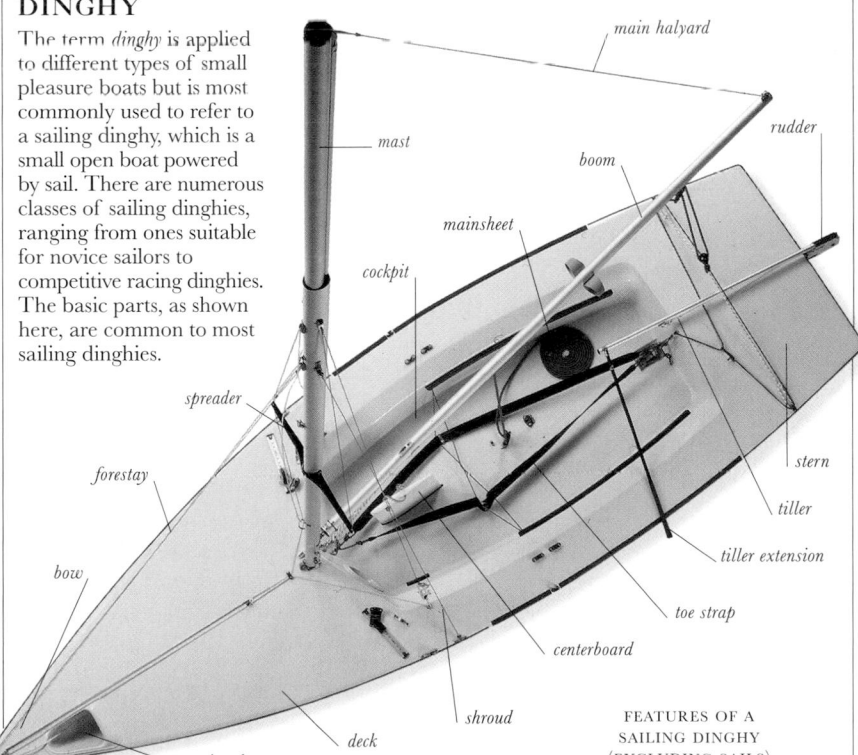

DINGHY

The term *dinghy* is applied to different types of small pleasure boats but is most commonly used to refer to a sailing dinghy, which is a small open boat powered by sail. There are numerous classes of sailing dinghies, ranging from ones suitable for novice sailors to competitive racing dinghies. The basic parts, as shown here, are common to most sailing dinghies.

main halyard
rudder
mast
boom
mainsheet
cockpit
spreader
stern
forestay
tiller
tiller extension
bow
toe strap
centerboard
shroud
deck
spinnaker chute

FEATURES OF A
SAILING DINGHY
(EXCLUDING SAILS)

din·ner /dínər/ n. **1** the main meal of the day, taken either at midday or in the evening. **2** a formal evening meal.

din·ner jack·et n. a man's, usu. black, formal jacket for evening wear.

di·no·saur /dínəsawr/ n. **1** ▶ an extinct reptile of the Mesozoic era. **2** a large, unwieldy system or organization, esp. one not adapting to new conditions. □□ **di·no·sau·ri·an** adj. & n.

dint /dint/ n. & v. a dent. ● v.tr. mark with dints. □ **by dint of** by force or means of.

di·oc·e·san /dīósisən/ adj. & n. ● adj. of or concerning a diocese. ● n. the bishop of a diocese.

di·o·cese /díəsis, -sees, -seez/ n. a district under the pastoral care of a bishop.

di·ode /díōd/ n. Electronics **1** ▼ a semiconductor allowing the flow of current in one direction only and having two terminals. ▷ RADIO. **2** a thermionic valve having two electrodes.

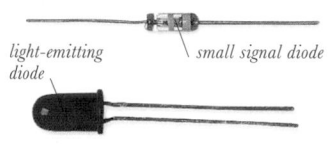

light-emitting diode   small signal diode

DIODES

di·oe·cious /dī-éeshəs/ adj. **1** Bot. having male and female organs on separate plants. **2** Zool. having the two sexes in separate individuals (cf. MONOECIOUS).

Di·o·nys·i·ac /díəníseeak/ adj. (also **Di·o·ny·sian** /-níshən, -nízhən, -níseeən/) **1** wildly sensual; unrestrained. **2** (in Greek mythology) of or relating to Dionysus, the Greek god of wine, or his worship.

di·op·ter /dīóptər/ n. Optics a unit of refractive power of a lens, equal to the reciprocal of its focal length in meters.

di·op·tric /dīóptrik/ adj. Optics **1** serving as a medium for sight; assisting sight by refraction (dioptric glass; dioptric lens). **2** of refraction; refractive.

di·op·trics /dīóptriks/ n. Optics the part of optics dealing with refraction.

di·o·ram·a /díərámə, -ráamə/ n. **1** a scenic painting in which changes in color and direction of illumination simulate a sunrise, etc. **2** a small representation of a scene with three-dimensional figures, viewed through a window, etc. **3** a small-scale model or movie set.

di·o·rite /díərīt/ n. ▶ a coarse-grained, plutonic igneous rock containing quartz. □□ **di·o·rit·ic** /-rítik/ adj.

di·ox·ide /dīóksīd/ n. Chem. an oxide containing two atoms of oxygen (carbon dioxide).

DIP /dip/ n. Computing a form of integrated circuit consisting of a small plastic or ceramic slab with two parallel rows of pins.

dip. abbr. diploma.

quartz

DIORITE SEEN THROUGH A MICROSCOPE

dip /dip/ v. & n. ● v. (**dipped**, **dipping**) **1** tr. put or let down briefly into liquid, etc. **2** intr. **a** go below a surface or level (the Sun dipped below the horizon). **b** (of a level of income, activity, etc.) decline slightly (profits dipped in May). **3** intr. extend downward; take or have a downward slope (the road dips after the curve). **4** intr. go under water and emerge quickly. **5** intr. (foll. by into) **a** read briefly from (a book, etc.). **b** take a cursory interest in (a subject). **6** (foll. by into) **a** intr. put a hand, ladle, etc., into a container to take something out. **b** tr. put (a hand, etc.) into a container to do this. **c** intr. spend from or make use of one's resources (dipped into our savings). **7** tr. & intr. lower or be lowered, esp. in salute. **8** tr. color (a fabric) by immersing it in dye. **9** tr. wash (sheep) by immersion in a vermin-killing liquid.

10 tr. make (a candle) by immersing a wick briefly in hot tallow. **11** tr. baptize by immersion. **12** tr. (often foll. by up, out of) remove or scoop up (liquid, grain, etc., or something from liquid). ● n. **1** an act of dipping or being dipped. **2** a liquid into which something is dipped. **3** a brief swim in the ocean, lake, etc. **4** a brief downward slope in a road, etc. **5** a sauce or dressing into which food is dipped before eating. **6** a depression in the skyline.

diph·the·ri·a /difthéereeə, dip-/ n. an acute infectious bacterial disease with inflammation of a mucous membrane esp. of the throat.

diph·thong /dífthawng, -thong, díp-/ n. **1** a speech sound in one syllable in which the articulation begins as for one vowel and moves as for another (as in coin, loud, and side). **2 a** a digraph representing the sound of a diphthong or single vowel (as in feat). **b** a compound vowel character; a ligature (as æ).

di·plod·o·cus /diplódəkəs, dī-/ n. a giant plant-eating dinosaur of the order Sauropoda, with a long neck and tail.

dip·loid /díployd/ adj. & n. Biol. ● adj. (of an organism or cell) having two complete sets of chromosomes per cell. ● n. a diploid cell or organism. ▷ MEIOSIS

di·plo·ma /diplōmə/ n. (pl. **diplomas**) **1** a certificate of qualification awarded by a college, etc. **2** a document conferring an honor or privilege. **3** (pl. also **diplomata** /-mətə/) a state paper; an official document; a charter.

di·plo·ma·cy /diplōməsee/ n. **1 a** the management of international relations. **b** expertise in this. **2** adroitness in personal relations; tact.

dip·lo·mat /dípləmat/ n. **1** an official representing a country abroad; a member of a diplomatic service. **2** a tactful person.

dip·lo·mate /dípləmayt/ n. a person who holds a diploma, esp. in medicine.

dip·lo·mat·ic /dípləmátik/ adj. **1 a** of or involved in diplomacy. **b** skilled in diplomacy. **2** tactful. **3** (of an edition, etc.) exactly reproducing the original. □□ **dip·lo·mat·i·cal·ly** adv.

dip·lo·mat·ic im·mu·ni·ty n. the exemption of diplomatic staff abroad from arrest, taxation, etc.

di·pole /dípōl/ n. **1** Physics two equal and oppositely charged or magnetized poles separated by a distance. **2** Chem. a molecule in which a concentration of positive charges is separated from a concentration of negative charges. **3** an aerial consisting of a horizontal metal rod with a connecting wire at its center.

dip·per /dípər/ n. **1** a diving bird, Cinclus cinclus. **2** a ladle.

dip·py /dípee/ adj. (**dippier**, **dippiest**) sl. crazy; silly.

dip·so /dípsō/ n. (pl. **-os**) colloq. a dipsomaniac.

dip·so·ma·ni·a /dípsəmáyneeə/ n. an abnormal craving for alcohol. □□ **dip·so·ma·ni·ac** /-máyneeak/ n.

dip·stick /dípstik/ n. a graduated rod for measuring the depth of a liquid, esp. in a vehicle's engine.

DIP switch n. an arrangement of switches on a printer for selecting a printing mode.

dip·ter·ous /díptərəs/ adj. **1** (of an insect) of the order Diptera, having two membranous wings, e.g., the fly, gnat, or mosquito. **2** Bot. having two winglike appendages.

dip·tych /díptik/ n. **1** ▶ a painting on two hinged panels which may be closed like a book. **2** an ancient writing tablet consisting of two hinged leaves with waxed inner sides.

DIPTYCH: INTERIOR OF THE WILTON DIPTYCH (c.1395)

dire /dīr/ adj. **1 a** calamitous; dreadful (in dire straits). **b** ominous (dire warnings). **2** urgent (in dire need). □□ **dire·ly** adv.

di·rect /dirékt, dī-/ adj., adv., & v. ● adj. **1** extending or moving in a straight line or by the shortest route; not crooked or circuitous. **2 a** straightforward; going straight to the point. **b** frank; not ambiguous. **3** without intermediaries or the intervention of other factors (direct rule; made a direct approach). **4** (of descent) lineal; not collateral. **5** complete; greatest possible (the direct opposite). ● adv. **1** without an intermediary or intervening factor (dealt with them direct). **2** frankly; without evasion. **3** by a direct route (send it direct to Chicago). ● v.tr. **1** control; guide; govern the movements of. **2** (foll. by to + infin., or that + clause) give a formal order or command to. **3** (foll. by to) **a** address (a letter, etc.). **b** tell or show (a person) the way to a destination. **4** (foll. by at, to, toward) **a** point, aim, or cause (a blow or missile) to move in a certain direction. **b** point or address (one's attention, a remark, etc.). **5** guide as an adviser, as a principle, etc. (I do as duty directs me). **6 a** (also absol.) supervise the performing, staging, etc., of (a movie, play, etc.). **b** supervise the performance of (an actor, etc.). **7** (also absol.) guide the performance of (a group of musicians). □□ **di·rect·ness** n.

di·rect ac·cess n. the facility of retrieving data immediately from any part of a computer file.

di·rect ad·dress n. Computing an address (see ADDRESS n. 1c) which specifies the location of data to be used in an operation.

di·rect cur·rent n. an electric current flowing in one direction only. ▷ CIRCUIT. ¶ Abbr.: **DC**, **dc**.

di·rec·tion /dirékshən, dī-/ n. **1** the act or process of directing; supervision. **2** (usu. in pl.) an order or instruction; esp. each of a set guiding use of equipment, etc. **3 a** the course or line along which a person or thing moves or looks, or which must be taken to reach a destination. **b** (in pl.) guidance on how to reach a destination. **c** the point to or from which a person or thing moves or looks. **4** the tendency or scope of a theme, subject, or inquiry. □□ **di·rec·tion·less** adj.

di·rec·tion·al /dirékshənəl, dī-/ adj. **1** of or indicating direction. **2** Electronics **a** concerned with the transmission of radio or sound waves in a particular direction. **b** (of equipment) designed to receive radio or sound waves most effectively from a particular direction or directions. □□ **di·rec·tion·al·i·ty** /-álitee/ n. **di·rec·tion·al·ly** adv.

di·rec·tion find·er n. a device for determining the source of radio waves, esp. as an aid in navigation.

di·rec·tive /diréktiv, dī-/ n. & adj. ● n. a general instruction from one in authority. ● adj. serving to direct.

di·rect·ly /diréktlee, dī-/ adv. **1 a** at once; without delay. **b** presently; shortly. **2** exactly; immediately (directly opposite; directly after lunch). **3** in a direct manner.

di·rect ob·ject n. Gram. the primary object of the action of a transitive verb.

DINOSAUR

Dinosaurs were the dominant land vertebrates for most of the Mesozoic era (248–65 million years ago). They are separated into two groups according to the structure of the pelvis: ornithischian (bird-hipped) dinosaurs had a pubis that slanted backward; most saurischian (lizard-hipped) dinosaurs had a forward-slanting pubis. Examples of dinosaurs from subgroups within these two main groups are shown below.

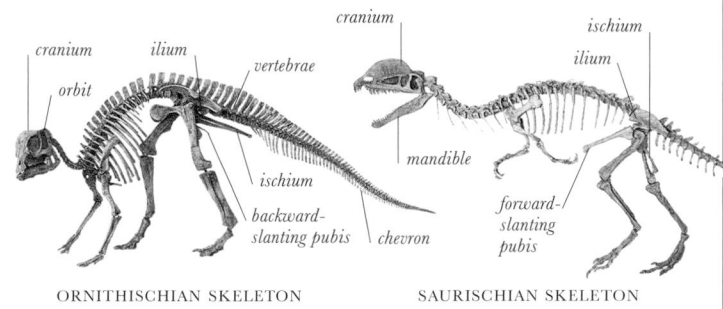

ORNITHISCHIAN SKELETON

SAURISCHIAN SKELETON

D

EXAMPLES OF DINOSAURS

ORNITHISCHIANS

PACHYCEPHALOSAURIA
(*Stegoceras*)

CERATOPSIA
(*Triceratops*)

STEGOSAURIA
(*Stegosaurus*)

ANKYLOSAURIA
(*Euoplocephalus*)

ORNITHOPODA
(*Iguanodon*)

SAURISCHIANS

COELUROSAURIA
(*Compsognathus*)

ORNITHOMIMOSAURIA
(*Gallimimus*)

CARNOSAURIA
(*Tyrannosaurus*)

SAUROPODA
(*Barosaurus*)

DEINONYCHOSAURIA
(*Deinonychus*)

di·rec·tor /diréktər, dī-/ *n.* **1** a person who directs or controls something. **2** a member of the managing board of a commercial company. **3** a person who directs a movie, etc. **4** a person acting as spiritual adviser. **5** = CONDUCTOR 1. □□ **di·rec·to·ri·al** /-táwreeəl/ *adj.* **di·rec·tor·ship** *n.* (esp. in sense 2).

di·rec·to·rate /diréktərət, dī-/ *n.* **1** a board of directors. **2** the office of director.

di·rec·to·ry /diréktəree, dī-/ *n.* (*pl.* **-ies**) **1** a book listing a particular group of individuals or organizations with various details. **2** a computer file listing other files or programs, etc.

dirge /dərj/ *n.* **1** a lament for the dead. **2** any mournful song or lament.

dir·i·gi·ble /dirijibəl, diríj-/ *adj.* & *n.* ● *adj.* capable of being guided. ● *n.* a dirigible balloon or airship.

dirk /dərk/ *n.* a long dagger, esp. as formerly worn by Scottish Highlanders.

dirn·dl /dərnd'l/ *n.* **1** ▼ a woman's dress with close-fitting bodice, tight waistband, and full skirt. **2** a full skirt of this kind.

close-fitting bodice

full skirt

DIRNDL DRESSES

dirt /dərt/ *n.* **1** unclean matter that soils. **2 a** earth; soil. **b** earth; cinders, etc., used to make a surface for a road, etc. (usu. *attrib.*: *dirt track*). **3 a** foul or malicious words or talk. **b** scurrilous information; scandal; gossip; the lowdown. **4** excrement. **5** a dirty condition. **6** a person or thing considered worthless. □ **do a person dirt** *sl.* harm or injure a person's reputation maliciously. **eat dirt 1** suffer insults, etc., without retaliating. **2** make a humiliating confession. **treat like dirt** treat (a person) contemptuously.

dirt bike *n.* a motorcycle designed for use on unpaved roads and tracks, esp. in scrambling.

dirt cheap *adj.* & *adv. colloq.* extremely cheap.

dirt poor *adj.* extremely poor; lacking basic necessities.

dirt track *n.* a course made of rolled cinders, soil, etc., for motorcycle racing or flat racing.

dirt·y /dərtee/ *adj.* & *v.* ● *adj.* (**dirtier, dirtiest**) **1** soiled; unclean. **2** causing one to become dirty (*a dirty job*). **3** sordid; lewd (*dirty joke*). **4** unpleasant; nasty. **5** dishonest; unfair (*dirty play*). **6** (of weather) rough; stormy. **7** (of a color) not pure nor clear; dingy. **8** *colloq.* (of a nuclear weapon) producing considerable radioactive fallout. ● *v.tr.* & *intr.* (**-ies, -ied**) make or become dirty. □ **the dirty end of the stick** *colloq.* the difficult or unpleasant part of an undertaking, situation, etc. □□ **dirt·i·ness** *n.*

dirt·y dog *n. colloq.* a scoundrel; a despicable person.

dirt·y lin·en *n.* (also **dirty laundry** or **wash**) *colloq.* intimate secrets, esp. of a scandalous nature.

dirt·y look *n. colloq.* a look of disapproval, anger, or disgust.

dirt·y trick *n.* **1** a dishonorable and deceitful act. **2** (in *pl.*) underhand political activity, esp. to discredit an opponent.

dirt·y word *n.* **1** an offensive or indecent word. **2** a word for something which is disapproved of (*profit is a dirty word*).

dirt·y work *n.* **1** unpleasant tasks. **2** dishonorable or illegal activity.

dis var. of DISS.

dis- /dis/ *prefix* forming nouns, adjectives, and verbs: **1** expressing negation (*dishonest*). **2** indicating reversal or absence of an action or state (*disengage*; *disbelieve*). **3** indicating removal of a thing or quality (*dismember*; *disable*). **4** indicating separation (*distinguish*; *dispose*). **5** indicating completeness or intensification of the action (*disembowel*; *disgruntled*). **6** indicating expulsion from (*disbar*).

dis·a·bil·i·ty /dísəbílitee/ *n.* (*pl.* **-ies**) **1** physical incapacity. **2** a lack of some asset, quality, or attribute, that prevents one's doing something. **3** a legal disqualification.

dis·a·ble /disáybəl/ *v.tr.* **1** render unable to function. **2** (often as **disabled** *adj.*) deprive of or reduce the power to walk or do other normal activities, esp. by crippling. □□ **dis·a·ble·ment** *n.*

dis·a·buse /dísəbyóoz/ *v.tr.* **1** (foll. by *of*) free from a mistaken idea. **2** disillusion; undeceive.

dis·ad·van·tage /dísədvántij/ *n.* & *v.* ● *n.* **1** an unfavorable circumstance or condition. **2** damage to one's interest or reputation. ● *v.tr.* cause disadvantage to. □ **at a disadvantage** in an unfavorable position or aspect.

dis·ad·van·taged /dísədvántijd/ *adj.* placed in unfavorable circumstances (esp. of a person lacking the normal social opportunities).

dis·ad·van·ta·geous /disádvəntáyjəs, dísad-/ *adj.* **1** involving disadvantage. **2** derogatory.

dis·af·fect·ed /dísəféktid/ *adj.* **1** disloyal, esp. to one's superiors. **2** estranged; no longer friendly; discontented.

dis·af·fec·tion /dísəfékshən/ *n.* **1** disloyalty. **2** political discontent.

dis·af·fil·i·ate /dísəfíleeayt/ *v.* **1** *tr.* end the affiliation of. **2** *intr.* end one's affiliation. **3** *tr.* & *intr.* detach. □□ **dis·af·fil·i·a·tion** /-leeáyshən/ *n.*

dis·a·gree /dísəgrée/ *v.intr.* (**-agrees, -agreed, -agreeing**) (often foll. by *with*) **1** hold a different opinion. **2** quarrel. **3** (of factors or circumstances) not correspond. **4** have an adverse effect upon (a person's health, digestion, etc.). □□ **dis·a·gree·ment** *n.*

dis·a·gree·a·ble /dísəgrééəbəl/ *adj.* **1** unpleasant. **2** bad-tempered. □□ **dis·a·gree·a·bly** *adv.*

dis·al·low /dísəlów/ *v.tr.* refuse to allow or accept as valid; prohibit. □□ **dis·al·low·ance** *n.*

dis·am·big·u·ate /dísambígyōo-ayt/ *v.tr.* remove ambiguity from. □□ **dis·am·big·u·a·tion** /-áyshən/ *n.*

dis·ap·pear /dísəpeér/ *v.intr.* **1** cease to be visible; pass from sight. **2** cease to exist or be in circulation or use (*rotary telephones had all but disappeared*). □□ **dis·ap·pear·ance** *n.*

dis·ap·point /dísəpóynt/ *v.tr.* **1** (also *absol.*) fail to fulfill a desire or expectation of (a person). **2** frustrate (hopes, etc.). □ **be disappointed** (foll. by *with, at, in*, or *to* + infin., or *that* + clause) fail to have one's expectation, etc., fulfilled in some regard (*was disappointed in you; disappointed to be last*). □□ **dis·ap·point·ed·ly** *adv.* **dis·ap·point·ing** *adj.* **dis·ap·point·ing·ly** *adv.*

dis·ap·point·ment /dísəpóyntmənt/ *n.* **1** an event, thing, or person that disappoints. **2** a feeling of distress, vexation, etc., resulting from this (*I cannot hide my disappointment*).

dis·ap·pro·ba·tion /dísáprəbáyshən/ *n.* strong disapproval.

dis·ap·prove /dísəpróov/ *v.* **1** *intr.* (usu. foll. by *of*) have or express an unfavorable opinion. **2** *tr.* be

displeased with. □□ **dis·ap·prov·al** *n.* **dis·ap·prov·ing** *adj.* **dis·ap·prov·ing·ly** *adv.*

dis·arm /disaárm/ *v.* **1** *tr.* **a** take weapons away from (often foll. by *of*: *were disarmed of their rifles*). **b** *Fencing*, etc., deprive of a weapon. **2** *tr.* deprive (a ship, etc.) of its means of defense. **3** *intr.* (of a nation, etc.) disband or reduce its military forces. **4** *tr.* remove the fuse from (a bomb, etc.). **5** *tr.* deprive of the power to injure. **6** *tr.* pacify or allay the hostility or suspicions of; mollify; placate. □□ **dis·arm·er** *n.* **dis·arm·ing** *adj.* (esp. in sense 6). **dis·arm·ing·ly** *adv.*

dis·ar·ma·ment /disaárməmənt/ *n.* the reduction by a nation of its military forces and weapons.

dis·ar·range /dísəráynj/ *v.tr.* bring into disorder.

dis·ar·ray /dísəráy/ *n.* & *v.* ● *n.* (often prec. by *in, into*) disorder; confusion. ● *v.tr.* throw into disorder.

dis·ar·tic·u·late /dísaartíkyəlayt/ *v.tr.* & *intr.* separate at the joints. □□ **dis·ar·tic·u·la·tion** /-láyshən/ *n.*

dis·as·sem·ble /dísəsémbəl/ *v.tr.* take (a machine, etc.) to pieces. □□ **dis·as·sem·bly** *n.*

dis·as·so·ci·ate /dísəsósheeayt, -seeayt/ *v.tr.* & *intr.* = DISSOCIATE. □□ **dis·as·so·ci·a·tion** /-áyshən/ *n.*

dis·as·ter /dizástər/ *n.* **1** a great or sudden misfortune. **2 a** a complete failure. **b** a person or enterprise ending in failure. □□ **dis·as·trous** *adj.* **dis·as·trous·ly** *adv.*

dis·a·vow /dísəvów/ *v.tr.* disclaim knowledge of, responsibility for, or belief in. □□ **dis·a·vow·al** *n.*

dis·band /disbánd/ *v.* **1** *intr.* (of an organized group, etc.) cease to work or act together; disperse. **2** *tr.* cause (such a group) to disband. □□ **dis·band·ment** *n.*

dis·bar /disbaár/ *v.tr.* (**disbarred, disbarring**) deprive (an attorney) of the right to practice. □□ **dis·bar·ment** *n.*

dis·be·lieve /dísbileév/ *v.* **1** *tr.* be unable or unwilling to believe (a person or statement). **2** *intr.* have no faith. □□ **dis·be·lief** /-leéf/ *n.* **dis·be·liev·er** *n.* **dis·be·liev·ing·ly** *adv.*

dis·bud /disbúd/ *v.tr.* (**disbudded, disbudding**) remove buds from.

dis·burse /disbərs/ *v.* **1** *tr.* expend (money). **2** *tr.* defray (a cost). **3** *intr.* pay money. □□ **dis·burse·ment** *n.*

disc var. of DISK.

dis·calced /diskálst/ *adj.* (of a friar or a nun) barefoot or wearing only sandals.

dis·card *v.* & *n.* ● *v.tr.* /diskaárd/ **1** reject or get rid of as unwanted or superfluous. **2** (also *absol.*) *Cards* remove or put aside (a card) from one's hand. ● *n.* /dískaard/ (often in *pl.*) a discarded item, esp. a card in a card game.

dis·car·nate /diskaárnət, -nayt/ *adj.* having no physical body; separated from the flesh.

dis·cern /disərn/ *v.tr.* **1** perceive clearly with the mind or the senses. **2** make out by thought or by gazing, listening, etc. □□ **dis·cern·i·ble** *adj.* **dis·cern·i·bly** *adv.*

dis·cern·ing /disərning/ *adj.* having or showing good judgment or insight.

dis·cern·ment /disərnmənt/ *n.* good judgment or insight.

dis·charge *v.* & *n.* ● *v.* /dischaárj/ **1** *tr.* **a** let go or release, esp. from a duty, commitment, or period of confinement. **b** relieve (a bankrupt) of residual liability. **2** *tr.* dismiss from office, employment, etc. **3** *tr.* **a** fire (a gun, etc.). **b** (of a gun, etc.) fire (a bullet, etc.). **4 a** *tr.* (also *absol.*) pour out or cause to pour out (pus, liquid, etc.) (*the wound was discharging*). **b** *tr.* throw; eject (*discharged a stone at the gopher*). **c** *tr.* utter (abuse, etc.). **d** *intr.* (foll. by *into*) (of a river, etc.) flow into. **5** *tr.* **a** carry out; perform (a duty or obligation). **b** relieve oneself of (a financial commitment) (*discharged his debt*). **6** *tr. Law* cancel (an order of court). **7** *tr. Physics* release an electrical charge from. **8** *tr.* **a** relieve (a ship, etc.) of its cargo. **b** unload (a cargo). ● *n.* /dischaarj, dischaárj/ **1** the act or an instance of discharging; the process of being discharged. **2** a dismissal. **3 a** a release, exemption, acquittal, etc. **b** a written certificate of release, etc. **4** an act of firing a gun, etc. **5 a** an emission (of pus, liquid, etc.). **b** the liquid or matter so discharged. **6** (usu. foll. by *of*) **a** the payment (of a debt). **b** the performance (of a duty, etc.). **7** *Physics* **a** the release of a quantity of electric charge from an object. **b** a flow of electricity through the air or other gas, esp. when accompanied by the emission of light. **c** the conversion of chemical energy in a cell into electrical energy. **8** the unloading (of a ship or a cargo). ▫▫ **dis·charg·er** *n.* (in sense 7 of *v.*).

dis·ci·ple /disípəl/ *n.* **1** a follower or pupil of a leader, teacher, philosophy, etc. (*a disciple of Zen Buddhism*). **2** any early believer in Christ, esp. one of the twelve Apostles. ▫▫ **dis·ci·ple·ship** *n.*

dis·ci·pli·nar·i·an /dísiplináireeən/ *n.* a person who upholds or practices firm discipline (*a strict disciplinarian*).

dis·ci·pli·nar·y /dísiplinéree/ *adj.* of, promoting, or enforcing discipline.

dis·ci·pline /dísiplin/ *n.* & *v.* ● *n.* **1 a** control or order exercised over people or animals. **b** the system of rules used to maintain this control. **c** the behavior of groups subjected to such rules (*poor discipline in the ranks*). **2 a** a mental, moral, or physical training. **b** adversity as used to bring about such training (*left the course because he couldn't take the discipline*). **3** a branch of instruction or learning. **4** punishment. **5** *Eccl.* mortification by physical self-punishment, esp. scourging. ● *v.tr.* **1** punish; chastise. **2** bring under control by training in obedience.

dis·claim /diskláym/ *v.tr.* **1** deny or disown (*disclaim all responsibility*). **2** (often *absol.*) *Law* renounce a legal claim to (property, etc.).

dis·claim·er /diskláymər/ *n.* a renunciation or disavowal, esp. of responsibility.

dis·close /disklṓz/ *v.tr.* **1** make known (*disclosed the truth*). **2** expose to view.

dis·clo·sure /disklṓzhər/ *n.* **1** the act or an instance of disclosing; the process of being disclosed. **2** something disclosed; a revelation.

dis·co /dískō/ *n.* & *v. colloq.* ● *n.* (*pl.* **-os**) = DISCOTHEQUE. ● *v.intr.* (**-oes, -oed**) **1** attend a discotheque. **2** dance to disco music (*discoed the night away*).

dis·cog·ra·phy /diskógrəfee/ *n.* (*pl.* **-ies**) **1** a descriptive catalog of recordings. **2** the study of recordings.

dis·coid /dískoyd/ *adj.* disk-shaped.

dis·col·or /diskúlər/ *v.tr.* & *intr.* spoil the color of; stain; tarnish. ▫▫ **dis·col·or·a·tion** *n.*

dis·com·bob·u·late /dískəmbóbyəlayt/ *v.tr. joc.* disturb; disconcert.

dis·com·fit /diskúmfit/ *v.tr.* **1** disconcert or baffle. **2** thwart. ▫▫ **dis·com·fi·ture** *n.*

dis·com·fort /diskúmfərt/ *n.* & *v.* ● *n.* **1 a** a lack of ease; slight pain (*tight collar caused discomfort*). **b** mental uneasiness (*his presence caused her discomfort*). **2** a lack of comfort. ● *v.tr.* make uneasy.

dis·com·mode /dískəmṓd/ *v.tr.* inconvenience (a person, etc.).

dis·com·pose /dískəmpṓz/ *v.tr.* disturb the composure of. ▫▫ **dis·com·po·sure** /-pṓzhər/ *n.*

dis·co mu·sic *n.* popular dance music characterized by a heavy bass rhythm.

dis·con·cert /dískənsə́rt/ *v.tr.* **1** (often as **disconcerted** *adj.*) disturb the composure of; fluster (*disconcerted by his expression*). **2** spoil or upset (plans, etc.). ▫▫ **dis·con·cert·ing** *adj.* **dis·con·cert·ing·ly** *adv.*

dis·con·nect /dískənékt/ *v.tr.* **1** (often foll. by *from*) break the connection of (things, ideas, etc.). **2** put (an electrical device) out of action by disconnecting the parts, esp. by pulling out the plug.

dis·con·nect·ed /dískənéktid/ *adj.* **1** not connected; detached; separated. **2** (of speech, writing, argument, etc.) incoherent and illogical.

dis·con·nec·tion /dískənékshən/ *n.* the act or an instance of disconnecting; the state of being disconnected.

dis·con·so·late /diskónsələt/ *adj.* **1** forlorn or inconsolable. **2** unhappy or disappointed. ▫▫ **dis·con·so·late·ly** *adv.*

dis·con·tent /dískəntént/ *n.*, *adj.*, & *v.* ● *n.* lack of contentment; restlessness; dissatisfaction. ● *adj.* dissatisfied (*was discontent with his lot*). ● *v.tr.* (esp. as **discontented** *adj.*) make dissatisfied. ▫▫ **dis·con·tent·ed·ly** *adv.* **dis·con·tent·ment** *n.*

dis·con·tin·ue /dískəntínyoo/ *v.* (**-continues, -continued, -continuing**) **1** *intr.* & *tr.* cease or cause to cease to exist or be made (*a discontinued line*). **2** *tr.* give up; cease from (*discontinued his visits*). **3** *tr.* cease taking or paying (a newspaper, a subscription, etc.). ▫▫ **dis·con·tin·u·ance** *n.* **dis·con·tin·u·a·tion** *n.*

dis·con·tin·u·ous /dískəntínyooəs/ *adj.* lacking continuity in space or time; intermittent. ▫▫ **dis·con·ti·nu·i·ty** /-kontinóo-itee, -nyóo-/ *n.* **dis·con·tin·u·ous·ly** *adv.*

dis·cord *n.* & *v.* ● *n.* /dískawrd/ **1** disagreement; strife. **2** harsh clashing noise; clangor. **3** *Mus.* **a** a lack of harmony between notes sounding together. **b** an unpleasing or unfinished chord needing to be completed by another. ● *v.intr.* /diskáwrd/ **1** (usu. foll. by *with*) **a** disagree or quarrel. **b** be different or inconsistent. **2** jar; clash; be dissonant.

dis·cord·ant /diskáwrd'nt/ *adj.* (usu. foll. by *to*, *from*, *with*) **1** disagreeing; at variance. **2** (of sounds) not in harmony; dissonant. ▫▫ **dis·cord·ance** /-d'ns/ *n.* **dis·cord·ant·ly** *adv.*

dis·co·theque /dískəték/ *n.* **1** a club, etc., for dancing to recorded popular music. **2 a** the professional lighting and sound equipment used at a discotheque. **b** a business that provides this. **3** a party with dancing to popular music, esp. using such equipment.

dis·count *n.* & *v.* ● *n.* /dískownt/ **1** a deduction from a bill or amount due. **2** a deduction from the amount of a bill of exchange, etc., by a person who gives value for it before it is due. **3** the act or an instance of discounting. ● *v.tr.* /diskównt/ **1** disregard as unreliable or unimportant (*discounted his story*). **2** reduce the effect of (an event, etc.) by previous action. **3** deduct (esp. an amount from a bill, etc.). **4** give or get the present worth of (a bill not yet due). ▫ **at a discount 1** below the nominal or usual price (cf. PREMIUM). **2** not in demand; depreciated. ▫▫ **dis·count·er** *n.*

dis·coun·te·nance /diskówntinəns/ *v.tr.* **1** (esp. in *passive*) disconcert. **2** refuse to countenance; show disapproval of.

dis·cour·age /diskə́rij, -kúr-/ *v.tr.* **1** deprive of courage, confidence, or energy. **2** (usu. foll. by *from*) dissuade (*discouraged her from going*). **3** inhibit or seek to prevent (an action, etc.) by showing disapproval (*smoking is discouraged*). ▫▫ **dis·cour·age·ment** *n.* **dis·cour·ag·ing·ly** *adv.*

dis·course *n.* & *v.* ● *n.* /dískawrs/ **1** *literary* **a** a conversation; talk. **b** a dissertation or treatise on an academic subject. **c** a lecture or sermon. **2** *Linguistics* a connected series of utterances; a text. ● *v.intr.* /diskórs/ **1** talk; converse. **2** (usu. foll. by *of*, *on*, *upon*) speak or write at length.

dis·cour·te·ous /diskə́rteeəs/ *adj.* impolite; rude. ▫▫ **dis·cour·te·ous·ly** *adv.*

dis·cour·te·sy /diskə́rtəsee/ *n.* (*pl.* **-ies**) **1** bad manners; rudeness. **2** an impolite act or remark.

dis·cov·er /diskúvər/ *v.tr.* **1** (often foll. by *that* + clause) **a** find out or become aware of. **b** be the first to find or find out (*who discovered America?*). **c** devise or pioneer (*discover new techniques*). **2** give (check) in a game of chess by removing one's own obstructing piece. **3** (in show business) find and promote as a new singer, actor, etc. ▫▫ **dis·cov·er·a·ble** *adj.* **dis·cov·er·er** *n.*

dis·cov·er·y /diskúvəree/ *n.* (*pl.* **-ies**) **1 a** the act or process of discovering or being discovered. **b** an instance of this (*the discovery of a new planet*). **2** a person or thing discovered.

dis·cred·it /diskrédit/ *n.* & *v.* ● *n.* **1** harm to reputation (*brought discredit on the enterprise*). **2** a person or thing causing this (*he is a discredit to his family*). **3** lack of credibility (*throws discredit on her story*). **4** the loss of commercial credit. ● *v.tr.* **1** harm the good reputation of. **2** cause to be disbelieved. **3** refuse to believe.

dis·cred·it·a·ble /diskréditəbəl/ *adj.* bringing discredit; shameful. ▫▫ **dis·cred·it·a·bly** *adv.*

dis·creet /diskréet/ *adj.* (**discreeter, discreetest**) **1 a** circumspect. **b** tactful; trustworthy. **2** unobtrusive (*a discreet touch of rouge*). ▫▫ **dis·creet·ly** *adv.*

dis·crep·an·cy /diskrépənsee/ *n.* (*pl.* **-ies**) **1** difference; inconsistency. **2** an instance of this. ▫▫ **dis·crep·ant** *adj.*

dis·crete /diskréet/ *adj.* individually distinct; separate; discontinuous. ▫▫ **dis·crete·ly** *adv.* **dis·crete·ness** *n.*

dis·cre·tion /diskréshən/ *n.* **1** being discreet; discreet behavior (*treats confidences with discretion*). **2** prudence; self-preservation. **3** the freedom to act and think as one wishes (*it is within his discretion to leave*). **4** *Law* a court's freedom to decide a sentence, etc. ▫ **at discretion** as one pleases. **at the discretion of** to be settled or disposed of according to the judgment or choice of. **discretion is the better part of valor** reckless courage is often self-defeating. **use one's discretion** act according to one's own judgment. **years** (or **age**) **of discretion** the esp. legal age at which a person is able to manage his or her own affairs. ▫▫ **dis·cre·tion·ar·y** *adj.*

dis·crim·i·nate /diskríminayt/ *v.* **1** *intr.* (often foll. by *between*) make or see a distinction; differentiate. **2** *intr.* make a distinction, esp. unjustly. **3** *intr.* (foll. by *against*) select for unfavorable treatment. **4** *tr.* (usu. foll. by *from*) make or see or constitute a difference in or between (*many things discriminate one person from another*). **5** *intr.* (esp. as **discriminating** *adj.*) observe distinctions carefully; have good judgment. **6** *tr.* mark as distinctive; be a distinguishing feature of. ▫▫ **dis·crim·i·na·tive** /-nətiv/ *adj.* **dis·crim·i·na·tor** *n.* **dis·crim·i·na·to·ry** /-nətáwree/ *adj.*

dis·crim·i·nat·ing /diskríminayting/ *adj.* **1** able to discern distinctions. **2** having good taste.

dis·crim·i·na·tion /diskrímináyshən/ *n.* **1** unfavorable treatment based on prejudice. **2** good taste or judgment in artistic matters, etc. **3** the power of discriminating or observing differences. **4** a distinction made with the mind or in action.

dis·cur·sive /diskə́rsiv/ *adj.* **1** rambling or digressive. **2** *Philos.* proceeding by argument or reasoning (opp. INTUITIVE). ▫▫ **dis·cur·sive·ly** *adv.* **dis·cur·sive·ness** *n.*

dis·cus /dískəs/ *n.* (*pl.* **discuses**) **1** a heavy, thick-centered disk thrown in ancient Greek games. **2** ► a similar disk thrown in modern field events.

metal rim
center weight
DISCUS

dis·cuss /diskús/ *v.tr.* **1** hold a conversation about (*discussed their vacations*). **2** examine by argument, esp. written; debate. ▫▫ **dis·cus·sant** *n.*

dis·cus·sion /diskúshən/ *n.* **1** a conversation, esp. on specific subjects; a debate (*had a discussion about what they should do*). **2** an examination by argument, written or spoken.

dis·dain /disdáyn/ *n.* & *v.* ● *n.* scorn; contempt. ● *v.tr.* **1** regard with disdain. **2** think oneself superior to; reject (*disdained his offer*; *disdained to enter*; *disdained answering*).

dis·dain·ful /disdáynfool/ *adj.* showing disdain or contempt. ▫▫ **dis·dain·ful·ly** *adv.*

dis·ease /dizéez/ *n.* **1** an unhealthy condition of the body or the mind. **2** a corresponding physical

D

condition of plants. **3** a particular kind of disease with special symptoms or location.

dis·eased /dizéezd/ *adj.* **1** affected with disease. **2** abnormal; disordered.

dis·em·bark /dísimbáark/ *v.tr. & intr.* put or go ashore or land from a ship or an aircraft. □□ **dis·em·bar·ka·tion** *n.*

dis·em·bar·rass /dísimbárəs/ *v.tr.* **1** (usu. foll. by *of*) relieve (of a load, etc.). **2** free from embarrassment.

dis·em·bod·y /dísimbódee/ *v.tr.* (**-ies, -ied**) (esp. as **disembodied** *adj.*) separate or free from the body or a concrete form (*disembodied spirit*).

dis·em·bogue /dísimbóg/ *v.tr. & intr.* (**disembogues, disembogued, disemboguing**) (of a river, etc.) pour forth (waters) at the mouth.

dis·em·bow·el /dísimbówəl/ *v.tr.* remove the bowels or entrails of.

dis·en·chant /dísinchánt/ *v.tr.* free from enchantment; disillusion. □□ **dis·en·chant·ment** *n.*

dis·en·cum·ber /dísinkúmbər/ *v.tr.* free from encumbrance.

dis·en·fran·chise var. of DISFRANCHISE.

dis·en·gage /dísingáyj/ *v.* **1 a** *tr.* detach, free, loosen, or separate (parts, etc.) (*disengaged the clutch*). **b** *refl.* detach oneself; get loose (*disengaged ourselves from their company*). **2** *tr. Mil.* remove (troops) from a battle or a battle area. **3** *intr.* become detached. **4** *intr.* (as **disengaged** *adj.*) **a** unoccupied; free; vacant. **b** uncommitted.

dis·en·gage·ment /dísingáyjmənt/ *n.* **1 a** the act of disengaging. **b** an instance of this. **2** freedom from ties; detachment. **3** the dissolution of an engagement to marry. **4** ease of manner or behavior.

dis·en·tan·gle /dísintánggəl/ *v.* **1** *tr.* **a** unravel; untwist. **b** free from complications; extricate (*disentangled her from the difficulty*). **2** *intr.* become disentangled. □□ **dis·en·tan·gle·ment** *n.*

dis·en·ti·tle /dísintít'l/ *v.tr.* (usu. foll. by *to*) deprive of any rightful claim.

dis·e·qui·lib·ri·um /díseekwilíbreeəm/ *n.* a lack or loss of equilibrium; instability.

dis·es·tab·lish /dísistáblish/ *v.tr.* **1** deprive (a church) of government support. **2** depose from an official position. **3** terminate the establishment of. □□ **dis·es·tab·lish·ment** *n.*

dis·fa·vor /disfáyvər/ *n. & v.* ● *n.* **1** disapproval or dislike. **2** the state of being disliked (*fell into disfavor*). ● *v.tr.* regard or treat with disfavor.

dis·fig·ure /disfígyər/ *v.tr.* spoil the beauty of; deform; deface. □□ **dis·fig·ure·ment** *n.*

dis·fran·chise /dísfránchīz/ *v.tr.* (also **dis·en·fran·chise** /disinfránchīz/) **1 a** deprive (a person) of the right to vote. **b** deprive (a place) of the right to send a representative to parliament. **2** deprive (a person) of rights as a citizen or of a franchise held. □□ **dis·fran·chise·ment** *n.*

dis·gorge /disgáwrj/ *v.tr.* **1** eject from the throat or stomach. **2** pour forth; discharge. □□ **dis·gorge·ment** *n.*

dis·grace /disgráys/ *n. & v.* ● *n.* **1** shame; ignominy (*brought disgrace on his family*). **2** a dishonorable, inefficient, or shameful person, thing, state of affairs, etc. (*the bus service is a disgrace*). ● *v.tr.* **1** bring shame or discredit on. **2** degrade from a position of honor; dismiss from favor. □ **in disgrace** out of favor.

dis·grace·ful /disgráysfool/ *adj.* shameful; dishonorable; degrading. □□ **dis·grace·ful·ly** *adv.*

dis·grun·tled /disgrúnt'ld/ *adj.* discontented; sulky. □□ **dis·grun·tle·ment** *n.*

dis·guise /disgíz/ *v. & n.* ● *v.tr.* **1** (often foll. by *as*) alter the appearance, sound, smell, etc., of, so as to conceal the identity; make unrecognizable. **2** misrepresent or cover up (*disguised their intentions*). ● *n.* **1 a** a costume, false beard, makeup, etc., used to alter the appearance so as to conceal or deceive. **b** any action, manner, etc., used for deception. **2 a** the act or practice of disguising; the conceal-

ment of reality. **b** an instance of this. □ **in disguise 1** wearing a concealing costume, etc. **2** appearing to be the opposite (*a blessing in disguise*).

dis·gust /disgúst/ *n. & v.* ● *n.* (usu. foll. by *at, for*) **1** strong aversion; repugnance. **2** strong distaste for (some item of) food, drink, medicine, etc.; nausea. ● *v.tr.* cause disgust in (*their behavior disgusts me; was disgusted to find a slug*). □ **in disgust** as a result of disgust (*left in disgust*). □□ **dis·gust·ed·ly** *adv.*

dis·gust·ing /disgústing/ *adj.* arousing aversion or indignation (*disgusting behavior*). □□ **dis·gust·ing·ly** *adv.*

dish /dish/ *n. & v.* ● *n.* **1 a** a shallow container for cooking or serving food. **b** the food served in a dish (*all the dishes were delicious*). **c** a particular kind of food (*a meat dish*). **2** (in *pl.*) dirty plates, utensils, cooking pots, etc., after a meal. **3 a** a dish-shaped object, or cavity. **b** = SATELLITE DISH. **4** *sl.* a sexually attractive person. ● *v.tr.* **1** put (food) into a dish ready for serving. **2** *colloq.* outmaneuver. **3** make concave or dish-shaped. □ **dish out** *sl.* distribute. **dish up 1** serve or prepare to serve (food). **2** *colloq.* seek to present (facts, argument, etc.) attractively. □□ **dish·ful** *n.* (*pl.* **-fuls**).

dis·ha·bille /disəbéel, -béé/ *n.* (also **des·ha·bille** /dezəbéel, -béé/) a state of being only partly or carelessly clothed.

dis·har·mo·ny /dis-haármənee/ *n.* a lack of harmony; discord. □□ **dis·har·mo·ni·ous** /-mōneeəs/ *adj.*

dish·cloth /díshklawth, -kloth/ *n.* a usu. open-weave cloth for washing dishes.

dis·heart·en /dis-haárt'n/ *v.tr.* cause to lose courage or confidence; make despondent. □□ **dis·heart·en·ing·ly** *adv.* **dis·heart·en·ment** *n.*

di·shev·eled /dishévəld/ *adj.* untidy; ruffled; disordered. □□ **di·shev·el** *v.tr.* **di·shev·el·ment** *n.*

dis·hon·est /disónist/ *adj.* fraudulent or insincere. □□ **dis·hon·est·ly** *adv.* **dis·hon·es·ty** /disónistee/ *n.* (*pl.* **-ies**)

dis·hon·or /disónər/ *n. & v.* ● *n.* **1** a state of shame or disgrace. **2** something that causes dishonor. ● *v.tr.* **1** treat without honor or respect. **2** disgrace (*dishonored his name*). **3** refuse to accept or pay (a check or a bill of exchange).

dis·hon·or·a·ble /disónərəbəl/ *adj.* **1** causing disgrace; ignominious. **2** unprincipled. □□ **dis·hon·or·a·bly** *adv.*

dish·pan /díshpan/ *n.* a large, deep, usu. circular pan for washing dishes.

dish·wash·er /díshwoshər, -wawshər/ *n.* **1** a machine for automatically washing dishes. **2** a person employed to wash dishes.

dish·wa·ter /díshwawtər, -woter/ *n.* water in which dishes have been washed. □ **dull as dishwater** extremely dull; boring.

dis·il·lu·sion /dísilóōzhən/ *n. & v.* ● *n.* freedom from illusions. ● *v.tr.* disenchant. □□ **dis·il·lu·sion·ment** *n.*

dis·in·cen·tive /dísinséntiv/ *n. & adj.* ● *n.* **1** something that tends to discourage a particular action, etc. **2** *Econ.* a source of discouragement to productivity or progress. ● *adj.* tending to discourage.

dis·in·cline /dísinklín/ *v.tr.* (usu. foll. by *to* + infin. or *for*) **1** make unwilling or reluctant. **2** (as **disinclined** *adj.*) unwilling; averse. □□ **dis·in·cli·na·tion** /dísinklináyshən/ *n.*

dis·in·fect /dísinfékt/ *v.tr.* cleanse (a wound, a room, clothes, etc.) of infection, esp. with a disinfectant. □□ **dis·in·fec·tion** /-fékshən/ *n.*

dis·in·fect·ant /dísinféktənt/ *n. & adj.* ● *n.* a usu. commercially produced chemical liquid that destroys germs. ● *adj.* causing disinfection.

dis·in·fest /dísinfést/ *v.tr.* rid of vermin, infesting insects, etc.

dis·in·fla·tion /dísinfláyshən/ *n. Econ.* a policy designed to counteract inflation without causing deflation. □□ **dis·in·fla·tion·ar·y** *adj.*

dis·in·for·ma·tion /dísinfərmáyshən/ *n.* false information, intended to mislead.

dis·in·gen·u·ous /dísinjényōōs/ *adj.* having secret motives; insincere. □□ **dis·in·gen·u·ous·ly** *adv.* **dis·in·gen·u·ous·ness** *n.*

dis·in·her·it /dísinhérit/ *v.tr.* reject as one's heir; deprive of the right of inheritance. □□ **dis·in·her·i·tance** *n.*

dis·in·te·grate /disíntigrayt/ *v.* **1** *tr. & intr.* **a** separate into component parts or fragments. **b** lose or cause to lose cohesion. **2** *intr. colloq.* deteriorate mentally or physically. **3** *intr. & tr. Physics* undergo or cause to undergo disintegration. □□ **dis·in·te·gra·tor** *n.*

dis·in·te·gra·tion /disíntigráyshən/ *n.* **1** the act or an instance of disintegrating. **2** *Physics* any process in which a nucleus emits a particle or particles or divides into smaller nuclei.

dis·in·ter /dísintér/ *v.tr.* (**disinterred, disinterring**) **1** remove (esp. a corpse) from the ground; unearth. **2** find after a protracted search (*disinterred the letter from the back of the drawer*). □□ **dis·in·ter·ment** *n.*

dis·in·ter·est /disíntrist, -íntərist/ *n.* **1** impartiality. **2** *disp.* lack of interest; unconcern.

dis·in·ter·est·ed /disíntristid, -íntəri-/ *adj.* **1** not influenced by one's own advantage. **2** *disp.* uninterested. □□ **dis·in·ter·est·ed·ly** *adv.* **dis·in·ter·est·ed·ness** *n.*

dis·in·vest /dísinvést/ *v.intr.* (foll. by *from*, or *absol.*) reduce or dispose of one's investment (in a place, company, etc.). □□ **dis·in·vest·ment** *n.*

dis·jec·ta mem·bra /disjéktə mémbrə/ *n.pl.* scattered remains; fragments, esp. of written work.

dis·join /disjóyn/ *v.tr.* separate or disunite.

dis·joint /disjóynt/ *v. & adj.* ● *v.tr.* **1** take apart at the joints. **2** (as **disjointed** *adj.*) (esp. of conversation) incoherent. **3** disturb the working or connection of. ● *adj.* (of two or more sets) having no elements in common. □□ **dis·joint·ed·ly** *adv.* **dis·joint·ed·ness** *n.*

dis·junc·tion /disjúngkshən/ *n.* **1** the process of disjoining; separation. **2** an instance of this.

dis·junc·tive /disjúngktiv/ *adj. & n.* ● *adj.* **1** involving separation. **2** *Gram.* (esp. of a conjunction) expressing a choice between two words, etc. ● *n. Gram.* a disjunctive conjunction or other word. □□ **dis·junc·tive·ly** *adv.*

disk /disk/ *n.* (also **disc**) **1 a** a flat thin circular object. **b** a round, flat or apparently flat surface (*the sun's disk*). **c** a mark of this shape. **2** ▼ a layer of cartilage between vertebrae. **3 a** a phonograph record. **b** = COMPACT DISC. **4 a** (in full **magnetic disc**) a computer storage device consisting of

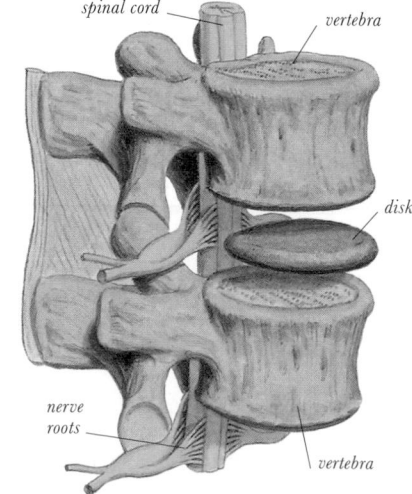

spinal cord   *vertebra*

disk

nerve roots

vertebra

DISK: SECTION OF THE HUMAN SPINE SHOWING AN INTERVERTEBRAL DISK

several flat, circular, magnetically coated plates formed into a rotatable disk. ▷ COMPUTER, HARD DISK. **b** (in full **optical disc** or **disk**) a smooth nonmagnetic disk with large storage capacity for data recorded and read by laser.

disk brake *n.* (often **disc brake**) a brake employing the friction of pads against a disk. ▷ BRAKE

disk drive *n. Computing* a mechanism for rotating a disk and reading or writing data from or to it. ▷ COMPUTER

disk·ette /diskét/ *n. Computing* = FLOPPY DISK.

disk har·row *n.* ▼ a harrow with cutting edges consisting of a row of concave disks set at an oblique angle.

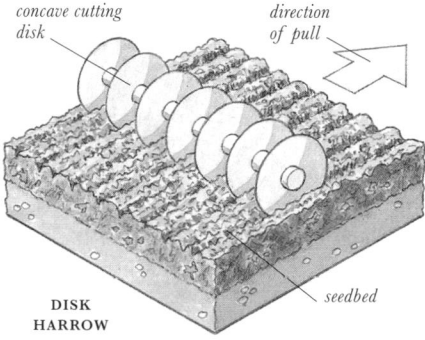

concave cutting disk   direction of pull

seedbed

DISK HARROW

disk jock·ey *n.* (also **disc jock·ey**) the presenter of a selection of phonograph records, compact discs, etc., of popular music.

dis·like /dislík/ *v. & n.* ● *v.tr.* have an aversion or objection to; not like. ● *n.* **1** a feeling of repugnance or not liking. **2** an object of dislike. □□ **dis·lik·a·ble** *adj.* (also **dis·like·a·ble**).

dis·lo·cate /dislôkayt, dislô-/ *v.tr.* **1** disturb the normal connection of (esp. a joint in the body). **2** disrupt; put out of order. **3** displace. □□ **dis·lo·ca·tion** /dislôkáyshən/ *n.*

dis·lodge /dislój/ *v.tr.* remove from an established or fixed position. □□ **dis·lodg·ment** *n.* (also **dis·lodge·ment**).

dis·loy·al /dislóyəl/ *adj.* (often foll. by *to*) **1** not loyal; unfaithful. **2** untrue to one's allegiance. □□ **dis·loy·al·ly** *adv.* **dis·loy·al·ty** *n.*

dis·mal /dízməl/ *adj.* **1** causing or showing gloom; miserable. **2** dreary or somber. **3** *colloq.* feeble or inept (*a dismal performance*). □□ **dis·mal·ly** *adv.*

dis·man·tle /dismánt'l/ *v.tr.* **1** take to pieces; pull down. **2** deprive of defenses or equipment. **3** (often foll. by *of*) strip of covering or protection. □□ **dis·man·tle·ment** *n.* **dis·man·tler** *n.*

dis·mast /dismást/ *v.tr.* deprive (a ship) of masts; break down the mast or masts of.

dis·may /dismáy/ *v. & n.* ● *v.tr.* fill with consternation or anxiety; reduce to despair. ● *n.* **1** consternation or anxiety. **2** depression or despair.

dis·mem·ber /dismémbər/ *v.tr.* **1** tear or cut the limbs from. **2** divide up (a country, etc.). □□ **dis·mem·ber·ment** *n.*

dis·miss /dismís/ *v.* **1 a** *tr.* cause to leave one's presence; disperse (an assembly or army). **b** *intr.* (of an assembly, etc.) break ranks. **2** *tr.* discharge from employment, office, etc., esp. dishonorably. **3** *tr.* put out of one's thoughts (*dismissed him from memory*). **4** *tr.* treat summarily (*dismissed his application*). **5** *tr. Law* refuse further hearing to (a case). **6** *tr. Cricket* put (a batsman or a side) out. **7** *intr.* (in *imper.*) *Mil.* a word of command at the end of drilling. □□ **dis·miss·al** *n.* **dis·miss·i·ble** *adj.*

dis·mis·sive /dismísiv/ *adj.* tending to dismiss from consideration. □□ **dis·mis·sive·ly** *adv.* **dis·mis·sive·ness** *n.*

dis·mount *v. & n.* ● *v.* /dismównt/ **1 a** *intr.* alight from a horse, bicycle, etc. **b** *tr.* (usu. in *passive*) throw from a horse; unseat. **2** *tr.* remove (a thing) from its

mounting (esp. a gun from its carriage). ● *n.* /dismównt, dís-/ the act of dismounting.

dis·o·be·di·ent /disəbéedeeənt/ *adj.* disobeying; rebellious. □□ **dis·o·be·di·ence** /-deeəns/ *n.* **dis·o·be·di·ent·ly** *adv.*

dis·o·bey /disəbáy/ *v.tr.* (also *absol.*) fail or refuse to obey; disregard (orders); break (rules).

dis·o·blige /disəblíj/ *v.tr.* **1** refuse to consider the convenience or wishes of. **2** (as **disobliging** *adj.*) uncooperative.

dis·or·der /disáwrdər/ *n. & v.* ● *n.* **1** a lack of order; confusion. **2** a riot; a commotion. **3** *Med.* a usu. minor ailment or disease. ● *v.tr.* **1** throw into confusion; disarrange. **2** *Med.* upset.

dis·or·der·ly /disáwrdərlee/ *adj.* **1** untidy; confused. **2** unruly; riotous. **3** *Law* contrary to public order or morality. □□ **dis·or·der·li·ness** *n.*

dis·or·gan·ize /disáwrgənīz/ *v.tr.* **1** destroy the system or order of. **2** (as **disorganized** *adj.*) lacking organization or system. □□ **dis·or·gan·i·za·tion** *n.*

dis·o·ri·ent /disáwreeənt/ *v.tr.* **1** confuse (a person) as to his or her bearings. **2** (often as **disoriented** *adj.*) confuse (a person) (*disoriented by his unexpected behavior*).

dis·o·ri·en·tate /disáwrieəntayt/ *v.tr.* = DISORIENT. □□ **dis·o·ri·en·ta·tion** /-táyshən/ *n.*

dis·own /disón/ *v.tr.* **1** refuse to recognize; repudiate; disclaim. **2** renounce one's connection with or allegiance to.

dis·par·age /dispárij/ *v.tr.* **1** speak slightingly of; depreciate. **2** bring discredit on. □□ **dis·par·age·ment** *n.* **dis·par·ag·ing·ly** *adv.*

dis·pa·rate /díspərət, dispár-/ *adj. & n.* ● *adj.* essentially different in kind; without comparison or relation. ● *n.* (in *pl.*) things so unlike that there is no basis for their comparison. □□ **dis·pa·rate·ly** *adv.* **dis·pa·rate·ness** *n.* **dis·par·i·ty** /dispáritee/ *n.* (*pl.* **-ies**).

dis·pas·sion·ate /dispáshənət/ *adj.* free from passion; calm; impartial. □□ **dis·pas·sion·ate·ly** *adv.* **dis·pas·sion·ate·ness** *n.*

dis·patch /dispách/ *v. & n.* (also **des·patch**) ● *v.tr.* **1** send off to a destination or for a purpose. **2** perform (business, a task, etc.) promptly. **3** kill; execute. **4** *colloq.* eat (food, a meal, etc.) quickly. ● *n.* **1** the act or an instance of sending. **2** the act or an instance of killing. **3** (also /dispách/) **a** an official written message on state or esp. military affairs. **b** a report sent in by a newspaper's correspondent. **4** promptness (*done with dispatch*). □□ **dis·patch·er** *n.*

dis·pel /dispél/ *v.tr.* (**dispelled, dispelling**) dissipate; disperse; scatter.

dis·pen·sa·ble /dispénsəbəl/ *adj.* **1** able to be done without; unnecessary. **2** (of a law, etc.) able to be relaxed in special cases. □□ **dis·pen·sa·bil·i·ty** *n.*

dis·pen·sa·ry /dispénsəree/ *n.* (*pl.* **-ies**) **1** a place where medicines, etc., are dispensed. **2** a public or charitable institution for medical advice and the dispensing of medicines.

dis·pen·sa·tion /dispensáyshən/ *n.* **1 a** the act or an instance of dispensing or distributing. **b** (foll. by *with*) the state of doing without (a thing). **c** something distributed. **2** (usu. foll. by *from*) exemption from a penalty, duty or religious observance; an instance of this. **3** a religious or political system obtaining in a nation, etc. **4 a** the ordering or management of the world by providence. **b** a specific example of such ordering (of a community, a person, etc.). □□ **dis·pen·sa·tion·al** *adj.*

dis·pense /dispéns/ *v.* **1** *tr.* distribute; deal out. **2** *tr.* administer (a sacrament, justice, etc.). **3** *tr.* make up and give out (medicine, etc.) according to a doctor's prescription. **4** *tr.* (usu. foll. by *from*) grant a dispensation to (a person) from an obligation, esp. a religious observance. **5** *intr.* (foll. by *with*) **a** do without; render needless. **b** give exemption from (a rule).

dis·pens·er /dispénsər/ *n.* a person, thing, or automatic machine that dispenses something, e.g., medicine, good advice, cash.

dis·per·sant /dispérsənt/ *n. Chem.* an agent used to disperse small particles in a medium.

dis·perse /dispérs/ *v.* **1** *intr. & tr.* go, send, drive, or distribute in different directions or over a wide area. **2 a** *intr.* (of people at a meeting, etc.) leave and go their various ways. **b** *tr.* cause to do this. **3** *tr.* send to or station at separate points. **4** *tr.* disseminate. □□ **dis·per·sal** *n.* **dis·pers·er** *n.* **dis·pers·i·ble** *adj.* **dis·per·sive** *adj.*

dis·per·sion /dispérzhən, -shən/ *n.* **1** the act or an instance of dispersing; the process of being dispersed. **2** *Chem.* a mixture of one substance dispersed in another. **3** *Statistics* the extent to which values of a variable differ from the mean. **4** (**the Dispersion**) **a** the dispersion of the Jews among the Gentiles mainly in the 8th–6th c. BC. **b** Jews dispersed in this way.

dis·pir·it /dispírit/ *v.tr.* **1** (esp. as **dispiriting** *adj.*) make despondent; discourage. **2** (as **dispirited** *adj.*) dejected; discouraged. □□ **dis·pir·it·ed·ly** *adv.* **dis·pir·it·ed·ness** *n.* **dis·pir·it·ing·ly** *adv.*

dis·place /displáys/ *v.tr.* **1** shift from its accustomed place. **2** remove from office. **3** take the place of; oust.

dis·placed per·son *n.* a person who is forced to leave his or her home country because of war, persecution, etc.; a refugee.

dis·place·ment /displáysmənt/ *n.* **1 a** the act or an instance of displacing; the process of being displaced. **b** an instance of this. **2** *Physics* the amount of a fluid displaced by a solid floating or immersed in it. **3** *Psychol.* **a** the substitution of one idea or impulse for another. **b** the unconscious transfer of strong unacceptable emotions from one object to another. **4** the amount by which a thing is shifted from its place.

dis·play /displáy/ *v. & n.* ● *v.tr.* **1** expose to view; exhibit. **2** show ostentatiously. **3** reveal (*displayed his ignorance*). ● *n.* **1** the act or an instance of displaying. **2** an exhibition or show. **3** ostentation; flashiness. **4** ▼ the distinct behavior of some birds and fish, esp. used to attract a mate. **5 a** the presentation of signals or data on a visual display unit, etc. **b** the information so presented. □□ **dis·play·er** *n.*

puffed out throat feathers

fanned tail

DISPLAY: COURTSHIP DISPLAY OF A MALE CAPERCAILLIE (*Tetrao urogallus*)

dis·please /displéez/ *v.tr.* make indignant or angry; offend; annoy. □ **be displeased** (often foll. by *at, with*) be indignant or dissatisfied; disapprove. □□ **dis·pleas·ing** *adj.* **dis·pleas·ing·ly** *adv.*

dis·pleas·ure /displézhər/ *n.* disapproval; anger; dissatisfaction.

dis·port /dispáwrt/ *v.intr. & refl.* frolic; gambol; enjoy oneself.

D

D

dis·pos·a·ble /dispőzəbəl/ *adj. & n.* ● *adj.* **1** intended to be used once and then thrown away. **2** that can be got rid of, made over, or used. **3** (esp. of assets) at the owner's disposal. ● *n.* a thing designed to be thrown away after one use. □□ **dis·pos·a·bil·i·ty** *n.*

dis·pos·a·ble in·come *n.* income after taxes, etc., available for spending.

dis·pos·al /dispőzəl/ *n.* (usu. foll. by *of*) **1** the act or an instance of disposing of something. **2** the arrangement, disposition, or placing of something. **3** control or management (of a person, business, etc.). **4** (esp. as **waste disposal**) the disposing of garbage. □ **at one's disposal 1** available for one's use. **2** subject to one's orders or decisions.

dis·pose /dispőz/ *v.* **1** *tr.* (usu. foll. by *to*, or *to* + *infin.*) **a** make willing; incline (*disposed him to the idea*). **b** give a tendency to (*disposed to buckle*). **2** *tr.* place suitably (*disposed the pictures in sequence*). **3** *tr.* (as **disposed** *adj.*) have a specified mental inclination (usu. in *comb.*: *ill-disposed*). **4** *intr.* determine the course of events (*man proposes, God disposes*). □ **dispose of 1 a** deal with. **b** get rid of. **c** finish. **d** kill. **e** distribute; dispense; bestow. **2** sell. **3** prove (a claim, an argument, an opponent, etc.) to be incorrect. **4** consume (food). □□ **dis·pos·er** *n.*

dis·po·si·tion /dispəzíshən/ *n.* **1 a** (often foll. by *to*) a natural tendency; an inclination. **b** a person's temperament. **2 a** setting in order; arranging. **b** the relative position of parts; an arrangement. **3** (usu. in *pl.*) **a** *Mil.* the stationing of troops ready for attack or defense. **b** preparations; plans. **4 a** a bestowal by deed or will. **b** control; the power of disposing. **5** ordinance; dispensation.

dis·pos·sess /dispəzés/ *v.tr.* **1** dislodge; oust (a person). **2** (usu. foll. by *of*) deprive. □□ **dis·pos·ses·sion** /-zéshən/ *n.*

dis·proof /dispróof/ *n.* **1** something that disproves. **2 a** refutation. **b** an instance of this.

dis·pro·por·tion /disprəpáwrshən/ *n.* **1** a lack of proportion. **2** an instance of this. □□ **dis·pro·por·tion·al** *adj.* **dis·pro·por·tion·al·ly** *adv.*

dis·pro·por·tion·ate /disprəpáwrshənət/ *adj.* **1** lacking proportion. **2** relatively too large, long, etc. □□ **dis·pro·por·tion·ate·ly** *adv.* **dis·pro·por·tion·ate·ness** *n.*

dis·prove /dispróov/ *v.tr.* prove false. □□ **dis·prov·a·ble** *adj.*

dis·put·a·ble /dispyóotəbəl/ *adj.* open to question; uncertain. □□ **dis·put·a·bly** *adv.*

dis·pu·ta·tion /dispyətáyshən/ *n.* **1 a** disputing; debating. **b** an argument; a controversy. **2** a formal debate.

dis·pu·ta·tious /dispyətáyshəs/ *adj.* fond of or inclined to argument. □□ **dis·pu·ta·tious·ly** *adv.* **dis·pu·ta·tious·ness** *n.*

dis·pute /dispyóot/ *v. & n.* ● *v.* **1** *intr.* (usu. foll. by *with*, *against*) **a** debate; argue. **b** quarrel. **2** *tr.* discuss, esp. heatedly (*disputed whether it was true*). **3** *tr.* question the truth or correctness or validity of (a statement, alleged fact, etc.). **4** *tr.* contend for; strive to win (*disputed the crown*). **5** *tr.* resist (a landing, advance, etc.). ● *n.* **1** a controversy; a debate. **2** a quarrel. **3** a disagreement leading to industrial action. □ **beyond** (or **past** or **without**) **dispute 1** certainly; indisputably. **2** certain; indisputable. **in dispute 1** being argued about. **2** (of a workforce) involved in industrial action. □□ **dis·pu·tant** /-spyóot'nt/ *n.* **dis·put·er** *n.*

dis·qual·i·fy /diskwólifī/ *v.tr.* (**-ies**, **-ied**) **1** (often foll. by *from*) debar from a competition or pronounce ineligible as a winner. **2** (often foll. by *for*, *from*) make or pronounce ineligible or unsuitable (*his age disqualifies him for the job*). **3** (often foll. by *from*) incapacitate legally; pronounce unqualified (*disqualified from practicing as a doctor*). □□ **dis·qual·i·fi·ca·tion** /diskwólifikáyshən/ *n.*

dis·qui·et /diskwíət/ *v. & n.* ● *v.tr.* worry. ● *n.* anxiety; unrest. □□ **dis·qui·et·ing** *adj.* **dis·qui·et·ing·ly** *adv.*

dis·qui·e·tude /diskwíətōōd, -tyōōd/ *n.* a state of uneasiness; anxiety.

dis·qui·si·tion /diskwizíshən/ *n.* a long or elaborate treatise or discourse.

dis·re·gard /dísrigaard/ *v. & n.* ● *v.tr.* **1** pay no attention to; ignore. **2** treat as of no importance. ● *n.* (often foll. by *of*, *for*) indifference; neglect.

dis·re·pair /dísripáir/ *n.* poor condition due to neglect.

dis·rep·u·ta·ble /disrépyətəbəl/ *adj.* **1** of bad reputation; discreditable. **2** not respectable in appearance; dirty; untidy. □□ **dis·rep·u·ta·ble·ness** *n.* **dis·rep·u·ta·bly** *adv.*

dis·re·pute /dísripyóot/ *n.* a lack of good reputation or respectability; discredit.

dis·re·spect /dísrispékt/ *n.* a lack of respect; discourtesy. □□ **dis·re·spect·ful** *adj.* **dis·re·spect·ful·ly** *adv.*

dis·robe /disrőb/ *v.tr. & refl.* (also *absol.*) **1** undress. **2** divest (oneself or another) of office, authority, etc.

dis·rupt /disrúpt/ *v.tr.* **1** interrupt the flow or continuity of (a meeting, speech, etc.); bring disorder to. **2** separate forcibly; shatter. □□ **dis·rupt·er** *n.* (also **dis·rup·tor**). **dis·rup·tion** /-rúpshən/ *n.* **dis·rup·tive** *adj.* **dis·rup·tive·ly** *adv.* **dis·rup·tive·ness** *n.*

diss /dis/ *v.tr. sl.* put (a person) down verbally; badmouth.

dis·sat·is·fy /disátisfī/ *v.tr.* (**-ies**, **-ied**) (often as **dissatisfied** *adj.*) make discontented; fail to satisfy. □□ **dis·sat·is·fac·tion** /-fákshən/ *n.* **dis·sat·is·fied·ly** *adv.*

dis·sect /disékt, dī-/ *v.tr.* **1** cut into pieces. **2** cut up (a plant or animal) to examine its parts, structure, etc., or (a corpse) for a post mortem. **3** analyze; criticize or examine in detail. □□ **dis·sec·tion** /-sékshən/ *n.* **dis·sec·tor** *n.*

dis·sem·ble /disémbəl/ *v.* **1** *intr.* talk or act hypocritically. **2** *tr.* **a** disguise or conceal (a feeling, intention, act, etc.). **b** simulate (*dissembled grief in public*). □□ **dis·sem·blance** *n.* **dis·sem·bler** *n.*

dis·sem·i·nate /diséminayt/ *v.tr.* scatter about; spread (esp. ideas) widely. □□ **dis·sem·i·na·tion** /-náyshən/ *n.* **dis·sem·i·na·tor** *n.*

dis·sen·sion /disénshən/ *n.* disagreement giving rise to discord.

dis·sent /disént/ *v. & n.* ● *v.intr.* (often foll. by *from*) **1** think differently; disagree; express disagreement. **2** differ in religious opinion, esp. from the doctrine of an established or orthodox church. ● *n.* **1 a** a difference of opinion. **b** an expression of this. **2** the refusal to accept the doctrines of an established or orthodox church; nonconformity. □□ **dis·sent·ing** *adj.*

dis·sent·er /diséntər/ *n.* a person who dissents.

dis·sen·tient /disénshənt/ *adj. & n.* ● *adj.* disagreeing with a majority or official view. ● *n.* a person who dissents.

dis·ser·ta·tion /disərtáyshən/ *n.* a detailed discourse on a subject, esp. one submitted in partial fulfillment of the requirements of a degree or diploma.

dis·serv·ice /dis-sárvis/ *n.* an ill turn; an injury, esp. done when trying to help.

dis·sev·er /disévər/ *v.tr. & intr.* sever; divide into parts. □□ **dis·sev·er·ance** *n.* **dis·sev·er·ment** *n.*

dis·si·dent /dísid'nt/ *adj. & n.* ● *adj.* disagreeing, esp. with an established government, system, etc. ● *n.* a dissident person. □□ **dis·si·dence** /dísid'ns/ *n.*

dis·sim·i·lar /disímilər/ *adj.* (often foll. by *to*) unlike; not similar. □□ **dis·sim·i·lar·i·ty** /-láritee/ *n.* (*pl.* **-ies**).

dis·sim·i·late /disímilayt/ *v.* (often foll. by *to*) *Phonet.* **1** *tr.* change (a sound or sounds in a word) to another when the word originally had the same sound repeated, as in *cinnamon*, orig. *cinnamom*. **2** *intr.* (of a sound) be changed in this way. □□ **dis·sim·i·la·tion** /-láyshən/ *n.* **dis·sim·i·la·to·ry** /-lətáwree/ *adj.*

dis·sim·u·late /disímyəlayt/ *v.tr. & intr.* dissemble. □□ **dis·sim·u·la·tion** /-láyshən/ *n.*

dis·si·pate /dísipayt/ *v.* **1 a** *tr.* cause (a cloud, vapor, fear, darkness, etc.) to disappear or disperse. **b** *intr.* disperse; scatter; disappear. **2** *intr. & tr.* break up; bring or come to nothing. **3** *tr.* squander or fritter away (money, energy, etc.). **4** *intr.* (as **dissipated** *adj.*) dissolute. □□ **dis·si·pa·tive** *adj.* **dis·si·pa·tor** *n.*

dis·si·pa·tion /dísipáyshən/ *n.* **1** intemperate, dissolute or debauched living. **2** (usu. foll. by *of*) wasteful expenditure (*dissipation of resources*). **3** scattering, dispersion, or disintegration. **4** a frivolous amusement.

dis·so·ci·ate /disősheeayt, -seeayt/ *v.tr. & intr.* (usu. foll. by *from*) disconnect or become disconnected; separate (*dissociated her from their guilt*). □ **dissociate oneself from 1** declare oneself unconnected with. **2** decline to support or agree with (a proposal, etc.). □□ **dis·so·ci·a·tion** /disőseeáyshən, -shee-/ *n.* **dis·so·ci·a·tive** /-sheeətiv, -seeətiv/ *adj.*

dis·sol·u·ble /disólyəbəl/ *adj.* able to be disintegrated, loosened, or disconnected; soluble. □□ **dis·sol·u·bil·i·ty** *n.* **dis·sol·u·bly** *adv.*

dis·so·lute /dísəlōot/ *adj.* lax in morals; licentious. □□ **dis·so·lute·ly** *adv.* **dis·so·lute·ness** *n.*

dis·so·lu·tion /dísəlṓshən/ *n.* **1** disintegration; decomposition. **2** (usu. foll. by *of*) the undoing or relaxing of a bond, esp.: **a** a marriage. **b** a partnership. **c** an alliance. **3** the dismissal or dispersal of an assembly, esp. of a parliament at the end of its term. **4** death. **5** bringing or coming to an end; fading away; disappearance. **6** dissipation; debauchery.

dis·solve /dizólv/ *v. & n.* ● *v.* **1** *tr. & intr.* make or become liquid, esp. by immersion or dispersion in a liquid. **2** *intr. & tr.* disappear or cause to disappear gradually. **3 a** *tr.* dismiss (an assembly, esp. parliament). **b** *intr.* (of an assembly) be dissolved (cf. DISSOLUTION 3). **4** *tr.* annul (a partnership, marriage, etc.). **5** *intr.* (of a person) become emotionally overcome. **6** *intr.* (often foll. by *into*) *Cinematog.* change gradually (from one picture into another). ● *n. Cinematog.* the act or process of dissolving a picture. □□ **dis·solv·a·ble** *adj.*

dis·so·nant /dísənənt/ *adj.* **1** *Mus.* harsh-toned; inharmonious. **2** incongruous. □□ **dis·so·nance** /-nəns/ *n.* **dis·so·nant·ly** *adv.*

dis·suade /diswáyd/ *v.tr.* (often foll. by *from*) discourage (a person); persuade against (*dissuaded her from continuing*; *was dissuaded from his belief*). □□ **dis·sua·sion** /-swáyzhən/ *n.* **dis·sua·sive** *adj.*

dis·sym·me·try /dis-símitree/ *n.* (*pl.* **-ies**) **1 a** lack of symmetry. **b** an instance of this. **2** symmetry as of mirror images or the left and right hands (esp. of crystals with two corresponding forms). □□ **dis·sym·met·ri·cal** /dís-simétrikəl/ *adj.*

dis·taff /distaf/ *n.* **a** ▶ a cleft stick holding wool or flax wound for spinning by hand. **b** the corresponding part of a spinning wheel.

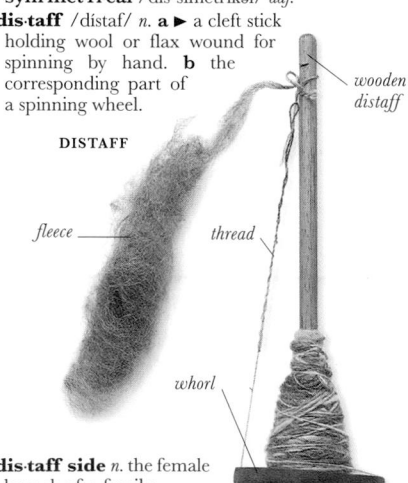

DISTAFF

wooden distaff

fleece

thread

whorl

dis·taff side *n.* the female branch of a family.

dis·tance /dístəns/ *n. & v.* ● *n.* **1** remoteness. **2 a** a space or interval between two things. **b** the length of this (*a distance of twenty miles*). **3** a distant point or place. **4** aloofness; reserve. **5** a remoter field of vision

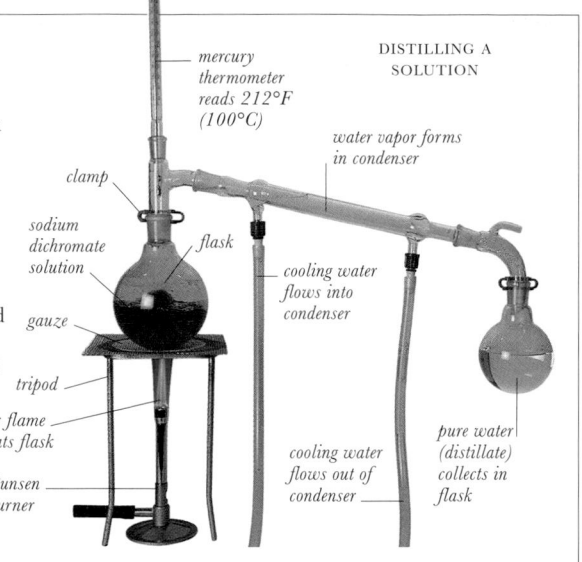

DISTILL

To distill a liquid it must be heated to the boiling point. In the demonstration shown here, a solution of sodium dichromate is heated in a flask. The solvent, in this case water, boils away from the solution leaving sodium dichromate crystals. The water vapor passes into a condenser, where it is cooled and becomes liquid again. The distillation is continued until the components of the mixture have been completely separated. The purified liquid is known as distillate.

DISTILLING A SOLUTION

mercury thermometer reads 212°F (100°C)

water vapor forms in condenser

clamp

sodium dichromate solution

flask

gauze

tripod

cooling water flows into condenser

cooling water flows out of condenser

pure water (distillate) collects in flask

gas flame heats flask

Bunsen burner

D

(*in the distance*). **6** an interval of time (*can't remember at this distance*). **7 a** the full length of a race, etc. **b** *Boxing* the scheduled length of a fight. ● *v.tr.* (often *refl.*) place far off (*distanced herself from them*). **2** leave far behind in a race or competition. □ **at a distance** far off. **go the distance 1** *Boxing* complete a fight without being knocked out. **2** complete a hard task; endure an ordeal. **keep one's distance** maintain one's reserve. **within walking distance** near enough to reach by walking.

dis·tant /dístənt/ *adj.* **1 a** far away in space or time. **b** (usu. *predic.*; often foll. by *from*) at a specified distance (*three miles distant*). **2** remote in position, time, etc. (*distant prospect; distant relation*). **3** reserved; cool (*a distant nod*). **4** abstracted (*a distant stare*). **5** faint; vague (*a distant memory*). □□ **dis·tant·ly** *adv.*

dis·taste /dístáyst/ *n.* (usu. foll. by *for*) dislike; aversion. □□ **dis·taste·ful** *adj.* **dis·taste·ful·ly** *adv.* **dis·taste·ful·ness** *n.*

dist. atty. *abbr.* district attorney.

dis·tem·per[1] /dístémpər/ *n. & v.* ● *n.* **1** a kind of paint using glue or size instead of an oil base. **2** a method of mural and poster painting using this. ● *v.tr.* paint with distemper.

dis·tem·per[2] /dístémpər/ *n.* a disease of esp. dogs, causing fever, coughing, and catarrh.

dis·tend /dísténd/ *v.tr. & intr.* swell out by pressure from within (*distended stomach*). □□ **dis·ten·si·ble** /-sténsibəl/ *adj.* **dis·ten·si·bil·i·ty** /-sténsibílitee/ *n.* **dis·ten·sion** /-sténshən/ *n.*

dis·tich /dístik/ *n. Prosody* a verse couplet.

dis·till /dístíl/ *v.* **1** *tr. Chem.* ▲ purify (a liquid) by vaporizing then condensing it with cold and collecting the result. **2** *tr.* **a** *Chem.* extract the essence of (a plant, etc.) usu. by heating it in a solvent. **b** extract the essential meaning or implications of (an idea, etc.). **3** *tr.* make (whiskey, essence, etc.) by distilling raw materials. **4** *tr.* (foll. by *off, out*) *Chem.* drive (the volatile constituent) off or out by heat. **5** *tr. & intr.* come as or give forth in drops; exude. **6** *intr.* undergo distillation. □□ **dis·til·late** /dístilit, -áyt/ *n.* **dis·til·la·tion** /dístiláyshən/ *n.* **dis·til·la·to·ry** *adj.*

dis·till·er /dístílər/ *n.* a person who distills, esp. a manufacturer of alcoholic liquor.

dis·till·er·y /dístíləree/ *n.* (*pl.* **-ies**) a place where alcoholic liquor is distilled.

dis·tinct /dístíngkt/ *adj.* **1** (often foll. by *from*) **a** not identical; separate; individual. **b** different in kind or quality; unlike. **2 a** clearly perceptible; plain. **b** clearly understandable; definite. **3** unmistakable; decided (*a distinct impression of being watched*). □□ **dis·tinct·ly** *adv.* **dis·tinct·ness** *n.*

dis·tinc·tion /dístíngkshən/ *n.* **1 a** the act or an instance of discriminating or distinguishing. **b** the difference made by distinguishing. **2 a** something that differentiates, e.g., a mark, name, or title. **b** the fact of being different. **3** special consideration or honor. **4** excellence; eminence. **5** a grade in an examination denoting great excellence (*passed with distinction*). □ **distinction without a difference** a merely nominal or artificial distinction.

dis·tinc·tive /dístíngktiv/ *adj.* distinguishing; characteristic. □□ **dis·tinc·tive·ly** *adv.* **dis·tinc·tive·ness** *n.*

dis·tin·gué /dístanggáy, deestangáy/ *adj.* (*fem.* **distinguée** *pronunc.* same) having a distinguished air, features, manner, etc.

dis·tin·guish /dístínggwish/ *v.* **1** *tr.* (often foll. by *from*) **a** see or point out the difference of (*cannot distinguish one from the other*). **b** constitute such a difference (*the mole distinguishes him from his twin*). **c** draw distinctions between; differentiate. **2** *tr.* be a mark or property of; characterize (*distinguished by her greed*). **3** *tr.* discover by listening, looking, etc. (*could distinguish two voices*). **4** *tr.* (usu. *refl.*; often foll. by *by*) make prominent or noteworthy (*distinguished himself by winning first prize*). **5** *tr.* (often foll. by *into*) divide; classify. **6** *intr.* (foll. by *between*) make or point out a difference between. □□ **dis·tin·guish·a·ble** *adj.*

dis·tin·guished /dístínggwisht/ *adj.* **1** (often foll. by *for, by*) of high standing; eminent; famous. **2** having an air of distinction, dignity, etc.

Dis·tin·guished Fly·ing Cross *n.* a US military decoration for heroism or extraordinary achievement in aerial flight.

Dis·tin·guished Serv·ice Cross *n.* a US Army decoration for extraordinary heroism in combat.

Dis·tin·guished Serv·ice Med·al *n.* a US military decoration for exceptionally meritorious service in a duty of great responsibility.

dis·tort /dístáwrt/ *v.tr.* **1 a** put out of shape; make crooked or unshapely. **b** distort the appearance of, esp. by curved mirrors, etc. **2** misrepresent (*facts*). □□ **dis·tort·ed·ly** *adv.* **dis·tort·ed·ness** *n.* **dis·tor·tion** /dístáwrshən/ *n.*

dis·tract /dístrákt/ *v.tr.* **1** (often foll. by *from*) draw away the attention of. **2** bewilder; perplex. **3** (as

---

distracted *adj.*) troubled or distraught. **4** amuse, esp. in order to take the attention from pain. □□ **dis·tract·ed·ly** *adv.*

dis·trac·tion /dístrákshən/ *n.* **1 a** the act of distracting, esp. the mind. **b** something that distracts. **2** a relaxation; an amusement. **3** a lack of concentration. **4** confusion; perplexity. **5** frenzy; madness. □ **to distraction** almost to a state of madness.

dis·train /dístráyn/ *v.intr. Law* (usu. foll. by *upon*) impose distraint (on a person, goods, etc.). □□ **dis·train·er** *n.* **dis·train·ment** *n.* **dis·trai·nor** *n.*

dis·traint /dístráynt/ *n. Law* the seizure of chattels to make a person pay rent, etc.

dis·trait /dístráy/ *adj.* (*fem.* **distraite** /-stráyt/) not paying attention; distraught.

dis·traught /dístráwt/ *adj.* distracted with worry, fear, etc.; extremely agitated.

dis·tress /dístrés/ *n. & v.* ● *n.* **1** severe pain, sorrow, anguish, etc. **2** the lack of money or comforts. **3** *Law* = DISTRAINT. **4** breathlessness; exhaustion. ● *v.tr.* **1** subject to distress. **2** cause anxiety to; make unhappy. □ **in distress 1** suffering or in danger. **2** (of a ship, aircraft, etc.) in danger or damaged. □□ **dis·tress·ful** *adj.* **dis·tress·ing·ly** *adv.*

dis·tressed /dístrést/ *adj.* **1** suffering from distress. **2** impoverished (*in distressed circumstances*). **3** (of furniture, leather, etc.) having simulated marks of age and wear.

dis·trib·u·tar·y /dístríbyəteree/ *n.* (*pl.* **-ies**) a branch of a river or glacier that does not return to the main stream after leaving it (as in a delta). ▷ DELTA

dis·trib·ute /dístríbyoot/ *v.tr.* **1** give shares of; deal out. **2** spread about; scatter. **3** divide into parts; arrange; classify. □□ **dis·trib·ut·a·ble** *adj.*

dis·tri·bu·tion /dístríbyooshən/ *n.* **1** the act or an instance of distributing; the process of being distributed. **2** *Econ.* **a** the dispersal of goods, etc., among consumers, brought about by commerce. **b** the extent to which different groups, classes, or individuals share in the total production or wealth of a community. **3** *Statistics* the way in which a characteristic is spread over members of a class. □□ **dis·tri·bu·tion·al** *adj.*

dis·tri·bu·tive /dístríbyətiv/ *adj. & n.* ● *adj.* **1** of, concerned with, or produced by distribution. **2** *Logic & Gram.* (of a pronoun, etc.) referring to each individual of a class, not to the class collectively (e.g., *each*, *either*). ● *n.* a distributive word. □□ **dis·tri·bu·tive·ly** *adv.*

dis·trib·u·tor /dístríbyətər/ *n.* **1** a person or thing that distributes. **2** an agent who supplies goods. **3** *Electr.* ◀ a device in an internal-combustion engine for passing current to each spark plug in turn.

dis·trict /dístrikt/ *n. & v.* ● *n.* **1** (often *attrib.*) a territory marked off for special administrative purposes. **2** an area which has common characteristics; a region (*the wine-growing district*). ● *v.tr.* divide into districts.

dis·trict at·tor·ney *n.* the prosecuting officer of a district.

dis·trust /dístrúst/ *n. & v.* ● *n.* a lack of trust; doubt; suspicion. ● *v.tr.* have no trust or confidence in; doubt. □□ **dis·trust·ful** *adj.* **dis·trust·ful·ly** *adv.*

dis·turb /dístúrb/ *v.tr.* **1** break the rest, calm, or quiet of; interrupt. **2 a** agitate; worry (*your story disturbs me*). **b** irritate. **3** move from a settled position; disarrange (*the papers had been disturbed*). **4** (as **disturbed** *adj.*) *Psychol.* emotionally or mentally unstable or abnormal. □□ **dis·turb·er** *n.* **dis·turb·ing** *adj.* **dis·turb·ing·ly** *adv.*

dis·tur·bance /dístúrbəns/ *n.* **1** the act or an instance of disturbing; the process of being disturbed.

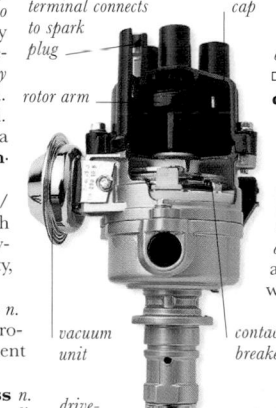

cap

terminal connects to spark plug

rotor arm

vacuum unit

contact breaker

drive-shaft

DISTRIBUTOR WITH CUTAWAY CAP

2 a tumult; an uproar. **3** agitation; worry. **4** an interruption.

di·sul·fide /dīsúlfīd/ *n. Chem.* a binary chemical containing two atoms of sulfur in each molecule.

dis·un·ion /disyŏ̅o̅nyən/ *n.* a lack of union; separation; dissension. □□ **dis·u·nite** /dísyŏ̅o̅nít/ *v.tr. & intr.* **dis·u·ni·ty** *n.*

dis·use *n. & v.* ● *n.* /disyŏ̅o̅s/ **1** lack of use or practice; discontinuance. **2** a disused state. ● *v.tr.* /disyŏ̅o̅z/ (esp. as **disused** *adj.*) cease to use. □ **fall into disuse** cease to be used.

di·syl·la·ble /dísíləbəl, di-/ *n.* (also **dis·syl·la·ble**) *Prosody* a word or metrical foot of two syllables. □□ **di·syl·lab·ic** /-lábik/ *adj.*

ditch /dich/ *n. & v.* **1** a long, narrow excavated channel esp. for drainage or to mark a boundary. **2** a watercourse, stream, etc. ● *v.* **1** *intr.* make or repair ditches. **2** *tr.* provide with ditches; drain. **3** *tr. sl.* leave in the lurch; abandon. **4** *tr. colloq.* **a** bring (an aircraft) down on water in an emergency. **b** drive (a vehicle) into a ditch. **5** *intr. colloq.* (of an aircraft) make a forced landing on water. **6** *tr. sl.* defeat; frustrate. **7** *tr.* derail (a train). □□ **ditch·er** *n.*

ditch·wa·ter /díchwawtər/ *n.* stagnant water in a ditch. □ **dull as ditchwater** = *dull as dishwater* (see DISHWATER).

di·the·ism /dítheeizəm/ *n. Theol.* **1** a belief in two gods; dualism. **2** a belief in equal independent ruling principles of good and evil. □□ **di·the·ist** *n.*

dith·er /díthər/ *v. & n.* ● *v.intr.* hesitate; be indecisive. ● *n. colloq.* **1** a state of agitation or apprehension. **2** a state of hesitation; indecisiveness. □ **in a dither** *colloq.* in a state of extreme agitation or vacillation. □□ **dith·er·er** *n.* **dith·er·y** *adj.*

dith·y·ramb /díthiram, -ramb/ *n.* **1 a** a wild choral hymn in ancient Greece. **b** a bacchanalian song. **2** any passionate or inflated poem, etc. □□ **dith·y·ram·bic** /-rámbik/ *adj.*

dit·sy /dítsee/ *adj.* (also **ditsier** or **ditzier, ditsiest** or **ditziest**) *colloq.* silly; foolishly giddy; scatterbrained.

dit·ta·ny /dít'nee/ *n.* (*pl.* **-ies**) any herb of the genus *Dictamnus*, formerly used medicinally.

dit·to /dítō/ *n. & v.* ● *n.* (*pl.* **-os**) **1** (in accounts, lists, etc.) the aforesaid; the same. Often represented by " under the word or sum to be repeated. **2** *colloq.* (replacing a word or phrase to avoid repetition) the same (*came in late last night and ditto the night before*). **3** a similar thing; a duplicate. ● *v.tr.* (**-oes, -oed**) repeat (another's action or words).

dit·tog·ra·phy /ditógrəfee/ *n.* (*pl.* **-ies**) **1** a copyist's mistaken repetition of a letter, word, or phrase. **2** an example of this. □□ **dit·tog·ra·phic** /dítəgráfik/ *adj.*

dit·to marks *n.pl.* quotation marks representing "ditto."

dit·ty /dítee/ *n.* (*pl.* **-ies**) a short simple song.

ditz /dits/ *n. sl.* a ditsy person.

dit·zy var. of DITSY.

di·u·re·sis /díəréesis/ *n. Med.* an increased excretion of urine.

di·u·ret·ic /díərétik/ *adj. & n.* ● *adj.* causing increased output of urine. ● *n.* a diuretic drug.

di·ur·nal /dī-ə́rnəl/ *adj.* **1** of or during the day; not nocturnal. **2** daily; of each day. **3** *Astron.* occupying one day. **4** *Zool.* (of animals) active in the daytime. **5** *Bot.* (of plants) open only during the day. □□ **di·ur·nal·ly** *adv.*

div. *abbr.* division.

di·va /déevə/ *n.* (*pl.* **divas** or **dive** /-vay/) a great or famous woman singer; a prima donna.

di·va·lent /dívʹáylənt/ *adj. Chem.* **1** having a valence of two; bivalent. **2** having two valencies. □□ **di·va·lence** *n.*

---

di·van /diván, dī-/ *n.* **1** a long, low, padded seat set against a wall; a backless sofa. **2** a bed consisting of a base and mattress, usu. with no board at either end.

di·var·i·cate /dīvárikayt, dee-/ *v.intr.* diverge; branch; separate widely. □□ **di·var·i·cate** /-kət/ *adj.* **di·var·i·ca·tion** /-káyshən/ *n.*

dive /dīv/ *v. & n.* ● *v.* (**dived** or **dove** /dōv/) **1** *intr.* plunge head first into water, esp. as a sport. **2** *intr.* **a** *Aeron.* (of an aircraft) plunge steeply downward at speed. **b** *Naut.* (of a submarine) submerge. **c** (of a person) plunge downward. **3** *intr.* (foll. by *into*) *colloq.* **a** put one's hand into (a pocket, handbag, vessel, etc.) quickly and deeply. **b** occupy oneself suddenly and enthusiastically with (a subject, meal, etc.). **4** *tr.* (foll. by *into*) plunge (a hand, etc.) into. ● *n.* **1** an act of diving; a plunge. **2 a** the submerging of a submarine. **b** the steep descent of an aircraft. **3** a sudden darting movement. **4** *colloq.* a disreputable nightclub, etc. **5** *Boxing sl.* a pretended knockout (*took a dive in the second round*). □ **dive in** *colloq.* help oneself (to food).

dive-bomb *v.tr.* bomb (a target) while diving in an aircraft. □□ **dive-bomb·er** *n.*

div·er /dívər/ *n.* **1** a person who dives. **2 a** ◄ a person who wears a diving suit to work under water for long periods. ▷ SCUBA DIVING. **b** a pearl diver, etc. **3** any of various diving birds, esp. large waterbirds of the family Gaviidae.

di·verge /divə́rj/ *v.* **1** *intr.* **a** proceed in a different direction or in different directions from a point. **b** take a different course or different courses (*their interests diverged*). **2** *intr.* **a** (often foll. by *from*) depart from a set course. **b** differ markedly. **3** *tr.* cause to diverge; deflect. □□ **di·ver·gence** /-jəns/ *n.* **di·ver·gen·cy** *n.* **di·ver·gent** *adj.* **di·ver·gent·ly** *adv.*

di·vers /dívərz/ *adj. archaic* or *literary* more than one; sundry; several.

di·verse /divə́rs, dī-/ *adj.* unlike in nature or qualities; varied. □□ **di·verse·ly** *adv.*

di·ver·si·fy /divə́rsifī, dī-/ *v.* (**-ies, -ied**) **1** *tr.* make diverse; vary; modify. **2** *tr. Commerce* **a** spread (investment) over several enterprises or products, esp. to reduce the risk of loss. **b** introduce a spread of investment in (an enterprise, etc.). **3** *intr.* (often foll. by *into*) esp. *Commerce* (of a firm, etc.) expand the range of products handled. □□ **di·ver·si·fi·ca·tion** /-fikáyshən/ *n.*

di·ver·sion /divə́rzhən, dī-/ *n.* **1 a** the act of diverting. **b** an instance of this. **2 a** the diverting of attention deliberately. **b** a stratagem for this purpose (*created a diversion*). **3** a recreation or pastime. □□ **di·ver·sion·ar·y** *adj.*

di·ver·si·ty /divə́rsitee, dī-/ *n.* (*pl.* **-ies**) **1** being diverse; variety. **2** a different kind; a variety.

di·vert /divə́rt, dī-/ *v.tr.* **1** (often foll. by *from, to*) **a** deflect. **b** distract. **2** (often as **diverting** *adj.*) entertain; amuse. □□ **di·vert·ing·ly** *adv.*

di·ver·tic·u·lum /dívertíkyələm/ *n.* (*pl.* **diverticula** /-lə/) *Anat.* a blind tube forming at weak points in a cavity or passage, esp. of the alimentary tract. □□ **di·ver·tic·u·lo·sis** /-lósis/ *n.*

di·ver·ti·men·to /divə́rtiméntō, diváir-/ *n.* (*pl.* **divertimenti** /-tee/ or **-os**) *Mus.* a light and entertaining composition.

di·ver·tisse·ment /divártismənt, deevaírteesmón/ *n.* **1** a diversion; an entertainment. **2** a short ballet, etc., between acts or longer pieces.

di·vest /divést, dī-/ *v.tr.* **1** (usu. foll. by *of*; often *refl.*) unclothe; strip (*divested himself of his jacket*). **2** deprive; dispossess; free; rid. □□ **di·vest·ment** *n.*

di·vide /divíd/ *v. & n.* ● *v.* **1** *tr. & intr.* (often foll. by *in, into*) separate or be separated into parts; break

---

up; split. **2** *tr. & intr.* (often foll. by *out*) distribute; deal; share. **3** *tr.* **a** cut off; separate; part. **b** mark out into parts (*a ruler divided into inches*). **c** specify different kinds of, classify (*people can be divided into two types*). **4** *tr.* cause to disagree (*religion divided them*). **5** *Math.* **a** *tr.* find how many times (a number) contains another (*divide 20 by 4*). **b** *intr.* (of a number) be contained in (a number) without a remainder (*4 divides into 20*). **c** *intr.* be susceptible of division (*10 divides by 2 and 5*). **d** *tr.* find how many times (a number) is contained in another (*divide 4 into 20*). **6** *intr. Math.* do division (*can divide well*). **7** *Parl.* **a** *intr.* (of a legislative assembly, etc.) part into two groups for voting (*the House divided*). **b** *tr.* so divide (a parliament, etc.) for voting. ● *n.* **1** a dividing or boundary line (*the divide between rich and poor*). **2** a watershed. □ **divided against itself** formed into factions.

div·i·dend /dívidend/ *n.* **1 a** a sum of money paid by a company to shareholders. **b** a similar sum payable to winners in a betting pool or to members of a cooperative. **c** an individual's share of a dividend. **2** *Math.* a number to be divided. **3** a benefit from any action (*their long training paid dividends*).

di·vid·er /divídər/ *n.* **1** a screen, piece of furniture, etc., dividing a room into two parts. **2** (in *pl.*) a measuring compass, esp. with a screw for setting small intervals.

div·i·na·tion /dívináyshən/ *n.* **1** supposed insight into the future or the unknown gained by supernatural means. **2 a** a skillful and accurate forecast. **b** a good guess. □□ **di·vin·a·to·ry** /-vínətáwree/ *adj.*

di·vine /divín/ *adj., v., & n.* ● *adj.* (**diviner, divinest**) **1 a** of, from, or like God or a god. **b** sacred (*divine service*). **2 a** more than humanly excellent, gifted, or beautiful. **b** *colloq.* excellent; delightful. ● *v.* **1** *tr.* discover by guessing, intuition, inspiration, or magic. **2** *tr.* foresee; predict; conjecture. **3** *intr.* practice divination. **4** *intr.* dowse. ● *n.* **1** a cleric, usu. an expert in theology. **2** (**the Divine**) providence or God. □□ **di·vine·ly** *adv.* **di·vin·er** *n.* **di·vi·nize** /díviníz/ *v.tr.*

div·ing bell *n.* ▶ an open-bottomed box or bell, supplied with air, in which a person can descend into deep water.

div·ing board *n.* an elevated board used for diving from.

div·ing suit *n.* a watertight suit usu. with a helmet and an air supply, worn for working under water.

di·vin·ing rod /divíning/ *n.* = DOWSING ROD.

di·vin·i·ty /divínitee/ *n.* (*pl.* **-ies**) **1** the state or quality of being divine. **2 a** a god; a divine being. **b** (as **the Divinity**) God. **3** the study of religion.

di·vis·i·ble /divízibəl/ *adj.* **1** capable of being divided, physically or mentally. **2** (foll. by *by*) *Math.* containing (a number) several times without a remainder (*15 is divisible by 3*). □□ **di·vis·i·bil·i·ty** /-bílitee/ *n.*

di·vi·sion /divízhən/ *n.* **1** the act or an instance of dividing; the process of being divided. **2** *Math.* the process of dividing one number by another. **3** disagreement or discord (*division of opinion*). **4** *Parl.* the separation of members of a legislative body into two sets for counting votes. **5 a** one of two or more parts into

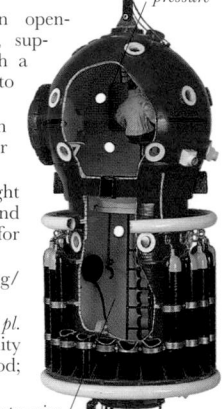

DIVING BELL: CUTAWAY MODEL OF 1965 SEATASK DIVING BELL

---

umbilical supplies air and electricity

helmet

weight belt

wetsuit

DIVER: OIL-RIG DIVER

chamber at normal air pressure

decompression chamber

entry hatch

D

which a thing is divided. **b** the point at which a thing is divided. **6** a major unit of administration or organization, esp.: **a** a group of army brigades or regiments. **b** *Sports* a grouping of teams within a league. **7** a district defined for administrative purposes. □□ **di·vi·sion·al** *adj.* **di·vi·sion·al·ly** *adv.*

di·vi·sive /divísiv/ *adj.* tending to divide, esp. in opinion; causing disagreement. □□ **di·vi·sive·ly** *adv.* **di·vi·sive·ness** *n.*

di·vi·sor /divízər/ *n. Math.* **1** a number by which another is to be divided. **2** a number that divides another without a remainder.

di·vorce /diváwrs/ *n. & v.* ● *n.* **1 a** the legal dissolution of a marriage. **b** a legal decree of this. **2** a severance or separation (*a divorce between thought and feeling*). ● *v.* **1 a** *tr.* (usu. as **divorced** *adj.*) (often foll. by *from*) legally dissolve the marriage of (*a divorced couple; he wants to get divorced from her*). **b** *intr.* separate by divorce (*they divorced*). **c** *tr.* end one's marriage with (*divorced him*). **2** *tr.* (often foll. by *from*) detach; separate (*divorced from reality*).

di·vor·cé /divawrsáy/ *n.* a divorced man.

di·vor·cée /divawrsáy/ *n.* a divorced woman.

div·ot /dívət/ *n.* a piece of turf cut out by a golf club in making a stroke.

di·vulge /divúlj, dī-/ *v.tr.* disclose; reveal (a secret, etc.). □□ **div·ul·ga·tion** /-vulgáyshən/ *n.* **di·vulge·ment** *n.* **di·vul·gence** *n.*

div·vy /dívee/ *n. & v. colloq.* ● *n.* (*pl.* **-ies**) a distribution. ● *v.tr.* (**-ies, -ied**) (often foll. by *up*) share out.

Di·wa·li /deewaalee/ *n.* a Hindu festival with illuminations, held between September and November.

Dix·ie /díksee/ *n.* the southern states of the US.

dix·ie /díksee/ *n.* a large iron cooking pot used by campers, etc.

Dix·ie·land /díkseeland/ *n.* **1** = DIXIE. **2** a kind of jazz with a strong, two-beat rhythm and collective improvisation.

diz·zy /dízee/ *adj. & v.* ● *adj.* (**dizzier, dizziest**) **1 a** giddy; unsteady. **b** lacking mental stability; confused. **2** causing giddiness. ● *v.tr.* **1** make dizzy. **2** bewilder. □□ **diz·zi·ly** *adv.* **diz·zi·ness** *n.*

DJ *abbr.* **1** disk jockey. **2** district judge.

djel·la·ba /jaláaba/ *n.* (also **djel·la·bah, jel·la·ba**) ► a loose, hooded, usu. woolen cloak worn or as worn by Arab men.

dl *abbr.* deciliter(s).

D.Litt. *abbr.* Doctor of Letters.

DM *abbr.* (also **D-mark**) deutsche mark.

dm *abbr.* decimeter(s).

D.Mus. *abbr.* Doctor of Music.

DMZ *abbr.* demilitarized zone.

DNA *abbr.* ▲ deoxyribonucleic acid, the self-replicating material present in nearly all living organisms, esp. as a constituent of chromosomes, which is the carrier of genetic information.

do¹ /dōō/ *v. & n.* ● *v.* (*3rd sing. present* **does** /duz/; *past* **did** /did/; *past part.* **done** /dun/) **1** *tr.* perform; carry out; achieve (*did his homework; there's a lot to do*). **2** *tr.* **a** produce; make (*she was doing a painting; I did a translation*). **b** provide (*do you do lunches?*). **3** *tr.* bestow; grant; have a specified effect on (*a walk would do you good; do me a favor*). **4** *intr.* act; behave; proceed (*do as I do; she would do well to accept the offer*). **5** *tr.* work at; study; be occupied with (*what does your father do?; we're doing Chaucer next term*). **6 a** *intr.* be suitable or acceptable; suffice (*a sandwich will do until we get home; that will never do*). **b** *tr.* satisfy; be suitable for (*that hotel will do me nicely*). **7** *tr.* deal with; put in order (*the garden needs doing; the barber will do you next; I must do my hair before we go*). **8** *intr.* **a** fare; get on (*the patients were doing excellently; he did badly in the test*). **b** perform; work (*could do better*). **9** *tr.* **a** solve; work out (*we did the puzzle*). **b** (*prec. by*

DJELLABA

DNA

DNA is a nucleic acid that constitutes the genes in virtually all living organisms. It governs cell growth and is responsible for the transmission of genetic information from one generation to the next. A DNA molecule consists of two strands that spiral around each other to form a double helix. The strands are held together by subunits called bases, which always pair in specific ways: adenine with thymine and cytosine with guanine.

MODEL OF A DNA MOLECULE

sugar-phosphate backbone

adenine-thymine base pair

double helix

cytosine-guanine base pair

D

---

can or *be able to*) be competent at (*can you do cartwheels?; I never could do algebra*). **10** *tr.* **a** traverse (a certain distance) (*we did fifty miles today*). **b** travel at a specified speed (*he overtook us doing about eighty*). **11** *tr. colloq.* act or behave like (*did a Houdini*). **12** *intr.* **a** *colloq.* finish (*are you done annoying me?; I'm done in the bathroom*). **b** (as **done** *adj.*) be over (*the day is done*). **13** *tr.* produce or give a performance of (*we've never done Pygmalion*). **14** *tr.* cook, esp. to the right degree (*do it in the oven; the potatoes aren't done yet*). **15** *intr.* in progress (*what's doing?*). **16** *tr.* visit; see the sights of (*we did all the art galleries*). **17** *tr. colloq.* **a** (often as **done** *adj.*; often foll. by *in*) exhaust; tire out (*the climb has completely done me*). **b** beat up; defeat; kill. **c** ruin (*now you've done it*). **18** *tr.* (foll. by *into*) translate or transform (*the book was done into French*). **19** *tr. sl.* rob (*they did a liquor store downtown*). **20** *tr. sl.* undergo (a specified term of imprisonment) (*he did two years for fraud*). **21** *tr. coarse sl.* have sexual intercourse with. **22** *tr. sl.* take (a drug). ● *v.aux.* **1 a** (except with *be, can, may, ought, shall, will*) in questions and negative statements (*do you understand?; I don't smoke*). **b** (except with *can, may, ought, shall, will*) in negative commands (*don't be silly; do not come tomorrow*). **2** *ellipt.* or in place of verb or verb and object (*you know her better than I do; I wanted to go and I did so; tell me, do!*). **3** forming emphatic present and past tenses (*I do want to; do tell me; they did go but she was out*). **4** in inversion for emphasis (*rarely does it happen; did she but know it*). ● *n.* (*pl.* **dos** or **do's**) *colloq.* an elaborate event, party, or operation. □ **be done with** see DONE. **do away with** *colloq.* **1** abolish. **2** kill. **do battle** enter into combat. **do one's best** see BEST. **do one's bit** see BIT¹. **do by** treat in a specified way (*do as you would be done by*). **do credit to** see CREDIT. **do down** *colloq.* **1** cheat; swindle. **2** get the better of; overcome. **do for 1** be satisfactory or sufficient for. **2** *colloq.* (esp. as **done for** *adj.*) destroy; ruin; kill (*he knew he was done for*). **do the honors** see HONOR. **do in 1** *sl.* a kill. **b** ruin; do injury to. **2** *colloq.* exhaust; tire out. **do justice to** see JUSTICE. **do nothing for** (or **to**) *colloq.* detract from the appearance or quality of. **do or die** persist regardless of danger. **do a person out of** *colloq.* unjustly deprive a person of; swindle out of (*he was done out of his pension*). **do over 1** *sl.* attack; beat up. **2** *colloq.* redecorate, refurbish. **3** *colloq.* do again. **do proud** see PROUD. **dos and don'ts** rules of behavior. **do something for** (or **to**) *colloq.* enhance the appearance or quality of (*that carpet does something for the room*). **do to** = *do by.* **do to death** see DEATH. **do the trick** see TRICK. **do up 1** fasten; secure. **2** *colloq.* **a** refurbish; renovate. **b** adorn; dress up. **do well for oneself** prosper. **do well out of** profit by. **do with** (prec. by *could*) would be glad to have; would profit by (*I could do with a rest*). **do without** manage without; forgo (also *absol.: we shall just have to do*

without). **have nothing to do with 1** have no connection or dealings with (*our problem has nothing to do with the latest news; he had nothing more to do with his father*). **2** be no business or concern of (*the decision has nothing to do with her*). **have to do** (or **something to do**) **with** be connected with (*his limp has to do with a car accident*).

do² /dō/ *n.* (also **doh**) *Mus.* **1** (in tonic sol-fa) the first and eighth notes of a major scale. **2** the note C in the fixed-do system.

DOA *abbr.* dead on arrival (at a hospital, etc.).

do·a·ble /dōōəbəl/ *adj.* that can be done.

Do·ber·man /dóbərmən/ *n.* (in full **Doberman pins·cher** /pínshər/) a large dog of a German breed with a smooth coat. ▷ DOG

doc /dok/ *n. colloq.* doctor.

do·cent /dósənt/ *n.* a well-informed guide, as in a museum.

doc·ile /dósəl/ *adj.* submissive; easily managed. □□ **doc·ile·ly** *adv.* **do·cil·i·ty** /-sílitee/ *n.*

dock¹ /dok/ *n. & v.* ● *n.* **1** an artificially enclosed body of water for the loading, unloading, and repair of ships. **2** (in *pl.*) a range of docks with wharves and offices; a dockyard. **3** a ship's berth; a wharf. ● *v.* **1** *tr. & intr.* bring or come into a dock. **2** *tr.* join (spacecraft) together in space. **b** *intr.* (of spacecraft) be joined. **3** *tr.* provide with a dock or docks.

dock² /dok/ *n.* the enclosure in a criminal court for the accused. □ **in the dock** on trial.

dock³ /dok/ *n.* any weed of the genus *Rumex*, with broad leaves.

dock⁴ /dok/ *v. & n.* ● *v.tr.* **1** cut short (an animal's tail). **2 a** (often foll. by *from*) deduct (a part) from wages, supplies, etc. **b** reduce (wages, etc.) in this way. ● *n.* the solid, bony part of an animal's tail.

dock·age /dókij/ *n.* **1** the charge made for using docks. **2** dock accommodation. **3** the berthing of vessels in docks.

dock·et /dókit/ *n. & v.* ● *n.* **1** a list of causes for trial or persons having causes pending. **2** a list of things to be done. ● *v.tr.* label with a docket.

dock·side /dóksīd/ *n.* the area adjacent to a dock.

dock·yard /dókyaard/ *n.* an area with docks and equipment for building and repairing ships, esp. for naval use.

Doc Mar·tens *n.pl.* (also **Doctor Martens, Dr. Martens**) *Trademark* ► a type of heavy usu. laced boot or shoe with a cushioned sole (named after *Dr. K. Maertens*, the German inventor of the sole).

doc·tor /dóktər/ *n. & v.* ● *n.* **1 a** a qualified practitioner of medicine; a physician. **b** a qualified dentist or veterinary

DOC MARTENS™

surgeon. **2** a person who holds a doctorate (*Doctor of Civil Law*). **3** *colloq.* a person who carries out repairs. ● *v. colloq.* **1 a** *tr.* treat medically. **b** *intr.* (esp. as **doctoring** *n.*) practice as a physician. **2** *tr.* patch up (machinery, etc.); mend. **3** *tr.* adulterate. **4** *tr.* tamper with; falsify. **5** *tr.* confer a degree of doctor on. □ **(just) what the doctor ordered** *colloq.* something beneficial or desirable. □□ **doc·tor·ly** *adj.*

doc·tor·al /dóktərəl/ *adj.* of or for a degree of doctor.

doc·tor·ate /dóktərət/ *n.* the highest university degree in any faculty, often honorary.

Doc·tor of Phi·los·o·phy *n.* a doctorate in a discipline other than education, law, medicine, or sometimes theology.

doc·tri·naire /dóktrináir/ *adj. & n.* ● *adj.* seeking to apply a theory or doctrine in all circumstances without regard to practical considerations. ● *n.* a doctrinaire person. □□ **doc·tri·nair·ism** *n.*

doc·tri·nal /dóktrinəl/ *adj.* of or inculcating a doctrine or doctrines. □□ **doc·tri·nal·ly** *adv.*

doc·trine /dóktrin/ *n.* **1** what is taught; a body of instruction. **2 a** a principle of religious or political, etc., belief. **b** a set of such principles; dogma. □□ **doc·trin·ism** *n.* **doc·trin·ist** *n.*

doc·u·dra·ma /dókyōōdraamə, -drámə/ *n.* a dramatized television movie based on real events.

doc·u·ment *n. & v.* ● *n.* /dókyəmənt/ a piece of written or printed matter that provides a record or evidence of events, an agreement, ownership, identification, etc. ● *v.tr.* /dókyəment/ **1** prove by or provide with documents or evidence. **2** record in a document.

doc·u·men·ta·ry /dókyəméntəree/ *adj. & n.* ● *adj.* **1** consisting of documents (*documentary evidence*). **2** providing a factual record or report. ● *n.* (*pl.* **-ies**) a documentary film, etc.

doc·u·men·ta·tion /dókyəmentáyshən/ *n.* **1** the accumulation, classification, and dissemination of information. **2** the material collected or disseminated. **3** the collection of documents relating to a process or event.

dod·der /dódər/ *v.intr.* tremble or totter, esp. from age. □□ **dod·der·er** *n.*

dod·dered /dódərd/ *adj.* (of a tree, esp. an oak) having lost its top or branches.

dod·der·y /dódəree/ *adj.* tending to tremble or totter, esp. from age.

dodeca- /dódekə/ *comb. form* twelve.

do·dec·a·gon /dōdékəgon/ *n.* ◄ a plane figure with twelve sides.

do·dec·a·he·dron /dódekəheédrən/ *n.* ▼ a solid figure with twelve faces. □□ **do·dec·a·he·dral** *adj.*

dodge /doj/ *v. & n.* ● *v.* **1** *intr.* (often foll. by *about, behind, around*) move quickly to one side or quickly change position, to elude a pursuer, blow, etc. (*dodged behind the chair*). **2** *tr.* **a** evade by cunning or trickery. **b** elude (a pursuer, blow, etc.) by a sideward movement, etc. ● *n.* **1** a quick movement to avoid or evade something. **2** a clever trick or expedient.

DODECAGON

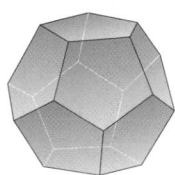

DODECAHEDRON

dodg·er /dójər/ *n.* **1** a person who dodges, esp. an artful or elusive person. **2** a screen on a ship's bridge, etc., as protection from spray, etc. **3** a small handbill. **4** (in full **corn dodger**) **a** esp. *southern US* a small, hard cornmeal cake. **b** esp. *S. Atlantic US* a boiled cornmeal dumpling.

dodg·y /dójee/ *adj.* (**dodgier, dodgiest**) *colloq.* awkward; unreliable; tricky.

do·do /dódō/ *n.* (*pl.* **-oes** or **-os**) **1** ◄ any large flightless bird of the extinct family Raphidae, formerly native to Mauritius. **2** an old-fashioned, stupid, or inactive person. □ **as dead as the** (or **a**) **dodo 1** completely or unmistakably dead. **2** entirely obsolete.

DODO (*Raphus cucullatus*)

doe /dō/ *n.* a female fallow deer, reindeer, hare, or rabbit.

do·er /dōōər/ *n.* **1** a person who does something. **2** one who acts rather than merely thinking or thinking.

does *3rd sing. present of* DO¹.

doe·skin /dóskin/ *n.* **1 a** the skin of a doe fallow deer. **b** leather made from this. **2** a fine cloth resembling it.

doesn't /dúzənt/ *contr.* does not.

doff /dawf, dof/ *v.tr. literary* take off (one's hat, clothing).

dog /dawg, dog/ *n. & v.* ● *n.* **1** ▶ any four-legged, flesh-eating animal of the genus *Canis*, of many breeds, domesticated and wild, kept as pets or for work or sport. **2** the male of the dog, or of the fox (also **dog fox**) or wolf (also **dog wolf**). **3 a** *colloq.* a despicable person. **b** *colloq.* a person or fellow of a specified kind (*a lucky dog*). **c** *sl. derog.* an unattractive or slovenly woman. **4** a mechanical device for gripping. **5** *sl.* something poor; a failure. **6** = FIREDOG. ● *v.tr.* (**dogged, dogging**) follow closely and persistently; pursue; track. □ **die like a dog** die miserably or shamefully. **go to the dogs** *sl.* deteriorate, be ruined. **not a dog's chance** no chance at all. **put on the dog** *colloq.* behave pretentiously. □□ **dog·like** *adj.*

dog bis·cuit *n.* a hard, thick biscuit for feeding dogs.

dog days *n.pl.* the hottest period of the year.

doge /dōj/ *n. hist.* the chief magistrate of Venice or Genoa.

dog-eared *adj.* (of a book, etc.) with the corners worn or battered with use.

dog-eat-dog *adj. colloq.* ruthlessly competitive.

dog·fight /dáwgfīt, dóg-/ *n.* **1** a close combat between fighter aircraft. **2** uproar; a fight like that between dogs.

dog·fish /dáwgfish, dóg-/ *n.* (*pl.* same or **dogfishes**) ◄ any of various small sharks, esp. of the families Squalidae or Scyliorhinidae. ▷ EGG, SHARK

dog·ged /dáwgid, dóg-/ *adj.* tenacious; grimly persistent. □□ **dog·ged·ly** *adv.* **dog·ged·ness** *n.*

dog·ger·el /dáwgərəl, dóg-/ *n.* poor or trivial verse.

dog·gie var. of DOGGY *n.*

dog·gie bag *n.* (also **dog·gy bag**) a bag given to a customer in a restaurant or to a guest at a party, etc., for putting leftovers in to take home.

dog·gone /dáwg-gon, dóg-/ *adj., adv., & int. sl.* ● *adj. & adv.* damned. ● *int.* expressing annoyance.

dog·gy /dáwgee, dógee/ *adj. & n.* (also **dog·gie**) (*pl.* **-ies**) ● *adj.* of or like a dog. ● *n.* little dog; a pet name for a dog.

dog·house /dáwghows, dóg-/ *n.* a dog's shelter. □ **in the doghouse** *sl.* in disgrace or disfavor.

do·gie /dógee/ *n.* a motherless or neglected calf.

dog in the man·ger *n.* a person who prevents others from using something, although that person has no use for it.

dog·leg /dáwgleg, dóg-/ *n., adj., & v.* ● *n.* something with a sharp, abrupt bend, as a road. ● *adj.* (also **dog·leg·ged**) bent like a dog's hind leg. ● *v.intr.* (**-legged, -legging**) proceed around a dogleg or on a dogleg course.

dog·ma /dáwgmə, dóg-/ *n.* **1 a** a principle, tenet,

DOGFISH: LESSER-SPOTTED DOGFISH (*Scyliorhinus canicula*)

or system of these, esp. as laid down by the authority of a church. **b** such principles collectively. **2** an arrogant declaration of opinion.

dog·mat·ic /dawgmátik, dog-/ *adj.* **1 a** (of a person) given to asserting or imposing personal opinions; arrogant. **b** intolerantly authoritative. **2 a** of or in the nature of dogma; doctrinal. **b** based on a priori principles, not on induction. □□ **dog·mat·i·cal·ly** *adv.*

dog·ma·tism /dáwgmətizəm, dóg-/ *n.* a tendency to be dogmatic. □□ **dog·ma·tist** *n.*

do-gooder /dōōgoōdər/ *n.* a well-meaning but unrealistic philanthropist or reformer.

dog pad·dle *n.* an elementary swimming stroke like that of a dog. □□ **dog-pad·dle** *v.intr.*

dog rose *n.* ▶ a wild rose, *Rosa canina*.

dog's life *n.* a life of misery or harassment.

dogs of war *n.pl. poet.* the havoc accompanying war.

Dog Star *n.* the chief star of the constellation Canis Major or Minor, esp. Sirius.

dog tag *n.* **1** a usu. metal plate attached to a dog's collar, giving owner's address, etc. **2** an identification tag, esp. as worn by a member of the military.

DOG ROSE (*Rosa canina*)

dog-tired *adj.* tired out.

dog·tooth /dáwgtooth, dóg-/ *n.* ▼ a small pointed ornament or molding esp. in Norman and Early English architecture.

dogtooth ornament

DOGTOOTH ORNAMENT IN A ROUND ARCH

dog·watch /dáwgwoch, dóg-/ *n. Naut.* either of two short watches (4–6 or 6–8 p.m.).

dog·wood /dáwgwood, dóg-/ *n.* **1** ▶ any of various shrubs of the genus *Cornus*, esp. the wild cornel with dark red branches, greenish-white flowers, and purple berries. **2** any of various similar trees. **3** the wood of the dogwood.

doh var. of DO².

DOI *abbr.* Department of the Interior.

doi·ly /dóylee/ *n.* (also **doy·ley**) (*pl.* **-ies** or **-eys**) a small ornamental mat of paper, lace, etc., on a plate for cakes, etc.

do·ing /dōōing/ *n.* **1 a** (usu. in *pl.*) an action (*famous for his doings; it was my doing*). **b** activity; effort (*it takes a lot of doing*). **2** *colloq.* a scolding;

DOGWOOD (*Cornus alba*)

DOG

Dogs belong to the family Canidae, which includes wolves, jackals, and foxes. All modern domestic dogs (*Canis familiaris*) are descended from the gray wolf (*Canis lupus*). There are now more than 300 different breeds of domestic dog, and these are often classified into various types, according to the task for which they were originally bred. These tasks included herding, hunting, and guarding. However, many breeds are now kept mainly as pets, irrespective of their original function.

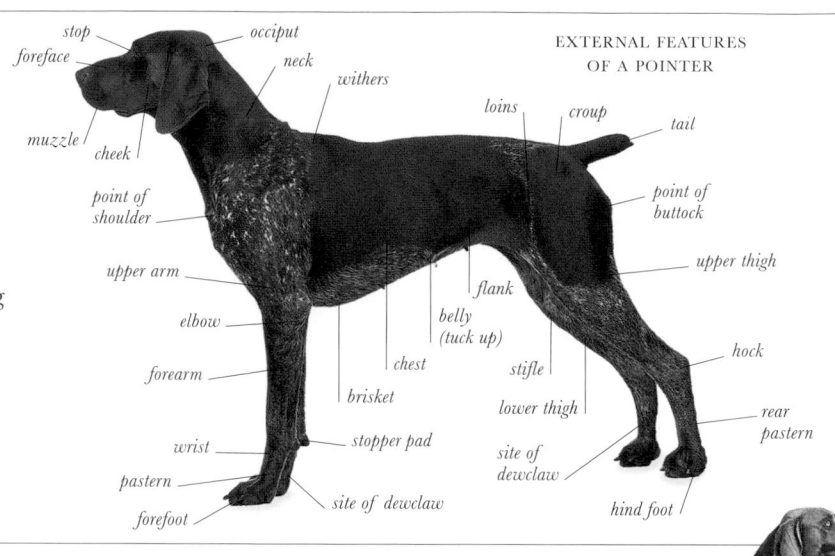

EXTERNAL FEATURES OF A POINTER

stop · occiput · foreface · neck · withers · loins · croup · tail · muzzle · cheek · point of shoulder · upper arm · elbow · forearm · wrist · pastern · forefoot · brisket · stopper pad · site of dewclaw · chest · belly (tuck up) · flank · stifle · lower thigh · site of dewclaw · point of buttock · upper thigh · hock · rear pastern · hind foot

TYPES OF DOG

WORKING DOGS

ALASKAN MALAMUTE

DOBERMAN

HOUNDS

BEAGLE

AFGHAN HOUND

HERDING DOGS

ROUGH COLLIE

CARDIGAN WELSH CORGI

OLD ENGLISH SHEEPDOG

SPORTING DOGS

STANDARD POODLE

WEIMARANER

GOLDEN RETRIEVER

TERRIERS

KERRY BLUE

AIREDALE

TOY DOGS

GERMAN SPITZ

PEKINGESE

SHIH TZU

D

a beating. **3** (in *pl.*) *sl.* things needed; adjuncts; things whose names are not known (*have we got all the doings?*).

do-it-your·self *adj. & n.* ● *adj.* (of work, esp. building, painting, decorating, etc.) done or to be done by an amateur at home. ● *n.* such work.

Dol·by /dólbee/ *n.* Trademark an electronic system of noise reduction used in tape recording to reduce hiss.

dol·ce vi·ta /dólchay véetə/ *n.* a life of pleasure and luxury.

dol·drums /dóldrəmz/ *n.pl.* (usu. prec. by *the*) **1** low spirits. **2** a period of inactivity. **3** an equatorial ocean region of calms, sudden storms, and light unpredictable winds. ▷ TRADE WIND

dole¹ /dōl/ *n. & v.* ● *n.* **1** (usu. prec. by *the*) *Brit. colloq.* benefit claimable by the unemployed from the government. **2 a** charitable distribution. **b** a charitable (esp. sparing, niggardly) gift of food, clothes, or money. ● *v.tr.* (usu. foll. by *out*) deal out sparingly. □ **on the dole** *colloq.* receiving welfare, etc., payments from the government.

dole² /dōl/ *n. poet.* grief; woe; lamentation.

dole·ful /dólfŏŏl/ *adj.* **1** mournful; sad. **2** dreary; dismal. □□ **dole·ful·ly** *adv.* **dole·ful·ness** *n.*

doll /dol/ *n. & v.* ● *n.* **1** a small model of a human figure as a child's toy. **2 a** *colloq.* a pretty but silly young woman. **b** *sl.* a young woman, esp. an attractive one. **3** a ventriloquist's dummy. ● *v.tr. & intr.* (foll. by *up*; often *refl.*) dress up smartly.

dol·lar /dólər/ *n.* **1** the chief monetary unit in the US, Canada, and Australia. **2** the chief monetary unit of certain countries in the Pacific, West Indies, SE Asia, Africa, and S. America.

dol·lar sign *n.* the sign $, used to indicate currency in dollars.

doll·house /dólhows/ *n.* **1** a miniature toy house for dolls. **2** a very small house.

dol·lop /dóləp/ *n. & v.* ● *n.* a shapeless lump of food, etc. ● *v.tr.* (usu. foll. by *out*) serve out in large, shapeless quantities.

dol·ly /dólee/ *n. & v.* ● *n.* (*pl.* **-ies**) **1** a child's name for a doll. **2** a movable platform for a movie camera. **3** *Cricket colloq.* an easy catch or hit. **4** a stick for stirring in clothes washing. **5** = CORN DOLLY. ● *v.* (**-ies, -ied**) **1** *tr.* (foll. by *up*) dress up smartly. **2** *intr.* (foll. by *in, up*) move a cine-camera up to a subject, or out from it.

dol·man sleeve /dólmən/ *n.* a loose sleeve cut in one piece with the body of the coat, etc.

dol·men /dólmən/ *n.* a megalithic tomb with a large, flat stone laid on upright ones. ▷ QUOIT

do·lo·mite /dóləmīt, dól-/ *n.* ◀ a mineral or rock of calcium magnesium carbonate. □□ **dol·o·mit·ic** /-mítik/ *adj.*

quartz matrix

curved crystal faces

dolomite crystals

DOLOMITE

do·lor /dōlər/ *n. literary* sorrow; distress.

dol·or·ous /dólərəs/ *adj. literary* or *joc.* **1** distressing; painful; doleful; dismal. **2** distressed; sad. □□ **dol·or·ous·ly** *adv.*

dol·phin /dólfin/ *n.* **1** ▼ any of various porpoiselike aquatic mammals of the family Delphinidae having a slender, beaklike

---

DOLPHIN

Dolphins are aquatic mammals belonging to the order Cetacea and generally have beaklike snouts and streamlined bodies. They can be broadly divided into oceanic and river dolphins. Oceanic dolphins, which belong to the family Delphinidae, are distributed throughout all oceans; some species are coastal or partly riverine. River dolphins, which belong to the family Platanistidae, are found in the largest rivers of Asia and South America. One species of dolphin, the franciscana, is closely related to the river dolphins but lives in coastal waters.

INTERNAL ANATOMY OF
A DOLPHIN

spinal cord · *stomach* · *aorta* · *brain* · *kidney* · *testis* · *rectum* · *blowhole* · *melon* · *esophagus* · *trachea* · *heart* · *lung* · *liver* · *urinogenital opening* · *anus*

EXAMPLES OF DOLPHINS

OCEANIC DOLPHINS

ATLANTIC WHITE-SIDED DOLPHIN
(*Lagenorhynchus acutus*)

COMMON DOLPHIN
(*Delphinus delphis*)

PACIFIC WHITE-SIDED DOLPHIN
(*Lagenorhynchus obliquidens*)

WHITE-BEAKED DOLPHIN
(*Lagenorhynchus albirostris*)

BOTTLENOSE DOLPHIN
(*Tursiops truncatus*)

RIVER DOLPHINS

FRANCISCANA
(*Pontoporia blainvillei*)

BOUTO
(*Inia geoffrensis*)

INDUS RIVER DOLPHIN
(*Platanista minor*)

snout. ▷ CETACEAN. **2** (in general use) = DORADO 1. **3** a pile or buoy for mooring. **4** a structure for protecting the pier of a bridge.

dol·phin·ar·i·um /dólfináireeəm/ n. (*pl.* **dolphin-ariums**) an aquarium for dolphins.

dolt /dōlt/ n. a stupid person. □□ **dolt·ish** *adj.*

Dom /dom/ n. **1** a title prefixed to the names of some Roman Catholic dignitaries, and Benedictine and Carthusian monks. **2** the Portuguese equivalent of Don (see DON[1] 2a, b).

do·main /dōmáyn/ n. **1** an area under one rule; a realm. **2** an estate or lands under one control. **3** a sphere of control or influence.

do·main name n. *Computing* the part of a network address which identifies it as belonging to a particular domain.

do·maine /dōmáyn/ n. a vineyard.

dome /dōm/ n. & v. ● n. **1 a** ▼ a rounded vault as a roof, with a circular, elliptical, or polygonal base. ▷ FAÇADE. **b** the revolving, openable hemispherical roof of an observatory. **2 a** a natural vault or canopy (of the sky, trees, etc.). **b** the rounded summit of a hill, etc. **3** *Geol.* a dome-shaped structure. **4** *sl.* the head. ● v.tr. (usu. as **domed** *adj.*) cover with or shape as a dome. □□ **dome·like** *adj.*

do·mes·tic /dəméstik/ *adj.* & n. ● *adj.* **1** of the home, household, or family affairs. **2 a** of one's own country, not foreign or international. **b** homegrown or homemade. **3** (of an animal) kept by or living with humans. **4** fond of home life. ● n. a household servant. □□ **do·mes·ti·cal·ly** *adv.*

do·mes·ti·cate /dəméstikayt/ v.tr. **1** tame (an animal) to live with humans. **2** accustom to home life and management. **3** naturalize (a plant or animal).

do·mes·ti·ca·ble /-kəbəl/ *adj.* **do·mes·ti·ca·tion** /-káyshən/ n.

do·mes·tic·i·ty /dómǝstísitee/ n. **1** the state of being domestic. **2** domestic or home life.

do·mes·tic sci·ence n. the study of household management.

dom·i·cile /dómisīl, -sil, dó-/ n. & v. (also **dom·i·cil** /-sil/) ● n. **1** a dwelling place; one's home. **2** *Law* **a** a place of permanent residence. **b** the fact of residing. **3** the place at which a bill of exchange is made payable. ● v.tr. **1** (usu. as **domiciled** *adj.*) (usu. foll. by *at, in*) establish or settle in a place. **2** (usu. foll. by *at*) make (a bill of exchange) payable at a certain place.

dom·i·cil·i·ar·y /dómisílee-eree/ *adj.* of a dwelling place (esp. of a doctor's, official's, etc., visit to a person's home).

dom·i·nant /dóminənt/ *adj.* & n. ● *adj.* **1** dominating; prevailing; most influential. **2** (of a high place) prominent; overlooking others. **3 a** (of an allele) expressed even when inherited from only one parent. **b** (of an inherited characteristic) appearing in an individual even when its allelic counterpart is also inherited (cf. RECESSIVE). ▷ MENDELISM. ● n. *Mus.* the fifth note of the diatonic scale of any key. □□ **dom·i·nance** /dóminəns/ n. **dom·i·nant·ly** *adv.*

dom·i·nate /dóminayt/ v. **1** tr. & (foll. by *over*) intr. exercise control over (*fear dominated them for years*). **2** intr. (of a person, sound, feature of a scene, etc.) be the most influential or conspicuous. **3** tr. & (foll. by *over*) intr. (of a building, etc.) overlook. □□ **dom·i·na·tion** /dómináyshən/ n. **dom·i·na·tor** n.

dom·i·neer /dóminéer/ v.intr. (often as **domineering** *adj.*) behave in an arrogant and overbearing way. □□ **dom·i·neer·ing·ly** *adv.*

Do·min·i·can /dəmínikən/ *adj.* & n. ● *adj.* **1** of or relating to St. Dominic or the order of preaching friars which he founded. **2** of or relating to either of two female religious orders founded on Dominican principles. ● n. a Dominican friar, nun, or sister.

do·min·ion /dəmínyən/ n. **1** sovereignty; control. **2** the territory of a sovereign or government; a domain.

dom·i·no /dóminō/ n. (*pl.* **-oes** or **-os**) **1 a** any of 28 small oblong pieces marked with 0–6 dots in each half. **b** (in *pl.*, usu. treated as *sing.*) a game played with these. **2** a loose cloak with a mask for the upper part of the face.

dom·i·no the·o·ry n. the theory that a political event, etc., in one country will cause similar events in neighboring countries, like a row of falling dominoes.

don[1] /don/ n. **1** a university teacher, esp. a senior member of a college at Oxford or Cambridge. **2** (**Don**) **a** a Spanish title prefixed to a forename. **b** a Spanish gentleman; a Spaniard.

don[2] /don/ v.tr. (**donned, donning**) put on (clothing).

do·nate /dónayt, dōnáyt/ v.tr. give or contribute (money, etc.), esp. to a charity. □□ **do·na·tor** n.

do·na·tion /dōnáyshən/ n. **1** the act or an instance of donating. **2** something, esp. money, donated.

done /dun/ *past part.* of DO[1]. *adj.* **1** *colloq.* socially acceptable (*the done thing*). **2** (often *in, up*) *colloq.* tired out. **3** (esp. as *int.* in reply to an offer, etc.) accepted. □ **be done with** be finished with. **done for** *colloq.* in serious trouble. **have done** have ceased or finished. **have done with** be rid of; have finished dealing with.

do·nee /dōneé/ n. the recipient of a gift.

don·gle /dáwnggəl, dóng-/ n. *Computing sl.* a security attachment required by a computer to enable protected software to be used.

don·jon /dónjən, dún-/ n. the great tower or innermost keep of a castle.

Don Juan /don waán, hwaán, jóoən/ n. a seducer of women; a libertine.

don·key /dóngkee, dúng-, dáwng-/ n. (*pl.* **-eys**) **1** a domestic ass. **2** *colloq.* a stupid or foolish person.

don·key's years *n.pl. colloq.* a very long time.

don·key·work /dónkeewərk, dúng-, dáwng-/ n. the laborious part of a job; drudgery.

don·nish /dónish/ *adj.* like or resembling a college don, esp. in supposed pedantry. □□ **don·nish·ly** *adv.* **don·nish·ness** n.

do·nor /dónər/ n. **1** a person who gives or donates something (e.g., to a charity). **2** one who provides blood for a transfusion, semen for insemination, or an organ or tissue for transplantation.

do·nor card n. an official card authorizing use of organs for transplant, carried by the donor.

don't /dōnt/ *contr.* & n. ● *contr.* do not. ● n. a prohibition (*dos and don'ts*).

do·nut var. of DOUGHNUT.

doo·dad /dóódad/ n. **1** a fancy article; a trivial ornament. **2** a gadget or thingamajig.

doo·dle /dóód'l/ v. & n. ● v.intr. scribble or draw, esp. absentmindedly. ● n. a scrawl or drawing so made. □□ **doo·dler** n.

doo·dle·bug /dóód'lbug/ n. **1** any of various insects, esp. the larva of an ant lion. **2** an unscientific device for locating minerals. **3** *colloq.* a robot bomb.

doo·hick·ey /dóóhikee/ n. (*pl.* **-eys** or **-ies**) *US colloq.* a small object, esp. mechanical.

doom /dōom/ n. & v. ● n. **1 a** a grim fate or destiny. **b** death or ruin. **2 a** a condemnation; a judgment or sentence. **b** the Last Judgment (*the crack of doom*). ● v.tr. **1** (usu. foll. by *to*) condemn or destine (*doomed to destruction*). **2** (esp. as **doomed** *adj.*) consign to misfortune or destruction.

dooms·day /dóómzday/ n. the day of the Last Judgment. □ **till doomsday** for ever.

doom·watch /dóómwoch/ n. organized vigilance or observation to avert danger, esp. from environmental pollution. □□ **doom·watch·er** n.

D

DOME

Domes are curved roofs first built on palaces, capitols, and religious buildings as striking symbols of the building's status. They can be categorized according to the shape of the dome. The framework of the dome, such as the one shown here, often has very complex bracing systems. The shape of the base depends on the plan of the walls on which the dome is constructed, known as the drum.

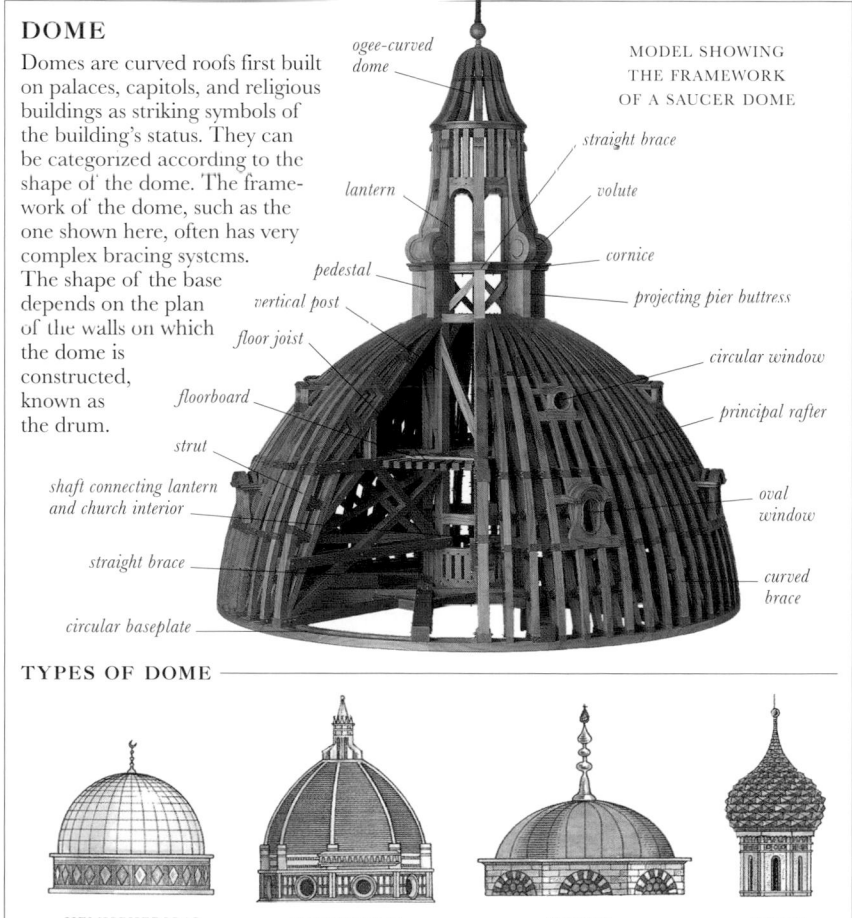

MODEL SHOWING
THE FRAMEWORK
OF A SAUCER DOME

ogee-curved dome

straight brace

volute

lantern

cornice

pedestal

projecting pier buttress

vertical post

floor joist

circular window

floorboard

principal rafter

strut

shaft connecting lantern and church interior

oval window

straight brace

curved brace

circular baseplate

TYPES OF DOME

HEMISPHERICAL   POLYHEDRAL   SAUCER   ONION

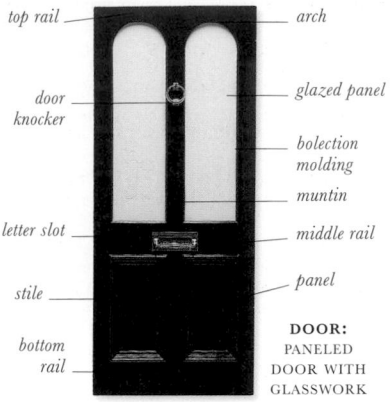

DOOR: PANELED DOOR WITH GLASSWORK

top rail — arch
door knocker
glazed panel
bolection molding
muntin
letter slot — middle rail
stile — panel
bottom rail

DOPPLER EFFECT

DEMONSTRATION OF THE DOPPLER EFFECT

The changing pitch of the siren of a passing police car is an example of the Doppler effect on sound waves. As the car moves toward you, the sound waves are short and reach you more frequently, and so the pitch rises. As the car moves away, the waves are longer and reach you less frequently, and so the pitch drops. The siren is, in fact, constantly producing sound of the same frequency.

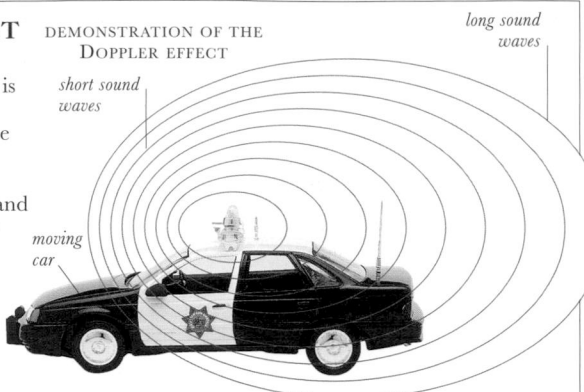

short sound waves
long sound waves
moving car

door /dawr/ *n.* **1 a** ▲ a hinged, sliding, or revolving barrier for closing and opening an entrance to a building, room, cupboard, etc. **b** this as representing a house, etc. (*lives two doors away*). **2 a** an entrance or exit; a doorway. **b** a means of access or approach. □ **close the door to** exclude the opportunity for. **lay** (or **lie**) **at the door of** impute (or be imputable) to. **leave the door open** ensure that an option remains available. **next door to 1** in the next house to. **2** nearly; near to. **open the door to** create an opportunity for. **out of doors** in or into the open air. □□ **doored** *adj.* (also in *comb.*).

door·bell /dáwrbel/ *n.* a bell in a house, etc., rung by visitors outside to signal their arrival.

door·frame /dáwrfraym/ *n.* the framework of a doorway.

door·knob /dáwrnob/ *n.* a knob for turning to release the latch of a door.

door·man /dáwrman, -mən/ *n.* (*pl.* **-men**) a person on duty at the door to a large building.

door·mat /dáwrmat/ *n.* **1** a mat at an entrance for wiping mud, etc., from the shoes. **2** a feebly submissive person.

door·nail /dáwrnayl/ *n.* a nail with which doors were studded for strength or ornament. □ **dead as a doornail** completely or unmistakably dead.

door·post /dáwrpōst/ *n.* each of the uprights of a doorframe.

door prize *n.* a prize awarded usu. by lottery at a dance, party, charity event, etc.

door·step /dáwrstep/ *n.* a step leading up to the outer door of a house, etc. □ **on one's** (or **the**) **doorstep** very close.

door·stop /dáwrstop/ *n.* a device for keeping a door open or to prevent it from striking a wall, etc., when opened.

door-to-door *adj.* (of selling, etc.) done at each house in turn.

door·way /dáwrway/ *n.* an opening filled by a door.

doo-wop /dóōwop/ *n.* a style of pop music involving close harmony vocals and nonsense phrases.

doo·zy /dóōzee/ *n.* (*pl.* **doozies**) *colloq.* one that is outstanding of its kind (*a mistake that was a doozy*).

dope /dōp/ *n.* & *v.* ● *n.* **1** a varnish applied to the cloth surface of airplane parts. **2** a thick liquid used as a lubricant, etc. **3** a substance added to gasoline, etc., to increase its effectiveness. **4 a** *sl.* a narcotic; a stupefying drug. **b** a drug, etc., given to a horse or greyhound, or taken by an athlete, to affect performance. **5** *sl.* a stupid person. **6** *sl.* **a** information about a subject, esp. if not generally known. **b** misleading information. ● *v.* **1** *tr.* administer dope to; drug. **2** *tr.* apply dope to. **3** *intr.* take addictive drugs. □ **dope out** *sl.* discover. □□ **dop·er** *n.*

dope·y /dōpee/ *adj.* (also **dop·y**) (**dopier, dopiest**) *colloq.* **1 a** half asleep. **b** stupefied by or as if by a drug. **2** stupid; silly. □□ **dop·i·ly** *adv.* **dop·i·ness** *n.*

dop·pel·gäng·er /dópəlgangər/ *n.* an apparition or double of a living person.

Dop·pler ef·fect /dóplər/ *n.* (also **Dop·pler shift**) *Physics* ▲ an increase (or decrease) in the frequency of sound, light, or other waves as the source and observer move toward (or away) from each other.

dop·y var. of DOPEY.

do·ra·do /dəráádō/ *n.* (*pl.* **-os**) **1** ▼ a blue and silver marine fish, *Coryphaena hippurus*. **2** a brightly colored freshwater fish, *Salminus maxillosus*, native to S. America.

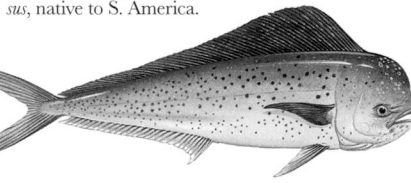

DORADO (*Coryphaena hippurus*)

do-rag /dóōrag/ *n.* *black sl.* a scarf or cloth worn to protect one's hairstyle.

Dor·ic /dáwrik, dór-/ *adj.* **1** (of a dialect) broad; rustic. **2** *Archit.* ▼ of the oldest, sturdiest, and simplest of the Greek orders. ▷ COLUMN

dork /dawrk/ *n.* *sl.* a dull, slow-witted, or oafish person. □□ **dork·y** *adj.*

dorm /dawrm/ *n.* *colloq.* dormitory.

dor·mant /dáwrmənt/ *adj.* **1** lying inactive; sleeping. **2 a** (of a volcano, etc.) temporarily inactive. **b** (of potential faculties, etc.) in abeyance. **3** (of plants) alive but not actively growing. □□ **dor·man·cy** *n.*

dor·mer /dáwrmər/ *n.* (in full **dormer window**) a projecting upright window in a sloping roof. ▷ CHÂTEAU

dor·mi·to·ry /dáwrmitáwree/ *n.* (*pl.* **-ies**) **1** a sleeping room with several beds, esp. in a school or institution. ▷ MONASTERY. **2** a university or college hall of residence or hostel.

dor·mouse /dáwrmows/ *n.* (*pl.* **dormice** /-mīs/) ► any small, mouselike hibernating rodent of the family Gliridae.

DORMOUSE: COMMON DORMOUSE (*Muscardinus avellanarius*)

dor·sal /dáwrsəl/ *adj. Anat.*, *Zool.*, & *Bot.* **1** of, on, or near the back (cf. VENTRAL). ▷ FISH. **2** ridge-shaped. □□ **dor·sal·ly** *adv.*

do·ry¹ /dáwree/ *n.* (*pl.* **-ies**) any of various marine fish having a compressed body and flat head, esp. the John Dory, used as food. ▷ JOHN DORY

do·ry² /dáwree/ *n.* (*pl.* **-ies**) a flat-bottomed fishing boat with high sides.

DOS /dos, daws/ *n. Computing* a software operating system for personal computers.

dos·age /dósij/ *n.* **1** the giving of medicine in doses. **2** the size of a dose.

dose /dōs/ *n.* & *v.* ● *n.* **1** an amount of a medicine or drug taken at one time. **2** a quantity of something administered or allocated (e.g., work, praise, punishment, etc.). **3** the amount of ionizing radiation received by a person or thing. **4** *sl.* a venereal infection. ● *v.tr.* **1** treat (a person or animal) with doses of medicine. **2** give a dose or doses to. **3** adulterate or blend (esp. wine with spirit).

do·sim·e·ter /dōsímitər/ *n.* a device used to measure an absorbed dose of ionizing radiation. □□ **do·si·met·ric** /-métrik/ *adj.* **do·sim·e·try** *n.*

dos·si·er /dósee-ay, dáw-/ *n.* a set of documents, esp. about a person, event, or subject.

DORIC

The Doric order, which dates from the 7th century BC, is the oldest of the three main ancient Greek architectural orders. Doric temples have fluted columns with plain capitals and no bases. The friezes are decorated with carved panels called triglyphs, which are separated by plainer panels called metopes.

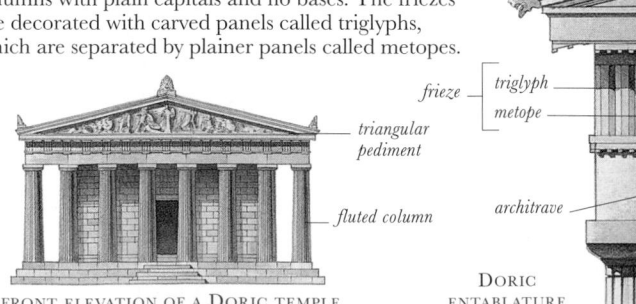

FRONT ELEVATION OF A DORIC TEMPLE

DORIC ENTABLATURE

acroterion
triangular pediment
frieze
triglyph
metope
fluted column
architrave
plain capital

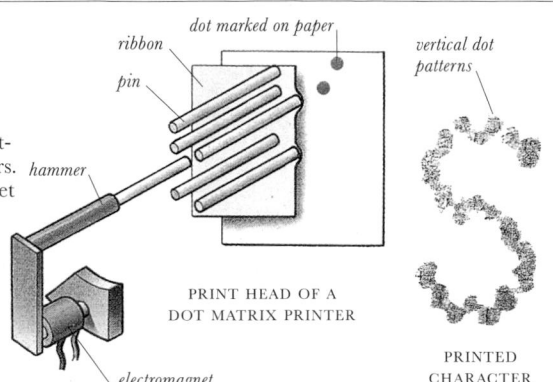

DOT MATRIX PRINTER

A dot matrix printer is a computer printer that uses pins or wires arranged in a matrix pattern to form printed characters. A signal from an electromagnet causes the hammer to hit a pin. The pin strikes an inked ribbon, making a dot on the paper. The pins are activated in different combinations so that each character is made up of a pattern of vertical dots.

dot marked on paper
ribbon
pin
vertical dot patterns
hammer

PRINT HEAD OF A
DOT MATRIX PRINTER

electromagnet

PRINTED CHARACTER

---

dot /dot/ *n. & v.* ● *n.* **1 a** a small spot, speck, or mark. **b** such a mark as part of an *i* or *j*, as a full stop, etc. **c** a decimal point. **2** *Mus.* a dot used to denote the lengthening of a note or rest, or to indicate staccato. **3** the shorter signal of the two used in Morse code (cf. DASH *n.* 6). **4** a tiny or apparently tiny object (*a dot on the horizon*). ● *v.tr.* (**dotted, dotting**) **1 a** mark with a dot or dots. **b** place a dot over (a letter). **2** *Mus.* mark (a note or rest) to show that the time value is increased by half. **3** (often foll. by *about*) scatter like dots. **4** partly cover as with dots (*an ocean dotted with ships*). □ **dot the i's and cross the t's** *colloq.* **1** be minutely accurate; emphasize details. **2** add the final touches to a task. **on the dot** exactly on time.

dot·age /dṓtij/ *n.* feeble-minded senility (*in his dotage*).

dot-com *n.* a company that conducts its business on the Internet.

do·tard /dṓtərd/ *n.* a person who is feeble-minded, esp. from senility.

dote /dōt/ *v.intr.* **1** (foll. by *on, upon*) be foolishly or excessively fond of. **2** be silly or feeble-minded, esp. from old age.

dot ma·trix print·er *n. Computing* ▲ a printer with characters formed from dots printed by configurations of the tips of small wires.

dot·ted line *n.* a line of dots on a document.

dot·ty /dótee/ *adj.* (**dottier, dottiest**) *colloq.* **1** feeble-minded; silly. **2** eccentric. **3** absurd. **4** (foll. by *about, on*) infatuated with; obsessed by. □□ **dot·ti·ly** *adv.* **dot·ti·ness** *n.*

dou·ble /dúbəl/ *adj., adv., n., & v.* ● *adj.* **1 a** consisting of two parts or things. **b** consisting of two identical parts. **2** twice as much or many (*double the amount; double the number; double thickness*). **3** having twice the usual size, quantity, strength, etc. (*double whiskey*). **4** designed for two people (*double bed*). **5 a** having some part double. **b** (of a flower) having more than one circle of petals. **c** (of a domino) having the same number of pips on each half. **6** having two different roles or interpretations, esp. implying confusion or deceit (*double meaning; leads a double life*). **7** *Mus.* lower in pitch by an octave (*double bassoon*). ● *adv.* **1** at or to twice the amount, etc. (*counts double*). **2** two together (*sleep double*). ● *n.* **1 a** a double quantity or thing; twice as much or many. **b** *colloq.* a double measure of liquor. **2 a** a person who looks exactly like another. **b** an understudy. **c** a wraith. **3** (in *pl.*) *Sports* (esp. tennis) a game between two pairs

scroll
fingerboard
shoulder
bridge
soundhole
sound-board
tail-piece
spike

DOUBLE BASS

---

of players. **4** *Sports* a pair of victories over the same team, a pair of championships at the same game, etc. **5** a system of betting in which the winnings and stake from the first bet are transferred to a second. **6** *Bridge* the doubling of an opponent's bid. **7** *Darts* a hit on the narrow ring enclosed by the two outer circles of a dartboard. **8** a sharp turn, esp. of the tracks of a hunted animal, or the course of a river. ● *v.* **1** *tr. & intr.* make or become twice as much or many; increase twofold; multiply by two. **2** *tr.* amount to twice as much as. **3 a** *tr.* fold or bend (paper, cloth, etc.) over on itself. **b** *intr.* become folded. **4 a** *tr.* (of an actor) play (two parts) in the same piece. **b** *intr.* (often foll. by *for*) be understudy, etc. **5** *intr.* (usu. foll. by *as*) play a twofold role. **6** *intr.* turn sharply in flight or pursuit. **7** *tr. Naut.* sail around (a headland). **8** *tr. Bridge* make a call increasing the value of the points to be won or lost on (an opponent's bid). **9** *Mus.* **a** *intr.* (often foll. by *on*) play two or more musical instruments (*the clarinettist doubles on tenor sax*). **b** *tr.* add the same note in a higher or lower octave to (a note). **10** *tr.* clench (a fist). **11** *intr.* move at twice the usual speed; run. **12** *Billiards* **a** *intr.* rebound. **b** *tr.* cause to rebound. □ **double back** take a new direction opposite to the previous one. **double or nothing** a gamble to decide whether a player's loss or debt be doubled or canceled. **double up 1 a** bend or curl up. **b** cause to do this. **2** be overcome with pain or laughter. **3** share or assign to a room, etc., with another or others. **4** fold or become folded. **5** use winnings from a bet as stake for another. **on the double** hurrying. □□ **dou·bler** *n.* **dou·bly** *adv.*

dou·ble a·gent *n.* one who spies simultaneously for two rival countries, etc.

dou·ble-bar·reled *adj.* **1** (of a gun) having two barrels. ▷ SHOTGUN. **2** twofold.

dou·ble bass *n.* **1** ◄ the largest and lowest-pitched instrument of the violin family. ▷ ORCHESTRA, STRINGED. **2** (also **dou·ble bass·ist**) its player.

dou·ble bill *n.* a program with two principal items.

dou·ble-blind *adj. & n.* ● *adj.* (of a test or experiment) in which neither the tester nor the subject has knowledge of identities, etc., that might lead to bias. ● *n.* such a test or experiment.

dou·ble boil·er *n.* a saucepan with a detachable upper compartment heated by boiling water in the lower one.

dou·ble-book *v.tr.* accept two reservations simultaneously for (the same seat, room, etc.).

dou·ble-breast·ed *adj.* (of a coat, etc.) having two fronts overlapping across the body.

dou·ble-check *v.tr.* verify twice or in two ways.

dou·ble chin *n.* a chin with a fold of loose flesh below it. □□ **dou·ble-chinned** *adj.*

---

dou·ble-cross *v. & n.* ● *v.tr.* deceive or betray (a person one is supposedly helping). ● *n.* an act of double-crossing. □□ **dou·ble-cross·er** *n.*

dou·ble-deal·ing *n. & adj.* ● *n.* deceit. ● *adj.* practicing deceit. □□ **dou·ble-deal·er** *n.*

dou·ble-deck·er *n.* **1** esp. *Brit.* a bus having an upper and lower deck. **2** *colloq.* anything consisting of two layers.

dou·ble Dutch *n.* a synchronized jump-rope game using two outstretched ropes swung in opposite directions.

dou·ble ea·gle *n.* **1** a figure of a two-headed eagle. **2** *Golf* a score of three strokes under par at any hole.

dou·ble-edged *adj.* **1** having two functions or (often contradictory) applications. **2** (of a knife, etc.) having two cutting edges.

dou·ble en·ten·dre /dúbəl aantaándrə, dōōblaan taándrə/ *n.* **1** a word or phrase open to two interpretations, one usu. risqué or indecent. **2** humor using such words or phrases.

dou·ble ex·po·sure *n. Photog.* the accidental or deliberate repeated exposure of a plate, film, etc.

dou·ble fea·ture *n.* a movie program with two full-length films.

dou·ble glaz·ing *n.* **1** a window consisting of two layers of glass with a space between them, designed to reduce loss of heat and exclude noise. **2** the provision of this.

dou·ble-head·er /dúbəlhedər/ *n.* **1** a train pulled by two locomotives coupled together. **2 a** two games (esp. baseball), etc., in succession between the same opponents. **b** two games (esp. basketball), etc., in succession between different opponents.

dou·ble he·lix *n.* a pair of parallel helices with a common axis, esp. in the structure of the DNA molecule. ▷ DNA

dou·ble in·dem·ni·ty *n.* a clause in a life-insurance policy providing double payment to the beneficiary if the insured person dies accidentally.

dou·ble-joint·ed *adj.* having joints that allow unusual bending.

dou·ble knit *n.* (of fabric) knit of two joined layers for extra thickness.

dou·ble neg·a·tive *n. Gram.* a negative statement containing two negative elements (e.g., *didn't say nothing*). ¶ Considered ungrammatical in standard English.

dou·ble-park *v.tr. & intr.* park (a vehicle) alongside one that is already parked at the roadside.

dou·ble play *n. Baseball* putting out two runners.

dou·ble pneu·mo·nia *n.* pneumonia affecting both lungs.

dou·ble stand·ard *n.* **1** a rule or principle applied more strictly to some people than to others. **2** bimetallism.

dou·blet /dúblit/ *n.* **1** either of a pair of similar things. **2** *hist.* a man's short, close-fitting jacket.

dou·ble take *n.* a delayed reaction to a situation, etc., immediately after one's first reaction.

dou·ble-talk *n.* verbal expression that is ambiguous or misleading.

dou·ble-think /dúbəlthingk/ *n.* the capacity to accept contrary opinions at the same time.

dou·bloon /dublōōn/ *n.* **1** *hist.* ► a Spanish gold coin. **2** (in *pl.*) *sl.* money.

doubt /dowt/ *n. & v.* ● *n.* **1** a feeling of uncertainty; an undecided state of mind (*be in no doubt about; have no doubt that*). **2** (often foll. by *of, about*) an inclination to disbelieve. **3** an uncertain state of things. **4** a lack of full proof or clear indication (*benefit of the doubt*). ● *v.* **1** *tr.* (often foll. by *whether, if, that* + clause; also foll. (after *neg.* or *interrog.*) by *but, but that*) feel uncertain or undecided about (*I doubt that you are right*). **2** *tr.* hesitate to believe. **3** *intr.* (often foll. by *of*) feel

DOUBLOONS

D

uncertain or undecided; have doubts (*never doubted of success*). **4** *tr.* call in question. □ **beyond doubt** certainly. **in doubt** open to question. **no doubt** certainly; probably; admittedly. **without doubt** (or **a doubt**) certainly. □□ **doubt·er** *n.*

doubt·ful /dówtfŏol/ *adj.* **1** feeling doubt. **2** causing doubt. **3** unreliable (*a doubtful ally*). □□ **doubt·ful·ly** *adv.*

doubt·ing Thom·as /tómɐs/ *n.* an incredulous or skeptical person (after John 20:24–29).

doubt·less /dówtlis/ *adv.* (often qualifying a sentence) **1** certainly; no doubt. **2** probably. □□ **doubt·less·ly** *adv.*

douche /dŏosh/ *n. & v.* ● *n.* **1** a jet of liquid applied to a body part for cleansing or medicinal purposes. **2** a device for producing such a jet. ● *v.* **1** *tr.* treat with a douche. **2** *intr.* use a douche.

dough /dō/ *n.* **1** a thick mixture of flour, etc., and liquid, for baking. **2** *sl.* money.

dough·boy /dóboy/ *n.* **1** *colloq.* a United States infantryman, esp. in World War I. **2** a boiled dumpling.

dough·nut /dónut/ *n.* (also **do·nut**) a small fried cake of sweetened dough, usu. in the form of a ball or ring.

dough·ty /dówtee/ *adj.* (**doughtier, doughtiest**) *archaic* or *joc.* valiant.

dough·y /dóee/ *adj.* (**doughier, doughiest**) **1** having the form or consistency of dough. **2** pale and sickly in color.

Doug·las fir /dúglɐs/ *n.* (also **Doug·las pine** or **spruce**) ▼ any large conifer of the genus *Pseudotsuga*, of western N. America.

DOUGLAS FIR (*Pseudotsuga menziesii*)

linear leaf

cone

mature tree

dour /dŏor, dowr/ *adj.* severe; stern; obstinate. □□ **dour·ly** *adv.*

douse /dows/ *v.tr.* (also **dowse**) **1 a** throw water over. **b** plunge into water. **2** extinguish (a light).

dove[1] /duv/ *n.* **1** any bird of the family Columbidae, with short legs, small head, and large breast. **2** a gentle or innocent person. **3** *Polit.* an advocate of peace or peaceful policies. **4** (**Dove**) *Relig.* a representation of the Holy Spirit (John 1:32). **5** a soft gray color.

dove[2] /dōv/ *past* and *past part.* of DIVE.

dove·cote /dúvkōt, -kot/ *n.* (also **dove·cot**) a shelter for domesticated pigeons.

dove·tail /dúvtayl/ *n. & v.* ● *n.* **1** ▶ a joint formed by a mortise with a tenon shaped like a dove's spread tail. **2** such a tenon. ● *v.* **1** *tr.* join together by means of a dovetail. **2** *tr. & intr.* (often foll. by *into, with*) fit readily together; combine neatly or compactly.

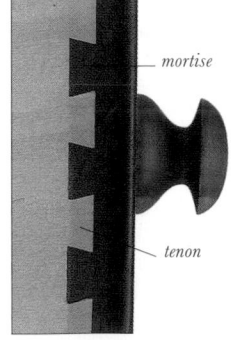

mortise

tenon

DOVETAIL JOINTS IN A DRAWER SIDE

dow·a·ger /dówɐjɐr/ *n.* **1** a widow with a title or property derived from her late husband (*Queen dowager; dowager duchess*). **2** *colloq.* a dignified elderly woman.

dow·dy /dówdee/ *adj. & n.* ● *adj.* (**dowdier, dowdiest**) **1** (of clothes) unattractively dull. **2** dressed in dowdy clothes. ● *n.* (*pl.* **-ies**) a dowdy woman. □□ **dow·di·ly** *adv.* **dow·di·ness** *n.*

dow·el /dówɐl/ *n. & v.* ● *n.* a headless peg holding together components of a structure. ● *v.tr.* fasten with a dowel.

dow·el·ing /dówɐling/ *n.* round rods for cutting into dowels.

dow·er /dówɐr/ *n.* **1** a widow's share for life of her husband's estate. **2** *archaic* a dowry.

Dow–Jones av·er·age /dowjónz/ *n.* (also **Dow–Jones index**) a figure indicating the relative price of shares on the New York Stock Exchange.

down[1] /down/ *adv., prep., adj., v., & n.* ● *adv.* **1** into or toward a lower place (*fall down; knelt down*). **2** in a lower place or position (*blinds were down*). **3** to or in a place regarded as lower, esp. southward. **4 a** in or into a low or weaker position, mood, or condition (*hit a man when he's down; many down with colds*). **b** in a position of loss or disadvantage (*our team was three goals down; $5 down on the transaction*). **c** (of a computer system) out of action. **5** from an earlier to a later time (*customs handed down; down to 1600*). **6** to a finer or thinner consistency or a smaller amount or size (*grind down; water down; boil down*). **7** cheaper (*bread is down; stocks are down*). **8** into a more settled state (*calm down*). **9** in writing; in or into recorded or listed form (*copy it down; I got it down on tape; you are down to speak next*). **10** (of part of a larger whole) paid; dealt with (*$5 down, $20 to pay; three down, six to go*). **11** *Naut.* **a** with the current or wind. **b** (of a ship's helm) with the rudder to windward. **12** inclusively of the lower limit in a series (*read down to the third paragraph*). **13** (as *int.*) lie down, put (something) down, etc. **14** (of a crossword clue or answer) read vertically (*cannot do five down*). **15** downstairs, esp. after rising (*is not down yet*). **16** swallowed (*could not get the pill down*). **17** *Football* (of the ball) no longer in play. ● *prep.* **1** downward along, through, or into. **2** from top to bottom of. **3** along (*walk down the road; cut down the middle*). **4** at or in a lower part of (*situated down the river*). ● *adj.* **1** directed downward. **2** *colloq.* unhappy; depressed. ● *v.tr. colloq.* **1** knock or bring down. **2** swallow. ● *n.* **1** an act of putting down (as an opponent in wrestling). **2** a reverse of fortune (*ups and downs*). **3** *colloq.* a period of depression. **4** *Football* **a** one of a series of plays (up to four) in which the offensive team must advance the ball 10 yards in order to keep the ball. **b** the declaring of the ball as no longer in play. □ **be** (or **have a**) **down on** *colloq.* disapprove of; show animosity toward. **be down to 1** be attributable to. **2** be the responsibility of. **3** have used up everything except (*down to their last can of rations*). **down on one's luck** *colloq.* **1** temporarily unfortunate. **2** dispirited by misfortune. **down to the ground** *colloq.* completely. **down with** *int.* expressing rejection of a specified person or thing.

down[2] /down/ *n.* **1 a** the first covering of young birds. **b** ▶ a bird's underplumage. **c** a layer of fine, soft feathers. **2** fine, soft hair, esp. on the face. **3** short, soft hairs on some leaves, fruit, seeds, etc. **4** a fluffy substance, e.g., thistledown.

down-and-out *adj. & n.* ● *adj.* (**down and out** when *predic.*) **1** penniless; destitute. **2** *Boxing* unable to resume the fight. ● *n.* a destitute person.

DOWN FEATHERS FROM A DUCK

down-at-the-heels *adj.* (also **down-at-heel, down-at-the-heel**) shabby; slovenly.

down·beat /dównbeet/ *n. & adj.* ● *n. Mus.*

an accented beat, usu. the first of the bar. ● *adj.* **1** pessimistic; gloomy. **2** relaxed.

down·cast /dównkast/ *adj. & n.* ● *adj.* **1** (of eyes) looking downward. **2** dejected. ● *n.* a shaft dug in a mine for extra ventilation.

down·draft /dówndraft/ *n.* a downward draft, esp. one down a chimney into a room.

down·er /dównɐr/ *n. sl.* **1** a depressant or tranquilizing drug. **2** a depressing person or experience; a failure. **3** = DOWNTURN.

down·fall /dównfawl/ *n.* **1 a** a fall from prosperity or power. **b** the cause of this. **2** a sudden heavy fall of rain, etc.

down·grade *v. & n.* ● *v.tr.* /dówngráyd/ **1** make lower in rank or status. **2** speak disparagingly of. ● *n.* /dówngrayd/ **1** a descending slope of a road or railroad. **2** deterioration.

down·heart·ed /dównháartid/ *adj.* dejected; in low spirits. □□ **down·heart·ed·ly** *adv.* **down·heart·ed·ness** *n.*

down·hill *adv., adj., & n.* ● *adv.* /dównhíl/ in a descending direction. ● *adj.* /dównhíl/ **1** sloping down; descending. **2** declining; deteriorating. ● *n.* /dównhíl/ **1** *Skiing* a downhill race. ▷ SKI. **2** a downward slope. **3** a decline. □ **go downhill** *colloq.* decline; deteriorate.

down in the mouth *adj. colloq.* looking unhappy; dejected.

down·load /dównlōd/ *v.tr. Computing* transfer (data) from one storage device or system to another.

down-mar·ket *adj. & adv. colloq.* toward or relating to the cheaper sector of the market.

down pay·ment *n.* a partial payment made at the time of purchase.

down·play /dównpláy/ *v.tr.* play down; minimize the importance of.

down·pour /dównpawr/ *n.* a heavy fall of rain.

down·right /dównrīt/ *adj. & adv.* ● *adj.* **1** plain; straightforward. **2** utter (*a downright lie; downright nonsense*). ● *adv.* thoroughly (*downright rude*).

down·riv·er /downrívɐr/ *adv. & adj.* towards or situated at a point nearer the mouth of a river.

down·scale /dównskáyl/ *v. & adj.* ● *v.tr.* reduce or restrict in size, scale, or extent. ● *adj.* at the lower end of a scale; inferior.

down·shift /dównshift/ *v.intr. & tr.* shift (an automotive vehicle) into a lower gear.

down·side /dównsīd/ *n.* a downward movement of share prices, etc.

down·size /dównsīz/ *v.tr.* (**downsized, downsizing**) **1** reduce in size. **2** cut back on the number of employees in (a company).

down·spout /dównspowt/ *n.* a pipe to carry rainwater from a roof. ▷ HOUSE

Down's syn·drome /downz/ *n. Med.* (also **Down syn·drome**) a congenital disorder characterized by mental retardation and physical abnormalities (cf. MONGOLISM).

down·stage /dównstayj/ *n., adj., & adv. Theatr.* ● *n.* the frontmost portion of the stage. ● *adj. & adv.* at or to the front of the stage. ▷ THEATER

down·stairs *adv., adj., & n.* ● *adv.* /dównstáirz/ **1** down a flight of stairs. **2** to or on a lower floor. ● *adj.* /dównstairz/ (also **down·stair**) situated downstairs. ● *n.* /dównstáirz/ the lower floor.

down·state /dównstáyt/ *adj., n., & adv.* ● *adj.* of or in a southern part of a state, esp. a part remote from large cities, esp. the southern. ● *n.* a downstate area. ● *adv.* in a downstate area.

down·stream /dównstréem/ *adv. & adj.* ● *adv.* in the direction of the flow of a stream, etc. ● *adj.* moving downstream.

down·time /dówntīm/ *n.* time during which a machine, esp. a computer, is out of action or unavailable for use.

down-to-earth *adj.* practical; realistic.

down·town /dówntówn/ *adj., n., & adv.* ● *adj.* of or in the lower or more central part, or the business part, of a town or city. ● *n.* a downtown area. ● *adv.* in or into a downtown area.

down·trod·den /dówntród'n/ *adj.* oppressed; badly treated.

down·turn /dówntərn/ *n.* a decline, esp. in economic activity.

down un·der *adv. colloq.* (also **Down Un·der**) in the antipodes, esp. Australia.

down·ward /dównwərd/ *adv. & adj.* ● *adv.* (also **down·wards**) toward what is lower, inferior, less important, or later. ● *adj.* moving, extending, pointing, or leading downward. □□ **down·ward·ly** *adv.*

down·wind /dównwínd/ *adj. & adv.* in the direction in which the wind is blowing.

down·y /dównee/ *adj.* (**downier**, **downiest**) **1** of, like, or covered with down. **2** soft and fluffy.

dow·ry /dówree/ *n.* (*pl.* **-ies**) **1** property or money brought by a bride to her husband. **2** a talent; a natural gift.

dowse[1] /dowz/ *v.intr.* search for underground water or minerals by holding a stick or rod which dips abruptly when over the right spot. □□ **dows·er** *n.*

dowse[2] *var. of* DOUSE.

dows·ing rod *n.* (also **di·vin·ing rod**) a stick or rod used in dowsing.

dox·ol·o·gy /doksóləjee/ *n.* (*pl.* **-ies**) a liturgical formula of praise to God.

doy·en /dóyen, dóyən, dwáayaN/ *n.* (*fem.* **doyenne** /dóyén, dwaayén/) the senior member of a body of colleagues, esp. the senior ambassador at a court.

doz. *abbr.* dozen.

doze /dōz/ *v. & n.* *v.intr.* sleep lightly; be half asleep. ● *n.* a short, light sleep. □ **doze off** fall lightly asleep.

doz·en /dúzən/ *n.* **1** (prec. by *a* or a number) (*pl.* **dozen**) twelve (*a dozen eggs; two dozen packages; ordered three dozen*). **2** a set or group of twelve (*packed in dozens*). **3** *colloq.* about twelve, a fairly large indefinite number. **4** (in *pl.*; usu. foll. by *of*) *colloq.* very many (*made dozens of mistakes*). **5** (**the dozens**) a game or ritualized exchange of verbal insults. □ **by the dozen** in large quantities.

doz·y /dózee/ *adj.* (**dozier**, **doziest**) drowsy; tending to doze. □□ **doz·i·ly** *adv.* **doz·i·ness** *n.*

D.Ph. *abbr.* Doctor of Philosophy.

DPT *abbr.* (vaccination against) diphtheria, pertussis, and tetanus.

Dr. *abbr.* **1** Doctor. **2** Drive. **3** debtor.

dr. *abbr.* **1** dram(s). **2** drachma(s).

drab[1] /drab/ *adj. & n.* *adj.* (**drabber**, **drabbest**) **1** dull; uninteresting. **2** of a dull brownish color. ● *n.* **1** drab color. **2** monotony. □□ **drab·ly** *adv.* **drab·ness** *n.*

drab[2] /drab/ *see* DRIBS AND DRABS.

drach·ma /drákmə/ *n.* (*pl.* **drachmas** or **drachmai** /-mī/ or **drachmae** /-mee/) **1** (until the introduction of the euro in 2002) the chief monetary unit of Greece. **2** a silver coin of ancient Greece.

dra·co·ni·an /drəkṓneeən, dray-/ *adj.* (also **dra·con·ic** /-kónik/) (esp. of laws and their application) very harsh or severe.

draft /draft/ *n. & v.* *n.* **1 a** a preliminary written version of a speech, document, etc. **b** a rough preliminary outline of a scheme. **c** a sketch of work to be carried out. **2 a** a written order for payment of money by a bank. **b** the drawing of money by means of this. **3** (foll. by *on*) a demand made on a person's confidence, friendship, etc. **4 a** a party detached from a larger group for a special purpose. **b** the selection of this. **5** compulsory military service. **6** a reinforcement. **7** a current of air in a confined space. **8** pulling; traction. **9** *Naut.* the depth of water needed to float a ship. **10** the drawing of liquor from a cask, etc. **11 a** a single act of drinking. **b** the amount drunk in this. **c** a dose of liquid medicine. **12 a** the drawing in of a fishing net. **b** the fish taken at one

drawing. ● *v.tr.* **1** prepare a draft of (a document, scheme, etc.). **2** select for a special purpose. **3** conscript for military service. □□ **draft·ee** /-tée/ *n.* **draft·er** *n.*

draft beer *n.* beer drawn from a cask.

draft horse *n.* ▼ a horse used for pulling heavy loads. ▷ HORSE

DRAFT HORSE: SHIRE-HORSES PULLING A PLOW

drag /drag/ *v. & n.* ● *v.* (**dragged**, **dragging**) **1** *tr.* pull along with effort. **2 a** *tr.* allow (one's feet, tail, etc.) to trail along the ground. **b** trail along the ground. **c** *intr.* (of time, etc.) go or pass heavily or slowly or tediously. **3 a** *intr.* (usu. foll. by *for*) use a grapnel or drag (to find a drowned person or lost object). **b** *tr.* search the bottom of (a river, etc.) with grapnels, nets, or drags. **4** *tr.* (often foll. by *to*) *colloq.* take (a person to a place, etc., esp. against his or her will). **5** *intr.* (foll. by *on, at*) draw on (a cigarette, etc.). **6** *intr.* (often foll. by *on*) continue at tedious length. ● *n.* **1 a** an obstruction to progress. **b** *Aeron.* the longitudinal retarding force exerted by air. **c** slow motion; impeded progress. **d** an iron shoe for retarding a horse-drawn vehicle downhill. **2** *colloq.* a boring or dreary person, duty, performance, etc. **3 a** a lure drawn before hounds as a substitute for a fox. **b** a hunt using this. **4** an apparatus for dredging or recovering drowned persons, etc., from under water. **5** = DRAGNET. **6** *sl.* a draw on a cigarette, etc. **7** *sl.* **a** women's clothes worn by men. **b** a party at which

these are worn. **c** clothes in general. **8** an act of dragging. **9** *sl.* (in full **drag race**) an acceleration race between cars. **10** *sl.* influence; pull. **11** *sl.* a street or road (*the main drag*). □ **drag one's feet** (or **heels**) be deliberately slow or reluctant to act. **drag in** introduce (a subject) irrelevantly. **drag out** protract. **drag through the mud** see MUD. **drag up** *colloq.* deliberately mention (an unwelcome subject).

drag·net /drágnet/ *n.* **1** a net drawn through a river or across ground to trap fish or game. **2** a systematic hunt for criminals, etc.

drag·o·man /drágəmən/ *n.* (*pl.* **dragomans** or **dragomen**) an interpreter or guide.

drag·on /drágən/ *n.* **1** a mythical monster like a reptile, usu. with wings and able to breathe out fire. **2** a fierce woman. **3** (in full **flying dragon**) a lizard, *Draco volans*, with a long tail and membranous winglike structures.

drag·on·fly /drágənflī/ *n.* (*pl.* **-ies**) ▼ any of various insects of the order Odonata, having a long, slender body and two pairs of large transparent wings.

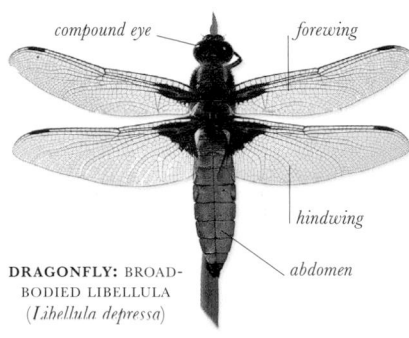

compound eye   *forewing*
hindwing
abdomen

DRAGONFLY: BROAD-BODIED LIBELLULA (*Libellula depressa*)

dra·goon /drəgōon/ *n. & v.* ● *n.* **1** a cavalry man (originally a mounted infantryman armed with a carbine). **2** a rough, fierce fellow. **3** a variety of pigeon. ● *v.tr.* **1** (foll. by *into*) coerce into doing something. **2** persecute, esp. with troops.

drag queen *n. sl.* a male transvestite.

drag race *n.* = DRAG *n.* 9.

drag·ster /drágstər/ *n.* ▼ a car built or modified to take part in drag races.

DRAGSTER

A dragster is a high-powered, single-seat car that is raced on a straight quarter-mile track. There are several classes of design, engine, and fuel. The fastest, known as "top-fuelers," run on rocket fuel and can complete the course in less than five seconds.

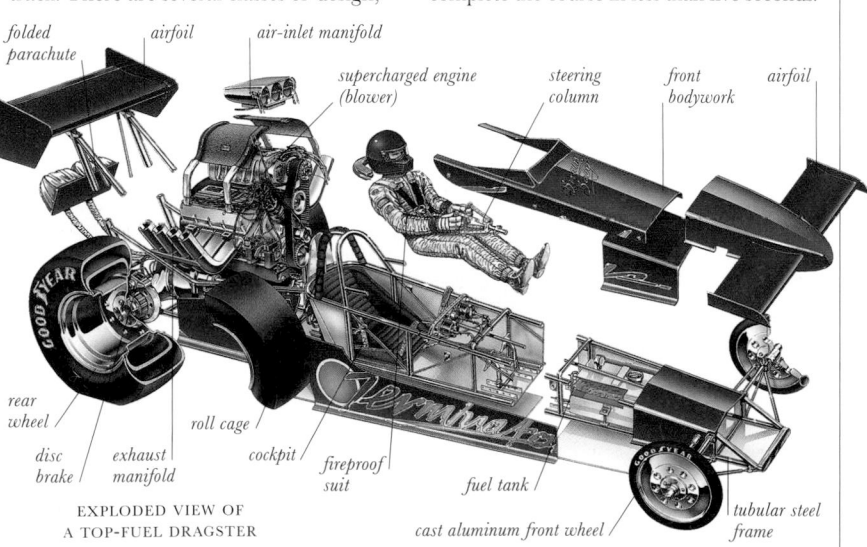

folded parachute   *airfoil*   *air-inlet manifold*   *supercharged engine (blower)*   *steering column*   *front bodywork*   *airfoil*

rear wheel   *disc brake*   *exhaust manifold*   *roll cage*   *cockpit*   *fireproof suit*   *fuel tank*   *cast aluminum front wheel*   *tubular steel frame*

EXPLODED VIEW OF A TOP-FUEL DRAGSTER

D

drain /drayn/ *v. & n.* • *v.* **1** *tr.* draw off liquid from, esp.: **a** make (land, etc.) dry by providing an outflow for moisture. **b** (of a river) carry off the superfluous water of (a district). **c** remove purulent matter from (an abscess). **2** *tr.* (foll. by *off, away*) draw off (liquid), esp. by a pipe. **3** *intr.* (foll. by *away, off, through*) flow or trickle away. **4** *intr.* (of a wet cloth, a vessel, etc.) become dry as liquid flows away (*put it there to drain*). **5** *tr.* (often foll. by *of*) exhaust or deprive (a person or thing) of strength, resources, etc. **6** *tr.* **a** drink (liquid) to the dregs. **b** empty (a vessel) by drinking the contents. • *n.* **1 a** a channel, conduit, or pipe carrying off liquid, esp. an artificial conduit for water or sewage. **b** a tube for drawing off the discharge from an abscess, etc. **2** a constant outflow, withdrawal, or expenditure (*a great drain on my resources*). □ **down the drain** *colloq.* lost; wasted.

drain·age /dráynij/ *n.* **1** the process or means of draining (*the land has poor drainage*). **2** a system of drains, artificial or natural. **3** what is drained off, esp. sewage.

drain·board /dráynbawrd/ *n.* a sloping surface beside a sink, on which washed dishes, etc., are left to drain.

drain·er /dráynər/ *n.* **1** a device for draining; anything on which things are put to drain. **2** a person who drains.

drain·pipe /dráynpīp/ *n.* a pipe for carrying off water, sewage, etc., from a building. ▷ HOUSE

drake /drayk/ *n.* a male duck. ▷ DUCK

dram /dram/ *n.* **1** a small drink of liquor. **2** apothecaries' weight or measure equivalent to one eighth of an ounce or (in full **fluid dram**) one eighth of a fluid ounce.

dra·ma /drámə, draáamə/ *n.* **1** a play for acting on stage or for broadcasting. **2** the art of writing and presenting plays. **3** an exciting or emotional event, set of circumstances, etc. **4** dramatic quality (*the drama of the situation*).

dra·mat·ic /drəmátik/ *adj.* **1** of drama or the study of drama. **2** (of an event, circumstance, etc.) sudden and exciting or unexpected. **3** vividly striking. **4** (of a gesture, etc.) theatrical; overdone; absurd. □□ **dra·mat·i·cal·ly** *adv.*

dra·mat·ic i·ro·ny = TRAGIC IRONY.

dra·mat·ics /drəmátiks/ *n.pl.* (often treated as *sing.*) **1** the production and performance of plays. **2** exaggerated or showy behavior.

dram·a·tis per·so·nae /drámətis pərsṓnee, draáamətis pərsṓnī/ *n.pl.* (often treated as *sing.*) **1** the characters in a play. **2** a list of these.

dram·a·tist /drámətist, draáamə-/ *n.* a writer of dramas.

dram·a·tize /drámətīz, draáamə-/ *v.* **1 a** *tr.* adapt (a novel, etc.) to form a stage play. **b** *intr.* admit of such adaptation. **2** *tr.* make a drama or dramatic scene of. **3** *tr.* (also *absol.*) express or react to in a dramatic way. □□ **dram·a·ti·za·tion** *n.*

Dram·bu·ie /drambo͞oee/ *n. Trademark* a sweet Scotch whisky liqueur.

drank *past* of DRINK.

drape /drayp/ *v. & n.* • *v.tr.* **1** hang, cover loosely, or adorn with cloth, etc. **2** arrange (clothes or hangings) carefully in folds. • *n.* **1** (often in *pl.*) a curtain or drapery. **2** a piece of drapery. **3** the way in which a garment or fabric hangs.

dra·per·y /dráypəree/ *n.* (*pl.* **-ies**) **1** clothing or hangings arranged in folds. **2** (often in *pl.*) a curtain or hanging. **3** the arrangement of clothing in sculpture or painting.

dras·tic /drástik/ *adj.* having a strong or far-reaching effect; severe. □□ **dras·ti·cal·ly** *adv.*

drat /drat/ *v. & int. colloq.* • *v.tr.* (**dratted**, **dratting**) (usu. as an exclam.)) curse; confound (*drat the thing!*). • *int.* expressing anger or annoyance. □□ **drat·ted** *adj.*

draw /draw/ *v. & n.* • *v.* (*past* **drew** /dro͞o/; *past part.* **drawn** /drawn/) **1** *tr.* pull or cause to move toward or after one. **2** *tr.* pull (a thing) up, over, or across. **3** *tr.* pull (curtains, etc.) open or shut. **4** *tr.* take (a person) aside, esp. to talk to. **5** *tr.* attract; bring to oneself or to something; take in (*drew a deep breath; I felt drawn to her; drew my attention to the matter; the match drew large crowds*). **6** *intr.* (foll. by *at, on*) suck smoke from (a cigarette, pipe, etc.). **7** *tr.* **a** (also *absol.*) take out; remove (e.g., a tooth, a gun from a holster). **b** select by taking out (e.g., a playing card from a deck). **8** *tr.* obtain or take from a source (*draw a salary; draw inspiration*). **9** *tr.* trace (a line, mark, furrow, or figure). **10 a** *tr.* produce (a picture) by tracing lines and marks. **b** *tr.* represent (a thing) by this means. **c** *absol.* make a drawing. **11** *tr.* (also *absol.*) finish (a contest or game) with neither side winning. **12** *intr.* make one's or its way; proceed; move; come (*drew near the bridge; draw to a close; drew ahead of the field; the time draws near*). **13** *tr.* infer; deduce (a conclusion). **14** *tr.* **a** elicit; evoke. **b** bring about; entail (*draw criticism*). **c** induce (a person) to reveal facts, feelings, or talent (*refused to be drawn*). **d** (foll. by *to* + infin.) induce (a person) to do something. **e** *Cards* cause to be played (*drew all the trumps*). **15** *tr.* haul up (water) from a well. **16** *tr.* bring out or extract (liquid, etc., from a vessel or a wound). **17** *tr.* extract a liquid essence from. **18** *intr.* (of a chimney or pipe) promote or allow a draft. **19** *intr.* (of tea) infuse. **20 a** *tr.* obtain by lot (*drew the winning number*). **b** *absol.* draw lots. **21** *intr.* (foll. by *on*) make a demand on a person, a person's skill, memory, imagination, etc. **22** *tr.* write out (a bill, check, or draft) (*drew a check on the bank*). **23** *tr.* (foll. by *up*) frame (a document) in due form; compose. **24** *tr.* formulate or perceive (a comparison or distinction). **25** *tr.* (of a ship) require (a specified depth of water) to float in. **26** *tr.* disembowel (*hang, draw, and quarter; draw the fowl before cooking it*). **27** *tr. Hunting* search (cover) for game. **28** *tr.* drag (a badger or fox) from a hole. **29** *tr.* protract; stretch; elongate (*long-drawn agony*). • *n.* **1** an act of drawing. **2 a** a person or thing that draws custom, attention, etc. **b** the power to attract attention. **3** the drawing of lots, esp. a raffle. **4** a drawn game. **5** a suck on a cigarette, etc. **6** the act of removing a gun from its holster in order to shoot (*quick on the draw*). **7** strain; pull. **8** the movable part of a drawbridge. □ **draw back** withdraw from an undertaking. **draw a bead on** see BEAD. **draw a blank** see BLANK. **draw a person's fire** attract hostility, criticism, etc., away from a more important target. **draw in 1 a** (of successive days) become shorter because of the changing seasons. **b** (of a day) approach its end. **c** (of successive evenings or nights) start earlier because of the changing seasons. **2** persuade to join; entice. **3** (of a train, etc.) arrive at a station. **draw in one's horns** become less assertive or ambitious; draw back. **draw the line at** set a limit (of tolerance, etc.) at. **draw lots** see LOT. **draw off 1** withdraw (troops). **2** drain off (a liquid), esp. without disturbing sediment. **draw out 1** prolong. **2** elicit. **3** induce to talk. **4** (of successive days) become longer. **5** lead out, detach, or array (troops). **draw one's sword against** attack. **quick on the draw** quick to act or react.

DRAWING OF QUEEN JANE SEYMOUR (1536) BY HANS HOLBEIN THE YOUNGER

draw·back /dráwbak/ *n.* a thing that impairs satisfaction; a disadvantage.

draw·bridge /dráwbrij/ *n.* a bridge, esp. over water, hinged at one end so that it may be raised to prevent passage or to allow ships, etc., to pass. ▷ CASTLE

draw·ee *n.* **1** /dráwée/ *n.* the person on whom a draft or bill is drawn.

draw·er *n.* **1** /dráwər/ a person or thing that draws, esp. a person who draws a check, etc. **2** /drawr/ a boxlike storage compartment without a lid, sliding in and out of a frame, table, etc. (*chest of drawers*). **3** (in *pl.*) /drawrz/ an undergarment worn next to the body below the waist. □□ **draw·er·ful** *n.* (*pl.* **-fuls**).

draw·ing /dráwing/ *n.* **1 a** the art of representing by line. **b** delineation without color or with a single color. **c** the art of representing with pencils, pens, crayons, etc., rather than paint. **2** ◄ a picture produced in this way.

draw·ing board *n.* a board for spreading drawing paper on. □ **back to the drawing board** *colloq.* back to begin afresh (after earlier failure).

draw·ing pa·per *n.* stout paper for drawing pictures, etc., on.

draw·ing room /dráwingro͞om, -ro͝om/ *n.* **1** a room for comfortable sitting or entertaining in a private house. **2** a private compartment in a train.

drawl /drawl/ *v. & n.* • *v.* **1** *intr.* speak with drawn-out vowel sounds. **2** *tr.* utter in this way. • *n.* a drawling utterance or way of speaking. □□ **drawl·er** *n.*

drawn /drawn/ *past part.* of DRAW. *adj.* **1** looking strained from fear, anxiety, or pain. **2** (of butter) melted. **3** (of a position in chess, etc.) that will result in a draw if both players make the best moves available.

draw·sheet /dráwsheet/ *n.* a sheet that can be taken from under a patient without remaking the bed.

draw·string /dráwstring/ *n.* a string that can be pulled to tighten the mouth of a bag, the waist of a garment, etc.

dray[1] /dray/ *n.* a low cart without sides for heavy loads.

dray[2] *n.* var. of DREY.

dread /dred/ *v., n., & adj.* • *v.tr.* **1** (foll. by *that*, or *to* + infin.) fear greatly. **2** shrink from; look forward to with great apprehension. **3** be in great fear of. • *n.* **1** great fear; apprehension; awe. **2** an object of fear or awe. • *adj.* **1** dreaded. **2** *archaic* awe-inspiring; revered.

dread·ful /drédfo͝ol/ *adj. & adv.* • *adj.* **1** terrible; inspiring fear or awe. **2** *colloq.* troublesome; disagreeable; very bad. • *adv. colloq.* dreadfully; very. □□ **dread·ful·ly** *adv.* **dread·ful·ness** *n.*

dread·locks /drédloks/ *n.pl.* **1** a Rastafarian hairstyle in which the hair is twisted into tight braids or ringlets hanging down on all sides. **2** hair dressed in this way.

dread·nought /drédnawt/ *n.* (usu. **Dreadnought**) *Brit. hist.* **1** a type of heavily armed battleship greatly superior to all its predecessors (from the name of the first, launched in 1906). **2** *archaic* a fearless person.

dream /dreem/ *n. & v.* • *n.* **1 a** a series of pictures or events in the mind of a sleeping person. **b** the act or time of seeing this. **c** (in full **waking dream**) a similar experience of one awake. **2** a daydream or fantasy. **3** an ideal, aspiration, or ambition, esp. of a nation. **4** a beautiful or ideal person or thing. **5** a state of mind without proper perception of reality (*goes about in a dream*). • *v.* (*past* and *past part.* **dreamed** or **dreamt** /dremt/) **1** *intr.* experience a dream. **2** *tr.* imagine in or as if in a dream. **3** (usu. with *neg.*) **a** *intr.* (foll. by *of*) contemplate the possibility of; have any conception or intention of (*would not dream of upsetting them*). **b** *tr.* (often foll. by *that* + clause) think of as a possibility (*never dreamed that he would come*). **4** *tr.* (foll. by *away*) spend (time) unprofitably. **5** *intr.* be inactive or unpractical. **6** *intr.* fall into a reverie. □ **dream up** imagine; invent. **like a dream** *colloq.* easily; effortlessly. □□ **dream·ful** *adj.* **dream·less** *adj.* **dream·like** *adj.*

dream·boat /dréembōt/ *n. colloq.* **1** a very attractive or ideal person, esp. of the opposite sex. **2** a very desirable or ideal thing.

dream·er /dréemər/ *n.* **1** a person who dreams. **2** a romantic or unpractical person.

dream·land /dréemland/ *n.* an ideal or imaginary land.

dream·y /dréemee/ *adj.* (**dreamier, dreamiest**) **1** given to daydreaming; fanciful; unpractical. **2** dreamlike; vague; misty. **3** *colloq.* delightful; marvelous. **4** *poet.* full of dreams. □□ **dream·i·ly** *adv.* **dream·i·ness** *n.*

drear /dreer/ *adj. poet.* = DREARY.

drear·y /dréeree/ *adj.* (**drearier, dreariest**) dismal; dull; gloomy. □□ **drear·i·ly** *adv.* **drear·i·ness** *n.*

dredge[1] /drej/ *v. & n.* ● *v.* **1** *tr.* **a** (often foll. by *up*) bring up (lost or hidden material) as if with a dredge (*don't dredge all that up again*). **b** (often foll. by *away, up, out*) bring up or clear (mud, etc.) from a river, harbor, etc. with a dredge. **2** *tr.* clean (a harbor, river, etc.) with a dredge. **3** *intr.* use a dredge. ● *n.* an apparatus used to scoop up oysters, specimens, etc., or to clear mud, etc., from a riverbed or seabed.

dredge[2] /drej/ *v.tr.* sprinkle with flour, sugar, etc.

dredg·er[1] /dréjər/ *n.* **1** a machine used for dredging rivers, etc.; a dredge. **2** a boat containing this.

dredg·er[2] /dréjər/ *n.* a container with a perforated lid used for sprinkling flour, sugar, etc.

dreg /dreg/ *n.* **1** (usu. in *pl.*) **a** a sediment; grounds, lees, etc. **b** a worthless part; refuse (*the dregs of humanity*). **2** a small remnant (*not a dreg*). □ **drain** (or **drink**) **to the dregs** consume leaving nothing (*drained life to the dregs*). □□ **dreg·gy** *adj. colloq.*

drench /drench/ *v. & n.* ● *v.tr.* **1** wet thoroughly (*was drenched by the rain*). **2** saturate; soak (in liquid). ● *n.* a soaking; a downpour.

dress /dres/ *v. & n.* ● *v.* **1 a** *tr.* clothe; array (*dressed in rags; dressed her quickly*). **b** *intr.* wear clothes of a specified kind or in a specified way (*dresses well*). **2** *intr.* **a** put on clothes. **b** put on formal or evening clothes, esp. for dinner. **3** *tr. Med.* a treat (a wound) with ointment, etc. **b** apply a dressing to (a wound). **4** *tr.* **a** clean and prepare (poultry, etc.) for cooking or eating. **b** add a dressing to (a salad, etc.). **5** *tr.* apply manure, etc., to a field, garden, etc. **6** *tr.* finish the surface of (fabric, building stone, etc.). **7** *tr.* groom (one's hair, a horse, etc.). **8** *Mil.* **a** *tr.* correct the alignment of (troops, etc.). **b** *intr.* (of troops) come into alignment. ● *n.* **1** a one-piece woman's garment consisting of a bodice and skirt. **2** clothing, esp. a whole outfit. (*fussy about his dress*). **3** formal or ceremonial costume (*evening dress*). **4** an external covering; the outward form (*birds in their winter dress*). □ **dress down** *colloq.* **1** reprimand or scold. **2** dress casually, esp. for an informal affair. **dress up 1** dress (oneself or another) elaborately for a special occasion. **2** dress in fancy dress. **3** decorate or adorn (*dress up the room*). **4** disguise (unwelcome facts) by embellishment.

dres·sage /drisáazh, dre-/ *n.* the training of a horse in obedience and deportment, esp. for competition.

dress cir·cle *n.* the first gallery in a theater, in which evening dress was formerly required.

dress code *n.* a set of rules, usu. written, describing acceptable dress, as at a school, restaurant, etc.

dress·er[1] /drésər/ *n.* a dressing table or chest of drawers; a bureau.

dress·er[2] /drésər/ *n.* **1** a person who assists actors to dress, takes care of their costumes, etc. **2** a person who dresses elegantly or in a specified way (*a snappy dresser*).

dress·ing /drésing/ *n.* **1** in senses of DRESS *v.* **2 a** an accompaniment to salads, usu. a mixture of oil with other ingredients; a sauce or seasoning (*French dressing*). **b** stuffing, esp. for poultry. **3 a** a bandage for a wound. **b** ointment, etc., used to dress a wound. **4** compost, etc., spread over land (*a top dressing of peat*).

dress·ing-down *n. colloq.* a scolding; a severe reprimand.

dress·ing gown *n.* = ROBE *n.* 2.

dress·ing room *n.* a room for changing clothes, etc., in a clothing store, theater, sports facility, etc.

dress·ing table *n.* a table with a mirror, drawers, etc., used while applying makeup, etc.

dress·mak·er /drésmaykər/ *n.* a person who makes clothes professionally. □□ **dress·mak·ing** *n.*

dress re·hears·al *n.* the final rehearsal of a play, etc., wearing costume.

dress·y /drésee/ *adj.* (**dressier, dressiest**) **1 a** fond of smart clothes. **b** overdressed. **c** (of clothes) stylish or elaborate. **2** overelaborate (*the design is rather dressy*). □□ **dress·i·ness** *n.*

drew *past* of DRAW.

drey /dray/ *n. Brit.* (also **dray**) ▼ a squirrel's nest.

DREY: CROSS SECTION OF A GRAY SQUIRREL'S DREY

inner lining

gray squirrel

tree fork

drib·ble /dríbəl/ *v. & n.* ● *v.* **1** *intr.* allow saliva to flow from the mouth. **2** *intr. & tr.* flow or allow to flow in drops or a trickling stream. **3** *tr.* (also *absol.*) **a** *Basketball* bounce (the ball) repeatedly, esp. to retain control of it. **b** *esp. Soccer & Hockey* move (the ball, puck, etc.) forward with slight touches of the feet, the stick, etc. ● *n.* **1** the act or an instance of dribbling. **2** a small trickling stream. □□ **drib·bler** *n.* **drib·bly** *adj.*

dribs and drabs /dríbz ənd drábz/ *n.pl. colloq.* small scattered amounts (*did the work in dribs and drabs*).

dried *past* and *past part.* of DRY.

dri·er[1] *compar.* of DRY.

dri·er[2] /dríər/ *n.* (also **dry·er**) **1** a machine for drying the hair, laundry, etc. **2** a substance mixed with oil paint or ink to promote drying.

dri·est *superl.* of DRY.

drift /drift/ *n. & v.* ● *n.* **1 a** a slow movement or variation. **b** such movement caused by a slow current. **2** the intention, meaning, scope, etc., of what is said, etc. (*didn't understand his drift*). **3** a large mass of snow, sand, etc., accumulated by the wind. **4** esp. *derog.* a state of inaction. **5 a** *Naut.* a ship's deviation from its course, due to currents. **b** *Aeron.* an aircraft's deviation due to side winds. **c** a projectile's deviation due to its rotation. **d** a controlled slide of a racing car, etc. **6** *Mining* a horizontal passage following a mineral vein. **7** a large mass of esp. flowering plants (*a drift of bluebells*). **8** *Geol.* **a** material deposited by the wind, a current of water, etc. (**Drift**) Pleistocene ice detritus, e.g., boulder clay. **9** the movement of cattle, esp. a gathering on an appointed day to determine ownership, etc. ● *v.* **1** *intr.* be carried by or as if by a current of air or water. **2** *intr.* move or progress passively, casually, or aimlessly (*drifted into teaching*). **3 a** *tr. & intr.* pile or be piled by the wind into drifts. **b** *tr.* cover (a field, a road, etc.) with drifts. **4** *tr.* (of a current) carry. □□ **drift·age** *n.*

drift·er /dríftər/ *n.* **1** an aimless or rootless person. **2** a boat used for drift-net fishing.

drift net *n.* a large net for herrings, etc., allowed to drift with the tide.

drift·wood /dríftwŏŏd/ *n.* wood, etc., driven or deposited by water.

drill[1] /dril/ *n. & v.* ● *n.* **1** ▼ a pointed, esp. revolving, steel tool or machine used for boring cylindrical holes, sinking wells, etc. ▷ OIL PLATFORM, PNEUMATIC. **2 a** esp. *Mil.* instruction or training in military exercises. **b** rigorous discipline or methodical instruction, esp. when learning or performing tasks. **c** routine procedure to be followed in an emergency (*fire drill*). **d** a routine or exercise (*drills in irregular verb patterns*). **3** *colloq.* a recognized procedure (*I expect you know the drill*). **4** a gastropod that bores into the shells of young oysters and other shellfish. ● *v.* **1** *tr.* (also *absol.*) **a** (of a person or a tool) make a hole with a drill through or into (wood, metal, etc.). **b** make (a hole) with a drill. **2** *tr. & intr. esp. Mil.* subject to or undergo discipline by drill. **3** *tr.* impart (knowledge, etc.) by a strict method. **4** *tr. sl.* shoot with a gun (*drilled him full of holes*). □□ **drill·er** *n.*

D

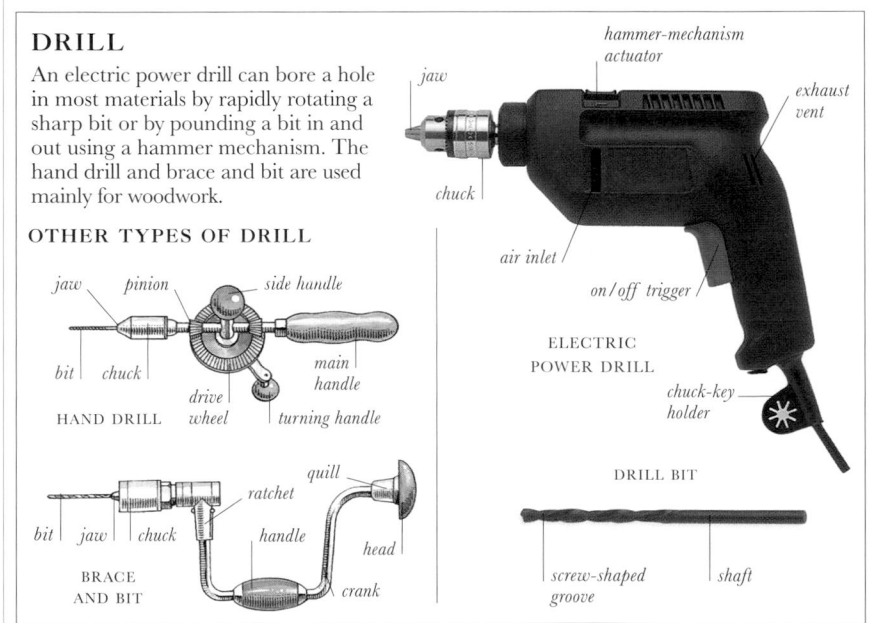

DRILL

An electric power drill can bore a hole in most materials by rapidly rotating a sharp bit or by pounding a bit in and out using a hammer mechanism. The hand drill and brace and bit are used mainly for woodwork.

OTHER TYPES OF DRILL

jaw — pinion — side handle

bit — chuck

drive wheel — main handle — turning handle

HAND DRILL

bit — jaw — chuck — ratchet — quill — handle — head — crank

BRACE AND BIT

jaw — hammer-mechanism actuator

chuck — air inlet — exhaust vent — on/off trigger

chuck-key holder

ELECTRIC POWER DRILL

screw-shaped groove — shaft

DRILL BIT

drill[2] /dril/ *n.* & *v.* ● *n.* **1** ▼ a machine used for making furrows, sowing, and covering seed. **2** a small furrow for sowing seed in. **3** a ridge with such furrows on top. **4** a row of plants so sown. ● *v.tr.* **1** sow (seed) with a drill. **2** plant (the ground) in drills.

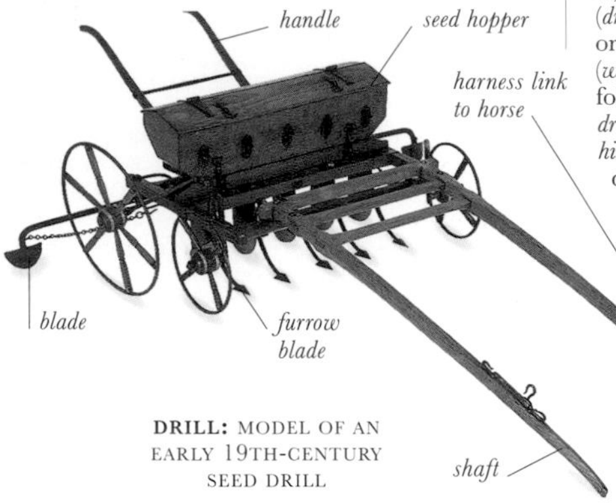

DRILL: MODEL OF AN EARLY 19TH-CENTURY SEED DRILL

drill[3] /dril/ *n.* a W. African baboon related to the mandrill.

drill[4] /dril/ *n.* a coarse twilled cotton or linen fabric.

drill·mas·ter /drílmastər/ *n.* **1** *Mil.* one who instructs or leads others (often recruits) in military drill. **2** a rigorous, exacting, or severe instructor.

drill press *n.* a drilling machine with a vertical bit that is lowered into the item being drilled.

drill rig *n.* (also **drilling rig**) a structure with equipment for drilling an oil well. ▷ OIL PLATFORM

drill ser·geant 1 *Mil.* a noncommissioned officer who trains soldiers, esp. new recruits. **2** a strict disciplinarian.

drink /dringk/ *v.* & *n.* ● *v.* (*past* **drank** /drangk/; *past part.* **drunk** /drungk/) **1 a** *tr.* swallow (a liquid). **b** *tr.* swallow the liquid contents of (a vessel). **c** *intr.* swallow liquid; take drafts (*drank from the stream*). **2** *intr.* take alcohol, esp. to excess (*I have heard that she drinks*). **3** *tr.* (of a plant, porous material, etc.) absorb (moisture). **4** *refl.* bring (oneself, etc.) to a specified condition by drinking (*drank himself into a stupor*). **5** *tr.* (usu. foll. by *away*) spend (wages, etc.) on drink (*drank away the money*). ● *n.* **1 a** a liquid for drinking (*milk is a high-cholesterol drink*). **b** a draft or specified amount of this (*had a drink of milk*). **2 a** a portion, glass, etc., of alcohol (*have a drink*). **b** excessive indulgence in alcohol (*drink is his vice*). **3** (as **the drink**) *colloq.* the sea. □ **drink in** listen to closely or eagerly (*drank in his every word*). **drink to** toast; wish success to. **drink a person under the table** remain sober longer than one's drinking companion. **drink up** drink the whole of; empty. **strong drink** alcohol, esp. liquor. □□ **drink·a·ble** *adj.* **drink·er** *n.*

drip /drip/ *v.* & *n.* ● *v.* (**dripped**, **dripping**) **1** *intr.* & *tr.* fall or let fall in drops. **2** *intr.* (often foll. by *with*) be so wet as to shed drops (*dripped with sweat*). ● *n.* **1 a** the act or an instance of dripping (*the steady drip of rain*). **b** a drop of liquid (*a drip of paint*). **c** a sound of dripping. **2** *colloq.* a stupid, dull, or ineffective person. **3** (in full **drip-feed**) *Med.* the drip-by-drip intravenous administration of a solution of salt, sugar, etc. **4** *Archit.* a projection, esp. from a windowsill, keeping the rain off the walls.

drip-dry *v.* (**-dries**, **-dried**) **1** *intr.* (of fabric, etc.) dry crease-free when hung up to drip. **2** *tr.* leave (a garment, etc.) hanging up to dry. *adj.* able to be drip-dried. **dripping wet** very wet.

drip·ping /dríping/ *n.* (usu. *pl.*) **1** fat melted from roasted meat and used for cooking or as a spread. **2** water, grease, etc., dripping from anything.

drip·py /drípee/ *adj.* (**drippier**, **drippiest**) **1** tending to drip. **2** *sl.* ineffectual; sloppily sentimental. □□ **drip·pi·ly** *adv.* **drip·pi·ness** *n.*

drip·stone /drípstōn/ *n.* **1** *Archit.* a stone, etc., projection that deflects rain, etc., from walls. **2** calcium carbonate in the form of stalagmites and stalactites. ▷ CAVE

drive /drīv/ *v.* & *n.* ● *v.* (*past* **drove** /drōv/; *past part.* **driven** /drívən/) **1** *tr.* (usu. foll. by *away*, *back*, *in*, *out*, *to*, etc.) urge in some direction, esp. forcibly (*drove back the wolves*). **2** *tr.* **a** (usu. foll. by *to* + infin., or *to* + verbal noun) compel or constrain forcibly (*was driven to complain*; *drove her to stealing*). **b** (often foll. by *to*) force into a specified state (*drove him mad*; *driven to despair*). **c** (often *refl.*) urge to overwork (*drives himself too hard*). **3 a** *tr.* (also *absol.*) operate and direct the course of (a vehicle, a locomotive, etc.) (*drove a sports car*; *drives well*). **b** *tr.* & *intr.* convey or be conveyed in a vehicle (*drove them to the station*; *drove to the station in a bus*). **c** *tr.* (also *absol.*) be licensed or competent to drive (a vehicle) (*does he drive?*). **d** *tr.* (also *absol.*) urge and direct the course of (an animal drawing a vehicle or plow). **4** *tr.* (of wind, water, etc.) carry along, propel, send, or cause to go in some direction (*pure as the driven snow*). **5** *tr.* **a** (often foll. by *into*) force (a stake, nail, etc.) into place by blows (*drove the nail home*). **b** *Mining* bore (a tunnel, horizontal cavity, etc.). **6** *tr.* effect or conclude forcibly (*drove a hard bargain*; *drove her point home*). **7** *tr.* (of steam or other power) set or keep (machinery) going. **8** *intr.* (usu. foll. by *at*) work hard; dash, rush, or hasten. **9** *tr.* *Baseball* & *Tennis* hit (the ball) hard from a freely swung bat or racket. **10** *tr.* (often *absol.*) *Golf* strike (a ball) with a driver from the tee. **11** *tr.* & *intr.* herd cattle, etc.; deal in cattle, etc. **12** *tr.* chase or frighten (game, wild beasts, an enemy in warfare, etc.) from a large area to a smaller, to kill or capture; corner. ● *n.* **1** an act of driving in a motor vehicle; a journey or excursion in such a vehicle (*went for a drive*; *lives an hour's drive from us*). **2 a** the capacity for achievement; motivation and energy (*lacks the drive needed to succeed*). **b** *Psychol.* an inner urge to attain a goal or satisfy a need (*unconscious emotional drives*). **3** a usu. landscaped street or road. **4** *Golf* a driving stroke of the club. **5** an organized effort to achieve a usu. charitable purpose (*a famine-relief drive*). **6 a** the transmission of power to machinery, the wheels of a motor vehicle, etc. (*belt drive*; *front-wheel drive*). **b** the position of a steering wheel in a motor vehicle (*left-hand drive*). **c** *Computing* = DISK DRIVE. **7** an act of driving game, cattle, an enemy, etc. □ **drive at** seek, intend, or mean (*what is he driving at?*). **drive out** take the place of; oust; exorcize; cast out (evil spirits, etc.). **driving range** *Golf* an area for practicing drives. **driving wheel** a wheel communicating motive power in machinery. □□ **driv·a·ble** *adj.*

drive-by *attrib.adj.* (of a crime, etc.) carried out from a moving vehicle.

drive-in *attrib.adj.* (of a bank, movie theater, etc.) able to be used while sitting in one's car. *n.* such a bank, movie theater, etc.

driv·el /drívəl/ *n.* & *v.* ● *n.* silly nonsense; twaddle. ● *v.* **1** *intr.* run at the mouth or nose; dribble. **2** *intr.* talk childishly or idiotically. **3** *tr.* (foll. by *away*) fritter; squander away. □□ **driv·el·er** *n.*

driv·en *past part.* of DRIVE.

driv·er /drívər/ *n.* **1** (often in *comb.*) a person who drives a vehicle (*bus driver*). **2** *Golf* a club with a flat face and wooden head, used for driving from the tee. ▷ GOLF. **3** *Electr.* a device or part of a circuit providing power for output. **4** *Mech.* a wheel, etc., receiving power directly and transmitting motion to other parts. **5** a person who herds cattle, etc. □ **in the driver's seat** in charge. □□ **driv·er·less** *adj.*

driv·er's li·cense *n.* a license permitting a person to drive a motor vehicle.

drive·shaft /drívshaft/ *n.* a rotating shaft that transmits power to machinery. ▷ CAR

drive·train /drívtrayn/ *n.* the components in an automotive vehicle that connect the transmission with the driving wheels.

drive·way /drívway/ *n.* a usu. private road from a public street, etc., to a house, garage, etc.

driz·zle /drízəl/ *n.* & *v.* ● *n.* very fine rain. ● *v.intr.* (esp. of rain) fall in very fine drops (*it's drizzling again*). □□ **driz·zly** *adj.*

drogue /drōg/ *n.* **1** *Naut.* **a** a buoy at the end of a harpoon line. **b** a sea anchor. **2** *Aeron.* a truncated cone of fabric used as a brake, a target for gunnery, a wind sock, etc.

droid /droyd/ *n.* (in science fiction) a robot.

droll /drōl/ *adj.* **1** quaintly amusing. **2** strange; odd; surprising. □□ **droll·er·y** *n.* (*pl.* **-ies**). **drol·ly** *adv.* **droll·ness** *n.*

-drome /drōm/ *comb. form* forming nouns denoting: **1** a place for running, racing, or other forms of movement (*hippodrome*). **2** a thing that runs or proceeds in a certain way (*palindrome*; *syndrome*).

drom·e·dar·y /drómideree, drúm-/ *n.* (*pl.* **-ies**) a one-humped camel bred for riding and racing. ▷ CAMEL

drone /drōn/ *n.* & *v.* ● *n.* **1** a nonworking male of certain bees, as the honeybee, whose sole function is to mate with fertile females. **2** an idler. **3** a deep humming sound. **4** a monotonous speech or speaker. **5 a** a pipe, esp. of a bagpipe, sounding a continuous note of fixed low pitch. ▷ BAGPIPE. **b** the note emitted by this. **6** a remote-controlled pilotless aircraft or missile. ● *v.* **1** *intr.* make a deep humming sound. **2** *intr.* & *tr.* speak or utter monotonously. **3 a** *intr.* be idle. **b** *tr.* (often foll. by *away*) idle away (one's time, etc.).

drool /dro͞ol/ *v.* & *n.* ● *v.intr.* **1** drivel; slobber. **2** (often foll. by *over*) show much pleasure or infatuation. ● *n.* slobbering; driveling.

droop /dro͞op/ *v.* & *n.* ● *v.* **1** *intr.* & *tr.* hang or allow to hang down; languish, decline, or sag, esp. from weariness. **2** *intr.* be dejected; flag. ● *n.* **1** a drooping attitude. **2** a loss of spirit or enthusiasm.

droop·y /dro͞opee/ *adj.* (**droopier**, **droopiest**) **1** drooping. **2** dejected; gloomy. □□ **droop·i·ly** *adv.* **droop·i·ness** *n.*

drop /drop/ *n.* & *v.* ● *n.* **1 a** a small, round or pear-shaped portion of liquid that hangs or falls or adheres to a surface (*drops of dew*; *tears fell in large drops*). **b** a very small amount of usu. drinkable liquid (*just a drop left in the glass*). **c** a glass, etc., of alcoholic liquor (*take a drop with us*). **2 a** an abrupt fall or slope. **b** the amount of this (*a drop of fifteen feet*). **c** an act of falling or dropping (*had a nasty drop*). **d** a reduction in prices, temperature, etc. **e** a deterioration or worsening (*a drop in status*). **3** something resembling a drop, esp.: **a** a pendant or earring. **b** a crystal ornament on a chandelier, etc. **c** (often in *comb.*) a candy or lozenge (*lemon drop*; *cough drop*). **4** something that drops or is dropped, esp.: **a** *Theatr.* a painted curtain or scenery let down on to the stage. **b** a platform or trapdoor on a gallows, the opening of which causes the victim to fall. **5** *Med.* **a** the smallest separable quantity of a liquid. **b** (in *pl.*) liquid medicine to be measured in drops (*eye drops*). **6** a minute quantity (*not a drop of pity*). **7** *sl.* **a** a hiding place for stolen or illicit goods. **b** a secret place where documents, etc., may be left or passed on in espionage. **8** a box for letters, etc. ● *v.* (**dropped**, **dropping**) **1** *intr.* & *tr.* fall or let fall in drops (*tears dropped on to the book*; *dropped the soup down her shirt*). **2** *intr.* & *tr.* fall or allow to fall; relinquish; let go (*dropped the box*; *the egg dropped from my hand*). **3 a** *intr.* & *tr.* sink or cause to sink or fall to the ground from exhaustion, a blow, a wound, etc. **b** *intr.* die. **4 a** *intr.* & *tr.* cease or cause to cease; lapse or let lapse; abandon (*the connection dropped*; *drop everything and come at once*). **b** *tr.* *colloq.* cease to associate with. **5** *tr.* set down (a passenger, etc.) (*drop me at the station*). **6** *tr.* & *intr.* utter or be uttered casually (*dropped a hint*; *the remark dropped into the conversation*). **7** *tr.* send casually (*drop me a postcard*). **8 a** *intr.* & *tr.* fall or allow to fall in direction, amount, condition, degree, pitch, etc. (*his voice dropped*; *we dropped the price by $20*). **b** *intr.* (of a person) jump down lightly; let oneself fall. **c** *tr.*

remove (clothes, esp. pants) rapidly, allowing them to fall to the ground. **9** *tr. colloq.* lose (money, esp. in gambling). **10** *tr.* **a** omit (*drop this article*). **b** omit (a letter, esp. 'h,' a syllable, etc.) in speech. **11** *tr.* (as **dropped** *adj.*) in a lower position than usual (*dropped handlebars; dropped waist*). **12** *tr.* give birth to (esp. a lamb, a kitten, etc.). **13** *tr. Sports* lose (a game, a point, a contest, a match, etc.). **14** *tr. Aeron.* deliver (supplies, etc.) by parachute. **15** *tr. Football* **a** send (a ball) by a drop-kick. **b** score points by a dropkick. **16** *tr. colloq.* dismiss or exclude (*was dropped from the team*). □ **at the drop of a hat** given the slightest excuse. **drop anchor** anchor ship. **drop asleep** fall gently asleep. **drop away** decrease or depart gradually. **drop back** (or **behind** or **to the rear**) fall back; get left behind. **drop dead!** *sl.* an exclamation of intense scorn. **drop in** (or **by**) *colloq.* call casually as a visitor. **a drop in the ocean** (or **bucket**) a very small amount, esp. compared with what is needed or expected. **drop it!** *sl.* stop (talking or referring to) that! **drop off 1** decline gradually. **2** *colloq.* fall asleep. **3** = sense 5 of *v.* **drop out** *colloq.* cease to participate, esp. in a race, a course of study, or in conventional society. **have the drop on** *colloq.* have the advantage over. **ready to drop** extremely tired. □□ **drop·let** *n.*

drop cur·tain *n. Theatr.* a painted curtain or scenery.

drop-leaf *adj.* (of a table, etc.) having a hinged flap.

drop·kick /drópkik/ *n. Football* a kick made by dropping the ball and kicking it on the bounce.

drop·out /drópowt/ *n. colloq.* a person who has dropped out, esp. from school.

drop·per /drópər/ *n.* a device for administering liquid, esp. medicine, in drops. ▷ MEDICINE

drop·pings /drópingz/ *n.pl.* the dung of animals or birds.

drop shot *n.* (in tennis) a shot dropping abruptly over the net.

drop·sy /drópsee/ *n.* (*pl.* **-ies**) = EDEMA. □□ **drop·si·cal** /-sikəl/ *adj.*

dro·soph·i·la /drəsófilə/ *n.* any fruit fly of the genus *Drosophila*, used extensively in genetic research.

dross /draws, dros/ *n.* **1** rubbish; refuse. **2 a** the scum separated from metals in melting. **b** foreign matter mixed with anything; impurities. □□ **dross·y** *adj.*

drought /drowt/ *n.* **1** the continuous absence of rain; dry weather. **2** the prolonged lack of something. □□ **drought·y** *adj.*

drove[1] *past of* DRIVE.

drove[2] /drōv/ *n.* **1 a** a large number (of people, etc.) moving together; a crowd; a multitude; a shoal. **b** (in *pl.*) *colloq.* a great number (*people arrived in droves*). **2** a herd or flock being driven or moving together.

drown /drown/ *v.* **1** *tr. & intr.* kill or be killed by submersion in liquid. **2** *tr.* submerge; flood; drench (*drowned the fields in six feet of water*). **3** *tr.* (often foll. by *in*) deaden (grief, etc.) with drink (*drowned his sorrows*). **4** *tr.* (often foll. by *out*) make (a sound) inaudible by means of a louder sound. □ **like a drowned rat** *colloq.* extremely wet and bedraggled.

drowse /drowz/ *v. intr.* be dull and sleepy or half asleep.

drow·sy /drówzee/ *adj.* (**drowsier, drowsiest**) **1** half asleep. **2** lulling. **3** sluggish. □□ **drow·si·ly** *adv.* **drow·si·ness.**

drub /drub/ *v.tr.* (**drubbed, drubbing**) **1** thump; belabor. **2** beat in a fight. □□ **drub·bing** *n.*

drudge /druj/ *n. & v.* ● *n.* a servile worker, esp. at menial tasks; a hack. ● *v.intr.* (often foll. by *at*) work slavishly (at menial, hard, or dull work). □□ **drudg·er·y** /drújəree/ *n.*

drug /drug/ *n. & v.* ● *n.* **1** a medicinal substance. **2** a narcotic, hallucinogen, or stimulant, esp. one causing addiction. ● *v.* (**drugged, drugging**) **1** *tr.* add a drug to (food or drink). **2** *tr.* **a** administer a drug to. **b** stupefy with a drug. **3** *intr.* take drugs as an addict.

drug ad·dict *n.* a person who is addicted to a narcotic drug.

drug·gie /drúgee/ *n. colloq.* (also **drug·gy**) (*pl.* **-ies**) a drug addict.

drug·gist /drúgist/ *n.* a pharmacist.

drug·push·er /drúgpoosher/ *n.* a person who sells esp. addictive drugs illegally.

drug·store /drúgstawr/ *n.* a pharmacy also selling miscellaneous drugs, cosmetics, and often light refreshments.

Dru·id /drooid/ *n.* (*fem.* **Druidess**) **1** an ancient Celtic priest, magician, or soothsayer of Gaul, Britain, or Ireland. **2** a member of a Welsh, etc., Druidic order. □□ **Dru·id·ic** /-ídik/ *adj.* **Dru·id·ism** *n.*

drum /drum/ *n. & v.* ● *n.* **1 a** ▼ a percussion instrument or toy made of a hollow cylinder or hemisphere covered at one or both ends with stretched skin or parchment and sounded by striking. ▷ PERCUSSION. **b** (often in *pl.*) percussion section (*the drums are playing too loud*). **c** a sound made by or resembling that of a drum. **2** something resembling a drum in shape, esp.: **a** a cylindrical container or receptacle for oil, etc. **b** a cylinder or barrel in machinery on which something is wound, etc. **c** *Archit.* a stone block forming a section of a shaft. **3** *Zool. & Anat.* the eardrum. ● *v.* (**drummed, drumming**) **1** *intr. & tr.* play on a drum. **2** *tr. & intr.* beat, tap, or thump (knuckles, feet, etc.) continuously (on something). **3** *intr.* (of a bird or an insect) make a loud, hollow noise with quivering wings. □ **drum into** drive (a lesson) into (a person) by persistence. **drum out** *Mil.* dismiss with ignominy. **drum up** summon, gather, or call up (*needs to drum up more support*).

drum and bass *n.* a type of dance music consisting largely of electronic drums and bass.

drum·beat /drúmbeet/ *n.* the sound of a drum being beaten.

drum brake *n.* a brake in which shoes on a vehicle press against the drum on a wheel. ▷ BRAKE

drum·head /drúmhed/ *n.* **1** the skin or membrane of a drum. **2** an eardrum. **3** (*attrib.*) improvised (*drumhead court-martial*).

drum·lin /drúmlin/ *Geol.* a long, oval mound of boulder clay molded by glacial action.

drum ma·jor *n.* the leader of a marching band.

drum ma·jor·ette *n.* a female member of a baton-twirling parading group.

drum·mer /drúmər/ *n.* a person who plays a drum or drums.

drum set *n.* ▼ a set of drums, cymbals, etc.

crash cymbal   tom-tom   ride cymbal

snare drum

floor tom

high hat cymbal

tripod   bass drum   beater   pedal   lug   **DRUM SET**

drum·stick /drúmstik/ *n.* **1** a stick used for beating a drum. **2** the lower joint of the leg of a cooked chicken, turkey, etc.

drunk /drungk/ *adj. & n.* ● *adj.* **1** rendered incapable by alcohol (*blind drunk; dead drunk; drunk as a skunk*). **2** (often foll. by *with*) overcome with joy, success, power, etc. ● *n.* **1** a habitually drunk person. **2** *sl.* a drinking bout; a period of drunkenness.

drunk·ard /drúngkərd/ *n.* a person who is drunk, esp. habitually.

drunk driver *n.* a person who drives a vehicle with an excess of alcohol in the blood. □□ **drunk driving** *adj.*

drunk·en /drúngkən/ *adj.* (usu. *attrib.*) **1** = DRUNK *adj.* **2** caused by or exhibiting drunkenness (*a drunken brawl*). □□ **drunk·en·ly** *adv.* **drunk·en·ness** *n.*

drupe /droop/ *n.* any fleshy or pulpy fruit enclosing a stone containing one or a few seeds, e.g., an olive, plum, or peach. ▷ FRUIT

drupe·let /drooplit/ *n.* a small drupe usu. in an aggregate fruit, e.g., a blackberry or raspberry.

druth·ers /drúthərz/ *n.pl. colloq.* preference; choice (*if I had my druthers, I'd stay at home*).

Druze /drooz/ *n.* (often *attrib.*) (also **Druse**) a member of a political or religious sect linked with Islam and living near Mt. Lebanon (**Druze militia**).

dry /drī/ *adj., v., & n.* ● *adj.* (**drier** /dríər/; **driest** /drí-ist/) **1** free from moisture, not wet, esp.: **a** with any moisture having evaporated, drained, or been wiped away (*the clothes are not dry yet*). **b** (of the eyes) free from tears. **c** (of a climate, etc.) with insufficient rainfall; not rainy (*a dry spell*). **d** (of a river, well, etc.) dried up; not yielding water. **e** (of a liquid) having disappeared by evaporation, etc. **f** not connected with or for use without moisture (*dry shampoo*). **g** (of a shave) with an electric razor. **2** (of wine, etc.) not sweet (*dry sherry*). **3 a** meager, plain, or bare (*dry facts*). **b** uninteresting; dull (*dry as dust*). **4** (of a sense of humor, a joke, etc.) subtle, ironic, and quietly expressed; not obvious. **5** (of a country, legislation, etc.) prohibiting the sale of alcoholic drink. **6** (of toast, bread, etc.) without butter, margarine, etc. **7** (of provisions, groceries, etc.) solid; not liquid (*dry goods*). **8** impassive; unsympathetic; hard; cold. **9** (of a cow, etc.) not yielding milk. **10** *colloq.* thirsty or thirst-making (*this is dry work*). ● *v.* (**dries, dried**) **1** *tr. & intr.* make or become dry by wiping, evaporation, draining, etc. **2** *tr.* (usu. as **dried** *adj.*) preserve (food, etc.) by removing the moisture (*dried fruit*). **3** *intr.* (often foll. by *up*) *Theatr. colloq.* forget one's lines. **4** *tr. & intr.* (often foll. by *off*) cease or cause (a cow, etc.) to cease yielding milk. ● *n.* (*pl.* **dries**) a prohibitionist. □ **dry out 1** become fully dry. **2** (of a drug addict, alcoholic, etc.) undergo treatment to cure addiction. **dry up 1** make utterly dry. **2** (of a well, etc.) cease to yield water. **3** *colloq.* (esp. in *imper.*) cease talking. □□ **dry·ish** *adj.* **dryly** *adv.* **dry·ness** *n.*

dry·ad /dríad, drí-əd/ *n. Mythol.* a nymph inhabiting a tree; a wood nymph.

dry bat·ter·y *n. Electr.* an electric battery consisting of dry cells. ▷ BATTERY

dry cell *n. Electr.* a cell in which the electrolyte is absorbed in a solid and cannot be spilled. ▷ BATTERY

dry-clean *v.tr.* clean (clothes, etc.) with organic solvents without using water.

dry clean·er *n.* an individual or a business that specializes in dry cleaning.

dry cough *n.* a cough not producing phlegm.

dry cure *v.tr.* cure (meat, etc.) without pickling in liquid.

dry dock *n.* an enclosure for the building or repairing of ships, from which water can be pumped out.

dry·er var. of DRIER[2].

D

D

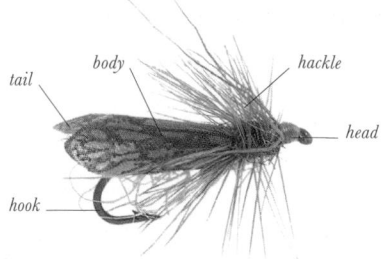

DRY FLY REPRESENTING
A MAYFLY

dry fly *n. Fishing* ▲ an artificial fly that is floated on the water's surface. □□ **dry-fly** *adj., v.intr.* (**-flies, -flied**).

dry goods *n.* fabric, thread, clothing, etc., esp. as distinct from hardware, groceries, etc.

dry ice *n.* solid carbon dioxide.

dry land *n.* land as opposed to the sea, etc.

dry mea·sure *n.* a measure of capacity for dry goods.

dry rot *n.* **1** a decayed state of wood when not ventilated, caused by certain fungi. **2** these fungi.

dry run *n. colloq.* a rehearsal.

dry-shod *adj. & adv.* without wetting the shoes.

dry·wall /dríwawl/ *n.* = PLASTERBOARD.

DSC *abbr.* Distinguished Service Cross.

D.Sc. *abbr.* Doctor of Science.

DSM *abbr.* Distinguished Service Medal.

DST *abbr.* daylight saving(s) time.

DT *abbr.* (also **DT's** /deétéez/) delirium tremens.

DTP *abbr.* desktop publishing.

du·al /dʊ́əl, dyʊ́əl/ *adj. & n.* ● *adj.* **1** of two; twofold. **2** divided in two; double (*dual ownership*). **3** *Gram.* (in some languages) denoting two persons or things (additional to singular and plural). ● *n.* (also **du·al num·ber**) *Gram.* a dual form of a noun, verb, etc. □ **dual control** (of a vehicle or an aircraft) having two sets of controls, one of which is used by the instructor. **dual in-line package** *Computing* see DIP. □□ **du·al·i·ty** /-álitee/ *n.* **du·al·ly** *adv.*

du·al·ism /dʊ́əlizəm, dyʊ́-/ *n.* **1** being twofold; duality. **2** *Philos.* the theory that in any domain of reality there are two independent underlying principles, e.g., mind and matter, form and content. **3** *Theol.* **a** the theory that the forces of good and evil are equally balanced in the universe. **b** the theory of the dual (human and divine) personality of Christ. □□ **du·al·ist** *n.* **du·al·is·tic** *adj.* **du·al·is·ti·cal·ly** *adv.*

dub[1] /dub/ *v.tr.* (**dubbed, dubbing**) **1** make (a person) a knight by touching his shoulders with a sword. **2** give (a person) a nickname or title (*dubbed him a crank*).

dub[2] /dub/ *v.tr.* (**dubbed, dubbing**) **1** provide (a movie, etc.) with an alternative soundtrack, esp. in a different language. **2** add (sound effects or music) to a movie or a broadcast. **3** combine (soundtracks) into one. **4** transfer or make a copy of (a soundtrack).

dub·bin /dúbin/ *n.* (also **dub·bing** /dúbing/) prepared grease for softening and waterproofing leather.

du·bi·e·ty /dʊʊbíətee, dyʊʊ-/ *n.* (*pl.* **-ies**) *literary* **1** a feeling of doubt. **2** a doubtful matter.

du·bi·ous /dʊʊbeeəs, dyʊʊ-/ *adj.* **1** hesitating or doubting (*dubious about going*). **2** of questionable value or truth (*a dubious claim*). **3** unreliable; suspicious (*dubious company*). **4** of doubtful result (*a dubious undertaking*). □□ **du·bi·ous·ly** *adv.* **du·bi·ous·ness** *n.*

du·cal /dʊ́kəl, dyʊ́-/ *adj.* of, like, or bearing the title of a duke.

duc·at /dúkət/ *n. hist.* a gold coin, formerly current in most European countries.

duch·ess /dúchis/ *n.* (as a title usu. **Duchess**) **1** a duke's wife or widow. **2** a woman holding the rank of duke in her own right.

DUCK

More than 100 species of ducks are found throughout the world. Most ducks nest on or beside fresh water, but some species spend much of their life on estuaries or shallow seas. Many ducks dive underwater to feed on mollusks or plant material. Surface-feeding ducks, including the mallard, sieve food from mud or water, or immerse only the front part of their body to reach food.

EXTERNAL FEATURES
OF A MALE MALLARD
(*Anas platyrhynchos*)

broad flat bill — white-bordered speculum (wing patch) — waterproof plumage — webbed front toes — hind toe

EXAMPLES OF OTHER DUCKS

EIDER DUCK
(*Somateria mollissima*)

NORTHERN SHOVELER
(*Anas clypeata*)

HARLEQUIN DUCK
(*Histrionicus histrionicus*)

WOOD DUCK
(*Aix sponsa*)

TORRENT DUCK
(*Merganetta armata*)

LONG-TAILED DUCK
(*Clangula hyemalis*)

---

duch·esse /dʊʊshés, dúchis/ *n.* **1** a soft heavy kind of satin. **2** a dressing table with a pivoting mirror.

duch·esse lace *n.* a kind of Brussels bobbin lace.

duch·y /dúchee/ *n.* (*pl.* **-ies**) **1** the territory of a duke or duchess; a dukedom. **2** (often as **the Duchy**) the royal dukedom of Cornwall or Lancaster, each with certain estates, revenues, and jurisdiction of its own.

duck[1] /duk/ *n.* (*pl.* same or **ducks**) **1** ▲ any of various swimming birds of the family Anatidae, esp. the domesticated form of the mallard or wild duck. **2** the female of this (opp. DRAKE). **3** the flesh of a duck as food. □ **like a duck to water** adapting very readily. **like water off a duck's back** *colloq.* (of remonstrances, etc.) producing no effect.

duck[2] /duk/ *v. & n.* ● *v.* **1** *intr. & tr.* plunge, dive, or dip under water and emerge (*ducked him in the pool*). **2** *intr. & tr.* bend (the head or the body) quickly to avoid a blow or being seen, or as a bow or curtsy; bob (*ducked out of sight*). **3** *tr. & intr. colloq.* avoid or dodge; withdraw (from) (*ducked out of the engagement*). **4** *intr. Bridge* lose a trick deliberately by playing a low card. ● *n.* **1** a quick dip or swim. **2** a quick lowering of the head, etc. □□ **duck·er** *n.*

duck[3] /duk/ *n.* **1** a strong, untwilled linen or cotton fabric used for small sails and the outer clothing of sailors. **2** (in *pl.*) pants made of this (*white ducks*).

duck[4] /duk/ *n. colloq.* an amphibious landing craft.

duck·bill /dúkbil/ *n.* (also **duck-billed plat·y·pus**) = PLATYPUS.

duck·ing stool *n. hist.* a chair fastened to the end of a pole, which could be plunged into a pond, used formerly for ducking public offenders, etc.

duck·board /dúkbawrd/ *n.* (usu. in *pl.*) a path of wooden slats placed over muddy ground or in a trench.

duck hawk *n.* a N. American peregrine falcon.

duck·ling /dúkling/ *n.* **1** a young duck. **2** its flesh as food.

ducks and drakes *n.* a game of making a flat stone skim along the surface of water.

duck's ass *n. coarse sl.* a haircut with the hair on the back of the head shaped like a duck's tail (usu. abbr. as **DA**).

duck soup *n. sl.* an easy task.

duck·weed /dúkweed/ *n.* ▼ any of various aquatic plants, esp. of the genus *Lemna*, growing on the surface of still water.

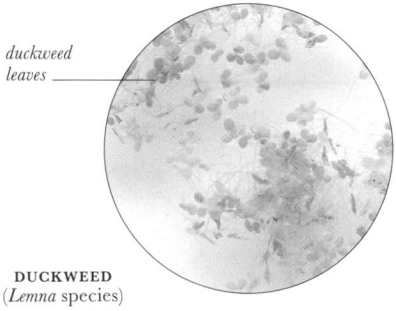

duckweed leaves

DUCKWEED
(*Lemna* species)

duck·y /dúkee/ *adj. colloq.* fine; wonderful; sweet; splendid.

duct /dukt/ *n. & v.* ● *n.* **1** a channel or tube for conveying fluid, cable, etc. **2 a** a tube in the body conveying secretions such as tears, etc. **b** *Bot.* a tube formed by cells that have lost their intervening end walls, holding air, water, etc. ● *v.tr.* convey through a duct.

duc·tile /dúktəl, -tīl/ *adj.* **1** (of a metal) capable of being drawn into wire; pliable, not brittle. **2** (of a substance) easily molded. **3** (of a person) docile; gullible. □□ **duc·til·i·ty** /-tílitee/ *n.*

duct·ing /dúkting/ *n.* **1** a system of ducts. **2** material in the form of a duct or ducts.

duct·less /dúktlis/ *adj.* lacking or not using a duct or ducts.

duct·less gland *n.* a gland secreting directly into the bloodstream.

duct tape *n. N. Amer.* strong cloth-backed waterproof adhesive tape.

duct·work /dúktwərk/ *n.* a series of interlinked ducts, as for a ventilation system.

dud /dud/ *n. & adj. sl.* ● *n.* **1** a futile or ineffectual person or thing (*a dud at the job*). **2** a counterfeit article. **3** a shell, etc., that fails to explode. **4** (in *pl.*) clothes. ● *adj.* **1** useless; worthless; unsatisfactory or futile. **2** counterfeit.

dude /dood, dyood/ *n. sl.* **1** a fastidious aesthetic person, usu. male; a dandy. **2** a vacationer on a dude ranch. **3** a fellow; a guy.

dude ranch *n.* a cattle ranch converted to a vacation resort for tourists, etc.

dudg·eon /dújən/ *n.* a feeling of offense; resentment. □ **in high dudgeon** very angry or angrily.

due /doo, dyoo/ *adj., n., & adv.* ● *adj.* **1** (*predic.*) owing or payable (*our thanks are due to him; $500 was due on the 15th*). **2** merited; fitting (*her due reward*). **3** proper; adequate. **4** (*predic.*; foll. by *to*) to be ascribed to (a cause, an agent, etc.) (*the discovery was due to Edison*). **5** (*predic.*) intended to arrive at a certain time (*a train is due at 7:30*). **6** (foll. by *to* + *infin.*) under an obligation or agreement to do something (*due to speak tonight*). ● *n.* **1** a person's right; what is owed to a person (*a fair hearing is my due*). **2** (in *pl.*) **a** what one owes (*pays his dues*). **b** a legally demandable toll or fee (*harbor dues*). ● *adv.* (of a point of the compass) exactly, directly (*went due east*). □ **due to** *disp.* because of; owing to (*was late due to an accident*) (cf. sense 4 of *adj.*). **fall** (or **become**) **due** (of a bill, etc.) be immediately payable. **in due course 1** at about the appropriate time. **2** in the natural order.

du·el /dóoəl, dyóoəl/ *n. & v.* ● *n.* **1** *hist.* a contest with deadly weapons between two people to settle a point of honor. **2** any contest between two people, causes, animals, etc. ● *v.intr.* fight a duel or duels. □□ **du·el·er** *n.* **du·el·ist** *n.*

duen·de /dóo-énday/ *n.* **1** an evil spirit. **2** inspiration.

du·en·na /dóo-énə, dyóo-/ *n.* an older woman acting as a governess and companion in charge of girls, esp. in a Spanish family.

due proc·ess *n.* a course of legal proceedings in accordance with a state's or nation's legal system, such that individual rights are protected.

du·et /doo-ét, dyoo-/ *n.* **1** *Mus.* a performance by two voices, instrumentalists, etc. **b** a composition for two performers. **2** a dialogue. □□ **du·et·tist** *n.*

duff /duf/ *n. sl.* buttocks (*get off your duff!*).

duf·fel /dúfəl/ *n.* (also **duf·fle**) **1** a coarse woolen cloth with a thick nap. **2** a sportsman's or camper's equipment.

duf·fel bag *n.* a cylindrical canvas bag closed by a drawstring.

duf·fer /dúfər/ *n. sl.* an inefficient, useless, or stupid person.

duf·fle (or **duf·fel**) **coat** *n.* ◀ a hooded overcoat of heavy woolen fabric, usu. fastened with toggles.

hood
wooden toggle
DUFFLE COAT

dug[1] *past* and *past part.* of DIG.

dug[2] /dug/ *n.* the udder, breast, teat, or nipple of a female animal.

du·gong /dóogawng, -gong/ *n.* (*pl.* same or **dugongs**) ▼ a marine mammal, *Dugong dugon*, of Asian seas and coasts.

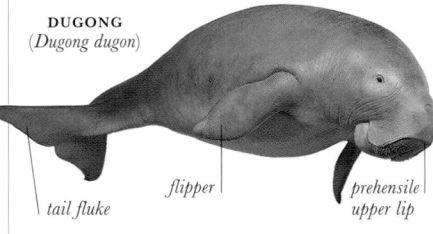

DUGONG
(*Dugong dugon*)

tail fluke　*flipper*　*prehensile upper lip*

dug·out /dúgowt/ *n.* **1 a** a roofed shelter esp. for troops in trenches. **b** an underground air-raid or nuclear shelter. **c** *Baseball* a roofed seating area for players, facing the field. **2** a canoe made from a hollowed tree trunk.

duke /dook, dyook/ *n.* (as a title usu. **Duke**) **1 a** a person holding the highest hereditary title of the nobility. **b** a sovereign prince ruling a duchy or small state. **2** (usu. in *pl.*) *sl.* the hand; the fist (*put up your dukes!*).

duke·dom /dóokdəm, dyóok-/ *n.* **1** a territory ruled by a duke. **2** the rank of duke.

dul·cet /dúlsit/ *adj.* (esp. of sound) sweet and soothing.

dul·ci·mer /dúlsimər/ *n.* a musical instrument with strings of graduated length stretched over a sounding board or box, played by being struck with hammers.

dul·ci·tone /dúlsitōn/ *n. Mus.* a keyboard instrument with steel tuning forks which are struck by hammers.

du·li·a /dōolía, dyōo-/ *n. RC Ch.* the reverence accorded to saints and angels.

dull /dul/ *adj. & v.* ● *adj.* **1** slow to understand; stupid. **2** tedious; boring. **3** (of the weather) overcast; gloomy. **4 a** (esp. of a knife edge, etc.) blunt. **b** (of color, light, sound, or taste) not bright, shining, vivid, or keen. **5** (of a pain, etc.) usu. prolonged and indistinct (*a dull ache*). **6 a** (of a person, an animal, trade, etc.) sluggish, slow-moving. **b** (of a person) listless; depressed (*he's a dull fellow since the accident*). **7** (of the ears, eyes, etc.) without keen perception. ● *v.tr. & intr.* make or become dull. □ **dull the edge of** make less sensitive, interesting, effective, amusing, etc.; blunt. □□ **dull·ish** *adj.* **dull·ness** *n.* (also **dul·ness**). **dul·ly** *adv.*

dull·ard /dúlərd/ *n.* a stupid person.

dull-wit·ted *adj.* = DULL *adj.* 1.

dulse /duls/ *n.* an edible seaweed, *Rhodymenia palmata*, with red wedge-shaped fronds.

du·ly /dóolee, dyóo-/ *adv.* **1** in due time or manner. **2** rightly; properly; fitly.

dumb /dum/ *adj.* **1 a** (of a person) unable to speak, usu. because of a congenital defect or deafness. **b** (of an animal) naturally unable to speak (*our dumb friends*). **2** silenced by surprise, shyness, etc. **3** taciturn or reticent, esp. insultingly (*dumb insolence*). **4** (of an action, etc.) performed without speech. **5** (often in *comb.*) giving no sound; without voice or some other property normally belonging to things of the name (*a dumb piano*). **6** *colloq.* stupid; ignorant. **7** having no voice in government; inarticulate (*the dumb masses*). **8** (of a computer terminal, etc.) able only to transmit data to or receive data; not programmable (opp. INTELLIGENT). □□ **dumb·ly** /dúmlee/ *adv.* **dumb·ness** /dúmnis/ *n.*

dumb·bell /dúmbel/ *n.* **1** a short bar with a weight at each end, used for exercise, muscle-building, etc. **2** *sl.* a stupid person.

dumb·found /dúmfównd/ *v.tr.* (also **dum·found**;

esp. as **dumbfounded** *adj.*) strike dumb; confound; nonplus.

dum·bo /dúmbō/ *n.* (*pl.* **-os**) *sl.* a stupid person; a fool.

dumb·size /dúmsīz/ *v.tr.* (of a company) reduce staff numbers to unreasonably low levels, with the result that work can no longer be carried out effectively.

dumb·struck /dúmstruk/ *adj.* greatly shocked or surprised and so lost for words.

dumb·wait·er /dúmwaytər/ *n.* **1** a small elevator for carrying food, plates, etc., between floors. **2** a movable table, esp. with revolving shelves, used in a dining room.

dum·dum /dúmdum/ *n.* (in full **dumdum bullet**) a kind of soft-nosed bullet that expands on impact and inflicts a severe wound.

dum·my /dúmee/ *n., adj., & v.* ● *n.* (*pl.* **-ies**) **1** a model of a human being, esp.: **a** a ventriloquist's doll. **b** a figure used to model clothes in a store window, etc. **c** a target used for firearms practice. **2** (often *attrib.*) **a** a counterfeit object used to replace or resemble a real or normal one. **b** a prototype, esp. in publishing. **3** *colloq.* a stupid person. **4** a person taking no significant part; a figurehead. **5** an imaginary fourth player at whist, whose hand is turned up and played by a partner. **6** *Bridge* **a** the partner of the declarer, whose cards are exposed after the first lead. **b** this player's hand. **7** (of the ears, eyes, etc.). **7** *Mil.* a blank round of ammunition. **8** *colloq.* a dumb person. ● *adj.* sham; counterfeit. □ **dummy up** *sl.* keep quiet; give no information.

dum·my run *n.* **1** a practice attack, etc.; a trial run. **2** a rehearsal.

dump /dump/ *n. & v.* ● *n.* **1 a** a place for depositing trash, garbage, etc. **b** a heap of trash, garbage, etc. **2** *colloq.* an unpleasant or dreary place. **3** *Mil.* a temporary store of ammunition, provisions, etc. **4** an accumulated pile of ore, earth, etc. **5** *Computing* **a** a printout of stored data. **b** the process or result of dumping data. ● *v.tr.* **1** put down firmly or clumsily (*dumped the shopping on the table*). **2** deposit or dispose of (trash, etc.). **3** *colloq.* abandon; desert. **4** *Mil.* leave (ammunition, etc.) in a dump. **5** *Econ.* send (goods unsalable at a high price in the home market) to a foreign market for sale at a low price. **6** *Computing* **a** copy (stored data) to a different location. **b** reproduce the contents of (a store) externally. □ **dump on** *sl.* criticize or abuse; get the better of.

dump·er /dúmpər/ *n.* a person or thing that dumps.

dump·ling /dúmpling/ *n.* **1** a small ball of usu. shortening, flour, and water, boiled in stew or water, and eaten. **b** a dessert consisting of apple or other fruit enclosed in dough and baked. **2** a small fat person.

dumps /dumps/ *n.pl. colloq.* depression; melancholy (*in the dumps*).

Dump·ster /dúmpstər/ *n. Trademark* a large trash receptacle designed to be hoisted and emptied into a truck.

dump truck *n.* a truck with a body that tilts or opens at the back for unloading.

dump·y /dúmpee/ *adj.* (**dumpier, dumpiest**) short and stout. □□ **dump·i·ly** *adv.*

dun[1] /dun/ *adj. & n.* ● *adj.* dull grayish brown. ● *n.* **1** a dun color. **2** a dun horse. **3** (in full **dun fly**) a dark fishing fly.

dun[2] /dun/ *n. & v.* ● *n.* **1** a debt collector; an importunate creditor. **2** a demand for payment. ● *v.tr.* (**dunned, dunning**) importune for payment of a debt; pester.

dunce /duns/ *n.* a person slow at learning; a dullard.

dunce cap *n.* (also **dunce's cap**) a paper cone formerly put on the head of a dunce at school as a mark of disgrace.

dun·der·head /dúndərhed/ *n.* a stupid person. □□ **dun·der·head·ed** *adj.*

D

D

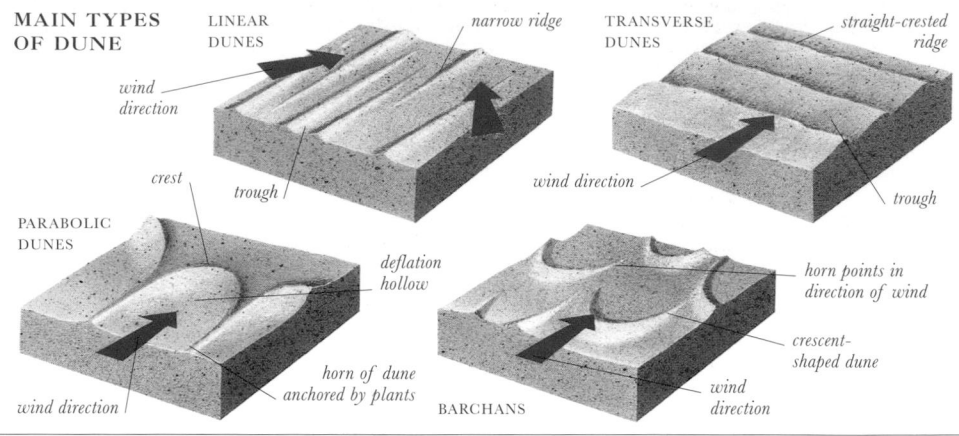

DUNE

Dunes form in different ways depending on the amount of sand available, the variability of wind direction, and the amount of vegetation cover. Linear dunes form where sand is scarce and the wind variable. Transverse dunes form at right angles to the wind in areas where there is abundant sand. Parabolic dunes are common on coasts, where there is abundant sand and the wind is strong. Barchans form on hard, flat plains with little sand.

MAIN TYPES OF DUNE

LINEAR DUNES — *narrow ridge* — *wind direction*

TRANSVERSE DUNES — *straight-crested ridge* — *wind direction* — *trough*

PARABOLIC DUNES — *crest* — *trough* — *deflation hollow* — *horn of dune anchored by plants* — *wind direction*

BARCHANS — *horn points in direction of wind* — *crescent-shaped dune* — *wind direction*

---

dune /doon, dyoon/ *n.* ▲ a mound or ridge of loose sand, etc., formed by the wind. ▷ ERODE

dung /dung/ *n. & v.* ● *n.* the excrement of animals; manure. ● *v.tr.* apply dung to; manure (land).

dun·ga·ree /dúnggərée/ *n.* **1** (in *pl.*) **a** overalls, etc., usu. made of blue denim, worn esp. by workers. **b** blue jeans. **2** a coarse E. Indian calico.

dung bee·tle *n.* ◀ any of a family of beetles whose larvae develop in dung.

dun·geon /dúnjən/ *n.* a strong underground cell for prisoners.

dung·hill /dúnghil/ *n.* a heap of dung or refuse, esp. in a farmyard.

dunk /dungk/ *v.tr.* **1** dip (a doughnut, etc.) into milk, coffee, etc. before eating. **2** immerse; dip (*was dunked in the river*).

dunk shot *n. Basketball* a shot made by a player jumping up and thrusting the ball down through the basket.

DUNG BEETLE

dun·lin /dúnlin/ *n.* a long-billed sandpiper, *Calidris alpina*.

dun·nage /dúnij/ *n. Naut.* **1** mats, brushwood, etc., stowed under or among cargo to prevent wetting or chafing. **2** *colloq.* miscellaneous baggage.

dun·nock /dúnək/ *n. Brit.* ▶ a small European songbird, *Prunella modularis*.

du·o /doo-o, dyoo-o/ *n.* (*pl.* **-os**) **1** a pair of actors, entertainers, singers, etc. **2** *Mus.* a duet.

du·o·dec·i·mal /doo-ōdésiməl, dyoo-/ *adj. & n.* ● *adj.* relating to or using a system of numerical notation that has 12 as a base. ● *n.* **1** the duodecimal system. **2** duodecimal notation. □□ **du·o·dec·i·mal·ly** *adv.*

du·o·de·num /doo-ōdeénəm, dyoo-, doo-ód'nəm, dyoo-/ *n. Anat.* ▲ the first part of the small intestine immediately below the stomach. ▷ DIGESTION. □□ **du·o·de·nal** *adj.* **du·o·de·ni·tis** /-nítis/ *n.*

du·o·logue /doo-əlawg, -log, dyoo-/ *n.* **1** a conversation between two people. **2** a play or part of a play for two actors.

du·op·o·ly /doo-ópəlee, dyoo-/ *n.* (*pl.* **-ies**) *Econ.* the possession of trade in a commodity, etc., by only two sellers.

du·o·tone /doo-ōtōn, dyoo-/ *n. & adj. Printing* ● *n.* **1** a halftone illustration in two colors from the same original with different screen angles. **2** the process of making a duotone. ● *adj.* in two colors.

dupe /doop, dyoop/ *n. & v.* ● *n.* a victim of deception. ● *v.tr.* make a fool of; cheat. □□ **dup·er·y** *n.*

du·pi·on /doopeeən, dyoo-/ *n.* **1** a rough silk fabric

DUNNOCK
(*Prunella modularis*)

---

woven from the threads of double cocoons. **2** an imitation of this with other fibers.

du·ple /doopəl, dyoo-/ *adj.* of two parts.

du·plex /doopleks, dyoo-/ *n. & adj.* ● *n.* **1** an apartment on two levels. **2** a house subdivided for two families. ● *adj.* **1** having two elements; twofold. **2 a** (of an apartment) two-story. **b** (of a house) for two families. **3** *Computing* (of a circuit) allowing the transmission of signals in both directions simultaneously (opp. SIMPLEX).

du·pli·cate *adj., n., & v.* ● *adj.* /dooplikət, dyoo-/ **1** exactly like something already existing; copied (esp. in large numbers). **2 a** having two corresponding parts. **b** existing in two examples; paired. **c** doubled. ● *n.* /doopli kət, dyoo-/ **1 a** one of two identical things, esp. a copy of an original. **b** one of two or more specimens of a thing exactly or almost identical. **2** *Law* a second copy of a letter or document. **3** (in full **duplicate bridge** or **whist**) a form of bridge or whist in which the same hands are played successively by different players. ● *v.tr.* /dooplikayt, dyoo-/ **1** multiply by two; double. **2 a** make or be an exact copy of. **b** make or supply copies of (*duplicated the leaflet for distribution*). **3** repeat (an action, etc.), esp. unnecessarily. □ **in duplicate** consisting of two exact copies. □□ **du·pli·ca·ble** /dooplikəbəl, dyoo-/ *adj.* **du·pli·ca·tion** /-káyshən/ *n.*

du·pli·ca·tor /dooplikaytər, dyoo-/ *n.* **1** a machine for making copies of a document, leaflet, etc. **2** a person or thing that duplicates.

du·plic·i·ty /dooplísitee, dyoo-/ *n.* double-dealing; deceitfulness. □□ **du·plic·i·tous** *adj.*

du·ra·ble /doorəbəl, dyoor-/ *adj. & n.* ● *adj.* **1** capable of lasting; hard-wearing. **2** (of goods) not for immediate consumption; able to be kept. ● *n.* (in *pl.*) durable goods. □□ **du·ra·bil·i·ty** *n.* **du·ra·bly** *adv.*

du·ra ma·ter /doorə máytər, má·a-, doorə/ *n. Anat.* the tough outermost membrane enveloping the brain and spinal cord (see MENINX). ▷ EYE, HEAD

du·ra·tion /dooráyshən, dyoor-/ *n.* **1** the length of time for which something continues. **2** a specified length of time (*after the duration of a minute*). □ **for the duration 1** until the end of something obstructing normal activities, as a war. **2** for a very long time. □□ **du·ra·tion·al** *adj.*

du·ress /doorés, dyoo-/ *n.* **1** compulsion, esp. imprisonment, threats, or violence, illegally used to force a person to act against his or her will (*under duress*). **2** imprisonment.

du·ri·an /dooreeən/ *n.* **1** a large tree, *Durio zibethinus*, native to SE Asia, bearing oval spiny fruits containing a creamy pulp with a fetid smell and an agreeable taste. **2** this fruit.

dur·ing /dooring, dyoor-/ *prep.* **1** throughout (*read during the meal*). **2** at some point in (*came in during the day*).

---

dur·ra /doorə/ *n.* (also **dhur·ra**) a kind of sorghum, *Sorghum vulgare*, native to Asia, Africa, and the US.

du·rum /doorəm, dyoo-/ *n.* a kind of wheat, *Triticum turgidum*, yielding a flour used for pasta.

dusk /dusk/ *n.* **1** the darker stage of twilight. **2** shade; gloom.

dusk·y /dúskee/ *adj.* (**duskier**, **duskiest**) **1** shadowy; dim. **2** dark-colored, darkish. □□ **dusk·i·ly** *adv.* **dusk·i·ness** *n.*

dust /dust/ *n. & v.* ● *n.* **1 a** a finely powdered earth, dirt, etc. **b** fine powder of any material (*pollen dust*; *gold dust*). **c** a cloud of dust. **2** a dead person's remains (*honored dust*). **3** confusion or turmoil (*raised quite a dust*). **4** the ground; the earth (*kissed the dust*). ● *v.* **1** *tr.* (also *absol.*) clear (furniture, etc.) of dust, etc., by wiping, brushing, etc. **2** *tr.* **a** sprinkle (esp. a

---

DUODENUM

The duodenum digests food that enters it from the stomach; this flow is controlled by the pyloric sphincter. Pancreatic juice containing enzymes breaks down the food and neutralizes stomach acids. Bile from the liver emulsifies (splits up) fats for later digestion. Ducts running from the pancreas and liver to the duodenum unite to form a passageway called the ampulla of Vater.

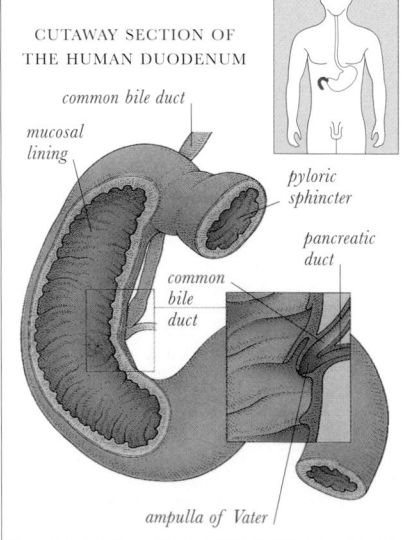

CUTAWAY SECTION OF THE HUMAN DUODENUM

common bile duct

mucosal lining

pyloric sphincter

pancreatic duct

common bile duct

ampulla of Vater

cake) with powder, dust, sugar, etc. **b** sprinkle or strew (sugar, powder, etc.). **3** *tr.* make dusty. □ **dust off 1** remove the dust from. **2** use and enjoy again after a long period of neglect. **in the dust 1** humiliated. **2** dead. **when the dust settles** when things quiet down. □□ **dust·less** *adj.*

dust bowl *n.* an area denuded of vegetation by drought or erosion and reduced to desert.

dust·cov·er /dústkuvər/ *n.* **1** a cloth put over furniture to protect it from dust. **2** = DUST JACKET.

dust dev·il *n.* a whirlwind visible as a column of dust.

dust·er /dústər/ *n.* **1 a** a cloth for dusting furniture, etc. **b** a person or contrivance that dusts. **2** a woman's light, loose, full-length coat.

dust jack·et *n.* a usu. decorated paper cover used to protect a book from dirt, etc.

dust·pan /dústpan/ *n.* a small pan into which dust, etc., is brushed from the floor.

dust storm *n.* a storm with clouds of dust carried in the air.

dust·y /dústee/ *adj.* (**dustier**, **dustiest**) **1** full of, covered with, or resembling dust. **2** uninteresting. **3** (of a color) dull. □□ **dust·i·ly** *adv.* **dust·i·ness** *n.*

Dutch /duch/ *adj. & n.* ● *adj.* of, relating to, or associated with the Netherlands. ● *n.* **1** the language of the Netherlands. **2** (prec. by *the*; treated as *pl.*) the people of the Netherlands. □ **go Dutch** share expenses equally.

Dutch auc·tion *n.* a sale, usu. public, of goods in which the price is reduced by the auctioneer until a buyer is found.

Dutch door *n.* a door divided into two parts horizontally allowing independent opening.

Dutch elm dis·ease *n.* a disease affecting elms caused by the fungus *Ceratocystis ulmi*, first found in the Netherlands.

Dutch·man /dúchmən/ *n.* (*pl.* **-men**; *fem.* **Dutchwoman**, *pl.* **-women**) a native or national of the Netherlands; a person of Dutch descent.

Dutch treat *n.* a party, outing, etc. to which each person makes a contribution.

Dutch un·cle *n.* a person giving advice with benevolent firmness.

du·te·ous /dóōteeəs, dyóō-/ *adj. literary* (of a person or conduct) dutiful; obedient. □□ **du·te·ous·ly** *adv.* **du·te·ous·ness** *n.*

du·ti·a·ble /dóōteeəbəl, dyóō-/ *adj.* liable to customs or other duties.

du·ti·ful /dóōtifŏol, dyóō-/ *adj.* doing or observant of one's duty. □□ **du·ti·ful·ly** *adv.* **du·ti·ful·ness** *n.*

du·ty /dóōtee, dyóō-/ *n.* (*pl.* **-ies**) **1 a** a moral or legal obligation; a responsibility. **b** the binding force of what is right (*strong sense of duty*). **c** what is required of one (*do one's duty*). **2** payment to the public revenue, esp.: **a** that levied on the import of goods (*customs duty*). **b** that levied on the transfer of property, licenses, etc. (*death duty*). **3** a job or function (*his duties as caretaker*). **4** the behavior due to a superior; deference; respect. □ **do duty for** serve as or pass for (something else). **on** (or **off**) **duty** engaged (or not) in one's work.

du·ty-bound *adj.* obliged by duty.

du·ty-free *adj.* (of goods) on which duty is not leviable.

du·ty-free shop *n.* a store at an airport, etc., at which duty-free goods can be bought.

du·vet /dóōváy/ *n.* a thick, soft quilt with a detachable cover, used instead of a top sheet and blankets.

DVD *abbr.* digital versatile disk.

dwarf /dwawrf/ *n. & v.* ● *n.* (*pl.* **dwarfs** or **dwarves** /dwawrvz/) **1** *Offens.* a person of abnormally small stature. **b** an animal or plant much below the ordinary size. **2** a small mythological being with supernatural powers. **3** (in full **dwarf star**) a small usu. dense star. ▷ STAR. **4** (*attrib.*) **a** of a kind very small in size (*dwarf bean*). **b** puny; stunted. ● *v.tr.* **1** stunt in growth. **2** cause (something similar or comparable) to seem small or insignificant. □□ **dwarf·ish** *adj.*

dweeb /dweeb/ *n. sl.* a studious or tedious person.

dwell /dwel/ *v. & n.* ● *v.intr.* (*past* and *past part.* **dwelled** or **dwelt**) **1** *literary* (usu. foll. by *in, at, near, on,* etc.) live; reside (*dwelt in the forest*). **2** (of a horse) be slow in raising its feet; pause before taking a fence. ● *n.* a slight, regular pause in the motion of a machine. □ **dwell on** (or **upon**) **1** write, brood, or speak at length on. **2** prolong (a note, a syllable, etc.). □□ **dwell·er** *n.*

dwell·ing /dwéling/ *n.* (also **dwell·ing place**) *formal* a house; a residence; an abode.

dwin·dle /dwínd'l/ *v.intr.* **1** become gradually smaller; shrink. **2** lose importance; decline.

Dy *symb. Chem.* the element dysprosium.

dyb·buk /díbŏok/ *n.* (in Jewish folklore) a malevolent wandering spirit able to possess the body of a living person.

dye /dī/ *n. & v.* ● *n.* **1 a** ▼ a substance used to change the color of hair, fabric, wood, etc. **b** a color produced by this. **2** (in full **dyestuff**) a substance yielding a dye, esp. for coloring materials in solution. ● *v.tr.* (**dyeing**) **1** impregnate with dye. **2** make (a thing) a specified color with dye (*dyed it yellow*).

dyed-in-the-wool *adj.* **1** out and out; inveterate. **2** (of a fabric) made of yarn dyed in its raw state.

dy·ing /dí-ing/ *adj.* connected with, or at the time of, death (*his dying words*). □ **to one's dying day** for the rest of one's life.

dyke[1] var. of DIKE[1].

dyke[2] /dīk/ *n.* (also **dike**) *sl.* a lesbian.

dy·nam·ic /dīnámik/ *adj. & n.* ● *adj.* (also **dy·nam·i·cal**) **1** energetic; active; potent. **2** *Physics* **a** concerning motive force (opp. STATIC). **b** concerning force in actual operation. **3** of or concerning dynamics. **4** *Mus.* relating to the volume of sound. ● *n.* **1** an energizing or motive force. **2** *Mus.* = DYNAMICS 3. □□ **dy·nam·i·cal·ly** *adv.*

dy·nam·ics /dīnámiks/ *n.pl.* **1** (usu. treated as *sing.*) **a** *Mech.* the branch of mechanics concerned with the motion of bodies under the action of forces (cf. STATICS). ▷ GRAVITY. **b** the branch of any science in which forces or changes are considered (*aerodynamics; population dynamics*). **2** the motive forces, physical or moral, affecting behavior and change in any sphere. **3** *Mus.* the varying degree of volume of sound in musical performance. □□ **dy·nam·i·cist** /-məsist/ *n.* (in sense 1).

dy·na·mism /dínəmizəm/ *n.* energizing or dynamic action or power.

dy·na·mite /dínəmīt/ *n. & v.* ● *n.* **1** a high explosive consisting of nitroglycerine mixed with an absorbent. **2** a potentially dangerous person, thing, or situation. **3** *sl.* a narcotic, esp. heroin. ● *v.tr.* charge or shatter with dynamite. □□ **dy·na·mit·er** *n.*

dy·na·mo /dínəmō/ *n.* (*pl.* **-os**) **1** a machine converting mechanical into electrical energy, esp. by rotating coils of copper wire in a magnetic field. **2** *colloq.* an energetic person.

dy·nas·ty /dínəstee/ *n.* (*pl.* **-ies**) **1** a line of hereditary rulers. **2** a succession of leaders in any field. □□ **dy·nas·tic** /-nástik/ *adj.* **dy·nas·ti·cal·ly** *adv.*

dyne /dīn/ *n. Physics* a unit of force that, acting on a mass of one gram, increases its velocity by one centimeter per second every second along the direction that it acts. ¶ Abbr.: **dyn**.

dys·en·ter·y /dísənteree/ *n.* a disease with inflammation of the intestines, causing severe diarrhea with blood and mucus. □□ **dys·en·ter·ic** *adj.*

dys·func·tion /dísfúngkshən/ *n.* an abnormality or impairment of function. □□ **dys·func·tion·al** *adj.*

dys·graph·i·a /disgráfeeə/ *n.* an inability to write coherently. □□ **dys·graph·ic** *adj.*

dys·lex·i·a /dislékseeə/ *n.* an abnormal difficulty in reading and spelling, caused by a brain condition. □□ **dys·lex·ic** *adj. & n.* **dys·lec·tic** /-léktik/ *adj. & n.*

dys·men·or·rhe·a /dísmenəréeə/ *n.* painful or difficult menstruation.

dys·morph·i·a /dismáwrfeeə/ *n. Med.* deformity or abnormality in the shape or size of a specified part of the body.

dys·pep·sia /dispépseeə/ *n.* indigestion. □□ **dys·pep·tic** /dispéptik/ *adj. & n.*

dys·pha·sia /disfáyzhə, -zheeə/ *n. Med.* lack of coordination in speech, owing to brain damage. □□ **dys·pha·sic** /-zik, -sik/ *adj.*

dys·pho·ri·a /disfáwreeə/ *n.* a state of unease or mental discomfort. □□ **dys·phor·ic** /-fáwrik/ *adj.*

dys·pla·sia /displáyzhə, -zheeə/ *n. Med.* abnormal growth of tissues, etc. □□ **dys·plas·tic** /-plástik/ *adj.*

dysp·ne·a /dispnéeə/ *n. Med.* difficult or labored breathing. □□ **dysp·ne·ic** *adj.*

dys·pro·si·um /disprózeeəm/ *n. Chem.* a naturally occurring soft metallic element of the lanthanide series. ¶ Symb.: **Dy**.

dys·to·pi·a /distópeeə/ *n.* an imaginary place or society in which everything is bad.

dys·tro·phy /dístrəfee/ *n.* defective nutrition. □□ **dys·troph·ic** /distrófik, -trō-/ *adj.*

dys·u·ri·a /disyŏoreeə/ *n.* painful or difficult urination.

D

DYE

A dye is a substance that is used to give color to another material. Synthetic dyes are made by adding sulfur or chlorine to the colorless chemicals derived from distilling petroleum or coal tar. Natural dyes, as shown below, are produced by grinding vegetable or animal material and mixing the resulting powder with water.

EXAMPLES OF NATURAL DYES

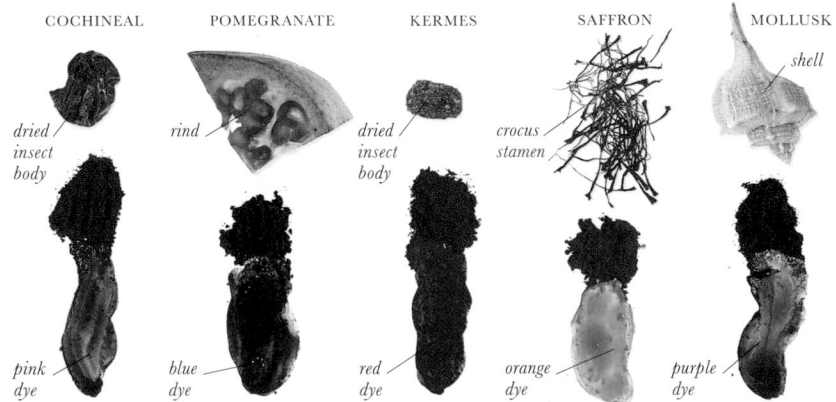

COCHINEAL　　POMEGRANATE　　KERMES　　SAFFRON　　MOLLUSK

shell

dried insect body　　*rind*　　*dried insect body*　　*crocus stamen*

pink dye　　*blue dye*　　*red dye*　　*orange dye*　　*purple dye*

E

E[1] /ee/ *n.* (also **e**) (*pl.* **Es** or **E's**) **1** the fifth letter of the alphabet. **2** *Mus.* the third note of the diatonic scale of C major. ▷ NOTATION

E[2] *abbr.* (also **E.**) **1** east; eastern. **2** English. **3** energy.

e *symb.* **1** *Math.* the base of natural logarithms, equal to approx. 2.71828. **2** used on packaging (in conjunction with specification of weight, size, etc.) to indicate compliance with EEC regulations.

e- /ee, e/ *prefix* form of EX-[1] 1 before some consonants.

ea. *abbr.* each.

each /eech/ *adj. & pron.* ● *adj.* every one of two or more persons or things, regarded and identified separately (*each person*; *five in each class*). ● *pron.* each person or thing (*each of us*; *have two books each*). □ **each and every** every single.

each oth·er *pron.* one another (*they hate each other*; *they wore each other's hats*).

ea·ger /éegər/ *adj.* **1 a** full of keen desire; enthusiastic. **b** (of passions, etc.) keen; impatient. **2** keen; strongly desirous (*eager to learn*; *eager for news*). □□ **ea·ger·ly** *adv.* **ea·ger·ness** *n.*

ea·ger bea·ver *n. colloq.* a very or excessively diligent person.

ea·gle /éegəl/ *n.* **1 a** ▼ any of various large birds of prey of the family Accipitridae, with keen vision and powerful flight. ▷ RAPTOR. **b** a figure of an eagle, esp. as a symbol of the US, or formerly as a Roman or French ensign. **2** *Golf* a score of two strokes under par at any hole. **3** *US* a gold coin worth ten dollars.

ea·gle eye *n.* keen sight; watchfulness. □□ **eagle-eyed** *adj.*

Ea·gle Scout *n.* the highest rank a Boy Scout can attain.

ea·glet /éeglit/ *n.* a young eagle.

ear[1] /eer/ *n.* **1** ▲ the organ of hearing and balance in humans and other vertebrates, esp. the external part of this. ▷ INNER EAR. **2** the faculty for discriminating sounds (*an ear for music*). **3** listening; attention. □ **all ears** listening attentively. **have a person's ear** receive a favorable hearing. **have** (or **keep) an ear to the ground** be alert to rumors or the trend of opinion. **out on one's ear** dismissed ignominiously. **up to one's ears** (often foll. by *in*) *colloq.* deeply involved or occupied. □□ **eared** *adj.* (also in *comb.*). **ear·less** *adj.*

ear[2] /eer/ *n.* the seed-bearing head of a cereal plant.

ear·ache /éerayk/ *n.* a pain in the ear.

ear·bash /éerbash/ *v.tr.* esp. *Austral. sl.* talk inordinately to; harangue.

ear·drum /éerdrum/ *n.* the membrane of the middle ear. ▷ EAR

ear·ful /éerfool/ *n.* (*pl.* **-fuls**) *colloq.* **1** a large quantity of talk. **2** a strong reprimand.

earl /ərl/ *n.* a British nobleman ranking between a marquess and a viscount (cf. COUNT[2]). □□ **earl·dom** *n.*

Earl Grey *n.* a kind of China tea flavored with bergamot.

ear·lobe /éerlōb/ *n.* the lower soft pendulous external part of the ear.

ear·ly /ə́rlee/ *adj., adv., & n.* ● *adj. & adv.* (**earlier, earliest**) **1** before the due, usual, or expected time (*was early for my appointment*; *arrived early*). **2 a** not far on in the day or night, or in time (*early evening*; *at the earliest opportunity*). **b** prompt (*early payment appreciated*; *at your earliest convenience*). **3 a** not far on in a period, development, or process of evolution; being the first stage (*Early English architecture*; *the early Christians*; *early spring*). **b** of the distant past (*early man*). **c** not far on in a sequence (*the early chapters*). **4 a** of childhood, esp. the preschool years (*early learning*). **b** (of a piece of writing, music, etc.) immature; youthful (*an early work*). **5** flowering, etc., before other varieties. ● *n.* (*pl.* **-ies**) (usu. in *pl.*) an early fruit or vegetable, esp. potatoes. □ **at the earliest** (often placed after a specified time) not before (*will arrive on Monday at the earliest*). **early** (or **earlier) on** one who arrives, gets up, etc., early. □□ **ear·li·ness** *n.*

ear·ly bird *n. colloq.* one who arrives, gets up, etc., early.

ear·mark /éermaark/ *n. & v.* ● *n.* **1** an identifying mark. **2** an owner's mark on the ear of an animal. ● *v.tr.* **1** set aside (money, etc.) for a special purpose. **2** mark (sheep, etc.) with such an identifying mark.

ear·muff /éermuf/ *n.* a wrap or cover for the ears, protecting them from cold, noise, etc.

earn /ərn/ *v.tr.* **1** (also *absol.*) **a** (of a person) obtain (income) in return for labor or services (*earn a weekly wage*). **b** (of capital invested) bring in as interest or profit. **2 a** deserve; obtain as the reward for hard work or merit (*earned our admiration*; *earn one's keep*). **b** incur (a reproach, reputation, etc.).

earned in·come *n.* income derived from wages, etc. (opp. *unearned income*).

earn·er /ə́rnər/ *n.* a person or thing that earns.

ear·nest[1] *adj. & n.* ● *adj.* intensely serious; not trifling or joking. ● *n.* seriousness. □ **in** (or **in real) earnest** serious(ly), not joking(ly); with determination. □□ **ear·nest·ly** *adv.* **ear·nest·ness** *n.*

EAR

The ear has three main parts: the outer, middle, and inner ear. The outer ear consists of the pinna and the auditory canal. The middle ear is filled with air and contains three tiny bones called ossicles: the anvil, hammer, and stirrup. The inner ear contains the semicircular canals and the cochlea.

temporal bone — *helix* — *eardrum* — *semicircular canal* — *antihelix* — *inner ear* — *ossicles* — *cartilage* — *cochlea* — *vestibular nerve* — *outer ear* — *cochlear nerve* — *auditory canal* — *Eustachian tube* — *pinna (auricle)* — *artery* — *temporal muscle* — *middle ear* — *mastoid process* — *lobe*

SECTION THROUGH THE HUMAN EAR

EAGLE

Eagles are the most powerful birds of prey. Like other raptors, eagles grasp and kill prey with their huge talons and use their hooked bills to tear through and eat flesh. There are more than 50 species of eagle found all over the world.

binocular vision — *hooked bill*

EXTERNAL FEATURES OF A BALD EAGLE (*Haliaeetus leucocephalus*)

powerful wings

talon

EXAMPLES OF OTHER EAGLES

GOLDEN EAGLE (*Aquila chrysaetos*)

TAWNY EAGLE (*Aquila rapax*)

AFRICAN HAWK EAGLE (*Hieraaetus spilogaster*)

EARTH

The fifth largest planet in the solar system, Earth is the only planet known to support life. The Earth has four main layers: a solid, metal inner core with a temperature of about 7,200°F (4,000°C); a molten, metal outer core; a mantle composed largely of a rock called peridotite; and the crust, of which there are two different types: continental and oceanic.

continental crust · molten outer core · solid inner core · oceanic crust

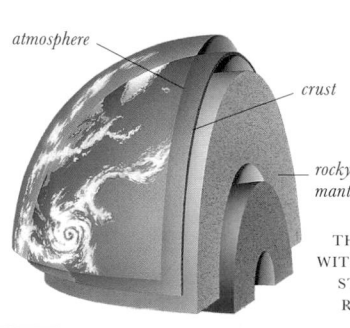
atmosphere · crust · rocky mantle

THE EARTH, WITH INTERNAL STRUCTURE REVEALED

SOLAR SYSTEM · Earth · Sun

ear·nest² /ɔ́rnist/ *n.* **1** money paid as an installment, esp. to confirm a contract, etc. **2** a token or foretaste (*in earnest of what is to come*).

earn·ings /ɔ́rningz/ *n.pl.* money earned.

ear·phone /ɛ́ərfōn/ *n.* a device applied to the ear to aid hearing or receive radio or telephone communications.

ear·piece /ɛ́ərpees/ *n.* the part of a telephone, etc., applied to the ear during use. ▷ RECEIVER

ear·pierc·ing *adj.* loud and shrill.

ear·plug /ɛ́ərplug/ *n.* a piece of plastic, etc., placed in the ear to protect against cold air, water, or noise.

ear·ring /ɛ́əring/ *n.* a piece of jewelry worn in or on (esp. the lobe of) the ear.

ear·shot /ɛ́ərshot/ *n.* the distance over which something can be heard (esp. *within* or *out of earshot*).

ear·split·ting /ɛ́ərspliting/ *adj.* excessively loud.

earth /ɔrth/ *n.* & *v.* ● *n.* **1 a** (also **Earth**) ▲ one of the planets of the solar system orbiting about the Sun between Venus and Mars; the planet on which we live. ▷ SOLAR SYSTEM **b** land and sea, as distinct from sky. **2 a** dry land; the ground (*fell to earth*). **b** soil; clay; mold. **c** bodily matter (*earth to earth*). **3** *Relig.* the present abode of mankind, as distinct from heaven or hell; the world. **4** the hole of a badger, fox, etc. **5** (prec. by *the*) *colloq.* a huge amount; everything (*cost the earth*; *want the earth*). ● *v.* **1** *tr.* (foll. by *up*) cover (the roots and lower stems of plants) with heaped-up earth. **2 a** *tr.* drive (a fox) to its earth. **b** *intr.* (of a fox, etc.) run to its earth. **3** *tr. Brit. Electr.* = GROUND¹ *v.* 5. □ **come back** (or **down**) **to earth** return to realities. **gone to earth** in hiding. **on earth** *colloq.* **1** existing anywhere (*the happiest man on Earth*; *looked like nothing on Earth*). **2** as an intensifier (*what on earth?*). □□ **earth·ward** *adj.* & *adv.* **earth·wards** *adv.*

EARTHENWARE: TRADITIONAL GREEK EARTHENWARE POT

earth·bound /ɔ́rthbound/ *adj.* **1** attached to the Earth or earthly things. **2** moving toward the Earth.

earth·en /ɔ́rthən/ *adj.* **1** made of earth. **2** made of baked clay.

earth·en·ware /ɔ́rthənwair/ *n.* & *adj.* ● *n.* ◄ pottery, vessels, etc., made of clay fired to a porous state, which can be made impervious to liquids by the use of a glaze (cf. PORCELAIN). ● *adj.* made of fired clay.

earth·ling /ɔ́rthling/ *n.* an inhabitant of the Earth, esp. as regarded in fiction by outsiders.

earth·ly /ɔ́rthlee/ *adj.* **1 a** of the Earth; terrestrial. **b** of human life on earth. **2** (usu. with *neg.*) *colloq.* remotely possible or conceivable (*is no earthly use*). □ **not an earthly** *colloq.* no chance whatever. □□ **earth·li·ness** *n*

earth·quake /ɔ́rthkwayk/ *n.* **1 ▼** a convulsion of the superficial parts of the earth due to the release of accumulated stress as a result of faults in strata or volcanic action. **2** a social, etc., disturbance.

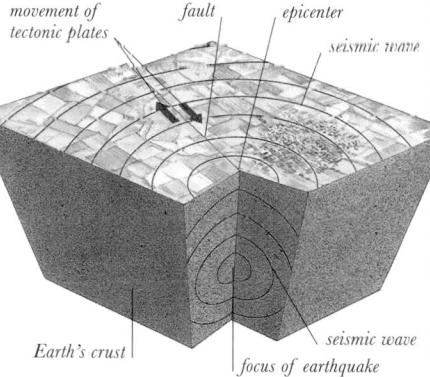
movement of tectonic plates · fault · epicenter · seismic wave · Earth's crust · seismic wave · focus of earthquake

EARTHQUAKE: CROSS SECTION OF THE EARTH'S CRUST DURING AN EARTHQUAKE

earth sci·ences *n.pl.* the sciences concerned with the earth or part of it, or its atmosphere (e.g., geology, oceanography, meteorology).

earth-shat·ter·ing *adj. colloq.* having a traumatic or devastating effect. □□ **earth-shat·ter·ing·ly** *adv.*

earth·work /ɔ́rthwərk/ *n.* **1** an artificial bank of earth in fortification or road building, etc. **2** the process of excavating soil in civil engineering work.

earth·worm /ɔ́rthwərm/ *n.* any of various annelid worms, esp. of the genus *Lumbricus* or *Allolobophora*, living and burrowing in the ground. ▷ ANNELID

earth·y /ɔ́rthee/ *adj.* (**earthier, earthiest**) **1** of or like earth or soil. **2** somewhat coarse or crude; unrefined (*earthy humor*). □□ **earth·i·ly** *adv.* **earth·i·ness** *n.*

ear·wax /ɛ́ərwaks/ *n.* a yellow waxy secretion produced by the ear. Also called cerumen.

ear·wig /ɛ́ərwig/ *n.* any small elongate insect of the order Dermaptera, with a pair of terminal appendages in the shape of forceps. ▷ INSECT

ease /eez/ *n.* & *v.* ● *n.* **1** absence of difficulty; facility; effortlessness (*did it with ease*). **2** freedom or relief from pain, embarrassment, or constraint. ● *v.* **1** *tr.* relieve from pain or anxiety, etc. (often foll. by *of*: *eased my mind*; *eased me of the burden*). **2** *intr.* (often foll. by *off, up*) **a** become less painful or burdensome. **b** relax; begin to take it easy. **c** slow down; moderate one's behavior, habits, etc. **3** *intr. Meteorol.* become less severe (*the wind will ease tonight*). **4 a** *tr.* relax; slacken. **b** *tr. & intr.* (foll. by *through, along,* etc.) move or be moved carefully into place (*eased it into the hole*). **5** *intr.* (often foll. by *off*) *Stock Exch.* (of shares, etc.) descend in price or value. □ **at ease 1** free from anxiety or constraint. **2** *Mil.* **a** in a relaxed attitude, with the feet apart. **b** the order to stand in this way. **at one's ease** free from embarrassment, awkwardness, or undue formality. □□ **eas·er** *n.*

ea·sel /éezəl/ *n.* ► a standing frame, usu. of wood, for supporting an artist's work, a blackboard, etc.

ease·ment /éezmənt/ *n. Law* a right of way or a similar right over another's land.

eas·i·ly /éezilee/ *adv.* **1** without difficulty. **2** by far (*easily the best*). **3** very probably (*it could easily snow*).

east /eest/ *n., adj., & adv.* ● *n.* **1 a** the point of the horizon where the Sun rises at the equinoxes. **b** the compass point corresponding to this. **c** the direction in which this lies. ▷ COMPASS. **2** (usu. **the East**) **a** the regions or countries lying to the east of Europe. **b** the formerly Communist nations of eastern Europe. **3** the eastern part of a country, town, etc. **4** (**East**) *Bridge* a player occupying the position designated "east." ● *adj.* **1** toward, at, near, or facing east. **2** coming from the east (*east wind*). ● *adv.* **1** toward, at, or near the east. **2** (foll. by *of*) further east than (*east of the Rockies*). □ **to the east** (often foll. by *of*) in an easterly direction.

east·bound /éestbownd/ *adj.* traveling or leading eastward.

Eas·ter /éestər/ *n.* **1** (also **Eas·ter Sun·day** or **Eas·ter Day**) the festival (held on a Sunday in March or April) commemorating Christ's resurrection. **2** the season in which this occurs, esp. the weekend from Good Friday to the following Monday.

Eas·ter egg *n.* **1** an egg that is dyed and often decorated as part of the Easter celebration. **2** an artificial chocolate egg given at Easter.

east·er·ly /éestərlee/ *adj., adv., & n.* ● *adj. & adv.* **1** in an eastern position or direction. **2** (of a wind) blowing from the east. ● *n.* (*pl.* **-ies**) a wind blowing from the east. ▷ TRADE WIND

east·ern /éestərn/ *adj.* **1** of or in the east; inhabiting the east. **2** lying or directed toward the east. **3** (**Eastern**) of or in the Far, Middle, or Near East. □□ **east·ern·most** *adj.*

East·ern·er /éestərnər/ *n.* a native or inhabitant of the east; esp. in the US.

eastern hem·i·sphere *n.* (also **Eastern Hemisphere**) the half of the Earth containing Europe, Asia, and Africa.

East In·dies *n.pl.* the islands, etc., east of India, esp. the Malay archipelago.

east·ing /éesting/ *n. Naut.,* etc., the distance traveled or the angle of longitude measured eastward from either a defined north-south grid line or a meridian.

east-north·east *n.* the direction or compass point midway between east and northeast.

east-south·east *n.* the direction or compass point midway between east and southeast.

east·ward /éestwərd/ *adj., adv., & n.* ● *adj. & adv.* (also **east·wards**) toward the east. ● *n.* an eastward direction or region. □□ **east·ward·ly** *adj. & adv.*

E

EASEL: ARTIST'S STUDIO EASEL

E

eas·y /éezee/ *adj., adv., & int.* (**easier, easiest**) ● *adj.* **1** not difficult; achieved without great effort. **2 a** free from pain, discomfort, anxiety, etc. **b** comfortably off; affluent (*easy circumstances*). **3** free from embarrassment, awkwardness, or constraint (*an easy manner*). **4 a** not strict; tolerant. **b** compliant; obliging; easily persuaded (*an easy touch*). ● *adv.* with ease; in an effortless or relaxed manner. ● *int.* go carefully; move gently. □ **easy come easy go** *colloq.* what is easily obtained is soon lost or spent. **easy does it** *colloq.* go carefully. **easy on the eye** (or **ear**, etc.) *colloq.* pleasant to look at (or listen to, etc.). **go easy** (foll. by *with, on*) be sparing or cautious. **I'm easy** *colloq.* I have no preference. **of easy virtue** (of a woman) sexually promiscuous. **take it easy 1** proceed gently or carefully. **2** relax; avoid overwork. □□ **eas·i·ness** *n.*

eas·y chair *n.* a large comfortable chair, usu. an armchair.

eas·y·go·ing /éezeegóing/ *adj.* **1** placid and tolerant; relaxed in manner; accepting things as they are. **2** (of a horse) having an easy gait.

eas·y lis·ten·ing *n.* popular music that is tuneful and undemanding.

eas·y street *n. colloq.* a situation of ease or affluence.

eas·y terms *n.pl.* payment by installments.

easy touch *n. sl.* a person who readily parts with money.

eat /eet/ *v.* (*past* **ate** /ayt/, esp. *Brit.* /et/; *past part.* **eaten** /éet'n/) **1 a** *tr.* take into the mouth, chew, and swallow (food). **b** *intr.* consume food; take a meal. **c** *tr.* devour (*eaten by a lion*). **2** *intr.* (foll. by (*away*) *at, into*) **a** destroy gradually, esp. by corrosion, erosion, disease, etc. **b** begin to consume or diminish (resources, etc.). **3** *tr. colloq.* trouble; vex (*what's eating you?*). □ **eat dirt** see DIRT. **eat one's heart out** suffer from excessive longing or envy. **eat humble pie** see HUMBLE. **eat out** have a meal away from home, esp. in a restaurant. **eat out of a person's hand** be entirely submissive to a person. **eat salt with** see SALT. **eat up 1** (also *absol.*) eat or consume completely. **2** use or deal with rapidly or wastefully (*eats up time; eats up the miles*). **3** encroach upon or annex (*eating up the neighboring countries*). **4** absorb; preoccupy (*eaten up with pride*). **eat one's words** admit that one was wrong.

eat·a·ble /éetəbəl/ *adj. & n.* ● *adj.* that is in a condition to be eaten (cf. EDIBLE). ● *n.* (usu. in *pl.*) food.

eat·er /éetər/ *n.* a person who eats (*a big eater*).

eat·er·y /éetəree/ *n.* (*pl.* **-ies**) *colloq.* a restaurant, esp. a diner, luncheonette, etc.

eat·ing /éeting/ *adj.* **1** suitable for eating (*eating apple*). **2** used for eating (*eating room*).

eats /eets/ *n.pl. colloq.* food.

eau de co·logne /ṓdəkəlṓn/ *n.* an alcohol-based perfume of a kind made orig. at Cologne, Germany.

eaves /eevz/ *n.pl.* the underside of a projecting roof. ▷ ROOF

eaves·drop /éevzdrop/ *v.intr.* (**-dropped, -dropping**) listen secretly to a private conversation. □□ **eaves·drop·per** *n.*

ebb /eb/ *n. & v.* ● *n.* **1** the movement of the tide out to sea (also *attrib.: ebb tide*). **2** the process of declining or diminishing; the state of being in decline. ● *v.intr.* (often foll. by *away*) **1** (of tidewater) flow out to sea; recede; drain away. **2** decline; run low (*his life was ebbing away*). □ **at a low ebb** in a poor condition or state of decline. **on the ebb** in decline.

E·bon·ics /eebóniks/ *n.pl.* the English used by black Americans, regarded as a language in its own right.

eb·on·ite /ébənīt/ *n.* = VULCANITE.

eb·on·y /ébənee/ *n. & adj.* ● *n.* (*pl.* **-ies**) **1** a heavy, hard, dark wood used for furniture. **2** any of various trees of the genus *Diospyros* producing this. ● *adj.* **1** made of ebony. **2** black like ebony.

e-book /ée-bŏŏk/ *n.* ▲ an electronic version of a printed book which can be read on a personal computer, personal digital assistant, or handheld device.

ECHINODERM

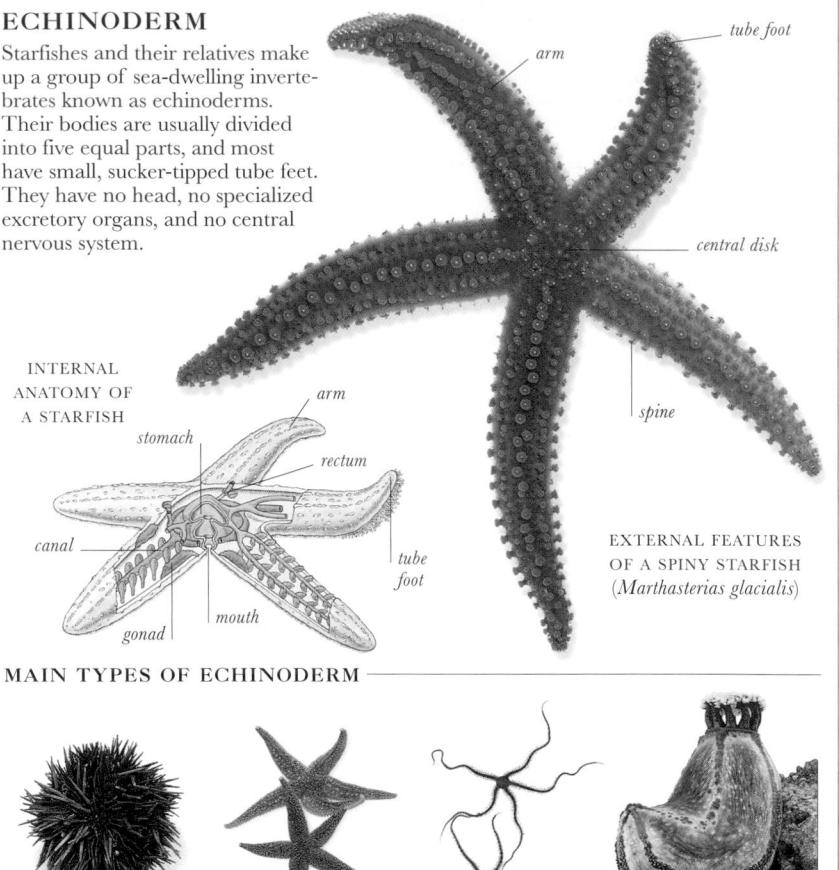

Starfishes and their relatives make up a group of sea-dwelling invertebrates known as echinoderms. Their bodies are usually divided into five equal parts, and most have small, sucker-tipped tube feet. They have no head, no specialized excretory organs, and no central nervous system.

INTERNAL ANATOMY OF A STARFISH

arm
stomach
rectum
canal
tube foot
gonad
mouth

tube foot
arm
central disk
spine

EXTERNAL FEATURES OF A SPINY STARFISH (*Marthasterias glacialis*)

MAIN TYPES OF ECHINODERM

ECHINOIDEA
(heart urchins, sand dollars, sea urchins)
▷ SEA URCHIN

ASTEROIDEA
(starfish)
▷ STARFISH

OPHIUROIDEA
(brittle stars)

HOLOTHUROIDEA
(sea cucumbers)
▷ SEA CUCUMBER

e·bul·lient /ibúlyənt, ibŏŏl-/ *adj.* exuberant; high-spirited. □□ **e·bul·lience** /-yəns/ *n.* **e·bul·lien·cy** *n.* **e·bul·lient·ly** *adv.*

EC *abbr.* **1** European Community. **2** executive committee.

ec·cen·tric /ikséntrik, ek-/ *adj. & n.* ● *adj.* **1** odd or capricious in behavior or appearance. **2 a** not placed or not having its axis, etc., placed centrally. **b** (often foll. by *to*) (of a circle) not concentric (to another). **c** (of an orbit) not circular. ▷ ORBIT.
● *n.* **1** an eccentric person.

E-BOOK ON A HANDHELD COMPUTER

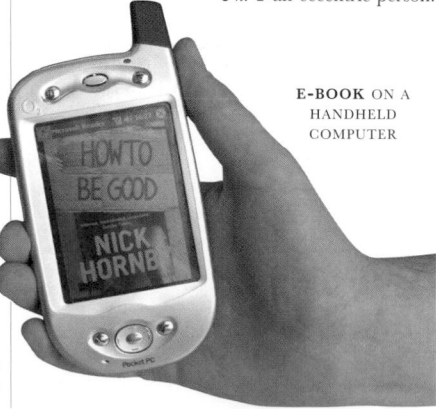

2 *Mech.* an eccentric contrivance for changing rotary into backward-and-forward motion. □□ **ec·cen·tri·cal·ly** *adv.* **ec·cen·tric·i·ty** /éksentrísitee/ *n.* (*pl.* **-ies**).

ec·cle·si·as·tic /ikleezeeástik/ *n. & adj.* ● *n.* a priest or clergyman. ● *adj.* = ECCLESIASTICAL. □□ **ec·cle·si·as·ti·cism** /-tisizəm/ *n.*

ec·cle·si·as·ti·cal /ikleezeeástikəl/ *adj.* of the church or the clergy. □□ **ec·cle·si·as·ti·cal·ly** *adv.*

ECG *abbr.* electrocardiogram.

ech·e·lon /éshəlon/ *n.* **1** a level or rank in an organization, in society, etc.; those occupying it (often in *pl.*: *the upper echelons*). **2** *Mil.* a formation of troops, ships, aircraft, etc., in parallel rows with the end of each row projecting further than the one in front (*in echelon*).

e·chid·na /ikídnə/ *n.* any of several egg-laying, insectivorous mammals native to Australia and New Guinea, with a covering of spines, and having a long snout and long claws.

e·chi·no·derm /ikínədərm/ *n.* ▲ any marine invertebrate of the phylum Echinodermata, usu. having a spiny skin, e.g., starfish and sea urchins.

e·chi·noid /ikínoyd/ *n.* a sea urchin. ▷ SEA URCHIN

ech·o /ékō/ *n. & v.* ● *n.* (*pl.* **-oes** or **-os**) **1 a** the repetition of a sound by the reflection of sound waves. **b** the secondary sound produced. **2 a** reflected radio or radar beam. ▷ RADAR. **3** a close imitation or repetition of something already done. **4** a person who slavishly repeats the words or opinions of another. **5** (often in *pl.*) circumstances or events reminiscent of or remotely connected with earlier ones. ● *v.* (**-oes, -oed**) **1** *intr.* **a** (of a place) resound with an echo. **b** (of a sound) be repeated; resound. **2** *tr.* repeat (a sound) by an echo. **3** *tr.* **a** repeat (another's words). **b** imitate the words, opinions, or actions of (a person). □□ **ech·o·er** *n.* **ech·o·less** *adj.*

ech·o·car·di·o·gram /ékōkáardeeəgram/ *n. Med.* a record produced by echocardiography.

ech·o·car·di·og·ra·phy /ékōkáardeeógrəfee/ *n. Med.* the use of ultrasound waves to investigate the action of the heart. □□ **ech·o·car·di·o·graph** /-deeəgraf/ *n.* **ech·o·car·di·o·gra·pher** *n.*

ech·o cham·ber *n.* an enclosure with sound-reflecting walls.

ech·o·gram /ékōgram/ *n.* a record made by an echo sounder.

ech·o·graph /ékōgraf/ *n.* a device for automatically recording echograms.

e·cho·ic /ekóik/ *adj. Phonet.* (of a word) imitating the sound it represents; onomatopoeic. □□ **e·cho·i·cal·ly** *adv.*

ech·o·lo·ca·tion /ékōlōkáyshən/ *n.* ▼ the location of objects by reflected sound.

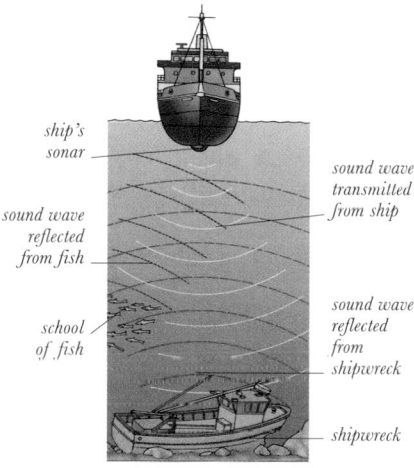

ECHOLOCATION: SHIP DETECTING UNDERWATER OBJECTS BY ECHOLOCATION

ech·o sound·er *n.* sounding apparatus for determining the depth of the sea beneath a ship by measuring the time taken for an echo to be received. □□ **echo-sound·ing** *n.*

ech·o·vi·rus /ékōvīrəs/ *n.* (also **ECHO vi·rus**) any of a group of enteroviruses sometimes causing mild meningitis, encephalitis, etc.

é·clair /aykláir/ *n.* a small, elongated light pastry filled with cream.

ec·lamp·si·a /iklámpseeə/ *n.* a condition involving convulsions leading to coma, occurring esp. in pregnant women. □□ **ec·lamp·tic** *adj.*

é·clat /aykláa/ *n.* **1** brilliant display; dazzling effect. **2** social distinction; conspicuous success.

ec·lec·tic /ikléktik/ *adj. & n.* ● *adj.* deriving ideas, tastes, style, etc., from various sources. ● *n.* an eclectic person. □□ **ec·lec·ti·cal·ly** *adv.* **ec·lec·ti·cism** /-tisizəm/ *n.*

e·clipse /iklíps/ *n. & v.* ● *n.* **1** ▲ the obscuring of the light from one celestial body by the passage of another between it and the observer. **2** a deprivation of light or the period of this. **3** a rapid or sudden loss of importance or prominence, esp. in relation to another or a newly arrived person or thing. ● *v.tr.* **1** (of a celestial body) obscure the light from or to (another). **2** deprive of prominence or importance; outshine; surpass. □□ **e·clips·er** *n.*

ECLIPSE

A lunar eclipse occurs when the Earth passes between the Sun and the full Moon, so that the Earth's shadow falls on the Moon. This darkens the Moon for the duration of the eclipse. A solar eclipse occurs when the new Moon passes directly between the Earth and the Sun. A solar eclipse is said to be total or partial depending on whether the observer is in the umbra or penumbra of the Moon's shadow.

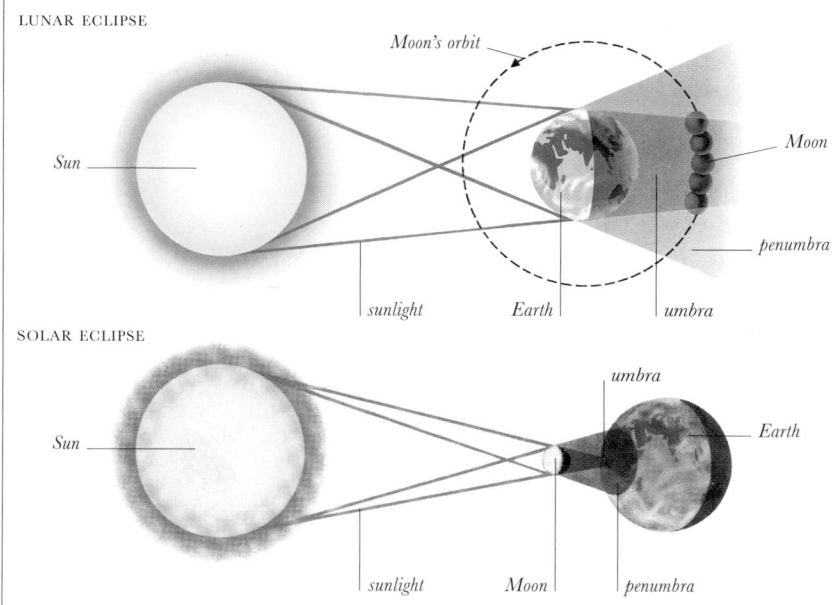

LUNAR ECLIPSE

Moon's orbit · *Sun* · *Moon* · *penumbra* · *sunlight* · *Earth* · *umbra*

SOLAR ECLIPSE

Sun · *umbra* · *Earth* · *sunlight* · *Moon* · *penumbra*

---

e·clip·tic /iklíptik/ *n. & adj.* ● *n.* the Sun's apparent path among the stars during the year. ● *adj.* of an eclipse or the ecliptic.

ec·logue /éklawg, -log/ *n.* a short poem, esp. a pastoral dialogue.

eco- /ékō, éekō/ *comb. form* ecology; ecological.

ecol. *abbr.* **1** ecological. **2** ecologist. **3** ecology.

E. co·li /eékōlī/ *n.* a species of anaerobic bacteria in the large intestine of humans and other animals; it is toxic in large quantities. ¶ Abbr. for **Esch·e·rich·i·a coli.**

e·col·o·gy /ikóləjee/ *n.* **1** the branch of biology dealing with the relations of organisms to one another and to their physical surroundings. **2** (in full **human ecology**) the study of the interaction of people with their environment. □□ **e·co·log·i·cal** /ékələjikəl, éekə-/ *adj.* **ec·o·log·i·cal·ly** *adv.* **e·col·o·gist** *n.*

e-com·merce /ee-cómərs/ *n.* commercial transactions conducted electronically on the Internet.

econ. *abbr.* **1** economics. **2** economy.

ec·o·nom·ic /ékənómik, éekə-/ *adj.* **1** of or relating to economics. **2** maintained for profit. **3** adequate to repay or recoup expenditure with some profit (*an economic rent*). **4** considered or studied with regard to economics (*economic geography*).

ec·o·nom·i·cal /ékənómikəl, éekə-/ *adj.* sparing in the use of resources. □□ **ec·o·nom·i·cal·ly** *adv.*

ec·o·nom·ics /ékənómiks, éekə-/ *n.pl.* (often treated as *sing.*) **1 a** the science of the production and distribution of wealth. **b** the application of this to a particular subject. **2** the condition of a country, etc., as regards material prosperity.

e·con·o·mist /ikónəmist/ *n.* **1** an expert in or student of economics. **2** a person who manages financial or economic matters.

e·con·o·mize /ikónəmīz/ *v.intr.* **1** be economical; make economies; reduce expenditure. **2** (foll. by *on*) use sparingly; spend less on. □□ **e·con·o·mi·za·tion** *n.* **e·con·o·miz·er** *n.*

e·con·o·my /ikónəmee/ *n.* (*pl.* **-ies**) **1 a** the wealth and resources of a community. **b** a particular kind of this (*a capitalist economy*). **c** the administration or condition of an economy. **2 a** the careful management of (esp. financial) resources; frugality. **b** (often in *pl.*) an instance of this. **3** sparing use. **4** (also **e·con·o·my class**) the cheapest class of air travel. **5** (*attrib.*) (also **e·con·o·my-size**) (of goods) consisting of a large quantity for a proportionally lower cost.

ec·o·sphere /ékōsfeer, éekə-/ *n.* the region of space including planets where conditions are such that living things can exist.

ec·o·sys·tem /ékōsistəm, éekō-/ *n.* a biological community of interacting organisms and their physical environment. ▷ SOIL.

ec·ru /ékrōō, áykrōō/ *n.* the color of unbleached linen; light fawn.

ec·sta·sy /ékstəsee/ *n.* (*pl.* **-ies**) **1** an overwhelming feeling of joy or rapture. **2** *sl.* methylene dioxymethamphetamine, a powerful stimulant and hallucinatory drug. □□ **ec·sta·tic** /ikstátik, ek-/ *adj.* **ec·stat·i·cal·ly** *adv.*

ECT *abbr.* electroconvulsive therapy.

ecto- /éktō/ *comb. form* outside.

ec·to·derm /éktōdərm/ *n. Biol.* the outermost layer of an animal embryo in early development.

ec·to·gen·e·sis /éktōjénisis/ *n. Biol.* the production of structures outside the organism. □□ **ec·to·ge·net·ic** /-jinétik/ *adj.* **ec·to·gen·ic** /-jénik/ *adj.* **ec·tog·e·nous** /éktójinəs/ *adj.*

ec·to·morph /éktəmawrf/ *n.* a person with a lean body build. (cf. ENDOMORPH, MESOMORPH). ▷ MESOMORPH. □□ **ec·to·mor·phic** *adj.* **ec·to·morph·y** *n.*

-ectomy /éktəmee/ *comb. form* denoting a surgical operation in which a part of the body is removed.

ec·top·ic /ektópik/ *adj. Med.* in an abnormal place or position.

ec·top·ic preg·nan·cy *n.* a pregnancy occurring outside the uterus.

E

E

EDENTATE

Although the word *edentate* means "without teeth," the only members of the scientific order Edentata that do not have teeth are the anteaters. Other edentates lack incisors and canines but have peglike molars and premolars.

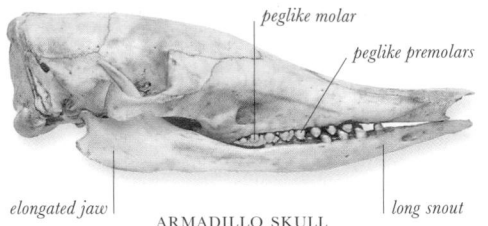

peglike molar
peglike premolars
elongated jaw
ARMADILLO SKULL
long snout

EXAMPLES OF EDENTATES

GIANT ARMADILLO
(*Priodontes maximus*)

SOUTHERN
TAMANDUA
(*Tamandua
tetradactyla*)

THREE-TOED
SLOTH
(*Bradypus
tridactylus*)

GIANT ANTEATER
(*Myrmecophaga
tridactyla*)

---

ec·to·plasm /éktəplazəm/ n. **1** the dense outer layer of the cytoplasm (cf. ENDOPLASM). **2** the supposed viscous substance exuding from the body of a spiritualistic medium during a trance. □□ **ec·to·plas·mic** adj.

ECU (also **e·cu** /ékyōō/) n. European currency unit.

ec·u·men·i·cal /ékyōōménikəl/ adj. **1** of or representing the whole Christian world. **2** seeking or promoting worldwide Christian unity. □□ **e·cu·men·i·cal·ism** n. (also **ec·u·me·nism** /ékyəminizəm, ikyōōmənizəm/) **ec·u·men·i·cal·ly** adv.

ec·ze·ma /éksimə, égzi-, igzée-/ n. inflammation of the skin, with itching and discharge from blisters. □□ **ec·zem·a·tous** /igzémətəs, egzém-, -zée-/ adj.

ed. abbr. **1** edited by. **2** edition. **3** editor. **4** educated; education.

-ed[1] /əd, id/ suffix forming adjectives: **1** from nouns, meaning 'having, wearing, affected by, etc.' (*talented*; *trousered*; *diseased*). **2** from phrases of adjective and noun (*good-humored*; *three-cornered*).

-ed[2] /əd, id/ suffix forming: **1** the past tense and past participle of weak verbs (*needed*; *risked*). **2** participial adjectives (*escaped prisoner*; *a pained look*).

E·dam /éedəm, éedam/ n. a round Dutch cheese, usu. pale yellow with a red rind.

e·daph·ic /idáfik/ adj. **1** Bot. of the soil. **2** Ecol. produced or influenced by the soil.

ed·dy /édee/ n. & v. ● n. (pl. **-ies**) **1** a circular movement of water causing a small whirlpool. **2** a movement of wind, fog, or smoke resembling this. ● v.tr. & intr. (**-ies**, **-ied**) whirl around in eddies.

e·del·weiss /áyd'lvīs/ n. an Alpine plant, *Leontopodium alpinum*, with woolly white bracts around the flower heads.

e·de·ma /ideémə/ n. a condition characterized by an excess of watery fluid collecting in the cavities or tissues of the body. Also called **dropsy**. □□ **e·dem·a·tose** /idémətōs, idée-/ adj. **e·dem·a·tous** adj.

E·den /éedən/ n. (also **Garden of Eden**) a place or state of great happiness; paradise (with reference to the abode of Adam and Eve in the biblical account of the Creation).

e·den·tate /idéntayt/ adj. & n. ● adj. having no or few teeth. ● n. ▲ any mammal, esp. of the order Edentata, having no or few teeth, e.g., an anteater or sloth.

edge /ej/ n. & v. ● n. **1** a boundary line or margin of an area or surface. **2** a narrow surface of a thin object. **3** the meeting line of two surfaces of a solid. **4 a** the sharpened side of the blade of a cutting instrument or weapon. **b** the sharpness of this (*the knife has lost its edge*). **5** the area close to a steep drop (*along the edge of the cliff*). **6** anything compared to an edge, esp. the crest of a ridge. **7 a** (as a personal attribute) incisiveness. **b** keenness; excitement (esp. as an element in an otherwise routine situation). **8** an advantage; superiority. ● v. **1** tr. & intr. (often foll. by *in*, *into*, *out*, etc.) move gradually or furtively toward an objective (*edged it into the corner*; *they all edged toward the door*). **2** tr. **a** provide with an edge or border. **b** form a border to. **c** trim the edge of. **3** tr. sharpen (a knife, tool, etc.). □ **have the edge on** (or **over**) have a slight advantage over. **on edge 1** tense and restless or irritable. **2** eager; excited. **on the edge of** almost involved in or affected by. **set a person's teeth on edge** (of a taste or sound) cause an unpleasant nervous sensation. **take the edge off** dull; weaken; make less effective or intense. □□ **edge·less** adj. **edg·er** n.

edge·wise /éjwiz/ adv. (also esp. Brit. **edgeways** /-wayz/) **1** with the edge uppermost or toward the viewer. **2** edge to edge. □ **get a word in edgewise** contribute to a conversation when the dominant speaker pauses briefly.

edg·ing /éjing/ n. **1** something forming an edge or border, e.g., a fringe or lace. **2** the process of making an edge.

edg·y /éjee/ adj. (**edgier**, **edgiest**) irritable; nervously anxious. □□ **edg·i·ly** adv. **edg·i·ness** n.

ed·i·ble /édibəl/ adj. & n. ● adj. fit or suitable to be eaten (cf. EATABLE). ● n. (in pl.) food. □□ **ed·i·bil·i·ty** n.

e·dict /éedikt/ n. an order proclaimed by authority. □□ **e·dic·tal** /eedíkt'l/ adj.

ed·i·fice /édifis/ n. **1** a building, esp. a large imposing one. **2** a complex organizational or conceptual structure.

ed·i·fy /édifī/ v.tr. (**-ies**, **-ied**) (of a circumstance, experience, etc.) instruct and improve morally or intellectually. □□ **ed·i·fi·ca·tion** /-fikáyshən/ n. **ed·i·fy·ing** adj. **ed·i·fy·ing·ly** adv.

ed·it /édit/ v. & n. ● v.tr. **1** a assemble, prepare, modify, or condense (written material, esp. the work of another or others) for publication. **b** prepare an edition of (an author's work). **2** be in overall charge of the content and arrangement of (a newspaper, journal, etc.). **3** take extracts from and collate (movies, tape recordings, etc.) to form a unified sequence. **4 a** prepare (data) for processing by a computer. **b** alter (a text entered in a word processor, etc.). **5 a** reword to correct, or to alter the emphasis. **b** (foll. by *out*) remove (part) from a text, etc. ● n. **1 a** a piece of editing. **b** an edited item. **2** a facility for editing.

e·di·tion /idíshən/ n. **1 a** one of the particular forms in which a literary work, etc., is published (*paperback edition*; *pocket edition*). **b** a copy of a book in a particular form (*a first edition*). **2** a whole number of copies of a book, newspaper, etc., issued at one time. **3** a particular version or instance of a broadcast, esp. of a regular program or feature. **4** a person or thing similar to or resembling another (*a miniature edition of her mother*).

ed·i·tor /éditər/ n. **1** a person who edits material for publication or broadcasting. **2** a person who directs the preparation of a newspaper or periodical, or a particular section of one (*sports editor*). **3** a person who selects or commissions material for publication. **4** a person who edits film, sound track, etc. **5** a computer program for modifying data. □□ **ed·i·tor·ship** n.

ed·i·to·ri·al /éditáwreeəl/ adj. & n. ● adj. **1** of or concerned with editing or editors. **2** written or approved by an editor. ● n. a newspaper article written by or on behalf of an editor, esp. one giving an opinion on a topical issue. □□ **ed·i·to·ri·al·ist** n. **ed·i·to·ri·al·ize** v.intr. **ed·i·to·ri·al·ly** adv.

EDP abbr. electronic data processing.

EDT abbr. eastern daylight time.

ed·u·cate /éjəkayt/ v.tr. (also absol.) **1** give intellectual, moral, and social instruction to (a pupil, esp. a child), esp. as a formal and prolonged process. **2** provide education for. **3** (often foll. by *in*, or *to* + infin.) train or instruct for a particular purpose. □□ **ed·u·ca·ble** /-kəbəl/ adj. **ed·u·ca·bil·i·ty** /-kəbílitee/ n. **ed·u·cat·a·ble** adj. **ed·u·ca·tive** adj. **ed·u·ca·tor** n.

ed·u·cat·ed /éjəkaytid/ adj. **1** having had an education, esp. to a higher level than average. **2** resulting from a (good) education (*an educated accent*). **3** based on experience or study (*an educated guess*).

ed·u·ca·tion /éjəkáyshən/ n. **1 a** the act or process of educating or being educated; systematic instruction. **b** the knowledge gained from this. **2** a particular kind of or stage in education (*a classical education*; *further education*). **3 a** development of character or mental powers. **b** a stage in or aspect of this (*travel will be an education for you*). □□ **ed·u·ca·tion·al** adj. **ed·u·ca·tion·al·ist** n. **ed·u·ca·tion·al·ly** adv. **ed·u·ca·tion·ist** n.

e·duce /idóos, idyóos/ v.tr. **1** bring out or develop from latent or potential existence; elicit. **2** infer; elicit a principle, number, etc., from data. □□ **e·duc·i·ble** adj. **e·duc·tion** /idúkshen/ n. **e·duc·tive** /idúktiv/ adj.

Ed·ward·i·an /edwáwrdeeən, -waár-/ adj. & n. ● adj. of, characteristic of, or associated with the reign of King Edward VII of England (1901–10). ● n. a person belonging to this period.

-ee /ee/ suffix forming nouns denoting: **1** the person affected by the verbal action (*addressee*; *employee*). **2** a person concerned with or described as (*absentee*; *refugee*). **3** an object of smaller size (*bootee*).

EEC abbr. European Economic Community.

EEG abbr. electroencephalogram.

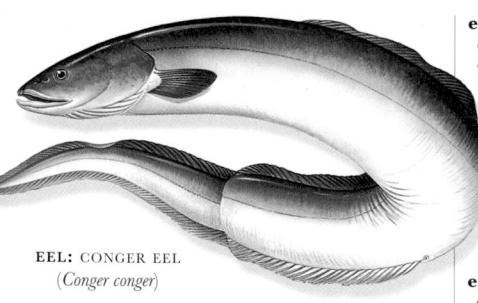

EEL: CONGER EEL
(Conger conger)

eel /eel/ *n.* **1** ▲ any of various snakelike fish, with slender body and poorly developed fins. ▷ FISH. **2** a slippery or evasive person or thing. □□ **eel·like** *adj.* **eel·y** *adj.*

eel·grass /éelgras/ *n.* **1** any marine plant of the genus *Zostera*, with long ribbonlike leaves. **2** any submerged freshwater plant of the genus *Vallisneria*.

eel·worm /éelwərm/ *n.* any of various small nematode worms infesting plant roots.

EEOC *abbr.* Equal Employment Opportunity Commission.

ee·rie /éeree/ *adj.* (**eerier**, **eeriest**) gloomy and strange; weird; frightening (*an eerie silence*). □□ **ee·ri·ly** *adv.* **ee·ri·ness** *n.*

ef- /if, ef/ *prefix* assim. form of EX-¹ 1 before *f*.

ef·face /ifáys/ *v.* **1** *tr.* rub or wipe out (a mark, etc.). **2** *tr.* (in abstract senses) obliterate; wipe out (*effaced it from his memory*). **3** *tr.* utterly surpass; eclipse (*success has effaced all previous attempts*). **4** *refl.* treat or regard oneself as unimportant (*self-effacing*). □□ **ef·face·ment** *n.*

ef·fect /ifékt/ *n. & v.* ● *n.* **1** the result or consequence of an action, etc.; the significance or implication of this. **2** efficacy (*had little effect*). **3** an impression produced on a spectator, hearer, etc. (*my words had no effect*). **4** (in *pl.*) property; luggage. **5** (in *pl.*) the lighting, sound, etc., used to accompany a play, movie, broadcast, etc. **6** *Physics* a physical phenomenon, usually named after its discoverer (*Doppler effect*). **7** the state of being operative. ● *v.tr.* **1** bring about; accomplish. **2** cause to exist or occur. □ **bring** (or **carry**) **into effect** accomplish. **for effect** to create an impression. **give effect to** make operative. **in effect** for practical purposes; in reality. **take effect** become operative. **to the effect that** the general substance or gist being. **to that effect** having that result or implication.

ef·fec·tive /iféktiv/ *adj. & n.* ● *adj.* **1** having a definite or desired effect. **2** powerful in effect; impressive. **3 a** actual; existing in fact rather than officially or theoretically (*took effective control in their absence*). **b** actually usable; realizable; equivalent in its effect (*effective money; effective demand*). **4** coming into operation (*effective as of May 1*). ● *n.* a soldier available for service. □□ **ef·fec·tive·ly** *adv.* **ef·fec·tive·ness** *n.*

ef·fec·tu·al /ifékchŏŏəl/ *adj.* **1** capable of producing the required result or effect; answering its purpose. **2** valid. □□ **ef·fec·tu·al·i·ty** /-chŏŏálitee/ *n.* **ef·fec·tu·al·ly** *adv.* **ef·fec·tu·al·ness** *n.*

ef·fem·i·nate /ifémimət/ *adj.* (of a man) feminine in appearance or manner; unmasculine. □□ **ef·fem·i·na·cy** *n.* **ef·fem·i·nate·ly** *adv.*

ef·fer·ent /éfərənt/ *adj. Physiol.* conducting outward (*efferent nerves; efferent vessels*). □□ **ef·fer·ence** /-rəns/ *n.*

ef·fer·vesce /éfərvés/ *v.intr.* **1** give off bubbles of gas; bubble. **2** (of a person) be lively. □□ **ef·fer·ves·cence** *n.* **ef·fer·ves·cen·cy** *n.* **ef·fer·ves·cent** *adj.*

ef·fete /iféet/ *adj.* **1 a** feeble and incapable. **b** effeminate. **2** worn out; exhausted of its essential quality or vitality. □□ **ef·fete·ness** *n.*

ef·fi·ca·cious /éfikáyshəs/ *adj.* (of a thing) producing or sure to produce the desired effect. □□ **ef·fi·ca·cious·ly** *adv.* **ef·fi·ca·cious·ness** *n.* **ef·fi·ca·cy** /éfikəsee/ *n.*

ef·fi·cien·cy /ifíshənsee/ *n.* (*pl.* **-ies**) **1** the state or quality of being efficient. **2** *Mech. & Physics* the ratio of useful work performed to the total energy expended or heat taken in.

ef·fi·cient /ifíshənt/ *adj.* **1** productive with minimum waste or effort. **2** (of a person) capable; acting effectively. □□ **ef·fi·cient·ly** *adv.*

ef·fi·gy /éfijee/ *n.* (*pl.* **-ies**) a sculpture or model of a person. □ **in effigy** in the form of a (usu. crude) representation of a person.

ef·flu·ence /éfloōəns/ *n.* **1** a flowing out (of light, electricity, etc.). **2** that which flows out.

ef·flu·ent /éfloōənt/ *adj. & n.* ● *adj.* flowing forth or out. ● *n.* **1** sewage or industrial waste discharged into a river, the sea, etc. **2** a stream or lake flowing from a larger body of water.

ef·flu·vi·um /iflóōveeəm/ *n.* (*pl.* **effluvia** /-veeə/) an unpleasant or noxious odor or exhaled substance affecting the lungs or the sense of smell, etc.

ef·flux /éfluks/ *n.* = EFFLUENCE. □□ **ef·flux·ion** /eflúkshən/ *n.*

ef·fort /éfərt/ *n.* **1** strenuous physical or mental exertion. **2** a vigorous or determined attempt. **3** *Mech.* a force exerted. ▷ LEVER. **4** *colloq.* the result of an attempt; something accomplished (*not bad for a first effort*). □□ **ef·fort·ful** *adj.*

ef·fort·less /éfərtlis/ *adj.* **1** seemingly without effort; natural; easy. **2** requiring no effort (*effortless contemplation*). □□ **ef·fort·less·ly** *adv.* **ef·fort·less·ness** *n.*

ef·fron·ter·y /ifrúntəree/ *n.* (*pl.* **-ies**) **1** shameless insolence; impudent audacity (esp. *have the effrontery to*). **2** an instance of this.

ef·ful·gent /ifúljənt/ *adj. literary* radiant; shining brilliantly. □□ **ef·ful·gence** /-jəns/ *n.* **ef·ful·gent·ly** *adv.*

ef·fuse *adj. & v.* ● *adj.* /ifyōōs/ *Bot.* (of an inflorescence, etc.) spreading loosely. ● *v.tr.* /ifyōōz/ **1** pour forth (liquid, light, etc.). **2** give out (ideas, etc.).

ef·fu·sion /ifyōōzhən/ *n.* **1** a copious outpouring. **2** usu. *derog.* an unrestrained flow of speech or writing.

ef·fu·sive /ifyōōsiv/ *adj.* gushing; demonstrative; exuberant (*effusive praise*). □□ **ef·fu·sive·ly** *adv.* **ef·fu·sive·ness** *n.*

EFL *abbr.* English as a foreign language.

EFTA /éftə/ *n.* European Free Trade Association.

e.g. *abbr.* for example.

e·gal·i·tar·i·an /igálitáireeən/ *adj. & n.* ● *adj.* **1** of or relating to the principle of equal rights and opportunities for all (*an egalitarian society*). **2** advocating this principle. ● *n.* a person who advocates or supports egalitarian principles. □□ **e·gal·i·tar·i·an·ism** *n.*

egg¹ /eg/ *n.* **1 a** ▼ the spheroidal reproductive body produced by females of animals such as birds, reptiles, fish, etc., enclosed in a protective layer and capable of developing into a new individual. **b** the egg of the domestic hen, used for food. **2** *Biol.* the female reproductive cell in animals and plants.

EGG

An egg develops from a single cell. After fertilization, it has the capacity to develop into a new individual. Development may take place inside the mother's body or outside, in which case the egg has a protective covering, such as a shell. The eggs of birds and reptiles contain enough yolk to sustain the embryo until it hatches. Pores in the shell allow the embryo to exchange oxygen and carbon dioxide with the atmosphere.

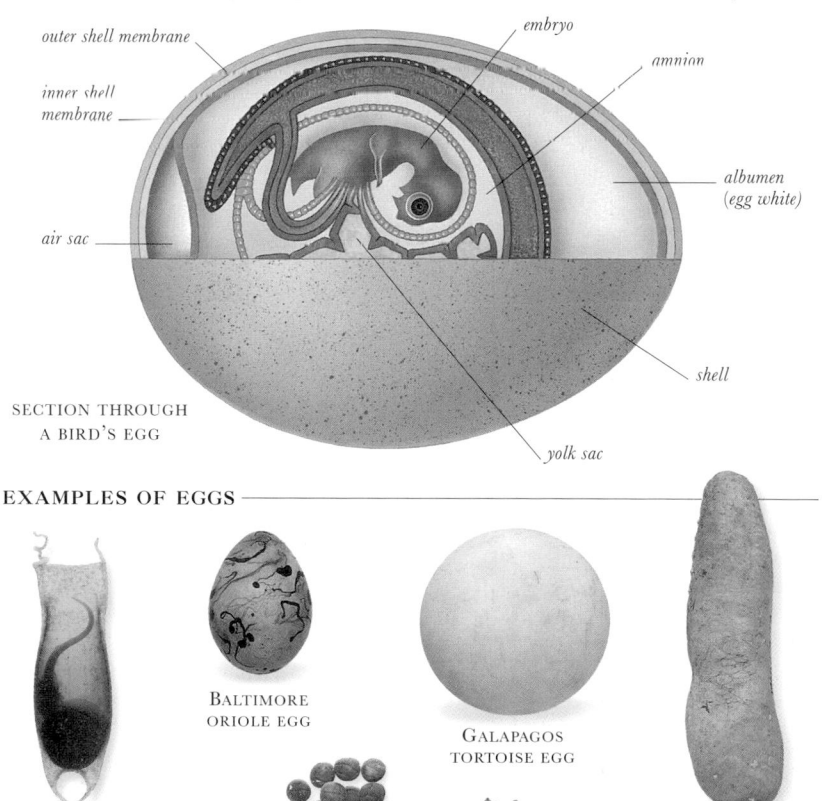

SECTION THROUGH A BIRD'S EGG

outer shell membrane — *inner shell membrane* — *air sac* — *embryo* — *amnion* — *albumen (egg white)* — *shell* — *yolk sac*

EXAMPLES OF EGGS

DOGFISH EGG (MERMAID'S PURSE)

BALTIMORE ORIOLE EGG

TOAD EGGS

GALAPAGOS TORTOISE EGG

LADYBUG EGGS

GROUND PYTHON EGG

E

E

3 *colloq.* a person or thing qualified in some way (*a tough egg*). □ **have** (or **put**) **all one's eggs in one basket** *colloq.* risk everything on a single venture. **with egg on one's face** *colloq.* made to look foolish. □□ **egg·less** *adj.* **egg·y** *adj.* (**eggier, eggiest**).

egg[2] /eg/ *v.tr.* (foll. by *on*) urge (*egged them on to do it*).

egg·cup /égkup/ *n.* a cup for holding a boiled egg.

egg·head /éghed/ *n. colloq.* an intellectual; an expert.

egg·nog /égnog/ *n.* a drink made from a mixture of eggs, cream, and flavorings, often with alcohol.

egg·plant /égplant/ *n.* **1** a tropical plant, *Solanum melongena*, having erect or spreading branches bearing purple or white egg-shaped fruit. ▷ VEGETABLE. **2** ● this fruit eaten as a vegetable. **3** the dark purple color of this fruit.

egg·shell /égshel/ *n. & adj.* ● *n.* **1** the shell of an egg. **2** anything very fragile. **3** a pale yellowish-white color. ● *adj.* **1** (of china) thin and fragile. **2** (of paint) with a slight gloss finish.

egg tim·er *n.* a device for timing the cooking of an egg.

egg white *n.* the white of an egg.

e·go /éegō/ *n.* (*pl.* **-os**) **1** *Metaphysics* a conscious thinking subject. **2** *Psychol.* the part of the mind that reacts to reality and has a sense of individuality. **3** self-esteem.

EGGPLANT

e·go·cen·tric /éegōséntrik, égō–/ *adj.* **1** centered in the ego. **2** self-centered; egoistic. □□ **e·go·cen·tri·cal·ly** *adv.* **e·go·cen·tric·i·ty** /-trísitee/ *n.*

e·go·ism /éegōizəm, égō–/ *n.* **1** an ethical theory that treats self-interest as the foundation of morality. **2** systematic selfishness. **3** self-opinionatedness. **4** = EGOTISM. □□ **e·go·ist** *n.* **e·go·is·tic** *adj.* **e·go·is·ti·cal** *adj.*

e·go·ma·ni·a /éegōmáyneeə, égō–/ *n.* morbid egotism. □□ **e·go·ma·ni·ac** *n.* **e·go·ma·ni·a·cal** /-mənîəkəl/ *adj.*

e·go·tism /éegōtizəm, égə–/ *n.* **1** the practice of talking about oneself. **2** an exaggerated opinion of oneself. **3** selfishness. □□ **e·go·tist** *n.* **e·go·tis·tic** *adj.* **e·go·tis·ti·cal** *adj.* **e·go·tis·ti·cal·ly** *adv.* **e·go·tize** *v.intr.*

e·go trip *n. colloq.* activity, etc., devoted entirely to one's own interests or feelings.

e·gre·gious /igréejəs/ *adj.* **1** outstandingly bad; shocking (*egregious folly; an egregious ass*). **2** *archaic* or *joc.* remarkable. □□ **e·gre·gious·ly** *adv.*

e·gress /éegres/ *n.* **1 a** a going out. **b** the right of going out. **2** an exit; a way out.

e·gret /éegrit/ *n.* any of various herons of the genus *Egretta* or *Bulbulcus*, usu. having long white feathers in the breeding season.

E·gyp·tian /ijípshən/ *adj. & n.* ● *adj.* **1** of or relating to Egypt in NE Africa. **2** of or for Egyptian antiquities (*Egyptian room*). ● *n.* **1** a native of ancient or modern Egypt; a national of the Arab Republic of Egypt. **2** the Hamitic language used in ancient Egypt until the 3rd c. AD. □□ **E·gyp·tian·ize** *v.tr.* **E·gyp·tian·i·za·tion** *n.*

E·gyp·tol·o·gy /éejiptóləjee/ *n.* the study of the language, history, and culture of ancient Egypt. □□ **E·gyp·tol·o·gist** *n.*

eh /ay/ *int. colloq.* **1** expressing inquiry or surprise. **2** inviting assent. **3** asking for something to be repeated or explained.

ei·der /ídər/ *n.* **1** (in full **eider duck**) any of various large northern ducks, esp. of the genus *Somateria*. ▷ DUCK. **2** = EIDERDOWN 1.

ei·der·down /ídərdown/ *n.* **1** small, soft feathers from the breast of the eider duck. **2** a quilt stuffed with down (orig. from the eider) or some other soft material, esp. as the upper layer of bedclothes.

eight /ayt/ *n. & adj.* ● *n.* **1** one more than seven, or two less than ten; the product of two units and four units. **2** a symbol for this (8, viii, VIII). **3** a figure resembling the form of 8. **4** a size, etc., denoted by eight. **5** an eight-oared rowing boat or its crew. **6** the time of eight o'clock (*is it eight yet?*). **7** a card with eight pips. ● *adj.* that amount to eight.

eight·een /áytéen/ *n. & adj.* ● *n.* **1** one more than seventeen, or eight more than ten; the product of two units and nine units. **2** a symbol for this (18, xviii, XVIII). **3** a size, etc., denoted by eighteen. **4** a set or team of eighteen individuals. ● *adj.* that amount to eighteen. □□ **eight·eenth** *adj. & n.*

eight·een-wheel·er *n.* a large tractor-trailer with eighteen wheels.

eight·fold /áytfōld/ *adj. & adv.* **1** eight times as much or as many. **2** consisting of eight parts. **3** amounting to eight.

eighth /ayt-th, ayth/ *n. & adj.* ● *n.* **1** the position in a sequence corresponding to the number 8 in the sequence 1–8. **2** something occupying this position. **3** one of eight equal parts of a thing. ● *adj.* that is the eighth. □□ **eighth·ly** *adv.*

eighth note *n. Mus.* a note having the time value of an eighth of a whole note and represented by a large dot with a hooked stem. Also called esp. *Brit.* QUAVER.

eight·some /áytsəm/ *n.* **1** (in full **eightsome reel**) a lively Scottish reel for eight dancers. **2** the music for this.

eight·y /áytee/ *n. & adj.* ● *n.* (*pl.* **-ies**) **1** the product of eight and ten. **2** a symbol for this (80, lxxx, LXXX). **3** (in *pl.*) the numbers from 80 to 89, esp. the years of a century or of a person's life. ● *adj.* that amount to eighty. □□ **eight·i·eth** *adj. & n.* **eight·y·fold** *adj. & adv.*

ein·stein·i·um /ínstíneeəm/ *n. Chem.* a transuranic radioactive metallic element produced artificially from plutonium. ¶ Symb.: **Es**.

ei·ther /éethər, îthər/ *adj., pron., adv., & conj.* ● *adj. & pron.* **1** one or the other of two (*either of you can go; you may have either book*). **2** each of two (*houses on either side of the road; either will do*). ● *adv. & conj.* **1** as one possibility (*is either black or white*). **2** as one choice or alternative; which way you will (*either come in or go out*). **3** (with *neg.* or *interrog.*) any more than the other (*I didn't like it either; if you do not go, I shall not either*). **b** moreover (*there is no time to lose, either*). □ **either or** *n.* an unavoidable choice between alternatives. **either way** in either case or event.

e·jac·u·late *v. & n.* ● *v.tr.* /ijákyəlayt/ (also *absol.*) **1** utter suddenly (words esp. of prayer or other emotion). **2** eject (fluid, etc., esp. semen) from the body. ● *n.* /ijákyələt/ semen that has been ejaculated from the body. □□ **e·jac·u·la·tion** /-láyshən/ *n.* **e·jac·u·la·tor** *n.* **e·jac·u·la·to·ry** /ijákyələtáwree/ *adj.*

e·ject /ijékt/ *v.tr.* **1 a** send or drive out precipitately or by force, esp. from a building or other property; compel to leave. **b** dismiss from employment or office. **2 a** eject (the pilot, etc.) to be propelled from an aircraft or spacecraft in an emergency. **b** (*absol.*) (of the pilot, etc.) be ejected in this way (*they both ejected at 1,000 feet*). **3** cause to be removed or drop out (e.g., a spent cartridge from a gun). **4** dispossess (a tenant, etc.) by legal process. **5** dart forth; emit. □□ **e·jec·tive** *adj.* **e·ject·ment** *n.*

e·jec·tion /ijékshən/ *n.* the act or an instance of ejecting; the process of being ejected.

e·jec·tion seat *n.* a device for the automatic ejection of the pilot, etc., of an aircraft or spacecraft in an emergency.

e·jec·tor /ijéktər/ *n.* a device for ejecting.

e·jec·tor seat *n.* = EJECTION SEAT.

eke /eek/ *v.tr.* □ **eke out 1** (foll. by *with, by*) supplement; make the best use of (defective means, etc.). **2** contrive to make (a livelihood) or support (an existence).

EKG *abbr.* electrocardiogram.

e·lab·o·rate *adj. & v.* ● *adj.* /ilábərət/ **1** carefully or minutely worked out. **2** highly developed or complicated. ● *v.* /ilábərayt/ **1 a** *tr.* work out or explain in detail. **b** *tr.* make more intricate or ornate. **c** *intr.* (often foll. by *on*) go into details (*I need not elaborate*). **2** *tr.* produce by labor. **3** *tr.* (of a

---

ELASMOBRANCH

The elasmobranchs form the main group of cartilaginous fish. They have five to seven prominent gill slits that open directly into the water, instead of being protected by a gill cover as in the bony fish. They have tough, usually gray skin covered in denticles (small toothlike scales). Elasmobranchs have numerous teeth that can be lost during feeding but are continually replaced (as often as once a week).

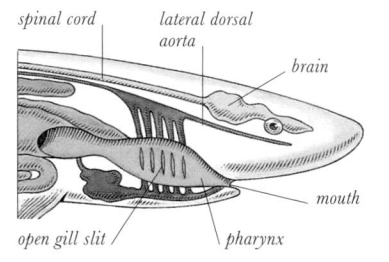

spinal cord   *lateral dorsal aorta*   *brain*   *mouth*   *open gill slit*   *pharynx*

INTERNAL ANATOMY OF A SHARK'S HEAD

MAIN TYPES OF ELASMOBRANCH

SHARKS
great white shark
(*Carcharodon carcharias*)

RAYS
thornback ray
(*Raja clavata*)

natural agency) produce (a substance, etc.) from its elements or sources. □□ **e·lab·o·rate·ly** *adv.* **e·lab·o·rate·ness** *n.* **e·lab·o·ra·tion** /-ráyshən/ *n.* **e·lab·o·ra·tive** *adj.* **e·lab·o·ra·tor** *n.*

é·lan /aylóN, aylón/ *n.* vivacity; dash.

e·land /éélənd/ *n.* any antelope of the genus *Taurotragus*, native to Africa, having spirally twisted horns, esp. the largest of living antelopes *T. derbianus*.

e·lapse /iláps/ *v.intr.* (of time) pass by.

e·las·mo·branch /ilázməbrangk/ *n.* (*pl.* **-branchs**) *Zool.* ◀ any cartilaginous fish of the subclass Chondrichthyes, e.g., sharks, skates, rays. ▷ CARTILAGINOUS FISH, RAY, SHARK

e·las·mo·sau·rus /ilázməsáwrəs/ *n.* ▼ a large extinct marine reptile with paddlelike limbs and tough crocodilelike skin.

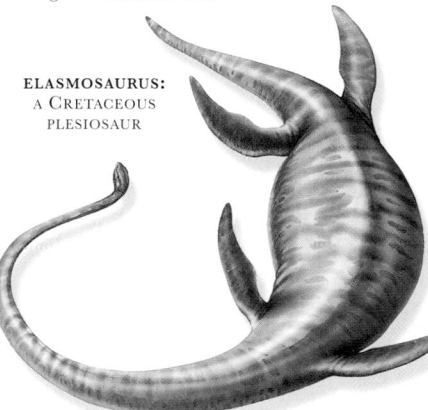

ELASMOSAURUS:
A CRETACEOUS
PLESIOSAUR

e·las·tic /ilástik/ *adj. & n.* ● *adj.* **1** able to resume its normal bulk or shape spontaneously after contraction, dilatation, or distortion. **2** springy. **3** (of a person or feelings) buoyant. **4** flexible; adaptable (*elastic conscience*). **5** *Econ.* (of demand) variable according to price. **6** *Physics* (of a collision) involving no decrease of kinetic energy. ● *n.* **1** elastic cord or fabric, usu. woven with strips of rubber. **2** (in full **elastic band**) = RUBBER BAND. □□ **e·las·ti·cal·ly** *adv.* **e·las·tic·i·ty** /ílastísitee, eelas-/ *n.* **e·las·ti·cize** /ilástisīz/ *v.tr.*

e·las·ti·cat·ed /ilástikaytid/ *adj.* (of a fabric) made elastic by weaving with rubber thread.

e·las·to·mer /ilástəmər/ *n.* a natural or synthetic rubber or rubberlike plastic. □□ **e·las·to·mer·ic** /-mérik/ *adj.*

e·late /iláyt/ *v.tr.* **1** (esp. as **elated** *adj.*) inspirit; stimulate. **2** make proud. □□ **e·lat·ed·ly** *adv.* **e·lat·ed·ness** *n.* **e·la·tion** /-láyshən/ *n.*

E layer /éélayər/ *n.* a layer of the ionosphere able to reflect medium-frequency radio waves.

el·bow /élbō/ *n. & v.* ● *n.* **1 a** the joint between the forearm and the upper arm. ▷ JOINT. **b** the part of the sleeve of a garment covering the elbow. **2** an elbow-shaped bend or corner; a short piece of piping bent through a right angle. ● *v.tr.* (foll. by *in, out, aside*, etc.) **1** thrust or jostle (a person or oneself). **2** make (one's way) by thrusting or jostling. **3** nudge or poke with the elbow. □ **at one's elbow** close at hand. **give a person the elbow** *colloq.* send a person away; dismiss or reject a person. **out at the elbows 1** (of a coat) worn out. **2** (of a person) ragged; poor.

el·bow grease *n. colloq.* vigorous polishing; hard work.

el·bow·room /élbōrōom/ *n.* plenty of room to move or work in.

eld·er[1] /éldər/ *adj. & n.* ● *attrib.adj.* (of two indicated persons, esp. when related) senior; of a greater age (*my elder brother*). ● *n.* (often prec. by *the*) **1** the older or more senior of two indicated (esp. related) persons (*which is the elder?; is my elder by ten years*). **2** (in *pl.*) **a** persons of greater age or seniority (*respect your elders*). **b** persons venerable because of age. **3** a person

advanced in life. **4** *hist.* a member of a senate or governing body. **5** an official in the early Christian, Presbyterian, or Mormon churches. □□ **eld·er·ship** *n.*

eld·er[2] /éldər/ *n.* any shrub or tree of the genus *Sambucus*, with white flowers and usu. blue-black or red berries.

el·der·ber·ry /éldərberee/ *n.* (*pl.* **-ies**) ▶ the berry of the elder, esp. common elder (*Sambucus nigra*) used for making jelly, wine, etc.

eld·er·ly /éldərlee/ *adj. & n.* ● *adj.* **1** somewhat old. **2** (of a person) past middle age. ● *n.* (*collect.*) (prec. by *the*) elderly people. □□ **eld·er·li·ness** *n.*

eld·er states·man *n.* an influential experienced person, esp. a politician, of advanced age.

eld·est /éldist/ *adj. & n.* ● *adj.* first-born or oldest surviving (member of a family, son, daughter, etc.). ● *n.* (often prec. by *the*) the eldest of three or more indicated (*who is the eldest?*).

El Do·ra·do /éldəráadō/ *n.* (*pl.* **-os**) **1** any imaginary country or city abounding in gold. **2** a place of great abundance.

el·dritch /éldrich/ *adj. Sc.* **1** weird. **2** hideous.

elec. *abbr.* **1** electric. **2** electrical. **3** electricity.

el·e·cam·pane /élikampáyn/ *n.* **1** a sunflowerlike plant, *Inula helenium*, with bitter aromatic leaves and roots. **2** an esp. candied confection flavored with this.

e·lect /ilékt/ *v. & adj.* ● *v.tr.* **1** (usu. foll. by *to* + infin.) choose (*the principles they elected to follow*). **2** choose (a person) by vote (*elected a new chairman*). **3** *Theol.* (of God) choose (persons) in preference to others for salvation. ● *adj.* **1** chosen. **2** select; choice. **3** *Theol.* chosen by God. **4** (after a noun designating office) chosen but not yet in office (*president elect*).

e·lec·tion /ilékshən/ *n.* **1** the process of electing or being elected. **2** the act or an instance of electing.

e·lec·tion·eer /ílékshənéer/ *v. & n.* ● *v.intr.* take part in an election campaign. ● *n.* a person who electioneers.

e·lec·tive /iléktiv/ *adj. & n.* ● *adj.* **1 a** (of an office or its holder) filled or appointed by election. **b** (of authority) derived from election. **2** (of a body) having the power to elect. **3** having a tendency to act on or be concerned with some things rather than others (*elective affinity*). **4** (of a course of study) chosen by the student; optional. **5** (of a surgical operation, etc.) optional; not urgently necessary. ● *n.* an elective course of study. □□ **e·lec·tive·ly** *adv.*

e·lec·tor /iléktər/ *n.* **1** a person who has the right of voting. **2** a member of the electoral college. □□ **e·lec·tor·ship** *n.*

e·lec·tor·al /iléktərəl/ *adj.* relating to or ranking as electors. □□ **e·lec·tor·al·ly** *adv.*

e·lec·tor·al col·lege *n.* **1** a body of persons representing each of the states of the US, who cast votes for the election of the president and vice president. **2** a body of electors.

e·lec·tor·ate /iléktərət/ *n.* a body of electors.

E·lec·tra com·plex /iléktrə/ *n. Psychol.* a daughter's subconscious sexual attraction to her father and hostility toward her mother, corresponding to the Oedipus complex in a son.

e·lec·tric /iléktrik/ *adj. & n.* ● *adj.* **1** of, worked by, or charged with electricity; producing or capable of generating electricity. ▷ CIRCUIT. **2** causing or charged with sudden and dramatic excitement (*the news had an electric effect; the atmosphere was electric*). ● *n.* **1** an electric light, vehicle, etc. **2** (in *pl.*) electrical equipment. □□ **e·lec·tri·cal·ly** *adv.*

e·lec·tri·cal /iléktrikəl/ *adj.* **1** of or concerned with or of the nature of electricity. **2** operating by electricity. **3** suddenly or dramatically exciting (*the effect was electrical*).

e·lec·tric blan·ket *n.* a blanket that can be heated electrically by an internal element.

e·lec·tric blue *n.* a steely or brilliant light blue.

e·lec·tric chair *n.* an electrified chair used for capital punishment.

e·lec·tric eel *n.* an eellike freshwater fish, *Electrophorus electricus*, native to S. America, that kills its prey by electric shock.

e·lec·tric eye *n. colloq.* a photoelectric cell operating a relay when the beam of light illuminating it is obscured.

e·lec·tri·cian /ilektríshən, éélek-/ *n.* a person who installs or maintains electrical equipment, esp. professionally.

e·lec·tric·i·ty /ilektrísitee, éélek-/ *n.* **1** a form of energy resulting from the existence of charged particles (electrons, protons, etc.), either statically as an accumulation of charge or dynamically as a current. **2** the branch of physics dealing with electricity. **3** a supply of electric current for heating, lighting, etc. **4** a state of heightened emotion; excitement; tension.

e·lec·tri·fy /iléktrifī/ *v.tr.* (**-ies**, **-ied**) **1** charge (a body) with electricity. **2** convert to the use of electric power. **3** cause dramatic or sudden excitement in. □□ **e·lec·tri·fi·ca·tion** /-fikáyshən/ *n.* **e·lec·tri·fi·er** *n.*

e·lec·tro /iléktrō/ *n. & v.* ● *n.* (*pl.* **-os**) **1** = ELECTROTYPE *n.* **2** = ELECTROPLATE *n.* ● *v.tr.* (**-oes**, **-oed**) *colloq.* **1** = ELECTROTYPE *v.* **2** = ELECTROPLATE *v.*

electro- /iléktrō/ *comb. form Electr.* of, relating to, or caused by electricity (*electrocute; electromagnet*).

e·lec·tro·car·di·o·gram /iléktrōkáardeeəgram/ *n.* a record of the heartbeat traced by an electrocardiograph.

e·lec·tro·car·di·o·graph /iléktrōkáardeeəgraf/ *n.* an instrument recording the electric currents generated by a person's heartbeat. □□ **e·lec·tro·car·di·o·graph·ic** *adj.* **e·lec·tro·car·di·og·ra·phy** /-deeógrəfee/ *n.*

e·lec·tro·con·vul·sive /iléktrōkənvúlsiv/ *adj.* (of a therapy) employing the use of the convulsive response to the application of electric shocks.

e·lec·tro·cute /iléktrəkyōōt/ *v.tr.* **1** kill by electricity (as a form of capital punishment). **2** cause death of by electric shock. □□ **e·lec·tro·cu·tion** /-kyōōshən/ *n.*

e·lec·trode /iléktrōd/ *n.* a conductor through which electricity enters or leaves an electrolyte, gas, vacuum, etc. ▷ BATTERY, ELECTROPLATE

e·lec·tro·dy·nam·ics /iléktrōdīnámiks/ *n.pl.* (usu. treated as *sing.*) the branch of mechanics concerned with electric current applied to motive forces. □□ **e·lec·tro·dy·nam·ic** *adj.*

e·lec·tro·en·ceph·a·lo·gram /iléktrōinséfələgram/ *n.* a record of the brain's activity traced by an electroencephalograph.

e·lec·tro·en·ceph·a·lo·graph /iléktrōinséfələgraf/ *n.* an instrument recording the electrical activity of the brain. □□ **e·lec·tro·en·ceph·a·log·ra·phy** /-lógrəfee/ *n.*

e·lec·trol·y·sis /ilektrólisis, éelek-/ *n.* **1** *Chem.* the decomposition of a substance by the application of an electric current. ▷ ELECTROPLATE. **2** *Med.* this process applied to the destruction of tumors, hair roots, etc. □□ **e·lec·tro·lyt·ic** /iléktrōlítik/ *adj.* **e·lec·tro·lyt·i·cal** *adj.* **e·lec·tro·lyt·i·cal·ly** *adv.*

e·lec·tro·lyte /iléktrəlīt/ *n.* **1** a substance that conducts electricity when molten or in solution, esp. in an electric cell or battery. ▷ BATTERY, ELECTROPLATE. **2** a solution of this.

e·lec·tro·lyze /iléktrəlīz/ *v.tr.* subject to or treat by electrolysis. □□ **e·lec·tro·lyz·er** *n.*

e·lec·tro·mag·net /iléktrōmágnit/ *n.* a soft metal core made into a magnet by the passage of electric current through a coil surrounding it. ▷ MRI, RECEIVER

e·lec·tro·mag·net·ic /iléktrōmágnétik/ *adj.* having both an electrical and a magnetic character or properties. □□ **e·lec·tro·mag·net·i·cal·ly** *adv.*

ELDERBERRY:
COMMON ELDER
(*Sambucus nigra*)

E

E

e·lec·tro·mag·ne·tic ra·di·a·tion ▼ a kind of radiation including visible light, radio waves, gamma rays, X rays, etc., in which electric and magnetic fields vary simultaneously.

e·lec·tro·mag·net·ism /iléktrōmágnitizəm/ *n.* **1** ▼ the magnetic forces produced by electricity. **2** the study of this.

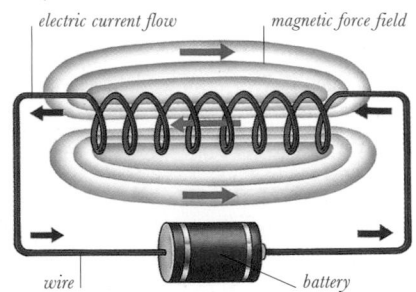

ELECTROMAGNETISM: DEMONSTRATION OF MAGNETISM PRODUCED BY ELECTRIC CURRENT

e·lec·tro·me·chan·i·cal /iléktrōmikánikəl/ *adj.* relating to the application of electricity to mechanical processes, devices, etc.

e·lec·trom·e·ter /ilektrómitər, éelek-/ *n.* an instrument for measuring electrical potential without drawing any current from the circuit. □□ **e·lec·tro·met·ric** /-métrik/ *adj.* **e·lec·trom·e·try** *n.*

e·lec·tro·mo·tive /iléktrōmótiv/ *adj.* producing or tending to produce an electric current.

e·lec·tron /iléktron/ *n.* a stable elementary particle with a charge of negative electricity, found in all atoms and acting as the primary carrier of electricity in solids. ▷ ATOM

e·lec·tron·ic /ilektrónik, éelek-/ *adj.* **1 a** produced by or involving the flow of electrons. **b** of or relating to electrons or electronics. **2** (of a device) using electronic components. **3 a** (of music) produced by electronic means, and usu. recorded on tape. **b** (of a musical instrument) producing sounds by electronic means. □□ **e·lec·tron·i·cal·ly** *adv.*

e·lec·tron·i·ca /ilektrónikə/ *n.* **1** a popular style of music deriving from techno and rave and having a more ambient, esoteric, or cerebral quality. **2** electronic devices or technology considered collectively.

e·lec·tron·ic mail *n.* messages distributed by electronic means, esp. from one computer system to one or more recipients: also called E-MAIL.

e·lec·tron·ics /ilektróniks, éelek-/ *n.pl.* (usu. treated as *sing.*) **1** a branch of physics and technology concerned with the behavior and movement of electrons in a vacuum, gas, semiconductor, etc. **2** the circuits used in this.

e·lec·tron mi·cro·scope *n.* a microscope with high magnification and resolution, employing electron beams in place of light and using electron lenses.

e·lec·tron·volt /iléktronvōlt/ *n.* a unit of energy equal to the work done on an electron in accelerating it through a potential difference of one volt. ¶ Abbr.: **eV**.

e·lec·tro·pho·re·sis /iléktrōfəreésis/ *n. Physics & Chem.* the movement of colloidal particles in a fluid under the influence of an electric field. □□ **e·lec·tro·pho·ret·ic** /-férétik/ *adj.*

e·lec·tro·plate /iléktrəplayt/ *v. & n.* ● *v.tr.* ▶ coat by electrolytic deposition with chromium, silver, etc. ● *n.* electroplated articles. □□ **e·lec·tro·plat·er** *n.*

e·lec·tro·scope /iléktrəskōp/ *n.* an instrument for detecting and measuring electricity, esp. as an indication of the ionization of air by radioactivity. ▷ STATIC ELECTRICITY. □□ **e·lec·tro·scop·ic** /-skópik/ *adj.*

e·lec·tro·shock /iléktrōshok/ *attrib.adj.* (of medical treatment) by means of electric shocks.

e·lec·tro·stat·ic /iléktrōstátik/ *adj.* of or relating to stationary electric charges or electrostatics.

e·lec·tro·stat·ics /iléktrōstátiks/ *n.pl.* (treated as *sing.*) the study of stationary electric charges or fields as opposed to electric currents.

e·lec·tro·tech·nol·o·gy /iléktrōteknóləjee/ *n.* the science of the application of electricity in technology. □□ **e·lec·tro·tech·nic** /-téknik/ *adj.* **e·lec·tro·tech·ni·cal** *adj.* **e·lec·tro·tech·nics** *n.*

e·lec·tro·ther·a·py /iléktrōthérəpee/ *n.* the treatment of diseases by the use of electricity. □□ **e·lec·tro·thera·peu·tic** /-pyōótik/ *adj.* **e·lec·tro·ther·a·peu·ti·cal** *adj.* **e·lec·tro·ther·a·pist** *n.*

e·lec·tro·ther·mal /iléktrōthɔ́rməl/ *adj.* relating to heat electrically derived.

el·e·gant /éligənt/ *adj.* **1** graceful in appearance or manner. **2** tasteful; refined. **3** (of a mode of life, etc.) of refined luxury. **4** ingeniously simple and pleasing. **5** excellent. □□ **el·e·gance** /-gəns/ *n.* **el·e·gant·ly** *adv.*

el·e·gi·ac /élijíək, iléejeeak/ *adj.* **1** (of a meter) used for elegies. **2** mournful. □□ **el·e·gi·a·cal·ly** *adv.*

el·e·gize /élijīz/ *v.* **1** *intr.* (often foll. by *upon*) write an elegy. **2** *intr.* write in a mournful strain. **3** *tr.* write an elegy upon. □□ **el·e·gist** *n.*

el·e·gy /élijee/ *n.* (*pl.* **-ies**) **1** a song of lament, esp. for the dead. **2** a poem in elegiac meter.

el·e·ment /élimənt/ *n.* **1** a component part or group; a contributing factor or thing. **2** *Chem. & Physics* any of the hundred or so substances that cannot be resolved by chemical means into simpler substances. **3 a** any of the four substances (earth, water, air, and fire) in ancient and medieval philosophy. **b** any of these as a being's natural abode or environment. **c** a person's appropriate or preferred sphere of operation. **4** *Electr.* a resistance wire that heats up in an electric heater, cooker, etc.; an electrode. **5** (in *pl.*) atmospheric agencies, esp. wind and storm. **6** (in *pl.*) the rudiments of learning or of

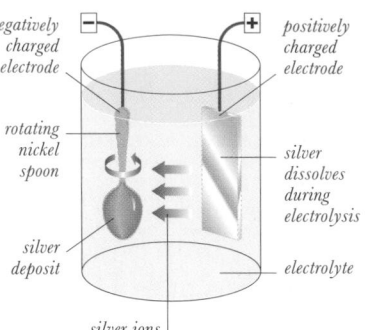

ELECTROPLATE: ELECTROPLATING A SPOON WITH SILVER

a branch of knowledge. **7** (in *pl.*) the bread and wine of the Eucharist. **8** *Math. & Logic* an entity that is a single member of a set. □ **in** (or **out of**) **one's element** in (or out of) one's accustomed or preferred surroundings.

el·e·men·tal /éliment'l/ *adj. & n.* ● *adj.* **1** of the four elements. **2** of the powers of nature (*elemental worship*). **3** comparable to a force of nature (*elemental grandeur*). **4** uncompounded (*elemental oxygen*). **5** essential. ● *n.* an entity or force thought to be physically manifested by occult means. □□ **el·e·men·tal·ism** *n.* (in senses 1, 2).

el·e·men·ta·ry /éliméntəree, -tree/ *adj.* **1 a** dealing with or arising from the simplest facts of a subject; rudimentary; introductory. **b** simple. **2** *Chem.* not decomposable.

el·e·men·ta·ry school *n.* a school in which elementary subjects are taught to young children.

el·e·phant /élifənt/ *n.* (*pl.* same or **elephants**) ▶ the largest living land animal, of which three species survive, the African (*Loxodonta africana*), the African Forest (*Loxodonta cyclotis*), and the Indian (*Elephas maximus*), all with a trunk and long curved ivory tusks. □□ **el·e·phan·toid** /-fantóyd/ *adj.*

el·e·phan·ti·a·sis /élifəntíəsis/ *n.* gross enlargement of the body, due to lymphatic obstruction.

el·e·phan·tine /élifánteen, -tīn, éləfən-/ *adj.* **1** of elephants. **2 a** huge. **b** clumsy; unwieldy.

el·e·phant seal *n.* any large seal of the genus *Mirounga*, the male of which has a proboscis.

el·e·vate /élivayt/ *v.tr.* **1** bring to a higher position. **2** raise; lift. **3** raise the axis of (a gun). **4** raise (a railroad, etc.) above ground level. **5** exalt in rank, etc. **6** (usu. as **elevated** *adj.*) **a** raise the spirits of; elate. **b** raise morally or intellectually (*elevated style*).

el·e·va·tion /éliváyshən/ *n.* **1 a** the process of elevating or being elevated. **b** the angle with the horizontal, esp. of a gun or of the direction of a heavenly body. **c** the height above a given level, esp. sea level. **d** a raised area; a swelling on the skin. **2 a** a drawing or diagram made by projection on a vertical plane (cf. PLAN). **b** a flat drawing of the front, side, or back of a house, etc. **3** *Ballet* **a** the capacity of a dancer to attain height in springing movements. **b** the action of tightening the muscles and uplifting the body. □□ **el·e·va·tion·al** *adj.* (in sense 2).

el·e·va·tor /élivaytər/ *n.* **1** a hoisting machine. **2** *Aeron.* the movable part of a tailplane for changing the pitch of an aircraft. ▷ AIRCRAFT. **3 a** a platform or compartment housed in a shaft for raising and lowering persons or things to different floors of a building or different levels of a mine, etc. **b** a place for lifting and storing quantities of grain. **4** that which elevates, esp. a muscle that raises a limb.

ELECTROMAGNETIC RADIATION

Electromagnetic radiation is a form of energy that travels through space and matter. There are many types of radiation, all of which are identical except for their wavelengths and energy. Radio waves, for example, have long wavelengths and low energy, while X rays have shorter wavelengths and higher energy.

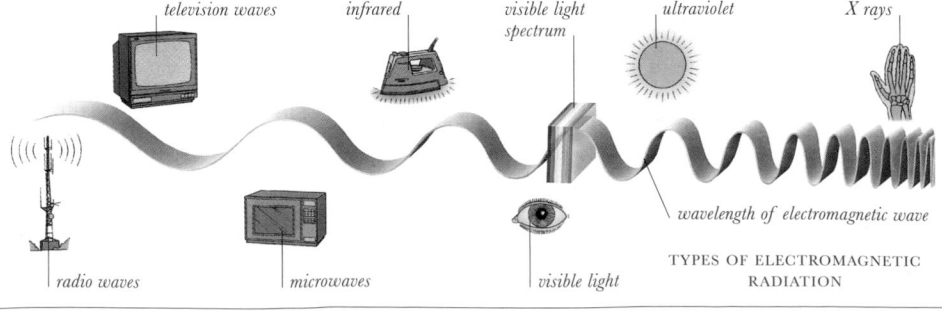

TYPES OF ELECTROMAGNETIC RADIATION

ELEPHANT

The Indian and African elephants are two of the three surviving species of the order Proboscidea (meaning animals with a proboscis or trunk). Elephants are herbivorous, highly intelligent, and extremely social, living in matriarchal herds.

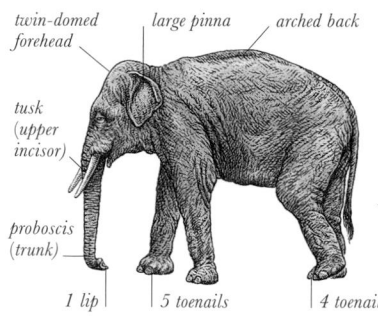

twin-domed forehead — large pinna — arched back

tusk (upper incisor)

proboscis (trunk)

1 lip   5 toenails   4 toenails

INDIAN ELEPHANT (*Elephas maximus*)

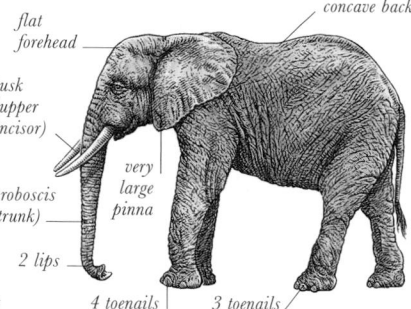

flat forehead — concave back

tusk (upper incisor)

very large pinna

proboscis (trunk)

2 lips

4 toenails   3 toenails

AFRICAN ELEPHANT (*Loxodonta africana*)

E

e·lev·en /ilévən/ *n. & adj.* ● *n.* **1** one more than ten; the sum of six units and five units. **2** a symbol for this (11, xi, XI). **3** a size, etc., denoted by eleven. **4** a set or team of eleven individuals. **5** the time of eleven o'clock. ● *adj.* that amount to eleven.

e·lev·en·fold /ilévənfōld/ *adj. & adv.* **1** eleven times as much or as many. **2** consisting of eleven parts.

e·lev·enth /ilévənth/ *n. & adj.* ● *n.* **1** the position in a sequence corresponding to the number 11 in the sequence 1–11. **2** something occupying this position. **3** one of eleven equal parts of a thing. **4** *Mus.* **a** an interval or chord spanning an octave and a third in the diatonic scale. **b** a note separated from another by this interval. ● *adj.* that is the eleventh.

e·lev·enth hour *n.* the last possible moment.

elf /elf/ *n.* (*pl.* **elves** /elvz/) **1** a mythological being, esp. one that is small and mischievous. **2** a sprite or little creature. □□ **elf·ish** *adj.* **elv·ish** *adj.*

elf·in /élfin/ *adj.* of elves; elflike; tiny; dainty.

elf·lock /élflok/ *n.* (usu. in *pl.*) a tangled mass of hair.

e·lic·it /ilísit/ *v.tr.* **1** draw out; evoke (an admission, response, etc.). **2** draw forth (what is latent). □□ **e·lic·i·ta·tion** *n.* **e·lic·i·tor** *n.*

e·lide /ilíd/ *v.tr.* omit (a vowel or syllable) by elision.

el·i·gi·ble /élijibəl/ *adj.* **1** (often foll. by *for*) fit or entitled to be chosen (*eligible for a rebate*). **2** desirable or suitable, esp. as a partner in marriage. □□ **el·i·gi·bil·i·ty** *n.*

e·lim·i·nate /ilíminayt/ *v.tr.* **1 a** remove; get rid of. **b** kill; murder. **2** exclude from consideration; ignore as irrelevant. **3** exclude from further participation in a competition, etc., on defeat. □□ **e·lim·i·na·ble** /-nəbəl/ *adj.* **e·lim·i·na·tion** /-náyshən/ *n.* **e·lim·i·na·tor** *n.* **e·lim·i·na·to·ry** /-nətáwree/ *adj.*

e·li·sion /ilízhən/ *n.* **1** the omission of a vowel or syllable in pronouncing (as in *I'm, let's, e'en*). **2** the omission of a passage in a book, etc.

e·lite /ayléet, əléet/ *n. & adj.* ● *n.* **1** (prec. by *the*) the best of a group. **2** a select group or class. ● *adj.* of or belonging to an elite; exclusive.

e·lit·ism /ayléetizəm, əleet-/ *n.* **1** advocacy of or reliance on leadership or dominance by a select group. **2** a sense of belonging to an elite. □□ **e·lit·ist** *n. & adj.*

e·lix·ir /iliksər/ *n.* *Alchemy* **a** a preparation supposedly able to change metals into gold. **b** (in full **elixir of life**) a preparation supposedly able to prolong life indefinitely. **c** a supposed remedy for all ills. **2** *Pharm.* an aromatic solution used as a medicine or flavoring.

E·liz·a·be·than /ilízəbéethən/ *adj. & n.* ● *adj.* of the time of England's Queen Elizabeth I (1558–1603) or of Queen Elizabeth II (1952–). ● *n.* a person of the time of Queen Elizabeth I or II.

elk /elk/ *n.* (*pl.* same or **elks**) ◀ **1** a large deer, *Alces alces*, of N. Europe and Asia; a moose. **2** a wapiti.

e·llipse /ilíps/ *n.* ▼ a regular oval, traced by a point moving in a plane so that the sum of its distances from two other points is constant, or resulting when a cone is cut by a plane that does not intersect the base and makes a smaller angle with the base than the side of the cone makes (cf. HYPERBOLA).

el·lip·sis /ilípsis/ *n.* (*pl.* **ellipses** /-seez/) **1** the omission from a sentence of words needed to complete the construction or sense. **2** the omission of a sentence at the end of a paragraph. **3** a set of three dots, etc., indicating an omission.

el·lip·soid /ilípsoyd/ *n.* a solid of which all the plane sections normal to one axis are circles and all the other plane sections are ellipses. □□ **el·lip·soi·dal** /-sóyd'l/ *adj.*

el·lip·tic /ilíptik/ *adj.* (also **el·lip·ti·cal**) of, relating to, or having the form of an ellipse or ellipsis. □□ **el·lip·ti·cal·ly** *adv.* **el·lip·tic·i·ty** /éliptísitee/ *n.*

elm /elm/ *n.* **1** ▶ any tree of the genus *Ulmus*, esp. *U. procera* with rough serrated leaves. **2** (in full **elmwood**) the wood of the elm. □□ **elm·y** *adj.*

El Ni·ño /el néenyō/ *n.* an irregularly occurring and complex cycle of climatic changes affecting the Pacific region.

el·o·cu·tion /éləkyóoshən/ *n.* **1** the art of clear and expressive speech, esp. of distinct pronunciation and articulation. **2** a particular style of speaking. □□ **el·o·cu·tion·ar·y** *adj.* **el·o·cu·tion·ist** *n.*

e·lon·gate /iláwnggayt, -long-/ *tr.* lengthen; prolong. □□ **e·lon·ga·tion** /ilawnggáyshən, ilong-, éelawng-, éelong-/ *n.*

ELK
(*Alces alces*)

serrated leaf

ELM
(*Ulmus × hollandica*)

e·lon·gat·ed *adj.* **1** long in relation to its width. **2** that has been made longer.

e·lope /ilṓp/ *v.intr.* **1** run away to marry secretly, esp. without parental consent. **2** run away with a lover. □□ **e·lope·ment** *n.*

el·o·quence /éləkwəns/ *n.* **1** fluent and effective use of language. **2** rhetoric.

el·o·quent /éləkwənt/ *adj.* **1** possessing or showing eloquence. **2** (often foll. by *of*) clearly expressive or indicative. □□ **el·o·quent·ly** *adv.*

else /els/ *adv.* **1** (prec. by indef. or interrog. pron.) besides; in addition (*someone else; nowhere else; who else*). **2** instead; other; different (*what else could I say?; he did not love her, but someone else*). **3** otherwise; if not (*run, (or) else you will be late*).

else·where /éls-hwair, -wáir/ *adv.* in or to some other place.

e·lu·ci·date /ilōōsidáyt/ *v.tr.* throw light on; explain. □□ **e·lu·ci·da·tion** /-dáyshən/ *n.* **e·lu·ci·da·tive** *adj.* **e·lu·ci·da·to·ry** *adj.*

e·lude /ilōōd/ *v.tr.* **1** escape adroitly from (a danger, difficulty, pursuer, etc.); dodge. **2** avoid compliance with (a law, request, etc.) or fulfillment of (an obligation). **3** (of a fact, solution, etc.) escape from or baffle (a person's memory or understanding). □□ **e·lu·sion** /ilōōzhən/ *n.* **e·lu·so·ry** /-lōōsəree/ *adj.*

e·lu·sive /ilōōsiv/ *adj.* **1** difficult to find or catch; tending to elude. **2** difficult to remember or recall. **3** (of an answer, etc.) avoiding the point raised; seeking to elude. □□ **e·lu·sive·ly** *adv.* **e·lu·sive·ness** *n.*

el·ver /élvər/ *n.* a young eel.

elves *pl.* of ELF.

elv·ish see ELF.

E·ly·si·um /ilízeeəm, ilízh-/ *n.* **1** (also **E·ly·sian fields**) (in Greek mythology) the abode of the blessed after death. **2** a place or state of ideal happiness. □□ **e·ly·si·an** or **E·ly·sian** *adj.*

el·y·tron /élitron/ *n.* (*pl.* **elytra** /-trə/) the outer hard, usu. brightly colored wing case of a coleopterous insect. ▷ BEETLE

em /em/ *n.* *Printing* **1** a unit for measuring the amount of printed matter in a line, usually equal to the nominal width of capital M. **2** a unit of measurement equal to 12 points.

'em /əm/ *pron. colloq.* them (*let 'em all come*).

e·ma·ci·ate /imáysheeayt/ *v.tr.* (esp. as **emaciated** *adj.*) make abnormally thin or feeble. □□ **e·ma·ci·a·tion** /-áyshən/ *n.*

e·mail /éemayl/ *n.* (also **e-mail**) = ELECTRONIC MAIL.

em·a·nate /émənayt/ *v.* **1** *intr.* (usu. foll. by *from*) (of an idea, rumor, etc.) issue; originate (from a source). **2** *intr.* (usu. foll. by *from*) (of gas, light, etc.) proceed; issue. **3** *tr.* emit; send forth.

em·a·na·tion /émənáyshən/ *n.* **1** the act or process of emanating. **2** something that emanates from a source (esp. of virtues, qualities, etc.). □□ **em·a·na·tive** *adj.*

e·man·ci·pate /imánsipayt/ *v.tr.* **1** free from restraint, esp. legal, social, or political. **2** (usu. as **emancipated** *adj.*) cause to be less inhibited by moral or social convention. **3** free from slavery. □□ **e·man·ci·pa·tion** /-páyshən/ *n.* **e·man·ci·pa·tor** *n.* **e·man·ci·pa·to·ry** *adj.*

e·mas·cu·late *v. & adj.* ● *v.tr.* /imáskyəlayt/ **1** deprive of force or vigor; make feeble or ineffective. **2** castrate. ● *adj.* /imáskyələt/ **1** deprived of force or vigor. **2** castrated. **3** effeminate. □□ **e·mas·cu·la·tion** /-láyshən/ *n.* **e·mas·cu·la·to·ry** /-lətawree/ *adj.*

em·balm /embáam, im-/ *v.tr.* **1** preserve (a corpse) from decay orig. with spices, now by means of arterial injection. **2** preserve from oblivion. □□ **em·balm·er** *n.* **em·balm·ment** *n.*

ellipse

cone

base

ELLIPSE

em·bank /embángk, im-/ *v.tr.* shut in or confine (a river, etc.) with an artificial bank.

em·bank·ment /embángkmənt, im-/ *n.* an earth or stone bank for keeping back water, or for carrying a road or railroad.

em·bar·go /embáargō/ *n. & v.* ● *n.* (*pl.* **-oes**) **1** an order of a government forbidding foreign ships to enter, or any ships to leave, its ports. **2** an official suspension of commerce or other activity (*be under an embargo*). **3** an impediment. ● *v.tr.* (**-oes**, **-oed**) **1** place (ships, trade, etc.) under embargo. **2** seize (a ship, goods) for government service.

em·bark /embáark, im-/ *v.* **1** *tr. & intr.* (often foll. by *for*) put or go on board a ship or aircraft (to a destination). **2** *intr.* (foll. by *on, upon*) engage in an activity or undertaking. □□ **em·bar·ka·tion** *n.* (in sense 1).

em·bar·rass /embárəs, im-/ *v.tr.* **1 a** cause (a person) to feel awkward or self-conscious or ashamed. **b** (as **embarrassed** *adj.*) having or expressing a feeling of awkwardness or self-consciousness. **2** (as **embarrassed** *adj.*) encumbered with debts. **3** hamper; impede. □□ **em·bar·rass·ed·ly** *adv.* **em·bar·rass·ing** *adj.* **em·bar·rass·ing·ly** *adv.* **em·bar·rass·ment** *n.*

em·bas·sy /émbəsee/ *n.* (*pl.* **-ies**) **1 a** the residence or offices of an ambassador. **b** the ambassador and staff attached to an embassy. **2** a deputation or mission to a foreign country.

em·bat·tle /embát'l, im-/ *v.tr.* **1 a** set (an army, etc.) in battle array. **b** fortify against attack. **2** provide (a building or wall) with battlements. **3** (as **embat·tled** *adj.*) **a** prepared or arrayed for battle. **b** involved in a conflict or difficult undertaking.

em·bed /embéd, im-/ *v.tr.* (also **imbed**) (**-bedded**, **-bedding**) **1** (esp. as **embedded** *adj.*) fix firmly in a surrounding mass (*embedded in concrete*). **2** (of a mass) surround so as to fix firmly. **3** place in or as in a bed. □□ **em·bed·ment** *n.*

em·bel·lish /embélish, im-/ *v.tr.* **1** beautify; adorn. **2** add interest to (a narrative) with fictitious additions. □□ **em·bel·lish·er** *n.* **em·bel·lish·ment** *n.*

em·ber /émbər/ *n.* **1** (usu. in *pl.*) a small piece of glowing coal or wood in a dying fire. **2** an almost extinct residue of a past activity, feeling, etc.

em·ber day /émbər/ *n.pl.* any of the days in the quarterly three-day periods traditionally reserved for fasting and prayer in the Christian Church, now associated with ordinations.

em·bez·zle /embézəl, im-/ *v.tr.* (also *absol.*) divert (money, etc.) fraudulently to one's own use. □□ **em·bez·zle·ment** *n.* **em·bez·zler** *n.*

em·bit·ter /embítər, im-/ *v.tr.* **1** arouse bitter feelings in (a person). **2** make more bitter or painful. **3** render (a person or feelings) hostile. □□ **em·bit·ter·ment** *n.*

em·bla·zon /embláyzən, im-/ *v.tr.* **1 a** portray conspicuously, as on a heraldic shield. **b** adorn (a shield) with heraldic devices. **2** adorn brightly and conspicuously. **3** celebrate; extol. □□ **em·bla·zon·ment** *n.*

em·blem /émbləm/ *n.* **1** a symbol or representation typifying or identifying an institution, quality, etc. ▷ INSIGNIA. **2** (foll. by *of*) (of a person) the type (*the very emblem of courage*). **3** a heraldic device or symbolic object as a distinctive badge. □□ **em·blem·at·ic** /-mátik/ *adj.* **em·blem·at·i·cal** *adj.* **em·blem·at·i·cal·ly** *adv.* **em·ble·ma·tize** /imblémətīz/ *v.tr.*

em·bod·y /embódee, im-/ *v.tr.* (**-ies**, **-ied**) **1** give a concrete or discernible form to (an idea, concept, etc.). **2** (of a thing or person) be an expression of (an idea, etc.). **3** express tangibly (*courage embodied in heroic actions*). **4** include; comprise. □□ **em·bod·i·ment** *n.*

em·bold·en /embóldən, im-/ *v.tr.* (often foll. by *to* + infin.) make bold; encourage.

em·bo·lism /émbəlizəm/ *n.* an obstruction of any artery by a clot of blood, air bubble, etc.

em·bo·lus /émbələs/ *n.* (*pl.* **emboli** /-lī/) an object causing an embolism.

EMBOSS: EMBOSSED TUDOR ROSE

em·boss /embós, im-/ *v.tr.* **1** ▲ carve or mold in relief. **2** form figures, etc., so that they stand out on (a surface). **3** make protuberant.

em·brace /embráys, im-/ *v. & n.* ● *v.tr.* **1 a** hold (a person) closely in the arms, esp. as a sign of affection. **b** (*absol.* of two people) hold each other closely. **2** clasp; enclose. **3** accept eagerly (an offer, opportunity, etc.). **4** adopt (a course of action, doctrine, cause, etc.). **5** include; comprise. **6** take in with the eye or mind. ● *n.* an act of embracing; holding in the arms. □□ **em·brace·a·ble** *adj.* **em·brace·ment** *n.* **em·brac·er** *n.*

em·bra·sure /embráyzhər, im-/ *n.* **1** the beveling of a wall at the sides of a door or window. **2** a small opening in a parapet of a fortified building. □□ **em·bra·sured** *adj.*

em·bro·ca·tion /émbrōkáyshən/ *n.* a liquid used for rubbing on the body to relieve muscular pain, etc.

em·broi·der /embróydər, im-/ *v.tr.* **1** (also *absol.*) **a** decorate (cloth, etc.) with needlework. **b** create (a design) in this way. **2** add interest to (a narrative) with fictitious additions. □□ **em·broi·der·er** *n.*

em·broi·der·y /embróydəree, im-/ *n.* (*pl.* **-ies**) **1** the art of embroidering. **2** embroidered work; a piece of this. **3** unnecessary or extravagant ornament.

em·broil /embróyl, im-/ *v.tr.* **1** (often foll. by *with*) involve (a person) in conflict or difficulties. **2** bring (affairs) into a state of confusion. □□ **em·broil·ment** *n.*

em·bry·o /émbreeō/ *n.* (*pl.* **-os**) **1 a** an unborn or unhatched offspring. ▷ EGG. **b** ▼ a human offspring in the first eight weeks from conception. **2** a rudimentary plant contained in a seed. **3** a thing in a rudimentary stage. **4** (*attrib.*) undeveloped; immature. □ **in embryo** undeveloped. □□ **em·bry·oid** /-breeoyd/ *adj.* **em·bry·o·nal** /émbreeənəl, émbreeónəl/ *adj.* **em·bry·on·ic** /émbreeónik/ *adj.* **em·bry·on·i·cal·ly** *adv.*

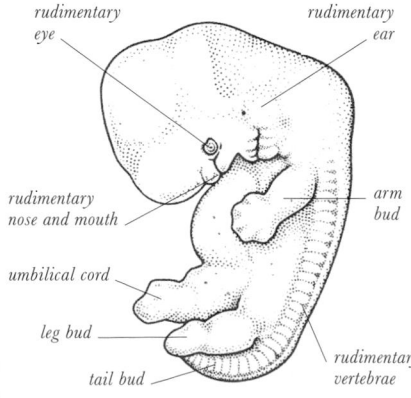

rudimentary eye

rudimentary ear

rudimentary nose and mouth

arm bud

umbilical cord

leg bud

tail bud

rudimentary vertebrae

EMBRYO: SIX-WEEK-OLD HUMAN EMBRYO

em·bry·o·gen·e·sis /émbreeōjénisis/ *n.* the formation of an embryo.

em·bry·ol·o·gy /émbreeóləjee/ *n.* the study of embryos. □□ **em·bry·o·log·ic** /-breeəlójik/ *adj.* **em·bry·o·log·i·cal** *adj.* **em·bry·o·log·i·cal·ly** *adv.* **em·bry·ol·o·gist** *n.*

em·cee /émsee/ *n. & v. colloq.* ● *n.* a master of ceremonies. ● *v.tr. & intr.* (**emcees, emceed**) act as a master of ceremonies.

e·mend /iménd/ *v.tr.* edit (a text, etc.) to remove errors and corruptions. □□ **e·men·da·tion** /éemendáyshən/ *n.* **e·men·da·to·ry** *adj.*

em·er·ald /émərəld, émrəld/ *n.* **1** a bright-green precious stone, a variety of beryl. ▷ GEM, MATRIX. **2** (also **em·er·ald green**) the color of this.

Em·er·ald Isle *n. literary* Ireland.

e·merge /imárj/ *v.intr.* (often foll. by *from*) **1** come up or out into view, esp. when formerly concealed. **2** come up out of a liquid. **3** (of facts, circumstances, etc.) come to light; become known, esp. as a result of inquiry, etc. **4** become recognized or prominent (*emerged as a leading contender*). **5** (of a question, difficulty, etc.) become apparent. **6** survive (an ordeal, etc.) with a specified result (*emerged unscathed*). □□ **e·mer·gence** *n.*

e·mer·gen·cy /imárjənsee/ *n.* (*pl.* **-ies**) **1** a sudden state of danger, conflict, etc., requiring immediate action. **2 a** a medical condition requiring immediate treatment. **b** a patient with such a condition. **3** (*attrib.*) characterized by or for use in an emergency.

e·mer·gen·cy med·i·cal tech·ni·cian *n.* a person trained and licensed to provide basic medical assistance in emergencies. ¶ Abbr.: **EMT.**

e·mer·gen·cy room *n.* the part of a hospital that treats those requiring immediate medical attention.

e·mer·gent /imárjənt/ *adj.* **1** becoming apparent; emerging. **2** (of a nation) newly formed or made independent.

e·mer·i·tus /iméritəs/ *adj.* retired and retaining one's title as an honor (*emeritus professor*).

em·er·y /émaree/ *n.* **1** a coarse corundum used for polishing metal, etc. **2** (*attrib.*) covered with emery.

em·er·y board *n.* a strip of thin wood or board coated with emery or another abrasive, used as a nail file.

e·met·ic /imétik/ *adj. & n.* ● *adj.* that causes vomiting. ● *n.* an emetic medicine.

EMF *abbr.* electromotive force.

em·i·grant /émigrənt/ *n. & adj.* ● *n.* a person who emigrates. ● *adj.* emigrating.

em·i·grate /émigrayt/ *v. intr.* leave one's own country to settle in another. □□ **em·i·gra·tion** /-gráyshən/ *n.* **em·i·gra·to·ry** /-grətáwree/ *adj.*

é·mi·gré /émigray/ *n.* (also **emigré**) an emigrant, esp. a political exile.

em·i·nence /éminəns/ *n.* **1** distinction; recognized superiority. **2** a piece of rising ground. **3** (**Eminence**) a title used in addressing or referring to a cardinal (*Your Eminence; His Eminence*).

é·mi·nence grise /áymeenóns gréez/ *n.* (*pl.* **éminences grises** *pronunc.* same) **1** a person who exercises power or influence without holding office. **2** a confidential agent.

em·i·nent /éminənt/ *adj.* **1** distinguished; notable. **2** (of qualities) remarkable in degree. □□ **em·i·nent·ly** *adv.*

em·i·nent do·main *n.* sovereign control over all property in a government jurisdiction, with the right of expropriation.

e·mir /eméer/ *n.* a title of various Muslim rulers.

e·mir·ate /iméerit, -ayt, aymér-, émərit/ *n.* the rank, domain, or reign of an emir.

em·is·sar·y /émiseree/ *n.* (*pl.* **-ies**) a person sent on a special, usu. diplomatic, mission.

e·mis·sion /imíshən/ *n.* **1** (often foll. by *of*) the process or an act of emitting. **2** a thing emitted.

e·mis·sive /imísiv/ *adj.* having the power to radiate light, heat, etc. □□ **em·is·siv·i·ty** /éemisivitee/ *n.*

e·mit /imít/ *v.tr.* (**emitted, emitting**) **1 a** send out (heat, light, vapor, etc.). **b** discharge from the body. **2** utter (a cry, etc.). □□ **e·mit·ter** *n.*

Em·men·ta·ler /émməntaalər/ *n.* (also **Em·men·tha·ler** or **Em·men·tal** or **Em·men·thal**) a kind of hard Swiss cheese with many holes in it, similar to Gruyère. ▷ CHEESE

em·mer /émər/ *n.* ► a kind of wheat, *Triticum dicoccum*, grown mainly for fodder.

Em·my /émee/ *n.* (*pl.* **-ies**) one of the statuettes awarded annually for outstanding programming, production, and performing in television.

EMMER
(*Triticum dicoccum*)

e·mol·lient /imólyənt/ *adj. & n.* ● *adj.* that softens or soothes the skin. ● *n.* an emollient agent. □□ **e·mol·lience** /-yəns/ *n.*

e·mol·u·ment /imólyəmənt/ *n.* a salary, fee, or profit from employment or office.

e·mote /imốt/ *v.intr. colloq.* show excessive emotion. □□ **e·mot·er** *n.*

e·mo·ti·con /imốtikon/ *n.* ▼ a representation of a facial expression such as a smile, formed with keyboard characters and used in electronic communications to convey the writer's feelings.

:-) :-(;-)

EMOTICON: SHOWING HAPPY, SAD, WINKING

e·mo·tion /imốshən/ *n.* a strong mental or instinctive feeling such as love or fear.

e·mo·tion·al /imốshənəl/ *adj.* **1** of or relating to the emotions. **2** (of a person) liable to excessive emotion. **3** expressing or based on emotion (*an emotional appeal*). **4** likely to excite emotion (*an emotional issue*). □□ **e·mo·tion·al·ism** *n.* **e·mo·tion·al·i·ty** /-álitee/ *n.* **e·mo·tion·al·ize** *v.tr.* **e·mo·tion·al·ly** *adv.*

e·mo·tive /imốtiv/ *adj.* **1** of or characterized by emotion. **2** tending to excite emotion. **3** arousing feeling; not purely descriptive. □□ **e·mo·tive·ly** *adv.* **e·mo·tive·ness** *n.* **e·mo·tiv·i·ty** /émōtívitee/ *n.*

em·pan·el /empánəl, im-/ *var. of* IMPANEL.

em·pa·thize /émpəthīz/ *v. Psychol.* **1** *intr.* (usu. foll. by *with*) exercise empathy. **2** *tr.* treat with empathy.

em·pa·thy /émpəthee/ *n. Psychol.* the power of identifying oneself mentally with (and so fully comprehending) a person or object of contemplation. □□ **em·pa·thet·ic** /-thétik/ *adj.* **em·pa·thet·i·cal·ly** *adv.* **em·path·ic** /empáthik/ *adj.* **em·path·i·cal·ly** *adv.*

em·per·or /émpərər/ *n.* the sovereign of an empire. □□ **em·per·or·ship** *n.*

em·per·or pen·guin *n.* ► the largest known penguin, *Aptenodytes forsteri*, of the Antarctic. ▷ PENGUIN

em·pha·sis /émfəsis/ *n.* (*pl.* **emphases** /-seez/) **1** special importance or prominence attached to a thing, fact, idea, etc. (*emphasis on economy*). **2** stress laid on a word or words to indicate special meaning or importance. **3** vigor or intensity of expression, feeling, action, etc. **4** prominence; sharpness of contour.

em·pha·size /émfəsīz/ *v.tr.* **1** bring (a thing, fact, etc.) into special prominence. **2** lay stress on (a word in speaking).

EMPEROR PENGUIN
(*Aptenodytes forsteri*)

em·phat·ic /emfátik/ *adj.* **1** (of language, tone, or gesture) forcibly expressive. **2** of words: **a** bearing the stress. **b** used to give emphasis. **3** expressing oneself with emphasis. **4** (of an action or process) forcible; significant. □□ **em·phat·i·cal·ly** *adv.*

em·phy·se·ma /émfiseémə, -zeémə/ *n.* enlargement of the air sacs of the lungs causing breathlessness.

em·pire /émpīr/ *n.* **1** an extensive group of lands or countries under a single supreme authority, esp. an emperor. **2** supreme dominion. **3** a large commercial organization, etc., owned or directed by one person or group.

em·pir·ic /empírik, im-/ *adj. & n.* ● *adj.* = EMPIRICAL. ● *n. archaic* **1** a person relying solely on experiment. **2** a quack doctor. □□ **em·pir·i·cism** /-sizəm/ *n.* **em·pir·i·cist** *n.*

em·pir·i·cal /empírikəl, im-/ *adj.* **1** based on or acting on observation or experiment, not on theory. **2** *Philos.* regarding sense-data as valid information. **3** deriving knowledge from experience alone. □□ **em·pir·i·cal·ly** *adv.*

em·place·ment /émplaysmənt, im-/ *n.* a platform or defended position where a gun is placed for firing.

em·ploy /emplóy, im-/ *v. & n.* ● *v.tr.* **1** use the services of (a person) in return for payment; keep (a person) in one's service. **2** (often foll. by *for, in, on*) use (a thing, time, energy, etc.) esp. to good effect. **3** (often foll. by *in*) keep (a person) occupied. ● *n.* the state of being employed, esp. for wages. □ **in the employ of** employed by. □□ **em·ploy·a·ble** *adj.* **em·ploy·a·bil·i·ty** *n.* **em·ploy·er** *n.*

em·ploy·ee /émplóyee, -plóyee/ *n.* (also **em·ploy·e**) a person employed for wages or salary.

em·ploy·ment /emplóymənt, im-/ *n.* **1** the act of employing or the state of being employed. **2** a person's regular trade or profession.

em·ploy·ment a·gen·cy *n.* a business that finds employers or employees for those seeking them.

em·po·ri·um /empáwreeəm/ *n.* (*pl.* **-ums** or **empo·ria** /-reeə/) **1** a large retail store selling a wide variety of goods. **2** a center of commerce; a market.

em·pow·er /empówər, im-/ *v.tr.* (foll. by *to* + infin.) **1** authorize; license. **2** give power to; make able. □□ **em·pow·er·ment** *n.*

em·press /émpris/ *n.* **1** the wife or widow of an emperor. **2** a woman emperor.

emp·ty /émptee/ *adj., v., & n.* ● *adj.* (**emptier, emptiest**) **1** containing nothing. **2** (of a space, place, house, etc.) unoccupied; uninhabited; deserted; unfurnished. **3** (of a transport vehicle, etc.) without a load, passengers, etc. **4 a** meaningless; hollow; insincere (*empty threats; an empty gesture*). **b** without substance or purpose (*an empty existence*). **c** (of a person) lacking sense or knowledge; vacant; foolish. **5** *colloq.* hungry. **6** (foll. by *of*) devoid; lacking. ● *v.* (**-ies, -ied**) **1** *tr.* **a** make empty; remove the contents of. **b** (foll. by *of*) deprive of certain contents (*emptied the room of its chairs*). **c** remove (contents) from a container, etc. **2** *tr.* (often foll. by *into*) transfer (the contents of a container). **3** *intr.* become empty. **4** *intr.* (usu. foll. by *into*) (of a river) discharge itself (into the sea, etc.). ● *n.* (*pl.* **-ies**) *colloq.* a container (esp. a bottle) left empty of its contents. □□ **emp·ti·ly** *adv.* **emp·ti·ness** *n.*

emp·ty-hand·ed /émptee hándid/ *adj.* **1** bringing or taking nothing. **2** having achieved or obtained nothing.

emp·ty-head·ed /émptee hedid/ *adj.* foolish; lacking common sense.

emp·ty nest·er *n. colloq.,* chiefly *N. Amer.* a parent whose children have grown up and left home.

EMT *abbr.* emergency medical technician.

e·mu /eémyoō/ *n.* a large flightless bird, *Dromaius novaehollandiae*, native to Australia, and capable of running at high speed.

e.m.u. *abbr.* electromagnetic unit(s).

em·u·late /émyəlayt/ *v.tr.* **1** try to equal or

excel. **2** imitate zealously. **3** rival. □□ **em·u·la·tion** /-láyshən/ *n.* **em·u·la·tive** *adj.* **em·u·la·tor** *n.*

e·mul·si·fi·er /imúlsifīər/ *n.* **1** any substance that stabilizes an emulsion, esp. a food additive used to stabilize processed foods. **2** an apparatus used for producing an emulsion.

e·mul·si·fy /imúlsifī/ *v.tr.* (**-ies, -ied**) convert into an emulsion. □□ **e·mul·si·fi·a·ble** *adj.* **e·mul·si·fi·ca·tion** /-fikáyshən/ *n.*

e·mul·sion /imúlshən/ *n.* **1** a fine dispersion of one liquid in another, esp. as paint, medicine, etc. **2** a mixture of a silver compound suspended in gelatin, etc., for coating plates or films. □□ **e·mul·sion·ize** *v.tr.* **e·mul·sive** /-siv/ *adj.*

en /en/ *n. Printing* a unit of measurement equal to half an em.

en·a·ble /enáybəl/ *v.tr.* **1** (foll. by *to* + infin.) give (a person, etc.) the means or authority to do something. **2** make possible. **3** esp. *Computing* make (a device) operational. □□ **en·a·bler** *n.*

en·act /enákt, in-/ *v.tr.* **1 a** (often foll. by *that* + clause) ordain; decree. **b** make (a bill, etc.) law. **2** play (a part or scene on stage or in life). □□ **en·ac·tion** /-ákshən/ *n.* **en·ac·tive** *adj.*

en·act·ment /enáktmənt, in-/ *n.* **1** a law enacted. **2** the process of enacting.

en·am·el /ináməl/ *n. & v.* ● *n.* **1** ▼ a glasslike opaque or semitransparent coating on metallic or other hard surfaces for ornament or as a preservative lining. **2 a** a smooth, hard coating. **b** a cosmetic simulating this. **3** the hard, glossy natural coating over the crown of a tooth. ▷ TOOTH. **4** painting done in enamel. ● *v.tr.* **1** inlay or encrust (a metal, etc.) with enamel. **2** portray (figures, etc.) with enamel. □□ **e·nam·el·er** *n.* **e·nam·el·work** *n.*

ENAMEL: 13TH-CENTURY
ENAMELED PORCELAIN MOSQUE LAMP

en·am·or /inámər/ *v.tr.* (usu. in *passive*; foll. by *of*) **1** inspire with love or liking. **2** charm; delight.

en·an·ti·o·mer /enánteeəmər/ *n. Chem.* a molecule with a mirror image. □□ **en·an·ti·o·mer·ic** /-mérik/ *adj.*

en bloc /on bláwk/ *adv.* in a block; all at the same time; wholesale.

en·camp /enkámp/ *v.tr. & intr.* **1** settle in a military camp. **2** lodge in the open in tents.

en·camp·ment /enkámpmənt, in-/ *n.* **1** a place where troops, etc., are encamped. **2** the process of setting up a camp.

en·cap·su·late /enkápsəlayt, -syoō-, in-/ *v.tr.* **1** enclose in or as in a capsule. **2** summarize; express the essential features of. □□ **en·cap·su·la·tion** /-láyshən/ *n.*

en·case /enkáys, in-/ *v.tr.* (also **incase**) **1** put into a case. **2** surround as with a case. □□ **en·case·ment** *n.*

en·caus·tic /enkáwstik, in-/ *adj. & n.* ● *adj.* **1** (in painting, ceramics, etc.) using pigments mixed with hot wax, which are burned in as an inlay. **2** (of bricks and tiles) inlaid with differently colored clays burned in. ● *n.* **1** the art of encaustic painting. **2** a painting done with this technique.

E

E

en·ceph·a·li·tis /enséfəlítis/ *n.* inflammation of the brain. □□ **en·ceph·a·lit·ic** /-lítik/ *adj.*

encephalo- /enséfəlō/ *comb. form* brain.

en·ceph·a·lo·gram /enséfələgram/ *n.* an X ray photograph of the brain.

en·ceph·a·lo·graph /enséfələgraf/ *n.* an instrument for recording the electrical activity of the brain.

en·ceph·a·lop·a·thy /enséfəlópəthee/ *n.* disease of the brain.

en·chain /encháyn, in-/ *v.tr.* **1** fetter. **2** hold fast (the attention, etc.). □□ **en·chain·ment** *n.*

en·chant /enchánt, in-/ *v.tr.* **1** charm; delight. **2** bewitch. □□ **en·chant·ed·ly** *adv.* **en·chant·ing** *adj.* **en·chant·ing·ly** *adv.* **en·chant·ment** *n.*

en·chant·er /enchántər, in-/ *n.* (*fem.* **enchantress**) a person who enchants, esp. by supposed use of magic.

en·chi·la·da /énchiláadə/ *n.* a tortilla with chili sauce and usu. a filling, esp. meat.

en·ci·pher /ensífər, in-/ *v.tr.* **1** write (a message, etc.) in cipher. **2** convert into coded form using a cipher. □□ **en·ci·pher·ment** *n.*

en·cir·cle /ensúrkəl, in-/ *v.tr.* **1** (usu. foll. by *with*) surround; encompass. **2** form a circle around. □□ **en·cir·cle·ment** *n.*

encl. *abbr.* **1** enclosed. **2** enclosure.

en·clave /énklayv, ón-/ *n.* **1** a portion of territory of one country surrounded by territory of another or others, as viewed by the surrounding territory (cf. EXCLAVE). **2** a group of people who are culturally, intellectually, or socially distinct from those surrounding them.

en·close /enklóz, in-/ *v.tr.* (also **inclose**) **1** (often foll. by *with*, *in*) **a** surround with a wall, fence, etc. **b** shut in on all sides. **2** fence in (common land) so as to make it private property. **3** put in a receptacle (esp. in an envelope together with a letter). **4** (usu. as **enclosed** *adj.*) seclude (a religious community) from the outside world.

en·clo·sure /enklózhər, in-/ *n.* (also **inclosure**) **1** the act of enclosing, esp. of common land. **2** a thing enclosed with a letter.

en·code /enkód, in-/ *v.tr.* put (a message, etc.) into code or cipher. □□ **en·cod·er** *n.*

en·co·mi·um /enkómeeəm/ *n.* (*pl.* **encomiums** or **encomia** /-meeə/) a formal or high-flown expression of praise.

en·com·pass /enkúmpəs, in-/ *v.tr.* **1** surround or form a circle about, esp. to protect or attack. **2** contain. □□ **en·com·pass·ment** *n.*

en·core /óngkawr/ *n.*, *v.*, *& int.* ● *n.* **1** a call by an audience or spectators for the repetition of an item, or for a further item. **2** such an item. ● *v.tr.* **1** call for the repetition of (an item). **2** call back (a performer) for this. ● *int.* also /-kór/ again; once more.

en·coun·ter /enkówntər, in-/ *v. & n.* ● *v.tr.* **1** meet by chance or unexpectedly. **2** meet as an adversary. **3** meet with; experience (problems, opposition, etc.). ● *n.* **1** a meeting by chance. **2** a meeting in conflict.

en·cour·age /enkə́rij, -kúr-, in-/ *v.tr.* **1** give courage, confidence, or hope to. **2** (foll. by *to* + infin.) urge; advise. **3** stimulate by help, reward, etc. **4** promote or assist (an enterprise, opinion, etc.). □□ **en·cour·age·ment** *n.* **en·cour·ag·er** *n.* **en·cour·ag·ing** *adj.* **en·cour·ag·ing·ly** *adv.*

en·croach /enkróch, in-/ *v.intr.* **1** (foll. by *on*, *upon*) intrude, esp. on another's territory or rights. **2** advance gradually beyond due limits. □□ **en·croach·er** *n.* **en·croach·ment** *n.*

en·crust /enkrúst, in-/ *v.* (also **incrust**) **1** *tr.* cover with a crust. **2** *tr.* overlay with an ornamental crust of precious material. **3** *intr.* form a crust. □□ **en·crust·ment** *n.*

en·crus·ta·tion var. of INCRUSTATION.

en·crypt /enkrípt, in-/ *v.tr.* **1** convert (data) into code, esp. to prevent unauthorized access. **2** conceal by this means. □□ **en·cryp·tion** /-krípshən/ *n.*

en·cum·ber /enkúmbər, in-/ *v.tr.* **1** be a burden to. **2** hamper; impede. **3** burden (a person or estate) with debts, esp. mortgages. **4** fill or block (a place), esp. with lumber. □□ **en·cum·ber·ment** *n.*

en·cum·brance /enkúmbrəns, in-/ *n.* **1** a burden. **2** an impediment. **3** a mortgage or other charge on property. **4** an annoyance.

en·cyc·li·cal /ensíklikəl/ *n. & adj.* ● *n.* a papal letter sent to all bishops of the Roman Catholic Church. ● *adj.* (of a letter) for wide circulation.

en·cy·clo·pe·di·a /ensíkləpéedeeə/ *n.* (also **en·cy·clo·pae·di·a**) a book, often in several volumes, giving information on many subjects, or on many aspects of one subject, usu. arranged alphabetically.

en·cy·clo·pe·dic /ensíkləpéedik/ *adj.* (also **en·cy·clo·pae·dic**) (of knowledge or information) comprehensive.

en·cyst /ensíst, in-/ *v.tr. & intr. Biol.* enclose or become enclosed in a cyst. □□ **en·cys·ta·tion** /-táyshən/ *n.* **en·cyst·ment** *n.*

end /end/ *n. & v.* ● *n.* **1 a** the extreme limit. **b** an extremity of a line, or of the greatest dimension of an object. **c** the furthest point (*to the ends of the earth*). **2** the surface bounding a thing at either extremity; an extreme part. **3 a** a conclusion; finish (*no end to his misery*). **b** the latter or final part. **c** death; destruction; downfall (*met an untimely end*). **d** result; outcome. **e** an ultimate state or condition. **4 a** a thing one seeks to attain; a purpose (*will do anything to achieve her ends*; *to what end?*). **b** the object for which a thing exists. **5** a remnant; a piece left over (*a board end*). **6** (prec. by *the*) *colloq.* the limit of endurability. **7** the half of a sports field or court occupied by one team or player. **8** the part or share with which a person is concerned (*no football at my end*). **9** *Football* a player at the extremity of the offensive or defensive line. ● *v.* **1** *tr. & intr.* bring or come to an end. **2** *tr.* put an end to; destroy. **3** *intr.* (foll. by *in*) have as its result (*will end in tears*). **4** *intr.* (foll. by *by*) do or achieve eventually (*ended by marrying an heiress*). □ **at an end** exhausted or completed. **at the end of one's tether** see TETHER. **come to an end 1** be completed or finished. **2** become exhausted. **end it all** (or **end it**) *colloq.* commit suicide. **end of the road** the point at which a hope or endeavor has to be abandoned. **end of the world** the cessation of mortal life. **end on** with the end facing one, or with the end adjoining the end of the next object. **end to end** with the end of each of a series adjoining the end of the next. **end up** reach a specified state, action, or place eventually (*ended up a drunk*; *ended up making a fortune*). **in the end** finally; after all. **keep one's end up** do one's part despite difficulties. **make ends** (or **both ends**) **meet** live within one's income. **no end** *colloq.* to a great extent; very much. **no end of** *colloq.* much or many of. **on end 1** upright (*hair stood on end*). **2** continuously (*for three weeks on end*). **put an end to 1** stop (an activity, etc.). **2** abolish; destroy.

en·dan·ger /endáynjər, in-/ *v.tr.* place in danger. □□ **en·dan·ger·ment** *n.*

en·dear /endeér, in-/ *v.tr.* (usu. foll. by *to*) make dear to or beloved by.

en·dear·ing /endeéring, in-/ *adj.* inspiring affection. □□ **en·dear·ing·ly** *adv.*

en·dear·ment /endeérmənt, in-/ *n.* **1** an expression of affection. **2** liking; affection.

en·deav·or /endévər, in-/ *v. & n.* ● *v. intr.* (foll. by *to* + infin.) try earnestly. ● *n.* (often foll. by *at*, or *to* + infin.) effort directed toward a goal; an earnest attempt.

en·dem·ic /endémik/ *adj. & n.* ● *adj.* regularly or only found among a particular people or in a certain region. ● *n.* an endemic disease or plant. □□ **en·dem·i·cal·ly** *adv.* **en·de·mic·i·ty** /éndimísitee/ *n.* **en·de·mism** *n.*

end·game /éndgaym/ *n.* the final stage of a game (esp. chess), when few pieces remain.

end·ing /énding/ *n.* **1** an end or final part, esp. of a story. **2** an inflected final part of a word.

en·dive /éndīv, óndeev/ *n.* **1 ▶** a curly-leaved plant, *Cichorium endivia*, used in salads. **2** a chicory crown.

ENDIVE
(*Cichorium endivia*)

end·less /éndlis/ *adj.* **1** infinite; without end; eternal. **2** continual; incessant (*tired of their endless complaints*). **3** *colloq.* innumerable. **4** (of a belt, chain, etc.) having the ends joined for continuous action over wheels, etc. □□ **end·less·ly** *adv.* **end·less·ness** *n.*

end·most /éndmōst/ *adj.* nearest the end.

en·do·car·di·tis /éndōkaardítis/ *n.* inflammation of the lining of the heart.

en·do·crine /éndōkrin, -kreen, -krīn/ *adj.* **▼** (of a gland) secreting directly into the blood.

en·do·cri·nol·o·gy /éndōkrinóləjee/ *n.* the study of the structure and physiology of endocrine glands. □□ **en·do·cri·no·log·i·cal** /-nəlójikəl/ *adj.* **en·do·cri·nol·o·gist** *n.*

en·dog·a·my /endógəmee/ *n.* **1** *Anthropol.* marrying within the same tribe. **2** *Bot.* pollination from the same plant. □□ **en·dog·a·mous** *adj.*

en·dog·e·nous /endójinəs/ *adj.* growing or originating from within. □□ **en·do·gen·e·sis** /éndəjénisis/ *n.* **en·dog·e·ny** /endójinee/ *n.*

en·do·me·tri·um /éndōméetreeəm/ *n. Anat.* the membrane lining the uterus. □□ **en·do·me·tri·tis** /éndōmitrítis/ *n.*

en·do·morph /éndōmawrf/ *n.* **1** a person with a soft, round body build and a high proportion of fat tissue (cf. ECTOMORPH, MESOMORPH). ▶ MESOMORPH. **2** *Mineral.* a mineral enclosed within another. □□ **en·do·mor·phic** *adj.* **en·do·mor·phy** *n.*

ENDOCRINE

Endocrine glands produce hormones that the body needs in order to grow properly and work smoothly. The hormones are secreted directly into the circulatory system and carried in the bloodstream to specific target tissues.

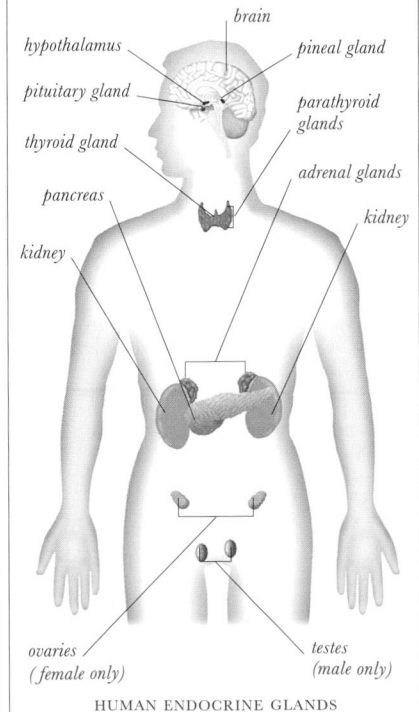

brain
hypothalamus
pineal gland
pituitary gland
parathyroid glands
thyroid gland
adrenal glands
pancreas
kidney
kidney
ovaries
(female only)
testes
(male only)

HUMAN ENDOCRINE GLANDS

en·do·plasm /éndōplazəm/ n. the inner fluid layer of the cytoplasm (cf. ECTOPLASM).

en·dor·phin /endáwrfin/ n. Biochem. a peptide neurotransmitter occurring naturally in the brain and having pain-relieving properties.

en·dorse /endáwrs, in-/ v.tr. (also **indorse**) **1 a** confirm (a statement or opinion). **b** declare one's approval of. **2** sign or write on the back of (a document), esp. the back of (a bill, check, etc.) as the payee or to specify another as payee. **3** write (an explanation or comment) on the back of a document. □□ **en·dors·a·ble** adj. **en·dor·see** /éndawrsée/ n. **en·dors·er** n.

en·dorse·ment /endáwrsmənt, in-/ n. **1** the act or an instance of endorsing. **2** something used to endorse a document, etc., esp. a signature.

en·do·scope /éndəskōp/ n. Surgery ▼ an instrument for viewing the internal parts of the body. □□ **en·do·scop·ic** /-skópik/ adj. **en·do·scop·i·cal·ly** adv. **en·dos·co·pist** /endóskəpist/ n. **en·dos·co·py** /endóskəpee/ n.

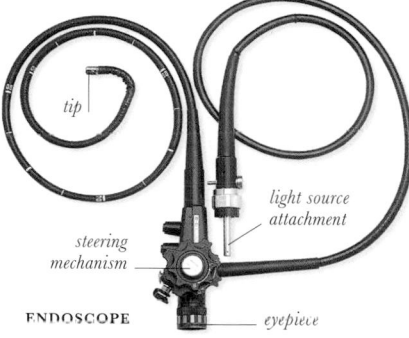

tip

light source attachment

steering mechanism

ENDOSCOPE

eyepiece

en·do·skel·e·ton /éndōskélitən/ n. an internal skeleton, as found in vertebrates.

en·do·sperm /éndəspərm/ n. albumen enclosed with the germ in seeds.

en·dow /endów, in-/ v.tr. **1** bequeath or give a permanent income to (a person, institution, etc.). **2** (esp. as **endowed** adj.) (usu. foll. by with) provide (a person) with talent, ability, etc. □□ **en·dow·er** n.

en·dow·ment /endówmənt, in-/ n. **1** the act or an instance of endowing. **2** assets, esp. property or income, which a person or body is endowed. **3** (usu. in pl.) skill, talent, etc., with which a person is endowed. **4** (attrib.) denoting forms of life insurance involving payment by the insurer of a fixed sum on a specified date, or on the death of the insured person if earlier.

end·pa·per /éndpaypər/ n. a usu. blank leaf of paper at the beginning and end of a book, fixed to the inside of the cover. ▷ BOOK

end·point /éndpoynt/ n. (also **end point**) Math. a point or value that marks the end of a ray or one of the ends of a line segment or interval.

en·due /endόō, -dyόō, in-/ v.tr. (also **indue**) (foll. by with) invest or provide (a person) with qualities, powers, etc.

en·dur·ance /endóōrəns, -dyόōr-, in-/ n. **1** the power or habit of enduring (beyond endurance). **2** the ability to withstand prolonged strain (endurance test). **3** the act of enduring.

en·dure /endóōr, -dyόōr, in-/ v. **1** tr. undergo (a difficulty, hardship, etc.). **2** tr. a tolerate (a person) (cannot endure him). **b** (esp. with neg.; foll. by to + infin.) bear. **3** intr. (often as **enduring** adj.) remain in existence; last. **4** tr. submit to. □□ **en·dur·a·ble** adj. **en·dur·a·bil·i·ty** n. **en·dur·ing·ly** adv.

end·ways /éndwayz/ adv. **1** with its end uppermost or foremost or turned toward the viewer. **2** end to end.

end·wise /éndwīz/ adv. = ENDWAYS.

end zone n. Football the area at each end of a football field where points are scored. ▷ FOOTBALL

ENE abbr. east-northeast.

en·e·ma /énimə/ n. (pl. **enemas** or **enemata** /inémətə/) **1** the injection of liquid or gas into the rectum, esp. to expel its contents. **2** a fluid or syringe used for this.

en·e·my /énimee/ n. (pl. **-ies**) **1** a person or group actively opposing or hostile to another, or to a cause, etc. **2 a** a hostile nation or army, esp. in war. **b** a member of this. **c** a hostile ship or aircraft. **3** (usu. foll. by of, to) an adversary or opponent. **4** a thing that harms or injures. **5** (attrib.) of or belonging to an enemy (destroyed by enemy action).

en·er·get·ic /énərjétik/ adj. **1** strenuously active. **2** forcible; vigorous. **3** powerfully operative. □□ **en·er·get·i·cal·ly** adv.

en·er·gize /énərjīz/ v.tr. **1** infuse energy into (a person or work). **2** provide energy for the operation of (a device). □□ **en·er·giz·er** n.

en·er·gy /énərjee/ n. (pl. **-ies**) **1** force; vigor; capacity for activity. **2** (in pl.) individual powers in use (devote your energies to this). **3** Physics the capacity of matter or radiation to do work. **4** the means of doing work by utilizing matter or radiation.

en·er·vate v. & adj. ● v.tr. /énərvayt/ deprive of vigor or vitality. ● adj. /inárvət/ enervated. □□ **en·er·va·tion** /-váyshən/ n.

en·fant ter·ri·ble /aanfaan teréeblə/ n. a person who causes embarrassment by indiscreet or unruly behavior.

en·fee·ble /enféebəl, in-/ v.tr. make feeble. □□ **en·fee·ble·ment** n.

en·fi·lade /énfiláyd, -láad/ n. & v. ● n. gunfire directed along a line from end to end. ● v.tr. direct an enfilade at (troops, a road, etc.).

en·fold /enfōld, in-/ v.tr. (also **infold**) **1** (usu. foll. by in, with) wrap up; envelop. **2** clasp; embrace.

en·force /enfáwrs, in-/ v.tr. **1** compel observance of (a law, etc.). **2** (foll. by on, upon) impose (an action, conduct, one's will). **3** persist in (a demand or argument). □□ **en·force·a·ble** adj. **en·force·a·bil·i·ty** n. **en·force·ment** n. **en·forc·er** n.

en·fran·chise /enfránchīz, in-/ v.tr. **1** give a person the right to vote. **2** give (a town, city, etc.) municipal or parliamentary rights. **3** hist. free (a slave, etc.). □□ **en·fran·chise·ment** n.

ENG abbr. electronic news gathering.

en·gage /en-gáyj, in-/ v. **1** tr. employ or hire (a person). **2** tr. a (usu. in passive) employ busily; occupy (are you engaged tomorrow?). **b** hold fast (a person's attention). **3** tr. (usu. in passive) bind by a promise, esp. of marriage. **4** tr. (foll. by to + infin.) bind by a contract. **5** tr. arrange beforehand to occupy (a room, seat, etc.). **6** (usu. foll. by with) Mech. **a** tr. interlock (parts of a gear, etc.); cause (a part) to interlock. **b** intr. (of a part, gear, etc.) interlock. **7 a** intr. (usu. foll. by with) (of troops, etc.) come into battle. **b** tr. bring (troops) into battle. **c** tr. come into battle with (an enemy, etc.). **8** intr. take part (engage in politics). **9** intr. (foll. by that + clause or to + infin.) pledge oneself.

en·ga·gé /oN-gazháy/ adj. (of a writer, artist, etc.) morally committed.

en·gaged /en-gáyjd, in-/ adj. **1** under a promise to marry. **2 a** occupied; busy. **b** reserved; booked.

en·gage·ment /en-gáyjmənt, in-/ n. **1** the act or state of engaging or being engaged. **2** an appointment with another person. **3** a betrothal. **4** an encounter between hostile forces.

en·gag·ing /en-gáyjing, in-/ adj. attractive; charming. □□ **en·gag·ing·ly** adv.

en·gen·der /enjéndər, in-/ v.tr. give rise to; bring about (a feeling, etc.).

en·gine /énjin/ n. **1** a mechanical contrivance consisting of several parts working together, esp. as a source of power. ▷ INTERNAL-COMBUSTION ENGINE, JET ENGINE, STEAM ENGINE. **2 a** a railroad locomotive. **b** = FIRE ENGINE. **c** = STEAM ENGINE. **3** archaic a machine or instrument, esp. a contrivance used in warfare. □□ **en·gined** adj. (also in comb.).

en·gi·neer /énjinéer/ n. & v. ● n. **1** a person qualified in a branch of engineering, esp. as a professional. **2** = CIVIL ENGINEER. **3** a person who makes or is in charge of engines. **4** the operator or supervisor of an engine, esp. a railroad locomotive. **5** a person who designs and constructs military works; a soldier trained for this purpose. **6** (foll. by of) a skillful or artful contriver. ● v. **1** tr. arrange, contrive, or bring about, esp. artfully. **2** intr. act as an engineer. **3** tr. construct or manage as an engineer.

en·gi·neer·ing /énjinéering/ n. the application of science to the design, building, and use of machines, constructions, etc.

Eng·lish /íngglish/ adj. & n. ● adj. of or relating to England or its people or language. ● n. **1** the language of England, now used in many varieties in the British Isles, the United States, and most Commonwealth or ex-Commonwealth countries, and often internationally. **2** (prec. by the; treated as pl.) the people of England. □□ **Eng·lish·ness** n.

Eng·lish horn n. Mus. **1** ▶ an alto woodwind instrument of the oboe family. ▷ ORCHESTRA, WOODWIND. **2** its player.

Eng·lish·man /íngglishmən/ n. (pl. **-men**) a person who is English by birth or descent.

Eng·lish muf·fin n. a flat round bread-dough muffin, usu. baked on a griddle, served sliced and toasted.

Eng·lish·wom·an /ínglishwŏŏmən/ n. (pl. **-women**) a woman who is English by birth or descent.

en·gorge /en-gáwrj, in-/ v.tr. **1** (in passive) **a** be crammed. **b** Med. be congested with blood. **2** devour greedily. □□ **en·gorge·ment** n.

engr. abbr. **1** engineer. **2** engraved. **3** engraver. **4** engraving.

en·grain /en-gráyn, in-/ v.tr. **1** implant (a habit, belief, or attitude) ineradicably in a person (see also INGRAINED). **2** cause (dye, etc.) to sink deeply into a thing.

en·grained /en-gráynd, in-/ adj. inveterate (see also INGRAINED).

en·grave /en-gráyv, in-/ v.tr. **1** (often foll. by on) inscribe, cut, or carve (a text or design) on a hard surface. **2** (often foll. by with) inscribe or ornament (a surface) in this way. **3** cut (a design) as lines on a metal plate, block, etc., for printing. **4** (often foll. by on) impress deeply on a person's memory, etc. □□ **en·grav·er** n.

en·grav·ing /en-gráyving, in-/ n. ◀ a print made from an engraved plate, block, or other surface.

en·gross /en-grós, in-/ v.tr. **1** absorb the attention of; occupy fully. **2** make a fair copy of a legal document. **3** reproduce (a document, etc.) in larger letters or larger format. **4** archaic monopolize (a conversation, etc.). □□ **en·gross·ing** adj. (in sense 1). **en·gross·ment** n.

en·gulf /en-gúlf, in-/ v.tr. (also **ingulf**) **1** flow over and swamp; overwhelm. **2** swallow or plunge into a gulf. □□ **en·gulf·ment** n.

double reed

crook

upper joint

conical wooden tube

key

middle joint

bell joint

bulb-shaped bell

ENGLISH HORN

1523

ENGRAVING: DETAIL FROM METAL PLATE ENGRAVING OF ST. SIMON (1523) BY ALBRECHT DÜRER

E

E

en·hance /enháns, in-/ *v.tr.* heighten or intensify (qualities, powers, value, etc.); improve (something already of good quality). □□ **en·hance·ment** *n.* **en·hanc·er** *n.*

en·har·mon·ic /énhaarmónik/ *adj. Mus.* of or having intervals smaller than a semitone. □□ **en·har·mon·i·cal·ly** *adv.*

e·nig·ma /inígmə/ *n.* **1** a puzzling thing or person. **2** a riddle or paradox. □□ **en·ig·mat·ic** /énigmátik/ *adj.* **en·ig·mat·i·cal** *adj.* **en·ig·mat·i·cal·ly** *adv.* **e·nig·mat·ize** /inígmətīz/ *v.tr.*

en·join /enjóyn, in-/ *v.tr.* **1** (foll. by *to* + infin.) command or order (a person). **2** (usu. foll. by *from*) *Law* prohibit (a person) by order. □□ **en·join·ment** *n.*

en·joy /enjóy, in-/ *v.tr.* **1** take delight or pleasure in. **2** have the use or benefit of. **3** experience (*enjoy poor health*). □ **enjoy oneself** experience pleasure. □□ **en·joy·er** *n.* **en·joy·ment** *n.*

en·joy·a·ble /enjóyəbəl, in-/ *adj.* pleasant; giving enjoyment. □□ **en·joy·a·bil·i·ty** *n.* **en·joy·a·ble·ness** *n.* **en·joy·a·bly** *adv.*

en·keph·al·in /enkéfəlin/ *n. Biochem.* either of two morphinelike peptides occurring naturally in the brain and thought to control levels of pain.

en·kin·dle /enkíndəl, in-/ *v.tr. literary* **1 a** cause (flames) to flare up. **b** stimulate (feeling, passion, etc.). **2** inflame with passion.

en·large /enláarj, in-/ *v.* **1** *tr. & intr.* make or become larger or wider. **2 a** *tr.* describe in greater detail. **b** *intr.* (usu. foll. by *upon*) expatiate. **3** *tr. Photog.* produce an enlargement of (a negative).

en·large·ment /enláarjmənt, in-/ *n.* **1** the act or an instance of enlarging; the state of being enlarged. **2** *Photog.* a print that is larger than the negative from which it is produced.

en·larg·er /enláarjər, in-/ *n. Photog.* an apparatus for enlarging or reducing negatives or positives.

en·light·en /enlít'n, in-/ *v.tr.* **1 a** (often foll. by *on*) instruct or inform (a person) about a subject. **b** (as **enlightened** *adj.*) well-informed; knowledgeable. **2** (esp. as **enlightened** *adj.*) free from prejudice or superstition.

en·light·en·ment /enlít'nmənt, in-/ *n.* **1** the act or an instance of enlightening; the state of being enlightened. **2** (**the Enlightenment**) the 18th-c. philosophy emphasizing reason and individualism rather than tradition.

en·list /enlíst, in-/ *v.* **1** *intr. & tr.* enroll in the armed services. **2** *tr.* secure as a means of help or support. □□ **en·list·er** *n.* **en·list·ment** *n.*

en·list·ed man *n.* a soldier or sailor below the rank of officer.

en·liv·en /enlívən, in-/ *v.tr.* **1** give life or spirit to. **2** make cheerful; brighten (a picture or scene). □□ **en·liv·en·er** *n.* **en·liv·en·ment** *n.*

en masse /on más/ *adv.* **1** all together. **2** in a mass.

en·mesh /enmésh, in-/ *v.tr.* entangle in or as in a net. □□ **en·mesh·ment** *n.*

en·mi·ty /énmitee/ *n.* (*pl.* **-ies**) **1** the state of being an enemy. **2** a feeling of hostility.

en·no·ble /enṓbəl, in-/ *v.tr.* **1** make (a person) a noble. **2** make noble; elevate. □□ **en·no·ble·ment** *n.*

en·nui /onweé/ *n.* mental weariness from lack of occupation or interest; boredom.

e·nol·o·gy /eenóləjee/ *n.* the study of wines. □□ **e·no·log·i·cal** /éenəlójikəl/ *adj.* **e·nol·o·gist** *n.*

e·nor·mi·ty /ináwrmitee/ *n.* (*pl.* **-ies**) **1** extreme wickedness. **2** an act of extreme wickedness. **3** a serious error. **4** *disp.* great size; enormousness.

e·nor·mous /ináwrməs/ *adj.* very large; huge. □□ **e·nor·mous·ly** *adv.* **e·nor·mous·ness** *n.*

e·nough /inúf/ *adj., n., adv., & int.* ● *adj.* as much or as many as required (*we have enough apples*). ● *n.* an amount or quantity that is enough (*we have enough of everything now*). ● *adv.* **1** to the required degree; adequately (*are you warm enough?*). **2** fairly (*she sings well enough*). **3** very; quite (*you know well enough what I mean; oddly enough*). ● *int.* that is enough (in various

senses, esp. to put an end to an action, thing said, etc.). □ **have had enough of** want no more of; be satiated with or tired of.

en pas·sant /ón pasón/ *adv.* by the way.

en·quire var. of INQUIRE.

en·quir·y var. of INQUIRY.

en·rage /enráyj, in-/ *v.tr.* (often foll. by *at, by, with*) make furious. □□ **en·rage·ment** *n.*

en·rap·ture /enrápchər, in-/ *v.tr.* give intense delight to.

en·rich /enrích, in-/ *v.tr.* **1** make rich or richer. **2** make richer in quality, flavor, nutritive value, etc. **3** add to the contents of (a collection, museum, or book). **4** increase the content of an isotope in (material), esp. enrich uranium with isotope U-235. □□ **en·rich·ment** *n.*

en·riched u·ra·ni·um *n.* uranium containing an increased proportion of the fissile isotope U-235.

en·robe /enrṓb, in-/ *v.intr.* put on a robe, vestment, etc.

en·roll /enrṓl, in-/ *v.* (also **en·rol**) (**enrolled, enrolling**) **1** *intr.* enter one's name on a list, esp. as a commitment to membership. **2** *tr.* **a** write the name of (a person) on a list. **b** (usu. foll. by *in*) incorporate (a person) as a member of a society, etc. □□ **en·roll·ee** /-leé/ *n.* **en·roll·er** *n.*

en·roll·ment /enrṓlmənt, in-/ *n.* (also **en·rol·ment**) **1** the act or an instance of enrolling; the state of being enrolled. **2** the number of persons enrolled, esp. at a school or college.

en route /on rōōt/ *adv.* (usu. foll. by *to, for*) on the way.

en·sconce /enskóns, in-/ *v.tr.* (usu. *refl.* or in *passive*) establish or settle comfortably, safely, or secretly.

en·sem·ble /onsómbəl/ *n.* **1 a** a thing viewed as the sum of its parts. **b** the general effect of this. **2** a set of clothes worn together; an outfit. **3** a group of actors, dancers, musicians, etc., performing together, esp. subsidiary dancers in ballet, etc. **4** *Mus.* a concerted passage for an ensemble.

en·shrine /enshrín, in-/ *v.tr.* **1** enclose in or as in a shrine. **2** serve as a shrine for. **3** preserve or cherish. □□ **en·shrine·ment** *n.*

en·shroud /enshrówd, in-/ *v.tr. literary* **1** cover with or as with a shroud. **2** cover completely; hide from view.

en·sign /énsin, -sīn/ *n.* **1** ▼ a banner or flag, esp. the military or naval flag of a nation. ▷ SHIP. **2 a** *hist.* the lowest commissioned infantry officer. **b** the lowest commissioned officer in the US Navy or US Coast Guard.

ENSIGN: BRITISH RED ENSIGN

en·slave /ensláyv, in-/ *v.tr.* make (a person) a slave. □□ **en·slave·ment** *n.* **en·slav·er** *n.*

en·snare /ensnáir, in-/ *v.tr.* catch in or as in a snare; entrap. □□ **en·snare·ment** *n.*

en·sue /ensṓo, in-/ *v.intr.* **1** happen afterward. **2** (often foll. by *from, on*) occur as a result.

en suite /on sweét/ *adv.* forming a single unit (*bedroom with bathroom en suite*).

en·sure /enshṓor, in-/ *v.tr.* **1** (often foll. by *that* + clause) make certain. **2** (usu. foll. by *to, for*) secure (a thing for a person, etc.). **3** (usu. foll. by *against*) make safe. □□ **en·sur·er** *n.*

ENT *abbr.* ear, nose, and throat.

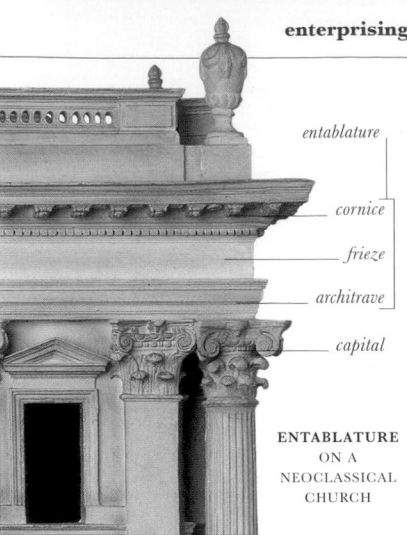

entablature
cornice
frieze
architrave
capital

ENTABLATURE
ON A
NEOCLASSICAL
CHURCH

en·tab·la·ture /entáblachər, in-/ *n. Archit.* ▲ the upper part of a classical building supported by columns or a colonnade, comprising architrave, frieze, and cornice. ▷ COLUMN, DORIC

en·tail /entáyl, in-/ *v.tr.* **1 a** necessitate or involve unavoidably (*the work entails much effort*). **b** give rise to; involve. **2** *Law* bequeath (property, etc.) so that it remains within a family. □□ **en·tail·ment** *n.*

en·tan·gle /entánggəl, in-/ *v.tr.* **1** cause to get caught in a snare or among obstacles. **2** cause to become tangled. **3** involve in difficulties or illicit activities. **4** make (a thing) tangled or intricate; complicate.

en·tan·gle·ment /entánggəlmənt, in-/ *n.* **1** the act or condition of entangling or being entangled. **2 a** a thing that entangles. **b** *Mil.* an extensive barrier erected to obstruct an enemy's movements. **3** a compromising (esp. amorous) relationship.

en·tente /aantáant, ontónt/ *n.* **1** = ENTENTE CORDIALE. **2** a group of nations in such a relation.

en·tente cor·diale /ontónt kawrdyaál/ *n.* a friendly understanding between nations, esp. (often **Entente Cordiale**) that reached in 1904 between Britain and France.

en·ter /éntər/ *v.* **1 a** *intr.* (often foll. by *into*) go or come in. **b** *tr.* go or come into. **c** *intr.* come on stage (as a direction: *enter Macbeth*). **2** *tr.* penetrate; go through; spread through (*a bullet entered his chest*). **3** *tr.* (often foll. by *up*) write (a name, details, etc.) in a list, book, etc. **4 a** *intr.* register or announce oneself as a competitor (*entered the long jump*). **b** *tr.* become a competitor in (an event). **c** *tr.* record the name of (a person, etc.) as a competitor (*entered two horses for the Kentucky Derby*). **5** *tr.* **a** become a member of (a society, etc.). **b** enroll as a member or prospective member of a society, school, etc.; admit or obtain admission for. **6** *tr.* make known; present for consideration (*entered a protest*). **7** *tr.* put into an official record. **8** *intr.* (foll. by *into*) **a** engage in (conversation, relations, an undertaking, etc.). **b** subscribe to; bind oneself by (an agreement, etc.). **c** form part of (one's calculations, plans, etc.). **9** *intr.* (foll. by *on, upon*) **a** begin; undertake; begin to deal with (a subject). **b** assume the functions of (an office). **c** assume possession of (property). **10** *intr.* (foll. by *up*) complete a series of entries in (account books, etc.). □□ **en·ter·er** *n.*

en·ter·ic /entérik/ *adj. & n.* ● *adj.* of the intestines. ● *n.* (in full **enteric fever**) typhoid. □□ **en·ter·i·tis** /éntərítis/ *n.*

entero- /éntərō/ *comb. form* intestine.

en·ter·prise /éntərprīz/ *n.* **1** an undertaking, esp. a bold or difficult one. **2** (as a personal attribute) readiness to engage in such undertakings (*has no enterprise*). **3** a business firm. □□ **en·ter·pris·er** *n.*

en·ter·pris·ing /éntərprīzing/ *adj.* **1** ready to engage in enterprises. **2** resourceful; imaginative; energetic. □□ **en·ter·pris·ing·ly** *adv.*

en·ter·tain /éntərtáyn/ v.tr. **1** amuse; occupy agreeably. **2 a** receive or treat as a guest. **b** (absol.) receive guests (they entertain a great deal). **3** give attention or consideration to (an idea, feeling, or proposal).

en·ter·tain·er /éntərtáynər/ n. a person who entertains, esp. professionally on stage, etc.

en·ter·tain·ing /éntərtáyning/ adj. amusing; diverting.

en·ter·tain·ment /éntərtáynmənt/ n. **1** the act or an instance of entertaining; the process of being entertained. **2** a public performance or show. **3** diversions or amusements for guests, etc. **4** amusement (much to my entertainment). **5** hospitality.

en·ter·tain·ment cen·ter n. a piece of furniture, usu. with several shelves to accommodate a television, video cassette recorder, stereo system, etc.

en·thrall /enthráwl, in-/ v.tr. (also **en·thral, in·thral, inthrall**) (-**thralled, -thralling**) **1** (often as **enthralling** adj.) captivate; please greatly. **2** enslave. □□ **en·thrall·ment** n.

en·throne /enthrón, in-/ v.tr. **1** install (a king, bishop, etc.) on a throne, esp. ceremonially. **2** exalt. □□ **en·throne·ment** n.

en·thuse /enthooz, in-/ v.intr. & tr. colloq. be or make enthusiastic.

en·thu·si·asm /enthoozeeazəm, in-/ n. **1** (often foll. by for, about) **a** strong interest or admiration. **b** great eagerness. **2** an object of enthusiasm.

en·thu·si·ast /enthoozeeast, in-/ n. (often foll. by for) a person who is full of enthusiasm.

en·thu·si·as·tic /enthoozeeástik, in-/ adj. having or showing enthusiasm. □□ **en·thu·si·as·ti·cal·ly** adv.

en·tice /entís, in-/ v.tr. (often foll. by from, into, or to + infin.) persuade by the offer of pleasure or reward. □□ **en·tice·ment** n. **en·tic·er** n. **en·tic·ing·ly** adv.

en·tire /entír, in-/ adj. **1** whole; complete. **2** not broken or decayed. **3** unqualified; absolute (an entire success). **4** in one piece; continuous. **5** not castrated.

en·tire·ly /entírlee, in-/ adv. **1** wholly; completely (the stock is entirely exhausted). **2** solely; exclusively (did it entirely for my benefit).

en·tire·ty /entírtee, in-/ n. (pl. **-ies**) **1** completeness. **2** (usu. foll. by of) the sum total. □ **in its entirety** in its complete form; completely.

en·ti·tle /entítəl, in-/ v.tr. **1 a** (usu. foll. by to) give (a person, etc.) a just claim. **b** (foll. by to + infin.) give (a person, etc.) a right. **2** give (a book, etc.) the title of. □□ **en·ti·tle·ment** n.

en·ti·ty /éntitee/ n. (pl. **-ies**) **1** a thing with distinct existence, as opposed to a quality or relation. **2** a thing's existence regarded distinctly; a thing's essential nature. □□ **en·ti·ta·tive** /-titáytiv/ adj.

en·tomb /entoom, in-/ v.tr. **1** place in or as in a tomb. **2** serve as a tomb for. □□ **en·tomb·ment** n.

en·to·mol·o·gy /éntəmóljee/ n. the study of the forms and behavior of insects. □□ **en·to·mo·log·i·cal** /-məlójikəl/ adj. **en·to·mol·o·gist** n.

en·tou·rage /óntooráazh/ n. **1** people attending an important person. **2** surroundings.

en·tr'acte /aantrákt, óntrakt/ n. **1** an interval between two acts of a play. **2** a piece of music or a dance performed during this.

en·trails /éntraylz, -trəlz/ n.pl. **1** the bowels and intestines of a person or animal. ▷ INTESTINE. **2** the innermost parts (entrails of the earth).

en·trance[1] /éntrəns/ n. **1** the act or an instance of going or coming in. **2** a door, passage, etc., by which one enters. **3** right of admission. **4** the coming of an actor on stage. **5** Mus. = ENTRY 8. **6** (foll. by into, upon) entering into office, etc. **7** (in full **entrance fee**) a fee paid for admission to a society, club, exhibition, etc.

en·trance[2] /entráns, in-/ v.tr. **1** enchant; delight. **2** put into a trance. **3** (often foll. by with) overwhelm with strong feeling. □□ **en·trance·ment** n. **en·tranc·ing** adj. **en·tranc·ing·ly** adv.

en·trant /éntrənt/ n. a person who enters (esp. an examination, profession, etc.).

en·trap /entráp, in-/ v.tr. (**entrapped, entrapping**) **1** catch in or as in a trap. **2** (often foll. by into + verbal noun) beguile or trick. □□ **en·trap·per** n.

en·trap·ment /entrápmənt, in-/ n. **1** the act or an instance of entrapping; the process of being entrapped. **2** Law inducement to commit a crime, esp. by the authorities to secure a prosecution.

en·treat /entreet, in-/ v.tr. **1** (foll. by to + infin. or that + clause) ask (a person) earnestly. **2** ask earnestly for (a thing). □□ **en·treat·ing·ly** adv.

en·treat·y /entreetee, in-/ n. (pl. **-ies**) an earnest request; a supplication.

en·tre·côte /óntrəkōt/ n. a boned steak cut off the sirloin.

en·trée /óntray/ n. (also **en·tree**) **1** Cookery **a** esp. US the main dish of a meal. **b** Brit. a dish served between the fish and meat courses. **2** the right or privilege of admission.

en·trench /entrénch, in-/ v. (also **intrench**) **1** tr. establish firmly (in a defensible position, in office, etc.). **2** tr. surround (a post, army, town, etc.) with a trench as a fortification. **3** tr. apply extra safeguards to (rights, etc., guaranteed by legislation). **4** intr. entrench oneself. **5** intr. (foll. by upon) encroach; trespass. □ **entrench oneself** adopt a well-defended position. □□ **en·trench·ment** n.

en·tre·pôt /óntrəpō/ n. **1** a warehouse for temporary storage of goods in transit. **2** a commercial center for import and export, and for collection and distribution.

en·tre·pre·neur /óntrəprənóor/ n. a person who undertakes an enterprise or business, with the chance of profit or loss. □□ **en·tre·pre·neur·i·al** adj. **en·tre·pre·neur·i·al·ism** n. (also **en·tre·pre·neur·ism**). **en·tre·pre·neur·i·al·ly** adv. **en·tre·pre·neur·ship** n.

en·trism var. of ENTRYISM.

en·tro·py /éntrəpee/ n. **1** Physics a measure of the unavailability of a system's thermal energy for conversion into mechanical work. **2** Physics a measure of the disorganization or degradation of the universe. **3** a measure of the rate of transfer of information in a message, etc. □□ **en·tro·pic** /-trópik/ adj. **en·tro·pi·cal·ly** adv.

en·trust /entrúst, in-/ v.tr. (also **in·trust**) **1** (foll. by to) give responsibility for (a person or a thing) to a person in whom one has confidence. **2** (foll. by with) assign responsibility for a thing to (a person). □□ **en·trust·ment** n.

en·try /éntree/ n. (pl. **-ies**) **1 a** the act or an instance of going or coming in. **b** the coming of an actor on stage. **c** ceremonial entrance. **2** liberty to go or come in. **3 a** a place of entrance; a door, gate, etc. **b** a lobby. **4** Brit. a passage between buildings. **5** the mouth of a river. **6 a** an item entered (in a diary, list, account book, etc.). **b** the recording of this. **7 a** a person or thing competing in a race, contest, etc. **b** a list of competitors. **8** the start or resumption of music for a particular instrument in an ensemble.

en·try·ism /éntreeizəm/ n. (also **entrism**) infiltration into a political organization to change or subvert its policies or objectives. □□ **en·trist** n. **en·try·ist** n.

en·try-lev·el adj. suitable for a beginner or first-time user.

en·twine /entwín, in-/ v. (also **in·twine** /in-/) **1** tr. & intr. (foll. by with, about, around) twine together (a thing with or around another). **2** tr. (as **entwined** adj.) entangled. **3** tr. interweave. □□ **en·twine·ment** n.

e·nu·mer·ate /inoomərayt, inyoo-/ v.tr. **1** specify (items); mention one by one. **2** count; establish the number of. □□ **e·nu·mer·a·ble** adj. **e·nu·mer·a·tion** /-ráyshən/ n. **e·nu·mer·a·tive** /-raytiv, -rətiv/ adj.

e·nu·mer·a·tor /inooməraytər, inyoo-/ n. a person who enumerates. **2** a person employed in census taking.

e·nun·ci·ate /inúnseeayt/ v.tr. **1** pronounce (words) clearly. **2** express (a proposition or theory) in definite terms. **3** proclaim. □□ **e·nun·ci·a·tion** /-áyshən/ n. **e·nun·ci·a·tive** /-seeətiv/ adj. **e·nun·ci·a·tor** n.

e·nu·re·sis /ényŏoréesis/ n. Med. involuntary urination, esp. while sleeping. □□ **e·nu·ret·ic** /-rétik/ adj. & n.

en·vel·op /envéləp, in-/ v.tr. (**enveloped, enveloping**) (often foll. by in) **1** wrap up or cover completely. **2** make obscure; conceal (was enveloped in mystery). □□ **en·vel·op·ment** n.

en·ve·lope /énvəlōp, ón-/ n. **1** a folded paper container, usu. with a sealable flap, for a letter, etc. **2** a wrapper or covering. **3** the structure within a balloon or airship containing the gas. ▷ HOT-AIR BALLOON, ZEPPELIN. **4** the outer metal or glass housing of a vacuum tube, electric light, etc.

en·ven·om /envénəm, in-/ v.tr. **1** put poison on or into; make poisonous. **2** infuse venom or bitterness into (feelings, words, or actions).

en·vi·a·ble /énveeəbəl/ adj. (of a person or thing) exciting or likely to excite envy. □□ **en·vi·a·bly** adv.

en·vi·ous /énveeəs/ adj. (often foll. by of) feeling or showing envy. □□ **en·vi·ous·ly** adv.

en·vi·ron·ment /envírənmənt, -vÍərn-, in-/ n. **1** physical surroundings and conditions, esp. as affecting people's lives. **2** conditions or circumstances of living. **3** Ecol. external conditions affecting the growth of plants and animals. **4** a structure designed to be experienced from inside as a work of art. **5** Computing the overall structure within which a user, computer, or program operates. □□ **en·vi·ron·men·tal** /-mént'l/ adj. **en·vi·ron·men·tal·ly** adv.

en·vi·ron·men·tal·ist /envírənmént'list, -vÍərn-, in-/ n. **1** a person who is concerned with or advocates the protection of the environment. **2** a person who considers that environment has the primary influence on the development of a person or group. □□ **en·vi·ron·men·tal·ism** n.

en·vi·ron·ment-friend·ly adj. not harmful to the environment.

en·vi·rons /envírənz, -vÍərnz, in-/ n.pl. a surrounding district, esp. around an urban area.

en·vis·age /envíziy, in-/ v.tr. **1** have a mental picture of (a thing not yet existing). **2** contemplate or conceive, esp. as a possibility or desirable future event. □□ **en·vis·age·ment** n.

en·vi·sion /envízhən, in-/ v.tr. envisage; visualize.

en·voy /énvoy, ón-/ n. **1** a messenger or representative, esp. on a diplomatic mission. **2** (in full **envoy extraordinary**) a minister plenipotentiary, ranking below ambassador and above chargé d'affaires.

en·vy /énvee/ n. & v. ● n. (pl. **-ies**) **1** a feeling of discontented or resentful longing aroused by another's better fortune, etc. **2** the object or ground of this feeling (their house is the envy of the neighborhood). ● v.tr. (**-ies, -ied**) feel envy of (a person, circumstances, etc.) (I envy you your position). □□ **en·vi·er** n.

en·zyme /énzīm/ n. Biochem. a protein acting as a catalyst in a specific biochemical reaction. □□ **en·zy·mat·ic** /-zīmátik/ adj. **en·zy·mic** adj. **en·zy·mol·o·gy** /-zīmóljee/ n.

E·o·cene /éeəseen/ adj. & n. Geol. ● adj. of or relating to the second epoch of the Tertiary period. ● n. this epoch or system.

e·o·li·an /ee-ólee-ən/ adj. wind-borne.

e·o·lith·ic /éeəlíthik/ adj. Archaeol. of the period preceding the Paleolithic age.

e.o.m. abbr. (also **E.O.M.**) end of month.

e·on /éeon/ n. (also **aeon**) **1** a very long or indefinite period. **2** an age of the universe. **3** a billion years.

e·o·sin /éeəsin/ n. a red fluorescent dyestuff used esp. as a stain in optical microscopy.

EP abbr. **1** European plan. **2** extended play.

Ep. abbr. Epistle.

EPA abbr. Environmental Protection Agency.

ep·act /éepakt/ n the number of days by which the solar year exceeds the lunar year.

E

E

fringed epaulet

ep·au·let /épəlét/ *n.* (also **ep·au·lette**) ◀ an ornamental shoulder piece on a coat, dress, etc., esp. on a uniform.

épée /aypáy, épay/ *n.* a sharp-pointed dueling sword, used (with the end blunted) in fencing. ▷ FENCING. □□ **é·pée·ist** *n.*

e·pergne /ipə́rn, aypə́rn/ *n.* an ornament for the center of a dinner-table, holding flowers or fruit.

EPAULET ON A GRENADIER OFFICER'S COAT

e·phed·ra /ifédrə/ *n.* any evergreen shrub of the genus *Ephedra*, with trailing stems and scalelike leaves.

e·phed·rine /ifédrin, éfədreen/ *n.* an alkaloid drug found in some ephedras, causing constriction of the blood vessels and widening of the bronchial passages, used to relieve asthma, etc.

e·phem·er·a[1] /ifémərə/ *n.* (*pl.* **ephemera** or **ephemerae** /-ree/ or **ephemeras**) **1 a** an insect living only a day or a few days. **b** any insect of the order Ephemeroptera, e.g., the mayfly. **2** = EPHEMERON 1.

e·phem·er·a[2] *pl.* of EPHEMERON 1.

e·phem·er·al /ifémərəl/ *adj.* **1** lasting or of use for only a short time; transitory. **2** lasting only a day. **3** (of an insect, flower, etc.) lasting a day or a few days. □□ **e·phem·er·al·i·ty** /-rálitee/ *n.* **e·phem·er·al·ly** *adv.* **e·phem·er·al·ness** *n.*

e·phem·er·is /iféməris/ *n.* (*pl.* **ephemerides** /éfimérideez/) *Astron.* an astronomical almanac or table of the predicted positions of celestial bodies.

e·phem·er·ist /ifémərist/ *n.* a collector of ephemera.

e·phem·er·on /ifémərən/ *n.* **1** (*pl.* **ephemera** /-rə/) (usu. in *pl.*) **a** a thing (esp. a printed item) of short-lived interest or usefulness. **b** a short-lived thing. **2** (*pl.* **ephemerons**) = EPHEMERA[1] 1.

ep·ic /épik/ *n. & adj.* ● *n.* **1** a long poem narrating the adventures or deeds of one or more heroic or legendary figures, e.g., the *Iliad, Paradise Lost.* **2** an imaginative work of any form, embodying a nation's conception of its history. **3** a book or motion picture based on an epic narrative or heroic in type or scale. **4** a subject fit for recital in an epic. ● *adj.* **1** of or like an epic. **2** grand; heroic. □□ **ep·i·cal** *adj.* **ep·i·cal·ly** *adv.*

ep·i·cene /épiseen/ *adj. & n.* ● *adj.* **1** *Gram.* denoting either sex without change of gender. **2** of, for, or used by both sexes. **3** having characteristics of both sexes. **4** having no characteristics of either sex. **5** effete; effeminate. ● *n.* an epicene person.

ep·i·cen·ter /épisentər/ *n.* **1** *Geol.* the point at which an earthquake reaches the Earth's surface. ▷ EARTHQUAKE. **2** the central point of a difficulty. □□ **ep·i·cen·tral** /-séntrəl/ *adj.*

ep·i·cure /épikyŏŏr/ *n.* a person with refined tastes, esp. in food and drink. □□ **ep·i·cur·ism** *n.*

Ep·i·cu·re·an /épikyŏŏréeən, -kyŏŏree-/ *n. & adj.* ● *n.* **1** a disciple or student of the Greek philosopher Epicurus (d. 270 BC). **2** (**epicurean**) a person devoted to (esp. sensual) enjoyment. ● *adj.* **1** of or concerning Epicurus or his ideas. **2** (**epicurean**) characteristic of an epicurean. □□ **Ep·i·cu·re·an·ism** *n.*

ep·i·dem·ic /épidémik/ *n. & adj.* ● *n.* **1** a widespread occurrence of a disease in a community at a particular time. **2** such a disease. **3** (foll. by *of*) a wide prevalence of something. ● *adj.* in the nature of an epidemic (cf. ENDEMIC). □□ **ep·i·dem·i·cal·ly** *adv.*

ep·i·de·mi·ol·o·gy /épideemeeóləjee/ *n.* the study of the incidence and distribution of diseases. □□ **ep·i·de·mi·o·log·i·cal** /-meeəlójikəl/ *adj.* **ep·i·de·mi·ol·o·gist** *n.*

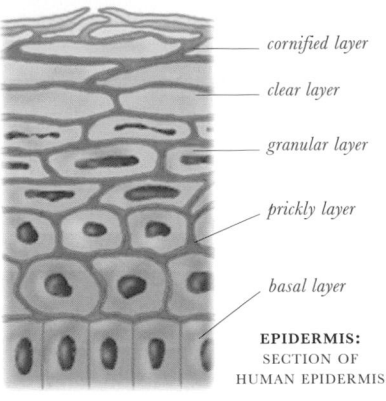

cornified layer

clear layer

granular layer

prickly layer

basal layer

EPIDERMIS: SECTION OF HUMAN EPIDERMIS

ep·i·der·mis /épidə́rmis/ *n.* **1** ▲ the outer cellular layer of the skin. ▷ SKIN. **2** *Bot.* the outer layer of cells of leaves, stems, roots, etc. □□ **ep·i·der·mal** *adj.* **ep·i·der·mic** *adj.* **ep·i·der·moid** *adj.*

ep·i·did·y·mis /épidídimis/ *n.* (*pl.* **epididymides** /-didímideez/) *Anat.* a convoluted duct behind the testis, along which sperm passes to the vas deferens. ▷ REPRODUCTIVE ORGANS

ep·i·du·ral /épidŏŏrəl, -dyŏŏr-/ *adj. & n.* ● *adj.* **1** *Anat.* on or around the dura mater. **2** (of an anesthetic) introduced into the space around the dura mater of the spinal cord. ● *n.* an epidural anesthetic, used esp. in childbirth.

ep·i·fau·na /épifawnə/ *n.* animals living on the seabed, either attached to animals, plants, etc., or free-living.

ep·i·glot·tis /épiglótis/ *n. Anat.* a flap of cartilage at the root of the tongue, depressed during swallowing to cover the windpipe. ▷ HEAD, TONGUE. □□ **ep·i·glot·tal** *adj.* **ep·i·glot·tic** *adj.*

ep·i·gram /épigram/ *n.* **1** a short poem with a witty ending. **2** a saying or maxim, esp a proverbial one. **3 a** a pointed remark or expression, esp. a witty one. **b** the use of concise witty remarks. □□ **ep·i·gram·mat·ic** /-grəmátik/ *adj.* **ep·i·gram·mat·i·cal·ly** *adv.* **ep·i·gram·ma·tist** /-grámətist/ *n.*

ep·i·graph /épigraf/ *n.* an inscription.

e·pig·ra·phy /ipígrəfee/ *n.* the study of (esp. ancient) inscriptions. □□ **ep·i·graph·ic** /épigráfik/ *adj.* **ep·i·graph·i·cal·ly** *adv.* **e·pig·ra·phist** /-pígrəfist/ *n.*

ep·i·late /épilayt/ *v.tr.* remove hair from. □□ **ep·i·la·tion** /-láyshən/ *n.*

ep·i·lep·sy /épilepsee/ *n.* a nervous disorder with convulsions and often loss of consciousness. □□ **ep·i·lep·tic** /épiléptik/ *adj. & n.*

ep·i·logue /épilawg, -og/ *n.* (also **ep·i·log**) **1 a** the concluding part of a literary work. **b** an appendix. **2** a speech or short poem addressed to the audience by an actor at the end of a play.

ep·i·neph·rine /épinéfrin/ *n.* a hormone secreted by the adrenal glands, affecting circulation and muscular action, and causing excitement and stimulation. Also called **adrenaline**.

e·piph·a·ny /ipífənee/ *n.* (*pl.* **-ies**) **1 (Epiphany) a** the manifestation of Christ to the Magi. **b** the festival commemorating this on January 6. **2** any manifestation of a god or demigod. □□ **ep·i·phan·ic** /épifánik/ *adj.*

ep·i·phyte /épifīt/ *n.* ▼ a plant growing but not parasitic on another, e.g., a moss. □□ **ep·i·phyt·ic** /-fitik/ *adj.*

e·pis·co·pa·cy /ipískəpəsee/ *n.* (*pl.* **-ies**) **1** government of a church by bishops. **2** (prec. by *the*) the bishops.

e·pis·co·pal /ipískəpəl/ *adj.* **1** of a bishop or bishops. **2** (of a Church) constituted on the principle of government by bishops. □□ **e·pis·co·pal·ism** *n.* **e·pis·co·pal·ly** *adv.*

E·pis·co·pal Church *n.* a Protestant Church in the US and Scotland, with elected bishops.

e·pis·co·pa·lian /ipískəpáyleeən/ *adj. & n.* ● *adj.* **1** of or advocating government of a church by bishops. **2** of or belonging to an episcopal church or (**Episcopalian**) the Episcopal Church. ● *n.* **1** an adherent of episcopacy. **2** (**Episcopalian**) a member of the Episcopal Church. □□ **e·pis·co·pa·lian·ism** *n.*

e·pis·co·pate /ipískəpət/ *n.* **1** the office or tenure of a bishop. **2** (prec. by *the*) the bishops collectively.

e·pi·si·ot·o·my /ipéezeeótəmee/ *n.* (*pl.* **-ies**) a surgical cut made at the opening of the vagina during childbirth.

ep·i·sode /épisōd/ *n.* **1** one event or a group of events as part of a sequence. **2** each of the parts of a serial story or broadcast. **3** an incident or set of incidents in a narrative. **4** an incident that is distinct but contributes to a whole (*a romantic episode in her life*). □□ **ep·i·sod·ic** /épisódik/ **ep·i·sod·i·cal** /-sódikəl/ *adj.* **ep·i·sod·i·cal·ly** *adv.*

e·pis·te·mol·o·gy /ipístimóləjee/ *n.* the theory of knowledge, esp. with regard to its methods and validation. □□ **e·pis·te·mo·log·i·cal** /-məlójikəl/ *adj.* **e·pis·te·mo·log·i·cal·ly** *adv.* **e·pis·te·mol·o·gist** *n.*

e·pis·tle /ipísəl/ *n.* **1** *formal* or *joc.* a letter, esp. a long

---

EPIPHYTE

Epiphytes, such as bromeliads and orchids, live above ground on other plants. However, they are not parasitic, but obtain their nutrients from rainwater and organic debris such as leaf litter.

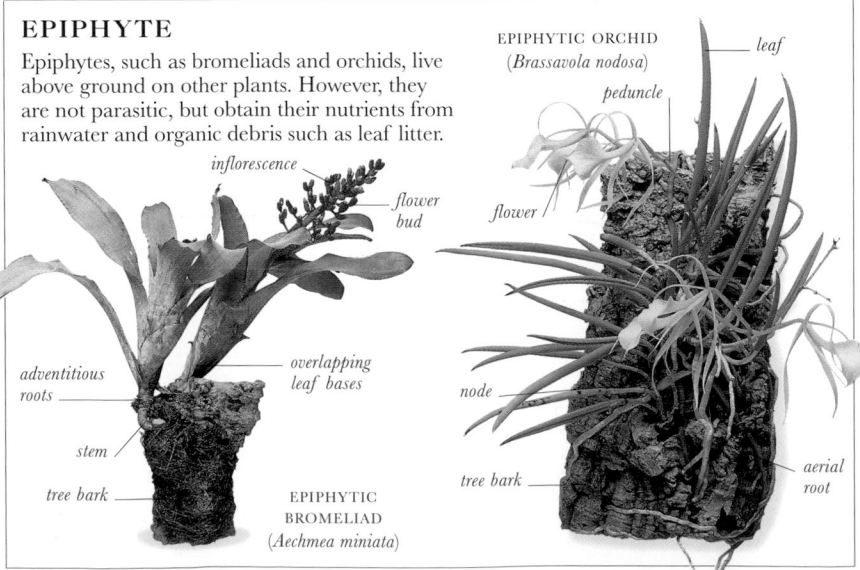

EPIPHYTIC ORCHID (*Brassavola nodosa*)

leaf

peduncle

flower

node

tree bark

aerial root

inflorescence

flower bud

adventitious roots

overlapping leaf bases

stem

tree bark

EPIPHYTIC BROMELIAD (*Aechmea miniata*)

one on a serious subject. **2** (**Epistle**) **a** any of the letters of the apostles in the New Testament. **b** an extract from an Epistle read in a church service. **3** a poem or other literary work in the form of a letter or series of letters.

e·pis·to·lar·y /ipístəleree/ *adj.* **1** in the style or form of a letter or letters. **2** of, carried by, or suited to letters.

ep·i·style /épistīl/ *n. Archit.* = ARCHITRAVE 1.

ep·i·taph /épitaf/ *n.* words written in memory of a person who has died, esp. as a tomb inscription.

ep·i·the·li·um /épitheéleeəm/ *n.* (*pl.* **epithelia** /-leeə/ or **epitheliums**) the tissue forming the outer layer of the body surface and lining many hollow structures. ▷ NOSE, SKIN. □□ **ep·i·the·li·al** *adj.*

ep·i·thet /épithet/ *n.* **1** an adjective or other descriptive word expressing a quality or attribute. **2** such a word as a term of abuse. □□ **ep·i·thet·ic** /-thétik/ *adj.* **ep·i·thet·i·cal** *adj.* **ep·i·thet·i·cal·ly** *adv.*

e·pit·o·me /ipítəmee/ *n.* **1** a person or thing embodying a quality, class, etc. **2** a thing representing another in miniature. **3** a summary of a written work. □□ **e·pit·o·mist** *n.*

e·pit·o·mize /ipítəmīz/ *v.tr.* **1** be a perfect example of (a quality, etc.). **2** make an epitome of (a work). □□ **e·pit·o·mi·za·tion** *n.*

ep·och /épək, éepok/ *n.* **1** a period of history or of a person's life marked by notable events. **2** the beginning of an era. **3** *Geol.* a division of a period, corresponding to a set of strata. □□ **ep·och·al** *adj.*

ep·o·nym /épənim/ *n.* **1** a person (real or imaginary) after whom a discovery, place, etc., is named. **2** the name given. □□ **ep·on·y·mous** /ipónimas/ *adj.*

ep·ox·ide /ipóksīd/ *n. Chem.* a compound containing an oxygen atom bonded in a triangular arrangement to two carbon atoms.

ep·ox·y /ipóksee/ *adj. Chem.* relating to or derived from an epoxide.

ep·ox·y res·in *n.* a synthetic thermosetting resin containing epoxy groups.

ep·si·lon /épsilon/ *n.* the fifth letter of the Greek alphabet (E, ε).

Ep·som salts /épsəm/ *n.pl.* a preparation of magnesium sulfate used as a purgative, etc.

eq·ua·ble /ékwəbəl/ *adj.* **1** even; not varying. **2** uniform and moderate (*an equable climate*). **3** (of a person) not easily angered. □□ **eq·ua·bil·i·ty** /-bíli-tee/ *n.* **eq·ua·bly** *adv.*

e·qual /éekwəl/ *adj., n., & v.* ● *adj.* **1** (often foll. by *to, with*) the same in quantity, quality, size, rank, etc. **2** evenly balanced (*an equal contest*). **3** having the same rights (*human beings are essentially equal*). **4** uniform in application or effect. ● *n.* a person or thing equal to another, esp. in rank, status, or characteristic quality (*he has no equal; is the equal of any man*). ● *v.tr.* be equal to in number, quality, etc. **2** achieve something that is equal to. □ **be equal to** have the ability or resources for. □□ **e·qual·i·ty** /ikwólitee/ *n.*

e·qual·ize /éekwəlīz/ *v.* **1** *tr. & intr.* make or become equal. **2** *intr.* reach one's opponent's score in a game, after being behind. □□ **e·qual·i·za·tion** *n.*

e·qual·iz·er /éekwəlīzər/ *n.* **1** an equalizing score or goal, etc., in a game. **2** *sl.* a weapon, esp. a gun.

e·qual·ly /éekwəlee/ *adv.* **1** in an equal manner (*treated them all equally*). **2** to an equal degree (*is equally important*). ¶ In sense 2 construction with *as* (*equally as important*) is often found, but is disputed.

e·qual op·por·tu·ni·ty *n.* (often in *pl.*) the opportunity or right to be employed, paid, etc., without discrimination on grounds of sex, race, etc.

e·qual sign *n.* (also **equals sign**) the symbol =.

e·qua·nim·i·ty /éekwənímitee, ékwə-/ *n.* mental composure; evenness of temper, esp. in misfortune. □□ **e·quan·i·mous** /ikwánimas/ *adj.*

e·quate /ikwáyt/ *v.* **1** *tr.* (usu. foll. by *to, with*) regard as equal or equivalent. **2** *intr.* (foll. by *with*) **a** be equal or equivalent to. **b** agree or correspond. □□ **e·quat·a·ble** *adj.*

e·qua·tion /ikwáyzhən/ *n.* **1** the process of equating or making equal; the state of being equal. **2** *Math.* a statement that two mathematical expressions are equal (indicated by the sign =). **3** *Chem.* a formula indicating a chemical reaction. □□ **e·qua·tion·al** *adj.*

e·qua·tor /ikwáytər/ *n.* **1** ▼ an imaginary line around the Earth or other body, equidistant from the poles. **2** *Astron.* = CELESTIAL EQUATOR. □□ **e·qua·to·ri·al** /ékwətáwreeəl, éekwə-/ *adj.* **e·qua·to·ri·al·ly** *adv.*

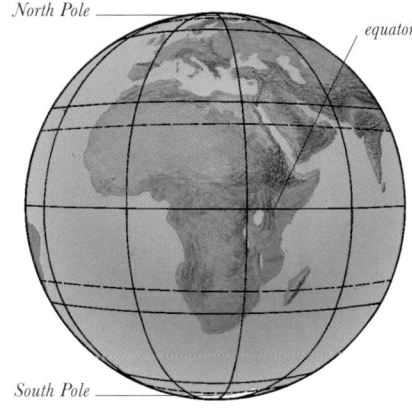

North Pole   *equator*

South Pole

EQUATOR

eq·uer·ry /ékwəree/ *n.* (*pl.* **-ies**) **1** an officer of the British royal household attending members of the royal family. **2** *hist.* an officer of a prince's or noble's household having charge over the horses.

e·ques·tri·an /ikwéstreeən/ *adj. & n.* ● *adj.* **1** of or relating to horses and horseback riding. **2** on horseback. ● *n.* (*fem.* **equestrienne** /-tree-én/) a rider or performer on horseback. □□ **e·ques·tri·an·ism** *n.*

equi- /éekwee, ékwi/ *comb. form* equal.

e·qui·an·gu·lar /éekweeángyələr, ékwee-/ *adj.* having equal angles.

e·qui·dis·tant /éekwidístənt, ékwi-/ *adj.* at equal distances. □□ **e·qui·dis·tant·ly** *adv.*

e·qui·lat·er·al /éekwilátərəl, ékwi-/ *adj.* having all its sides equal in length.

e·qui·li·brist /ikwílibrist/ *n.* an acrobat, esp. on a high rope.

e·qui·lib·ri·um /éekwilíbreeəm, ékwi-/ *n.* (*pl.* **equilibriums** or **equilibria** /-reeə/) **1** a state of physical balance. **2** a state of mental or emotional equanimity. **3** a state in which the energy in a system is evenly distributed and forces, influences, etc., balance each other.

e·quine /éekwīn, ékwīn/ *adj.* of or like a horse.

e·qui·noc·tial /éekwinókshəl, ékwi-/ *adj. & n.* ● *adj.* **1** happening at or near the time of an equinox (*equinoctial gales*). **2** of or relating to equal day and night. **3** at or near the (terrestrial) equator. ● *n.* (in full **equinoctial line**) = CELESTIAL EQUATOR.

e·qui·nox /éekwinoks, ékwi-/ *n.* the time or date (twice each year) at which the Sun crosses the celestial equator, when day and night are of equal length.

e·quip /ikwíp/ *v.tr.* (**equipped, equipping**) supply with what is needed. □□ **e·quip·per** *n.*

e·qui·page /ékwipij/ *n.* **1 a** requisites for an undertaking. **b** an outfit for a special purpose. **2** a carriage and horses with attendants.

e·quip·ment /ikwípmənt/ *n.* **1** the necessary articles, clothing, etc., for a purpose. **2** the process of equipping or being equipped.

e·qui·poise /éekwipoyz, ékwi-/ *n. & v.* ● *n.* **1** equilibrium; a balanced state. **2** a counterbalancing thing. ● *v.tr.* counterbalance.

eq·ui·ta·ble /ékwitəbəl/ *adj.* **1** fair; just. **2** *Law* valid in equity as distinct from law. □□ **eq·ui·ta·ble·ness** *n.* **eq·ui·ta·bly** *adv.*

eq·ui·ta·tion /ékwitáyshən/ *n.* the art and practice of horsemanship and horseback riding.

eq·ui·ty /ékwitee/ *n.* (*pl.* **-ies**) **1** fairness. **2** the application of the principles of justice to correct or supplement the law. **3 a** the value of the shares issued by a company. **b** (in *pl.*) stocks and shares not bearing fixed interest. **4** the net value of a mortgaged property after the deduction of charges.

e·quiv·a·lent /ikwívələnt/ *adj. & n.* *adj.* **1** (often foll. by *to*) equal in value, amount, etc. **2** corresponding. **3** (of words) having the same meaning. **4** having the same result. ● *n.* an equivalent thing, amount, word, etc. □□ **e·quiv·a·lence** /-ləns/ *n.* **e·quiv·a·len·cy** *n.* **e·quiv·a·lent·ly** *adv.*

e·quiv·o·cal /ikwívəkəl/ *adj.* **1** of double or doubtful meaning. **2** of uncertain nature. **3** (of a person, character, etc.) suspect. □□ **e·quiv·o·cal·i·ty** /-káli-tee/ *n.* **e·quiv·o·cal·ly** *adv.* **e·quiv·o·cal·ness** *n.*

e·quiv·o·cate /ikwívəkayt/ *v.intr.* use ambiguity to conceal the truth. □□ **e·quiv·o·ca·tion** /-káyshən/ *n.* **e·quiv·o·ca·tor** *n.* **e·quiv·o·ca·to·ry** *adj.*

ER *abbr.* emergency room.

Er *symb. Chem.* the element erbium.

er /ər/ *int.* expressing hesitation or a pause in speech.

ERA *abbr.* **1** *Baseball* earned run average. **2** Equal Rights Amendment.

e·ra /éerə, érə/ *n.* **1** a system of chronology reckoning from a noteworthy event (*the Christian era*). **2** a distinct period of time, esp. regarded historically (*the pre-Roman era*). **3** a date at which an era begins. **4** *Geol.* a major division of time.

e·rad·i·cate /irádikayt/ *v.tr.* root out; destroy completely; get rid of. □□ **e·rad·i·ca·ble** *adj.* **e·rad·i·ca·tion** /-káyshən/ *n.* **e·rad·i·ca·tor** *n.*

e·rase /iráys/ *v.tr.* **1** rub out. **2** remove all traces of (*erased it from my memory*). **3** remove recorded material from (a magnetic medium). □□ **e·ras·a·ble** *adj.* **e·ra·sure** *n.*

e·ras·er /iráysər/ *n.* a thing that erases, esp. a piece of rubber or plastic used for removing pencil and ink marks.

er·bi·um /árbeeəm/ *n. Chem.* a soft, silvery, metallic element of the lanthanide series. ¶ *Symb.*: **Er.**

ere /air/ *prep. & conj. poet.* or *archaic* before (of time) (*ere noon; ere they come*).

e·rect /irékt/ *adj. & v.* ● *adj.* **1** upright; vertical. **2** (of the penis, clitoris, or nipples) enlarged and rigid, esp. in sexual excitement. **3** (of hair) bristling; standing up from the skin. ● *v.tr.* **1** raise; set upright. **2** build. **3** establish (*erect a theory*). □□ **e·rect·a·ble** *adj.* **e·rect·ly** *adv.* **e·rect·ness** *n.* **e·rec·tor** *n.*

e·rec·tile /irékt'l, -tīl/ *adj.* that can be erected or become erect.

e·rec·tion /irékshən/ *n.* **1** the act or an instance of erecting; the state of being erected. **2** a building or structure. **3** *Physiol.* an enlarged and erect state of erectile tissue, esp. of the penis.

E re·gion *n.* the part of the ionosphere that contains the E layer.

er·e·mite /érimīt/ *n.* a hermit or recluse (esp. Christian). □□ **er·e·mit·ic** /-mítik/ *adj.* **er·e·mit·i·cal** *adj.*

erg /ərg/ *n. Physics* a unit of work or energy.

er·go /árgō, ér-/ *adv.* therefore.

er·go·cal·cif·er·ol /árgōkalsífə-rōl, -rol/ *n.* = CALCIFEROL.

er·go·nom·ics /árgonómiks/ *n.* the study of the efficiency of persons in their working environment. □□ **er·go·nom·ic** *adj.* **er·gon·o·mist** /ergón-əmist/ *n.*

er·got /árgot, -got/ *n.* **1** a disease of rye and other cereals caused by the fungus *Claviceps purpurea.* **2** this fungus.

er·i·ca /érikə/ *n.* ▶ any shrub or heath of the genus *Erica*, with small leathery leaves and bell-like flowers. □□ **er·i·ca·ceous** /-káyshəs/ *adj.*

ERICA:
DORSET HEATH
(*Erica ciliaris*)

E

ERODE

The wearing away and removal of land surfaces by water, wind, or ice is known as erosion. It has the greatest impact in areas of little or no surface vegetation, such as deserts.

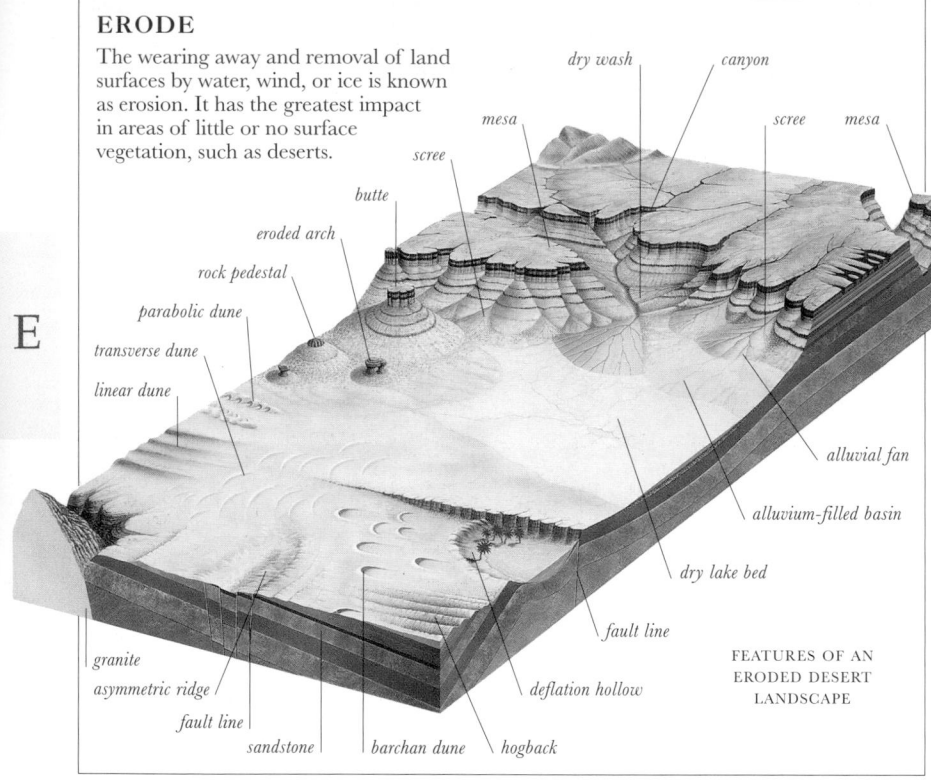

dry wash *canyon* *mesa* *scree* *mesa* *scree* *butte* *eroded arch* *rock pedestal* *parabolic dune* *transverse dune* *linear dune* *alluvial fan* *alluvium-filled basin* *dry lake bed* *fault line* *granite* *asymmetric ridge* *fault line* *sandstone* *barchan dune* *hogback* *deflation hollow*

FEATURES OF AN
ERODED DESERT
LANDSCAPE

er·mine /árminʔ/ n. (pl. same or **ermines**) **1** the stoat, esp. when in its white winter fur. **2** its white fur, used as trimming for the robes of judges, peers, etc. **3** *Heraldry* a white fur marked with black spots. □□ **er·mined** adj.

erne /ern/ (also **ern**) a sea eagle.

e·rode /iród/ v.tr. & intr. ▲ wear away; destroy or be destroyed gradually. □□ **e·rod·i·ble** adj. **e·ro·sion** /iróʒhən/ n. **e·ro·sive** adj.

e·rog·e·nous /irójinəs/ adj. **1** (esp. of a part of the body) sensitive to sexual stimulation. **2** giving rise to sexual desire or excitement.

e·rot·ic /irótik/ adj. of or causing sexual love, esp. tending to arouse sexual desire or excitement. □□ **e·rot·i·cal·ly** adv.

e·rot·i·ca /irótikə/ n.pl. erotic literature or art.

e·rot·i·cism /irótisizəm/ n. **1** erotic nature or character. **2** the use of or response to erotic images or stimulation.

er·o·tism /érətizəm/ n. = eroticism.

eroto- /irótō, irŏ-/ comb. form erotic; eroticism.

e·ro·to·gen·ic /irótəjénik, irŏ-/ adj. = EROGENOUS.

e·ro·to·ma·ni·a /irótəmáyneeə, irŏ-/ n. **1** excessive or morbid erotic desire. **2** a preoccupation with sexual passion. □□ **e·ro·to·ma·ni·ac** /-neeak/ n.

err /ər, er/ v.intr. **1** be mistaken or incorrect. **2** do wrong; sin. □ **err on the right side** act so that the least harmful of possible errors is the most likely to occur. **err on the side of** act with a specified bias (*errs on the side of generosity*).

er·rand /érənd/ n. **1** a short journey, esp. on another's behalf, to take a message, collect goods, etc. **2** the object of such a journey.

er·rant /érənt/ adj. **1** erring; deviating from an accepted standard. **2** *literary* or *archaic* traveling in search of adventure (*knight errant*). □□ **er·ran·cy** /-ənsee/ n. (in sense 1). **er·rant·ry** n. (in sense 2).

er·rat·ic /irátik/ adj. **1** inconsistently variable in conduct, opinions, etc. **2** uncertain in movement. □□ **er·rat·i·cal·ly** adv.

er·ra·tum /iráːtəm, irát-/ n. (pl. **errata** /-tə/) an error in printing or writing.

er·ro·ne·ous /irŏneeəs/ adj. incorrect; arising from error. □□ **er·ro·ne·ous·ly** adv. **er·ro·ne·ous·ness** n.

er·ror /érər/ n. **1** a mistake. **2** the condition of being wrong in conduct or judgment. **3** a wrong opinion or judgment. **4** the amount by which something is incorrect or inaccurate in a calculation or measurement. □□ **er·ror·less** adj.

er·satz /érzaats, -saats, erzáats, -sáats/ adj. substitute; imitation (esp. of inferior quality).

Erse /ərs/ adj. & n. ● adj. Irish or Highland Gaelic. ● n. the Gaelic language.

erst /ərst/ adv. archaic formerly; of old.

erst·while /árst-hwīl, -wīl/ adj. former; previous.

er·u·dite /éryədīt, érə-/ adj. **1** (of a person) learned. **2** (of writing, etc.) showing great learning. □□ **er·u·dite·ly** adv. **er·u·di·tion** /-díshən/ n.

e·rupt /irúpt/ v.intr. **1** break out suddenly or dramatically. **2** (of a volcano) become active and eject lava, etc. **3 a** (of a rash, boil, etc.) appear on the skin. **b** (of the skin) produce a rash, etc. **4** (of the teeth) break through the gums. □□ **e·rup·tion** /-rúpshən/ n. **e·rup·tive** adj.

er·y·sip·e·las /érisípiləs/ n. *Med.* a streptococcal infection producing inflammation and a deep red color on the skin.

er·y·the·ma /érithéemə/ n. a superficial reddening of the skin, usu. in patches.

erythro- /iríthrō/ comb. form red.

e·ryth·ro·cyte /iríthrəsīt/ n. a red blood cell. ▷ BLOOD. □□ **e·ryth·ro·cyt·ic** /-sítik/ adj.

Es symb. *Chem.* the element einsteinium.

-es[1] /iz/ suffix forming plurals of nouns ending in sibilant sounds (such words in -e dropping the e) (*kisses; cases; boxes; churches*).

-es[2] /iz, z/ suffix forming the 3rd person sing. present of verbs ending in sibilant sounds (such words in -e dropping the e) and ending in -o (but not -oo) (*goes; places; pushes*).

ESA abbr. European Space Agency.

es·ca·late /éskəlayt/ v. **1** intr. & tr. increase or develop (usu. rapidly) by stages. **2** tr. cause to become more intense. □□ **es·ca·la·tion** /-láyshən/ n.

es·ca·la·tor /éskəlaytər/ n. a moving staircase consisting of a circulating belt forming steps.

es·cal·lo·ni·a /éskəlŏneeə/ n. any evergreen shrub of the genus *Escallonia*, bearing rose-red flowers.

es·ca·lope /éskəlŏp/ n. a thin slice of meat without any bone, esp. veal.

es·ca·pade /éskəpáyd/ n. a piece of daring or reckless behavior.

es·cape /iskáyp/ v. & n. ● v. **1** intr. (often foll. by *from*) get free of the restriction or control of a place, person, etc. **2** intr. (of a gas, liquid, etc.) leak from a container or pipe, etc. **3** intr. succeed in avoiding danger, punishment, etc. **4** tr. get completely free of (a person, grasp, etc.). **5** tr. elude (a commitment, danger, etc.). **6** tr. elude the notice or memory of (*the name escaped me*). **7** tr. (of words, etc.) issue unawares from (a person's lips). ● n. **1** the act or an instance of escaping; avoidance of danger, injury, etc. **2** the state of having escaped (*a narrow escape*). **3** a means of escaping (often attrib.: *escape hatch*). **4** a leakage of gas, etc. **5** a temporary relief from reality or worry. □□ **es·cap·a·ble** adj. **es·cap·er** n.

es·cape clause n. *Law* a clause specifying the conditions under which a contracting party is free from an obligation.

es·cap·ee /iskaypée/ n. a person, esp. a prisoner, who has escaped.

es·cape·ment /iskáypmənt/ n. **1** the part of a clock or watch that connects and regulates the motive power. **2** the part of the mechanism in a piano that enables the hammer to fall back immediately after striking the string.

es·cape ve·loc·i·ty n. the minimum velocity needed to escape from the gravitational field of a body.

es·cape wheel n. a toothed wheel in the escapement of a watch or clock.

es·cap·ism /iskáypizəm/ n. the tendency to seek distraction and relief from reality, esp. in the arts or through fantasy. □□ **es·cap·ist** n. & adj.

es·cap·ol·o·gy /éskəpóləjee/ n. the methods and techniques of escaping from confinement, esp. as a form of entertainment. □□ **es·cap·ol·o·gist** n.

es·car·got /eskaargŏ/ n. an edible snail.

es·carp·ment /iskáarpmənt/ n. (also **es·carp**) *Geol.* a long, steep slope at the edge of a plateau, etc.

es·cha·tol·o·gy /éskətóləjee/ n. the part of theology concerned with death and final destiny. □□ **es·cha·to·log·i·cal** /-təlójikəl/ adj. **es·cha·tolo·gist** n.

es·cheat /ischéet/ n. hist. **1** the reversion of property to the state, or (in feudal law) to a lord, on the owner's dying without legal heirs. **2** property affected by this.

es·chew /eschŏo/ v.tr. literary avoid; abstain from. □□ **es·chew·al** n.

esch·scholt·zi·a /eshŏltseeə/ n. any yellow-flowering plant of the genus *Eschscholtzia*, esp. the Californian poppy.

es·cort n. & v. ● n. /éskawrt/ **1** one or more persons, vehicles, ships, etc., accompanying a person, vehicle, etc., esp. for protection or security or as a mark of rank or status. **2** a person accompanying a person of the opposite sex socially. ● v.tr. /iskáwrt/ act as an escort to.

es·cri·toire /éskritwáar/ n. a writing desk with drawers, etc.

es·crow /éskrō/ n. & v. *Law* ● n. **1** money, property, or a written bond, kept in the custody of a third party until a specified condition has been fulfilled. **2** the status of this (*in escrow*). ● v.tr. place in escrow.

es·cu·lent /éskŏlent/ adj. & n. ● adj. fit to eat; edible. ● n. an edible substance.

es·cu·do /eskŏodō/ n. (pl. **-os**) the principal monetary unit of Portugal and Cape Verde (replaced in Portugal by the euro in 2002).

es·cutch·eon /iskúchən/ n. **1** a shield or emblem bearing a coat of arms. **2** the protective plate around a keyhole or door handle.

Esd. *abbr.* Esdras (Apocrypha).

ESE *abbr.* east-southeast.

-ese /eez/ *suffix* forming adjectives and nouns denoting: **1** an inhabitant or language of a country or city (*Japanese; Milanese; Viennese*). ¶ Plural forms are the same. **2** often *derog.* character or style, esp. of language (*officialese*).

es·ker /éskər/ *n.* *Geol.* a long ridge of postglacial gravel in river valleys. ▷ VALLEY

Es·ki·mo /éskimō/ *n. & adj.* ● *n.* (*pl.* same or **-os**) **1** a member of a people inhabiting N. Canada, Alaska, Greenland, and E. Siberia. **2** the language of this people. ● *adj.* of or relating to the Eskimos or their language. ¶ The term *Inuit* is preferred by the people themselves.

ESL *abbr.* English as a second language.

e·soph·a·gus /isófəgəs, ee–/ *n.* (*pl.* **esophagi** /-gī, -jī/) ▼ the part of the alimentary canal from the mouth to the stomach; the gullet. ▷ DIGESTION. □□ **e·so·pha·ge·al** /isófəjéeəl, eesəfájeeəl/ *adj.*

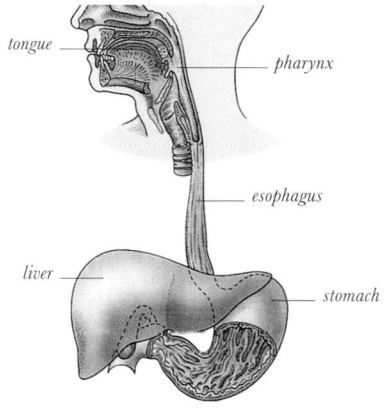

ESOPHAGUS: HUMAN ALIMENTARY CANAL
SHOWING THE ESOPHAGUS

tongue

pharynx

esophagus

liver

stomach

es·o·ter·ic /ésətérik/ *adj.* **1** intelligible only to those with special knowledge. **2** (of a belief, etc.) intended only for the initiated. □□ **es·o·ter·i·cal** *adj.* **es·o·ter·i·cal·ly** *adv.* **es·o·ter·i·cism** /-rəsizəm/ *n.* **es·o·ter·i·cist** *n.*

ESP *abbr.* extrasensory perception.

es·pa·drille /éspədril/ *n.* a light canvas shoe with a plaited fiber sole.

es·pal·ier /ispályər, -yay/ *n.* **1** a latticework along which the branches of a tree or shrub are trained to grow flat against a wall, etc. **2** ▶ a tree or shrub trained in this way.

es·par·to /espáartō/ *n.* (*pl.* **-os**) (in full **esparto grass**) a coarse grass, *Stipa tenacissima*, native to Spain and N. Africa, with tough, narrow leaves, used to make ropes, wickerwork, and good-quality paper.

ESPALIER

es·pe·cial /ispéshəl/ *adj.* **1** notable; exceptional. **2** attributed or belonging chiefly to one person or thing (*your especial charm*).

es·pe·cial·ly /ispéshəlee, espésh-/ *adv.* chiefly; much more than in other cases.

Es·pe·ran·to /éspərántō, -ráan-/ *n.* an artificial universal language devised in 1887, based on roots common to the chief European languages. □□ **Es·pe·ran·tist** *n.*

es·pi·o·nage /éspeeənaazh/ *n.* the practice of spying or of using spies.

es·pla·nade /ésplənáad, -náyd/ *n.* **1** a long, open level area for walking on, esp. beside the ocean. **2** a level space separating a fortress from a town.

es·pous·al /ispówzəl, -səl/ *n.* **1** (foll. by *of*) the espousing of a cause, etc. **2** *archaic* a marriage or betrothal.

es·pouse /ispówz/ *v.tr.* **1** adopt or support (a cause, doctrine, etc.). **2** *archaic* **a** (usu. of a man) marry. **b** (usu. foll. by *to*) give (a woman) in marriage.

es·pres·so /esprésō/ *n.* (also **ex·pres·so** /eksprésō/) (*pl.* **-os**) **1** strong, concentrated black coffee made under steam pressure. **2** a machine for making this.

es·prit /espreé/ *n.* sprightliness; wit.

es·prit de corps /espreé də káwr/ *n.* a feeling of devotion to and pride in the group one belongs to.

es·py /ispī/ *v.tr.* (**-ies, -ied**) *literary* catch sight of.

Esq. *abbr.* esquire.

-esque /esk/ *suffix* forming adjectives meaning 'in the style of' or 'resembling' (*romanesque; Schumannesque; statuesque*).

Es·qui·mau /éskimō/ *n.* (*pl.* **-aux** /-mōz/) = ESKIMO.

es·quire /éskwīr, iskwír/ *n.* **1** (usu. as abbr. **Esq.**) **a** a title appended to a man's surname when no other form of address is used, esp. as a form of address for letters. **b** a title placed after the name of an attorney (male or female), esp. in correspondence. **2** *archaic* = SQUIRE.

-ess /is/ *suffix* forming nouns denoting females (*actress; lioness; mayoress*).

es·say *n. & v.* ● *n.* /ésay/ **1** a composition, usu. short and in prose, on any subject. **2** (often foll. by *at, in*) *formal* an attempt. ● *v.tr.* /esáy/ *formal* attempt; try. □□ **es·say·ist** *n.*

es·sence /ésəns/ *n.* **1** fundamental nature or inherent characteristics. **2 a** an extract obtained by distillation, etc. **b** a perfume. **3** the constituent of a plant that determines its chemical properties. **4** an abstract entity; the reality underlying a phenomenon or all phenomena. □ **in essence** fundamentally. **of the essence** indispensable.

es·sen·tial /isénshəl/ *adj. & n.* ● *adj.* **1** absolutely necessary; indispensable. **2** fundamental; basic. **3** of or constituting the essence of a person or thing. **4** (of a disease) with no known external stimulus or cause; idiopathic. ● *n.* (esp. in *pl.*) a basic or indispensable element or thing. □□ **es·sen·ti·al·i·ty** /-sheeálitee/ *n.* **es·sen·tial·ly** *adv.*

es·sen·tial oil *n.* a volatile oil derived from a plant, etc., with its characteristic odor.

EST *abbr.* **1** eastern standard time. **2** electroshock treatment.

es·tab·lish /istáblish/ *v.tr.* **1** set up or consolidate (a business, system, etc.) on a permanent basis. **2** (foll. by *in*) settle (a person or oneself) in some capacity. **3** (esp. as **established** *adj.*) achieve permanent acceptance for (a custom, belief, practice, institution, etc.). **4** place beyond dispute (a fact, etc.). □□ **es·tab·lish·er** *n.*

es·tab·lish·ment /istáblishmənt/ *n.* **1** the act or an instance of establishing; the process of being established. **2 a** a business organization or public institution. **b** a place of business. **c** a residence. **3 a** the staff or equipment of an organization. **b** a household. **4** any organized body permanently maintained. **5** a church system organized by law. **6** (**the Establishment**) **a** the group in a society exercising authority or influence, and seen as resisting change. **b** any influential or controlling group (*the literary Establishment*).

es·tate /istáyt/ *n.* **1** a property consisting of an extensive area of land usu. with a large house. **2** *Brit.* a housing development. **3** all of a person's assets and liabilities, esp. at death. **4** a property where rubber, tea, grapes, etc., are cultivated. **5** (in full **estate of the realm**) an order or class form-

ing (or regarded as) a part of the body politic. **6** *archaic* or *literary* a state or position in life (*the estate of holy matrimony*).

es·teem /istéem/ *v. & n.* ● *v.tr.* **1** (usu. in *passive*) have a high regard for. **2** *formal* consider (*esteemed it an honor*). ● *n.* high regard; favor (*held them in esteem*).

es·ter /éstər/ *n.* *Chem.* any of a class of organic compounds produced by replacing the hydrogen of an acid by an alkyl, etc., radical, many of which occur naturally as oils and fats. □□ **es·ter·i·fy** /estérifī/ *v.tr.* (**-ies, -ied**).

es·thete var. of AESTHETE.

es·thet·ic var. of AESTHETIC.

es·ti·ma·ble /éstiməbəl/ *adj.* worthy of esteem.

es·ti·mate *n. & v.* ● *n.* /éstimət/ **1** an approximate judgment. **2** a price specified as that likely to be charged for work to be undertaken. **3** opinion; judgment; estimation. ● *v.tr.* (also *absol.*) /éstimayt/ **1** form an estimate of. **2** (foll. by *that* + clause) make a rough calculation. **3** (often foll. by *at*) form an estimate; adjudge. **4** fix (a price, etc.) by estimate. □□ **es·ti·ma·tor** *n.*

es·ti·ma·tion /éstimáyshən/ *n.* **1** the process or result of estimating. **2** judgment of worth (*in my estimation*).

es·ti·val /éstəvəl, estívəl/ *adj.* (also **aestival**) *formal* belonging to or appearing in summer.

es·ti·vate /éstəvayt/ *v.intr.* (also **aes·ti·vate**) *Zool.* spend the summer or dry season in a state of torpor.

Es·to·ni·an /estóneeən/ *n. & adj* ● *n.* **1 a** a native of Estonia, a Baltic republic. **b** a person of Estonian descent. **2** the language of Estonia. ● *adj.* of or relating to Estonia or its people or language.

es·trange /istráynj/ *v.tr.* (usu. in *passive*; often foll. by *from*) cause to turn away in feeling or affection; alienate. □□ **es·trange·ment** *n.*

es·tro·gen /éstrəjən/ *n.* **1** any of various steroid hormones developing and maintaining female characteristics of the body. **2** this hormone produced artificially. □□ **es·tro·gen·ic** /-jénik/ *adj.* **es·tro·gen·i·cal·ly** /-jénikəlee/ *adv.*

es·trus /éstrəs/ *n.* (also **es·trum**) a recurring period of sexual receptivity in many female mammals. □□ **es·trous** *adj.*

es·tu·a·r·y /és-chooeree/ *n.* (*pl.* **-ies**) a wide tidal mouth of a river. ▷ COASTLINE. □□ **es·tu·a·rine** /-ərīn, -əreen/ *adj.*

ET *abbr.* extraterrestrial.

ETA *abbr.* estimated time of arrival.

e·ta /áytə, éetə/ *n.* the seventh letter of the Greek alphabet (Η, η).

et al. /et ál/ *abbr.* and others.

etc. *abbr.* = ET CETERA.

et cet·er·a /et sétərə, sétrə/ *adv. & n.* (also **et·cet·er·a**) ● *adv.* **1 a** and the rest; and similar things or people. **b** or similar things or people. **2** and so on. ● *n.* (in *pl.*) the usual sundries or extras.

etch /ech/ *v. & n.* ● *v.* **1 a** *tr.* reproduce (a picture, etc.) by engraving a design on a metal plate with acid. **b** *tr.* engrave (a plate) in this way. **2** *intr.* practice this craft. **3** *tr.* (foll. by *on, upon*) impress deeply (esp. on the mind). ● *n.* the action or process of etching. □□ **etch·er** *n.*

etch·ing /éching/ *n.* **1** a print made from an etched plate. **2** the art of producing these plates.

ETD *abbr.* estimated time of departure.

e·ter·nal /itórnəl/ *adj.* **1** existing always; without an end or (usu.) beginning in time. **2** essentially unchanging (*eternal truths*). **3** *colloq.* constant; seeming not to cease (*your eternal nagging*). □ **the Eternal** God. □□ **e·ter·nal·i·ty** /-nálitee/ *n.* **e·ter·nal·ize** *v.tr.* **e·ter·nal·ly** *adv.*

E·ter·nal Cit·y *n.* (prec. by *the*) Rome.

e·ter·nal tri·an·gle *n.* a relationship of three people involving sexual rivalry.

e·ter·ni·ty /itórnitee/ *n.* (*pl.* **-ies**) **1** infinite or unending (esp. future) time. **2** *Theol.* endless life after death. **3** the state of being eternal. **4** *colloq.* (often prec. by *an*) a very long time.

E

E

eth·ane /éthayn/ *n. Chem.* a gaseous hydrocarbon of the alkane series, occurring in natural gas.

eth·a·nol /éthənawl, -nol/ *n. Chem.* = ALCOHOL 1.

eth·ene /étheen/ *n. Chem.* = ETHYLENE.

e·ther /éethər/ *n.* **1** *Chem.* a colorless volatile organic liquid used as an anesthetic or solvent. Also called **diethyl ether**. **b** any of a class of organic compounds with a similar structure to this, having an oxygen joined to two alkyl, etc., groups. **2** a clear sky; the upper regions of air. **3** *hist.* **a** a medium formerly assumed to permeate space. **b** a medium through which electromagnetic waves were formerly thought to be transmitted. □□ **e·ther·ic** /eethérik/ *adj.*

e·the·re·al /itheéreeəl/ *adj.* **1** light; airy. **2** highly delicate, esp. in appearance. **3** heavenly; celestial. □□ **e·the·re·al·i·ty** /-reeálitee/ *n.* **e·the·re·al·ly** *adv.*

eth·ic /éthik/ *n. & adj.* ● *n.* a set of moral principles (*the Quaker ethic*). ● *adj.* = ETHICAL.

eth·i·cal /éthikəl/ *adj.* **1** relating to morals. **2** morally correct; honorable. **3** (of a medicine or drug) not advertised to the general public, and usu. available only on a doctor's prescription. □□ **eth·i·cal·i·ty** /-kálitee/ *n.* **eth·i·cal·ly** *adv.*

eth·ics /éthiks/ *n.pl.* (also treated as *sing.*) **1** the science of morals in human conduct. **2 a** moral principles. **b** a set of these (*medical ethics*). □□ **eth·i·cist** /éthisist/ *n.*

E·thi·o·pi·an /éetheeópeeən/ *n. & adj.* ● *n.* **1** a native or national of Ethiopia in NE Africa. **2** a person of Ethiopian descent. ● *adj.* of or relating to Ethiopia.

eth·nic /éthnik/ *adj. & n.* ● *adj.* **1 a** (of a social group) having a common national or cultural tradition. **b** (of clothes, etc.) resembling those of a non-European exotic people. **2** denoting origin by birth or descent rather than nationality (*ethnic Turks*). **3** relating to race or culture (*ethnic group*; *ethnic origins*). ● *n.* **1** a member of an (esp. minority) ethnic group. **2** (in *pl.*, usu. treated as *sing.*) = ETHNOLOGY. □□ **eth·ni·cal·ly** *adv.* **eth·nic·i·ty** /-nísitee/ *n.*

eth·nic cleans·ing *n. euphem.* the practice of mass expulsion or killing of people from opposing ethnic or religious groups within a certain area.

ethno- /éthnō/ *comb. form* ethnic; ethnological.

eth·no·cen·tric /éthnōséntrik/ *adj.* evaluating other races and cultures by criteria specific to one's own. □□ **eth·no·cen·tri·cal·ly** *adv.* **eth·no·cen·tric·i·ty** /-trísitee/ *n.* **eth·no·cen·trism** *n.*

eth·nog·ra·phy /ethnógrəfee/ *n.* the scientific description of races and cultures of mankind. □□ **eth·nog·ra·pher** *n.* **eth·no·graph·ic** /-nəgráfik/ *adj.* **eth·no·graph·i·cal** *adj.*

eth·nol·o·gy /ethnóləjee/ *n.* the comparative scientific study of human peoples. □□ **eth·no·log·ic** /-nəlójik/ *adj.* **eth·no·log·i·cal** *adj.* **eth·nol·o·gist** *n.*

e·thol·o·gy /eethóləjee/ *n.* **1** the science of animal behavior. **2** the science of character formation in human behavior. □□ **e·tho·log·i·cal** /éethəlójikəl/ *adj.* **e·thol·o·gist** *n.*

e·thos /éethos/ *n.* the characteristic spirit or attitudes of a community, people, or system, or of a literary work, etc.

eth·yl /éthil/ *n.* (*attrib.*) *Chem.* the univalent radical derived from ethane by removal of a hydrogen atom (*ethyl alcohol*).

eth·yl·ene /éthileen/ *n. Chem.* a gaseous hydrocarbon of the alkene series, occurring in natural gas and used in the manufacture of polyethylene. Also called **ethene**.

e·ti·o·late /éeteeəláyt/ *v.tr.* **1** make (a plant) pale by excluding light. **2** give a sickly hue to (a person). □□ **e·ti·o·la·tion** /-láyshən/ *n.*

e·ti·ol·o·gy /éeteeóləjee/ *n.* **1** the assignment of a cause or reason. **2** the philosophy of causation. **3** *Med.* the science of the causes of disease. □□ **e·ti-**

o·log·ic /-teeəlójik/ *adj.* **e·ti·o·log·i·cal** /-teeəlójikəl/ *adj.* **e·ti·o·log·i·cal·ly** /-teeəlójikəlee/ *adv.*

et·i·quette /étiket, -kit/ *n.* **1** the conventional rules of social behavior. **2 a** the customary behavior of members of a profession toward each other. **b** the unwritten code governing this (*medical etiquette*).

E·trus·can /itrúskən/ *adj. & n.* ● *adj.* of ancient Etruria in Italy. ● *n.* **1** a native of Etruria. **2** the language of Etruria.

et seq. *abbr.* (also **et seqq.**) and the following (pages, etc.).

-ette /et/ *suffix* forming nouns meaning: **1** small (*kitchenette*; *cigarette*). **2** imitation or substitute (*leatherette*; *flannelette*). **3** often *offens.* female (*usherette*; *suffragette*).

é·tude /áytood, -tyood/ *n.* a short musical composition designed to improve the technique of the player.

et·y·mol·o·gy /étimóləjee/ *n.* (*pl.* **-ies**) **1 a** the sources of the formation of a word and the development of its meaning. **b** an account of these. **2** the branch of linguistic science concerned with etymologies. □□ **et·y·mo·log·i·cal** /-məlójikəl/ *adj.* **et·y·mo·log·i·cal·ly** *adv.* **et·y·mol·o·gist** *n.*

e·ty·mon /étimon/ *n.* a word or form from which a later word is derived.

EU *abbr.* European Union.

Eu *symb. Chem.* the element europium.

eu- /yoo/ *comb. form* well; easily.

eu·ca·lyp·tus /yóokəlíptəs/ *n.* (also **eu·ca·lypt**) (*pl.* **eucalypti** /-tī/ or **eucalyptuses** or **eucalypts**) **1** ▼ any tree of the genus *Eucalyptus*, native to Australasia, cultivated for its wood and for the oil from its leaves. **2** (in full **eucalyptus oil**) this oil used as an antiseptic, etc.

Eu·cha·rist /yóokərist/ *n.* **1** the Christian sacrament commemorating the Last Supper, in which bread and wine are consecrated and consumed. **2** the consecrated elements, esp. the bread (*receive the Eucharist*). □□ **Eu·cha·ris·tic** *adj.*

eu·clid·e·an /yóoklídeeən/ *adj.* (also **Eu·clid·e·an**) of or relating to Euclid, 3rd-c. BC Alexandrian geometrician.

eu·gen·ics /yoojéniks/ *n.pl.* (also treated as *sing.*) the science of improving the population by controlled breeding for desirable inherited characteristics. □□ **eu·gen·ic** *adj.* **eu·gen·i·cal·ly** *adv.* **eu·gen·i·cist** /yoojénisist/ *n.* **eu·ge·nist** /yóojinist/ *n.*

eu·kar·y·ote /yóokáreeōt/ *n.* (also **eu·car·y·ote**) *Biol.* an organism consisting of a cell or cells in which the genetic material is contained within a distinct nucleus (cf. PROKARYOTE). □□ **eu·kar·y·ot·ic** /-reeótik/ *adj.*

eu·lo·gize /yóoləjīz/ *v.tr.* praise in speech or writing. □□ **eu·lo·gist** /-jist/ *n.* **eu·lo·gis·tic** *adj.* **eu·lo·gis·ti·cal·ly** *adv.*

eu·lo·gy /yóoləjee/ *n.* (*pl.* **-ies**) **1** a speech or writing in praise of a person. **b** an expression of praise. **2** a funeral oration in praise of a person.

eu·nuch /yóonək/ *n.* **1** a castrated man, esp. one formerly employed at an Oriental harem or court. **2** a person lacking effectiveness (*political eunuch*).

eu·on·y·mus /yoo-óniməs/ *n.* any tree of the genus *Euonymus*, e.g., the spindle tree.

eu·phe·mism /yóofimizəm/ *n.* **1** a mild or vague expression substituted for one thought to be too harsh or direct (e.g., *pass over* for *die*). **2** the use of such expressions. □□ **eu·phe·mis·tic** *adj.* **eu·phe·mis·ti·cal·ly** *adv.* **eu·phe·mize** *v.tr. & intr.*

eu·pho·ni·ous /yoofóneeəs/ *adj.* **1** sounding pleasant; harmonious. **2** concerning euphony. □□ **eu·pho·ni·ous·ly** *adv.*

eu·pho·ni·um /yoofóneeəm/ *n.* ► a brass wind instrument of the tuba family. ▷ BRASS

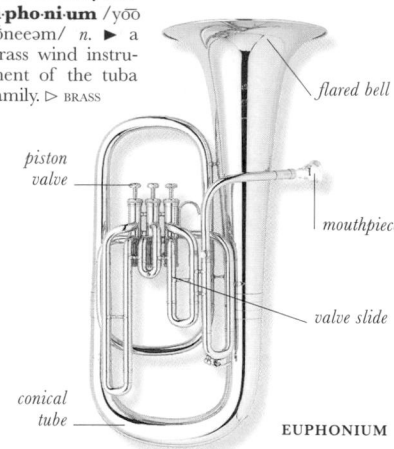

flared bell

piston valve

mouthpiece

valve slide

conical tube

EUPHONIUM

eu·pho·ny /yóofənee/ *n.* (*pl.* **-ies**) **1 a** pleasantness of sound, esp. of a word or phrase. **b** a pleasant sound. **2** the tendency to make a phonetic change for ease of pronunciation.

eu·phor·bi·a /yoofáwrbeeə/ *n.* any plant of the genus *Euphorbia*, including spurges. ▷ SUCCULENT

eu·pho·ri·a /yoofáwreeə/ *n.* a feeling of well-being, esp. one based on overconfidence or overoptimism. □□ **eu·phor·ic** /-fáwrik, fór-/ *adj.* **eu·phor·i·cal·ly** *adv.*

Eur·a·sian /yooráyzhən/ *adj. & n.* ● *adj.* **1** of mixed European and Asian parentage. **2** of Europe and Asia. ● *n.* a Eurasian person.

Eur·at·om /yoorátəm/ *n.* European Atomic Energy Community.

eu·re·ka /yooreékə/ *int. & n.* ● *int.* I have found it! (announcing a discovery, etc.). ● *n.* the exultant cry of 'eureka'.

eu·rhyth·mic var. of EURYTHMIC.

eu·rhyth·mics var. of EURYTHMICS.

eur·o /yóorō/ *n.* the single European currency, which replaced the national currencies of France, Germany, Spain, Italy, Greece, Portugal, Luxembourg, Austria, Finland, the Republic of Ireland, Belgium, and the Netherlands in 2002. ▷ BANKNOTE

Euro- /yóorō/ *comb. form* Europe; European.

Eu·ro·crat /yóorōkrat/ *n.* usu. *derog.* a bureaucrat in the administration of the European Community.

Eu·ro·dol·lar /yóorōdolər/ *n.* a dollar held in a bank in Europe.

Eu·ro·pe·an /yóorəpeeən/ *adj. & n.* ● *adj.* **1** of or in Europe. **2 a** descended from natives of Europe. **b** originating in or characteristic of Europe. **3 a** happening in or extending over Europe. **b** concerning Europe as a whole rather than its individual countries. **4** of or relating to the European Economic Community. ● *n.* **1 a** a native or inhabitant of Europe. **b** a person descended from natives of Europe. **c** a white person. **2** a person concerned with European matters. □□ **Eu·ro·pe·an·ism** *n.* **Eu·ro·pe·an·ize** *v.tr. & intr.* **Eu·ro·pe·an·i·za·tion** *n.*

Eu·ro·pe·an Com·mu·ni·ty *n.* (also **European Economic Community**) an economic and political association of certain European countries as a unit with internal free trade and common external tariffs.

eu·ro·pi·um /yoorópeeəm/ *n. Chem.* a soft, silvery metallic element of the lanthanide series, occurring naturally in small quantities. ¶ Symb.: **Eu**.

eu·rhyth·mic /yoorithmik/ *adj.* (also **eu·rhyth·mic**) of or in harmonious proportion.

eu·ryth·mics /yoorithmiks/ *n.pl.* (also treated as *sing.*) (also **eu·rhyth·mics**) harmony of bodily movement, esp. as developed with music and dance into a system of education.

EUCALYPTUS:
MOUNT WELLINGTON PEPPERMINT
(*Eucalyptus coccifera*)

Eu·sta·chian tube /yōōstáyshən, -keeən/ *n. Anat.* a tube leading from the pharynx to the cavity of the middle ear. ▷ EAR

eu·sta·sy /yōōstəsee/ *n.* a change in sea level throughout the world caused by tectonic movements, melting of glaciers, etc. □□ **eu·stat·ic** /-státik/ *adj.*

eu·tec·tic /yōōtéktik/ *adj. & n. Chem.* ● *adj.* (of a mixture, alloy, etc.) having the lowest freezing point of any possible proportions of its constituents. ● *n.* a eutectic mixture.

eu·tha·na·sia /yōōthənáyzhə/ *n.* **1** the bringing about of a gentle and easy death in the case of incurable and painful disease. **2** such a death.

eu·troph·ic /yōōtrófik, -trófik/ *adj.* (of a lake, etc.) rich in nutrients and therefore supporting a dense plant population, which kills animal life by depriving it of oxygen. □□ **eu·troph·i·cate** *v.tr.* **eu·troph·i·ca·tion** *n.* **eu·tro·phy** /yōōtrəfee/ *n.*

eV *abbr.* electronvolt.

EVA *abbr. Astronaut.* extravehicular activity.

e·vac·u·ate /ivákyoo-ayt/ *v.tr.* **1 a** remove (people) from a place of danger. **b** empty (a place) in this way. **2** make empty (a vessel of air, etc.). **3** (of troops) withdraw from (a place). **4 a** empty (the bowels or other bodily organ). **b** discharge (feces, etc.). □□ **e·vac·u·a·tion** /-áyshən/ *n.*

e·vac·u·ee /ivákyoo-ée/ *n.* a person evacuated from a place of danger.

e·vade /iváyd/ *v.tr.* **1 a** escape from, avoid, esp. by guile or trickery. **b** avoid doing (one's duty, etc.). **c** avoid answering (a question). **2 a** fail to pay (tax due). **b** defeat the intention of (a law, etc.). **3** (of a thing) elude or baffle (a person). □□ **e·vad·er** *n.*

e·val·u·ate /ivályoo-ayt/ *v.tr.* **1** assess; appraise. **2 a** find or state the number or amount of. **b** find a numerical expression for. □□ **e·val·u·a·tion** /-áyshən/ *n.* **e·val·u·a·tive** *adj.* **e·val·u·a·tor** *n.*

e·va·nesce /évənés/ *v.intr.* **1** fade from sight. **2** become effaced.

e·va·nes·cent /évənésənt/ *adj.* quickly fading. □□ **e·va·nes·cence** /-səns/ *n.*

e·van·gel·i·cal /éevanjélikəl, évən-/ *adj. & n.* ● *adj.* **1** of or according to the teaching of the gospel or the Christian religion. **2** of the Protestant school maintaining that the doctrine of salvation by faith in the Atonement is the essence of the gospel. ● *n.* a member of the evangelical school. □□ **e·van·gel·i·cal·ism** *n.* **e·van·gel·i·cal·ly** *adv.*

e·van·gel·ism /ivánjəlizəm/ *n.* **1** the preaching of the gospel. **2** zealous advocacy of a cause or doctrine.

e·van·gel·ist /ivánjəlist/ *n.* **1** any of the writers of the four Gospels. **2** a preacher of the gospel. **3** a lay person doing missionary work.

e·van·gel·is·tic /ivánjəlístik/ *adj.* **1** = EVANGELICAL. **2** of preachers of the gospel. **3** of the four evangelists.

e·van·gel·ize /ivánjəlīz/ *v.tr.* **1** (also *absol.*) preach the gospel to. **2** convert (a person) to Christianity. □□ **e·van·ge·li·za·tion** *n.* **e·van·ge·liz·er** *n.*

e·vap·o·rate /ivápərayt/ *v.* **1** *intr.* turn from solid or liquid into vapor. ▷ MATTER. **2** *intr. & tr.* lose or cause to lose moisture as vapor. **3** *intr. & tr.* disappear or cause to disappear (*our courage evaporated*). □□ **e·vap·o·ra·tion** /-ráyshən/ *n.* **e·vap·o·ra·tive** /-vápərətiv, -raytiv/ *adj.* **e·vap·o·ra·tor** *n.*

e·vap·o·rat·ed milk *n.* milk concentrated by partial evaporation.

e·va·sion /iváyzhən/ *n.* **1** the act of evading. **2 a** subterfuge or a prevaricating excuse. **b** an evasive answer.

e·va·sive /iváysiv/ *adj.* **1** seeking to evade something. **2** not direct in one's answers, etc. **3** enabling or effecting evasion (*evasive action*). **4** (of a person) habitually practicing evasion. □□ **e·va·sive·ly** *adv.* **e·va·sive·ness** *n.*

eve /eev/ *n.* **1** the evening or day before a church festival or any date or event (*Christmas Eve, the eve of the funeral*). **2** the time just before anything (*the eve of the election*). **3** *archaic* evening.

e·ven /éevən/ *adj., adv., & v.* ● *adj.* (**evener, evenest**) **1** level. **2 a** uniform in quality; constant. **b** equal in number or amount or value, etc. **c** equally balanced. **3** (usu. foll. by *with*) in the same plane or line. **4** (of a person's temper, etc.) equable; calm. **5 a** (of a number) divisible by two without a remainder. **b** bearing such a number (*no parking on even days*). **c** not involving fractions; exact (*in even dozens*). ● *adv.* **1** used to invite comparison of the stated assertion, negation, etc., with an implied one that is less strong or remarkable (*never even opened* [let alone read] *the letter*; *does he even suspect* [not to say realize] *the danger?* **2** used to introduce an extreme case (*even you must realize it*; *it might even cost $100*). **3** (sometimes foll. by *with* or *though*) in spite of; notwithstanding (*even with the delays, we arrived on time*). ● *v. tr. & intr.* (often foll. by *up* or *out*) make or become even. □ **even as** at the very moment that. **even now 1** now as well as before. **2** at this very moment. **even so 1** notwithstanding that; nevertheless. **2** quite so. **3** in that case as well as in others. **get** (or **be**) **even with** have one's revenge on. **on an even keel 1** (of a ship or aircraft) not listing. **2** (of a plan or person) untroubled. □□ **e·ven·ly** *adv.* **e·ven·ness** *n.*

e·ven·hand·ed /éevənhándid/ *adj.* impartial. □□ **e·ven·hand·ed·ly** *adv.* **e·ven·hand·ed·ness** *n.*

eve·ning /éevning/ *n. & int.* **1** the end part of the day, esp. from about 6 p.m. to bedtime (*this evening*; *during the evening*; *evening meal*). **2** this time spent in a particular way (*had a lively evening*). **3** a time compared with this, esp. the last part of a person's life. ● *int.* = *good evening* (see GOOD *adj.* 14).

eve·ning prim·rose *n.* ▶ any plant of the genus *Oenothera* with pale yellow flowers that open in the evening.

eve·ning star *n.* a planet, esp. Venus, conspicuous in the west after sunset.

e·ven mon·ey *n.* **1** betting odds offering the gambler the chance of winning the amount he or she staked. **2** equally likely to happen or not (*it's even money he'll fail to arrive*).

e·ven·song /éevənsawng, -song/ *n.* a service of evening prayer esp. in the Anglican Church.

e·ven-ste·ven (also **-Steven**) *colloq.* even; equal; level.

e·vent /ivént/ *n.* **1** a thing that happens. **2 a** the fact of a thing's occurring. **b** a result or outcome. **3** an item in a sports program, or the program as a whole. **4** *Physics* a single occurrence of a process, e.g., the ionization of one atom. **5** something on the result of which money is staked. □ **in any event** (or **at all events**) whatever happens. **in the event** as it turns (or turned) out. **in the event of** if (a specified thing) happens. **in the event that** *disp.* if it happens that.

e·vent·ful /ivéntfool/ *adj.* marked by noteworthy events. □□ **e·vent·ful·ly** *adv.* **e·vent·ful·ness** *n.*

e·vent ho·ri·zon *n. Astron.* a notional boundary around a black hole beyond which no light or other radiation can escape. ▷ BLACK HOLE

e·ven·tide /éevəntīd/ *n. archaic* or *poet.* = EVENING.

e·ven·tu·al /ivénchooəl/ *adj.* occurring or existing in due course or at last. □□ **e·ven·tu·al·ly** *adv.*

e·ven·tu·al·i·ty /ivénchoo-álitee/ *n.* (*pl.* -**ies**) a possible event or outcome.

e·ven·tu·ate /ivénchoo-ayt/ *v.intr. formal* **1** turn out in a specified way as the result. **2** (often foll. by *in*) result.

ev·er /évər/ *adv.* **1** at all times; always (*ever hopeful*; *ever after*). **2** at any time (*have you ever been to Paris?*; *as good as ever*). **3** as an emphatic word: **a** in any way; at all (*when will they ever learn?*). **b** (prec. by *as*) in any manner possible (*be as quick as ever you can*). **4** (in *comb.*) constantly (*ever-present*). **5** (foll. by *so, such*) esp. *Brit. colloq.* very; very much (*is ever so easy*). **6** (foll. by compar.) constantly; increasingly (*grew ever larger*). □ **ever since** throughout the period since. **for ever 1** for all future time. **2** *colloq.* for a long time (cf. FOREVER).

ev·er·green /évərgreen/ *adj. & n.* ● *adj.* **1** always green or fresh. **2** (of a plant) retaining green leaves throughout the year. ● *n.* an evergreen plant (cf. DECIDUOUS). ▷ TREE

ev·er·last·ing /évərlásting/ *adj. & n.* ● *adj.* **1** lasting for ever. **2** lasting for a long time, esp. so as to become unwelcome. **3** (of flowers) keeping their shape and color when dried. ● *n.* eternity. □□ **ev·er·last·ing·ly** *adv.* **ev·er·last·ing·ness** *n.*

ev·er·more /évərmáwr/ *adv.* for ever; always.

eve·ry /évree/ *adj.* **1** each single (*heard every word*; *watched her every move*). **2** each at a specified interval in a series (*comes every four days*). **3** all possible (*there is every prospect of success*). □ **every bit as** *colloq.* (in comparisons) quite as (*every bit as good*). **every now and again** (or **now and then**) from time to time. **every one** each one (see also EVERYONE). **every other** each second in a series (*every other day*). **every so often** occasionally. **every which way** *colloq.* **1** in all directions. **2** in a disorderly manner.

eve·ry·bod·y /évreebodee, -budee/ *pron.* every person.

eve·ry·day /évreedáy/ *adj.* **1** occurring every day. **2** suitable for or used on ordinary days (*wear your everyday clothes*). **3** commonplace; usual. **4** mundane; mediocre; inferior.

eve·ry·man /évreeman/ *n.* (also **Eve·ry·man**) the ordinary or typical human being; the "man in the street."

eve·ry·one /évreewun/ *pron.* everybody.

eve·ry·thing /évreething/ *pron.* **1** all things; all the things of a group or class. **2** *colloq.* a great deal (*gave me everything*). **3** an essential consideration (*speed is everything*). □ **have everything** *colloq.* possess all the desired attributes, etc.

eve·ry·where /évreewhair, -wair/ *adv.* **1** in every place. **2** *colloq.* in many places.

e·vict /ivíkt/ *v.tr.* expel (a tenant) from a property by legal process. □□ **e·vic·tion** /-víkshən/ *n.*

ev·i·dence /évidəns/ *n. & v.* ● *n.* **1** (often foll. by *for, of*) the available facts, circumstances, etc., indicating whether or not a thing is true or valid. **2** *Law* **a** information tending to prove a fact or proposition. **b** statements or proofs admissible as testimony in a court of law. **3** clearness; obviousness. ● *v.tr.* be evidence of. □ **call in evidence** *Law* summon (a person) as a witness. **in evidence** noticeable; conspicuous.

ev·i·dent /évidənt/ *adj.* **1** plain or obvious. **2** seeming; apparent (*his evident anxiety*).

ev·i·den·tial /évidénshəl/ *adj.* of or providing evidence. □□ **ev·i·den·tial·ly** *adv.*

ev·i·dent·ly /évidəntlee, -déntlee/ *adv.* **1** as shown by evidence. **2** seemingly; as it appears (*was evidently unwilling to go*).

e·vil /éevəl/ *adj. & n.* ● *adj.* **1** morally bad; wicked. **2** harmful or tending to harm. **3** disagreeable (*has an evil temper*). **4** unlucky; causing misfortune (*evil days*). ● *n.* **1** an evil thing; an instance of something evil. **2** wickedness. □□ **e·vil·ly** *adv.* **e·vil·ness** *n.*

e·vil eye *n.* a gaze superstitiously believed to be able to cause harm.

e·vince /ivíns/ *v.tr.* **1** indicate or make evident. **2** show that one has (a quality). □□ **e·vin·ci·ble** *adj.*

e·vis·cer·ate /ivísərayt/ *v.tr. formal* **1** disembowel. **2** empty or deprive of essential contents. □□ **e·vis·cer·a·tion** /-ráyshən/ *n.*

E

EVENING PRIMROSE (*Oenothera biennis*)

E

EVOLUTION

Evolution is a process by which living things change over time, and thus adapt to the conditions of their environment. For example, fossils reveal that the modern horse evolved from smaller ancestors; the earliest horse, *Hyracotherium*, was about the size of a small dog. Evolution can also bring about a reduction in size and a loss of redundant features, such as wings.

EVOLUTION OF THE HORSE

HYRACOTHERIUM
(50 million years ago)

MESOHIPPUS
(30 million years ago)

MERYCHIPPUS
(20 million years ago)

EQUUS
(modern horse)

e·voc·a·tive /ivókətiv/ *adj.* tending to evoke (esp. feelings or memories). □□ **e·voc·a·tive·ly** *adv.*

e·voke /ivók/ *v.tr.* **1** inspire or draw forth (memories, feelings, a response, etc.). **2** summon (a supposed spirit from the dead). □□ **ev·o·ca·tion** /évəkáyshən, éevō–/ *n.* **e·vok·er** *n.*

ev·o·lu·tion /évəlóoshən/ *n.* **1** gradual development. **2** ▲ a process by which species develop from earlier forms, as an explanation of their origins. **3** the appearance or presentation of events, etc., in due succession (*the evolution of the plot*). **4** a change in the disposition of troops or ships. **5** the giving off or evolving of gas, heat, etc. **6** an opening out. **7** the unfolding of a curve. □□ **ev·o·lu·tion·al** *adj.* **ev·o·lu·tion·al·ly** *adv.* **ev·o·lu·tion·ar·y** *adj.* **ev·o·lu·tion·ar·i·ly** *adv.*

ev·o·lu·tion·ist /évəlóoshənist/ *n.* a person who believes in evolution as explaining the origin of species. □□ **ev·o·lu·tion·ism** *n.*

e·volve /ivólv/ *v.* **1** *intr. & tr.* develop gradually by a natural process. **2** *tr.* devise (a theory, plan, etc.). **3** *intr. & tr.* unfold; open out. **4** *tr.* give off (gas, heat, etc.). □□ **e·volve·ment** *n.*

ewe /yoo/ *n.* a female sheep.

ew·er /yoóər/ *n.* a large water jug with a wide mouth.

ex[1] /eks/ *prep.* **1** (of goods) sold from (*ex factory*). **2** (of stocks or shares) without; excluding.

ex[2] /eks/ *n. colloq.* a former husband or wife.

ex- /eks/ *prefix* (also **e-** before some consonants, **ef-** before *f*) **1** forming verbs meaning: **a** out; forth (*exclude*; *exit*). **b** upward (*extol*). **c** thoroughly (*excruciate*). **d** bring into a state (*exasperate*). **e** remove or free from (*expatriate*, *exonerate*). **2** forming nouns from titles of office, status, etc., meaning 'formerly' (*ex-president*; *ex-wife*).

ex·ac·er·bate /igzásərbayt/ *v.tr.* **1** make (pain, anger, etc.) worse. **2** irritate (a person). □□ **ex·ac·er·ba·tion** /–báyshən/ *n.*

ex·act /igzákt/ *adj. & v.* ● *adj.* **1** accurate; correct in all details (*an exact description*). **2 a** precise. **b** (of a person) tending to precision. ● *v.tr.* (often foll. by *from*, *of*) **1** demand and enforce payment of (money, etc.). **2 a** demand; insist on. **b** (of circumstances) require urgently. □□ **ex·ac·ti·tude** *n.* **ex·act·ness** *n.*

ex·act·ing /igzákting/ *adj.* **1** making great demands. **2** calling for much effort. □□ **ex·act·ing·ly** *adv.*

ex·ac·tion /igzákshən/ *n.* **1** the act or an instance of exacting; the process of being exacted. **2 a** an illegal or exorbitant demand; an extortion. **b** a sum or thing exacted.

ex·act·ly /igzáktlee/ *adv.* **1** accurately; precisely; in an exact manner (*worked it out exactly*). **2** in exact terms (*exactly when did it happen?*). **3** (said in reply) quite so; I quite agree. **4** just; in all respects. □ **not exactly** *colloq.* **1** by no means. **2** not precisely.

ex·ag·ger·ate /igzájərayt/ *v.tr.* **1** (also *absol.*) give an impression of (a thing) that makes it seem larger or greater, etc., than it really is. **2** enlarge or alter beyond normal or due proportions (*spoke with*

exaggerated politeness). □□ **ex·ag·ger·at·ed·ly** *adv.* **ex·ag·ger·a·tion** /–ráyshən/ *n.* **ex·ag·ger·a·tor** *n.*

ex·alt /igzáwlt/ *v.tr.* **1** raise in rank or power, etc. **2** praise highly. **3** (usu. as **exalted** *adj.*) **a** make lofty or noble (*exalted aims*). **b** make rapturously excited. **4** (as **exalted** *adj.*) elevated in rank or character; eminent; celebrated. **5** stimulate (a faculty, etc.) to greater activity; intensify; heighten. □□ **ex·alt·ed·ly** *adv.* **ex·alt·ed·ness** *n.*

ex·al·ta·tion /égzawltáyshən/ *n.* **1** the act or an instance of exalting; the state of being exalted. **2** elation; rapturous emotion.

ex·am /igzám/ *n.* = EXAMINATION.

ex·am·i·na·tion /igzámináyshən/ *n.* **1** the act or an instance of examining; the state of being examined. **2** a detailed inspection. **3** the testing of the proficiency or knowledge of candidates for a qualification by questions. **4** an instance of examining or being examined medically. **5** *Law* the formal questioning of the accused or of a witness in court.

ex·am·ine /igzámin/ *v.* **1** *tr.* inquire into the nature or condition, etc., of. **2** *tr.* look closely at. **3** *tr.* test the proficiency of. **4** *tr.* check the health of (a patient). **5** *tr. Law* formally question (the accused or a witness) in court. **6** *intr.* (foll. by *into*) inquire. □□ **ex·am·in·a·ble** *adj.* **ex·am·in·ee** /–née/ *n.* **ex·am·in·er** *n.*

ex·am·ple /igzámpəl/ *n.* **1** a thing characteristic of its kind or illustrating a general rule. **2** a person, thing, or piece of conduct, regarded in terms of its fitness to be imitated (*must set him an example*; *you are a bad example*). **3** a circumstance or treatment seen as a warning to others; a person so treated (*shall make an example of you*). **4** a problem or exercise designed to illustrate a rule. □ **for example** by way of illustration.

ex·as·per·ate /igzáaspərayt/ *v.tr.* **1** (often as **exasperated** *adj.* or **exasperating** *adj.*) irritate intensely. **2** make (a pain, ill feeling, etc.) worse. □□ **ex·as·per·at·ed·ly** *adv.* **ex·as·per·at·ing·ly** *adv.* **ex·as·per·a·tion** /–ráyshən/ *n.*

ex ca·the·dra /éks kəthéedrə/ *adj. & adv.* with full authority (esp. of a papal pronouncement).

ex·ca·vate /ékskəvayt/ *v.tr.* **1 a** ▶ make (a hole or channel) by digging. **b** dig out material from (the ground). **2** reveal or extract by digging. **3** (also *absol.*) *Archaeol.* dig systematically to explore (a site). □□ **ex·ca·va·tion** /–váyshən/ *n.* **ex·ca·va·tor** *n.*

ex·ceed /ikséed/ *v.tr.* **1** be more or greater than. **2** go beyond or do more than is warranted by (a set limit, esp. of one's instructions or rights). **3** surpass.

ex·ceed·ing /ikséeding/ *adj.* **1** surpassing in amount or degree. **2** preeminent.

ex·ceed·ing·ly /ikséeding-lee/ *adv.* **1** very; to a great extent. **2** surpassingly; preeminently.

ex·cel /iksél/ *v.* (**excelled**, **excelling**) (often foll. by *in*, *at*) **1** *tr.* be superior to. **2** *intr.* be preeminent (*excels at games*).

ex·cel·lence /éksələns/ *n.* **1** the state of excelling; surpassing merit or quality. **2** the activity, etc., in which a person excels.

Ex·cel·len·cy /éksələnsee/ *n.* (*pl.* **-ies**) (usu. prec. by *Your*, *His*, *Her*, *Their*) a title used in addressing or

referring to certain high officials, e.g., ambassadors, governors, etc.

ex·cel·lent /éksələnt/ *adj.* extremely good. □□ **ex·cel·lent·ly** *adv.*

ex·cel·si·or /iksélseeər/ *n.* soft wood shavings used for stuffing, packing, etc.

ex·cept /iksépt/ *v., prep., & conj.* ● *v.tr.* (often as **excepted** *adj.* placed after object) exclude from a general statement, condition, etc. (*excepted him from the amnesty*; *present company excepted*). ● *prep.* (often foll. by *for* or *that*) not including; other than (*all failed except her*; *is all right except that it is too long*). ● *conj. archaic* unless (*except he be born again*).

ex·cept·ing /iksépting/ *prep.* = EXCEPT *prep.*

ex·cep·tion /iksépshən/ *n.* **1** the act or an instance of excepting; the state of being excepted. **2** a thing that has been or will be excepted. **3** an instance that does not follow a rule. □ **take exception** (often foll. by *to*) object; be resentful (about). **with the exception of** except; not including.

ex·cep·tion·a·ble /iksépshənəbəl/ *adj.* open to objection. □□ **ex·cep·tion·a·bly** *adv.*

ex·cep·tion·al /iksépshənəl/ *adj.* **1** forming an exception. **2** unusual; not typical (*exceptional circumstances*). **3** unusually good; outstanding. □□ **ex·cep·tion·al·i·ty** /–nálitee/ *n.* **ex·cep·tion·al·ly** *adv.*

ex·cerpt *n. & v.* ● *n.* /éksərpt/ a short extract from a book, motion picture, piece of music, etc. ● *v.tr.* /iksérpt/ (also *absol.*) **1** take an excerpt or excerpts from (a book, etc.). **2** take (an extract) from a book, etc. □□ **ex·cerpt·i·ble** *adj.* **ex·cerp·tion** /–sérpshən/ *n.*

ex·cess /iksés, ékses/ *n. & adj.* ● *n.* **1** the state or an instance of exceeding. **2** the amount by which one quantity or number exceeds another. **3** exceeding of a proper or permitted limit. **4 a** the overstepping of the accepted limits of moderation, esp. intemperance in eating or drinking. **b** (in *pl.*) outrageous or immoderate behavior. **5** an extreme or improper degree or extent (*an excess of cruelty*). **6** part of an insurance claim to be paid by the insured. ● *attrib.adj.* usu. /ékses/ **1** that exceeds a limited or prescribed amount (*excess weight*). **2** required as extra payment (*excess postage*). □ **in** (or **to**) **excess** exceeding the proper amount or degree. **in excess of** more than; exceeding.

ex·ces·sive /iksésiv/ *adj.* **1** too much or too great. **2** more than what is normal or necessary. □□ **ex·ces·sive·ly** *adv.* **ex·ces·sive·ness** *n.*

ex·change /ikscháynj/ *n. & v.* ● *n.* **1** the act or an instance of giving one thing and receiving another in its place. **2 a** the giving of money for its equivalent in the money of the same or another country. **b** the fee or percentage charged for this. **3** the central telephone office of a district, where connections are effected. **4** a place where merchants, bankers, etc., gather to transact business. **5 a** an office where certain information is given or a service provided, usu. involving two parties. **b** an employment office. **6** a system of settling debts without the use of money, by bills of exchange (see BILL OF EXCHANGE). **7 a** a short conversation, esp. a disagreement or quarrel. **b** a sequence of letters between correspondents. **8** (*attrib.*) forming part of an exchange, e.g., of personnel between institutions (*an exchange student*). ● *v.* **1** *tr.* (often foll. by *for*) give or receive (one thing) in place of another. **2** *tr.* give and receive as equivalents (e.g., things or people, blows, information, etc.). **3** *intr.* (often foll. by *with*) make an exchange. □ **in exchange** (often foll. by *for*) as a thing exchanged (for). □□ **ex·change·a·ble** *adj.* **ex·change·a·bil·i·ty** *n.* **ex·chang·er** *n.*

ex·change rate *n.* the value of one currency in terms of another.

ex·cheq·uer /ikschékər/ *n.* **1** *Brit.* the former government department in charge of national revenue. ¶ Its functions now belong to the Treasury, although the name formally survives, esp. in the title *Chancellor of the Exchequer*. **2** a royal or national treasury. **3** the money of a private individual or group.

ex·cise[1] /éksīz/ *n. & v.* ● *n.* **1** a duty or tax levied on goods and commodities produced or sold within the country of origin. **2** a tax levied on certain licenses. ● *v.tr.* **1** charge excise on (goods). **2** force (a person) to pay excise.

ex·cise[2] /iksíz/ *v.tr.* **1** remove (a passage of a book, etc.). **2** cut out (an organ, etc.) by surgery. □□ **ex·ci·sion** /iksízhən/ *n.*

ex·cit·a·ble /iksítəbəl/ *adj.* **1** (esp. of a person) easily excited. **2** (of an organism, tissue, etc.) responding to a stimulus, or susceptible to stimulation. □□ **ex·cit·a·bil·i·ty** *n.* **ex·cit·a·bly** *adv.*

ex·cite /iksít/ *v.tr.* **1 a** rouse the feelings or emotions of (a person). **b** bring into play; rouse up (feelings, faculties, etc.). **c** arouse sexually. **2** provoke; bring about (an action or active condition). **3** promote the activity of (an organism, tissue, etc.) by stimulus. **4** *Physics* put (an atom, etc.) into a state of higher energy. □□ **ex·cit·ant** /éksit'nt, iksít'nt/ *adj. & n.* **ex·ci·ta·tion** /éksitáyshən/ *n.* **ex·cit·a·to·ry** /-tətawree/ *adj.* **ex·cit·ed·ly** *adv.* **ex·cit·ed·ness** *n.* **ex·cite·ment** *n.* **ex·cit·er** *n.* (esp. in sense 4).

ex·cit·ing /iksíting/ *adj.* arousing great interest or enthusiasm; stirring. □□ **ex·cit·ing·ly** *adv.*

ex·claim /ikskláym/ *v.* **1** *intr.* cry out suddenly, esp.

in anger, surprise, pain, etc. **2** *tr.* (foll. by *that*) utter by exclaiming.

ex·cla·ma·tion /ékskləmáyshən/ *n.* **1** the act or an instance of exclaiming. **2** words exclaimed.

ex·cla·ma·tion point *n.* (also esp. *Brit.* **exclamation mark**) a punctuation mark (!) indicating an exclamation.

ex·clam·a·to·ry /iksklámətawree/ *adj.* of or serving as an exclamation.

ex·clude /iksklóod/ *v.tr.* **1** shut or keep out (a person or thing) from a place, group, privilege, etc. **2** expel and shut out. **3** remove from consideration. **4** prevent the occurrence of; make impossible (*excluded all doubt*). □□ **ex·clud·a·ble** *adj.* **ex·clud·er** *n.*

ex·clu·sion /iksklóozhən/ *n.* the act or an instance of excluding; the state of being excluded. □ **to the exclusion of** so as to exclude. □□ **ex·clu·sion·ar·y** *adj.*

ex·clu·sive /iksklóosiv/ *adj. & n.* ● *adj.* **1** excluding other things. **2** (*predic.*; foll. by *of*) not including; except for. **3** tending to exclude others, esp. socially; select. **4** catering for few or select customers; high-class. **5 a** (of a commodity) not obtainable elsewhere. **b** (of a newspaper article) not published elsewhere. **6** (*predic.*; foll. by *to*) restricted or limited to; existing or available only in. **7** (of terms, etc.) excluding all but what is specified. **8** employed or followed or held to the exclusion of all else (*my exclusive occupation; exclusive rights*). ● *n.* an article or story published by only one newspaper or periodical. □□ **ex·clu·sive·ly** *adv.* **ex·clu·sive·ness** *n.* **ex·clu·siv·i·ty** /éksklóosivitee/ *n.*

ex·cog·i·tate /ekskójitayt/ *v.tr.* think out; contrive. □□ **ex·cog·i·ta·tion** /-táyshən/ *n.*

ex·com·mu·ni·cate *v., adj., & n. Eccl.* ● *v.tr.* /ékskəmyóonikayt/ officially exclude (a person) from participation in the sacraments, or from formal communion with the church. ● *adj.* /ékskəmyóonikət/ excommunicated. ● *n.* /ékskəmyóonikət/ an excommunicated person. □□ **ex·com·mu·ni·ca·tion** /-káyshən/ *n.*

ex-con /ékskón/ *n. colloq.* an ex-convict.

ex·co·ri·ate /ckskáwrecayt/ *v.tr.* **1 a** remove part of

the skin of (a person, etc.) by abrasion. **b** strip or peel off (skin). **2** censure severely. □□ **ex·co·ri·a·tion** /-áyshən/ *n.*

ex·cre·ment /ékskrimənt/ *n.* (in *sing.* or *pl.*) feces. □□ **ex·cre·men·tal** /-mént'l/ *adj.*

ex·cres·cence /ikskrésəns/ *n.* **1** an abnormal or morbid outgrowth on the body or a plant. **2** an ugly addition. □□ **ex·cres·cent** /-sənt/ *adj.*

ex·cre·ta /ikskréetə/ *n.pl.* waste discharged from the body, esp. feces and urine.

ex·crete /ikskréet/ *v.tr.* (also *absol.*) (of an animal or plant) separate and expel (waste matter). □□ **ex·cre·tion** /-kréeshən/ *n.* **ex·cre·to·ry** /ékskrətáwree/ *adj.*

ex·cru·ci·at·ing *adj.* causing acute mental or physical pain. □□ **ex·cru·ci·at·ing·ly** *adv.*

ex·cul·pate /ékskulpayt, ikskúl-/ *v.tr. formal* **1** free from blame. **2** (foll. by *from*) clear (a person) of a charge. □□ **ex·cul·pa·tion** /-páyshən/ *n.* **ex·cul·pa·to·ry** /-kúlpətawree/ *adj.*

ex·cur·sion /ikskárzhən/ *n.* a short journey for pleasure, with return to the starting point. □□ **ex·cur·sion·ar·y** *adj.* **ex·cur·sion·ist** *n.*

ex·cuse *v. & n.* ● *v.tr.* /ikskyóoz/ **1** attempt to lessen the blame attaching to (a person, act, or fault). **2** (of a fact) serve in mitigation of (a person or act). **3** obtain exemption for (a person or oneself). **4** (foll. by *from*) release (a person) from a duty, etc. (*excused from kitchen duties*). **5** overlook or forgive (a fault or offense). **6** (foll. by *for*) forgive (a person) for a fault. **7** not insist upon (what is due). **8** *refl.* apologize for leaving. ● *n.* **1** a reason put forward to mitigate or justify an offense, fault, etc. **2** an apology (*made my excuses*). **3** (foll. by *for*) a poor or inadequate example of. **4** the action of excusing; indulgence; pardon. □ **be excused** be allowed to leave a room, etc., e.g., to go to the bathroom. **excuse me** a polite apology for an interruption, etc., or for disagreeing. □□ **ex·cus·a·ble** /-kyóozəbəl/ *adj.* **ex·cus·a·bly** *adv.* **ex·cus·a·to·ry** /-kyóozətawree/ *adj.*

ex div·i·dend /eks dívidend/ *adj. & adv.* (of stocks or shares) not including the previously announced dividend.

ex·ec /igzék/ *n.* an executive.

ex·e·cra·ble /éksikrəbəl/ *adj.* abominable; detestable. □□ **ex·e·cra·bly** *adv.*

ex·e·crate /éksikrayt/ *v.* **1** *tr.* express or feel abhorrence for. **2** *tr.* curse (a person or thing). **3** *intr.* utter curses. □□ **ex·e·cra·tion** /-kráyshən/ *n.* **ex·e·cra·to·ry** /-krətawree/ *adj.*

ex·e·cute /éksikyóot/ *v.tr.* **1 a** carry out a sentence of death on (a condemned person). **b** kill as a political act. **2** carry into effect; perform (a plan, duty, command, operation, etc.). **3 a** carry out a design for (a product of art or skill). **b** perform (a musical composition, dance, etc.). **4** make (a legal instrument) valid by signing, sealing, etc. **5** put into effect (a judicial sentence, the terms of a will, etc.). □□ **ex·e·cut·a·ble** *adj.*

ex·e·cu·tion /éksikyóoshən/ *n.* **1** the carrying out of a sentence of death. **2** the act or an instance of carrying out or performing something. **3** technique or style of performance in the arts, esp. music. **4 a** seizure of the property or person of a debtor in default of payment. **b** a judicial writ enforcing a judgment. □□ **ex·e·cu·tion·ar·y** *adj.*

ex·e·cu·tion·er /éksikyóoshənər/ *n.* an official who carries out a sentence of death.

ex·ec·u·tive /igzékyətiv/ *n. & adj.* ● *n.* **1** a person or body with managerial or administrative responsibility in a business organization, etc. **2** a branch of a government or organization concerned with executing laws, agreements, etc., or with other administration or management. ● *adj.* **1** concerned with executing laws, agreements, etc., or with other administration or management. **2** relating to or having the function of executing. □□ **ex·ec·u·tive·ly** *adv.*

ex·ec·u·tor /igzékyətər/ *n.* (*fem.* **executrix** /-triks/, *pl.* **-trices** /-tríseez/ or **-trixes**) a person ap-

E

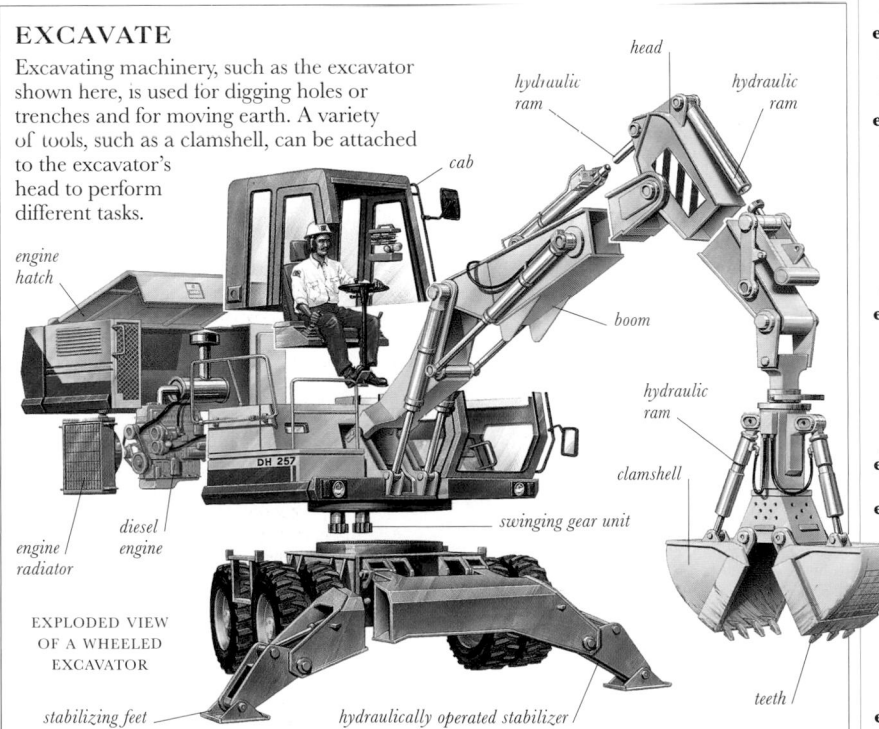

EXCAVATE

Excavating machinery, such as the excavator shown here, is used for digging holes or trenches and for moving earth. A variety of tools, such as a clamshell, can be attached to the excavator's head to perform different tasks.

engine hatch
cab
head
hydraulic ram
hydraulic ram
boom
engine radiator
diesel engine
hydraulic ram
clamshell
swinging gear unit
stabilizing feet
hydraulically operated stabilizer
teeth
DH 257

EXPLODED VIEW
OF A WHEELED
EXCAVATOR

E

pointed by a testator to carry out the terms of his or her will. ▫▫ **ex·ec·u·tor·ship** *n.* **ex·ec·u·to·ry** *adj.*

ex·e·ge·sis /éksijéesis/ *n.* (*pl.* **exegeses** /-seez/) critical explanation of a text, esp. of Scripture. ▫▫ **ex·e·gete** /éksijeet/ *n.* **ex·e·get·ic** /-jétik/ *adj.* **ex·e·get·i·cal** *adj.*

ex·em·plar /igzémplər, -plaar/ *n.* **1** a model or pattern. **2** a typical parallel instance.

ex·em·pla·ry /igzémpləree/ *adj.* **1** fit to be imitated; outstandingly good. **2 a** serving as a warning. **b** *Law* (of damages) exceeding the amount needed for simple compensation. **3** illustrative; representative. ▫▫ **ex·em·pla·ri·ly** *adv.*

ex·em·pli·fy /igzémplifī/ *v.tr.* (**-ies**, **-ied**) **1** illustrate by example. **2** be an example of. ▫▫ **ex·em·pli·fi·ca·tion** /-fikáyshən/ *n.*

ex·empt /igzémpt/ *adj.*, *n.*, *& v.* ● *adj.* **1** free from an obligation or liability, etc., imposed on others. **2** (foll. by *from*) not liable to. ● *n.* a person who is exempt, esp. from payment of tax. ● *v.tr.* (usu. foll. by *from*) free from an obligation, esp. one imposed on others. ▫▫ **ex·emp·tion** /-zémpshən/ *n.*

ex·er·cise /éksərsīz/ *n.* *& v.* ● *n.* **1** activity requiring physical effort, done esp. as training or to sustain or improve health. **2** mental or spiritual activity, esp. as practice to develop a skill. **3** (often in *pl.*) a particular task or set of tasks devised as practice in a technique, etc. **4 a** the use or application of a mental faculty, right, etc. **b** practice of an ability, quality, etc. **5** (often in *pl.*) military drill or maneuvers. **6** (foll. by *in*) a process directed at or concerned with something specified (*was an exercise in public relations*). ● *v.* **1** *tr.* use or apply (a faculty, right, influence, restraint, etc.). **2** *tr.* perform (a function). **3 a** *intr.* take (esp. physical) exercise; do exercises. **b** *tr.* provide (an animal) with exercise. **c** *tr.* train (a person). **4** *tr.* **a** tax the powers of. **b** perplex; worry. ▫▫ **ex·er·cis·a·ble** *adj.* **ex·er·cis·er** *n.*

ex·ert /igzárt/ *v.tr.* **1** exercise; bring to bear (a quality, influence, etc.). **2** *refl.* (often foll. by *for*, or *to* + infin.) use one's efforts or endeavors; strive. ▫▫ **ex·er·tion** /-zárshən/ *n.*

ex·e·unt /ékseeənt, -ōōnt/ *v.intr.* (as a stage direction) (actors) leave the stage.

ex·fo·li·ate /eksfṓleeayt/ *v.intr.* **1** (of bone, the skin, a mineral, etc.) come off in scales or layers. **2** ► (of a tree) throw off layers of bark. ▫▫ **ex·fo·li·a·tion** /-áyshən/ *n.* **ex·fo·li·a·tive** *adj.*

EXFOLIATE: PEELING BIRCH BARK

ex gra·ti·a /eks gráysheeə/ *adv.* *& adj.* ● *adv.* as a favor rather than from an (esp. legal) obligation. ● *adj.* granted on this basis.

ex·ha·la·tion /éks-həláyshən/ *n.* **1 a** an expiration of air. **b** a puff of breath. **2** a mist; vapor.

ex·hale /eks-háyl/ *v.* **1** *tr.* (also *absol.*) breathe out (esp. air or smoke) from the lungs. **2** *tr.* *& intr.* give off or be given off in vapor.

ex·haust /igzáwst/ *v.* *& n.* ● *v.tr.* **1** consume or use up the whole of. **2** (often as **exhausted** *adj.* or **exhausting** *adj.*) tire out. **3** study or expound on (a subject) completely. **4** (often foll. by *of*) empty (a vessel, etc.) of its contents. **5** (often as **exhausted** *adj.*) drain of strength or resources; (of land) make barren. ● *n.* **1 a** a waste gases, etc., expelled from an engine after combustion. **b** (also **ex·haust pipe**) the pipe or system by which these are expelled. ▷ CAR, OFFROAD. **c** the process of expulsion of these gases. **2 a** the production of an outward current of air by the creation of a partial vacuum. **b** an apparatus for this. ▫▫ **ex·haust·er** *n.* **ex·haust·i·ble** *adj.*

ex·haus·tion /igzáwschən/ *n.* **1** the action or process of draining or emptying something; the state of being depleted or emptied. **2** a total loss of strength or vitality. **3** the process of establishing a conclusion by eliminating alternatives.

ex·haus·tive /igzáwstiv/ *adj.* **1** thorough; comprehensive. **2** tending to exhaust a subject. ▫▫ **ex·haus·tive·ly** *adv.* **ex·haus·tive·ness** *n.*

ex·hib·it /igzíbit/ *v.* *& n.* ● *v.tr.* **1** show or reveal publicly (for amusement, in competition, etc.). **2 a** show; display. **b** manifest (a quality). **3** submit for consideration. ● *n.* **1** a thing or collection of things in an exhibition. **2** a document or other item produced in a court of law as evidence. ▫▫ **ex·hib·i·to·ry** *adj.*

ex·hi·bi·tion /éksibíshən/ *n.* **1** a display (esp. public) of works of art, industrial products, etc. **2** the act or an instance of exhibiting; the state of being exhibited. ▫ **make an exhibition of oneself** behave so as to appear ridiculous or foolish.

ex·hi·bi·tion·ism /éksibíshənizəm/ *n.* **1** a tendency toward display or extravagant behavior. **2** *Psychol.* a mental condition characterized by the compulsion to display one's genitals indecently in public. ▫▫ **ex·hi·bi·tion·ist** *n.* **ex·hi·bi·tion·is·tic** *adj.* **ex·hi·bi·tion·is·ti·cal·ly** *adv.*

ex·hib·i·tor /igzíbitər/ *n.* a person who provides an item or items for an exhibition.

ex·hil·a·rate /igzílərayt/ *v.tr.* (often as **exhilarating** *adj.* or **exhilarated** *adj.*) affect with great liveliness or joy; raise the spirits of. ▫▫ **ex·hil·a·rat·ing·ly** *adv.* **ex·hil·a·ra·tion** /-ráyshən/ *n.*

ex·hort /igzáwrt/ *v.tr.* (often foll. by *to* + infin.) urge or advise strongly or earnestly. ▫▫ **ex·hor·ta·tion** /égzawrtáyshən/ *n.* **ex·hort·a·to·ry** /-tətáwree/ *adj.* **ex·hort·er** *n.*

ex·hume /igzóōm, -zyóōm, eks-hyóōm/ *v.tr.* dig out; unearth (esp. a buried corpse). ▫▫ **ex·hu·ma·tion** *n.*

ex hy·poth·e·si /éks hīpóthəsee/ *adv.* according to the hypothesis proposed.

ex·i·gen·cy /éksijənsee, igzíj-/ *n.* (*pl.* **-ies**) (also **ex·i·gence** /éksijəns/) **1** an urgent need or demand. **2** an emergency. ▫▫ **ex·i·gent** /éksijənt/ *adj.*

ex·ig·u·ous /igzígyōōəs, iksíg-/ *adj.* scanty; small. ▫▫ **ex·i·gu·i·ty** /éksigyóōitee/ *n.* **ex·ig·u·ous·ly** *adv.*

ex·ile /éksīl, égzīl/ *n.* *& v.* ● *n.* **1** expulsion from one's native land or (**internal exile**) native town, etc. **2** long absence abroad, esp. enforced. **3** a person expelled or long absent from his or her native country. ● *v.tr.* (foll. by *from*) officially expel (a person) from his or her native country or town, etc. ▫▫ **ex·il·ic** /-sílik, -zílik/ *adj.*

ex·ist /igzíst/ *v.intr.* **1** have a place as part of objective reality. **2 a** have being under specified conditions. **b** (foll. by *as*) exist in the form of. **3** (of circumstances, etc.) occur; be found. **4** live with no pleasure under adverse conditions (*felt he was merely existing*). **5** continue in being; maintain life (*can hardly exist on this salary*). **6** be alive; live.

ex·ist·ence /igzístəns/ *n.* **1** the fact or condition of being or existing. **2** continued being; the manner of one's existing or living, esp. under adverse conditions (*a wretched existence*). **3** an existing thing. **4** all that exists.

ex·ist·ent /igzístənt/ *adj.* existing; actual; current.

ex·is·ten·tial /égzisténshəl/ *adj.* **1** of or relating to existence. **2** *Logic* (of a proposition, etc.) affirming or implying the existence of a thing. **3** *Philos.* concerned with existence, esp. with human existence as viewed by existentialism. ▫▫ **ex·is·ten·tial·ly** *adv.*

ex·is·ten·tial·ism /égzisténshəlizəm/ *n.* a philosophical theory emphasizing the existence of the individual person as a free and responsible agent determining his or her own development. ▫▫ **ex·is·ten·tial·ist** *n.*

ex·it /égzit, éksit/ *n.* *& v.* ● *n.* **1** a passage or door by which to leave a room, building, etc. **2 a** the act of going out. **b** the right to go out. **3** a place where vehicles can leave a highway or major road. **4** the departure of an actor from the stage. **5** death. ● *v.intr.* **1** go out of a room, building, etc. **2** (as a stage direction) (an actor) leaves the stage (*exit Macbeth*).

ex·it per·mit *n.* (or **visa**, etc.) authorization to leave a particular country.

ex·it poll *n.* a survey usu. of voters leaving voting booths, used to predict an election's outcome, analyze voting patterns, etc.

ex·o·crine /éksəkrin, -kreen, -krīn/ *adj.* (of a gland) secreting through a duct (cf. ENDOCRINE).

ex·o·dus /éksədəs/ *n.* **1** a mass departure of people. **2** (**Exodus**) *Bibl.* **a** the departure of the Israelites from Egypt. **b** the book of the Old Testament relating this.

ex of·fi·ci·o /eksəfísheeō/ *adv.* *& adj.* by virtue of one's office or status.

ex·og·a·my /eksógəmee/ *n.* **1** *Anthropol.* marriage of a man outside his own tribe. **2** *Biol.* the fusion of reproductive cells from distantly related or unrelated individuals. ▫▫ **ex·og·a·mous** *adj.*

ex·og·e·nous /eksójinəs/ *adj.* *Biol.* growing or originating from outside. ▫▫ **ex·og·e·nous·ly** *adv.*

ex·on·er·ate /igzónərayt/ *v.tr.* (often foll. by *from*) **1** free or declare free from blame, etc. **2** release from a duty, etc. ▫▫ **ex·on·er·a·tion** /-ráyshən/ *n.*

ex·or·bi·tant /igzáwrbit'nt/ *adj.* (of a price, demand, etc.) grossly excessive. ▫▫ **ex·or·bi·tance** /-təns/ *n.* **ex·or·bi·tant·ly** *adv.*

ex·or·cize /éksawrsīz, -sər-/ *v.tr.* **1** expel (a supposed evil spirit) by invocation, etc. **2** (often foll. by *of*) free (a person or place) of a supposed evil spirit. ▫▫ **ex·or·cism** /-sízəm/ *n.* **ex·or·cist** *n.*

ex·o·skel·e·ton /éksōskélit'n/ *n.* ► a rigid external covering for the body in certain animals, esp. arthropods. ▷ ARTHROPOD. ▫▫ **ex·o·skel·e·tal** *adj.*

ex·ot·ic /igzótik/ *adj.* *& n.* ● *adj.* **1** introduced from a foreign (esp. tropical) country (*exotic fruits*). **2** attractively or remarkably strange or unusual; bizarre. **3** (of a fuel, metal, etc.) of a kind newly brought into use. ● *n.* an exotic person or thing. ▫▫ **ex·ot·i·cal·ly** *adv.* **ex·ot·i·cism** /-tisizəm/ *n.*

ex·ot·i·ca /igzótikə/ *n.pl.* remarkably strange or rare objects.

ex·ot·ic danc·er *n.* a striptease dancer.

ex·pand /ikspánd/ *v.* **1** *tr.* *& intr.* increase in size or importance. **2** *intr.* (often foll. by *on*) give a fuller description or account. **3** *intr.* become more genial or effusive. **4** *tr.* set or write out in full. **5** *tr.* *& intr.* spread out flat. ▫▫ **ex·pand·a·ble** *adj.* **ex·pand·er** *n.*

ex·panse /ikspáns/ *n.* **1** a wide continuous area or extent of land, space, etc. **2** an amount of expansion.

ex·pan·sion /ikspánshən/ *n.* **1** the act or an instance of expanding; the state of being expanded. **2** enlargement of the scale or scope of (esp. commercial) operations. **3** increase in the amount of a country's territory or area of control. **4** an increase in the volume of fuel, etc., on combustion in the cylinder of an engine. **5** the action of making or becoming greater in area, bulk, capacity, etc.; dilatation; the degree of this (*alternate expansion and contraction of the muscle*). ▫▫ **ex·pan·sion·ar·y** *adj.* **ex·pan·sion·ism** *n.* **ex·pan·sion·ist** *n.* **ex·pan·sion·is·tic** *adj.* (all in senses 2, 3).

ex·pan·sive /ikspánsiv/ *adj.* **1** able or tending to expand. **2** extensive; wide-ranging. **3** (of a person, feelings, or speech) effusive; open. ▫▫ **ex·pan·sive·ly** *adv.* **ex·pan·sive·ness** *n.* **ex·pan·siv·i·ty** /-sívitee/ *n.*

ex·pa·ti·ate /ikspáysheeayt/ *v.intr.* (usu. foll. by *on*, *upon*) speak or write at length or in detail. ▫▫ **ex·pa·ti·a·tion** /-áyshən/ *n.*

ex·pa·tri·ate *adj.*, *n.*, *& v.* ● *adj.* /ékspáytreeət/ **1** living abroad. **2** exiled. ● *n.* /ekspáytreeət/ an expatriate person. ● *v.tr.* /ekspáytreeayt/ **1** expel (a person) from his or her native country. **2** *refl.* withdraw (oneself) from one's citizenship or allegiance. ▫▫ **ex·pa·tri·a·tion** /-áyshən/ *n.*

ex·pect /ikspékt/ *v.tr.* **1** (often foll. by *to* + infin.,

EXOSKELETON

Many animals do not have a bony internal skeleton, but instead have a hard outer casing called an exoskeleton. The exoskeleton has the same function as an internal skeleton, providing strength and support; it also protects the soft, inner organs. To permit growth, some animals periodically shed their exoskeletons and grow new, larger ones.

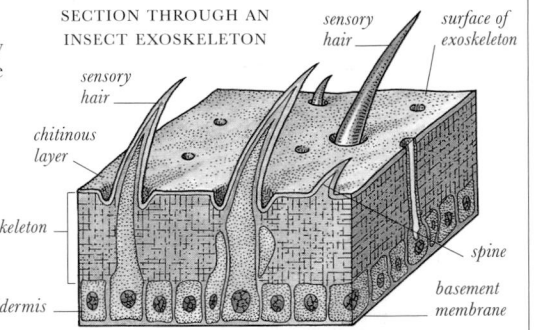

SECTION THROUGH AN INSECT EXOSKELETON

sensory hair · surface of exoskeleton · sensory hair · chitinous layer · exoskeleton · spine · epidermis · basement membrane

EXAMPLES OF ANIMALS WITH EXOSKELETONS

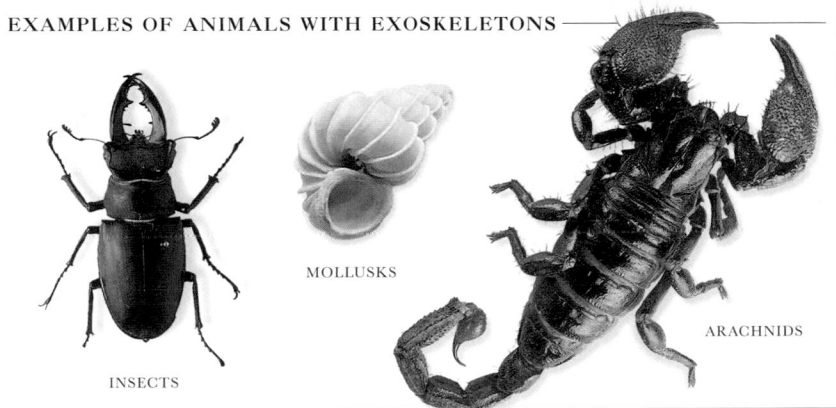

INSECTS · MOLLUSKS · ARACHNIDS

---

or *that* + clause) **a** regard as likely. **b** (often foll. by *of*) look for as appropriate or one's due (from a person) (*I expect cooperation*). **2** *colloq.* (often foll. by *that* + clause) think; suppose (*I expect we'll be on time*). □ **be expecting** *colloq.* be pregnant. □□ **ex·pect·a·ble** *adj.*

ex·pect·an·cy /ikspéktansee/ *n.* (*pl.* **-ies**) **1** a state of expectation. **2** a prospect, esp. of future possession. **3** (foll. by *of*) a prospective chance.

ex·pect·ant /ikspéktant/ *adj. & n.* ● *adj.* **1** (often foll. by *of*) expecting. **2** having the expectation of possession, status, etc. **3** (*attrib.*) expecting a baby (said of the mother or father). ● *n.* **1** one who expects. **2** a candidate for office, etc. □□ **ex·pect·ant·ly** *adv.*

ex·pec·ta·tion /ékspektáyshən/ *n.* **1** the act or an instance of expecting or looking forward. **2** something expected or hoped for. **3** (foll. by *of*) the probability of an event. **4** (in *pl.*) one's prospects of inheritance.

ex·pec·to·rant /ikspéktərənt/ *adj. & n.* ● *adj.* causing the coughing out of phlegm, etc. ● *n.* an expectorant medicine.

ex·pec·to·rate /ikspéktərayt/ *v.tr.* (also *absol.*) cough or spit out (phlegm, etc.) from the chest or lungs. □□ **ex·pec·to·ra·tion** /-ráyshən/ *n.*

ex·pe·di·ent /ikspéedeeənt/ *adj. & n.* ● *adj.* **1** advantageous; advisable on practical rather than moral grounds. **2** suitable; appropriate. ● *n.* a means of attaining an end. □□ **ex·pe·di·ence** /-əns/ *n.* **ex·pe·di·en·cy.** **ex·pe·di·ent·ly** *adv.*

ex·pe·dite /ékspidīt/ *v.tr.* **1** assist the progress of; hasten (an action, process, etc.). **2** accomplish (business) quickly. □□ **ex·pe·dit·er** *n.*

ex·pe·di·tion /ékspidíshən/ *n.* **1** a journey or voyage for a particular purpose, esp. exploration, scientific research, or war. **2** the personnel or ships, etc., undertaking this. **3** promptness; speed.

ex·pe·di·tion·ar·y /ékspidíshəneree/ *adj.* of or used in an expedition, esp. military.

ex·pe·di·tious /ékspidíshəs/ *adj.* **1** acting or done with speed and efficiency. **2** suited for speedy performance. □□ **ex·pe·di·tious·ly** *adv.*

ex·pel /ikspél/ *v.tr.* (**expelled**, **expelling**) (often foll. by *from*) **1** deprive (a person) of the membership of or involvement in (a school, society, etc.). **2** force out or eject (a thing from its container, etc.). **3** order or force to leave a building, etc. □□ **ex·pel·lee** /-lée/ *n.* **ex·pel·ler** *n.*

ex·pend /ikspénd/ *v.tr.* spend or use up (money, time, etc.).

ex·pend·a·ble /ikspéndəbəl/ *adj.* **1** that may be sacrificed or dispensed with, esp. to achieve a purpose. **2 a** not regarded as worth preserving or saving. **b** unimportant; insignificant. **3** not normally reused. □□ **ex·pend·a·bil·i·ty** *n.*

ex·pend·i·ture /ikspéndichər/ *n.* **1** the process or an instance of spending or using up. **2** a thing (esp. a sum of money) expended.

ex·pense /ikspéns/ *n.* **1** cost incurred; payment of money. **2** (usu. in *pl.*) **a** costs incurred in doing a particular job, etc. (*will pay your expenses*). **b** an amount paid to reimburse this (*offered me $40 per day expenses*). **3** a thing that is a cause of much expense (*the house is a real expense to run*). □ **at the expense of** so as to cause loss or damage or discredit to.

ex·pense ac·count *n.* a list of an employee's expenses payable by the employer.

ex·pen·sive /ikspénsiv/ *adj.* **1** costing much. **2** making a high charge. **3** causing much expense (*has expensive tastes*). □□ **ex·pen·sive·ly** *adv.* **ex·pen·sive·ness** *n.*

ex·pe·ri·ence /ikspéereeəns/ *n. & v.* ● *n.* **1** actual observation of or practical acquaintance with facts or events. **2** knowledge or skill resulting from this. **3 a** an event regarded as affecting one (*an unpleasant experience*). **b** the fact or process of being so affected (*learned by experience*). ● *v.tr.* **1** have experience of; undergo. **2** feel or be affected by (an emotion, etc.). □□ **ex·pe·ri·ence·a·ble** *adj.*

ex·pe·ri·enced /ikspéereeənst/ *adj.* **1** having had much experience. **2** skilled from experience (*an experienced driver*).

ex·pe·ri·en·tial /ikspéereeénshəl/ *adj.* involving or based on experience. □□ **ex·pe·ri·en·tial·ly** *adv.*

ex·per·i·ment /ikspérimənt/ *n. & v.* ● *n.* **1** a proce-

dure adopted on the chance of its succeeding, for testing a hypothesis, etc., or to demonstrate a known fact. **2** (foll. by *of*) a test or trial of. ● *v.intr.* (often foll. by *on*, *with*) make an experiment. □□ **ex·per·i·men·ta·tion** *n.* **ex·per·i·ment·er** *n.*

ex·per·i·men·tal /ikspérimént'l/ *adj.* **1** based on or making use of experiment (*experimental psychology*). **2 a** used in experiments. **b** serving or resulting from (esp. incomplete) experiment; tentative; provisional. **3** based on experience, not on authority or conjecture. □□ **ex·per·i·men·tal·ism** *n.* **ex·per·i·men·tal·ist** *n.* **ex·per·i·men·tal·ly** *adv.*

ex·pert /ékspərt/ *adj. & n.* ● *adj.* **1** (often foll. by *at*, *in*) having special knowledge or skill in a subject. **2** involving or resulting from this (*expert evidence*; *an expert piece of work*). ● *n.* (often foll. by *at*, *in*) a person having special knowledge or skill. □□ **ex·pert·ly** *adv.* **ex·pert·ness** *n.*

ex·per·tise /ékspərtéez/ *n.* expert skill, knowledge, or judgment.

ex·per·tize /ékspərtīz/ *v.* **1** *intr.* give an expert opinion. **2** *tr.* give an expert opinion concerning.

ex·pi·ate /ékspeeayt/ *v.tr.* **1** pay the penalty for (wrongdoing). **2** make amends for. □□ **ex·pi·a·tion** /-áyshən/ *n.* **ex·pi·a·to·ry** /-peeatawree/ *adj.*

ex·pi·ra·tion /ékspəráyshən/ *n.* **1** breathing out. **2** the end of the validity or duration of something.

ex·pire /ikspír/ *v.intr.* **1** (of a period of time, validity, etc.) come to an end. **2** (of a document, authorization, etc.) cease to be valid. **3** (of a person) from the lungs. □□ **ex·pir·a·to·ry** *adj.* (in sense 4).

ex·pi·ry /ikspíree/ *n.* **1** expiration. **2** death.

ex·plain /ikspláyn/ *v.tr.* **1** make clear or intelligible (also *absol.*: *let me explain*). **2** (foll. by *that* + clause) say by way of explanation. **3** account for (one's conduct, etc.). □ **explain away** minimize the significance of (a difficulty or mistake) by explanation. **explain oneself 1** make one's meaning clear. **2** give an account of one's motives or conduct. □□ **ex·plain·a·ble** *adj.* **ex·plain·er** *n.*

ex·pla·na·tion /éksplənáyshən/ *n.* **1** the act or an instance of explaining. **2** a statement or circumstance that explains something. **3** a declaration made with a view to mutual understanding.

ex·plan·a·to·ry /iksplánətawree/ *adj.* serving or intended to serve to explain. □□ **ex·plan·a·to·ri·ly** *adv.*

ex·ple·tive /éksplətiv/ *n.* a swearword or other expression, used in an exclamation.

ex·pli·ca·ble /éksplikəbəl, iksplík-/ *adj.* that can be explained.

ex·pli·cate /éksplikayt/ *v.tr.* **1** develop the meaning of (an idea, principle, etc.). **2** explain (esp. a literary text). □□ **ex·pli·ca·tion** /-káyshən/ *n.* **ex·pli·ca·tive** /éksplikaytiv, iksplíkətiv/ *adj.* **ex·pli·ca·tor** *n.* **ex·pli·ca·to·ry** /éksplikátawree, iksplik-/ *adj.*

ex·plic·it /iksplísit/ *adj.* **1** expressly stated; leaving nothing merely implied. **2** (of knowledge, a notion, etc.) definite; clear. **3** (of a person, book, etc.) outspoken. □□ **ex·plic·it·ly** *adv.* **ex·plic·it·ness** *n.*

ex·plode /iksplód/ *v.* **1 a** *intr.* (of gas, gunpowder, a bomb, a boiler, etc.) expand suddenly with a loud noise owing to a release of internal energy. **b** *tr.* cause (a bomb, etc.) to explode. **2** *intr.* give vent suddenly to emotion, esp. anger. **3** *intr.* (of a population, etc.) increase suddenly or rapidly. **4** *tr.* show (a theory, etc.) to be baseless. **5** *tr.* (as **exploded** *adj.*) (of a drawing, etc.) showing the components of a mechanism as if separated but in the normal relative positions. □□ **ex·plod·er** *n.*

ex·ploit *n. & v.* ● *n.* /éksployt/ a daring feat. ● *v.tr.* /iksplóyt/ **1** make use of (a resource, etc.); derive benefit from. **2** usu. *derog.* utilize or take advantage of (esp. a person) for one's own ends. □□ **ex·ploit·a·ble** *adj.* **ex·ploi·ta·tion** *n.* **ex·ploi·ta·tive** /iksplóytətiv/ *adj.* **ex·ploit·er** *n.* **ex·ploi·tive** *adj.*

ex·plo·ra·tion /ékspləráyshən/ *n.* **1** an act or instance of exploring. **2** the process of exploring. □□ **ex·plo·ra·tion·al** *adj.*

E

E

EXPRESSIONISM

Expressionism is an artistic concept that distorts the representation of reality to express an inner vision. This approach is the direct opposite of that adopted by the Impressionists, who placed a strong emphasis on imitating nature. Expressionism is particularly associated with an early-20th-century artistic movement in northern and central Europe. Germany became the center of expressionism, and one of the leading expressionist groups, Der Blaue Reiter ("The Blue Rider"), whose leaders included Wassily Kandinsky and Paul Klee, was formed there. In literature, expressionism is seen as a revolt against realism and naturalism, and writers such as August Strindberg, Franz Kafka, and James Joyce were associated with the movement.

Self-portrait Screaming (1910),
EGON SCHIELE

TIMELINE

| 1500 | 1550 | 1600 | 1650 | 1700 | 1750 | 1800 | 1850 | 1900 | 1950 | 2000 |

ex·plor·a·to·ry /ikspláwrətawree/ *adj.* **1** (of discussion, etc.) preliminary. **2** of or concerning exploration or investigation (*exploratory surgery*).

ex·plore /iksplávr/ *v.tr.* **1** travel through (a country, etc.) in order to learn about it. **2** inquire into. **3** *Surgery* examine (a part of the body) in detail. □□ **ex·plor·a·tive** /-rətiv/ *adj.* **ex·plor·er** /iksplávrər/ *n.*

ex·plo·sion /iksplṓzhən/ *n.* **1** the act or an instance of exploding. **2** a loud noise caused by something exploding. **3 a** a sudden outburst of noise. **b** a sudden outbreak of feeling, esp. anger. **4** a rapid or sudden increase.

ex·plo·sive /iksplṓsiv/ *adj. & n.* ● *adj.* **1** able or tending or likely to explode. **2** likely to cause a violent outburst, etc.; (of a situation, etc.) dangerously tense. ● *n.* an explosive substance. □□ **ex·plo·sive·ly** *adv.* **ex·plo·sive·ness** *n.*

ex·po /ékspō/ *n.* (also **Ex·po**) (*pl.* **-os**) a large international exhibition.

ex·po·nent /ikspṓnənt/ *n.* **1** a person who favors or promotes an idea, etc. **2** a representative or practitioner of an activity, profession, etc. **3** a person who explains or interprets something. **4** *Math.* a raised symbol or expression beside a numeral indicating how many times it is to be multiplied by itself (e.g., $2^3 = 2 \times 2 \times 2$).

ex·po·nen·tial /ékspənénshəl/ *adj.* **1** *Math.* of or indicated by a mathematical exponent. **2** (of an increase, etc.) more and more rapid. □□ **ex·po·nen·tial·ly** *adv.*

ex·port *v. & n.* ● *v.tr.* /ekspáwrt, éks-/ send out (goods or services) esp. for sale in another country. ● *n.* /ékspawrt/ **1** the process of exporting. **2 a** an exported article or service. **b** (in *pl.*) an amount exported (*exports exceeded $50 billion*). **3** (*attrib.*) suitable for export, esp. of better quality. □□ **ex·port·a·ble** *adj.* **ex·port·a·bil·i·ty** *n.* **ex·por·ta·tion** *n.* **ex·port·er** *n.*

ex·pose /ikspṓz/ *v.tr.* **1** leave uncovered or unprotected, esp. from the weather. **2** (foll. by *to*) a cause to be liable to or in danger of (*was exposed to great danger*). **b** lay open to the action or influence of; introduce to. **3** (as **exposed** *adj.*) **a** (foll. by *to*) open to; unprotected from (*exposed to the east*). **b** vulnera-

ble; risky. **4** *Photog.* subject (film) to light, esp. by operation of a camera. **5** reveal the identity or fact of (esp. a person or thing disapproved of or guilty of crime, etc.). **6** disclose; make public. **7** exhibit; display. **8** put up for sale. □ **expose oneself** display one's body, esp. the genitals, publicly and indecently. □□ **ex·pos·er** *n.*

ex·po·sé /ekspōzáy/ *n.* (also **ex·pose**) **1** an orderly statement of facts. **2** the act or an instance of revealing something discreditable.

ex·po·si·tion /ékspəzíshən/ *n.* **1** an explanatory statement or account. **2** an explanation or commentary. **3** *Mus.* the part of a movement in which the principal themes are first presented. **4** a large public exhibition. □□ **ex·po·si·tion·al** *adj.*

ex·pos·i·tor /ikspózitər/ *n.* an expounder or interpreter. □□ **ex·pos·i·to·ry** *adj.*

ex·pos·tu·late /ikspóschəlayt/ *v.intr.* (often foll. by *with* a person) make a protest; remonstrate. □□ **ex·pos·tu·la·tion** /-láyshən/ *n.* **ex·pos·tu·la·to·ry** /-lətawree/ *adj.*

ex·po·sure /ikspṓzhər/ *n.* **1** (foll. by *to*) the act or condition of exposing or being exposed. **2** the condition of being exposed to the elements, esp. in severe conditions (*died from exposure*). **3** the revelation of an identity or fact, esp. when concealed or likely to find disapproval. **4** *Photog.* **a** the action of exposing film, etc., to the light. **b** the duration of this action. **c** the area of film, etc., affected by it. **5** an aspect or outlook (*has a fine southern exposure*). **6** experience, esp. of a specified kind of work.

ex·pound /ikspównd/ *v.tr.* **1** set out in detail (a doctrine, etc.). **2** explain or interpret. □□ **ex·pound·er** *n.*

ex·press¹ /iksprés/ *v.tr.* **1** represent or make known (thought, feelings, etc.) in words or by gestures, conduct, etc. **2** *refl.* say what one thinks or means. **3** esp. *Math.* represent by symbols. **4** squeeze out (liquid or air). □□ **ex·press·er** *n.* **ex·press·i·ble** *adj.*

ex·press² /iksprés/ *adj., adv., n., & v.* ● *adj.* **1** operating at high speed. **2** also /ékspres/ definitely stated. **3 a** done, made, or sent for a special purpose. **b** (of messages or goods) delivered by a special messenger or service. ● *adv.* **1** at high speed. **2** by express messenger or train. ● *n.* **1 a** an express train or messenger. **b** an express rifle. **2** a company

undertaking the transport of packages, etc. ● *v.tr.* send by express messenger or delivery. □□ **ex·press·ly** *adv.* (in senses 2 and 3a of *adj.*)

ex·pres·sion /ikspréshən/ *n.* **1** the act or an instance of expressing. **2 a** a word or phrase expressed. **b** manner or means of expressing in language; wording; diction. **3** *Math.* a collection of symbols expressing a quantity. **4** a person's facial appearance or intonation of voice, esp. as indicating feeling. **5** depiction of feeling, movement, etc., in art. **6** conveying of feeling in the performance of a piece of music. □□ **ex·pres·sion·al** *adj.* **ex·pres·sion·less** *adj.* **ex·pres·sion·less·ly** *adv.* **ex·pres·sion·less·ness** *n.*

ex·pres·sion·ism /ikspréshənizəm/ *n.* ◀ a style of painting, music, drama, etc., in which an artist or writer seeks to express emotional experience rather than impressions of the external world. □□ **ex·pres·sion·ist** *n. & adj.* **ex·pres·sion·is·tic** *adj.* **ex·pres·sion·is·ti·cal·ly** *adv.*

ex·pres·sive /iksprésiv/ *adj.* **1** full of expression (*an expressive look*). **2** (foll. by *of*) serving to express (*words expressive of contempt*). □□ **ex·pres·sive·ly** *adv.* **ex·pres·sive·ness** *n.* **ex·pres·siv·i·ty** /-sívitee/ *n.*

ex·pres·so var. of ESPRESSO.

ex·press train *n.* a fast train, stopping at few intermediate stations.

ex·press·way /iksprésway/ *n.* a divided highway for high-speed traffic.

ex·pro·pri·ate /eksprṓpreeayt/ *v.tr.* **1** take away (property) from its owner. **2** (foll. by *from*) dispossess. □□ **ex·pro·pri·a·tion** /-áyshən/ *n.* **ex·pro·pri·a·tor** *n.*

ex·pul·sion /ikspúlshən/ *n.* the act or an instance of expelling; the process of being expelled. □□ **ex·pul·sive** /-púlsiv/ *adj.*

ex·punge /ikspúnj/ *v.tr.* (foll. by *from*) erase; remove (esp. a passage from a book or a name from a list). □□ **ex·pung·er** *n.*

ex·pur·gate /ékspərgayt/ *v.tr.* **1** remove matter thought to be objectionable from (a book, etc.). **2** remove (such matter). □□ **ex·pur·ga·tion** /-gáyshən/ *n.* **ex·pur·ga·tor** *n.*

ex·qui·site /ékskwizit, ikskwízit/ *adj. & n.* ● *adj.* **1** extremely beautiful or delicate. **2** acute; keenly felt (*exquisite pleasure*). **3 a** keen; highly sensitive or discriminating (*exquisite taste*). **b** elaborately devised or accomplished; consummate; perfect. ● *n.* a person of refined (esp. affected) tastes. □□ **ex·qui·site·ly** *adv.* **ex·qui·site·ness** *n.*

ex-serv·ice /éks-sárvis/ *adj. Brit.* **1** having formerly been a member of the armed forces. **2** relating to former servicemen and -women.

ex-serv·ice·man /éks-sárvismən/ *n.* (*pl.* **-men**) a former member of the armed forces.

ex-serv·ice·wom·an /éks-sárviswŏŏmən/ *n.* (*pl.* **-women**) a former woman member of the armed forces.

ex·tant /ékstənt, ekstánt/ *adj.* (esp. of a document, etc.) still existing; surviving.

ex·tem·po·ra·ne·ous /ikstémpəráyneeəs/ *adj.* spoken or done without preparation. □□ **ex·tem·po·ra·ne·ous·ly** *adv.*

ex·tem·po·rar·y /ikstémpəreree/ *adj.* = EXTEMPORANEOUS. □□ **ex·tem·po·rar·i·ly** /-ráirəlee/ *adv.*

ex·tem·po·re /ikstémpəree/ *adj. & adv.* **1** without preparation. **2** offhand.

ex·tem·po·rize /ikstémpərīz/ *v.tr.* (also *absol.*) compose or produce (music, a speech, etc.) without preparation; improvise. □□ **ex·tem·po·ri·za·tion** *n.*

ex·tend /iksténd/ *v.* **1** *tr. & intr.* lengthen or make larger in space or time. **2 a** *tr.* stretch or lay out at full length. **b** *tr. & intr.* (often foll. by *over*) (cause to) stretch or span over a period of time. **3** *intr. & tr.* (foll. by *to, over*) reach or be or make continuous over a certain area. **4** *intr.* (foll. by *to*) have a certain scope (*the permit does not extend to camping*). **5** *tr.* offer or accord (an invitation, hospitality, kindness, etc.). **6** *tr.* (usu. *refl.* or in *passive*) tax the powers of (an athlete, horse, etc.) to the utmost. □□ **ex·tend·a·ble**

adj. **ex·tend·a·bil·i·ty** *n.* **ex·tend·i·ble** *adj.* **ex·tend·i·bil·i·ty** *n.* **ex·ten·si·ble** /-sténsibəl/ *adj.* **ex·ten·si·bil·i·ty** *n.*

ex·tend·ed fam·i·ly *n.* **1** a family group that includes relatives living in one household. **2** all the members of a family, including cousins, in-laws, etc.

ex·tend·ed-play *adj.* (of a phonograph record) playing for longer than most singles, usu. at 45 r.p.m.; (of a videocassette recording) playing at the slowest recordable speed.

ex·tend·er /iksténdər/ *n.* **1** a person or thing that extends. **2** a substance added to paint, ink, glue, etc., to dilute its color or increase its bulk.

ex·ten·sion /iksténshən/ *n.* **1** the act or an instance of extending; the process of being extended. **2** prolongation; enlargement. **3** a part enlarging or added on to a main structure or building. **4** an additional part of anything. **5 a** a subsidiary telephone on the same line as the main one. **b** its number. **6 a** an additional period of time. **b** permission for the sale of alcoholic drinks until later than usual, granted to licensed premises on special occasions. **7** extramural instruction by a university or college (*extension course*). **8** extent; range. □□ **ex·ten·sion·al** *adj.*

ex·ten·sive /iksténsiv/ *adj.* **1** covering a large area in space or time. **2** having a wide scope; far-reaching. **3** *Agriculture* involving cultivation from a large area, with a minimum of special resources. □□ **ex·ten·sive·ly** *adv.* **ex·ten·sive·ness** *n.*

ex·ten·sor /iksténsər/ *n.* (in full **extensor muscle**) *Anat.* a muscle that extends or straightens out part of the body (cf. FLEXOR).

ex·tent /ikstént/ *n.* **1** the space over which a thing extends. **2** the width or limits of application; scope (*to a great extent*).

ex·ten·u·ate /ikstényōō-ayt/ *v.tr.* (often as **extenuating** *adj.*) lessen the seeming seriousness of (guilt or an offense) by reference to some mitigating factor. □□ **ex·ten·u·at·ing·ly** *adv.* **ex·ten·u·a·tion** /-áyshən/ *n.* **ex·ten·u·a·to·ry** /-yōōətáwree/ *adj.*

ex·te·ri·or /ikstéereeər/ *adj.* & *n.* • *adj.* **1 a** of or on the outer side (opp. INTERIOR). **b** (foll. by *to*) situated on the outside of (a building, etc.). **c** coming from outside. **2** *Cinematog.* outdoor. • *n.* **1** the outward aspect or surface of a building, etc. **2** the apparent behavior or demeanor of a person. **3** *Cinematog.* an outdoor scene. □□ **ex·te·ri·or·i·ty** /-ree-áwritee, -ree-ór-/ *n.* **ex·te·ri·or·ize** *v.tr.* **ex·te·ri·or·ly** *adv.*

ex·ter·mi·nate /ikstármínayt/ *v.tr.* **1** destroy utterly (esp. something living). **2** get rid of; eliminate (a pest, disease, etc.). □□ **ex·ter·mi·na·tion** /-náyshən/ *n.* **ex·ter·mi·na·tor** *n.* **ex·ter·mi·na·to·ry** /-nətáwree/ *adj.*

ex·ter·nal /ikstárnəl/ *adj.* & *n.* • *adj.* **1 a** of or situated on the outside or visible part. **b** coming or derived from the outside or an outside source. **2** relating to a country's foreign affairs. **3** outside the conscious subject (*the external world*). **4** (of medicine, etc.) for use on the outside of the body. **5** for or concerning students taking the examinations of a university without attending it. • *n.* (in *pl.*) **1** the outward features or aspect. **2** external circumstances. **3** inessentials. □□ **ex·ter·nal·i·ty** /-nálitee/ *n.* (*pl.* **-ies**). **ex·ter·nal·ly** *adv.*

ex·ter·nal·ize /ikstárnəlīz/ *v.tr.* give or attribute external existence to. □□ **ex·ter·nal·i·za·tion** *n.*

ex·tinct /ikstíngkt/ *adj.* **1** (of a family, class, or species) that has died out. **2 a** (of fire, etc.) no longer burning. **b** (of a volcano) that no longer erupts. **3** (of life, hope, etc.) terminated; quenched. **4** (of an office, etc.) obsolete. **5** (of a title of nobility) having no qualified claimant.

ex·tinc·tion /ikstíngkshən/ *n.* **1** the act of making extinct; the state of being or process of becoming extinct. **2** the act of extinguishing; the state of being extinguished. **3** total destruction or annihilation. □□ **ex·tinc·tive** *adj.*

ex·tin·guish /ikstínggwish/ *v.tr.* **1** cause (a flame, light, etc.) to die out; put out. **2** make extinct; annihilate; destroy. **3** put an end to; terminate; obscure utterly (a feeling, quality, etc.). **4 a** abolish; wipe out (a debt). **b** *Law* render void. **5** *colloq.* reduce to silence (*the argument extinguished the opposition*). □□ **ex·tin·guish·a·ble** *adj.* **ex·tin·guish·ment** *n.*

ex·tin·guish·er /ikstínggwishər/ *n.* a person or thing that extinguishes, esp. = FIRE EXTINGUISHER.

ex·tir·pate /ékstərpayt/ *v.tr.* root out; destroy completely. □□ **ex·tir·pa·tion** /-páyshən/ *n.* **ex·tir·pa·tor** *n.*

ex·tol /ikstṓl/ *v.tr.* (**extolled**, **extolling**) praise enthusiastically.

ex·tort /ikstáwrt/ *v.tr.* obtain by force, threats, persistent demands, etc.

ex·tor·tion /ikstáwrshən/ *n.* **1** the act or an instance of extorting, esp. money. **2** illegal exaction. □□ **ex·tor·tion·er** *n.* **ex·tor·tion·ist** *n.*

ex·tor·tion·ate /ikstáwrshənət/ *adj.* (of a price, etc.) exorbitant. □□ **ex·tor·tion·ate·ly** *adv.*

ex·tra /ékstrə/ *adj., adv., & n.* • *adj.* additional; more than is usual or necessary or expected. • *adv.* **1** more than usually. **2** additionally (*was charged extra*). • *n.* **1** an extra thing. **2** a thing for which an extra charge is made; such a charge. **3** a person engaged temporarily to fill out a scene in a motion picture or play, esp. as one of a crowd. **4** a special issue of a newspaper, etc.

extra- /ékstrə/ *comb. form* **1** outside; beyond (*extramarital*). **2** beyond the scope of (*extracurricular*).

ex·tract *v.* & *n.* • *v.tr.* /ikstrákt/ **1** remove or take out, esp. by effort or force (anything firmly rooted). **2** obtain (money, an admission, etc.) with difficulty or against a person's will. **3** obtain (a natural resource) from the earth. **4** select or reproduce for quotation or performance (a passage of writing, music, etc.). **5** obtain (juice, etc.) by suction, pressure, distillation, etc. **6** derive (pleasure, etc.). **7** *Math.* find (the root of a number). • *n.* /ékstrakt/ **1** a short passage taken from a book, piece of music, etc.; an excerpt. **2** a preparation containing the active principle of a substance in concentrated form (*malt extract*). □□ **ex·tract·a·ble** *adj.* **ex·trac·tive** *adj.*

ex·trac·tion /ikstrákshən/ *n.* **1** the act or an instance of extracting; the process of being extracted. **2** the removal of a tooth. **3** origin; lineage; descent (*of German extraction*). **4** something extracted; an extract.

ex·trac·tor /ikstráktər/ *n.* **1** a person or machine that extracts. **2** (*attrib.*) (of a device) that extracts bad air, etc., or ventilates a room (*extractor fan*).

ex·tra·cur·ric·u·lar /ékstrəkəríkyələr/ *adj.* (of a subject of study) not included in the normal curriculum.

ex·tra·dit·a·ble /ékstrədītəbəl/ *adj.* **1** liable to extradition. **2** (of a crime) warranting extradition.

ex·tra·dite /ékstrədīt/ *v.tr.* hand over (a person accused or convicted of a crime) to the country, state, etc., in which the crime was committed. □□ **ex·tra·di·tion** *n.*

ex·tra·mar·i·tal /ékstrəmárit'l/ *adj.* (esp. of sexual relations) occurring outside marriage. □□ **ex·tra·mar·i·tal·ly** *adv.*

ex·tra·mu·ral /ékstrəmyŏŏrəl/ *adj.* **1** taught or conducted off the premises of a university, college, or school. **2** additional to normal teaching or studies, esp. for nonresident students. □□ **ex·tra·mu·ral·ly** *adv.*

ex·tra·ne·ous /ikstráyneeəs/ *adj.* **1** of external origin. **2** (often foll. by *to*) **a** separate from the object to which it is attached, etc. **b** external to; irrelevant or unrelated to. **c** inessential; superfluous. □□ **ex·tra·ne·ous·ly** *adv.* **ex·tra·ne·ous·ness** *n.*

ex·traor·di·naire /ikstrawrdənáir/ *adj.* outstanding in a particular capacity.

ex·traor·di·nar·y /ikstráwrd'neree, ékstrəáwr-/ *adj.* **1** unusual or remarkable; out of the usual course. **2** unusually great (*an extraordinary talent*). **3** so exceptional as to provoke astonishment or admiration. **4 a** (of an official, etc.) additional; specially employed (*envoy extraordinary*). **b** (of a meeting) specially convened. □□ **ex·traor·di·nar·i·ly** *adv.* **ex·traor·di·nar·i·ness** *n.*

ex·trap·o·late /ikstrápəlayt/ *v.tr.* (also *absol.*) **1** *Math.* & *Philos.* **a** calculate approximately from known values, data, etc. (others which lie outside the range of those known). **b** calculate on the basis of (known facts) to estimate unknown facts, esp. extend (a curve) on a graph. **2** infer more widely from a limited range of known facts. □□ **ex·trap·o·la·tion** /-láyshən/ *n.* **ex·trap·o·la·tive** *adj.*

ex·tra·sen·so·ry per·cep·tion /ékstrəsénsəree/ *n.* a person's supposed faculty of perceiving by means other than the known senses, eg. by telepathy, clairvoyance, etc.

ex·tra·ter·res·tri·al /ékstrətəréstreeəl/ *adj.* & *n.* • *adj.* **1** outside the Earth or its atmosphere. **2** (in science fiction) from outer space. • *n.* (in science fiction) a being from outer space.

ex·trav·a·gant /ikstrávəgənt/ *adj.* **1** spending (esp. money) excessively; immoderate or wasteful in use of resources. **2** exorbitant; costing much. **3** exceeding normal restraint or sense; unreasonable; absurd (*extravagant claims*). □□ **ex·tra·va·gance** /ikstrávəgəns/ *n.* **ex·trav·a·gant·ly** *adv.*

ex·trav·a·gan·za /ikstrávəgánzə/ *n.* **1** a fanciful literary, musical, or dramatic composition. **2** a spectacular theatrical or television production.

ex·treme /ikstréem/ *adj.* & *n.* • *adj.* **1** reaching a high or the highest degree; exceedingly great or intense (*extreme old age; in extreme danger*). **2 a** severe; stringent; lacking restraint or moderation (*take extreme measures; an extreme reaction*). **b** (of a person, opinion, etc.) going to great lengths; advocating immoderate measures. **3** outermost (*the extreme edge*). **4** *Polit.* on the far left or right of a party. **5** utmost; last. • *n.* **1** (often in *pl.*) one or other of two things as remote or as different as possible. **2** a thing at either end of anything. **3** the highest degree of anything. **4** *Math.* the first or the last term of a ratio or series. □ **go to extremes** take an extreme course of action. **go to the other extreme** take a diametrically opposite course of action. **in the extreme** to an extreme degree. □□ **ex·treme·ly** *adv.* **ex·treme·ness** *n.*

ex·trem·ist /ikstréemist/ *n.* (also *attrib.*) a person who holds extreme or fanatical political or religious views. □□ **ex·trem·ism** *n.*

ex·trem·i·ty /ikstrémitee/ *n.* (*pl.* **-ies**) **1** the extreme point; the very end. **2** (in *pl.*) the hands and feet. **3** a condition of extreme adversity or difficulty. **4** excessiveness; extremeness.

ex·tre·mum /ikstréeməm/ *n.* (*pl.* **ex·tre·ma** /-mə/) *Math.* the maximum or minimum value of a function. □□ **ex·tre·mal** *adj.*

ex·tri·cate /ékstrikayt/ *v.tr.* (often foll. by *from*) free or disentangle from a constraint or difficulty. □□ **ex·tri·ca·ble** *adj.* **ex·tri·ca·tion** /-káyshən/ *n.*

ex·trin·sic /ekstrínsik, -zik/ *adj.* **1** not inherent or intrinsic; not essential (opp. INTRINSIC). **2** (often foll. by *to*) extraneous; lying outside; not belonging (to). **3** originating or operating from without. □□ **ex·trin·si·cal·ly** *adv.*

ex·tro·vert /ékstrəvərt/ *n.* & *adj.* • *n.* **1** *Psychol.* a person predominantly concerned with external things or objective considerations. **2** an outgoing or sociable person. • *adj.* typical or characteristic of an extrovert. □□ **ex·tro·ver·sion** /-várzhən/ *n.* **ex·tro·vert·ed** *adj.*

ex·trude /ikstróōd/ *v.tr.* **1** (foll. by *from*) thrust or force out. **2** shape metal, plastics, etc., by forcing them through a die. □□ **ex·tru·sion** /-tróōzhən/ *n.* **ex·tru·sile** /-tróōsəl, -sīl/ *adj.* **ex·tru·sive** /-tróōsiv/ *adj.*

ex·u·ber·ant /igzóōbərənt/ *adj.* **1** lively, high-spirited. **2** (of a plant, etc.) prolific; growing copiously. **3** (of feelings, etc.) abounding; lavish; effusive. □□ **ex·u·ber·ance** /-rəns/ *n.* **ex·u·ber·ant·ly** *adv.*

E

E

EYE

The human eye is contained in a bony socket in the skull. Light rays that enter the pupil are focused by the cornea and lens to form an image on the retina. These images are converted into electrical impulses, which are transmitted along the optic nerve to the brain.

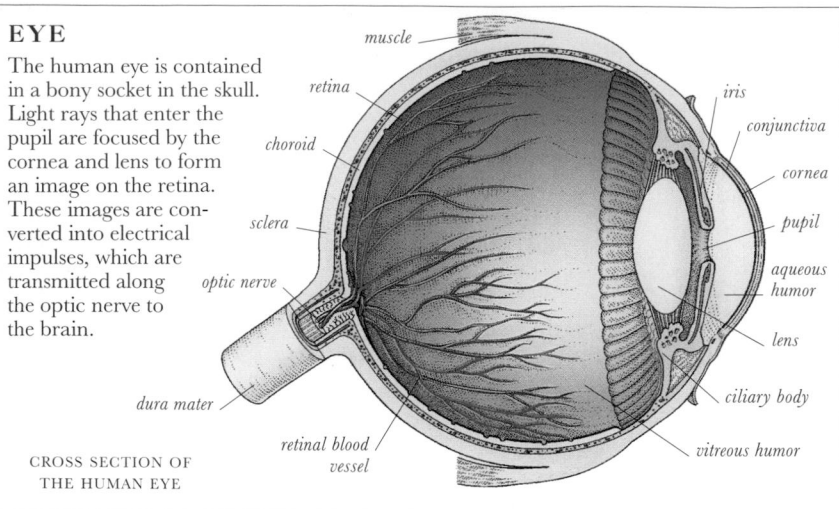

CROSS SECTION OF THE HUMAN EYE

muscle · retina · iris · conjunctiva · choroid · cornea · sclera · pupil · optic nerve · aqueous humor · lens · ciliary body · dura mater · retinal blood vessel · vitreous humor

---

ex·ude /igzŏŏd, iksŏŏd/ *v.* **1** *tr. & intr.* (of a liquid, moisture, etc.) escape or cause to escape gradually; ooze out; give off. **2** *tr.* emit (a smell). **3** *tr.* display (an emotion, etc.) freely or abundantly (*exuded displeasure*). □□ **ex·u·date** /éksyŏŏdayt, éksə-/ *n.* **ex·u·da·tion** *n.* **ex·u·da·tive** *adj.*

ex·ult /igzúlt/ *v.intr.* (often foll. by *at, in, over,* or *to* + infin.) **1** be greatly joyful. **2** (often foll. by *over*) have a feeling of triumph (over a person). □□ **ex·ult·an·cy** /-tənsee/ *n.* **ex·ul·ta·tion** /égzultáyshən, éksul-/ *n.* **ex·ult·ant** *adj.* **ex·ult·ant·ly** *adv.* **ex·ult·ing·ly** *adv.*

-ey /ee/ *suffix* var. of -Y².

eye /ī/ *n. & v.* ● *n.* **1 a** ▲ the organ of sight in humans and other animals. ▷ HEAD, SIGHT. **b** the light-detecting organ in some invertebrates. **2** the eye characterized by the color of the iris (*has blue eyes*). **3** the region around the eye (*eyes red from crying*). **4** a glass or plastic ball serving as an artificial eye. **5** (in *sing.* or *pl.*) sight; the faculty of sight (*demonstrate to the eye*). **6** a particular visual faculty or talent; visual appreciation; perspicacity (*cast an expert eye over*). **7 a** (in *sing.* or *pl.*) a look, gaze, or glance, esp. as indicating the disposition of the viewer (*a friendly eye*). **b** (the **eye**) a flirtatious or sexually provocative glance. **8** mental awareness; consciousness. **9** a person or animal, etc., that sees on behalf of another. **10 a** = ELECTRIC EYE. **b** = PRIVATE EYE. **11** a thing like an eye, esp.: **a** a spot on a peacock's tail. **b** the leaf bud of a potato. **12** the center of something circular, e.g., a flower or target. **13** the relatively calm region at the center of a storm or hurricane. ▷ HURRICANE. **14** an aperture in an implement, esp. a needle, for the insertion of something, e.g., thread. **15** a ring or loop for a bolt or hook, etc., to pass through. ● *v.tr.* (**eyes, eyed, eyeing** or **eying**) watch or observe closely, esp. admiringly or with curiosity or suspicion. □ **all eyes 1** watching intently. **2** general attention (*all eyes were on us*). **before one's** (or **one's very**) **eyes** right in front of one. **an eye for an**

eye retaliation in kind (Exodus 21:24). **have an eye for 1** be quick to notice. **2** be partial to. **have eyes for** be interested in; wish to acquire. **have an eye to** have as one's objective; prudently consider. **have one's eye on** wish or plan to procure. **hit a person in the eye** (or **between the eyes**) *colloq.* be very obvious or impressive. **keep an eye on 1** pay attention to. **2** look after; take care of. **keep an eye open** (or **out**) (often foll. by *for*) watch carefully. **keep one's eyes open** (or **peeled** or **skinned**) watch out; be on the alert. **make eyes** (or **sheep's eyes**) (foll. by *at*) look amorously or flirtatiously at. **open a person's eyes** be enlightening or revealing to a person. **see eye to eye** (often foll. by *with*) be in full agreement. **set eyes on** catch sight of. **take one's eyes off** (usu. in *neg.*) stop watching; stop paying attention to. **under the eye of** under the supervision or observation of. **up to the** (or **one's**) **eyes in 1** deeply engaged or involved in; inundated with (*up to the eyes in work*). **2** to the utmost limit (*mortgaged up to the eyes*). **with one's eyes open** deliberately; with full awareness. **with one's eyes shut** (or **closed**) **1** easily; with little effort. **2** without awareness; unobservant (*goes around with his eyes shut*). **with an eye to** with a view to; prudently considering. **with one eye on** directing one's attention partly to. **with one eye shut** *colloq.* easily; with little effort (*could do this with one eye shut*). □□ **eyed** *adj.* (also in *comb.*). **eye·less** *adj.*

eye·ball /íbawl/ *n. & v.* ● *n.* the ball of the eye within the lids and socket. ● *v. sl.* **1** *tr.* look or stare at. **2** *intr.* look or stare. □ **eyeball to eyeball** *colloq.* confronting closely. **to** (or **up to**) **the eyeballs** *colloq.* completely (permeated, soaked, etc.).

eye·bright /íbrīt/ *n.* ▶ any plant of the genus *Euphrasia,* formerly used as a remedy for weak eyes.

eye·brow /íbrow/ *n.* the line of hair growing on the ridge above the eye socket. □ **raise one's eyebrows** show surprise, disbelief, or mild disapproval.

eye-catch·ing *adj. colloq.* striking; attractive.

eye con·tact *n.* looking directly into another person's eyes.

eye·ful /ífŏŏl/ *n.* (*pl.* **-fuls**) *colloq.* **1** a long, steady look. **2** a visually striking person or thing. **3** anything thrown or blown into the eye.

eye·glass /íglas/ *n.* **1** a lens for correcting or assisting defective sight. **2** (in *pl.*) a pair of these, usu. set into a frame that rests on the nose and has side pieces that curve over the ears.

eye·lash /ílash/ *n.* each of the hairs growing on the edges of the eyelids. □ **by an eyelash** by a very small margin.

eye·let /ílit/ *n.* **1** a small hole in paper, leather, cloth, etc., for string or rope, etc., to pass through. **2** a metal ring reinforcement for this. **3** a small eye, esp. the ocellus on a butterfly's wing. **4** a form of decoration in embroidery. **5** a small hole for observation, shooting through, etc.

eye lev·el *n.* the level seen by the eyes looking horizontally (*put it at eye level*).

eye·lid /ílid/ *n.* the upper or lower fold of skin closing to cover the eye.

eye·lin·er /ílīnər/ *n.* a cosmetic applied as a line around the eye. ▷ MAKEUP

eye-o·pen·er *n. colloq.* **1** an enlightening experience; an unexpected revelation. **2** an alcoholic drink taken on waking up.

eye·piece /ípees/ *n.* the lens or lenses at the end of a microscope, telescope, etc., to which the eye is applied. ▷ CAMCORDER, TELESCOPE

eye·shade /íshayd/ *n.* a device, esp. a visor, to protect the eyes, esp. from strong light.

eye shad·ow *n.* a colored cosmetic applied to the skin around the eyes. ▷ MAKEUP

eye·shot /íshot/ *n.* seeing distance (*out of eyeshot*).

eye·sight /ísīt/ *n.* the faculty or power of seeing.

eye·sore /ísawr/ *n.* a visually offensive or ugly thing, esp. a building.

EYEBRIGHT (*Euphrasia* species)

eye·stalk /ístawk/ *n. Zool.* a movable stalk carrying the eye, esp. in crabs, shrimps, etc.

eye·strain /ístrayn/ *n.* fatigue of the (internal or external) muscles of the eye.

eye·tooth /ítŏŏth/ *n.* a canine tooth just under or next to the eye, esp. in the upper jaw.

eye·wash /íwosh, íwawsh/ *n.* **1** lotion for the eye. **2** *sl.* nonsense; bunkum; pretentious or insincere talk.

eye·wear /íwair/ *n.* spectacles, goggles, or lenses for improving eyesight or protecting the eyes.

eye·wit·ness /íwítnis/ *n.* a person who has seen a thing happen and can give evidence of it.

ey·rie var. of AERIE.

F

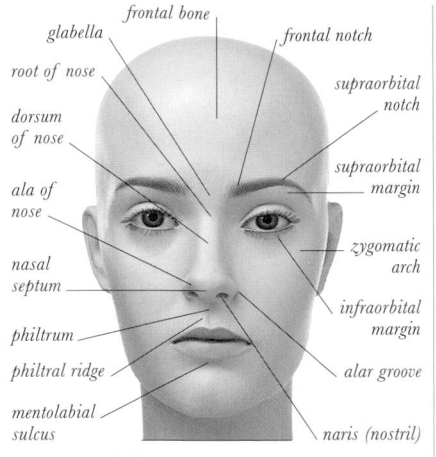

FACE: EXTERNAL FEATURES

frontal bone
glabella
frontal notch
root of nose
supraorbital notch
dorsum of nose
supraorbital margin
ala of nose
zygomatic arch
nasal septum
infraorbital margin
philtrum
alar groove
philtral ridge
mentolabial sulcus
naris (nostril)

F[1] /ef/ *n.* (also **f**) (*pl.* **Fs** or **F's**) **1** the sixth letter of the alphabet. **2** *Mus.* the fourth note of the diatonic scale of C major. ▷ NOTATION.

F[2] *abbr.* (also **F.**) **1** Fahrenheit. **2** farad(s). **3** female. **4** *Biol.* filial generation.

F[3] *symb. Chem.* the element fluorine.

f *abbr.* (also **f.**) **1** female. **2** feminine. **3** following page, etc. **4** *Mus.* forte. **5** folio. **6** focal length (cf. F-NUMBER).

fa /faa/ *n.* (also **fah**) *Mus.* **1** (in tonic sol-fa) the fourth note of a major scale. **2** the note F in the fixed-do system.

FAA *abbr.* Federal Aviation Administration.

fab /fab/ *adj. colloq.* fabulous; marvelous.

fa·ble /fáybəl/ *n. & v.* ● *n.* **1 a** a story, esp. a supernatural one, not based on fact. **b** a tale, esp. with animals as characters, conveying a moral. **2** (*collect.*) myths and legendary tales (*in fable*). **3 a** a false statement; a lie. **b** a thing only supposed to exist. ● *v.tr.* (as **fabled** *adj.*) celebrated in fable; famous; legendary.

fab·ric /fábrik/ *n.* **1 a** a woven material; a textile. **b** other material resembling woven cloth. **2** a structure or framework, esp. the walls, floor, and roof of a building. **3** (in abstract senses) the essential structure of a thing (*the fabric of society*).

fab·ri·cate /fábrikayt/ *v.tr.* **1** construct esp. from prepared components. **2** invent or concoct (a story, etc.). **3** forge (a document). □□ **fab·ri·ca·tion** /fábrikáyshən/ *n.* **fab·ri·ca·tor** *n.*

fab·u·list /fábyəlist/ *n.* **1** a composer of fables. **2** a liar.

fab·u·lous /fábyələs/ *adj.* **1** incredible; exaggerated; absurd (*fabulous wealth*). **2** *colloq.* marvelous (*looking fabulous*). **3 a** celebrated in fable. **b** legendary; mythical. □□ **fab·u·lous·ly** *adv.* **fab·u·lous·ness** *n.*

fa·çade /fəsáad/ *n.* **1** ▼ the face of a building, esp. its principal front. **2** an outward appearance or front, esp. a deceptive one.

face /fays/ *n. & v.* ● *n.* **1** ▲ the front of the head from the forehead to the chin. **2 a** the expression of the facial features (*had a happy face*). **b** an expression of disgust; a grimace (*make a face*). **3** coolness; effrontery. **4** the surface of a thing, esp.: **a** the visible part of a celestial body. **b** a side of a mountain, etc. (*the north face*). **c** the (usu. vertical) surface of a coal seam, excavation, etc. **d** *Geom.* each surface of a solid. **e** the façade of a building. **f** the plate of a clock or watch. **5 a** the functional side of a tool, etc. **b** the distinctive side of a playing card. **c** the obverse of a coin. **6** = TYPEFACE. **7 a** the outward appearance or aspect (*the unacceptable face of capitalism*). **b** outward show, disguise, pretense (*put on a brave face*). **8** a person, esp. conveying some quality or association (*a face from the past*). **9** credibility or respect; good reputation; dignity (*lose face*). ● *v.* **1** *tr. & intr.* look or be positioned toward or in a certain direction (*facing the window; the room faces north*). **2** *tr.* be opposite (*facing page 20*). **3** *tr.* **a** meet resolutely or defiantly (*face one's critics*). **b** not shrink from (*face the facts*). **4** *tr.* present itself to (*the problem that faces us*). **5** *tr.* **a** cover the surface of (a thing) with a coating, etc. **b** put a facing on (a garment). **6** *intr. & tr.* turn or cause to turn in a certain direction. □ **face down** (or **downward**) with the face or surface turned toward the ground, floor, etc. **face a person down** overcome a person by a show of determination or by browbeating. **face facts** (or **the facts**) recognize the truth. **face the music** *colloq.* stand up to

unpleasant consequences, esp. criticism. **face to face** (often foll. by *with*) confronting each other. **face up** (or **upward**) with the face or surface turned upward to view. **face up to** accept bravely; confront. **have the face** be shameless enough. **in one's** (or **the**) **face 1** straight against one; as one approaches. **2** confronting. **in the face of 1** despite. **2** confronted by. **in your face** demanding attention. **let's face it** *colloq.* we must be honest and realistic about it. **on the face of it** as it would appear. **put a bold** (or **brave**) **face on it** accept difficulty, etc., cheerfully or with courage. **put one's face on** *colloq.* apply makeup to one's face. **put a good face on** make (a matter) look good. **put a new face on** alter the aspect of. **save face** preserve esteem. **save a person's face** enable a person to save face; forbear from humiliating a person. **show one's face** see SHOW. **set one's face against** oppose with determination. **to a person's face** openly in a person's presence. □□ **faced** *adj.* (also in *comb.*). **fac·ing** *adj.* (also in *comb.*).

face card *n. Cards* ► a king, queen, or jack.

face·less /fáyslis/ *adj.* **1** without identity. **2** lacking character. **3** without a face. □□ **face·less·ly** *adv.* **face·less·ness** *n.*

face-lift *n.* **1** (also **face-lifting**) cosmetic surgery to remove wrinkles, etc. **2** a procedure to improve the appearance of a thing.

fac·er /fáysər/ *n. colloq.* **1** a blow in the face. **2** one that faces.

face-sav·ing *n.* preserving one's reputation, credibility, etc.

fac·et /fásit/ *n.* **1** a particular aspect of a thing. **2** ◄ one side of a a cut gem, a bone, etc. ▷ COMPOUND EYE. □□ **fac·et·ed** *adj.* (also in *comb.*)

fa·ce·ti·ae /fəséeshee-ee/ *n.* pleasantries; witticisms.

fa·ce·tious /fəséeshəs/ *adj.* **1** characterized by flippant or inappropriate humor. **2** intending to be amusing, esp. inappropriately. □□ **fa·ce·tious·ly** *adv.* **fa·ce·tious·ness** *n.*

face val·ue *n.* **1** the nominal value as printed or stamped on money. **2** the superficial appearance or implication of a thing.

fa·cia var. of FASCIA.

fa·cial /fáyshəl/ *adj. & n.* ● *adj.* of or for the face. ● *n.* a beauty treatment for the face. □□ **fa·cial·ly** *adv.*

-facient /fáyshənt/ *comb. form* forming adjectives and nouns indicating an action or state produced (*abortifacient*).

fa·ci·es /fáyshee-eez, -sheez/ *n.* (*pl.* same) **1** *Med.* the appearance or facial expression of an individual. **2** *Geol.* the character of rock, etc., expressed by its composition, fossil content, etc.

fac·ile /fásil/ *adj.* usu. *derog.* **1** easily achieved but of little value. **2** (of speech, writing, etc.) fluent; glib. □□ **fac·ile·ly** *adv.* **fac·ile·ness** *n.*

fa·cil·i·tate /fəsílitayt/ *v.tr.* make easy or less difficult or more easily achieved. □□ **fa·cil·i·ta·tion** /-táyshən/ *n.* **fa·cil·i·ta·tive** *adj.* **fa·cil·i·ta·tor** *n.*

fa·cil·i·ty /fəsílitee/ *n.* (*pl.* **-ies**) **1** ease; absence of difficulty. **2** dexterity; aptitude (*facility of expression*). **3** (esp. in *pl.*) an opportunity, the equipment, or the resources for doing something. **4** a plant, installation, or establishment. **5** *euphem.* (in *pl.*) a (public) toilet.

FACE CARDS

king
queen
jack

F

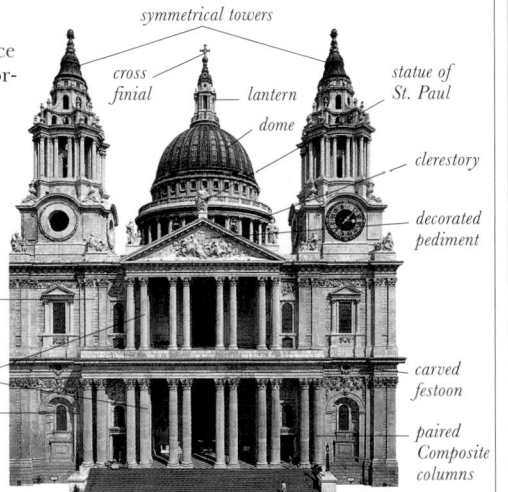

FACET: MANY-FACETED CUT DIAMOND

facet

FAÇADE

A building's façade offers a unified face to the world, while providing an opportunity for architectural expression. Types of façades vary greatly among building styles, from the formal ordering of classical architecture to the intricate detailing of Gothic buildings or the theatricality of the baroque. The dramatic interest of the façade shown here is achieved by the use of classical motifs, such as the dome, pediment, and columns, which are drawn together symmetrically around the grand entrance.

WEST FAÇADE OF ST. PAUL'S CATHEDRAL, ENGLAND (1675–1710)

symmetrical towers
cross finial
lantern
statue of St. Paul
dome
clerestory
decorated pediment
Composite pilaster
two-tiered portico
niche
carved festoon
paired Composite columns

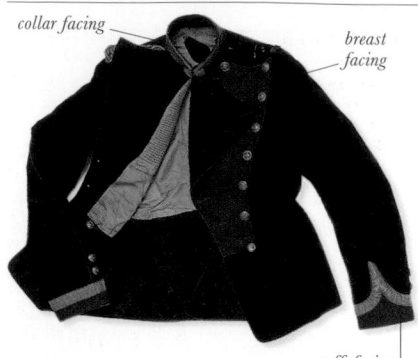

collar facing

breast facing

cuff facing

FACINGS ON A MILITARY JACKET

F

fac·ing /fáysing/ n. **1 a** a layer of material covering part of a garment, etc., for contrast or strength. **b** (in pl.) ▲ the cuffs, collar, etc., of a military jacket. **2** an outer layer covering the surface of a wall, etc.

fac·sim·i·le /faksímilee/ n. & v. ● n. **1** an exact copy, esp. of writing, a picture, etc. (often attrib.: facsimile edition). **2 a** a production of an exact copy of a document, etc., by electronic scanning and transmission (see also FAX). **b** a copy produced in this way. ● v.tr. (**facsimiled, facsimileing**) make a facsimile of. □ **in facsimile** as an exact copy.

fact /fakt/ n. **1** a thing that is known to have occurred, to exist, or to be true. **2** a datum of experience (often foll. by an explanatory clause or phrase: the fact that fire burns). **3** (usu. in pl.) a piece of evidence. **4** truth; reality. **5** a thing assumed as the basis for argument or inference. □ **before** (or **after**) **the fact** before (or after) the committing of a crime. **a fact of life** something that must be accepted. **facts and figures** precise details. **in** (or **in point of) fact 1** in reality; as a matter of fact. **2** (in summarizing) in short.

fac·tion¹ /fákshən/ n. **1** a small organized dissenting group within a larger one, esp. in politics. **2** a state of dissension within an organization. □□ **fac·tion·al** /fákshənəl/ adj. **fac·tion·al·ize** v.tr. & intr. **fac·tion·al·ly** adv.

fac·tion² /fákshən/ n. a book, movie, etc., using real events as a basis for a fictional narrative or dramatization.

-faction /fákshən/ comb. form forming nouns of action from verbs in -fy (petrifaction; satisfaction).

fac·tious /fákshəs/ adj. characterized by or inclined to faction. □□ **fac·tious·ly** adv. **fac·tiousness** n.

fac·ti·tious /faktíshəs/ adj. **1** contrived; not genuine (factitious value). **2** not natural (factitious joy). □□ **fac·ti·tious·ly** adv. **fac·ti·tious·ness** n.

fac·ti·tive /fáktitiv/ adj. Gram. (of a verb) having a sense of regarding or designating, and taking a complement as well as an object (e.g., appointed me captain).

fac·toid /fáktoyd/ n. an assumption or speculation that is reported and repeated so often that it becomes accepted as fact.

fac·tor /fáktər/ n. & v. ● n. **1** a circumstance, fact, or influence contributing to a result. **2** Math. a whole number, etc., that when multiplied with another produces a given number. **3** Biol. a gene, etc., determining hereditary character. **4** (foll. by identifying number) Med. any of several substances in the blood contributing to coagulation (factor eight). **5 a** a merchant buying and selling on commission. **b** Sc. a land agent or steward. **c** an agent or a deputy. **6** an agent or company that buys a manufacturer's invoices and takes responsibility for collecting the payments due on them; a backer. ● v.tr. **1** Math. resolve into factors or components. **2** tr. sell (one's receivable debts) to a factor. □□ **fac·tor·ize** /fáktərīz/ v.tr. & intr.

fac·tor·age /fáktərij/ n. **1** commission or charges payable to a factor. **2** the business of a factor.

fac·to·ri·al /faktáwreeəl/ n. & adj. Math. ● n. **1** the product of a number and all the whole numbers below it (four factorial = 4 x 3 x 2 x 1). ¶ Symb.: ! (as in 4!). **2** the product of a series of factors in an arithmetical progression. ● adj. of a factor or factorial. □□ **fac·to·ri·al·ly** adv.

fac·to·ry /fáktəree/ n. (pl. **-ies**) **1** a building or buildings containing equipment for manufacturing machinery or goods. **2** (usu. derog.) a place producing mass quantities or a low quality of goods, etc. (a degree factory).

factory farming n. a system of rearing livestock using industrial or intensive methods.

fac·to·ry ship n. ▼ a fishing ship with facilities for immediate processing of the catch.

fac·to·tum /faktótəm/ n. (pl. **factotums**) an employee who does all kinds of work.

facts of life n.pl. (prec. by the) information about sexual functions and practices.

fac·tu·al /fákchŏŏəl/ adj. **1** based on or concerned with fact. **2** actual; true. □□ **fac·tu·al·i·ty** /-chŏŏálitee/ n. **fac·tu·al·ly** adv. **fac·tu·al·ness** n.

fac·tum /fáktəm/ n. (pl. **factums** or **facta** /-tə/) Law **1** an act or deed. **2** a statement of the facts.

fac·ture /fákchər/ n. the quality or manner of execution of an artwork, etc.

fac·u·la /fákyələ/ n. (pl. **faculae** /-lee/) Astron. a bright spot or streak on the Sun. □□ **fac·u·lar** adj. **fac·u·lous** adj.

fac·ul·ta·tive /fákəltaytiv/ adj. **1** Law enabling an act to take place. **2** that may occur. **3** Biol. not restricted to a particular function, mode of life, etc. **4** of a faculty. □□ **fac·ul·ta·tive·ly** adv.

fac·ul·ty /fákəltee/ n. (pl. **-ies**) **1** an aptitude or ability for a particular activity. **2** an inherent mental or physical power. **3 a** the teaching staff of a university, college, or secondary school. **b** a department of a university, etc., teaching a specific branch of learning (faculty of modern languages).

fad /fad/ n. **1** a craze. **2** a peculiar notion or idiosyncrasy. □□ **fad·dish** adj. **fad·dish·ly** adv. **fad·dish·ness** n. **fad·dism** n. **fad·dist** n.

fade /fayd/ v. & n. ● v. **1** intr. & tr. lose or cause to lose color. **2** intr. lose freshness or strength; (of flowers, etc.) droop; wither. **3** intr. **a** (of color, light, etc.) grow pale or dim. **b** (of sound) grow faint. **4** intr. (of a feeling, etc.) diminish. **5** intr. (foll. by away, out) (of a person, etc.) disappear or depart gradually. **6** tr. (foll. by in, out) Cinematog. & Broadcasting **a** cause (a picture) to come gradually in or out of view on a screen, or to merge into another shot. **b** make (the sound) more or less audible. ● n. the action or an instance of fading. □ **fade away** colloq. languish; grow thin. □□ **fade·less** adj. **fad·er** n. (in sense 6 of v.).

FACTORY SHIP

Factory ships are equipped not only for catching fish but also for the immediate processing and freezing of the catch. The fish are gutted and cleaned in the factory area and then stored in ice. The freshness of the fish is secured by this immediate freezing, so the vessel can stay out at sea for many weeks, trawling for more catches.

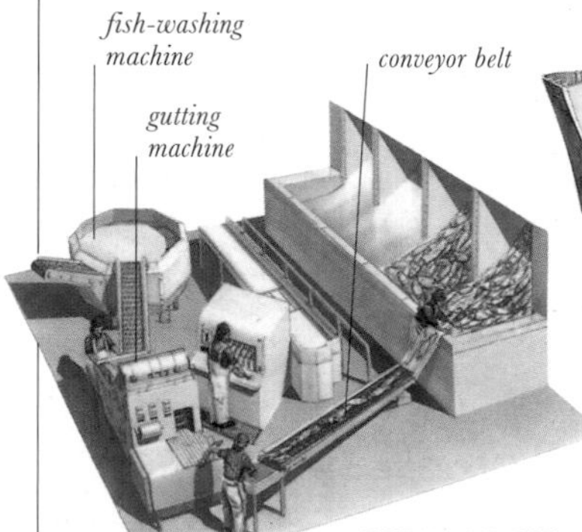

fishing lights

radio mast

search-light

radar scanner

stern gantry

pulley

pulley

midwater-fishing towing block

bow gantries

seabed-fishing towing block

pilothouse

upper deck

fish-washing machine

conveyor belt

trawl warps

net drum

fish chute

net

trawl net storage

gutting machine

engine room

trawl winches

fish hold

ice storage

processing area

rudder

propeller

DETAIL OF THE PROCESSING AREA

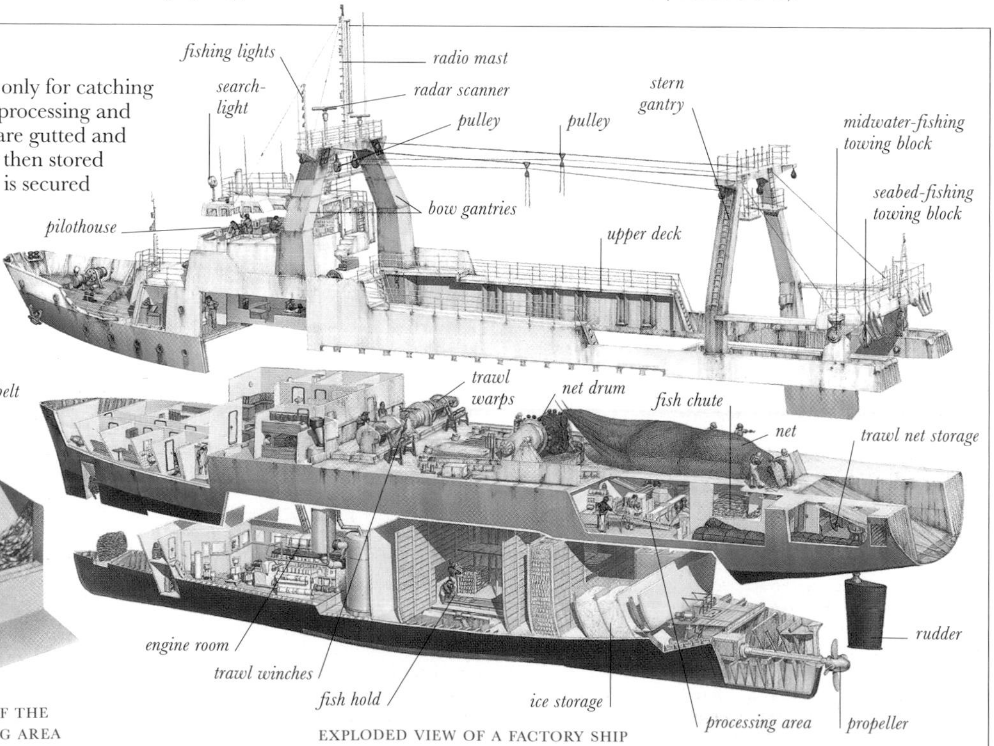

EXPLODED VIEW OF A FACTORY SHIP

fade-in *n.* *Cinematog.* & *Broadcasting* the action or an instance of fading in a picture or sound.

fade-out *n.* **1** *colloq.* disappearance; death. **2** *Cinematog.* & *Broadcasting* the action or an instance of fading out a picture or sound.

fa·do /faadō/ *n.* a type of popular Portuguese song, usually with a melancholy theme.

fae·rie /fáiree/ *n.* (also **faery**) *archaic* **1** fairyland; the fairies, esp. as represented by Spenser (*the Faerie Queene*). **2** (*attrib.*) visionary; imagined.

fag /fag/ *n.* *sl.* often *offens.* a male homosexual.

fag·got /fágət/ *n.* **1** *sl. derog.* often *offens.* a male homosexual. **2** a bunch of herbs. □□ **fag·got·y** *adj.*

fag·ot /fágət/ *n. & v.* ● *n.* (also **fag·got**) **1** a bundle of sticks or twigs bound together as fuel. **2** a bundle of iron rods for heat treatment. ● *v.tr.* (**fagoted**, **fagoting**) **1** bind in or make into fagots. **2** join by fagoting (see FAGOTING).

fag·ot·ing /fágəting/ *n.* (also **fag·got·ing**) **1** embroidery in which threads are fastened together like a fagot. **2** the joining of materials in a similar manner.

fah var. of FA.

Fahr. *abbr.* Fahrenheit.

Fahr·en·heit /fárənhīt/ *adj.* of a scale of temperature on which water freezes at 32° and boils at 212° under standard conditions.

fa·ience /fī-óns, fay-/ *n.* decorated and glazed earthenware and porcelain.

fail /fayl/ *v. & n.* ● *v.* **1** *intr.* not succeed. **2 a** *tr. & intr.* be unsuccessful in (an examination, etc.). **b** *tr.* (of a commodity, etc.) not pass (a test of quality). **c** *tr.* reject (a candidate, etc.); adjudge or grade as unsuccessful. **3** *intr.* be unable to; neglect to (*failed to appear*). **4** *tr.* disappoint; let down. **5** *intr.* (of supplies, crops, etc.) be or become insufficient. **6** *intr.* become weaker; cease functioning (*the engine has failed*). **7** *intr.* **a** (of an enterprise) collapse. **b** become bankrupt. ● *n.* a failure in an examination. □ **without fail** for certain; whatever happens.

failed /fayld/ *adj.* **1** not good enough (*a failed actor*). **2** deficient; broken down (*a failed crop*).

fail·ing /fáyling/ *n. & prep.* ● *n.* a fault or shortcoming; a weakness, esp. in character. ● *prep.* in default of; if not.

fail-safe *adj.* reverting to a safe condition in the event of a breakdown, etc.

fail·ure /fáylyər/ *n.* **1** lack of success. **2** an unsuccessful person, thing, or attempt. **3** nonperformance; nonoccurrence. **4** breaking down or ceasing to function (*heart failure*). **5** running short of supply, etc. **6** bankruptcy.

fain /fayn/ *adj. & adv. archaic* ● *predic.adj.* (foll. by *to* + infin.) **1** willing under the circumstances to. **2** left with no alternative but to. ● *adv.* gladly (esp. *would fain*).

faint /faynt/ *adj., v., & n.* ● *adj.* **1** indistinct; dim; not clearly perceived. **2** (of a person) weak or dizzy; inclined to faint. **3** slight; remote; inadequate (*a faint chance*). **4** halfhearted (*faint praise*). **5** timid (*a faint heart*). ● *v.intr.* **1** lose consciousness. **2** become faint. ● *n.* a sudden loss of consciousness. □ **not have the faintest** *colloq.* have no idea. □□ **faint·ness** *n.*

faint-heart·ed *adj.* cowardly; timid. □□ **faint-heart·ed·ly** *adv.* **faint-heart·ed·ness** *n.*

faint·ly /fáyntlee/ *adv.* **1** very slightly (*faintly amused*). **2** indistinctly; feebly.

fair[1] /fair/ *adj. & adv.* ● *adj.* **1** just; equitable; in accordance with the rules. **2** blond; light or pale in color or complexion. **3 a** of (only) moderate quality or amount; average. **b** considerable; satisfactory (*a fair chance of success*). **4** (of weather) fine and dry; (of the wind) favorable. **5** clean; clear; unblemished (*fair copy*). **6** beautiful; attractive. ● *adv.* in a fair manner (*play fair*). □ **fair and square** *adv. & adj.* **1** exactly. **2** straightforward; honest; aboveboard. **fair enough** *colloq.* that is reasonable or acceptable. **fair's fair** *colloq.* all involved should act fairly. **in a fair way to** likely to. □□ **fair·ish** *adj.* **fair·ness** *n.*

fair[2] /fair/ *n.* **1** a gathering of stalls, amusements, etc., for public entertainment. **2** a periodical gathering for the sale of goods, often with entertainments. **3** an exhibition of farm products, usu. held annually, with competitions, entertainments, etc. **4** an exhibition, esp. to promote particular products.

fair game *n.* a thing or person one may legitimately pursue, exploit, etc.

fair·ground /fáirgrownd/ *n.* an outdoor area where a fair is held.

Fair Isle /fáir īl/ *n.* (also *attrib.*) ◄ a piece of clothing knitted in a characteristic multicolored design.

fair·lead /fáirleed/ *n. Naut.* a device to guide rope, etc.

fair·ly /fáirlee/ *adv.* **1** in a fair manner. **2** moderately (*fairly good*). **3** to a noticeable degree (*fairly narrow*). **4** utterly; completely (*fairly beside himself*). **5** actually (*fairly jumped for joy*).

fair-mind·ed *adj.* just; impartial. □□ **fair-mind·ed·ly** *adv.* **fair-mind·ed·ness** *n.*

fair play *n.* reasonable treatment or behavior.

fair sex *n.* (prec. by *the*) women.

fair·wa·ter /fáirwawtər, -wotər/ *n.* a structure on a ship, etc., assisting its passage through water.

fair·way /fáirway/ *n.* **1** a navigable channel. **2** ▼ the part of a golf course between a tee and its green, kept free of rough grass. ▷ GOLF

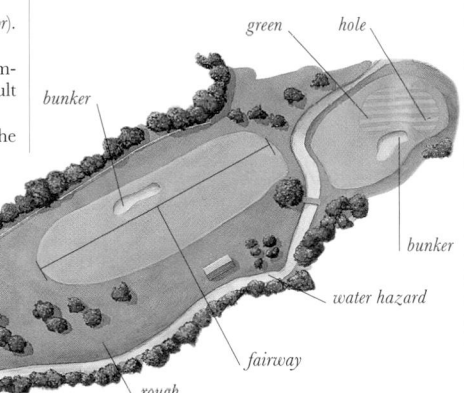

FAIRWAY ON A GOLF COURSE

green *hole* *bunker* *bunker* *water hazard* *fairway* *rough* *teeing-off area*

fair-weath·er friend *n.* a friend or ally who is unreliable in times of difficulty.

fair·y /fáiree/ *n. & adj.* ● *n.* (*pl.* **-ies**) **1** a small imaginary being with magical powers. **2** *sl. derog.* a male homosexual. ● *adj.* of fairies; fairylike; delicate; small. □□ **fair·y·like** *adj.*

fair·y god·moth·er *n.* a benefactress.

fair·y·land /fáireeland/ *n.* **1** the imaginary home of fairies. **2** an enchanted region.

fair·y ring *n.* a ring of mushrooms or darker grass caused by fungi.

fair·y tale *n.* (also **fairy story**) **1** a tale about fairies or other fantastic creatures. **2** an incredible story; a fabrication.

fait ac·com·pli /fet aakawɴplée, -komplée/ *n.* (*pl.* **faits accomplis** *pronunc.* same) a thing that has been done and is past altering.

faith /fayth/ *n.* **1** complete trust or confidence. **2** firm belief, esp. without logical proof. **3 a** religious belief. **b** spiritual apprehension of divine truth apart from proof. **c** things believed or to be believed. **4** duty or commitment to fulfill a trust, promise, etc. (*keep faith*). **5** (*attrib.*) concerned with a supposed ability to cure by faith rather than treatment.

faith·ful /fáythfool/ *adj.* **1** showing faith. **2** (often foll. by *to*) loyal; trustworthy. **3** accurate; true to fact (*a faithful account*). **4** thorough in performing one's duty; conscientious. **5** (**the Faithful**) the believers in a religion. □□ **faith·ful·ness** *n.*

faith·ful·ly /fáythfoolee/ *adv.* in a faithful manner. □ **yours faithfully** a formula for ending a business or formal letter.

faith heal·er *n.* one who uses religious faith and prayer to heal. □□ **faith heal·ing** *n.*

faith·less /fáythlis/ *adj.* **1** false; unreliable; disloyal. **2** without religious faith. □□ **faith·less·ly** *adv.* **faith·less·ness** *n.*

fa·ji·tas /faaheétas, fə-/ *n.pl. Mexican Cooking* thin strips of fried or broiled meat, usu. seasoned with salsa.

fake /fayk/ *n., adj., & v.* ● *n.* **1** a thing or person that is not genuine. **2** a trick. **3** *Sport* a feint. ● *adj.* counterfeit; not genuine. ● *v.tr.* **1** make (a false thing) appear genuine; forge; counterfeit. **2** make a pretense of having (a feeling, illness, etc.). **3** *Sport* feint. **4** improvise (*I'm not exactly sure, but I can fake it*). □□ **fak·er** *n.* **fak·er·y** *n.*

fa·kir /fəkéer, fáykeer/ *n.* (also **fa·quir**) a Muslim or Hindu religious mendicant or ascetic.

fa·la·fel /fəláafəl/ *n.* (also **fe·la·fel**) (in Near Eastern countries) a spicy dish of fried patties made from mashed chick peas or beans.

fal·chion /fáwlchən/ *n. hist.* a broad curved sword with a convex edge.

fal·ci·form /fálsifawrm/ *adj. Anat.* curved like a sickle.

fal·con /fálkən, fáwl-/ *n.* ▼ any diurnal bird of prey of the family Falconidae, sometimes trained to hunt small game for sport. ▷ RAPTOR

FALCON:
LANNER FALCON
(*Falco biarmicus*)

fal·con·er /fálkənər, fáwl-/ *n.* **1** a keeper and trainer of hawks. **2** a person who hunts with hawks.

fal·con·et /fálkənit, fáwl-/ *n.* **1** *hist.* a light cannon. **2** *Zool.* a small falcon.

fal·con·gen·tle *n.* a female falcon.

fal·con·ry /fálkənree, fáwl-/ *n.* the breeding and training of hawks; the sport of hawking.

fall /fawl/ *v. & n.* ● *v.intr.* (*past* **fell** /fel/; *past part.* **fallen** /fáwlən/) **1 a** descend rapidly from a higher to a lower level (*fell from the top floor*). **b** drop or be dropped (*supplies fell by parachute*). **2 a** (often foll. by *over* or *down*) cease to stand; come suddenly to the ground. **b** collapse forward or downward, esp. of one's own volition (*fell into my arms*). **3** become detached and descend or disappear. **4** take a downward direction: **a** (of hair, clothing, etc.) hang down. **b** (of ground, etc.) slope. **c** (foll. by *into*) (of a river, etc.) discharge into. **5 a** find a lower level; sink lower. **b** subside; abate. **6** (of a barometer, etc.) show a lower reading. **7** occur (*darkness fell*). **8** decline (*demand is falling*; *standards have fallen*). **9 a** (of the face) show dismay. **b** (of the eyes or a glance) look downward. **10 a** lose power or status (*the* *government will fall*). **b** lose esteem, moral integrity, etc. **11** commit sin; yield to temptation. **12** take or have a particular direction or place (*his eye fell on me*). **13 a** find a place; be naturally divisible (*the subject falls into three parts; the accent falls on the first syllable*). **b** (foll. by *under, within*) be classed among. **14** occur at a specified time (*Easter falls early this year*). **15** come by chance or duty (*it fell to me to answer*). **16 a** pass into a specified condition (*fall into decay; fell ill*). **b** become (*fall asleep*). **17 a** (of a position, etc.) be overthrown or captured; succumb to attack. **b** be defeated; fail. **18** die (*fall in battle*). **19** (foll. by *on, upon*) **a** attack. **b** meet with. **c** embrace or embark on avidly. **20** (foll. by *to* + verbal noun) begin (*fell to wondering*). **21** (foll. by *to*) lapse; revert (*revenues fall to the state*). ● *n.* **1** the act or an instance of falling; a sudden rapid descent. **2** that which falls or has fallen, e.g., snow, etc. **3** the recorded amount of rainfall, etc. **4** a decline or diminution; depreciation in price, value, demand, etc. **5** downfall (*the fall of Rome*). **6 a** succumbing to temptation. **b** (**the Fall**) the biblical sin of Adam and its consequences. **7** (of material, land, light, etc.) a downward direction; a slope. **8** (also **Fall**) autumn. **9** (esp. in *pl.*) a waterfall, cataract, or cascade. **10** *Mus.* a cadence. **11 a** a wrestling bout; a throw in wrestling that keeps the opponent on the ground for a specified time. **b** a controlled act of falling in judo, etc. **12 a** the birth of young of certain animals. **b** the number of young born. **13** a rope of a hoisting tackle. □ **fall apart** (or **to pieces**) **1** break into pieces. **2** (of a situation, etc.) be reduced to chaos. **3** lose one's capacity to cope. **fall away 1** (of a surface) incline abruptly. **2** gradually vanish. **3** desert; revolt. **fall back** retreat. **fall back on** have recourse to in difficulty. **fall behind 1** lag. **2** be in arrears. **fall down** (often foll. by *on*) *colloq.* fail; fail to deliver (payment, etc.). **fall flat** fail to achieve expected success or evoke a desired response. **fall for** *colloq.* **1** be captivated or deceived by. **2** yield to the charms or merits of. **fall foul of** come into conflict with. **fall in 1 a** take one's place in military formation. **b** (as *int.*) the order to do this. **2** collapse inward. **fall in love** see LOVE. **fall into line 1** take one's place in the ranks. **2** conform with others. **fall into place** begin to make sense or cohere. **fall in with 1** meet by chance. **2** agree with; accede to; humor. **3** coincide with. **fall off 1** (of demand, etc.) decrease. **2** withdraw. **fall out 1** quarrel. **2** (of the hair, etc.) become detached. **3** *Mil.* come out of formation. **4** result; come to pass; occur. **fall out of** gradually discontinue (a habit, etc.). **fall over oneself** *colloq.* **1** be eager or competitive. **2** stumble through haste, confusion, etc. **fall short 1** be or become inadequate. **2** (of a missile, etc.) not reach its target. **fall short of** fail to reach or obtain. **fall through** come to nothing; miscarry. **fall to** begin an activity, e.g., eating or working.

fal·la·cy /fálǝsee/ *n.* (*pl.* **-ies**) **1** a mistaken belief, esp. based on unsound argument. **2** faulty reasoning; misleading or unsound argument. □□ **fal·la·cious** /fǝláyshǝs/ *adj.* **fal·la·cious·ly** *adv.* **fal·la·cious·ness** *n.*

fall·back /fáwlbak/ *n.* (also *attrib.*) an alternative resource, as in an emergency.

fall·en *past part.* of FALL *v.* *adj.* **1** (*attrib.*) having lost one's honor or reputation. **2** killed in war.

fall·fish /fáwlfish/ *n.* a N. American freshwater fish, *Semotilus corporalis.*

fall guy *sl.* **1** an easy victim. **2** a scapegoat.

fal·li·ble /fálibǝl/ *adj.* **1** capable of making mistakes. **2** liable to be erroneous. □□ **fal·li·bil·i·ty** *n.* **fal·li·bly** *adv.*

fall·ing star *n.* a meteor.

fall-off /fáwlawf/ *n.* a decrease, deterioration, withdrawal, etc.

Fal·lo·pi·an tube /fǝlópeeǝn/ *n. Anat.* ▶ either of two tubes in female mammals along which ova travel to the uterus. ▷ OVARY

fall-out /fáwlowt/ *n.* **1** radioactive debris caused by a nuclear explosion or accident. **2** the adverse side effects of a situation, etc.

fal·low¹ /fálō/ *adj. & n.* ● *adj.* **1 a** (of land) plowed and harrowed but left unsown. **b** uncultivated. **2** (of an idea, etc.) potentially useful but not yet in use. ● *n.* fallow or uncultivated land. □□ **fal·low·ness** *n.*

fal·low² /fálō/ *adj.* of a pale brownish or reddish yellow.

false /fawls/ *adj. & adv.* ● *adj.* **1** not according with fact; incorrect. **2 a** spurious; artificial (*false gods; false teeth; false modesty*). **b** acting as such, esp. deceptively (*a false lining*). **3** illusory (*a false economy*). **4** improperly so called (*false acacia*). **5** deceptive. **6** (foll. by *to*) deceitful, treacherous, or unfaithful. **7** illegal (*false imprisonment*). ● *adv.* in a false manner (esp. *play false*). □□ **false·ly** *adv.* **false·ness** *n.* **fal·si·ty** *n.* (*pl.* **-ies**).

false a·larm *n.* an alarm given needlessly.

false e·co·no·my *n.* an apparent financial saving that in fact leads to greater expenditure.

false·hood /fáwls-hŏod/ *n.* **1** the state of being false, esp. untrue. **2** a false or untrue thing. **3 a** the act of lying. **b** a lie or lies.

false pre·tens·es *n.pl.* misrepresentations made with intent to deceive (esp. *under false pretenses*).

false start *n.* **1** an invalid start in a race. **2** an unsuccessful attempt to begin something.

false step *n.* a slip; a mistake.

fal·set·to /fawlsétō/ *n.* (*pl.* **-os**) **1** a method of voice production used by male singers, esp. tenors, to sing notes higher than their normal range. **2** a singer using this method.

fal·sies /fáwlseez/ *n.pl. colloq.* padded material to increase the apparent size of the breasts.

fal·si·fy /fáwlsifī/ *v.tr.* (**-ies, -ied**) **1** fraudulently alter or make false (a document, evidence, etc.). **2** misrepresent. **3** make wrong; pervert. **4** show to be false. **5** disappoint (a hope, fear, etc.). □□ **fal·si·fi·a·ble** *adj.* **fal·si·fi·ca·tion** *n.*

fal·ter /fáwltǝr/ *v.* **1** *intr.* stumble; go unsteadily. **2** *intr.* lose courage. **3** *tr. & intr.* speak hesitatingly. □□ **fal·ter·er** *n.* **fal·ter·ing·ly** *adv.*

Fa·lun Gong /fáloōn góng/ *n.* (also **Fa·lun Dafa**) a spiritual exercise and meditation regime with similarities to t'ai chi ch'uan, practiced predominantly in China.

fame /faym/ *n.* **1** renown; the state of being famous. **2** reputation.

famed /faymd/ *adj.* (foll. by *for*) famous; much spoken of (*famed for its good food*).

fa·mil·ial /fǝmílyǝl, -leeǝl/ *adj.* of, occurring in, or characteristic of a family or its members.

fa·mil·iar /fǝmílyǝr/ *adj. & n.* ● *adj.* **1 a** (often foll. by *to*) well known; no longer novel. **b** often encountered or experienced. **2** (foll. by *with*) knowing a thing well or in detail (*am familiar with all the problems*). **3** (often foll. by *with*) **a** well acquainted (with a person); intimate. **b** sexually intimate. **4** excessively informal. **5** unceremonious. **6** (of animals) tame. ● *n.* **1** a close friend or associate. **2** (in full **familiar spirit**) a demon

supposedly attending and obeying a witch, etc. □□ **fa·mil·iar·ly** *adv.*

fa·mil·iar·i·ty /fǝmíleeáritee, -yár-/ *n.* (*pl.* **-ies**) **1** the state of being well known. **2** (foll. by *with*) close acquaintance. **3** a close relationship. **4 a** sexual intimacy. **b** (in *pl.*) acts of physical intimacy. **5** informal behavior, esp. excessively so.

fa·mil·iar·ize /fǝmílyǝrīz/ *v.tr.* **1** (foll. by *with*) make (a person) conversant or well acquainted. **2** make (a thing) well known. □□ **fa·mil·iar·i·za·tion** *n.*

fam·i·ly /fámilee/ *n.* (*pl.* **-ies**) **1** a set of relations, living together or not. **2 a** the members of a household. **b** a person's children. **c** (*attrib.*) serving the needs of families (*family butcher*). **3 a** all the descendants of a common ancestor. **b** a group of peoples from a common stock. **4** all the languages ultimately derived from a particular early language, regarded as a group. **5** a brotherhood of persons or nations united by political or religious ties. **6** a group of objects distinguished by common features. **7** *Math.* a group of curves, etc., obtained by varying one quantity. **8** *Biol.* a group of related genera of organisms within an order in taxonomic classification. □ **in the** (or **a**) **family way** *colloq.* pregnant.

fam·i·ly name *n.* a surname.

fam·i·ly plan·ning *n.* birth control.

fam·i·ly tree *n.* a chart showing relationships and lines of descent.

fam·ine /fámin/ *n.* **1** extreme scarcity of food. **2** a shortage of something specified (*water famine*).

fam·ish /fámish/ *v.tr. & intr.* (usu. in *passive*) **1** reduce or be reduced to extreme hunger. **2** *colloq.* (esp. as **famished** *adj.*) feel very hungry.

fa·mous /fáymǝs/ *adj.* **1** (often foll. by *for*) celebrated; well known. **2** *colloq.* excellent. □□ **fa·mous·ly** *adv.* **fa·mous·ness** *n.*

fan¹ /fan/ *n. & v.* ● *n.* **1** an apparatus, usu. with rotating blades, giving a current of air for ventilation, etc. **2** ◄ a device, usu. folding and forming a semicircle when spread out, for agitating the air to cool oneself. **3** anything spread out like a fan. ▷ VAULT. ● *v.* (**fanned, fanning**) **1** *tr.* **a** blow a current of air on, with or as with a fan. **b** agitate (the air) with a fan. **2** *tr.* (of a breeze) blow gently on. **3** *tr.* **a** winnow (grain). **b** winnow away (chaff). **4** *intr. & tr.* (usu. foll. by *out*) spread out in the shape of a fan. **5 a** *tr.* strike (a batter) out. **b** *intr.* strike out. □□ **fan·like** *adj.*

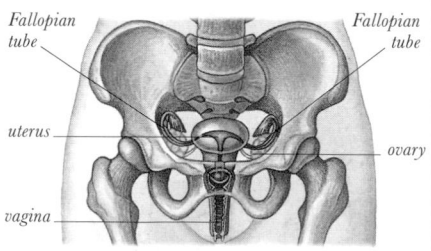

FAN: 19TH-CENTURY EUROPEAN FAN

fan² /fan/ *n.* a devotee of a particular activity, performer, etc.

fa·nat·ic /fǝnátik/ *n. & adj.* ● *n.* a person filled with excessive and often misguided enthusiasm for something. ● *adj.* excessively enthusiastic. □□ **fa·nat·i·cal** *adj.* **fa·nat·i·cal·ly** *adv.* **fa·nat·i·cism** /-ti-sizǝm/ *n.* **fa·nat·i·cize** /-tisīz/ *v.intr. & tr.*

fan belt *n.* ▼ a belt that drives a fan to cool the radiator in a motor vehicle.

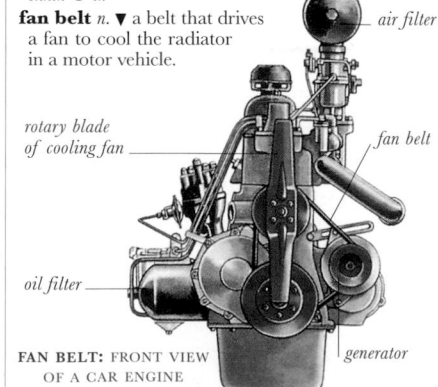

FALLOPIAN TUBES IN THE FEMALE HUMAN BODY

Fallopian tube   *Fallopian tube*   *uterus*   *ovary*   *vagina*

rotary blade of cooling fan   *air filter*   *fan belt*   *oil filter*   *generator*

FAN BELT: FRONT VIEW OF A CAR ENGINE SHOWING THE FAN BELT

FANG

In venomous snakes, the fangs are usually folded back against the roof of the mouth, swinging forward only when needed to attack prey. Venom stored in a sac at the back of the mouth passes along a tube to be released through a tiny hole close to the fang's point.

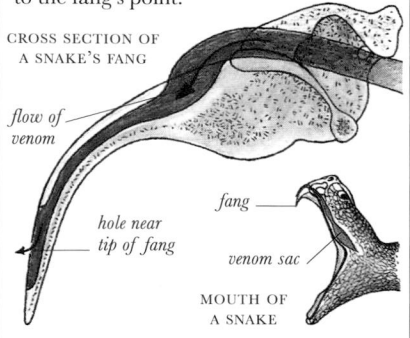

CROSS SECTION OF
A SNAKE'S FANG

flow of venom

fang

hole near tip of fang

venom sac

MOUTH OF
A SNAKE

fan·ci·er /fánseeər/ n. a connoisseur or follower of some activity or thing (*dog fancier*).

fan·ci·ful /fánsifool/ adj. **1** existing only in the imagination or fancy. **2** whimsical; capricious. **3** fantastically designed, etc. □□ **fan·ci·ful·ly** adv. **fan·ci·ful·ness** n.

fan club n. an organized group of devotees.

fan·cy /fánsee/ n., adj., & v. ● n. (pl. **-ies**) **1** an individual taste or inclination. **2** a caprice or whim. **3** a thing favored, e.g., a horse to win a race. **4** an arbitrary supposition. **5 a** the faculty of using imagination or of inventing imagery. **b** a mental image. **6** delusion; unfounded belief. **7** (prec. by *the*) those who have a certain hobby; fanciers, esp. patrons of boxing. ● adj. (usu. *attrib.*) (**fancier, fanciest**) **1** ornamental; not plain. **2** capricious; whimsical; extravagant (*at a fancy price*). **3** based on imagination, not fact. **4 a** (of foods, etc.) above average quality. **b** of superior skill. **5** (of flowers, etc.) particolored. **6** (of an animal) bred for particular points of beauty, etc. ● v.tr. (**-ies, -ied**) **1** (foll. by *that* + clause) be inclined to suppose. **2** *Brit. colloq.* feel a desire for (*do you fancy a drink?*). **3** *Brit. colloq.* find sexually attractive. **4** (in *imper.*) an exclamation of surprise (*fancy their doing that!*). **5 a** picture to oneself. **b** (as **fancied** adj.) having no basis in fact; imaginary. □ **catch** (or **take**) **the fancy of** please; appeal to. □□ **fan·ci·a·ble** adj. (in sense 3 of v.). **fan·ci·ly** adv. **fan·ci·ness** n.

fan·cy-free adj. without (esp. emotional) commitments.

fan·cy·man *sl. derog.* **1** a woman's lover. **2** a pimp.

fan·cy·work /fánseewərk/ n. ornamental sewing, etc.

fan·dan·go /fandánggō/ n. (pl. **-oes** or **-os**) **1 a** a lively Spanish dance for two. **b** the music for this. **2** tomfoolery.

fan·fare /fánfair/ n. **1** a short showy or ceremonious sounding of trumpets, etc. **2** an elaborate display; a burst of publicity.

fang /fang/ n. **1** a canine tooth, esp. of a dog or wolf. ▷ CARNIVORE. **2 ▲** the tooth of a venomous snake, by which poison is injected. **3** the root of a tooth or its prong. **4** *colloq.* a person's tooth. □□ **fanged** adj. (also in *comb.*).

fan·light /fánlīt/ n. ▶ a small, orig. semicircular window over a door or another window.

fan mail n. letters from fans.

fan·ny /fánee/ n. (pl. **-ies**) **1** *sl.* the buttocks. **2** *Brit. coarse sl.* the female genitals. ¶ Usually considered a taboo word in *Brit.* use.

fanny pack n. a pouch for personal items, worn on a belt around the waist or hips.

fan·tail /fántayl/ n. a pigeon with a broad tail. □□ **fan-tailed** adj.

fan-tan /fántan/ n. **1** a Chinese gambling game in which players try to guess the remainder after the banker has divided a number of hidden objects into four groups. **2** a card game in which players build on sequences of sevens.

fan·ta·sia /fantáyzhə, -zheə, fántəzéeə/ n. a musical or other composition free in form and often in improvisatory style, or that is based on several familiar tunes.

fan·ta·size /fántəsīz/ v. **1** *intr.* have a fantasy or fanciful vision. **2** *tr.* imagine; create a fantasy about. □□ **fan·ta·sist** n.

fan·tas·tic /fantástik/ adj. (also **fan·tas·ti·cal**) **1** *colloq.* excellent; extraordinary. **2** extravagantly fanciful. **3** grotesque or bizarre in design, etc. □□ **fan·tas·ti·cal·i·ty** /-kálitee/ n. **fan·tas·ti·cal·ly** adv.

fan·ta·sy /fántəsee, -zee/ n. (pl. **-ies**) **1** the faculty of inventing images, esp. extravagant or visionary ones. **2** a fanciful mental image; a daydream. **3** a whimsical speculation. **4** a fantastic invention or composition. **5** fabrication; pretense; make-believe (*his account was pure fantasy*).

FAQ abbr. Computing frequently asked questions.

far /faar/ adv. & adj. (**farther, farthest** or **further, furthest**) ● adv. **1** at or to or by a great distance (*far away; far off; far out*). **2** a long way (off) in space or time (*are you traveling far?; we talked far into the night*). **3** to a great extent or degree; by much (*far better; far too early*). ● adj. **1** situated at or extending over a great distance in space or time; remote (*a far country*). **2** more distant (*the far end of the hall*). **3** extreme (*far right militants*). □ **as far as 1** to the distance of (a place). **2** to the extent that (*travel as far as you like*). **by far 1** by a great amount. **2** (as an intensifier) without doubt. **far and away** by a very large amount. **far and near** everywhere. **far and wide** over a large area. **far be it from me** (foll. by *to* + infin.) I am reluctant to (esp. express criticism, etc.). **far from** very different from; tending to the opposite of (*the problem is far from being solved*). **go far 1** achieve much. **2** contribute greatly. **3** be adequate. **go too far** go beyond the limits of what is reasonable, polite, etc. **how far** to what extent. **so far 1** to such an extent or distance; to this point. **2** until now. **so** (or **in so**) **far as** (or **that**) to the extent that. **so far so good** progress has been satisfactory up to now.

far·ad /fárəd, -ad/ n. *Electr.* a unit of capacitance, such that one coulomb of charge causes a potential difference of one volt. ¶ Abbr.: **F**.

far·a·day /fárəday/ n. (also **Faraday's constant**) *Electr.* the quantity of electric charge carried by one mole of electrons.

fa·rad·ic /fərádik/ adj. (also **fa·ra·da·ic** /fárədáyik/) *Electr.* inductive; induced.

far·an·dole /fárəndōl/ n. **1** a lively Provençal dance.

far·a·way /fáarəwáy/ adj. **1** remote; long past. **2** (of a look) dreamy. **3** (of a voice) sounding as if from a distance.

farce /faars/ n. **1 a** a broadly comic dramatic work based on ludicrously improbable events. **b** this branch of drama. **2** absurdly futile proceedings.

far·ceur /faarsŕr/ n. **1** a joker or wag. **2** an actor or writer of farces.

far·ci·cal /fáarsikəl/ adj. **1** extremely ludicrous or futile. **2** of or like farce. □□ **far·ci·cal·ly** adv.

far cry n. a long way.

fare /fair/ n. & v. ● n. **1 a** the price a passenger has to pay to be conveyed by bus, train, etc. **b** a passenger paying to travel in a public vehicle. **2** a range of food. ● v.intr. **1** progress; get on (*how did you fare?*). **2** happen; turn out. **3** journey; go; travel.

Far East n. (prec. by *the*) China, Japan, and other countries of E. Asia. □□ **Far East·ern** adj.

fare·well /fáirwél/ int. & n. ● int. good-bye; adieu. ● n. **1** leave-taking; departure (also *attrib.: a farewell kiss*). **2** parting good wishes.

far-fetched adj. (of an explanation, etc.) strained; unconvincing.

far-flung adj. **1** extending far; widely distributed. **2** remote; distant.

far gone adj. **1** advanced in time. **2** *colloq.* in an advanced state of illness, drunkenness, etc. **3** *colloq.* in a dilapidated state; beyond help.

fa·ri·na /fəréenə/ n. **1** the flour or meal of cereal, nuts, or starchy roots. **2** a powdery substance. □□ **far·i·na·ceous** /fárináyshəs/ adj.

farm /faarm/ n. & v. ● n. **1** an area of land and its buildings used under one management for growing crops, rearing animals, etc. **2** a place or establishment for breeding a particular type of animal, growing fruit, etc. (*trout farm; mink farm*). **3** = FARM-HOUSE. **4** a place with many tanks for the storage of oil or oil products. ● v. **1 a** *tr.* use (land) for growing crops, rearing animals, etc. **b** *intr.* be a farmer; work on a farm. **2** *tr.* breed (fish, etc.) commercially. **3** *tr.* (often foll. by *out*) **a** delegate or subcontract (work) to others. **b** contract (the collection of taxes) to another for a fee. **c** arrange for (a person) to be looked after by another, with payment. **4** *tr.* lease the labor or services of (a person) for hire. **5** *tr.* contract to maintain and care for (a person, esp. a child) for a fixed sum. □□ **farm·ing** n.

farm·er /fáarmər/ n. **1** a person who cultivates a farm. **2** a person to whom the collection of taxes is contracted for a fee. **3** a person who looks after children or performs other services for payment.

farm hand n. a worker on a farm.

farm·house /fáarmhows/ n. a dwelling place attached to a farm.

farm·land /fáarmland/ n. land used or suitable for farming.

farm·stead /fáarmsted/ n. a farm and its buildings.

farm·yard /fáarmyaard/ n. a yard attached to a farmhouse.

far·o /fáirō/ n. a gambling card game in which bets are placed on the order of appearance of the cards.

far-off adj. remote.

far-out adj. **1** distant. **2** avant-garde; unconventional.

far·ra·go /fəráagō, -ráy-/ n. (pl. **-oes**) a medley or hodgepodge. □□ **far·rag·i·nous** /-ráajinəs/ adj.

far-reach·ing adj. **1** widely applicable. **2** having important consequences or implications.

far·ri·er /fáreeər/ n. a smith who shoes horses. □□ **far·ri·er·y** n.

far·row /fárō/ n. & v. ● n. **1** a litter of pigs. **2** the birth of a litter. ● v.tr. (also *absol.*) (of a sow) produce (pigs).

far·ru·ca /fərŏŏkə/ n. a type of flamenco dance.

far-see·ing /fáarséeing/ adj. shrewd in judgment; prescient.

Far·si /fáarsee/ n. the modern Persian language.

far·sight·ed /fáarsítid/ adj. **1** having foresight; prudent. **2** able to see clearly only what is comparatively distant. ▷ SIGHT. □□ **far·sight·ed·ly** adv. **far·sight·ed·ness** n.

fart /faart/ v. & n. *coarse sl.* ● v.intr. **1** emit intestinal gas from the anus. **2** (foll. by *around*) behave foolishly. ● n. **1** an emission of intestinal gas from the anus. **2** an unpleasant person. ¶ Usually considered a taboo word.

far·ther /fáarthər/ adv. & adj. (also **fur·ther** /fŕrthər/) ● adv. **1** to or at a more advanced point in space or time (*unsafe to proceed farther*). **2** at a

FANLIGHT ABOVE A
GEORGIAN FRONT DOOR

F

F

greater distance (*nothing was farther from his thoughts*). ● *adj.* more distant or advanced (*on the farther side*). □□ **far·ther·most** *adj.*

far·thest /fáarthist/ *adj. & adv.* (also **fur·thest** /fúr-thist/) ● *adj.* most distant. ● *adv.* to or at the greatest distance. □ **at the farthest** (or **at farthest**) at the greatest distance; at the latest; at most.

far·thing /fáarthing/ *n.* **1** ◄ (in the UK) a former coin and monetary unit worth a quarter of an old penny. **2** the least possible amount (*it doesn't matter a farthing*).

far·thin·gale /fáarthinggayl/ *n. hist.* ▼ a hooped petticoat.

FARTHING

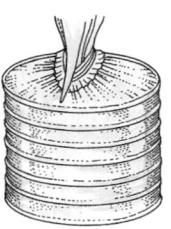 

WHEEL-SHAPED FARTHINGALE   BELL-SHAPED FARTHINGALE

FARTHINGALES

fas·ces /fáseez/ *n.pl.* **1** *Rom.Hist.* a bundle of rods with a projecting ax blade, carried as a symbol of a magistrate's power. **2** *hist.* (in Fascist Italy) emblems of authority.

fas·ci·a /fáyshə/ *n.* **1** a stripe or band. **2** *Archit.* **a** a long flat surface between moldings on the architrave in classical architecture. **b** a flat surface, usu. of wood, covering the ends of rafters. **3** /fásheeə/ *Anat.* a thin sheath of fibrous connective tissue.

fas·ci·cle /fásikəl/ *n.* (also **fas·ci·cule** /-kyool/) a separately published installment of a book.

fas·ci·nate /fásinayt/ *v.tr.* **1** capture the interest of; attract irresistibly. **2** paralyze (a victim) with fear. □□ **fas·ci·nat·ed** *adj.* **fas·ci·nat·ing** *adj.* **fas·ci·nat·ing·ly** *adv.* **fas·ci·na·tion** /-náyshən/ *n.*

Fas·cism /fáshizəm/ *n.* **1** the totalitarian principles and organization of the extreme right-wing nationalist movement in Italy (1922–43). **2** (also **fascism**) **a** any similar nationalist and authoritarian movement. **b** *disp.* any system of extreme right-wing or authoritarian views. □□ **Fas·cist** *n. & adj.* (also **fas·cist**). **Fas·cis·tic** *adj.* (also **fas·cis·tic**).

fash·ion /fáshən/ *n. & v.* ● *n.* **1** the current popular custom or style, esp. in dress. **2** a manner of doing something (*in a peculiar fashion*). **3** (in *comb.*) in a specified manner (*in a peaceable fashion*). **4** fashionable society (*a woman of fashion*). ● *v.tr.* (often foll. by *into*) make into a particular or the required form. □ **after** (or **in**) **a fashion** as well as is practicable, though not satisfactorily. **in** (or **out of**) **fashion** fashionable (or not fashionable).

fash·ion·a·ble /fáshənəbəl/ *adj.* **1** following, suited to, or influenced by the current fashion. **2** characteristic of or favored by those who are leaders of social fashion. □□ **fash·ion·a·ble·ness** *n.* **fash·ion·a·bly** *adv.*

fash·ion·is·ta /fashonéestə/ *n. colloq.* **1** a designer of haute couture. **2** a devoted follower of fashion.

fast[1] /fast/ *adj. & adv.* ● *adj.* **1** rapid; quick-moving. **2** capable of high speed (*a fast car*). **3** enabling or causing or intended for high speed (*the fast lane*). **4** (of a clock, etc.) showing a time ahead of the correct time. **5** (of a field, etc., in a sport) likely to make the ball bounce quickly. **6 a** (of photographic film) needing only a short exposure. **b** (of a lens) having a large aperture. **7 a** firmly fixed or attached. **b** secure; firmly established (*a fast friendship*).

8 (of a color) not fading. **9** (of a person) immoral; dissipated. ● *adv.* **1** quickly; in quick succession. **2** firmly; tightly (*stand fast; eyes fast shut*). **3** soundly; completely (*fast asleep*). **4** close; immediately (*fast on their heels*). **5** in a dissipated manner; extravagantly; immorally. □ **pull a fast one** (often foll. by *on*) *colloq.* try to deceive or gain an unfair advantage.

fast[2] /fast/ *v. & n.* ● *v.intr.* abstain from all or some kinds of food or drink. ● *n.* an act or period of fasting.

fast·back /fástbak/ *n.* **1** an automobile with the rear sloping continuously down to the bumper. **2** such a back.

fast breed·er *n.* (also **fast breeder reactor**) a reactor using fast neutrons to produce the same fissile material as it uses.

fast·en /fásən/ *v.* **1** *tr.* make or become fixed or secure. **2** *tr.* (foll. by *in, up*) lock securely; shut in. **3** *tr.* **a** (foll. by *on, upon*) direct (a look, thoughts, etc.) fixedly or intently. **b** focus or direct the attention fixedly upon (*fastened him with her eyes*). **4** *tr.* (foll. by *on, upon*) fix (a designation or imputation, etc.). **5** *intr.* (foll. by *on, upon*) **a** take hold of. **b** single out. □□ **fast·en·er** *n.*

fast·en·ing /fásəning/ *n.* a device that fastens something; a fastener.

fast food *n.* food that can be prepared and served quickly and easily, esp. in a snack bar or restaurant.

fas·tid·i·ous /fastídeeəs/ *adj.* **1** very careful in matters of choice or taste; fussy. **2** easily disgusted; squeamish. □□ **fas·tid·i·ous·ly** *adv.* **fas·tid·i·ous·ness** *n.*

fas·ti·gi·ate /fástíjeeət/ *adj. Bot.* **1** ► having a conical or tapering outline. **2** having parallel upright branches.

fast·ness /fástnis/ *n.* **1** a stronghold or fortress. **2** the state of being secure.

fast-talk *v.tr. colloq.* persuade by rapid or deceitful talk.

fast track *n.* a course or situation leading to rapid advancement or promotion, as in a career.

fat /fat/ *n., adj., & v.* ● *n.* **1** ▼ a natural oily or greasy substance occurring esp. in animal bodies. **2** the part of anything containing this. **3** excessive presence of fat in a person or animal. **4** *Chem.* any of a group of natural esters of glycerol and various fatty acids existing as solids at room temperature. **5** overabundance or excess. ● *adj.* (**fatter**, **fattest**) **1** (of a person or animal) having excessive fat. **2** (of an animal) made plump for slaughter; fatted. **3** containing much fat. **4** greasy; oily; unctuous. **5** (of land or

FASTIGIATE OUTLINE OF A SPANISH FIR TREE

resources) fertile; rich; yielding abundantly. **6 a** thick; substantial in content (*a fat book*). **b** substantial as an asset or opportunity (*a fat check*). **7** *colloq. iron.* very little; not much (*a fat chance*). **8** *Baseball* (of a pitch) easy to hit. ● *v.tr. & intr.* (**fatted**, **fatting**) make or become fat. □ **the fat is in the fire** trouble is imminent. **kill the fatted calf** celebrate, esp. at a prodigal's return (Luke 15). **live off** (or **on**) **the fat of the land** have the best of everything. □□ **fat·less** *adj.* **fat·ly** *adv.* **fat·ness** *n.* **fat·tish** *adj.*

fa·tal /fáytəl/ *adj.* **1** causing or ending in death (*a fatal accident*). **2** (often foll. by *to*) destructive; ruinous; ending in disaster (*was fatal to their chances; made a fatal mistake*). **3** fateful. □□ **fa·tal·ly** *adv.*

fa·tal·ism /fáyt'lizəm/ *n.* **1** the belief that all events are predetermined and therefore inevitable. **2** a submissive attitude to events as being inevitable. □□ **fa·tal·ist** *n.* **fa·tal·is·tic** *adj.* **fa·tal·is·ti·cal·ly** /-lístiklee/ *adv.*

fa·tal·i·ty /fətálətee, fay-/ *n.* (*pl.* **-ies**) **1 a** an occurrence of death by accident or in war, etc. **b** a person killed in this way. **2** a fatal influence. **3** a predestined liability to disaster. **4** subjection to or the supremacy of fate. **5** a disastrous event; a calamity.

fat cat *n. sl.* **1** a wealthy person, esp. as a benefactor. **2** a highly paid executive or official.

fat cit·y *n.* a situation or condition of ease, prosperity, comfort, etc. (*since winning the lottery, she's living in fat city*).

fate /fayt/ *n. & v.* ● *n.* **1** a power regarded as predetermining events unalterably. **2 a** the future regarded as determined by such a power. **b** an individual's appointed lot. **c** the ultimate condition or end of a person or thing (*that sealed our fate*). **3** death; destruction. **4** (usu. **Fate**) a goddess of destiny. ● *v.tr.* **1** (usu. in *passive*) preordain (*was fated to win*). **2** (as **fated** *adj.*) **a** doomed to destruction. **b** unavoidable; preordained; fateful. □ **fate worse than death** see DEATH.

fate·ful /fáytfool/ *adj.* **1** important; decisive; having far-reaching consequences. **2** controlled as if by fate. **3** causing or likely to cause disaster. **4** prophetic. □□ **fate·ful·ly** *adv.*

fat·head /fat-hed/ *n. colloq.* a stupid person. □□ **fat·head·ed** *adj.* **fat·head·ed·ness** *n.*

fa·ther /fáathər/ *n. & v.* **1 a** a man in relation to a child born from his fertilization of an ovum. **b** a man who has continuous care of a child, esp. by adoption. **2** any male animal in relation to its offspring. **3** (usu. in *pl.*) a forefather. **4** an originator or early leader. **5** a person who deserves special

FAT

Fat – also known as adipose tissue – is an important component of all animal bodies. Most fat is stored just beneath the skin, although various internal organs, such as the kidneys, heart, and liver, are also protected by a surrounding layer of fat. The purpose of fat is threefold: it is a highly concentrated reserve of energy; it acts as insulation against the loss of body heat; and it provides a buffer to absorb shock in areas of the body that experience frequent impact or pressure, such as the buttocks.

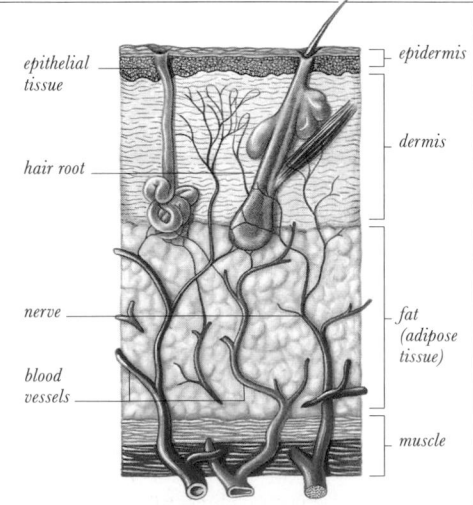

CROSS SECTION OF HUMAN SKIN WITH HEAVY CONCENTRATION OF FAT

epithelial tissue — epidermis

hair root — dermis

nerve — fat (adipose tissue)

blood vessels — muscle

respect (*the father of his country*). **6** (**Fathers** or **Fathers of the Church**) early Christian theologians. **7** (also **Father**) **a** (often as a title or form of address) a priest. **b** a religious leader. **8** (**the Father**) (in Christian belief) the first person of the Trinity. **9** (**Father**) a venerable person, esp. as a title in personifications (*Father Time*). **10** the oldest member or doyen. **11** (usu. in *pl.*) the leading men or elders in a city, etc. (*city fathers*). ● *v.tr.* **1** beget; be the father of. **2** behave as a father toward. **3** originate (a scheme, etc.). **4** appear as or admit that one is the father or originator of. **5** (foll. by *on*) assign the paternity of (a child, book, etc.) to a person. □□ **fa·ther·hood** *n.* **fa·ther·less** *adj.*

fa·ther fig·ure *n.* an older man who is respected like a father.

fa·ther-in-law *n.* (*pl.* **fathers-in-law**) the father of one's husband or wife.

fa·ther·land /fáathərland/ *n.* one's native country.

fa·ther·ly /fáathərlee/ *adj.* **1** like or characteristic of a father in affection, care, etc. (*fatherly concern*). **2** of or proper to a father. □□ **fa·ther·li·ness** *n.*

fath·om /fáthəm/ *n. & v.* ● *n.* (*pl.* often **fathom** when prec. by a number) a measure of six feet, esp. used in taking depth soundings. ● *v.tr.* **1** comprehend. **2** measure the depth of (water). □□ **fath·om·a·ble** *adj.* **fath·om·less** *adj.*

fa·tigue /fətéeg/ *n. & v.* ● *n.* **1** extreme tiredness after exertion. **2** weakness in materials, esp. metal, caused by repeated variations of stress. **3** a reduction in the efficiency of a muscle, organ, etc., after prolonged activity. **4 a** a nonmilitary duty in the army, often as a punishment. **b** (in full **fatigue party**) a group of soldiers ordered to do fatigues. **c** (in *pl.*) work clothing worn by soldiers on fatigue duty. ● *v.tr.* (**fatigues, fatigued, fatiguing**) **1** cause fatigue in; tire; exhaust. **2** (as **fatigued** *adj.*) weary; listless.

fat·so /fátsō/ *n.* (*pl.* **-oes**) *sl. joc.* or *offens.* a fat person.

fat·ten /fát'n/ *v.* **1** *tr. & intr.* make or become fat. **2** *tr.* enrich (soil).

fat·ty /fátee/ *adj. & n.* ● *adj.* (**fattier, fattiest**) **1** like fat; oily; greasy. **2** consisting of or containing fat; adipose. **3** marked by abnormal deposition of fat. ● *n.* (*pl.* **-ies**) *colloq.* usu. *offens.* a fat person. □□ **fat·ti·ness** *n.*

fat·ty ac·id *n. Chem.* any of a class of organic compounds consisting of a hydrocarbon chain and a terminal carboxyl group.

fat·u·ous /fáchŏŏəs/ *adj.* vacantly silly; purposeless; idiotic. □□ **fa·tu·i·ty** /fətŏŏitee, tyŏŏ-/ *n.* (*pl.* **-ies**). **fat·u·ous·ly** *adv.* **fat·u·ous·ness** *n.*

fat·wa /fátwaa/ *n.* (in Islamic countries) an authoritative ruling on a religious matter.

fau·bourg /fōbŏŏrg/ *n.* a suburb, esp. of a French city or New Orleans.

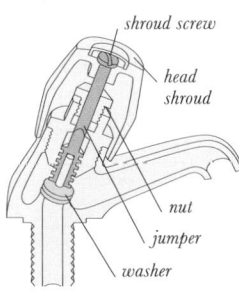

FAUCET: CROSS SECTION
OF A FAUCET

shroud screw
head shroud
nut
jumper
washer

fau·cet /fáwsit/ *n.* ◄ a device by which a flow of liquid from a pipe or vessel can be controlled.

fault /fawlt/ *n. & v.* ● *n.* **1** a defect or imperfection of character or of structure, appearance, etc. **2** a break in an electric circuit. **3** a transgression, offense, or thing wrongly done. **4 a** *Tennis*, etc., a service of the ball not in accordance with the rules. **b** (in show jumping) a penalty for an error. **5** responsibility for wrongdoing, error, etc. (*it will be your own fault*). **6** a defect regarded as the cause of something wrong (*the fault lies in the teaching methods*). **7** *Geol.* ▲ an extended break in the continuity of strata or a vein. ▷ EARTHQUAKE, MOUNTAIN. ● *v.* **1** *tr.* find fault with; blame. **2** *tr.* declare to be faulty. **3** *tr. Geol.* break

---

FAULT

A fault is the result of a fracture in the Earth's crust, in which different forces acting upon the rock layers on either side of the fracture cause movement between them. Different combinations of forces at work and angles of fracture (measured by the degree of dip and angle of hade) give rise to a series of fault descriptions. The principal types are shown here.

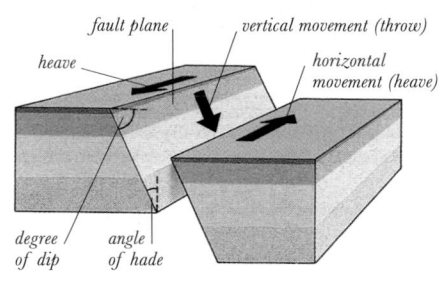

fault plane   *vertical movement (throw)*
heave   *horizontal movement (heave)*
degree of dip   *angle of hade*

MOVEMENT OF AN OBLIQUE-SLIP FAULT

TYPES OF FAULT

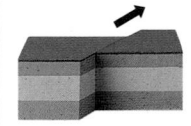  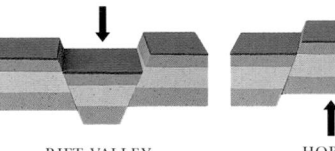

WRENCH FAULT   REVERSE FAULT   RIFT VALLEY   HORST

---

the continuity of (strata). **4** *intr.* commit a fault. **5** *intr. Geol.* show a fault. □ **at fault** guilty; to blame. **find fault** (often foll. by *with*) make an adverse criticism; complain. **to a fault** (usu. of a commendable quality, etc.) excessively (*generous to a fault*).

fault·find·er /fáwltfīndər/ *n.* a person given to continually finding fault. □□ **fault·find·ing** *n. & adj.*

fault·less /fáwltlis/ *adj.* without fault; free from defect or error. □□ **fault·less·ly** *adv.* **fault·less·ness** *n.*

fault·y /fáwltee/ (**faultier, faultiest**) *adj.* having faults; imperfect. □□ **fault·i·ly** *adv.* **fault·i·ness** *n.*

faun /fawn/ *n.* ► a Roman rural deity with a human face and torso and a goat's horns, legs, and tail.

FAUN: ANCIENT
ROMAN FIGURE OF
A FAUN

fau·na /fáwnə/ *n.* (*pl.* **faunas** or **faunae** /-nee/) **1** the animal life of a region or geological period (cf. FLORA). **2** a treatise on or list of this. □□ **fau·nal** *adj.*

faute de mieux /fốt də myố/ *adv.* for want of a better alternative.

fau·teuil /fốtil, fōtố-i/ *n.* an armchair with open sides and upholstered arms.

fauv·ism /fốvizəm/ *n.* ▼ a style of painting with vivid use of color. □□ **fauv·ist** *n*

faux /fō/ *adj.* imitation; counterfeit (*faux emeralds*).

faux pas /fō paá/ *n.* (*pl.* same, *pronunc.* /paaz/) **1** a tactless mistake; a blunder. **2** a social indiscretion.

fave /fayv/ *n. & adj. sl.* = FAVORITE.

fa·ve·la /fəvélə/ *n.* a Brazilian shack, slum, or shantytown.

FAUVISM

Fauvism was a short-lived but influential movement that developed from postimpressionism. Whereas painters before the fauvists had used color primarily to imitate visual appearance, Henri Matisse, André Derain, and Maurice de Vlaminck (the main exponents of fauvism) attempted to free color from its representational purpose, and use it instead as an expression of feeling. In this painting by Matisse, the green of the shadows in the interior and the red of the masts in the background are based not on observation but on emotional response to the moment. The fauvists' approach to color had a profound effect on expressionism and the development of abstractionism.

The Open Window (1905),
HENRI MATISSE

TIMELINE

| 1500 | 1550 | 1600 | 1650 | 1700 | 1750 | 1800 | 1850 | 1900 | 1950 | 2000 |

F

fa·vor /fáyvər/ *n. & v.* ● *n.* **1** an act of kindness (*did it as a favor*). **2** approval; goodwill; friendly regard (*gained their favor; look with favor on*). **3** partiality; too lenient or generous treatment. **4** aid; support (*under favor of night*). **5** a thing given or worn as a mark of favor or support, e.g., a badge or a knot of ribbons. **6** a small present or token given out, as at a party. ● *v.tr.* **1** regard or treat with favor or partiality. **2** give support or approval to; promote; prefer. **3 a** be to the advantage of (a person). **b** facilitate (a process, etc.). **4** tend to confirm (an idea or theory). **5** (foll. by *with*) oblige (*favor me with a reply*). **6** (as **favored** *adj.*) **a** having special advantages. **b** preferred; favorite. **7** *colloq.* resemble in features. **8** treat gingerly or gently. (*favored her injured wrist*). □ **in favor 1** meeting with approval. **2** (foll. by *of*) **a** in support of. **b** to the advantage of. **out of favor** lacking approval.

fa·vor·a·ble /fáyvərəbəl/ *adj.* **1 a** well-disposed; propitious. **b** approving. **2** giving consent (*a favorable answer*). **3** promising; auspicious (*a favorable aspect*). **4** (often foll. by *to*) helpful; suitable. □□ **fa·vor·a·ble·ness** *n.* **fa·vor·a·bly** *adv.*

fa·vor·ite /fáyvərit, fáyvrit/ *adj. & n.* ● *adj.* preferred to all others (*my favorite book*). ● *n.* **1** a particularly favored person. **2** *Sports* a competitor thought most likely to win.

fa·vor·ite son *n.* **1** a person preferred as the presidential candidate by delegates from the candidate's home state. **2** a celebrity particularly popular in his hometown.

fa·vor·it·ism /fáyvəritizəm, fáyvri-/ *n.* the unfair favoring of one person or group at the expense of another.

fawn[1] /fawn/ *n., adj., & v.* ● *n.* **1** a deer in its first year. **2** a light yellowish brown. ● *adj.* fawn colored. ● *v.tr.* (also *absol.*) (of a deer) bring forth (young). □ **in fawn** (of a deer) pregnant.

fawn[2] /fawn/ *v.intr.* **1** (often foll. by *on*) (of a person) behave servilely; cringe. **2** (of an animal, esp. a dog) show extreme affection. □□ **fawn·ing** *adj.* **fawn·ing·ly** *adv.*

fax /faks/ *n. & v.* ● *n.* **1** facsimile transmission (see FACSIMILE *n.* 2). **2 a** a copy produced by this. **b** ▼ a machine for transmitting and receiving these. ● *v.tr.* transmit in this way.

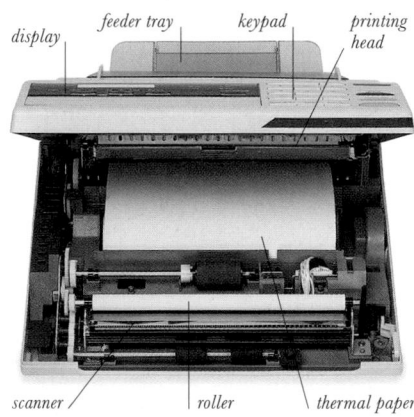

FAX MACHINE, WITH INTERNAL MECHANISM REVEALED

display   feeder tray   keypad   printing head   scanner   roller   thermal paper

fay /fay/ *n. literary* a fairy.

faze /fayz/ *v.tr.* (often as **fazed** *adj.*) *colloq.* disconcert; disorient.

FBI *abbr.* Federal Bureau of Investigation.

FCC *abbr.* Federal Communications Commission.

F clef *n.* = BASS CLEF.

fcp *abbr.* foolscap.

FD *abbr.* fire department.

FDA *abbr.* Food and Drug Administration.

FDIC *abbr.* Federal Deposit Insurance Corporation.

Fe *symb. Chem.* the element iron.

fe·al·ty /féeəltee/ *n.* (*pl.* **-ies**) **1** *hist.* **a** a feudal tenant's or vassal's fidelity to a lord. **b** an acknowledgment of this. **2** allegiance.

fear /feer/ *n. & v.* ● *n.* **1 a** an unpleasant emotion caused by exposure to danger, expectation of pain, etc. **b** a state of alarm (*be in fear*). **2** a cause of fear (*all fears removed*). **3** (often foll. by *of*) dread or fearful respect (for) (*had a fear of heights*). **4** anxiety for the safety of (*in fear of their lives*). **5** danger; likelihood (of something unwelcome) (*there is little fear of failure*). ● *v.* **1 a** *tr.* feel fear about or toward (a person or thing). **b** *intr.* feel fear. **2** *intr.* (foll. by *for*) feel anxiety or apprehension about (*feared for my life*). **3** *tr.* have uneasy expectation of (*fear the worst*). **4** *tr.* (usu. foll. by *that* + clause) apprehend with fear or regret (*I fear that you are wrong*). **5** *tr.* **a** (foll. by *to* + infin.) hesitate. **b** (in verbal noun) shrink from: be apprehensive about (*he feared meeting his ex-wife*). **6** *tr.* show reverence toward. □ **for fear of** (or **that**) to avoid the risk of (or that). **never fear** there is no danger of that.

fear·ful /féerfŏŏl/ *adj.* **1** (usu. foll. by *of*, or *that* + clause) afraid. **2** terrible; awful. **3** *colloq.* extremely unwelcome or unpleasant (*a fearful row*). □□ **fear·ful·ly** *adv.* **fear·ful·ness** *n.*

fear·less /féerlis/ *adj.* **1** courageous; brave. **2** (foll. by *of*) without fear. □□ **fear·less·ly** *adv.* **fear·less·ness** *n.*

fear·some /féersəm/ *adj.* **1** appalling or frightening. **2** timid; fearful. □□ **fear·some·ly** *adv.* **fear·some·ness** *n.*

fea·si·ble /féezibəl/ *adj.* **1** practicable; possible. **2** *disp.* likely; probable (*it is feasible that they will get the job*). □□ **fea·si·bil·i·ty** /féezibílitee/ *n.* **fea·si·bly** *adv.*

feast /feest/ *n. & v.* ● *n.* **1** a large or sumptuous meal, esp. with entertainment. **2** a gratification to the senses or mind. **3 a** an annual religious celebration. **b** a day dedicated to a particular saint. ● *v.* **1** *intr.* partake of a feast; eat and drink sumptuously. **2** *tr.* **a** regale. **b** pass (time) in feasting. □ **feast one's eyes on** take pleasure in beholding. □□ **feast·er** *n.*

feat /feet/ *n.* a noteworthy act or achievement.

feath·er /féthər/ *n. & v.* ● *n.* **1** ▶ any of the appendages growing from a bird's skin, with a horny hollow stem and fine strands. **2** one or more of these as decoration etc. **3** (*collect.*) **a** plumage. **b** game birds. ● *v.* **1** *tr.* cover or line with feathers. **2** *tr. Rowing* turn (an oar) so that it passes through the air edgewise. **3** *tr. Aeron. & Naut.* **a** cause to rotate in such a way as to lessen the air or water resistance. **b** vary the angle of incidence of (helicopter blades). □ **a feather in one's cap** an achievement to one's credit. **feather one's nest** enrich oneself. **in fine** (or **high**) **feather** *colloq.* in good spirits. □□ **feath·ered** *adj.* (also in *comb.*). **feath·er·i·ness** *n.* **feath·er·less** *adj.* **feath·er·y** *adj.*

feath·er bed *n. & v.tr.* ● *n.* a bed with a mattress stuffed with feathers. ● *v.tr.* (**featherbed**) (**-bed·ded, -bed·ding**) provide with (esp. financial) advantages.

feath·er·bed·ding /féthərbeding/ *n.* the employment of excess staff, esp. due to union rules.

feath·er·brain /féthərbrayn/ *n.* (also **feather·head**) a silly or absent-minded person. □□ **feath·er·brained** /féthərbraynd/ *adj.* (also **feath·erheaded**)

feath·er·edge /féthərej/ *n.* the thin edge of a wedge-shaped board.

feath·er·ing /féthəring/ *n.* **1** bird's plumage. **2** the feathers of an arrow. **3** a featherlike structure in an animal's coat. **4** *Archit.* cusps in tracery.

feath·er·stitch /féthərstich/ *n.* ornamental zigzag sewing.

feath·er·weight /féthərwayt/ *n.* **1 a** any of various weight classes in certain sports intermediate between bantamweight and lightweight. **b** a boxer,

etc., of this weight. **2** a very light person or thing. **3** (usu. *attrib.*) an unimportant thing.

fea·ture /féechər/ *n. & v.* ● *n.* **1** a distinctive or characteristic part of a thing. **2** (usu. in *pl.*) (a distinctive part of) the face. **3 a** a distinctive or regular article in a newspaper or magazine. **b** a special attraction at an event, etc. **4 a** (in full **feature film**) a full-length movie intended as the main item at a showing. **b** (in full **feature program**) a broadcast devoted to a particular topic. ● *v.* **1** *tr.* make a special display or attraction of; give special prominence to. **2** *tr. & intr.* have as or be an important actor, participant, or topic in a movie, broadcast, etc. **3** *intr.* be a feature. □□ **fea·tured** *adj.* (also in *comb.*). **fea·ture·less** *adj.*

Feb. *abbr.* February.

feb·ri·fuge /fébrifyŏoj/ *n.* a medicine or treatment that reduces fever; a cooling drink.

fe·brile /fébral, fée-/ *adj.* of or relating to fever; feverish. □□ **fe·bril·i·ty** /fibrílitee/ *n.*

Feb·ru·ar·y /fébrŏŏeree, fébyŏŏ-/ *n.* (*pl.* **-ies**) the second month of the year.

fe·ces /féeseez/ *n.pl.* waste matter discharged from the bowels. □□ **fe·cal** /féekəl/ *adj.*

feck·less /féklis/ *adj.* **1** feeble; ineffective. **2** unthinking; irresponsible (*feckless gaiety*). □□ **feck·less·ly** *adv.* **feck·less·ness** *n.*

fec·u·lent /fékyələnt/ *adj.* **1** murky; filthy. **2** containing sediments or dregs. □□ **fec·u·lence** *n.*

fe·cund /féekənd, fék-/ *adj.* **1** prolific; fertile. **2** fertilizing. □□ **fe·cun·di·ty** /fikúnditee/ *n.*

fe·cun·date /féekəndayt, fék-/ *v.tr.* **1** make fruitful. **2** = FERTILIZE 2. □□ **fe·cun·da·tion** /-dáyshən/ *n.*

Fed /fed/ *n. sl.* **1** a federal agent or official, esp. a member of the FBI. **2 a** the Federal Reserve System. **b** the Federal Reserve Board.

fed *past* and *past part.* of FEED.

fe·da·yeen /fédaayéen/ *n.pl.* Arab guerrillas operating esp. against Israel.

fed·er·al /fédərəl/ *adj.* **1** of a system of government in which several states form a unity but remain independent in internal affairs. **2** relating to or affecting such a federation. **3 a** of or relating to central government (*federal laws*). **b** (also **Federal**) favoring centralized government. **4** (**Federal**) of or loyal to the Union army and federal government in the US Civil War. **5** comprising an association of largely independent units. □□ **fed·er·al·ism** *n.* **fed·er·al·ist** *n.* **fed·er·al·ize** *v.tr.* **fed·er·al·i·za·tion** *n.* **fed·er·al·ly** *adv.*

Fed·er·al Re·serve Sys·tem *n.* a national system of reserve cash available to banks.

fed·er·ate *v. & adj.* ● *v.tr. & intr.* /fédərayt/ organize or be organized on a federal basis. ● *adj.* /fédərət/ having a federal organization. □□ **fed·er·a·tive** /fédəraytiv, -rətiv/ *adj.*

fed·er·a·tion /fédəráyshən/ *n.* **1** a federal group of states. **2** a federated society or group. **3** the act or an instance of federating. □□ **fed·er·a·tion·ist** *n.*

fe·do·ra /fidáwrə/ *n.* a soft felt hat with a low crown creased lengthways.

fed up *adj.* (or **fed to death**) (often foll. by *with*) discontented or bored, esp. from a surfeit of something (*am fed up with the rain*).

fee /fee/ *n. & v.* ● *n.* **1** a payment made to a professional person or to a professional or public body in exchange for advice or services. **2** money paid as part of a special transaction, for a privilege, admission to a society, etc. (*enrollment fee*). **3** (in *pl.*) money regularly paid for continuing services. **4** *Law* an inherited estate, unlimited (**fee simple**) or limited (**fee tail**) as to the category of heir. ● *v.tr.* (**fee'd** or **feed**) **1** pay a fee to. **2** engage for a fee.

fee·ble /féebəl/ *adj.* **1** weak; infirm. **2** lacking energy, force, or effectiveness. **3** dim; indistinct. **4** deficient in character or intelligence. □□ **fee·ble·ness** *n.* **fee·blish** *adj.* **fee·bly** *adv.*

fee·ble·mind·ed /féebəlmíndid/ *adj.* **1** unintelligent. **2** mentally deficient. □□ **fee·ble·mind·ed·ly** *adv.* **fee·ble·mind·ed·ness** *n.*

FEATHER

Essential for insulation and flight, feathers grow from birds' outer skin and are made up of hollow fibers. The sleek outer wing feathers and a small group of feathers called the alula are shaped to maximize lift. Inner wing feathers (the main and lesser coverts) provide overall contouring. Fluffy down feathers insulate the body from cold and heat. Tail feathers are used to steer a course and aid balance; sometimes they are also used in courtship. The color of feathers often depends on their use – either as camouflage or for a courtship display.

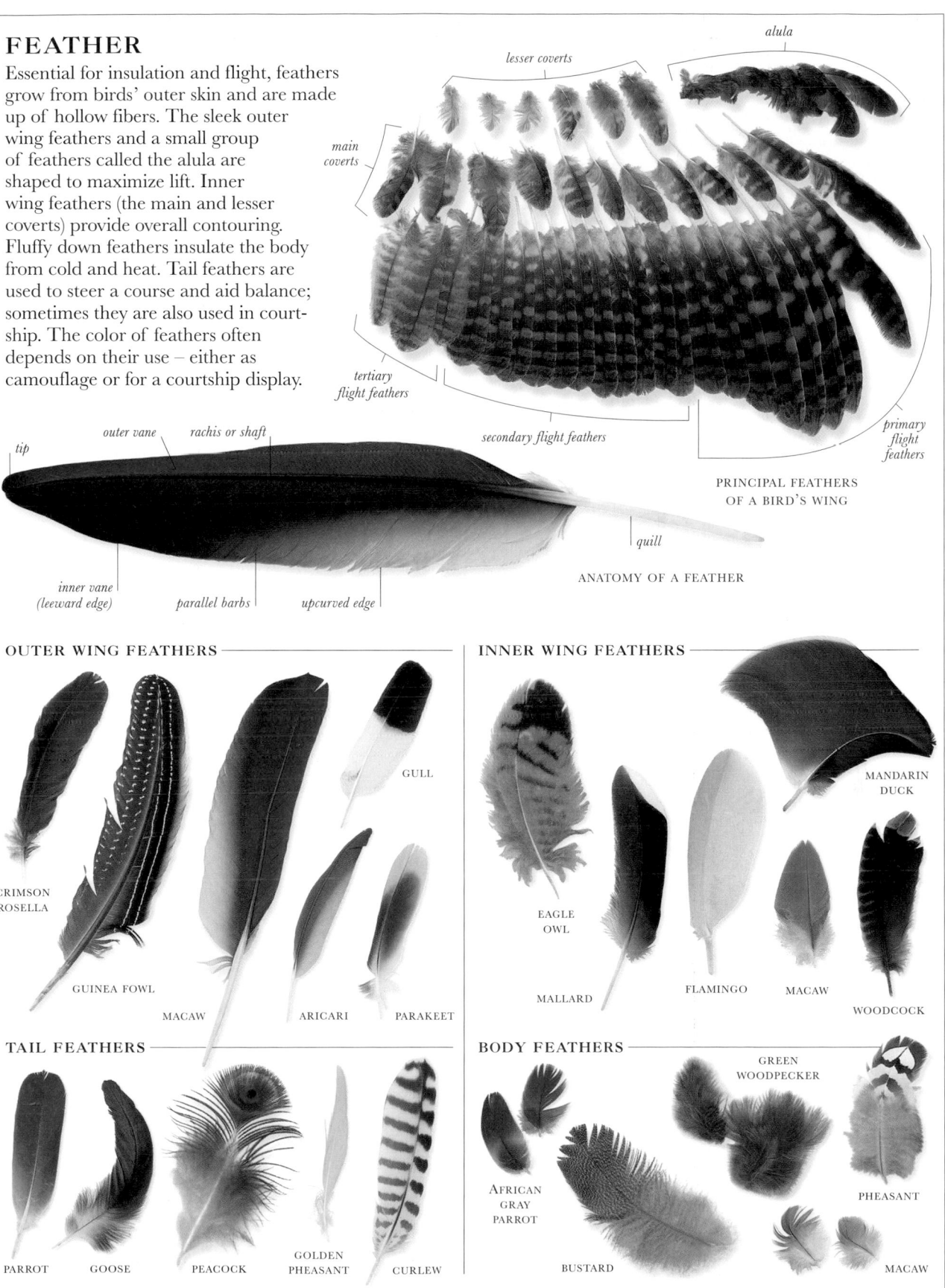

lesser coverts

alula

main coverts

tertiary flight feathers

secondary flight feathers

primary flight feathers

PRINCIPAL FEATHERS OF A BIRD'S WING

tip

outer vane

rachis or shaft

inner vane (leeward edge)

parallel barbs

upcurved edge

quill

ANATOMY OF A FEATHER

OUTER WING FEATHERS

GULL

CRIMSON ROSELLA

GUINEA FOWL

MACAW

ARICARI

PARAKEET

INNER WING FEATHERS

MANDARIN DUCK

EAGLE OWL

MALLARD

FLAMINGO

MACAW

WOODCOCK

TAIL FEATHERS

PARROT

GOOSE

PEACOCK

GOLDEN PHEASANT

CURLEW

BODY FEATHERS

GREEN WOODPECKER

AFRICAN GRAY PARROT

BUSTARD

PHEASANT

MACAW

feed /feed/ *v.* & *n.* ● *v.* (*past* and *past part.* **fed** /fed/) **1** *tr.* **a** supply with food. **b** put food into the mouth of. **2** *tr.* **a** give as food, esp. to animals. **b** graze (cattle). **3** *tr.* serve as food for. **4** *intr.* (usu. foll. by *on*) take food; eat. **5** *tr.* nourish; make grow. **6 a** *tr.* maintain supply of raw material, fuel, etc., to (a fire, machine, etc.). **b** *tr.* (foll. by *into*) supply (material) to a machine, etc. **c** *tr.* supply or send (an electronic signal) for broadcast, etc. **d** *intr.* (often foll. by *into*) (of a river, etc.) flow into another body of water. **e** *tr.* insert further coins into (a meter) to continue its function, validity, etc. **7** *intr.* (foll. by *on*) **a** be nourished by. **b** derive benefit from. **8** *tr.* use (land) as pasture. **9** *tr.* *Theatr. sl.* supply (an actor, etc.) with cues. **10** *tr.* *Sports* send passes to (a player) in a basketball game, soccer or hockey match, etc. **11** *tr.* gratify (vanity, etc.). **12** *tr.* provide (advice, information, etc.) to. ● *n.* **1** an amount of food, esp. for animals. **2** the act or an instance of feeding; the giving of food. **3** *colloq.* a meal. **4** pasturage; green crops. **5 a** a supply of raw material to a machine, etc. **b** the provision of this or a device for it. **c** an electronic signal fed to a television or radio station. **6** the charge of a gun. **7** *Theatr. sl.* an actor who supplies another with cues. □ **feed back** produce feedback. **feed the fishes 1** meet one's death by drowning. **2** be seasick. **feed up 1** fatten. **2** satiate. □□ **feed·a·ble** *adj.*

feed·back /féedbak/ *n.* **1** information about the result of an experiment, etc.; response. **2** *Electronics* the return of a fraction of the output signal from one stage of a circuit, amplifier, etc., to the input of the same or a preceding stage. **3** *Biol.*, etc., the modification or control of a process or system by its results or effects.

feed bag *n.* a bag containing fodder, hung on a horse's head.

feed·er /féedər/ *n.* **1** a person or thing that feeds. **2** a person who eats in a specified manner. **3** a tributary stream. **4** a branch road, railroad line, etc., linking outlying districts with a main communication system. **5** *Electr.* a main conductor carrying electricity to a distribution point. **6** a hopper or feeding apparatus in a machine.

feel /feel/ *v.* & *n.* ● *v.* (*past* and *past part.* **felt** /felt/) **1** *tr.* **a** examine or search by touch. **b** (*absol.*) have the sensation of touch (*was unable to feel*). **2** *tr.* perceive or ascertain by touch; have a sensation of (*could feel the warmth*; *felt that it was cold*). **3** *tr.* **a** undergo; experience (*shall feel my anger*). **b** exhibit or be conscious of (an emotion, sensation, conviction, etc.). **4 a** *intr.* have a specified feeling or reaction (*felt strongly about it*). **b** *tr.* be emotionally affected by (*felt the rebuke deeply*). **5** *tr.* (usu. foll. by *that* + clause) have a vague or unreasoned impression (*I feel that I am right*). **6** *tr.* consider; think (*I feel it is useful to go*). **7** *intr.* seem (*the air feels chilly*). **8** *intr.* be consciously; consider oneself (*I feel happy*; *do not feel well*). **9** *intr.* **a** (foll. by *with*) have sympathy with. **b** (foll. by *for*) have pity or compassion for. **10** *tr.* (often foll. by *up*) *sl.* fondle the breasts or genitals of. ● *n.* **1** the act or an instance of feeling; testing by touch. **2** the sensation characterizing a material, situation, etc. **3** the sense of touch. □ **feel free** (often foll. by *to* + infin.) not be reluctant or hesitant (*do feel free to criticize*). **feel like** have a wish for; be inclined toward. **feel oneself** be fit or confident, etc. **feel out** investigate cautiously. **feel up to** be ready to face or deal with. **feel one's way** proceed carefully; act cautiously. **get the feel of** become accustomed to using. **make one's influence** (or **presence**, etc.) **felt** assert one's influence; make others aware of one's presence, etc.

feel·er /féelər/ *n.* **1** an organ in certain animals for testing things by touch or for searching for food. **2** a tentative proposal (*put out feelers*).

feel·ing /féeling/ *n.* & *adj.* ● *n.* **1 a** the capacity to feel; a sense of touch (*lost all feeling in his arm*). **b** a physical sensation. **2 a** (often foll. by *of*) a particular emotional reaction (*a feeling of despair*). **b** (in *pl.*) emotional susceptibilities (*hurt my feelings*; *had strong feelings about it*). **c** intense emotion (*said it with such feeling*). **3** a particular sensitivity (*had a feeling for literature*). **4 a** an opinion or notion, esp. a vague or irrational one (*had a feeling she would be there*). **b** vague awareness (*had a feeling of safety*). **c** sentiment (*the general feeling was against it*). **5** readiness to feel sympathy or compassion. **6 a** the general emotional response produced by a work of art, piece of music, etc. **b** emotional commitment or sensibility in artistic execution (*played with feeling*). ● *adj.* **1** sensitive; sympathetic. **2** showing emotion or sensitivity. □□ **feel·ing·less** *adj.* **feel·ing·ly** *adv.*

feet *pl.* of FOOT.

feign /fayn/ *v.* **1** *tr.* simulate; pretend to be affected by (*feign madness*). **2** *intr.* indulge in pretense.

feint /faynt/ *n.* & *v.* ● *n.* **1** a sham attack or blow, etc. **2** pretense. ● *v.intr.* make a feint.

feist·y /fístee/ *adj.* (**feistier, feistiest**) *sl.* **1** aggressive; exuberant. **2** touchy. □□ **feist·i·ness** *n.*

fe·la·fel var. of FALAFEL.

feld·spar /féldspaar/ *n.* *Mineral.* ▼ any of a group of aluminum silicates of potassium, sodium, or calcium. ▷ AGGREGATE. **feld·spath·oid** /féldspəthoyd, félspə-/ *n.* □□ **feld·spath·ic** /-spáthik/ *adj.*

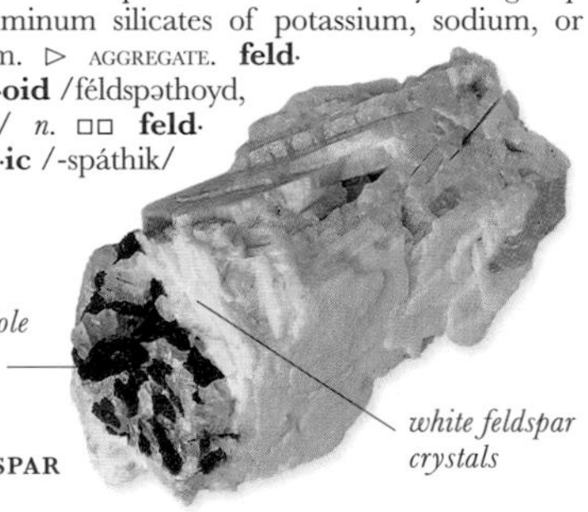
amphibole crystals
white feldspar crystals

FELDSPAR

fe·lic·i·tate /fəlísitayt/ *v.tr.* congratulate. □□ **fe·lic·i·ta·tion** /-táyshən/ *n.* (usu. in *pl.*).

fe·lic·i·tous /fəlísitəs/ *adj.* strikingly apt; pleasantly ingenious. □□ **fe·lic·i·tous·ly** *adv.* **fe·lic·i·tous·ness** *n.*

fe·lic·i·ty /fəlísitee/ *n.* (*pl.* **-ies**) **1** intense happiness; being happy. **2** a cause of happiness. **3 a** a capacity for apt expression. **b** an appropriate or well-chosen phrase. **4** a fortunate trait.

fe·line /féelīn/ *adj.* & *n.* ● *adj.* **1** of or relating to the cat family. **2** catlike. ● *n.* an animal of the cat family Felidae. □□ **fe·lin·i·ty** /filínitee/ *n.*

fell[1] *past* of FALL *v.*

fell[2] /fel/ *v.* & *n.* ● *v.tr.* **1** cut down (esp. a tree). **2** strike or knock down (a person or animal). **3** stitch down (the edge of a seam) to lie flat. ● *n.* an amount of timber cut. □□ **fell·er** *n.*

fell[3] /fel/ *n.* *No. of Engl.* **1** a hill. **2** a stretch of hills or moorland.

fell[4] /fel/ *adj. poet.* or *rhet.* **1** fierce; ruthless. **2** terrible; destructive. □ **at** (or **in**) **one fell swoop** in a single action.

fell[5] /fel/ *n.* an animal's hide or skin with its hair.

fel·la·ti·o /filáysheeō, feláateeō/ *n.* oral stimulation of the penis. □□ **fel·late** /filáyt/ *v.tr.*

fell·er /félər/ *n.* = FELLOW 1, 2. (see also FELL[2]).

fel·loe /félō/ *n.* (also **felly** /félee/) (*pl.* **-oes** or **-ies**) the outer circle (or a section of it) of a wheel, to which the spokes are fixed.

fel·low /félō/ *n.* **1** *colloq.* a man or boy (*poor fellow!*; *my dear fellow*). **2** *derog.* a person regarded with contempt. **3** (usu. in *pl.*) a comrade (*were separated from their fellows*). **4** a counterpart or match; the other of a pair. **5** an equal; one of the same class. **6** a contemporary. **7 a** *Brit.* an incorporated senior member of a college. **b** a selected graduate receiving a stipend for a period of research. **c** a member of the governing body in some universities. **8** a member of a learned society. **9** (*attrib.*) belonging to the same class or activity (*fellow soldier*).

fel·low feel·ing *n.* sympathy from common experience.

fel·low·ship /félōship/ *n.* **1** companionship; friendliness. **2** participation; sharing; community of interest. **3** a body of associates. **4** a brotherhood or fraternity. **5** a guild or corporation. **6** a financial grant to a scholar.

fel·low trav·el·er *n.* **1** a person who travels with another. **2** a sympathizer with the Communist Party.

fel·on /félən/ *n.* a person who has committed a felony.

fe·lo·ni·ous /filṓneeəs/ *adj.* **1** criminal. **2** *Law* **a** of or involving felony. **b** who has committed felony. □□ **fe·lo·ni·ous·ly** *adv.*

fel·o·ny /félənee/ *n.* (*pl.* **-ies**) a crime regarded by the law as grave, and usu. involving violence.

felt[1] /felt/ *n.* & *v.* ● *n.* **1** a kind of cloth made by rolling and pressing wool, etc., or by weaving and shrinking it. **2** a similar material made from other fibers. ● *v.* **1** *tr.* make into felt; mat together. **2** *tr.* cover with felt. **3** *intr.* become matted. □□ **felt·y** *adj.*

felt[2] *past* and *past part.* of FEEL.

felt-tip pen *n.* (also **felt-tipped pen, felt-tip**) a pen with a writing point made of felt or fiber.

fe·luc·ca /filúkə, -lṓōkə/ *n.* a small Mediterranean coasting vessel with oars or lateen sails or both.

FEMA /féemə/ *abbr.* Federal Emergency Management Agency.

fe·male /féemayl/ *adj.* & *n.* ● *adj.* **1** of the sex that can bear offspring or produce eggs. **2** (of plants or their parts) fruit-bearing. **3** of or consisting of women or female animals or female plants. **4** (of a screw, socket, etc.) hollow to receive a corresponding inserted part. ● *n.* a female person, animal, or plant. □□ **fe·male·ness** *n.*

fe·male im·per·son·a·tor *n.* a male performer impersonating a woman.

fem·i·nine /féminin/ *adj.* & *n.* ● *adj.* **1** of or characteristic of women. **2** having qualities associated with women. **3** womanly; effeminate. **4** *Gram.* of or denoting the gender proper to women's names. ● *n.* *Gram.* a feminine gender or word. □□ **fem·i·nine·ly** *adv.* **fem·i·nine·ness** *n.* **fem·i·nin·i·ty** /-nínitee/ *n.*

fem·i·nism /féminizəm/ *n.* **1** the advocacy of women's rights on the ground of the equality of the sexes. **2** *Med.* the development of female characteristics in a male person. □□ **fem·i·nist** *n.* (in sense 1).

fe·min·i·ty /femínitee/ *n.* = *femininity* (see FEMININE).

fem·i·nize /féminīz/ *v.tr.* & *intr.* make or become feminine or female. □□ **fem·i·ni·za·tion** *n.*

femme fa·tale /fém fətál, -táal, fay-/ *n.* (*pl.* **femmes fatales** *pronunc.* same) a seductively attractive woman.

femto- /fémtō/ *comb. form* denoting a factor of 10^{-15} (*femtometer*).

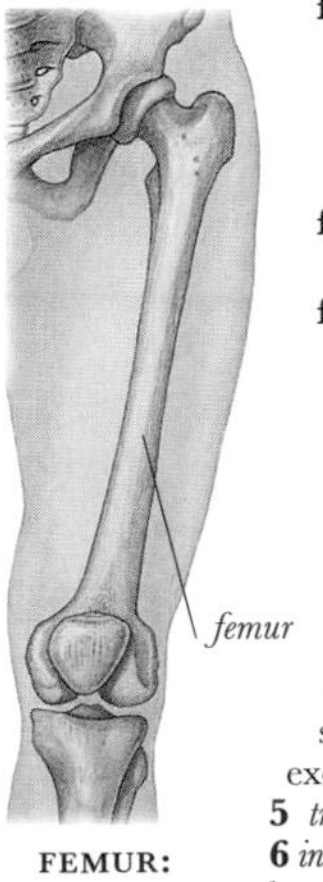
femur

FEMUR: HUMAN THIGH SHOWING THE FEMUR

fe·mur /féemər/ *n.* (*pl.* **femurs** or **femora** /fémərə/) *Anat.* ◀ the thigh bone, the thick bone between the hip and the knee. ▷ HIP JOINT, SKELETON. □□ **fem·o·ral** /fémərəl/ *adj.*

fen /fen/ *n.* a low marshy or flooded area of land.

fence /fens/ *n.* & *v.* ● *n.* **1** a barrier or railing enclosing an area of ground. **2** a large upright obstacle in steeplechasing or show jumping. ▷ SHOW JUMPING. **3** *sl.* a receiver of stolen goods. **4** a guard or guide in machinery. ● *v.* **1** *tr.* surround with or as with a fence. **2** *tr.* **a** (foll. by *in*, *off*) enclose or separate with or as with a fence. **b** (foll. by *up*) seal with or as with a fence. **3** *tr.* (foll. by *from*, *against*) screen; shield; protect. **4** *tr.* (foll. by *out*) exclude with or as with a fence; keep out. **5** *tr.* (also *absol.*) *sl.* deal in (stolen goods). **6** *intr.* practice the sport of fencing. **7** *intr.* (foll. by *with*) evade answering (a person or question). □ **sit on the fence** remain neutral or undecided in a dispute, etc. □□ **fenc·er** *n.*

FENCING

The sport of fencing developed from traditional swordsmanship and was one of the events included in the first modern Olympic Games in 1896. Competition bouts take place within a restricted area 46 ft (14 m) long by 6 ft (2 m) wide, using three types of regulation-length swords: the saber, the foil, and the épée. Points are awarded for hits to specific target areas on the body. In the modern sport, these are registered electronically. Protective jackets, masks, and gloves are essential for the competitors' safety.

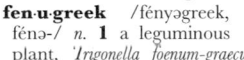

FENCING ATTIRE

- face mask
- protective glove
- foil
- metallic overjacket registers hits
- breeches
- stockings
- high-grip shoes
- electronic-monitor connection

TYPES OF SWORDS

SABER
(34½ in./88 cm)

FOIL
(35 in./90 cm)

ÉPÉE
(35 in./90 cm)

---

fenc·ing /fénsing/ *n.* **1** a set or extent of fences. **2** material for making fences. **3** ▲ the art or sport of swordplay.

fend /fend/ *v.* **1** *intr.* (foll. by *for*) look after (esp. oneself). **2** *tr.* (usu. foll. by *off*) ward off.

fend·er /féndər/ *n.* **1** a low frame bordering a fireplace. **2** *Naut.* a piece of old timber, matting, etc., hung over a vessel's side to protect it against impact. **3 a** a thing used to keep something off, prevent a collision, etc. **b** a device or enclosure over or around the wheel of a motor vehicle, bicycle, etc.

fe·nes·tra /finéstrə/ *n.* (*pl.* **fenestrae** /-tree/) **1** *Anat.* a small hole or opening in a bone, etc., esp. one of two (**fenestra ovalis** /ōváylis/, **fenestra rotunda**) in the inner ear. **2** a perforation in a surgical instrument. **3** a hole made by surgical fenestration.

fe·nes·trate /fénistrayt, finés-/ *adj. Bot. & Zool.* having small windowlike perforations or transparent areas.

fen·es·tra·tion /fénistráyshən/ *n.* **1** *Archit.* ◄ the arrangement of windows in a building. **2** a surgical operation in which a new opening is formed, esp. in the bony labyrinth of

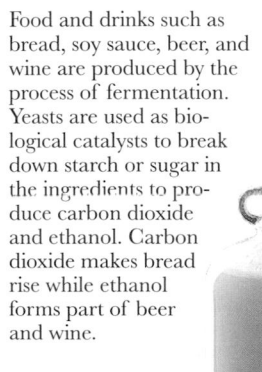

FENESTRATION: TIERED FENESTRATION IN A GERMAN TOWN HOUSE

the inner ear, as a form of treatment in some cases of deafness.

feng shui /feng shōoee, shwáy/ *n.* (in Chinese thought) a system of laws considered to govern spatial arrangement in relation to the flow of energy, and whose effects are taken into account when designing buildings.

fen·nec /fénik/ *n.* ► a small fox, *Vulpes zerda*, native to N. Africa, having large pointed ears.

fen·nel /fénəl/ *n.* **1** a yellow-flowered fragrant umbelliferous plant, *Foeniculum vulgare*, with leaves or leaf stalks used in salads, soups, etc. ▷ HERB. **2** the seeds of this used as flavoring.

FENNEC
(*Vulpes zerda*)

fen·u·greek /fényəgreek, fénə-/ *n.* **1** a leguminous plant, *Trigonella foenum-graecum*, having aromatic seeds. **2** these seeds used as flavoring.

fe·ral /féerəl, térəl/ *adj.* **1** untamed; uncultivated. **2** (of an animal) in a wild state after escape from captivity or domestication.

fe·ri·al /féereeəl, féreeəl/ *adj. Eccl.* **1** (of a day) ordinary; not appointed for a festival or fast. **2** (of a service, etc.) for use on a ferial day.

fer·ment *n. & v.* ● *n.* /fárment/ **1** agitation; excitement; tumult. **2 a** fermentation. **b** a fermenting agent. ● *v.* /fərmént/ **1** *intr. & tr.* undergo or subject to fermentation. **2** *intr. & tr.* effervesce or cause to effervesce. **3** *tr.* excite; stir up. □□ **fer·ment·a·ble** *adj.* **fer·ment·er** /-méntər/ *n.*

fer·men·ta·tion /fárməntáyshən/ *n.* **1** ◄ the breakdown of a substance by microorganisms, such as

yeasts and bacteria, esp. of sugar to ethyl alcohol in making beers, wines, and spirits. **2** agitation; excitement. □□ **fer·ment·a·tive** /-méntətiv/ *adj.*

fer·mi·on /fármeeon/ *n. Physics* a subatomic particle, such as a nucleon, which has a spin of a half integer.

fer·mi·um /fármeeəm, fér-/ *n. Chem.* a transuranic radioactive metallic element produced artificially. ¶ Symb.: **Fm**.

fern /fərn/ *n.* (*pl.* same or **ferns**) ▼ any flowerless plant of the order Filicales, usu. having feathery fronds. □□ **fern·er·y** *n.* (*pl.* **-ies**). **fern·y** *adj.*

fe·ro·cious /fəróshəs/ *adj.* fierce; savage; wildly cruel. □□ **fe·ro·cious·ly** *adv.* **fe·ro·cious·ness** *n.* **fe·roc·i·ty** /fərósitee/ *n.*

-ferous /fárəs/ *comb. form* (usu. **-iferous**) forming adjectives with the sense 'bearing,' 'having' (*auriferous; odoriferous*). □□ **-ferously** *suffix forming adverbs.* **-ferousness** *suffix forming nouns.*

fer·rate /férayt/ *n. Chem.* a salt of (the hypothetical) ferric acid.

fer·ret /férit/ *n. & v.* ● *n.* **1** a small semidomesticated polecat, *Mustela putorius furo*, used in catching rabbits, rats, etc. **2** a person who searches assiduously. ● *v.* **1** *intr.* hunt with ferrets. **2** *intr.* rummage; search out. **3** *tr.* (often foll. by *about, away, out,* etc.) **a** clear out (holes or an area of ground) with ferrets. **b** take or drive away (rabbits, etc.) with ferrets. **4** *tr.* (foll. by *out*) search out (secrets, criminals, etc.). □□ **fer·ret·er** *n.* **fer·ret·y** *adj.*

fer·ric /férik/ *adj.* **1** of iron. **2** *Chem.* containing iron in a trivalent form (cf. FERROUS 2).

Fer·ris wheel /féris/ *n.* ► a carnival ride consisting of a tall revolving vertical wheel with passenger cars suspended on its outer edge.

fer·rite /férīt/ *n. Chem.* a magnetic subtance, a compound of ferric oxide and another metallic oxide.

FERRIS WHEEL

ferro- /féro/ *comb. form Chem.* **1** iron, esp. in ferrous compounds (*ferrocyanide*). **2** (of alloys) containing iron (*ferromanganese*).

fer·ro·con·crete /férōkónkreet/ *n.* concrete reinforced with steel.

fer·ro·e·lec·tric /férōiléktrik/ *adj. & n. Physics* ● *adj.* exhibiting permanent electric polarization that varies in strength with the applied electric field. ● *n.* a ferroelectric substance. □□ **fer·ro·e·lec·tric·i·ty** /-trísitee/ *n.*

fer·ro·mag·net·ism /férōmágnitizəm/ *n. Physics* a phenomenon in which there is a high susceptibility to magnetization, the strength of which varies with

F

FERMENTATION

Food and drinks such as bread, soy sauce, beer, and wine are produced by the process of fermentation. Yeasts are used as biological catalysts to break down starch or sugar in the ingredients to produce carbon dioxide and ethanol. Carbon dioxide makes bread rise while ethanol forms part of beer and wine.

- airlock
- demijohn
- fermenting mixture of grape juice, sugar, and yeast

FERMENTATION OF WINE

FERN

A mature fern plant, or sporophyte, typically has divided fronds. Reproductive structures (sori) form on the fronds' undersides and liberate spores into the air. The shed spores develop into gametophytes – simplified plants that produce male and female cells. Following fertilization, these give rise to new sporophytes.

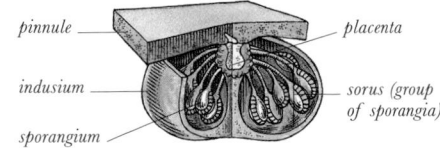

- pinnule
- indusium
- sporangium
- placenta
- sorus (group of sporangia)

SECTION THROUGH A MATURE SORUS

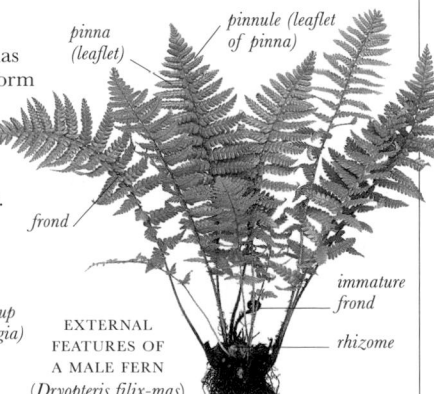

- pinna (leaflet)
- pinnule (leaflet of pinna)
- frond
- immature frond
- rhizome

EXTERNAL FEATURES OF A MALE FERN
(*Dryopteris filix-mas*)

F

the applied magnetizing field, and which may persist after removal of the applied field. □□ **fer·ro·mag·net·ic** /-magnétik/ *adj.*

fer·rous /férəs/ *adj.* **1** containing iron (*ferrous and nonferrous metals*). **2** *Chem.* containing iron in a divalent form (cf. FERRIC 2).

fer·ru·gi·nous /fərōōjinəs/ *adj.* **1** of or containing iron rust, or iron as a chemical constituent. **2** rust-colored; reddish brown.

fer·rule /férŏol/ *n.* **1** a ring or cap strengthening the end of a stick or tube. **2** a band strengthening or forming a joint.

fer·ry /féree/ *n. & v.* ● *n.* (*pl.* **-ies**) **1** ▼ a boat or aircraft, etc., for conveying passengers and goods, esp. across water and as a regular service. **2** the service itself or the place where it operates. ● *v.* (**-ies, -ied**) **1** *tr. & intr.* convey in a boat, etc. across water. **2** *intr.* (of a boat, etc.) pass to and fro across water. **3** *tr.* transport from one place to another, esp. as a regular service. □□ **fer·ry·man** /-mən/ *n.* (*pl.* **-men**).

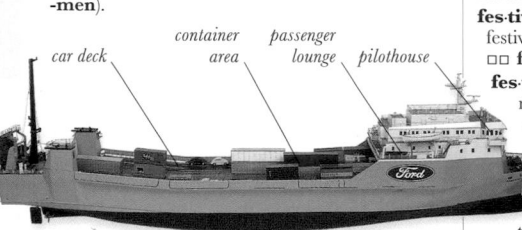

FERRY: MODERN CARGO AND PASSENGER FERRY

container area   passenger lounge   pilothouse   car deck

fer·tile /fərt'l/ *adj.* **1 a** (of soil) producing abundant vegetation or crops. **b** fruitful. **2 a** (of a seed, egg, etc.) capable of becoming a new individual. **b** (of animals and plants) able to conceive young or produce fruit. **3** (of the mind) inventive. **4** (of nuclear material) able to become fissile by the capture of neutrons. □□ **fer·til·i·ty** /-tílitee/ *n.*

fer·ti·li·za·tion /fərt'līzayshən/ *n.* **1** *Biol.* ▼ the fusion of male and female gametes during sexual reproduction to form a zygote. **2 a** the act or an instance of fertilizing. **b** the process of being fertilized.

fer·ti·lize /fərt'līz/ *v.tr.* **1** make (soil, etc.) fertile or productive. **2** cause (an egg, female animal, or plant) to develop a new individual by introducing male reproductive material. □□ **fer·ti·liz·a·ble** *adj.*

fer·ti·liz·er /fərt'līzər/ *n.* a chemical or natural substance added to soil to make it more fertile.

FERTILIZATION

Human fertilization begins when a sperm penetrates the corona radiata surrounding the ovum. A chemical change is then triggered, preventing the entry of other sperm. The sperm's flagellum (tail) is discarded, while its head, containing the nucleus and genetic material, continues toward the center of the ovum.

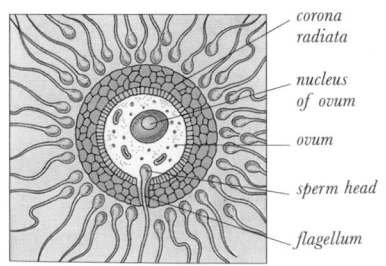

corona radiata
nucleus of ovum
ovum
sperm head
flagellum

HUMAN SPERM ENTERING THE OVUM

fer·vent /fúrvənt/ *adj.* **1** ardent; impassioned; intense. **2** hot; glowing. □□ **fer·ven·cy** *n.* **fer·vent·ly** *adv.*

fer·vid /fúrvid/ *adj.* **1** ardent; intense. **2** hot; glowing. □□ **fer·vid·ly** *adv.*

fer·vor /fúrvər/ *n.* **1** vehemence; passion; zeal. **2** a glowing condition; intense heat.

fes·cue /féskyōō/ *n.* any grass of the genus *Festuca*, valuable for pasture and fodder.

fes·tal /fést'l/ *adj.* **1** joyous; merry. **2** engaging in holiday activities. **3** of a feast. □□ **fes·tal·ly** *adv.*

fes·ter /féstər/ *v.* **1** *tr. & intr.* make or become septic. **2** *intr.* cause continuing annoyance. **3** *intr.* rot; stagnate.

fes·ti·val /féstivəl/ *n.* (also *attrib.*) **1** a day or period of celebration. **2** a concentrated series of concerts, plays, etc., held regularly in a town, etc.

fes·ti·val of lights *n.* **1** = HANUKKAH. **2** = DIWALI.

fes·tive /féstiv/ *adj.* **1** of or characteristic of a festival. **2** joyous. **3** fond of feasting; jovial. □□ **fes·tive·ly** *adv.* **fes·tive·ness** *n.*

fes·tiv·i·ty /festívitee/ *n.* (*pl.* **-ies**) **1** gaiety; rejoicing. **2 a** a festive celebration. **b** (in *pl.*) festive proceedings.

fes·toon /festōōn/ *n. & v.* ● *n.* a chain of flowers, leaves, ribbons, etc., hung in a curve as a decoration. ▷ FAÇADE. ● *v.tr.* (often foll. by *with*) adorn with or form into festoons; decorate elaborately. □□ **fes·toon·er·y** *n.*

Fest·schrift /féstshrift/ *n.* (also **fest·schrift**) (*pl.* **-schriften** or **-schrifts**) a collection of writings published in honor of a scholar.

fet·a /fétə/ *n.* a crumbly white ewe's milk or goat's milk cheese, made esp. in Greece. ▷ CHEESE

fetch /fech/ *v. & n.* ● *v.tr.* **1** go for and bring back (a person or thing) (*fetch a doctor*). **2** be sold for (a price) (*fetched $10*). **3** cause (blood, tears, etc.) to flow. **4** draw (breath). **5** *colloq.* give (a blow, slap, etc.) (*fetched him a slap on the face*). **6** excite the emotions of; delight or irritate. ● *n.* **1** an act of fetching. **2** a dodge or trick. □ **fetch and carry** run backward and forward with things; be a servant. **fetch up** *colloq.* arrive; come to rest.

fetch·ing /féching/ *adj.* attractive. □□ **fetch·ing·ly** *adv.*

fête /fayt, fet/ *n. & v.* ● *n.* **1** a festival. **2** *Brit.* an outdoor function with the sale of goods, amusements, etc. **3** a saint's day. ● *v.tr.* honor or entertain lavishly.

fet·id /fétid, féetid/ *adj.* (also **foe·tid**) stinking. □□ **fet·id·ly** *adv.* **fet·id·ness** *n.*

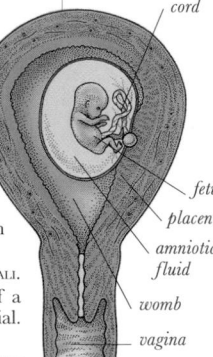

cannon bone
fetlock
pastern

FETLOCK

fet·ish /fétish/ *n.* **1** *Psychol.* a thing abnormally stimulating or attracting sexual desire. **2 a** an object worshiped for its supposed inherent magical powers or as being inhabited by a spirit. **b** a thing evoking irrational devotion or respect. □□ **fet·ish·ism** *n.* **fet·ish·ist** *n.* **fet·ish·is·tic** /-shístik/ *adj.*

fet·lock /fétlok/ *n.* ◀ part of the back of a horse's leg above the hoof where a tuft of hair grows. ▷ HORSE

fe·tor /féetər/ *n.* a stench.

fet·ter /fétər/ *n. & v.* ● *n.* **1 a** ▶ a shackle for holding a prisoner by the ankles. **b** any shackle or bond. **2** (in *pl.*) captivity. **3** a restraint. ● *v.tr.* **1** put into fetters. **2** restrict; impede.

FETTER: 18TH-CENTURY ANKLE FETTERS

umbilical cord

fet·tle /fét'l/ *n. & v.* ● *n.* condition or trim (*in fine fettle*). ● *v.tr.* **1** trim or clean (the rough edge of a metal casting, pottery before firing, etc.). **2** line (a hearth, furnace, etc.) with loose sand or gravel.

fet·tuc·ci·ne /fetəchéenee/ *n.* (also **fet·tuc·ci·ni**) pasta in the form of long flat ribbons.

fe·tus /féetəs/ *n.* ◀ an unborn or unhatched offspring of a mammal, esp. a human one more than eight weeks after conception. □□ **fe·tal** *adj.* **fe·ti·cide** /-tisīd/ *n.*

fetus
placenta
amniotic fluid
womb
vagina

FETUS: NINE-WEEK-OLD HUMAN FETUS IN THE WOMB

feud /fyōōd/ *n. & v.* ● *n.* **1** prolonged mutual hostility, esp. between two families, tribes, etc., with murderous assaults in revenge for a previous injury. **2** a prolonged or bitter quarrel or dispute. ● *v.intr.* conduct a feud. □□ **feud·ist** *n.*

feu·dal /fyōōd'l/ *adj.* **1** of, according to, or resembling the feudal system. **2** of a feud or fief. **3** outdated (*had a feudal attitude*). □□ **feu·dal·ism** *n.* **feu·dal·ist** *n.* **feu·dal·is·tic** *adj.*

feu·dal·i·ty /fyōōdálitee/ *n.* (*pl.* **-ies**) **1** the feudal system or its principles. **2** a feudal holding; a fief.

feu·dal sys·tem *n.* the social system in medieval Europe whereby a vassal held land from a superior in exchange for allegiance and service.

feu·da·to·ry /fyōōdətáwree/ *adj. & n.* ● *adj.* (often foll. by *to*) feudally subject; under overlordship. ● *n.* (*pl.* **-ies**) a feudal vassal.

feud·ist /fyōōdist/ ● *n.* a person who is conducting a feud.

fe·ver /féevər/ *n. & v.* ● *n.* **1 a** an abnormally high body temperature, often with delirium, and a disease characterized by this (*scarlet fever; typhoid fever*). **2** nervous excitement; agitation. ● *v.tr.* (esp. as **fevered** *adj.*) affect with fever or excitement.

fe·ver·few /féevərfyōō/ *n.* ▶ an aromatic bushy European plant, *Tanacetum parthenium*, with feathery leaves and white daisylike flowers, formerly used to reduce fever.

fe·ver·ish /féevərish/ *adj.* **1** having the symptoms of a fever. **2** excited; fitful; restless. **3** (of a place) infested by fever; feverous. □□ **fe·ver·ish·ly** *adv.* **fe·ver·ish·ness** *n.*

fe·ver·ous /féevərəs/ *adj.* feverish.

fe·ver pitch *n.* a state of extreme excitement.

FEVERFEW (*Tanacetum parthenium*)

few /fyōō/ *adj. & n.* ● *adj.* not many (*few doctors smoke; visitors are few*). ● *n.* (as *pl.*) **1** (prec. by *a*) some but not many (*a few words should be added; a few of his friends were there*). **2** a small number; not many (*many are called but few are chosen*). **3** (prec. by *the*) **a** the minority. **b** the elect. □ **every few** once in every small group of (*every few days*). **few and far between** scarce. **no fewer than** as many as (a specified number). **not a few** a considerable number. **some few** some but not all many.

fey /fay/ *adj.* **1 a** strange; otherworldly; whimsical. **b** clairvoyant. **2** *Sc.* **a** fated to die soon. **b** overexcited or elated, as formerly associated with the state of mind of a person about to die. □□ **fey·ly** *adv.* **fey·ness** *n*

FEZ

fez /fez/ n. (pl. **fezzes**) ◀ a flat-topped conical red cap with a tassel, worn by men in some Muslim countries. □□ **fez·zed** adj.

ff abbr. Mus. fortissimo.

ff. abbr. **1** following pages, etc. **2** folios.

FHA abbr. Federal Housing Administration.

fi·a·cre /fiáakər/ ● n. hist. a small four-wheeled carriage.

fi·an·cé /féeonsáy, fónsay/ n. (fem. **fiancée** pronunc. same) a person to whom another is engaged to be married.

fi·an·chet·to /féeoncētó/ n. & v. Chess ● n. (pl. **-oes**) the development of a bishop to a long diagonal of the board. ● v.tr. (**-oes**, **-oed**) develop (a bishop) in this way.

fi·as·co /feeáskō/ n. (pl. **-os**) a ludicrous or humiliating failure or breakdown.

fi·at /féeot, -at, -aat, fíat, fíot/ n. **1** an authorization. **2** a decree or order.

fib /fib/ n. & v. n. a trivial or venial lie. ● v.intr. (**fibbed**, **fibbing**) tell a fib. □□ **fib·ber** n. **fib·ster** n.

fi·ber /fíbər/ n. **1** Biol. any of the threads or filaments forming animal or vegetable tissue and textile substances. **2** a piece of glass in the form of a thread. **3 a** a substance formed of fibers. **b** a substance that can be spun, woven, or felted. **4** the structure or character of something (lacks moral fiber). **5** dietary material that is resistant to the action of digestive enzymes; roughage. □□ **fi·bered** adj. (also in comb.). **fi·ber·less** adj. **fi·bri·form** /fíbrifawrm/ adj.

fi·ber·board /fíbərbawrd/ n. a building material made of wood or other plant fibers compressed into boards.

fi·ber·glass /fíbərglas/ n. **1** a textile fabric made from woven glass fibers. **2** ● a plastic reinforced by glass fibers. ● v.tr. repair or reinforce with fiberglass.

fi·ber op·tics n. (treated as sing.) optics employing thin glass fibers, usu. for the transmission of light, esp. modulated to carry signals.

Fi·bo·nac·ci se·ries /féebonáachee/ ● n. Math. a series of numbers in which each number (**Fibonacci number**) is the sum of the two preceding numbers, esp. 1, 1, 2, 3, 5, 8, etc.

fi·bril /fíbril, fib-/ n. **1** a small fiber. **2** a subdivision of a fiber. □□ **fi·bril·lar** adj. **fi·bril·lar·y** adj.

fi·bril·late /fíbrilayt, fī-/ v. **1** intr. **a** (of a fiber) split up into fibrils. **b** (of a muscle, esp. in the heart) undergo a quivering movement in fibrils. **2** tr. break (a fiber) into fibrils. □□ **fi·bril·la·tion** /-láyshən/ n.

fi·brin /fíbrin/ ● n. an insoluble protein formed during blood clotting from fibrinogen. □□ **fi·bri·noid** adj.

fi·brin·o·gen /fībrínəjən/ n. a soluble blood plasma protein that produces fibrin when acted upon by the enzyme thrombin.

fibro- /fíbrō/ comb. form fiber.

fi·broid /fíbroyd/ adj. & n. ● adj. **1** of or characterized by fibrous tissue. **2** resembling or containing fibers. ● n. a benign tumor of muscular and fibrous tissues, one or more of which may develop in the wall of the uterus.

fi·bro·in /fíbrōin/ n. a protein that is the chief constituent of silk.

fi·bro·sis /fībrósis/ n. Med. a thickening and scarring of connective tissue, usu. as a result of injury or disease. □□ **fi·brot·ic** /-brótik/ adj.

fi·bro·si·tis /fībrəsítis/ n. an inflammation of fibrous connective tissue, usu. rheumatic. □□ **fi·bro·si·tic** /-sítik/ adj.

fi·brous /fíbrəs/ adj. consisting of or like fibers. □□ **fi·brous·ness** n.

fib·u·la /fíbyələ/ n. (pl. **fibulae** /-lee/ or **fibulas**) Anat. ▶ the smaller and outer of the two bones between the knee and the ankle in terrestrial vertebrates. ▷ SKELETON. □□ **fib·u·lar** adj.

FICA /fíkə/ abbr. Federal Insurance Contributions Act.

fiche /feesh/ n. (pl. same or **fiches**) a microfiche.

fi·chu /físhōō, feeshōō/ n. a woman's small triangular shawl of lace, etc., for the shoulders and neck.

fick·le /fíkəl/ adj. inconstant or changeable, esp. in loyalty. □□ **fick·le·ness** n. **fick·ly** adv.

fic·tile /fíktəl, -til/ adj. **1** made of earth or clay by a potter. **2** of pottery.

fic·tion /fíkshən/ n. **1** an invented idea or statement or narrative. **2** literature, esp. novels, describing imaginary events and people. **3** a conventionally accepted falsehood (polite fiction). **4** the act or process of inventing imaginary things. □□ **fic·tion·al** adj. **fic·tion·al·i·ty** /-nálitee/ n. **fic·tion·al·ize** v.tr. **fic·tion·al·i·za·tion** n. **fic·tion·al·ly** adv. **fic·tion·ist** n.

fic·ti·tious /fiktíshəs/ adj. **1** imaginary; unreal. **2** counterfeit; not genuine. **3** (of a name or character) assumed. **4** of or in novels. □□ **fic·ti·tious·ly** adv. **fic·ti·tious·ness** n.

fic·tive /fíktiv/ adj. **1** creating or created by imagination. **2** not genuine. □□ **fic·tive·ness** n.

fid·dle /fíd'l/ n. & v. ● n. **1** a stringed instrument played with a bow, esp. a violin. **2** Brit. colloq an instance of cheating or fraud. **3** a fiddly task. ● v. **1** intr. **a** (often foll. by with) play restlessly. **b** (often foll. by about) move aimlessly. **c** act idly or frivolously. **d** (usu. foll. by with) make minor adjustments; tinker. **2** tr. Brit. sl. **a** cheat; swindle. **b** falsify. **c** get by cheating. **3 a** intr. play the fiddle. **b** tr. play (a tune, etc.) on the fiddle. □ **as fit as a fiddle** in very good health. **play second** (or **first**) **fiddle** take a subordinate (or leading) role.

fid·dle-de-dee /fíd'ldeedée/ int. & n. nonsense.

fid·dle-fad·dle /fíd'lfad'l/ n., v., int., & adj. ● n. trivial matters. ● v.intr. fuss; trifle. ● int. nonsense! ● adj. (of a person or thing) petty; fussy.

fid·dle·head /fíd'lhed/ n. **1** a scroll like carving at a ship's bow. **2** the coiled frond of some ferns eaten as a vegetable.

FIBERGLASS: 1950s FIBERGLASS CHAIR

fid·dler /fídlər/ n. **1** a fiddle player. **2** (in full **fiddler crab**) any small N. American crab of the genus Uca, the male having one of its claws enlarged and held in a position like a violinist's arm.

fid·dle·stick /fíd'lstik/ n. **1** (in pl.; as int.) nonsense! **2** colloq. a bow for a fiddle.

fid·dling /fídling/ adj. **1 a** petty; trivial. **b** contemptible; futile. **2** Brit. colloq. = FIDDLY. **3** that fiddles.

fid·dly /fídlee/ adj. (**fiddlier**, **fiddliest**) esp. Brit. colloq. intricate, awkward, or tiresome to do or use.

fi·de·ism /féedayizəm, fídee-/ n. the doctrine that all or some knowledge depends on faith or revelation. □□ **fi·de·ist** n. **fi·de·is·tic** adj.

fi·del·i·ty /fidélitee/ n. **1** (often foll. by to) faithfulness; loyalty. **2** strict conformity to truth or fact. **3** exact correspondence to the original. **4** precision in reproduction of sound or video (high fidelity).

fidg·et /fíjit/ v. & n. ● v. (**fidgeted**, **fidgeting**) **1** intr. move or act restlessly or nervously, usu. while maintaining basically the same posture. **2** intr. be uneasy; worry. **3** tr. make (a person) uneasy or uncomfortable. ● n. **1** a person who fidgets. **2** (usu. in pl.) **a** bodily uneasiness seeking relief in spasmodic movements; such movements. **b** a restless mood. □□ **fidg·et·y** adj. **fidg·et·i·ness** n.

fi·du·cial /fidóóshəl, -dyōō-, fī-/ adj. Surveying, Astron., etc., (of a line, point, etc.) assumed as a fixed basis of comparison; a standard reference.

fi·du·ci·ar·y /fidóóshee-eree, -shəree, -dyōō-, fī-/ adj. & n. ● adj. **1 a** of a trust, trustee, or trusteeship. **b** held or given in trust. **2** (of a paper currency) depending for its value on public confidence or securities. ● n. (pl. **-ies**) a trustee.

fie /fī/ int. expressing disgust, shame, etc.

fief /feef/ n. **1** a piece of land held under the feudal system or in fee. **2** a person's sphere of operation or control.

fief·dom /féefdəm/ n. a fief.

field /feeld/ n. & v. **1** an area of open land, esp. one used for pasture or crops. **2** an area rich in some natural product (gas field; diamond field). **3** a piece of land for a specified purpose, esp. **a** an area marked out for a game or sport (football field), or **b** an airfield. **4 a** the participants in a contest or sport. **b** all the competitors in a race or all except those specified. **5** Cricket **a** the side fielding. **b** a fielder. **6** an expanse of ice, snow, sea, sky, etc. **7 a** a battlefield. **b** the scene of a campaign. **c** (attrib.) (of artillery, etc.) light and mobile for use on campaign. **d** a battle. **8** an area of operation or activity; a subject of study. **9 a** the region in which a force is effective (gravitational field; magnetic field). **b** the force exerted in such an area. **10** a range of perception (field of view; filled the field of the telescope). **11** Math. a system subject to two operations analogous to those for the multiplication and addition of real numbers. **12** (attrib.) **a** (of an animal or plant) found in the countryside; wild (field mouse). **b** carried out or working in the natural environment, not in a laboratory, etc. (field test). **13** the background of a picture, coin, flag, etc. **14** Computing a part of a database record, representing an item of data. ● v. **1** Baseball, Cricket, etc. **a** intr. act as a fielder. **b** tr. catch (and return) (the ball). **2** tr. select (a team or individual) to play in a game. **3** tr. deal with (a succession of questions, etc.). □ **in the field 1** campaigning. **2** working, etc., away from one's laboratory, headquarters, etc. **play the field** colloq. avoid exclusive attachment to one person or activity, etc. **take the field 1** begin a battle. **2** (of a sports team) go on to a field to begin a game.

field day n. **1** wide scope for action or success; a time occupied with exciting events (when crowds form, pickpockets have a field day). **2** Mil. an exercise, esp. in maneuvering. **3** a day spent in exploration, scientific investigation, etc., in the natural environment. **4** an all-day sports or athletics meet, esp. at a school.

field·er /féeldər/ n. Baseball, etc. a member of the team that is fielding. ▷ BASEBALL.

field glas·ses n.pl. binoculars for outdoor use.

field goal n. **1** Football a score of three points by a kick from the field. **2** Basketball a goal scored when the ball is in normal play.

field hock·ey n. a field game played between two teams with curved sticks and a small hard ball. ▷ HOCKEY

field hos·pi·tal n. a temporary hospital near a battlefield.

Field Mar·shal n. Brit. an army officer of the highest rank.

field mouse n. **1** ▼ a small rodent, Apodemus sylvaticus, with beady eyes, prominent ears, and a long tail. **2** various similar rodents inhabiting fields.

fibula

FIBULA: HUMAN LOWER LEG SHOWING THE FIBULA

FIELD MICE (Apodemus sylvaticus)

F

297

F

field of vi·sion *n.* all that comes into view when the eyes are turned in some direction.

field·work /féeldwərk/ *n.* the practical work of a surveyor, collector of scientific data, sociologist, etc., conducted in the natural environment rather than a laboratory, office, etc. □□ **field·work·er** *n.*

fiend /feend/ *n.* **1 a** an evil spirit; a demon. **b** (prec. by *the*) the Devil. **2 a** a very wicked or cruel person. **b** a person causing mischief or annoyance. **3** (with a qualifying word) *sl.* a devotee or addict (*a fitness fiend*). **4** something difficult or unpleasant. □□ **fiend·ish** *adj.* **fiend·ish·ly** *adv.* **fiend·ish·ness** *n.* **fiend·like** *adj.*

fierce /feers/ *adj.* (**fiercer**, **fiercest**) **1** vehemently aggressive or frightening in temper or action; violent. **2** intense; ardent. **3** unpleasantly strong or intense (*fierce heat*). **4** (of a mechanism) not smooth or easy in action. □□ **fierce·ly** *adv.* **fierce·ness** *n.*

fi·e·ri fa·ci·as /fīrī fáysheeəs, -shəs, fīree/ *n. Law* a writ to a sheriff for executing a judgment.

fier·y /fíree/ *adj.* (**fierier**, **fieriest**) **1 a** consisting of or flaming with fire. **b** (of an arrow, etc.) fire-bearing. **2** bright red. **3** hot as fire. **b** acting like fire; producing a burning sensation. **4 a** flashing; ardent (*fiery eyes*). **b** spirited; irritable (*fiery temper*). **c** (of a horse) mettlesome. □□ **fier·i·ly** *adv.* **fier·i·ness** *n.*

fi·es·ta /fee-éstə/ *n.* **1** a holiday or festivity. **2** a religious festival in Spanish-speaking countries.

FIFA /féefə/ *abbr.* International Football Federation.

fife /fīf/ *n. & v.* ● *n.* **1** a kind of small shrill flute used in military music. **2** its player. ● *v.* **1** *intr.* play the fife. **2** *tr.* play (an air, etc.) on the fife. □□ **fif·er** *n.*

fif·teen /fíftéen/ *n. & adj.* ● *n.* **1** one more than fourteen. **2** a symbol for this (15, xv, XV). **3** a size, etc., denoted by fifteen. **4** a team of fifteen players, esp. in rugby. ● *adj.* that amount to fifteen. □□ **fif·teenth** *adj. & n.*

fifth /fifth/ *n. & adj.* ● *n.* **1** the position in a sequence corresponding to that of the number 5 in the sequence 1–5. **2** something occupying this position. **3** the fifth person, etc., in a race or competition. **4** any of five equal parts of a thing. **5** *Mus.* **a** an interval or chord spanning five consecutive notes in the diatonic scale (e.g., C to G). **b** a note separated from another by this interval. **6 a** a fifth of a gallon of liquor. **b** a bottle containing this. **7** (**the Fifth**) the Fifth Amendment to the US Constitution. ● *adj.* that is the fifth. □ **take the Fifth** exercise the right guaranteed by the Fifth Amendment to the Constitution of refusing to answer questions in order to avoid incriminating oneself. □□ **fifth·ly** *adv.*

fifth col·umn *n.* a group working for an enemy within a country at war, etc. □□ **fifth col·umn·ist** *n.*

fifth gen·er·a·tion *n. Computing* a stage in computer design involving machines that make use of artificial intelligence.

fifth wheel *n.* **1** an extra wheel of a carriage. **2** a superfluous person or thing. **3** a horizontal turntable over the front axle of a carriage as an extra support to prevent its tipping. **4** a round coupling device to connect a tractor and trailer.

fif·ty /fíftee/ *n. & adj.* ● *n.* (*pl.* **-ies**) **1** the product of five and ten. **2** a symbol for this (50, 1 (letter), L). **3** (in *pl.*) the numbers from 50 to 59, esp. the years of a century or of a person's life. **4** a set of fifty persons or things. **5** a large indefinite number (*have fifty things to tell you*). **6** a fifty-dollar bill. ● *adj.* that amount to fifty. □□ **fif·ti·eth** *adj. & n.* **fif·ty·fold** *adj. & adv.*

fif·ty-fif·ty *adj. & adv.* ● *adj.* equal; with equal shares or chances (*on a fifty-fifty basis*). ● *adv.* equally; half and half (*go fifty-fifty*).

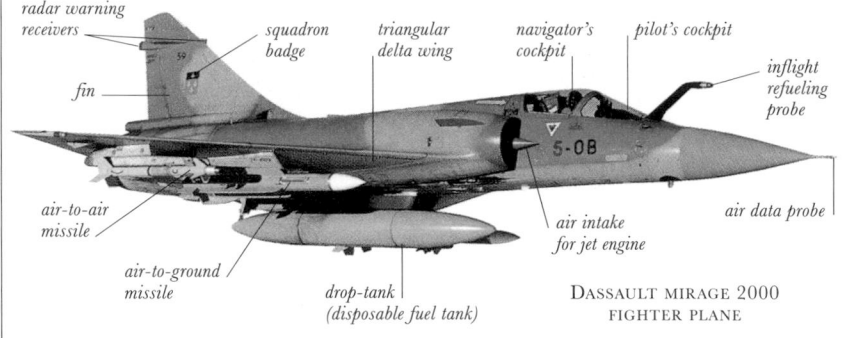

FIGHTER

Fighters are fast and highly maneuverable aircraft. On-board computers help the pilot control and navigate the plane and launch its weaponry. Fighters are capable of carrying air-to-air and air-to-ground missiles for airborne, land, and sea targets. Their defensive systems include electronic beams and flares for confusing enemy fire.

radar warning receivers

fin

squadron badge

triangular delta wing

navigator's cockpit

pilot's cockpit

inflight refueling probe

air-to-air missile

air-to-ground missile

drop-tank (disposable fuel tank)

air intake for jet engine

air data probe

DASSAULT MIRAGE 2000 FIGHTER PLANE

---

fig[1] /fig/ *n.* **1 a** ◄ a soft pear-shaped fruit with many seeds, eaten fresh or dried. ▷ FRUIT. **b** (in full **fig tree**) any deciduous tree of the genus *Ficus*, esp. *F. carica*, having broad leaves and bearing figs. **2** a valueless thing (*don't care a fig for*).

seeds

FIG: COMMON FIG (*Ficus carica*)

fig[2] /fig/ *n. & v.* ● *n.* **1** dress or equipment (*in full fig*). **2** condition or form (*in good fig*). ● *v.tr.* (**figged**, **figging**) **1** (foll. by *out*) dress up (a person). **2** (foll. by *out, up*) make (a horse) lively.

fig. *abbr.* figure.

fight /fīt/ *v. & n.* ● *v.* (*past* and *past part.* **fought** /fawt/) **1** *intr.* **a** (often foll. by *against, with*) contend or struggle in war, battle, single combat, etc. **b** (often foll. by *with*) argue; quarrel. **2** *tr.* content with (an opponent) in this way. **3** *tr.* take part in or engage in (a battle, war, duel, boxing match, etc.). **4** *tr.* contend about (an issue, an election); maintain (a lawsuit, cause, etc.) against an opponent. **5** *intr.* campaign or strive determinedly to achieve something. **6** *tr.* strive to overcome (disease, fire, fear, etc.). **7** *tr.* make (one's way) by fighting. **8** *tr.* cause (cocks or dogs) to fight. **9** *tr.* handle (troops, a ship, etc.) in battle. ● *n.* **1 a** a combat, esp. unpremeditated, between two or more persons, animals, or parties. **b** a boxing match. **c** a battle. **d** an argument **2** a conflict or struggle; a vigorous effort in the face of difficulty. **3** power or inclination to fight (*has no fight left*). □ **fight back 1** counterattack. **2** suppress (one's feelings, tears, etc.). **fight down** suppress (one's feelings, tears, etc.). **fight for 1** fight on behalf of. **2** fight to secure (a thing). **fight off** repel with effort. **fight out** (usu. **fight it out**) settle (a dispute, etc.) by fighting. **fight shy of** avoid; be unwilling to approach (a person, task, etc.). **put up a fight** (or **make a fight of it**) offer resistance.

fight·er /fítər/ *n.* **1** a person or animal that fights. **2** ▲ a fast military aircraft designed for attacking other aircraft.

fight·er-bomb·er *n.* an aircraft serving as both fighter and bomber.

fight·ing chance *n.* an opportunity to succeed by great effort.

fight·ing words *n.pl. colloq.* words likely to start a fight.

fig·ment /fígmənt/ *n.* a thing invented or existing only in the imagination.

fig·u·ra·tion /fígyəráyshən/ *n.* **1 a** the act of formation. **b** a mode of formation; a form. **c** a shape or outline. **2 a** ornamentation by designs. **b** *Mus.* ornamental patters of scales, arpeggios, etc.

fig·ur·a·tive /fígyərətiv/ *adj.* **1 a** metaphorical, not literal. **b** metaphorically so called. **2** characterized by or addicted to figures of speech. **3** of pictorial or sculptural representation. **4** emblematic; serving as a type. □□ **fig·ur·a·tive·ly** *adv.* **fig·ur·a·tive·ness** *n.*

fig·ure /fígyər/ *n. & v.* ● *n.* **1 a** the external form or shape of a thing. **b** bodily shape (*has a model's figure*). **2 a** a person as seen in outline but not identified. **b** a person as contemplated mentally (*a public figure*). **3** appearance as giving a certain impression (*cut a poor figure*). **4 a** a representation of the human form in drawing, sculpture, etc. **b** an image or likeness. **c** an emblem or type. **5** *Geom.* a two-dimensional space enclosed by a line or lines, or a three-dimensional space enclosed by a surface or surfaces. **6 a** a numerical symbol, esp. any of the ten in Arabic notation. **b** a number so expressed. **c** an amount of money; a value (*cannot put a figure on it*). **d** (in *pl.*) arithmetical calculations. **7** a diagram or illustrative drawing. **8** a decorative pattern. **9 a** a division of a set dance. **b** (in skating) a prescribed pattern of movements from a stationary position. **10** *Mus.* a short succession of notes producing a single impression. **11** (in full **figure of speech**) a recognized form of rhetorical expression, esp. metaphor or hyperbole. **12** *Gram.* a permitted deviation from the usual rules of construction, e.g., ellipsis. ● *v.* **1** *intr.* appear or be mentioned, esp. prominently. **2** *tr.* represent in a diagram or picture. **3** *tr.* imagine; picture mentally. **4 a** *tr.* embellish with a pattern (*figured satin*). **b** *tr. Mus.* embellish with figures. **c** *intr.* perform a figure in skating or dancing. **5** *tr.* mark with numbers or prices. **6 a** *tr.* calculate. **b** *intr.* do arithmetic. **7** *tr.* be a symbol of; represent typically. **8 a** *tr.* understand; ascertain; consider. **b** *intr. colloq.* be likely or understandably (*that figures*). □ **figure on** count on; expect. **figure out 1** work out by arithmetic or logic. **2** estimate. **3** understand. □□ **fig·ure·less** *adj.*

fig·ure-head /fígyərhed/ *n* **1** a normal leader or head without real power. **2** ▼ a carving, usu. a bust or a full-length figure, at a ship's prow.

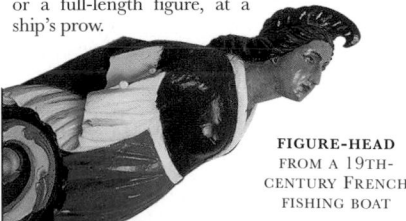

FIGURE-HEAD FROM A 19TH-CENTURY FRENCH FISHING BOAT

fig·ure skat·ing *n.* the sport of performing jumps and spins, etc., in a dancelike performance while ice skating, and also including skating in prescribed patterns from a stationary position. □□ **fig·ure ska·ter** *n.*

fig·ur·ine /fígyəréen/ *n.* a statuette.

fig·wort /fígwərt, -wawrt/ *n.* ► any aromatic green-flowered plant of the genus *Scrophularia*, once believed to be useful against scrofula.

fil·a·gree var. of FILIGREE.

fil·a·ment /fíləmənt/ *n.* **1** a slender threadlike body or fiber (esp. in animal or vegetable structures). **2** a wire or thread in an electric bulb or vacuum tube, heated or made incandescent by an electric current. ▷ LIGHTBULB. □□ **fil·a·men·ta·ry** /-méntəree/ *adj.* **fil·a·ment·ed** *adj.* **fil·a·men·tous** /-méntəs/ *adj.*

fil·a·ri·a·sis /fíləríəsis/ *n.* a disease common in the tropics, caused by the presence of parasitic nematode worms in the lymph vessels.

fil·a·ture /fíləchər/ *n.* **1** the action of reeling silk from cocoons. **2** an establishment for this.

fil·bert /fílbərt/ *n.* **1** the cultivated hazel, *Corylus maxima*, bearing edible ovoid nuts. **2** this nut.

filch /filch/ *v.tr.* pilfer; steal. □□ **filch·er** *n.*

file[1] /fīl/ *n. & v.* ● *n.* **1** a folder, box, etc., for holding loose papers. **2** a set of papers kept in this. **3** *Computing* a collection of (usu. related) data stored under one name. ● *v.tr.* **1** place (papers) in a file or among (esp. public) records. **2** submit (a petition for divorce, an application for a patent, etc.). **3** (of a reporter) send (a story, information, etc.) to a newspaper. □□ **fil·er** *n.*

file[2] /fīl/ *n. & v.* ● *n.* a line of persons or things one behind another. ● *v.intr.* walk in a file.

file[3] /fīl/ *n. & v.* ● *n.* a tool with a roughened surface for smoothing or shaping wood, fingernails, etc. ● *v.tr.* smooth or shape with a file. □ **file away** remove (roughness, etc.) with a file. □□ **fil·er** *n.*

fi·let mi·gnon /filáy minyón/ *n.* a small tender piece of beef from the end of the tenderloin.

fil·i·al /fíleeəl/ *adj.* **1** of or due from a son or daughter. **2** *Biol.* bearing the relation of offspring (cf. F[2] 4). □□ **fil·i·al·ly** *adv.*

fil·i·bus·ter /fílibustər/ *n. & v.* ● *n.* **1** the obstruction of progress in a legislative assembly, esp. by prolonged speaking. **2** a person who engages in filibuster. ● *v.* **1** *intr.* act as filibuster. **2** *tr.* act in this way against (a motion, etc.). □□ **fil·i·bus·ter·er** *n.*

fil·i·gree /fíligree/ *n.* (also **fil·a·gree** /fílə-/) **1** fine metal openwork. **2** anything delicate resembling this. □□ **fil·i·greed** *adj.*

fil·ing /fíling/ *n.* (usu. in *pl.*) a particle rubbed off by a file.

fil·ing cab·i·net *n.* a case with drawers for storing documents.

Fil·i·pi·no /filipéenō/ *n. & adj.* ● *n.* (*pl.* **-os**; *fem.* **Filipina** /-nə/) a native or inhabitant of the Philippines, a group of islands in the SW Pacific. ● *adj.* of or relating to the Philippines or the Filipinos.

fill /fil/ *v. & n.* ● *v.* **1** *tr. & intr.* (often foll. by *with*) make or become full. **2** *tr.* occupy completely; spread over or through; pervade. **3** *tr.* block up (a cavity or hole in a tooth) with cement, amalgam, gold, etc. **4** *tr.* make level or raise the level of (low-lying land). **5** *tr.* appoint a person to hold (a vacant post). **6** *tr.* hold (a position); discharge the duties of (an office). **7** *tr.* carry out or supply (an order, commission, etc.). **8** *tr.* occupy (vacant time). **9** *intr.* (of a sail) be distended by wind. **10** *tr.* (usu. as **filling** *adj.*) (esp. of food) satisfy; satiate. **11** *tr.* satisfy; fulfill (a need or requirement). **12** *tr.* stock abundantly. ● *n.* **1** (prec. by possessive) as much as one wants or can bear (*eat your fill*). **2** enough to fill something (*a fill of tobacco*). **3** earth, etc., used to fill a cavity. □ **fill the bill** be suitable or adequate. **fill in 1** add information to complete (a document, blank check, etc.). **2 a** complete (a drawing, etc.) within an outline. **b** fill (an outline) in this way. **3** fill (a hole, etc.) completely. **4** (often foll. by *for*) act as a substitute. **5** occupy oneself during (time between other activities). **6** *colloq.* inform (a person) more fully. **fill out 1** enlarge to the required size. **2** become enlarged or plump. **3** add information to complete (a document, etc.). **fill up 1** make or become completely full. **2** fill the fuel tank of (a car, etc.). **3** provide what is needed to occupy vacant parts or places or deal with deficiencies in.

fill·er /fílər/ *n.* **1** material or an object used to fill a cavity or increase bulk. **2** an item filling space in a newspaper, etc. **3** paper for filling a binder or notebook. **4** a person or thing that fills.

fil·let /fílit/ *n. & v.* ● *n.* **1** (usu. /filáy/) **a** a fleshy boneless piece of meat from near the loins or the ribs. ▷ CUT. **b** (in full **fillet steak**) the tenderloin. **c** a boned longitudinal section of a fish. **2 a** a headband, ribbon, string, or narrow band, for binding the hair or worn around the head. **b** a band or bandage. **3 a** a thin narrow strip. **b** a raised rim or ridge. **4** *Archit.* **a** a narrow flat band separating two moldings. ▷ WINDOW. **b** a small band between the flutes of a column. ● *v.tr.* (**filleted, filleting**) **1** (also /filáy, filay/) **a** remove bones from (fish or meat). **b** divide (fish or meat) into fillets. **2** bind or provide with a fillet or fillets. **3** encircle with an ornamental band. □□ **fil·let·er** *n.*

fill·ing /fíling/ *n.* **1** any material that is used to fill, esp.: **a** a piece of material used to fill a cavity in a tooth. **b** the edible substance between the bread in a sandwich or between the pastry crusts in a pie. **2** weft.

fill·ing sta·tion *n.* an establishment selling automotive fuel, etc., to motorists.

fil·lip /fílip/ *n.* a stimulus or incentive.

fil·ly /fílee/ *n.* (*pl.* **-ies**) **1** a young female horse, usu. before it is four years old. **2** *colloq.* a girl or young woman.

film /film/ *n. & v.* ● *n.* **1** a thin coating or covering layer. **2** *Photog.* ▼ a strip or sheet of plastic or other flexible base coated with light-sensitive emulsion for exposure in a camera. ▷ CAMERA. **3 a** a representation of a story, episode, etc., on a film, with the illusion of movement; a movie. **b** a story represented in this way; a movie. **c** (in *pl.*) the movie industry. **4** a slight veil or haze, etc. **5** a dimness or morbid growth affecting the eyes. **6** a fine thread or filament. ● *v.* **1 a** *tr.* make a photographic film of (a scene, person, etc.). **b** *tr.* (also *absol.*) make a movie or television film of (a book, etc.). **c** *intr.* be (well or ill) suited for reproduction on film. **2** *tr. & intr.* cover or become covered with or as with a film.

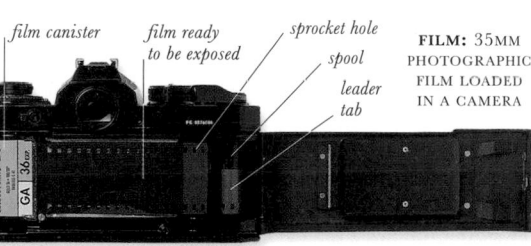

FILM: 35MM PHOTOGRAPHIC FILM LOADED IN A CAMERA

film canister

film ready to be exposed

sprocket hole

spool

leader tab

film·go·er /fílmgōər/ *n.* a person who frequents movie theaters.

film·ic /fílmik/ *adj.* of or relating to movies or cinematography.

film·mak·er /fílmaykər/ *n.* a person who makes motion pictures.

film noir /film nwáar/ *n.* a style of film marked by a mood of pessimism, fatalism, and menace.

film·og·ra·phy /filmógrəfee/ *n.* (*pl.* **-ies**) a list of movies by one director, etc., or on one subject.

film·set /fílmset/ *v.tr.* (**-setting**; *past* and *past part.* **-set**) *Printing* set (material for printing) by filmsetting. □□ **film·set·ter** *n.*

film·set·ting /fílmseting/ *n.* = PHOTOCOMPOSITION.

film·strip /fílmstrip/ *n.* a series of transparencies in a strip for projection as still pictures. ▷ PROJECTOR

film·y /fílmee/ *adj.* (**filmier, filmiest**) **1** thin and translucent. **2** covered with or as with a film. □□ **film·i·ly** *adv.* **film·i·ness** *n.*

fi·lo /féelō/ *n.* (also **phyllo**) dough that can be stretched into very thin layers; pastry made from this dough.

fils /fees/ *n.* (added to a surname to distinguish a son from a father) the son; junior (cf. PÈRE).

fil·ter /fíltər/ *n. & v.* ● *n.* **1** ▼ a porous device for removing impurities or solid particles from a liquid or gas passed through it. **2** = FILTER TIP. **3** ▼ a screen or attachment for absorbing or modifying light, X rays, etc. ▷ POLARIZE. **4** a device for suppressing electrical or sound waves of frequencies not required. **5** *Brit.* an arrangement for filtering traffic. ● *v.* **1** *tr. & intr.* pass or cause to pass through a filter. **2** *tr.* (foll. by *out*) remove (impurities, etc.) by means of a filter. **3** *intr.* (foll. by *through, into*) make way gradually. **4** *intr.* (foll. by *out*) leak or cause to leak.

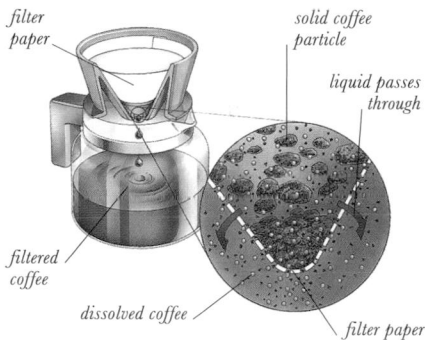

filter paper

solid coffee particle

liquid passes through

filtered coffee

dissolved coffee

filter paper

FILTER (*n.*1): COFFEE FILTER.

FILTER (*n.*3)

Photographic filters are used to modify the light passing through a lens. In the examples below, each color filter allows light of predominantly the same color through the lens, distorting the film's hues.

PICTURE TAKEN WITHOUT A FILTER

YELLOW FILTER

ORANGE FILTER

BLUE FILTER

F

FIGWORT: VARIEGATED WATER FIGWORT (*Scrophularia auriculata* 'VARIEGATA')

F

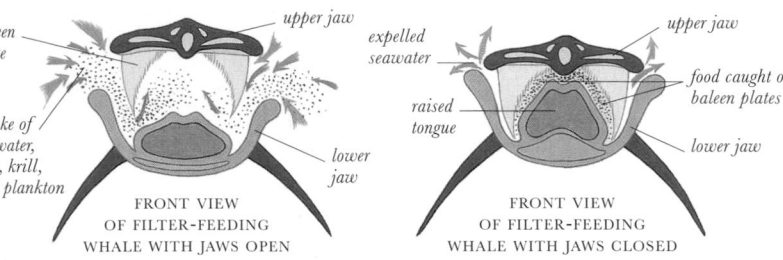

FILTER FEEDING

Baleen whales are the largest filter feeders. They have modified mucous membrane plates (baleen) in their mouths, which look like huge fringed brushes. The whale draws seawater into its mouth and then expels it through the baleen, keeping food such as fish or krill trapped inside. The whale then wipes the plates clean with its tongue.

baleen plate
upper jaw
intake of seawater, fish, krill, and plankton
lower jaw

FRONT VIEW OF FILTER-FEEDING WHALE WITH JAWS OPEN

expelled seawater
upper jaw
raised tongue
food caught on baleen plates
lower jaw

FRONT VIEW OF FILTER-FEEDING WHALE WITH JAWS CLOSED

fil·ter·a·ble /fíltərəbəl/ *adj.* (also **fil·tra·ble** /fíltrəbəl/) **1** *Med.* (of a virus) able to pass through a filter that retains bacteria. **2** that can be filtered.

fil·ter feed·ing *n. Zool.* ▲ feeding by filtering out plankton or nutrients suspended in water. ▷ WHALE. □□ **fil·ter feed·er** *n.*

fil·ter tip 1 a filter attached to a cigarette for removing impurities from the inhaled smoke. **2** a cigarette with this. □□ **fil·ter-tipped** *adj.*

filth /filth/ *n.* **1** repugnant or extreme dirt. **2** vileness; corruption; obscenity. **3** foul or obscene language.

filth·y /filthee/ *adj. & adv.* ● *adj.* (**filthier, filthiest**) **1** extremely or disgustingly dirty. **2** obscene. **3** vile; disgraceful. ● *adv.* **1** filthily (*filthy dirty*). **2** *colloq.* extremely (*filthy rich*). □□ **filth·i·ly** *adv.* **filth·i·ness** *n.*

filth·y lu·cre *n.* **1** dishonorable gain (Tit. 1:11). **2** *joc.* money.

fil·tra·ble var. of FILTERABLE.

fil·trate /fíltrayt/ *v. & n.* ● *v.tr.* filter. ● *n.* filtered liquid. □□ **fil·tra·tion** /-tráyshən/ *n.*

fin[1] /fin/ *n.* **1** an organ on various parts of the body of many aquatic vertebrates and some invertebrates, including fish and cetaceans, for propelling, steering, and balancing. ▷ CETACEAN, FISH. **2** a small projecting surface or attachment on an aircraft, rocket, or automobile for ensuring aerodynamic stability. ▷ AIRCRAFT, SPACECRAFT. **3** an underwater swimmer's flipper. **4** a sharp lateral projection on the share or colter of a plow. **5** a finlike projection on any device, for improving heat transfer, etc. □□ **fin·less** *adj.* **finned** *adj.* (also in *comb.*).

fin[2] /fin/ *n. sl.* a five-dollar bill.

fi·na·gle /fináygəl/ *v.intr. & tr. colloq.* act or obtain dishonestly or deviously. □□ **fi·na·gler** *n.*

fi·nal /fínəl/ *adj. & n.* ● *adj.* **1** situated at the end; coming last. **2** conclusive; decisive; unalterable; putting an end to doubt. **3** concerned with the purpose or end aimed at. ● *n.* (also in *pl.*) the last or deciding heat or game in sports or in a competition. □□ **fi·nal·ly** *adv.*

fi·na·le /fináalee, -nálee/ *n.* **1 a** the last movement of an instrumental composition. **b** a piece of music closing an act in an opera. **2** the close of a drama, etc. **3** a conclusion.

fi·nal·ist /fínəlist/ *n.* a competitor in the final of a competition, etc.

fi·nal·i·ty /fináilitee, fə-/ *n.* (*pl.* **-ies**) **1** the quality or fact of being final. **2** the belief that something is final. **3** a final act, state, or utterance. **4** the principle of final cause viewed as operative in the universe.

fi·nal·ize /fínəlīz/ *v.tr.* **1** put into final form. **2** complete; bring to an end. **3** approve the final form or details of. □□ **fi·nal·i·za·tion** *n.*

fi·nal so·lu·tion *n.* the Nazi policy (1941–45) of exterminating European Jews.

fi·nance /fináns, fī-, fínans/ *n. & v.* ● *n.* **1** the management of (esp. public) money. **2** monetary support for an enterprise. **3** (in *pl.*) the money resources of a government, company, or person. ● *v.tr.* provide capital for (a person or enterprise).

fi·nan·cial /fináns͟hal, fī-/ *adj.* of finance. □□ **fi·nan·cial·ly** *adv.*

fin·an·cier /fínənséer, fənan-, fínən-/ *n.* a person engaged in large-scale finance.

fin·back /fínbak/ *n.* (or **fin whale**) a rorqual, *Balaenoptera physalus.*

finch /finch/ *n.* ▶ any small seed-eating passerine bird of the family Fringillidae (esp. one of the genus *Fringilla*), including crossbills, canaries, and chaffinches. ▷ SONGBIRD

find /fīnd/ *v. & n.* ● *v.tr.* (*past* and *past part.* **found** /fownd/) **1 a** discover by chance or effort (*found a key*). **b** become aware of. **2 a** get possession of by chance (*found a treasure*). **b** obtain; receive (*idea found acceptance*). **c** succeed in obtaining (*cannot find the money*). **d** summon up (*found courage to protest*). **3 a** seek out and provide (*will find you a book*). **b** supply; furnish (*each finds his own equipment*). **4** ascertain by study or calculation or inquiry (*could not find the answer*). **5 a** perceive or experience (*find no sense in it; find difficulty in breathing*). **b** (often in *passive*) recognize or discover to be present (*the word is not found in Shakespeare*). **c** regard or discover from experience (*finds Canada too cold; you'll find it pays*). **6** *Law* decide in favor of (a jury, judge, etc.) decide and declare (*found him guilty*). **7** reach by a natural or normal process (*water finds its own level*). **8 a** (of a letter) reach (a person). **b** (of an address) be adequate to enable a letter, etc., to reach (a person). ● *n.* **1** a discovery of treasure, minerals, etc. **2** a thing or person discovered, esp. of value. □ **find against** *Law* decide against (a person); judge to be guilty. **find fault** see FAULT. **find favor** prove acceptable. **find one's feet 1** become able to walk. **2** develop one's independent ability. **find for** *Law* decide in favor of (a person); judge to be innocent. **find oneself 1** discover that one is (*woke to find myself in the hospital*). **2** discover one's own talents, strengths, etc. **find out 1** discover or detect (a wrongdoer, etc.). **2** (often foll. by *about*) get information. **3** discover (*find out where we are*). **4** (often foll. by *about*) discover the truth, a fact, etc. (*he never found out*). **5** devise. **6** solve. **find one's way 1** (often foll. by *to*) manage to reach a place. **2** (often foll. by *into*) be brought or get. □□ **find·a·ble** *adj.*

find·er /fíndər/ *n.* **1** a person who finds. **2** a small telescope attached to a large one to locate an object for observation. **3** the viewfinder of a camera.

find·ers keep·ers *n. colloq.* whoever finds a thing is entitled to keep it.

fin de siè·cle /faN də see-éklə/ *adj.* relating to or characteristic of the end of a century, esp. the 19th century.

find·ing /fínding/ *n.* (often in *pl.*) a conclusion reached by an inquiry.

fine[1] /fīn/ *adj., n., adv., & v.* ● *adj.* **1** of high quality. **2 a** excellent; of notable merit (*a fine painting*). **b** good; satisfactory (*that will be fine*). **c** fortunate (*has been a fine thing for him*). **d** well conceived or expressed (*a fine saying*). **3 a** pure; refined. **b** (of gold or silver) containing a specified proportion of pure metal. **4** of handsome appearance or size; imposing; dignified (*fine buildings*). **5** in good health (*I'm fine, thank you*). **6** (of weather, etc.) bright and clear with sunshine; free from rain. **7 a** thin; sharp. **b** in small particles. **c** worked in slender thread. **d** (esp. of print) small. **e** (of a pen) narrow-pointed. **8** *Cricket* behind the wicket and near the line of flight of the ball. **9** tritely complimentary; euphemistic (*call things by fine names*). **10** ornate; showy; smart. **11** fastidious; dainty; pretending refinement; (of speech or writing) affectedly ornate. **12 a** capable of delicate perception or discrimination. **b** perceptible only with difficulty (*a fine distinction*). **13 a** delicate; subtle; exquisitely fashioned. **b** (of feelings) refined; elevated. **14** (of wine or other goods) of a high standard; conforming to a specified grade. ● *n.* (in *pl.*) very small particles in mining, milling, etc. ● *adv.* **1** finely. **2** *colloq.* very well (*suits me fine*). ● *v.* **1** (often foll. by *down*) **a** make (beer or wine) clear. **b** *intr.* (of liquid) become clear. **2** *tr. & intr.* (often foll. by *away, down, off*) make or become finer, thinner, or less coarse; dwindle or taper, or cause to do so. □ **cut it fine** allow very little margin of time, etc. **not to put too fine a point on it** (as a parenthetic remark) to speak bluntly. □□ **fine·ly** *adv.* **fine·ness** *n.*

fine[2] /fīn/ *n. & v.* ● *n.* a sum of money exacted as a penalty. ● *v.tr.* punish by a fine (*fined him $5*). □ **in fine** to sum up; in short. □□ **fin·a·ble** /fínəbəl/ *adj.*

fine arts *n.pl.* those appealing to the mind or to the sense of beauty, as poetry, music, and esp. painting, sculpture, and architecture.

fine print *n.* detailed printed information, esp. in legal documents, instructions, etc.

fin·er·y /fínəree/ *n.* showy dress or decoration.

fines herbes /feen áirb, feenz/ *n.pl.* mixed herbs used in cooking.

fi·nesse /finés/ *n. & v.* ● *n.* **1** refinement. **2** subtle or delicate manipulation. **3** *Cards* an attempt to win a trick with a card that is not the highest held. ● *v.intr. & tr.* use or achieve by finesse.

fine-tooth comb *n.* a comb with narrow close-set teeth. □ **go over with a fine-tooth comb** check or search thoroughly.

fine-tune *v.tr.* make small adjustments to.

fin·ger /fínggər/ *n. & v.* ● *n.* **1** any of the terminal projections of the hand (including or excluding the thumb). ▷ HAND. **2** the part of a glove, etc. intended to cover a finger. **3 a** a finger-like object (*chicken finger*). **b** a long narrow structure. **4** *colloq.* a measure of liquor in a glass, based on the breadth of a finger. ● *v.tr.* **1** touch, feel, or handle with the fingers. **2** *Mus.* **a** play (a passage) with fingers used in a particular way. **b** play upon (an instrument) with the fingers. **3** *sl.* indicate (a victim, or a criminal to the police). □ **have a finger in** (or **in the pie**) be (esp. officiously) concerned in (the matter). **lay a finger on** touch however slightly. **point the finger at** *colloq.* accuse; blame. **put one's finger on** locate or identify exactly. **put the finger on** *sl.* **1** inform against. **2** identify (an intended victim). **slip through one's fingers** escape. **twist** (or **wind** or **wrap**) **around one's finger** (or **little finger**) persuade (a person) without difficulty; dominate (a person) completely. □□ **fin·gered** *adj.* (also in *comb.*). **fin·ger·less** *adj.*

FINCH:
ZEBRA FINCHES
(*Poephia guttata*)

fin·ger·board /fínggərbawrd/ n. a flat strip at the top end of a stringed instrument, against which the strings are pressed to determine tones. ▷ SITAR, STRINGED.

fin·ger bowl n. a small bowl for rinsing the fingers at the table.

fin·ger·ing /fínggəring/ n. **1** a manner or technique of using the fingers, esp. to play an instrument. **2** an indication of this in a musical score.

fin·ger·nail /fínggərnayl/ n. the nail at the tip of each finger. ▷ NAIL.

fin·ger paint n. & v. ● n. paint that can be applied with the fingers. ● v.intr. apply paint with the fingers.

fin·ger·print /fínggərprint/ n. & v. ● n. **1** an impression made on a surface by the fine ridges on the fingertips. **2** a distinctive characteristic. ● v.tr. record the fingerprints of (a person).

fin·ger·spell·ing /fínggər-spéling/ n. a form of sign language in which individual letters are formed by the fingers to spell out words.

fin·ger·tip /fínggərtip/ n. the tip of a finger. ▷ NAIL. □ **have at one's fingertips** be thoroughly familiar with (a subject, etc.).

fin·i·al /fíneeəl/ n. Archit. **1** ▼ an ornament finishing off the apex of a roof, pediment, gable, tower corner, canopy, etc. ▷ CHURCH. **2** the topmost part of a pinnacle.

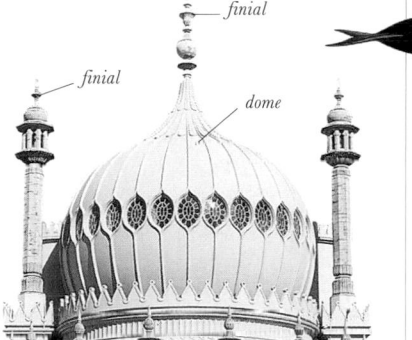

FINIALS ON A REGENCY PAVILION

fin·i·cal /fínikəl/ adj. = FINICKY. **fin·i·cal·ness** n.

fin·ick·y /fínikee/ adj. **1** overly particular; fastidious. **2** needing much care or attention to detail. □□ **fin·ick·i·ness** n.

fin·is /fínis, feenée, fínis/ n. **1** (at the end of a book) the end. **2** the end of anything, esp. of life.

fin·ish /fínish/ v. & n. ● v. **1** tr. **a** (often foll. by off) bring to an end; come to the end of; complete. **b** (usu. foll. by off) colloq. kill; overcome completely. **c** (often foll. by off, up) consume or get through the whole or the remainder of (food or drink) (finish your dinner). **2** intr. **a** come to an end; cease. **b** reach the end, esp. of a race. **c** = finish up. **3** tr. **a** complete the manufacture of (cloth, woodwork, etc.) by surface treatment. **b** put the final touches to; make perfect or highly accomplished (finished manners). **c** prepare (a girl) for entry into fashionable society. ● n. **1 a** the end; the last stage. **b** the point at which a race, etc., ends. **c** the death of a fox in a hunt (be in at the finish). **2** a method, material, or texture used for surface treatment of wood, cloth, etc. (mahogany finish). **3** what serves to give completeness. **4** an accomplished or completed state. □ **fight to the finish** fight until one party is completely beaten. **finish off** provide with an ending. **finish up** (often foll. by in, by) end in something, end by doing something (the plan finished up in the wastebasket; finished up by apologizing). **finish with** have no more to do with; complete one's use of or association with.

fin·ish·er /fínishər/ n. **1** a person who finishes something. **2** a worker or machine doing the last operation in a manufacturing process. **3** colloq. a discomfiting thing, a crushing blow, etc.

fin·ish·ing touch n. (usu. in pl.) the final details completing and enhancing a piece of work, etc.

fin·ish·ing school n. a private school where girls are prepared for entry into fashionable society.

fi·nite /fínīt/ adj. **1** limited; bounded; not infinite. **2** Gram. (of a part of a verb) having a specific number and person. **3** not infinitely small. □□ **fi·nite·ly** adv. **fi·nite·ness** n. **fin·i·tude** /fínitood, -tyood/ n.

fi·nit·ism /fínītizəm/ n. belief in the finiteness of the world, God, etc. □□ **fi·nit·ist** /-tist/ n.

fink /fingk/ n. & v. sl. ● n. **1** an unpleasant person. **2** an informer. **3** a strikebreaker. ● v.intr. (foll. by on) inform on.

Finn /fin/ n. a native or inhabitant of Finland; a person of Finnish descent.

fin·nan /fínən/ n. (in full **finnan haddie** or **haddock**) a haddock cured with the smoke of green wood, turf, or peat.

Finn·ish /fínish/ adj. & n. ● adj. of the Finns or their language. ● n. the language of the Finns.

fin·ny /fínee/ adj. **1** having fins; like a fin. **2** poet. of or teeming with fish.

fi·no /feénō/ n. (pl. **-os**) a light-colored dry sherry.

fin whale n. ▼ a large rorqual, Balaenoptera physalus, with a prominent dorsal fin.

dorsal fin

FIN WHALE (Balaenoptera physalus)

fiord var. of FJORD. ▷ COASTLINE.

fip·ple /fípəl/ n. a plug at the mouth end of a wind instrument.

fir /fər/ n. **1** (in full **fir tree**) any evergreen coniferous tree, esp. of the genus Abies, with needles borne singly on the stems (cf. PINE[1]). ▷ CONIFER. **2** the wood of the fir.

fire /fīr/ n. & v. ● n. **1 a** the state or process of combustion, in which substances combine chemically with oxygen from the air and usu. give out bright light and heat. **b** the active principle operative in this. **c** flame or incandescence. **2** a conflagration; a destructive burning (forest fire). **3** burning fuel in a fireplace, furnace, etc. **4** firing of guns. **5 a** fervor; spirit; vivacity. **b** poetic inspiration; lively imagination. **6** burning heat; fever. **7** luminosity; glow (St. Elmo's fire). ● v. **1 a** tr. discharge (a gun, etc.). **b** tr. propel (a missile) from a gun, etc. **c** tr. propel (a missile) with force or high speed. **d** intr. (often foll. by at, into, on) fire a gun or missile. **e** tr. produce (a broadside, salute, etc.) by discharge of guns. **f** intr. (of a gun, etc.) be discharged. **2** tr. cause (explosive) to explode. **3** tr. deliver or utter in rapid succession (fired insults at us). **4** tr. sl. dismiss (an employee) from a job. **5** tr. **a** set fire to with the intention of destroying. **b** kindle (explosives). **6** intr. catch fire. **7** intr. (of an internal-combustion engine, or a cylinder in one) undergo ignition of its fuel. **8** tr. supply (a furnace, engine, boiler, or power station) with fuel. **9** tr. **a** stimulate (the imagination or emotion). **b** fill (a person) with enthusiasm. **10** tr. **a** bake or dry (pottery, bricks, etc.). **b** cure (tea or tobacco) by artificial heat. **11** intr. become heated or excited. **12** tr. cause to glow or redden. □ **catch fire** begin to burn. **fire away** colloq. begin; go ahead. **fire up 1** start up, as an engine. **2** show sudden anger. **on fire 1** burning. **2** excited. **set fire to** (or **set on fire**) ignite; kindle; cause to burn. **take fire** catch fire. **under fire 1** being shot at. **2** being rigorously criticized or questioned. □□ **fire·less** adj. **fir·er** n.

fire a·larm n. a device for giving warning of fire.

fire and brim·stone n. the supposed torments of hell.

fire·arm /fíraarm/ n. (usu. in pl.) a gun, esp. a pistol or rifle.

fire·back /fírbak/ n. **a** the back wall of a fireplace. **b** an iron sheet for this.

fire·ball /fírbawl/ n. **1** a large meteor. **2** a ball of flame, esp. from a nuclear explosion. **3** an energetic person.

fire·bomb /fírbom/ n. an incendiary bomb.

fire·box /fírboks/ n. the fuel chamber of a steam engine or boiler. ▷ STEAM ENGINE.

fire·brand /fírbrand/ n. **1** a piece of burning wood. **2** a cause of trouble, esp. a person causing unrest.

fire·break /fírbrayk/ n. an obstacle to the spread of fire in a forest, etc., esp. an open space.

fire·brick /fírbrik/ n. a fireproof brick used in a grate.

fire·bug /fírbug/ n. colloq. a pyromaniac.

fire·clay /fírklay/ n. clay capable of withstanding high temperatures, often used to make firebricks.

fire·crack·er /fírkrakər/ n. an explosive firework.

fire·damp /fírdamp/ n. a miners' name for methane, which is explosive when mixed in certain proportions with air.

fire de·part·ment n. an organized body of fire-fighters trained and employed to extinguish fires.

fire·dog /fírdawg, -dog/ n. a metal support for burning wood or for a grate or fire irons.

fire door n. a fire-resistant door to prevent the spread of fire.

fire drill n. **1** a rehearsal of the procedures to be used in case of fire. **2** a primitive device for kindling fire with a stick and wood.

fire en·gine n. a vehicle carrying equipment for fighting large fires.

fire es·cape n. a vehicle carrying equipment for fighting large fires.

fire ex·tin·guish·er n. ▼ an apparatus for discharging liquid chemicals, water, or foam to extinguish a fire.

fire·fight·er /fírfītər/ n. a person whose task is to extinguish fires.

fire·fly /fírflī/ n. (pl. **-flies**) any soft-bodied beetle of the family Lampyridae, emitting phosphorescent light, including glowworms.

fire·guard /fírgaard/ n. **1** a fire screen. **2** a firebreak.

F

FIRE EXTINGUISHER

The water-filled fire extinguisher shown contains a canister of high-pressure gas. When the operating lever is depressed, a pin punctures the canister, releasing gas into the main cylinder. The pressure of the gas forces the water through the discharge tube and out of the nozzle.

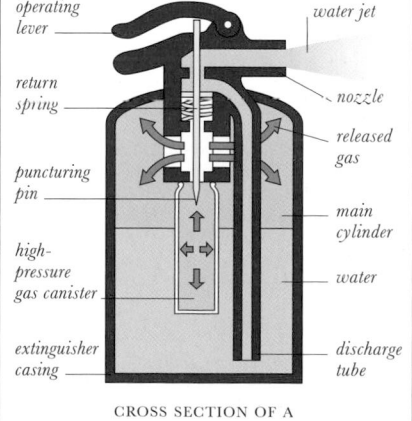

operating lever *water jet*
return spring *nozzle*
released gas
puncturing pin
main cylinder
high-pressure gas canister *water*
extinguisher casing *discharge tube*

CROSS SECTION OF A
WATER-FILLED FIRE EXTINGUISHER

FISH

There are over 20,000 species of fish, divided into three groups: bony fish, cartilaginous fish, and jawless fish. Bony fish, which are the most numerous, have skeletons of bone, and swim bladders (gas-filled organs) to keep them afloat. Cartilaginous fish, such as sharks, rays, and ratfish, are mostly marine hunters; they have skeletons made of cartilage and sandpaperlike skin. The primitive jawless fish have suckerlike mouths and include lampreys and hagfish.

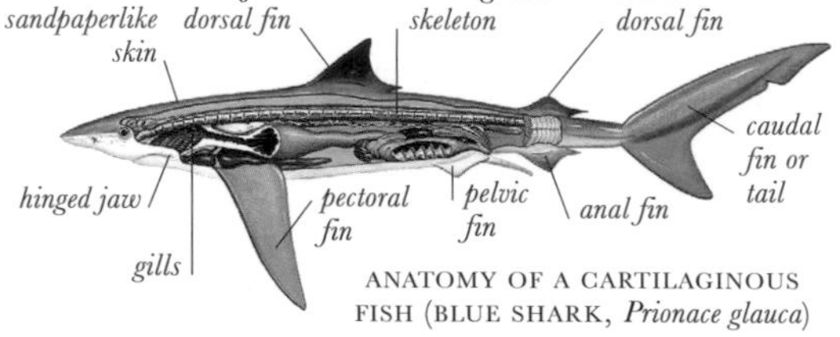

ANATOMY OF A CARTILAGINOUS FISH (BLUE SHARK, *Prionace glauca*)

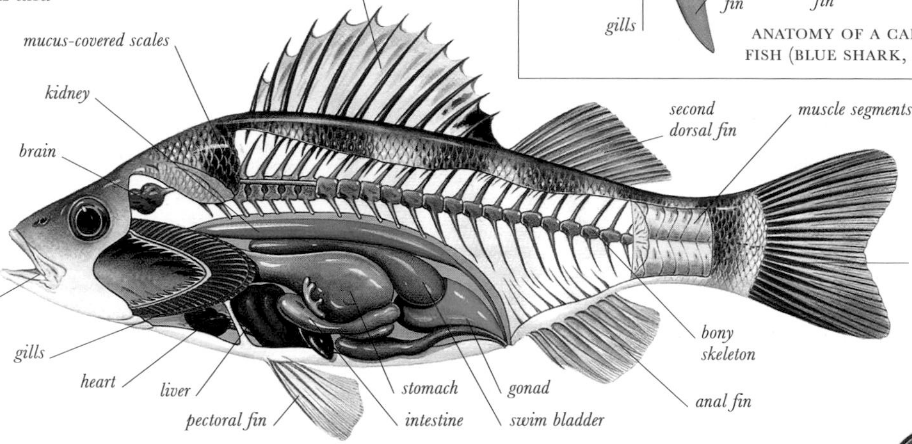

sandpaperlike skin · *first dorsal fin* · *cartilaginous skeleton* · *second dorsal fin* · *caudal fin or tail* · *anal fin* · *pelvic fin* · *pectoral fin* · *gills* · *hinged jaw*

ANATOMY OF A BONY FISH (YELLOW PERCH, *Perca flavescens*)

first dorsal fin · *mucus-covered scales* · *kidney* · *brain* · *second dorsal fin* · *muscle segments* · *caudal fin or tail* · *hinged jaw* · *gills* · *heart* · *liver* · *pectoral fin* · *stomach* · *intestine* · *gonad* · *swim bladder* · *bony skeleton* · *anal fin*

EXAMPLES OF FISH

BONY FISH

MANDARINFISH
(*Synchiropus splendidus*)

TAILBAR LIONFISH
(*Pterois radiata*)

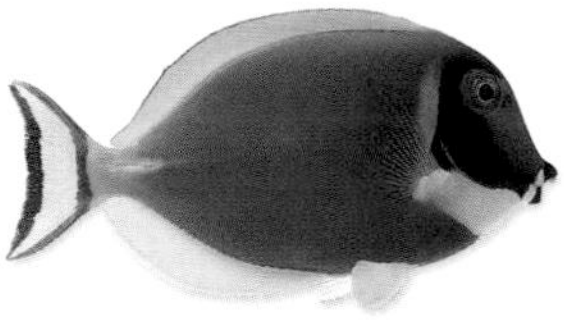

POWDER BLUE SURGEONFISH
(*Acanthurus leucosternon*)

SEAHORSES
(*Hippocampus kuda*)
▷ SEAHORSE

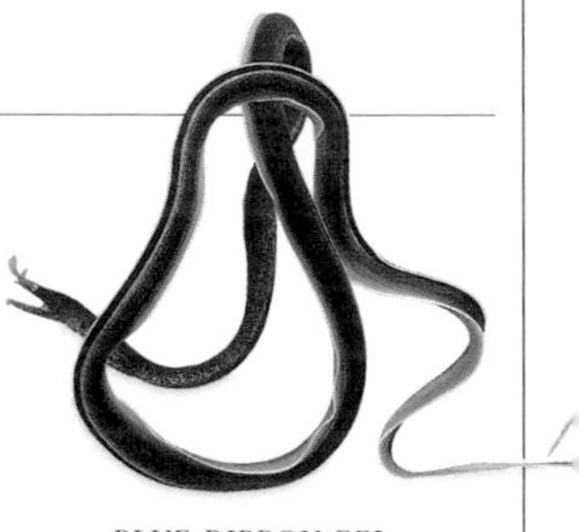

BLUE RIBBON EEL
(*Rhinomuraena amboinensis*)
▷ EEL

CARTILAGINOUS FISH

HORN SHARK
(*Heterodontus francisci*)
▷ SHARK

RATFISH
(*Chimaera monstrosa*)

BLONDE RAY
(*Raja brachyura*)
▷ RAY

JAWLESS FISH

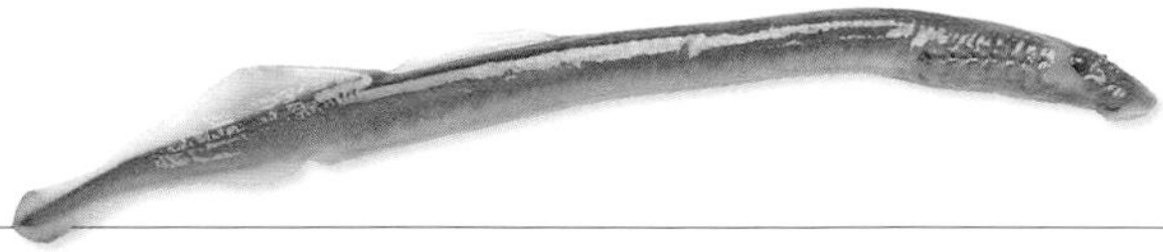

LAMPREY
(*Lampetra fluviatilis*)

---

fire·house /fírhows/ *n.* a fire station.

fire·light /fírlīt/ *n.* light from a fire in a fireplace.

fire·man /fírmən/ *n.* (*pl.* **-men**) a member of a fire department; a person employed to extinguish fires.

fire·place /fírplays/ *n. Archit.* **1** a place for a domestic fire, esp. a grate at the base of a chimney. **2** ▶ a structure surrounding this. **3** the area in front of this.

fire·pow·er /fírpowar/ *n.* **1** the destructive capacity of guns, etc. **2** financial,

mantelpiece or surround · *mantel shelf* · *chimney* · *grate* · *ashpan* · *hearth*

FIREPLACE

intellectual, or emotional strength.

fire·proof /fírproof/ *adj. & v.* ● *adj.* able to resist fire or great heat. ● *v.tr.* make fireproof.

fire screen *n* a protective screen or grid placed in front of a fireplace.

fire·side /fírsīd/ *n.* **1** the area around a fireplace. **2** a person's home or home life.

fire·side chat *n.* an informal talk.

fire storm *n.* **1** a high wind or storm following a very intense fire. **2** a sudden outburst, esp. of criticism, etc.

fire·trap /fírtrap/ *n.* a building without proper provision for escape in case of fire.

fire·wall /fírwawl/ *n.* **1** a wall or partition designed to stop the spread of fire. **2** *Computing* a part of a computer system or network which is designed to block unauthorized access while permitting outward communication.

fire·wa·ter /fírwawtər/ *n. colloq.* strong alcoholic liquor.

fire·weed /fírweed/ *n.* any of several plants that spring up on burned land, esp. willow herb.

fire·wood /fírwŏŏd/ *n.* wood for use as fuel.

fire·work /fírwərk/ *n.* **1** a device containing combustible chemicals that cause explosions or spectacular effects. **2** (in *pl.*) **a** an outburst of passion, esp. anger. **b** a display of wit or brilliance.

fir·ing /fíring/ *n.* **1** the discharging of guns. **2** material for a fire; fuel. **3** the heating process that hardens clay into pottery, etc.

firing line *n.* **1** the front line in a battle. **2** the leading part in an activity, etc.

firing squad *n.* a group detailed to shoot a condemned person.

fir·kin /fə́rkin/ *n.* a small cask for liquids, butter, fish, etc.

firm[1] /fərm/ *adj., adv., & v.* ● *adj.* **1 a** of solid or compact structure. **b** fixed; stable. **c** steady; not shaking. **2 a** resolute; determined. **b** not easily shaken (*firm belief*). **c** steadfast; constant (*a firm friend*). **3 a** (of an offer, etc.) not liable to cancellation after acceptance. **b** (of a decree, law, etc.) established; immutable. **4** *Commerce* (of prices or goods) maintaining their level or value. ● *adv.* firmly (*stand firm; hold firm to*). ● *v.* **1** *tr.* & *intr.* make or become firm, secure, compact, or solid. **2** *tr.* fix (plants) firmly in the soil. □□ **firm·ly** *adv.* **firm·ness** *n.*

firm[2] /fərm/ *n.* **1** a business concern. **2** the partners in such a concern.

fir·ma·ment /fə́rməmənt/ *n. literary* the sky regarded as a vault or arch. □□ **fir·ma·men·tal** /-mént'l/ *adj.*

firm·ware /fə́rmwair/ *n. Computing* a permanent kind of software programmed into a read-only memory.

first /fərst/ *adj., n., & adv.* ● *adj.* **1 a** earliest in time or order. **b** coming next after a specified or implied time (*shall take the first train; the first cuckoo*). **2** foremost in position, rank, or importance (*first mate*). **3** *Mus.* performing the highest or chief of two or more parts for the same instrument or voice. **4** most willing or likely (*should be the first to admit the problem*). **5** basic or evident (*first principles*). ● *n.* **1** (prec. by *the*) the person or thing first mentioned or occurring. **2** the first occurrence of something notable. **3** *Brit.* **a** a place in the first class in an examination. **b** a person having this. **4** the first day of a month. **5** first gear. **6 a** first place in a race. **b** the winner of this. **7** (in *pl.*) goods of the best quality. **8** first base. ● *adv.* **1** before any other person or thing (*first of all; first and foremost; first come first served*). **2** before someone or something else (*must get this done first*). **3** for the first time (*when did you first see her?*). **4** in preference; sooner (*will see him damned first*). □ **at first** at the beginning. **at first hand** directly from the original source. **first and last** taking one thing with another; on the whole. **first off** *colloq.* at first; first of all (*first off, lets make a list*). **first or last** sooner or later. **from the first** from the beginning. **from first to last** throughout. **get to first base** achieve the first step toward an objective. **in the first place** as the first consideration. **of the first water** see WATER.

first aid *n.* help given to an injured person until proper medical treatment is available.

first base *n. Baseball* **1** the base touched first by a base runner. **2 a** the fielder stationed nearest first base. **b** the position nearest first base.

first-born *adj. & n.* ● *adj.* eldest. ● *n.* the eldest child of a person.

first class *n.* **1** a set of persons or things grouped together as the best. **2** the best accommodation in a train, ship, etc. **3** the class of mail given priority in handling. **4** *Brit.* **a** the highest division in an examination list. **b** a place in this.

first-class *adj. & adv.* ● *adj.* **1** belonging to or traveling by the first class. **2** of the best quality; very good. ● *adv.* by the first class (*travels first-class*).

first cous·in see COUSIN.

first day cov·er *n.* an envelope with stamps postmarked on their first day of issue.

first-de·gree *adj. Med.* denoting burns that affect only the surface of the skin, causing reddening.

first gear *n.* the lowest gear in a series.

first·hand /fə́rst-hánd/ *attrib. adj. & adv.* from the original source; direct.

First La·dy *n.* the wife of the US President.

first light *n.* the time when light first appears in the morning.

first·ly /fə́rstlee/ *adv.* (in enumerating topics, arguments, etc.) in the first place; first (cf. FIRST *adv.*).

first mate *n.* (on a merchant ship) the officer second in command to the master.

first name *n.* a personal name other than a surname.

first of·fend·er *n.* a criminal against whom no previous conviction is recorded.

first per·son see PERSON 3.

first-rate *adj. & adv.* ● *adj.* of the highest class; excellent. ● *adv. colloq.* **1** very well (*feeling first-rate*). **2** excellently.

first thing *n. & adv.* ● *n.* even the most elementary fact or principle (*does not know the first thing about it*). ● *adv. colloq.* before anything else; very early in the morning (*shall do it first thing*). □ **first things first** the most important things before any others (*we must do first things first*).

firth /fərth/ *n.* (also **frith** /frith/) **1** a narrow inlet of the sea. **2** an estuary.

fis·cal /fískəl/ *adj. & n.* ● *adj.* of public revenue; of financial matters. ● *n.* a legal official in some countries. □□ **fis·cal·ly** *adv.*

fis·cal year *n.* a year as reckoned for taxing or accounting.

fish[1] /fish/ *n. & v.* ● *n.* (*pl.* same or **fishes**) **1** ◀ a vertebrate cold-blooded animal with gills and fins living wholly in water. **2** any animal living wholly in water, e.g., cuttlefish, shellfish, jellyfish. **3** the flesh of fish as food. **4** *colloq.* a person remarkable in some way (usu. unfavorable) (*an odd fish*). **5** (**the Fish** or **Fishes**) the zodiacal sign or constellation Pisces. ▷ PISCES. ● *v.* **1** *intr.* try to catch fish. **2** *tr.* fish for (a certain kind of fish) or in (a certain stretch of water). **3** *intr.* (foll. by *for*) **a** search for in water or

a concealed place. **b** seek by indirect means (*fishing for compliments*). **4** *tr.* (foll. by *up*, *out*, etc.) retrieve with careful or awkward searching. □ **drink like a fish** drink excessively. **fish out of water** a person in an unsuitable or unwelcome environment or situation. **other fish to fry** other matters to attend to. □□ **fish·like** *adj.*

fish[2] /fish/ *n. & v.* ● *n.* **1** a flat plate of iron, wood, etc., to strengthen a beam or joint. **2** *Naut.* a piece of wood used to strengthen a mast, etc. ● *v.tr.* **1** mend or strengthen (a spar, etc.) with a fish. **2** join (rails) with a fishplate.

fish bowl *n.* a usu. round glass bowl for keeping pet fish in.

fish·er /físhər/ *n.* **1** any animal that catches fish, esp. the marten, *Martes pennanti*, valued for its fur. ▷ MUSTELID. **2** *archaic* a fisherman.

fish·er·man /físhərmən/ *n.* (*pl.* **-men**) **1** a person who catches fish. **2** a fishing boat.

fish·er·y /físhəree/ *n.* (*pl.* **-ies**) **1** a place where fish or other aquatic animals are caught or reared. **2** the occupation or industry of catching or rearing fish or other aquatic animals.

fish-eye lens *n. Photog.* a very wide-angle lens with a curved front.

fish fin·ger *n. Brit.* = FISH STICK.

fish hook /fish-hŏŏk/ *n.* a barbed hook for catching fish.

fish·ing /físhing/ *n.* ▼ the activity of catching fish, esp. for food or as recreation.

fish·ing line *n.* a long thread with a baited hook, sinker, float, etc., used for catching fish. ▷ FISHING

fish·ing rod *n.* a long tapering usu. jointed rod to which a fishing line is attached. ▷ FISHING

fish meal *n.* ground dried fish used as fertilizer or animal feed.

fish·mon·ger /físhmunggər, -mong-/ *n.* esp. *Brit.* a dealer in fish.

fish·net /físhnet/ *n.* (often *attrib.*) an open-meshed fabric (*fishnet stockings*).

F

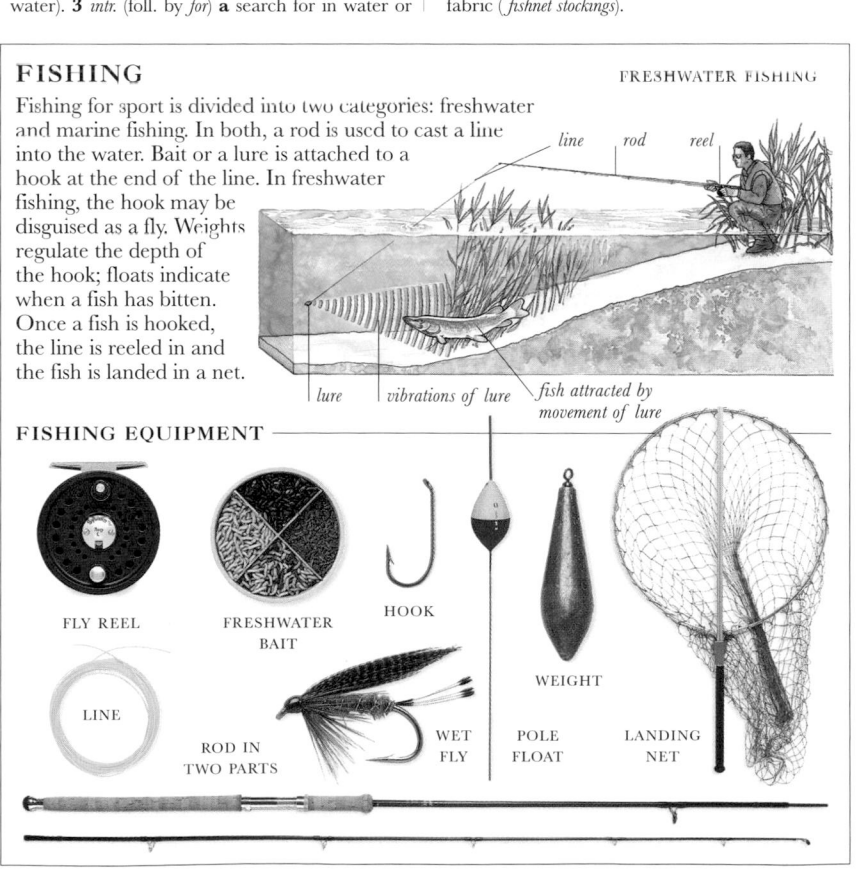

FISHING

Fishing for sport is divided into two categories: freshwater and marine fishing. In both, a rod is used to cast a line into the water. Bait or a lure is attached to a hook at the end of the line. In freshwater fishing, the hook may be disguised as a fly. Weights regulate the depth of the hook; floats indicate when a fish has bitten. Once a fish is hooked, the line is reeled in and the fish is landed in a net.

FRESHWATER FISHING

line   rod   reel

lure   vibrations of lure   fish attracted by movement of lure

FISHING EQUIPMENT

FLY REEL

FRESHWATER BAIT

HOOK

LINE

ROD IN TWO PARTS

WET FLY

WEIGHT

POLE FLOAT

LANDING NET

F

fish·plate /físhplayt/ n. **a** a flat piece of iron, etc., connecting railroad rails. **b** a flat piece of metal with ends like a fish's tail, used to position masonry.

fish·pond /físhpond/ n. a pond or pool in which fish are kept.

fish stick n. a small oblong piece of fish in batter or breadcrumbs.

fish sto·ry n. colloq. an exaggerated account.

fish·tail /físhtayl/ n. & v. • n. a device, etc., shaped like a fish's tail. • v.intr. move the tail of a vehicle from side to side.

fish·wife /físhwíf/ n. (pl. **-wives**) **1** an ill-mannered or noisy woman. **2** a woman who sells fish.

fish·y /físhee/ adj. (**fishier**, **fishiest**) **1 a** smelling or tasting like fish. **b** like that of a fish. **c** (of an eye) dull; vacant-looking. **d** consisting of fish (a fishy repast). **2** sl. of dubious character; questionable; suspect. □□ **fish·i·ness** n.

fis·sile /físəl, -īl/ adj. **1** capable of undergoing nuclear fission. **2** tending to split.

fis·sion /físhən/ n. & v. • n. **1** Physics the spontaneous or impact-induced splitting of a heavy atomic nucleus, accompanied by a release of energy. **2** Biol. the division of a cell into new cells as a mode of reproduction. • v.intr. & tr. undergo or cause to undergo fission. □□ **fis·sion·a·ble** adj.

fis·sure /físhər/ n. & v. • n. **1** an opening, usu. long and narrow, made esp. by cracking, splitting, or separation of parts. **2** Bot. & Anat. a narrow opening in an organ, etc., esp. a depression between convolutions of the brain. **3** a cleavage. • v.tr. & intr. split or crack.

fist /fist/ n. & v. • n. **1** a tightly closed hand. **2** sl. handwriting (writes a good fist; I know his fist). **3** sl. a hand (give us your fist). • v.tr. close into a fist. □ **make a good** (or **poor**, etc.) **fist** (foll. by at, of) colloq. make a good (or poor, etc.) attempt at. □□ **fist·ed** adj. (also in comb.). **fist·ful** n. (pl. **-fuls**).

fist·fight /fístfīt/ n. a fight with bare fists.

fist·i·cuffs /fístikufs/ n.pl. fighting with the fists.

fis·tu·la /físchələ/ n. (pl. **fistulas** or **fistulae** /-lee/) **1** an abnormal or surgically made passage between a hollow organ and the body surface or between two hollow organs. **2** a natural pipe or spout in whales, insects, etc. □□ **fis·tu·lar** adj. **fis·tu·lous** adj.

fit[1] /fit/ adj., v., n., & adv. • adj. (**fitter**, **fittest**) **1 a** (usu. foll. by for, or to + infin.) well suited. **b** (foll. by to + infin.) qualified; competent; worthy. **c** (foll. by for, or to + infin.) in a suitable condition; ready. **d** (foll. by for) good enough (a dinner fit for a king). **e** (foll. by to + infin.) sufficiently exhausted, troubled, or angry (fit to drop). **2** in good health or athletic condition. **3** proper; becoming; right (it is fit that). • v. (**fitted**, **fitting**) **1 a** tr. (also absol.) be of the right shape and size for (the key doesn't fit the lock; these shoes don't fit). **b** tr. make, fix, or insert (a thing) so that it is of the right size or shape (fitted shelves in the alcoves). **c** intr. (often foll. by in, into) (of a component) be correctly positioned (that piece fits here). **d** tr. find room for (can't fit another person on the bench). **2** tr. (foll. by for, or to + infin.) **a** make suitable; adapt. **b** make competent (fitted him to be a priest). **3** tr. (usu. foll. by with) supply; furnish (fitted the boat with a new rudder). **4** tr. fix in place (fit a lock on the door). **5** tr. try on (a garment). **6** tr. befit; become (the punishment fits the crime). • n. the way in which a garment, component, etc., fits (a bad fit; a tight fit). • adv. (foll. by to + infin.) colloq. in a suitable manner; appropriately (was laughing fit to bust). □ **fit the bill** = fill the bill. **fit in 1** (often foll. by with) be compatible or accommodating (tried to fit in with their plans). **2** find space or time for (the dentist fitted me in at the last minute). **fit out** (or **up**) (often foll. by with) equip. **see** (or **think**) **fit** (often foll. by to + infin.) decide or choose a specified course of action). □□ **fit·ly** adv. **fit·ness** n.

fit[2] /fit/ n. **1** a sudden seizure of epilepsy, hysteria, apoplexy, fainting, or paralysis, with unconsciousness or convulsions. **2** a sudden brief attack of an illness or of symptoms (fit of coughing). **3** a sudden short bout or burst (fit of energy; fit of giggles). **4** colloq.

an attack of strong feeling (fit of rage). **5** a capricious impulse; a mood (when the fit was on him). □ **by** (or **in**) **fits and starts** spasmodically. **give a person a fit** colloq. surprise or outrage him or her. **have a fit** colloq. be greatly surprised or outraged. **in fits** laughing uncontrollably.

fit·ful /fítfŏŏl/ adj. spasmodic or intermittent. □□ **fit·ful·ly** adv. **fit·ful·ness** n.

fit·ted /fítid/ adj. **1** made or shaped to fill a space or cover something closely or exactly (a fitted sheet). **2** esp. Brit. built-in (fitted cupboards).

fit·ter /fítər/ n. **1** a person who supervises the cutting, fitting, altering, etc., of garments. **2** a mechanic who fits together and adjusts machinery.

fit·ting /fíting/ n. & adj. • n. **1** the process or an instance of having a garment, etc., fitted (needed several fittings). **2 a** (in pl.) the fixtures and furnishings of a building. **b** a piece of apparatus or a detachable part of a machine, fixture, etc. • adj. proper; becoming; right. □□ **fit·ting·ly** adv. **fit·ting·ness** n.

five /fīv/ n. & adj. • n. **1** one more than four or one half of ten; the sum of three units and two units. **2** a symbol for this (5, v, V). **3** a size, etc., denoted by five. **4** a set or team of five individuals. **5** five o'clock (is it five yet?). **6** a card with five pips. **7** a five-dollar bill. • adj. that amount to five.

five-and-dime n. N. Amer. a shop selling a wide variety of inexpensive goods.

five o'clock shad·ow n. beard growth visible on a man's face in the latter part of the day.

fiv·er /fívər/ n. colloq. **1** a five-dollar bill. **2** Brit. a five-pound note.

five-star adj. of the highest class.

fix /fiks/ v. & n. • v. **1** tr. make firm or stable; fasten; secure (fixed a picture to the wall). **2** tr. decide; settle; specify (a price, date, etc.). **3** tr. mend; repair. **4** tr. implant in the mind (couldn't get the rules fixed in his head). **5** tr. & (foll. by on, upon) direct steadily; set (one's eyes, gaze, attention, or affection). **b** attract and hold (a person's attention, eyes, etc.). **c** (foll. by with) single out with one's eyes, etc. **6** tr. place definitely; establish. **7** tr. determine the exact nature, position, etc., of; refer (a thing or person) to a definite place or time; identify, locate. **8 a** tr. make (eyes, features, etc.) rigid. **b** intr. (of eyes, features, etc.) become rigid. **9** tr. colloq. prepare (food or drink) (fixed me a drink). **10 a** tr. congeal. **b** intr. become congealed. **11** tr. colloq. punish; kill; silence; deal with (a person). **12** tr. colloq. **a** secure the support of (a person) fraudulently, esp. by bribery. **b** arrange the result of (a race, match, etc.) fraudulently. **13** sl. **a** tr. inject (a person, esp. oneself) with a narcotic. **b** intr. take an injection of a narcotic. **14** tr. make (a color, photographic image, or microscope specimen) fast or permanent. **15** tr. (of a plant or microorganism) assimilate (nitrogen or carbon dioxide). **16** tr. castrate or spay (an animal). **17** tr. arrest changes or development in (a language or literature). **18** tr. determine the incidence of (liability, etc.). **19** (as **fixed** adj.) **a** permanently placed; stationary. **b** without moving; rigid; (of a gaze, etc.) steady or intent. **c** definite. **d** sl. dishonest; fraudulent. • n. **1** colloq. a dilemma or predicament. **2 a** the act of finding one's position by bearings or astronomical observations. **b** a position found in this way. **3** sl. a dose of a narcotic drug to which one is addicted. **4** sl. bribery. □ **be fixed** (usu. foll. by for) be disposed or affected (regarding) (how are you fixed for Friday?). **fix on** (or **upon**) choose; decide on. **fix up 1** arrange; organize; prepare. **2** accommodate. **3** (often foll. by with) provide (a person) with (fixed me up with a job). **4** restore; refurbish (fixed up the old house). □□ **fix·a·ble** adj. **fix·ed·ly** /fíksidlee/ adv. **fix·ed·ness** /fíksidnis/ n.

fix·ate /fíksayt/ v.tr. **1** direct one's gaze on. **2** Psychol. **a** (usu. in passive; often foll. by on, upon) cause (a person) to acquire an abnormal attachment to persons or things (was fixated on his son). **b** arrest (part

of the libido) at an immature stage, causing such attachment.

fix·a·tion /fiksáyshən/ n. **1** the act or an instance of being fixated. **2** an obsession; concentration on a single idea. **3** fixing or being fixed. **4** coagulation. **5** the process of assimilating a gas to form a solid compound.

fix·a·tive /fíksətiv/ adj. & n. • adj. tending to fix or secure. • n. a substance used to fix colors, hair, microscope specimens, etc.

fixed-do attrib.adj. Mus. applied to a system of sight-singing in which C is called 'do,' D is called 're,' etc., irrespective of the key in which they occur.

fixed in·come n. income deriving from a pension, investment at fixed interest, etc.

fixed star n. Astron. a star so far from the Earth as to appear motionless.

fix·er /fíksər/ n. **1** a person or thing that fixes. **2** Photog. a substance used for fixing a photographic image, etc. **3** colloq. a person who makes arrangements, esp. of an illicit kind.

fix·ings /fíksingz/ n.pl. **1** apparatus or equipment. **2** the trimmings for a dish. **3** the trimmings of a dress, etc.

fix·i·ty /fíksitee/ n. **1** a fixed state. **2** stability; permanence.

fix·ture /fíkschər/ n. **1 a** something fixed in position. **b** an attached appliance, apparatus, etc. (electrical fixture). **c** (usu. predic.) colloq. a person or thing confined to or established in one place (he seems to be a fixture). **2** (in pl.) Law articles attached to a house or land and regarded as legally part of it.

fizz /fiz/ v. & n. • v.intr. **1** make a hissing or spluttering sound. **2** (of a drink) effervesce. • n. effervescence.

fiz·zle /fízəl/ v. & n. • v.intr. make a feeble hissing sound. • n. such a sound. □ **fizzle out** end feebly (the party fizzled out at 10 o'clock).

fizz·y /fízee/ adj. (**fizzier**, **fizziest**) effervescent; carbonated. □□ **fizz·i·ly** adv. **fizz·i·ness** n.

fjord /fyawrd/ n. (also **fiord**) a long narrow inlet of sea between high cliffs, as in Norway. ▷ COASTLINE

FL abbr. Florida (in official postal use).

fl. abbr. **1** floor. **2** floruit. **3** fluid.

Fla. abbr. Florida.

flab /flab/ n. colloq. fat; flabbiness.

flab·ber·gast /flábərgast/ v.tr. (esp. as **flabbergasted** adj.) colloq. overwhelm with astonishment; dumbfound.

flab·by /flábee/ adj. (**flabbier**, **flabbiest**) **1** (of flesh, etc.) hanging down; limp; flaccid. **2** (of language or character) feeble. □□ **flab·bi·ly** adv. **flab·bi·ness** n.

flac·cid /flásid, fláksid/ adj. **1 a** (of flesh, etc.) hanging loose or wrinkled; limp; flabby. **b** (of plant tissue) soft; less rigid. **2** relaxed; drooping. **3** lacking vigor; feeble. □□ **flac·cid·i·ty** /-síditee/ n. **flac·cid·ly** adv.

flack[1] /flak/ n. & v. sl. • n. a publicity agent. • v.intr. act as a publicity agent.

flack[2] var. of FLAK.

flag[1] /flag/ n. & v. • n. **1** ▶ a piece of cloth, usu. oblong or square, attachable by one edge to a pole or rope and used as a country's emblem or as a standard, signal, etc. **2** a small toy, device, etc., resembling a flag. **3** Naut. a flag carried by a flagship as an emblem of an admiral's rank afloat. • v. (**flagged**, **flagging**) **1** intr. **a** grow tired; lose vigor; lag (his energy flagged after the first lap). **b** hang down; droop. **2** tr. **a** place a flag on or over. **b** mark out with or as if with a flag or flags (they flagged the site of the accident). **3** tr. (often foll. by that) **a** inform (a person) by flag signals. **b** communicate (information) by flagging. □ **flag down** signal to (a vehicle or driver) to stop. **keep the flag flying** continue the fight. **put the flag out** celebrate victory, success, etc. **show the flag 1** make an official visit to a foreign port, etc. **2** ensure that notice is taken of one's country, oneself, etc.; make a patriotic display. □□ **flag·ger** n.

FLAG

For centuries flags have been used as patriotic rallying points, emblems, or signals. All countries have their own flags, as do many organizations. Flags are usually made from strongly colored fabric and are usually rectangular or square. A flag is divided into four quarters, called cantons: those near the flagstaff are the hoist cantons; those farthest away are the fly cantons. Ships use flags to communicate at sea via the international code of signals (shown below). Flags that represent a letter of the alphabet also convey a specific message.

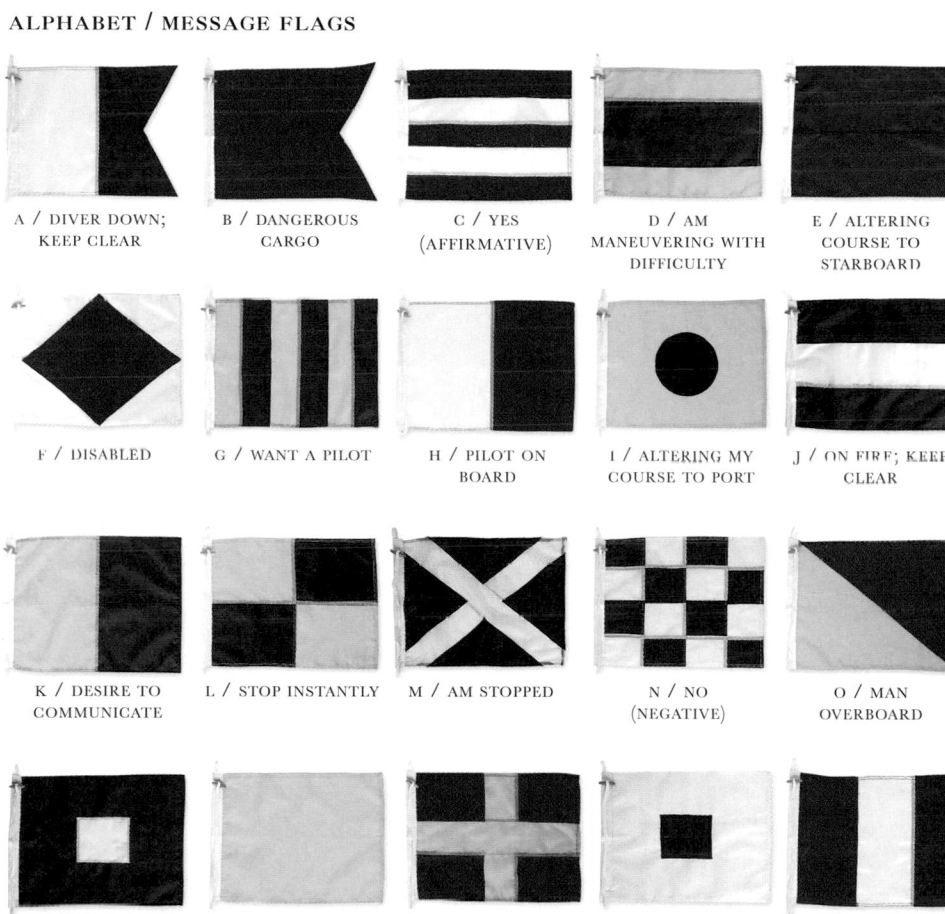

truck
becket
toggle
upper hoist canton
upper fly canton
chief mullet
tack line
bunting cloth
mullet (five-pointed star)
roundel
base mullet
lower hoist canton
lower fly canton
canvas sleeve
flagstaff
halyard

PARTS OF A FLAG (NATIONAL FLAG OF GRENADA)

INTERNATIONAL CODE OF SIGNALS

ALPHABET / MESSAGE FLAGS

A / DIVER DOWN; KEEP CLEAR

B / DANGEROUS CARGO

C / YES (AFFIRMATIVE)

D / AM MANEUVERING WITH DIFFICULTY

E / ALTERING COURSE TO STARBOARD

F / DISABLED

G / WANT A PILOT

H / PILOT ON BOARD

I / ALTERING MY COURSE TO PORT

J / ON FIRE; KEEP CLEAR

K / DESIRE TO COMMUNICATE

L / STOP INSTANTLY

M / AM STOPPED

N / NO (NEGATIVE)

O / MAN OVERBOARD

P / ABOUT TO SAIL

Q / REQUEST PRATIQUE

R / NO MEANING

S / ENGINES GOING ASTERN

T / KEEP CLEAR OF ME

U / YOU ARE RUNNING INTO DANGER

V / REQUIRE ASSISTANCE

W / REQUIRE MEDICAL ASSISTANCE

X / STOP YOUR INTENTIONS

Y / AM DRAGGING ANCHOR

Z / REQUIRE A TUG

NUMBER FLAGS

1
2
3
4
5
6
7
8
9
0

F

FLAG:
YELLOW FLAG
(*Iris pseudacorus*)

flag² /flag/ *n. & v.* ● *n.* (also **flag·stone**) **1** a flat usu. rectangular stone slab used for paving. **2** (in *pl.*) a pavement made of these. ● *v.tr.* (**flagged, flagging**) pave with flags.

flag³ /flag/ *n.* **1** ◄ any plant with a bladed leaf (esp. several of the genus *Iris*) growing on moist ground. **2** the long slender leaf of such a plant.

Flag Day *n.* June 14, the anniversary of the adoption of the Stars and Stripes in 1777.

flag·el·lant /flájələnt, fləjélənt/ *n. & adj.* ● *n.* **1** a person who scourges himself or herself or others as a religious discipline. **2** a person who engages in flogging as a sexual stimulus. ● *adj.* of or concerning flagellation.

flag·el·late¹ /flájəlayt/ *v.tr.* scourge; flog (cf. FLAGELLANT). □□ **flag·el·la·tion** /-láyshən/ *n.*

flag·el·late² /flájilit, -layt/ *adj. & n.* ● *adj.* having flagella (see FLAGELLUM). ● *n.* a protozoan having one or more flagella.

fla·gel·lum /fləjéləm/ *n.* (*pl.* **flagella** /-lə/) **1** *Biol.* a long lashlike appendage found principally on microscopic organisms. ▷ ALGA, BACTERIUM, SPERMATOZOON. **2** *Bot.* a runner; a creeping shoot. □□ **fla·gel·lar** /-lər/ *adj.*

flag·eo·let¹ /fláiélét, -láy/ *n.* **1** ▼ a small flute blown at the end, like a recorder but with two thumb holes. **2** an organ stop having a similar sound.

mouthpiece   *finger hole*

blowhole

FLAGEOLET: CARVED NATIVE AMERICAN FLAGEOLET

flag·eo·let² /fláiəláy, -lét/ *n.* a kind of French kidney bean.

fla·gi·tious /fləjíshəs/ *adj.* deeply criminal; utterly villainous. □□ **fla·gi·tious·ly** *adv.* **fla·gi·tious·ness** *n.*

flag·man /flágmən/ *n.* (*pl.* **-men**) a person who signals with or as with a flag, e.g., in highway construction.

flag·on /flágən/ *n.* **1** a large bottle in which wine, cider, etc., are sold, usu. holding 1.13 liters. **2** a large vessel usu. with a handle, spout, and lid, to hold wine, etc.

flag·pole /flágpōl/ *n.* a pole on which a flag may be hoisted. ▷ FLAG

fla·grant /fláygrənt/ *adj.* (of an offense or an offender) glaring; notorious; scandalous. □□ **fla·gran·cy** /-grənsee/ *n.* **fla·grant·ly** *adv.*

flag·ship /flágship/ *n.* **1** a ship having an admiral on board. **2** something that is held to be the best or most important of its kind; a leader.

flag·staff /flágstaf/ *n.* = FLAGPOLE.

flag·stone /flágstōn/ *n.* = FLAG².

flag·wav·er *n.* a populist agitator; a patriotic chauvinist. □□ **flag·wav·ing** *n.*

flail /flayl/ *n. & v.* ● *n.* a threshing tool consisting of a wooden staff with a short heavy stick swinging from it. ● *v.* **1** *tr.* beat or strike with or as if with a flail. **2** *intr.* wave or swing wildly.

flair /flair/ *n.* **1** an instinct for selecting or performing what is excellent, useful, etc. **2** talent or ability, esp. artistic or stylistic.

flak /flak/ *n.* (also **flack**) **1** antiaircraft fire. **2** adverse criticism; abuse.

flake /flayk/ *n. & v.* ● *n.* **1 a** a small thin light piece of snow. **b** a similar piece of another material. **2 a** thin broad piece of material peeled or split off. **3** *Archaeol.* a piece of hard stone chipped off and used as a tool. **4** a natural division of the flesh of some fish. **5** the dogfish or other shark as food. **6** *sl.* a crazy or eccentric person. ● *v.tr. & intr.* (often foll.

by *away, off*) **1** take off or come away in flakes. **2** sprinkle with or fall in snowlike flakes. □ **flake out** *colloq.* **1** fall asleep or drop from exhaustion; faint. **2** act strangely.

flak jack·et *n.* ► a protective jacket reinforced with bulletproof material, worn by soldiers, etc.

flak·y /fláykee/ *adj.* (**flakier, flakiest**) **1** of or like flakes; separating easily into flakes. **2** *sl.* crazy; eccentric. □□ **flak·i·ly** *adv.* **flak·i·ness** *n.*

flam·bé /flaambáy/ *adj.* (of food) covered with alcohol and set alight briefly.

flam·boy·ant /flambóyənt/ *adj.* **1** ostentatious; showy. **2** floridly decorated. **3** gorgeously colored. □□ **flam·boy·ance** /-əns/ *n.* **flam·boy·ant·ly** *adv.*

flame /flaym/ *n. & v.* ● *n.* **1 a** ignited gas (*the fire burned with a steady flame*). **b** one portion of this (*the flame flickered and died*). **c** (usu. in *pl.*) visible combustion (*burst into flames*). **2 a** a bright light; brilliant coloring. **b** a brilliant orange-red color. **3 a** a strong passion, esp. love (*fan the flame*). **b** *colloq.* a boyfriend or girlfriend. ● *v.* **1** *intr. & tr.* (often foll. by *away, forth, out, up*) emit or cause to emit flames. **2** *intr.* (often foll. by *out, up*) **a** (of passion) break out. **b** (of a person) become angry. **3** *intr.* shine or glow like flame (*leaves flamed in the autumn sun*). **4** *tr.* send (a signal) by means of flame. **5** *tr.* subject to the action of flame. □ **flame out** (of a jet engine) lose power through imperfect combustion in the combustion chamber. **go up in flames** be consumed by fire. □□ **flame·less** *adj.* **flame·like** *adj.* **flam·y** *adj.*

FLAK JACKET

fla·men /fláymən/ *n. Rom.Hist.* a priest serving a particular deity.

fla·men·co /fləméngkō/ *n.* (*pl.* **-os**) **1** a style of music played (esp. on the guitar) and sung by Spanish gypsies. **2** a dance performed to this music.

flame·proof /fláymprōof/ *adj.* treated so as to be nonflammable.

flame·throw·er /fláymthrōər/ *n.* a weapon for throwing a spray of flame.

flam·ing /fláyming/ *adj.* **1** emitting flames. **2** very hot (*flaming day*). **3** *colloq.* **a** passionate (*a flaming argument*). **b** expressing annoyance, or as an intensifier (*that flaming idiot*). **4** bright colored (*flaming red hair*).

fla·min·go /fləmínggō/ *n.* (*pl.* **-os** or **-oes**) ► any tall web-footed wading bird of the family Phoenicopteridae, with pink, scarlet, and black plumage.

flam·ma·ble /flámmabəl/ *adj.* easily set on fire; inflammable. ¶ Often used because *inflammable* can be mistaken for a negative (the true negative being *nonflammable*). □□ **flam·ma·bil·i·ty** *n.*

flan /flan/ *n.* **1 a** an open pastry case with a savory or sweet filling. **b** a custard topped with caramel glaze. **2** a disk of metal from which a coin, etc., is made.

flange /flanj/ *n. & v. Engin.* ● *n.* a projecting flat rim, collar, or rib, used for strengthening or attachment. ● *v.tr.* provide with a flange.

flank /flangk/ *n. & v.* ● *n.* **1 a** the side of the body between the ribs and the hip. **b** the side of an animal carved as meat (*flank of beef*). **2** the side of a mountain, building, etc. **3** the right or left side of an army or other body of persons. ● *v.tr.* **1** (often in *passive*) be situated at both sides of (*a road flanked by mountains*). **2** *Mil.* **a** guard or strengthen on the flank. **b** menace the flank of.

flank·er /flángkər/ *n.* **1** *Mil.* a fortification guarding or menacing the flank. **2** anything that flanks another thing. **3 a** *Football* an offensive back posi-

FLAMINGO: LESSER FLAMINGO (*Phoeniconaias minor*)

tioned outside the tackle and behind the line of scrimmage. **b** *Rugby* a flank forward.

flan·nel /flánəl/ *n.* **1** a kind of woven wool fabric, usu. with a slight nap. **2** (in *pl.*) flannel garments, esp. underwear or trousers.

flan·nel·board /flánəlbawrd/ *n.* a piece of flannel used as a base for paper or cloth cutouts, used as a toy or a teaching aid.

flan·nel·ette /flánəlét/ *n.* a napped cotton fabric similar to flannel.

flap /flap/ *v. & n.* ● *v.* (**flapped, flapping**) **1 a** *tr.* move (wings, the arms, etc.) up and down when flying, or as if flying. **b** *intr.* (of wings, the arms, etc.) move up and down. **2** *intr. colloq.* be agitated or panicky. **3** *intr.* (esp. of curtains, loose cloth, etc.) swing or sway about; flutter. **4** *tr.* (usu. foll. by *away, off*) strike (flies, etc.) with something broad; drive. **5** *intr. colloq.* (of ears) listen intently. ● *n.* **1** a piece of cloth, wood, paper, etc., hinged or attached by one side only and often used to cover a gap, e.g., the folded part of an envelope, a table leaf. **2** one up-and-down motion of a wing, an arm, etc. **3** *colloq.* a state of agitation; panic (*don't get into a flap*). **4** a hinged or sliding section of a wing used to control lift and drag. **5** a light blow with something broad. **6** an open mushroom top. □□ **flap·py** *adj.*

flap·doo·dle /flápdōōd'l/ *n. colloq.* nonsense.

flap·jack /flápjak/ *n.* a pancake.

flap·per /flápər/ *n.* **1** a person or thing that flaps. **2** an instrument that is flapped to kill flies, scare birds, etc. **3** a person who panics easily. **4** *sl.* (in the 1920s) a young unconventional or lively woman.

flare /flair/ *v. & n.* ● *v.* **1** *intr. & tr.* widen or cause to widen, esp. toward the bottom (*flared trousers*). **2** *intr. & tr.* burn or cause to burn suddenly with a bright unsteady flame. **3** *intr.* burst into anger; burst forth. ● *n.* **1 a** a dazzling irregular flame or light. **b** a sudden outburst of flame. **2 a** a signal light used at sea. **b** ► a bright light used as a signal. **c** a flame dropped from an aircraft to illuminate a target, etc. **3** *Astron.* a sudden burst of radiation from a star. ▷ SUN. **4 a** a gradual widening, esp. of a skirt or trousers. **b** (in *pl.*) wide-bottomed trousers. **5** *Photog.* unnecessary illumination on a lens caused by internal reflection, etc. □ **flare up 1** burst into a sudden blaze. **2** become suddenly angry or active.

flare-up *n.* an outburst of flame, anger, activity, etc.

flare

firing pin

case containing firing mechanism

FLARE WITH FIRING MECHANISM

flash /flash/ *v. & n.* ● *v.* **1** *intr. & tr.* emit or reflect or cause to emit or reflect light briefly, suddenly, or intermittently; gleam or cause to gleam. **2** *intr.* break suddenly into flame; give out flame or sparks. **3** *tr.* send or reflect like a sudden flame or blaze (*his eyes flashed fire*). **4** *intr.* **a** burst suddenly into view or perception (*the explanation flashed upon me*). **b** move swiftly (*the train flashed through the station*). **5** *tr.* **a** send (news, etc.) by radio, telegraph, etc. (*flashed a message to her*). **b** signal to (a person) by shining lights or headlights briefly. **6** *tr. colloq.* show ostentatiously (*flashed her engagement ring*). **7** *intr.* (of water) rush along; rise and flow. **8** *intr. sl.* indecently expose oneself. ● *n.* **1** a sudden bright light or flame, e.g., of lightning. **2** a very brief time; an instant (*all over in a flash*). **3 a** a brief, sudden burst of feeling (*a flash of hope*). **b** a sudden display (of wit, understanding, etc.). **4** = NEWS FLASH.

5 *Photog.* = FLASHLIGHT 2. **6 a** a rush of water, esp. down a weir to take a boat over shallows. **b** a contrivance for producing this. **7** vulgar display; ostentation. **8** a bright patch of color. **9** *Cinematog.* the momentary exposure of a scene. **10** excess plastic or metal oozing from a mold during molding. □ **flash in the pan** a promising start followed by failure (from the priming of old guns). **flash over** *Electr.* make an electric circuit by sparking across a gap.

flash·back /fláshbak/ *n.* a scene in a movie, novel, etc., set in a time earlier than the main action.

flash·board /fláshbawrd/ *n.* a board used for increasing the depth of water behind a dam.

flash bulb *n.* a bulb for a photographic flashlight.

flash burn *n.* a burn caused by sudden intense radiation, esp. from a nuclear explosion.

flash card *n.* a card containing a small amount of information, held up for pupils to see, as an aid to learning.

flash·cube /fláshkyoob/ *n. Photog.* a set of four flash bulbs arranged as a cube and operated in turn.

flash·er /fláshər/ *n.* **1** *sl.* a person, esp. a man, who indecently exposes himself. **2 a** an automatic device for switching lights rapidly on and off. **b** a sign or signal using this. **3** a person or thing that flashes.

flash flood *n.* a sudden local flood due to heavy rain, etc.

flash·gun /fláshgun/ *n. Photog.* ◄ a device used to operate a photographic flashlight.

flash·ing /fláshing/ *n.* a usu. metallic strip used to prevent water penetration at the junction of a roof with a wall, chimney, etc.

flash·light /fláshlīt/ *n.* **1** a battery-operated portable light. **2** a light giving an intense flash, used for photographing by night, indoors, etc. **3** a flashing light used for signals and in lighthouses.

flash·o·ver /fláshōvər/ *n. Electr.* an instance of flashing over.

flash point *n.* **1** the temperature at which vapor from oil, etc., will ignite in air. **2** the point at which anger, indignation, etc., becomes uncontrollable.

flash·y /fláshee/ *adj.* (**flashier, flashiest**) showy; gaudy; cheaply attractive. □□ **flash·i·ly** *adv.* **flash·i·ness** *n.*

flask /flask/ *n.* ► **1** a narrow-necked bulbous bottle for wine, etc., or as used in chemistry. **2** a small flat bottle for brandy, etc.

flat[1] /flat/ *adj., adv., n., & v.* ● *adj.* (**flatter, flattest**) **a** horizontally level (*a flat roof*). **b** even; smooth; unbroken; without projection or indentation (*a flat stomach*). **c** with a level surface and little depth; shallow (*a flat cap; a flat heel*). **2** unqualified; downright (*a flat refusal*). **3 a** dull; lifeless; monotonous (*spoke in a flat tone*). **b** dejected. **4** (of a carbonated drink) having lost its effervescence; stale. **5** *Mus.* **a** below true or normal pitch (*the violins are flat*). **b** (of a key) having a flat or flats in the signature. **c** (as B, E, etc., **flat**) a half step lower than B, E, etc. ▷ NOTATION. **6** *Photog.* lacking contrast. **7 a** (of paint, etc.) not glossy; matte. **b** (of a tint) uniform. **8** (of a tire) punctured; deflated. **9** (of a market, prices, etc.) inactive; sluggish. **10** of or relating to flat racing. ● *adv.* **1** lying at full length; spread out (*lay flat on the floor; flat against the wall*). **2** *colloq.* **a** completely; absolutely (*flat broke*). **b** exactly (*in five*

minutes flat). **3** *Mus.* below the true or normal pitch (*always sings flat*). ● *n.* **1** the flat part of anything (*the flat of the hand*). **2** level ground, esp. a plain or swamp. **3** *Mus.* **a** a note lowered a half step below natural pitch. **b** the sign (♭) indicating this. **4** (as **the flat**) *Brit.* **a** flat racing. **b** the flat racing season. **5** *Theatr.* a flat section of scenery mounted on a frame. **6** *colloq.* a flat tire. **7** a shallow planter box for starting seedlings. ● *v.tr.* (**flatted, flatting**) **1** make flat; flatten (esp. in technical use). **2** *Mus.* make (a note) flat. □ **fall flat** fail to live up to expectations; not win applause. **flat out 1** at top speed. **2** without hesitation or delay. **3** using all one's strength, energy, or resources. **that's flat** *colloq.* let there be no doubt about it. □□ **flat·ly** *adv.* **flat·ness** *n.* **flat·tish** *adj.*

flat[2] /flat/ *n.* esp. *Brit.* = APARTMENT 1. □□ **flat·let** *n.*

flat·boat /flátbōt/ *n.* (or **flat-bot·tomed boat**) a boat with a flat bottom for transport in shallow water.

flat·car /flátkaar/ *n.* a railroad car without raised sides or ends.

flat·fish /flátfish/ *n.* (*pl.* usu. same) ▼ any marine fish of various families having an asymmetric appearance with both eyes on one side of a flattened body, including sole, turbot, plaice, etc.

FLATFISH:
PACIFIC HALIBUT
(*Hippoglossus stenolepis*)

flat·foot /flátfoot/ *n.* **1** (*pl.* **flat feet**) a foot with a less than normal arch. **2** (*pl.* **-foots** or **-feet**) *sl.* a police officer.

flat·foot·ed /flátfootid/ *adj.* **1** having flat feet. **2** *colloq.* downright; positive. **3** *colloq.* unprepared; off guard (*was caught flat-footed*). □□ **flat·foot·ed·ly** *adv.* **flat·foot·ed·ness** *n.*

flat·i·ron /flátīərn/ *n.* an iron heated externally and used for pressing clothes, etc.

flat·line /flátlīn/ *v.intr. colloq.* die.

flat rate *n.* a rate that is the same in all cases.

flat·ten /flát'n/ *v.* **1** *tr. & intr.* make or become flat. **2** *tr. colloq.* **a** humiliate. **b** knock down. □ **flatten out** bring an aircraft parallel to the ground. □□ **flat·ten·er** *n.*

flat·ter /flátər/ *v.tr.* **1** compliment unduly, esp. for gain or advantage. **2** usu. *refl.; usu.* foll. by *that* + clause) congratulate or delude (oneself, etc.) (*I flatter myself that I can sing*). **3 a** (of a color, a style, etc.) make (a person) appear to the best advantage. **b** (esp. of a portrait, a painter, etc.) represent too favorably. **4** make (a person) feel honored. **5** inspire (a person) with hope, esp. unduly (*was flattered into thinking himself invulnerable*). **6** please or gratify (the ear, the palate, etc.). □□ **flat·ter·er** *n.* **flat·ter·ing** *adj.* **flat·ter·ing·ly** *adv.*

flat·ter·y /flátəree/ *n.* (*pl.* **-ies**) **1** exaggerated or insincere praise. **2** the act or an instance of flattering.

flat·top *n.* **1** *Aeron. sl.* an aircraft carrier. **2** *sl.* a man's short flat haircut.

flat·u·lent /fláchələnt/ *adj.* **1 a** causing formation of gas in the alimentary canal. **b** caused by or suffering from this. **2** (of speech, etc.) inflated; pretentious. □□ **flat·u·lence** *n.* **flat·u·lent·ly** *adv.*

fla·tus /fláytəs/ *n.* wind in or from the stomach or bowels.

flat·ware /flátwair/ *n.* **1** forks, knives, spoons, etc.; cutlery. **2** plates, saucers, etc. (cf. HOLLOWWARE).

flat·worm /flátwərm/ *n.* any worm of the phylum Platyhelminthes, having a flattened body and no

FLASK USED FOR
CHEMICAL EXPERIMENT

body cavity or blood vessels, including turbellaria, flukes, etc.

flaunt /flawnt/ *v. & n.* ● *v.tr. & intr.* **1** (often *refl.*) display ostentatiously; show off; parade (*liked to flaunt his gold cuff links; flaunted themselves before the crowd*). ¶ Often confused with *flout.* **2** wave or cause to wave proudly (*flaunted the banner*). ● *n.* an act or instance of flaunting.

flau·tist /fláwtist, flów-/ *n.* a flute player.

fla·vo·noid /fláyvənoyd/ *n. Chem.* any of a class of compounds including several white or yellow plant pigments.

fla·vor /fláyvər/ *n. & v.* ● *n.* **1** a distinctive mingled sensation of smell and taste (*a cheesy flavor*). **2** an indefinable characteristic quality (*music with a romantic flavor*). **3** (usu. foll. by *of*) a slight admixture of a quality (*the flavor of failure hangs over the enterprise*). **4** = FLAVORING. ● *v.tr.* give flavor to; season. □ **flavor of the month** (or **week**) a temporary trend or fashion. □□ **fla·vor·ful** *adj.* **fla·vor·less** *adj.* **fla·vor·some** *adj.*

fla·vor·ing /fláyvəring/ *n.* a substance used to flavor food or drink.

flaw /flaw/ *n. & v.* ● *n.* **1** an imperfection; a blemish (*has a character without a flaw*). **2** a crack or similar fault (*the cup has a flaw*). **3** *Law* an invalidating defect in a legal matter. ● *v.tr. & intr.* crack; damage; spoil. □□ **flawed** *adj.* **flaw·less** *adj.* **flaw·less·ly** *adv.* **flaw·less·ness** *n.*

flax /flaks/ *n.* **1 a** a blue-flowered plant, *Linum usitatissimum*, cultivated for its textile fiber and its seeds (see LINSEED). **b** a plant resembling this. **2** ► flax fibers.

flax·en /fláksən/ *adj.* **1** of flax. **2** (of hair) colored like dressed flax; pale yellow.

flax·seed /flákseed/ *n.* linseed.

flay /flay/ *v.tr.* **1** strip the skin or hide off, esp. by beating. **2** criticize severely. **3** peel off (skin, bark, peel, etc.).

FLAX FIBERS

F layer /éf layər/ *n.* the highest and most strongly ionized region of the ionosphere.

flea /flee/ *n.* **1** ► a small wingless jumping insect of the order Siphonaptera, feeding on blood. ▷ INSECT. **2 a** (in full **flea beetle**) a small jumping beetle infesting hops, cabbages, etc. **b** (in full **water flea**) daphnia. □ **a flea in one's ear** a sharp reproof.

laterally
compressed
body

strong
rear legs

FLEA

flea·bag /fléebag/ *n. sl.* a shabby or unattractive place or thing.

flea·bane /fléebayn/ *n.* any of various composite plants of the genus *Inula* or *Pulicaria*, supposed to drive away fleas.

flea·bite /fléebīt/ *n.* **1** the bite of a flea. **2** a trivial injury or inconvenience.

flea-bit·ten *adj.* **1** bitten by or infested with fleas. **2** shabby.

flea cir·cus *n.* a show of performing fleas.

flea col·lar *n.* an insecticidal collar for pets.

flea mar·ket *n.* a market selling secondhand goods, etc.

flea·wort /fléewawrt/ *n.* any of various plants supposed to drive away fleas.

fleck /flek/ *n. & v.* ● *n.* **1** a small patch of color or light (*eyes with green flecks*). **2** a small particle or speck. **3** a spot on the skin; a freckle. ● *v.tr.* mark with flecks.

flec·tion var. of FLEXION.

fled *past* and *past part.* of FLEE.

fledge /flej/ *v.* **1** *intr.* (of a bird) grow feathers. **2** *tr.* provide (an arrow) with feathers. **3** *tr.* bring up (a young bird) until it can fly. **4** *tr.* (as **fledged** *adj.*) **a** able to fly. **b** independent; mature. **5** *tr.* deck or provide with feathers or down.

F

F

fledg·ling /fléjling/ *n*. **1** a young bird. **2** an inexperienced person.

flee /flee/ *v.* (*past* and *past part.* **fled** /fled/) **1** *intr.* (often foll. by *from*, *before*) **a** run away. **b** seek safety by fleeing. **2** *tr.* run away from; leave abruptly; shun (*fled the room*; *fled his attentions*). **3** *intr.* vanish.

fleece /flees/ *n. & v.* ● *n.* **1 a** ▼ the woolly covering of a sheep or a similar animal. **b** the amount of wool sheared from a sheep at one time. **2** something resembling a fleece, esp.: **a** a woolly or rough head of hair. **b** a soft warm fabric with a pile, used for lining coats, etc. **c** a white cloud, a blanket of snow, etc. ● *v.tr.* **1** (often foll. by *of*) strip (a person) of money, valuables, etc.; swindle. **2** remove the fleece from (a sheep, etc.); shear. **3** cover as if with a fleece (*a sky fleeced with clouds*). □□ **fleeced** *adj*. (also in *comb.*).

FLEECE BEING SHEARED FROM A SHEEP

fleec·y /fléesee/ *adj.* (**fleecier, fleeciest**) **1** of or like a fleece. **2** covered with a fleece. □□ **fleec·i·ness** *n*.

fleet[1] /fleet/ *n*. **1 a** a number of warships under one commander. **b** (prec. by *the*) all the warships and merchant ships of a nation. **2** a number of ships, aircraft, buses, trucks, taxis, etc., operating together or owned by one proprietor.

fleet[2] /fleet/ *adj.* swift; nimble. □□ **fleet·ly** *adv.* **fleet·ness** *n*.

Fleet Ad·mi·ral *n*. an admiral of the highest rank in the US navy.

fleet·ing /fléeting/ *adj.* transitory; brief. □□ **fleet·ing·ly** *adv.*

Flem·ing /fléming/ *n*. **1** a native of medieval Flanders in the Low Countries. **2** a member of a Flemish-speaking people inhabiting N. and W. Belgium (see also **Walloon**).

Flem·ish /flémish/ *adj. & n.* ● *adj.* of or relating to Flanders. ● *n.* the language of the Flemings.

flense /flens/ *v.tr.* (also **flench** /flench/, **flinch** /flinch/) **1** cut up (a whale or seal). **2** flay (a seal).

flesh /flesh/ *n. & v.* ● *n.* **1 a** the soft, esp. muscular, substance between the skin and bones of an animal or a human. **b** plumpness; fat (*has put on flesh*). **c** *archaic* meat, esp. excluding poultry, game, and offal. **2** the body as opposed to the mind or the soul, esp. considered as sinful. **3** the pulpy substance of a fruit or a plant. **4 a** the visible surface of the human body with ref. to its color or appearance. **b** (also **flesh col·or**) a yellowish pink color. **5** animal or human life. ● *v.tr.* embody in flesh. □ **all flesh** all human and animal life. **flesh out** make or become substantial. **in the flesh** in bodily form; in person. **lose** (or **put on**) **flesh** grow thinner or fatter. **make a person's flesh creep** (or **crawl**) frighten or horrify a person, esp. with tales of the supernatural, etc. **sins of the flesh** unchastity. **the way of all flesh** experience common to all humankind. □□ **flesh·less** *adj*.

flesh and blood *n. & adj.* ● *n.* **1** the body or its substance. **2** humankind. **3** human nature, esp. as being fallible. ● *adj.* actually living, not imaginary or supernatural. □ **one's own flesh and blood** near relatives; descendants.

flesh·ings /fléshingz/ *n.pl.* an actor's flesh-colored tights.

flesh·ly /fléshlee/ *adj.* (**fleshlier, fleshliest**) **1** (of desire, etc.) bodily; sensual. **2** mortal; not divine. **3** worldly.

flesh·pots /fléshpots/ *n.pl.* luxurious living (Exod. 16:3).

flesh·y /fléshee/ *adj.* (**fleshier, fleshiest**) **1** plump; fat. **2** of flesh; without bone. **3** (of plant or fruit tissue) pulpy. **4** like flesh. □□ **flesh·i·ness** *n*.

fleur-de-lis /flórdəlée/ *n.* (also **fleur-de-lys**) (*pl.* **fleurs-** *pronunc.* same) **1** the iris flower. **2** *Heraldry* **a** ▶ a lily composed of three petals bound together near their bases. **b** the former royal arms of France.

fleu·ret /flŏŏrét/ *n*. an ornament like a small flower.

fleu·ry /flŏŏree, flŏŏree/ *adj.* (also **flo·ry** /flóree/) *Heraldry* decorated with fleurs-de-lis.

flew *past of* FLY[1].

flex /fleks/ *v.* **1** *tr. & intr.* bend (a joint, limb, etc.) or be bent. **2** *tr. & intr.* move (a muscle) or (of a muscle) be moved to bend a joint.

flex·i·ble /fléksibəl/ *adj.* **1** able to bend without breaking; pliable. **2** manageable. **3** adaptable; variable (*works flexible hours*). □□ **flex·i·bil·i·ty** *n*. **flex·i·bly** *adv.*

flex·ile /fléksəl, -sīl/ *adj. archaic* **1** supple; mobile. **2** tractable; manageable. **3** versatile. □□ **flex·il·i·ty** /-silitee/ *n*.

flex·ion /flékshən/ *n.* (also **flec·tion**) **1 a** the act of bending or the condition of being bent, esp. of a limb or joint. **b** a bent part; a curve. **2** *Gram.* inflection. **3** *Math.* = FLEXURE.

flex·i·time /fléksitīm/ *n.* var. of FLEXTIME.

flex·og·ra·phy /fleksógrəfee/ *n. Printing* a rotary letterpress technique using rubber or plastic plates and synthetic inks or dyes for printing on fabrics, plastics, etc., as well as on paper. □□ **flex·o·graph·ic** /-səgráfik/ *adj.*

flex·or /fléksər/ *n.* (in full **flexor muscle**) a muscle that bends part of the body (cf. EXTENSOR).

flex·time /flékstīm/ *n.* **1** a system of working a set number of hours with the starting and finishing times chosen within agreed limits by the employee. **2** the hours worked in this way.

flex·u·ous /flékshŏŏəs/ *adj.* full of bends; winding. □□ **flex·u·os·i·ty** /-yŏŏ-ósitee/ *n*. **flex·u·ous·ly** *adv.*

flex·ure /flékshər/ *n.* **1** the act of bending or the condition of being bent. **b** a bend, curve, or turn. **2** *Math.* the curving of a line, surface, or solid, esp. from a straight line, plane, etc. **3** *Geol.* the bending of strata under pressure. □□ **flex·u·ral** *adj.*

flib·ber·ti·gib·bet /flíbərteejíbit/ *n.* a gossiping, frivolous, or restless person.

flick /flik/ *n. & v.* ● *n.* **1 a** a light, sharp blow with a whip, etc. **b** the sudden release of a bent finger or thumb, esp. to propel a small object. **2** a sudden movement or jerk. **3** a quick turn of the wrist in playing games, esp. in throwing or striking a ball. **4** a slight, sharp sound. **5** *colloq.* **a** a movie. **b** (in *pl.*; prec. by *the*) the movies. ● *v.* **1** *tr.* (often foll. by *away*, *off*) strike or move with a flick (*flicked the ash off his cigar*). **2** *tr.* give a flick with (a whip, towel, etc.). **3** *intr.* make a flicking movement or sound. □ **flick through** = *flip through*.

flick·er[1] /flíkər/ *v. & n.* ● *v.intr.* **1** (of light) shine unsteadily. **2** (of a flame) burn unsteadily, alternately flaring and dying down. **3 a** (of a flag, a reptile's tongue, an eyelid, etc.) move or wave to and fro; quiver; vibrate. **b** (of the wind) blow lightly and unsteadily. **4** (of hope, etc.) increase and decrease unsteadily. ● *n.* a flickering movement, light, thought, etc. □ **flicker out** die away after a final flicker.

flick·er[2] /flíkər/ *n.* any woodpecker of the genus *Colaptes*, a ground-feeder native to N. America.

fli·er /flíər/ *n.* (also **fly·er**) *colloq.* **1** an airman or airwoman. **2** a thing that flies in a specified way (*a poor flier*). **3** a fast-moving animal or vehicle. **4** an ambitious or outstanding person. **5** (usu. **fly·er**) a small handbill. **6** a speculative investment. **7** a flying jump.

flight[1] /flīt/ *n.* **1 a** the act or manner of flying through the air (*studied swallows' flight*). **b** the movement or passage of a projectile, etc., through the air (*the flight of an arrow*). **2 a** a journey made through the air or in space. **b** a timetabled journey made by an airline. **c** a military air unit of two or more aircraft. **3 a** a flock of birds, insects, etc. **b** a migration. **4** (usu. foll. by *of*) a series, esp. of stairs between floors, or of hurdles across a race track. **5** a mental or verbal excursion or sally (of wit, etc.) (*a flight of fancy*). **6** the trajectory and pace of a ball in games. **7** the distance that a bird, aircraft, or missile can fly. **8** (usu. foll. by *of*) a volley (*a flight of arrows*). **9** the tail of a dart. ▷ DART. □ **in the first** (or **top**) **flight** taking a leading place. **take** (or **wing**) **one's flight** fly.

flight[2] /flīt/ *n.* **1 a** the act or manner of fleeing. **b** a hasty retreat. **2** *Econ.* the selling of currency, investments, etc., in anticipation of a fall in value (*flight from the dollar*). □ **put to flight** cause to flee. **take** (or **take to**) **flight** flee.

flight at·tend·ant *n.* an airline employee who attends to passengers' safety and comfort during flights.

flight bag *n.* a small, zippered, shoulder bag carried by air travelers.

flight deck *n.* **1** the deck of an aircraft carrier used for takeoff and landing. **2** the forward compartment occupied by the pilot, navigator, etc., in an aircraft.

flight·less /flítlis/ *adj.* ▶ (of a bird, etc.) naturally unable to fly.

FLEUR-DE-LIS

FLIGHTLESS BIRD: OSTRICH (*Struthio camelus*)

flight re·cord·er *n.* /ri-káwrdər/ ▶ a device in an aircraft to record technical details during a flight, which may be used in the event of an accident to discover its cause.

flight·y /flítee/ *adj.* (**flightier, flightiest**) **1** frivolous; fickle; changeable. **2** crazy. □□ **flight·i·ly** *adv.* **flight·i·ness** *n*.

flim·flam /flímflam/ *n. & v.* ● *n.* **1** a trifle; nonsense; idle talk. **2** humbug; deception. ● *v.tr.* cheat; deceive. □□ **flim·flam·mer** *n.* **flim·flam·mer·y** /-məree/ *n.* (*pl.* **-ies**)

flim·sy /flímzee/ *adj.* (**flimsier, flimsiest**) **1** insubstantial; easily damaged (*a flimsy structure*). **2** (of an excuse, etc.) unconvincing (*a flimsy pretext*). **3** paltry; trivial; superficial (*a flimsy play*). **4** (of clothing) thin (*a flimsy blouse*). □□ **flim·si·ly** *adv.* **flim·si·ness** *n*.

flinch /flinch/ *v. & n.* ● *v.intr.* **1** draw back in pain or expectation of a blow, etc.; wince. **2** (often foll. by *from*) give way; shrink; turn aside (*flinched from his duty*). ● *n.* an act or instance of flinching. □□ **flinch·ing·ly** *adv.*

fling /fling/ *v. & n.* ● *v.* (*past* and *past part.* **flung** /flung/) **1** *tr.* throw or hurl (an object) forcefully. **2** *refl.* **a** (usu. foll. by *into*) rush headlong (into a person's arms, a train, etc.). **b** (usu. foll. by *into*) embark wholeheartedly (on an enterprise). **c** (usu. foll. by *on*) throw (oneself) on a person's mercy, etc. **3** *tr.* utter (words) forcefully. **4** *tr.* (usu. foll. by *out*) suddenly spread (the arms). **5** *tr.* (foll. by *on*, *off*) put on or take off (clothes) carelessly or rapidly. **6** *intr.* go angrily or violently; rush (*flung out of the room*). **7** *tr.* put or send suddenly or violently (*was flung into jail*). **8** *tr.* (foll. by *away*) discard thoughtlessly (*flung away their reputation*). ● *n.* **1** an act or instance of flinging; a throw. **2 a** a spell of indulgence or wild behavior (*he's had his fling*). **b** *colloq.* an attempt (*give it a fling*). **3** a brief or casual romance. **4** an impetuous, whirling Scottish dance, esp. the Highland fling. □ **have a fling at 1** make an attempt at. **2** jeer at. □□ **fling·er** *n*.

FLIGHT RECORDER

Most modern aircraft, whether military or civilian, carry a flight data recorder, often known as a "black box." The box records data from the main operating systems of the aircraft and tapes conversations inside the flight deck. Data is stored on magnetic tape inside a strong titanium case, which protects it from impact and fire damage.

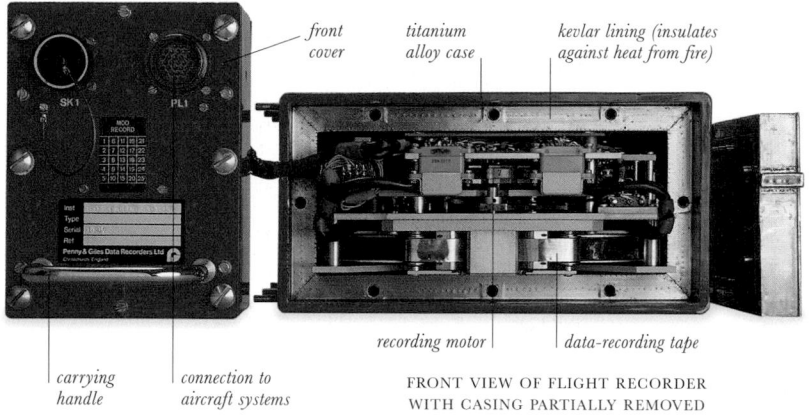

FRONT VIEW OF FLIGHT RECORDER
WITH CASING PARTIALLY REMOVED

front cover · *titanium alloy case* · *kevlar lining (insulates against heat from fire)* · *recording motor* · *data-recording tape* · *carrying handle* · *connection to aircraft systems*

---

flint /flint/ n. **1 a** a hard gray stone of nearly pure silica occurring naturally as nodules or bands in chalk. **b** ◀ a piece of this, esp. as flaked or shaped to form a primitive tool or weapon. **2** a piece of hard alloy of rare Earth metals used to give an igniting spark in a cigarette lighter, etc. **3** a piece of flint used with steel to produce fire. **4** anything hard and unyielding. □□ **flint·y** adj. (**flintier, flintiest**).

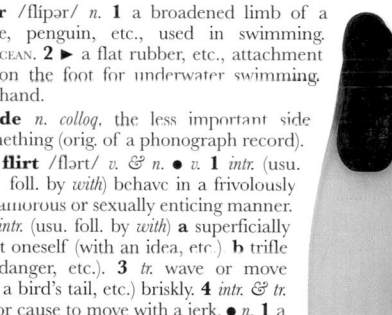

FLINT
BLADE

flint·lock /flintlok/ n. hist. **1** ▼ an old type of gun fired by a spark from a flint. ▷ BLUNDERBUSS. **2** the lock producing such a spark.

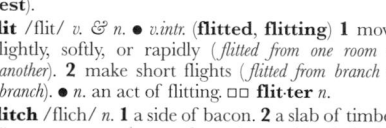

cock (holds flint) · *barrel* · *brass butt* · *trigger* · *ramrod*

FLINTLOCK
PISTOL

flip[1] /flip/ v., n., & adj. ● v. (**flipped, flipping**) **1** tr. **a** flick (a coin, ball, etc.) so that it spins in the air. **b** remove (a small object) from a surface with a flick of the fingers. **2** tr. **a** flick (a person's ear, cheek, etc.) lightly or smartly. **b** move (a whip, etc.) with a sudden jerk. **3** tr. turn or turn over. **4** intr. **a** make a flicking noise with the fingers. **b** (foll. by at) strike smartly at. **5** intr. move about with sudden jerks. **6** intr. sl. (often foll. by out) become suddenly angry, excited, or enthusiastic. ● n. **1** a smart light blow; a flick. **2** a somersault, esp. while in the air. **3** an act of flipping over (gave the stone a flip). **4** colloq. **a** a short pleasure flight in an aircraft. **b** a quick tour, etc. ● adj. colloq. glib; flippant. □ **flip one's lid** sl. **1** lose self-control. **2** go crazy. **flip through 1** turn over (cards, pages, etc.). **2 a** turn over (cards, pages, etc.). **b** look cursorily through (a book, etc.).

flip[2] /flip/ n. a drink of heated beer and liquor.

flip chart n. a large pad erected on a stand and bound so that one page can be turned over at the top to reveal the next.

flip-flop /flipflop/ n. & v. ● n. **1** ▶ a usu. rubber sandal with a thong between the big and second toe. **2** a backward somersault. **3** an electronic switching circuit changed from one stable state to another, or through an unstable state back to its stable state, by a triggering pulse. **4** an esp. sudden change of direction, attitude, policy, etc. ● v.intr. (**-flopped, -flopping**) **1** move with a sound or motion suggested by "flip-flop." **2** to change direction, attitude, policy, etc., esp. suddenly.

flip·pant /flipənt/ adj. treating serious things lightly; disrespectful. □□ **flip·pan·cy** /-pənsee/ n. **flip·pant·ly** adv.

flip·per /flipər/ n. **1** a broadened limb of a tortoise, penguin, etc., used in swimming. ▷ CETACEAN. **2** ▶ a flat rubber, etc., attachment worn on the foot for underwater swimming. **3** sl. a hand.

flip side n. colloq. the less important side of something (orig. of a phonograph record).

flirt /flərt/ v. & n. ● v. **1** intr. (usu. foll. by with) behave in a frivolously amorous or sexually enticing manner. **2** intr. (usu. foll. by with) **a** superficially interest oneself (with an idea, etc.). **b** trifle (with danger, etc.). **3** tr. wave or move (a fan, a bird's tail, etc.) briskly. **4** intr. & tr. move or cause to move with a jerk. ● n. **1** a person who indulges in flirting. **2** a quick movement; a sudden jerk. □□ **flir·ta·tion** n. **flir·ta·tious** adj. **flir·ta·tious·ly** adv. **flir·ta·tious·ness** n. **flirt·y** adj. (**flirtier, flirtiest**).

flit /flit/ v. & n. ● v.intr. (**flitted, flitting**) **1** move lightly, softly, or rapidly (flitted from one room to another). **2** make short flights (flitted from branch to branch). ● n. an act of flitting. □□ **flit·ter** n.

flitch /flich/ n. **1** a side of bacon. **2** a slab of timber from a tree trunk, usu. from the outside. **3** (in full **flitch plate**) a strengthening plate in a beam, etc.

flit·ter /flitər/ v.intr. flit about; flutter.

FLIP-FLOP:
PAIR OF RUBBER
FLIP-FLOPS

thong

float /flōt/ v. & n. ● v. **1** intr. & tr. **a** rest or move or cause (a buoyant object) to rest or move on the surface of a liquid without sinking. **b** get afloat or set (a stranded ship) afloat. **2** intr. drift (the clouds floated high up). **3** intr. colloq. **a** move in a leisurely or casual way. **b** (often foll. by before) hover before the eye or mind (the prospect of lunch floated before them). **4** intr. (often foll. by in) move or be suspended freely in a liquid or a gas. **5** tr. **a** bring (a company, etc.) into being. **b** offer (stock, shares, etc.) on the stock market. **6** Commerce **a** intr. (of currency) be allowed to have a fluctuating exchange rate. **b** tr. cause (currency) to float. **c** intr. (of an acceptance) be in circulation. **7** tr. (of water, etc.) support; bear along (a buoyant object). **8** intr. & tr. circulate or cause (a rumor or idea) to circulate. **9** tr. put forward as a proposal. **10** waft (a buoyant object) through the air. ● n. **1** a thing that floats, esp.: **a** a raft. **b** a cork or other buoyant object on a fishing line as an indicator of a fish biting. **c** a cork supporting the edge of a fishing net. **d** the hollow or inflated part or organ supporting a fish, etc., in the water. **e** a hollow structure fixed underneath an aircraft enabling it to float on water. **f** a floating device on the surface of water, fuel, etc., controlling the flow. **2** Brit. a small vehicle or cart, esp. one powered by electricity (milk float). **3** a platform mounted on a truck or trailer and carrying a display in a parade, etc. **4 a** an amount of money outstanding but not yet collected by a bank, etc., such as checks written but not yet collected on. **b** the time between the writing of a check, etc., and the actual collection of funds. **5** a tool used for smoothing plaster or concrete. □□ **float·a·ble** adj. **float·a·bil·i·ty** /-təbílitee/ n. **float·er** /flótər/ n.

float·a·tion var. of FLOTATION.

float·ing /flóting/ adj. not settled in a definite place; variable (the floating population).

float·ing rib n. any of the lower ribs, which are not attached to the breastbone.

float·y /flótee/ adj. (esp. of a woman's garment or a fabric) light and airy.

floc·cu·late /flókyəlayt/ v.tr. & intr. form into flocculent masses. □□ **floc·cu·la·tion** /-láyshən/ n.

floc·cule /flókyōol/ n. a small portion of matter resembling a tuft of wool.

floc·cu·lent /flókyələnt/ adj. **1** like tufts of wool. **2** downy. **3** Chem. (of precipitates) loosely massed. □□ **floc·cu·lence** /-ləns/ n.

flock[1] /flok/ n. & v. ● n. **1 a** a number of animals of one kind, esp. birds, feeding or traveling together. **b** a number of domestic animals kept together. **2** a large crowd of people. **3 a** a Christian congregation or body of believers, esp. in relation to one minister. **b** a family of children, a number of pupils, etc. ● v.intr. **1** congregate; mass. **2** (usu. foll. by to, in, out, together) go together in a crowd (thousands flocked to the polls).

flock[2] /flok/ n. **1** a lock or tuft of wool, cotton, etc. **2 a** (also in pl.; often attrib.) material for quilting and stuffing made of wool refuse or torn-up cloth (a flock pillow). **b** powdered wool or cloth.

floe /flō/ n. a sheet of floating ice.

flog /flawg, flog/ v. (**flogged, flogging**) **1** tr. **a** beat with a whip, stick, etc. **b** make work through violent effort (flogged the engine). **2** sl. sell or promote aggressively. **3** tr. (usu. foll. by into, out of) drive (a quality, knowledge, etc.) into or out of a person, esp. by physical punishment. □ **flog** (also **beat**) **a dead horse** waste energy on something unalterable. **flog to death** colloq. talk about at tedious length. □□ **flog·ger** n.

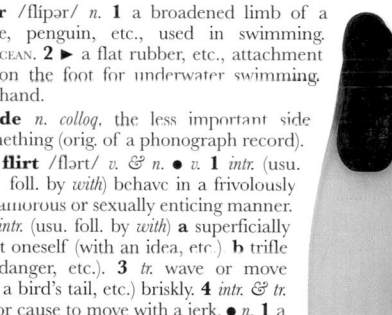

FLIPPER

flood /flud/ n. & v. ● n. **1 a** an overflowing or influx of water beyond its normal confines, esp. over land; an inundation. **b** the water that overflows. **2 a** an outpouring of water; a torrent (a flood of rain). **b** something resembling a torrent (a flood of tears). **c** an abundance or excess. **3** the inflow of the tide (also in comb.: flood tide). **4** colloq. a floodlight. **5** (**the Flood**) the flood described in Genesis. ● v. **1** tr. **a** cover with or overflow in a flood (rain flooded the cellar). **b** overflow as if with a flood (the market was flooded with foreign goods). **2** tr. irrigate (flooded the rice paddies). **3** tr. deluge with water. **4** intr. (often foll. by in, through) arrive in great quantities. **5** intr. become inundated (the bathroom flooded). **6** tr. overfill (a carburetor) with fuel. **7** intr. experience a uterine hemorrhage. **8** tr. (of rain, etc.) fill (a river) to overflowing. □ **flood out** drive out (of one's home, etc.) with a flood.

F

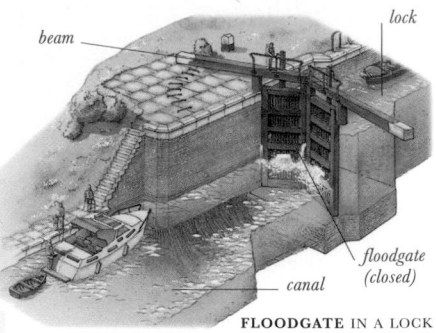

FLOODGATE IN A LOCK

beam · lock · floodgate (closed) · canal

flood·gate /flúdgayt/ *n.* **1** ▲ a gate opened or closed to admit or exclude water, esp. the lower gate of a lock. **2** (usu. in *pl.*) a last restraint holding back tears, etc.

flood·light /flúdlīt/ *n. & v.* ● *n.* **1** a large powerful light (usu. one of several) to illuminate a building, stage, etc. **2** the illumination so provided. ● *v.tr.* illuminate with floodlights.

flood·plain /flúdplayn/ *n.* flat terrain alongside a river that is subject to inundation when the river floods.

flood tide *n.* the periodical exceptional rise of the tide because of lunar or solar attraction.

flood·wa·ter /flúdwawtər, -wo-/ *n.* the water overflowing as the result of a flood.

floor /flawr/ *n. & v.* ● *n.* **1 a** the lower surface of a room. **b** the boards, etc., of which it is made. **2 a** the bottom of the sea, a cave, etc. **b** any level area. **3** all the rooms, etc., on the same level of a building; a story. **4 a** (in a legislative assembly) the part of the house in which members sit and speak. **b** the right to speak next in debate (*gave him the floor*). **5** *Stock Exch.* the large central hall where trading takes place. **6** the minimum of prices, wages, etc. **7** *colloq.* the ground. ● *v.tr.* **1** furnish with a floor; pave. **2** knock (a person) down. **3** *colloq.* confound; baffle. **4** *colloq.* get the better of. **5** serve as the floor of (*leopard skins floored the hall*). **6** cause a vehicle to accelerate rapidly. □ **from the floor** (of a speech, etc.) given by a member of the audience, not by those on the platform, etc. **take the floor 1** begin to dance. **2** speak in a debate. □□ **floor·less** *adj.*

floor·board /fláwrbawrd/ *n.* a long wooden board used for flooring.

floor·cloth /fláwrklawth, -kloth/ *n.* **1** a cloth for washing the floor. **2** a heavy cloth or covering for a floor.

floor·ing /fláwring/ *n.* the boards, etc., of which a floor is made.

floor lamp *n.* a lamp with a base that rests on the floor.

floor plan *n.* a diagram of the rooms, etc., on one floor of a building.

floor show *n.* an entertainment presented at a nightclub, etc.

floor·walk·er /fláwrwawkər/ *n.* a person employed in a retail store who assists customers and supervises other workers.

floo·zy /flóōzee/ *n.* (also **floo·zie**) (*pl.* **-ies**) *colloq.* a girl or a woman, esp. a disreputable one.

flop /flop/ *v., n., & adv.* ● *v.intr.* (**flopped**, **flop·ping**) **1** sway about heavily or loosely (*hair flopped over his face*). **2** move in an ungainly way (*flopped along in flippers*). **3** (often foll. by *down, on, into*) sit, kneel, lie, or fall awkwardly or suddenly. **4** *sl.* (esp. of a play, movie, etc.) fail; collapse (*flopped on Broadway*). **5** *sl.* sleep. **6** make a dull sound as of a soft

body landing, or of a flat thing slapping water. ● *n.* **1 a** a flopping movement. **b** the sound made by it. **2** *sl.* a failure. **3** *sl.* a place to sleep, esp. cheaply. **4** a piece of cow dung. ● *adv.* with a flop.

flop·house /flop-hows/ *n.* a cheap hotel or rooming house.

flop·py /flópee/ *adj. & n.* ● *adj.* (**floppier**, **floppiest**) tending to flop; not firm or rigid. ● *n.* (*pl.* **-ies**) (in full **floppy disk**) *Computing* a flexible removable magnetic disk for the storage of data. □□ **flop·pi·ly** *adv.* **flop·pi·ness** *n.*

flo·ra /fláwrə/ *n.* (*pl.* **floras** or **florae** /-ree/) **1** the plants of a particular region or period (cf. FAUNA). **2** a treatise on or list of these.

flo·ral /fláwrəl/ *adj.* **1** of flowers. **2** decorated with or depicting flowers. **3** of flora or floras. □□ **flo·ral·ly** *adv.*

Flor·en·tine /fláwrənteen, -tīn, flór-/ *adj. & n.* ● *adj.* **1** of or relating to Florence in Italy. **2** (**florentine** /-teen/) (of a dish) served on a bed of spinach. ● *n.* a native or citizen of Florence.

flo·res·cence /flawrésəns/ *n.* flowering.

flo·ret /fláwrit/ *n. Bot.* **1** ◄ each of the small flowers making up a composite flower head. ▷ INFLORESCENCE. **2** each of the flowering stems of a head of cauliflower, broccoli, etc. **3** a small flower.

flo·ri·ate /fláwriyayt/ *v.tr.* decorate with flower designs, etc.

flo·ri·bun·da /fláwribúndə/ *n.* a plant, esp. a rose, bearing dense clusters of flowers.

flor·id /fláwrid, flór-/ *adj.* **1** ruddy (*a florid complexion*). **2** (of a book, music, etc.) elaborately ornate. **3** flowery. □□ **flo·rid·i·ty** *n.* **flor·id·ly** *adv.* **flor·id·ness** *n.*

flo·ri·le·gi·um /fláwriléejeeəm/ *n.* (*pl.* **florilegia** /-jeeə/ or **florilegiums**) an anthology.

flor·in /fláwrin, flór-/ *n. hist.* **1 a** ◄ a British silver or alloy two-shilling coin of the 19th–20th c. **b** an English gold coin of the 14th c. **2** a foreign coin of gold or silver, esp. a Dutch guilder.

flo·rist /fláwrist, flór-/ *n.* a person who deals in or grows flowers. □□ **flo·rist·ry** *n.*

flo·ris·tic /flawrístik/ *adj.* relating to the study of the distribution of plants. □□ **flo·ris·ti·cal·ly** *adv.* **flo·ris·tics** *n.*

flo·ru·it /fláwrōoit, flór-/ *v. & n.* ● *v.intr.* (he or she) was alive and working; flourished (of a painter, writer, etc., whose exact dates are unknown). ● *n.* the period or date at which a person lived or worked.

floss /flaws, flos/ *n. & v.* ● *n.* **1** ► the rough silk enveloping a silkworm's cocoon. **2** untwisted silk thread used in embroidery. **3** = DENTAL FLOSS. ● *v.tr.* (also *absol.*) clean (the teeth) with dental floss.

floss·y /fláwsee, flósee/ *adj.* (**flossier**, **flossiest**) **1** of or like floss. **2** *colloq.* fancy; showy.

flo·tage /flótij/ *n.* **1** the act or state of floating. **2 a** floating objects or masses; flotsam. **b** *Brit.* the right of appropriating flotsam. **3 a** ships, etc., afloat on a river. **b** the part of a ship above the water line. **4** buoyancy; floating power.

flo·ta·tion /flótáyshən/ *n.* (also **float·a·tion**) **1** the process of launching or financing a commercial enterprise. **2** the separation of the components of crushed ore, etc., by their different capacities to float. **3** the capacity to float. □ **center of flotation** the center of gravity in a floating body.

flo·til·la /flōtílə/ *n.* **1** a small fleet. **2** a fleet of small ships.

flot·sam /flótsəm/ *n.* wreckage found floating.

flot·sam and jet·sam *n.* **1** odds and ends; rubbish. **2** vagrants, etc.

flounce[1] /flowns/ *v. & n.* ● *v.intr.* (often foll. by *away, off, out*) go or move with an agitated or impatient motion. ● *n.* a flouncing movement.

flounce[2] /flowns/ *n. & v.* ● *n.* a wide frill. ● *v.tr.* trim with a flounce or flounces.

floun·der[1] /flówndər/ *v. & n.* ● *v.intr.* **1** struggle in mud, or as if in mud, or when wading. **2** perform a task badly or without knowledge. ● *n.* an act of floundering. □□ **floun·der·er** *n.*

floun·der[2] /flówndər/ *n.* **1** an edible flatfish, *Pleuronectes flesus*, native to European shores. **2** any of various flatfish native to N. American shores.

flour /flowr/ *n. & v.* ● *n.* **1** ▼ a meal or powder obtained by grinding and usu. sifting grain, esp. wheat. **2** any fine powder. ● *v.tr.* **1** sprinkle with flour. **2** grind into flour. □□ **flour·y** *adj.* (**flourier**, **flouriest**). **flour·i·ness** *n.*

wheat flour · whole grain flour · rye flour

FLOUR: COMMON FLOUR TYPES

flour·ish /flórish, flúr-/ *v. & n.* ● *v.* **1** *intr.* **a** grow vigorously; thrive. **b** prosper. **c** be in one's prime. **d** be in good health. **e** (as **flourishing** *adj.*) successful; prosperous. **2** *intr.* (usu. foll. by *in, at, about*) spend one's life; be active (at a specified time) (*flourished in the Middle Ages*) (cf. FLORUIT). **3** *tr.* show ostentatiously (*flourished her checkbook*). **4** *tr.* wave (a weapon, etc.) vigorously. ● *n.* **1** an ostentatious gesture with a weapon, a hand, etc. **2** an ornamental curving decoration of handwriting. **3** a rhetorical embellishment. **4** *Mus.* **a** a fanfare played by brass instruments. **b** an ornate musical passage. **c** an extemporized addition played esp. at the beginning or end of a composition. □□ **flour·ish·er** *n.*

flout /flowt/ *v.* **1** *tr.* express contempt for (the law, rules, etc.) by word or action; mock. ¶ Often confused with *flaunt.* **2** *intr.* (often foll. by *at*) mock or scoff.

flow /flō/ *v. & n.* ● *v.intr.* **1** glide along as a stream. **2 a** (of a liquid, esp. water) gush out; spring. **b** (of blood, liquid, etc.) be spilled. **3** (of blood, money, electric current, etc.) circulate. **4** (of people or things) come or go in large numbers or smoothly (*traffic flowed along the highway*). **5** (of talk, literary style, etc.) proceed easily and smoothly. **6** (of a garment, hair, etc.) hang easily or gracefully. **7** (often foll. by *from*) result from (*his failure flows from his diffidence*). **8** (esp. of the tide) be in flood. **9** (of wine) be poured out copiously. **10** (of a rock or metal) undergo a permanent change of shape under stress. ● *n.* **1 a** a flowing movement in a stream. **b** a flowing liquid. **c** a copious outpouring (*a continuous flow of complaints*). **d** a hardened mass that formerly flowed (*walked out onto the lava flow*). **2** the rise of a tide or a river (*ebb and flow*). **3** menstruation.

flow chart 1 a diagram of the movement or action in a complex activity. **2** a graphical representation of a computer program in relation to its sequence of functions (as distinct from the data it processes).

flow·er /flówər/ *n. & v.* ● *n.* **1** the part of a plant from which the fruit or seed is developed. **2** ► the reproductive organ in a plant containing one or more pistils or stamens or both, and usu. a corolla

ray floret · disk florets

FLORET: COMPOSITE FLOWER HEAD (SUNFLOWER) SHOWING FLORETS

FLORIN: BRITISH FLORIN (1849)

floss · silkworm in cocoon

FLOSS AROUND A COCOON

FLOWER

Flowers are the sites of sexual reproduction in flowering plants (angiosperms). The male reproductive organ is the stamen; the female structure consists of the ovary, style, and stigma. Flowering plants fall into two categories: dicotyledons and monocotyledons (known as dicots and monocots). In dicot flowers, there is a distinction between the outer sepals, which are typically green, and the petals, which are usually larger and colorful. In monocot flowers, the petals and sepals are similar, and are known collectively as tepals. Flowers also vary in their shape, growth habit, coloration, and petal arrangements.

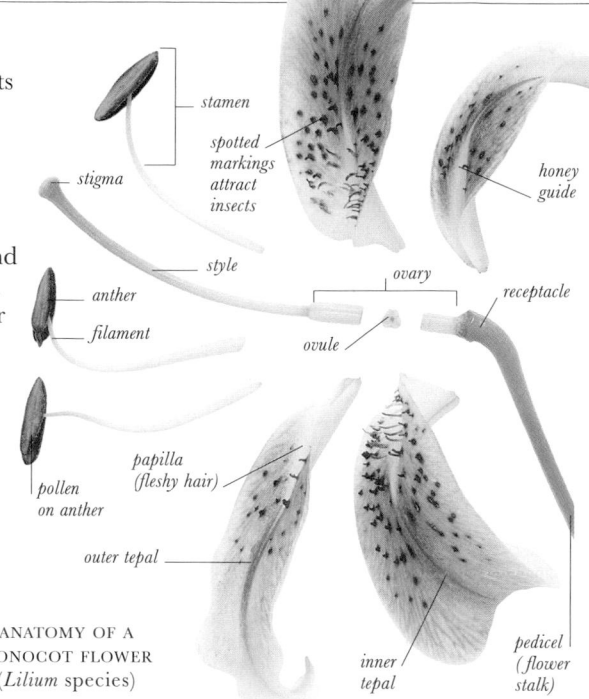

stamen

spotted markings attract insects

honey guide

stigma

style

ovary

receptacle

anther

filament

ovule

papilla (fleshy hair)

pollen on anther

outer tepal

ANATOMY OF A MONOCOT FLOWER (*Lilium* species)

inner tepal

pedicel (flower stalk)

DICOT AND MONOCOT FLOWER FEATURES

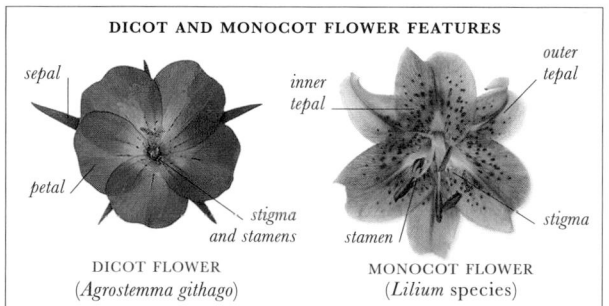

sepal

inner tepal

outer tepal

petal

stigma and stamens

stamen

stigma

DICOT FLOWER (*Agrostemma githago*)

MONOCOT FLOWER (*Lilium* species)

FLOWER HABITS

ERECT

NODDING

PENDENT

FLOWER COLORATION

SELF-COLORED

BICOLORED

PICOTEE

STRIPED

PETAL ARRANGEMENTS

RECURVED

REFLEXED

FUSED

SINGLE

SEMI-DOUBLE

DOUBLE

FLOWER SHAPES

CRUCIFORM

STELLATE

SAUCER-SHAPED

CUP-SHAPED

BELL-SHAPED

TUBULAR

FUNNEL-SHAPED

SALVERFORM

TRUMPET-SHAPED

ROSETTE

POMPON

PEALIKE

PITCHER-SHAPED

SLIPPER-SHAPED

and calyx. **3** a blossom, esp. on a stem and used in bunches for decoration. **4** a plant cultivated or noted for its flowers. **5** (in *pl.*) ornamental phrases (*flowers of speech*). **6** the finest time, group, example, etc.; the peak. ● *v.* **1** *intr.* (of a plant) produce flowers; bloom or blossom. **2** *intr.* reach a peak. **3** *tr.* cause or allow (a plant) to flower. **4** *tr.* decorate with worked flowers or a floral design. □ **the flower of** the best or best part of. **in flower** with the flowers out. □□ **flow·ered** *adj.* (also in *comb.*). **flow·er·less** *adj.* **flow·er·like** *adj.*

flow·er·et /flówrit/ *n.* a small flower.

flow·er girl *n.* a girl who carries flowers at a wedding as an attendant to the bride.

flow·er·ing /flówring/ *adj.* (of a plant) capable of producing flowers.

flow·er peo·ple *n.pl.* (esp. in the 1960s) hippies carrying or wearing flowers as symbols of peace and love.

flow·er·pot /flówərpot/ *n.* a pot in which a plant may be grown.

flow·er pow·er *n.* (esp. in the 1960s) the ideas of the flower people regarded as an instrument in changing the world.

flow·er·y /flówəree/ *adj.* **1** decorated with flowers or floral designs. **2** (of literary style, etc.) highly embellished; ornate. **3** full of flowers (*a flowery meadow*). □□ **flow·er·i·ness** *n.*

flow·ing /flóing/ *adj.* **1** (of literary style, etc.) fluent; easy. **2** (of a line or contour) smoothly continuous; not abrupt. **3** (of hair, a garment, etc.) unconfined. □□ **flow·ing·ly** *adv.*

flown *past part.* of FLY[1].

fl. oz. *abbr.* fluid ounce(s).

FLQ *abbr.* Front de Libération du Québec.

flu /floo/ *n.* *colloq.* influenza.

flub /flub/ *v.* & *n.* *colloq.* ● *v.tr.* & *intr.* (**flubbed, flubbing**) botch; bungle. ● *n.* something badly or clumsily done.

fluc·tu·ate /flúkchoo-ayt/ *v.intr.* vary irregularly; vacillate; rise and fall, move to and fro. □□ **fluc·tu·a·tion** /-áyshən/ *n.*

flue /floo/ *n.* **1** a smoke duct in a chimney. **2** a channel for conveying heat, esp. a hot-air passage in a wall; a tube for heating water in some kinds of boiler.

flu·ent /flóoənt/ *adj.* **1 a** (of speech or literary style) flowing naturally and readily. **b** having command of a foreign language (*is fluent in German*). **c** able to speak quickly and easily. **2** flowing easily or gracefully (*the fluent line of her arabesque*). □□ **flu·en·cy** /flóoənsee/ *n.* **flu·ent·ly** *adv.*

fluff /fluf/ *n.* & *v.* ● *n.* **1** soft, light, feathery material coming off blankets, etc. **2** soft fur or feathers. **3** *sl.* a mistake in delivering theatrical lines, in playing music, etc. ● *v.* **1** *tr.* & *intr.* (often foll. by *up*) shake into or become a soft mass. **2** *tr.* & *intr.* *colloq.* make a mistake in (a theatrical part, a game, playing music, etc.); blunder (*fluffed his opening line*). **3** *tr.* make into fluff. **4** *tr.* put a soft surface on (the flesh side of leather).

fluff·y /lúfee/ *adj.* (**fluffier, fluffiest**) **1** of or like fluff. **2** covered in fluff; downy. **3** nonintellectual; frivolous; superficial. □□ **fluff·i·ly** *adv.* **fluff·i·ness** *n.*

flu·gel·horn /flóogəlhawrn/ *n.* (also **flue·gel·horn**) ▼ a valved brass wind instrument similar to a cornet. ▷ BRASS

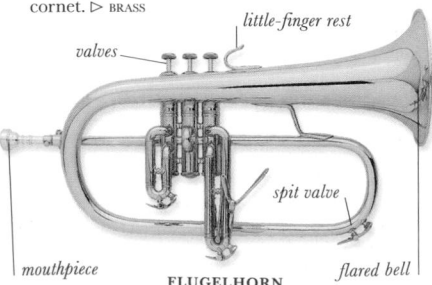

little-finger rest
valves
mouthpiece
spit valve
flared bell
FLUGELHORN

flu·id /flóoid/ *n.* & *adj.* ● *n.* a substance, esp. a gas or liquid, lacking definite shape and capable of flowing and yielding to the slightest pressure. ● *adj.* **1** able to flow and alter shape freely. **2** constantly changing (*the situation is fluid*). **3** (of a clutch, coupling, etc.) in which liquid is used to transmit power. □□ **flu·id·i·fy** /-ídifī/ *v.tr.* (**-ies, -ied**). **flu·id·i·ty** /-íditee/ *n.* **flu·id·ly** *adv.* **flu·id·ness** *n.*

flu·id·ize /flóoidīz/ *v.tr.* cause (a finely divided solid) to acquire the characteristics of a fluid. □□ **flu·id·i·za·tion** /-dizáyshən/ *n.*

fluid ounce *n.* a unit of capacity equal to one-sixteenth of a pint (approx. 0.034 liter).

flu·i·dram /flóoidram/ *n.* a fluid dram.

fluke[1] /flook/ *n.* & *v.* ● *n.* **1** a lucky accident (*won by a fluke*). **2** a chance breeze. ● *v.tr.* achieve by a fluke (*fluked that shot*).

fluke[2] /flook/ *n.* **1** any parasitic flatworm of the class Digenea or Monogenea, including liver flukes and blood flukes. **2** a flatfish, esp. a flounder.

fluke[3] /flook/ *n.* **1** *Naut.* a broad triangular plate on the arm of an anchor. **2** ▼ the barbed head of a lance, harpoon, etc. **3** *Zool.* either of the lobes of a whale's tail. ▷ CETACEAN

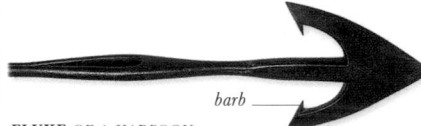

barb

FLUKE OF A HARPOON

fluk·y /flóokee/ *adj.* (**flukier, flukiest**) obtained more by chance than skill. □□ **fluk·i·ly** *adv.* **fluk·i·ness** *n.*

flume /floom/ *n.* **1** an artificial channel conveying water, typically used for transporting logs. **2** a water slide or chute at a swimming pool or amusement park.

flum·mer·y /flúmeree/ *n.* (*pl.* **-ies**) **1** empty compliments; trifles. **2** any of various sweet dishes made with beaten eggs, sugar, etc.

flum·mox /flúməks/ *v.tr.* *colloq.* confound; disconcert.

flump /flump/ *v.* (often foll. by *down*) **1** *intr.* fall or move heavily. **2** *tr.* set or throw down with a heavy thud.

flung *past* and *past part.* of FLING.

flunk /flungk/ *v.* & *n.* *colloq.* ● *v.* **1** *tr.* **a** fail (an examination, etc.). **b** fail (an examination candidate). **2** *intr.* (often foll. by *out*) fail utterly; give up. ● *n.* an instance of flunking. □ **flunk out** be dismissed from school, etc., after failing an examination, course, etc.

flun·ky /flúngkee/ *n.* (also **flun·key**) (*pl.* **-ies** or **-eys**) usu. *derog.* **1** a liveried servant. **2** a toady. **3** a person who does menial work.

fluo·resce /floorés, flaw-/ *v.intr.* be or become fluorescent.

fluo·res·cence /flŏorésəns, flaw-/ *n.* **1** ▲ the visible or invisible radiation produced from certain substances as a result of incident radiation of a shorter wavelength. **2** the property of absorbing light of short (invisible) wavelength and emitting light of longer (visible) wavelength.

fluo·res·cent /flŏorésənt, flaw-/ *adj.* (of a substance) having or showing fluorescence.

fluo·res·cent lamp *n.* (also **fluo·res·cent bulb**) a lamp or bulb radiating largely by fluorescence.

fluor·i·date /flóoridayt, flaw-/ *v.tr.* add traces of fluoride to (drinking water, etc.). □□ **fluor·i·da·tion** /flŏoridáyshən, flaw-/ *n.* (also **fluor·i·di·za·tion**).

fluor·ide /flóorīd, flaw-/ *n.* any binary compound of fluorine.

fluor·i·nate /flŏorinayt, flaw-/ *v.tr.* **1** = FLUORIDATE. **2** introduce fluorine into (a compound). □□ **fluor·i·na·tion** /-náyshən/ *n.*

FLUORESCENCE

Fluorescence is a type of luminescence. In the demonstration shown here, a bright light is shone into a test tube containing sodium fluorescein, which appears red in ambient light conditions. The fluorescein in the solution transforms energy from the flashlight, emitting it as a bright green fluorescent light.

test tube

flashlight

fluorescent green light emitted

fluorescein appears red in ambient light

solution of sodium fluorescein

DEMONSTRATION OF FLUORESCENCE

fluor·ine /flóoreen, fláw-/ *n.* a poisonous pale yellow gaseous element of the halogen group. ¶ Symb.: **f.**

fluor·ite /flóorīt, fláw-/ *n.* ◄ a mineral form of calcium fluoride.

fluoro- /flóorō, fláw-/ *comb. form* **1** fluorine (*fluorocarbon*). **2** fluorescence (*fluoroscope*).

fluor·o·car·bon /flŏorōkáarbən, fláw-/ *n.* a compound in which fluorine atoms replace the hydrogen atoms of a hydrocarbon.

fluor·o·scope /flóorōskōp, fláw-/ *n.* an instrument with a fluorescent screen on which X-ray images may be viewed without developing X-ray photographs.

fluor·o·spar /flóorspaar, flóor-/ *n.* = FLUORITE.

FLUORITE

flur·ry /flóree, flúree/ *n.* & *v.* ● *n.* (*pl.* **-ies**) **1** a gust or squall (esp. of snow). **2** a sudden burst of activity. **3** nervous agitation (*a flurry of speculation*). ● *v.tr.* (**-ies, -ied**) confuse by haste or nervousness; agitate.

flush[1] /flush/ *v.* & *n.* ● *v.* **1** *intr.* **a** redden; flush (*he flushed with embarrassment*). **b** glow with a warm color (*sky flushed pink*). **2** *tr.* (usu. as **flushed** *adj.*) cause to glow, blush, or be elated (often foll. by *with*: *flushed with pride*). **3** *tr.* **a** cleanse (a drain, toilet, etc.) by a rushing flow of water. **b** (often foll. by *away, down*) dispose of (an object) in this way (*flushed away the cigarette*). **4** *intr.* rush out; spurt. **5** *tr.* flood (*the river flushed the meadow*). **6** *intr.* (of a plant) throw out fresh shoots. ● *n.* **1 a** a blush. **b** a glow of light or color. **2 a** a rush of water. **b** the cleansing of a drain, toilet, etc., by flushing. **3 a** a rush of emotion. **b** the elation produced by a victory, etc. (*the flush of triumph*). **4** sudden abundance. **5** freshness; vigor (*in the first flush of womanhood*). **6 a** a feverish temperature. **b** facial redness, esp. caused by fever, alcohol, etc. **7** a fresh growth of grass, etc. □□ **flush·er** *n.*

flush[2] /flush/ *adj.* & *v.* ● *adj.* **1** (often foll. by *with*) in the same plane; level (*the sink is flush with the counter*). **2** (usu. *predic.*) *colloq.* **a** having plenty of money. **b** (of money) abundant; plentiful. **3** full to overflowing; in flood. ● *v.tr.* **1** make (surfaces) level. **2** fill in (a joint) level with a surface. □□ **flush·ness** *n.*

flush[3] /flush/ *n.* a hand of cards all of one suit.

flush[4] /flush/ *v.* **1** *tr.* cause (esp. a game bird) to fly up. **2** *intr.* (of a bird) fly up and away. □ **flush out 1** reveal. **2** drive out.

flus·ter /flústər/ *v. & n.* ● *v.* **1** *tr. & intr.* make or become nervous or confused (*was flustered by the noise*). **2** *tr.* confuse with drink; half-intoxicate. **3** *intr.* bustle. ● *n.* a confused or agitated state.

mouth-piece
blow-hole
thumb keys
key

flute /floot/ *n. & v.* ● *n.* **1 a** ◀ a high-pitched woodwind instrument, having holes along it stopped by the fingers or keys, and held horizontally. ▷ ORCHESTRA, WOODWIND. **b** an organ stop having a similar sound. **c** any of various wind instruments resembling a flute. **d** a flute player. **2 a** *Archit.* an ornamental vertical groove in a column. **b** a trumpet-shaped frill on a dress, etc. **c** any similar cylindrical groove. **3** a tall narrow wineglass. ● *v.* **1** *intr.* play the flute. **2** *intr.* speak, sing, or whistle in a fluting way. **3** *tr.* make flutes or grooves in. **4** *tr.* play (a tune, etc.) on a flute. □□ **flute·like** *adj.* **flut·ing** *n.* **flut·ist** *n.* (cf. FLAUTIST). **flut·y** *adj.* (in sense 1a of *n.*).

flut·ter /flútər/ *v. & n.* ● *v.* **1 a** *intr.* flap the wings in flying or trying to fly. **b** *tr.* flap (the wings). **2** *intr.* fall with a quivering motion. **3** *intr. & tr.* move or cause to move irregularly (*the wind fluttered the flag*). **4** *intr.* go about restlessly. **5** *tr.* agitate; confuse. **6** *intr.* (of a pulse or heartbeat) beat irregularly. **7** *intr.* tremble with excitement. ● *n.* **1 a** the act of fluttering. **b** an instance of this. **2 a** tremulous state of excitement; (*was in a flutter; caused a flutter with his behavior*). **3** an abnormally rapid but regular heartbeat. **4** *Electronics* a rapid variation of pitch, esp. of recorded sound (cf. WOW[2]). **5** a vibration. □□ **flut·ter·y** *adj.*

flu·vi·al /flóoveeəl/ *adj.* of, found in, or produced by a river or rivers.

flu·vi·om·e·ter /flóoveeómitər/ *n.* an instrument for measuring the rise and fall of rivers.

flux /fluks/ *n. & v.* ● *n.* **1** a process of flowing or flowing out. **2** an issue or discharge. **3** continuous change (*in a state of flux*). **4** *Metallurgy* a substance mixed with a metal, etc., to promote fusion. **5** *Physics* **a** the rate of flow of any fluid across a given area. **b** the amount of fluid crossing an area in a given time. **6** *Physics* the amount of radiation or particles incident on an area in a given time. **7** *Electr.* the total electric or magnetic field passing through a surface. ● *v.* **1** *tr. & intr.* make or become fluid. **2** *tr.* **a** fuse. **b** treat with a fusing flux.

fly[1] /flī/ *v. & n.* ● *v.* (**flies**; *past* **flew** /floo/; *past part.* **flown** /flōn/) **1** *intr.* move through the air under control, esp. with wings. **2** (of an aircraft or its occupants): **a** *intr.* travel through the air or through space. **b** *tr.* traverse (*flew the Atlantic*). **3** *tr.* **a** control the flight of (esp. an aircraft). **b** transport in an aircraft. **4 a** *tr.* cause to fly or remain aloft. **b** *intr.* (of a flag, hair, etc.) wave or flutter. **5** *intr.* pass or rise quickly through the air or over an obstacle. **6** *intr.* pass swiftly (*time flies*). **7** *intr.* **a** flee. **b** *colloq.* depart hastily. **8** *intr.* be forced off suddenly (*sent me flying*). **9** *intr.* (foll. by *at, upon*) **a** hasten or spring violently. **b** attack or criticize fiercely. **10** *tr.* flee from. **11** *intr.* *Baseball* hit a fly ball. ● *n.* (*pl.* **-ies**) **1** (*Brit.* usu. in *pl.*) **a** a flap on a garment, esp. pants, to cover a fastening. **b** this fastening. **2 a** a fabric cover pitched over a tent for extra protection from rain, etc. **b** a flap at the entrance of a tent. ▷ TENT. **3** (in *pl.*) the space over the proscenium in a theater. **4** the act or an instance of flying. **5** *Baseball* a batted ball hit high in the air. **6** a speed-regulating device in clockwork and machinery. □ **fly high 1** pursue a high ambition. **2** excel; prosper. **fly in the face of** openly disregard or disobey. **fly into a rage** (or **temper**, etc.) become suddenly or violently angry. **fly off the handle** *colloq.* lose one's temper suddenly and unexpectedly. □□ **fly·a·ble** *adj.*

fly[2] /flī/ *n.* (*pl.* **flies**) **1** ▼ any insect of the order Diptera with two usu. transparent wings. **2** any other winged insect. **3** a disease of plants or animals caused by flies. **4** a natural or artificial fly used as bait in fishing. ▷ DRY FLY. □ **fly in the ointment** a minor irritation that spoils enjoyment. **fly on the wall** an unnoticed observer. **like flies** in large numbers.

fly·a·way /flíəway/ *adj.* (of hair, etc.) tending to fly out or up.

fly ball *n.* = FLY[1] *n.* 5.

fly·blown /flíblōn/ *adj.* tainted, esp. by flies.

fly-by-night *adj.* **1** unreliable. **2** short-lived.

fly-by-wire *adj.* a semi-automatic, computer-regulated system for controlling an aircraft or spacecraft.

fly·catch·er /flíkachər/ *n.* ◀ any bird of the families Tyrannidae and Muscicapidae, catching insects, esp. in short flights from a perch.

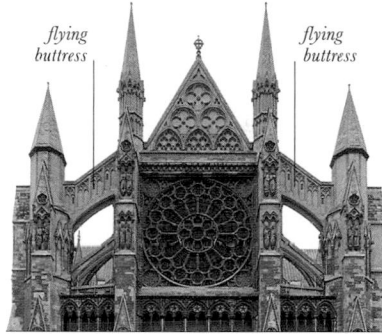

FLYCATCHER: JAPANESE BLUE FLYCATCHER (*Cyanoptila cyanomelana*)

fly·er var. of FLIER.

fly-fish *v.intr.* fish with a fly (sense 4 of FLY[2]).

fly·ing /flí-ing/ *adj. & n.* ● *adj.* **1** fluttering or waving in the air. **2** hasty; brief (*a flying visit*). **3** designed for rapid movement. **4** (of an animal) able to make very long leaps by using winglike membranes, etc. ● *n.* flight, esp. in an aircraft. □ **with flying colors** with distinction.

fly·ing but·tress *n.* ▼ a buttress slanting from a separate column, usu. forming an arch with the wall it supports. ▷ GOTHIC.

flying buttress   *flying buttress*

FLYING BUTTRESS: ELEVATION OF WESTMINSTER ABBEY, ENGLAND, SHOWING FLYING BUTTRESSES

fly·ing fish *n.* (*pl.* **fish** or **fishes**) ▼ any tropical fish of the family Exocoetidae, with winglike pectoral fins for gliding through the air.

FLYING FISH (*Exocetus volitans*)   *pectoral fin*

fly·ing sau·cer *n.* any unidentified, esp. circular, flying object, popularly supposed to have come from space.

fly·ing squir·rel *n.* any of various squirrels, esp. of the genera *Glaucomys Pteromys*, with skin joining the fore and hind limbs for gliding from tree to tree.

fly·leaf /flíleef/ *n.* (*pl.* **-leaves**) a blank leaf at the beginning or end of a book.

fly·o·ver /flíōvər/ *n.* **1** a ceremonial flight of aircraft past a person or a place. **2** *Brit.* a bridge carrying one road or railroad over another.

fly·pa·per /flípaypər/ *n.* sticky treated paper for catching flies.

fly·sheet /flísheet/ *n.* a tract or circular of two or four pages.

fly swat·ter *n.* an implement for killing flies and other insects, usu. consisting of a flat mesh square attached to a handle.

fly·trap /flítrap/ *n.* any of various plants that catch flies, esp. the Venus flytrap.

fly·weight /flíwayt/ *n.* **1** a weight in certain sports intermediate between light flyweight and bantamweight. **2** a boxer, wrestler, etc., of this weight.

FLUTE: MODERN METAL FLUTE

F

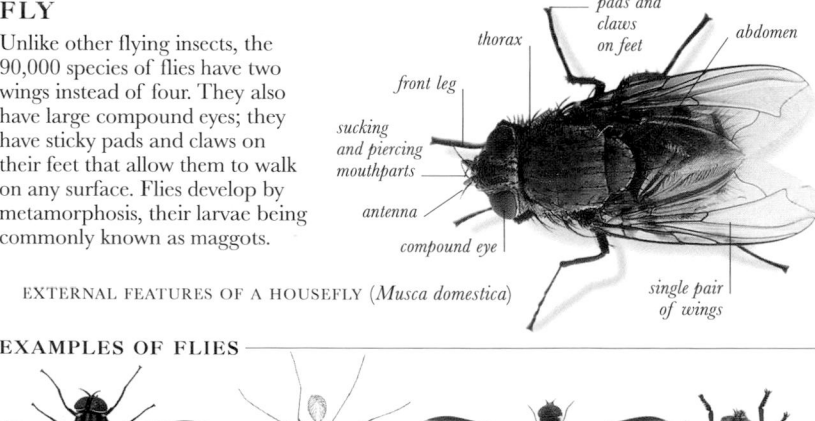

FLY

Unlike other flying insects, the 90,000 species of flies have two wings instead of four. They also have large compound eyes; they have sticky pads and claws on their feet that allow them to walk on any surface. Flies develop by metamorphosis, their larvae being commonly known as maggots.

thorax
pads and claws on feet
abdomen
front leg
sucking and piercing mouthparts
antenna
compound eye
single pair of wings

EXTERNAL FEATURES OF A HOUSEFLY (*Musca domestica*)

EXAMPLES OF FLIES

SOUTH AMERICAN FLY (*Pantophthalmus bellardii*)

CRANE FLY (*Holorusia* species)

AFRICAN BEE FLY (*Ligyra venus*)

ROBBER FLY (*Mallophora atra*)

F

fly·wheel /flíhweel, -weel/ *n.* ▶ a heavy wheel on a revolving shaft used to regulate machinery or accumulate power. ▷ INTERNAL-COMBUSTION ENGINE

tip of revolving shaft

flywheel   piston   gas

drive belt

generator

FLYWHEEL IN A GENERATOR

FM *abbr.* **1** frequency modulation. **2** Field Marshal.

Fm *symb. Chem.* the element fermium.

FNMA /fáneemáy/ *n.* Federal National Mortgage Association.

f-number /éf numbər/ *n.* (also **f-stop**) *Photog.* the ratio of the focal length to the effective diameter of a lens.

foal /fōl/ *n. & v.* • *n.* the young of a horse or related animal. • *v.tr.* give birth to (a foal). □ **in** (or **with**) **foal** (of a mare, etc.) pregnant.

foam /fōm/ *n. & v.* • *n.* **1** a mass of small bubbles formed on or in liquid by agitation, fermentation, etc. **2** a froth of saliva or sweat. **3** a substance resembling these, e.g., rubber or plastic in a cellular mass. **4** the sea. • *v.intr.* **1** emit foam; froth. **2** run with foam. **3** (of a vessel) be filled and overflow with foam. □ **foam at the mouth** be very angry. □□ **foam·less** *adj.* **foam·y** *adj.* (**foamier, foami·est**).

foam rub·ber *n.* a light, spongy foam used for mattresses, pillows, cushions, etc.

fob[1] /fob/ *n. & v.* • *n.* **1** (in full **fob chain**) a chain attached to a watch for carrying in a waistcoat or pocket. **2** a small pocket for carrying a watch. **3** a tab on a key ring. • *v.tr.* (**fobbed, fobbing**) put in one's fob; pocket.

fob[2] /fob/ *v.tr.* (**fobbed, fobbing**) cheat; deceive. □ **fob off 1** (often foll. by *with* a thing) deceive into accepting something inferior. **2** (often foll. by *on to* a person) palm or pass off (an inferior thing).

f.o.b. *abbr.* free on board.

fo·cal /fōkəl/ *adj.* of, at, or in terms of a focus.

fo·cal·ize /fōkəlīz/ *v.tr.* = FOCUS *v.* □□ **fo·cal·i·za·tion** /-lizáyshən/ *n.*

fo·cal length *n.* the distance between the center of a mirror or lens and its focus. ▷ LENS

fo·cal point *n* = FOCUS *n.* 1.

fo'c's'le var. of FORECASTLE.

fo·cus /fōkəs/ *n. & v.* • *n.* (*pl.* **focuses** or **foci** /fōsī/) **1** *Physics* **a** the point at which rays or waves meet after reflection or refraction. ▷ SIGHT. **b** the point from which diverging rays or waves appear to proceed. **2 a** *Optics* the point at which an object must be situated for an image of it given by a lens or mirror to be well defined. **b** the adjustment of

the eye or a lens necessary to produce a clear image. **c** a state of clear definition (*out of focus*). **3** the center of interest or activity (*focus of attention*). **4** *Geom.* one of the points from which the distances to any point of a given curve are connected by a linear relation. **5** *Med.* the principal site of an infection or other disease. **6** *Geol.* the place of origin of an earthquake. • *v.* (**focused, focusing** or **focussed, focussing**) **1** *tr.* bring into focus. **2** *tr.* adjust the focus of (a lens, the eye, etc.). **3** *tr. & intr.* (often foll. by *on*) concentrate or be concentrated on. **4** *intr. & tr.* converge or make converge to a focus. □□ **fo·cus·er** *n.*

fo·cus group *n.* a group that meets to discuss a particular problem, issue, etc.

fod·der /fódər/ *n. & v.* • *n.* dried hay or straw, etc., for cattle, etc. • *v.tr.* give fodder to.

foe /fō/ *n.* an enemy or opponent.

foet·id var. of FETID.

fog /fawg, fog/ *n. & v.* • *n.* **1** ▼ a thick cloud of water droplets or smoke suspended in the atmosphere at or near the Earth's surface. **2** *Photog.* cloudiness on a developed negative, etc., obscuring the image. **3** an uncertain or confused position or state. • *v.* (**fogged, fogging**) **1** *tr.* **a** (often foll. by *up*) cover with fog or condensed vapor. **b** bewilder or confuse. **2** *intr.* (often foll. by *up*) become covered with fog or condensed vapor. **3** *tr. Photog.* make (a negative, etc.) obscure or cloudy. □ **in a fog** puzzled; at a loss.

fog bank *n.* a mass of fog at sea.

fog·bound /fáwgbownd, fóg-/ *adj.* unable to proceed because of fog.

fog·bow /fáwgbō, fóg-/ *n.* a manifestation like a rainbow, produced by light on fog.

fo·gey var. of FOGY.

fog·gy /fáwgee, fógee/ *adj.* (**foggier, foggiest**) **1** (of the atmosphere) thick or obscure with fog. **2** of or like fog. **3** vague; confused; unclear. □ **not have the foggiest** *colloq.* have no idea at all. □□ **fog·gi·ness** *n.*

fog·horn /fáwghawrn, fóg-/ *n.* **1** a deep-sounding instrument for warning ships in fog. **2** *colloq.* a loud penetrating voice.

fo·gy /fōgee/ *n.* (also **fo·gey**) (*pl.* **-ies** or **-eys**) a dull old-fashioned person (esp. *old fogy*). □□ **fo·gy·dom** *n.* **fo·gy·ish** *adj.*

foi·ble /fóybəl/ *n.* a minor weakness or idiosyncrasy.

foie gras /fwaa gráá/ *n. colloq.* = PÂTÉ DE FOIE GRAS.

foil[1] /foyl/ *v.tr.* frustrate; baffle; defeat.

foil[2] /foyl/ *n.* **1 a** metal hammered or rolled into a thin sheet (*tin foil*). **b** a sheet of this or another material attached to mirror glass as a reflector. **c** a leaf of foil placed under a precious stone, etc., to brighten or color it. **2** a person or thing that enhances the qualities of another by contrast.

foil[3] /foyl/ *n.* ▶ light blunt-edged sword with a button on its point used in fencing. ▷ FENCING

foil[4] /foyl/ *n.* = HYDROFOIL.

foist /foyst/ *v.tr.* **1** (foll. by *on, upon*) impose (an unwelcome person or thing). **2** (foll. by *on, upon*) falsely fix the authorship of (a composition). **3** (foll. by *in, into*) introduce surreptitiously or unwarrantably.

fol. *abbr.* folio.

fold[1] /fōld/ *v. & n.* • *v.* **1** *tr.* **a** bend or close (a flexible thing) over upon itself. **b** (foll. by *back, over, down*) bend a part of (a flexible thing) in the manner specified (*fold down the flap*). **2** *intr.* become or be able to be folded. **3** *tr.* (foll. by *away, up*) make compact by folding. **4** *intr. colloq.* **a** collapse; disintegrate. **b** (of an enterprise) fail; go bankrupt. **5** *tr. poet.* embrace (esp. *fold in the arms* or *to the breast*). **6** *tr.* (foll. by *about, around*) clasp (the arms); wrap; envelop. **7** *tr.* (foll. by *in*) mix (an ingredient with others) using a gentle cutting and turning motion. • *n.* **1** the act or an instance of folding. **2** a line made by or for folding. **3** a folded part. **4** a hollow among hills. **5** *Geol.* a curvature of strata. ▷ MOUNTAIN. □ **fold one's arms** place one's arms across the chest, side by side or entwined. □□ **fold·a·ble** *adj.*

button

FOIL

fold[2] /fōld/ *n.* **1** = SHEEPFOLD. **2** a body of believers or members of a church.

fold·a·way /fōldəway/ *adj.* adapted or designed to be folded away.

fold·er /fōldər/ *n.* **1** a folding cover or holder for loose papers. **2** a folded leaflet.

fold·ing mon·ey *n. colloq.* paper money.

fo·li·a·ceous /fōlee-áyshəs/ *adj.* **1** of or like leaves. **2** having organs like leaves. **3** laminated.

fo·li·age /fōleeij/ *n.* **1** leaves; leafage. **2** a design in art resembling leaves.

fo·li·ar /fōleeər/ *adj.* of or relating to leaves.

fo·li·ate *adj. & v.* • *adj.* /fōleeət/ **1** leaflike. **2** having leaves. **3** (in *comb.*) having a specified number of leaflets (*trifoliate*). • *v.* /fōleeayt/ **1** *intr.* split into laminae. **2** *tr.* number leaves (not pages) of (a volume) consecutively. □□ **fo·li·a·tion** /-áyshən/ *n.*

fo·lic ac·id /fōlik, fól-/ *n.* a vitamin of the B complex, found in leafy green vegetables, liver, and kidney, a deficiency of which causes pernicious anemia.

fo·li·o /fōleeō/ *n. & adj.* • *n.* (*pl.* **-os**) **1** a leaf of paper, etc., esp. one numbered only on the front. **2 a** a leaf number of a book. **b** a page number of a book. **3** a sheet of paper folded once making two leaves of a book. **4** a book made of such sheets. • *adj.* (of a book) made of folios, of the largest size. □ **in folio** made of folios.

fo·li·ole /fōleeōl/ *n.* a division of a compound leaf; a leaflet.

folk /fōk/ *n.* (*pl.* **folk** or **folks**) **1** (treated as *pl.*) people in general or of a specified class (*few folks about*; *townsfolk*). **2** (in *pl.*) (usu. **folks**) one's parents or relatives. **3** (treated as *sing.*) a people. **4** (treated as *sing.*) *colloq.* traditional music, esp. a style featuring acoustic guitar. **5** (*attrib.*) of popular origin; traditional (*folk art*).

folk dance *n.* **1** a dance of traditional origin. **2** the music for such a dance.

folk·lore /fōklawr/ *n.* the traditional beliefs and stories of a people; the study of these. □□ **folk·lor·ic** *adj.* **folk·lor·ist** *n.* **folk·lor·is·tic** *adj.*

folk mu·sic *n.* FOLK 4.

folk sing·er *n.* a singer of folk songs.

folk song *n.* a song of popular or traditional origin or style.

folk·sy /fōksee/ *adj.* (**folksier, folksiest**) **1** friendly; sociable; informal. **2 a** having the characteristics of folk art, culture, etc. **b** ostensibly or artificially folkish. □□ **folk·si·ness** *n.*

folk tale *n.* a popular or traditional story.

FOG

There are two main types of fog. Advection fog occurs at sea when warm, moist air flows over cold sea water. The water vapor in the air condenses to form a layer of fog.

Radiation fog occurs on land on cool, clear nights. As the ground loses its heat, it may cool the air nearby, creating fog. Mist is a light fog, while smog is fog with pollutants.

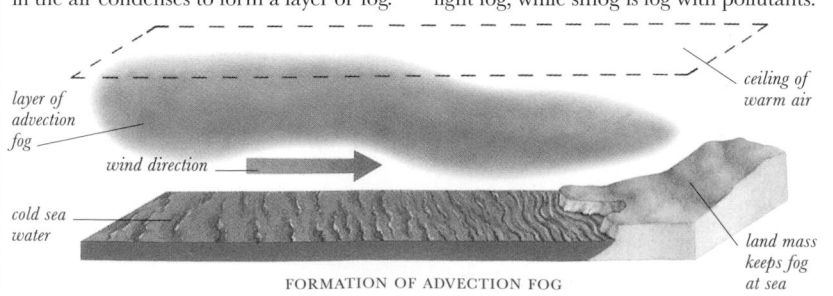

layer of advection fog

wind direction

cold sea water

ceiling of warm air

land mass keeps fog at sea

FORMATION OF ADVECTION FOG

FOLD

Folds in the Earth's surface occur when the tectonic plates of the Earth's crust collide, causing the rock strata to deform. The strata are squeezed horizontally and vertically, and the scale and severity of folding can vary greatly. The type of fold produced depends on the strength of the forces, the rock's resilience, and the arrangement of the strata. Various characteristic fold types are shown here.

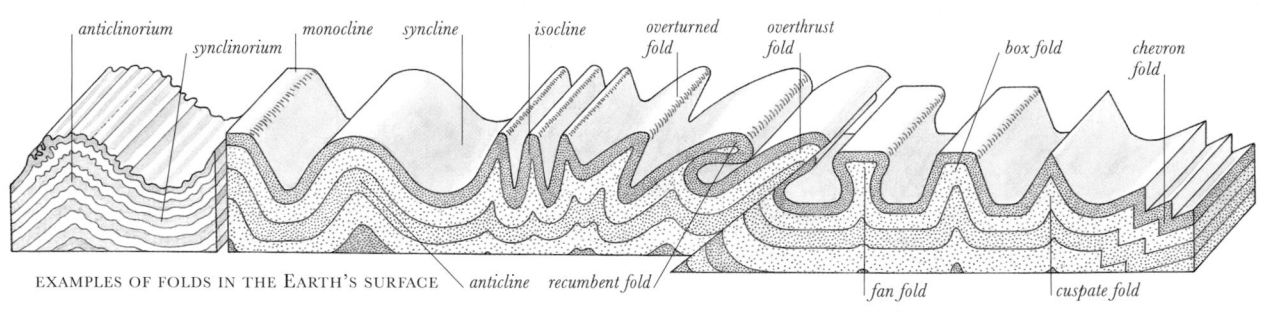

anticlinorium   *synclinorium*   *monocline*   *syncline*   *isocline*   *overturned fold*   *overthrust fold*   *box fold*   *chevron fold*

EXAMPLES OF FOLDS IN THE EARTH'S SURFACE   *anticline*   *recumbent fold*   *fan fold*   *cuspate fold*

F

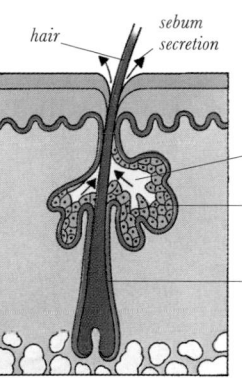

hair   *sebum secretion*   *sebum*   *sebaceous gland*   *follicle*

FOLLICLE: CROSS SECTION OF A HUMAN HAIR FOLLICLE

fol·li·cle /fólikəl/ *n.* **1** ◄ a small sac or vesicle. **2** a small sac-shaped secretory gland or cavity. ▷ SKIN, OVARY. □□ **fol·lic·u·lar** /fəlíkyələr/ *adj.*

fol·low /fólō/ *v.* **1** *tr.* or (foll. by *after*) *intr.* go or come after (a person or thing proceeding ahead *tr.* go along (a route, path, etc.). **3** *tr. & intr.* come after in order or time. **4** *tr.* take as a guide or leader. **5** *tr.* conform to (*follow your example*). **6** *tr.* practice (a trade or profession). **7** *tr.* undertake (a course of study, etc.). **8** *tr.* understand the meaning or tendency of (a speaker or argument). **9** *tr.* maintain awareness of the current state or progress of (events, etc., in a particular sphere) **10** *tr.* (foll. by *with*) provide with a sequel or successor. **11** *intr.* happen after something else; ensue. **12** *intr.* **a** be necessarily true as a result of something else. **b** (foll. by *from*) be a result of. □ **follow one's nose** trust to instinct. **follow on** continue. **follow out** carry out; adhere precisely to (instructions, etc.). **follow suit 1** *Cards* play a card of the suit led. **2** conform to another person's actions. **follow through 1** continue (an action, etc.) to its conclusion. **2** *Sports* continue the movement of a stroke after the ball has been struck. **follow up 1** (foll. by *with*) pursue; develop; supplement. **2** make further investigation of.

fol·low·er /fólōər/ *n.* **1** an adherent or devotee. **2** a person or thing that follows.

fol·low·ing /fólōing/ *prep., n., & adj.* ● *prep.* coming after in time; as a sequel to. ● *n.* a body of adherents or devotees. ● *adj.* that follows or comes after.

fol·low-my-lead·er *n.* (also **fol·low the lead·er**) a game in which players must do as the leader does.

fol·low-through *n.* the action of following through.

fol·low-up *n.* a subsequent or continued action, measure, experience, etc.

fol·ly /fólee/ *n.* (*pl.* **-ies**) **1** foolishness; lack of good sense. **2** a foolishact, behavior, idea, etc. **3** ◄ an ornamental building, usu. a tower or mock Gothic ruin. **4** (in

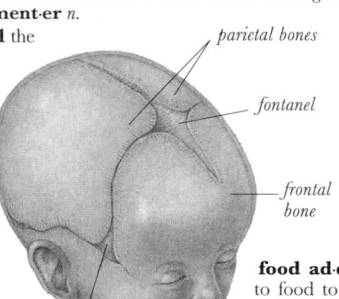

pl.) *Theatr.* **a** a revue with glamorous female performers, esp. scantily clad. **b** the performers.

fo·ment /fōmént/ *v.tr.* **1** instigate or stir up (trouble, sedition, etc.). **2 a** bathe with warm or medicated liquid. **b** apply warmth to. □□ **fo·ment·er** *n.*

fo·men·ta·tion /fōmentáyshən/ *n.* **1** the act or an instance of fomenting. **2** materials prepared for application to a wound, etc.

fond /fond/ *adj.* **1** (foll. by *of*) having affection or a liking for. **2** affectionate; loving; doting. **3** (of beliefs, etc.) foolishly optimistic or credulous; naive. □□ **fond·ly** *adv.* **fond·ness** *n.*

fon·dant /fóndənt/ *n.* a soft creamy candy of flavored sugar.

fon·dle /fónd'l/ *v.tr.* touch or stroke lovingly; caress. □□ **fon·dler** *n.*

fon·due /fondóo, -dyóo/ *n.* **1** a dish of flavored melted cheese. **2** a dish of small pieces of food cooked at the table by dipping in hot melted chocolate, cheese, etc.

parietal bones   *fontanel*   *frontal bone*   *fontanel*

FONTANEL: INFANT'S SKULL SHOWING FONTANELS

font¹ /font/ *n.* **1** a receptacle in a church for baptismal water. ▷ CHURCH. **2** the reservoir for oil in a lamp.

font² /font/ *Printing* a set of type of one face or size.

fon·ta·nel /fóntənél/ *n.* ◄ a membranous space in an infant's skull at the angles of the parietal bones.

food /food/ *n.* **1** a nutritious substance, esp. solid in form, ingested to maintain life and growth. **2** ideas as a resource for or stimulus to mental work (*food for thought*).

food ad·di·tive *n.* a substance added to food to enhance its color, flavor, or presentation, or for any other nonnutritional purpose.

food chain *n. Ecol.* ▼ a series of organisms each dependent on the next for food.

food·ie /foodee/ *n.* (also **food·y**) (*pl.* **-ies**) *colloq.* a person who is particular about food; a gourmet.

FOOD CHAIN

A food chain is a pathway that shows how energy and nutrients pass between living things. Each chain links a single series of species, with different food chains interconnecting to form food webs. In a food chain, each species occupies a particular position, known as a trophic level. The marine food web here shows a number of separate food chains, with a total of five trophic levels. In each chain, the first level is occupied by plantlike planktonic organisms, which make food by photosynthesis. These "producers" supply food that can then be passed on to "consumers" – animals that either eat the producers or each other. Few food chains have more than five trophic levels, because a large amount of energy is lost each time that food is passed on.

killer whale (highest trophic level)   *seabird*   *seal*   *minke whale*   *fish*   *squid*   *movement of food and energy*   *krill*   *plankton (lowest trophic level)*

MARINE FOOD CHAINS

FOLLY: 18TH-CENTURY ENGLISH GARDEN FOLLY

food poi·son·ing *n.* illness due to bacteria or other toxins in food.

food pro·ces·sor *n.* ▼ a machine for chopping and mixing food materials.

filling funnel
working bowl
driveshaft
controls
motor block

FOOD PROCESSOR

food pyr·a·mid *n.* **1** an ecological model of the food chain, with green plants at the base and predators at the apex. **2** a dietary model of recommended foods, with carbohydrates at the base and fats and sugars at the apex.

food·stuff /foŏdstuf/ *n.* any substance suitable as food.

fool[1] /foŏl/ *n., v., & adj.* ● *n.* **1** a person who acts unwisely or imprudently; a stupid person. **2** *hist.* a jester; a clown. **3** a dupe. **4** (often foll. by *for*) a devotee or fan (*a fool for the ballet*). ● *v.* **1** *tr.* deceive so as to cause to appear foolish. **2** *tr.* (foll. by *into* + verbal noun, or *out of*) trick; cause to do something foolish. **3** *tr.* play tricks on; dupe. **4** *intr.* act in a joking, frivolous, or teasing way. **5** *intr.* (foll. by *around*) behave in a playful or silly way. ● *adj. colloq.* foolish; silly. **act** (or **play**) **the fool** behave in a silly way. **make a fool of** make (a person or oneself) look foolish; trick or deceive. **no** (or **nobody's**) **fool** a shrewd or prudent person.

fool[2] /foŏl/ *n. esp. Brit.* a dessert of usu. stewed fruit crushed and mixed with cream, custard, etc.

fool·er·y /foŏləree/ *n.* (*pl.* **-ies**) **1** foolish behavior. **2** a foolish act.

fool·har·dy /foŏlhaardee/ *adj.* (**foolhardier, foolhardiest**) rashly or foolishly bold; reckless. □□ **fool·har·di·ly** *adv.* **fool·har·di·ness** *n.*

fool·ish /foŏlish/ *adj.* (of a person, action, etc.) lacking good sense or judgment; unwise. □□ **fool·ish·ly** *adv.* **fool·ish·ness** *n.*

fool·proof /foŏlproŏf/ *adj.* (of a procedure, mechanism, etc.) so straightforward or simple as to be incapable of misuse or mistake.

fool's gold *n.* ◄ iron pyrites.

fool's par·a·dise *n.* happiness founded on an illusion.

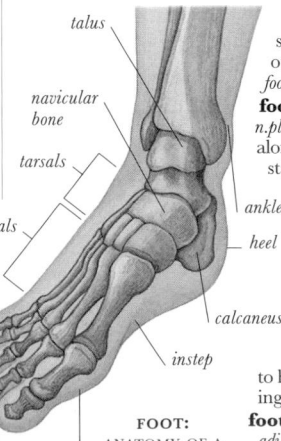

iron pyrites

FOOL'S GOLD

foot /foŏt/ *n. & v.* ● *n.* (*pl.* **feet** /feet/) **1 a** ► the lower extremity of the leg below the ankle. ▷ ANKLE. **b** the part of a sock, etc., covering the foot. **2 a** the lower or lowest part of a page, stairs, etc. **b** the lower end of a table. **c** the end of a bed where the user's feet normally rest. **3** the base, often projecting, of anything extending vertically. **4** a step, pace, or tread; a manner of walking (*fleet of foot*). **5** (*pl.* **feet** or **foot**) a unit of linear measure equal to 12 inches (30.48 cm). **6** *Prosody* **a** a group of syllables (one usu. stressed) constituting a metrical unit. **b** a simi-

lar unit of speech, etc. **7** *Brit. hist.* infantry (*a regiment of foot*). **8** *Zool.* the locomotive or adhesive organ of invertebrates. ▷ GASTROPOD, MOLLUSK, RAZOR CLAM. **9** *Bot.* the part by which a petal is attached. **10** a device on a sewing machine for holding the material steady as it is sewn. **11** (*pl.* **foots**) dregs; oil refuse. **12** (usu. in *pl.*) footlights. ● *v.tr.* **1** (usu. as **foot it**) a traverse (esp. a long distance) by foot. **b** dance. **2** pay (a bill, esp. one considered large). □ **at a person's feet** as a person's disciple or subject. **feet of clay** a fundamental weakness in a person otherwise revered. **get one's feet wet** begin to participate. **have one's** (or **both**) **feet on the ground** be practical. **have a foot in the door** have a prospect of success. **have one foot in the grave** be near death or very old. **my foot!** *int.* expressing strong contradiction. **not put a foot wrong** make no mistakes. **off one's feet** so as to be unable to stand, or in a state compared with this (*was rushed off my feet*). **on foot** walking; not riding, etc. **put one's feet up** *colloq.* take a rest. **put one's foot down** *colloq.* **1** be firmly insistent or repressive. **2** accelerate a motor vehicle. **put one's foot in it** *colloq.* commit a blunder or indiscretion. **set foot in** (or **on**) enter; go into. □□ **foot·ed** *adj.* (also in *comb.*). **foot·less** *adj.*

foot·age /foŏtij/ *n.* **1** length or distance in feet. **2** an amount of film made for showing, broadcasting, etc.

foot-and-mouth dis·ease *n.* a contagious viral disease of cattle, etc.

foot·ball /foŏtbawl/ *n. & v.* ● *n.* **1** ► any of several outdoor games between two teams played with a ball on a field with goals at each end. ¶ In N. America generally American football is referred to; elsewhere usu. soccer or rugby is meant. **2** a large inflated ball of a kind used in these. **3** a topical issue or problem that is the subject of continued argument or controversy. ● *v.intr.* play football. □□ **foot·ball·er** *n.*

foot·board /foŏtbawrd/ *n.* **1** a board to support the feet or a foot. **2** an upright board at the foot of a bed.

foot·brake /foŏtbrayk/ *n.* a brake operated by the foot in a motor vehicle.

foot·bridge /foŏtbrij/ *n.* a bridge for use by pedestrians.

foot·er /foŏtər/ *n.* (in *comb.*) a person or thing of so many feet in length or height (*six-footer*).

foot·fall /foŏtfawl/ *n.* the sound of a footstep.

foot·hill /foŏt-hil/ *n.* (often in *pl.*) any of the low hills around the base of a mountain.

foot·hold /foŏt-hōld/ *n.* **1** a place, esp. in climbing, where a foot can be supported securely. **2** a secure initial position or advantage.

foot·ing /foŏting/ *n.* **1** a foothold; a secure position (*lost his footing*). **2** the basis on which an enterprise is established or operates; relative position or status; the position or status of a person in relation to others (*on an equal footing*).

foot·lights /foŏtlīts/ *n.pl.* a row of lights along the front of a stage. ▷ THEATER

foot·ling /foŏtling/ *adj. colloq.* trivial; silly.

foot·lock·er /foŏtlokər/ *n.* a small trunk usu. kept at the foot of a soldier's or camper's bunk to hold items of clothing or equipment.

foot·loose /foŏtloŏs/ *adj.* free to go where or act as one pleases.

foot·man /foŏtmən/ *n.* (*pl.* **-men**) **1** a liveried servant attending at the door, at table, or on a carriage. **2** *hist.* an infantryman.

foot·mark /foŏtmaark/ *n.* a footprint.

foot·note /foŏtnōt/ *n. & v.* ● *n.* a note printed at the foot of a page. ● *v.tr.* supply with a footnote or footnotes.

foot·pad /foŏtpad/ *n. hist.* an unmounted highwayman.

foot·path /foŏtpath/ *n.* **1** a trail or path for pedestrians (in the woods, etc.). **2** *Brit.* a path for pedestrians; a pavement.

foot·print /foŏtprint/ *n.* **1** the impression left by a foot or shoe. **2** *Computing* the area of desk space, etc., occupied by a computer or other piece of hardware. **3** the ground area covered by a communications satellite or affected by noise, etc., from aircraft.

foot·rest /foŏtrest/ *n.* a support for the feet or a foot.

foot·sie /foŏtsee/ *n. colloq.* amorous play with the feet.

foot sol·dier *n.* a soldier who fights on foot.

foot·sore /foŏtsawr/ *adj.* having sore feet, esp. from walking.

foot·step /foŏtstep/ *n.* **1** a step taken in walking. **2** the sound of this. □ **follow** (or **tread**) **in a person's footsteps** do as another person did before.

foot·stool /foŏtstoŏl/ *n.* a stool for resting the feet on when sitting.

foot·wear /foŏtwair/ *n.* shoes, socks, etc.

foot·work /foŏtwərk/ *n.* the use of the feet, esp. skillfully, in sports, dancing, etc.

fop /fop/ *n.* an affectedly elegant or fashionable man; a dandy. □□ **fop·per·y** *n.* **fop·pish** *adj.* **fop·pish·ly** *adv.* **fop·pish·ness** *n.*

for /fawr, fər/ *prep. & conj.* ● *prep.* **1** in the interest or to the benefit of; intended to go to (*these flowers are for you; wish to see it for myself*). **2** in defense, support, or favor of (*fight for one's rights*). **3** suitable or appropriate to (*a dance for beginners; not for me to say*). **4** in respect of or with reference to (*usual for ties to be worn; don't care for him at all; ready for bed*). **5** representing or in place of (*here for my uncle*). **6** in exchange against (*swapped it for a bigger one*). **7 a** as the price of (*give me $5 for it*). **b** at the price of (*bought it for $5*). **c** to the amount of (*a bill for $100*). **8** as the penalty of (*fined them heavily for it*). **9** in requital of (*that's for upsetting my sister*). **10** as a reward for (*here's $5 for your trouble*). **11 a** with a view to; in the hope or quest of; in order to get (*go for a walk; did it for the money*). **b** on account of (*could not speak for laughing*). **12** corresponding to (*word for word*). **13** to reach; in the direction of; toward (*left for Rome*). **14** conducive or conducively to; in order to achieve (*take the pills for a sound night's sleep*). **15** starting at (a specified time) (*we set the meeting for eight*). **16** through or over (a distance or period); during (*walked for miles; sang for two hours*). **17** in the character of; as being (*for the last time; know it for a lie*). **18** because of; on account of (*could not see for tears; rewarded for good behavior*). **19** in spite of; notwithstanding (*for all your fine words*). **20** considering or making due allowance in respect of (*good for a beginner*). **21** in order to be (*gone for a soldier*). ● *conj.* because; since; seeing that. □ **o** (or **oh**) **for** I wish I had.

for·age /fáwrij, fór-/ *n. & v.* ● *n.* **1** food for horses and cattle. **2** the act or an instance of searching for food. ● *v.* **1** *intr.* go searching; rummage (esp. for food). **2** *tr.* obtain food from; plunder. **3** *tr.* **a** get by foraging. **b** supply with food. □□ **for·ag·er** *n.*

for·age cap /kap/ *n.* an infantry undress cap.

fo·ra·men /fəráymen/ *n.* (*pl.* **foramina** /-rámina/) *Anat.* an opening, hole, or passage, esp. in a bone.

for·as·much as /fáwrəzmúch/ *conj. archaic* because; since.

for·ay /fáwray, fór-/ *n. & v.* ● *n.* **1** a sudden attack; a raid or incursion. **2** an attempt or venture, esp. into a field not one's own. ● *v.intr.* make or go on a foray.

talus
navicular bone
tarsals
metatarsals
phalanges
ankle
heel
calcaneus
instep
ball

FOOT:
ANATOMY OF A HUMAN FOOT

FOOTBALL

The term *football* is applied to various games around the world. In American football, two teams with 11 players on the field score points by crossing the opponent's goal line, either by passing the ball or carrying it across for a touchdown (six points), or by kicking it between the goalposts for a field goal (three points). In Australian Rules football, 18 players on each side score goals (six points) through the inner goalposts, or "behinds" (one point) between the inner and outer goalposts. Association Football (soccer) is played by two teams, each of 11 players, who attempt to get the ball into the opponent's goal, usually by kicking it.

AMERICAN FOOTBALL

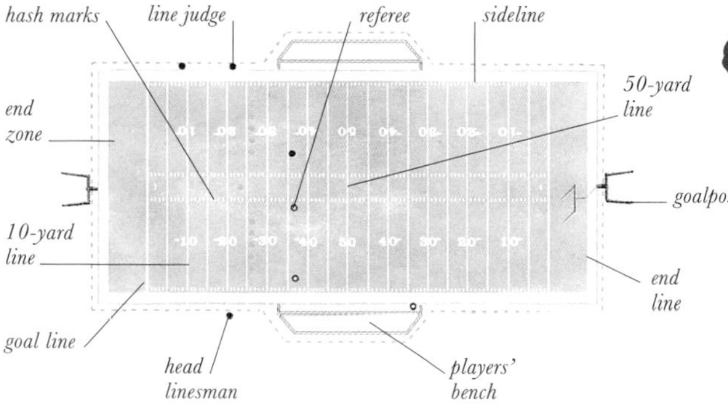

hash marks
line judge
referee
sideline
end zone
50-yard line
10-yard line
goalpost
goal line
end line
head linesman
players' bench

FOOTBALL FIELD

laces
brown pebbled leather
rigid plastic helmet
face mask

FOOTBALL

shoulder pad

upper arm pad
chest protector

elbow pad
tail-bone pad
rib pad
pants
hip pad

fingerless glove

cleat
thigh pad

knee pad

AUSTRALIAN RULES FOOTBALL

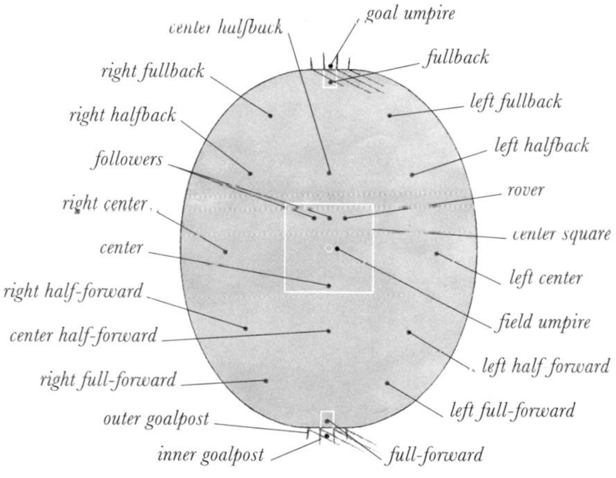

center halfback
goal umpire
right fullback
fullback
right halfback
left fullback
followers
left halfback
right center
rover
center
center square
right half-forward
left center
center half-forward
field umpire
right full-forward
left half forward
outer goalpost
left full-forward
inner goalpost
full-forward

FOOTBALL FIELD

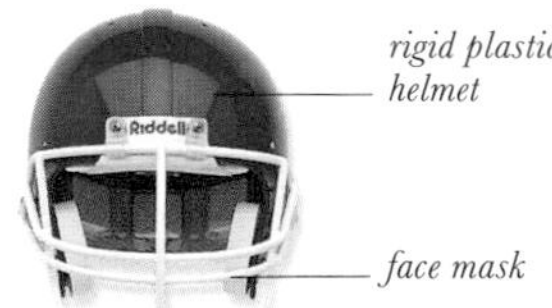

FOOTBALL SHOES

PROTECTIVE EQUIPMENT

ASSOCIATION FOOTBALL (SOCCER)

corner flag
center circle
right forward
center forward
right midfielder
right halfback
goal area
right defender
goal
goalkeeper
penalty spot
center midfielder
penalty area
left defender
left halfback
referee
center line
left forward
left midfielder
assistant referee

SOCCER FIELD

ball size number
manufacturer's name
team badge

Mitre
MULTIPLEX

SOCCER BALL

Motta

sponsor's logo
team shirt
long socks
team shorts

cleat

SOCCER SHOE

team crest

SOCCER UNIFORM

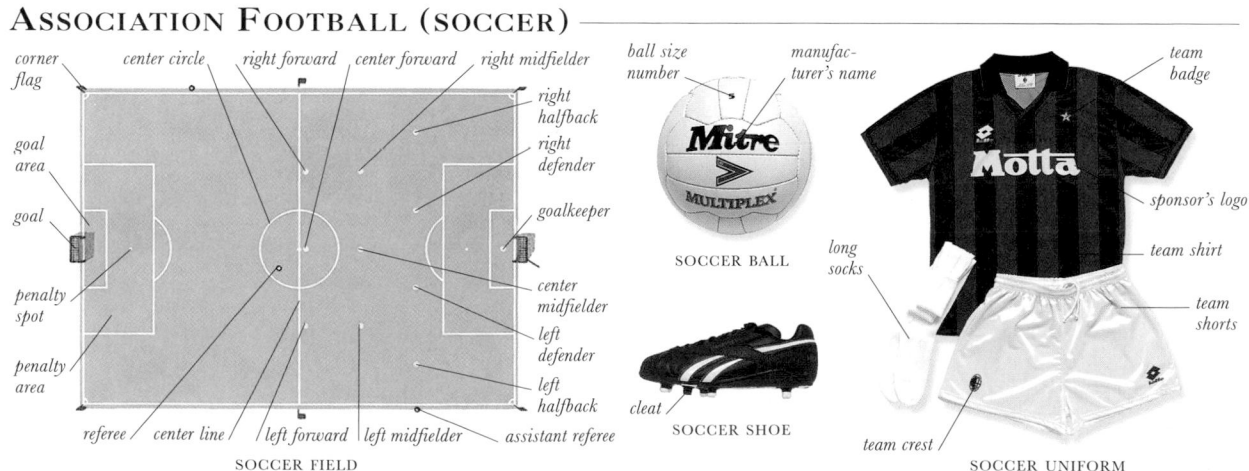

F

for·bade (also **for·bad**) *past* of FORBID.

for·bear[1] /fáwrbáir/ *v.intr. & tr. (past* **forbore** /-báwr/; *past part.* **forborne** /-báwrn/) (often foll. by *from,* or *to* + infin.) *literary* abstain or desist (from) (*could not forbear (from) speaking out*; *forbore to mention it*).

for·bear[2] var. of FOREBEAR.

for·bear·ance /fawrbáirəns/ *n.* patient self-control; tolerance.

for·bid /fərbíd, fawr-/ *v.tr.* (**forbidding**; *past* **for·bade**, -bád, -báyd/ *or* **forbad** /-bád/; *past part.* **forbidden** /-bíd'n/) **1** (foll. by *to* + infin.) order not (*I forbid you to go*). **2** refuse to allow (a thing, or a person to have a thing) (*I forbid it*; *was forbidden any wine*). **3** refuse a person entry to (*the gardens are forbidden to children*).

for·bid·den fruit *n.* something desired or enjoyed all the more because not allowed.

for·bid·ding /fərbíding, fawr-/ *adj.* uninviting; repellent; stern. □□ **for·bid·ding·ly** *adv.*

for·bore *past* of FORBEAR[1].

for·borne *past part.* of FORBEAR[1].

force /fawrs/ *n. & v.* ● *n.* **1** power; exerted strength or impetus; intense effort. **2** coercion or compulsion, esp. with the use or threat of violence. **3 a** military strength. **b** (in *pl.*) troops; fighting resources. **c** an organized body of people, esp. soldiers, police, or workers. **4** binding power; validity. **5** effect; precise significance (*the force of their words*). **6 a** mental or moral strength; influence; efficacy (*force of habit*). **b** vividness of effect (*described with much force*). **7** *Physics* **a** an influence tending to cause the motion of a body. **b** the intensity of this. **8** a person or thing regarded as exerting influence (*is a force for good*). ● *v.* **1** *tr.* constrain (a person) by force. **2** *tr.* make a way through or into by force. **3** *tr.* (usu. with prep. or adv.) drive or propel violently or against resistance (*the wind forced them back*). **4** *tr.* (foll. by *on, upon*) impose or press (on a person) (*forced their views on us*). **5** *tr.* **a** cause or produce by effort (*forced a smile*). **b** attain by strength or effort (*forced an entry*; *must force a decision*). **6** *tr.* strain or increase to the utmost; overstrain. **7** *tr.* artificially hasten the development or maturity of (a plant). **8** *tr.* seek or demand quick results from; accelerate the process of (*force the pace*). □ **by force of** by means of. **force the bidding** (at an auction) make bids to raise the price rapidly. **force a person's hand** make a person act prematurely or unwillingly. **force the issue** render an immediate decision necessary. **in force 1** valid; effective. **2** in great strength or numbers. **join forces** combine efforts. □□ **force·a·ble** *adj.* **forc·er** *n.*

forced la·bor *n.* compulsory labor, esp. under harsh conditions.

forced march *n.* a long and vigorous march, esp. by troops.

force-feed *v.tr.* (*past. & past part.* **-fed** /-fed/) force (esp. a prisoner) to take food.

force field *n.* (in science fiction) an invisible barrier of force.

force·ful /fáwrsfŏŏl/ *adj.* **1** vigorous; powerful. **2** (of speech) compelling; impressive. □□ **force·ful·ly** *adv.* **force·ful·ness** *n.*

force ma·jeure /fáwrs mazhŏ́r/ *n.* **1** irresistible compulsion or coercion. **2** unforeseeable events excusing a person from the fulfillment of a contract.

force·meat /fáwrsmeet/ *n.* meat, etc., chopped and seasoned for use as a stuffing or a garnish.

for·ceps /fáwrseps/ *n.* (*pl.* same) **1** ▼ surgical pincers, used for grasping and holding. **2** *Bot. & Zool.* an organ or structure resembling forceps.

FORCEPS:
SPENCER WELLS
ARTERY FORCEPS

for·ci·ble /fáwrsibəl/ *adj.* done by or involving force; forceful. □□ **for·ci·ble·ness** *n.* **for·ci·bly** *adv.*

ford /fawrd/ *n. & v.* ● *n.* a shallow place where a river or stream may be crossed by wading or in a vehicle. ● *v.tr.* cross (water) at a ford. □□ **ford·a·ble** *adj.* **ford·less** *adj.*

fore /fawr/ *adj., n., int.* ● *adj.* situated in front. ● *n.* the front part, esp. of a ship; the bow. ● *int. Golf* a warning to persons in the path of a ball. □ **come to the fore** take a leading part. **to the fore** in front; conspicuous.

fore and aft *adv. & adj.* ● *adv.* at bow and stern; all over the ship. ● *adj.* (**fore-and-aft**) (of a sail or rigging) set lengthwise, not on the yards.

fore·arm[1] /fáwraarm/ *n.* **1** the part of the arm from the elbow to the wrist or the fingertips. ▷ RADIUS. **2** the corresponding part in a fore-leg or wing.

fore·arm[2] /fawraárm/ *v.tr.* prepare or arm beforehand.

fore·bear /fáwrbair/ *n.* (also **for·bear**) (usu. in *pl.*) an ancestor.

fore·bode /fawrbód/ *v.tr.* **1** betoken; be an advance warning of (an evil or unwelcome event). **2** have a presentiment of (usu. evil).

fore·bod·ing /fawrbóding/ *n.* an expectation of trouble or evil; a presage or omen.

fore·cast /fáwrkast/ *v. & n.* ● *v.tr.* (*past* and *past part.* **-cast** *or* **-casted**) predict; estimate or calculate beforehand. ● *n.* a calculation or estimate of something future, esp. coming weather. □□ **fore·cast·er** *n.*

fore·cas·tle /fóksəl/ *n.* (also **fo'c's'le**) *Naut.* ▼ the forward part of a ship.

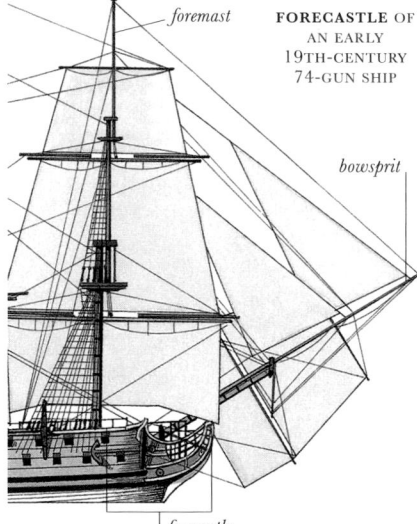

foremast

FORECASTLE OF
AN EARLY
19TH-CENTURY
74-GUN SHIP

bowsprit

forecastle

fore·close /fawrklóz/ *v.tr.* **1** (also *absol.*; foll. by *on*) stop (a mortgage) from being redeemable or (a mortgager) from redeeming, esp. as a result of defaults in payment. **2** exclude; prevent. **3** shut out; bar. □□ **fore·clo·sure** /-klózhər/ *n.*

fore·court /fáwrkawrt/ *n.* **1** an enclosed space in front of a building. **2** *Tennis* the part of the court between the service line and the net.

fore·doom /fawrdŏ́om/ *v.tr.* (often foll. by *to*) doom or condemn beforehand.

fore·fa·ther /fáwrfaathər/ *n.* (usu. in *pl.*) **1** an ancestor. **2** a member of a past generation of a family or people.

fore·fin·ger /fáwrfinggər/ *n.* the finger next to the thumb.

fore·foot /fáwrfŏŏt/ *n.* (*pl.* **-feet**) either of the front feet of a four-footed animal.

fore·front /fáwrfrunt/ *n.* **1** the foremost part. **2** the leading position.

fore·gath·er var. of FOREGATHER.

fore·go[1] /fáwrgó/ *v.tr. & intr.* (**-goes**; *past* **-went** /-wént/; *past part.* **-gone** /-gón/) precede in place or time. □□ **fore·go·er** *n.*

fore·go[2] var. of FORGO.

fore·go·ing /fawrgóing/ *adj.* preceding; previously mentioned.

fore·gone con·clu·sion *n.* an easily foreseen or predictable result.

fore·ground /fáwrgrownd/ *n.* **1** the part of a view that is nearest the observer. **2** the most conspicuous position.

fore·hand /fáwrhand/ *n. Tennis,* etc. **1** ◀ a stroke played with the palm of the hand facing the opponent. **2** (*attrib.*) (also **fore·hand·ed**) of or made with a forehand.

FOREHAND TENNIS
STROKE

fore·head /fáwrid, -hed, fór-/ *n.* the part of the face above the eyebrows.

for·eign /fáwrin, fór-/ *adj.* **1** of or from or situated in or characteristic of a country or a language other than one's own. **2** dealing with other countries (*foreign service*). **3** of another district, society, etc. **4** (often foll. by *to*) unfamiliar; strange; uncharacteristic (*his behavior is foreign to me*). **5** coming from outside (*a foreign body lodged in my eye*). □□ **for·eign·ness** *n.*

for·eign·er /fáwrinər, fór-/ *n.* **1** a person born in or coming from a foreign country or place. **2** *dial.* a person not native to a place. **3 a** a foreign ship. **b** an imported animal or article.

for·eign ex·change *n.* **1** the currency of other countries. **2** dealings in these.

for·eign le·gion *n.* a body of foreign volunteers in an army (esp. the French army).

for·eign min·is·ter *n.* (also **for·eign sec·re·tar·y**) (in some governments) a government minister in charge of his or her country's relations with other countries.

fore·judge /fáwrjúj/ *v.tr.* judge or determine before knowing the evidence.

fore·know /fáwrnó/ *v.tr.* (*past* **-knew** /-nŏŏ, -nyŏŏ/; *past part.* **-known** /-nón/) know beforehand; have prescience of.

fore·knowl·edge *n.* prior knowledge of an event, etc.

fore·land /fáwrland/ *n.* **1** a cape or promontory. **2** a piece of land in front of something.

fore·leg /fáwrleg/ *n.* each of the front legs of a quadruped.

fore·limb /fáwrlim/ *n.* any of the front limbs of an animal.

fore·lock /fáwrlok/ *n.* ▶ a lock of hair growing just above the forehead.

fore·man /fáwrmən/ *n.* (*pl.* **-men**) **1** a worker with supervisory responsibilities. **2** the member of a jury who presides over its deliberations and speaks on its behalf.

fore·mast /fáwrmast, -məst/ *n.* the forward (lower) mast of a ship. ▷ MAN-OF-WAR, SCHOONER

forelock

FORELOCK
ON A HORSE

fore·most /fáwrmóst/ *adj. & adv.* ● *adj.* **1** the chief or most notable. **2** the most advanced in position; the front. ● *adv.* before anything else in position; in the first place (*first and foremost*).

fore·name /fáwrnaym/ *n.* a first name.

fore·noon /fáwrnŏŏn/ *n.* the part of the day before noon.

fo·ren·sic /fərénsik, -zik/ *adj.* **1** of or used in connection with courts of law (*forensic science*). **2** *disp.* of

FORESHORTEN

In this diagram, the figure on the right is foreshortened, appearing to recede toward the horizon. This effect can be achieved by dividing up the side view of the figure at the left edge of the picture plane. The divisions are joined to the vanishing point on the horizon. Where these lines intersect with the picture plane, horizontal lines can be plotted, providing the divisions for foreshortening the figure.

DEMONSTRATION OF FORESHORTENING

picture plane (edge-on)   *horizon line*   *vanishing point*

plotted horizontal lines

fore-shortened figure

side view of figure

F

or involving forensic science (*sent for forensic examination*). □□ **fo·ren·si·cal·ly** *adv.*

fo·ren·sic med·i·cine *n.* the application of medical knowledge to legal problems.

fore·or·dain /fáwrawrdáyn/ *v.tr.* predestinate; ordain beforehand. □□ **fore·or·di·na·tion** /-d'náy-shən/ *n.*

fore·paw /fáwrpaw/ *n.* either of the front paws of a quadruped.

fore·play /fáwrplay/ *n.* stimulation preceding sexual intercourse.

fore·run /fáwr-rún/ *v.tr.* (**-running**; *past* **-ran** /-rán/; *past part.* **-run**) **1** go before. **2** foreshadow.

fore·run·ner /fáwr-runər/ *n.* **1** a predecessor. **2** an advance messenger.

fore·sail /fáwrsayl, səl/ *n. Naut.* the principal sail on a foremast. ▷ MAN-OF-WAR, SCHOONER

fore·see /fáwrsée/ *v.tr.* (*past* **-saw** /-sáw/; *past part.* **-seen** /-séen/) (often foll. by *that* + clause) see or be aware of beforehand. □□ **fore·see·a·ble** *adj.* **fore·see·a·bil·i·ty** *n.*

fore·shad·ow /fáwrshádō/ *v.tr.* be a warning or indication of (a future event).

fore·shore /fáwrshawr/ *n.* the part of the shore between high- and low-water marks.

fore·short·en /fáwrsháwrt'n/ *v.tr.* ▲ show or portray (an object) with the apparent shortening due to visual perspective.

fore·sight /fáwrsīt/ *n.* **1** regard or provision for the future. **2** the process of foreseeing. **3** the front sight of a gun. **4** *Surveying* a sight taken forward. □□ **fore·sight·ed** /-sītid/ *adj.* **fore·sight·ed·ly** *adv.* **fore·sight·ed·ness** *n.*

fore·skin /fáwrskin/ *n.* the fold of skin covering the end of the penis. Also called PREPUCE.

for·est /fáwrist, fór-/ *n. & v.* **1 a** (often *attrib.*) a large area covered chiefly with trees and undergrowth. **b** the trees growing in it. **c** a large number or dense mass of vertical objects (*a forest of masts*). **2** a district formerly a forest but now cultivated. ● *v.tr.* **1** plant with trees. **2** convert into a forest.

fore·stall /fáwrstáwl/ *v.tr.* **1** act in advance of in order to prevent. **2** anticipate (the action of another, or an event). **3** deal with beforehand.

fore·stay /fáwrstay/ *n. Naut.* a stay from the head of the foremast to the ship's deck to support the foremast. ▷ DINGHY, RIGGING

for·est·er /fáwristər, fór-/ *n.* **1** a person in charge of a forest or skilled in forestry. **2** a person or animal living in a forest.

for·est rang·er *n.* a government official who protects and preserves forests.

for·est·ry /fáwristree, fór-/ *n.* **1** the science or management of forests. **2** wooded country; forests.

fore·taste *n. & v.* ● *n.* /fáwrtayst/ partial enjoyment or suffering in advance; anticipation. ● *v.tr.* /fáwrtáyst/ taste beforehand; anticipate the experience of.

fore·tell /fáwrtél/ *v.tr.* (*past* and *past part.* **-told** /-tốld/) **1** tell of (an event, etc.) before it takes place; predict; prophesy. **2** presage; be a precursor of. □□ **fore·tell·er** *n.*

fore·thought /fáwrthawt/ *n.* **1** care or provision for the future. **2** previous thinking or devising. **3** deliberate intention.

fore·to·ken *n. & v.* ● *n.* /fáwrtōkən/ a sign of something to come. ● *v.tr.* /fáwrtōkən/ portend; indicate beforehand.

fore·told *past* and *past part.* of FORETELL.

fore·top·mast *n.* /fawrtópmast, -məst/ *Naut.* the mast above the foremast.

for·ev·er /fərévar, fawr-/ *adv.* continually; persistently (*is forever complaining*).

fore·warn /fáwrwáwrn/ *v.tr.* warn beforehand.

fore·went *past* of FOREGO[1], FOREGO[2].

fore·wom·an /fáwrwŏŏmən/ *n.* (*pl.* **-women**) **1** a female worker with supervisory responsibilities. **2** a woman who presides over a jury's deliberations and speaks on its behalf.

fore·word /fáwrwərd/ *n.* introductory remarks at the beginning of a book, often by a person other than the author.

fo·rex /fáwreks/ *abbr.* foreign exchange.

for·feit /fáwrfit/ *n., adj., & v.* ● *n.* **1** a penalty for a breach of contract or neglect; a fine. **2 a** a trivial fine for a breach of rules in clubs, etc., or in a game. **b** (in *pl.*) a game in which forfeits are exacted. **3** something surrendered as a penalty. **4** the process of forfeiting. ● *adj.* lost or surrendered as a penalty. ● *v.tr.* (**forfeited, forfeiting**) lose the right to, be deprived of, or have to pay as a penalty. □□ **for·feit·a·ble** *adj.* **for·fei·ture** /-fichər/ *n.*

for·fend /fawrfénd/ *v.tr.* **1** protect by precautions. **2** *archaic* avert; keep off.

for·gath·er /fáwrgáthər/ *v.intr.* (also **fore·gath·er**) assemble; meet together; associate.

for·gave *past* of FORGIVE.

forge[1] /fawrj/ *v. & n.* ● *v.tr.* **1 a** write (a document or signature) in order to pass it off as written by another. **b** make (money, etc.) in fraudulent imitation. **2** fabricate; invent. **3** ◀ shape (esp. metal) by heating and hammering. ● *n.* **1** a

blacksmith's workshop; a smithy. **2 a** a furnace or hearth for melting or refining metal. **b** a workshop containing this. □□ **forge·a·ble** *adj.* **forg·er** *n.*

forge[2] /fawrj/ *v.intr.* move forward gradually or steadily. □ **forge ahead 1** take the lead in a race. **2** progress rapidly.

for·ger·y /fáwrjəree/ *n.* (*pl.* **-ies**) **1** the act or an instance of forging a document, etc. **2** a forged document.

for·get /fərgét/ *v.* (**forgetting**; *past* **forgot** /-gót/; *past part.* **forgotten** /-gót'n/ or esp. *US* **forgot**) **1** *tr. & (*often foll. by *about*) *intr.* lose the remembrance of; not remember (a person or thing). **2** *tr.* (foll. by clause or *to* + infin.) not remember; neglect (*forgot to come; forgot how to do it*). **3** *tr.* inadvertently omit to bring or mention or attend to. **4** *tr.* (also *absol.*) put out of mind; cease to think of (*forgive and forget*). □ **forget oneself 1** neglect one's own interests. **2** act unbecomingly or unworthily. □□ **for·get·ta·ble** *adj.*

for·get·ful /fərgétfŏŏl/ *adj.* **1** apt to forget; absentminded. **2** (often foll. by *of*) forgetting; neglectful. □□ **for·get·ful·ly** *adv.* **for·get·ful·ness** *n.*

for·get-me-not *n.* ◀ any plant of the genus *Myosotis*, esp. *M. alpestris* with small yellow-eyed bright blue flowers.

for·give /fərgív/ *v.tr.* (also *absol.* or with double object) (*past* **forgave**; *past part.* **forgiven**) **1** cease to feel angry or resentful toward; pardon (an offender or offense). **2** remit or let off (a debt or debtor). □□ **for·giv·a·ble** *adj.* **for·giv·a·bly** *adv.* **for·giv·er** *n.*

FORGET-ME-NOT:
WOOD FORGET-ME-NOT
(*Myosotis sylvatica*)

for·give·ness /fərgívnis/ *n.* **1** the act of forgiving; the state of being forgiven. **2** readiness to forgive.

for·giv·ing /fərgíving/ *adj.* inclined readily to forgive. □□ **for·giv·ing·ly** *adv.*

for·go /fáwrgố/ *v.tr.* (also **fore·go**) (**-goes**; *past* **-went** /-wént/; *past part.* **-gone** /-gáwn, -gón/) **1** abstain from; go without; relinquish. **2** omit or decline to take or use (a pleasure, advantage, etc.).

for·got *past & esp. US past part.* of FORGET.

for·got·ten *past part.* of FORGET.

fork /fawrk/ *n. & v.* ● *n.* **1** an instrument with two or more prongs used in eating or cooking. **2** a similar much larger instrument used for digging, lifting, etc. **3** any pronged device or component (*tuning fork*). ▷ TUNING FORK. **4** a forked support for a bicycle wheel. ▷ OFF-ROAD. **5 a** a divergence of anything, e.g., a stick, road, or a river, into two parts. **b** the place where this occurs. **c** either of the two parts (*take the left fork*). **6** a flash of forked lightning. ● *v.* **1** *intr.* form a fork or branch by separating into two parts. **2** *intr.* take one or other road, etc., at a fork (*fork left for Danbury*). **3** *tr.* dig or lift, etc., with a fork. □ **fork out** (or **over** or **up**) *sl.* hand over or pay, usu. reluctantly.

forked /fawrkt/ *adj.* **1** having a fork or forklike end or branches. **2** divergent; cleft. **3** (in *comb.*) having so many prongs (*three-forked*).

forked light·ning *n.* a lightning flash in the form of a zigzag or branching line.

fork·lift /fáwrklift/ *n.* a vehicle with a horizontal fork in front for lifting and carrying loads.

fork lunch *n. Brit.* a light meal eaten with a fork at a buffet, etc.

for·lorn /fawrláwrn/ *adj.* **1** sad and abandoned or lonely. **2** in a pitiful state; of wretched appearance. □□ **for·lorn·ly** *adv.* **for·lorn·ness** *n.*

forlorn hope *n.* **1** a faint remaining hope or chance. **2** a desperate enterprise.

form /fawrm/ *n. & v.* ● *n.* **1 a** a shape; an arrangement of parts. **b** the outward aspect (esp. apart from color) or shape of a body. **2** a person or animal as visible or tangible (*the familiar form of the teacher*). **3** the mode in which a thing exists or manifests itself (*took the form of a book*). **4** a species, kind, or variety. **5 a** a printed document with blank spaces for information to be inserted. **b** a regularly

FORGE: BLACKSMITH FORGING
METAL ON AN ANVIL

F

drawn document. **6** a class or grade, as in some private schools or a British school. **7** a customary method; what is usually done (*common form*). **8** a set order of words; a formula. **9** behavior according to a rule or custom. **10** (prec. by *the*) correct procedure (*knows the form*). **11 a** (of an athlete, horse, etc.) condition of health and training (*is in top form*). **b** *Racing* details of previous performances. **12** general state or disposition (*was in great form*). **13** formality or mere ceremony. **14** *Gram.* **a** one of the ways in which a word may be spelled or pronounced or inflected. **b** the external characteristics of words apart from meaning. **15** arrangement and style in literary or musical composition. **16** *Philos.* the essential nature of a species or thing. **17** *Brit.* a long bench without a back. **18** a hare's lair. ● *v.* **1** *tr.* make or fashion into a certain shape or form. **2** *intr.* take a certain shape; be formed. **3** *tr.* be the material of; make up or constitute (*together form a unit*; *forms part of the structure*). **4** *tr.* train or instruct. **5** *tr.* develop or establish as a concept, institution, or practice (*form an idea*; *formed an alliance*). **6** *tr.* (foll. by *into*) embody; organize. **7** *tr.* articulate (a word). **8** *tr. & intr.* (often foll. by *up*) esp. *Mil.* bring or be brought into a certain arrangement or formation. **9** *tr.* construct (a new word) by derivation, inflection, etc.

for·mal /fáwrməl/ *adj. & n.* ● *adj.* **1** used or done or held in accordance with rules, convention, or ceremony (*formal dress*; *a formal occasion*). **2** ceremonial; required by convention (*a formal offer*). **3** precise or symmetrical (*a formal garden*). **4** prim or stiff in manner. **5** perfunctory; having the form without the spirit. **6** valid or correctly so called because of its form; explicit (*a formal agreement*). **7** in accordance with recognized forms or rules. **8** of or concerned with (outward) form or appearance, esp. as distinct from content or matter. **9** *Logic* concerned with the form and not the matter of reasoning. **10** *Philos.* of the essence of a thing; essential not material. ● *n.* **1** evening dress. **2** an occasion on which evening dress is worn. □□ **for·mal·ly** *adv.*

form·al·de·hyde /fawrmáldihīd/ *n.* a colorless pungent gas used as a disinfectant and preservative and in the manufacture of synthetic resins.

for·ma·lin /fáwrməlin/ *n.* a colorless solution of formaldehyde in water used as a preservative for biological specimens, etc.

for·mal·ism /fáwrməlizəm/ *n.* **1 a** excessive adherence to prescribed forms. **b** the use of forms without regard to inner significance. **2** *derog.* an artist's concentration on form at the expense of content. □□ **for·mal·ist** *n.* **for·mal·is·tic** *adj.*

for·mal·i·ty /fawrmálitee/ *n.* (*pl.* **-ies**) **1 a** a formal or ceremonial act, requirement of etiquette, regulation, or custom. **b** a thing done simply to comply with a rule. **2** the rigid observance of rules or convention. **3** ceremony; elaborate procedure. **4** being formal; precision of manners.

for·mal·ize /fáwrməlīz/ *v.tr.* **1** give definite shape or legal formality to. **2** make ceremonious, precise, or rigid; imbue with formalism. □□ **for·mal·i·za·tion** /-lizáyshən/ *n.*

for·mant /fáwrmənt/ *n.* **1** the characteristic pitch constituent of a vowel. **2** a morpheme occurring only in combination in a word or word stem.

for·mat /fáwrmat/ *n. & v.* ● *n.* **1** the shape and size of a book, periodical, etc. **2** the style or manner of arrangement or procedure. **3** *Computing* a defined structure for holding data, etc., in a record for processing or storage. ● *v.tr.* (**formatted**, **formatting**) **1** arrange or put into a format. **2** *Computing* prepare (a storage medium) to receive data.

for·ma·tion /fawrmáyshən/ *n.* **1** the act or an instance of forming; the process of being formed. **2** a thing formed. **3** a structure or arrangement of parts. **4** a particular arrangement, e.g., of troops, aircraft in flight, etc. **5** *Geol.* an assemblage of rocks or series of strata having some common characteristic. □□ **for·ma·tion·al** *adj.*

for·ma·tive /fáwrmətiv/ *adj.* serving to form or fashion; of formation. □□ **for·ma·tive·ly** *adv.*

for·mer[1] /fáwrmər/ *attrib.adj.* **1** of or occurring in the past or an earlier period (*in former times*). **2** having been previously (*her former husband*). **3** (prec. by *the*; often *absol.*) the first or first mentioned of two.

form·er[2] /fáwrmər/ *n.* **1** a person or thing that forms. **2** *Electr.* a frame or core for winding a coil on. **3** *Aeron.* a transverse strengthening member in a wing or fuselage. **4** esp. *Brit.* (in *comb.*) a pupil of a specified form in a school (*fourth-former*).

for·mer·ly /fáwrmərlee/ *adv.* in the past; in former times.

For·mi·ca /fawrmíkə/ *n. Trademark* a hard durable plastic laminate used for working surfaces, cupboard doors, etc.

for·mic ac·id /fáwrmik/ *n.* a colorless irritant volatile acid emitted by some ants.

for·mi·ca·tion /fáwrmikáyshən/ a sensation as of ants crawling over the skin.

for·mi·da·ble /fáwrmidəbəl, *disp.* formídəbəl/ *adj.* **1** inspiring fear or dread. **2** inspiring respect or awe. **3** likely to be hard to overcome, resist, or deal with. □□ **for·mi·da·ble·ness** *n.* **for·mi·da·bly** *adv.*

form·less /fáwrmlis/ *adj.* shapeless; without determinate or regular form. □□ **form·less·ly** *adv.* **form·less·ness** *n.*

form let·ter *n.* a standardized letter to deal with frequently occurring matters.

for·mu·la /fáwrmyələ/ *n.* (*pl.* **formulas** or (esp. in senses 1, 2) **formulae** /-lee/) **1** *Chem.* a set of chemical symbols showing the constituents of a substance and their relative proportions. **2** *Math.* a mathematical rule expressed in symbols. **3 a** a fixed form of words, esp. one used on social or ceremonial occasions. **b** a rule unintelligently or slavishly followed. **c** a form of words embodying agreement, etc. **4 a** a list of ingredients; a recipe. **b** an infant's liquid food preparation. **5** a classification of racing car, esp. by the engine capacity. □□ **for·mu·la·ic** /-láyik/ *adj.* **for·mu·lar·ize** /-lərīz/ *v.tr.* **for·mu·lize** *v.tr.*

for·mu·lar·y /fáwrmyəleree/ *n.* (*pl.* **-ies**) **1** a collection of formulas or set forms, esp. for religious use. **2** *Pharm.* a compendium of formulae used in the preparation of medicinal drugs.

for·mu·late /fáwrmyəlayt/ *v.tr.* **1** express in a formula. **2** express clearly and precisely. **3** create or devise (a plan, etc.). **4** develop or prepare following a formula. □□ **for·mu·la·tion** /-láyshən/ *n.*

for·mu·lism /fáwrmyəlizəm/ *n.* adherence to or dependence on conventional formulas. □□ **for·mu·list** *n.* **for·mu·lis·tic** *adj.*

form·work /fáwrmwərk/ *n.* a temporary structure, usu. of wood, used to hold concrete during setting.

for·ni·cate /fáwrnikayt/ *v.intr.* (of people not married or not married to each other) have sexual intercourse voluntarily. □□ **for·ni·ca·tion** /-káyshən/ *n.* **for·ni·ca·tor** *n.*

for·sake /fərsáyk, fawr-/ *v.tr.* (*past* **forsook** /-sook/; *past part.* **forsaken** /-sáykən/) **1** give up; renounce. **2** withdraw one's help, friendship, or companionship from; desert; abandon. □□ **for·sak·en·ness** *n.* **for·sak·er** *n.*

for·sooth /fərsóoth, fawr-/ *adv. archaic* or *joc.* truly; in truth; no doubt.

for·swear /fáwrswáir/ *v.tr.* (*past* **forswore** /-swáwr/; *past part.* **forsworn** /-swáwrn/) **1** abjure; renounce on oath. **2** (in *refl.* or *passive*) swear falsely; commit perjury.

FORSYTHIA
(*Forsythia* × *intermedia* 'Lynwood')

for·syth·i·a /fawrsíthee-ə/ *n.* ◀ any ornamental shrub of the genus *Forsythia*, bearing bright yellow flowers in early spring.

fort /fawrt/ *n.* **1** ▶ a fortified building or position. **2** *hist.* a trading post, orig. fortified.

forte[1] /fawrt, fáwrtay/ *n.* a thing in which a person excels.

for·te[2] /fórtay/ *adj., adv., & n. Mus.* ● *adj.* performed loudly. ● *adv.* loudly. ● *n.* a passage to be performed loudly.

for·te·pia·no /fórtaypyáanō, -pyáanō/ *n.* (*pl.* **-os**) *Mus.* = PIANOFORTE esp. with ref. to an instrument of the 18th to early 19th c.

forth /fawrth/ *adv. archaic* except in set phrases and after certain verbs, e.g. *bring, come, go,* and *set.* **1** forward; into view. **2** onward in time (*from this time forth*; *henceforth*). **3** forward. **4** out from a starting point (*set forth*). □ **and so forth** and so on; and the like.

forth·com·ing /fáwrthkúming/ *attrib. adj.* **1 a** about or likely to appear or become available. **b** approaching. **2** produced when wanted (*no reply was forthcoming*). **3** (of a person) informative; responsive. □□ **forth·com·ing·ness** *n.*

forth·right /fáwrthrīt/ *adj. & adv.* ● *adj.* **1** direct and outspoken. **2** decisive. ● *adv.* in a direct manner; bluntly. □□ **forth·right·ly** *adv.* **forth·right·ness** *n.*

forth·with /fáwrthwith, -wíth/ *adv.* immediately; without delay.

for·ti·fi·ca·tion /fáwrtifikáyshən/ *n.* **1** the act or an instance of fortifying; the process of being fortified. **2** *Mil.* **a** the art or science of fortifying. **b** (usu. in *pl.*) defensive works fortifying a position.

for·ti·fy /fáwrtifī/ *v.tr.* (**-ies, -ied**) **1** provide or equip with defensive works. **2** strengthen or invigorate physically, mentally, or morally. **3** strengthen the structure of. **4** strengthen (wine) with alcohol. **5** increase the nutritive value of (food, esp. with vitamins). □□ **for·ti·fi·a·ble** *adj.* **for·ti·fi·er** *n.*

for·tis·si·mo /fawrtísimō/ *adj., adv., & n. Mus.* ● *adj.* performed very loudly. ● *adv.* very loudly. ● *n.* (*pl.* **-os** or **fortissimi** /-mee/) a passage to be performed very loudly.

for·ti·tude /fáwrtitood, -tyood/ *n.* courage in pain or adversity.

fort·night /fáwrtnīt/ *n.* two weeks.

fort·night·ly /fáwrtnītlee/ *adj., adv., & n.* esp. *Brit.* ● *adj.* done, produced, or occurring once a fortnight. ● *adv.* every fortnight. ● *n.* (*pl.* **-ies**) a magazine, etc., issued every fortnight.

For·tran /fáwrtran/ *n.* (also **FORTRAN**) *Computing* a high-level programming language used esp. for scientific calculations.

for·tress /fáwrtris/ *n.* a military stronghold, esp. a strongly fortified town.

for·tu·i·tous /fawrtóoitəs, -tyóo-/ *adj.* due to or characterized by chance. □□ **for·tu·i·tous·ly** *adv.* **for·tu·i·tous·ness** *n.*

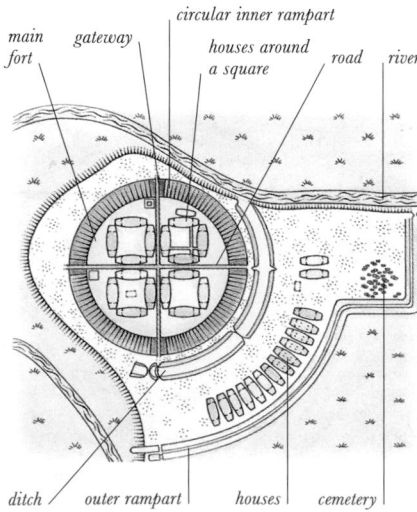

FORT: LAYOUT OF A CIRCULAR VIKING FORT

circular inner rampart
main fort   *gateway*   *houses around a square*   *road*   *river*
ditch   *outer rampart*   *houses*   *cemetery*

for·tu·nate /fáwrchənət/ *adj.* **1** lucky; prosperous. **2** auspicious; favorable.

for·tu·nate·ly /fáwrchənətlee/ *adv.* **1** luckily; successfully. **2** (qualifying a whole sentence) it is fortunate that.

for·tune /fáwrchən/ *n.* **1 a** chance or luck as a force in human affairs. **b** a person's destiny. **2** (**Fortune**) this force personified, often as a deity. **3** (in *sing.* or *pl.*) the good or bad luck that befalls a person or an enterprise. **4** good luck. **5** prosperity; a prosperous condition. **6** (also *colloq.* **small fortune**) great wealth; a huge sum of money. □ **make a** (or **one's**) **fortune** acquire wealth or prosperity. **tell a person's fortune** make predictions about a person's future.

for·tune hunt·er *n. colloq.* a person seeking wealth by marriage.

for·tune-tel·ler *n.* a person who claims to predict future events in a person's life. □□ **for·tune-tell·ing** *n.*

for·ty /fáwrtee/ *n. & adj.* ● *n.* (*pl.* **-ies**) **1** the product of four and ten. **2** a symbol for this (40, xl, XL). **3** (in *pl.*) the numbers from 40 to 49, esp. the years of a century or of a person's life. ● *adj.* that amount to forty. □□ **for·ti·eth** *adj. & n.* **for·ty·fold** *adj. & adv.*

for·ty-nin·er *n.* a seeker for gold, etc., esp. in the California gold rush of 1849.

for·ty winks *n.pl. colloq.* a short sleep.

fo·rum /fáwrəm/ *n.* **1** a place of or meeting for public discussion. **2** a periodical, etc., giving an opportunity for discussion. **3** a court or tribunal. **4** *hist.* ▼ a public square or marketplace in an ancient Roman city.

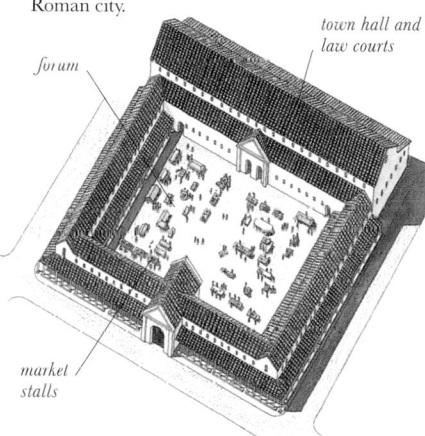

forum

town hall and law courts

market stalls

FORUM: ROMAN LONDON'S FORUM, C.3RD CENTURY BC

for·ward /fáwrwərd/ *adj., n., adv., & v.* ● *adj.* **1** lying in one's line of motion. **2 a** onward or toward the front. **b** *Naut.* belonging to the fore part of a ship. **3** precocious; bold in manner; presumptuous. **4** *Commerce* relating to future produce, delivery, etc. (*forward contract*). **5 a** advanced; progressing toward or approaching maturity or completion. **b** (of a plant, etc.) well advanced or early. ● *n.* an attacking player in soccer, hockey, etc. ● *adv.* **1** to the front; into prominence. **2** in advance; ahead (*sent them forward*). **3** onward so as to make progress (*not getting any farther forward*). **4** toward the future; continuously onward (*from this time forward*). **5** (also **forwards**) **a** in the direction one is facing. **b** in the normal direction of motion or of traversal. **c** with continuous forward motion (*rushing forward*). **6** *Naut. & Aeron.* in, near, or toward the bow or nose. ● *v.tr.* **1 a** send (a letter, etc.) on to a further destination. **b** esp. *Brit.* dispatch (goods, etc.). **2** help to advance; promote. □□ **for·ward·er** *n.* **for·ward·ly** *adv.* **for·ward·ness** *n.* (esp. in sense 3 of *adj.*).

for·ward-look·ing *adj.* progressive; favoring change.

for·wards var. of FORWARD *adv.* 5.

FOSSIL

For an organism's remains to be fossilized, the natural process of decay must be arrested. Rapid burial is essential to isolate the remains from air and water. If the organism's cavities are filled with hard minerals, the dead organism becomes more resistant than the sediment around it and is said to be fossilized. Fossilization may also occur through refrigeration (organisms in ice) or carbonization (e.g., leaves in coal). Organisms sometimes leave cast-type fossils (e.g., footprints in mud) or become preserved in amber (the fossilized resin of a plant).

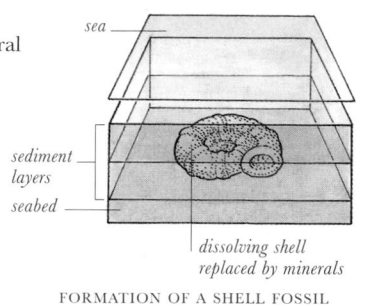

sea

sediment layers

seabed

dissolving shell replaced by minerals

FORMATION OF A SHELL FOSSIL

EXAMPLES OF FOSSILS

  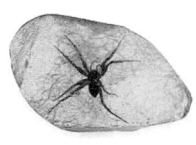  

CLYPEASTER IN SAND   DICROIDIUM LEAF IN MUDSTONE   SPIDER TRAPPED IN AMBER   BEETLE IN TAR AND SAND   AMMONITE IN IRON PYRITES

for·went *past* of FORGO.

fos·sa /fósə/ *n.* (*pl.* **fossae** /-see/) *Anat.* a shallow depression or cavity.

fosse /fos/ *n.* **1** a long narrow trench or excavation, esp. in a fortification. **2** *Anat.* = FOSSA.

fos·sil /fósəl/ *n. & adj.* ● *n.* **1** ▲ the remains or impression of a (usu. prehistoric) plant or animal in rock (often *attrib.: fossil shells*). **2** *colloq.* an antiquated or unchanging person or thing. ● *adj.* **1** of or like a fossil. **2** antiquated. □□ **fos·sil·if·er·ous** /fósilífərəs/ *adj.* **fos·sil·ize** *v.tr. & intr.* **fos·sil·i·za·tion** *n.*

fos·sil fu·el *n.* ► a natural fuel such as coal or gas formed from the remains of living organisms.

fos·so·ri·al /fosáwreeəl/ *adj.* **1** (of animals) burrowing. **2** (of limbs, etc.) used in burrowing.

fos·ter /fáwstər, fós-/ *v. & adj.* ● *v.tr.* **1 a** promote the growth or development of. **b** encourage or harbor (a feeling). **2** (of circumstances) be favorable to. **3** bring up (a child that is not one's own by birth). **4** cherish; have affectionate regard for (an idea, scheme, etc.). ● *adj.* **1** having a family connection by fostering and not by birth (*foster brother; foster parent*). **2** concerned with fostering a child (*foster care; foster home*). □□ **fos·ter·age** *n.* (esp. in sense 3 of *v.*). **fos·ter·er** *n.*

fouet·té /fwetáy/ *n. Ballet* a quick whipping movement of the raised leg.

fought *past* and *past part.* of FIGHT.

foul /fowl/ *adj., n., adv., & v.* ● *adj.* **1** offensive to the senses; loathsome; stinking. **2** dirty; soiled; filthy. **3** *colloq.* revolting; disgusting. **4 a** containing or charged with noxious matter (*foul air*). **b** clogged; choked. **5** disgustingly abusive or offensive (*foul language; foul deeds*). **6** unfair; against the rules of a game, etc. (*by foul means or foul*). **7** (of the weather) wet; rough; stormy. **8** (of a rope, etc.) entangled. **9** (of a ship's bottom) overgrown with weeds, barnacles, etc. ● *n.* **1** *Sports* an unfair or invalid stroke or action. **2** *Baseball* a batted ball not hit into fair territory. **3** a collision or entanglement. **4** a foul thing. ● *adv.* unfairly. ● *v.* **1** *tr. & intr.* make or become foul or dirty. **2** *tr.* (of an animal) make dirty with excrement. **3 a** *tr. Sports* commit a foul against (a player). **b** *intr.* commit a foul. **4** *tr. & intr. Sports* hit a ball foul. **5 a** *tr.* (often foll. by *up*) cause (an anchor, cable, etc.) to become entangled or muddled. **b** *intr.* become entangled. **6** *tr.* jam or block (a crossing, railway line, or traffic). **7** *tr.* (usu. foll. by *up*) *colloq.* spoil or bungle. □□ **foul·ly** *adv.* **foul·ness** *n.*

fou·lard /foōláard/ *n.* **1** a thin soft material of silk or silk and cotton. **2** an article made of this.

foul play *n.* **1** unfair play in games. **2** treacherous or violent activity, esp. murder.

foul shot *n.* = FREE THROW.

foul-up *n.* a muddled or bungled situation.

found[1] *past* and *past part.* of FIND.

found[2] /fownd/ *v.* **1** *tr.* **a** establish (esp. with an endowment). **b** originate or initiate (an institution). **2** *tr.* be the original builder or begin the building of (a town, etc.). **3** *tr.* lay the base of (a building, etc.). **4** (foll. by *on, upon*) **a** *tr.* construct or base (a story, theory, rule, etc.) according to a specified principle or ground. **b** *intr.* have a basis in.

FOSSIL FUEL

Decaying organic matter produces gases that are usually lost to the atmosphere. If plant and animal remains are trapped in sediment, however, they may form fossil fuels. Land plants buried in mud may form a layer of peat, which over millions of years is compressed to form coal. Oil and natural gas can be produced by marine life decaying under sediment.

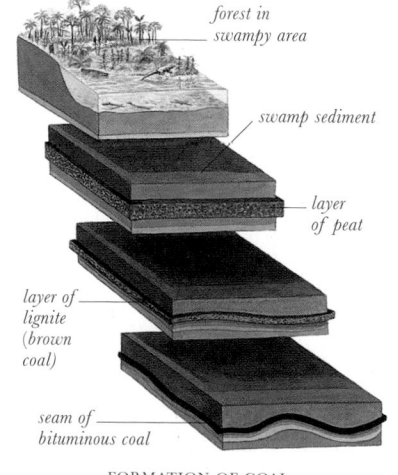

forest in swampy area

swamp sediment

layer of peat

layer of lignite (brown coal)

seam of bituminous coal

FORMATION OF COAL

F

F

found[3] /fownd/ *v.tr.* **1 a** melt and mold (metal). **b** fuse (materials for glass). **2** make by founding. □□ **found·er** *n.*

foun·da·tion /fowndáyshən/ *n.* **1 a** the solid ground or base on which a building rests. **b** (usu. in *pl.*) the lowest load-bearing part of a building, usu. below ground level. ▷ HOUSE. **2** a body or ground on which other parts are overlaid. **3** a basis or underlying principle (*the report has no foundation*). **4 a** the act or an instance of establishing or constituting (esp. an endowed institution). **b** such an institution, e.g., a college or hospital. **5** (in full **foundation garment**) a woman's supporting undergarment, e.g., a corset. □□ **foun·da·tion·al** *adj.*

found·er[1] /fówndər/ *n.* a person who founds an institution.

found·er[2] /fówndər/ *v.* **1 a** *intr.* (of a ship) fill with water and sink. **b** *tr.* cause (a ship) to founder. **2** *intr.* (of a plan, etc.) fail. **3** *intr.* (of earth, a building, etc.) fall down or in. **4** *intr.* (of a horse or its rider) fall to the ground, fall from lameness, stick fast in mud, etc.

found·ing fa·ther *n.* a person associated with a founding, esp. (usu. *cap.*) an American statesman at the time of the Revolution.

found·ling /fówndling/ *n.* an abandoned infant of unknown parentage.

found·ry /fówndree/ *n.* (*pl.* **-ies**) a workshop for or a business of casting metal.

fount[1] /fownt/ *n. poet.* a spring or fountain; a source.

fount[2] /fownt, font/ *n. Brit.* = FONT[2].

foun·tain /fówntin/ *n.* **1 a** a jet or jets of water made to spout for ornamental purposes or for drinking. **b** a structure provided for this. **2** a structure for the constant public supply of drinking water. **3** a natural spring of water. **4** a source (in physical or abstract senses). **5** = SODA FOUNTAIN. **6** a reservoir for oil, ink, etc. □□ **foun·tained** *adj.* (also in *comb.*).

foun·tain·head /fówntn-hed/ *n.* an original source.

foun·tain pen *n.* a pen with a reservoir or cartridge holding ink. ▷ PEN

four /fawr/ *n. & adj.* ● *n.* **1** one more than three. **2** a symbol for this (4, iv, IV). **3** a size, etc., denoted by four. **4** a four-oared rowing boat or its crew. **5** four o'clock (*is it four yet?*). **6** a card with four pips. ● *adj.* that amount to four. □ **on all fours** on hands and knees.

four·chette /foorshét/ *n. Anat.* a thin fold of skin at the back of the vulva.

four-eyes *n. sl.* a person wearing glasses.

four flush *n. Cards* a poker hand of little value, having four cards of the same suit and one of another.

four-flush·er *n.* a bluffer, one who makes false claims.

four·fold /fáwrfōld/ *adj. & adv.* **1** four times as much or as many. **2** consisting of four parts. **3** amounting to four.

four-leaf clover *n.* (also **four-leaved clover**) a clover leaf with four leaflets thought to bring good luck.

four-let·ter word *n.* any of several short words referring to sexual or excretory functions, regarded as coarse or offensive.

four-post·er *n.* a bed with a post at each corner supporting a canopy.

four·score /fáwrskáwr/ *n. archaic* eighty.

four·some /fáwrsəm/ *n.* **1** a group of four persons. **2** a golf match with four players.

four·square /fáwrskwáir/ *adj. & adv.* ● *adj.* **1** solidly based. **2** steady; resolute; forthright. **3** square shaped. ● *adv.* steadily; resolutely.

four-stroke *adj.* (of an internal-combustion engine) having a cycle of four strokes (intake, compression, combustion, and exhaust).

four·teen /fáwrteén/ *n. & adj.* ● *n.* **1** one more than thirteen. **2** a symbol for this (14, xiv, XIV). **3** a size, etc., denoted by fourteen. ● *adj.* that amount to fourteen. □□ **four·teenth** *adj. & n.*

fourth /fawrth/ *n. & adj.* ● *n.* **1** the position in a sequence corresponding to that of the number 4 in the sequence 1–4. **2** something occupying this position. **3** the fourth person, etc., in a race or competition. **4** each of four equal parts of a thing; a quarter. **5** the fourth in a sequence of gears. **6** *Mus.* **a** an interval or chord spanning four consecutive notes in the diatonic scale (e.g., C to F). **b** a note separated from another by this interval. **7** (**Fourth**) the Fourth of July. ● *adj.* that is the fourth. □□ **fourth·ly** *adv.*

fourth es·tate *n.* the press; journalism.

four-wheel drive *n.* drive powering all four wheels of a vehicle.

fo·ve·a /fóveeə/ *n.* (*pl.* **foveae** /-vee-ee/) *Anat.* a small depression or pit, esp. the pit in the retina of the eye for focusing images. □□ **fo·ve·al** *adj.* **fo·ve·ate** /-veeayt/ *adj.*

fowl /fowl/ *n. & v.* (*pl.* same or **fowls**) ● *n.* **1** any domestic cock or hen kept for eggs and flesh. ▷ BANTAM. **2** the flesh of birds, esp. a domestic cock or hen, as food. ● *v.intr.* catch or hunt wildfowl. □□ **fowl·er** *n.* **fowl·ing** *n.*

Fox /foks/ *n.* **1 a** a N. American people native to the northeastern US. **b** a member of this people. **2** the language of this people.

fox /foks/ *n. & v.* ● *n.* **1 a** ◀ any of various wild flesh-eating mammals of the dog family, esp. of the genus *Vulpes*, with a bushy tail, and red or gray fur. **b** the fur of a fox. **2** a cunning or sly person. **3** *sl.* an attractive young woman or man. ● *v.* **1 a** *intr.* act craftily. **b** *tr.* deceive; baffle; trick. **2** *tr.* (usu. as **foxed** *adj.*) discolor (the leaves of a book, engraving, etc.) with brownish marks. □□ **fox·ing** *n.* (in sense 2 of *v.*). **fox·like** *adj.*

FOX: RED FOX
(*Vulpes vulpes*)

fox·glove /fóksgluv/ *n.* any tall plant of the genus *Digitalis*, with erect spikes of purple or white flowers like glove fingers.

fox·hole /fóks-hōl/ *n.* **1** *Mil.* a hole in the ground used as a shelter. **2** a place of refuge or concealment.

fox·hound /fóks-hownd/ *n.* a kind of hound bred and trained to hunt foxes.

fox hunt /fóks-hunt/ *n. & v.* ● *n.* **1** the hunting of foxes with hounds. **2** a particular group of people engaged in this. ● *v.intr.* engage in a foxhunt. □□ **fox·hunt·er** *n.* **fox·hunt·ing** *n. & adj.*

fox·tail /fókstayl/ *n.* any of several grasses of the genus *Alopecurus*, with brushlike spikes.

fox ter·ri·er *n.* a terrier of a short-haired breed.

fox·trot /fókstrot/ *n. & v.* ● *n.* **1** a ballroom dance with slow and quick steps. **2** the music for this. ● *v.intr.* (**foxtrotted, foxtrotting**) perform this dance.

fox·y /fóksee/ *adj.* (**foxier, foxiest**) **1** of or like a fox. **2** sly or cunning. **3** reddish brown. **4** (of paper) damaged, esp. by mildew. **5** *sl.* sexually attractive. □□ **fox·i·ly** *adv.* **fox·i·ness** *n.*

foy·er /fóyər, fóyay, fwaáyay/ *n.* the entrance hall or other large area in a hotel, theater, etc.

Fr *symb. Chem.* the element francium.

Fr. *abbr.* (also **Fr**) **1** Father. **2** French.

fr. *abbr.* franc(s).

fra·cas /fráykəs/ *n.* (*pl.* same, *pronunc.* /-kaaz/) a noisy disturbance or quarrel.

frac·tal /fráktəl/ *n. & adj. Math.* ● *n.* ▶ a curve or geometrical figure, each part of which has the same statistical character as the whole. ● *adj.* relating to or of the nature of a fractal or fractals.

FRACTAL: COMPUTER GENERATED FRACTAL

FRACTIONAL

Fractional distillation is the process used to separate complex mixtures, such as crude oil, into their component parts. In the diagram below, crude oil is heated and pumped into a fractionating tower. Vapors from the oil cool as they rise. At each tier, a different compound of the crude oil reaches the temperature at which it condenses, and so collects on trays. The resultant liquids are then drained off through pipes.

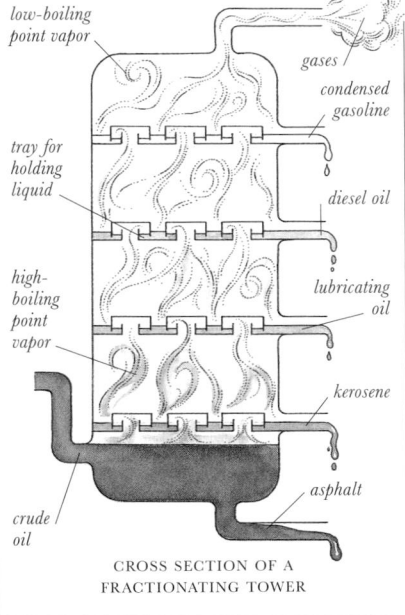

low-boiling point vapor

gases

condensed gasoline

tray for holding liquid

diesel oil

high-boiling point vapor

lubricating oil

kerosene

crude oil

asphalt

CROSS SECTION OF A
FRACTIONATING TOWER

frac·tion /frákshən/ *n.* **1** a numerical quantity that is not a whole number (e.g., 0.5, $\frac{1}{2}$). **2** a small, esp. very small, part, piece, or amount. **3** a portion of a mixture separated by distillation, etc. **4** *Polit.* any organized dissenting group. □□ **frac·tion·ary** *adj.* **frac·tion·ize** *v.*

frac·tion·al /frákshənəl/ *adj.* **1** of or relating to a fraction. **2** very slight; incomplete. **3** *Chem.* ▲ relating to the separation of parts of a mixture by making use of their different physical properties (*fractional distillation, fractional crystallization*). □□ **frac·tion·al·ize** *n.* **frac·tion·al·ly** *adv.*

frac·tion·ate /frákshənayt/ *v.tr.* **1** break up into parts. **2** separate by fractional distillation, etc. □□ **frac·tion·a·tion** /-náyshən/ *n.*

frac·tious /frákshəs/ *adj.* **1** irritable; peevish. **2** unruly. □□ **frac·tious·ly** *adv.* **frac·tious·ness** *n.*

frac·ture /frákchər/ *n. & v.* ● *n.* **1 a** ▶ breakage or breaking, esp. of a bone or cartilage. **b** the result of breaking; a crack or split. **2** the surface appearance of a freshly broken rock or mineral. ● *v.intr. & tr. Med.* undergo or cause to undergo a fracture. **2** break or cause to break.

frag·ile /frájil, -jīl/ *adj.* **1** easily broken; weak. **2** of delicate frame or constitution; not strong. □□ **frag·ile·ly** *adv.* **fra·gil·i·ty** /frəjílitee/ *n.*

frag·ment *n. & v.* ● *n.* /frágmənt/ **1** a part broken off; a detached piece. **2** an isolated or incomplete part. **3** the remains of an otherwise lost or destroyed book or work of art. ● *v.tr. & intr.* /fragmént/ break or separate into fragments. □□ **frag·men·tal** /-mént'l/ *adj.* **frag·ment·ize** *v.tr.*

FRACTURE

There are several types of bone fractures, determined by the degree and direction of the force applied. A straight-on force may cause a different break from an oblique one; more than one break may occur; or only one side of the bone may be broken.

TYPES OF FRACTURE

TRANSVERSE FRACTURE — *right-angled break*

OBLIQUE FRACTURE — *angled break*

SPIRAL FRACTURE — *twisted break*

IMPACTED FRACTURE — *compression break*

COMMINUTED FRACTURE — *multiple break*

GREENSTICK FRACTURE — *one-sided break*

frag·men·tar·y /frágmənteree/ *adj.* **1** consisting of fragments. **2** disconnected. □□ **frag·men·tar·i·ly** *adv.*

frag·men·ta·tion /frágməntáyshən/ *n.* the process or an instance of breaking into fragments.

frag·men·ta·tion bomb *n.* a bomb designed to break up into small rapidly-moving fragments when exploded.

fra·grance /fráygrəns/ *n.* (also **fragrancy** *pl.* **-ies**) **1** sweetness of smell. **2** a sweet scent.

fra·grant /fráygrənt/ *adj.* sweet-smelling. □□ **fra·grant·ly** *adv.*

frail /frayl/ *adj.* **1** fragile; delicate. **2** in weak health. **3** morally weak. **4** transient; insubstantial. □□ **frail·ly** *adv.* **frail·ness** *n.*

frail·ty /fráyltee/ *n.* (*pl.* **-ies**) **1** the condition of being frail. **2** liability to err or yield to temptation. **3** a fault, weakness, or foible.

frame /fraym/ *n.* & *v.* ● *n.* **1** a case or border enclosing a picture, window, door, etc. **2** the basic rigid supporting structure of anything, e.g., of a building, motor vehicle, or aircraft. **3** (in *pl.*) the structure of spectacles holding the lenses. **4** a human or animal body, esp. with reference to its size or structure. **5** a framed work or structure (*the frame of heaven*). **6 a** an established order, plan, or system (*the frame of society*). **b** construction; constitution; build. **7** a temporary state (esp. in **frame of mind**). **8** a single complete image or picture on a movie or video film or transmitted in a series of lines by television. **9 a** a triangular structure for positioning the balls in pool, etc. **b** the balls positioned in this way. **c** a round of play in bowling, etc. **10** *Hort.* a boxlike structure of glass, etc., for protecting plants. **11** a removable box of slats for the building of a honeycomb in a beehive. **12** *sl.* = FRAME-UP. ● *v.tr.* **1 a** set in or provide with a frame. **b** serve as a frame for. **2** construct by a combination of parts or in accordance with a design or plan. **3** formulate the essentials of (a complex thing, idea, etc.). **4** (foll. by *to*, *into*) adapt or fit. **5** *colloq.* concoct a false charge or evidence against; devise a plot with regard to. **6** articulate (words). □□ **fram·a·ble** *adj.* (also **frame·a·ble**) **frame·less** *adj.* **fram·er** *n.*

frame of ref·er·ence *n.* **1** a set of standards or principles governing behavior, thought, etc. **2** *Geom.* a system of geometrical axes for defining position.

frame-up *n. colloq.* a conspiracy, esp. to make an innocent person appear guilty.

frame·work /fráymwərk/ *n.* **1** an essential supporting structure. **2** a basic system.

franc /frangk/ *n.* the chief monetary unit of France, Belgium, Switzerland, Luxembourg, and several other countries (replaced in France, Belgium, and Luxembourg by the euro in 2002).

fran·chise /fránchīz/ *n.* & *v.* ● *n.* **1 a** the right to vote in governmental elections. **b** the principle of qualification for this. **2** full membership of a corporation or nation; citizenship. **3** authorization granted by a company to sell its goods or services in a particular way. **4** *hist.* legal immunity or exemption from a burden or jurisdiction. **5** a right or privilege granted to a person or corporation. **6** a professional sports team, esp. as part of a league. ● *v.tr.* grant a franchise to. □□ **fran·chi·see** /-zée/ *n.* **fran·chis·er** *n.* (also **fran·chi·sor**).

Fran·cis·can /fransískən/ *n.* & *adj.* ● *n.* a friar, sister, or lay member of an order founded by St. Francis of Assisi (see also **grey friar**). ● *adj.* of St. Francis or his order.

fran·ci·um /fránseeəm/ *n. Chem.* a radioactive metallic element occurring naturally in uranium and thorium ores. ¶ Symb.: **Fr.**

Franco- /frángkō/ *comb. form* **1** French; French and (*Franco-German*). **2** regarding France or the French (*Francophile*).

Fran·co·phile /frángkəfīl/ *n.* a person who is fond of France or the French.

fran·co·phone /frángkəfōn/ *n.* & *adj.* ● *n.* a French-speaking person. ● *adj.* French-speaking.

fran·gi·ble /fránjibəl/ *adj.* breakable; fragile.

fran·gi·pane /fránjipayn/ *n.* **1 a** an almond-flavored cream or paste. **b** a flan filled with this. **2** = FRANGIPANI.

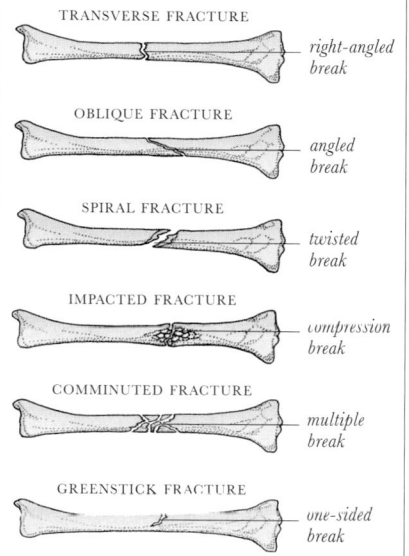

FRANGIPANI
(*Plumeria rubra*)

fran·gi·pan·i /fránjipánee, -páanee/ *n.* (*pl.* **frangipanis**) **1** ◄ any tree or shrub of the genus *Plumeria*, native to tropical America, esp. *P. rubra* with clusters of fragrant white, pink, or yellow flowers. **2** the perfume from this plant.

fran·glais /fróⁿglay/ *n.* a version of French using many words and idioms borrowed from English.

Frank /frangk/ *n.* **1** a member of the Germanic nation or coalition that conquered Gaul in the 6th c. **2** (in the Levant) a person of Western nationality. □□ **Frank·ish** *adj.*

frank /frangk/ *adj.*, *v.*, & *n.* ● *adj.* **1** candid; outspoken (*a frank opinion*). **2** undisguised; avowed (*frank admiration*). **3** ingenuous; open (*a frank face*). ● *v.tr.* stamp (a letter) with an official mark to record the payment of postage. ● *n.* **1** a franking mark. **2** a franked cover. □□ **frank·er** *n.* **frank·ness** *n.*

Frank·en·stein /frángkənstīn/ *n.* (in full **Frankenstein's monster**) a thing that becomes terrifying to its maker; a monster.

frank·furt·er /frángkfərtər/ *n.* a seasoned sausage made of beef and pork.

frank·in·cense /frángkinsens/ *n.* an aromatic gum resin used for burning as incense.

Frank·lin stove /frángklin/ *n.* a cast-iron stove having the general shape of an open fireplace but often placed so as to be freestanding.

frank·ly /frángklee/ *adv.* **1** in a frank manner. **2** (qualifying a whole sentence) to be frank.

fran·tic /frántik/ *adj.* **1** wildly excited; frenzied. **2** characterized by great hurry or anxiety; desperate; violent. **3** *colloq.* extreme; very great. □□ **fran·ti·cal·ly** *adv.* **fran·tic·ly** *adv.* **fran·tic·ness** *n.*

frap·pé /frapáy/ *adj.* & *n.* ● *adj.* (esp. of wine) iced, cooled. ● *n.* **1** an iced drink. **2** a soft semi-frozen drink or dessert.

Fras·ca·ti /fraskáatee/ *n.* a white wine produced in the Frascati region of Italy.

frass /fras/ *n.* **1** a fine powdery refuse left by insects boring. **2** the excrement of insect larvae.

frat /frat/ *n. colloq.* a student fraternity.

fra·ter·nal /frətərnəl/ *adj.* **1** of a brother or brothers. **2** suitable to a brother; brotherly. **3** (of twins) developed from separate ova and not necessarily similar. **4** of or concerning a fraternity (see FRATERNITY 3). □□ **fra·ter·nal·ism** *n.* **fra·ter·nal·ly** *adv.*

fra·ter·ni·ty /frətərnitee/ *n.* (*pl.* **-ies**) **1** a male students' society in a university or college. **2** a group or company with common interests, or of the same professional class. **3** a religious brotherhood. **4** brotherliness.

frat·er·nize /frátərnīz/ *v.intr.* (often foll. by *with*) **1** associate; make friends. **2** (of troops) enter into friendly relations with enemy troops or the inhabitants of an occupied country. □□ **frat·er·ni·za·tion** *n.*

frat·ri·cide /frátrisīd/ *n.* **1** the killing of one's brother or sister. **2** a person who does this. □□ **frat·ri·cid·al** /-síd'l/ *adj.*

Frau /frow/ *n.* (*pl.* **Frauen** /frówən/) (often as a title) a married or widowed German woman.

fraud /frawd/ *n.* **1** criminal deception. **2** a dishonest artifice or trick. **3** a person or thing not fulfilling what is claimed or expected of it.

fraud·u·lent /fráwjələnt/ *adj.* **1** characterized or achieved by fraud. **2** guilty of fraud. □□ **fraud·u·lence** /-ləns/ *n.* **fraud·u·lent·ly** *adv.*

fraught /frawt/ *adj.* **1** (foll. by *with*) filled or attended with (*fraught with danger*). **2** *colloq.* causing or affected by great anxiety or distress.

Fräu·lein /fróylīn, frów-/ *n.* (often as a title or form of address) an unmarried (esp. young) German woman.

Fraun·ho·fer lines /frównhōfər/ *n.pl.* the dark lines visible in solar and stellar spectra.

frax·i·nel·la /fráksinélə/ *n.* ► an aromatic plant *Dictamnus albus*, having foliage that emits an ethereal flammable oil. Also called **dittany**, **gas plant**.

fray[1] /fray/ *v.* **1** *tr.* & *intr.* wear through or become worn, esp. (of woven material) unweave at the edges. **2** *intr.* (of nerves, temper, etc.) become strained.

fray[2] /fray/ *n.* **1** conflict; fighting (*eager for the fray*). **2** a noisy quarrel or brawl.

fra·zil /fráyzil/ *n.* ice crystals that form in a stream or on its bed.

FRAXINELLA
(*Dictamnus albus*)

fraz·zle /frázəl/ *n.* & *v. colloq.* ● *n.* a worn or exhausted state (*burned to a frazzle*). ● *v.tr.* (usu. as **frazzled** *adj.*) wear out; exhaust.

freak /freek/ *n.* & *v.* ● *n.* **1** (also **freak of nature**) a monstrosity; an abnormally developed individual or thing. **2** (often *attrib.*) an abnormal, irregular, or bizarre occurrence (*a freak storm*). **3** *colloq.* **a** an unconventional person. **b** a person with a specified enthusiasm (*health freak*). **c** a person who undergoes hallucinations; a drug addict (see sense 2 of *v.*). **4 a** a caprice or vagary. **b** capriciousness. ● *v.* (often foll. by *out*) *colloq.* **1** *intr.* & *tr.* become or make very angry. **2** *intr.* & *tr.* undergo or cause to undergo hallucinations, etc. esp. from use of narcotics. **3** *intr.* adopt a wildly unconventional lifestyle.

freak·ish /fréekish/ *adj.* **1** of or like a freak. **2** bizarre, unconventional. □□ **freak·ish·ly** *adv.* **freak·ish·ness** *n.*

freak·y /fréekee/ *adj.* (**freakier**, **freakiest**) = FREAKISH. □□ **freak·i·ly** *adv.* **freak·i·ness** *n.*

F

F

freck·le /frékəl/ *n. & v.* ● *n.* (often in *pl.*) a light brown spot on the skin, usu. caused by exposure to the sun. ● *v.* **1** *tr.* (usu. as **freckled** *adj.*) spot with freckles. **2** *intr.* be spotted with freckles. □□ **freck·ly** /fréklee/ *adj.*

free /free/ *adj., adv., & v.* ● *adj.* (**freer** /frée-ər/; **freest** /frée-ist/) **1** not in bondage to or under the control of another; having personal rights and social and political liberty. **2** (of a nation or its citizens) subject neither to foreign domination nor to despotic government; having national and civil liberty (*a free press; a free society*). **3 a** unrestricted; not restrained or fixed. **b** not confined or imprisoned. **c** released from ties or duties. **d** unrestrained as to action; independent (*set free*). **4** (foll. by *of*, *from*) **a** exempt from (*free of tax*). **b** not containing or subject to a specified (usu. undesirable) thing (*free of preservatives; free from disease*). **5** (foll. by *to* + infin.) able to take a specified action (*free to choose*). **6** unconstrained (*free gestures*). **7 a** costing nothing. **b** not subject to tax, duty, or fees. **8 a** clear of engagements (*are you free tomorrow?*). **b** not occupied or in use (*the bathroom is free now*). **c** clear of obstructions. **9** spontaneous; unforced (*free compliments*). **10** open to all comers. **11** lavish; profuse (*very free with their money*). **12** frank; unreserved. **13** (of a literary, sporting, etc., style) not observing the strict laws of form. **14** (of a translation) conveying the broad sense. **15** forward; impudent. **16** (of talk, stories, etc.) slightly indecent. **17** *Physics* **a** not modified by an external force. **b** not bound in an atom or molecule. **18** *Chem.* not combined (*free oxygen*). **19** (of power or energy) disengaged or available. ● *adv.* **1** in a free manner. **2** without cost or payment. ● *v.tr.* **1** make free; set at liberty. **2** (foll. by *of*, *from*) relieve from (something undesirable). **3** disengage; disentangle. □ **free and easy** informal; unceremonious. □□ **free·ly** *adv.* **free·ness** *n.*

-free /free/ *comb. form* free of or from (*duty-free; trouble-free*).

free a·gent *n.* a person with freedom of action.

free·base /frée-bays/ *n. & v. sl.* ● *n.* cocaine that has been purified by heating with ether, and is taken by inhaling the fumes or smoking the residue. ● *v.tr.* purify (cocaine) for smoking or inhaling.

free·bie /frée-bee/ *n. colloq.* a thing provided free of charge.

free·board /frée-bawrd/ *n.* ▶ the part of a ship's side between the water-line and the deck.

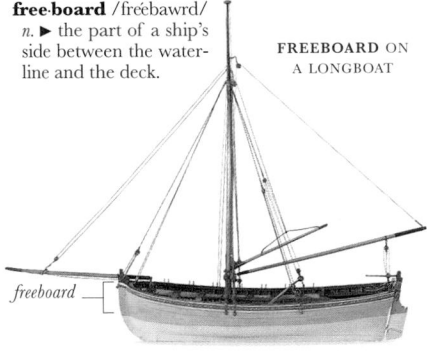

FREEBOARD ON
A LONGBOAT

freeboard

free·boot·er /frée-boōtər/ *n.* a pirate or buccaneer. □□ **free·boot** *v.intr.*

free·born /frée-bawrn/ *adj.* inheriting a citizen's rights and liberty.

freed·man /fréedmən/ *n.* (*pl.* **-men**) an emancipated slave.

free·dom /frée-dəm/ *n.* **1** the condition of being free or unrestricted. **2** personal or civic liberty. **3** the power of self-determination. **4** the state of being free to act (often foll. by *to* + infin.: *we have the freedom to leave*). **5** frankness; outspokenness. **6** (foll. by *from*) the condition of being exempt from or not subject to (a defect, burden, etc.). **7** (foll. by *of*) **a** full or honorary participation in (membership, privileges, etc.). **b** unrestricted use of (facilities, etc.). **8** a privilege possessed by a city or corporation. **9** facility or ease in action. **10** boldness of conception.

free·dom fight·er *n.* a person who takes part in violent resistance to an established political system, etc.

free en·ter·prise *n.* a system in which private business operates in competition and largely free of government control.

free fall *n.* movement under the force of gravity only, esp.: **1** the part of a parachute descent before the parachute opens. **2** the movement of a spacecraft in space without thrust from the engines.

free-for-all *n.* a fight, contest, argument, etc., open to all and usu. without rules.

free-form *attrib.adj.* of an irregular shape or structure.

free·hand /frée-hand/ *adj. & adv.* ● *adj.* (of a drawing or plan, etc.) done by hand without special instruments. ● *adv.* in a freehand manner.

free hand *n.* freedom to act at one's own discretion (see also FREEHAND).

free-hand·ed *adj.* generous. □□ **free-hand·ed·ly** *adv.* **free-hand·ed·ness** *n.*

free·hold /frée-hōld/ *n. & adj.* ● *n.* **1** tenure of land or property in fee simple or fee tail or for life. **2** esp. *Brit.* land or property or an office held by such tenure. ● *adj.* held by or having the status of freehold. □□ **free·hold·er** *n.*

free·lance /frée-lans/ *n., v., & adv.* ● *n.* **1** (also **free·lanc·er**) a person, usu. self-employed, offering services on a temporary basis. **2** (*attrib.*) (*a freelance editor*). ● *v.intr.* act as a freelance. ● *adv.* as a freelance.

free·load·er /frée-lōdər/ *n. sl.* a person who eats, drinks, or lives at others' expense; a sponger. □□ **free·load** /-lód/ *v.intr.*

free love *n.* sexual relations according to choice and unrestricted by marriage.

free·man /frée-mən/ *n.* (*pl.* **-men**) **1** a person who has the freedom of a city, company, etc. **2** a person who is not a slave.

free mar·ket *n.* a market in which prices are determined by unrestricted competition.

free·mar·tin /frée-maartin/ *n.* a hermaphrodite or imperfect female calf of oppositely sexed twins.

Free·ma·son /frée-maysən/ *n.* a member of an international fraternity for mutual help, with elaborate secret rituals. □□ **Free·ma·son·ry** /frée-maysənree/ *n.*

free port *n.* **1** a port area where goods in transit are exempt from customs duty. **2** a port open to all traders.

fre·er *compar.* of FREE.

free rad·i·cal *n. Chem.* an unchanged atom or group of atoms with one or more unpaired electrons.

free-range *adj.* (of hens, etc.) kept in natural conditions with freedom of movement.

free rein see REIN.

free·si·a /fréezhə, -zeeə/ *n.* ▶ any bulbous plant of the genus *Freesia*, native to Africa, having fragrant colored flowers.

free speech *n.* the right to express opinions freely.

free-spok·en *adj.* speaking candidly; not concealing one's opinions.

fre·est *superl.* of FREE.

free-stand·ing *adj.* not supported by another structure.

free·style /frée-stīl/ *adj. & n.* ● *adj.* (of a contest) in which all styles are allowed, esp.: **1** *Swimming* in which any stroke may be used. **2** *Wrestling* with few restrictions on the holds permitted. ● *n.* = CRAWL *n.* 3.

free-think·er /frée-thíngkər/ *n.* a person who rejects dogma or authority. □□ **free-think·ing** *n. & adj.*

free throw *n. Basketball* an unhindered shot at the

basket made by a player after a foul has been called against the opposing team.

free verse *n.* verse without a fixed metrical pattern.

free·ware /frée-wair/ *n. Computing* software that is distributed free and without technical support to users.

free·way /frée-way/ *n.* **1** an express highway, esp. with controlled access. **2** a toll-free highway.

free·wheel /frée-weel/ *v.intr.* **1** move freely with gears disengaged, esp. downhill. **2** move or act without constraint or effort.

free will *n.* **1** the power of acting without the constraint of necessity or fate. **2** the ability to act at one's own discretion (*of my own free will*).

free world *n.* the noncommunist countries, esp. during the Cold War.

freeze /freez/ *v. & n.* ● *v.* (*past* **froze** /frōz/; *past part.* **frozen** /frōzən/) **1** *tr. & intr.* **a** turn or be turned into ice or another solid by cold. **b** (often foll. by *over, up*) make or become rigid as a result of the cold. **2** *intr.* be or feel very cold. **3** *tr. & intr.* cover or become covered with ice. **4** *intr.* (foll. by *to, together*) adhere by frost. **5** *tr.* preserve (food) by refrigeration below the freezing point. **6** *tr. & intr.* **a** make or become motionless or powerless through fear, etc. **b** react or cause to react with sudden detachment. **7** *tr.* stiffen or harden, or injure or kill, by chilling (*frozen to death*). **8** *tr.* make (assets, etc.) unrealizable. **9** *tr.* fix or stabilize (prices, etc.) at a certain level. **10** *tr.* arrest (an action) at a stage of development. **11** *tr.* = FREEZE-FRAME *v.* ● *n.* **1** a state of frost; a period of very cold weather. **2** the fixing or stabilization of prices, etc. **3** = FREEZE-FRAME *n.* □ **freeze out** *colloq.* exclude by competition or boycott, etc. **freeze up** obstruct or be obstructed by the formation of ice. □□ **freez·a·ble** *adj.* **fro·zen·ly** *adv.*

freeze-dry *v.tr.* (**-dries**, **-dried**) freeze and dry by the sublimation of ice in a high vacuum.

freeze-frame *n. & v.* ● *n.* (also *attrib.*) the facility of stopping a videotape, etc., in order to view a motionless image; a film shot in which movement is arrested by repetition of a frame. ● *v.tr.* use freeze-frame on (an image, etc.).

freez·er /frée-zər/ *n.* a refrigerated compartment, cabinet, or room for preserving food at very low temperatures; = DEEP FREEZE *n.* 1

freeze-up *n.* a period or conditions of extreme cold.

freez·ing point *n.* the temperature at which a liquid, esp. water, freezes.

freight /frayt/ *n. & v.* ● *n.* **1** the transport of goods in containers or by air or land or, esp. *Brit.*, water. **2** goods transported; cargo. **3** a charge for transportation of goods. **4** the lease of a ship or aircraft for transporting goods. **5** a load or burden. ● *v.tr.* **1** transport (goods) as freight. **2** load with freight. **3** lease out (a ship) for the carriage of goods and passengers.

FREESIA
(*Freesia* 'Everett')

freight·age /fráytij/ *n.* **1 a** the transportation of freight. **b** the cost of this. **2** freight transported.

freight car *n.* a railroad car used for transporting freight.

freight·er /fráytər/ *n.* **1** a ship or aircraft designed to carry freight. **2** a person who loads or charters and loads a ship. **3** a person who consigns goods for carriage inland. **4** a person whose business is to receive and forward freight.

French /french/ *adj. & n.* ● *adj.* **1** of or relating to France or its people or language. **2** having the characteristics attributed to the French people. ● *n.* **1** the language of France, also used in Belgium, Switzerland, Canada, and elsewhere. **2** (prec. by *the;* treated as *pl.*) the people of France. **3** *colloq.* bad language (*excuse my French*). **4** *colloq.* dry vermouth (*gin and French*). □□ **French·i·fy** /frénchifī/ *v.tr.* (**-ies**, **-ied**) **French·ness** *n.*

French bread *n.* white bread in a long crisp loaf.

French Ca·na·di·an *n. & adj.* ● *n.* a Canadian whose principal language is French. ● *adj.* of or relating to French-speaking Canadians.

French cuff *n.* a double cuff formed by turning back a long cuff and fastening it.

French curve *n.* a template used for drawing curved lines.

French door *n.* a door with glass panes throughout its length.

French dress·ing *n.* **1** a creamy orange salad dressing, usu. made with tomato. **2** a salad dressing of vinegar and oil, usu. seasoned.

French fries *n.pl.* (also **French fried po·ta·toes**) strips of potato, deep-fried.

French horn *n.* ◀ a coiled brass wind instrument with a wide bell. ▷ BRASS

French kiss *n* a kiss with one partner's tongue inserted in the other's mouth.

French leave *n.* absence without permission.

French·man /frénchmən/ *n.* (*pl.* **-men**) a man who is French by birth or descent.

French toast *n.* bread dipped in egg and milk and sautéed.

French·wom·an /frénchwŏŏmən/ *n.* (*pl.* **-women**) a woman who is French by birth or descent.

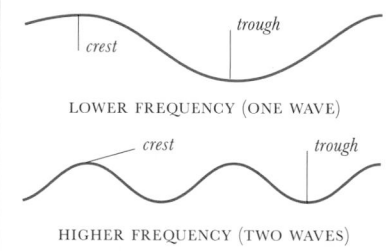

mouthpiece
finger keys
valves
coiled tubing
wide bell

FRENCH HORN

fre·net·ic /frənétik/ *adj.* **1** frantic; frenzied. **2** fanatic. □□ **fre·net·i·cal·ly** *adv.*

fren·u·lum /frényələm/ *n.* (*pl.* **-la** /-lə/) *Anat.* a small frenum.

fre·num /frénəm/ *n.* (*pl.* **-na** /-nə/) *Anat.* a fold of mucous membrane or skin, esp. under the tongue, checking the motion of an organ.

fren·zy /frénzee/ *n. & v.* ● *n.* (*pl.* **-ies**) **1** mental derangement; wild excitement or agitation. **2** delirious fury. ● *v.tr.* (**-ies, -ied**) (usu. as **frenzied** *adj.*) drive to frenzy; infuriate. □□ **fren·zied·ly** *adv.*

Fre·on /fréeon/ *n. Trademark* any of a group of halogenated hydrocarbons containing fluorine, chlorine, and sometimes bromine, used in aerosols, refrigerants, etc. (see also CFC).

fre·quen·cy /fréekwənsee/ *n.* (*pl.* **-ies**) **1** commonness of occurrence. **2 a** frequent occurrence. **b** the process of being repeated at short intervals. **3** *Physics* ▲ the rate of recurrence of a vibration, cycle, etc.; the number of repetitions in a given time.

fre·quen·cy mod·u·la·tion *n. Electronics* a modulation in which the frequency of the carrier wave is varied. ¶ Abbr.: **FM**.

fre·quent /fréekwənt/ *adj. & v.* ● *adj.* **1** occurring often or in close succession. **2** habitual (*a frequent caller*). **3** found near together; abundant. **4** (of the pulse) rapid. ● *v.tr.* /also frikwént/ attend or go to habitually. □□ **fre·quen·ta·tion** *n.* **fre·quent·er** /frikwéntər/ *n.* **fre·quent·ly** /fréekwəntlee/ *adv.*

fre·quen·ta·tive /frikwéntətiv/ *adj. & n. Gram.* ● *adj.* expressing frequent repetition or intensity of action. ● *n.* a verb or verbal form or conjugation expressing this (e.g., *chatter, twinkle*).

fres·co /fréskō/ *n.* (*pl.* **-os** or **-oes**) **1** ▶ a painting done in watercolor on a wall or ceiling while the plaster is still wet. **2** this method of painting (esp. *in fresco*). □□ **fres·coed** *adj.*

fresh /fresh/ *adj., adv., & n.* ● *adj.* **1** newly made or obtained (*fresh sandwiches*). **2 a** other; different; not previously known or used (*start a fresh page*). **b** additional (*fresh supplies*). **3** (foll. by *from*) lately arrived from. **4** not stale or faded (*fresh memories*). **5** (of food) not preserved by salting, freezing, etc. **6** not salty (*fresh water*). **7 a** pure; untainted; invigorating

---

FREQUENCY

In physics, frequency refers to the number of periodic vibrations, oscillations, or waves that occur per unit of time. The unit of frequency is the hertz (Hz); one hertz is equivalent to one cycle per second. The human ear can hear sounds from vibrations in the range 20–20,000 Hz.

crest   *trough*

LOWER FREQUENCY (ONE WAVE)

crest   *trough*

HIGHER FREQUENCY (TWO WAVES)

(*fresh air*). **b** bright and pure in color (*a fresh complexion*). **8** (of the wind) brisk. **9** alert; vigorous (*never felt fresher*). **10** *colloq.* **a** cheeky. **b** amorously impudent. **11** young and inexperienced. ● *adv.* newly; recently (esp. in *comb.*: *fresh-baked*). ● *n.* the fresh part of the day, etc. (*in the fresh of the morning*). □□ **fresh·ly** *adv.* **fresh·ness** *n.*

fresh·en /fréshən/ *v.* **1** *tr. & intr.* make or become fresh or fresher. **2** *intr. & tr.* (foll. by *up*) **a** wash, change one's clothes, etc. **b** revive; refresh; renew.

fresh·er /fréshər/ *n. Brit. colloq.* = FRESHMAN.

fresh·et /tréshit/ *n.* **1** a rush of fresh water flowing into the sea. **2** the flood of a river.

fresh·man /fréshmən/ *n.* (*pl.* **-men**) a first-year student at a high school, college, or university.

fresh·wa·ter /fréshwawtər, -wotər/ *adj.* **1** of or found in fresh water; not of the sea. **2** (esp. of a school or college) rustic or provincial.

fret[1] /fret/ *v.* (**fretted, fretting**) **1** *intr.* **a** be greatly and visibly worried or distressed. **b** be irritated or resentful. **2** *tr.* **a** cause anxiety or distress to. **b** irritate; annoy. **3** *tr.* wear or consume by gnawing or rubbing. **4** *tr.* form (a channel or passage) by wearing away.

fret[2] /fret/ *n. & v.* ● *n.* an ornamental pattern made of continuous combinations of straight lines joined usu. at right angles. ● *v.tr.* (**fretted, fretting**) **1** embellish or decorate with a fret. **2** adorn (esp. a ceiling) with carved or embossed work.

fret[3] /fret/ *n.* each of a sequence of bars or ridges on the fingerboard of some stringed musical instru-

---

ments (esp. the guitar) fixing the positions of the fingers to produce the desired notes. ▷ GUITAR, SITAR. □□ **fret·less** *adj.*

fret·ful /frétfŏol/ *adj.* visibly anxious or distressed. □□ **fret·ful·ly** *adv.* **fret·ful·ness** *n.*

fret·saw /frétsaw/ *n.* a saw consisting of a narrow blade stretched on a frame, for cutting thin wood in patterns.

fret·work /frétwərk/ *n.* ornamental work in wood, done with a fretsaw.

Freud·i·an /fróydeeən/ *adj. & n. Psychol.* ● *adj.* of or relating to the Austrian psychologist Sigmund Freud (d. 1939) or his methods of psychoanalysis. ● *n.* a follower of Freud or his methods. □□ **Freud·i·an·ism** *n.*

Freud·i·an slip *n.* an unintentional error regarded as revealing subconscious feelings.

Fri. *abbr.* Friday.

fri·a·ble /fríəbəl/ *adj.* easily crumbled. □□ **fri·a·bil·i·ty** *n.* **fri·a·ble·ness** *n.*

fri·ar /fríər/ *n.* a member of certain religious orders of men, esp. the four mendicant orders (Augustinians, Carmelites, Dominicans, and Franciscans). □□ **fri·ar·ly** *adj.*

fri·ar·y /fríəree/ *n.* (*pl.* **-ies**) a convent of friars.

fric·as·see /fríkəsée/ *n. & v.* ● *n.* a dish of stewed or fried pieces of meat served in a thick white sauce. ● *v.tr.* (**fricassees, fricasseed**) make a fricassee of.

fric·a·tive /fríkətiv/ *adj. & n. Phonet.* ● *adj.* made by the friction of breath in a narrow opening. ● *n.* a consonant made in this way, e.g., *f* and *th*.

fric·tion /fríkshən/ *n.* **1** the action of one object rubbing against another. **2** the resistance an object encounters in moving over another. **3** a clash of wills, temperaments, or opinions. **4** (in *comb.*) of devices that transmit motion by frictional contact (*friction clutch; friction disk*). □□ **fric·tion·al** *adj.* **fric·tion·less** *adj.*

Fri·day /fríday, -dee/ *n. & adv.* ● *n.* the sixth day of the week, following Thursday. ● *adv. colloq.* **1** on Friday. **2** (**Fridays**) on Fridays; each Friday.

fridge /frij/ *n. colloq.* = REFRIGERATOR.

friend /frend/ *n. & v.* ● *n.* **1 a** a person with whom one enjoys mutual affection and regard (usu. exclusive of sexual or family bonds). **2** a sympathizer, helper, or patron (*no friend to virtue*). **3** a person who is not an enemy or who is on the same side (*friend or foe?*). **4 a** a person already mentioned (*my friend at the next table*). **b** a person known by sight. **c** used as a polite or ironic form of address. **5** (usu. in *pl.*) a regular contributor to an institution. **6** (**Friend**) a member of the Society of Friends; a Quaker. **7** a helpful thing or quality. ● *v.tr.* befriend; help. □ **be friends with** be friendly with. □□ **friend·ed** *adj.* **friend·less** *adj.*

FRESCO

A fresco is a form of wall painting in which pigments mixed with water are applied to a layer of fresh, damp plaster known as *intonaco*. As the *intonaco* dries, it absorbs the pigments, and so the painting becomes part of the wall. The earliest frescoes were found in Knossos, Crete (*c.*1750–1400 BC), but the art form reached its greatest height under the Italian Renaissance masters.

The Angel Appearing to Zacharias (detail) (1485–90), DOMENICO GHIRLANDAIO

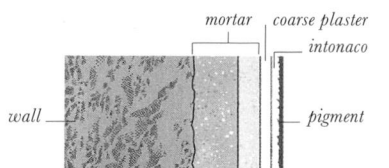

mortar   *coarse plaster*
intonaco
wall   *pigment*

CROSS SECTION OF A FRESCO

F

friend·ly /fréndlee/ *adj. & adv.* ● *adj.* (**friendlier,
friendliest**) **1** acting as or like a friend; well-disposed; kindly. **2 a** (often foll. by *with*) on amicable terms. **b** not hostile. **3** characteristic of friends; showing or prompted by kindness. **4** favorably disposed; ready to approve or help. **5 a** (of a thing) serviceable; convenient; opportune. **b** = USER-FRIENDLY. ● *adv.* in a friendly manner. □□ **friend·li·ly** *adv.* **friend·li·ness** *n.*

friend·ly fire *n. Mil.* fire coming from one's own side, esp. as the cause of accidental injury to one's forces.

friend·ship /fréndship/ *n.* **1** being friends; the relationship between friends. **2** a friendly disposition felt or shown.

fri·er var. of FRYER.

frieze /freez/ *n.* **1** *Archit.* the part of an entablature between the architrave and the cornice. ▷ ENTABLATURE. **2** *Archit.* ▼ a horizontal band of sculpture filling this. **3** a band of decoration elsewhere, esp. along a wall near the ceiling.

FRIEZE: 8TH-CENTURY ROMAN FRIEZE

frig[1] /frig/ *v. & n. coarse sl.* ● *v.* (**frigged, frigging**) **1 a** *tr. & intr.* have sexual intercourse (with). **b** masturbate. **2** *tr.* (usu. as an exclamation) = FUCK *v.* 3. **3** *intr.* (foll. by *around, about*) mess around; fool around. **4** *intr.* (foll. by *off*) go away. ● *n.* an act of frigging.

frig[2] /frij/ *n. colloq.* = REFRIGERATOR.

frig·ate /frígit/ *n.* **1 a** a naval vessel between a destroyer and a cruiser in size. **b** *Brit.* a similar ship between a corvette and a destroyer in size. **2** *hist.* a warship.

frig·ate bird *n.* any marine bird of the family Fregatidae, found in tropical seas, with a wide wingspan and deeply forked tail. ▷ SEABIRD

fright /frīt/ *n. & v.* ● *n.* **1 a** sudden or extreme fear. **b** an instance of this (*gave me a fright*). **2** a person or thing looking grotesque or ridiculous. ● *v.tr.* frighten. □ **take fright** become frightened.

fright·en /frítən/ *v.* **1** *tr.* fill with fright; terrify. **2** *tr.* (foll. by *away, off, out of, into*) drive or force by fright. **3** *intr.* become frightened (*I frighten easily*). □□ **fright·en·ing** *adj.* **fright·en·ing·ly** *adv.*

fright·en·er /frítnər/ *n.* a person or thing that frightens.

fright·ful /frítfool/ *adj.* **1 a** dreadful; shocking. **b** ugly. **2** *colloq.* extremely bad (*a frightful idea*). **3** *colloq.* very great; extreme. □□ **fright·ful·ly** *adv.* **fright·ful·ness** *n.*

frig·id /fríjid/ *adj.* **1 a** lacking friendliness or enthusiasm. **b** dull; insipid. **c** chilling; depressing. **2** (of a woman) sexually unresponsive. **3** (esp. of climate or air) cold. □□ **fri·gid·i·ty** /-jíditee/ *n.* **fri·gid·ly** *adv.* **fri·gid·ness** *n.*

fri·jo·les /freehólays/ *n.pl.* beans.

frill /fril/ *n. & v.* ● *n.* **1 a** a strip of material with one side gathered or pleated and the other left loose with a fluted appearance, used as an ornamental edging. **b** a similar paper ornament on a lamb chop, etc. **c** a natural fringe of feathers, hair, etc.,

erect frill

FRILLED LIZARD
(*Chlamydosaurus kingii*)

on esp. a bird or a plant. **2** (in *pl.*) **a** unnecessary embellishments or accomplishments. **b** airs; affectation (*put on frills*). ● *v.tr.* **1** decorate with a frill. **2** form into a frill. □□ **frilled** *adj.* **frill·y** /frílee/ *adj.* (**frillier, frilliest**). **frill·i·ness** *n.*

frilled liz·ard *n.* (also **frill liz·ard** or **frill-necked liz·ard**) ◀ a large N. Australian lizard, *Chlamydosaurus kingii*, with an erectile membrane around the neck.

fringe /frinj/ *n. & v.* ● *n.* **1 a** an ornamental bordering of threads left loose or formed into tassels or twists. **b** such a border made separately. **c** any border or edging. **2 a** *Brit.* a portion of the front hair hanging over the forehead; bangs. **b** a natural border of hair, etc., in an animal or plant. **3** an outer edge or margin; the outer limit of an area, population, etc. (often *attrib.*: *fringe theater*). **4** a thing, part, or area of secondary or minor importance. **5 a** a band of contrasting brightness or darkness produced by diffraction or interference of light. **b** a strip of false color in an optical image. **6** a fringe benefit. ● *v.tr.* **1** adorn or encircle with a fringe. **2** serve as a fringe to. □□ **fringe·less** *adj.*

fringe ben·e·fit *n.* an employee's benefit supplementing a money wage or salary.

fring·ing reef *n.* a coral reef that fringes the shore.

frip·per·y /frípəree/ *n.* (*pl.* **-ies**) **1** showy, tawdry, or unnecessary ornament. **2** a knickknack or trifle.

Fris·bee /frízbee/ *n. Trademark* a molded plastic disk for sailing through the air as an outdoor game.

Fri·sian /frízhən, free-/ *adj. & n.* ● *adj.* of Friesland (an area comprising the NW Netherlands and adjacent islands). ● *n.* **1** a native or inhabitant of Friesland. **2** the language of Friesland.

frisk /frisk/ *v. & n.* ● *v.* **1** *intr.* leap or skip playfully. **2** *tr. sl.* feel over or search (a person) for a weapon, etc. (usu. rapidly). ● *n.* **1** a playful leap or skip. **2** *sl.* the frisking of a person.

frisk·y /frískee/ *adj.* (**friskier, friskiest**) lively; playful. □□ **frisk·i·ly** *adv.* **frisk·i·ness** *n.*

fris·son /freesón/ *n.* an emotional thrill.

frith var. of FIRTH.

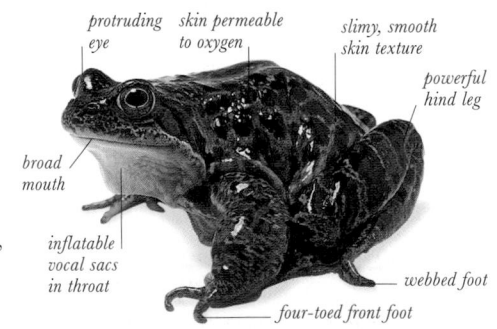

FRITILLARY (*Fritillaria imperialis*)

frit·il·lar·y /frít'leree/ *n.* (*pl.* **-ies**) **1** ▲ any liliaceous plant of the genus *Fritillaria*, having pendent bell-like flowers. **2** any of various butterflies, esp. of the genus *Argynnis*, having reddish-brown wings checkered with black.

frit·ta·ta /fritáatə/ *n.* an Italian dish made with fried beaten eggs, resembling a Spanish omelette.

frit·ter[1] /frítər/ *v.tr.* (usu. foll. by *away*) waste (money, energy, etc.) triflingly.

frit·ter[2] /frítər/ *n.* a piece of fruit, meat, etc., coated in batter and deep-fried (*apple fritter*).

frit·to mi·sto /fréetō méestō/ *n.* a mixed grill.

fritz /frits/ *n.* □ **on the fritz** *sl.* out of order; unsatisfactory.

friv·o·lous /frívələs/ *adj.* **1** paltry; trifling. **2** lacking seriousness; given to trifling; silly. □□ **fri·vol·i·ty** /-vólitee/ *n.* (*pl.* **-ies**). **friv·o·lous·ly** *adv.* **friv·o·lous·ness** *n.*

frizz /friz/ *v. & n.* ● *v.tr.* form (hair, etc.) into a mass of small curls. ● *n.* **1 a** a frizzed hair. **b** a row of curls. **2** a frizzed state. □□ **friz·zi·ness** *n.* **friz·zy** /frízee/ *adj.* (**frizzier, frizziest**)

friz·zle[1] /frízəl/ *v.intr. & tr.* **1** fry, toast, or grill, with a sputtering noise. **2** (often foll. by *up*) burn or shrivel.

FROG

Frogs are amphibians of the order Anura, which includes toads and consists of about 2,500 species. Frogs characteristically have squat bodies, smooth skin, strong hind legs for leaping, and webbed feet. Most reproduce in water, laying eggs that develop into larvae (tadpoles). They are the most widespread amphibians, with habitats ranging from lakes, marshes, and rain forests to mountains and deserts.

protruding eye *skin permeable to oxygen* *slimy, smooth skin texture* *powerful hind leg* *broad mouth* *inflatable vocal sacs in throat* *webbed foot* *four-toed front foot*

EXTERNAL FEATURES OF A COMMON FROG (*Rana temporaria*)

EXAMPLES OF OTHER FROGS

TOMATO FROG
(*Dyscophus antongilii*)

WHITE'S TREEFROG
(*Litoria caerulea*)

POISON DART FROG
(*Dendrobates species*)

frieze *cornice* *architrave*

friz·zle[2] /frízəl/ *v. & n.* ● *v.* **1** *tr.* form (hair) into tight curls. **2** *intr.* (often foll. by *up*) (of hair, etc.) curl tightly. ● *n.* frizzled hair.

friz·zly /frízlee/ *adj.* in tight curls.

fro /frō/ *adv.* back (now only in *to and fro*: see TO).

frock /frok/ *n.* **1** *esp. Brit.* a woman's or girl's dress. **2 a** a monk's or priest's long gown with loose sleeves. **b** priestly office. **3** a smock.

frog[1] /frawg, frog/ *n.* **1** ▼ any of various small amphibians of the order Anura, having a tailless smooth-skinned body with legs developed for jumping. ▷ SPAWN, TOAD. **2** (**Frog**) *sl. offens.* a French person. **3** a hollow in the top face of a brick for holding the mortar. **4** the nut of a violin bow, etc. □ **frog in the** (or **one's**) **throat** *colloq.* hoarseness. □□ **frog·gy** *adj.*

frog[2] /frawg, frog/ *n.* an elastic horny substance in the sole of a horse's foot.

frog[3] /frawg, frog/ *n.* **1** an ornamental coat fastening of a spindle-shaped button and loop. **2** an attachment to a belt to support a sword, bayonet, etc. □□ **frogged** *adj.* **frog·ging** *n.*

frog·fish /fráwgfish, fróg-/ *n.* = ANGLERFISH.

frog·hop·per /fráwghopər, fróg-/ *n.* any jumping insect of the family Cercopidae, sucking sap and as larvae producing a protective mass of froth.

frog·man /fráwgman, fróg-, -mən/ *n.* (*pl.* **-men**) a person equipped with a rubber suit, flippers, and an oxygen supply for underwater swimming.

frog·march /fráwgmaarch, fróg-/ *v. & n.* ● *v.tr.* **1** hustle (a person) forward holding and pinning the arms from behind (*frogmarched me out of the room*). **2** carry (a person) in a frogmarch. ● *n.* the carrying of a person face downward by four others each holding a limb.

frol·ic /frólik/ *v. & n.* ● *v.intr.* (**frolicked, frolicking**) play about cheerfully; gambol. ● *n.* **1** cheerful play. **2** a prank. **3** a merry party. **4** an outburst of gaiety. **5** merriment. □□ **frol·ick·er** *n.*

frol·ic·some /fróliksəm/ *adj.* merry; playful. □□ **frol·ic·some·ly** *adv.* **frol·ic·some·ness** *n.*

from /frum, from, frəm/ *prep.* expressing separation or origin, followed by: **1** a person, place, time, etc., that is the starting point of motion or action, or of extent in place or time (*rain comes from the clouds; dinner is served from 8*). **2** a place, object, etc., whose distance or remoteness is reckoned (*ten miles from Los Angeles; apart from its moral aspect*). **3 a** a source (*a man from Idaho; draw a conclusion from premises*). **b** a giver or sender (*presents from their parents*). **4 a** a thing or person avoided, escaped, lost, etc. (*released him from prison*). **b** a person or thing deprived (*took his gun from him*). **5** a reason, cause, or motive (*died from fatigue*). **6** a thing distinguished or unlike (*know black from white*). **7** a lower limit (*tickets from $5*). **8** a state changed for another (*raised the penalty from a fine to imprisonment*). **9** an adverb or preposition of time or place (*from long ago; from under the bed*). **10** the position of a person who observes or considers (*saw it from the roof*). **11** a model (*painted it from nature*). □ **from now on** henceforward. **from time to time** occasionally.

frond /frond/ *n. Bot.* ◀ a large usu. divided leaf in esp. ferns and palms. ▷ FERN

fron·deur /frondőr/ *n.* a political rebel.

front /frunt/ *n., adj., & v.* ● *n.* **1** the side or part normally nearer to or toward the spectator or the direction of motion (*the front of the car*). **2** any face of a building, esp. that of the main entrance. **3** *Mil.* **a** the foremost line or part of an army, etc. **b** line of battle. **c** the part of the ground toward a real or imaginary enemy. **d** a scene of actual fighting. **e** the direction in which a formed line faces. **4 a** a sector of activity regarded as

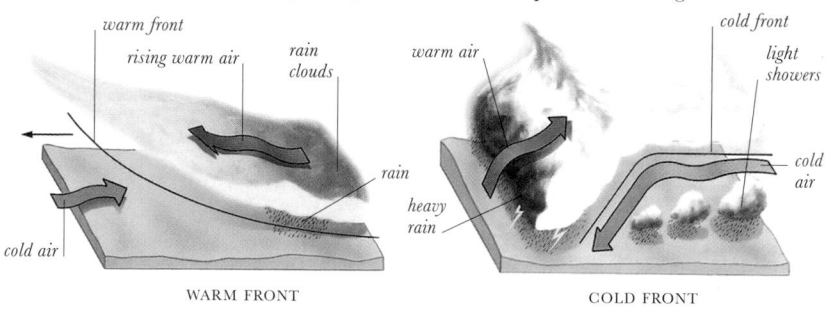

FRONT

In meteorology, a front is the meeting point between two air masses of different temperature. In a warm front, warm air gradually rises over cold air, bringing steady rain.

In a cold front, a mass of cold air undercuts warm air, forcing it to rise sharply. Short, heavy rain showers occur, followed by lowered temperatures and light showers.

warm front
rising warm air
rain clouds
rain
cold air
WARM FRONT

warm air
cold front
light showers
rain
heavy rain
cold air
COLD FRONT

resembling a military front. **b** an organized political group. **5 a** demeanor; bearing. **b** outward appearance. **6** a forward or conspicuous position (*come to the front*). **7 a** a bluff. **b** a pretext. **8** a person, etc., serving to cover subversive or illegal activities. **9** *Meteorol.* ▲ the forward edge of an advancing mass of cold or warm air. ▷ WEATHER CHART. **10** (prec. by *the*) the audience or auditorium of a theater. **11** a face. **12 a** the breast of a man's shirt. **b** a false shirtfront. **13** impudence. ● *attrib.adj.* **1** of the front. **2** situated in front. ● *v.* **1** *intr.* (foll. by *on, to, toward, upon*) have the front facing or directed. **2** *intr.* (foll. by *for*) *sl.* act as a front or cover for. **3** *tr* furnish with a front (*fronted with stone*). **4** *tr* lead (a band). **5** *tr.* **a** stand opposite to; front toward. **b** have its front on the side of (a street, etc.). □ **in front 1** in an advanced position. **2** facing the spectator. **in front of 1** ahead of. **2** in the presence of; confronting. **on the front burner** see BURNER. □□ **front·less** *adj.* **front·ward** *adj. & adv.* **front·wards** *adv.*

front·age /frúntij/ *n.* **1** the front of a building. **2 a** land abutting on a street or on water. **b** the land between the front of a building and the road. **3** extent of front (*a store with little frontage*).

fron·tal[1] /frúnt'l/ *adj.* **1 a** of, at, or on the front (*a frontal attack*). **b** of the front as seen by an onlooker (*a frontal view*). **2** of the forehead (*frontal bone*). □□ **front·al·ly** *adv.*

fron·tal[2] /frúnt'l/ *n.* **1** a covering for the front of an altar. **2** the façade of a building.

fron·tier /frúnteer/ *n.* **1 a** the border between two countries. **b** the district on each side of this. **2** the limits of attainment or knowledge in a subject. **3** the borders between settled and unsettled country.

fron·tiers·man /frúnteerzmən/ *n.* (*pl.* **-men**) a person living in the region of a frontier, esp. between settled and unsettled country.

fron·tis·piece /frúntispees/ *n.* an illustration facing the title page of a book or of one of its divisions.

front·line /frúntlin/ *adj.* **1** *Mil.* relating to or located at a front line. **2** relating to the forefront of any activity.

front line *n. Mil.* = FRONT *n.* 3.

front man *n.* a person acting as a front or cover.

front mat·ter *n. Printing* the title page, preface, etc., preceding the text proper.

front of·fice *n.* **1** the executives or executive branch of an organization. **2** a main office.

fron·ton /frónton, -tón/ *n.* **1** a jai alai court. **2** a pediment.

front page *n.* the first page of a newspaper, esp. as containing important or remarkable news.

front run·ner *n.* **1** the contestant most likely to succeed. **2** an athlete or horse running best when in the lead.

front-wheel drive *n.* an automobile drive system in which power is transmitted from the engine to the front wheels.

frost /frawst, frost/ *n. & v.* ● *n.* **1 a** a white frozen dew coating esp. the ground at night (*windows covered with frost*). **b** a consistent temperature below freezing point causing frost to form. **2** a chilling or dispiriting atmosphere. ● *v.* **1** *intr.* (usu. foll. by *over, up*) become covered with frost. **2** *tr.* **a** cover with or as if with frost, powder, etc. **b** injure (a plant, etc.) with frost. **3** *tr.* give a roughened or finely granulated surface to (*frosted glass*). **4** *tr.* cover or decorate (a cake, etc.) with icing. □□ **frost·less** *adj.*

frost·bite /fráwstbīt, fróst-/ *n.* injury to body tissues, esp. the nose, fingers, or toes, due to freezing.

frost heave *n. Geol.* an upthrust of soil or pavement caused by the freezing of moist soil underneath.

frost·ing /fráwsting, fróst-/ *n.* **1** icing. **2** a rough surface on glass, etc.

frost·y /fráwstee, fróst-/ *adj.* (**frostier, frostiest**) **1** cold with frost. **2** covered with or as with hoarfrost. **3** unfriendly in manner. □□ **frost·i·ly** *adv.* **frost·i·ness** *n.*

froth /frawth, froth/ *n. & v.* ● *n.* **1 a** a collection of small bubbles; foam. **b** scum. **2 a** idle talk or ideas. **b** anything unsubstantial or of little worth. ● *v.* **1** *intr.* emit or gather froth. **2** *tr.* cause (beer, etc.) to foam. □□ **froth·i·ly** *adv.* **froth·i·ness** *n.* **froth·y** *adj.* (**frothier, frothiest**).

frou·frou /fróōfroō/ *n.* **1** a rustling, esp. of a dress. **2** frilly ornamentation.

fro·ward /fróərd/ *adj. archaic* perverse; difficult to deal with. □□ **fro·ward·ly** *adv.* **fro·ward·ness** *n.*

frown /frown/ *v. & n.* ● *v.* **1** *intr.* wrinkle one's brows, esp. in displeasure or deep thought. **2** *intr.* (foll. by *at, on, upon*) express disapproval. **3** *intr.* (of a thing) present a gloomy aspect. **4** *tr.* compel with a frown (*frowned them into silence*). **5** *tr.* express (defiance, etc.) with a frown. ● *n.* **1** an action of frowning. **2** a look expressing severity, disapproval, or deep thought. □□ **frown·ing·ly** *adv.*

frowz·y /frówzee/ *adj.* (also **frows·y**) (**-ier, -iest**) **1** fusty. **2** slatternly; dingy. □□ **frowz·i·ness** *n.*

froze *past* of FREEZE.

fro·zen *past part.* of FREEZE.

FRS *abbr.* Federal Reserve System.

fruc·tif·er·ous /fruktífərəs, frŏŏk-/ *adj.* bearing fruit.

fruc·ti·fi·ca·tion /frúktifikáyshən, frŏŏk-/ *n. Bot.* **1** the process of fructifying. **2** any spore-bearing structure, esp. in ferns, fungi, and mosses.

fruc·ti·fy /frúktifī, frŏŏk-/ *v.* (**-ies, -ied**) **1** *intr.* bear fruit. **2** *tr.* make fruitful.

fruc·tose /frúktōs, frŏŏk-/ *n. Chem.* a simple sugar found in honey and fruits. Also called **levulose**.

fru·gal /frŏŏgəl/ *adj.* **1** (often foll. by *of*) sparing or economical, esp. as regards food. **2** sparingly used

FROND OF THE MALE FERN
(*Dryopteris filix-mas*)

FRUIT

A fruit is the part of a plant that holds the seeds and aids in their dispersal. It develops from the ovary of a flower that has been pollinated, and can be juicy and colorful or hard and dry. There are two broad categories: succulent and dry fruits. Of the succulent fruits, berries typically have a combined mesocarp and endocarp layer and many seeds; drupes usually have a fleshy mesocarp and one seed surrounded by a woody endocarp. Aggregate fruits such as blackberries are made up of small drupes. False fruits develop from parts of the flower as well as the ovary. Dry fruits may be dehiscent (splitting open to scatter seeds) or indehiscent (falling without breaking apart).

DEVELOPMENT OF A FRUIT (MELON)

insect pollinates flower

flower shrivels and dies

remains of flower

ovary begins to swell

fruit grows and ripens

combined mesocarp and endocarp layer

seeds

cortex

exocarp

pedicel (remains of flower stalk)

exocarp

FEATURES OF A BERRY (KIWI FRUIT, *Actinidia deliciosa*)

SUCCULENT FRUITS

EXAMPLES OF BERRIES

GRAPES
(*Vitis vinifera*)

MELON
(*Cucumis melo*)

GOOSEBERRY
(*Ribes grossularia*)

LEMON
(*Citrus limon*)

TOMATO
(*Lycopersicon esculentum*)

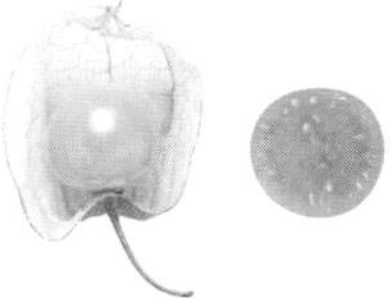

CAPE GOOSEBERRY
(*Physalis peruviana*)

EXAMPLES OF DRUPES AND AGGREGATE FRUITS

PEACH (DRUPE)
(*Prunus persica*)

MANGO (DRUPE)
(*Mangifera indica*)

BLACKBERRY (AGGREGATE FRUIT)
(*Rubus fruticosus*)

ACCESSORY FRUITS

PSEUDOCARP
strawberry
(*Fragaria × ananassa*)

SYCONIUM
fig
(*Ficus carica*)

POME
apple
(*Malus sylvestris*)

DRY FRUITS

DEHISCENT FRUITS

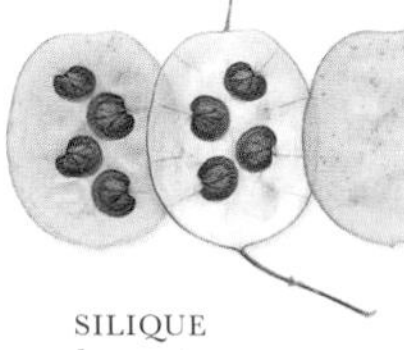

SILIQUE
honesty
(*Lunaria annua*)

FOLLICLE
larkspur
(*Delphinium* species)

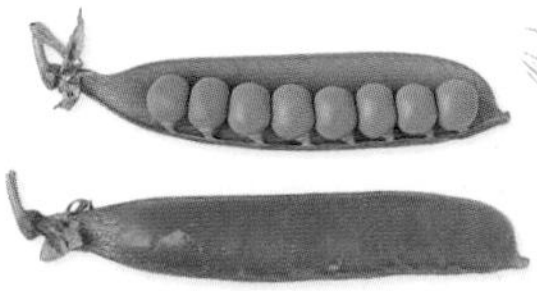

POD OR LEGUME
pea
(*Pisum sativum*)

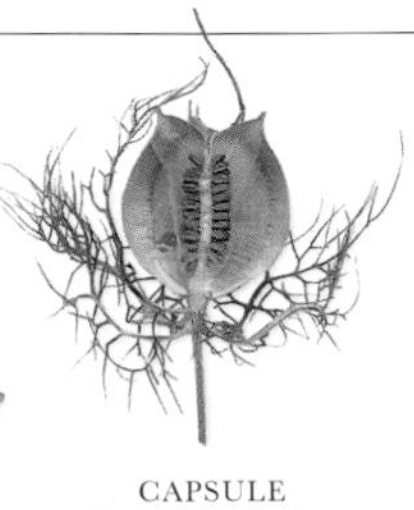

CAPSULE
love-in-a-mist
(*Nigella damascena*)

INDEHISCENT FRUITS

ACHENE (CLUSTER)
field marigold
(*Calendula arvensis*)

NUT
acorn
(*Quercus* species)

or supplied; meager; costing little. □□ **fru·gal·i·ty** /-gálitee/ n. **fru·gal·ly** adv. **fru·gal·ness** n.

fru·giv·o·rous /frōojívərəs/ adj. feeding on fruit.

fruit /frōot/ n. & v. • n. **1 a** ◄ the usu. sweet and fleshy edible product of a plant or tree, containing seed. **b** (in sing.) these in quantity (eats fruit). **2** the seed of a plant or tree with its covering, e.g., an acorn, pea pod, cherry, etc. **3** (usu. in pl.) vegetables, grains, etc., used for food (fruits of the earth). **4** (usu. in pl.) the result of action, etc. (fruits of his labors). **5** derog. sl. a male homosexual. **6** Bibl. an offspring (the fruit of the womb). • v.intr. & tr. bear or cause to bear fruit. □□ **fruit·ed** adj. (also in comb.).

fruit·ar·i·an /frōotáireeən/ n. a person who eats only fruit.

fruitbat n. ▼ any large bat of the suborder Mega-chiroptera, feeding on fruit. ▷ BAT

FRUITBAT
(Pteropus species)

fruit·cake /frōotkayk/ n. **1** a cake containing dried fruit. **2** sl. an eccentric or mad person.

fruit·er /frōotər/ n. **1** a tree producing fruit, esp. with reference to its quality (a poor fruiter). **2** a fruit grower. **3** a ship carrying fruit.

fruit·er·er /frōotərər/ n. esp. Brit. a dealer in fruit.

fruit fly n. (pl. **flies**) any of various flies, esp. of the genus Drosophila, having larvae that feed on fruit.

fruit·ful /frōotfool/ adj. **1** producing much fruit. **2** successful; beneficial; remunerative. **3** producing offspring, esp. prolifically. □□ **fruit·ful·ly** adv. **fruit·ful·ness** n.

fru·i·tion /frōo-íshən/ n. **1 a** the bearing of fruit. **b** the production of results. **2** the realization of aims or hopes. **3** enjoyment.

fruit·less /frōotlis/ adj. **1** not bearing fruit. **2** useless; unsuccessful. □□ **fruit·less·ly** adv. **fruit·less·ness** n.

fruit·y /frōotee/ adj. (**fruitier, fruitiest**) **1 a** of fruit. **b** tasting or smelling like fruit. **2** (of a voice, etc.) of full rich quality. **3** sl. crazy; silly. **4** offens. sl. homosexual. □□ **fruit·i·ly** adv. **fruit·i·ness** n.

frump /frump/ n. a dowdy, unattractive, old-fashioned woman. □□ **frump·ish** adj. **frump·ish·ly** adv.

frump·y /frúmpee/ adj. (**frumpier, frumpiest**) dowdy, unattractive, and old-fashioned. □□ **frump·i·ly** adv. **frump·i·ness** n.

frus·trate /frústrayt/ v.tr. **1** make (efforts) ineffective. **2** prevent (a person) from achieving a purpose. **3** (as **frustrated** adj.) **a** discontented because unable to achieve one's desire. **b** sexually unfulfilled. **4** disappoint (a hope). □□ **frus·trat·ed·ly** /-stráytidlee/ adv. **frus·trat·ing** adj. **frus·trat·ing·ly** adv. **frus·tra·tion** /-stráyshən/ n.

fry[1] /frī/ n. & v. • v. (**fries, fried**) **1** tr. & intr. cook or be cooked in hot fat. **2** tr. & intr. sl. electrocute or be electrocuted. **3** tr. (as **fried** adj.) sl. drunk. **4** intr. colloq. be very hot. • n. (pl. **fries**) **1** a French fry. **2** a social gathering serving fried food. **3** a dish of fried food, esp. meat. **4** various internal parts of animals usu. eaten fried (lamb's fry). □ **fry up** cook in a frying pan. **out of the frying pan into the fire** from a bad situation to a worse one.

fry[2] /frī/ n.pl. **1** young or newly hatched fish. **2** the

young of other creatures produced in large numbers, e.g., bees or frogs.

fry·er /fríər/ n. (also **fri·er**) **1** a person who fries. **2** a vessel for frying, esp. deep frying. **3** a young chicken suitable for frying.

fry·ing pan n. (also **fry pan**) a shallow pan used in frying.

FSH abbr. follicle-stimulating hormone.

FSLIC abbr. Federal Savings and Loan Insurance Corporation.

f-stop /éf stop/ var. of F-NUMBER.

Ft. abbr. Fort.

ft. abbr. foot, feet.

FTC abbr. Federal Trade Commission.

FTP abbr. Computing file transfer protocol, a standard for the exchange of program and data files across a network.

fuch·sia /fyōoshə/ n. any shrub of the genus Fuchsia, with drooping red or purple or white flowers.

fuck /fuk/ v., int., & n. coarse sl. • v. **1** tr. & intr. have sexual intercourse (with). **2** intr. (foll. by around, about) mess around; fool around. **3** tr. (usu. as exclam.) curse; confound (fuck the thing!). **4** intr. (as **fucking** adj., adv.) used as an intensive to express annoyance, etc. • int. expressing anger or annoyance. • n. **1 a** an act of sexual intercourse. **b** a partner in sexual intercourse. **2** the slightest amount (don't give a fuck). □ **fuck off** go away. **fuck up** make a mess of. ¶ A highly taboo word. □□ **fuck·er** n. (often as a term of abuse).

fuck-up coarse sl. n. a mess or muddle.

fu·cus /fyōokəs/ n. (pl. **fuci** /fyōosī/) any seaweed of the genus Fucus, with flat leathery fronds. □□ **fu·coid** adj.

fud·dle /fúd'l/ v. confuse or stupefy, esp. with alcoholic liquor.

fud·dy-dud·dy /fúdeedúdee/ adj. & n. sl. • adj. old-fashioned or quaintly fussy. • n. (pl. **-ies**) a fuddy-duddy person.

fudge /fuj/ n. & v. • n. **1** a soft toffee-like candy made with milk, sugar, butter, etc. **2** nonsense. **3** a piece of dishonesty or faking. **4** a piece of late news inserted in a newspaper page. • v. **1** tr. put together in a makeshift or dishonest way; fake. **2** tr. deal with incompetently. **3** intr. practice such methods.

fueh·rer var. of FUHRER.

fu·el /fyōoəl/ n. & v. • n. **1** material burned or used as a source of heat or power. **2** food as a source of energy. **3** material used as a source of nuclear energy. **4** anything that sustains or inflames emotion or passion. • v. **1** tr. supply with fuel. **2** tr. inflame (an argument, feeling, etc.) (liquor fueled his anger). **3** intr. take in or get fuel.

fu·el cell n. a cell producing an electric current direct from a chemical reaction.

fu·el in·jec·tion n. the direct introduction of fuel under pressure into the combustion units of an internal-combustion engine.

fu·gal /fyōogəl/ adj. of the nature of a fugue.

-fuge /fyōoj/ comb. form forming adjectives and nouns denoting expelling or dispelling (febrifuge; vermifuge).

fu·gi·tive /fyōojitiv/ adj. & n. • adj. **1** fleeing. **2** transient; fleeting. **3** (of literature) of passing interest; ephemeral. **4** flitting; shifting. • n. **1** (often foll. by from) one who flees. **2** an exile or refugee.

fu·gle /fyōogəl/ v.intr. act as a fugleman.

fu·gle·man /fyōogəlmən/ n. (pl. **-men**) **1** hist. a soldier placed in front of a regiment, etc., while drilling to show the motions and time. **2** a leader, organizer, or spokesman.

fugue /fyōog/ n. **1** Mus. a contrapuntal composition in which a short melody or phrase is introduced by one part and successively taken up by others and developed by interweaving the parts. **2** Psychol. loss of awareness of one's identity, often coupled with flight from one's usual environment.

füh·rer /fyōorər/ n. (also **fueh·rer**) a leader, esp. a tyrannical one.

ful·crum /foolkrəm, fúl-/ n. (pl. **fulcra** /-rə/ or **fulcrums**) ► the point against which a lever is placed to get a purchase or on which it turns or is supported. ▷ LEVER, SCALE

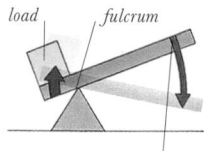

load   fulcrum

FULCRUM   effort

ful·fill /foolfíl/ v.tr. (**fulfilled, fulfilling**) **1** carry out (a prophecy or promise). **2** satisfy (a desire or prayer). **3 a** execute; obey (a command or law). **b** perform; carry out (a task). **4** comply with (conditions). **5** answer (a purpose). **6** bring to an end; finish; complete (a period or piece of work). □ **fulfill oneself** develop one's gifts and character to the full. □□ **ful·fill·ment** n.

full[1] /fool/ adj., adv. & n. • adj. **1** (often foll. by of) holding all its limits will allow (the bucket is full; full of water). **2** having eaten to one's limits or satisfaction. **3** abundant; copious; satisfying (led a full life; the book is very full on this point). **4** (foll. by of) having or holding an abundance of; showing marked signs of (full of interest; full of mistakes). **5** (foll. by of) **a** engrossed in thinking about (full of himself). **b** unable to refrain from talking about (full of the news). **6** complete; perfect (full membership; full daylight; waited a full hour). **7 a** (of tone or color) deep and clear. **b** (of light) intense. **c** (of motion, etc.) vigorous (a full pulse; at full gallop). **8** plump; rounded (a full figure). **9** (of clothes) made of much material arranged in folds. **10** (of the heart, etc.) overcharged with emotion. • adv. **1** very (you know full well). **2** quite; fully (full six miles). **3** exactly (hit him full on the nose). **4** more than sufficiently (full early). • n. **1** height; acme (season is past the full). **2** the state or time of full moon. **3** the whole; the complete amount. □ **at full length 1** lying stretched out. **2** without abridgment. **come full circle** see CIRCLE. **full speed** (or **steam**) **ahead!** an order to proceed at maximum speed or to pursue a course of action energetically. **full tilt** see TILT. **full up** colloq. completely full. **in full 1** without abridgment. **2** to or for the full amount (paid in full). **in full swing** at the height of activity. **in full view** entirely visible. **to the full** to the utmost extent.

full[2] /fool/ v.tr. cleanse and thicken (cloth).

full·back /foolbak/ n. **1** an offensive player in the backfield in football. **2** a defensive player, or a position near the goal, in soccer, field hockey, etc. ▷ FOOTBALL, RUGBY

full-blood·ed adj. **1** vigorous; hearty; sensual. **2** not hybrid. □□ **full-blood·ed·ly** adv. **full-blood·ed·ness** n.

full-blown adj. fully developed.

full-bod·ied adj. rich in quality, tone, etc.

full-court press n. Basketball a defensive strategy in which the team with the ball is closely guarded the full length of the court.

full-fledged adj. mature.

full-fron·tal adj. **1** (of nudity or a nude figure) with full exposure at the front. **2** unrestrained; explicit.

full-grown adj. having reached maturity.

full house n. **1** a maximum attendance at a theater, etc. **2** Poker a hand with three of a kind and a pair.

full-length adj. **1** not shortened. **2** (of a mirror, portrait, etc.) showing the whole height of the human figure.

full moon n. **1** the Moon with its whole disk illuminated. **2** the time when this occurs.

full·ness /foolnis/ n. (also **ful·ness**) **1** being full. **2** (of sound, color, etc.) richness; volume; body. **3** all that is contained (in the world, etc.). □ **the fullness of time** the appropriate or destined time.

full-scale adj. not reduced in size; complete.

full-serv·ice adj. (of a bank, service station, etc.) providing a wide range of service.

full time n. the total normal duration of work, etc.

full-time adj. occupying or using the whole of the available working time.

F

FUNGUS

Neither plants nor animals, fungi form a separate kingdom. They absorb food from living or dead organic matter and reproduce by spores. There are three main divisions. Basidiomycota, which includes mushrooms and toadstools, embraces species that pro- duce spores in microscopic structures called basidia. Ascomycota is a varied division of some 30,000 species, which bear spores in microscopic structures called asci. Zygo- mycota includes moldlike fungi that live on decaying plant and animal matter.

EXAMPLES OF FUNGUS TYPES

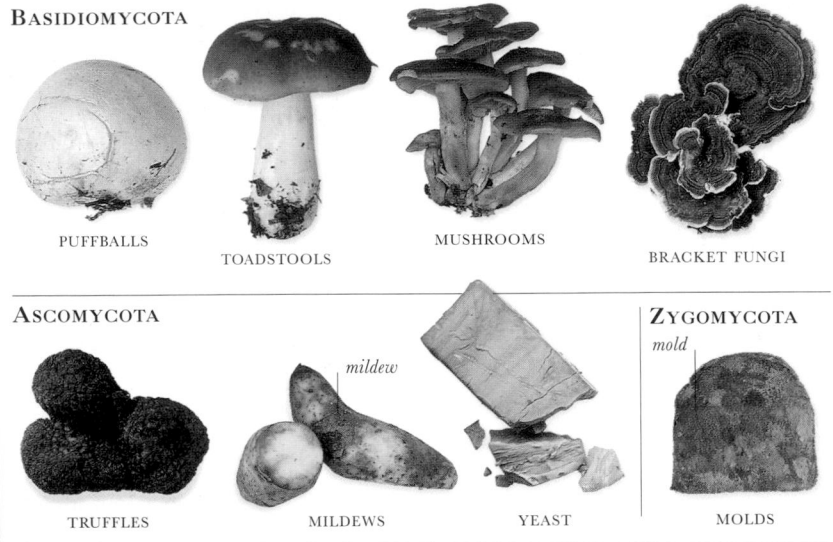

BASIDIOMYCOTA

PUFFBALLS

TOADSTOOLS

MUSHROOMS

BRACKET FUNGI

ASCOMYCOTA

mildew

TRUFFLES

MILDEWS

YEAST

ZYGOMYCOTA

mold

MOLDS

full-tim·er *n.* a person who holds a full-time job.

ful·ly /fŏŏlee/ *adv.* **1** completely; entirely (*am fully aware*). **2** no less or fewer than (*fully 60*).

ful·mar /fŏŏlmər/ *n.* any medium-sized seabird of the genus *Fulmarus*, with stout body, robust bill, and rounded tail.

ful·mi·nant /fúlminənt, fŏŏl-/ *adj.* **1** fulminating. **2** *Med.* (of a disease or symptom) developing suddenly.

ful·mi·nate /fúlminayt, fŏŏl-/ *v.intr.* **1** (often foll. by *against*) express censure loudly and forcefully. **2** explode violently; flash like lightning (*fulminating mercury*). **3** *Med.* (of a disease or symptom) develop suddenly. □□ **ful·mi·na·tion** /-náyshən/ *n.*

ful·ness var. of FULLNESS.

ful·some /fŏŏlsəm/ *adj.* **1** disgusting by excess of flattery, servility, or expressions of affection; excessive; cloying. **2** *disp.* copious. ¶ In *fulsome praise,* *fulsome* means 'excessive,' not 'generous.' □□ **ful·some·ly** *adv.* **ful·some·ness** *n.*

fum·ble /fúmbəl/ *v. & n.* ● *v.* **1** *intr.* (often foll. by *at, with, for, after*) use the hands awkwardly; grope about. **2** *tr.* **a** handle clumsily or nervously. **b** *Football* drop (the ball). ● *n.* an act of fumbling. □□ **fum·bler** *n.* **fum·bling·ly** *adv.*

fume /fyŏŏm/ *n. & v.* ● *n.* **1** (usu. in *pl.*) exuded gas or smoke or vapor, esp. when harmful or unpleasant. **2** a fit of anger (*in a fume*). ● *v.* **1 a** *intr.* emit fumes. **b** *tr.* give off as fumes. **2** *intr.* (often foll. by *at*) be affected by (esp. suppressed) anger (*was fuming at their inefficiency*). **3** *tr.* **a** fumigate. **b** subject to fumes (to darken tints in oak, photographic film, etc.). □□ **fum·y** *adj.* (in sense 1 of *n.*).

fu·mi·gate /fyŏŏmigayt/ *v.tr.* **1** disinfect or purify with fumes. **2** apply fumes to. □□ **fu·mi·gant** /-gənt/ *n.* **fu·mi·ga·tion** /-gáyshən/ *n.* **fu·mi·ga·tor** *n.*

fun /fun/ *n. & adj.* ● *n.* **1** amusement, esp. lively or playful. **2** a source of this. **3** (in full **fun and games**) exciting or amusing goings-on. ● *adj. disp. colloq.* amusing; enjoyable (*a fun thing to do*). □ **for fun** (or **for the fun of it**) not for a serious purpose.

have fun enjoy oneself. **in fun** as a joke; not seriously. **make fun of** tease; ridicule.

fun·board /fúnbawrd/ *n.* a type of windsurfing board that is less stable but faster than a standard board. ▷ WINDSURFING

func·tion /fúngkshən/ *n. & v.* ● *n.* **1 a** an activity proper to a person or institution. **b** a mode of action or activity by which a thing fulfills its purpose. **c** an official or professional duty. **2 a** a public ceremony or occasion. **b** a social gathering, esp. a large, formal, or important one. **3** *Math.* a variable quantity regarded in relation to another or others in terms of which it may be expressed or on which its value depends (*x is a function of y and z*). ● *v.intr.* fulfill a function; operate; be in working order. □□ **func·tion·less** *adj.*

func·tion·al /fúngkshənəl/ *adj.* **1** of or serving a function. **2** designed or intended to be practical rather than attractive. **3** *Physiol.* **a** (esp. of disease) of or affecting only the functions of an organ, etc., not structural or organic. **b** (of mental disorder) having no discernible organic cause. **c** (of an organ) having a function, not functionless or rudimentary. **4** *Math.* of a function. □□ **func·tion·al·i·ty** /-nálitee/ *n.* **func·tion·al·ly** *adv.*

func·tion·ar·y /fúngkshəneree/ *n.* (*pl.* **-ies**) a person who has to perform official functions or duties; an official.

fund /fund/ *n. & v.* ● *n.* **1** a permanent stock of something ready to be drawn upon (*a fund of knowledge*). **2** a stock of money, esp. one set apart for a purpose. **3** (in *pl.*) money resources. ● *v.tr.* **1** provide with money. **2** convert (a floating debt) into a more or less permanent debt at fixed interest. **3** put into a fund.

fun·da·ment /fúndəmənt/ *n. joc.* the buttocks or anus.

fun·da·men·tal /fúndəmént'l/ *adj. & n.* ● *adj.* of, affecting, or serving as a base or foundation; essential; primary (*a fundamental change; the fundamental*

rules). ● *n.* (usu. in *pl.*) a fundamental principle. □□ **fun·da·men·tal·ly** *adv.*

fun·da·men·tal·ism /fúndəméntəlizəm/ *n.* **1** (also **Fun·da·men·tal·ism**) strict maintenance of traditional Protestant beliefs. **2** strict maintenance of ancient or fundamental doctrines of any religion, esp. Islam. □□ **fun·da·men·tal·ist** *n.*

fund-rais·er *n.* a person who seeks financial support for a cause, enterprise, etc. □□ **fund-rais·ing** *n.*

fu·ner·al /fyŏŏnərəl/ *n. & adj.* ● *n.* **1 a** the burial or cremation of a dead person with its ceremonies. **b** a burial or cremation procession. **c** a burial or cremation service. **2** *sl.* one's (usu. unpleasant) concern (*that's your funeral*). ● *attrib.adj.* of or used, etc., at a funeral (*funeral oration*).

fu·ner·al di·rec·tor *n.* an undertaker.

fu·ner·al par·lor *n.* (also **funeral home**) an establishment where the dead are prepared for burial or cremation.

fu·ner·ar·y /fyŏŏnəreree/ *adj.* of or used at a funeral or funerals.

fu·ne·re·al /fyŏŏnéereeəl/ *adj.* **1** of or appropriate to a funeral. **2** dismal; dark. □□ **fu·ne·re·al·ly** *adv.*

fun·fair /fúnfair/ *n. Brit.* = AMUSEMENT PARK.

fun·gi *pl.* of FUNGUS.

fun·gi·cide /fúnjisīd, fúnggi-/ *n.* a fungus-destroying substance. □□ **fun·gi·cid·al** /-síd'l/ *adj.*

fun·goid /fúnggoyd/ *adj. & n.* ● *adj.* resembling a fungus in texture or in rapid growth. ● *n.* a fungoid plant.

fun·gous /fúnggəs/ *adj.* **1** having the nature of a fungus. **2** springing up like a mushroom; transitory.

fun·gus /fúnggəs/ *n.* (*pl.* **fungi** /-gī, -jī/ or **fun·guses**) **1** ◀ any of a group of unicellular, multicellular, or multinucleate nonphotosynthetic organisms feeding on organic matter, which include molds, yeast, mushrooms, and toadstools. **2** anything similar usu. growing suddenly and rapidly. **3** *Med.* a spongy morbid growth. □□ **fun·gal** /fúnggəl/ *adj.* **fun·gi·form** /fúnjifawrm, fúnggi-/ *adj.* **fun·giv·or·ous** /funjívərəs, funggív-/ *adj.*

fu·nic·u·lar /fyŏŏníkyələr, fə-/ *adj. & n.* ● *adj.* **1** ▶ (of a railway, esp. on a mountainside) operating by cable with ascending and descending cars counterbalanced. **2** of a rope or its tension. ● *n.* a funicular railway.

weight of descending car helps pull up ascending car

cable

FUNICULAR
IN OPERATION

funk[1] /fungk/ *n.* fear; panic. □ **in a funk** dejected.

funk[2] /fungk/ *n. sl.* **1** funky music. **2** a strong smell.

funk·y /fúngkee/ *adj.* (**funkier, funkiest**) *sl.* **1** (esp. of jazz or rock music) earthy, bluesy, with a heavy rhythmical beat. **2** fashionable. **3** odd; unconventional. **4** having a strong smell. □□ **funk·i·ly** *adv.* **funk·i·ness** *n.*

fun·nel /fúnəl/ *n. & v.* ● *n.* **1** a tube or pipe widening at the top, for pouring liquid, powder, etc., into a small opening. **2** a metal chimney on a steam engine or ship. **3** something resembling a funnel in shape or use. ● *v.tr. & intr.* (**funneled, funneling; funnelled, funnelling**) guide or move through or as through a funnel. □□ **fun·nel·like** *adj.*

fun·ny /fúnee/ *adj. & n.* ● *adj.* (**funnier, funniest**) **1** amusing; comical. **2** strange; perplexing; hard to account for. **3** *colloq.* slightly unwell, eccentric, etc. ● *n.* (*pl.* **-ies**) (usu. in *pl.*) *colloq.* **1** a comic strip in a newspaper. **2** a joke. □□ **fun·ni·ly** *adv.* **fun·ni·ness** *n.*

fun·ny bone *n.* the part of the elbow over which the ulnar nerve passes.

fun·ny busi·ness *n.* **1** *sl.* misbehavior or deception. **2** comic behavior, comedy.

fun·ny farm *n. sl.* a mental hospital.

fun·ny mon·ey *n. colloq.* **1** counterfeit money. **2** foreign currency. **3** inflated currency.

fun·ny pa·per *n.* a newspaper, etc., containing humorous matter.

fun run *n. colloq.* an uncompetitive run, esp. for sponsored runners in support of a charity.

fur /fər/ *n. & v.* ● *n.* **1 a** the short fine soft hair of certain animals, distinguished from the longer hair. **b** the skin of such an animal with the fur on it. **2 a** the coat of certain animals as material for making, trimming, or lining clothes. **b** a trimming or lining made of the dressed coat of such animals, or of material imitating this. **c** a garment made of or trimmed or lined with fur. **3 a** a coating formed on the tongue in sickness. **b** a crust adhering to a surface, e.g., a deposit from wine. ● *v.* (**furred**, **furring**) **1** *tr.* (esp. as **furred** *adj.*) **a** line or trim (a garment) with fur. **b** provide (an animal) with fur. **c** clothe (a person) with fur. **d** coat (a tongue, the inside of a kettle, etc.) with fur. **2** *intr.* (often foll. by *up*) (of a kettle, etc.) become coated with fur. □ **make the fur fly** *colloq.* cause a disturbance; stir up trouble. □□ **fur·less** *adj.*

fur·be·low /fɔ́rbilō/ *n. & v.* ● *n.* **1** ▼ a gathered strip or pleated border of a skirt or petticoat. **2** (in *pl.*) *derog.* showy ornaments. ● *v.tr.* adorn with a furbelow or furbelows.

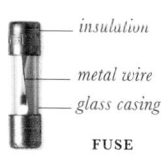

fur·bish /fɔ́r-bish/ *v.tr.* (often foll. by *up*) **1** remove rust from; polish; burnish. **2** give a new look to; renovate; revive (something antiquated).

furbelow

FURBELOW ON AN
EDWARDIAN PETTICOAT

fur·cate /fɔ́rkayt/ *adj. & v.* ● *adj.* also /fɔ́rkət/ forked; branched. ● *v.intr.* form a fork; divide. □□ **fur·ca·tion** /-káyshən/ *n.*

fu·ri·ous /fyŏŏreeəs/ *adj.* **1** extremely angry. **2** full of fury. **3** raging; violent; intense. □ **fast and furious** ● *adv.* **1** rapidly. **2** eagerly; uproariously. ● *adj.* (of mirth, etc.) eager; uproarious. □□ **fu·ri·ous·ly** *adv.*

furl /fərl/ *v.* **1** *tr.* roll up and secure (a sail, umbrella, flag, etc.). **2** *intr.* become furled. **3** *tr.* **a** close (a fan). **b** fold up (wings). **c** draw away (a curtain).

fur·long /fɔ́rlawng, -long/ *n.* an eighth of a mile, 220 yards.

fur·lough /fɔ́rlō/ *n. & v.* ● *n.* leave of absence, esp. granted to a member of the services or to a missionary. ● *v.* **1** *tr.* grant furlough to. **2** *intr.* spend furlough. **3** lay off.

fur·nace /fɔ́rnis/ *n.* **1** an enclosed structure for intense heating by fire. **2** a very hot place.

fur·nish /fɔ́rnish/ *v.tr.* **1** provide (a house, etc.) with all necessary contents, esp. movable furniture. **2** (foll. by *with*) cause to have possession or use of. **3** provide; afford; yield.

fur·nished /fɔ́rnisht/ *adj.* (of a house, etc.) rented with furniture.

fur·nish·er /fɔ́rnishər/ *n.* **1** a person who sells furniture. **2** a person who furnishes.

fur·nish·ings /fɔ́rnishingz/ *n.pl.* the furniture and utensils, etc., in a house, room, etc.

fur·ni·ture /fɔ́rnichər/ *n.* **1** the movable equipment of a house, room, etc., e.g., tables, chairs, and beds. **2** *Naut.* a ship's equipment. **3** accessories, e.g., the handles and lock of a door. □ **part of the furniture** *colloq.* a person or thing that goes unnoticed or is taken for granted.

fu·ror /fyŏŏrawr, -ər/ *n.* **1** an uproar; an outbreak of fury. **2** a wave of enthusiastic admiration; a craze.

fur·ri·er /fɔ́reeər/ *n.* a dealer in furs.

fur·row /fɔ́rō, fúr-/ *n. & v.* ● *n.* **1** a narrow trench made by a plow. **2** a rut, groove, or deep wrinkle. **3** a ship's track. ● *v.tr.* **1** plow. **2 a** make furrows, grooves, etc., in. **b** mark with wrinkles.

fur·ry /fɔ́ree, fúree/ *adj.* (**furrier**, **furriest**) **1** of or like fur. **2** covered with or wearing fur. □□ **fur·ri·ness** *n.*

fur·ther /fɔ́rthər/ *adv., adj., & v.* ● *adv.* **1** = FARTHER. **2** to a greater extent; more (*will inquire further*). **3** in addition (*I may add further*). ● *adj.* **1** = FARTHER. **2** more; additional (*threats of further punishment*). ● *v.tr.* promote; favor (a scheme, undertaking, movement, or cause). □ **till further notice** (or **orders**) to continue until explicitly changed. □□ **fur·ther·most** *adj.*

fur·ther·ance /fɔ́rthərəns/ *n.* furthering or being furthered; the advancement of a scheme, etc.

fur·ther·more /fɔ́rthərmáwr/ *adv.* in addition; besides.

fur·thest var. of FARTHEST.

fur·tive /fɔ́rtiv/ *adj.* **1** done by stealth; clandestine; meant to escape notice. **2** sly; stealthy. **3** stolen; taken secretly. **4** thievish; pilfering. □□ **fur·tive·ly** *adv.* **fur·tive·ness** *n.*

fu·ry /fyŏŏree/ *n* (*pl.* **-ies**) **1 a** wild and passionate anger. **b** a fit of rage (*in a blind fury*). **c** impetuosity in battle, etc. **2** violence of a storm, disease, etc. **3** (**Fury**) (usu. in *pl.*) (in Greek mythology) each of three goddesses sent from Tartarus to avenge crime. **4** an avenging spirit. **5** an angry or spiteful woman. □ **like fury** *colloq.* with great force or effect.

fuse¹ /fyŏŏz/ *v. & n.* ● *v.* **1** *tr. & intr.* melt with intense heat. **2** *tr. & intr.* blend or amalgamate into one whole by or as by melting. **3** *tr.* provide (a circuit, plug, etc.) with a fuse. **4** *Brit.* **a** *intr.* (of an appliance) cease to function when a fuse blows. **b** *tr.* cause (an appliance) to do this. ● *n.* ◄ a device or component for protecting an electric circuit, containing a strip of wire of easily melted metal and placed in the circuit so as to break it by melting when an excessive current passes through.

insulation
metal wire
glass casing

FUSE

fuse² /fyŏŏz/ *n. & v.* (also **fuze**) ● *n.* **1** a device for igniting a bomb or explosive charge, consisting of a tube or cord, etc., filled or saturated with combustible matter. **2** a component in a shell, mine, etc., designed to detonate an explosive charge. ● *v.tr.* fit a fuse to. □□ **fuse·less** *adj.*

fuse box *n.* a box housing the fuses for circuits in a building.

fu·se·lage /fyŏŏsəláazh, -lij, -zə-/ *n.* the body of an airplane. ▷ SPACECRAFT

fu·si·ble /fyŏŏzibəl/ *adj.* that can be easily fused or melted.

fu·si·form /fyŏŏzifawrm/ *adj. Bot. & Zool.* shaped like a spindle or cigar, tapering at both ends.

fu·sil /fyŏŏzil/ *n. hist.* a light musket.

fu·sil·ier /fyŏŏzileer/ *n.* (also **fu·sil·eer**) **1** a member of any of several British regiments formerly armed with fusils. **2** *hist.* ► a soldier armed with a fusil.

fu·sil·lade /fyŏŏsiláyd, -láad, -zi-/ *n.* **1 a** a continuous discharge of firearms. **b** a wholesale execution by this means. **2** a sustained outburst of criticism, etc.

fu·sil·li /fyŏŏzílee/ *n.* pasta pieces in the form of short spirals.

fu·sion /fyŏŏzhən/ *n.* **1** the act or an instance of fusing or melting. **2** a fused mass. **3** the blending of different things into one. **4** a coalition. **5** *Physics* = NUCLEAR FUSION.

fu·sion bomb *n.* a bomb involving nuclear fusion, esp. a hydrogen bomb.

fuss /fus/ *n. & v.* ● *n.* **1** excited commotion; bustle. **2 a** excessive concern about a trivial thing. **b** abundance of petty detail. **3** a sustained protest or dispute. **4** a person who fusses. ● *v. intr.* **a** make a fuss. **b** busy oneself restlessly with trivial things. **c** move fussily. □ **make a fuss** complain vigorously. **make a fuss over** treat (a person or animal) with great or excessive attention. □□ **fuss·er** *n.*

fuss·pot /fúspot/ *n. colloq.* a person given to fussing.

fuss·y /fúsee/ *adj.* (**fussier**, **fussiest**) **1** inclined to fuss. **2** full of unnecessary detail or decoration. **3** fastidious. □□ **fuss·i·ly** *adv.* **fuss·i·ness** *n.*

fus·tian /fúschən/ *n. & adj.* ● *n.* **1** thick twilled cotton cloth with a short nap, usu. dyed in dark colors. **2** bombast. ● *adj.* made of fustian.

fus·ty /fústee/ *adj.* (**fustier**, **fustiest**) **1** stale-smelling; musty. **2** stuffy. **3** antiquated; old-fashioned. □□ **fus·ti·ly** *adv.* **fus·ti·ness** *n.*

fu·tile /fyŏŏtʼl, -tīl/ *adj.* **1** useless; ineffectual. **2** frivolous. □□ **fu·tile·ly** *adv.* **fu·til·i·ty** /-tilitee/ *n.*

fu·ton /fŏŏton/ *n.* **1** a Japanese quilted mattress rolled out on the floor for use as a bed. **2** a type of low wooden bed using this kind of mattress.

fu·ture /fyŏŏchər/ *adj. & n.* ● *adj.* **1 a** going or expected to happen or be or become (*his future career*). **b** that will be something specified (*my future wife*). **c** that will be after death (*a future life*). **2 a** of time to come (*future years*). **b** *Gram.* (of a tense or participle) describing an event yet to happen. ● *n.* **1** time to come (*past, present, and future*). **2** what will happen in the future (*the future is uncertain*). **3** the future condition of a person, country, etc. **4** a prospect of success, etc. (*there's no future in it*). **5** *Gram.* the future tense. **6** (in *pl.*) *Stock Exch.* **a** goods and stocks sold for future delivery. **b** contracts for these. □ **for the future** from now onward. **in future** = *for the future.*

fu·ture per·fect *n. Gram.* a tense giving the sense *will have done*.

fu·tur·ism /fyŏŏchərizəm/ *n.* a movement in art, literature, music, etc., with violent departure from traditional forms so as to express movement and growth.

fu·tur·ist /fyŏŏchərist/ *n.* (often *attrib.*) **1** an adherent of futurism. **2** a believer in human progress. **3** a student of the future.

fu·tur·is·tic /fyŏŏchəristik/ *adj.* **1** suitable for the future; ultramodern. **2** of futurism. **3** relating to the future. □□ **fu·tur·is·ti·cal·ly** *adv.*

fu·tu·ri·ty /fyŏŏtŏŏritee, -tyŏŏr-, -chŏŏr-/ *n.* (*pl.* **-ies**) **1** future time. **2** (in *sing.* or *pl.*) future events.

fu·tur·ol·o·gy /fyŏŏchəróləjee/ *n.* systematic forecasting of the future. □□ **fu·tur·ol·o·gist** *n.*

fuze var. of FUSE².

fuzz /fuz/ *n.* **1** fluff. **2** fluffy or frizzled hair. **3** *sl.* **a** the police. **b** a policeman.

fuzz·y /fúzee/ *adj.* (**fuzzier**, **fuzziest**) **1 a** like fuzz. **b** fluffy. **c** frizzy. **2** blurred; indistinct. □□ **fuzz·i·ly** *adv.* **fuzz·i·ness** *n.*

fuzz·y log·ic *n.* a form of logic in which predicates can have fractional values rather than simply being true or false.

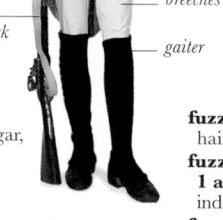

shako
cockade
bayonet
coat (habit)
fusil (flintlock musket)
breeches
gaiter

FUSILIER:
FRENCH FUSILIER
(1807–12)

F

G

G[1] /jee/ *n.* (also **g**) (*pl.* **Gs** or **G's**) **1** the seventh letter of the alphabet. **2** *Mus.* the fifth note in the diatonic scale of C major. ▷ NOTATION

G[2] *abbr.* **1** gauss. **2** giga-. **3** gravitational constant. **4** *sl.* = GRAND *n.* 2.

g *abbr.* (also **g.**) **1** gelding. **2** gram(s). **3** gravity.

GA *abbr.* Georgia (in official postal use).

Ga *symb. Chem.* the element gallium.

Ga. *abbr.* Georgia (US).

gab /gab/ *n. & v. colloq.* ● *n.* talk; chatter. ● *v.intr.* talk incessantly; chatter. □ **gift of gab** the facility of speaking eloquently.

gab·ar·dine /gábərdéen/ *n.* (also **gab·er·dine**) **1** a smooth durable twilled cloth esp. of worsted or cotton. **2** *Brit.* a garment made of this, esp. a raincoat.

gab·ble /gábəl/ *v. & n.* ● *v.* **1** *intr.* talk volubly or inarticulately. **2** *tr.* utter too fast. ● *n.* fast unintelligible talk. □□ **gab·bler** *n.*

gab·bro /gábrō/ *n.* (*pl.* **-os**) a dark granular plutonic rock of crystalline texture. □□ **gab·bro·ic** /-brôik/ *adj.* **gab·broid** *adv.*

gab·by /gábee/ *adj.* (**gabbier**, **gabbiest**) *colloq.* talkative.

gab·er·dine /gábərdéen/ *n.* var. of GABARDINE.

ga·bi·on /gáybeeən/ *n.* a cylindrical wicker or metal basket for filling with earth or stones, used in engineering or (formerly) in fortification. □□ **ga·bi·on·age** *n.*

ga·ble /gáybəl/ *n.* **1 a** the triangular upper part of a wall at the end of a ridged roof. ▷ HALF-TIMBERED, ROOF. **b** (in full **gable end**) a gable-topped wall. **2** a gable-shaped canopy over a window or door. □□ **ga·bled** *adj.* (also in *comb.*).

gad[1] /gad/ *v.intr.* (**gadded**, **gadding**) (foll. by *about*) go about idly or in search of pleasure.

gad[2] /gad/ *int.* (also **by gad**) an expression of surprise or emphatic assertion.

gad·a·bout /gádəbowt/ *n.* a person who gads about; an idle pleasure seeker.

Gad·a·rene /gádəreen/ *adj.* involving or engaged in headlong or suicidal rush or flight.

proboscis

gad·fly /gádflī/ *n.* (*pl.* **-flies**) **1** ◀ a cattle-biting fly. **2** an irritating person.

GADFLY: ORIENTAL HORSEFLY

gadg·et /gájit/ *n.* any small and usu. ingenious mechanical or electronic device or tool. □□ **gadg·et·ry** *n.*

ga·doid /gáydoyd, gád-/ *n. & adj.* ● *n.* any marine fish of the cod family Gadidae, including haddock and whiting. ● *adj.* belonging to or resembling the Gadidae.

gad·o·lin·ite /gád'linīt/ *n.* a dark crystalline mineral consisting of ferrous silicate of beryllium.

gad·o·lin·i·um /gád'líneeəm/ *n. Chem.* a soft silvery metallic element of the lanthanide series. ¶ Symb.: **Gd**.

ga·droon /gədróōn/ *n.* a decoration on silverware, etc., consisting of convex curves in a series forming an ornamental edge like inverted fluting.

GALAXY

Galaxies are classified as spiral, irregular, or elliptical. Spiral galaxies vary in the size and structure of the central hub and spiral arms; of these, barred spiral galaxies – to which our galaxy, the Milky Way, may belong – have a central bar consisting of millions of stars revolving in unison around the galaxy axis. Spiral and irregular galaxies hold gas from which new stars are created. Elliptical galaxies contain old red stars and practically no gas.

MAIN TYPES OF GALAXY

SPIRAL GALAXY

BARRED SPIRAL GALAXY

IRREGULAR GALAXY

ELLIPTICAL GALAXY

---

gad·wall /gádwawl/ *n.* a brownish gray freshwater duck, *Anas strepera*.

gad·zooks /gadzōōks/ *int. archaic* an expression of surprise, etc.

Gael /gayl/ *n.* **1** a Scottish Celt. **2** a Gaelic-speaking Celt.

Gael·ic /gáylik, gálik/ *n. & adj.* ● *n.* any of the Celtic languages spoken in Ireland, Scotland, and the Isle of Man. ● *adj.* of or relating to the Celts or the Celtic languages.

Gael·tacht /gáyltəkht/ *n.* any of the regions in Ireland where the vernacular language is Irish.

hook

gaff /gaf/ *n. & v.* ● *n.* **1 a** ◀ a stick with an iron hook for landing large fish. **b** a barbed fishing spear. **2** a spar to which the head of a fore-and-aft sail is bent. ▷ SCHOONER, SHIP. ● *v.tr.* seize (a fish) with a gaff.

gaffe /gaf/ *n.* a blunder; an indiscreet act or remark.

gaf·fer /gáfər/ *n.* **1** *Brit. sl.* an old fellow. **2** *colloq.* the chief electrician in a movie or television production unit.

gaff·er tape *n.* strong cloth-backed waterproof adhesive tape.

gag /gag/ *n. & v.* ● *n.* **1** a piece of cloth, etc., thrust into or held over the mouth to prevent speaking or crying out. **2** a joke or comic scene. **3** an actor's interpolation in a dramatic dialogue. **4** a thing or circumstance restricting free speech. **5** a joke or hoax. ● *v.* (**gagged**, **gagging**) **1** *tr.* apply a gag to. **2** *tr.* deprive of free speech. **3 a** *intr.* choke or retch. **b** *tr.* cause to do this. **4** *intr. Theatr.* make gags.

ga·ga /gáagaa/ *adj. sl.* **1** senile. **2** fatuous; slightly crazy.

gage[1] /gayj/ *n.* **1** a pledge; a thing deposited as security. **2 a** a challenge to fight. **b** a symbol of this, esp. a glove thrown down.

gage[2] var. of GAUGE.

gag·gle /gágəl/ *n.* **1** a flock of geese. **2** *colloq.* a disorderly group of people.

gag·man /gágman/ *n.* a deviser, writer, or performer of theatrical gags.

gag·ster /gágstər/ *n.* = GAGMAN.

gai·e·ty /gáyətee/ *n.* **1** the state of being merry; mirth. **2** merrymaking. **3** a bright appearance.

gail·lar·di·a /gaylaárdeeə/ *n.* ▶ any composite plant of the genus *Gaillardia*.

gai·ly /gáylee/ *adv.* **1** in a lighthearted manner. **2** with a bright appearance.

gain /gayn/ *v. & n.* ● *v.* **1** *tr.* obtain or secure (usu. something desired or favorable) (*gain an advantage*;

GAFF: TELESCOPIC GAFF (EXTENDED)

GAILLARDIA
(*Gaillardia* × *grandiflora* 'Kobold')

---

gain recognition). **2** *tr.* acquire (a sum) as profits; earn. **3** *tr.* obtain as an increment or addition (*gain weight*). **4** *intr.* (foll. by *in*) make a specified advance or improvement (*gained in stature*). **5** *intr. & tr.* (of a clock, etc.) become fast, or be fast by (a specified amount of time). **6** *intr.* (often foll. by *on*, *upon*) come closer to a person or thing pursued. **7** *tr.* **a** bring over to one's views. **b** (foll. by *over*) win by persuasion, etc. **8** *tr.* reach (a desired place). ● *n.* **1** something gained, achieved, etc. **2** an increase of possessions, etc.; a profit or improvement. **3** the acquisition of wealth. **4** (in *pl.*) sums of money acquired by trade, etc.; winnings. **5** an increase in amount. □ **gain ground** see GROUND[1]. □□ **gain·a·ble** *adj.* **gain·er** *n.* **gain·ings** *n.pl.*

gain·ful /gáynfŏŏl/ *adj.* **1** (of employment) paid. **2** lucrative. □□ **gain·ful·ly** *adv.* **gain·ful·ness** *n.*

gain·say /gáynsáy/ *v.tr.* (*past and past part.* **gainsaid** /-séd/) deny; contradict.

'gainst /genst/ *prep. poet.* = AGAINST.

gait /gayt/ *n.* a manner of running or walking.

gait·er /gáytər/ *n.* ▶ a covering of cloth, leather, etc., covering the lower leg and part of the foot, used to protect against snow, mud, etc. □□ **gait·ered** *adj.*

MUD GAITER

GAITERS USED FOR LEG PROTECTION

SNOW GAITER

gal /gal/ *n. sl.* a girl.

gal. *abbr.* gallon(s).

ga·la /gáylə, gáalə, gálə/ *n.* **1** (often *attrib.*) a festive or special occasion (*a gala performance*). **2** *Brit.* a festive gathering for sports.

ga·lac·ta·gogue /gəláktəgawg, -gog/ *adj. & n.* ● *adj.* inducing a flow of milk. ● *n.* a galactagogue substance.

ga·lac·tic /gəláktik/ *adj.* of or relating to a galaxy, esp. the Milky Way.

ga·la·go /gəláygō, -láa-/ *n.* (*pl.* **-os**) any small tree-climbing primate of the genus *Galago*, found in southern Africa, with large eyes and ears and a long tail. Also called **bushbaby**.

Gal·a·had /gáləhad/ *n.* a person characterized by nobility, integrity, courtesy, etc.

gal·an·tine /gáləteen/ *n.* white meat or fish boned, cooked, pressed, and served cold in aspic, etc.

gal·a·vant var. of GALLIVANT.

gal·ax·y /gáləksee/ *n.* (*pl.* **-ies**) **1** ◄ any of many independent systems of stars, dust, etc., held together by gravitational attraction. **2** (**the Galaxy**) the galaxy of which the solar system is a part. **3** (**the Galaxy**) the Milky Way.

gal·ba·num /gálbənəm/ *n.* a bitter aromatic gum resin produced from certain Asian plants.

gale /gayl/ *n.* **1** a very strong wind, esp. (on the Beaufort scale) one of 32–63 m.p.h. ▷ BEAUFORT SCALE. **2** an outburst, esp. of laughter.

ga·lea /gáyleeə/ *n.* (*pl.* **galeae** /-lee-ee/ or **-as**) *Bot. & Zool.* a structure like a helmet in shape, form, or function. □□ **ga·le·ate** /-lee-ayt/ *adj.* **ga·le·at·ed** *adj.*

ga·le·na /gəléenə/ *n.* ◄ a bluish, gray, or black mineral ore of lead sulfide. ▷ ORE

ga·len·ic var. of GALENICAL.

ga·len·i·cal /gəlénikəl/ *adj.* (also **ga·len·ic** /-lénik/) **1** of or relating to Galen, a Greek physician of the 2nd c. AD, or his methods. **2** made of natural as opposed to synthetic components.

Gal·i·le·an[1] /gálilàyən, -léeən/ *adj.* of or relating to Galileo, Italian astronomer d. 1642, or his methods.

Gal·i·le·an[2] /gálileeən/ *adj. & n.* ● *adj.* **1** of Galilee in Palestine. **2** Christian. ● *n.* **1** a native of Galilee. **2** a Christian. **3** (prec. by *the*) *derog.* Christ.

gal·i·pot /gálipot/ *n.* a hardened deposit of resin formed on the stem of the cluster pine.

gall[1] /gawl/ *n.* **1** *sl.* impudence. **2** asperity; rancor. **3** bitterness; anything bitter (*gall and wormwood*). **4** the bile of animals. **5** the gallbladder and its contents.

gall[2] /gawl/ *n. & v.* ● *n.* **1** a sore on the skin made by chafing. **2** **a** mental soreness or vexation. **b** a cause of this. **3** a place rubbed bare. ● *v.tr.* **1** rub sore; injure by rubbing. **2** vex; annoy; irritate. □□ **gall·ing·ly** *adv.*

gall[3] /gawl/ *n.* **1** ◄ a growth produced by insects or fungus, etc., on plants and trees, esp. on oak. **2** (*attrib.*) of insects producing galls.

gal·lant *adj. & n.* ● *adj.* /gálənt/ **1** brave; chivalrous. **2 a** (of a ship, horse, etc.) grand; stately. **b** *archaic* finely dressed. **3** /gálənt, gəlánt, -láant/ **a** markedly attentive to women. **b** concerned with sexual love ● *n.* /gálənt, gəlánt, -láant/ **1** a ladies' man; a paramour. **2** *archaic* a man of fashion; a fine gentleman. □□ **gal·lant·ly** /gáləntlee/ *adv.*

gal·lant·ry /gáləntree/ *n.* (*pl.* **-ies**) **1** bravery; dashing courage. **2** courtliness; devotion to women. **3** a polite act or speech. **4** the conduct of a gallant; sexual intrigue.

gall·blad·der *n.* ▲ the vessel storing bile after its secretion by the liver and before release into the intestine. ▷ DIGESTION

gal·le·on /gáleeən/ *n. hist.* **1** a ship of war (usu. Spanish). **2** a large Spanish merchant ship. **3** a vessel shorter and higher than a galley.

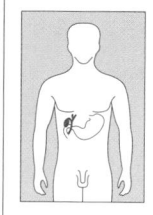
GALENA: CUBIC CRYSTALS

cross section through gall

wasp larva

exterior of gall

GALLS FORMED ON AN OAK TREE

GALLINULE
(*Gallinula chloropus*)

GALLBLADDER

Together with the hepatic ducts and the bile ducts, the gallbladder forms part of the human biliary system. Bile, an alkaline fluid secreted by the liver, drains through the hepatic ducts to the gallbladder, where it is stored in concentrated form. When food is consumed, the gallbladder releases bile via the cystic duct and common bile duct to the stomach, where the bile aids in the digestion of fats.

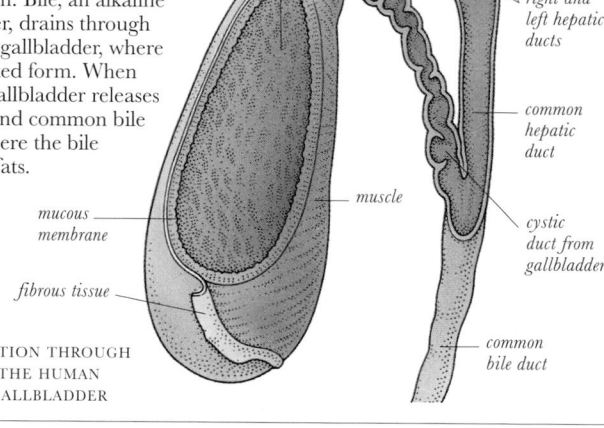

gallbladder

right and left hepatic ducts

common hepatic duct

muscle

cystic duct from gallbladder

mucous membrane

fibrous tissue

common bile duct

SECTION THROUGH THE HUMAN GALLBLADDER

gal·le·ri·a /gáləréeə/ *n.* a collection of small shops under a single roof.

gal·ler·y /gáləree/ *n.* (*pl.* **-ies**) **1** a room or building for showing works of art. **2** a balcony, esp. a platform projecting from the inner wall of a church, etc. (*minstrels' gallery*). ▷ ROMANESQUE. **3 a** the highest balcony in a theater. **b** its occupants. **4 a** a covered space for walking in, partly open at the side. **b** a long narrow passage in the thickness of a wall or supported on corbels, open toward the interior of the building. **5** a long narrow room or corridor. **6** *Mil. & Mining* a horizontal underground passage. **7** a group of spectators at a golf match, etc. □ **play to the gallery** seek to win approval by appealing to popular taste. □□ **gal·ler·ied** *adj.*

gal·ler·y·ite /gáləree-īt/ *n.* a person occupying a seat in a gallery; a spectator at a play, tennis match, etc.

gal·ley /gálee/ *n.* (*pl.* **-eys**) **1** *hist.* **a** a low flat single-decked vessel using sails and oars, and usu. rowed by slaves or criminals. **b** an ancient Greek or Roman warship with one or more banks of oars. **2** a ship's or aircraft's kitchen. **3** *Printing* (in full **galley proof**) a proof in the form of long single-column strips, not in sheets or pages.

gal·ley slave *n.* **1** *hist.* a person condemned to row in a galley. **2** a drudge.

gal·liard /gályaard/ *n. hist.* **1** a lively dance usu. in triple time for two persons. **2** the music for this.

Gal·lic /gálik/ *adj.* **1** French or typically French. **2** of the Gauls. □□ **Gal·li·cize** /-lisīz/ *v.tr. & intr.*

gal·lic ac·id /gálik/ *n. Chem.* an acid extracted from gallnuts, etc., formerly used in making ink.

Gal·li·cism /gálisizəm/ *n.* a French idiom adopted in another language.

gal·li·mau·fry /gálimáwfree/ *n.* (*pl.* **-ies**) a heterogeneous mixture; a jumble.

gal·li·mi·mus /galimīməs/ *n.* an ostrichlike dinosaur of the late Cretaceous period.

gal·li·na·ceous /gálináyshəs/ *adj.* of or relating to the order Galliformes, which includes domestic poultry, pheasants, partridges, etc.

gal·li·nule /gálinōōl, -nyōōl/ *n.* **1** ◄ a small aquatic bird, *Gallinula chloropus*, with long legs and a short reddish-yellow bill. **2.** any of various similar birds of the genus *Porphyrula* or *Porphyrio*.

gal·li·um /gáleeəm/ *n. Chem.* a soft bluish white metallic element occurring naturally in coal, bauxite, and kaolin. ¶ Symb.: **Ga**.

gal·li·vant /gálivant/ *v.intr. colloq.* **1** gad about. **2** flirt.

Gallo- /gálō/ *comb. form* **1** French; relating to France. **2** Gaul (*Gallo-Roman*).

gal·lon /gálən/ *n.* **1 a** a measure of capacity equivalent to four quarts (3785 cc). **b** (in full **imperial gallon**) *Brit.* a measure of capacity equal to eight pints and equivalent to four quarts (4546 cc). **2** (usu. in *pl.*) *colloq.* a large amount. □□ **gal·lon·age** *n.*

gal·loon /gəlōōn/ *n.* a narrow braid of gold, silver, silk, cotton, nylon, etc., for trimming dresses, etc.

gal·lop /gáləp/ *n. & v.* ● *n.* **1** the fastest pace of a horse or other quadruped, with all the feet off the ground together in each stride. **2** a ride at this pace. **3** *Brit.* a track or ground for this. ● *v.* (**galloped**, **galloping**) **1 a** *intr.* go at the pace of a gallop. **b** *tr.* make (a horse, etc., or its rider) gallop. **2** *intr.* (foll. by *through*, *over*) read, recite, or talk at great speed. **3** *intr.* progress rapidly (*galloping inflation*). □□ **gal·lop·er** *n.*

gal·lo·way /gáləway/ *n.* **1** an animal of a breed of hornless black beef cattle from Galloway in SW Scotland. **2** this breed.

gal·lows /gálōz/ *n.pl.* (usu. treated as *sing.*) **1** a structure, usu. of two uprights and a crosspiece, for the hanging of criminals. **2** (prec. by *the*) execution by hanging.

gal·lows hu·mor *n.* grim and ironic humor.

gall·stone /gáwlstōn/ *n.* a small hard mass forming in the gallbladder.

gall wasp *n.* ◄ a gall-forming insect of the hymenopteran superfamily Cynipoidea.

GALL WASP: MARBLE GALL WASP (*Andricus kollari*)

Gal·lup poll /gáləp/ *n.* an opinion poll.

gal·lus·es /gáləsiz/ *n.pl. dial. & old-fashioned* suspenders.

ga·loot /gəlōōt/ *n. colloq.* a person, esp. a strange or clumsy one.

gal·op /gáləp/ *n. & v.* ● *n.* **1** a lively dance in duple time. **2** the music for this. ● *v.intr.* (**galoped**, **galoping**) perform this dance.

ga·lore /gəláwr/ *adv.* in abundance (placed after noun: *flowers galore*).

ga·losh /gəlósh/ *n.* (usu. in *pl.*) a waterproof overshoe of rubber.

ga·lumph /gəlúmf/ *v.intr. colloq.* **1** move clumsily. **2** go prancing in triumph.

gal·van·ic /galvánik/ *adj.* **1 a** sudden and remarkable (*a galvanic effect*). **b** full of energy. **2** producing

G

an electric current by chemical action. □□ **gal·van·i·cal·ly** *adv.*

gal·va·nism /gálvənizəm/ *n.* **1** electricity produced by chemical action. **2** the use of electricity for medical purposes. □□ **gal·va·nist** *n.*

gal·va·nize /gálvənīz/ *v.tr.* **1** (often foll. by *into*) rouse forcefully, esp. by shock or excitement. **2** stimulate by or as if by electricity. **3** coat (iron) with zinc (usu. without the use of electricity) as a protection against rust. □□ **gal·va·ni·za·tion** *n.* **gal·va·niz·er** *n.*

gal·va·nom·e·ter /gálvənómitər/ *n.* ▼ an instrument for detecting and measuring small electric currents. □□ **gal·va·no·met·ric** /-nəmétrik/ *adj.*

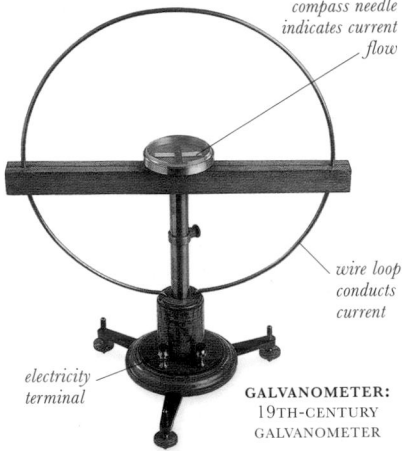

compass needle indicates current flow

wire loop conducts current

electricity terminal

GALVANOMETER: 19TH-CENTURY GALVANOMETER

gam·bit /gámbit/ *n.* **1** a chess opening in which a player sacrifices a piece or pawn to secure an advantage. **2** an opening move in a discussion, etc. **3** a trick or device.

gam·ble /gámbəl/ *v. & n.* ● *v.* **1** *intr.* play games of chance for money, esp. for high stakes. **2** *tr.* a bet (a sum of money) in gambling. **b** (often foll. by *away*) lose (assets) by gambling. **3** *intr.* take great risks in the hope of substantial gain. **4** *intr.* (foll. by *on*) act in the hope of (*gambled on fine weather*). ● *n.* **1** a risky undertaking or attempt. **2** an act of gambling. □□ **gam·bler** *n.*

gam·boge /gambój, -bŏ̄ozh/ *n.* ► a gum resin used as a yellow pigment and as a purgative.

gam·bol /gámbəl/ *v. & n.* ● *v.intr.* (**gamboled, gamboling;** also **gambolled, gambolling**) skip or frolic playfully. ● *n.* a playful frolic.

gam·brel /gámbrəl/ *n.* (in full **gambrel roof**) a roof with gables and with each face having two slopes, the lower one steeper.

game[1] /gaym/ *n., adj., & v.* ● *n.* **1** a form or spell of play or sport, esp. a competitive one played according to rules. **2** a single portion of play forming a scoring unit in some contests, e.g., bridge or tennis. **3** (in *pl.*) **a** *Brit.* athletics or sports as organized in a school, etc. **b** a meeting for athletic, etc., contests (*Olympic Games*). **4** a winning score in a game; the state of the score in a game. **5** the equipment for a game. **6** one's level of achievement in a game, as specified (*played a good game*). **7 a** a piece of fun (*was only playing a game with you*). **b** (in *pl.*) jokes; tricks (*none of your games!*). **8** a scheme, etc., regarded as a game (*so that's your game*). **9** a policy or line of action. **10** (collect.) **a** wild animals or birds hunted for sport or food. **b** the flesh of these. **11** a hunted animal. ● *adj.* **1** eager and willing. **2** (foll. by *for*, or *to* + infin.) having the spirit or energy. ● *v.intr.* esp. *Brit.* play at games of chance for money; gamble. □ **the game is up** the scheme is revealed. **off** (or **on**) **one's game** playing badly (or well). **play the**

game behave fairly. □□ **game·ly** *adv.* **game·ness** *n.* **game·ster** *n.*

game[2] /gaym/ *adj.* (of a leg, arm, etc.) lame; crippled.

game·keep·er /gáymkeepər/ *n.* a person employed to protect game.

game·lan /gáməlan/ *n.* **1** ▼ a type of orchestra found in SE Asia, with a wide range of percussion instruments. **2** a kind of xylophone used in this.

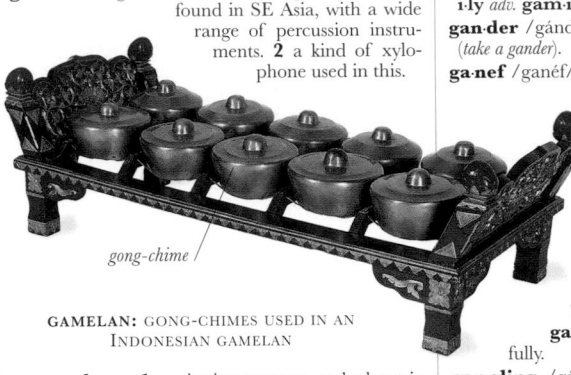

gong-chime

GAMELAN: GONG-CHIMES USED IN AN INDONESIAN GAMELAN

game plan *n.* **1** a winning strategy worked out in advance for a particular game. **2** a plan of campaign, esp. in politics.

game point *n. Tennis*, etc., a point which, if won, would win the game.

game show *n.* a program on television in which people compete to win prizes.

games·man·ship /gáymzmənship/ *n.* the art or practice of winning games or other contests by gaining a psychological advantage over an opponent.

gam·e·tan·gi·um /gámitánjeeəm/ *n.* (*pl.* **gametangia** /-jeeə/) *Bot.* an organ in which gametes are formed.

gam·ete /gámeet, gəmeét/ *n. Biol.* a mature germ cell able to unite with another in sexual reproduction. □□ **ga·met·ic** /gəmétik/ *adj.*

game theory *n.* (also **games theory**) the mathematical analysis of conflict in war, economics, games of skill, etc.

gameto- /gəmeétō/ *comb. form Biol.* gamete.

ga·me·to·cyte /gəmeétōsīt/ *n. Biol.* any cell that is in the process of developing into one or more gametes.

gam·e·to·gen·e·sis /gəmeétəjénisis/ *n. Biol.* the process by which cells undergo meiosis to form gametes. ▷ MEIOSIS

ga·me·to·phyte /gəmeétəfīt/ *n.* the gamete-producing form of a plant that has alternation of generations between this and the asexual form. ▷ BRYOPHYTE. □□ **ga·me·to·phyt·ic** /-fítik/ *adj.*

game war·den *n.* an official locally supervising game and hunting.

gam·in /gámin/ *n.* **1** a street urchin. **2** an impudent child.

gam·ine /gámeen/ *n.* **1** a girl gamin. **2** a girl with mischievous or boyish charm.

gam·ma /gámə/ *n.* **1** the third letter of the Greek alphabet (Γ, γ). **2** *Brit.* a third-class mark given for a piece of work or in an examination. **3** the third member of a series.

gam·ma ra·di·a·tion *n.* (also **gamma rays**) electromagnetic radiation of very short wavelength.

gam·mon[1] /gámən/ *n. & v.* ● *n.* **1** the bottom piece of a side of bacon including a hind leg. **2** esp. *Brit.* the ham of a pig cured like bacon. ● *v.tr.* cure (bacon).

gam·mon[2] /gámən/ *n. & v.* ● *n.* a victory in backgammon in which the opponent removes no pieces from the board. ● *v.tr.* defeat in this way.

gam·ut /gámət/ *n.* **1** the whole series or range or scope of anything (*the whole gamut of crime*). **2** *Mus.* **a** the whole series of notes used in medieval or modern music. **b** a major diatonic scale.

gam·y /gáymee/ *adj.* (**gamier, gamiest**) **1** having the flavor or scent of game kept till it is high. **2** scandalous; sensational. **3** = GAME[1] *adj.* □□ **gam·i·ly** *adv.* **gam·i·ness** *n.*

gan·der /gándər/ *n.* **1** a male goose. **2** *sl.* a glance (*take a gander*).

ga·nef /ganéf/ *n. colloq.*, chiefly *US* a dishonest or unscrupulous person.

gang /gang/ *n.* **1 a** a band of persons acting or going about together. **b** *colloq.* such a band pursuing antisocial purposes. **2** a set of workers, slaves, or prisoners. □ **gang up** *colloq.* **1** (often foll. by *with*) act in concert. **2** (foll. by *on*) combine against.

gang·land /gángland, -lənd/ *n.* the world of organized crime.

gan·gle /gánggəl/ *v.intr.* move ungracefully.

gan·gling /gánggling/ *adj.* (of a person) loosely built; lanky.

gan·gli·on /gánggleeən/ *n.* (*pl.* **ganglia** /-leeə/ or **ganglions**) **1 a** an enlargement or knot on a nerve, etc., containing an assemblage of nerve cells. **b** a mass of gray matter in the central nervous system forming a nerve nucleus. ▷ NERVOUS SYSTEM. **2** *Med.* a cyst, esp. on a tendon sheath. □□ **gan·gli·on·at·ed** *adj.* **gan·gli·on·ic** /-leeónik/ *adj.*

gang·ly /gánglee/ *adj.* (**ganglier, gangliest**) = GANGLING.

gang·plank /gángplangk/ *n.* a movable plank usu. with cleats nailed on it for boarding or disembarking from a ship, etc.

gan·grene /gánggreen/ *n. & v.* ● *n.* **1** *Med.* death and decomposition of a part of the body tissue, usu. resulting from obstructed circulation. **2** moral corruption. ● *v.tr. & intr.* affect or become affected with gangrene. □□ **gan·gre·nous** /gánggrinəs/ *adj.*

gang·sta /gángstə/ *n. black sl.* a gang member.

gang·ster /gángstər/ *n.* a member of a gang of violent criminals. □□ **gang·ster·ism** *n.*

gangue /gang/ *n.* valueless earth, rock, etc., in which ore is found.

gang·way /gángway/ *n. & int.* ● *n.* **1 a** an opening in the bulwarks for a gangplank by which a ship is entered or left. **b** a bridge laid from ship to shore. **c** a passage on a ship. **2** a temporary bridge on a building site, etc. ● *int.* make way!

gan·ja /gáanjə/ *n.* marijuana.

gan·net /gánit/ *n.* **1** any sea bird of the genus *Morus*, catching fish by plunge-diving. ▷ SEABIRD. **2** *Brit. sl.* a greedy person. □□ **gan·net·ry** *n.* (*pl.* **-ies**).

gan·oid /gánoyd/ *adj. & n.* ● *adj.* **1** (of fish scales) enameled; smooth and bright. **2** having ganoid scales. ● *n.* a fish having ganoid scales.

gant·let var. of GAUNTLET[2].

gan·try /gántree/ *n.* (*pl.* **-ies**) **1** an overhead structure supporting a traveling crane, or railroad or road signals. ▷ FACTORY SHIP. **2** a structure supporting a space rocket prior to launching.

gaol *Brit.* var. of JAIL.

gaol·er *Brit.* var. of JAILER.

gap /gap/ *n.* **1** an unfilled space or interval; a break in continuity. **2** a wide (usu. undesirable) divergence in views, etc. (*generation gap*). **3** a gorge or pass. □□ **gap·py** *adj.*

gape /gayp/ *v. & n.* ● *v.intr.* **1 a** open one's mouth wide, esp. in amazement or wonder. **b** be or become wide open. **2** (foll. by *at*) gaze curiously or wondrously. **3** split. ● *n.* **1** an open-mouthed stare. **2** a yawn. **3 a** an expanse of open mouth or beak. **b** the part of a beak that opens. **4** a rent or opening. □□ **gap·ing·ly** *adv.*

gape·worm /gáypwərm/ *n.* a nematode worm, *Syngamus tracheae*, that infests the trachea and bronchi of birds and causes the gapes.

gar /gaar/ *n.* **1** any mainly marine fish of the family Belonidae, having long beaklike jaws. Also called **needlefish**. **2** ▼ any similar freshwater fish of the genus *Lepisosteus*. Also called **garfish** or **garpike**.

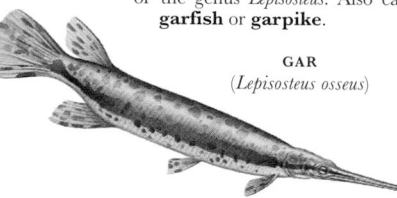

GAR
(*Lepisosteus osseus*)

ga·rage /gəráa<u>zh</u>, -ráaj/ *n. & v.* ● *n.* **1** a building for the storage of a motor vehicle or vehicles. **2** an establishment selling gasoline, etc., or repairing and selling motor vehicles. ● *v.tr.* keep (a motor vehicle) in a garage.

ga·ram ma·sa·la /gáarəm mə-sáálə/ *n.* ◄ a mixture of spices used in Indian cookery.

garb /gaarb/ *n. & v.* ● *n.* **1** clothing, esp. of a distinctive kind. **2** the way a person is dressed. ● *v.tr.* **1** (usu. in *passive* or *refl.*) put (esp. distinctive) clothes on (a person). **2** attire.

gar·bage /gáarbij/ *n.* **1 a** refuse; filth. **b** domestic waste, esp. food wastes. **2** foul or inferior literature, etc. **3** nonsense. **4** incomprehensible or meaningless data.

GARAM MASALA

gar·ble /gáarbəl/ *v.tr.* **1** unintentionally distort or confuse (facts, messages, etc.). **2 a** mutilate in order to misrepresent. **b** make (usu. unfair or malicious) selections from (facts, statements, etc.). □□ **gar·bler** *n.*

gar·board /gáarbərd/ *n.* (in full **garboard strake**) the first range of planks or plates laid on a ship's bottom next to the keel.

gar·den /gáard'n/ *n. & v.* ● *n.* **1 a** a piece of ground used for growing esp. flowers or vegetables. **b** a piece of ground, usu. partly grassed and adjoining a private house, used for growing flowers, fruit, or vegetables, and as a place of recreation. **2** (esp. in *pl.*) ornamental grounds laid out for public enjoyment. **3** a similar place with the service of refreshments (*tea garden*). **4** (*attrib.*) **a** (of plants) cultivated, not wild. **b** for use in a garden (*garden seat*). **5** (usu. in *pl.* prec. by a name) *Brit.* a street, square, etc. (*Onslow Gardens*). **6** an especially fertile region. **7** a large public hall. ● *v.intr.* cultivate or work in a garden. □□ **gar·den·ing** *n.*

gar·den·er /gáardnər/ *n.* a person who gardens or is employed to tend a garden.

gar·de·nia /gaardéenyə/ *n.* ◄ any tree or shrub of the genus *Gardenia*, with large white or yellow flowers and usu. a fragrant scent.

gar·fish /gáarfish/ *n.* (*pl.* same) = GAR.

gar·gan·tu·an /gaargánchooən/ *adj.* enormous; gigantic.

gar·get /gáargit/ *n.* **1** inflammation of a cow's or ewe's udder. **2** pokeweed.

GARDENIA
(*Gardenia augusta* 'Veitchii')

gar·gle /gáargəl/ *v. & n.* ● *v.* **1** *tr.* (also *absol.*) wash (one's mouth and throat), esp. for medicinal purposes, with a liquid kept in motion by breathing through it. **2** *intr. Brit.* make a sound as when doing this. ● *n.* **1** a liquid used for gargling. **2** *Brit. sl.* an alcoholic drink.

gar·goyle /gáargoyl/ *n.* ► a grotesque carved human or animal face or figure projecting from the gutter of building as a spout. ▷ CHURCH

gar·i·bal·di /gáribáwldee/ *n.* (*pl.* **garibaldis**) a kind of woman's or child's loose blouse.

gar·ish /gáirish/ *adj.* **1** obtrusively bright. **2** gaudy; over-decorated. □□ **gar·ish·ly** *adv.* **gar·ish·ness** *n.*

gar·land /gáarlənd/ *n. & v.* ● *n.* **1 a** wreath of flowers, leaves, etc., worn on the head or hung as a decoration. **2** a prize or distinction. ● *v.tr.* **1** adorn with garlands. **2** crown with a garland.

gar·lic /gáarlik/ *n.* **1** ◄ any of various alliaceous plants, esp. *Allium sativum*. **2** the strong-smelling pungent bulb of this plant, used in cooking. □□ **gar·lick·y** *adj.*

gar·ment /gáarmənt/ *n.* **1 a** an article of dress. **b** (in *pl.*) clothes. **2** the outward and visible covering of anything.

gar·ner /gáarnər/ *v. & n.* ● *v.tr.* **1** collect. **2** store; deposit. ● *n. literary* a storehouse or granary.

gar·net /gáarnit/ *n.* ► a vitreous silicate mineral, esp. a transparent deep red kind used as a gem.

gar·nish /gáarnish/ *v. & n.* ● *v.tr.* **1** decorate or embellish (esp. food). **2** garnishee. ● *n.* (also **gar·nish·ing**) a decoration, esp. to food.

garlic bulb

GARLIC
(*Allium sativum*)

gar·nish·ee /gáarnishée/ *v. & n. Law* ● *v.tr.* (**garnishees, garnisheed**) **1** legally seize (money, etc.) **2** serve notice on (a person) for the purpose of seizing money. ● *n.* a person garnished.

gar·pike /gáarpīk/ *n.* = GAR.

gar·ret /gárit/ *n.* **1** a top floor or attic room, esp. a dismal or unfurnished one. **2** an attic.

gar·ri·son /gárisən/ *n. & v.* ● *n.* **1** the troops stationed in a fortress, etc., to defend it. **2** the building occupied by them. ● *v.tr.* **1** provide (a place) with or occupy as a garrison. **2** place on garrison duty.

gar·rote /gərót/ *v. & n.* (also **ga·rotte; gar·rotte**) ● *v.tr.* execute or kill by strangulation, esp. with an iron or wire collar, etc. ● *n.* an apparatus used for this.

GARGOYLE: REPLICA
OF A GOTHIC-STYLE
GARGOYLE

spout

gar·ru·lous /gárələs, gáryə-/ *adj.* **1** talkative, esp. on trivial matters. **2** wordy. □□ **gar·ru·li·ty** /gəróōlitee/ *n.* **gar·ru·lous·ly** *adv.* **gar·ru·lous·ness** *n.*

gar·ter /gáartər/ *n.* **1** a band worn to keep a sock or stocking up. **2** a strap hanging from a girdle, etc., for holding up a stocking.

gar·ter belt *n.* a belt with hanging straps for holding up stockings.

gar·ter snake *n.* ► any water snake of the genus *Thamnophis*, native to N. America, having lengthwise stripes.

gar·ter stitch *n.* a plain knitting stitch or pattern, forming ridges in alternate rows. ▷ KNITTING

GARTER SNAKE
(*Thamnophis* species)

G

gas /gas/ *n. & v.* ● *n.* (*pl.* **gases**) **1** any airlike substance which moves freely to fill any space available, irrespective of its quantity. ▷ MATTER. **2** such a substance used as a domestic or industrial fuel (also *attrib.: gas stove*). **3** nitrous oxide or another gas used as an anesthetic (esp. in dentistry). **4** a gas or vapor used in warfare. **5** *colloq.* **a** gasoline. **b** a motor vehicle's accelerator. **6** *sl.* pointless idle talk. **7** *sl.* an amusing thing or person. ● *v.* (**gases, gassed, gassing**) **1** *tr.* expose to gas, esp. to kill or make unconscious. **2** *intr.* give off gas. **3** *tr.* (usu. foll. by *up*) *colloq.* fill (the tank of a motor vehicle) with gasoline. **4** *intr. colloq.* talk idly.

gas·bag /gásbag/ *n.* **1** a container of gas, esp. for holding the gas for a balloon or airship. **2** *sl.* an idle talker.

gas cham·ber *n.* an airtight chamber that can be filled with poisonous gas to kill people or animals.

gas·e·ous /gásseəs, gáshəs/ *adj.* of or like gas. □□ **gas·e·ous·ness** *n.*

gas field *n.* ▼ an area yielding natural gas.

gas-guz·zler *n. colloq.* a motor vehicle that gets relatively poor gas mileage.

gash /gash/ *n. & v.* ● *n.* **1** a long deep slash or wound. **2 a** a cleft such as might be made by a slashing cut. **b** the act of making such a cut. ● *v.tr.* make a gash in.

gas·hold·er /gás-hōldər/ *n.* a large receptacle for storing gas.

GAS FIELD

Natural gas (largely methane) and oil are usually found together. Both derive from microscopic marine organisms buried in layers of sediment and broken down over millions of years. Less dense than water, the two fuels may rise through permeable rocks to collect beneath a stratum of cap rock, often in folds created by movements in the Earth's crust. The site of natural gas and oil can thus be accurately predicted by studying rock formations.

CROSS SECTION SHOWING
THE GEOLOGIC
FORMATION OF A GAS FIELD

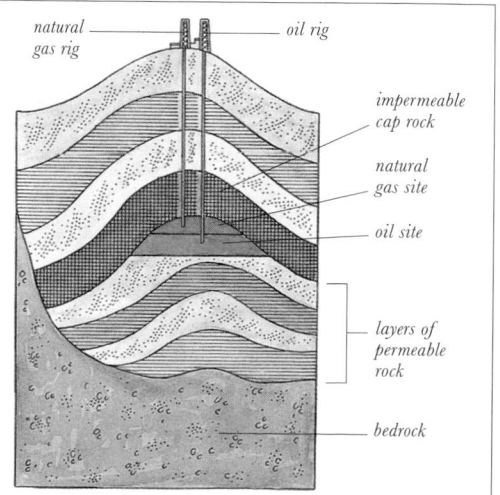

natural gas rig — *oil rig*
impermeable cap rock
natural gas site
oil site
layers of permeable rock
bedrock

G

gas·i·fy /gásifī/ *v.tr. & intr.* (**-ies, -ied**) convert or be converted into gas. □□ **gas·i·fi·ca·tion** /-fikáyshən/ *n.*

gas·ket /gáskit/ *n.* a sheet or ring of rubber, etc., shaped to seal the junction of metal surfaces. □ **blow a gasket** *sl.* lose one's temper.

gas·kin /gáskin/ *n.* the thigh of a horse's hind leg. ▷ HORSE

gas·light /gáslīt/ *n.* **1** a jet of burning gas, usu. heating a mantle, to provide light. **2** light emanating from this.

gas mask *n.* ◀ a respirator used as a defense against poison gas.

gas·o·line /gásəléen/ *n.* (also **gas·o·lene**) a volatile flammable liquid blended from petroleum and natural gas and used as a fuel.

gas·om·e·ter /gasómitər/ *n. Brit.* a large tank in which gas is stored for distribution by pipes to users.

gasp /gasp/ *v. & n.* ● *v.* **1** *intr.* catch one's breath with an open mouth as in astonishment. **2** *intr.* (foll. by *for*) strain to obtain by gasping (*gasped for air*). **3** *tr.* (often foll. by *out*) utter with gasps. ● *n.* a convulsive catching of breath.

gas·ser /gásər/ *n.* **1** *colloq.* an idle talker. **2** *sl.* a very attractive or impressive person or thing.

gas sta·tion *n.* a filling station.

gas·sy /gásee/ *adj.* (**gassier, gassiest**) **1 a** of or like gas. **b** full of gas. **2** *colloq.* (of talk, etc.) pointless; verbose. □□ **gas·si·ness** *n.*

gas·trec·to·my /gastréktəmee/ *n.* (*pl.* **-ies**) a surgical operation in which the whole or part of the stomach is removed.

gas·tric /gástrik/ *adj.* of the stomach.

gas·tric juice *n.* a thin clear virtually colorless acid fluid secreted by the stomach glands and active in promoting digestion.

gas·tri·tis /gastrítis/ *n.* inflammation of the lining of the stomach.

gastro- /gástrō/ *comb. form* (also **gastr-** before a vowel) stomach.

GAS MASK
(*c.*1990)

rubber hood   eyepiece   breathing tube

air filter

gas·tro·en·ter·ic /gástrōentérik/ *adj.* of or relating to the stomach and intestines.

gas·tro·en·ter·i·tis /gástrō-éntərítis/ *n.* inflammation of the stomach and intestines.

gas·tro·nome /gástrənōm/ *n.* a gourmet.

gas·tron·o·my /gastrónəmee/ *n.* the practice, study, or art of eating and drinking well. □□ **gas·tro·nom·ic** /gástrənómik/ *adj.* **gas·tro·nom·i·cal** *adj.* **gas·tro·nom·i·cal·ly** *adv.*

gas·tro·pod /gástrəpod/ *n.* ▼ any mollusk of the class Gastropoda that moves along by means of a large muscular foot, e.g., a snail, slug, etc. □□ **gas·trop·o·dous** /gastrópədəs/ *adj.*

gas·tro·scope /gástrəskōp/ *n.* an optical instrument used for inspecting the interior of the stomach.

gas·tru·la /gástrələ/ *n.* (*pl.* **gastrulae** /-lee/) *Zool.* an embryonic stage developing from the blastula.

gas·works /gáswərks/ *n.* a place where gas is manufactured and processed.

gat¹ /gat/ *n. sl.* a revolver or other firearm.

gat² /gat/ *archaic past of* GET *v.*

gate /gayt/ *n. & v.* ● *n.* **1** a barrier, usu. hinged, used to close an opening made for entrance and exit through a wall, fence, etc. **2** such an opening, esp. in the wall of a city, enclosure, or large building. **3** a means of entrance or exit. **4** a numbered place of access to aircraft at an airport. **5 a** an electrical signal that causes or controls the passage of other signals. **b** an electrical circuit with an output which depends on the combination of several inputs. **6** a device regulating the passage of water in a lock, etc. **7 a** the number of people entering by payment at the gates of a sports stadium, etc. **b** (in full **gate money**) the proceeds taken for admission. **8** = STARTING GATE. ● *v.tr.* (as **gated** *adj.*) (of a road) having a gate or gates to control the movement of traffic or animals.

ga·teau /gatṓ, gaa-/ *n.* (*pl.* **gateaus** or **gateaux** /-tṓz/) any of various rich cakes, usu. containing cream or fruit.

gate·crash·er /gáytkrashər/ *n.* an uninvited guest at a party, etc. □□ **gate·crash** *v.tr. & intr.*

gate·fold /gáytfōld/ *n.* a page in a book or magazine, etc., that folds out to be larger than the page format.

gate·house /gáyt-hows/ *n.* **1** a house standing by a gateway, esp. to a large house or park. ▷ MONASTERY. **2** *hist.* a room over a city gate, often used as a prison.

gate·keep·er /gáytkeepər/ *n.* an attendant at a gate, controlling entrance and exit.

gate·leg /gáytleg/ *n.* (in full **gateleg table**) a table with drop leaves supported by legs swung open like a gate. □□ **gate·legged** *adj.*

gate·man /gáytmən/ *n.* (*pl.* **-men**) = GATEKEEPER.

gate·post /gáytpōst/ *n.* a post on which a gate is hung or against which it shuts.

gate·way /gáytway/ *n.* **1** an entrance with or opening for a gate. **2** a frame or structure built over a gate. **3** an entrance or exit.

gath·er /gáthər/ *v. & n.* ● *v.* **1** *tr. & intr.* bring or come together; assemble. **2** *tr.* (usu. foll. by *up*) **a** bring together from scattered places. **b** take up together from the ground, etc. **c** draw into a smaller compass. **3** *tr.* acquire by gradually collecting. **4** *tr.* **a** pick a quantity of (flowers, etc.). **b** collect (grain, etc.) as a harvest. **5** *tr.* (often foll. by *that* + clause) infer or understand. **6** *tr.* be affected by the accumulation or increase of (*gather speed*). **7** *tr.* (often foll. by *up*) summon up (one's thoughts, energy, etc.) for a purpose. **8** *tr.* gain or recover (one's breath). **9** *tr.* **a** draw (material, or one's brow) together in folds or wrinkles. **b** pucker or draw together (part of a dress) by running a thread through. **10** *intr.* come to a head; develop a purulent swelling. ● *n.* (in *pl.*) a part of a garment that is gathered or drawn in. □ **gather way** (of a ship) begin to move. □□ **gath·er·er** *n.*

gath·er·ing /gáthəring/ *n.* **1** an assembly or meeting. **2** a purulent swelling. **3** a group of leaves taken together in bookbinding.

Gat·ling /gátling/ *n.* (in full **Gatling gun**) a machine gun with clustered barrels.

ga·tor /gáytər/ *n.* (also **ga·ter**) *colloq.* an alligator.

GATT /gat/ *abbr.* (also **Gatt**) General Agreement on Tariffs and Trade.

gauche /gōsh/ *adj.* **1** socially awkward. **2** tactless. □□ **gauche·ly** *adv.* **gauche·ness** *n.*

gau·che·rie /gṓshəree/ *n.* **1** gauche manners. **2** a gauche action.

gau·cho /gówchō/ *n.* (*pl.* **-os**) ▼ a cowboy from the S. American pampas.

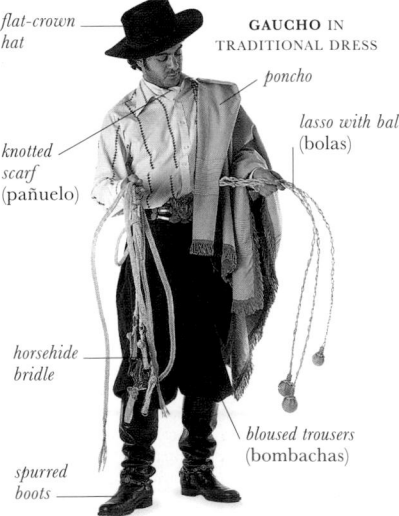

GAUCHO IN TRADITIONAL DRESS

flat-crown hat

poncho

lasso with balls (bolas)

knotted scarf (pañuelo)

horsehide bridle

bloused trousers (bombachas)

spurred boots

gaud /gawd/ *n.* a gaudy thing; a showy ornament.

gaud·y /gáwdee/ *adj.* (**gaudier, gaudiest**) tastelessly bright or showy. □□ **gaud·i·ly** *adv.* **gaud·i·ness** *n.*

gauge /gayj/ *n. & v.* (also **gage**) ● *n.* **1** a standard measure, esp.: **a** the capacity of a barrel. **b** the fineness of a textile. **c** the diameter of a bullet. **d** the thickness of sheet metal. **2** any of various instruments for measuring this, or for measuring other dimensions or properties. **3** the distance between a pair of rails or the wheels on one axle. **4** the capacity,

---

GASTROPOD

All gastropods, whether marine or land-dwelling, move on a single flat, muscular foot and are equipped with tentacles and a radula – a rasping, tonguelike organ. Marine gastropods respire through gills, while many freshwater and land gastropods have lungs. Most are cased in a protective shell.

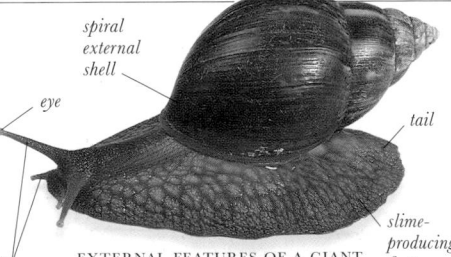

spiral external shell

eye

tail

tentacles

slime-producing foot

EXTERNAL FEATURES OF A GIANT AFRICAN SNAIL (*Achatina fulica*)

EXAMPLES OF OTHER GASTROPODS

GREAT POND SNAIL (*Lymnaea stagnalis*)

COMMON PERIWINKLE (*Littorina littorea*)

DOG WHELK (*Nucella lapillus*)

LETTUCE SLUG (*Elysia crispata*)

SEA LEMON (*Archidoris pseudoargus*)

LARGE BLACK SLUG (*Arion ater*)

extent, or scope of something. **5** a means of estimating. **6** *Naut.* a relative position with respect to the wind. ● *v.tr.* **1** measure exactly (esp. objects of standard size). **2** determine the capacity or content of. **3** estimate or form a judgment of (a person, situation, etc.). □□ **gaug·er** *n.*

Gaul /gawl/ *n.* a native or inhabitant of ancient Gaul.

gau·lei·ter /gówlītər/ *n.* **1** an official governing a district under Nazi rule. **2** a local or petty tyrant.

Gaul·ish /gáwlish/ *adj. & n.* ● *adj.* of or relating to the ancient Gauls. ● *n.* their language.

Gaull·ism /gólizəm, gáw-/ *n.* **1** the principles and policies of Charles de Gaulle, French military and political leader (d. 1970), characterized by their conservatism, nationalism, and advocacy of centralized government. **2** adherence to these. □□ **Gaull·ist** *n.*

gaunt /gawnt/ *adj.* **1** lean; haggard. **2** grim or desolate in appearance. □□ **gaunt·ly** *adv.* **gaunt·ness** *n.*

gaunt·let[1] /gáwntlit/ *n.* **1** a stout glove with a long loose wrist. **2** *hist.* ◄ an armored glove. ▷ ARMOR. **3** a chalz **down the gauntlet**).

gaunt·let[2] /gáwntlit/ *n.* □ **run the gauntlet 1** be subjected to harsh criticism. **2** pass between two rows

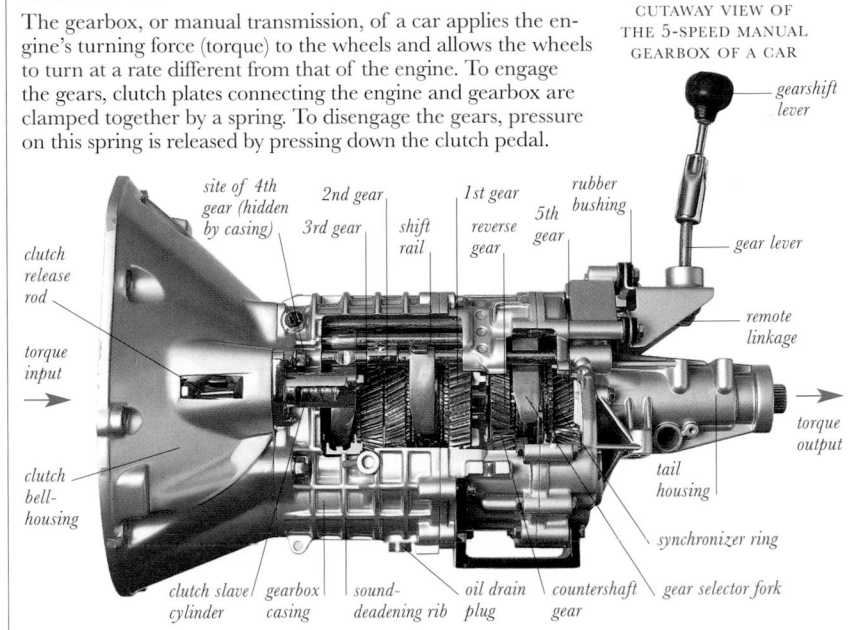

GAUNTLETS FROM A 16TH-CENTURY ITALIAN SUIT OF ARMOR

of people and receive blows from them, as a punishment or ordeal.

gauss /gows/ *n.* (*pl.* same or **gausses**) a unit of magnetic induction, equal to one ten-thousandth of a tesla.

Gauss·i·an dis·tri·bu·tion /gówseeən/ *n. Statistics* = NORMAL DISTRIBUTION.

gauze /gawz/ *n.* **1** a thin transparent fabric of silk, cotton, etc. **2** a fine mesh of wire, etc. **3** a slight haze.

gauz·y /gáwzee/ *adj.* (**gauzier, gauziest**) **1** like gauze; thin and translucent. **2** flimsy; delicate. □□ **gauz·i·ly** *adv.* **gauz·i·ness** *n.*

gave past of GIVE.

gav·el /gávəl/ *n. & v.* ● *n.* a small hammer used by an auctioneer, or for calling a meeting, courtroom, etc., to order.

ga·votte /gəvót/ *n.* **1** an old French dance in moderately quick 4/4 time. **2** the music for this.

gawk /gawk/ *v. & n.* ● *v.intr. colloq.* stare stupidly. ● *n.* an awkward or bashful person. □□ **gawk·ish** *adj.*

gawk·y /gáwkee/ *adj.* (**gawkier, gawkiest**) awkward or ungainly. □□ **gawk·i·ly** *adv.* **gawk·i·ness** *n.*

gawp /gawp/ *v.intr. Brit. colloq.* stare stupidly or obtrusively. □□ **gawp·er** *n.*

gay /gay/ *adj. & n.* ● *adj.* **1** lighthearted and carefree. **2 a** homosexual. **b** intended for or used by homosexuals (*a gay bar*). ¶ Generally informal in use, but often favored by esp. male homosexuals with ref. to themselves. **3** brightly colored; showy, brilliant (*a gay scarf*). ● *n.* a homosexual, esp. male. □□ **gay·ness** *n.*

ga·za·ni·a /gəzáyneeə/ *n.* any herbaceous plant of the genus *Gazania*, with showy yellow or orange daisy-shaped flowers.

gaze /gayz/ *v. & n.* ● *v.intr.* (foll. by *at, into*, etc.) look fixedly. ● *n.* a fixed or intent look. □□ **gaz·er** *n.*

GEARBOX

The gearbox, or manual transmission, of a car applies the engine's turning force (torque) to the wheels and allows the wheels to turn at a rate different from that of the engine. To engage the gears, clutch plates connecting the engine and gearbox are clamped together by a spring. To disengage the gears, pressure on this spring is released by pressing down the clutch pedal.

CUTAWAY VIEW OF THE 5-SPEED MANUAL GEARBOX OF A CAR

gearshift lever · *site of 4th gear (hidden by casing)* · *2nd gear* · *3rd gear* · *1st gear* · *5th gear* · *reverse gear* · *shift rail* · *rubber bushing* · *gear lever* · *clutch release rod* · *torque input* · *remote linkage* · *clutch bell-housing* · *torque output* · *tail housing* · *synchronizer ring* · *clutch slave cylinder* · *gearbox casing* · *sound-deadening rib* · *oil drain plug* · *countershaft gear* · *gear selector fork*

G

---

ga·ze·bo /gəzéebō/ *n.* (*pl.* **-os** or **-oes**) a summerhouse or turret designed to give a wide view.

ga·zelle /gəzél/ *n.* ◄ any of various small graceful soft-eyed antelopes of Asia or Africa, esp. of the genus *Gazella*.

ga·zette /gəzét/ *n.* a newspaper.

gaz·et·teer /gázitéer/ *n.* a geographical index or dictionary.

ga·zill·ion /gəzílyən/ *n. N. Amer. colloq.* a very large number or quantity.

gaz·pa·cho /gəspaáchō/ *n.* (*pl.* **-os**) a Spanish soup made with tomatoes, oil, garlic, onions, etc., and served cold.

GB *abbr.* Great Britain.

GDP *abbr.* gross domestic product.

GDR *abbr. hist.* German Democratic Republic.

gear /geer/ *n. & v.* ● *n.* **1** (often in *pl.*) a set of toothed wheels that work together to transmit and control motion from an engine, esp. to the road wheels of a vehicle. ▷ DERAILLEUR, GEARBOX. **2** a particular function or state of adjustment of engaged gears (*second gear*). **3** a mechanism of wheels, levers, etc., usu. for a special purpose (*winding gear*). **4** a particular apparatus or mechanism, as specified (*landing gear*). **5** equipment or tackle for a special purpose. **6** *colloq.* **a** clothing, esp. when modern or fashionable. **b** possessions in general. **7** goods; household utensils. **8** rigging. **9** a harness for a draft animal. ● *v.* **1** *tr.* (foll. by *to*) adjust or adapt to suit a special purpose or need. **2** *tr.* (often foll. by *up*) equip with gears. **3** *tr.* (foll. by *up*) make ready or prepared. **4** *tr.* put (machinery) in gear. **5** *intr.* **a** *Brit.* be in gear. **b** (foll. by *with*) work smoothly with. □ **be geared** (or **all geared**) **up** *colloq.* be ready or enthusiastic. **in gear** with a gear engaged. **out of gear 1** with no gear engaged. **2** out of order.

gear·box /géerboks/ *n.* **1** the casing that encloses a set of gears. **2** ▲ a set of gears with its casing, esp. in a motor vehicle; a transmission. ▷ CLUTCH, SYNCHROMESH

gear·ing /géering/ *n.* **1** a set or arrangement of gears in a machine. **2** *Brit. Commerce* = LEVERAGE 5.

gear·shift /géershift/ *n.* a lever used to engage or change gear, esp. in a motor vehicle.

gear·wheel /géerhweel, -weel/ *n.* **1** a toothed wheel in a set of gears. ▷ OBSERVATORY. **2** (in a bi-

---

cycle) the cogwheel driven directly by the chain. ▷ BICYCLE

geck·o /gékō/ *n.* (*pl.* **-os** or **-oes**) ► any of various house lizards found in warm climates, with adhesive feet for climbing vertical surfaces. ▷ LIZARD

gee[1] /jee/ *int.* (also **gee whiz** /wiz/) *colloq.* a mild expression of surprise, etc.

gee[2] /jee/ *int.* (often foll. by *up*) a command to a horse, etc., esp. to turn to the right or to go faster.

gee[3] /jee/ *n. sl.* (usu. in *pl.*) a thousand dollars.

geek /geek/ *n. sl.* **1** a person who is socially inept or tediously conventional; a dupe. **2** a carnival performer who bites the heads off live chickens.

geese *pl.* of GOOSE.

gee·zer /géezər/ *n. sl.* a person, esp. an old man.

Ge·hen·na /gihénə/ *n.* **1** (in the New Testament) hell. **2** a place of burning, torment, or misery.

Gei·ger count·er /gígər/ *n.* ▼ a device for measuring radioactivity by detecting and counting ionizing particles.

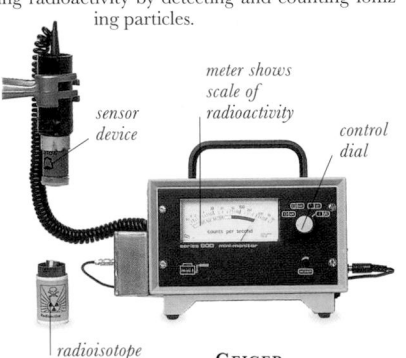

meter shows scale of radioactivity · *sensor device* · *control dial* · *radioisotope in lead box*

GEIGER COUNTER

GAZELLE: THOMSON'S GAZELLE (*Gazella thomsoni*)

GECKO: TOKAY GECKO (*Gekko gecko*)

GEM

Some 50 minerals are commonly used as gems. Normally, the surface of a gem is cut into flat faces, known as facets. The lapidary who cuts the stone aims to display its best features, most notably its color, clarity, and size. However, some aspects may be compromised to preserve the weight – and thus the value – of the gem.

MAIN TYPES OF CUT

BRILLIANT CUTS

ROUND

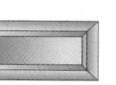

OVAL

STEP CUTS

TABLE

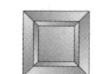

SQUARE

OCTAGONAL

BAGUETTE

OVAL

SIMPLE CUT

CABOCHON

MIXED CUTS

CUSHION

MIXED

FANCY CUTS

PENDELOQUE

SCISSORS

MARQUISE

YELLOW/BROWN GEMS

CARNELIAN

SARDONYX

CITRINE

HESSONITE

CASSITERITE

AMBER

FIRE OPAL

HYPERSTHENE

GREEN GEMS

JADEITE

EMERALD

HIDDENITE

MALACHITE

PERIDOT

MOLDAVITE

BLUE/VIOLET GEMS

SAPPHIRE

LAPIS LAZULI

AMETHYST

TURQUOISE

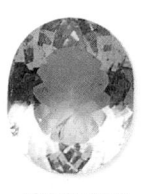

AQUAMARINE

SODALITE

RED/PINK GEMS

RUBY

RHODONITE

KUNZITE

PYROPE

COLORLESS GEMS

DIAMOND

ROCK CRYSTAL

SCHEELITE

PETALITE

WHITE GEMS

PEARL

MILKY QUARTZ

BLACK GEMS

JET

SCHORL

IRIDESCENT GEMS

FIRE AGATE

OPAL

LABRADORITE

G

gei·sha /gáyshə, gée-/ n. (pl. same or **geishas**) a Japanese hostess trained in entertaining men with dance and song.

gel /jel/ n. & v. ● n. **1** a semisolid colloidal suspension or jelly, of a solid dispersed in a liquid. **2** a gelatinous hair-styling preparation. ● v.intr. (**gelled**, **gelling**) form a gel.

gel·a·tin /jélətin/ n. (also **gel·a·tine** /-teen/) a virtually colorless, tasteless, transparent, water-soluble protein derived from collagen and used in food preparation, photography, etc. □□ **gel·at·i·nize** /jilát´nīz/ v.tr. & intr. **ge·lat·i·ni·za·tion** /jilát´nizáyshən/ n.

ge·lat·i·nous /jilát´nəs/ adj. **1** of or like gelatin. **2** of a jellylike consistency. □□ **ge·lat·i·nous·ly** adv.

ge·la·tion /jiláyshən/ n. solidification by freezing.

ge·la·to /jəláatō/ n. a kind of Italian ice cream.

geld /geld/ v.tr. **1** deprive (usu. a male animal) of the ability to reproduce. **2** castrate or spay; excise the testicles or ovaries of.

geld·ing /gélding/ n. a gelded animal, esp. a male horse.

gel·id /jélid/ adj. **1** icy; ice cold. **2** chilly; cool.

gel·ig·nite /jélignīt/ n. an explosive made from nitroglycerine, cellulose nitrate, sodium or potassium nitrate, and wood pulp.

gem /jem/ n. & v. ● n. **1** ◀ a precious or semi-precious stone, esp. when cut and polished or engraved. **2** an object or person of great beauty or worth. ● v.tr. (**gemmed**, **gemming**) adorn with or as with gems. □□ **gem·like** adj.

Ge·ma·ra /gimáarə, -máwrə, -maaráa/ n. a rabbinical commentary forming the second part of the Talmud.

gem·i·nate adj. & v. ● adj. /jéminət/ combined in pairs. ● v.tr. /jéminayt/ **1** double; repeat. **2** arrange in pairs. □□ **gem·i·na·tion** n.

Gem·i·ni /jémini, -nee/ n. **1** ▼ a constellation, traditionally regarded as contained in the figures of twins. **2** a the third sign of the zodiac (the Twins). ▷ ZODIAC. **b** a person born when the Sun is in this sign. □□ **Gem·i·ne·an** /jéminéeən, -níən/ n. & adj.

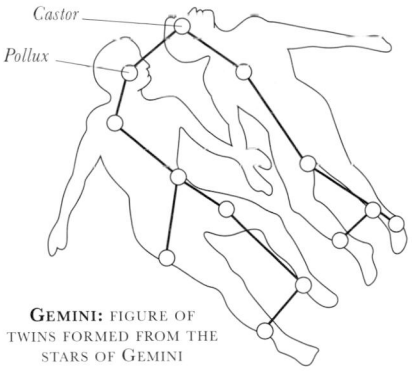

GEMINI: FIGURE OF
TWINS FORMED FROM THE
STARS OF GEMINI

gem·ma /jémə/ n. (pl. **gemmae** /-mee/) a small cellular body in cryptogams that separates from the mother plant and starts a new one; an asexual spore.

gem·mif·er·ous /jemífərəs/ adj. **1** producing precious stones. **2** bearing buds.

gem·ol·o·gy /jemóləjee/ n. (also **gem·mol·o·gy**) the study of gems. □□ **gem·ol·o·gist** or **gem·mol·o·gist** n.

gem·stone /jémstōn/ n. a precious stone used as a gem.

Gen. abbr. General.

-gen /jən/ comb. form **1** Chem. that which produces (hydrogen; antigen). **2** Bot. growth (endogen; exogen; acrogen).

gen·darme /zhondáarm/ n. **1** a police officer, esp. in France. **2** a soldier, mounted or on foot, employed in police duties, esp. in France. **3** a rocktower on a mountain, occupying and blocking an arête.

GENE

Genes, transmitted from parents and previous forebears, determine the heritable characteristics of animals and plants. Consisting of a specific sequence of DNA building blocks, the nucleotides, genes are arranged along chromosomes in the nuclei of sperm and egg cells, which fuse during fertilization. A new individual is thus created, possessing a blend of genetic information from each parent.

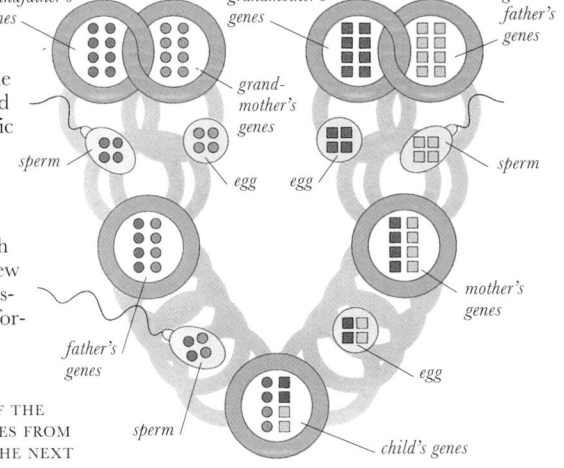

DEMONSTRATION OF THE
TRANSMISSION OF GENES FROM
ONE GENERATION TO THE NEXT

gen·der /jéndər/ n. **1 a** the grammatical classification of nouns and related words, roughly corresponding to the two sexes and sexlessness. **b** each of the classes of nouns (see MASCULINE, FEMININE, NEUTER, COMMON adj. 6). **2** (of nouns and related words) the property of belonging to such a class. **3** colloq. a person's sex.

gen·der bend·er n. a person or thing not conforming to sexual stereotypes.

gene /jeen/ n. ▲ a unit of heredity composed of DNA or RNA and forming part of a chromosome, etc., that determines a particular characteristic of an individual. ▷ DNA

ge·ne·a·log·i·cal /jéeneeəlójikəl/ adj. **1** of or concerning genealogy. **2** tracing family descent. □□ **ge·ne·a·log·i·cal·ly** adv.

ge·ne·al·o·gy /jéeneeáləjee/ n. (pl. **-ies**) **1 a** a line of descent traced continuously from an ancestor. **b** an account of this. **2** the study and investigation of lines of descent. **3** a plant's or animal's line of development from earlier forms. □□ **ge·ne·a·lo·gist** n. **ge·ne·a·lo·gize** v.tr. & intr.

gene pool n. the stock of different genes in an interbreeding population.

gen·er·a pl. of GENUS.

gen·er·al /jénərəl/ adj. & n. ● adj. **1 a** completely or almost universal. **b** including or affecting all or nearly all parts or cases of things. **2** prevalent; widespread; usual. **3** not partial, particular, local, or sectional. **4** not limited in application; relating to whole classes or all cases. **5** including points common to the individuals of a class and neglecting the differences (a general term). **6** not restricted or specialized (general knowledge). **7 a** roughly corresponding or adequate. **b** sufficient for practical purposes. **8** not detailed (a general resemblance; a general idea). **9** vague; indefinite (spoke only in general terms). **10** chief or principal; having overall authority (general manager; Secretary General). ● n. **1 a** an army officer ranking next above lieutenant general. **b** = BRIGADIER GENERAL, LIEUTENANT GENERAL, MAJOR GENERAL. **2** a commander of an army. **3** a tactician or strategist of specified merit (a great general). **4** the head of a religious order, e.g., of the Jesuits or Dominicans or the Salvation Army. **5** (prec. by the) archaic the public. □ **in general 1** as a normal rule; usually. **2** for the most part. □□ **gen·er·al·ness** n.

gen·er·al e·lec·tion n. the election of representatives to a legislature from constituencies throughout the country.

gen·er·al head·quar·ters n. the headquarters of a military commander.

gen·er·al·is·si·mo /jénərəlísimō/ n. (pl. **-os**) the commander of a combined military force in some countries consisting of army, navy, and air force units.

gen·er·al·ist /jénərəlist/ n. a person competent in several different fields or activities (opp. SPECIALIST).

gen·er·al·i·ty /jénərálitee/ n. (pl. **-ies**) **1** a statement or principle, etc., having general validity or force. **2** applicability to a whole class of instances. **3** vagueness; lack of detail. **4** (foll. by of) the main body or majority.

gen·er·al·i·za·tion /jénərəlizáyshən/ n. **1** a general notion or proposition obtained by inference from particular cases. **2** the act of generalizing.

gen·er·al·ize /jénərəlīz/ v. **1** intr. **a** speak in general or indefinite terms. **b** form general principles or notions. **2** tr. reduce to a general statement, principle, or notion. **3** tr. give a general character to. **4** tr. infer (a law or conclusion) by induction. **5** tr. Math. & Philos. express in a general form; extend the application of. **6** tr. (in painting) render only the typical characteristics of. **7** tr. bring into general use. □□ **gen·er·al·iz·a·ble** adj. **gen·er·al·iz·a·bil·i·ty** n. **gen·er·al·iz·er** n.

gen·er·al·ly /jénərəlee/ adv. **1** usually; in most cases. **2** in a general sense; without regard to particulars or exceptions (generally speaking). **3** for the most part; extensively (not generally known). **4** in most respects (they were generally well-behaved).

gen·er·al of the ar·my (or **air force**) n. the officer of the highest rank in the army or air force.

gen·er·al prac·ti·tion·er n. a doctor working in the community and treating cases of all kinds in the first instance.

gen·er·al store n. a store, usu. located in a rural area, that carries a wide variety of items, as food, clothing, etc., without being divided into departments.

gen·er·ate /jénərayt/ v.tr. **1** bring into existence. **2** produce (electricity). □□ **gen·er·a·ble** /-rəbəl/ adj.

gen·er·a·tion /jénəráyshən/ n. **1** all the people born at a particular time, regarded collectively (my generation; the next generation). **2** a single step in descent or pedigree (have known them for three generations). **3** a stage in (esp. technological) development (fourth-generation computers). **4** the average time in which children are ready to take the place of their parents (usu. figured at about 30 years). **5** production by natural or artificial process, esp. the production of electricity or heat. **6 a** procreation; the propagation of species. **b** the act of begetting or being begotten. □□ **gen·er·a·tion·al** adj.

gen·er·a·tion gap n. difference of outlook or opinion between those of different generations.

Gen·er·a·tion X n. term used for people born from about 1965 to 1975 (fr. a novel by Douglas Coupland).

G

G

gen·er·a·tive /jénərətiv, -raytiv/ *adj.* **1** of or concerning procreation. **2** able to produce; productive.

gen·er·a·tor /jénəraytər/ *n.* **1** a machine for converting mechanical into electrical energy. ▷ HYDROELECTRIC, NUCLEAR POWER. **2** an apparatus for producing gas, steam, etc.

ge·ner·ic /jinérik/ *adj.* **1** characteristic of or relating to a class; general. **2** *Biol.* characteristic of or belonging to a genus. **3** (of goods, esp. a drug) having no brand name. □□ **ge·ner·i·cal·ly** *adv.*

gen·er·ous /jénərəs/ *adj.* **1** giving or given freely. **2** magnanimous; noble-minded. **3** ample; abundant (*a generous portion*). □□ **gen·er·os·i·ty** /-rósitee/ *n.* **gen·er·ous·ly** *adv.*

gen·e·sis /jénisis/ *n.* **1** the origin, or mode of formation, of a thing. **2** (**Genesis**) the first book of the Old Testament.

gen·et /jénit/ *n.* **1** ▼ any catlike mammal of the genus *Genetta*, native to Africa and S. Europe, with spotted fur and a long ringed bushy tail. **2** the fur of the genet.

GENET:
COMMON GENET
(*Genetta genetta*)

gene ther·a·py *n. Med.* the introduction of normal genes into cells in place of defective or missing ones in order to correct genetic disorders.

ge·net·ic /jinétik/ *adj.* **1** of genetics or genes; inherited. **2** of, in, or concerning origin; causal. □□ **ge·net·i·cal·ly** *adv.*

ge·net·i·cal·ly mod·i·fied *adj.* (of an organism) containing genetic material that has been artificially altered so as to produce a desired characteristic.

ge·net·ic code *n. Biochem.* the means by which genetic information is stored as sequences of nucleotide bases in the chromosomal DNA.

ge·net·ic en·gi·neer·ing *n.* the deliberate modification of the characteristics of an organism by the manipulation of DNA.

ge·net·ic fin·ger·print·ing *n.* (also **ge·net·ic pro·fil·ing**) the analysis of characteristic patterns in DNA as a means of identifying individuals.

ge·net·ics /jinétiks/ *n.pl.* (usu. treated as *sing.*) the study of heredity and the variation of inherited characteristics. □□ **ge·net·i·cist** /-tisist/ *n.*

Ge·ne·va Con·ven·tion /jinéevə/ *n.* an international agreement first made at Geneva in 1864 and later revised, governing the status and treatment of prisoners and the sick, wounded, and dead in battle.

ge·ni·al /jéeneeəl/ *adj.* **1** jovial; sociable; kindly; cheerful. **2** (of the climate) mild and warm; conducive to growth. **3** cheering; enlivening. □□ **ge·ni·al·i·ty** /-neeálitee/ *n.* **gen·ial·ly** *adv.*

-genic /jénik/ *comb. form* forming adjectives meaning: **1** producing (*carcinogenic; pathogenic*). **2** well suited to (*photogenic; radiogenic*). **3** produced by (*iatrogenic*). □□ **-genically** *suffix* forming adverbs.

ge·nie /jéenee/ *n.* (*pl.* usu. **genii** /jéenee-ī/) a jinni, goblin, or familiar spirit of Arabian folklore.

ge·ni·i *pl.* of GENIE, GENIUS.

ge·nis·ta /jinístə/ *n.* any almost leafless shrub of the genus *Genista*, with a profusion of yellow pea-shaped flowers, e.g., dyer's broom.

gen·i·tal /jénit'l/ *adj. & n.* ● *adj.* of or relating to animal reproduction. ● *n.* (in *pl.*) the external reproductive organs. ▷ REPRODUCTIVE ORGANS

gen·i·ta·li·a /jénitáyleeə/ *n.pl.* the genitals.

gen·i·tive /jénitiv/ *n. & adj. Gram.* ● *n.* the case of nouns and pronouns (and words in grammatical agreement with them) corresponding to *of, from*, and other prepositions and indicating possession or close association. ● *adj.* of or in the genitive. □□ **gen·i·ti·val** /-tívəl/ **gen·i·ti·val·ly** *adv.*

genito- /jénitō/ *comb. form* genital.

gen·i·to·u·ri·nar·y /jénitōyŏŏrinəree/ *adj.* of the genital and urinary organs. ▷ REPRODUCTIVE ORGANS, URINARY SYSTEM

gen·ius /jéenyəs/ *n.* (*pl.* **geniuses** or **genii** /-nee-ī/) **1** (*pl.* **geniuses**) **a** an exceptional intellectual or creative power or other natural ability or tendency. **b** a person having this. **2** the tutelary spirit of a person, place, institution, etc. **3** a person or spirit regarded as powerfully influencing a person for good or evil. **4** the prevalent feeling or associations, etc., of a nation, age, etc.

ge·ni·zah /gənéezə, -neezáá/ *n.* a room attached to a synagogue and housing damaged, discarded, or heretical books, etc., and sacred relics.

Gen·o·a jib *n.* (also **gen·o·a**, **jen·ny**) a large jib or foresail used esp. on yachts.

gen·o·cide /jénəsīd/ *n.* the deliberate extermination of a people or nation. □□ **gen·o·cid·al** /-síd'l/ *adj.*

ge·nome /jéenōm/ *n.* **1** the haploid set of chromosomes of an organism. **2** the genetic material of an organism.

ge·no·mics /jinŏmiks, jinómiks/ *n.* the branch of molecular biology concerned with the structure, function, evolution, and mapping of genomes.

gen·o·type /jéenətīp/ *n. Biol.* the genetic constitution of an individual. □□ **gen·o·typ·ic** /-típik/ *adj.*

-genous *comb. form* forming adjectives meaning 'produced' (*endogenous*).

gen·re /zhónrə/ *n.* **1** a kind or style, esp. of art or literature (e.g., novel, drama, satire). **2** (in full **genre painting**) the painting of scenes from ordinary life.

gens /jenz/ *n.* (*pl.* **gentes** /jénteez/) **1** *Rom.Hist.* a group of families sharing a name and claiming a common origin. **2** *Anthropol.* a number of people sharing descent through the male line.

gent /jent/ *n. colloq.* (often *joc.*) **1** a gentleman. **2** (**the Gents**) *Brit. colloq.* a men's public toilet.

gen·teel /jentéel/ *adj.* **1** affectedly or ostentatiously refined or stylish. **2** often *iron.* of or appropriate to the upper classes. □□ **gen·teel·ly** *adv.*

gen·tian /jénshən/ *n.* ▼ any plant of the genus *Gentiana* or *Gentianella*, found esp. in mountainous regions, and having usu. vivid blue flowers.

gen·tile /jéntīl/ *adj. & n.* (also **Gentile**) ● *adj.* **1** not Jewish. **2** (in the Mormon Church) not Mormon. ● *n.* **1** a person who is not Jewish. **2** (in the Mormon Church) a person who is not Mormon.

gen·til·i·ty /jentilitee/ *n.* **1** social superiority. **2** good manners.

gen·tle /jént'l/ *adj.* (**gentler, gentlest**) **1** mild or kind in temperament. **2** moderate; not severe or drastic (*a gentle rebuke; a gentle breeze*). **3** (of birth, pursuits, etc.) honorable; of or fit for people of good social position. **4** quiet

GENTIAN: SPRING
GENTIAN (*Gentiana verna*)

requiring patience (*gentle art*). □□ **gen·tle·ness** *n.* **gent·ly** *adv.*

gent·le·folk /jént'lfōk/ *n.pl. literary* people of good family.

gent·le·man /jént'lmən/ *n.* (*pl.* **-men**) **1** a man (in polite or formal use). **2** a chivalrous or well-bred man. **3** a man of good social position or of wealth and leisure (*country gentleman*). **4** esp. *Brit.* a man of gentle birth attached to a royal household (*gentleman in waiting*). **5** (in *pl.* as a form of address) a male audience or the male part of an audience.

gent·le·man·ly /jént'lmənlee/ *adj.* like a gentleman in looks or behavior; befitting a gentleman. □□ **gent·le·man·li·ness** *n.*

gent·le·man's (or **-men's**) **a·gree·ment** *n.* one which is binding in honor but not legally enforceable.

gent·le·wom·an /jént'lwŏŏmən/ *n.* (*pl.* **-women**) *archaic* a woman of good birth.

gen·too /jéntōō/ *n.* a penguin, *Pygoscelis papua*, esp. abundant in the Falkland Islands.

gen·tri·fi·ca·tion /jéntrifikáyshən/ *n.* the social advancement of an inner urban area by the refurbishing of buildings and arrival of affluent middle-class residents, usu. displacing poorer inhabitants. □□ **gen·tri·fy** /-fī/ *v.tr.* (**-ies, -ied**)

gen·try /jéntree/ *n.pl.* the people next below the nobility in position and birth.

gen·u·flect /jényəflekt/ *v.intr.* bend the knee, esp. in worship or as a sign of respect. □□ **gen·u·flec·tion** /-flékshən/ *n.* **gen·u·flec·tor** *n.*

gen·u·ine /jényōō-in/ *adj.* **1** actually coming from its stated or reputed source. **2** properly so called; not sham. **3** purebred. **4** (of a person) free from affectation or hypocrisy; honest. □□ **gen·u·ine·ly** *adv.* **gen·u·ine·ness** *n.*

ge·nus /jéenəs/ *n.* (*pl.* **genera** /jénərə/) **1** *Biol.* a taxonomic grouping of organisms having common characteristics distinct from those of other genera, usu. containing several or many species and being one of a series constituting a taxonomic family. **2** a kind or class having common characteristics. **3** *Logic* kinds of things including subordinate kinds or species.

-geny /jənee/ *comb. form* forming nouns meaning 'mode of production or development of' (*ontogeny; pathogeny*).

geo- /jée-ō/ *comb. form* earth.

ge·o·bot·a·ny /jéeōbót'nee/ *n.* the study of the geographical distribution of plants. □□ **ge·o·bot·a·nist** *n.*

ge·o·cen·tric /jéeōséntrik/ *adj.* **1** considered as viewed from the center of the Earth. **2** having the Earth as the center. □□ **ge·o·cen·tri·cal·ly** *adv.*

ge·o·chem·is·try /jéeōkémistree/ *n.* the chemistry of the Earth and its rocks, minerals, etc. □□ **ge·o·chem·i·cal** /-mikəl/ *adj.* **ge·o·chem·ist** /-mist/ *n.*

ge·o·chro·nol·o·gy /jéeōkrənóləjee/ *n.* **1** the study and measurement of geological time by means of geological events. **2** the ordering of geological events. □□ **ge·o·chron·o·log·i·cal** /-krónəlójikəl/ *adj.* **ge·o·chro·nol·o·gist** *n.*

ge·ode /jée-ōd/ *n.* **1** ▼ a small cavity lined with crystals or other mineral matter. **2** a rock containing such a cavity. □□ **ge·od·ic** /jee-ódik/ *adj.*

quartz crystals   *agate*   *geode*

GEODE FORMED WITHIN AGATE
(BANDED CHALCEDONY)

ge·o·des·ic /jéeədéezik, -désik/ *adj.* (also **ge·o·det·ic** /-détik/) **1** of or relating to geodesy. **2** of, involving, or consisting of a geodesic line.

ge·o·des·ic dome *n.* ▶ a dome constructed of short struts along geodesic lines.

ge·o·des·ic line *n.* the shortest possible line between two points on a curved surface.

ge·od·e·sy /jeeódisee/ *n.* the branch of mathematics dealing with the shape and area of the Earth. □□ **ge·od·e·sist** *n.*

ge·o·det·ic var. of GEODESIC.

geog. *abbr.* **1** geographer. **2** geographic. **3** geographical. **4** geography.

ge·o·graph·ic /jéeəgráfik/ *adj.* (also **ge·o·graph·i·cal** /-gráfikəl/) of or relating to geography. □□ **ge·o·graph·i·cal·ly** *adv.*

ge·o·graph·ic in·for·ma·tion sys·tem(s) *n.* a computerized system utilizing precise locational data for mapping, navigation, etc. ¶ Abbr.: **GIS**.

ge·og·ra·phy /jeeógrəfee/ *n.* **1** the study of the Earth's physical features, resources, and climate, and the physical aspects of its population. **2** the main physical features of an area. **3** the layout or arrangement of any set of constituent elements. □□ **ge·og·ra·pher** *n.*

geol. *abbr.* **1** geologic. **2** geological. **3** geologist. **4** geology.

ge·ol·o·gy /jeeóləjee/ *n.* **1** the science of the Earth, including the composition, structure, and origin of its rocks. ▷ ROCK CYCLE. **2** this science applied to any other planet. **3** the geological features of a district. □□ **ge·o·log·ic** /jéeəlójik/ *adj.* **ge·o·log·i·cal** *adj.* **ge·o·log·i·cal·ly** *adv.* **ge·ol·o·gist** /-óləjist/ *n.*

geom. *abbr.* **1** geometric. **2** geometrical. **3** geometry.

ge·o·mag·net·ism /jéeōmágnitizəm/ *n.* the study of the magnetic properties of the Earth. □□ **ge·o·mag·net·ic** /-magnétik/ *adj.*

ge·o·man·cy /jéeōmánsee/ *n.* divination from the configuration of a handful of earth or random dots, lines, or figures. □□ **ge·o·man·tic** /-mántik/ *adj.*

ge·om·e·ter /jeeómitər/ *n.* **1** a person skilled in geometry. **2** (also **ge·om·e·trid**) any moth, esp. of the family Geometridae, having twiglike larvae which move in a looping fashion, seeming to measure the ground.

ge·o·met·ric /jeeəmétrik/ *adj.* (also **ge·o·met·ri·cal**) **1** of, according to, or like geometry. **2** (of a design, etc.) characterized by or decorated with regular lines and shapes. □□ **ge·o·met·ri·cal·ly** *adv.*

ge·o·met·ric pro·gres·sion *n.* a progression of numbers with a constant ratio between each number and the one before (as 1, 3, 9, 27, 81).

ge·om·e·trid /jeeómitrid/ *n.* = GEOMETER 2.

ge·om·e·try /jeeómitree/ *n.* **1** the branch of mathematics concerned with the properties and relations of points, lines, surfaces, and solids. **2** the relative arrangement of objects or parts. □□ **ge·om·e·tri·cian** /jéeəmitríshən/ *n.*

ge·o·mor·phol·o·gy /jéeōmawrfóləjee/ *n.* the study of the physical features of the surface of the Earth and their relation to its geological structures. □□ **ge·o·mor·pho·log·i·cal** /-fəlójikəl/ *adj.* **ge·o·mor·phol·o·gist** *n.*

ge·oph·a·gy /jeeófəjee/ *n.* the practice of eating earth.

ge·o·phys·ics /jée-ōfiziks/ *n.* the physics of the Earth. □□ **ge·o·phys·i·cal** *adj.* **ge·o·phys·i·cist** /-zisist/ *n.*

ge·o·pol·i·tics /jée-ōpólitiks/ *n.* **1** the politics of a country as determined by its geographical features. **2** the study of this. □□ **ge·o·po·lit·i·cal** /-pəlítikəl/ *adj.* **ge·o·po·lit·i·cal·ly** *adv.* **ge·o·pol·i·ti·cian** /-tíshən/ *n.*

George Cross /jawrj/ *n.* (also **George Med·al**) (in the UK) a decoration for bravery awarded esp. to civilians, instituted in 1940 by King George VI.

geor·gette /jawrjét/ *n.* a thin silk or crêpe dress material.

Geor·gian[1] /jáwrjən/ *adj. & n.* ● *adj.* of or relating to the state of Georgia. ● *n.* a native of Georgia.

Geor·gian[2] /jáwrjən/ *adj.* **1** of or characteristic of the time of Kings George I–IV (1714–1830). **2** of or characteristic of the time of Kings George V and VI (1910–52).

Geor·gian[3] /jáwrjən/ *adj. & n.* ● *adj.* of or relating to Georgia in the Caucasus. ● *n.* **1** a native of Georgia; a person of Georgian descent. **2** the language of Georgia.

ge·o·sphere /jéeəsfeer/ *n.* **1** the solid surface of the Earth. **2** any of the almost spherical concentric regions of the Earth and its atmosphere.

ge·o·sta·tion·ar·y /jée-ōstáyshənəree/ *adj.* = GEOSYNCHRONOUS.

ge·o·stroph·ic /jée-ōstrófik/ *adj.* *Meteorol.* depending upon the rotation of the Earth.

ge·o·syn·chro·nous /jée-ōsíngkrənəs/ *adj.* ▶ (of an artificial satellite of the Earth) moving in an orbit equal to the Earth's period of rotation. Also called **geostationary**.

ge·o·ther·mal /jée-ōthɔ́rməl/ *adj.* relating to, originating from, or produced by the internal heat of the Earth.

ge·ot·ro·pism /jeeótrəpizəm/ *n.* plant growth in relation to gravity. ■ **negative geotropism** the tendency of stems, etc., to grow away from the center of the Earth. **positive geotropism** the tendency of roots to grow toward the center of the Earth. □□ **ge·o·tro·pic** /jéeətrópik, -ōtrópik/ *adj.*

ge·ra·ni·um /jəráyneeəm/ *n.* **1** ◀ any herb or shrub of the genus *Geranium* bearing fruit shaped like the bill of a crane. **2** (in general use) a cultivated pelargonium.

ger·ber·a /jɔ́rbərə/ *n.* any composite plant of the genus *Gerbera* of Africa or Asia, esp. the Transvaal daisy.

ger·bil /jɔ́rbil/ *n.* ▶ a mouselike desert rodent of the subfamily Gerbillinae, with long hind legs. ▷ RODENT

ger·e·nuk /gérənook/ *n.* an antelope, *Litocranius walleri*, native to E. Africa, with a very long neck and small head.

ger·i·at·ric /jéreeátrik/ *adj. & n.* ● *adj.* **1** of or relating to old people. **2** *colloq.* old; outdated. ● *n.* an old person, esp. one receiving special care.

ger·i·at·rics /jéreeátriks/ *n.pl.* (usu. treated as *sing.*) a branch of medicine or social science dealing with the health and care of old people. □□ **ger·i·a·tri·cian** /-ətríshən/ *n.*

germ /jɔrm/ *n.* **1** a microorganism, esp. one which causes disease. **2 a** a portion of an organism capable of developing into a new one; the rudiment of an animal or plant. **b** an embryo of a seed (*wheat germ*). **3** an original idea, etc., from which something may develop.

Ger·man /jɔ́rmən/ *n. & adj.* ● *n.* **1** a native or inhabitant of Germany; a person of German descent. **2** the language of Germany, also used in Austria and Switzerland. ● *adj.* of or relating to Germany or its people or language.

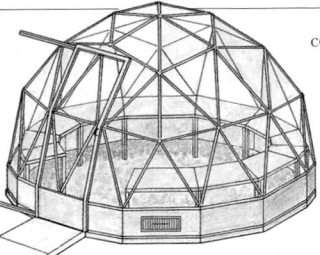

GEODESIC DOME: DOME-SHAPED GREENHOUSE

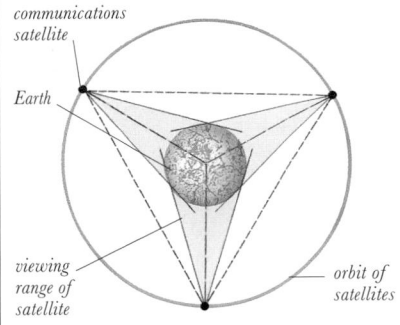

GEOSYNCHRONOUS

A satellite placed 22,296 miles (35,880 km) above the equator takes 24 hours to travel its orbit ▪ the time it takes the Earth to spin on its axis – and so seems to hover over the Earth's surface. Three evenly spaced satellites can thus view the entire globe.

communications satellite

Earth

viewing range of satellite

orbit of satellites

VIEWING RANGE OF SATELLITES IN GEOSYNCHRONOUS ORBIT (NOT TO SCALE)

G

ger·man /jɔ́rmən/ *adj.* (placed after *brother*, *sister*, or *cousin*) **1** having the same parents. **2** having the same grandparents on one side.

ger·mane /jərmáyn/ *adj.* (usu. foll. by *to*) relevant (to a subject under consideration). □□ **ger·mane·ly** *adv.* **ger·mane·ness** *n.*

Ger·man·ic /jərmánik/ *adj. & n.* ● *adj.* **1** having German characteristics. **2** *hist.* of the Germans. **3** of the Scandinavians, Anglo-Saxons, or Germans. **4** of the languages or language group called Germanic. ● *n.* **1** the branch of Indo-European languages including English, German, Dutch, and the Scandinavian languages. **2** the (unrecorded) early language from which other Germanic languages developed.

ger·man·ic /jərmánik/ *adj.* *Chem.* of or containing germanium, esp. in its tetravalent state.

Ger·man·ist /jɔ́rmənist/ *n.* an expert in or student of the language, literature, and civilization of Germany, or Germanic languages.

ger·ma·ni·um /jərmáyneeəm/ *n.* *Chem.* a lustrous brittle semimetallic element occurring naturally in sulfide ores and used in semiconductors. ¶ Symb.: **Ge**.

Ger·man·ize /jɔ́rmənīz/ *v.tr. & intr.* adopt or cause to adopt German customs, etc. □□ **Ger·man·i·za·tion** *n.* **Ger·man·i·zer** *n.*

Ger·man mea·sles *n.* a contagious disease, rubella, with symptoms like mild measles.

Ger·man shep·herd *n.* **1** a large breed of dog bred from the wolfhound, used in police work, as guide dogs for the blind, etc. **2** ▶ a dog of this breed.

fruit

GERANIUM: HEDGEROW CRANESBILL (*Geranium pyrenaicum*)

GERBIL: PALLID GERBIL (*Meriones unguiculatus*)

GERMAN SHEPHERD

G

GERMINATE

A germinating seed absorbs water and swells. Food stored in the cotyledons (seed leaves) or endosperm allows the embryo to grow. In hypogeal germination, cotyledons remain below ground as the shoot develops. In epigeal germination (right), cotyledons are borne above the soil on an epicotyl. As the cotyledons turn green, they begin to produce food through photosynthesis, withering as the true leaves unfurl.

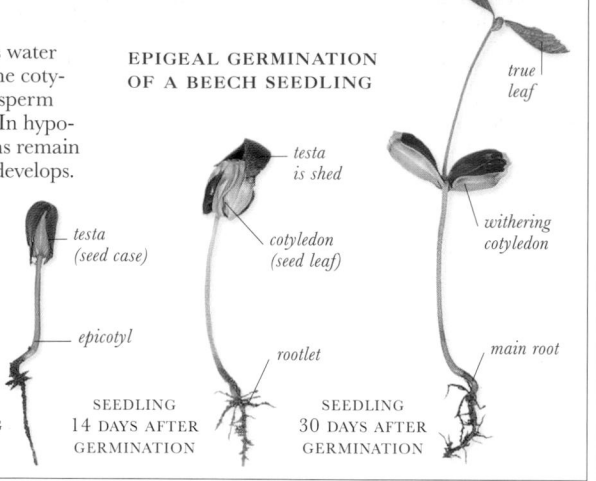

EPIGEAL GERMINATION OF A BEECH SEEDLING

true leaf

testa is shed

cotyledon (seed case)

cotyledon (seed leaf)

withering cotyledon

epicotyl

rootlet

main root

GERMINATING SEEDLING

SEEDLING 14 DAYS AFTER GERMINATION

SEEDLING 30 DAYS AFTER GERMINATION

ger·mi·cide /jə́rmisīd/ *n.* a substance destroying germs, esp. those causing disease. □□ **ger·mi·cid·al** /-síd'l/ *adj.*

ger·mi·nal /jə́rminəl/ *adj.* **1** relating to or of the nature of a germ or germs (see GERM 1). **2** in the earliest stage of development. **3** productive of new ideas. □□ **ger·mi·nal·ly** *adv.*

ger·mi·nate /jə́rminayt/ *v.* **1 a** *intr.* ▲ sprout, bud, or put forth shoots. **b** *tr.* cause to sprout or shoot. **2 a** *tr.* cause (ideas, etc.) to originate. **b** *intr.* come into existence. □□ **ger·mi·na·tion** /-náyshən/ *n.*

germ war·fare *n.* the systematic spreading of microorganisms to cause disease in an enemy population.

ger·on·tol·o·gy /jərontóləjee/ *n.* the scientific study of old age, the process of aging, and the special problems of old people. □□ **ge·ron·to·log·i·cal** /-təlójikəl/ *adj.* **ger·on·tol·o·gist** *n.*

-gerous /jərəs/ *comb. form* forming adjectives meaning 'bearing'.

ger·ry·man·der /jérimándər/ *v.tr.* **1** manipulate the boundaries of (a constituency, etc.) so as to give undue influence to some party or class. **2** manipulate (a situation, etc.) to gain advantage. □□ **ger·ry·man·der·er** *n.*

ger·und /jérənd/ *n. Gram.* a form of a verb functioning as a noun, orig. in Latin ending in *-ndum* (declinable), in English ending in *-ing* and used distinctly as a part of a verb (e.g., *do you mind my asking?*).

ge·run·dive /jərúndiv/ *n. Gram.* a form of a Latin verb, ending in *-ndus* (declinable) and functioning as an adjective meaning 'that should or must be done,' etc.

GESSO: DESIGN DRAWN INTO GESSO

ges·so /jésō/ *n.* (*pl.* **-oes**) ◄ plaster of Paris or gypsum as used in painting or sculpture.

ge·stalt /gəshtaált, -staált, -shtáwlt, -stawlt/ *n. Psychol.* an organized whole that is perceived as more than the sum of its parts. □□ **ge·stalt·ism** *n.* **ge·stalt·ist** *n.*

Ge·sta·po /gestaápō, -shtaá-/ *n.* **1** the German secret police under Nazi rule. **2** *derog.* an organization compared to this.

ges·tate /jéstáyt/ *v.tr.* **1** carry (a fetus) in gestation. **2** develop (an idea, etc.).

ges·ta·tion /jestáyshən/ *n.* **1 a** ► the process of carrying or being carried in the womb between conception and birth. **b** this period. **2** the private development of a plan, idea, etc.

ges·tic·u·late /jestíkyəlayt/ *v.* **1** *intr.* use gestures

instead of or in addition to speech. **2** *tr.* express with gestures. □□ **ges·tic·u·la·tion** /-láyshən/ *n.* **ges·tic·u·la·tive** /-lətawree/ *adj.* **ges·tic·u·la·to·ry** /-lətáwree/ *adj.*

ges·ture /jés-chər/ *n. & v.* ● *n.* **1** a significant movement of a limb or the body. **2** the use of such movements, esp. as a rhetorical device. **3** an action to evoke a response or convey intention, usu. friendly. ● *v.tr. & intr.* gesticulate. □□ **ges·tur·al** *adj.*

ge·sund·heit /gəzŏŏnt-hīt/ *int.* expressing a wish of good health, esp. to a person who has sneezed.

get /get/ *v.* (**getting**; *past* **got** /got/; *past part.* **got** /got/, **gotten** /gót'n/) **1** *tr.* come into the possession of (*get a job*; *got $200 a week*). **2** *tr.* fetch; obtain (*get my book for me*; *got a new car*). **3** *tr.* go to catch (a bus, train, etc.). **4** *tr.* prepare (a meal, etc.). **5** *intr. & tr.* reach or cause to reach a certain state; become or cause to become (*get rich*; *get one's feet wet*). **6** *tr.* obtain as a result of calculation. **7** *tr.* contract (a disease, etc.). **8** *tr.* establish or be in communication with via telephone or radio; receive (a radio signal). **9** *tr.* experience or suffer; have inflicted on one; receive as one's lot or penalty (*got four years in prison*). **10 a** *tr.* succeed in bringing, placing, etc. (*get it around the corner*; *get it onto the agenda*; *flattery will get you nowhere*). **b** *intr. & tr.* succeed or cause to succeed in coming or going (*will get you there somehow*; *got absolutely nowhere*). **11** *tr.* (prec. by *have*) **a** possess (*haven't got a penny*). **b** (foll. by *to* + infin.) be bound (*have got to see you*). **12** *tr.* (foll. by *to* + infin.) induce (*got them to help*

me). **13** *tr. colloq.* understand (a person or an argument) (*have you got that?*; *do you get me?*). **14** *tr. colloq.* inflict punishment or retribution on, esp. in retaliation (*I'll get you for that*). **15** *tr. colloq.* **a** annoy. **b** affect emotionally. **c** attract; obsess. **d** amuse. **16** *tr.* (foll. by *to* + infin.) develop an inclination as specified (*am getting to like it*). **17** *intr.* (foll. by verbal noun) begin (*get going*). **18** *tr.* (esp. in *past* or *perfect*) catch in an argument; corner. **19** *tr.* establish (an idea) in one's mind. □ **get about** (or **around**) **1** travel extensively; go from place to place. **2** manage to walk (esp. after illness). **3** (of news) be circulated. **get across 1** manage to communicate (an idea). **2** (of an idea) be communicated successfully. **3** *Brit. colloq.* annoy; irritate. **get ahead** be or become successful. **get along** (or **on**) (foll. by *together*, *with*) live harmoniously. **get around** (*Brit.* **round**) **1** successfully coax or cajole (a person) esp. to secure a favor. **2** evade (a law, etc.). **get around to** deal with (a task, etc.) in due course. **get at 1** reach; get hold of. **2** *colloq.* imply (*what are you getting at?*). **3** *colloq.* try to upset or irritate. **get away 1** escape. **2** (foll. by *with*) escape blame or punishment for. **get back at** *colloq.* retaliate against. **get by** *colloq.* **1** just manage, even with difficulty. **2** be acceptable. **get down 1** descend (from a vehicle, ladder, etc.). **2** record in writing. **get a person down** depress or deject him or her. **get down to** begin working on or discussing. **get even** (often foll. by *with*) achieve revenge; act in retaliation. **get his** (or **hers**, etc.) *sl.* **1** be killed. **2** be avenged. **get hold** (or **ahold**) **of 1** grasp (physically). **2** make contact with (a person). **3** acquire. **get in 1** enter. **2** be elected. **get into** become interested or involved in. **get it** *sl.* **1** understand. **2** be punished or in trouble. **get it into one's head** (foll. by *that* & clause) firmly believe or maintain. **get off 1** *colloq.* be acquitted; escape with little or no punishment. **2** leave. **3** alight; alight from (a bus, etc.). **4** go, or cause to go, to sleep. **get a person off** *colloq.* cause a person to be acquitted. **get off on** *sl.* be excited or aroused by. **get on 1** make progress; manage. **2** enter (a bus, etc.). **get on to** *colloq.* **1** make contact with. **2** become aware of. **get out 1** leave or escape. **2** manage to go outdoors. **3** alight from a vehicle. **4** become known. **5** succeed in uttering, publishing, etc. **6** *Brit.* solve (a puzzle, etc.). **get out of 1** avoid or escape (a duty, etc.). **2** abandon (a habit) gradually. **get over 1** recover from (an illness, upset, etc.). **2** overcome (a difficulty). **3** manage to communicate (an idea, etc.). **get a thing over** (or **over with**) complete (a tedious task) promptly. **get one's own back** *colloq.* have one's revenge. **get rid of** see RID. **get somewhere** make progress. **get there** *colloq.* **1** succeed.

GESTATION

Length of gestation has some relation to the adult size of an animal. While human gestation lasts 40 weeks, an elephant's gestation period is 22 months. Human gestation is divided into trimesters. By the end of the first trimester, the body systems, organs, nerves, and muscles of the fetus are well developed. During the second trimester, the fetus grows hair, sucks its thumb, and coughs. In the third trimester, most babies lie head down, awaiting birth.

STAGES OF HUMAN GESTATION

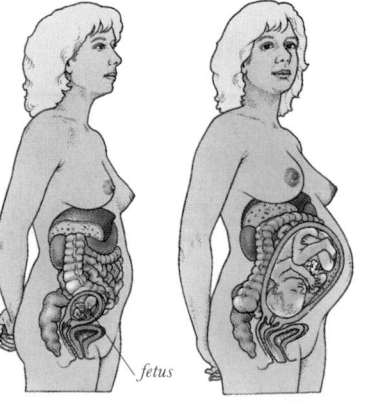

fetus

FIRST TRIMESTER

SECOND TRIMESTER

THIRD TRIMESTER

2 understand what is meant. **get through 1** pass or assist in passing (an examination, an ordeal, etc.). **2** finish or use up (esp. resources). **3** make contact by telephone. **4** (foll. by *to*) succeed in making (a person) listen or understand. **get to 1** reach. **2** = *get down to*. **get together** gather; assemble. **get up 1** rise or cause to rise from sitting, etc., or from bed after sleeping or an illness. **2** ascend or mount, e.g., on horseback. **3** (of fire, wind, or the sea) begin to be strong or agitated. **4** prepare or organize. **5** enhance or refine one's knowledge of (a subject). **6** work up (a feeling, e.g., anger). **7** produce or stimulate (*get up steam; get up speed*). **8** (often *refl.*) dress or arrange elaborately; make presentable; arrange the appearance of. **9** (foll. by *to*) esp. *Brit. colloq.* indulge or be involved in (*always getting up to mischief*). **have got it bad** *sl.* be obsessed or affected emotionally. □□ **get·ta·ble** *adj.*

get·a·way /gétəway/ *n.* an escape, esp. after committing a crime.

get-go /gét-gō/ *n. colloq.*, chiefly *N. Amer.* the very beginning.

get-rich-quick *adj.* designed to make a lot of money fast.

get·ter /gétər/ *n.* **1** in senses of GET. **2** *Physics* a substance used to remove residual gas from a vacuum tube.

get-to·geth·er *n. colloq.* a social gathering.

get-up *n. colloq.* a style or arrangement of dress, etc., esp. an elaborate one.

get-up-and-go *n. colloq.* energy; enthusiasm.

gew·gaw /gyoōgaw, goō-/ *n.* a gaudy plaything or ornament; a bauble.

gey·ser /gízər/ *n.* ▼ an intermittently gushing hot spring that throws up a tall column of water.

Gha·na·ian /gáaneeən/ *adj. & n.* ● *adj.* of or relating to Ghana in W. Africa. ● *n.* a native or inhabitant of Ghana; a person of Ghanaian descent.

ghast·ly /gástlee/ *adj. & adv.* ● *adj.* (**ghastlier, ghastliest**) **1** horrible; frightful. **2** *colloq.* objectionable; unpleasant. **3** deathlike; pallid. ● *adv.* in a ghastly or sickly way (*ghastly pale*). □□ **ghast·li·ness** *n.*

ghat /gaat, gat/ *n.* in India. **1** steps leading down to a river. **2** a landing place. **3** a mountain pass.

Gha·zi /gáazee/ *n.* (*pl.* **Ghazis**) a Muslim fighter against non-Muslims.

ghee /gee/ *n.* (also **ghi**) clarified butter esp. from the milk of a buffalo or cow.

ghe·rao /gerów/ *n.* (*pl.* **-os**) (in India and Pakistan) coercion of employers, by which their workers prevent them from leaving the premises until certain demands are met.

gher·kin /górkin/ *n.* a small variety of cucumber, or a young green cucumber, used for pickling.

ghet·to /gétō/ *n.* (*pl.* **-os**) **1** a part of a city, esp. a slum area, occupied by a minority group or groups. **2** *hist.* the Jewish quarter in a city. **3** a segregated group or area.

ghet·to blast·er *n. sl.* a large portable radio, often with cassette player or CD player, esp. used to play loud pop music.

ghi var. of GHEE.

ghost /gōst/ *n. & v.* ● *n.* **1** the supposed apparition of a dead person or animal. **2** a mere semblance (*not a ghost of a chance*). **3** a secondary image produced by defective television reception or by a telescope. ● *v.* **1** *intr.* (often foll. by *for*) act as ghostwriter. **2** *tr.* act as ghostwriter of (a work). □□ **ghost·like** *adj.*

ghost·ing /gṓsting/ *n.* the appearance of a "ghost" (see GHOST *n.* 3) in a television picture.

ghost·ly /gṓstlee/ *adj.* (**ghostlier, ghostliest**) like a ghost. □□ **ghost·li·ness** *n.*

ghost town *n.* a deserted town with few or no remaining inhabitants.

ghost·write /gṓstrīt/ *v.tr. & intr.* act as ghostwriter (of).

ghost·writ·er *n.* a person who writes on behalf of the credited author of a work.

ghoul /goōl/ *n.* **1** a person morbidly interested in death, etc. **2** an evil spirit or phantom. **3** a spirit in Muslim folklore preying on corpses. □□ **ghoul·ish** *adj.* **ghoul·ish·ly** *adv.* **ghoul·ish·ness** *n.*

GHQ *abbr.* General Headquarters.

GI /jée-í/ *n. & adj.* ● *n.* an enlisted soldier in the US armed forces, esp. the army. ● *adj.* of, for, or characteristic of US soldiers. ▷ INFANTRYMAN

gi·ant /jíənt/ *n. & adj.* ● *n.* **1** an imaginary or mythical being of human form but superhuman size. **2** (in Greek mythology) one of such beings who fought against the gods. **3** an abnormally tall or large person, animal, or plant. **4** a person of exceptional ability, courage, etc. **5** a large star. ● *attrib.adj.* **1** gigantic; monstrous. **2** (of a plant or animal) of a very large kind. □□ **gi·ant·ism** *n.* **gi·ant·like** *adj.*

giaour /jówr/ *n. derog.* or *literary* a non-Muslim, esp. a Christian (orig. a Turkish name).

gib /gib, jib/ *n.* a wood or metal bolt, wedge, or pin for holding a machine part, etc., in place.

gib·ber /jíbər/ *v. & n.* ● *v.intr.* chatter incoherently. ● *n.* such speech.

gib·ber·el·lin /jíbərélin/ *n.* one of a group of plant hormones that stimulate the growth of leaves and shoots.

gib·ber·ish /jíbərish/ *n.* unintelligible or meaningless speech; nonsense.

gib·bet /jíbit/ *n. hist.* **1** a gallows. **2** ◄ an upright post with an arm on which the bodies of executed criminals were left hanging in chains, irons, or an iron cage as a warning or deterrent to others.

gib·bon /jíbən/ *n.* any small ape of the genus *Hylobates*, native to SE Asia.

gib·bous /jíbəs/ *adj.* **1** convex or protuberant. **2** (of a moon or planet) having the bright part greater than a semicircle and less than a circle. ▷ LUNAR MONTH

gibe /jīb/ *v. & n.* (also **jibe**) ● *v.intr.* (often foll. by *at*) jeer; mock. ● *n.* an instance of gibing. □□ **gib·er** *n.*

gib·lets /jíblits/ *n.pl.* the liver, gizzard, neck, etc., of a bird, usu. removed and kept separate when the bird is prepared for cooking.

gid·dy /gídee/ *adj. & v.* ● *adj.* (**giddier, giddiest**) **1** having a sensation of whirling and a tendency to fall, stagger, or spin around. **2** *a* overexcited. *b* excitable; frivolous. **3** tending to make one giddy. ● *v.tr. & intr.* (**-ies, -ied**) make or become giddy. □□ **gid·di·ly** *adv.* **gid·di·ness** *n.*

gift /gift/ *n. & v.* ● *n.* **1** a thing given. **2** a natural ability or talent. **3** the power to give (*in his gift*). **4** the act or an instance of giving. **5** *colloq.* an easy task. ● *v.tr.* bestow as a gift. □ **look a gift horse in the mouth** (usu. *neg.*) find fault with what has been given.

gift cer·tif·i·cate *n.* (also *Brit.* **gift token** or **voucher**) a certificate used as a gift and exchangeable for goods.

gift·ed /gíftid/ *adj.* exceptionally talented or intelligent. □□ **gift·ed·ness** *n.*

gift-wrap *v.tr.* (**wrapped, wrapping**) wrap attractively as a gift.

gig¹ /gig/ *n.* **1** a light two-wheeled one-horse carriage. **2** a light ship's boat for rowing or sailing. **3** a rowing boat esp. for racing.

gig² /gig/ *n. & v. colloq.* ● *n.* an engagement of an entertainer, esp. a musician, usu. for a single appearance. ● *v.intr.* (**gigged, gigging**) perform a gig.

gig³ /gig/ *n.* a kind of fishing spear.

giga- /gígə, jígə/ *comb. form* denoting a factor of 10^9.

gig·a·bit /gígəbit, jígə-/ *n. Computing* a unit of information equal to one billion (10^9) bits.

gig·a·byte /gígəbīt, jígə-/ *n. Computing* a unit of information equal to one billion (10^9) bytes.

gi·ga·me·ter /gígəmeetər, jígə-/ *n.* a metric unit equal to 10^9 meters.

gi·gan·tic /jīgántik/ *adj.* **1** very large; enormous. **2** like or suited to a giant. □□ **gi·gan·ti·cal·ly** *adv.*

gi·gan·tism /jīgántizəm/ *n.* abnormal largeness.

gig·gle /gígəl/ *v. & n.* ● *v.intr.* laugh in half-suppressed spasms. ● *n.* such a laugh. □□ **gig·gler** *n.* **gig·gly** *adj.* (**gigglier, giggliest**).

GIGO /gígō/ *n. Computing abbr.* garbage *in*, garbage *out*, an informal rule stating that the quality of the data input determines the quality of the results.

gig·o·lo /jígəlō, zhíg-/ *n.* (*pl.* **-os**) **1** a young man paid by an older woman to be her escort or lover. **2** a professional male dancing partner or escort.

gig·ot /jígət, zheegó/ *n.* a leg of mutton or lamb.

gigue /zheeg/ *n.* **1** = JIG 1. **2** *Mus.* a lively piece of music in double or triple time, forming the last movement of a suite.

criminal's skull

GIBBET: 18TH-CENTURY GIBBET CAGE

G

GEYSER

A geyser field occurs in a geothermal area, where trapped water is heated by energy within subterranean volcanic rocks. The eruption cycle begins as water seeps into chambers corroded into the rock. Intense heat causes the water in each chamber to boil and vaporize. Rising pressure then forces overlying water upward through vents to the eye of the geyser, followed by steam. As pressure drops, the eruption dies, recommencing as the chambers refill.

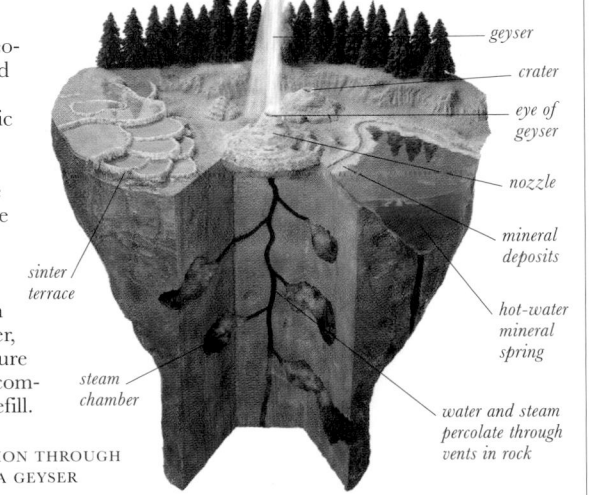

geyser
crater
eye of geyser
nozzle
mineral deposits
hot-water mineral spring
water and steam percolate through vents in rock
sinter terrace
steam chamber

SECTION THROUGH A GEYSER

G

Gi·la mon·ster /héelə/ *n.* a large venomous lizard, *Heloderma suspectum*, of the southwestern US, having orange, yellow, and black scales like beads.

gild[1] /gild/ *v.tr.* (*past part.* **gilded** or as adj. in sense 1 **gilt**) **1** cover thinly with gold. **2** tinge with a golden color or light. □ **gild the lily** try to improve what is already beautiful or excellent. □□ **gild·er** *n.*

gild[2] var. of GUILD.

gild·ing /gílding/ *n.* **1** the act of applying gilt. **2** ► material used in applying gilt.

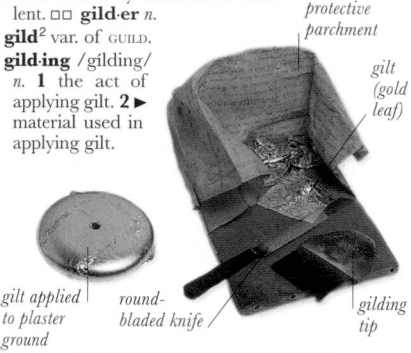

GILDING: MATERIALS REQUIRED FOR GILDING

protective parchment
gilt (gold leaf)
gilding tip
gilt applied to plaster ground
round-bladed knife

gill[1] /gil/ *n.* (usu. in *pl.*) **1** ▼ the respiratory organ in fishes and other aquatic animals. **2** the vertical radial plates on the underside of mushrooms and other fungi. ▷ MUSHROOM. **3** the flesh below a person's jaws and ears. □□ **gilled** *adj.* (also in *comb.*).

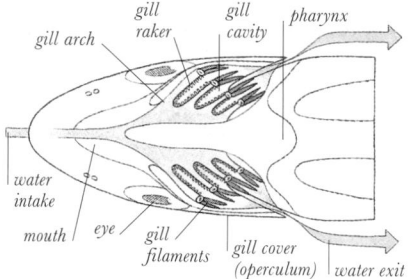

gill raker
gill cavity
pharynx
gill arch
water intake
mouth
eye
gill filaments
gill cover (operculum)
water exit

GILL: INTERNAL ANATOMY OF A FISH'S HEAD AND GILLS

gill[2] /jil/ *n.* a unit of liquid measure, equal to a quarter of a pint.

gil·ly·flow·er /jíleeflowr, gílee-/ *n.* **1** (in full **clove gillyflower**) a clove-scented pink. **2** any of various similarly scented flowers such as the wallflower.

gilt[1] /gilt/ *adj. & n.* ● *adj.* **1** covered thinly with gold. **2** gold-colored. ● *n.* gold or a goldlike substance applied in a thin layer to a surface.

gilt[2] /gilt/ *n.* a young unbred sow.

gim·bals /gímbəlz, jim-/ *n.pl.* ▼ a contrivance, usu. of rings and pivots, for keeping a stove or instruments such as a compass and chronometer horizontal at sea, in the air, etc.

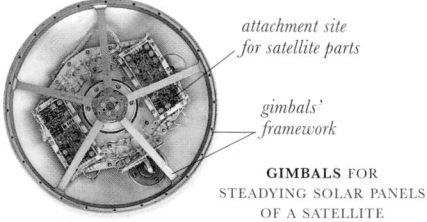

attachment site for satellite parts
gimbals' framework

GIMBALS FOR STEADYING SOLAR PANELS OF A SATELLITE

gim·crack /jímkrak/ *adj. & n.* ● *adj.* showy but flimsy and worthless. ● *n.* a cheap showy ornament; a knick-knack. □□ **gim·crack·er·y** *n.* **gim·crack·y** *adj.*

gim·let /gímlit/ *n.* a small tool with a screw tip for boring holes.

gim·mick /gímik/ *n. colloq.* a trick or device, esp. to attract publicity or trade. □□ **gim·mick·ry** *n.* **gim·mick·y** *adj.*

gimp[1] /gimp/ *n.* (also **guimp, gymp**) **1** a twist of silk, etc., with cord or wire running through it, used esp. as trimming. **2** fishing line of silk, etc., bound with wire.

gimp[2] /gimp/ *n. & v. sl.* ● *n.* a lame person or leg. ● *v.intr.* walk with a lame gait.

gin[1] /jin/ *n.* an alcoholic spirit distilled from grain or malt and flavored with juniper berries.

gin[2] /jin/ *n.* **1** a machine for separating cotton from its seeds. **2** a snare or trap. □□ **gin·ner** *n.*

gin·ger /jínjər/ *n., adj., & v.* ● *n.* **1 a** a hot spicy root usu. powdered for use in cooking, or preserved in syrup, or candied. ▷ SPICE. **b** the plant, *Zingiber officinale*, of SE Asia, having this root. **2** a light reddish yellow color. ● *adj.* of a ginger color. ● *v.tr.* **1** flavor with ginger. **2** (foll. by *up*) rouse or enliven. □□ **gin·ger·y** *adj.*

gin·ger ale *n.* a carbonated nonalcoholic clear drink flavored with ginger extract.

gin·ger·bread /jínjərbred/ *n.* a cake made with molasses or syrup and flavored with ginger.

gin·ger·ly /jínjərlee/ *adv. & adj.* ● *adv.* in a careful or cautious manner. ● *adj.* showing great care or caution.

gin·ger·snap /jínjərsnap/ *n.* a thin brittle cookie flavored with ginger.

ging·ham /gíng-əm/ *n.* a plain-woven cotton cloth, esp. checked.

gin·gi·va /jínjívə, jinjívə/ *n.* (*pl.* **gingivae** /-vee/) the gums. □□ **gin·gi·val** /-jívəl, -jivəl/ *adj.*

gin·gi·vi·tis /jínjivítis/ *n.* inflammation of the gums.

ging·ko var. of GINKGO.

gin·gly·mus /jínggliməs, ging-/ *n.* (*pl.* **ginglymi** /-mī/) *Anat.* a hingelike joint in the body with motion in one plane only, e.g., the elbow or knee.

gink /gingk/ *n. sl.* often *derog.* a fellow; a man.

gink·go /gíngkgō/ *n.* (also **ging·ko**) (*pl.* **-os** or **-oes**) ► an orig. Chinese and Japanese tree, *Ginkgo biloba*, with fan-shaped leaves and yellow flowers. Also called **maidenhair tree**.

gin rum·my *n.* a form of the card game rummy.

gin·seng /jínseng/ *n.* **1** any of several medicinal plants of the genus *Panax*, found in E. Asia and N. America. **2** ► the root of this.

Gip·sy var. of GYPSY.

gi·raffe /jiráf/ *n.* (*pl.* same or **giraffes**) ▲ a ruminant mammal, *Giraffa camelopardalis* of Africa, the tallest living animal, with a long neck and forelegs and a skin of dark patches separated by lighter lines.

gir·an·dole /jírəndōl/ *n.* **1** a revolving cluster of fireworks. **2** a branched candle bracket or candlestick. **3** an earring or pendant with a large central stone surrounded by small ones.

gir·a·sol /jírəsawl, -sol/ *n.* (also **gir·a·sole** /-sōl/) **1** a kind of opal reflecting a reddish glow; a fire opal. **2** (usu. **gir·a·sole**) = JERUSALEM ARTICHOKE.

gird[1] /gərd/ *v.tr.* (*past* and *past part.* **girded** or **girt**) **1** encircle or secure with a belt or band. **2** secure (clothes) on the body with a girdle or belt. **3** enclose or encircle. **4** (foll. by *around*) place (cord, etc.) around. □ **gird** (or **up**) **one's loins** prepare for action.

gird[2] /gərd/ *v. & n.* ● *v.intr.* (foll. by *at*) jeer or gibe. ● *n.* a gibe or taunt.

gird·er /gárdər/ *n.* a large iron beam or compound structure for bearing loads.

gir·dle /gárd'l/ *n. & v.* ● *n.* **1** a belt or cord worn around the waist. **2** a woman's corset extending from waist to thigh. **3** the bony support for a limb (*pelvic girdle*). ● *v.tr.* surround with a girdle.

girl /gərl/ *n.* **1** a female child. **2** *colloq.* a young woman. **3** *colloq.* a girlfriend. **4** *derog.* a female servant. □□ **girl·hood** *n.*

girl Fri·day *n.* a female helper or follower (cf. MAN FRIDAY).

girl·friend /gárlfrend/ *n.* **1** a regular female companion or lover. **2** a female friend.

girl·ie /gárlee/ *adj. colloq.* (of a magazine, etc.) depicting young women in erotic poses.

girl·ish /gárlish/ *adj.* of or like a girl. □□ **girl·ish·ly** *adv.* **girl·ish·ness** *n.*

Girl Scout *n.* a member of an organization of girls, esp. the Girl Scouts of America, that promotes character, outdoor activities, community service, etc.

gi·ro /jírō/ *n. & v.* ● *n.* (*pl.* **-os**) **1** a system of credit transfer between banks, post offices, etc., in Europe. **2** a payment by giro. ● *v.tr.* (**-oes, -oed**) pay by giro.

girt[1] *past part.* of GIRD[1].

girt[2] var. of GIRTH.

girth /gərth/ *n.* (also **girt** /gərt/) **1** the distance around a thing. **2** a band around the body of a horse to secure the saddle, etc. ▷ SHOW JUMPING

GIS *abbr.* geographic information system(s).

gist /jist/ *n.* the substance or essence of a matter.

git·tern /gítərn/ *n.* a medieval stringed instrument, a forerunner of the guitar.

give /giv/ *v. & n.* ● *v.* (*past* **gave** /gayv/; *past part.* **given** /gívən/) **1** *tr.* (also *absol.*) hand over as a present (*gave them her old curtains*). **2** *tr.* **a** transfer the ownership of, bequeath (*gave him $200 in her will*). **b** transfer, esp. temporarily or for safe keeping; hand over (*gave the dog to hold*). **c** administer (medicine). **d** deliver (a message) (*give her my best wishes*). **3** *tr.* (usu. foll. by *for*) **a** pay (*gave him $30 for the bicycle*). **b** sell (*gave him the bicycle for $30*). **4** *tr.* **a** confer; grant (a benefit, an honor, etc.). **b** accord; bestow (one's affections, confidence, etc.). **c** administer (one's approval, blame, etc.); offer (esp. something unpleasant) (*gave him a talking-to; gave him my blessing*). **d** pledge (*gave his word*). **5** *tr.* **a** perform (an action, etc.) (*gave him a kiss; gave a*

GIRAFFE

The world's tallest animal, giraffes live among the acacias of the African savanna. The sole giraffe species contains eight subspecies, differing in their coat markings.

horn
mane
hoof

RETICULATED GIRAFFE
(*Giraffa camelopardalis reticulata*)

TYPES OF MARKING

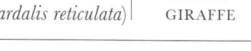

ROTHSCHILD'S GIRAFFE

MASAI GIRAFFE

GINKGO: MAIDENHAIR TREE
(*Ginkgo biloba*)

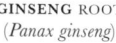

GINSENG ROOT
(*Panax ginseng*)

jump). **b** utter (gave a shriek). **6** tr. allot; assign (was given the contract). **7** tr. (in passive; foll. by to) be inclined to or fond of (is given to speculation). **8** tr. yield as a product or result (the lamp gives a bad light; the field gives fodder for twenty cows). **9** intr. **a** yield to pressure; become relaxed; lose firmness (this elastic doesn't give properly). **b** collapse (the roof gave under the pressure). **10** intr. (usu. foll. by of) grant; bestow (gave freely of his time). **11** tr. **a** commit, consign, or entrust (give him into custody; give her into your care). **b** sanction the marriage of (a daughter, etc.). **12** tr. devote; dedicate (gave his life to croquet). **13** tr. (usu. absol.) colloq. tell what one knows (What happened? Come on, give!). **14** tr. show; hold out (gives no sign of life). **15** tr. Theatr. read, recite etc. (gave them Hamlet's soliloquy). **16** tr. impart; be a source of (gave its name to the battle). **17** tr. allow (esp. a fixed amount of time) (can give you five minutes). **18** tr. (usu. foll. by for) value (something) (gives nothing for their opinions). **19** tr. concede (I give you the victory). **20** tr. deliver (a judgment, etc.) authoritatively (gave his verdict). **21** tr. toast (a person, cause, etc.) (I give you our President). **22** tr. provide (a party etc.) as host (gave a banquet). ● n. **1** capacity to yield under pressure. **2** ability to adapt (no give in his attitudes). □ **give and take** v.tr. exchange (words, blows, or concessions). ● n. an exchange of words, etc. **give as good as one gets** retort adequately in words or blows. **give away 1** transfer as a gift. **2** hand over (a bride) ceremonially to a bridegroom. **3** expose to detection. **give back** return (something) to its previous owner or in exchange. **give birth (to)** see BIRTH. **give chase** pursue a person, animal, etc. **give the game away** reveal a secret. **give a hand** = lend a hand (see HAND). **give a person his or her due** acknowledge, esp. grudgingly, a person's abilities, etc. **give in** cease fighting or arguing. **give me** I prefer (give me the Greek islands). **give off** emit (vapor, etc.). **give oneself** (of a woman) yield sexually. **give oneself airs** act pretentiously. **give oneself up to 1** abandon oneself to. **2** addict oneself to. **give onto** (or **into**) (of a window, corridor, etc.) overlook or lead into. **give or take** colloq. add or subtract (a specified amount or number) in estimating. **give out 1** announce; emit. **2** break down from exhaustion, etc. **3** run short. **give rise to** cause. **give a person to understand** inform authoritatively. **give up 1** resign; surrender. **2** part with. **3** deliver (a wanted person, etc.). **4** pronounce incurable or insoluble. **5** cease (an activity). **give up the ghost** archaic or colloq. die. **give way** see WAY. **give a person what for** colloq. scold severely. **not give a damn** colloq. not care at all. **what gives?** colloq. what is the news? ▷ **giv·er** n.

give·a·way /gívəway/ n. colloq. **1** an inadvertent betrayal or revelation. **2** an act of giving away. **3** a free gift; a low price.

giv·en /gívən/ adj. & n. ● adj. as previously stated or assumed; granted; specified (given that he is a liar, we cannot trust him; a given number of people). **2** Law (of a document) signed and dated (given this day the 30th of June). ● n. a known fact or situation.

giz·mo /gízmō/ n. (also **gis·mo**) (pl. **-os**) sl. a gadget.

giz·zard /gízərd/ n. **1** the second part of a bird's stomach, for grinding food. ▷ BIRD. **2** a muscular stomach of some fish, insects, mollusks, and other invertebrates.

gla·bel·la /gləbélə/ n. (pl. **glabellae** /-lee/) the smooth part of the forehead above and between the eyebrows. □□ **gla·bel·lar** adj.

gla·brous /gláybrəs/ adj. free from hair or down; smooth-skinned.

gla·cé /glasáy/ adj. **1** (of fruit, esp. cherries) preserved in sugar. **2** (of cloth, leather, etc.) smooth; polished.

gla·cial /gláyshəl/ adj. **1** of ice; icy. **2** Geol. characterized or produced by the presence or agency of ice. **3** colloq. exceptionally slow. **4** Chem. forming icelike crystals upon freezing (glacial acetic acid). □□ **gla·cial·ly** adv.

GLACIER

A valley glacier forms from snow that collects in bowl-shaped basins called cirques. The snow compresses into ice, which slowly creeps downhill under its own weight, gathering moraine (rocky debris) in its path and gradually eroding a U-shaped valley. If ice at the snout melts faster than the advance of the glacier, then the glacier retreats. Meltwater streams deposit sand and gravel, but flush finer sediment onto an outwash plain.

MODEL OF A GLACIER IN A VALLEY

G

gla·ci·at·ed /gláyshee-aytid, -see-/ adj. **1** marked or polished by the action of ice. **2** covered or having been covered by glaciers or ice sheets. □□ **gla·ci·a·tion** /-áyshən/ n.

gla·cier /gláyshər/ n. ▲ a mass of land ice formed by the accumulation of snow on high ground. ▷ CIRQUE, OUTWASH, VALLEY

gla·ci·ol·o·gy /gláyshee-óləjee, -see-/ n. the science of the internal dynamics and effects of glaciers. □□ **gla·ci·o·log·i·cal** /-əlójikəl/ adj. **gla·ci·ol·o·gist** n.

gla·cis /gláysis, glás-/ n. (pl. same /-siz, -seez/) a bank sloping down from a fort, on which attackers are exposed to the defenders' missiles, etc.

glad /glad/ adj. (**gladder**, **gladdest**) **1** (predic.) pleased (shall be glad to come). **2 a** marked by, filled with, or expressing joy (a glad expression). **b** (of news, events, etc.) giving joy (glad tidings). **3** (of objects) bright; beautiful. □□ **glad·ly** adv. **glad·ness** n. **glad·some** adj. poet.

glad·den /glád'n/ v.tr. make glad.

glade /glayd/ n. an open space in a wood or forest.

glad·i·a·tor /gládee-aytər/ n. **1** hist. a man trained to fight with a sword at ancient Roman shows. **2** a person defending or opposing a cause. □□ **glad·i·a·to·ri·al** /-deeətáwreeəl/ adj.

glad·i·o·lus /gládeeóləs/ n. (pl. **gladioli** /-lī/ or **gladioluses**) ▶ any iridaceous plant of the genus Gladiolus with sword-shaped leaves and brightly colored flower spikes.

glad rags n.pl. colloq. best clothes.

Glad·stone bag /gládstōn, -stən/ n. a suitcase that opens flat into two equal compartments.

Glag·o·lit·ic /glágəlítik/ adj. of or relating to the alphabet ascribed to St. Cyril and formerly used in writing some Slavonic languages.

glair /glair/ n. (also **glaire**) **1** white of egg. **2** an adhesive preparation made from this, used in bookbinding, etc. □□ **glair·e·ous** adj. **glair·y** adj.

glaive /glayv/ n. archaic poet. **1** a broadsword. **2** any sword.

glam·or·ize /glámərīz/ v.tr. (also **glam·our·ize**) make glamorous or attractive. □□ **glam·or·i·za·tion** n.

glam·our /glámər/ n. (also **glam·or**) **1** physical attractiveness, esp. when achieved by makeup, etc. **2** alluring or exciting beauty or charm (the glamour of New York). □□ **glam·or·ous** adj. **glam·or·ous·ly** adv.

glance[1] /glans/ v. & n. ● v. **1** intr. cast a momentary look (glanced up at the sky). **2** intr. (esp. of a weapon) bounce (off an object). **3** intr. (of talk or a talker) pass quickly over a subject (glanced over the question of payment). **4** intr. (of a bright object or light) flash or gleam (the sun glanced off the knife). **5** tr. (esp. of a weapon) strike (an object) obliquely. ● n. **1** a brief look. **2** a flash or gleam (a glance of sunlight). □ **at a glance** immediately upon looking. **glance over** (or **through**) read cursorily. □□ **glanc·ing·ly** adv.

glance[2] /glans/ n. any lustrous sulfide ore (copper glance; lead glance).

gland[1] /gland/ n. **1 a** an organ in an animal body secreting substances for use in the body or for ejection. **b** a structure resembling this, such as a lymph gland. ▷ ENDOCRINE, LYMPHATIC SYSTEM. **2** Bot. a secreting cell or group of cells on the surface of a plant structure.

gland[2] /gland/ n. a sleeve used to produce a seal around a moving shaft.

gland·ers /glándərz/ n.pl. (also treated as sing.) a contagious disease of horses.

glan·du·lar /glánjələr/ adj. of or relating to a gland or glands.

glan·du·lar fe·ver n. an infectious viral disease characterized by swelling of the lymph glands and prolonged lassitude. Also called **infectious mononucleosis**.

glans /glanz/ n. (pl. **glandes** /glándeez/) the rounded part forming the end of the penis or clitoris. ▷ REPRODUCTIVE ORGANS

glare[1] /glair/ v. & n. ● v. **1** intr. look fiercely. **2** intr. shine dazzlingly. **3** tr. express (hate, defiance, etc.) by a look. ● n. **1 a** strong fierce light, esp. sunshine. **b** oppressive public attention (the glare of fame). **2** a fierce look. □□ **glar·y** adj.

glare[2] /glair/ adj. (esp. of ice) smooth and glassy.

glar·ing /gláiring/ adj. **1** obvious; conspicuous (a glaring error). **2** shining oppressively. **3** staring fiercely. □□ **glar·ing·ly** adv.

glas·nost /gláɑsnost, -nawst/ n. (in the former Soviet Union) the policy of more open government and wider dissemination of information.

GLADIOLUS
(Gladiolus
'Beau Rivage')

G

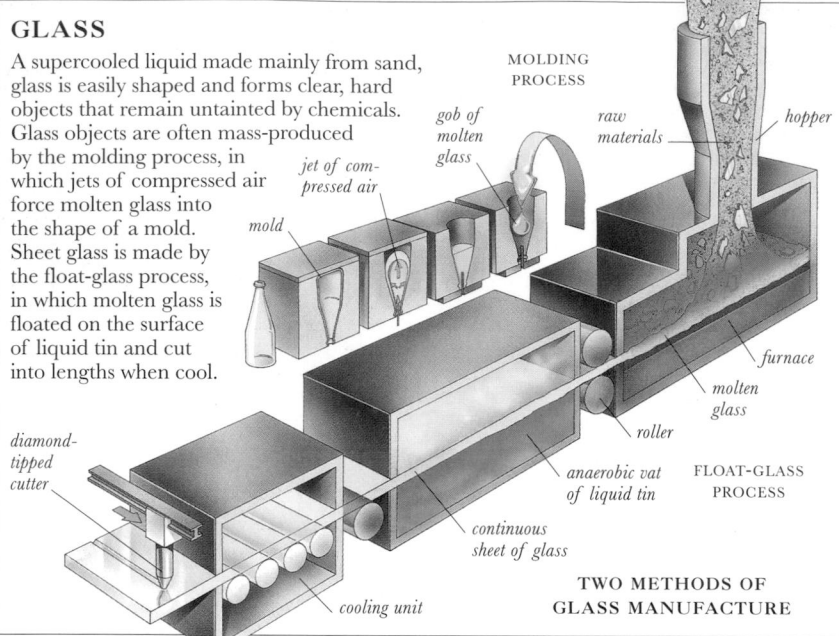

GLASS

A supercooled liquid made mainly from sand, glass is easily shaped and forms clear, hard objects that remain untainted by chemicals. Glass objects are often mass-produced by the molding process, in which jets of compressed air force molten glass into the shape of a mold. Sheet glass is made by the float-glass process, in which molten glass is floated on the surface of liquid tin and cut into lengths when cool.

MOLDING PROCESS

gob of molten glass

jet of compressed air

raw materials

hopper

mold

furnace

molten glass

roller

diamond-tipped cutter

anaerobic vat of liquid tin

FLOAT-GLASS PROCESS

continuous sheet of glass

cooling unit

TWO METHODS OF GLASS MANUFACTURE

---

glass /glas/ n., v., & adj. ● n. **1 a** (often attrib.) ▲ a hard, brittle, usu. transparent or shiny substance, made by fusing sand with soda and lime and sometimes other ingredients. **b** a substance of similar properties. **2** (often collect.) an object or objects made from glass, esp.: **a** a drinking vessel. **b** esp. Brit. a mirror. **c** an hourglass. **d** a window. **e** a greenhouse (rows of lettuce under glass). **f** glass ornaments. **g** a barometer. **h** Brit. a glass disk covering a watch face. **i** a magnifying lens. **j** a monocle. **3** (in pl.) **a** eyeglasses. **b** field glasses; opera glasses. **4** the amount of liquid contained in a glass; a drink (he likes a glass). ● v.tr. (usu. as **glassed** adj.) fit with glass. ● adj. of or made from glass. □□ **glass·ful** n. (pl. **-fuls**). **glass·like** adj.

glass·blow·er /glásblōər/ n. a person who blows semimolten glass to make glassware. □□ **glass·blow·ing** n.

glass ceil·ing n. a barrier hindering promotion to high executive positions.

glass cut·ter n. **1** a worker who cuts glass. **2** a tool used for cutting glass.

glass·house /glás-hows/ n. a building where glass is made.

glass·ine /glaseén/ n. a glossy transparent paper.

glass·mak·ing /glásmayking/ n. the manufacture of glass.

glass·ware /gláswair/ n. articles made from glass, esp. drinking glasses, etc.

glass·wort /gláswort/ n. any plant of the genus Salicornia or Salsola formerly burned for use in glassmaking. ▷ HALOPHYTE

glass·y /glásee/ adj. (**glassier, glassiest**) **1** of or resembling glass, esp. in smoothness. **2** (of the eye, the expression, etc.) abstracted; dull; fixed (fixed her with a glassy stare). □□ **glass·i·ly** adv. **glass·i·ness** n.

Glau·ber's salt /glówbərz/ n. (also **Glau·ber's salts**) a crystalline hydrated form of sodium sulfate used esp. as a laxative.

glau·co·ma /glawkṓmə, glou-/ n. an eye condition with increased pressure within the eyeball, causing gradual loss of sight.

glau·cous /gláwkəs/ adj. **1** ▶ of a dull grayish green or blue. **2** covered with a powdery bloom as of grapes.

glaze /glayz/ v. & n. ● v. **1** tr. **a** fit (a window, picture, etc.) with glass. **b** provide (a building) with glass windows. **2** tr. **a** cover (pottery, etc.) with a glaze. **b** fix (paint) on pottery with a glaze. **3** tr. cover (pastry, meat, etc.) with a glaze. **4** intr. (often foll. by over) (of the eyes) become fixed or glassy. **5** tr. cover (cloth, paper, etc.) with a glaze or other similar finish. **6** tr. give a glassy surface to, e.g., by rubbing. ● n. **1** a vitreous substance, used to glaze pottery. **2** a smooth shiny coating on food. **3** a thin topcoat of transparent paint used to modify the tone of the underlying color. **4** a smooth surface formed by glazing.

gla·zier /gláyzhər/ n. a person whose trade is glazing windows, etc.

glaz·ing /gláyzing/ n. **1** the act or an instance of glazing. **2** windows (see also DOUBLE GLAZING). **3** material used to produce a glaze.

gleam /gleem/ n. & v. ● n. **1** a faint light (a gleam of sunlight). **2** a faint, sudden, or temporary show (not a gleam of hope). ● v.intr. **1** emit gleams. **2** shine with a faint brightness. **3** (of a quality) be indicated (amusement gleamed in his eyes).

glean /gleen/ v. **1** tr. collect or scrape together (news, facts, gossip, etc.) in small quantities. **2 a** tr. (also absol.) gather (ears of grain, etc.) after the harvest. **b** tr. strip (a field, etc.) after a harvest. □□ **glean·er** n.

glean·ings /gléeningz/ n.pl. things gleaned, esp. facts.

glebe /gleeb/ n. **1** a piece of land serving as part of a clergyman's benefice and providing income. **2** poet. earth; land; a field.

glee /glee/ n. **1** mirth; delight. **2** a song for three or more voices, singing different parts simultaneously.

glee club n. a chorus for singing part-songs or other usu. short choral works.

glee·ful /gléefŏol/ adj. joyful. □□ **glee·ful·ly** adv.

Gleich·schal·tung /glíkh-shaltoong/ n. the standardization of political, economic, and social institutions in authoritarian countries.

glen /glen/ n. a narrow valley.

glen·gar·ry /glengáree/ n. (pl. **-ies**) ▶ a brimless Scottish cap with a cleft down the center and usu. two ribbons hanging at the back.

GLAUCOUS
FOLIAGE OF A EUCALYPTUS TREE

---

gle·noid cav·i·ty /gléenoyd/ n. a shallow depression on a bone, esp. the scapula and temporal bone, receiving the projection of another bone to form a joint.

gley /glay/ n. a sticky waterlogged soil, gray to blue in color.

glib /glib/ adj. (**glibber, glibbest**) fluent and voluble but insincere and shallow. □□ **glib·ly** adv. **glib·ness** n.

glide /glīd/ v. & n. ● v. **1** intr. move with a smooth continuous motion. **2** intr. (of an aircraft) fly without engine power. **3** intr. of time, etc.: **a** pass gently and imperceptibly. **b** (often foll. by into) pass and change gradually and imperceptibly (night glided into day). **4** intr. move quietly or stealthily. **5** tr. cause to glide (breezes glided the boat on its course). **6** tr. traverse or fly in a glider. ● n. **1 a** the act of gliding. **b** an instance of this. **2** Phonet. a gradually changing sound made in passing from one position of the speech organs to another. **3** a gliding dance or dance step. **4** a flight in a glider.

glid·er /glīdər/ n. **1** ▼ an aircraft that flies without an engine. ▷ AIRCRAFT. **2** a person or thing that glides.

air brake

hinged elevator

canopy

tailplane

towing hook

cantilevered fin

rudder

GLIDER:
SCHLEICHER K23 GLIDER

glim /glim/ n. **1** a faint light. **2** archaic sl. a candle; a lantern.

glim·mer /glímər/ v. & n. ● v.intr. shine faintly. ● n. **1** a feeble light. **2** (usu. foll. by of) a faint gleam (of hope, understanding, etc.). **3** a glimpse.

glim·mer·ing /glíməring/ n. **1** = GLIMMER n. **2** an act of glimmering.

glimpse /glimps/ n. & v. ● n. **1** a momentary view (caught a glimpse of her). **2** a faint and transient appearance (glimpses of the truth). ● v. tr. see faintly (glimpsed his face in the crowd).

glint /glint/ v. & n. ● v.intr. & tr. flash or cause to flash; glitter; sparkle (eyes glinted with amusement; the sword glinted fire). ● n. a brief flash of light.

glis·sade /glisáad, -sáyd/ n. & v. ● n. **1** an act of sliding down a steep slope of snow or ice, usu. on the feet with the support of an ice ax, etc. **2** a gliding step in ballet. ● v.intr. perform a glissade.

glis·san·do /glisáandō/ n. (pl. **glissandi** /-dee/ or **-os**) Mus. a continuous slide of adjacent notes upward or downward.

glis·ten /glísən/ v. & n. ● v.intr. shine; glitter. ● n. a glitter; a sparkle.

glis·ter /glístər/ v. & n. archaic ● v.intr. sparkle; glitter. ● n. a sparkle.

glitch /glich/ n. colloq. a sudden irregularity or malfunction.

glit·ter /glítər/ v. & n. ● v.intr. **1** shine, esp. with a bright reflected light; sparkle. **2** (usu. foll. by with) **a** be showy (glittered with diamonds). **b** be ostentatious or flashily brilliant (glittering rhetoric). ● n. **1** a gleam; a sparkle. **2** showiness; splendor. **3** tiny pieces of sparkling material as on Christmas tree decorations. □□ **glit·ter·y** adj.

glit·te·ra·ti /glítəráatee/ n.pl. sl. the fashionable set of literary or show business people.

glitz /glits/ n. sl. extravagant but superficial display; show business glamour.

glitz·y /glítsee/ adj. (**glitzier, glitziest**) sl. extravagant; ostentatious; tawdry.

GLENGARRY:
WORLD WAR I SCOTTISH
BATTALION GLENGARRY

ribbon

GLOBAL WARMING

For millions of years, gases in the Earth's atmosphere have trapped sufficient heat from solar radiation to sustain life. However, an increase in human activity may now be raising levels of "greenhouse gases" such as carbon dioxide, so that excess heat is trapped in the atmosphere.

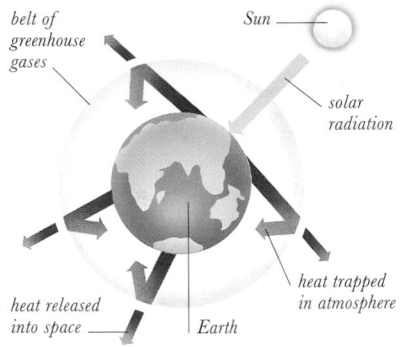

belt of greenhouse gases

Sun

solar radiation

heat released into space

Earth

heat trapped in atmosphere

DEMONSTRATION OF GLOBAL WARMING

gloam·ing /glṓming/ n. poet. twilight; dusk.

gloat /glōt/ v. & n. ● v.intr. (often foll. by over) contemplate with malice, triumph, etc. (gloated over his collection). ● n. **1** the act of gloating. **2** a look of triumphant satisfaction.

glob /glob/ n. a mass or lump of semiliquid substance.

glob·al /glṓbəl/ adj. **1** worldwide (global conflict). **2** relating to or embracing a group of items, etc.; total. □□ **glob·al·ly** adv.

glob·al warm·ing n. ▲ the increase in temperature of the Earth's atmosphere caused by the greenhouse effect.

globe /glōb/ n. **1 a** (prec. by the) the planet Earth. **b** a planet, star, or sun. **c** any spherical body. **2** a spherical representation of the Earth or of the constellations with a map on the surface. **3** a golden sphere as an emblem of sovereignty. **4** any spherical glass vessel. □□ **globe·like** adj. **glo·boid** adj. & n. **glo·bose** /-bōs/ adj.

globe ar·ti·choke n. ▶ the partly edible head of the artichoke plant.

globe·fish /glṓbfish/ n. = PUFFER 2.

globe·flow·er /glṓbflowər/ n. any ranunculaceous plant of the genus Trollius with globular usu. yellow flowers.

glob·u·lar /glóbyələr/ adj. **1** globe-shaped; spherical. **2** composed of globules.

glob·ule /glóbyōōl/ n. a small globe or round particle; a drop.

glob·u·lin /glóbyəlin/ n. any of a group of proteins found in plant and animal tissues responsible for the transport of molecules, etc.

glock·en·spiel /glókənspeel, -shpeel/ n. a musical instrument consisting of a series of bells or metal bars or tubes struck by hammers.

glom /glom/ v. sl. (**glommed**, **glomming**) **1** tr. steal; grab. **2** intr. (usu. foll. by on to) steal; grab.

glom·er·ate /glómərət/ adj. Bot. & Anat. compactly clustered.

glom·er·ule /glómərōōl/ n. a clustered flower head.

glom·er·u·lus /glōméryələs/ n. (pl. **glomeruli** /-lī/) a cluster of small organisms, tissues, or blood vessels, esp. a group of capillaries in the kidney. □□ **glo·mer·u·lar** adj.

gloom /glōōm/ n. & v. ● n. **1** darkness; obscurity.

GLOBE ARTICHOKE
(*Cynara scolymus*)

2 melancholy; despondency. **3** poet. a dark place. ● v. **1** intr. be gloomy or melancholy. **2** intr. (of the sky, etc.) be dull or threatening. **3** intr. appear obscurely. **4** tr. make dark or dismal.

gloom·y /glṓomee/ adj. (**gloomier**, **gloomiest**) **1** dark; unlighted. **2** depressed; sullen. **3** dismal; depressing. □□ **gloom·i·ly** adv. **gloom·i·ness** n.

glop /glop/ n. sl. a liquid or sticky mess, esp. unappealing or inedible food.

Glo·ri·a /gláwreeə/ n. **1** any of various doxologies beginning with Gloria, esp. the hymn beginning with Gloria in excelsis Deo (Glory be to God in the highest). **2** an aureole.

glo·ri·fy /gláwrifī/ v.tr. (**-ies**, **-ied**) **1** make glorious. **2** transform into something more splendid. **3** extol; praise. **4** (as **glorified** adj.) seeming to be better than in reality (just a glorified office boy). □□ **glo·ri·fi·ca·tion** n.

glo·ri·ole /gláwreeōl/ n. an aureole; a halo.

glo·ri·ous /gláwreeəs/ adj. **1** possessing glory. **2** conferring glory. **3** colloq. splendid; magnificent; delightful (a glorious day). □□ **glo·ri·ous·ly** adv.

glo·ry /gláwree/ n. & v. (pl. **-ies**) **1** high renown or fame. **2** adoring praise (Glory to the Lord). **3** resplendent majesty or magnificence (the glory of Versailles). **4** a thing that brings renown or praise. **5** the bliss and splendor of heaven. **6** an aureole; a halo. ● v.intr. pride oneself; exult (glory in their skill). □ **glory be!** **1** a devout ejaculation. **2** colloq. an exclamation of surprise or delight.

gloss¹ /glaws, glos/ n. & v. ● n. **1** a surface shine or luster. **b** an instance of this. **2 a** deceptively attractive appearance. **b** an instance of this. **3** (in full **gloss paint**) paint formulated to give a hard glossy finish (cf. MATTE). ● v.tr. make glossy. □ **gloss over 1** seek to conceal beneath a false appearance. **2** conceal by mentioning briefly.

gloss² /glaws, glos/ n. & v. ● n. **1 a** an explanatory word or phrase inserted between the lines or in the margin of a text. **b** a comment, explanation, interpretation, or paraphrase. **2** a misrepresentation of another's words. **3 a** a glossary. **b** an interlinear translation or annotation. ● v. **1** (also **gloze**) tr. **a** add a gloss or glosses to (a text, word, etc.). **b** read a different sense into; explain away. **2** intr. (often foll. by on) make (esp. unfavorable) comments. **3** intr. write or introduce glosses.

glos·sal /gláwsəl, glós-/ adj. Anat. of the tongue; lingual.

glos·sa·ry /gláwsəree, glós-/ n. (pl. **-ies**) (also **gloss**) an alphabetical list of terms relating to a specific subject or text.

glos·sa·tor /glawsáytər, glo-/ n. **1** a writer of glosses or glossaries. **2** hist. a commentator on, or interpreter of, medieval law texts.

glos·seme /gláwseem, glós-/ n. any meaningful feature of a language that cannot be analyzed into smaller meaningful units.

glos·si·tis /glawsítis, glo-/ n. inflammation of the tongue.

glos·sog·ra·pher /glawsógrəfər, glo-/ n. a writer of glosses or commentaries.

glos·so·la·ryn·ge·al /gláwsōlarinjeeəl, glós-/ adj. of the tongue and larynx.

gloss·y /gláwsee, glós-/ adj. & n. ● adj. (**glossier**, **glossiest**) **1** having a shine. **2** (of paper, etc.) smooth and shiny. **3** (of a magazine, etc.) printed on such paper. ● n. (pl. **-ies**) colloq. **1** a glossy magazine. **2** a photograph with a glossy surface. □□ **gloss·i·ly** adv. **gloss·i·ness** n.

glot·tal /glót'l/ adj. of or produced by the glottis.

glot·tis /glótis/ n. ▶ the space at the upper end of the windpipe and between the vocal cords.

glove /gluv/ n. & v. ● n. **1** a covering for the hand, worn esp. for protection against cold or dirt, and usu. having separate fingers. **2** a padded protective glove, esp.: **a** a boxing glove. **b** Baseball a fielder's glove. ● v.tr. cover or provide with a glove. □□ **glov·er** n.

glove box n. **1** a box for gloves. **2** a closed chamber with sealed-in gloves for handling radioactive material, etc. **3** = GLOVE COMPARTMENT.

glove com·part·ment n. a recess or cabinet for small articles in the dashboard of a motor vehicle.

glow /glō/ v. & n. ● v.intr. **1 a** throw out light and heat without flame; be incandescent. **b** shine like something heated in this way. **2** (of the cheeks) redden, esp. from cold or exercise. **3 a** (of the body) be heated; sweat. **b** express or experience strong emotion (glowed with pride). **4** show a warm color (the painting glows with warmth). **5** (as **glowing** adj.) expressing pride or satisfaction (a glowing report). ● n. **1** a glowing state. **2** a bright warm color. **3** ardor; passion. **4** a feeling induced by good health, exercise, etc. □□ **glow·ing·ly** adv.

glow·er /glowr/ v. & n. ● v.intr. stare or scowl. ● n. a glowering look.

glow plug n. a device in a diesel engine that heats air and fuel entering a cylinder in order to facilitate combustion in a cold engine.

glow·worm /glṓwərm/ n. any beetle of the genus Lampyris whose wingless female emits light from the abdomen.

glox·in·i·a /gloksíneeə/ n. any tropical plant of the genus Gloxinia, native to S. America, with large bell flowers of various colors.

gloze /glōz/ v. **1** tr. GLOSS², 1. **2** = gloss over (see GLOSS¹).

glu·ca·gon /glṓōkəgon/ n. a hormone formed in the pancreas that aids the breakdown of glycogen to glucose in the liver.

glu·cose /glṓōkōs/ n. **1** a simple sugar containing six carbon atoms, found mainly in the form of dextrose. Glucose is an important energy source in living organisms and obtainable from some carbohydrates by hydrolysis. ¶ Chem. formula: $C_6H_{12}O_6$. **2** a syrup containing glucose sugars from the incomplete hydrolysis of starch.

glu·co·side /glṓōkəsīd/ n. a compound giving glucose and other products upon hydrolysis. □□ **glu·co·sid·ic** /-sídik/ adj.

glue /glōō/ n. & v. ● n. an adhesive substance used for sticking objects or materials together. ● v.tr. (**glues**, **glued**, **gluing** or **glueing**) **1** fasten or join with glue. **2** keep or put very close (an eye glued to the keyhole). □□ **glue·like** adj. **glu·er** n. **glue·y** /glṓō-ee/ adj. (**gluier**, **gluiest**).

glue·pot /glṓōpot/ n. **1** a pot with an outer vessel holding water to heat glue. **2** colloq. an area of sticky mud, etc.

glug /glug/ n. & v. ● n. a hollow, usu. repetitive gurgling sound. ● v.intr. make a gurgling sound as of water from a bottle.

glum /glum/ adj. (**glummer**, **glummest**) looking or feeling dejected; sullen; displeased. □□ **glum·ly** adv. **glum·ness** n.

glu·on /glṓō-on/ n. Physics any of a group of elementary particles that are thought to bind quarks together.

glut /glut/ v. & n. ● v.tr. (**glutted**, **glutting**) **1** feed (a person, one's stomach, etc.) or indulge (an appetite, a desire, etc.) to the full; satiate; cloy. **2** fill to excess; choke up. **3** Econ. overstock (a market).

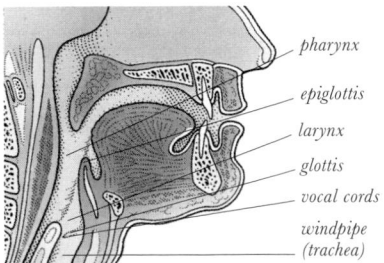

pharynx

epiglottis

larynx

glottis

vocal cords

windpipe (trachea)

GLOTTIS: INTERNAL FEATURES OF THE HUMAN HEAD SHOWING THE GLOTTIS

G

• *n.* **1** *Econ.* supply exceeding demand. **2** full indulgence.

glu·ta·mate /glo͞otəmayt/ *n.* any salt or ester of glutamic acid, esp. a sodium salt used to enhance the flavor of food.

glu·tam·ic ac·id /gloōtámik/ *n.* a naturally occurring amino acid, a constituent of many proteins.

glu·ten /glo͞otən/ *n.* a mixture of proteins present in cereal grains.

glu·te·us /glo͞oteeəs/ *n.* (*pl.* **glutei** /-teeī/) ▼ any of the three muscles in each buttock. ▫▫ **glu·te·al** *adj.*

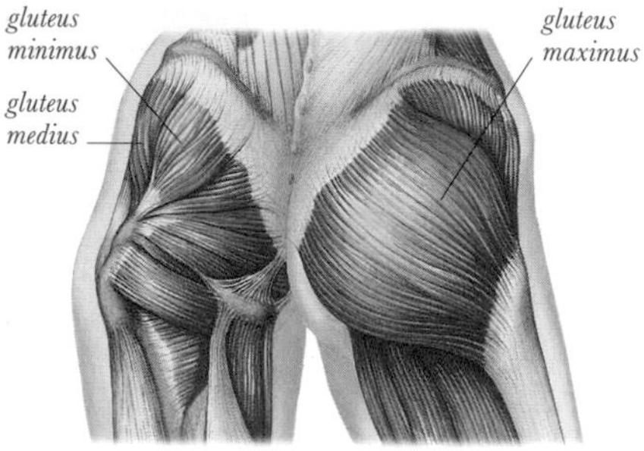

GLUTEUS MUSCLES IN THE HUMAN BUTTOCKS

glu·ti·nous /glo͞ot'nəs/ *adj.* sticky; like glue.

glut·ton /glút'n/ *n.* **1** an excessively greedy eater. **2** *colloq.* a person insatiably eager (*a glutton for work*). **3** a carnivorous animal, *Gulo gulo*, of the weasel family. Also called **wolverine.** ▫ **glutton for punishment** a person eager to take on hard tasks. ▫▫ **glut·ton·ous** *adj.*

glut·ton·y /glút'nee/ *n.* habitual greed or excess in eating.

glyc·er·ide /glísərīd/ *n.* any fatty acid ester of glycerol.

glyc·er·in /glísərin/ *n.* (also **glyc·er·ine**) = GLYCEROL.

glyc·er·ol /glísərawl, -rol/ *n.* a colorless sweet viscous liquid formed as a byproduct in the manufacture of soap, used as an emollient and laxative, in explosives, etc.

gly·cine /glíseen/ *n.* the simplest naturally occurring amino acid, a general constituent of proteins.

glyco- /glíkō/ *comb. form* sugar.

gly·co·gen /glíkəjən/ *n.* a polysaccharide serving as a store of carbohydrates, esp. in animal tissues, and yielding glucose on hydrolysis.

gly·co·gen·e·sis /glíkəjénisis/ *n.* the formation of glycogen from sugar.

gly·col /glíkawl, -kol/ *n.* an alcohol, esp. ethylene glycol. ▫▫ **gly·col·ic** /-kólik/ *adj.* **gly·col·lic** *adj.*

gly·col·y·sis /glīkólisis/ *n.* the breakdown of glucose by enzymes.

gly·co·pro·tein /glíkōprṓteen/ *n.* any of a group of compounds consisting of a protein combined with a carbohydrate.

gly·co·side /glíkəsīd/ *n.* any compound giving sugar and other products on hydrolysis. ▫▫ **gly·co·sid·ic** /-sídik/ *adj.*

gly·cos·u·ri·a /glíkəsyo͝oreeə, -sho͝or-/ *n.* a condition characterized by an excess of sugar in the urine, associated with diabetes, kidney disease, etc. ▫▫ **gly·cos·u·ric** *adj.*

glyph /glif/ *n.* **1** a sculptured character or symbol. **2** a vertical groove, esp. that on a Greek frieze.

glyp·tic /glíptik/ *adj.* of or concerning carving, esp. on precious stones.

glyp·tog·ra·phy /gliptógrəfee/ *n.* the art or scientific study of engraving gems.

GM *abbr.* **1** General Motors. **2** general manager. **3** (in the UK) George Medal.

gm *abbr.* gram(s).

G-man /jéeman/ *n.* (*pl.* **G-men**) **1** *US colloq.* an FBI agent. **2** *Ir.* a political detective.

GMT *abbr.* Greenwich Mean Time.

gnarled /naarld/ *adj.* (also **gnarl·y** /naárlee/) (of a tree, hands, etc.) knobbly; twisted; rugged.

gnash /nash/ *v.* **1** *tr.* grind (the teeth). **2** *intr.* (of the teeth) strike together.

gnat /nat/ *n.* **1** any small two-winged biting fly of the genus *Culex*, esp. *C. pipiens*. **2** an insignificant annoyance. **3** a tiny thing.

gnath·ic /náthik/ *adj.* of or relating to the jaws.

gnaw /naw/ *v.* (*past part.* **gnawed** or **gnawn**) **1 a** *tr.* bite persistently. **b** *intr.* (often foll. by *at, into*) bite; nibble. **2 a** *intr.* (often foll. by *at, into*) (of a destructive agent, pain, fear, etc.) consume; torture. **b** *tr.* consume, torture, etc., with pain, fear, etc. (*was gnawed by doubt*). **3** *tr.* (as **gnawing** *adj.*) persistent; worrying.

gneiss /nīs/ *n.* ► a usu. coarse-grained metamorphic rock principally of feldspar, quartz, and ferromagnesian minerals. ▷ METAMORPHIC, ROCK CYCLE

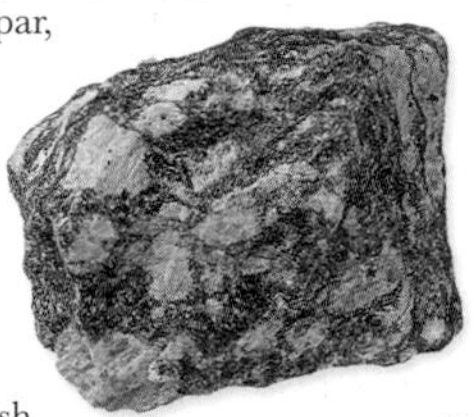

GNEISS: AUGEN GNEISS

GNMA /jínee may/ *n.* Government National Mortgage Association.

gnoc·chi /nyáwkee/ *n.pl.* an Italian dish of small dumplings usu. made from potato, semolina flour, etc., or from spinach and cheese.

gnome[1] /nōm/ *n.* **1 a** a dwarfish legendary creature supposed to guard the earth's treasures underground. **b** a figure of a gnome, esp. as a garden ornament. **2** (esp. in *pl.*) *colloq.* a person with sinister influence, esp. financial (*gnomes of Zurich*). ▫▫ **gnom·ish** *adj.*

gnome[2] /nōm, nṓmee/ *n.* a maxim; an aphorism.

gno·mic /nṓmik/ *adj.* of, consisting of, or using aphorisms.

gno·mon /nṓmon, -mən/ *n.* **1** ► the rod or pin, etc., on a sundial that shows the time by the position of its shadow. **2** *Astron.* a column, etc., used in observing the Sun's meridian altitude. ▫▫ **gno·mon·ic** /-mónik/ *adj.*

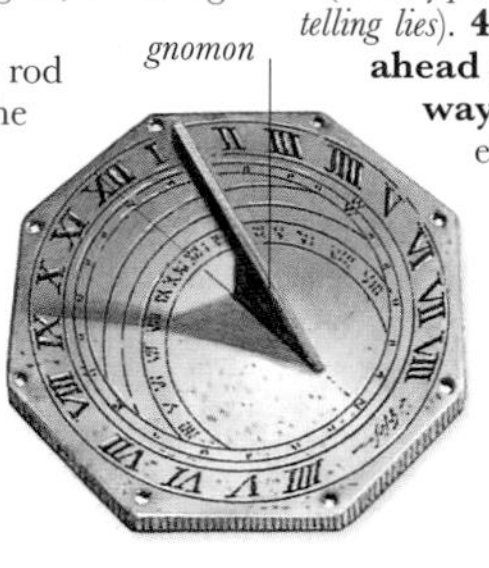

GNOMON ON AN 18TH-CENTURY SUNDIAL

gno·sis /nṓsis/ *n.* knowledge of spiritual mysteries.

gnos·tic /nóstik/ *adj.* & *n.* • *adj.* **1** relating to knowledge, esp. esoteric mystical knowledge. **2** (**Gnostic**) concerning the Gnostics. • *n.* (**Gnostic**) (usu. in *pl.*) a Christian heretic of the 1st–3rd c. claiming gnosis. ▫▫ **Gnos·ti·cism** /-tisizəm/ *n.*

GNP *abbr.* gross national product.

gnu /no͞o, nyo͞o/ *n.* any antelope of the genus *Connochaetes*, native to S. Africa, with a large erect head and brown stripes on the neck and shoulders. Also called **wildebeest**.

go[1] /gō/ *v., n.,* & *adj.* • *v.* (*3rd sing. present* **goes** /gōz/; *past* **went** /went/; *past part.* **gone** /gon/) **1** *intr.* **a** start moving or be moving from one place or point in time to another. **b** (foll. by *to* + infin., or *and* + verb) proceed in order to (*went to find him*). **c** (foll. by *and* + verb) *colloq.* expressing annoyance (*you went and told him*). **2** *intr.* (foll. by verbal noun) make a special trip for; participate in (*went skiing*). **3** *intr.* lie in a certain direction (*the road goes to the shore*). **4** *intr.* leave (*they had to go*). **5** *intr.* move, work, etc. (*the clock doesn't go*). **6** *intr.* **a** make a specified movement (*go like this*). **b** make a sound (of a specified kind) (*the gun went bang*). **c** *colloq.* say (*so he goes to me, "Why didn't you like it?"*). **7** *intr.* be in a specified state (*go hungry*). **8** *intr.* **a** pass into a specified condition (*gone bad*). **b** *colloq.* die. **c** proceed or escape in a specified condition (*the crime went unnoticed*). **9** *intr.* (of time or distance) pass; elapse; be traversed (*ten days to go before Easter*). **10** *intr.* **a** have a specified content or wording (*the tune goes like this*). **b** be current or accepted (*so the story goes*). **c** be suitable; fit (*the shoes don't go with the hat*). **d** be regularly kept (*the forks go here*). **e** fit (*this won't go into the cupboard*). **11** *intr.* **a** turn out; proceed (*things went well*). **b** be successful (*make the party go*). **c** progress (*we've still got a long way to go*). **12** *intr.* **a** be sold (*went cheap*). **b** (of money) be spent (*$200 went on a new jacket*). **13** *intr.* **a** be relinquished or abolished (*the car will have to go*). **b** fail; decline (*his sight is going*). **14** *intr.* be acceptable or permitted (*anything goes*). **15** *intr.* be guided by; judge or act on (*have nothing to go on*). **16** *intr.* attend or travel to regularly (*goes to school*). **17** *intr.* (foll. by pres. part.) *colloq.* proceed (often foolishly) to do (*went running to the police*). **18** *intr.* proceed to a certain point (*will go so far and no further*). **19** *intr.* (of a number) be capable of being contained in another (*6 into 5 won't go*). **20** *tr. Cards* bid; declare (*has gone two spades*). **21** *intr.* be allotted or awarded (*the job went to his rival*). **22** *intr.* (foll. by *to, toward*) amount to (*12 inches go to make a foot*). **23** *intr.* (in *imper.*) begin motion (a starter's order in a race) (*ready, set, go!*). **24** *intr.* refer or appeal (*go to him for help*). **25** *intr.* take up a specified profession (*went on the stage*). **26** *intr.* (usu. foll. by *by, under*) be known or called (*goes by the name of Droopy*). **27** *tr. colloq.* proceed to (*go jump in the lake*). **28** *intr.* (foll. by *for*) apply to (*that goes for me too*). • *n.* (*pl.* **goes**) **1** the act of going. **2** spirit; animation (*she has a lot of go in her*). **3** vigorous activity (*it's all go*). **4** *colloq.* a success (*made a go of it*). **5** *colloq.* a turn; an attempt (*I'll have a go; it's my go*). **6** permission; approval; go-ahead (*gave us a go on the new project*). • *adj. colloq.* functioning properly (*all systems are go*). ▫ **from the word go** *colloq.* from the very beginning. **give it a go** *colloq.* make an effort to succeed. **go about 1** busy oneself with. **2** be socially active. **3** (foll. by *pres. part.*) make a habit of doing (*goes about telling lies*). **4** *Naut.* change to an opposite tack. **go ahead** proceed without hesitation. **go all the way 1** win a contest, one's ultimate goal, etc. **2** engage in sexual intercourse. **go along with** agree to; take the same view as. **go around 1** spin, revolve. **2** be long enough to encompass. **3** (of food, etc.) suffice for everybody. **4** (usu. foll. by *to*) visit informally. **5** (foll. by *with*) be regularly in the company of. **6** = *go about* 3. **7** = *go on* 4. **go at** take in hand energetically; attack. **go away** depart, esp. from home for a vacation, etc. **go back 1** return. **2** extend backward (in time or space). **3** (foll. by *to*) have a history extending back to. **go back on** fail to keep (one's word etc.). **go bail** see BAIL[1]. **go begging** see BEG. **go by 1** pass. **2** be dependent on. **go by default** see DEFAULT. **go-devil** an instrument used to clean the inside of pipes, etc. **go down 1 a** (of an amount) become less (*the coffee has gone down a lot*). **b** subside (*the flood went down*) **c** decrease in price. **2 a** (of a ship) sink. **b** (of the Sun) set. **3** (usu. foll. by *to*) be continued to a specified point. **4** fail; (of a computer network, etc.) cease to function. **5** be recorded in writing. **6** be swallowed. **7** (often foll. by *with*) be received (in a specified way). **8** fall (before a conqueror). **go Dutch** see DUTCH. **go far** be very successful. **go for 1** go to fetch. **2** be accounted as (*went for nothing*). **3** prefer; choose (*that's the one I go for*). **4** *colloq.* strive to attain (*go for it!*). **5** *colloq.* attack (*the dog went for him*). **go for broke** see BROKE. **go great guns** see GUN. **go halves** (or **shares**) (often foll. by *with*) share equally. **go in 1** enter a room, house, etc. **2** (usu. foll. by *for*) enter as a competitor. **3** (of the Sun, etc.) become obscured by cloud. **go in for** take as one's object, style, etc. **going, gone!** an auctioneer's announcement that bidding is closing or closed. **go into 1** enter (a profession, etc.). **2** take part in. **3** investigate. **4** allow oneself to pass into (hysterics, etc.). **5** dress oneself in (mourning, etc.). **go a long way 1** have a great effect. **2** (of food, money, etc.) last a long time; buy much. **3** = *go far*. **go off 1** explode. **2** leave the stage. **3** gradually cease to be felt. **4** (esp. of foodstuffs) deteriorate; decompose. **5** go to sleep; become unconscious. **6** die. **7** be gotten rid of by sale, etc. **8** sound, as an

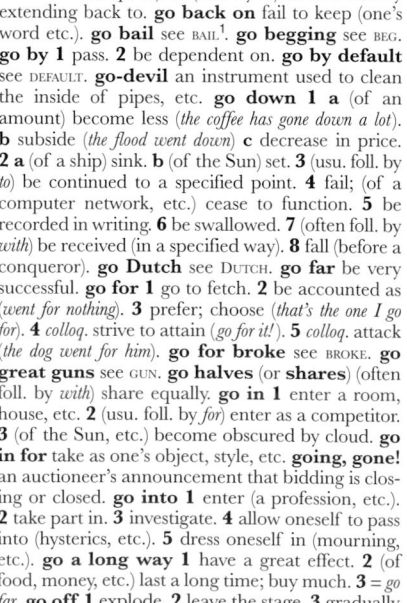

alarm, etc. **go off well** (or **badly**, etc.) (of an enterprise, etc.) be received or accomplished well (or badly, etc.). **go on 1** continue; persevere (*went on trying*). **2** *colloq.* **a** talk at great length. **b** (foll. by *at*) admonish (*went on and on at him*). **3** (foll. by *to* + infin.) proceed (*went on to become a star*). **4** happen. **5** conduct oneself (*shameful, the way they went on*). **6** *Theatr.* appear on stage. **7** (of a garment) be large enough for its wearer. **8** take one's turn to do something. **9** (*also Brit.* **go upon**) *colloq.* use as evidence (*police don't have anything to go on*). **10** *colloq.* (esp. in *neg.*) **a** concern oneself about. **b** care for (*don't go much on red hair*). **go out 1** leave a room, house, etc. **2** be broadcast. **3** be extinguished. **4** (often foll. by *with*) be courting. **5** (of a government) leave office. **6** cease to be fashionable. **7** (usu. foll. by *to*) depart, esp. to a colony, etc. **8** *colloq.* lose consciousness. **9** (of workers) strike. **10** (usu. foll. by *to*) (of the heart, etc.) expand with sympathy, etc., toward (*my heart goes out to them*). **11** *Golf* play the first nine holes in a round. **12** *Cards* be the first to dispose of one's hand. **13** (of a tide) turn to low tide. **go over 1** inspect the details of; rehearse. **2** (often foll. by *to*) change one's allegiance or religion. **3** (of a play, etc.) be received in a specified way (*went over well in Dallas*). **go round** = go around. **go through 1** be dealt with or completed. **2** discuss in detail; scrutinize in sequence. **3** perform (a ceremony, a recitation, etc.). **4** undergo. **5** *colloq.* use up; spend (money, etc.). **6** make holes in. **7** (of a book) be successively published (in so many editions). **go through with** not leave unfinished. **go to the bar** become a lawyer. **go to blazes** (or **hell**, etc.) *sl.* an exclamation of dismissal, contempt, etc. **go together 1** match; fit. **2** be courting. **go to it!** *colloq.* begin work! **go to show** (or **prove**) serve to demonstrate (or prove). **go to town** see TOWN. **go under** sink. **go up 1** increase in price. **2** be consumed (in flames, etc.). **go well** (often foll. by *with*) turn out well. **go with 1** be harmonious with. **2** agree to. **3 a** be a pair with. **b** be courting. **4** follow the drift of. **go without** manage without (also *absol.*: *we shall just have to go without*). **go with the tide** (or **times**) do as others do. **have a go at 1** *esp. Brit.* attack; criticize. **2** attempt; try. **on the go** *colloq.* **1** in constant motion. **2** constantly working. **to go** (of food, etc.) to be eaten or drunk off the premises. **who goes there?** a sentry's challenge.

go² /gō/ *n.* a Japanese board game of territorial possession and capture.

goad /gōd/ *n. & v.* ● *n.* **1** a spiked stick used for urging cattle forward. **2** anything that torments, incites, or stimulates. ● *v.tr.* **1** urge on with a goad. **2** (usu. foll. by *into*) irritate; stimulate (*goaded him into retaliating*).

go-a·head *n.* permission to proceed; approval; authorization.

goal /gōl/ *n.* **1** the object of a person's ambition or effort; a destination; an aim (*fame is his goal*; *Washington was our goal*). **2 a** *Football* a pair of posts with a crossbar between which the ball has to be kicked to score a field goal. ▷ FOOTBALL. **b** *Soccer, Ice Hockey,* etc., ▼ a cage or basket used similarly. **c** a point or points won (*scored 3 goals*). **3** a point marking the end of a race. □ **in goal** in the position of goalkeeper. □□ **goal·less** *adj.*

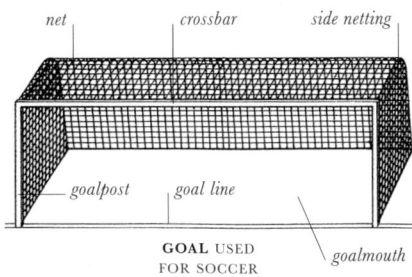

net   *crossbar*   *side netting*

goalpost   *goal line*

GOAL USED FOR SOCCER   *goalmouth*

goal·ball /gṓlbawl/ *n.* a team ball game for blind and visually handicapped players.

goal·ie /gṓlee/ *n. colloq.* = GOALKEEPER.

goal·keep·er /gṓlkeepər/ *n.* a player stationed to protect the goal in various sports. ▷ FOOTBALL, HOCKEY

goal line *n.* *Football, Soccer,* etc., a line between each pair of goalposts, extended to form the end boundary of a field of play (cf. TOUCHLINE). ▷ GOAL, RUGBY

goal·mouth /gṓlmowth/ *n.* *Soccer, Ice Hockey* the space between or near the goalposts. ▷ GOAL

goal·post /gṓlpōst/ *n.* either of the two upright posts of a goal. ▷ GOAL. □ **move the goalposts** alter the basis or scope of a procedure during its course, so as to fit adverse circumstances encountered.

goal·tend·er /gṓl-tendər/ *n.* a hockey goalkeeper.

goat /gōt/ *n.* **1 a** ► a hardy shorthaired domesticated mammal, *Capra aegagrus,* having horns and (in the male) a beard, and kept for its milk and meat. ▷ UNGULATE. **b** either of two similar mammals, the mountain goat and the Spanish goat. **2** any other mammal of the genus *Capra,* including the ibex. **3** a lecherous man. **4** (**the Goat**) the zodiacal sign or constellation Capricorn. ▷ CAPRICORN. **5** a scapegoat. □ **get a person's goat** *colloq.* irritate a person. □□ **goat·ish** *adj.* **goat·y** *adj.*

goat god *n.* Pan.

goat·ee /gōtée/ *n.* a small pointed beard like that of a goat.

goats·beard /gṓtsbeerd/ *n.* **1** a meadow plant, *Tragopogon pratensis.* **2** a herbaceous plant, *Aruncus dioicus,* with long spikes of white flowers.

goat·herd /gṓt-hərd/ *n.* a person who tends goats.

goat·skin /gṓtskin/ *n.* **1** the skin of a goat. **2** a garment or bottle made out of goatskin.

gob¹ /gob/ *n.* *esp. Brit. sl.* the mouth.

gob² /gob/ *n. & v. sl.* ● *n.* **1** a lump or clot of slimy matter. **2** (in *pl.*) large amounts (*gobs of cash*) ● *v.intr.* (**gobbed, gobbing**) spit.

gob³ /gob/ *n. sl.* a sailor.

gob·bet /góbit/ *n.* **1** a piece or lump of raw meat, flesh, food, etc. **2** an extract from a text, esp. one set for translation or comment in an examination.

gob·ble¹ /góbəl/ *v.tr. & intr.* eat hurriedly and noisily. □□ **gob·bler** *n.*

gob·ble² /góbəl/ *v.intr.* **1** (of a male turkey) make a characteristic swallowing sound in the throat. **2** make such a sound when speaking, esp. when excited, angry, etc.

gob·ble·dy·gook /góbəldeegōōk/ *n.* (also **gob·ble·de·gook**) *colloq.* pompous or unintelligible jargon.

gob·bler /góblər/ *n. colloq.* a male turkey.

Gob·e·lin /góbəlin, gṓbəlin, gawblán/ *n.* (in full **Gobelin tapestry**) **1** a tapestry made at the Gobelins factory. **2** a tapestry imitating this.

gobe·mouche /góbmōōsh/ *n.* (*pl.* **gobemouches** *pronunc.* same) a gullible listener.

go-be·tween *n.* an intermediary.

gob·let /góblit/ *n.* **1** ► a drinking vessel with a foot and a stem, usu. of glass. **2** *archaic* a metal or glass bowl-shaped drinking cup without handles.

gob·lin /góblin/ *n.* a mischievous, ugly, dwarflike creature of folklore.

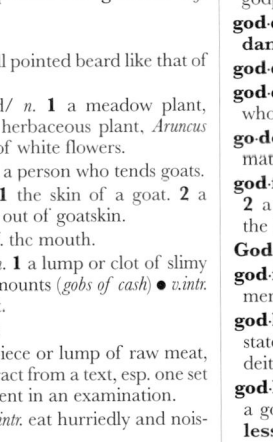

GOAT: MALE BAGOT GOAT

beard

GOBY: BUMBLEBEE FISH (*Brachygobius doriae*)

sucker

go·by /gṓbee/ *n.* (*pl.* **-ies**) ▲ any small marine fish of the family Gobiidae, having ventral fins joined to form a sucker or disk.

go-cart *n.* **1** a handcart; a stroller. **2** = GO-KART.

god /god/ *n.* **1 a** (in many religions) a superhuman being or spirit worshiped as having power over nature, human fortunes, etc. **b** an image, idol, animal, or other object worshiped as divine or symbolizing a god. **2** (**God**) (in Christian and other monotheistic religions) the creator and ruler of the universe. **3 a** an adored, admired, or influential person. **b** something worshiped like a god (*makes a god of success*). **4** *Theatr.* (in *pl.*) **a** the gallery. **b** the people sitting in it. □ **for God's sake!** see SAKE¹. **God the Father, Son, and Holy Spirit** (or **Ghost**) (in the Christian tradition) the Persons of the Trinity. **in God's name** an appeal for help. **in the name of God** an expression of surprise or annoyance. **my** (or **oh**) **God!** an exclamation of surprise, anger, etc. **play God** assume importance or superiority. **thank God!** an exclamation of pleasure or relief. **with God** dead and in heaven. □□ **god·hood** *n.* **god·ship** *n.* **god·ward** *adj. & adv.* **god·wards** *adv.*

god-aw·ful *adj. sl.* extremely unpleasant, nasty, etc.

god·child /gódchīld/ *n.* a person in relation to a godparent.

god·damn /gódám/ *adj.* (or **god·dam** or **god·damned** /-dámd/) *sl.* accursed.

god·daugh·ter /góddawtər/ *n.* a female godchild.

god·dess /gódis/ *n.* **1** a female deity. **2** a woman who is adored.

go·det /gōdét, góday/ *n.* a triangular piece of material inserted in a dress, glove, etc.

god·fa·ther /gódfaathər/ *n.* **1** a male godparent. **2** a person directing an illegal organization, esp. the Mafia.

God-fear·ing *adj.* earnestly religious.

god·for·sak·en /gódfərsaykən/ *adj.* devoid of all merit; dismal; dreary.

god·head /gódhed/ *n.* (also **God·head**) **1 a** the state of being God or a god. **b** divine nature. **2** a deity. **3** (**the Godhead**) God.

god·less /gódlis/ *adj.* **1** impious; wicked. **2** without a god. **3** not recognizing a god or gods. □□ **god·less·ness** *n.*

god·like /gódlīk/ *adj.* **1** resembling God or a god. **2** befitting to a god.

god·ly /gódlee/ *adj.* religious; pious; devout. □□ **god·li·ness** *n.*

god·moth·er /gódmuthər/ *n.* a female godparent.

go·down /gṓdown/ *n.* a warehouse in parts of E. Asia.

god·par·ent /gódpairənt/ *n.* a person who presents a child at baptism and responds on the child's behalf.

god·send /gódsend/ *n.* an unexpected but welcome event or acquisition.

god·son /gódsun/ *n.* a male godchild.

God·speed /gódspeed/ *int.* an expression of good wishes to a person starting a journey.

god·wit /gódwit/ *n.* any wading bird of the genus *Limosa,* with long legs and a long straight or slightly upcurved bill.

go·er /gṓər/ *n.* **1** a person or thing that goes (*a slow goer*). **2** (often in *comb.*) a person who attends (*a churchgoer*).

goes *3rd sing. present* of GO¹.

GOBLET

G

G

go·est /gṓist/ *archaic 2nd sing. present* of GO[1].

go·eth /gṓith/ *archaic 3rd sing. present* of GO[1].

Goe·the·an /gṓteeən/ *adj. & n.* (also **Goe·thi·an**) ● *adj.* of, relating to, or characteristic of the German writer J. W. von Goethe (d. 1832). ● *n.* an admirer or follower of Goethe.

go·fer /gṓfər/ *n. sl.* a person who runs errands, esp. on a movie set or in an office.

gof·fer /gófər/ *v. & n.* ● *v.tr.* make wavy, flute, or crimp (a lace edge, a trimming, etc.) with heated irons. ● *n.* an iron used for goffering.

go-get·ter *n. colloq.* an aggressively enterprising person.

gog·gle /gógəl/ *v., adj., & n.* ● *v.* **1** *intr.* **a** (often foll. by *at*) look with wide-open eyes. **b** (of the eyes) be rolled about; protrude. **2** *tr.* turn (the eyes) sideways or from side to side. ● *adj.* (usu. *attrib.*) (of the eyes) protuberant or rolling. ● *n.* (in *pl.*) **a** eyeglasses for protecting the eyes from glare, dust, water, etc. **b** *colloq.* eyeglasses. **2** (in *pl.*) a sheep disease; the staggers. **3** a goggling expression.

go-go *adj. colloq.* **1** (of a dancer, music, etc.) in pop music style, lively, and rhythmic. **2** unrestrained; energetic. **3** (of investment) speculative.

Goi·del /góyd'l/ *n.* a Celt who speaks Irish Gaelic, Scottish Gaelic, or Manx. □□ **Goi·del·ic** /-délik/ *adj.*

go·ing /gṓing/ *n. & adj.* ● *n.* **1 a** the act or process of going. **b** an instance of this. **2 a** the condition of the ground for walking, riding, etc. **b** progress affected by this (*found the going hard*). ● *adj.* **1** in or into action (*set the clock going*). **2** esp. *Brit.* existing; available (*there's hot soup going*). **3** current; prevalent (*the going rate*). □ **get going** start steadily talking, working, etc. (*can't stop him when he gets going*). **going for one** *colloq.* acting in one's favor (*he's got a lot going for him*). **going on fifteen**, etc. approaching one's fifteenth, etc., birthday. **going to** intending or intended to; about to (*it's going to sink!*). **to be going on with** for the time being. **while the going is good** while conditions are favorable.

go·ing con·cern *n.* a thriving business.

go·ing-o·ver *n.* **1** *colloq.* an inspection or overhaul. **2** *sl.* a beating. **3** *colloq.* a scolding.

go·ings-on /gṓingzón, -áwn/ *n.pl.* behavior, esp. morally suspect.

goi·ter /góytər/ *n.* (*Brit.* **goitre**) *Med.* a swelling of the neck resulting from enlargement of the thyroid gland. □□ **goit·rous** /-trəs/ *adj.*

go-kart *n.* a miniature racing car.

Gol·con·da /golkóndə/ *n.* a mine or source of wealth, advantages, etc.

GOLD IN QUARTZ MATRIX

quartz crystals　*gold*

gold /gōld/ *n. & adj.* ● *n.* **1** ◀ a yellow, malleable, ductile, high density metallic element resistant to chemical reaction, occurring naturally in quartz veins and gravel, and precious as a monetary medium, in jewelry, etc. ▷ METAL. ¶ Symb.: **Au**. **2** the color of gold. **3 a** coins or articles made of gold. **b** wealth. **4** something precious, beautiful, or brilliant (*all that glitters is not gold*). **5** = GOLD MEDAL. **6** the bull's-eye of an archery target. ● *adj.* **1** made wholly or chiefly of gold. **2** colored like gold.

gold brick *n. sl.* **1** a thing with only a surface appearance of value. **2** a lazy person.

gold·crest /gṓldkrest/ *n.* a small bird, *Regulus regulus*, with a golden crest.

gold dig·ger *n.* **1** *sl.* **a** a woman who wheedles money out of men. **b** a woman who strives to marry a rich man. **2** a person who digs for gold.

gold dust *n.* **1** gold in fine particles as often found naturally. **2** ◀ a plant, *Aurinia saxatile*, with many small yellow flowers.

GOLD DUST
(*Aurinia saxatile*)

gold·en /gṓldən/ *adj.* **1 a** made or consisting of gold. **b** yielding gold. **2** colored like gold (*golden hair*). **3** precious; valuable (*a golden memory*).

gold·en age *n.* **1** a supposed past age when people were happy and innocent. **2** the period of a nation's greatest prosperity, literary merit, etc.

gold·en-ag·er *n.* an old person.

gold·en boy (or **girl**) *colloq. n.* a popular or successful person.

gold·en calf *n.* wealth as an object of worship (Exod. 32).

Gold·en De·li·cious *n.* a variety of apple.

gold·en ea·gle *n.* a large eagle, *Aquila chrysaetos*, with yellow-tipped head feathers. ▷ EAGLE

Gold·en Fleece *n.* (in Greek mythology) a fleece of gold sought and won by Jason.

gold·en goose *n.* a continuing source of wealth or profit.

gold·en old·ie *n. colloq.* an old hit record or movie, etc., that is still well known and popular.

gold·en re·triev·er *n.* a retriever with a thick, golden-colored coat. ▷ DOG

gold·en·rod /gṓldənrod/ *n.* any plant of the genus *Solidago* with a rodlike stem and small bright yellow flowerheads.

gold·en rule *n.* a basic principle of action, esp. "do unto others as you would have them do unto you".

Gold·en State *n.* California.

gold·finch /gṓldfinch/ *n.* ► any of various brightly colored songbirds of the genus *Carduelis*.

GOLDFINCH
(*Carduelis carduelis*)

gold·fish /gṓldfish/ *n.* ▼ a small reddish golden Chinese carp kept for ornament, *Carassius auratus*.

GOLDFISH:
FANTAIL GOLDFISH
(*Carassius auratus*)

gold·fish bowl *n.* **1** a globular glass container for goldfish. **2** a situation lacking privacy.

gold leaf *n.* gold beaten into a very thin sheet. ▷ GILDING

gold med·al *n.* a medal of gold, usu. awarded as first prize.

gold mine *n.* **1** a place where gold is mined. **2** *colloq.* a source of wealth.

gold plate *n.* **1** vessels made of gold. **2** material plated with gold. □□ **gold-plate** *v.tr.*

gold rush *n.* a rush to a newly discovered gold field.

gold·smith /gṓldsmith/ *n.* a worker in gold; a manufacturer of gold articles.

gold stand·ard *n.* a system by which the value of a currency is defined in terms of gold.

go·lem /gṓləm/ *n.* **1** a clay figure supposedly brought to life in Jewish legend. **2** an automaton; a robot.

golf /golf, gawlf/ *n. & v.* ● *n.* ► a game in which a small hard ball is driven with clubs into a series of 18 or 9 holes with the fewest possible strokes. ▷ FAIRWAY. ● *v.intr.* play golf.

golf ball *n.* **1** a ball used in golf. ▷ GOLF. **2** a small

ball used in some electric typewriters to carry the type.

golf cart *n.* **1** a cart used for carrying golf clubs. **2** a motorized cart for golfers and equipment.

golf club *n.* **1** a club used in golf. ▷ GOLF. **2** an association for playing golf. **3** the premises used by a golf club.

golf course *n.* the course on which golf is played. ▷ GOLF

golf·er /gólfər/ *n.* a golf player.

Gol·gi bod·y /gáwljee/ *n.* (also **Gol·gi ap·pa·rat·us**) *Biol.* an organelle of vesicles and folded membranes within the cytoplasm of most eukaryotic cells, involved esp. in the secretion of substances.

gol·li·wog /góleewog/ *n.* a black-faced brightly dressed soft doll with fuzzy hair.

gol·lop /góləp/ *v. & n. colloq.* ● *v.tr.* (**golloped**, **golloping**) swallow hastily or greedily. ● *n.* a hasty gulp.

gol·ly[1] /gólee/ *int.* expressing surprise.

gol·ly[2] /gólee/ *n.* (*pl.* **-ies**) *colloq.* = GOLLIWOG.

go·mer /gṓmər/ *n. US* **1** *Mil. sl.* an inept or stupid colleague, esp. a trainee. **2** *colloq.* (used by doctors) a troublesome patient, esp. an elderly one.

-gon *comb. form* forming nouns denoting plane figures with a specified number of angles (*hexagon*; *polygon*; *n-gon*).

go·nad /gṓnad/ *n.* an animal organ producing gametes, e.g., the testis or ovary. ▷ REPRODUCTIVE ORGANS. □□ **go·nad·al** /-nád'l/ *adj.*

go·nad·o·troph·ic hor·mone /gōnádətrófik, -trófik/ *n.* (also **go·nad·o·trop·ic** /-trópik, trópik/) *Biochem.* any of various hormones stimulating the activity of the gonads.

go·nad·o·tro·phin /gōnádətrófin, -trófin/ *n.* (also **go·na·do·tro·pin**) = GONADOTROPHIC HORMONE.

gon·do·la /góndələ, gondólə/ *n.* **1** ► a light flat-bottomed boat used on Venetian canals, worked by one oar at the stern. **2** a car suspended from an airship or balloon. **3** an island of shelves used to display goods in a supermarket. **4** a car attached to a ski lift.

gon·do·lier /góndəleér/ *n.* the oarsman on a gondola. ▷ GONDOLA

gone /gawn, gon/ *adj.* **1 a** lost; hopeless. **b** dead. **2** *colloq.* pregnant for a specified time (*three months gone*). **3** *sl.* completely enthralled or entranced. □ **be gone** depart. **gone on** *sl.* infatuated with.

gon·er /gáwnər,gon/ *n. sl.* a person or thing that is doomed, ended, irrevocably lost, etc.; a dead person.

gong /gawng, gon/ *n.* **1** ► a metal disk with a turned rim, giving a resonant note when struck. ▷ ORCHESTRA. **2** a saucer-shaped bell. **3** *Brit. sl.* a medal.

go·ni·om·e·ter /gṓneeómitər/ *n.* an instrument for measuring angles. □□ **go·ni·om·e·try** *n.* **go·ni·o·met·ric** /-neeəmétrik/ *adj.* **go·ni·o·met·ri·cal** *adj.*

gon·o·coc·cus /gónəkókəs/ *n.* (*pl.* **gonococci** /-kókī, -kóksī/) a bacterium, *Neisseria gonorrhoeae*, that causes gonorrhea. □□ **gon·o·coc·cal** *adj.*

gon·or·rhe·a /gónəreéə/ *n.* a venereal disease with inflammatory discharge from the urethra or vagina.

goo /gσ̄o/ *n.* **1** a sticky or viscous substance. **2** sickly sentiment.

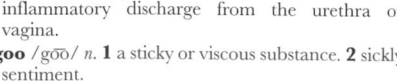

GONG: TRADITIONAL GONG FROM BORNEO

central boss　　*beater*

GOLF

Now a popular international sport, golf was established in Scotland by the 16th century. Players use wooden or metal clubs, each with a different function, to hit a ball from a level area called a tee, down a fairway – marked with hazards such as bunkers (sandpits) and rough (uncut grass) – onto a putting green, and into a hole. Competing individually or in teams, players move from one hole to the next, trying to advance the ball using as few strokes as possible.

GOLFER PREPARING TO
TAKE A FULL SWING

club shaft

club face

golf ball

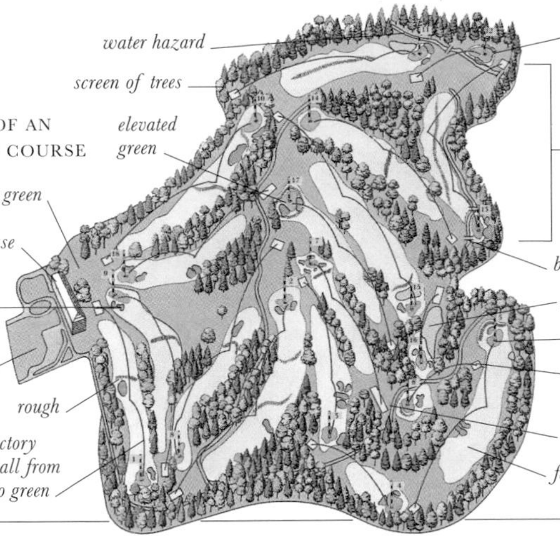

FEATURES OF AN
18-HOLE GOLF COURSE

water hazard

screen of trees

elevated green

putting green

clubhouse

bunker

practice area

rough

trajectory of ball from tee to green

putting green

dogleg hole

bridge

pond

hole

tee

pathway

fairway

EXAMPLES OF GOLF CLUBS

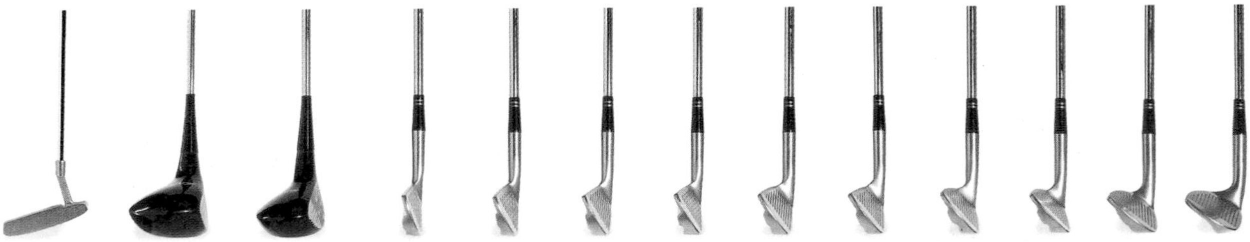

PUTTER   DRIVER   5 WOOD   DRIVING IRON   3 IRON   4 IRON   5 IRON   6 IRON   7 IRON   8 IRON   9 IRON   PITCHING WEDGE   SAND WEDGE

G

good /good/ *adj., n., & adv.* ● *adj.* (**better**, **best**) **1** having the right or desired qualities. **2 a** (of a person) efficient; competent (*good at math*). **b** (of a thing) reliable; efficient (*good brakes*). **c** (of health, etc.) strong (*good eyesight*). **3 a** kind (*good of you to come*). **b** morally excellent (*a good deed*). **c** charitable (*good works*). **d** well-behaved (*a good child*). **4** enjoyable, agreeable (*a good party*). **5** thorough; considerable (*a good wash*). **6 a** not less than (*waited a good hour*). **b** considerable in number, quality, etc. (*a good many people*). **7** beneficial (*good for you*). **8 a** valid; sound (*a good reason*). **b** financially sound (*his credit is good*). **9** in exclamations of surprise (*good heavens!*). **10** right; proper (*thought it good to have a try*). **11** fresh; eatable. **12** (sometimes patronizing) commendable; worthy (*good old George*). **13** well shaped; attractive (*good looks*). **14** in courteous greetings and farewells (*good afternoon*). ● *n.* **1** (only in *sing.*) what is beneficial or morally right (*only good can come of it*). **2** (only in *sing.*) a desirable end or object (*a future good*). **3** (in *pl.*) **a** movable property or merchandise. **b** *Brit.* things to be transported, as distinct from passengers; freight. **c** (prec. by *the*) *colloq.* what one has undertaken to supply (esp. deliver the goods). **d** (prec. by *the*) *sl.* the real thing; the genuine article. **4** proof, esp. of guilt. **5** (as *pl.*; prec. by *the*) virtuous people. ● *adv. colloq.* well (*doing pretty good*). □ **as good as** practically (*he as good as told me*). **be so good as** (or **be good enough**) **to** (often in a request) be kind and do (a favor) (*be so good as to open the window*). **be (a certain amount) to the good** have as net profit or advantage. **do good** show kindness. **do a person good** be beneficial to. **for good (and all)** finally; permanently. **good and** *colloq.* used as an intensifier before an adj. or adv. (*was good and angry*). **good for you!** (or **him!, her!**, etc.) exclamation of approval toward a person. **have a good mind** see

MIND. **have the goods on a person** *sl.* have advantageous information about a person. **have a good time** enjoy oneself. **in a person's good books** see BOOK. **in good faith** with honest or sincere intentions. **in good time 1** with no risk of being late. **2** (also **all in good time**) in due course but without haste. **make good 1** make up for; compensate for. **2** fulfill (a promise); effect (a purpose). **3** demonstrate the truth of (a statement). **4** gain and hold (a position). **5** replace or restore (a thing lost or damaged). **6** (*absol.*) accomplish what one intended. **to the good** having as profit or benefit. □□ **good·ish** *adj.*

Good Book *n.* the Bible.

good-bye /goodbí/ *int. & n.* (also **good·bye**, **good-by** or **goodby**) ● *int.* expressing good wishes on parting, ending a telephone conversation, etc. ● *n.* (*pl.* **good-byes**) the saying of "good-bye"; a parting; a farewell.

good for *adj.* **1** beneficial to. **2** able to perform; inclined for (*good for a ten-mile walk*). **3** able to be trusted to pay (*is good for $100*).

good-for-noth·ing *adj. & n.* ● *adj.* worthless. ● *n.* a worthless person.

Good Fri·day *n.* the Friday before Easter commemorating the crucifixion of Christ.

good-heart·ed *adj.* kindly; well-meaning.

good-hu·mored /goodhyóomərd/ *adj.* genial; cheerful. □□ **good-hu·mored·ly** *adv.*

good-look·er *n.* a handsome or attractive person.

good-look·ing *adj.* handsome; attractive.

good luck *n. & int.* ● *n.* good fortune; happy chance. ● *int.* exclamation of well-wishing.

good·ly /goodlee/ *adj.* (**goodlier**, **goodliest**) **1** comely; handsome. **2** of imposing size, etc.

good·man /goodmən/ *n.* (*pl.* **-men**) *archaic* the head of a household.

good-na·tured /goodnáychərd/ *adj.* kind; patient. □□ **good-na·tured·ly** *adv.*

good·ness /goodnis/ *n. & int.* ● *n.* **1** excellence, esp. moral. **2** kindness (*had the goodness to wait*).

GONDOLA

Gondolas, built from nine different woods, have plied the canals of Venice, Italy, for over 1,000 years. Once used to transport goods from markets to residences (*palazzi*), gondolas now serve largely as pleasure craft for tourists or to ferry Venetians to such events as weddings and funerals.

TRADITIONAL
VENETIAN GONDOLA

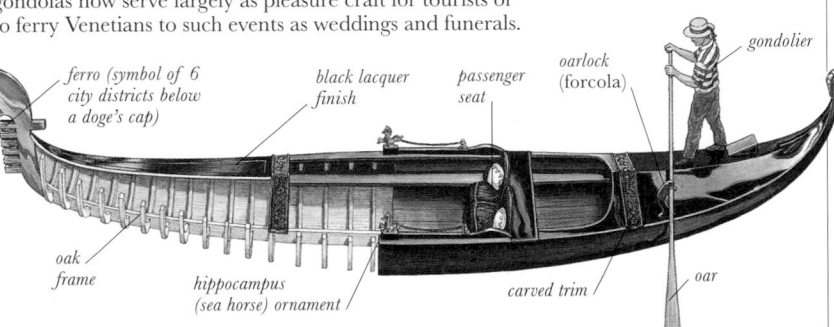

ferro (symbol of 6 city districts below a doge's cap)

black lacquer finish

passenger seat

oarlock (forcola)

gondolier

oak frame

hippocampus (sea horse) ornament

carved trim

oar

3 what is beneficial in a thing (*vegetables with all the goodness boiled out*). ● *int.* (as a substitution for "God") expressing surprise, anger, etc.

good·tem·pered /gŏŏdtémpərd/ *adj.* not easily annoyed.

good·wife /gŏŏdwīf/ *n.* (*pl.* **-wives**) *archaic* the mistress of a household.

good·will /gŏŏdwíl/ *n.* **1** kindly feeling. **2** the established reputation of a business, etc., as enhancing its value. **3** cheerful consent or acquiescence.

good will *n.* the intention and hope that good will result (see also GOODWILL).

good word *n.* (often in phr. **put in a good word for**) words in recommendation or defense.

good·y /gŏŏdee/ *n. & int.* ● *n.* (also **good·ie**) (*pl.* **-ies**) **1** (usu. in *pl.*) something good or attractive, esp. to eat. **2** *colloq.* a good or favored person, esp. a hero in a story, movie, etc. **3** = GOODY-GOODY *n.* ● *int.* expressing childish delight.

good·y-good·y *n. & adj.* ● *n.* a smug or obtrusively virtuous person. ● *adj.* obtrusively or smugly virtuous.

goo·ey /gŏŏ-ee/ *adj.* (**gooier, gooiest**) *sl.* **1** viscous; sticky. **2** sickly; sentimental.

goof /gŏŏf/ *n. & v. sl.* ● *n.* **1** a foolish person. **2** a mistake. ● *v.* **1** *tr.* bungle. **2** *intr.* blunder. **3** *intr.* (often foll. by *off*) idle.

goof·ball /gŏŏfbawl/ *n. sl.* a silly, ridiculous, or inept person.

goof·y /gŏŏfee/ *adj.* (**goofier, goofiest**) *sl.* stupid; silly. □□ **goof·i·ly** *adv.* **goof·i·ness** *n.*

goo·gol /gŏŏgawl/ *n.* ten raised to the hundredth power (10^{100}). ¶ Not in formal use.

gook /gŏŏk, gŏŏk/ *n. sl. offens.* a foreigner, esp. a person from E. Asia.

goon /gŏŏn/ *n. sl.* **1** a stupid person. **2** a person hired by racketeers, etc., to terrorize political or industrial opponents.

goop /gŏŏp/ *n. colloq.* a viscous substance.

goopy /gŏŏpee/ *adj. colloq.* thick; viscous.

goos·an·der /gŏŏsándər/ *n.* a large diving duck, *Mergus merganser*, with a narrow serrated bill; a common merganser.

goose /gŏŏs/ *n. & v.* ● *n.* (*pl.* **geese** /gees/) **1 a** ◀ any of various large water birds of the family Anatidae, with short legs, webbed feet, and a broad bill. ▷ WATERFOWL. **b** the female of this (opp. GANDER). **c** the flesh of a goose as food. **2** *colloq.* a simpleton. ● *v.tr. sl.* poke (a person) between the buttocks.

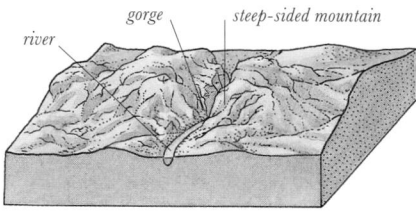

GOOSE: CHINESE GANDER

goose·ber·ry /gŏŏsberee, -bəree, gŏŏz-/ *n.* (*pl.* **-ies**) **1** a round edible yellowish green berry. ▷ FRUIT. **2** the thorny shrub, *Ribes grossularia*, bearing this fruit.

goose bumps *n.pl.* (also **goose flesh**) a bristling state of the skin produced by cold or fright.

goose egg *n.* a zero score in a game.

goose·foot /gŏŏsfŏŏt/ *n.* (*pl.* **-foots**) any plant of the genus *Chenopodium*, having leaves shaped like the foot of a goose.

goose·grass /gŏŏsgras/ *n.* cleavers.

goose step *n.* a military marching step in which the knees are kept stiff.

GOP *abbr.* Grand Old Party (the Republican Party).

go·pher¹ /gŏfər/ *n.* **1** (in full **pocket gopher**) any burrowing rodent of the family Geomyidae, native to N. America. **2** a N. American ground squirrel. **3** a tortoise, *Gopherus polyphemus*, native to the southern US.

go·pher² /gŏfər/ *n.* **1** *Bibl.* a tree from the wood of which Noah's ark was made. **2** (in full **gopher wood**) a tree, *Cladrastis lutea*, yielding yellowish timber.

go·ral /gáwrəl/ *n.* a goat antelope, *Nemorhaedus goral*, native to mountainous regions of N. India, having short horns curving to the rear.

Gor·di·an knot /gáwrdeeən/ *n.* **1** an intricate knot. **2** a difficult problem or task. □ **cut the Gordian knot** solve a problem by force or by evasion.

Gor·don set·ter /gáwrd'n/ *n.* **1** a setter of a black and tan breed, used as a gun dog. **2** this breed.

gore¹ /gawr/ *n.* **1** blood shed and clotted. **2** slaughter; carnage.

gore² /gawr/ *v.tr.* pierce with a horn, tusk, etc.

gore³ /gawr/ *n. & v.* ● *n.* **1** a wedge-shaped piece in a garment. **2** a triangular piece in an umbrella, etc. ● *v.tr.* shape with a gore.

gorge /gawrj/ *n. & v.* ● *n.* **1** ▼ a narrow opening between hills or a rocky ravine. ▷ RIVER. **2** an act of gorging. **3** the contents of the stomach. ● *v.* **1** *intr.* feed greedily. **2** *tr.* **a** (often *refl.*) satiate. **b** devour greedily. □ **one's gorge rises at** one is sickened by.

GORGE: SECTION THROUGH A GORGE CUT BY A RIVER

[labels: river, gorge, steep-sided mountain]

gor·geous /gáwrjəs/ *adj.* **1** richly colored; sumptuous. **2** *colloq.* very pleasant (*gorgeous weather*). **3** *colloq.* strikingly beautiful. □□ **gor·geous·ly** *adv.*

gor·get /górjit/ *n.* **1** *hist.* **a** a piece of armor for the throat. ▷ ARMOR. **b** a woman's wimple. **2** ◀ a patch of color on the throat of a bird, insect, etc.

GORGET OF A CONGO PEAFOWL (*Afropavo congensis*)

[label: gorget]

Gor·gon /gáwrgən/ *n.* **1** (in Greek mythology) each of three snake-haired sisters (esp. Medusa) with the power to turn anyone who looked at them to stone. **2** a frightening or repulsive person, esp. a woman.

gor·go·ni·an /gawrgṓneeən/ *n. & adj.* ● *n.* a usu. brightly colored horny coral of the order Gorgonacea, having a treelike skeleton bearing polyps, e.g., a sea fan. ● *adj.* of or relating to the Gorgonacea.

gor·gon·ize /gáwrgənīz/ *v.tr.* **1** stare at like a gorgon. **2** paralyze with terror, etc.

Gor·gon·zo·la /gáwrgənzṓlə/ *n.* a type of rich cheese with bluish green veins. ▷ CHEESE

go·ril·la /gərílə/ *n.* the largest anthropoid ape, *Gorilla gorilla*, native to central Africa, having a large head, short neck, and prominent mouth. ▷ PRIMATE

gor·man·dize /gáwrməndīz/ *v. & n.* ● *v.* **1** *intr. & tr.* eat or devour voraciously. **2** *intr.* indulge in good eating. ● *n.* = GOURMANDISE. □□ **gor·mand·iz·er** *n.*

gorm·less /gáwrmlis/ *adj.* esp. *Brit. colloq.* foolish; lacking sense. □□ **gorm·less·ly** *adv.*

gorse /gawrs/ *n.* ▶ any spiny yellow-flowered shrub of the genus *Ulex*.

GORSE (*Ulex parviflorus*)

gor·y /gáwree/ *adj.* (**gorier, goriest**) **1** involving bloodshed; blood thirsty (*a gory movie*). **2** covered in gore. □□ **gor·i·ly** *adv.* **gor·i·ness** *n.*

gosh /gosh/ *int.* expressing surprise.

gos·hawk /gós-hawk/ *n.* a large short-winged hawk, *Accipiter gentilis*.

gos·ling /gózling/ *n.* a young goose.

gos·pel /góspəl/ *n.* **1** the teaching or revelation of Christ. **2** (**Gospel**) **a** the record of Christ's life and teaching in the first four books of the New Testament. **b** each of these books. **c** a portion from one of them read at a service. **d** a similar book in the Apocrypha. **3** a thing regarded as absolutely true (*take my word as gospel*). **4** a principle one acts on or advocates. **5** (in full **gospel music**) African-American evangelical religious singing.

gos·pel truth *n.* something considered to be unquestionably true.

gos·sa·mer /gósəmər/ *n. & adj.* ● *n.* **1** a filmy substance of small spiders' webs. **2** delicate filmy material. ● *adj.* light and flimsy.

gos·sip /gósip/ *n. & v.* ● *n.* **1 a** unconstrained talk or writing esp. about persons or social incidents. **b** idle talk; groundless rumor. **2** an informal chat, esp. about persons or social incidents. **3** a person who indulges in gossip. ● *v.intr.* (**gossiped, gossiping**) talk or write gossip.

gos·sip col·umn *n.* a section of a newspaper devoted to gossip about well-known people. □□ **gos·sip col·umn·ist** *n.*

gos·sip·mon·ger /gósipmongər/ *n.* a perpetrator of gossip.

got *past* and *past part.* of GET.

Goth /goth/ *n.* **1** a member of a Germanic tribe that invaded the Roman Empire in the 3rd–5th c. **2** an uncivilized or ignorant person.

Goth·ic /góthik/ *adj. & n.* ● *adj.* **1** of the Goths or their language. **2** ▶ in the style of architecture prevalent in W. Europe in the 12th–16th c., characterized by pointed arches. **3** (of a novel, etc.) in a style popular in the 18th–19th c., with supernatural events. **4** *Printing* (of type) old-fashioned German, black letter, or sans serif. ● *n.* **1** the Gothic language. **2** Gothic architecture. **3** *Printing* ▼ Gothic type. □□ **Goth·i·cism** /-thisizəm/ *n.* **Goth·i·cize** /-thisīz/ *v.tr. & intr.*

[Gothic script: Incipit liber Bresith, quem Principio creauit deus]

GOTHIC TYPE FROM A 15TH-CENTURY GERMAN BIBLE

got·ta /gótə/ *colloq.* have got to (*we gotta go*).

got·ten *past part.* of GET.

Göt·ter·däm·mer·ung /gótərdámərung, gótərdémərŏŏng/ *n.* **1** the twilight (i.e., downfall) of the gods. **2** the complete downfall of a regime, etc.

gouache /gwaash, gŏŏ-aásh/ *n.* **1** ▼ a method of painting in opaque pigments ground in water and thickened with a gluelike substance. **2** these pigments. **3** a picture painted in this way.

[label: white gouache]

GOUACHE USED TO EMPHASIZE FORM IN A WATERCOLOR PAINTING

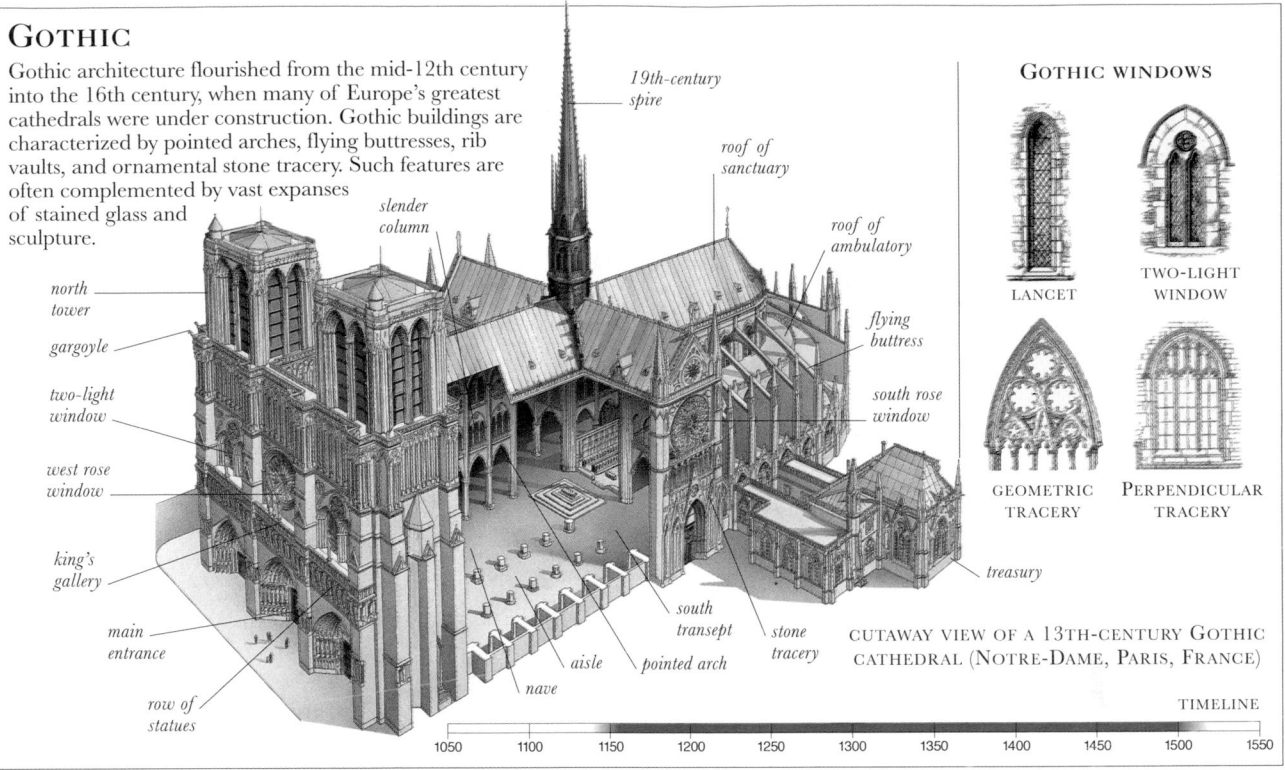

GOTHIC

Gothic architecture flourished from the mid-12th century into the 16th century, when many of Europe's greatest cathedrals were under construction. Gothic buildings are characterized by pointed arches, flying buttresses, rib vaults, and ornamental stone tracery. Such features are often complemented by vast expanses of stained glass and sculpture.

19th-century spire
roof of sanctuary
roof of ambulatory
slender column
flying buttress
north tower
gargoyle
south rose window
two-light window
west rose window
king's gallery
treasury
main entrance
south transept
stone tracery
aisle *pointed arch*
row of statues
nave

CUTAWAY VIEW OF A 13TH-CENTURY GOTHIC CATHEDRAL (NOTRE-DAME, PARIS, FRANCE)

GOTHIC WINDOWS

LANCET

TWO-LIGHT WINDOW

GEOMETRIC TRACERY

PERPENDICULAR TRACERY

TIMELINE

1050   1100   1150   1200   1250   1300   1350   1400   1450   1500   1550

G

Gou·da /góŏdə, gów-/ *n.* a flat round usu. Dutch cheese with a yellow rind.

gouge /gowj/ *n. & v.* ● *n.* **1** ▼ a chisel with a concave blade, used in woodworking, sculpture, and surgery. **2** an indentation or groove made with or as with this. ● *v.* **1** *tr.* cut with or as with a gouge. **2** *tr.* **a** (foll. by *out*) force out (esp. an eye with the thumb) with or as with a gouge. **b** force out the eye of (a person). **3** *tr. colloq.* swindle; extort money from; overcharge. □□ **goug·er** *n.*

concave blade

GOUGE: CARPENTER'S GOUGE

gou·lash /góŏlaash, -lash/ *n.* a highly seasoned Hungarian dish of meat and vegetables, usu. flavored with paprika.

gou·ra·mi /góŏraámee, góŏrəmee/ *n.* **1 a** a large freshwater fish, *Osphronemus goramy*, native to SE Asia, used as food. **b** any small fish of the family Osphronemidae, usu. kept in aquariums. **2** any small brightly colored freshwater fish of the family Belontiidae, usu. kept in aquariums. Also called **labyrinth fish**.

gourd /góŏrd/ *n.* **1 a** any of various fleshy usu. large fruits with a hard skin. **b** any of various climbing or trailing plants of the family Cucurbitaceae bearing this fruit. Also called **cucurbit**. **2** ▶ the hollow hard skin of the gourd fruit, dried and used as a drinking vessel, water container, etc. □□ **gourd·ful** *n.* (*pl.* **-fuls**).

gour·mand /góŏrmaánd/ *n. & adj.* ● *n.* **1** a glutton. **2** *disp.* a gourmet. ● *adj.* gluttonous; fond of eating, esp. to excess. □□ **gour·mand·ism** *n.*

gour·man·dise /góŏrmɔnde͡ez/ *n.* the habits of a gourmand; gluttony.

gour·met /góŏrmáy/ *n.* a connoisseur of good or delicate food.

gout /gowt/ *n.* **1** a disease with inflammation of the smaller joints, esp. the toe, as a result of excess uric acid salts in the blood. **2 a** a drop, esp. of blood. **b** a splash or spot. □□ **gout·y** *adj.*

GOURD: TRADITIONAL AFRICAN WATER CONTAINER

Gov. *abbr.* **1** Government. **2** Governor.

gov. *abbr.* governor.

gov·ern /gúvərn/ *v.* **1 a** *tr.* rule or control with authority; conduct the policy and affairs of. **b** *intr.* be in government. **2 a** *tr.* influence or determine (a person or a course of action). **b** *intr.* be the predominating influence. **3** *tr.* be a standard or principle for. **4** *tr.* check or control (esp. passions). **5** *tr. Gram.* (esp. of a verb or preposition) have (a noun or pronoun or its case) depending on it. □□ **gov·ern·a·ble** *adj.* **gov·ern·a·bil·i·ty** *n.*

gov·ern·ance /gúvərnəns/ *n.* **1** the act or manner of governing. **2** the office of governing. **3** sway; control.

gov·ern·ess /gúvərnis/ *n.* a woman employed to teach children in a private household.

gov·ern·ess·y /gúvərnisee/ *adj.* characteristic of a governess; prim.

gov·ern·ment /gúvərnmənt/ *n.* **1** the act or manner of governing. **2** the system by which a nation is governed. **3 a** a body of persons governing a nation. **b** (usu. **Government**) a particular party in office. **4** the nation as an agent. □□ **gov·ern·men·tal** /-mént'l/ *adj.* **gov·ern·men·tal·ly** *adv.*

gov·er·nor /gúvərnər/ *n.* **1** a person who governs; a ruler. **2** the executive head of each state of the US. **3 a** *hist.* an official governing a province, town, etc. **b** *Brit.* a representative of the British crown in a colony. **4** an officer commanding a fortress or garrison. **5** the head or a member of a governing body of an institution. **6** *Mech.* an automatic regulator controlling the speed of an engine, etc. □□ **gov·er·nor·ate** /-rət, -rayt/ *n.* **gov·er·nor·ship** *n.*

Govt. *abbr.* Government.

gown /gown/ *n. & v.* ● *n.* **1** a loose flowing garment, esp. a long dress worn by a woman. **2** the official robe of an alderman, judge, cleric, etc. **3** a surgeon's robe, worn during surgery. ● *v.tr.* (usu. as **gowned** *adj.*) attire in a gown.

goy /goy/ *n.* (*pl.* **goyim** /góyim/ or **goys**) *sl.* sometimes *derog.* a Jewish name for a non-Jew. □□ **goy·ish** *adj.* (also **goy·isch**).

GP *abbr.* **1** general practitioner. **2** Grand Prix.

GPA *abbr.* grade point average.

GPO *abbr.* **1** General Post Office. **2** Government Printing Office.

gr *abbr.* (also **gr.**) **1** gram(s). **2** grain(s). **3** gross. **4** gray.

Graaf·i·an fol·li·cle /graáfeeən, gráf-/ *n.* a follicle in the mammalian ovary in which an ovum develops prior to ovulation.

grab /grab/ *v. & n.* ● *v.* (**grabbed, grabbing**) **1** *tr.* **a** seize suddenly. **b** capture; arrest. **2** *tr.* take greedily or unfairly. **3** *tr. sl.* attract the attention of; impress. **4** *intr.* (foll. by *at*) make a sudden snatch at. **5** *intr.* (of brakes) act harshly or jerkily. ● *n.* **1** a sudden attempt to seize. **2** a mechanical device for clutching. ▷ EXCAVATE. **3** the practice of grabbing. □ **up for grabs** *sl.* easily obtainable. □□ **grab·ber** *n.*

grab bag *n.* **1** a container from which one removes a mystery gift. **2** a miscellaneous group of items.

grab·ble /grábəl/ *v.intr.* **1** grope about; feel for something. **2** (often foll. by *for*) sprawl on all fours; scramble (for something).

grab·by /grábee/ *adj. colloq.* tending to grab; greedy; grasping.

gra·ben /graábən/ *n.* (*pl.* same or **grabens**) *Geol.* a depression of the Earth's surface between faults.

grace /grays/ *n. & v.* ● *n.* **1** attractiveness, esp. in elegance of proportion or manner. **2** courteous good will (*had the grace to apologize*). **3** an attractive feature (*social graces*). **4 a** (in Christian belief) the unmerited favor of God. **b** the state of receiving this. **c** a divinely given talent. **5** goodwill; favor (*fall from grace*). **6** delay granted as a favor (*a year's grace*). **7** a short thanksgiving before or after a meal. **8** (**Grace**) (in Greek mythology) each of three beautiful sister goddesses, bestowers of beauty and charm. **9** (**Grace**) (prec. by *His, Her, Your*) forms of description or address for a duke, duchess, or archbishop. ● *v.tr.* **1** enhance or embellish. **2** confer honor on (*graced us with his presence*). □ **with good** (or **bad**) **grace** as if willingly (or reluctantly).

grace·ful /gráysfŏŏl/ *adj.* having or showing elegance. □□ **grace·ful·ly** *adv.* **grace·ful·ness** *n.*

grace·less /gráyslis/ *adj.* lacking elegance or charm. □□ **grace·less·ly** *adv.*

grace pe·ri·od *n.* the time allowed by law for payment of an amount due.

grac·ile /grásil, -sīl/ *adj.* slender; gracefully slender.

gra·cil·i·ty /grəsílitee/ *n.* **1** slenderness. **2** (of literary style) unornamented simplicity.

gra·cious /gráyshəs/ *adj.* & *int.* ● *adj.* **1** indulgent and beneficent to others. **2** (of God) merciful; benign. **3** kindly; courteous. ● *int.* expressing surprise. □□ **gra·cious·ly** *adv.* **gra·cious·ness** *n.*

gra·cious liv·ing *n.* an elegant way of life.

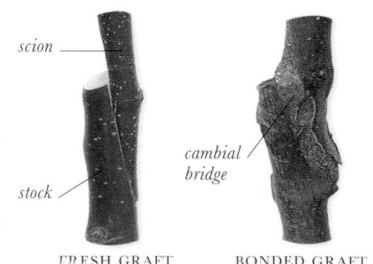

GRACKLE: COMMON
GRACKLE
(*Quiscalus quiscula*)

grack·le /grákəl/ *n.* **1** ◄ any of various orioles, esp. of the genus *Quiscalus*, native to America. **2** any of various mynahs, esp. of the genus *Gracula*, native to Asia.

grad /grad/ *n. colloq.* = GRADUATE *n.* 1.

gra·date /gráydayt/ *v.* **1** *v.intr.* & *tr.* pass or cause to pass by gradations from one shade to another. **2** *tr.* arrange in steps or grades of size, etc.

gra·da·tion /gráydáyshən/ *n.* (usu. in *pl.*) **1** a stage of transition or advance. **2 a** a certain degree in rank, intensity, etc. **b** an arrangement in such degrees. **3** (of paint, etc.) the gradual passing from one shade, tone, etc., to another.

grade /grayd/ *n.* & *v.* ● *n.* **1 a** a certain degree in rank, merit, proficiency, quality, etc. **b** a class of persons or things of the same grade. **2** a mark indicating the quality of a student's work. **3** a class in school, concerned with a particular year's work and usu. numbered from the first upwards. **4 a** a gradient or slope. **b** the rate of ascent or descent. **5 a** a variety of cattle produced by crossing native stock with a superior breed. **b** a group of animals at a similar level of development. **6** *Philol.* a relative position in a series of forms involving ablaut. ● *v.* **1** *tr.* arrange in or allocate to grades; class; sort. **2** *intr.* (foll. by *up, down, off, into,* etc.) pass gradually between grades, or into a grade. **3** *tr.* give a grade to (a student). **4** *tr.* blend so as to affect the grade of color with tints passing into each other. **5** *tr.* reduce (a road, etc.) to easy gradients. **6** *tr.* (often foll. by *up*) cross (livestock) with a better breed. □ **make the grade** *colloq.* reach the desired standard.

grade cross·ing *n.* a crossing of a roadway, etc., with a railroad track at the same level.

grade point *n.* the numerical equivalent of a scholastic letter grade. □ **grade point average** *n.*

grad·er /gráydər/ *n.* **1** a person or thing that grades. **2** (in *comb.*) a pupil of a specified grade in a school (*third grader*).

grade school *n.* elementary school.

gra·di·ent /gráydeeənt/ *n.* **1 a** a stretch of road, railroad, etc., that slopes. **b** the amount of such a slope. **2** the rate of rise or fall of temperature, pressure, etc., in passing from one region to another.

gra·din /gráydin/ *n.* (also **gra·dine** /-deen/) **1** each of a series of low steps or a tier of seats. **2** a ledge at the back of an altar.

grad·u·al /grájŏŏəl/ *adj.* & *n.* ● *adj.* **1** taking place or progressing by degrees. **2** not rapid or steep. ● *n. Eccl.* **1** a response sung or recited between the Epistle and Gospel in the Mass. **2** a book of music for the sung Mass. □□ **grad·u·al·ly** *adv.* **grad·u·al·ness** *n.*

grad·u·al·ism /grájŏŏəlizəm/ *n.* a policy of gradual reform rather than sudden change or revolution. □□ **grad·u·al·ist** *n.*

grad·u·ate *n.* & *v.* ● *n.* /grájŏŏət/ **1** a person who has been awarded an academic degree (also *attrib.: graduate student*). **2** a person who has completed a course of study. ● *v.* /grájŏŏ-áyt/ **1** *intr.* take an academic degree. **2** *intr.* **a** (foll. by *from*) be a graduate of a specified university. **b** (foll. by *in*) be a graduate in a specified subject. **3** *tr.* send out as a graduate from a university, etc. **4** *intr.* **a** (foll. by *to*) move up to (a higher grade of activity, etc.). **b** (foll. by *as, in*) gain specified qualifications. **5** *tr.* mark out in degrees. **6** *tr.* arrange in gradations; apportion (e.g., tax) according to a scale. **7** *intr.* (foll. by *into, away*) pass by degrees.

grad·u·ate school *n.* a division of a university for advanced work by graduates.

grad·u·a·tion /grájŏŏáyshən/ *n.* **1** the act of graduating. **2** a ceremony at which degrees are conferred. **3** each or all of the marks on a vessel or instrument indicating degrees of quantity, etc.

Grae·cism var. of GRECISM.

Grae·cize var. of GRECIZE.

Graeco- var. of GRECO-.

Grae·co-Ro·man var. of GRECO-ROMAN.

graf·fi·to /grəféetō/ *n.* (*pl.* **graffiti** /-tee/) **1** (usu. in *pl.*) a piece of writing or drawing scribbled, scratched, or sprayed on a surface. ¶ The plural form *graffiti* is sometimes used with a singular verb, even though it is not a mass noun in this sense, and so properly a plural construction is needed, e.g., *graffiti are an art form*.

GRAIN

Grain crops (cereals) are the most important of all the world's foods and have been cultivated since earliest times. Grain kernels are typically rich in starch, protein, and oil, while the husk contains vitamins and fiber. If kept dry, grains can be stored for months or years.

EXAMPLES OF DRIED GRAINS

WILD RICE
(*Zizania aquatica*)

OATS
(*Avena sativa*)

WHEAT
(*Triticum vulgare*)

BARLEY
(*Hordeum vulgare*)

CORN
(*Zea mays*)

MILLET
(*Panicum miliaceum*)

GRAFT

In many woody and herbaceous plants, a budded stem (scion) may be grafted onto a rootstock of another species or cultivar. Cells in the cambial layers of the two plants bond, creating a composite plant with improved characteristics.

WHIP-AND-TONGUE GRAFT

scion
cambial bridge
stock

FRESH GRAFT   BONDED GRAFT

---

graft[1] /graft/ *n.* & *v.* ● *n.* **1** *Bot.* **a** ▼ a shoot or scion inserted into a slit of stock, from which it receives sap. **b** the place where a graft is inserted. **2** *Surgery* a piece of living tissue, organ, etc., transplanted surgically. **3** *Brit. sl.* hard work. ● *v.* **1** *tr.* **a** (often foll. by *into, on, together,* etc.) insert (a scion) as a graft. **b** insert a graft on (a stock). **2** *intr.* insert a graft. **3** *tr. Surgery* transplant (living tissue). **4** *tr.* (foll. by *in, on*) insert or fix (a thing) permanently to another. **5** *intr. Brit. sl.* work hard. □□ **graft·er** *n.*

graft[2] /graft/ *n.* & *v. colloq.* ● *n.* **1** practices, esp. bribery, used to secure illicit gains in politics or business. **2** such gains. ● *v.intr.* seek or make such gains. □□ **graft·er** *n.*

gra·ham crack·er /gram, gráyəm/ *n.* a crisp, slightly sweet cracker made from whole wheat flour.

Grail /grayl/ *n.* (in full **Holy Grail**) (in medieval legend) the cup or platter used by Christ at the Last Supper, and in which Joseph of Arimathea received Christ's blood at the Cross, esp. as the object of quests by medieval knights.

grain /grayn/ *n.* & *v.* ● *n.* **1** ▲ a fruit or seed of a cereal. **2 a** (*collect.*) wheat or any related grass used as food. ▷ GRASS. **b** (*collect.*) their fruit. **c** any particular species of a cereal crop. **3 a** a small hard particle of salt, sand, etc. **b** a discrete particle or crystal, usu. small, in a rock or metal. **c** a piece of solid propellant for use in a rocket engine. **4** the smallest unit of weight in the troy system (equivalent to ¹⁄₄₈₀ of an ounce), and in the avoirdupois system (equivalent to ¹⁄₄₃₇.₅ of an ounce). **5** the smallest possible quantity (*a grain of truth*). **6 a** a roughness of surface. **b** *Photog.* a granular appearance on a photograph or negative. **7** the texture of wood, stone, etc. **8 a** a pattern of lines of fiber in wood or paper. **b** lamination or planes of cleavage in stone, coal, etc. **9** nature; tendency. ● *v.* **1** *tr.* paint in imitation of the grain of wood or marble. **2** *tr.* give a granular surface to. **3** *tr.* & *intr.* form into grains. □ **against the grain** (often in phr. **go against the grain**) contrary to one's natural inclination or feeling. **in grain** thorough; genuine; by nature; downright; indelible. □□ **grained** *adj.* (also in *comb.*).

grain el·e·va·tor *n.* a building in which grain is stored, usu. with mechanical devices for lifting and lowering the grain.

grain·y /gráynee/ *adj.* (**grainier, grainiest**) **1** granular. **2** resembling the grain of wood. **3** *Photog.* having a granular appearance. □□ **grain·i·ness** *n.*

gral·la·to·ri·al /grálətáwreeəl/ *adj. Zool.* of or relating to wading birds.

gram[1] /gram/ *n.* a metric unit of mass equal to one-thousandth of a kilogram.

gram[2] /gram/ *n.* any of various beans used as food, esp. the chickpea.

-gram /gram/ *comb. form* forming nouns denoting a thing written or recorded (*anagram; epigram*).

G

□□ **-grammatic** /grəmátik/ *comb. form* forming adjectives.

gram·i·na·ceous /gráminάyshəs/ *adj.* = GRAMINEOUS.

gram·in·e·ous /grəmíneeəs/ *adj.* of or like grass; grassy.

gram·i·niv·o·rous /grámínívərəs/ *adj.* feeding on grass, cereals, etc.

gram·ma·logue /grámələwg, -log/ *n.* a word represented by a single shorthand sign.

gram·mar /grámər/ *n.* **1** the study or rules of a language's inflections or other means of showing the relation between words (*Latin grammar*). **2** application of the rules of grammar (*bad grammar*). **3** a book on grammar. **4** the rudiments of an art or science. **5** *Brit. colloq.* = GRAMMAR SCHOOL. □□ **grammar·less** *adj.*

gram·mar·i·an /grəmáireeən/ *n.* an expert in grammar or linguistics; a philologist.

gram·mar school *n.* **1** *US* an elementary school. **2** *Brit. esp. hist.* a selective state-supported secondary school with a mainly academic curriculum. **3** *Brit. hist.* a school founded in or before the 16th c. for teaching Latin, later becoming a secondary school teaching academic subjects.

gram·mat·i·cal /grəmátikəl/ *adj.* **1** of or relating to grammar. **2** conforming to the rules of grammar. □□ **gram·mat·i·cal·ly** *adv.*

gram·o·phone /grámə fōn/ *n.* = PHONOGRAPH. □□ **gram·o·phon·ic** /-fónik/ *adj.*

gram·pus /grámpəs/ *n.* (*pl.* **grampuses**) ▼ a dolphin, *Grampus griseus*, with a blunt snout and long pointed black flippers.

pointed flippers   **GRAMPUS** (*Grampus griseus*)

Gram's stain /gramz/ *n.* (also **Gram stain**, **Gram's method**) *Biol.* a method of differentiating bacteria by staining with a dye, then attempting to remove the dye with a solvent, for purposes of identification. □ **Gram-positive** (or **-negative**) (of bacteria) that do (or do not) retain the dye.

gran /gran/ *n. colloq.* grandmother (cf. GRANNY).

gran·a·dil·la /gránədílə, -déeyə/ *n.* (also **gren·a·dil·la** /grén-/) ▶ a passionfruit.

gra·na·ry /gránəree, gráy-/ *n.* (*pl.* **-ies**) **1** a storehouse for threshed grain. **2** a region producing, and esp. exporting, much grain.

grand /grand/ *adj. & n.* ● *adj.* **1 a** imposing; dignified. **b** solemn in conception or expression. **2** main (*grand staircase*). **3** (**Grand**) of the highest rank, esp. in official titles (*Grand Inquisitor*). **4** *colloq.* excellent; enjoyable (*had a grand time*). **5** belonging to high society (*the grand folk at the manor*). **6** (in *comb.*) in family relationships, denoting the second degree of ascent or descent (*granddaughter*). ● *n.* **1** = GRAND PIANO. **2** (*pl.* same) *sl.* a thousand dollars or pounds sterling. □□ **grand·ly** *adv.* **grand·ness** *n.*

gran·dad /grándad/ *n.* (also **grand·dad**) *colloq.* **1** grandfather. **2** an elderly man.

gran·dam /grándam/ *n.* **1** (also **gran·dame**) *archaic* grandmother. **2** an old woman. **3** an ancestress.

grand·child /gránchīld, gránd-/ *n.* (*pl.* **-children**) a child of one's son or daughter.

grand·dad·dy /grándadee/ *n.* (also **grand·dad·dy**) (*pl.* **-dies**) **1** *colloq.* a grandfather. **2** the original and usu. most venerated of its kind (*the granddaddy of symphony orchestras*).

---

grand·daugh·ter /grándawtər/ *n.* a female grandchild.

grande dame /groND dáam/ *n.* a dignified woman of high rank.

gran·dee /grandée/ *n.* **1** a Spanish or Portuguese nobleman of the highest rank. **2** a person of high rank or eminence.

gran·deur /gránjər, -jōōr/ *n.* **1** majesty; splendor; dignity of appearance or bearing. **2** high rank; eminence. **3** nobility of character.

grand·fa·ther /gránfaathər, gránd-/ *n.* a male grandparent. □□ **grand·fa·ther·ly** *adj.*

grand·fa·ther clock *n.* a floor-standing pendulum clock in a tall wooden case. ▷ CLOCK

Grand Gui·gnol /groN geenyáwl/ *n.* a dramatic entertainment of a sensational or horrific nature.

gran·di·flo·ra /grándiflɔ́wrə/ *adj.* bearing large flowers.

gran·dil·o·quent /grandíləkwənt/ *adj.* **1** pompous in language. **2** given to boastful talk. □□ **gran·dil·o·quence** /-kwəns/ *n.* **gran·dil·o·quent·ly** *adv.*

gran·di·ose /grándeeós/ *adj.* **1** producing an imposing effect. **2** planned on an ambitious scale. □□ **gran·di·ose·ly** *adv.* **gran·di·os·i·ty** /-deeósitee/ *n.*

grand ju·ry *n. Law* a jury selected to examine the validity of an accusation prior to trial.

grand lar·ce·ny *n. Law* larceny in which the value of the stolen property exceeds a certain legally established limit.

grand·ma /gránmaa, gránd-/ *n. colloq.* grandmother.

grand mal /groN máal, gránd mál/ *n.* a serious form of epilepsy with loss of consciousness (cf. PETIT MAL).

grand·ma·ma /gránməmáa, -maamə, gránd-/ *n. archaic colloq.* = GRANDMA.

Grand Mar·ni·er /groN máarnyər/ *n. Trademark* an orange-flavored cognac-based liqueur.

grand·moth·er /gránmuthər, gránd-/ *n.* a female grandparent. □□ **grand·moth·er·ly** *adj.*

grand·moth·er clock *n.* a clock like a grandfather clock but in a shorter case.

grand·pa /gránpaa, gránd-/ *n. colloq.* grandfather.

grand·pa·pa /gránpəpáa, -paapə, gránd-/ *n. archaic colloq.* = GRANDPA.

grand·par·ent /gránpairənt, gránd-/ *n.* a parent of one's father or mother.

grand pi·a·no *n.* a large full-toned piano standing on three legs, with the body, strings, and soundboard arranged horizontally and in line with the keys. ▷ PIANO

Grand Prix /groN prée/ *n.* any of several important international automobile or motorcycle racing events.

grand siècle /groN syéklə/ *n.* the classical or golden age, esp. the 17th c. in France.

grand·sire /gránsīr, gránd-/ *n. archaic* grandfather; old man; ancestor.

grand slam *n.* **1** *Sports* the winning of all of a group of major championships. **2** *Bridge* the winning of all 13 tricks. **3** *Baseball* a home run hit with three runners on base.

grand·son /gránsun, gránd-/ *n.* a male grandchild.

grand·stand /gránstand, gránd-/ *n. & v.* ● *n.* the main stand for spectators at a racetrack, etc. ▷ RACETRACK. ● *v.tr.* perform ostentatiously to impress an audience; show off.

grand to·tal *n.* the final amount after everything is added up; the sum of other totals.

grange /graynj/ *n.* **1** *esp. Brit.* a country house with farm buildings. **2** (**Grange**) a farmer's social organization. **3** *archaic* a barn.

gran·if·er·ous /grəníf ərəs/ *adj.* producing grain or a

GRANADILLA: PURPLE PASSIONFRUIT (*Passiflora edulis*)

---

grainlike seed. □□ **gran·i·form** /gránifawrm/ *adj.*

gran·ite /gránit/ *n.* **1** ◀ a coarse, granular crystalline igneous rock composed of quartz, mica, hornblende, etc., used for building. ▷ IGNEOUS. **2** a determined or resolute quality, attitude, etc. □□ **gran·it·ic** /grənítik/ *adj.* **gran·it·oid** *adj. & n.*

GRANITE: PORPHYRITIC GRANITE

gran·iv·o·rous /grənívərəs/ *adj.* feeding on grain. □□ **gra·ni·vore** /gránivawr/ *n.*

gran·ny /gránee/ *n.* (also **gran·nie**) (*pl.* **-ies**) *colloq.* grandmother.

gran·ny knot *n.* ▶ a square knot crossed the wrong way and therefore insecure. ▷ KNOT

Gran·ny Smith /gránee smith/ *n.* an orig. Australian green variety of apple.

gra·no·la /grənólə/ *n.* a breakfast food consisting typically of a mixture of rolled oats, nuts, dried fruits, and brown sugar.

grant /grant/ *v. & n.* ● *v.tr.* **1 a** consent to fulfill (a request, etc.) (*granted all he asked*). **b** allow (a person) to have (a thing) (*granted me my freedom*). **c** (as **granted**) *colloq.* apology accepted; pardon given. **2** give formally; transfer legally. **3** (often foll. by *that* + clause) concede, esp. as a basis for argument. ● *n.* **1** the process of granting or a thing granted. **2** a sum of money given by the government for any of various purposes, esp. to finance education. **3** *Law* **a** a legal conveyance by written instrument. **b** formal conferment. □ **take for granted 1** assume something to be true or valid. **2** cease to appreciate through familiarity. □□ **grant·a·ble** *adj.* **gran·tee** /-tée/ *n.* (esp. in sense 2 of *v.*). **grant·er** *n.* **gran·tor** /-tór/ *n.* (esp. in sense 2 of *v.*).

Granth /grunt/ *n.* (also **Grunth**) ▼ the sacred scriptures of the Sikhs.

GRANNY KNOT

GRANTH: 20TH-CENTURY INDIAN GURU GRANTH SAHIB

gran tur·is·mo /gran tōōrízmō/ *n.* a high-performance model of car.

gran·u·lar /grányələr/ *adj.* **1** of grains or granules. **2** having a granulated surface. □□ **gran·u·lar·i·ty** /-láritee/ *n.*

gran·u·late /grányəlayt/ *v.* **1** *tr. & intr.* form into grains (*granulated sugar*). **2** *tr.* roughen the surface of. **3** *intr.* (of a wound, etc.) form small prominences at the beginning of healing; heal; join. □□ **gran·u·la·tion** /-láyshən/ *n.* **gran·u·la·tor** *n.*

gran·ule /grányōōl/ *n.* a small grain.

gran·u·lo·cyte /grányəlōsīt/ *n. Physiol.* any of various white blood cells having granules in their cytoplasm. □□ **gran·u·lo·cyt·ic** /-sítik/ *adj.*

grape /grayp/ *n.* **1** a berry (usu. green, purple, or black) growing in clusters on a vine, used as fruit and in making wine. ▷ FRUIT, VINE. **2** (prec. by *the*) *colloq.* wine. **3** = GRAPESHOT. **4** (in *pl.*) a diseased growth like a bunch of grapes on the pastern of a horse, etc., or on a pleura in cattle. □□ **grap·y** *adj.* (also **grap·ey**).

grape·fruit /gráypfrōōt/ *n.* (*pl.* same) **1** a large round yellow citrus fruit with an acid juicy pulp. ▷ CITRUS FRUIT. **2** the tree, *Citrus paradisi*, bearing this fruit.

G

GRAPE HYACINTH (*Muscari armeniacum*)

G

grape hya·cinth *n.* ▲ any liliaceous plant of the genus *Muscari*, with clusters of usu. blue flowers.

grape·shot /gráypshot/ *n. hist.* small balls used as charge in a cannon and scattering when fired.

grape·vine /gráypvīn/ *n.* **1** any of various vines of the genus *Vitis*. **2** *colloq.* the means of transmission of unofficial information or rumor (*heard it through the grapevine*).

graph[1] /graf/ *n. & v.* ● *n.* a diagram showing the relation between variable quantities, usu. of two variables, each measured along one of a pair of axes at right angles. ● *v.tr.* plot on a graph.

graph[2] /graf/ *n. Linguistics* a visual symbol, esp. a letter or letters, representing a unit of sound or other feature of speech.

-graph /graf/ *comb. form* forming nouns meaning: **1** a thing written or drawn, etc., in a specified way (*autograph*). **2** an instrument that records (*seismograph*).

graph·eme /gráfeem/ *n. Linguistics* **1** a class of letters, etc., representing a unit of sound. **2** a feature of a written expression that cannot be analyzed into smaller meaningful units. □□ **gra·phe·mat·ic** /-mátik/ *adj.* **gra·phe·mic** /grǝféemik/ *adj.* **gra·phe·mi·cal·ly** *adv.*

-grapher /grǝfǝr/ *comb. form* forming nouns denoting a person concerned with a subject (*geographer*; *radiographer*).

graph·ic /gráfik/ *adj. & n.* ● *adj.* **1** of or relating to the visual or descriptive arts, esp. writing and drawing. **2** vividly descriptive; conveying all (esp. unwelcome or unpleasant) details; unequivocal. **3** (of minerals) showing marks like writing on the surface or in a fracture. **4** = GRAPHICAL. ● *n.* a product of the graphic arts (cf. GRAPHICS). □□ **graph·i·cal·ly** *adv.* **graph·ic·ness** *n.*

-graphic /gráfik/ *comb. form* (also **-graphical** /gráfikǝl/) forming adjectives corresponding to nouns in *-graphy* (see -GRAPHY). □□ **-graphically** /gráfiklee/ *comb. form* forming adverbs.

graph·i·ca·cy /gráfikǝsee/ *n.* the ability to read a map, graph, etc., or to present information by means of diagrams.

graph·i·cal /gráfikǝl/ *adj.* **1** of or in the form of graphs (see GRAPH[1]). **2** graphic. □□ **graph·i·cal·ly** *adv.*

graph·i·cal us·er in·ter·face *n. Computing* a visual way of interacting with a computer using items suchs as windows, icons, and menus. ¶ Abbr.: **GUI**.

graph·ic arts *n.pl.* the visual and technical arts involving design, writing, drawing, etc.

graph·ic e·qual·iz·er *n.* a device for the separate control of the strength and quality of selected audio frequency bands.

graph·ics /gráfiks/ *n.pl.* (usu. treated as *sing.*) **1** the products of the graphic arts, esp. commercial design or illustration. **2** the use of diagrams in calculation and design. **3** (in full **computer graphics**) *Computing* a mode of processing and output in which a significant part of the information is in pictorial form.

graph·ite /gráfīt/ *n.* ► a crystalline allotropic form of carbon used as a solid lubricant, in pencils, etc. Also called **plumbago**. ▷ ALLOTROPE. □□ **gra·phit·ic** /-fítik/ *adj.* **graph·i·tize** /-fitīz/ *v.tr. & intr.*

graph·ol·o·gy /grǝfóləjee/ *n.* **1** the study of handwriting esp. as a supposed guide to character. **2** a system of graphic formulae. **3** *Linguistics* the study of systems of writing. □□ **graph·o·log·i·cal** /gráfǝlójikǝl/ *adj.* **graph·ol·o·gist** *n.*

graph pa·per *n.* paper printed with a network of lines as a basis for drawing graphs.

-graphy /grǝfee/ *comb. form* forming nouns denoting: **1** a descriptive science (*bibliography*; *geography*). **2** a technique of producing images (*photography*; *radiography*). **3** a style or method of writing, drawing, etc. (*calligraphy*).

grap·nel /grápnǝl/ *n.* **1** a device with iron claws, attached to a rope and used for dragging or grasping. **2** a small anchor with several flukes.

grap·pa /gráapǝ/ *n.* a brandy distilled from the fermented residue of grapes after they have been pressed in wine-making.

grap·ple /grápǝl/ *v. & n.* ● *v.* **1** *intr.* (often foll. by *with*) fight at close quarters. **2** *intr.* (foll. by *with*) try to manage a difficult problem, etc. **3** *tr.* **a** grip with the hands. **b** seize with or as with a grapnel. ● *n.* **1 a** a hold or grip in or as in wrestling. **b** a contest at close quarters. **2** a clutching instrument. □□ **grap·pler** *n.*

grap·to·lite /gráptǝlīt/ *n.* an extinct marine invertebrate animal found as a fossil in lower Paleozoic rocks.

grasp /grasp/ *v. & n.* ● *v.* **1** *tr.* **a** clutch at; seize greedily. **b** hold firmly. **2** *intr.* (foll. by *at*) try to seize. **3** *tr.* understand or realize (a fact or meaning). ● *n.* **1** a firm hold. **2** (foll. by *of*) **a** mastery or control (a *grasp of the situation*). **b** a mental hold (a *grasp of the facts*). □ **grasp at straws** see STRAW. □□ **grasp·a·ble** *adj.* **grasp·er** *n.*

grasp·ing /gráasping/ *adj.* avaricious; greedy. □□ **grasp·ing·ly** *adv.* **grasp·ing·ness** *n.*

grass /gras/ *n. & v.* ● *n.* **1 a** a vegetation belonging to a group of small plants with green blades that are eaten by cattle, horses, etc. **b** any species of this. **c** ▼ any plant of the family Gramineae, which includes cereals, reeds, and bamboos. **2** pasture land. **3** a lawn. **4** *sl.* marijuana. ● *v.tr.* **1** cover with turf. **2** *tr.* provide with pasture. □ **out to grass 1** to pasture. **2** in retirement. □□ **grass·less** *adj.* **grass·like** *adj.*

GRAPHITE

grass·hop·per /grás-hoppǝr/ *n.* a jumping and chirping plant-eating insect of the order Saltatoria. ▷ ORTHOPTERAN

grass·land /grásland/ *n.* a large open area covered with grass, esp. one used for grazing.

grass roots *n.pl.* **1** a fundamental level or source. **2** ordinary people; the rank and file of an organization, esp. a political party.

grass skirt *n. Polynesia* a skirt made of long grass and leaves fastened to a waistband.

grass snake *n.* **1** the common greensnake, *Opheodrys vernalis*. **2** *Brit.* the common ringed snake, *Natrix natrix*.

grass wid·ow (or **widower**) *n.* a person whose husband (or wife) is away for a prolonged period.

grass·y /grásee/ *adj.* (**grassier**, **grassiest**) **1** covered with or abounding in grass. **2** resembling grass. **3** of grass. □□ **grass·i·ness** *n.*

grate[1] /grayt/ *v.* **1** *tr.* reduce to small particles by rubbing on a serrated surface. **2** *intr.* (often foll. by *against, on*) rub with a harsh scraping sound. **3** *tr.* utter in a harsh tone. **4** *intr.* **a** sound harshly. **b** have an irritating effect. **5** *tr.* grind (one's teeth). **6** *intr.* creak.

grate[2] /grayt/ *n.* **1** the recess of a fireplace. **2** a metal frame confining fuel in a grate.

grate·ful /gráytfŏŏl/ *adj.* **1** feeling or showing gratitude. **2** pleasant, acceptable. □□ **grate·ful·ly** *adv.* **grate·ful·ness** *n.*

grat·er /gráytǝr/ *n.* a device for reducing cheese or other food to small particles.

grat·i·cule /gratikyŏŏl/ *n.* fine lines or fibers incorporated in a telescope or other optical instrument as a measuring scale or as an aid in locating objects.

grat·i·fy /grátifī/ *v.tr.* (**-fies**, **-fied**) **1 a** please; delight. **b** please by compliance; assent to the

---

GRASS

The grass family contains some 9,000 species, including both terrestrial and aquatic species. No other plant family has been so successful in colonizing a broad range of habitats across the world. Most grasses have inconspicuous flowers that are wind pollinated. Certain species (the cereals) are cultivated as food crops; others are used in horticulture.

EXTERNAL
FEATURES OF
COUCH GRASS
(*Agropyron repens*)

caryopsis
(dry fruit)

culm
(jointed
stem)

node

lamina
(blade)

sheathing
leaf base

round,
hollow stem

roots

MAIN TYPES OF GRASS

CEREALS
bread wheat
(*Triticum aestivum*)

GRASSES
winter wild oats
(*Avena sterilis*)

BAMBOOS
(*Arundinaria nitida*)

REEDS
cattail
(*Arundo donax*)

wish of. **2** yield to (a feeling or desire). □□ **grat·i·fi·ca·tion** *n.* **grat·i·fi·er** *n.* **grat·i·fy·ing** *adj.* **grat·i·fy·ing·ly** *adv.*

grat·ing[1] /gráyting/ *adj.* **1** sounding harsh. **2** having an irritating effect. □□ **grat·ing·ly** *adv.*

grat·ing[2] /gráyting/ *n.* **1** a framework of parallel or crossed metal bars. **2** *Optics* a set of parallel wires, lines ruled on glass, etc., for producing spectra by diffraction.

grat·is /grátis, graa-/ *adv. & adj.* free; without charge.

grat·i·tude /grátitõod, -tyõod/ *n.* being thankful; readiness to return kindness.

gra·tu·i·tous /grətõoitəs, tyõo-/ *adj.* **1** given or done free of charge. **2** uncalled-for; lacking good reason. □□ **gra·tu·i·tous·ly** *adv.* **gra·tu·i·tous·ness** *n.*

gra·tu·i·ty /grətõoitee, -tyõo-/ *n.* (*pl.* **-ies**) a tip.

grat·u·la·to·ry /gráchələtáwree/ *adj.* expressing congratulation.

gra·va·men /grəváymen/ *n.* (*pl.* **gravamens** or **gravamina** /-vámínə/) **1** the essence or most serious part of an argument. **2** a grievance.

grave[1] /grayv/ *n.* **1** a trench dug in the ground to receive a coffin for burial. **2** (prec. by *the*) death. □ **turn in one's grave** (of a dead person) be likely to have been shocked or angry if still alive.

grave[2] /grayv/ *adj. & n.* ● *adj.* **1 a** serious; weighty; important (*a grave matter*). **b** dignified; solemn; somber (*a grave look*). **2** extremely threatening (*grave danger*). ● *n.* /grayv/ = GRAVE ACCENT. □□ **grave·ly** *adv.* **grave·ness** *n.*

grave[3] /grayv/ *v.tr.* (*past part.* **graven** or **graved**) **1** (foll. by *in, on*) fix indelibly (on one's memory). **2** engrave.

grave[4] /grayv/ *v.tr.* clean (a ship's bottom) by burning off accretions and by tarring.

gra·ve[5] /gráavay/ *adj. & adv.* ● *adj.* slow and solemn. ● *adv.* slowly and solemnly.

grave ac·cent *n.* /graav, grayv/ a mark (`) placed over a vowel in some languages to denote pronunciation, length, etc., orig. indicating low or falling pitch.

grave·dig·ger /gráyvdigər/ *n.* a person who digs graves.

grav·el /grávəl/ *n. & v.* ● *n.* **1 a** a mixture of coarse sand and small waterworn or pounded stones, used for paths and roads. **b** *Geol.* a stratum of this. **2** *Med.* aggregations of crystals in the urinary tract. ● *v.tr.* (**graveled, graveling**; also **gravelled, gravelling**) **1** lay or strew with gravel. **2** perplex; puzzle.

grave·lax var. of GRAVLAX.

grav·el·ly /grávəlee/ *adj.* **1** of or like gravel. **2** having or containing gravel. **3** (of a voice) deep and rough sounding.

grav·en *past part.* of GRAVE[3].

grav·en im·age *n.* an idol.

grav·er /gráyvər/ *n.* **1** an engraving tool; a burin. **2** an engraver; a carver.

Graves' dis·ease /grayvz/ *n.* a type of goiter with characteristic swelling of the neck and protrusion of the eyes, resulting from an overactive thyroid gland.

grave·stone /gráyvstōn/ *n.* a stone (usu. inscribed) marking a grave.

grave·yard /gráyvyaard/ *n.* a burial ground.

grave·yard shift *n.* a work shift that usu. starts about midnight and ends about eight in the morning.

grav·id /grávid/ *adj. literary* or *Zool.* pregnant.

gra·vim·e·ter /grəvímitər/ *n.* an instrument for measuring the difference in the force of gravity from one place to another.

gravi·met·ric /grávimétrik/ *adj.* of or relating to the measurement of weight.

gra·vim·e·try /grəvímitree/ *n.* the measurement of weight.

grav·i·tas /grávitaas/ *n.* solemn demeanor; seriousness.

grav·i·tate /grávitayt/ *v. intr.* **1** (foll. by *to, toward*) be attracted to some source of influence. **2** sink by or as if by gravity.

grav·i·ta·tion /grávitáyshən/ *n. Physics* **1** a force of attraction between any particle of matter in the universe and any other. **2** the effect of this, esp. the falling of bodies to the Earth.

grav·i·ta·tion·al /grávitáyshənəl/ *adj.* of or relating to gravitation. □□ **grav·i·ta·tion·al·ly** *adv.*

grav·i·ty /grávitee/ *n.* **1 a** the force that attracts a body to the center of the Earth or other celestial body. **b** the degree of intensity of this measured by acceleration. **c** gravitational force. **2** the property of having weight. **3 a** importance; seriousness. **b** solemnity; sobriety.

grav·lax /grávlaaks/ *n.* (also **grave·lax**) filleted salmon cured by marination in salt, sugar, and dill.

gra·vure /grəvyóor/ *n.* = PHOTOGRAVURE.

gra·vy /gráyvee/ *n.* (*pl.* **-ies**) **a** the juices exuding from meat during and after cooking. **b** sauce for food, made by thickening these.

gra·vy train *n. sl.* a source of easy financial benefit.

gray[1] /gray/ *adj., n., & v.* (also **grey**) ● *adj.* **1** of a color intermediate between black and white. **2 a** (of the weather, etc.) dull; dismal. **b** bleak; (of a person) depressed. **3 a** (of hair) turning white with age, etc. **b** (of a person) having gray hair. **4** anonymous; nondescript. ● *n.* **1 a** a gray color or pigment. **b** gray clothes or material (*dressed in gray*). **2** a gray or white horse. ● *v.tr. & intr.* make or become gray. □□ **gray·ish** *adj.* **gray·ly** *adv.* **gray·ness** *n.*

gray[2] /gray/ *n. Physics* the SI unit of the absorbed dose of ionizing radiation, corresponding to one joule per kilogram. ¶ Abbr.: **Gy.**

gray a·re·a *n.* a situation sharing features of more than one category and not clearly attributable to any one category. an area in economic decline.

gray·beard /gráybeerd/ *n. archaic* **1** an old man. **2** a large jug for alcohol.

gray·ling /gráyling/ *n.* ▼ any silver-gray freshwater fish of the genus *Thymallus*, with a long high dorsal fin.

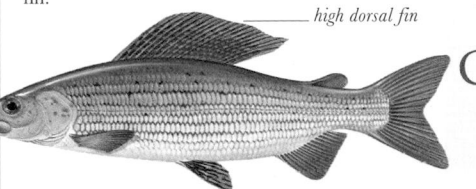

—— high dorsal fin

GRAYLING (*Thymallus thymallus*)

gray mat·ter *n.* **1** the darker tissues of the brain and spinal cord consisting of nerve cell bodies and branching dendrites. ▷ MENINX. **2** *colloq.* intelligence.

gray·wacke /gráywakə, -wak/ *n.* (*Brit.* **grey·wacke**) *Geol.* a dark and coarse-grained sandstone, usu. with an admixture of clay.

graze[1] /grayz/ *v.* **1** *intr.* (of cattle, etc.) eat growing grass. **2** *tr.* **a** feed (cattle, etc.) on growing grass. **b** feed on (grass). **3** *intr.* pasture cattle. □□ **graz·er** *n.*

graze[2] /grayz/ *v. & n.* ● *v.* **1** *tr.* scrape (the skin) so as to break the surface with only minor bleeding. **2 a** *tr.* touch lightly in passing. **b** *intr.* (foll. by *against, along*, etc.) move with a light passing contact. ● *n.* an act or instance of grazing.

gra·zier /gráyzhər/ *n.* a person who feeds cattle for market. □□ **gra·zier·y** *n.*

graz·ing /gráyzing/ *n.* grassland suitable for pasturage.

grease /grees/ *n. & v.* ● *n.* **1** oily or fatty matter esp. as a lubricant. **2** the melted fat of a dead animal. ● *v.tr.* also /greez/ lubricate with grease. □ **grease the palm of** *colloq.* bribe. **like greased lightning** *colloq.* very fast.

grease gun ▶ a device for pumping grease under pressure to a particular point.

grease mon·key *n. sl.* a mechanic who works on motor vehicles.

grease·paint /gréespaynt/ *n.* a waxy composition used as makeup for actors.

grease·proof /gréesprõof/ *adj.* impervious to the penetration of grease.

greas·er /gréesər/ *n.* **1** *sl.* a member of a gang of young street toughs. **3** *sl. offens.* a Mexican or Spanish-American.

greas·y /gréesee, gréezee/ *adj.* (**greas·ier, greasiest**) **1 a** of or like grease. **b** smeared with grease. **c** containing or having too much grease. **2 a** slippery. **b** (of a person or manner) unpleasantly unctuous. **c** objectionable. □□ **greas·i·ly** *adv.* **greas·i·ness** *n.*

greas·y spoon *n. sl.* an inexpensive small restaurant that serves fried food and that is often dirty or unsanitary.

G

GRAVITY

In 1687, Sir Isaac Newton postulated his theory that a gravitational force acts on all matter that has mass. Furthermore, the force between two objects depends not only on their physical mass but also on the distance between them. Thus if the Moon were twice its actual mass (as shown below), the gravitational force between the Earth and the Moon would be twice as large as it is. If the Moon were also half its actual distance from the Earth, the force of gravity would be four times as large.

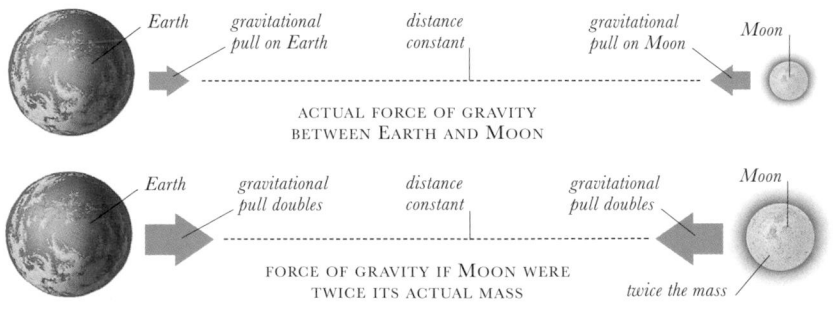

HOW GRAVITY CHANGES WITH MASS

Earth   *gravitational pull on Earth*   *distance constant*   *gravitational pull on Moon*   Moon

ACTUAL FORCE OF GRAVITY
BETWEEN EARTH AND MOON

Earth   *gravitational pull doubles*   *distance constant*   *gravitational pull doubles*   Moon

FORCE OF GRAVITY IF MOON WERE
TWICE ITS ACTUAL MASS   *twice the mass*

great /grayt/ *adj. & n.* ● *adj.* **1 a** of a size, amount, extent, or intensity considerably above the average. **b** also with implied surprise, contempt, etc. (*great stuff!*). **c** reinforcing other words denoting size, quantity, etc. (*a great big hole*). **2** important; worthy or most worthy of consideration. **3** grand; imposing (*a great occasion*). **4 a** (esp. of a public or historic figure) distinguished. **b** (as a title denoting the most important (*Alexander the Great*). **5 a** (of a person) remarkable in ability, character, etc. (*a great thinker*). **b** (of a thing) outstanding of its kind (*the Great Depression*). **6** (foll. by *at*) skilled; well-informed. **7** doing a thing habitually or extensively (*a great reader*). **8** (also **greater**) the larger of the species, etc. (*great auk*). **9** (**Greater**) (of a city, etc.) including adjacent urban areas (*Greater Boston*). **10** *colloq.* **a** very enjoyable or satisfactory; (*had a great time*). **b** (as an exclam.) fine; very good. **11** (in *comb.*) denoting one degree further removed upwards or downwards (*great-uncle*). ● *n.* a great or outstanding person or thing. □ **great and small** all classes or types. **great deal** see DEAL[1]. **the great majority** by far the most. **to a great extent** largely. □□ **great·ness** *n.*

Great Brit·ain *n.* England, Wales, and Scotland.

great·coat /gráytkōt/ *n.* a long heavy overcoat.

Great Dane *n.* ▼ a dog of a very large, short-haired breed.

GREAT DANE

Great Di·vide *n.* (prec. by *the*) **1** a vast continental divide or watershed between two drainage systems, esp. the Rocky Mountains of N. America. **2** the boundary between life and death.

great·heart·ed /gráyt-haártid/ *adj.* magnanimous; having a noble or generous mind. □□ **great·heart·ed·ness** *n.*

Great Lakes *n.pl.* (prec. by *the*) the Lakes Superior, Huron, Michigan, Erie, and Ontario, along the boundary of the US and Canada.

great·ly /gráytlee/ *adv.* by a considerable amount; much (*greatly admired*; *greatly superior*).

great tit *n.* a Eurasian songbird, *Parus major*, with black and white head markings.

great toe *n.* the big toe.

Great War *n.* World War I (1914–18).

greave /greev/ *n.* (usu. in *pl.*) armor for the shin. ▷ ARMOR

grebe /greeb/ *n.* any diving bird of the family Podicipedidae, with a long neck.

Gre·cian /gréeshən/ *adj.* (of architecture or facial outline) following Greek models or ideals.

Gre·cism /gréesizəm/ *n.* (also **Grae·cism**) **1** a Greek idiom, esp. as imitated in another language. **2 a** the Greek spirit, style, mode of expression, etc. **b** the imitation of these.

Gre·cize /gréesīz/ *v.tr.* (also **Grae·cize**) give a Greek character or form to.

Greco- /grékō/ *comb. form* (also **Graeco-**) Greek; Greek and.

Gre·co-Ro·man /grékō-rṓmən, gréko–/ *adj.* **1** of or relating to the Greeks and Romans. **2** *Wrestling* denoting a style attacking only the upper part of the body.

greed /greed/ *n.* an excessive desire, esp. for food or wealth.

greed·y /gréedee/ *adj.* (**greedier**, **greediest**) **1** having or showing an excessive appetite for food. **2** wanting wealth to excess. **3** (foll. by *for*, or *to* + infin.) very keen or eager. □□ **greed·i·ly** *adv.* **greed·i·ness** *n.*

Greek /greek/ *n. & adj.* ● *n.* **1 a** a native or inhabitant of modern Greece; a person of Greek descent. **b** a native or citizen of any of the ancient states of Greece. **2** the Indo-European language of Greece. ● *adj.* of Greece or its people or language. □□ **Greek·ness** *n.*

Greek cross *n.* a cross with four equal arms.

green /green/ *adj., n., & v.* ● *adj.* **1** of the color between blue and yellow in the spectrum. **2** covered with leaves or grass. **3** (of fruit, etc., or wood) unripe or unseasoned. **4** not dried, smoked, or tanned. **5** inexperienced; naive. **6 a** (of the complexion) sickly-hued. **b** jealous; envious. **7** young; flourishing. **8** not worn out (*a green old age*). **9** (also **Green**) concerned with protection of the environment as a political principle. ● *n.* **1** a green color or pigment. **2** green clothes or material. **3 a** a piece of common grassy land (*village green*). **b** a grassy area used for a special purpose (*putting green*). **c** *Golf* a putting green. ▷ GOLF. **4** (in *pl.*) green vegetables. **5** (also **Green**) a member or supporter of an environmentalist group or party. **6** *sl.* low-grade marijuana. **7** *sl.* money. **8** green foliage or growing plants. ● *v. tr. & intr.* make or become green. □□ **green·ish** *adj.* **green·ness** *n.*

green·back /gréenbak/ *n.* a US legal tender note.

green bean *n.* the green pods of a young kidney bean, eaten as a vegetable. Also STRING BEAN.

Green Be·ret *n. Mil.* a member of the U.S. Army Special Forces.

green·bot·tle /gréenbot'l/ *n.* any fly of the genus *Lucilia*, esp. *L. sericata* which lays eggs in the flesh of sheep.

green card *n.* **1** a work and residence permit issued to permanent resident aliens in the US. **2** *Brit.* an international insurance document for motorists.

green·er·y /gréenəree/ *n.* green foliage or growing plants.

green-eyed mon·ster *n.* jealousy.

green·field /gréenfeeld/ *n.* (*attrib.*) (of a site, in terms of its potential development) having no previous building development on it.

green·finch /gréenfinch/ *n.* ▶ a finch, *Carduelis chloris*, with green and yellow plumage.

green·fly /gréenflī/ *n.* (*pl.* **-flies**) **1** a green aphid. **2** these collectively.

green·gage /gréengayj/ *n.* a roundish green fine-flavored variety of plum.

green·gro·cer /gréengrṓsər/ *n.* a retailer of fruit and vegetables.

green·heart /gréenhaart/ *n.* **1** any of several tropical American trees, esp. *Ocotea rodiaei*. **2** the hard greenish wood of one of these.

green·horn /gréenhawrn/ *n.* an inexperienced person; a new recruit.

green·house /gréenhows/ *n.* ▼ a light structure with the sides and roof mainly of glass, for rearing delicate plants or hastening the growth of plants.

green·house ef·fect *n.* the trapping of the Sun's warmth in the lower atmosphere caused by an increase in carbon dioxide. ▷ GLOBAL WARMING

green·house gas *n.* any of various gases, esp. carbon dioxide, that contribute to the greenhouse effect. ▷ GLOBAL WARMING

green·ing /gréening/ *n.* any variety of apple that is green when ripe.

green·keep·er var. of GREENSKEEPER.

green light *n.* **1** a signal to proceed on a road, etc. **2** *colloq.* permission to go ahead with a project.

green pep·per *n.* the unripe fruit of *Capsicum annuum*.

green·room /gréenrōōm/ *n.* a room in a theater for actors and actresses who are off stage.

green·sand /gréensand/ *n.* **1** ▶ a greenish kind of sandstone, often imperfectly cemented. **2** a stratum largely formed of this sandstone.

green·shank /gréen-shangk/ *n.* a large sandpiper, *Tringa nebularia*.

green·sick /gréensik/ *adj.* affected with chlorosis. □□ **green·sick·ness** *n.*

GREENSAND

greens·keep·er /gréenzkéepər/ *n.* the keeper of a golf course.

green·stick frac·ture /gréenstik/ *n.* a bone fracture, esp. in children, in which one side of the bone is broken and one only bent. ▷ FRACTURE

green·stone /gréenstōn/ *n.* a greenish igneous rock containing feldspar and hornblende.

green·stuff /gréenstuf/ *n.* vegetation; green vegetables.

GREENFINCH
(*Carduelis chloris*)

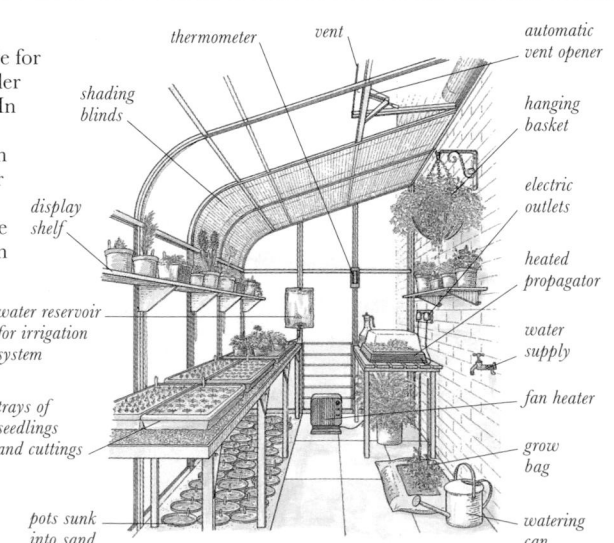

GREENHOUSE

A greenhouse is valuable for overwintering frost-tender plants in cold climates. In addition, plants may be raised from seed or from cuttings in open trays or in heated propagators. In summer, blinds can be used to shade plants from direct sun, and automatic vents can be fitted to control air circulation and humidity. In winter, a fan heater is useful for maintaining suitable temperature levels.

thermometer   *vent*   *automatic vent opener*

shading blinds   *hanging basket*

display shelf   *electric outlets*

heated propagator

water reservoir for irrigation system   *water supply*

fan heater

trays of seedlings and cuttings   *grow bag*

FEATURES OF A TYPICAL LEAN-TO GREENHOUSE   *pots sunk into sand*   *watering can*

G

green·sward /gréenswawrd/ *n. archaic* or *literary* **1** grassy turf. **2** an expanse of this.

green tea *n.* tea made from dried, not fermented, leaves.

green thumb *n.* skill in growing plants.

Green·wich Mean Time /grénich, gríníj/ *n.* (also **Green·wich Time**) the local time on the meridian of Greenwich, England, used as an international basis for reckoning time.

green·wood /gréenwŏŏd/ *n.* a wood in summer, esp. as the scene of outlaw life.

green·y /gréenee/ *adj.* greenish (*greeny-yellow*).

greet /greet/ *v.tr.* **1** address politely or welcomingly on meeting or arrival. **2** receive in a specified way. **3** (of a sight, etc.) become apparent to or noticed by. □□ **greet·er** *n.*

greet·ing /gréeting/ *n.* **1** the act or an instance of welcoming or addressing politely. **2** words, gestures, etc., used to greet a person. **3** (often in *pl.*) an expression of goodwill.

greet·ing card *n.* a decorative card sent to convey greetings.

gre·gar·i·ous /grigáireeəs/ *adj.* **1** fond of company. **2** living in flocks or communities. □□ **gre·gar·i·ous·ly** *adv.* **gre·gar·i·ous·ness** *n.*

Gre·go·ri·an cal·en·dar /grigáwreeən/ *n.* the calendar introduced in 1582 by Pope Gregory XIII.

Gre·go·ri·an chant /grigáwreeən/ *n.* plainsong ritual music, named after Pope Gregory I.

grem·lin /grémlin/ *n. colloq.* an imaginary mischievous sprite regarded as responsible for mechanical faults.

gre·nade /grináyd/ *n.* ▶ a small bomb thrown by hand (**hand grenade**) or shot from a rifle.

gren·a·dier /grénədéer/ *n. hist.* a soldier armed with grenades.

gren·a·dil·la var. of GRANADILLA.

gren·a·dine /grénədéen/ *n.* a syrup of pomegranates, etc., used in mixed drinks.

gres·so·ri·al /gresáwreeəl/ *adj. Zool.* **1** walking. **2** adapted for walking.

grew past of GROW.

grey var. of GRAY.

Grey Fri·ar *n.* a Franciscan friar.

grey·hound /gráyhownd/ *n.* **1** a dog of a tall slender breed capable of high speed. **2** this breed.

grey·lag /gráylag/ *n.* (in full **greylag goose**) a wild goose, *Anser anser*, native to Europe.

grid /grid/ *n.* **1** a framework of spaced parallel bars. **2** a system of numbered squares printed on a map and forming the basis of map references. **3** a network of lines, electrical power connections, etc. **4** a pattern of lines marking the starting places on a motor-racing track. **5** an arrangement of city streets in a rectangular pattern. □□ **grid·ded** *adj.*

grid·dle /gríd'l/ *n. & v.* ● *n.* a circular iron plate placed over a fire or otherwise heated for baking, etc. ● *v.tr.* cook with a griddle.

grid·i·ron /grídīərn/ *n.* **1** a cooking utensil of metal bars for broiling or grilling. **2** = GRID 5.

grid·lock /grídlok/ *n.* **1** a traffic jam affecting a network of streets. **2** a complete standstill in progress. □□ **gridlocked** *adj.*

grief /greef/ *n.* **1** intense sorrow or mourning. **2** the cause of this. □ **come to grief** meet with disaster. **good grief!** an exclamation of surprise, etc.

griev·ance /gréevəns/ *n.* a real or fancied cause for complaint.

grieve /greev/ *v.* **1** *tr.* cause great distress to. **2** *intr.* suffer grief, esp. at another's death.

griev·ous /gréevəs/ *adj.* **1** (of pain, etc.) severe. **2** causing suffering. **3** injurious. **4** flagrant; heinous. □□ **griev·ous·ly** *adv.* **griev·ous·ness** *n.*

grif·fin /grífin/ *n.* (also **gryph·on**) a mythical creature with an eagle's head and wings and a lion's body. ▷ CORINTHIAN

grif·fon /grífən/ *n.* **1** a dog of a small terrierlike breed with coarse or smooth hair. **2** (in full **griffon vulture**) a large S. European vulture, *Gyps fulvus*.

grill¹ /gril/ *n. & v.* ● *n.* **1** = GRIDIRON 1. **2** food cooked on a grill. **3** (in full **grill room**) a restaurant serving grilled food. ● *v.* **1** *tr. & intr.* cook or be cooked under a boiler or on a gridiron. **2** *tr. & intr.* subject or be subjected to extreme heat. **3** *tr.* subject to severe questioning. □□ **grill·ing** *n.* (in sense 3 of *v.*).

grill² var. of GRILLE.

gril·lage /grílij/ *n.* a heavy framework of crosstimbering or metal beams forming a foundation for building on difficult ground.

grille /gril/ *n.* (also **grill**) **1** a grating or latticed screen, used as a partition or to allow discreet vision. **2** a metal grid protecting the radiator of a motor vehicle.

grill·work /grílwərk/ *n.* metal fashioned to form a grille (*a balcony of ornate grillwork*).

grilse /grils/ *n.* a young salmon that has returned to fresh water from the sea for the first time.

grim /grim/ *adj.* (**grimmer**, **grimmest**) **1** of a stern or forbidding appearance. **2** harsh; severe. **3** ghastly; joyless (*has a grim truth in it*). **4** unpleasant; unattractive. □ **like grim death** with great determination. □□ **grim·ly** *adv.* **grim·ness** *n.*

grim·ace /grímos, grimáys/ *n. & v.* ● *n.* a distortion of the face made in disgust, etc., or to amuse. ● *v.intr.* make a grimace.

gri·mal·kin /grimálkin, -máwlkin/ *n. archaic* (esp. in fiction) **1** an old female cat. **2** a spiteful old woman.

grime /grīm/ *n. & v.* ● *n.* dirt ingrained in a surface. ● *v.tr.* blacken with grime.

grim·y /grímee/ *adj.* (**grimier**, **grimiest**) covered with grime. □□ **grim·i·ly** *adv.* **grim·i·ness** *n.*

grin /grin/ *v. & n.* ● *v.* (**grinned**, **grinning**) **1** *intr.* smile broadly, showing the teeth. **2** express by grinning. ● *n.* the act of grinning. □ **grin and bear it** take misfortune stoically. □□ **grin·ning·ly** *adv.*

Grinch /grinch/ *n. N. Amer. colloq.* a spoilsport or killjoy.

grind /grīnd/ *v. & n.* ● *v.* (*past* and *past part.* **ground** /grownd/) **1 a** *tr.* reduce to small particles by crushing. **b** *intr.* (of a machine, etc.) move with a crushing action. **2 a** *tr.* reduce, sharpen, or smooth by friction. **b** *tr. & intr.* rub or rub together gratingly. **3** *tr.* (often foll. by *down*) oppress (*grinding poverty*). **4** *intr.* **a** (often foll. by *away*) work or study hard. **b** (foll. by *out*) produce with effort. **c** (foll. by *on*) (of a sound) continue gratingly. **5** *tr.* turn the handle of e.g., a barrel organ, etc. **6** *intr. sl.* (of a dancer) rotate the hips. ● *n.* **1** the act of grinding. **2** *colloq.* hard dull work (*the daily grind*). **3** the size of ground particles. □ **grind to a halt** stop laboriously. □□ **grind·ing·ly** *adv.*

grind·er /gríndər/ *n.* **1** a person or thing that grinds, esp. a machine (often in *comb.*: *coffee grinder*). **2** a molar tooth. **3** *US dial.* a submarine sandwich.

grind·stone /gríndstōn/ *n.* **1** ▶ a thick revolving disk used for grinding. **2** a kind of stone used for this. □ **keep one's nose to the grindstone** work hard and continuously.

grin·go /grínggō/ *n.* (*pl.* **-os**) *colloq.* a foreigner, esp. a non-Hispanic N. American, in a Spanish-speaking country.

grip /grip/ *v. & n.* ● *v.* (**gripped**, **gripping**) **1 a** *tr.* grasp tightly. **b** *intr.* take a firm hold, esp. by friction. **2** *tr.* (of a feeling or emotion) deeply affect (a person). **3** *tr.* compel the attention of (*a gripping story*). ● *n.* **1 a** a firm hold. **b** a manner of grasping. **2** the power of holding attention. **3 a** mental or intellectual understanding. **b** effective control of a situation. (*lose one's grip*). **4 a** a part of a machine that grips or holds something. **b** a part by which a tool, weapon, etc., is held in the hand. **5** a traveling bag. **6** an assistant in a theater, movie studio, etc. □ **come** (or **get**) **to grips with** begin to deal with. **get a grip** (**on oneself**) recover one's self-control. □□ **grip·ping·ly** *adv.*

gripe /grīp/ *v. & n.* ● *v.* **1** *intr. colloq.* complain. **2** *tr.* affect with gastric pain. ● *n.* **1** (usu. in *pl.*) gastric or intestinal pain; colic. **2** *colloq.* a complaint. **b** the act of griping. **3** a grip or clutch. **4** (in *pl.*) *Naut.* lashings securing a boat in its place. □□ **grip·er** *n.* **grip·ing·ly** *adv.*

grippe /grip/ *n. archaic* or *colloq.* influenza.

gri·saille /grizí, -záyl/ *n.* **1** a method of painting in gray monochrome, often to imitate sculpture. **2** a painting or stained glass window of this kind.

gris·ly /grízlee/ *adj.* (**grislier**, **grisliest**) causing horror or fear. □□ **gris·li·ness** *n.*

grist /grist/ *n.* **1** grain to grind. **2** malt crushed for brewing. □ **grist to the** (or **a person's**) **mill** a source of profit or advantage.

gris·tle /grísəl/ *n.* tough flexible tissue in vertebrates. □□ **gris·tly** /grísee/ *adj.*

grit /grit/ *n. & v.* ● *n.* **1** particles of stone or sand, esp. as causing discomfort, etc. **2** coarse sandstone. **3** *colloq.* pluck; endurance. ● *v.* (**gritted**, **gritting**) **1** *tr.* spread grit on (icy roads, etc.). **2** *tr.* clench (the teeth). **3** *intr.* make a grating sound. □□ **grit·ter** *n.* **grit·ty** *adj.* (**grittier**, **grittiest**). **grit·ti·ness** *n.*

grits /grits/ *n.pl.* coarsely ground grain, esp. hominy prepared by boiling, then sometimes frying.

griz·zled /grízəld/ *adj.* having, or streaked with, gray hair.

griz·zly /grízlee/ *adj. & n.* ● *adj.* (**grizzlier**, **grizzliest**) gray, grayish, gray-haired. ● *n.* (*pl.* **-ies**) (in full **grizzly bear**) ▶ a variety of large brown bear found in N. America.

groan /grōn/ *v. & n.* ● *v.* **1 a** *intr.* make a deep sound expressing pain, grief, or disapproval. **b** *tr.* utter with groans. **2** *intr.* (usu. foll. by *under*, *beneath*, *with*) be loaded or oppressed. ● *n.* the sound made in groaning. □□ **groan·er** *n.*

groat /grōt/ *n. hist.* a silver coin worth four old English pence.

groats /grōts/ *n.pl.* hulled or crushed grain, esp. oats.

gro·cer /grósər/ *n.* a dealer in food and household provisions.

gro·cer·y /grósəree/ *n.* (*pl.* **-ies**) **1** a grocer's store. **2** (in *pl.*) provisions, esp. food.

grog /grog/ *n.* a drink of liquor (orig. rum) and water.

grog·gy /grógee/ *adj.* (**groggier**, **groggiest**) unsteady from being dazed or semiconscious. □□ **grog·gi·ly** *adv.* **grog·gi·ness** *n.*

grog·ram /grógrəm, grō-/ *n.* a coarse fabric of silk, mohair and wool, or a mixture of these.

GRENADE: CROSS SECTION OF A WORLD WAR II GRENADE

striker
explosive chamber
safety pin
body
detonator
percussion cap
fuse

GRIZZLY BEAR (*Ursus arctos horribilis*)

"eye" to hold shaft

GRINDSTONE FOR MILLING FLOUR

G

G

groin[1] /groyn/ *n. & v.* ● *n.* **1** the depression between the belly and the thigh. **2** *Archit.* **a** an edge formed by intersecting vaults. ▷ VAULT. **b** an arch supporting a vault. ● *v.tr. Archit.* build with groins.

groin[2] /groyn/ *n.* (also **groyne**) a wooden framework or low broad wall built out from a shore to check erosion of a beach. ▷ LONGSHORE DRIFT

grom·met /grómit/ *n.* **1** a metal, plastic, or rubber eyelet placed in a hole to protect or insulate a rope or cable, etc., passed through it.

grom·well /grómwəl/ *n.* any of various plants of the genus *Lithospermum*, with hard seeds formerly used in medicine.

groom /grōōm/ *n. & v.* ● *n.* **1** = BRIDEGROOM. **2** a person employed to take care of horses. ● *v.tr.* **1 a** curry or tend (a horse). **b** give a neat appearance to (a person, etc.). **2** (of an ape or monkey, etc.) clean and comb the fur of (its fellow) with the fingers. **3** prepare or train (a person) for a particular purpose or activity (*was groomed for the top job*).

groove /grōōv/ *n. & v.* ● *n.* **1 a** a channel or hollow, esp. one made to guide motion or receive a corresponding ridge. **b** a spiral track cut in a phonograph record. **2** an established routine or habit. ● *v.* **1** *tr.* make a groove in. **2** *intr. sl.* enjoy oneself. ¶ Often with ref. to popular music or jazz; now largely disused in general contexts. □ **in the groove** *sl.* doing or performing well.

groov·y /grōōvee/ *adj.* (**groovier, grooviest**) *sl.* or *joc.* fashionable and exciting. □□ **groov·i·ly** *adv.*

grope /grōp/ *v. & n.* ● *v.* **1** *intr.* (usu. foll. by *for*) feel about or search blindly. **2** *intr.* (foll. by *for, after*) search mentally. **3** *tr.* feel (one's way) toward something. **4** *tr. sl.* fondle clumsily for sexual pleasure. ● *n.* the process or an instance of groping. □□ **grop·er** *n.* **grop·ing·ly** *adv.*

gros·beak /grósbeek/ *n.* ◄ any of various finches of the families Cardinalidae and Fringillidae, having stout conical bills and usu. brightly colored plumage.

gro·schen /gróshən/ *n.* (until the introduction of the euro in 2002) an Austrian coin and monetary unit, one hundredth of a schilling.

GROSBEAK: JAPANESE
GROSBEAK FINCH
(*Eophona personata*)

gros·grain /grógrayn/ *n.* a corded fabric of silk, rayon, etc.

gros point /grō póynt, pwáɴ/ *n.* cross-stitch embroidery on canvas.

gross /grōs/ *adj., v., & n.* ● *adj.* **1** overfed; repulsively fat. **2** (of a person, manners, or morals) noticeably coarse or indecent. **3** flagrant; conspicuously wrong (*gross negligence*). **4** total; without deductions (*gross income*). **5 a** luxuriant; rank. **b** thick; solid; dense. **6** (of the senses, etc.) dull. **7** *sl.* repulsive; disgusting. ● *v.tr.* produce or earn as gross profit or income. ● *n.* (*pl.* same) twelve dozen. □ **gross out** *sl.* disgust, esp. by repulsive behavior. □□ **gross·ly** *adv.* **gross·ness** *n.*

gross do·mes·tic prod·uct *n.* the total value of goods produced and services provided in a country in one year.

gross na·tion·al prod·uct *n.* the gross domestic product plus the total of net income from abroad.

gro·tesque /grōtésk/ *adj. & n.* ● *adj.* **1** comically or repulsively distorted; monstrous; unnatural. **2** incongruous; ludicrous; absurd. ● *n.* **1** a decorative form interweaving human and animal features. **2** a comically distorted figure or design. **3** *Printing* a family of sans serif typefaces. □□ **gro·tesque·ly** *adv.* **gro·tesque·ness** *n.* **gro·tes·quer·ie** /-téskəree/ *n.*

grot·to /grótō/ *n.* (*pl.* **-oes** or **-os**) **1** a small picturesque cave. **2** an artificial ornamental cave. □□ **grot·toed** *adj.*

grouch /growch/ *v. & n. colloq.* ● *v.intr.* grumble. ● *n.* **1** a discontented person. **2** a fit of grumbling.

grouch·y /grówchee/ *adj.* (**grouchier, grouchiest**) *colloq.* discontented; grumpy. □□ **grouch·i·ly** *adv.* **grouch·i·ness** *n.*

ground[1] /grownd/ *n. & v.* ● *n.* **1 a** the surface of the Earth, esp. as contrasted with the air around it. **b** a part of this specified in some way (*low ground*). **2** soil; earth (*stony ground*). **3 a** a position, area, or distance on the Earth's surface. **b** the extent of a subject dealt with (*the book covers a lot of ground*). **4** (often in *pl.*) a motive or reason (*ground for concern*). **5** an area of a special kind or designated for special use (often in *comb.*: *fishing-grounds*). **6** (in *pl.*) an area of sometimes enclosed land attached to a house, etc. **7** an area or basis for consideration, agreement, etc. (*common ground; on firm ground*). **8 a** (in painting) the prepared surface giving the predominant color or tone. **b** (in embroidery, ceramics, etc.) the undecorated surface. **9** (in full **ground bass**) *Mus.* a short theme in the bass constantly repeated with the upper parts of the music varied. **10** (in *pl.*) solid particles, esp. of coffee, forming a residue. **11** *Electr.* the connection to the ground that completes an electrical circuit. **12** the bottom of the sea. **13** (*attrib.*) **a** (of animals) living on or in the ground; (of fish) living at the bottom of water; (of plants) dwarfish. **b** relating to the ground (*ground staff*). ● *v.* **1** *tr.* **a** refuse authority for (a pilot or an aircraft) to fly. **b** restrict (esp. a child) from certain activities, esp. as a form of punishment. **2 a** *tr.* run (a ship) aground. **b** *intr.* (of a ship) run aground. **3** *tr.* (foll. by *in*) instruct thoroughly (in a subject). **4** *tr.* (often as **grounded** *adj.*) (foll. by *on*) base (a conclusion, etc.) on. **5** *tr. Electr.* connect to the ground. **6** *intr.* alight on the ground. **7** *tr.* place (esp. weapons) on the ground. □ **break new** (or **fresh**) **ground** treat a subject previously not dealt with. **gain ground 1** advance steadily. **2** (foll. by *on*) catch (a person) up. **get in on the ground floor** become part of an enterprise in its early stages. **get off the ground** *colloq.* make a successful start. **give** (or **lose**) **ground 1** retreat; decline. **2** lose the advantage. **go to ground 1** (of a fox, etc.) enter its burrow, etc. **2** (of a person) become inaccessible for a prolonged period. **hold one's ground** not give way. **on the ground** at the point of production or operation. **thin on the ground** not numerous.

ground[2] *past* and *past part.* of GRIND.

ground ball *n. Baseball* a ball batted such that it bounces on the ground. Also **grounder.**

ground·break·ing /grówndbrayking/ *adj.* innovative; pioneering.

ground con·trol *n.* the personnel directing the landing, etc., of aircraft or spacecraft.

ground cov·er *n.* plants covering the surface of the soil, esp. low-growing spreading plants that inhibit the growth of weeds.

ground crew *n.* mechanics who maintain and service aircraft.

ground·er /grówndər/ *n. Baseball* = GROUND BALL.

ground·fish /grówndfish/ *n.* a fish, as cod, flounder, etc., that lives at the bottom of oceans, lakes, rivers, etc.

ground glass *n.* **1** glass made nontransparent by grinding, etc. **2** glass ground to a powder.

ground·hog /grówndhawg, -hog/ *n.* a woodchuck; a marmot.

ground·ing /grównding/ *n.* basic training or instruction in a subject.

ground·less /grówndlis/ *adj.* without motive or foundation. □□ **ground·less·ly** *adv.* **ground·less·ness** *n.*

ground·ling /grówndling/ *n.* **1 a** a creeping or dwarf plant. **b** an animal that lives near the ground, at the bottom of a lake, etc., esp. a groundfish. **2** a person on the ground as opposed to one in an aircraft. **3** a spectator or reader of inferior taste (with ref. to Shakesp. *Hamlet* III. ii. 11).

ground·nut /grówndnut/ *n.* **1 a** a N. American wild bean. **b** its edible tuber. **2** = PEANUT.

ground·sel /grówndsəl/ *n.* any composite plant of the genus *Senecio*, esp. *S. vulgaris*, used as a food for cage birds.

ground·sheet /grówndsheet/ *n.* a waterproof sheet for spreading on the ground, esp. in or under a tent.

grounds·keep·er /grówndzkeepər, grównz-/ *n.* a person who maintains the grounds of a sizable property, as a golf course or park.

ground speed *n.* an aircraft's speed relative to the ground.

ground swell *n.* **1** a heavy sea caused by a distant or past storm or an earthquake. **2** a build-up of opinion in a large section of the population.

ground·wa·ter /grówndwáwtər, -wotər/ *n.* water found in soil or in pores, crevices, etc., in rock.

ground·work /grówndwərk/ *n.* **1** preliminary or basic work. **2** a foundation or basis.

ground ze·ro *n.* **1** the point on the ground under an exploding bomb. **2** (**Ground Zero**) the site of the World Trade Center in New York, destroyed by terrorists on September 11 2001.

group /grōōp/ *n. & v.* ● *n.* **1** a number of persons or things located close together, or classed together. **2** a number of people working together or sharing beliefs. **3** a number of commercial companies under common ownership. **4** an ensemble playing popular music. **5** a division of an air force or air fleet. ● *v.* **1** *tr. & intr.* form or be formed into a group. **2** *tr.* (often foll. by *with*) place in a group or groups. **3** *tr.* form (colors, figures, etc.) into a well-arranged and harmonious whole. **4** *tr.* classify. □□ **group·age** *n.*

group dy·nam·ics *n. Psychol.* the field of social psychology concerned with the nature, development, and interactions of human groups.

group·er /grōōpər/ *n.* ▼ any marine fish of the family Serranidae, with heavy body, big head, and wide mouth.

GROUPER: NASSAU GROUPER
(*Epinephelus striatus*)

group·ie /grōōpee/ *n. sl.* an ardent follower of a touring pop group.

group·ing /grōōping/ *n.* **1** a process or system of allocation to groups. **2** the formation or arrangement so produced.

group ther·a·py *n.* therapy in which patients with a similar condition are brought together to assist one another psychologically.

grouse[1] /grows/ *n.* (*pl.* same) **1** ▼ any of various game birds of the family Tetraonidae, with a plump body. **2** the flesh of a grouse used as food.

GROUSE: HAZEL GROUSE
(*Bonasa bonasia*)

grouse[2] /grows/ *v. & n. colloq.* ● *v.intr.* grumble or complain pettily. ● *n.* a complaint. □□ **grous·er** *n.*

grout /growt/ *n. & v.* ● *n.* a thin fluid mortar for filling gaps in tiling, etc. ● *v.tr.* provide or fill with grout. □□ **grout·er** *n.*

grove /grōv/ *n.* a small wood or group of trees.

grov·el /gróvəl/ *v.intr.* (**groveled, groveling**; also **grovelled, grovelling**) **1** behave obsequiously in seeking favor or forgiveness. **2** lie prone in abject humility. □□ **grov·el·er** *n.* **grov·el·ing** *adj.* **grov·el·ing·ly** *adv.*

grow /grō/ *v.* (*past* **grew** /grōō/; *past part.* **grown** /grōn/) **1** *intr.* increase in size, height, quantity, degree, or in any way regarded as measurable (e.g., authority or reputation) (often foll. by *in*: *grew in stature*). **2** *intr.* **a** develop or exist as a living plant or natural product. **b** develop in a specific way or direction (*began to grow sideways*). **c** germinate; sprout. **3** *intr.* be produced; come naturally into existence. **4** *intr.* (as **grown** *adj.*) fully matured. **5** *intr.* **a** become gradually (*grow rich*). **b** (foll. by *to* + infin.) come by degrees (*grew to like it*). **6** *intr.* (foll. by *into*) **a** become; having grown or developed (*will grow into a fine athlete*). **b** become large enough for (*will grow into the coat*). **7** *intr.* (foll. by *on*) become gradually more favored by. **8** *tr.* **a** produce (plants, etc.) by cultivation. **b** bring forth. **c** cause (a beard, etc.) to develop. **9** *tr.* (in *passive*; foll. by *over, up*) be covered with a growth. □ **grow out of 1** become too large to wear (a garment). **2** become too mature to retain (a childish habit, etc.). **3** be the result of. **grow up 1** advance to maturity. **2** (of a custom) arise. □□ **grow·a·ble** *adj.*

grow·er /grōər/ *n.* **1** (often in *comb.*) a person growing produce (*fruit-grower*). **2** a plant that grows in a specified way (*a fast grower*).

grow·ing pains *n.pl* **1** early difficulties in the development of an enterprise, etc. **2** neuralgic pain in children's legs due to fatigue, etc.

growl /growl/ *v. & n.* ● *v. intr.* **1 a** (often foll. by *at*) (esp. of a dog) make a low guttural sound, usu. of anger. **b** murmur angrily. **2** rumble. ● *n.* **1** a growling sound. **2** an angry murmur. **3** a rumble.

growl·er /grówlər/ *n.* a person or thing that growls, esp. *sl.* a dog.

grown *past part.* of GROW.

grown-up *adj. & n.* ● *adj.* adult. ● *n.* an adult person.

growth /grōth/ *n.* **1** the act or process of growing. **2** an increase in size or value. **3** something that has grown or is growing. **4** *Med.* a morbid formation. **5** the cultivation of produce.

groyne var. of GROIN[2].

grub /grub/ *n. & v.* ● *n.* **1** the larva of an insect. **2** *colloq.* food. ● *v.* (**grubbed, grubbing**) **1** *tr. & intr.* dig superficially. **2** *tr.* **a** clear (the ground) of roots and stumps. **b** clear away (roots, etc.). **3** *tr.* (foll. by *up, out*) **a** fetch by digging (*grubbing up weeds*). **b** extract (information, etc.) by searching in books, etc. **4** *intr.* search; rummage. □□ **grub·ber** *n.*

grub·by /grúbee/ *adj.* (**grubbier, grubbiest**) **1** dirty; grimy. **2** of or infested with grubs. □□ **grub·bi·ly** *adv.* **grub·bi·ness** *n.*

grub·stake /grúbstayk/ *n. & v.* ● *n.* material or provisions supplied to an enterprise in return for a share in the resulting profits (orig. in prospecting for ore). ● *v.tr.* provide with a grubstake. □□ **grub·stak·er** *n.*

Grub Street /grúb/ *n.* (often *attrib.*) the world or class of literary hacks and impoverished authors.

grudge /gruj/ *n. & v.* ● *n.* a persistent feeling of ill will or resentment, esp. one due to an insult or injury (*bears a grudge against me*). ● *v.tr.* **1** be resentfully unwilling to give or allow (a thing). **2** reluctant to do (a thing) (*grudged paying so much*).

grudg·ing /grújing/ *adj.* reluctant. □□ **grudg·ing·ly** *adv.* **grudg·ing·ness** *n.*

gru·el /grōōəl/ *n.* a liquid food of oatmeal, etc., boiled in milk or water.

gru·el·ing /grōōling/ *adj. & n.* (also **gru·el·ling**) ● *adj.* extremely demanding, severe, or tiring. ● *n.* a harsh or exhausting experience; punishment. □□ **gruel·ing·ly** *adv.*

grue·some /grōōsəm/ *adj.* horrible; grisly; disgusting. □□ **grue·some·ly** *adv.* **grue·some·ness** *n.*

gruff /gruf/ *adj.* **1 a** (of a voice) low and harsh. **b** (of a person) having a gruff voice. **2** surly; laconic; rough-mannered. □□ **gruff·ly** *adv.* **gruff·ness** *n.*

grum·ble /grúmbəl/ *v. & n.* ● *v.* **1** *intr.* **a** (often foll. by *at, about, over*) complain peevishly. **b** be discontented. **2** *intr.* **a** utter a dull inarticulate sound; murmur; growl faintly. **b** rumble. **3** *tr.* (often foll. by *out*) utter complainingly. **4** *intr.* (as **grumbling** *adj.*) *colloq.* giving intermittent discomfort (*a grumbling appendix*). ● *n.* **1** a complaint. **2 a** a dull inarticulate sound. **b** a rumble. □□ **grum·bler** *n.* **grum·bling** *adj.* **grum·bling·ly** *adv.* **grum·bly** *adj.*

grump /grump/ *n. colloq.* **1** a grumpy person. **2** (in *pl.*) a fit of sulks. □□ **grump·ish** *adj.* **grump·ish·ly** *adv.*

grump·y /grúmpee/ *adj.* (**grumpier, grumpiest**) morosely irritable. □□ **grump·i·ly** *adv.* **grump·i·ness** *n.*

grunge /grunj/ *n. sl.* **1** grime; dirt. **2** an aggressive style of rock music characterized by a raucous guitar sound. **3** a style of clothing and appearance marked by studied dishevelment. □□ **grun·gy** *adj.*

grun·ion /grúnyən/ *n.* a Californian marine fish, *Leuresthes tenuis.*

grunt /grunt/ *n. & v.* ● *n.* **1** a low guttural sound made by a pig. **2** a sound resembling this. ● *v.* **1** *intr.* (of a pig) make a grunt. **2** *intr.* (of a person) make a low inarticulate sound resembling this, esp. to express discontent, fatigue, etc. **3** *tr.* utter with a grunt.

grunt·er /grúntər/ *n.* a person or animal that grunts, esp. a pig.

Gru·yère /grōō-yáir, gree-/ *n.* a firm pale cheese made from cow's milk. ▷ CHEESE

gryph·on var. of GRIFFIN.

GSA *abbr.* **1** General Services Administration. **2** Girl Scouts of America.

G-spot *n.* a sensitive area of the anterior wall of the vagina believed by some to be highly erogenous.

G-string /jéestring/ *n.* **1** *Mus.* a string sounding the note G. **2** a narrow strip of cloth covering only the genitals and attached to a string around the waist.

G suit /jéesōōt/ *n.* a garment with inflatable pressurized pouches, worn to withstand high acceleration.

GT *n.* a high-performance two-door automobile.

gua·ca·mo·le /gwáakəmólee/ *n.* a dish of mashed avocado mixed with chopped onion, tomatoes, chili peppers, and seasoning.

guai·ac var. of GUAIACUM 2.

guai·a·cum /gwíəkəm/ *n.* **1** any tree of the genus *Guaiacum*, native to tropical America. **2** (also **gua·i·ac** /gwíak/) **a** the hard dense oily timber of some of these, esp. *G. officinale*. Also called **lignum vitae**. **b** the resin from this used medicinally.

gua·na·co /gwənaakó/ *n.* (*pl.* **-os**) ◀ a llamalike camelid, *Lama guanicoe*, with a coat of soft pale brown hair used for wool.

gua·nine /gwáaneen/ *n. Biochem.* a purine derivative found in all living organisms as a component base of DNA and RNA. ▷ DNA

gua·no /gwaanó/ *n. & v.* (*pl.* **-os**) ● *n.* **1** the excrement of seabirds, used as manure. **2** an artificial manure, esp. that made from fish. ● *v.tr.* (**-oes, -oed**) fertilize with guano.

GUANACO
(Lama guanicoe)

Gua·ra·ni /gwáarənee/ *n.* **1** a member of a S. American Indian people. **2** the language of this people.

guar·an·tee /gárəntée/ *n. & v.* ● *n.* **1 a** a formal promise or assurance, esp. that an obligation will be fulfilled or that something is of a specified quality and durability. **b** a document giving such an undertaking. **2** = GUARANTY. **3** a person making a guaranty or giving a security. ● *v.tr.* (**guarantees, guaranteed**) **1 a** give or serve as a guarantee for. **b** assure the permanence, etc., of. **c** provide with a guarantee. **2** (foll. by *that* + clause, or *to* + infin.) give a promise. **3 a** (foll. by *to*) secure the possession of (a thing) for a person. **b** make (a person) secure against a risk or in possession of a thing.

guar·an·tor /gárəntawr, -tər/ *n.* a person who gives a guarantee or guaranty.

guar·an·ty /gárəntee/ *n.* (*pl.* **-ies**) **1** a written or other undertaking to answer for the payment of a debt or for the performance of an obligation by another person liable in the first instance. **2** a thing serving as security for a guaranty.

guard /gaard/ *v. & n.* ● *v.* **1** *tr.* (often foll. by *from, against*) watch over and defend or protect from harm. **2** *tr.* keep watch by (a door, etc.) so as to control entry or exit. **3** *tr.* supervise (prisoners, etc.). **4** *tr.* provide (machinery) with a protective device. **5** *tr.* keep (thoughts or speech) in check. **6** *tr.* provide with safeguards. **7** *intr.* (foll. by *against*) take precautions. ● *n.* **1** a state of vigilance or watchfulness. **2** a person who protects or keeps watch. **3** a body of soldiers, etc., serving to protect a place or person. **4** a person who keeps watch over prisoners. **5** a part of an army detached for some purpose (*advance guard*). **6** (in *pl.*) (usu. **Guards**) any of various bodies of troops nominally employed to guard a ruler. **7** a thing that protects. **8** (often in *comb.*) a device fitted to a machine, etc., to prevent injury (*fire guard*). □ **be on** (or **keep** or **stand**) **guard** (of a sentry, etc.) keep watch. **lower one's guard** reduce vigilance against attack. **off** (or **off one's**) **guard** unprepared for some surprise or difficulty. **on** (or **on one's**) **guard** prepared for all contingencies.

guard·ant /gaard'nt/ *adj. Heraldry* depicted with the body sideways and the face toward the viewer.

guard·ed /gaardid/ *adj.* (of a remark, etc.) cautious. □□ **guard·ed·ly** *adv.*

guard·house /gaardhows/ *n.* a building used to accommodate a military guard or to detain military prisoners temporarily.

guard·i·an /gaardeeən/ *n.* **1** a defender, protector, or keeper. **2** a person having legal custody of another person and his or her property when that person is incapable of managing his or her own affairs. **3** the superior of a Franciscan convent. □□ **guard·i·an·ship** *n.*

guard·i·an an·gel *n.* a spirit conceived as watching over a person or place.

guard·rail /gaardrayl/ *n.* a rail, e.g., a handrail, fitted as a support or to prevent an accident.

guard·room /gaardrōōm, -rōōm/ *n.* a room with the same purpose as a guardhouse.

guards·man /gaardzmən/ *n.* (*pl.* **-men**) a soldier belonging to a body of guards.

gua·va /gwaavə/ *n.* **1** a small tropical American tree, *Psidium guajava*, bearing an edible pale yellow fruit with pink juicy flesh. **2** ◀ this fruit.

gua·yu·le /gwīyōōlee/ *n.* **1** a silver-leaved shrub, *Parthenium argentatum*, native to Mexico. **2** a rubber substitute made from the sap of this plant.

GUAVA
(Psidium guajava)

gu·ber·na·to·ri·al /gōōbərnətáwreeəl, gyōō-/ *adj.* of or relating to a governor.

G

GUDGEON (*Gobio gobio*)

gudg·eon[1] /gújən/ *n.* ▲ a small European freshwater fish, *Gobio gobio*.

gudg·eon[2] /gújən/ *n.* **1** any of various kinds of pivot working a wheel, bell, etc. **2** the tubular part of a hinge into which the pin fits to effect the joint. **3** a socket at the stern of a boat, into which a rudder is fitted. **4** a pin holding two blocks of stone, etc., together.

guel·der rose /géldər/ *n.* ▶ a deciduous shrub, *Viburnum opulus*, with round bunches of creamy white flowers. Also called **snowball bush.**

gue·non /gənón/ *n.* any African monkey of the genus *Cercopithecus*, having a characteristic long tail, e.g., the vervet.

guer·don /górdən/ *n. & v. poet.* ● *n.* a reward or recompense. ● *v.tr.* give a reward to.

Guern·sey /górnzee/ *n.* (*pl.* **-eys**) **1 a** an animal of a breed of dairy cattle from Guernsey in the Channel Islands. **b** this breed. **2** (**guernsey**) **a** a thick (usu. blue) woolen sweater of a distinctive pattern. **b** *Austral.* a soccer or football shirt.

guer·ril·la /gərilə/ *n.* (also **gue·ril·la**) a member of a small independently acting (usu. politcial) group taking part in irregular fighting, esp. against larger regular forces.

guer·ril·la war *n.* (also **war·fare**) fighting by or with guerrillas.

guess /ges/ *v. & n.* ● *v.* **1** *tr.* (often *absol.*) estimate without calculation or measurement, or on the basis of inadequate data. **2** *tr.* form a hypothesis or opinion about; conjecture; think likely (*cannot guess how you did it*). **3** *tr.* conjecture or estimate correctly by guessing (*you have to guess the weight*). **4** *intr.* (foll. by *at*) make a conjecture about. ● *n.* an estimate or conjecture. □ **I guess** *colloq.* I suppose. □□ **guess·er** *n.*

guess-rope var. of GUEST-ROPE.

guess·ti·mate /géstimət/ *n.* (also **gues·ti·mate**) *colloq.* an estimate based on a mixture of guesswork and calculation.

guess·work /géswərk/ *n.* the process of or results got by guessing.

guest /gest/ *n. & v.* ● *n.* **1** a person invited to visit another's house or have a meal, etc., at the expense of the inviter. **2** a person lodging at a hotel, boarding house, etc. **3 a** an outside performer invited to take part with a regular body of performers. **b** a person who takes part by invitation in a radio or television program (often *attrib.*: *guest artist*). **4** (*attrib.*) **a** serving or set aside for guests (*guest room*). **b** acting as a guest (*guest speaker*). **5** an organism living in close association with another. ● *v.intr.* be a guest on a radio or television show. □ **be my guest** *colloq.* make what use you wish of the available facilities. □□ **guest·ship** *n.*

guest·house /gésthows/ *n.* a private house offering paid accommodation.

guest of hon·or *n.* the most important guest at an occasion.

guest-rope /géstrōp, gésrōp/ *n.* (also **guess-rope**) **1** a second rope fastened to a boat in tow to steady it. **2** a rope slung outside a ship to give a hold for boats coming alongside.

guff /guf/ *n. sl.* empty talk; nonsense.

guf·faw /gufáw/ *n. & v.* ● *n.* a loud or boisterous laugh. ● *v.* **1** *intr.* utter a guffaw. **2** *tr.* say with a guffaw.

GUELDER ROSE
(*Viburnum opulus*
'Roseum')

GUI /góo-ee/ *abbr. Computing* graphical user interface.

guid·ance /gíd'ns/ *n.* **1 a** advice or information aimed at resolving a problem, difficulty, etc. **b** leadership or direction. **2** the process of guiding or being guided.

guide /gīd/ *n. & v.* ● *n.* **1** a person who leads or shows the way, or directs the movements of a person or group. **2** a person who conducts travelers on tours, etc. **3** a professional mountain climber in charge of a group. **4** an adviser. **5** a directing principle or standard (*one's feelings are a bad guide*). **6** a book with essential information on a subject, esp. = GUIDEBOOK. **7** a thing marking a position or guiding the eye. **8** a soldier, vehicle, or ship whose position determines the movements of others. **9** *Mech.* **a** a bar, rod, etc., directing the motion of something. **b** a gauge, controlling a tool. **10** (**Guide**) *Brit.* a member of an organization similar to the Girl Scouts. ● *v.tr.* **1 a** act as guide to; lead or direct. **b** arrange the course of (events). **2** be the principle, motive, or ground of (an action, judgment, etc.). **3** direct the affairs of (a government, etc.).

guide·book /gídbŏok/ *n.* a book of information about a place for visitors.

guide dog *n.* a dog trained to guide a blind person.

guide·line /gídlīn/ *n.* a principle or criterion guiding or directing action.

guid·ed mis·sile *n.* a missile directed to its target by remote control or by equipment within itself.

gui·don /gíd'n/ *n.* a pennant narrowing to a point or fork at the free end, esp. one used as the standard of a military unit.

guild /gild/ *n.* (also **gild**) **1** an association of people for mutual aid or the pursuit of a common goal. **2** a medieval association of craftsmen or merchants.

guild·er /gíldər/ *n.* (until the intoduction of the euro in 2002) the chief monetary unit of the Netherlands.

guild·hall /gíldháwl/ *n.* **1** the meeting place of a

G

GUITAR

The first narrow-waisted guitars appeared in 15th-century Italy and Spain and were derived from stringed instruments of the ancient world. However, modern steel-string, flattop, and arch-top acoustic guitars originated in 19th-century North America at a similar time to the development of classical guitars in Spain. Electric guitars were the result of research into the artificial amplification of sound from musical instruments in the 1930s.

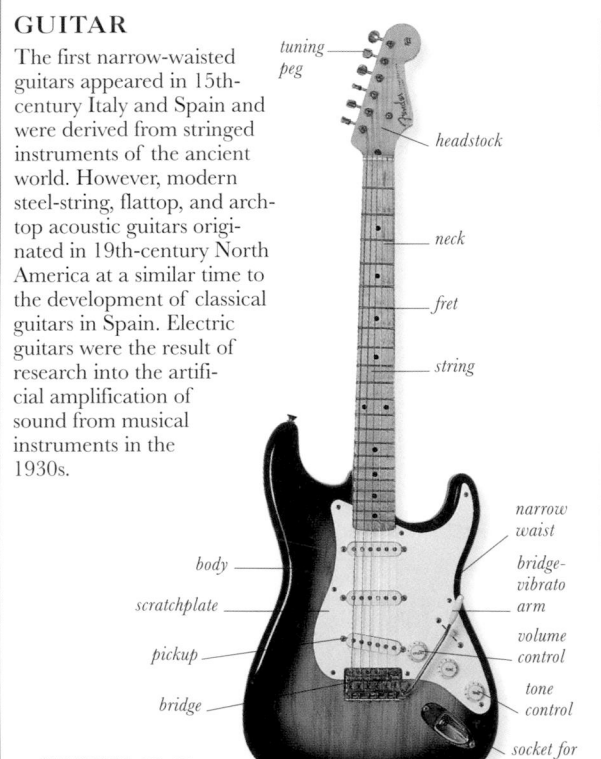

tuning peg
headstock
neck
fret
string
narrow waist
bridge-vibrato arm
volume control
tone control
socket for wire to amplifier
body
scratchplate
pickup
bridge

FEATURES OF AN ELECTRIC GUITAR

MAIN TYPES OF GUITAR

CLASSICAL GUITAR
Ramírez 1A
(late 19th century)

STEEL-STRING ACOUSTIC GUITAR
Martin D-45 (1988)

ARCHTOP SEMI-ACOUSTIC GUITAR
Gretsch Chet Atkins 6120 (1954)

ELECTRIC BASS GUITAR
Fender Precision (1957)

guild or corporation; (*Brit.*) a town hall. **2** (**the Guildhall**) the hall of the Corporation of the City of London, used for ceremonial occasions.

guile /gīl/ *n.* treachery; deceit; cunning or sly behavior. □□ **guile·ful** *adj.* **guile·less** *adj.* **guile·less·ly** *adv.*

guil·le·mot /gíləmot/ *n.* any fast-flying sea bird of the genus *Uria* or *Cepphus*, nesting on cliffs or islands.

guil·loche /gilṓsh, geeyósh/ *n.* an architectural or metalwork ornament imitating braided ribbons.

guil·lo·tine /gílətēn, géeə-/ *n. & v.* ● *n.* **1** ► a machine with a heavy knife blade dropping vertically in grooves, used for beheading. **2** a device for cutting paper, metal, etc. ● *v.tr.* use a guillotine on.

guilt /gilt/ *n.* **1** the fact of having committed a specified or implied offense. **2 a** culpability. **b** the feeling of this.

guilt com·plex *n. Psychol.* a mental obsession with the idea of having done wrong.

guilt·less /gíltlis/ *adj.* **1** (often foll. by *of*) innocent. **2** (foll. by *of*) not having knowledge or possession of. □□ **guilt·less·ly** *adv.*

guilt trip *n. colloq.* a feeling of guilt, esp. when self-indulgent or unjustified.

guilt·y /gíltee/ *adj.* (**guiltier, guiltiest**) **1** culpable of or responsible for a wrong. **2** conscious of or affected by guilt (*a guilty conscience*). **3** concerning guilt (*a guilty secret*). **4** (often foll. by *of*) **a** having committed a (specified) offense. **b** *Law* adjudged to have committed a specified offense, esp. by a verdict in a trial. □□ **guilt·i·ly** *adv.*

guimp var. of GIMP[1].

guin·ea /gínee/ *n.* **1** *Brit. hist.* the sum of 21 old shillings, used esp. in determining professional fees. **2** *hist.* a former British gold coin worth 21 shillings, first coined for the African trade.

guin·ea fowl *n.* any African fowl of the family Numididae, esp. *Numida meleagris*, with slate-colored white-spotted plumage.

guin·ea pig *n.* **1** a domesticated S. American cavy, *Cavia porcellus*, kept as a pet or for research in biology, etc. ▷ RODENT. **2** a person or thing used as a subject for experiment.

guise /gīz/ *n.* **1** an assumed appearance (*in the guise of*). **2** external appearance.

gui·tar /gitaár/ *n.* ◄ a usu. six-stringed musical instrument, played by plucking with the fingers or a plectrum. ▷ STRINGED. □□ **gui·tar·ist** *n.*

Gu·lag /gŏŏlag/ *n.* (**the Gulag**) a system of harsh labor camps maintained in the Soviet Union, 1930–55.

gulch /gulch/ *n.* a ravine, esp. one in which a torrent flows.

gules /gyŏŏlz/ *n. & adj.* (usu. placed after noun) *Heraldry* red.

gulf /gulf/ *n.* **1** ▼ a stretch of sea consisting of a deep

---

GUILLOTINE: REPLICA OF LATE 18TH-CENTURY FRENCH GUILLOTINE

guillotine blade
wooden frame
hole for victim's head
bench for victim to lie on

---

inlet with a narrow mouth. **2** (**the Gulf**) **a** the Gulf of Mexico. **b** the Persian Gulf. **3** a deep hollow. **4** a wide difference of feelings, opinion, etc.

Gulf Stream *n.* a warm current flowing from the Gulf of Mexico to Newfoundland where it is deflected into the Atlantic Ocean.

gull[1] /gul/ *n.* any of various long-winged seabirds of the family Laridae. ▷ SEABIRD

gull[2] /gul/ *v.tr.* (usu. in *passive*; foll. by *into*) dupe; fool.

Gul·lah /gúlə/ *n.* **1** a member of a group of African-Americans living on the coast of S. Carolina. **2** the Creole language spoken by them.

gul·let /gúlit/ *n.* **1** the food passage extending from the mouth to the stomach; the esophagus. **2** the throat.

gul·li·ble /gúlibəl/ *adj.* easily persuaded or deceived. □□ **gul·li·bil·i·ty** *n.*

gul·ly /gúlee/ *n.* (*pl.* **-ies**) **1** a waterworn ravine. **2** a gutter or drain.

gulp /gulp/ *v. & n.* ● *v.* **1** *tr.* swallow hastily, greedily, or with effort. **2** *intr.* swallow with difficulty. **3** *tr.* (foll. by *down, back*) stifle; suppress (esp. tears). ● *n.* **1** an act of gulping (*drained it in one gulp*). **2** an effort to swallow. **3** a large mouthful of a drink.

gum[1] /gum/ *n. & v.* ● *n.* **1 a** a viscous secretion of some trees and shrubs that hardens on drying but is soluble in water. **b** an adhesive substance made from this. **2** chewing gum. **3** = GUMDROP. **4** = GUM ARABIC. **5** = GUM TREE. **6** a secretion collecting in the corner of the eye. ● *v.* (**gummed, gumming**) **1** *tr.* smear or cover with gum. **2** *tr.* fasten with gum.

□ **gum up 1** (of a mechanism, etc.) become clogged or obstructed with stickiness. **2** *colloq.* interfere with the smooth running of (*gum up the works*).

gum[2] /gum/ *n.* (usu. in *pl.*) the firm flesh around the roots of the teeth. ▷ TOOTH

gum[3] /gum/ *n. colloq.* (in oaths) God (*by gum!*).

gum ar·a·bic *n.* a gum exuded by some kinds of acacia.

gum·bo /gúmbō/ *n.* (*pl.* **-os**) **1** okra. **2** a soup thickened with okra pods. **3** (**Gumbo**) a patois of African-Americans and Creoles spoken esp. in Louisiana.

gum·boil /gúmboyl/ *n.* a small abscess on the gums.

gum·boot /gúmbŏŏt/ *n.* a rubber boot.

gum·drop /gúmdrop/ *n.* a soft candy made with gelatin or gum arabic.

gum·ma /gúmə/ *n.* (*pl.* **gummas** or **gummata** /-mətə/) *Med.* a small soft swelling occurring in the connective tissue of the liver, brain, testes, and heart, and characteristic of the late stages of syphilis. □□ **gum·ma·tous** *adj.*

gum·my[1] /gúmee/ *adj.* (**gummier, gummiest**) **1** sticky. **2** exuding gum. □□ **gum·mi·ness** *n.*

gum·my[2] /gúmee/ *adj.* (**gummier, gummiest**) toothless.

gump·tion /gúmpshən/ *n. colloq.* **1** resourcefulness; initiative. **2** common sense.

gum·shoe /gúmshŏŏ/ *n.* **1** *sl.* a detective. **2** a galosh.

gum tree *n.* a tree exuding gum, esp. a eucalyptus.

gun /gun/ *n. & v.* ● *n.* **1** ▼ any kind of weapon consisting of a metal tube and often held in the hand with a grip at one end, from which bullets or other missiles are propelled with great force by a contained explosion. **2** a starting pistol. **3** a device for discharging insecticide, grease, electrons, etc., in the required direction (often in *comb.*: *grease gun*). **4** a gunman. **5** the firing of a gun. ● *v.* (**gunned, gunning**) **1** *tr.* (usu. foll. by *down*) shoot (a person) with a gun. **2** *tr. colloq.* accelerate (an engine or vehicle). **3** *intr.* go shooting. **4** *intr.* (foll. by *for*) seek out

---

G

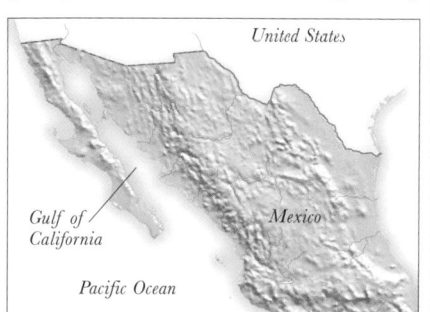

United States

Gulf of California

Mexico

Pacific Ocean

GULF OF **CALIFORNIA**, **MEXICO**

GUN

From small arms such as handguns to heavy artillery such as howitzers, all guns are classed by the width (caliber) of the barrel. Whatever the type, an explosion in one area propels a bullet or shell from the barrel toward its target. While many guns are intended for military action, some are used by police, and others by civilians for hunting, target practice, or self-defense.

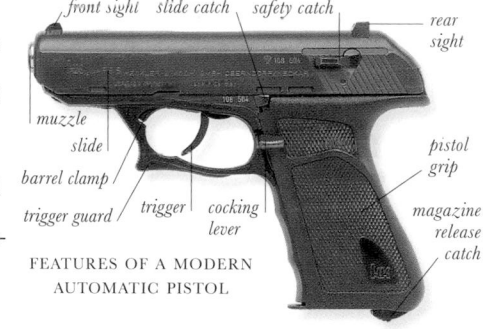

front sight   *slide catch*   *safety catch*   *rear sight*

muzzle
slide
barrel clamp
trigger guard   *trigger*   *cocking lever*
pistol grip
magazine release catch

FEATURES OF A MODERN AUTOMATIC PISTOL

EXAMPLES OF GUNS

REVOLVER
US .44 in. Smith & Wesson (1873)

SHORT-MAGAZINE RIFLE
British .303 in. Lee Enfield (1902)

SNIPER'S RIFLE
Japanese 6.5 mm type 97 (c.1937)

SILENCED AUTOMATIC PISTOL
British .22 in. (c.1939–45)

CARBINE
US 5.56 mm Colt Commando (1960s–90s)

SUBMACHINE GUN
German 9 mm Heckler and Koch (1990s)

determinedly to attack. □ **go great guns** *colloq.* proceed vigorously or successfully. **jump the gun** *colloq.* start before a signal is given, or before an agreed time. **stick to one's guns** *colloq.* maintain one's position under attack.

gun·boat /gúnbōt/ *n.* a small vessel with heavy guns.

gun·boat di·plo·ma·cy *n.* political negotiation supported by the threat of military force.

gun car·riage *n.* a wheeled support for a gun.

gun·cot·ton /gúnkotən/ *n.* an explosive used for blasting, made by steeping cotton in nitric and sulfuric acids.

gun crew *n.* a team manning a gun.

gun dog *n.* a dog trained to follow hunters using guns.

gun·fight /gúnfīt/ *n.* a fight with firearms. □□ **gun·fight·er** *n.*

gun·fire /gúnfīr/ *n.* **1** the firing of a gun, esp. repeatedly. **2** the noise from this.

gung-ho /gúnghṓ/ *adj.* enthusiastic; eager.

gunk /gungk/ *n. sl.* viscous or liquid material.

gun·lock /gúnlok/ *n.* a mechanism by which the charge of a gun is exploded.

gun·man /gúnmən/ *n.* (*pl.* **-men**) a man armed with a gun, esp. in committing a crime.

gun·met·al /gúnmetəl/ *n.* **1** a dull bluish gray color. **2** an alloy of copper and tin or zinc (formerly used for guns).

gun·nel var. of GUNWALE.

gun·ner /gúnər/ *n.* **1** an artillery

soldier (esp. *Brit.* as an official term for a private). **2** *Naut.* a warrant officer in charge of a battery, magazine, etc. **3** a member of an aircraft crew who operates a gun. **4** a person who hunts game with a gun.

gun·ner·a /gúnərə/ *n.* any plant of the genus *Gunnera* from S. America and New Zealand, having huge leaves and often grown for ornament.

gun·ner·y /gúnəree/ *n.* **1** the construction and management of large guns. **2** the firing of guns.

gun·ny /gúnee/ *n.* (*pl.* **-ies**) **1** coarse sacking, usu. of jute fiber. **2** a sack made of this.

gun·point /gúnpoynt/ *n.* the point of a gun. □ **at gunpoint** threatened with a gun or an ultimatum.

G

GYMNASTICS

While forms of gymnastics were popular in the ancient world, modern gymnastics date only from the early 19th century but are now practiced up to Olympic level. A gymnast combines set patterns of movement to display technique, as well as flexibility, strength, and agility. In artistic gymnastics, women perform exercises on the floor, beam, vault, and asymmetric bars; men perform on the floor, pommel horse, vault, rings, parallel bars, and horizontal bar. Rhythmic gymnastics are executed to music by women using ribbons, balls, hoops, ropes, or clubs. Sports acrobatics, evolved from acrobatic circus acts, feature balance work and tumbling.

swivel

wand

ribbon

raised arm

flexed hand

pointed toes

leotard

DEMONSTRATION OF AN ARABESQUE IN RHYTHMIC GYMNASTICS

EXAMPLES OF GYMNASTIC MOVEMENTS

BALANCES

V-SIT BALANCE

SHOULDER STAND BALANCE

ARABESQUE

TURNING MOVES

CARTWHEEL

HOOP WORK

HOOP JUMP

SHAPES

ARCH

STRADDLE SPLITS

BRIDGE

BALL WORK

BALL BALANCE

JUMPS AND LEAPS

STAG LEAP

TUCK JUMP

STRADDLE PIKE JUMP

STAR JUMP

SPORTS ACROBATICS

STAG BALANCE

STRADDLE LEVER BALANCE

COUNTER-BALANCE

SHOULDER BALANCE

gun·pow·der /gúnpowdər/ *n.* **1** ▶ an explosive made of saltpeter, sulfur, and charcoal. **2** a fine green tea of granular appearance.

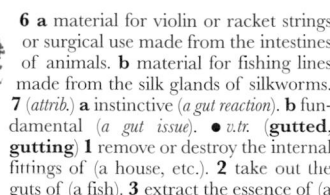

GUNPOWDER

gun·pow·er /gúnpowər/ *n.* the strength or quantity of available guns.

gun·run·ner /gúnrunər/ *n.* a person engaged in the illegal sale or importing of firearms. □□ **gun·run·ning** *n.*

gun·sel /gúnsəl/ *n. sl.* a criminal, esp. a gunman.

gun·ship /gúnship/ *n.* a heavily armed helicopter or other aircraft. ▷ HELICOPTER

gun·shot /gúnshot/ *n.* **1** a shot fired from a gun. **2** the range of a gun (*within gunshot*).

gun·sling·er /gúnslingər/ *n. sl.* a gunman. □□ **gun·sling·ing** *n.*

gun·smith /gúnsmith/ *n.* a person who makes and repairs small firearms.

gun·stock /gúnstok/ *n.* the wooden mounting of the barrel of a gun.

Gun·ter's chain /gúntərz/ *n. Surveying* **1** a measuring chain of 66 ft. **2** this length as a unit.

gun·wale /gúnəl/ *n.* (also **gun·nel**) the upper edge of the side of a boat or ship. ▷ TRIREME

gup·py /gúpee/ *n.* (*pl.* **-ies**) ▼ a freshwater fish, *Poecilia reticulata*, of the W. Indies and S. America, frequently kept in aquariums.

GUPPY:
BLONDE GUPPY
(*Poecilia reticulata*)

gur·gle /gɔ́rgəl/ *v. & n.* ● *v.* **1** *intr.* make a bubbling sound as of water from a bottle. **2** *tr.* utter with such a sound. ● *n.* a gurgling sound.

Gur·kha /gɔ́rkə/ *n.* **1** a member of the dominant Hindu people in Nepal. **2** a Nepalese soldier serving in the British army.

gur·nard /gɔ́rnərd/ *n.* (also **gur·net** /gɔ́rnit/) any marine fish of the family Triglidae, having a large spiny head with mailed sides.

gu·ru /gǒŏrōō/ *n.* **1** a Hindu spiritual teacher or head of a religious sect. **2 a** an influential teacher. **b** a revered mentor.

gush /gush/ *v. & n.* ● *v.* **1** *tr. & intr.* emit or flow in a sudden and copious stream. **2** *intr.* speak or behave with effusiveness. ● *n.* **1** a sudden or copious stream. **2** an effusive manner. □□ **gush·ing** *adj.* **gush·ing·ly** *adv.*

gush·er /gúshər/ *n.* **1** an oil well from which oil flows without being pumped. **2** an effusive person.

gush·y /gúshee/ *adj.* (**gushier**, **gushiest**) excessively effusive or sentimental.

gus·set /gúsit/ *n.* **1** a piece inserted into a garment, etc., to strengthen or enlarge a part. **2** a bracket strengthening an angle of a structure. □□ **gus·set·ed** *adj.*

gust /gust/ *n. & v.* ● *n.* **1** a sudden strong rush of wind. **2** a burst of rain, fire, smoke, or sound. **3** a passionate or emotional outburst. ● *v.intr.* blow in gusts.

gus·ta·tion /gustáyshən/ *n.* the act of tasting. □□ **gus·ta·to·ry** /gústətáwree/ *adj.*

gus·to /gústō/ *n.* (*pl.* **-oes**) zest; enjoyment or vigor in doing something.

gust·y /gústee/ *adj.* (**gustier**, **gustiest**) **1** characterized by or blowing in strong winds. **2** characterized by gusto. □□ **gust·i·ly** *adv.*

gut /gut/ *n. & v.* ● *n.* **1** the intestine. ▷ INTESTINE. **2** (in *pl.*) the bowel or entrails. **3** (in *pl.*) *colloq.* personal courage and determination; perseverance. **4** *colloq.* (in *pl.*) the belly as the source of appetite. **5** (in *pl.*) **a** the contents of anything. **b** the essence of a thing.

6 a material for violin or racket strings or surgical use made from the intestines of animals. **b** material for fishing lines made from the silk glands of silkworms. **7** (*attrib.*) **a** instinctive (*a gut reaction*). **b** fundamental (*a gut issue*). ● *v.tr.* (**gutted**, **gutting**) **1** remove or destroy the internal fittings of (a house, etc.). **2** take out the guts of (a fish). **3** extract the essence of (a book, etc.). □ **hate a person's guts** *colloq.* dislike a person intensely. **spill one's guts** *colloq.* reveal one's feelings, secrets, etc.; divulge previously untold information. **sweat** (or **work**) **one's guts out** *colloq.* work extremely hard.

gut·less /gútlis/ *adj. colloq.* lacking courage or determination.

guts·y /gútsee/ *adj.* (**gutsier**, **gutsiest**) *colloq.* **1** courageous. **2** greedy.

gut·ta-per·cha /gútəpɔ́rchə/ *n.* a tough plastic substance obtained from the latex of various Malaysian trees.

gut·tate /gútayt/ *adj. Biol.* having droplike markings.

gut·ter /gútər/ *n. & v.* ● *n.* **1** a shallow trough along the eaves of a house, or a channel at the side of a street, to carry off rainwater. ▷ HOUSE. **2** (prec. by *the*) a poor or degraded background or environment. **3** an open conduit. **4** a groove. **5** a track made by the flow of water. ● *v.intr.* **1** flow in streams. **2** (of a candle) melt away as the wax forms channels down the side.

gut·ter·ing /gútəring/ *n.* **1 a** the gutters of a building, etc. **b** a section or length of a gutter. **2** material for gutters.

gut·ter press *n.* esp. *Brit.* sensational journalism concerned esp. with the private lives of public figures.

gut·ter·snipe /gútərsnīp/ *n.* a street urchin.

gut·tur·al /gútərəl/ *adj. & n.* ● *adj.* **1** throaty; harsh sounding. **2 a** *Phonet.* (of a consonant) produced in the throat or by the back of the tongue and palate. **b** (of a sound) coming from the throat. **c** of the throat. ● *n. Phonet.* a guttural consonant (e.g., *k*, *g*).

guy[1] /gī/ *n. & v.* ● *n.* **1** *colloq.* a man; a fellow. **2** (usu. in *pl.*) a person of either sex. ● *v.tr.* ridicule.

guy[2] /gī/ *n. & v.* ● *n.* a rope or chain to secure a tent or steady a crane load, etc. ▷ TENT. ● *v.tr.* secure with a guy or guys.

guz·zle /gúzəl/ *v.tr. & intr.* eat, drink, or consume greedily. □□ **guz·zler** *n.*

gybe /jīb/ *v. & n.* var. of JIBE[2].

gym /jim/ *n. colloq.* **1** a gymnasium. **2** gymnastics.

gym·kha·na /jimkáánə/ *n.* a meeting for competition or display in a sport, esp. horse riding or automobile racing.

gym·na·si·um /jimnáyzeeəm/ *n.* (*pl.* **gymnasiums** or **gymnasia** /-zeeə/) **1** a room or building equipped for indoor sports, often including gymnastics. **2** a school in Germany or Scandinavia that prepares pupils for university entrance.

gym·nast /jímnast, -nəst/ *n.* an expert in gymnastics.

gym·nas·tic /jimnástik/ *adj.* of or involving gymnastics.

gym·nas·tics /jimnástiks/ *n.pl.* (also treated as *sing.*) **1** ◀ exercises developing or displaying physical agility and coordination. **2** other physical or mental agility.

gym·nos·o·phist /jimnósəfist/ *n.* a member of an ancient Hindu sect wearing little or no clothing and devoted to mystical contemplation. □□ **gym·nos·o·phy** *n.*

gym·no·sperm /jímnəspərm/ *n.* ▼ any of various plants having seeds unprotected by an ovary, including conifers, cycads, and ginkgos. □□ **gym·no·sper·mous** *adj.*

gymp var. of GIMP[1].

gy·nan·dro·morph /jinándrəmawrf, gī-/ *n. Biol.* an individual, esp. an insect, having male and female characteristics. □□ **gy·nan·dro·mor·phic** *adj.* **gy·nan·dro·morph·ism** *n.*

gy·nan·drous /jinándrəs, gī-/ *adj. Bot.* with stamens and pistil united in one column, as in orchids.

gyneco- /gínikō, jína-/ *comb. form* (*Brit.* **gynaeco-**) woman; women; female.

gy·ne·col·o·gy /gínikóləjee, jína-/ *n.* the science of the physiological functions and diseases of women. □□ **gyn·e·co·log·i·cal** *adj.* **gy·ne·col·o·gist** /-kóləjist/ *n.*

gyn·e·co·mas·ti·a /gínikōmásteeə, jína-/ *n. Med.* enlargement of a man's breasts, usu. due to hormone imbalance or hormone therapy.

gy·noe·ci·um /jɪnéeseeəm, -shee-, gī-/ *n.* (also **gy·nae·ci·um**) (*pl.* **-cia** /-seeə, -sheeə/) *Bot.* the carpels of a flower taken collectively.

-gynous /jinəs, ginəs/ *comb. form Bot.* forming adjectives meaning 'having specified female organs or pistils' (*monogynous*).

gyp /jip/ *v. & n. sl.* ● *v.tr.* (**gypped**, **gypping**) cheat; swindle. ● *n.* a swindle.

G

GYMNOSPERM

Mostly trees and shrubs, gymnosperms are made up of four phyla: conifers (the largest phylum), cycads, gnetophytes, and the ginkgo. Unlike angiosperms, gymnosperms produce seeds on the surface of specialized scales, which are often arranged in cones. Because the seeds do not develop inside a protective ovary, gymnosperms do not form fruits.

MAIN TYPES OF GYMNOSPERM

CONIFER CONE
AND SEED

seed

seed

wing

MATURE
FEMALE CONE

ovuliferous scale

SEED
(ENLARGED)

CONIFERS
bishop pine
(*Pinus muricata*) ▷ CONIFER

GNETOPHYTES
(*Welwitschia mirabilis*)

GINKGO
(*Ginkgo biloba*)

CYCADS
sago palm
(*Cycas revoluta*)

gyp·soph·i·la /jipsófilə/ *n.* any plant of the genus *Gypsophila*, native to the Mediterranean, with a profusion of small usu. white composite flowers, as baby's breath.

gyp·sum /jípsəm/ *n.* ◀ a hydrated form of calcium sulfate occurring naturally and used to make plaster of Paris and in the building industry.

Gyp·sy /jípsee/ *n.* (also **Gip·sy**) (*pl.* **-ies**) **1** a member of a nomadic people of Europe and N. America, of Hindu origin with dark skin and hair, and speaking a language related to Hindi. **2** (**gypsy**) a person resembling or living like a Gypsy.

GYPSUM: DESERT ROSE FORMATION

gyp·sy moth *n.* a kind of tussock moth, *Lymantria dispar*, of which the larvae are very destructive to foliage.

gy·rate /jírayt/ *v. & adj.* ● *v.intr.* (also /jīráyt/) go in a circle or spiral. ● *adj. Bot.* arranged in rings or convolutions. □□ **gy·ra·tion** /-ráyshən/ *n.* **gy·ra·tor** *n.* **gy·ra·to·ry** /-rətáwree/ *adj.*

gyre /jīr/ *v. & n. esp. poet.* ● *v.intr.* whirl or gyrate. ● *n.* a gyration.

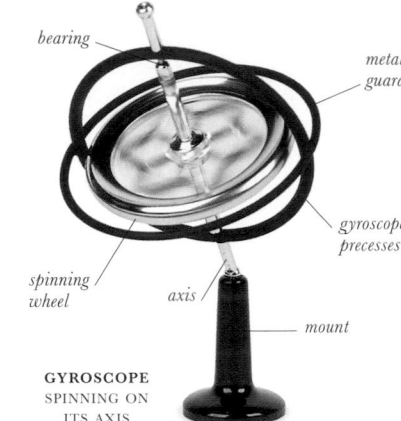

GYRFALCON
(*Falco rusticolus*)

gyr·fal·con /jórfalkən, -fawlkən/ *n.* (also **ger·fal·con**) ◀ a large falcon, *Falco rusticolus*, of the northern hemisphere.

gy·ro /jírō/ *n.* (*pl.* **-os**) *colloq.* **1** = GYROSCOPE. **2** = GYROCOMPASS.

gyro- /jírō/ *comb. form* rotation.

gy·ro·com·pass /jírōkumpəs, -kom-/ *n.* a nonmagnetic compass giving true north and bearings from it by means of a gyroscope.

gy·ro·graph /jírəgraf/ *n.* an instrument for recording revolutions.

gy·ro·mag·net·ic /jírōmagnétik/ *adj.* **1** *Physics* of the magnetic and mechanical properties of a rotating charged particle. **2** (of a compass) combining a gyroscope and a normal magnetic compass.

gy·ro·plane /jírəplayn/ *n.* a form of aircraft deriving its lift mainly from freely rotating overhead vanes.

gy·ro·scope /jírəskōp/ *n.* ▶ a rotating wheel whose axis is free to turn but maintains a fixed direction unless perturbed, esp. used for stabilization or with the compass in an aircraft, ship, etc. □□ **gy·ro·scop·ic** /-skópik/ *adj.*

gy·ro·sta·bi·liz·er /jírōstáybilīzər/ *n.* a gyroscopic device for maintaining the equilibrium of a ship, aircraft, platform, etc.

gy·rus /jírəs/ *n.* (*pl.* **gyri** /-rī/) a fold or convolution, esp. of the brain.

gyt·tja /yíchə/ *n. Geol.* a lake deposit of a usu. black organic sediment.

bearing

metal guard

gyroscope precesses

spinning wheel

axis

mount

GYROSCOPE
SPINNING ON
ITS AXIS

G

H

H[1] /aych/ *n.* (also **h**) (*pl.* **Hs** or **H's**) **1** the eighth letter of the alphabet. **2** anything having the form of an H (esp. in *comb.*: *H-girder*).

H[2] *abbr.* (also **H.**) **1** (of a pencil lead) hard. **2** (water) hydrant. **3** *sl.* heroin.

H[3] *symb. Chem.* the element hydrogen.

h. *abbr.* **1** hecto-. **2** height. **3** hot. **4** *Baseball* hit; hits.

Ha *symb. Chem.* the element hahnium.

ha[1] /haa/ *int.* (also **hah**) expressing surprise, suspicion, triumph, etc.

ha[2] *abbr.* hectare(s).

ha·be·as cor·pus /háybeeəs káwrpəs/ *n.* a writ requiring a person to be brought before a judge, esp. to investigate the lawfulness of his or her detention.

hab·er·dash·er /hábərdashər/ *n.* a dealer in men's clothing. □□ **hab·er·dash·er·y** *n.* (*pl.* **-ies**).

ha·bil·i·ment /həbílimənt/ *n.* (usu. in *pl.*) **1** clothes suited to a particular purpose. **2** *joc.* ordinary clothes.

hab·it /hábit/ *n. & v.* ● *n.* **1** a settled or regular tendency (*has a habit of ignoring me*). **2** a practice that is hard to give up. **3** a mental constitution. **4** *colloq.* an addictive practice, esp. of taking drugs. **5 a** ▼ the dress of a particular class, esp. of a religious order. **b** (in full **riding habit**) a woman's riding dress. **c** *archaic* dress; attire. **6** a bodily constitution. **7** *Biol. & Crystallog.* a mode of growth. ● *v.tr.* (usu. as **habited** *adj.*) clothe. □ **make a habit of** do regularly.

HABIT: BENEDICTINE MONK'S HABIT

hood
cloak
leather belt
linen shift beneath habit
rosary
woolen habit

hab·it·a·ble /hábitəbəl/ *adj.* that can be inhabited. □□ **hab·it·a·bil·i·ty** *n.* **hab·it·a·ble·ness** *n.* **hab·it·a·bly** *adv.*

hab·i·tant *n.* **1** /hábit'nt/ an inhabitant. **2** /ábeetóN/ **a** an early French settler in Canada or Louisiana. **b** a descendant of these early French settlers.

hab·i·tat /hábitat/ *n.* **1** the natural home of an organism. **2** a habitation.

hab·i·ta·tion /hábitáyshən/ *n.* **1** the process of in-

habiting (*fit for human habitation*). **2** a dwelling; a house or home.

hab·it-form·ing *adj.* causing addiction.

ha·bit·u·al /həbíchōoəl/ *adj.* **1** done constantly. **2** regular; usual. **3** given to a (specified) habit (*a habitual smoker*). □□ **ha·bit·u·al·ly** *adv.* **ha·bit·u·al·ness** *n.*

ha·bit·u·ate /həbíchōo-ayt/ *v.tr.* (often foll. by *to*) accustom. □□ **ha·bit·u·a·tion** /-áyshən/ *n.*

ha·bit·u·é /həbíchōo-áy/ *n.* a habitual visitor or resident.

ha·ček /háachek/ *n.* (also **háček**) a diacritic mark (ˇ) placed over letters to modify the sound in some Slavic and Baltic languages.

ha·chures /hashyŏor/ *n.pl.* parallel lines used in shading hills on maps, their closeness indicating the steepness of gradient.

ha·ci·en·da /háasee-éndə/ *n.* in Spanish-speaking countries: **1** an estate or plantation with a dwelling house. **2** a factory.

hack[1] /hak/ *v. & n.* ● *v.* **1** *tr.* cut or chop roughly. **2** *tr.* strike illegally at the legs of (an opponent) during a game. **3** *intr.* deliver cutting blows. **4** *tr.* cut (one's way) through thick foliage, etc. **5** *tr. colloq.* gain unauthorized access to (data in a computer). **6** *tr. sl.* **a** cope with. **b** tolerate. **c** (often followed by *off* or as **hacked off** *adj.*) annoy; disconcert. ● *n.* **1** a kick with the toe of a boot. **2** a wound, esp. from a kick. **3 a** a mattock. **b** a miner's pick.

hack[2] /hak/ *n., adj., & v.* ● *n.* **1 a** a horse for ordinary riding. **b** a horse let out for hire. **c** = JADE[2] 1. **2** a writer of mediocre literary work; *colloq.* usu. *derog.* a journalist. **3** a person hired to do dull routine work. **4** a taxi. ● *attrib.adj.* **1** used as a hack. **2** commonplace (*hack work*). ● *v.* **1** *intr.* ride on horseback at an ordinary pace. **2** *tr.* ride (a horse) in this way.

hack·er /hákər/ *n.* **1** a person or thing that hacks or cuts roughly. **2** *colloq.* **a** a person who is very adept at programming computers. **b** a person who uses computers to gain unauthorized access to data. **3** a golfer who plays poorly.

hack·ing cough *n.* a short dry frequent cough.

hack·le /hákəl/ *n.* **1** a long feather or series of feathers on the neck or saddle of a domestic fowl and other birds. **2** (in *pl.*) the erectile hairs along the back of a dog, which rise when it is angry or alarmed. □ **raise a person's hackles** cause a person to be angry.

hack·ney /háknee/ *n.* (*pl.* **-eys**) **1** a horse of average size for ordinary riding. **2** (*attrib.*) designating any of various vehicles for hire.

hack·neyed /hákneed/ *adj.* (of a phrase, etc.) made trite by overuse.

hack·saw /háksaw/ *n.* a saw with a narrow blade set in a frame, for cutting metal. ▷ SAW

had *past* and *past part.* of HAVE.

had·dock /hádək/ *n.* (*pl.* same) ▶ a marine fish, *Melanogrammus aeglefinus*, of the N. Atlantic, allied to cod, but smaller.

Ha·des /háydeez/ *n.* (in Greek mythology) the underworld; the abode of the spirits of the dead.

hadji var. of HAJJI.

hadn't /hád'nt/ *contr.* had not.

had·ron /hádron/ *n. Physics* any strongly interacting elementary particle. □□ **had·ron·ic** /-drónik/ *adj.*

haf·ni·um /háfneeəm/ *n. Chem.* a silvery metallic element occurring naturally with zirconium, used in tungsten alloys for filaments and electrodes. ¶ Symb.: **Hf**.

haft /haft/ *n. & v.* ● *n.* the handle of a dagger, knife, etc. ● *v.tr.* provide with a haft.

Hag. *abbr.* Haggai (Old Testament).

hag /hag/ *n.* **1** an ugly old woman. **2** a witch. □□ **hag·gish** *adj.*

hag·fish *n.* any jawless fish of the family Myxinidae,

with a rasplike tongue used for feeding on dead or dying fish.

hag·gard /hágərd/ *adj.* looking exhausted and distraught, esp. from fatigue, worry, privation, etc. □□ **hag·gard·ly** *adv.* **hag·gard·ness** *n.*

hag·gis /hágis/ *n.* ▶ a Scottish dish consisting of a sheep's or calf's offal mixed with suet, oatmeal, etc., and boiled in a bag made from the animal's stomach or in an artificial bag.

HAGGIS

hag·gle /hágəl/ *v. & n.* ● *v.intr.* (often foll. by *about*, *over*) bargain persistently. ● *n.* a dispute or wrangle. □□ **hag·gler** *n.*

hagio- /hágeeō, hágyeeō/ *comb. form* of saints or holiness.

Hag·i·og·ra·pha /hágeeógrəfə, hágyee-/ *n.pl.* the twelve books comprising the last of the three major divisions of the Hebrew Scriptures, along with the Law and the Prophets.

hag·i·og·ra·pher /hágeeógrəfər, hágyee-/ *n.* **1** a writer of the lives of saints. **2** a writer of any of the Hagiographa.

hag·i·og·ra·phy /hágeeógrəfee, hágyee-/ *n.* the writing of the lives of saints. □□ **hag·i·o·graph·ic** /-geeəgráfik/ *adj.* **hag·i·o·graph·i·cal** *adj.*

hag·i·ol·a·try /hágeeólətree, hágyee-/ *n.* the worship of saints.

hag·i·ol·o·gy /hágióləjee/ *n.* literature dealing with the lives and legends of saints. □□ **hag·i·o·log·i·cal** /-geeəlójikəl/ *adj.* **hag·i·ol·o·gist** *n.*

hag·rid·den /hágrid'n/ *adj.* afflicted by nightmares or anxieties.

hah var. of HA[1].

ha ha /háahaá/ *int.* repr. laughter.

ha-ha /háahaá/ *n.* a ditch with a wall on its inner side below ground level, forming a boundary to a park or garden without interrupting the view.

hahn·i·um /háaniəm/ *n. Chem.* an artificially produced radioactive element. ¶ Symb.: **Ha**.

haik /hīk, hayk/ *n.* (also **haick**) an outer covering for head and body worn by Arabs.

hai·ku /hīkoo/ *n.* (*pl.* same) a Japanese three line poem usu. consisting of 17 syllables. **2** an English imitation of this.

hail[1] /hayl/ *n. & v.* ● *n.* **1** pellets of frozen rain falling in showers from cumulonimbus clouds. **2** (foll. by *of*) a barrage or onslaught (of missiles, curses, questions, etc.). ● *v.* **1** *intr.* (prec. by *it* as subject) hail falls (*it is hailing*; *if it hails*). **2 a** *tr.* pour down (blows, words, etc.). **b** *intr.* come down forcefully.

HADDOCK
(*Melanogrammus aeglefinus*)

hail[2] /hayl/ *v., int., & n.* ● *v.* **1** *tr.* greet enthusiastically. **2** *tr.* signal to (*hailed a taxi*). **3** *tr.* acclaim (*hailed him king*; *was hailed as a prodigy*). **4** *intr.* (foll. by *from*) have one's home or origins in (a place) (*hails from Mexico*). ● *int. archaic* or *rhet.* expressing greeting. ● *n.* **1** a greeting or act of hailing. **2** distance as affecting the possibility of hailing (*within hail*; *within hailing distance*). □ **hail-fellow-well-met** jovially intimate, esp. too intimate.

Hail Mar·y *n.* the Ave Maria (see AVE).

H

HAILSTONE

A hailstone is an ice pellet that forms as air currents cause it to rise and fall within a cloud. As it falls, the pellet gathers an outer layer of moisture, which freezes as it rises again. Eventually, the pellet grows too heavy for the upcurrents to support it and falls to the ground as a hailstone.

FORMATION OF A
HAILSTONE
WITHIN A CLOUD

outermost
ice layer

down-
current

hailstone

upcurrent

ice pellet

---

hail·stone /háylstōn/ *n.* ▲ a pellet of hail.

hail·storm /háylstorm/ *n.* a period of heavy hail.

hair /hair/ *n.* **1 a** ▼ any of the fine threadlike strands growing from the skin of mammals, esp. from the human head. **b** these collectively (*his hair is falling out*). **c** a hairstyle or way of wearing the hair (*I like your hair today*). **2 a** an artificially produced hairlike strand, e.g., in a brush. **b** a mass of such hairs. **c** anything resembling a hair. **3** an elongated cell growing from the epidermis of a plant. **4** a very small quantity or extent (also *attrib.*: *a hair crack*). □ **get in a person's hair** *colloq.* annoy a person. **keep one's hair on** *Brit. colloq.* remain calm. **let one's hair down** *colloq.* abandon restraint. **make a person's hair stand on end** horrify a person. **not turn a hair** remain unmoved or unaffected. □□ **haired** *adj.* (also in *comb.*). **hair·less** *adj.* **hair·like** *adj.*

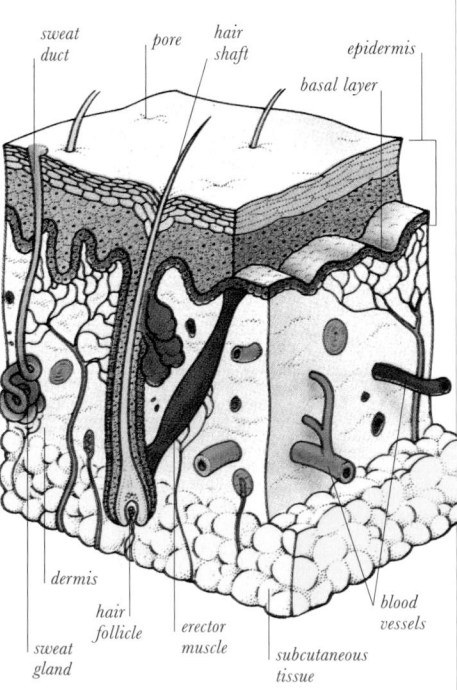

sweat
duct

pore

hair
shaft

epidermis

basal layer

dermis

hair
follicle

erector
muscle

subcutaneous
tissue

blood
vessels

sweat
gland

HAIR: SECTION THROUGH HUMAN
SKIN SHOWING HAIR

---

hair·ball /háirbawl/ *n.* (also **hair ball**) a ball of hair that accumulates in the stomach of a cat, etc., that grooms itself by licking its fur.

hair·band /háirband/ *n.* a band for securing or tying back one's hair.

hair·brush /háirbrush/ *n.* a brush for arranging or smoothing the hair.

hair·cloth /háirklawth, -kloth/ *n.* stiff cloth woven from hair.

hair·cut /háirkut/ *n.* **1** a cutting of the hair. **2** the style in which the hair is cut.

hair·do /háirdoō/ *n.* (*pl.* **-dos**) *colloq.* the style of a woman's hair.

hair·dress·er /háirdresər/ *n.* **1** a person who cuts and styles hair, esp. professionally. **2** the business or establishment of a hairdresser. □□ **hair·dress·ing** *n.*

hair dry·er *n.* (also **hair drier**) an electrical device for drying the hair by blowing warm air over it.

hair·line /háirlīn/ *n.* **1** the edge of a person's hair, esp. on the forehead. **2** a very thin line or crack, etc.

hair·net /háirnet/ *n.* a piece of fine mesh fabric for confining the hair.

hair of the dog *n.* further alcoholic drink to cure hangover from that drink.

hair·piece /háirpees/ *n.* a quantity or switch of detached hair used to augment a person's natural hair.

hair·pin /háirpin/ *n.* a U-shaped pin for fastening the hair.

hair·pin turn *n.* a sharp U-shaped bend in a road.

hair·rais·ing /háirrayzing/ *adj.* extremely alarming; terrifying.

hair's breadth *n.* a very small amount or margin.

hair·split·ting /háirspliting/ *adj. & n.* making over-fine distinctions; quibbling. □□ **hair·split·ter** *n.*

    hair spray *n.* a solution sprayed on the hair to keep it in place.

    hair·spring /háirspring/ *n.* a fine spring regulating the balance wheel in a watch.

    hair trig·ger *n.* a trigger of a firearm set for release at the slightest pressure.

    hair-trig·ger *adj.* reacting to the slightest pressure or provocation; likely to prompt such a reaction (*a hair-trigger situation*).

hair·y /háiree/ *adj.* (**hairier**, **hairiest**) **1** covered with hair. **2** having the feel of hair. **3** *sl.* alarmingly unpleasant. □□ **hair·i·ly** *adv.* **hair·i·ness** *n.*

hajj /haj/ *n.* (also **hadj**) the Islamic pilgrimage to Mecca.

hajj·i /hájee/ *n.* (also **hadj·i**) (*pl.* **-is**) a Muslim who has been to Mecca as a pilgrim: also (**Hajji**) used as a title.

---

hake /hayk/ *n.* any marine fish of the genus *Merluccius*, esp. *M. merluccius* with an elongate body and large head.

ha·lal /haaláal/ *v. & n.* (also **hal·lal**) ● *v.tr.* (**halalled**, **halalling**) kill (an animal) as prescribed by Muslim law. ● *n.* (often *attrib.*) meat prepared in this way.

hal·berd /hálbərd/ *n.* (also **hal·bert** /-bərt/) *hist.* a combined spear and battleax. ▷ ROUNDHEAD

hal·cy·on /hálseeən/ *adj.* **1** calm; peaceful (*halcyon days*). **2** (of a period) happy; prosperous.

hale[1] /hayl/ *adj.* strong and healthy (esp. in **hale and hearty**). □□ **hale·ness** *n.*

hale[2] /hayl/ *v.tr.* drag or draw forcibly.

half /haf/ *n., adj., & adv.* ● *n.* (*pl.* **halves** /havz/) **1** either of two equal or corresponding parts into which a thing is or might be divided. **2** *colloq.* = HALF-BACK. **3** either of two equal periods of play in sports. **4** *colloq.* a half-price fare or ticket, esp. for a child. ● *adj.* **1** of an amount or quantity equal to a half, or roughly a half (*half a pint*). **2** forming a half (*a half share*). ● *adv.* **1** (often in *comb.*) to the extent of half (*half-frozen*). **2** to a certain extent (esp. in phrases: *half dead*; *half inclined to agree*). **3** (in reckoning time) by the amount of half (an hour, etc.) (*half past two*). □ **at half cock** see COCK[1]. **by half** (prec. by *too* + *adj.*) excessively (*too clever by half*). **by halves** incompletely (*never does things by halves*). **half a chance** *colloq.* the slightest opportunity (esp. given half a chance). **half an eye** the slightest degree of perceptiveness. **half measures** an unsatisfactory compromise or inadequate policy. **the half of it** *colloq.* the important part of something (usu. after *neg.*: *you don't know the half of it*). **half the time** see TIME. **not half 1** not nearly (*not half long enough*). **2** *colloq.* not at all (*not half bad*).

half-and-half *adj.* being half one thing and half another.

half·back /háfbak/ *n.* (in some sports) a player between the linemen and fullbacks, or behind the forward line. ▷ FOOTBALL

half-baked *adj.* **1** incompletely planned. **2** (of enthusiasm, etc.) only partly committed. **3** foolish.

half-blood *n.* **1** a person having one parent in common with another. **2** this relationship. **3** = HALF BREED. □□ **half-blooded** *adj.*

half breed *n.* often *offens.* a person of mixed race.

half broth·er *n.* a brother with only one parent in common.

half-doz·en *n.* (also **half-a-dozen**) *colloq.* six, or about six.

half·heart·ed /háfháartid/ *adj.* lacking enthusiasm. □□ **half·heart·ed·ly** *adv.* **half·heart·ed·ness** *n.*

half hitch *n.* ▶ a noose or knot formed by passing the end of a rope around its standing part and then through the loop.

half hour *n.* **1** (also **half an hour**) a period of 30 minutes. **2** a point of time 30 minutes after any hour. □□ **half-hourly** *adv.*

HALF HITCH

half-inch *n.* a unit of length half as large as an inch.

half-life *n.* the time taken for the radioactivity or some other property of a substance to fall to half its original value.

half-mast *n.* the position of a flag halfway down the mast, as a mark of respect for a person who has died. □ **at half-mast** often *joc.* (of a garment) having slipped down.

half meas·ures *n.pl.* an unsatisfactory compromise or inadequate policy.

half moon *n.* **1** the Moon when only half its illuminated surface is visible from Earth. **2** the time when this occurs. **3** a semicircular object.

half note *n. Mus.* a note whose duration is one half of a whole note. ▷ NOTATION

half sis·ter *n.* a sister with only one parent in common.

half·tim·bered *adj. Archit.* ▶ having walls with a timber frame and a brick or plaster filling.

half-time *n. & adj.* ● *n.* **1** the time at which half of a game is completed. **2** a short interval occurring at this time. ● *adj.* working half the usual or normal hours.

half·tone *n.* **1** a reproduction printed from a block (produced by photographic means) in which the various tones of gray are produced from small and large black dots. **2** *Mus.* (**half tone**) a semitone.

half-truth *n.* a statement that conveys only part of the truth.

half·way /háfwáy/ *adv. & adj.* ● *adv.* **1** at a point equidistant between two others (*we were halfway to Chicago*). **2** to some extent; more or less (*is halfway decent*). ● *adj.* situated halfway (*reached a halfway point*).

half·way house *n.* **1** a compromise. **2** the halfway point in a progression. **3** a center for rehabilitating ex-prisoners, mental patients, or others unused to normal life. **4** an inn midway between two towns.

half·way line *n.* a line midway between the ends of a sports field, esp. in soccer.

half·wit /háfwit/ *n.* **1** *colloq.* an extremely stupid person. **2** a person who is mentally deficient. □□ **half·wit·ted** /wítid/ *adj.*

hal·i·but /hálibət/ *n.* (also **hol·i·but** /hól-/) (*pl.* same) ▼ any of various large marine flatfishes, commonly used as food.

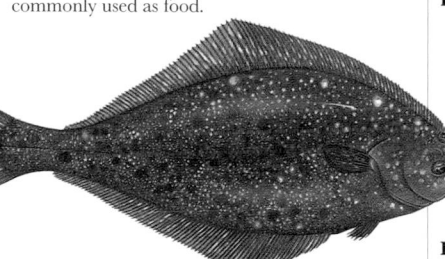

HALIBUT: PACIFIC HALIBUT
(*Hippoglossus stenolepis*)

hal·ide /hálid, háyl-/ *n. Chem.* a binary compound of a halogen with another group or element. **2** any organic compound containing a halogen.

hal·i·o·tis /háleeótis/ *n.* ◀ any edible gastropod mollusk of the genus *Haliotis* with an ear-shaped shell lined with mother-of-pearl.

hal·ite /hálīt, háy-/ *n.* rock salt.

hal·i·to·sis /hálitósis/ *n.* = BAD BREATH.

hall /hawl/ *n.* **1 a** a space or passage into which the front entrance of a house, etc., opens. **b** a corridor or passage in a building. **2** a large room or building for meetings, meals, concerts, etc. **3** a university residence for students. **4 a** (in an English college, a residence hall, etc.) a common dining room. **b** *Brit.* dinner in this. **5** the building of a guild (*Fishmongers' Hall*). **6** a large public room in a palace, etc.

HALIOTIS:
INNER SURFACE OF
A HALIOTIS SHELL

hal·le·lu·jah var. of ALLELUIA.

hall·mark /háwlmaark/ *n. & v.* ● *n.* **1** a mark used at Goldsmiths' Hall in London (and by the UK assay offices) for marking the standard of gold, silver, and platinum. **2** any distinctive feature, esp. of excellence. ● *v.tr.* **1** stamp with a hallmark. **2** designate as excellent.

plaster infill *timber frame* *pointed gable*

HALF-TIMBERED
17TH-CENTURY ENGLISH HOUSE

Hall of Fame *n.* a building with memorials to individuals who excelled in a sport, etc.

hal·loo /həlóō/ *int., n., & v.* ● *int.* **1** inciting dogs to the chase. **2** calling attention. **3** expressing surprise. ● *n.* the cry "halloo." ● *v.* (**halloos, hallooed**) **1** *intr.* cry "halloo," esp. to dogs. **2** *intr.* shout to attract attention. **3** *tr.* urge on (dogs, etc.) with shouts.

hal·low /hálō/ *v.tr.* **1** make holy; consecrate. **2** honor as holy.

Hal·low·een /hálōwéen/ *n.* (also **Hallowe'en**) the eve of All Saints' Day, Oct. 31, esp. as celebrated by children dressing in costumes and collecting treats door-to-door.

Hall·statt /háalshtaat/ *adj.* of or relating to the early Iron Age in Europe as attested by archaeological finds at Hallstatt in Upper Austria.

hal·lu·ces *pl.* of HALLUX.

hal·lu·ci·nate /həlóōsinayt/ *v.* **1** *tr.* produce illusions in the mind of (a person). **2** *intr.* experience hallucinations. □□ **hal·lu·ci·nant** /-nənt/ *adj. & n.* **hal·lu·ci·na·tor** *n.*

hal·lu·ci·na·tion /həlóōsináyshən/ *n.* the apparent perception of an object not actually present. □□ **hal·lu·ci·na·to·ry** /-sinátəwree/ *adj.*

hal·lu·ci·no·gen /həlóōsinəjən/ *n.* a drug causing hallucinations. □□ **hal·lu·ci·no·gen·ic** /-jénik/ *adj.*

hal·lux /háluks/ *n.* (*pl.* **halluces** /hályəseez/) **1** the big toe. **2** the innermost digit of the hind foot of vertebrates.

hall·way /háwlway/ *n.* an entrance hall or corridor.

halm var. of HAULM.

hal·ma /hálmə/ *n.* a game played by two or four persons on a board of 256 squares, with men advancing from one corner to the opposite corner by being moved over other men into vacant squares.

ha·lo /háylō/ *n. & v.* ● *n.* (*pl.* **-oes**) **1** a disk or circle of light shown in art surrounding the head of a sacred person. **2** the glory associated with an idealized person, etc. **3** a circle of light around a luminous body, esp. the Sun or Moon. **4** a circle or ring. ● *v.tr.* (**-oes, -oed**) surround with a halo.

hal·o·gen /hálōjən/ *n. Chem.* any of the group of nonmetallic elements: fluorine, chlorine, bromine, iodine, and astatine, which form halides (e.g., sodium chloride) by simple union with a metal. □□ **hal·o·gen·ic** /-jénik/ *adj.*

hal·on /háylon/ *n. Chem.* any of various gaseous compounds of carbon, bromine, and other halogens, used to extinguish fires.

hal·o·phyte /hálōfit/ *n.* ▶ a plant adapted to saline conditions.

halt[1] /hawlt/ *n. & v.* ● *n.* **1** a stop (usu. temporary) (*come to a halt*). **2** a temporary stoppage on a march or journey. ● *v.intr. & tr.* stop; come or bring to a halt. □ **call a halt (to)** decide to stop.

halt[2] /hawlt/ *v. & adj.* ● *v.intr.* **1** (esp. as **halting** *adj.*) lack smooth progress. **2** hesitate (*halt between two opinions*). ● *adj. archaic* lame. □□ **halt·ing·ly** *adv.*

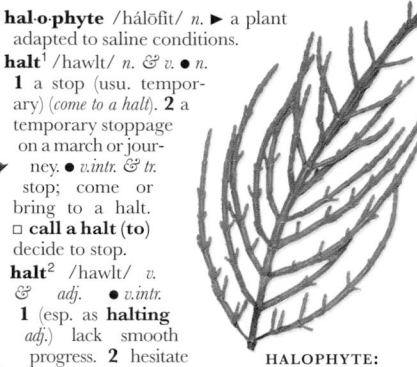

HALOPHYTE:
GLASSWORT
(*Salicornia europaea*)

halt·er /háwltər/ *n.* **1** a rope or strap with a noose or headstall for horses or cattle. **2 a** a strap around the back of a woman's neck holding her dress top and leaving her shoulders and back bare. **b** dress top held by this.

hal·va /háalvaa/ *n.* (also **hal·vah**) a sweet confection of ground sesame seeds and honey.

halve /hav/ *v.tr.* **1** divide into two parts or halves. **2** reduce by half. **3** share equally. **4** *Golf* use the same number of strokes as one's opponent in (a hole or match).

hal·yard /hályərd/ *n. Naut.* a rope or tackle for raising or lowering a sail or yard, etc. ▷ FLAG

ham /ham/ *n. & v.* ● *n.* **1 a** the upper part of a pig's leg salted and dried or smoked for food. **b** the meat from this. **2** the back of the thigh. **3** *sl.* (often *attrib.*) an inexpert or unsubtle actor or piece of acting. **4** (in full **radio ham**) *colloq.* the operator of an amateur radio station. ● *v.intr. & tr.* (often foll. by *up*) (**hammed, hamming**) *sl.* overact; act or treat emotionally or sentimentally.

ha·ma·dry·ad /hámədríyəd/ *n. Gk. & Rom. Mythol.* a nymph who lives in a tree and dies when it dies.

ham·burg·er /hámbərgər/ *n.* a patty of ground beef, usu. fried or grilled and eaten in a soft bread roll.

ham-fist·ed /hámfistid/ *adj. colloq.* clumsy. □□ **ham-fist·ed·ly** *adv.* **ham-fist·ed·ness** *n.*

Ham·it·ic /həmítik/ *n. & adj.* ● *n.* a group of African languages including ancient Egyptian and Berber. ● *adj.* **1** of or relating to this group of languages. **2** of or relating to the Hamites, a group of peoples in Egypt and N. Africa, by tradition descended from Noah's son Ham (Gen. 10:6 ff.).

ham·let /hámlit/ *n.* a small village.

ham·mer /hámər/ *n. & v.* ● *n.* **1 a** a tool with a heavy metal head at right angles to the handle, used for driving nails, etc. **b** a machine with a metal block serving the same purpose. **c** a similar contrivance, as for exploding the charge in a gun, etc. **2** an auctioneer's mallet, indicating by a rap that an article is sold. **3 a** a metal ball attached to a wire for throwing in an athletic contest. **b** the sport of throwing the hammer. ● *v.* **1 a** *tr. & intr.* hit or beat with or as with a hammer. **b** *intr.* strike loudly. **2** *tr.* **a** drive in (nails) with a hammer. **b** fasten by hammering (*hammered the lid down*). **3** *tr.* (often foll. by *in*) inculcate (ideas, knowledge, etc.) forcefully. **4** *tr. colloq.* utterly defeat. **5** *intr.* (foll. by *away at*) work hard at. □ **come under the hammer** be sold at auction.

hammer out 1 make flat or smooth by hammering. **2** work out the details of. **3** play (a tune, esp. on the piano) loudly or clumsily. □□ **ham·mer·ing** *n.* (esp. in sense 4 of *v.*).

ham·mer and sick·le *n.* ▶ the symbols of the industrial worker and the peasant used as the emblem of the former USSR and of international communism.

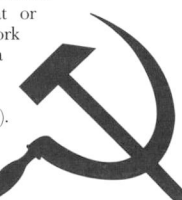

HAMMER AND
SICKLE

H

H

ham·mer·head /hámərhed/ *n.* any shark of the family Sphyrinidae, with a flattened head and eyes in lateral extensions of it. ▷ SHARK.

ham·mer·lock /hámərlok/ *n. Wrestling* a hold in which the arm is twisted and bent behind the back.

ham·mer·toe /hámərtō/ *n.* a deformity in which the toe is bent permanently downwards.

ham·mock /hámək/ *n.* a bed of canvas or rope network, suspended by cords.

Ham·mond or·gan *n. Trademark* a type of electronic organ.

ham·my /hámee/ *adj.* (**hammier**, **hammiest**) **1** of or like ham. **2** *colloq.* over-theatrical.

ham·per¹ /hámpər/ *n.* a large basket, usu. with a hinged lid and containing laundry or (esp. *Brit.*) food (*clothes hamper; picnic hamper*).

ham·per² /hámpər/ *v.tr.* **1** prevent the free movement or activity of. **2** impede; hinder.

ham·ster /hámstər/ *n.* any of various rodents of the subfamily Cricetinae, esp. *Cricetus cricetus*, having a short tail and large cheek pouches for storing food, kept as a pet or laboratory animal. ▷ RODENT

ham·string /hámstring/ *n. & v.* ● *n. Anat.* **1 ▼** each of five tendons at the back of the knee in humans. ▷ KNEE. **2** the great tendon at the back of the hock in quadrupeds. ● *v.tr.* (*past* and *past part.* **hamstrung** or **hamstringed**) **1** cripple by cutting the hamstrings of (a person or animal). **2** prevent the activity of.

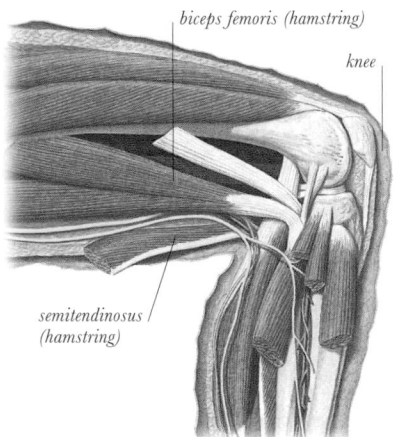

HAMSTRING: TWO OF THE HAMSTRING TENDONS IN THE HUMAN LEG

biceps femoris (hamstring)

knee

semitendinosus (hamstring)

hand /hand/ *n. & v.* ● *n.* **1 a ▶** the end part of the human arm beyond the wrist. **b** in other primates, the end part of a forelimb, also used as a foot. **2 a** (often in *pl.*) control; custody (*is in good hands*). **b** agency or influence (*suffered at their hands*). **c** a share in an action. **3** the pointer of a clock or watch. **4** the right or left side or direction relative to a person or thing. **5 a** a skill (*a hand for making pastry*). **b** a person skillful in some respect. **6** a person who does or makes something, esp. distinctively (*a picture by the same hand*). **7** an individual's writing or the style of this. **8** a person as the source of information (*at first hand*). **9** a pledge of marriage. **10** a manual laborer, esp. in a factory, on a farm, or on board ship. **11 a** the playing cards dealt to a player. **b** the player holding these. **c** a round of play. **12** *colloq.* applause (*a big hand*). **13** the unit of measure of a horse's height, equal to 4 inches (10.16 cm). **14** a forehock of pork. **15** a bunch of bananas. **16** (*attrib.*) **a** operated or held in the hand (*hand drill; hand luggage*). **b** done by hand and not by machine (*hand-knitted*). ● *v.tr.* **1** deliver; transfer. **2** convey verbally (*handed me a lot of abuse*). **3** *colloq.* give away too readily (*handed them the advantage*). □ **all hands 1** the entire crew of a ship. **2** the entire workforce. **at hand 1** close by. **2** about to happen. **by hand 1** by a person and not a machine. **2** delivered privately and not by the public mail. **from hand to mouth** satisfy-

HAND

The human hand is a sensitive tool with opposable fingers and thumb. A system of muscles and tendons in the forearm and hand flexes and extends a framework of 27 bones, allowing a wide range of precise movements.

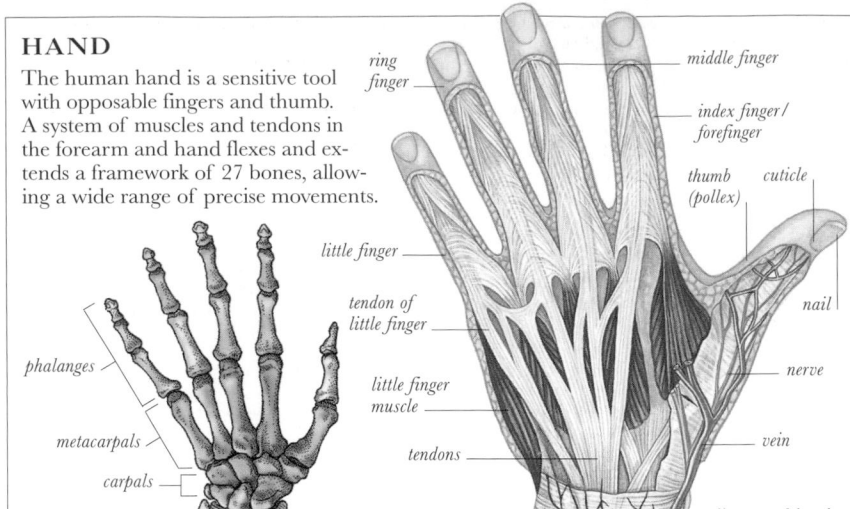

ring finger

middle finger

index finger/ forefinger

thumb (pollex)

cuticle

nail

little finger

tendon of little finger

nerve

little finger muscle

tendons

vein

phalanges

metacarpals

carpals

ligamental band around wrist

BONES OF THE HUMAN HAND

INTERNAL ANATOMY OF THE HUMAN HAND

ing only one's immediate needs (also *attrib.*: *a hand-to-mouth existence*). **get** (or **have** or **keep**) **one's hand in** become (or be or remain) practiced in something. **hand and foot** completely; satisfying all demands (*waited on them hand and foot*). **hand around** distribute. **hand down 1** pass the ownership of to another. **2 a** transmit (a decision) from a higher court, etc. **b** express (an opinion or verdict). **hand in glove** in collusion or association. **hand in hand** in close association. **hand it to** *colloq.* acknowledge the merit of. **hand on** pass (a thing) to the next in a series. **hand out 1** serve; distribute. **2** award, allocate (*the judges handed out stiff sentences*). **hand over** surrender possession of. **hands down** (esp. of winning) with no difficulty. **hands off** *int.* a warning not to touch or interfere with something. *adj.* not requiring manual use of controls. **hands on 1** *Computing* of or requiring personal operation at a keyboard. **2** involving or offering active participation rather than theory. **hands up!** an instruction to raise one's hands in surrender or to signify assent. **have** (or **take**) **a hand** (often foll. by *in*) share or take part. **have one's hands full** be fully occupied. **have one's hands tied** *colloq.* be unable to act. **hold one's hand** = *stay one's hand*. **in hand 1** receiving attention. **2** in reserve. **3** under one's control. **lay** (or **put**) **one's hands on** see LAY¹. **lend** (or **give**) **a hand** assist in an action or enterprise. **off one's hands** no longer one's responsibility. **on every hand** (or **all hands**) to or from all directions. **on hand** available. **on one's hands** resting on one as a responsibility. **on the one** (or **the other**) **hand** from one (or another) point of view. **out of hand 1** out of control. **2** peremptorily (*refused out of hand*). **put** (or **set**) **one's hand to** start work on; engage in. **stay one's hand** *archaic* or *literary* refrain from action. **to hand 1** within easy reach. **2** (of a letter) received. **turn one's hand to** undertake (as a new activity). □□ **hand·less** *adj.*

hand·bag /hándbag/ *n.* a small bag usu. with a handle or shoulder strap carried esp. by a woman and used to hold a wallet, cosmetics, etc.

hand·ball *n.* **1** /hándbawl/ one of several games with a ball thrown by hand among players or struck with an open hand against a wall. **2** /hándbáwl/ *Soccer* intentional touching of the ball with the hand or arm by a player other than the goalkeeper in the goal area, constituting a foul.

leather strap

larger bell produces lower note

smaller bell produces higher note

clapper

HANDBELLS

hand·bell /hándbel/ *n.* **▲** a small bell, usu. tuned to a particular note and rung by hand, esp. one of a set giving a range of notes.

hand·bill /hándbil/ *n.* a printed notice distributed by hand.

hand·book /hándbook/ *n.* a short manual or guidebook.

hand·brake /hándbrayk/ *n.* a hand-operated brake.

hand·cart /hándkaart/ *n.* a small cart pushed or drawn by hand.

hand·clap /hándklap/ *n.* a clapping of the hands.

hand·craft /hándkraft/ *n. & v.* ● *n.* = HANDICRAFT. ● *v.tr.* make by handicraft.

hand·cuff /hándkuf/ *n. & v.* ● *n.* (in *pl.*) **◄** a pair of lockable linked metal rings for securing a person's wrists. ● *v.tr.* put handcuffs on.

-handed /hándid/ *adj.* (in *comb.*) **1** for or involving a specified number of hands (in various senses) (*two-handed*). **2** using chiefly the hand specified (*left-handed*). □□ **-hand·ed·ly** *adv.* **-hand·ed·ness** *n.* (both in sense 2).

HANDCUFF: 19TH-CENTURY BRITISH HANDCUFFS

hand·ful /hándfool/ *n.* (*pl.* **-fuls**) **1** a quantity that fills the hand. **2** a small number or amount. **3** *colloq.* a troublesome person or task.

hand gre·nade *n.* see GRENADE.

hand glass *n.* **1** a magnifying glass held in the hand. **2** a small mirror with a handle.

hand·grip /hándgrip/ *n.* **1** a grasp with the hand. **2** a handle designed for easy holding.

hand·gun /hándgun/ *n.* a small firearm held in and fired with one hand. ▷ GUN

hand·hold /hándhōld/ *n.* something for the hands to grip on (in climbing, sailing, etc.).

hand·i·cap /hándeekap/ *n.* & *v.* ● *n.* **1 a** a disadvantage imposed on a superior competitor in order to make the chances more equal. **b** a race or contest in which this is imposed. **2** the number of strokes by which a golfer normally exceeds par for the course. **3** a thing that makes progress difficult. **4** a physical or mental disability. ● *v.tr.* (**handicapped**, **handicapping**) **1** impose a handicap on. **2** place at a disadvantage. □□ **hand·i·cap·per** *n.*

hand·i·capped /hándeekapt/ *adj.* having a physical or mental disability.

hand·i·craft /hándeekraft/ *n.* work that requires both manual and artistic skill.

hand·i·work /hándeewərk/ *n.* work done or a thing made by hand.

hand·ker·chief /hángkərchif, -cheef/ *n.* (*pl.* **handkerchiefs** or **-chieves** /-cheevz/) a square of cotton, linen, silk, etc., for wiping one's nose, etc.

han·dle /hánd'l/ *n.* & *v.* ● *n.* **1** the part by which a thing is held, carried, or controlled. **2** a fact that may be taken advantage of (*gave a handle to his critics*). **3** *colloq.* a personal title. **4** the feel of goods when handled. ● *v.tr.* **1** touch, operate, or move with the hands. **2** manage or deal with (*knows how to handle people*). **3** deal in (goods). **4** discuss or write about (a subject). □□ **han·dle·a·ble** *adj.* **han·dle·a·bil·i·ty** *n.* **han·dled** *adj.* (also in *comb.*).

han·dle·bar /hánd'lbaar/ *n.* (often in *pl.*) the steering bar of a bicycle, etc. ▷ BICYCLE

han·dle·bar mus·tache *n.* a thick mustache with curved ends.

han·dler /hándlər/ *n.* **1** a person who handles or deals in certain commodities. **2** a person who trains and looks after an animal (esp. a working or show dog).

hand·made /hándmáyd/ *adj.* made by hand and not by machine, esp. as designating superior quality.

hand·maid /hándmayd/ *n.* (also **hand·maid·en** /-máyd'n/) *archaic* a female servant or helper.

hand-me-down *n.* an article of clothing, etc., passed on from another person.

hand·out /hándowt/ *n.* **1** something given free to a needy person. **2** a statement given to the press, printed information given to a lecture audience, etc.

hand-o·ver-fist *adv. colloq.* with rapid progress.

hand·pick /hándpik/ *v.tr.* choose carefully or personally.

hand·rail /hándrayl/ *n.* a narrow rail for holding as a support on stairs, etc.

hand·saw /hándsaw/ *n.* a saw worked by one hand.

hand·set /hándset/ *n.* a telephone mouthpiece and earpiece forming one unit. ▷ TELEPHONE

hands-free *adj. attrib.* (esp. of a telephone) designed to be operated without using the hands.

hand·shake /hándshayk/ *n.* the shaking of a person's hand by another's hand as a greeting, etc.

hand·some /hánsəm/ *adj.* (**handsomer**, **handsomest**) **1** (of a person) good-looking. **2** (of a building, etc.) imposing; attractive. **3** generous (*a handsome present*). **b** (of a price, fortune, etc., as assets gained) considerable. □□ **hand·some·ness** *n.*

hand·some·ly /hánsəmlee/ *adv.* **1** generously. **2** finely; beautifully. **3** *Naut.* carefully.

hand·spring /hándspring/ *n.* an aerobatic flip in which one lands first on the hands and then on the feet.

hand·stand /hándstand/ *n.* balancing on one's hands with the feet in the air.

hand-to-hand *adj.* (of fighting) at close quarters.

hand·writ·ing /hándrīting/ *n.* **1** writing with a pen, pencil, etc. ▷ CALLIGRAPHY. **2** a person's particular style of writing. □□ **hand·writ·ten** /-rítən/ *adj.*

hand·y /hándee/ *adj.* (**handier**, **handiest**) **1** convenient to handle or use. **2** ready to hand. **3** clever with the hands. □□ **hand·i·ly** *adv.* **hand·i·ness** *n.*

hand·y·man /hándeeman/ *n.* (*pl.* **-men**) a person able or employed to do occasional domestic repairs and minor renovations.

hang /hang/ *v.* & *n.* ● *v.* (*past* and *past part.* **hung** /hung/ except in sense 7) **1** *tr.* **a** secure or cause to be supported from above. **b** (foll. by *up, on, onto,* etc.) attach loosely by suspending from the top. **2** *tr.* set up (a door, gate, etc.) on its hinges. **3** *tr.* place (a picture) on a wall or in an exhibition. **4** *tr.* attach (wallpaper) to a wall. **5** *tr.* (foll. by *on*) *colloq.* attach the blame for (a thing) to (a person) (*you can't hang that on me*). **6** *tr.* (foll. by *with*) decorate by hanging decorations, etc. (*a hall hung with tapestries*). **7** *tr.* & *intr.* (*past* and *past part.* **hanged**) **a** suspend or be suspended by the neck until dead, esp. as a form of capital punishment. **b** as a mild oath (*hang the expense*). **8** *tr.* let droop (*hang one's head*). **9** *tr.* suspend (meat or game) from a hook and leave it until dry or tender or high. **10** *intr.* be hung (in various senses). **11** *intr.* remain static in the air. **12** *intr.* be present, esp. threateningly (*a hush hung over the room*). **13** *intr.* (foll. by *on*) **a** be dependent on (*everything hangs on the discussions*). **b** listen closely to (*hangs on their every word*). ● *n.* **1** the way a thing hangs or falls. **2** a downward droop or bend. □ **get the hang of** *colloq.* understand the technique or meaning of. **hang around** (or *Brit.* **about**) **1** loiter or dally; not move away. **2** (foll. by *with*) associate with (a person, etc.). **hang back 1** show reluctance to act or move. **2** remain behind. **hang fire** be slow in taking action or in progressing. **hang heavily** (or **heavy**) (of time) pass slowly. **hang in** *colloq.* **1** persist; persevere. **2** linger. **hang loose** *colloq.* relax; stay calm. **hang on** *colloq.* **1** continue or persevere. **2** (often foll. by *to*) retain one's grip. **3** (foll. by *to*) fail to give back. **4 a** wait for a short time. **b** (in telephoning) continue to listen during a pause in the conversation. **hang out 1** hang from a window, clothesline, etc. **2** protrude or cause to protrude downwards. **3** (foll. by *of*) lean out of (a window, etc.). **4** *sl.* be often present. **5** (foll. by *with*) *sl.* be friends with. **hang together 1** make sense. **2** remain associated. **hang up 1** hang from a hook, peg, etc. **2** end a telephone conversation, esp. abruptly (*then he hung up on me*). **3** (usu. in *passive*, foll. by *on*) *sl.* be a psychological or emotional problem to (*is really hung up on her teacher*). **not care** (or **give**) **a hang** *colloq.* not care at all.

hang·ar /hángər/ *n.* a building for housing aircraft, etc. □□ **hang·a·rage** *n.*

hang·dog /hángdawg, -dog/ *adj.* having a dejected or guilty appearance; shamefaced.

hang·er /hángər/ *n.* **1** a person or thing that hangs. **2** (in full **coat hanger**) a shaped piece of wood or plastic, etc., from which clothes may be hung.

hang·er-on *n.* (*pl.* **hangers-on**) a follower or dependent.

hang glid·er *n.* a frame with a fabric airfoil stretched over it, from which the operator is suspended and controls flight by body movement. □ **hang gliding** *n.*

hang·ing /hánging/ *n.* & *adj.* ● *n.* **1 a** the act of executing by hanging a person. **b** (*attrib.*) meriting or causing this (*a hanging offense*). **2** (usu. in *pl.*) draperies hung on a wall, etc. ● *adj.* that hangs or is hung.

hang·man /hángmən/ *n.* (*pl.* **-men**) **1** an executioner who hangs condemned persons. **2** a game for two players, in which the tally of failed guesses is kept by drawing a representation of a figure hanging from a gallows.

hang·nail /hángnayl/ *n.* a piece of torn skin at the root of a fingernail.

hang·out /hángowt/ *n. sl.* a place one lives in or frequently visits.

hang·o·ver /hángōvər/ *n.* **1** a severe headache or other aftereffects caused by drinking an excess of liquor. **2** a survival from the past.

hang-up *n. sl.* an emotional problem or inhibition.

hank /hangk/ *n.* a coil of wool.

hank·er /hángkər/ *v.intr.* (foll. by *to* + infin., *for,* or *after*) long for; crave. □□ **hank·er·er** *n.* **hank·er·ing** *n.*

han·ky /hángkee/ *n.* (also **han·kie**) (*pl.* **-ies**) *colloq.* a handkerchief.

han·ky-pan·ky /hángkeepángkee/ *n. sl.* **1** naughtiness, esp. sexual misbehavior. **2** dishonest dealing; trickery.

Han·sen's dis·ease /hánsənz/ *n.* leprosy.

han·som /hánsəm/ *n.* (in full **hansom cab**) *hist.* ▼ a two-wheeled horse-drawn cab.

HANSOM CAB:
19TH-CENTURY
BRITISH HANSOM CAB

han·ta·vi·rus /hántəvīrəs/ *n.* a virus of a kind carried by rodents and causing various diseases characterized by fever and hemorrhaging.

Ha·nuk·kah /kҳáánəkə, háa-/ *n.* (also **Chanukkah**) the Jewish festival of lights, commemorating the purification of the Temple in 165 BC.

hap /hap/ *n. archaic* chance; luck.

hap·haz·ard /háphazərd/ *adj.* & *adv.* ● *adj.* done, etc., by chance; random. ● *adv.* at random. □□ **hap·haz·ard·ly** *adv.* **hap·haz·ard·ness** *n.*

hap·less /háplis/ *adj.* unlucky. □□ **hap·less·ly** *adv.* **hap·less·ness** *n.*

hap·loid /háployd/ *adj.* & *n. Biol.* ● *adj.* (of an organism or cell) with a single set of chromosomes. ● *n.* a haploid organism or cell. ▷ MEIOSIS

hap·pen /hápən/ *v.intr.* **1** occur (by chance or otherwise). **2** (foll. by *to* + infin.) have the (good or bad) fortune to (*I happened to meet her*). **3** (foll. by *to*) be the (esp. unwelcome) fate or experience of (*what happened to you?*). **4** (foll. by *on*) encounter or discover by chance. □ **as it happens** in fact; in reality (*as it happens, it turned out well*).

hap·pen·ing /hápəning/ *n.* & *adj.* **1** an event or occurrence. **2** an improvised or spontaneous theatrical, etc., performance. ● *adj. sl.* exciting; fashionable.

hap·pen·stance /hápənstans/ *n.* a thing that happens by chance.

hap·py /hápee/ *adj.* (**happier**, **happiest**) **1** feeling or showing pleasure or contentment. **2 a** fortunate. **b** (of words, behavior, etc.) apt; pleasing. **3** *colloq.* slightly drunk. **4** (in *comb.*) *colloq.* inclined to use excessively (*trigger-happy*). □□ **hap·pi·ly** *adv.* **hap·pi·ness** *n.*

hap·py-go-luck·y *adj.* cheerfully casual.

hap·py hour *n.* a period of the day when drinks are sold at reduced prices.

hap·py me·di·um *n.* a compromise; the avoidance of extremes.

ha·ra-ki·ri /hárəkéeree, háaree-/ *n.* ritual suicide by disembowelment with a sword, formerly practiced by samurai when disgraced or sentenced to death.

H

H

ha·rangue /həráng/ *n. & v.* ● *n.* a lengthy and earnest speech. ● *v.tr.* lecture or make a harangue to. □□ **ha·rangu·er** *n.*

ha·rass /hərás, háras/ *v.tr.* **1** trouble and annoy continually or repeatedly. **2** make repeated attacks on (an enemy or opponent). □□ **ha·rass·er** *n.* **ha·rass·ing·ly** *adv.* **ha·rass·ment** *n.*

har·bin·ger /háarbinjər/ *n. & v.* ● *n.* **1** a person or thing that announces or signals the approach of another. **2** a forerunner. ● *v.tr.* announce the approach of.

har·bor /háarbər/ *n. & v.* ● *n.* **1** a place of shelter for ships. **2** a place of refuge or protection. ● *v.* **1** *tr.* give shelter to (a criminal or wanted person). **2** *tr.* keep in one's mind, esp. resentfully (*harbor a grudge*). **3** *intr.* come to anchor in a harbor.

hard /háard/ *adj., adv., & n.* ● *adj.* **1** (of a substance, material, etc.) firm and solid; unyielding to pressure; not easily cut. **2 a** difficult to understand or explain (*a hard problem*). **b** difficult to accomplish (*a hard decision*). **c** (foll. by *to* + infin.) not easy (*hard to believe*). **3** difficult to bear (*a hard life*). **4** unfeeling; severely critical. **5** (of a season or the weather) severe (*a hard winter*). **6** harsh or unpleasant to the senses (*a hard voice*). **7 a** strenuous; enthusiastic; intense (*a hard worker*). **b** severe; uncompromising (*a hard bargain*; *hard words*). **c** *Polit.* extreme; most radical (*the hard right*). **8 a** (of liquor) strongly alcoholic. **b** (of drugs) potent and addictive. **c** (of radiation) highly penetrating. **d** (of pornography) highly suggestive and explicit. **9** (of water) containing mineral salts that make lathering difficult. **10** established; not disputable (*hard facts*; *hard data*). **11** *Stock Exch.* (of currency, prices, etc.) not likely to fall in value. **12** (of a consonant) guttural (as *c* in *cat*, *g* in *go*). **13** (of a shape, boundary, etc.) clearly defined; unambiguous. ● *adv.* **1** strenuously; intensely (*try hard*). **2** with difficulty or effort (*hard-earned*). **3** so as to be hard or firm (*the jelly set hard*). ● *n.* *Brit.* a sloping roadway across a foreshore. □ **be hard on 1** be difficult for. **2** be severe in one's treatment of. **3** be unpleasant to (the senses). **be hard put** (usu. foll. by *to* + infin.) find it difficult. **hard at it** *colloq.* busily working or occupied. **hard by** near; close by. **a hard case 1** *colloq.* an intractable person. **2** a case of hardship. **hard hit** badly affected. **hard·ish** *adj.* **hard·ness** *n.*

hard and fast *adj.* (of a rule or a distinction made) definite; unalterable; strict.

hard·back /háardbak/ *adj. & n.* ● *adj.* (of a book) bound in stiff covers. ● *n.* a hardback book.

hard·ball /háardbawl/ *n.* **1** = BASEBALL. **2** *sl.* uncompromising methods or dealings, esp. in politics (*play hardball*).

hard·bit·ten /háardbítən/ *adj. colloq.* tough and cynical.

hard·board /háardbawrd/ *n.* stiff board made of compressed and treated wood pulp.

hard-boiled *adj.* **1** (of an egg) boiled until the white and the yolk are solid. **2** (of a person) tough; shrewd.

hard cash *n.* negotiable coins and paper money.

hard cop·y *n.* printed material produced by computer, usu. on paper, suitable for ordinary reading.

hard core *n.* **1** an irreducible nucleus. **2** *colloq.* **a** the most active or committed members of a society, etc. **b** a conservative or reactionary minority.

hard-core *adj.* blatant; uncompromising, esp.: **1** (of pornography) explicit; obscene. **2** (of drug addiction) relating to hard drugs, esp. heroin. **3** *Brit.* solid material, esp. rubble, used to form the foundation of a road, etc.

hard·cov·er /hárdkəvər/ *adj. & n.* ● *adj.* bound between rigid boards (*a hardcover edition*). ● *n.* a hardcover book.

hard disk (**drive**) *n. Computing* ▶ a large-capacity rigid usu. magnetic storage disk. ▷ COMPUTER

hard·en /háardən/ *v.* **1** *tr. & intr.* make or become hard. **2** *intr. & tr.* become, or make (one's attitude, etc.), less sympathetic. **3** *intr.* (of prices, etc.) cease to fall or fluctuate. □□ **hard·en·er** *n.*

hard·en·ing /háardəning/ *n.* **1** the process of becoming hard. **2** (in full **hardening of the arteries**) *Med.* = ARTERIOSCLEROSIS.

hard hat *n.* **1** a protective helmet worn on building sites, etc. **2** *colloq.* a reactionary person.

hard·head·ed /háardhédid/ *adj.* practical; realistic; not sentimental. □□ **hard·head·ed·ly** *adv.* **hard·head·ed·ness** *n.*

hard-heart·ed /háardháartid/ *adj.* unfeeling; unsympathetic. □□ **hard-heart·ed·ly** *adv.* **hard-heart·ed·ness** *n.*

hard-hit·ting *adj.* aggressively critical.

har·di·hood /háardeehŏŏd/ *n.* boldness; daring.

hard line *n.* unyielding adherence to a firm policy. □□ **hard-liner** *n.* a person who adheres rigidly to a policy.

hard luck *n.* worse fortune than one deserves.

hard·ly /háardlee/ *adv.* **1** scarcely (*we hardly knew them*). **2** only with difficulty (*could hardly speak*). **3** harshly.

hard-nosed *adj. colloq.* realistic; uncompromising.

hard nut *n. sl.* a tough, aggressive person. □ **a hard nut to crack** *colloq.* a difficult problem.

hard of hear·ing *adj.* somewhat deaf.

hard·pan /háardpan/ *n. Geol.* a hardened layer of clay occurring in or below the soil profile.

hard-pressed *adj.* **1** closely pursued. **2** burdened with urgent business.

hard sell *n.* aggressive salesmanship or advertising.

hard·ship /háardship/ *n.* **1** severe suffering. **2** the circumstance causing this.

hard stuff *n. sl.* strong liquor, esp. whiskey.

hard up *adj.* **1** short of money. **2** (foll. by *for*) at a loss for; lacking.

hard·ware /háardwair/ *n.* **1** tools and household articles of metal, etc. **2** heavy machinery or armaments. **3** the mechanical and electronic components of a computer, etc.

hard·wear·ing /háardwáiring/ *adj.* able to stand much wear.

hard-wired *adj.* involving or achieved by permanently connected circuits designed to perform a specific function.

hard·wood /háardwŏŏd/ *n.* the wood from a deciduous broad-leaved tree. ▷ WOOD

hard·work·ing /háardwərking/ *adj.* diligent.

har·dy /háardee/ *adj.* (**hardier, hardiest**) **1** capable of enduring difficult conditions. **2** (of a plant) able to grow in the open air all year round. □□ **har·di·ness** *n.*

hare /hair/ *n. & v.* ● *n.* **1** any of various mammals of the family Leporidae, like a large rabbit, with tawny fur, long ears, short tail and hind legs longer than forelegs. ▷ LAGOMORPH. **2** (in full **electric hare**) a dummy hare propelled by electricity, used in greyhound racing. ● *v.intr.* run with great speed.

hare·bell /háirbel/ *n.* **1** ▶ a plant, *Campanula rotundifolia*, with slender stems and pale blue bell-shaped flowers. **2** = BLUEBELL.

hare-brained /háirbraynd/ *adj.* rash; foolish; wild.

Hare Krish·na /haree kríshnə/ *n.* a member of the International Society for Krishna Consciousness, a religious sect based on the worship of the Hindu god Krishna.

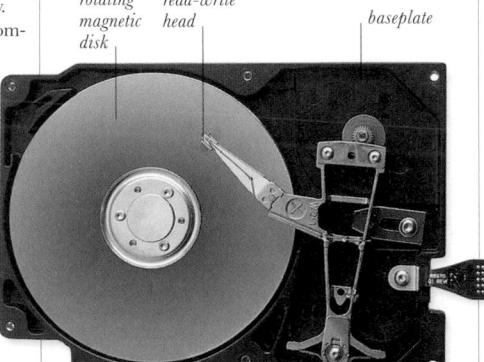

HAREBELL
(*Campanula rotundifolia*)

hare·lip /háirlip/ *n.* a congenital fissure of the upper lip. □□ **hare-lipped** *adj.*

har·em /háirəm, hár-/ *n.* **1** the women of a Muslim household, living in a separate part of the house. **2** their quarters.

har·i·cot /áarikō/ *n.* **1** (in full **haricot vert** /ver/) a variety of French bean with small white seeds. ▷ LEGUME. **2** the dried seed of this used as a vegetable.

hark /háark/ *v.intr.* (usu. in *imper.*) *archaic* listen attentively. □ **hark back** revert to a topic discussed earlier.

hark·en var. of HEARKEN.

har·le·quin /háarlikwin/ *n. & adj.* ● *n.* (**Harlequin**) a mute character in pantomime, usu. masked and dressed in a diamond-patterned costume. ● *adj.* in varied colors.

har·le·quin·ade /háarlikwináyd/ *n.* **1** the part of a pantomime featuring Harlequin. **2** a piece of buffoonery.

har·lot /háarlət/ *n. archaic* a prostitute. □□ **har·lot·ry** *n.*

harm /háarm/ *n. & v.* ● *n.* hurt; damage. ● *v.tr.* cause harm to. □ **out of harm's way** in safety.

harm·ful /háarmfŏŏl/ *adj.* causing or likely to cause harm. □□ **harm·ful·ly** *adv.* **harm·ful·ness** *n.*

harm·less /háarmlis/ *adj.* **1** unlikely to cause harm. **2** inoffensive. □□ **harm·less·ly** *adv.* **harm·less·ness** *n.*

har·mon·ic /haarmónik/ *adj. & n.* ● *adj.* **1** of or characterized by harmony. **2** *Mus.* **a** of or relating to harmony. **b** (of a tone) produced by vibration of a string, etc., in an exact fraction of its length. ● *n.* *Mus.* an overtone accompanying at a fixed interval (and forming a note with) a fundamental. □□ **har·mon·i·cal·ly** *adv.*

har·mon·i·ca /haarmónikə/ *n.* ◀ a small rectangular wind instrument held against the lips and moved from side to side to produce different notes by blowing or sucking.

har·mo·ni·ous /haarmốneeəs/ *adj.* **1** pleasant sounding; tuneful. **2** forming a pleasing or consistent whole. **3** free from any disagreement. □□ **har·mo·ni·ous·ly** *adv.* **har·mo·ni·ous·ness** *n.*

har·mo·ni·um /haarmốneeəm/ *n.* a keyboard instrument in which notes are produced by air driven through metal reeds by bellows operated by the feet.

har·mo·nize /háarmənīz/ *v.* **1** *tr.* add notes to (a melody) to produce harmony. **2** *tr. & intr.* (often foll. by *with*) bring into or be in harmony. **3** *intr.* make or form a pleasing or consistent whole. □□ **har·mo·ni·za·tion** *n.*

har·mo·ny /háarmənee/ *n.* (*pl.* **-ies**) **1 a** a combination of simultaneously sounded musical notes to produce chords and chord progressions, esp. as having a pleasing effect. **b** the study of this. **2 a** an apt or aesthetic arrangement of parts. **b** the pleasing effect of this. **3** agreement; concord. □ **in harmony 1** (of singing, etc.) producing chords; not discordant. **2** (often foll. by *with*) in agreement.

reed chamber

slide

HARMONICA

rotating magnetic disk   *read-write head*   *baseplate*

HARD DISK

HARNESS

A harness consists of three or more main elements. The bridle and reins are used by the driver to control the horse. The collar around its neck enables the horse to draw its load. Breeching straps allow it to brake or to reverse the load.

blinder · bridle · collar · saddle pad · rein · driver · beer cask · noseband · breeching strap · afterwale · pole · belly-band · loin strap · breeching strap · trace chain · trace chain

HEAVY HORSES HARNESSED TO A BREWER'S DRAY

har·ness /háarnis/ *n. & v.* ● *n.* **1** ▲ the equipment of straps and fittings by which a horse is fastened to a cart, etc., and controlled. **2** a similar arrangement for fastening a thing to a person's body, for restraining a young child, etc. ● *v.tr.* **1 a** put a harness on. **b** (foll. by *to*) attach by a harness. **2** make use of (natural resources) esp. to produce energy. □ **in harness** in the routine of daily work.

harp /haarp/ *n. & v.* ● *n.* ▼ a large upright musical instrument consisting of a frame housing a series of strings, played by plucking with the fingers. ▷ ORCHESTRA, STRINGED. ● *v.intr.* (foll by *on*) talk repeatedly and tediously about. □□ **harp·ist** *n*

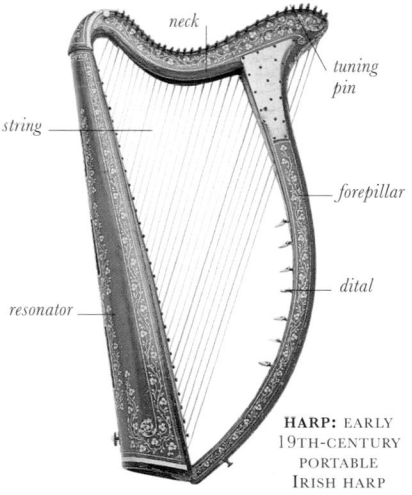

neck · tuning pin · string · forepillar · ditat · resonator

HARP: EARLY 19TH-CENTURY PORTABLE IRISH HARP

har·poon /haarpoốn/ *n. & v.* ● *n.* a barbed spearlike missile with a rope attached, for killing whales, etc. ● *v.tr.* spear with a harpoon. □□ **har·poon·er** *n*.

har·poon gun *n.* a gun for firing a harpoon.

harp seal *n.* a Greenland seal, *Phoca groenlandica*, with a harp-shaped dark mark on its back.

harp·si·chord /haárpsikawrd/ *n.* a keyboard instrument with horizontal strings which are plucked mechanically. □□ **harp·si·chord·ist** *n*.

har·py /haárpee/ *n.* (*pl.* **-ies**) **1** (in Greek and Roman mythology) a monster with a woman's head and body and bird's wings and claws. **2** a grasping unscrupulous person.

har·que·bus /haárkwibəs/ *n.* (also **arquebus** /aár-/) *hist.* an early type of portable gun supported on a tripod or on a forked rest.

har·ri·dan /hárid'n/ *n.* a bad-tempered woman.

har·ri·er[1] /háreeər/ *n.* a person who harries or lays waste.

har·ri·er[2] /háreeər/ *n.* **1** a hound used for hunting hares. **2** a cross-country runner or group of runners.

har·ri·er[3] /háreeər/ *n.* ▶ any bird of prey of the genus *Circus*, with long wings for swooping over the ground.

Har·ris tweed /háris/ *n.* a kind of tweed woven by hand in Harris in the Outer Hebrides of Scotland.

har·row /hárō/ *n. & v.* ● *n.* ▼ a heavy frame with iron teeth dragged over plowed land to break up clods, remove weeds, cover seed, etc. ● *v.tr.* **1** draw a harrow over (land). **2** (usu. as **harrowing** *adj.*) upset or distress greatly. □□ **har·row·er** *n.* **har·row·ing·ly** *adv.*

HARRIER: MARSH HARRIER (*Circus aeruginosus*)

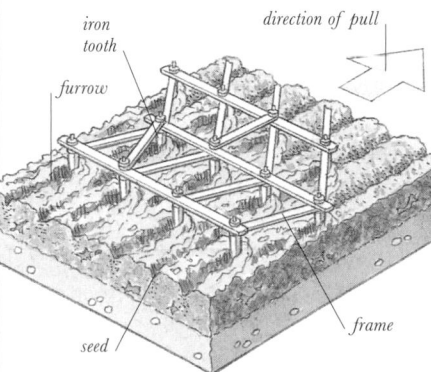

iron tooth · direction of pull · furrow · seed · frame

HARROW: ACTION OF A HARROW

har·ry /háree/ *v.tr.* (**-ies**, **-ied**) **1** ravage or despoil. **2** harass; worry.

harsh /haarsh/ *adj.* **1** unpleasantly rough or sharp. **2** severe; cruel. □□ **harsh·en** *v.tr. & intr.* **harsh·ly** *adv.* **harsh·ness** *n.*

hars·let var. of HASLET.

hart /haart/ *n.* esp. *Brit.* the male of the deer (esp. the red deer).

harte·beest /haártbeest, haárbeest/ *n.* any large African antelope of the genus *Alcelaphus*, with ringed horns bent back at the tips.

harts·horn /haárts-hawrn/ *n. archaic* **1** an ammonious substance obtained from the horns of a hart. **2** (in full **spirit of hartshorn**) an aqueous solution of ammonia.

har·um-scar·um /háirəmskáirəm/ *adj. & n. colloq.* ● *adj.* wild and reckless. ● *n.* such a person.

har·vest /haárvist/ *n. & v.* ● *n.* **1 a** the process of gathering in crops, etc. **b** the season when this takes place. **2** the season's yield. **3** the product of any action. ● *v.tr.* **1** gather as a harvest. **2** experience (consequences). □□ **har·vest·a·ble** *adj.*

har·vest·er /haárvistər/ *n.* **1** a reaper. **2** a reaping machine.

har·vest·man /haárvistmən/ *n.* (*pl.* **-men**) any of various arachnids of the family Opilionidae, with very long thin legs. ▷ ARACHNID.

har·vest mouse *n.* ▶ a small Eurasian rodent, *Micromys minutus*, that nests in the stalks of growing grain.

HARVEST MOUSE (*Micromys minutus*)

has 3rd sing. present of HAVE.

has-been /házbin/ *n. colloq.* a person who has lost a former importance.

hash[1] /hash/ *n. & v.* ● *n.* **1** a dish of cooked meat and potatoes cut into small pieces and recooked. **2 a** a mixture; a jumble. **b** a mess. **3** reused or recycled material. ● *v.tr.* (often foll. by *up*) **1** make (meat, etc.) into a hash. **2** recycle (old material). □ **make a hash of** *colloq.* make a mess of; bungle. **settle a person's hash** *colloq.* deal with and subdue a person.

hash[2] /hash/ *n. colloq.* hashish.

hash·ish /háshcesh, hashéésh/ *n.* a resinous product of the top leaves and tender parts of hemp, smoked or chewed for its narcotic effects.

Ha·sid /kháasid, kháw-, haá-/ *n.* (*pl.* **Hasidim** /-sidim, -séé-/) a member of any of several mystical Jewish sects, esp. one founded in the 18th c. □□ **Ha·sid·ic** /-sídik/ *adj.*

has·let /háslit, hávz-/ *n.* (also **harslet** /haár-/) pieces of offal cooked together and usu. compressed into a meat loaf.

hasn't /házənt/ *contr.* has not.

hasp /hasp/ *n. & v.* ● *n.* a hinged metal clasp that fits over a staple and can be secured by a padlock. ● *v.tr.* fasten with a hasp.

has·sle /hásəl/ *n. & v. colloq.* ● *n.* **1** a prolonged trouble or inconvenience. **2** an argument or involved struggle. ● *v.* **1** *tr.* harass; annoy. **2** *intr.* argue; quarrel.

has·sock /hásək/ *n.* a thick firm cushion for kneeling on, esp. in church.

haste /hayst/ *n. & v.* ● *n.* **1** urgency of movement or action. **2** excessive hurry. ● *v.intr. archaic* = HASTEN. □ **in haste** quickly; hurriedly. **make haste** hurry.

has·ten /háysən/ *v.* **1** *intr.* make haste; hurry. **2** *tr.* cause to occur sooner.

hast·y /háystee/ *adj.* (**hastier**, **hastiest**) **1** hurried; acting quickly. **2** said or done too quickly; rash. **3** quick-tempered. □□ **hast·i·ly** *adv.* **hast·i·ness** *n.*

H

H

hat /hat/ *n. & v.* ● *n.* **1** ▶ a covering for the head, often with a brim and worn out of doors. **2** *colloq.* a person's occupation or capacity, esp. one of several (*wearing his managerial hat*). ● *v.tr.* (**hatted, hatting**) cover or provide with a hat. □ **keep it under one's hat** *colloq.* keep it secret. **out of a hat** by random selection. **pass the hat** collect contributions of money. **take off one's hat to** (or **hats off to**) *colloq.* acknowledge admiration for. **throw one's hat in the ring** take up a challenge. □□ **hat·ful** *n.* (*pl.* **-fuls**). **hat·less** *adj.*

hat·band /hátband/ *n.* a band of ribbon around a hat above the brim. ▷ HAT

hat·box /hátboks/ *n.* a box to hold a hat, esp. for traveling.

hatch[1] /hach/ *n.* **1** an opening between two rooms, e.g., between a kitchen and a dining room for serving food. **2** an opening in an aircraft, spacecraft, etc. **3** *Naut.* **a** = HATCHWAY. **b** a trapdoor for this.

hatch[2] /hach/ *v. & n.* ● *v.* **1** *intr.* **a** (often foll. by *out*) (of a young bird or fish, etc.) emerge from the egg. **b** (of an egg) produce a young animal. **2** *tr.* incubate (an egg). **3** *tr.* (also foll. by *up*) devise (a plot, etc.). ● *n.* **1** the act or an instance of hatching. **2** a brood hatched.

hatch[3] /hach/ *v.tr.* mark (a surface) with close parallel lines. □□ **hatch·ing** *n.*

hatch·back /háchbak/ *c* a car with a sloping back hinged at the top to form a door. ▷ CAR

hatch·er·y /háchəree/ *n.* (*pl.* **-ies**) a place for hatching eggs, esp. of fish or poultry.

hatch·et /háchit/ *n.* a light short-handled ax.

hatch·et job *n. colloq.* a fierce destructive critique of a person, esp. in print.

hatch·et man *n. colloq.* **1** a hired killer. **2** a person employed to carry out a hatchet job.

hatch·ling /háchling/ *n.* a newly hatched young animal.

hatch·way /háchway/ *n.* an opening in a ship's deck for lowering cargo into the hold. ▷ SHIP

hate /hayt/ *v. & n.* ● *v.tr.* **1** dislike intensely. **2** *colloq.* **a** dislike. **b** (foll. by verbal noun or *to* + infin.) be reluctant (to do something). ● *n.* **1** hatred. **2** *colloq.* a hated person or thing. □□ **hate·a·ble** *adj.* (also **hat·a·ble**). **hat·er** *n.*

hate·ful /háytfŏŏl/ *adj.* arousing hatred. □□ **hate·ful·ly** *adv.* **hate·ful·ness** *n.*

hat·pin /hátpin/ *n.* a long pin, often decorative, for securing a hat to the head.

ha·tred /háytrid/ *n.* intense dislike or ill will.

hat·stand /hátstand/ *n.* a stand with hooks on which to hang hats.

hat·ter /hátər/ *n.* a maker or seller of hats.

hat trick *n. Sports* the scoring of three goals, etc., in a single game, match, etc.

haugh·ty /háwtee/ *adj.* (**haughtier, haughtiest**) arrogantly self-admiring. □□ **haugh·ti·ly** *adv.* **haugh·ti·ness** *n.*

haul /hawl/ *v. & n.* ● *v.* **1** *tr.* pull forcibly. **2** *tr.* transport by truck, cart, etc. **3** *intr.* turn a ship's course. **4** *tr. colloq.* (usu. foll. by *up*) bring for reprimand. ● *n.* **1** the act of hauling. **2** an amount acquired. **3** a distance to be traversed (*a short haul*). □ **haul over the coals** see COAL.

haul·age /háwlij/ *n.* **1** the commercial transport of goods. **2** a charge for this.

haul·er /háwlər/ *n.* **1** a person or thing that hauls. **2** a miner who takes coal from the workface to the bottom of the shaft. **3** a person or business engaged in the transport of goods.

haulm /hawm/ *n.* (also **halm**) **1** a stalk or stem. **2** the stalks or stems collectively of peas, beans, potatoes, etc., without the pods, etc.

haunch /hawnch/ *n.* **1** the fleshy part of the buttock with the thigh, esp. in animals. **2** the leg and loin of a deer, etc., as food.

haunt /hawnt/ *v. & n.* ● *v.tr.* **1** (of a ghost) visit (a place) regularly. **2** frequent (a place). **3** (of a memory, etc.) be persistently in the mind of. ● *n.*

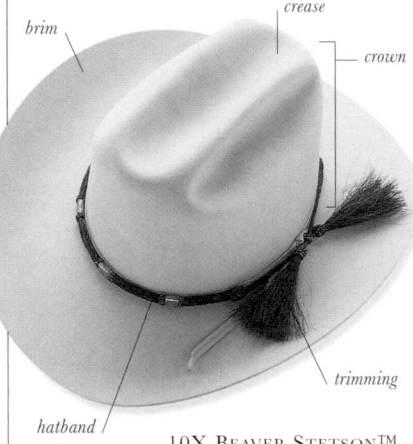

HAT

Hats were originally worn to provide protection from extremes of the weather or to signify the social status of the wearer. In addition to these functions, hats are viewed as fashion accessories.

brim

crease

crown

trimming

hatband

10X BEAVER STETSON™

EXAMPLES OF OTHER HATS

STRAW BOATER

BERET

TOP HAT

PANAMA

BASEBALL CAP

DERBY

1 (often in *pl.*) a place frequented by a person. **2** a place frequented by animals, esp. for food and drink. □□ **haunt·er** *n.*

haunt·ing /háwnting/ *adj.* (of a melody, etc.) wistful; evocative. □□ **haunt·ing·ly** *adv.*

Hau·sa /hówzə/ *n. & adj.* ● *n.* (*pl.* same or **Hausas**) **1 a** a people of W. Africa and the Sudan. **b** a member of this people. **2** the Hamitic language of this people, widely used in W. Africa. ● *adj.* of or relating to this people or language.

haute cou·ture /ót kŏŏtŏŏr/ *n.* high fashion; the leading fashion houses.

haute cui·sine /ót kwizeén/ *n.* cooking of a high standard.

hau·teur /hōtár/ *n.* haughtiness of manner.

have /hav/ *v. & n.* ● *v.* (*3rd sing. present* **has** /haz/; *past* and *past part.* **had** /had/) ● *v.tr.* **1** hold in possession as one's property or at one's disposal (*has a car*). **2** hold in a certain relationship (*has a sister*). **3** contain as a part or quality (*house has two floors*). **4 a** undergo; experience; (*has a headache*). **b** be subjected to a specified state (*had my car stolen*). **c** cause or invite (a person or thing) to be in a particular state or take a particular action (*had him dismissed*; *had my hair cut*). **5 a** engage in (an activity) (*had an argument*). **b** hold (a meeting, party, etc.). **6** eat or drink (*had a beer*). **7** (usu. in *neg.*) accept or tolerate (*I won't have it*). **8 a** let (a feeling, etc.) be present (*have nothing against them*). **b** show or feel (mercy, pity, etc.) toward another person (*have pity on him*). **c** (foll. by *to* + infin.) show by action that one is influenced by (a feeling etc.) (*have the goodness to leave now*). **9 a** give birth to (offspring). **b** conceive mentally (an idea, etc.). **10** receive; obtain (*had a letter from him*). **11** be burdened with or committed to (*has a job to do*). **12 a** have obtained (a qualification) (*has several degrees*). **b** know (a language) (*has no Latin*). **13** *sl.* **a** get the better of (*I had him there*). **b** (usu. in *passive*) cheat (*you were had*). **14** *coarse sl.* have sexual intercourse with. ● *v.aux.* (with *past part.* or *ellipt.*, to form the perfect, pluperfect, and future perfect tenses, and the conditional mood) (*have worked*; *had seen*; *will have been*). ● *n.* **1** (usu. in *pl.*) *colloq.* a person who has wealth or resources. **2** *Brit. sl.* a swindle. □ **had best**

see BEST. **had better** would find it prudent to. **had rather** see RATHER. **have a care** see CARE. **have done, have done with** see DONE. **have an eye for, have eyes for, have an eye to** see EYE. **have a good mind to** see MIND. **have got to** *colloq.* = *have to.* **have had it** *colloq.* **1** have missed one's chance. **2** (of a person) have passed one's prime; (of a thing) be worn out or broken. **3** have been killed, defeated, etc. **4** have suffered or endured enough. **have it 1** (foll. by *that* + clause) express the view that. **2** win a decision in a vote, etc. **3** have found the answer, etc. **have it in for** *colloq.* be hostile toward. **have it out** (often foll. by *with*) *colloq.* attempt to settle a dispute by discussion. **have it one's own way** see WAY. **have on 1** be wearing (clothes). **2** be committed to (an engagement). **have out** get (a tooth, etc.) extracted (*had her tonsils out*). **have to** be obliged to; must.

ha·ven /háyvən/ *n.* **1** a harbor. **2** a place of refuge.

have-not *n.* (usu. in *pl.*) *colloq.* a person lacking wealth or resources.

have·n't /hávənt/ *contr.* have not.

hav·er·sack /hávərsak/ *n.* a stout bag carried on the back or over the shoulder.

hav·oc /hávək/ *n.* great confusion or disorder. □ **play havoc with** *colloq.* cause great confusion or difficulty to.

haw /haw/ *n.* the hawthorn or its fruit.

Ha·wai·ian /həwiən/ *n. & adj.* ● *n.* **1 a** a native of Hawaii, an island or island group (comprising a US state) in the N. Pacific. **b** a person of Hawaiian descent. **2** the language of Hawaii. ● *adj.* of or relating to Hawaii, its people or language.

haw·finch /háwfinch/ *n.* any large stout finch of the genus *Coccothraustes*, with a thick beak for cracking seeds.

hawk[1] /hawk/ *n. & v.* ● *n.* **1** ◀ any of various diurnal birds of prey of the family Accipitridae, having a characteristic curved beak and a long tail. ▷ RAPTOR. **2** *Polit.* a person who advocates a warlike policy, esp. in foreign affairs. ● *v.intr.*

HAWK: HARRIS'S HAWK (*Parabuteo unicinctus*)

hunt game with a hawk. □□ **hawk·ish** *adj.* **hawk·ish·ness** *n.* **hawk·like** *adj.*

hawk² /hawk/ *v.* **1** *intr.* clear the throat noisily. **2** *tr.* (foll. by *up*) bring (phlegm, etc.) up from the throat.

hawk·er /háwkər/ *n.* a person who travels about selling goods.

hawk-eyed *adj.* keen-sighted.

hawk moth *n.* ▼ any moth of the family Sphingidae, having narrow forewings and a stout body. ▷ MOTH

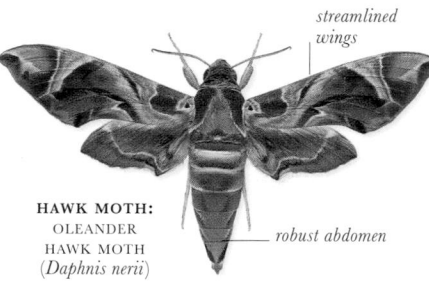

streamlined wings

HAWK MOTH:
OLEANDER
HAWK MOTH
(*Daphnis nerii*)

robust abdomen

hawks·bill /háwksbil/ *n.* (in full **hawksbill turtle**) a small turtle, *Eretmochelys imbricata*, yielding tortoiseshell.

hawk·weed /háwkweed/ *n.* ► any composite plant of the genus *Hieracium*, with yellow flowers.

haw·ser /háwzər/ *n. Naut.* a thick rope or cable for mooring a ship. ▷ ROPE

haw·thorn /háwthawrn/ *n.* any thorny shrub or tree of the genus *Crataegus*, esp. *C. monogyna*, with small dark red fruit.

hay /hay/ *n.* grass mown and dried for fodder. □ **make hay (while the sun shines)** seize opportunities for profit or enjoyment.

hay fe·ver *n.* a common allergy with respiratory symptoms, caused by pollen or dust.

HAWKWEED:
COMMON
HAWKWEED
(*Hieracium vulgatum*)

hay·mak·er /háymaykər/ *n.* **1** a person who tosses and spreads hay to dry after mowing. **2** an apparatus for shaking and drying hay. **3** *sl.* a forceful punch. □□ **hay·mak·ing** *n.*

hay·rick /háyrik/ *n.* = HAYSTACK.

hay·seed /háyseed/ *n.* **1** grass seed obtained from hay. **2** *colloq.* a yokel.

hay·stack /háystak/ *n.* a packed pile of hay with a pointed or ridged top.

hay·wire /háywīr/ *adj. colloq.* **1** out of control. **2** (of a person) erratic.

haz·ard /házərd/ *n. & v.* ● *n.* **1** a danger or risk. **2** a source of this. **3** chance. **4** *Golf* an obstruction in playing a shot, e.g., a bunker, water, etc. ● *v.tr.* **1** venture on (*hazard a guess*). **2** run the risk of. **3** expose to hazard.

haz·ard·ous /házərdəs/ *adj.* risky; dangerous. □□ **haz·ard·ous·ly** *adv.*

haze /hayz/ *n.* **1** obscuration of the atmosphere near the Earth by fine particles of water, smoke, or dust. **2** mental obscurity or confusion.

ha·zel /háyzəl/ *n.* **1** any shrub or small tree of the genus *Corylus*, esp. *C. avellana* bearing round brown edible nuts. **2** wood from the hazel. **3** a greenish brown color (esp. of the eyes).

ha·zel·nut /háyzəlnut/ *n.* the fruit of the hazel. ▷ NUT

ha·zy /háyzee/ *adj.* (**hazier, haziest**) **1** misty. **2** vague; indistinct. **3** confused; uncertain. □□ **ha·zi·ly** *adv.* **ha·zi·ness** *n.*

Hb *symb.* hemoglobin.

H-bomb /áychbom/ *n.* = HYDROGEN BOMB.

HC *abbr.* **1** Holy Communion. **2** (in the UK) House of Commons.

HCF *abbr.* highest common factor.

HDTV *abbr.* high-definition television.

HE *abbr.* **1** high explosive. **2** His Eminence. **3** His or Her Excellency.

He *symb. Chem.* the element helium.

he /hee/ *pron. & n.* ● *pron.* (*obj.* **him** /him/; *poss.* **his** /hiz/; *pl.* **they** /thay/) **1** the man or boy or male animal previously named or in question. **2** a person, etc., of unspecified sex (*if anyone comes he will have to wait*). ● *n.* **1** a male; a man. **2** (in *comb.*) male (*he-goat*).

head /hed/ *n., adj., & v.* ● *n.* **1** ▼ the upper part of the human body, or the foremost or upper part of an animal's body, containing the brain, mouth, and sense organs. **2 a** the head regarded as the seat of intellect. **b** intelligence (*use your head*). **c** mental aptitude (usu. foll. by *for: a good head for business*). **3** *colloq.* a headache. **4** a thing like a head in form or position, esp.: **a** the operative part of a tool. **b** the flattened top of a nail. **c** the ornamented top of a pillar. **d** a mass of flowers at the top of a stem. **e** the flat end of a drum. **f** the foam on top of a glass of beer. **g** the upper horizontal part of a window frame, etc. **5** life when regarded as vulnerable (*it cost him his head*). **6 a** a person in charge. **b** a position of leadership. **7** the forward part of something. **8** the upper end of something, e.g., a bed. **9** the top or highest part of something, e.g., a page. **10** a person regarded as a numerical unit (*$10 per head*). **11** (*pl.* same) **a** an individual animal as a unit. **b** (as *pl.*) a number of cattle (*20 head*). **12 a** the side of a coin bearing the image of a head. **b** (usu. in *pl.*) this side as a choice when tossing a coin. **13 a** the source of a river or stream. **b** the end of a lake at which a river enters it. **14** the height or length of a head as a measure. **15** the component of a machine that is in contact with or very close to what is being worked on, esp.: **a** the component on a tape recorder that touches the moving tape in play and converts the signals. **b** the part of a phonograph that holds the playing cartridge and stylus. **c** = PRINTHEAD. **16 a** a confined body of water, or steam in an engine, etc. **b** the pressure exerted by this. **17** a promontory (esp. in place-names) (*Nags Head*). **18** *Naut.* **a** the bow of a ship. **b** a ship's latrine. **19** a main topic for consideration. **20** *Journalism* = HEADLINE *n.* **21** a culmination or crisis. **22** the fully developed top of a boil, etc. **23** *sl.* a habitual taker of drugs. ● *attrib.adj.* chief or principal (*head gardener; head office*). ● *v.* **1** *tr.* be at the head or front of. **2** *tr.* be in charge of (*headed a small team*). **3** *tr.* **a** provide with a head or heading. **b** (of an inscription, etc.) serve as a heading for. **4 a** *intr.* face or move in a specified direction (often foll. by *for: heading for trouble*). **b** *tr.* direct in a specified direction. **5** *tr. Soccer* strike (the ball) with the head. **6 a** *tr.* (often foll. by *down*) cut the head off (a plant, etc.). **b** *intr.* (of a plant, etc.) form a head. □ **above one's head** beyond one's ability to understand. **come to a head** reach a crisis. **enter** (or **come into**) **one's head** *colloq.* occur to one. **from head to toe** (or **foot**) all over a person's body. **give a person his** or **her head** allow a person to act freely. **go out of one's head** go mad. **go to one's head** **1** (of liquor) make one slightly drunk. **2** (of success) make one conceited. **head and shoulders** *colloq.* by a considerable amount. **head in the sand** refusal to acknowledge an obvious danger or difficulty. **head off** **1** get ahead of so as to intercept and turn aside. **2** forestall. **head over heels 1** turning over completely in forward motion as in a somersault, etc. **2** topsy-turvy. **3** utterly; completely (*head over heels in love*). **hold up one's head** be confident or unashamed. **in one's head 1** in one's imagination. **2** by mental process. **keep one's head** remain calm. **keep one's head down** *colloq.* remain inconspicuous in dangerous times. **lose one's head** lose self-control. **make head or tail of** (usu. with *neg.* or *interrog.*) understand at all. **off one's head** *sl.* crazy. **off the top of one's head** *colloq.* impromptu. **on one's** (or **one's own**) **head** as one's sole responsibility. **out of one's head** *sl.* crazy. **over one's head 1** beyond one's ability to understand. **2** without one's knowledge or involvement. **3** with disregard for one's own (stronger) claim (*was promoted over their heads*). **put heads together** consult together. **put into a person's head** suggest to a person. **take** (or **get**) **it into one's head** (foll. by *that* + clause or *to* + infin.) form a definite idea or plan. **turn a person's head** make a person conceited. **with one's head in the clouds** see CLOUD. □□ **head·ed** *adj.* (also in *comb.*). **head·less** *adj.*

head·ache /hédayk/ *n.* **1** a continuous pain in the head. **2** *colloq.* **a** a worrying problem. **b** a troublesome person. □□ **head·ach·y** *adj.*

head·band /hédband/ *n.* a band worn around the head as decoration or to keep the hair off the face.

head·board /hédbawrd/ *n.* an upright panel forming the head of a bed.

H

HEAD

The head is the site of some of the human body's major sensory organs – the eyes, ears, nose, and tongue. Speech and facial gestures are the primary means of communication. Much of the internal volume of the head is taken up by the brain.

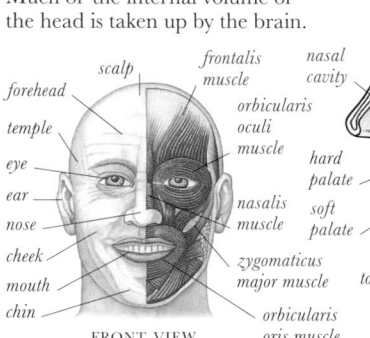

scalp
frontalis muscle
nasal cavity
forehead
temple
eye
ear
nose
cheek
mouth
chin
orbicularis oculi muscle
nasalis muscle
zygomaticus major muscle
orbicularis oris muscle

FRONT VIEW
OF THE HUMAN HEAD

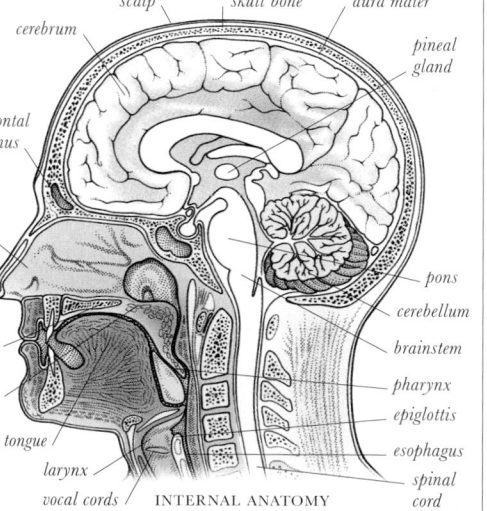

scalp
skull bone
dura mater
cerebrum
pineal gland
frontal sinus
hard palate
soft palate
tongue
larynx
vocal cords
pons
cerebellum
brainstem
pharynx
epiglottis
esophagus
spinal cord

INTERNAL ANATOMY
OF THE HUMAN HEAD

H

head·count /hédkownt/ *n.* **1** a counting of individual people. **2** a total number of people, esp. the number of people employed in a particular organization.

head·dress /héd-dres/ *n.* ▶ an ornamental covering or band for the head.

head·er /hédər/ *n.* **1** *Soccer* a shot made with the head. **2** *colloq.* a headlong fall. **3** a stone laid at right angles to the face of a wall. ▷ BRICK. **4** (in full **header tank**) a tank of water, etc., maintaining pressure in a plumbing system. **5** line or lines of information printed at the top of the page throughout a document.

head·gear /hédgeer/ *n.* a hat, headdress, or head covering.

head·hunt·ing /héd-hunting/ *n.* **1** the practice among some peoples of collecting the heads of dead enemies as trophies. **2** the practice of filling a (usu. senior) business position by approaching a suitable person employed elsewhere. □□ **head·hunt** *v.tr.* (also *absol.*). **head·hunt·er** *n.*

head·ing /héding/ *n.* **1 a** a title at the head of a page. **b** a division of a subject of discourse, etc. **2** a horizontal passage made in preparation for building a tunnel.

head·lamp /hédlamp/ *n.* = HEADLIGHT.

head·land /hédlənd/ *n.* a promontory. ▷ COASTLINE

head·light /hédlīt/ *n.* **1** a strong light at the front of a motor vehicle or train engine. **2** the beam from this.

head·line /hédlīn/ *n. & v.* ● *n.* **1** a heading at the top of an article or page, esp. in a newspaper. **2** (in *pl.*) the most important items of news in a newspaper or broadcast news bulletin. ● *v.tr.* give a headline to. □ **hit** (or **make**) **the headlines** *colloq.* be given prominent attention as news.

head·lin·er /hédlīnər/ *n.* a star performer.

head·lock /hédlok/ *n.* *Wrestling* a hold with an arm around the opponent's head.

head·long /hédlawng, -lóng/ *adv. & adj.* **1** with head foremost. **2** in a rush.

head·man /hédmən/ *n.* (*pl.* **-men**) the chief man of a tribe, etc.

head·mas·ter /hédmástər/ *n.* (*fem.* **headmistress** /-místris/) (esp. in the UK or in private schools in the US) the person in charge of a school.

head-on *adj.* **1** with the front foremost (*a head-on crash*). **2** in direct confrontation.

head·phone /hédfōn/ *n.* (usu. in *pl.*) a pair of earphones joined by a band placed over the head, for listening to audio equipment, etc.

head·quar·ters /hédkwáwrtərz/ *n.* (as *sing.* or *pl.*) the administrative center of an organization.

head·rest /hédrest/ *n.* a support for the head, esp. on a seat or chair.

head·room /hédrōōm, -rōōm/ *n.* **1** the space or clearance between the top of a vehicle and the underside of a bridge, etc. **2** the space above a driver's or passenger's head in a vehicle.

head·scarf /hédskaarf/ *n.* a scarf worn around the head and tied under the chin, instead of a hat.

head·set /hédset/ *n.* a set of headphones, often with a microphone attached.

head·ship /hédship/ *n.* the position of chief or leader.

head shrink·er *n. sl.* a psychiatrist.

head·square /hédskwair/ *n.* a rectangular scarf for wearing on the head.

head·stall /hédstawl/ *n.* the part of a halter that fits around a horse's head.

HEADDRESS:
NATIVE AMERICAN
WAR BONNET

head start *n.* an advantage granted or gained at an early stage.

head·stone /hédstōn/ *n.* a (usu. inscribed) stone set up at the head of a grave.

head·strong /hédstrawng, -strong/ *adj.* self-willed and obstinate.

head·wa·ter /hédwawtər, -woter/ *n.* (in *sing.* or *pl.*) streams flowing at the sources of a river.

head·way /hédway/ *n.* **1** progress. **2** the rate of progress of a ship. **3** = HEADROOM 1.

head wind *n.* a wind blowing from directly in front.

head·word /hédwərd/ *n.* a word forming a heading.

head·work /hédwərk/ *n.* mental work or effort.

head·y /hédee/ *adj.* (**headier, headiest**) **1** (of alcohol) potent; intoxicating. **2** (of success, etc.) likely to cause conceit. **3** (of a person, thing, or action) impetuous; violent. □□ **head·i·ly** *adv.* **head·i·ness** *n.*

heal /heel/ *v.* **1** *intr.* (often foll. by *up*) (of a wound or injury) become sound or healthy again. **2** *tr.* cause (a wound, disease, or person) to heal or be healed. **3** *tr.* put right (differences, etc.). **4** *tr.* alleviate (sorrow, etc.). □□ **heal·a·ble** *adj.* **heal·er** *n.*

heal-all *n.* **1** a universal remedy; a panacea. **2** a popular name of various medicinal plants.

health /helth/ *n.* **1** the state of being well in body or mind. **2** a person's mental or physical condition. **3** soundness (*the health of the nation*).

health food *n.* food thought to have health-giving qualities.

health·ful /hélthfōōl/ *adj.* conducive to good health; beneficial.

health main·te·nance or·ga·ni·za·tion *n.* an organization that provides medical care to subscribers who have paid in advance, usu. through a health insurance plan.

health spa *n.* a resort, club, gym, etc., providing facilities for exercise and conditioning.

health·y /hélthee/ *adj.* (**healthier, healthiest**) **1** having or promoting good health. **2** beneficial; helpful. □□ **health·i·ly** *adv.* **health·i·ness** *n.*

heap /heep/ *n. & v.* ● *n.* **1** a collection of things lying haphazardly one on another. **2** (esp. *Brit.* in *pl.*) *colloq.* a large number or amount (*heaps of time*). **3** *sl.* an old or dilapidated thing, esp. a motor vehicle. ● *v.* **1** *tr.* (foll. by *up, together*, etc.) collect or be collected in a heap. **2** *tr.* (foll. by *with*) load copiously. **3** *tr.* (foll. by *on, upon*) accord or offer copiously. **4** *tr.* (as **heaped** *adj.*) (of a spoonful, etc.) with the contents piled above the brim.

hear /heer/ *v.* (*past* and *past part.* **heard** /herd/) **1** *tr.* (also *absol.*) perceive (sound, etc.) with the ear. **2** *tr.* listen to (*heard them on the radio*). **3** *tr.* listen judicially to and judge. **4** *intr.* (foll. by *about, of,* or *that* + clause) be told or informed. **5** *intr.* (foll. by *from*) be contacted by. **6** *tr.* be ready to obey (an order). **7** *tr.* grant (a prayer). □ **have heard of** be aware of. **hear! hear!** *int.* expressing agreement (esp. with something said in a speech). **hear a person out** listen to all that a person says. **hear say** (or **tell**) (usu. foll. by *of,* or *that* + clause) be informed. **will not hear of** will not allow or agree to. □□ **hear·er** *n.*

hear·ing /héering/ *n.* **1** the faculty of perceiving sounds. **2** earshot (*within hearing*). **3** an opportunity to state one's case. **4** the listening to evidence in a court of law.

hear·ing aid *n.* ▶ a small device to amplify sound, worn by a partially deaf person.

hark·en /háarkən/ *v.intr.* (also **hark·en**) *archaic* or *literary* (foll. by *to*) listen.

hear·say /héersay/ *n.* rumor; gossip.

hearse /hərs/ *n.* a vehicle for conveying the coffin at a funeral.

heart /haart/ *n.* **1** ▼ a hollow muscular organ maintaining the circulation of blood by rhythmic contraction and dilation. ▷ CARDIOVASCULAR. **2** the breast. **3 a** the heart regarded as the center of

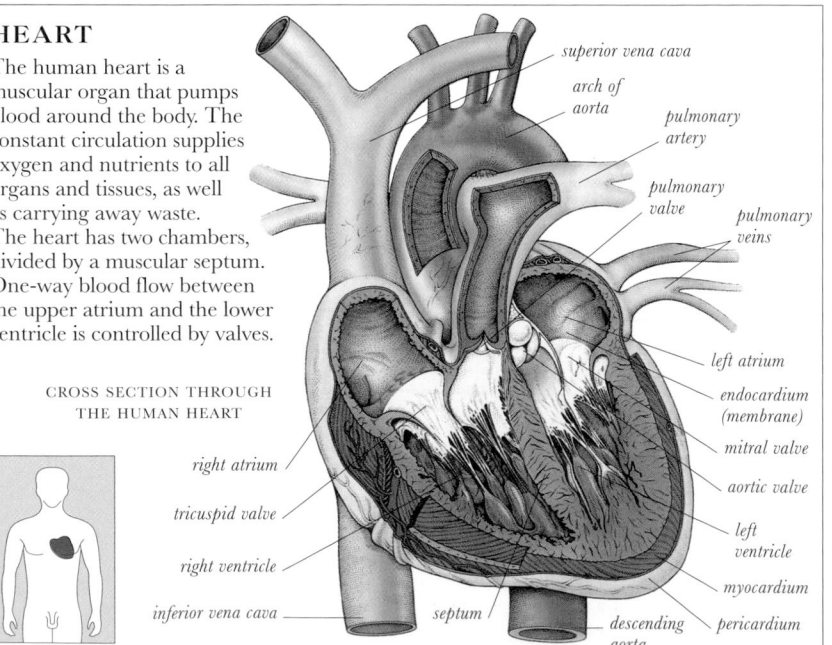

HEARING AID

plastic ear fitting

amplifier unit

volume control dial

battery casing

sound output tube

HEART

The human heart is a muscular organ that pumps blood around the body. The constant circulation supplies oxygen and nutrients to all organs and tissues, as well as carrying away waste. The heart has two chambers, divided by a muscular septum. One-way blood flow between the upper atrium and the lower ventricle is controlled by valves.

CROSS SECTION THROUGH
THE HUMAN HEART

superior vena cava
arch of aorta
pulmonary artery
pulmonary valve
pulmonary veins
left atrium
endocardium (membrane)
mitral valve
aortic valve
left ventricle
myocardium
pericardium
descending aorta
septum
inferior vena cava
right ventricle
tricuspid valve
right atrium

thought and emotion. **b** a person's capacity for feeling emotion (*has no heart*). **4 a** courage (*take heart*). **b** one's mood (*change of heart*). **5 a** the central or innermost part of something. **b** the vital part (*the heart of the matter*). **6** the close compact head of cabbage, etc. **7 a** a heart-shaped thing. **b** a conventional representation of a heart. **8 a** a playing card of a suit denoted by a red figure of a heart. **b** (in *pl.*) this suit. □ **after one's own heart** such as one likes or desires. **at heart 1** in one's inmost feelings. **2** basically; essentially. **break a person's heart** overwhelm a person with sorrow. **by heart** in or from memory. **close to** (or **near**) **one's heart 1** dear to one. **2** affecting one deeply. **from the heart** (or **the bottom of one's heart**) sincerely; profoundly. **give** (or **lose**) **one's heart** (often foll. by *to*) fall in love (with). **have the heart** (usu. with *neg.*; foll. by *to* + infin.) be insensitive or hardhearted enough. **heart to heart** candidly; intimately. **in one's heart of hearts** in one's inmost feelings. **take to heart** be much affected or distressed by. **to one's heart's content** see CONTENT[1]. **with all one's heart** sincerely; with all goodwill. □□ **-heart·ed** *adj.*

heart·ache /háartayk/ *n.* mental anguish or grief.

heart at·tack *n.* a sudden occurrence of coronary thrombosis usu. resulting in the death of part of a heart muscle.

heart·beat /háartbeet/ *n.* a pulsation of the heart.

heart·break /háartbrayk/ *n.* overwhelming distress. □□ **heart·break·er** *n.* **heart·break·ing** *adj.* **heart·bro·ken** *adj.*

heart·burn /háartbərn/ *n.* a burning sensation in the chest resulting from indigestion.

heart·en /háart'n/ *v.tr. & intr.* make or become cheerful. □□ **heart·en·ing·ly** *adv.*

heart·felt /háartfélt/ *adj.* sincere, deeply felt.

hearth /haarth/ *n.* **1 a** the floor of a fireplace. **b** the area in front of a fireplace. **2** this symbolizing the home. **3** the bottom of a blast furnace where molten metal collects.

hearth·rug /háarthrug/ *n.* a rug laid before a fireplace.

heart·i·ly /háartilee/ *adv.* **1** in a hearty manner; with goodwill or courage. **2** to a great degree (*am heartily sick of it*).

heart·land /háartland/ *n.* the central or most important part of an area.

heart·less /háartlis/ *adj.* unfeeling; pitiless. □□ **heart·less·ly** *adv.* **heart·less·ness** *n.*

heart of gold *n.* a generous nature.

heart-rend·ing *adj.* very distressing. □□ **heart-rend·ing·ly** *adv.*

hearts·ease /háartseez/ *n.* (also **heart's-ease**) ▶ any plant of the genus *Viola*, esp. a pansy.

heart·sick /háartsik/ *adj.* very despondent. □□ **heart·sick·ness** *n.*

heart·strings /háartstringz/ *n.pl.* one's deepest feelings or emotions.

heart·throb /háart-throb/ *n.* **1** beating of the heart. **2** *colloq.* a person for whom one has (esp. immature) romantic feelings.

heart-to-heart *adj. & n.* ● *adj.* (of a conversation, etc.) candid; intimate. ● *n.* a candid or personal conversation.

heart·warm·ing /háartwawrming/ *adj.* emotionally rewarding or uplifting.

heart·wood /háartwŏŏd/ *n.* the dense inner part of a tree trunk, yielding the hardest timber. ▷ WOOD

heart·y /háartee/ *adj.* (**heartier, heartiest**) **1** strong; vigorous. **2** spirited. **3** (of a meal or appetite) large. **4** warm; friendly. □□ **heart·i·ness** *n.*

heat /heet/ *n. & v.* ● *n.* **1 a** the condition of being hot. **b** the sensation or perception of this. **c** high temperature of the body. **2** *Physics* **a** a form of energy arising from the random motion of the molecules of bodies, which may be transferred by conduction, convection, or radiation. **b** the amount of this needed to cause a specific process, or evolved in a process (*heat of formation; heat of solution*). **3** hot weather. **4 a** warmth of feeling. **b** anger or excitement. **5** (foll. by *of*) the most intense period of an activity (*in the heat of the battle*). **6** a (usu. preliminary or trial) round in a race or contest. **7** the receptive period of the sexual cycle, esp. in female mammals. **8** pungency of flavor. ● *v.* **1** *tr. & intr.* make or become hot or warm. **2** *tr.* inflame; excite or intensify. □ **in the heat of the moment** during or resulting from intense activity, without pause for thought. **turn the heat on** *colloq.* concentrate an attack on (a person).

heat·ed /héetid/ *adj.* **1** angry; inflamed with passion or excitement. **2** made hot. □□ **heat·ed·ly** *adv.*

heat·er /héetər/ *n.* **1** a device for supplying heat to its environment. **2** a container with an element, etc., for heating the contents (*water heater*). **3** *sl.* a gun.

heat ex·haus·tion *n.* (also **heat prostration**) a condition caused by prolonged exposure to exercise in heat and characterized by faintness, nausea, and profuse sweating.

heath /heeth/ *n.* **1** an area of flattish uncultivated land with low shrubs. **2** a plant growing on a heath, esp. of the genus *Erica* or *Calluna*. □□ **heath·y** *adj.*

heath·en /héethən/ *n. & adj.* ● *n.* **1** a person who does not belong to a widely-held religion as regarded by those that do. **2** an unenlightened person; a person regarded as lacking culture or moral principles. **3** *Bibl.* a Gentile. ● *adj.* **1** of or relating to heathens. **2** having no religion. □□ **heath·en·dom** *n.* **heath·en·ism** *n.*

heath·er /héthər/ *n.* **1** an evergreen shrub, *Calluna vulgaris*, with purple bell-shaped flowers. **2** any of various shrubs growing esp. on moors and heaths. □□ **heath·er·y** *adj.*

heat·ing /héeting/ *n.* **1** the imparting or generation of heat. **2** equipment or devices used to provide heat, esp. to a building.

heat light·ning *n.* lightning seen as vivid flashes near the horizon, usu. without the sound of thunder.

heat-seek·ing *adj.* (of a missile, etc.) able to detect infrared radiation to guide it to its target.

heat·stroke /héetstrōk/ *n.* a feverish condition caused by excessive exposure to high temperature.

heat·wave /héetwayv/ *n.* a prolonged period of abnormally hot weather.

heave /heev/ *v. & n.* ● *v.* (*past* and *past part.* **heaved** or esp. *Naut.* **hove** /hōv/) **1** *tr.* lift or haul with great effort. **2** *tr.* utter with effort or resignation. **3** *tr. colloq.* throw. **4** *intr.* rise and fall rhythmically or spasmodically. **5** *intr.* retch. ● *n.* an instance of heaving. □ **heave in sight** *Naut.* or *colloq.* come into view. **heave to** esp. *Naut.* bring or be brought to a standstill. □□ **heav·er** *n.*

heave-ho *int. & n.* ● *int.* a sailors' cry, esp. on raising the anchor. ● *n. sl.* (usu. prec. by *the* or *the old*) a dismissal or rejection.

heav·en /hévən/ *n.* **1** a place regarded in some religions as the abode of God and the angels, and of the good after death, often characterized as above the sky. **2** a place or state of supreme bliss. **3** *colloq.* something delightful. **4** (usu. **Heaven**) **a** God; Providence. **b** (in *sing.* or *pl.*) an exclamation or mild oath (*by Heaven!*). **5** (**the heavens**) esp. *poet.* the sky as the abode of the Sun, Moon, and stars and regarded from Earth. □□ **heav·en·ward** *adj. & adv.* **heav·en·wards** *adv.*

heav·en·ly /hévənlee/ *adj.* **1** of heaven; divine. **2** of the heavens or sky. **3** *colloq.* very pleasing. □□ **heav·en·li·ness** *n.*

heav·en·ly bod·ies *n.pl.* the Sun, stars, planets, etc.

HEARTSEASE
(*Viola tricolor*)

heav·en-sent *adj.* providential; wonderfully opportune.

heav·y /hévee/ *adj., n., & adv.* ● *adj.* (**heavier, heaviest**) **1 a** of great or exceptionally high weight; difficult to lift. **b** (of a person) fat; overweight. **2** of great density. **3** abundant (*a heavy crop*). **4** severe; intense; extensive; excessive (*heavy fighting; a heavy sleep*). **5** doing something to excess (*a heavy drinker*). **6 a** striking or falling with force (*heavy blows; heavy rain*). **b** (of the sea) having large powerful waves. **7** (of machinery, artillery, etc.) very large of its kind; large in caliber, etc. **8** causing a strong impact (*a heavy fall*). **9** needing much physical effort (*heavy work*). **10** (foll. by *with*) laden. **11** carrying heavy weapons (*the heavy brigade*). **12 a** (of a writing, music, etc.) serious or somber in tone or attitude. **b** (of an issue, etc.) grave; important. **13 a** (of food) hard to digest. **b** (of a literary work, etc.) hard to understand. **14** (of temperament) dignified; stern. **15** (of bread, etc.) too dense from not having risen. **16** (of ground) difficult to traverse or work. **17** hard to endure (*heavy demands*). **18 a** coarse; ungraceful (*heavy features*). **b** unwieldy. ● *n.* (*pl.* **-ies**) **1** *colloq.* a large violent person. **2** a villainous or tragic role in a play, etc. ● *adv.* heavily (esp. in *comb.*: *heavy-laden*). □ **make heavy weather of** see WEATHER. □□ **heav·i·ly** *adv.* **heav·i·ness** *n.* **heav·y·ish** *adj.*

heav·y-du·ty *adj.* **1** intended to withstand hard use. **2** serious; grave.

heav·y-foot·ed *adj.* awkward; ponderous.

heav·y go·ing *n.* slow or difficult progress.

heav·y-hand·ed /hévihándid/ *adj.* **1** clumsy. **2** overbearing; oppressive. □□ **heav·y-hand·ed·ly** *adv.* **heav·y-hand·ed·ness** *n.*

heav·y-heart·ed *adj.* sad; doleful.

heav·y hit·ter *n.* (also **big hit·ter**) *colloq.* an important or powerful person.

heav·y in·dus·try *n.* industry producing metal, machinery, etc.

heav·y met·al *n.* **1** heavy guns. **2** metal of high density. **3** *colloq.* (often *attrib.*) a type of highly-amplified rock music with a strong beat.

heav·y sleep·er *n.* a person who sleeps deeply.

heav·y wa·ter *n.* a substance composed entirely or mainly of deuterium oxide.

heav·y·weight /héviwayt/ *n.* **1 a** a weight in certain sports, differing for professional and amateur boxers, wrestlers, and weightlifters. **b** a sports participant of this weight. **2** a person, animal, or thing of above average weight. **3** *colloq.* a person of influence or importance.

he·be /héebee/ *n.* ▶ any flowering shrub of the genus *Hebe*, with usu. overlapping scalelike leaves.

He·brew /héebrōō/ *n. & adj.* ● *n.* **1** a member of a Semitic people orig. centered in ancient Palestine. **2 a** the language of this people. **b** a modern form of this, used esp. in Israel. ● *adj.* **1** of or in Hebrew. **2** of the Hebrews.

heck /hek/ *int. colloq.* a mild exclamation of surprise or dismay.

HEBE
(*Hebe* 'Bowles')

heck·le /hékəl/ *v.tr.* interrupt and harass (a public speaker). □□ **heck·ler** *n.*

hec·tare /héktair/ *n.* a metric unit of square measure, equal to 100 ares (2.471 acres or 10,000 square meters). □□ **hec·tar·age** /-tərij/ *n.*

hec·tic /héktik/ *adj. & n.* ● *adj.* **1** busy and confused; excited. **2** having a hectic fever; morbidly flushed. ● *n.* **1** a hectic fever or flush. **2** a patient suffering from this. □□ **hec·ti·cal·ly** *adv.*

hec·to·gram /héktəgram/ *n.* a metric unit of mass, equal to one hundred grams.

hec·to·li·ter /héktəleetər/ *n.* a metric unit of capacity, equal to one hundred liters.

hec·to·me·ter /héktəmeetər, hektómitər/ *n.* a metric unit of length, equal to one hundred meters.

hec·tor /héktər/ *v.tr.* bully; intimidate. □□ **hec·tor·ing·ly** *adv.*

he'd /heed/ *contr.* **1** he had. **2** he would.

hedge /hej/ *n. & v.* ● *n.* **1** a fence or boundary formed by closely growing bushes or shrubs. **2** a protection against possible loss. ● *v.* **1** *tr.* surround or bound with a hedge. **2** *tr.* (foll. by *in*) enclose. **3 a** *tr.* reduce one's risk of loss on (a bet or speculation) by compensating transactions on the other side. **b** *intr.* avoid a definite decision or commitment. **4** *intr.* make hedges. □□ **hedg·er** *n.*

hedge·hog /héjhawg, -hog/ *n.* ◀ any small nocturnal mammal of the genus *Erinaceus*, esp. *E. europaeus*, having a piglike snout and a coat of spines, and rolling itself up into a ball for defense.

HEDGEHOG (*Erinaceus europaeus*)

hedge·hop /héjhop/ *v.intr.* fly at a very low altitude.

hedge·row /héjrō/ *n.* a row of bushes, etc., forming a hedge.

he·don·ism /héed'nizəm/ *n.* **1** belief in pleasure as the highest good and the proper aim of humans. **2** behavior based on this. □□ **he·don·ist** *n.* **he·don·is·tic** *adj.*

-hedron /héedrən, hédrən/ *comb. form* (*pl.* **-hedra**) forming nouns denoting geometrical solids with various numbers or shapes of faces (*rhombohedron*). □□ **-hedral** *comb. form* forming adjectives.

hee·bie·jee·bies /héebeejeébeez/ *n.pl.* (prec. by *the*) *sl.* a state of nervous depression or anxiety.

heed /heed/ *v. & n.* ● *v.tr.* attend to; take notice of.

● *n.* careful attention. □□ **heed·ful** *adj.* **heed·ful·ly** *adv.* **heed·ful·ness** *n.* **heed·less** *adj.* **heed·less·ly** *adv.* **heed·less·ness** *n.*

hee-haw /héehaw/ *n. & v.* ● *n.* the bray of a donkey. ● *v.intr.* emit a braying sound.

heel[1] /heel/ *n. & v.* ● *n.* **1** the back part of the foot below the ankle. ▷ ACHILLES TENDON. **2** the corresponding part in vertebrate animals. ▷ HORSE. **3 a** the part of a sock, etc., covering the heel. **b** the part of a shoe or boot supporting the heel. ▷ SHOE. **4** a thing like a heel in form or position, e.g., the part of the palm next to the wrist, or the part of a golf club near where the head joins the shaft. **5** *colloq.* a person regarded with contempt. ● *v.* **1** *tr.* fit or renew a heel on (a shoe or boot). **2** *intr.* touch the ground with the heel, as in dancing. □ **at heel 1** (of a dog) close behind. **2** (of a person, etc.) under control. **at** (or **on**) **the heels of** following closely after (a person or event). **cool** (or *Brit.* **kick**) **one's heels** be kept waiting. **take to one's heels** run away. **to heel 1** (of a dog) close behind. **2** (of a person, etc.) under control. **turn on one's heel** turn sharply around. □□ **heel·less** *adj.* **well-heeled** *adj. colloq.* wealthy.

heel[2] /heel/ *v. & n.* ● *v.* **1** *intr.* (of a ship, etc.) lean over owing to the pressure of wind or an uneven load (cf. LIST[2]). **2** *tr.* cause (a ship, etc.) to do this. ● *n.* the act or amount of heeling.

heel[3] /heel/ *v.tr.* (foll. by *in*) ► set (a plant) temporarily in the ground at an angle and cover its roots.

tree at angle — *moist soil*

trench

HEEL: TREE HEELED INTO A TRENCH

heel·ball /héelbawl/ *n.* **1** a mixture of hard wax and lampblack used by shoemakers for polishing. **2** this or a similar mixture used in brass-rubbing.

heel·tap /héeltap/ *n.* **1** a layer of leather, metal, etc., in a shoe heel. **2** liquor left at the bottom of a glass after drinking.

heft /heft/ *v.tr.* lift (something heavy), esp. to judge its weight.

heft·y /héftee/ *adj.* (**heftier**, **heftiest**) **1** (of a person) big and strong. **2** (of a thing) large; heavy; powerful; sizable; considerable. □□ **heft·i·ly** *adv.* **heft·i·ness** *n.*

Hegelian /haygáyleeən, hijeé-/ *adj. & n.* ● *adj.* of or relating to the German philosopher G.W.F. Hegel (d. 1831) or his philosophy of objective idealism. ● *n.* an adherent of Hegel or of his philosophy.

he·gem·o·ny /hijémənee, héjəmōnee/ *n.* leadership, esp. by one nation over others of a confederacy. □□ **hegemonic** *adj.*

he·gi·ra /hijírə, héjirə/ *n.* (also **he·ji·ra**, **hij·ra** /híjrə/) **1** (**Hegira**) Muhammad's departure from Mecca to Medina in AD 622. **2** the Muslim era reckoned from this date.

heif·er /héfər/ *n.* a young cow, esp. one that has not had more than one calf.

heigh /hay, hī/ *int.* expressing encouragement or inquiry.

heigh-ho /hí hō, háy-/ *int.* expressing boredom, resignation, etc.

height /hīt/ *n.* **1** the measurement from base to top or (of a standing person) from head to foot. **2** the elevation above ground or a recognized level (usu. sea level). **3** any considerable elevation (*situated at a height*). **4 a** a high place or area. **b** rising ground. **5** the top of something. **6** *Printing* the distance from the foot to the face of type. **7 a** the most intense part or period of anything (*the battle was at its height*). **b** an extreme instance or example (*the height of fashion*).

height·en /hítən/ *v.tr. & intr.* make or become higher or more intense.

HELICOPTER

Helicopters are lifted, propelled, and steered by powerful rotating blades (rotors). First developed in the 1920s, modern helicopters date from the advent of turbojet engines in 1955. They are now used for such widely diverse purposes as military gunships, for spraying crops, and for aerial observation, such as of traffic conditions. Helicopters are also used as rapid means of transportation in the form of air ambulances and air taxis to convey troops and oil-rig workers, victims of serious accidents, and busy officials.

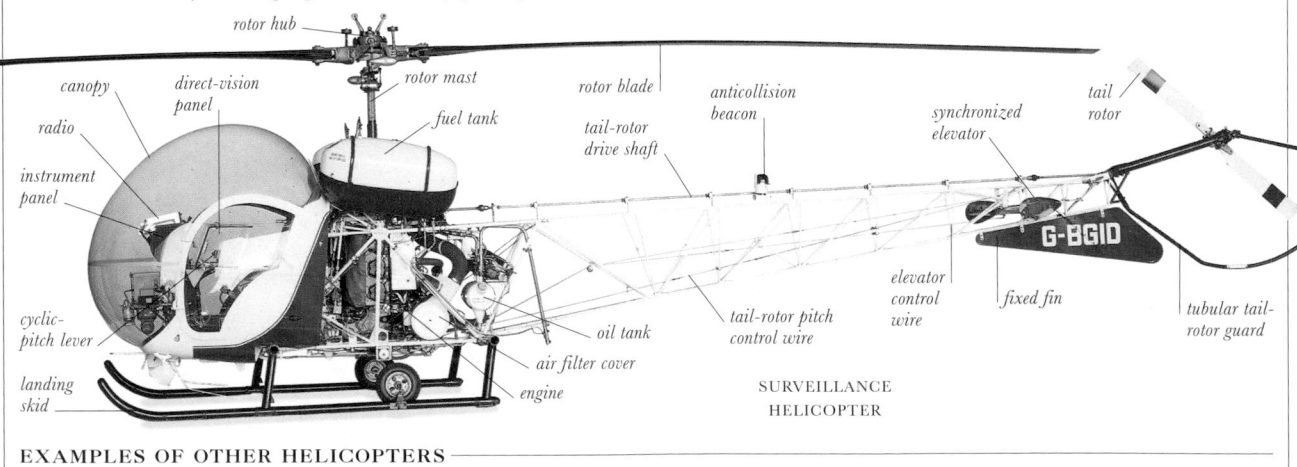

SURVEILLANCE HELICOPTER

EXAMPLES OF OTHER HELICOPTERS

MULTIPURPOSE HELICOPTER

MILITARY GUNSHIP

PERSONNEL CARRIER

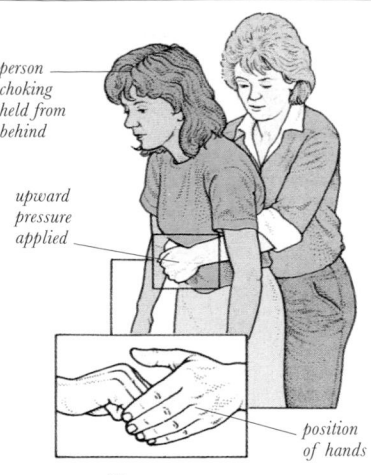

HEIMLICH MANEUVER

person choking held from behind

upward pressure applied

position of hands

Heim·lich ma·neu·ver /hímlik/ *n.* ▲ an emergency procedure for assisting a choking victim in which one applies sudden upward pressure with the fist against the victim's upper abdomen in order to dislodge the object causing the choking.

hei·nous /háynəs/ *adj.* (of a crime or criminal) utterly odious or wicked. □□ **hei·nous·ly** *adv.* **hei·nous·ness** *n.*

heir /air/ *n.* **1** a person entitled to property or rank as the legal successor of its former owner. **2** a person morally entitled to some thing, quality, etc., from a predecessor. □□ **heir·dom** *n.* **heir·less** *adj.* **heir·ship** *n.*

heir ap·par·ent *n.* an heir whose claim cannot be set aside by the birth of another heir.

heir·ess /áiris/ *n.* a female heir, esp. to great wealth or high title.

heir·loom /áirloom/ *n.* **1** a piece of personal property that has been in a family for several generations. **2** a piece of property received as part of an inheritance.

heist /hīst/ *n. & v. sl.* ● *n.* a robbery. ● *v.tr.* rob.

he·ji·ra var. of HEGIRA.

He·La /hélə/ *adj.* of a strain of human epithelial cells maintained in tissue culture.

held past and past part. of HOLD.

heli- /hélee/ *comb. form* helicopter (*heliport*).

he·li·an·thus /héeleeánthəs/ *n.* any plant of the genus *Helianthus*, including the sunflower and Jerusalem artichoke.

hel·i·cal /hélikəl, héeli-/ *adj.* having the form of a helix. □□ **hel·i·cal·ly** *adv.* **hel·i·coid** *adj. & n.*

hel·i·ces *pl.* of HELIX.

hel·i·chry·sum /hélikríəzəm, héeli-/ *n.* any composite plant of the genus *Helichrysum*, with flowers retaining their appearance when dried.

hel·i·cop·ter /hélikoptər/ *n.* ◀ a type of aircraft obtaining lift and propulsion from horizontally revolving overhead blades. ▷ AIRCRAFT

helio- /héeleeō/ *comb. form* the Sun.

he·li·o·cen·tric /héeleeōséntrik/ *adj.* **1** regarding the Sun as center. **2** considered as viewed from the Sun's center. □□ **he·li·o·cen·tri·cal·ly** *adv.*

he·li·o·gram /héeleeəgram/ *n.* a message sent by heliograph.

he·li·o·graph /héeleeəgraf/ *n. & v.* ● *n.* **1** ▶ a signaling apparatus reflecting sunlight in flashes from a movable mirror. **2** an apparatus for photographing the Sun. ● *v.tr.* send (a message) by heliograph. □□ **he·li·og·ra·phy** /-leeógrəfee/ *n.*

mirror

sight

tripod

HELIOGRAPH: LATE 19TH-CENTURY HELIOGRAPH

he·li·o·trope /héeleeətrōp/ *n.* **1** any plant of the genus *Heliotropium*, with fragrant purple flowers. **2** a light purple color.

hel·i·port /héleepawrt/ *n.* a place where helicopters take off and land.

he·li·um /héeleeəm/ *n. Chem.* a colorless, light, inert, gaseous element occurring in deposits of natural gas, used in airships and balloons and as a refrigerant. ¶ Symb.: **He**.

he·lix /héeliks/ *n.* (*pl.* **helices** /-seez, hél-/) **1** ▶ a spiral curve (like a corkscrew) or a coiled curve (like a watch spring). **2** *Geom.* a curve that cuts a line on a solid cone or cylinder, at a constant angle with the axis.

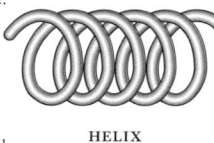

HELIX

hell /hel/ *n.* **1** in some religions, the abode of the dead, or of condemned sinners and devils. **2** a place or state of misery or wickedness. □ **beat** (or **knock**, etc.) **the hell out of** *colloq.* beat, etc., without restraint. **for the hell of it** *colloq.* for fun. **give a person hell** *colloq.* scold or punish a person. **hell of** *colloq.* extreme or outstanding example of (*a hell of a mess; one hell of a party*). **hell for leather** at full speed. **like hell** *colloq.* **1** not at all. **2** exceedingly. **play hell with** *colloq.* be upsetting or disruptive to. **what the hell** *colloq.* it is of no importance. □□ **hell-like** *adj.*

he'll /heel/ *contr.* he will; he shall.

hell-bent *adj.* (foll. by *on*) recklessly determined.

hell·cat /hélkat/ *n.* a spiteful violent woman.

hel·le·bore /hélibawr/ *n.* ▶ any evergreen plant of the genus *Helleborus*, having large white, green, or purplish flowers.

Hel·lene /héleen/ *n.* **1** a native of modern Greece. **2** an ancient Greek. □□ **Hel·len·ic** /helénik/ *adj.*

Hel·len·ism /hélinizəm/ *n.* Greek character or culture (esp. of ancient Greece). □□ **Hel·len·ize** *v.tr. & intr.* **Hel·len·i·za·tion** *n.*

Hel·len·ist /hélinist/ *n.* an expert on or admirer of Greek language or culture.

HELLEBORE
(*Helleborus lividus*)

Hel·len·is·tic /hélinístik/ *adj.* of or relating to Greek history, language, and culture from 4th–1st c. BC.

hell·fire /hélfīr/ *n.* the fire or fires regarded as existing in hell.

hell·hole /hélhōl/ *n. colloq.* an oppressive or unbearable place.

hell·hound /hélhownd/ *n.* a fiend.

hell·ish /hélish/ *adj. & adv.* ● *adj.* **1** of or like hell. **2** *colloq.* extremely unpleasant. ● *adv. Brit. colloq.* (as an intensifier) extremely (*hellish expensive*). □□ **hell·ish·ly** *adv.* **hell·ish·ness** *n.*

hel·lo /helō, hə-/ *int., n., & v.* (also esp. *Brit.* **hullo** /hə-/, **hallo** /hə-/) ● *int.* **1** an expression of informal greeting. **2** a cry used to call attention. ● *n.* (*pl.* **-os**) a cry of "hello." ● *v.intr.* (**-oes, -oed**) cry "hello."

hell-rais·er /-/ *n.* a person who causes trouble or creates chaos.

Hell's An·gel *n.* a member of a gang of motorcyclists notorious for their outrageous or violent behavior.

helm /helm/ *n. & v.* ● *n.* **1** a tiller or wheel by which a ship's rudder is controlled. **2** the amount by which this is turned (*more helm needed*). ● *v.tr.* steer or guide as if with a helm. □ **at the helm** in control; at the head (of an organization, etc.).

hel·met /hélmit/ *n.* ▶ any of various protective head coverings worn by soldiers, cyclists, etc. □□ **hel·met·ed** *adj.*

helms·man /hélmzmən/ *n.* (*pl.* **-men**) a person who steers a vessel.

hel·ot /hélət/ *n.* a serf (esp. **Helot**), of a class in ancient Sparta. □□ **hel·ot·ry** *n.*

HELMET: FOOTBALL PLAYER'S HELMET

help /help/ *v. & n.* ● *v.tr.* **1** provide (a person, etc.) with the means toward what is needed (*helped me with my work*). **2** (foll. by *up, down*, etc.) assist (a person) in moving, etc., as specified (*helped her into the chair*). **3** (often *absol.*) be of use to (a person) (*does that help?*). **4** contribute to alleviating (a pain or difficulty). **5** prevent or remedy (*it can't be helped*). **6** (usu. with *neg.*) **a** *tr.* refrain from (*could not help laughing*). **b** *refl.* refrain from acting (*couldn't help himself*). **7** *tr.* (often foll. by *to*) serve (a person with food) (*shall I help you to more rice?*). ● *n.* **1** the act of helping or being helped (*we need your help*). **2** a person or thing that helps. **3** a domestic servant. □ **help oneself** (often foll. by *to*) **1** serve oneself (with food). **2** take without seeking help; take without permission. **help a person out** give a person help, esp. in difficulty. □□ **help·er** *n.*

help·ful /hélpfool/ *adj.* (of a person or thing) giving help; useful. □□ **help·ful·ly** *adv.* **help·ful·ness** *n.*

help·ing /hélping/ *n.* a portion of food, esp. at a meal.

help·ing hand *n.* assistance.

help·less /hélplis/ *adj.* **1** lacking help or protection. **2** unable to act without help. □□ **help·less·ly** *adv.* **help·less·ness** *n.*

help·line /hélplīn/ *n.* a telephone service providing help with problems.

help·mate /hélpmayt/ *n.* a helpful companion (usu. a husband or wife).

hel·ter-skel·ter /héltərskéltər/ *adv., adj., & n.* ● *adv.* in disorderly haste. ● *adj.* characterized by disorderly haste. ● *n. Brit.* a tall spiral slide around a tower, at a fairground.

hem¹ /hem/ *n. & v.* ● *n.* the border of a piece of cloth, turned under and sewn down. ● *v.tr.* (**hemmed, hemming**) turn down and sew in the edge of (a piece of cloth, etc.). □ **hem in** confine; restrict the movement of.

hem² /hem, həm/ *int., n., & v.* ● *int.* (also **ahem**) calling attention or expressing hesitation by a slight cough or clearing of the throat. ● *n.* an utterance of this. ● *v.intr.* (**hemmed, hemming**) say *hem*; hesitate in speech. □ **hem and haw** hesitate in speaking.

he·mal /héeməl/ *adj. Anat.* **1** of or concerning the blood. **2** situated on the same side of the body as the heart and major blood vessels.

he-man *n.* (*pl.* **-men**) a masterful or virile man.

he·ma·tite /héemətīt, hém-/ *n.* (*Brit.* **hae·matite**) ▶ a ferric oxide ore. ▷ ORE

hemato- /héemətō, hém-/ *comb. form* (*Brit.* **haemato-**) blood.

he·mat·o·cele /himátəseel, héemətəseel, hém-/ *n. Med.* a swelling caused by blood collecting in a body cavity.

he·ma·tol·o·gy /héemətóləjee, hém-/ *n. Med.* the study of the physiology of the blood and blood-forming organs. □□ **he·ma·to·log·ic** /-təlójik/ *adj.* **he·ma·to·log·i·cal** *adj.* **he·ma·tol·o·gist** *n.*

HEMATITE

H

he·ma·to·ma /heemətṓmə/ *n. Med.* a solid swelling of clotted blood within the tissues.

hem·i·ple·gi·a /hémipléejə, -jeeə/ *n. Med.* paralysis of one side of the body. □□ **hem·i·ple·gic** *n. & adj.*

He·mip·ter·a /hemíptərə/ *n.pl.* ▶ an order of insects comprising the "true bugs," which have mouthparts adapted for piercing and sucking. ▷ INSECT. □□ **hem·ip·ter·an** *n. & adj.* **he·mip·ter·ous** /hemíptərəs/ *adj.*

hem·i·sphere /hémisfeer/ *n.* **1** half of a sphere. **2** ▼ a half of the Earth, esp. as divided by the equator (into *northern* and *southern hemispheres*) or by a line passing through the poles (into *eastern* and *western hemispheres*). □□ **hem·i·spher·ic** /-sféerik, -sférik/ *adj.* **hem·i·spher·i·cal** *adj.*

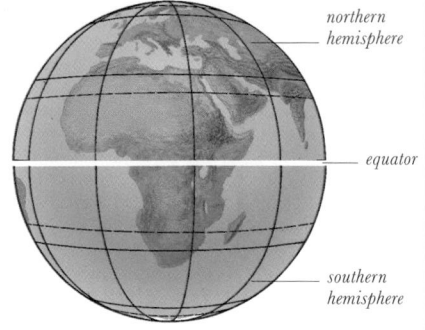

northern
hemisphere

equator

southern
hemisphere

HEMISPHERE: GLOBE DIVIDED INTO NORTHERN AND SOUTHERN HEMISPHERES

hem·line /hémlīn/ *n.* the line or level of the lower edge of a skirt, dress, or coat.

hem·lock /hémlok/ *n.* **1** a poisonous umbelliferous plant, *Conium maculatum*, with fernlike leaves and small white flowers. **2** a poisonous potion obtained from this.

he·mo·glo·bin /héeməglṓbin, hém-/ *n.* a red oxygen-carrying substance containing iron, present in the red blood cells of vertebrates.

he·mo·phil·i·a /héeməfileeə, hém-/ *n. Med.* a usu. hereditary disorder with a tendency to bleed severely from even a slight injury, through the failure of the blood to clot normally. □□ **he·mo·phil·ic** *adj.*

he·mo·phil·i·ac /héeməfileeak, -féelee-, hém-/ *n.* a person suffering from hemophilia.

hem·or·rhage /hémərij, hémrij/ *n. & v.* ● *n.* **1** an escape of blood from a ruptured blood vessel, esp. when profuse. **2** an extensive damaging loss, esp. of people or assets. ● *v.intr.* undergo a hemorrhage. □□ **he·mor·rhag·ic** /hémərájik/ *adj.*

hem·or·rhoid /héməroyd/ *n.* (usu. in *pl.*) swollen veins at or near the anus.

he·mos·ta·sis /himóstəsis, héemōstáysis, hém-/ *n.* the stopping of the flow of blood. □□ **he·mo·stat·ic** /héeməstátik/ *adj.*

hemp /hemp/ *n.* **1** (in full **Indian hemp**) a herbaceous plant, *Cannabis sativa*, native to Asia. **2** its fiber extracted from the stem and used to make rope and strong fabrics. ▷ ROPE. **3** any of several narcotic drugs made from the hemp plant (cf. CANNABIS, MARIJUANA). □□ **hempen** *adj.*

hem·stitch /hémstich/ *n. & v.* ● *n.* ▼ decorative stitch used to sew hems. ● *v.tr.* hem with this stitch. ▷ STITCH

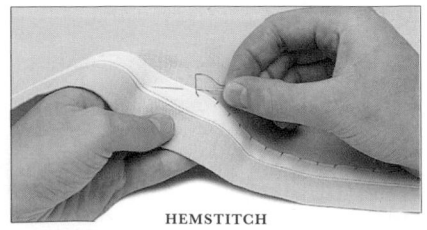

HEMSTITCH

HEMIPTERA

Hemipterans form a hugely varied group of insects, the "true bugs." All possess biting and sucking mouthparts, used to draw fluids from plant or animal tissues (most species are herbivorous). While the majority of hemipterans are terrestrial, the group also includes all aquatic bugs.

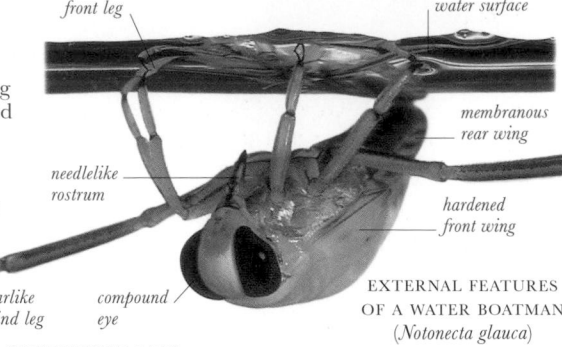

front leg

water surface

membranous
rear wing

needlelike
rostrum

hardened
front wing

oarlike
hind leg

compound
eye

EXTERNAL FEATURES
OF A WATER BOATMAN
(*Notonecta glauca*)

EXAMPLES OF OTHER HEMIPTERANS

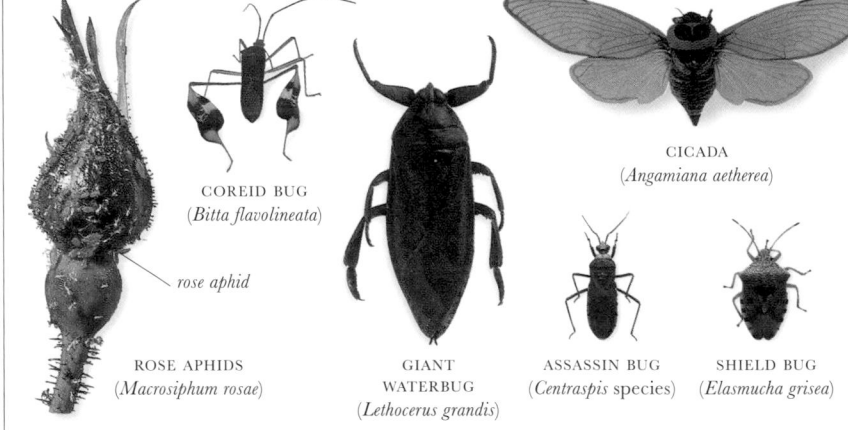

COREID BUG
(*Bitta flavolineata*)

rose aphid

ROSE APHIDS
(*Macrosiphum rosae*)

GIANT
WATERBUG
(*Lethocerus grandis*)

CICADA
(*Angamiana aetherea*)

ASSASSIN BUG
(*Centraspis* species)

SHIELD BUG
(*Elasmucha grisea*)

---

hen /hen/ *n.* **1** a female bird, esp. of a domestic fowl. **2** a female lobster or crab or salmon.

hence /hens/ *adv.* **1** from this time (*two years hence*). **2** for this reason (*hence we seem to be wrong*). **3** *archaic* from here.

hence·forth /hénsfáwrth/ *adv.* (also **hence·for·ward** /-fáwrwərd/) from this time onward.

hench·man /hénchmən/ *n.* (*pl.* **-men**) a trusted supporter or attendant.

henge /henj/ *n.* ▼ a prehistoric monument consisting of a circle of massive stone or wood uprights.

HENGE: STONEHENGE, ENGLAND, *C.* 2000 BC

hen·na /hénə/ *n.* **1** a tropical shrub, *Lawsonia inermis*, having small flowers. **2** the reddish dye from its shoots and leaves used to color hair.

hen·naed /hénəd/ *adj.* treated with henna.

hen·peck /hénpek/ *v.tr.* (of a woman) constantly harass (a man, esp. her husband).

hen·ry /hénree/ *n.* (*pl.* **-ies** or **henrys**) *Electr.* the SI unit of inductance that gives an electromotive force of one volt in a closed circuit with a uniform rate of change of current of one ampere per second. ¶ Abbr.: **H**.

---

he·or·tol·o·gy /hée-awrtóləjee/ *n.* the study of ecclesiatical festivals.

hep var. of HIP³.

hep·a·rin /hépərin/ *n. Biochem.* a substance produced in liver cells, etc., which is used as an anticoagulant in the treatment of thrombosis.

he·pat·ic /hipátik/ *adj.* **1** of or relating to the liver. ▷ CARDIOVASCULAR, LIVER. **2** dark brownish red.

hep·a·ti·tis /hépətítis/ *n.* inflammation of the liver.

hepta- /héptə/ *comb. form* seven.

hep·ta·gon /héptəgən/ *n.* ▶ a plane figure with seven sides and angles. □□ **hep·tag·o·nal** /-tágənəl/ *adj.*

hep·tath·lon /heptáthlon, -lən/ *n. Sports* a seven-event track and field competition, esp. for women.

hep·ta·va·lent /héptəváylənt/ *adj. Chem.* having a valence of seven; septivalent.

HEPTAGON

her /hər/ *pron. & poss.pron.* ● *pron. objective case* of SHE (*I like her*). ● *poss.pron.* (*attrib.*) of or belonging to her (*her house; her own business*).

her·ald /hérəld/ *n. & v.* ● *n.* **1** an official messenger bringing news. **2** a forerunner (*spring is the herald of summer*). ● *v.tr.* proclaim the approach of; usher in.

he·ral·dic /heráldik/ *adj.* of or concerning heraldry. □□ **he·ral·di·cal·ly** *adv.*

her·ald·ist /hérəldist/ *n.* an expert in heraldry.

her·ald·ry /hérəldree/ *n.* **1** the science or art of a herald, esp. in dealing with armorial bearings. **2** armorial bearings.

herb /ərb, hərb/ *n.* **1** any nonwoody seed-bearing plant that dies down to the ground after flowering. **2** ▶ any plant with leaves, seeds, or flowers used for flavoring, medicine, scent, etc. □ **give it the herbs** *Austral. colloq.* accelerate. □□ **her·bif·er·ous** /-bífərəs/ *adj.* **herb·like** *adj.*

HERB

Plants have been exploited since ancient times both as a source of food and medicine and to scent or cleanse the home. Many herbs are traditionally used to alleviate the symptoms of disease, either through herbal treatments such as aromatherapy or through homeopathy. In the domestic environment, fresh or dried herbs are used to flavor food, while herbal extracts provide a base for a wide variety of household compounds for cleaning, polishing, sterilizing, and laundering. Shown below is a small selection of the more familiar herbs.

CULINARY HERBS

THYME
garden thyme
(*Thymus vulgaris*)

ROSEMARY
(*Rosmarinus officinalis*)

MINT
water mint
(*Mentha aquatica*)

CORIANDER
(CILANTRO)
(*Coriandrum sativum*)

PARSLEY
curled parsley
(*Petroselinum crispum*)

BASIL
sweet basil
(*Ocimum basilicum*)

BORAGE
(*Borago officinalis*)

CALENDULA
(POT MARIGOLD)
(*Calendula officinalis*)

SAGE
common sage
(*Salvia officinalis*)

OREGANO
common oregano
(*Origanum vulgare*)

FENNEL
(*Foeniculum vulgare*)

BAY
(*Laurus nobilis*)

MEDICINAL HERBS

GERMAN CHAMOMILE
(*Matricaria recutita*)

TEA TREE
(*Melaleuca alternifolia*)

OPIUM POPPY
(*Papaver somniferum*)

AROMATIC HERBS

WORMWOOD
(*Artemisia absinthium*)

HYSSOP
(*Hyssopus officinalis*)

LAVENDER
(*Lavandula
angustifolia*)

HERMAPHRODITE

Although hermaphrodite plants and animals have both male and female organs, it is usual for individuals in a species to fertilize each other. This produces twice the number of possible offspring compared to unisexual reproduction and helps to maintain genetic diversity.

copulatory bursa

ovotestis

hermaphrodite duct

spermatheca

pistil (female organ)

stamens (male organs)

penis

vagina

spermoviduct

REPRODUCTIVE ORGANS OF A
HERMAPHRODITE FLOWER (POPPY)

REPRODUCTIVE ORGANS OF A
HERMAPHRODITE ANIMAL (SNAIL)

H

her·ba·ceous /hərbáyshəs, ər-/ *adj.* of or like herbs (see HERB 1).

herb·age /árbij, hár-/ *n.* **1** herbs collectively. **2** the succulent part of herbs, esp. as pasture.

herb·al /árbəl, hár-/ *adj. & n.* ● *adj.* of herbs in medicinal and culinary use. ● *n.* a book with descriptions and accounts of the properties of these.

herb·al·ist /árbəlist, hár-/ *n.* **1** a dealer in medicinal herbs. **2** a person skilled in herbs, esp. an early botanical writer.

her·bar·i·um /hərbáireeəm, ər-/ *n.* (*pl.* **herbaria** /-reeə/) **1** a systematically arranged collection of dried plants. **2** a book, room, or building for these.

herb·i·cide /hárbisīd, ár-/ *n.* a substance toxic to plants.

herb·i·vore /hárbivawr, ár-/ *n.* an animal that feeds on plants. □□ **her·biv·o·rous** /-bívərəs/ *adj.*

herb·y /árbee, hár-/ *adj.* (**herbier, herbiest**) **1** abounding in herbs. **2** of the nature of a herb.

Her·cu·le·an /hárkyəléeən, -kyoóleeən/ *adj.* having or requiring great strength.

herd /hərd/ *n. & v.* ● *n.* **1** a large number of animals, esp. cattle, feeding or traveling or kept together. **2** (often prec. by *the*) *derog.* a large number of people; a mob (*prefers not to follow the herd*). ● *v.* **1** *intr. & tr.* go or cause to go in a herd (*herded together for warmth*; *herded the cattle into the field*). **2** *tr.* tend (sheep, cattle, etc.). □□ **herd·er** *n.*

herds·man /hárdzmən/ *n.* (*pl.* **-men**) the owner or keeper of herds.

here /heer/ *adv., n., & int.* ● *adv.* **1** in or at or to this place. **2** indicating a person's presence or a thing offered (*here is your coat*; *my son here will show you*). **3** at this point in the argument, situation, etc. ● *n.* this place. ● *int.* **1** calling attention (*here, where are you going with that?*). **2** indicating one's presence in a roll call. □ **here goes!** *colloq.* an expression indicating the start of a bold act. **here's to** I drink to the health of. **neither here nor there** of no relevance.

here·a·bouts /héerəbówts/ *adv.* (also **here·a·bout**) near this place.

here·af·ter /heeráftər/ *adv. & n.* ● *adv.* **1** from now on. **2** in the world to come (after death). ● *n.* **1** the future. **2** life after death.

here and now *adv.* at this very moment; immediately.

here and there *adv.* in various places.

here·by /héerbí/ *adv.* by this means; as a result of this.

he·red·i·ta·ble /hiréd'itəbəl/ *adj.* that can be inherited.

he·red·i·tar·y /hiréditeree/ *adj.* **1** (of disease, instinct, etc.) able to be passed down from one generation to another. **2 a** descending by inheritance. **b** holding a position by inheritance.

3 the same as or resembling what one's parents had (*a hereditary hatred*). **4** of or relating to inheritance. □□ **he·red·i·tar·i·ly** *adv.*

he·red·i·ty /hiréditee/ *n.* **1** the passing on of physical or mental characteristics genetically from one generation to another. **2** these characteristics.

Her·e·ford /hárfərd, hérifərd/ *n.* an animal of a breed of red and white beef cattle.

here·in /héerín/ *adv. formal* in this matter, book, etc.

here·in·af·ter /héerináftər/ *adv. esp. Law formal* in a later part of this document.

here·of /heerúv, -óv/ *adv. formal* of this.

her·e·sy /hérəsee/ *n.* (*pl.* **-ies**) **1 a** belief or practice contrary to the orthodox doctrine of esp. the Christian church. **b** an instance of this. **2 a** opinion contrary to what is normally accepted or maintained. **b** an instance of this.

her·e·tic /hérətik/ *n.* **1** the holder of an unorthodox opinion. **2** a person believing in or practicing religious heresy. □□ **he·ret·i·cal** /hirétikəl/ *adj.* **he·ret·i·cal·ly** *adv.*

here·to /héertoō/ *adv. formal* to this matter.

here·to·fore /héertəfáwr/ *adv. formal* before this time.

here·up·on /héerəpón, -páwn/ *adv.* after this; in consequence of this.

here·with /héerwíth, -wíth/ *adv.* with this (esp. of an enclosure in a letter, etc.).

her·it·a·ble /hérítəbəl/ *adj.* **1** *Law* **a** (of property) capable of being inherited by heirs-at-law (cf. MOVABLE). **b** capable of inheriting. **2** *Biol.* (of a characteristic) transmissible from parent to offspring. □□ **her·it·a·bil·i·ty** *n.* **her·it·a·bly** *adv.*

her·it·age /hérítij/ *n.* **1** anything that is or may be inherited. **2** inherited circumstances, benefits, etc. (*a heritage of confusion*). **3** a nation's historic buildings, monuments, countryside, etc., esp. when regarded as worthy of preservation.

her·maph·ro·dite /hərmáfrədīt/ *n. & adj.* ● *n.* **1 a** *Zool.* ▲ an animal having both male and female sexual organs. **b** *Bot.* ▲ a plant having stamens and pistils in the same flower. **2** a human being in which both male and female sex organs are present, or in which the sex organs contain both ovarian and testicular tissue. ● *adj.* combining both sexes. □□ **her·maph·ro·dit·ic** /-dítik/ *adj.* **her·maph·ro·dit·i·cal** *adj.* **her·maph·ro·dit·ism** *n.*

her·me·neu·tic /hərminoótik, -nyoó-/ *adj.* concerning interpretation, esp. of Scripture or literary texts. □□ **her·me·neu·ti·cal** *adj.* **her·me·neu·ti·cal·ly** *adv.*

her·me·neu·tics /hərminoótiks, -nyoó-/ *n.pl.* (also treated as *sing.*) *Bibl.* interpretation, esp. of Scripture or literary texts.

her·met·ic /hərmétik/ *adj.* (also **her·met·i·cal**) **1** with an airtight closure. **2** protected from outside agencies. □□ **her·met·i·cal·ly** *adv.* **her·me·tism** /hérmitizəm/ *n.*

her·mit /hármit/ *n.* **1** an early Christian recluse. **2** any person living in solitude. □□ **her·mit·ic** /-mítik/ *adj.*

her·mit·age /hármitij/ *n.* **1** a hermit's dwelling. **2** a monastery.

her·mit crab *n.* ▼ any crab of the family Paguridae that lives in a cast-off mollusk shell for protection.

discarded mollusk shell

HERMIT CRAB
(*Dardanus megistos*)

her·ni·a /hárneeə/ *n.* (*pl.* **hernias** or **herniae** /-nee-ee/) the protrusion of part of an organ through the wall of the cavity containing it, esp. of the abdomen. □□ **her·ni·al** *adj.* **her·ni·at·ed** *adj.*

he·ro /heerō/ *n.* (*pl.* **-oes**) **1** a person noted or admired for nobility, courage, outstanding achievements, etc. **2** the chief male character in a poem, play, story, etc. **3** *Gk Antiq.* a man of superhuman qualities, favored by the gods; a demigod. **4** *dial.* = SUBMARINE SANDWICH.

he·ro·ic /hiróik/ *adj. & n.* ● *adj.* **1 a** of or fit for a hero. **b** like a hero. **2 a** (of language) grand; dramatic. **b** (of a work of art) heroic in scale or subject. ● *n.* (in *pl.*) **1** high-flown language or sentiments. **2** unduly bold behavior. □□ **he·ro·i·cal·ly** *adv.*

her·o·in /héroin/ *n.* a highly addictive analgesic drug derived from morphine.

her·o·ine /héroin/ *n.* **1** a woman admired for courage, outstanding achievements, etc. **2** the chief female character in a play, story, etc.

her·o·ism /héroizəm/ *n.* heroic conduct or qualities.

her·on /hérən/ *n.* ◄ any of various large wading birds of the family Ardeidae, esp. *Ardea cinerea*, with long legs and a long S-shaped neck. □□ **her·on·ry** *n.* (*pl.* **-ies**).

her·o·wor·ship *n. & v.* ● *n.* **1** idealization of an admired man. **2** *Gk Antiq.* worship of the ancient heroes. ● *v.tr.* (**-worshiped, -worshiping** or **-worshipped, -worshipping**) worship as a hero; idolize. □□ **hero-wor·ship·er** *n.*

her·pes /hárpeez/ *n.* a virus disease with outbreaks of blisters on the skin, etc. □□ **her·pet·ic** /-pétik/ *adj.*

her·pes sim·plex *n.* a viral infection which may produce blisters or conjunctivitis.

HERON:
PURPLE HERON
(*Ardea purpurea*)

her·pes zos·ter /zóstər/ = SHINGLES.

her·pe·tol·o·gy /hárpitóləjee/ *n.* the study of reptiles. □□ **her·pe·to·log·i·cal** /-təlójikəl/ *adj.* **her·pe·tol·o·gist** *n.*

Herr /hair/ *n.* (*pl.* **Herren** /hérən/) **1** the title of a German man; Mr. **2** a German man.

Her·ren·volk /hérənfawlk/ *n.* **1** the German nation characterized by the Nazis as born to mastery. **2** a group regarding itself as naturally superior.

her·ring /héring/ *n.* a N. Atlantic fish, *Clupea harengus*, coming near the coast in large shoals to spawn.

her·ring·bone /héringbōn/ *n.* ▼ a stitch with a zigzag pattern, resembling the pattern of a herring's bones.

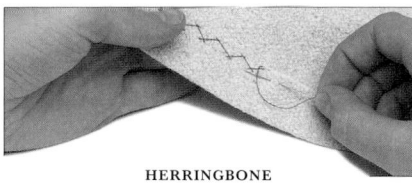

HERRINGBONE

hers /hərz/ *poss.pron.* the one or ones belonging to or associated with her (*it is hers; hers are over there*). □ **of hers** of or belonging to her (*a friend of hers*).

her·self /hərsélf/ *pron.* **1 a** *emphat. form* of SHE or HER (*she herself will do it*). **b** *refl. form* of HER (*she has hurt herself*). **2** in her normal state of body or mind (*does not feel quite herself today*). □ **be herself** act in her normal unconstrained manner. **by herself** see *by oneself*.

hertz /herts/ *n.* (*pl.* same) a unit of frequency, equal to one cycle per second.

he's /heez/ *contr.* **1** he is. **2** he has.

hes·i·tant /hézit'nt/ *adj.* hesitating; irresolute. □□ **hes·i·tance** /-təns/ *n.* **hes·i·tan·cy** *n.* **hes·i·tant·ly** *adv.*

hes·i·tate /hézitayt/ *v.intr.* **1** (often foll. by *about, over*) show or feel indecision or uncertainty (*hesitated over her choice*). **2** (often foll. by *to* + infin.) be reluctant (*I hesitate to inform against him*). □□ **hes·i·tat·ing·ly** *adv.* **hes·i·ta·tion** /-táyshən/ *n.*

hes·sian /héshən/ *n.* a strong coarse sacking made of hemp or jute.

het·er·o /hétərō/ *n.* (*pl.* **-os**) *colloq.* a heterosexual.

hetero- /hétərō/ *comb. form* other; different (often opp. HOMO-).

het·er·o·cy·clic /hétərōsíklik, -síklik/ *adj. Chem.* (of a compound) with a bonded ring of atoms of more than one kind.

het·er·o·dox /hétərədoks/ *adj.* (of a person, opinion, etc.) not orthodox. □□ **het·er·o·dox·y** *n.*

het·er·o·dyne /hétərədīn/ *adj. & v. Radio* ● *adj.* relating to the production of a lower frequency from the combination of two almost equal high frequencies. ● *v.intr.* produce a frequency in this way.

het·er·o·ge·ne·ous /hétərōjéeneeəs, -nyəs/ *adj.* **1** diverse in character. **2** varied in content. **3** *Math.* incommensurable through being of different kinds or degrees. □□ **het·er·o·ge·ne·i·ty** /-jinéeitee/ *n.* **het·er·o·ge·ne·ous·ly** *adv.* **het·er·o·ge·ne·ous·ness** *n.*

het·er·ol·o·gous /hétəróləgəs/ *adj.* not homologous. □□ **het·er·ol·o·gy** *n.*

het·er·o·mor·phic /hétərōmáwrfik/ *adj. Biol.* **1** of dissimilar forms. **2** (of insects) existing in different forms at different stages in their life cycle.

het·er·o·mor·phism /hétərōmáwrfizəm/ *n.* existing in various forms.

het·er·o·sex·u·al /hétərōsékshōōəl/ *adj. & n.* ● *adj.* **1** feeling or involving sexual attraction to persons of the opposite sex. **2** concerning heterosexual relations or people. ● *n.* a heterosexual person. □□ **het·er·o·sex·u·al·i·ty** /-shōōálitee/ *n.* **het·er·o·sex·u·al·ly** *adv.*

het up /hét úp/ *adj. colloq.* excited; overwrought.

heu·ris·tic /hyŏŏrístik/ *adj. & n.* ● *adj.* **1** allowing or assisting to discover. **2** *Computing* proceeding to a solution by trial and error. ● *n.* (in *pl.*, usu. treated as *sing.*) *Computing* the study and use of heuristic techniques in data processing. □□ **heu·ris·ti·cal·ly** *adv.*

HEW *abbr. US hist.* Department of Health, Education, and Welfare (1953–79).

hew /hyŏŏ/ *v.* (*past part.* **hewn** /hyŏŏn/ or **hewed**) **1** *tr.* **a** (often foll. by *down, away, off*) chop or cut (a thing) with an ax, a sword, etc. **b** cut (a block of wood, etc.) into shape. **2** *intr.* (often foll. by *at,*

among, etc.) strike cutting blows. **3** *intr.* (usu. foll. by *to*) conform. □ **hew one's way** make a way for oneself by hewing.

hex /heks/ *v. & n.* ● *v.* **1** *intr.* practice witchcraft. **2** *tr.* bewitch. ● *n.* **1** a magic spell. **2** a witch.

hexa- /héksə/ *comb. form* six.

hex·ad /héksad/ *n.* a group of six.

hex·a·dec·i·mal /héksədésiməl/ *adj. & n. esp. Computing* ● *adj.* relating to or using a system of numerical notation that has 16 rather than 10 as a base. ● *n.* the hexadecimal system; hexadecimal notation. □□ **hex·a·dec·i·mal·ly** *adv.*

hex·a·gon /héksəgon/ *n.* a plane figure with six sides and angles. □□ **hex·a·gon·al** /-ságənəl/ *adj.*

hex·a·gram /héksəgram/ *n.* **1** ▶ a figure formed by two intersecting equilateral triangles. **2** a figure of six lines.

HEXAGRAM

hex·a·he·dron /héksəheédrən/ *n.*

◀ a solid figure with six faces. □□ **hex·a·he·dral** *adj.*

HEXAHEDRON

hex·am·e·ter /heksámitər/ *n.* a line or verse of six metrical feet.

hex·ane /héksayn/ *n. Chem.* a liquid hydrocarbon of the alkane series.

hex·a·va·lent /héksəváylənt/ *adj.* having a valence of six; sexivalent.

hey /hay/ *int.* calling attention or expressing joy, surprise, inquiry, etc.

hey·day /háyday/ *n.* the flush or full bloom of youth, vigor, prosperity, etc.

HF *abbr.* high frequency.

Hf *symb. Chem.* the element hafnium.

hf. *abbr.* half.

Hg *symb. Chem.* the element mercury.

hg *abbr.* hectogram(s).

hgt. *abbr.* height.

hgwy. *abbr.* highway.

hh. *abbr.* hands (see HAND *n.* 13).

hhd. *abbr.* hogshead(s).

H-hour /áychowr/ *n.* the hour at which a military operation is scheduled to begin.

HHS *abbr.* (Department of) Health and Human Services.

HI *abbr.* **1** Hawaii (also in official postal use). **2** the Hawaiian Islands.

hi /hī/ *int.* expression of greeting.

hi·a·tus /hīáytəs/ *n.* (*pl.* **hiatuses**) **1** a break or gap, esp. in a series, account, or chain of proof. **2** *Prosody & Gram.* a break between two vowels coming together but not in the same syllable, as in *though oft the ear.* □□ **hi·a·tal** *adj.*

hi·ba·chi /həbáachee/ *n.* a small charcoal-burning brazier for grilling food.

hi·ber·nate /híbərnayt/ *v.intr.* **1** (of some animals) spend the winter in a dormant state. **2** remain inactive. □□ **hi·ber·na·tion** /-náyshən/ *n.* **hi·ber·na·tor** *n.*

Hi·ber·ni·an /hībérneeən/ *adj. & n. archaic poet.* ● *adj.* of or concerning Ireland. ● *n.* a native of Ireland.

hi·bis·cus /hibískəs/ *n.* ▶ any tree or shrub of the genus *Hibiscus*, cultivated for its large, brightly colored flowers. Also called **rose mallow.**

HIBISCUS: CHINESE HIBISCUS
(*Hibiscus rosa-sinensis*)

hic /hik/ *int.* expressing the sound of a hiccup, esp. a drunken hiccup.

hic·cup /híkup/ *n. & v.* (also **hic·cough**) ● *n.* **1** an involuntary spasm of the diaphragm and respiratory organs, with sudden closure of the glottis and characteristic coughlike sound. **2** a temporary or minor difficulty. ● *v. intr.* make a hiccup or series of hiccups.

hick /hik/ *n. colloq.* a country dweller; a provincial.

hick·ey /híkee/ *n.* (*pl.* **-eys**) *colloq.* a reddish mark on the skin produced by a sucking kiss.

hick·o·ry /híkəree/ *n.* (*pl.* **-ies**) **1** ▶ any N. American tree of the genus *Carya*, yielding tough heavy wood and bearing nutlike edible fruits (see PECAN). **2** the wood of these trees.

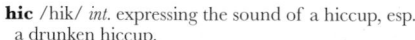

HICKORY:
SHAGBARK HICKORY
(*Carya ovata*)

male catkins

H

hid *past* of HIDE[1].

hi·dal·go /hidálgō, eetháalgō/ *n.* (*pl.* **-os**) a Spanish gentleman.

hid·den *past part.* of HIDE[1]

hid·den a·gen·da *n.* a secret motivation behind a policy, statement, etc.; an ulterior motive.

hide[1] /hīd/ *v.* (*past* **hid** /hid/; *past part.* **hidden** /hídən/ or *archaic* **hid**) **1** *tr.* put or keep out of sight. **2** *intr.* conceal oneself. **3** *tr.* (usu. foll. by *from*) keep (a fact) secret (*hid his real motive from her*). **4** *tr.* conceal (a thing) from sight (*trees hid the house*). □ **hide one's head** keep out of sight, esp. from shame. □□ **hid·den** *adj.* **hid·er** *n.*

hide[2] /hīd/ *n.* **1** the skin of an animal, esp. when tanned or dressed. **2** *colloq.* the human skin (*I'll tan your hide*). □□ **hid·ed** (also in *comb.*).

hide-and-seek *n.* **1** a children's game in which one or more players seek a child or children hiding. **2** a process of attempting to find an evasive person or thing.

hide·a·way /hídəway/ *n.* a hiding place or place of retreat.

hide·bound /hídbownd/ *adj.* **1 a** narrow-minded; bigoted. **b** (of the law, rules, etc.) constricted by tradition. **2** (of cattle) with the skin clinging close as a result of bad feeding.

hid·e·os·i·ty /hideeósitee/ *n.* (*pl.* **-ies**) **1** a hideous object. **2** hideousness.

hid·e·ous /hídeeəs/ *adj.* **1** frightful, repulsive, or revolting, to the senses or the mind (*a hideous monster; a hideous pattern*). **2** *colloq.* unpleasant. □□ **hid·e·ous·ly** *adv.* **hid·e·ous·ness** *n.*

hide·out *n. colloq.* a hiding place.

hid·ey-hole /hídeehōl/ *n. colloq.* a hiding place.

hid·ing[1] /híding/ *n. colloq.* a thrashing.

hid·ing[2] /híding/ *n.* **1** the act of hiding. **2** the state of remaining hidden (*go into hiding*).

hie /hī/ *v.intr. & refl.* (**hies, hied, hieing** or **hying**) *esp. archaic or poet.* go quickly (*hie to your chamber; hied him to the chase*).

hi·er·ar·chy /hí‌əraarkee/ *n.* (*pl.* **-ies**) **1 a** a system in which grades or classes of status or authority are ranked one above the other. **b** the hierarchical system (of government, management, etc.). **2 a** a priestly government. **b** a priesthood organized in grades. □□ **hi·er·ar·chic** *adj.* /-raárkik/ **hi·er·ar·chi·cal** *adj.*

hi·er·at·ic /hí‌ərátik/ *adj.* **1** of or concerning priests; priestly. **2** of the ancient Egyptian writing of abridged hieroglyphics as used by priests. □□ **hi·er·at·i·cal·ly** *adv.*

hiero- /hí‌ərō/ *comb. form* sacred; holy.

H

hi·er·o·glyph /hírəglif/ *n.* ▶ a picture of an object representing a word, syllable, or sound, as used in ancient Egyptian and other writing.

hi·er·o·glyph·ic /hírəglífik/ *adj. & n.* ● *adj.* **1** of or written in hieroglyphs. **2** symbolic. ● *n.* (in *pl.*) hieroglyphs; hieroglyphic writing.

hi-fi /hífi/ *adj. & n. colloq.* ● *adj.* of high fidelity. ● *n.* (*pl.* **hi-fis**) a set of equipment for high fidelity sound reproduction.

hig·gle·dy-pig·gle·dy /hígəldee-pígəldee/ *adv. & adj.* in confusion or disorder.

high /hī/ *adj., n., & adv.* ● *adj.* **1 a** of great vertical extent (*a high building*). **b** (*predic.*; often in *comb.*) of a specified height (*one inch high*). **2** far above ground or sea level, etc. (*a high altitude*). **3** extending above the normal or average level (*high boots*). **4** of exalted, esp. spiritual, quality (*high principles*). **5** of exalted rank (*high society*). **6 a** great; intense (*high praise; high temperature*). **b** greater than normal (*high prices*). **c** extreme in religious or political opinion (*high Tory*). **7** *colloq.* (often foll. by *on*) intoxicated by alcohol or esp. drugs. **8** (of a sound or note) of high frequency; shrill; at the top end of the scale. **9** (of a period, an age, a time, etc.) at its peak (*high noon; high summer; High Renaissance*). **10 a** (of meat) beginning to go bad; off. **b** (of game) well-hung and slightly decomposed. **11** *Geog.* (of latitude) near the North or South Pole. **12** *Phonet.* (of a vowel) close (see CLOSE¹ *adj.* 14). ● *n.* **1** a high, or the highest, level or figure. **2** an area of high barometric pressure. **3** *sl.* a eu-phoric drug-induced state. **4** top gear in a motor vehicle. **5** *colloq.* high school. ● *adv.* **1** far up; aloft (*flew the flag high*). **2** in or to a high degree. **3** at a high price. **4** (of a sound) at or to a high pitch (*sang high*). □ **from on high** from heaven or a high place. **high old** *colloq.* most enjoyable (*a high old time*). **high opinion of** a favorable opinion of. **in high feather** see FEATHER. **on high** in or to heaven or a high place. **on one's high horse** *colloq.* behaving superciliously or arrogantly. **run high 1** (of the sea) have a strong current with high tide. **2** (of feelings) be strong.

high and dry *adj.* **1** out of the current of events; stranded. **2** (of a ship) out of the water.

high and low *adv.* everywhere (*searched high and low*).

high and might·y *adj. colloq.* arrogant.

high·ball /híbawl/ *n.* a drink of liquor and soda, etc., served with ice in a tall glass.

high beam *n.* full, bright illumination from a motor vehicle's headlight.

high·born /híbáwrn/ *adj.* of noble birth.

high·boy /híboy/ *n.* a tall chest of drawers on legs.

high·brow /híbrow/ *adj. & n. colloq.* ● *adj.* intellectual; cultural. ● *n.* an intellectual or cultured person.

high chair *n.* an infant's chair with long legs and a tray, for use at meals.

high-class *adj.* of high quality.

high-con·cept *adj.* (esp. of a film or television plot) having a striking and easily communicable idea.

high·er court *n. Law* a court that can overrule the decision of another.

high·er-up *n. colloq.* a person of higher rank.

high·fa·lu·tin /hífəlootn/ *adj.* (also **high·fa·lu·ting** /-ing/) *colloq.* absurdly pompous or pretentious.

high fash·ion *n.* = HAUTE COUTURE.

high fi·del·i·ty *n.* the reproduction of sound with little distortion, giving a result very similar to the original.

high fi·nance *n.* financial transactions involving large sums.

---

high five *n.* gesture in which two people slap each other's raised palm, esp. out of elation.

high-flown *adj.* (of language, etc.) extravagant; bombastic.

high-fly·er *n.* (also **high-flier**) **1** an ambitious person. **2** a person or thing with great potential for achievement. □□ **high-fly·ing** *adj.*

high fre·quen·cy *n.* a frequency, esp. in radio, of 3 to 30 megahertz.

high gear *n.* a gear such that the driven end of a transmission revolves faster (or slower) than the driving end.

high-grade *adj.* of high quality.

high-hand·ed /híhándid/ *adj.* disregarding the feelings of others. □□ **high-hand·ed·ly** *adv.* **high-hand·ed·ness** *n.*

high-hat *adj. & v.* ● *adj.* supercilious; snobbish. ● *v.* (**-hatted**, **-hatting**) **1** *tr.* treat superciliously. **2** *intr.* assume a superior attitude.

high jinks *n.pl.* boisterous joking or merrymaking.

high jump *n.* an athletic event consisting of jumping as high as possible over a bar of adjustable height.

high·land /híland/ *n. & adj.* ● *n.* (usu. in *pl.*) **1** an area of high land. **2** (**the Highlands**) the mountainous part of Scotland. ● *adj.* of or in a highland or the Highlands. □□ **high·land·er** *n.* (also **High·land·er**).

High·land cat·tle *n.* **1** ▼ cattle of a shaggy-haired breed with long curved widely-spaced horns. **2** this breed.

HIGHLAND CATTLE: COW

high-lev·el *adj.* **1** (of negotiations, etc.) conducted by high-ranking people. **2** *Computing* (of a programming language) that is not machine-dependent and is usu. at a level of abstraction close to natural language.

high life *n.* (also **high living**) a luxurious existence ascribed to the upper classes.

high·light /hílīt/ *n. & v.* ● *n.* **1** (in a painting, etc.) a light area, or one seeming to reflect light. **2** a moment or detail of vivid interest; an outstanding feature. **3** (usu. in *pl.*) a bright tint in the hair produced by bleaching. ● *v.tr.* **1 a** draw attention to; bring into prominence. **b** mark with a highlighter. **2** create highlights in (the hair).

high·light·er /hílītər/ *n.* a marker pen that overlays color on a printed word, etc., leaving it legible and emphasized.

high·ly /hílee/ *adv.* **1** in a high degree (*highly amusing; highly probable; commend it highly*). **2** honorably; favorably (*think highly of him*). **3** in a high position or rank (*highly placed*). □ **highly-strung** = HIGH-STRUNG.

high-mind·ed /hímíndid/ *adj.* **1** having high moral principles. **2** proud. □□ **high-mind·ed·ly** *adv.* **high-mind·ed·ness** *n.*

high·ness /hínis/ *n.* **1** the state of being high (cf. HEIGHT). **2** (**Highness**) a title used in addressing and

---

referring to a prince or princess (*Her Highness; Your Royal Highness*).

high-oc·cu·pan·cy ve·hi·cle *n.* a commuter vehicle carrying several (or many) passengers.

high-oc·tane *adj.* (of gasoline, etc.) having good antiknock properties.

high-pitched *adj.* **1** (of a sound) high. **2** (of a roof) steep.

high-pow·ered *adj.* **1** having great power or energy. **2** important or influential.

high pres·sure *n.* **1** a high degree of activity or exertion. **2** a condition of the atmosphere with the pressure above average.

high priest *n.* **1** a chief priest, esp. in early Judaism. **2** the head of any cult.

high pro·file *n.* exposure to attention or publicity. □□ **high-pro·file** *adj.*

high-rank·ing *adj.* of high rank; senior.

high-rise *adj. & n.* ● *adj.* (of a building) having many stories. ● *n.* such a building.

high-risk *adj.* (usu. *attrib.*) involving or exposed to danger (*high-risk sports*).

high roll·er *n. sl.* a person who gambles large sums or spends freely.

high school *n.* a secondary school.

high seas *n.pl.* open seas not within any country's jurisdiction.

high sign *n. colloq.* a surreptitious gesture indicating that all is well or that the coast is clear.

high-speed *adj.* **1** operating at great speed. **2** (of steel) suitable for cutting tools even when red-hot.

high spir·its *n.pl.* vivacity; energy; cheerfulness. □□ **high-spir·it·ed** *adj.* **high-spir·it·ed·ness** *n.*

high-strung *adj.* very sensitive or nervous.

high·tail /hítayl/ *v.intr. colloq.* move at high speed, esp. in retreat.

high tech *n. & adj.* ● *n.* = HIGH TECHNOLOGY. ● *adj.* **1** (of interior design, etc.) imitating styles more usual in industry, etc., esp. using steel, glass, or plastic in a functional way. **2** employing, requiring, or involved in high technology.

high tech·nol·o·gy *n.* advanced technological development, esp. in electronics.

high ten·sion *n.* = HIGH-VOLTAGE.

high tide *n.* the time or level of the tide at its flow.

high time *n.* a time that is late or overdue (*it is high time they arrived*).

high tops *n.pl.* sports shoes or sneakers that cover the ankle.

high-volt·age *n.* electrical potential causing some danger of injury or damage.

high wa·ter *n.* **1** the tide at its fullest. **2** the time of this.

high-water mark *n.* the level reached at high water.

high·way /híway/ *n.* **1 a** a public road. **b** a main route (by land or water). **2** a direct course of action (*on the highway to success*).

high·way·man /híwaymən/ *n.* (*pl.* **-men**) *hist.* a robber of passengers, travelers, etc., usu. mounted.

high wire *n.* a high tightrope.

hi·jack /híjak/ *v. & n.* ● *v.tr.* **1** seize control of (a loaded truck, an aircraft in flight, etc.), usu. to force it to a different destination. **2** seize (goods) in transit. **3** take over (an organization, etc.) by force or subterfuge in order to redirect it. ● *n.* an instance of hijacking. □□ **hi·jack·er** *n.*

hij·ra var. of HEGIRA.

hike /hīk/ *n. & v.* ● *n.* **1** a long walk, esp. in the country or wilderness with backpacks, etc. **2** an increase (of prices, etc.). ● *v.* **1** *intr.* walk, esp. across country, for a long distance, esp. with boots, backpack, etc. **2** (usu. foll. by *up*) *tr.* hitch up (clothing, etc.); hoist; shove. **3** *tr.* increase (prices, etc.). □□ **hik·er** *n.*

hi·lar·i·ous /hiláireeəs/ *adj.* **1** exceedingly funny.

2 boisterously merry. □□ **hi·lar·i·ous·ly** *adv.* **hi·lar·i·ous·ness** *n.* **hi·lar·i·ty** /-lárítee/ *n.*

hill /hil/ *n.* **1** a naturally raised area of land, not as high as a mountain. **2** (often in *comb.*) a heap; a mound (*anthill; dunghill*). **3** a sloping piece of road. □ **old as the hills** very ancient. **over the hill** *colloq.* past the prime of life; declining.

hill·bil·ly /hílbilee/ *n.* (*pl.* **-ies**) *colloq.*, often *derog.* **1** a person from a remote or mountainous area, esp. in the Appalachian Mountains. **2** music of or like that originating in the Appalachian region.

hill·fort /hílfawrt/ *n.* ▼ a fort built on a hill.

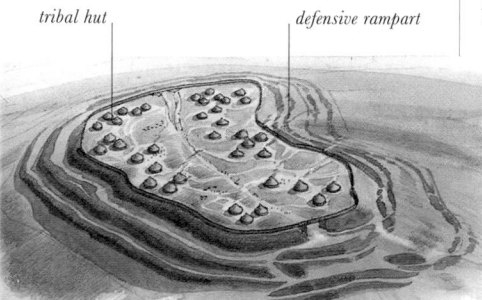

tribal hut

defensive rampart

HIILLFORT: IRON AGE HILLFORT, ENGLAND, *c.* 300 BC

hill·ock /hílək/ *n.* a small hill or mound. □□ **hill·ock·y** *adj.*

hill·side /hílsīd/ *n.* the sloping side of a hill.

hill·top /híltop/ *n.* the summit of a hill.

hill·walk·ing /hílwawking/ *n.* the pastime of walking in hilly country. □□ **hill·walk·er** *n.*

hill·y /hílee/ *adj.* (**hillier**, **hilliest**) having many hills. □□ **hill·i·ness** *n.*

hilt /hilt/ *n.* the handle of a sword, dagger, etc. ▷ SWORD. □ **up to the hilt** completely.

him /him/ *pron.* **1** objective case of HE (*I saw him*). **2** *colloq.* he (*it's him again; is taller than him*).

him·self /himsélf/ *pron.* **1 a** *emphat. form* of HE or HIM (*he himself will do it*). **b** *refl. form* of HIM (*he has hurt himself*). **2** in his normal state of body or mind (*does not feel quite himself today*). □ **be himself** act in his normal unconstrained manner. **by himself** see *by oneself.*

hind¹ /hīnd/ *adj.* (esp. of parts of the body) situated at the back (*hind leg*).

hind² /hīnd/ *n.* a female deer (usu. a red deer).

hind·er¹ /híndər/ *v.tr.* (also *absol.*) impede; delay; prevent.

hind·er² /híndər/ *adj.* rear; hind (*the hinder part*).

Hin·di /híndee/ *n. & adj.* ● *n.* **1** a group of spoken dialects of N. India. **2** a literary form of Hindustani with a Sanskrit-based vocabulary, an official language of India. ● *adj.* of or concerning Hindi.

hind·most /híndmōst/ *adj.* farthest behind.

hind·quar·ters /híndkwáwrtərz/ *n.pl.* the hind legs and adjoining parts of a quadruped.

hin·drance /híndrəns/ *n.* **1** the act of hindering. **2** a thing that hinders; an obstacle.

hind·sight /híndsīt/ *n.* wisdom after the event (*realized with hindsight that they were wrong*).

Hin·du /híndoo/ *n. & adj.* ● *n.* a follower of Hinduism. ● *adj.* of or concerning Hindus or Hinduism.

Hin·du·ism /híndooizm/ *n.* the main religious and social system of India, including belief in reincarnation and the worship of several gods. □□ **Hin·du·ize** *v.tr.*

Hin·du·sta·ni /híndoostáanee, -stánee/ *n. & adj.* ● *n.* a language based on Western Hindi, with elements of Arabic, Persian, etc., used as a lingua franca in much of India. ● *adj.* of or relating to Hindustan or its people, or Hindustani.

hinge /hinj/ *n. & v.* ● *n.* **1 a** a movable joint by which a door is hung on a side post. **b** *Biol.* a

natural joint performing a similar function, e.g., that of a bivalve shell. **2** a central point or principle on which everything depends. ● *v.* **1** *intr.* (foll. by *on*) depend (on a principle, an event, etc.) (*all hinges on his acceptance*). **2** *tr.* attach with or as if with a hinge. □□ **hinged** *adj.* **hinge·less** *adj.*

hin·ny /hínee/ *n.* (*pl.* **-ies**) the offspring of a female donkey and a male horse.

hint /hint/ *n. & v.* ● *n.* **1** a slight or indirect indication or suggestion (*took the hint and left*). **2** a small piece of practical information (*handy hints on cooking*). **3** a very small trace; a suggestion (*a hint of perfume*). ● *v.tr.* (often foll. by *that* + clause) suggest slightly (*hinted that they were near*). □ **hint at** give a hint of; refer indirectly to.

hin·ter·land /híntərland/ *n.* **1** the areas beyond a coastal district or a river's banks. **2** a remote area served by a port or other center.

hip¹ /hip/ *n.* a projection of the pelvis and upper thigh bone on each side of the body. ▷ HIP JOINT. □□ **hipped** *adj.* (also in comb.).

hip² /hip/ *n.* ► the fruit of a rose.

hip³ /hip/ *adj.* (also **hep** /hep/) (**hipper**, **hippest** or **hepper**, **heppest**) *sl.* following the latest fashion in music, clothes, etc. □□ **hip·ness** *n.*

hip⁴ /hip/ *int.* introducing a united cheer (*hip, hip, hooray*).

hip·bone /hípbōn/ *n.* a bone forming the hip.

hip-hop *n.* a style of urban youth rock music or the street subculture surrounding it (typically including graffiti art, rap, and break dancing).

hip-hug·gers *n.pl.* trousers hanging from the hips.

hip joint *n.* ▼ the articulation of the head of the thigh bone with the ilium. ▷ JOINT

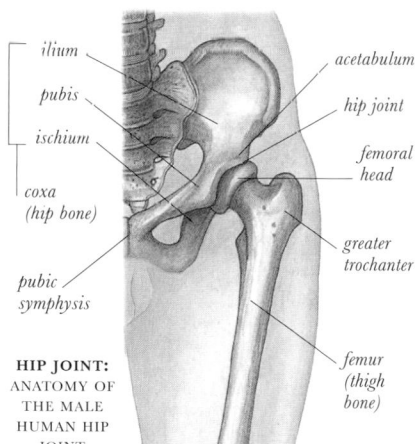

HIP:
ROSE HIPS
(*Rosa rugosa*)

ilium

pubis

ischium

coxa
(hip bone)

pubic
symphysis

acetabulum

hip joint

femoral
head

greater
trochanter

femur
(thigh
bone)

HIP JOINT:
ANATOMY OF
THE MALE
HUMAN HIP
JOINT

hip·pie /hípee/ *n.* (also **hip·py**) (*pl.* **-ies**) *colloq.* (esp. in the 1960s) a person with long hair, jeans, beads, etc., often associated with hallucinogenic drugs and a rejection of conventional values.

hip·po /hípō/ *n.* (*pl.* **-os**) *colloq.* a hippopotamus.

hip·po·cam·pus /hipōkámpəs/ *n. Anat.* a curving strand of tissue lying deep within the cerebral cortex in each hemisphere of the brain, that functions in the feeling and expression of emotions and in memory. ▷ BRAIN

Hip·po·crat·ic oath /hípəkrátik/ *n.* an oath taken by doctors affirming their obligations and proper conduct.

hip·po·drome /hípədrōm/ *n.* an arena used for equestrian or other sporting events.

hip·po·pot·a·mus /hipəpótəməs/ *n.* (*pl.* **hippopotamuses** or **hippopotami** /-mī/) a large thick-

skinned four-legged mammal, *Hippopotamus amphibius*, native to Africa, inhabiting rivers, lakes, etc.

hip·py¹ var. of HIPPIE.

hip·py² /hípee/ *adj.* having large hips.

hip roof *n.* (also **hipped**) ▼ a roof with the sides and the ends inclined.

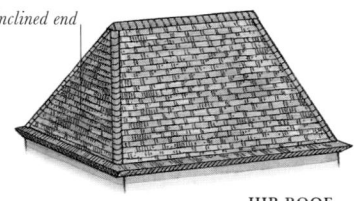

inclined end

HIP ROOF

hip·ster /hípstər/ *n. sl.* a person who is stylish or hip. □□ **hip·ster·ism** *n.*

hire /hīr/ *v. & n.* ● *v.tr.* **1** employ (a person). **2** (often foll. by *from*) procure the temporary use of (a thing) for an agreed payment. ● *n.* **1** hiring or being hired. **2** esp. *Brit.* payment for this. □ **for hire** ready to be hired. □□ **hir·a·ble** *adj.* (also **hire·a·ble**). **hir·er** *n.*

hired gun *n. N. Amer. colloq.* **1** an expert brought in to resolve legal or financial problems or disputes. **2** a lobbyist on behalf of others. **3** a bodyguard. **4** a mercenary or hired assassin.

hire·ling /hírling/ *n. usu. derog.* a person who works for hire.

hir·sute /hórsyoot/ *adj.* hairy; shaggy. □□ **hir·sute·ness** *n.*

his /hiz/ *poss.pron.* **1** (*attrib.*) of or belonging to him (*his house*). **2** the one or ones belonging to or associated with him (*it is his; his are over there*). □ **of his** of or belonging to him (*a friend of his*).

His·pan·ic /hispánik/ *adj. & n.* ● *adj.* **1** of or being a person of Latin-American or Spanish or Portuguese descent in the US. **2** of or relating to Spain or other Spanish-speaking countries. ● *n.* a Spanish-speaking person, esp. one of Latin-American descent, living in the US. □□ **His·pan·i·cize** /-nísīz/ *v.tr.*

hiss /his/ *v. & n.* ● *v.* **1** *intr. & tr.* (of a person, snake, etc.) make a sharp sibilant sound, esp. as a sign of disapproval (*audience booed and hissed*). **2** *tr.* whisper (a threat, etc.) angrily. ● *n.* **1** a sharp sibilant sound as of the letter *s*, esp. as an expression of disapproval. **2** *Electronics* unwanted interference at audio frequencies.

hiss·y fit /hísee fit/ *n. N. Amer. colloq.* an angry outburst; a temper tantrum.

his·ta·mine /hístəmin, -meen/ *n. Biochem.* an organic compound occurring in injured body tissues, etc., and also associated with allergic reactions. □□ **his·ta·min·ic** /-mínik/ *adj.*

his·to·gram /hístəgram/ *n. Statistics* ▼ a chart consisting of rectangles (usu. drawn vertically from a base line) whose areas and positions are proportional to the value or range of a number of variables.

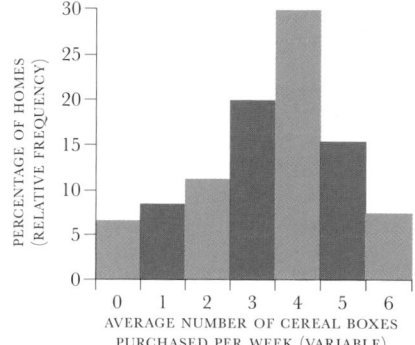

HISTOGRAM SHOWING RATE OF CEREAL
PURCHASES PER HOUSEHOLD

H

his·tol·o·gy /históləjee/ *n.* the study of the structure of tissues. □□ **his·to·log·i·cal** /hístəlójikəl/ *adj.* **his·tol·o·gist** /históləjist/ *n.*

his·tol·y·sis /histólisis/ *n.* the breaking down of tissues. □□ **his·to·lyt·ic** /-təlítik/ *adj.*

his·tone /hístōn/ *n. Biochem.* any of a group of proteins found in chromatin.

his·to·ri·an /hïstáwreeən/ *n.* **1** a writer of history. **2** a person learned in or studying history.

his·tor·ic /hïstáwrik, -stór-/ *adj.* **1** important in history or potentially so (*a historic moment*). **2** *Gram.* (of a tense) normally used in the narration of past events.

his·tor·i·cal /hïstáwrikəl, -stór-/ *adj.* **1** of or concerning history (*historical evidence*). **2** belonging to history, not to prehistory or legend. **3** (of the study of a subject) based on an analysis of its development over a period. **4** belonging to the past, not the present. **5** (of a novel, a movie, etc.) dealing or professing to deal with historical events. **6** in connection with history (*of purely historical interest*). □□ **his·tor·i·cal·ly** *adv.*

his·tor·i·cism /hïstáwrisizəm, -stór-/ *n.* **1** the theory that social and cultural phenomena are determined by history. **2** the belief that historical events are governed by laws. □□ **his·tor·i·cist** *n.*

his·to·ric·i·ty /hïstərísitee/ *n.* the historical genuineness of an event, etc.

his·to·ri·og·ra·pher /hïstáwreeógrəfər/ *n.* **1** an ex-

pert in historiography. **2** a writer of history, esp. an official historian.

his·to·ri·og·ra·phy /hïstáwreeógrəfee/ *n.* **1** the writing of history. **2** the study of historical writing. □□ **his·to·ri·o·graph·ic** /-reeəgráfik/ *adj.* **his·to·ri·o·graph·i·cal** *adj.*

his·to·ry /hístəree/ *n. (pl.* **-ies**) **1** a continuous, usu. chronological, record of important or public events. **2 a** the study of past events, esp. human affairs. **b** the total accumulation of past events, esp. relating to human affairs or a particular nation, person, thing, etc. (*the history of astronomy*). **3** an eventful past (*this house has a history*). **4 a** a systematic account of a past event or events, etc. **b** a similar account of natural phenomena. **5** a historical play. □ **make history** do something memorable.

his·tri·on·ic /hístreeónik/ *adj. & n.* ● *adj.* (of behavior) theatrical; dramatic. ● *n.* (in *pl.*) insincere and dramatic behavior designed to impress. □□ **his·tri·on·i·cal·ly** *adv.*

hit /hit/ *v. & n.* ● *v.* (**hitting**; *past* and *past part.* **hit**) **1** *tr.* **a** strike with a blow or a missile. **b** (of a moving body) strike (*the plane hit the ground*). **c** reach (a target, a person, etc.) with a directed missile (*hit the window with the ball*). **2** *tr.* cause to suffer or affect adversely. **3** *intr.* (often foll. by *at, against*) direct a blow. **4** *tr.* (often foll. by *against, on*) knock (a part of the body) (*hit his head on the door frame*). **5** *tr.* light upon (*he's hit the truth at last*) (see **hit on**). **6** *tr. colloq.* **a** encounter (*hit a snag*). **b** arrive at (*hit an all-time low*). **c** indulge in,

esp. liquor, etc. (*hit the bottle*). **7** *tr. sl.* rob or kill. **8** *tr.* occur forcefully to (*the seriousness of the situation only hit him later*). **9** *tr. Sports* **a** propel (a ball, etc.) with a bat, etc. **b** score (runs, etc.) in this way. **c** (usu. foll. by *for*) strike (a ball or a pitcher, etc.) for a specific hit, result, etc. **10** *tr.* represent exactly. ● *n.* **1 a** a blow; a stroke. **b** a collision. **2** a shot, etc., that hits its target. **3** *colloq.* a popular success in entertainment. **4** *sl.* **a** a murder or other violent crime. **b** a drug injection, etc. **7** a successful attempt. **8** *Baseball* = BASE HIT. □ **hit and run a** cause (accidental or willful) damage and escape or leave the scene before being discovered. **b** *Baseball* play in which a base runner begins running to the next base as the pitcher delivers the ball and the batter then tries to hit the thrown ball. **hit back** retaliate. **hit below the belt 1** esp. *Boxing* give a foul blow. **2** treat or behave unfairly. **hit home** make a salutary impression. **hit it off** (often foll. by *with*) agree or be congenial. **hit the nail on the head** state the truth exactly. **hit on** (or **upon**) find (what is sought), esp. by chance. **hit out** deal vigorous physical or verbal blows (*hit out at her enemies*). **hit the road** (or **trail**) *sl.* depart. **hit the roof** see ROOF. **make a hit** (usu. foll. by *with*) be successful or popular. □□ **hit·ter** *n.*

hitch /hich/ *v. & n.* ● *v.* **1 a** *tr.* fasten with a loop, hook, etc. (*hitched the horse to the cart*). **b** *intr.* (often foll. by *in, onto*, etc.) become fastened in this way (*the rod hitched in to the bracket*). **2** *tr.* move (a thing) with a jerk

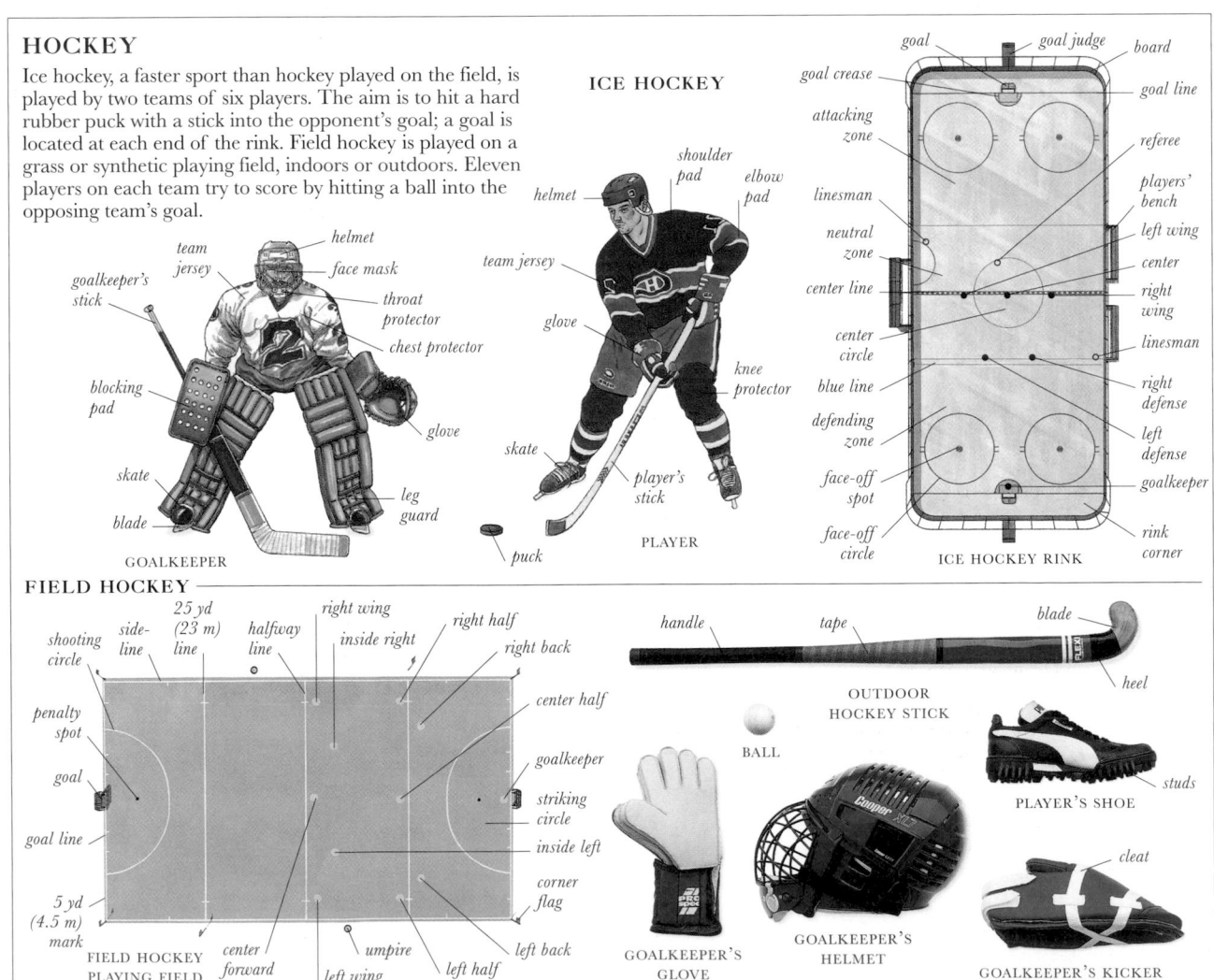

HOCKEY

Ice hockey, a faster sport than hockey played on the field, is played by two teams of six players. The aim is to hit a hard rubber puck with a stick into the opponent's goal; a goal is located at each end of the rink. Field hockey is played on a grass or synthetic playing field, indoors or outdoors. Eleven players on each team try to score by hitting a ball into the opposing team's goal.

ICE HOCKEY

GOALKEEPER — goalkeeper's stick, team jersey, helmet, face mask, throat protector, chest protector, blocking pad, glove, skate, blade, leg guard

PLAYER — helmet, shoulder pad, elbow pad, team jersey, glove, knee protector, skate, player's stick, puck

ICE HOCKEY RINK — goal, goal judge, board, goal crease, goal line, attacking zone, referee, linesman, players' bench, neutral zone, left wing, center, center line, right wing, center circle, linesman, blue line, right defense, defending zone, left defense, face-off spot, goalkeeper, face-off circle, rink corner

FIELD HOCKEY

FIELD HOCKEY PLAYING FIELD — 25 yd (23 m) line, right wing, right half, shooting circle, side-line, halfway line, inside right, right back, penalty spot, center half, goal, goalkeeper, goal line, striking circle, inside left, corner flag, 5 yd (4.5 m) mark, center forward, umpire, left back, left wing, left half

OUTDOOR HOCKEY STICK — handle, tape, blade, heel

BALL

GOALKEEPER'S GLOVE

GOALKEEPER'S HELMET

PLAYER'S SHOE — studs

GOALKEEPER'S KICKER — cleat

HOE

Every hoe has a sharp blade, fashioned in a particular shape to suit its purpose, whether for weeding, drawing up earth around plants, breaking up hard soil, or making seed drills.

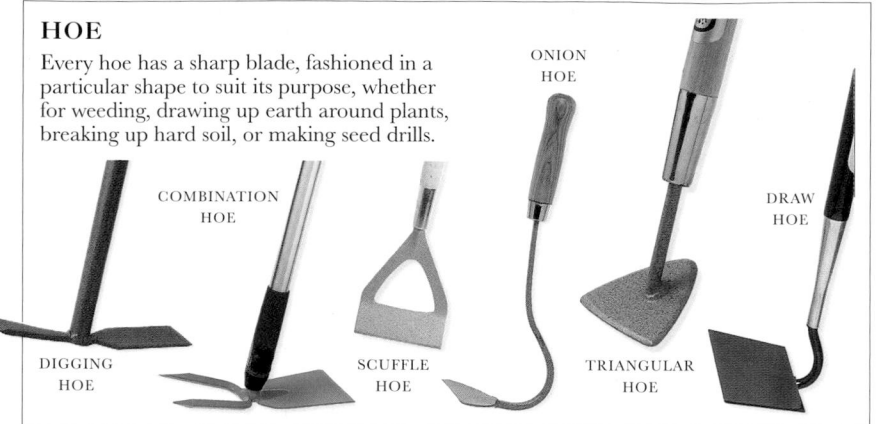

COMBINATION HOE

ONION HOE

DRAW HOE

DIGGING HOE

SCUFFLE HOE

TRIANGULAR HOE

(*hitched the pillow to a comfortable position*). **3** *colloq.* **a** *intr.* = HITCHHIKE. **b** *tr.* obtain (a ride) by hitchhiking. ● *n.* **1** a temporary obstacle. **2** an abrupt pull or push. **3** a noose or knot of various kinds. ▷ KNOT. **4** *colloq.* a free ride in a vehicle. □ **get hitched** *colloq.* marry. **hitch up** lift (esp. clothing) with a jerk. □□ **hitch·er** *n.*

hit-and-run *attrib. adj.* relating to or (of a person) committing an act or play of this kind.

hitch·hike /hích-hīk/ *v. & n.* ● *v.intr.* travel by seeking free rides in passing vehicles. ● *n.* a journey made by hitchhiking. □□ **hitch·hik·er** *n.*

hi-tech /hítek/ *adj.* = HIGH TECH.

hith·er /híthər/ *adv.* usu. *formal* or *literary* to or toward this place.

hith·er·to /híthərtōō/ *adv.* until this time; up to now.

hit list *n. sl.* a list of prospective victims.

hit man *n.* (*pl.* **hit men**) *sl.* a hired assassin.

hit-or-miss *adj.* aimed or done carelessly.

hit pa·rade *n. colloq.* a list of the current best-selling records of popular music.

Hit·tite /hítīt/ *n. & adj.* ● *n.* **1** a member of an ancient people of Asia Minor and Syria. **2** the extinct language of the Hittites. ● *adj.* of or relating to the Hittites or their language.

HIV *abbr.* human immunodeficiency virus, a retrovirus causing AIDS.

hive /hīv/ *n.* **1** a beehive. **2** a busy swarming place.

hives /hīvz/ *n.pl.* a skin eruption, esp. nettle rash.

hiya /híyə/ *int. colloq.* a word used in greeting.

hl *abbr.* hectoliter(s).

HM *abbr. Brit.* **1** Her (or His) Majesty('s). **2 a** headmaster. **b** headmistress.

hm *abbr.* hectometer(s).

h'm /hm/ *int. & n.* (also **hmm**) = HEM[2], HUM[2].

HMO *abbr.* health maintenance organization.

Ho *symb. Chem.* the element holmium.

ho /hō/ *int.* **1 a** an expression of surprise, triumph, or (often repeated as **ho! ho!**, etc.) derision. **b** (in *comb.*) (*heigh-ho*; *what ho*). **2** a call for attention.

hoa·gie /hṓgee/ *n.* (also **hoa·gy**) (*pl.* **-ies**) = SUBMARINE SANDWICH.

hoard /hawrd/ *n. & v.* ● *n.* **1** a stock or supply (esp. of money) stored for future use. **2** an amassed store of facts, etc. **3** *Archaeol.* an ancient store of treasure, etc. ● *v.* **1** *tr.* (often *absol.*; often foll. by *up*) amass (money, etc.) and put away. **2** *intr.* accumulate more than one's current requirements of food, etc., in a time of scarcity. □□ **hoard·er** *n.*

hoard·ing /háwrding/ *n.* a board fence erected around a building site, etc., often used for displaying posters, etc.

hoar·frost /háwrfrawst/ *n.* frozen water vapor deposited on vegetation, etc., in clear still weather.

hoarse /hawrs/ *adj.* **1** (of the voice) rough and deep. **2** having such a voice. □□ **hoarse·ly** *adv.* **hoars·en** *v.tr. & intr.* **hoarse·ness** *n.*

---

hoar·y /háwree/ *adj.* (**hoarier, hoariest**) **1 a** (of hair) gray or white with age. **b** having such hair. **2** old and trite (*a hoary joke*). □□ **hoar·i·ly** *adv.* **hoar·i·ness** *n.*

hoax /hōks/ *n. & v.* ● *n.* a humorous or malicious deception. ● *v.tr.* deceive (a person) with a hoax. □□ **hoax·er** *n.*

hob[1] /hob/ *n.* **1** a flat metal shelf at the side of a fireplace, used esp. for keeping things warm. **2** = HOBNAIL.

hob[2] /hob/ *n.* **1** a male ferret. **2** a hobgoblin. □ **play** (or **raise**) **hob** cause mischief.

hob·bit /hóbit/ *n.* a member of an imaginary race of half-sized people in stories by Tolkien.

hob·ble /hóbəl/ *v. & n.* ● *v.* **1** *intr.* walk lamely; limp. **2** *tr.* tie together the legs of (a horse, etc.) to prevent it from straying. ● *n.* **1** an uneven or infirm gait. **2** a rope, etc., used for hobbling a horse, etc. ▷ TROTTING. □□ **hob·bler** *n.*

hob·ble·de·hoy /hóbəldeehoy/ *n. colloq.* **1** a clumsy or awkward youth. **2** a hooligan.

hob·by[1] /hóbee/ *n.* (*pl.* **-ies**) a favorite leisure time activity or occupation. □□ **hob·by·ist** *n.*

hob·by[2] /hóbee/ *n.* (*pl.* **-ies**) any of several small long-winged falcons, esp. *Falco subbuteo.*

hob·by·horse /hóbeehawrs/ *n.* **1** a child's toy consisting of a stick with a horse's head. **2** a preoccupation; a favorite topic of conversation.

hob·gob·lin /hóbgoblin/ *n.* a mischievous imp; a bogy; a bugbear.

hob·nail /hóbnayl/ *n.* a heavy-headed nail used for boot soles. □□ **hob·nailed** *adj.*

hob·nob /hóbnob/ *v.intr.* (**hobnobbed, hobnobbing**) (usu. foll. by *with*) mix socially or informally.

ho·bo /hṓbō/ *n.* (*pl.* **-oes** or **-os**) a wandering worker; a tramp.

Hob·son's choice /hóbsənz/ *n.* a choice of taking the thing offered or nothing.

hock[1] /hok/ *n.* **1** the joint of a quadruped's hind leg between the knee and the fetlock. ▷ HORSE. **2** a knuckle of pork; the lower joint of a ham.

hock[2] /hok/ *n. Brit.* a German white wine from the Rhineland.

hock[3] /hok/ *v. & n. colloq.* ● *v.tr.* pawn; pledge. ● *n.* a pawnbroker's pledge. □ **in hock 1** in pawn. **2** in debt.

ho·cus /hṓkəs/ *v.tr.* (**hocussed, hocussing**; also **hocused, hocusing**) **1** take in; hoax. **2** stupefy (a person, animal, etc.) with drugs. **3** drug (liquor).

ho·cus-po·cus /hṓkəspṓkəs/ *n.* **1** deception; trickery. **2** a typical verbal formula used in conjuring.

hod /hod/ *n.* **1** a V-shaped open trough on a pole used for carrying bricks, mortar, etc. **2** a portable receptacle for coal.

hodge·podge /hójpoj/ *n.* a confused mixture, a jumble.

---

hoe /hō/ *n. & v.* ● *n.* ◀ a long-handled tool with a thin metal blade, used for weeding, etc. ● *v.* (**hoes, hoed, hoeing**) **1** *tr.* weed (crops); loosen (earth); dig up or cut down with a hoe. **2** *intr.* use a hoe. □□ **ho·er** *n.*

hoe·cake /hṓkayk/ *n.* a coarse cake of cornmeal orig. baked on the blade of a hoe.

hoe·down /hṓdown/ *n.* a lively dance or dance party, esp. one with square dancing.

hog /hawg, hog/ *n. & v.* ● *n.* **1 a** a domesticated pig, esp. one over 120 pounds and reared for slaughter. **b** any of several other pigs of the family Suidae, e.g., a warthog. **2** *colloq.* a greedy person. ● *v.* (**hogged, hogging**) *tr. colloq.* take greedily; hoard selfishly. □ **go the whole hog** *colloq.* do something completely or thoroughly. □□ **hog·ger** *n.* **hog·gish** *adj.* **hog·gish·ly** *adv.* **hog·gish·ness** *n.* **hog·like** *adj.*

ho·gan /hṓgaan, -gən/ *n.* a Navajo dwelling of logs, etc.

hog·back /háwgbak, hóg-/ *n.* (also **hog's back**) a steep-sided ridge of a hill. ▷ ERODE.

hog hea·ven *n. colloq.*, chiefly *N. Amer.* a place or condition of foolish or idle bliss.

Hog·ma·nay /hógmənáy/ *n. Sc.* **1** New Year's Eve. **2** a celebration on this day.

hog's back var. of HOGBACK.

hogs·head /háwgz-hed, hógz/ *n.* **1** a large cask. **2** a liquid or dry measure, usu. about 63 gallons.

hog-tie *v.tr.* **1** secure by fastening the hands and feet or all four feet together. **2** restrain; impede.

hog·wash /háwgwosh, -wawsh, hóg-/ *n.* **1** *colloq.* nonsense; rubbish. **2** kitchen swill, etc., for pigs.

hog·weed /háwgweed, hóg-/ *n.* ◀ any of various coarse weeds of the genus *Heracleum*, esp. *H. sphondylium.*

ho-hum /hṓhúm/ *int.* expressing boredom.

hoi pol·loi /hóy pəlóy/ *n.* (often prec. by *the*: see note below) the masses; the common people. ¶ Use with *the* is strictly unnecessary, since *hoi* = 'the,' but this construction is very common.

HOGWEED
(*Heracleum sphondylium*)

hoist /hoyst/ *v. & n.*
● *v.tr.* **1** raise or haul up. **2** raise by means of ropes and pulleys, etc. ● *n.* **1** an act of hoisting. **2** ▶ an apparatus for hoisting. **3** the part of a flag nearest the staff. □ **hoist with one's own petard** see PETARD. □□ **hoist·er** *n.*

hoi·ty-toi·ty /hóyteetóytee/ *adj.* haughty; petulant; snobbish.

hok·ey /hṓkee/ *adj.* (also **hok·y**) (**hokier, hokiest**) *sl.* sentimental; melodramatic; artificial. □□ **hok·ey·ness** *n.*

ho·key-po·key /hṓkeepṓkee/ *n. colloq.* **1** = HOCUS-POCUS. **2** a communal dance that is performed in a circle with synchronized shaking of the limbs in turn.

ho·kum /hṓkəm/ *n. sl.* **1** sentimental, popular, sensational, or unreal situations, dialogue, etc., in a movie or play. **2** bunkum; rubbish.

hok·y var. of HOKEY.

Hol·arc·tic /hōláarktik, -láartik/ *adj.* of or relating to the geographical distribution of animals in the whole northern or Arctic region.

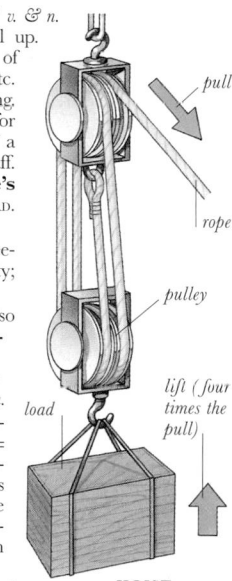

pull

rope

pulley

lift (*four times the pull*)

load

HOIST

H

hold[1] /hōld/ *v. & n.* • *v.* (*past* and *past part.* **held** /held/) **1** *tr.* **a** grasp (esp. in the hands or arms). **b** (also *refl.*) sustain (a thing, oneself, one's head, etc.) in a particular position (*hold it to the light*; *held himself erect*). **c** grasp so as to control (*hold the reins*). **2** *tr.* (of a vessel, etc.) contain or be capable of containing (*the pitcher holds two pints*). **3** *tr.* possess or have, esp.: **a** be the owner or tenant of (land, property, etc.) (*holds the farm from the trust*). **b** gain or have gained (a degree, record, etc.) (*holds the long-jump record*). **c** have the position of (a job or office). **d** have (a specified card) in one's hand. **e** keep possession of (a place, a person's thoughts, etc.) esp. against attack (*held the fort against the enemy*; *held his place in her estimation*). **4** *intr.* remain unbroken (*the roof held under the storm*). **5** *tr.* observe; conduct (a meeting, festival, conversation, etc.). **6** *tr.* **a** keep (a person, etc.) in a specified condition, place, etc. (*held her prisoner*). **b** detain, esp. in custody (*hold him until I arrive*). **7** *tr.* **a** engross (a person or a person's attention) (*the book held him for hours*). **b** dominate (*held the stage*). **8** *tr.* (foll. by *to*) make (a person, etc.) adhere to (terms, a promise, etc.). **9** *intr.* (of weather) continue fine. **10** *tr.* (often foll. by *to* + infin., or *that* + clause) believe (*held it to be self-evident*). **11** *tr.* regard with a specified feeling (*held him in contempt*). **12** *tr.* **a** cease (*hold your fire*). **b** *colloq.* withhold (*a burger please, and hold the onions!*). **13** *tr.* keep or reserve (*will you hold our seats please?*). **14** *tr.* be able to drink (liquor) without effect (*can hold his liquor*). **15** *tr.* (usu. foll. by *that* + clause) (of a judge, a court, etc.) lay down; decide. **16** *tr. Mus.* sustain (a note). **17** *intr. archaic* restrain oneself. • *n.* **1** a grasp (*catch hold of him*; *keep a hold on her*). **2** (often in *comb.*) a thing to hold by (*seized the handhold*). **3** (foll. by *on*, *over*) influence over (*has a strange hold over them*). **4** a manner of holding in wrestling, etc. **5** *archaic* a fortress. □ **hold (a thing) against (a person)** resent or regard it as discreditable to (a person). **hold aloof** avoid communication with people, etc. **hold back** **1** impede the progress of. **2** keep (a thing) for oneself. **3** (often foll. by *from*) hesitate. **hold one's breath** see BREATH. **hold court** preside over one's admirers, etc. **hold dear** regard with affection. **hold down** **1** repress. **2** *colloq.* be competent enough to keep (one's job, etc.). **hold everything!** (or **it!**) cease action or movement. **hold for ransom** **1** keep (a person) prisoner until a ransom is paid. **2** demand concessions from by threats of damaging action. **hold the fort** **1** act as a temporary substitute. **2** cope in an emergency. **hold forth** **1** offer (an inducement, etc.). **2** usu. *derog.* speak at length. **hold good** (or **true**) be valid; apply. **hold one's ground** see GROUND[1]. **hold a person's hand** give a person guidance or moral support. **hold hands** grasp one another by the hand as a sign of affection or for support. **hold one's head high** behave proudly and confidently. **hold one's horses** *colloq.* stop; slow down. **hold in** keep in check. **hold the line** **1** not yield. **2** maintain a telephone connection. **hold off** **1** delay; not begin. **2** keep one's distance. **hold on** **1** keep one's grasp on something. **2** wait a moment. **3** (when telephoning) not hang up. **hold out** **1** stretch forth (a hand, etc.). **2** offer (an inducement, etc.). **3** maintain resistance. **4** persist or last. **hold out for** continue to demand. **hold out on** *colloq.* refuse something to (a person). **hold over** postpone. **hold something over** threaten (a person) constantly with something. **hold one's own** see OWN. **hold together** **1** cohere. **2** cause to cohere. **hold one's tongue** *colloq.* be silent. **hold up** **1** **a** support; sustain. **b** maintain (the head, etc.) erect. **2** exhibit; display. **3** arrest the progress of. **4** stop and rob by violence or threats. **hold water** (of reasoning) be sound; bear examination. **hold with** (usu. with *neg.*) *colloq.* approve of (*don't hold with motorcycles*). **on hold** **1** temporarily deferred. **2** (of a telephone call or caller) holding on (see hold on 3 above). **take hold** (of a custom or habit) become established. **there is no holding him** (or **her**, etc.) he (or she, etc.) is high-spirited, determined, etc. **with no holds barred** with no restrictions. □□ **hold·a·ble** *adj.*

hold[2] /hōld/ *n.* a cavity in the lower part of a ship or aircraft in which the cargo is stored. ▷ FACTORY SHIP

hold·all /hṓldawl/ *n.* esp. *Brit.* a portable case for miscellaneous articles.

hold·er /hṓldər/ *n.* **1** (often in *comb.*) a device for holding something (*cigarette holder*). **2** **a** the possessor of a title, etc. **b** the occupant of an office, etc.

hold·ing /hṓlding/ *n.* **1** land held by lease. **2** stocks, property, etc., held.

hold·ing com·pa·ny *n.* a company created to hold the shares of other companies, which it then controls.

hold·up /hṓldəp/ *n.* **1** a stoppage or delay by traffic, fog, etc. **2** a robbery, esp. by the use of threats or violence.

hole /hōl/ *n. & v.* • *n.* **1** **a** an empty space in a solid body. **b** an aperture in or through something. **2** an animal's burrow. **3** a cavity or receptacle for a ball in various sports or games. ▷ GOLF. **4** *colloq.* a small, mean, or dingy abode. **5** *colloq.* an awkward situation. **6** *Golf* **a** a point scored by a player who gets the ball from tee to hole with the fewest strokes. **b** the terrain or distance from tee to hole. **7** a position from which an electron is absent, esp. acting as a mobile positive particle in a semiconductor. • *v.tr.* **1** make a hole or holes in. **2** pierce the side of (a ship). **3** put into a hole. **4** (also *absol.*; often foll. by *out*) send (a golf ball) into a hole. □ **hole up** *colloq.* hide oneself. **make a hole in** use a large amount of. □□ **hol·ey** *adj.*

hole in one *n. Golf* a shot that enters the hole from the tee.

hole in the wall *n.* a small dingy place (esp. of a business).

hol·i·day /hóliday/ *n. & v.* • *n.* **1** a day of festivity or recreation when no work is done, esp. a religious festival, etc. **2** esp. *Brit.* (often in *pl.*) = VACATION. **3** (*attrib.*) (of clothes, etc.) festive. • *v.intr.* esp. *Brit.* spend a holiday. □ **take a holiday** have a break from work.

ho·li·er-than-thou *adj. colloq.* self-righteous.

ho·li·ly /hṓlilee/ *adv.* in a holy manner.

ho·li·ness /hṓleenis/ *n.* **1** sanctity; the state of being holy. **2** (**Holiness**) a title used when referring to or addressing the Pope.

ho·lism /hṓlizəm/ *n.* (also **wholism**) **1** *Philos.* the theory that certain wholes are to be regarded as greater than the sum of their parts (cf. REDUCTIONISM). **2** *Med.* the treating of the whole person including mental and social factors rather than just the symptoms of a disease. □□ **ho·lis·tic** *adj.* **ho·lis·ti·cal·ly** *adv.*

hol·land /hólənd/ *n.* a smooth, hard-wearing, linen fabric.

hol·lan·daise sauce /hóləndáyz/ *n.* a creamy sauce of melted butter, egg yolks, and lemon juice or vinegar, served esp. with fish.

hol·ler /hólər/ *v. & n. colloq.* • *v.* **1** *intr.* make a loud cry or noise. **2** *tr.* express with a loud cry or shout. • *n.* a loud cry, noise, or shout.

hol·low /hólō/ *adj., n., v., & adv.* • *adj.* **1** **a** having a hole or cavity inside. **b** sunken (*hollow cheeks*). **2** (of a sound) echoing, as though made in or on a hollow container. **3** empty; hungry. **4** meaningless (*a hollow triumph*). **5** insincere; false (*a hollow laugh*; *hollow promises*). • *n.* **1** a hollow place; a hole. **2** a valley; a basin. • *v.tr.* (often foll. by *out*) make hollow; excavate. • *adv. colloq.* completely (*beaten hollow*). □ **in the hollow** (also **palm**) **of one's hand** entirely subservient to one. □□ **hol·low·ly** *adv.* **hol·low·ness** *n.*

hol·low·ware /hólōwair/ *n.* hollow articles of metal, china, etc., such as pots, kettles, pitchers, etc. (cf. FLATWARE).

hol·ly /hólee/ *n.* (*pl.* **-ies**) an evergreen shrub of the genus *Ilex*, often with prickly usu. dark green leaves and red berries.

HOLLYHOCK
(*Alcea rosea* 'Nigra')

hol·ly·hock /hóleehok/ *n.* ◀ a tall plant, *Alcea rosea*, with large showy flowers of various colors.

Hol·ly·wood /hóleewŏŏd/ *n.* the American movie industry or its products, with its principal center at Hollywood, California.

hol·mi·um /hṓlmeeəm/ *n. Chem.* a soft silvery metallic element of the lanthanide. ¶ Symb.: **Ho**.

holo- /hólō/ *comb. form* whole (*Holocene*; *holocaust*).

hol·o·caust /hóləkawst/ *n.* **1** a case of large-scale destruction, esp. by fire or nuclear war. **2** (**the Holocaust**) the mass murder of the Jews by the Nazis in World War II.

Hol·o·cene /hóləseen/ *adj. & n. Geol.* • *adj.* of or relating to the most recent epoch of the Quaternary period with evidence of human development. • *n.* this period or system. Also called **Recent**.

hol·o·gram /hóləgram/ *n. Physics* **1** ▶ a three-dimensional image formed by the interference of light beams from a coherent light source. **2** a photograph of the interference pattern, which when suitably illuminated produces a three-dimensional image.

hol·o·graph /hóləgraf/ *adj. & n.* • *adj.* wholly written by hand by the person named as the author. • *n.* a holograph document.

hol·og·ra·phy /həlógrəfee/ *n. Physics* the study or production of holograms. □□ **hol·o·graph·ic** /hóləgráfik/ *adj.* **hol·o·graph·i·cal·ly** *adv.*

hol·ster /hṓlstər/ *n.* a leather case for a pistol or revolver.

ho·ly /hṓlee/ *adj.* (**holier**, **holiest**) **1** morally and spiritually excellent or perfect, and to be revered. **2** belonging to, devoted to, or empowered by God. **3** consecrated; sacred. **4** used as an intensive and in trivial exclamations (*holy smoke!*).

Ho·ly Ghost *n.* = HOLY SPIRIT.

Ho·ly Grail *n.* see GRAIL.

ho·ly Joe *n. orig. Naut sl.* **1** a clergyman. **2** a pious person.

Ho·ly Land *n.* **1** W. Palestine, esp. Judaea. **2** a region similarly revered in non-Christian religions.

Ho·ly Ro·man Em·pire *n.* see ROMAN.

Ho·ly Spir·it *n.* the third person of the Christian Trinity, God as spiritually acting.

ho·ly war *n.* a war waged in support of a religious cause.

ho·ly wa·ter *n.* water dedicated to holy uses, or blessed by a priest.

Ho·ly Week *n.* the week before Easter.

hom·age /hómij/ *n.* acknowledgment of superiority; dutiful reverence (*pay homage to*).

hom·bre /ómbray/ *n.* a man.

Hom·burg /hómbərg/ *n.* ◀ a man's felt hat with a narrow curled brim and a lengthwise dent in the crown.

HOMBURG

home /hōm/ *n., adj., adv., & v.* • *n.* **1** **a** the place where one lives. **b** a dwelling house. **2** the members of a family collectively (*comes from a good home*). **3** the native land of a person or of a person's ancestors. **4** an institution for persons needing care, rest, or refuge (*nursing home*). **5** the place where a thing originates or is native or most common. **6** **a** the finishing point in a race. **b** (in games) the place where one is free from attack. **c** *Baseball* home plate. • *attrib. adj.* **1** **a** connected

HOLOGRAM

A hologram is made by lighting an object with a laser beam split in two. The reference beam is directed toward a photographic plate or film, while the object beam is aimed at the object itself. The plate or film is struck simultaneously by light from the reference beam and by the light of the object beam reflected from the object. A pattern forms on the plate as a result of interference between the two beams. An image appears only when this pattern is illuminated by laser light of the right wavelength.

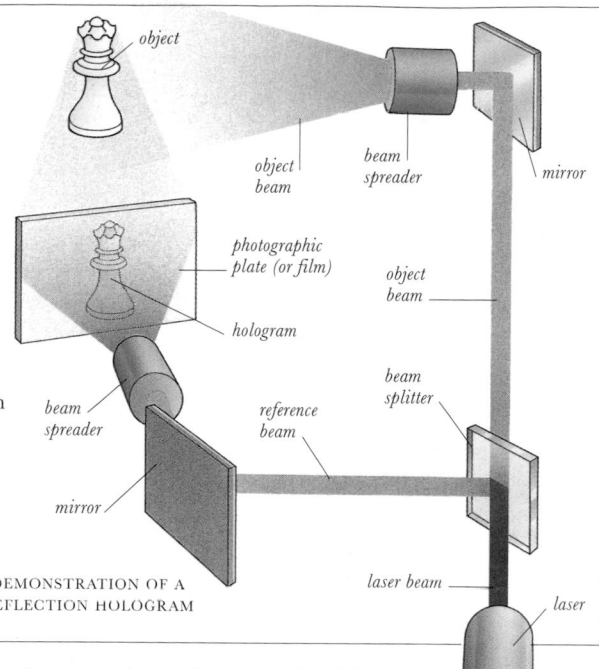

object
object beam
beam spreader
mirror
photographic plate (or film)
object beam
hologram
beam splitter
beam spreader
reference beam
mirror
laser beam
laser

DEMONSTRATION OF A
REFLECTION HOLOGRAM

---

with one's home. **b** carried on, done, or made at home. **2 a** carried on or produced in one's own country (*the home market*). **b** dealing with the domestic affairs of a country. **3** *Sports* played on one's own field, etc. (*home game*). ● *adv.* **1 a** to one's home or country (*go home*). **b** arrived at home (*is he home yet?*). **c** at home (*stay home*). **2 a** to the point aimed at (*the thrust went home*). **b** as far as possible (*drove the nail home*). ● *v.* **1** *intr.* (esp. of a trained pigeon) return home (cf. HOMING 1). **2** *intr.* (often foll. by *on*, *in on*) (of a vessel, missile, etc.) be guided by a landmark, radio beam, etc. **3** *tr.* provide with a home. □ **at home 1** in one's own house or native land. **2** at ease as if in one's own home (*make yourself at home*) **3** (usu. foll. by *in*, *on*, *with*) familiar or well informed. **4** available to callers. **come home to** become fully realized by. **come home to roost** see ROOST. **home away from home** a place other than one's home where one feels at home; a place providing homelike amenities. **home from home** = *home away from home*. **home, James!** *joc.* drive home quickly! □□ **home·like** *adj.*

home·boy /hṓmboy/ *n. colloq.* a person from one's own town or neighborhood.

home·com·ing /hṓmkəming/ *n.* **1** arrival at home. **2** a high school, college, or university game, dance, or other event to which alumni are invited to visit.

home ec·o·nom·ics *n.* the study of household management.

home·grown /hṓmgrōn/ *adj.* grown or produced at home.

home·land /hṓmland/ *n.* **1** one's native land. **2** *hist.* an area in S. Africa formerly reserved for a particular African people.

home·less /hṓmlis/ *adj. & n.* ● *adj.* lacking a home. ● *n.* (prec. by *the*) homeless people. □□ **home·less·ness** *n.*

home·ly /hṓmlee/ *adj.* (**homelier, homeliest**) **1** (of people or their features) not attractive in appearance. **2 a** simple; plain. **b** unpretentious. **c** primitive. **3** comfortable in the manner of a home; cozy. □□ **home·li·ness** *n.*

home·made /hṓmáyd/ *adj.* made at home.

home·mak·er /hṓmaykər/ *n.* a person who manages a household.

home mov·ie *n.* a film made at home or of one's own activities.

ho·me·o·path /hṓmeeəpath/ *n.* a person who practices homeopathy.

ho·me·op·a·thy /hṓmeeópəthee/ *n.* the treatment of disease by minute doses of drugs which in a healthy person would produce symptoms of the disease (cf. ALLOPATHY). □□ **ho·me·o·path·ic** /-meeəpáthik/ *adj.*

ho·me·o·sta·sis /hṓmeeōstáysis/ *n.* the maintenance of a stable equilibrium, esp. through physiological processes.

ho·me·o·therm /hṓmeeəthórm/ *n.* an organism that maintains its body temperature at a constant level by its metabolic activity. □□ **ho·me·o·ther·mal** *adj.* **ho·me·o·ther·mic** *adj.*

home·own·er /hṓmōnər/ *n.* a person who owns his or her own home.

home page *n.* a hypertext document on the World Wide Web, serving as an introductory focus of information relating to an organization or an individual.

home plate *n.* *Baseball* ▼ a plate beside which the batter stands and which the runner must touch in order to score a run.

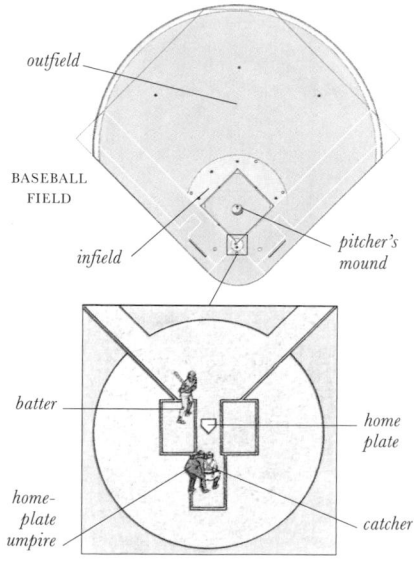

outfield
BASEBALL FIELD
infield
pitcher's mound
batter
home plate
home-plate umpire
catcher

HOME PLATE

---

ho·mer /hṓmər/ *n.* **1** *Baseball* a home run. **2** a homing pigeon.

home rule *n.* the government of a country or region by its own citizens.

home run *n.* **1** *Baseball* a hit that allows the batter to make a complete circuit of the bases. **2** any singular success.

home·sick /hṓmsik/ *adj.* depressed by missing one's home. □□ **home·sick·ness** *n.*

home·spun /hṓmspun/ *adj. & n.* ● *adj.* **1 a** (of cloth) made of yarn spun at home. **b** (of yarn) spun at home. **2** plain; simple; unsophisticated; homely. ● *n.* homespun cloth.

home·stead /hṓmsted/ *n.* **1** a house, esp. a farmhouse, and outbuildings. **2** *Austral. & NZ* the owner's residence on a sheep or cattle station. **3** an area of land (usu. 160 acres) granted to an early American settler as a home. □□ **home·stead·er** *n.*

home·style /hṓmstīl/ *adj.* (esp. of food) of a kind made or done at home; homey.

home stretch *n.* the concluding stretch of a racetrack. ▷ RACETRACK.

home town *n.* the town of one's birth or early life or present fixed residence.

home·ward /hṓmwərd/ *adv. & adj.* ● *adv.* (also **home·wards** /-wərdz/) toward home. ● *adj.* going or leading toward home.

home·work /hṓmwərk/ *n.* **1** work to be done at home, esp. by a school pupil. **2** preparatory work or study.

hom·ey /hṓmee/ *adj.* (also **hom·y**) (**homier, homiest**) suggesting home; cozy.

hom·i·cide /hṓmisīd, hṓ-/ *n.* **1** the killing of a human being by another. **2** a person who kills a human being. □□ **hom·i·cid·al** /-sīd'l/ *adj.*

hom·i·ly /hṓmilee/ *n.* (*pl.* **-ies**) **1** a sermon. **2** a tedious moralizing discourse. □□ **hom·i·list** *n.*

hom·ing /hṓming/ *attrib. adj.* **1** (of a pigeon) trained to fly home; bred for long-distance racing. **2** (of a device) for guiding to a target, etc.

hom·i·nid /hṓminid/ *n. & adj.* ● *n.* ▶ any member of the primate family Hominidae, including humans. ● *adj.* of or relating to this family.

hom·i·noid /hṓminoyd/ *adj. & n.* ● *adj.* like a human. ● *n.* an animal resembling a human.

hom·i·ny /hṓminee/ *n.* coarsely ground corn kernels soaked in lye then washed to remove the hulls.

ho·mo¹ /hṓmō/ *n.* any primate of the genus *Homo*, including modern humans.

ho·mo² /hṓmō/ *n.* (*pl.* **-os**) *offens. colloq.* a homosexual.

homo- /hṓmō/ *comb. form* same (often opp. HETERO-).

ho·mo·e·rot·ic /hṓmōərótik/ *adj.* homosexual.

ho·mo·ge·ne·ous /hṓməjéenees, -yəs/ *adj.* **1** of the same kind. **2** consisting of parts all of the same kind. **3** *Math.* containing terms all of the same degree. □□ **ho·mo·ge·ne·i·ty** /-jinéeitee/ *n.*

ho·mog·e·nize /həmójinīz/ *v.* **1** *tr. & intr.* make or become homogeneous. **2** *tr.* treat (milk) so that the fat droplets are emulsified and the cream does not separate. □□ **ho·mog·e·ni·za·tion** *n.* **ho·mog·e·niz·er** *n.*

HOMINID: MODEL OF AN AUSTRALOPITHECINE HOMINID

H

ho·mog·e·ny /həmójinee/ *n. Biol.* similarity due to common descent. □□ **ho·mog·e·nous** *adj.*

ho·mo·graft /hóməgraft, hóm-/ *n.* a graft of living tissue from one to another of the same species but different genotype.

ho·mo·graph /hóməgraf, hó-/ *n.* a word spelled like another but of different meaning or origin (e.g., POLE¹, POLE²).

ho·mol·o·gous /həmóləgəs/ *adj.* **1 a** having the same relation, relative position, etc. **b** corresponding. **2** *Biol.* (of organs, etc.) similar in position and structure but not necessarily in function. □□ **ho·mol·o·gy** *n.*

ho·mo·logue /hóməlawg, -log, hó-/ *n.* (also **ho·mo·log**) a homologous thing.

ho·mo·mor·phic /hóməmáwrfik, hóm-/ *adj.* of the same or similar form. □□ **ho·mo·mor·phism** *n.*

hom·o·nym /hómənim/ *n.* a word of the same spelling or sound as another but of different meaning. □□ **ho·mon·y·mous** /həmóniməs/ *adj.*

ho·mo·pho·bi·a /hóməfóbeeə/ *n.* a hatred or fear of homosexuals. □□ **ho·mo·phobe** /-əfób/ *n.* **ho·mo·pho·bic** *adj.*

ho·mo·phone /hóməfón, hó-/ *n.* **1** a word having the same sound as another but of different meaning or origin (e.g., *pair, pear*). **2** a symbol denoting the same sound as another.

ho·mo·phon·ic /hómófónik, hó-/ *adj. Mus.* in unison; characterized by movement of all parts to the same melody. □□ **ho·mo·phon·i·cal·ly** *adv.*

ho·moph·o·nous /həmófənəs/ *adj.* **1** (of music) homophonic. **2** (of a word or symbol) that is a homophone. □□ **ho·moph·o·ny** *n.*

ho·mop·ter·an /həmóptərən/ *n.* any insect of the suborder Homoptera, including aphids and cicadas, with wings of uniform texture. □□ **ho·mop·ter·ous** *adj.*

Ho·mo sa·pi·ens /hómō sáypee-enz/ *n.* modern humans regarded as a species.

ho·mo·sex·u·al /hóməséksh○○əl/ *adj. & n.* ● *adj.* **1** involving sexual attraction to persons of the same sex. **2** concerning homosexual relations or people. ● *n.* a homosexual person. □□ **ho·mo·sex·u·al·i·ty** /-sh○○álitee/ *n.* **ho·mo·sex·u·al·ly** *adv.*

ho·mun·cu·lus /həmúngkyələs/ *n.* (also **ho·mun·cule** /-kyōōl/) (*pl.* **homunculi** /-lī/ or **homuncules**) a little man; a manikin.

hom·y var. of HOMEY.

Hon. *abbr.* **1** Honorary. **2** Honorable.

hon /hun/ *n. colloq.* = HONEY 3.

hon·cho /hónchō/ *n. & v. sl.* ● *n.* (*pl.* **-os**) **1** a leader or manager; the person in charge. **2** an admirable man. ● *v.tr.* (**-oes, -oed**) be in charge of; oversee.

hone /hōn/ *n. & v.* ● *n.* **1** a whetstone, esp. for razors. **2** any of various stones used as material for this. ● *v.tr.* sharpen on or as on a hone.

hon·est /ónist/ *adj. & adv.* ● *adj.* **1** fair and just in character or behavior. **2** free of deceit and untruthfulness. **3** fairly earned (*an honest living*). **4** (of an act or feeling) showing fairness. **5** (of a thing) unadulterated; unsophisticated. ● *adv. colloq.* genuinely; really. □ **make an honest woman of** *colloq.* marry (esp. a pregnant woman).

hon·est·ly /ónistlee/ *adv.* **1** in an honest way. **2** really (*I don't honestly know*).

hon·est-to-God *adj. & adv.* (also **honest-to-goodness**) *colloq.* ● *adj.* genuine; real. ● *adv.* genuinely; really.

hon·es·ty /ónistee/ *n.* **1** being honest. **2** truthfulness. **3** ▶ a plant of the genus *Lunaria* with flat round semitransparent seed pods. ▷ SEED

hon·ey /húnee/ *n.* (*pl.* **-eys**) **1** a sweet sticky yellowish fluid made by bees and other insects from nectar collected from flowers. **2** the color of this. **3** (usu. as a form of address) darling; sweetheart.

HONESTY
(*Lunaria annua*)

hon·ey·bee /húneebee/ *n.* any of various bees of the genus *Apis*.

hon·ey·comb /húneekōm/ *n. & v.* ● *n.* **1** ▼ a structure of hexagonal cells of wax, made by bees to store honey and eggs. **2** a pattern arranged hexagonally. ● *v.tr.* **1** fill with cavities or tunnels. **2** mark with a honeycomb pattern.

HONEYCOMB AND WORKER BEES

hon·ey·dew /húneed○○, -dy○○/ *n.* **1** a variety of melon with smooth pale skin and sweet green flesh. **2** a sweet sticky substance found on leaves and stems, excreted by aphids.

hon·eyed /húneed/ *adj.* **1** of or containing honey. **2** sweet.

hon·ey·moon /húneem○○n/ *n. & v.* ● *n.* **1** a vacation spent together by a newly married couple. **2** an initial period of enthusiasm or goodwill. ● *v.intr.* (usu. foll. by *in, at*) spend a honeymoon. □□ **hon·ey·moon·er** *n.*

hon·ey mush·room /húnee múshr○○m, -r○○m/ *n.* ▶ a parasitic fungus, *Armillaria mellea*, with honey-colored edible toadstools.

hon·ey·suck·le /húneesukəl/ *n.* any climbing shrub of the genus *Lonicera* with fragrant yellow, pink, or red flowers.

hon·ey·trap /húneetrap/ *n.* a stratagem in which an attractive person entices another person into unwittingly revealing information.

honk /hawngk, hongk/ *n. & v.* ● *n.* **1** the cry of a wild goose. **2** the harsh sound of a car horn. ● *v.* **1** *intr.* emit or give a honk. **2** *tr.* cause to do this.

hon·ky /háwngkee, hóngkee/ *n.* (*pl.* **-ies**) *black sl. offens.* a white person.

hon·ky-tonk /háwngkeetawngk, hóngkeetongk/ *n. colloq.* **1** ragtime piano music. **2** a cheap or disreputable nightclub, bar, dancehall, etc.

hon·or /ónər/ *n. & v.* ● *n.* **1** high respect; glory. **2** adherence to what is right or to a conventional standard of conduct. **3** nobleness of mind; magnanimity (*honor among thieves*). **4** a thing conferred as a distinction, esp. an official award for bravery or achievement. **5** (foll. by *of* + verbal noun, or *to* + infin.) privilege; special right (*had the honor of being invited*). **6 a** exalted position. **b** (**Honor**) (prec. by *your, his*, etc.) a title of a judge, a mayor, or *Ir.* in rustic speech any person of rank. **7** (foll. by *to*) a person or thing that brings honor (*she is an honor to her profession*). **8 a** (of a woman) chastity. **b** the reputation for this. **9** (in *pl.*) **a** special distinction for proficiency in an examination. **b** a course of degree studies more specialized than for a standard course or degree. **10 a** *Bridge*

the ace, king, queen, jack, and ten, esp. of trumps, or the four aces at no trumps. **b** *Whist* the ace, king, queen, and jack, esp. of trumps. **11** *Golf* the right of driving off first as having won the last hole (*it is my honor*). ● *v.tr.* **1** respect highly. **2** confer honor on. **3** accept or pay (a bill or check) when due. **4** acknowledge. □ **do the honors** perform the duties of a host to guests, etc. **in honor of** as a celebration of. **on one's honor** (usu. foll. by *to* + infin.) under a moral obligation.

hon·or·a·ble /ónərəbəl/ *adj.* **1 a** worthy of honor. **b** bringing honor to its possessor. **c** showing honor. **d** consistent with honor. **2 a** *colloq.* (of the intentions of a man courting a woman) directed toward marriage. **2** (**Honorable**) a title given to certain government officials and members of Congress. □□ **hon·or·a·bly** *adv.*

hon·or·a·ble men·tion *n.* an award of merit to a candidate in an examination, a work of art, etc., not awarded a prize.

hon·or bright *colloq.* = on my honor.

hon·o·rar·i·um /ónəráireeəm/ *n.* (*pl.* **honorariums** or **honoraria** /-reeə/) a voluntary payment for professional services rendered without the normal fee.

hon·or·ar·y /ónəreree/ *adj.* **1 a** conferred as an honor, without the usual requirements, functions, etc. (*honorary degree*). **b** holding such a title or position (*honorary colonel*). **2** (of an office or its holder) unpaid (*honorary treasurer*). **3** (of an obligation) depending on honor, not legally enforceable.

hon·or·if·ic /ónərífik/ *adj. & n.* ● *adj.* **1** conferring honor. **2** (esp. of forms of speech) implying respect. ● *n.* an honorific form of words. □□ **hon·or·if·i·cal·ly** *adv.*

hon·or roll *n.* a list of people who have attained an honor, esp. a list of students who have received academic honors.

hon·ors of war *n.* privileges granted to a capitulating force, e.g., that of marching out with colors flying.

hon·or sys·tem *n.* a system of examinations, etc., without supervision, relying on the honor of those concerned.

hooch /h○○ch/ *n.* (also **hootch**) *colloq.* alcoholic liquor, esp. illicit whiskey.

hood¹ /h○○d/ *n. & v.* ● *n.* **1 a** a covering for the head and neck, whether part of a cloak, etc., or separate. **b** a separate hoodlike garment worn over a university gown or a surplice to indicate the wearer's degree. **2** the cover over the engine of a motor vehicle. ▷ CAR. **3** a canopy to protect users of machinery or to remove fumes, etc. **4** the hoodlike part of a cobra, seal, etc. **5** a leather covering for a hawk's head. ● *v.tr.* cover with a hood. □□ **hood·less** *adj.* **hood·like** *adj.*

hood² /h○○d/ *n. sl.* a gangster or gunman.

hood·ed /h○○did/ *adj.* having a hood; covered with a hood.

hood·lum /h○○dləm, h○○d-/ *n.* **1** a street hooligan; a young thug. **2** a gangster.

hoo·doo /h○○d○○/ *n. & v.* ● *n.* **1 a** bad luck. **b** a thing or person that brings or causes this. **2** voodoo. **3** a fantastic rock pinnacle or column of rock formed by erosion, etc. ● *v.tr.* (**hoodoos, hoodooed**) **1** make unlucky. **2** bewitch.

hood·wink /h○○dwingk/ *v.tr.* deceive; delude.

hoo·ey /h○○-ee/ *n. & int. sl.* nonsense; humbug.

hoof /h○○f, h○○f/ *n.* (*pl.* **hoofs** or **hooves** /h○○vz/) the horny part of the foot of a horse, antelope, and other ungulates. ▷ HORSE, UNGULATE. □ **hoof it** *sl.* go on foot. **on the hoof** (of cattle) not yet slaughtered. □□ **hoofed** *adj.* (also in *comb.*).

hoof·er /h○○fər, h○○f'ər/ *n. sl.* a professional dancer.

hoo-ha /h○○haa/ *n. sl.* a commotion; uproar.

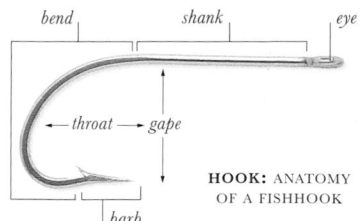

HOOK: ANATOMY OF A FISHHOOK

hook /hŏŏk/ *n. & v.* ● *n.* **1 a** a piece of metal or other material bent back at an angle or with a round bend, for catching hold or for hanging things on. **b** (in full **fishhook**) ▲ a bent piece of wire, usu. barbed and baited, for catching fish. **2** a curved cutting instrument (*reaping hook*). **3 a** a sharp bend, e.g., in a river. **b** a projecting point of land (*Hook of Holland*). **4 a** *Golf* a hooking stroke (see sense 5 of *v.*). **b** *Boxing* a short swinging blow with the elbow bent and rigid. ● *v.* **1** *tr.* **a** grasp with a hook. **b** secure with a hook or hooks. **2** (often foll. by *on, up*) **a** *tr.* attach with or as with a hook. **b** *intr.* be attached with a hook. **3** *tr.* catch with or as with a hook. **4** *tr. sl.* steal. **5** *tr.* (also *absol.*) *Golf* strike (the ball) so that it deviates toward the striker. **6** *tr. Boxing* strike (one's opponent) with the elbow bent and rigid. □ **be hooked on** *sl.* be addicted to or captivated by. **by hook or by crook** by fair means or foul. **hook, line, and sinker** entirely. **off the hook 1** *colloq.* no longer in trouble. **2** (of a telephone receiver) not on its rest, and so preventing incoming calls. □□ **hook·less** *adj.* **hook·let** *n.* **hook·like** *adj.*

hook·ah /hŏŏkə/ *n.* an oriental tobacco pipe with a long tube passing through water for cooling the smoke as it is drawn through.

hook and eye *n.* ▶ a small metal hook and loop as a fastener on a garment.

hooked /hŏŏkt/ *adj.* **1** hook-shaped (*hooked nose*). **2** furnished with a hook or hooks. **3** in senses of HOOK *v.*

HOOK AND EYE

hook·er /hŏŏkər/ *n. sl.* a prostitute.

hook·nose /hŏŏknōz/ *n.* an aquiline nose. □□ **hook·nosed** *adj.*

hook·up /hŏŏkəp/ *n.* a connection, esp. of broadcasting equipment.

hook·worm /hŏŏkwərm/ *n.* **1** any of various nematode worms, with hooklike mouthparts, infesting humans and animals. **2** a disease caused by one of these.

hook·y /hŏŏkee/ *n.* (also **hook·ey**) □ **play hooky** *sl.* play truant.

hoo·li·gan /hŏŏligən/ *n.* a young ruffian, esp. a member of a gang. □□ **hoo·li·gan·ism** *n.*

hoop¹ /hŏŏp/ *n. & v.* ● *n.* **1** a circular band of metal, wood, etc., esp. for binding the staves of casks, etc., or for forming part of a framework. **2 a** a circular usu. wood or plastic band used as a toy. **b** a large ring usu. with paper stretched over it for circus performers to jump through. **3** an arch through which the balls are hit in croquet. **4** (in *pl.*) the game of basketball. **5 a** band of contrasting color on a jockey's blouse, sleeves, or cap. ● *v.tr.* **1** bind with a hoop or hoops. **2** encircle with or as with a hoop. □ **be put** (or **go**) **through the hoop** (or **hoops**) undergo an ordeal.

hoop·la /hŏŏplaa/ *n.* **1** *sl.* excitement; commotion. **2** *sl.* pretentious nonsense.

hoo·poe /hŏŏpoo/ *n.* ◀ a salmon-pink bird, *Upupa epops*, with black and white wings and tail, a large erectile crest, and a long decurved bill.

HOOPOE
(*Upupa epops*)

hoo·ray /hŏŏráy/ *int.* = HURRAH.

hoose·gow /hŏŏsgow/ *n. sl.* a prison.

hoot /hŏŏt/ *n. & v.* ● *n.* **1** an owl's cry. **2** the sound made by a vehicle's horn or a steam whistle. **3** a shout expressing scorn or disapproval. **4** *colloq.* **a** laughter. **b** a cause of this. **5** (also **two hoots**) *sl.* anything at all (*doesn't matter two hoots*). ● *v.* **1** *intr.* **a** (of an owl) utter its cry. **b** (of a vehicle horn or steam whistle) make a hoot. **c** (often foll. by *at*) make loud sounds, esp. of scorn or colloq. merriment (*hooted with laughter*). **2** *tr.* **a** assail with scornful shouts. **b** (often foll. by *out, away*) drive away by hooting. **3** *tr.* sound (a vehicle horn or steam whistle).

hootch var. of HOOCH.

hoot·en·an·ny /hŏŏt'nanee/ *n.* (*pl.* **-ies**) *colloq.* an informal gathering with folk music.

hoot·er /hŏŏtər/ *n.* **1** *sl.* a nose. **2** (*pl.*) *coarse sl.* a women's breasts.

hooves *pl.* of HOOF.

hop¹ /hop/ *v. & n.* ● *v.* (**hopped, hopping**) **1** *intr.* (of a bird, etc.) spring with two or all feet at once. **2** *intr.* (of a person) jump on one foot. **3** *tr.* cross (a ditch, etc.) by hopping. **4** *tr. colloq.* **a** jump into (a vehicle). **b** obtain (a ride) in this way. **5** *tr.* (usu. as **hopping** *n.*) (esp. of aircraft) pass quickly from one (place of a specified type) to another (*island-hopping*). ● *n.* **1** a hopping movement. **2** *colloq.* an informal dance. **3** a short flight in an aircraft. □ **hop in** (or **out**) *colloq.* get into (or out of) a car, etc. **hopping mad** *colloq.* very angry.

hop² /hop/ *n. & v.* ● *n.* **1** ▶ a climbing plant, *Humulus lupulus*, cultivated for the cones borne by the female. **2** (in *pl.*) the ripe cones of this, used to give a bitter flavor to beer. **3** *sl.* opium or any other narcotic. ● *v.* (**hopped, hopping**) **1** *tr.* flavor with hops. **2** *intr.* produce or pick hops.

cone

HOP: COMMON HOP
(*Humulus lupulus*)

hope /hōp/ *n. & v.* ● *n.* **1** (in *sing.* or *pl.*; often foll. by *of, that*) expectation and desire combined (*hope of getting the job*). **2 a** a person, thing, or circumstance that gives cause for hope. **b** ground of hope; promise. **3** what is hoped for. ● *v.* **1** *intr.* (often foll. by *for*) feel hope. **2** *tr.* expect and desire. **3** *tr.* feel fairly confident. □ **hope against hope** cling to a mere possibility. **not a hope!** *colloq.* no chance at all. □□ **hop·er** *n.*

hope chest *n.* **1** a young woman's collection of clothes, linens, etc., in preparation for her marriage. **2** the chest in which it is stored.

hope·ful /hōpfŏŏl/ *adj. & n.* ● *adj.* **1** feeling hope. **2** causing or inspiring hope. **3** likely to succeed; promising. ● *n.* (in full **young hopeful**) **1** a person likely to succeed. **2** *iron.* a person likely to be disappointed. □□ **hope·ful·ness** *n.*

hope·ful·ly /hōpfŏŏlee/ *adv.* **1** in a hopeful manner. **2** *disp.* (qualifying a whole sentence) it is to be hoped.

hope·less /hōplis/ *adj.* **1** feeling no hope. **2** admitting no hope (*a hopeless case*). **3** inadequate; incompetent (*am hopeless at tennis*). □□ **hope·less·ly** *adv.* **hope·less·ness** *n.*

hop·head /hóp-hed/ *n. sl.* a drug addict.

Ho·pi /hŏpee/ *n.* **1 a** a N. American people native to northeastern Arizona. **b** a member of this people. **2** the language of this people.

hop·lite /hóplīt/ *n.* ▶ a heavily armed foot soldier of ancient Greece.

HOPLITE: ANCIENT GREEK
FOOT SOLDIER, *c.* 200 BC

hop·per¹ /hópər/ *n.* **1** a person who hops. **2** a hopping arthropod, esp. a flea or young locust. **3 a** a container tapering downward through which grain passes into a mill. ▷ DRILL. **b** a similar contrivance in various machines.

hop·per² /hópər/ *n.* a hop picker.

hop·ple /hópəl/ *v. & n.* ● *v.tr.* fasten together the legs of (a horse, etc.) to prevent it from straying, etc. ● *n.* an apparatus for this.

hop·sack /hópsak/ *n.* **1 a** a coarse material made from hemp, etc. **b** sacking for hops made from this. **2** a coarse fabric of a loose plain weave.

hop·scotch /hópskoch/ *n.* a children's game of hopping over squares or oblongs marked on the ground to retrieve a flat stone, etc.

hop, skip (or **step**), **and jump** *n.* = TRIPLE JUMP.

ho·ra·ry /háwrəree/ *adj. archaic* **1** of the hours. **2** occurring every hour; hourly.

horde /hawrd/ *n.* **1 a** usu. *derog.* a large group. **b** a moving swarm or pack (of insects, wolves, etc.). **2** a troop of nomads.

hore·hound /háwrhownd/ *n.* a herbaceous plant, *Marrubium vulgare*, with a white cottony covering on its stem and leaves.

ho·ri·zon /hərizən/ *n.* **1** the line at which the Earth and sky appear to meet. **2** limit of mental perception, experience, interest, etc. □ **on the horizon** (of an event) just imminent or becoming apparent.

hor·i·zon·tal /háwrizónt'l, hór-/ *adj. & n.* ● *adj.* **1 a** parallel to the plane of the horizon; at right angles to the vertical (*horizontal plane*). **b** (of machinery, etc.) having its parts working in a horizontal direction. **2 a** combining firms engaged in the same stage of production (*horizontal integration*). **b** involving social groups of equal status, etc. **3** of or at the horizon. ● *n.* a horizontal line, plane, etc.

hor·i·zon·tal sta·bi·liz·er *n.* a horizontal airfoil at the tail of an aircraft.

hor·mone /háwrmōn/ *n.* **1** *Biochem.* a regulatory substance produced in an organism and transported in tissue fluids such as blood or sap to stimulate cells or tissues into action. ▷ ENDOCRINE. **2** a synthetic substance with a similar effect. □□ **hor·mo·nal** /-mōnəl/ *adj.*

horn /hawrn/ *n. & v.* ● *n.* **1** a hard permanent outgrowth, often curved and pointed, on the head of cattle, giraffes, rhinoceroses, and other esp. hoofed mammals, found singly, in pairs, or one in front of the other. ▷ RHINOCEROS. **2** each of two deciduous branched appendages on the head of (esp. male) deer. **3** a hornlike projection on the head of other animals, e.g., a snail's tentacle. **4** the substance of which horns are composed. **5** anything resembling or compared to a horn in shape. **6** *Mus.* **a** = FRENCH HORN. **b** a wind instrument played by lip vibration, orig. made of horn, now usu. of brass. ▷ BRASS, ORCHESTRA. **7** an instrument sounding a warning or other signal (*car horn; foghorn*). **8** a receptacle or instrument made of horn. **9** a horn-shaped projection. **10** the extremity of the Moon or other crescent. **11** an arm or branch of a river, bay, etc. **12** *sl.* the telephone. ● *v.tr.* **1** (esp. as **horned** *adj.*) provide with horns. **2** gore with the horns. □ **horn in** *sl.* **1** (usu. foll. by *on*) intrude. **2** interfere. **on the horns of a dilemma** faced with a decision that involves equally unfavorable alternatives. □□ **horn·ist** *n.* (in sense 6 of *n.*). **horn·less** *adj.* **horn·like** *adj.*

horn·beam /háwrnbeem/ *n.* any tree of the genus *Carpinus*, with a smooth bark and a hard tough wood.

horn·bill /háwrnbil/ *n.* any bird of the family Bucerotidae, with a hornlike excrescence on its large red or yellow curved bill.

H

HORSE

Modern horses are ungulate (hoofed) mammals, descended from the first equine (*Eohippus*) over a period of 50 million years. While all modern horses belong to one species (*Equus caballus*), domestic forms are selectively bred for specific purposes such as riding, racing, or harness work.

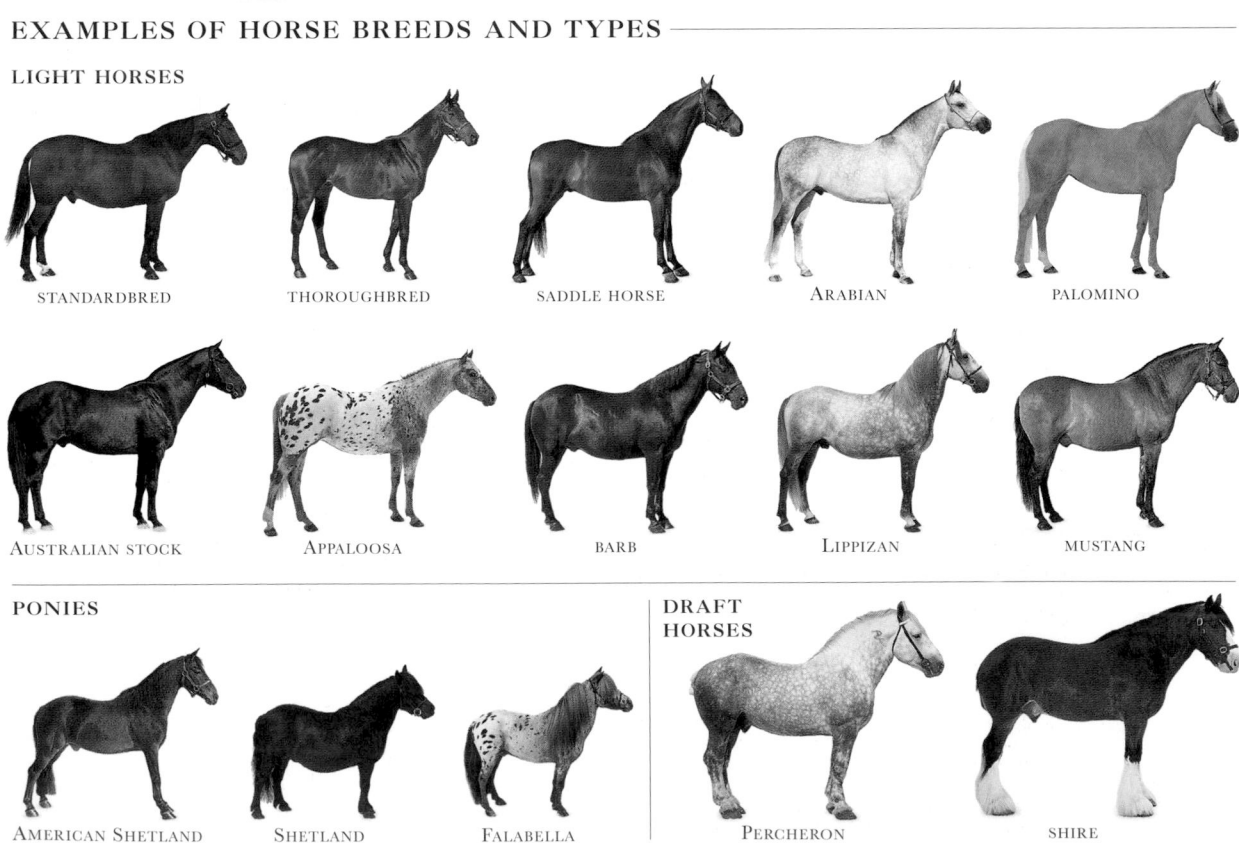

mane
crest
ear
forelock
forehead
eye
nose
croup
loin
back
withers
dock
throat-latch
cheek
chin groove
mouth
muzzle
neck
buttock
shoulder
breast
thigh
tail
stifle
flank
belly
chest
elbow
foreleg
gaskin
hock
chestnut
knee
cannonbone
fetlock
coronet
ergot
pastern
heel
hoof
pastern

EXTERNAL FEATURES OF
THE DOMESTIC HORSE
(*Equus caballus*)

EXAMPLES OF HORSE BREEDS AND TYPES

LIGHT HORSES

STANDARDBRED — THOROUGHBRED — SADDLE HORSE — ARABIAN — PALOMINO

AUSTRALIAN STOCK — APPALOOSA — BARB — LIPPIZAN — MUSTANG

PONIES

AMERICAN SHETLAND — SHETLAND — FALABELLA

DRAFT HORSES

PERCHERON — SHIRE

horn·blende /háwrnblend/ n. ► a dark brown, black, or green mineral occurring in many igneous and metamorphic rocks.

horned /hawrnd/ adj. having a horn.

horned owl n. an owl, Bubo virginianus, with hornlike feathers over the ears.

horned toad n. **1** ▼ an American lizard, Phrynosoma cornutum, covered with spiny scales. **2** any SE Asian toad of the family Pelobatidae, with horn-shaped extensions over the eyes.

HORNBLENDE

HORNED TOAD
(Phrynosoma cornutum)

spiny scales

horn

hor·net /háwrnit/ n. a large wasp, Vespa crabro. ▷ MIMESIS. ■ **stir up a hornets' nest** provoke or cause trouble or opposition.

horn of plen·ty n. a cornucopia.

horn·pipe /háwrnpīp/ n. **1** a lively dance (esp. associated with sailors). **2** the music for this.

horn-rimmed adj. (esp. of eyeglasses) having rims made of horn or a substance resembling it.

horn·swog·gle /háwrnswogəl/ v.tr. sl. cheat; hoax.

horn·wort /háwrnwərt/ n. any aquatic rootless plant of the genus Ceratophyllum, with forked leaves.

horn·y /háwrnee/ adj. (**hornier**, **horniest**) **1** of or like horn. **2** hard like horn. **3** sl. sexually excited. □□ **horn·i·ness** n.

ho·rol·o·gy /hawrólajee/ n. the art of measuring time or making clocks, watches, etc.; the study of this. □□ **ho·rol·o·ger** n. **hor·o·log·ic** /háwrəlójik/ adj. **hor·o·log·i·cal** adj. **hor·o·log·ist** /-ról ∂jist/ n.

hor·o·scope /háwrəskōp, hór-/ n. Astrol. **1** a forecast of a person's future based on a diagram showing the relative positions of the stars and planets at that person's birth. **2** such a diagram (cast a horoscope). **3** observation of the sky and planets at a particular moment, esp. at a person's birth. □□ **hor·o·scop·ic** /-skópik/ adj. **ho·ros·co·py** /həróskəpee/ n.

hor·ren·dous /həréndəs/ adj. horrifying; awful. □□ **hor·ren·dous·ly** adv. **hor·ren·dous·ness** n.

hor·ri·ble /háwribəl, hór-/ adj. **1** causing or likely to cause horror; hideous; shocking. **2** colloq. unpleasant; excessive (horrible weather). □□ **hor·ri·ble·ness** n. **hor·ri·bly** adv.

hor·rid /háwrid, hór-/ adj. **1** horrible; revolting. **2** colloq. unpleasant; disagreeable (horrid weather). **3** archaic. rough; bristling. □□ **hor·rid·ly** adv. **hor·rid·ness** n.

hor·rif·ic /hawrífik, hór-/ adj. horrifying. □□ **hor·rif·i·cal·ly** adv.

hor·ri·fy /háwrifī, hór-/ v.tr. (**-ies**, **-ied**) arouse horror in; shock. □□ **hor·ri·fi·ca·tion** n. **hor·ri·fy·ing** adj. **hor·ri·fy·ing·ly** adv.

hor·rip·i·la·tion /hawrípiláyshən, ho-/ n. = GOOSE BUMPS.

hor·ror /háwrər, hór-/ n. & adj. ● n. **1** a painful feeling of loathing and fear. **2 a** (often foll. by of) intense dislike. **b** (often foll. by at) colloq. intense dismay. **3 a** a person or thing causing horror. **b** colloq. a bad or mischievous person, etc. **4** (in pl.; prec. by the) a fit of horror or nervousness, esp. as in delirium tremens. **5** (in pl.) an exclamation of dismay. ● attrib. adj. (of literature, movies, etc.) designed to attract by arousing pleasurable feelings of horror.

hors de com·bat /áwr də kawNbáá/ adj. out of the fight; disabled.

hors d'oeuvre /awrdörvrə, -dörv/ n. an appetizer served at the beginning of a meal.

horse /hawrs/ n. & v. ● n. **1 a** ◄ a solid-hoofed plant-eating quadruped, Equus caballus, with flowing mane and tail, used for riding and to carry and pull loads. ▷ EVOLUTION, SHOW JUMPING. **b** any other four-legged mammal of the genus Equus, including asses and zebras. **c** (collect.; as sing.) cavalry. **2** a vaulting block. **3** a supporting frame esp. with legs (clothes-horse). **4** sl. heroin. ● v. **1** intr. (foll. by around) fool around. **2** tr. provide (a person or vehicle) with a horse or horses. **3** intr. mount or go on horseback. □ **from the horse's mouth** (of information, etc.) from the person directly concerned or another authoritative source. **to horse!** (as a command) mount your horses. □□ **horse·less** adj. **horse·like** adj.

horse-and-bug·gy adj. old-fashioned.

horse·back /háwrsbak/ n. the back of a horse, esp. as sat on in riding. □ **on horseback** mounted on a horse.

horse·bean /háwrsbeen/ n. a broad bean used as fodder.

horse·box /háwrsboks/ n. Brit. a closed vehicle for transporting a horse or horses.

horse chest·nut n. **1** any large ornamental tree of the genus Aesculus, with upright conical clusters of white or pink or red flowers. **2** the dark brown fruit of this.

horse·flesh /háwrsflesh/ n. **1** the flesh of a horse, esp. as food. **2** horses collectively.

horse·fly /háwrsflī/ n. (pl. **-flies**) any of various biting dipterous insects of the family Tabanidae troublesome esp. to horses.

Horse Guards n. **1** ◄ (in the UK) the cavalry brigade of the household troops. **2** the headquarters of such cavalry.

horse·hair /háwrs hair/ n. hair from the mane or tail of a horse, used for padding, etc.

horse·man /háwrsmən/ n. (pl. **-men**) **1** a rider on horseback. **2** a skilled rider.

horse·man·ship /háwrsmənship/ n. the art of riding on horseback; skill in doing this.

horse·play /háwrsplay/ n. boisterous play.

horse·pow·er /háwrspowər/ n. (pl. same) **1** a unit of power equal to 550 foot-pounds per second (about 750 watts). **2** the power of an engine, etc., measured in terms of this.

HORSE GUARDS: MOUNTED SENTRY OF THE HORSE GUARDS, LONDON, ENGLAND

horse race n. **1** a race between horses with riders. □□ **horse rac·ing** n.

horse·rad·ish /háwrsradish/ n. **1** a cruciferous plant, Armoracia rusticana, with long lobed leaves. **2** the pungent root of this, scraped or grated as a condiment, often made into a sauce.

horse sense n. colloq. plain common sense.

horse·shoe /háwrs-shōō/ n. **1** an iron shoe for a horse shaped like the outline of the hard part of the hoof. **2** a thing of this shape.

horse·shoe crab n. ► a large marine arthropod, Limulus polyphemus, with a horseshoe-shaped shell and a long tail-spine.

horse·tail /háwrs tayl/ n. **1** the tail of a horse. **2** ► any cryptogamous plant of the genus Equisetum, like a horse's tail, with a hollow jointed stem and scale-like leaves.

horse-trad·ing n. **1** dealing in horses. **2** shrewd bargaining.

horse·whip /háwrs-hwip, -wip/ n. & v. ● n. a whip used for driving horses. ● v.tr. (**-whipped**, **-whip·ping**) beat with a horsewhip.

horse·wom·an /háwrs-wōōmən/ n. (pl. **-women**) **1** a woman who rides on horseback. **2** a skilled woman rider.

hors·y /háwrsee/ adj. (**horsier**, **horsiest**) **1** of or like a horse. **2** concerned with or devoted to horses or horse racing. **3** colloq. large and clumsy. □□ **hors·i·ness** n.

hor·ta·tive /háwrtətiv/ adj. (also **hor·ta·to·ry** /háwrtətawree/) tending or serving to exhort. □□ **hor·ta·tion** /hawrtáyshən/ n.

hor·ti·cul·ture /háwrtikúlchər/ n. the art of garden cultivation. □□ **hor·ti·cul·tur·al** adj. **hor·ti·cul·tur·ist** n.

ho·san·na /hōzánə/ n. & int. a shout of adoration (Matt. 21: 9, 15, etc.).

hose /hōz/ n. & v. ● n. **1** (also Brit. **hose-pipe**) a flexible tube conveying water for watering plants, etc., putting out fires, etc. **2 a** (collect.; as pl.) stockings and socks (esp. in trade use). **b** hist. ► breeches (doublet and hose). ● v.tr. **1** (often foll. by down) water or spray or drench with a hose. **2** provide with hose.

ho·sier /hózhər/ n. a dealer in hosiery.

ho·sier·y /hózhəree/ n. stockings and socks.

hosp. abbr. **1** hospital. **2** hospice.

hos·pice /hóspis/ n. **1** a health care facility or program for people who are terminally ill. **2** a lodging for travelers, esp. one kept by a religious order.

hos·pi·ta·ble /hóspitəbəl, hospít-/ adj. **1** giving welcome and entertainment to strangers or guests. **2** disposed to welcome something readily; receptive. □□ **hos·pi·ta·bly** adv.

hos·pi·tal /hóspit'l/ n. **1** an institution providing medical and surgical treatment and nursing care for ill or injured people. **2** hist. **a** hospice. **b** an establishment of the Knights Hospitallers.

hos·pi·tal·er var. of HOSPITALLER.

hos·pi·tal·ism /hóspit'lizəm/ n. the adverse effects of a prolonged stay in the hospital.

hos·pi·tal·i·ty /hóspitálitee/ n. the friendly and generous reception and entertainment of guests or strangers.

hos·pi·tal·ize /hóspit'līz/ v.tr. send or admit (a patient) to hospital. □□ **hos·pi·tal·i·za·tion** n.

HORSETAIL: COMMON HORSETAIL (Equisetum arvense)

strobilus · sterile shoot · scalelike leaves · joint · photosynthetic stem · fertile stem · rhizome

H

HORSESHOE CRAB (Limulus polyphemus)

HOSE: 14TH-CENTURY ITALIAN DOUBLET AND HOSE

doublet · hose

H

hos·pi·tal·ler /hóspit'lər/ n. (also **hos·pi·tal·er**) a member of a charitable religious order.

host[1] /hōst/ n. **1** (usu. foll. by *of*) a large number of people or things. **2** *archaic* an army.

host[2] /hōst/ n. & v. ● n. **1** a person who receives or entertains another as a guest. **2** the landlord of an inn. **3** *Biol.* an animal or plant having a parasite or commensal. **4** an animal or person that has received a transplanted organ, etc. **5** the person who introduces and often interviews guests on a television or radio program. ● *v.tr.* act as host to (a person) or at (an event).

host[3] /hōst/ n. the bread consecrated in the Eucharist.

hos·ta /hósta/ n. ▼ any perennial garden plant of the genus *Hosta*, with green or variegated leaves and loose clusters of tubular lavender or white flowers.

HOSTA (*Hosta* 'Tall Boy')

hos·tage /hóstij/ n. **1** a person seized or held as security for the fulfillment of a condition. **2** a pledge or security. □ **a hostage to fortune** an acquisition, commitment, etc., regarded as endangered by unforeseen circumstances.

hos·tel /hóst'l/ n. **1** = YOUTH HOSTEL. **2** *Brit.* **a** a house of residence or lodging for students, nurses, etc. **b** a place providing temporary accommodation for the homeless, etc. **3** *archaic* an inn.

hos·tel·ing /hóst'ling/ n. the practice of staying in youth hostels, esp. while traveling. □□ **hos·tel·er** n.

hos·tel·ry /hóst'lree/ n. (*pl.* **-ies**) *archaic* or *literary* an inn.

host·ess /hóstis/ n. **1** a woman who receives or entertains a guest. **2** a woman employed to welcome and entertain customers at a nightclub, etc. **3** a stewardess on an aircraft, train, etc. (*air hostess*).

hos·tile /hóstəl, -tīl/ adj. **1** of an enemy. **2** (often foll. by *to*) unfriendly; opposed. □□ **hos·tile·ly** adv.

hos·tile wit·ness n. *Law* a witness who appears hostile to the party calling him or her and therefore untrustworthy.

hos·til·i·ty /hóstilitee/ n. (*pl.* **-ies**) **1** being hostile; enmity. **2** a state of warfare. **3** (in *pl.*) acts of warfare. **4** opposition (in thought, etc.).

hos·tler /hóslər, ós-/ n. **1** = OSTLER. **2** a person who services vehicles or machines, esp. train engines, when they are not in use.

hot /hot/ adj. & adv. ● adj. (**hotter**, **hottest**) **1 a** having a relatively high temperature. **b** (of food or drink) prepared by heating and served without cooling. **2** producing the sensation of heat (*hot flash*). **3** (of spices, etc.) pungent; piquant. **4** (of a person) feeling heat. **5 a** passionate; excited. **b** (often foll. by *for*, *on*) eager; keen (*in hot pursuit*). **c** lustful. **d** exciting. **6** (of news, etc.) fresh; recent. **7** *Hunting* (of the scent) fresh and strong. **8 a** (of a player) very skillful. **b** (of a competitor) strongly favored to win (*a hot favorite*). **c** (of a hit in ball games) difficult for an opponent to deal with. **d** *colloq.* currently popular or in demand. **9** (of music, esp. jazz) strongly rhythmical and emotional. **10 a** *sl.* (of goods) stolen, esp. easily identifiable and therefore difficult to dispose of. **b** *sl.* (of a person) wanted by the police. **11** *sl.* radioactive. **12** *colloq.* (of information) unusually reliable (*hot tip*). ● adv. eagerly. □ **have the hots for** *sl.* be sexually attracted to. **hot under the collar** angry or embarrassed. **make it** (or **things**) **hot for a person** persecute a person. **not so hot** *colloq.* only mediocre. □□ **hot·ly** adv. **hot·ness** n. **hot·tish** adj.

hot air n. *sl.* empty boastful talk.

hot-air bal·loon n. ▶ a balloon (see BALLOON n. 2) consisting of a bag in which air is heated by burners located below it, causing it to rise.
▷ AIRCRAFT

hot·bed /hótbed/ n. **1** a bed of earth heated by fermenting manure. **2** (foll. by *of*) an environment promoting the growth of something, esp. something unwelcome (*a hotbed of vice*).

hot·cake /hótkayk/ n. a pancake. □ **like hotcakes** quickly and in great quantity, esp. because of popularity (*the new CD is selling like hotcakes*).

hot-blood·ed adj. ardent; passionate.

hot-desk·ing n. the allocation of desks to office workers when they are required or on a rotating system.

hot·dog /hótdawg, -dog/ *v.intr. sl.* show off, esp. one's skills.

hot dog n. & int. **1 a** = FRANKFURTER. **b** a frankfurter sandwiched in a soft roll. **2** *sl.* a person who shows off skills. ● *int. sl.* expressing approval.

ho·tel /hōtél/ n. an establishment providing accommodation and meals for payment.

ho·te·lier /ōtelyáy, hōt'léər/ n. a hotel-keeper.

hot flash n. a sudden sensation of heat, esp. during menopause.

hot·foot /hótfŏot/ adv., v., & adj. ● adv. in eager haste. ● *v.tr.* hurry eagerly (esp. **hotfoot it**). ● adj. acting quickly.

hot·head /hót-hed/ n. an impetuous person.

hot·head·ed /hót-hédid/ adj. impetuous; excitable. □□ **hot·head·ed·ness** n.

hot·house /hót-hows/ n. & adj. ● n. **1** a heated building, usu. largely of glass, for rearing plants out of season or in a climate colder than is natural for them. **2** an environment that encourages the rapid growth or development of something. ● adj. (*attrib.*) characteristic of something reared in a hothouse; sheltered; sensitive.

hot line n. a direct exclusive line of communication, esp. for emergencies.

hot met·al n. a printing technique using type cast from molten metal.

hot mon·ey n. capital transferred at frequent intervals.

hot plate n. a heated metal plate, etc. (or a set of these), for cooking food or keeping it hot.

hot po·ta·to n. *colloq.* a controversial or awkward matter or situation.

hot rod n. a motor vehicle modified to have extra power and speed.

hot seat n. *sl.* **1** a position of difficult responsibility. **2** the electric chair.

hot·shot /hótshot/ n. & adj. *colloq.* ● n. an important or exceptionally able person. ● adj. (*attrib.*) important; able; expert.

hot spot n. **1** a small region or area that is relatively hot. **2** a lively or dangerous place.

hot spring n. a spring of naturally hot water.

hot stuff n. *colloq.* **1** a formidably capable person. **2** an important person or thing. **3** a sexually attractive person. **4** a spirited or passionate person. **5** a book, movie, etc., with a strongly erotic content.

hot-tem·pered adj. impulsively angry.

Hot·ten·tot /hót'ntot/ n. & adj. ● n. **1** a member of a pastoral black people of SW Africa. **2** their language. ● adj. of this people.

hot tub n. a tub of heated, circulating water for therapy or recreation, usu. able to accommodate several people.

hot wa·ter n. *colloq.* trouble or disgrace.

hot-wa·ter bot·tle n. (also **bag**) a container, usu. made of rubber, filled with hot water, esp. to warm a bed.

hot-wire adj. operated by the expansion of heated wire.

Hou·di·ni /hōōdéenee/ n. **1** an ingenious escape. **2** a person skilled at escaping (from H. Houdini, U.S. escapologist, d. 1926).

houm·mos var. of HUMMUS.

hound /hownd/ n. & v. ● n. **1 a** a dog used for hunting, esp. one able to track by scent. **b** (**the hounds**) a pack of foxhounds. **2** *colloq.* a despicable man. **3** a person keen in pursuit of something (usu. in *comb*.: *newshound*). ● *v.tr.* **1** harass or pursue relentlessly. **2** chase or pursue with a hound. **3** (foll. by *at*) set (a dog or person) on (a quarry). **4** urge on or nag (a person). □ **ride to hounds** go fox-hunting on horseback.

HOT-AIR BALLOON

envelope

cable

burner

basket

hound's-tooth n. a check pattern with notched corners suggestive of a canine tooth.

hour /owr/ n. **1** a twenty-fourth part of a day and night, 60 minutes. **2** a time of day; a point in time (*a late hour*). **3** (in *pl.*) this number of hours and minutes past midnight on the 24-hour clock (*will assemble at 20:00 hours*). **4 a** a period set aside for some purpose (*lunch hour*). **b** (in *pl.*) a fixed period of time for work, use of a building, etc. (*office hours*). **5** a short indefinite period of time (*an idle hour*). **6** the present time (*question of the hour*). **7** a time for action, etc. (*the hour has come*). **8** the distance traversed in one hour by a means of transport stated or implied (*we are an hour from San Francisco*). **9** *RC Ch.* **a** prayers to be said at one of seven fixed times of day (*book of hours*). **b** any of these times. **10** (prec. by *the*) each time o'clock of a whole number of hours (*buses leave on the hour*). □ **after hours** after closing time. **till all hours** till very late.

hour·glass /ówrglas/ n. ▶ a reversible device with two connected glass bulbs containing sand that takes an hour to pass from the upper to the lower bulb.

hou·ri /hŏoree/ n. a beautiful young woman, esp. in the Muslim Paradise.

hour·ly /ówrlee/ adj. & adv. ● adj. **1** done or occurring every hour (*on an hourly basis*). **2** frequent; continual. **3** reckoned hour by hour (*hourly wage*). ● adv. **1** every hour (*the train runs hourly*). **2** frequently; continually.

HOURGLASS

HOUSE

Most Western houses are built from local materials, such as timber, stone, brick, and concrete. Foundations, walls, and roof spaces, as in the house shown here, often conceal insulation and pipes for services such as electricity, drainage, water, gas, and heating. New technology offers alternative energy sources such as solar panels.

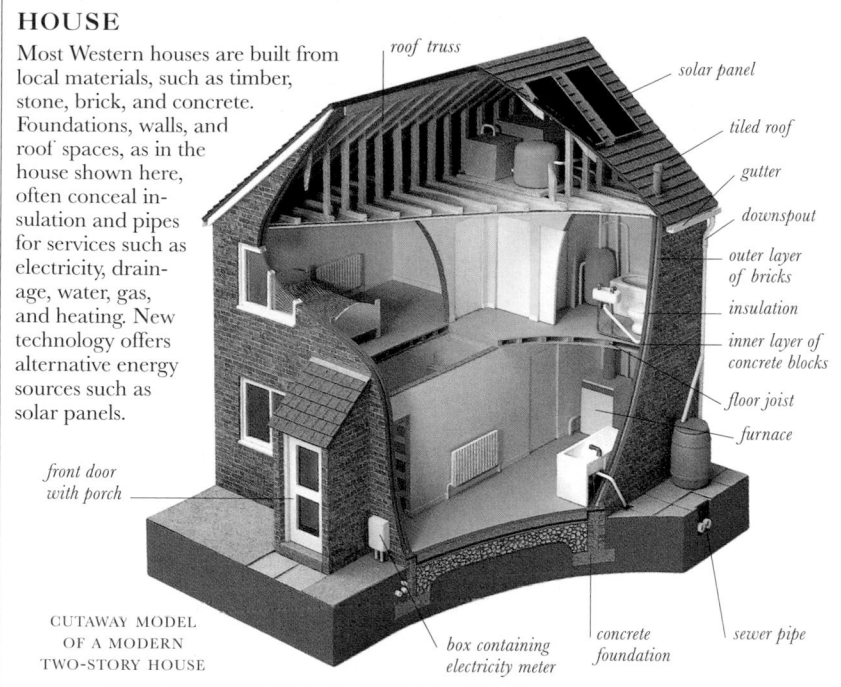

roof truss

solar panel

tiled roof

gutter

downspout

outer layer of bricks

insulation

inner layer of concrete blocks

floor joist

furnace

front door with porch

CUTAWAY MODEL OF A MODERN TWO-STORY HOUSE

box containing electricity meter

concrete foundation

sewer pipe

house *n. & v.* • *n.* /hows/ (*pl.* /hówziz, -siz/) **1 a** ▲ a building for human habitation. **b** (*attrib.*) (of an animal) kept in, frequenting, or infesting houses (*house cat, housefly*). **2** a building for a special purpose (*opera house; summer house*). **3** a building for keeping animals or goods (*henhouse*). **4 a** a religious community. **b** the buildings occupied by it. **5** esp. *Brit.* **a** a body of pupils living in the same building at a boarding school. **b** such a building. **c** a division of a day school for games, competitions, etc. **6** a family, esp. a royal family; a dynasty (*House of York*). **7** a business or institution. **8 a** a legislative or deliberative assembly. **b** the building where it meets. **c** (**the House**) the House of Representatives. **9 a** an audience in a theater, movie theater, etc. **b** a theater. **10** *Astrol.* a twelfth part of the heavens. **11** (*attrib.*) staying in a hospital as a member of the staff (*house surgeon*). **12 a** a place of public refreshment; a restaurant or inn (*coffeehouse*). **b** (*attrib.*) (of wine) selected by the management of a hotel, etc., to be offered at a special price. • *v.tr.* /howz/ **1** provide (a person, a population, etc.) with a house or other accommodation. **2** store (goods, etc.). **3** enclose or encase (a part or fitting). **4** fix in a socket, etc. □ **keep house** manage a household. **like a house on fire 1** vigorously; fast. **2** successfully. **on the house** at the management's expense; free. **play house** play at being a family in its home. **put** (or **set**) **one's house in order** make necessary reforms. **set up house** begin to live in a separate dwelling. □□ **house·ful** *n.* (*pl.* **-fuls**). **house·less** *adj.*

house ar·rest *n.* detention in one's own house, etc., not in prison.

house·boat /hówsbōt/ *n.* a boat fitted for living in.

house·bound /hówsbownd/ *adj.* unable to leave one's house due to illness, etc.

house·boy /hówsboy/ *n.* a boy or man who works as a servant in a house, hotel, etc.

house·break /hówsbrayk/ *v.tr.* train (a pet living indoors) to excrete outdoors. □□ **house·broken** *adj.*

house·break·er /hówsbraykər/ *n.* a person guilty of housebreaking.

house·break·ing /hówsbrayking/ *n.* the act of breaking into a building, esp. in daytime, to commit a crime.

house·bro·ken /hówsbrōkən/ *adj.* **1** (of animals) trained to be clean in the house. **2** *colloq.* well-mannered; courteous.

house·coat /hówskōt/ *n.* a woman's garment for informal wear in the house, usu. a long dresslike coat.

house·dress /hówsdres/ *n.* an inexpensive dress of simple design suitable for wear while doing housework.

house·fa·ther /hówsfaathər/ *n.* a man in charge of a house, esp. of a home for children or a dormitory, etc.

house·fly /hówsflī/ *n.* ▼ any fly of the family Muscidae, esp. *Musca domestica*, breeding in decaying organic matter and often entering houses.

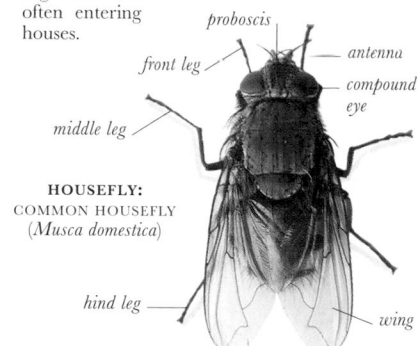

proboscis

front leg

antenna

compound eye

middle leg

HOUSEFLY: COMMON HOUSEFLY (*Musca domestica*)

hind leg

wing

house·guest /hówsgest/ *n.* a guest staying for some days in a private house.

house·hold /hóws-hōld/ *n.* **1** the occupants of a house regarded as a unit. **2** a house and its affairs.

house·hold·er /hóws-hōldər/ *n.* **1** a person who owns or rents a house. **2** the head of a household.

house·hold gods *n.pl.* gods presiding over a household, esp. (in Roman Antiquity) the lares and penates.

house·hold word *n.* (also **name**) **1** a familiar name or saying. **2** a familiar person or thing.

house·hus·band /hóws-həzbənd/ *n.* a husband who carries out the household duties traditionally carried out by a housewife.

house·keep /hówskeep/ *v.intr.* (*past* and *past part.* **-kept**) *colloq.* keep house.

house·keep·er /hówskeepər/ *n.* a person employed to manage a household.

house·keep·ing /hówskeeping/ *n.* **1** the management of household affairs. **2** money allowed for this. **3** operations of record keeping, etc., in an organization.

house·leek /hówsleek/ *n.* ▶ a succulent European plant, *Sempervivum tectorum*, with pink flowers, growing on walls and roofs.

house lights *n.pl.* the lights in the auditorium of a theater.

house·maid /hóws-mayd/ *n.* a female servant in a house. □ **housemaid's knee** inflammation of the kneecap, often due to excessive kneeling.

HOUSELEEK (*Sempervivum tectorum*)

house·man /hówsmən/ *n.* (*pl.* **-men**) = HOUSEBOY.

house mar·tin *n.* a black and white swallow-like bird, *Delichon urbica*, which builds a mud nest on house walls, etc.

house·mas·ter /hówsmastər/ *n.* (*fem.* **house·mistress** /-mistris/) the teacher in charge of a house at a boarding school.

house·moth·er /hówsməthər/ *n.* a woman in charge of a house, esp. of a home for children or a dormitory, etc.

house of cards *n.* **1** an insecure scheme, etc. **2** a structure built (usu. by a child) out of playing cards.

house of God *n.* a church; a place of worship.

house of ill re·pute *n. archaic* a brothel.

House of Rep·re·sen·ta·tives *n.* the lower house of the US Congress and other legislatures.

house·par·ent /hówsparənt/ *n.* a housemother or housefather.

house·plant /hówsplant/ *n.* a plant grown indoors.

house·room /hówsrōōm, -rŏŏm/ *n.* space or accommodation in one's house. □ **not give house-room** *Brit.* not have in any circumstances.

house·top /hówstop/ *n.* the roof of a house. □ **proclaim** (or **shout**, etc.) **from the housetops** announce publicly.

house·wares /hówswairz/ *n.pl.* small articles for furnishing a home, such as dishware, glassware, and small appliances.

house·warm·ing /hówswawrming/ *n.* a party celebrating a move to a new home.

house·wife /hówswīf/ *n.* (*pl.* **-wives**) **1** a married woman managing a household. **2** *Brit.* /húzif/ a case for holding needles, thread, etc. □□ **house·wife·ly** *adj.*

house·wif·er·y /hówswīfəree, -wīfree/ *n.* **1** housekeeping. **2** skill in household management and housekeeping.

house·work /hówswərk/ *n.* regular work done in housekeeping, e.g., cleaning and cooking.

hous·ing /hówzing/ *n.* **1 a** dwelling houses collectively. **b** the provision of these. **2** shelter; lodging. **3** a rigid casing, esp. for moving or sensitive parts of a machine. **4** the hole or niche cut in one piece of wood to receive some part of another in order to join them. □ **housing development** a residential area planned as a unit.

HOV *abbr.* high-occupancy vehicle.

hove *past* of HEAVE.

hov·el /húvəl, hóv-/ *n.* a small miserable dwelling.

hov·er /húvər, hóvər/ *v. & n.* • *v.intr.* **1** (of a bird, helicopter, etc.) remain in one place in the air. **2** (often foll. by *about, around*) wait close at hand; linger. **3** remain undecided. • *n.* **1** hovering. **2** a state of suspense. □□ **hov·er·er** *n.*

H

HOVERCRAFT

Mostly used for passenger transport, a hovercraft skims over land or water, propelled on a cushion of air. The air is sucked into inlets and pumped by fans beneath the hull where it is contained by an inflatable flexible skirt. The fastest models can travel at a speed of 75 m.p.h. (120 k.p.h.).

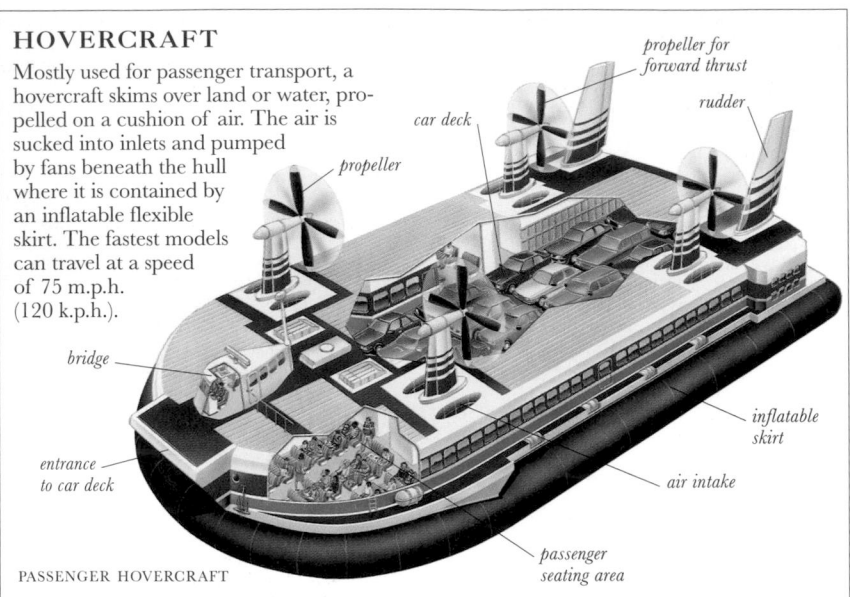

PASSENGER HOVERCRAFT

Labels: propeller for forward thrust; rudder; car deck; propeller; bridge; entrance to car deck; inflatable skirt; air intake; passenger seating area

H

hov·er·craft /húvərkraft, hóv-/ *n.* (*pl.* same) ▲ a vehicle or craft that travels over land or water on a cushion of air provided by a downward blast.

hov·er·port /húvərpawrt, hóv-/ *n.* a terminal for hovercraft.

how /how/ *adv., conj., & n.* ● *interrog.adv.* **1** by what means; in what way (*how do you do it?*). **2** in what condition, esp. of health (*how is the patient?*). **3 a** to what extent (*how far is it?*). **b** to what extent good or well, what . . . like (*how was the film?*). ● *rel.* adv. in whatever way (*do it how you like*). ● *conj.* that (*told us how he'd been in Canada*). ● *n.* the way a thing is done (*the how and why of it*). □ **how about 1** would you like. **2** what is to be done about. **3** what is the news about. **how are you? 1** what is your state of health? **2** = *how do you do?* **how come?** see COME. **how do you do?** a formal greeting. **how many** what number. **how much 1** what amount (*how much do I owe you?*). **2** what price (*how much is it?*). **how's that?** what is your explanation of that?

how·be·it /hówbéeit/ *adv. archaic* nevertheless.

how·dah /hówdə/ *n.* a seat, usu. with a canopy, for riding on the back of an elephant.

how·dy /hówdee/ *int.* = *how do you do?*

how·ev·er /hówévər/ *adv.* **1 a** in whatever way (*do it however you want*). **b** to whatever extent; no matter how (*however inconvenient*). **2** nevertheless. **3** *colloq.* (as an emphatic) in what way; by what means (*however did that happen?*).

how·itz·er /hówitsər/ *n.* a short cannon for high-angle firing of shells at low velocities.

howl /howl/ *n. & v.* ● *n.* **1** a long, loud, doleful cry uttered by a dog, wolf, etc. **2** a prolonged wailing noise, e.g., as made by a strong wind. **3** a loud cry of pain or rage. **4** a yell of derision or merriment. **5** *Electronics* a howling noise in a loudspeaker due to electrical or acoustic feedback. ● *v.* **1** *intr.* make a howl. **2** *intr.* weep loudly. **3** *tr.* utter (words) with a howl. □ **howl down** prevent (a speaker) from being heard by howls of derision.

howl·er /hówlər/ *n.* **1** *colloq.* a glaring mistake. **2** ▶ a S. American monkey of the genus *Alouatta*. **3** a person or animal that howls.

HOWLER: RED HOWLER
(*Alouatta seniculus*)

howl·ing /hówling/ *adj.* **1** that howls. **2** *sl.* extreme (*a howling shame*).

howl·ing der·vish see WHIRLING DERVISH.

how·so·ev·er /hówsō-évər/ *adv.* **1** in whatsoever way. **2** to whatsoever extent.

hoy /hoy/ *int.* used to call attention, drive animals, or *Naut.* hail.

hoy·a /hóyə/ *n.* any climbing shrub of the genus *Hoya*, with pink, white, or yellow waxy flowers.

h.p. *abbr.* **1** horsepower. **2** high pressure.

HQ *abbr.* headquarters.

HR *abbr.* (also **H.R.**) **1** House of Representatives. **2** home run. **3** home rule.

hr. *abbr.* hour.

hrs. *abbr.* hours.

HST *abbr.* Hawaii(an) Standard Time.

HT *abbr.* high tension.

HTML *n. Computing* Hypertext Mark-up Language.

HTTP *abbr. Computing* Hypertext Transport (or Transfer) Protocol.

hub /hub/ *n.* **1** the central part of a wheel, rotating on or with the axle, and from which the spokes radiate. ▷ DERAILLEUR. **2** a central point of interest, activity, etc.

hub·bub /húbub/ *n.* **1** a confused din. **2** a disturbance or riot.

hub·by /húbee/ *n.* (*pl.* **-ies**) *colloq.* a husband.

hub·cap /húbkap/ *n.* a cover for the hub of a vehicle's wheel. ▷ CAR

hu·bris /hyóobris/ *n.* **1** arrogant pride or presumption. **2** (in Greek tragedy) excessive pride toward or defiance of the gods, leading to nemesis □□ **hu·bris·tic** *adj.*

huck·le·ber·ry /húkəlberee/ *n.* (*pl.* **-ies**) **1** any low-growing N. American shrub of the genus *Gaylussacia*. **2** the blue or black soft fruit of this plant.

huck·ster /húkstər/ *n. & v.* ● *n.* **1** a mercenary person. **2** a publicity agent, esp. for broadcast material. **3** a peddler or hawker. ● *v.* **1** *intr.* bargain; haggle. **2** *tr.* carry on a petty traffic in. **3** *tr.* adulterate.

HUD /hud/ *abbr.* (Department of) Housing and Urban Development.

hud·dle /húd'l/ *v. & n.* ● *v.* **1** *tr. & intr.* (often foll. by *up*) crowd together; nestle closely. **2** *intr. & refl.* (often foll. by *up*) coil one's body into a small space. ● *n.* **1** a confused mass of people or things. **2** *colloq.* a close or secret conference (esp. in **go into a huddle**). **3** *Football* a gathering of the players of one team to receive instructions about the next play.

hue /hyōo/ *n.* **1** a color or tint. **2** a variety or shade of color. □□ **-hued** *adj.* **hue·less** *adj.*

hue and cry /hyōo/ *n.* a loud outcry.

hue·vos ranch·er·os /wevos rancháiros/ *n.* a dish of fried or poached eggs served on a tortilla with a spicy tomato sauce, originating in Mexico.

huff /huf/ *v. & n.* ● *v.* **1** *intr.* give out loud puffs of air, steam, etc. **2** *intr.* bluster loudly or threateningly. **3** *intr. & tr.* take or cause to take offense. **4** *tr. Checkers* remove (an opponent's man that could have made a capture) from the board as a forfeit. ● *n.* a fit of petty annoyance. □ **in a huff** annoyed and offended.

huff·y /húfee/ *adj.* (**huffier, huffiest**) **1** apt to take offense. **2** offended. □□ **huff·i·ly** *adv.* **huff·i·ness** *n.*

hug /hug/ *v. & n.* ● *v.tr.* (**hugged, hugging**) **1** squeeze tightly in one's arms, esp. with affection. **2** (of a bear) squeeze (a person) between its forelegs. **3** keep close to (the curb, etc.). **4** cherish or cling to (prejudices, etc.). ● *n.* **1** a strong clasp with the arms. **2** a squeezing grip in wrestling. □□ **hug·ga·ble** *adj.*

huge /hyōoj/ *adj.* **1** extremely large; enormous. **2** (of immaterial things) very great (*a huge success*). □□ **huge·ness** *n.*

huge·ly /hyōojlee/ *adv.* **1** enormously (*hugely successful*). **2** very much (*enjoyed it hugely*).

hug·ger-mug·ger /húgərmúgər/ *adj., adv. & n.* ● *adj. & adv.* **1** in secret. **2** confused; in confusion. ● *n.* **1** secrecy. **2** confusion.

Hu·gue·not /hyóogənot/ *n. hist.* a French Protestant.

huh /hə/ *int.* expressing disgust, surprise, etc.

hu·la /hōolə/ *n.* (also **hu·la-hu·la**) a Polynesian dance with flowing movements of the arms.

hu·la hoop *n.* a large hoop for spinning around the body with hula-like movements.

hu·la skirt *n.* a long grass skirt.

hulk /hulk/ *n.* **1 a** the body of a dismantled ship, used as a storage vessel, etc. **b** (in *pl.*) *hist.* this used as a prison. **2** *colloq.* a large clumsy-looking person or thing.

hulk·ing /húlking/ *adj. colloq.* bulky; large and clumsy.

hull[1] /hul/ *n. & v.* ● *n.* the body or frame of a ship, airship, flying boat, etc. ▷ SAILBOAT. ● *v.tr.* pierce the hull of (a ship) with gunshot, etc.

hull[2] /hul/ *n. & v.* ● *n.* **1** the outer covering of a fruit, esp. the pod of peas and beans, the husk of grain, or the green calyx of a strawberry. **2** a covering. ● *v.tr.* remove the hulls from (fruit, etc.).

hul·la·ba·loo /húləbəlōo/ *n.* (*pl.* **hullabaloos**) uproar or clamor.

hul·lo var. of HELLO.

hum /hum/ *v. & n.* ● *v.* (**hummed, humming**) **1** *intr.* make a low steady continuous sound like that of a bee. **2** *tr.* (also *absol.*) sing (a wordless tune) with closed lips. **3** *intr.* utter a slight inarticulate sound. **4** *intr. colloq.* be in an active state (*really made things hum*). ● *n.* **1** a humming sound. **2** an unwanted low-frequency noise caused by variation of electric current, usu. the alternating frequency of a power source, in an amplifier, etc. □□ **hum·ma·ble** *adj.*

hum·mer *n.*

hu·man /hyōomən/ *adj. & n.* ● *adj.* **1** of or belonging to the genus *Homo*. ▷ BODY. **2** consisting of human beings (*the human race*). **3** of or characteristic of people as opposed to God or animals or machines, esp. susceptible to weaknesses (*is only human*). **4** showing (esp. the better) qualities of man (*proved to be very human*). ● *n.* a human being. □□ **hu·man·ness** *n.*

hu·man be·ing *n.* any man or woman or child of the species *Homo sapiens*.

hu·mane /hyŏŏmáyn/ *adj.* **1** benevolent; compassionate. **2** inflicting the minimum of pain. **3** (of a branch of learning) tending to civilize or confer refinement. □□ **hu·mane·ly** *adv.* **hu·mane·ness** *n.*

hu·man in·ter·est *n.* (in a newspaper story, etc.) reference to personal experience and emotions, etc.

hu·man·ism /hyŏŏmənizəm/ *n.* **1** a system of thought concerned with human rather than divine or supernatural matters. **2** a belief or outlook emphasizing common human needs and concerned with human beings as responsible and progressive intellectual beings. **3** (often **Humanism**) literary culture, esp. that of the Renaissance humanists.

hu·man·ist /hyŏŏmənist/ *n.* **1** an adherent of humanism. **2** a humanitarian. □□ **hu·man·is·tic** *adj.* **hu·man·is·ti·cal·ly** *adv.*

hu·man·i·tar·i·an /hyŏŏmánitáireeən/ *n. & adj.* ● *n.* **1** a person who seeks to promote human welfare. **2** a philanthropist. ● *adj.* relating to humanitarians. □□ **hu·man·i·tar·i·an·ism** *n.*

hu·man·i·ty /hyŏŏmánitee/ *n.* (*pl.* **-ies**) **1 a** the human race. **b** human beings collectively. **c** the fact or condition of being human. **2** humaneness. **3** (in *pl.*) human attributes. **4** (in *pl.*) learning or literature concerned with human culture.

hu·man·ize /hyŏŏmənīz/ *v.tr.* **1** give a human character to. **2** make humane. □□ **hu·man·i·za·tion** *n.*

hu·man·kind /hyŏŏmənkínd/ *n.* human beings collectively.

hu·man·ly /hyŏŏmənlee/ *adv.* **1** by human means (*if humanly possible*). **2** in a human manner. **3** from a human point of view. **4** with human feelings.

hu·man na·ture *n.* the general characteristics and feelings of human beings.

hu·man re·sourc·es *n.* — PERSONNEL.

hu·man rights *n.pl.* rights held to be justifiably belonging to any person.

hum·ble /húmbəl/ *adj. & v.* ● *adj.* **1** having or showing a low estimate of one's own importance. **2** of low social or political rank (*humble origins*). **3** of modest pretensions, dimensions, etc. ● *v.tr.* **1** make humble; abase. **2** lower the rank or status of. □ **eat humble pie** make a humble apology. □□ **hum·ble·ness** *n.* **hum·bly** *adv.*

hum·ble-bee /húmbəlbee/ *n.* = BUMBLEBEE.

hum·bug /húmbug/ *n. & v.* ● *n.* **1** deceptive talk or behavior. **2** an impostor. ● *v.* (**humbugged, humbugging**) **1** *intr.* behave like an impostor. **2** *tr.* deceive; hoax. □□ **hum·bug·ger·y** /-búgəree/ *n.*

hum·ding·er /húmdingər/ *n. sl.* an excellent or remarkable person or thing.

hum·drum /húmdrum/ *adj.* **1** commonplace; dull. **2** monotonous.

hu·mec·tant /hyŏŏméktənt/ *adj. & n.* ● *adj.* retaining or preserving moisture. ● *n.* a substance, esp. a food additive, used to reduce loss of moisture.

hu·mer·al /hyŏŏmərəl/ *adj.* **1** of the humerus or shoulder. **2** worn on the shoulder.

hu·mer·us /hyŏŏmərəs/ *n.* (*pl.* **humeri** /-rī/) **1** ▶ the bone of the upper arm in humans. ▷ SKELETON. **2** the corresponding bone in other vertebrates.

shoulder

humerus

HUMERUS:
HUMAN ARM
SHOWING THE
HUMERUS

hu·mic /hyŏŏmik/ *adj.* of or consisting of humus.

hu·mid /hyŏŏmid/ *adj.* (of the air or climate) warm and damp. □□ **hu·mid·ly** *adv.*

hu·mid·i·fi·er /hyŏŏmídifiər/ *n.* a device for keeping the atmosphere moist in a room.

hu·mid·i·fy /hyŏŏmídifī/ *v.tr.* (**-ies, -ied**) make (air, etc.) humid or damp. □□ **hu·mid·i·fi·ca·tion** *n.*

hu·mid·i·ty /hyŏŏmíditee/ *n.* (*pl.* **-ies**) **1** a humid state. **2** moisture. **3** the degree of moisture, esp. in the atmosphere.

hu·mi·dor /hyŏŏmidawr/ *n.* a room or container for keeping cigars or tobacco moist.

hu·mil·i·ate /hyŏŏmílee-ayt/ *v.tr.* injure the dignity or self-respect of. □□ **hu·mil·i·at·ing** *adj.* **hu·mil·i·at·ing·ly** *adv.* **hu·mil·i·a·tion** /-áyshən/ *n.* **hu·mil·i·a·tor** *n.*

hu·mil·i·ty /hyŏŏmílitee/ *n.* **1** humbleness; meekness. **2** a humble condition.

hum·ming·bird /húmingbərd/ *n.* ▼ any tiny bird of the family Trochilidae that makes a humming sound by the vibration of its wings when it hovers.

HUMMINGBIRD:
FORK-TAILED
WOODNYMPH
(*Thalurania furcata*)

hum·mock /húmək/ *n.* **1** a hillock or knoll. **2** a piece of rising ground, esp. in a marsh. **3** a hump or ridge in an ice field. □□ **hum·mock·y** *adj.*

hum·mus /hŏŏməs/ *n.* (also **houm·mos**) a thick sauce or spread made from chickpeas.

hu·mon·gous /hyŏŏmónggəs, -múng-/ *adj.* (also **hu·mun·gous**) *sl.* extremely large.

hu·mor /hyŏŏmər/ *n. & v.* ● *n.* **1 a** the condition of being amusing or comical (less intellectual and more sympathetic than wit). **b** the expression of humor in literature, speech, etc. **2** (in full **sense of humor**) the ability to perceive or express humor. **3** a mood or state of mind (*bad humor*). **4** (in full **cardinal humor**) *hist.* each of the four chief fluids of the body (blood, phlegm, choler, melancholy), thought to determine a person's physical and mental qualities. ● *v.tr.* indulge (a person or taste, etc.). □ **out of humor** displeased. □□ **-hu·mored** *adj.* **hu·mor·less** *adj.* **hu·mor·less·ly** *adv.* **hu·mor·less·ness** *n.*

hu·mor·esque /hyŏŏmərésk/ *n.* a short lively piece of music.

hu·mor·ist /hyŏŏmərist/ *n.* **1** a facetious person. **2** a humorous talker or writer. □□ **hu·mor·is·tic** *adj.*

hu·mor·ous /hyŏŏmərəs/ *adj.* **1** showing humor or a sense of humor. **2** facetious; comic. □□ **hu·mor·ous·ly** *adv.* **hu·mor·ous·ness** *n.*

hump /hump/ *n. & v.* ● *n.* **1** a rounded protuberance on the back of a camel, etc., or as an abnormality on a person's back. **2** a rounded raised mass of earth, etc. **3** a critical point in an undertaking, etc. ● *v.tr.* **1 a** *colloq.* lift or carry (heavy objects, etc.) with difficulty. **b** esp. *Austral.* hoist up; shoulder (one's pack, etc.). **2** make hump-shaped. **3** annoy; depress. **4** *coarse sl.* have sexual intercourse with. ¶ In sense 4 usually considered a taboo word. □ **over the hump** over the worst; well begun. □□ **humped** *adj.*

hump·back /húmpbak/ *n.* **1 a** a deformed back with a hump. **b** a person having this. **2** ▶ a baleen whale, *Megaptera novaeangliae*, with a dorsal fin forming a hump. □□ **hump·backed** *adj.*

humph /humf/ *int. & n.* a sound expressing doubt or dissatisfaction.

hum·py /húmpee/ *adj.* (**humpier, humpiest**) **1** having a hump. **2** humplike.

hu·mus /hyŏŏməs/ *n.* the organic constituent of soil, usu. formed by the decomposition of plants and leaves. ▷ SOIL.

Hun /hun/ *n.* **1** a member of a warlike Asiatic people who invaded Europe in the 4th–5th c. **2** *offens.* a German (esp. in military contexts). □□ **Hun·nish** *adj.*

hunch /hunch/ *v. & n.* ● *v.* **1** *tr.* arch into a hump. **2** *tr.* thrust up to form a hump. ● *n.* **1** *colloq.* an intuitive feeling. **2** *colloq.* a hint. **3** a hump.

hunch·back /húnchbak/ *n.* = HUMPBACK. □□ **hunch·backed** *adj.*

hun·dred /húndrəd/ *n. & adj.* ● *n.* (*pl.* **hundreds** or (in sense 1) **hundred**) (in *sing.*, prec. by *a* or *one*) **1** the product of ten and ten. **2** a symbol for this (100, c, C). **3** a set of a hundred things. **4** (in *sing.* or *pl.*) *colloq.* a large number. **5** (in *pl.*) the years of a specified century (*the seventeen hundreds*). ● *adj.* **1** that amount to a hundred. **2** used to express whole hours in the 24-hour system (*thirteen hundred hours*). □ **a** (or **one**) **hundred percent** *adv.* entirely. ● *adj.* **1** entire. **2** fully recovered. □□ **hun·dred·fold** *adj. & adv.* **hun·dredth** *adj. & n.*

hun·dred·weight /húndrədwayt/ *n.* (*pl.* same or **-weights**) **1** (in full **short hundredweight**) a unit of weight equal to 100 lb. (about 45.4 kg). **2** (in full **long hundredweight**) *Brit.* a unit of weight equal to 112 lb. (about 50.8 kg). **3** (in full **metric hundredweight**) a unit of weight equal to 50 kg.

hung *past* and *past part.* of HANG.

Hun·gar·i·an /hunggáireeən/ *n. & adj.* ● *n.* **1 a** a native or inhabitant of Hungary in E. Europe. **b** a person of Hungarian descent. **2** the language of Hungary. ● *adj.* of or relating to Hungary or its people or language.

hun·ger /húnggər/ *n. & v.* ● *n.* **1** a feeling of discomfort, or an exhausted condition, caused by lack of food. **2** (often foll. by *for*) a strong desire. ● *v.intr.* **1** (often foll. by *for*) have a craving or strong desire. **2** feel hunger.

hun·ger strike *n.* the refusal of food as a form of protest, esp. by prisoners.

hung ju·ry *n.* a jury unable to reach unanimous agreement after extended deliberations.

hung-o·ver *adj. colloq.* suffering from a hangover.

hun·gry /húnggree/ *adj.* (**hungrier, hungriest**) **1** feeling hunger; needing food. **2** eager; craving. □□ **hun·gri·ly** *adv.* **hun·gri·ness** *n.*

hunk /hungk/ *n.* **1 a** a large piece cut off (*a hunk of bread*). **b** a thick or clumsy piece. **2** *colloq.* **a** a sexually attractive man. **b** a very large person. □□ **hunk·y** *adj.* (**hunk·i·er, hunk·i·est**)

hunk·er /húngkər/ *n. & v.* ● *n.pl.* the haunches. ● *v.intr.* (foll. by *down*) squat.

hunk·y-do·ry /húngkeedáwree/ *adj. colloq.* excellent.

hunt /hunt/ *v. & n.* ● *v.* **1** *tr.* (also *absol.*) **a** pursue and kill (wild animals, esp. game), *Brit.* esp. on horseback and with hounds, for sport or food. **b** (of an animal) chase (its prey). **2** *intr.* (foll. by *after, for*) seek; search (*hunting for a pen*). **3** *intr.* oscillate. **4** *tr.* (foll. by *away*, etc.) drive off by pursuit. **5** *tr.* scour (a district) in pursuit of game. **6** *tr.* (as **hunted** *adj.*) (of a look, etc.) expressing alarm or terror as of one being hunted. ● *n.* **1** the practice of hunting. **2 a** an association of people engaged in hunting with hounds. **b** an area where hunting takes place. □ **hunt down** pursue and capture. **hunt out** find by searching.

HUMPBACK
(*Megaptera novaeangliae*)

hump

HURRICANE

A typical hurricane is some 1,000 miles (1,500 km) across and consists of bands of cumulonimbus cloud arranged in spirals around the eye of the storm. Within these bands, warm air rises quickly, causing torrential rain and drawing in winds that may gust at up to 220 m.p.h. (360 k.p.h.). Hurricanes form over tropical oceans and die over the land.

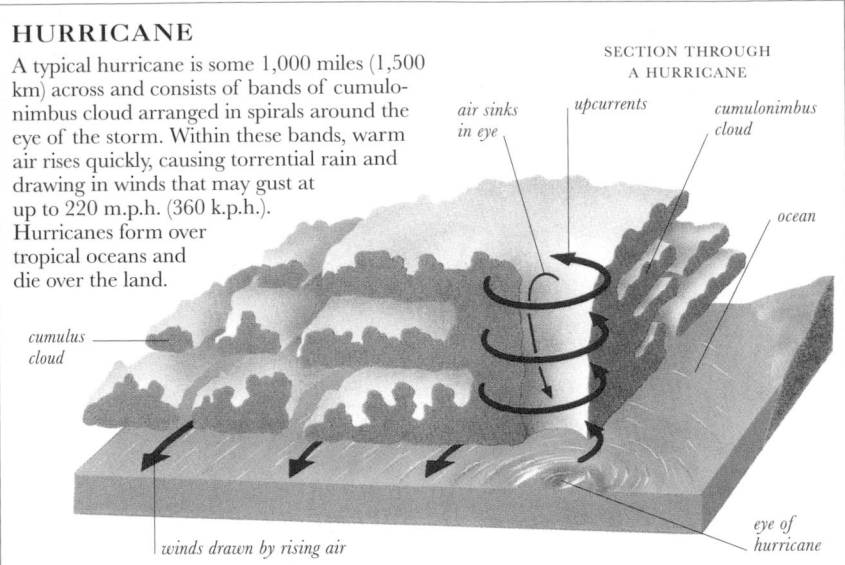

SECTION THROUGH A HURRICANE

air sinks in eye

upcurrents

cumulonimbus cloud

ocean

cumulus cloud

eye of hurricane

winds drawn by rising air

H

hunt·er /húntər/ *n.* **1 a** (*fem.* **huntress**) a person or animal that hunts. **b** a horse used in hunting. **2** a person who seeks something. **3** a watch with a hinged cover protecting the glass.

hunt·ing /húnting/ *n.* the practice of pursuing and killing wild animals.

Hun·ting·ton's cho·re·a /húntingt'nz/ *n. Med.* chorea accompanied by a progressive dementia.

hunts·man /húntsmən/ *n.* (*pl.* **-men**) **1** a hunter. **2** a hunt official in charge of hounds.

hur·dle /hárd'l/ *n. & v.* ● *n.* **1** *Track & Field* **a** each of a series of light frames to be cleared by runners in a race. **b** (in *pl.*) a hurdle race. **2** an obstacle or difficulty. **3** a portable rectangular frame used as a temporary fence, etc. ● *v.* **1** *Track & Field* **a** *intr.* run in a hurdle race. **b** *tr.* clear (a hurdle). **2** *tr.* fence off, etc., with hurdles. □□ **hurd·ler** *n.*

hur·dy-gur·dy /hárdeegárdee/ *n.* (*pl.* **-ies**) **1** a musical instrument with a droning sound, played by turning a handle. **2** *colloq.* a barrel organ.

hurl /hárl/ *v. & n.* ● *v.* **1** *tr.* throw with great force. **2** *tr.* utter (abuse, etc.) vehemently. ● *n.* a forceful throw.

Hur·ler's syn·drome /hárlərz/ *n. Med.* a defect in metabolism resulting in mental retardation, a protruding abdomen, and deformities of the bones, including an abnormally large head. Also called **gargoylism**.

hurl·y-burl·y /hárleebárlee/ *n.* boisterous activity; commotion.

Hu·ron /hyōōrən, -on/ *n.* **1 a** a N. American people native to the northeastern US. **b** a member of this people. **2** the language of this people.

hur·rah /hōōráa/ *int., n., & v.* (also **hur·ray** /hōōráy/) ● *int. & n.* an exclamation of joy or approval. ● *v.intr.* cry or shout "hurrah" or "hurray."

hur·ri·cane /hárikayn, húr-/ *n.* ▲ a storm with a violent wind, esp. a cyclone.

hur·ri·cane lamp *n.* an oil lamp designed to resist a high wind.

hur·ry /hóree, húree/ *n. & v.* ● *n.* (*pl.* **-ies**) **1 a** great haste. **b** (with *neg.* or *interrog.*) a need for haste (*what's the hurry?*). **2** (often foll. by *for,* or *to* + infin.) eagerness to get a thing done quickly. ● *v.* (**-ies, -ied**) **1** *intr.* move or act with great or undue haste. **2** *tr.* (often foll. by *away, along*) cause to move or proceed in this way. **3** *tr.* (as **hurried** *adj.*) hasty; done rapidly owing to lack of time. □ **hurry up** (or **along**) make or cause to make haste. **in a hurry 1** hurrying; rushed; in a rushed manner. **2** *colloq.* easily or readily (*you will not beat that in a hurry; shall not ask again in a hurry*). □□ **hur·ried·ly** *adv.* **hur·ried·ness** *n.*

hurt /hárt/ *v. & n.* ● *v.* (*past* and *past part.* **hurt**) **1** *tr.* (also *absol.*) cause injury to. **2** *tr.* cause mental distress to. **3** *intr.* suffer pain (*my arm hurts*). ● *n.* **1** bodily or material injury. **2** harm; wrong.

hurt·ful /hártfööl/ *adj.* causing (esp. mental) hurt. □□ **hurt·ful·ly** *adv.* **hurt·ful·ness** *n.*

hur·tle /hárt'l/ *v.* **1** *intr. & tr.* move or hurl rapidly or with a clattering sound. **2** *intr.* come with a crash.

hus·band /húzbənd/ *n. & v.* ● *n.* a married man, esp. in relation to his wife. ● *v.tr.* manage thriftily. □□ **hus·band·er** *n.* **hus·band·hood** *n.* **hus·band·less** *adj.* **hus·band·ly** *adj.*

hus·band·ry /húzbəndree/ *n.* **1** farming. **2 a** management of resources. **b** careful management.

hush /húsh/ *v., int., & n.* ● *v. tr. & intr.* make or become silent or muted. ● *int.* calling for silence. ● *n.* an expectant stillness or silence. □ **hush up** suppress public mention of (a scandal).

hush·a·by /húshəbī/ *int.* (also **hush·a·bye**) used to lull a child.

hush-hush /húsh-húsh/ *adj. colloq.* (esp. of an official plan or enterprise, etc.) highly secret or confidential.

hush mon·ey *n.* money paid to prevent the disclosure of a discreditable matter.

hush pup·py *n.* a deep-fried ball of cornmeal dough.

husk /húsk/ *n. & v.* ● *n.* **1** the dry outer covering of some fruits or seeds. ▷ MAST. **2** the worthless outside part of a thing. ● *v.tr.* remove a husk from.

husk·y[1] /húskee/ *adj.* (**huskier, huskiest**) **1** (of a person or voice) dry in the throat; hoarse. **2** of or full of husks. **3** dry as a husk. **4** strong; hefty. □□ **husk·i·ly** *adv.* **husk·i·ness** *n.*

husk·y[2] /húskee/ *n.* (*pl.* **-ies**) ▼ a dog of a powerful breed used in the Arctic for pulling sledges.

hus·sar /həzáar, -sáar/ *n.* **1** ▶ a soldier of a light cavalry regiment. **2** a Hungarian light horseman of the 15th c.

hus·sy /húsee, -zee/ *n.* (*pl.* **-ies**) *derog.* an impudent or immoral girl or woman.

hust·ings /hústingz/ *n.* political campaigning, esp. the appearances and activities involved with a campaign.

hus·tle /húsəl/ *v. & n.* ● *v.* **1** *tr.* push roughly. **2** *tr.* **a** (foll. by *into, out of,* etc.) force or deal with hurriedly or unceremoniously (*hustled them out of the room*). **b** (foll. by *into*) coerce hurriedly (*was hustled into agreeing*). **3** *intr.* push one's way; bustle. **4** *tr. sl.* **a** obtain by forceful action. **b** swindle. **5** *intr. sl.* engage in prostitution. ● *n.* **1** an act of hustling. **2** *colloq.* a fraud or swindle.

hus·tler /húslər/ *n. sl.* **1** an aggressive and enterprising individual, esp. an unscrupulous one. **2** a prostitute.

hut /hut/ *n. & v.* ● *n.* **1** a small simple or crude house or shelter. **2** *Mil.* a temporary wooden, etc., house for troops. ● *v.* (**hutted, hutting**) **1** *tr.* provide with huts. **2** *tr. Mil.* place (troops, etc.) in huts. **3** *intr.* lodge in a hut. □□ **hut·like** *adj.*

hutch /huch/ *n.* **1** a box or cage, usu. with a wire mesh front, for keeping small pet animals. **2** *derog.* a small house.

hut·ment /hútmənt/ *n. Mil.* an encampment of huts.

HWM *abbr.* high-water mark.

hwy. *abbr.* highway.

hy·a·cinth /híəsinth/ *n.* **1** any bulbous plant of the genus *Hyacinthus* with racemes of bell-shaped fragrant flowers. **2** = GRAPE HYACINTH. **3** the purplish blue color of the hyacinth flower. □□ **hy·a·cin·thine** /-sínthin, -īn/ *adj.*

Hy·a·des /híədeez/ *n.pl.* a group of stars in Taurus near the Pleiades, whose heliacal rising was once thought to foretell rain.

hy·ae·na var. of HYENA.

hy·a·lin /híəlin/ *n.* a clear glassy substance produced as a result of the degeneration of certain body tissues.

hy·a·line *adj. & n.* /híəlin, -līn/ ● *adj.* glasslike; vitreous; transparent. ● *n.* /híəléen, -lín/ *literary* a smooth sea, clear sky, etc.

hy·a·lite /híəlīt/ *n.* a colorless variety of opal.

hy·a·loid /híəloyd/ *adj. Anat.* glassy.

hy·brid /híbrid/ *n. & adj.* ● *n.* **1** *Biol.* the offspring of two plants or animals of different species or varieties. **2** often *offens.* a person of mixed racial origin. **3** a thing composed of incongruous elements. ● *adj.* **1** bred as a hybrid from different species or varieties. **2** *Biol.* heterogeneous. **3** of mixed character; derived from incongruous elements or unlike sources. □□ **hy·brid·ism** *n.* **hy·brid·i·ty** /-bríditee/ *n.*

hy·brid·ize /híbridīz/ *v.* **1** *tr.* subject (a species, etc.) to cross-breeding. **2** *intr.* **a** produce hybrids. **b** (of an animal or plant) interbreed. □□ **hy·brid·iz·a·ble** *adj.* **hy·brid·i·za·tion** *n.*

hy·da·tid /hídətid/ *n. Med.* **1** a cyst containing watery fluid (esp. one formed by, and containing, a tapeworm larva). **2** a tapeworm larva. □□ **hy·da·tid·i·form** /-tídiform/ *adj.*

hy·dra /hídrə/ *n.* **1** a freshwater polyp of the genus *Hydra* with tubular body and tentacles. **2** something that is hard to destroy.

HUSKY

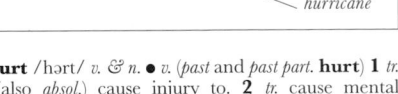

HUSSAR: 19TH-CENTURY FRENCH HUSSAR OFFICER

hy·dran·gea /hīdráynjə, -dran-/ *n.* ▼ any shrub of the genus *Hydrangea* with large white, pink, or blue flowers.

hy·drant /hídrənt/ *n.* a pipe (esp. in a street) with a nozzle to which a hose can be attached for drawing water from a water main.

hy·drate /hídrayt/ *n. & v.* ● *n. Chem.* a compound of water with another compound or with an element. ● *v.tr.* **1 a** combine chemically with water. **b** (as **hydrated** *adj.*) chemically bonded to water. **2** cause to absorb water. □□ **hy·dra·ta·ble** *adj.* **hy·dra·tion** /-dráyshən/ *n.* **hy·dra·tor** *n.*

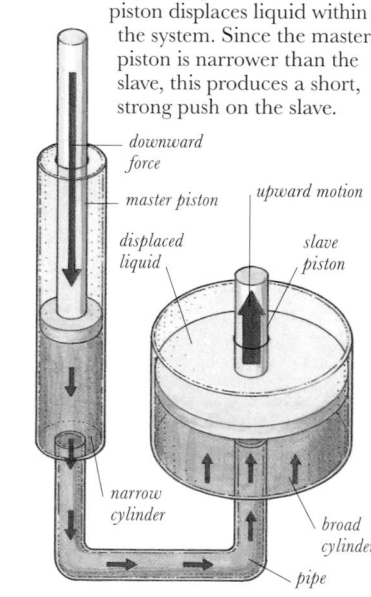

HYDRANGEA
(*Hydrangea macrophylla* 'Altona')

hy·drau·lic /hīdráwlik, -drólik/ *adj.* **1** (of water, oil, etc.) conveyed through pipes or channels, usu. by pressure. **2** ▶ (of a mechanism, etc.) operated by liquid moving in this manner (*hydraulic brakes*) ▷ SIMULATOR. **3** hardening under water (*hydraulic cement*). □□ **hy·drau·li·cal·ly** *adv.* **hy·drau·lic·i·ty** /-lísitee/ *n.*

hy·drau·lics /hīdráwliks, -dróliks/ *n.pl.* (usu. treated as *sing.*) the science of the conveyance of liquids through pipes, etc., esp. as motive power.

hy·dra·zine /hídrəzeen/ *n. Chem.* a colorless alkaline liquid which is a powerful reducing agent and is used as a rocket propellant.

hy·dride /hídrīd/ *n. Chem.* a binary compound of hydrogen with an element, esp. with a metal.

hy·dro /hídrō/ *n.* (*pl.* **-os**) *colloq.* a hydroelectric power plant.

hydro- /hídrō/ *comb. for* (also **hydr-** before a vowel) **1** having to do with water (*hydroelectric*). **2** *Med.* affected with an accumulation of serous fluid (*hydrocele*). **3** *Chem.* combined with hydrogen (*hydrochloric*).

hy·dro·car·bon /hídrəkaárbən/ *n. Chem.* a compound of hydrogen and carbon. ▷ ALKANE, ALKENE, ALKYNE

hy·dro·ceph·a·lus /hídrəséfələs/ *n. Med.* an abnormal amount of fluid within the brain, esp. in young children, which makes the head enlarge and can cause mental deficiency. □□ **hy·dro·ce·phal·ic** /-sifálik/ *adj.*

hy·dro·chlo·ric ac·id /hídrəkláwrik/ *n. Chem.* a solution of the colorless gas hydrogen chloride in water.

hy·dro·chlo·ride /hídrəkláwrīd/ *n. Chem.* a compound of an organic base with hydrochloric acid.

hy·dro·cor·ti·sone /hídrəkáwrtizōn/ *n. Biochem.* a steroid hormone produced by the adrenal cortex, used medicinally to treat inflammation and rheumatism.

hy·dro·cy·an·ic ac·id /hídrōsīánik/ *n. Chem.* a highly poisonous volatile liquid with a characteristic odor of bitter almonds. Also called **prussic acid**.

hy·dro·dy·nam·ics /hídrōdīnámiks/ *n.* the science of forces acting on or exerted by fluids (esp. liquids). □□ **hy·dro·dy·nam·ic** *adj.* **hy·dro·dy·nam·i·cal** *adj.* **hy·dro·dy·nam·i·cist** /-misist/ *n.*

hy·dro·e·lec·tric /hídrōiléktrik/ *adj.* **1** ▶ generating electricity by utilization of waterpower. **2** (of electricity) generated in this way. □□ **hy·dro·e·lec·tric·i·ty** /-trísitee/ *n.*

hy·dro·fluor·ic ac·id /hídrəflŏorik, fláwr-/ *n. Chem.* a solution of the colorless liquid hydrogen fluoride in water. ¶ Chem. formula: HF.

hy·dro·foil /hídrəfoyl/ *n.* **1** a boat equipped with a device consisting of planes for lifting its hull out of the water to increase its speed. **2** this device.

hy·dro·gen /hídrəjən/ *n. Chem.* a colorless gaseous element, the lightest of the elements and occurring in water and all organic compounds. ¶ Symb.: **H**. □□ **hy·drog·e·nous** /-drójinəs/ *adj.*

HYDRAULIC

A hydraulic system uses fluid to convert a small force to a large one, as in the brakes of a car. A long, weak push on the master piston displaces liquid within the system. Since the master piston is narrower than the slave, this produces a short, strong push on the slave.

— downward force
— master piston
— upward motion
displaced liquid
slave piston
narrow cylinder
broad cylinder
pipe

DEMONSTRATION OF A HYDRAULIC SYSTEM

hy·dro·gen·ate /hīdrójinayt, hídrəjənayt/ *v.tr.* charge with or cause to combine with hydrogen. □□ **hy·dro·gen·a·tion** /-náyshən/ *n.*

hy·dro·gen bomb *n.* an immensely powerful bomb utilizing the explosive fusion of hydrogen nuclei: also called **H-bomb**.

hy·dro·gen per·ox·ide *n.* a colorless viscous unstable liquid with strong oxidizing properties. ¶ Chem. formula: H_2O_2.

hy·drog·ra·phy /hīdrógrəfee/ *n.* the science of surveying and charting seas, lakes, rivers, etc. □□ **hy·drog·ra·pher** *n.* **hy·dro·graph·ic** /hídrəgráfik/ *adj.* **hy·dro·graph·i·cal** *adj.* **hy·dro·graph·i·cal·ly** *adv.*

hy·droid /hídroyd/ *adj. & n. Zool.* ▶ any usu. polypoid hydrozoan of the order Hydroida, including hydra. ▷ CNIDARIAN

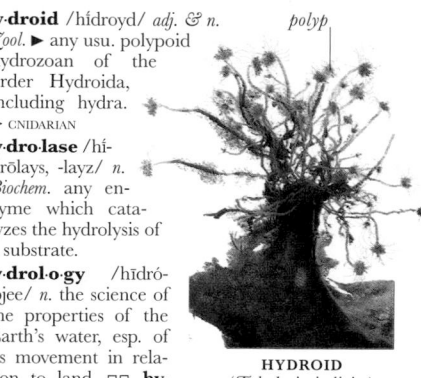

polyp

HYDROID
(*Tubularia indivisa*)

hy·dro·lase /hídrōlays, -layz/ *n. Biochem.* any enzyme which catalyzes the hydrolysis of a substrate.

hy·drol·o·gy /hīdróləjee/ *n.* the science of the properties of the Earth's water, esp. of its movement in relation to land. □□ **hy·dro·log·ic** /hídrəlójik/ *adj.* **hy·dro·log·i·cal** *adj.* **hy·dro·log·i·cal·ly** *adv.* **hy·drol·o·gist** /-róləjist/ *n.*

hy·drol·y·sis /hīdrólisis/ *n.* the chemical reaction of a substance with water, usu. resulting in decomposition. □□ **hy·dro·lyt·ic** /hídrəlítik/ *adj.*

hy·dro·lyze /hídrəlīz/ *v.tr. & intr.* subject to or undergo the chemical action of water.

hy·dro·ma·ni·a /hídrəmáyneeə/ *n.* a craving for water.

hy·dro·me·chan·ics /hídrōmikániks/ *n.* the mechanics of liquids; hydrodynamics.

hy·drom·e·ter /hīdrómitər/ *n.* an instrument for measuring the density of liquids. □□ **hy·dro·met·ric** /hídrəmétrik/ *adj.* **hy·drom·e·try** *n.*

hy·drop·a·thy /hīdrópəthee/ *n.* the (medically unorthodox) treatment of disease by external and internal application of water. □□ **hy·dro·path·ic** /hídrəpáthik/ *adj.* **hy·dro·a·thist** *n.*

hy·dro·phil·ic /hídrəfilik/ *adj.* **1** having an affinity for water. **2** wettable by water.

hy·dro·pho·bi·a /hídrəfóbeeə/ *n.* **1** a morbid aversion to water, esp. as a symptom of rabies in humans. **2** rabies, esp. in humans.

hy·dro·pho·bic /hídrəfóbik/ *adj.* **1** of or suffering from hydrophobia. **2 a** lacking an affinity for water. **b** not readily wettable.

hy·dro·plane /hídrəplayn/ *n. & v.* ● *n.* **1** a light fast motorboat designed to skim over the surface of water. **2** a finlike attachment which enables a submarine to rise and submerge in water. ● *v.intr.* (of a boat) skim over the surface of water with its hull lifted.

H

HYDROELECTRIC

In a hydroelectric power station, gravity forces water between two reservoirs via a turbine. The momentum of the surging water turns the turbine, which powers a generator to produce electricity.

CROSS SECTION OF A HYDROELECTRIC POWER STATION

high-voltage cable
rotor house
insulator
transformer
generator unit
switch gear with circuit breaker
generator rotor
gate
shaft
screen
turbine
blade
gate
afterbay
tailrace
outlet to lower reservoir
incoming water turns the turbine
inlet from upper reservoir
draft tube

H

hy·dro·pon·ics /hídrəpóniks/ *n.* the process of growing plants in sand, gravel, or liquid, without soil and with added nutrients. □□ **hy·dro·pon·ic** *adj.* **hy·dro·pon·i·cal·ly** *adv.*

hy·dro·sphere /hídrəsfeer/ *n.* the waters of the Earth's surface.

hy·dro·stat·ic /hídrəstátik/ *adj.* of the equilibrium of liquids and the pressure exerted by liquid at rest. □□ **hy·dro·stat·i·cal·ly** *adv.*

hy·dro·stat·ics /hídrəstátiks/ *n.pl.* (usu. treated as *sing.*) the branch of mechanics concerned with the hydrostatic properties of liquids.

hy·dro·ther·a·py /hídrəthérəpee/ *n.* the use of water in the treatment of disorders, usu. exercises in swimming pools. □□ **hy·dro·ther·a·pist** *n.*

hy·dro·ther·mal /hídrəthórməl/ *adj.* of the action of heated water on the Earth's crust. □□ **hy·dro·ther·mal·ly** *adv.*

hy·drous /hídrəs/ *adj. Chem.* & *Mineral.* containing water.

hy·drox·ide /hīdróksīd/ *n. Chem.* a metallic compound containing oxygen and hydrogen either in the form of the hydroxide ion (OH⁻) or the hydroxyl group (–OH).

hydroxy- /hīdróksee/ *comb. form Chem.* having a hydroxide ion or group.

hy·drox·yl /hīdróksil/ *n. Chem.* the univalent group containing hydrogen and oxygen, as -OH.

hy·dro·zo·an *n.* & *adj.* of any aquatic cnidarian of the class Hydrozoa of mainly marine polyp or medusoid forms, including hydra and Portuguese man-of-war.

hy·e·na /hī-éenə/ *n.* (also **hy·ae·na**) ▶ any flesh-eating mammal of the order Hyaenidae.

hy·giene /híjeen/ *n.* **1 a** a study, or set of principles, of maintaining health. **b** conditions or practices conducive to maintaining health. **2** sanitary science.

hy·gi·en·ic /híjénik, hījéenik/ *adj.* clean and sanitary. □□ **hy·gi·en·i·cal·ly** *adv.*

hy·gi·en·ics /hījéniks, hījéeniks/ *n.pl.* (usu. treated as *sing.*) = HYGIENE 1a.

hy·gien·ist /hījénist, -jée-, -híjeen-ist/ *n.* a specialist in the promotion and practice of cleanliness for the preservation of health.

hygro- /hígrō/ *comb. form* moisture.

hy·grol·o·gy /hīgróləjee/ *n.* the study of the humidity of the atmosphere, etc.

hy·grom·e·ter /hīgrómitər/ *n.* ▶ an instrument for measuring the humidity of the air or a gas. □□ **hy·gro·met·ric** /hígrəmét-rik/ *adj.* **hy·grom·e·try** *n.*

hy·gro·scope /hígrəskōp/ *n.* an instrument that indicates but does not measure the humidity of the air.

hy·gro·scop·ic /hígrəskópik/ *adj.* **1** of the hygroscope. **2** (of a substance) tending to absorb moisture from the air. □□ **hy·gro·scop·i·cal·ly** *adv.*

hy·ing *pres. part.* of HIE.

hy·men /hímən/ *n. Anat.* a membrane that partially closes the opening of the vagina and is usu. broken at the first occurrence of sexual intercourse.

HYENA: STRIPED HYENA (*Hyaena hyaena*)

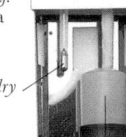

thermometers

bulb kept dry

bulb kept wet

HYGROMETER: WET AND DRY HYGROMETER

HYMENOPTERAN

Hymenopterans are a huge group of insects comprising ants, bees, and wasps, together with sawflies, gall wasps, ichneumon wasps, and other parasites. Most (except worker ants) have two pairs of membranous wings joined by tiny hooks, with veins forming largish cells. Many species live in social groups, each rank fulfilling specific functions.

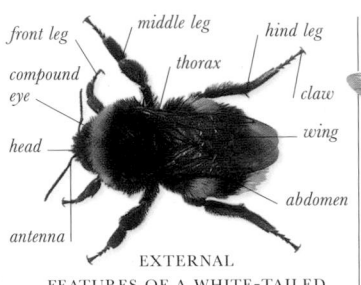

front leg   *middle leg*   *hind leg*
compound eye   *thorax*   *claw*
head   *wing*
abdomen
antenna

EXTERNAL FEATURES OF A WHITE-TAILED BUMBLEBEE (*Bombus lucorum*)

OTHER TYPES OF HYMENOPTERAN

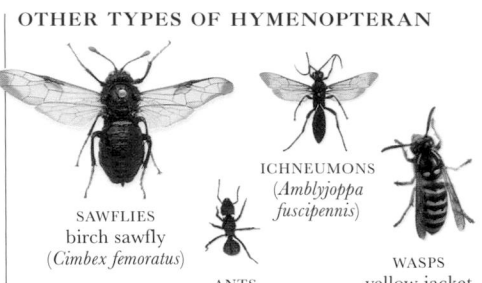

SAWFLIES birch sawfly (*Cimbex femoratus*)

ICHNEUMONS (*Amblyjoppa fuscipennis*)

ANTS (unidentified species)

WASPS yellow jacket (*Vespula vulgaris*)

---

hy·me·nop·ter·an /hímənóptərən/ *n.* ▲ any insect of the order *Hymenoptera* having four transparent wings, including bees, wasps, and ants. □□ **hy·me·nop·ter·ous** *adj.*

hymn /him/ *n.* & *v.* *n.* a song of praise, esp. to God in Christian worship, usu. a metrical composition sung in a religious service. ● *v.* **1** *tr.* praise in hymns. **2** *intr.* sing hymns.

hym·nal /hímnəl/ *n.* & *adj.* ● *n.* a hymnbook. ● *adj.* of hymns.

hymn·book /hímbo͞ok/ *n.* a book of hymns.

hym·no·dy /hímnədee/ *n.* (*pl.* **-ies**) **1 a** the singing of hymns. **b** the composition of hymns. **2** hymns collectively. □□ **hym·no·dist** *n.*

hym·nog·ra·pher /himnógrəfər/ *n.* a writer of hymns. □□ **hym·no·graph·y** *n.*

hy·os·cine /híəseen/ *n.* a poisonous alkaloid found in plants of the nightshade family, esp. of the genus *Scopolia*, and used as an antiemetic in motion sickness and a preoperative medication for examination of the eye. Also called **scopolamine**.

hype¹ /hīp/ *n.* & *v. sl.* ● *n.* **1** extravagant or intensive publicity promotion. **2** cheating; a trick. ● *v.tr.* **1** promote (a product) with extravagant publicity. **2** cheat; trick.

hype² /hīp/ *n. sl.* **1** a drug addict. **2** a hypodermic needle or injection. □ **hyped up** stimulated by or as if by a hypodermic injection.

hy·per /hípər/ *adj. sl.* excessively excited, nervous, stimulated, etc.

hyper- /hípər/ *prefix* meaning: **1** over; beyond; above (*hyperphysical*). **2** exceeding (*hypersonic*). **3** excessively; above normal (*hyperbole*; *hypersensitive*).

hy·per·ac·tive /hípəráktiv/ *adj.* (of a person, esp. a child) abnormally active. □□ **hy·per·ac·tiv·i·ty** /-tívitee/ *n.*

hy·per·bo·la /hīpárbələ/ *n.* (*pl.* **hyperbolas** or **hyperbolae** /-lee/) *Geom.* the plane curve of two equal branches, produced when a cone is cut by a plane that makes a larger angle with the base than the side of the cone (cf. ELLIPSE). ▷ CONIC SECTION

hy·per·bo·le /hīpárbəlee/ *n. Rhet.* an exaggerated statement not meant to be taken literally. □□ **hy·per·bol·i·cal** /hípərbólikəl/ *adj.* **hy·per·bol·i·cal·ly** *adv.*

hy·per·bol·ic /hípərbólik/ *adj. Geom.* of or relating to a hyperbola.

hy·per·crit·i·cal /hípərkrítikəl/ *adj.* excessively critical, esp. of small faults.

hy·per·e·mi·a /hípəréemeeə/ *n.* (*Brit.* **hy·per·ae·mi·a**) an excessive quantity of blood in the vessels supplying an organ or other part of the body. □□ **hy·per·e·mic** *adj.*

hy·per·es·the·si·a /hípəris-theezhə/ *n.* (*Brit.* **hy·per·aes·the·si·a**) an excessive physical sensibility, esp. of the skin. □□ **hy·per·es·thet·ic** /-thétik/ *adj.*

hy·per·fo·cal dis·tance /hípərfókəl/ *n.* the distance on which a camera lens can be focused to bring the maximum range of object distances into focus.

hy·per·gly·ce·mi·a /hípərglīseémeeə/ *n.* an excess of glucose in the bloodstream, often associated with diabetes mellitus. □□ **hy·per·gly·ce·mic** *adj.*

hy·per·gol·ic /hípərgólik/ *adj.* (of a rocket propellant) igniting instantly on contact with an oxidant, etc.

hy·per·i·cum /hīpérikəm/ *n.* any shrub of the genus *Hypericum* with five-petaled yellow flowers.

hy·per·link /hípərlingk/ *n. Computing* a link from a hypertext document to another location, activated by clicking on a highlighted word or image.

hy·per·sen·si·tive /hípərsénsitiv/ *adj.* excessively sensitive. □□ **hy·per·sen·si·tiv·i·ty** /-tívitee/ *n.*

hy·per·son·ic /hípərsónik/ *adj.* **1** relating to speeds of more than five times the speed of sound. **2** relating to sound frequencies above about a billion hertz.

hy·per·ten·sion /hípərténshən/ *n.* **1** abnormally high blood pressure. **2** a state of great emotional tension. □□ **hy·per·ten·sive** /-ténsiv/ *adj.*

hy·per·text /hípərtekst/ *n. Computing* computer software that links topics on the screen to related information, graphics, etc.

hy·per·ther·mi·a /hípərthórmeeə/ *n. Med.* the condition of having a body temperature greatly above normal.

hy·per·thy·roid·ism /hípərthíroydizəm/ *n. Med.* overactivity of the thyroid gland, resulting in an increased metabolic rate. □□ **hy·per·thy·roid** *adj.*

hy·per·ton·ic /hípərtónik/ *adj.* **1** (of muscles) having high tension. **2** (of a solution) having a greater osmotic pressure than another solution. □□ **hy·per·to·ni·a** /-tóneeə/ *n.* (in sense 1). **hy·per·to·nic·i·ty** /-tənisitee/ *n.*

hy·per·tro·phy /hīpártrəfee/ *n.* enlargement of an organ or part. □□ **hy·per·troph·ic** /-trófik, -trófik/ *adj.* **hy·per·troph·ied** *adj.*

hy·per·ven·ti·la·tion /hípərvént'láyshən/ *n.* breathing at an abnormally rapid rate.

hy·pha /hífə/ *n.* (*pl.* **hyphae** /-fee/) a filament in the mycelium of a fungus. □□ **hy·phal** *adj.*

hy·phen /hífən/ *n.* & *v.* ● *n.* the sign (-) used to join words semantically or syntactically (as in *pick-me-up*, *rock-forming*), to indicate the division of a word at the end of a line, or to indicate a missing or implied element (as in *man-* and *womankind*). ● *v.tr.* **1** write (a compound word) with a hyphen. **2** join (words) with a hyphen.

hy·phen·ate /hífənayt/ *v.tr.* = HYPHEN *v.* □□ **hy·phen·a·tion** /-náyshən/ *n.*

hypno- /hípnō/ *comb. form* sleep; hypnosis.

hyp·no·gen·e·sis /hipnōjénisis/ *n.* the induction of a hypnotic state.

hyp·nol·o·gy /hipnóləjee/ *n.* the science of the phenomena of sleep. □□ **hyp·nol·o·gist** *n.*

hyp·no·sis /hipnósis/ *n.* **1** a state like sleep in which the subject acts only on external suggestion. **2** artificially produced sleep.

hyp·no·ther·a·py /hípnōthérəpee/ *n.* the treatment of disease by hypnosis.

hyp·not·ic /hipnótik/ *adj. & n.* ● *adj.* **1** of or producing hypnosis. **2** (of a drug) soporific. ● *n.* **1** a thing, esp. a drug, that produces sleep. **2** a person under or open to the influence of hypnotism. □□ **hyp·not·i·cal·ly** *adv.*

hyp·no·tism /hípnətizəm/ *n.* the practice of hypnosis. □□ **hyp·no·tist** *n.*

hyp·no·tize /hípnətīz/ *v.tr.* **1** produce hypnosis in. **2** fascinate; capture the mind of (a person). □□ **hyp·no·tiz·a·ble** *adj.*

hy·po[1] /hípō/ *n. Photog.* the chemical sodium thiosulfate (incorrectly called hyposulfite) used as a photographic fixer.

hy·po[2] /hípō/ *n.* (*pl.* **-os**) *colloq.* = HYPODERMIC *n.*

hy·po·al·ler·gen·ic /hípōalərjénik/ *adj.* having little likelihood of causing an allergic reaction (*hypoallergenic foods; hypoallergenic cosmetics*).

hy·po·caust /hípəkawst/ *n.* ▼ a hollow space under the floor in ancient Roman houses, into which hot air was sent for heating a room or bath.

hot air   *heated bath*

fire   *hypocaust*   *floor support*

HYPOCAUST: CROSS SECTION OF AN ANCIENT ROMAN HYPOCAUST

hy·po·chon·dri·a /hípəkóndreeə/ *n.* **1** abnormal anxiety about one's health. **2** morbid depression without real cause.

hy·po·chon·dri·ac /hípəkóndreeak/ *n. & adj.* ● *n.* a person suffering from hypochondria. ● *adj.* (also **hy·po·chon·dri·a·cal** /-dríəkəl/) of hypochondria.

hy·po·co·ris·tic /hípəkərístik/ *adj. Gram.* of the nature of a pet name.

hy·po·cot·yl /hípəkót'l/ *n. Bot.* the part of the stem of an embryo plant beneath the stalks of the seed leaves or cotyledons and directly above the root.

hy·poc·ri·sy /hipókrisee/ *n.* (*pl.* **-ies**) **1** the assumption of moral standards to which one's own behavior does not conform; pretense. **2** an instance of this.

hyp·o·crite /hípəkrit/ *n.* a person given to hypocrisy. □□ **hyp·o·crit·i·cal** /-krítikəl/ *adj.* **hyp·o·crit·i·cal·ly** *adv.*

hy·po·cy·cloid /hípəsíkloyd/ *n. Math.* the curve traced by a point on the circumference of a circle rolling on the interior of another circle. □□ **hy·po·cy·cloid·al** /-síklóyd'l/ *adj.*

hy·po·der·mic /hípədórmik/ *adj. & n.* ● *adj. Med.* **1** of or relating to the area beneath the skin. **2 a** (of a drug, etc., or its application) injected beneath the skin. **b** (of a syringe, etc.) used to do this. ● *n.* a hypodermic injection or syringe. □□ **hy·po·der·mi·cal·ly** *adv.*

hy·po·gas·tri·um /hípəgástreeəm/ *n.* (*pl.* **hypogastria** /-treeə/) the part of the central abdomen that is situated below the region of the stomach. □□ **hy·po·gas·tric** *adj.*

hy·po·ge·an /hípəjéeən/ *adj.* (also **hy·po·ge·al** /-jéeəl/) **1** (existing or growing) underground. **2** (of seed germination) with the seed leaves remaining below the ground.

hy·po·gene /hípəjeen/ *adj. Geol.* produced under the surface of the Earth.

hy·po·ge·um /hípəjéeəm/ *n.* (*pl.* **hypogea** /-jéeə/) an underground chamber.

hy·po·gly·ce·mi·a /hípōglīséemeeə/ *n.* a deficiency of glucose in the bloodstream. □□ **hy·po·gly·ce·mic** *adj.*

hy·poid /hípoyd/ *n.* a gear with the pinion offset from the centerline of the wheel, to connect nonintersecting shafts.

hy·po·ma·ni·a /hípəmáyneeə/ *n.* a minor form of mania. □□ **hy·po·man·ic** /-mánik/ *adj.*

hy·pos·ta·sis /hīpóstəsis/ *n.* (*pl.* **hypostases** /-seez/) **1** *Med.* an accumulation of fluid or blood in the lower parts of the body or organs under the influence of gravity, in cases of poor circulation. **2** *Metaphysics* an underlying substance, as opposed to attributes or to that which is unsubstantial. **3** *Theol.* **a** the person of Christ, combining human and divine natures. **b** each of the three persons of the Trinity.

hy·po·stat·ic /hípəstátik/ *adj.* (also **hy·po·stat·i·cal**) *Theol.* relating to the three persons of the Trinity. □ **hypostatic union** the divine and human natures in Christ.

hy·po·style /hípəstīl/ *adj. Archit.* having a roof supported by pillars.

hy·po·tax·is /hípətáksis/ *n. Gram.* the subordination of one clause to another.

hy·po·ten·sion /hípəténshən/ *n.* abnormally low blood pressure. □□ **hy·po·ten·sive** *adj.*

hy·pot·e·nuse /hīpót'noos, -nyoos/ *n.* ▶ the side opposite the right angle of a right-angled triangle.

HYPOTENUSE   *right angle*
hypotenuse

hy·po·thal·a·mus /hípətháláməs/ *n.* (*pl.* **-mi** /-mī/) *Anat.* ▶ the region of the brain that controls thirst, hunger, etc. ▷ BRAIN, ENDOCRINE. □□ **hy·po·tha·lam·ic** /-thəlámik/ *adj.*

hy·po·ther·mi·a /hípōthórmeeə/ *n. Med.* the condition of having an abnormally low body temperature.

hy·poth·e·sis /hīpóthisis/ *n.* (*pl.* **hypotheses** /-seez/) **1** a proposition made as a basis for reasoning. **2** a supposition made as a starting point for further investigation from known facts. **3** a groundless assumption.

hy·poth·e·size /hīpóthisīz/ *v.* **1** *intr.* frame a hypothesis. **2** *tr.* assume as a hypothesis. □□ **hy·poth·e·sist** /-sist/ *n.* **hy·poth·e·siz·er** *n.*

hy·po·thet·i·cal /hípəthétikəl/ *adj.* **1** of or based on or serving as a hypothesis. **2** supposed but not necessarily real or true. □□ **hy·po·thet·i·cal·ly** *adv.*

hy·po·thy·roid·ism /hípōthíroydizəm/ *n. Med.* subnormal activity of the thyroid gland, resulting in cretinism. □□ **hy·po·thy·roid** *n. & adj.*

hy·po·ven·ti·la·tion /hípōvént'láyshən/ *n.* breathing at an abnormally slow rate.

hy·pox·i·a /hīpókseeə/ *n. Med.* a deficiency of oxygen reaching the tissues. □□ **hy·pox·ic** *adj.*

hy·rax /híraks/ *n.* ▼ any small mammal of the order *Hyracoidea*.

HYRAX: ROCK HYRAX
(*Procavia capensis*)

hys·sop /hísəp/ *n.* any small bushy aromatic herb of the genus *Hyssopus*, formerly used medicinally. ▷ HERB

hys·ter·ec·to·my /hístəréktəmee/ *n.* (*pl.* **-ies**) the surgical removal of the uterus.

hys·ter·e·sis /hístəréesis/ *n. Physics* the lagging behind of an effect when its cause varies in amount, etc.

hys·te·ri·a /histéreeə, -stéer-/ *n.* **1** a wild uncontrollable emotion or excitement. **2** a disturbance of the nervous system, of psychoneurotic origin.

hys·ter·ic /histérik/ *n. & adj.* ● *n.* **1** (in *pl.*) **a** a fit of hysteria. **b** *colloq.* overwhelming mirth (*we were in hysterics*). **2** a hysterical person. ● *adj.* = HYSTERICAL.

hys·ter·i·cal /histérikəl/ *adj.* **1** of or affected with hysteria. **2** uncontrolledly emotional. **3** *colloq.* extremely funny. □□ **hys·ter·i·cal·ly** *adv.*

Hz *abbr.* hertz.

hypothalamus

HYPOTHALAMUS: SITE OF THE HYPOTHALAMUS IN THE HUMAN BRAIN

H

I

I[1] /ī/ *n.* (also **i**) (*pl.* **Is** or **I's**) **1** the ninth letter of the alphabet. **2** (as a Roman numeral) 1.

I[2] /ī/ *pron.* (*obj.* **me**; *poss.* **my**, **mine**; *pl.* **we**) used by a speaker or writer to refer to himself or herself.

I[3] *symb. Chem.* the element iodine.

I[4] *abbr.* (also **I.**) **1** Island(s). **2** Isle(s).

IA *abbr.* Iowa (in official postal use).

Ia. *abbr.* Iowa.

IAEA *abbr.* International Atomic Energy Agency.

i·amb /íamb/ *n. Prosody* a foot consisting of one short (or unstressed) followed by one long (or stressed) syllable.

i·am·bic /īámbik/ *adj. & n. Prosody* ● *adj.* of or using iambuses. ● *n.* (usu. in *pl.*) iambic verse.

i·am·bus /íámbəs/ *n.* (*pl.* **iambuses** or **-bi** /-bī/) an iamb.

i·a·tro·gen·ic /íãtrəjénik/ *adj.* (of a disease, etc.) caused by medical examination or treatment.

ib. var. of IBID.

I beam *n.* a girder of I-shaped section.

I·be·ri·an /ībeéreeən/ *adj. & n.* ● *adj.* of ancient Iberia, the peninsula now comprising Spain and Portugal; of Spain and Portugal. ● *n.* **1** a native of ancient Iberia. **2** any of the languages of ancient Iberia.

i·bex /íbeks/ *n.* (*pl.* same or **ibexes**) a wild goat, *Capra ibex*, esp. of mountainous areas of Europe, N. Africa, and Asia, with thick curved ridged horns.

ibid. /íbid/ *abbr.* (also **ib.**) in the same book or passage, etc.

i·bis /íbis/ *n.* (*pl.* same or **ibises**) ▼ any wading bird of the family Threskiornithidae with a curved bill, long neck, and long legs.

IBIS:
SCARLET IBIS
(*Eudocimus ruber*)

IBM *abbr.* International Business Machines.

IBRD *abbr.* International Bank for Reconstruction and Development (also known as the **World Bank**).

i·bu·pro·fen /íbyoōprófən/ *n.* an anti-inflammatory medication used to relieve pain and reduce fever.

IC *abbr.* **1** integrated circuit. **2** intensive care.

i/c *abbr.* **1** in charge. **2** in command. **3** internal combustion.

ICAO *abbr.* International Civil Aviation Organization.

ICBM *abbr.* intercontinental ballistic missile.

ICC *abbr.* **1** Interstate Commerce Commission. **2** International Claims Commission. **3** Indian Claims Commission.

ice /īs/ *n. & v.* ● *n.* **1 a** frozen water, a brittle transparent crystalline solid. **b** a sheet of this on the

ICEBERG

In the southern hemisphere, broad, tabular icebergs are formed when sections detach themselves from the floating edges of the ice sheets that extend from Antarctica. In the northern hemisphere, icebergs form when wind and tidal action cause large chunks of ice to break away from glaciers. All icebergs are made up of frozen freshwater, as opposed to seawater, and only the top 12 percent is visible above sea level.

SOUTHERN-HEMISPHERE ICEBERG

glacier
crevasse
tabular iceberg
snout
coastal shelf
sea level

NORTHERN-HEMISPHERE ICEBERG

glacier
irregularly shaped iceberg
sea level
seabed

surface of water (*fell through the ice*). **2** *Brit.* a portion of ice cream, sherbet, etc. (*would you like an ice?*). **3** *sl.* diamonds. ● *v.* **1** *tr.* mix with or cool in ice (*iced drinks*). **2** *tr. & intr.* (often foll. by *over, up*) **a** cover or become covered with ice. **b** freeze. **3** *tr.* cover (a cake, etc.) with icing. **4** *sl.* kill. □ **on ice 1** (of an entertainment, sport, etc.) performed by skaters. **2** *colloq.* held in reserve; awaiting further attention. **on thin ice** in a risky situation.

ice age *n.* a glacial period, esp. (the **Ice Age**) in the Pleistocene epoch.

ice·berg /ísbərg/ *n.* **1** ▲ a large floating mass of ice detached from a glacier or ice sheet and carried out to sea. **2** an unemotional or cold-blooded person. □ **the tip of the iceberg** a small perceptible part of something (esp. a difficulty) the greater part of which is hidden.

ice·berg let·tuce *n.* any of various crisp lettuces with a freely blanching head.

ice·bound /ísbownd/ *adj.* confined by ice.

ice·box /ísboks/ *n.* **1** a compartment in a refrigerator for making and storing ice. **2** a refrigerator.

ice·break·er /ísbraykər/ *n.* **1** a boat or ship used for breaking ice on a river, the sea, etc. **2** something that serves to relieve inhibitions, start a conversation, etc.

ice cap *n.* a permanent covering of ice, e.g., in polar regions.

ice-cold *adj.* as cold as ice.

ice cream *n.* a sweet creamy frozen food, usu. flavored.

ice cube *n.* a small block of ice made in a refrigerator.

ice hock·ey *n.* a form of hockey played on ice with a puck. ▷ HOCKEY

Ice·land·er /ísləndər/ *n.* **1** a native or national of Iceland, an island in the N. Atlantic. **2** a person of Icelandic descent.

Ice·lan·dic /īslándik/ *adj. & n.* ● *adj.* of or relating to Iceland. ● *n.* the language of Iceland.

Ice·land moss /íslənd/ *n.* (also **Ice·land li·chen**) a mountain and moorland lichen, *Cetraria islandica*, with edible branching fronds.

Ice·land pop·py /íslənd/ *n.* an arctic poppy, *Papaver nudicaule*, with red or yellow flowers.

ice skate *n.* a skate consisting of a boot with a blade beneath, for skating on ice. □□ **ice-skate** *v.intr.* **ice-skat·er** *n.*

I Ching /eé chíng/ *n.* an ancient Chinese manual of divination based on symbolic trigrams and hexagrams.

ich·neu·mon /iknoōmən, -nyoō-/ *n.* (in full **ich-neumon fly**) any small hymenopterous insect of the family Ichneumonidae, depositing eggs in or on the larva of another insect as food for its own larva. ▷ OVIPOSITOR

ich·nog·ra·phy /iknógrəfee/ *n.* (*pl.* **-ies**) **1** the ground-plan of a building, map of a region, etc. **2** a drawing of this.

i·chor /íkawr, íkər, *n.* **1** (in Greek mythology) fluid flowing like blood in the veins of the gods. **2** *poet.* bloodlike fluid. □□ **i·chor·ous** /íkərəs/ *adj.*

ichthyo- /íktheeō/ *comb. form* fish.

ich·thy·oid /íkthee-oyd/ *adj. & n.* ● *adj.* fishlike. ● *n.* any fishlike vertebrate.

ich·thy·o·lite /íktheeəlít/ *n.* a fossil fish.

ich·thy·ol·o·gy /íkteeóləjee/ *n.* the study of fishes. □□ **ich·thy·ol·og·i·cal** /-theeəlójikəl/ *adj.* **ich·thy·ol·o·gist** *n.*

ich·thy·oph·a·gous /íktheeófəgəs/ *adj.* fish-eating. □□ **ich·thy·oph·a·gy** /-ófəjee/ *n.*

ich·thy·o·saur /íktheeəsáwr/ *n.* (also **ich·thy·o·saur·us** /íktheeəsáwrəs/) ▼ any extinct marine reptile of the order Ichthyosauria, with long head, tapering body, four flippers, and usu. a large tail.

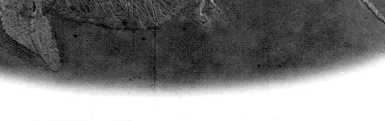

ICHTHYOSAUR: FOSSILIZED ICHTHYOSAUR SKELETON (*Ichthyosaurus megacephalus*)

ich·thy·o·sis /íktheeósis/ *n.* a skin disease that causes the epidermis to become dry and horny like fish scales. □□ **ich·thy·ot·ic** /-theeótik/ *adj.*

i·ci·cle /ísikəl/ *n.* a hanging tapering piece of ice, formed by the freezing of dripping water.

ic·ing /ísing/ *n.* **1** a coating of sugar, etc., on a cake or cookie. **2** the formation of ice on a ship or aircraft. □ **icing on the cake** an attractive though inessential addition or enhancement.

ick·y /íkkee/ *adj. colloq.* **1** sickly. **2** (as a general term of disapproval) nasty; repulsive.

i·con /íkon/ *n.* (also **i·kon**) **1** a devotional painting or carving, usu. on wood, of Christ or another holy figure, esp. in the Eastern Church. ▷ ICONOSTASIS **2** an image or statue. **3** *Computing* a symbol or graphic representation that appears on the monitor in a program, option, or window, esp. one of several for selection. **4** *Linguistics* a sign which has a characteristic in common with the thing it signifies.

i·con·ic /īkónik/ *adj.* **1** of or having the nature of an image or portrait. **2** (of a statue) following a conventional type. **3** *Linguistics* that is an icon. □□ **i·con·i·ci·ty** /íkənísitee/ *n.* (esp. in sense 3).

i·con·i·fy /īkónəfī/ *v.tr. Computing* reduce (a window on a VDU screen) to an icon.

icono- /īkónō/ *comb. form* an image or likeness.

i·con·o·clasm /īkónəklazəm/ *n.* **1** the breaking of images. **2** the assailing of cherished beliefs.

i·con·o·clast /īkónōklast/ *n.* **1** a person who attacks cherished beliefs. **2** a person who destroys images used in religious worship, esp. *hist.* during the 8th–9th c. in the churches of the East, or as a Puritan of the 16th–17th c. □□ **i·con·o·clas·tic** /-klástik/ *adj.* **i·con·o·clas·ti·cal·ly** *adv.*

i·con·og·ra·phy /īkənógrəfee/ *n.* (*pl.* **-ies**) **1** the illustration of a subject by drawings or figures. **2 a** the study of portraits, esp. of an individual. **b** the study of artistic images or symbols. **3** a treatise on pictures or statuary. □□ **i·co·nog·ra·pher** *n.* **i·con·o·graph·ic** /-nəgráfik/ *adj.* **i·con·o·graph·i·cal** *adj.* **i·con·o·graph·i·cal·ly** *adv.*

i·co·nol·o·gy /īkənóləjee/ *n.* **1** an artistic theory developed from iconography (see ICONOGRAPHY 2b). **2** symbolism.

i·con·o·sta·sis /íkənóstəsis/ *n.* (*pl.* **iconostases** /-seéz/) ▼ (in the Eastern Church) a screen bearing icons and separating the sanctuary from the nave.

iconostasis   *doorway to sanctuary*   *icon*

ICONOSTASIS IN A 19TH-CENTURY GREEK CHURCH

i·co·sa·he·dron /īkósəheédrən, -īkós-/ *n.* ▶ a solid figure with 20 faces. □□ **i·co·sa·he·dral** *adj.*

ic·ter·us /íktərəs/ *n. Med.* = JAUNDICE. □□ **ic·ter·ic** /iktérik/ *adj.*

ic·tus /íktəs/ *n.* (*pl.* **ictuses** or same) **1** *Prosody* rhythmical or metrical stress. **2** *Med.* a stroke or seizure; a fit.

ICOSAHEDRON

ICU *abbr.* intensive care unit.

i·cy /ísee/ *adj.* (**icier, iciest**) **1** very cold. **2** covered with or abounding in ice. **3** (of a tone or manner) unfriendly; hostile (*an icy stare*). □□ **i·ci·ly** *adv.* **i·ci·ness** *n.*

ID *abbr.* **1** identification, identity (*ID card*). **2** Idaho (in official postal use).

I'd /īd/ *contr.* **1** I had. **2** I should; I would.

id /id/ *n. Psychol.* the inherited instinctive impulses of the individual as part of the unconscious.

IDA *abbr.* International Development Association.

i·de·a /īdeéə/ *n.* **1** a conception or plan formed by mental effort (*have you any ideas?*). **2 a** a mental impression or notion; a concept. **b** a vague belief or fancy (*had an idea you were married; had no idea where you were*). **c** an opinion; an outlook or point of view (*had some funny ideas about marriage*). **3** an intention, purpose, or essential feature (*the idea is to make money*). **4** an archetype or pattern as distinguished from its realization in individual cases. □ **get** (or **have**) **ideas** *colloq.* be ambitious, rebellious, etc. **have no idea** *colloq.* **1** not know at all. **2** be completely incompetent. **not one's idea of** *colloq.* not what one regards as (*not my idea of a pleasant evening*). **put ideas into a person's head** suggest ambitions, etc., he or she would not otherwise have had. **that's an idea** *colloq.* that proposal, etc., is worth considering.

i·de·al /īdeéəl/ *adj. & n.* ● *adj.* **1 a** answering to one's highest conception. **b** perfect or supremely excellent. **2 a** existing only in idea. **b** visionary. **3** embodying an idea. **4** relating to or consisting of ideas; dependent on the mind. ● *n.* **1** a perfect type, or a conception of this. **2 a** an actual thing as a standard for imitation. **b** (often in *pl.*) a moral principle or standard of behavior. □□ **i·de·al·ly** *adv.*

i·de·al gas *n.* a hypothetical gas consisting of molecules occupying negligible space and without attraction for each other, thereby obeying simple laws.

i·de·al·ism /īdeéəlizəm/ *n.* **1** the practice of forming or following after ideals, esp. unrealistically. **2** the representation of things in ideal or idealized form. **3** imaginative treatment. □□ **i·de·al·ist** *n.* **i·de·al·is·tic** *adj.* **i·de·al·is·ti·cal·ly** *adv.*

i·de·al·ize /īdeéəlīz/ *v.tr.* **1** regard or represent (a thing or person) in ideal form or character. **2** exalt in thought to ideal perfection or excellence. □□ **i·de·al·i·za·tion** *n.* **i·de·al·iz·er** *n.*

i·dée fixe /eeday feéks/ *n.* (*pl.* **idées fixes** *pronunc.* same) an idea dominating the mind; an obsession.

i·den·ti·cal /īdéntikəl/ *adj.* **1** (often foll. by *with*) (of different things) agreeing in every detail. **2** (of one thing viewed at different times) one and the same. **3** (of twins) developed from a single fertilized ovum, therefore of the same sex and usu. very similar in appearance. **4** *Logic & Math.* expressing an identity. □□ **i·den·ti·cal·ly** *adv.* **i·den·ti·cal·ness** *n.*

i·den·ti·fi·ca·tion /īdéntifikáyshən/ *n.* **1 a** the act or an instance of identifying; recognition; pinpointing. **b** association of oneself with the feelings, situation, characteristics, etc., of another person or group of people. **2** a means of identifying a person. **3** (*attrib.*) serving to identify (esp. the bearer) (*identification card*).

i·den·ti·fi·er /īdéntifīər/ *n.* **1** a person or thing that identifies. **2** *Computing* a sequence of characters used to identify or refer to a set of data.

i·den·ti·fy /īdéntifī/ *v.* (**-ies, -ied**) **1** *tr.* establish the identity of; recognize. **2** *tr.* establish or select by consideration or analysis of the circumstances (*identify the best method of solving the problem*). **3** *tr.* (foll. by *with*) associate (a person or oneself) inseparably or very closely (with a party, policy, etc.). **4** *tr.* (often foll. by *with*) treat (a thing) as identical. **5** *intr.* (foll. by *with*) **a** regard oneself as sharing characteristics of (another person). **b** associate oneself. □□ **i·den·ti·fi·a·ble** /-fíəbəl/ *adj.* **i·den·ti·fi·a·bly** *adv.*

i·den·ti·ty /īdéntitee/ *n.* (*pl.* **-ies**) **1 a** the quality or condition of being a specified person or thing. **b** individuality; personality (*felt he had lost his identity*). **2** identification or the result of it (*a case of mistaken identity; identity card*). **3** the state of being the same in substance, nature, qualities, etc.; absolute sameness (*no identity of interests between them*). **4** *Algebra* **a** the equality of two expressions for all values of the quantities expressed by letters. **b** an equation expressing this, e.g., $(x + 1)^2 = x^2 + 2x + 1$. **5** a transformation that leaves an object unchanged.

i·den·ti·ty cri·sis *n.* a temporary period during which an individual experiences a feeling of loss or breakdown of identity.

id·e·o·gram /ídeeəgram/ *n.* ▼ a character symbolizing the idea of a thing without indicating the sequence of sounds in its name (e.g., a numeral, and many Chinese characters).

CHINESE CHARACTER FOR TREE

ROMAN NUMERAL TWO

WHEELCHAIR ACCESS SIGN

AIRPORT SYMBOL

IDEOGRAMS

id·e·o·graph /ídeeəgraf/ *n.* = IDEOGRAM. □□ **id·e·o·graph·ic** *adj.* **id·e·og·ra·phy** /ídeeógrəfee/ *n.*

id·e·o·logue /ídeeəlawg, -log, idee-/ *n.* **1** a theorist; a visionary. **2** an adherent of an ideology.

id·e·ol·o·gy /ídeeóləjee, idee-/ *n.* (*pl.* **-ies**) **1** the system of ideas at the basis of an economic or political theory (*Marxist ideology*). **2** the manner of thinking characteristic of a class or individual (*bourgeois ideology*). **3** visionary speculation6. □□ **id·e·o·log·i·cal** /-əlójikəl/ *adj.* **id·e·o·log·i·cal·ly** *adv.* **id·e·ol·o·gist** /-deeól-/ *n.*

ides /īdz/ *n.pl.* the eighth day after the nones in the ancient Roman calendar (the 15th day of March, May, July, October; the 13th of other months).

id·i·o·cy /ídeeəsee/ *n.* (*pl.* **-ies**) **1** utter foolishness; idiotic behavior or an idiotic action. **2** extreme mental imbecility.

id·i·o·lect /ídeeəlekt/ *n.* the speech habits peculiar to a particular person.

id·i·om /ídeeəm/ *n.* **1** a group of words established by usage and having a meaning not deducible from those of the individual words (as in *at the drop of a hat, see the light*). **2** a form of expression peculiar to a language, person, or group of people. **3 a** the language of a people or country. **b** the specific character of this. **4** a characteristic mode of expression in music, art, etc.

id·i·o·mat·ic /ídeeəmátik/ *adj.* **1** relating to or conforming to idiom. **2** characteristic of a particular language. □□ **id·i·o·mat·i·cal·ly** *adv.*

id·i·op·a·thy /ídeeópəthee/ *n. Med.* any disease or condition of unknown cause or that arises spontaneously. □□ **id·i·o·path·ic** /ídeeəpáthik/ *adj.*

id·i·o·syn·cra·sy /ídeeōsíngkrəsee/ *n.* (*pl.* **-ies**) **1** a mental constitution, view or feeling, or mode of behavior, peculiar to a person. **2** anything highly individualized or eccentric. **3** a mode of expression peculiar to an author. **4** *Med.* a physical condition peculiar to a person. □□ **id·i·o·syn·crat·ic** /-krátik/ *adj.* **id·i·o·syn·crat·i·cal·ly** *adv.*

id·i·ot /ídeeət/ *n.* **1** *colloq.* a stupid person; an utter fool. **2** a person deficient in mind and permanently incapable of rational conduct. □□ **id·i·ot·ic** /ídeeótik/ *adj.* **id·i·ot·i·cal·ly** /ídeeótiklee/ *adv.*

id·i·ot sa·vant /ídyō savóN/ *n.* a mentally handicapped person who displays brilliance in a specific area, esp. one involving memory.

i·dle /íd'l/ *adj. & v.* ● *adj.* (**idler, idlest**) **1** lazy; indolent. **2** not in use; not working; unemployed. **3** (of time, etc.) unoccupied. **4** having no special basis or purpose (*idle rumor; idle curiosity*). **5** useless. **6** (of an action, thought, or word) ineffective; worthless; vain. ● *v.* **1 a** *intr.* (of an engine) run slowly without doing any work. **b** *tr.* cause (an engine) to idle. **2** *intr.* be idle. **3** *tr.* (foll. by *away*) pass (time, etc.) in idleness. □□ **i·dle·ness** *n.* **i·dler** /ídlər/ *n.* **i·dly** *adv.*

i·dler /ídlər/ *n.* a habitually lazy person.

i·dol /íd'l/ *n.* **1** an image of a deity, etc., used as an object of worship. **2** *Bibl.* a false god. **3** a person or thing that is the object of excessive or supreme adulation (*movie idol*).

IGNEOUS

Molten magma cooling slowly within batholiths and other intrusions in rock creates coarse- and intermediate-grained igneous rocks, such as granite and dolerite. Finer-grained basalt is commonly formed by volcanic lava cooling more quickly on the Earth's surface. Lava that is subject to a very rapid chilling gives rise to obsidian, which is composed of crystals so small that the rock's appearance is of smooth glass.

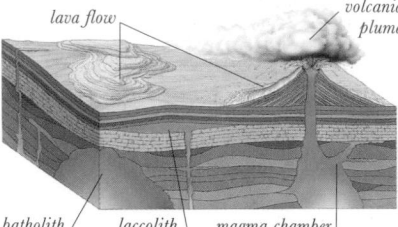

SECTION OF THE EARTH'S CRUST SHOWING
VOLCANIC FEATURES

lava flow · volcanic plume · batholith · laccolith · magma chamber

EXAMPLES OF IGNEOUS ROCKS

DOLERITE · PINK GRANITE · BASALT · SNOWFLAKE OBSIDIAN

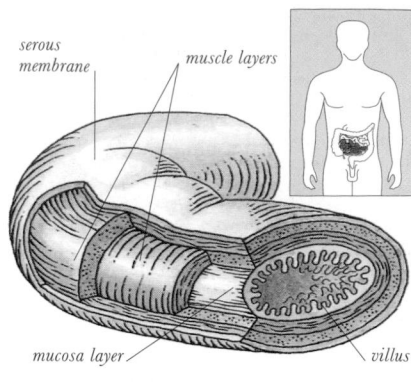

serous membrane · muscle layers · mucosa layer · villus

ILEUM: CUTAWAY SECTION
OF THE HUMAN ILEUM

I

i·dol·a·ter /īdólətər/ n. (fem. **idolatress** /-tris/) **1** a worshiper of idols. **2** (often foll. by *of*) a devoted admirer. □□ **i·dol·a·trous** adj.

i·dol·a·try /īdólətree/ n. **1** the worship of idols. **2** great adulation.

i·dol·ize /íd'līz/ v. **1** tr. venerate or love extremely or excessively. **2** tr. make an idol of. **3** intr. practice idolatry. □□ **i·dol·i·za·tion** n. **i·dol·iz·er** n.

i·dyll /íd'l/ n. (also **i·dyl**) **1** a short description in verse or prose of a picturesque scene or incident, esp. in rustic life. **2** an episode suitable for such treatment, usu. a love story. □□ **i·dyll·ist** n. **i·dyl·lize** v.tr.

i·dyl·lic /īdílik/ adj. **1** blissfully peaceful and happy. **2** of or like an idyll. □□ **i·dyl·li·cal·ly** adv.

i.e. abbr. that is to say.

if /if/ conj. & n. ● conj. **1** introducing a conditional clause: **a** on the condition or supposition that; in the event that (*if he comes I will tell him; if you are tired we will rest*). **b** (with past tense) implying that the condition is not fulfilled (*if I were you; if I knew I would say*). **2** even though (*I'll finish it, if it takes me all day*). **3** whenever (*if I am not sure I ask*). **4** whether (*see if you can find it*). **5 a** expressing wish or surprise (*if I could just try!; if it isn't my old hat!*). **b** expressing a request (*if you wouldn't mind opening the door?*). **6** with implied reservation, and perhaps not (*very rarely if at all*). **7** (with reduction of the protasis to its significant word) if there is or it is, etc. (*took little if any*). **8** despite being (*a useful if cumbersome device*). ● n. a condition or supposition (*too many ifs about it*). □ **if only 1** even if for no other reason than (*I'll come if only to see her*). **2** (often ellipt.) an expression of regret (*if only I had thought of it; if only I could swim!*). **if so** if that is the case.

if·fy /ífee/ adj. (**iffier**, **iffiest**) colloq. uncertain; doubtful.

ig·loo /íglōō/ n. an Eskimo dome-shaped dwelling, esp. one built of snow.

ig·ne·ous /ígneeəs/ adj. **1** of fire; fiery. **2** Geol. ▲ (esp. of rocks) produced by volcanic or magmatic action. ▷ ROCK CYCLE

ig·nis fat·u·us /ígnis fáchŏŏəs/ n. (pl. **ignes fatui** /ígneez fáchŏŏ-ī/) a will-o'-the-wisp.

ig·nite /ignít/ v. **1** tr. set fire to; cause to burn. **2** intr. catch fire. **3** tr. Chem. heat to the point of combustion or chemical change. **4** tr. provoke or excite (feelings, etc.). □□ **ig·nit·a·ble** adj. **ig·nit·a·bil·i·ty** /-təbílitee/ n. **ig·nit·i·ble** adj. **ig·nit·i·bil·i·ty** /-tibílitee/ n.

ig·ni·ter /ignítər/ n. **1** a device for igniting a fuel mixture in an engine. ▷ ROCKET. **2** a device for causing an electric arc.

ig·ni·tion /igníshən/ n. **1** a mechanism for, or the action of, starting the combustion of fuel in the cylinder of an internal-combustion engine. **2** the act or an instance of igniting or being ignited.

ig·no·ble /ignṓbəl/ adj. (**ignobler**, **ignoblest**) **1** dishonorable; mean; base. **2** of low birth, position, or reputation. □□ **ig·no·bil·i·ty** n. **ig·no·bly** adv.

ig·no·min·i·ous /ígnəmíneeəs/ adj. **1** causing or deserving ignominy. **2** humiliating. □□ **ig·no·min·i·ous·ly** adv. **ig·no·min·i·ous·ness** n.

ig·no·min·y /ígnəminee/ n. dishonor; infamy.

ig·no·ra·mus /ígnəráyməs/ n. (pl. **ignoramuses** or **ignorami**) an ignorant person.

ig·no·rance /ígnərəns/ n. (often foll. by *of*) lack of knowledge (about a thing).

ig·no·rant /ígnərənt/ adj. **1 a** lacking knowledge or experience. **b** (foll. by *of*, *in*) uninformed (about a fact or subject). **2** colloq. ill-mannered; uncouth. □□ **ig·no·rant·ly** adv.

ig·nore /ignáwr/ v.tr. **1** refuse to take notice of or accept. **2** intentionally disregard. □□ **ig·nor·er** n.

i·gua·na /igwaánə/ n. ◄ any of various large lizards of the family Iguanidae native to America, the W. Indies, and the Pacific islands, having a dorsal crest and throat appendages. ▷ LIZARD

IGUANA:
COMMON IGUANA
(*Iguana iguana*)

i·guan·o·don /igwaánə-don/ n. a large extinct plant-eating dinosaur of the genus *Iguanodon*, with forelimbs smaller than hind limbs. ▷ DINOSAUR

i·ke·ba·na /íkəbaánə/ n. the art of Japanese flower arrangement, with formal display according to strict rules.

IHS abbr. Jesus.

i·kon var. of ICON.

IL abbr. Illinois (in official postal use).

il- /il/ prefix assim. form in in-, in before *l*.

i·lang-i·lang var. of YLANG-YLANG.

il·e·a pl. of ILEUM.

il·e·um /íleeəm/ n. (pl. **ilea** /íleeə/) Anat. ▲ the third and last portion of the small intestine. ▷ INTESTINE. □□ **il·e·ac** adj.

i·lex /íleks/ n. **1** any tree or shrub of the genus *Ilex*, esp. the common holly. **2** the holm oak.

il·i·ac /íleeak/ adj. of the lower body or ilium (*iliac artery*). ▷ CARDIOVASCULAR

il·i·um /íleeəm/ n. (pl. **ilia** /íleeə/) **1** the bone forming the upper part of each half of the human pelvis. ▷ HIP JOINT, SKELETON. **2** the corresponding bone in animals.

ilk /ilk/ n. **1** a family, class, or set (*not of the same ilk as you*). **2** (in **of that ilk**) Sc. of the same (landed estate or place) (*Guthrie of that ilk* = of Guthrie).

Ill. abbr. Illinois.

ill. abbr. **1** illustrated. **2** illustration. **3** illustrator.

I'll /īl/ contr. I shall; I will.

ill /il/ adj., adv., & n. ● adj. **1** (usu. predic.; often foll. by *with*) out of health; sick (*is ill*; *was taken ill with pneumonia*; *mentally ill people*). **2** (of health) unsound; disordered. **3** wretched; unfavorable (*ill fortune*; *ill luck*). **4** harmful (*ill effects*). **5** hostile; unkind (*ill feeling*). **6** archaic morally bad. **7** faulty; unskillful (*ill taste*; *ill management*). **8** (of manners or conduct) improper. ● adv. **1** badly; wrongly (*ill-matched*). **2 a** imperfectly (*ill-provided*). **b** scarcely (*can ill afford to do it*). **3** unfavorably (*it would have gone ill with them*). ● n. **1** injury; harm. **2** evil; the opposite of good. □ **ill at ease** embarrassed; uneasy. **speak ill of** say something unfavorable about.

ill-ad·vised adj. **1** (of a person) foolish or imprudent. **2** (of a plan, etc.) not well formed or considered. □□ **ill-ad·vis·ed·ly** /-ədvízidlee/ adv.

il·la·tive /iláytiv, ílətiv/ adj. **1 a** (of a word) stating or introducing an inference. **b** inferential. **2** Gram. (of a case) denoting motion into. □□ **il·la·tive·ly** adv.

ill-be·haved adj. having bad manners or conduct.

ill-bred adj. badly brought up; rude.

il·le·gal /ileégəl/ adj. **1** not legal. **2** contrary to law. □□ **il·le·gal·i·ty** /-gálitee/ n. (pl. **-ies**). **il·le·gal·ly** adv.

il·leg·i·ble /iléjibəl/ adj. not legible. □□ **il·leg·i·bil·i·ty** n. **il·leg·i·bly** adv.

il·le·git·i·mate adj. & n. ● adj. /ilijítimət/ **1** (of a child) born of parents not married to each other. **2** not authorized by law; unlawful. **3** improper. **4** wrongly inferred. **5** physiologically abnormal. ● n. /ilijítimət/ a person whose position is illegitimate, esp. by birth. □□ **il·le·git·i·ma·cy** /-məsee/ n. **il·le·git·i·mate·ly** adv.

ill-e·quipped adj. (often foll. by *to* + infin.) not adequately equipped or qualified.

ill-fat·ed adj. destined to or bringing bad fortune.

ill-fa·vored adj. unattractive; displeasing; objectionable.

ill-found·ed adj. (of an idea, etc.) not well founded; baseless.

ill-got·ten adj. gained by wicked or unlawful means.

ill hu·mor n. moroseness; irritability. □□ **ill-hu·mored** adj.

il·lib·er·al /ilíbərəl/ *adj.* **1** intolerant; narrow-minded. **2** without liberal culture. **3** not generous; stingy. **4** vulgar; sordid. □□ **il·lib·er·al·i·ty** /-álitee/ *n.* (*pl.* **-ies**). **il·lib·er·al·ly** *adv.*

il·lic·it /ilísit/ *adj.* **1** unlawful; forbidden (*illicit dealings*). **2** secret; furtive (*an illicit cigarette*). □□ **il·lic·it·ly** *adv.* **il·lic·it·ness** *n.*

il·lim·it·a·ble /ilímitəbəl/ *adj.* limitless.

il·lit·er·ate /ilítərət/ *adj. & n.* ● *adj.* **1** unable to read. **2** uneducated. ● *n.* an illiterate person. □□ **il·lit·er·a·cy** *n.* **il·lit·er·ate·ly** *adv.* **il·lit·er·ate·ness** *n.*

ill-man·nered *adj.* having bad manners; rude.

ill na·ture *n.* churlishness; unkindness. □□ **ill-na·tured** *adj.* **ill-na·tured·ly** *adv.*

ill·ness /ílnis/ *n.* **1** a disease, ailment, or malady. **2** the state of being ill.

il·log·i·cal /ilójikəl/ *adj.* devoid of or contrary to logic. □□ **il·log·i·cal·i·ty** /-kálitee/ *n.* (*pl.* **-ies**). **il·log·i·cal·ly** *adv.*

ill-starred *adj.* unlucky; destined to failure.

ill tem·per *n.* moroseness. □□ **ill-tem·pered** *adj.*

ill-timed *adj.* done or occurring at an inappropriate time.

ill-treat *v.tr.* treat badly; abuse. □□ **ill-treat·ment** *n.*

il·lu·mi·nant /ilóominənt/ *n. & adj.* ● *n.* a means of illumination. ● *adj.* serving to illuminate. □□ **il·lu·mi·nance** /-nəns/ *n.*

il·lu·mi·nate /ilóominayt/ *v.tr.* **1** light up; make bright. **2** decorate (buildings, etc.) with lights as a sign of festivity. **3** ▼ decorate (an initial letter, a manuscript, etc.) with gold, silver, or brilliant colors. **4** help to explain (a subject, etc.). **5** enlighten spiritually or intellectually. **6** shed luster on. □□ **il·lu·mi·nat·ing** *adj.* **il·lu·mi·nat·ing·ly** *adv.* **il·lu·mi·na·tion** /-náyshən/ *n.* **il·lu·mi·na·tive** /-náytiv, -nətiv/ *adj.* **il·lu·mi·na·tor** *n.*

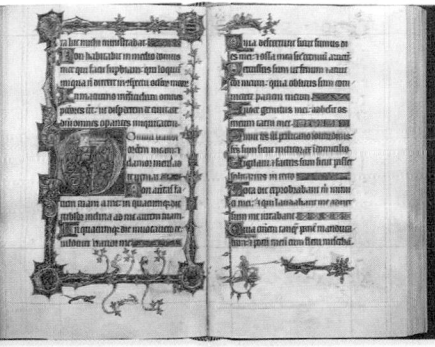

ILLUMINATE: 14TH-CENTURY ILLUMINATED MANUSCRIPT

il·lu·mine /ilóomin/ *v.tr. literary* **1** light up; make bright. **2** enlighten spiritually.

ill-use *v.tr.* = ILL-TREAT. □□ **ill use** *n.*

il·lu·sion /ilóozhən/ *n.* **1** deception; delusion. **2** a misapprehension of the true state of affairs. **3 a** the faulty perception of an external object. **b** an instance of this. **4** a figment of the imagination. **5** = OPTICAL ILLUSION. □ **be under the illusion** (foll. by *that* + clause) believe mistakenly. □□ **il·lu·sion·al** *adj.*

il·lu·sion·ist /ilóozhənist/ *n.* a person who produces illusions; a magician. □□ **il·lu·sion·ism** *n.* **il·lu·sion·is·tic** *adj.*

il·lu·sive /ilóosiv/ *adj.* = ILLUSORY.

il·lu·so·ry /ilóosəree, -zəree/ *adj.* **1** deceptive (esp. as regards value or content). **2** having the character of an illusion. □□ **il·lu·so·ri·ly** *adv.* **il·lu·so·ri·ness** *n.*

il·lus·trate /íləstrayt/ *v.tr.* **1 a** provide (a book, newspaper, etc.) with pictures. **b** elucidate (a description, etc.) by drawings or pictures. **2** serve as an example of. **3** explain or make clear, esp. by examples.

il·lus·tra·tion /íləstráyshən/ *n.* **1** a drawing or picture illustrating a book, magazine article, etc. **2** an example serving to elucidate. **3** the act or an instance of illustrating. □□ **il·lus·tra·tion·al** *adj.*

il·lus·tra·tive /ilústrətiv, íləstray-/ *adj.* (often foll. by *of*) serving as an explanation or example. □□ **il·lus·tra·tive·ly** *adv.*

il·lus·tra·tor /íləstraytər/ *n.* a person who makes illustrations, esp. for magazines, books, advertising copy, etc.

il·lus·tri·ous /ilústreeəs/ *adj.* distinguished; renowned. □□ **il·lus·tri·ous·ly** *adv.* **il·lus·tri·ous·ness** *n.*

ill will *n.* bad feeling; animosity.

ill wind *n.* an unfavorable or untoward circumstance (with ref. to the proverb *it's an ill wind that blows nobody good*).

ILO *abbr.* International Labor Organization.

I'm /īm/ *contr.* I am.

im·age /ímij/ *n. & v.* ● *n.* **1** a representation of the external form of an object, e.g., a statue (esp. of a saint, etc., as an object of veneration). **2** the character or reputation of a person or thing as generally perceived. **3** an optical appearance or counterpart produced by light or other radiation from an object reflected in a mirror, refracted through a lens, etc. **4** semblance; likeness (*God created man in His own image*). **5** a person or thing that closely resembles another (*is the image of his father*). **6** a typical example. **7** a simile or metaphor. **8 a** a mental representation. **b** an idea or conception. **9** *Math.* a set formed by mapping from another set. ● *v.tr.* **1** make an image of; portray. **2** reflect; mirror. **3** describe or imagine vividly. **4** typify.

im·age·ry /ímijree/ *n.* **1** figurative illustration, esp. as used by an author for particular effects. **2** images collectively. **3** statuary; carving. **4** mental images collectively.

im·ag·in·a·ble /imájinəbəl/ *adj.* that can be imagined (*the greatest difficulty imaginable*). □□ **i·mag·i·na·bly** *adv.*

im·ag·i·nar·y /imájinéree/ *adj.* **1** existing only in the imagination. **2** *Math.* being the square root of a negative quantity. □□ **im·ag·i·nar·i·ly** *adv.*

im·ag·i·na·tion /imájináyshən/ *n.* **1** a mental faculty forming images or concepts of external objects not present to the senses. **2** the ability of the mind to be creative or resourceful. **3** the process of imagining.

im·ag·i·na·tive /imájinətiv/ *adj.* **1** having or showing in a high degree the faculty of imagination. **2** given to using the imagination. □□ **im·ag·i·na·tive·ly** *adv.* **im·ag·i·na·tive·ness** *n.*

im·ag·ine /imájin/ *v.tr.* **1 a** form a mental image or concept of. **b** picture to oneself (something nonexistent or not present to the senses). **2** (often foll. by *to* + infin.) think or conceive (*imagined them to be soldiers*). **3** guess (*cannot imagine what they are doing*). **4** (often foll. by *that* + clause) suppose; be of the opinion (*I imagine you will need help*). □□ **i·mag·in·er** *n.*

im·ag·in·ings /imájiningz/ *n.pl.* fancies; fantasies.

im·ag·ism /íməjizəm/ *n.* a movement in early 20th-c. poetry which sought clarity of expression through the use of precise images. □□ **im·ag·ist** *n.* **im·ag·is·tic** *adj.*

i·ma·go /imáygō, imáa-/ *n.* (*pl.* **-oes** or **imagines** /imájineez/) *Zool.* the final and fully developed stage of an insect after all metamorphoses, e.g., a butterfly or beetle. ▷ METAMORPHOSIS

i·mam /imaám/ *n.* **1** a leader of prayers in a mosque. **2** a title of various Islamic leaders, esp. of one succeeding Muhammad as leader of Islam. □□ **i·mam·ate** /-mayt/ *n.*

im·bal·ance /imbáləns/ *n.* **1** lack of balance. **2** disproportion.

im·be·cile /ímbisil, -səl/ *n. & adj.* ● *n.* **1** a person of abnormally weak intellect, esp. an adult with a mental age of about five. **2** *colloq.* a stupid person. ● *adj.* mentally weak; stupid; idiotic. □□ **im·be·cile·ly** *adv.* **im·be·cil·ic** /-sílik/ *adj.* **im·be·cil·i·ty** /-silitee/ *n.* (*pl.* **-ies**).

im·bed var. of EMBED.

im·bibe /imbíb/ *v.tr.* **1** (also *absol.*) drink (esp. alcoholic liquor). **2 a** absorb or assimilate (ideas, etc.). **b** absorb (moisture, etc.). **3** inhale (air, etc.). □□ **im·bib·er** *n.* **im·bi·bi·tion** /ímbibíshən/ *n.*

im·bri·cate /ímbrəkayt/ *adj.* (also **im·bri·cat·ed**) arranged in an overlapping manner like roof tiles.

im·bro·glio /imbrólyō/ *n.* (*pl.* **-os**) **1** a confused or complicated situation. **2** a confused heap.

im·bue /imbyōō/ *v.tr.* (**imbues, imbued, imbuing**) (often foll. by *with*) **1** inspire or permeate (with feelings, opinions, or qualities). **2** saturate. **3** dye.

IMF *abbr.* International Monetary Fund.

im·i·tate /ímitayt/ *v.tr.* **1** follow the example of; copy the action(s) of. **2** mimic. **3** make a copy of; reproduce. **4** be (consciously or not) like. □□ **im·i·ta·ble** *adj.* **im·i·ta·tor** *n.*

im·i·ta·tion /ímitáyshən/ *n. & adj.* ● *n.* **1** the act or an instance of imitating or being imitated. **2** a copy. **3** *Mus.* the repetition of a phrase, etc., usu. at a different pitch, in another part or voice. ● *adj.* made in imitation of something genuine; counterfeit; fake (*imitation leather*).

im·i·ta·tive /ímitaytiv/ *adj.* **1** (often foll. by *of*) imitating; following a model or example. **2** counterfeit. **3** of a word: **a** that reproduces a natural sound (e.g., *fizz*). **b** whose sound is thought to correspond to the appearance, etc., of the object or action described (e.g., *blob*). □□ **im·i·ta·tive·ly** *adv.* **im·i·ta·tive·ness** *n.*

im·mac·u·late /imákyələt/ *adj.* **1** pure; spotless; perfectly clean or neat and tidy. **2** perfectly or extremely well executed (*an immaculate performance*). **3** free from fault; innocent. □□ **im·mac·u·la·cy** *n.* **im·mac·u·late·ly** *adv.* **im·mac·u·late·ness** *n.*

Im·mac·u·late Con·cep·tion *n. RC Ch.* the doctrine that God preserved the Virgin Mary from the taint of original sin from the moment she was conceived.

im·ma·nent /ímənənt/ *adj.* **1** (often foll. by *in*) indwelling; inherent. **2** (of the Supreme Being) permanently pervading the universe (opp. TRANSCENDENT). □□ **im·ma·nence** /-nəns/ *n.* **im·ma·nen·cy** *n.* **im·ma·nent·ism** *n.* **im·ma·nent·ist** *n.*

im·ma·te·ri·al /iməteereeəl/ *adj.* **1** of no essential consequence; unimportant. **2** not material; incorporeal.

im·ma·ture /iməchōōr, -tōōr, -tyōōr/ *adj.* **1** not mature or fully developed. **2** lacking emotional or intellectual development. **3** unripe. □□ **im·ma·ture·ly** *adv.* **im·ma·tur·i·ty** *n.*

im·meas·ur·a·ble /imézhərəbəl/ *adj.* not measurable; immense. □□ **im·meas·ur·a·bly** *adv.*

im·me·di·ate /iméedeeət/ *adj.* **1** occurring or done at once or without delay (*an immediate reply*). **2** nearest; not separated by others (*the immediate vicinity; the immediate future; my immediate neighbor*). **3** most pressing or urgent; of current concern (*our immediate concern was to get him to the hospital*). **4** (of a relation or action) having direct effect; without an intervening medium or agency (*the immediate cause of death*). **5** (of knowledge, reactions, etc.) intuitive; gained or exhibited without reasoning. □□ **im·me·di·a·cy** *n.* **im·me·di·ate·ness** *n.*

im·me·di·ate·ly /iméedeeətlee/ *adv. & conj.* ● *adv.* **1** without pause or delay. **2** without intermediary. ● *conj. Brit.* as soon as.

im·me·mo·ri·al /imimáwreeəl/ *adj.* **1** ancient beyond memory or record. **2** very old. □□ **im·me·mo·ri·al·ly** *adv.*

im·mense /iméns/ *adj.* **1** immeasurably large or great; huge. **2** very great; considerable (*made an immense difference*). **3** *colloq.* very good. □□ **im·mense·ness** *n.* **im·men·si·ty** *n.*

im·mense·ly /ménslee/ *adv.* **1** very much (*enjoyed myself immensely*). **2** to an immense degree.

im·merse /imə́rs/ *v.tr.* **1 a** (often foll. by *in*) dip; plunge. **b** cause (a person) to be completely under water. **2** (often *refl.* or in *passive*; often foll. by *in*) absorb or involve deeply. **3** (often foll. by *in*) bury; embed.

I

im·mer·sion /imə́rzhən, -shən/ n. **1** the act or an instance of immersing; the process of being immersed. **2** baptism by immersing the whole person in water. **3** mental absorption. **4** Astron. the disappearance of a celestial body behind another or in its shadow.

im·mi·grant /ímigrənt/ n. & adj. ● n. a person who immigrates. ● adj. **1** immigrating. **2** of or concerning immigrants.

im·mi·grate /ímigrayt/ v. **1** intr. come as a permanent resident to a country other than one's native land. **2** tr. bring in (a person) as an immigrant. □□ **im·mi·gra·tion** /-gráyshən/ n. **im·mi·gra·to·ry** adj.

im·mi·nent /íminənt/ adj. **1** (of an event, esp. danger) impending; about to happen. **2** archaic overhanging. □□ **im·mi·nence** /-nəns/ n. **im·mi·nent·ly** adv.

im·mis·ci·ble /imísibəl/ adj. (often foll. by with) that cannot be mixed. □□ **im·mis·ci·bil·i·ty** n. **im·mis·ci·bly** adv.

im·mit·tance /imít'ns/ n. Electr. admittance or impedance (when not distinguished).

im·mix·ture /imíks-chər/ n. **1** the process of mixing up. **2** (often foll. by in) being involved.

im·mo·bile /imṓbəl, -beel, -bīl/ adj. **1** not moving. **2** not able to move or be moved. □□ **im·mo·bil·i·ty** /-bílitee/ n.

im·mo·bi·lize /imṓbilīz/ v.tr. **1** make or keep immobile. **2** make (a vehicle or troops) incapable of being moved. **3** keep (a limb or patient) restricted in movement for healing purposes. **4** restrict the free movement of. **5** withdraw (coins) from circulation to support paper currency. □□ **im·mo·bi·li·za·tion** n. **im·mo·bi·liz·er** n.

im·mod·er·ate /imódərət/ adj. excessive; lacking moderation. □□ **im·mod·er·ate·ly** adv. **im·mod·er·ate·ness** n. **im·mod·er·a·tion** /-ráyshən/ n.

im·mod·est /imódist/ adj. **1** lacking modesty; forward; impudent. **2** lacking due decency. □□ **im·mod·est·ly** adv. **im·mod·es·ty** n.

im·mo·late /íməlayt/ v.tr. **1** kill or offer as a sacrifice. **2** literary sacrifice (a valued thing). □□ **im·mo·la·tion** /-láyshən/ n. **im·mo·la·tor** n.

im·mor·al /imáwrəl, imór-/ adj. **1** not conforming to accepted standards of morality (cf. AMORAL). **2** morally wrong (esp. in sexual matters). **3** depraved; dissolute. □□ **im·mo·ral·i·ty** /-álitee/ n. (pl. **-ies**). **im·mor·al·ly** adv.

im·mor·tal /imáwrt'l/ adj. & n. ● adj. **1 a** living forever; not mortal. **b** divine. **2** unfading; incorruptible. **3** likely or worthy to be famous for all time. ● n. **1 a** an immortal being. **b** (in pl.) the gods of antiquity. **2** a person (esp. an author) of enduring fame. **3** (**Immortal**) a member of the French Academy. □□ **im·mor·tal·i·ty** /-tálitee/ n. **im·mor·tal·ize** v.tr. **im·mor·tal·i·za·tion** n. **im·mor·tal·ly** adv.

im·mov·a·ble /imṓvəbəl/ adj. & n. (also **im·move·a·ble**) ● adj. **1** that cannot be moved. **2** steadfast; unyielding. **3** emotionless. **4** not subject to change (immovable law). **5** motionless. **6** Law (of property) consisting of land, houses, etc. ● n. (in pl.) Law immovable property. □□ **im·mov·a·bil·i·ty** n. **im·mov·a·ble·ness** n. **im·mov·a·bly** adv.

im·mune /imyoon/ adj. **1 a** (often foll. by against, from, to) protected against an infection owing to the presence of specific antibodies, or through inoculation or inherited or acquired resistance. **b** relating to immunity (immune mechanism). **2** (foll. by from, to) free or exempt from or not subject to (some undesirable factor or circumstance).

im·mune re·sponse n. the reaction of the body to the introduction into it of an antigen. ▷ INFLAMMATION

im·mu·ni·ty /imyōonitee/ n. (pl. **-ies**) **1** Med. the ability of an organism to resist infection, by means of the presence of circulating antibodies and white blood cells. **2** freedom or exemption from an obligation, penalty, or unfavorable circumstance.

im·mu·nize /imyənīz/ v.tr. make immune, esp. to

infection, usu. by inoculation. □□ **im·mu·ni·za·tion** n. **im·mu·niz·er** n.

immuno- /ímyənō/ comb. form immunity to infection.

im·mu·no·de·fi·cien·cy /ímyənōdifíshənsee, imyōo-/ n. a reduction in a person's normal immune defenses.

im·mu·no·gen·ic /ímyənōjénik, imyōo-/ adj. Biochem. of, relating to, or possessing the ability to elicit an immune response.

im·mu·no·glob·u·lin /ímyənōglóbyəlin, imyōo-/ n. Biochem. any of a group of structurally related proteins which function as antibodies.

im·mu·nol·o·gy /ímyənóləjee/ n. the scientific study of immunity. □□ **im·mu·no·log·ic** /-nəlójik/ adj. **im·mu·no·log·i·cal** /-nəlójikəl/ adj. **im·mu·no·log·i·cal·ly** adv. **im·mu·nol·o·gist** /-nóləjist/ n.

im·mu·no·sup·pressed /ímyənōsəprést, imyōo-/ adj. (of an individual) rendered partially or completely unable to react immunologically.

im·mu·no·sup·pres·sion /ímyənōsəpréshən, imyōo-/ n. Biochem. the partial or complete suppression of the immune response of an individual, esp. in order to maintain the survival of an organ after a transplant operation. □□ **im·mu·no·sup·pres·sant** n.

im·mu·no·sup·pres·sive /ímyənōsəprésiv, imyōo-/ adj. & n. ● adj. partially or completely suppressing the immune response of an individual. ● n. an immunosuppressive drug.

im·mu·no·ther·a·py /ímyənōthérəpee, imyōo-/ n. Med. the prevention or treatment of disease with substances that stimulate the immune response.

im·mure /imyōor/ v.tr. **1** enclose within walls; imprison. **2** refl. shut oneself away. □□ **im·mure·ment** n.

im·mu·ta·ble /imyōotəbəl/ adj. **1** unchangeable. **2** not subject to variation in different cases. □□ **im·mu·ta·bil·i·ty** /-bílitee/ n. **im·mu·ta·bly** adv.

imp /imp/ n. **1** a mischievous child. **2** a small mischievous devil or sprite.

im·pact n. & v. ● n. /ímpakt/ **1** (often foll. by on, against) the action of one body coming forcibly into contact with another. **2** a strong effect or influence. ● v. /impákt/ **1** tr. (often foll. by in, into) press or fix firmly. **2** tr. (as **impacted** adj.) **a** (of a tooth) wedged between another tooth and the jaw. **b** (of a fractured bone) with the parts crushed together. ▷ FRACTURE. **c** (of feces) lodged in the intestine. **3** intr. **a** (foll. by against, on) come forcibly into contact with a (larger) body or surface. **b** (foll. by on) have a pronounced effect. □□ **im·pac·tion** /-pákshən/ n.

im·pair /impáir/ v.tr. damage or weaken. □□ **im·pair·ment** n.

im·pal·a /impáalə, -pálə/ n. (pl. same) a small antelope, Aepyceros melampus, of S. and E. Africa, capable of long high jumps.

im·pale /impáyl/ v.tr. (foll. by on, upon, with) transfix or pierce with a sharp instrument. □□ **im·pale·ment** n.

im·pal·pa·ble /impálpəbəl/ adj. **1** not easily grasped by the mind; intangible. **2** imperceptible to the touch. **3** (of powder) very fine; not containing grains that can be felt. □□ **im·pal·pa·bil·i·ty** /-bílitee/ n. **im·pal·pa·bly** adv.

im·pan·el /impán'l/ v.tr. (also **empanel**) (**-paneled**, **-paneling**; esp. Brit. **-panelled**, **-panelling**) enroll or enter on a panel (those eligible for jury service). □□ **im·pan·el·ment** n.

im·part /impáart/ v.tr. (often foll. by to) **1** communicate (news, etc.). **2** give a share of (a thing).

im·par·tial /impáarshəl/ adj. treating all sides in a dispute, etc., equally; unprejudiced; fair. □□ **im·par·ti·al·i·ty** /-sheeálitee/ n. **im·par·tial·ly** adv.

im·pas·sa·ble /impásəbəl/ adj. that cannot be traversed. □□ **im·pas·sa·bil·i·ty** n. **im·pas·sa·ble·ness** n. **im·pas·sa·bly** adv.

im·passe /ímpas/ n. a position from which progress is impossible; deadlock.

im·pas·si·ble /impásibəl/ adj. **1** impassive. **2** incapable of feeling or emotion. **3** incapable of suffering injury. □□ **im·pas·si·bil·i·ty** n. **im·pas·si·ble·ness** n. **im·pas·si·bly** adv.

im·pas·sioned /impáshənd/ adj. deeply felt; ardent (an impassioned plea).

im·pas·sive /impásiv/ adj. **1 a** deficient in or incapable of feeling emotion. **b** undisturbed by passion; serene. **2** without sensation. **3** not subject to suffering. □□ **im·pas·sive·ly** adv. **im·pas·sive·ness** n. **im·pas·siv·i·ty** /-sívitee/ n.

im·pas·to /impástō, -páas-/ n. Art **1** the process of laying on paint thickly. **2** this technique of painting.

im·pa·tiens /impáyshənz/ n. ◀ any plant of the genus Impatiens, including several species popularly as touch-me-not.

im·pa·tient /impáyshənt/ adj. **1 a** (often foll. by at, with) lacking patience or tolerance. **b** (of an action) showing a lack of patience. **2** (often foll. by for, or to + infin.) restlessly eager. **3** (foll. by of) intolerant. □□ **im·pa·tience** /-shəns/ n. **im·pa·tient·ly** adv.

IMPATIENS (Impatiens walleriana cultivar)

im·peach /impéech/ v.tr. **1** charge (the holder of a public office) with misconduct. **2** Brit. charge with a crime against the government, esp. treason. **3** call in question; disparage (a person's integrity, etc.). □□ **im·peach·a·ble** adj. **im·peach·ment** n.

im·pec·ca·ble /impékəbəl/ adj. **1** (of behavior, performance, etc.) faultless; exemplary. **2** not liable to sin. □□ **im·pec·ca·bil·i·ty** n. **im·pec·ca·bly** adv.

im·pe·cu·ni·ous /ímpikyōoneeəs/ adj. having little or no money. □□ **im·pe·cu·ni·os·i·ty** /-neeósitee/ n. **im·pe·cu·ni·ous·ness** n.

im·ped·ance /impéed'ns/ n. Electr. the total effective resistance of an electric circuit, etc., to alternating current, arising from ohmic resistance and reactance.

im·pede /impéed/ v.tr. retard by obstructing; hinder.

im·ped·i·ment /impédimənt/ n. **1** a hindrance or obstruction. **2** a defect in speech, e.g., a lisp or stammer. □□ **im·ped·i·men·tal** /-mént'l/ adj.

im·ped·i·men·ta /impédiméntə/ n.pl. **1** encumbrances. **2** traveling equipment, esp. of an army.

im·pel /impél/ v.tr. (**impelled**, **impelling**) **1** drive, force, or urge into action. **2** drive forward; propel. □□ **im·pel·lent** adj. & n. **im·pel·ler** n.

im·pend /impénd/ v.intr. **1** be about to happen. **2** often foll. by over) **a** (of a danger) be threatening. **b** hang; be suspended. □□ **im·pend·ing** adj.

im·pen·e·tra·ble /impénitrəbəl/ adj. **1** that cannot be penetrated. **2** inscrutable; unfathomable. **3** inaccessible to ideas, influences, etc. □□ **im·pen·e·tra·bil·i·ty** n. **im·pen·e·tra·ble·ness** n. **im·pen·e·tra·bly** adv.

im·pen·i·tent /impénit'nt/ adj. not repentant or penitent. □□ **im·pen·i·tence** n. **im·pen·i·ten·cy** n. **im·pen·i·tent·ly** adv.

im·per·a·tive /impérətiv/ adj. & n. ● adj. **1** urgent. **2** obligatory. **3** commanding; peremptory. **4** Gram. (of a mood) expressing a command (e.g., come here!). ● n. **1** Gram. the imperative mood. **2** a command. □□ **im·per·a·ti·val** /-ətívəl/ adj. **im·per·a·tive·ly** adv. **im·per·a·tive·ness** n.

im·per·cep·ti·ble /impərséptibəl/ adj. **1** that cannot be perceived. **2** very slight, gradual, or subtle. □□ **im·per·cep·ti·bil·i·ty** n. **im·per·cep·ti·bly** adv.

im·per·fect /impə́rfikt/ adj. & n. ● adj. **1** not fully formed or done; faulty; incomplete. **2** Gram. (of a tense) denoting a (usu. past) action in progress but not completed at the time in question (e.g., they were singing). **3** Mus. (of a cadence) ending on the dominant chord. ● n. the imperfect tense. □□ **im·per·fect·ly** adv.

im·per·fec·tion /ímpərfékshən/ *n.* **1** incompleteness. **2 a** faultiness. **b** a fault or blemish.

im·per·fec·tive /ímpərféktiv/ *adj.* & *n. Gram.* ● *adj.* (of a verb aspect, etc.) expressing an action without reference to its completion (opp. PERFECTIVE). ● *n.* an imperfective aspect or form of a verb.

im·pe·ri·al /impeéreeəl/ *adj.* **1** of or characteristic of an empire or comparable sovereign state. **2 a** of or characteristic of an emperor. **b** supreme in authority. **c** majestic; august. **d** magnificent. **3** (of nonmetric weights and measures) used or formerly used by statute in the UK (*imperial gallon*). □□ **im·pe·ri·al·ly** *adv.*

im·pe·ri·al·ism /impeéreeəlizəm/ *n.* **1** an imperial rule or system. **2** usu. *derog.* a policy of acquiring dependent territories or extending a country's influence through trade, diplomacy, etc. □□ **im·pe·ri·al·is·tic** *adj.* **im·pe·ri·al·is·ti·cal·ly** *adv.* **im·pe·ri·al·ize** *v.tr.*

im·pe·ri·al·ist /impeéreeəlist/ *n.* & *adj.* ● *n.* usu. *derog.* an advocate or agent of imperial rule or of imperialism. ● *adj.* of or relating to imperialism or imperialists.

im·per·il /impéril/ *v.tr.* (**imperiled, imperiling**) bring or put into danger.

im·pe·ri·ous /impeéreeəs/ *adj.* **1** overbearing; domineering. **2** urgent; imperative. □□ **im·pe·ri·ous·ly** *adv.* **im·pe·ri·ous·ness** *n.*

im·per·ish·a·ble /impérishəbəl/ *adj.* that cannot perish. □□ **im·per·ish·a·bil·i·ty** *n.* **im·per·ish·a·ble·ness** *n.* **im·per·ish·a·bly** *adv.*

im·per·ma·nent /impə́rmənənt/ *adj.* not permanent; transient. □□ **im·per·ma·nence** /-nəns/ *n.* **im·per·ma·nen·cy** *n.* **im·per·ma·nent·ly** *adv.*

im·per·me·a·ble /impə́rmeeəbəl/ *adj.* **1** that cannot be penetrated. **2** *Physics* that does not permit the passage of fluids. □□ **im·per·me·a·bil·i·ty** *n.*

im·per·mis·si·ble /impərmísibəl/ *adj.* not allowable. □□ **im·per·mis·si·bil·i·ty** *n.*

im·per·son·al /impə́rsənəl/ *adj.* **1** having no personality. **2** having no personal feeling or reference. **3** *Gram.* **a** (of a verb) used only with a formal subject (usu. *it*) and expressing an action not attributable to a definite subject (e.g., *it is snowing*). **b** (of a pronoun) = INDEFINITE 3. □□ **im·per·son·al·i·ty** /-álitee/ *n.* **im·per·son·al·ly** *adv.*

im·per·son·ate /impə́rsənayt/ *v.tr.* **1** pretend to be (another person) for the purpose of entertainment or fraud. **2** act (a character). □□ **im·per·son·a·tion** /-náyshən/ *n.* **im·per·son·a·tor** *n.*

im·per·ti·nent /impə́rt'nənt/ *adj.* **1** rude or insolent; lacking proper respect. **2** out of place; absurd. **3** esp. *Law* irrelevant; intrusive. □□ **im·per·ti·nence** /-nəns/ *n.* **im·per·ti·nent·ly** *adv.*

im·per·turb·a·ble /impərtə́rbəbəl/ *adj.* not excitable; calm. □□ **im·per·turb·a·bil·i·ty** *n.* **im·per·turb·a·ble·ness** *n.* **im·per·turb·a·bly** *adv.*

im·per·vi·ous /impə́rveeəs/ *adj.* (usu. foll. by *to*) **1** not responsive to an argument, etc. **2** not affording passage to a fluid. □□ **im·per·vi·ous·ly** *adv.* **im·per·vi·ous·ness** *n.*

im·pe·ti·go /impitígō/ *n.* a contagious bacterial skin infection forming pustules and yellow crusty sores. □□ **im·pe·tig·i·nous** /impitíjinəs/ *adj.*

im·pet·u·ous /impéchōōəs/ *adj.* **1** acting or done rashly or with sudden energy. **2** moving forcefully or rapidly. □□ **im·pet·u·os·i·ty** /-ósitee/ *n.* **im·pet·u·ous·ly** *adv.* **im·pet·u·ous·ness** *n.*

im·pe·tus /impitəs/ *n.* **1** the force or energy with which a body moves. **2** a driving force or impulse.

im·pi·e·ty /impíətee/ *n.* (*pl.* **-ies**) **1** a lack of piety or reverence. **2** an act, etc. showing this.

im·pinge /impínj/ *v.tr.* (usu. foll. by *on, upon*) **1** make an impact; have an effect. **2** encroach. □□ **im·pinge·ment** *n.*

im·pi·ous /impeeəs, impí-/ *adj.* **1** not pious. **2** wicked; profane. □□ **im·pi·ous·ly** *adv.* **im·pi·ous·ness** *n.*

imp·ish /ímpish/ *adj.* of or like an imp; mischievous. □□ **imp·ish·ly** *adv.* **imp·ish·ness** *n.*

im·plac·a·ble /implákəbəl/ *adj.* that cannot be appeased; inexorable. □□ **im·plac·a·bil·i·ty** *n.* **im·plac·a·bly** *adv.*

im·plant *v.* & *n.* ● *v.tr.* /implánt/ **1** (often foll. by *in*) insert or fix. **2** (often foll. by *in*) instill (a principle, idea, etc.) in a person's mind. **3** plant. **4** *Med.* **a** insert (tissue, etc.) in a living body. **b** (in *passive*) (of a fertilized ovum) become attached to the wall of the womb. ● *n.* /ímplant/ **1** a thing implanted. **2** a thing implanted in the body, e.g., a piece of tissue or a capsule containing material for radium therapy. □□ **im·plan·ta·tion** *n.*

im·plau·si·ble /impláwzibəl/ *adj.* not plausible. □□ **im·plau·si·bil·i·ty** *n.* **im·plau·si·bly** *adv.*

im·ple·ment *n.* & *v.* ● *n.* /ímplimənt/ **1** a tool, instrument, or utensil. **2** (in *pl.*) equipment; articles of furniture, dress, etc. **3** *Law* performance of an obligation. ● *v.tr.* /ímpliment/ **1 a** put (a decision, plan, etc.) into effect. **b** fulfill (an undertaking). **2** complete (a contract, etc.). □□ **im·ple·men·ta·tion** *n.*

im·pli·cate *v.* & *n.* ● *v.tr.* /ímplikayt/ **1** (often foll. by *in*) show (a person) to be concerned or involved (in a charge, crime, etc.). **2** (in *passive*; often foll. by *in*) be affected or involved. **3** lead to as a consequence or inference. ● *n.* /ímplikət/ a thing implied. □□ **im·pli·ca·tive** /ímplikaytiv, implíkə-/ *adj.* **im·pli·ca·tive·ly** *adv.*

im·pli·ca·tion /implikáyshən/ *n.* **1** what is involved in or implied by something else. **2** the act of implicating or implying. □ **by implication** by what is implied or suggested rather than by formal expression.

im·plic·it /implísit/ *adj.* **1** implied though not plainly expressed. **2** (often foll. by *in*) virtually contained. **3** absolute; unquestioning; unreserved (*implicit obedience*). **4** *Math.* (of a function) not expressed directly in terms of independent variables. □□ **im·plic·it·ly** *adv.* **im·plic·it·ness** *n.*

im·plode /implṓd/ *v.intr.* & *tr.* burst or cause to burst inward. □□ **im·plo·sion** /-plṓzhən/ *n.* **im·plo·sive** /-plṓsiv/ *adj.*

im·plore /impláwr/ *v.tr.* **1** (often foll. by *to* + infin.) entreat (a person). **2** beg earnestly for. □□ **im·plor·ing** *adj.* **im·plor·ing·ly** *adv.*

im·ply /implí/ *v.tr.* (**-ies, -ied**) **1** (often foll. by *that* + clause) strongly suggest the truth or existence of (a thing not expressly asserted). **2** insinuate; hint (*what are you implying?*). **3** signify. □□ **im·plied** *adj.* **im·pli·ed·ly** *adv.*

im·po·lite /impəlít/ *adj.* (**impolitest**) ill-mannered; uncivil; rude. □□ **im·po·lite·ly** *adv.* **im·po·lite·ness** *n.*

im·pol·i·tic /impólitik/ *adj.* **1** inexpedient; unwise. **2** not politic. □□ **im·pol·i·tic·ly** *adv.*

im·pon·der·a·ble /impóndərəbəl/ *adj.* & *n.* ● *adj.* that cannot be estimated or assessed in any definite way. ● *n.* (usu. in *pl.*) something difficult or impossible to assess. □□ **im·pon·der·a·bil·i·ty** *n.* **im·pon·der·a·bly** *adv.*

im·port *v.* & *n.* ● *v.tr.* /impáwrt, ím-/ **1** bring in (esp. foreign goods or services) to a country. **2** (often foll. by *that* + clause) **a** imply; indicate; signify. **b** express; make known. ● *n.* /ímpawrt/ **1** the process of importing. **2 a** an imported article or service. **b** (in *pl.*) an amount imported (*imports exceeded $50 billion*). **3** what is implied; meaning. **4** importance. □□ **im·port·a·ble** *adj.* **im·por·ta·tion** *n.* **im·port·er** /-páwrtər/ *n.* (all in sense 1 of *v.*).

im·por·tance /impáwrt'ns/ *n.* **1** the state of being important. **2** weight; significance. **3** personal consequence; dignity.

im·por·tant /impáwrt'nt/ *adj.* **1** (often foll. by *to*) of great effect or consequence; momentous. **2** (of a person) having high rank or status, or great authority. **3** pretentious; pompous. **4** (*absol.* in parenthetic construction) what is a more important point or matter (*they are willing and, more important, able*). ¶ Use of *importantly* here is *disp.* □□ **im·por·tant·ly** *adv.* (see note above).

im·por·tu·nate /impáwrchənət/ *adj.* **1** making persistent or pressing requests. **2** (of affairs) urgent. □□ **im·por·tu·nate·ly** *adv.* **im·por·tu·ni·ty** /-tṓōnətee, -tyṓō-/ *n.*

im·por·tune /ímpáwrtōōn, -tyōōn, impáwrchən/ *v.tr.* **1** solicit (a person) pressingly. **2** solicit for an immoral purpose.

im·pose /impṓz/ *v.* **1** *tr.* (often foll. by *on, upon*) require (a tax, duty, charge, or obligation) to be paid or undertaken (by a person, etc.). **2** *tr.* enforce compliance with. **3** *intr.* & *refl.* (foll. by *on, upon,* or *absol.*) demand the attention or commitment of (a person); take advantage of (*I do not want to impose on you any longer*; *I did not want to impose*). **4** *tr.* (often foll. by *on, upon*) palm (a thing) off on (a person).

im·pos·ing /impṓzing/ *adj.* impressive or formidable, esp. in appearance. □□ **im·pos·ing·ly** *adv.* **im·pos·ing·ness** *n.*

im·po·si·tion /impəzíshən/ *n.* **1** the act or an instance of imposing; the process of being imposed. **2** an unfair or resented demand or burden. **3** a tax or duty.

im·pos·si·bil·i·ty /impósibílitee/ *n.* (*pl.* **-ies**) **1** the fact or condition of being impossible. **2** an impossible thing or circumstance.

im·pos·si·ble /impósibəl/ *adj.* **1** not possible; that cannot be done, occur, or exist (*it is impossible to alter them*; *such a thing is impossible*). **2** (loosely) not easy; not convenient; not easily believable. **3** *colloq.* (of a person or thing) outrageous; intolerable. □□ **im·pos·si·bly** *adv.* I

impost[1] /ímpōst/ *n.* **1** a tax; duty; tribute. **2** a weight carried by a horse in a handicap race.

impost[2] /ímpōst/ *n.* the upper course of a pillar, carrying an arch.

im·pos·tor /impóstər/ *n.* (also **im·post·er**) **1** a person who assumes a false character or pretends to be someone else. **2** a swindler.

im·pos·ture /impós-chər/ *n.* the act or an instance of fraudulent deception.

im·po·tent /ímpət'nt/ *adj.* **1 a** powerless; lacking all strength. **b** helpless. **c** ineffective. **2 a** (esp. of a male) unable, esp. for a prolonged period, to achieve a sexual erection or orgasm. **b** *colloq.* unable to procreate; infertile. □□ **im·po·tence** /-t'ns/ *n.* **im·po·ten·cy** *n.* **im·po·tent·ly** *adv.*

im·pound /impównd/ *v.tr.* **1** confiscate. **2** take possession of. **3** shut up (animals) in a pound. **4** shut up (a person or thing) as in a pound. **5** (of a dam, etc.) collect or confine (water). □□ **im·pound·er** *n.* **im·pound·ment** *n.*

im·pov·er·ish /impóvərish/ *v.tr.* (often as **impoverished** *adj.*) **1** make poor. **2** exhaust the strength or natural fertility of. □□ **im·pov·er·ish·ment** *n.*

im·prac·ti·ca·ble /impráktikəbəl/ *adj.* **1** impossible in practice. **2** (of a road, etc.) impassable. **3** (of a person or thing) unmanageable. □□ **im·prac·ti·ca·bil·i·ty** /-bílitee/ *n.* **im·prac·ti·ca·ble·ness** *n.* **im·prac·ti·ca·bly** *adv.*

im·prac·ti·cal /impráktikəl/ *adj.* **1** not practical. **2** not practicable. □□ **im·prac·ti·cal·i·ty** /-kálitee/ *n.* **im·prac·ti·cal·ly** *adv.*

im·pre·ca·tion /imprikáyshən/ *n.* **1** a spoken curse; a malediction. **2** the act of uttering an imprecation. □□ **im·pre·ca·to·ry** /-kətáwree/ *adj.*

im·pre·cise /imprisís/ *adj.* not precise. □□ **im·pre·cise·ly** *adv.* **im·pre·cise·ness** *n.* **im·pre·ci·sion** /-sízhən/ *n.*

im·preg·na·ble /imprégnəbəl/ *adj.* **1** (of a fortified position) that cannot be taken by force. **2** resistant to attack or criticism. □□ **im·preg·na·bil·i·ty** /-bílitee/ *n.* **im·preg·na·bly** *adv.*

im·preg·nate /imprégnayt/ *v.tr.* **1** (often foll. by *with*) fill or saturate. **2** (often foll. by *with*) imbue; fill (with feelings, moral qualities, etc.). **3 a** make (a female) pregnant. **b** *Biol.* fertilize (a female reproductive cell or ovum). □□ **im·preg·na·tion** /-náyshən/ *n.*

im·pre·sa·ri·o /imprisaáreeō, -sáir-/ *n.* (*pl.* **-os**) an organizer of public entertainments, esp. the manager of an operatic, theatrical, or concert company.

im·press[1] *v. & n.* ● *v.tr.* /imprés/ **1** (often foll. by *with*) **a** affect or influence deeply. **b** evoke a favorable opinion or reaction from (a person) (*was most impressed with your efforts*). **2** (often foll. by *on*) emphasize (an idea, etc.) (*must impress on you the need to be prompt*). **3** (often foll. by *on*) **a** imprint or stamp. **b** apply (a mark, etc.) with pressure. **4** make a mark or design on (a thing) with a stamp, seal, etc. ● *n.* /ímpres/ **1** the act or an instance of impressing. **2** a mark made by a seal, stamp, etc. **3** a characteristic mark or quality. **4** = IMPRESSION 1. □□ **im·pres·si·ble** /-présibəl/ *adj.*

im·press[2] /imprés/ *v.tr. hist.* **1** force (men) to serve in the army or navy. **2** seize (goods, etc.) for public service. □□ **im·press·ment** *n.*

im·pres·sion /impréshən/ *n.* **1** an effect produced (esp. on the mind or feelings). **2** a notion or belief (esp. a vague or mistaken one) (*my impression is they are afraid*). **3** an imitation of a person or sound, esp. done to entertain. **4 a** the impressing of a mark. **b** a mark impressed. **5** an unaltered reprint from standing type or plates (esp. as distinct from *edition*). **6 a** the number of copies of a book, newspaper, etc., issued at one time. **b** the printing of these. **7** a print taken from a wood engraving. □□ **im·pres·sion·al** *adj.*

im·pres·sion·a·ble /impréshənəbəl/ *adj.* easily influenced; susceptible to impressions. □□ **im·pres·sion·a·bil·i·ty** /-bílitee/ *n.* **im·pres·sion·a·bly** *adv.*

im·pres·sion·ism /impréshənizəm/ *n.* **1** ▶ a style or movement in art concerned with expression of feeling by visual impression, esp. from the effect of light on objects. **2** a style of music or writing that seeks to describe a feeling or experience rather than achieve accurate depiction or systematic structure.

im·pres·sion·ist /impréshənist/ *n.* an entertainer who impersonates famous people, etc.

im·pres·sion·is·tic /impréshənístik/ *adj.* **1** in the style of impressionism. **2** subjective; unsystematic. □□ **im·pres·sion·is·ti·cal·ly** *adv.*

im·pres·sive /imprésiv/ *adj.* **1** impressing the mind or senses, esp. so as to cause approval or admiration. **2** (of language, a scene, etc.) tending to excite deep feeling. □□ **im·pres·sive·ly** *adv.* **im·pres·sive·ness** *n.*

im·pri·ma·tur /imprimáatər, -máytər, -tŏŏr/ *n.* **1** *RC Ch.* an official license to print (an ecclesiastical or religious book, etc.). **2** official approval.

im·print *v. & n.* ● *v.tr.* /imprínt/ **1** (often foll. by *on*) impress or establish firmly, esp. on the mind. **2 a** (often foll. by *on*) make a stamp or impression of (a figure, etc.) on a thing. **b** make an impression on (a thing) with a stamp, etc. ● *n.* /ímprint/ **1** an impression or stamp. **2** the printer's or publisher's name and other details printed in a book.

im·print·ing /imprínting/ *n.* **1** in senses of IMPRINT *v.* **2** *Zool.* the development in a young animal of a pattern of recognition and trust for its own species.

im·pris·on /imprízən/ *v.tr.* **1** put into prison. **2** confine; shut up. □□ **im·pris·on·ment** *n.*

im·prob·a·ble /impróbəbəl/ *adj.* **1** not likely to be true or to happen. **2** difficult to believe. □□ **im·prob·a·bil·i·ty** *n.* **im·prob·a·bly** *adv.*

im·pro·bi·ty /impróbitee/ *n.* (*pl.* **-ies**) **1** wickedness; lack of moral integrity. **2** dishonesty. **3** a wicked or dishonest act.

im·promp·tu /imprómptŏŏ, -tyŏŏ/ *adj., adv., & n.* ● *adj. & adv.* extempore; unrehearsed. ● *n.* **1** an extempore performance or speech. **2** a short piece of usu. solo instrumental music, often songlike.

im·prop·er /imprópər/ *adj.* **1 a** unseemly; indecent. **b** not in accordance with accepted rules of behavior. **2** inaccurate; wrong. **3** not properly so called. □□ **im·prop·er·ly** *adv.*

im·prop·er frac·tion *n.* a fraction in which the numerator is greater than or equal to the denominator.

im·pro·pri·e·ty /imprəprí‿itee/ *n.* (*pl.* **-ies**) **1** lack of propriety; indecency. **2** an instance of improper conduct, etc. **3** incorrectness. **4** unfitness.

Emerging in Paris during the 1860s, impressionism was an artistic movement that drew inspiration from the simplicity of everyday life. Many of the movement's leading artists, such as Monet, Cézanne, Pissarro, and Renoir, painted in the open air, working quickly to create an "impression" of what they saw. These artists attempted to capture with paint the natural, transient effects of light and color.

The Waterlily Pond (1899), CLAUDE MONET

TIMELINE

1500	1550	1600	1650	1700	1750	1800	1850	1900	1950	2000

im·prove /improov/ *v.* **1 a** *tr. & intr.* make or become better. **b** *intr.* (foll. by *on, upon*) produce something better than. **2** *absol.* (as **improving** *adj.*) giving moral benefit (*improving literature*). □□ **im·prov·er** *n.*

im·prove·ment /improovmənt/ *n.* **1** the act or an instance of improving or being improved. **2** something that improves, esp. an addition or alteration that adds to value. **3** something that has been improved.

im·prov·i·dent /impróvid'nt/ *adj.* **1** lacking foresight or care for the future. **2** not frugal; thriftless. **3** heedless; incautious. □□ **im·prov·i·dence** /-d'ns/ *n.* **im·prov·i·dent·ly** *adv.*

im·pro·vise /imprəvīz/ *v.tr.* (also *absol.*) **1** compose or perform (music, verse, etc.) extempore. **2** provide or construct (a thing) extempore. □□ **im·prov·i·sa·tion** /-izáyshən/ *n.* **im·prov·i·sa·tion·al** *adj.* **im·prov·i·sa·to·ri·al** /impróvizətáwreeəl/ *adj.* **im·pro·vi·sa·to·ry** *adj.* **im·pro·vis·er** *n.*

im·pru·dent /impróod'nt/ *adj.* rash; indiscreet. □□ **im·pru·dence** /-d'ns/ *n.* **im·pru·dent·ly** *adv.*

im·pu·dent /ímpyəd'nt/ *adj.* **1** insolently disrespectful; impertinent. **2** shamelessly presumptuous. **3** unblushing. □□ **im·pu·dence** /-d'ns/ *n.* **im·pu·dent·ly** *adv.*

im·pugn /impyŏŏn/ *v.tr.* challenge or call in question (a statement, action, etc.). □□ **im·pugn·a·ble** *adj.* **im·pugn·ment** *n.*

im·pulse /ímpuls/ *n.* **1** the act or an instance of impelling; a push. **2** an impetus. **3** *Physics* **a** an indefinitely large force acting for a very short time but producing a finite change of momentum (e.g., the blow of a hammer). **b** the change of momentum produced by this or any force. **4** a wave of excitation in a nerve. **5** a sudden desire or tendency to act without reflection (*did it on impulse*).

im·pulse buy·ing *n.* the unpremeditated buying of goods as a result of a whim or impulse.

im·pul·sion /impúlshən/ *n.* **1** the act or an instance of impelling. **2** a mental impulse. **3** impetus.

im·pul·sive /impúlsiv/ *adj.* **1** (of a person or conduct, etc.) apt to be affected or determined by sudden impulse. **2** tending to impel. **3** *Physics* acting as an impulse. □□ **im·pul·sive·ly** *adv.* **im·pul·sive·ness** *n.*

im·pu·ni·ty /impyŏŏnitee/ *n.* exemption from punishment or from the injurious consequences of an action. □ **with impunity** without having to suffer the normal injurious consequences (of an action).

im·pure /impyŏŏr/ *adj.* **1** mixed with foreign matter; adulterated. **2 a** dirty. **b** ceremonially unclean. **3** unchaste. **4** (of a color) mixed with another color. □□ **im·pure·ly** *adv.* **im·pure·ness** *n.*

im·pu·ri·ty /impyŏŏritee/ *n.* (*pl.* **-ies**) **1** the quality or condition of being impure. **2** an impure thing or constituent.

im·pute /impyŏŏt/ *v.tr.* (foll. by *to*) regard (esp. something undesirable) as being done or caused or possessed by. □□ **im·put·a·ble** *adj.* **im·pu·ta·tion** *n.* **im·pu·ta·tive** /-tətiv/ *adj.*

IN *abbr.* Indiana (in official postal use).

In *symb. Chem.* the element indium.

in /in/ *prep., adv., & adj.* ● *prep.* **1** expressing inclusion or position within limits of space, time, circumstance, etc. (*in Nebraska; in bed; in the rain*). **2** during the time of (*in the night; in 1989*). **3** within the time of (*will be back in two hours*). **4 a** with respect to (*blind in one eye; good in parts*). **b** as a kind of (*the latest thing in luxury*). **5** as a proportionate part of (*one in three failed; a gradient of one in six*). **6** with the form or arrangement of (*packed in tens; falling in folds*). **7** as a member of (*in the army*). **8** concerned with (*is in politics*). **9** as or regarding the content of (*there is something in what you say*). **10** within the ability of (*does he have it in him?*). **11** having the condition of; affected by (*in bad health; in danger*). **12** having as a purpose (*in search of; in reply to*). **13** by means of or using as material (*drawn in pencil; modeled in bronze*). **14 a** using as the language of expression (*written in French*). **b** (of music) having as its key (*symphony in C*). **15** (of a word) having as a beginning or ending (*words beginning in un-*). **16** wearing as dress (*in blue; in a suit*). **17** with the identity of (*found a friend in Mary*). **18** (of an animal) pregnant with (*in calf*). **19** into (with a verb of motion or change: *put it in the box; cut it in two*). **20** introducing an indirect object after a verb (*believe in; engage in; share in*). **21** forming adverbial phrases (*in any case; in reality; in short*). ● *adv.* expressing position within limits, or motion to such a position: **1** into a room, house, etc. (*come in*). **2** at home, in one's office, etc. (*is not in*). **3** so as to be enclosed or confined (*locked in*). **4** in a publication (*is the advertisement in?*). **5** in or to the inward side (*rub it in*). **6 a** in fashion, season, or office (*long skirts are in; strawberries are not yet in*). **b** elected (*the Democrat got in*). **7** exerting favorable action or influence (*their luck was in*). **8** (of transport) at the platform, etc. (*the train is in*). **9** (of a season, harvest, order, etc.) having arrived or been received. **10** denoting effective action (*join in*). **11** (of the tide) at the highest point. **12** (in *comb.*) *colloq.* denoting prolonged or concerted action, esp. by large numbers (*sit-in; teach in*). ● *adj.* **1** internal; living in; inside (*in-patient*). **2** fashionable; esoteric (*the in thing to do*). **3** confined to or shared by a group of people (*in-joke*). □ **in all** see ALL. **in at** present at; contributing to (*in at the kill*). **in for 1** about to undergo (*esp. something unpleasant*). **2** competing in or for. **3** involved in; committed to. **in on** sharing in; privy to (a secret, etc.). **ins and outs** (often foll. by *of*) all the details (of a procedure, etc.). **in that** because; in so far as. **in with** on good terms with.

in. *abbr.* inch(es).

in·a·bil·i·ty /ínəbílitee/ *n.* **1** the state of being unable. **2** a lack of power or means.

in ab·sen·ti·a /ín absénshə/ *adv.* in (his, her, or their) absence.

in·ac·ces·si·ble /ínaksésibəl/ *adj.* **1** not accessible; that cannot be reached. **2** (of a person) not open to advances or influence; unapproachable. □□ **in·ac·ces·si·bil·i·ty** *n.* **in·ac·ces·si·ble·ness** *n.* **in·ac·ces·si·bly** *adv.*

in·ac·cu·rate /ínákyərət/ *adj.* not accurate. □□ **in·ac·cu·ra·cy** *n.* (*pl.* **-ies**). **in·ac·cu·rate·ly** *adv.*

in·ac·tion /ínákshən/ *n.* **1** lack of action. **2** sluggishness; inertness.

in·ac·ti·vate /ináktivayt/ *v.tr.* make inactive or inoperative. □□ **in·ac·ti·va·tion** /-váyshən/ *n.*

in·ac·tive /ináktiv/ *adj.* **1** not active or inclined to act. **2** passive. **3** indolent. □□ **in·ac·tive·ly** *adv.* **in·ac·tiv·i·ty** /-tívitee/ *n.*

in·ad·e·quate /ínádikwət/ *adj.* (often foll. by *to*) **1** not adequate; insufficient. **2** (of a person) incompetent; unable to deal with a situation. □□ **in·ad·e·qua·cy** /-kwəsee/ *n.* (*pl.* **-ies**). **in·ad·e·quate·ly** *adv.*

in·ad·mis·si·ble /ínədmísibəl/ *adj.* that cannot be admitted or allowed. □□ **in·ad·mis·si·bil·i·ty** *n.* **in·ad·mis·si·bly** *adv.*

in·ad·vert·ent /ínədvə́rt'nt/ *adj.* **1** (of an action) unintentional. **2 a** not properly attentive. **b** negligent. □□ **in·ad·vert·ence** /-t'ns/ *n.* **in·ad·vert·en·cy** *n.* **in·ad·vert·ent·ly** *adv.*

in·ad·vis·a·ble /ínədvízəbəl/ *adj.* not advisable. □□ **in·ad·vis·a·bil·i·ty** *n.*

in·al·ien·a·ble /ináyleeənəbəl/ *adj.* that cannot be transferred to another; not alienable. □□ **in·al·ien·a·bil·i·ty** *n.* **in·al·ien·a·bly** *adv.*

in·al·ter·a·ble /ináwltərəbəl/ *adj.* not alterable; that cannot be changed. □□ **in·al·ter·a·bil·i·ty** /-bílitee/ *n.* **in·al·ter·a·bly** *adv.*

in·am·o·ra·to /ínáməráətō/ *n.* (*pl.* **-os**; *fem.* inamorata /-tə/) a lover.

in·ane /ináyn/ *adj.* **1** silly; senseless. **2** empty; void. □□ **in·ane·ly** *adv.* **in·ane·ness** *n.* **in·an·i·ty** /-ánitee/ *n.* (*pl.* **-ies**).

in·an·i·mate /inánimət/ *adj.* **1** not animate; not endowed with (esp. animal) life. **2** lifeless; showing no sign of life. **3** spiritless; dull. □□ **in·an·i·mate·ly** *adv.* **in·an·i·ma·tion** /-máyshən/ *n.*

in·a·ni·tion /ínəníshən/ *n.* emptiness, esp. exhaustion from lack of nourishment.

in·ap·pli·ca·ble /ínáplikəbəl, ínəplík-/ *adj.* (often foll. by *to*) not applicable; unsuitable. □□ **in·ap·pli·ca·bil·i·ty** *n.* **in·ap·pli·ca·bly** *adv.*

in·ap·po·site /ínápəzit/ *adj.* not apposite; out of place. □□ **in·ap·po·site·ly** *adv.* **in·ap·po·site·ness** *n.*

in·ap·pro·pri·ate /ínəprṓpreeət/ *adj.* not appropriate. □□ **in·ap·pro·pri·ate·ly** *adv.* **in·ap·pro·pri·ate·ness** *n.*

in·apt /inápt/ *adj.* **1** not apt or suitable. **2** unskillful. □□ **in·apt·i·tude** *n.* **in·apt·ly** *adv.* **in·apt·ness** *n.*

in·ar·gu·a·ble /ináargyōōbəl/ *adj.* that cannot be argued about or disputed. □□ **in·ar·gu·a·bly** *adv.*

in·ar·tic·u·late /ínaartíkyələt/ *adj.* **1** unable to speak distinctly or express oneself clearly. **2** (of speech) not articulate; indistinctly pronounced. **3** dumb. **4** esp. *Anat.* not jointed. □□ **in·ar·tic·u·late·ly** *adv.* **in·ar·tic·u·late·ness** *n.*

in·as·much /ínəzmúch/ *adv.* (foll. by *as*) **1** since; because. **2** to the extent that.

in·at·ten·tive /ínəténtiv/ *adj.* **1** not paying due attention; heedless. **2** neglecting to show courtesy. □□ **in·at·ten·tion** *n.* **in·at·ten·tive·ly** *adv.* **in·at·ten·tive·ness** *n.*

in·au·di·ble /ináwdibəl/ *adj.* that cannot be heard. □□ **in·au·di·bil·i·ty** *n.* **in·au·di·bly** *adv.*

in·au·gu·ral /ináwgyərəl/ *adj. & n.* ● *adj.* **1** of inauguration. **2** (of a lecture, etc.) given by a person being inaugurated. ● *n.* an inaugural speech, etc.

in·au·gu·rate /ináwgyərayt/ *v.tr.* **1** admit (a person) formally to office. **2** initiate the public use of (a building, etc.). **3** begin; introduce. **4** enter with ceremony upon (an undertaking, etc.). □□ **in·au·gu·ra·tion** /-ráyshən/ *n.* **in·au·gu·ra·tor** *n.* **in·au·gu·ra·to·ry** /-rətáwree/ *adj.*

in·aus·pi·cious /ínawspíshəs/ *adj.* **1** ill-omened; unpropitious. **2** unlucky. □□ **in·aus·pi·cious·ly** *adv.* **in·aus·pi·cious·ness** *n.*

in·be·tween *adj. attrib. colloq.* intermediate (*at an in-between stage*).

in·board /ínbawrd/ *adv. & adj.* ● *adv.* within the sides of or toward the center of a ship, aircraft, or vehicle. ● *adj.* situated inboard.

in·born /ínbáwrn/ *adj.* existing from birth; implanted by nature.

in·bred /ínbréd/ *adj.* **1** inborn. **2** produced by inbreeding.

in·breed·ing /ínbréeding/ *n.* breeding from closely related animals or persons. □□ **in·breed** *v.tr. & intr.* (*past* and *past part.* **inbred**).

in·built /ínbílt/ *adj.* incorporated as part of a structure.

inc. *abbr.* **1** (esp. **Inc.**) Incorporated. **2** incomplete.

In·ca /íngkə/ *n.* a member of a Native American people in Peru before the Spanish conquest. □□ **In·ca·ic** /ingkáyik/ *adj.* **In·can** *adj.*

in·cal·cu·la·ble /ínkálkyələbəl/ *adj.* **1** too great for

INCANDESCENT

Heat produces the illumination in an incandescent light source. In a lightbulb an electrical current runs through a fine filament, heating it to more than 4500°F (2482°C). The heat caused by the current makes the filament glow white-hot, producing a strong source of light.

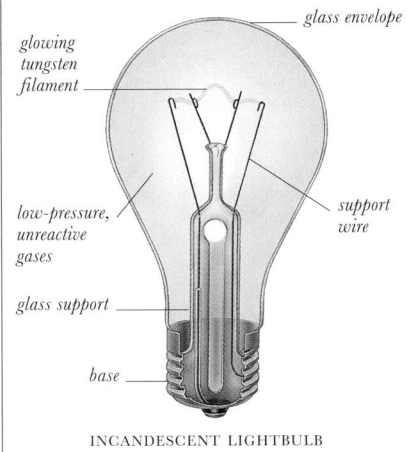

glass envelope

glowing tungsten filament

support wire

low-pressure, unreactive gases

glass support

base

INCANDESCENT LIGHTBULB

calculation. **2** unpredictable. □□ **in·cal·cu·la·bil·i·ty** *n.* **in·cal·cu·la·bly** *adv.*

in cam·er·a see CAMERA.

in·can·des·cent /ínkandésənt/ *adj.* **1** glowing with heat. **2** shining brightly. **3** ▲ (of an electric or other light) produced by a glowing white-hot filament. □□ **in·can·desce** *v. intr. & tr.* **in·can·des·cence** /-səns/ *n.* **in·can·des·cent·ly** *adv.*

in·can·ta·tion /ínkantáyshən/ *n.* **1 a** a magical formula. **b** the use of this. **2** a spell or charm. □□ **in·can·ta·tion·al** *adj.* **in·can·ta·to·ry** /-kántətáwree/ *adj.*

in·ca·pa·ble /ínkáypəbəl/ *adj.* **1** (often foll. by *of*) **a** not capable. **b** lacking the required quality or characteristic (favorable or adverse) (*incapable of hurting anyone*). **2** not capable of rational conduct or of managing one's own affairs (*drunk and incapable*). □□ **in·ca·pa·bil·i·ty** *n.* **in·ca·pa·bly** *adv.*

in·ca·pac·i·tate /ínkəpásitayt/ *v.tr.* **1** render incapable or unfit. **2** disqualify. □□ **in·ca·pac·i·tant** *n.* **in·ca·pac·i·ta·tion** /-táyshən/ *n.*

in·ca·pac·i·ty /ínkəpásitee/ *n.* (*pl.* **-ies**) **1** inability; lack of the necessary power or resources. **2** legal disqualification. **3** an instance of incapacity.

in·car·cer·ate /inkáarsərayt/ *v.tr.* imprison or confine. □□ **in·car·cer·a·tion** /-ráyshən/ *n.* **in·car·cer·a·tor** *n.*

in·car·nate *adj. & v.* ● *adj.* /inkáarnət, -nayt/ **1** (of a person, spirit, quality, etc.) embodied in flesh, esp. in human form (*is the devil incarnate*). **2** represented in a recognizable or typical form (*folly incarnate*). ● *v.tr.* /inkáarnayt/ **1** embody in flesh. **2** put (an idea, etc.) into concrete form; realize. **3** (of a person, etc.) be the living embodiment of (a quality).

in·car·na·tion /ínkaarnáyshən/ *n.* **1 a** embodiment in (esp. human) flesh. **b** (**the Incarnation**) *Theol.* the embodiment of God the Son in human flesh as Jesus Christ. **2** (often foll. by *of*) a living type of (a quality, etc.).

in·cau·tious /inkáwshəs/ *adj.* heedless; rash. □□ **in·cau·tion** *n.* **in·cau·tious·ly** *adv.* **in·cau·tious·ness** *n.*

in·cen·di·ar·y /inséndee-eree/ *adj. & n.* ● *adj.* **1** (of a bomb) designed to cause fires. **2 a** of or relating to the malicious setting on fire of property. **b** guilty of this. **3** tending to stir up strife; inflammatory. ● *n.* (*pl.* **-ies**) **1** an incendiary bomb or device. **2** an incendiary person. □□ **in·cen·di·a·rism** *n.*

in·cense[1] /ínsens/ *n. & v.* ● *n.* **1** a gum or spice producing a sweet smell when burned. **2** the smoke of this, esp. in religious ceremonial. ● *v.tr.* **1** treat or perfume (a person or thing) with incense. **2** burn incense to (a deity, etc.). **3** suffuse with fragrance. □□ **in·cen·sa·tion** *n.*

in·cense[2] /ínsens/ *v.tr.* (often foll. by *at, with, against*) enrage; make angry.

in·cen·tive /inséntiv/ *n. & adj.* ● *n.* **1** (often foll. by *to*) a motive or incitement, esp. to action. **2** a payment or concession to stimulate greater output by workers. ● *adj.* serving to motivate or incite.

in·cep·tion /insépshən/ *n.* a beginning.

in·cep·tive /inséptiv/ *adj. & n.* ● *adj.* **1 a** beginning. **b** initial. **2** *Gram.* (of a verb) that denotes the beginning of an action. ● *n.* an inceptive verb.

in·cer·ti·tude /insórtitōod, -tyōod/ *n.* uncertainty; doubt.

in·ces·sant /insésənt/ *adj.* unceasing; continual; repeated. □□ **in·ces·san·cy** *n.* **in·ces·sant·ly** *adv.* **in·ces·sant·ness** *n.*

in·cest /ínsest/ *n.* sexual intercourse between persons regarded as too closely related to marry each other.

in·ces·tu·ous /inséschōoəs/ *adj.* **1** involving or guilty of incest. **2** (of human relations generally) excessively restricted or resistant to wider influence. □□ **in·ces·tu·ous·ly** *adv.* **in·ces·tu·ous·ness** *n.*

inch[1] /inch/ *n. & v.* ● *n.* **1** a unit of linear measure equal to one-twelfth of a foot (2.54 cm). **2 a** (as a unit of rainfall) a quantity that would cover a horizontal surface to a depth of 1 inch. **b** (of atmospheric or other pressure) an amount that balances the weight of a column of mercury 1 inch high. **3** (as a unit of map scale) so many inches representing 1 mile on the ground (*a 4-inch map*). **4** a small amount (usu. with *neg.: would not yield an inch*). ● *v.tr. & intr.* move gradually in a specified way (*inched forward*). □ **every inch 1** entirely (*looked every inch a judge*). **2** the whole distance or area (*combed every inch of the garden*). **inch by inch** gradually; bit by bit. **within an inch of** almost to the point of.

inch[2] /inch/ *n.* esp. *Sc.* a small island (esp. in place-names).

in·cho·ate /inkóit/ *adj. & v.* ● *adj.* **1** just begun. **2** undeveloped; rudimentary; unformed. ● *v.tr.* begin; originate. □□ **in·cho·ate·ly** *adv.* **in·cho·ate·ness** *n.* **in·cho·a·tion** /-áyshən/ *n.* **in·cho·a·tive** /-kóətiv/ *adj.*

in·ci·dence /ínsidəns/ *n.* **1** (often foll. by *of*) the fact, manner, or rate, of occurrence or action. **2** the range, scope, or extent of influence of a thing. **3** *Physics* the falling of a line, or of a thing moving in a line, upon a surface. **4** the act or an instance of coming into contact with a thing.

in·ci·dent /ínsidənt/ *n. & adj.* ● *n.* **1 a** an event or occurrence. **b** a minor or detached event attracting general attention or noteworthy in some way. **2** a hostile clash, esp. of troops of countries at war (*a frontier incident*). **3** a distinct piece of action in a play or a poem. **4** *Law* a privilege, burden, etc., attaching to an obligation or right. ● *adj.* **1 a** (often foll. by *to*) apt or liable to happen; naturally attaching or dependent. **b** (foll. by *to*) *Law* attaching to. **2** (often foll. by *on, upon*) (of light, etc.) falling or striking.

in·ci·den·tal /ínsidéntəl/ *adj.* **1** (often foll. by *to*) **a** having a minor role in relation to a more important thing, event, etc. **b** not essential. **c** casual; happening by chance. **2** (foll. by *to*) liable to happen. **3** (foll. by *on, upon*) following as a subordinate event.

in·ci·den·tal·ly /ínsidént'lee/ *adv.* **1** by the way; as an unconnected remark. **2** in an incidental way.

in·ci·den·tal mu·sic *n.* music used as a background to the action of a play, motion picture, broadcast, etc.

in·cin·er·ate /insínərayt/ *v.tr.* **1** consume (a body, etc.) by fire. **2** reduce to ashes. □□ **in·cin·er·a·tion** /-ráyshən/ *n.*

in·cin·er·a·tor /insínəraytər/ *n.* a furnace or apparatus for burning, esp. refuse to ashes.

in·cip·i·ent /insípeeənt/ *adj.* **1** beginning. **2** in an

initial stage. □□ **in·cip·i·ence** /-əns/ *n.* **in·cip·i·en·cy** *n.* **in·cip·i·ent·ly** *adv.*

in·cise /insíz/ *v.tr.* **1** make a cut in. **2** engrave.

in·ci·sion /insízhən/ *n.* **1** a cut; a division produced by cutting; a notch. **2** the act of cutting into a thing.

in·ci·sive /insísiv/ *adj.* **1** mentally sharp; acute. **2** clear and effective. **3** cutting; penetrating. □□ **in·ci·sive·ly** *adv.* **in·ci·sive·ness** *n.*

in·ci·sor /insízər/ *n.* a ▶ cutting tooth, esp. at the front of the mouth. ▷ DENTITION, TOOTH

in·cite /insít/ *v.tr.* (often foll. by *to*) urge or stir up. □□ **in·ci·ta·tion** *n.* **in·cite·ment** *n.* **in·cit·er** *n.*

in·ci·vil·i·ty /insivílitee/ *n.* (*pl.* **-ies**) **1** rudeness; discourtesy. **2** a rude or discourteous act.

in·clem·ent /inklémənt/ *adj.* (of the weather or climate) severe, esp. cold or stormy. □□ **in·clem·en·cy** *n.* (*pl.* **-ies**). **in·clem·ent·ly** *adv.*

in·cli·na·tion /inklináyshən/ *n.* **1** (often foll. by *to*) a disposition or propensity. **2** (often foll. by *for*) a liking or affection. **3** a leaning, slope, or slant. **4** the difference of direction of two lines or planes, esp. as measured by the angle between them. **5** the dip of a magnetic needle.

in·cline *v. & n.* ● *v.* /inklín/ **1** *tr.* (usu. in *passive*; often foll. by *to, for,* or *to* + infin.) **a** make (a person, feelings, etc.) willing or favorably disposed (*am inclined to think so; does not incline me to agree*). **b** give a specified tendency to (a thing) (*the door is inclined to bang*). **2** *intr.* **a** be disposed (*I incline to think so*). **b** (often foll. by *to, toward*) tend. **3** *intr. & tr.* lean or turn away from a given direction, esp. the vertical. **4** *tr.* bend (the head, body, or oneself) forward or downward. ● *n.* /ínklín/ **1** a slope. **2** an inclined plane. □□ **in·clin·er** *n.*

in·clined plane *n.* ▼ a sloping plane (esp. as a means of reducing the force needed to raise a load).

in·clude /inklōod/ *v.tr.* **1** comprise or reckon in as part of a whole; place in a class or category. **2** (as **including** *prep.*) if we include (*six members, including the chairperson*). **3** treat or regard as so included. **4** (as **included** *adj.*) shut in; enclosed. □ **include out** *colloq.* or *joc.* specifically exclude. □□ **in·clud·a·ble** *adj.* **in·clud·i·ble** *adj.* **in·clu·sion** /-klōozhən/ *n.*

in·clu·sive /inklōosiv/ *adj.* **1** (often foll. by *of*) including, comprising. **2** with the inclusion of the extreme limits stated (*pages 7 to 26 inclusive*). **3** including all the normal services, etc. (*a hotel offering inclusive terms*). □□ **in·clu·sive·ly** *adv.* **in·clu·sive·ness** *n.*

in·clu·sive lan·guage *n.* language that is deliberately nonsexist, esp. avoiding the use of masculine pronouns to cover both men and women.

in·cog·ni·to /ínkognéetō, -kógni-/ *adj., adv., & n.* ● *adj. & adv.* with one's name or identity kept secret (*was traveling incognito*). ● *n.* (*pl.* **-os**) **1** a person who is incognito. **2** the pretended identity of such a person.

in·cog·ni·zant /inkógnizənt/ *adj.* (foll. by *of*) unaware; not knowing. □□ **in·cog·ni·zance** /-zəns/ *n.*

in·co·her·ent /inkōhéerənt/ *adj.* **1** (of a person) unable to speak intelligibly. **2** (of speech, etc.) lacking logic or consistency. **3** *Physics* (of waves) having no definite or stable phase relationship. □□ **in·co·her·ence** /-əns/ *n.* **in·co·her·en·cy** *n.* (*pl.* **-ies**). **in·co·her·ent·ly** *adv.*

in·com·bus·ti·ble /ínkəmbústibəl/ *adj.* that cannot be burned or consumed by fire. □□ **in·com·bus·ti·bil·i·ty** *n.*

in·come /ínkum/ *n.* the money or other assets received, esp. periodically or in a year, from one's business, lands, work, investments, etc.

in·com·er /ínkumər/ *n.* **1** a person who comes in. **2** an intruder. **3** a successor.

in·come tax *n.* a tax levied on income.

in·com·ing /ínkuming/ *adj. & n.* ● *adj.* **1** coming in (*the incoming tide; incoming telephone calls*). **2** succeeding another person or persons (*the incoming tenant*). ● *n.* **1** (usu. in *pl.*) revenue; income. **2** the act of arriving or entering.

in·com·men·su·ra·ble /ínkəménsərəbəl, -shərəbəl/ *adj.* (often foll. by *with*) **1** not comparable in respect of magnitude. **2** incapable of being measured. **3** *Math.* (of a magnitude or magnitudes) having no common factor, integral or fractional. **4** *Math.* irrational. □□ **in·com·men·su·ra·bil·i·ty** *n.* **in·com·men·su·ra·bly** *adv.*

in·com·men·su·rate /ínkəménsərət, -shərət/ *adj.* **1** (often foll. by *with, to*) out of proportion; inadequate. **2** = INCOMMENSURABLE. □□ **in·com·men·su·rate·ly** *adv.* **in·com·men·su·rate·ness** *n.*

in·com·mode /ínkəmṓd/ *v.tr.* **1** hinder; inconvenience. **2** trouble; annoy.

in·com·mo·di·ous /ínkəmṓdeeəs/ *adj.* not affording

upper central incisors

lateral incisor

lateral incisor

lateral incisors

lateral incisors

lower central incisors

INDIVIDUAL INCISOR

INCISOR

PLAN OF HUMAN DENTITION

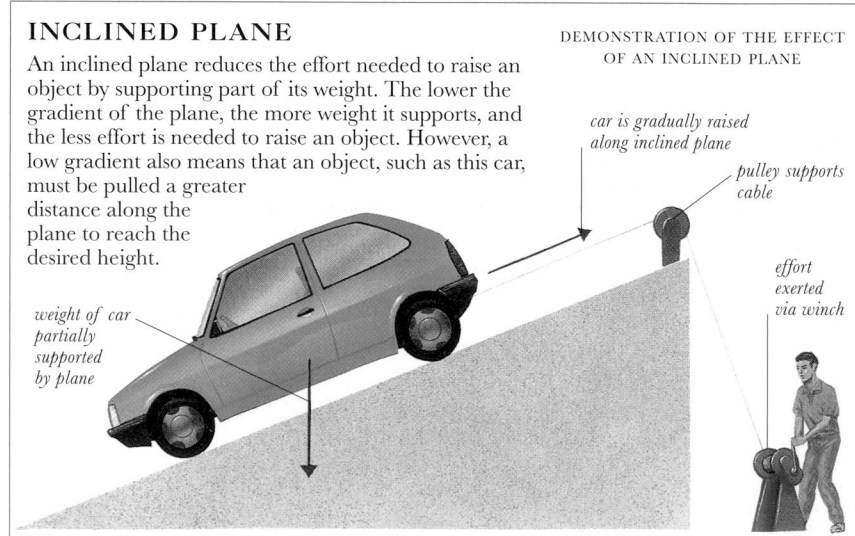

INCLINED PLANE

An inclined plane reduces the effort needed to raise an object by supporting part of its weight. The lower the gradient of the plane, the more weight it supports, and the less effort is needed to raise an object. However, a low gradient also means that an object, such as this car, must be pulled a greater distance along the plane to reach the desired height.

DEMONSTRATION OF THE EFFECT OF AN INCLINED PLANE

car is gradually raised along inclined plane

pulley supports cable

effort exerted via winch

weight of car partially supported by plane

good accommodation; uncomfortable. □□ **in·com·mo·di·ous·ly** adv. **in·com·mo·di·ous·ness** n.

in·com·mu·ni·ca·ble /ínkəmyōōnikəbəl/ adj. that cannot be communicated or shared. □□ **in·com·mu·ni·ca·bil·i·ty** n. **in·com·mu·ni·ca·ble·ness** n. **in·com·mu·ni·ca·bly** adv.

in·com·mu·ni·ca·do /ínkəmyōōnikáadō/ adj. without or deprived of the means of communication with others.

in·com·mu·ni·ca·tive /ínkəmyōōnikətiv, -káytiv/ adj. not communicative; taciturn. □□ **in·com·mu·ni·ca·tive·ly** adv. **in·com·mu·ni·ca·tive·ness** n.

in·com·mut·a·ble /ínkəmyōōtəbəl/ adj. **1** not changeable. **2** not commutable. □□ **in·com·mut·a·bly** adv.

in·com·pa·ra·ble /ínkómpərəbəl/ adj. **1** without an equal; matchless. **2** (often foll. by with, to) not to be compared. □□ **in·com·pa·ra·bil·i·ty** n. **in·com·pa·ra·ble·ness** n. **in·com·pa·ra·bly** adv.

in·com·pat·i·ble /ínkəmpátibəl/ adj. **1** opposed in character; discordant. **2** (often foll. by with) inconsistent. **3** (of persons) unable to live, work, etc., together in harmony. **4** (of drugs) not suitable for taking at the same time. **5** (of equipment, machinery, etc.) not capable of being used in combination. □□ **in·com·pat·i·bil·i·ty** n. **in·com·pat·i·ble·ness** n. **in·com·pat·i·bly** adv.

in·com·pe·tent /ínkómpit'nt/ adj. & n. ● adj. **1** (often foll. by to + infin.) not qualified or able to perform a particular task or function. **2** showing a lack of skill (an incompetent performance). ● n. an incompetent person. □□ **in·com·pe·tence** /-t'ns/ n. **in·com·pe·ten·cy** n. **in·com·pe·tent·ly** adv.

in·com·plete /ínkómpléet/ adj. not complete. □□ **in·com·plete·ly** adv. **in·com·plete·ness** n.

in·com·pre·hen·si·ble /ínkómprihénsibəl/ adj. (often foll. by to) that cannot be understood. □□ **in·com·pre·hen·si·bil·i·ty** n. **in·com·pre·hen·si·ble·ness** n. **in·com·pre·hen·si·bly** adv.

in·com·pre·hen·sion /ínkómprihénshən/ n. failure to understand.

in·con·ceiv·a·ble /ínkənséevəbəl/ adj. **1** that cannot be imagined. **2** colloq. very remarkable. □□ **in·con·ceiv·a·bil·i·ty** n. **in·con·ceiv·a·ble·ness** n. **in·con·ceiv·a·bly** adv.

in·con·clu·sive /ínkənklōōsiv/ adj. (of an argument, evidence, or action) not decisive or convincing. □□ **in·con·clu·sive·ly** adv. **in·con·clu·sive·ness** n.

in·con·gru·ous /ínkónggrōōəs/ adj. **1** out of place; absurd. **2** (often foll. by with) disagreeing; out of keeping. □□ **in·con·gru·i·ty** /-grōōitee/ n. (pl. -ies). **in·con·gru·ous·ly** adv. **in·con·gru·ous·ness** n.

in·con·se·quent /ínkónsikwənt/ adj. **1** not following naturally; irrelevant. **2** lacking logical sequence. **3** disconnected. □□ **in·con·se·quence** /-kwəns/ n. **in·con·se·quent·ly** adv.

in·con·se·quen·tial /ínkónsikwénshəl, ínkon-/ adj. **1** unimportant. **2** = INCONSEQUENT. □□ **in·con·se·quen·ti·al·i·ty** /-sheeálitee/ n. (pl. -ies). **in·con·se·quen·tial·ly** adv. **in·con·se·quen·tial·ness** n.

in·con·sid·er·a·ble /ínkənsídərəbəl/ adj. **1** of small size, value, etc. **2** not worth considering. □□ **in·con·sid·er·a·ble·ness** n. **in·con·sid·er·a·bly** adv.

in·con·sid·er·ate /ínkənsídərət/ adj. **1** (of a person or action) thoughtless; rash. **2** lacking in regard for the feelings of others. □□ **in·con·sid·er·ate·ly** adv. **in·con·sid·er·ate·ness** n. **in·con·sid·er·a·tion** /-ráyshən/ n.

in·con·sist·ent /ínkənsístənt/ adj. **1** acting at variance with one's own principles or former conduct. **2** (often foll. by with) not in keeping; discordant; incompatible. □□ **in·con·sist·en·cy** n. (pl. -ies). **in·con·sist·ent·ly** adv.

in·con·sol·a·ble /ínkənsóləbəl/ adj. (of a person, grief, etc.) that cannot be consoled or comforted. □□ **in·con·sol·a·bil·i·ty** /-bílitee/ n. **in·con·sol·a·ble·ness** n. **in·con·sol·a·bly** adv.

in·con·spic·u·ous /ínkənspíkyōōəs/ adj. not conspicuous; not easily noticed. □□ **in·con·spic·u·ous·ly** adv. **in·con·spic·u·ous·ness** n.

in·con·stant /ínkónstənt/ adj. **1** (of a person) fickle; changeable. **2** frequently changing; variable; irregular. □□ **in·con·stan·cy** n. (pl. -ies). **in·con·stant·ly** adv.

in·con·test·a·ble /ínkəntéstəbəl/ adj. that cannot be disputed. □□ **in·con·test·a·bil·i·ty** /-bílitee/ n. **in·con·test·a·bly** adv.

in·con·ti·nent /ínkóntinənt/ adj. **1** unable to control movements of the bowels or bladder or both. **2** lacking self-restraint (esp. in regard to sexual desire). **3** (foll. by of) unable to control. □□ **in·con·ti·nence** /-nəns/ n. **in·con·ti·nent·ly** adv.

in·con·tro·vert·i·ble /ínkóntrəvártibəl/ adj. indisputable; indubitable. □□ **in·con·tro·vert·i·bil·i·ty** n. **in·con·tro·vert·i·bly** adv.

in·con·ven·ience /ínkənveényəns/ n. & v. ● n. **1** lack of suitability to personal requirements or ease. **2** a cause or instance of this. ● v.tr. cause inconvenience to.

in·con·ven·ient /ínkənveényənt/ adj. **1** unfavorable to ease or comfort; not convenient. **2** awkward; troublesome. □□ **in·con·ven·ient·ly** adv.

in·cor·po·rate v. & adj. ● v. /inkáwrpərayt/ **1** tr. (often foll. by in, with) unite; form into one body or whole. **2** intr. become incorporated. **3** tr. combine (ingredients) into one substance. **4** tr. admit as a member of a company, etc. **5** tr. **a** constitute as a legal corporation. **b** (as **incorporated** adj.) forming a legal corporation. ● adj. /inkáwrpərət/ **1** (of a company, etc.) formed into a legal corporation. **2** embodied. □□ **in·cor·po·ra·tion** /-áyshən/ n. **in·cor·po·ra·tor** n.

in·cor·po·re·al /ínkawrpáwreeəl/ adj. **1** not composed of matter. **2** of immaterial beings. □□ **in·cor·po·re·al·i·ty** /-reeálitee/ n. **in·cor·po·re·al·ly** adv. **in·cor·po·re·i·ty** /-pəreéitee/ n.

in·cor·rect /ínkərékt/ adj. **1** not in accordance with fact; wrong. **2** (of style, etc.) improper; faulty. □□ **in·cor·rect·ly** adv. **in·cor·rect·ness** n.

in·cor·ri·gi·ble /inkáwrijibəl, -kór-/ adj. **1** (of a person or habit) incurably bad or depraved. **2** not readily improved. □□ **in·cor·ri·gi·bil·i·ty** n. **in·cor·ri·gi·ble·ness** n. **in·cor·ri·gi·bly** adv.

in·cor·rupt·i·ble /ínkərúptibəl/ adj. **1** that cannot be corrupted, esp. by bribery. **2** that cannot decay; everlasting. □□ **in·cor·rupt·i·bil·i·ty** /-bílitee/ n. **in·cor·rupt·i·bly** adv.

in·crease v. & n. ● v. /inkrées/ **1** tr. & intr. make or become greater in size, amount, etc., or more numerous. **2** intr. advance (in quality, attainment, etc.). **3** tr. intensify (a quality). ● n. /inkrees/ **1** the act or process of becoming greater or more numerous; growth; enlargement. **2** (of people, animals, or plants) growth in numbers; multiplication. **3** the amount or extent of an increase. □ **on the increase** increasing, esp. in frequency. □□ **in·creas·a·ble** adj. **in·creas·er** n. **in·creas·ing·ly** adv.

in·cred·i·ble /inkrédibəl/ adj. **1** that cannot be believed. **2** colloq. hard to believe; amazing. □□ **in·cred·i·bil·i·ty** n. **in·cred·i·ble·ness** n. **in·cred·i·bly** adv.

in·cred·u·lous /inkréjələs/ adj. (often foll. by of) unwilling to believe. □□ **in·cre·du·li·ty** /ínkridōō-litee, -dyōō-/ n. **in·cred·u·lous·ly** adv. **in·cred·u·lous·ness** n.

in·cre·ment /ínkrimənt/ n. an increase or addition, esp. one of a series on a fixed scale. □□ **in·cre·men·tal** /- mént'l/ adj.

in·crim·i·nate /inkríminayt/ v.tr. **1** tend to prove the guilt of (incriminating evidence). **2** involve in an accusation. **3** charge with a crime. □□ **in·crim·i·na·tion** /-náyshən/ n. **in·crim·i·na·to·ry** /-nətáwree/ adj.

in-crowd n. (**the in-crowd**) colloq. a small group of people that are particularly fashionable or popular.

in·crus·ta·tion /ínkrustáyshən/ n. **1** the process of encrusting or state of being encrusted. **2** a hard coating, esp. of fine material. **3** a deposit on a surface.

in·cu·bate /íngkyəbayt/ v. **1** tr. sit on or artificially heat (eggs) in order to bring forth young birds, etc. **2** tr. cause the development of (bacteria, etc.) by creating suitable conditions. **3** intr. sit on eggs; brood.

in·cu·ba·tion /íngkyəbáyshən/ n. **1 a** the act of incubating. **b** brooding. **2** Med. (in full **in·cu·ba·tion pe·ri·od**) the period between exposure to an infection and the appearance of the first symptoms. □□ **in·cu·ba·tion·al** adj. **in·cu·ba·tive** adj. **in·cu·ba·to·ry** /íngkyəbətáwree/ adj.

in·cu·ba·tor /íngkyəbaytər/ n. **1** an apparatus used to provide a suitable temperature and environment for a premature baby or one of low birthweight. **2** ▾ an apparatus used to hatch eggs or grow microorganisms.

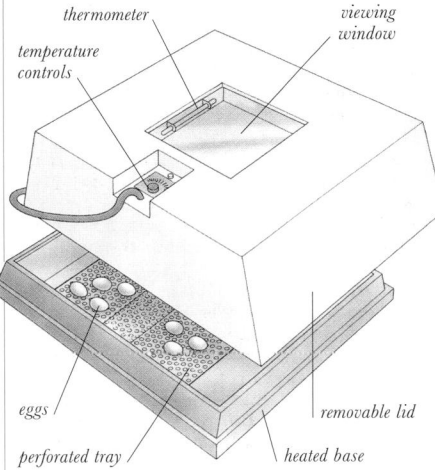

thermometer

temperature controls

viewing window

eggs

removable lid

perforated tray

heated base

INCUBATOR FOR HATCHING BIRDS' EGGS

in·cu·bus /íngkyəbəs/ n. (pl. **incubi** /-bī/ or **incubuses**) **1** an evil spirit supposed to descend on sleeping persons. **2** a nightmare. **3** a person or thing that oppresses like a nightmare.

in·cu·des pl. of INCUS.

in·cul·cate /inkúlkayt/ v.tr. (often foll. by upon, in) urge or impress (a fact, habit, or idea) persistently. □□ **in·cul·ca·tion** /-káyshən/ n. **in·cul·ca·tor** n.

in·cul·pate /inkúlpayt/ v.tr. **1** involve in a charge. **2** accuse; blame. □□ **in·cul·pa·tion** /-páyshən/ n. **in·cul·pa·tive** /inkúlpətiv/ adj. **in·cul·pa·to·ry** /-pətáwree/ adj.

in·cum·ben·cy /inkúmbənsee/ n. (pl. -ies) the office, tenure, or sphere of an incumbent.

in·cum·bent /inkúmbənt/ adj. & n. ● adj. **1** (foll. by on, upon) resting as a duty (it is incumbent on you to warn them). **2** (often foll. by on) lying; pressing. **3** currently holding office (the incumbent president). ● n. the holder of an office or post, esp. an elected official.

in·cu·nab·u·lum /ínkyənábyələm/ n. (pl. **incunabula** /-lə/) a book printed at an early date, esp. before 1501.

in·cur /inkór/ v.tr. (**incurred, incurring**) suffer, experience, or become subject to (something unpleasant) as a result of one's own behavior, etc. (incurred huge debts). □□ **in·cur·ra·ble** adj.

in·cur·a·ble /inkyōōrəbəl/ adj. & n. ● adj. that cannot be cured. ● n. a person who cannot be cured. □□ **in·cur·a·bil·i·ty** n. **in·cur·a·ble·ness** n. **in·cur·a·bly** adv.

in·cur·sion /inkórzhən, -shən/ n. an invasion or attack, esp. when sudden or brief. □□ **in·cur·sive** /-kórsiv/ adj.

in·cus /íngkəs/ n. (pl. **incudes** /-kyōōdeez/) the small anvil-shaped bone in the middle ear, in contact with the malleus and stapes.

Ind. abbr. **1** Independent. **2** Indiana. **3 a** India. **b** Indian.

in·debt·ed /indétid/ adj. (usu. foll. by to) **1** owing gratitude or obligation. **2** owing money. □□ **in·debt·ed·ness** n.

in·de·cent /indéesənt/ adj. **1** offending against recognized standards of decency. **2** unbecoming; highly unsuitable (with indecent haste). □□ **in·de·cen·cy** n. (pl. -ies). **in·de·cent·ly** adv.

I

in·de·cent ex·po·sure *n.* the intentional act of publicly and indecently exposing one's body, esp. the genitals.

in·de·ci·pher·a·ble /indisífərəbəl/ *adj.* that cannot be deciphered.

in·de·ci·sion /índisízhən/ *n.* lack of decision; hesitation.

in·de·ci·sive /índisísiv/ *adj.* **1** not decisive. **2** undecided; hesitating. ▫▫ **in·de·ci·sive·ly** *adv.* **in·de·ci·sive·ness** *n.*

in·de·clin·a·ble /índiklínəbəl/ *adj. Gram.* **1** that cannot be declined. **2** having no inflections.

in·dec·o·rous /indékərəs/ *adj.* **1** improper. **2** in bad taste. ▫▫ **in·dec·o·rous·ly** *adv.* **in·dec·o·rous·ness** *n.*

in·deed /indéed/ *adv. & int.* ● *adv.* **1** in truth; really; yes; that is so (*they are, indeed, a remarkable family*). **2** expressing emphasis or intensification (*indeed it is*). **3** admittedly (*there are indeed exceptions*). **4** in point of fact (*if indeed such a thing is possible*). ● *int.* expressing irony, contempt, incredulity, etc.

in·de·fat·i·ga·ble /indifátigəbəl/ *adj.* (of a person, quality, etc.) that cannot be tired out; unwearying; unremitting. ▫▫ **in·de·fat·i·ga·bil·i·ty** *n.* **in·de·fat·i·ga·bly** *adv.*

in·de·fen·si·ble /índifénsibəl/ *adj.* that cannot be defended or justified. ▫▫ **in·de·fen·si·bil·i·ty** *n.* **in·de·fen·si·bly** *adv.*

in·de·fin·a·ble /índifínəbəl/ *adj.* that cannot be defined or exactly described. ▫▫ **in·de·fin·a·bly** *adv.*

in·def·i·nite /indéfinit/ *adj.* **1** vague; undefined. **2** unlimited. **3** *Gram.* not determining the person, thing, time, etc., referred to. ▫▫ **in·def·i·nite·ness** *n.*

in·def·i·nite ar·ti·cle *n. Gram.* the word (e.g., *a, an, some* in English) preceding a noun and implying lack of specificity (*bought me a book; government is an art*).

in·def·i·nite·ly /indéfinitlee/ *adv.* **1** for an unlimited time (*was postponed indefinitely*). **2** in an indefinite manner.

in·de·his·cent /índihísənt/ *adj. Bot.* (of fruit) not splitting open when ripe. ▫▫ **in·de·his·cence** /-səns/ *n.*

in·del·i·ble /indélibəl/ *adj.* **1** that cannot be rubbed out or (in abstract senses) removed. **2** (of ink, etc.) that makes indelible marks. ▫▫ **in·del·i·bil·i·ty** *n.* **in·del·i·bly** *adv.*

in·del·i·cate /indélikət/ *adj.* **1** coarse; unrefined. **2** tactless. **3** tending to indecency. ▫▫ **in·del·i·ca·cy** *n.* (*pl.* **-ies**). **in·del·i·cate·ly** *adv.*

in·dem·ni·fy /indémnifī/ *v.tr.* (**-ies**, **-ied**) **1** (often foll. by *from, against*) protect or secure (a person) in respect of harm, a loss, etc. **2** (often foll. by *for*) secure (a person) against legal responsibility for actions. **3** (often foll. by *for*) compensate (a person) for a loss, expenses, etc. ▫▫ **in·dem·ni·fi·ca·tion** /-fikáyshən/ *n.* **in·dem·ni·fi·er** *n.*

in·dem·ni·ty /indémnitee/ *n.* (*pl.* **-ies**) **1 a** compensation for loss incurred. **b** a sum paid for this, esp. a sum exacted by a victor in war, etc., as one condition of peace. **2** security against loss. **3** legal exemption from penalties, etc., incurred.

in·dent[1] /indént/ *v. & n.* ● *v.* **1** *tr.* start (a line of print or writing) further from the margin than other lines, e.g., to mark a new paragraph. **2** *tr.* **a** divide (a document drawn up in duplicate) into its two copies with a zigzag line dividing them and ensuring identification. **b** draw up (usu. a legal document) in exact duplicate. **3** *tr.* make toothlike notches in. **4** *tr.* form deep recesses in (a coastline, etc.). ● *n. also* /índent/ **1** indentation. **2** an indented line. **3** *Brit.* **a** an order (esp. from abroad) for goods. **b** an official requisition for stores. **4** an indenture. ▫▫ **in·den·ta·tion** *n.* **in·dent·er** *n.* **in·den·tor** *n.*

in·dent[2] /indént/ *v.tr.* **1** make a dent in. **2** impress (a mark, etc.).

in·den·tion /indénshən/ *n.* **1** the indenting of a line in printing or writing. **2** an indentation.

in·den·ture /indénchər/ *n. & v.* ● *n.* **1** an indented document (see INDENT[1] *v.* 2). **2** (usu. in *pl.*) a sealed agreement or contract. **3** a formal list, certificate, etc. ● *v.tr. hist.* bind (a person) by indentures, esp. as an apprentice. ▫▫ **in·den·ture·ship** *n.*

in·de·pend·ence /índipéndəns/ *n.* **1** (often foll. by *of, from*) the state of being independent. **2** independent income.

In·de·pend·ence Day *n.* a day celebrating the anniversary of national independence; in the US July 4.

in·de·pend·en·cy /índipéndənsee/ *n.* (*pl.* **-ies**) **1** an independent state, territory, etc. **2** = INDEPENDENCE.

in·de·pend·ent /índipéndənt/ *adj. & n.* ● *adj.* **1 a** (often foll. by *of*) not depending on authority or control. **b** self-governing. **2 a** not depending on another person for one's opinion or livelihood. **b** (of income or resources) making it unnecessary to earn one's living. **3** unwilling to be under an obligation to others. **4** *Polit.* (usu. **Independent**) not belonging to or supported by a party. **5** not depending on something else for its validity, efficiency, value, etc. (*independent proof*). **6** (of broadcasting, a school, etc.) not supported by public funds. ● *n.* (usu. **Independent**) a person who is politically independent. ▫▫ **in·de·pend·ent·ly** *adv.*

in-depth *attrib.adj.* thorough; done in depth.

in·de·scrib·a·ble /índiskríbəbəl/ *adj.* **1** too unusual or extreme to be described. **2** vague; indefinite. ▫▫ **in·de·scrib·a·bil·i·ty** *n.* **in·de·scrib·a·bly** *adv.*

in·de·struct·i·ble /índistrúktibəl/ *adj.* that cannot be destroyed. ▫▫ **in·de·struct·i·bil·i·ty** *n.* **in·de·struct·i·bly** *adv.*

in·de·ter·mi·na·ble /índitérminəbəl/ *adj.* **1** that cannot be ascertained. **2** (of a dispute, etc.) that cannot be settled. ▫▫ **in·de·ter·mi·na·bly** *adv.*

in·de·ter·mi·nate /índitérminət/ *adj.* **1** not fixed in extent, character, etc. **2** left doubtful; vague. **3** *Math.* (of a quantity) not limited to a fixed value by the value of another quantity. ▫▫ **in·de·ter·mi·na·cy** *n.* **in·de·ter·mi·nate·ly** *adv.* **in·de·ter·mi·nate·ness** *n.*

in·de·ter·mi·na·tion /índitérmináyshən/ *n.* **1** lack of determination. **2** the state of being indeterminate.

in·dex /índeks/ *n. & v.* ● *n.* (*pl.* **indexes** or esp. in technical use **indices** /índiseez/) **1** an alphabetical list of names, subjects, etc., with references, usu. at the end of a book. **2** (in full **index number**) a number showing the variation of prices or wages as compared with a chosen base period (*retail price index; Dow-Jones index*). **3** *Math.* **a** the exponent of a number. **b** the power to which it is raised. **4 a** a pointer, esp. on an instrument, showing a quantity, a position on a scale, etc. ▷ SEXTANT. **b** an indicator of a trend, direction, tendency, etc. **c** (usu. foll. by *of*) a sign, token, or indication of something. **5** *Physics* a number expressing a physical property, etc., in terms of a standard (*refractive index*). **6** *Computing* a set of items each of which specifies one of the records of a file and contains information about its address. ● *v.tr.* **1** provide (a book, etc.) with an index. **2** enter in an index. **3** relate (wages, etc.) to the value of a price index. ▫▫ **in·dex·a·tion** *n.* **in·dex·er** *n.* **in·dex·i·ble** /-déksibəl/ *adj.* **in·dex·i·cal** *adj.* **in·dex·less** *adj.*

in·dex fin·ger *n.* the forefinger.

in·di·a ink /índeeə/ *n.* (also **In·di·a ink**) **1** a black pigment made orig. in China and Japan. **2** a dark ink made from this, used esp. in drawing and technical graphics.

In·di·an /índeeən/ *n. & adj.* ● *n.* **1 a** a native or national of India. **b** a person of Indian descent. **2** (in full **American Indian**) a member of the aboriginal peoples of America or their descendants. **3** any of the languages of the aboriginal peoples of America. ● *adj.* **1** of or relating to India, or to the subcontinent comprising India, Pakistan, and Bangladesh. **2** of or relating to the aboriginal peoples of America.

In·di·an clubs *n.pl.* ► a pair of bottle-shaped clubs swung to exercise the arms in gymnastics.

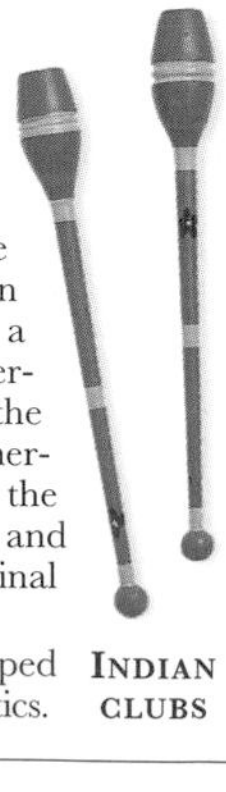

INDIAN CLUBS

In·di·an corn *n.* = CORN[1] *n.* 1.

In·di·an el·e·phant *n.* the elephant, *Elephas maximus*, of India, which is smaller than the African elephant. ▷ ELEPHANT

In·di·an O·cean *n.* the ocean between Africa to the west, and Australia to the east. ▷ OCEAN

In·di·an sum·mer *n.* **1** a period of unusually dry, warm weather sometimes occurring in late autumn. **2** a late period of life characterized by comparative calm.

In·di·a pa·per *n.* **1** a soft absorbent kind of paper orig. imported from China, used for proofs of engravings. **2** a very thin, tough, opaque printing paper.

in·di·a rub·ber /índeeərúbər/ *n.* (also **In·di·a rub·ber**) = RUBBER[1] 2.

in·di·cate /índikayt/ *v.tr.* (often foll. by *that* + clause) **1** point out; make known; show. **2** be a sign or symptom of; express the presence of. **3** (often in *passive*) suggest; call for; require or show to be necessary (*stronger measures are indicated*). **4** admit to or state briefly (*indicated his disapproval*). **5** (of a gauge, etc.) give as a reading.

in·di·ca·tion /índikáyshən/ *n.* **1 a** the act or an instance of indicating. **b** something that suggests or indicates; a sign or symptom. **2** something indicated or suggested, esp., in *Med.*, a remedy or treatment that is suggested by the symptoms. **3** a reading given by a gauge or instrument.

in·dic·a·tive /indíkətiv/ *adj. & n.* ● *adj.* **1** (foll. by *of*) suggestive; serving as an indication. **2** *Gram.* (of a mood) denoting simple statement of a fact. ● *n. Gram.* **1** the indicative mood. **2** a verb in this mood. ▫▫ **in·dic·a·tive·ly** *adv.*

in·di·ca·tor /índikaytər/ *n.* **1** a person or thing that indicates. **2** a device indicating the condition of a machine, etc. **3** a recording instrument attached to an apparatus, etc.

in·dic·a·to·ry /indíkətawree/ *adj.* = INDICATIVE *adj.* 1.

in·di·ces *pl.* of INDEX.

in·dict /indít/ *v.tr.* accuse (a person) formally by legal process. ▫▫ **in·dict·ee** /-tée/ *n.* **in·dict·er** *n.*

in·dict·a·ble /indítəbəl/ *adj.* **1** (of an offense) rendering the person who commits it liable to be charged with a crime. **2** (of a person) so liable.

in·dict·ment /indítmənt/ *n.* **1** the act of indicting. **2 a** a formal accusation. **b** a legal process in which this is made. **c** a document containing a charge. **3** something that serves to condemn or censure.

in·dif·fer·ence /indífrəns/ *n.* **1** lack of interest or attention. **2** unimportance (*a matter of indifference*). **3** neutrality.

in·dif·fer·ent /indífrənt/ *adj.* **1** neither good nor bad; average; mediocre. **2 a** not especially good. **b** fairly bad. **3** (often prec. by *very*) decidedly inferior. **4** (foll. by *to*) having no partiality for or against; having no interest in or sympathy for. ▫▫ **in·dif·fer·ent·ly** *adv.*

in·dig·e·nize /indíjinīz/ *v.tr.* **1** make indigenous; subject to native influence. **2** subject to increased use of indigenous people in government, etc. ▫▫ **in·dig·e·ni·za·tion** *n.*

in·dig·e·nous /indíjinəs/ *adj.* **1 a** (esp. of flora or fauna) originating naturally in a region. **b** (of people) born in a region. **2** (foll. by *to*) belonging naturally to a place. ▫▫ **in·dig·e·nous·ly** *adv.* **in·dig·e·nous·ness** *n.*

in·di·gent /índijənt/ *adj.* needy; poor. ▫▫ **in·di·gence** /-jəns/ *n.*

in·di·gest·i·ble /índijéstibəl/ *adj.* **1** difficult or impossible to digest. **2** too complex or awkward to read or comprehend easily. ▫▫ **in·di·gest·i·bil·i·ty** *n.* **in·di·gest·i·bly** *adv.*

in·di·ges·tion /índijés-chən/ *n.* **1** difficulty in digesting food. **2** pain or discomfort caused by this. ▫▫ **in·di·ges·tive** *adj.*

in·dig·nant /indígnənt/ *adj.* feeling or showing scornful anger or a sense of injured innocence. ▫▫ **in·dig·nant·ly** *adv.*

in·dig·na·tion /índignáyshən/ *n.* scornful

anger at supposed unjust or unfair conduct or treatment.

in·dig·ni·ty /indígnitee/ *n.* (*pl.* **-ies**) **1** unworthy treatment. **2** a slight or insult. **3** the humiliating quality of something (*the indignity of my position*).

in·di·go /indígō/ *n.* (*pl.* **-os**) **1 a** a natural blue dye obtained from the indigo plant. **b** a synthetic form of this dye. **2** ▶ any plant of the genus *Indigofera*. **3** (in full **indigo blue**) a color between blue and violet in the spectrum.

in·di·rect /indirékt, -dī-/ *adj.* **1** not going straight to the point. **2** (of a route, etc.) not straight. **3** not directly sought or aimed at (*an indirect result*). **4** (of lighting) from a concealed source and diffusely reflected. □□ **in·di·rect·ly** *adv.* **in·di·rect·ness** *n.*

in·di·rect ob·ject *n. Gram.* a person or thing affected by a verbal action but not primarily acted on (e.g., *him* in *give him the book*).

in·dis·cern·i·ble /indisárnibəl/ *adj.* that cannot be discerned or distinguished from another. □□ **in·dis·cern·i·bil·i·ty** *n.* **in·dis·cern·i·bly** *adv.*

in·dis·creet /indiskreét/ *adj.* **1** not discreet; revealing secrets. **2** injudicious; unwary. □□ **in·dis·creet·ly** *adv.* **in·dis·creet·ness** *n.*

in·dis·cre·tion /indiskréshən/ *n.* **1** lack of discretion; indiscreet conduct. **2** an indiscreet action, remark, etc.

in·dis·crim·i·nate /indiskríminət/ *adj.* **1** making no distinctions. **2** confused; promiscuous. □□ **in·dis·crim·i·nate·ly** *adv.* **in·dis·crim·i·nate·ness** *n.* **in·dis·crim·i·na·tion** /-náyshən/ *n.* **in·dis·crim·i·na·tive** *adj.*

in·dis·pen·sa·ble /indispénsəbəl/ *adj.* **1** (often foll. by *to, for*) that cannot be dispensed with; necessary. **2** (of a law, duty, etc.) that is not to be set aside. □□ **in·dis·pen·sa·bil·i·ty** *n.* **in·dis·pen·sa·ble·ness** *n.* **in·dis·pen·sa·bly** *adv.*

in·dis·posed /indispốzd/ *adj.* **1** slightly unwell. **2** averse or unwilling. □□ **in·dis·po·si·tion** *n.*

in·dis·put·a·ble /indispyóotəbəl/ *adj.* **1** that cannot be disputed. **2** unquestionable. □□ **in·dis·put·a·bil·i·ty** *n.* **in·dis·put·a·ble·ness** *n.* **in·dis·put·a·bly** *adv.*

in·dis·sol·u·ble /indisólyəbəl/ *adj.* **1** that cannot be dissolved or decomposed. **2** lasting; stable (*an indissoluble bond*). □□ **in·dis·sol·u·bil·i·ty** *n.* **in·dis·sol·u·bly** *adv.*

in·dis·tinct /indistíngkt/ *adj.* **1** not distinct. **2** confused; obscure. □□ **in·dis·tinct·ly** *adv.* **in·dis·tinct·ness** *n.*

in·dis·tin·guish·a·ble /indistínggwishəbəl/ *adj.* (often foll. by *from*) not distinguishable. □□ **in·dis·tin·guish·a·ble·ness** *n.* **in·dis·tin·guish·a·bly** *adv.*

in·dite /indít/ *v.tr. formal or joc.* **1** put (a speech, etc.) into words. **2** write (a letter, etc.).

in·di·um /índeeəm/ *n. Chem.* a soft, silvery-white metallic element occurring naturally in sphalerite, etc., used for electroplating and in semiconductors. ¶ Symb.: **In.**

in·di·vid·u·al /indivíjōōəl/ *adj. & n.* ● *adj.* **1** single. **2** particular; special; not general. **3** having a distinct character. **4** characteristic of a particular person. **5** designed for use by one person. ● *n.* **1** a single member of a class. **2** a single human being as distinct from a family or group. **3** *colloq.* a person (*a most unpleasant individual*).

in·di·vid·u·al·ism /indivíjōōəlizəm/ *n.* **1** the habit or principle of being independent and self-reliant. **2** a social theory favoring the free action of individuals. **3** self-centered feeling or conduct; egoism. □□ **in·di·vid·u·al·ist** *n.* **in·di·vid·u·al·is·tic** *adj.* **in·di·vid·u·al·is·ti·cal·ly** *adv.*

in·di·vid·u·al·i·ty /indivíjōō-álitee/ *n.* (*pl.* **-ies**) **1** individual character, esp. when strongly marked. **2** (in *pl.*) individual tastes, etc. **3** separate existence.

in·di·vid·u·al·ize /indivíjōōəlīz/ *v.tr.* **1** give an individual character to. **2** specify. □□ **in·di·vid·u·al·i·za·tion** *n.*

in·di·vid·u·al·ly /indivíjōōəlee/ *adv.* **1** personally; in an individual capacity. **2** in a distinctive manner. **3** one by one; not collectively.

in·di·vid·u·al re·tire·ment ac·count *n.* a savings account that allows tax owed on interest to be deferred. ¶ Abbr.: **IRA**

in·di·vid·u·ate /indivíjōō-ayt/ *v.tr.* individualize; form into an individual.

in·di·vis·i·ble /indivízibəl/ *adj.* **1** not divisible. **2** not distributable among a number. □□ **in·di·vis·i·bil·i·ty** *n.* **in·di·vis·i·bly** *adv.*

Indo- /índō/ *comb. form* Indian; Indian and.

in·doc·tri·nate /indóktrinayt/ *v.tr.* teach to accept (esp. partisan or tendentious) ideas uncritically. □□ **in·doc·tri·na·tion** /-náyshən/ *n.* **in·doc·tri·na·tor** *n.*

In·do-Eu·ro·pe·an /índō-yŏŏrəpeéən/ *adj. & n.* ● *adj.* **1** of or relating to the family of languages spoken over the greater part of Europe and Asia as far as N. India. **2** of or relating to the hypothetical parent language of this family. ● *n.* **1** the Indo-European family of languages. **2** the hypothetical parent language of all languages belonging to this family.

in·do·lent /índələnt/ *adj.* **1** lazy; wishing to avoid activity or exertion. **2** *Med.* causing no pain (*an indolent tumor*). □□ **in·do·lence** /-ləns/ *n.* **in·do·lent·ly** *adv.*

in·dom·i·ta·ble /indómitəbəl/ *adj.* **1** that cannot be subdued; unyielding. **2** stubbornly persistent. □□ **in·dom·i·ta·bil·i·ty** *n.* **in·dom·i·ta·ble·ness** *n.* **in·dom·i·ta·bly** *adv.*

In·do·ne·sian /indəneézhən, -shən/ *n. & adj.* ● *n.* **1** a native or national of Indonesia in SE Asia. **2** a person of Indonesian descent. ● *adj.* of or relating to Indonesia or its people or language.

in·door /índawr/ *adj.* situated, carried on, or used within a building or under cover (*indoor antenna*; *indoor games*).

in·doors /índáwrz/ *adv.* into or within a building.

in·dorse var. of ENDORSE.

in·drawn /índráwn/ *adj.* **1** (of breath, etc.) drawn in. **2** aloof.

in·du·bi·ta·ble /indoóbitəbəl, -dyoó-/ *adj.* that cannot be doubted. □□ **in·du·bi·ta·bly** *adv.*

in·duce /indoós, -dyoós/ *v.tr.* **1** (often foll. by *to* + infin.) prevail on; persuade. **2** bring about; give rise to. **3** *Med.* bring on (labor) artificially, esp. by use of drugs. **4** *Electr.* produce (a current) by induction. **5** *Physics* cause (radioactivity) by bombardment. **6** infer; derive as a deduction. □□ **in·duc·er** *n.* **in·duc·i·ble** *adj.*

in·duce·ment /indoósmənt, -dyoós-/ *n.* **1** (often foll. by *to*) an attraction that leads one on. **2** a thing that induces.

in·duct /indúkt/ *v.tr.* (often foll. by *to, into*) **1** introduce formally into possession of a benefice. **2** install into a room, office, etc. **3** introduce; initiate. **4** enlist (a person) for military service. □□ **in·duc·tee** /indúkteé/ *n.*

in·duc·tance /indúktəns/ *n. Electr.* the property of an electric circuit that causes an electromotive force to be generated by a change in the current flowing.

in·duc·tion /indúkshən/ *n.* **1** the act or an instance of inducting or inducing. **2** *Med.* the process of bringing on (esp. labor) by artificial means. **3 a** *Logic* the inference of a general law from particular instances (cf. DEDUCTION). **b** *Math.* a means of proving a theorem by showing that, if it is true of any particular case, it is true of the next case in a series, and then showing that it is indeed true in one particular case. **c** (foll. by *of*) the production of (facts) to prove a general statement. **4** (often *attrib.*) a formal introduction to a new job, position, etc. (*attended an induction course*). **5** *Electr.* **a** the production of an electric or magnetic state by the proximity (without contact) of an electrified or magnetized body. **b** ▼ the production of an electric current in a conductor by a change of magnetic field. ▷ ELECTROMAGNETISM. **6** the drawing of a fuel mixture into the cylinders of an internal-combustion engine. **7** enlistment for military service.

in·duc·tive /indúktiv/ *adj.* **1** (of reasoning, etc.) of or based on induction. **2** of electric or magnetic induction. □□ **in·duc·tive·ly** *adv.* **in·duc·tive·ness** *n.*

in·duc·tor /indúktər/ *n.* **1** *Electr.* a component (in a circuit) which possesses inductance. **2** a person who inducts a member of the clergy.

in·due var. of ENDUE.

in·dulge /indúlj/ *v.* **1** *intr.* (often foll. by *in*) take pleasure freely. **2** *tr.* yield freely to (a desire, etc.). **3** *tr.* gratify the wishes of; favor (*indulged them with money*). **4** *intr. colloq.* take alcoholic liquor. □□ **in·dulg·er** *n.*

in·dul·gence /indúljəns/ *n.* **1 a** the act of indulging. **b** the state of being indulgent. **2** something indulged in. **3** *RC Ch.* the remission of temporal punishment in purgatory, still due for sins after absolution. **4** a privilege granted.

in·dul·gent /indúljənt/ *adj.* **1** ready or too ready to overlook faults, etc. **2** indulging or tending to indulge. □□ **in·dul·gent·ly** *adv.*

in·dus·tri·al /indústreeəl/ *adj. & n.* ● *adj.* **1** of or relating to industry or industries. **2** designed or suitable for industrial use (*industrial alcohol*). **3** characterized by highly developed industries (*the industrial nations*). ● *n.* (in *pl.*) shares in industrial companies. □□ **in·dus·tri·al·ly** *adv.*

in·dus·tri·al·ism /indústreeəlizəm/ *n.* a social or economic system in which manufacturing industries are prevalent.

in·dus·tri·al·ist /indústreeəlist/ *n.* a person engaged in the management of industry.

in·dus·tri·al·ize /indústreeəlīz/ *v.* **1** *tr.* introduce industries to (a country or region, etc.). **2** *intr.* become industrialized. □□ **in·dus·tri·al·i·za·tion** *n.*

in·dus·tri·al park *n.* an area of land developed for a complex of factories and other businesses, usu. separate from an urban center.

in·dus·tri·al rev·o·lu·tion *n.* the rapid development of a nation's industry (esp. the **Industrial Revolution**, in the late 18th and early 19th c.).

in·dus·tri·ous /indústreeəs/ *adj.* diligent; hard-working. □□ **in·dus·tri·ous·ly** *adv.* **in·dus·tri·ous·ness** *n.*

I

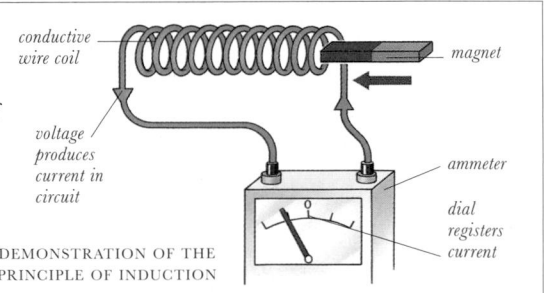

INDIGO
(*Indigofera decora*)

INDUCTION

Electromagnetic induction occurs when a magnet moves near a coil of wire. The effect of the induction is to produce an electric voltage whose strength depends upon the speed of motion and the strength of the magnet, as well as upon the number of turns of the coil.

conductive wire coil — *magnet*

voltage produces current in circuit

ammeter

dial registers current

DEMONSTRATION OF THE PRINCIPLE OF INDUCTION

in·dus·try /índəstree/ *n.* (*pl.* **-ies**) **1 a** a branch of trade or manufacture. **b** trade and manufacture collectively (*incentives to industry*). **2** concerted or copious activity (*the building was a hive of industry*). **3 a** diligence. **b** *colloq.* the diligent study of a particular topic (*the Shakespeare industry*). **4** habitual employment in useful work.

In·dy *n.* /índee/ a form of motor racing, usu. at very high speeds on oval circuits.

In·dy car *n.* ▼ a car used in Indy racing.

in·e·bri·ate *v., adj., & n.* ● *v.tr.* /inéebreeayt/ **1** make drunk; intoxicate. **2** excite. ● *adj.* /inéebreeət/ drunken. ● *n.* /inéebreeət/ a drunken person, esp. a habitual drunkard. □□ **in·e·bri·a·tion** /-áyshən/ *n.* **in·e·bri·e·ty** /ínibrīətee/ *n.*

in·ed·i·ble /inédibəl/ *adj.* not edible, esp. not suitable for eating (cf. UNEATABLE). □□ **in·ed·i·bil·i·ty** *n.*

in·ed·u·ca·ble /inéjəkəbəl/ *adj.* incapable of being educated. □□ **in·ed·u·ca·bil·i·ty** *n.*

in·ef·fa·ble /inéfəbəl/ *adj.* **1** unutterable; too great for description in words. **2** that must not be uttered. □□ **in·ef·fa·bil·i·ty** *n.* **in·ef·fa·bly** *adv.*

in·ef·fec·tive /iniféktiv/ *adj.* **1** not producing any effect or the desired effect. **2** (of a person) inefficient; not achieving results. **3** lacking artistic effect. □□ **in·ef·fec·tive·ly** *adv.* **in·ef·fec·tive·ness** *n.*

in·ef·fec·tu·al /inifékchōōəl/ *adj.* **1 a** without effect. **b** not producing the desired or expected effect. **2** (of a person) lacking the ability to achieve results (*an ineffectual leader*). □□ **in·ef·fec·tu·al·i·ty** /-álitee/ *n.* **in·ef·fec·tu·al·ly** *adv.* **in·ef·fec·tu·al·ness** *n.*

in·ef·fi·ca·cious /inefikáyshəs/ *adj.* (of a remedy, etc.) not producing the desired effect. □□ **in·ef·fi·ca·cious·ly** *adv.* **in·ef·fi·ca·cious·ness** *n.* **in·ef·fi·ca·cy** /inéfikəsee/ *n.*

in·ef·fi·cient /inifíshənt/ *adj.* **1** not efficient. **2** (of a person) not fully capable; not well qualified. □□ **in·ef·fi·cien·cy** *n.* **in·ef·fi·cient·ly** *adv.*

in·e·las·tic /inilástik/ *adj.* **1** not elastic. **2** unadaptable; inflexible; unyielding. □□ **in·e·las·ti·cal·ly** *adv.* **in·e·las·tic·i·ty** /-lastísitee/ *n.*

in·el·e·gant /inéligənt/ *adj.* **1** ungraceful. **2 a** unrefined. **b** (of a style) unpolished. □□ **in·el·e·gance** /-gəns/ *n.* **in·el·e·gant·ly** *adv.*

in·el·i·gi·ble /inélijibəl/ *adj.* **1** not eligible. **2** undesirable. □□ **in·el·i·gi·bil·i·ty** *n.* **in·el·i·gi·bly** *adv.*

in·e·luc·ta·ble /inilúktəbəl/ *adj.* **1** irresistible. **2** inescapable. □□ **in·e·luc·ta·bil·i·ty** *n.* **in·e·luc·ta·bly** *adv.*

in·ept /inépt/ *adj.* **1** unskillful. **2** absurd; silly. **3** out of place. □□ **in·ept·i·tude** *n.* **in·ept·ly** *adv.* **in·ept·ness** *n.*

in·e·qua·ble /inékwəbəl/ *adj.* **1** not fairly distributed. **2** not uniform.

in·e·qual·i·ty /inikwólitee/ *n.* (*pl.* **-ies**) **1 a** lack of equality in any respect. **b** an instance of this. **2** the state of being variable.

in·eq·ui·ta·ble /inékwitəbəl/ *adj.* unfair; unjust. □□ **in·eq·ui·ta·bly** *adv.*

in·eq·ui·ty /inékwitee/ *n.* (*pl.* **-ies**) unfairness; bias.

in·e·rad·i·ca·ble /inirádikəbəl/ *adj.* that cannot be eradicated. □□ **in·e·rad·i·ca·bly** *adv.*

in·ert /inэ́rt/ *adj.* **1** without inherent power of action, motion, or resistance. **2** without active chemical or other properties. **3** sluggish; slow. □□ **in·ert·ly** *adv.* **in·ert·ness** *n.*

in·ert gas *n.* = NOBLE GAS.

in·er·tia /inэ́rshə/ *n.* **1** *Physics* a property of matter by which it continues in its existing state of rest or uniform motion in a straight line, unless that state is changed by an external force. **2** inertness; sloth. □□ **in·er·tial** *adj.* **in·er·tia·less** *adj.*

in·es·ca·pa·ble /iniskáypəbəl/ *adj.* that cannot be escaped or avoided. □□ **in·es·cap·a·bil·i·ty** *n.* **in·es·cap·a·bly** *adv.*

in·es·sen·tial /inisénshəl/ *adj. & n.* ● *adj.* **1** not necessary. **2** dispensable. ● *n.* an inessential thing.

in·es·ti·ma·ble /inéstiməbəl/ *adj.* too great, intense, precious, etc., to be estimated. □□ **in·es·ti·ma·bly** *adv.*

in·ev·i·ta·ble /inévitəbəl/ *adj.* **1 a** unavoidable; sure to happen. **b** that is bound to occur or appear. **2** *colloq.* that is tiresomely familiar. **3** (of character drawing, the development of a plot, etc.) so true to nature, etc., as to preclude alternative treatment or solution; convincing. □□ **in·ev·i·ta·bil·i·ty** *n.* **in·ev·i·ta·ble·ness** *n.* **in·ev·i·ta·bly** *adv.*

in·ex·act /inigzákt/ *adj.* not exact. □□ **in·ex·act·i·tude** /-titōod, -tyōod/ *n.* **in·ex·act·ly** *adv.* **in·ex·act·ness** *n.*

in·ex·cus·a·ble /inikskyōōzəbəl/ *adj.* (of a person, action, etc.) that cannot be excused or justified. □□ **in·ex·cus·a·bly** *adv.*

in·ex·haust·i·ble /inigzáwstibəl/ *adj.* **1** that cannot be exhausted or used up. **2** that cannot be worn out. □□ **in·ex·haust·i·bil·i·ty** *n.* **in·ex·haust·i·bly** *adv.*

in·ex·o·ra·ble /inéksərəbəl/ *adj.* **1** relentless. **2** (of a person or attribute) that cannot be persuaded by request or entreaty. □□ **in·ex·o·ra·bil·i·ty** /-bílitee/ *n.* **in·ex·o·ra·bly** *adv.*

in·ex·pen·sive /inikspénsiv/ *adj.* **1** not expensive; cheap. **2** offering good value for the price. □□ **in·ex·pen·sive·ly** *adv.* **in·ex·pen·sive·ness** *n.*

in·ex·pe·ri·ence /inikspéereeəns/ *n.* lack of experience, or of the resulting knowledge or skill. □□ **in·ex·pe·ri·enced** *adj.*

in·ex·pert /inékspərt/ *adj.* unskillful; lacking expertise. □□ **in·ex·pert·ly** *adv.* **in·ex·pert·ness** *n.*

in·ex·pli·ca·ble /iniksplíkəbəl, inéks-/ *adj.* that cannot be explained or accounted for. □□ **in·ex·pli·ca·bil·i·ty** *n.* **in·ex·pli·ca·bly** *adv.*

in·ex·plic·it /iniksplísit/ *adj.* not definitely or clearly expressed. □□ **in·ex·plic·it·ly** *adv.* **in·ex·plic·it·ness** *n.*

in·ex·press·i·ble /iniksprésibəl/ *adj.* that cannot be expressed in words. □□ **in·ex·press·i·bly** *adv.*

in ex·tre·mis /ín ekstréemis, -tré-/ *adj.* **1** at the point of death. **2** in great difficulties.

in·ex·tri·ca·ble /inékstrikəbəl, inikstrík-/ *adj.* **1** (of a circumstance) that cannot be escaped from. **2** (of a knot, problem, etc.) that cannot be unraveled or solved. **3** intricately confused. □□ **in·ex·tri·ca·bil·i·ty** *n.* **in·ex·tri·ca·bly** *adv.*

inf. *abbr.* **1** infantry. **2** inferior. **3** infinitive.

in·fal·li·ble /infálibəl/ *adj.* **1** incapable of error. **2** (of a method, test, proof, etc.) unfailing; sure to succeed. □□ **in·fal·li·bil·i·ty** /-bílitee/ *n.* **in·fal·li·bly** *adv.*

in·fa·mous /ínfəməs/ *adj.* **1** notoriously bad; having a bad reputation. **2** abominable. □□ **in·fa·mous·ly** *adv.* **in·fa·my** /ínfəmee/ *n.* (*pl.* **-ies**).

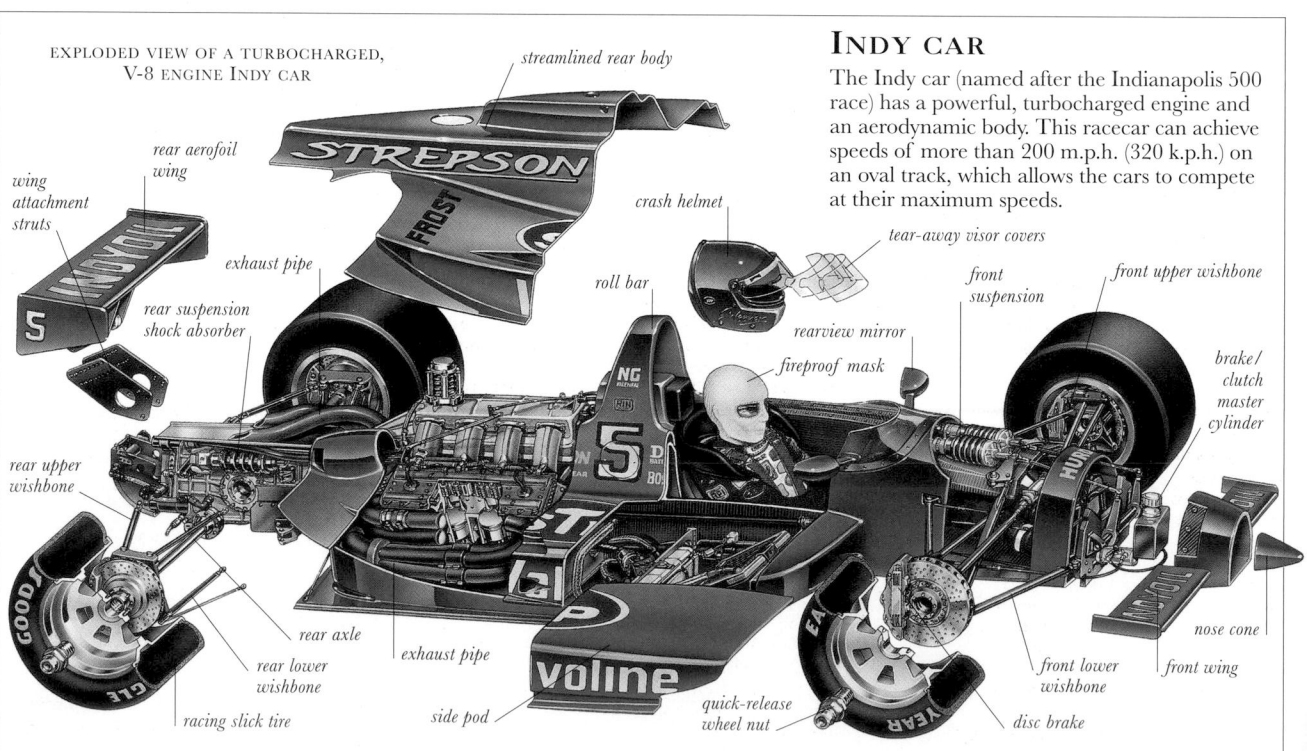

EXPLODED VIEW OF A TURBOCHARGED, V-8 ENGINE INDY CAR

INDY CAR

The Indy car (named after the Indianapolis 500 race) has a powerful, turbocharged engine and an aerodynamic body. This racecar can achieve speeds of more than 200 m.p.h. (320 k.p.h.) on an oval track, which allows the cars to compete at their maximum speeds.

streamlined rear body · crash helmet · tear-away visor covers · front suspension · front upper wishbone · rearview mirror · fireproof mask · brake/clutch master cylinder · rear aerofoil wing · roll bar · wing attachment struts · exhaust pipe · rear suspension shock absorber · rear upper wishbone · rear axle · rear lower wishbone · racing slick tire · side pod · exhaust pipe · quick-release wheel nut · front lower wishbone · front wing · disc brake · nose cone

in·fan·cy /ínfənsee/ n. (pl. **-ies**) **1** early childhood; babyhood. **2** an early state in the development of an idea, undertaking, etc.

in·fant /ínfənt/ n. **1 a** a child during the earliest period of its life. **b** Brit. a schoolchild below the age of seven years. **2** (esp. attrib.) a thing in an early stage of its development.

in·fan·ti·cide /infántisīd/ n. **1** the killing of an infant soon after birth. **2** the practice of killing newborn infants. **3** a person who kills an infant. □□ **in·fan·ti·cid·al** /-síd'l/ adj.

in·fan·tile /ínfəntīl/ adj. **1 a** like or characteristic of a child. **b** childish; immature (infantile humor). **2** in its infancy.

in·fan·tile pa·ral·y·sis n. poliomyelitis.

in·fan·try /ínfəntree/ n. (pl. **-ies**) a body of soldiers who march and fight on foot; foot soldiers collectively.

in·fan·try·man /ínfəntreemən/ n. (pl. **-men**) ▼ a soldier of an infantry unit.

covered helmet
flashlight
unit badge
name tape
wide-brimmed hat
camouflage trousers
M16 rifle
water bottle
equipment belt
storage pocket
Desert boot

INFANTRYMAN IN US
DESERT COMBAT UNIFORM

in·farct /ínfaarkt/ n. Med. a localized area of dead tissue caused by an inadequate blood supply. □□ **in·farc·tion** /-fáarkshən/ n.

in·fat·u·ate /infáchoō-ayt/ v.tr. (usu. as **infatuated** adj.) **1** (often foll. by with) inspire with intense, usu. transitory fondness or admiration. **2** affect with extreme folly. □□ **in·fat·u·a·tion** /-áyshən/ n.

in·fect /infékt/ v.tr. **1** contaminate (air, water, etc.) with harmful organisms or noxious matter. **2** affect (a person) with disease, etc. **3** instill bad feeling or opinion into (a person). □□ **in·fec·tor** n.

in·fec·tion /infékshən/ n. **1 a** the process of infecting or state of being infected. **b** an instance of this; an infectious disease. **2** communication of disease, esp. by the agency of air or water, etc. **3 a** moral contamination. **b** the diffusive influence of example, sympathy, etc.

in·fec·tious /infékshəs/ adj. **1** infecting with disease. **2** (of a disease) liable to be transmitted by air, water, etc. **3** (of emotions, etc.) apt to spread; quickly affecting others. □□ **in·fec·tious·ly** adv. **in·fec·tious·ness** n.

in·fec·tive /inféktiv/ adj. **1** capable of infecting with disease. **2** infectious. □□ **in·fec·tive·ness** n.

in·fe·lic·i·tous /ínfilísitəs/ adj. not felicitous; unfortunate. □□ **in·fe·lic·i·tous·ly** adv.

in·fe·lic·i·ty /ínfilísitee/ n. (pl. **-ies**) **1 a** inaptness of expression, etc. **b** an instance of this. **2 a** unhappiness. **b** a misfortune.

in·fer /infər/ v.tr. (**inferred**, **inferring**) (often foll. by that + clause) **1** deduce or conclude from facts

and reasoning. **2** disp. imply; suggest. □□ **in·fer·a·ble** adj. (also **infer(r)ible**).

in·fer·ence /ínfərəns/ n. **1** the act or an instance of inferring. **2** Logic **a** the forming of a conclusion from premises. **b** a thing inferred. □□ **in·fer·en·tial** /-rénshəl/ adj. **in·fer·en·tial·ly** adv.

in·fe·ri·or /inféereeər/ adj. & n. ● adj. **1** (often foll. by to) **a** lower; in a lower position. **b** of lower rank, quality, etc. **2** poor in quality. **3** (of figures or letters) written or printed below the line. ● n. **1** a person inferior to another, esp. in rank. **2** an inferior letter or figure. □□ **in·fe·ri·or·ly** adv.

in·fe·ri·or·i·ty /inféeree-áwritee, -ór-/ n. the state of being inferior.

in·fe·ri·or·i·ty com·plex n. an unrealistic feeling of general inadequacy caused by actual or supposed inferiority in one sphere, sometimes marked by aggressive behavior in compensation.

in·fer·nal /infərnəl/ adj. **1 a** of hell or the underworld. **b** hellish; fiendish. **2** colloq. detestable; tiresome. □□ **in·fer·nal·ly** adv.

in·fer·no /infərnō/ n. (pl. **-os**) **1** a raging fire. **2** a scene of horror or distress.

in·fer·tile /infərt'l/ adj. not fertile. □□ **in·fer·til·i·ty** /-tílitee/ n.

in·fest /infést/ v.tr. (of harmful persons or things, esp. vermin or disease) overrun (a place) in large numbers. □□ **in·fes·ta·tion** n.

in·fi·del /infid'l, -del/ n. & adj. ● n. a person who does not believe in religion or in a particular religion; an unbeliever. ● adj. **1** that is an infidel. **2** of unbelievers.

in·fi·del·i·ty /ínfidélitee/ n. (pl. **-ies**) **1 a** disloyalty or unfaithfulness, esp. to a husband or wife. **b** an instance of this. **2** disbelief in Christianity or another religion.

in·field /ínfeeld/ n. **1** Baseball **a** the area enclosed by the three bases and home plate. ▷ BASEBALL. **b** the four fielders stationed near the bases. **2** farmland around or near a homestead. **3 a** arable land. **b** land regularly manured and cropped. □□ **in·field·er** n. (in sense 1).

in·fight·ing /ínfīting/ n. **1** hidden conflict or competitiveness within an organization. **2** boxing at closer quarters than arm's length. □□ **in·fight·er** n.

in·fill /ínfil/ n. & v. ● n. **1** material used to fill a hole, gap, etc. **2** the placing of buildings to occupy the space between existing ones. ● v.tr. fill in (a cavity, etc.).

in·fil·trate /ínfiltrayt/ v. **1** tr. **a** gain entrance or access to surreptitiously and by degrees (as spies, etc.). **b** cause to do this. **2** tr. permeate by filtration. **3** tr. (often foll. by into, through) introduce (fluid) by filtration. □□ **in·fil·tra·tion** /-tráyshən/ n. **in·fil·tra·tor** n.

in·fi·nite /ínfinit/ adj. & n. ● adj. **1** boundless; endless. **2** very great. **3** (usu. with pl.) innumerable; very many (infinite resources). **4** Math. **a** greater than any assignable quantity or countable number. **b** (of a series) that may be continued indefinitely. **5** Gram. (of a verb part) not limited by person or number, e.g., infinitive, gerund, and participle. ● n. **1** (**the Infinite**) God. **2** (**the Infinite**) infinite space. □□ **in·fi·nite·ly** adv. **in·fi·nite·ness** n.

in·fin·i·tes·i·mal /ínfinitésiməl/ adj. & n. ● adj. infinitely or very small. ● n. an infinitesimal amount. □□ **in·fin·i·tes·i·mal·ly** adv.

in·fin·i·tive /infinitiv/ n. a form of a verb expressing the verbal notion without reference to a particular subject, tense, etc. (e.g., see in we came to see, let him see). □□ **in·fin·i·ti·val** /-tívəl/ adj. **in·fin·i·ti·val·ly** /-tívəlee/ adv.

in·fin·i·ty /infínitee/ n. (pl. **-ies**) **1** the state of being infinite. **2** an infinite number or extent. **3** infinite distance. **4** Math. infinite quantity. ¶ Symb.: ∞

in·firm /infərm/ adj. **1** physically weak, esp. through age. **2** (of a person, mind, judgment, etc.) weak; irresolute. □□ **in·fir·mi·ty** n. (pl. **-ies**). **in·firm·ly** adv.

in·fir·ma·ry /infərməree/ n. (pl. **-ies**) **1** a hospital.

2 a place for those who are ill in a monastery, school, etc. ▷ MONASTERY

in·fix /infíks/ v.tr. (often foll. by in) **1** fix (a thing in another). **2** impress (a fact, etc., in the mind). □□ **in·fix·a·tion** n.

in fla·gran·te de·lic·to /in fləgrántee dilíktō/ adv. in the very act of committing an offense.

in·flame /infláym/ v. tr. & intr. (often foll. by with, by) provoke or become provoked to strong feeling, esp. anger. **2** Med. **a** intr. become hot, reddened, and sore. **b** tr. (esp. as **inflamed** adj.) cause inflammation or fever in (a body, etc.); make hot. **3** tr. aggravate. **4** intr. & tr. catch or set on fire. **5** tr. light up with or as if with flames. □□ **in·flam·er** n.

in·flam·ma·ble /inflámməbəl/ adj. & n. ● adj. **1** easily set on fire; flammable. **2** easily excited. ● n. (usu. in pl.) a flammable substance. □□ **in·flam·ma·bil·i·ty** n. **in·flam·ma·ble·ness** n. **in·flam·ma·bly** adv.

in·flam·ma·tion /ínfləmáyshən/ n. **1** the act or an instance of inflaming. **2** Med. ▼ a localized physical condition with heat, swelling, redness, and usu. pain, esp. as a reaction to injury or infection.

in·flam·ma·to·ry /inflámmətáwree/ adj. **1** (esp. of speeches, leaflets, etc.) tending to cause anger, etc. **2** of or tending to inflammation of the body.

in·flat·a·ble /infláytəbəl/ adj. & n. ● adj. that can be inflated. ● n. an inflatable plastic or rubber object.

in·flate /infláyt/ v.tr. **1** distend (a balloon, etc.) with air. **2** (usu. foll. by with; usu. in passive) puff up (a person with pride, etc.). **3 a** (often absol.) bring about inflation (of the currency). **b** raise (prices) artificially. **4** (as **inflated** adj.) (esp. of language, sentiments, etc.) bombastic. □□ **in·flat·ed·ly** adv. **in·flat·ed·ness** n. **in·flat·er** n. **in·fla·tor** n.

in·fla·tion /infláyshən/ n. **1 a** the act or condition of inflating or being inflated. **b** an instance of this. **2** Econ. **a** a general increase in prices and fall in the purchasing value of money. **b** an increase in available currency regarded as causing this. □□ **in·fla·tion·ar·y** adj. **in·fla·tion·ism** n. **in·fla·tion·ist** n. & adj.

in·flect /inflékt/ v. **1** tr. change the pitch of (a voice, a musical note, etc.). **2** Gram. **a** tr. change the form of (a word) to express tense, gender, number, mood, etc. **b** intr. (of a word, language, etc.) undergo such change. **3** tr. bend inward; curve. □□ **in·flec·tive** adj.

in·flec·tion /inflékshən/ n. (also esp. Brit. **inflexion**) **1 a** the act or condition of inflecting or being inflected. **b** an instance of this. **2** Gram. **a** the process or practice of inflecting words. **b** an inflected form of a word. **c** a suffix, etc., used to inflect, e.g., -ed. **3** a

I

INFLAMMATION

Damage to the skin or a localized infection induces an influx of phagocytic blood cells and proteins to the affected area to fight bacteria or repair tissue damage. The increased supply of blood causes the redness and swelling of inflammation.

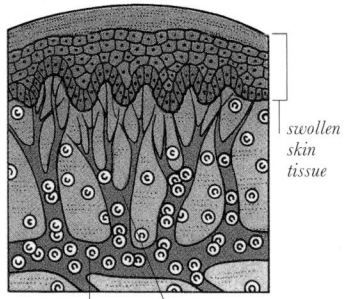

swollen skin tissue

phagocytic cells   enlarged blood vessels

CROSS SECTION OF INFLAMED HUMAN SKIN

modulation of the voice. □□ **in·flec·tion·al** *adj.* **in·flec·tion·al·ly** *adv.* **in·flec·tion·less** *adj.*

in·flex·i·ble /infléksibəl/ *adj.* **1** unbendable. **2** stiff; immovable; obstinate. **3** unchangeable; inexorable. □□ **in·flex·i·bil·i·ty** *n.* **in·flex·i·bly** *adv.*

in·flict /inflíkt/ *v.tr.* (usu. foll. by *on, upon*) **1** administer; deal (a stroke, wound, defeat, etc.). **2** (also *refl.*) often *joc.* impose (suffering, a penalty, oneself, one's company, etc.) on (*shall not inflict myself on you any longer*). □□ **in·flict·a·ble** *adj.* **in·flict·er** *n.* **in·flic·tion** *n.*

in·flight /inflīt/ *attrib.adj.* occurring or provided during an aircraft flight.

in·flo·res·cence /inflərésəns/ *n.* **1** *Bot.* **a** ▶ the complete flower head of a plant including stems, stalks, bracts, and flowers. **b** the arrangement of this. **2** the process of flowering.

in·flow /inflō/ *n.* **1** a flowing in. **2** something that flows in. □□ **in·flow·ing** *n. & adj.*

in·flu·ence /inflōōəns/ *n. & v.* ● *n.* **1** (usu. foll. by *on, upon*) the effect a person or thing has on another. **2** (usu. foll. by *over, with*) moral ascendancy or power. **3** a thing or person exercising such power (*is a good influence on them*). ● *v.tr.* exert influence on; have an effect on. □ **under the influence** *colloq.* affected by alcoholic drink. □□ **in·flu·ence·a·ble** *adj.*

in·flu·en·tial /inflōō-énshəl/ *adj.* having a great influence or power (*influential in the financial world*). □□ **in·flu·en·tial·ly** *adv.*

in·flu·en·za /inflōō-énzə/ *n.* a highly contagious virus infection causing fever, severe aching, and catarrh, often occurring in epidemics. □□ **in·flu·en·zal** *adj.*

in·flux /influks/ *n.* a continual stream of people or things.

in·fo /infō/ *n. colloq.* information.

in·fo·mer·cial /infōmárshəl/ *n.* a television program promoting a commercial product.

in·form /infáwrm/ *v.* **1** *tr.* (usu. foll. by *of, about, on*, or *that, how* + clause) tell (*informed them of their rights*; *informed us that the train was late*). **2** *intr.* (usu. foll. by *against, on*) give incriminating information about a person to the authorities. **3** *tr.* impart its quality to; permeate. □□ **in·form·ant** *n.*

in·for·mal /infáwrməl/ *adj.* **1** without ceremony or formality (*just an informal chat*). **2** (of language, clothing, etc.) everyday; normal. □□ **in·for·mal·i·ty** /-málitee/ *n.* (*pl.* **-ies**) **in·for·mal·ly** *adv.*

in·for·mat·ics /infərmátiks/ *n.pl.* (usu. treated as *sing.*) the science of processing data for storage and retrieval; information science.

in·for·ma·tion /infərmáyshən/ *n.* **1 a** something told; knowledge. **b** (usu. foll. by *on, about*) items of knowledge; news. **2** *Law* (usu. foll. by *against*) a charge or complaint lodged with a court or magistrate. **3 a** the act of informing or telling. **b** an instance of this. □□ **in·for·ma·tion·al** *adj.* **in·for·ma·tion·al·ly** *adv.*

in·for·ma·tion (su·per)high·way *n.* a putative worldwide computer network offering information, shopping, and other services.

in·form·a·tive /infáwrmətiv/ *adj.* (also **in·for·ma·to·ry** /infáwrmətáwree/) giving information; instructive. □□ **in·form·a·tive·ly** *adv.* **in·form·a·tive·ness** *n.*

in·formed /infáwrmd/ *adj.* **1** knowing the facts; instructed (*his answers show that he is badly informed*). **2** educated; intelligent. □□ **in·form·ed·ly** /infáwrmidlee/ *adv.* **in·form·ed·ness** /infáwrmidnis/ *n.*

in·form·er /infáwrmər/ *n.* **1** a person who informs against another. **2** a person who informs or advises.

in·fo·tain·ment /infōtáynmənt/ *n.* **1** factual information presented in dramatized form on television. **2** a television program mixing news and entertainment.

in·fra /infrə/ *adv.* below, further (in a book or writing).

infra- /infrə/ *comb. form* **1** below. **2** *Anat.* below or under a part of the body.

in·frac·tion /infrákshən/ *n.* esp. *Law* a violation or infringement. □□ **in·fract** *v.tr.* **in·frac·tor** *n.*

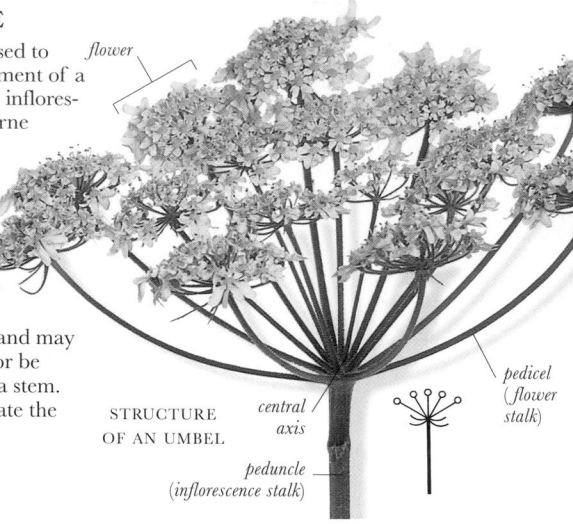

INFLORESCENCE

The term inflorescence is used to describe the flower arrangement of a plant. The simplest form of inflorescence is a solitary flower borne on a single stem. A capitulum (head) often looks similar but consists of a disklike pad that supports a number of densely packed smaller flowers (florets). The flowers in other types of inflorescence may be stalked or stalkless, and may radiate from a single point or be arranged at intervals along a stem. The examples shown illustrate the structure of each type of inflorescence.

flower

STRUCTURE OF AN UMBEL

central axis

pedicel (flower stalk)

peduncle (inflorescence stalk)

EXAMPLES OF OTHER INFLORESCENCES

SOLITARY   CLUSTER   CAPITULUM   CYME

SPIKE   RACEME   CORYMB   PANICLE

in·fran·gi·ble /infránjibəl/ *adj.* **1** unbreakable. **2** inviolable. □□ **in·fran·gi·bil·i·ty** *n.* **in·fran·gi·ble·ness** *n.* **in·fran·gi·bly** *adv.*

in·fra·red /infrəréd/ *adj.* **1** having a wavelength just greater than the red end of the visible light spectrum but less than that of radio waves. ▷ ELECTROMAGNETIC RADIATION. **2** of or using such radiation. ▷ THERMOGRAM

in·fra·son·ic /infrəsónik/ *adj.* of or relating to sound waves with a frequency below the lower limit of human audibility. □□ **in·fra·son·i·cal·ly** *adv.*

in·fra·struc·ture /infrəstrukchər/ *n.* **1 a** the basic structural foundations of a society or enterprise; a substructure or foundation. **b** roads, bridges, sewers, etc., regarded as a country's economic foundation. **2** permanent installations as a basis for military, etc., operations.

in·fre·quent /infréekwənt/ *adj.* not frequent. □□ **in·fre·quen·cy** *n.* **in·fre·quent·ly** *adv.*

in·fringe /infrínj/ *v.* **1** *tr.* **a** act contrary to; violate (a law, an oath, etc.). **b** act in defiance of (another's rights, etc.). **2** *intr.* (usu. foll. by *on, upon*) encroach; trespass. □□ **in·fringe·ment** *n.* **in·fring·er** *n.*

in·fu·ri·ate *v. & adj.* ● *v.tr.* /infyŏoreeayt/ fill with fury; enrage. ● *adj.* /infyŏoreeət/ *literary* excited to fury; frantic. □□ **in·fu·ri·at·ing** *adj.* **in·fu·ri·at·ing·ly** *adv.* **in·fu·ri·a·tion** /-áyshən/ *n.*

in·fuse /infyŏoz/ *v.* **1** *tr.* (usu. foll. by *with*) imbue; pervade (*anger infused with resentment*). **2** *tr.* steep (herbs, tea, etc.) in liquid to extract the content. **3** *tr.* (usu. foll. by *into*) instill (grace, spirit, life, etc.). **4** *intr.* undergo infusion (*let it infuse for five minutes*). □□ **in·fus·a·ble** *adj.* **in·fus·er** *n.* **in·fu·sive** /-fyŏosiv/ *adj.*

in·fu·sion /infyŏozhən/ *n.* **1** a liquid obtained by infusing. **2** an infused element; an admixture. **3** *Med.* a slow injection of a substance into a vein or tissue. **4 a** the act of infusing. **b** an instance of this.

in·gath·er /in-gáthər/ *v.tr.* gather in; assemble.

in·ge·ni·ous /injéenyəs/ *adj.* **1** clever at inventing, constructing, organizing, etc.; skillful; resourceful. **2** (of a machine, theory, etc.) cleverly contrived. □□ **in·gen·ious·ly** *adv.* **in·gen·ious·ness** *n.*

in·ge·nue /ánzhənŏo/ *n.* (also **ingénue**) **1** an innocent or unsophisticated young woman. **2** *Theatr.* **a** such a part in a play. **b** the actress who plays this part.

in·ge·nu·i·ty /injinŏoitee, -nyŏo-/ *n.* skill in devising or contriving; ingeniousness.

in·gen·u·ous /injényŏoəs/ *adj.* **1** innocent; artless.

2 open; frank. □□ **in·gen·u·ous·ly** *adv.* **in·gen·u·ous·ness** *n.*

in·gest /injést/ *v.tr.* **1** take in (food, etc.); eat. **2** absorb (facts, knowledge, etc.). □□ **in·ges·tion** /injés-chən/ *n.* **in·ges·tive** *adj.*

in·gle·nook /ínggəlnŏŏk/ *n.* a space within the opening on either side of a large fireplace; chimney corner.

in·glo·ri·ous /in-gláwreeəs/ *adj.* **1** shameful; ignominious. **2** not famous. □□ **in·glo·ri·ous·ly** *adv.* **in·glo·ri·ous·ness** *n.*

in·go·ing /ín-gōing/ *adj.* **1** going in; entering. **2** penetrating; thorough.

in·got /ínggət/ *n.* a usu. oblong piece of cast metal, esp. of gold, silver, or steel.

in·grain *adj. & v.* ● *adj.* /ín-grayn/ inherent; ingrained. ● *v.tr.* /in-gráyn/ cause to become embedded.

in·grained /ín-gráynd/ *attrib.adj.* **1** deeply rooted; inveterate. **2** thorough. **3** (of dirt, etc.) deeply embedded. □□ **in·grain·ed·ly** /-gráynidlee/ *adv.*

in·gra·ti·ate /in-gráysheeayt/ *v.refl.* (usu. foll. by *with*) bring oneself into favor. □□ **in·gra·ti·at·ing** *adj.* **in·gra·ti·at·ing·ly** *adv.* **in·gra·ti·a·tion** /-áyshən/ *n.*

in·grat·i·tude /in-grátitŏŏd, -tyŏŏd/ *n.* a lack of due gratitude.

in·gre·di·ent /in-gréedeeənt/ *n.* a component part or element in a recipe, mixture, or combination.

in·gress /ín-gres/ *n.* the act or right of going in or entering. □□ **in·gres·sion** /-gréshən/ *n.*

in·group /ín-grŏŏp/ *n.* a small exclusive group of people with a common interest.

in·grow·ing /in-grōing/ *adj.* growing inward, esp. (of a toenail) growing into the flesh. □□ **in·grown** *adj.* **in·growth** *n.*

in·hab·it /in-hábit/ *v.tr.* (of a person or animal) dwell in; occupy (a region, town, house, etc.). □□ **in·hab·it·a·bil·i·ty** /-təbílitee/ *n.* **in·hab·it·a·ble** *adj.* **in·hab·it·ant** *n.* **in·hab·i·ta·tion** /-táyshən/ *n.*

in·hal·ant /in-háylənt/ *n.* a medicinal preparation for inhaling.

in·hale /in-háyl/ *v.tr.* (often *absol.*) breathe in (air, gas, tobacco smoke, etc.). □□ **in·ha·la·tion** /-həláyshən/ *n.*

in·hal·er /in-háylər/ *n.* ▶ a portable device used for relieving esp. asthma by inhaling.
▷ MEDICINE

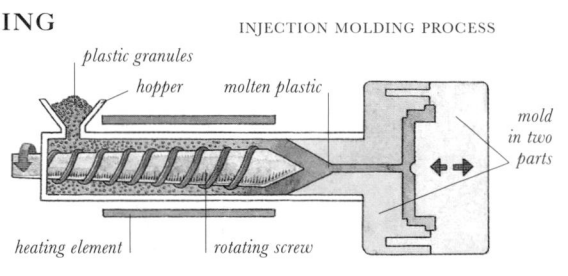

canister

plastic outer casing

nozzle

mouthpiece

INHALER

in·har·mo·ni·ous /ínhaarmṓneeəs/ *adj.* esp. *Mus.* not harmonious. □□ **in·har·mo·ni·ous·ly** *adv.*

in·here /in-héer/ *v.intr.* (often foll. by *in*) **1** exist essentially or permanently in (*goodness inheres in that child*). **2** (of rights, etc.) be vested in (a person, etc.).

in·her·ent /in-héerənt, inhér-/ *adj.* (often foll. by *in*) **1** existing in something, esp. as a permanent or characteristic attribute. **2** vested in (a person, etc.) as a right or privilege. □□ **in·her·ence** /-rəns/ *n.* **in·her·ent·ly** *adv.*

in·her·it /in-hérit/ *v.* **1** *tr.* receive (property, rank, title, etc.) by legal descent or succession. **2** *tr.* derive (a quality or characteristic) genetically from one's ancestors. **3** *absol.* succeed as an heir (*a younger son rarely inherits*). □□ **in·her·i·tor** *n.*

in·her·it·a·ble /in-héritəbəl/ *adj.* **1** capable of being inherited. **2** capable of inheriting. □□ **in·her·it·a·bil·i·ty** /-bílitee/ *n.*

in·her·it·ance /in-hérit'ns/ *n.* **1** something inherited. **2 a** the act of inheriting. **b** an instance of this.

in·hib·it /in-híbit/ *v.tr.* **1** hinder, restrain, or prevent (an action or progress). **2** (as **inhibited** *adj.*) subject to inhibition. **3** (usu. foll. by *from* + verbal noun) forbid or prohibit (a person). □□ **in·hib·i·tive** *adj.* **in·hib·i·tor** *n.* **in·hib·i·to·ry** *adj.*

in·hi·bi·tion /inhibíshən/ *n.* **1** *Psychol.* a restraint on the direct expression of an instinct. **2** *colloq.* an

emotional resistance to a thought, an action, etc. (*has inhibitions about singing in public*). **3** *Law* an order forbidding alteration to property rights. **4 a** the act of inhibiting. **b** the process of being inhibited.

in·hos·pi·ta·ble /ínhospítəbəl, inhóspi-/ *adj.* **1** not hospitable. **2** (of a region, coast, etc.) not affording shelter, etc. □□ **in·hos·pi·ta·ble·ness** *n.* **in·hos·pi·ta·bly** *adv.*

in-house *adj. & adv.* ● *adj.* /ínhóws/ done or existing within an institution, company, etc. (*an in-house project*). ● *adv.* /inhóws/ internally, without outside assistance.

in·hu·man /inhyŏŏmən/ *adj.* **1** (of a person, conduct, etc.) brutal; unfeeling; barbarous. **2** not of a human type. □□ **in·hu·man·ly** *adv.*

in·hu·mane /inhyŏŏmáyn/ *adj.* not humane. □□ **in·hu·mane·ly** *adv.*

in·hu·man·i·ty /inhyŏŏmánitee/ *n.* (*pl.* **-ies**) **1** brutality; barbarousness; callousness. **2** an inhumane act.

in·im·i·cal /inímikəl/ *adj.* (usu. foll. by *to*) **1** hostile. **2** harmful. □□ **in·im·i·cal·ly** *adv.*

in·im·i·ta·ble /inímitəbəl/ *adj.* impossible to imitate. □□ **in·im·i·ta·bil·i·ty** *n.* **in·im·i·ta·ble·ness** *n.* **in·im·i·ta·bly** *adv.*

in·iq·ui·ty /iníkwitee/ *n.* (*pl.* **-ies**) **1** wickedness; unrighteousness. **2** a gross injustice. □□ **in·iq·ui·tous** *adj.* **in·iq·ui·tous·ly** *adv.* **in·iq·ui·tous·ness** *n.*

in·i·tial /iníshəl/ *adj., n., & v.* ● *adj.* of, existing, or occurring at the beginning (*initial stage; initial expenses*). ● *n.* **1** the letter at the beginning of a word. **2** (usu. in *pl.*) the first letter or letters of the words of a (esp. a person's) name or names. ● *v.tr.* (**initialed, initialing**; esp. *Brit.* **initialled, initialling**) mark or sign with one's initials. □□ **in·i·tial·ly** *adv.*

in·i·tial·ize /iníshəlīz/ *v.tr. Computing* set to the value or put in the condition appropriate to the start of an operation. □□ **in·i·tial·i·za·tion** *n.*

in·i·ti·ate *v., n., & adj.* ● *v.tr.* /inísheeayt/ **1** begin; set going; originate. **2 a** (usu. foll. by *into*) admit (a person) into a society, an office, a secret, etc., esp. with a ritual. **b** (usu. foll. by *in, into*) instruct (a person) in science, art, etc. ● *n.* /inísheeət/ a person who has been newly initiated. ● *adj.* /inísheeət/ (of a person) newly initiated (*an initiate member*). □□ **in·i·ti·a·tion** /-sheeáyshən/ *n.* **in·i·ti·a·tor** *n.* **in·i·ti·a·to·ry** /inísheeətáwree/ *adj.*

in·i·ti·a·tive /iníshətiv, inísheeətiv/ *n. & adj.* ● *n.* **1** the ability to initiate things; enterprise (*I'm afraid he lacks all initiative*). **2** a first step; origination (*a peace initiative*). **3** the power or right to begin something. ● *adj.* beginning; originating. ● **on one's own initiative** without being prompted by others. **take the initiative** (usu. foll. by *in* + verbal noun) be the first to take action.

in·ject /injékt/ *v.tr.* **1** *Med.* **a** (usu. foll. by *into*) drive or force (a solution, medicine, etc.) by or as if by a syringe. **b** (usu. foll. by *with*) fill (a cavity, etc.) by injecting. **c** administer medicine, etc., to (a person) by injection. **2** place or insert (an object, a quality, etc.) into something (*may I inject a note of realism?*). □□ **in·ject·a·ble** *adj. & n.* **in·jec·tor** *n.*

in·jec·tion /injékshən/ *n.* **1 a** the act of injecting.

b an instance of this. **2** a liquid or solution (to be) injected.

in·jec·tion mold·ing *n.* ▼ the shaping of rubber or plastic articles by injecting heated material into a mold.

in·ju·di·cious /injŏŏdíshəs/ *adj.* unwise; ill-judged. □□ **in·ju·di·cious·ly** *adv.* **in·ju·di·cious·ness** *n.*

in·junc·tion /injúngkshən/ *n.* **1** an authoritative warning or order. **2** *Law* a judicial order restraining a person from an act or compelling redress to an injured party. □□ **in·junc·tive** *adj.*

in·jure /ínjər/ *v.tr.* **1** do physical harm or damage to; hurt. **2** harm or impair (*illness might injure her chances*). **3** do wrong to. □□ **in·jur·er** *n.*

in·jured /ínjərd/ *adj.* **1** harmed or hurt (*the injured passengers*). **2** offended; wronged (*in an injured tone*).

in·ju·ri·ous /injŏŏreeəs/ *adj.* **1** hurtful. **2** (of language) insulting; libelous. **3** wrongful. □□ **in·ju·ri·ous·ly** *adv.* **in·ju·ri·ous·ness** *n.*

in·ju·ry /ínjəree/ *n.* (*pl.* **-ies**) **1 a** a physical harm or damage. **b** an instance of this (*suffered head injuries*). **2** esp. *Law* **a** a wrongful action or treatment. **b** an instance of this. **3** damage to one's good name, etc.

in·jus·tice /injústis/ *n.* **1** a lack of fairness or justice. **2** an unjust act. ● **do a person an injustice** judge a person unfairly.

ink /ingk/ *n. & v.* ● *n.* **1 a** a colored fluid used for writing with a pen, marking with a rubber stamp, etc. **b** a thick paste used in printing, duplicating, in ballpoint pens, etc. **2** *Zool.* a black liquid ejected by a cuttlefish, octopus, etc., to confuse a predator. ● *v.tr.* **1** (usu. foll. by *in, over*, etc.) mark with ink. **2** cover (type, etc.) with ink before printing. **3** apply ink to.

ink-jet print·er *n.* a computer-controlled printer in which minute droplets of ink are projected onto the paper.

ink·ling /ingkling/ *n.* (often foll. by *of*) a slight knowledge or suspicion; a hint.

ink pad *n.* an ink-soaked pad, usu. in a box, used for inking a rubber stamp, etc.

ink·well /ingkwel/ *n.* a pot for ink usu. housed in a hole in a desk.

ink·y /ingkee/ *adj.* (**inkier, inkiest**) of, as black as, or stained with ink. □□ **ink·i·ness** *n.*

in·laid *past* and *past part.* of INLAY.

in·land /ínlənd, ínland/ *adj., n., & adv.* ● *adj.* **1** situated in the interior of a country. **2** esp. *Brit.* carried on within the limits of a country; domestic (*inland trade*). ● *n.* the parts of a country remote from the sea or frontiers; the interior. ● *adv.* in or toward the interior of a country. □□ **in·land·er** *n.* **in·land·ish** *adj.*

in-law /ínlaw/ *n.* (often in *pl.*) a relative by marriage.

in·lay *v. & n.* ● *v.tr.* /ínláy/ (*past* and *past part.* **inlaid** /ínláyd/) **1 a** (usu. foll. by *in*) embed (a thing in another) so that the surfaces are even. **b** (usu. foll. by *with*) ornament (a thing with inlaid work). **2** (as **inlaid** *adj.*) (of a piece of furniture, etc.) ornamented by inlaying. ● *n.* /ínlay/ **1** inlaid work. **2** material inlaid. □□ **in·lay·er** *n.*

in·let /ínlet, -lit/ *n.* **1** a small arm of the sea, a lake, or a river. **2** a piece inserted, esp. in dressmaking, etc. **3** a way of entry.

I

INJECTION MOLDING

In the process of injection molding, plastic granules are fed through a hopper to be heated in a chamber. A screw in the chamber rotates, forcing the molten plastic into a mold, where it quickly cools and solidifies into the shape required.

INJECTION MOLDING PROCESS

plastic granules
hopper
molten plastic
mold in two parts
heating element
rotating screw

INNER EAR

Inside the human inner ear the cochlea, a fluid-filled spiral, converts sound waves into electrical impulses, which are transmitted via the cochlear nerve to the brain. Three semicircular canals, also containing fluid, aid our sense of balance. The canals are connected to the brain via the vestibular nerve.

vestibular nerves attached to lateral and anterior canals

lateral semicircular canal

posterior semicircular canal

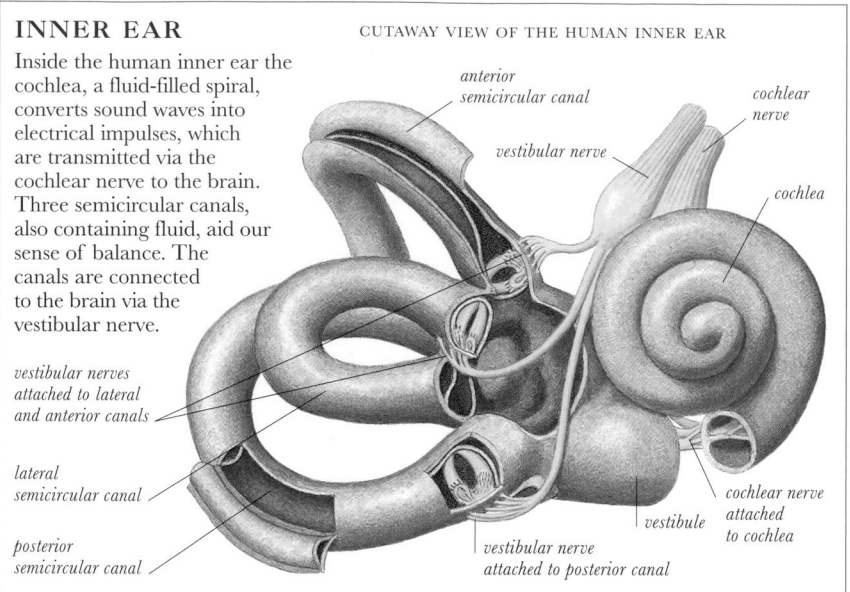

CUTAWAY VIEW OF THE HUMAN INNER EAR

anterior semicircular canal

vestibular nerve

cochlear nerve

cochlea

cochlear nerve attached to cochlea

vestibule

vestibular nerve attached to posterior canal

I

in·line /ínlín/ *adj.* **1** having parts arranged in a line. **2** constituting an integral part of a continuous sequence of operations or machines.

in lo·co pa·ren·tis /in lṓkō pəréntis/ *adv.* in the place or position of a parent.

in·mate /ínmayt/ *n.* (usu. foll. by *of*) **1** an occupant of a hospital, prison, institution, etc. **2** an occupant of a house, etc., esp. one of several.

in me·mo·ri·am /in mimáwreeəm/ *prep. & n.* ● *prep.* in memory of (a dead person). ● *n.* a written article or notice, etc., in memory of a dead person; an obituary.

in·most /ínmōst/ *adj.* **1** most inward. **2** most intimate; deepest.

inn /in/ *n.* **1** a public house providing alcoholic liquor for consumption on the premises, and sometimes accommodation, etc. **2** *hist.* a house providing accommodation, esp. for travelers.

in·nards /ínərdz/ *n.pl. colloq.* **1** entrails. **2** works (of an engine, etc.).

in·nate /ináyt, ínayt/ *adj.* **1** inborn; natural. **2** *Philos.* originating in the mind. □□ **in·nate·ly** *adv.* **in·nate·ness** *n.*

in·ner /ínər/ *adj.* (usu. *attrib.*) **1** further in; inside; interior (*the inner compartment*). **2** (of thoughts, feelings, etc.) deeper; more secret. □□ **in·ner·ly** *adv.* **in·ner·most** *adj.* **in·ner·ness** *n.*

in·ner cir·cle *n.* an intimate, usu. influential small group of people.

in·ner cit·y *n.* the central most densely populated area of a city (also with hyphen) *attrib.: inner-city housing*).

in·ner ear *n.* ▲ the semicircular canals and cochlea, which form the organs of balance and hearing. ▷ EAR

in·ner plan·et *n.* any of the four planets closest to the Sun (i.e., Mercury, Venus, Earth, and Mars) (cf. outer planet).

in·ner tube *n.* a separate inflatable tube inside the cover of a pneumatic tire.

in·ning /íning/ *n.* **1** *Baseball* **a** a division of a game in which the two teams alternate as offense and defense and during which each team is allowed three outs. **b** a single turn at bat for a team until they make three outs. **2** a similar division of play in other games, as horseshoes.

inn·keep·er /ínkeepər/ *n.* a person who keeps an inn.

in·no·cent /ínəsənt/ *adj. & n.* ● *adj.* **1** free from moral wrong; sinless. **2** (usu. foll. by *of*) not guilty (of a crime, etc.). **3 a** simple; guileless; naive. **b** pretending to be guileless. **4** harmless. **5** (foll. by *of*) *colloq.* without; lacking (*appeared, innocent of shoes*). ● *n.* an innocent person, esp. a young child. □□ **in·no·cence** /-səns/ *n.* **in·no·cen·cy** *n.* **in·no·cent·ly** *adv.*

in·noc·u·ous /inókyōōəs/ *adj.* **1** not injurious; harmless. **2** inoffensive. □□ **in·no·cu·i·ty** /ínəkyōō-itee/ *n.* **in·noc·u·ous·ly** *adv.* **in·noc·u·ous·ness** *n.*

in·no·vate /ínəvayt/ *v.intr.* **1** bring in new methods, ideas, etc. **2** (often foll. by *in*) make changes. □□ **in·no·va·tion** /-váyshən/ *n.* **in·no·va·tion·al** /-váyshənəl/ *adj.* **in·no·va·tor** *n.* **in·no·va·tive** *adj.* **in·no·va·tive·ness** *n.* **in·no·va·to·ry** /-vəytáwree/ *adj.*

in·nox·ious /inókshəs/ *adj.* harmless. □□ **in·nox·ious·ly** *adv.* **in·nox·ious·ness** *n.*

in·nu·en·do /ínyōō-éndō/ *n.* (*pl.* **-os** or **-oes**) **1** an allusive or oblique remark or hint, usu. disparaging. **2** a remark with a double meaning, usu. suggestive.

In·nu·it var. of INUIT.

in·nu·mer·a·ble /inōōmərəbəl, inyōō-/ *adj.* too many to be counted. □□ **in·nu·mer·a·bil·i·ty** /-bílitee/ *n.* **in·nu·mer·a·bly** *adv.*

in·nu·mer·ate /inōōmərət, inyōō-/ *adj.* having no knowledge of or feeling for mathematical operations; not numerate. □□ **in·nu·mer·a·cy** /-rəsee/ *n.*

in·oc·u·late /inókyəlayt/ *v.tr.* treat (a person or animal) with a small quantity of the agent of a disease, in the form of vaccine or serum, usu. by injection, to promote immunity against the disease. □□ **in·oc·u·la·ble** *adj.* **in·oc·u·la·tion** /-láyshən/ *n.* **in·oc·u·la·tive** *adj.* **in·oc·u·la·tor** *n.*

in·of·fen·sive /ínəfénsiv/ *adj.* not objectionable; harmless. □□ **in·of·fen·sive·ly** *adv.* **in·of·fen·sive·ness** *n.*

in·op·er·a·ble /inópərəbəl/ *adj.* **1** *Surgery* that cannot suitably be operated on (*inoperable cancer*). **2** that cannot be operated; inoperative. □□ **in·op·er·a·bil·i·ty** *n.* **in·op·er·a·bly** *adv.*

in·op·er·a·tive /inópərətiv/ *adj.* not working or taking effect.

in·op·por·tune /inópərtōōn, -tyōōn/ *adj.* not appropriate, esp. as regards time; unseasonable. □□ **in·op·por·tune·ly** *adv.* **in·op·por·tune·ness** *n.*

in·or·di·nate /ináwrd'nət/ *adj.* **1** immoderate; excessive. **2** intemperate. **3** disorderly. □□ **in·or·di·nate·ly** *adv.*

in·or·gan·ic /ínawrgánik/ *adj.* **1** *Chem.* (of a compound) not organic, usu. of mineral origin. **2** without organized physical structure. **3** not arising by natural growth; extraneous. **4** *Philol.* not explainable by normal etymology. □□ **in·or·gan·i·cal·ly** *adv.*

in·pa·tient /ínpayshənt/ *n.* a patient who stays in the hospital while under treatment.

in·put /ínpōōt/ *n. & v.* ● *n.* **1** what is put in or taken in, or operated on by any process or system. **2** *Electronics* **a** a place where, or a device through which, energy, information, etc., enters a system (*a tape recorder with inputs for microphone and radio*). **b** energy supplied to a device or system; an electrical signal. **3** the information fed into a computer. **4** the action or process of putting in or feeding in. **5** a contribution of information, etc. ● *v.tr.* (**inputting**; *past* and *past part.* **input** or **inputted**) (often foll. by *into*) **1** put in. **2** *Computing* supply (data, programs, etc., to a computer, program, etc.). □ **input-**(or **input/**)**output** *Computing*, etc. of, relating to, or for input and output. □□ **in·put·ter** *n.*

in·quest /ínkwest, íng-/ *n.* **1** *Law* **a** an inquiry by a coroner's court into the cause of a death. **b** a judicial inquiry to ascertain the facts relating to an incident, etc. **c** a coroner's jury. **2** *colloq.* a discussion analyzing the outcome of a game, an election, etc.

in·qui·e·tude /inkwí-itōōd, -tyōōd/ *n.* uneasiness of mind or body.

in·quire /inkwír, ing-/ *v.* **1** *intr.* (often foll. by *of*) seek information formally; make a formal investigation. **2** *intr.* (foll. by *about, after, for*) ask about a person, a person's health, etc. **3** *intr.* (foll. by *for*) ask about the availability of. **4** *tr.* ask for information as to (*inquired whether we were coming*). **5** *tr.* (foll. by *into*) investigate; look into. □□ **in·quir·er** *n.*

in·quir·y /inkwíree, ing-, ínkwəree, íng-/ *n.* (*pl.* **-ies**) **1** an investigation, esp. an official one. **2** the act or an instance of asking or seeking information.

in·qui·si·tion /ínkwizíshən, íng-/ *n.* **1** usu. *derog.* an intensive search or investigation. **2** a judicial or official inquiry. **3** (**the Inquisition**) *RC Ch. hist.* an ecclesiastical tribunal for the suppression of heresy, esp. in Spain, operating through torture and execution. □□ **in·qui·si·tion·al** *adj.*

in·quis·i·tive /inkwízitiv, ing-/ *adj.* **1** unduly curious; prying. **2** seeking knowledge; inquiring. □□ **in·quis·i·tive·ly** *adv.* **in·quis·i·tive·ness** *n.*

in·quis·i·tor /inkwízitər, ing-/ *n.* **1** an official investigator. **2** *hist.* an officer of the Inquisition.

in re /in rée, ráy/ *prep.* = RE¹.

in·road /ínrōd/ *n.* **1** (often in *pl.*) **a** (usu. foll. by *on, into*) an encroachment; a using up of resources, etc. (*makes inroads on my time*). **b** (often foll. by *in, into*) progress; an advance (*making inroads into a difficult market*). **2** a hostile attack; a raid.

INS *abbr.* (US) Immigration and Naturalization Service.

in·sane /insáyn/ *adj.* **1** not of sound mind; mad. **2** *colloq.* extremely foolish; irrational. □□ **in·sane·ly** *adv.* **in·sane·ness** *n.* **in·san·i·ty** /-sánitee/ *n.* (*pl.* **-ies**).

in·sa·tia·ble /insáyshəbəl/ *adj.* **1** unable to be satisfied. **2** (usu. foll. by *of*) extremely greedy. □□ **in·sa·tia·bil·i·ty** *n.* **in·sa·tia·bly** *adv.*

in·scribe /inskríb/ *v.tr.* **1 a** (usu. foll. by *in, on*) write or carve (words, etc.) on stone, metal, paper, a book, etc. **b** (usu. foll. by *with*) mark (a sheet, tablet, etc.) with characters. **2** (usu. foll. by *to*) write an informal dedication (to a person) in or on (a book, etc.). **3** enter the name of (a person) on a list or in a book. □□ **in·scrib·a·ble** *adj.* **in·scrib·er** *n.*

in·scrip·tion /inskrípshən/ *n.* **1** words inscribed, esp. on a monument, coin, stone, or in a book, etc. **2 a** the act of inscribing, esp. the informal dedication of a book, etc. **b** an instance of this. □□ **in·scrip·tion·al** *adj.* **in·scrip·tive** *adj.*

in·scru·ta·ble /inskrōōtəbəl/ *adj.* wholly mysterious; impenetrable. □□ **in·scru·ta·bil·i·ty** *n.* **in·scru·ta·ble·ness** *n.* **in·scru·ta·bly** *adv.*

in·sect /ínsekt/ *n.* **1 a** ▶ any arthropod of the class Insecta, having a head, thorax, abdomen, two antennae, three pairs of thoracic legs, and usu. one or two pairs of thoracic wings. ▷ EXOSKELETON. **b** (loosely) any other small segmented invertebrate animal. **2** an insignificant or contemptible person or creature. □□ **in·sec·tile** /-séktəl, -tīl/ *adj.*

INSECT

Insects are small, land-dwelling arthropods, characterized by three pairs of jointed legs and by three distinct body sections: the head, thorax, and abdomen. They have one pair of antennae (comprising the scape, pedicel, and flagellum in this longhorn beetle), compound eyes, and often one or two pairs of wings. Insects have a hard outer casing, an exoskeleton, instead of an internal skeleton.

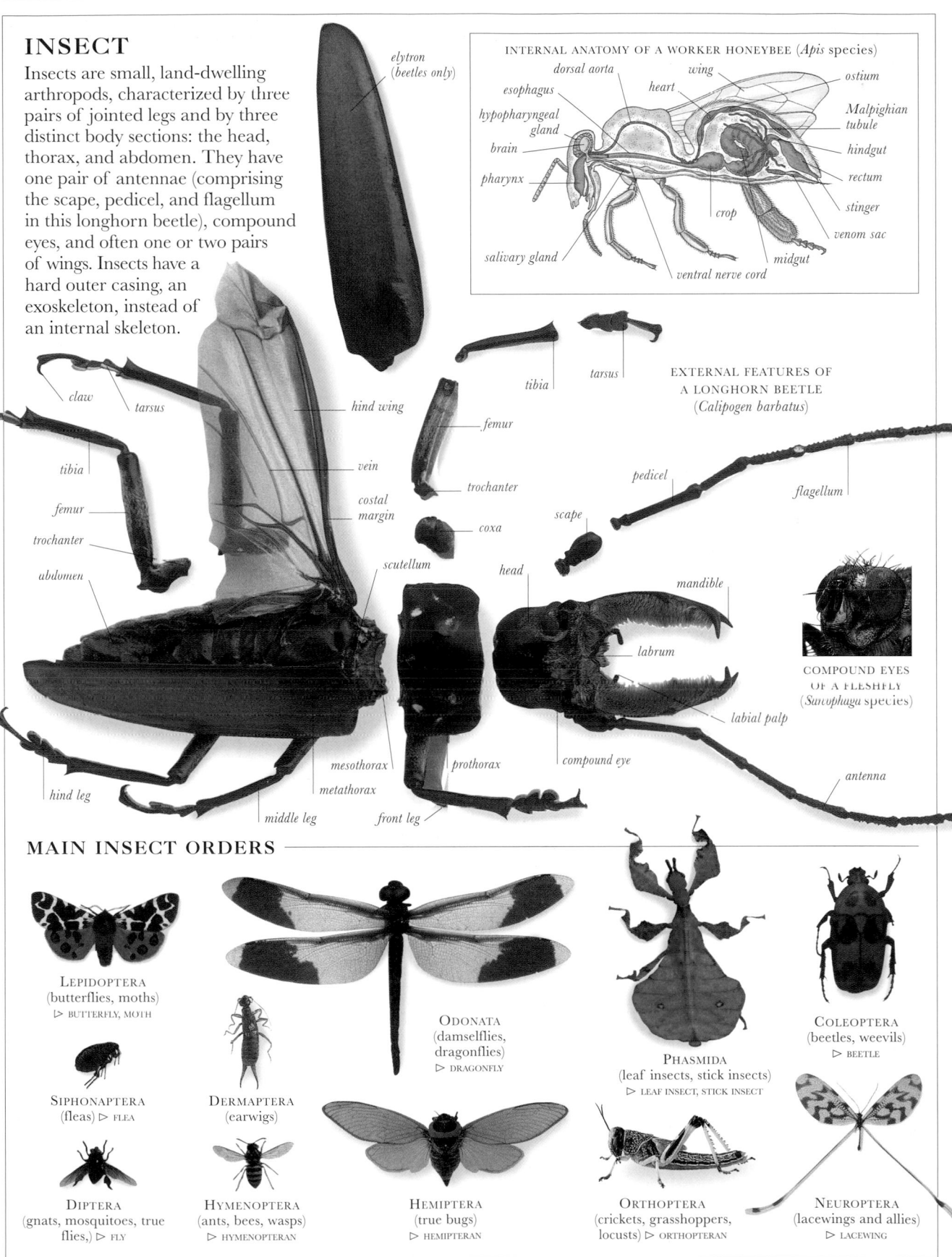

elytron (beetles only)

INTERNAL ANATOMY OF A WORKER HONEYBEE (*Apis* species)

dorsal aorta
wing
esophagus
heart
ostium
hypopharyngeal gland
Malpighian tubule
brain
hindgut
pharynx
rectum
crop
stinger
salivary gland
venom sac
ventral nerve cord
midgut

hind wing
vein
costal margin
femur
trochanter
tibia
tarsus
coxa
scape
pedicel
flagellum

EXTERNAL FEATURES OF A LONGHORN BEETLE (*Calipogen barbatus*)

claw
tarsus
tibia
femur
trochanter
abdomen
scutellum
head
mandible
labrum

COMPOUND EYES OF A FLESHFLY (*Sarcophaga* species)

hind leg
middle leg
mesothorax
metathorax
prothorax
front leg
compound eye
labial palp
antenna

MAIN INSECT ORDERS

LEPIDOPTERA (butterflies, moths)
▷ BUTTERFLY, MOTH

ODONATA (damselflies, dragonflies)
▷ DRAGONFLY

PHASMIDA (leaf insects, stick insects)
▷ LEAF INSECT, STICK INSECT

COLEOPTERA (beetles, weevils)
▷ BEETLE

SIPHONAPTERA (fleas) ▷ FLEA

DERMAPTERA (earwigs)

DIPTERA (gnats, mosquitoes, true flies,) ▷ FLY

HYMENOPTERA (ants, bees, wasps)
▷ HYMENOPTERAN

HEMIPTERA (true bugs)
▷ HEMIPTERAN

ORTHOPTERA (crickets, grasshoppers, locusts) ▷ ORTHOPTERAN

NEUROPTERA (lacewings and allies)
▷ LACEWING

in·sec·ti·cide /inséktisīd/ n. a substance used for killing insects. □□ **in·sec·ti·cid·al** /-síd'l/ adj.

in·sec·ti·vore /inséktivawr/ n. 1 ▼ any mammal of the order Insectivora feeding on insects, etc., e.g., a hedgehog or mole. 2 any plant that captures and absorbs insects. □□ **in·sec·tiv·o·rous** /-tívərəs/ adj.

in·se·cure /insikyŏŏr/ adj. 1 (of a person or state of mind) uncertain; lacking confidence. 2 a unsafe; not firm or fixed. b (of ice, ground, etc.) liable to give way. c lacking security; unprotected. □□ **in·se·cure·ly** adv. **in·se·cu·ri·ty** n.

in·sem·i·nate /inséminayt/ v.tr. 1 introduce semen into (a female) by natural or artificial means. 2 sow (seed, etc.). □□ **in·sem·i·na·tion** /-náyshən/ n. **in·sem·i·na·tor** n.

in·sen·sate /insénsayt/ adj. 1 without physical sensation; unconscious. 2 without sensibility; unfeeling. 3 stupid. □□ **in·sen·sate·ly** adv.

in·sen·si·bil·i·ty /insénsibilitee/ n. 1 unconsciousness. 2 a lack of mental feeling or emotion; hardness. 3 (often foll. by to) indifference.

in·sen·si·ble /insénsibəl/ adj. 1 a without one's mental faculties; unconscious. b (of the extremities, etc.) numb; without feeling. 2 (usu. foll. by of, to) unaware; indifferent (insensible of her needs). 3 without emotion; callous. 4 too small or gradual to be perceived; inappreciable. □□ **in·sen·si·bly** adv.

in·sen·si·tive /insénsitiv/ adj. (often foll. by to) 1 unfeeling; boorish; crass. 2 not sensitive to physical stimuli. □□ **in·sen·si·tive·ly** adv. **in·sen·si·tive·ness** n. **in·sen·si·tiv·i·ty** /-tívitee/ n.

in·sen·ti·ent /insénshənt/ adj. not sentient; inanimate. □□ **in·sen·ti·ence** /-shəns/ n.

in·sep·a·ra·ble /inséparabəl/ adj. 1 (esp. of friends) unable or unwilling to be separated. 2 Gram. (of a prefix, or a verb in respect of it) unable to be used as a separate word, e.g., dis-, mis-, un-. □□ **in·sep·a·ra·bil·i·ty** n. **in·sep·a·ra·bly** adv.

in·sert v. & n. ● v.tr. /insórt/ 1 (usu. foll. by in, into, between, etc.) place, fit, or thrust (a thing) into another. 2 (usu. foll. by in, into) introduce (a letter, word, article, advertisement, etc.) into a newspaper, etc. ● n. /insərt/ something inserted, e.g., a loose page in a magazine, a piece of cloth in a garment, a motion-picture cut-in. □□ **in·sert·a·ble** adj. **in·sert·er** n.

in·ser·tion /insórshən/ n. 1 the act or an instance of inserting. 2 an amendment, etc., inserted in writing or printing. 3 each appearance of an advertisement in a newspaper, etc. 4 an ornamental section of needlework inserted into plain material (lace insertions).

in·ser·vice /insərvis/ adj. (of training) intended for those actively engaged in the profession or activity concerned.

in·set n. & v. ● n. /ínset/ 1 a an extra page or pages inserted in a folded sheet or in a book; an insert. b a small map, photograph, etc., inserted within the border of a larger one. 2 a piece let into a dress, etc. ● v.tr. /insét/ (**insetting**; past and past part. **inset** or **insetted**) 1 put in as an inset. 2 decorate with an inset. □□ **in·set·ter** n.

in·shore /ínsháwr/ adv. & adj. at sea but close to the shore.

in·side n., adj., adv., & prep. ● n. /ínsíd/ 1 a the inner side or surface of a thing. b the inner part; the interior. 2 (of a roadway, etc.) the side or lane nearer the center. 3 (usu. in pl.) colloq. a the stomach and bowels (something wrong with my insides). b the operative part of a machine, etc. 4 colloq. a position affording inside information (knows someone on the inside). ● adj. /ínsíd/ 1 situated on or in, or derived from, the inside; (of information, etc.) available only to those on the inside. 2 Soccer nearer to the center of the field (inside forward). ● adv. /insíd/ 1 on, in, or to the inside. 2 sl. in prison. ● prep. /insíd/ 1 on the inner side of; within (inside the house). 2 in less than (inside an hour). □ **inside of** colloq. in less than (a week, etc.).

in·side job n. colloq. a crime committed by a person living or working on the premises burgled, etc.

in·side out adj. with the inner surface turned outward. □ **know a thing inside out** know a thing thoroughly. **turn inside out 1** turn the inner surface of outward. 2 colloq. ransack; cause confusion in.

in·sid·er /insídər/ n. 1 a person who is within a society, organization, etc. 2 a person privy to a secret, esp. when using it to gain advantage.

in·sid·er trad·ing n. Stock Exch. the illegal practice of trading to one's own advantage through having access to confidential information.

in·side track n. 1 the track which is shorter, because of the curve. 2 a position of advantage.

in·sid·i·ous /insídeeəs/ adj. 1 proceeding or progressing inconspicuously but harmfully (an insidious disease). 2 treacherous; crafty. □□ **in·sid·i·ous·ly** adv. **in·sid·i·ous·ness** n.

in·sight /ínsīt/ n. (usu. foll. by into) 1 the capacity of understanding hidden truths, etc., esp. of character or situations. 2 an instance of this. □□ **in·sight·ful** adj. **in·sight·ful·ly** adv.

in·sig·ni·a /insígneeə/ n. (treated as sing. or pl. (formerly with sing. **insigne**); usu. foll. by of) 1 ▼ badges (wore his insignia of office). 2 distinguishing marks.

INSIGNIA: WORLD WAR I PRUSSIAN
MILITARY INSIGNIA

battle honor commemoration
COLBERG 1807
eagle emblem

in·sig·nif·i·cant /ínsignífikənt/ adj. 1 unimportant; trifling. 2 (of a person) undistinguished. 3 meaningless. □□ **in·sig·nif·i·cance** /-kəns/ n. **in·sig·nif·i·can·cy** n. **in·sig·nif·i·cant·ly** adv.

in·sin·cere /insinseér/ adj. not sincere; not candid. □□ **in·sin·cere·ly** adv. **in·sin·cer·i·ty** /-séritee/ n. (pl. **-ies**).

in·sin·u·ate /insínyŏŏ-ayt/ v.tr. 1 (often foll. by that + clause) convey indirectly or obliquely; hint (insinuated that she was lying). 2 (often refl.; usu. foll. by into) a introduce (oneself, a person, etc.) into favor, office, etc., by subtle manipulation. b introduce (a thing, an idea, oneself, etc.) subtly or deviously into a place (insinuated himself into their inner circle). □□ **in·sin·u·a·tion** /-áyshən/ n. **in·sin·u·a·tive** adj. **in·sin·u·a·tor** n. **in·sin·u·a·to·ry** /-sínyŏŏətáwree/ adj.

in·sip·id /insípid/ adj. 1 lacking vigor or interest; dull. 2 lacking flavor; tasteless. □□ **in·si·pid·i·ty** /-píditee/ n. **in·sip·id·ly** adv. **in·sip·id·ness** n.

in·sist /insíst/ v.tr. (usu. foll. by that + clause; also absol.) maintain or demand positively and assertively (insisted that he was innocent). □ **insist on** demand or maintain (I insist on being present). □□ **in·sist·er** n. **in·sist·ing·ly** adv.

in·sist·ent /insístənt/ adj. 1 (often foll. by on) insisting; demanding positively or continually (is insistent on taking me with him). 2 obtruding itself on the attention (the insistent rattle of the window frame). □□ **in·sist·ence** /-təns/ n. **in·sist·en·cy** n. **in·sist·ent·ly** adv.

in si·tu /in seetŏŏ, sí-/ adv. 1 in its place. 2 in its original place.

in·so·bri·e·ty /insəbrí-itee/ n. intemperance, esp. in drinking.

in·so·far as /insōfaár az/ conj. to the extent that.

in·sole /ínsōl/ n. 1 a removable sole worn in a boot or shoe for warmth, etc. 2 the fixed inner sole of a boot or shoe. ▷ SHOE

in·so·lent /ínsələnt/ adj. offensively contemptuous or arrogant; insulting. □□ **in·so·lence** /-ləns/ n. **in·so·lent·ly** adv.

in·sol·u·ble /insólyəbəl/ adj. 1 incapable of being solved. 2 incapable of being dissolved. □□ **in·sol·u·bil·i·ty** n. **in·sol·u·bil·ize** /-bilīz/ v.tr. **in·sol·u·ble·ness** n. **in·sol·u·bly** adv.

in·solv·a·ble /insólvəbəl/ adj. = INSOLUBLE.

in·sol·vent /insólvənt/ adj. & n. ● adj. 1 unable to pay one's debts. 2 relating to insolvency (insolvent laws). ● n. a debtor. □□ **in·sol·ven·cy** n.

in·som·ni·a /insómneeə/ n. habitual sleeplessness; inability to sleep. □□ **in·som·ni·ac** /-neeak/ n. & adj.

in·so·much /ínsōmúch/ adv. 1 (foll. by that + clause) to such an extent. 2 (foll. by as) inasmuch.

in·sou·ci·ant /insŏŏseeant, ANSŏŏsyaán/ adj. carefree; unconcerned. □□ **in·sou·ci·ance** /-seəns/ n. **in·sou·ci·ant·ly** adv.

in·spect /inspékt/ v.tr. 1 look closely at or into. 2 examine (a document, etc.) officially. □□ **in·spec·tion** /-spékshən/ n.

in·spec·tor /inspéktər/ n. 1 a person who inspects. 2 an official employed to supervise a service, a machine, etc., and make reports. 3 a police officer usu. ranking just below a superintendent. □□ **in·spec·tor·ate** /-tərəət/ n. **in·spec·to·ri·al** /-táwreeəl/ adj. **in·spec·tor·ship** n.

in·spi·ra·tion /ínspiráyshən/ n. 1 a a supposed creative force or influence on poets, artists, musicians, etc., stimulating the production of works of art. b a person, principle, faith, etc., stimulating artistic or moral fervor and creativity. 2 a sudden brilliant, creative, or timely idea. 3 a drawing in of breath; the act of inhalation. □□ **in·spi·ra·tion·al** adj. **in·spi·ra·tion·ism** n. **in·spi·ra·tion·ist** n.

in·spire /inspír/ v.tr. 1 stimulate or arouse (a person) to esp. creative activity, esp. by supposed divine or supernatural agency (your faith inspired him; inspired by God). 2 a (usu. foll. by with) animate (a person) with a feeling. b (usu. foll. by into) instill (a feeling) into a person, etc. c (usu. foll. by in) create (a feeling) in a person. 3 prompt; give rise to (the poem was inspired by the autumn). 4 (as **inspired** adj.) a (of a work of art, etc.) as if prompted by or emanating from a supernatural source; characterized by inspiration (an inspired speech). b (of a guess) intuitive but accurate. □□ **in·spir·a·to·ry** /-rətáwree/ adj. **in·spir·ed·ly** /-ridlee/ adv. **in·spir·er** n. **in·spir·ing** adj. **in·spir·ing·ly** adv.

inst. abbr. 1 instance. 2 institute. 3 institution. 4 instrument.

in·sta·bil·i·ty /ínstəbilitee/ n. (pl. **-ies**) 1 a lack of stability. 2 Psychol. unpredictability in behavior, etc. 3 an instance of instability.

in·stall /instáwl/ v.tr. (**installed**, **installing**) 1 place (equipment, etc.) in position ready for use. 2 place (a person) in an office or rank with ceremony. 3 establish (oneself, a person, etc.) in a place, condition, etc. (installed herself at the head of the table). □□ **in·stall·er** n.

---

in·sec·ti·vore illustration:
INSECTIVORE: EUROPEAN MOLE (Talpa europaea)
elongated snout
sensitive vibrissae (whiskers)

in·stal·la·tion /ìnstəláyshən/ *n.* **1 a** the act or an instance of installing. **b** the process or an instance of being installed. **2** a piece of apparatus, a machine, etc., installed or the place where it is installed.

in·stall·ment /instáwlmənt/ *n.* (esp. *Brit.* **instalment**) **1** a sum of money due as one of several usu. equal payments for something, spread over an agreed period of time. **2** any of several parts, esp. of a television or radio serial or a magazine story, published or shown in sequence at intervals.

in·stall·ment plan *n.* payment by installments.

in·stance /ínstəns/ *n.* & *v.* • *n.* **1** an example or illustration of (*just another instance of his lack of determination*). **2** a particular case (*that's not true in this instance*). **3** *Law* a legal suit. • *v.tr.* cite (a fact, case, etc.) as an instance. □ **at the instance of** at the request or suggestion of. **for instance** as an example. **in the first** (or **second**, etc.) **instance** in the first (or second, etc.) place; at the first (or second, etc.) stage of a proceeding.

in·stant /ínstənt/ *adj.* & *n.* • *adj.* **1** occurring immediately (*gives an instant result*). **2 a** (of food, etc.) ready for immediate use, with little or no preparation. **b** prepared hastily and with little effort (*I have no instant solution*). **3** urgent; pressing. • *n.* **1** a precise moment of time, esp. the present (*come here this instant; told you the instant I heard*). **2** a short space of time (*was there in an instant; not an instant too soon*).

in·stan·ta·ne·ous /ínstəntáyneeəs/ *adj.* **1** occurring or done in an instant or instantly. **2** *Physics* existing at a particular instant. □□ **in·stan·ta·ne·i·ty** /ínstəntənée-itee/ *n.* **in·stan·ta·ne·ous·ly** *adv.* **in·stan·ta·ne·ous·ness** *n.*

in·stan·ti·ate /instánsheeayt/ *v.tr.* represent by an instance. □□ **in·stan·ti·a·tion** /-áyshən/ *n.*

in·stant·ly /ínstəntlee/ *adv.* **1** immediately; at once. **2** *archaic* urgently; pressingly.

in·stant re·play *n.* the immediate repetition of part of a videotaped sports event, often in slow motion.

in·stead /instéd/ *adv.* **1** (foll. by *of*) as a substitute or alternative to; in place of (*instead of this one; stayed instead of going*). **2** as an alternative (*took me instead*).

in·step /ínstep/ *n.* **1** the inner arch of the foot between the toes and the ankle. **2** the part of a shoe, etc., fitting over or under this.

in·sti·gate /ínstigayt/ *v.tr.* **1** bring about by incitement or persuasion; provoke (*who instigated the inquiry?*). **2** (usu. foll. by *to*) urge on; incite (a person, etc.) to esp. an evil act. □□ **in·sti·ga·tion** /-gáyshən/ *n.* **in·sti·ga·tive** *adj.* **in·sti·ga·tor** *n.*

in·still /instíl/ *v.tr.* (esp. *Brit.* **instil**) (**instilled, instilling**) (often foll. by *into*) **1** introduce (a feeling, idea, etc.) into a person's mind, etc., gradually. **2** put (a liquid) into something in drops. □□ **in·stil·la·tion** *n.* **in·still·er** *n.* **in·still·ment** *n.*

in·stinct *n.* & *adj.* • *n.* /ínstingkt/ **1 a** an innate, usu. fixed, pattern of behavior in most animals in response to certain stimuli. **b** a similar propensity in human beings to act without conscious intention; innate impulsion. **2** (usu. foll. by *for*) unconscious skill; intuition. • *predic.adj.* /instíngkt/ (foll. by *with*) imbued; filled (with life, beauty, force, etc.). □□ **in·stinc·tu·al** /-stíngkchōōəl/ *adj.* **in·stinc·tu·al·ly** *adv.*

in·stinc·tive /instíngktiv/ *adj.* **1** relating to or prompted by instinct. **2** apparently unconscious or automatic (*an instinctive reaction*). □□ **in·stinc·tive·ly** *adv.*

in·sti·tute /ínstitōōt, -tyōōt/ *n.* & *v.* • *n.* **1** a society or organization for the promotion of science, education, etc. **2** a building used by an institute. • *v.tr.* **1** establish; found. **2 a** initiate (an inquiry, etc.). **b** begin (proceedings) in a court. **3** (usu. foll. by *to*, *into*) appoint (a person) as a cleric in a church, etc.

in·sti·tu·tion /ínstitōōshən, -tyōō-/ *n.* **1** the act or an instance of instituting. **2 a** a society or organization founded esp. for charitable, religious, educational, or social purposes. **b** a building used by an institution. **3** an established law, practice, or custom. **4** *colloq.* (of a person, a custom, etc.) a familiar object. **5** the establishment of a cleric, etc., in a church.

in·sti·tu·tion·al /ínstitōōshənəl, -tyōō-/ *adj.* **1** of or like an institution. **2** typical of institutions, esp. in being regimented or unimaginative (*the food was dreadfully institutional*). **3** (of religion) expressed or organized through institutions (churches, etc.). □□ **in·sti·tu·tion·al·ism** *n.* **in·sti·tu·tion·al·ly** *adv.*

in·sti·tu·tion·al·ize /ínstitōōshənəlīz, -tyōō-/ *v.tr.* **1** (as **institutionalized** *adj.*) (of a prisoner, a long-term patient, etc.) made apathetic and dependent after a long period in an institution. **2** place or keep (a person) in an institution. **3** convert into an institution; make institutional. □□ **in·sti·tu·tion·al·i·za·tion** *n.*

in·struct /instrúkt/ *v.tr.* **1** (often foll. by *in*) teach (a person) a subject, etc. (*instructed her in French*). **2** (usu. foll. by *to* + infin.) direct; command (*instructed him to fill in the hole*). **3** (often foll. by *of*, or *that*, etc. + clause) inform (a person) of a fact, etc. **4** *Law* (of a judge) give information (esp. clarification of legal principles) to (a jury).

in·struc·tion /instrúkshən/ *n.* **1** (often in *pl.*) a direction; an order (*gave him his instructions*). **2** teaching; education (*took a course of instruction*). **3** *Law* (in *pl.*) directions issued to a jury, etc. **4** *Computing* a direction in a computer program defining and effecting an operation. □□ **in·struc·tion·al** *adj.*

in·struc·tive /instrúktiv/ *adj.* tending to instruct; conveying a lesson; enlightening (*found the experience instructive*). □□ **in·struc·tive·ly** *adv.* **in·struc·tive·ness** *n.*

in·struc·tor /instrúktər/ *n.* (*fem.* **instructress** /-strúktris/) **1** a person who instructs; a teacher, demonstrator, etc. **2** a university teacher ranking below assistant professor. □□ **in·struc·tor·ship** *n.*

in·stru·ment /ínstrəmənt/ *n.* & *v.* • *n.* **1** a tool or implement, esp. for delicate or scientific work. **2** (in full **musical instrument**) a device for producing musical sounds by vibration, wind, percussion, etc. ▷ BRASS, PERCUSSION, STRINGED, WOODWIND. **3 a** a thing used in performing an action (*the meeting was an instrument in his success*). **b** a person made use of (*is merely their instrument*). **4** a measuring device, esp. in an airplane, serving to determine its position in darkness, etc. **5** a formal, esp. legal, document. • *v.tr.* **1** arrange (music) for instruments. **2** equip with instruments (for measuring, recording, controlling, etc.).

in·stru·men·tal /ínstrəméntʼl/ *adj.* & *n.* • *adj.* **1** (usu. foll. by *to*, *in*, or *in* + verbal noun) serving as an instrument or means (*was instrumental in finding the money*). **2** (of music) performed on instruments, without singing (cf. VOCAL). **3** of, or arising from, an instrument (*instrumental error*). **4** *Gram.* of or in the instrumental. • *n.* **1** a piece of music performed by instruments, not by the voice. **2** *Gram.* the case of nouns and pronouns (and words in grammatical agreement with them) indicating a means or instrument. □□ **in·stru·men·tal·ist** *n.* **in·stru·men·tal·i·ty** /-mentálitee/ *n.* **in·stru·men·tal·ly** *adv.*

in·stru·men·ta·tion /ínstrəmentáyshən/ *n.* **1 a** the arrangement or composition of music for a particular group of musical instruments. **b** the instruments used in any one piece of music. **2 a** the design, provision, or use of instruments in industry, science, etc. **b** such instruments collectively.

in·stru·ment pan·el *n.* (also **in·stru·ment board**) ► a surface, esp. in a car or airplane, containing the dials, etc., of measuring devices.

in·sub·or·di·nate /ínsəbáwrdʼnət/ *adj.* disobedient; rebellious. □□ **in·sub·or·di·nate·ly** *adv.* **in·sub·or·di·na·tion** /-náyshən/ *n.*

in·sub·stan·tial /ínsəbstánshəl/ *adj.* **1** lacking solidity or substance. **2** not real. □□ **in·sub·stan·ti·al·i·ty** /-sheeálitee/ *n.* **in·sub·stan·tial·ly** *adv.*

in·suf·fer·a·ble /insúfərəbəl/ *adj.* **1** intolerable. **2** unbearably arrogant or conceited, etc. □□ **in·suf·fer·a·ble·ness** *n.* **in·suf·fer·a·bly** *adv.*

in·suf·fi·cient /ínsəfíshənt/ *adj.* not sufficient; inadequate. □□ **in·suf·fi·cien·cy** *n.* **in·suf·fi·cient·ly** *adv.*

in·su·lar /ínsələr, ínsyə-/ *adj.* **1 a** of or like an island. **b** separated or remote, like an island. **2** ignorant of or indifferent to cultures, peoples, etc., outside one's own experience; narrow-minded. □□ **in·su·lar·ism** *n.* **in·su·lar·i·ty** /-láritee/ *n.* **in·su·lar·ly** *adv.*

in·su·late /ínsəlayt, ínsyə-/ *v.tr.* **1** prevent the passage of electricity, heat, or sound from (a thing, room, etc.) by interposing nonconductors. **2** detach (a person or thing) from its surroundings; isolate. □□ **in·su·la·tion** /-láyshən/ *n.*

in·su·la·tor /ínsəlaytər, ínysə-/ *n.* **1** a thing or substance used for insulation against electricity, heat, or sound. ▷ CORD, HOUSE, SOLAR PANEL. **2** an insulating device to support telegraph wires, etc. **3** a device preventing contact between electrical conductors.

in·su·lin /ínsəlin/ *n.* *Biochem.* a hormone produced in the pancreas by the islets of Langerhans, regulating the amount of glucose in the blood, and the lack of which causes diabetes.

in·sult *v.* & *n.* • *v.tr.* /insúlt/ **1** speak to or treat with scornful abuse or indignity. **2** offend the self-respect or modesty of. • *n.* /ínsult/ **1** an insulting remark or action. **2** *colloq.* something so worthless or contemptible as to be offensive. □□ **in·sult·er** *n.* **in·sult·ing·ly** *adv.*

in·su·per·a·ble /insōōpərəbəl/ *adj.* **1** (of a barrier) impossible to surmount. **2** (of a difficulty, etc.) impossible to overcome. □□ **in·su·per·a·bil·i·ty** *n.* **in·su·per·a·bly** *adv.*

in·sup·port·a·ble /ínsəpáwrtəbəl/ *adj.* **1** unable to be endured. **2** unjustifiable. □□ **in·sup·port·a·ble·ness** *n.* **in·sup·port·a·bly** *adv.*

in·sur·ance /inshŏŏrəns/ *n.* **1** the act or an instance of insuring. **2 a** a sum paid for this; a premium. **b** a sum paid out as compensation for theft, damage, loss, etc. **3** = INSURANCE POLICY. **4** a measure taken to provide for a possible contingency (*take an umbrella as insurance*).

in·sur·ance pol·i·cy *n.* **1** a contract of insurance. **2** a document detailing such a policy and constituting a contract.

in·sure /inshŏŏr/ *v.tr.* **1** (often foll. by *against*; also *absol.*) secure the contractual payment of a sum of money in the event of loss or damage to (property, life, a person, etc.) by regular payments or premiums (*insured the house for $100,000; we have insured against flood damage*). **2** (of the owner of a property, an insurance company, etc.) secure the payment of (a sum of money) in this way. **3** (usu. foll. by *against*) provide for (a possible contingency) (*insured themselves against the rain by taking umbrellas*). **4** = ENSURE. □□ **in·sur·a·ble** *adj.* **in·sur·a·bil·i·ty** /-shŏŏrəbílitee/ *n.*

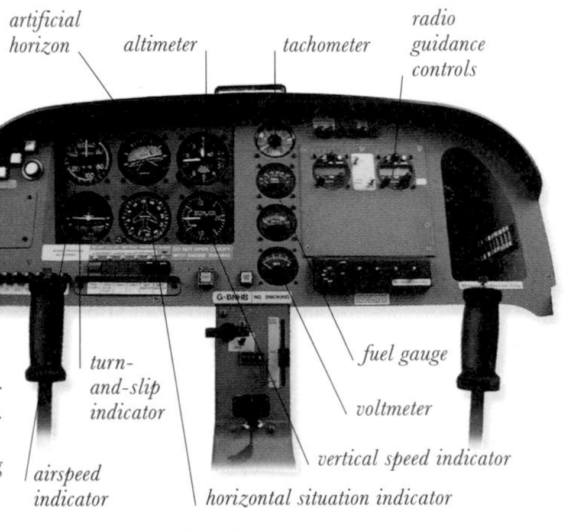
artificial horizon
altimeter
tachometer
radio guidance controls
turn-and-slip indicator
fuel gauge
voltmeter
vertical speed indicator
airspeed indicator
horizontal situation indicator

INSTRUMENT PANEL OF A LIGHT AIRCRAFT

in·sured /inshŏŏrd/ *adj. & n.* ● *adj.* covered by insurance. ● *n.* (usu. prec. by *the*) a person, etc., covered by insurance.

in·sur·er /inshŏŏrər/ *n.* **1** a person or company offering insurance policies for premiums; an underwriter. **2** a person that insures.

in·sur·gent /insɔ́rjənt/ *adj. & n.* ● *adj.* **1** rising in active revolt. **2** (of the sea, etc.) rushing in. ● *n.* a rebel; a revolutionary. ▫▫ **in·sur·gence** /-jəns/ *n.* **in·sur·gen·cy** *n.* (*pl.* **-ies**).

in·sur·mount·a·ble /ínsərmówntəbəl/ *adj.* unable to be surmounted or overcome. ▫▫ **in·sur·mount·a·bly** *adv.*

in·sur·rec·tion /ínsərékshən/ *n.* a rising in open resistance to established authority; a rebellion. ▫▫ **in·sur·rec·tion·ar·y** *adj.* **in·sur·rec·tion·ist** *n.*

int. *abbr.* **1** interior. **2** internal. **3** international.

in·tact /intákt/ *adj.* **1** entire; unimpaired. **2** untouched. ▫▫ **in·tact·ness** *n.*

in·tagl·io /intályō, -taál-/ *n.* (*pl.* **-os**) **1** a gem with an incised design (cf. CAMEO). **2** an engraved design. **3** ► a carving, esp. incised, in hard material. **4** a process of printing from an engraved design. ▷ PRINTING

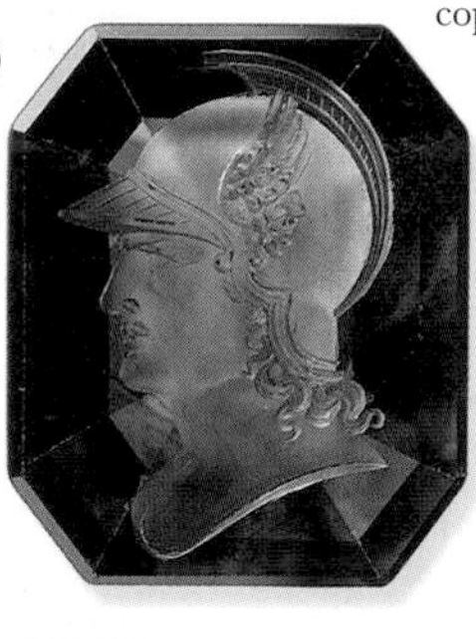

INTAGLIO: REPRODUCTION ROMAN INTAGLIO SEAL

in·take /íntayk/ *n.* **1 a** the action of taking in. **b** an instance of this. **2** a number or the amount taken in or received. **3** a place where water is taken into a channel or pipe from a river, or fuel or air enters an engine, etc.

in·tan·gi·ble /intánjibəl/ *adj. & n.* ● *adj.* **1** unable to be touched; not solid. **2** unable to be grasped mentally. ● *n.* something that cannot be precisely measured or assessed. ▫▫ **in·tan·gi·bil·i·ty** *n.* **in·tan·gi·bly** *adv.*

in·tar·si·a /intaárseeə/ *n.* the craft of using wood inlays, esp. as practiced in 15th-c. Italy.

in·te·ger /íntijər/ *n.* **1** a whole number. **2** a thing complete in itself.

in·te·gral /íntigrəl, intégrəl/ *adj. & n.* ● *adj.* **1 a** of a whole or necessary to the completeness of a whole. **b** forming a whole (*integral design*). **c** whole; complete. **2** *Math.* **a** of or denoted by an integer. **b** involving only integers, esp. as coefficients of a function. ● *n.* /íntigrəl/ *Math.* **1** a quantity of which a given function is the derivative, either containing an indeterminate additive constant (**indefinite integral**), or calculated as the difference between its values at specified limits (**definite integral**). **2** a function satisfying a given differential equation. ▫▫ **in·te·gral·i·ty** /-grálitee/ *n.* **in·te·gral·ly** *adv.*

in·te·gral cal·cu·lus *n.* mathematics concerned with finding integrals, their properties and application, etc. (cf. DIFFERENTIAL CALCULUS).

in·te·grate /íntigrayt/ *v.* **1** *tr.* **a** combine (parts) into a whole. **b** complete (an imperfect thing) by the addition of parts. **2** *tr. & intr.* bring or come into equal participation in or membership of society, a school, etc. **3** *tr.* desegregate, esp. racially (a school, etc.). **4** *tr. Math.* find the integral of. ▫▫ **in·te·gra·ble** /íntigrəbəl/ *adj.* **in·te·gra·bil·i·ty** *n.* **in·te·gra·tive** /íntigraytiv/ *adj.* **in·te·gra·tor** *n.*

in·te·gra·ted cir·cuit *n. Electronics* a small chip, etc., of material replacing several separate components in a conventional electrical circuit.

in·te·gra·tion /íntigráyshən/ *n.* **1** the act or an instance of integrating. **2** the intermixing of persons previously segregated. ▫▫ **in·te·gra·tion·ist** *n.*

in·teg·ri·ty /intégritee/ *n.* **1** moral uprightness; honesty. **2** wholeness; soundness.

in·teg·u·ment /intégyəmənt/ *n.* a natural outer covering, as a skin, husk, rind, etc. ▫▫ **in·teg·u·men·tal** /-mént'l/ *adj.* **in·teg·u·men·ta·ry** /-méntəree/ *adj.*

in·tel /íntel/ *n. Mil. colloq.* military intelligence; information.

in·tel·lect /íntilekt/ *n.* **1 a** the faculty of reasoning, knowing, and thinking, as distinct from feeling. **b** the understanding or mental powers (of a particular person, etc.) (*his intellect is not great*). **2** a clever or knowledgeable person.

in·tel·lec·tu·al /íntilékchōōəl/ *adj. & n.* ● *adj.* **1** of or appealing to the intellect. **2** possessing a high level of understanding or intelligence; cultured. **3** requiring, or given to the exercise of, the intellect. ● *n.* a person possessing a highly developed intellect. ▫▫ **in·tel·lec·tu·al·i·ty** /-chōōálitee/ *n.* **in·tel·lec·tu·al·ize** *v.tr. & intr.* **in·tel·lec·tu·al·ly** *adv.*

in·tel·lec·tu·al·ism /íntilékchōōəlizəm/ *n.* **1** the exercise, esp. when excessive, of the intellect at the expense of the emotions. **2** *Philos.* the theory that knowledge is wholly or mainly derived from pure reason. ▫▫ **in·tel·lec·tu·al·ist** *n.*

in·tel·lec·tu·al prop·er·ty *n. Law* intangible property that is the result of creativity, e.g. patents or copyrights.

in·tel·li·gence /intélijəns/ *n.* **1 a** the intellect; the understanding. **b** (of a person or an animal) quickness of understanding; wisdom. **2 a** the collection of information, esp. of military or political value. **b** people employed in this. **c** information; news. **3** an intelligent or rational being.

in·tel·li·gence quo·tient *n.* a number denoting the ratio of a person's intelligence to the normal or average.

in·tel·li·gent /intélijənt/ *adj.* **1** having or showing intelligence, esp. of a high level. **2** quick of mind; clever. **3 a** (of a device or machine) able to vary its behavior in response to varying situations and requirements and past experience. **b** (esp. of a computer terminal) having its own data-processing capability; incorporating a microprocessor (opp. DUMB). ▫▫ **in·tel·li·gent·ly** *adv.*

in·tel·li·gent·si·a /intélijéntseeə/ *n.* **1** the class of intellectuals regarded as possessing culture and political initiative. **2** people doing intellectual work; intellectuals.

in·tel·li·gi·ble /intélijibəl/ *adj.* able to be understood; comprehensible. ▫▫ **in·tel·li·gi·bil·i·ty** *n.* **in·tel·li·gi·bly** *adv.*

in·tem·per·ate /intémpərət/ *adj.* **1** (of a person, conduct, or speech) immoderate; unbridled; violent (*used intemperate language*). **2 a** given to excessive indulgence in alcohol. **b** excessively indulgent in one's appetites. ▫▫ **in·tem·per·ance** /-rəns/ *n.* **in·tem·per·ate·ly** *adv.* **in·tem·per·ate·ness** *n.*

in·tend /inténd/ *v.tr.* **1** have as one's purpose; propose (*we intend to go; we intend that it shall be done*). **2** (usu. foll. by *for, as*) design or destine (a person or a thing) (*I intend for him to go; I intend it as a warning*). **3** mean (*what does he intend by that?*). **4** (in *passive*; foll. by *for*) **a** be meant for a person to have or use, etc. (*they are intended for the children*). **b** be meant to represent (*the picture is intended for you*).

in·tend·ed /inténdid/ *adj. & n.* ● *adj.* **1** done on purpose; intentional. **2** designed; meant. ● *n. colloq.* the person one intends to marry; one's fiancé or fiancée (*is this your intended?*). ▫▫ **in·tend·ed·ly** *adv.*

in·tense /inténs/ *adj.* (**intenser, intensest**) **1** (of a quality, etc.) existing in a high degree; violent; forceful (*intense cold*). **2** (of a person) feeling, or apt to feel, strong emotion (*very intense about her music*). **3** (of a feeling or action, etc.) extreme (*intense joy; intense thought*). ▫▫ **in·tense·ly** *adv.* **in·tense·ness** *n.*

in·ten·si·fi·er /inténsifīər/ *n.* **1** a person or thing that intensifies. **2** *Gram.* = INTENSIVE *n.*

in·ten·si·fy /inténsifī/ *v.* (**-ies, -ied**) *tr. & intr.* make or become intense or more intense. ▫▫ **in·ten·si·fi·ca·tion** *n.*

in·ten·si·ty /inténsitee/ *n.* (*pl.* **-ies**) **1** the quality or an instance of being intense. **2** esp. *Physics* the measurable amount of some quality, e.g., force, brightness, a magnetic field, etc.

in·ten·sive /inténsiv/ *adj. & n.* ● *adj.* **1** thorough; vigorous; directed to a single point, area, or subject (*intensive study; intensive bombardment*). **2** of or relating to intensity as opposed to extent; producing intensity. **3** serving to increase production in relation to costs (*intensive farming methods*). **4** (usu. in *comb.*) *Econ.* making much use of (*a labor-intensive industry*). **5** *Gram.* (of an adjective, adverb, etc.) expressing intensity; giving force, as *really* in *my feet are really cold.* ● *n. Gram.* an intensive adjective, adverb, etc. ▫▫ **in·ten·sive·ly** *adv.* **in·ten·sive·ness** *n.*

in·ten·sive care *n.* medical treatment with constant monitoring, etc., of a dangerously ill patient (also (with hyphen) *attrib.*: *intensive-care unit*).

in·tent /intént/ *n. & adj.* ● *n.* (usu. without article) intention; a purpose (*with intent to defraud; my intent to reach the top; with evil intent*). ● *adj.* **1** (usu. foll. by *on*) **a** resolved; bent; determined (*was intent on succeeding*). **b** attentively occupied (*intent on his books*). **2** (esp. of a look) earnest; eager; meaningful. ▫ **to (or for) all intents and purposes** practically; virtually. ▫▫ **in·tent·ly** *adv.* **in·tent·ness** *n.*

in·ten·tion /inténshən/ *n.* **1** (often foll. by *to* + infin., or *of* + verbal noun) a thing intended; an aim or purpose (*it was not her intention to interfere; have no intention of staying*). **2** the act of intending (*done without intention*). **3** *colloq.* (usu. in *pl.*) a person's, esp. a man's, designs in respect to marriage (*are his intentions strictly honorable?*). ▫▫ **in·ten·tioned** *adj.* (usu. in *comb.*).

in·ten·tion·al /inténshənəl/ *adj.* done on purpose. ▫▫ **in·ten·tion·al·i·ty** /-álitee/ *n.* **in·ten·tion·al·ly** *adv.*

in·ter /intɔ́r/ *v.tr.* (**interred, interring**) deposit (a corpse, etc.) in the earth, a tomb, etc.; bury.

inter- /íntər/ *comb. form* **1** between; among (*intercontinental*). **2** mutually; reciprocally (*interbreed*).

in·ter·act /íntərákt/ *v.intr.* act reciprocally; act on each other. ▫▫ **in·ter·ac·tant** *adj. & n.* **in·ter·ac·tion** *n.*

in·ter·ac·tive /íntəráktiv/ *adj.* **1** reciprocally active; acting upon or influencing each other. **2** (of a computer or other electronic device) allowing a two-way flow of information between it and a user, responding to the user's input. ▫▫ **in·ter·ac·tive·ly** *adv.*

in·ter a·li·a /íntər áyleeə, aáleeə/ *adv.* among other things.

in·ter·breed /íntərbreéd/ *v.* (*past* and *past part.* **-bred** /-bréd/) **1** *intr. & tr.* breed or cause to breed with members of a different race or species to produce a hybrid. **2** *tr.* breed within one family, etc., in order to produce desired characteristics.

in·ter·ca·lar·y /intɔ́rkəléree, -káləree/ *adj.* **1 a** (of a day or a month) inserted in the calendar to harmonize it with the solar year, e.g., Feb. 29 in leap years. **b** (of a year) having such an addition. **2** interpolated; intervening.

in·ter·cede /íntərseéd/ *v.intr.* (usu. foll. by *with*) interpose or intervene on behalf of another; plead (*they interceded with the governor for his life*). ▫▫ **in·ter·ced·er** *n.*

in·ter·cept /íntərsépt/ *v.tr.* **1** seize, catch, or stop (a person, message, vehicle, ball, etc.) going from one place to another. **2** (usu. foll. by *from*) cut off (light, etc.). **3** check or stop (motion, etc.). ▫▫ **in·ter·cep·tion** /-sépshən/ *n.* **in·ter·cep·tive** /-séptiv/ *adj.*

in·ter·cep·tor /íntərséptər/ *n.* **1** an aircraft used to intercept enemy raiders. **2** a person or thing that intercepts.

in·ter·ces·sion /íntərséshən/ *n.* **1** the act of interceding, esp. by prayer. **2** an instance of this. **3** a prayer. ▫▫ **in·ter·ces·sion·al** *adj.* **in·ter·ces·sor** *n.* **in·ter·ces·so·ri·al** /-sesáwreeəl/ *adj.* **in·ter·ces·so·ry** *adj.*

in·ter·change *v. & n.* ● *v.tr.* /íntərcháynj/ **1** (of two people) exchange (things) with each other. **2** put each of (two things) in the other's place; alternate. ● *n.* /íntərchaynj/ **1** (often foll. by *of*) a reciprocal

exchange between two people, etc. **2** alternation (*the interchange of woods and fields*). **3** a road junction designed so that traffic streams do not intersect. □□ **in·ter·change·a·ble** *adj.* **in·ter·change·a·bil·i·ty** /-cháynjəbilitee/ *n.* **in·ter·change·a·ble·ness** *n.* **in·ter·change·a·bly** *adv.*

in·ter·ci·ty /íntərsítee/ *adj.* existing or traveling between cities.

in·ter·com /íntərkom/ *n. colloq.* a system of intercommunication by radio or telephone between or within offices, aircraft, etc.

in·ter·com·mu·ni·cate /íntərkəmyóonikayt/ *v.intr.* **1** communicate reciprocally. **2** (of rooms, etc.) have free passage into each other; have a connecting door. □□ **in·ter·com·mu·ni·ca·tion** /-káyshən/ *n.* **in·ter·com·mu·ni·ca·tive** /-kaytiv, -kətiv/ *adj.*

in·ter·con·nect /íntərkənékt/ *v.tr. & intr.* connect with each other. □□ **in·ter·con·nec·tion** /-nékshən/ *n.*

in·ter·con·ti·nen·tal /íntərkóntinént'l/ *adj.* connecting or traveling between continents. □□ **in·ter·con·ti·nen·tal·ly** *adv.*

in·ter·cool·ing /íntərkóoling/ *n.* the cooling of gas between successive compressions, esp. in a car or truck engine. □□ **in·ter·cool** *v.tr.* **in·ter·cool·er** *n.*

in·ter·cos·tal /íntərkóst'l/ *adj.* between the ribs (of the body or a ship). □□ **in·ter·cos·tal·ly** *adv.*

in·ter·course /íntərkawrs/ *n.* **1** communication or dealings between individuals, nations, etc. **2** = SEXUAL INTERCOURSE. **3** communion between human beings and God.

in·ter·crop /íntərkróp/ *v.tr.* (also *absol.*) (**-cropped**, **-cropping**) raise (a crop) among plants of a different kind, usu. in the space between rows. □□ **in·ter·crop·ping** *n.*

in·ter·cut /íntərkút/ *v.tr.* (**-cutting**; *past* and *past part.* **-cut**) *Cinematog.* alternate (shots) with contrasting shots by cutting.

in·ter·de·nom·i·na·tion·al /íntərdinómináyshənəl/ *adj.* concerning more than one (religious) denomination. □□ **in·ter·de·nom·i·na·tion·al·ly** *adv.*

in·ter·de·part·men·tal /íntərdeépaartmént'l/ *adj.* concerning more than one department. □□ **in·ter·de·part·men·tal·ly** *adv.*

in·ter·de·pend /íntərdipénd/ *v.intr.* depend on each other. □□ **in·ter·de·pend·ence** *n.* **in·ter·de·pend·en·cy** *n.* **in·ter·de·pend·ent** *adj.*

in·ter·dict *n. & v.* ● *n.* /íntərdikt/ **1** an authoritative prohibition. **2** *RC Ch.* a sentence debarring a person, or esp. a place, from ecclesiastical functions and privileges. ● *v.tr.* /íntərdíkt/ **1** prohibit (an action). **2** forbid the use of. **3** (usu. foll. by *from* + verbal noun) restrain (a person). **4** (usu. foll. by *to*) forbid (a thing) to a person. □□ **in·ter·dic·tion** /-díkshən/ *n.* **in·ter·dic·to·ry** /-díktəree/ *adj.*

in·ter·dis·ci·pli·nar·y /íntərdísiplinéree/ *adj.* of or between more than one branch of learning.

in·ter·est /íntərist, -trist/ *n. & v.* ● *n.* **1 a** a feeling of curiosity or concern (*have no interest in fishing*). **b** a quality exciting curiosity or holding the attention (*this magazine lacks interest*). **c** the power of an issue, action, etc., to hold the attention; noteworthiness; importance (*findings of no particular interest*). **2** a subject, hobby, etc., in which one is concerned (*his interests are gardening and sports*). **3** advantage or profit, esp. when financial (*it is in your interest to go*; *look after your own interests*). **4** money paid for the use of money lent, or for not requiring the repayment of a debt. **5** (usu. foll. by *in*) **a** a financial stake (in an undertaking, etc.). **b** a legal concern, title, or right (in property). **6 a** a party or group having a common interest (*the mining interest*). **b** a principle in which a party or group is concerned. **7** the selfish pursuit of one's own welfare; self-interest. ● *v.tr.* **1** excite the curiosity or attention of (*your story interests me greatly*). **2** (usu. foll. by *in*) cause (a person) to take a personal interest or share (*can I interest you in a weekend cruise?*). **3** (as **interested** *adj.*) having a private interest; not impartial or disinterested (*an interested party*). □ **in the interest** (or **interests**) **of**

as something that is advantageous to. **lose interest** become bored or boring. □□ **in·ter·est·ed·ly** *adv.* **in·ter·est·ed·ness** *n.*

in·ter·est·ing /íntristing, -təresting/ *adj.* causing curiosity; holding the attention. □□ **in·ter·est·ing·ly** *adv.* **in·ter·est·ing·ness** *n.*

in·ter·face /íntərfays/ *n. & v.* ● *n.* **1** esp. *Physics* a surface forming a common boundary between two regions. **2** a point where interaction occurs between two systems, processes, subjects, etc. (*the interface between psychology and education*). **3** esp. *Computing* **a** an apparatus for connecting two pieces of equipment so that they can be operated jointly. **b** a means by which a user interacts with a program or utilizes an application. ● *v.tr. & intr.* (often foll. by *with*) connect with (another piece of equipment, etc.) by an interface.

in·ter·fac·ing /íntərfaysing/ *n.* a stiffish material, esp. buckram, between two layers of fabric in collars, etc.

in·ter·fere /íntərféer/ *v.intr.* **1** (usu. foll. by *with*) **a** (of a person) meddle; obstruct a process, etc. **b** (of a thing) be a hindrance; get in the way. **2** (usu. foll. by *in*) take part or intervene, esp. without invitation or necessity. **3** (foll. by *with*) *euphem.* molest or assault sexually. **4** *Physics* (of light or other waves) combine so as to cause interference. □□ **in·ter·fer·er** *n.* **in·ter·fer·ing** *adj.* **in·ter·fer·ing·ly** *adv.*

in·ter·fer·ence /íntərféerəns/ *n.* **1** (usu. foll. by *with*) **a** the act of interfering. **b** an instance of this. **2** the fading or disturbance of received radio signals by the interference of waves from different sources, or esp. by atmospherics or unwanted signals. **3** *Physics* ▼ the combination of two or more wave motions to form a resultant wave in which the displacement is reinforced or canceled. □□ **in·ter·fe·ren·tial** /-fərénshəl/ *adj.*

in·ter·fer·on /íntərféeron/ *n. Biochem.* any of various proteins that can inhibit the development of a virus in a cell, etc.

in·ter·file /íntərfíl/ *v.tr.* **1** file (two sequences) together. **2** file (one or more items) into an existing sequence.

in·ter·fuse /íntərfyóoz/ *v.* **1** *tr.* **a** (usu. foll. by *with*) mix (a thing) with; intersperse. **b** blend (things) together. **2** *intr.* (of two things) blend with each other. □□ **in·ter·fu·sion** /-fyóozhən/ *n.*

in·ter·ga·lac·tic /íntərgəláktik/ *adj.* of or situated between two or more galaxies. □□ **in·ter·ga·lac·ti·cal·ly** *adv.*

in·ter·gla·cial /íntərgláyshəl/ *adj.* between glacial periods.

in·ter·gov·ern·men·tal /íntərgúvərnmént'l/ *adj.* concerning or conducted between two or more governments. □□ **in·ter·gov·ern·men·tal·ly** *adv.*

in·ter·im /íntərim/ *n. & adj.* ● *n.* the intervening time (*in the interim he had died*). ● *adj.* intervening; provisional; temporary.

in·te·ri·or /intéereeər/ *adj. & n.* ● *adj.* **1** inner (opp. EXTERIOR). **2** remote from the coast or frontier; inland. **3** internal; domestic (opp. FOREIGN). **4** (usu. foll. by *to*) situated further in or within. **5** existing in the mind or soul; inward. **6** drawn, photographed, etc., within a building. **7** coming from inside. ● *n.* **1** the interior part; the inside. **2** the interior part of a country or region. **3 a** the home affairs of a country. **b** a department dealing with these (*Secretary of the Interior*). **4** a representation of the inside of a building or a room (*Dutch interior*). **5** the inner nature; the soul. □□ **in·te·ri·or·ize** *v.tr.* **in·te·ri·or·ly** *adv.*

interj. *abbr.* interjection.

in·ter·ject /íntərjékt/ *v.tr.* **1** utter (words) abruptly or parenthetically. **2** interrupt with. □□ **in·ter·jec·to·ry** *adj.*

in·ter·jec·tion /íntərjékshən/ *n.* an exclamation, esp. as a part of speech (e.g., *ah!*, *dear me!*). □□ **in·ter·jec·tion·al** *adj.*

in·ter·lace /íntərláys/ *v.* **1** *tr.* bind intricately together; interweave. **2** *tr.* mingle; intersperse. **3** *intr.* cross each other intricately. □□ **in·ter·lace·ment** *n.*

in·ter·lard /íntərláard/ *v.tr.* (usu. foll. by *with*) mix (writing or speech) with unusual words or phrases.

in·ter·leaf /íntərléef/ *n.* (*pl.* **-leaves**) an extra (usu. blank) leaf between the leaves of a book.

in·ter·leave /íntərléev/ *v.tr.* insert (usu. blank) leaves between the leaves of (a book, etc.).

in·ter·leu·kin /íntərlóokin/ *n. Biochem.* any of several glycoproteins produced by leukocytes for regulating immune responses.

in·ter·li·brar·y /íntərlíbreree/ *adj.* between libraries (esp. *interlibrary loan*).

in·ter·line /íntərlín/ *v.tr.* put an extra lining between the ordinary lining and the fabric of (a garment).

in·ter·lin·ing /íntərlíning/ *n.* material used to interline a garment.

in·ter·link /íntərlíngk/ *v.tr. & intr.* link or be linked together.

in·ter·lock /íntərlók/ *v., adj., & n.* ● *v.* **1** *intr.* engage with each other by overlapping or by the fitting together of projections and recesses. **2** *tr.* (usu. in *passive*) lock or clasp within each other. ● *adj.* (of a fabric) knitted with closely interlocking stitches. ● *n.* a device or mechanism for connecting or coordinating the function of different components. □□ **in·ter·lock·er** *n.*

in·ter·loc·u·tor /íntərlókyətər/ *n.* (*fem.* **interlocutrix** /-triks/) a person who takes part in a dialogue or conversation. □□ **in·ter·lo·cu·tion** /-ləkyóoshən/ *n.*

in·ter·loc·u·to·ry /íntərlókyətawree/ *adj.* of dialogue or conversation.

in·ter·lop·er /íntərlópər/ *n.* **1** an intruder. **2** a person who interferes in others' affairs, esp. for profit. □□ **in·ter·lope** *v.intr.*

INTERFERENCE

Interference is caused by waves acting upon one another. In this demonstration, two waves on water radiate in a circular pattern. Their paths cross and cancel out in the central area, but farther away from the epicenter, the waves interfere constructively and combine to produce a new pattern.

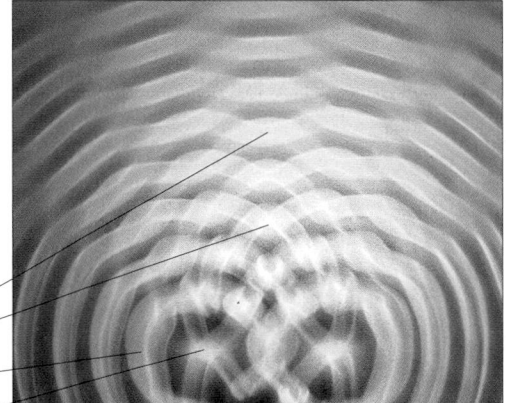

combined wave pattern
wave patterns cancel out
radiating wave pattern
epicenter of wave

DEMONSTRATION OF WAVE INTERFERENCE

in·ter·lude /íntərlōōd/ *n.* **1 a** a pause between the acts of a play. **b** something performed or done during this pause. **2 a** an intervening time, space, or event that contrasts with what goes before or after. **b** a temporary amusement or entertaining episode. **3** a piece of music played between other pieces, the verses of a hymn, etc.

in·ter·mar·riage /íntərmárij/ *n.* **1** marriage between people of different races, castes, families, etc. **2** (loosely) marriage between near relations.

in·ter·mar·ry /íntərmáree/ *v.intr.* (**-ies, -ied**) (foll. by *with*) (of races, castes, families, etc.) become connected by marriage.

in·ter·me·di·ar·y /íntərmeédee-eree/ *n. & adj.* ● *n.* (*pl.* **-ies**) an intermediate person or thing, esp. a mediator. ● *adj.* acting as mediator; intermediate.

in·ter·me·di·ate *adj., n., & v.* ● *adj.* /íntərmeédeeət/ coming between two things in time, place, order, character, etc. ● *n.* /íntərmeédeeət/ **1** an intermediate thing. **2** a chemical compound formed by one reaction and then used in another, esp. during synthesis. ● *v.intr.* /íntərmeédeeáyt/ (foll. by *between*) act as intermediary; mediate. □□ **in·ter·me·di·a·cy** /-deeəsee/ *n.* **in·ter·me·di·ate·ly** *adv.* **in·ter·me·di·ate·ness** *n.* **in·ter·me·di·a·tion** /-deeáyshən/ *n.* **in·ter·me·di·a·tor** /-deeaytər/ *n.*

in·ter·ment /íntərmənt/ *n.* the burial of a corpse, esp. with ceremony.

in·ter·mez·zo /íntərmétsō/ *n.* (*pl.* **intermezzi** /-see/ or **-os**) **1 a** a short connecting instrumental movement in an opera or other musical work. **b** a similar piece performed independently. **c** a short piece for a solo instrument. **2** a short, light dramatic or other performance inserted between the acts of a play.

in·ter·mi·na·ble /íntərminəbəl/ *adj.* **1** endless. **2** tediously long or habitual. **3** with no prospect of

an end. □□ **in·ter·mi·na·ble·ness** *n.* **in·ter·mi·na·bly** *adv.*

in·ter·min·gle /íntərmínggəl/ *v.tr. & intr.* (often foll. by *with*) mix together; mingle.

in·ter·mis·sion /íntərmíshən/ *n.* **1** a pause or cessation. **2** an interval between parts of a play, motion picture, concert, etc. **3** a period of inactivity.

in·ter·mit /íntərmít/ *v.* (**intermitted, intermitting**) **1** *intr.* esp. *Med.* stop or cease activity briefly (e.g., of a fever, or a pulse). **2** *tr.* suspend; discontinue for a time.

in·ter·mit·tent /íntərmít'nt/ *adj.* occurring at intervals; not continuous or steady. □□ **in·ter·mit·tence** /-mít'ns/ *n.* **in·ter·mit·ten·cy** *n.* **in·ter·mit·tent·ly** *adv.*

in·ter·mix /íntərmíks/ *v.tr. & intr.* mix together. □□ **in·ter·mix·a·ble** *adj.* **in·ter·mix·ture** *n.*

in·tern *n. & v.* ● *n.* /íntərn/ (also **in·terne**) a recent graduate of medical school who works in a hospital as an assistant physician or surgeon. ● *v.* **1** *tr.* /intə́rn/ confine; oblige (a prisoner, alien, etc.) to reside within prescribed limits. **2** *intr.* /íntərn/ serve as an intern. □□ **in·tern·ment** /-tə́rn-/ *n.* **in·tern·ship** /íntərn-/ *n.*

in·ter·nal /íntə́rnəl/ *adj. & n.* ● *adj.* **1** of or situated in the inside or invisible part. **2** relating or applied to the inside of the body (*internal injuries*). **3** of a nation's domestic affairs. **4** (of a student) attending a university, etc., as well as taking its examinations. **5** used or applying within an organization. **6 a** of the inner nature of a thing; intrinsic. **b** of the mind or soul. ● *n.* (in *pl.*) intrinsic qualities. □□ **in·ter·nal·i·ty** /-nálitee/ *n.* **in·ter·nal·ize** *v.tr.* **in·ter·nal·i·za·tion** *n.* **in·ter·nal·ly** *adv.*

in·ter·nal-com·bus·tion en·gine *n.* ▼ an engine with its motive power generated by the explosion of gases or vapor with air in a cylinder.

in·ter·nal med·i·cine *n.* a branch of medicine specializing in the diagnosis and nonsurgical treatment of diseases.

internat. *abbr.* international.

in·ter·na·tion·al /íntərnáshənəl/ *adj. & n.* ● *adj.* **1** existing, involving, or carried on between two or more nations. **2** agreed on or used by all or many nations (*international date line; international driver's license*). ● *n.* **1 a** a contest, esp. in sport, between teams representing different countries. **b** a member of such a team. **2 a** (**International**) any of four associations founded (1864–1936) to promote socialist or communist action. **b** a member of any of these. □□ **in·ter·na·tion·al·i·ty** /-nálitee/ *n.* **in·ter·na·tion·al·ly** *adv.*

in·ter·na·tion·al date line *n.* (also **International Date Line**) see DATELINE 1.

in·ter·na·tion·al·ism /íntərnáshənəlizəm/ *n.* **1** the advocacy of a community of interests among nations. **2** (**Internationalism**) the principles of any of the Internationals. □□ **in·ter·na·tion·al·ist** *n.*

in·ter·na·tion·al·ize /íntərnáshənəlīz/ *v.tr.* **1** make international. **2** bring under the protection or control of two or more nations. □□ **in·ter·na·tion·al·i·za·tion** /-lizáyshən/ *n.*

in·ter·na·tion·al sys·tem of u·nits *n.* a system of physical units based on the meter, kilogram, second, ampere, kelvin, candela, and mole, with prefixes to indicate multiplication or division by a power of ten.

in·ter·na·tion·al u·nit *n.* a standard quantity of a vitamin, etc.

in·terne var. of INTERN *n.*

in·ter·ne·cine /íntərneéseen, -néseen/ *adj.* mutually destructive.

in·tern·ee /interneé/ *n.* a person interned.

In·ter·net /íntərnét/ *n.* a communications network enabling the linking of computers worldwide for data interchange.

in·ter·nun·cial /íntərnúnshəl/ *adj.* (of nerves) communicating between different parts of the system.

in·ter·o·ce·an·ic /íntərōsheeánik/ *adj.* between or connecting two oceans.

in·ter·pel·late /intə́rpəlayt/ *v.tr.* (in European parliaments) interrupt the order of the day by demanding an explanation from (the minister concerned). □□ **in·ter·pel·la·tion** /-láyshən/ *n.* **in·ter·pel·la·tor** *n.*

in·ter·pen·e·trate /íntərpénitrayt/ *v.* **1** *intr.* (of two things) penetrate each other. **2** *tr.* pervade; penetrate thoroughly. □□ **in·ter·pen·e·tra·tion** /-tráyshən/ *n.* **in·ter·pen·e·tra·tive** *adj.*

in·ter·per·son·al /íntərpə́rsənəl/ *adj.* (of relations) occurring between persons, esp. reciprocally. □□ **in·ter·per·son·al·ly** *adv.*

in·ter·plan·e·tar·y /íntərplániteree/ *adj.* **1** between planets. **2** relating to travel between planets.

in·ter·play /íntərplay/ *n.* **1** reciprocal action. **2** the operation of two things on each other.

In·ter·pol /íntərpōl/ *n.* International Criminal Police Organization.

in·ter·po·late /intə́rpəlayt/ *v.tr.* **1 a** insert (words) in a book, etc., esp. to give false impressions as to its date, etc. **b** make such insertions in (a book, etc.). **2** interject (a remark) in a conversation. **3** estimate (values) from known ones in the same range. □□ **in·ter·po·la·tion** /-láyshən/ *n.* **in·ter·po·la·tive** /-lətiv/ *adj.* **in·ter·po·la·tor** *n.*

in·ter·pose /íntərpóz/ *v.* **1** *tr.* (often foll. by *between*) place or insert (a thing) between others. **2** *tr.* say (words) as an interruption. **3** *tr.* exercise or advance (a veto or objection) so as to interfere. **4** *intr.* (foll. by *between*) intervene (between parties). □□ **in·ter·po·si·tion** *n.*

in·ter·pret /intə́rprit/ *v.* (**interpreted, interpreting**) **1** *tr.* explain the meaning of (foreign or abstruse words, a dream, etc.). **2** *tr.* make out or bring out the meaning of (creative work). **3** *intr.* act as an interpreter, esp. of foreign languages. **4** *tr.*

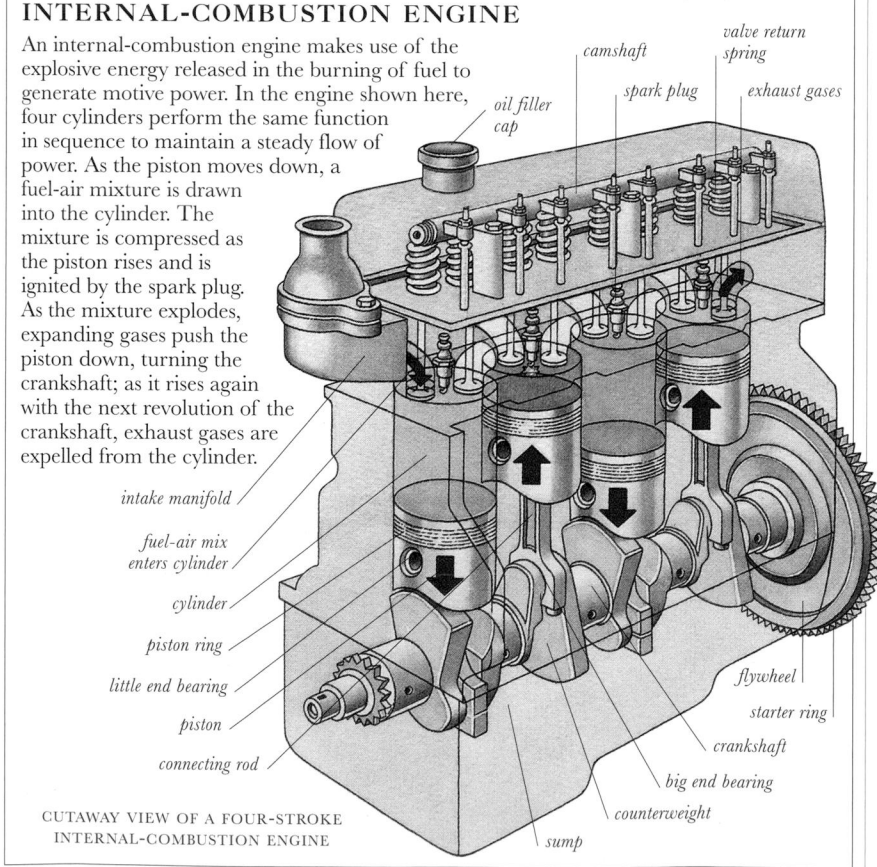

INTERNAL-COMBUSTION ENGINE

An internal-combustion engine makes use of the explosive energy released in the burning of fuel to generate motive power. In the engine shown here, four cylinders perform the same function in sequence to maintain a steady flow of power. As the piston moves down, a fuel-air mixture is drawn into the cylinder. The mixture is compressed as the piston rises and is ignited by the spark plug. As the mixture explodes, expanding gases push the piston down, turning the crankshaft; as it rises again with the next revolution of the crankshaft, exhaust gases are expelled from the cylinder.

camshaft
valve return spring
oil filler cap
spark plug
exhaust gases
intake manifold
fuel-air mix enters cylinder
cylinder
piston ring
little end bearing
piston
connecting rod
flywheel
starter ring
crankshaft
big end bearing
counterweight
sump

CUTAWAY VIEW OF A FOUR-STROKE INTERNAL-COMBUSTION ENGINE

explain or understand (behavior, etc.) in a specified manner (*interpreted his gesture as mocking*). □□ **in·ter·pret·a·ble** *adj.* **in·ter·pret·a·bil·i·ty** *n.* **in·ter·pre·ta·tion** *n.* **in·ter·pre·ta·tion·al** *adj.* **in·ter·pre·ta·tive** /-táytiv/ *adj.* **in·ter·pre·tive** *adj.* **in·ter·pre·tive·ly** *adv.*

in·ter·pret·er /intə́rpritər/ *n.* a person who interprets, esp. one who translates speech orally.

in·ter·ra·cial /intərráyshəl/ *adj.* existing between or affecting different races. □□ **in·ter·ra·cial·ly** *adv.*

in·ter·reg·num /intərrégnəm/ *n.* (*pl.* **interregnums** or **interregna** /-nə/) **1** an interval when the normal government is suspended, esp. between successive reigns or regimes. **2** an interval or pause.

in·ter·re·late /intəriláyt/ *v.tr.* relate (two or more things) to each other. □□ **in·ter·re·la·tion** /-láyshən/ *n.* **in·ter·re·la·tion·ship** *n.*

interrog. *abbr.* interrogative.

in·ter·ro·gate /intérəgayt/ *v.tr.* ask questions of (a person) esp. closely, thoroughly, or formally. □□ **in·ter·ro·ga·tor** *n.*

in·ter·ro·ga·tion /intérəgáyshən/ *n.* **1** the act or an instance of interrogating; the process of being interrogated. **2** a question or inquiry. □□ **in·ter·ro·ga·tion·al** *adj.*

in·ter·rog·a·tive /intərrógətiv/ *adj. & n.* ● *adj.* **1 a** of or like a question; used in questions. **b** *Gram.* (of an adjective or pronoun) asking a question (e.g., *who?*, *which?*). **2** having the form or force of a question. **3** suggesting inquiry (*an interrogative tone*). ● *n.* an interrogative word (e.g., *what?*, *why?*). □□ **in·ter·rog·a·tive·ly** *adv.*

in·ter·rog·a·to·ry /intərrógətáwree/ *adj. & n.* ● *adj.* questioning; of or suggesting inquiry (*an interrogatory eyebrow*). ● *n.* (*pl.* **-ies**) a formal set of questions, esp. *Law* one formally put to an accused person, etc.

in·ter·rupt /intərúpt/ *v.tr.* **1** act so as to break the continuous progress of (an action, speech, a person speaking, etc.). **2** obstruct (a person's view, etc.). **3** break or suspend the continuity of. □□ **in·ter·rupt·i·ble** *adj.* **in·ter·rup·tion** /-rúpshən/ *n.* **in·ter·rup·tive** *adj.* **in·ter·rup·to·ry** *adj.*

in·ter·rupt·er /intərúptər/ *n.* (also **in·ter·rup·tor**) **1** a person or thing that interrupts. **2** a device for interrupting, esp. an electric circuit.

in·ter·sect /intərsékt/ *v.* **1** *tr.* divide (a thing) by passing or lying across it. **2** *intr.* (of lines, roads, etc.) cross or cut each other.

in·ter·sec·tion /intərsékshən/ *n.* **1** the act of intersecting. **2** a place where two roads intersect. **3** a point or line common to lines or planes that intersect. □□ **in·ter·sec·tion·al** *adj.*

in·ter·sex /intərseks/ *n.* **1** the abnormal condition of being intermediate between male and female. **2** an individual in this condition.

in·ter·sex·u·al /intərsékshooəl/ *adj.* **1** existing between the sexes. **2** of intersex. □□ **in·ter·sex·u·al·i·ty** /-álitee/ *n.* **in·ter·sex·u·al·ly** *adv.*

in·ter·space *n. & v.* ● *n.* /intərspáys/ an interval of space or time. ● *v.tr.* /intərspáys/ put interspaces between.

in·ter·sperse /intərspɔ́rs/ *v.tr.* **1** (often foll. by *between, among*) scatter; place here and there. **2** (foll. by *with*) diversify (a thing or things with others so scattered). □□ **in·ter·sper·sion** /-pɔ́rzhən/ *n.*

in·ter·state *adj. & n.* ● *adj.* /intərstáyt/ existing or carried on between states, esp. of the US. ● *n.* /intərstayt/ a limited access highway that is part of the US Interstate Highway System.

in·ter·stel·lar /intərstélər/ *adj.* occurring or situated between stars.

in·ter·stice /intɔ́rstis/ *n.* **1** an intervening space. **2** a chink or crevice.

in·ter·sti·tial /intərstíshəl/ *adj.* of, forming, or occupying interstices. □□ **in·ter·sti·tial·ly** *adv.*

in·ter·ti·dal /intərtíd'l/ *adj.* of or relating to the area which is covered at high tide and uncovered at low tide.

in·ter·twine /intərtwín/ *v.* **1** *tr.* (often foll. by *with*)

entwine (together). **2** *intr.* become entwined. □□ **in·ter·twine·ment** *n.*

in·ter·val /intərvəl/ *n.* **1** an intervening time or space. **2** *Brit.* a pause or break, esp. between the parts of a theatrical or musical performance. **3** the difference in pitch between two sounds. **4** the distance between persons or things in respect of qualities. □ **at intervals** here and there; now and then. □□ **in·ter·val·lic** /-válik/ *adj.*

in·ter·vene /intərvéen/ *v.intr.* (often foll. by *between, in*) **1** occur in time between events. **2** interfere; come between so as to prevent or modify the result or course of events. **3** be situated between things. **4** come in as an extraneous factor or thing. □□ **in·ter·ven·er** *n.* **in·ter·ven·ient** *adj.* **in·ter·ve·nor** *n.*

in·ter·ven·tion /intərvénshən/ *n.* **1** the act or an instance of intervening. **2** interference, esp. by a state in another's affairs. **3** mediation.

in·ter·ven·tion·ist /intərvénshənist/ *n.* a person who favors intervention. □□ **in·ter·ven·tion·ism** *n.*

in·ter·view /intərvyōō/ *n. & v.* ● *n.* **1** an oral examination of an applicant for employment, a college place, etc. **2** a conversation between a reporter, etc., and a person of public interest, used as a basis of a broadcast or publication. **3** a meeting of persons face to face, esp. for consultation. ● *v.tr.* **1** hold an interview with. **2** question to discover the opinions or experience of (a person). □□ **in·ter·view·ee** /-vyōō-ée/ *n.* **in·ter·view·er** *n.*

in·ter·war /intərwáwr/ *adj.* existing in the period between two wars, esp. the two world wars.

in·ter·weave /intərwéev/ *v.tr.* (*past* **-wove** /-wóv/; *past part.* **-woven** /-wóvən/) **1** (often foll. by *with*) weave together. **2** blend intimately.

in·ter·wind /intərwínd/ *v.tr. & intr.* (*past and past part.* **wound** /-wównd/) wind together.

in·ter·work /intərwórk/ *v.* **1** *intr.* work together or interactively. **2** *tr.* interweave.

in·tes·tate /intéstayt, -tət/ *adj. & n.* ● *adj.* (of a person) not having made a will before death. ● *n.* a person who has died intestate. □□ **in·tes·ta·cy** /-téstəsee/ *n.*

in·tes·tine /intéstin/ *n.* (in *sing.* or *pl.*) ▼ the lower part of the alimentary canal from the end of the stomach to the anus. ▷ DIGESTION. □□ **in·tes·ti·nal** *adj.*

INTESTINE: STRUCTURE OF THE HUMAN INTESTINE

transverse colon (large intestine)
duodenum (small intestine)
stomach
descending colon (large intestine)
jejunum (small intestine)
appendix
rectum
anus
ascending colon (large intestine)
ileum (small intestine)

in·thrall var. of ENTHRALL.

in·ti·ma·cy /intiməsee/ *n.* (*pl.* **-ies**) **1** the state of being intimate. **2** an intimate act, esp. sexual intercourse. **3** an intimate remark; an endearment.

in·ti·mate[1] /intimət/ *adj. & n.* ● *adj.* **1** closely acquainted; familiar; close (*an intimate friend; an intimate relationship*). **2** private and personal (*intimate thoughts*).

3 (usu. foll. by *with*) having sexual relations. **4** (of knowledge) detailed; thorough. **5** (of a relationship between things) close. **6** (of mixing, etc.) thorough. **7** essential; intrinsic. **8** (of a place, etc.) friendly; promoting close personal relationships. ● *n.* a very close friend. □□ **in·ti·mate·ly** *adv.*

in·ti·mate[2] /intimayt/ *v.tr.* **1** (often foll. by *that* + clause) state or make known. **2** imply; hint. □□ **in·ti·ma·tion** /-máyshən/ *n.*

in·tim·i·date /intímidayt/ *v.tr.* frighten or overawe, esp. to subdue or influence. □□ **in·tim·i·da·tion** /-dáyshən/ *n.* **in·tim·i·da·tor** *n.*

in·to /intōō/ *prep.* **1** expressing motion or direction to a point on or within (*walked into a tree; ran into the house*). **2** expressing direction of attention or concern (*will look into it*). **3** expressing a change of state (*turned into a dragon; separated into groups; forced into cooperation*). **4** *colloq.* interested in; knowledgeable about (*is really into art*).

in·tol·er·a·ble /intólərəbəl/ *adj.* that cannot be endured. □□ **in·tol·er·a·ble·ness** *n.* **in·tol·er·a·bly** *adv.*

in·tol·er·ant /intólərənt/ *adj.* not tolerant, esp. of views, beliefs, or behavior differing from one's own. □□ **in·tol·er·ance** /-rəns/ *n.* **in·tol·er·ant·ly** *adv.*

in·to·na·tion /intənáyshən/ *n.* **1** modulation of the voice; accent. **2** the act of intoning. **3** accuracy of pitch in playing or singing (*has good intonation*) □□ **in·to·na·tion·al** *adj.*

in·tone /intón/ *v.tr.* **1** recite (prayers, etc.) with prolonged sounds, esp. in a monotone. **2** utter with a particular tone. □□ **in·ton·er** *n.*

in to·to /in tótō/ *adv.* completely.

in·tox·i·cant /intóksikənt/ *adj. & n.* ● *adj.* intoxicating. ● *n.* an intoxicating substance.

in·tox·i·cate /intóksikayt/ *v.tr.* **1** make drunk. **2** excite or elate beyond self-control. □□ **in·tox·i·ca·tion** /-káyshən/ *n.*

in·tox·i·cat·ing /intóksikayting/ *adj.* **1** liable to cause intoxication; alcoholic. **2** exhilarating; exciting. □□ **in·tox·i·cat·ing·ly** *adv.*

intr. *abbr.* intransitive.

intra- /intrə/ *prefix* forming adjectives usu. from adjectives, meaning 'on the inside, within' (*intra-mural*).

in·trac·ta·ble /intráktəbəl/ *adj.* **1** hard to control or deal with. **2** difficult; stubborn (*an intractable patient*). □□ **in·trac·ta·bil·i·ty** *n.* **in·trac·ta·ble·ness** *n.* **in·trac·ta·bly** *adv.*

in·tra·dos /intrədos, -dōs, intráydos, -dōs/ *n.* the lower or inner curve of an arch. ▷ ARCH, WINDOW

in·tra·mu·ral /intrəmyōōrəl/ *adj.* **1** situated or done within walls. **2** forming part of normal university or college studies. □□ **in·tra·mu·ral·ly** *adv.*

in·tra·net /intrənet/ *n.* *Computing* a local or private network communicating with World Wide Web browsing software.

in·tran·si·gent /intránsijənt, -tránz-/ *adj. & n.* ● *adj.* uncompromising; stubborn. ● *n.* an intransigent person. □□ **in·tran·si·gence** /-jəns/ *n.* **in·tran·si·gen·cy** *n.* **in·tran·si·gent·ly** *adv.*

in·tran·si·tive /intránsitiv, -tránz-/ *adj.* (of a verb or sense of a verb) that does not take or require a direct object (whether expressed or implied), e.g., *look* in *look at the sky* (opp. TRANSITIVE). □□ **in·tran·si·tive·ly** *adv.* **in·tran·si·tiv·i·ty** /-tívitee/ *n.*

in·tra·u·ter·ine /intrəyōōtərin, -rīn/ *adj.* within the uterus.

in·tra·u·ter·ine de·vice *n.* a device inserted into the uterus that provides birth control by preventing implantation. Abbr.: **IUD**.

in·tra·ve·nous /intrəvéenəs/ *adj.* in or into a vein or veins. □□ **in·tra·ve·nous·ly** *adv.*

in·trep·id /intrépid/ *adj.* fearless; very brave. □□ **in·tre·pid·i·ty** /-tripíditee/ *n.* **in·trep·id·ly** *adv.*

in·tri·cate /intrikit/ *adj.* very complicated; perplexingly detailed or obscure. □□ **in·tri·ca·cy** /-kəsee/ *n.* (*pl.* **-ies**). **in·tri·cate·ly** *adv.*

I

in·trigue v. & n. ● v. /intréeg/ (**intrigues, in·trigued, intriguing**) **1** intr. (foll. by with) **a** carry on an underhand plot. **b** use secret influence. **2** tr. arouse the curiosity of; fascinate. ● n. /intréeg, in-/ **1** an underhand plot or plotting. **2** archaic a secret love affair. □□ **in·tri·guer** /intréegər/ n. **in·tri·guing** /intréeging/ adj. (esp. in sense 2 of v.). **in·tri·guing·ly** adv.

in·trin·sic /intrínzik/ adj. inherent; essential; belonging naturally (opp. EXTRINSIC). □□ **in·trin·si·cal·ly** adv.

in·tro /íntrō/ n. (pl. **-os**) colloq. an introduction.

intro- /íntrō/ comb. form into (introgression).

intro. abbr. **1** introduction. **2** introductory.

in·tro·duce /íntrədōos, -dyōos/ v.tr. **1** (foll. by to) make (a person or oneself) known by name to another, esp. formally. **2** announce or present to an audience. **3** bring (a custom, idea, etc.) into use. **4** bring (a piece of legislation) before a legislative assembly. **5** (foll. by to) draw the attention or extend the understanding of (a person) to a subject. **6** insert; place in. **7** bring in; usher in; bring forward. **8** begin; occur just before the start of. □□ **in·tro·duc·er** n. **in·tro·duc·i·ble** adj.

in·tro·duc·tion /íntrədúkshən/ n. **1** the act or an instance of introducing; the process of being introduced. **2** a formal presentation of one person to another. **3** an explanatory section at the beginning of a book, etc. **4** a preliminary section in a piece of music, often thematically different from the main section. **5** an introductory treatise on a subject.

in·tro·duc·to·ry /íntrədúktəree/ adj. serving as an introduction; preliminary.

in·tro·spec·tion /íntrəspékshən/ n. the examination or observation of one's own mental and emotional processes, etc. □□ **in·tro·spec·tive** adj. **in·tro·spec·tive·ly** adv. **in·tro·spec·tive·ness** n.

in·tro·vert /íntrəvərt/ n. & adj. ● n. **1** Psychol. a person predominantly concerned with his or her own thoughts and feelings rather than with external things. **2** a shy, inwardly thoughtful person. ● adj. (also **in·tro·vert·ed** /-tid/) typical or characteristic of an introvert. □□ **in·tro·ver·sion** /-vŕzhən, -shən/ n. **in·tro·ver·sive** /-vŕsiv/ adj. **in·tro·vert·ed** adj. **in·tro·ver·tive** /-vərtiv/ adj.

in·trude /intrōod/ v. (foll. by on, upon, into) **1** intr. come uninvited or unwanted; force oneself abruptly on others. **2** tr. thrust or force (something unwelcome) on a person. □□ **in·trud·ing·ly** adv.

in·trud·er /intrōodər/ n. a person who intrudes, esp. into a building with criminal intent.

in·tru·sion /intrōozhən/ n. **1** the act or an instance of intruding. **2** an unwanted interruption, etc. **3** Geol. ▼ an influx of molten rock between or through strata, etc., but not reaching the surface. ▷ IGNEOUS

flat intrusion (sill)   lens-shaped intrusion (laccolith)   rock strata within crust

Earth's surface

INTRUSION: CROSS SECTION OF THE EARTH'S CRUST SHOWING INTRUSIONS

in·tru·sive /intrōosiv/ adj. **1** that intrudes or tends to intrude. **2** characterized by intrusion. □□ **in·tru·sive·ly** adv. **in·tru·sive·ness** n.

in·trust var. of ENTRUST.

in·tu·it /intōoit, -tyōo-/ v. **1** tr. know by intuition. **2** intr. receive knowledge by direct perception.

in·tu·i·tion /íntōo-íshən, -tyōo-/ n. **1** immediate apprehension by the mind without reasoning. **2** immediate apprehension by a sense. **3** immediate insight. □□ **in·tu·i·tion·al** adj.

in·tu·i·tive /intōoitiv, -tyōo-/ adj. **1** of, characterized by, or possessing intuition. **2** perceived by intuition. □□ **in·tu·i·tive·ly** adv. **in·tu·i·tive·ness** n.

in·tu·mesce /íntōomés, -tyōo-/ v.intr. swell up. □□ **in·tu·mes·cence** n. **in·tu·mes·cent** adj.

in·twine var. of ENTWINE.

In·u·it /ínyōo-it/ n. (also **In·nu·it**) (pl. same or **Inuits**) a N. American Eskimo.

in·un·date /ínəndayt/ v.tr. (often foll. by with) **1** flood. **2** overwhelm (inundated with inquiries). □□ **in·un·da·tion** /-dáyshən/ n.

in·ure /inyōor/ v. tr. (often in passive; foll. by to) accustom (a person) to something esp. unpleasant. □□ **in·ure·ment** n.

in u·ter·o /in yōotərō/ adv. in the womb; before birth.

in vac·u·o /in vákyōo-ō/ adv. in a vacuum.

in·vade /inváyd/ v.tr. (often absol.) **1** enter (a country, etc.) under arms to control or subdue it. **2** swarm into. **3** (of a disease) attack (a body, etc.). **4** encroach upon (a person's rights, esp. privacy). □□ **in·vad·er** n.

in·vag·i·nate /inváijinayt/ v.tr. **1** put in a sheath. **2** turn (a tube) inside out. □□ **in·vag·i·na·tion** /-náyshən/ n.

in·va·lid[1] /ínvalid/ n. & v. ● n. **1** a person enfeebled or disabled by illness or injury. **2** (attrib.) **a** of or for invalids (invalid car; invalid diet). **b** being an invalid (caring for her invalid mother). ● v. tr. (often foll. by out, etc.) remove from active service (one who has become an invalid). **2** tr. (usu. in passive) disable (a person) by illness. **3** intr. become an invalid. □□ **in·va·lid·ism** n.

in·val·id[2] /inválid/ adj. not valid, esp. having no legal force. □□ **in·val·id·ly** adv.

in·val·i·date /inválidayt/ v.tr. **1** make (esp. an argument, etc.) invalid. **2** remove the validity or force of (a treaty, contract, etc.). □□ **in·val·i·da·tion** /-dáyshən/ n.

in·va·lid·i·ty /ínvəlíditee/ n. **1** lack of validity. **2** bodily infirmity.

in·val·u·a·ble /invályōoəbəl/ adj. above valuation; inestimable. □□ **in·val·u·a·ble·ness** n. **in·val·u·a·bly** adv.

in·var·i·a·ble /inváireeəbəl/ adj. **1** unchangeable. **2** always the same. **3** Math. constant; fixed. □□ **in·var·i·a·bil·i·ty** /-bílitee/ n. **in·var·i·a·ble·ness** n. **in·var·i·a·bly** adv.

in·var·i·ant /inváireeənt/ adj. & n. ● adj. invariable. ● n. Math. a function that remains unchanged when a specified transformation is applied. □□ **in·var·i·ance** /-reeəns/ n.

in·va·sion /inváyzhən/ n. **1** the act of invading or process of being invaded. **2** an entry of a hostile army into a country. □□ **in·va·sive** /-váysiv/ adj.

in·vec·tive /invéktiv/ n. **1 a** strongly attacking words. **b** the use of these. **2** abusive rhetoric.

in·veigh /inváy/ v.intr. (foll. by against) speak or write with strong hostility.

in·vei·gle /inváygəl, -vée-/ v.tr. (foll. by into, or to + infin.) entice; persuade by guile. □□ **in·vei·gle·ment** n.

in·vent /invént/ v.tr. **1** create by thought; devise; originate (a new method, an instrument, etc.). **2** concoct (a false story, etc.). □□ **in·vent·a·ble** adj. **in·ven·tor** n.

in·ven·tion /invénshən/ n. **1** the process of inventing. **2** a thing invented; a contrivance, esp. one for which a patent is granted. **3** a fictitious story. **4** inventiveness.

in·ven·tive /invéntiv/ adj. **1** able or inclined to invent; original in devising. **2** showing ingenuity of devising. □□ **in·ven·tive·ly** adv. **in·ven·tive·ness** n.

in·ven·to·ry /ínvəntáwree/ n. & v. ● n. (pl. **-ies**) **1** a complete list of goods in stock, house contents, etc. **2** the goods listed in this. **3** the total of a firm's commercial assets. ● v.tr. (**-ies, -ied**) **1** make an inventory of. **2** enter (goods) in an inventory.

in·verse /ínvərs, -vŕs/ adj. & n. ● adj. inverted in position, order, or relation. ● n. **1** the state of being inverted. **2** (often foll. by of) a thing that is the opposite or reverse of another. □□ **in·verse·ly** adv.

in·verse pro·por·tion n. (also **in·verse ra·tio**) a relation between two quantities such that one increases in proportion as the other decreases.

in·ver·sion /invŕzhən, -shən/ n. **1** the act of turning upside down or inside out. **2** the reversal of a normal order, position, or relation. **3** the reversal of the order of words, for rhetorical effect. **4** the reversal of the normal variation of air temperature with altitude. **5** the process or result of inverting. □□ **in·ver·sive** /-vŕsiv/ adj.

in·vert /invŕt/ v.tr. **1** turn upside down. **2** reverse the position, order, or relation of. **3** Mus. change the relative position of the notes of (a chord or interval) by placing the lowest note higher, usu. by an octave. **4** subject to inversion. □□ **in·vert·er** n. **in·vert·i·ble** adj. **in·vert·i·bil·i·ty** n.

in·ver·te·brate /invŕtibrət, -brayt/ adj. & n. ● adj. **1** (of an animal) not having a backbone. **2** lacking firmness of character. ● n. ▶ an invertebrate animal.

in·vest /invést/ v. **1** tr. (often foll. by in) apply or use (money), esp. for profit. **2** intr. (foll. by in) **a** put money for profit (into stocks, etc.). **b** colloq. buy (invested in a new car). **3** tr. **a** (foll. by with) provide or endue (a person with qualities, insignia, or rank). **b** (foll. by in) attribute or entrust (qualities or feelings to a person). □□ **in·vest·a·ble** adj. **in·vest·i·ble** adj. **in·ves·tor** n.

in·ves·ti·gate /invéstigayt/ v. **1** tr. **a** inquire into; examine; study carefully. **b** make an official inquiry into. **2** intr. make a systematic inquiry or search. □□ **in·ves·ti·ga·tor** n. **in·ves·ti·ga·to·ry** /-gətáwree/ adj.

in·ves·ti·ga·tion /invéstigáyshən/ n. **1** the process or an instance of investigating. **2** a formal examination or study.

in·ves·ti·ga·tive /invéstigaytiv/ adj. seeking or serving to investigate, esp. (of journalism) inquiring intensively into controversial issues.

in·ves·ti·ture /invéstichōor, -chər/ n. **1** the formal investing of a person with honors or rank, esp. a ceremony at which a sovereign confers honors. **2** (often foll. by with) the act of enduing (with attributes).

in·vest·ment /invéstmənt/ n. **1** the act or process of investing. **2** money invested. **3** property, etc., in which money is invested.

in·vet·er·ate /invétərət/ adj. **1** (of a person) confirmed in an (esp. undesirable) habit, etc. (an inveterate gambler). **2** (of a habit, etc.) long-established. □□ **in·vet·er·a·cy** /-rəsee/ n. **in·vet·er·ate·ly** adv.

in·vid·i·ous /invídeeəs/ adj. (of an action, conduct, attitude, etc.) likely to excite resentment or indignation against the person responsible, esp. by real or seeming injustice (an invidious position; an invidious task). □□ **in·vid·i·ous·ly** adv. **in·vid·i·ous·ness** n.

in·vig·or·ate /invígərayt/ v.tr. give vigor or strength to. □□ **in·vig·or·at·ing** adj. **in·vig·or·at·ing·ly** adv. **in·vig·or·a·tion** /-ráyshən/ n.

in·vin·ci·ble /invínsibəl/ adj. unconquerable; that cannot be defeated. □□ **in·vin·ci·bil·i·ty** n. **in·vin·ci·ble·ness** n. **in·vin·ci·bly** adv.

in·vi·o·la·ble /invíələbəl/ adj. not to be violated or profaned. □□ **in·vi·o·la·bil·i·ty** /-bílitee/ n. **in·vi·o·la·bly** adv.

in·vi·o·late /invíələt/ adj. not violated or profaned. □□ **in·vi·o·la·cy** /-ləsee/ n. **in·vi·o·late·ly** adv. **in·vi·o·late·ness** n.

in·vis·i·ble /invízibəl/ adj. **1** not visible to the eye, either characteristically or because hidden. **2** too small to be seen or noticed. **3** artfully concealed (invisible mending). □□ **in·vis·i·bil·i·ty** n. **in·vis·i·ble·ness** n. **in·vis·i·bly** adv.

INVERTEBRATE

The animal kingdom may be divided into two main groups: vertebrates, which have backbones, and invertebrates, which do not. The latter constitutes by far the larger group. It includes animals such as cnidarians, which have soft, jellylike bodies, and insects and crustaceans, which have a hard outer casing called an exoskeleton. Insects make up the largest number of invertebrates.

EXAMPLES OF INVERTEBRATES

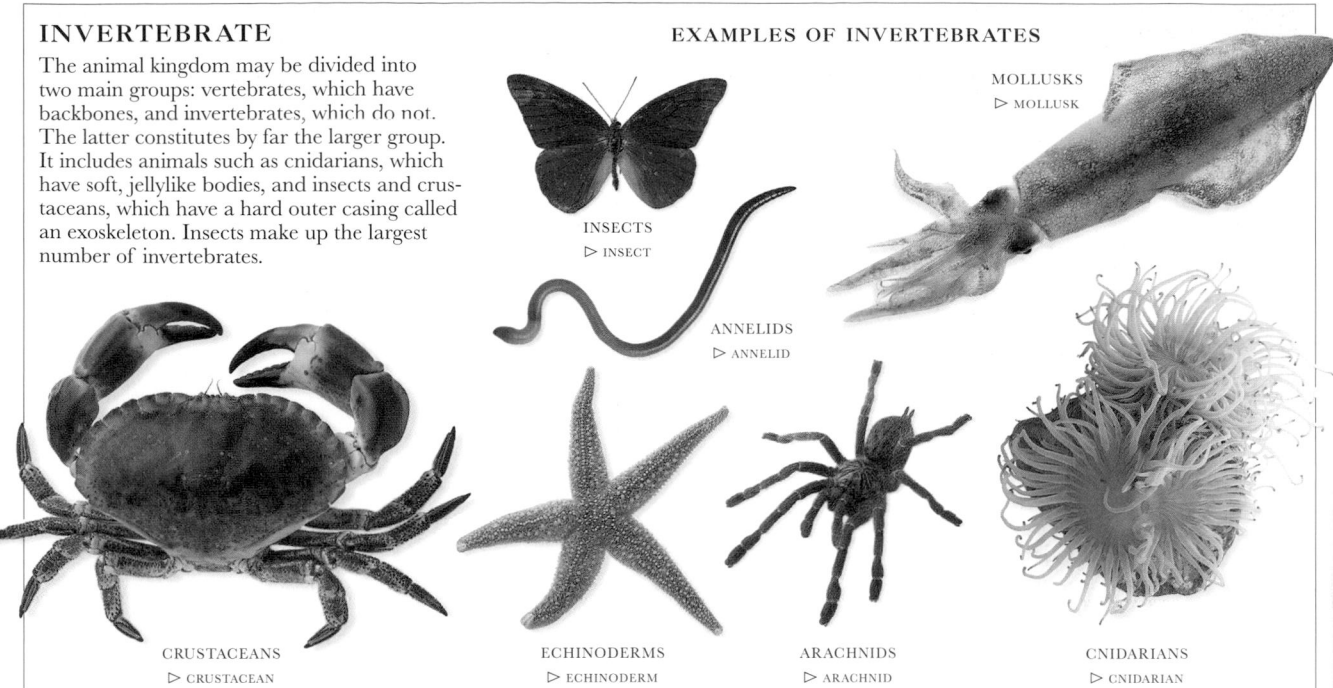

INSECTS
▷ INSECT

ANNELIDS
▷ ANNELID

MOLLUSKS
▷ MOLLUSK

CRUSTACEANS
▷ CRUSTACEAN

ECHINODERMS
▷ ECHINODERM

ARACHNIDS
▷ ARACHNID

CNIDARIANS
▷ CNIDARIAN

I

---

in·vi·ta·tion /ínvitáyshən/ *n.* **1 a** the process of inviting or fact of being invited, esp. to a social occasion. **b** the spoken or written form in which a person is invited. **2** the action or an act of enticing; attraction; allurement.

in·vite *v. & n.* ● *v.* /invít/ **1** *tr.* (often foll. by *to*, or *to* + infin.) ask (a person) courteously to come, or to do something (*were invited to lunch*; *invited them to reply*). **2** *tr.* make a formal courteous request for (*invited comments*). **3** *tr.* tend to call forth unintentionally (*something unwanted*). **4 a** *tr.* attract. **b** *intr.* be attractive. ● *n.* /ínvīt/ *colloq.* an invitation. □□ **in·vi·tee** /-tée/ *n.* **in·vit·er** *n.*

in·vit·ing /invíting/ *adj.* **1** attractive. **2** enticing; tempting. □□ **in·vit·ing·ly** *adv.* **in·vit·ing·ness** *n.*

in vi·tro /in véetrō/ *adv. Biol.* (of processes or reactions) taking place in a test tube or other laboratory environment.

in vi·vo /in véevō/ *adv. Biol.* (of processes) taking place in a living organism.

in·vo·ca·tion /ínvəkáyshən/ *n.* **1** the act or an instance of invoking, esp. in prayer. **2** an appeal to a supernatural being or beings, e.g., the Muses, for psychological or spiritual inspiration. □□ **in·voc·a·to·ry** /invókətáwree/ *adj.*

in·voice /ínvoys/ *n. & v.* ● *n.* an itemized bill for goods or services. ● *v.tr.* **1** make an invoice of (goods and services). **2** send an invoice to (a person).

in·voke /invók/ *v.tr.* **1** call on (a deity, etc.) in prayer or as a witness. **2** appeal to (the law, a person's authority, etc.). **3** summon (a spirit) by charms. **4** ask earnestly for (vengeance, help, etc.). □□ **in·vo·ca·ble** *adj.* **in·vok·er** *n.*

in·vo·lu·cre /ínvəlōōkər/ *n.* a membranous covering or envelope.

in·vol·un·tar·y /invóləntéree/ *adj.* **1** done without the exercise of the will; unintentional. **2** (of a limb, muscle, or movement) not under the control of the will. □□ **in·vol·un·tar·i·ly** /-térilee/ *adv.* **in·vol·un·tar·i·ness** *n.*

in·vo·lute /ínvəlōōt/ *adj.* **1** involved; intricate. **2** ◄ curled spirally. **3** *Bot.* rolled inward at the edges.

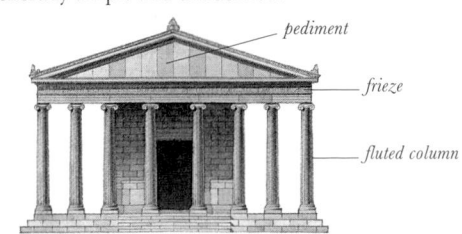

INVOLUTE
SHELL

in·vo·lut·ed /ínvəlōōtid/ *adj.* **1** complicated; abstruse. **2** = INVOLUTE *adj.* 2.

in·vo·lu·tion /ínvəlōōshən/ *n.* **1** the process of involving. **2** an entanglement. **3** intricacy. **4** curling inward. **5** a part that curls upward.

in·volve /invólv/ *v.tr.* **1** (often foll. by *in*) cause (a person or thing) to participate, or share the experience or effect (in a situation, etc.). **2** imply; entail; make necessary. **3** (foll. by *in*) implicate (a person in a crime, etc.). **4** include or affect in its operations. **5** (as **involved** *adj.*) **a** (often foll. by *in*) concerned or interested. **b** complicated in thought or form.

in·volve·ment /invólvmənt/ *n.* **1** (often foll. by *in, with*) the act or an instance of involving; the process of being involved. **2** financial embarrassment. **3** a complicated affair or concern.

in·vul·ner·a·ble /invúlnərəbəl/ *adj.* that cannot be wounded or hurt, physically or mentally. □□ **in·vul·ner·a·bil·i·ty** *n.* **in·vul·ner·a·bly** *adv.*

in·ward /ínwərd/ *adj. & adv.* ● *adj.* **1** directed toward the inside; going in. **2** situated within. **3** mental; spiritual. ● *adv.* (also **in·wards**) **1** toward the inside. **2** in the mind or soul. □□ **in·ward·ly** *adv.*

in·wrought /ínráwt/ *adj.* **1 a** (often foll. by *with*) (of a fabric) decorated (with a pattern). **b** (often foll. by *in, on*) (of a pattern) wrought (in or on a fabric). **2** closely blended.

I/O *abbr. Computing* input/output.

IOC *abbr.* International Olympic Committee.

i·o·dine /íədīn, -din, -deen/ *n.* **1** *Chem.* a non-metallic element of the halogen group, forming black crystals and a violet vapor, used in medicine and photography, and important as an essential element for living organisms. ¶ Symb.: **I**. **2** a solution of this in alcohol used as a mild antiseptic.

i·o·dize /íədīz/ *v.tr.* treat or impregnate with iodine. □□ **i·o·di·za·tion** *n.*

i·on /íən, íon/ *n.* an atom or group of atoms that has lost one or more electrons (= CATION), or gained one or more electrons (= ANION). □□ **i·on·ic** *adj.* **i·on·i·cal·ly** *adv.*

I·on·ic /īónik/ *adj. & n.* ● *adj.* **1** ▼ of the order of Greek architecture characterized by a column with scroll shapes on either side of the capital. ▷ COLUMN. **2** of the ancient Greek dialect used in Ionia. ● *n.* the Ionic dialect.

IONIC

The term *Ionic* applies to one of the classical architectural orders. It is especially attributable to temple architecture and is characterized by the use of fluted columns, volutes (spiral scrolls) on each capital, and a continuous, sculpted frieze. The triangular pediment on the main façade is generally simple and unadorned.

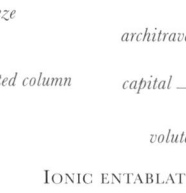

pediment

frieze

fluted column

FRONT ELEVATION OF AN IONIC TEMPLE

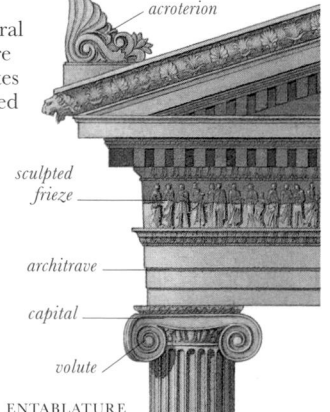

acroterion

sculpted frieze

architrave

capital

volute

IONIC ENTABLATURE

i·on·i·za·tion /ī̄ənizáyshən/ *n.* the process of producing ions as a result of solvation, heat, radiation, etc.

i·on·ize /ī́ənīz/ *v.tr. & intr.* convert or be converted into an ion or ions. □□ **i·on·iz·a·ble** *adj.*

i·on·iz·er /ī́ənīzər/ *n.* any thing which produces ionization, esp. a device used to improve the quality of the air in a room, etc.

i·on·o·sphere /ī̄ónəsfeer/ *n.* ▼ an ionized region of the atmosphere above the mesosphere, extending to about 600 miles (1,000 km) above the Earth's surface and able to reflect radio waves, allowing long-distance transmission around the Earth. ▷ ATMOSPHERE. (cf. TROPOSPHERE) □□ **i·on·o·spher·ic** /-sféerik, -sfér-/ *adj.*

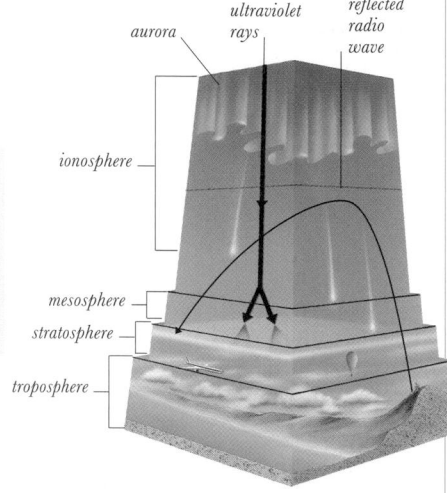

IONOSPHERE: SECTION THROUGH THE
LOWER DIVISIONS OF THE EARTH'S ATMOSPHERE

aurora
ultraviolet rays
reflected radio wave
ionosphere
mesosphere
stratosphere
troposphere

i·o·ta /ī-ṓtə/ *n.* **1** the ninth letter of the Greek alphabet (I, ι). **2** (usu. with *neg.*) the smallest possible amount.

IOU /í-ō-yṓo/ *n.* a signed document acknowledging a debt.

IPA *abbr.* International Phonetic Alphabet (or Association).

ip·e·cac /ípikak/ *n. colloq.* ipecacuanha.

ip·e·cac·u·an·ha /ípikákyṓo-áanə/ *n.* the root of a S. American shrub, *Cephaelis ipecacuanha*, used as an emetic and purgative.

ip·si·lat·er·al /ípsilátərəl/ *adj.* belonging to or occurring on the same side of the body.

ip·so fac·to /ípsō fáktō/ *adv.* **1** by that very fact or act. **2** thereby.

IQ *abbr.* intelligence quotient.

IR *abbr.* infrared.

Ir *symb. Chem.* the element iridium.

IRA *abbr.* **1** individual retirement account. **2** Irish Republican Army.

I·ra·ni·an /iráyneeən/ *adj. & n.* ● *adj.* **1** of or relating to Iran (formerly Persia) in the Middle East. **2** of the Indo-European group of languages including Persian, Pashto, Avestan, and Kurdish. ● *n.* **1** a native or national of Iran. **2** a person of Iranian descent.

I·ra·qi /iráakee/ *adj. & n.* ● *adj.* of or relating to Iraq in the Middle East. ● *n.* (*pl.* **Iraqis**) **1 a** a native or national of Iraq. **b** a person of Iraqi descent. **2** the form of Arabic spoken in Iraq.

i·ras·ci·ble /irásibəl/ *adj.* irritable; hot-tempered. □□ **i·ras·ci·bil·i·ty** *n.* **i·ras·ci·bly** *adv.*

i·rate /īráyt/ *adj.* angry, enraged. □□ **i·rate·ly** *adv.* **i·rate·ness** *n.*

IRC *abbr. Computing* Internet Relay Chat.

ire /īr/ *n. literary* anger. □□ **ire·ful** *adj.*

ir·i·da·ceous /íridáyshəs/ *adj. Bot.* of or relating to the family Iridaceae of plants growing from bulbs, corms, or rhizomes, e.g., iris, crocus, and gladiolus.

ir·i·des·cent /íridésənt/ *adj.* **1** showing rainbowlike luminous or gleaming colors. **2** changing color with position. □□ **ir·i·des·cence** /-səns/ *n.* **ir·i·des·cent·ly** *adv.*

ir·id·i·um /irídeeəm/ *n. Chem.* a hard, white metallic element of the transition series used esp. in alloys. ¶ Symb.: **Ir**.

i·ris /ī́ris/ *n.* **1** the flat, circular colored membrane behind the cornea of the eye, with a circular opening (pupil) in the center. ▷ EYE. **2** ► any herbaceous plant of the genus *Iris*, usu. with tuberous roots, sword-shaped leaves, and showy flowers. **3** (in full **iris diaphragm**) an adjustable diaphragm of thin overlapping plates for regulating the size of a central hole esp. for the admission of light to a lens.

standard (inner tepal)
stigmatic lip
beard
fall (outer tepal)

IRIS
(*Iris* 'Banbury Beauty')

I·rish /ī́rish/ *adj. & n.* ● *adj.* of or relating to Ireland; of or like its people. ● *n.* **1** the Celtic language of Ireland. **2** (prec. by *the*; treated as *pl.*) the people of Ireland.

I·rish cof·fee *n.* coffee mixed with Irish whiskey and served with cream on top.

I·rish·man /ī́rishmən/ *n.* (*pl.* **-men**) a person who is Irish by birth or descent.

I·rish Sea *n.* the sea between England and Wales and Ireland.

I·rish set·ter *n.* a silky-haired, dark red breed of setter.

I·rish wolf·hound *n.* ▼ a large, often greyish hound of a rough-coated breed.

IRISH WOLFHOUND

I·rish·wom·an /ī́rishwŏomən/ *n.* (*pl.* **-women**) a woman who is Irish by birth or descent.

i·ri·tis /īrī́tis/ *n.* inflammation of the iris.

irk /ərk/ *v.tr.* (usu. *impers.*; often foll. by *that* + clause) irritate; bore; annoy.

irk·some /ə́rksəm/ *adj.* tedious; annoying; tiresome. □□ **irk·some·ly** *adv.* **irk·some·ness** *n.*

i·ro·ko /irṓkō/ *n.* (*pl.* **-os**) **1** either of two African trees, *Chlorophora excelsa* or *C. regia*. **2** the light-colored hardwood from these trees. ▷ WOOD

i·ron /ī́ərn/ *n., adj., & v.* ● *n.* **1** *Chem.* a silver-white ductile metallic element occurring naturally as hematite, magnetite, etc., much used for tools and implements, and an essential element in all living organisms. ▷ BLAST FURNACE, METAL. ¶ Symb.: **Fe**. **2** this as a type of unyieldingness or a symbol of firmness (*man of iron*; *will of iron*). **3** a tool or implement made of iron (*branding iron*; *curling iron*). **4** a household, now usu. electrical, implement with a flat base which is heated to smooth clothes, etc. **5** a golf club with an iron or steel sloping face used for lofting the ball. ▷ GOLF. **6** (usu. in *pl.*) a fetter (*clapped in irons*). **7** (usu. in *pl.*) a stirrup. **8** (often in *pl.*) an iron support for a malformed leg. **9** a preparation of iron as a tonic or dietary supplement (*iron pills*). ● *adj.* **1** made of iron. **2** very robust. **3** unyielding; merciless (*iron determination*). ● *v.tr.* **1** smooth (clothes, etc.) with an iron. **2** furnish or cover with iron. **3** shackle with irons. □ **in irons** handcuffed, chained, etc. **iron in the fire** an undertaking, opportunity, or commitment (usu. in *pl.*: *too many irons in the fire*). **iron out** remove or smooth over (difficulties, etc.). □□ **i·ron·er** *n.* **i·ron·less** *adj.* **i·ron·like** *adj.*

I·ron Age *n. Archaeol.* the period following the Bronze Age when iron replaced bronze in the making of implements and weapons.

i·ron·clad *adj. & n.* ● *adj.* /ī́ərnklád/ **1** clad or protected with iron. **2** impregnable; rigorous. ● *n.* /ī́ərnklad/ *hist.* an early name for a 19th-c. warship built of iron or protected by iron plates.

I·ron Cross *n.* ► the highest German military decoration for bravery.

I·ron Cur·tain *n. hist.* a notional barrier to the passage of people and information between the former Soviet bloc and the West.

i·ron hand *n.* firmness or inflexibility (cf. VELVET GLOVE).

i·ron·ic /īrónik/ *adj.* (also **i·ron·i·cal**) **1** using or displaying irony. **2** in the nature of irony. □□ **i·ron·i·cal·ly** *adv.*

i·ron·ing board *n.* a flat surface usu. on legs and of adjustable height on which clothes, etc., are ironed.

i·ron·ist /ī́rənist/ *n.* a person who uses irony. □□ **i·ron·ize** *v.intr.*

IRON CROSS

i·ron lung *n.* a rigid case fitted over a patient's body, used for administering prolonged artificial respiration by means of mechanical pumps.

i·ron maid·en *n. hist.* an instrument of torture consisting of a coffin-shaped box lined with iron spikes.

i·ron mold *n.* a spot caused by iron rust or an ink stain, esp. on fabric.

i·ron·stone /ī́ərnstōn/ *n.* **1** ► any rock containing a substantial proportion of an iron compound. **2** a kind of hard, white, opaque stoneware.

i·ron·ware /ī́ərnwair/ *n.* various articles made of iron, esp. implements used in the home.

i·ron·wood /ī́ərnwŏod/ *n.* **1** any of various tough-timbered trees and shrubs, esp. American hornbeam *Carpinus caroliniana*. **2** the wood from these trees.

IRONSTONE:
HEMATITE

i·ron·work /ī́ərnwərk/ *n.* **1** things made of iron. **2** work in iron.

i·ron·works /ī́ərnwərks/ *n.* (as *sing.* or *pl.*) a place where iron is smelted or iron goods are made.

i·ro·ny /ī́rənee/ *n.* (*pl.* **-ies**) **1** an expression of meaning, often humorous or sarcastic, by the use of language of a different or opposite tendency. **2** an ill-timed or perverse arrival of an event or circumstance that is in itself desirable. **3** the use of language with one meaning for a privileged audience and another for those addressed or concerned.

Ir·o·quoi·an /írəkwóyən/ *n. & adj.* ● *n.* **1** a language family of eastern N. America, including Cherokee and Mohawk. **2** a member of the Iroquois people. ● *adj.* of or relating to the Iroquois or the Iroquoian language family or one of its members.

Ir·o·quois /írəkwoy/ n. & adj. ● n. (pl. same) **1 a** a Native American confederacy of five (later six) peoples formerly inhabiting New York State. **b** a member of any of these peoples. **2** any of the languages spoken by these peoples. ● adj. ▶ of or relating to the Iroquois or their languages.

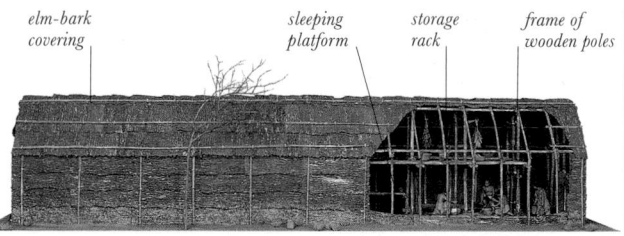

elm-bark covering · sleeping platform · storage rack · frame of wooden poles

IROQUOIS: CUTAWAY OF AN EIGHT-FAMILY IROQUOIS LONGHOUSE

ir·ra·di·ant /iráydeeənt/ adj. literary shining brightly. □□ **ir·ra·di·ance** /-əns/ n.

ir·ra·di·ate /iráydee-áyt/ v.tr. **1** subject to (any form of) radiation. **2** shine upon; light up. **3** throw light on (a subject). □□ **ir·ra·di·a·tive** /-deeətiv/ adj.

ir·ra·di·a·tion /iráydee-áyshən/ n. **1** the process of irradiating. **2** shining; illumination. **3** the apparent extension of the edges of an illuminated object seen against a dark background.

ir·ra·tion·al /iráshənəl/ adj. **1** illogical; unreasonable. **2** not endowed with reason. **3** Math. (of a root, etc.) not rational; not able to be expressed as a ratio between two integers; not commensurate with the natural numbers (e.g., a nonterminating decimal). □□ **ir·ra·tion·al·i·ty** /-álitee/ n. **ir·ra·tion·al·ize** v.tr. **ir·ra·tion·al·ly** adv.

ir·re·claim·a·ble /iríkláyməbəl/ adj. that cannot be reclaimed or reformed. □□ **ir·re·claim·a·bly** adv.

ir·rec·on·cil·a·ble /irékənsíləbəl/ adj. & n. ● adj. **1** implacably hostile. **2** (of ideas, etc.) incompatible. ● n. **1** an uncompromising opponent of a political measure, etc. **2** (usu. in pl.) any of two or more items, ideas, etc., that cannot be made to agree. □□ **ir·rec·on·cil·a·bil·i·ty** n. **ir·rec·on·cil·a·ble·ness** n. **ir·rec·on·cil·a·bly** adv.

ir·re·cov·er·a·ble /iríkúvərəbəl/ adj. that cannot be recovered or remedied. □□ **ir·re·cov·er·a·bly** adv.

ir·re·cu·sa·ble /iríkyőozəbəl/ adj. that must be accepted.

ir·re·deem·a·ble /irídéeməbəl/ adj. **1** that cannot be redeemed. **2** hopeless; absolute. □□ **ir·re·deem·a·bil·i·ty** n. **ir·re·deem·a·bly** adv.

ir·re·duc·i·ble /irídőosibəl, -dyőo-/ adj. **1** that cannot be reduced or simplified. **2** (often foll. by to) that cannot be brought to a desired condition. □□ **ir·re·duc·i·bil·i·ty** n. **ir·re·duc·i·bly** adv.

ir·re·frag·a·ble /iréfrəgəbəl/ adj. **1** (of a statement, argument, or person) unanswerable; indisputable. **2** (of rules, etc.) inviolable.

ir·ref·u·ta·ble /iréfyətəbəl, írifyőo-/ adj. that cannot be refuted. □□ **ir·ref·u·ta·bil·i·ty** n. **ir·ref·u·ta·bly** adv.

ir·reg·u·lar /irégyələr/ adj. & n. ● adj. **1** not regular; unsymmetrical; uneven; varying in form. **2** (of a surface) uneven. **3** contrary to a rule, moral principle, or custom; abnormal. **4** uneven in duration, order, etc. **5** (of troops) not belonging to the regular army. **6** Gram. (of a verb, noun, etc.) not inflected according to the usual rules. **7** disorderly. ● n. (in pl.) irregular troops. □□ **ir·reg·u·lar·i·ty** /-láritee/ n. (pl. **-ies**). **ir·reg·u·lar·ly** adv.

ir·rel·e·vant /irélivənt/ adj. (often foll. by to) not relevant; not applicable (to a matter in hand). □□ **ir·rel·e·vance** /-vəns/ n. **ir·rel·e·van·cy** n. **ir·rel·e·vant·ly** adv.

ir·re·li·gious /irílijəs/ adj. **1** indifferent or hostile to religion. **2** lacking a religion. □□ **ir·re·li·gious·ly** adv. **ir·re·li·gious·ness** n.

ir·re·me·di·a·ble /iríméedeeəbəl/ adj. that cannot be remedied. □□ **ir·re·me·di·a·bly** adv.

ir·re·mis·si·ble /irímísibəl/ adj. **1** unpardonable. **2** unalterably obligatory. □□ **ir·re·mis·si·bly** adv.

ir·re·mov·a·ble /irímőovəbəl/ adj. that cannot be removed, esp. from office. □□ **ir·re·mov·a·bil·i·ty** n. **ir·re·mov·a·bly** adv.

ir·rep·a·ra·ble /irépərəbəl/ adj. (of an injury, loss, etc.) that cannot be rectified or made good. □□ **ir·rep·a·ra·bil·i·ty** n. **ir·rep·a·ra·ble·ness** n. **ir·rep·a·ra·bly** adv.

ir·re·place·a·ble /iripláysəbəl/ adj. **1** that cannot be replaced. **2** of which the loss cannot be made good. □□ **ir·re·place·a·bly** adv.

ir·re·press·i·ble /iriprésibəl/ adj. that cannot be repressed or restrained. □□ **ir·re·press·i·bil·i·ty** n. **ir·re·press·i·ble·ness** n. **ir·re·press·i·bly** adv.

ir·re·proach·a·ble /iriprōchəbəl/ adj. faultless; blameless. □□ **ir·re·proach·a·bil·i·ty** n. **ir·re·proach·a·ble·ness** n. **ir·re·proach·a·bly** adv.

ir·re·sist·i·ble /irizístibəl/ adj. **1** too strong or convincing to be resisted. **2** delightful; alluring. □□ **ir·re·sist·i·bil·i·ty** n. **ir·re·sist·i·ble·ness** n. **ir·re·sist·i·bly** adv.

ir·res·o·lute /irézəlōot/ adj. **1** hesitant; undecided. **2** lacking in resoluteness. □□ **ir·res·o·lute·ly** adv. **ir·res·o·lute·ness** n. **ir·res·o·lu·tion** /-lőoshən/ n.

ir·re·solv·a·ble /irizólvəbəl/ adj. **1** that cannot be resolved into its components. **2** (of a problem) that cannot be solved.

ir·re·spec·tive /irispéktiv/ adj. (foll. by of) not taking into account; regardless of. □□ **ir·re·spec·tive·ly** adv.

ir·re·spon·si·ble /irispónsibəl/ adj. **1** acting or done without due sense of responsibility. **2** not responsible for one's conduct. □□ **ir·re·spon·si·bil·i·ty** n. **ir·re·spon·si·bly** adv.

ir·re·spon·sive /irispónsiv/ adj. (often foll. by to) not responsive. □□ **ir·re·spon·sive·ly** adv. **ir·re·spon·sive·ness** n.

ir·re·triev·a·ble /iritréevəbəl/ adj. that cannot be retrieved or restored. □□ **ir·re·triev·a·bil·i·ty** n. **ir·re·triev·a·bly** adv.

ir·rev·er·ent /irévərənt/ adj. lacking reverence. □□ **ir·rev·er·ence** /-rəns/ n. **ir·rev·er·en·tial** /-rénshəl/ adj. **ir·rev·er·ent·ly** adv.

ir·re·vers·i·ble /irivársibəl/ adj. not reversible or alterable. □□ **ir·re·vers·i·bil·i·ty** n. **ir·re·vers·i·bly** adv.

ir·rev·o·ca·ble /irévəkəbəl, irivōk-/ adj. **1** unalterable. **2** gone beyond recall. □□ **ir·rev·o·ca·bil·i·ty** /-bílitee/ n. **ir·rev·o·ca·bly** adv.

ir·ri·gate /írigayt/ v.tr. **1 a** water (land) by means of channels. **b** (of a stream, etc.) supply (land) with water. **2** Med. supply (a wound, etc.) with a constant flow of liquid. **3** refresh as with moisture. □□ **ir·ri·ga·ble** adj. **ir·ri·ga·tion** /-gáyshən/ n. **ir·ri·ga·tive** adj. **ir·ri·ga·tor** n.

ir·ri·ta·ble /íritəbəl/ adj. **1** easily annoyed or angered. **2** (of an organ, etc.) very sensitive to contact. □□ **ir·ri·ta·bil·i·ty** n. **ir·ri·ta·bly** adv.

ir·ri·tant /írit'nt/ adj. & n. ● adj. causing irritation. ● n. an irritant substance. □□ **ir·ri·tan·cy** n.

ir·ri·tate /íritayt/ v.tr. **1** excite to anger; annoy. **2** stimulate discomfort or pain in (a part of the body). **3** Biol. stimulate (an organ) to action. □□ **ir·ri·tat·ed·ly** adv. **ir·ri·tat·ing** adj. **ir·ri·tat·ing·ly** adv. **ir·ri·ta·tion** /-táyshən/ n. **ir·ri·ta·tive** adj. **ir·ri·ta·tor** n.

ir·rupt /irúpt/ v.intr. (foll. by into) enter forcibly or violently. □□ **ir·rup·tion** /irúpshən/ n.

IRS abbr. Internal Revenue Service.

Is. abbr. **1 a** Island(s). **b** Isle(s). **2** (also **Isa.**) Isaiah (Old Testament).

is 3rd sing. present of BE.

ISBN abbr. international standard book number.

is·che·mi·a /iskéemeeə/ n. (esp. Brit. **ischaemia**)

Med. a reduction of the blood supply to part of the body. □□ **is·che·mic** adj.

is·chi·um /ískeeəm/ n. (pl. **ischia** /-keeə/) the curved bone forming the base of each half of the pelvis. □□ **is·chi·al** adj.

ISDN abbr. integrated services digital network.

i·sin·glass /ízinglas/ n. **1** a kind of gelatin obtained from fish, esp. sturgeon, and used in making jellies, glue, etc. **2** mica.

isl. abbr. island.

Is·lam /islaam, íz-, islaám, iz-/ n. **1** a monotheistic religious faith regarded as revealed through Muhammad as the Prophet of Allah. **2** collectively, those countries in which Islam is the principal religion. □□ **Is·lam·ic** adj. **Is·lam·ism** n. **Is·lam·ist** n. **Is·lam·ize** v.tr. **Is·lam·i·za·tion** /-mizáyshən/ n.

is·land /íland/ n. **1** a piece of land surrounded by water. **2** anything compared to an island, esp. in being surrounded in some way. **3 a** a detached or isolated thing. **b** Physiol. a detached portion of tissue or group of cells (cf. ISLET).

is·land·er /ílandər/ n. a native or inhabitant of an island.

isle /īl/ n. poet. (and in place-names) an island or peninsula, esp. a small one.

is·let /ílit/ n. **1** a small island. **2** Anat. a portion of tissue structurally distinct from surrounding tissues.

is·lets of Lang·er·hans /láanggərhaans, -háanz/ n.pl. Physiol. groups of pancreatic cells secreting insulin and glucagon.

ism /ízəm/ n. colloq. usu. derog. any distinctive but unspecified doctrine or practice of a kind with a name ending in -ism.

isn't /íznt/ contr. is not.

ISO abbr. International Standardization Organization.

iso- /ísō/ comb. form **1** equal (isometric). **2** Chem. isomeric, esp. of a hydrocarbon with a branched chain of carbon atoms (isobutane).

i·so·bar /ísəbaar/ n. a line on a map connecting positions having the same atmospheric pressure at a given time or on average over a given period. ▷ WEATHER CHART. □□ **i·so·bar·ic** /-bárik/ adj.

i·so·cheim /ísəkīm/ n. a line on a map connecting places having the same average temperature in winter.

i·so·chro·mat·ic /ísōkrōmátik/ adj. of the same color.

i·soch·ro·nous /ísókrənəs/ adj. **1** occurring at the same time. **2** occupying equal time. □□ **i·soch·ro·nous·ly** adv.

i·so·cli·nal /ísəklín'l/ adj. (also **i·so·clin·ic** /-klínik/) **1** Geol. (of a fold) in which the two limbs are parallel. **2** corresponding to equal values of magnetic dip.

i·so·gloss /ísəglaws, -glos/ n. a line on a map marking an area having a distinct linguistic feature.

i·so·hy·et /ísōhí-it/ n. a line on a map connecting places having the same amount of rainfall in a given period.

i·so·late /ísəlayt/ v.tr. **1 a** place apart or alone, cut off from society. **b** place (a patient thought to be contagious or infectious) in quarantine. **2 a** identify and separate for attention (isolated the problem). **b** Chem. separate (a substance) from a mixture. **3** insulate (electrical apparatus). □□ **i·so·la·ble** /ísələbəl/ adj. **i·so·lat·a·ble** adj. **i·so·la·tor** n.

i·so·lat·ed /ísəlaytid/ adj. **1** lonely; cut off from society or contact; remote (feeling isolated; an isolated farmhouse). **2** untypical; unique (an isolated example).

i·so·lat·ing /ísəlayting/ adj. (of a language) having each element as an independent word without inflections.

i·so·la·tion /ísəláyshən/ n. the act or an instance of isolating; the state of being isolated or separated. □ **in isolation** considered singly and not relatively.

i·so·la·tion·ism /ísəláyshənizəm/ n. the policy of holding aloof from the affairs of other countries or groups esp. in politics. □□ **i·so·la·tion·ist** n.

ISOMER

Compounds that have the same molecular formula, but a different configuration of atoms, are known as isomers. Butane and 2-methylpropane, for example, both have the chemical formula C_4H_{10}, but their atoms link up in different ways. As a result, each isomeric form has different physical and chemical properties.

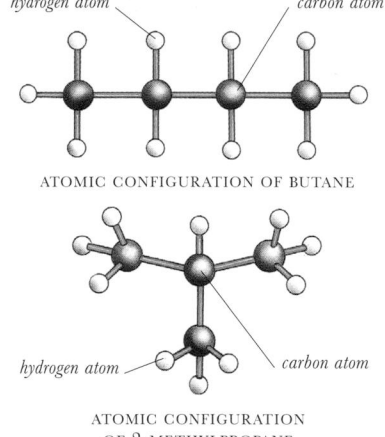

ATOMIC CONFIGURATION OF BUTANE

ATOMIC CONFIGURATION
OF 2-METHYLPROPANE

ISOTOPE

Isotopes are different forms of the same element. They have identical chemical properties and occupy the same place on the periodic table, but each isotopic form has a different number of neutrons in the nucleus of its atoms, giving each form a different mass. Hydrogen, for example, exists in three isotopic forms (see below).

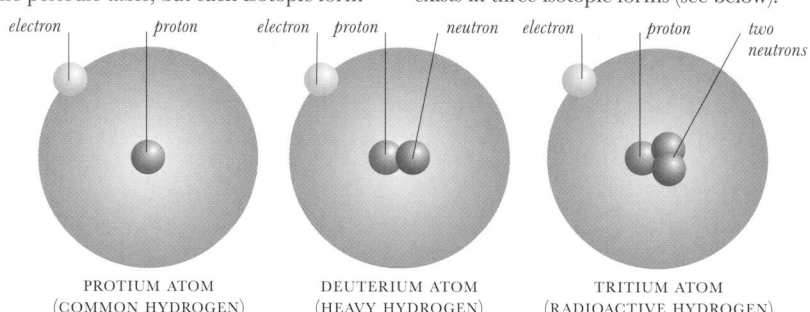

PROTIUM ATOM
(COMMON HYDROGEN)

DEUTERIUM ATOM
(HEAVY HYDROGEN)

TRITIUM ATOM
(RADIOACTIVE HYDROGEN)

i·so·mer /ísəmər/ *n.* **1** *Chem.* ▲ one of two or more compounds with the same molecular formula but a different arrangement of atoms and different properties. **2** *Physics* one of two or more atomic nuclei that have the same atomic number and the same mass number but different energy states. □□ **i·so·mer·ic** /-mérik/ *adj.* **i·som·er·ism** /īsómərizəm/ *n.* **i·som·er·ize** *v.*

i·so·met·ric /ísəmétrik/ *adj.* **1** of equal measure. **2** *Physiol.* (of muscle action) developing tension while the muscle is prevented from contracting. **3** (of a drawing, etc.) with the plane of projection at equal angles to the three principal axes of the object shown. **4** *Math.* (of a transformation) without change of shape or size. □□ **i·so·met·ri·cal·ly** *adv.* **i·som·e·try** /īsómitree/ *n.* (in sense 4).

i·so·met·rics /ísəmétriks/ *n.pl.* a system of physical exercises in which muscles are caused to act against each other or against a fixed object.

i·so·mor·phic /ísəmáwrfik/ *adj.* (also **i·so·mor·phous** /-fəs/) **1** exactly corresponding in form and relations. **2** *Crystallog.* having the same form. □□ **i·so·morph** *n.* **i·so·mor·phism** *n.*

i·so·pod /ísəpod/ *n.* any crustacean of the order *Isopoda,* including sowbugs and slaters, often parasitic and having a flattened body with seven pairs of legs.

i·sos·ce·les /īsósileez/ *adj.* (of a triangle) having two sides equal.

i·sos·ta·sy /īsóstəsee/ *n. Geol.* the general state of equilibrium of the Earth's crust, with the rise and fall of land relative to sea. □□ **i·so·stat·ic** /ísəstátik/ *adj.*

i·so·therm /ísəthərm/ *n.* **1** a line on a map connecting places having the same temperature at a given time or on average over a given period. **2** a curve for changes in a physical system at a constant temperature. □□ **i·so·ther·mal** *adj.* **i·so·ther·mal·ly** *adv.*

i·so·ton·ic /ísətónik/ *adj.* **1** having the same osmotic pressure. **2** *Physiol.* (of muscle action) taking place with normal contraction. □□ **i·so·ton·i·cal·ly** *adv.* **i·so·to·nic·i·ty** /-tənísitee/ *n.*

i·so·tope /ísətōp/ *n. Chem.* ▲ one of two or more forms of an element differing from each other in relative atomic mass, and in nuclear but not chem-

ical properties. □□ **i·so·top·ic** /-tópik/ *adj.* **i·so·top·i·cal·ly** *adv.* **i·sot·o·py** /īsótəpee, ísətópee/ *n.*

i·so·trop·ic /ísōtrópik, -tróp-/ *adj.* having the same physical properties in all directions. □□ **i·so·trop·i·cal·ly** *adv.* **i·sot·ro·py** /īsótrəpee/ *n.*

ISP *abbr.* Internet service provider.

Is·rae·li /izráylee/ *adj. & n.* ● *adj.* of or relating to the modern state of Israel in the Middle East. ● *n.* **1** a native or national of Israel. **2** a person of Israeli descent.

Is·ra·el·ite /ízreeəlīt, -rəlīt/ *n. hist.* a native of ancient Israel; a Jew.

is·sue /íshoo/ *n. & v.* ● *n.* **1 a** a giving out or circulation of shares, notes, stamps, etc. **b** a quantity of coins, supplies, copies of a newspaper or book, etc., circulated or put on sale at one time. **c** an item or amount given out or distributed. **d** each of a regular series of a magazine, etc. (*the May issue*). **2 a** an outgoing; an outflow. **b** a way out; an outlet, esp. the place of the emergence of a stream, etc. **3** a point in question; an important subject of debate or litigation. **4** a result; an outcome; a decision. **5** *Law* children; progeny (*without male issue*). ● *v.* (**issues**, **issued**, **issuing**) **1** *intr.* (often foll. by *out, forth*) *literary* go or come out. **2** *tr.* **a** send forth; publish; put into circulation. **b** supply, esp. officially or authoritatively (usu. foll. by *to*): *issued orders to the staff*). **3** *intr.* **a** (often foll. by *from*) be derived or result. **b** (foll. by *in*) end; result. **4** *intr.* (foll. by *from*) emerge from a condition. □ **at issue 1** under discussion; in dispute. **2** at variance. **join issue** identify and submit an issue for formal argument (foll. by *with, on*). **make an issue of** make a fuss about; turn into a subject of contention. □□ **is·sue·a·ble** *adj.* **is·su·ance** *n.* **is·sue·less** *adj.* **is·su·er** *n.*

isth·mus /ísməs/ *n.* **1** ▼ a narrow piece of land connecting two larger bodies of land. **2** *Anat.* a narrow part connecting two larger parts. □□ **isth·mi·an** *adj.*

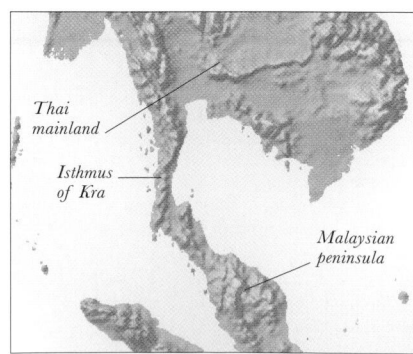

Thai mainland

Isthmus of Kra

Malaysian peninsula

ISTHMUS BETWEEN THAILAND AND MALAYSIA

IT *abbr.* information technology.

It. *abbr.* Italian.

it /it/ *pron.* (*poss.* **its**; *pl.* **they**) **1** the thing (or occas. the animal or child) previously named or in question (*took a stone and threw it*). **2** the person in question (*Who is it? It is I; is it a boy or a girl?*). **3** as the subject of an impersonal verb (*it is raining; it is winter; it is Tuesday; it is two miles to Denver*). **4** as a substitute for a deferred subject or object (*it is intolerable, this delay; it is silly to talk like that; I take it that you agree*). **5** as a substitute for a vague object (*tough it out; run for it!*). **6** as the antecedent to a relative word (*it was an owl I heard*). **7** exactly what is needed (*absolutely it*). **8** the extreme limit of achievement. **9** *colloq.* sexual intercourse; sex appeal. **10** (in children's games) a player who has to perform a required feat, esp. to catch the others. □ **that's it** *colloq.* that is: **1** what is required. **2** the difficulty. **3** the end; enough. **this is it** *colloq.* **1** the expected event is at hand. **2** this is the difficulty.

Ital. *abbr.* Italian.

ital. *abbr.* italic (type).

I·tal·ian /itályən/ *n. & adj.* ● *n.* **1 a** a native or national of Italy. **b** a person of Italian descent. **2** the Romance language used in Italy and parts of Switzerland. ● *adj.* of or relating to Italy or its people or language.

I·tal·ian·ate /itályənayt/ *adj.* of Italian style or appearance.

i·tal·ic /itálik/ *adj. & n.* ● *adj.* **1 a** *Printing* of the sloping kind of letters now used esp. for emphasis or distinction and in foreign words. **b** (of handwriting) compact and pointed like early Italian handwriting. ▷ CALLIGRAPHY. **2** (**Italic**) of ancient Italy. ● *n.* **1** a letter in italic type. **2** this type.

i·tal·i·cize /itálisīz/ *v.tr.* print in italics. □□ **i·tal·i·ci·za·tion** *n.*

itch /ich/ *n. & v.* ● *n.* **1** an irritation in the skin. **2** an impatient desire; a hankering. **3** (prec. by *the*) (in general use) scabies. ● *v.intr.* **1** feel an irritation in the skin, causing a desire to scratch it. **2** (usu. foll. by *to* + infin.) (of a person) feel a desire to do something (*am itching to tell you the news*).

itch·y /íchee/ *adj.* (**itchier**, **itchiest**) having or causing an itch. □□ **itch·i·ness** *n.*

it'd /ítəd/ *contr. colloq.* **1** it had. **2** it would.

i·tem /ítəm/ *n.* **1 a** any of a number of enumerated or listed things. **b** an entry in an account. **2** an article, esp. one for sale (*household items*). **3** a separate or distinct piece of news, information, etc.

i·tem·ize /ítəmīz/ *v.tr.* state or list item by item. □□ **i·tem·i·za·tion** *n.* **i·tem·iz·er** *n.*

it·er·ate /ítərayt/ *v.tr.* repeat; state repeatedly. □□ **it·er·a·tion** /-áyshən/ *n.* **it·er·a·tive** /ítərəytiv, -rətiv/ *adj. Gram.* = FREQUENTATIVE. □□ **it·er·a·tive·ly** *adv.*

I

i·tin·er·ant /ītínərənt, itín-/ *adj. & n.* ● *adj.* traveling from place to place. ● *n.* an itinerant person; a tramp. □□ **i·tin·er·a·cy** *n.* **i·tin·er·an·cy** *n.*

i·tin·er·ar·y /ītínəreree, itín-/ *n. & adj.* ● *n.* (*pl.* **-ies**) **1** a detailed route. **2** a record of travel. **3** a guidebook. ● *adj.* of roads or traveling.

it'll /it'l/ *contr. colloq.* it will; it shall.

its /its/ *poss.pron.* of it; of itself (*can see its advantages*).

it's /its/ *contr.* **1** it is. **2** it has.

it·self /itsélf/ *pron.* emphatic and refl. form of IT. □ **by itself** apart from its surroundings, automatically, spontaneously. **in itself** viewed in its essential qualities (*not in itself a bad thing*).

it·ty-bit·ty /íteebítee/ *adj.* (also **it·sy-bit·sy** /ítsee-bítsee/) *colloq.* usu. *derog.* tiny; insubstantial; slight.

IUD *abbr.* intrauterine (contraceptive) device.

IV *abbr.* intravenous(ly).

I've /īv/ *contr.* I have.

IVF *abbr.* in vitro fertilization.

i·vied /íveed/ *adj.* overgrown with ivy.

i·vo·ry /ívəree, ívree/ *n.* (*pl.* **-ies**) **1** ▶ a hard, creamy-white substance composing the main part of the tusks of an elephant, hippopotamus, walrus, and narwhal. ▷ ELEPHANT. **2** the color of this. **3** (usu. in *pl.*) **a** an article made of ivory. **b** *sl.* anything made of or resembling ivory, esp. a piano key or a tooth. □□ **i·vo·ried** *adj.*

IVORY: 20TH-CENTURY INDIAN IVORY BROOCH

i·vo·ry tow·er *n.* a state of seclusion or separation from the ordinary world and the harsh realities of life.

i·vy /ívee/ *n.* (*pl.* **-ies**) **1** ▶ a climbing evergreen shrub, *Hedera helix*, with usu. dark-green, shining five-angled leaves. **2** any of various other climbing plants including ground ivy and poison ivy.

I·vy League *n.* a group of prestigious universities in the eastern US.

IVY (*Hedera helix* 'White Knight')

I

J

J[1] /jay/ *n.* (also **j**) (*pl.* **Js** or **J's**) the tenth letter of the alphabet.

J[2] *symb.* (also **J.**) joule(s).

jab /jab/ *v. & n.* ● *v.tr.* (**jabbed**, **jabbing**) **1 a** poke roughly. **b** stab. **2** (foll. by *into*) thrust (a thing) hard or abruptly. ● *n.* **1** an abrupt blow with one's fist or a pointed implement. **2** *colloq.* a hypodermic injection, esp. a vaccination.

jab·ber /jábər/ *v. & n.* ● *v.* **1** *intr.* chatter volubly and incoherently. **2** *tr.* utter (words) fast and indistinctly. ● *n.* meaningless jabbering; a gabble.

jab·ber·wock·y /jábərwokee/ *n.* (*pl.* **-ies**) a piece of nonsensical writing or speech, esp. for comic effect.

jab·i·ru /jábiroo/ *n.* a large stork, *Jabiru mycteria*, of Central and S. America.

ja·bot /zhabó, ja-/ *n.* ▶ an ornamental frill or ruffle of lace, etc., on the front of a shirt or blouse.

jabot

JABOT:
18TH-CENTURY
GENTLEMAN'S JABOT

ja·ca·na /zhaakənáa, -sənáa/ *n.* any of various small tropical wading birds of the family Jacanidae, with elongated toes and hind claws which enable them to walk on floating leaves, etc. ▷ WADING BIRD

jac·a·ran·da /jákərándə/ *n.* **1** any tropical American tree of the genus *Jacaranda*, with trumpet-shaped blue flowers. **2** any tropical American tree of the genus *Dalbergia*, with hard scented wood.

ja·cinth /jáysinth, jás-/ *n.* ▶ a reddish-orange variety of zircon used as a gem.

jack /jak/ *n. & v.* ● *n.* **1** a device for lifting heavy objects, esp. the axle of a vehicle, off the ground while changing a wheel, etc. **2** ▼ a playing card with a picture of a man, esp. a soldier, page, or knave, etc. **3** a ship's flag, esp. one flown from the bow and showing nationality. **4** a device using a single plug to connect an electrical circuit. **5** a white ball in lawn bowling, at which players aim. **6 a** (also **jack·stone**) a small piece of metal, etc., used with others in tossing games. **b** (in *pl.*) a game with a ball and jacks. **7** (**Jack**) the familiar form of *John*, typifying the common man or the male of a species (*I'm all right, Jack*). **8** *sl.* money. **9** = LUMBERJACK. **10** = STEEPLEJACK. **11** any of various marine perchlike fish of the family Carangidae, including the amberjack. ● *v.tr.* **1** (usu. foll. by *up*) raise with or as with a jack (in *n.* sense 1). **2** (usu. foll. by *up*) *colloq.* raise, e.g., prices. **3** (foll. by *off*) **a** go away; depart. **b** *coarse sl.* masturbate.

JACINTH

JACKS ON
PLAYING CARDS

□ **every man jack** each and every person. **jack in** (or **up**) esp. *Brit. sl.* abandon an attempt, etc.

jack·al /jákəl/ *n.* **1** any of various wild doglike mammals of the genus *Canis*, esp. *C. aureus*, found in Africa and S. Asia, usu. hunting or scavenging for food in packs. **2** *colloq.* **a** a person who does preliminary drudgery for another. **b** a person who assists another's immoral behavior.

jack·ass /jákas/ *n.* **1** a male ass. **2** a stupid person.

jack·boot /jákboot/ *n.* **1** a large boot reaching above the knee. **2** this as a symbol of fascism or military oppression. □□ **jack·boot·ed** *adj.*

jack·daw /jákdaw/ *n.* ▼ a small gray-headed crow, *Corvus monedula*.

JACKDAW
(*Corvus monedula*)

jack·et /jákit/ *n. & v.* ● *n.* **1 a** a sleeved, short outer garment. **b** a thing worn esp. around the torso for protection or support (*life jacket*). **2** a casing or covering, e.g., as insulation around a boiler. **3** = DUST JACKET. **4** the skin of a potato, esp. when baked whole. **5** an animal's coat. ● *v.tr.* cover with a jacket.

jack·fish /jákfish/ *n.* (*pl.* same) = PIKE[1].

Jack Frost *n.* frost personified.

jack·fruit /jákfroot/ *n.* **1** an East Indian tree, *Artocarpus heterophyllus*, bearing fruit resembling breadfruit. **2** this fruit.

jack·ham·mer /ják-hamər/ *n.* a pneumatic hammer or drill.

jack-in-the-box *n.* a toy figure that springs out of a box when it is opened.

jack-in-the-pul·pit *n.* a N. American plant having an upright flower spike and an over-arching hood-like spathe.

jack·knife /jáknīf/ *n. & v.* ● *n.* (*pl.* **-knives**) **1** a large pocketknife. **2** a dive in which the body is first bent at the waist and then straightened. ● *v.intr.* (**-knifed**, **-knifing**) (of an articulated vehicle) fold against itself in an accidental skidding movement.

jack-of-all-trades *n.* a person who can do many different kinds of work.

jack-o'-lan·tern *n.* **1** a will-o'-the wisp. **2** a lantern made esp. from a pumpkin with holes cut into it for facial features.

jack·pot /jákpot/ *n.* a large prize or amount of winnings, esp. accumulated in a game or lottery, etc. □ **hit the jackpot** *colloq.* **1** win a large prize. **2** have remarkable luck or success.

jack·rab·bit /jákrabit/ *n.* any of various large prairie hares of the genus *Lepus* with very long ears and hind legs.

Jack Rus·sell /jak rúsəl/ *n.* **1** a terrier of a breed with short legs. **2** this breed.

jack·straw /jákstraw/ *n.* **1** a splinter of wood, straw, etc., esp. one of a bundle, pile, etc. **2** (in *pl.*) a game in which a heap of jack-straws is to be removed one at a time without moving the others.

Jac·o·be·an /jákəbee'ən/ *adj. & n.* ● *adj.* **1** of or relating to the reign of James I of England. **2** (of furniture) in the style prevalent then, esp. of the color of dark oak. ● *n.* a Jacobean person.

Jac·o·bin /jákəbin/ *n.* **1** *hist.* a member of a radical democratic club established in Paris in 1789, in the wake of the French Revolution. **2** an extreme political radical.

Jac·o·bite /jákəbīt/ *n. hist.* a supporter of James II of England after his removal from the throne in 1688, or of his family, the Stuarts. □□ **Jac·o·bit·i·cal** /-bítikəl/ *adj.* **Jac·o·bit·ism** *n.*

Ja·cob's lad·der /jáykəbz/ *n.* **1** ▼ a plant, *Polemonium caeruleum*, with corymbs of blue or white flowers, and leaves suggesting a ladder. **2** a rope ladder with wooden rungs.

ladderlike leaves

JACOB'S LADDER
(*Polemonium caeruleum*)

Jac·quard /jákaard, jəkaárd/ *n.* **1** an apparatus using perforated cards that record a pattern and are fitted to a loom to mechanize the weaving of figured fabrics. **2** (in full **Jacquard loom**) a loom fitted with this. **3** a fabric or article made with this, with an intricate variegated pattern.

Ja·cuz·zi /jəkoozee/ *n.* (*pl.* **Jacuzzis**) *Trademark* a large bath with underwater jets of water to massage the body.

jade[1] /jayd/ *n.* **1** ▶ a hard, usu. green stone composed of silicates of calcium and magnesium, or of sodium and aluminum, used for ornaments and implements. **2** the green color of jade.

jade[2] /jayd/ *n.* **1** an inferior or worn-out horse. **2** *derog.* a disreputable woman.

jad·ed /jáydid/ *adj.* tired or worn out; surfeited. □□ **jad·ed·ly** *adv.* **jad·ed·ness** *n.*

jade·ite /jáydīt/ *n.* a green, blue, or white sodium aluminum silicate form of jade. ▷ GEM

JADE: 18TH-CENTURY MEXICAN JADE MASK

jae·ger /yáygər/ *n.* **1** (also **yager**) hunter. **2** (also /jáy-/) any large predatory seabird of the family Stercorariidae that pursues other birds and makes them disgorge the fish they have caught.

jag[1] /jag/ *n. & v.* ● *n.* a sharp projection of rock, etc. ● *v.tr.* (**jagged**, **jagging**) **1** cut or tear unevenly. **2** make indentations in. □□ **jag·ger** *n.*

jag[2] /jag/ *n. sl.* **1** a drinking bout; a spree. **2** a period of indulgence in an activity, emotion, etc.

jag·ged /jágid/ *adj.* **1** with an unevenly cut or torn edge. **2** deeply indented; with sharp points. □□ **jag·ged·ly** *adv.* **jag·ged·ness** *n.*

jag·uar /jágwaar/ *n.* ▼ a large, flesh-eating spotted feline, *Panthera onca*, of Central and S. America.

JAGUAR (*Panthera onca*)

ja·gua·run·di /jágwərúndee/ n. (pl. **jaguarundis**) a long-tailed slender feline, *Felis yaguarondi*, of Central and S. America.

jai a·lai /hí lī, əlí/ n. an indoor court game somewhat resembling handball in which the ball is propelled with large curved wicker baskets.

jail /jayl/ n. & v. (also *Brit.* **gaol** *pronunc.* same) ● n. **1** a place to which persons are committed by a court for detention. **2** confinement in a jail. ● v.tr. put in jail.

jail·bait /jáylbayt/ n. *sl.* a girl under the age of consent.

jail·bird /jáylbərd/ n. (also *Brit.* **gaolbird**) a prisoner or habitual criminal.

jail·break /jáylbrayk/ n. (also *Brit.* **gaolbreak**) an escape from jail.

jail·er /jáylər/ n. (also **jail·or**, *Brit.* **gaoler**) a person in charge of a jail or of the prisoners in it.

Jain /jīn/ n. & adj. (also **Jai·na**) ● n. an adherent of a non-brahminical Indian religion. ● adj. of or relating to this religion. □□ **Jain·ism** n. **Jain·ist** n.

jake /jayk/ adj. *sl.* all right; satisfactory.

ja·la·pe·ño /halapáynyō, -peén-/ n.  a variety of hot pepper commonly used in Mexican and other highly spiced cooking.

ja·lop·y /jəlópee/ n. (pl. **-ies**) *colloq.* a dilapidated old motor vehicle.

jal·ou·sie /jáləsee/ n. a blind or shutter made of a row of angled slats to keep out rain, etc., and control the influx of light.

JALAPEÑO
PEPPER

jam[1] /jam/ v. & n. ● v.tr. & intr. (**jammed**, **jamming**) **1 a** tr. (usu. foll. by *into*) squeeze or wedge into a space. **b** intr. become wedged. **2 a** tr. cause (machinery or a component) to become wedged or immovable so that it cannot work. **b** intr. become jammed in this way. **3** tr. push or cram together in a compact mass. **4** intr. (foll. by *in, onto*) push or crowd (*they jammed onto the bus*). **5** tr. **a** block (a passage, road, etc.) by crowding or obstructing. **b** (foll. by *in*) obstruct the exit of (*we were jammed in*). **6** tr. (usu. foll. by *on*) apply (brakes, etc.) forcefully or abruptly. **7** tr. make (a radio transmission) unintelligible by causing interference. **8** intr. *colloq.* (in jazz, etc.) extemporize with other musicians. ● n. **1** a squeeze or crush. **2** a crowded mass (*traffic jam*). **3** *colloq.* an awkward situation or predicament. **4** a stoppage (of a machine, etc.) due to jamming. **5** (in full **jam session**) *colloq.* improvised playing by a group of jazz musicians. □□ **jam·mer** n.

jam[2] /jam/ n. & v. ● n. **1** a conserve of fruit and sugar boiled to a thick consistency. **2** *Brit. colloq.* something easy or pleasant (*money for jam*). ● v.tr. (**jammed**, **jamming**) **1** spread jam on. **2** make (fruit, etc.) into jam.

jamb /jam/ n. *Archit.* a side post or surface of a doorway, window, or fireplace.

jam·ba·lay·a /júmbəlíə/ n. a dish of rice with shrimp, chicken, etc.

jam·bo·ree /jámbəreé/ n. **1** a celebration or merrymaking. **2** a large rally of Boy Scouts or Girl Scouts.

jam-packed adj. *colloq.* full to capacity.

Jan. abbr. January.

jane /jayn/ n. *sl.* a woman (*a plain jane*).

Jane Doe n. *US* **1** *Law* an anonymous female party, typically the plaintiff, in a legal action. **2** *colloq.* a hypothetical average woman.

jan·gle /jánggəl/ v. & n. ● v. **1** intr. & tr. make, or cause (a bell, etc.) to make, a harsh metallic sound. **2** tr. irritate (the nerves, etc.) by discordant sound or speech, etc. ● n. a harsh metallic sound.

Jang·lish /jángglish/ n. = JAPLISH.

jan·is·sar·y /jániseree/ n. (also **jan·i·zar·y** /-zeree/) (pl. **-ies**) **1** *hist.* a member of the Turkish infantry forming the Sultan's guard in the 14th–19th c. **2** a devoted follower or supporter.

jan·i·tor /jánitər/ n. **1** a caretaker of a building. **2** *Brit.* a doorman. □□ **jan·i·to·ri·al** /-táwreeəl/ adj.

Jan·u·ar·y /jányōoeree/ n. (pl. **-ies**) the first month of the year.

Jap /jap/ n. & adj. *colloq.* often *offens.* = JAPANESE.

ja·pan /jəpán/ n. & v. ● n. **1** ▼ a hard, usu. black varnish, esp. of a kind originally from Japan. **2** work in a Japanese style. ● v.tr. (**japanned**, **japanning**) **1** varnish with japan. **2** make black and glossy as with japan.

*japanned
finish*

JAPAN: JAPANNED AND LACQUERED
ANTIQUE SCREEN

Jap·a·nese /jápəneéz/ n. & adj. ● n. (pl. same) **1 a** a native or national of Japan. **b** a person of Japanese descent. **2** the language of Japan. ● adj. of or relating to Japan, its people, or its language.

Jap·a·nese bee·tle n. an iridescent green and brown beetle that is a garden and crop pest.

jape /jayp/ n. & v. ● n. a practical joke. ● v.intr. play a joke. □□ **jap·er·y** n.

Jap·lish /jáplish/ n. a blend of Japanese and English, used in Japan.

ja·pon·i·ca /jəpónikə/ n. a camellia, *Camellia japonica*, with variously colored waxy flowers.

jar[1] /jaar/ n. **1** a container of glass, earthenware, plastic, etc., usu. cylindrical. **2** the contents of this. □□ **jar·ful** n. (pl. **-fuls**).

jar[2] /jaar/ v. & n. ● v. (**jarred**, **jarring**) **1** intr. (often foll. by *on*) (of sound, words, manner, etc.) sound discordant or grating (on the nerves, etc.). **2 a** tr. (foll. by *against, on*) strike or cause to strike with vibration or a grating sound. **b** intr. (of a body affected) vibrate gratingly. **3** tr. send a shock through (a part of the body) (*the fall jarred his neck*). **4** intr. (often foll. by *with*) (of an opinion, fact, etc.) be at variance; be in conflict or in dispute. ● n. **1** a jarring sound or sensation. **2** a physical shock or jolt. **3** lack of harmony; disagreement.

jar[3] /jaar/ n. □ **on the jar** ajar.

jar·di·niere /jáard'neér, zhaárdinyáir/ n. (also **jardinière**) **1** an ornamental pot or stand for the display of growing plants. **2** a dish of mixed vegetables.

jar·gon /jaárgon/ n. **1** words or expressions used by a particular group or profession (*medical jargon*). **2** barbarous or debased language. **3** gibberish. □□ **jar·gon·ic** /-gónik/ adj. **jar·gon·is·tic** adj. **jar·gon·ize** v.tr. & intr.

jas·mine /jázmin/ n. (also **jes·sa·mine** /jésəmin/) ► any of various fragrant ornamental shrubs of the genus *Jasminum* usu. with white or yellow flowers.

JASMINE:
YELLOW JASMINE
(*Jasminum humile*)

jas·per /jáspər/ n. ► an opaque variety of quartz, usu. red, yellow, or brown in color.

JASPER:
RED JASPER

ja·to /jáytō/ n. (pl. **-os**) *Aeron.* **1** jet-assisted takeoff. **2** an auxiliary power unit providing extra thrust at takeoff.

jaun·dice /jáwndis/ n. & v. ● n. **1** *Med.* a condition with yellowing of the skin or whites of the eyes, often caused by obstruction of the bile duct or by liver disease. **2** disordered (esp. mental) vision. **3** envy. ● v.tr. **1** affect with jaundice. **2** (esp. as **jaundiced** adj.) affect (a person) with envy, resentment, or jealousy.

jaunt /jawnt/ n. & v. ● n. a short excursion for enjoyment. ● v.intr. take a jaunt.

jaun·ty /jáwntee/ adj. (**jauntier, jauntiest**) **1** cheerful and self-confident. **2** sprightly. □□ **jaun·ti·ly** adv. **jaun·ti·ness** n.

Ja·van /jaávən/ n. & adj. = JAVANESE.

Jav·a·nese /jávəneéz, jaá-/ n. & adj. ● n. (pl. same) **1 a** a native of Java in Indonesia. **b** a person of Javanese descent. **2** the language of Java. ● adj. of or relating to Java, its people, or its language.

jave·lin /jávəlin, jávlin/ n. **1** a light spear thrown in a competitive sport or as a weapon. **2** the athletic event or sport of throwing the javelin.

jaw /jaw/ n. & v. ● n. **1 a** each of the upper and lower bony structures in vertebrates forming the framework of the mouth and containing the teeth. ▷ VERTEBRATE. **b** the parts of certain invertebrates used for the ingestion of food. **2 a** (in *pl.*) the mouth with its bones and teeth. **b** the narrow mouth of a valley, channel, etc. **c** the gripping parts of a tool or machine. **d** gripping power (*jaws of death*). **3** *colloq.* **a** talkativeness; tedious talk. **b** a sermonizing talk; a lecture. ● v. *colloq.* **1** intr. speak, esp. at tedious length. **2** tr. **a** persuade by talking. **b** admonish or lecture.

jaw·bone /jáwbōn/ n. **1** each of the two bones forming the lower jaw in most mammals. ▷ VERTEBRATE. **2** these two combined into one in other mammals.

jaw·break·er /jáwbraykər/ n. *colloq.* a word that is very long or hard to pronounce. **2** a round, very hard candy.

jaw-drop·ping adj. *colloq.* amazing.

jay /jay/ n. & v. **1 a** ▼ a noisy chattering European bird, *Garrulus glandarius*, with vivid pinkish-brown, blue, black, and white plumage. ▷ PASSERINE. **b** any other bird of the subfamily Garrulinae. **2** a person who chatters impertinently.

JAY: EURASIAN JAY
(*Garrulus glandarius*)

jay·walk /jáywawk/ v.intr. cross or walk in the street or road without regard for traffic. □□ **jay·walk·er** n.

jazz /jaz/ n. & v. ● n. **1** music of American origin characterized by improvisation, syncopation, and usu. a regular or forceful rhythm. **2** *sl.* pretentious talk or behavior, nonsensical stuff (*all that jazz*). ● v.intr. play or dance to jazz. □ **jazz up** brighten or enliven. □□ **jazz·er** n.

jazz·y /jázee/ adj. (**jazzier, jazziest**) **1** of or like jazz. **2** vivid; unrestrained; showy. □□ **jazz·i·ly** adv. **jazz·i·ness** n.

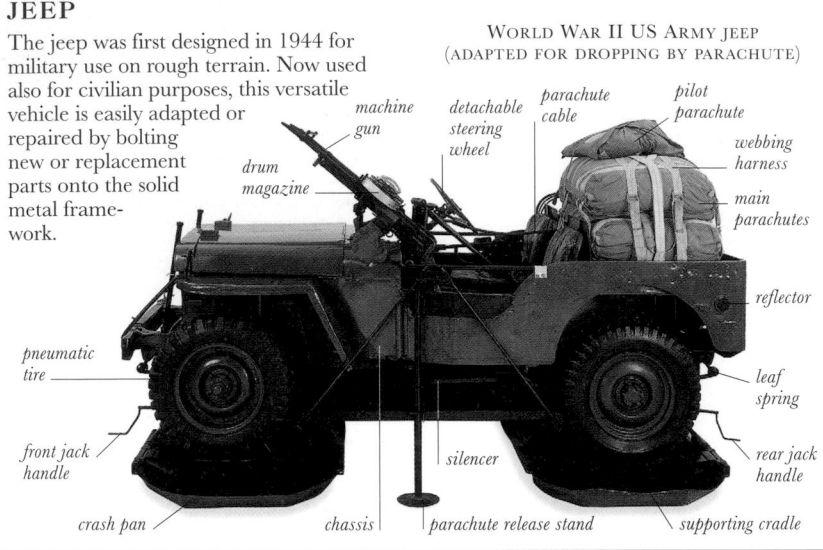

JEEP

The jeep was first designed in 1944 for military use on rough terrain. Now used also for civilian purposes, this versatile vehicle is easily adapted or repaired by bolting new or replacement parts onto the solid metal framework.

WORLD WAR II US ARMY JEEP
(ADAPTED FOR DROPPING BY PARACHUTE)

machine gun · drum magazine · detachable steering wheel · parachute cable · pilot parachute · webbing harness · main parachutes · reflector · leaf spring · rear jack handle · pneumatic tire · front jack handle · silencer · crash pan · chassis · parachute release stand · supporting cradle

JCS *abbr.* (also **J.C.S.**) Joint Chiefs of Staff.

jct. *abbr.* junction.

jeal·ous /jélэs/ *adj.* **1** (often foll. by *of*) fiercely protective (of rights, etc.). **2** afraid, suspicious, or resentful of rivalry in love or affection. **3** (often foll. by *of*) envious or resentful (of a person or a person's advantages, etc.). **4** (of God) intolerant of disloyalty. **5** (of inquiry, supervision, etc.) vigilant. □□ **jeal·ous·ly** *adv.*

jeal·ous·y /jélэsee/ *n.* (*pl.* **-ies**) **1** a jealous state or feeling. **2** an instance of this.

jean /jeen/ *n.* twilled cotton cloth.

jeans /jeenz/ *n.pl.* pants made of jean or (more usually) denim, for informal wear.

jeep /jeep/ *n.* (also *Trademark* **Jeep**) ▲ a small, sturdy, esp. military motor vehicle with four-wheel drive.

jee·pers /jéepэrz/ *int. sl.* expressing surprise, etc.

jeer /jeer/ *v. & n.* ● *v.* **1** *intr.* (usu. foll. by *at*) scoff derisively. **2** *tr.* scoff at; deride. ● *n.* a scoff or taunt. □□ **jeer·ing·ly** *adv.*

jeez /jeez/ *int. sl.* a mild expression of surprise, discovery, etc. (cf. GEE[1]).

je·fe /héfay/ *n. US colloq.* a boss or leader; a person in charge of something.

je·had var. of JIHAD.

Je·ho·vah /jэhóvэ/ *n.* the Hebrew name of God in the Old Testament.

Je·ho·vah's Wit·ness *n.* a member of a millenarian Christian sect rejecting the supremacy of government and religious institutions over personal conscience, faith, etc.

je·june /jijóon/ *adj.* **1** intellectually unsatisfying; shallow. **2** puerile. **3** (of ideas, writings, etc.) meager; scanty; dry and uninteresting. **4** (of the land) barren; poor. □□ **je·june·ly** *adv.* **je·june·ness** *n.*

je·ju·num /jijóonэm/ *n. Anat.* the part of the small intestine between the duodenum and ileum. ▷ INTESTINE

Jek·yll and Hyde /jékil эnd híd/ *n.* a person alternately displaying opposing good and evil personalities.

jell /jel/ *v.intr. colloq.* **1 a** set as a jelly. **b** (of ideas, etc.) take a definite form. **2** (of two different things) cohere.

jel·la·ba var. of DJELLABA.

jel·ly /jélee/ *n. & v.* ● *n.* (*pl.* **-ies**) **1 a** a gelatinous preparation of fruit juice, etc., for use as a jam or a condiment (*grape jelly*). **b** esp. *Brit.* a soft, stiffish, semitransparent preparation of boiled sugar and fruit juice or milk, etc., often cooled in a mold and eaten as a dessert. **c** a similar preparation derived from meat, bones, etc., and gelatin (*marrowbone jelly*). **2** any substance of a similar consistency. **3** an inexpensive sandal or shoe made of molded plastic. **4** *Brit. sl.* gelignite. ● *v.* (**-ies, -ied**) **1** *intr. & tr.* set or cause to set as a jelly; congeal. **2** *tr.* set (food) in a jelly (*jellied eels*). □□ **jel·ly·like** *adj.*

jel·ly bag *n.* a bag for straining juice from fruit to make jelly.

jel·ly bean *n.* a chewy, gelatinous candy in the shape of a bean with a hard sugar coating.

jel·ly·fish /jéleefish/ *n.* (*pl.* usu. same) **1** ▼ a marine coelenterate of the class Scyphozoa having an umbrella-shaped jellylike body and stinging tentacles. ▷ CNIDARIAN. **2** *colloq.* a feeble person.

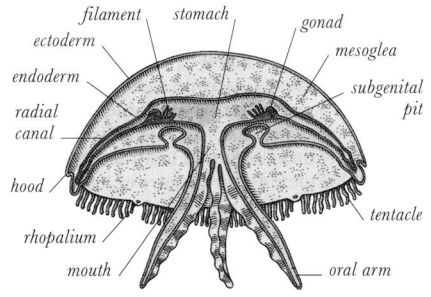

filament · stomach · gonad · ectoderm · mesoglea · endoderm · subgenital pit · radial canal · hood · tentacle · rhopalium · mouth · oral arm

JELLYFISH: ANATOMY OF A JELLYFISH

jel·ly roll *n.* a rolled sponge cake with a jelly filling.

je ne sais quoi /zhэ nэ say kwáa/ *n.* an indefinable something.

jen·net /jénit/ *n.* a small Spanish horse.

jen·ny /jénee/ *n.* (*pl.* **-ies**) **1** *hist.* = SPINNING JENNY. **2** a female donkey or ass. **3** a locomotive crane. □ **jenny wren** a popular name for a female wren.

jeop·ard·ize /jépэrdīz/ *v.tr.* endanger; put into jeopardy.

jeop·ard·y /jépэrdee/ *n.* **1** danger, esp. of severe harm or loss. **2** *Law* danger resulting from being on trial for a criminal offense.

Jer. *abbr.* Jeremiah (Old Testament).

jerbil esp. *Brit.* var. of GERBIL.

jer·bo·a /jэrbóэ/ *n.* ▶ any small desert rodent of the family Dipodidae with long hind legs and the ability to make long jumps.

JERBOA (*Jaculus jaculus*)

jer·e·mi·ad /jérimíad/ *n.* a doleful complaint or lamentation; a list of woes.

Jer·e·mi·ah /jérimíэ/ *n.* a dismal prophet; a denouncer of the times.

jerk[1] /jэrk/ *n. & v.* ● *n.* **1** a sharp sudden pull, twist, twitch, start, etc. **2** a spasmodic muscular twitch. **3** *sl.* a fool; a stupid or contemptible person. ● *v.* **1** *intr.* move with a jerk. **2** *tr.* pull, thrust, twist, etc., with a jerk. **3** *tr.* throw with a suddenly arrested motion. **4** *tr. Weight Lifting* raise (a weight) from shoulder level to above the head. □ **jerk off** *coarse sl.* masturbate. ¶ Usually considered a taboo use. □□ **jerk·er** *n.*

jerk[2] /jэrk/ *v.tr.* cure (beef) by cutting it in long slices and drying it in the sun.

jer·kin /jэ́rkin/ *n.* **1** a sleeveless jacket. **2** *hist.* a man's close-fitting jacket, often of leather.

jerk·y /jэ́rkee/ *adj.* (**jerkier, jerkiest**) **1** having sudden abrupt movements. **2** spasmodic. □□ **jerk·i·ly** *adv.* **jerk·i·ness** *n.*

jer·o·bo·am /jérэbóэm/ *n.* a wine bottle of 4–12 times the ordinary size.

jer·ry /jéree/ *n.* (*pl.* **-ies**) *Brit. sl.* a chamber pot.

jer·ry-build·er /jéribildэr/ *n.* a builder of unsubstantial houses, etc., with poor-quality materials. □□ **jer·ry-build·ing** *n.* **jer·ry-built** *adj.*

jer·ry can /jérikan/ *n.* (also **jer·ry-can, jer·ri·can**) a flat-sided 5-gallon container (orig. German) for liquids, esp. fuel or water.

jer·ry·man·der esp. *Brit.* var. of GERRYMANDER.

jer·sey /jэ́rzee/ *n.* (*pl.* **-eys**) **1 a** a knitted, usu. woolen pullover or similar garment. **b** a plain-knitted (orig. woolen) fabric. **2** (**Jersey**) a light brown dairy cow from Jersey.

Je·ru·sa·lem ar·ti·choke /jэróosэlэm/ *n.* **1** a species of sunflower, *Helianthus tuberosus*, with edible underground tubers. **2** ▶ this tuber used as a vegetable.

jess /jes/ *n. & v.* ● *n.* a short strap of leather, silk, etc., put around the leg of a hawk in falconry. ● *v.tr.* put jesses on (a hawk, etc.).

jes·sa·mine var. of JASMINE.

jest /jest/ *n. & v.* ● *n.* **1 a** a joke. **b** fun. **2 a** raillery; banter. **b** an object of derision (*a standing jest*). ● *v.intr.* **1** joke; make jests. **2** fool about; play or act triflingly. □ **in jest** in fun. □□ **jest·ful** *adj.*

jest·er /jéstэr/ *n.* a professional joker or fool at a medieval court, etc., traditionally wearing a cap and bells and carrying a scepter.

Jes·u·it /jézhōoit, jézōo-, jézyōo-/ *n.* a member of the Society of Jesus, a Roman Catholic order founded by St. Ignatius Loyola and others in 1534.

Jes·u·it·i·cal /jézhōo-ítikэl, jézōo-, -yōo-/ *adj.* **1** of or concerning the Jesuits. **2** often *offens.* dissembling or equivocating, in the manner once associated with Jesuits. □□ **Jes·u·it·i·cal·ly** *adv.*

Je·sus /jéezэs/ *n.* the name of the central figure of the Christian religion d. *c.* AD 30.

jet[1] /jet/ *n. & v.* ● *n.* **1** a stream of water, steam, gas, flame, etc., shot out esp. from a small opening. **2** a spout or nozzle for emitting water, etc., in this

JERKIN: 16TH-CENTURY LEATHER JERKIN

punched design

tuber

JERUSALEM ARTICHOKE (*Helianthus tuberosus*)

JET ENGINE

The simplest type of jet engine, the turbojet, produces thrust by burning a combination of fuel and air, which releases a powerful stream of hot exhaust gases. This also turns a turbine, which runs an air compressor, which in turn forces more air into the combustion chamber. In a turbofan jet engine, a low-pressure turbine drives a fan that forces air through bypass ducts to join the exhaust stream, producing dual thrust. A turboprop jet engine spins a propeller and expels exhaust gases, both producing thrust.

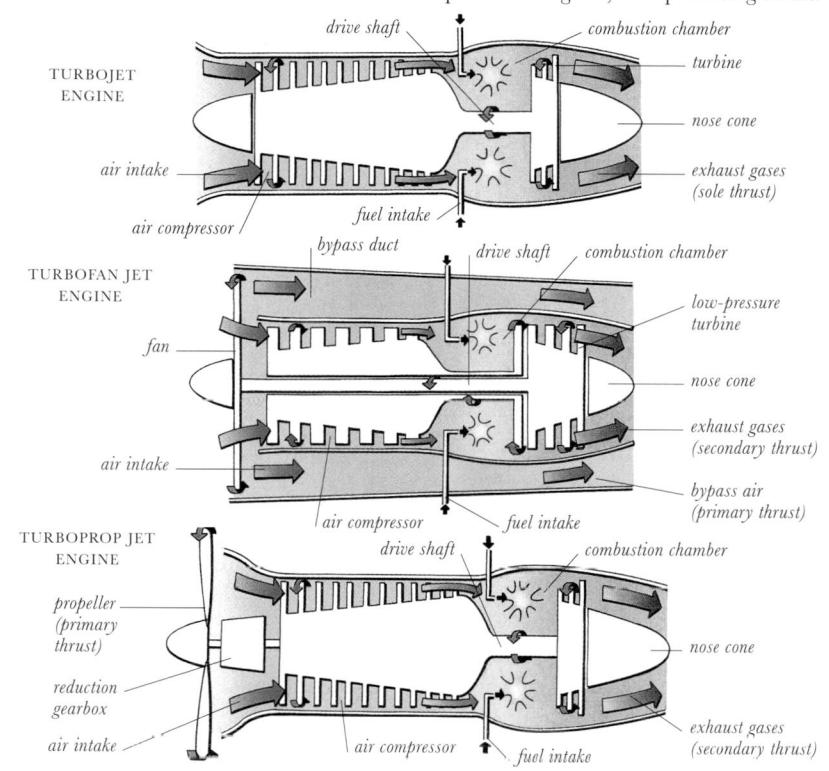

TURBOJET ENGINE — drive shaft, combustion chamber, turbine, nose cone, exhaust gases (sole thrust), fuel intake, air compressor, air intake

TURBOFAN JET ENGINE — bypass duct, drive shaft, combustion chamber, low-pressure turbine, nose cone, exhaust gases (secondary thrust), bypass air (primary thrust), fuel intake, air compressor, air intake, fan

TURBOPROP JET ENGINE — drive shaft, combustion chamber, nose cone, exhaust gases (secondary thrust), fuel intake, air compressor, air intake, reduction gearbox, propeller (primary thrust)

way. **3 a ▲** a jet engine. **b** an aircraft powered by one or more jet engines. ● *v.* (**jetted, jetting**) **1** *intr.* spurt out in jets. **2** *tr. & intr. colloq.* send or travel by jet.

jet² /jet/ *n.* **1 a** ▼ a hard black variety of lignite capable of being carved and highly polished. ▷ GEM. **b** (*attrib.*) made of this. **2** (in full **jet-black**) a deep glossy black color.

jet·é /zhətáy/ *n. Ballet* a spring or leap with one leg forward and the other stretched backward.

jet en·gine *n.* ▲ an engine using jet propulsion for forward thrust, esp. of an aircraft.

jet lag *n.* extreme tiredness and other bodily effects felt after a long flight involving marked differences of local time.

JET: MODERN TURKISH JET NECKLACE

jet-pro·pelled *adj.* **1** having jet propulsion. **2** (of a person, etc.) very fast.

jet pro·pul·sion *n.* propulsion by the backward ejection of a high-speed jet of gas, etc.

jet·sam /jétsəm/ *n.* discarded material washed ashore, esp. that thrown overboard to lighten a ship, etc. (cf. FLOTSAM).

jet set *n. colloq.* wealthy people frequently traveling by air, esp. for pleasure. □□ **jet-set·ter** *n.*

jet stream *n.* **1** a narrow current of very strong winds encircling the globe several miles above the earth. **2** the stream of exhaust from a jet engine.

jet·ti·son /jétisən, -zən/ *v. & n.* ● *v.tr.* **1 a** throw (esp. heavy material) overboard to lighten a ship, hot-air balloon, etc. **b** drop (goods) from an aircraft. **2** abandon; get rid of (something no longer wanted). ● *n.* the act of jettisoning.

jet·ty /jétee/ *n.* (*pl.* **-ies**) **1** a pier or breakwater constructed to protect or defend a harbor, coast, etc. **2** a landing pier.

Jew /jōo/ *n.* a person of Hebrew descent or whose religion is Judaism.

jew·el /jōoəl/ *n. & v.* ● *n.* **1 a** a precious stone. **b** this as used for its hardness as a bearing in watchmaking. **2** a personal ornament containing a jewel or jewels. **3** a precious person or thing. ● *v.tr.* (**jeweled, jeweling**; esp. *Brit.* **jewelled, jewelling**) **1** (esp. as **jeweled** *adj.*) adorn or set with jewels. **2** (in watchmaking) set with jewels. □□ **jew·el·like** *adj.*

jew·el box *n.* a plastic case for a compact disc or CD-ROM.

jew·el·er /jōoələr/ *n.* (esp. *Brit.* **jeweller**) a maker of or dealer in jewels or jewelry.

jew·el·er's rouge *n.* finely ground rouge for polishing.

jew·el·ry /jōoəlree/ *n.* (esp. *Brit.* **jewellery** /jōoəlree/) jewels or other ornamental objects, esp. for personal adornment, regarded collectively.

jew·el·ry box *n.* a box in which jewelry is kept.

Jew·ish /jōoish/ *adj.* **1** of or relating to Jews. **2** of Judaism. □□ **Jew·ish·ly** *adv.* **Jew·ish·ness** *n.*

Jew·ry /jōoree/ *n.* (*pl.* **-ies**) **1** Jews collectively. **2** *hist.* a Jews' quarter in a town, etc.

Jew's (or **Jews'**) **harp** *n.* a small lyre-shaped musical instrument held between the teeth and struck with the finger.

Jez·e·bel /jézəbel/ *n.* a shameless or immoral woman.

jg *abbr.* (also **J.G.**) *US Navy* junior grade.

jib¹ /jib/ *n. & v.* ● *n.* **1** a triangular staysail from the outer end of the jibboom to the top of the foremast or from the bowsprit to the masthead. ▷ SCHOONER, SHIP. **2** the projecting arm of a crane. ● *v.tr. & intr.* (**jibbed, jibbing**) (of a sail, etc.) pull or swing around from one side of the ship to the other; jibe.

jib² /jib/ *v.intr.* (**jibbed, jibbing**) esp. *Brit.* **1 a** (of an animal, esp. a horse) stop and refuse to go on; move backward or sideways instead of going on. **b** (of a person) refuse to continue. **2** (foll. by *at*) show aversion to (a person or course of action). □□ **jib·ber** *n.*

jib·ba /jíbə/ *n.* (also **jib·bah**) a long coat worn by Muslims.

jibe¹ var. of GIBE.

jibe² /jīb/ *v. & n.* (*Brit.* **gybe**) ● *v.* **1** *intr.* (of a fore-and-aft sail or boom) swing across in wearing or running before the winds. **2** *tr.* cause (a sail) to do this. **3** *intr.* (of a ship or its crew) change course so that this happens. ● *n.* a change of course causing jibing.

jibe³ /jīb/ *v.intr.* (usu. foll. by *with*) *colloq.* agree; be in accord.

jiff /jif/ *n.* (also **jif·fy**, *pl.* **-ies**) *colloq.* a short time; a moment (*in a jiffy; half a jiff*).

jig /jig/ *n. & v.* ● *n.* **1 a** a lively dance with leaping movements. **b** the music for this, usu. in triple time. **2** a device that holds a piece of work and guides the tools operating on it. ● *v.* (**jigged, jigging**) **1** *intr.* dance a jig. **2** *tr. & intr.* move quickly and jerkily up and down. **3** *tr.* work on or equip with a jig or jigs.

jig·ger¹ /jígər/ *n.* **1** *Naut.* **a** a small tackle consisting of a double and single block with a rope. **b** a small sail at the stern. **c** a small smack having this. **2** *sl.* a gadget. **3** *Golf* an iron club with a narrow face. **4** *Billiards colloq.* a cue rest. **5 a** a measure of spirits, etc. **b** a small glass holding this. **6** a person or thing that jigs.

jig·ger² /jígər/ *n.* **1** = CHIGOE. **2** = CHIGGER 2.

jig·gered /jígərd/ *adj. colloq.* (as a mild oath) confounded (*I'll be jiggered*).

jig·gle /jígəl/ *v.* (often foll. by *about*, etc.) **1** *tr.* shake lightly; rock jerkily. **2** *intr.* fidget. □□ **jig·gly** *adj.*

jig·gy /jígee/ *adj. chiefly US colloq.* **1** trembling, esp. as the result of drug withdrawal; jittery or fidgety. **2** mentally disturbed; crazy. **3** uninhibited, often in a sexual manner. **4** attractive or stylish.

jig·saw /jígsaw/ *n.* **1 a** (in full **jigsaw puzzle**) a puzzle consisting of a picture on board or wood, etc., cut into irregular interlocking pieces to be reassembled. **b** a mental puzzle resolvable by assembling various pieces of information. **2** ▶ a machine saw with a fine blade enabling it to cut curved lines in a sheet of wood, metal, etc. ▷ SAW

JIGSAW

fine blade

ji·had /jihaád/ *n.* (also **je·had**) a holy war undertaken by Muslims against unbelievers.

jil·lion /jílyən/ *n. colloq.* a very large indefinite number.

jilt /jilt/ *v. & n.* ● *v.tr.* abruptly reject or abandon (a lover, etc.). ● *n.* a person (esp. a woman) who jilts a lover.

jim crow /jim krṓ/ *n.* (also **Jim Crow**) **1** the practice of segregating blacks. **2** *offens.* a black person. **3** an implement for straightening iron bars or bending rails by screw pressure. □□ **jim crow·ism** *n.* (in sense 1).

jim·my /jímee/ *n. & v.* (*Brit.* **jemmy** /jémee/) ● *n.* (*pl.* **-ies**) a burglar's short crowbar, usu. made in sections. ● *v.tr.* (**-ies, -ied**) force open with a jimmy.

jim·son·weed /jímsənweed/ *n.* = THORN APPLE.

jin·gle /jínggəl/ *n. & v.* ● *n.* **1** a mixed noise as of bells or light metal objects being shaken together.

J

2 a a repetition of the same sound in words, esp. as an aid to memory or to attract attention. **b** a short verse of this kind used in advertising, etc. ● *v.intr. & tr.* make or cause to make a jingling sound. □□ **jin·gly** *adj.* (**jinglier, jingliest**).

jin·go /jínggō/ *n.* (*pl.* **-oes**) a supporter of policy favoring war; a blustering patriot. □□ **jin·go·ism** *n.* **jin·go·ist** *n.* **jin·go·is·tic** /-gō-ístik/ *adj.*

jin·ni /jínee, jinée/ *n.* (also **jinn, djinn** /jin/) (*pl.* **jinn** or **jinns, djinn** or **djinns**) (in Muslim mythology) an intelligent being lower than the angels, able to appear in human and animal forms, and having power over people.

jinx /jingks/ *n. & v. colloq.* ● *n.* a person or thing that seems to cause bad luck. ● *v.tr.* (often in *passive*) subject (a person) to an unlucky force.

jit·ney /jítnee/ *n. N. Amer. colloq.* a bus or other vehicle carrying passengers for a low fare (originally five cents).

jit·ter /jítər/ *n. & v. colloq.* ● *n.* (**the jitters**) extreme nervousness. ● *v.intr.* be nervous; act nervously. □□ **jit·ter·y** *adj.* **jit·ter·i·ness** *n.*

jit·ter·bug /jítərbug/ *n. & v.* ● *n.* **1** a nervous person. **2** *hist.* **a** a fast popular dance. **b** a person fond of dancing this. ● *v.intr.* (**-bugged, -bugging**) dance the jitterbug.

jiu·jit·su var. of JUJUTSU.

jive /jīv/ *n. & v.* ● *n.* **1** a jerky lively style of dance esp. popular in the 1950s. **2** music for this. **3** *sl.* talk, conversation, esp. when misleading or pretentious. ● *v.intr.* **1** dance the jive. **2** play jive music. □□ **jiv·er** *n.*

job /job/ *n. & v.* ● *n.* **1** a piece of work, esp. one done for hire or profit. **2** a paid position of employment. **3** *colloq.* anything one has to do. **4** *colloq.* a difficult task (*had a job to find them*). **5** a product of work, esp. if well done. **6** *Computing* an item of work regarded separately. **7** *sl.* a crime, esp. a robbery. **8** a transaction in which private advantage prevails over duty or public interest. **9** a state of affairs or set of circumstances (*is a bad job*). ● *v.* (**jobbed, jobbing**) **1 a** *intr.* do jobs; do piecework. **b** *tr.* (usu. foll. by *out*) let or deal with for profit; subcontract. **2 a** *intr.* deal in stocks. **b** *tr.* buy and sell (stocks or goods) as a middleman. **3 a** *intr.* turn a position of trust to private advantage. **b** *tr.* deal corruptly with (a matter). **4** *tr. sl.* swindle. □ **jobs for the boys** *colloq.* profitable situations, etc., to reward one's supporters. **make a job** (or **good job**) **of** do thoroughly or successfully. **on the job** *colloq.* **1** at work; in the course of doing a piece of work. **2** *coarse* engaged in sexual intercourse. **out of a job** unemployed.

job ac·tion *n.* any action, esp. a strike, taken by employees as a protest.

job·ber /jóbər/ *n.* **1 a** a wholesaler. **b** *derog.* a broker (see BROKER 2). **2** *Brit.* before 1986, a principal or wholesaler dealing on the stock exchange. **3** a person who jobs.

job·ber·y /jóbəree/ *n.* corrupt dealing.

job con·trol lan·guage *n. Computing* a language enabling the user to determine the tasks to be undertaken by the operating system.

job·less /jóblis/ *adj.* without a job; unemployed. □□ **job·less·ness** *n.*

job lot *n.* a miscellaneous group of articles, esp. bought together.

job-shar·ing *n.* an arrangement by which a full-time job is done jointly by several part-time employees who share the remuneration.

jock[1] /jok/ *n. colloq.* a jockey.

jock[2] /jok/ *n. sl.* **1** = JOCK-STRAP. **2** an athlete.

jock·ey /jókee/ *n. & v.* ● *n.* (*pl.* **-eys**) ▶ a rider in horse races, esp. a professional one. ● *v.* (**-eys, -eyed**) **1** *tr.* **a** trick or cheat (a person). **b** outwit. **2** (foll. by *away,*

out, in, etc.) draw (a person) by trickery. **3** *intr.* cheat. □ **jockey for position** try to gain an advantageous position, esp. by skillful maneuvering or unfair action. □□ **jock·ey·dom** *n.* **jock·ey·ship** *n.*

jock·strap /jókstrap/ *n.* a support or protection for the male genitals, worn esp. by athletes.

jo·cose /jōkós/ *adj.* **1** playful in style. **2** fond of joking; jocular. □□ **jo·cose·ly** *adv.* **jo·cose·ness** *n.* **jo·cos·i·ty** /-kósitee/ *n.* (*pl.* **-ies**).

joc·u·lar /jókyələr/ *adj.* **1** merry; fond of joking. **2** of the nature of a joke; humorous. □□ **joc·u·lar·i·ty** /-láritee/ *n.* (*pl.* **-ies**). **joc·u·lar·ly** *adv.*

joc·und /jókənd, jó-/ *adj. literary* merry; cheerful; sprightly. □□ **jo·cun·di·ty** /jəkúnditee/ *n.* (*pl.* **-ies**). **joc·und·ly** *adv.*

jodh·purs /jódpərz/ *n.pl.* long breeches for riding, etc., close-fitting from the knee to the ankle. ▷ SHOW JUMPING

Joe Blow /jō blō/ *n. colloq.* a hypothetical average man.

jo·ey /jóee/ *n.* (*pl.* **-eys**) *Austral.* **1** a young kangaroo. **2** a young animal.

jog /jog/ *v. & n.* ● *v.* (**jogged, jogging**) **1** *intr.* run at a slow pace, esp. as physical exercise. **2** *intr.* (of a horse) move at a jog trot. **3** *intr.* (often foll. by *on, along*) proceed laboriously; trudge. **4** *intr.* go on one's way. **5** *intr.* proceed; get through the time (*we must jog on somehow*). **6** *intr.* move up and down with an unsteady motion. **7** *tr.* nudge (a person), esp. to arouse attention. **8** *tr.* shake with a push or jerk. **9** *tr.* stimulate (a person's or one's own memory). ● *n.* **1** a shake, push, or nudge. **2** a slow walk or trot.

jog·ger /jógər/ *n.* a person who jogs, esp. one who runs for physical exercise.

jog·gle /jógəl/ *v. & n.* ● *v.tr. & intr.* shake or move by or as if by repeated jerks. ● *n.* **1** a slight shake. **2** the act or action of joggling.

john /jon/ *n. sl.* a toilet or bathroom.

John Bull /jon bŏŏl/ *n.* a personification of England or the typical Englishman.

John Doe *n.* **1** *Law,* chiefly *N. Amer.* an anonymous party in a legal action. **2** *N. Amer. colloq.* a name used to represent a person in a hypothetical situation.

John Do·ry /jon dáwree/ *n.* (*pl.* **-ies**) ▶ a European marine fish, *Zeus faber,* with a laterally flattened body and a black spot on each side.

John Hop /jon hóp/ *n. Austral. sl.* a police officer.

john·ny /jónee/ *n.* (*pl.* **-ies**) **1** *colloq.* (also **Johnny**) a fellow; a man. **2** *sl.* a short-sleeved, collarless gown worn by patients in hospitals, examining rooms, etc.

john·ny-come-late·ly *n. colloq.* a recently arrived person.

joie de vi·vre /zhwáa də véevrə/ *n.* a feeling of healthy and exuberant enjoyment of life.

join /joyn/ *v. & n.* ● *v.* **1** *tr.* (often foll. by *to, together*) put together; fasten; unite (one thing or person to another or several together). **2** *tr.* connect (points) by a line, etc. **3** *tr.* become a member of (an association, society, organization, etc.). **4** *tr.* take one's place with or in (a company, group, procession, etc.). **5** *tr.* **a** come into the company of (a person). **b** (foll. by *in*) take part with (others) in an activity, etc. (*joined me in condemnation of the outrage*). **c** (foll. by *for*) share the company of for a specified

occasion (*may I join you for lunch?*). **6** *intr.* (often foll. by *with, to*) come together; be united. **7** *intr.* (often foll. by *in*) take part with others in an activity, etc. **8** *tr.* be or become connected or continuous with (*the Gila River joins the Colorado at Yuma*). ● *n.* a point, line, or surface at which two or more things are joined. □ **join battle** begin fighting. **join forces** combine efforts. **join hands 1 a** clasp each other's hands. **b** clasp one's hands together. **2** combine in an action or enterprise. **join up 1** enlist for military service. **2** (often foll. by *with*) unite; connect. □□ **join·a·ble** *adj.*

join·der /jóyndər/ *n. Law* the act of bringing together.

join·er /jóynər/ *n.* **1** a person who makes furniture and light woodwork. **2** *colloq.* a person who readily joins societies, etc. □□ **join·er·y** *n.* (in sense 1).

joint /joynt/ *n., adj., & v.* ● *n.* **1 a** a place at which two things are joined together. **b** a point at which, or a contrivance by which, two parts of an artificial structure are joined. **2** ▶ a structure in an animal body by which two bones are fitted together. **3 a** any of the parts into which an animal carcass is divided for food. **b** any of the parts of which a body is made up. **4** *sl.* a place of meeting for drinking, etc. **5** *sl.* a marijuana cigarette. **6** the part of a stem from which a leaf or branch grows. **7** a piece of flexible material forming the hinge of a book cover. **8** *Geol.* a fissure in a mass of rock. ● *adj.* **1** held or done by, or belonging to, two or more persons, etc., in conjunction (*a joint mortgage; joint action*). **2** sharing with another in some action, state, etc. (*joint author; joint favorite*). ● *v.tr.* **1** connect by joints. **2** divide (a body or member) at a joint or into joints. **3** fill up the joints of (masonry, etc.) with mortar, etc.; trim the surface of (a mortar joint). **4** prepare (a board, etc.) for being joined to another by planing its edge. □ **out of joint 1** (of a bone) dislocated. **2 a** out of order. **b** inappropriate. □□ **joint·less** *adj.* **joint·ly** *adv.*

Joint Chiefs of Staff *n.pl. Mil.* a military advisory group made up of the Army Chief of Staff, the Air Force Chief of Staff, the Marine Corps commandant, and the Chief of Naval Operations.

joint stock *n.* capital held jointly; a common fund.

join·ture /jóynchər/ *n. & v.* ● *n.* an estate settled on a wife for the period during which she survives her husband. ● *v.tr.* provide (a wife) with a jointure.

joist /joyst/ *n.* each of a series of parallel supporting beams of lumber, steel, etc., used in floors, ceilings, etc. ▷ HOUSE. □□ **joist·ed** *adj.*

jo·jo·ba /hōhṓbə/ *n.* ▶ a plant, *Simmondsia chinensis,* with seeds yielding an oily extract used in cosmetics, etc.

joke /jōk/ *n. & v.* ● *n.* **1 a** a thing said or done to excite laughter. **b** a witticism or jest. **2** a ridiculous thing, person, or circumstance. ● *v.* **1** *intr.* make jokes. **2** *tr.* poke fun at; banter. □ **no joke** *colloq.* a serious matter. □□ **jok·ing·ly** *adv.* **jok·ey** *adj.* (also **jok·y**). **jok·i·ly** *adv.* **jok·i·ness** *n.*

jok·er /jókər/ *n.* **1** a person who jokes. **2** *sl.* a fellow; a man. **3** a playing card usu. with a figure of a jester, used in some games. **4** an unexpected factor or resource.

joke·smith /jóksmith/ *n.* a skilled user or inventor of jokes.

jol·li·fy /jólifī/ *v.tr. & intr.* (**-ies, -ied**) make or be merry, esp. in drinking. □□ **jol·li·fi·ca·tion** *n.*

jol·li·ty /jólitee/ *n.* (*pl.* **-ies**) **1** merrymaking; festiveness. **2** (in *pl.*) festivities.

jockey cap

racing-silk jacket

whip

riding boots

JOCKEY

JOHN DORY
(*Zeus faber*)

JOJOBA
(*Simmondsia chinensis*)

leaves

seeds

JOINT

Joints are classified by their structure and by the manner of articulation between the bones that they link. Fixed or slightly movable joints, such as those between the vertebrae in the spine, are held in place by fibrous tissue (ligaments) or cartilage. In synovial joints, articulating bone surfaces are enclosed in a fibrous capsule and covered with smooth cartilage, allowing more flexible movement.

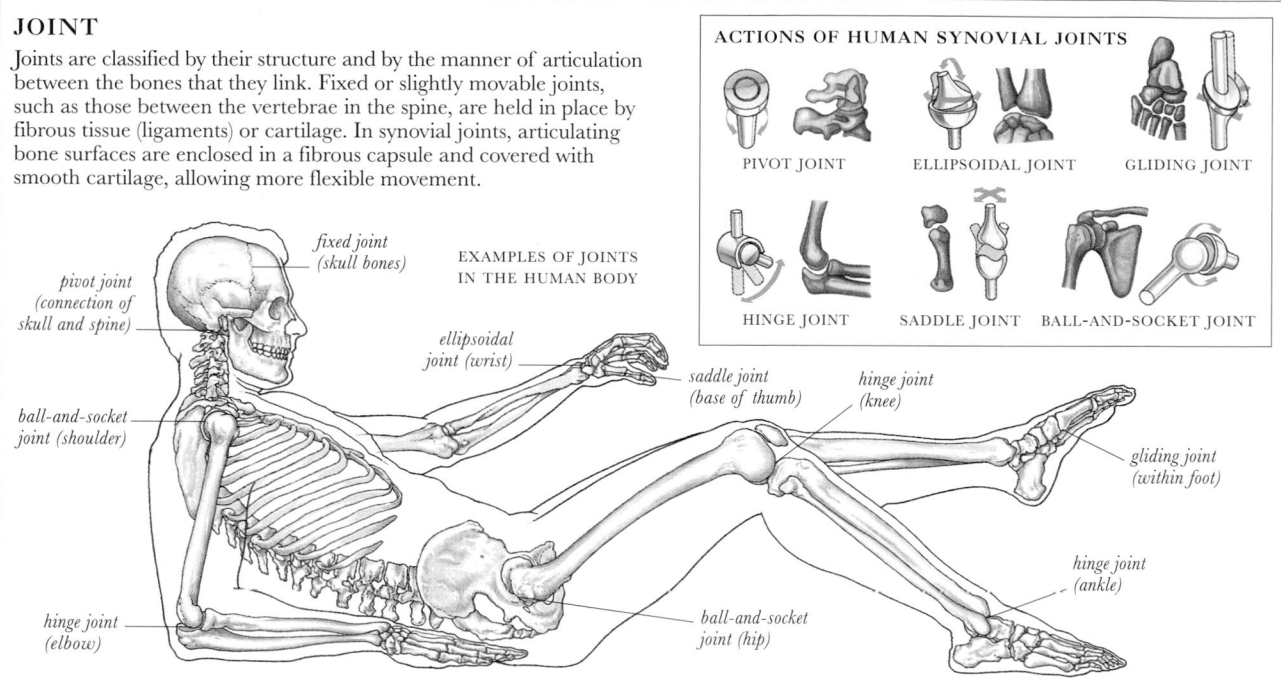

ACTIONS OF HUMAN SYNOVIAL JOINTS

PIVOT JOINT ELLIPSOIDAL JOINT GLIDING JOINT

HINGE JOINT SADDLE JOINT BALL-AND-SOCKET JOINT

EXAMPLES OF JOINTS IN THE HUMAN BODY

pivot joint (connection of skull and spine)

fixed joint (skull bones)

ellipsoidal joint (wrist)

saddle joint (base of thumb)

hinge joint (knee)

ball-and-socket joint (shoulder)

gliding joint (within foot)

hinge joint (ankle)

hinge joint (elbow)

ball-and-socket joint (hip)

J

jol·ly¹ /jólee/ *adj., adv., v., & n.* ● *adj.* (**jollier, jolliest**) **1** cheerful and good-humored; merry. **2** festive; jovial. **3** slightly drunk. ● *adv.* esp. *Brit. colloq.* very (*they were jolly unlucky*). ● *v.tr.* (**-ies, -ied**) **1** (usu. foll. by *along*) *colloq.* coax or humor (a person) in a friendly way. **2** chaff; banter. ● *n.* (*pl.* **-ies**) *colloq.* a party or celebration; an outing. □□ **jol·li·ly** *adv.* **jol·li·ness** *n.*

jol·ly² /jólee/ *n.* (*pl.* **-ies**) (in full **jolly boat**) a clinker-built ship's boat smaller than a cutter.

Jol·ly Rog·er *n.* a pirates' black flag, usu. with the skull and crossbones.

jolt /jōlt/ *v. & n.* ● *v.* **1** *tr.* disturb or shake from the normal position (esp. in a moving vehicle) with a jerk. **2** *tr.* give a mental shock to; perturb. **3** *intr.* (of a vehicle) move along with jerks, as on a rough road. ● *n.* **1** such a jerk. **2** a surprise or shock. □□ **jolt·y** *adj.* (**joltier, joltiest**).

jon·quil /jóngkwil/ *n.* a bulbous plant, *Narcissus jonquilla*, with clusters of small fragrant yellow flowers.

Jor·da·ni·an /jawrdáyneeən/ *adj. & n.* ● *adj.* of or relating to the kingdom of Jordan in the Middle East. ● *n.* **1** a native or national of Jordan. **2** a person of Jordanian descent.

josh /josh/ *n. & v. sl.* ● *n.* a good-natured or teasing joke. ● *v.* **1** *tr.* tease or banter. **2** *intr.* indulge in ridicule. □□ **josh·er** *n.*

Josh·u·a tree *n.* a tall branching yucca of SW North America, with clusters of spiky leaves.

jos·tle /jósəl/ *v. & n.* ● *v.* **1** *tr.* push against; elbow. **2** *tr.* (often foll. by *away, from*, etc.) push (a person) abruptly or roughly. **3** *intr.* (foll. by *against*) knock or push, esp. in a crowd. **4** *intr.* (foll. by *with*) struggle; have a rough exchange. ● *n.* **1** the act or an instance of jostling. **2** a collision.

jot /jot/ *v. & n.* ● *v.tr.* (**jotted, jotting**) (usu. foll. by *down*) write briefly or hastily. ● *n.* (usu. with *neg.* expressed or implied) a very small amount (*not one jot*).

jot·ter /jótər/ *n.* a small pad or notebook for making notes, etc.

jot·ting /jóting/ *n.* (usu. in *pl.*) a note; something jotted down.

joule /jōōl/ *n.* the SI unit of work or energy equal to the work done by a force of one newton when its point of application moves one meter in the direction of action of the force, equivalent to a watt-second. ¶ Symb.: **J**.

jounce /jowns/ *v.tr. & intr.* bump; bounce; jolt.

jour·nal /jɔ́rnəl/ *n.* **1** a newspaper or periodical. **2** a daily record of events. **3** *Naut.* a logbook. **4** a book in which business transactions are entered, with a statement of the accounts to which each is to be debited and credited. **5** the part of a shaft or axle that rests on bearings.

jour·nal·ese /jɔ́rnəléez/ *n.* a hackneyed style of language characteristic of some newspaper writing.

jour·nal·ism /jɔ́rnəlizəm/ *n.* the business or practice of writing and producing newspapers.

jour·nal·ist /jɔ́rnəlist/ *n.* a person employed to report for or edit a newspaper, journal, or newscast. □□ **jour·nal·is·tic** *adj.* **jour·nal·is·ti·cal·ly** /-istikəlee/ *adv.*

jour·ney /jɔ́rnee/ *n. & v.* ● *n.* (*pl.* **-eys**) **1** an act of going from one place to another, esp. at a long distance. **2** the distance traveled in a specified time (*a day's journey*). **3** the traveling of a vehicle along a route at a stated time. ● *v.intr.* (**-eys, -eyed**) make a journey. □□ **jour·ney·er** *n.*

jour·ney·man /jɔ́rneemən/ *n.* (*pl.* **-men**) **1** a qualified mechanic or artisan who works for another. **2** *derog.* a reliable but not outstanding worker.

jour·no /jə́wnō/ *n. colloq.* a journalist.

joust /jowst/ *n. & v. hist.* ● *n.* ▼ a combat between two knights on horseback with lances. ● *v.intr.* engage in a joust. □□ **joust·er** *n.*

Jove /jōv/ *n.* (in Roman mythology) Jupiter. □ **by Jove!** an exclamation of surprise or approval.

jo·vi·al /jṓveeəl/ *adj.* **1** merry. **2** convivial. **3** hearty and good-humored. □□ **jo·vi·al·i·ty** /-álitee/ *n.* **jo·vi·al·ly** *adv.*

jowl¹ /jowl/ *n.* **1** the jaw or jawbone. **2** the cheek (*cheek by jowl*). □□ **-jowled** *adj.* (in *comb.*).

JOUST

In 15th-century Europe, knights practiced the skills of battle by jousting. A knight would try to unhorse his opponent or break his lance against the other's shield. A jousting horse (destrier) carried some 420 lb (190 kg) of knight, armor, and saddle.

surcoat

vamplate

lance

chain-mail armor

gauntlet

crest

helm

high saddle board

REENACTMENT OF A 15TH-CENTURY EUROPEAN JOUST

stirrup

caparison

jowl² /jowl/ *n.* **1** the external loose skin on the throat or neck when prominent. **2** the dewlap of oxen, wattle of a bird, etc. □□ **jowl·y** *adj.*

joy /joy/ *n. & v.* ● *n.* **1** (often foll. by *at, in*) a vivid emotion of pleasure; extreme gladness. **2** a thing that causes joy. ● *v. esp. poet.* **1** *intr.* rejoice. **2** *tr.* gladden. □□ **joy·less** *adj.* **joy·less·ly** *adv.*

joy·ful /jóyfŏol/ *adj.* full of, showing, or causing joy. □□ **joy·ful·ly** *adv.* **joy·ful·ness** *n.*

joy·ous /jóyəs/ *adj.* (of an occasion, circumstance, etc.) characterized by pleasure or joy; joyful. □□ **joy·ous·ly** *adv.* **joy·ous·ness** *n.*

joy·ride /jóyrīd/ *n. & v. colloq.* ● *n.* a ride for pleasure in an automobile, esp. without the owner's permission. ● *v.intr.* (*past* **-rode** /-rōd/; *past part.* **-ridden** /-rid'n/) go for a joyride. □□ **joy·rid·er** *n.*

joy·stick /jóystik/ *n.* **1** *colloq.* the control column of an aircraft. **2** a lever that can be moved in several directions to control the movement of an image on a computer monitor.

JP *abbr.* **1** justice of the peace. **2** jet propulsion.

Jr. *abbr.* junior.

ju·bi·lant /jŏobilənt/ *adj.* exultant; rejoicing; joyful. □□ **ju·bi·lance** /-ləns/ *n.* **ju·bi·lant·ly** *adv.*

ju·bi·la·tion /jŏobəláyshən/ *n.* a feeling of great happiness and triumph.

ju·bi·lee /jŏobileé/ *n.* **1** a time or season of rejoicing. **2** an anniversary, esp. the 25th or 50th.

Ju·da·ic /jŏodáyik/ *adj.* of or characteristic of the Jews or Judaism.

Ju·da·ism /jŏodeeizəm, -day-/ *n.* **1** the religion of the Jews, with a belief in one God and a basis in Mosaic and rabbinical teachings. **2** the Jews collectively. □□ **Ju·da·ist** *n.*

Ju·das /jŏodəs/ *n.* a person who betrays a friend.

Judeo- /jŏodáy-ō, -dée-ō/ *comb. form* (esp. *Brit.* **Judaeo-**) Jewish; Jewish and.

judge /juj/ *n. & v.* ● *n.* **1** a public officer appointed to hear and try causes in a court of justice. **2** a person appointed to decide a dispute or contest. **3 a** a person who decides a question. **b** a person regarded in terms of capacity to decide on the merits of a thing or question (*am no judge of that*; *a good judge of art*). ● *v.* **1** *tr.* a try (a cause) in a court of justice. **b** pronounce sentence on (a person). **2** *tr.* form an opinion about; estimate, appraise. **3** *tr.* act as a judge of (a dispute or contest). **4** *tr.* (often foll. by *to* + infin. or *that* + clause) conclude, consider, or suppose. **5** *intr.* **a** form a judgment. **b** act as judge. □□ **judge·like** *adj.* **judge·ship** *n.*

judg·ment /jújmənt/ *n.* (also **judge·ment**) **1** the critical faculty; discernment (*an error of judgment*). **2** good sense. **3** an opinion or estimate (*in my judgment*). **4** the sentence of a court of justice; a deci-

sion by a judge. **5** often *joc.* a misfortune viewed as a deserved recompense (*it is a judgment on you for getting up late*). **6** criticism. □ **against one's better judgment** contrary to what one really feels to be advisable.

Judg·ment Day *n.* the day on which the Last Judgment is believed to take place.

judg·men·tal /jujmént'l/ *adj.* (also **judge·men·tal**) **1** of or concerning or by way of judgment. **2** condemning; critical. □□ **judg·men·tal·ly** *adv.*

ju·di·ca·ture /jŏodikəchər/ *n.* **1** the administration of justice. **2** a judge's office or term of office. **3** judges collectively; judiciary. **4** a court of justice.

ju·di·cial /jŏodíshəl/ *adj.* **1** of, done by, or proper to a court of law. **2** having the function of judgment (*a judicial assembly*). **3** of or proper to a judge. **4** expressing a judgment; critical. **5** impartial. **6** regarded as a divine judgment. □□ **ju·di·cial·ly** *adv.*

ju·di·ci·ar·y /jŏodíshee-eree, -díshəree/ *n.* (*pl.* **-ies**) the judges of a nation's judicial branch collectively.

ju·di·cious /jŏodíshəs/ *adj.* **1** sensible; prudent. **2** sound in discernment and judgment. □□ **ju·di·cious·ly** *adv.* **ju·di·cious·ness** *n.*

ju·do /jŏodō/ *n.* ▼ a sport of unarmed combat derived from jujitsu. □□ **ju·do·ist** *n.*

jug /jug/ *n. & v.* ● *n.* **1 a** a deep vessel for holding liquids, with a handle and often with a spout or lip shaped for pouring. **b** the contents of this; a jugful. **2** a large jar with a narrow mouth. **3** *sl.* prison. **4** (in *pl.*) *coarse sl.* a woman's breasts. ● *v.tr.* (**jugged**, **jugging**) **1** (usu. as **jugged** *adj.*) stew or boil (a hare or rabbit) in a covered vessel. **2** *sl.* imprison. □□ **jug·ful** *n.* (*pl.* **-fuls**).

jug·ger·naut /júgərnawt/ *n.* **1** esp. *Brit.* a large heavy motor vehicle, esp. a tractor-trailer truck. **2** huge or overwhelming force or object. **3** (**Juggernaut**) an institution or notion to which persons blindly sacrifice themselves or others.

jug·gle /júgəl/ *v. & n.* ● *v.* **1 a** *intr.* (often foll. by *with*) perform feats of dexterity, esp. by tossing objects in the air and catching them, keeping several in the air at the same time. **b** *tr.* perform such feats with. **2** *tr.* continue to deal with (several activities) at once, esp. with ingenuity. **3** *intr.* (foll. by *with*) & *tr.* **a** deceive or cheat. **b** misrepresent (facts). **c** rearrange adroitly. ● *n.* **1** a piece of juggling. **2** a fraud.

jug·gler /júglər/ *n.* **1** a person who juggles. **2** a trickster or impostor. □□ **jug·gler·y** *n.*

jug·u·lar /júgyələr/ *adj.* **1** of the neck or throat. **2** (of fish) having ventral fins in front of the pectoral fins.

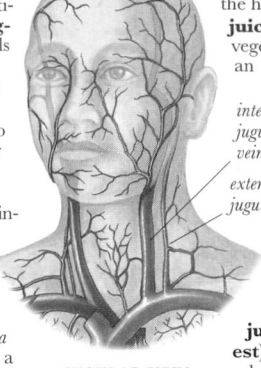

JUGULAR VEIN

internal jugular vein

external jugular vein

jug·u·lar vein *n.* ◀ any of several large veins in the neck which carry blood from the head. ▷ CARDIOVASCULAR

juice /jŏos/ *n.* **1** the liquid part of vegetables or fruits. **2** the fluid part of an animal body or substance, esp. a secretion (*gastric juice*). **3** the essence or spirit of anything. **4** *colloq.* gasoline, etc., or electricity as a source of power. **5** *sl.* alcoholic liquor. □□ **juice·less** *adj.*

juic·er /jŏosər/ *n.* **1** a kitchen tool or appliance for extracting the juice from fruits and vegetables. **2** *sl.* an alcoholic.

juic·y /jŏosee/ *adj.* (**juicier, juiciest**) **1** full of juice; succulent. **2** *colloq.* substantial or interesting; racy; scandalous. **3** *colloq.* profitable. □□ **juic·i·ly** *adv.* **juic·i·ness** *n.*

ju·jit·su /jŏojítsŏo/ *n.* (also **jiu·jit·su**) a Japanese system of unarmed combat and physical training.

ju·ju /jŏojōo/ *n.* **1** ▶ a charm or fetish of some W. African peoples. **2** a supernatural power attributed to this.

ju·jube /jŏojōob/ *n.* **1 a** any plant of the genus *Zizyphus* bearing edible acidic berry-like fruits. **b** this fruit. **2** a small lozenge or candy of gelatin, etc., flavored with or imitating this.

juke·box /jŏokboks/ *n.* a machine that automatically plays a selected musical recording when a coin is inserted.

Jul. *abbr.* July.

JU-JU: MODERN WEST AFRICAN JU-JU

ju·lep /jŏolip/ *n.* **1 a** a sweet drink, esp. as a vehicle for medicine. **b** a medicated drink as a mild stimulant, etc. **2** iced and flavored spirits and water (*mint julep*).

Jul·ian /jŏolyən/ *adj.* of or associated with Julius Caesar.

Jul·ian cal·en·dar *n.* a calendar introduced by Julius Caesar, in which the year consisted of 365 days, every fourth year having 366 (cf. GREGORIAN CALENDAR).

ju·li·enne /jŏolee-én/ *n. & adj.* ● *n.* foodstuff, esp. vegetables, cut into short, thin strips. ● *adj.* cut into thin strips.

Ju·ly /jŏolí/ *n.* (*pl.* **Julies** or **Julys**) the seventh month of the year.

jum·ble /júmbəl/ *v. & n.* ● *v.* **1** *tr.* (often foll. by *up*) confuse; mix up. **2** *intr.* move about in disorder. ● *n.* **1** a confused state or heap; a muddle. **2** *Brit.* articles collected for a jumble sale. □□ **jum·bly** *adj.*

jum·bo /júmbō/ *n. & adj. colloq.* ● *n.* (*pl.* **-os**) **1** a large animal (esp. an elephant), person, or thing. **2** (in full **jumbo jet**) a large airliner with capacity for several hundred passengers. ● *adj.* **1** very large of its kind. **2** extra large (*jumbo packet*).

jump /jump/ *v. & n.* ● *v.* **1** *intr.* move off the ground or other surface (usu. upward, at least initially) by sudden muscular effort in the legs. **2** *intr.* (often foll. by *up, from, in, out*, etc.) move suddenly or hastily in a specified way (*we jumped into the car*). **3** *intr.* give a sudden bodily movement from shock or excitement, etc. **4** *intr.* undergo a rapid change, esp. an advance in status. **5** *intr.* (often foll. by *about*) change or move rapidly from one idea or subject to another. **6 a** *intr.* rise or increase suddenly (*prices jumped*). **b** *tr.* cause to do this. **7 a** *tr.* a pass over (an obstacle, barrier, etc.) by jumping. **b** move or pass over (an intervening thing)

J

JUDO

Judo is a system of unarmed combat developed in East Asia. Competitors attempt to throw, pin, or master their opponent during a controlled bout on a regulation mat. Colored belts indicate the student's level of proficiency.

judge
scorer
time-keepers
contestant

contestant
referee
contest area
danger area
safety area

JUDO MAT (SHIAIJO)

cotton jacket

black belt

cotton trousers

JUDO OUTFIT (JUDOGI)

to a point beyond. **8** *tr.* skip or pass over (a passage in a book, etc.). **9** *tr.* cause (a thing, or an animal, esp. a horse) to jump. ▷ SHOW JUMPING. **10** *intr.* (foll. by *to, at*) reach a conclusion hastily. **11** *tr.* (of a train) leave (the rails) owing to a fault. **12** *tr.* esp. *Brit.* ignore and pass (a red traffic light, etc.). **13** *tr.* get on or off (a train, etc.) quickly, esp. illegally or dangerously. **14** *tr.* pounce on or attack (a person) unexpectedly. **15** *tr.* take summary possession of (a claim allegedly abandoned or forfeit by the former occupant). ● *n.* **1** the act or an instance of jumping. **2** a sudden bodily movement caused by shock or excitement. **3** an abrupt rise in amount, price, value, status, etc. **4** an obstacle to be jumped, esp. by a horse. **5 a** a sudden transition. **b** a gap in a series, logical sequence, etc. □ **get** (or **have**) **the jump on** *colloq.* get (or have) an advantage over (a person) by prompt action. **jump at** accept eagerly. **jump bail** see BAIL.¹ **jump down a person's throat** *colloq.* reprimand or contradict a person fiercely. **jump the gun** see GUN. **jump on** *colloq.* attack or criticize severely and without warning. **jump ship** (of a seaman) desert. **jump to it** *colloq.* act promptly and energetically. **one jump ahead** one stage further on than a rival, etc. **on the jump** *colloq.* on the move; in a hurry. □□ **jump·a·ble** *adj.*

jump·er¹ /júmpər/ *n.* a sleeveless one-piece dress usu. worn over a blouse or shirt.

jump·er² /júmpər/ *n.* a person or animal that jumps.

jump·er ca·bles *n.pl.* a pair of electrical cables attached to a battery and used to start a motor vehicle with a weak or discharged battery.

jump·ing bean /júmping/ *n.* the seed of a Mexican plant that jumps with the movement of the larva inside.

jump·ing jack /júmping/ *n.* **1** a jumping exercise performed by alternating the position of standing feet together with arms at sides with the position of standing feet apart with arms extended and hands above the head. **2** a toy figure of a man, with movable limbs.

jump-jet *n.* a jet aircraft that can take off and land vertically.

jump rope *n.* a length of rope revolved over the head and under the feet while jumping as a game or exercise.

jump·suit /júmpsoōt/ *n.* a one-piece garment for the whole body, of a kind orig. worn by paratroopers.

jump·y /júmpee/ *adj.* (**jumpier, jumpiest**) **1** nervous; easily startled. **2** making sudden movements, esp. of nervous excitement. □□ **jump·i·ly** *adv.* **jump·i·ness** *n.*

Jun. *abbr.* **1** June. **2** Junior.

junc·tion /júngkshən/ *n.* **1** a point at which two or more things are joined. **2** a place where two or more railroad lines or roads meet, unite, or cross. **3** the act or an instance of joining. **4** *Electronics* a region of transition in a semiconductor between regions where conduction is mainly by electrons and regions where it is mainly by holes.

junc·tion box *n.* a box containing a junction of electric cables, etc.

junc·ture /júngkchər/ *n.* **1** a critical convergence of events; a critical point of time (*at this juncture*). **2** a place where things join. **3** an act of joining.

June /joōn/ *n.* the sixth month of the year.

June bug *n.* ▼ any of several large brown scarab beetles, esp. *Phyllophaga fusca*.

june·teenth /joōntéenth/ *n.* (in the US) a festival held annually on the nineteenth of June by African-Americans (esp. in the southern states), to commemo-

JUNE BUG

rate emancipation from slavery in Texas on that day in 1865.

Jung·i·an /yoōngeeən/ *adj. & n.* ● *adj.* relating to Carl Jung, the Swiss psychologist, 1875–1961, or his work. ● *n.* a follower of Jung or his work.

jun·gle /júnggəl/ *n.* **1 a** land overgrown with underwood or tangled vegetation, esp. in the tropics. **b** an area of such land. **2** a wild tangled mass. **3** a place of bewildering complexity or confusion, or of a struggle for survival (*blackboard jungle*). □ **law of the jungle** a state of ruthless competition. □□ **jun·gled** *adj.* **jun·gly** *adj.*

jun·gle gym *n.* a playground structure with bars, ladders, etc., for children to climb.

jun·ior /joōnyər/ *adj. & n.* ● *adj.* **1** less advanced in age. **2** (foll. by *to*) inferior in age, standing, or position. **3** the younger (esp. appended to a name for distinction from an older person of the same name). **4** of less or least standing; of the lower or lowest position (*junior partner*). **5** *Brit.* (of a school) having pupils in a younger age-range, usu. 7–11. **6** of the year before the final year at college, high school, etc. ● *n.* **1** a junior person. **2** one's inferior in length of service, etc. **3** a junior student. **4** *colloq.* a young male child, esp. in relation to his family.

jun·ior col·lege *n.* a college offering a two-year course, esp. in preparation for senior college.

jun·ior high school *n.* school attended between elementary and high school and usu. consisting of grades seven and eight or seven, eight, and nine.

ju·ni·per /joōnipər/ *n.* ◀ any evergreen shrub or tree of the genus *Juniperus*, esp. *J. communis* with prickly leaves and dark purple berrylike cones.

junk¹ /jungk/ *n. & v.* ● *n.* **1** discarded articles; rubbish. **2** anything regarded as of little value. **3** *sl.* a narcotic drug, esp. heroin. ● *v.tr.* discard as junk.

leaves

berries

JUNIPER
(*Juniperus communis*)

junk² /jungk/ *n.* ▶ a flat-bottomed sailing vessel of the China seas, with a prominent stem and lugsails.

junk bond *n. Stock Exch.* a bond bearing high interest but deemed to be a risky investment.

junk·et /júngkit/ *n. & v.* ● *n.* **1** a dish of sweetened and flavored curds. **2** a feast. **3** an official's tour at public expense. ● *v.intr.* feast; picnic. □□ **jun·ket·ing** *n.*

junk food *n.* food with low nutritional value.

junk·ie /júngkee/ *n. sl.* a drug addict.

junk mail *n.* unsolicited advertising matter sent through the mail.

junk·yard /júngkyard/ *n.* a yard in which junk is collected and sometimes resold.

Ju·no·esque /joōnō-esk/ *adj.* (of a woman) tall and shapely.

jun·ta /hoōntə, júntə/ *n.* a political or military clique or faction taking power after a revolution or coup d'état.

Ju·pi·ter /joōpitər/ *n.* ▼ the largest planet of the solar system, orbiting about the Sun between Mars and Saturn. ▷ SOLAR SYSTEM

Ju·ras·sic /joōrásik/ *adj. & n. Geol.* ● *adj.* of or relating to the second period of the Mesozoic era with evidence of many large dinosaurs, the first birds (including *Archaeopteryx*), and mammals. ● *n.* this era or system.

JUNK:
TRADITIONAL
CHINESE JUNK

J

JUPITER

Jupiter is the largest, most massive planet in the solar system. Its rapid rate of rotation in 9 hours 55 minutes causes the clouds in its atmosphere to form dark, low-altitude "belts" and bright, high-altitude "zones" – both with huge storm systems which encircle the planet parallel with the equator. Jupiter has two faint rings and is orbited by 16 known moons, of which Ganymede, Callisto, Io, and Europa (the Galileans) are the largest.

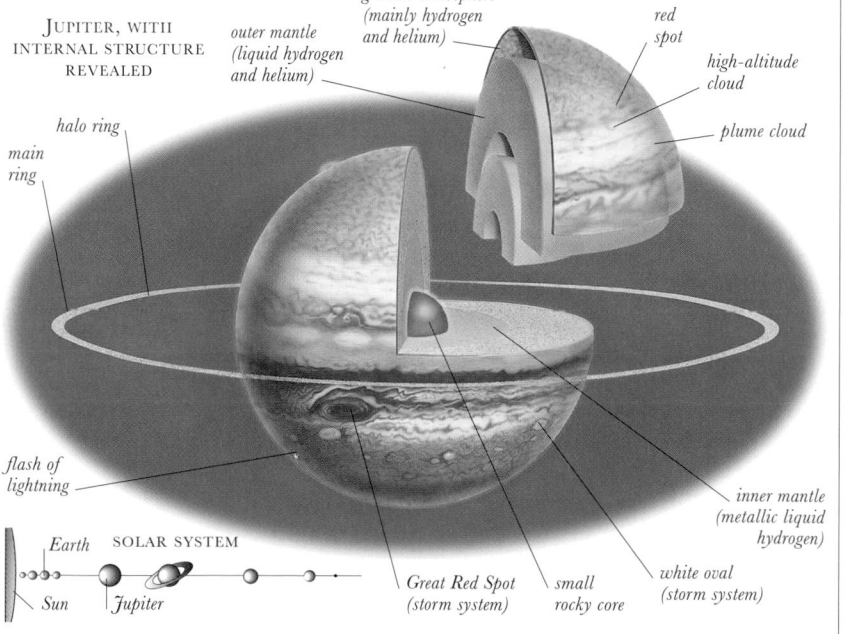

JUPITER, WITH INTERNAL STRUCTURE REVEALED

gaseous atmosphere (mainly hydrogen and helium)
red spot
high-altitude cloud
plume cloud
outer mantle (liquid hydrogen and helium)
halo ring
main ring
flash of lightning
Earth
Sun
Jupiter
SOLAR SYSTEM
Great Red Spot (storm system)
small rocky core
white oval (storm system)
inner mantle (metallic liquid hydrogen)

ju·rid·i·cal /jŏŏrídikəl/ *adj.* **1** of judicial proceedings. **2** relating to the law. □□ **ju·rid·i·cal·ly** *adv.*

ju·ris·dic·tion /jŏŏrisdíkshən/ *n.* **1** (often foll. by *over, of*) the administration of justice. **2 a** legal or other authority. **b** the extent of this; the territory it extends over. □□ **ju·ris·dic·tion·al** *adj.*

ju·ris·pru·dence /jŏŏrisprŏŏd'ns/ *n.* **1** the science or philosophy of law. **2** skill in law. □□ **ju·ris·pru·dent** /-dənt/ *adj. & n.* **ju·ris·pru·den·tial** /-dénshəl/ *adj.*

ju·rist /jŏŏrist/ *n.* **1** an expert in law. **2** a legal writer. **3** a lawyer. □□ **ju·ris·tic** /-rístik/ *adj.* **ju·ris·ti·cal** /-rístikəl/ *adj.*

ju·ror /jŏŏrər/ *n.* **1** a member of a jury. **2** a person who takes an oath.

ju·ry /jŏŏree/ *n.* (*pl.* **-ies**) **1** a body of persons sworn to render a verdict on the basis of evidence submitted to them in a court of justice. **2** a body of persons selected to award prizes in a competition.

ju·ry·man /jŏŏreemən/ *n.* (*pl.* **-men**) a member of a jury.

ju·ry-rigged /jŏŏreerigd/ *adj.* having temporary makeshift rigging.

ju·ry·wom·an /jŏŏreewŏŏmən/ *n.* (*pl.* **-women**) a woman member of a jury.

just /just/ *adj. & adv.* ● *adj.* **1** acting or done in accordance with what is morally right or fair. **2** (of treatment, etc.) deserved (*a just reward*). **3** (of feelings, opinions, etc.) well-grounded (*just resentment*). **4** right in amount, etc.; proper. ● *adv.* **1** exactly (*just what I need*). **2** exactly or nearly at this or that moment; a little time ago (*I have just seen them*). **3** *colloq.* simply; merely (*we were just good friends*; *it just doesn't make sense*). **4** barely; no more than (*I just managed it*; *just a minute*). **5** *colloq.* positively (*it is just splendid*). **6** quite (*not just yet*; *it is just as well*

that I checked). **7** *colloq.* really; indeed (*won't I just tell him!*). **8** in questions, seeking precise information (*just how did you manage?*). □ **just about** *colloq.* almost exactly; almost completely. **just in case 1** lest. **2** as a precaution. **just now 1** at this moment. **2** a little time ago. **just so 1** exactly arranged (*they like everything just so*). **2** it is exactly as you say. □□ **just·ly** *adv.* **just·ness** *n.*

jus·tice /jústis/ *n.* **1** just conduct. **2** fairness. **3** the exercise of authority in the maintenance of right. **4** judicial proceedings (*was duly brought to justice*). **5 a** a magistrate. **b** a judge, esp. of a supreme court. □ **do justice to** treat fairly or appropriately; show due appreciation of. **do oneself justice** perform in a manner worthy of one's abilities. □□ **jus·tice·ship** *n.* (in sense 5).

jus·tice of the peace *n.* a local magistrate appointed to preserve the peace in a county, town, etc., hear minor cases, grant licenses, perform marriages, etc.

jus·ti·ci·ar·y /justíshee-eree/ *n. & adj.* ● *n.* (*pl.* **-ies**) an administrator of justice. ● *adj.* of the administration of justice.

jus·ti·fi·a·ble /jústifíəbəl/ *adj.* that can be justified or defended. □□ **jus·ti·fi·a·bil·i·ty** *n.* **jus·ti·fi·a·ble·ness** *n.* **jus·ti·fi·a·bly** *adv.*

jus·ti·fy /jústifī/ *v.tr.* (**-ies, -ied**) **1** show the justice or rightness of (a person, act, etc.). **2** demonstrate the correctness of (an assertion, etc.). **3** adduce adequate grounds for (conduct, a claim, etc.). **4 a** (esp. in *passive*) (of circumstances) be such as to justify. **b** vindicate. **5** (as **justified** *adj.*) just; right (*am justified in assuming*). **6** *Printing* adjust (a line of type) to fill a space evenly. □□ **jus·ti·fi·ca·tion** /-fikáyshən/ *n.* **jus·tif·i·ca·to·ry** /-stífikətáwree/ *adj.* **jus·ti·fi·er** *n.*

jut /jut/ *v. & n.* ● *v.intr.* (**jutted, jutting**) (often foll. by *out, forth*) protrude; project. ● *n.* a projection; a protruding point.

Jute /jōot/ *n.* a member of a Low-German tribe that settled in Britain in the 5th–6th c.

jute /jōot/ *n.* ▶ a rough fiber made from the bark of E. Indian plants of the genus *Corchorus*, used for making twine and rope, and woven into sacking, mats, etc.

ju·ve·nile /jŏŏvənīl/ *adj. & n.* ● *adj.* **1 a** young; youthful. **b** of or for young persons. **2** suited to or characteristic of youth. **3** often *derog.* immature. ● *n.* **1** a young person. **2** *Commerce* a book intended for young people. **3** an actor playing the part of a youthful person. □□ **ju·ve·nile·ly** *adv.* **ju·ve·nil·i·ty** /-nílitee/ *n.*

JUTE: HANK OF RAW JUTE FIBERS

ju·ve·nile court a court for the trial of children usu. under 18.

ju·ve·nile de·lin·quen·cy *n.* offenses committed by a person or persons below the age of legal responsibility. □□ **ju·ve·nile de·lin·quent** *n.*

ju·ve·nil·i·a /jŏŏvəníleeə/ *n.pl.* works produced by an author or artist in youth.

jux·ta·pose /júkstəpōz/ *v.tr.* **1** place (things) side by side. **2** (foll. by *to, with*) place (a thing) beside another. □□ **jux·ta·po·si·tion** /-pəzíshən/ *n.* **jux·ta·po·si·tion·al** /-pəzíshənəl/ *adj.*

JV *abbr.* junior varsity.

J

K

K[1] /kay/ *n.* (also **k**) (*pl.* **Ks** or **K's**) the eleventh letter of the alphabet.

K[2] *abbr.* (also **K.**) **1** kelvin(s). **2** King; King's. **3** (also **k**) (prec. by a numeral) **a** *Computing* a unit of 1,024 (i.e., 2[10]) bytes or bits, or loosely 1,000. **b** 1,000. **4** *Baseball* strikeout.

K[3] *symb. Chem.* the element potassium.

k *abbr.* **1** kilo-. **2** knot(s).

kab·ba·la var. of CABALA.

ka·bob /kəbób/ *n.* (also **ke·bab, ke·bob**) (usu. in *pl.*) small pieces of meat, vegetables, etc., packed closely on a skewer and broiled.

ka·bu·ki /kəbŏŏkee/ *n.* a form of popular traditional Japanese drama with highly stylized song, acted by males only.

Kad·dish /kaadish/ *n. Judaism* **1** a Jewish mourner's prayer. **2** a doxology in the synagogue service.

ka·di var. of QADI.

Kaf·fir /káfər/ *n.* **1** a member of the Xhosa-speaking peoples of S. Africa. **2** the language of these peoples.

woolen coils
kaffiyeh

KAFFIYEH

kaf·fi·yeh /kəféeə/ *n.* (also **kef·fi·yeh**) ▶ a Bedouin Arab's kerchief worn as a headdress.

Kaf·ka·esque /káafkǎésk/ *adj.* (of a situation, atmosphere, etc.) impenetrably oppressive, nightmarish, in a manner characteristic of the fictional world created by Franz Kafka, German-speaking novelist (d. 1924).

kaf·tan var. of CAFTAN.

kail var. of KALE.

kail·yard var. of KALEYARD.

kai·ser /kízər/ *n. hist.* an emperor, esp. the German emperor, the emperor of Austria, or the head of the Holy Roman Empire. □□ **kai·ser·ship** *n.*

kal·an·cho·e /kalənkóee/ *n.* a succulent plant of the mainly African genus *Kalanchoe*, which includes several house plants, some producing miniature plants from the edges of the leaves.

kale /kayl/ *n.* (also **kail**) **1** ◀ a variety of cabbage, esp. one with wrinkled leaves and no compact head. Also called **curly kale**. **2** *sl.* money.

ka·lei·do·scope /kəlídəskōp/ *n.* **1** a tube containing mirrors and pieces of colored glass, paper, plastic, etc., whose reflections produce changing patterns when the tube is rotated. **2** a constantly changing group of bright or interesting objects. □□ **ka·lei·do·scop·ic** /-skópik/ *adj.* **ka·lei·do·scop·i·cal** *adj.*

kal·ends var. of CALENDS.

kale·yard /káyl-yaard/ *n.* (also **kail·yard**) *Sc.* a kitchen garden.

KALE (*Brassica oleracea acephala*)

kal·pa /kálpə/ *n. Hinduism* & *Buddhism* the period between the beginning and the end of the world considered as the day of Brahma (4,320 million human years).

Ka·ma /kaamə/ *n.* the Hindu god of love.

Ka·ma Su·tra /sŏŏtrə/ *n.* an ancient Sanskrit treatise on the art of erotic love.

ka·mi·ka·ze /kámikaazee/ *n.* & *adj.* ● *n. hist.* **1** a Japanese aircraft loaded with explosives and deliberately crashed by its pilot onto its target. **2** the pilot of such an aircraft. ● *adj.* **1** of or relating to a kamikaze. **2** reckless; dangerous; potentially self-destructive.

kam·pong /kaampáwng, -póng/ *n.* a Malayan enclosure or village.

Kam·pu·che·an /kámpŏŏchéeən/ *n.* & *adj.* = CAMBODIAN.

Kan. *abbr.* Kansas.

ka·na /kaanə/ *n.* any of various Japanese syllabaries.

kan·ga·roo /kánggərŏŏ/ *n.* a plant-eating marsupial of the genus *Macropus*, native to Australia and New Guinea, with a long tail and strongly developed hindquarters enabling it to travel by jumping. ▷ MARSUPIAL

kan·ga·roo court *n.* an improperly constituted or illegal court held by a mob, etc.

kan·gar·oo rat *n.* any burrowing rodent of the genus *Dipodomys*, having elongated hind feet.

kan·ji /káanjee/ *n.* Japanese writing using Chinese characters.

Kans. *abbr.* Kansas.

Kan·sa /káanzə, -sə/ *n.* **1 a** a N. American people native to eastern Kansas. **b** a member of this people. **2** the language of this people. Also called **Kaw**.

ka·o·lin /káyəlin/ *n.* a fine, soft, white clay produced by the decomposition of other clays or feldspar, used esp. for making porcelain and in medicines. Also called **china clay**. □□ **ka·o·lin·ic** /-línik/ *adj.* **ka·o·lin·ize** *v.tr.*

ka·on /káyon/ *n. Physics* an unstable meson created from a high-energy particle collision.

ka·pell·meis·ter /kəpélmīstər/ *n.* (*pl.* same) the conductor of an orchestra, opera, choir, etc., esp. in German contexts.

ka·pok /káypok/ *n.* ▶ a fine, fibrous, cottonlike substance found surrounding the seeds of a tropical tree, *Ceiba pentandra*, used for stuffing cushions, soft toys, etc.

Ka·po·si's sar·co·ma /kápəseez, kapó-/ *n. Med.* a malignant neoplasm of connective tissue marked by bluish-red lesions on the skin; often associated with AIDS.

kapok

KAPOK SEED POD (*Ceiba pentandra*)

kap·pa /kápə/ *n.* the tenth letter of the Greek alphabet (Κ, κ).

ka·put /kaapŏŏt/ *predic.adj. sl.* broken; ruined; done for.

kar·a·kul /kárəkŏŏl/ *n.* (also **Kar·a·kul, caracul**) **1** a variety of Asian sheep with a dark curled fleece when young. **2** fur made from or resembling this. Also called **Persian lamb**.

kar·a·o·ke /káreeŏkee, kárə-/ *n.* a form of entertainment in which people sing popular songs as soloists against a prerecorded backing.

kar·at /kárət/ *n.* (*Brit.* **carat**) a measure of purity of gold, pure gold being 24 karats.

ka·ra·te /kəraatee/ *n.* a Japanese system of unarmed combat using the hands and feet as weapons.

kar·ma /kaarmə/ *n. Buddhism* & *Hinduism* **1** the sum of a person's actions in previous states of existence, viewed as deciding his or her fate in future existences. **2** destiny. □□ **kar·mic** *adj.*

karst /kaarst/ *n.* a limestone region with underground drainage and many cavities and passages caused by the dissolution of the rock.

kart /kaart/ *n.* a small unsprung racing vehicle with a tubular frame and a rear-mounted engine.

karyo- /káreeō/ *comb. form Biol.* denoting the nucleus of a cell.

kar·y·o·ki·ne·sis /káreeōkinéesis/ *n. Biol.* the division of a cell nucleus during mitosis.

kar·y·o·type /káreeətīp/ *n.* the number and structure of the chromosomes in the nucleus of a cell.

Kas·bah var. of CASBAH.

ka·tab·o·lism esp. *Brit.* var. of CATABOLISM.

ka·ta·ka·na /kátəkaanə/ *n.* an angular form of Japanese kana.

ka·ty·did /káytee-did/ *n.* ▶ any of various green grasshoppers of the family Tettigoniidae, native to the US.

kau·ri /kówree/ *n.* (*pl.* **kauris**) a coniferous New Zealand tree, *Agathis australis*, which produces valuable timber and a resin.

KATYDID: FALSE LEAF KATYDID (*Ommatopia pictifolia*)

ka·va /kaavə/ *n.* **1** a Polynesian shrub, *Piper methysticum*. **2** an intoxicating drink made from the crushed roots of this.

kay·ak /kíak/ *n.* **1** ▼ an Eskimo canoe for one paddler, consisting of a light wooden frame covered with skins. **2** a small covered canoe resembling this.

KAYAK

The Inuit of northern Canada, Alaska, Russia, and Greenland traditionally used kayaks to hunt sea mammals such as seals and whales. Kayaks were completely enclosed with waterproof sealskin except for an opening for the hunter to climb in at the top.

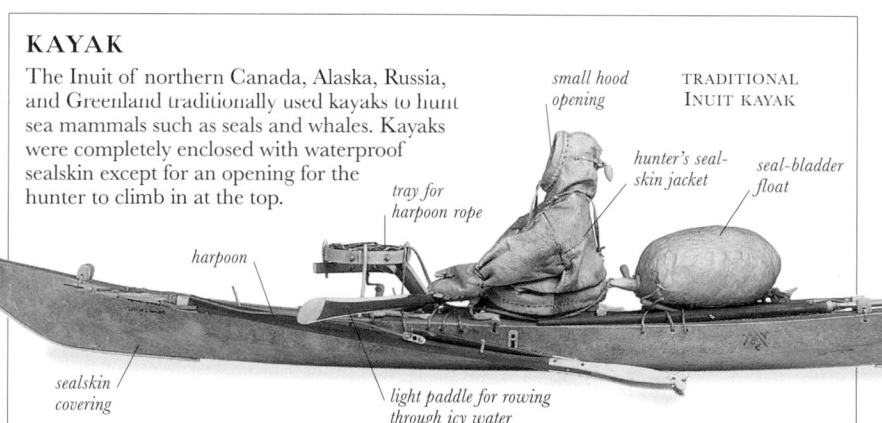

small hood opening — TRADITIONAL INUIT KAYAK
hunter's sealskin jacket
seal-bladder float
tray for harpoon rope
harpoon
sealskin covering
light paddle for rowing through icy water

K

kay·o /káyṓ, káyṓ/ *v. & n. colloq.* ● *v.tr.* (**-oes, -oed**) knock out; stun by a blow. ● *n.* (*pl.* **-os**) a knockout.

ka·zoo /kəzōō/ *n.* a toy musical instrument into which the player sings or hums.

KC *abbr.* **1** Kansas City. **2** Knights of Columbus.

kc *abbr.* kilocycle(s).

KE *abbr.* kinetic energy.

ke·a /kéeə, káyə/ *n.* ► a parrot, *Nestor notabilis*, of New Zealand, with brownish-green and red plumage.

ke·bab var. of KABOB.

ke·bob var. of KABOB.

kedge /kej/ *v. & n.* ● *v.* **1** *tr.* move (a ship) by means of a hawser attached to a small anchor that is dropped at some distance away. **2** *intr.* (of a ship) move in this way. ● *n.* (in full **kedge anchor**) a small anchor for this purpose.

ked·ger·ee /kéjərée/ *n.* **1** an E. Indian dish of rice, lentils, onions, eggs, etc. **2** a European dish of fish, rice, hard-boiled eggs, etc.

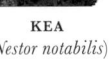

KEA
(*Nestor notabilis*)

keek /keek/ *v. & n. Sc.* ● *v.intr.* peep. ● *n.* a peep.

keel /keel/ *n. & v.* ● *n.* **1** the lengthwise timber or steel structure along the base of a ship, airship, or some aircraft, on which the framework of the whole is built up. ▷ SAILBOAT. **2** *poet.* a ship. **3** a ridge along the breastbone of many birds; a carina. **4** *Bot.* a prow-shaped pair of petals in a corolla, etc. ● *v.* **1** (often foll. by *over*) **a** *intr.* turn over or fall down. **b** *tr.* cause to do this. **2** *tr. & intr.* turn keel upward. □□ **keel·less** *adj.*

keel·haul /kéelhawl/ *v.tr.* **1** *hist.* drag (a person) through the water under the keel of a ship as a punishment. **2** scold or rebuke severely.

keel·son /kéelsən/ *n.* (also **kel·son** /kélsən/) a line of timber fastening a ship's floor timbers to its keel.

keen[1] /keen/ *adj.* **1** (of a person, desire, or interest) eager; ardent. **2** (foll. by *on*) much attracted by; fond of or enthusiastic about. **3 a** (of the senses) sharp; highly sensitive. **b** (of memory, etc.) clear; vivid. **4** (of a person) intellectually acute; (of a remark, etc.) quick; sharp; biting. **5 a** having a sharp edge or point. **b** (of an edge, etc.) sharp. **6** (of a sound, light, etc.) penetrating; vivid; strong. **7** (of a wind, frost, etc.) piercingly cold. **8** (of a pain, etc.) acute; intense. □□ **keen·ly** *adv.* **keen·ness** *n.*

keen[2] /keen/ *n. & v.* ● *n.* an Irish funeral song accompanied with wailing. ● *v.* **1** *intr.* utter the keen. **2** *tr.* bewail (a person) in this way. **3** *tr.* utter in a wailing tone. □□ **keen·er** *n.*

keep /keep/ *v. & n.* ● *v.* (*past* and *past part.* **kept** /kept/) **1** *tr.* have continuous charge of; retain possession of; save or hold on to. **2** *tr.* (foll. by *for*) retain or reserve for a future occasion or time (*will keep it for tomorrow*). **3** *tr. & intr.* retain or remain in a specified condition, position, course, etc. (*keep cool; keep them happy*). **4** *tr.* put or store in a regular place (*knives are kept in this drawer*). **5** *tr.* (foll. by *from*) cause to avoid or abstain from something. **6** *tr.* detain; cause to be late (*what kept you?*). **7** *tr.* **a** observe or pay due regard to (a law, custom, etc.) (*keep one's word*). **b** honor or fulfill (a commitment, undertaking, etc.). **c** respect the commitment implied by (a secret, etc.). **d** act fittingly on the occasion of (*keep the Sabbath*). **8** *tr.* own and look after (animals) for amusement or profit. **9** *tr.* **a** provide for the sustenance of (a person, family, etc.). **b** (foll. by *in*) maintain (a person) with a supply of. **10** *tr.* manage (a shop, business, etc.). **11** *tr.* **a** maintain (accounts, a diary, etc.) by making the requisite entries. **b** maintain (a house) in proper order. **12** *tr.* have (a

commodity) regularly on sale (*do you keep buttons?*). **13** *tr.* **a** confine or detain (a person, animal, etc.). **b** guard or protect (a person or place, a goal in soccer, etc.). **14** *tr.* preserve in being; continue to have (*keep order*). **15** *intr.* (foll. by verbal noun) continue or do repeatedly or habitually (*why do you keep saying that?*). **16** *tr.* continue to follow (a way or course). **17** *intr.* **a** (esp. of perishable commodities) remain in good condition. **b** (of news or information, etc.) admit of being withheld for a time. **18** *tr.* esp. *Brit.* remain in (one's bed, room, house, etc.). **19** *tr.* retain one's place in (a seat or saddle, one's ground, etc.) against opposition or difficulty. **20** *tr.* maintain (a person) in return for sexual favors (*a kept woman*). ● *n.* **1** maintenance or the essentials for this (esp. food) (*earn your keep*). **2** charge or control (*is in your keep*). **3** *hist.* ▼ a tower or stronghold. ▷ CASTLE. □ **for keeps** *colloq.* (esp. of something received or won) permanently; indefinitely. **keep at** persist or cause to persist with. **keep away** (often foll. by *from*) avoid being near. **2** prevent from being near. **keep back 1** remain or keep at a distance. **2** retard the progress of. **3** conceal; decline to disclose. **4** retain; withhold (*kept back $50*). **keep down 1** hold in subjection. **2** keep low in amount. **3** lie low; stay hidden. **4** manage not to vomit (food eaten). **keep one's feet** manage not to fall. **keep one's hair on** see HAIR. **keep one's hand in** see HAND. **keep in mind** take into account having remembered. **keep in with** remain on good terms with. **keep kosher** see KOSHER. **keep off 1** stay or cause to stay away from. **2** ward off; avert. **3** abstain from. **4** avoid (a subject). **keep on 1** continue to do something; do continually (*kept on laughing*). **2** continue to use or employ. **3** (foll. by *at*) pester or harass. **keep out 1** keep or remain outside. **2** exclude. **keep to 1** adhere to (a course, schedule, etc.). **2** observe (a promise). **3** confine oneself to. **keep to oneself 1** avoid contact with others. **2** refuse to disclose or share. **keep together** remain or keep in harmony. **keep track of** see TRACK[1] *v.* **keep under** hold in subjection. **keep up 1** maintain (progress, etc.). **2** prevent (prices, one's spirits, etc.) from sinking. **3** keep in repair, in an efficient or proper state, etc. **4** carry on (a correspondence, etc.). **5** prevent (a person) from going to bed, esp. when late. **6** (often foll. by *with*) manage not to fall behind. **keep up with the Joneses** strive to compete socially with one's neighbors. **keep one's word** see WORD. □□ **keep·a·ble** *adj.*

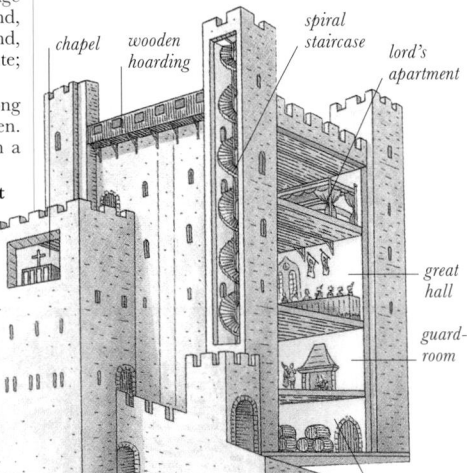

KEEP: 11TH-CENTURY ENGLISH CASTLE KEEP

(labels: chapel; wooden hoarding; spiral staircase; lord's apartment; great hall; guardroom; storeroom)

keep·er /kéepər/ *n.* **1** a person who keeps or looks after something or someone. **2 a** = GAMEKEEPER. **b** a person in charge of animals in a zoo. **3 a** = WICKET-KEEPER. **b** = GOALKEEPER. **4** a bar of soft iron across the poles of a horseshoe magnet to maintain its strength.

keep·ing /kéeping/ *n.* **1** custody; charge (*in safe keeping*). **2** agreement; harmony (*not in keeping with good taste*).

keep·sake /kéepsayk/ *n.* a thing kept for the sake of or in remembrance of the giver.

kef /kef, keef/ *n.* (also **kif** /kif/) **1** a drowsy state induced by marijuana, etc. **2** the enjoyment of idleness. **3** a substance smoked to produce kef.

kef·fi·yeh var. of KAFFIYEH.

keg /keg/ *n.* a small barrel of less than 30 gallons (usu. 5–10 gallons).

keg par·ty *n.* a party at which keg beer is served.

keis·ter /kéestər/ *n. sl.* **1** the buttocks. **2** a suitcase, satchel, handbag, etc.

kelp /kelp/ *n.* **1** any of several large, broad-fronded brown seaweeds, esp. of the genus *Laminaria*, suitable for use as manure. **2** the calcined ashes of seaweed formerly used in glassmaking and soap manufacture because of their high content of sodium, potassium, and magnesium salts.

kel·pie /kélpee/ *n. Sc.* **1** a water spirit, usu. in the form of a horse, reputed to delight in the drowning of travelers, etc. **2** an Australian sheepdog orig. bred from a Scottish collie.

kel·son var. of KEELSON.

Kelt var. of CELT.

kelt /kelt/ *n.* a salmon or sea trout after spawning.

kel·ter var. of KILTER.

kel·vin /kélvin/ *n.* the SI unit of thermodynamic temperature, equal in magnitude to the degree celsius. ¶ Abbr.: **K.**

Kel·vin scale *n.* a scale of temperature with absolute zero as zero.

kempt /kempt/ *adj.* combed; neatly kept.

ken /ken/ *n. & v.* ● *n.* range of sight or knowledge (*it's beyond my ken*). ● *v.tr.* (**kenning**; *past* and *past part.* **kenned** or **kent**) *Sc. & No. of Engl.* **1** recognize at sight. **2** know.

ken·do /kéndō/ *n.* ► a Japanese form of fencing with bamboo swords.

ken·nel /kénəl/ *n. & v.* ● *n.* **1** a small shelter for a dog. **2** (in *pl.*) a breeding or boarding establishment for dogs. **3** a mean dwelling. ● *v.* (**kenneled, kenneling**; esp. *Brit.* **kennelled, kennelling**) **1** *tr.* put into or keep in a kennel. **2** *intr.* live in or go to a kennel.

kent *past* and *past part.* of KEN.

Ken·yan /kényən, kéen-/ *adj. & n.* ● *adj.* of or relating to Kenya in E. Africa. ● *n.* **1** a native or national of Kenya. **2** a person of Kenyan descent.

kep·i /képee, káypee/ *n.* (*pl.* **kepis**) ► a French military cap with a horizontal peak.

kept *past* and *past part.* of KEEP.

ker·a·tin /kérətin/ *n.* a fibrous protein which occurs in hair, feathers, hooves, claws, horns, etc.

ker·a·tin·ize /kérətinīz/ *v.tr. & intr.* cover or become covered with a deposit of keratin. □□ **ker·a·tin·i·za·tion** *n.*

ker·a·tose /kérətōs/ *adj.* (of sponge) composed of a horny substance.

KEPI OF A
CONFEDERATE ARMY
INFANTRYMAN

kerb *Brit.* var. of CURB 2.

kerb·stone *Brit.* var. of CURBSTONE.

ker·chief /kárchif, -cheef/ *n.* **1** a cloth used to cover the head. **2** *poet.* a handkerchief. □□ **ker·chiefed** *adj.*

kerf /kərf/ *n.* **1** a slit made by cutting, esp. with a saw. **2** the cut end of a felled tree.

ker·fuf·fle /kərfúfəl/ *n.* esp. *Brit. colloq.* a fuss or commotion.

ker·mes /kármeez/ *n.* **1** the female of a bug, *Kermes ilicis*, with a berrylike appearance. **2** (in full **kermes oak**) an evergreen oak, *Quercus coccifera*, of S. Europe and N. Africa, on which this insect feeds.

KENDO

Kendo, meaning "way of the sword," derives from the art of kenjutsu, practiced by Japanese warriors in the 14th century. Today it is an internationally recognized martial art, in which points are awarded for striking the opponent's body showing the correct technique and spiritual attitude. Bouts take place on a wooden square and last up to five minutes.

practice sword (shinai)
mask (men)
headcloth (hachimaki)
shoulder protector
throat protector
jacket (kendo-gi)
breastplate (do)
padded glove (kote)
apron (tare)
divided skirt (hakama)

DEMONSTRATION OF KENDO SWORDPLAY

3 a red dye made from the dried bodies of these insects. ▷ DYE. **4** (in full **kermes mineral**) a bright red hydrous trisulfide of antimony.

kern /kərn/ *n. Printing* the part of a metal type projecting beyond its body or shank. □□ **kerned** *adj.*

ker·nel /kərnəl/ *n.* **1** a central, softer, usu. edible part within a hard shell of a nut, fruit stone, seed, etc. ▷ NUT. **2** the whole seed of a cereal. **3** the nucleus or essential part of anything.

ker·o·sene /kérəseen/ *n.* (also **ker·o·sine**) a liquid mixture obtained by distillation from petroleum or shale, used esp. as a fuel or solvent.

ker·ry /kéree/ *n.* (also **Kerry**) (*pl.* **-ies**) **1** an animal of a breed of small, black dairy cattle. **2** this breed.

ker·sey /kərzee/ *n.* (*pl.* **-eys**) **1** a kind of coarse narrow cloth woven from long wool, usu. ribbed. **2** a variety of this.

ker·sey·mere /kərzee-meer/ *n.* a twilled fine woolen cloth.

kes·ki·dee var. of KISKADEE.

kes·trel /késtrəl/ *n.* ▶ any small falcon, esp. *Falco tinnunculus*, that hovers while searching for its prey. ▷ NEST.

KESTREL
(*Falco tinnunculus*)

ketch /kech/ *n.* ▼ a two-masted, fore-and-aft rigged sailing boat with a mizzenmast stepped forward of the rudder and smaller than its foremast.

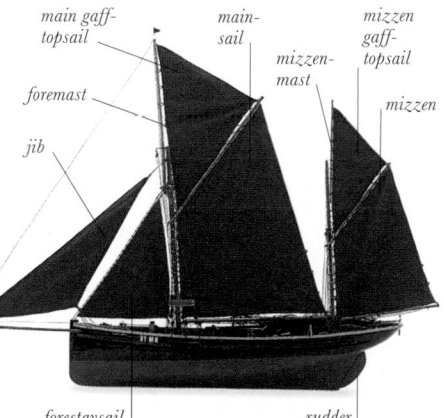

main gaff-topsail
mainsail
mizzen gaff-topsail
mizzenmast
mizzen
foremast
jib
forestaysail
rudder

KETCH: EARLY 20TH-CENTURY BRITISH KETCH

ketch·up /kéchup, káchup/ *n.* (also **catchup, catsup** /kátsəp/) a spicy sauce made from tomatoes, mushrooms, vinegar, etc., used as a condiment.

ke·tone /kéetōn/ *n.* any of a class of organic compounds in which two hydrocarbon groups are linked by a carbonyl group, e.g. propanone (acetone). □□ **ke·ton·ic** /kitónik/ *adj.*

ke·to·sis /keetōsis/ *n.* a condition characterized by raised levels of ketone bodies in the body, associated with fat metabolism and diabetes. □□ **ke·tot·ic** /-tótik/ *adj.*

ket·tle /két'l/ *n.* **1** a vessel, usu. of metal with a lid, spout, and handle, for boiling water in. **2** (in full **kettle hole**) a depression in the ground in a glaciated area. □ **a fine** (or **pretty**) **kettle of fish** an awkward state of affairs. □□ **ket·tle·ful** *n.* (*pl.* **-fuls**).

ket·tle·drum /két'ldrum/ *n.* a large drum shaped like a bowl with a membrane adjustable for tension (and so pitch) stretched across. ▷ PERCUSSION. □□ **ket·tle·drum·mer** *n.*

keV *abbr.* kilo-electronvolt.

Kev·lar /kévlaar/ *n. Trademark* a synthetic fiber of high tensile strength used esp. as a reinforcing agent in the manufacture of rubber products, e.g., tires.

Kew·pie /kyōōpee/ *n. Trademark* a small, chubby doll with a curl or topknot.

key[1] /kee/ *n., adj., & v.* ● *n.* (*pl.* **keys**) **1** an instrument, usu. of metal, for moving the bolt of a lock forward or backward to lock or unlock. **2** a similar implement for operating a switch in the form of a lock. **3** an instrument for grasping screws, pegs, nuts, etc., esp. one for winding a clock, etc. **4** a lever depressed by the finger in playing the organ, piano, flute, concertina, etc. ▷ PIANO. **5** (often in *pl.*) each of several buttons for operating a typewriter, word processor, or computer terminal, etc. **6** what gives or precludes the opportunity for or access to something. **7** a place that by its position gives control of a sea, territory, etc. **8 a** a solution or explanation. **b** a word or system for solving a cipher or code. **c** an explanatory list of symbols used in a map, table, etc. **d** a book of solutions to mathematical problems, etc. **e** a literal translation of a book written in a foreign language. **f** the first move in a chess-problem solution. **9** *Mus.* a system of notes definitely related to each other, based on a particular note, and predominating in a piece of music; tone or pitch (*a study in the key of C major*). **10** a tone or style of thought or expression. **11** a piece of wood or metal inserted between others to secure them. **12** the part of a first coat of wall plaster that passes

between the laths and so secures the rest. **13** the roughness of a surface, helping the adhesion of plaster, etc. **14** the samara of a sycamore, etc. **15** a mechanical device for making or breaking an electric circuit, e.g., in telegraphy. ● *adj.* essential; of vital importance (*the key element in the problem*). ● *v.tr.* (**keys, keyed**) **1** (foll. by *in, on,* etc.) fasten with a pin, wedge, bolt, etc. **2** (often foll. by *in*) enter (data) by means of a keyboard. **3** roughen (a surface) to help the adhesion of plaster, etc. **4** (foll. by *to*) align or link (one thing to another). **5** regulate the pitch of the strings of (a violin, etc.). **6** word (an advertisement in a particular periodical) so that answers to it can be identified (usu. by varying the form of address given). □ **key up** (often foll. by *to,* or *to +* infin.) make (a person) nervous or tense; excite. □□ **key·er** *n.* **key·less** *adj.*

key[2] /kee/ *n.* a low-lying island or reef, esp. off the Florida coast (cf. CAY).

key·board /kéebawrd/ *n. & v.* ● *n.* **1** a set of keys on a typewriter, computer, piano, etc.; the keys of a computer terminal regarded as a person's place of work. ▷ COMPUTER, PIANO. **2** an electronic musical instrument with keys arranged as on a piano. ● *v.tr. & intr.* enter (data) by means of a keyboard; work at a keyboard. □□ **key·board·er** *n.* **key·board·ist** *n.*

key·hole /kéehōl/ *n.* a hole by which a key is put into a lock.

Keynes·i·an /káynzeeən/ *adj. & n.* ● *adj.* of or relating to the economic theories of J. M. Keynes (d. 1946), esp. regarding government control of the economy through money and taxation. ● *n.* an adherent of these theories. □□ **Keynes·i·an·ism** *n.*

key·note /kéenōt/ *n.* **1** a prevailing tone or idea (*the keynote of the whole occasion*). **2** (*attrib.*) intended to set the prevailing tone at a meeting or conference (*keynote address*). **3** *Mus.* the note on which a key is based.

key·pad /kéepad/ *n.* a miniature keyboard or set of buttons for operating a portable electronic device, telephone, etc.

key·punch /kéepunch/ *n. & v.* ● *n.* a device for transferring data by means of punched holes or notches on a series of cards or paper tape. ● *v.tr.* transfer (data) by means of a keypunch. □□ **key·punch·er** *n.*

key ring *n.* a ring for keeping keys on.

key sig·na·ture *n. Mus.* any of several combinations of sharps or flats after the clef at the beginning of each staff indicating the key of a composition. ▷ NOTATION.

key·stone /kéestōn/ *n.* **1** the central principle of a system, policy, etc., on which all the rest depends. **2** a central stone at the summit of an arch locking the whole together. ▷ ARCH.

key·stroke /kéestrōk/ *n.* a single depression of a key on a keyboard, esp. as a measure of work.

key·word /kéewərd/ *n.* (also **Key word**) **1** the key to a cipher, etc. **2 a** a word of great significance. **b** a significant word used in indexing.

kg *abbr.* kilogram(s).

KGB /káyjeebée/ *n.* the state security police of the former USSR from 1954.

khad·dar /káadər/ *n.* homespun cloth of India.

khak·i /kákee, káa-/ *adj. & n.* ● *adj.* dust-colored; dull brownish-yellow. ● *n.* (*pl.* **khakis**) **1 a** khaki fabric of twilled cotton or wool, used esp. in military dress. **b** (in *pl.*) a garment, esp. pants or a military uniform, made of this fabric. **2** the dull brownish-yellow color of this.

kham·sin /kámsin/ *n.* an oppressive, hot southerly or southeasterly wind blowing in Egypt in spring.

khan /kaan, kan/ *n.* a title given to rulers and officials in Central Asia, Afghanistan, etc. □□ **khan·ate** *n.*

Khmer /kmair/ *n. & adj.* ● *n.* **1** a native of the ancient Khmer kingdom in SE Asia, or of modern Cambodia. **2** the language of this people. ● *adj.* of the Khmers or their language.

K

K

khur·ta var. of KURTA.

kHz *abbr.* kilohertz.

kib·ble /kíbəl/ *v. & n.* ● *v.tr.* grind coarsely. ● *n.* coarsely ground pellets of meal, etc., used as a dry pet food.

kib·butz /kibŏŏts/ *n.* (*pl.* **kibbutzim** /-bŏŏtseém/) a communal, esp. farming, settlement in Israel.

kib·butz·nik /kibŏŏtsnik/ *n.* a member of a kibbutz.

kib·itz /kíbits/ *v.intr. colloq.* act as a kibitzer.

kib·itz·er /kíbitsər/ *n. colloq.* **1** an onlooker at cards, etc., esp. one who offers unwanted advice. **2** a busy-body; a meddler.

ki·bosh /kíbosh/ *n.* (also *Brit.* **kybosh**) *sl.* nonsense. □ **put the kibosh on** put an end to; finally dispose of.

kick /kik/ *v. & n.* ● *v.* **1** *tr.* strike or propel forcibly with the foot or hoof, etc. **2** *intr.* (usu. foll. by *at, against*) **a** strike out with the foot. **b** express annoyance at or dislike of (treatment, a proposal, etc.); rebel against. **3** *tr. sl.* give up (a habit). **4** *tr.* (often foll. by *out*, etc.) expel or dismiss forcibly. **5** *refl.* be annoyed with oneself (*I'll kick myself if I'm wrong*). **6** *tr. Football* score (a goal) by a kick. **7** *intr. Cricket* (of a ball) rise sharply from the field. ● *n.* **1 a** a blow with the foot or hoof, etc. **b** the delivery of such a blow. **2** *colloq.* **a** a sharp stimulant effect, esp. of alcohol (*has some kick in it*). **b** (often in *pl.*) a pleasurable thrill (*did it just for kicks; got a kick out of flying*). **3** strength; resilience (*have no kick left*). **4** *colloq.* a specified temporary interest or enthusiasm (*on a jogging kick*). **5** the recoil of a gun when discharged. □ **kick about** (or **around**) *colloq.* **1 a** drift idly from place to place. **b** be unused or unwanted. **2 a** treat roughly or scornfully. **b** discuss (an idea) unsystematically. **kick the bucket** *sl.* die. **kick one's heels** see HEEL. **kick in 1** knock down (a door, etc.) by kicking. **2** *sl.* contribute (esp. money); pay one's share. **kick in the pants** (or **teeth**) *colloq.* a humiliating punishment or setback. **kick off 1 a** *Football*, etc. begin or resume play. **b** *colloq.* begin. **2** remove (shoes, etc.) by kicking. **kick over the traces** see TRACE². **kick up** (or **kick up a fuss**, **dust**, etc.) create a disturbance; object or register strong disapproval. **kick up one's heels** frolic. **kick a person upstairs** shelve a person by giving him or her a promotion or a title. □□ **kick·a·ble** *adj.* **kick·er** *n.*

Kick·a·poo /kíkəpŏŏ/ *n.* **1 a** a N. American people native to the upper Midwest. **b** a member of this people. **2** the language of this people.

kick·back /kíkbak/ *n. colloq.* **1** the force of a recoil. **2** payment for collaboration.

kick drum *n. colloq.* a bass drum played using a pedal. ▷ DRUM SET

kick·off /kíkawf/ *n.* **1** *Football & Soccer* the start or resumption of play. **2** the start of something, esp. a campaign, drive, or project.

kick·stand /kíkstand/ *n.* a rod attached to a bicycle or motorcycle and kicked into a vertical position to support the vehicle when stationary.

kick-start *v.tr.* **1** start (a motorcycle, etc.) by the downward thrust of a pedal. **2** start or restart (a process, etc.) by providing some initial impetus. □□ **kick start·er** *n.*

kid¹ /kid/ *n. & v.* ● *n.* **1** a young goat. **2** the leather made from its skin. **3** *colloq.* a child or young person. ● *v.intr.* (**kidded, kidding**) (of a goat) give birth. □ **handle with kid gloves** handle in a gentle, delicate, or gingerly manner.

kid² /kid/ *v.* (**kidded, kidding**) *colloq.* **1** *tr. & also refl.* deceive; trick (*don't kid yourself; kidded his mother that he was ill*). **2** *tr. & intr.* tease (*only kidding*). □ **no kidding** *sl.* that is the truth. □□ **kid·der** *n.* **kid·ding·ly** *adv.*

kid·die /kídee/ *n.* (also **kid·dy**) (*pl.* **-ies**) *sl.* = KID¹ *n.* 3.

---

kid·do /kídō/ *n.* (*pl.* **-os**) *sl.* = KID¹ *n.* 3.

kid·nap /kídnap/ *v.tr.* (**kidnapped, kidnapping** or **kidnaped, kidnaping**) **1** carry off (a person, etc.) by illegal force or fraud esp. to obtain a ransom. **2** steal (a child). □□ **kid·nap·per** *n.*

kid·ney /kídnee/ *n.* (*pl.* **-eys**) **1 ▲** either of a pair of organs in the abdominal cavity of mammals, birds, and reptiles, which remove nitrogenous wastes from the blood and excrete urine. ▷ ENDOCRINE, URINARY SYSTEM. **2** the kidney of a sheep, ox, or pig as food. **3** temperament; nature.

kidney bean *n.* **1** a dwarf French bean. **2** a scarlet runner bean. ▷ LEGUME

kid·ney ma·chine *n.* = ARTIFICIAL KIDNEY.

kid stuff *n. sl.* something very simple.

kiel·ba·sa /keelbáasə, kib-/ *n.* a variety of smoked, garlic-flavored sausage.

kie·sel·guhr /kéezəlgŏŏr/ *n.* a soft friable porous form of diatomite forming deposits in lakes and ponds and used as a filter, filler, insulator, etc., in various manufacturing processes.

kif var. of KEF.

ki·lim *n.* **▼** a pileless woven carpet, rug, etc., made in Turkey, Kurdistan, and neighboring areas. *attrib. adj.* designating such a carpet, rug, etc.

KILIM: MODERN TURKISH KILIM

kill¹ /kil/ *v. & n.* ● *v.tr.* **1 a** deprive of life or vitality; put to death; cause the death of. **b** (*absol.*) cause or bring about death (*must kill to survive*). **2** destroy; put an end to (feelings, etc.) (*overwork killed my enthusiasm*). **3** *refl.* (often foll. by pres. part.) *colloq.* **a** overexert oneself (*don't kill yourself lifting them all at once*). **b** laugh heartily. **4** *colloq.* overwhelm (a person) with amusement, delight, etc. (*the things he says really kill me*). **5** switch off (a spotlight, engine, etc.). **6** *colloq.* delete (a line paragraph, etc.) from a computer file. **7** *colloq.* cause pain or discomfort to (*my feet are killing me*). **8** pass (time, or a specified amount of it) usu. while waiting for a specific event (*had an hour to kill before the interview*). **9** defeat (a bill in Congress, etc.). **10** *colloq.* consume the entire contents of (a bottle of wine, etc.). **11 a** *Tennis*, etc., hit (the ball) so skillfully that it cannot be returned. **b** stop (the ball) dead. **12** neutralize or render ineffective (taste, sound, color, etc.) (*thick carpet killed the sound of footsteps*). ● *n.* **1** an act of killing (esp. an animal). **2** an animal or animals killed, esp. by a sportsman. **3** *colloq.* the destruction or disablement of an enemy aircraft, submarine, etc. □ **dressed to kill** dressed showily, alluringly, or impressively. **kill off 1** get rid of or destroy completely (esp. a number of persons or things). **2** (of an author) bring about the death of (a fictional character). **kill or cure** (usu. *attrib.*) (of a remedy, etc.) drastic; extreme. **kill two birds with one stone** achieve two aims at once. **kill with kindness** spoil (a person) with overindulgence.

kill² /kil/ *n. esp. New York State dial.* a stream, creek, or tributary river.

kill·deer /kíldeer/ *n.* a large American plover, *Charadrius vociferus*, with a plaintive song.

kill·er /kílər/ *n.* **1 a** a person, animal, or thing that kills. **b** a murderer. **2** *colloq.* **a** an impressive, formidable, or excellent thing (*this one is quite difficult, but the next one is a real killer*). **b** a hilarious joke. **c** a decisive blow (*his home run proved to be the killer*).

kill·er app /kílər áp/ *n. colloq.* a feature, function, or application of a new technology or product which is presented as virtually indispensable or much superior to rival products.

kill·er bee *n.* a very aggressive honeybee, *Apis mellifera adansonii*, orig. from Africa.

kill·er cell *n. Immunology* a cell that attacks and destroys a cell (as a tumor cell) that bears a specific antigen on its surface.

kill·er in·stinct *n.* **1** an innate tendency to kill. **2** a ruthless streak.

kill·er whale *n.* a voracious cetacean, *Orcinus orca*, with a white belly and prominent dorsal fin.

kil·li·fish /kíleefish/ *n.* **1 ▼** any small fresh- or brackish-water fish of the family Cyprinodontidae, many of which are brightly colored. **2** a brightly colored tropical aquarium fish, *Pterolebias peruensis*.

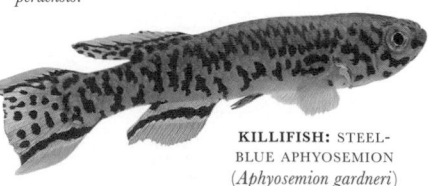

KILLIFISH: STEEL-BLUE APHYOSEMION (*Aphyosemion gardneri*)

kill·ing /kíling/ *n. & adj.* ● *n.* **1 a** the causing of death. **b** an instance of this. **2** a great (esp. financial) success (*make a killing*). ● *adj. colloq.* **1** overwhelmingly funny. **2** exhausting; very strenuous. □□ **kill·ing·ly** *adv.*

kill·joy /kíljoy/ *n.* a person who throws gloom over or prevents other people's enjoyment.

kiln /kiln, kil/ *n.* ▼ a furnace or oven for burning, baking, or drying, esp. for calcining lime or firing pottery, etc.

insulated lining   *shelving*

KILN STACKED WITH POTTERY FOR FIRING

ki·lo /kéelō/ *n.* (*pl.* **-os**) **1** a kilogram. **2** a kilometer.

kilo- /kílō/ *comb. form* denoting a factor of 1,000 (esp. in metric units). ¶ Abbr.: **k**, or **K** in *Computing.*

kil·o·byte /kíləbīt/ *n. Computing* 1,024 (i.e. 2¹⁰) bytes as a measure of memory size.

kil·o·cal·o·rie /kíləkàləree/ *n.* = CALORIE 2.

kil·o·cy·cle /kíləsīkəl/ *n.* a former measure of frequency, equivalent to 1 kilohertz. ¶ Abbr.: **kc**.

kil·o·gram /kíləgram/ *n.* (also *Brit.* **-gramme**) the SI unit of mass, equivalent to the international standard kept at Sèvres near Paris (approx. 2.205 lb.). ¶ Abbr.: **kg**.

kil·o·hertz /kíləhərts/ *n.* a measure of frequency equivalent to 1,000 cycles per second.¶ Abbr.: **kHz**.

kil·o·joule /kíləjool/ *n.* 1,000 joules, esp. as a measure of the energy value of foods. ¶ Abbr.: **kJ**.

kil·o·li·ter /kíləleetər/ *n.* (*Brit.* **-litre**) 1,000 liters (equivalent to 220 imperial gallons). ¶ Abbr.: **kl**.

kil·o·me·ter /kílómitər, kíləmeetər/ *n.* (*Brit.* **kilometre**) a metric unit of measurement equal to 1,000 meters (approx. 0.62 miles). ¶ Abbr.: **km**. □□ **kil·o·met·ric** /kíləmétrik/ *adj.*

kil·o·ton /kílətun/ *n.* a unit of explosive power equivalent to 1,000 tons of TNT.

kil·o·volt /kíləvōlt/ *n.* 1,000 volts. ¶ Abbr.: **kV**.

kil·o·watt /kíləwot/ *n.* 1,000 watts. ¶ Abbr.: **kW**.

kil·o·watt-hour /kíləwot-ówr/ *n.* a measure of electrical energy equivalent to a power consumption of 1,000 watts for one hour. ¶ Abbr.: **kWh**.

kilt /kilt/ *n. & v.* ● *n.* **1** a skirtlike garment, usu. of pleated tartan cloth and reaching to the knees. **2** a similar garment worn by women and children. ● *v.tr.* **1** tuck up (skirts) around the body. **2** (esp. as **kilted** *adj.*) gather in vertical pleats. □□ **kilt·ed** *adj.*

kil·ter /kíltər/ *n.* good working order (esp. *out of kilter*).

kim·ber·lite /kímbərlīt/ *n. Mineral.* a rare igneous blue-tinged rock sometimes containing diamonds, found in South Africa and Siberia.

ki·mo·no /kimónō/ *n.* (*pl.* **-os**) ▶ a long, loose Japanese robe worn with a sash. □□ **ki·mo·noed** *adj.*

KIMONO: TRADITIONAL JAPANESE KIMONO (SASH NOT SHOWN)

kin /kin/ *n. & adj.* ● *n.* one's relatives or family. ● *predic.adj.* (of a person) related (*we are kin; he is kin to me*) (see also AKIN). □ **kith and kin** see KITH. **near of kin** closely related by blood, or in character. □□ **kin·less** *adj.*

-kin /kin/ *suffix* forming diminutive nouns (*catkin; manikin*).

kin·cob /kínkob/ *n.* a rich fabric of India embroidered with gold or silver.

kind¹ /kīnd/ *n.* **1 a** a race or species (*humankind*). **b** a natural group of animals, plants, etc. (*the wolf kind*). **2** class; type; sort; variety (*what kind of job are you looking for?*). ¶ In sense 2, *these* (or *those*) *kind* is often encountered when followed by a plural, as in *I don't like these kind of things*, but *this kind* and *these kinds* are usually preferred. **3** each of the elements of the Eucharist (*communion under* (or *in*) *both kinds*). **4** the manner or fashion natural to a person, etc. (*act after their kind; true to kind*). □ **kind of** *colloq.* to some extent (*felt kind of sorry; I kind of expected it*). **a kind of** used to imply looseness, vagueness, exaggeration, etc., in the term used (*a kind of Jane Austen of our times; I suppose he's a kind of doctor*). **in kind 1** in the same form; likewise (*was insulted and replied in kind*). **2** (of payment) in goods or labor as opposed to money (*received their wages in kind*). **3** in character or quality (*differ in degree but not in kind*). **nothing of the kind 1** not at all like the thing in question. **2** (expressing denial) not at all. **of its kind** within the limitations of its own class (*good of its kind*). **of a kind 1** *derog.* scarcely deserving the name (*a choir of a kind*). **2** similar in some important respect (*they're two of a kind*). **one's own kind** those with whom one has much in common.

kind² /kīnd/ *adj.* **1** of a friendly, generous, benevolent, or gentle nature. **2** (usu. foll. by *to*) showing friendliness, affection, or consideration. **3** affectionate.

kind·a /kíndə/ *colloq.* = *kind of* (see KIND¹ 2).

kin·der·gar·ten /kíndərgaart'n/ *n.* an establishment or class for preschool learning.

kind·heart·ed /kíndháartid/ *adj.* of a kind disposition. □□ **kind·heart·ed·ly** *adv.* **kind·heart·ed·ness** *n.*

kin·dle /kínd'l/ *v.* **1** *tr.* light or set on fire (a flame, fire, substance, etc.). **2** *intr.* catch fire, burst into flame. **3** *tr.* arouse or inspire (*kindle enthusiasm for the project; kindle jealousy in a rival*). **4** *intr.* (usu. foll. by *to*) respond; react (*to a person, an action, etc.*). **5** *intr.* become animated, glow with passion, etc. (*her imagination kindled*). **6** *tr. & intr.* make or become bright (*kindle the embers to a glow*). □□ **kin·dler** *n.*

kin·dling /kíndling/ *n.* small sticks, etc., for lighting fires.

kind·ly¹ /kíndlee/ *adv.* **1** in a kind manner (*spoke to the child kindly*). **2** often *iron.* used in a polite request or demand (*kindly acknowledge this letter; kindly leave me alone*). □ **look kindly upon** regard sympathetically. **take a thing kindly** like or be pleased by it. **take kindly to** be pleased by or endeared to (a person or thing). **thank kindly** thank very much.

kind·ly² /kíndlee/ *adj.* (**kindlier**, **kindliest**) **1** kind; kindhearted. **2** (of climate, etc.) pleasant; genial. □□ **kind·li·ly** *adv.* **kind·li·ness** *n.*

kind·ness /kíndnis/ *n.* **1** the state or quality of being kind. **2** a kind act.

kin·dred /kíndrid/ *n. & adj.* ● *n.* **1** one's relations, referred to collectively. **2** a relationship by blood. **3** a resemblance or affinity in character. ● *adj.* **1** related by blood or marriage. **2** allied or similar in character (*other kindred symptoms*).

kin·dred spir·it *n.* a person whose character and outlook have much in common with one's own.

kin·e·mat·ics /kínimátiks/ *n.pl.* (usu. treated as *sing.*) the branch of mechanics concerned with the motion of objects without reference to the forces which cause the motion. □□ **kin·e·mat·ic** *adj.* **kin·e·mat·i·cal·ly** *adv.*

kin·e·mat·o·graph var. of CINEMATOGRAPH.

ki·ne·sics /kinéesiks, -ziks/ *n.pl.* (usu. treated as *sing.*) **1** the study of body movements and gestures that contribute to communication. **2** these movements; body language.

ki·ne·si·ol·o·gy /kinéeseeóləjee, -zee-/ *n.* the study of the mechanics of body movements.

ki·net·ic /kinétik, kī-/ *adj.* of or due to motion. □□ **ki·net·i·cal·ly** *adv.*

ki·net·ic en·er·gy *n.* the energy of motion.

ki·net·ics /kinétiks, kī-/ *n.pl.* **1** = DYNAMICS 1a. **2** (usu. treated as *sing.*) the branch of physical chemistry concerned with measuring and studying the rates of chemical reactions.

kin·folk /kínfōk/ *n.pl.* (also **kin·folks**, **kins·folk**) one's relations by blood.

king /king/ *n. & v.* ● *n.* **1** (as a title usu. **King**) a male sovereign, esp. the hereditary ruler of an independent nation. **2** a person or thing preeminent in a specified field or class (*railroad king*). **3** a large (or the largest) kind of plant, animal, etc. (*king penguin*). **4** *Chess* the piece on each side that the opposing side has to checkmate to win. ▷ CHESS. **5** a piece in checkers with extra capacity of moving, made by crowning an ordinary piece that has reached the opponent's baseline. **6** ▲ a playing card bearing a representation of a king and usu. ranking next below an ace. **7** (**Kings** or **Books of Kings**) two Old Testament books dealing with history, esp. of the kingdom of Judah. ● *v.tr.* make (a person) king. □ **king it 1** play or act the king. **2** (usu. foll. by *over*) govern; control. □□ **king·hood** *n.* **king·less** *adj.* **king·like** *adj.* **king·ly** *adj.* **king·li·ness** *n.* **king·ship** *n.*

KING OF HEARTS

K

king·bird /kíngbərd/ *n.* any flycatcher of the genus *Tyrannus*, with olive-gray plumage and long pointed wings.

king·bolt /kíngbōlt/ *n.* = KINGPIN 1.

King Charles span·iel *n.* ▼ a spaniel of a small black and tan breed.

KING CHARLES SPANIEL

king co·bra *n.* a large and venomous hooded Indian snake, *Ophiophagus hannah.*

king crab *n.* **1** = HORSESHOE CRAB. **2** any of various large edible spider crabs.

king·dom /kíngdəm/ *n.* **1** an organized community headed by a king. **2** the territory subject to a king. **3 a** the spiritual reign attributed to God (*Thy kingdom come*). **b** the sphere of this (*kingdom of heaven*). **4** a domain belonging to a person, animal, etc. **5** a province of nature (*the vegetable kingdom*). **6** a specified mental or emotional province (*kingdom of the heart; kingdom of fantasy*). **7** *Biol.* the highest category in taxonomic classification. □ **kingdom come**

colloq. eternity; the next world. **till kingdom come** *colloq.* for ever. □□ **king·domed** *adj.*

king·fish /kíngfish/ *n.* any of various large fish, esp. the opah or mulloway.

king·fish·er /kíngfishər/ *n.* any bird of the family Alcedinidae, esp. *Alcedo atthis*, with a long sharp beak and brightly colored plumage, which dives for fish in rivers, etc.

King James Bi·ble *n.* = AUTHORIZED VERSION.

king·let /kínglit/ *n.* **1** a petty king. **2** any of various small birds of the family Regulidae, esp. the gold-crest.

king·mak·er /kíngmaykər/ *n.* a person who makes kings, leaders, etc., through the exercise of political influence, orig. with ref. to the Earl of Warwick in the reign of Henry VI of England.

king·pin /kíngpin/ *n.* **1 a** a main or large bolt in a central position. **b** a vertical bolt used as a pivot. **2** an essential person or thing, esp. in a complex system; the most important person in an organization.

king-size *adj.* (also **king-sized**) larger than normal; very large.

king's ran·som *n.* a fortune.

kink /kingk/ *n. & v.* ● *n.* **1 a** a short backward twist in wire or tubing, etc., such as may cause an obstruction. **b** a tight wave in human or animal hair. **2** a mental twist or quirk. ● *v.intr. & tr.* form or cause to form a kink.

kin·ka·jou /kíngkəjoo/ *n.* ◄ a Central and S. American nocturnal fruit-eating mammal, *Potos flavus*, with a prehensile tail and living in trees.

kink·y /kíngkee/ *adj.* (**kinkier**, **kinkiest**) **1** *colloq.* **a** given to or involving abnormal sexual behavior. **b** (of clothing, etc.) bizarre in a sexually provocative way. **2** strange; eccentric. **3** having kinks or twists. □□ **kink·i·ly** *adv.* **kink·i·ness** *n.*

kins·folk var. of KINFOLK.

kin·ship /kínship/ *n.* **1** blood relationship. **2** the sharing of characteristics or origins.

kins·man /kínzmən/ *n.* (*pl.* **-men**; *fem.* **kinswoman**, *pl.* **-women**) **1** a blood relation or *disp.* a relation by marriage. **2** a member of one's own tribe or people.

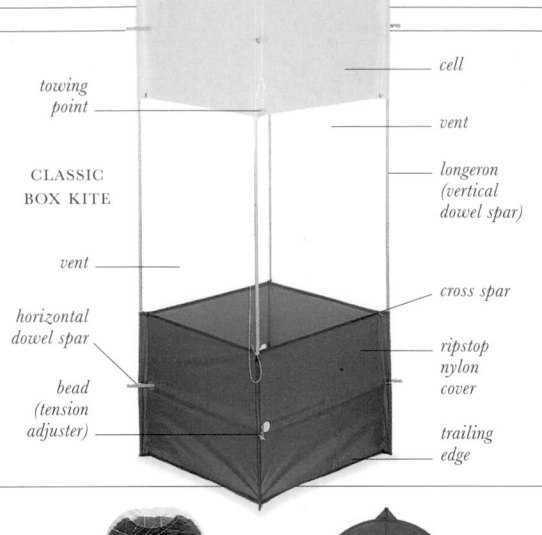

KINKAJOU
(*Potos flavus*)

ki·osk /kéeosk, -ósk/ *n.* **1** a light, open-fronted booth or cubicle from which food, newspapers, tickets, etc., are sold. **2** *Brit.* a telephone booth. **3** a building in which refreshments are served in a park, zoo, etc.

Ki·o·wa /kíəwə/ *n.* **1 a** a N. American people native to the southwest. **b** a member of this people. **2** the language of this people.

kip /kip/ *n. & v. Brit. sl.* ● *n.* **1** a sleep or nap. **2** a bed or cheap motel, etc. **3** (also **kip-house** or **-shop**) a brothel. ● *v.intr.* (**kipped**, **kipping**) **1** sleep; take a nap. **2** (foll. by *down*) lie or settle down to sleep.

kip·per /kípər/ *n. & v.* ● *n.* **1** a kippered fish, esp. herring. **2** a male salmon in the spawning season. ● *v.tr.* cure (a herring, etc.) by splitting open, salting, and drying in the open air or smoke.

Kir /keer/ *n.* a drink made from dry white wine and crème de cassis.

kirk /kurk/ *n. Sc. & N. England* a church.

kirsch /keersh/ *n.* (also **kirsch·was·ser** /kéershvaasər/) a brandy distilled from the fermented juice of cherries.

kis·ka·dee /kískədée/ *n.* (also **kes·ki·dee** /késkidée/) a tyrant flycatcher, *Pitangus sulphuratus*, of Central and S. America, with brown and yellow plumage.

KITE

Kites were first developed more than 2,500 years ago by the ancient Chinese who used them for aerial reconnaissance in battle and to bear archers aloft over the enemy. Today, kites are flown both as a pastime and as a sport. A basic kite consists of a nylon-covered frame supported by spars. Launched and held aloft by rising wind currents, the kite is controlled from the ground by a flying line.

towing point
cell
vent
CLASSIC BOX KITE
longeron (vertical dowel spar)
vent
cross spar
horizontal dowel spar
ripstop nylon cover
bead (tension adjuster)
trailing edge

OTHER TYPES OF KITE

DELTA KITE

FLAT KITE

STUNT KITE

AIRFOIL KITE

TRI-D KITE

---

kis·met /kízmet/ *n.* destiny; fate.

kiss /kis/ *v. & n.* ● *v.* **1** *tr.* touch with the lips, esp. as a sign of love, affection, greeting, or reverence. **2** *tr.* express (greeting or farewell) in this way. **3** *absol.* (of two persons) touch each others' lips in this way. **4** *tr.* (also *absol.*) (of a billiard ball, etc., in motion) lightly touch (another ball). ● *n.* **1** a touch with the lips in kissing. **2** the slight impact when one billiard ball, etc., lightly touches another. **3** a usu. droplet-shaped piece of candy or small cookie. □ **kiss and tell** recount sexual exploits. **kiss a person's ass** (or **butt**) *coarse sl.* act obsequiously toward a person. **kiss away** remove (tears, etc.) by kissing. **kiss the dust** submit abjectly; be overthrown. **kiss good-bye to** *colloq.* accept the loss of. **kiss the ground** prostrate oneself as a token of homage. **kiss off** *sl.* **1** dismiss; get rid of. **2** go away; die. □□ **kiss·a·ble** *adj.*

kiss·er /kísər/ *n.* **1** a person who kisses. **2** (orig. *Boxing*) *sl.* the mouth; the face.

kiss·ing cous·in *n.* (also **kiss·ing kin**) a distant relative (given a formal kiss on occasional meetings).

kiss of death *n.* an apparently friendly act which causes ruin.

kiss of life *n.* mouth-to-mouth resuscitation.

kiss of peace *n. Eccl.* a ceremonial kiss, esp. during the Eucharist, as a sign of unity.

kiss·y /kísee/ *adj. colloq.* given to kissing (*not the kissy type*).

kist var. of CIST.

Ki·swa·hi·li /kíswaahéelee/ *n.* one of the six languages preferred for use in Africa by the Organization for African Unity.

kit[1] /kit/ *n.* **1** a set of articles, equipment, or clothing needed for a specific purpose (*first-aid kit; bicycle-*

repair kit). **2** a set of all the parts needed to assemble an item, e.g., a piece of furniture, a model, etc. □ **the whole kit and caboodle**.

kit[2] /kit/ *n.* **1** a kitten. **2** a young fox, badger, etc.

kit[3] /kit/ *n. hist.* a small fiddle, esp. as used by a dancing master.

kit bag *n.* a large, usu. cylindrical bag used for carrying a soldier's, traveler's, or sportsman's equipment.

kitch·en /kíchin/ *n.* **1** the room or area where food is prepared and cooked. **2** (*attrib.*) of or belonging to the kitchen (*kitchen knife; kitchen table*). **3** *sl.* the percussion section of an orchestra. □ **everything but the kitchen sink** everything imaginable.

kitch·en cab·i·net *n.* a group of unofficial advisers thought to be unduly influential.

kitch·en·ette /kíchinét/ *n.* a small kitchen or part of a room fitted as a kitchen.

kitch·en·ware /kíchinwair/ *n.* the utensils used in the kitchen.

kite /kīt/ *n. & v.* ● *n.* **1** ▲ a toy consisting of a light framework with thin material stretched over it, flown in the wind at the end of a long string. **2** any of various soaring birds of prey esp. of the genus *Milvus* with long wings and usu. a forked tail. **3** *Brit. sl.* an airplane. **4** *sl.* a fraudulent check, bill, or receipt. **5** *Geom.* a quadrilateral figure symmetrical about one diagonal. **6** *sl.* a letter or note, esp. one that is illicit or surreptitious. **7** (in *pl.*) the highest sail of a ship, set only in a light wind. ● *v.* **1** *intr.* soar like a kite. **2** *tr.* (also *absol.*) originate or pass (fraudulent checks, bills, or receipts). **3** *tr.* (also *absol.*) raise (money by dishonest means) (*kite a loan*).

kith /kith/ *n.* □ **kith and kin** friends and relations.

kitsch /kich/ *n.* (often *attrib.*) garish, pretentious, or sentimental art, usu. vulgar and worthless (*kitsch*

K

plastic models of the Lincoln Memorial). □□ **kitsch·y** *adj.* (**kitschier, kitschiest**). **kitsch·i·ness** *n.*

kit·ten /kít'n/ *n. & v.* ● *n.* **1** a young cat. **2** a young ferret, etc. ● *v.intr. & tr.* (of a cat, etc.) give birth or give birth to. □ **have kittens** *colloq.* be extremely upset, anxious, or nervous.

kitten heel *n.* a type of low heel on a woman's shoe.

kit·ten·ish /kít'nish/ *adj.* **1** like a young cat; playful and lively. **2** flirtatious. □□ **kit·ten·ish·ly** *adv.* **kit·ten·ish·ness** *n.*

kit·ti·wake /kíteewayk/ *n.* either of two small gulls, *Rissa tridactyla* and *R. brevirostris,* nesting on sea cliffs.

kit·ty[1] /kítee/ *n.* (*pl.* **-ies**) **1** a fund of money for communal use. **2** the pool in some card games.

kit·ty[2] /kítee/ *n.* (*pl.* **-ies**) a pet name or a child's name for a kitten or cat.

kit·ty-cor·ner var. of CATERCORNERED.

Kit·ty Lit·ter *n. Trademark* a granular clay used in boxes to absorb pet (esp. cat) waste.

ki·wi /kéewee/ *n.* (*pl.* **kiwis**) **1** ▼ a flightless New Zealand bird of the genus *Apteryx* with hairlike feathers and a long bill. Also called **apteryx**. **2** (**Kiwi**) *colloq.* a New Zealander, esp. a soldier or member of a national sports team.

KIWI:
BROWN KIWI
(*Apteryx australis*)

ki·wi fruit *n.* ◄ the fruit of a climbing plant, *Actinidia chinensis,* having a thin hairy skin, green flesh, and black seeds. Also called **Chinese goose-berry**.

kJ *abbr.* kilojoule(s).

KKK *abbr.* Ku Klux Klan.

kl *abbr.* kiloliter(s).

Klax·on /kláksən/ *n.* a loud horn, orig. on a motor vehicle.

Kleen·ex /kléeneks/ *n.* (*pl.* same or **Kleenexes**) *Trademark* an absorbent disposable paper tissue, used esp. as a handkerchief.

KIWI FRUIT
(*Actinidia chinensis*)

Klein bot·tle /klīn/ *n. Math.* a closed surface with only one side, formed by passing the neck of a tube through the side of the tube to join the hole in the base.

klep·to·crat /kléptōkrat/ *n.* a ruler who uses his or her power to steal a country's resources.

klep·to·ma·ni·a /kléptəmáyneeə/ *n.* a recurrent urge to steal, usu. without regard for need or profit. □□ **klep·to·ma·ni·ac** *n. & adj.*

klieg /kleeg/ *n.* (also **klieg light**) a powerful lamp in a movie studio, etc.

klip·spring·er /klípspringər/ *n.* a S. African dwarf antelope, *Oreotragus oreotragus,* which can bound up and down rocky slopes.

Klon·dike /klóndīk/ *n.* a source of valuable material.

kludge /kloōj/ *n. sl.* **1** an ill-assorted collection of poorly matching parts. **2** *Computing* a machine, system, or program that has been badly put together.

klutz /kluts/ *n. sl.* **1** a clumsy awkward person. **2** a fool. □□ **klutz·y** *adj.*

klys·tron /klístron/ *n.* an electron tube that generates or amplifies microwaves by velocity modulation.

km *abbr.* kilometer(s).

K-me·son /kaymézon, -més-, -méezon, -son/ *n.* = KAON.

kmph *abbr.* kilometers per hour.

kmps *abbr.* kilometers per second.

kn. *abbr. Naut.* knot(s).

knack /nak/ *n.* **1** an acquired or intuitive faculty of doing a thing adroitly. **2** a trick or habit of action or speech, etc. (*has a knack of offending people*).

knack·wurst var. of KNOCKWURST.

knag /nag/ *n.* **1** a knot in wood; the base of a branch. **2** a short dead branch. **3** esp. *Brit.* a peg for hanging things on. □□ **knag·gy** *adj.*

knap /nap/ *v.tr.* (**knapped, knapping**) **1** break (stones for roads or building, flints, or *Austral.* ore) with a hammer. **2** *archaic* knock; rap; snap asunder. □□ **knap·per** *n.*

knap·sack /nápsak/ *n.* a soldier's or hiker's bag with shoulder straps, carried on the back, and usu. made of canvas or weatherproof material.

knap·weed /nápweed/ *n.* ► any of various plants of the genus *Centaurea,* having thistlelike purple flowers.

knar /naar/ *n.* a knot or protuberance in a tree trunk, root, etc.

knave /nayv/ *n.* **1** a rogue; a scoundrel. **2** = JACK[1] *n.* 2. □□ **knav·er·y** *n.* (*pl.* **-ies**). **knav·ish** *adj.* **knav·ish·ly** *adv.* **knav·ish·ness** *n.*

knaw·el /náwəl/ *n.* any low-growing plant of the genus *Scleranthus.*

knead /need/ *v.tr.* **1 a** work (a yeast mixture, clay, etc.) into dough, paste, etc., by pressing and folding. **b** make (bread, pottery, etc.) in this way. **2** blend or weld together. **3** massage (muscles, etc.) as if kneading. □□ **knead·a·ble** *adj.* **kneader** *n.*

KNAPWEED:
COMMON
KNAPWEED
(*Centaurea nigra*)

knee /nee/ *n. & v.* ● *n.* **1 a** (often *attrib.*) ▼ the joint between the thigh and the lower leg in humans. ▷ JOINT. **b** the corresponding joint in other animals. **c** the area around this. **d** the upper surface of the thigh of a sitting person; the lap. **2** the part of a garment covering the knee. **3** anything resembling a knee in shape or position, esp. a piece of wood or iron bent at an angle, a sharp turn in a graph, etc. ● *v.tr.* (**knees, kneed, kneeing**) **1** touch or strike with the knee (*kneed him in the groin*). **2** *colloq.* cause (pants) to bulge at the knee. □ **bring a person to his** or **her knees** reduce a person to submission. **on** (or

on one's) **bended knee** (or **knees**) kneeling, esp. in supplication, submission, or worship.

knee·cap /néekap/ *n. & v.* ● *n.* **1** the convex bone in front of the knee joint. ▷ KNEE. **2** a protective covering for the knee. ● *v.tr.* (**-capped, -capping**) *colloq.* shoot (a person) in the knee or leg as a punishment, esp. for betraying a terrorist group. □□ **knee·cap·ping** *n.*

knee-deep *adj.* **1** (usu. foll. by *in*) **a** immersed up to the knees. **b** deeply involved. **2** so deep as to reach the knees.

knee·hole /néehōl/ *n.* a space for the knees, esp. under a desk.

knee jerk *n.* a sudden involuntary kick caused by a blow on the tendon just below the knee.

knee-jerk *attrib.adj.* predictable; automatic; stereotyped.

kneel /neel/ *v.intr.* (*past* and *past part.* **knelt** /nelt/ or **kneeled**) fall or rest on the knees or a knee.

kneel·er /néelər/ *n.* **1** a hassock or cushion used for kneeling, esp. in church. **2** a person who kneels.

knee·pan /néepan/ *n.* the kneecap.

knell /nel/ *n. & v.* ● *n.* **1** the sound of a bell, esp. when rung solemnly for a death or funeral. **2** an announcement, event, etc., regarded as a solemn warning of disaster. ● *v.* **1** *intr.* **a** (of a bell) ring solemnly, esp. for a death or funeral. **b** make a dolcful or ominous sound. **2** *tr.* proclaim by or as by a knell (*knelled the death of all their hopes*).

knelt *past* and *past part.* of KNEEL.

Knes·set /knéset/ *n.* the parliament of modern Israel.

knew *past* of KNOW.

knick·er·bock·er /níkərbokər/ *n.* **1** (in *pl.*) = KNICKERS 1. **2** (**Knickerbocker**) **a** a New Yorker. **b** a descendant of the original Dutch settlers in New York.

knick·ers /níkərz/ *n.pl.* **1** ► loose-fitting pants gathered at the knee or calf. **2** *Brit.* = PANTIES. **3** (as *int.*) *Brit. sl.* an expression of contempt.

knick·knack /níknak/ *n.* **1** a useless and usu. worthless ornament; a trinket. **2** a small, dainty article of furniture, dress, etc. □□ **knick·knack·er·y** *n.* **knick·knack·ish** *adj*

knife /nīf/ *n. & v.* ● *n.* (*pl.* **knives** /nīvz/) **1 a** a metal blade used as a cutting tool with usu. one long, sharp edge fixed rigidly in a handle or hinged (cf. PENKNIFE). **b** a similar tool used as a weapon. **2** a cutting blade forming part of a machine. ● *v.tr.* **1** cut or stab with a knife. **2** *sl.* bring about the defeat of (a person) by underhand means. □ **get one's knife into** treat maliciously or vindictively; persecute. **that one could cut with a knife** *colloq.* (of an accent, atmosphere, etc.) very obvious, oppressive, etc. **under the knife** undergoing a surgical operation or operations. □□ **knife·like** *adj.* **knif·er** *n.*

knickers

KNICKERS:
1920S PLUS-TWO
KNICKERS

knife pleat *n.* a narrow flat pleat on a skirt, etc., usu. overlapping another.

knife·point /nīfpoynt/ *n.* the point of a knife. □ **at knifepoint** threatened with a knife or an ultimatum, etc.

knight /nīt/ *n. & v.* ● *n.* **1** a man awarded a non-hereditary title (*Sir*) by a sovereign in recognition of merit or service. **2** *hist.* **a** a man, usu. noble, raised esp. by a sovereign to honorable military rank after service as a page and squire. ▷ JOUST, TABARD. **b** a military follower or attendant, esp. of a lady as her champion in a war or tournament. **3** a man devoted to the service of a woman, cause, etc. **4** *Chess* a piece usu. shaped like a horse's head. ▷ CHESS. ● *v.tr.* confer a knighthood on. □□ **knight·hood** *n.* **knight·like** *adj.* **knight·ly** *adj. & adv. poet.* **knight·li·ness** *n.*

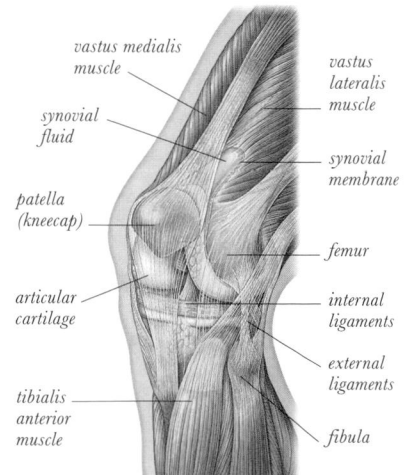

vastus medialis muscle

vastus lateralis muscle

synovial fluid

synovial membrane

patella (kneecap)

femur

articular cartilage

internal ligaments

external ligaments

tibialis anterior muscle

fibula

KNEE: HUMAN LEG SHOWING THE KNEE

KNIT

The earliest known samples of true knitting date from 7th-century Arabia. Modern knitting still consists of the creation of a continuous looped fabric using a length of yarn and two or more eyeless needles. The combination of knit, purl, and other stitches, together with colored yarns and needles of varying size, can produce an enormous diversity of sophisticated effects and textures.

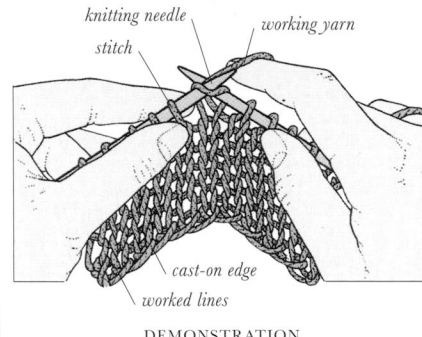

DEMONSTRATION
OF THE KNIT STITCH

TYPES OF KNITTING STITCH

GARTER STITCH

STOCKINETTE STITCH

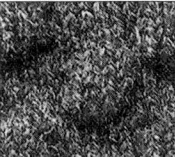

BERRY STITCH

DOUBLE MOSS STITCH

BASKETWEAVE
STITCH

SIX-STITCH
CABLE

K

knight-er·rant n. **1** a medieval knight wandering in search of chivalrous adventures. **2** a man of a chivalrous or quixotic nature. □□ **knight-er·rant·ry** n.

knish /knish/ n. a dumpling of flaky dough filled with potato, meat, cheese, etc., and baked or fried.

knit /nit/ v. & n. ● v. (**knitting**; past and past part. **knitted** or (esp. in senses 2–4) **knit**) **1** tr. (also absol.) **a** ▲ make (a garment, blanket, etc.) by interlocking loops of yarn with knitting needles. **b** make (a garment, etc.) with a knitting machine. **c** make (a plain stitch) in knitting (knit one, purl one). **2 a** tr. contract (the forehead) in vertical wrinkles. **b** intr. (of the forehead) contract; frown. **3** tr. & intr. (often foll. by together) make or become close or compact, esp. by common interests, etc. (a close-knit group). **4** intr. (often foll. by together) (of parts of a broken bone) become joined; heal. ● n. knitted material or a knitted garment. □□ **knit·ter** n.

knit·ting /níting/ n. **1** a garment, etc., in the process of being knitted. **2 a** the act of knitting. **b** an instance of this.

knit·ting ma·chine n. a machine used for mechanically knitting garments, etc.

knit·ting nee·dle n. a thin pointed rod of steel, wood, plastic, etc., used esp. in pairs for knitting. ▷ KNITTING

knit·wear /nítwair/ n. knitted garments.

knives pl. of KNIFE.

knob /nob/ n. & v. ● n. **1 a** a rounded protuberance, esp. at the end or on the surface of a thing. **b** a handle of a door, drawer, etc., shaped like a knob. **c** a knob-shaped attachment for pulling, turning, etc. (press the knob under the desk). **2** Brit. a small, usu. round, piece (of butter, coal, sugar, etc.). ● v. (**knobbed**, **knobbing**) **1** tr. provide with knobs. **2** intr. (usu. foll. by out) bulge. □□ **knob·by** adj. **knob·like** adj.

knob·ble /nóbəl/ n. a small knob. □□ **knob·bly** adj.

knock /nok/ v. & n. ● v. **1 a** tr. strike (a hard surface) with an audible sharp blow (knocked the table three times). **b** intr. strike, esp. a door, to gain admittance (can you hear someone knocking?; knocked at the door). **2** tr. make (a hole, a dent, etc.) by knocking (knock a hole in the fence). **3** tr. (usu. foll. by in, out, off, etc.) drive (a thing, a person, etc.) by striking (knocked the ball into

the hole; knocked those ideas out of his head; knocked her hand away). **4** tr. sl. criticize. **5** intr. **a** (of a motor or other engine) make a thumping or rattling noise, esp. as the result of a loose bearing. **b** (of a vehicle engine) emit a series of high-pitched explosive sounds caused by faulty combustion. ● n. **1** an act of knocking. **2** a sharp rap, esp. at a door. **3** an audible sharp blow. **4** the sound of knocking, esp. in a motor engine. □ **knock about** (or **around**) **1** strike repeatedly; treat roughly. **2** lead a wandering adventurous life; wander aimlessly. **3** be present without design or volition (there's a cup knocking about somewhere). **4** (usu. foll. by with) be associated socially (knocks about with his brother). **knock the bottom out of** prove (a thing) worthless. **knock down 1** strike (esp. a person) to the ground with a blow. **2** demolish. **3** (usu. foll. by to) (at an auction) dispose of (an article) to a bidder by a knock with a hammer (knocked the Picasso down to him for a million). **4** colloq. lower the price of (an article). **5** take (machinery, furniture, etc.) to pieces for transportation. **6** sl. steal. **knock one's head against** come into collision with (unfavorable facts or conditions). **knock into a cocked hat** see COCK¹. **knock into the middle of next week** colloq. send (a person) flying, esp. with a blow. **knock into shape** see SHAPE. **knock off 1** strike off with a blow. **2** colloq. **a** finish work (knocked off at 5:30). **b** finish (work) (knocked off work early). **3** colloq. dispatch (business). **4** colloq. rapidly produce (a work of art, verses, etc.). **5** (often foll. by from) deduct (a sum) from a price, bill, etc. **6** sl. steal from (knocked off a liquor store). **7** Brit. coarse sl. offens. have sexual intercourse with (a woman). **8** sl. kill. **knock on** (or **knock**) **wood** knock something wooden with the knuckles to avert bad luck. **knock out 1** make (a person) unconscious by a blow on the head. **2** knock down (a boxer) for a count of 10, thereby winning the contest. **3** defeat, esp. in a knockout competition. **4** sl. astonish. **5** (refl.) colloq. exhaust (knocked themselves out swimming). **6** colloq. make or write (a plan, etc.) hastily. **knock sideways** colloq. disconcert; astonish. **knock together** put together or assemble hastily or roughly. **knock up 1** make or arrange hastily. **2** damage or mar. **3 a** become exhausted or ill. **b** exhaust or make ill. **4** Brit. arouse (a person) by a knock at the door. **5** coarse sl. make pregnant. **take a** (or **the**) **knock** esp. Brit. be hard hit financially or emotionally.

knock·a·bout /nókəbowt/ attrib.adj. **1** (of comedy) boisterous; slapstick. **2** (of clothes) suitable for rough use.

knock·down /nókdown/ adj. & n. ● adj. **1** (of a blow, misfortune, argument, etc.) overwhelming. **2** Brit. (of a price) very low. **3** (of a price at auction) reserve. **4** (of furniture, etc.) easily dismantled and reassembled. ● n. **1** a knockdown item. **2** sl. an introduction to a person.

knock·er /nókər/ n. **1** a metal or wooden instrument hinged to a door for knocking to call attention. **2** a person or thing that knocks. **3** (in pl.) coarse sl. a woman's breasts.

knock-knees n.pl. a condition in which the legs curve inward at the knee. □□ **knock-kneed** adj.

knock·out /nókowt/ n. **1** the act of making unconscious by a blow. **2** Boxing, etc., a blow that knocks an opponent out. **3** a competition in which the loser in each round is eliminated (also attrib.: a knock-out round). **4** colloq. an outstanding or irresistible person or thing.

knock·wurst /náakwərst/ n. a variety of thick, seasoned sausage.

knoll /nōl/ n. a small hill or mound.

knop /nop/ n. **1** a knob, esp. ornamental. **2** an ornamental loop or tuft in yarn.

knot¹ /not/ n. & v. ● n. **1 a** ▶ an intertwining of a rope, string, tress of hair, etc., with another, itself, or something else to join or fasten together. **b** a set method of tying a knot (a reef knot). **c** a ribbon, etc., tied as an ornament and worn on a dress, etc. **d** a tangle in hair, knitting, etc. **2 a** a unit of a ship's or aircraft's speed equivalent to one nautical mile per hour (see NAUTICAL MILE). **b** a division marked by knots on a log line, as a measure of speed. **c** colloq. a nautical mile. **3** (usu. foll. by of) a group or cluster (a small knot of journalists at the gate). **4** something forming or maintaining a union; a bond or tie, esp. of wedlock. **5** a hard lump of tissue in an animal or human body. **6 a** a knob or protuberance in a stem, branch, or root. **b** a hard mass formed in a tree trunk at the intersection with a branch. **c** a round cross-grained piece in lumber where a branch has been cut through. **d** a node on the stem of a plant. **7** a difficulty; a problem. **8** a central point in a problem or the plot of a story, etc. ● v. (**knotted**, **knotting**) **1** tr. tie (a string, etc.) in a knot. **2** tr. entangle. **3** tr. esp. Brit. knit (the brows). **4** tr. unite closely or intricately (knotted together in intrigue). **5 a** intr. make knots for fringing. **b** tr. make (a fringe) with knots. □ **tie in knots** colloq. baffle or confuse completely. **tie the knot** get married. □□ **knot·less** adj. **knot·ter** n. **knot·ting** n. (esp. in sense 5 of v.).

knot² /not/ n. a small sandpiper, *Calidris canutus*.

knot·grass /nótgras/ n. **1** ▶ a common weed, *Polygonum aviculare*, with creeping stems and small pink flowers. **2** = POLY-GONUM. Also called **knotweed**.

knot·hole /nót-hōl/ n. a hole in a piece of lumber where a knot has fallen out.

knot·ty /nótee/ adj. (**knot·tier, knot·tiest**) **1** full of knots. **2** hard to explain; puzzling (a knotty problem). □□ **knot·ti·ly** adv. **knot·ti·ness** n.

knot·weed /nótweed/ n. = POLY-GONUM.

knot·work /nótwərk/ n. ornamental work representing or consisting of intertwined cords.

KNOTGRASS
(*Polygonum aviculare*)

know /nō/ v. & n. ● v. (past **knew** /nōō, nyōō/; past part. **known** /nōn/) **1** tr. (often foll. by that, how, what, etc.) **a** have in the mind; have learned; be able to recall (knows a lot about cars; knows what to do). **b** (also absol.) be aware of (a fact) (he knows I am waiting; I think she knows). **c** have a good command of (a subject or language) (knew German; knows his multiplication tables). **2** tr. be

KNOT

Early people first tied knots in single-strand fibers, and later into longer, thicker ropes. Modern knot types suit specific purposes. Stopper knots prevent lines from sliding through the hands and may add weight to the end of a throwing line. Binding knots are used to fasten tightly around an object or to tie sails. Bends join two ropes of similar or different weight, while quick-release hitches can secure rope to a pole or ring or may tether animals. Loop knots may be dropped over an object, threaded through a ring, or tied around the wrist or waist.

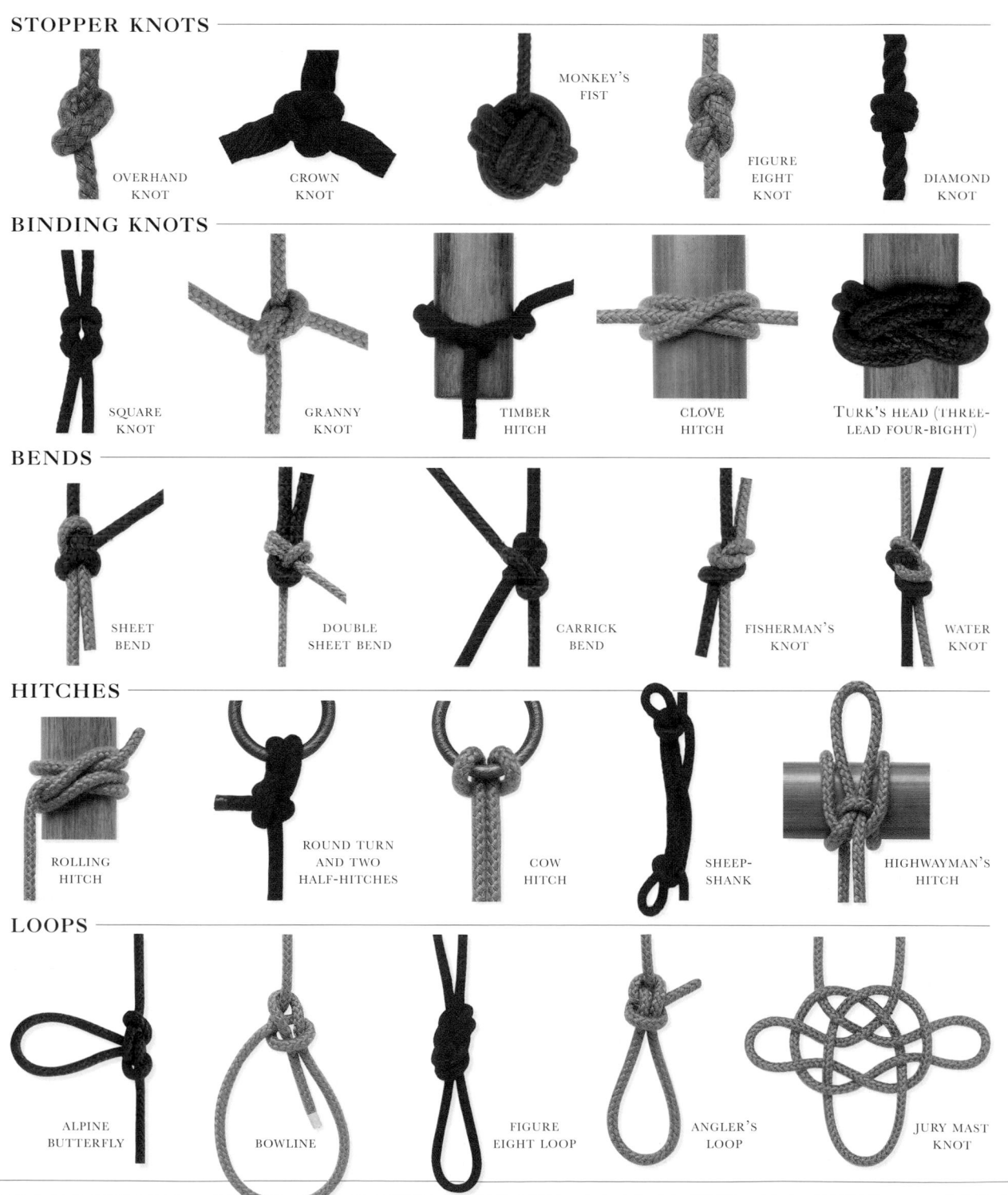

STOPPER KNOTS

OVERHAND KNOT

CROWN KNOT

MONKEY'S FIST

FIGURE EIGHT KNOT

DIAMOND KNOT

BINDING KNOTS

SQUARE KNOT

GRANNY KNOT

TIMBER HITCH

CLOVE HITCH

TURK'S HEAD (THREE-LEAD FOUR-BIGHT)

BENDS

SHEET BEND

DOUBLE SHEET BEND

CARRICK BEND

FISHERMAN'S KNOT

WATER KNOT

HITCHES

ROLLING HITCH

ROUND TURN AND TWO HALF-HITCHES

COW HITCH

SHEEP-SHANK

HIGHWAYMAN'S HITCH

LOOPS

ALPINE BUTTERFLY

BOWLINE

FIGURE EIGHT LOOP

ANGLER'S LOOP

JURY MAST KNOT

K

acquainted or friendly with (a person or thing). **3** *tr.* **a** recognize; identify (*I knew him at once; knew him to be an Englishman*). **b** (foll. by *to* + infin.) be aware of (a person or thing) as being or doing what is specified (*knew them to be rogues*). **c** (foll. by *from*) be able to distinguish (one from another) (*did not know him from Adam*). **4** *tr.* be subject to (*her joy knew no bounds*). **5** *tr.* have personal experience of (fear, etc.). **6** *tr.* (as **known** *adj.*) **a** publicly acknowledged (*a known thief; a known fact*). **b** *Math.* (of a quantity, etc.) having a value that can be stated. **7** *intr.* have understanding or knowledge. **8** *tr. archaic* have sexual intercourse with. • *n.* (in phr. **in the know**) *colloq.* well-informed; having special knowledge. □ **all one knows** (or **knows how**) **1** all one can (*did all she knew to stop it*). **2** *adv.* to the utmost of one's power (*tried all she knew*). **before one knows where one is** with baffling speed. **be not to know 1** have no way of learning (*wasn't to know they'd arrive late*). **2** be not to be told (*she's not to know about the party*). **don't I know it!** *colloq.* an expression of rueful assent. **don't you know** *colloq.* or *joc.* an expression used for emphasis (*such a bore, don't you know*). **for all I know** so far as my knowledge extends. **have been known to** be known to have done (*they have been known to not turn up*). **I knew it!** I was sure that this would happen. **know about** have information about. **know best** be or claim to be better informed, etc., than others. **know better than** (foll. by *that*, or *to* + infin.) be wise, well-informed, or well-mannered enough to avoid (specified behavior, etc.). **know by name 1** have heard the name of. **2** be able to give the name of. **know by sight** recognize the appearance (only) of. **know how** know the way to do something. **know of** be aware of; have heard of (*not that I know of*). **know the ropes** (or **one's stuff**) be fully knowledgeable or experienced. **know a thing or two** be experienced or shrewd. **know what's what** have adequate knowledge of the world, life, etc. **know who's who** be aware of who or what each person is. **not know that ...** *colloq.* be fairly sure that something is not the case (*I don't know that I want to go*). **not know what hit one** be suddenly injured, killed, disconcerted, etc. **not want to know** refuse to take any notice of. **what do you know** *colloq.* an expression of surprise. **you know** *colloq.* **1** an expression implying something generally known or known to the hearer (*you know, the store on the corner*). **2** an expression used as a gap-filler in conversation. **you know something** (or **what**)? I am going to tell you something. **you never know** nothing in the future is certain. □□ **know·a·ble** *adj.* **know·er** *n.*

know-how *n.* **1** practical knowledge; technique; expertise. **2** natural skill or invention.

know·ing /nṓing/ *n. & adj.* • *n.* the state of being aware or informed of any thing. • *adj.* **1** usu. *derog.* cunning; sly. **2** showing knowledge; shrewd. □ **there is no knowing** no one can tell. □□ **know·ing·ness** *n.*

know·ing·ly /nṓinglee/ *adv.* **1** consciously; intentionally (*had never knowingly injured him*). **2** in a knowing manner (*smiled knowingly*).

know-it-all *n. colloq.* a person who acts as if he or she knows everything.

knowl·edge /nólij/ *n.* **1 a** (usu. foll. by *of*) awareness or familiarity gained by experience (of a person, fact, or thing) (*have no knowledge of their character*). **b** a person's range of information (*is not within his knowledge*). **c** specific information; facts or intelligence about something (*received knowledge of their imminent departure*). **2 a** (usu. foll. by *of*) a theoretical or practical understanding of a subject, language, etc. **b** the sum of what is known (*every branch of knowledge*). **c** learning; scholarship. **3** *Philos.* true, justified belief; certain understanding, as opp. to opinion. **4** = CARNAL KNOWLEDGE. □ **to my knowledge 1** so far as I know. **2** as I know for certain.

knowl·edge·a·ble /nólijəbəl/ *adj.* (also **knowl·edge·a·ble**) well-informed; intelligent. □□ **knowl·edge·a·bil·i·ty** *n.* **knowl·edge·a·ble·ness** *n.* **knowl·edge·a·bly** *adv.*

---

know-noth·ing *n.* an ignorant person.

Know-noth·ing par·ty *n.* *US Hist.* a short-lived 19th-century political party advocating intolerance toward immigrants and Roman Catholics esp. as political candidates.

known past part. of KNOW.

knuck·le /núkəl/ *n. & v.* • *n.* **1** the bone at a finger joint, esp. that adjoining the hand. **2 a** a projection of the carpal or tarsal joint of a quadruped. **b** a joint of meat consisting of this with the adjoining parts, esp. of bacon or pork. • *v.tr.* strike, press, or rub with the knuckles. □ **knuckle down** (often foll. by *to*) **1** apply oneself seriously (to a task, etc.). **2** give in; submit. **knuckle under** give in; submit. **rap** (or **over**) **the knuckles** see RAP¹. □□ **knuck·ly** *adj.*

knuck·le·ball /núkəlbawl/ *n.* *Baseball* a pitch delivered with the ball held by the knuckles or fingernails such that the thrown ball has minimal spin and moves erratically. □□ **knuck·le·ball·er** *n.*

knuck·le·bone /núkəlbōn/ *n.* **1** bone forming a knuckle. **2** the bone of a sheep or other animal corresponding to or resembling a knuckle. **3** a knuckle of meat. **4** (in *pl.*) animal knucklebones used in the game of jacks. **5** (in *pl.*) the game of jacks.

knuck·le·head /núkəlhed/ *n.* *colloq.* a slow-witted or stupid person.

knuck·le sand·wich *n. sl.* a punch in the mouth

knur /nər/ *n.* **1** a hard excrescence on the trunk of a tree. **2** a hard concretion.

knurl /nərl/ *n.* a small projecting knob, ridge, etc. □□ **knurled** /nərld/ *adj.*

KO *abbr.* **1** knockout. **2** kickoff.

ko·a /kṓə/ *n.* **1** a Hawaiian tree, *Acacia koa*, which produces dark red wood. **2** this wood.

ko·a·la /kō-áálə/ *n.* an Australian bearlike marsupial, *Phascolarctos cinereus*, having thick, gray fur and feeding on eucalyptus leaves. ▷ MARSUPIAL. ¶ The fuller form *koala bear* is now considered incorrect.

Kö·chel list·ing /kárshəl, kṓkhəl/ *n.* *Mus.* (also **Köchel number**) a number given to each of Mozart's compositions.

KO'd /kayṓd, káyōd/ *adj.* knocked out.

Ko·di·ak /kṓdeeak/ *n.* (in full **Kodiak bear**) a large Alaskan brown bear, *Ursus arctos middendorffi*.

ko·el /kṓəl/ *n.* a dark-colored cuckoo, *Eudynamys scolopacea*.

kohl /kōl/ *n.* a black powder, usu. antimony sulfide or lead sulfide, used as eye makeup esp. in Eastern countries.

kohl·ra·bi /kōlráábee/ *n.* (*pl.* **kohlrabies**) ▼ a variety of cabbage with an edible turniplike swollen stem.

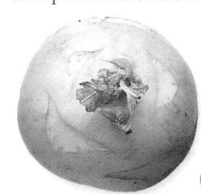

KOHLRABI STEMS
(*Brassica oleracea gongyloides*)

ko·la var. of COLA.

ko·lin·sky /kəlínskee/ *n.* (*pl.* **-ies**) **1** the Siberian mink, *Mustela sibirica*. **2** the fur of this.

Ko·mo·do drag·on /kəmṓdō/ *n.* (also **Ko·mo·do liz·ard**) ▶ a large monitor lizard, *Varanus komodoensis*, native to the E. Indies.

Kom·so·mol /kómsəmáwl/ *n. hist.* **1** an organization for Communist youth in the former Soviet Union. **2** a member of this.

koo·doo var. of KUDU.

---

kook·a·bur·ra /kŏŏkəbərə, -burə/ *n.* ▶ any Australian kingfisher of the genus *Dacelo*, esp. *D. novaeguineae*, which makes a strange laughing cry. Also called **laughing jackass**.

kook·y /kṓkee/ *adj.* (**kookier, kooki·est**) *sl.* crazy or eccentric. □□ **kook·i·ly** *adv.* **kook·i·ness** *n.*

kop /kop/ *n. S.Afr.* a prominent hill or peak.

ko·peck /kṓpek, kópek/ *n.* (also **ko·pek, copeck**) a Russian coin and monetary unit worth one-hundredth of a ruble.

Ko·ran /kərán, -ráán, kaw-/ *n.* (also **Qur'an** /kə-/) ▼ the Islamic sacred book, believed to be the word of God as dictated to Muhammad and written down in Arabic. □□ **Ko·ran·ic** *adj.*

KOOKABURRA:
LAUGHING
KOOKABURRA
(*Dacelo
novaeguineae*)

KORAN: 15TH-CENTURY TURKISH KORAN

Ko·re·an /kəréeən, kaw-/ *n. & adj.* • *n.* **1** a native or national of N. or S. Korea in SE Asia. **2** the language of Korea. • *adj.* of or relating to Korea or its people or language.

ko·sher /kṓshər/ *adj. & n.* • *adj.* **1** (of food or premises in which food is sold, cooked, or eaten) fulfilling the requirements of Jewish law. **2** *colloq.* correct; genuine; legitimate. • *n.* kosher food. □ **keep kosher** adhere to kosher practices.

ko·tow var. of KOWTOW.

kow·tow /kowtṓw/ *n. & v.* (also **ko·tow** /kōtṓw/) • *n. hist.* the Chinese custom of kneeling and touching the ground with the forehead in worship or submission. • *v.intr.* **1** *hist.* perform the kowtow. **2** (usu. foll. by *to*) act obsequiously.

KP *n. Mil. colloq.* **1** enlisted person detailed to help the cooks. **2** kitchen duty.

k.p.h. *abbr.* kilometers per hour.

Kr *symb. Chem.* the element krypton.

kraal /kraal/ *n. S.Afr.* **1** ▲ a village of huts enclosed by a fence. **2** an enclosure for cattle or sheep.

kraft /kraft/ *n.* (in full **kraft paper**) a kind of strong smooth brown wrapping paper.

**KOMODO
DRAGON**
(*Varanus
komodoensis*)

KRAAL

A typical kraal is composed of a meeting area, animal pens, and enclosures for the householder and each of his wives. Linked by passageways, each enclosure contains a sleeping hut, kitchen, granary, and storehouse. The kraal site is inhabited for about ten years.

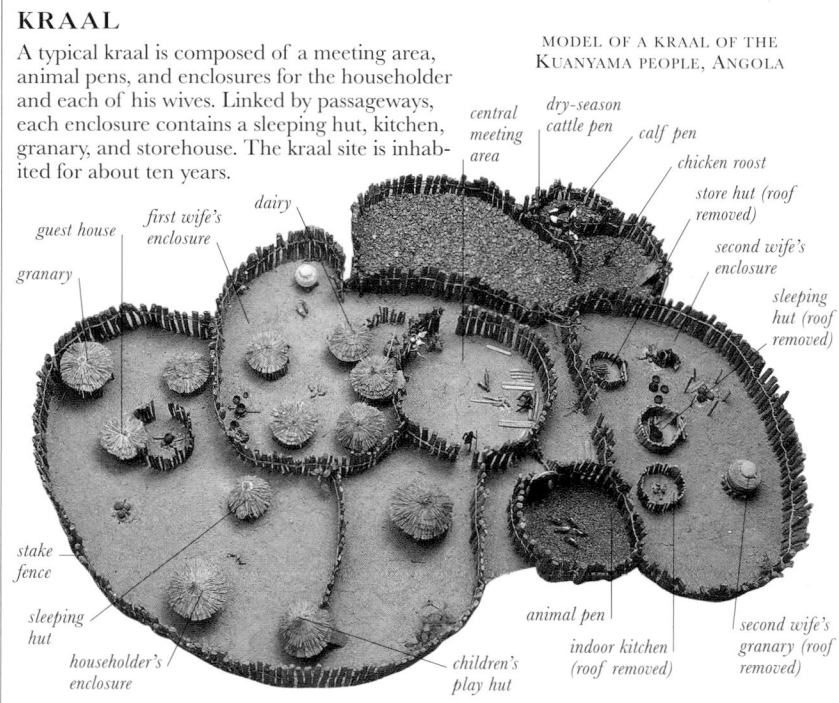

MODEL OF A KRAAL OF THE KUANYAMA PEOPLE, ANGOLA

guest house · granary · first wife's enclosure · dairy · central meeting area · dry-season cattle pen · calf pen · chicken roost · store hut (roof removed) · second wife's enclosure · sleeping hut (roof removed) · stake fence · sleeping hut · householder's enclosure · children's play hut · animal pen · indoor kitchen (roof removed) · second wife's granary (roof removed)

KUKRI: TRADITIONAL GURKHA KNIFE

KUMQUAT
(*Fortunella japonica*)

K

---

krait /krīt/ *n.* any venomous snake of the genus *Bungarus* of E. Asia.

kra·ken /kráakən/ *n.* a large mythical sea monster said to appear off the coast of Norway.

krans /kraans/ *n.* *S.Afr.* a precipitous or overhanging wall of rocks.

kraut /krowt/ *n.* **1** *colloq.* sauerkraut. **2** (also **Kraut**) *sl. offens.* a German.

krem·lin /krémlin/ *n.* **1** a citadel within a Russian city or town. **2** (**the Kremlin**) **a** the citadel in Moscow. **b** the Russian or former USSR government housed within it.

krieg·spiel /kreégshpeel/ *n.* (also **Krieg·spiel**) **1** a war game in which blocks representing armies, etc., are moved about on maps. **2** a form of chess with an umpire, in which each player has only limited information about the opponent's moves.

krill /kril/ *n.* ▶ tiny planktonic crustaceans found in the seas around the Antarctic and eaten by baleen whales.

kris /krees/ *n.* (also **crease, creese**) a Malay or Indonesian dagger with a wavy blade.

Krish·na·ism /kríshnəizəm/ *n.* *Hinduism* the worship of Krishna as an incarnation of Vishnu.

KRILL: ANTARCTIC KRILL (*Euphausia superba*)

kro·mes·ky /krəméskee/ *n.* (*pl.* **-ies**) a croquette of ground meat or fish, rolled in bacon and fried.

kro·na /krónə/ *n.* **1** (*pl.* **kronor** /krónər, -nawr/) the chief monetary unit of Sweden. **2** (*pl.* **kronur** /krónər/) the chief monetary unit of Iceland.

kro·ne /krónə/ *n.* (*pl.* **kroner** /krónər/) the chief monetary unit of Denmark and of Norway.

Kru·ger·rand /króogərand, -raant/ *n.* (also **kru·ger·rand**) a S. African gold coin depicting President Kruger.

krumm·horn /krúmhawrn/ *n.* (also **krum·horn, crumhorn**) a medieval wind instrument with a double reed and a curved end.

kryp·ton /krípton/ *n.* *Chem.* an inert gaseous element of the noble gas group, forming a small portion of the Earth's atmosphere and used in fluorescent lamps, etc. ¶ Symb.: **Kr**.

KS *abbr.* Kansas (in official postal use).

Kshat·ri·ya /kshátreeə/ *n.* a member of the second of the four great Hindu castes, the military caste.

kt. *abbr.* **1** karat(s). **2** kiloton(s). **3** knots.

ku·dos /kóodoz, -dōs, -dos, kyóo-/ *n.* *colloq.* glory; renown.

ku·du /kóodoo/ *n.* (also **koo·doo**) either of two African antelopes, *Tragelaphus strepsiceros* or *T. imberbis*, with white stripes and corkscrew-shaped ridged horns.

kud·zu /kóodzoo, kúd-/ *n.* (in full **kudzu vine**) a quick-growing climbing plant *Pueraria thunbergiana*, with reddish-purple flowers.

Ku·fic /kóofik, kyóo-/ *n.* & *adj.* (also **Cufic**) ● *n.* an early angular form of the Arabic alphabet found chiefly in decorative inscriptions. ● *adj.* of or in this type of script.

Ku Klux Klan /kóo kluks klán, kyóo-/ *n.* a secret society founded in the southern US, orig. formed after the Civil War and dedicated to white supremacy. □□ **Ku Klux Klans·man** *n.* (*pl.* **-men**).

---

kuk·ri /kóokree/ *n.* (*pl.* **kukris**) ▲ a curved knife broadening toward the point, used by Gurkhas.

ku·lak /kóolák, -laák/ *n. hist.* a peasant working for personal profit in Soviet Russia.

küm·mel /kíməl, kö-/ *n.* a sweet liqueur flavored with caraway and cumin seeds.

kum·quat /kúmkwot/ *n.* (also **cumquat**) **1** ▶ an orangelike fruit with a sweet rind and acid pulp, used in preserves. **2** any shrub or small tree of the genus *Fortunella* yielding this.

kung fu /kung fóo, kóong/ *n.* the Chinese form of karate.

Kurd /kərd/ *n.* a member of a mainly pastoral Aryan Islamic people living in Kurdistan (contiguous areas of Iraq, Iran, and Turkey).

kur·dai·tcha /kərdíchə/ *n. Austral.* **1** the tribal use of a bone in spells intended to cause sickness or death. **2** a man empowered to point the bone at a victim.

Kurd·ish /kórdish/ *adj.* & *n.* ● *adj.* of or relating to the Kurds or their language. ● *n.* the Iranian language of the Kurds.

kur·ta /kórtə/ *n.* (also **khur·ta**) a loose shirt or tunic worn by esp. Hindu men and women.

kV *abbr.* kilovolt(s).

kvass /kvaas/ *n.* a Russian fermented beverage, low in alcohol, made from rye flour or bread with malt.

kvetch /kvech/ *n.* & *v.i.* ● *n.* an objectionable person, esp. one who complains a great deal. ● *v.intr.* complain; whine. □□ **kvetch·er** *n.*

kW *abbr.* kilowatt(s).

KWAC /kwak/ *n.* Computing, etc., keyword and context.

kwash·i·or·kor /kwóoshee-áwrkawr/ *n.* a form of malnutrition caused by a protein deficiency of diet, esp. in young children in the tropics.

kWh *abbr.* kilowatt-hour(s).

KY *abbr.* Kentucky (in official postal use).

Ky. *abbr.* Kentucky.

ky·a·nite /kíənīt/ *n.* a blue crystalline mineral of aluminum silicate. □□ **ky·a·nit·ic** /-nítik/ *adj.*

ky·an·ize /kíənīz/ *v.tr.* treat (wood) with a solution of corrosive sublimate to prevent decay.

ky·bosh var. of KIBOSH.

kyle /kīl/ *n.* (in Scotland) a narrow channel between islands or between an island and the mainland.

ky·mo·graph /kíməgraf/ *n.* an instrument for recording variations in pressure, e.g., in sound waves or in blood within blood vessels. □□ **ky·mo·graph·ic** *adj.*

ky·pho·sis /kīfósis/ *n.* *Med.* excessive outward curvature of the spine, causing hunching of the back. □□ **ky·phot·ic** /-fótik/ *adj.*

Kyr·i·e /kéereeay/ (in full **Kyrie eleison** /ilíáyizon, -son, eláy-/) *n.* **1 a** a short repeated invocation used in the RC and Greek Orthodox churches, esp. at the beginning of the Mass. **b** a response sometimes used in the Anglican communion service. **2** a musical setting of the Kyrie.

L

L¹ /el/ *n.* (also **l**) (*pl.* **Ls** or **L's**) **1** the twelfth letter of the alphabet. **2** (as a Roman numeral) 50. **3** a thing shaped like an L, esp. a joint connecting two pipes at right angles.

L² *abbr.* (also **L.**) **1** Lake. **2** Latin. **3** Liberal. **4** large. **5** *Biol.* Linnaeus. **6** lire.

l *abbr.* (also **l.**) **1** left. **2** line. **3** liter(s). **4** length. **5** *archaic* pound(s) (money).

£ *abbr.* (preceding a numeral) pound or pounds (of money).

LA *abbr.* **1** Los Angeles. **2** Louisiana (in official postal use).

La *symb. Chem.* the element lanthanum.

La. *abbr.* Louisiana.

la /laa/ *n. Mus.* **1** (in tonic sol-fa) the sixth note of a major scale. **2** the note A in the fixed-do system.

laa·ger /láagər/ *n. & v.* ● *n.* **1** esp. *S.Afr.* a camp or encampment, esp. formed by a circle of wagons. **2** *Mil.* a park for armored vehicles. ● *v.* **1** *tr.* **a** form (vehicles) into a laager. **b** encamp (people) in a laager. **2** *intr.* encamp.

Lab. *abbr.* **1** *Brit.* Labour Party. **2** Labrador.

lab /lab/ *n. colloq.* a laboratory.

lab·a·rum /lábərəm/ *n.* **1** a symbolic banner. **2** Constantine the Great's imperial standard, with Christian symbols added to Roman military symbols.

lab·da·num /lábdənəm/ *n.* (also **lad·a·num** /ládənəm/) a gum resin from plants of the genus *Cistus*, used in perfumery, etc.

lab·e·fac·tion /lábifákshən/ *n. literary* a shaking, weakening, or downfall.

la·bel /láybəl/ *n. & v.* ● *n.* **1** a usu. small piece of paper, card, linen, metal, etc., for attaching to an object and giving its name, information about it, instructions for use, etc. **2** esp. *derog.* a short classifying phrase or name applied to a person, a work of art, etc. **3 a** a small fabric label sewn into a garment bearing the maker's name. **b** the logo, title, or trademark of esp. a fashion or recording company (*brought it out under their own label*). **c** the piece of paper in the center of a phonograph record describing its contents, etc. **4** an adhesive stamp on a parcel, etc. **5** a word placed before, after, or in the course of a dictionary definition, etc., to specify its subject, register, nationality, etc. **6** *Archit.* a dripstone. **7** *Heraldry* the mark of an eldest son, consisting of a superimposed horizontal bar with usu. three downward projections. ● *v.tr.* (**labeled**, **labeling**; esp. *Brit.* **labelled**, **labelling**) **1** attach a label to. **2** (usu. foll. by *as*) assign to a category (*labeled them as irresponsible*). **3 a** replace (an atom) by an atom of a usu. radioactive isotope as a means of identification. **b** replace an atom in (a molecule) or atoms in the molecules of (a substance). **4** (as **labeled** *adj.*) made identifiable by the replacement of atoms. □□ **la·bel·er** *n.*

la·bi·a *pl.* of LABIUM.

la·bi·al /láybeeəl/ *adj. & n.* ● *adj.* **1 a** of the lips. **b** *Zool.* of, like, or serving as a lip, a liplike part, or a labium. **2** *Dentistry* designating the surface of a tooth adjacent to the lips. **3** *Phonet.* (of a sound) requiring partial or complete closure of the lips (e.g., *p*,

b, *f*, *v*, *m*, *w*; and vowels in which lips are rounded, e.g., *oo* in moon). ● *n. Phonet.* a labial sound. □ **labial pipe** *Mus.* an organ pipe having lips; a flue pipe. □□ **la·bi·al·ism** *n.* **la·bi·al·ize** *v.tr.* **la·bi·al·ly** *adv.*

la·bi·ate /láybeeət, -ayt/ *n. & adj.* ● *n.* any plant of the family Labiatae, including mint and rosemary, having square stems and a corolla or calyx divided into two parts suggesting lips. ● *adj.* **1** *Bot.* of or relating to the Labiatae. **2** *Bot. & Zool.* like a lip or labium.

la·bile /láybīl, -bil/ *adj. Chem.* (of a compound) unstable; liable to displacement or change, esp. if an atom or group is easily replaced by other atoms or groups. □□ **la·bil·i·ty** /ləbílitee, lay-/ *n.*

labio- /láybeeō/ *comb.form* of the lips.

la·bi·o·den·tal /láybeeōdént'l/ *adj.* (of a sound) made with the lips and teeth, e.g., *f* and *v*.

la·bi·o·ve·lar /láybeeōvéélər/ *adj.* (of a sound) made with the lips and soft palate, e.g., *w*.

la·bi·um /láybeeəm/ *n.* (*pl.* **labia** /-beeə/) **1** (usu. in *pl.*) *Anat.* each of the two pairs of skin folds that enclose the vulva. ▷ REPRODUCTIVE ORGANS. **2** the lower lip in the mouthparts of an insect or crustacean. **3** a lip, esp. the lower one of a labiate plant's corolla.

la·bor /láybər/ *n. & v.* (*Brit.* **labour**) ● *n.* **1 a** physical or mental work; exertion. **b** such work considered as supplying the needs of a community. **2** workers, esp. manual, considered as a class or political force. **3** the process of childbirth, esp. the period from the start of uterine contractions to delivery. **4** a particular task, esp. of a difficult nature. ● *v.* **1** *intr.* work hard; exert oneself. **2** *intr.* (usu. foll. by *for*, or *to* + infin.) strive for a purpose. **3** *tr.* **a** elaborate needlessly (*I will not labor the point*). **b** (as **labored** *adj.*) not spontaneous or fluent. **4** *intr.* (often foll. by *under*) suffer under (a disadvantage or delusion) (*labored under universal disapproval*). **5** *intr.* proceed with trouble or difficulty (*labored slowly up the hill*). **6** *intr.* (of a ship) roll or pitch heavily.

lab·o·ra·to·ry /lábrətáwree/ *n.* (*pl.* **-ies**) a room or building fitted out for scientific experiments, research, or the manufacture of drugs and chemicals.

la·bor camp *n.* a prison camp enforcing a regime of hard labor.

La·bor Day *adj.* the first Monday in September (or in some other countries May 1), celebrated in honor of working people.

la·bor·er /láybərər/ *n.* **1** a person doing unskilled, usu. manual, work for wages. **2** a person who labors.

la·bor-in·ten·sive *adj.* (of a form of work) needing a large workforce.

la·bo·ri·ous /ləbáwreeəs/ *adj.* **1** needing hard work or toil (*a laborious task*). **2** (esp. of literary style) pedestrian; not fluent. □□ **la·bo·ri·ous·ly** *adv.* **la·bo·ri·ous·ness** *n.*

la·bor·sav·ing /láybərsáyving/ *adj.* (of an appliance, etc.) designed to reduce or eliminate work.

la·bor un·ion *n.* an organized association of workers, often in a trade or profession, formed to protect and further their rights and interests.

la·bour etc. *Brit.* var. of LABOR.

La·bour Par·ty *n.* **1** a British political party formed to represent the interests of ordinary working people. **2** any similar political party in other countries.

Lab·ra·dor /lábrədawr/ *n.* (in full **Labrador retriever**) **1** a retriever of a breed with a black or golden coat. **2** this breed.

la·bur·num /ləbárnəm/ *n.* any small tree of the genus *Laburnum* with racemes of golden flowers yielding poisonous seeds. Also called **golden chain**.

LABURNUM:
COMMON LABURNUM
(*Laburnum anagyroides*)

lab·y·rinth /lábərinth/ *n.* **1** a complicated network of passages, etc.; a maze. **2** an intricate or tangled arrangement. □□ **lab·y·rin·thi·an** /-ríntheeən/ *adj.* **lab·y·rin·thine** /-rínthin, -thīn/ *adj.*

LAC *abbr.* leading aircraftsman.

lac /lak/ *n.* a resinous substance secreted as a protective covering by an Asian insect.

lace /lays/ *n. & v.* ● *n.* **1** ▼ a fine open fabric made by weaving thread in patterns and used esp. to trim blouses, underwear, etc. **2** a cord or leather strip passed through eyelets or hooks on opposite sides of a shoe, corset, etc., pulled tight and fastened. **3** braid used for trimming esp. dress uniform (*gold lace*). ● *v.* **1** *tr.* (usu. foll. by *up*) **a** fasten or tighten with a lace or laces. **b** compress the waist of (a person) with a laced corset. **2** *tr.* flavor or fortify (coffee, beer, etc.) with a dash of liquor. **3** *tr.* (usu. foll. by *with*) **a** streak with color (*cheek laced with blood*). **b** interlace or embroider (fabric) with thread, etc. **4** *tr. & (foll. by into*) *intr. colloq.* lash; beat; defeat. **5** *tr.* (often foll. by *through*) pass (a shoelace, etc.) through. **6** *tr.* trim with lace.

LACE: DETAIL OF 19TH-CENTURY ENGLISH LACE

lace·mak·er /láysmaykər/ *n.* a person who makes lace, esp. professionally. □□ **lace·mak·ing** *n.*

lac·er·ate /lásərayt/ *v.tr.* **1** mangle or tear (esp. flesh or tissue). **2** cause pain to (the feelings, etc.). □□ **lac·er·a·ble** *adj.* **lac·er·a·tion** /-ráyshən/ *n.*

lace-up *n. & adj.* ● *n.* a shoe fastened with a lace. ● *attrib.adj.* (of a shoe, etc.) fastened with a lace or laces.

lace·wing /láyswing/ *n.* ▼ a neuropterous insect. ▷ INSECT

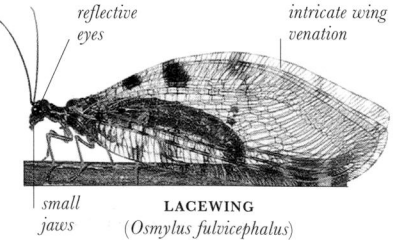

reflective eyes

intricate wing venation

small jaws

LACEWING
(*Osmylus fulvicephalus*)

lach·es /láchiz/ *n. Law* delay in performing a legal duty, asserting a right, claiming a privilege, etc.

lach·ry·mal /lákriməl/ *adj* (also **lac·ri·mal**) **1** *literary* of or for tears. **2** (usu. as **lacrimal**) *Anat.* concerned in the secretion of tears (*lacrimal canal*; *lacrimal duct*). ▷ TEAR DUCT

lach·ry·ma·tion /lákrimáyshən/ *n.* (also **lac·ri·ma·tion**) *formal* the flow of tears. **lach·ry·ma·to·ry** /lákrimətawree/ *adj. formal* of or causing tears.

lach·ry·mose /lákrimōs/ *adj. formal* given to weeping; tearful. □□ **lach·ry·mose·ly** *adv.*

lac·ing /láysing/ *n.* **1** lace trimming, esp. on a uniform. **2** a laced fastening on a shoe or corsets. **3** *colloq.* a beating. **4** a dash of spirits in a beverage.

lack /lak/ *n. & v.* ● *n.* (usu. foll. by *of*) an absence, want, or deficiency. ● *v.tr.* be without or deficient in (*lacks courage*). □ **for lack of** owing to the absence of. **lack for** lack.

lack·a·dai·si·cal /lákədáyzikəl/ *adj.* **1** listless; idle. **2** feebly sentimental and affected. □□ **lack·a·dai·si·cal·ly** *adv.*

lack·er var. of LACQUER.

lack·ey /lákee/ *n.* (also **lac·quey**) (*pl.* **-eys**) **1** *derog.* **a** a servile political follower. **b** an obsequious parasitical person. **2 a** a (usu. liveried) footman or manservant. **b** a servant.

lack·ing /láking/ *adj.* **1** absent or deficient. **2** *colloq.* deficient in intellect; mentally subnormal.

lack·lus·ter /láklustər/ *adj.* **1** lacking in vitality, force, or conviction. **2** (of the eye) dull.

la·con·ic /ləkónik/ *adj.* **1** (of a style of speech or writing) brief; concise; terse. **2** (of a person) laconic in speech, etc. □□ **la·con·i·cal·ly** *adv.* **la·con·i·cism** /-sizəm/ *n.* **lac·o·nism** /lákənizəm/ *n.*

lac·quer /lákər/ *n. & v.* (also **lack·er**) ● *n.* **1 a** sometimes colored liquid made of shellac dissolved in alcohol, or of synthetic substances, that dries to form a hard protective coating for wood, brass, etc. **2** the sap of the lacquer tree, *Rhus verniciflua*, used to varnish wood, etc. ● *v.tr.* coat with lacquer. □□ **lac·quer·er** *n.*

lac·quey var. of LACKEY.

lac·ri·mal var. of LACHRYMAL.

lac·ri·ma·tion var. of LACHRYMATION.

la·crosse /ləkráws, -krós/ *n.* ▶ a game like hockey, but with a ball driven by, caught, and carried in a crosse.

lac·tate[1] /láktayt/ *v.intr.* (of mammals) secrete milk. □□ **lac·ta·tion** /-táyshən/ *n.*

lac·tate[2] /láktayt/ *n. Chem.* any salt or ester of lactic acid.

lac·te·al /lákteeəl/ *adj. & n.* ● *adj.* **1** of milk. **2** conveying chyle or other milky fluid. ● *n.* (in *pl.*) the lymphatic vessels of the small intestine which absorb digested fats.

lac·tes·cence /laktésəns/ *n.* **1** a milky form or appearance. **2** a milky juice.

lac·tes·cent /laktésənt/ *adj.* **1** milky. **2** yielding a milky juice.

lac·tic /láktik/ *adj. Chem.* of, relating to, or obtained from milk.

lac·tic ac·id *n.* a carboxylic acid formed in sour milk, and produced in the muscle tissues during strenuous exercise.

lac·tif·er·ous /laktífərəs/ *adj.* yielding milk or milky fluid.

lacto- /láktō/ *comb. form* milk.

lac·to·ba·cil·lus /láktōbəsíləs/ *n.* (*pl.* **-bacilli** /-lī/) *Biol.* any rod-shaped bacterium of the genus *Lactobacillus*, producing lactic acid.

lac·tose /láktōs/ *n. Chem.* a sugar that occurs in milk, and is less sweet than sucrose.

la·cu·na /ləkyōonə/ *n.* (*pl.* **lacunae** /-nee/ or **lacunas**) **1** a hiatus, blank, or gap. **2** a missing portion or empty page, esp. in an ancient manuscript, etc. **3** *Anat.* a cavity or depression, esp. in bone. □□ **la·cu·nar** *adj.* **la·cu·nar·y** /lákyōonéree, ləkyōonaree/ *adj.* **la·cu·nose** *adj.*

la·cus·trine /ləkústrin/ *adj. formal* or *Biol.* **1** of or relating to lakes. **2** living or growing in or beside a lake.

LACW *abbr.* leading aircraftswoman.

lac·y /láysee/ *adj.* (**lacier**, **laciest**) of or resembling lace fabric. □□ **lac·i·ly** *adv.* **lac·i·ness** *n.*

lad /lad/ *n.* **1** a boy or youth. **2** a young son.

lad·der /ládər/ *n.* **1** a set of horizontal bars of wood or metal fixed between two uprights and used for climbing up or down. **2 a** a hierarchical structure. **b** such a structure as a means of advancement, promotion, etc.

lad·der·back *n.* an upright chair with a back resembling a ladder.

lad·der stitch *n.* transverse bars in embroidery.

LACROSSE

Lacrosse is played as a 12-a-side game for women and a 10-a-side game for men. Each team aims to score goals by propelling the ball into the opposing team's goal net. The women's field has no absolute boundaries, but the men's field has clearly defined sidelines and endlines. The ball is kept in play by being carried, thrown, or batted with the crosse, or rolled or kicked, in any direction. In both games, play can continue beyond the goal areas.

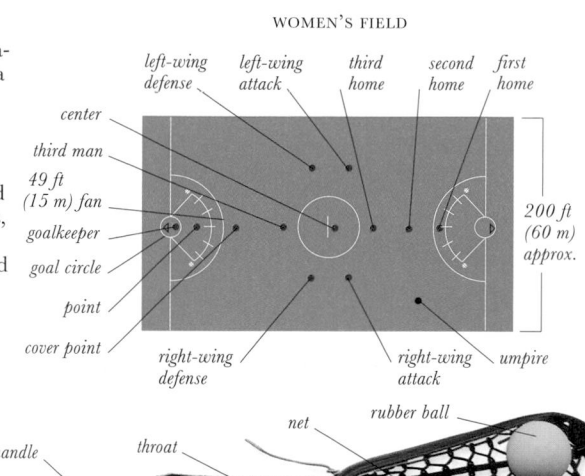

WOMEN'S FIELD

left-wing defense · left-wing attack · third home · second home · first home · center · third man · 49 ft (15 m) fan · goalkeeper · goal circle · point · cover point · right-wing defense · right-wing attack · umpire · 200 ft (60 m) approx.

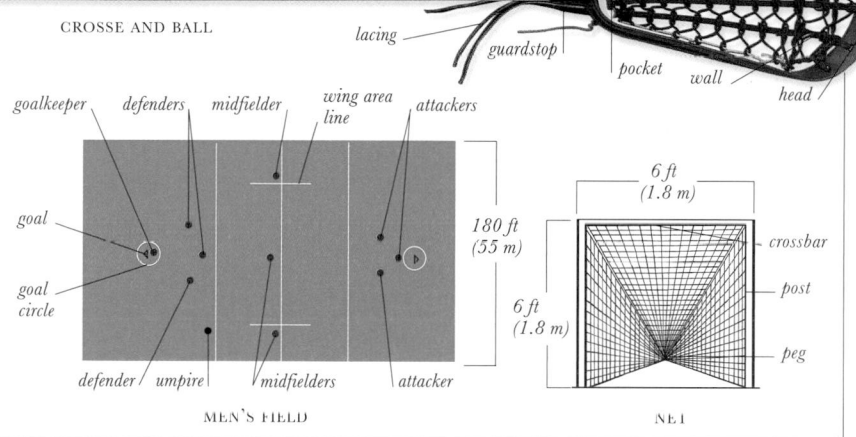

CROSSE AND BALL

handle · throat · net · rubber ball · lacing · guardstop · pocket · wall · head

goalkeeper · defenders · midfielder · wing area line · attackers · goal · goal circle · 180 ft (55 m) · defender · umpire · midfielders · attacker · MEN'S FIELD

6 ft (1.8 m) · crossbar · post · peg · 6 ft (1.8 m) · NET

L

---

lad·die /ládee/ *n. colloq.* a young boy or lad.

lade /layd/ *v.* (*past part.* **laden** /láyd'n/) **1** *tr.* **a** put cargo on board (a ship). **b** ship (goods) as cargo. **2** *intr.* (of a ship) take on cargo. **3** *tr.* (as **laden** *adj.*) (usu. foll. by *with*) **a** (of a vehicle, donkey, person, tree, table, etc.) heavily loaded. **b** (of the conscience, spirit, etc.) painfully burdened with sorrow, etc.

la·di·da /láadeedáá/ *adj. & n. colloq.* (also **la·de·da**) ● *adj.* pretentious or snobbish, esp. in manner or speech. ● *n.* **1** a la-di-da speech or manners. **2** la-di-da speech or manners.

la·dies *pl.* of LADY.

ladies' man *n.* (also **lady's man**) a man fond of female company; a seducer.

lad·ing /láyding/ *n.* **1** a cargo. **2** the act or process of lading.

la·dle /láyd'l/ *n. & v.* ● *n.* **1** a large, long-handled spoon with a cup-shaped bowl used for serving esp. soups and gravy. ▷ UTENSIL. **2** a vessel for transporting molten metal in a foundry. ● *v.tr.* (often foll. by *out*) transfer (liquid) from one receptacle to another. □ **ladle out** distribute, esp. lavishly. □□ **la·dle·ful** *n.* (*pl.* **-fuls**). **la·dler** *n.*

la·dy /láydee/ *n.* (*pl.* **-ies**) **1 a** a woman regarded as being of superior social status or as having the refined manners associated with this (cf. GENTLEMAN). **b** (**Lady**) a title used by peeresses, wives, and widows of knights, etc. **2** (often *attrib.*) a female person or animal (*ask that lady over there*; *lady butcher*; *lady dog*). **3** *colloq.* **a** a wife. **b** a man's girlfriend. **4** a ruling woman (*lady of the house*). **5** (in *pl.* as a form of address) a female audience or the female part of an audience. □□ **la·dy·hood** *n.*

hardened forewing (elytron) · flexible hind wing

LADYBUG
(*Anatis ocellata*)

la·dy·bug /láydeebug/ *n.* ◀ a coleopterous insect of the family Coccinellidae, with wing covers usu. of a reddish-brown color with black spots. ▷ BEETLE, EGG

la·dy·fern ▷ a slender fern, *Athyrium filix-femina*.

la·dy·fin·ger /láydeefinggər/ *n.* a finger-shaped sponge cake.

la·dy-in-wait·ing *n.* (*pl.* **ladies-in-waiting**) a lady attending a queen or princess.

la·dy-kill·er *n.* **1** a man very attractive to women. **2** a practiced and habitual seducer.

la·dy·like /láydeelīk/ *adj.* **1 a** with the modesty, manners, etc., of a lady. **b** befitting a lady. **2** (of a man) effeminate.

la·dy·love /láydeeluv/ *n.* a man's sweetheart.

la·dy·ship /láydeeship/ *n.* □ **her** (or **your**) **ladyship** (*pl.* **their** or **your ladyships**) **1** a respectful form of reference or address to a titled lady or ladies. **2** *iron.* a form of reference or address to a woman thought to be giving herself airs.

la·dy's man var. of LADIES' MAN.

la·dy's slip·per *n.* ▶ any orchidaceous plant of the genus *Cypripedium*, with a usu. yellow or pink slipper-shaped lip on its flowers.

LADY'S SLIPPER
(*Cypripedium calceolus*)

lip

LAGOMORPH

The order Lagomorpha includes rabbits, hares, and pikas. Lagomorphs have long ears, powerful hind legs for jumping, forelimbs adapted for burrowing, and a small tail. They are closely related to rodents and share many characteristics with them, including chisel-shaped incisors (four in the upper jaw and two in the lower) that grow continually; they also share the habit of eating their feces to extract more nutrients from their plant diet.

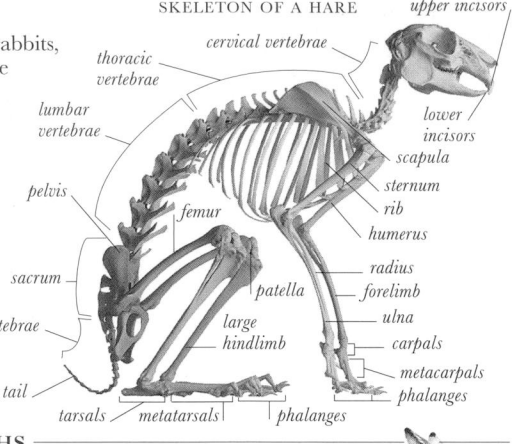

SKELETON OF A HARE

upper incisors, *cervical vertebrae*, *thoracic vertebrae*, *lumbar vertebrae*, *lower incisors*, *scapula*, *sternum*, *rib*, *humerus*, *pelvis*, *femur*, *radius*, *forelimb*, *ulna*, *sacrum*, *patella*, *large hindlimb*, *caudal vertebrae*, *carpals*, *metacarpals*, *phalanges*, *tail*, *tarsals*, *metatarsals*, *phalanges*

EXAMPLES OF LAGOMORPHS

PIKA
(*Ochotona princeps*)

COMMON RABBIT
(*Oryctolagus cuniculus*)

ARCTIC HARE
(*Lepus arcticus*)

lag[1] /lag/ *v. & n.* ● *v.intr.* (**lagged, lagging**) (often foll. by *behind*) fall behind; not keep pace. ● *n.* a delay.

lag[2] /lag/ *v. & n.* ● *v.tr.* (**lagged, lagging**) enclose or cover in lagging. ● *n.* **1** the non-heat-conducting cover of a boiler, etc. **2** a piece of this.

la·ger /láagər/ *n.* a kind of beer, effervescent and light in color and body.

lag·gard /lágərd/ *n. & adj.* ● *n.* a dawdler. ● *adj.* dawdling; slow. □□ **lag·gard·ly** *adj. & adv.*

lag·ging /láging/ *n.* material providing heat insulation for a boiler, pipes, etc.

lag·o·morph /lágəmawrf/ *n. Zool.* ▲ any mammal of the order Lagomorpha, including hares and rabbits.

la·goon /ləgóon/ *n.* **1** a stretch of salt water separated from the sea by a low sandbank, coral reef, etc. **2** the enclosed water of an atoll. ▷ ATOLL. **3** a small freshwater lake near a larger lake or river. **4** an artificial pool for the treatment of effluent or to accommodate an overspill from surface drains during heavy rain.

la·har /láahaar/ *n.* a mudflow composed mainly of volcanic debris.

la·ic /láyik/ *adj. & n.* ● *adj.* nonclerical; lay; secular; temporal. ● *n. formal* a lay person; a noncleric. □□ **la·i·cal** *adj.* **la·i·cal·ly** *adv.*

laid *past* and *past part.* of LAY[1].

laid-back *adj. colloq.* relaxed; unbothered; easy-going.

laid up *adj.* confined to bed or the house.

lain *past part.* of LIE[1].

lair /lair/ *n. & v.* ● *n.* **1 a** a wild animal's resting place. **b** a person's hiding place (*tracked him to his lair*). **2** a place where domestic animals lie down. ● *v.* **1** *intr.* go to or rest in a lair. **2** *tr.* place (an animal) in a lair.

laird /laird/ *n. Sc.* a landed proprietor. □□ **laird·ship** *n.*

lais·sez-faire /lésayfáir/ *n.* (also **lais·ser-faire**) the theory or practice of governmental abstention from interference in the workings of the market, etc.

la·i·ty /láy-itee/ *n.* (usu. prec. by *the*; usu. treated as *pl.*) **1** lay people, as distinct from the clergy. **2** nonprofessionals.

lake[1] /layk/ *n.* ▼ a large body of water surrounded by land.

lake[2] /layk/ *n.* **1** a reddish coloring orig. made from lac (*crimson lake*). **2** a complex formed by the action of dye and mordants applied to fabric to fix color. **3** any insoluble product of a soluble dye and mordant.

Lake Dis·trict *n.* (prec. by *the*) the region of many lakes in NW England.

lake·side /láyksīd/ *attrib.adj.* beside a lake.

lal·la·tion /laláyshən/ *n.* **1** the pronunciation of *r* as *l*. **2** imperfect speech, esp. that of young children.

lam /lam/ *v.* (**lammed, lamming**) *sl.* **1** *tr.* thrash; hit. **2** *intr.* (foll. by *into*) hit (a person, etc.) hard with a stick, etc.

la·ma /láamə/ *n.* a Tibetan or Mongolian Buddhist monk.

La·marck·ism /ləmáarkizəm/ *n.* the theory of evolution based on the supposed inheritance of acquired characteristics, devised by Jean Baptiste de Lamarck, the French naturalist, 1744–1829.

la·ma·ser·y /láaməseree/ *n.* (*pl.* **-ies**) a monastery of lamas.

lamb /lam/ *n. & v.* ● *n.* **1** a young sheep. **2** the flesh of a lamb as food. ▷ CUT. **3** a mild or gentle person, esp. a young child. ● *v.* **1 a** *tr.* (in *passive*) (of a lamb) be born. **b** *intr.* (of a ewe) give birth to lambs. **2** *tr.* tend (lambing ewes). □ **The Lamb** (or **The Lamb of God**) a name for Christ (John 1:29) (cf. AGNUS DEI). **like a lamb** meekly; obediently.

lam·ba·da /ləmbáadə/ *n.* a fast erotic Brazilian dance in which couples dance with their hips touching each other.

lam·baste /lambáyst/ *v.tr.* (also **lam·bast** /-bást/) *colloq.* **1** thrash; beat. **2** criticize severely.

lamb·da /lámdə/ *n.* **1** the eleventh letter of the Greek alphabet (Λ, λ). **2** (as λ) the symbol for wavelength.

lam·bent /lámbənt/ *adj.* **1** (of a flame or a light) playing on a surface with a soft radiance. **2** (of the eyes, sky, etc.) softly radiant. **3** (of wit, etc.) lightly brilliant. □□ **lam·ben·cy** *n.*

lamb·skin /lámskin/ *n.* a prepared skin from a lamb with the wool on or as leather.

lame /laym/ *adj. & v.* ● *adj.* **1** disabled, esp. in the foot or leg; limping. **2 a** (of an excuse, etc.) unconvincing; unsatisfactory. **b** (of verse, etc.) halting. ● *v.tr.* make lame; disable. □□ **lame·ly** *adv.* **lame·ness** *n.*

la·mé /lamáy/ *n. & adj.* ● *n.* a fabric with gold or silver threads interwoven. ● *adj.* (of fabric, etc.) having such threads.

lame·brain /láymbrayn/ *n. colloq.* a stupid person.

lame duck *n.* **1** a disabled or weak person. **2** a defaulter in the stock market. **3** an official (esp. the president) in the final period of office, after the election of a successor.

la·mel·la /ləmélə/ *n.* (*pl.* **lamellae** /-lee/ or **lamellas**) **1** a thin layer, membrane, scale, or platelike tissue or part, esp. in bone tissue. **2** *Bot.* a membranous fold in a chloroplast. □□ **la·mel·lar** *adj.* **la·mel·late** /ləmélayt, lámə-/ *adj.*

la·ment /ləmént/ *n. & v.* ● *n.* **1** a passionate expression of grief. **2** a song or poem of mourning or sorrow. ● *v.tr.* (also *absol.*) **1** express or feel grief for or about; regret (*lamented the loss of his ticket*). **2** (as **lamented** *adj.*) a conventional expression referring to a recently dead person (*your late lamented father*). □ **lament for** (or **over**) mourn or regret. □□ **lam·en·ta·tion** /láməntáyshən/ *n.* **la·ment·er** *n.* **la·ment·ing·ly** *adv.*

LAKE

Natural lakes are formed when the supply of water to a basin (for instance by rain or streams) is greater than the amount of water lost by evaporation and seepage. In some cases, the formation of natural barriers, such as glacial moraines or landslides, provides a dam, allowing water to accumulate. In others, seepage is reduced by the presence of impermeable rocks under the lake bed. Lakes tend to be classified according to the mode of origin of their basin; for example, glacial, alluvial, volcanic, or fault-related.

EXAMPLES OF LAKE TYPES

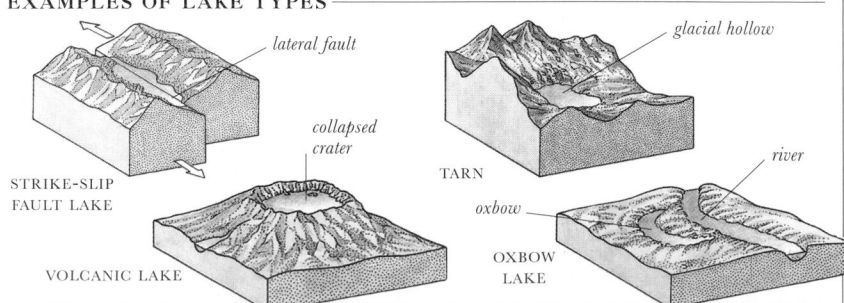

lateral fault, *glacial hollow*, *collapsed crater*, *river*, STRIKE-SLIP FAULT LAKE, TARN, *oxbow*, VOLCANIC LAKE, OXBOW LAKE

lam·en·ta·ble /ləméntəbəl, lámənt-/ *adj.* deplorable; regrettable. □□ **lam·en·ta·bly** *adv.*

lam·i·na /láminə/ *n.* (*pl.* **laminae** /-nee/ or **laminas**) a thin plate or scale, e.g., of bone, stratified rock, or vegetable tissue. □□ **lam·i·nar** /láminər/ *adj.*

lam·i·nate *v., n., & adj.* ● *v.* /láminayt/ **1** *tr.* beat or roll (metal) into thin plates. **2** *tr.* overlay with metal plates, a plastic layer, etc. **3** *tr.* manufacture by placing layer on layer. **4** *tr. & intr.* split into layers or leaves. ● *n.* /láminət/ a laminated structure or material. ● *adj.* /láminət/ in the form of lamina or laminae. □□ **lam·i·na·tion** /-náyshən/ *n.* **lam·i·na·tor** *n.*

Lam·mas /láməs/ *n.* (in full **Lammas Day**) the first day of August, formerly observed as harvest festival.

lam·mer·gei·er /lámərgīər/ *n.* (also **lam·mer·gey·er**) ▼ a large vulture, *Gypaetus barbatus*, with a very large wingspan and dark, beardlike feathers on either side of its beak.

LAMMERGEIER
(*Gypaetus barbatus*)

beardlike feathers

lamp /lamp/ *n. & v.* ● *n.* **1** a device for producing a steady light, esp.: **a** an electric bulb, and usu. its holder (*bedside lamp*). **b** an oil lamp. **c** a usu. glass holder for a candle. **d** a gas jet and mantle. **2** a source of spiritual or intellectual inspiration. **3** a device producing esp. ultraviolet or infrared radiation as a treatment for various complaints. ● *v.* **1** *intr. poet.* shine. **2** *tr.* supply with lamps; illuminate. **3** *tr. sl.* look at. □□ **lamp·less** *adj.*

lamp·black /lámpblak/ *n.* a pigment made from soot.

lamp chim·ney *n.* a glass cylinder enclosing and making a draft for an oil lamp's flame.

lamp·light /lámplīt/ *n.* light given by a lamp or lamps.

lamp·light·er /lámplītər/ *n. hist.* **1** a person who lights street lamps. **2** a spill for lighting lamps.

lam·poon /lampōón/ *n. & v.* ● *n.* a satirical attack on a person, etc. ● *v.tr.* satirize. □□ **lam·poon·ist** *n.*

lamp·post /lámp-pōst/ *n.* a tall post supporting an outdoor light.

lam·prey /lámpree, -pray/ *n.* (*pl.* **-eys**) ▼ any eellike aquatic vertebrate of the family Petromyzonidae, without scales, paired fins, or jaws, but having a sucker mouth. ▷ FISH

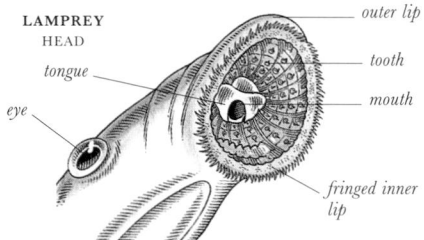

LAMPREY
HEAD

outer lip
tooth
tongue
mouth
eye
fringed inner lip

lamp·shade /lámpshayd/ *n.* a translucent cover for a lamp used to soften or direct its light.

LAN /lan/ *n. Computing* local area network.

Lan·cas·tri·an /langkástreeən/ *n. & adj.* ● *n.* **1** a native of Lancashire or Lancaster in NW England. **2** *hist.* a follower of the House of Lancaster in the Wars of the Roses (cf. YORKIST). ● *adj.* of or concerning Lancashire or Lancaster, or the House of Lancaster.

lance /lans/ *n. & v.* ● *n.* **1 a** a long weapon with a wooden shaft and a pointed steel head, used by a horseman in charging. ▷ JOUST. **b** a similar weapon used for spearing a fish. **2** a metal pipe supplying oxygen to burn metal. **3** = LANCER. ● *v.tr.* **1** *Surgery* prick or cut open with a lancet. **2** pierce with a lance.

lan·ce·o·late /lánseeəlayt/ *adj.* shaped like a lance head, tapering to each end. ▷ LEAF

lanc·er /lánsər/ *n.* **1** *hist.* a soldier of a cavalry regiment armed with lances. **2** (in *pl.*) **a** a quadrille for 8 or 16 pairs. **b** the music for this.

lan·cet /lánsit/ *n.* a small, broad, two-edged surgical knife with a sharp point.

lan·cet arch *n.* ▶ a narrow arch with a pointed head. ▷ ARCH, CATHEDRAL

LANCET ARCH

land /land/ *n. & v.* ● *n.* **1** the solid part of the Earth's surface (opp. SEA, WATER, AIR). **2 a** an expanse of country; ground. **b** such land in relation to its use, etc., or (often prec. by *the*) as a basis for agriculture (*works on the land*). **3** a country, nation, or state (*land of hope and glory*). **4 a** a landed property. **b** (in *pl.*) estates. **5** the space between the rifling grooves in a gun. **6** a strip of plow land or pastureland parted from others by drain furrows. ● *v.* **1 a** *tr. & intr.* set or go ashore. **b** *intr.* (often foll. by *at*) disembark. **2** *tr.* bring (an aircraft, etc.) to the ground or the surface of water. **3** *intr.* (of an aircraft, parachutist, etc.) alight on the ground or water. **4** *tr.* bring (a fish) to land. **5** *tr. & intr.* (also *refl.*; often foll. by *up*) *colloq.* bring to, reach, or find oneself in a certain situation, place, or state. **6** *tr. colloq.* present (a person, etc.) a blow, etc. (*landed him one in the eye*). **b** (foll. by *with*) present (a person) with (a problem, etc.). **7** *tr.* set down (a person, cargo, etc.) from a vehicle, ship, etc. **8** *tr. colloq.* win or obtain (a prize, job, etc.). □ **how the land lies** what is the state of affairs. in **the land of the living** *joc.* still alive. **land on one's feet** attain a good position, job, etc., by luck. □□ **land·less** *adj.* **land·ward** *adj. & adv.*

länd·ler /léndlər/ *n.* (*pl.* **länd·ler** or **länd·lers**) **1** an Austrian dance in triple time, a precursor of the waltz. **2** the music for a ländler.

lan·dau /lándow, -daw/ *n.* ▶ a four-wheeled enclosed carriage with a removable front cover and a back cover that can be raised and lowered.

land bridge *n.* a neck of land joining two large landmasses.

land·ed /lándid/ *adj.* **1** owning land (*landed gentry*). **2** consisting of, including, or relating to land (*landed property*).

land·fall /lándfawl/ *n.* the approach to land, esp. for the first time on a sea or air journey.

land·fill /lándfil/ *n.* **1** waste material, etc., used to landscape or reclaim areas of ground. **2** the process of disposing of rubbish in this way. **3** landfill site a place where rubbish is disposed of by burying it in the ground.

land·form /lándfawrm/ *n.* a natural feature of the Earth's surface.

land·hold·er /lándhōldər/ *n.* the proprietor or, esp., the tenant of land.

land·ing /lánding/ *n.* **1 a** the act or process of coming to land. **b** an instance of this. **c** (also **land·ing place**) a place where ships, etc., land. **2 a** a platform between two flights of stairs. **b** a passage leading to upstairs rooms.

land·ing craft *n.* any of several types of craft esp. designed for putting troops and equipment ashore.

land·ing gear *n.* the undercarriage of an aircraft. ▷ AIRCRAFT

land·ing stage *n.* a platform, often floating, on which goods and passengers are disembarked.

land·la·dy /lándlaydee/ *n.* (*pl.* **-ies**) **1** a woman who rents land, a building, etc., to a tenant. **2** a woman who keeps a boardinghouse, an inn, etc.

land·line /lándlīn/ *n.* a means of telecommunication over land.

land·locked /lándlokt/ *adj.* almost or entirely enclosed by land.

land·lord /lándlawrd/ *n.* **1** a man who rents land, a building, etc., to a tenant. **2** a man who keeps a boardinghouse, an inn, etc.

land·lub·ber /lándlubər/ *n.* a person unfamiliar with the sea or sailing.

land·mark /lándmaark/ *n.* **1 a** a conspicuous object in a district, etc. **b** an object marking the boundary of an estate, country, etc. **2** an event, change, etc., marking a stage or turning point in history, etc. **3** *attrib.* serving as a landmark; signifying an important change, development, etc.

land·mass /lándmas/ *n.* a large area of land.

land mine *n.* **1** an explosive mine laid in or on the ground. **2** a parachute mine.

land·own·er /lándōnər/ *n.* an owner of land. □□ **land·own·ing** *adj. & n.*

land·scape /lándskayp/ *n. & v.* ● *n.* **1** natural or imaginary scenery, as seen in a broad view. **2** (often *attrib.*) a picture representing this; the genre of landscape painting. **3** (in graphic design, etc.) a format in which the width of an illustration, etc., is greater than the height (cf. PORTRAIT). ● *v.tr.* (also *absol.*) improve (a piece of land) by landscape gardening. □□ **land·scap·ist** *n.*

land·scape gar·den·ing *n.* the laying out of esp. extensive grounds to resemble natural scenery. □□ **land·scape gar·den·er** *n.*

land·slide /lándslīd/ *n.* **1** the sliding down of a mass of land from a mountain, cliff, etc. **2** an overwhelming majority for one side in an election.

land·slip /lándslip/ *n.* = LANDSLIDE 1.

lands·man /lándzmən/ *n.* (*pl.* **-men**) a nonsailor.

lane /layn/ *n.* **1** a narrow, often rural, road, street, or path. **2** a division of a road for a stream of traffic. **3** a strip of track or water for a runner, rower,

LANDAU:
STEAM-DRIVEN LANDAU
CARRIAGE, 1854

chimney *back cover* *landau body* *front cover* *driver's seat* *steering tiller* *brake lever*

coke hopper *chauffeur's seat* *water tank* *step* *iron rim* *wooden spoke* *steam chest* *twin-cylinder steam engine* *steam pipe* *wheel hub* *towing hook*

L

or swimmer in a race. **4** a path or course prescribed for or regularly followed by a ship, aircraft, etc. **5** a gangway.

lang·lauf /láanglowf/ n. cross-country skiing; a cross-country skiing race.

lan·gouste /loɴgóost, lónggōost/ n. a crawfish or spiny lobster.

lan·gous·tine /lóɴgoostéen, lánggo-/ n. any of several varieties of small lobsters, used as food.

lan·guage /lánggwij/ n. **1** the method of human communication, either spoken or written, consisting of the use of words in an agreed way. **2** the language of a particular community or country, etc. **3 a** the faculty of speech. **b** a style of expression; the use of words, etc. (*his language was poetic*). **c** (also **bad language**) coarse, crude, or abusive speech. **4** a system of symbols and rules for writing computer programs or algorithms. **5** any method of expression (*the language of mime; sign language*). **6** a professional or specialized vocabulary. **7** literary style.

lan·guage lab·o·ra·to·ry n. a room equipped with tape recorders, etc., for learning a foreign language.

lan·guid /lánggwid/ adj. **1** lacking vigor; idle; inert. **2** (of ideas, etc.) lacking force; uninteresting. **3** (of trade, etc.) slow-moving; sluggish. **4** faint; weak. □□ **lan·guid·ly** adv. **lan·guid·ness** n.

lan·guish /lánggwish/ v.intr. **1** be or grow feeble; lose or lack vitality. **2** put on a sentimentally tender or languid look. □ **languish for** droop or pine for. **languish under** suffer under (esp. depression, confinement, etc.). □□ **lan·guish·ment** n.

lan·guor /lánggər/ n. **1** lack of energy or alertness; idleness. **2** faintness; fatigue. **3** a soft or tender mood or effect. **4** an oppressive stillness (of the air, etc.). □□ **lan·guor·ous** adj. **lan·guor·ous·ly** adv.

la·ni·ar·y /láynee-eree, lán-/ adj. & n. ● adj. (of a tooth) adapted for tearing; canine. ● n. (pl. **-ies**) a laniary tooth.

la·nif·er·ous /lənífərəs/ adj. wool-bearing.

lank /langk/ adj. **1** (of hair, grass, etc.) long, limp, and straight. **2** thin and tall. **3** shrunken; spare. □□ **lank·ly** adv. **lank·ness** n.

lank·y /lángkee/ adj. (**lankier, lankiest**) (of limbs, a person, etc.) ungracefully thin and long or tall. □□ **lank·i·ly** adv. **lank·i·ness** n.

lan·o·lin /lánəlin/ n. a fat found naturally on sheep's wool and used purified for cosmetics, etc.

lan·tern /lántərn/ n. **1 a** a lamp with a transparent usu. glass case protecting a candle flame, etc. **b** a similar electric, etc., lamp. **c** its case. **2** a raised structure on a dome, room, etc., glazed to admit light or ventilation. ▷ DOME. **3** the light chamber of a lighthouse. **4** = MAGIC LANTERN.

lan·tern fish n. any marine fish of the family Myctophidae, having small light organs on the head and body.

lan·tern slide n. ▶ a slide for projection by a magic lantern, etc.

lan·tern jaws n.pl. long thin jaws and chin, giving a hollow look to the face. □□ **lan·tern-jawed** adj.

lan·tha·nide /lánthənīd/ n. Chem. an element of the lanthanide series.

lan·tha·nide se·ries n. a series of 15 metallic elements from lanthanum to lutetium in the periodic table, having similar chemical properties: also called **rare earths** (see RARE[1]).

LANTERN SLIDE IN A MAGIC LANTERN

chimney

magic lantern

slide

lens

lan·tha·num /lánthənəm/ n. Chem. a silvery metallic element of the lanthanide series which occurs naturally and is used in the manufacture of alloys. ¶ Symb.: **La**.

la·nu·go /lənŏŏgō, -nyŏŏ-/ n. fine, soft hair, esp. that which covers the body and limbs of a human fetus.

lan·yard /lányərd/ n. **1** a cord hanging around the neck or looped around the shoulder, esp. of a scout or sailor, etc., to which a knife, etc., may be attached. **2** Naut. ◀ a short rope or line used for securing, tightening, etc. **3** a cord attached to a breech mechanism for firing a gun.

deadeye

lanyard

deadeye

LANYARD BETWEEN DEADEYES

La·od·i·ce·an /layódəséeən/ adj. & n. ● adj. lukewarm or halfhearted, esp. in religion or politics. ● n. such a person.

La·o·tian /layóshən, lóushən/ n. & adj. ● n. **1 a** a native or national of Laos in SE Asia. **b** a person of Laotian descent. **2** the language of Laos. ● adj. of or relating to Laos or its people or language.

lap[1] /lap/ n. **1 a** the front of the body from the waist to the knees of a sitting person. **b** the clothing, esp. a skirt, covering the lap. **c** the front of a skirt held up to catch or contain something. **2** a hollow among hills. **3** a hanging flap on a garment, a saddle, etc. □ **in** (or **on**) **a person's lap** as a person's responsibility. **in the lap of the gods** (of an event, etc.) open to chance; beyond human control. **in the lap of luxury** in extremely luxurious surroundings. □□ **lap·ful** n. (pl. **-fuls**)

lap[2] /lap/ n. & v. ● n. **1 a** one circuit of a racetrack, etc. **b** a section of a journey, etc. (*on the last lap*). **2 a** an amount of overlapping. **b** an overlapping or projecting part. **3 a** a layer or sheet (of cotton, etc., being made) wound on a roller. **b** a single turn of rope, thread, etc., around a drum or reel. **4** a rotating disk for polishing a gem or metal. ● v. (**lapped, lapping**) **1** tr. lead or overtake (a competitor) by one or more laps. **2** tr. (often foll. by *about, around*) coil, fold, or wrap (a garment, etc.) around. **3** tr. (usu. foll. by *in*) enfold or wrap (a person) in clothing, etc. **4** tr. (as **lapped** adj.) (usu. foll. by *in*) enfolded caressingly. **5** tr. surround (a person) with an influence, etc. **6** intr. (usu. foll. by *over*) project; overlap. **7** tr. cause to overlap. **8** tr. polish (a gem, etc.) with a lap.

lap[3] /lap/ v. & n. ● v. (**lapped, lapping**) **1** tr. **a** (also *absol.*) (usu. of an animal) drink (liquid) with the tongue. **b** (usu. foll. by *up, down*) consume greedily. **c** (usu. foll. by *up*) consume (gossip, praise, etc.) greedily. **2 a** tr. (of water) move or beat upon (a shore) with a rippling sound as of lapping. **b** intr. (of waves, etc.) move in ripples; make a lapping sound. ● n. **1 a** the process or an act of lapping. **b** the amount of liquid taken up. **2** the sound of wavelets on a beach. **3** liquid food for dogs. **4** sl. **a** a weak beverage. **b** any liquor.

lap·a·ro·scope /lápərəskŏp/ n. Surgery a fiber-optic instrument inserted through the abdominal wall to give a view of the organs in the abdomen. □□ **lap·a·ros·co·py** /-róskəpee/ n. (pl. **-ies**).

lap·a·rot·o·my /lápərótəmee/ n. (pl. **-ies**) a surgical incision into the abdominal cavity for exploration or diagnosis.

lap danc·ing n. erotic dancing in which the dancer performs a striptease near to or on the lap of a paying customer.

lap·dog /lápdawg/ n. a small pet dog.

la·pel /ləpél/ n. the part of a coat, jacket, etc., folded back against

the front around the neck opening. □□ **la·pelled** or **la·peled** adj.

lap·i·dar·y /lápideree/ adj. & n. ● adj. **1** concerned with stone or stones. **2** engraved upon stone. **3** (of writing style) dignified and concise, suitable for inscriptions. ● n. (pl. **-ies**) a cutter, polisher, or engraver of gems.

la·pil·li /ləpíli/ n.pl. stone fragments ejected from volcanoes.

lap·is laz·u·li /lápis lázŏŏlee, lázyə-, lázhə-/ n. **1** ▶ a blue mineral containing sodium aluminum silicate and sulfur, used as a gemstone. ▷ GEM. **2** a bright blue pigment formerly made from this. **3** its color.

LAPIS LAZULI

lap joint n. the joining of rails, shafts, etc., by halving the thickness of each at the joint and fitting them together.

Lap·land·er /láplandər/ n. **1** a native or national of Lapland. **2** a person of this descent.

Lapp /lap/ n. & adj. ● n. **1** a member of a nomadic Mongol people of northern Scandinavia. **2** the language of this people. ● adj. of or relating to the Lapps or their language.

lap·pet /lápit/ n. **1** a small flap or fold of a garment, etc. **2** a hanging or loose piece of flesh, such as a lobe or wattle.

Lap·pish /lápish/ adj. & n. ● adj. = LAPP adj. ● n. the Lapp language.

lapse /laps/ n. & v. ● n. **1** a slight error; a slip of memory, etc. **2** a weak or careless decline into an inferior state. **3** (foll. by *of*) an interval or passage of time (*after a lapse of three years*). **4** Law the termination of a right or privilege through disuse or failure to follow appropriate procedures. ● v.intr. **1** fail to maintain a position or standard. **2** (foll. by *into*) fall back into an inferior or previous state. **3** (of a right or privilege, etc.) become invalid because it is not used or claimed or renewed. **4** (as **lapsed** adj.) (of a person or thing) that has lapsed.

lapse rate n. Meteorol. the rate at which the temperature falls with increasing altitude.

lap·top /láptop/ n. (often *attrib.*) ▼ a microcomputer that is portable and suitable for use while traveling.

foldaway LCD screen

QWERTY keyboard

mobile telephone

CD-ROM tray

modem cable

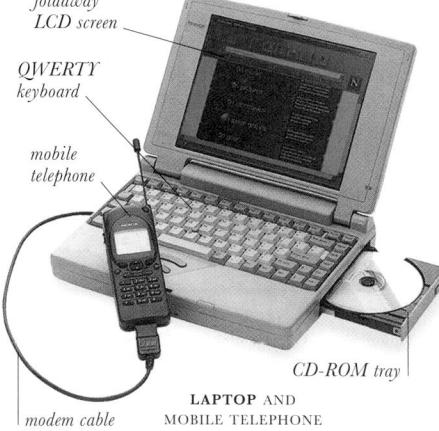

LAPTOP AND MOBILE TELEPHONE

lap-weld v. & n. ● v.tr. weld with overlapping edges. ● n. such a weld.

lap·wing /lápwing/ n. a plover, *Vanellus vanellus*, with black and white plumage, crested head, and a shrill cry.

lar·board /láarbərd/ n. & adj. Naut. archaic = PORT[3].

lar·ce·ny /láarsənee/ n. (pl. **-ies**) the theft of personal property. □□ **lar·ce·nist** n. **lar·ce·nous** adj.

L

LARCH:
EUROPEAN LARCH
(*Larix decidua*)

needles

cone

larch /laarch/ *n.* **1** ◄ a deciduous coniferous tree of the genus *Larix*, with bright foliage and producing tough wood. **2** (in full **larchwood**) its wood. ▷ WOOD

lard /laard/ *n. & v.* ● *n.* the internal fat of the abdomen of pigs, esp. when rendered for use in cooking and pharmacy. ● *v.tr.* **1** insert strips of fat or bacon in (meat, etc.) before cooking. **2** (foll. by *with*) embellish (talk or writing) with foreign or technical terms.

lard·er /laardər/ *n.* **1** a room or cupboard for storing food. **2** a wild animal's store of food, esp. for winter.

lar·doon /laardoon/ *n.* (also **lar·don** /-d'n/) a strip of fat bacon used to lard meat.

large /laarj/ *adj. & n.* ● *adj.* **1** of considerable or relatively great size or extent. **2** of the larger kind (*the large intestine*). **3** of wide range; comprehensive. **4** pursuing an activity on a large scale (*large farmer*). ● *n.* (**at large**) **1** at liberty. **2** as a body or whole (*the people at large*). **3** (of a narration, etc.) at full length and with all details. **4** without a specific target (*scatters insults at large*). **5** representing a whole area and not merely a part of it (*councilwoman at large*). □ **in large** on a large scale. **large as life** see LIFE. **larger than life** see LIFE. □□ **large·ness** *n.* **larg·ish** *adj.*

LARVA

The larva represents the second stage in the life cycle of those insects, such as wasps, butterflies, beetles, and flies, that undergo complete metamorphosis. It follows the egg stage and precedes the pupal and adult stages. A larva often has a different diet from the adult. It does not have wings and may also lack legs. During the larval stage, which may last several years, the insect grows by periodically shedding its hard outer skin, or exoskeleton, and replacing it with a new, larger skin underneath.

EXAMPLES OF INSECT LARVAE

CADDIS FLY LARVA
(*Glyphotaelius pellucidus*)

SWALLOWTAIL
LARVA
(*Papilio machaon*)

FLOUR BEETLE LARVA
(*Tenebrio molitor*)

LASER

A laser consists of a tube containing a substance known as a lasing medium, which may be solid, liquid, or gaseous. A power source, such as a flash tube, excites the atoms of the lasing medium, causing them to emit light in the form of photons. These photons are reflected backward and forward between mirrors at either end of the tube, colliding with other atoms and releasing more photons as they go. Some photons pass through the half-silvered mirror, emerging from the tube as a thin beam of coherent light, with waves all of the same color.

CUTAWAY VIEW OF A
HELIUM-NEON LASER

waves of red light · *flash tube* · *photon* · *half-silvered mirror* · *gaseous lasing medium* · *mirror*

large in·tes·tine *n.* the cecum, colon, and rectum collectively. ▷ DIGESTION

large·ly /laarjlee/ *adv.* to a great extent; principally (*is largely due to laziness*).

large-scale *adj.* made or occurring on a large scale or in large amounts.

lar·gesse /laarzhés/ *n.* (also **lar·gess**) **1** money or gifts freely given, esp. on an occasion of rejoicing, by a person in high position. **2** generosity; beneficence.

lar·ghet·to /laargétō/ *adv., adj., & n. Mus.* ● *adv. & adj.* in a fairly slow tempo. ● *n.* (*pl.* **-os**) a larghetto passage or movement.

lar·go /laargō/ *adv., adj., & n. Mus.* ● *adv. & adj.* in a slow tempo and dignified in style. ● *n.* (*pl.* **-os**) a largo passage or movement.

lar·i·at /láreeət/ *n.* **1** a lasso. **2** a tethering rope, esp. used by cowboys.

lark[1] /laark/ *n.* **1** any small bird of the family Alaudidae with brown plumage, elongated hind claws and tuneful song. **2** any of various similar birds.

lark[2] /laark/ *n. & v. colloq.* ● *n.* a frolic or spree; an amusing incident. ● *v.intr.* (foll. by *about*) play tricks; frolic. □□ **lark·y** *adj.* **lark·i·ness** *n.*

lark·spur /laarkspur/ *n.* any of various plants of the genus *Consolida*, with a spur-shaped calyx.

lar·va /laarvə/ *n.* (*pl.* **larvae** /-vee/) **1** ◄ the stage of development of an insect between egg and pupa, e.g., a caterpillar. ▷ METAMORPHOSIS. **2** an immature form of other animals that undergo

some metamorphosis, e.g. a tadpole. □□ **lar·val** *adj.*

la·ryn·ge·al /lərínjəl, -jeeəl/ *adj.* **1** of or relating to the larynx. **2** *Phonet.* (of a sound) made in the larynx.

lar·yn·gi·tis /lárinjítis/ *n.* inflammation of the larynx.

lar·ynx /láringks/ *n.* (*pl.* **larynges** /lərínjeez/ or **larynxes**) the hollow muscular organ forming an air passage to the lungs and holding the vocal cords. ▷ RESPIRATION

la·sa·gna /ləzaanyə/ *n.* (also **la·sa·gne**) pasta in the form of sheets or wide ribbons. ▷ PASTA

las·car /láskər/ *n.* an E. Indian sailor.

las·civ·i·ous /ləsíveeəs/ *adj.* **1** lustful. **2** inciting to or evoking lust. □□ **las·civ·i·ous·ly** *adv.* **las·civ·i·ous·ness** *n.*

lase /layz/ *v.intr.* **1** function as or in a laser. **2** (of a substance) undergo the physical processes employed in a laser.

la·ser /láyzər/ *n.* ▲ a device that generates an intense beam of coherent monochromatic radiation in the infrared, visible, or ultraviolet region of the electromagnetic spectrum, by stimulated emission of photons from an excited source. ▷ HOLOGRAM

la·ser disc *n.* a disk on which signals and data are recorded to be reproduced by directing a laser beam on to the surface.

la·ser print·er *n.* ▼ a printer in which a laser is used to form a pattern of dots on a photosensitive drum corresponding to the pattern of print required.

LASER PRINTER

Laser printers produce permanent high-resolution images made up of tiny dots. The image to be printed is represented by a binary code signal that causes a laser beam to turn on and off intermittently. Guided by a spinning mirror, this on-off beam focuses via lenses onto a rotating drum. As the beam scans across the drum, it changes a negative charge of static electricity into a positive charge. Particles of ink adhere to the positively charged areas of the drum, building up a complete image that is transferred onto paper in the form of a printed document.

DEMONSTRATION
OF HOW A LASER
PRINTER WORKS

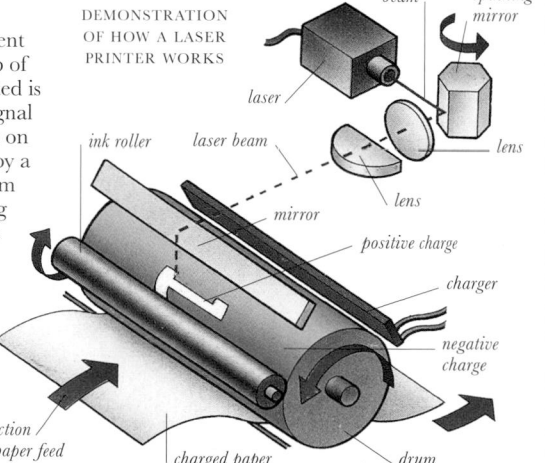

beam · *spinning mirror* · *laser* · *lens* · *ink roller* · *laser beam* · *lens* · *mirror* · *positive charge* · *charger* · *negative charge* · *direction of paper feed* · *charged paper* · *drum*

L

la·ser·vi·sion /láyzərvizhən/ *n.* a system for the reproduction of video signals recorded on a disk with a laser.

lash /lash/ *v. & n.* ● *v.* **1** *intr.* make a sudden whip-like movement. **2** *tr.* beat with a whip, etc. **3** *intr.* pour or rush with great force. **4** *intr.* (foll. by *at*, *against*) strike violently. **5** *tr.* castigate in words. **6** *tr.* urge on as with a lash. **7** *tr.* (foll. by *down*, *together*, etc.) fasten with a cord, rope, etc. **8** *tr.* (of rain, wind, etc.) beat forcefully upon. ● *n.* **1 a** a sharp blow made by a whip, rope, etc. **b** (prec. by *the*) punishment by beating with a whip, etc. **2** the flexible end of a whip. **3** (usu. in *pl.*) an eyelash. □ **lash out** (often foll. by *at*) speak or hit out angrily. □□ **lash·less** *adj.*

lash·ing /láshing/ *n.* **1** a beating. **2** cord used for lashing.

LASIK /láyzik/ *n.* corrective eye surgery in which a flap of the corneal surface is raised and a thin layer of underlying tissue is removed using a laser.

lass /las/ *n.* Brit. a girl or young woman.

Las·sa fe·ver /lásə/ *n.* an acute and often fatal febrile viral disease of tropical Africa.

las·si·tude /lásitōod, -tyōod/ *n.* **1** languor; weariness. **2** disinclination to exert or interest oneself.

las·so /láso, lasōo/ *n. & v.* ● *n.* (*pl.* **-os** or **-oes**) ◄ a rope with a noose at one end, used esp. in N. America for catching cattle, etc. ● *v.tr.* (**-oes**, **-oed**) catch with a lasso. □□ **las·so·er** *n.*

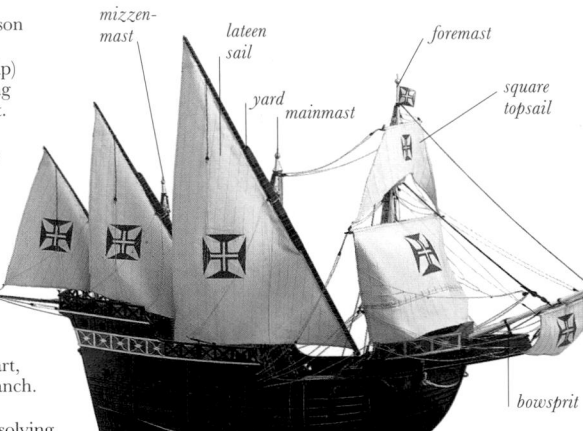

LASSO

last[1] /last/ *adj., adv., & n.* ● *adj.* **1** after all others; coming at or belonging to the end. **2 a** most recent; next before a specified time (*last Christmas*). **b** preceding (*got on at the last station*). **3** only remaining (*the last cookie*). **4** (prec. by *the*) least likely or suitable (*the last person I'd want*). **5** the lowest in rank (*the last place*). ● *adv.* **1** after all others (esp. in *comb.*: *last-mentioned*). **2** on the last occasion before the present (*when did you last see him?*). **3** (esp. in enumerating) lastly. ● *n.* **1** a person or thing that is last, last-mentioned, etc. **2** (prec. by *the*) the last mention or sight, etc. (*shall never hear the last of it*). **3** the last performance of certain acts (*breathed his last*). **4** (prec. by *the*) **a** the end or last moment. **b** death. □ **at last** (or **long last**) in the end; after much delay. **on one's last legs** see LEG. **pay one's last respects** see RESPECT. **to** (or **till**) **the last** till the end; esp. till death.

last[2] /last/ *v.intr.* **1** remain unexhausted or adequate or alive for a specified or considerable time (*enough food to last us a week*). **2** continue for a specified time (*the journey lasts an hour*). □ **last out** remain adequate or in existence for the whole of a period previously stated or implied.

last[3] /last/ *n.* a shoemaker's model for shaping or repairing a shoe or boot.

last ditch *n.* a place of final desperate defense (often (with hyphen) *attrib.*).

last-gasp *adj. colloq.* at the last possible moment.

last·ing /lásting/ *adj.* **1** continuing; permanent. **2** durable. □□ **last·ing·ly** *adv.*

last·ly /lástlee/ *adv.* finally; in the last place.

last name *n.* = SURNAME.

last rites *n.pl.* sacred rites for a person about to die.

last straw *n.* (prec. by *the*) a slight addition to a burden or difficulty that makes it finally unbearable.

Last Sup·per *n.* that of Christ and his disciples on the eve of the Crucifixion, as recorded in the New Testament.

last word *n.* (prec. by *the*) **1** a final or definitive statement. **2** (often foll. by *in*) the latest fashion.

---

lat. *abbr.* latitude.

latch /lach/ *n. & v.* ● *n.* **1** a bar with a catch and lever used as a fastening for a gate, etc. **2** a springlock preventing a door from being opened from the outside without a key after being shut. ● *v.tr. & intr.* fasten or be fastened with a latch. □ **latch on** (often foll. by *to*) *colloq.* **1** attach oneself (to). **2** understand.

late /layt/ *adj. & adv.* ● *adj.* **1** after the due or usual time; occurring or done after the proper time. **2 a** far on in the day or night or in a specified time or period. **b** far on in development. **3** flowering or ripening toward the end of the season. **4** (prec. by *the* or *my*, *his*, etc.) no longer alive or having the specified status (*the late president*). **5** of recent date (*the late storms*). **6** (as **latest**, prec. by *the*) fashionable, up to date. ● *adv.* **1** after the due or usual time (*arrived late*). **2** far on in time (*this happened later on*). **3** at or till a late hour. **4** at a late stage of development. **5** formerly but not now (*a family late of New England*). □ **at the latest** as the latest time envisaged (*by six at the latest*). **late in the day** *colloq.* at a late stage in the proceedings, esp. too late to be useful. **the latest** the most recent news, fashion, etc. □□ **late·ness** *n.*

late·com·er /láytkumər/ *n.* a person who arrives late.

la·teen /lətéen/ *adj.* ► (of a ship) rigged with a triangular sail on a long yard at an angle of 45° to the mast. ▷ DHOW

late·ly /láytlee/ *adv.* not long ago; recently; in recent times.

la·tent /láyt'nt/ *adj.* **1** concealed; dormant. **2** existing but not developed or manifest. □□ **la·ten·cy** *n.* **la·tent·ly** *adv.*

lat·er·al /látərəl/ *adj. & n.* ● *adj.* **1** of, at, toward, or from the side or sides. **2** descended from a brother or sister of a person in direct line. ● *n.* a side part, etc., esp. a lateral shoot or branch. □□ **lat·er·al·ly** *adv.*

lat·er·al think·ing *n.* a method of solving problems indirectly or by apparently illogical methods.

lat·er·ite /látərīt/ *n.* a red or yellow iron-bearing clay, friable and hardening in air, used for making roads in the tropics. □□ **lat·er·it·ic** /-rítik/ *adj.*

la·tex /láyteks/ *n.* (*pl.* **latices** /-tiseez/ or **latexes**) **1** a milky fluid of mixed composition found in various plants and trees, esp. the rubber tree. **2** a synthetic product resembling this.

lath /lath/ *n. & v.* ● *n.* (*pl.* **laths** /laths, lathz/) a thin flat strip of wood, esp. each of a series forming a framework or support for plaster, etc. ● *v.tr.* attach laths to (a wall or ceiling).

lathe /layth/ *n.* a machine for shaping wood, metal, etc., by means of a rotating drive which turns the piece being worked on against changeable cutting tools.

lath·er /láthər/ *n. & v.* ● *n.* **1** a froth produced by agitating soap, etc., and water. **2** frothy sweat, esp. of a horse. **3** a state of agitation. ● *v.* **1** *intr.* (of soap, etc.) form a lather. **2** *tr.* cover with lather. **3** *intr.* (of a horse, etc.) develop or become covered with lather. **4** *tr. colloq.* thrash. □□ **lath·er·y** *adj.*

lat·i·ces *pl.* of LATEX.

Lat·in /lát'n/ *n. & adj.* ● *n.* **1** the Italic language of ancient Rome and its empire, originating in Latium. **2** *Rom. Hist.* an inhabitant of ancient Latium in Central Italy. ● *adj.* **1** of or in Latin. **2** of the countries or peoples using languages developed from Latin. **3** *Rom.Hist.* of or relating to ancient Latium or its inhabitants. **4** of the Roman Catholic Church. □□ **Lat·in·ism** *n.* **Lat·in·ist** *n.*

Lat·in A·mer·i·ca *n.* the parts of Central and S. America where Spanish

---

or Portuguese is the main language. □□ **Lat·in A·mer·i·can** *n. & adj.*

Lat·in·ate /lát'nayt/ *adj.* having the character of Latin.

Lat·in·ize /lát'nīz/ *v.* **1** *tr.* give a Latin or Latinate form to. **2** *tr.* translate into Latin. **3** *tr.* make conformable to the ideas, customs, etc., of the ancient Romans, Latin peoples, or Latin Church. **4** *intr.* use Latin forms, idioms, etc. □□ **Lat·in·i·za·tion** *n.* **Lat·in·iz·er** *n.*

La·ti·no /lətéenō/ *n.* (*pl.* **Latinos**; *fem.* **Latina** /-nə/, *pl.* **Latinas**) **1** a native or inhabitant of Latin America. **2** a person of Spanish-speaking or Latin-American descent.

lat·i·tude /látitōod, -tyōod/ *n.* **1** *Geog.* **a** the angular distance on a meridian north or south of the equator, expressed in degrees and minutes. ▷ LONGITUDE. **b** (usu. in *pl.*) regions or climes, esp. with reference to temperature (*warm latitudes*). **2** freedom from narrowness; liberality of interpretation. **3** tolerated variety of action or opinion. **4** *Astron.* the angular distance of a celestial body or point from the ecliptic. □□ **lat·i·tu·di·nal** /-tōod'nəl, -tyōod-/ *adj.* **lat·i·tu·di·nal·ly** *adv.*

mizzen-mast   **lateen sail**   **foremast**

yard   **mainmast**   **square topsail**

bowsprit

LATEEN: 15TH-CENTURY PORTUGUESE LATEEN SHIP

lat·i·tu·di·nar·i·an /látitōod'náireeən, -tyōod-/ *adj. & n.* ● *adj.* allowing latitude esp. in religion. ● *n.* a person with a latitudinarian attitude. □□ **lat·i·tu·di·nar·i·an·ism** *n.*

la·trine /lətréen/ *n.* a communal toilet, esp. in a barracks, etc.

lat·te /láatay/ *n.* a drink of frothy steamed milk to which a shot of espresso coffee is added.

lat·ter /látər/ *adj.* **1 a** denoting the second-mentioned of two, or *disp.* the last-mentioned of three or more. **b** (prec. by *the*; usu. *absol.*) the second- or last-mentioned person or thing. **2** nearer to the end (*the latter part of the year*). **3** recent. **4** belonging to the end of a period, of the world, etc.

Lat·ter-day Saints *n.pl.* the Mormons' name for themselves.

lat·ter·ly /látərlee/ *adv.* **1** in the latter part of life or of a period. **2** recently.

lat·tice /látis/ *n.* **1** a structure of crossed laths or bars with spaces between, used as a fence, etc. **2** *Crystallog.* a regular periodic arrangement of atoms, ions, or molecules. □□ **lat·ticed** *adj.* **lat·tic·ing** *n.*

lat·tice win·dow *n.* ◄ a window with small panes set in diagonally crossing strips of lead.

LATTICE WINDOW

Lat·vi·an /látveeən/ *n. & adj.* ● *n.* **1 a** a native of Latvia, a Baltic republic.

LAVA

Magma (molten rock) emerging from a volcanic eruption is called lava. Magma bubbles up from a magma chamber deep under the ground and flows out through a vent. There are two main kinds of lava flow, both of which take their name from Hawaiian words. Aa (pronounced *ah-ah*) flows are viscous and are covered in sharp angular blocks called scoria. Pahoehoe (*pa-hōee-hōee*) flows are less viscous and form a wrinkled skin with a ropelike appearance, caused by the lava flowing beneath.

EXAMPLES OF LAVA

AA LAVA   PAHOEHOE LAVA

CROSS SECTION OF A VOLCANO, SHOWING LAVA FLOW

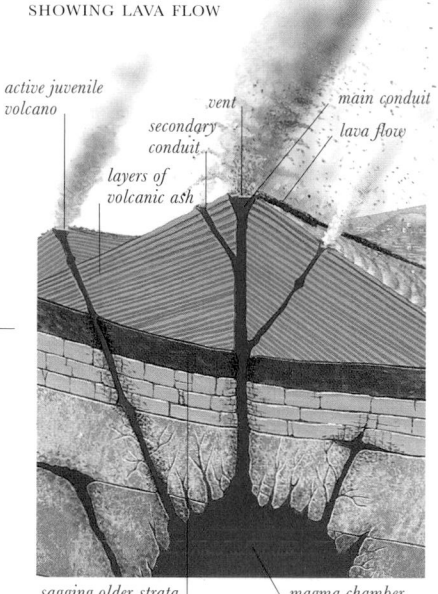

active juvenile volcano

vent

secondary conduit

main conduit

lava flow

layers of volcanic ash

sagging older strata   *magma chamber*

---

b a person of Latvian descent. **2** the language of Latvia. ● *adj.* of or relating to Latvia or its people or language.

laud /lawd/ *v. & n.* ● *v.tr.* praise or extol, esp. in hymns. ● *n.* **1** *literary* praise, a hymn of praise. **2** (in *pl.*) the traditional morning prayer of the Roman Catholic Church.

laud·a·ble /láwdəbəl/ *adj.* commendable; praiseworthy. □□ **laud·a·bly** *adv.*

lau·da·num /láwd'nəm/ *n.* a solution containing morphine and prepared from opium, formerly used as a narcotic painkiller.

lau·da·tion /lawdáyshən/ *n. formal* praise.

laud·a·to·ry /láwdətawree/ *adj.* expressing praise.

laugh /laf/ *v. & n.* ● *v.* **1** *intr.* make the spontaneous sounds and movements usual in expressing lively amusement, scorn, derision, etc. **2** *tr.* express by laughing. **3** *tr.* bring (a person) into a certain state by laughing (*laughed them into agreeing*). **4** *intr.* (foll. by *at*) ridicule; make fun of. **5** *intr.* (**be laughing**) *colloq.* be in a fortunate or successful position. ● *n.* **1** the sound or act or manner of laughing. **2** *colloq.* a comical or ridiculous person or thing. □ **have the last laugh** be ultimately the winner. **laugh in a person's face** show open scorn for a person. **laugh off** get rid of (embarrassment or humiliation) with a jest. **laugh out of court** deprive of a hearing by ridicule. **laugh out of the other side of one's mouth (or on the other side of one's face)** change from enjoyment or amusement to displeasure, shame, apprehension, etc. **laugh up one's sleeve** be secretly or inwardly amused.

laugh·a·ble /láfəbəl/ *adj.* ludicrous; highly amusing. □□ **laugh·a·bly** *adv.*

laugh·ing /láfing/ *n. & adj.* ● *n.* laughter. ● *adj.* in senses of LAUGH *v.* □ **no laughing matter** something serious. □□ **laugh·ing·ly** *adv.*

laughing gas *n.* nitrous oxide as an anesthetic.

laughing hy·e·na *n.* a hyena, *Crocuta crocuta*, whose howl is compared to a fiendish laugh.

laugh·ing·stock /láfingstok/ *n.* a person or thing open to general ridicule.

laugh·ter /láftər/ *n.* the act or sound of laughing.

laugh track *n.* recorded laughter added to a comedy show, esp. a television situation comedy.

launch[1] /lawnch/ *v. & n.* ● *v.* **1** *tr.* set (a vessel) afloat. **2** *tr.* hurl or send forth (a weapon, rocket, etc.). **3** *tr.* start or set in motion (an enterprise, a

person on a course of action, etc.). **4** *tr.* formally introduce (a new product) with publicity, etc. **5** *intr.* (often foll. by *out, into,* etc.) **a** make a start, esp. on an ambitious enterprise. **b** burst into strong language, etc. ● *n.* the act or an instance of launching.

launch[2] /lawnch/ *n.* **1** a motorboat, used esp. for pleasure. **2** a man-of-war's largest boat.

launch·er /láwnchər/ *n.* a structure or device to hold a rocket during launching.

launch·pad /láwnchpad/ *n.* (also **launch·ing pad**) a platform from which rockets are launched.

laun·der /láwndər, laán-/ *v. & n.* ● *v.tr.* **1** wash and iron (clothes, linen, etc.). **2** *colloq.* transfer (funds) to conceal a dubious or illegal origin. ● *n.* a channel for conveying liquids, esp. molten metal. □□ **laun·der·er** *n.*

laun·der·ette /lawndərét, laán-/ *n.* (also **laun·drette**) = LAUNDROMAT.

laun·dro·mat /láwndrəmat, laán-/ *n. Trademark* an establishment with coin-operated washing machines and dryers for public use.

laun·dry /láwndree, laán-/ *n.* (*pl.* **-ies**) **1** an establishment for washing clothes or linen. **2** clothes or linen for laundering or newly laundered.

laundry list *n. colloq.* a lengthy and often random list of items (*a laundry list of weekend projects*).

lau·re·ate /láwreeət, lór-/ *adj. & n.* ● *adj.* **1** wreathed with laurel as a mark of honor. **2** consisting of laurel; laurellike. ● *n.* **1** a person who is honored for outstanding achievement (*Nobel laureate*). **2** = POET LAUREATE. □□ **lau·re·ate·ship** *n.*

lau·rel /láwrəl, lór-/ *n. & v.* ● *n.* **1** = BAY[2]. **2 a** (in *sing.* or *pl.*) ▶ the foliage of the bay tree used as an emblem of victory or distinction in poetry, usu. formed into a wreath or crown. **b** (in *pl.*) honor or distinction. **3** any plant with dark-green glossy leaves like a bay tree. ● *v.tr.* wreathe with laurel. □ **look to one's laurels** beware of losing one's preeminence. **rest on one's laurels** be satisfied with what one has done and not seek further success.

lav /lav/ *n. colloq.* lavatory.

LAUREL

la·va /laávə, lávə/ *n.* **1** ◀ the molten matter which flows from a volcano. ▷ VOLCANO. **2** the solid substance which it forms on cooling.

la·vage /ləvaázh, lávij/ *n. Med.* the washing out of a body cavity, such as the colon or stomach, with water or a medicated solution.

la·va lamp *n.* a transparent electric lamp containing a viscous liquid in which a suspended waxy substance rises and falls in constantly changing shapes.

la·va·tion /ləváyshən/ *n. formal* washing.

lav·a·to·ry /lávətawree/ *n.* (*pl.* **-ies**) **1** a sink or wash basin in a bathroom. **2** a room or compartment with a toilet and wash basin. **3** *Brit.* a flush toilet.

lav·en·der /lávindər/ *n. & adj.* ● *n.* **1 a** ▶ any small evergreen shrub of the genus *Lavandula*, with narrow leaves and blue, purple, or pink aromatic flowers. **b** its flowers and stalks dried and used to scent linen, clothes, etc. ▷ HERB. **2** a pale blue color with a trace of red. ● *adj.* **1** pale blue with a trace of red. **2** having the fragrance of lavender flowers.

la·ver /láyvər/ *n.* any of various edible seaweeds, esp. *Porphyra umbilicaulis*, having sheetlike fronds.

LAVENDER (*Lavandula angustifolia* 'Munstead')

lav·ish /lávish/ *adj. & v.* ● *adj.* **1** giving or producing in large quantities; profuse. **2** generous; unstinting. **3** excessive; overabundant. ● *v.tr.* (often foll. by *on*) bestow or spend (money, praise, etc.) abundantly. □□ **lav·ish·ly** *adv.* **lav·ish·ness** *n.*

law /law/ *n.* **1 a** a rule enacted or customary in a community and recognized as enjoining or prohibiting certain actions and enforced by the imposition of penalties (*an environmental protection law*). **b** a body of such rules (*the law of the land; forbidden under state law*). **2** the controlling influence of laws; respect for laws (*law and order*). **3** laws collectively as a social system or subject of study (*was reading law*). **4** (with defining word) any of the specific branches or applications of law (*commercial law*). **5** binding force or effect (*their word is law*). **6** (prec. by *the*) **a** the legal profession. **b** *colloq.* the police. **7** the statute and common law (opp. EQUITY). **8** (in *pl.*) jurisprudence. **9 a** the judicial remedy; litigation. **b** courts of law as providing this (*go to law*). **10** a rule of action or procedure, e.g., in a game, form of art, etc. **11** a regularity in natural occurrences, esp. as formulated or propounded in particular instances (*the law of gravity; Parkinson's law*). **12 a** divine commandments. **b** (**Law of Moses**) the precepts of the Pentateuch. □ **at** (or **in**) **law** according to the laws. **be a law unto oneself** do what one feels is right; disregard custom. **lay down the law** be dogmatic or authoritarian. **take the law into one's own hands** redress a grievance by one's own means, esp. by force.

law-a·bid·ing *adj.* obedient to the laws.

law·break·er /láwbraykər/ *n.* a person who breaks the law. □□ **law·break·ing** *n. & adj.*

law·court /láwkawrt/ *n. Brit.* a court of law.

law·ful /láwfŏŏl/ *adj.* conforming with, permitted by, or recognized by law. □□ **law·ful·ly** *adv.* **law·ful·ness** *n.*

law·giv·er /láwgivər/ *n.* a person who lays down laws.

law·less /láwlis/ *adj.* **1** having no laws or enforcement of them. **2** disregarding laws. **3** unbridled; uncontrolled. □□ **law·less·ly** *adv.* **law·less·ness** *n.*

law·mak·er /láwmaykər/ *n.* a legislator.

law·man /láwman/ *n.* (*pl.* **-men**) a law-enforcement officer, esp. a sheriff or policeman.

L

lawn[1] /lawn/ *n.* a piece of grass kept mown and smooth in a yard, garden, park, etc.

lawn[2] /lawn/ *n.* a fine linen or cotton fabric used for clothes. □□ **lawn·y** *adj.*

lawn mow·er *n.* ▼ a machine for cutting the grass on a lawn.

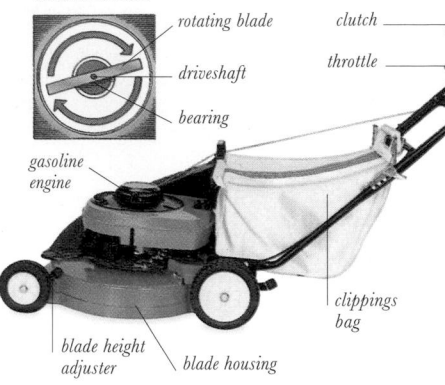

ROTARY BLADE

rotating blade   clutch

driveshaft   throttle

bearing

gasoline engine

clippings bag

blade height adjuster   blade housing

LAWN MOWER: GAS-POWERED ROTARY LAWN MOWER

lawn ten·nis *n.* the usual form of tennis, played with a soft ball on outdoor grass or a hard court.

law of av·er·ag·es *n.* the principle that if one of two extremes occurs the other will also tend to so as to maintain the normal average.

law of na·ture *n.* = NATURAL LAW 2.

law of suc·ces·sion *n.* the law regulating inheritance.

law·ren·ci·um /lɔrénseeəm, law-/ *n.* *Chem.* an artificially made transuranic radioactive metallic element. ¶ Symb.: **Lw**.

law·suit /láwsōōt/ *n.* the process or an instance of making a claim in a court of law.

law·yer /láwyər, lóyər/ *n.* a member of the legal profession. □□ **law·yer·ly** *adj.*

lax /laks/ *adj.* **1** lacking care, concern, or firmness. **2** loose, relaxed; not compact. □□ **lax·i·ty** *n.* **lax·ly** *adv.* **lax·ness** *n.*

lax·a·tive /láksətiv/ *adj. & n.* ● *adj.* tending to stimulate or facilitate evacuation of the bowels. ● *n.* a laxative medicine.

lay[1] /lay/ *v. & n.* ● *v.* (*past* and *past part.* **laid** /layd/) **1** *tr.* place on a surface, esp. horizontally or in the proper or specified place. **2** *tr.* put or bring into a certain or the required position or state (*lay a carpet*). **3** *intr.* *dial.* or *erron.* lie. ¶ This use, incorrect in standard English, is probably partly encouraged by confusion with *lay* as the past of *lie*, as in *the dog lay on the floor* which is correct; *the dog is laying on the floor* is not correct. **4** *tr.* make by laying (*lay the foundations*). **5** *tr.* (often *absol.*) (of a hen bird) produce (an egg). **6** *tr.* **a** cause to subside or lie flat. **b** deal with to remove (a ghost, fear, etc.). **7** *tr.* place or present for consideration (a case, proposal, etc.). **8** *tr.* set down as a basis or starting point. **9** *tr.* (usu. foll. by *on*) attribute or impute (blame, etc.). **10** *tr.* locate (a scene, etc.) in a certain place. **11** *tr.* prepare or make ready (a plan or a trap). **12** *tr.* prepare (a table) for a meal. **13** *tr.* place or arrange the material for (a fire). **14** *tr.* put down as a wager; stake. **15** *tr.* (foll. by *with*) coat or strew (a surface). **16** *tr. sl. offens.* have sexual intercourse with (esp. a woman). ● *n.* **1** the way, position, or direction in which something lies. **2** *sl. offens.* a partner (esp. female) in sexual intercourse. **3** the direction or amount of twist in rope strands. □ **in lay** (of a hen) laying eggs regularly. **lay about one 1** hit out on all sides. **2** criticize indiscriminately. **lay aside 1** put to one side. **2** cease to practice or consider. **3** save (money, etc.) for future needs. **lay at the door of** see DOOR. **lay bare** expose; reveal. **lay a charge** make an accusation. **lay claim to** claim as one's own. **lay**

down 1 put on the ground. **2** relinquish; give up (an office). **3** formulate or insist on (a rule or principle). **4** pay or wager (money). **5** store (wine) in a cellar. **6** set down on paper. **7** sacrifice (one's life). **8** convert (land) into pasture. **9** record (esp. popular music). **lay down the law** see LAW. **lay hands on 1** seize or attack. **2** place one's hands on or over, esp. in confirmation, ordination, or spiritual healing. **lay one's hands on** obtain; acquire; locate. **lay hold of** seize or grasp. **lay in** provide oneself with a stock of. **lay into** *colloq.* punish or scold severely. **lay it on thick** (or **with a trowel**) *colloq.* flatter or exaggerate grossly. **lay low** overthrow, kill, or humble. **lay off 1** discharge (workers) temporarily because of a shortage of work. **2** *colloq.* desist. **lay on 1** spread on (paint, etc.). **2** inflict (blows). **3** impose (a penalty, obligation, etc.). **lay open 1** break the skin of. **2** (foll. by *to*) expose (to criticism, etc.). **lay out 1** spread out. **2** expose to view. **3** prepare (a corpse) for burial. **4** *colloq.* knock unconscious. **5** prepare a layout. **6** expend (money). **7** *refl.* (foll. by *to* + infin.) take pains (to do something) (*laid themselves out to help*). **lay store by** see STORE. **lay to rest** bury in a grave. **lay up 1** store; save. **2** put (a ship, etc.) out of service. **lay waste** see WASTE.

lay[2] /lay/ *adj.* **1 a** nonclerical. **b** not ordained into the clergy. **2 a** not professionally qualified, esp. in law or medicine. **b** of or done by such persons.

lay[3] /lay/ *n.* **1** a short lyric or narrative poem meant to be sung. **2** a song.

lay[4] *past of* LIE[1].

lay·a·bout /láyəbowt/ *n.* a habitual loafer or idler.

lay-by /láybī/ *n.* (*pl.* **lay-bys**) an area at the side of a canal or railroad where vehicles may stop.

lay·er /láyər/ *n. & v.* ● *n.* **1** a thickness of matter, esp. one of several, covering a surface. **2** a person or thing that lays. **3** a hen that lays eggs. **4** ▶ a shoot fastened down to take root while attached to the parent plant. ● *v.tr.* **1 a** arrange in layers. **b** cut (hair) in layers. **2** propagate (a plant) as a layer. □□ **lay·ered** *adj.*

lay·ette /layét/ *n.* a set of clothing, toilet articles, and bedclothes for a newborn child.

lay fig·ure /lay/ *n.* **1** a dummy or jointed figure of a human body used by artists for arranging drapery on, etc. **2** an unrealistic character in a novel, etc. **3** a person lacking in individuality.

lay·man /láymən/ *n.* (*pl.* **-men**; *fem.* **laywoman**, *pl.* **-women**) **1** any nonordained member of a church. **2** a person without professional or specialized knowledge in a particular subject.

lay·off /láyawf/ *n. n.* **1** a temporary discharge of workers. **2** a period when this is in force.

lay of the land *n.* (prec. by *the*) the current state of affairs.

lay·out /láyowt/ *n.* **1** the disposing or arrangement of a site, ground, etc. **2** the way in which plans, printed matter, etc., are arranged or set out. **3** something arranged or set out in a particular way. **4** the makeup of a book, newspaper, etc.

lay·o·ver /láyōvər/ *n.* a period of rest or waiting before a further stage in a journey, etc.; a stop over.

lay·wom·an see LAYMAN.

laz·ar /lázər, láy-/ *n.* *archaic* a poor and diseased person, esp. a leper.

laze /layz/ *v. & n.* ● *v.* **1** *intr.* spend time lazily or idly. **2** *tr.* (often foll. by *away*) pass (time) in this way. ● *n.* a spell of lazing.

la·zy /láyzee/ *adj.* (**lazier, laziest**) **1** disinclined to work; doing little work. **2** of or inducing idleness. **3** (of a river, etc.) slow-moving. □□ **la·zi·ly** *adv.* **la·zi·ness** *n.*

la·zy·bones /láyzeebōnz/ *n.* (*pl.* same) *colloq.* a lazy person.

la·zy eye *n.* an eye with poor vision due to underuse, esp. the unused eye in a squint.

lb. *abbr.* a pound or pounds (weight).

LC *abbr.* (also **L.C.** or **l.c.**) **1** landing craft. **2** left center. **3** letter of credit. **4** (**LC** or **L.C.**) Library of Congress. **5** lowercase. **6** in the passage, etc., cited.

LCD *abbr.* **1** liquid crystal display. **2** lowest (or least) common denominator.

LCM *abbr.* lowest (or least) common multiple.

Ld. *abbr.* Lord.

lea /lee, láy/ *n.* *poet.* (also **ley**) a piece of meadow or pasture or arable land.

leach /leech/ *v.* **1** *tr.* make (a liquid) percolate through some material. **2** *tr.* subject (bark, ore, ash, or soil) to the action of percolating fluid. **3** *tr. & intr.* (foll. by *away, out*) remove (soluble matter) or be removed in this way.

lead[1] /leed/ *v., n., & adj.* ● *v.* (*past* and *past part.* **led** /led/) **1** *tr.* cause to go with one, esp. by guiding or showing the way or by going in front. **2** *tr.* **a** direct the actions or opinions of. **b** (often foll. by *to*, or *to* + infin.) guide by persuasion or example or argument (*what led you to that conclusion?*; *was led to think you may be right*). **3** *tr.* (also *absol.*) provide access to; bring to a certain position or destination (*this door leads you into a small room*; *the road leads to Atlanta*; *the path leads uphill*). **4** *tr.* pass or go through (a life, etc., of a specified kind) (*led a miserable existence*). **5** *tr.* **a** have the first place in (*lead the dance*; *leads the world in sugar production*). **b** (*absol.*) go first; be ahead in a race or game. **c** (*absol.*) be preeminent in some field. **6** *tr.* be in charge of (*leads a team of researchers*). **7** *tr.* **a** direct by example. **b** set (a fashion). **c** be the principal player of (a group of musicians). **8** *tr.* (also *absol.*) begin a round of play at cards by playing (a card) or a card of (a particular suit). **9** *intr.* (foll. by *to*) have as an end or outcome; result in (*what does all this lead to?*). **10** *intr.* (foll. by *with*) *Boxing* make an attack (with a particular hand or blow). **11 a** *intr.* (foll. by *with*) (of a newspaper) use a particular item as the main story (*led with the stock-market crash*). **b** *tr.* (of a story) be the main feature of (a newspaper or part of it) (*the governor's wedding will lead the front page*). **12** *tr.* (foll. by *through*) make (a liquid, strip of material, etc.) pass through a pulley, channel, etc. ● *n.* **1** guidance given by going in front; example. **2 a** a leading place; the leadership (*is in the lead*; *take the lead*). **b** the amount by which a competitor is ahead of the others (*a lead of ten yards*). **3** a clue, esp. an early indication of the resolution of a problem (*is the first real lead in the case*). **4** a strap or cord for leading a dog, etc. **5** esp. *Brit.* a conductor (usu. a wire) conveying electric current from a source to an appliance. **6 a** the chief part in a play, etc. **b** the person playing this. **7** (in full **lead story**) the item of news given the greatest prominence in a newspaper or magazine. **8 a** the act or right of playing first in a game or round of cards. **b** the card led. **9** the distance advanced by a screw in one turn. **10 a** an artificial watercourse, esp. one leading to a mill. **b** a channel of water in an icefield. ● *attrib.adj.* leading; principal; first. □ **lead astray** see ASTRAY. **lead by the nose** cajole (a person) into compliance. **lead-in 1** an introduction, opening, etc. **2** a wire leading in from outside, esp. from an aerial to a receiver or transmitter. **lead off 1 a** begin; make a start. **b** *Baseball* be the first batter in the batting order or the inning. **2** *colloq.* lose one's temper. **lead on 1** entice into going further than was intended. **2** mislead or deceive. **lead up the garden path** *colloq.* give someone misleading clues or signals; deceive. **lead up to 1** form an introduction to; precede; prepare for. **2** direct one's talk gradually or cautiously to a particular topic, etc. **lead the way** see WAY. □□ **lead·a·ble** *adj.*

LAYER   runner   peg   roots

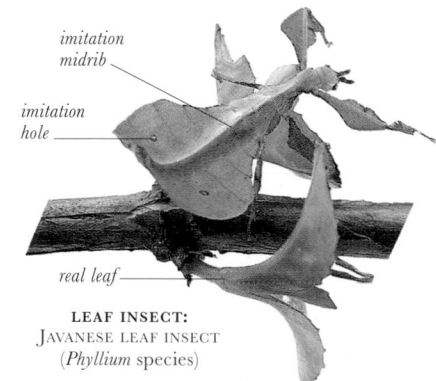

LEAD BETWEEN INVERTED METAL
TYPE ON A COMPOSING STICK

type   lead   composing stick

lead[2] /led/ *n. & v.* ● *n.* **1** *Chem.* a heavy, bluish-gray soft ductile metallic element used in building and the manufacture of alloys. ▷ ORE. ¶ Symb.: **Pb**. **2 a** graphite. **b** a thin length of this in a pencil. **3** *Printing* ▲ a blank space between lines of print (orig. with ref. to the metal strip used to give this space). **4** (*attrib.*) made of lead. ● *v.tr.* **1** cover, weight, or frame (a roof or window panes) with lead. **2** *Printing* separate lines of (printed matter) with leads. **3** add a lead compound to (gasoline, etc.). □□ **lead·less** *adj.*

lead bal·loon *n.* a failure; an unsuccessful venture.

lead·en /léd'n/ *adj.* **1** of or like lead. **2** heavy; slow; burdensome (*leaden limbs*). **3** inert; depressing (*leaden rule*). **4** lead-colored (*leaden skies*). □□ **lead·en·ly** *adv.* **lead·en·ness** *n.*

lead·er /léedər/ *n.* **1 a** a person or thing that leads. **b** a person followed by others. **2 a** the principal player in a music group or of the first violins in an orchestra. **b** a conductor of an orchestra. **3** a short strip of nonfunctioning material at each end of a reel of film or recording tape for connection to the spool. **4** a shoot of a plant at the apex of a stem or of the main branch. **5** (in *pl.*) *Printing* a series of dots or dashes across the page to guide the eye, esp. in tabulated material. **6** the horse placed at the front in a team or pair. □□ **lead·er·less** *adj.* **lead·er·ship** *n.*

lead·ing[1] /léeding/ *adj. & n.* ● *adj.* chief; most important. ● *n.* guidance; leadership.

lead·ing[2] /léding/ *n.* *Printing* = LEAD[2] *n.* 3.

lead·ing ques·tion *n.* a question that prompts the answer wanted.

lead time *n.* the time between the initiation and completion of a production process.

leaf /leef/ *n. & v.* ● *n.* (*pl.* **leaves** /leevz/) **1 a** ▼ each of several flattened usu. green structures of a plant, usu. on the side of a stem or branch. ▷ SUCCULENT. **b** other similar plant structures, e.g., bracts, sepals, and petals (*floral leaf*). **2 a** foliage regarded collectively. **b** the state of having leaves out (*a tree in leaf*). **3** the leaves of tobacco or tea. **4** a single thickness of paper, esp. in a book with each side forming a page. **5** a very thin sheet of metal, esp. gold or silver. **6 a** the hinged part or flap of a door, shutter, table, etc. **b** an extra section inserted to extend a table. ● *v.* **1** *intr.* put forth leaves. **2** *tr.* (foll. by *through*) turn over the pages of (a book, etc.). □□ **leaf·age** *n.* **leafed** *adj.* (also in *comb.*). **leaf·less** *adj.* **leaf·like** *adj.*

leaf in·sect *n.* ▶ any insect of the family Phyllidae, having a flattened body leaflike in appearance.

leaf·let /léeflit/ *n. & v.* ● *n.* **1** a young leaf. **2** *Bot.* any division of a compound leaf. **3** a sheet of paper giving information. ● *v.tr.* (**leafleted, leafleting; leafletted, leafletting**) distribute leaflets to.

leaf·y /léefee/ *adj.* (**leafier, leafiest**) **1** having many leaves; (of a place) rich in foliage; verdant. **2** resembling a leaf. □□ **leaf·i·ness** *n.*

league[1] /leeg/ *n. & v.* ● *n.* **1** people, countries, groups, etc., combining for a purpose. **2** an agreement to combine in this way. **3** a group of sports organizations that compete for a championship. ● *v.intr.* (**leagues, leagued, leaguing**) (often foll. by *together*) join in a league. □ **in league** allied; conspiring.

imitation midrib

imitation hole

real leaf

LEAF INSECT:
JAVANESE LEAF INSECT
(*Phyllium* species)

L

LEAF

A typical leaf consists of a thin flat lamina (blade) supported by a network of veins, a petiole (leafstalk), and a leaf base, where the petiole joins the stem. Leaves can be classified as simple, where the lamina is a single unit, or compound, where the lamina is divided into separate leaflets. Compound leaves may be pinnate, with pinnae (leaflets) on both sides of a rachis (main axis), or palmate, with leaflets arising from a single point at the tip of the petiole. Conifer leaves are usually simple and slender, with a tough waxy surface. Unlike more delicate leaves, they often last for several years.

apex
midrib
margin
lateral vein
petiole
leaf base
lamina

SIMPLE LEAF

terminal pinna
pinna
rachis
petiolule (leaflet stalk)
petiole

COMPOUND LEAF

EXAMPLES OF LEAF TYPES AND SHAPES

CONIFEROUS

COMBLIKE
(pectinate)

NEEDLELIKE
(acicular)

SCALELIKE

LOBED OR DIVIDED

PINNATIFID

DIGITATE
(5-palmate)

BIPINNATE
(2-pinnate)

PALMATELY
LOBED

PINNATE

TRIPINNATE
(3-pinnate)

SHAPES

LANCE-SHAPED
(lanceolate)

SPOON-SHAPED
(spathulate)

ELLIPTIC

HEART-SHAPED
(cordate)

KIDNEY-SHAPED
(reniform)

INVERSELY HEART-SHAPED
(obcordate)

TRIANGULAR
(deltoid)

ARROW-SHAPED
(sagittate)

FAN-SHAPED
(flabellate)

league[2] /leeg/ *n. archaic* a measure of traveling distance by land, usu. about three miles.

League of Wom·en Vot·ers *n.* an Amer. nonpartisan organization that promotes and sponsors programs, etc., that encourage voter awareness and participations.

lea·guer /léégər/ *n.* a member of a league.

leak /leek/ *n. & v.* • *n.* **1 a** a hole in a pipe, container, etc., caused by wear or damage, through which matter, esp. liquid or gas, passes accidentally in or out. **b** the matter passing in or out through this. **c** the act or an instance of leaking. **2 a** a similar escape of electrical charge. **b** the charge that escapes. **3** the intentional disclosure of secret information. • *v.* **1 a** *intr.* (of liquid, gas, etc.) pass in or out through a leak. **b** *tr.* lose or admit (liquid, gas, etc.) through a leak. **2** *tr.* intentionally disclose (secret information). **3** *intr.* (often foll. by *out*) (of a secret, secret information) become known. □ **take a leak** *sl.* urinate. □□ **leak·er** *n.*

leak·age /léékij/ *n.* **1** the action or result of leaking. **2** what leaks in or out. **3** an intentional disclosure of secret information.

leak·y /léékee/ *adj.* (**leakier, leakiest**) **1** having a leak or leaks. **2** given to letting out secrets. □□ **leak·i·ness** *n.*

lean[1] /leen/ *v. & n.* • *v.* (*past* and *past part.* **leaned** /leend, lent/ or **leant** /lent/) **1** *intr. & tr.* (often foll. by *across, back, over,* etc.) be or place in a sloping position. **2** *intr. & tr.* (foll. by *against, on, upon*) rest or cause to rest for support against, etc. **3** *intr.* (foll. by *on, upon*) rely on. **4** *intr.* (foll. by *to, toward*) be inclined or partial to. • *n.* a deviation from the perpendicular; an inclination (*has a decided lean to the right*). □ **lean on** *colloq.* put pressure on (a person) to act in a certain way. **lean over backward** see BACKWARD.

lean[2] /leen/ *adj. & n.* • *adj.* **1** (of a person or animal) thin; having no superfluous fat. **2** (of meat) containing little fat. **3 a** meager (*lean crop*). **b** not nourishing (*lean diet*). **4** unremunerative. • *n.* the lean part of meat. □□ **lean·ly** *adv.* **lean·ness** *n.*

lean·ing /léening/ *n.* a tendency or partiality.

lean-to *n.* (*pl.* **-tos**) **1** a building with its roof leaning against a larger building or a wall. **2** a shed with an inclined roof usu. leaning against trees, posts, etc.

lean years *n.pl.* years of scarcity.

leap /leep/ *v. & n.* • *v.* (*past* and *past part.* **leaped** /leept, lept/ or **leapt** /lept/) **1** *intr.* jump or spring forcefully. **2** *tr.* jump across. **3** *intr.* (of prices, etc.) increase dramatically. **4** *intr.* hurry; rush; proceed without pausing for thought (*leaped to the wrong conclusion; leapt to their defense*). • *n.* a forceful jump. □ **by leaps and bounds** with startlingly rapid progress. **leap at 1** rush toward; pounce upon. **2** accept eagerly. **leap to the eye** be immediately apparent. □□ **leap·er** *n.*

leap·frog /léépfrawg, -frog/ *n. & v.* • *n.* a game in which players in turn vault with parted legs over another who is bending down. • *v.* (**-frogged, -frogging**) **1** *intr.* (foll. by *over*) perform such a vault. **2** *tr.* vault over in this way. **3** *tr. & intr.* (of two or more people, vehicles, etc.) overtake alternately.

leap of faith *n.* an act or instance of accepting something on the basis of belief or trust, not reason or fact.

leap year *n.* a year, occurring once in four, with 366 days (including Feb. 29).

learn /lərn/ *v.* (*past* and *past part.* **learned** /lərnd, lərnt/) **1** *tr.* gain knowledge of or skill in by study, experience, or being taught. **2** *tr.* (foll. by *to* + infin.) acquire or develop a particular ability (*learn to swim*). **3** *tr.* commit to memory (*will try to learn your names*). **4** *intr.* (foll. by *of*) be informed about. **5** *tr.* (foll. by *that, how,* etc. + clause) become aware of by information or from observation. **6** *intr.* receive instruction; acquire knowledge or skill. □ **learn one's lesson** see LESSON. □□ **learn·a·ble** *adj.* **learn·a·bil·i·ty** /lə́rnəbílitee/ *n.*

learn·ed /lə́rnid/ *adj.* **1** having much knowledge acquired by study. **2** showing or requiring learning (*a learned work*). **3** studied or pursued by learned persons. **4** scholarly (*a learned journal*). **5** as a courteous description of a lawyer or colleague in certain formal contexts (*my learned friend*). □□ **learn·ed·ly** *adv.* **learn·ed·ness** *n.*

learn·er /lə́rnər/ *n.* a person who is learning a subject or skill.

learn·ing /lə́rning/ *n.* knowledge acquired by study.

learn·ing curve *n.* **1** a graph showing the time needed to acquire a new skill, knowledge of a subject, etc. **2** the time represented by such a graph.

learn·ing dis·a·bil·i·ty *n.* a disorder (such as dyslexia) that interferes with the learning process in a child of usu. normal intelligence.

lease /lees/ *n. & v.* • *n.* an agreement by which the owner of a building or land allows another to use it for a specified time, usu. in return for payment. • *v.tr.* grant or take on lease. □ **a new lease on life** a substantially improved prospect of living, or of use after repair. □□ **leas·a·ble** *adj.* **leas·er** *n.*

lease·back /léésbak/ *n.* the leasing of a property back to the vendor.

lease·hold /lées-hōld/ *n. & adj.* • *n.* **1** the holding of property by lease. **2** property held by lease. • *adj.* held by lease. □□ **lease·hold·er** *n.*

leash /leesh/ *n. & v.* • *n.* a thong for holding a dog; a dog's lead. • *v.tr.* **1** put a leash on. **2** restrain. □ **straining at the leash** eager to begin.

least /leest/ *adj., n., & adv.* • *adj.* **1** smallest; slightest; most insignificant. **2** (prec. by *the*; esp. with *neg.*) any at all (*it does not make the least difference*). **3** (of a species or variety) very small (*least tern*). • *n.* the least amount. • *adv.* in the least degree. □ **at least 1** at all events; anyway. **2** (also **at the least**) not less than. **in the least** (or **the least**) (usu. with *neg.*) in the smallest degree; at all (*not in the least offended*). **to say the least** (or **the least of it**) used to imply the moderation of a statement (*that is doubtful to say the least*).

least com·mon mul·ti·ple *n.* = LOWEST COMMON MULTIPLE.

leath·er /lé*th*ər/ *n. & v.* • *n.* **1 a** material made from the skin of an animal by tanning or a similar process. **b** (*attrib.*) made of leather. **2** a piece of leather for polishing with. **3** the leather part or parts of something. **4** *sl.* a football. **5** (in *pl.*) leather clothes. **6** a thong (*stirrup-leather*). • *v.tr.* **1** cover with leather. **2** polish or wipe with leather. **3** beat; thrash.

leath·ern /lé*th*ərn/ *n. archaic* made of leather.

leath·er·back /lé*th*ərbak/ *n.* ▼ a large marine turtle, *Dermochelys coriacea*, having a thick leathery carapace.

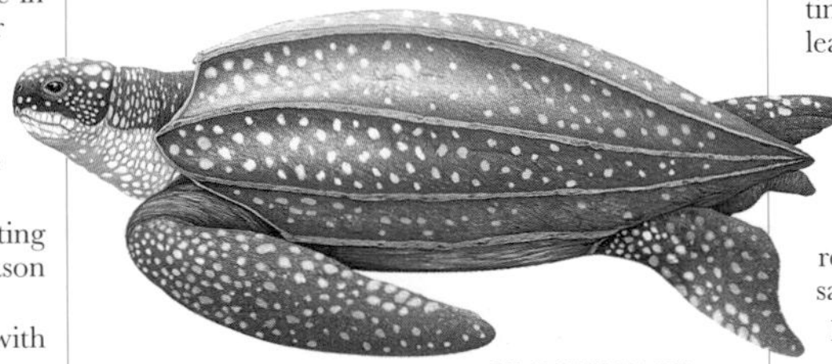

LEATHERBACK
(*Dermochelys coriacea*)

leath·er·ette /lé*th*ərét/ *n.* imitation leather.

leath·er·jack·et /lé*th*ərjakət/ *n.* **1** any of various tough-skinned marine fish of the family Monacanthidae. **2** any marine fish of the genus *Oligoplites*, family Carangidae, esp. *O. saurus*.

leath·er·neck /lé*th*ərnek/ *n. sl.* a US Marine (with reference to the leather collar formerly worn by them).

leath·er·y /lé*th*əree/ *adj.* **1** like leather. **2** (esp. of meat, etc.) tough. □□ **leath·er·i·ness** *n.*

leave[1] /leev/ *v.* (*past* and *past part.* **left** /left/) **1 a** *tr.* go away from. **b** *intr.* (often foll. by *for*) depart. **2** *tr.* cause to or let remain; depart without taking (*has left his gloves; left a slimy trail*). **3** *tr.* (also *absol.*) cease to reside at or attend or belong to or work for (*has left the school; I am leaving for another firm*). **4** *tr.* abandon; forsake; desert. **5** *tr.* have remaining after one's death (*leaves a wife and two children*). **6** *tr.* bequeath. **7** *tr.* (foll. by *to* + infin.) allow (a person or thing) to do something without interference or assistance (*leave the future to take care of itself*). **8** *tr.* (foll. by *to*) commit or refer to another person (*leave that to me; nothing was left to chance*). **9** *tr.* **a** abstain from consuming or dealing with. **b** (in *passive*; often foll. by *over*) remain over. **10** *tr.* **a** deposit or entrust (a thing) to be attended to, collected, delivered, etc., in one's absence (*left a message with his assistant*). **b** depute (a person) to perform a function in one's absence. **11** *tr.* allow to remain or cause to be in a specified state or position (*left the door open*). **12** *tr.* pass (an object) so that it is in a specified relative direction (*leave the church on the left*). □ **be left with 1** retain (a feeling, etc.). **2** be burdened with (a responsibility, etc.). **be well left** be well provided for by a legacy, etc. **get left** *colloq.* be deserted. **have left** have remaining. **leave alone 1** refrain from disturbing; not interfere with. **2** not have dealings with. **leave be** *colloq.* refrain from disturbing; not interfere with. **leave behind 1** go away without. **2** leave as a consequence or a visible sign of passage. **3** pass. **leave a person cold** (or **cool**) not impress or excite a person. **leave go** *colloq.* relax one's hold. **leave hold of** cease holding. **leave it at that** *colloq.* abstain from comment or further action. **leave much** (or **a lot**, etc.) **to be desired** be highly unsatisfactory. **leave off 1** come to or make an end. **2** discontinue (*leave off work; leave off talking*). **3** not wear. **leave out** omit; not include. **leave a person to himself** or **herself 1** not attempt to control a person. **2** leave a person solitary. **left at the gate (post)** beaten from the start of a race. **left for dead** abandoned as being beyond rescue. □□ **leav·er** *n.*

leave[2] /leev/ *n.* **1** (often foll. by *to* + infin.) permission. **2 a** (in full **leave of absence**) permission to be absent from duty. **b** the period for which this lasts. □ **by** (or **with**) **your leave** often *iron.* an expression of apology for taking a liberty or making an unwelcome statement. **on leave** legitimately absent from duty. **take one's leave (of)** bid farewell (to). **take leave of one's senses** see SENSE. **take leave to** venture or presume to.

leaved /leevd/ *adj.* **1** having leaves. **2** (in *comb.*) having a leaf or leaves of a specified kind or number (*red-leaved maple*).

leav·en /lévən/ *n. & v.* • *n.* **1** a substance added to dough to make it ferment and rise, esp. yeast, or fermenting dough reserved for the purpose. **2 a** a pervasive transforming influence. **b** (foll. by *of*) a tinge or admixture. • *v.tr.* **1** ferment (dough) with leaven. **2 a** permeate and transform. **b** (foll. by *with*) modify with a tempering element.

leaves *pl.* of LEAF.

leav·ings /léévingz/ *n.pl.* things left over, esp. as worthless.

Leb·a·nese /lébənééz/ *adj. & n.* • *adj.* of or relating to Lebanon in the Middle East. • *n.* (*pl.* same) **1** a native or national of Lebanon. **2** a person of Lebanese descent.

lech /lech/ *v. & n. colloq.* • *v.intr.* feel lecherous; behave lustfully. • *n.* **1** a strong desire, esp. sexual. **2** a lecher.

lech·er /léchər/ *n.* a lecherous man.

lech·er·ous /léchərəs/ *adj.* lustful; having strong or excessive sexual desire. □□ **lech·er·ous·ly** *adv.* **lech·er·ous·ness** *n.*

lech·er·y /léchəree/ *n.* unrestrained indulgence of sexual desire.

lec·i·thin /lésithin/ *n.* **1** any of a group of phospholipids found naturally in animals, egg yolk, and some higher plants. **2** a preparation of this used to emulsify foods, etc.

lec·tern /léktərn/ *n.* **1** ▶ a stand for holding a book in a church or chapel. **2** a similar stand for a lecturer, etc.

lec·tion /lékshən/ *n.* a reading of a text found in a particular copy or edition.

lec·tion·ar·y /lékshənéree/ *n.* (*pl.* **-ies**) **1** a list of portions of Scripture appointed to be read at divine service. **2** a book containing such portions.

lec·ture /lékchər/ *n. & v.* ● *n.* **1** a discourse giving information about a subject to a class or other audience. **2** a long, serious speech, esp. as a scolding or reprimand. ● *v.* **1** *intr.* (often foll. by *on*) deliver a lecture or lectures. **2** *tr.* talk seriously or reprovingly to (a person). **3** *tr.* instruct or entertain (a class or other audience) by a lecture.

lec·tur·er /lékchərər/ *n.* a person who lectures, esp. as a teacher in higher education.

lec·ture·ship /lékchərship/ *n.* the office of lecturer.

LED *abbr.* ▼ light-emitting diode; a device used to display the time, meter readings, etc. ▷ DIODE

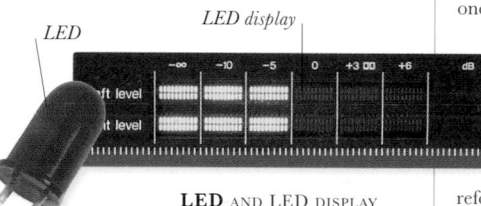

LED AND LED DISPLAY
ON A STEREO SYSTEM

led *past* and *past part.* of LEAD[1].

le·der·ho·sen /láydərhózən/ *n.pl.* leather shorts as worn in Bavaria, etc.

ledge /lej/ *n.* **1** a narrow horizontal surface projecting from a wall, etc. **2** a shelflike projection on the side of a rock or mountain. **3** a ridge of rocks, esp. below water. **4** *Mining* a stratum of metal-bearing rock. □□ **ledged** *adj.* **ledg·y** *adj.*

ledg·er /léjər/ *n.* **1** a tall, narrow book in which a firm's accounts are kept, esp. one which is the principal book of a set and contains debtor-and-creditor accounts. **2** a flat gravestone. **3** a horizontal timber in scaffolding, parallel to the face of the building.

ledg·er line *n.* **1** ▼ a short line added for notes above or below the range of a staff. **2** a kind of fishing tackle in which a lead weight keeps the bait on the bottom.

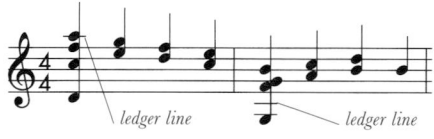

LEDGER LINES ABOVE AND BELOW A
MUSICAL STAFF

lee /lee/ *n.* **1** shelter given by a neighboring object (*under the lee of*). **2** (in full **lee side**) the sheltered side; the side away from the wind (opp. WEATHER SIDE).

leech[1] /leech/ *n.* **1** ▶ any freshwater or terrestrial annelid worm of the class *Hirudinea* with suckers at both ends, esp. *Hirudo medicinalis*, a bloodsucking parasite of vertebrates formerly much used medically. **2** a person who extorts profit from or sponges on others. □ **like a leech** persistently or clingingly present.

leech[2] /leech/ *n. archaic* or *joc.* a physician; a healer.

leek /leek/ *n.* an alliaceous plant, *Allium porrum*, with flat overlapping leaves forming a cylindrical bulb, used as food. ▷ VEGETABLE.

anterior / sucker

dorsal surface

segment

posterior sucker

LEECH
(*Hirudo medicinalis*)

leer /leer/ *v. & n.* ● *v.intr.* look slyly or lasciviously or maliciously. ● *n.* a leering look. □□ **leer·ing·ly** *adv.*

leer·y /léeree/ *adj.* (**leerier**, **leeriest**) *sl.* **1** knowing; sly. **2** (foll. by *of*) wary. □□ **leer·i·ness** *n.*

lees /leez/ *n.pl.* **1** the sediment of wine, etc. **2** dregs; refuse.

lee·ward /léeward, *Naut.* lóoərd/ *adj., adv., & n.* ● *adj.* on or toward the side sheltered from the wind (opp. WINDWARD). ● *n.* the leeward region, side, or direction (*to leeward*).

lee·ward·ly /léewərdlee, lóoərdlee/ *adj.* (of a ship) apt to drift to leeward.

lee·way /léeway/ *n.* **1** the sideways drift of a ship to leeward of the desired course. **2 a** allowable deviation or freedom of action. **b** margin of safety. □ **make up leeway** recover lost time, etc.

left[1] /left/ *adj., adv., & n.* (opp. RIGHT). ● *adj.* **1** on or toward the side of the human body which corresponds to the position of west if one regards oneself as facing north. **2** on or toward the part of an object which is analogous to a person's left side or (with opposite sense) which is nearer to an observer's left hand. **3** (also **Left**) *Polit.* of the Left. ● *adv.* on or to the left side. ● *n.* **1** the left hand part or region or direction. **2** *Boxing* **a** the left hand. **b** a blow with this. **3 a** (often **Left**) *Polit.* a group or section favoring liberalism, social reform, etc. **b** the more advanced or innovative section of any group. **4** the side of a stage which is to the left of a person facing the audience. **5** (esp. in marching) the left foot. **6** the left wing of an army. □ **have two left feet** be clumsy. **left and right** = *right and left* (see RIGHT). □□ **left·ish** *adj.*

left[2] *past* and *past part.* of LEAVE[1].

left field *n. Baseball* the part of the outfield to the left of the batter as he or she faces the pitcher.

left-hand *adj.* **1** on or toward the left side of a person or thing (*left-hand drive*). **2** done with the left hand (*left-hand blow*). **3 a** (of rope) twisted counterclockwise. **b** (of a screw) = LEFT-HANDED 4c.

left-hand·ed /léft-hándid/ *adj.* **1** using the left hand by preference as more serviceable than the right. **2** (of a tool, etc.) made to be used with the left hand. **3** (of a blow) struck with the left hand. **4 a** turning to the left; toward the left. **b** (of a racecourse) turning counterclockwise. **c** (of a screw) advanced by turning to the left (counterclockwise). **5** awkward; clumsy. **6 a** (of a compliment) ambiguous. **b** of doubtful sincerity or validity. □□ **left-hand·ed·ly** *adv.* **left-hand·ed·ness** *n.*

left-hand·er /léft-hándər/ *n.* **1** a left-handed person. **2** a left-handed blow.

left·ie var. of LEFTY.

left·ism /léftizəm/ *n. Polit.* the principles or policy of the left. □□ **left·ist** *n. & adj.*

left·most /léftmōst/ *adj.* furthest to the left.

left·o·ver /léftōvər/ *adj. & n.* ● *adj.* remaining over; not used up or disposed of. ● *n.* (in *pl.*) items (esp. of food) remaining after the rest has been used.

left·ward /léftwərd/ *adv. & adj.* ● *adv.* (also **left·wards** /-wərdz/) toward the left. ● *adj.* going toward or facing the left.

left wing *n.* **1** the liberal or socialist section of a political party. **2** the left side of a soccer, etc., team on the field. ▷ RUGBY. **3** the left side of an army. □□ **left-wing** *adj.* **left-wing·er** *n.*

left·y /léftee/ *n.* (also **left·ie**) (*pl.* **-ies**) *colloq.* **1** *Polit.* a left-winger. **2** a left-handed person.

leg /leg/ *n.* **1 a** each of the limbs on which a person or animal walks and stands. **b** the part of this from the hip to the ankle. **2** a leg of an animal or bird as food. ▷ CUT. **3** an artificial leg (*wooden leg*). **4** a part of a garment covering a leg or part of a leg. **5 a** a support of a chair, table, bed, etc. **b** a long, thin support or

prop, esp. a pole. **6** *Cricket* the half of the field (as divided lengthways through the pitch) in which the striker's feet are placed (opp. OFF). **7 a** a section of a journey. **b** a section of a relay race. **c** a stage in a competition. **d** one of two or more games constituting a round. **8** one branch of a tripod, etc. **9** *Naut.* a run made on a single tack. □ **feel** (or **find**) **one's legs** become able to stand or walk. **give a person a leg up** help a person to mount a horse, etc., or get over an obstacle or difficulty. **have no legs** *colloq.* (of a golf ball, etc.) have not enough momentum to reach the desired point. **keep one's legs** not fall. **leg it** *colloq.* walk or run fast. **not have a leg to stand on** be unable to support one's argument by facts or sound reasons. **on one's last legs** near death or the end of one's usefulness, etc. **on one's legs 1** (also **on one's hind legs**) standing, esp. to make a speech. **2** well enough to walk about. **take to one's legs** run away. □□ **leg·ged** /legd, légid/ *adj.* (also in *comb.*).

leg·a·cy /légəsee/ *n.* (*pl.* **-ies**) **1** a gift left in a will. **2** something handed down by a predecessor (*legacy of corruption*).

le·gal /léegəl/ *adj.* **1** of or based on law; concerned with law; falling within the province of law. **2** appointed or required by law. **3** permitted by law; lawful. **4** recognized by law, as distinct from equity. □□ **le·gal·ly** *adv.*

le·gal age *n.* age at which a person assumes adult rights and privileges by law.

le·gal aid *n.* payment from public funds allowed, in cases of need, to help pay for legal advice or proceedings.

le·gal·ese /léegəléez/ *n. colloq.* the technical language of legal documents.

le·gal fic·tion *n.* an assumption of the truth of something, though unproven or unfounded, for legal purposes.

le·gal·ism /léegəlizəm/ *n.* excessive adherence to law or formula. □□ **le·gal·ist** *n.* **le·gal·is·tic** /-lístik/ *adj.* **le·gal·is·ti·cal·ly** /-lístikəlee/ *adv.*

le·gal·i·ty /ligálitee, leegál-/ *n.* (*pl.* **-ies**) **1** lawfulness. **2** legalism. **3** (in *pl.*) obligations imposed by law.

le·gal·ize /léegəlīz/ *v.tr.* **1** make lawful. **2** bring into harmony with the law. □□ **le·gal·i·za·tion** *n.*

le·gal ten·der *n.* currency that cannot legally be refused in payment of a debt.

leg·ate /légət/ *n.* **1** a member of the clergy representing the Pope. **2** *Rom.Hist.* **a** a deputy of a general. **b** a governor or deputy governor of a province. □□ **leg·ate·ship** *n.* **leg·a·tine** /-teen, -tīn/ *adj.*

leg·a·tee /légətée/ *n.* the recipient of a legacy.

le·ga·tion /ligáyshən/ *n.* **1** a body of deputies. **2 a** the office and staff of a diplomatic minister. **b** the official residence of a diplomatic minister. **3** a legateship. **4** the sending of a legate or deputy.

le·ga·to /ligaátō/ *adv., adj., & n. Mus.* ● *adv. & adj.* in a smooth flowing manner. (cf. STACCATO). ● *n.* (*pl.* **-os**) **1** a legato passage. **2** legato playing.

le·ga·tor /ligáytər/ *n.* the giver of a legacy.

leg·end /léjənd/ *n.* **1 a** a traditional story sometimes popularly regarded as historical but unauthenticated; a myth. **b** such stories collectively. **c** a popular but unfounded belief. **d** *colloq.* a subject of such beliefs (*became a legend in his own lifetime*). **2 a** an inscription, esp. on a coin or medal. **b** *Printing* a caption. **c** wording on a map, etc., explaining the symbols used. **3** *hist.* **a** the story of a saint's life. **b** a collection of lives of saints or similar stories.

leg·end·ar·y /léjəndəree/ *adj.* **1** of or connected with legends. **2** described in a legend. **3** *colloq.* remarkable. **4** based on a legend. □□ **leg·end·ar·i·ly** *adv.*

leg·er·de·main /léjərdəmáyn/ *n.* **1** sleight of hand. **2** trickery; sophistry.

leg·er line *n.* = LEDGER LINE.

leg·ging /léging/ *n.* **1** (usu. in *pl.*) a stout protective outer covering for the leg from the knee to the

L

LEGIONARY

Legionaries were Roman citizens who served as foot soldiers in the ancient Roman army. They enlisted voluntarily to serve in the legions for 20–25 years, and their rigorous training made them the backbone of the army. Their distinctive uniform included the belt (*cingulum*), which was the legionary's badge of office, a segmented cuirass (*lorica segmentata*), a tunic, and a helmet (*cassis*). The *cingulum* was made of decorated leather strips and gave protection to the groin in battle. Strong, well-ventilated military sandals (*caligae*) were patterned with iron hobnails and were essential for long marches.

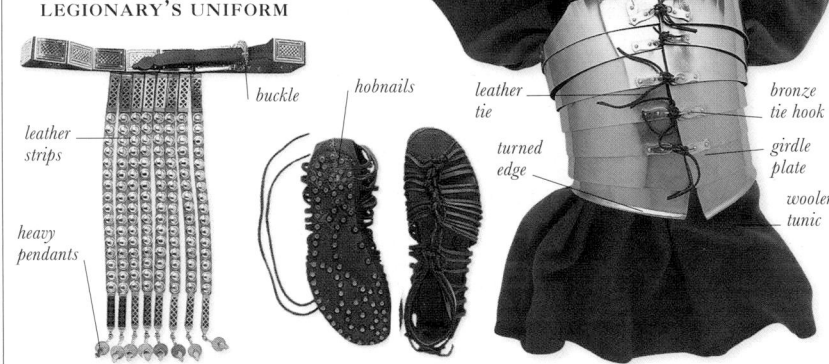

HELMET (*CASSIS*)

plume holder
brow guard
neck guard
boss
cheek guard
embossed rivet
shoulder plate
leather tie
bronze tie hook
turned edge
girdle plate
woolen tunic

LEGIONARY'S UNIFORM

buckle
hobnails
leather strips
heavy pendants

BELT (*CINGULUM*)   SANDALS (*CALIGAE*)   CUIRASS (*LORICA SEGMENTATA*)

L

---

ankle. **2** (pl.) a close-fitting stretch garment covering the legs and the lower part of the torso.

leg·gy /légee/ *adj.* (**leggier, leggiest**) **1 a** long-legged. **b** (of a woman) having attractively long legs. **2** long-stemmed. □□ **leg·gi·ness** *n.*

leg·i·ble /léjibəl/ *adj.* (of handwriting, print, etc.) clear enough to read; readable. □□ **leg·i·bil·i·ty** *n.* **leg·i·bly** *adv.*

le·gion /léejən/ *n. & adj.* ● *n.* **1** a division of 3,000–6,000 men in the ancient Roman army. **2** a large organized body. **3** a vast host, multitude, or number. ● *predic.adj.* great in number (*his good works have been legion*).

le·gion·ar·y /léejəneree/ *adj. & n.* ● *adj.* of a legion or legions. ● *n.* (*pl.* **-ies**) ▲ a member of a legion.

le·gioned /léejənd/ *adj. poet.* arrayed in legions.

le·gion·el·la /léejənélə/ *n.* the bacterium *Legionella pneumophila*, which causes legionnaires' disease.

le·gion·naire /léejənáir/ *n.* **1** a member of a foreign legion. **2** a member of the American Legion.

  le·gion·naires' dis·ease *n.* a form of bacterial pneumonia first identified after an outbreak at an American Legion meeting in 1976.

leg i·ron *n.* ◀ a shackle or fetter for the leg.

leg·is·late /léjislayt/ *v.intr.* **1** make laws. **2** (foll. by *for*) make provision by law.

  leg·is·la·tion /léjisláyshən/ *n.* **1** the process of making laws. **2** laws collectively.

  leg·is·la·tive /léjislaytiv/ *adj.* of or empowered to make laws. □□ **leg·is·la·tive·ly** *adv.*

LEG IRON

leg·is·la·tor /léjislaytər/ *n.* **1** a member of a legislative body. **2** a lawgiver.

leg·is·la·ture /léjislaychər/ *n.* the legislative body of a nation or state.

le·git /lijít/ *adj. & n. colloq.* ● *adj.* legitimate. ● *n.* **1** legitimate drama. **2** an actor in legitimate drama.

le·git·i·mate *adj. & v.* ● *adj.* /lijítimət/ **1 a** born of parents lawfully married to each other. **b** (of a parent, birth, descent, etc.) with, of, through, etc., a legitimate child. **2** lawful; proper; regular. **3** logically admissible. **4 a** (of a sovereign's title) based on strict hereditary right. **b** (of a sovereign) having a legitimate title. **5** constituting or relating to serious drama as distinct from musical comedy, revue, etc. ● *v.tr.* /lijítimayt/ **1** make legitimate by decree, enactment, or proof. **2** justify. □□ **le·git·i·ma·cy** /-məsee/ *n.* **le·git·i·mate·ly** /-mətlee/ *adv.* **le·git·i·ma·tion** /-máyshən/ *n.*

le·git·i·ma·tize /lijítimətīz/ *v.tr.* legitimize. □□ **le·git·i·ma·ti·za·tion** *n.*

le·git·i·mize /lijítimīz/ *v.tr.* **1** make legitimate. **2** serve as a justification for. □□ **le·git·i·mi·za·tion** *n.*

pedicel
receptacle
remains of stamen
pericarp
remains of style and stigma

remains of sepal
remains of sepal
pericarp
seed (pea)
funicle

LEGUME: PEA POD (*Pisum sativum*)

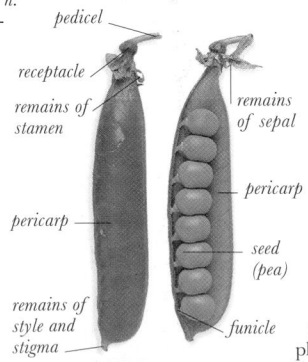

leg·less /léglis/ *adj.* **1** having no legs. **2** *sl.* drunk, esp. too drunk to stand.

Le·go /légō/ *n. Trademark* a construction toy consisting of interlocking plastic building blocks.

leg-of-mut·ton sleeve *n.* a sleeve which is full and loose on the upper arm but close-fitting on the forearm.

leg·room /légrōom/ *n.* space for the legs of a seated person.

leg·ume /légyōom/ *n.* **1** ◀ the seedpod of a leguminous plant. **2** any seed, pod, or other edible part of a leguminous plant used as food.

le·gu·mi·nous /ligyōōminəs/ *adj.* of or like the family Leguminosae, including peas and beans, having seeds in pods.

leg warm·er *n.* either of a pair of tubular knitted garments covering the leg from ankle to thigh.

leg·work /légwərk/ *n.* work which involves a lot of walking, traveling, or physical activity.

lehr /leer/ *n.* (also **leer**) a furnace used for the annealing of glass.

lei /láy-ee, lay/ *n.* a garland of flowers usu. worn on the head or shoulders.

Leib·niz·i·an /líbnítseeən/ *adj. & n.* ● *adj.* of or relating to the philosophy of G.W. Leibniz, German philosopher (d. 1716), esp. regarding matter as a multitude of monads and assuming a preestablished harmony between spirit and matter. ● *n.* a follower of this philosophy.

Leices·ter /léstər/ *n.* a kind of mild firm cheese, usu. orange-colored and orig. made in Leicestershire, England.

leish·man·i·a·sis /léeshmənī́əsis/ *n.* any of several diseases caused by parasitic protzoans of the genus *Leishmania* transmitted by the bite of sandflies.

leis·ter /léestər/ *n. & v.* ● *n.* a pronged spear, used to spear fish. ● *v.tr.* pierce with a leister.

lei·sure /léezhər, lézh-/ *n.* **1** free time; time at one's own disposal. **2** enjoyment of free time. **3** (usu. foll. by *for*, or *to* + infin.) opportunity afforded by free time. □ **at leisure 1** not occupied. **2** in an unhurried manner. **at one's leisure** when one has time.

lei·sured /léezhərd, lézh-/ *adj.* having ample leisure.

lei·sure·ly /léezhərlee, lézh-/ *adj. & adv.* ● *adj.* having leisure; acting or done at leisure; unhurried; relaxed. ● *adv.* without hurry. □□ **lei·sure·li·ness** *n.*

lei·sure·wear /léezhərwair, lézh-/ *n.* informal clothes, especially sportswear.

leit·mo·tiv /lítmōtéef/ *n.* (also **leit·mo·tif**) a recurrent theme associated throughout a musical, literary, etc., composition with a particular person, idea, or situation.

lek[1] /lek/ *n.* the chief monetary unit of Albania.

lek[2] /lek/ *n.* a patch of ground used by groups of certain birds during the breeding season as a setting for the males' display and their meeting with the females.

LEM /lem/ *abbr.* lunar excursion module.

lem·an /lémən/ *n.* (*pl.* **lemans**) *archaic* **1** a lover or sweetheart. **2** an illicit lover, esp. a mistress.

lem·ma /lémə/ *n.* (*pl.* **lemmas** or **lemmata** /-mətə/) **1** an assumed or demonstrated proposition used in an argument or proof. **2 a** a heading indicating the subject or argument of a literary composition, a dictionary entry, etc. **b** a heading indicating the subject or argument of an annotation. **3** a motto appended to a picture, etc.

lem·ming /léming/ *n.* any small arctic rodent of the genus *Lemmus*, esp. *L. lemmus* of Norway which is reputed to rush headlong into the sea and drown during periods of mass migration.

lem·on /lémən/ *n.* **1 a** a pale-yellow, thick-skinned, oval citrus fruit with acidic juice. ▷ BERRY. **b** a tree of the species *Citrus limon* which produces this fruit. **2** a pale-yellow color. **3** *colloq.* a person or thing regarded as feeble or unsatisfactory or disappointing. □□ **lem·on·y** *adj.*

lem·on·ade /lémənáyd/ *n.* **1** a beverage made from sweetened lemon juice. **2** a synthetic substitute for this.

lem·on balm *n.* ▶ a bushy plant, *Melissa officinalis*, with leaves smelling and tasting of lemon.

LEMON BALM: GOLDEN LEMON BALM (*Melissa officinalis* 'Aurea')

lem·on sole /lémən/ *n.*
▶ a flatfish, *Microstomus kitt,* of the plaice family.

le·mur /léemər/ *n.* ▼ any arboreal primate of the family Lemuridae native to Madagascar, with a pointed snout and long tail.

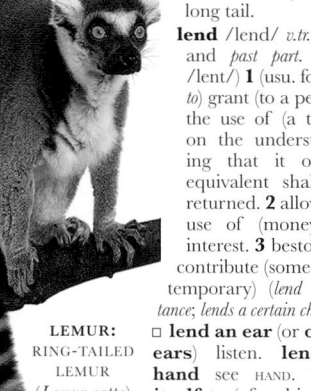

LEMON SOLE
(*Microstomus kitt*)

LEMUR:
RING-TAILED
LEMUR
(*Lemur catta*)

lend /lend/ *v.tr.* (*past* and *past part.* **lent** /lent/) **1** (usu. foll. by *to*) grant (to a person) the use of (a thing) on the understanding that it or its equivalent shall be returned. **2** allow the use of (money) at interest. **3** bestow or contribute (something temporary) (*lend assistance; lends a certain charm*). □ **lend an ear** (or **one's ears**) listen. **lend a hand** see HAND. **lend itself to** (of a thing) be suitable for. **lend oneself to** accommodate oneself to (a policy or purpose). □□ **lend·a·ble** *adj.*

lend·er *n.* **lend·ing** *n.*

lend·ing li·brar·y *n.* a library from which books may be temporarily taken away.

length /length, lengkth/ *n.* **1** measurement or extent from end to end; the greater of two or the greatest of three dimensions of a body. **2** extent in, of, or with regard to, time (*a stay of some length; the length of a speech*). **3** the distance a thing extends (*at arm's length; ships a cable's length apart*). **4** the length of a horse, boat, etc., as a measure of the lead in a race. **5** a long stretch or extent (*a length of hair*). **6** a degree of thoroughness in action (*went to great lengths; prepared to go to any length*). **7** a piece of material of a certain length (*a length of cloth*). **8** *Prosody* the quantity of a vowel or syllable. **9** the extent of a garment in a vertical direction when worn. **10** the full extent of one's body. □ **at length 1** (also **at full** or **great**, etc., **length**) in detail. **2** after a long time; at last.

length·en /léngthən, léngk-/ *v.tr. & intr.* make or become longer. □□ **length·en·er** *n.*

length·ways /léngthwayz, léngkth-/ *adv.* lengthwise.

length·wise /léngthwīz, léngkth-/ *adv. & adj.* ● *adv.* in a direction parallel to a thing's length. ● *adj.* lying or moving lengthways.

length·y /léngthee, léngkthee/ *adj.* (**lengthier**, **lengthiest**) **1** of unusual length. **2** (of speech, writing, style, a speaker, etc.) tedious; prolix. □□ **length·i·ly** *adv.* **length·i·ness** *n.*

le·ni·ent /léenyənt/ *adj.* **1** merciful; tolerant; not disposed to severity. **2** (of punishment, etc.) mild. □□ **le·ni·ence** /-yəns/ *n.* **le·ni·en·cy** *n.* **le·ni·ent·ly** *adv.*

Len·in·ism /léninizəm/ *n.* Marxism as interpreted and applied by Lenin.

len·i·tive /lénitiv/ *adj. & n.* ● *adj. Med.* soothing. ● *n.* **1** *Med.* a soothing drug or appliance. **2** a palliative.

len·i·ty /lénitee/ *n.* (*pl.* **-ies**) *literary* **1** mercifulness. **2** an act of mercy.

le·no /léenō/ *n.* (*pl.* **-os**) an openwork fabric with the warp threads twisted in pairs before weaving.

lens /lenz/ *n.* **1** a piece of a transparent substance with one or (usu.) both sides curved for concentrating or dispersing light rays, esp. in optical instruments. ▷ EYE, TELESCOPE. **2** ▼ a combination of lenses used in photography. ▷ APERTURE. **3** *Physics* a device for focusing or otherwise modifying the direction of movement of light, sound, electrons, etc. □□ **lensed** *adj.* **lens·less** *adj.*

Lent /lent/ *n. Eccl.* the period from Ash Wednesday to Holy Saturday, devoted to fasting and penitence in commemoration of Christ's fasting in the wilderness.

lent *past* and *past part.* of LEND.

Lent·en /léntən/ *adj.* of, in, or appropriate to Lent.

Lent·en fare *n.* a meager meal, esp. one without meat.

len·ti·cel /léntisel/ *n. Bot.* any of the raised pores in the stems of woody plants that allow gas exchange between the atmosphere and the internal tissues.

len·tic·u·lar /lentíkyələr/ *adj.* **1** shaped like a lentil or a biconvex lens. **2** of the lens of the eye.

len·til /léntəl/ *n.* **1** a leguminous plant, *Lens culinaris*, yielding edible biconvex seeds. **2** this seed, esp. used as food with the husk removed. ▷ PULSE.

len·to /léntō/ *adj. & adv. Mus.* ● *adj.* slow. ● *adv.* slowly.

len·toid /léntoyd/ *adj.* = LENTICULAR 1.

LENS

Camera lenses can be divided into three broad groups: wide-angle, standard, and telephoto. Extreme wide-angle lenses of focal length 6–8 mm, known as fish-eyes, give a distorted image, with vertical and horizontal lines bowed. A standard lens of 50 mm often has a wide maximum aperture. Its angle of view is similar to that of the human eye. Telephoto lenses of 80–1,200 mm are useful for detailed images of distant subjects or when it is not possible to move close enough to use a shorter lens. The illustration and sequence of photographs below, which are all taken from the same viewpoint, show that, as the focal length of a lens increases, so the angle of view decreases.

STANDARD 50 MM CAMERA LENS

L

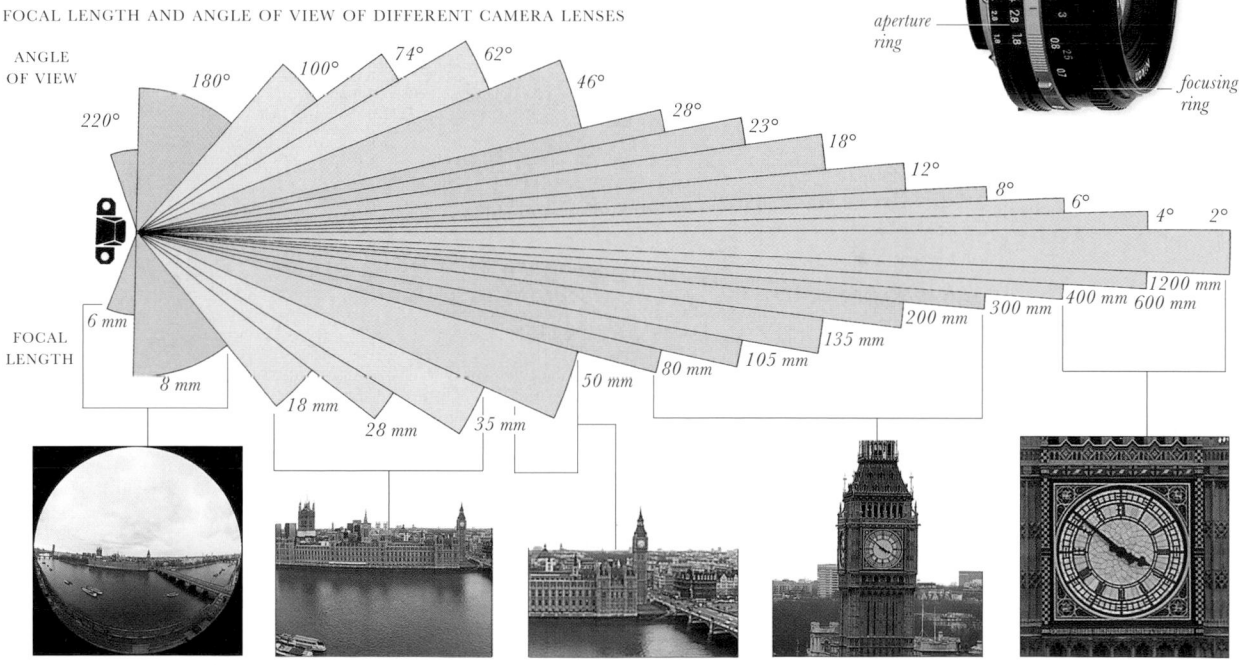

FOCAL LENGTH AND ANGLE OF VIEW OF DIFFERENT CAMERA LENSES

ANGLE OF VIEW

FOCAL LENGTH

FISH-EYE LENS   WIDE-ANGLE LENS   STANDARD LENS   TELEPHOTO LENS   EXTREME TELEPHOTO LENS

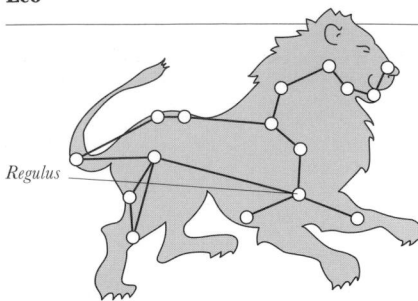

LEO: FIGURE OF A LION FORMED FROM THE STARS OF LEO

Le·o /lée-ō/ n. (pl. **-os**) **1** ▲ a constellation, traditionally regarded as contained in the figure of a lion. **2 a** the fifth sign of the zodiac (the Lion). ▷ ZODIAC. **b** a person born when the Sun is in this sign.

le·o·nine /lée·ənīn/ adj. **1** like a lion. **2** of or relating to lions.

leop·ard /lépərd/ n. (fem. **leopardess** /-dis/) **1** ▼ a large African or Asian feline, *Panthera pardus*, with either a black-spotted, yellowish-fawn or all black coat. Also called **panther**. **2** (attrib.) spotted like a leopard (*leopard moth*).

LEOPARD
(*Panthera pardus*)

lep·o·rine /lépərīn/ adj. of or like hares.

le·o·tard /lée·ətaard/ n. **1** ▶ a close-fitting one-piece garment worn by ballet dancers, acrobats, etc. **2** = TIGHTS.

lep·er /lépər/ n. **1** a person suffering from leprosy. **2** a person shunned on moral grounds.

lep·i·dop·ter·ous /lépidóptərəs/ adj. of the order Lepidoptera of insects, with four scale-covered wings, including butterflies and moths. □□ **lep·i·dop·ter·an** adj. & n. **lep·i·dop·ter·ist** n.

lep·re·chaun /léprəkon, -kawn/ n. a small mischievous sprite in Irish folklore.

lep·ro·sy /léprəsee/ n. a contagious bacterial disease that affects the skin, mucous membranes, and nerves, causing disfigurement. Also called **Hansen's disease**. □□ **lep·rous** /léprəs/ adj.

lep·tin /léptin/ n. Biochem. a protein produced by fatty tissue which is believed to regulate fat storage in the body.

LEOTARD

les·bi·an /lézbeeən/ n. & adj. ● n. a homosexual woman. ● adj. **1** of homosexuality in women. **2** (**Lesbian**) of Lesbos. □□ **les·bi·an·ism** n.

lese-maj·es·ty /leez májistee/ n. (also **lèse-maj·es·té** /layz mázhestay/) **1** treason. **2** an insult to a sovereign or ruler. **3** presumptuous conduct.

le·sion /léezhən/ n. **1** damage. **2** injury. **3** Med. a morbid change in the functioning or texture of an organ, etc.

less /les/ adj., adv., n., & prep. ● adj. **1** smaller in extent, degree, duration, number, etc. (*of less importance; in a less degree*). **2** of smaller quantity, not so much (opp. MORE) (*find less difficulty; eat less meat*). **3** disp. fewer (*eat less cookies*). **4** of lower rank, etc. (*no less a person than*). ● adv. to a smaller extent; in a lower degree. ● n. a smaller amount or quantity or number (*cannot take less; for less than $10*). ● prep. minus (*made $1,000 less tax*). □ **in less than no time** joc. very quickly or soon. **much less** with even greater force of denial (*do not suspect him of negligence, much less of dishonesty*).

les·see /lesée/ n. (often foll. by *of*) a person who holds a property by lease. □□ **les·see·ship** n.

less·en /lésən/ v.tr. & intr. make or become less; diminish.

less·er /lésər/ adj. (usu. attrib.) not so great as the other or the rest (*the lesser evil; the lesser celandine*).

les·son /lésən/ n. **1 a** an amount of teaching given at one time. **b** the time assigned to this. **2** (in pl.; foll. by *in*) systematic instruction (*gives lessons in dancing*). **3** a thing learned or to be learned by a pupil; an assignment. **4 a** an occurrence, example, rebuke, or punishment, that serves to warn or encourage (*let that be a lesson to you*). **b** a thing inculcated by experience or study. **5** a passage from the Bible read aloud during a church service. □ **learn one's lesson** profit from or bear in mind a particular (usu. unpleasant) experience. **teach a person a lesson** punish a person, esp. as a deterrent.

les·sor /lésawr/ n. a person who lets a property by lease.

lest /lest/ conj. **1** in order that not; for fear that (*lest we forget*). **2** that (*afraid lest we should be late*).

let¹ /let/ v. (**letting**; past and past part. **let**) **1** tr. **a** allow to; not prevent or forbid (*we let them go*). **b** cause to (*let me know; let it be known*). **2** tr. (foll. by *into*) **a** allow to enter. **b** make acquainted with (a secret, etc.). **c** inlay in. **3** tr. allow or cause (liquid or air) to escape (*let blood*). **4** tr. award (a contract for work). **5** aux. supplying the first and third persons of the imperative in exhortations (*let us pray*), commands (*let it be done at once; let there be light*), assumptions (*let AB be equal to CD*), and permission or challenge (*let him do his worst*). □ **let alone 1** not to mention (*hasn't got a television, let alone a VCR*). **2** = let be. **let be** not interfere with, attend to, or do. **let down 1** lower. **2** fail to support or satisfy; disappoint. **3** lengthen (a garment). **let down gently** avoid humiliating abruptly. **let drop** (or **fall**) drop (esp. a word or hint) intentionally or by accident. **let fly 1** (often foll. by *at*) attack physically or verbally. **2** discharge (a missile). **let go 1** release. **2 a** (often foll. by *of*) lose or relinquish one's hold. **b** lose hold of. **3** cease to think or talk about. **let oneself go 1** give way to enthusiasm, impulse, etc. **2** neglect one's appearance or habits. **let in 1** allow to enter (*let the dog in; let in a flood of light; this would let in all sorts of evils*). **2** (usu. foll. by *for*) involve (a person, often oneself) in loss or difficulty. **3** (foll. by *on*) allow (a person) to share privileges, information, etc. **4** inlay (a thing) in another. **let oneself in** unassistedly enter another person's home, office, etc., usu. with permission. **let loose** release or unchain (a dog, fury, a maniac, etc.). **let me see** see SEE¹. **let off 1 a** fire (a gun). **b** explode (a bomb or firework). **2** allow or cause (steam, liquid, etc.) to escape. **3** allow to alight from a vehicle, etc. **4 a** not punish or compel. **b** (foll. by *with*) punish lightly. **let off steam** see STEAM. **let on** colloq. **1** reveal a secret. **2** pretend (*let on that he had succeeded*). **let out 1** allow to go out. **2** release from restraint. **3** (often foll. by *that* + clause) reveal (a secret, etc.). **4** make (a garment) looser. **5** exculpate. **6** give vent or expression to; emit (a sound, etc.). **let rip** see RIP¹. **let slip** see SLIP¹. **let through** allow to pass. **let up** colloq. **1** become less intense or severe. **2** relax one's efforts.

let² /let/ n. **1** (in tennis, squash, etc.) an obstruction of a ball or a player, requiring the ball to be served again. **2** archaic (except in **without let or hindrance**) obstruction; hindrance.

let·down /létdown/ n. **1** a disappointment. **2** the release of milk in a nursing mother as a reflex response to suckling or massage.

le·thal /léethəl/ adj. causing or sufficient to cause death. □□ **le·thal·i·ty** /-álitee/ n. **le·thal·ly** adv.

leth·ar·gy /léthərjee/ n. **1** lack of energy. **2** Med. morbid drowsiness. □□ **le·thar·gic** /lithaárjik/ adj. **le·thar·gi·cal·ly** adv.

Le·the /léethee/ n. **1** (in Greek mythology) a river in Hades producing forgetfulness of the past. **2** (also **lethe**) such forgetfulness. □□ **Le·the·an** adj.

let's /lets/ contr. let us (*let's go now*).

let·ter /létər/ n. & v. ● n. **1 a** a character representing one or more of the simple or compound sounds used in speech. **b** (in pl.) colloq. the initials of a degree, etc., after the holder's name. **c** a school or college initial as a mark of proficiency in sports, etc. **2 a** a written, typed, or printed communication, usu. sent by mail or messenger. **b** (in pl.) an addressed legal or formal document for any of various purposes. **3** the precise terms of a statement; the strict verbal interpretation (opp. SPIRIT n. 6) (*according to the letter of the law*). **4 a** literature. **b** acquaintance with books; erudition. **c** authorship (*the profession of letters*). **5** Printing **a** types collectively. **b** a font of type. ● v.tr. **1 a** inscribe letters on. **b** impress a title, etc., on (a book cover, etc.). **2** classify with letters. □ **to the letter** with adherence to every detail.

let·ter bomb n. a terrorist explosive device in the form of or enclosed in a posted envelope.

let·ter car·ri·er n. one who delivers mail, usu. as an employee of the postal service.

let·tered /létərd/ adj. well-read or educated.

let·ter·head /létərhed/ n. **1** a printed heading on stationery. **2** stationery with this.

let·ter·ing /létəring/ n. **1** the process of inscribing letters. **2** letters inscribed.

let·ter of cred·it n. a letter from a banker authorizing a person to draw money up to a specified amount, usu. from another bank.

let·ter-per·fect adj. **1** Theatr. knowing one's part perfectly. **2** precise; verbatim.

let·ter·press /létərpres/ n. ▼ printing from raised type, not from lithography or other planographic processes.

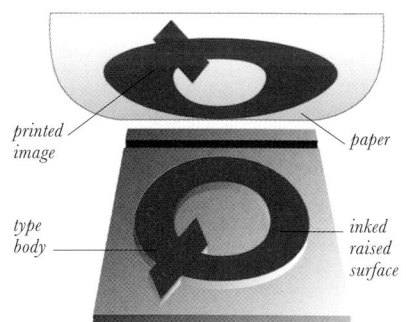

printed image   *paper*   *type body*   *inked raised surface*

LETTERPRESS

let·ter-qual·i·ty adj. of the quality of printing suitable for a business letter; producing print of this quality.

let·tuce /létis/ n. **1** a composite plant, *Lactuca sativa*, with crisp edible leaves used in salads. ▷ VEGETABLE. **2** any of various plants resembling this.

let·up /létup/ n. colloq. **1** a reduction in intensity. **2** a relaxation of effort.

leu·ke·mi·a /lookéemeeə/ n. Med. any of a group of malignant diseases in which the bone marrow and other blood-forming organs produce increased numbers of leukocytes. □□ **leu·ke·mic** adj.

leuko- /lookō/ comb. form white.

leu·ko·cyte /lookəsīt/ n. **1** a white blood cell. **2** any blood cell that contains a nucleus.

Le·vant /livánt/ n. (prec. by *the*) the eastern part of the Mediterranean with its islands and neighboring countries.

Le·van·tine /lévəntīn, -teen, ləván-/ *adj. & n.* ● *adj.* of or trading to the Levant. ● *n.* a native or inhabitant of the Levant.

le·va·tor /liváytər/ *n.* a muscle that lifts a body part.

lev·ee[1] /lévee, livée/ *n.* **1** an assembly of visitors or guests, esp. at a formal reception. **2** *hist.* a reception of visitors on rising from bed.

lev·ee[2] /lévee/ *n.* **1** an embankment against river floods. **2** ▼ a natural embankment built up by a river. **3** a landing place.

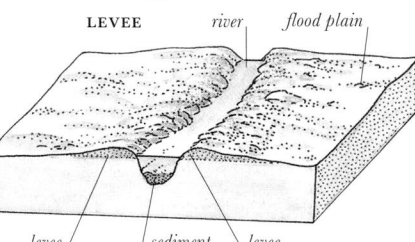

LEVEE

river   *flood plain*

levee   *sediment*   *levee*

lev·el /lévəl/ *n., adj., & v.* ● *n.* **1** a horizontal line or plane. **2** a height or value reached; a position on a scale (*eye level; sugar level in the blood; danger level*). **3** a social, moral, or intellectual standard (*at age six, he could read at a fifth-grade level*). **4** a plane of rank or authority (*discussions at cabinet level*). **5 a** an instrument giving a line parallel to the plane of the horizon for testing whether things are horizontal. Also called **spirit level.** ▷ SPIRIT LEVEL. **b** *Surveying* an instrument for giving a horizontal line of sight. **6** a more or less level surface. **7** a flat tract of land. **8** a floor or story in a building, ship, etc. ● *adj.* **1** having a flat and even surface; not bumpy (*a level road*). **2** horizontal; perpendicular to the plumb line. **3** (often foll. by *with*) **a** on the same horizontal plane as something else. **b** having equality with something else. **c** (of a spoonful, etc.) with the contents flat with the brim. **4** even, uniform, equable, or well-balanced in quality, style, temper, judgment, etc. **5** (of a race) having the leading competitors close together. ● *v.* **1** *tr.* make level, even, or uniform. **2** *tr.* (often foll. by *to* (or *with*) *the ground*) raze or demolish. **3** *tr.* (also *absol.*) aim (a missile or gun). **4** *tr.* (also *absol.*; foll. by *at, against*) direct (an accusation, criticism, or satire). **5** *tr.* abolish (distinctions). **6** *intr.* (usu. foll. by *with*) *sl.* be frank or honest (*please level with me*). **7** *tr.* place on the same level. **8** *tr.* (also *absol.*) *Surveying* ascertain differences in the height of (land). □ **do one's level best** *colloq.* do one's utmost. **find its** (or **its own**) **level** (of a liquid) reach the same height in receptacles or regions which communicate with each other. **find one's level** reach the right social, intellectual, etc., place in relation to others. **level down** bring down to a standard. **level off** make or become level or smooth. **level out** make or become level; remove differences from. **on the level** *colloq. adv.* honestly; without deception. *adj.* honest; truthful. **on a level with 1** in the same horizontal plane as. **2** equal with. □□ **lev·el·ly** *adv.* **lev·el·ness** *n.*

lev·el·head·ed /lévəlhédid/ *adj.* mentally well-balanced; sensible. □□ **lev·el·head·ed·ly** *adv.* **lev·el·head·ed·ness** *n.*

lev·el·er /lévələr/ *n.* **1** a person who advocates the abolition of social distinctions. **2** (**Leveler**) *hist.* an extreme radical dissenter in 17th-c. England. **3** a person or thing that levels.

lev·er /lévər, léev-/ *n. & v.* ● *n.* **1** a bar resting on a pivot, used to help lift a heavy or firmly fixed object. **2** *Mech.* ▶ a simple machine consisting of a rigid bar pivoted about a fulcrum (fixed point) which can be acted upon by a force (effort) in order to move a load. **3** a projecting handle moved to operate a mechanism. **4** a means of exerting moral pressure. ● *v.* **1** *intr.* use a lever. **2** *tr.* (often foll. by *away, out, up*, etc.) lift, move, or act on with a lever.

lev·er·age /lévərij, léev-/ *n.* **1** the action of a lever; a

way of applying a lever. **2** the power of a lever; the mechanical advantage gained by use of a lever. **3** a means of accomplishing a purpose; power; influence. **4** a set or system of levers. **5** *Commerce* the use of a relatively small investment or value in equity to acquire or control a much larger investment.

lev·er·aged buy·out *n.* the buyout of a company by its management using outside capital.

lev·er·et /lévərit/ *n.* a young hare, esp. one in its first year.

lev·i·a·ble /léveeəbəl/ *adj.* that which may be levied.

le·vi·a·than /livíəthən/ *n.* **1** *Bibl.* a sea monster. **2** anything very large or powerful, esp. a ship. **3** an autocratic monarch or state (in allusion to a book by Hobbes, 1651).

lev·i·gate /lévigayt/ *v.tr.* **1** reduce to a fine, smooth powder. **2** make a smooth paste of. □□ **lev·i·ga·tion** /-gáyshən/ *n.*

Le·vis /léevīz/ *n.pl. Trademark* a type of (orig. blue) denim jeans or overalls reinforced with rivets.

lev·i·tate /lévitayt/ *v.* **1** *intr.* rise and float in the air (esp. with reference to spiritualism). **2** *tr.* cause to do this. □□ **lev·i·ta·tion** /-táyshən/ *n.*

lev·i·ty /lévitee/ *n.* **1** lack of serious thought; frivolity. **2** inconstancy. **3** undignified behavior.

lev·u·lose /lévyəlōs/ *n.* = FRUCTOSE.

lev·y /lévee/ *v. & n.* ● *v.tr.* (**-ies, -ied**) **1 a** impose (a rate or toll). **b** raise (contributions or taxes). **c** (also *absol.*) raise (a sum of money) by legal execution or process (*the debt was levied on the debtor's goods*). **d** seize (goods) in this way. **e** extort (*levy blackmail*). **2** enlist or enroll (troops, etc.). **3** (usu. foll. by *upon, against*) wage; proceed to make (war). ● *n.* (*pl.* **-ies**) **1 a** the collecting of a contribution, tax, etc., or of property to satisfy a legal judgment. **b** a contribution, tax, etc., levied. **2 a** the act or an instance of enrolling troops, etc. **b** (in *pl.*) persons enrolled. **c** a body of persons enrolled. **d** the number of persons enrolled. □□ **le·vi·a·ble** *adj.*

lewd /lood/ *adj.* **1** lascivious. **2** indecent; obscene. □□ **lewd·ly** *adv.* **lewd·ness** *n.*

lew·is /lóois/ *n.* an iron contrivance for gripping heavy blocks of stone or concrete for lifting.

lex·eme /lékseem/ *n. Linguistics* a basic lexical unit of a language comprising one or several words, the elements of which do not separately convey the meaning of the whole.

lex·i·cal /léksikəl/ *adj.* **1** of the words of a language. **2** of or as of a lexicon. □□ **lex·i·cal·ly** *adv.*

lex·i·cog·ra·phy /léksikógrəfee/ *n.* the compiling of dictionaries. □□ **lex·i·cog·ra·pher** *n.* **lex·i·co·graph·ic** /-kəgráfik/ *adj.* **lex·i·co·graph·i·cal** *adj.*

lex·i·col·o·gy /léksikóləjee/ *n.* the study of the

form, history, and meaning of words. □□ **lex·i·co·log·i·cal** /-kəlójikəl/ *adj.* **lex·i·col·o·gist** /-kól-əjist/ *n.*

lex·i·con /léksikon/ *n.* **1** a dictionary, esp. of Greek, Hebrew, Syriac, or Arabic. **2** the vocabulary of a person, language, branch of knowledge, etc.

lex·ig·ra·phy /leksígrəfee/ *n.* a system of writing in which each character represents a word.

lex·is /léksis/ *n.* **1** words; vocabulary. **2** the total stock of words in a language.

lex lo·ci /leks lósī, -kee, -kī/ *n. Law* the law of the country in which a transaction is performed, a tort is committed, or a property is situated.

lex ta·li·o·nis /léks taleeónis/ *n.* the law of retaliation, whereby a punishment resembles the offense commited, in kind and degree.

ley[1] /lay/ see LEA.

ley[2] /lay, lee/ *n.* the supposed straight line of a prehistoric track, usu. between hilltops.

Ley·den jar /líd'n/ *n.* an early form of capacitor consisting of a glass jar with layers of metal foil on the outside and inside.

LF *abbr.* low frequency.

LH *abbr. Biochem.* luteinizing hormone.

l.h. *abbr. Biochem.* left hand.

LI *abbr.* Long Island.

Li *symb. Chem.* the element lithium.

li·a·bil·i·ty /líəbílitee/ *n.* (*pl.* **-ies**) **1** the state of being liable. **2** a person or thing that is troublesome as an unwelcome responsibility; a handicap. **3** what a person is liable for, esp. (in *pl.*) debts.

li·a·ble /líəbəl/ *predic.adj.* **1** legally bound. **2** (foll. by *to*) subject to (a tax or penalty). **3** (foll. by *to* + infin.) under an obligation. **4** (foll. by *to*) exposed or open to (something undesirable). **5** *disp.* (foll. by *to* + infin.) apt; likely (*it is liable to rain*). **6** (foll. by *for*) answerable.

li·aise /lee-áyz/ *v.intr.* (foll. by *with, between*) *colloq.* establish cooperation; act as a link.

li·ai·son /lee-áyzon, lée-ay-/ *n.* **1 a** communication or cooperation, esp. between military forces or units. **b** a person who initiates such. **2** an illicit sexual relationship. **3** the binding or thickening agent of a sauce. **4** the sounding of an ordinarily silent final consonant before a word beginning with a vowel (or a mute *h* in French).

li·ai·son of·fi·cer *n.* an officer acting as a link between allied forces or units of the same force.

li·a·na /lee-áanə/ *n.* (also **li·ane** /-áan/) any of several climbing and twining plants of tropical forests. ▷ RAIN FOREST

li·ar /líər/ *n.* a person who tells a lie or lies, esp. habitually.

LEVER

Levers multiply effort to give mechanical advantage. There are three classes of lever, each with a different arrangement of load, effort, and fulcrum. The force on the load is multiplied by the ratio of the distances of effort and load from the fulcrum. A class 1 lever has the fulcrum between load and effort. A class 2 lever has the load between fulcrum and effort. A class 3 lever has the effort applied between load and fulcrum; it reduces the force on the load while increasing the distance it moves.

CLASSES OF LEVER

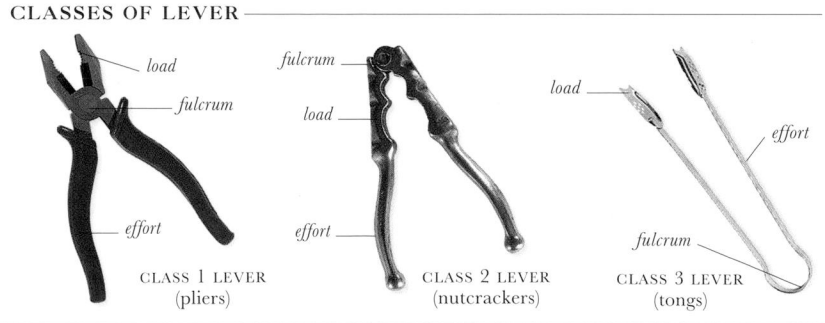

CLASS 1 LEVER (pliers)   CLASS 2 LEVER (nutcrackers)   CLASS 3 LEVER (tongs)

load   *fulcrum*   *effort*   *fulcrum*   *load*   *effort*   *load*   *effort*   *fulcrum*

L

li·as /lĩəs/ *n.* **1** (**Lias**) *Geol.* the lower strata of the Jurassic system of rocks, consisting of shales and limestones rich in fossils. **2** a blue limestone rock found in SW England. □□ **li·as·sic** /lĩásik/ *adj.* (in sense 1).

Lib. *abbr.* Liberal.

lib /lib/ *n. colloq.* liberation (*women's lib*).

li·ba·tion /lĩbáyshən/ *n.* **1 a** the pouring out of a drink offering to a god. **b** such a drink offering. **2** *joc.* a drink.

lib·ber /lίbər/ *n. colloq.* an advocate of women's liberation.

li·bel /lίbəl/ *n. & v.* ● *n.* **1** *Law* **a** a published false statement damaging to a person's reputation (cf. SLANDER). **b** the act of publishing this. **2 a** a false and defamatory written statement. **b** (foll. by *on*) a thing that brings discredit by misrepresentation, etc. (*the portrait is a libel on him*; *the book is a libel on human nature*). **3 a** (in civil and ecclesiastical law) the plaintiff's written declaration. **b** *Sc. Law* a statement of the grounds of a charge. ● *v.tr.* **1** defame by libelous statements. **2** accuse falsely and maliciously. **3** *Law* publish a libel against. □□ **li·bel·er** *n.*

li·bel·ous /lίbələs/ *adj.* containing or constituting a libel. □□ **li·bel·ous·ly** *adv.*

lib·er·al /lίbərəl, lίbrəl/ *adj. & n.* ● *adj.* **1** given freely; ample; abundant. **2** (often foll. by *of*) giving freely; generous; not sparing. **3** open-minded; not prejudiced. **4** not strict or rigorous; (of interpretation) not literal. **5** for general broadening of the mind; not professional or technical (*liberal studies*). **6 a** favoring individual liberty and political and social reform. **b** (**Liberal**) of or characteristic of Liberals or a Liberal party. **7** *Theol.* regarding many traditional beliefs as dispensable, invalidated by modern thought, or liable to change (*liberal Protestant*; *liberal Judaism*). ● *n.* **1** a person of liberal views. **2** (**Liberal**) a supporter or member of a Liberal party. □□ **lib·er·al·ism** *n.* **lib·er·al·ly** *adv.*

lib·er·al arts *n.pl.* the arts as distinct from science and technology.

lib·er·al·i·ty /lίbərálitee/ *n.* **1** free giving; munificence. **2** freedom from prejudice; breadth of mind.

lib·er·al·ize /lίbərəlīz, lίbrə-/ *v.tr. & intr.* make or become more liberal or less strict. □□ **lib·er·al·i·za·tion** *n.*

lib·er·ate /lίbərayt/ *v.tr.* **1** (often foll. by *from*) set at liberty; set free. **2** free (a country, etc.) from an oppressor or an enemy occupation. **3** (often as **liberated** *adj.*) free (a person) from rigid social conventions, esp. in sexual behavior. **4** *sl.* steal. **5** *Chem.* release (esp. a gas) from a state of combination. □□ **lib·er·a·tor** *n.*

lib·er·a·tion /lίbəráyshən/ *n.* the act or an instance of liberating; the state of being liberated. □□ **lib·er·a·tion·ist** *n.*

lib·er·tar·i·an /lίbərtáireeən/ *n.* an advocate of liberty. □□ **lib·er·tar·i·an·ism** *n.*

lib·er·tine /lίbərteen, -tin/ *n. & adj.* ● *n.* **1** a dissolute or licentious person. **2** a free thinker on religion. **3** a person who follows his or her own inclinations. ● *adj.* **1** licentious; dissolute. **2** free-thinking. **3** following one's own inclinations. □□ **lib·er·tin·ism** /-nízəm/ *n.*

lib·er·ty /lίbərtee/ *n.* (*pl.* **-ies**) **1 a** freedom from captivity, imprisonment, slavery, or despotic control. **b** a personification of this. **2 a** the right or power to do as one pleases. **b** (foll. by *to* + infin.) right; power; opportunity; permission. **c** *Philos.* freedom from control by fate or necessity. **3 a** (usu. in *pl.*) a right, privilege, or immunity, enjoyed by prescription or grant. **b** (in *sing.* or *pl.*) *hist.* an area having such privileges, etc., esp. a district controlled by a city though outside its boundary or an area outside a prison where some prisoners might reside. **4** setting aside of rules or convention. □ **at liberty 1** free; not imprisoned (*set at liberty*). **2** (foll. by *to* + infin.) entitled; permitted. **3** available; disengaged. **take liberties 1** (often foll. by *with*) behave in an unduly familiar manner. **2** (foll.

by *with*) deal freely or superficially with rules or facts. **take the liberty** (foll. by *to* + infin., or *of* + verbal noun) presume; venture.

li·bid·i·nous /libídənəs/ *adj.* lustful.

li·bi·do /libéedō, -bí-/ *n.* (*pl.* **-os**) *Psychol.* psychic drive or energy, esp. that associated with sexual desire. □□ **li·bid·i·nal** /libídənəl/ *adj.*

Li·bra /léébrə, lí-/ *n.* **1** ▶ a constellation, traditionally regarded as contained in the figure of scales (the Balance or Scales). ▷ ZODIAC. **b** a person born when the Sun is in this sign. □□ **Li·bran** *n. & adj.*

li·brar·i·an /lībráireeən/ *n.* a person in charge of, or an assistant in, a library. □□ **li·brar·i·an·ship** *n.*

li·brar·y /lίbreree/ *n.* (*pl.* **-ies**) **1 a** a collection of books, etc., for use by the public or by members of a group. **b** a person's collection of books. **2** a room or building containing a collection of books (for reading or reference rather than for sale). **3 a** a similar collection of films, records, computer software, etc. **b** the place where these are kept. **4** a series of books issued by a publisher in similar bindings, etc., usu. as a set. **5** a public institution charged with the care of a collection of books, films, etc.

li·bra·tion /lībráyshən/ *n.* an apparent oscillation of a heavenly body, esp. the Moon, by which the parts near the edge of the disk are alternately in view and out of view.

li·bret·to /librétō/ *n.* (*pl.* **-os** or **libretti** /-tee/) the text of an opera or other long musical vocal work. □□ **li·bret·tist** *n.*

Lib·ri·um /lίbreeəm/ *n. Trademark* a white crystalline drug used as a tranquilizer.

Lib·y·an /lίbeeən, lίbyən/ *adj. & n.* ● *adj.* **1** of or relating to modern Libya in N. Africa. **2** of ancient N. Africa west of Egypt. **3** of or relating to the Berber group of languages. ● *n.* **1 a** a native or national of modern Libya. **b** a person of Libyan descent. **2** an ancient language of the Berber group.

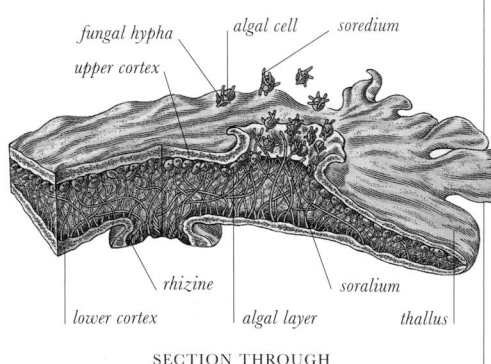

LIBRA: FIGURE OF SCALES FORMED FROM THE STARS OF LIBRA

lice *pl.* of LOUSE.

li·cense /lίsəns/ *n. & v.* ● *n.* **1** a permit from an authority to own or use something (esp. a dog, gun, television set, or vehicle), do something (esp. marry, print something, preach, or drive on a public road), or carry on a business (esp. in alcoholic liquor). **2** permission (*have I your license to remove the fence?*). **3 a** liberty of action, esp. when excessive; abuse of freedom. **b** licentiousness. **4** a writer's or artist's irregularity in grammar, meter, perspective, etc., or deviation from fact, esp. for effect (*poetic license*). ● *v.tr.* **1** grant a license to (a person). **2** authorize the use of (premises) for a certain purpose, esp. the sale and consumption of alcoholic liquor. **3** authorize the publication of (a book, etc.) or the performance of (a play). **4** *archaic* allow. □□ **li·cens·a·ble** *adj.* **li·cen·sor, li·cen·ser** *n.*

li·cen·see /lίsənseé/ *n.* the holder of a license, esp. to sell alcoholic liquor.

license plate *n.* the usu. metal plate of a motor vehicle that attests to its registration.

li·cen·ti·ate /līsénsheeət/ *n.* **1** a holder of a certificate of competence to practice a certain profession. **2** a licensed preacher not yet having an appointment, esp. in a Presbyterian church.

li·cen·tious /līsénshəs/ *adj.* **1** immoral in sexual relations. □□ **li·cen·tious·ly** *adv.* **li·cen·tious·ness** *n.*

li·chee var. of LITCHI.

li·chen /līkən/ *n.* **1** ▼ any plant organism of the group Lichenes, composed of a fungus and an alga in symbiotic association, growing on and coloring rocks, tree trunks, roofs, walls, etc. **2** any of several types of skin disease in which small, round, hard lesions occur close together. □□ **li·chened** *adj.* (in sense 1). **li·chen·ol·o·gy** *n.* (in sense 1). **li·chen·ous** *adj.* (in sense 2).

LICHEN

Lichens are symbiotic partnerships between algae and fungi: the algae live among the tiny threads formed by the fungus and supply it with food, which is produced by photosynthesis. Although they grow very slowly, lichens are extremely long-lived. They reproduce by means of spores or soredia (powdery vegetative fragments). Of the six forms of lichen, the three most common are foliose (leafy), crustose (flat and crusty), and fruticose (shrublike). Some lichens, such as *Cladonia floerkeana*, are a combination of forms.

fungal hypha   algal cell   soredium

upper cortex

rhizine   soralium

lower cortex   algal layer   thallus

SECTION THROUGH FOLIOSE LICHEN

EXAMPLES OF LICHENS

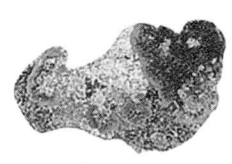

CRUSTOSE (*Caloplaca heppiana*)

FRUTICOSE (*Cladonia portentosa*)

squamulose thallus

moss   fruticose thallus

SQUAMULOSE (SCALY) AND FRUTICOSE THALLUS (*Cladonia floerkeana*)

lich-gate /líchgayt/ *n.* (also **lych-gate**) ▶ a roofed gateway to a churchyard where a coffin awaits the clergyman's arrival. ▷ CHURCH

LICH-GATE

lic·it /lísit/ *adj.* not forbidden; lawful. □□ **lic·it·ly** *adv.*

lick /lik/ *v. & n.* ● *v.* **1** *tr.* pass the tongue over. **2** *tr.* bring into a specified condition or position by licking (*licked it all up; licked it clean*). **3 a** *tr.* (of a flame, waves, etc.) play lightly over. **b** *intr.* move gently or caressingly. **4** *tr. colloq.* **a** defeat; excel. **b** surpass the comprehension of (*has got me licked*). **5** *tr. colloq.* thrash. ● *n.* **1** an act of licking with the tongue. **2** = SALT LICK. **3** *colloq.* a fast pace (*at a lick; at full lick*). **4** *colloq.* **a** a small amount; quick treatment with (foll. by *of: a lick of paint*). **b** a quick wash. **5** a smart blow with a stick, etc. □ **a lick and a promise** *colloq.* a hasty performance of a task, esp. of washing oneself. **lick a person's boots** (or **shoes**) be servile. **lick into shape** see SHAPE. **lick one's lips** (or **chops**) **1** look forward with relish. **2** show one's satisfaction. **lick one's wounds** be in retirement after defeat. □□ **lick·er** *n.* (also in *comb.*).

lick·er·ish /líkərish/ *adj.* (also **liqu·or·ish**) **1** lecherous. **2 a** fond of fine food. **b** greedy; longing.

lick·e·ty-split /líkəteesplít/ *adv. colloq.* at full speed; headlong.

lick·ing /líking/ *n. colloq.* **1** a thrashing. **2** a defeat.

lick·spit·tle /líkspit'l/ *n.* a toady.

lic·o·rice /líkərish, -ris/ *n.* **1** a black root extract used as a candy and in medicine. **2** ◀ the leguminous plant, *Glycyrrhiza glabra*, from which it is obtained.

LICORICE:
WILD LICORICE
(Glycyrrhiza glabra)

lid /lid/ *n.* **1** a hinged or removable cover, esp. for the top of a container. **2** = EYELID. □ **put a lid on** be quiet about; keep secret. **take the lid off** *colloq.* expose (a scandal, etc.) □□ **lid·ded** *adj.* (also in *comb.*). **lid·less** *adj.*

lie[1] /lī/ *v. & n.* ● *v.intr.* (**lying** /lī-ing/; *past* **lay** /lay/; *past part.* **lain** /layn/) **1** be in or assume a horizontal position on a supporting surface; be at rest on something. **2** (of a thing) rest flat on a surface (*snow lay on the ground*). **3** (of abstract things) remain undisturbed or undiscussed, etc. (*let matters lie*). **4 a** be kept or remain or be in a specified state or place (*lie hidden; lie in wait; malice lay behind those words; they lay dying; the books lay unread; the money is lying in the bank*). **b** (of abstract things) exist; reside; be in a certain position or relation (foll. by *in, with*, etc.: *the answer lies in education; my sympathies lie with the family*). **5 a** be situated or stationed (*the village lay to the east; the ships are lying off the coast*). **b** (of a road) lead (*the road lies over mountains*). **c** be spread out to view (*the desert lay before us*). **6** (of the dead) be buried in a grave. **7** (foll. by *with*) *archaic* have sexual intercourse. **8** *Law* be admissible or sustainable (*the objection will not lie*). **9** (of a game bird) not rise. ● *n.* **1 a** the way or direction or position in which a thing lies. **b** *Golf* the position of a golf ball when about to be struck. **2** the place of cover of an animal or a bird. □ **as far as in me lies** to the best of my power. **let lie** not raise (a controversial matter, etc.) for discussion, etc. **lie about** (or **around**) be left carelessly out of place. **lie ahead** be going to happen; be in store. **lie back** recline so as to rest. **lie heavy** cause discomfort or anxiety. **lie in** remain in bed in the morning. **lie in state** (of a deceased great personage) be laid in a public place of honor before burial. **lie low 1** keep quiet

or unseen. **2** be discreet about one's intentions. **lie off** *Naut.* stand some distance from shore or from another ship. **lie over** be deferred. **lie to** *Naut.* come almost to a stop facing the wind. **lie up** (of a ship) go into dock or be out of commission. **lie with** (often foll. by *to* + infin.) be the responsibility of (a person) (*it lies with you to answer*). **take lying down** (usu. with *neg.*) accept (defeat, rebuke, etc.) without resistance or protest, etc.

lie[2] /lī/ *n. & v.* ● *n.* **1** an intentionally false statement (*tell a lie; pack of lies*). **2** imposture; false belief (*live a lie*). ● *v.* (**lies, lied, lying** /lī-ing/) **1** *intr.* **a** tell a lie or lies (*they lied to me*). **b** (of a thing) be deceptive (*the camera cannot lie*). **2** *tr.* (usu. *refl.*; foll. by *into, out of*) get (oneself) into or out of a situation by lying (*lied themselves into trouble; lied my way out of danger*). □ **give the lie to** serve to show the falsity of (a supposition, etc.).

lied /leed, leet/ *n.* (*pl.* **lieder** /léedər/) a type of German song, esp. of the Romantic period.

lie de·tec·tor *n.* an instrument for determining whether a person is telling the truth by testing for physiological changes considered to be symptomatic of lying.

liege /leej, leezh/ *adj. & n.* usu. *hist.* ● *adj.* (of a superior) entitled to receive or (of a vassal) bound to give feudal service or allegiance. ● *n.* **1** (in full **liege lord**) a feudal superior or sovereign. **2** (usu. in *pl.*) a vassal or subject.

lien /leen, léeən/ *n. Law* a right over another's property to protect a debt charged on that property.

lieu /loo/ *n.* □ **in lieu 1** instead. **2** (foll. by *of*) in the place of.

lieut. *abbr.* lieutenant.

lieu·ten·ant /looténənt/ *n.* **1** a deputy. **2 a** an army officer next in rank below captain. **b** a naval officer next in rank below lieutenant commander. **3** a police officer next in rank below captain. □□ **lieu·ten·an·cy** *n.* (*pl.* **-ies**).

lieu·ten·ant colo·nel *n.* an army officer ranking below colonel and above a major.

lieu·ten·ant com·man·der *n.* a naval officer ranking below a commander and above a lieutenant.

lieu·ten·ant gen·er·al *n.* an army officer ranking below a general and above a major general.

lieu·ten·ant gov·er·nor *n.* (in the US) the elected official next in rank to a state's governor.

life /līf/ *n.* (*pl.* **lives** /līvz/) **1** the condition that distinguishes active animals and plants from inorganic matter, including the capacity for growth, functional activity, and continual change preceding death. **2 a** living things and their activity (*insect life; is there life on Mars?*). **b** human presence or activity (*no sign of life*). **3 a** the period during which life lasts, or the period from birth to the present time or from the present time to death (*have done it all my life; will regret it all my life; life membership*). **b** the duration of a thing's existence or of its ability to function (*the battery has a life of two years*). **4 a** a person's state of

existence as a living individual (*sacrificed their lives; took many lives*). **b** a living person (*many lives were lost*). **5 a** an individual's occupation, actions, or fortunes; the manner of one's existence (*that would make life easy; start a new life*). **b** a particular aspect of this (*love life; private life*). **6** the business and pleasures of the world (*travel is the best way to see life*). **7** a human's earthly or supposed future existence. **8 a** energy; liveliness (*full of life; put some life into it!*). **b** an animating influence (*was the life of the party*). **c** (of an inanimate object) power; force; ability to perform its intended function. **9** the living form or model (*drawn from life*). **10** a biography. **11** *colloq.* a sentence of imprisonment for life (*they were all serving life*). **12** a chance; a fresh start (*cats have nine lives; gave the player three lives*). □ **come to life 1** emerge from unconsciousness or inactivity; begin operating. **2** (of an inanimate object) assume an imaginary animation. **for dear** (or **one's**) **life** as if or in order to escape death (*hanging on for dear life; run for your life*). **for life** for the rest of one's life. **for the life of** (foll. by pers. pron.) even if (one's) life depended on it (*cannot for the life of me remember*). **give one's life 1** (foll. by *for*) die; sacrifice oneself. **2** (foll. by *to*) dedicate oneself. **large as life** *colloq.* in person, esp. prominently (*stood there large as life*). **larger than life 1** exaggerated. **2** (of a person) having an exuberant personality. **lose one's life** be killed. **a matter of life and** (or **or**) **death** a matter of vital importance. **not on your life** *colloq.* most certainly not. **save a person's life 1** prevent a person's death. **2** save a person from serious difficulty. **take one's life in one's hands** take a crucial personal risk. **to the life** true to the original.

life-and-death *adj.* vitally important; desperate (*a life-and-death struggle*).

life·blood /lífblud/ *n.* **1** the blood, as being necessary to life. **2** the vital factor or influence.

life·boat /lífbōt/ *n.* **1** ▼ a specially constructed boat launched from land to rescue those in distress at sea. ▷ BOAT. **2** a ship's small boat for use in emergency. ▷ SHIP

LIFEBOAT: SELF-RIGHTING
ARUN CLASS LIFEBOAT

masthead light *steering position* *binnacle* *pilothouse* *air-intake pipe* *bollard* *winch* *anchor*
life raft *radar* *rescue craft* *davit*
rudder *propeller* *sloping recovery deck* *rubber fender* *fast-planing hull*

life bu·oy *n.* a buoyant support for keeping a person afloat.

life cy·cle *n.* the series of changes in the life of an organism including reproduction.

life ex·pec·tan·cy *n.* the average period that a person may expect to live.

life-form *n.* an organism.

life-giv·ing *adj.* that sustains life or uplifts and revitalizes.

life·guard /lífgaard/ *n.* an expert swimmer employed to rescue bathers from drowning.

life in·sur·ance *n.* insurance for a sum to be paid on the death of the insured person.

L

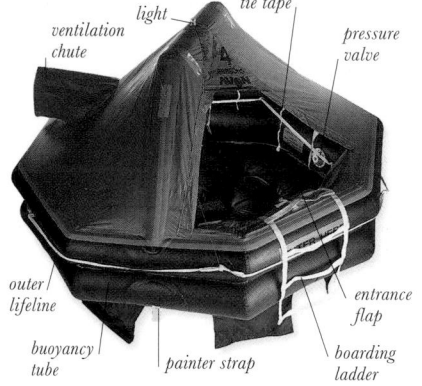

LIFE JACKET

life jack·et *n.* ◄ a buoyant jacket for keeping a person afloat.

life·less /líflis/ *adj.* **1** lacking life; no longer living **2** unconscious. **3** lacking movement or vitality. □□ **life·less·ly** *adv.* **life·less·ness** *n.*

life·like /líflīk/ *adj.* closely resembling the person or thing represented.

life·line /líflīn/ *n.* **1 a** a rope, etc., used for lifesaving. **b** a diver's signaling line. **2** a sole means of communication or transport. **3** a fold in the palm of the hand, regarded as significant in palmistry. **4** an emergency telephone counseling service.

life·long /líflawng, -long/ *adj.* lasting a lifetime.

life pre·serv·er *n.* a life jacket, etc.

lif·er /lífər/ *n. sl.* **1** a person serving a life sentence. **2** a person committed to a long or lifetime career in a profession, esp. the military.

life raft *n.* ▼ an inflatable or log, etc., raft for use in an emergency instead of a boat.

LIFE RAFT

life·sav·er /lífsayvər/ *n.* a person or thing that saves one from serious difficulty.

life sci·ences *n.pl.* biology and related subjects.

life sen·tence *n.* **1** a sentence of imprisonment for life. **2** an illness or commitment, etc., perceived as a continuing threat to one's freedom.

life-size *adj.* (also **life-sized**) of the same size as the person or thing represented.

life·style /lífstīl/ *n.* the particular way of life of a person or group.

life-sup·port *adj.* (of equipment) allowing vital functions to continue in an adverse environment or during severe disablement.

life·time /líftīm/ *n.* **1** the duration of a person's life. **2** the duration of a thing or its usefulness. **3** *colloq.* an exceptionally long time. □ **of a lifetime** such as does not occur more than once in a person's life (*the chance of a lifetime; the journey of a lifetime*).

life·work /lífwǒrk/ *n.* a task, profession, etc., pursued throughout one's lifetime.

lift /lift/ *v. & n.* ● *v.* **1** *tr.* (often foll. by *up, off, out*, etc.) raise or remove to a higher position. **2** *intr.* go up; be raised; yield to an upward force (*the window will not lift*). **3** *tr.* give an upward direction to (the eyes or face). **4** *tr.* **a** elevate to a higher plane of thought or feeling (*the news lifted their spirits*). **b** make less heavy or dull; add interest to. **c** enhance; improve (*lifted their game after halftime*). **5** *intr.* (of a cloud, fog, etc.) rise; disperse. **6** *tr.* remove (a barrier or restriction). **7** *tr.* transport (supplies, troops, etc.) by air. **8** *tr.*

colloq. **a** steal. **b** plagiarize (a passage of writing, etc.). **9** *Phonet.* **a** *tr.* make louder; raise the pitch of. **b** *intr.* (of the voice) rise. **10** *tr. esp. Brit.* dig up (esp. potatoes, etc., at harvest). **11** *intr.* (of a floor) swell upward, bulge. **12** *tr.* hold or have on high (*the church lifts its spire*). **13** *tr.* hit (a ball) into the air. **14** *tr.* (usu. in *passive*) perform cosmetic surgery on (esp. the face or breasts) to reduce sagging. ● *n.* **1** the act of lifting or process of being lifted. **2** a free ride in another person's vehicle (*gave them a lift*). **3 a** *Brit.* = ELEVATOR 3a. **b** an apparatus for carrying persons up or down a mountain, etc. (see SKI LIFT). **4 a** transport by air (see AIRLIFT *n.*). **b** a quantity of goods transported by air. **5** the upward pressure that air exerts on an airfoil. ▷ AIRFOIL. **6** a supporting or elevating influence; a feeling of elation. **7** a layer of leather in the heel of a boot or shoe, esp. to correct shortening of a leg or increase height. **8 a** a rise in the level of the ground. **b** the extent to which water rises in a canal lock. □ **lift a finger** (or **hand**, etc.) (in *neg.*) make the slightest effort (*didn't lift a finger to help*). **lift off** (of a spacecraft or rocket) rise from the launching pad. **lift up one's head** hold one's head high with pride. **lift up one's voice** sing out. □□ **lift·a·ble** *adj.* **lift·er** *n.*

lift-off /líftawf/ *n.* the vertical takeoff of a spacecraft or rocket.

lig·a·ment /lígəmənt/ *n.* **1** *Anat.* a short band of tough, flexible, fibrous connective tissue linking bones together. **2** any membranous fold keeping an organ in position. □□ **lig·a·men·tal** /-mént'l/ *adj.* **lig·a·men·ta·ry** /-méntəree/ *adj.* **lig·a·men·tous** /-méntəs/ *adj.*

lig·and /lígənd, lig-/ *n. Chem.* an ion or molecule attached to a metal atom by bonding in which both electrons are supplied by one atom.

li·gate /lígayt/ *v.tr. Surgery* tie up (a bleeding artery, etc.). □□ **li·ga·tion** /-gáyshən/ *n.*

li·ga·ture /lígəchər/ *n. & v.* ● *n.* **1** a tie or bandage. **2** *Mus.* ▼ a slur; a tie. **3** *Printing* two or more letters joined, e.g., *æ*. **4** a bond; a thing that unites. **5** the act of tying or binding. ● *v.tr.* bind or connect with a ligature.

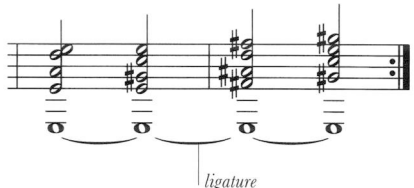

ligature

LIGATURES BELOW A MUSICAL STAFF

light[1] /līt/ *n., v., & adj.* ● *n.* **1** ▼ the natural agent (electromagnetic radiation of wavelength between about 390 and 740 nm) that stimulates sight and makes things visible. ▷ ELECTROMAGNETIC RADIATION. **2** the medium or condition of the space in which this is present. **3** an appearance of brightness (*saw a distant light*). **4 a** a source of light. **b** (in *pl.*) illuminations. **5** (often in *pl.*) a traffic light (*went through a red light; stop at the lights*). **6 a** the amount or quality of illumination in a place (*bad light stopped play*). **b** one's fair or usual share of this (*you are standing in my light*). **7 a** a flame or spark serving to ignite (*struck a light*). **b** a device producing this (*have you got a light?*). **8** the aspect in which a thing is regarded (*appeared in a new light*). **9 a** mental illumination; elucidation; enlightenment. **b** hope; happiness; a happy outcome. **c** spiritual illumination by divine truth. **10** vivacity, enthusiasm, or inspiration visible in a person's face, esp. in the eyes. **11** (in *pl.*) a person's mental powers or ability (*according to one's lights*). **12** an eminent person (*a leading light*). **13 a** the bright part of a thing; a highlight. **b** the bright parts of a picture, etc., esp. suggesting illumination (*light and shade*). **14 a** a window or opening in a wall to let light in. **b** the perpendicular division of a mullioned window. ▷ WINDOW. **c** a pane of glass, esp. in the side or roof of a greenhouse. **15** *Law* the light falling on windows, the obstruction of which by a neighbor is illegal. ● *v.* (*past* **lit** /lit/; *past part.* **lit** or (*attrib.*) **lighted**) **1** *tr. & intr.* set burning or begin to burn; ignite. **2** *tr.* provide with light or lighting. **3** *tr.* show (a person) the way or surroundings with a light. **4** *intr.* (usu. foll. by *up*) (of the face or eyes) brighten with animation. ● *adj.* **1** well provided with light; not dark. **2** (of a color) pale (*light blue; a light-blue ribbon*). □ **bring** (or **come**) **to light** reveal or be revealed. **in a good** (or **bad**) **light** giving a favorable (or unfavorable) impression. **in** (**the**) **light of** having regard to; drawing information from. **light of one's life** usu. *joc.* a much-loved person. **light up 1** *colloq.* begin to smoke a cigarette, etc. **2** switch on lights or lighting; illuminate a scene. **lit up** *colloq.* drunk. **out like a light** deeply asleep or unconscious. **throw** (or **shed**) **light on** help to explain. □□ **light·ish** *adj.* **light·less** *adj.* **light·ness** *n.*

light[2] /līt/ *adj., adv., & v.* ● *adj.* **1** not heavy. **2 a** relatively low in weight, amount, density, intensity, etc. (*light arms; light traffic; light metal; light rain; a light breeze*). **b** deficient in weight (*light coin*). **c** (of an isotope, etc.) having not more than the usual mass. **3 a** carrying or suitable for small loads (*light aircraft*). **b** (of a ship) unladen. **c** carrying only light arms, armaments, etc. (*light brigade; light infantry*). **d** (of a

---

LIGHT

Visible, or white, light is a form of electromagnetic radiation occurring between infrared and ultraviolet waves in the electromagnetic spectrum. White light is a mixture of many different colors of light, each with its own wavelength. When white light passes through a prism, it is refracted and split up into its various wavelengths, so that all the colors can be seen separately. These colors make up the visible spectrum. Our eyes detect colors by recognizing the different wavelengths of visible light.

DETAIL FROM THE ELECTROMAGNETIC SPECTRUM

infrared waves *visible light* *ultraviolet waves* *X rays*

WHITE LIGHT REFRACTED BY A PRISM

visible spectrum *prism* *white light*

L

locomotive) with no train attached. **4 a** (of food, a meal, etc.) small in amount; easy to digest (*had a light lunch*). **b** (of drink) not heavy on the stomach or strongly alcoholic. **5 a** (of entertainment, music, etc.) intended for amusement, rather than edification; not profound. **b** frivolous; thoughtless; trivial (*a light remark*). **6** (of sleep or a sleeper) easily disturbed. **7** easily borne or done (*light duties*). **8** nimble; quick-moving (*a light step; light of foot; a light rhythm*). **9** (of a building, etc.) graceful; elegant. **10** (of type) not heavy or bold. **11 a** free from sorrow; cheerful (*a light heart*). **b** giddy (*light in the head*). **12** (of soil) not dense; porous. **13** (of pastry, sponge cake, etc.) fluffy and well-aerated during cooking and with the fat fully absorbed. **14** (of a woman) unchaste or wanton; fickle. ● *adv.* **1** in a light manner (*tread light; sleep light*). **2** with a minimum load or minimum luggage (*travel light*). ● *v.intr.* (*past* and *past part.* **lit** /lit/ or **lighted**) (foll. by *on, upon*) come upon or find by chance. □ **light into** *colloq.* attack. **light out** *colloq.* depart. **make light of** treat as unimportant. **make light work of** do a thing quickly and easily. □□ **light·ish** *adj.* **light·ness** *n.*

light box *n.* a box with a translucent top and containing an electric light, providing an evenly lighted flat surface for viewing transparencies.

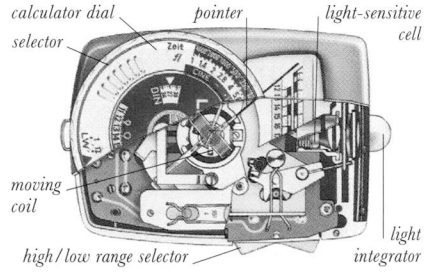

light bulb /lítbulb/ *n.* ◄ a glass bulb containing an inert gas and a metal filament, providing light when an electric current is passed through.

tungsten filament
inert gas
seal
electrical wire
screw fitting
terminal

LIGHTBULB

light-e·mit·ting di·ode see LED.

light·en[1] /lít'n/ *v.* **1 a** *tr.* & *intr.* make or become lighter in weight. **b** *tr.* reduce the weight or load of. **2** *tr.* bring relief to (the heart, mind, etc.). **3** *tr.* mitigate (a penalty).

light·en[2] /lít'n/ *v.* **1 a** *tr.* shed light on. **b** *tr.* & *intr.* make or grow lighter or brighter. **2** *intr.* **a** shine brightly; flash. **b** emit lightning (*it is lightening*).

light·er[1] /lítər/ *n.* a device for lighting cigarettes, etc.

light·er[2] /lítər/ *n.* a boat, usu. flat-bottomed, for transferring goods from a ship to a wharf or another ship.

light·er·age /lítərij/ *n.* **1** the transference of cargo by means of a lighter. **2** a charge made for this service.

light·er-than-air *adj.* (of an aircraft) weighing less than the air it displaces.

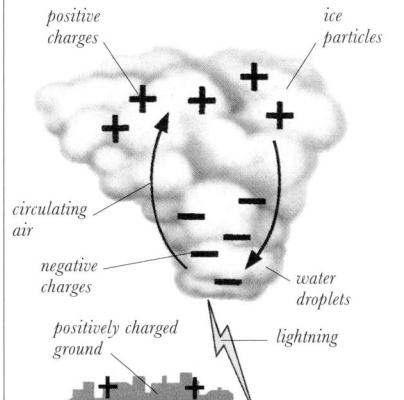

weather vane
ventilation ball
beacon
guardrail
bedroom (inside)
winch room (inside)
entrance door

LIGHTHOUSE

light-fin·gered *adj.* given to stealing.

light-foot·ed *adj.* nimble. □□ **light-foot·ed·ly** *adv.*

light-head·ed *n.* giddy; delirious. □□ **light-head·ed·ly** *adj.* **light-head·ed·ness** *adv.*

light-heart·ed /lít-haartid/ *adj.* **1** cheerful. **2** (unduly) casual; thoughtless. □□ **light-heart·ed·ly** *adv.* **light-heart·ed·ness** *n.*

light heav·y·weight *n.* **1** the weight in some sports between middleweight and heavyweight. **2** a sportsman of this weight.

light·house /lít-hows/ *n.* ◄ a tower or other structure containing a beacon light to warn or guide ships at sea.

light in·dus·try *n.* the manufacture of small or light articles.

light·ing /líting/ *n.* **1** equipment in a room or street, etc., for producing light. **2** the arrangement or effect of lights.

light·ly /lítlee/ *adv.* in a light (esp. frivolous or unserious) manner. □ **get off lightly** escape with little or no punishment. **take lightly** not be serious about (a thing).

light me·ter *n.* ▼ an instrument for measuring the intensity of the light, esp. to show the correct photographic exposure.

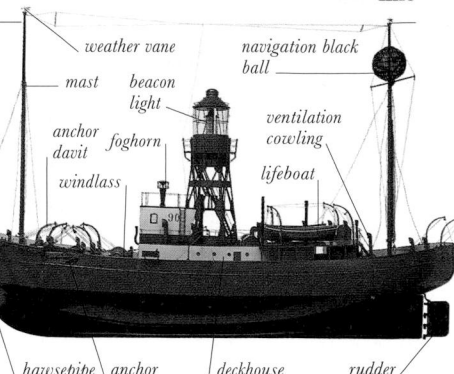

calculator dial
pointer
light-sensitive cell
selector
moving coil
high/low range selector
light integrator

LIGHT METER: CUTAWAY VIEW OF AN ANALOG LIGHT METER

light·ning /lítning/ *n.* & *adj.* ● *n.* ▼ a flash of bright light produced by an electric discharge between clouds or between clouds and the ground. ● *attrib.adj.* very quick (*with lightning speed*).

light·ning bug *n.* = FIREFLY.

light·ning rod *n.* (also **light·ning con·duc·tor**) a metal rod or wire fixed to an exposed part of a building or to a mast to divert lightning into the earth or sea.

light·proof /lítproof/ *adj.* able to block out light completely (*a lightproof envelope*).

LIGHTNING

Lightning begins inside thunderclouds, when water and ice particles are thrown together by air currents, creating static electricity. Positive charges collect at the top of the cloud, negative charges at the bottom. Eventually the difference between the positive and negative charges is large enough to overcome the insulation of the air in between. A lightning bolt leaps between the two – or between the cloud and the positively charged ground – to neutralize the charge.

FORMATION OF LIGHTNING WITHIN A THUNDERCLOUD (CUMULONIMBUS)

positive charges
ice particles
circulating air
negative charges
water droplets
positively charged ground
lightning

---

weather vane
navigation black ball
mast
beacon light
anchor davit
foghorn
ventilation cowling
windlass
lifeboat
hawsepipe
anchor
deckhouse
rudder

LIGHTSHIP: 1930s BRITISH LIGHTSHIP

light·ship /lítship/ *n.* ▲ a moored or anchored ship with a beacon light.

light·some /lítsəm/ *adj.* gracefully light; nimble; merry. □□ **light·some·ly** *adv.* **light·some·ness** *n.*

light touch *n.* delicate or tactful treatment.

light·weight /lítwayt/ *adj.* & ● *adj.* **1** of below average weight. **2** of little importance or influence. ● *n.* **1** a lightweight person, animal, or thing. **2 a** weight in certain sports intermediate between featherweight and welterweight. **b** a sportsman of this weight.

light·wood /lítwood/ *n.* wood used for kindling, esp. pine.

light-year *n.* **1** *Astron.* the distance light travels in one year, nearly 6 trillion miles. **2** (in *pl.*) *colloq.* a long distance or great amount.

lig·ne·ous /lígneeəs/ *adj.* **1** (of a plant) woody (opp. HERBACEOUS). **2** of the nature of wood.

lig·nin /lígnin/ *n. Bot.* a complex organic polymer deposited in the cell walls of many plants making them rigid and woody.

lig·ni·fy /lígnifī/ *v.tr.* & *intr.* (**-ies, -ied**) *Bot.* make or become woody by the deposition of lignin.

lig·nite /lígnīt/ *n.* a soft brown coal showing traces of plant structure, intermediate between bituminous coal and peat. ▷ COAL

lig·no·caine /lígnəkayn/ *n. Pharm.* a local anesthetic for the gums, mucous membranes, or skin, usu. given by injection.

li·gus·trum /ligústrəm/ *n.* = PRIVET.

lik·a·ble /líkəbəl/ *adj.* (also **like·a·ble**) pleasant; easy to like. □□ **lik·a·ble·ness** *n.* **lik·a·bly** /-blee/ *adv.*

like[1] /līk/ *adj., prep., adv., conj., & n.* ● *adj.* (often governing a noun as if a transitive participle such as *resembling*) (**more like, most like**) **1 a** having some or all of the qualities of another or each other or an original (*in like manner; as like as two peas; is very like her brother*). **b** resembling in some way, such as (*good writers like Poe*). **c** (usu. in pairs correlatively) as one is so will the other be (*like mother, like daughter*). **2** characteristic of (*it is not like them to be late*). **3** in a suitable state or mood for (*felt like working; felt like a cup of coffee*). ● *prep.* in the manner of; to the same degree as (*drink like a fish; sell like hotcakes; acted like an idiot*). ● *adv.* **1** archaic likely (*they will come, like enough*). **2** *sl.* so to speak (*did a quick getaway, like; as I said, like, I'm no Shakespeare*). ● *conj. colloq. disp.* **1** as (*cannot do it like you do*). **2** as if (*ate like they were starving*). ● *n.* **1** a counterpart; an equal; a similar person or thing (*shall not see its like again; compare like with like*). **2** (prec. by *the*) a thing or things of the same kind (*will never do the like again*). □ **and the like** and similar things (*music, painting, and the like*). **be nothing like** (usu. with compl.) be in no way similar or comparable or adequate. **like** (or **as like**) **as not** *colloq.* probably. **like so** *colloq.* like this; in this manner. **the likes of** *colloq.* a person such as (*I wouldn't trust the likes of him*). **more like it** *colloq.* nearer what is required.

like[2] /līk/ *v.* & *n.* ● *v.tr.* **1 a** find agreeable or enjoyable (*like reading; like the sea; like to dance*). **b** be fond of (a person). **2 a** choose to have; prefer (*like my coffee*

L

L

black; do not like such things discussed). **b** wish for or be inclined to (*would like a cup of tea*). **3** (usu. in *interrog.*; prec. by *how*) feel about; regard (*how would you like it if it happened to you?*). ● *n.* (in *pl.*) the things one likes or prefers. □ **I like that!** *iron.* as an exclamation expressing affront. **like it or not** *colloq.* whether it is acceptable or not.

-like /līk/ *comb. form* forming adjectives from nouns, meaning 'similar to, characteristic of' (*doglike; tortoiselike*). ¶ In (esp. polysyllabic) formations intended as nonce words, or not generally current, a hyphen is often used (*celebration-like*). Nouns ending in *-ll* always require it (*shell-like*).

like·a·ble var. of LIKABLE.

like·li·hood /līkleehŏŏd/ *n.* probability. □ **in all likelihood** very probably.

like·ly /līklee/ *adj. & adv.* ● *adj.* (**likelier, likeliest**) **1** probable; such as well might happen or be true (*it is not likely that they will come; the most likely place is California; a likely story*). **2** (foll. by *to* + infin.) to be reasonably expected (*he is not likely to come now*). **3** promising; apparently suitable (*this is a likely spot; three likely candidates*). ● *adv.* probably (*is very likely true*). □ **as likely as not** probably. **not likely!** *colloq.* certainly not; I refuse. □□ **like·li·ness** *n.*

like·mind·ed *adj.* having the same tastes, opinions, etc. □□ **like·mind·ed·ly** *adv.* **like·mind·ed·ness** *n.*

lik·en /līkən/ *v.tr.* (foll. by *to*) point out the resemblance of (a person or thing to another).

like·ness /līknis/ *n.* **1** (foll. by *between, to*) resemblance. **2** (foll. by *of*) a semblance or guise (*in the likeness of a ghost*). **3** a portrait or representation (*is a good likeness*).

like·wise /līkwīz/ *adv.* **1** also; moreover. **2** similarly (*do likewise*).

lik·ing /līking/ *n.* **1** what one likes; one's taste (*is it to your liking?*). **2** (foll. by *for*) regard or fondness; taste or fancy (*had a liking for chocolate*).

li·lac /līlək, -lok, -lak/ *n. & adj.* ● *n.* **1** any shrub or small tree of the genus *Syringa*, esp. *S. vulgaris* with fragrant pale pinkish-violet or white blossoms. **2** a pale pinkish-violet color. ● *adj.* of this color.

lil·i·a·ceous /lilee-ayshəs/ *adj.* **1** of or relating to the family Liliaceae of plants with elongated leaves growing from a corm, bulb, or rhizome. **2** lilylike.

lil·li·pu·tian /lilipyŏŏshən/ *n. & adj.* (also **Lil·li·pu·tian**) ● *n.* a diminutive person or thing. ● *adj.* diminutive.

lilt /lilt/ *n. & v.* ● *n.* **1 a** a light springing rhythm or gait. **b** a song or tune marked by this. **2** (of the voice) a characteristic cadence or inflection. ● *v.intr.* (esp. as **lilting** *adj.*) move or speak, etc., with a lilt.

lil·y /lilee/ *n.* (*pl.* **-ies**) **1 a** any bulbous plant of the genus *Lilium* with large, trumpet-shaped flowers on a tall, slender stem. **b** any of several other plants of the family Liliaceae with similar flowers. **c** the water lily. **2** a person or thing of special whiteness or purity. **3** a heraldic fleur-de-lis. **4** (*attrib.*) **a** delicately white (*a lily hand*). **b** pallid.

lil·y-liv·ered *adj.* cowardly.

lil·y of the val·ley *n.* ▼ any liliaceous plant of the genus *Convallaria*, with racemes of white, bell-shaped, fragrant flowers.

LILY OF THE VALLEY (*Convallaria majalis*)

lil·y pad *n.* a floating leaf of a water lily.

lil·y-white *adj.* **1** as white as a lily. **2** faultless.

li·ma bean /līmə/ *n.* **1** a tropical American bean plant, *Phaseolus lunatus*, having large, flat, greenish-white edible seeds. **2** the seed of this plant. ▷ PULSE

limb [1] /lim/ *n.* **1** any of the projecting parts of a person's or animal's body used for contact or movement. **2** a large branch of a tree. **3** a branch of a cross. **4** a spur of mountain. **5** a clause

of a sentence. □ **out on a limb 1** isolated; stranded. **2** at a disadvantage. **tear limb from limb** violently dismember. **with life and limb** (esp. escape) without grave injury. □□ **limbed** *adj.* (also in *comb.*). **limb·less** *adj.*

limb [2] /lim/ *n.* **1** *Astron.* **a** a specified edge of the Sun, Moon, etc. **b** the graduated edge of a quadrant, etc. **2** *Bot.* the broad part of a petal, sepal, or leaf.

lim·ber [1] /limbər/ *adj. & v.* ● *adj.* **1** lithe; agile; nimble. **2** flexible. ● *v.* (usu. foll. by *up*) **1** *tr.* make (oneself or a part of the body, etc.) supple. **2** *intr.* warm up in preparation for athletic, etc., activity. □□ **lim·ber·ness** *n.*

lim·ber [2] /limbər/ *n. & v.* ● *n.* ▼ the detachable front part of a gun carriage. ● *v.* **1** *tr.* attach a limber to (a gun, etc.). **2** *intr.* fasten together the two parts of a gun carriage.

coupling wheel
spade
ammunition chest   *gunpowder bags*   *explosive shells*

LIMBER OF A MID-19TH-CENTURY GUN CARRIAGE

lim·bic sys·tem /limbik sistəm/ *n.* a complex system of nerves and networks in the brain, controlling the basic emotions and drives.

lim·bo [1] /limbō/ *n.* (*pl.* **-os**) **1** (in some Christian beliefs) the supposed abode of the souls of unbaptized infants, and of the just who died before Christ. **2** an intermediate state or condition of awaiting a decision, etc. **3** prison; confinement. **4** a state of neglect or oblivion.

lim·bo [2] /limbō/ *n.* (*pl.* **-os**) a W. Indian dance in which the dancer bends backward to pass under a horizontal bar that is progressively lowered.

lime [1] /līm/ *n. & v.* ● *n.* **1** (in full **quicklime**) a white caustic alkaline substance (calcium oxide) obtained by heating limestone. **2** = BIRDLIME. ● *v.tr.* treat (wood, skins, land, etc.) with lime. □□ **lime·less** *adj.* **lim·y** *adj.* (**lim·i·er, lim·i·est**).

lime [2] /līm/ *n.* **1 a** a round citrus fruit like a lemon but greener, smaller, and more acid. ▷ CITRUS FRUIT. **b** the tree, *Citrus aurantiifolia*, bearing this. **2** (in full **lime juice**) the juice of limes as a drink. **3** (in full **lime green**) a pale green color like a lime.

lime [3] /līm/ *n.* a European linden, esp. *Tilia europaea*.

lime·kiln /līmkiln, -kil/ *n.* a kiln for heating limestone.

lime·light /līmlīt/ *n.* **1** an intense white light used formerly in theaters. **2** (prec. by *the*) the full glare of publicity; the focus of attention.

lim·er·ick /limərik, limrik/ *n.* a humorous or comic form of five-line stanza with a rhyme scheme *aabba*.

lime·stone /līmstōn/ *n.* *Geol.* ◀ a sedimentary rock composed mainly of calcium carbonate. ▷ SEDIMENT

LIMESTONE: OOLITIC LIMESTONE

lim·ey /limee/ *n.* (also **Limey**) (*pl.* **-eys**) *sl. offens.* a British person (orig. a sailor) or ship.

lim·it /limit/ *n. & v.* ● *n.* **1** a point, line, or level beyond which something does not or may not extend or pass. **2** (often in *pl.*) the boundary of an area. **3** the greatest or smallest amount permissible or possible. **4** *Math.* a quantity that a function or sum of a series can be made to approach as closely as desired. ● *v.tr.* **1** set or serve as a limit to. **2** (foll. by *to*) restrict. □ **be the limit** *colloq.* be intolerable or extremely irritating. **within limits** moderately; with some degree of freedom. **without limit** with no restriction. □□ **lim·it·a·ble** *adj.* **lim·it·er** *n.*

lim·i·ta·tion /limitáyshən/ *n.* **1** the act or an instance of limiting; the process of being limited. **2** a condition of limited ability (often in *pl.*: *know one's limitations*). **3** a limiting circumstance (often in *pl.*: *has its limitations*). **4** a legally specified period beyond which an action cannot be brought, or a property right is not to continue.

lim·it·ed /limitid/ *adj.* **1** confined within limits. **2** not great in scope or talents (*has limited experience*). **3 a** few; scanty; restricted (*limited accommodation*). **b** restricted to a few examples (*limited edition*). □□ **lim·it·ed·ness** *n.*

lim·it·less /limitlis/ *adj.* **1** extending or going on indefinitely (*a limitless expanse*). **2** unlimited (*limitless generosity*). □□ **lim·it·less·ly** *adv.* **lim·it·less·ness** *n.*

limn /lim/ *v.tr.* **1** *archaic* paint (esp. a miniature portrait). **2** *hist.* illuminate (manuscripts). □□ **lim·ner** /limnər/ *n.*

lim·nol·o·gy /limnóləjee/ *n.* the study of the physical phenomena of lakes and other fresh waters. □□ **lim·no·log·i·cal** /-nəlójikəl/ *adj.* **lim·nol·o·gist** /-nól-/ *n.*

lim·o /limō/ *n.* (*pl.* **-os**) *colloq.* a limousine.

lim·ou·sine /limə́zeen/ *n.* a large, luxurious automobile.

limp [1] /limp/ *v. & n.* ● *v.intr.* **1** walk lamely. **2** (of a damaged ship, aircraft, etc.) proceed with difficulty. **3** (of verse) be defective. ● *n.* a lame walk. □□ **limp·ing·ly** *adv.*

limp [2] /limp/ *adj.* **1** not stiff or firm; easily bent. **2** without energy or will. **3** (of a book) having a soft cover. □□ **limp·ly** *adv.* **limp·ness** *n.*

lim·pet /limpit/ *n.* **1** ▶ any of various marine gastropod mollusks with a shallow conical shell and a broad muscular foot that sticks tightly to rocks. **2** a clinging person.

LIMPET

lim·pet mine *n.* a mine designed to be attached to a ship's hull and set to explode after a certain time.

lim·pid /limpid/ *adj.* **1** (of water, eyes, etc.) clear; transparent. **2** (of writing) easily comprehended. □□ **lim·pid·i·ty** /-píditee/ *n.* **lim·pid·ly** *adv.* **lim·pid·ness** *n.*

limp-wrist·ed *adj.* *sl. offens.* effeminate; weak.

lin·age /līnij/ *n.* **1** the number of lines in printed or written matter. **2** payment by the line.

linch·pin /linchpin/ *n.* **1** a pin passed through the end of an axle to keep a wheel in position. **2** a person or thing vital to an enterprise, organization, etc.

lin·dane /lindayn/ *n.* *Chem.* a colorless, crystalline, chlorinated derivative of cyclohexane used as an insecticide.

lin·den /lindən/ *n.* **1** ▶ any ornamental tree of the genus *Tilia*, with heart-shaped leaves and fragrant yellow blossoms. **2** the wood of this.

flower cluster

LINDEN: LITTLE-LEAF LINDEN (*Tilia cordata*)

line[1] /līn/ *n. & v.* ● *n.* **1** a continuous mark or band made on a surface (*drew a line*). **2** use of lines in art, esp. draftsmanship or engraving (*boldness of line*). **3** a thing resembling such a mark, esp. a furrow or wrinkle. **4** *Mus.* **a** each of (usu. five) horizontal marks forming a stave in musical notation. **b** a sequence of notes or tones forming a melody. **5 a** a straight or curved continuous extent of length without breadth. **b** the track of a moving point. **6 a** a contour or outline, esp. as a feature of design (*the sculpture's clean lines*). **b** a facial feature (*the cruel line of his mouth*). **7 a** (on a map or graph) a curve connecting all points having a specified common property. **b** (**the Line**) the Equator. **8 a** a limit or boundary. **b** a mark limiting the area of play, the starting or finishing point in a race, etc. **c** the boundary between a credit and a debit in an account. **9 a** a row of persons or things. **b** a direction as indicated by them (*line of march*). **10 a** a row of printed or written words. **b** a portion of verse written in one line. **11** (in *pl.*) **a** a piece of poetry. **b** the words of an actor's part. **c** a specified amount of text, etc., to be written out as a school punishment. **12** a short letter or note (*drop me a line*). **13** a length of cord, etc., usu. serving a specified purpose, esp. a fishing line or clothesline. **14 a** a wire or cable for a telephone or telegraph. **b** a connection by means of this (*am trying to get a line*). **15 a** a single track of a railroad. **b** one branch or route of a railroad system. **16 a** a regular succession of buses, ships, etc., plying between certain places. **b** a company conducting this (*shipping line*). **17** a connected series of persons following one another in time (esp. several generations of a family) (*a long line of craftsmen*). **18 a** a course or manner of procedure, conduct, etc. (*along these lines*). **b** policy (*the party line*). **c** conformity (*bring them into line*). **19** a direction, course, or channel (*lines of communication*). **20** a department of activity; a branch of business (*not my line*). **21** a class of commercial goods (*a new line of hats*). **22** *colloq.* a false or exaggerated account (*gave me a line about missing the bus*). **23 a** a connected series of military defenses, etc. (*behind enemy lines*). **b** an arrangement of soldiers or ships side by side (*ship of the line*). **24** each of the very narrow horizontal sections forming a television picture. **25** a narrow range of

the spectrum that is noticeably brighter or darker than the adjacent parts. **26** the level of the base of most letters in printing and writing. **27** (as a measure) one twelfth of an inch. ● *v.* **1** *tr.* mark with lines. **2** *tr.* cover with lines (*a face lined with pain*). **3** *tr. & intr.* position or stand at intervals along. □ **all along the line** at every point. **bring into line** make conform. **come into line** conform. **end of the line** the point at which further effort is unproductive or one can go no further. **get a line on** *colloq.* learn something about. **in line for** likely to receive. **in the line of** in the course of (esp. duty). **in** (or **out of**) **line with** in (or not in) alignment or accordance with. **lay** (or **put**) **it on the line** speak frankly. **line up 1** arrange or be arranged in a line or lines. **2** organize (*had a job lined up*). **on the line 1** at risk (*put my reputation on the line*). **2** speaking on the telephone. **3** (of a picture in an exhibition) hung with its center about level with the spectator's eye. **out of line 1** not in alignment; discordant.

2 inappropriate; (of behavior, etc.) improper. **step out of line** behave inappropriately.

line[2] /līn/ *v.tr.* **1 a** cover the inside surface of (a garment, box, etc.) with a layer of usu. different material. **b** serve as a lining for. **2** cover as if with a lining (*shelves lined with books*). **3** *colloq.* fill, esp. plentifully. □ **line one's pocket** (or **purse**) make money, usu. by corrupt means.

lin·e·age /línee-ij/ *n.* lineal descent; ancestry; pedigree.

lin·e·al /líneeəl/ *adj.* **1** in the direct line of descent or ancestry. **2** linear; of or in lines. □□ **lin·e·al·ly** *adv.*

lin·e·a·ment /líneeəmənt/ *n.* (usu. in *pl.*) a distinctive feature or characteristic, esp. of the face.

lin·e·ar /líneeər/ *adj.* **1 a** of or in lines. **b** of length (*linear extent*). **2** long and narrow and of uniform breadth. **3** involving one dimension only. □□ **lin·e·ar·i·ty** /-neeáritee/ *n.* **lin·e·ar·ize** *v.tr.* **lin·e·ar·ly** *adv.*

lin·e·ar e·qua·tion *n.* an equation between two variables that gives a straight line when plotted on a graph.

lin·e·a·tion /línee-áyshən/ *n.* **1** a marking with or drawing of lines. **2** a division into lines.

line danc·ing *n.* a type of country and western dancing in which a line of dancers follow a choreographed pattern of steps.

line drive *n. Baseball* a hard-hit ball that travels nearly parallel to the ground.

line·man /línmən/ *n.* (*pl.* **-men**) **1** a person who repairs and maintains railroad lines. **2** *Football* a player positioned along the line of scrimmage.

lin·en /línin/ *n. & adj.* ● *n.* **1** cloth woven from flax. **2** (*collect.*) articles made or orig. made of linen, as sheets, cloths, etc. ● *adj.* made of linen or flax. □ **wash one's dirty linen in public** be indiscreet about one's domestic quarrels, etc.

line of fire *n.* the expected path of gunfire, a missile, etc.

line of vi·sion *n.* the straight line along which an observer looks.

line print·er *n.* a machine that prints output from a computer a line at a time.

lin·er[1] /línər/ *n.* ▼ a ship or aircraft, etc., carrying passengers on a regular line.

docking bridge | second-class lounge | baggage crane | lifeboat | funnel | first-class lounge | first-class promenade decks | cowl | bridge | observation room

rudder | keel | propeller

LINER: EARLY 20TH-CENTURY STEAM-POWERED LINER

lin·er[2] /línər/ *n.* a removable lining.

lin·er notes *n.pl.* printed information packaged with records, cassette tapes, and compact disks.

lines·man /línzmən/ *n.* (*pl.* **-men**) (in games played on a field or court) an umpire's or referee's assistant who decides whether a ball falls within the playing area or not.

line·up /línup/ *n.* **1** a line of people for inspection. **2** an arrangement of persons on a team, or of nations, etc., in an alliance.

ling[1] /ling/ *n.* ▼ a long slender marine fish, *Molva molva*, of N. Europe, used as food.

LING: COMMON LING (*Molva molva*)

ling[2] /ling/ *n.* any of various heathers, esp. *Calluna vulgaris*.

lin·ger /línggər/ *v.intr.* **1 a** be slow or reluctant to depart. **b** stay about. **c** (foll. by *over, on,* etc.) dally. **2** (esp. of an illness) be protracted. **3** (foll. by *on*) (of a dying person or custom) be slow in dying. □□ **lin·ger·er** *n.* **lin·ger·ing** *adj.* **lin·ger·ing·ly** *adv.*

lin·ge·rie /láánzhəráy, lánzhərée/ *n.* women's underwear and nightclothes.

lin·go /línggō/ *n.* (*pl.* **-oes**) *colloq.* **1** a foreign language. **2** the vocabulary of a special subject or group of people.

lin·gua fran·ca /línggwə frángkə/ *n.* (*pl.* **lingua francas** or **linguae francae** /-gwee fránkee/) **1** a language adopted as a common language between speakers whose native languages are different. **2** a system for mutual understanding.

lin·gual /línggwəl/ *adj.* **1** of or formed by the tongue. **2** of speech or languages. □□ **lin·gual·ly** *adv.*

lin·gui·form /línggwifawrm/ *adj. Bot., Zool., & Anat.* tongue-shaped.

lin·gui·ne /línggwéenee/ *n.* (also **lin·gui·ni**) a variety of pasta made in slender flattened strips.

lin·guist /línggwist/ *n.* a person skilled in languages or linguistics.

lin·guis·tic /linggwístik/ *adj.* of or relating to language or the study of languages. □□ **lin·guis·ti·cal·ly** *adv.*

lin·guis·tics /linggwístiks/ *n.* the scientific study of language and its structure.

lin·i·ment /línimənt/ *n.* an embrocation, usu. made with oil.

lin·ing /líning/ *n.* **1** a layer of material used to line a surface, etc. **2** an inside layer or surface, etc.

link /lingk/ *n. & v.* ● *n.* **1** one loop or ring of a chain, etc. **2 a** a connecting part; one in a series. **b** a state or means of connection. **3** a means of contact by radio or telephone between two points. **4** a means of travel or transport between two places. **5** = CUFF LINK. **6** a measure equal to one-hundredth of a surveying chain (7.92 inches). ● *v.* **1** *tr.* (foll. by *together, to, with*) connect or join. **2** *tr.* clasp or intertwine (hands or arms). **3** *intr.* (foll. by *on, to, in to*) be joined; attach oneself to (a system, company, etc.). □ **link up** (foll. by *with*) connect or combine.

link·age /língkij/ *n.* **1** a connection. **2** a system of links; a linking or link.

links /lingks/ *n.pl.* (treated as *sing.* or *pl.*) a golf course, esp. one having undulating ground, coarse grass, etc.

link·up /língkup/ *n.* an act or result of linking up.

Lin·nae·an /linéeən, -náyən/ *adj. & n.* (also **Lin·ne·an**) ● *adj.* of or relating to the Swedish naturalist Linnaeus or his system of classification of plants and animals. ● *n.* a follower of Linnaeus. ¶ Spelled *Linnean* in *Linnean Society*.

lin·net /línit/ *n.* a finch, *Acanthis cannabina*, with brown and gray plumage.

li·no·cut /línōkut/ *n.* **1** ▼ a design carved in relief on a block of linoleum. **2** ▼ a print made from this. □□ **li·no·cut·ting** *n.*

li·no·le·um /línóleeəm/ *n.* a material consisting of a canvas backing thickly coated with a preparation of linseed oil and powdered cork, etc., used esp. as a floor covering. □□ **li·no·le·umed** *adj.*

design cut in linoleum

print

Lin·o·type /línətīp/ *n. Printing propr.* a composing machine producing lines of words as single strips of metal, used esp. for newspapers.

LINOCUT

L

lin·seed /línseed/ *n.* the seed of flax.

lin·seed oil *n.* oil extracted from linseed and used esp. in paint and varnish.

lin·sey-wool·sey /línzeewŏolzee/ *n.* a fabric of coarse wool woven on a cotton warp.

lint /lint/ *n.* **1 a** a fabric, orig. of linen, with a raised nap on one side, used for dressing wounds. **2** fluff. □□ **lint·y** *adj.*

lin·tel /lint'l/ *n. Archit.* ▶ a horizontal supporting piece of wood, stone, etc., across the top of a door or window. □□ **lin·teled** *adj.*

lint·er /líntər/ *n.* **1** a machine for removing the short fibers from cottonseed after ginning. **2** (in *pl.*) these fibers.

li·on /líən/ *n.* **1** (*fem.* **lioness** /-nis/) ▼ a large feline, *Panthera leo*, of Africa and S. Asia, with a tawny coat. ▷ CARNIVORE. **2** (**the Lion**) the zodiacal sign or constellation Leo. ▷ LEO. **3** a brave or celebrated person. **4** the lion as a national emblem of Great Britain or as a representation in heraldry. □□ **li·on·like** *adj.*

canine teeth

mane (males only)

LION AND **LIONESS** (*Panthera leo*)

li·on·heart /líənhaart/ *n.* a courageous person (esp. as a sobriquet of Richard I of England). □□ **li·on·heart·ed** *adj.*

li·on·ize /líəniz/ *v.tr.* treat as a celebrity. □□ **li·on·i·za·tion** *n.* **li·on·iz·er** *n.*

li·on's share *n.* (prec. by *the*) the largest or best part.

lip /lip/ *n. & v.* ● *n.* **1 a** either of the two fleshy parts forming the edges of the mouth opening. **b** a thing resembling these. **c** = LABIUM. **2** the edge of a cup, vessel, etc., esp. the part shaped for pouring from. **3** *colloq.* impudent talk. ● *v.tr.* (**lipped, lipping**) **1 a** touch with the lips; apply the lips to. **b** touch lightly. **2** *Golf* **a** hit a ball just to the edge of (the cup). **b** (of a ball) reach the edge of (the cup) but fail to drop in. □ **bite one's lip** repress an emotion; stifle laughter, a retort, etc. **curl one's lip** express scorn. **hang on a person's lips** listen attentively to a person. **lick one's lips** see LICK. **pass a person's lips** be eaten, drunk, spoken, etc. **smack one's lips** part the lips noisily in relish or anticipation, esp. of food. □□ **lip·less** *adj.* **lip·like** *adj.* **lipped** *adj.* (also in *comb.*).

li·pase /lípays, líp-/ *n. Biochem.* an enzyme that catalyzes the decomposition of fats.

lip·ec·to·my /ləpéktəmee/ *n.* any surgical procedure carried out to remove unwanted body fat, usu. by suction.

lip·gloss /lípglos, -glaws/ *n.* a cosmetic preparation for adding shine or color to the lips.

lip·id /lípid/ *n. Chem.* any of a group of organic compounds that are insoluble in water but soluble in organic solvents, including fatty acids, oils, waxes, and steroids.

lip·oid /lípoyd/ *adj.* resembling fat.

lip·o·pro·tein /lípōprōteen, lí-/ *n. Biochem.* any of a group of proteins that are combined with fats or other lipids.

lip·o·some /lípōsōm, lí-/ *n. Biochem.* a minute artificial spherical sac usu. of a phospholipid membrane enclosing an aqueous core.

lip·o·suc·tion /lípōsúkshən, lí-/ *n.* a technique in cosmetic surgery for removing excess fat from under the skin by suction.

lip·py /lípee/ *adj.* (**lippier, lippiest**) *colloq.* **1** insolent; impertinent. **2** talkative. **lip-read** *v.intr.* (*past* and *past part.* **-read** /-red/) practice lipreading. □□ **lip-read·er** *n.*

lip·read·ing /lípreeding/ *n.* (esp. of a deaf person) the practice of understanding (speech) entirely from observing a speaker's lip movements.

lip service *n.* an insincere expression of support, etc.

lip·stick /lípstik/ *n.* a small stick of cosmetic for coloring the lips. ▷ MAKEUP

lip-sync *v.intr.* synchronize lip movements to recorded sound to appear to be singing or talking.

li·quate /líkwáyt/ *v.tr.* separate or purify (metals) by liquefying. □□ **li·qua·tion** /-áyshən/ *n.*

liq·ue·fy /líkwifī/ *v.tr. & intr.* (also **liq·ui·fy**) (**-ies, -ied**) *Chem.* make or become liquid. □□ **liq·ue·fa·cient** /-fáyshənt/ *adj. & n.* **liq·ue·fac·tion** /-fákshən/ *n.* **liq·ue·fi·a·ble** *adj.* **liq·ue·fi·er** *n.*

li·queur /likór, -kyŏor/ *n.* any of several strong, sweet alcoholic liquors, variously flavored, usu. drunk after a meal.

liq·uid /líkwid/ *adj. & n.* ● *adj.* **1** having a consistency like that of water or oil, flowing freely but of constant volume. ▷ MATTER. **2** having the qualities of water in appearance (*liquid blue; a liquid luster*). **3** (of a gas, e.g., air, hydrogen) reduced to a liquid state by intense cold. **4** (of sounds) clear and pure; harmonious; fluent. **5** (of assets) easily converted into cash; having ready cash or liquid assets. **6** not fixed; fluid (*liquid opinions*). ● *n.* **1** a liquid substance. **2** *Phonet.* the sound of *l* or *r*. □□ **liq·uid·ly** *adv.* **liq·uid·ness** *n.*

liq·ui·date /líkwidayt/ *v.* **1 a** *tr.* wind up the affairs of (a company or firm) by ascertaining liabilities and apportioning assets. **b** *intr.* (of a company) be liquidated. **2** *tr.* clear or pay off (a debt). **3** *tr.* put an end to or get rid of (esp. by violent means). □□ **liq·ui·da·tion** /-áyshən/ *n.* **liq·ui·da·tor** /-aytər/ *n.*

liquid crys·tal *n.* a turbid liquid with some order in its molecular arrangement.

liq·uid crys·tal dis·play *n.* ▶ a form of visual display in electronic devices, in which the reflectivity of a matrix of liquid crystals changes as a signal is applied. ▷ SEWING MACHINE

liquid crystal display

LIQUID CRYSTAL DISPLAY ON A **CALCULATOR**

liq·uid·i·ty /likwíditee/ *n.* (*pl.* **-ies**) **1** the state of being liquid. **2 a** availability of liquid assets. **b** (in *pl.*) liquid assets.

liq·uid·ize /líkwidīz/ *v.tr.* reduce (esp. food) to a liquid or puréed state.

liq·uid·iz·er /líkwidīzər/ *n.* a machine for liquidizing.

liq·uid meas·ure *n.* a unit for measuring the volume of liquids.

liq·ui·fy var. of LIQUEFY.

liq·uor /líkər/ *n. & v.* ● *n.* **1** an alcoholic (esp. distilled) drink. **2** water used in brewing. **3** other liquid, esp. that produced in cooking. **4** *Pharm.* a solution of a specified drug in water. ● *v.tr.* **1** dress (leather) with grease or oil. **2** steep (malt, etc.) in water.

liq·uor·ish /líkərish/ *adj.* **1** = LICKERISH. **2** fond of or

indicating a fondness for liquor. □□ **liq·uor·ish·ly** *adv.* **liq·uor·ish·ness** *n.*

li·ra /léerə/ *n.* (*pl.* **lire** /léere/ or **liras**) **1** (until the introduction of the euro in 2002) the chief monetary unit of Italy. **2** the chief monetary unit of Turkey.

lisle /līl/ *n.* (in full **lisle thread**) a fine, smooth cotton thread for stockings, etc.

lisp /lisp/ *n. & v.* ● *n.* **1** a speech defect in which *s* is pronounced like *th* in *thick* and *z* is pronounced like *th* in *this*. **2** a rippling of waters; a rustling of leaves. ● *v.intr. & tr.* speak or utter with a lisp. □□ **lisp·er** *n.* **lisp·ing** *adj.*

lis·some /lísəm/ *adj.* (also **lis·som**) lithe; supple; agile. □□ **lis·some·ly** *adv.* **lis·some·ness** *n.*

list[1] /list/ *n. & v.* ● *n.* **1** a number of connected items, names, etc., written or printed together usu. consecutively to form a record or aid to memory. **2** (in *pl.*) **a** palisades enclosing an area for a tournament. **b** the scene of a contest. ● *v.tr.* **1 a** make a list of. **b** enumerate; name one by one as if in a list. **2** enter in a list. **3** (as **listed** *adj.*) (of securities) approved for dealings on the stock exchange. □□ **list·a·ble** *adj.*

list[2] /list/ *v. & n.* ● *v.intr.* (of a ship, etc.) lean over to one side, esp. owing to a leak or shifting cargo (cf. HEEL[2]). ● *n.* the process or an instance of listing.

lis·ten /lísən/ *v.intr.* **1 a** make an effort to hear something. **b** attentively hear a person speaking. **2** (foll. by *to*) **a** give attention with the ear (*listened to my story*). **b** respond to advice or a request or to the person expressing it. **3** (also **lis·ten out**) (often foll. by *for*) seek to hear by waiting alertly. □ **listen in 1** eavesdrop. **2** listen to a radio or television broadcast.

lis·ten·a·ble /lísənəbəl/ *adj.* easy or pleasant to listen to. □□ **lis·ten·a·bil·i·ty** *n.*

lis·ten·er /lísənər, lísnər/ *n.* **1** a person who listens. **2** a person receiving broadcast radio programs.

lis·ten·ing post *n.* a station for intercepting electronic communications.

lis·te·ri·a /listéereeə/ *n.* any motile rodlike bacterium of the genus *Listeria*, esp. *L. monocytogenes* infecting humans and animals eating contaminated food.

list·ing /lísting/ *n.* **1** a list or catalog (see LIST[1] 1). **2** the drawing up of a list.

list·less /lístlis/ *adj.* lacking energy or enthusiasm. □□ **list·less·ly** *adv.* **list·less·ness** *n.*

list price *n.* the price of something as shown in a published list.

lit *past* and *past part.* of LIGHT[1], LIGHT[2].

lit·a·ny /lít'nee/ *n.* (*pl.* **-ies**) **1 a** a series of petitions for use in church services or processions. **b** (**the Litany**) that contained in the Book of Common Prayer. **2** a tedious recital (*a litany of woes*).

spiny skin

li·tchi /léechee/ *n.* (also **li·chee**, **ly·chee**) **1** ▶ a sweet, fleshy fruit with a thin, spiny skin. **2** the tree, *Nephelium litchi*, orig. from China, bearing this.

li·ter /léetər/ *n.* a metric unit of capacity, formerly defined as the volume of one kilogram of water under standard conditions, now equal to 1 cubic decimeter (about 1.057 quarts).

LITCHI (*Nephelium litchi*)

lit·er·a·cy /lítərəsee/ *n.* the ability to read and write.

lit·er·al /lítərəl/ *adj. & n.* ● *adj.* **1** taking words in their usual or primary sense without metaphor or allegory. **2** following the letter, text, or exact or original words (*literal translation*). **3** (in full **literal-minded**) (of a person) prosaic. **4 a** not exaggerated (*the literal truth*). **b** so called without exaggeration (*a literal extermination*). **5** *colloq. disp.* so called with some exaggeration or using metaphor (*a literal avalanche of mail*). **6** of, in, or expressed by a letter

L

LINTEL ON A GEORGIAN **DOORFRAME**

lintel

or the letters of the alphabet. **7** *Algebra* not numerical. ● *n. Printing* a misprint of a letter. □□ **lit·er·al·ize** *v.tr.* **lit·er·al·ly** *adv.* **lit·er·al·ness** *n.*

lit·er·al·ism /lítərəlizəm/ *n.* insistence on a literal interpretation. □□ **lit·er·al·ist** *n.*

lit·er·ar·y /lítəreree/ *adj.* **1** of, constituting, or occupied with books or written composition. **2** well informed about literature. **3** (of a word or idiom) used chiefly in literary works or other formal writing. □□ **lit·er·ar·i·ly** /-áirilee/ *adv.* **lit·er·ar·i·ness** *n.*

lit·er·ate /lítərət/ *adj.* able to read and write. ● *n.* a literate person. □□ **lit·er·ate·ly** *adv.*

lit·er·a·ti /lítəráatee/ *n.pl.* **1** men of letters. **2** the learned class.

lit·er·a·tim /lítəráytim, -ráa-/ *adv.* letter for letter; textually; literally.

lit·er·a·tion /lítəráyshən/ *n.* the representation of sounds, etc., by a letter or group of letters.

lit·er·a·ture /lítərəchər, -chŏŏr/ *n.* **1** written works, esp. those whose value lies in beauty of language or in emotional effect. **2** the realm of letters. **3** the writings of a country or period. **4** literary production. **5** *colloq.* printed matter, leaflets, etc. **6** the material in print on a particular subject (*there is a considerable literature on geraniums*).

lithe /lith/ *adj.* flexible; supple. □□ **lithe·ly** *adv.* **lithe·ness** *n.* **lithe·some** *adj.*

lith·ic /líthik/ *adj.* **1** of, like, or made of stone. **2** *Med.* of a calculus.

lith·i·um /lítheeəm/ *n. Chem.* a soft, silver-white metallic element. ¶ Symb.: **Li.**

lith·o /lítho/ *n. & v. colloq.* ● *n.* = LITHOGRAPHY. ● *v.tr.* (**-oes, -oed**) produce by lithography.

litho- /lítho/ *comb. form* stone.

lith·o·graph /líthəgraf/ *n. & v.* ● *n.* a lithographic print. ● *v.tr.* **1** print by lithography. **2** write or engrave on stone.

lith·og·ra·phy /lithógrəfee/ *n.* ▼ a process of obtaining prints from a stone or metal surface so treated that what is to be printed can be inked but the remaining area rejects ink. ▷ PRINTING. □□ **lith·og·ra·pher** *n.* **lith·o·graph·ic** /líthəgráfik/ *adj.* **lith·o·graph·i·cal·ly** *adv.*

li·thol·o·gy /lithóləjee/ *n.* the science of the nature and composition of rocks. □□ **lith·o·log·i·cal** /líthəlójikəl/ *adj.*

lith·o·phyte /líthəfīt/ *n. Bot.* a plant that grows on stone.

lith·o·sphere /líthəsfeer/ *n.* **1** ▼ the layer including the Earth's crust and upper mantle. ▷ EARTH. **2** solid earth (opp. HYDROSPHERE, ATMOSPHERE). □□ **lith·o·spher·ic** /-sféerik, -sfér-/ *adj.*

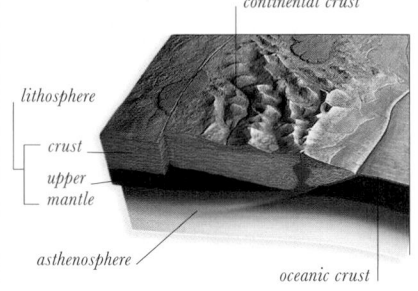

continental crust

lithosphere

crust

upper
mantle

asthenosphere

oceanic crust

LITHOSPHERE: SECTION OF THE EARTH'S
UPPER LAYERS SHOWING THE LITHOSPHERE

li·thot·o·my /lithótəmee/ *n.* (*pl.* **-ies**) the surgical removal of a stone from the urinary tract, esp. the bladder. □□ **li·thot·o·mist** *n.* **li·thot·o·mize** *v.tr.*

lith·o·trip·sy /líthətripsee/ *n.* (*pl.* **-ies**) a treatment using ultrasound to shatter a stone in the bladder into small particles that may then be passed through the urethra. □□ **lith·o·trip·ter** /-triptər/ *n.* **lith·o·trip·tic** *adj.*

Lith·u·a·ni·an /líthōō-áyneeən/ *n. & adj.* ● *n.* **1 a** a native of Lithuania, a Baltic republic. **b** a person of Lithuanian descent. **2** the language of Lithuania. ● *adj.* of or relating to Lithuania or its people or language.

lit·i·gant /lítigənt/ *n. & adj.* ● *n.* a party to a lawsuit. ● *adj.* engaged in a lawsuit.

lit·i·gate /lítigayt/ *v.* **1** *intr.* go to law. **2** *tr.* contest (a point) in a lawsuit. □□ **lit·i·ga·ble** /-gəbəl/ *adj.* **lit·i·ga·tion** /-gáyshən/ *n.* **lit·i·ga·tor** *n.*

lit·i·gious /litíjəs/ *adj.* **1** given to litigation. **2** disputable in a court of law; offering matter for a lawsuit. **3** of lawsuits. □□ **li·ti·gious·ly** *adv.* **li·ti·gious·ness** *n.*

lit·mus /lítməs/ *n.* a dye obtained from lichens that is red under acid conditions and blue under alkaline conditions.

lit·mus pa·per *n.* a paper stained with litmus to be used as a test for acids or alkalis.

lit·mus test *n.* **1** a test for acids and alkalis using litmus paper. **2** a simple test to establish true character.

li·to·tes /lítəteez, lít-, lītóteez/ *n.* ironical understatement, esp. the expressing of an affirmative by the negative of its contrary (e.g., *I won't be sorry* for *I will be glad*).

Litt.D. *abbr.* Doctor of Letters.

lit·ter /lítər/ *n. & v.* ● *n.* **1 a** refuse, esp. paper, discarded in a public place. **b** odds and ends lying about. **2** disorderly accumulation of papers, etc. **3** the young animals brought forth at a birth. **4** a vehicle containing a couch shut in by curtains and carried on men's shoulders or by beasts of burden. **5** a framework with a couch for transporting the sick and wounded. **6 a** straw, rushes, etc., as bedding, esp. for animals. **b** straw and dung in a farmyard. ● *v.tr.* **1** make (a place) untidy with litter. **2** scatter untidily and leave lying about. **3** give birth to (whelps, etc.). **4** (often foll. by *down*) **a** provide (a horse, etc.) with litter as bedding. **b** spread litter or straw on (a floor) or in (a stable).

lit·te·rae hu·ma·ni·o·res /lítərī hōōmáneeáwrez, lítəree/ *n.* the formal study of the humanities.

lit·té·ra·teur /lítəraatór/ *n.* a literary person.

lit·ter·bug /lítərbug/ *n.* a person who carelessly leaves litter in a public place.

lit·tle /lít'l/ *adj., n., & adv.* ● *adj.* (**littler, littlest**; **less** /les/ or **lesser** /lésər/; **least** /leest/) **1** small in size, amount, degree, etc.; often used to convey affectionate or emotional overtones (*a friendly little guy; a silly little fool*). **2 a** short in stature (*a little man*). **b** of short distance or duration (*wait a little while*). **3** (prec. by *a*) a certain though small amount of (*give me a little butter*). **4** trivial (*exaggerates every little difficulty*). **5** not much; inconsiderable (*gained little advantage from it*). **6** operating on a small scale (*the little storekeeper*). **7** as a distinctive epithet: **a** of a smaller or the smallest size, etc. (*little finger*). **b** that is the smaller or smallest of the name (*little auk*). **8** young or younger (*my little sister*). **9** as of a child, evoking tenderness, amusement, etc. (*we know their little ways*). **10** mean; contemptible (*you little sneak*). ● *n.* **1** only a small amount (*did what little I could*). **2** (usu. prec. by *a*) **a** a certain but no great amount (*every little bit helps*). **b** a short time or distance (*after a little*). ● *adv.* (**less, least**) **1** to a small extent only (*little-known authors*). **2** hardly (*they little thought*). **3** (prec. by *a*) somewhat (*is a little deaf*). □ **in little** on a small scale. **little by little** by degrees. **little or nothing** hardly anything. **no little** considerable. **not a little** much; a great deal. *adv.* extremely (*not a little concerned*). □□ **lit·tle·ness** *n.*

Lit·tle Bear *n.* = LITTLE DIPPER.

Lit·tle Dip·per *n.* the constellation of seven bright stars in Ursa Minor in the shape of a dipper.

lit·tle fin·ger *n.* the smallest finger, at the outer end of the hand.

lit·tle grebe *n.* a small waterbird of the grebe family, *Tachybaptus ruficollis.*

Lit·tle League *n.* an international organization that promotes youth baseball and softball. □□ **Lit·tle Lea·guer** *n.*

lit·tle man *n.* esp. *joc.* (as a form of address) a boy.

lit·tle peo·ple *n.pl.* **1** (prec. by *the*) fairies. **2** midgets.

lit·tle slam *n. Bridge* the winning of 12 tricks.

lit·tle wom·an *n. colloq.* often *derog.* one's wife.

lit·to·ral /lítərəl/ *adj. & n.* ● *adj.* of or on the shore of the sea, a lake, etc. ● *n.* a region lying along a shore.

li·tur·gi·cal /litórjikəl/ *adj.* of or related to liturgies or public worship. □□ **li·tur·gi·cal·ly** *adv.* **lit·ur·gist** /lítərjist/ *n.*

lit·ur·gy /lítərjee/ *n.* (*pl.* **-ies**) **1 a** a form of public worship. **b** a set of formularies for this. **c** public worship in accordance with a prescribed form.

LITHOGRAPHY

In traditional lithographic printing, a reverse image is drawn on a stone plate with a greasy medium and fixed by applying an acidic solution. The plate is then dampened and rolled with ink, which adheres only to the greasy areas and is repelled by the water. Paper is laid onto the inked block and pressure is applied by a press, transferring the inked image to the paper. Today, most printed articles are produced by offset lithography, in which the image is transferred from a dampened and inked metal plate to an intermediate "offset" roller before being reproduced on paper.

IMAGE DRAWN
ON STONE

LITHOGRAPHIC
PRINT

TRADITIONAL LITHOGRAPHIC EQUIPMENT

CRAYON
AND
HOLDER

LITHOGRAPHIC
PENCIL

TUSCHE
PEN

ROLLER

ERASING
STICK

L

L

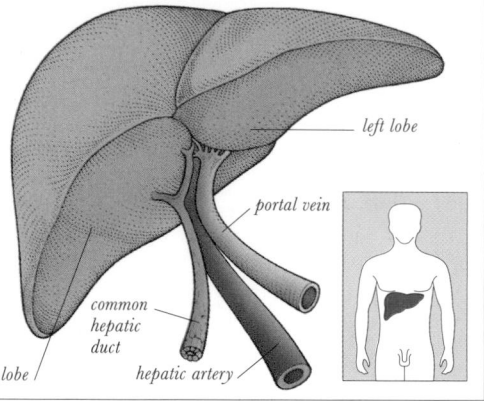

LIVER

Nutrients absorbed from the intestine reach the liver via the portal vein, and are processed and redistributed according to the body's requirements. Hence the liver regulates the levels of glucose, fats, and proteins in the blood. It also removes toxins, breaks down aging red blood cells, and produces bile, which is stored in the gall bladder for discharge into the duodenum where it assists the absorption and digestion of fats.

STRUCTURE OF THE
HUMAN LIVER

left lobe

portal vein

common hepatic duct

right lobe   *hepatic artery*

---

2 (**the Divine Liturgy**) the Communion office of the Orthodox Church.

liv·a·ble /lívəbəl/ *adj.* (also **live·a·ble**) **1** (of a house, climate, etc.) fit to live in. **2** (of a life) worth living. **3** (of a person) easy to live with. □□ **liv·a·bil·i·ty** *n.*

live[1] /liv/ *v.* **1** *intr.* have (esp. animal) life; be or remain alive. **2** *intr.* (foll. by *on*) subsist or feed. **3** *intr.* (foll. by *on, off*) depend for subsistence (*lives off the family*). **4** *intr.* (foll. by *on, by*) sustain one's position or repute (*lives by his wits*). **5** *tr.* **a** (with compl.) spend; experience (*lived a happy life*). **b** express in one's life (*was living a lie*). **6** *intr.* conduct oneself in a specified way (*live quietly*). **7** *intr.* arrange one's expenditure, etc. (*live modestly*). **8** *intr.* make or have one's abode. **9** *intr.* (foll. by *in*) spend the daytime (*the room does not seem to be lived in*). **10** *intr.* (of a person or thing) survive. **11** *intr.* (of a ship) escape destruction. **12** *intr.* enjoy life intensely or to the full (*you haven't lived till you've drunk champagne*). □ **live and let live** condone others' failings so as to be similarly tolerated. **live down** (usu. with *neg.*) cause (past guilt, etc.) to be forgotten. **live in** (of a domestic employee) reside on the premises of one's work. **live it up** *colloq.* live gaily and extravagantly. **live out 1** survive (a danger, difficulty, etc.). **2** (of a domestic employee) reside away from one's place of work. **live through** survive; remain alive at the end of. **live to** survive and reach (*lived to a great age*). **live to oneself** live in isolation. **live together** share a home and have a sexual relationship. **live up to** honor or fulfill. **live with 1** share a home with. **2** tolerate. **long live ...!** an exclamation of loyalty (to a person, etc., specified).

live[2] /līv/ *adj.* **1** (*attrib.*) that is alive; living. **2** (of a broadcast) heard or seen at the time of its performance, not from a recording. **3** not obsolete or exhausted (*disarmament is still a live issue*). **4** expending or still able to expend energy, esp.: **a** (of coals) glowing; burning. **b** (of a shell) unexploded. **c** (of a match) unkindled. **d** (of a wire, etc.) connected to a source of electrical power. **5** (of rock) not detached, seeming to form part of the earth's frame. **6** (of a wheel, etc., in machinery) moving or imparting motion.

live·a·ble var. of LIVABLE.

live-in *attrib.adj.* **1** (of a domestic employee) living in (*live-in maid*). **2** (of a sexual partner) cohabiting.

live·li·hood /lívleehŏŏd/ *n.* a means of living; sustenance.

live·long /lívlawng, -long/ *adj. poet.* or *rhet.* in its entire length or apparently so (*the livelong day*).

live·ly /lívlee/ *adj.* (**livelier**, **liveliest**) **1** full of life; vigorous; energetic. **2** brisk (*a lively pace*). **3** stimulating (*a lively discussion*). **4** vivacious; jolly; sociable. **5** *joc.* exciting; dangerous; difficult (*the press is making things lively for them*). **6** (of a color) bright and vivid. **7** lifelike; realistic (*a lively description*). **8** (of a boat, etc.) rising lightly to the waves. □□ **live·li·ly** *adv.* **live·li·ness** *n.*

liv·en /lívən/ *v.tr. & intr.* (often foll. by *up*) *colloq.* brighten; cheer.

liv·er[1] /lívər/ *n.* **1 a** ▲ a large lobed glandular organ in the abdomen of vertebrates, functioning in many metabolic processes. ▷ DIGESTION. **b** a similar organ in other animals. **2** the flesh of an animal's liver as food. ▷ CUT. **3** a dark reddish-brown color.

liv·er[2] /lívər/ *n.* a person who lives in a specified way (*a clean liver*).

liv·er·ish /lívərish/ *adj.* **1** suffering from a disorder of the liver. **2** peevish; glum. **3** resembling liver. □□ **liv·er·ish·ly** *adv.* **liv·er·ish·ness** *n.*

Liv·er·pud·li·an /lívərpúdleeən/ *n. & adj.* ● *n.* a native of Liverpool, England. ● *adj.* of or relating to Liverpool.

liv·er spot(s) *n.(pl.)* brownish pigmentation of the skin, esp. of older people.

liv·er·wort /lívərwərt, -wawrt/ *n.* any small leafy or thalloid bryophyte of the class Hepaticae, of which some have liver-shaped parts. ▷ BRYOPHYTE

liv·er·wurst /lívərwərst, -vərst/ *n.* a sausage containing cooked liver, etc.

liv·er·y /lívəree/ *n.* (*pl.* **-ies**) **1** ▶ distinctive clothing worn by a servant, official member of a guild, etc. **2** an establishment from which horses or vehicles can be hired. **3** a distinctive marking or outward appearance (*birds in their winter livery*). **4** a distinctive color scheme in which the vehicles, etc., of a particular company are painted. □ **at livery** (of a horse) kept for the owner and fed and groomed for a fixed charge. □□ **liv·er·ied** *adj.* (esp. in senses 3, 4).

liv·er·y sta·ble *n.* a stable where horses are kept at livery or let out for hire.

lives *pl.* of LIFE.

live·stock /lívstok/ *n.* (usu. treated as *pl.*) animals, esp. on a farm, regarded as an asset.

live wire *n.* an energetic and forceful person.

liv·id /lívid/ *adj.* **1** *colloq.* furiously angry. **2 a** of a bluish leaden color. **b** discolored as by a bruise. □□ **li·vid·i·ty** /-víditee/ *n.* **liv·id·ly** *adv.* **liv·id·ness** *n.*

liv·ing /líving/ *n. & adj.* ● *n.* **1** a livelihood or means of maintenance (*made my living as a journalist; what does she do for a living?*). **2** *Brit. Eccl.* a position as a vicar or rector with an income or property. ● *adj.* **1** contemporary; now existent (*the greatest living poet*). **2** (of a likeness or image of a person) exact. **3** (of a language) still in vernacular use. **4** (of water) perennially flowing. **5** (of rock, etc.) = LIVE[2] 5. □ **within living memory** within the memory of people still living.

liv·ing death *n.* a state of hopeless misery.

liv·ing room *n.* a room for general day use.

liv·ing wage *n.* a wage that affords the means of normal subsistence.

---

liv·ing will *n.* a written statement of a person's desire not to be kept alive by artificial means in the event of terminal illness or accident.

lix·iv·i·ate /liksívee-ayt/ *v.tr.* separate (a substance) into soluble and insoluble constituents by the percolation of liquid. □□ **lix·iv·i·a·tion** /-áyshən/ *n.*

liz·ard /lízərd/ *n.* ▶ any reptile of the suborder Lacertilia, having usu. a long body and tail and a rough or scaly hide. ▷ REPTILE

'll *v.* (usu. after pronouns) shall; will (*I'll; that'll*).

lla·ma /láːmə, yáa-/ *n.*
1 ▶ a S. American ruminant, *Lama glama*, kept as a beast of burden and for its soft, woolly fleece. **2** the wool from this animal.

LLAMA
(*Lama glama*)

lla·no /láːnō, yáa-/ *n.* (*pl.* **-os**) a treeless grassy plain or steppe, esp. in S. America.

LLB *abbr.* Bachelor of Laws.

LLD *abbr.* Doctor of Laws.

LLM *abbr.* Master of Laws.

Lloyd's /loydz/ *n.* an incorporated society of insurance underwriters in London.

lm *abbr.* lumen(s).

lo /lō/ *int. archaic* calling attention to an amazing sight. □ **lo and behold** *joc.* a formula introducing a surprising or unexpected fact.

loach /lōch/ *n.* ▶ any small edible freshwater fish of the family Cobitidae.

load /lōd/ *n. & v.* ● *n.* **1 a** what is carried or is to be carried; a burden. **b** an amount usu. or actually carried (often in *comb.: a busload of tourists; a truckload of bricks*). **2** a unit of measure or weight of certain substances. **3** a burden or commitment of work, responsibility, etc. **4** (in *pl.*; often foll. by *of*) *colloq.* plenty; a lot. **5 a** *Electr.* the amount of power supplied by a generating system at any given time. **b** *Electronics* an impedance or circuit that receives or develops the output of a transistor or other device. **6** the weight or force borne by the supporting part of a structure. **7** a material object or force acting as a weight or clog. **8** the resistance of machinery to motive power. ● *v.* **1** *tr.* **a** put a load on or aboard (a person, ship, etc.). **b** place (a load or cargo) aboard a ship, etc. **2** *intr.* (often foll. by *up*) (of a ship, vehicle, or person) take a load aboard. **3** *tr.* (often foll. by *with*) **a** add weight to. **b** oppress. **4** *tr.* strain the bearing-capacity of (*a table loaded with food*). **5** *tr.* (also **load up**) (foll. by *with*) **a** supply overwhelmingly (*loaded us with work*). **b** assail overwhelmingly (*loaded us with abuse*). **6** *tr.* charge (a firearm) with ammunition. **7** *tr.* insert (the required operating medium) in a device, e.g., film in a camera, etc. **8** *tr.* add an extra charge to (an insurance premium) in the case of a poorer risk. **9** *tr.* **a** weight with lead. **b** give a bias to (dice, a roulette wheel, etc.) with weights. □ **get a load of** *sl.* listen attentively to.

load·ed /lōdid/ *adj.* **1** bearing or carrying a load. **2** *sl.* **a** wealthy. **b** drunk. **c** drugged. **3** (of dice, etc.) weighted or given a bias. **4** (of a question or statement) charged with some hidden or improper implication.

load·er /lōdər/ *n.* **1** a loading machine. **2** (in *comb.*) a gun, machine, truck, etc., loaded in a specified

---

LIVERY:
FOOTMAN IN
19TH-CENTURY
LIVERY

LOACH:
CLOWN LOACH
(*Botia macracantha*)

LIZARD

Numbering approximately 3,500 species, lizards make up more than half of the world's reptiles. They are grouped into 17 families, with representatives of the ten principal families shown below. The typical lizard has a long tail, a broad head, movable eyelids, scaly skin, and four splayed legs. In some species, such as the glass lizards, the legs are reduced or completely absent. Many are good climbers, and some – including chameleons and geckos – are especially adapted to life in trees. Most lizards also have special fracture points along their tails; if the lizard is attacked, the tail can be shed and then regenerated. Apart from some iguanas (which eat plants) and monitor lizards (which often eat carrion), the majority of lizards feed on small animals.

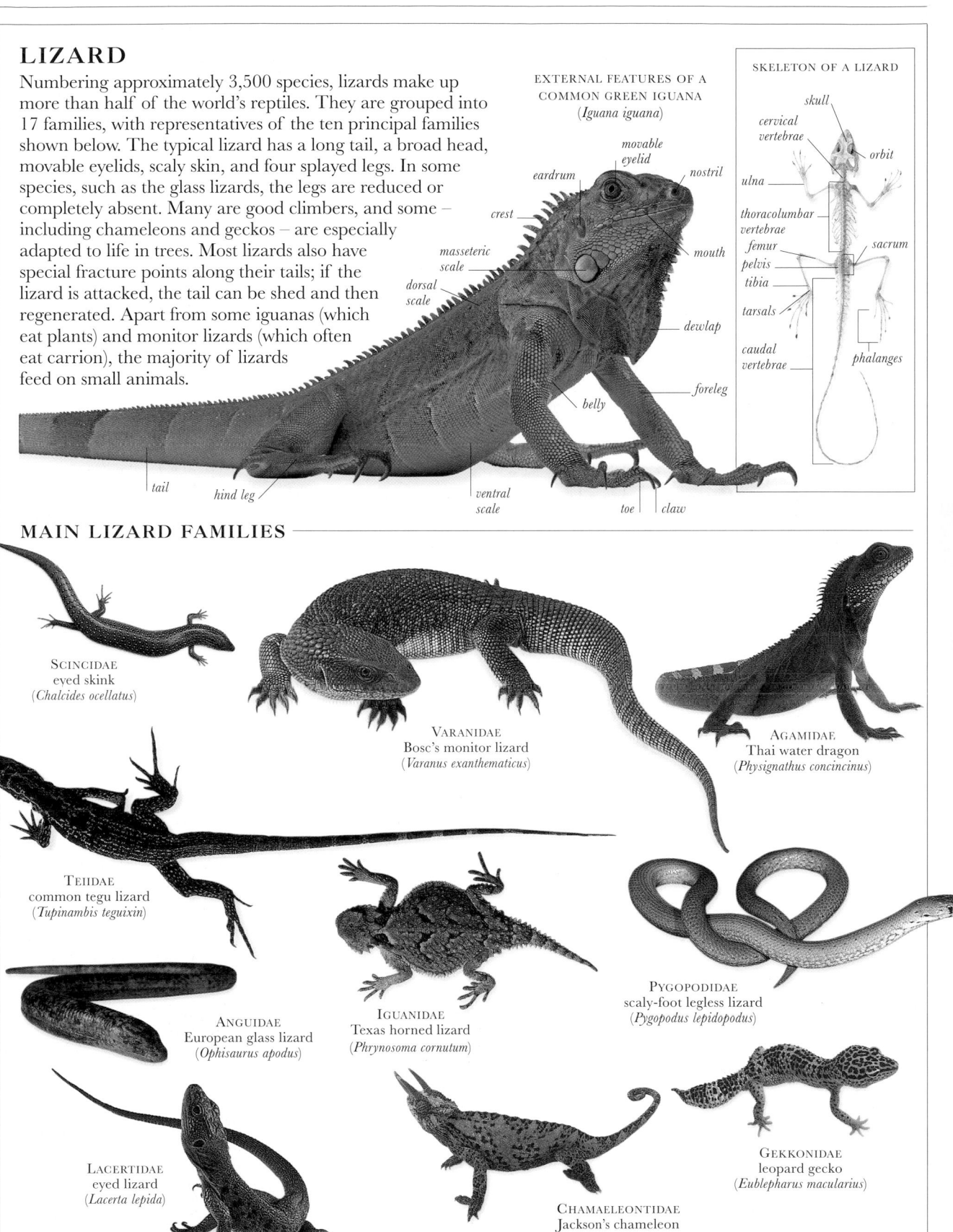

EXTERNAL FEATURES OF A
COMMON GREEN IGUANA
(*Iguana iguana*)

movable eyelid
nostril
eardrum
crest
masseteric scale
mouth
dorsal scale
dewlap
tail
hind leg
ventral scale
belly
foreleg
toe
claw

SKELETON OF A LIZARD

skull
cervical vertebrae
orbit
ulna
thoracolumbar vertebrae
femur
sacrum
pelvis
tibia
tarsals
caudal vertebrae
phalanges

L

MAIN LIZARD FAMILIES

SCINCIDAE
eyed skink
(*Chalcides ocellatus*)

VARANIDAE
Bosc's monitor lizard
(*Varanus exanthematicus*)

AGAMIDAE
Thai water dragon
(*Physignathus concincinus*)

TEIIDAE
common tegu lizard
(*Tupinambis teguixin*)

ANGUIDAE
European glass lizard
(*Ophisaurus apodus*)

IGUANIDAE
Texas horned lizard
(*Phrynosoma cornutum*)

PYGOPODIDAE
scaly-foot legless lizard
(*Pygopodus lepidopodus*)

GEKKONIDAE
leopard gecko
(*Eublepharus macularius*)

LACERTIDAE
eyed lizard
(*Lacerta lepida*)

CHAMAELEONTIDAE
Jackson's chameleon
(*Chamaeleo jacksoni*)

477

way (*breechloader*). **3** an attendant who loads guns at a shoot. □□ **-loading** *adj.* (in *comb.*) (in sense 2).

load·ing /lṓding/ *n.* **1** *Electr.* the maximum current or power taken by an appliance. **2** an increase in an insurance premium due to a factor increasing the risk involved (see LOAD *v.* 8).

load·star var. of LODESTAR.

load·stone var. of LODESTONE.

loaf[1] /lōf/ *n.* (*pl.* **loaves** /lōvz/) **1** a portion of baked bread, usu. of a standard size or shape. **2** (often in *comb.*) other food formed into a particular shape (*meat loaf*).

loaf[2] /lōf/ *v.* **1** *intr.* (often foll. by *about, around*) spend time idly. **2** *tr.* (foll. by *away*) waste (time) idly. **3** *intr.* saunter.

loaf·er /lṓfər/ *n.* **1** an idle person. **2** (**Loafer**) *Trademark* a leather shoe shaped like a moccasin with a flat heel.

loam /lōm/ *n.* **1** a fertile soil of clay and sand containing decayed vegetable matter. **2** a paste of clay and water with sand, chopped straw, etc., used in making bricks, plastering, etc. □□ **loam·y** *adj.* **loam·i·ness** *n.*

loan /lōn/ *n.* & *v.* ● *n.* **1** something lent, esp. a sum of money to be returned normally with interest. **2** the act of lending or state of being lent. **3** a word, custom, etc., adopted by one people from another. ● *v.tr.* lend (esp. money). □ **on loan** acquired or given as a loan. □□ **loan·a·ble** *adj.* **loan·ee** /lōneé/ *n.* **loan·er** *n.*

loan shark *n. colloq.* a person who lends money at exorbitant rates of interest.

loan·word /lṓnwərd/ *n.* a word adopted, usu. with little modification, from a foreign language.

loath /lōth, lōth/ *predic.adj.* (also **loth**) (usu. foll. by *to* + infin.) disinclined; reluctant (*loath to admit it*). □ **nothing loath** *adj.* quite willing.

loathe /lōth/ *v.tr.* regard with disgust; detest. □□ **loath·ing** *n.*

loath·some /lṓthsəm, lóth-/ *adj.* arousing hatred or disgust; offensive; repulsive. □□ **loath·some·ness** *n.*

loaves *pl.* of LOAF[1].

lob /lob/ *v.* & *n.* ● *v.tr.* (**lobbed, lobbing**) **1** hit or throw (a ball or missile, etc.) slowly or in a high arc. **2** send (an opponent) a lobbed ball. ● *n.* **1** a ball struck in a high arc. **2** a stroke producing this result.

lo·bar /lṓbər, -baar/ *adj.* **1** of the lungs (*lobar pneumonia*). **2** of, relating to, or affecting a lobe.

lo·bate /lṓbayt/ *adj. Biol.* having a lobe or lobes. □□ **lo·ba·tion** /-áyshən/ *n.*

lob·by /lóbee/ *n.* & *v.* ● *n.* (*pl.* **-ies**) **1** a porch, anteroom, entrance hall, or corridor. **2** *Brit.* **a** (in the House of Commons) a large hall used esp. for interviews between members of Parliament and the public. **b** (also **division lobby**) each of two corridors to which members of Parliament retire to vote. **3** a body of persons seeking to influence legislators on behalf of a particular interest (*the tobacco lobby*). ● *v.* (**-ies, -ied**) **1** *tr.* solicit the support of (an influential person). **2** *tr.* (of members of the public) seek to influence (the members of a legislature). **3** *intr.* frequent a parliamentary lobby. **4** *tr.* (foll. by *through*) get (a bill, etc.) through a legislature, by interviews, etc., in the lobby. □□ **lob·by·er** *n.* **lob·by·ism** *n.* **lob·by·ist** *n.*

lobe /lōb/ *n.* **1** a roundish and flattish projecting or pendulous part, often each of two or more such parts divided by a fissure (*lobes of the brain*). **2** = EARLOBE. □□ **lobed** *adj.* **lobe·less** *adj.*

lo·bec·to·my /lōbéktəmee/ *n.* (*pl.* **-ies**) *Surgery* the excision of a lobe of an organ such as the thyroid gland, lung, etc.

lo·bel·ia /lōbéelyə/ *n.* any plant of the genus *Lobelia*, with blue, scarlet, white, or purple flowers having a deeply cleft corolla.

lo·bot·o·my /ləbótəmee/ *n.* (*pl.* **-ies**) *Surgery* see PREFRONTAL LOBOTOMY.

lob·scouse /lóbskows/ *n.* a sailor's dish of meat stewed with vegetables and ship's biscuit.

lob·ster /lóbstər/ *n.* & *v.* ● *n.* **1** ▼ any large marine crustacean of the family Nephropidae, with two pincerlike claws as the first pair of ten limbs. **2** its flesh as food. ● *v.intr.* catch lobsters.

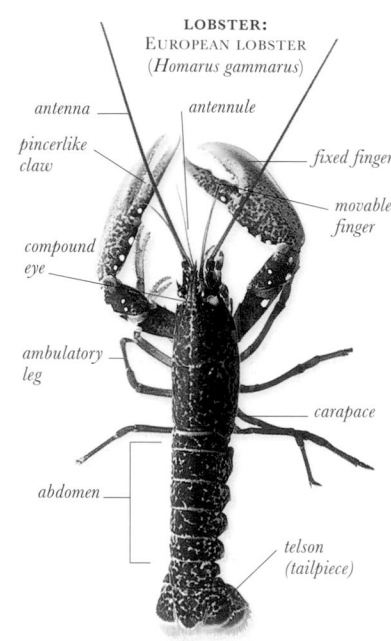

LOBSTER:
EUROPEAN LOBSTER
(*Homarus gammarus*)

antenna — antennule
pincerlike claw — fixed finger
— movable finger
compound eye
ambulatory leg — carapace
abdomen
telson (tailpiece)

lob·ster pot *n.* a basket in which lobsters are trapped.

lob·worm /lóbwərm/ *n.* **1** a large earthworm used as fishing bait. **2** = LUGWORM.

lo·cal /lṓkəl/ *adj.* & *n.* ● *adj.* **1** belonging to or existing in a particular place or places. **2** peculiar to or only encountered in a particular place or places. **3** of or belonging to the neighborhood (*the local doctor*). **4** of or affecting a part and not the whole (*local pain*). **5** in regard to place. ● *n.* a local person or thing, esp.: **1** an inhabitant of a particular place regarded with reference to that place. **2** a local train, bus, etc. **3** a local anesthetic. **4** a local branch of a labor union. □□ **lo·cal·ize** /lṓkəlīz/ *v.tr.* **lo·cal·ly** *adv.* **lo·cal·ness** *n.*

lo·cal ar·e·a net·work *n. Computing* a system for linking telecommunications or computer equipment in several offices, a group of buildings, etc. ¶ Abbr.: **LAN.**

lo·cal col·or *n.* characteristics distinctive of a place, esp. as depicted in literature, film, etc.

lo·cale /lōkál/ *n.* a scene or locality, esp. with reference to an event or occurrence taking place there.

lo·cal gov·ern·ment *n.* a system of administration of a county, etc., by the elected representatives of those who live there.

lo·cal·ism /lṓkəlizəm/ *n.* **1** preference for what is local. **2** a local idiom, custom, etc. **3 a** attachment to a place. **b** a limitation of ideas, etc., resulting from this.

lo·cal·i·ty /lōkálitee/ *n.* (*pl.* **-ies**) **1** a district or neighborhood. **2** the site or scene of something, esp. in relation to its surroundings. **3** the position of a thing; the place where it is.

lo·cal time *n.* **1** time measured from the Sun's transit over the meridian of a place. **2** the time as reckoned in a particular place, esp. with reference to an event recorded there.

lo·cal train *n.* a train stopping at all the stations on its route.

lo·cate /lṓkayt, lōkáyt/ *v.* **1** *tr.* discover the exact place or position of (*locate the enemy's camp*). **2** *tr.* establish or install in a place or in its proper place. **3** *tr.* state the locality of. **4** *tr.* (in *passive*) be situated. **5** *intr.* (often foll. by *in*) take up residence or business (in a place). □□ **lo·cat·a·ble** *adj.* **lo·cat·er** *n.* **lo·ca·tor** *n.*

lo·ca·tion /lōkáyshən/ *n.* **1** a particular place. **2** the act of locating or process of being located. **3** an actual place or natural setting featured in a motion picture, etc. (*filmed on location*).

loc·a·tive /lṓkətiv/ *n.* & *adj. Gram.* ● *n.* the case of nouns, pronouns, and adjectives, expressing location. ● *adj.* of or in the locative.

loc. cit. /lók sít/ *abbr.* in the passage already cited.

loch /lok, lokh/ *n. Sc.* **1** a lake. **2** an arm of the sea, esp. when narrow or partially landlocked.

lo·ci *pl.* of LOCUS.

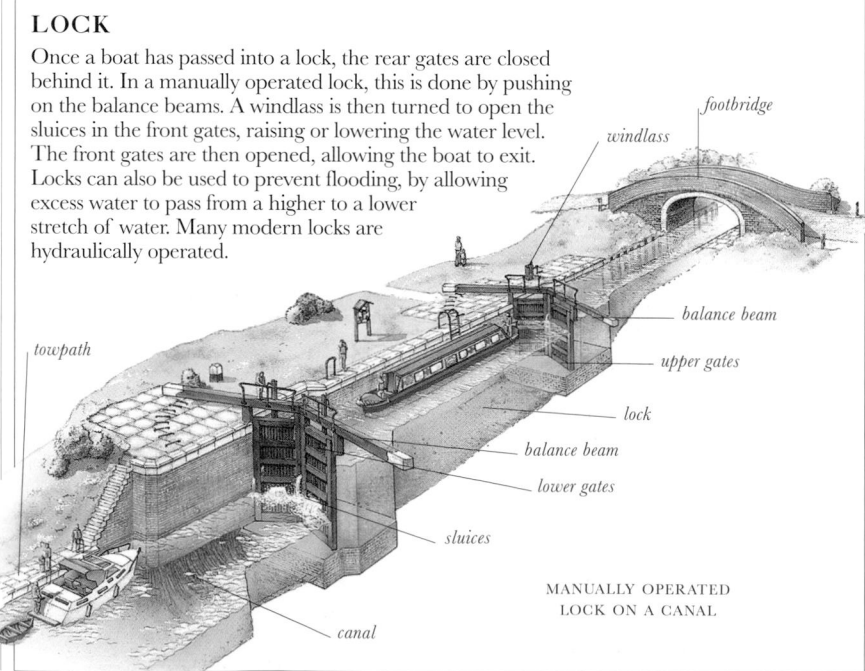

LOCK

Once a boat has passed into a lock, the rear gates are closed behind it. In a manually operated lock, this is done by pushing on the balance beams. A windlass is then turned to open the sluices in the front gates, raising or lowering the water level. The front gates are then opened, allowing the boat to exit. Locks can also be used to prevent flooding, by allowing excess water to pass from a higher to a lower stretch of water. Many modern locks are hydraulically operated.

footbridge
windlass
balance beam
upper gates
lock
balance beam
lower gates
towpath
sluices
canal

MANUALLY OPERATED
LOCK ON A CANAL

L

lo·ci clas·si·ci *pl.* of LOCUS CLASSICUS.

lock[1] /lok/ *n. & v.* ● *n.* **1** a mechanism for fastening a door, lid, etc., with a bolt that requires a key or a combination of movements (see COMBINATION LOCK), to work it. ▷ MORTISE LOCK. **2** ▼ a confined section of a canal or river where the water level can be changed by the use of gates and sluices. **3 a** the turning of the front wheels of a vehicle. **b** (in full **full lock**) the maximum extent of this. **4** an interlocked or jammed state. **5** *Wrestling* a hold that keeps an opponent's limb fixed. **6** an appliance to keep a wheel from revolving or slewing. **7** a mechanism for exploding the charge of a gun. **8** = AIRLOCK 2. ● *v.* **1 a** *tr.* fasten with a lock. **b** *tr.* (foll. by *up*) shut and secure by locking. **c** *intr.* (of a door, window, etc.) have the means of being locked. **2** *tr.* (foll. by *up, in, into*) enclose by locking or as if by locking. **3** *tr.* (often foll. by *up, away*) allocate inaccessibly (*capital locked up in land*). **4** *tr.* (foll. by *in*) hold fast (in sleep or enchantment, etc.). **5** *tr.* (usu. in *passive*) (of land, hills, etc.) enclose. **6** *tr. & intr.* make or become rigidly fixed or immovable. **7** *intr. & tr.* become or cause to become caught. **8** *tr.* (often in *passive*; foll. by *in*) entangle in an embrace or struggle. □ **lock on to** locate or cause to locate by radar, etc., and then track. **lock out 1** keep (a person) out by locking the door. **2** (of an employer) submit (employees) to a lockout. **under lock and key** securely locked up. □□ **lock·a·ble** *adj.* **lock·less** *adj.*

lock[2] /lok/ *n.* **1 a** a portion of hair that coils or hangs together. **b** (in *pl.*) the hair of the head. **2** a tuft of wool or cotton. □□ **-locked** *adj.* (in *comb.*).

lock·age /lókij/ *n.* **1** the amount of rise and fall effected by canal locks. **2** a toll for the use of a lock. **3** the construction or use of locks. **4** locks collectively; the aggregate of locks constructed.

lock·down /lókdown/ *n. N. Amer.* the confining of prisoners to their cells.

lock·er /lókər/ *n.* **1** a small lockable cupboard or compartment, esp. each of several for public use. **2** *Naut.* a chest or compartment for clothes, ammunition, etc. **3** a person or thing that locks.

lock·er room *n.* a room containing lockers (in sense 1), esp. in a sports facility.

lock·et /lókit/ *n.* **1** ◀ a small ornamental case holding a portrait, lock of hair, etc., and usu. hung from the neck. **2** a metal plate or band on a scabbard.

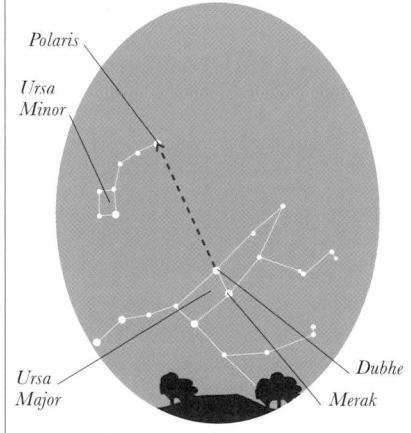

LOCKET:
LATE 19TH-CENTURY
LOCKET

lock·jaw /lókjaw/ *n.* = TRISMUS. ¶ Not in technical use.

lock·keep·er /lókkeepər/ *n.* a keeper of a lock on a river or canal.

lock·knit *adj.* knitted with an interlocking stitch.

lock·nut /lóknut/ *n. Mech.* a nut screwed down on another to keep it tight.

lock·out /lókowt/ *n.* the exclusion of employees by their employer from their place of work until certain terms are agreed to.

lock·smith /lóksmith/ *n.* a maker and repairer of locks.

lock·stitch /lókstich/ *n.* a stitch made by a sewing machine by firmly locking together two threads or stitches.

lock, stock, and bar·rel *n. & adv.* ● *n.* the whole of a thing. ● *adv.* completely.

lock·up /lókup/ *n.* **1** a house or room for the temporary detention of prisoners. **2 a** the locking up of premises for the night. **b** the time of doing this. **3 a** the unrealizable state of invested capital. **b** an amount of capital locked up.

lo·co /lókō/ *adj. & n.* ● *adj. sl.* crazy. ● *n.* (*pl.* **-os** or **-oes**) **1** *colloq.* = LOCOWEED. **2** *sl.* a crazy person; maniac.

LOCOMOTIVE ENGINE

Trains are pulled by powerful engine units called locomotives. In a steam locomotive, pressure from the steam moves a piston back and forth, which turns the wheels via a connecting rod. In a diesel-electric locomotive, air is drawn into the engine cylinders and is compressed to increase its temperature; a small amount of diesel fuel is then injected into it. The resulting combustion drives the generator to produce electricity, which is fed to electric motors. In electric locomotives, electric current is picked up either from a catenary (overhead cable) via a pantograph, or from a third rail.

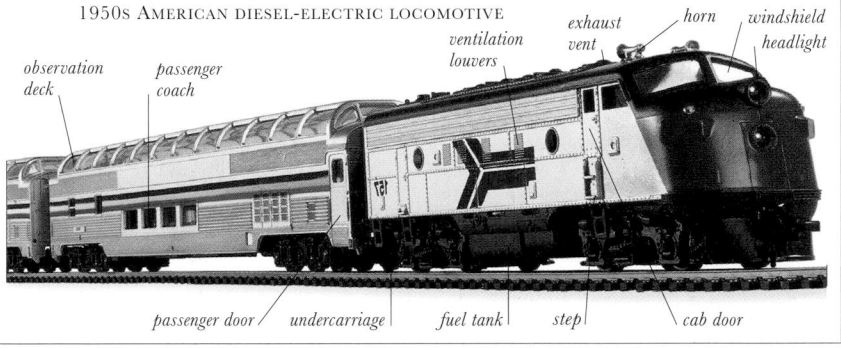

1950S AMERICAN DIESEL-ELECTRIC LOCOMOTIVE

exhaust vent — *horn* — *windshield* — *headlight* — *ventilation louvers* — *observation deck* — *passenger coach* — *passenger door* — *undercarriage* — *fuel tank* — *step* — *cab door*

lo·co·mo·tion /lókəmóshən/ *n.* **1** motion or the power of motion from one place to another. **2** travel; a means of traveling, esp. an artificial one.

lo·co·mo·tive /lókəmótiv/ *n. & adj.* ● *n.* (in full **locomotive engine**) ▲ an engine powered by steam, diesel fuel, or electricity, used for pulling trains. ▷ TRAIN. ● *adj.* **1** of or relating to or effecting locomotion. **2** having the power of or given to locomotion; not stationary.

lo·co·mo·tor /lókəmótər/ *adj.* of or relating to locomotion.

lo·co·weed /lókōweed/ *n.* a poisonous leguminous plant of the southwestern US, causing brain disease in cattle eating it.

loc·u·lus /lókyələs/ *n.* (*pl.* **loculi** /-lī/) *Zool., Anat., & Bot.* each of a number of small separate cavities. □□ **loc·u·lar** *adj.*

lo·cus /lókəs/ *n.* (*pl.* **loci** /lósī, -kee, -kī/) **1** a position or point, esp. in a text, treatise, etc. **2** *Math.* a curve, etc., formed by all the points satisfying a particular equation of the relation between coordinates, or by a point, line, or surface moving according to mathematically defined conditions. **3** *Biol.* the position of a gene, mutation, etc., on a chromosome.

lo·cus clas·si·cus /lókəs-klásikəs/ *n.* (*pl.* **loci classici** /klásisī, -kī/) the best known or most authoritative passage on a subject.

lo·cus stan·di /lókəs-stándī/ *n.* a recognized or identifiable (esp. legal) status.

lo·cust /lókəst/ *n.* **1** ▼ any of various African and Asian grasshoppers of the family Acrididae, migrating in swarms. ▷ ORTHOPTERAN. **2** a cicada. **3** (in full **locust bean**) a carob. **4** (in full **locust tree**) **a** a carob tree. **b** = ACACIA 2.

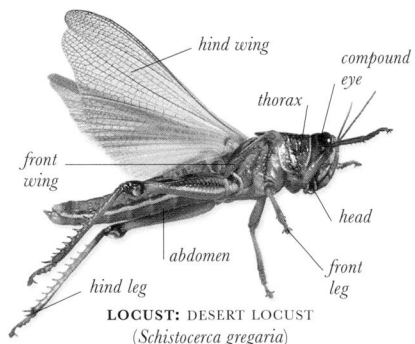

hind wing — *compound eye* — *thorax* — *front wing* — *head* — *abdomen* — *front leg* — *hind leg*

LOCUST: DESERT LOCUST
(*Schistocerca gregaria*)

lo·cu·tion /lōkyóoshən/ *n.* **1** a word or phrase, esp. considered in regard to style or idiom. **2** style of speech.

lode /lōd/ *n.* a vein of metal ore.

lo·den /lṓd'n/ *n.* **1** a thick, waterproof woolen cloth. **2** the dark green color in which this is often dyed.

lode·star /lṓdstaar/ *n.* (also **load·star**) **1** ▼ a star that a ship, etc., is steered by, esp. the pole star. **2 a** a guiding principle. **b** an object of pursuit.

lode·stone /lṓdstōn/ *n.* (also **load·stone**) **1** ▶ magnetic oxide of iron; magnetite. **2 a** a piece of this used as a magnet. **b** a thing that attracts.

iron filings

LODESTONE WITH
ATTRACTED
IRON FILINGS

LODESTAR

In the northern hemisphere, the lodestar Polaris can be used to locate north, since it remains fixed almost directly above the North Pole. The stars Merak and Dubhe, in Ursa Major, act as pointers to Polaris.

POSITION OF THE LODESTAR POLARIS

Polaris — *Ursa Minor* — *compound* — *Ursa Major* — *Dubhe* — *Merak*

L

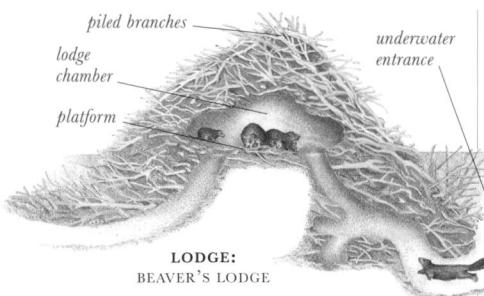

piled branches
lodge chamber
platform
underwater entrance

LODGE:
BEAVER'S LODGE

lodge /loj/ *n. & v.* ● *n.* **1** a small house at the gates of a park or on the grounds of a large house, occupied by a gatekeeper, etc. **2** any large house or hotel, esp. in a resort. **3** a house occupied in the hunting or shooting season. **4 a** a porter's room or quarters at the gate of a college or other large building. **b** the residence of a head of a college, esp. at Cambridge University in England. **5** the members or the meeting place of a branch of a society such as the Freemasons. **6** *Brit.* a local branch of a labor union. **7** ▲ a beaver's or otter's lair. **8** a type of Native American dwelling; a wigwam. ● *v.* **1** *tr.* deposit in court or with an official a formal statement of (complaint or information). **2** *tr.* deposit (money, etc.) for security. **3** *tr.* bring forward (an objection, etc.). **4** (foll. by *in, with*) place (power, etc.) in a person or group. **5** *tr. & intr.* make or become fixed without further movement (*the bullet lodged in his brain; the tide lodges mud in the cavities*). **6** *tr.* **a** provide with sleeping quarters. **b** receive as a guest or inmate. **c** establish as a resident in a house or room or rooms. **7** *intr.* reside or live, esp. as a guest paying for accommodations. **8** *tr.* serve as a habitation for; contain. **9** *tr.* (in *passive*; foll. by *in*) be contained in. **10 a** *tr.* (of wind or rain) flatten (crops). **b** *intr.* (of crops) be flattened in this way.

lodge·pole pine /lójpōl/ *n.* a straight-trunked pine tree (*Pinus contorta*) that grows in the mountains of western North America, widely grown for timber and traditionally used by some American Indians in the construction of lodges.

lodg·er /lójər/ *n.* a person receiving accommodations in another's house for payment.

lodg·ing /lójing/ *n.* **1** temporary accommodations. **2** (in *pl.*) esp. *Brit.* a room or rooms (other than in a hotel) rented for lodging in. **3** a dwelling place.

lodg·ing house *n.* a house in which lodgings are let.

lod·i·cule /lódikyōol/ *n. Bot.* a small green or white scale below the ovary of a grass flower.

lo·ess /lṓis, les, lus/ *n.* a deposit of fine, light-colored windblown dust found esp. in the basins of large rivers.

loft /lawft, loft/ *n. & v.* ● *n.* **1** the space under the roof of a house, above the ceiling of the top floor; an attic. **2** a room over a stable, esp. for hay and straw. **3** a gallery in a church or hall (*organ loft*). **4** an upstairs room. **5** a pigeon house. **6** *Golf* **a** a backward slope in a club head. **b** a lofting stroke. ● *v.tr.* **1 a** send (a ball, etc.) high up. **b** clear (an obstacle) in this way. **2** (esp. as **lofted** *adj.*) give a loft to (a golf club).

loft·er /láwftər, lóf-/ *n.* a golf club for lofting the ball.

loft·y /láwftee, lóf-/ *adj.* (**loftier, loftiest**) **1** *literary* (of things) of imposing height; towering; soaring (*lofty heights*). **2** consciously haughty, aloof, or dignified (*lofty contempt*). **3** sublime (*lofty ideals*). □□ **loft·i·ly** *adv.* **loft·i·ness** *n.*

log[1] /lawg, log/ *n. & v.* ● *n.* **1** an unhewn piece of a felled tree, or a similar rough mass of wood, esp. cut for firewood. **2 a** a float attached to a line wound on a reel for gauging the speed of a ship. **b** any other apparatus for the same purpose. **3** a record of events occurring during and affecting the voyage of a ship or aircraft (including the rate of a ship's progress

shown by a log: see sense 2). **4** any systematic record of things done, experienced, etc. **5** = LOGBOOK. ● *v.tr.* (**logged, logging**) **1 a** enter (the distance made or other details) in a logbook. **b** enter details about (a person or event) in a logbook. **c** (of a ship) achieve (a certain distance). **2 a** enter (information) in a regular record. **b** attain (a cumulative total of time, etc., recorded in this way) (*logged 50 hours on the computer*). **3** cut into logs. □ **like a log 1** in a helpless or stunned state (*the blow to the head made him fall like a log*). **2** without stirring (*slept like a log*). **log in** = log on. **log on** (or **off**) go through the procedures to begin (or conclude) use of a computer system.

log[2] /lawg, log/ *n.* a logarithm (esp. prefixed to a number or algebraic symbol whose logarithm is to be indicated).

lo·gan /lṓgən/ *n.* (in full **logan stone**) a poised heavy stone rocking at a touch.

lo·gan·ber·ry /lṓgənberee/ *n.* (*pl.* **-ies**) **1** ▶ a hybrid, *Rubus loganobaccus*, between a blackberry and a raspberry with dull red acid fruits. **2** the fruit of this plant.

log·a·rithm /láwgərithəm, lóg-/ *n.* **1** one of a series of arithmetic exponents tabulated to simplify computation by making it possible to use addition and subtraction instead of multiplication and division. **2** the power to which a fixed number or base (see BASE[1] 7) must be raised to produce a given number (*the logarithm of 1,000 to base 10 is 3*). ¶ Abbr.: **log.** □□ **log·a·rith·mic** /-ríthmik/ *adj.* **log·a·rith·mi·cal·ly** *adv.*

log·book /láwgbŏok, lóg-/ *n.* a book containing a detailed record or log.

log cab·in *n.* a hut built of logs.

loge /lōzh/ *n.* (in a theater, etc.) **1** the front section of the first balcony. **2** a private box or enclosure.

log·ger /láwgər, lóg-/ *n.* a lumberjack.

log·ger·head /láwgərhed, lóg-/ *n.* **1** an iron instrument with a ball at the end heated for melting tar, etc. **2** ▼ any of various large-headed animals, esp. a turtle (*Caretta caretta*). □ **at loggerheads** (often foll. by *with*) disagreeing or disputing.

LOGGERHEAD TURTLE
(*Caretta caretta*)

log·gia /lójeeə, láwj-/ *n.* **1** an open-sided gallery or arcade. **2** an open-sided extension of a house.

log·ging /láwging, lóg-/ *n.* the work of cutting and preparing forest timber.

log·ic /lójik/ *n.* **1 a** the science of reasoning, proof, thinking, or inference. **b** a particular scheme of or treatise on this. **2 a** a chain of reasoning (*I don't follow your logic*). **b** the correct or incorrect use of reasoning (*your logic is flawed*). **c** ability in reasoning (*argues with great learning and logic*). **d** arguments (*is not governed by logic*). **3 a** the inexorable force or compulsion of a thing (*the logic of events*). **b** the necessary consequence of (an argument, decision, etc.). **4 a** principles underlying the arrangements of elements in a computer or electronic device so as to perform a specified task. **b** logical operations collectively. □□ **lo·gi·cian** /ləjíshən/ *n.*

-logic /lójik/ *comb. form* (also **-logical** /lójikəl/) forming adjectives corresponding esp. to nouns ending in *-logy* (*analogic; theological*).

log·i·cal /lójikəl/ *adj.* **1** of logic or formal argument. **2** not contravening the laws of thought; correctly reasoned. **3** deducible or defensible on

the grounds of consistency; reasonably to be believed or done. **4** capable of correct reasoning. □□ **log·i·cal·i·ty** /-kálitee/ *n.* **log·i·cal·ly** *adv.*

log·i·cal at·om·ism *Philos. n.* the theory that all propositions can be analyzed into simple independent elements.

log·i·cal ne·ces·si·ty *n.* the compulsion to believe that of which the opposite is inconceivable.

log·i·cal pos·i·tiv·ism *n.* (or **empiricism**) a form of positivism in which symbolic logic is used and linguistic problems of meaning are emphasized.

lo·gi·on /lógeeon, -jee-/ *n.* (*pl.* **logia** /-geeə-/) a saying attributed to Christ, esp. one not recorded in the canonical Gospels.

lo·gis·tics /ləjístiks/ *n.pl.* **1** the organization of moving, lodging, and supplying troops and equipment. **2** the detailed organization and implementation of a plan or operation. □□ **lo·gis·tic** *adj.* **lo·gis·ti·cal** *adj.* **lo·gis·ti·cal·ly** *adv.*

log·jam /láwgjam, lóg-/ *n.* **1** a crowded mass of logs in a river. **2** a deadlock.

lo·go /lṓgō/ *n.* (*pl.* **-os**) *colloq.* **1** = LOGOTYPE 2. **2** a motto, esp. of a commercial product, etc.

log·o·gram /láwgəgram, lóg-/ *n.* a sign or character representing a word, esp. in shorthand.

log·or·rhe·a /láwgəréeə, lóg-/ *n.* an excessive flow of words, esp. in mental illness.

Lo·gos /lṓgos, lógos/ *n. Theol.* the Word of God, associated with the second person of the Trinity.

lo·go·type /láwgətīp, lóg-/ *n. Printing* a single piece of type that prints a word or group of separate letters.

log·roll·ing /láwgrōling, lóg-/ *n.* **1** *colloq.* the practice of exchanging favors, esp. (in politics) of exchanging votes to mutual benefit. **2** a sport in which two contestants stand on a floating log and try to knock each other off. □□ **log·roll** *v.intr. & tr.* **log·roll·er** *n.*

log·wood /láwgwŏod, lóg-/ *n.* **1** a W. Indian tree, *Haematoxylon campechianum*. **2** the wood of this, producing a substance used in dyeing.

loin /loyn/ *n.* **1** (in *pl.*) the part of the body on both sides of the spine between the false ribs and the hipbones. **2** a cut of meat that includes the loin vertebrae. ▷ CUT

loin·cloth /lóynklawth, -kloth/ *n.* a cloth worn around the loins, esp. as a sole garment.

loi·ter /lóytər/ *v.* **1** *intr.* hang around; linger idly. **2** *intr.* travel indolently and with long pauses. **3** *tr.* (foll. by *away*) pass (time, etc.) in loitering. □□ **loi·ter·er** *n.*

loll /lol/ *v.* **1** *intr.* stand, sit, or recline in a lazy attitude. **2** *intr.* (foll. by *out*) (of the tongue) hang out. **3** *tr.* (foll. by *out*) hang (one's tongue) out. **4** *tr.* let (one's head or limbs) rest lazily on something. □□ **loll·er** *n.*

lol·la·pa·loo·za /loləpəlṓzə/ *n.* (also **la·la·pa·loo·za**) *N. Amer. colloq.* a particularly impressive or attractive person or thing.

lol·li·pop /lóleepop/ *n.* a large, usu. flat, round candy on a small stick.

lol·lop /lóləp/ *v.intr. colloq.* flop about.

lol·ly /lólee/ *n.* (*pl.* **-ies**) *colloq.* a lollipop.

Lom·bard·y pop·lar /lómberdee, lúm-/ *n.* a variety of poplar with an especially tall slender form.

lo·ment /lṓment/ *n. Bot.* a kind of pod that breaks up into one-seeded joints when mature. □□ **lo·men·ta·ceous** /-táyshəs/ *adj.*

Lon·don·er /lúndənər/ *n.* a native or inhabitant of London.

lone /lōn/ *attrib.adj.* **1** (of a person) solitary; without a companion or supporter. **2** (of a place) unfrequented; uninhabited; lonely. **3** *literary* feeling or causing to feel lonely.

lone·ly /lṓnlee/ *adj.* (**lonelier, loneliest**) **1** solitary;

LOGANBERRY
(*Rubus loganobaccus*)

L

companionless; isolated. **2** (of a place) unfrequented. **3** sad because without friends or company. □□ **lone·li·ness** *n.*

lone·ly heart *n.* a lonely person (in sense 3).

lon·er /lṓnər/ *n.* a person or animal that prefers not to associate with others.

lone·some /lṓnsəm/ *adj.* **1** solitary; lonely. **2** feeling lonely or forlorn. **3** causing such a feeling. □ **by** (or **on**) **one's lonesome** all alone. □□ **lone·some·ness** *n.*

lone wolf *n.* a person who prefers to act alone.

long¹ /lawng, long/ *adj., n., & adv.* ● *adj.* (**longer** /láwnggər, lóng-/; **longest** /láwnggist, lóng-/) **1** measuring much from end to end in space or time (*a long line; a long journey; a long time ago*). **2** (following a measurement) in length or duration (*three miles long*). **3** relatively great in extent or duration (*a long meeting*). **4 a** consisting of a large number of items (*a long list*). **b** seemingly more than the stated amount; tedious; lengthy (*ten long miles; tired after a long day*). **5** of elongated shape. **6 a** lasting or reaching far back or forward in time (*a long friendship*). **b** (of a person's memory) retaining things for a long time. **7** far-reaching; acting at a distance; involving a great interval or difference. **8** *Phonet. & Prosody* of a vowel or syllable: **a** having the greater of the two recognized durations. **b** stressed. **c** (of a vowel in English) having the pronunciation shown in the name of the letter (as in *pile* and *cute*, which have a long *i* and *u*, as distinct from *pill* and *cut*). **9** (of odds or a chance) reflecting or representing a low level of probability. **10** *Stock Exch.* **a** (of stocks) bought in large quantities in advance, with the expectation of a rise in price. **b** (of a broker, etc.) buying, etc., on this basis. **11** (of a bill of exchange) maturing at a distant date. **12** (of a cold drink) large and refreshing. **13** *colloq.* (of a person) tall. **14** (foll. by *on*) *colloq.* well supplied with. ● *n.* **1** a long interval or period (*shall not be away for long; it will not take long*). **2** *Phonet.* **a** a long syllable or vowel. **b** a mark indicating that a vowel is long. **3 a** a long-dated stock. **b** a person who buys this. ● *adv.* (**longer** /lónggər/; **longest** /lónggist/) **1** by or for a long time (*long before; long ago; long live the king!*). **2** (following nouns of duration) throughout a specified time (*all day long*). **3** (in *compar.*; with *neg.*) after an implied point of time (*shall not wait any longer*). □ **as** (or **so**) **long as 1** during the whole time that. **2** provided that; only if. **at long last** see LAST¹. **before long** fairly soon (*shall see you before long*). **be long** (often foll. by *pres. part.* or *in* + verbal noun) take a long time; be slow (*I won't be long*). **in the long run 1** over a long period. **2** eventually; finally. **long ago** in the distant past. **the long and the short of it 1** all that can or need be said. **2** the eventual outcome. **long in the tooth** rather old (orig. of horses, from the recession of the gums with age). □□ **long·ish** *adj.*

long² /lawng, long/ *v.intr.* (foll. by *for* or *to* + infin.) have a strong wish or desire for.

long. *abbr.* longitude.

long·board /láwngbawrd, lóng-/ *n.* a type of surfboard.

long·boat /láwngbōt, lóng-/ *n.* a sailing ship's largest boat.

long·bow /láwngbō, lóng-/ ◄ *n.* a bow drawn by hand and shooting a long feathered arrow.

long·case clock *n.* a grandfather clock.

long-dis·tance *adj.* **1** (of a telephone call, public transport, etc.) between distant places. **2** (of a weather forecast) long-range.

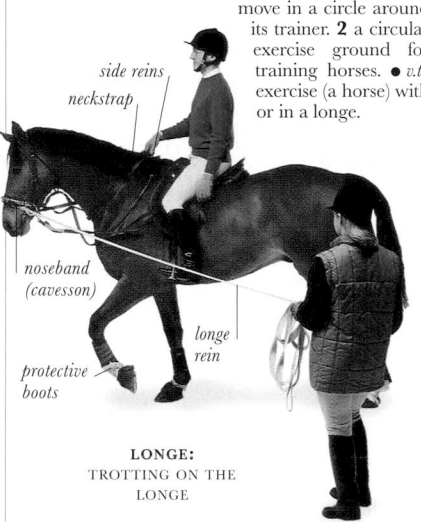

side reins
neckstrap
noseband (cavesson)
longe rein
protective boots

LONGE:
TROTTING ON THE
LONGE

long di·vi·sion *n.* division of numbers with details of the calculations written down.

long-drawn *adj.* (also **long-drawn-out**) prolonged, esp. unduly.

longe /lonj/ *n. & v.* (also **lunge** /lunj/) ● *n.* **1** ▲ a long rope on which a horse is held and made to move in a circle around its trainer. **2** a circular exercise ground for training horses. ● *v.tr.* exercise (a horse) with or in a longe.

lon·gev·i·ty /lonjévitee, lawn-/ *n.* long life.

lon·ge·ron /lónjərən/ *n.* a longitudinal member of a plane's fuselage.

long face *n.* a dismal or disappointed expression. □□ **long-faced** *adj.*

long·hair /láwnghair, lóng-/ *n.* a person characterized by the associations of long hair, esp. a hippie or intellectual.

long·hand /láwnghand, lóng-/ *n.* ordinary handwriting (as opposed to shorthand or typing or printing).

long haul *adj.* **1** the transport of goods or passengers over a long distance. **2** a prolonged effort or task.

long·head·ed /láwnghedid, lóng-/ *adj.* shrewd; far-seeing. □□ **long·head·ed·ness** *n.*

long·horn /láwnghawrn, lóng-/ *n.* **1** ► one of a breed of cattle with long horns. **2** any beetle of the family Cerambycidae with long antennae.

long·house /láwnghows, lóng-/ *n.* a tribal communal dwelling, esp. in N. America and the Far East.

lon·gi·corn /lónjikawrn/ *n.* a longhorn beetle.

long·ing /láwnging, lóng-/ *n. & adj.* ● *n.* a feeling of intense desire. ● *adj.* having or showing this feeling. □□ **long·ing·ly** *adv.*

lon·gi·tude /lónjitōōd, -tyōōd, lawn-/ *n.* **1** *Geog.* ▲ the angular distance east or west from a standard meridian such as Greenwich to the meridian of any place. ¶ Symb.: λ. **2** *Astron.* the angular distance of a celestial body north or south of the ecliptic measured along a great circle through the body and the poles of the ecliptic.

long johns *n.pl. colloq.* = LONG UNDERWEAR.

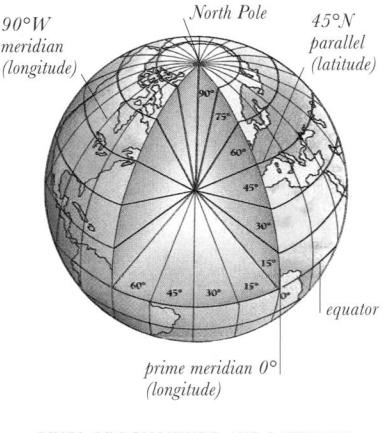

LONGHORN
COW

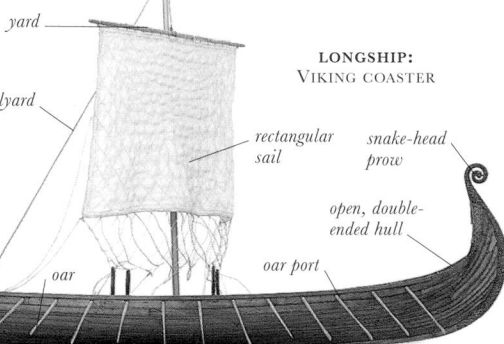

LONGITUDE

Lines of longitude, or meridians, are imaginary lines drawn around the Earth from the North Pole to the South Pole. Positions of longitude are given in degrees east or west of the prime meridian, which passes through Greenwich, England. In contrast, lines of latitude, or parallels, are drawn around the Earth parallel to the equator. Positions of latitude are given in degrees north or south of the equator.

90°W meridian (longitude)
North Pole
45°N parallel (latitude)
equator
prime meridian 0° (longitude)

LINES OF LONGITUDE AND LATITUDE
ON A GLOBE OF THE EARTH

L

long jump *n.* a track-and-field contest of jumping as far as possible along the ground in one leap.

long-life *adj. Brit.* (of consumable goods) treated to preserve freshness.

long-lived *adj.* having a long life; durable.

long meas·ure *n.* **1** *archaic* linear measure (of miles, meters, etc.). **2** (also **long meter**) *Mus.* **a** a hymn stanza of four lines with eight syllables each. **b** a quatrain of iambic tetrameters with alternate lines rhyming.

long-play·ing *adj.* (of a phonograph record) playing for about 20–30 minutes on each side.

long-range *adj.* **1** extending a long distance. **2** extending far into the future.

long-run·ning *adj.* continuing for a long time.

long·ship /láwngship, lóng-/ *n. hist.* ▼ a long, narrow warship with many rowers, used esp. by the Vikings.

masthead
yard
halyard
rectangular sail
snake-head prow
snake-tail stern
open, double-ended hull
tiller
oar
oar port
steering oar
keel

LONGSHIP:
VIKING COASTER

LONGBOW:
15TH-CENTURY
LONGBOW AND
ARCHER

string
stave
arrow

LONGSHORE DRIFT

Longshore drift is the movement of sand and pebbles along the shoreline, caused by the ebb and flow of waves and by the wind. This continual movement means that a beach in winter may consist of coarse pebbles, but the same beach in summer may be sandy. In places where longshore drift is strong, it can wash sand across a bay or river mouth, depositing it to form a spit. To reduce the amount of beach matter being washed away in this manner, barriers, called groins, are often built at right angles out into the water.

river mouth   *hook*

sand spit

sand and pebbles

beach matter buildup

groin

receding wave

angled approaching wave

PROCESS OF LONGSHORE DRIFT ON A BEACH

---

long·shore /láwngshawr, lóng-/ *adj.* **1** existing on or frequenting the shore. **2** directed along the shore.

long·shore drift *n.* ▲ the movement of material along a coast by waves that approach it at an angle to the shore but recede directly away from it.

long·shore·man /láwngshawrmən, lóng-/ *n.* (*pl.* **-men**) a person employed to load and unload ships.

long shot *n.* **1** a wild guess or venture. **2** a bet at long odds. **3** *Cinematog.* a shot including objects at a distance. □ **not by a long shot** by no means.

long·sight·ed /láwngsítid, lóng-/ *adj.* **1** able to see clearly only what is comparatively distant. **2** having imagination or foresight. □□ **long·sight·ed·ness** *n.*

long-sleeved *adj.* with sleeves reaching to the wrist.

long·spur /lawng·spər/ *n.* ▶ a N. American bunting of the genus *Calcarius*.

long-stand·ing *adj.* that has long existed; not recent.

long-suf·fer·ing *adj.* bearing provocation patiently. □□ **long-suf·fer·ing·ly** *adv.*

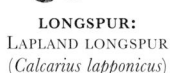

LONGSPUR: LAPLAND LONGSPUR (*Calcarius lapponicus*)

long suit *n.* **1** ▼ many cards of one suit in a hand (esp. more than 3 or 4 in a hand of 13). **2** a thing at which one excels.

LONG SUIT OF HEARTS IN A MIXED HAND

---

long-term *adj.* occurring in or relating to a long period of time (*long-term plans*).

long·time /láwngtīm, lóng-/ *adj.* that has been such for a long time.

lon·gueur /lawngŏr, long-/ *n.* **1** a tedious passage in a book, etc. **2** a tedious stretch of time.

long un·der·wear *n.* a warm, close-fitting undergarment with ankle-length legs and often a long-sleeved top.

long·ways /láwngwayz, lóng-/ *adv.* (also **long·wise** /-wīz/) = LENGTHWISE.

long-wind·ed /láwngwíndid, lóng-/ *adj.* **1** (of speech or writing) tediously lengthy. **2** able to run a long distance without rest. □□ **long-wind·ed·ly** *adv.* **long-wind·ed·ness** *n.*

lon·i·ce·ra /lənísərə/ *n.* **1** a dense evergreen shrub, *Lonicera nitidum*, much used as hedging. **2** = HONEYSUCKLE.

loo[1] /lōō/ *n. Brit. colloq.* a toilet.

loo[2] /lōō/ *n.* **1** a card game with penalties paid to the pool. **2** this penalty.

loo·fah /lōōfə/ *n.* (also **luf·fa** /lúfə/) **1** ▶ a climbing gourdlike plant, *Luffa cylindrica*, native to Asia, producing edible marrow-like fruits. **2** the dried fibrous vascular system of this fruit used as a sponge.

look /lŏŏk/ *v., n., & int.* ● *v.* **1 a** *intr.* (often foll. by *at*) use one's sight; turn one's eyes in some direction. **b** *tr.* turn one's eyes on; contemplate or examine (*looked me in the eyes*). **2** *intr.* **a** make a visual or mental search (*I'll look in the morning*). **b** (foll. by *at*) consider; examine (*we must look at the facts*). **3** *intr.* (foll. by *for*) **a** search for. **b** hope or be on the watch for. **c** expect. **4** *intr.* inquire (*when one looks deeper*). **5** *intr.* have a specified appearance; seem (*look a fool*; *look foolish*). **6** *intr.* (foll. by *to*) **a** consider; take care of; be careful about (*look to the future*). **b** rely on (a person or thing) (*you can look to me for support*). **c** expect. **7** *intr.* (foll. by *into*) investigate or examine. **8** *tr.* (foll. by *what*, *where*, etc. + clause) ascertain or observe by sight (*look where we are*). **9** *intr.* (of a thing) face or be turned, or have or afford an outlook, in a specified direction. **10** *tr.* express, threaten, or show (an emotion, etc.) by one's looks. **11** *intr.* (foll. by *that* + clause) take care; make sure. **12** *intr.* (foll. by *to* + infin.) expect (*am looking to finish this today*). ● *n.* **1** an act of looking; a glance (*a scornful look*). **2** (in *sing.* or

---

pl.) the appearance of a face; a person's expression or personal aspect. **3** the (esp. characteristic) appearance of a thing (*the place has a European look*). ● *int.* (also **look here!**) calling attention, expressing a protest, etc. □ **look after 1** attend to; take care of. **2** follow with the eye. **3** seek for. **look alive** (or **lively**) *colloq.* be brisk and alert. **look around 1** look in every or another direction. **2** examine the objects of interest in a place. **3** examine the possibilities, etc., with a view to deciding on a course of action. **look as if** suggest by appearance the belief that (*it looks as if he's gone*). **look back 1** (foll. by *on*, *upon*, *to*) turn one's thoughts to (something past). **2** (usu. with *neg.*) cease to progress (*since then we have never looked back*). **look before you leap** avoid precipitate action. **look daggers at** see DAGGER. **look down on** (or **upon** or **look down one's nose at**) regard with contempt or a feeling of superiority. **look for trouble** see TROUBLE. **look forward to** await (an expected event) eagerly or with specified feelings. **look in** make a short visit or call. **look a person in the eye** (or **eyes** or **face**) look directly and unashamedly at him or her. **look like 1** have the appearance of. **2** threaten or promise (*it looks like rain*). **3** indicate the presence of (*it looks like woodworm*). **look on 1** (often foll. by *as*) regard (*looks on you as a friend*). **2** be a spectator; avoid participation. **look oneself** appear in good health (esp. after illness, etc.). **look out 1** direct one's sight out of a window, etc. **2** (often foll. by *for*) be vigilant or prepared. **3** (foll. by *on*, *over*, etc.) have or afford a specified outlook. **4** *Brit.* search for and produce (*shall look one out for you*). **look over 1** inspect or survey (*looked over the house*). **2** examine (a document, etc.), esp. cursorily (*I'll look it over*). **look sharp** act promptly; make haste. **look through 1** examine the contents of, esp. cursorily. **2** penetrate (a pretense or pretender) with insight. **3** ignore by pretending not to see (*I waved, but you just looked through me*). **look up 1** search for (esp. information in a book). **2** *colloq.* go to visit (a person). **3** raise one's eyes. **4** improve, esp. in price, prosperity, or well-being (*things are looking up*). **look a person up and down** scrutinize a person keenly or contemptuously. **look up to** respect or venerate. **not like the look of** find alarming or suspicious. □□ **-looking** *adj.* (in comb.).

look·a·like a person or thing closely resembling another (*an Elvis look-alike*).

look·er /lŏŏkər/ *n.* **1** a person having a specified appearance (*a good-looker*). **2** *colloq.* an attractive person.

look·er-on *n.* a person who is a mere spectator.

look·ing glass /lŏŏking glas/ *n.* a mirror for looking at oneself.

look·out /lŏŏkowt/ *n.* **1** a watch or looking out (*on the lookout for bargains*). **2 a** a post of observation. **b** a person or party or boat stationed to keep watch. **3** a view over a landscape. **4** *colloq.* a person's own concern.

look-see *n. colloq.* a survey or inspection.

look·up /lŏŏkup/ *n.* the action of systematic electronic information retrieval.

loom[1] /lōōm/ *n.* an apparatus for weaving yarn or thread into fabric. ▷ WEAVE

loom[2] /lōōm/ *v.intr.* (often foll. by *up*) **1** come into sight dimly, esp. as a vague and often threatening shape. **2** (of an event or prospect) be ominously close.

brown peel

fibrous fruit

LOOFAH: SMOOTH LOOFAH (*Luffa cylindrica*)

loon /lōōn/ *n.* **1** an aquatic diving bird with a sharp bill. **2** *colloq.* a crazy person (cf. LOONY).

loon·y /lōōnee/ *n. & adj. sl.* ● *n.* (*pl.* **-ies**) a mad or silly person; a lunatic. ● *adj.* (**loonier**, **looniest**) crazy; silly. □□ **loon·i·ness** *n.*

loon·y bin *n. sl.* a mental home or hospital.

loop /lōōp/ *n. & v.* ● *n.* **1 a** a figure produced by a

L

curve, or a doubled thread, etc., that crosses itself. **b** anything forming this figure. ▷ KNOT. **2** a similarly shaped attachment or ornament formed of cord or thread, etc., and fastened at the crossing. **3** a ring or curved piece of material as a handle, etc. **4** a contraceptive coil. **5** a railroad or telegraph line that diverges from a main line and joins it again. **6** a maneuver in which an airplane describes a vertical loop. **7** *Skating* a maneuver describing a curve that crosses itself, made on a single edge. **8** *Electr.* a complete circuit for a current. **9** an endless strip of tape or film allowing continuous repetition. **10** *Computing* a programmed sequence of instructions that is repeated until or while a condition is satisfied. ● *v.* **1** *tr.* form (thread, etc.) into a loop or loops. **2** *tr.* enclose with or as with a loop. **3** *tr.* (often foll. by *up, back, together*) fasten or join with a loop or loops. **4** *intr.* **a** form a loop. **b** move in looplike patterns. **5** *intr.* (also **loop the loop**) *Aeron.* perform an aerobatic loop.

loop·er /lōopər/ *n.* **1** a caterpillar of the geometer moth, which progresses by arching itself into loops. **2** a device for making loops. **3** *Baseball* a shallow fly ball that drops for a hit.

loop·hole /lōop-hōl/ *n.* **1** a means of evading a rule, etc., without infringing the letter of it. **2** ◀ a narrow vertical slit in a wall. ▷ NORMAN

LOOPHOLE IN A CASTLE WALL

loop·y /lōopee/ *adj.* (**loopier, loopiest**) **1** *sl.* crazy. **2** having many loops.

loose /lōos/ *adj., n., & v.* ● *adj.* **1 a** not or no longer held by bonds or restraint. **b** (of an animal) not confined or tethered, etc. **2** detached or detachable from its place (*has come loose*). **3** not held together or contained or fixed. **4** not specially fastened or packaged (*loose papers; had her hair loose*). **5** hanging partly free (*a loose end*). **6** slack; relaxed; not tense or tight. **7** not compact or dense (*loose soil*). **8** (of language, concepts, etc.) inexact; conveying only the general sense. **9** (preceding an agent noun) doing the expressed action in a loose or careless manner (*a loose thinker*). **10** morally lax; dissolute (*loose living*). **11** (of the tongue) likely to speak indiscreetly. **12** (of the bowels) tending to diarrhea. **13** *Sports* **a** (of a ball) in play but not in any player's possession. **b** (of play, etc.) with the players not close together. **14** *Cricket* **a** (of bowling) inaccurately pitched. **b** (of fielding) careless or bungling. **15** (in *comb.*) loosely (*loose-flowing; loose-fitting*). ● *n.* **1** a state of freedom or unrestrainedness. **2** loose play in soccer (*in the loose*). **3** free expression. ● *v.tr.* **1** release; set free; free from constraint. **2** untie or undo (something that constrains). **3** free the bowels from moorings. **4** relax (*loosed my hold on it*). **5** discharge (a bullet or arrow, etc.). □ **at loose ends** (of a person) unoccupied, esp. temporarily. **on the loose 1** escaped from captivity. **2** having a free enjoyable time. **play fast and loose** ignore one's obligations; be unreliable; trifle. □□ **loose·ly** *adv.* **loose·ness** *n.* **loos·ish** *adj.*

loose change *n.* money as coins in the pocket, etc., for casual use.

loose-leaf *adj. & n.* ● *adj.* (of a notebook, manual, etc.) with each leaf separate and removable. ● *n.* a loose-leaf notebook, etc.

loose-limbed *adj.* having supple limbs.

loos·en /lōosən/ *v.* **1** *tr. & intr.* make or become less tight or compact or firm. **2** *tr.* make (a regime, etc.) less severe. **3** *tr.* release (the bowels) from constipation. **4** *tr.* relieve (a cough) from dryness. □ **loosen a person's tongue** make a person talk freely. **loosen up** = *limber up* (see LIMBER[1]). □□ **loos·en·er** *n.*

loose·strife /lōos-strīf/ *n.* **1** any marsh plant of the genus *Lysimachia*, esp. the golden or yellow loosestrife, *L. vulgaris*. **2** any plant of the genus *Lythrum*, esp. the purple loosestrife, *L. salicaria*, with racemes of star-shaped purple flowers.

loot /lōot/ *n. & v.* ● *n.* **1** goods taken from an enemy; booty; spoils. **2** illicit gains made by an official. **3** *sl.* money. ● *v.tr.* **1** rob (premises) or steal (goods) left unprotected, esp. after riots. **2** plunder or sack (a city, building, etc.). **3** carry off as booty. □□ **loot·er** *n.*

lop[1] /lop/ *v.* (**lopped, lopping**) **1** *tr.* **a** (often foll. by *off, away*) cut or remove (a part or parts) from a whole, esp. branches from a tree. **b** remove branches from (a tree). **2** *tr.* (often foll. by *off, away*) remove (items) as superfluous. **3** *intr.* (foll. by *at*) make lopping strokes on (a tree, etc.). □□ **lop·per** *n.*

lop[2] /lop/ *v.* (**lopped, lopping**) **1** *intr. & tr.* hang limply. **2** *intr.* (foll. by *about*) slouch; dawdle; hang about. **3** *intr.* move with short bounds. **4** *tr.* (of an animal) let (the ears) hang.

lope /lōp/ *v. & n.* ● *v.intr.* (esp. of animals) run with a long bounding stride. ● *n.* a long bounding stride.

lop-eared *adj.* (of an animal) having drooping ears.

lop·sid·ed /lópsídid/ *adj.* with one side lower or smaller than the other. □□ **lop·sid·ed·ly** *adv.* **lop·sid·ed·ness** *n.*

lo·qua·cious /lōkwáyshəs/ *adj.* **1** talkative. **2** (of birds or water) chattering; babbling. □□ **lo·qua·cious·ly** *adv.* **lo·qua·cious·ness** *n.* **lo·quac·i·ty** /-kwásitee/ *n.*

lo·quat /lókwot/ *n.* **1** a rosaceous tree, *Eriobotrya japonica*, bearing small, yellow egg-shaped fruits. **2** this fruit.

lo·ran /láwran/ *n.* a system of long-distance navigation in which position is determined from the intervals between signal pulses received from widely spaced radio transmitters (acronym for *long-range* navigation).

lord /lawrd/ *n., int., & v.* ● *n.* **1** a master or ruler. **2** *hist.* a feudal superior, esp. of a manor. **3** (in the UK) a peer of the realm or a person entitled to the title Lord. **4** (**Lord**) (often prec. by *the*) a name for God or Christ. **5** (**Lord**) **a** a prefixed as the designation of a marquess, earl, viscount, or baron. **b** prefixed to the Christian name of the younger son of a duke or marquess. **6** *Astrol.* the ruling planet (of a sign, house, or chart). ● *int.* (**Lord**) expressing surprise, dismay, etc. ● *v.tr.* confer the title of Lord upon. □ **live like a lord** live sumptuously. **lord it over** domineer. **lord over** (usu. in *passive*) domineer; rule over. □□ **lord·like** *adj.*

lord·ling /láwrdling/ *n.* usu. *derog.* a minor lord.

lord·ly /láwrdlee/ *adj.* (**lordlier, lordliest**) **1** haughty; imperious. **2** suitable for a lord. □□ **lord·li·ness** *n.*

lord·ship /láwrdship/ *n.* **1** (usu. **Lordship**) a title used in addressing or referring to a man with the rank of Lord or (in the UK) a judge or a bishop (*Your Lordship; His Lordship*). **2** (foll. by *of, over*) dominion, rule, or ownership. **3** the condition of being a lord.

Lord's Prayer the prayer taught by Jesus to his disciples.

Lord·y /láwrdee/ *int.* = LORD *int.*

lore /lawr/ *n.* a body of traditions and knowledge on a subject or held by a particular group (*herbal lore; gypsy lore*).

lor·gnette /lawrnyét/ *n.* (in *sing.* or *pl.*) ▶ a pair of eyeglasses or opera glasses held by a long handle.

LORGNETTE: LATE 19TH-CENTURY TORTOISESHELL LORGNETTE

lor·i·cate /láwrikayt, -kit, lór-/ *adj. & n. Zool.* ● *adj.* having a defensive armor of bone, plates, scales, etc. ● *n.* an animal with this.

lor·i·keet /láwrikeet, lór-/ *n.* any of various small, brightly colored parrots of the subfamily Loriinae. ▷ PARROT

LORIS: SLENDER LORIS (*Loris tardigradus*)

lo·ris /láwris/ *n.* (*pl.* same) ▲ either of two small, tailless nocturnal primates, *Loris tardigradus* of S. India (**slender loris**), and *Nycticebus coucang* of the E. Indies (**slow loris**).

lorn /lawrn/ *adj. literary* desolate; forlorn; abandoned.

lor·ry /láwree, lór-/ *n. Brit.* (*pl.* **-ies**) **1** a large strong motor vehicle for transporting goods, etc.; a truck. **2** a long flat low wagon. **3** a railway freight car.

lo·ry /láwree/ *n.* (*pl.* **-ies**) any of various brightly colored Australasian parrots of the subfamily Loriinae.

lose /lōoz/ *v.* (*past* and *past part.* **lost** /lawst, lost/) **1** *tr.* be deprived of or cease to have, esp. by negligence or misadventure. **2** *tr.* **a** be deprived of (a person, esp. a close relative) by death. **b** suffer the loss of (a baby) in childbirth. **3** *tr.* become unable to find; fail to keep in sight or follow or mentally grasp (*lose one's way*). **4** *tr.* let or have pass from one's control or reach (*lose one's chance*). **5** *tr.* be defeated in (a game, race, lawsuit, battle, etc.). **6** *tr.* evade; get rid of (*lost our pursuers*). **7** *tr.* fail to obtain, catch, or perceive (*lose a train; lose a word*). **8** *tr.* forfeit (a stake, deposit, right to a thing, etc.). **9** *tr.* spend (time, efforts, etc.) to no purpose (*lost no time in sounding the alarm*). **10** *intr.* **a** suffer loss or detriment. **b** be worse off, esp. financially. **11** *tr.* cause (a person) the loss of (*will lose you your job*). **12** *intr. & tr.* (of a timepiece) become slow; become slow by (a specified amount of time). **13** *tr.* (in *passive*) **a** disappear; perish; be dead (*was lost in the war*). **b** fall; be damned (*souls lost to drunkenness and greed*). **14** (as **lost** *adj.*) **a** gone, stray; mislaid; forgotten (*lost valuables; a lost art*). **b** dead; destroyed (*lost comrades*). **c** damned; fallen (*lost souls in hell*). □ **be lost** (or **lose oneself**) **in** be engrossed in. **be lost on** be wasted on, or not noticed or appreciated by. **be lost to** be no longer affected by or accessible to. **be lost without** have great difficulty if deprived of (*am lost without my diary*). **get lost** *sl.* (usu. in *imper.*) go away. **lose one's balance 1** fail to remain stable; fall. **2** fail to retain one's composure. **lose one's cool** *colloq.* lose one's composure. **lose face** be humiliated; lose one's credibility. **lose ground** see GROUND[1]. **lose one's head** see HEAD. **lose heart** be discouraged. **lose one's heart** see HEART. **lose one's nerve** become timid or irresolute. **lose out** (often foll. by *on*) *colloq.* be unsuccessful; not get a fair chance or advantage (in). **lose sleep over a thing** lie awake worrying about a thing. **lose one's temper** become angry. **lose time** allow time to pass with something unachieved, etc. **lose touch** see TOUCH. **lose track of** see TRACK[1]. **lose the** (or **one's**) **way** become lost; fail to reach one's destination.

los·er /lōozər/ *n.* **1** a person or thing that loses or has lost (esp. a contest or game). **2** *colloq.* a person who regularly fails.

los·ing bat·tle *n.* a contest or effort in which failure seems certain.

loss /laws, los/ *n.* **1** the act or an instance of losing; being lost. **2** a person, thing, or amount lost. **3** the detriment or disadvantage resulting from losing (*it's no great loss*). □ **at a loss** (sold, etc.) for less than was paid for it. **be at a loss** be puzzled or uncertain. **be at a loss for words** not know what to say.

L

LOST-WAX PROCESS

In lost-wax casting, wax rods (runners and risers) are attached to a wax-covered clay model, creating channels for bronze to flow in. These are held in place with nails. The model is then encased in plaster and baked in a mold. The wax melts away through the channels, and the molten bronze is poured in. When the bronze has cooled, the mold is broken open. The runners and risers are then sawed off, and the clay core removed.

STAGES IN THE LOST-WAX PROCESS OF CASTING

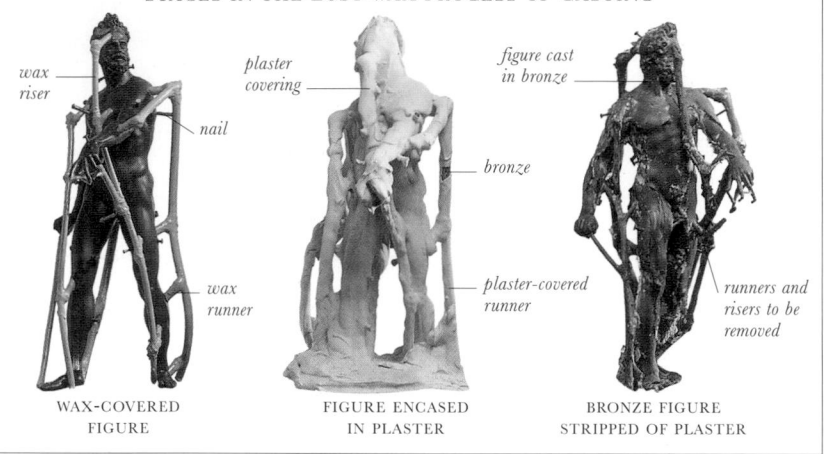

wax riser

nail

wax runner

plaster covering

bronze

plaster-covered runner

figure cast in bronze

runners and risers to be removed

WAX-COVERED FIGURE

FIGURE ENCASED IN PLASTER

BRONZE FIGURE STRIPPED OF PLASTER

L

loss lead·er *n.* an item sold at a loss to attract customers.

lost *past* and *past part.* of LOSE.

lost cause *n.* **1** an enterprise, etc., with no chance of success. **2** a person one can no longer hope to influence.

lost gen·er·a·tion *n.* **1** a generation with many of its men killed in war, esp. (**the Lost Generation**) that of the World War I era. **2** an emotionally and culturally unstable generation coming to maturity.

lost-wax pro·cess *n.* ▲ a method of bronze casting using a clay core and a wax coating placed in a mold: the wax is melted in the mold and bronze poured into the space left, producing a hollow bronze figure when the core is discarded.

lot /lot/ *n. & v.* ● *n.* **1** *colloq.* (prec. by *a* or in *pl.*) **a** a large number or amount. **b** *colloq.* much (*a lot warmer*; *smiles a lot*; *is lots better*). **2 a** each of a set of objects used in making a chance selection. **b** this method of deciding (*chosen by lot*). **3** a share, or the responsibility resulting from it. **4** a person's destiny, fortune, or condition. **5** a plot; an allotment of land (*parking lot*). **6** an article or set of articles for sale at an auction, etc. **7** a number or quantity of associated persons or things. ● *v.tr.* (**lotted**, **lotting**) divide into lots. □ **cast** (or **draw**) **lots** decide by means of lots. **throw in one's lot with** decide to share the fortunes of. **the** (or **the whole**) **lot** the whole number or quantity. **a whole lot** *colloq.* very much (*is a whole lot better*).

lo·thar·i·o /lōtháireeō/ *n.* (also **Lothario**) (*pl.* **-os**) a rake or libertine.

lo·tion /lṓshən/ *n.* a medicinal or cosmetic liquid applied externally.

lot·ter·y /lótəree/ *n.* (*pl.* **-ies**) **1** a means of raising money by selling numbered tickets and giving prizes to the holders of numbers drawn at random. **2** a thing whose success is governed by chance.

lot·to /lótō/ *n.* a game of chance like bingo, but with numbers drawn instead of called.

lo·tus /lṓtəs/ *n.* **1** (in Greek mythology) a legendary plant inducing luxurious languor when eaten. **2 a** ◄ any water lily of the genus *Nelumbo*, esp. *N. nucifera* of India, with large pink flowers. **b** this flower used symbolically in Hinduism and Buddhism. **3** an Egyptian water lily, *Nymphaea lotus*, with white flowers. **4** any plant of the genus *Lotus*, e.g., bird's-foot trefoil.

LOTUS: RED LOTUS (*Nelumbo nucifera*)

lo·tus-eat·er *n.* a person given to indolent enjoyment.

lo·tus po·si·tion *n.* ► a cross-legged position of meditation with the feet resting on the thighs.

louche /lōōsh/ *adj.* disreputable; shifty.

loud /lowd/ *adj. & adv.* ● *adj.* **1 a** strongly audible, esp. noisily or oppressively so. **b** able or liable to produce loud sounds (*a loud engine*). **c** clamorous; insistent (*loud complaints*). **2** (of colors, design, etc.) gaudy; obtrusive. **3** (of behavior) aggressive and noisy. ● *adv.* in a loud manner. □ **out loud 1** aloud. **2** loudly (*laughed out loud*). □□ **loud·en** *v.tr. & intr.* **loud·ish** *adj.* **loud·ly** *adv.* **loud·ness** *n.*

LOTUS POSITION

loud·mouth /lówdmowth/ *n. colloq.* a noisily self-assertive, vociferous person. □□ **loud·mouthed** *adj.*

loud·speak·er /lówdspeékər/ *n.* ▼ an apparatus that converts electrical impulses into sound, esp. music and voice. ▷ RADIO

lough /lok, lokh/ *n. Ir.* = LAKE.

lounge /lownj/ *v. & n.* ● *v.intr.* **1** recline comfortably and casually; loll. **2** stand or move about idly. ● *n.* **1** a place for lounging, esp.: **a** a bar or other public room (e.g., in a hotel). **b** a place in an airport, etc., with seats for waiting passengers. **c** *Brit.* a sitting room in a house. **2** a spell of lounging.

lounge liz·ard *n. colloq.* **1** a person, esp. a man, who frequents bars, etc. **2** an idler in fashionable society.

loung·er /lównjər/ *n.* **1** a person who lounges. **2** a piece of furniture for relaxing on. **3** a casual garment for wearing when relaxing.

loupe /lōōp/ *n.* ► a small magnifying glass used by jewelers, etc.

lour var. of LOWER³.

louse /lows/ *n. & v.* ● *n.* **1** (*pl.* **lice** /līs/) **a** a parasitic insect, *Pediculus humanus*, infesting the human hair and skin and transmitting various diseases. ▷ PARASITE. **b** any insect of the order Anoplura or Mallophaga parasitic on mammals, birds, fish, or plants. **2** *sl.* (*pl.* **louses**) a contemptible or unpleasant person. ● *v.tr.* remove lice from. □ **louse up** *sl.* make a mess of.

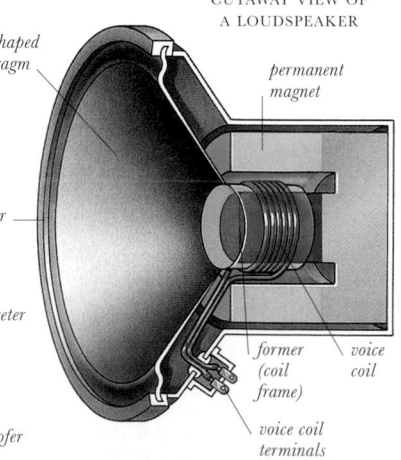

lens

protective case

LOUPE

lous·y /lówzee/ *adj.* (**lousier**, **lousiest**) **1** infested with lice. **2** *colloq.* very bad; disgusting (also as a term of general disparagement). **3** *colloq.* (often foll. by *with*) well supplied; teeming (with). □□ **lous·i·ly** *adv.* **lous·i·ness** *n.*

lout /lowt/ *n.* a rough, crude, or ill-mannered person. □□ **lout·ish** *adj.* **lout·ish·ly** *adv.* **lout·ish·ness** *n.*

lou·ver /lṓōvər/ *n.* **1** a set, or each of a set, of overlapping slats designed to admit air and some light and exclude rain. **2** a domed structure on a roof with side openings for ventilation, etc. □□ **lou·vered** *adj.*

lou·ver boards *n.* the slats or boards making up a louver.

lov·a·ble /lúvəbəl/ *adj.* (also **love·a·ble**) inspiring or deserving of love or affection. □□ **lov·a·ble·ness** *n.* **lov·a·bly** *adv.*

LOUDSPEAKER

A loudspeaker produces sound waves from electrical signals. The signals pass through a voice coil, which is attached to a cone-shaped diaphragm. The coil acts as an electromagnet, and around it is a strong permanent magnet. When the current flows one way, the magnetic forces push the electromagnet and the cone outward. When the current flows the other way, the cone is pulled inward. The vibrations of the cone produce sound waves.

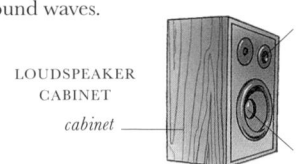

LOUDSPEAKER CABINET

cabinet

CUTAWAY VIEW OF A LOUDSPEAKER

cone-shaped diaphragm

collar

tweeter

woofer

permanent magnet

former (coil frame)

voice coil

voice coil terminals

LOVAGE
(*Levisticum officinale*)

lov·age /lúvij/ *n.* **1** ◄ a S. European herb, *Levisticum officinale*, used for flavoring, etc. **2** a white-flowered umbelliferous plant, *Ligusticum scoticum*.

lov·at /lúvət/ *n.* (also *attrib.*) a muted green color found esp. in tweed and woolen garments.

love /luv/ *n. & v.* ● *n.* **1** deep affection or fondness. **2** sexual passion. **3** sexual relations. **4** a beloved one; a sweetheart (often as a form of address). **5** *colloq.* a person of whom one is fond. **6** affectionate greetings (*give him my love*). **7** (often **Love**) a representation of Cupid. **8** (in some games) no score; nil. ● *v.tr.* **1** (also *absol.*) feel love or deep fondness for. **2** delight in; admire; greatly cherish. **3** *colloq.* like very much (*loves books*). **4** (foll. by verbal noun, or *to* + infin.) be inclined, esp. as a habit; greatly enjoy (*children love dressing up*). □ **fall in love** (often foll. by *with*) develop a great (esp. sexual) love (for). **for love** for pleasure not profit. **for the love of** for the sake of. **in love** (often foll. by *with*) deeply enamored (of). **make love** (often foll. by *to*) **1** have sexual intercourse (with). **2** *archaic* pay amorous attention (to). **not for love or money** *colloq.* not in any circumstances. **out of love** no longer in love.

love·a·ble var. of LOVABLE.

love af·fair *n.* **1** a romantic or sexual relationship between two people in love. **2** a passion for something.

love bird /lúvbərd/ *n.* **1** ► any of various African and Madagascan parrots, genus *Agapornis personata*. **2** (in *pl.*) a pair of lovers who display much affection.

love child *n.* a child born out of wedlock.

love-hate re·la·tion·ship *n.* an intensely emotional relationship in which one or each party has ambivalent feelings of love and hate for the other.

love-in /lúvin/ *n. colloq.* (esp. among hippies in the 1960s) a gathering at which people are encouraged to express friendship and physical attraction.

love·less /lúvlis/ *adj.* without love; unloving or unloved or both. □□ **love·less·ly** *adv.* **love·less·ness** *n.*

love let·ter *n.* a letter expressing feelings of sexual love.

love life *n.* one's amorous or sexual relationships.

love·lorn /lúvlawrn/ *adj.* pining from unrequited love.

love·ly /lúvlee/ *adj. & n.* ● *adj.* (**lovelier, loveliest**) **1** exquisitely beautiful. **2** *colloq.* pleasing; delightful. ● *n.* (*pl.* **-ies**) *colloq.* a pretty woman. □ **lovely and** *colloq.* delightfully (*lovely and warm*). □□ **love·li·ness** *n.*

love·mak·ing /lúvmayking/ *n.* **1** amorous sexual activity, esp. sexual intercourse. **2** *archaic* courtship.

love nest *n.* a place of intimate lovemaking.

lov·er /lúvər/ *n.* **1** a person in love with another. **2** a person with whom another is having sexual relations. **3** (in *pl.*) a couple in love or having sexual relations. **4** a person who likes or enjoys something specified (*a music lover; a lover of words*).

love seat *n.* an armchair or small sofa for two.

love·sick /lúvsik/ *adj.* languishing with romantic love. □□ **love·sick·ness** *n.*

love-y-dove·y /lúveedúvee/ *adj. colloq.* fondly affectionate, esp. unduly sentimental.

lov·ing /lúving/ *adj. & n.* ● *adj.* feeling or showing love; affectionate. ● *n.* affection; active love. □□ **lov·ing·ly** *adv.* **lov·ing·ness** *n.*

lov·ing cup *n.* **1** a two-handled drinking cup passed around at banquets, etc. **2** a loving cup presented as a trophy.

low[1] /lō/ *adj., n., & adv.* ● *adj.* **1** of less than average height; not high or tall or reaching far up (*a low wall*). **2 a** situated close to ground or sea level, etc.; not elevated in position (*low altitude*). **b** (of the Sun) near the horizon. **c** (of latitude) near the equator. **3** of or in humble rank or position (*of low birth*). **4** of small or less than normal amount or extent or intensity (*low price; low temperature; low in calories*). **5** small or reduced in quantity (*stocks are low*). **6** coming below the normal level (*a dress with a low neck*). **7 a** dejected; lacking vigor (*feeling low; in low spirits*). **b** poorly nourished; indicative of poor nutrition. **8** (of a sound) not shrill or loud or high-pitched. **9** not exalted or sublime; commonplace. **10** unfavorable (*a low opinion*). **11** abject; mean; vulgar (*low cunning; low slang*). **12** (in *compar.*) situated on less high land or to the south. **13** (of a geographical period) earlier. ● *n.* **1** a low or the lowest level or number (*the dollar has reached a new low*). **2** an area of low pressure. ● *adv.* **1** in or to a low position or state. **2** in a low tone (*speak low*). **3** (of a sound) at or to a low pitch. □□ **low·ish** *adj.* **low·ness** *n.*

low[2] /lō/ *n. & v.* ● *n.* a sound made by cattle; a moo. ● *v.intr.* utter this sound.

low-ball *n. & v.* ● *n. Cards* a type of poker. ● *v.tr. & intr.* underestimate or underbid a price (usu. for a service) deliberately.

low beam *n.* an automobile headlight providing short-range illumination.

low·boy /lóboy/ *n.* a low chest or table with drawers and short legs.

low·brow /lóbrow/ *adj. & n.* ● *adj.* not highly intellectual or cultured. ● *n.* a lowbrow person. □□ **low·browed** *adj.*

Low Coun·tries *n.pl.* the Netherlands, Belgium, and Luxembourg.

low-cut *adj.* (of a dress, etc.) made with a low neckline.

low-down *adj. & n.* ● *adj.* abject; mean; dishonorable. ● *n. colloq.* (usu. foll. by *on*) the relevant information (about).

low·er[1] /lóər/ *adj. & adv.* ● *adj.* (*compar.* of LOW[1]). **1** less high in position or status. **2** situated below another part (*lower lip; lower atmosphere*). **3 a** situated on less highland (*Lower Egypt*). **b** situated to the south (*Lower California*). **4** (of a mammal, plant, etc.) evolved to a relatively small degree (e.g., a platypus or fungus). ● *adv.* in or to a lower position, status, etc. □□ **low·er·most** *adj.*

low·er[2] /lóər/ *v.* **1** *tr.* let or haul down. **2** *tr. & intr.* make or become lower. **3** *tr.* reduce the height or pitch or elevation of (*lower your voice; lower one's eyes*). **4** *tr.* degrade. **5** *tr. & intr.* diminish.

low·er[3] /lowər/ *v. & n.* (also **lour**) ● *v.intr.* **1** frown; look sullen. **2** (of the sky, etc.) look dark and threatening. ● *n.* **1** a scowl. **2** a gloomy look (of the sky, etc.). □□ **low·er·y** *adj.*

low·er·case /lóərkays/ *n., adj., & v.* ● *n.* small letters. ● *adj.* of or having small letters. ● *v.tr.* print or write in lowercase.

low·er class *n.* working-class people and their families. □□ **low·er-class** *adj.*

low·er court *n.* a court whose decisions may be overruled by another court on appeal.

low·er house *n.* the usu. larger body in a legislature, esp. in Britain, the House of Commons.

low·est com·mon mul·ti·ple *n.* the least quantity that is a multiple of two or more given quantities.

low fre·quen·cy *n.* (in radio) 30–300 kilohertz.

low gear *n.* a gear such that the driven end of a transmission revolves slower than the driving end.

low-grade *adj.* of low quality or strength.

low-key *adj.* lacking intensity or prominence; restrained.

LOVEBIRD:
MASKED LOVEBIRD
(*Agapornis personata*)

low·land /lóland/ *n. & adj.* ● *n.* **1** (usu. in *pl.*) low-lying country. **2** (**Lowland**) (usu. in *pl.*) the region of Scotland lying south and east of the Highlands. ● *adj.* of or in lowland or the Scottish Lowlands. □□ **low·land·er** *n.* (also **Low·land·er**).

low-lev·el *adj. Computing* (of a programming language) close in form to machine language.

low life *n.* **1** disreputable or criminal people or activities. **2** (**low-life**) *colloq.* a disreputable or criminal person.

low·light /lólīt/ *n.* **1** a monotonous or dull period; a feature of little prominence (*one of the lowlights of the evening*). **2** (usu. in *pl.*) a dark tint in the hair produced by dyeing.

low·ly /lólee/ *adj.* (**lowlier, lowliest**) **1** humble in feeling, behavior, or status. **2** modest; unpretentious. **3** (of an organism) evolved to only a slight degree. □□ **low·li·ness** *n.*

low-ly·ing *adj.* at low altitude (above sea level, etc.).

low-mind·ed /lómíndid/ *adj.* vulgar or ignoble in mind or character. □□ **low-mind·ed·ness** *n.*

low-pitched *adj.* **1** (of a sound) low. **2** (of a roof) having only a slight slope.

low pres·sure *n.* **1** little demand for activity or exertion. **2** an atmospheric condition with pressure below average.

low pro·file *n.* avoidance of attention or publicity. □□ **low-pro·file** *adj.*

low spir·its *n.pl.* dejection; depression. □□ **low-spir·it·ed** *adj.* **low-spir·it·ed·ness** *n.*

low tide *n.* the time or level of the tide at its ebb.

low wa·ter the tide at its lowest.

low-wa·ter mark *n.* **1** the level reached at low water. **2** a minimum recorded level or value, etc.

lux /loks/ *n.* smoked salmon.

loy·al /lóyal/ *adj.* **1** (often foll. by *to*) true or faithful (to duty, love, or obligation). **2** steadfast in allegiance; devoted to the legitimate sovereign or government of one's country. **3** showing loyalty. □□ **loy·al·ly** *adv.*

loy·al·ist /lóyalist/ *n.* **1** a person who remains loyal to the legitimate sovereign, etc. **2** (**Loyalist**) a *hist.* a resident of N. America who supported Great Britain during the American Revolution. **b** a supporter of Parliamentary union between Great Britain and Northern Ireland. □□ **loy·al·ism** *n.*

loy·al·ty /lóyaltee/ *n.* (*pl.* **-ies**) **1** the state of being loyal. **2** (often in *pl.*) a feeling or application of loyalty.

loz·enge /lózinj/ *n.* **1** a rhombus or diamond figure. **2** a small sweet or medicinal tablet for dissolving in the mouth. **3** ► a lozenge-shaped cut on a gemstone.

LOZENGE

LP *abbr.* **1** long-playing (phonograph record). **2** low pressure.

LSD *abbr.* lysergic acid diethylamide.

Lt. *abbr.* **1** lieutenant. **2** light.

Ltd. *abbr.* limited.

Lu *symb. Chem.* the element lutetium.

lube /loob/ *colloq.*, chiefly *N. Amer., Austral., & NZ n. & v.* ● *n.* a lubricant. ● *v.tr.* lubricate.

lu·bri·cant /lóobrikant/ *n. & adj.* ● *n.* a substance used to reduce friction. ● *adj.* lubricating.

lu·bri·cate /lóobrikayt/ *v.tr.* **1** reduce friction in (machinery, etc.) by applying oil or grease, etc. **2** make slippery or smooth with oil or grease. □□ **lu·bri·ca·tion** /-káyshən/ *n.* **lu·bri·ca·tive** *adj.* **lu·bri·ca·tor** *n.*

lu·bri·cious /lóobríshəs/ *adj.* (also **lu·bri·cous** /lóobrikəs/) **1** slippery; smooth; oily. **2** lewd; prurient. **3** evasive. □□ **lu·bric·i·ty** /-brísitee/ *n.*

lu·cid /lóosid/ *adj.* **1** expressing or expressed clearly; easy to understand. **2** of or denoting intervals of sanity between periods of insanity or dementia. □□ **lu·cid·i·ty** /-síditee/ *n.* **lu·cid·ly** *adv.*

L

Lu·ci·fer /lóosifər/ *n.* Satan.

luck /luk/ *n.* **1** chance regarded as the bringer of good or bad fortune. **2** circumstances of life (beneficial or not) brought by this. **3** good fortune; success due to chance (*in luck; out of luck*). □ **for luck** to bring good fortune. **no such luck** *colloq.* unfortunately not. **try one's luck** make a venture. **with luck** if all goes well. **worse luck** *colloq.* unfortunately.

luck·i·ly /lúkilee/ *adv.* **1** (qualifying a whole sentence or clause) fortunately (*luckily there was enough food*). **2** in a lucky or fortunate manner.

luck·less /lúklis/ *adj.* having no luck; unfortunate. □□ **luck·less·ness** *n.*

luck·y /lúkee/ *adj.* (**luckier, luckiest**) **1** having or resulting from good luck, esp. as distinct from skill or design or merit. **2** bringing good luck (*a lucky mascot*). **3** fortunate; appropriate (*a lucky guess*).

lu·cra·tive /lóokrətiv/ *adj.* profitable; yielding financial gain. □□ **lu·cra·tive·ly** *adv.* **lu·cra·tive·ness** *n.*

lu·cre /lóokər/ *n. derog.* financial profit or gain.

Lud·dite /lúdīt/ *n. & adj.* ● *n.* **1** *hist.* a member of any of the bands of English artisans who rioted against mechanization and destroyed machinery (1811–16). **2** a person opposed to increased industrialization or new technology. ● *adj.* of the Luddites or their beliefs. □□ **Lud·dism** *n.* **Lud·dit·ism** *n.*

lu·di·crous /lóodikrəs/ *adj.* absurd or ridiculous; laughable. □□ **lu·di·crous·ly** *adv.* **lu·di·crous·ness** *n.*

luff /luf/ *n. & v.* (also **loof** /loof/) *Naut.* ● *n.* the edge of the fore-and-aft sail next to the mast or stay. ● *v.tr.* (also *absol.*) **1** steer (a ship) nearer the wind. **2** turn (the helm) so as to achieve this. **3** obstruct (an opponent in yacht racing) by sailing closer to the wind. **4** raise or lower (the jib of a crane or derrick).

luf·fa var. of LOOFAH.

lug[1] /lug/ *v. & n.* ● *v.* (**lugged, lugging**) **1** *tr.* drag or tug (a heavy object) with effort or violence. **b** (usu. foll. by *around, about*) carry (something heavy) around with one. **2** *tr.* (usu. foll. by *in, into*) introduce (a subject, etc.) irrelevantly. **3** *tr.* (usu. foll. by *along, to*) force (a person) to join in an activity. **4** *intr.* (usu. foll. by *at*) pull hard. ● *n.* **1** a hard or rough pull. **2** (in *pl.*) affectation (*put on lugs*).

lug[2] /lug/ *n.* **1** *colloq.* an ear. **2** a projection on an object by which it may be carried, fixed in place, etc. **3** *sl.* a lout; a sponger; a stupid person.

luge /loozh/ *n. & v.* ● *n.* a light toboggan for one or two people. ● *v.intr.* ride on a luge.

lug·gage /lúgij/ *n.* suitcases, bags, etc., to hold a traveler's belongings.

lug·ger /lúgər/ *n.* ▼ a small ship carrying two or three masts with a lugsail on each.

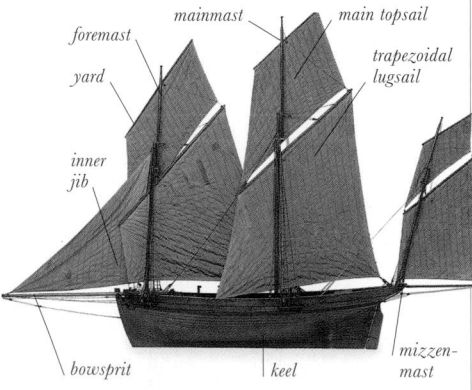

LUGGER: FRENCH LUGGER (*c.*1800)

mainmast
foremast
main topsail
yard
trapezoidal lugsail
inner jib
bowsprit
keel
mizzenmast

lug nut *n.* a nut that attaches to a heavy bolt, esp. as used to attach a wheel to a motor vehicle.

lug·sail /lúgsayl, -səl/ *n. Naut.* a quadrilateral sail that is bent on and hoisted from a yard.

lu·gu·bri·ous /loogóobreeəs, -gyóo-/ *adj.* doleful; mournful; dismal. □□ **lu·gu·bri·ous·ly** *adv.* **lu·gu·bri·ous·ness** *n.*

lug·worm /lúgwərm/ *n.* ▶ any polychaete worm of the genus *Arenicola*, living in muddy sand and often used as bait by fishermen.

LUGWORM:
BROWN LUGWORMS
(*Arenicola* species)

luke·warm /lóokwáwrm/ *adj.* **1** moderately warm; tepid. **2** unenthusiastic; indifferent. □□ **luke·warm·ly** *adv.* **luke·warm·ness** *n.*

lull /lul/ *v. & n.* ● *v.* **1** *tr.* soothe or send to sleep gently. **2** *tr.* (usu. foll. by *into*) deceive (a person) into confidence (*lulled into a false sense of security*). **3** *tr.* allay (suspicions, etc.) usu. by deception. **4** *intr.* (of noise, a storm, etc.) abate or fall quiet. ● *n.* a temporary quiet period in a storm or in any activity.

lull·a·by /lúləbī/ *n. & v.* ● *n.* (*pl.* **-ies**) **1** a soothing song to send a child to sleep. **2** the music for this. ● *v.tr.* (**-ies, -ied**) sing to sleep.

lum·ba·go /lumbáygō/ *n.* rheumatic pain in the muscles of the lower back.

lum·bar /lúmbər, -baar/ *adj. Anat.* relating to the loin, esp. the lower back area. ▷ VERTEBRA

lum·bar punc·ture *n.* the withdrawal of spinal fluid from the lower back with a hollow needle, usu. for diagnosis.

lum·ber[1] /lúmbər/ *v.intr.* (usu. foll. by *along, past, by*, etc.) move in a slow, clumsy, noisy way. □□ **lum·ber·ing** *adj.*

lum·ber[2] /lúmbər/ *n. & v.* ● *n.* **1** logs or timber cut and prepared for use. **2 a** disused articles of furniture, etc., inconveniently taking up space. **b** useless or cumbersome objects. ● *v.* **1** *intr.* cut and prepare forest timber for transport. **2** *tr.* **a** (usu. foll. by *with*) leave (a person, etc.) with something unwanted or unpleasant (*always lumbering me with the cleaning*). **b** (as **lumbered** *adj.*) in an unwanted or inconvenient situation (*afraid of being lumbered*). **3** *tr.* (usu. foll. by *together*) heap or group together carelessly. **4** *tr.* (usu. foll. by *up*) obstruct. □□ **lum·ber·er** *n.* (in sense 1 of *v.*). **lum·ber·ing** *n.* (in sense 1 of *v.*).

lum·ber·jack /lúmbərjak/ *n.* (also **lum·ber·man** /-mən/ *pl.* **-men**) one who fells, prepares, or conveys lumber.

lum·ber·jack·et *n.* a jacket, usu. of warm checked material, of the kind worn by lumberjacks.

lum·bri·cal mus·cle /lúmbrikəl/ *n.* any of the muscles flexing the fingers or toes.

lu·men /lóomən/ *n. Physics* the SI unit of luminous flux. ¶ Abbr.: **lm**.

lu·mi·nance /lóominəns/ *n. Physics* the intensity of light emitted from a surface per unit area in a given direction.

lu·mi·nar·y /lóomineree/ *n.* (*pl.* **-ies**) **1** *literary* a natural light-giving body, esp. the Sun or Moon. **2** a person as a source of intellectual light or moral inspiration. **3** a prominent member of a group or gathering (*a host of show-business luminaries*).

lu·mi·nes·cence /lóominésəns/ *n.* the emission of light by a substance other than as a result of incandescence. □□ **lu·mi·nes·cent** /-sənt/ *adj.*

lu·mi·nous /lóominəs/ *adj.* **1** full of or shedding light. **2** phosphorescent; visible in darkness (*luminous paint*). **3** (esp. of a writer or a writer's work) throwing light on a subject. **4** of visible radiation (*luminous intensity*). □□ **lu·mi·nos·i·ty** /-nósitee/ *n.* **lu·mi·nous·ly** *adj.*

lum·mox /lúməks/ *n. colloq.* a clumsy or stupid person.

lump[1] /lump/ *n. & v.* ● *n.* **1** a compact shapeless or unshapely mass. **2** *sl.* a quantity or heap. **3 a** tumor, swelling, or bruise. **4** a heavy, dull, or ungainly person. ● *v.* **1** *tr.* (usu. foll. by *together, with, in with, under*, etc.) mass together or group indiscriminately. **2** *tr.* carry or throw carelessly (*lumping crates around the yard*). **3** *intr.* become lumpy (*the gravy is lumping*). **4** *intr.* (usu.

foll. by *along*) proceed heavily or awkwardly. **5** *intr.* (usu. foll. by *down*) sit down heavily. □ **lump in the throat** a feeling of pressure in the throat, caused by emotion. □□ **lump·er** *n.* (in sense 2 of *v.*).

lump[2] /lump/ *v.tr. colloq.* endure or suffer (a situation) ungraciously. □ **like it or lump it** put up with something whether one likes it or not.

lump·ec·to·my /lumpéktəmee/ *n.* (*pl.* **-ies**) the surgical removal of a usu. cancerous lump from the breast.

lump·en /lúmpən/ *adj.* **1** lumpy and misshapen. **2** boorish and stupid. **3** (in Marxist contexts) uninterested in revolutionary advancement.

lump·fish /lúmpfish/ *n.* (*pl.* **-fishes** or **-fish**) ▼ a spiny-finned fish, *Cyclopterus lumpus*, of the N. Atlantic, with modified pelvic fins for clinging to objects.

pelvic fins
LUMPFISH
(*Cyclopterus lumpus*)

lump·ish /lúmpish/ *adj.* **1** heavy and clumsy. **2** stupid; lethargic. □□ **lump·ish·ly** *adv.* **lump·ish·ness** *n.*

lump sum *n.* **1** a sum covering a number of items. **2** money paid down at once (opp. INSTALLMENT).

lump·y /lúmpee/ *adj.* (**lumpier, lumpiest**) **1** full of or covered with lumps. **2** (of water) cut up by the wind into small waves. □□ **lump·i·ly** *adv.* **lump·i·ness** *n.*

lu·na·cy /lóonəsee/ *n.* (*pl.* **-ies**) **1** insanity. **2** *Law* such mental unsoundness as interferes with civil rights or transactions. **3** great folly or eccentricity; a foolish act.

luna moth /lóonə/ *n.* a large N. American moth, *Actias luna*, with crescent-shaped spots on its pale green wings.

lu·nar /lóonər/ *adj.* **1** of, relating to, or determined by the Moon. **2** concerned with travel to the Moon and related research. **3** (of light, glory, etc.) pale; feeble. **4** crescent-shaped; lunate. **5** of or containing silver.

lu·nar mod·ule *n.* a small craft used for traveling between the Moon's surface and a spacecraft in orbit around the Moon. ▷ SPACECRAFT

lu·nar month *n.* **1** ▲ the period of the Moon's revolution, esp. the interval between new moons of about 29½ days. ▷ MOON. **2** (in general use) a period of four weeks.

lu·nar year *n.* a period of 12 lunar months.

lu·nate /lóonayt/ *adj.* crescent-shaped.

lu·na·tic /lóonətik/ *n. & adj.* ● *n.* **1** an insane person. **2** someone foolish or eccentric. ● *adj.* mad; foolish.

lu·na·tic asy·lum *n. hist.* a mental home or hospital.

lu·na·tic fringe *n.* an extreme or eccentric minority group.

lu·na·tion /loonáyshən/ *n.* the interval between new moons, about 29½ days.

lunch /lunch/ *n. & v.* ● *n.* **1** the meal eaten in the middle of the day. **2** a light meal eaten at any time. ● *v.* **1** *intr.* eat one's lunch. **2** *tr.* provide lunch for. □ **out to lunch** *sl.* unaware; incompetent. □□ **lunch·er** *n.*

lunch·box /lúnchboks/ *n.* a container for a packed lunch.

lunch·eon /lúnchən/ *n. formal* lunch.

lunch·eon·ette /lúnchənét/ *n.* a small restaurant or snack bar serving light lunches.

L

LUNAR MONTH

As the Moon orbits the Earth, the amount of the sunlit side visible from the Earth changes, so that the Moon appears to take on different shapes, or phases. The time it takes for the Moon to go through all its different phases, from a new moon, when we see only a glimpse of the sunlit side, to a full moon, when we see all of its sunlit side, is called a lunar month. Although it takes the Moon 27.3 days to circle the Earth, a lunar month lasts 29.53 days, since the Earth moves as well as the Moon.

PHASES OF THE MOON

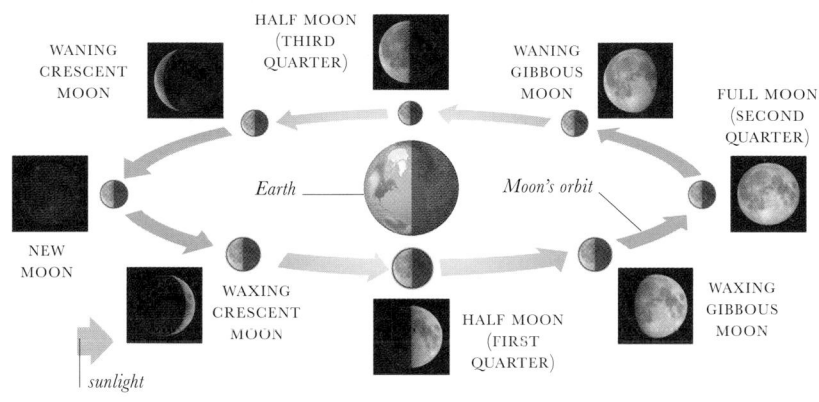

WANING CRESCENT MOON

HALF MOON (THIRD QUARTER)

WANING GIBBOUS MOON

FULL MOON (SECOND QUARTER)

Earth

Moon's orbit

NEW MOON

WAXING CRESCENT MOON

HALF MOON (FIRST QUARTER)

WAXING GIBBOUS MOON

sunlight

LUNETTE

lunch·time /lúnchtīm/ *n.* the time (usu. around noon) at which lunch is eaten.

lune /lōōn/ *n. Geom.* a crescent-shaped figure formed on a sphere or plane by two arcs intersecting at two points.

lu·nette /lōōnét/ *n.* **1** an arched aperture in a domed ceiling to admit light. **2** ◀ a crescent-shaped or semicircular space or alcove that contains a painting, statue, etc. **3** a watch crystal of flattened shape. **4** a ring through which a hook is placed to attach a vehicle to the vehicle towing it. **5** a temporary fortification with two faces forming a salient angle, and two flanks. **6** *RC Ch.* a holder for the consecrated host in a monstrance.

lung /lung/ *n.* ▼ either of the pair of respiratory organs, which bring air into contact with the blood in humans and many other vertebrates. ▷ RESPIRATION. □□ **lunged** *adj.* **lung·ful** *n.* (*pl.* **-fuls**). **lung·less** *adj.*

lunge /lunj/ *n. & v. ● n.* **1** a sudden movement forward. **2** a thrust with a sword, etc., esp. the basic attacking move in fencing. **3** a movement forward by bending the front leg at the knee while keeping the back leg straight ● *v* **1** *intr* make a lunge **2** *intr* (usu. foll. by *at*, *out*) deliver a blow from the shoul-

LUNG

During inhalation, air enters the lungs via the trachea, and ultimately penetrates to microscopic thin-walled air sacs (alveoli). The trachea divides into two main bronchi, one feeding into each lung, where they subdivide into smaller tubes (secondary and tertiary bronchi), and tubules (bronchioles) that lead to the alveoli. In the alveoli, oxygen passes into the bloodstream to be transported to the body's tissues, while waste carbon dioxide is exchanged, to be removed by exhalation.

trachea (windpipe)

right primary bronchus

rib

lobes

terminal bronchioles

alveoli

left primary bronchus

tertiary bronchus

secondary bronchus

diaphragm

lobes

pleura

CROSS SECTION OF THE HUMAN LUNGS

der in boxing. **3** *tr.* drive (a weapon, etc.) violently in some direction.

lunge² var. of LONGE.

lung·fish /lúngfish/ *n.* (*pl.* **fishes** or **-fish**) ▼ any freshwater fish of the order Dipnoi, having gills and a modified swim bladder used as lungs, and able to estivate to survive drought.

LUNGFISH: AUSTRALIAN LUNGFISH
(*Neoceratodus forsteri*)

lung·wort /lúngwort, -wawrt/ *n.* **1** any herbaceous plant of the genus *Pulmonaria*, esp. *P. officinalis* with white-spotted leaves likened to a diseased lung. **2** a lichen, *Lobaria pulmonaria*, used as a remedy for lung disease.

lunk /lungk/ *n.* (also **lunk·head**) *colloq.* a slow-witted person.

lu·pine¹ /lōōpin/ *n.* (also **lu·pin**) **1** ◀ any plant of the genus *Lupinus*, with long tapering spikes of blue, purple, pink, white, or yellow flowers. **2** (in *pl.*) seeds of the lupine.

lu·pine² /lōōpīn/ *adj.* of or like a wolf or wolves.

lu·pus /lōōpəs/ *n.* any of various ulcerous skin diseases, esp. lupus vulgaris, a tuberculosis of the skin. □□ **lu·poid** *adj.* **lu·pous** *adj.*

LUPINE
(*Lupinus*
'Chandelier')

lurch¹ /lərch/ *n. & v. ● n.* a stagger; a sudden unsteady movement or leaning. ● *v.intr.* stagger; move suddenly and unsteadily.

lurch² /lərch/ *n.* □ **leave in the lurch** desert (a friend, etc.) in difficulties.

lurch·er /lə́rchər/ *n.* **1** *Brit.* ▶ a crossbred dog, usu. a retriever, collie, or sheepdog crossed with a greyhound, used esp. for hunting and by poachers. **2** *archaic* a petty thief, swindler, or spy.

lure /lōōr/ *v. & n. ● v.tr.* **1** (usu. foll. by *away*, *into*) entice (a person, animal, etc.) usu. with some form of bait. **2** attract back again or recall (a person, animal, etc.) with the promise of a reward. ● *n.* **1** ▼ a thing used to entice, e.g., artificial bait for fishing. **2** (usu. foll. by *of*) the attractive or compelling qualities (of a pursuit, etc.). **3** a falconer's apparatus for recalling a hawk. □□ **lur·ing** *adj.* **lur·ing·ly** *adv.*

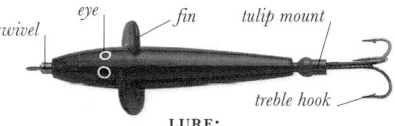

LURCHER:
SHORT-HAIRED LURCHER

eye

swivel

fin

tulip mount

treble hook

LURE:
DEVON MINNOW FISHING LURE

Lur·ex /lōōreks/ *n. Trademark* **1** a type of yarn that incorporates a glittering metallic thread. **2** fabric made from this yarn.

lu·rid /lōōrid/ *adj.* **1** vivid or glowing in color (*lurid orange*). **2** of an unnatural glare (*lurid nocturnal brilliance*). **3** sensational, horrifying, or terrible (*lurid details*). □ **cast a lurid light on** explain or reveal (facts or character) in a horrific, sensational, or shocking way. □□ **lu·rid·ly** *adv.* **lu·rid·ness** *n.*

lurk /lərk/ *v.intr.* **1** linger furtively or unobtrusively. **2 a** lie in ambush. **b** (usu. foll. by *in*, *under*, *about*,

L

etc.) hide, esp. for sinister purposes. **3** (as **lurking** *adj.*) latent; semiconscious (*a lurking suspicion*). □□ **lurk·er** *n.*

lus·cious /lúshəs/ *adj.* **1 a** richly sweet in taste or smell. **b** *colloq.* delicious. **2** (of literary style, music, etc.) overrich in sound, imagery, or voluptuous suggestion. **3** voluptuously attractive. □□ **lus·cious·ly** *adv.* **lus·cious·ness** *n.*

lush[1] /lush/ *adj.* **1** (of vegetation, esp. grass) luxuriant and succulent. **2** luxurious. □□ **lush·ly** *adv.* **lush·ness** *n.*

lush[2] /lush/ *n. & v. sl.* ● *n.* **1** alcohol; liquor. **2** an alcoholic; a drunkard. ● *v.* **1** *tr. & intr.* drink (alcohol). **2** *tr.* ply with alcohol.

lust /lust/ *n. & v.* ● *n.* **1** strong sexual desire. **2 a** (usu. foll. by *for, of*) a passionate desire for (*a lust for power*). **b** (usu. foll. by *of*) a passionate enjoyment of (*the lust of battle*). **3** (usu. in *pl.*) a sensuous appetite regarded as sinful (*the lusts of the flesh*). ● *v.intr.* (usu. foll. by *after, for*) have a strong or excessive (esp. sexual) desire. □□ **lust·ful** *adj.* **lust·ful·ly** *adv.* **lust·ful·ness** *n.*

lus·ter /lústər/ *n. & v.* ● *n.* **1** gloss; sheen. **2** a shining or reflective surface. **3 a** a thin metallic coating giving an iridescent glaze to ceramics. **b** = LUSTER-WARE. **4** a radiance or attractiveness; splendor; glory; distinction (of achievements, etc.) (*add luster to; shed luster on*). **5 a** a prismatic glass pendant on a chandelier, etc. **b** a cut-glass chandelier or candelabra. **6** any fabric with a sheen or gloss. ● *v.tr.* put luster on (pottery, a cloth, etc.). □□ **lus·ter·less** *adj.* **lus·trous** *adj.* **lus·trous·ly** *adv.* **lus·trous·ness** *n.*

lus·ter·ware /lústərwair/ *n.* ceramics with an iridescent glaze.

lus·tral /lústrəl/ *adj.* relating to or used in ceremonial purification.

lust·y /lústee/ *adj.* (**lustier, lustiest**) **1** healthy and strong. **2** vigorous or lively. □□ **lust·i·ly** *adv.* **lust·i·ness** *n.*

lu·ta·nist var. of LUTENIST.

lute[1] /loot/ *n.* ▼ a guitarlike instrument with a long neck and a pear-shaped body. ▷ STRINGED

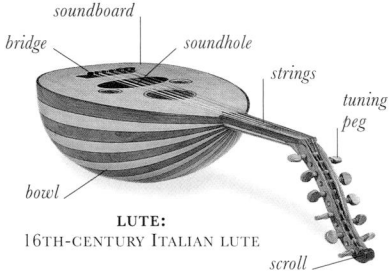

LUTE:
16TH-CENTURY ITALIAN LUTE

soundboard
bridge
soundhole
strings
tuning peg
bowl
scroll

lute[2] /loot/ *n. & v.* ● *n.* **1** clay or cement used to stop a hole, make a joint airtight, coat a crucible, protect a graft, etc. **2** a rubber seal for a jar, etc. ● *v.tr.* apply lute to.

lu·te·ci·um var. of LUTETIUM.

lu·te·nist /loot'nist/ *n.* (also **lu·ta·nist**) a lute player.

lu·te·ti·um /looteeshəm/ *n.* (also **lu·te·ci·um**) *Chem.* a silvery metallic element of the lanthanide series. ¶ Symb.: **Lu.**

Lu·ther·an /loothərən/ *n. & adj.* ● *n.* **1** a follower of Martin Luther, Ger. religious reformer d. 1546. **2** a member of the Lutheran Church, which accepts the Augsburg confession of 1530, with justification by faith alone as a cardinal doctrine. ● *adj.* of or characterized by the theology of Martin Luther. □□ **Lu·ther·an·ism** *n.*

lut·ing /looting/ *n.* = LUTE[2] *n.*

lutz /luts/ *n.* a jump in figure skating in which the skater takes off from the outside back edge of one skate and lands, after a complete rotation in the air, on the outside back edge of the opposite skate.

lux /luks/ *n.* (*pl.* same or **luxes**) *Physics* the SI unit

---

LYMPHATIC SYSTEM

The lymphatic system removes excess fluid from the body's tissues and returns it to the circulatory system. It also helps the body fight infection. It consists of lymph vessels, lymph nodes, and associated lymphoid organs such as the spleen and tonsils. Lymph vessels form a network of tubes that extend all over the body. From lymph capillaries – the smallest vessels – lymph flows into larger vessels called lymphatics, which are studded with nodes. These nodes are collections of lymph tissue that act as filters and contain spaces (sinuses) where many scavenging white blood cells (macrophages) ingest bacteria and other foreign matter and debris. When an infection occurs, specialized white blood cells (lymphocytes) are released from the lymph nodes to fight infection.

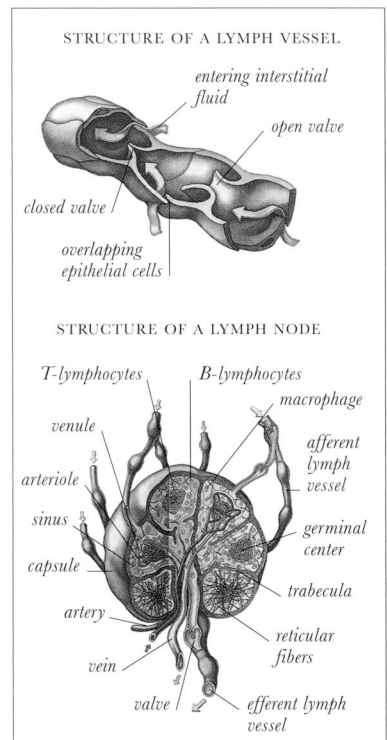

STRUCTURE OF A LYMPH VESSEL

entering interstitial fluid
open valve
closed valve
overlapping epithelial cells

STRUCTURE OF A LYMPH NODE

T-lymphocytes
B-lymphocytes
venule
macrophage
arteriole
afferent lymph vessel
sinus
germinal center
capsule
artery
trabecula
vein
reticular fibers
valve
efferent lymph vessel

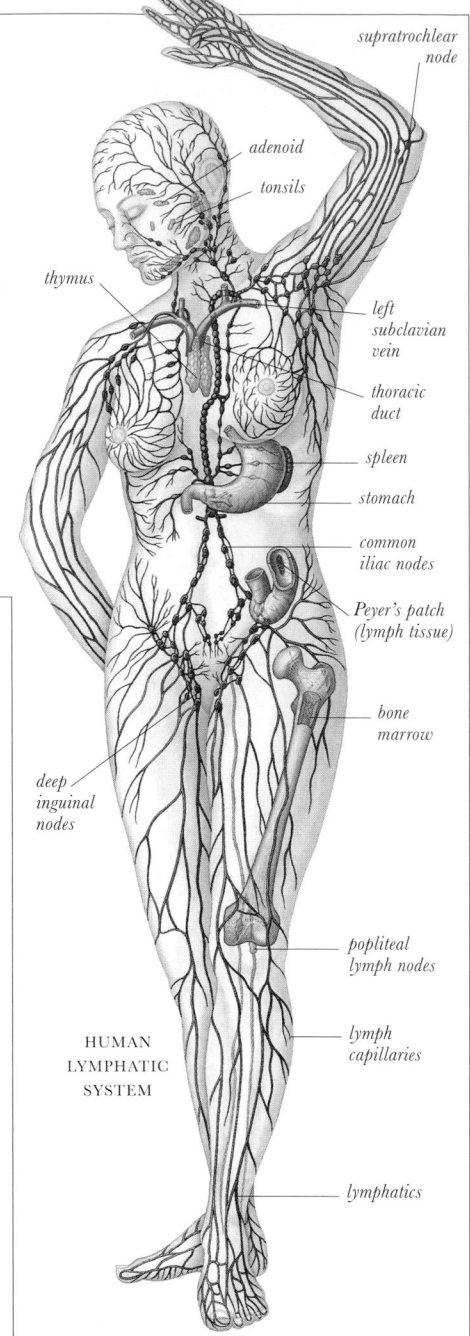

supratrochlear node
adenoid
tonsils
thymus
left subclavian vein
thoracic duct
spleen
stomach
common iliac nodes
Peyer's patch (lymph tissue)
deep inguinal nodes
bone marrow
popliteal lymph nodes
lymph capillaries
lymphatics

HUMAN LYMPHATIC SYSTEM

---

of illumination, equivalent to one lumen per square meter. ¶ Abbr.: **lx.**

luxe /looks, luks/ *n.* luxury (cf. DELUXE).

lux·u·ri·ant /lugzhŏoreeənt, lukshŏor-/ *adj.* **1** (of vegetation, etc.) lush; profuse in growth. **2** exuberant (*luxuriant imagination*). **3** (of literary or artistic style) florid; richly ornate. □□ **lux·u·ri·ance** /-eeəns/ *n.* **lux·u·ri·ant·ly** *adv.*

lux·u·ri·ate /lugzhŏoreeayt, lukshŏor-/ *v.intr.* **1** (foll. by *in*) take self-indulgent delight in; enjoy in a luxurious manner. **2** relax in comfort.

lux·u·ri·ous /lugzhŏoreeəs, lukshŏor-/ *adj.* **1** supplied with luxuries. **2** extremely comfortable. **3** self-indulgent; voluptuous. □□ **lux·u·ri·ous·ly** *adv.* **lux·u·ri·ous·ness** *n.*

lux·u·ry /lúgzhəree, lúkshəree/ *n.* (*pl.* **-ies**) **1** choice

or costly surroundings, possessions, food, etc. (*a life of luxury*). **2** something desirable for comfort or enjoyment, but not indispensable. **3** (*attrib.*) providing great comfort; expensive (*a luxury apartment; a luxury vacation*).

Lw *symb. Chem.* the element lawrencium.

lx *abbr.* lux.

ly·can·thro·py /līkánthrəpee/ *n.* **1** the mythical transformation of a person into a wolf (see also WEREWOLF). **2** a form of madness involving the delusion of being a wolf, with changed appetites, voice, etc. □□ **ly·can·thrope** /līkánthrōp, līkán-/ *n.*

ly·ce·um /līseeəm/ *n.* a literary institution, lecture hall, concert hall, etc.

ly·chee var. of LITCHI.

lych-gate var. of LICH-GATE.

L

Ly·cra /líkrə/ *n. Trademark* an elastic polyurethane fiber or fabric used esp. for close-fitting sports clothing.

lye /lī/ *n.* **1** water that has been made alkaline by lixiviation of vegetable ashes. **2** any strong alkaline solution, esp. of potassium hydroxide used for washing or cleansing.

ly·ing[1] /lí-ing/ *pres. part. & n.* ● *pres. part.* of LIE[1]. ● *n.* a place to lie (*a dry lying*).

ly·ing[2] /lí-ing/ *pres. part. & adj.* ● *pres. part.* of LIE[2]. ● *adj.* deceitful; false. □□ **ly·ing·ly** *adv.*

Lyme dis·ease /līm/ *n.* a disease transmitted by ticks, usually characterized by rash, fever, fatigue, and joint pain.

lymph /limf/ *n. Physiol.* a colorless fluid containing white blood cells, drained from the tissues and conveyed through the body in the lymphatic system. ▷ LYMPHATIC SYSTEM. **2** this fluid used as a vaccine. **3** exudation from a sore, etc. □□ **lym·phoid** *adj.* **lym·phous** *adj.*

lym·phat·ic /limfátik/ *adj. & n.* ● *adj.* **1** of or secreting or conveying lymph. **2** (of a person) pale, flabby, or sluggish. ● *n.* a veinlike vessel conveying lymph.

lym·phat·ic sys·tem *n.* ◄ a network of vessels conveying lymph.

lymph node *n.* (also **lymph gland**) a small mass of tissue in the lymphatic system where lymph is purified and lymphocytes are formed. ▷ LYMPHATIC SYSTEM

lym·pho·cyte /límfəsīt/ *n.* a form of leukocyte occurring in the blood, in lymph, etc. ▷ BLOOD, LYMPHATIC SYSTEM. □□ **lym·pho·cyt·ic** /-sítik/ *adj.*

lym·pho·ma /limfṓmə/ *n.* (*pl.* **lymphomas** or **lymphomata** /-mətə/) any malignant tumor of the lymph nodes, excluding leukemia.

lynch /linch/ *v.tr.* (of a body of people) put (a person) to death for an alleged offense without a legal trial. □□ **lynch·er** *n.* **lynch·ing** *n.*

lynch law *n.* the procedure of a self-constituted illegal court that punishes or executes.

lynch mob *n.* a group of people intent on lynching someone.

lynch·pin var. of LINCHPIN.

lynx /lingks/ *n.* **1** ▼ a medium-sized feline, *Lynx lynx*, with short tail, spotted fur, and tufted ear tips. **2** its fur. □□ **lynx·like** *adj.*

lynx-eyed *adj.* keen-sighted.

lyre /līr/ *n. Gk Antiq.* an ancient stringed instrument like a small U-shaped harp, played usu. with a plectrum and accompanying the voice.

lyre·bird /lírbərd/ *n.* any Australian bird of the family Menuridae, the male of which has a lyre-shaped tail display.

lyr·ic /lírik/ *adj. & n.* ● *adj.* **1** (of poetry) expressing the writer's emotions,

LYNX
(*Lynx lynx*)

usu. briefly and in stanzas. **2** (of a poet) writing in this manner. **3** of or for the lyre. **4** meant to be sung; fit to be expressed in song; songlike (*lyric drama*; *lyric opera*). ● *n.* **1** a lyric poem. **2** (in *pl.*) lyric verses. **3** (usu. in *pl.*) the words of a song.

lyr·i·cal /lírikəl/ *adj.* **1** = LYRIC *adj.* 1, 2. **2** resembling, couched in, or using language appropriate to, lyric poetry. □□ **lyr·i·cal·ly** *adv.*

lyr·i·cism /lírisizəm/ *n.* **1** the character or quality of being lyric. **2** a lyrical expression.

lyr·i·cist /lírisist/ *n.* a person who writes the words to a song.

ly·ser·gic ac·id di·eth·yl·am·ide /līsə́rjik ásid dī-éthilámīd/ *n.* a powerful hallucinogenic drug. ¶ Abbr.: **LSD**.

ly·sin /lísin/ *n. Biol.* a protein in the blood able to cause lysis.

ly·sine /líseen/ *n. Biochem.* an amino acid present in protein and essential in the diet of vertebrates.

ly·sis /lísis/ *n.* (*pl.* **lyses** /-seez/) *Biol.* the disintegration of a cell.

lyt·ic /lítik/ *adj.* of, relating to, or causing lysis.

L

M

M[1] /em/ *n.* (*pl.* **Ms** or **M's**) **1** the thirteenth letter of the alphabet. **2** (as a Roman numeral) 1,000.

M[2] *abbr.* (also **M.**) **1** Master. **2** *Monsieur.* **3** mega-. **4** *Chem.* molar. **5** Mach. **6** *Mus.* major.

m *abbr.* (also **m.**) **1 a** masculine. **b** male. **2** married. **3** mile(s). **4** meter(s). **5** million(s). **6** minute(s). **7** *Physics* mass. **8** *Currency* mark(s). **9** milli-.

'm *n. colloq.* madam (in *yes'm*, etc.).

MA *abbr.* **1** Master of Arts. **2** Massachusetts (in official postal use).

ma /maa/ *n. colloq.* mother.

ma'am /mam/ *n.* madam.

maar /maar/ *n.* a crater created by a volcanic explosion and typically forming a lake.

Mac /mak/ *n.* man (esp. as a form of address).

mac /mak/ *n.* (also **mack**) *colloq.* mackintosh.

ma·ca·bre /məkáabər/ *adj.* (also **ma·ca·ber**) grim, gruesome.

mac·ad·am /məkádəm/ *n.* **1** material for making roads with successive layers of compacted broken stone (named for J. L. *McAdam,* Brit. surveyor d.1836, who advocated its use). **2** a road made from such material. □□ **mac·ad·am·ize** *v.tr.*

mac·a·da·mi·a /mákədáymeeə/ *n.* any Australian evergreen tree of the genus *Macadamia,* esp. *M. ternifolia,* bearing edible nutlike seeds (named for J. *Macadam,* Australian chemist d. 1865).

ma·caque /məkák/ *n.* ► any monkey of the genus *Macaca,* including the rhesus monkey and Barbary ape having prominent cheek pouches and usu. a long tail.

MACAQUE
(*Macaca* species)

mac·a·ro·ni /mákərőnee/ *n.* **1** a tubular variety of pasta. **2** (*pl.* **macaronies**) *hist.* an 18th-c. British dandy affecting Continental fashions.

mac·a·ron·ic /mákərónik/ *n. & adj.* ● *n.* (in *pl.*) burlesque verses containing Latin (or other foreign words) and vernacular words with Latin, etc., terminations. ● *adj.* (of verse) of this kind.

mac·a·roon /mákərőőn/ *n.* a small light cake or cookie made with egg white, sugar, and ground almonds or coconut.

Ma·cas·sar /məkásər/ *n.* (in full **Ma·cas·sar oil**) a kind of oil formerly used as a dressing for the hair.

ma·caw /məkáw/ *n.* ◄ any long-tailed brightly colored parrot of the genus *Ara* or *Anodorhynchus,* native to S. and Central America. ▷ PARROT

MACAW:
SCARLET MACAW
(*Ara macao*)

Mac·ca·bees /mákəbeez/ *n.pl.* (in full **Books of the Maccabees**) four books of Jewish history and theology, of which the first and second are in the Apocrypha. □□ **Mac·ca·bean** /-béeən/ *adj.*

mac·chi·a·to /makeeáatō/ *n.* espresso coffee with a dash of frothy steamed milk.

Mace /mays/ *n. Trademark* a chemical spray used to disable an attacker temporarily. □□ **mace** *v.*

mace[1] /mays/ *n.* **1** ► a heavy club usu. having a metal head and spikes used esp. in the Middle Ages. **2** a ceremonial staff of office.

mace[2] /mays/ *n.* the fibrous layer between a nutmeg's shell and its husk, dried and ground as a spice. ▷ SPICE

ma·cé·doine /másidwaan/ *n.* mixed vegetables or fruit, esp. cut up small or in jelly.

mac·er·ate /másərayt/ *v.* **1** *tr. & intr.* make or become soft by soaking. **2** *intr.* waste away, as by fasting. □□ **mac·er·a·tion** /-ráyshən/ *n.* **mac·er·a·tor** *n.*

Mc·Guf·fin /məgúfin/ *n.* an object or device in a film or a book which serves merely as a trigger for the plot.

Mach /maak, mak/ *n.* (in full **Mach number**) the ratio of the speed of a body to the speed of sound in the surrounding medium. □ **Mach one** (or **two**, etc.) the speed (or twice the speed) of sound.

ma·chet·e /məshétee, məchétee/ *n.* a broad heavy knife used in Central America and the W. Indies as an implement and weapon.

Mach·i·a·vel·li·an /mákeeəvéleeən/ *adj.* elaborately cunning; scheming, unscrupulous (for N. dei *Machiavelli,* Florentine statesman and political writer d. 1527). □□ **mach·i·a·vel·li·an·ism** *n.*

ma·chic·o·late /məchíkəlayt/ *v.tr.* (usu. as **ma·chic·o·lat·ed** *adj.*) furnish (a parapet, etc.) with openings between supporting corbels for dropping stones, etc., on attackers. □□ **ma·chic·o·la·tion** /-láyshən/ *n.*

ma·chin·a·ble /məsheenəbəl/ *adj.* capable of being cut by machine tools. □□ **ma·chin·a·bil·i·ty** *n.*

mach·i·nate /mákinayt, másh-/ *v.intr.* lay plots; intrigue. □□ **mach·i·na·tion** *n.*

ma·chine /məsheen/ *n. & v.* ● *n.* **1** an apparatus applying mechanical power, having several parts each with a definite function. **2** a particular kind of machine, esp. a vehicle, a piece of electrical or electronic apparatus, etc. **3** an instrument that transmits a force or directs its application. **4** the controlling system of an organization, etc. (*the party machine*). **5** a person who acts mechanically. ● *v.tr.* make or operate on with a machine.

ma·chine code *n.* (also **ma·chine lan·guage**) a computer language to which a particular computer can respond directly.

ma·chine gun *n.* ► an automatic gun giving continuous fire. ▷ GUN

ma·chine-read·a·ble *adj.* in a form that a computer can process.

ma·chin·er·y /məsheenəree/ *n.* (*pl.* **-ies**) **1** machines collectively. **2** the components of a machine; a mechanism. **3** (foll. by *of*) an organized system. **4** (foll. by *for*) the means devised or available (*the machinery for decision making*).

ma·chine tool *n.* a mechanically operated tool. □□ **ma·chine-tooled** *adj.*

ma·chin·ist /məsheenist/ *n.* **1** a person who operates a machine, esp. a machine tool. **2** a person who makes machinery.

ma·chis·mo /məcheezmō, -chízmō/ *n.* exaggeratedly assertive manliness; a show of masculinity.

Mach num·ber see MACH.

ma·cho /máachō/ *adj. & n.* ● *adj.* showily manly or virile. ● *n.* (*pl.* **-os**) **1** a macho man. **2** = MACHISMO.

mac·in·tosh var. of MACKINTOSH.

mack var. of MAC.

mack·er·el /mákərəl, mákrəl/ *n.* (*pl.* same or **mackerels**) ▼ a N. Atlantic marine fish, *Scomber scombrus,* with a greenish-blue body, used for food.

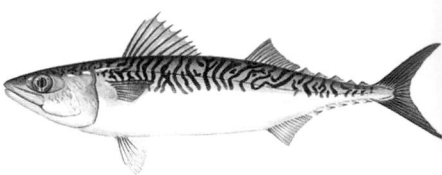

MACKEREL: ATLANTIC MACKEREL
(*Scomber scombrus*)

mack·er·el shark *n.* any of the sharks of the family Lamnidae, incl. the mako and the great white.

mack·er·el sky *n.* a sky dappled with rows of white fleecy clouds, like the pattern on a mackerel's back.

mack·in·tosh /mákintosh/ *n.* (also **mac·in·tosh**) **1** a waterproof, esp. rubberized, coat. **2** cloth waterproofed with rubber.

ma·cle /mákəl/ *n.* **1** a twin crystal. **2** a dark spot in a mineral.

ma·cra·mé /mákrəmáy/ *n.* **1** the art of knotting cord or string in patterns to make decorative articles. **2** ► articles made in this way.

mac·ro /mákrō/ *n.* (also **macro·in·struc·tion**) *Computing* a series of abbreviated instructions expanded automatically when needed.

macro- /mákrō/ *comb. form* **1** long. **2** large; large-scale.

mac·ro·bi·ot·ic /mákrōbītótik/ *adj. & n.* ● *adj.* relating to or following a diet intended to prolong life, comprising pure vegetable foods, brown rice, etc. ● *n.* (in *pl.*; treated as *sing*) the use or theory of such a dietary system.

MACRAMÉ:
DOUBLE-KNOTTED
MACRAMÉ CHAIN

mac·ro·cosm /mákrōkozəm/ *n.* **1** the universe. **2** the whole of a complex structure. □□ **mac·ro·cos·mic** /-kózmik/ *adj.* **mac·ro·cos·mi·cal·ly** /-kózmiklee/ *adv.*

mac·ro·ec·o·nom·ics /mákrō-éekənómiks, -ék-/ *n.* the study of large-scale or general economic factors. □□ **mac·ro·ec·o·nom·ic** *adj.*

mac·ro·in·struc·tion /mákrō-instrúkshən/ *n.* = MACRO.

front sight *cocking handle* *recoil spring* *adjustable butt*

9 mm parabellum round

follower and spring

trigger

safety catch / firing selector

30-round magazine

MACHINE GUN: GERMAN 9 MM SUBMACHINE GUN
WITH INNER MECHANISM REVEALED

MACE:
18TH-CENTURY
INDIAN SPIKED
MACE

mac·ro·mol·e·cule /mákrōmólikyōōl/ *n. Chem.* a molecule containing a very large number of atoms. □□ **mac·ro·mo·lec·u·lar** /-mɘlékyɘlɘr/ *adj.*

ma·cron /máykraan, mák-/ *n.* a diacritical mark (ˉ) over a long or stressed vowel.

mac·ro·phage /mákrɘfayj/ *n.* a large phagocytic white blood cell usually occurring at points of infection.

mac·ro·pho·tog·ra·phy /mákrōfɘtógrɘfee/ *n.* photography producing photographs larger than life.

mac·ro·scop·ic /mákrɘskópik/ *adj.* **1** visible to the naked eye. **2** regarded in terms of large units. □□ **mac·ro·scop·i·cal·ly** *adv.*

mac·u·la /mákyɘlɘ/ *n.* (*pl.* **maculae** /-lee/) **1** a dark spot, esp. a permanent one, in the skin. **2** (in full **macula lutea** /lōōteeɘ/) the region of greatest visual acuity in the retina. □□ **mac·u·lar** *adj.*

mad /mad/ *adj. & v.* ● *adj.* (**madder, maddest**) **1** insane; having a disordered mind. **2** (of a person, conduct, or idea) wildly foolish. **3** (often foll. by *about*) wildly excited or infatuated (*mad about football; is chess-mad*). **4** *colloq.* angry. **5** (of an animal) rabid. **6** wildly lighthearted. ● *v.* (**madded, madding**) **1** *intr. archaic* be mad; act madly (*the madding crowd*). □ **as mad as a hatter** wildly eccentric. **like mad** *colloq.* with great energy, intensity, or enthusiasm. □□ **mad·ness** *n.*

mad·am /mádɘm/ *n.* **1** a polite or respectful form of address or mode of reference to a woman. **2** a woman brothel-keeper. **3** *Brit colloq.* a conceited or precocious girl or young woman.

Mad·ame /mɘdáam, mádɘm/ *n.* **1** (*pl.* **Mesdames** /maydáam, -dám/) a title or form of address used of or to a French-speaking woman, corresponding to Mrs. or madam. **2** (**madame**) = MADAM 1.

mad·cap /mádkap/ *adj. & n.* ● *adj.* **1** wildly impulsive. **2** undertaken without forethought. ● *n.* a wildly impulsive person.

mad·den /mád'n/ *v.* **1** *tr. & intr.* make or become mad. **2** *tr.* irritate intensely. □□ **mad·den·ing** *adj.* **mad·den·ing·ly** *adv.*

mad·der /mádɘr/ *n.* **1** ◄ a herbaceous plant, *Rubia tinctorum*, with yellowish flowers. **2** a red dye obtained from the root of the madder plant, or its synthetic substitute.

made /mayd/ **1** *past* and *past part.* of MAKE. **2** *adj.* (usu. in *comb.*) **a** (of a person or thing) built or formed (*well-made; strongly made*). **b** successful (*a self-made man*). □ **have it made** *colloq.* be sure of success. **made for** ideally suited to. **made of** consisting of. **made of money** *colloq.* very rich.

Ma·dei·ra /mɘdeérɘ/ *n.* an amber-colored fortified white wine from the island of Madeira off the coast of N. Africa.

mad·e·leine /mádɘlin/ *n.* a small shell-shaped sponge cake.

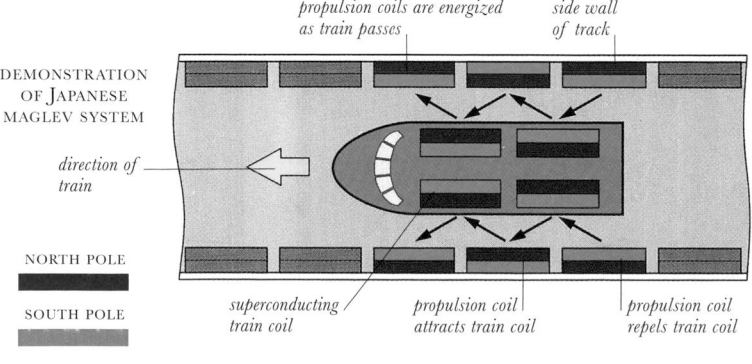

Mad·e·moi·selle /mádɘmɘzél, mádmwɘ-/ *n.* (*pl.* **-s** or **Mesdemoiselles** /máydmwɘ-/) **1** a title or form of address used of or to an unmarried French-speaking woman, corresponding to Miss. **2** (**mademoiselle**) **a** a young Frenchwoman **b** a French governess.

made to meas·ure *adj.* (*attrib.* **made-to-measure**) (of a suit, etc.) made to a specific customer's measurements.

made to or·der *adj.* (*attrib.* **made-to-order**) **1** made according to individual requirements. **2** exactly as wanted.

mad·house /mádhows/ *n.* **1** *archaic* or *colloq.* a home or hospital for the mentally disturbed. **2** *colloq.* a scene of extreme confusion or uproar.

MADDER: WILD
MADDER
(*Rubia tinctorum*)

---

mad·ly /mádlee/ *adv.* **1** in a mad manner. **2** *colloq.* **a** passionately. **b** extremely.

mad·man /mádmɘn, -man/ *n.* (*pl.* **-men**) a man who is insane or who behaves insanely.

Ma·don·na /mɘdónɘ/ *n. Eccl.* **1** (prec. by *the*) a name for the Virgin Mary. **2** a picture or statue of the Madonna.

Ma·don·na lil·y *n.* the white lily *Lilium candidum*, as shown in many pictures of the Madonna.

mad·ras /mádrɘs, mɘdrás/ *n.* a strong, lightweight cotton fabric with colored or white stripes, checks, etc.

mad·ri·gal /mádrigɘl/ *n.* **1** a usu. 16th-c. or 17th-c. part song for several voices, usu. arranged in elaborate counterpoint and without instrumental accompaniment. **2** a short love poem. □□ **mad·ri·gal·i·an** /-gáyleeɘn/ *adj.* **mad·ri·gal·ist** *n.*

mad·wom·an /mádwŏŏmɘn/ *n.* (*pl.* **-women**) a woman who is insane or who behaves insanely.

Mae·ce·nas /mīseénɘs/ *n.* a generous patron, esp. of literature, art, or music.

mael·strom /máylstrɘm/ *n.* **1** a great whirlpool. **2** a state of confusion.

mae·nad /meénad/ *n.* **1** a bacchante. **2** a frenzied woman.

ma·es·to·so /mīstósō/ *adj., adv., & n. Mus.* ● *adj. & adv.* to be performed majestically. ● *n.* (*pl.* **-os**) a piece of music to be performed in this way.

maes·tro /místrō/ *n.* (*pl.* **maestri** /-stree/ or **-os**) **1** a distinguished musician, esp. a conductor. **2** a great performer in any sphere.

Ma·fi·a /máafeeɘ, máf-/ *n.* **1** an organized body of criminals, orig. in Sicily, now also in Italy, the US, and elsewhere. **2** (**mafia**) a group regarded as exerting a hidden sinister influence.

Ma·fi·o·so /máafeeósō, máf-/ *n.* (*pl.* **Mafiosi** /-see/) a member of the Mafia.

mag /mag/ *n. colloq.* a magazine (periodical).

mag·a·zine /mágɘzéen/ *n.* **1** a periodical publication containing articles, stories, etc., usu. with illustrations. **2** a chamber for holding a supply of cartridges to be fed automatically to the breech of a gun. ▷ GUN, MACHINE GUN. **3** a similar device feeding a camera, slide projector, etc. **4** a store for arms, ammunition, and provisions for use in war. **5** a store for explosives.

mage /mayj/ *n. archaic* **1** a magician. **2** a wise and learned person.

ma·gen·ta /mɘjéntɘ/ *n. & adj.* ● *n.* **1** a brilliant mauvish-crimson color. **2** an aniline dye of this color. ● *adj.* of or colored with magenta.

---

mag·got /mágɘt/ *n.* **1** the soft-bodied larva of a dipterous insect, esp. the housefly or bluebottle. **2** *archaic* a whimsical fancy. □□ **mag·got·y** *adj.*

ma·gi *pl.* of MAGUS.

ma·gi·an /máyjeeɘn/ *adj. & n.* ● *adj.* of the magi or Magi. ● *n.* **1** a magus or Magus. **2** a magician. □□ **ma·gi·an·ism** *n.*

mag·ic /májik/ *n., adj., & v.* ● *n.* **1 a** the supposed art of influencing the course of events by the occult control of nature or of the spirits. **b** witchcraft. **2** conjuring tricks. **3** an inexplicable or remarkable influence producing surprising results. **4** an enchanting quality or phenomenon. ● *adj.* **1** of or resulting from magic. **2** producing surprising results. **3** *colloq.* wonderful, exciting. ● *v.tr.* (**magicked, magicking**) change or create by magic, or apparently so. □ **like magic** very effectively or rapidly.

mag·ic bul·let *n.* a medicine or treatment that is curative without incurring adverse side effects.

mag·ic car·pet *n.* a mythical carpet able to transport a person to any desired place.

mag·ic lan·tern *n.* a simple form of image projector using slides.

Mag·ic Mark·er *n. Trademark* a felt-tipped pen.

mag·ic mush·room *n. sl.* a mushroom producing psilocybin.

mag·i·cal /májikɘl/ *adj.* **1** of or relating to magic. **2** resembling magic; produced as if by magic. **3** wonderful, enchanting. □□ **mag·i·cal·ly** *adv.*

ma·gi·cian /mɘjíshɘn/ *n.* **1** a person skilled in or practicing magic. **2** a person who performs magic tricks for entertainment. **3** a person with exceptional skill.

mag·is·te·ri·al /májistéereeɘl/ *adj.* **1** imperious. **2** invested with authority. **3** of or conducted by a magistrate. **4** (of a work, opinion etc.) highly authoritative. □□ **mag·is·te·ri·al·ly** *adv.*

mag·is·te·ri·um /májistéereeɘm/ *n. RC Ch.* the official teaching of a bishop or pope.

mag·is·tra·cy /májistrɘsee/ *n.* (*pl.* **-ies**) **1** the office or authority of a magistrate. **2** magistrates collectively.

mag·is·trate /májistrayt, -strɘt/ *n.* **1** a civil officer administering the law. **2** an official conducting a court for minor cases and preliminary hearings (*magistrates' court*). □□ **mag·is·trate·ship** *n.* **mag·is·tra·ture** /-chɘr/ *n.*

mag·lev /máglev/ *n.* (usu. *attrib.*) ▼ magnetic levitation, a system in which trains glide above the track in a magnetic field.

M

MAGLEV

Still at an experimental stage, maglev trains are projected to travel up to 311 m.p.h. (500 k.p.h.) by superconducting electromagnets. In one system in Japan, coils in the track wall are fed an alternating electric current as the train passes. Each coil alternately attracts and repels the train coils, driving the vehicle forward. Other coils on the track wall and on the train interact to lift and guide it along the track.

DEMONSTRATION OF JAPANESE MAGLEV SYSTEM

propulsion coils are energized as train passes

side wall of track

direction of train

NORTH POLE

SOUTH POLE

superconducting train coil

propulsion coil attracts train coil

propulsion coil repels train coil

MAGMA

Magma originates far beneath the surface of the Earth, where rocks are melted by intensely high temperatures. The molten magma may collect in a reservoir underground before emerging through a vent or fissure in the Earth's surface, in a volcanic eruption. When it reaches the surface, where it flows out as lava, it cools and solidifies to form extrusive igneous rock. Magma does not always erupt on to the surface, but may solidify underground to form an intrusion of igneous rock, which appears on the surface only when overlying rocks are eroded. The fierce heat from rising magma is one of the forces that transforms other rocks by metamorphism.

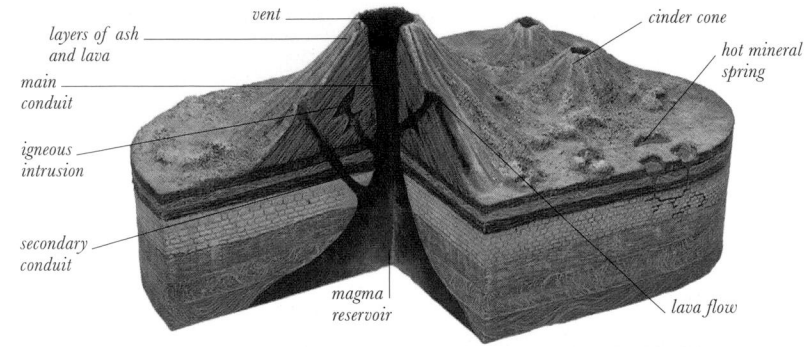

layers of ash and lava

vent

cinder cone

hot mineral spring

main conduit

igneous intrusion

secondary conduit

magma reservoir

lava flow

MODEL OF A VOLCANO SHOWING UNDERLYING MAGMA RESERVOIR

mag·ma /mágmə/ n. (pl. **magmata** /-mətə/ or **magmas**) **1** ▲ fluid or semifluid material from which igneous rock is formed by cooling. ▷ ROCK CYCLE, SEABED, VOLCANO. **2** a crude pasty mixture of mineral or organic matter. □□ **mag·mat·ic** /-mátik/ adj.

Mag·na Car·ta /mágnə kaártə/ n. (also **Mag·na Char·ta**) **1** a charter of liberty and political rights obtained from King John of England in 1215. **2** any similar document of rights.

mag·na cum lau·de /magnə koom lówday/ adv. & adj. chiefly N. Amer. with great distinction.

mag·nan·i·mous /magnánimǝs/ adj. nobly generous; not petty in feelings or conduct. □□ **mag·na·nim·i·ty** /mágnǝnímitee/ n. **mag·nan·i·mous·ly** adv.

mag·nate /mágnayt, -nǝt/ n. a wealthy and influential person (shipping magnate; financial magnate).

mag·ne·sia /magnéezhǝ, -shǝ, -zyǝ/ n. **1** Chem. magnesium oxide. **2** (in general use) hydrated magnesium carbonate, a white powder used as an antacid and laxative. □□ **mag·ne·sian** adj.

mag·ne·site /mágnisīt/ n. a white or gray mineral form of magnesium carbonate.

mag·ne·si·um /magnéezeeǝm/ n. Chem. a silvery metallic element used for making light alloys and important as an essential element in living organisms. ¶ Symb.: **Mg**.

mag·net /mágnit/ n. **1** a piece of iron, steel, alloy, ore, etc., having properties of attracting or repelling iron. ▷ ALTERNATING CURRENT. **2** a lodestone. **3** a person or thing that attracts.

mag·net·ic /magnétik/ adj. **1 a** having the properties of a magnet. **b** producing, produced by, or acting by magnetism. **2** capable of being attracted by or acquiring the properties of a magnet. **3** very attractive or alluring (a magnetic personality). □□ **mag·net·i·cal·ly** adv.

mag·net·ic field n. ▶ a region of variable force around magnets, magnetic materials, or current-carrying conductors. ▷ ELECTROMAGNETISM

mag·net·ic north n. the point indicated by the north end of a compass needle.

mag·net·ic pole n. **1** each of the points near the extremities of the axis of rotation of the Earth or another body where a magnetic needle dips vertically. **2** each of the regions of an artificial or natural magnet, from which the magnetic forces appear to originate.

mag·net·ic res·o·nance im·ag·ing n. a non-invasive diagnostic technique employing a scanner to obtain computerized images of internal body tissue. ¶ Abbr.: **MRI**. ▷ MRI

mag·net·ic tape n. a tape coated with magnetic material for recording sound or pictures or for the storage of information. ▷ TAPE

mag·net·ism /mágnitizǝm/ n. **1 a** magnetic phenomena and their study. **b** the property of producing these phenomena. **2** personal charm.

mag·net·ite /mágnitīt/ n. magnetic iron oxide.

mag·net·ize /mágnitīz/ v.tr. **1** give magnetic properties to. **2** make into a magnet. **3** attract as or like a magnet. □□ **mag·net·i·za·tion** n.

mag·ne·to /magnéetō/ n. (pl. **-os**) an electric generator using permanent magnets and producing high voltage, esp. for the ignition of an internal-combustion engine.

mag·ne·to·e·lec·tric /magnéetō-iléktrik/ adj. (of an electric generator) using permanent magnets. □□ **mag·ne·to·e·lec·tric·i·ty** /-trísitee/ n.

mag·ne·to·graph /magnéetǝgraf/ n. an instrument for recording measurements of magnetic quantities.

mag·ne·tom·e·ter /mágnitómitǝr/ n. an instrument measuring magnetic forces, esp. the Earth's magnetism. ▷ SPACECRAFT. □□ **mag·ne·tom·e·try** n.

mag·ne·to·sphere /magnéetǝsfeer/ n. the region surrounding a planet, star, etc., in which its magnetic field is effective.

mag·ne·tron /mágnitron/ n. an electron tube for amplifying or generating microwaves, with the flow of electrons controlled by an external magnetic field.

mag·net school n. a public school that draws students from throughout a district, offering superior facilities, specialized courses, etc.

mag·nif·i·cat /magnífikat/ n. **1** a song of praise. **2** (**Magnificat**) the hymn of the Virgin Mary (Luke 1:46–55) used as a canticle.

mag·nif·i·cent /magnífisǝnt/ adj. **1** splendid, stately. **2** sumptuously constructed or adorned. **3** colloq. fine, excellent. □□ **mag·nif·i·cence** /-sǝns/ n. **mag·nif·i·cent·ly** adv.

mag·nif·i·co /magnífikō/ n. (pl. **-oes**) a high ranking, eminent, or powerful person.

mag·ni·fy /mágnifī/ v.tr. (**-ies**, **-ied**) **1** make (a thing) appear larger than it is, as with a lens. **2** exaggerate. **3** intensify. **4** archaic extol, glorify. □□ **mag·ni·fi·a·ble** adj. **mag·ni·fi·ca·tion** /mágnifikáyshǝn/ n. **mag·ni·fi·er** n.

mag·ni·fy·ing glass n. a lens used to produce an enlarged image.

mag·nil·o·quent /magnílǝkwǝnt/ adj. **1** grand or grandiose in speech. **2** boastful. □□ **mag·nil·o·quence** /-kwǝns/ n. **mag·nil·o·quent·ly** adv.

mag·ni·tude /mágnitood, -tyood/ n. **1** largeness. **2** size. **3** importance. **4 a** the degree of brightness of a star. **b** a class of stars arranged according to this (of the third magnitude). □ **of the first magnitude** very important.

mag·no·lia /magnōlyǝ/ n. **1** ▶ any tree or shrub of the genus Magnolia, cultivated for its dark-green foliage and large waxlike flowers in spring. **2** a pale creamy-pink color.

mag·num /mágnǝm/ n. (pl. **magnums**) **1** a wine bottle of about twice the standard size. **2 a** a cartridge or shell that is especially powerful or large. **b** (often attrib.) a cartridge or gun adapted so as to be more powerful than its caliber suggests.

MAGNOLIA
(Magnolia x veitchii)

mag·num o·pus /mágnǝm ópǝs/ n. **1** a great work of art, literature, etc. **2** the most important work of an artist, writer, etc.

MAGNETIC FIELD

Magnetism is invisible, but lines of magnetic force around a magnet (the magnetic field) can be demonstrated. When unmagnetized magnetic material comes near a magnet, it becomes temporarily magnetized, with north and south poles that are attracted to the magnet's opposite poles. Here, temporarily magnetized iron filings swivel to align with the magnet's field, clustering around the poles where the force is strongest. The compass needles, which are already magnetized, show this effect in a similar way.

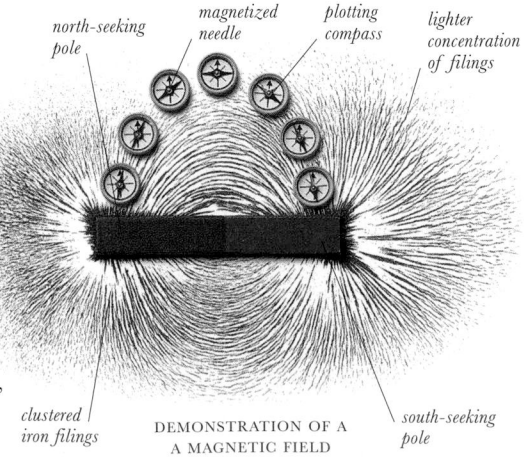

north-seeking pole

magnetized needle

plotting compass

lighter concentration of filings

clustered iron filings

south-seeking pole

DEMONSTRATION OF A A MAGNETIC FIELD

mag·pie /mágpī/ *n.* **1** ▶ a Eurasian crow, *Pica pica* or a N. American crow, *P. nuttalli* with a long pointed tail and black-and-white plumage. **2** any of various birds with plumage like a magpie, esp. *Gymnorhina tibicen* of Australia. **3** an idle chatterer. **4** a person who collects things indiscriminately.

MAGPIE: BLACK-BILLED MAGPIE
(*Pica pica*)

mag·uey /mágway/ *n.* an agave plant, esp. one yielding pulque.

ma·gus /máygəs/ *n.* (*pl.* **magi** /máyjī/) **1** a member of a priestly caste of ancient Persia. **2** a sorcerer. **3** (**the Magi**) the "wise men" from the east who brought gifts to the infant Christ (Matt. 2:1).

Mag·yar /mágyaar/ *n. & adj.* ● *n.* **1** a member of a Ural-Altaic people now predominant in Hungary. **2** the language of this people. ● *adj.* of or relating to this people or language.

ma·ha·ra·ja /máahəráajə, -zhə-/ *n.* (also **ma·ha·ra·jah**) *hist.* a title of some princes of India.

ma·ha·ra·ni /máahəráanee/ *n.* (also **ma·ha·ra·nee**) *hist.* a maharaja's wife or widow.

ma·ha·ri·shi /máahəréeshi/ *n.* a great Hindu sage or spiritual leader.

ma·hat·ma /məháatmə, -hát-/ *n.* (esp. in India) a person regarded with reverence; a sage.

Ma·hi·can /məhéekən/ *n. & adj.* (also **Mo·hi·can** /mō-/) ● *n.* **1** a N. American people native to the upper Hudson River Valley of New York state. **2** a member of this people. ● *adj.* of or relating to this people.

mah-jongg /maajóng, -jáwng, -zhóng, -zháwng/ *n.* (also **mahjong**) a Chinese game for four resembling rummy and played with 136 or 144 pieces called tiles.

mahl·stick var. of MAULSTICK.

ma·hog·a·ny /məhógənee/ *n.* (*pl.* **-ies**) **1 a** a reddish-brown wood used for furniture. ▷ WOOD. **b** the color of this. **2** any tropical tree of the genus *Swietenia*, esp. *S. mahogani*, yielding this wood.

ma·ho·ni·a /məhôneeə/ *n.* ▼ any evergreen shrub of the genus *Mahonia*, with yellow bell-shaped or globular flowers.

MAHONIA:
OREGON GRAPE
(*Mahonia aquifolium*)

berries

ma·hout /məhówt/ *n.* (esp. in India) an elephant driver.

maid /mayd/ *n.* **1** a female domestic servant. **2** *archaic* or *poet.* a girl or young woman.

maid·en /máyd'n/ *n. & adj.* ● *n.* **1** *archaic* or *poet.* a girl; a young unmarried woman. **2** (often *attrib.*) **a** a horse that has never won a race. **b** a race open only to such horses. ● *adj.* **1** unmarried (*maiden aunt*). **2** being or involving the first attempt at or occurrence (*maiden speech; maiden voyage*). **3** (of a female animal) unmated. □□ **maid·en·hood** *n.* **maid·en·ly** *adj.*

maid·en·hair /máyd'nhair/ *n.* (in full **maidenhair fern**) a fern of the genus *Adiantum*, esp. *A. capillus-veneris*, with delicate fronds.

maid·en·head /máyd'nhed/ *n.* **1** virginity. **2** the hymen.

maid·en name *n.* a wife's surname before marriage.

maiden pink *n.* a widespread plant, *Dianthus deltoides*, with pink or reddish flowers.

maid of hon·or *n.* **1** a principal bridesmaid. **2** an unmarried lady attending a queen or princess.

maid·serv·ant /máydservənt/ *n.* a female servant.

mai·gre /máygər/ *adj. RC Ch.* **1** (of a day) on which abstinence from meat is ordered. **2** (of food) suitable for eating on maigre days.

mail[1] /mayl/ *n. & v.* ● *n.* **1 a** letters and parcels, etc., conveyed by the postal system. **b** the postal system. **c** one complete delivery or collection of mail. **d** one delivery of letters to one place, esp. to a business on one occasion. **2** (usu. **the mails**) the system that delivers the mail. **3** a vehicle carrying mail. ● *v.tr.* send by mail.

mail[2] /mayl/ *n. & v.* ● *n.* **1** armor made of rings, chains, or plates. ▷ CHAIN MAIL, VIKING. **2** the protective shell, scales, etc., of an animal. ● *v.tr.* clothe with or as if with mail. □□ **mailed** *adj.*

mail·bag /máylbag/ *n.* a large sack or bag for carrying mail.

mail·box /máylboks/ *n.* **1** a public receptacle for depositing mail. **2** a private receptacle for at-home pickup and delivery of mail. **3** a computer file in which electronic mail is stored.

mail car·ri·er *n.* a person who delivers mail.

mail·er /máylər/ *n.* **1** chiefly *N. Amer.* the sender of a letter or package by mail. **2** *Computing* a program that sends email messages.

mail·ing list *n.* a list of people to whom advertising matter, information, etc., is to be mailed.

mail·lot /maayố/ *n.* **1** tights for dancing, gymnastics, etc. **2** a woman's one-piece bathing suit. **3** a jersey.

mail·man /máylmən/ *n.* (*pl.* **-men**) a mail carrier.

mail or·der *n.* an order for goods sent by mail.

mail·room /máylrōōm, -rŏŏm/ *n.* a room for sorting incoming and outgoing mail in a business or an organization.

maim /maym/ *v.tr.* **1** cripple, disable, mutilate. **2** harm, impair (*emotionally maimed by neglect*).

main /mayn/ *adj. & n.* ● *adj.* **1** chief; principal (*the main part; the main point*). **2** exerted to the full (*by main force*). ● *n.* **1** a principal channel, duct, etc., for water, sewage, etc. (*water main*). **2** *archaic* or *poet.* **a** the ocean or oceans (*the Spanish Main*). **b** the mainland. □ **in the main** for the most part. **with might and main** with all one's force.

main course *n.* **1** the chief course of a meal. **2** *Naut.* the mainsail.

main drag *n. US colloq.* = MAIN STREET.

main·frame /máynfraym/ *n.* **1** the central processing unit and primary memory of a computer. **2** (often *attrib.*) a large computer system.

main·land /máynlənd/ *n.* a large continuous extent of land, excluding neighboring islands, etc. □□ **main·land·er** *n.*

main·line /máynlīn/ *v. sl.* **1** *intr.* take drugs intravenously. **2** *tr.* inject (drugs) intravenously. □□ **main·lin·er** *n.*

main line *n.* **1** a chief railroad line. **2** *sl.* a principal vein (cf. MAINLINE). **3** a chief road or street.

main·ly /máynlee/ *adv.* for the most part; chiefly.

main man *n. N. Amer. colloq.* a close and trusted friend.

main·mast /máynmast, -məst/ *n. Naut.* the principal mast of a ship. ▷ RIGGING, SHIP

main·sail /máynsayl, -səl/ *n. Naut.* **1** (in a square-rigged vessel) the lowest sail on the mainmast. **2** (in a fore-and-aft-rigged vessel) a sail set on the after part of the mainmast.

main·spring /máynspring/ *n.* **1** the principal spring of a mechanical watch, clock, etc. **2** a chief motive power; an incentive.

main·stay /máynstay/ *n.* **1** a chief support (*has been his mainstay since his trouble*). **2** *Naut.* a stay from the maintop to the foot of the foremast. ▷ RIGGING

main·stream /máynstreem/ *n.* **1** (often *attrib.*) the prevailing trend in opinion, fashion, etc. **2** a type of jazz based on the 1930s swing style and consisting esp. of solo improvisation on chord sequences. **3** the principal current of a river.

main street *n.* the principal street of a town.

main·tain /mayntáyn/ *v.tr.* **1** cause to continue; keep up, preserve (a state of affairs, an activity, etc.) (*maintained friendly relations*). **2** (often foll. by *in*; *refl.*) support (life, a condition, etc.) by work, nourishment, expenditure, etc. (*maintained him in comfort; maintained themselves by fishing*). **3** (often foll. by *that* + clause) assert (an opinion, statement, etc.) as true (*maintained that she was the best; his story was true, he maintained*). **4** preserve or provide for the preservation of (a building, machine, road, etc.) in good repair. **5** give aid to (a cause, party, etc.). **6** provide means for (a garrison, etc., to be equipped). □□ **main·tain·er** *n.* **main·tain·a·ble** *adj.* **main·tain·a·bil·i·ty** *n.*

main·te·nance /máyntənəns/ *n.* **1** the process of maintaining or being maintained. **2** the provision of the means to support life.

main·top /máyntop/ *n. Naut.* a platform above the head of the lower mainmast.

main-top·mast /mayntópmast, -məst/ *n. Naut.* a mast above the head of the lower mainmast.

ma·iol·i·ca var. of MAJOLICA.

mai·son·ette /máyzənét/ *n.* (also **mai·son·nette**) **1** a part of a house, apartment building, etc., forming separate living accommodation, usu. on two floors and having a separate entrance. **2** a small house.

maî·tre d'hô·tel /métrə dōtél, máyt-/ *n.* (*pl.* **maîtres d'hôtel** *pronunc.* same) **1** (also **maitre d'**) a headwaiter. **2** the manager, head steward, etc., of a hotel.

maize /mayz/ *n.* **1** esp. *Brit.* = CORN[1] *n.* 1. **2** a pale golden-yellow color.

Maj. *abbr.* Major.

ma·jes·tic /məjéstik/ *adj.* stately and dignified; imposing. □□ **ma·jes·ti·cal·ly** *adv.*

maj·es·ty /májistee/ *n.* (*pl.* **-ies**) **1** impressive stateliness, dignity, or authority. **2 a** royal power. **b** (**Majesty**) part of several titles given to a sovereign or a sovereign's wife or widow or used in addressing them (*Your Majesty; Her Majesty the Queen Mother*).

ma·jol·i·ca /məyólikə, məjól-/ *n.* (also **ma·iol·i·ca**) **1** a 19th-c. trade name for earthenware with colored decoration on an opaque white glaze. **2** ◀ a white tin-glazed earthenware decorated with metallic colors, orig. popular in the Mediterranean area during the Renaissance.

MAJOLICA: 16TH-
CENTURY ITALIAN
MAJOLICA BOWL

ma·jor /máyjər/ *adj., n., & v.* ● *adj.* **1** important, large, serious, significant (*a major road; a major war; the major consideration must be their health*). **2** (of an operation) serious. **3** *Mus.* **a** (of a scale) having intervals of a semitone between the third and fourth, and seventh and eighth degrees. **b** (of an interval) greater by a semitone than a minor interval (*major third*). **c** (of a key) based on a major scale. **4** of full legal age. **5** *Brit.* (appended to a surname, esp. in public schools) the elder of two brothers (*Smith major*). ● *n.* **1 a** an army officer

M

next below lieutenant colonel and above captain. **b** a person in charge of a section of band instruments (*drum major*). **2** a person of full legal age. **3** *US* **a** a student's most emphasized subject or course. **b** a student specializing in a specified subject (*a philosophy major*). ● *v.intr.* (foll. by *in*) study or qualify in as a special subject (*majored in theology*).

ma·jor·do·mo /máyjərdṓmō/ *n.* (*pl.* **-os**) **1** the chief official of an Italian or Spanish princely household. **2** a house steward; a butler.

ma·jor gen·er·al *n.* an officer next below a lieutenant general.

ma·jor·i·ty /məjáwritee, -jór-/ *n.* (*pl.* **-ies**) **1** (usu. foll. by *of*) the greater number or part. ¶ Strictly used only with countable nouns, e.g., *a majority of people*, and not with mass nouns, e.g., *a majority of the work*. **2** *Polit.* **a** the number by which the votes cast for one party, candidate, etc., exceed those of the next (*won by a majority of 151*). **b** a party, etc., receiving the greater number of votes. **3** full legal age (*attained his majority*). **4** the rank of major. □ **the great majority 1** much the greater number. **2** *euphem.* the dead (*has joined the great majority*). **in the majority** esp. *Polit.* belonging to or constituting a majority party, etc.

ma·jor league *n.* a professional league of highest classification in baseball, etc.

ma·jus·cule /májəskyōōl/ *n. & adj.* ● *n. Paleog.* **1** a large letter, whether capital or uncial. **2** large lettering. adj. of, written in, or concerning majuscules. □□ **ma·jus·cu·lar** /məjúskyələr/ *adj.*

make /mayk/ *v. & n.* ● *v.* (*past* and *past part.* **made** /mayd/) **1** *tr.* construct; create; form from parts or other substances. **2** *tr.* (often foll. by *to* + infin.) cause or compel (*make him repeat it*). **3** *tr.* **a** cause to exist; bring about (*made a noise*). **b** cause to become or seem (*made him angry*). **c** appoint; designate (*made him a cardinal*). **4** *tr.* prepare; draw up (*made her will*). **5** *tr.* amount to (*makes a difference; 2 and 2 make 4*). **6** *tr.* **a** undertake or agree to (an aim or purpose) (*made a promise*). **b** execute or perform (a bodily movement, a speech, etc.) (*made a face*). **7** *tr.* gain, acquire, procure (money, a profit, etc.). **8** *tr.* prepare (tea,

coffee, a dish, etc.) for consumption. **9** *tr.* **a** arrange bedding neatly on (a bed). **b** arrange and ignite materials for (a fire). **10** *intr.* **a** proceed (*made toward the river*). **b** (foll. by *to* + infin.) begin an action (*he made to go*). **11** *tr. colloq.* **a** arrive at (a place) or in time for (a train, etc.) (*made the six o'clock train*). **b** manage to attend (*couldn't make the meeting last week; can make any day except Friday*). **c** achieve a place in (*made the first team*). **d** achieve the rank of (*made colonel in three years*). **12** *tr.* establish or enact (a distinction, rule, law, etc.). **13** *tr.* estimate as (*I'd make the time to be 7 o'clock*). **14** *tr.* secure the success or advancement of (*it made my day*). **15** *tr.* accomplish (a distance, score, etc.) (*made 60 m.p.h. on the freeway*). **16** *tr.* **a** become by development or training (*made a great leader*). **b** serve as (*a log makes a useful seat*). **17** *tr.* (usu. foll. by *out*) cause to appear as (*makes him out a liar*). **18** *tr.* form in the mind (*I make no judgment*). **19** *tr.* (foll. by *it* + compl.) **a** determine, establish, or choose (*let's make it Tuesday*). **b** bring to (a chosen value, etc.) (*decided to make it a dozen*). **20** *tr. sl.* have sexual relations with. **21** *Cards* **a** win (a trick). **b** play (a card) to advantage. **c** win the number of tricks that fulfills (a contract). **d** shuffle (a deck of cards) for dealing. **22** *tr. Electr.* complete or close (a circuit) (opp. BREAK[1] 10). ● *n.* **1** (esp. of a product) a type, origin, brand, etc., of manufacture (*different make of car*). **2** a kind of mental, moral, or physical structure or composition. **3** an act of shuffling cards. □ **make against** be unfavorable to. **make as if** (or **though**) (foll. by *to* + infin. or conditional) act as if (*made as if to leave*). **make away with 1** get rid of; kill. **2** squander. **3** = make off with. **make believe** pretend. **make conversation** talk politely. **make a day** (or **night**, etc.) **of it** devote a whole day (or night, etc.) to an activity. **make do 1** manage with the means available. **2** (foll. by *with*) manage with (something) as an inferior substitute (*make do with a smaller staff*). **make an example of** punish as a warning to others. **make a fool of** see FOOL[1]. **make for 1** tend to result in (happiness, etc.). **2** proceed toward (a place). **3** assault; attack. **4** confirm (an opinion). **make friends** (often foll. by *with*) become friendly. **make fun of** see FUN. **make**

good see GOOD. **make a habit of** see HABIT. **make a hash of** see HASH[1]. **make hay** see HAY[1]. **make head or tail** (or **heads or tails**) **of** see HEAD. **make headway** advance, progress. **make it 1** *colloq.* succeed in reaching, esp. in time. **2** *colloq.* be successful. **3** (usu. foll. by *with*) *sl.* have sexual intercourse (with). **make it up 1** be reconciled, esp. after a quarrel. **2** fill in a deficit. **make it up to** remedy negligence, an injury, etc., to (a person). **make light of** see LIGHT[2]. **make love** see LOVE. **make a meal of** see MEAL[1]. **make merry** see MERRY. **make money** acquire wealth or an income. **make the most of** see MOST. **make much** (or **little** or **the best**) **of 1** derive much (or little, etc.) advantage from. **2** give much (or little, etc.) attention, importance, etc., to. **make no bones about** see BONE. **make nothing of 1** do without hesitation. **2** treat as a trifle. **3** be unable to understand, use, or deal with. **make of 1** construct from. **2** conclude to be the meaning or character of (*can you make anything of it?*). **make off** (or **away**) **with** carry away; steal. **make oneself scarce** see SCARCE. **make or break** cause the success or ruin of. **make out 1 a** distinguish by sight or hearing. **b** decipher (handwriting, etc.). **2** understand (*can't make him out*). **3** assert; pretend (*made out he liked it*). **4** *colloq.* make progress; fare (*how did you make out?*). **5** (usu. foll. by *to, in favor of*) draw up; write out (*made out a check to her*). **6** prove or try to prove (*how do you make that out?*). **7** (often foll. by *with*). *colloq.* **a** engage in sexual play or petting. **b** form a sexual relationship. **make over 1** transfer the possession of (a thing) to a person. **2** refashion, restyle. **make a point of** see POINT. **make time 1** (usu. foll. by *for* or *to* + infin.) find an occasion when time is available. **2** (usu. foll. by *with*) *sl.* make sexual advances (to a person). **make up 1** serve or act to overcome (a deficiency). **2** complete (an amount, a party, etc.). **3** compensate. **4** be reconciled. **5** put together; compound; prepare (*made up the medicine*). **6** sew together. **7** get (a sum of money, a company, etc.) together. **8** concoct (a story). **9** (of parts) compose (a whole). **10 a** apply cosmetics. **b** apply cosmetics to. **11** settle (a dispute). **12** prepare (a bed) for use with fresh sheets, etc. **13** *Printing* arrange (type) in pages. **14** compile (a list, an account, etc.). **make up one's mind** decide, resolve. **make up to** curry favor with; court. **make way 1** (often foll. by *for*) allow room for others to proceed. **2** achieve progress. **make one's way** proceed. **on the make** *colloq.* **1** intent on gain. **2** looking for sexual partners.

make-be·lieve (also **make-be·lief**) *n. & adj.* ● *n.* pretense. ● *adj.* pretended.

make·o·ver /máykōvər/ *n.* a complete transformation or restyling.

mak·er /máykər/ *n.* **1** (often in *comb.*) a person or thing that makes. **2** (**our, the**, etc., **Maker**) God.

make·shift /máykshift/ *adj. & n.* ● *adj.* temporary; serving for the time being. ● *n.* a temporary substitute or device.

make·up /máykəp/ *n.* **1** ◀ cosmetics for the face, etc., either generally or to create an actor's appearance or disguise. **2** the appearance of the face, etc., when cosmetics have been applied (*his makeup was not convincing*). **3** *Printing* the making up of a type. **4** *Printing* the type made up. **5** a person's character, temperament, etc. **6** the composition or constitution of a thing.

make·weight /máykwayt/ *n.* **1** a small quantity or thing added to make up the full weight. **2** an unimportant extra person. **3** an unimportant point added to make an argument seem stronger.

mak·ing /máyking/ *n.* **1** in senses of MAKE *v.* **2** (in *pl.*) **a** earnings; profit. **b** (foll. by *of*) essential qualities or ingredients (*has the makings of a general*). **c** *colloq.* paper and tobacco for rolling a cigarette. □ **be the making of** ensure the success or favorable development of. **in the making** in the course of being made or formed.

MAKEUP

Since early times, people have used face and body paints for adornment and camouflage, and in religious ceremonies and rituals. Modern cosmetics provide a huge range of products designed specifically to enhance the color and shape of the face, eyes, and lips.

EXAMPLES OF MAKEUP

FOUNDATION

FACE POWDER

BLUSHER

EYE PENCILS

LIP PENCILS

EYELINER   MASCARA   EYESHADOW

LIPSTICK

M

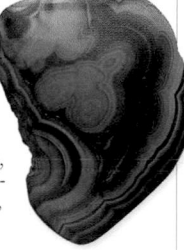

MAKO
(*Isurus oxyrinchus*)

ma·ko /máykō, máakō/ *n.* (*pl.* **-os**) ▲ a blue shark, *Isurus oxyrinchus*. ▷ SHARK

mal- /mal/ *comb. form* **1** bad; badly (*malpractice*; *maltreat*). **2** faulty; faultily (*malfunction*).

mal·ab·sorp·tion /málǝbsáwrpshǝn, -záwrp-/ *n.* imperfect absorption of food by the small intestine.

ma·lac·ca /mǝláke/ *n.* (in full **malacca cane**) a rich-brown cane from the stem of the palm tree *Calamus scipionum*, used for walking sticks, etc.

mal·a·chite /málǝkīt/ *n.* ► a bright-green mineral of hydrous copper carbonate, used for ornament. ▷ GEM

mal·a·col·o·gy /málǝkólǝjee/ *n.* the study of mollusks.

mal·a·dap·tive /málǝdáptiv/ *adj.* (of an individual, species, etc.) failing to adjust adequately to the environment, and undergoing emotional, behavioral, physical, or mental repercussions. □□ **mal·a·dap·ta·tion** /máladaptáy-shǝn/ *n.*

MALACHITE:
BANDED VARIETY

mal·ad·just·ed /málǝjústid/ *adj.* **1** not correctly adjusted. **2** (of a person) unable to adapt to or cope with the demands of a social environment. □□ **mal·ad·just·ment** *n.*

mal·ad·min·is·ter /málǝdmínistǝr/ *v.tr.* manage badly. □□ **mal·ad·min·is·tra·tion** /-stráyshǝn/ *n.*

mal·a·droit /málǝdróyt/ *adj.* clumsy; bungling. □□ **mal·a·droit·ly** *adv.* **mal·a·droit·ness** *n.*

mal·a·dy /málǝdee/ *n.* (*pl.* **-ies**) **1** an ailment; a disease. **2** a morbid or depraved condition.

ma·la fi·de /máylǝ fídee, máalaa féede/ *adj. & adv.* ● *adj.* acting or done in bad faith ● *adv.* in bad faith.

Mal·a·gas·y /málǝgásee/ *adj. & n.* ● *adj.* of or relating to Madagascar, an island in the Indian Ocean. ● *n.* the language of Madagascar.

ma·laise /mǝláyz/ *n.* **1** a non-specific bodily discomfort not associated with the development of a disease. **2** a feeling of uneasiness.

mal·a·mute /málǝmyoot/ *n.* (also **malemute**) any of an Alaskan breed of large sled dogs.

mal·an·ders /málǝndǝrz/ *n.pl.* (also **mallenders**) a dry scabby eruption behind a horse's knee.

mal·a·pert /málǝpǝrt/ *adj. & n. archaic* ● *adj.* impudent; saucy. ● *n.* an impudent or saucy person.

mal·a·prop·ism /málǝpropizǝm/ *n.* (also **mal·a·prop** /mál ǝprop/) the use of a word in mistake for one sounding similar, to comic effect, e.g., *allegory* for *alligator*.

mal·a·pro·pos /málǝprǝpó/ *adv., adj., & n.* ● *adv.* inopportunely; inappropriately. ● *adj.* inopportune; inappropriate. ● *n.* something inappropriately said, done, etc.

ma·lar /máylǝr/ *adj. & n.* ● *adj.* of the cheek. ● *n.* (also **malar bone**) a bone of the cheek.

ma·lar·i·a /mǝláireeǝ/ *n.* a recurrent fever caused by a protozoan parasite of the genus *Plasmodium*, introduced by the bite of a mosquito. □□ **ma·lar·i·al** *adj.* **ma·lar·i·ous** *adj.*

ma·lar·key /mǝláarkee/ *n. colloq.* humbug; nonsense.

mal·a·thi·on /málǝthíǝn/ *n.* an insecticide containing phosphorus, with low toxicity to plants.

Ma·lay /máylay, mǝláy/ *n. & adj.* ● *n.* **1 a** a member of a people predominating in Malaysia and Indonesia. **b** a person of Malay descent. **2** the language of this people, the official language of Malaysia. ● *adj.* of or relating to this people or language. □□ **Ma·lay·an** *n. & adj.*

mal·con·tent /málkǝntent/ *n. & adj.* ● *n.* a discontented person; a rebel. ● *adj.* discontented or rebellious.

male /mayl/ *adj. & n.* ● *adj.* **1** of the sex that can beget offspring by fertilization or insemination. (*male child*; *male dog*) **2** of men or male animals, plants, etc.; masculine. (*the male sex*; *a male-voice choir*) **3 a** (of plants or their parts) containing only fertilizing organs. **b** (of plants) thought of as male because of color, shape, etc. **4** (of parts of machinery, etc.) designed to enter or fill the corresponding female part (*a male plug*). ● *n.* a male person or animal. □□ **male·ness** *n.*

male chau·vin·ist (**pig**) *n.* a man who is prejudiced against women or regards women as inferior.

mal·e·dic·tion /málidíkshǝn/ *n.* **1** a curse. **2** the utterance of a curse.

mal·e·fac·tor /málifaktǝr/ *n.* a criminal; an evildoer.

ma·lef·ic /mǝléfik/ *adj. literary* (of magical arts, etc.) harmful; baleful. □□ **ma·lef·i·cence** /-sǝns/ *n.* **ma·lef·i·cent** /mǝléfisǝnt/ *adj.*

mal·ev·o·lent /mǝlévǝlǝnt/ *adj.* wishing evil to others. □□ **ma·lev·o·lence** /-lǝns/ *n.* **ma·lev·o·lent·ly** *adv.*

mal·fea·sance /malféezǝns/ *n. Law* evildoing. □□ **mal·fea·sant** /-zǝnt/ *n. & adj.*

mal·for·ma·tion /málformáyshǝn/ *n.* faulty formation. □□ **mal·formed** /-fáwrmd/ *adj.*

mal·func·tion /málfúngkshǝn/ *n. & v.* ● *n.* a failure to function in a normal or satisfactory manner. ● *v.intr.* fail to function normally or satisfactorily.

mal·ice /mális/ *n.* **1 a** the intention to do evil. **b** a desire to tease, esp. cruelly. **2** *Law* wrongful intention, esp. as increasing guilt. □□ **ma·li·cious** /mǝlíshǝs/ *adj.* **ma·li·cious·ly** *adv.* **ma·li·cious·ness** *n.*

mal·ice a·fore·thought *n.* (also **malice prepense**) *Law* the intention to commit a crime, esp. murder.

ma·lign /mǝlín/ *adj. & v.* ● *adj.* **1** (of a thing) injurious. **2** (of a disease) malignant. **3** malevolent. ● *v.tr.* speak ill of; slander. □□ **ma·lig·ni·ty** /mǝlígnitee/ *n.* (*pl.* **-ies**). **ma·lign·ly** /-línlee/ *adv.*

ma·lig·nant /mǝlígnǝnt/ *adj.* **1 a** (of a disease) very virulent or infectious (*malignant cholera*). **b** (of a tumor) tending to invade normal tissue and recur after removal; cancerous. **2** harmful; feeling or showing intense ill will. □□ **ma·lig·nan·cy** *n.* (*pl.* **-ies**). **ma·lig·nant·ly** *adv.*

ma·lin·ger /mǝlínggǝr/ *v.intr.* exaggerate or feign illness in order to escape duty, work, etc. □□ **ma·lin·ger·er** *n.*

mall /mawl/ *n.* **1** a sheltered walk or promenade. **2** an enclosed shopping center.

mal·lard /málǝrd/ *n.* (*pl.* same or **mallards**) **1** ▼ a wild duck or drake, *Anas platyrhynchos*, of the northern hemisphere. ▷ DUCK. **2** the flesh of the mallard.

MALE

MALLARD
(*Anas platyrhynchos*)

FEMALE

mal·le·a·ble /máleeǝbǝl/ *adj.* **1** (of metal, etc.) that can be shaped by hammering. **2** adaptable; pliable; flexible. □□ **mal·le·a·bil·i·ty** *n.* **mal·le·a·bly** *adv.*

mal·lee /málee/ *n. Austral.* **1** any of several types of eucalyptus, esp. *Eucalyptus dumosa*, that flourish in arid areas. **2** a scrub formed by mallee.

mal·le·o·lus /mǝléeǝlǝs/ *n.* (*pl.* **malleoli** /-lī/) *Anat.* a bone with the shape of a hammerhead, esp. each of those forming a projection on either side of the ankle.

mal·let /málit/ *n.* **1** ► a hammer, usu. of wood. **2** a long-handled wooden hammer for striking a croquet or polo ball. ▷ CROQUET, POLO STICK

mal·le·us /máleeǝs/ *n.* (*pl.* **mallei** /-lee-ī/) *Anat.* a small bone in the middle ear transmitting the vibrations of the tympanum to the incus.

mal·low /málō/ *n.* any plant of the genus *Malva*, with hairy leaves and pink or purple flowers.

mall rat *n. N. Amer. colloq.* a young person who frequents shopping malls to socialize.

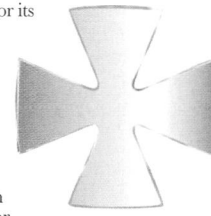

MALLET

malm /maam/ *n.* **1** a soft chalky rock. **2** a loamy soil produced by the disintegration of this rock. **3** a fine-quality brick made originally from malm, marl, or a similar chalky clay.

malm·sey /máamzee/ *n.* a strong sweet wine orig. from Greece, now chiefly from Madeira.

mal·nour·ished /málnórisht, -núr-/ *adj.* suffering from malnutrition. □□ **mal·nour·ish·ment** /-nór-ishmǝnt, -núr-/ *n.*

mal·nu·tri·tion /málnōōtríshǝn, -nyōō-/ *n.* a dietary condition resulting from the absence of foods necessary for health; insufficient nutrition.

mal·oc·clu·sion /málǝklōōzhǝn/ *n. Dentistry* faulty contact of opposing teeth when the jaws are closed.

mal·o·dor·ous /málódǝrǝs/ *adj.* having an unpleasant smell.

mal·prac·tice /malpráktis/ *n.* improper, negligent, or criminal professional conduct, as by a medical practitioner.

malt /mawlt/ *n. & v.* ● *n.* barley or other grain that is steeped, germinated, and dried, esp. for brewing ● *v.* **1** *tr.* convert (grain) into malt. **2** *intr.* (of seeds) become malt when germination is checked by drought. □□ **malt·y** /máwltee/ *adj.* (**maltier**, **maltiest**). **malt·i·ness** *n.*

mal·tase /mawltáys, -táyz/ *n. Biochem.* an enzyme found esp. in the small intestine that converts maltose into glucose.

malt·ed milk *n.* **1** a drink combining milk, a malt preparation, and ice cream or flavoring. **2** the powdered malt preparation used to make this.

Mal·tese /máwltéez, -tées/ *n. & adj.* ● *n.* **1** (*pl.* same) **a** a native or national of Malta. **b** a person of Maltese descent. **2** the language of Malta. ● *adj.* of or relating to Malta or its people or language.

Maltese cross *n.* ► a cross with arms of equal length broadening from the center, often indented at the ends.

Mal·thu·sian /malthōō-zhǝn, -zeeǝn/ *adj. & n.* ● *adj.* of or relating to T. R. Malthus, English clergyman and economist (d. 1834) or his theories, esp. that sexual restraint should be exercised as a means of preventing an increase of the population beyond its means of subsistence. ● *n.* a follower of Malthus. □□ **Mal·thu·sian·ism** *n.*

MALTESE CROSS

malt liq·uor *n.* a kind of strong beer.

malt·ose /máwltōs, -tōz/ *n. Chem.* a sugar produced by the hydrolysis of starch under the action of the enzymes in malt, saliva, etc.

mal·treat /máltréet/ *v.tr.* ill-treat. □□ **mal·treat·er** *n.* **mal·treat·ment** *n.*

M

MAMMAL

Mammals, a class of about 4,000 species living in a variety of habitats, are unique in their possession of mammary glands, which produce milk to feed their young. Another distinctive feature is hair, which can be in the form of fur, wool, whiskers, prickles, or spines – although some species have lost their hair in the course of evolution. Mammals are divided into three unequal subgroups. The largest of these is the placental mammals, whose young grow inside the mother's body where they are fed, via the placenta, from her blood. The young of marsupials leave the womb at an early stage, but continue to develop in the mother's pouch. Monotremes, comprising just three species, are the only egg-laying mammals.

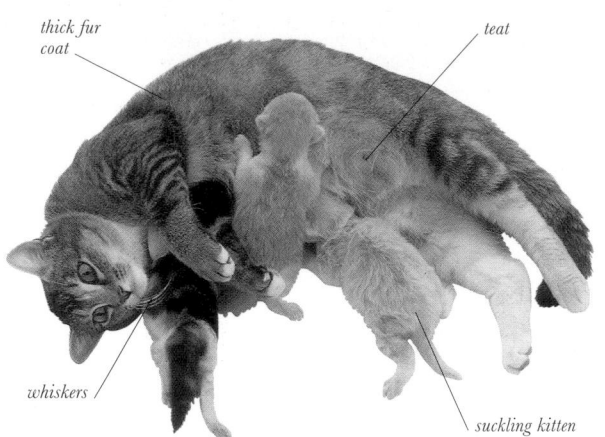

thick fur coat   *teat*

whiskers   *suckling kitten*

DOMESTIC CAT AND SUCKLING KITTENS

MAMMAL ORDERS

PLACENTAL MAMMALS

PROBOSCIDEA
(elephants)
▷ ELEPHANT

PERISSODACTYLA
(horses, rhinos, tapirs)
▷ HORSE, RUMINANT, UNGULATE

PINNIPEDIA
(seals, sea lions, walruses)
▷ PINNIPED, SEAL

CETACEA
(dolphins, porpoises, whales)
▷ CETACEAN, DOLPHIN, PORPOISE, WHALE

TUBULIDENTATA
(aardvark)

PRIMATES
(apes, humans, monkeys)
▷ PRIMATE, PROSIMIAN

DERMOPTERA
(flying lemurs)

LAGOMORPHA
(hares, pikas, rabbits)
▷ LAGOMORPH

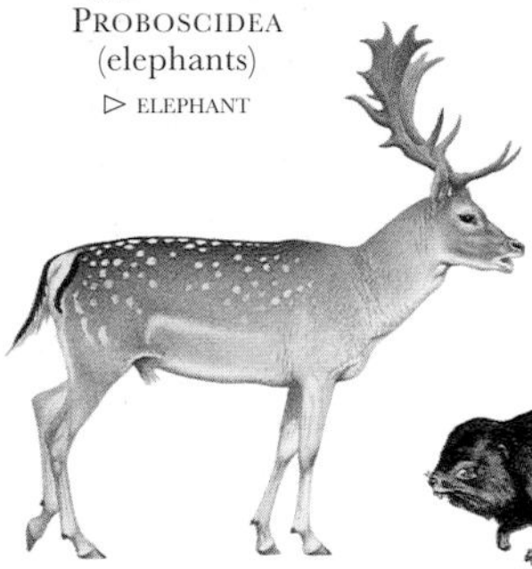

ARTIODACTYLA
(antelope, cattle, deer, goats)
▷ DEER, RUMINANT, UNGULATE

HYRACOIDEA
(hyraxes)
▷ HYRAX

SCANDENTIA
(tree shrews)

INSECTIVORA
(hedgehogs, moles, shrews)
▷ INSECTIVORE, SHREW

RODENTIA
(beavers, porcupines, rats, squirrels)
▷ RODENT

CHIROPTERA
(bats)
▷ BAT

SIRENIA
(dugong, manatees)

XENARTHRA
(anteaters, armadillos, sloths)

PHOLIDOTA
(pangolins)

CARNIVORA
(bears, cats, dogs, hyenas, mustelids)
▷ BEAR, CARNIVORE, CAT, DOG, MUSTELID

MONOTREMES

MONOTREMATA
(platypus, spiny anteaters)
▷ PLATYPUS

MARSUPIALS

MARSUPIALIA
(kangaroos, koalas, opossums, wombats)
▷ MARSUPIAL

M

malt whis·key *n.* whiskey made from malted barley.

mal·ver·sa·tion /málvərsáyshən/ *n. formal* **1** corrupt behavior in a position of trust. **2** (often foll. by *of*) corrupt administration (of public money, etc.).

ma·ma /máamə, məmáá/ *n. colloq.* (esp. as a child's term) mother.

mam·ba /máambə/ *n.* any venomous African snake of the genus *Dendroaspis,* esp. the green mamba (*D. angusticeps*) or black mamba (*D. polylepis*).

mam·bo /máambō/ *n. & v.* ● *n.* (*pl.* **-os**) **1** a Latin American dance like the rumba. **2** the music for this. ● *v.intr.* (**-oes, -oed**) perform the mambo.

mam·ma[1] /máamə/ *n.* (also **mom·ma**) *colloq.* (esp. as a child's term) mother.

mam·ma[2] /máamə/ *n.* (*pl.* **mammae** /-mee/) **1** a milk-secreting organ of female mammals. **2** a corresponding nonsecretory structure in male mammals. □□ **mam·mi·form** *adj.*

mam·mal /máməl/ *n.* ◄ any vertebrate of the class Mammalia, the females of which possess milk-secreting mammae for the nourishment of the young. □□ **mam·ma·li·an** /-máylien/ *adj. & n.*

mam·ma·ry /mámeree/ *adj.* of the human female breasts or milk-secreting organs of other mammals. ▷ BREAST

mam·mog·ra·phy /mamógrəfee/ *n. Med.* an X-ray technique of diagnosing and locating abnormalities of the breasts.

mam·mon /mámən/ *n.* (also **Mammon**) **1** wealth regarded as a god or as an evil influence. **2** the worldly rich.

mam·moth /máməth/ *n. & adj.* ● *n.* ► any large extinct elephant of the genus *Mammuthus,* with a hairy coat and curved tusks. ● *adj.* huge.

mam·my /mámee/ *n.* (*pl.* **-ies**) **1** a child's word for mother. **2** *formerly southern US* an African-American nursemaid or nanny in charge of white children.

Man. *abbr.* Manitoba.

man /man/ *n. & v.* ● *n.* (*pl.* **men** /men/) **1** an adult human male. **2 a** a person (*no man is perfect*). **b** the human race (*man is mortal*). **3** a person showing characteristics associated with males (*she's more of a man than he is*). **4** a worker; an employee (*the manager spoke to the men*). **5 a** (usu. in *pl.*) soldiers, sailors, etc., esp. nonofficers (*was in command of 200 men*). **b** an individual (*fought to the last man*). **c** (usu. prec. by *the,* or *poss. pron.*) a person fulfilling requirements (*I'm your man*). **6 a** a husband (*man and wife*). **b** *colloq.* a boyfriend or lover. **7 a** a human being of a specified historical period or character (*Renaissance man*). **b** a type of prehistoric man named after the place where the remains were found (*Peking man*). **8** any one of a set of pieces used in playing chess, etc. **9** (as second element in *comb.*) a man of a specified nationality, profession, etc. (*Dutchman; clergyman*). **10** an expression of impatience, etc., used in addressing a male (*nonsense, man!*). **b** *colloq.* a general mode of address (*blew my mind, man!*). **11** (prec. by *a*) one (*what can a man do?*). **12** a person pursued (*the police have so far not caught their man*). **13** (**the Man**) *sl.* **a** the police. **b** *sl.* a person with power or authority. **14** (in *comb.*) a ship of a specified type (*merchantman; Indiaman*). ● *v.tr.* (**manned, manning**) **1** supply (a ship, factory, etc.) with a person or people for work or defense, etc. **2** work or service or defend (a specified piece of equipment, a fortification, etc.) (*man the pumps*). **3** *Naut.* place men at (a part of a ship). **4** fill (a post or office). **5** (usu. *refl.*) fortify the spirits or courage of (*manned herself for the task*). □ **as one man** in unison; in agreement. **be a man** be courageous. **be one's own man 1** be free to act; be

independent. **2** be in full possession of one's faculties, etc. **separate** (or **sort out**) **the men from the boys** *colloq.* find those who are truly virile, competent, etc. **to a man** all without exception.

man a·bout town *n.* a fashionable man of leisure.

man·a·cle /mánəkəl/ *n. & v.* ● *n.* (usu. in *pl.*) **1** a fetter or shackle for the hand. **2** a restraint. ● *v.tr.* fetter with manacles.

man·age /mánij/ *v.* **1** *tr.* organize; regulate; be in charge of (a business, household, etc.). **2** *tr.* (often foll. by *to* + infin.) succeed in achieving (*managed a smile*). **3** *intr.* **a** (often foll. by *with*) succeed in one's aim, esp. against heavy odds (*managed with one assistant*). **b** meet one's needs with limited resources, etc. (*manages on a pension*). **4** *tr.* maintain control over (*cannot manage their teenage son*). **5** *tr.* (also *absol.;* often prec. by *can, be able to*) **a** cope with (*can you manage by yourself?*). **b** be free to attend on (a certain day) or at (a certain time) (*can you manage Thursday?*). **6** *tr.* handle or wield (a tool, weapon, etc.). **7** *tr.* take or have charge or control of (an animal or animals, esp. cattle).

man·age·a·ble /mánijəbəl/ *adj.* able to be easily managed, controlled, or accomplished, etc. □□ **man·age·a·bil·i·ty** *n.* **man·age·a·ble·ness** *n.* **man·age·a·bly** *adv.*

man·aged care *n.* health care administered by a health maintenance organization or similar system, intended to limit hospital and practioner fees.

man·age·ment /mánijmənt/ *n.* **1** managing or being managed. **2 a** the professional administration of business concerns, etc. **b** the people engaged in this.

man·age·ment in·for·ma·tion sys·tem *n.* *Computing* a computer system used in business for processing data related to management activities.

man·ag·er /mánijər/ *n.* **1** a person controlling or administering a business or part of a business. **2** a person controlling the affairs, training, etc., of a person or team in sports, entertainment, etc. **3** a person regarded in terms of skill in management (*a good manager*). □□ **man·a·ge·ri·al** /mánijée·reeəl/ *adj.* **man·a·ge·ri·al·ly** /-jée·reeəlee/ *adv.* **man·a·ger·ship** *n.*

man·ag·ing /mánijing/ *adj.* **1** (in *comb.*) having executive authority (*managing partner*). **2** (*attrib.*) fond of controlling affairs, etc.

ma·ña·na /mənyáanə/ *adv. & n.* ● *adv.* in the indefinite future (esp. to indicate procrastination). ● *n.* an indefinite future time.

man·a·tee /mánətée/ *n.* any large aquatic plant-eating mammal.

Man·cu·ni·an /mangkyōoneeən/ *n. & adj.* ● *n.* a native of Manchester in NW England. ● *adj.* of or relating to Manchester.

man·da·la /mándələ, mún-/ *n.* a symbolic circular figure representing the universe in various religions.

man·da·mus /mandáyməs/ *n. Law* a judicial writ issued as a command to an inferior court, or ordering a person to perform a public or statutory duty.

man·da·rin[1] /mándərin/ *n.* **1** (**Mandarin**) the official language of China. **2** *hist.* a Chinese official. **3 a** a party leader; a bureaucrat. **b** a powerful member of the establishment. **4 a** a nodding Chinese figure, usu. of porcelain. **b** porcelain, etc., decorated with Chinese figures in mandarin dress.

man·da·rin[2] /mándərin/ *n.* (in full **mandarin orange**) **1** a small flattish deep-colored orange with a loose skin. ▷ CITRUS FRUIT. **2** the tree, *Citrus reticulata,* yielding this. Also called **tangerine.**

man·date /mándayt/ *n. & v.* ● *n.* **1** an official command or instruction. **2** support for a policy or course of action, regarded by a victorious party, etc., as derived from the wishes of the people in an

election. **3** a commission to act for another. ● *v.tr.* instruct (a delegate) to act or vote in a certain way.

man·da·to·ry /mándətáwree/ *adj.* **1** of or conveying a command. **2** compulsory. □□ **man·da·to·ri·ly** *adv.*

man-day see MAN-HOUR.

man·di·ble /mándibəl/ *n.* **1** ▼ the jaw, esp. the lower jaw in mammals and fishes. ▷ MAXILLA, SKULL. **2** the upper or lower part of a bird's beak. ▷ BIRD. **3** either half of the crushing organ in an arthropod's mouthparts. ▷ INSECT. □□ **man·dib·u·lar** /-díbyələr/ *adj.*

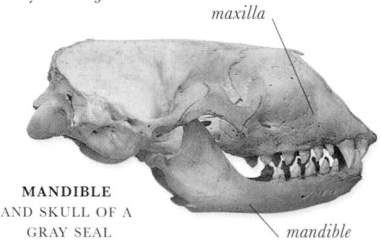

maxilla

MANDIBLE
AND SKULL OF A
GRAY SEAL

mandible

man·do·lin /mándəlin/ *n.* (also **man·do·line**) a musical instrument resembling a lute, having paired metal strings plucked with a plectrum. □□ **man·do·lin·ist** *n.*

man·drake /mándrayk/ *n.* **1** ▼ a poisonous plant, *Mandragora officinarum,* having emetic and narcotic properties. **2** = MAY-APPLE.

MANDRAKE
(*Mandragora officinarum*)

M

man·drel /mándrəl/ *n.* **1** a shaft in a lathe to which work is fixed while being turned. **2** a cylindrical rod around which metal or other material is forged or shaped.

man·drill /mándril/ *n.* ► a large W. African baboon, *Papio* (or *Mandrillus*) *sphinx.*

man·du·cate /mánjōokayt/ *v.tr. literary* chew; eat. □□ **man·du·ca·tion** /-káyshən/ *n.* **man·du·ca·to·ry** /-kətáwree/ *adj.*

mane /mayn/ *n.* **1** long hair growing in a line on the neck of a horse, lion, etc. ▷ HORSE. **2** *colloq.* a person's long hair. □□ **maned** *adj.* (also in *comb.*). **mane·less** *adj.*

MANDRILL
(*Mandrillus sphinx*)

man·ège /manézh/ *n.* (also **ma·nege**) **1** a riding school. **2** the movements of a trained horse. **3** horsemanship.

ma·nes /máanayz, máyneez/ *n.pl.* **1** the deified souls of dead ancestors. **2** (as *sing.*) the revered ghost of a dead person.

ma·neu·ver /mənōovər/ *n. & v.* (*Brit.* **manoeu·vre**) ● *n.* **1** a planned and controlled movement or series of moves. **2** (in *pl.*) a large-scale exercise of troops, warships etc. **3 a** an often deceptive planned or controlled action designed to gain an objective. **b** a skillful plan. ● *v.* **1** *intr. & tr.* perform or cause to perform a maneuver (*maneuvered the car into the space*). **2** *intr. & tr.* perform or cause (troops, etc.) to perform military maneuvers. **3 a** *tr.* (usu. foll. by *into, out, away*) force, drive, or manipulate (a person, thing, etc.) by scheming or adroitness. **b** *intr.* use artifice. □□ **ma·neu·ver·a·ble** *adj.* **ma·neu·ver·a·bil·i·ty** /-vrəbílitee, -vərə-/ *n.* **ma·neu·ver·er** *n.*

MAMMOTH: WOOLLY MAMMOTH
(*Mammuthus* species)

M

man Fri·day a helper or follower (after *Man Friday* in Defoe's *Robinson Crusoe*).

man·ful /mánfŏŏl/ *adj.* brave; resolute. □□ **man·ful·ly** *adv.* **man·ful·ness** *n.*

man·ga /mángə/ *n.* Japanese cartoons, comic books, and animated films with a science-fiction or fantasy theme.

man·ga·nese /mánggənéez/ *n.* **1** *Chem.* a gray brittle metallic element used with steel to make alloys. ¶ Symb.: **Mn**. **2** (in full **manganese oxide**) the black mineral oxide of this used in the manufacture of glass. □□ **man·ga·nous** /mánggənəs/ *adj.*

mange /maynj/ *n.* a skin disease in hairy and woolly animals, caused by an arachnid parasite and occasionally communicated to people.

man·ger /máynjər/ *n.* a long open box or trough for horses or cattle to eat from.

man·gle[1] /mánggəl/ *v.tr.* hack, cut, or mutilate.

man·gle[2] /mánggəl/ *n. & v.* ● *n.* a machine having two or more usu. heated revolving cylinders between which clothes, etc., are squeezed and pressed. ● *v.tr.* press (clothes, etc.) in a mangle.

man·go /mánggō/ *n.* (*pl.* **-oes** or **-os**) **1** a fleshy yellowish-red fruit, eaten ripe or used green for pickles, etc. ▷ FRUIT. **2** the E. Indian evergreen tree, *Mangifera indica*, bearing this.

man·go·steen /mánggəsteen/ *n.* **1** a white juicy-pulped fruit with a thick reddish-brown rind. **2** the E. Indian tree, *Garcinia mangostana*, bearing this.

man·grove /mánggrōv/ *n.* ▼ any tropical tree or shrub of the genus *Rhizophora*, growing in tidal-shore mud with many tangled roots above ground.

MANGROVE SWAMP

man·gy /máynjee/ *adj.* (**mangier**, **mangiest**) **1** (esp. of a domestic animal) having mange. **2** squalid; shabby. □□ **man·gi·ly** *adv.* **man·gi·ness** *n.*

man·han·dle /mánhánd'l/ *v.tr. colloq.* handle (someone or something) roughly.

man·hole /mánhōl/ *n.* a covered opening in a floor, pavement, etc., for workers to gain access.

man·hood /mánhŏŏd/ *n.* **1** the state of being a man rather than a child or woman. **2 a** manliness; courage. **b** a man's sexual potency. **3** the men of a country, etc. **4** the state of being human.

man-hour *n.* (also **man-day**, etc.) an hour (or day, etc.) regarded in terms of the amount of work that could be done by one person within this period.

man·hunt /mánhunt/ *n.* an organized search for a person, esp. a criminal.

ma·ni·a /máyneeə/ *n.* **1** *Psychol.* mental illness marked by periods of great excitement and violence. **2** (often foll. by *for*) excessive enthusiasm.

-mania /máyneeə/ *comb. form* **1** *Psychol.* denoting a special type of mental abnormality or obsession (*megalomania*). **2** denoting extreme enthusiasm or admiration (*bibliomania*).

ma·ni·ac /máyneeak/ *n. & adj.* ● *n.* **1** *colloq.* a person exhibiting extreme symptoms of wild behavior, etc.; a madman. **2** *colloq.* an obsessive enthusiast. ● *adj.* of or behaving like a maniac. □□ **ma·ni·a·cal** /mənÍəkəl/ *adj.* **ma·ni·a·cal·ly** /mənÍəklee/ *adv.*

-maniac /máyneeak/ *comb. form* forming adjectives and nouns meaning 'affected with -mania' or 'a person affected with -mania'.

man·ic /mánik/ *adj.* of or affected by mania. □□ **man·i·cal·ly** *adv.*

man·ic-de·pres·sive *adj., & n. Psychol.* ● *adj.* affected by or relating to a mental disorder with alternating periods of elation and depression. ● *n.* a person having such a disorder.

Ma·ni·che·ism /manikée-izəm/ *n.* a religious system with Christian, Gnostic, and pagan elements, founded in Persia in the 3rd century by Manes and based on a belief in an ancient conflict between light and darkness.

man·i·cure /mánikyŏŏr/ *n. & v.* ● *n.* a cosmetic treatment of the hands and fingernails. ● *v.tr.* give a manicure to (the hands or a person). □□ **man·i·cur·ist** *n.*

man·i·fest[1] /mánifest/ *adj. & v.* ● *adj.* clear or obvious to the eye or mind. ● *v.* **1** *tr.* display or show (a quality, feeling, etc.) by one's acts, etc. **2** *tr.* show plainly to the eye or mind. **3** *tr.* be evidence of. **4** *refl.* (of a thing) reveal itself. **5** *intr.* (of a ghost) appear. □□ **man·i·fes·ta·tion** /-stáyshən/ *n.* **man·i·fest·ly** *adv.*

man·i·fest[2] /mánifest/ *n. & v.* ● *n.* **1** a cargo list for the use of customs officers. **2** a list of passengers in an aircraft or of cars, etc., in a freight train. ● *v.tr.* record (names, cargo, etc.) in a manifest.

Man·i·fest Des·ti·ny *n.* 19th-c. doctrine asserting that the United States was destined to expand westward to the Pacific and to exert economic and social control throughout N. America.

man·i·fes·to /mániféstō/ *n.* (*pl.* **-os** or **-oes**) a public declaration of policy and aims esp. political or social.

man·i·fold /mánifōld/ *adj. & n.* ● *adj. literary* **1** many and various. **2** having various forms, parts, applications, etc. ● *n.* **1** a manifold thing. **2** *Mech.* a pipe or chamber branching into several openings. □□ **man·i·fold·ly** *adv.* **man·i·fold·ness** *n.*

man·i·kin /mánikin/ *n.* (also **man·ni·kin**) **1** a little man. **2** an anatomical model of the body.

Ma·nil·a /mənílə/ *n.* (also **Ma·nil·la**) **1** (in full **Manila hemp**) the strong fiber of a Philippine tree, *Musa textilis*, used for rope, etc. **2** (also **manila**) a strong brown paper made from Manila hemp. **3** a cigar or cheroot made in Manila.

man in the street *n.* (also **man on the street**) an ordinary average person.

man·i·oc /máneeok/ *n.* **1** cassava. **2** the flour made from it.

man·i·ple /mánipəl/ *n. Rom.Hist.* a subdivision of a legion, containing 120 or 60 men.

ma·nip·u·late /mənípyəlayt/ *v.tr.* **1** handle, treat, or use, esp. skillfully. **2** manage (a person, situation, etc.) to one's own advantage, esp. unfairly or unscrupulously. **3** manually examine and treat (a part of the body). **4** *Computing* alter, edit, or move (text, data, etc.). □□ **ma·nip·u·la·ble** /-ləbəl/ *adj.* **ma·nip·u·la·tion** /-láyshən/ *n.* **ma·nip·u·la·tor** *n.* **ma·nip·u·la·to·ry** /-lətáwree/ *adj.*

ma·nip·u·la·tive /mənípyəlative/ *adj.* **1** characterized by unscrupulous exploitation for one's own ends. **2** of or concerning manipulation. □□ **ma·nip·u·la·tive·ly** *adv.* **ma·nip·u·la·tive·ness** *n.*

Manit. *abbr.* Manitoba.

MAN-OF-WAR

By the 18th century, large, heavily armed wooden sailing ships, known as men-of-war, were being built for northern European navies that were engaged in the battle for control of the oceans and of the lucrative trade routes. The ships were classified according to how many guns they carried, the largest vessels being armed with more than 100 guns. The ships went into battle in single file so that broadsides from the multiple gun decks would have maximum effect on the enemy.

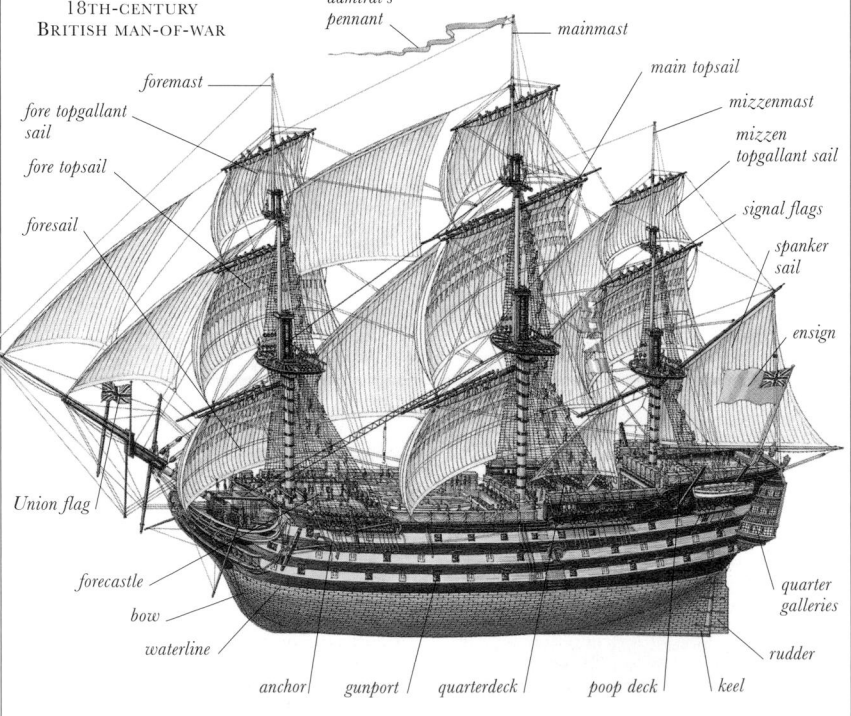

18TH-CENTURY BRITISH MAN-OF-WAR

admiral's pennant · mainmast · main topsail · mizzenmast · mizzen topgallant sail · signal flags · spanker sail · ensign · foremast · fore topgallant sail · fore topsail · foresail · Union flag · forecastle · bow · waterline · anchor · gunport · quarterdeck · poop deck · keel · rudder · quarter galleries

man·i·tou /mánitōō/ *n.* **1** a good or evil spirit as an object of reverence. **2** something regarded as having supernatural power.

man·kind *n.* **1** /mánkínd/ the human species. **2** /mánkīnd/ male people, as distinct from female.

man·ly /mánlee/ *adj.* (**manlier, manliest**) **1** having qualities regarded as admirable in a man, such as courage, frankness, etc. **2** befitting a man. □□ **man·li·ness** *n.*

man-made *adj.* (esp. of a textile fiber) artificial; synthetic.

man·na /mánə/ *n.* **1** the substance miraculously supplied as food to the Israelites in the wilderness (Exod. 16). **2** an unexpected benefit (esp. *manna from heaven*). **3** spiritual nourishment, esp. the Eucharist.

manned /mand/ *adj.* (of an aircraft, spacecraft, etc.) having a human crew.

man·ne·quin /mánikin/ *n.* **1** a fashion model. **2** a model of the human form, for fitting or displaying garments.

man·ner /mánər/ *n.* **1** a way a thing is done or happens. **2** (in *pl.*) **a** a social behavior (*it is bad manners to stare*). **b** polite or well-bred behavior (*he has no manners*). **3** a person's outward bearing, etc. (*has an imperious manner*). **4** a style in literature, art, etc. (*in the manner of Rembrandt*). □ **to the manner born** *colloq.* naturally at ease in a specified job, situation etc. □□ **man·ner·less** *adj.* (in sense of 2b).

man·nered /mánərd/ *adj.* **1** (in *comb.*) behaving in a specified way (*ill-mannered*). **2** (of a style, artist, etc.) showing idiosyncratic mannerisms. **3** (of a person) eccentrically affected in behavior.

man·ner·ism /mánərizəm/ *n.* **1** a habitual gesture or way of speaking, etc. **2 a** excessive addiction to a distinctive style in art or literature. **b** a stylistic trick. **3** a style of Italian art preceding the Baroque, characterized by lengthened figures. □□ **man·ner·ist** *n.* **man·ner·is·tic** /-rístik/ *adj.*

man·ner·ly /mánərlee/ *adj.* & *adv.* ● *adj.* well-mannered; polite. ● *adv.* politely. □□ **man·ner·li·ness** *n.*

man·ni·kin var. of MANIKIN.

man·nish /mánish/ *adj.* **1** (of a woman) masculine in appearance or manner. **2** characteristic of a man. □□ **man·nish·ly** *adv.* **man·nish·ness** *n.*

man of let·ters *n.* a scholar; an author.

man-of-war *n.* (*pl.* **men-of-war**) ◀ an armed ship, esp. of a specified country.

ma·nom·e·ter /mənómitər/ *n.* a pressure gauge for gases and liquids. □□ **man·o·met·ric** /mánəmétrik/ *adj.*

man on the street see MAN IN THE STREET.

man·or /mánər/ *n.* (also **man·or house**) **1** a large country house with lands. **2** the house of the lord of the manor. □□ **ma·no·ri·al** /mənáwreeəl/ *adj.*

man·pow·er /mánpowr/ *n.* **1** the power generated by a person working. **2** the number of people available or required for work, service, etc.

man·qué /maaNkáy/ *adj.* (placed after noun) that might have been but is not (*a comic actor manqué*).

man·sard /mánsaard/ *n.* ▼ a roof that has four sloping sides, each of which becomes steeper halfway down.

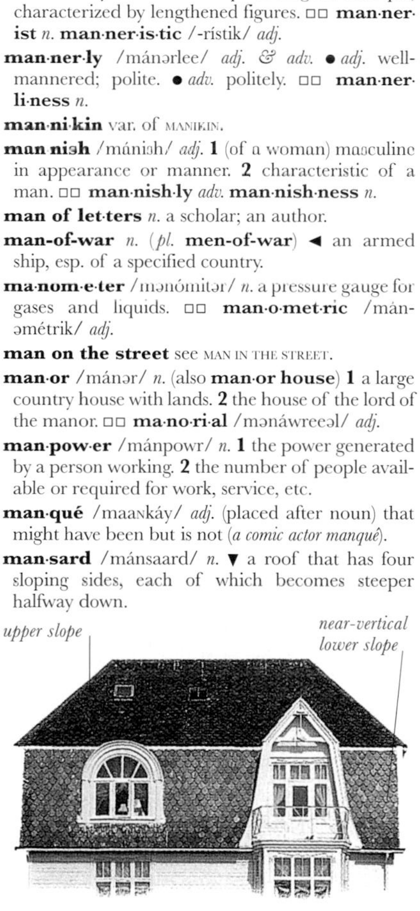
upper slope
near-vertical lower slope

MANSARD ROOF

manse /mans/ *n.* **1** the house of a minister, esp. a Presbyterian **2** a mansion.

man·serv·ant /mánservənt/ *n.* (*pl.* **menservants**) a male servant.

man·sion /mánshən/ *n.* a large house.

man-size *adj.* (also **man·sized**) **1** of the size of a man; very large. **2** big enough for a man.

man·slaugh·ter /mánslawtər/ *n.* **1** the killing of one human being by another. **2** *Law* the unlawful killing of a human being without malice aforethought.

man·ta /mántə/ *n.* **1** esp. *SW US* & *Latin Amer.* a cloak or shawl made from a square cloth. **2** any large ray of the family Mobulidae, esp. *Manta birostris*, having winglike pectoral fins and a whiplike tail. ▷ RAY

man·tel /mánt'l/ *n.* **1** = MANTELPIECE 1. **2** = MANTELSHELF.

man·tel·et /mánt'lit/ *n.* (also **man·tlet** /mántlit/) **1** *hist.* a woman's short loose sleeveless mantle. **2** a protective screen for gunners, etc.

man·tel·piece /mánt'lpees/ *n.* **1** a structure of wood, marble, etc., above and around a fireplace. **2** = MANTELSHELF.

man·tel·shelf /mánt'lshelf/ *n.* a shelf above a fireplace.

man·tic /mántik/ *adj.* *formal* of or concerning divination or prophecy.

man·til·la /mantílə, -téeə/ *n.* a lace scarf worn by Spanish women over the hair and shoulders.

man·tis /mántis/ *n.* (*pl.* same or **mantises**) any insect of the family Mantidae, feeding on other insects, etc.

man·tle /mánt'l/ *n.* & *v.* ● *n.* **1** a loose sleeveless cloak. **2** a covering (*a mantle of snow*). **3** responsibility or authority, esp. as passing from one person to another. **4** a fragile lacelike tube fixed around a gas jet to give an incandescent light. **5** an outer fold of skin enclosing a mollusk's viscera. **6** a bird's back, scapulars, and wing coverts, esp. if of a distinctive color. **7** the region between the crust and the core of the Earth. ▷ EARTH. ● *v.* **1** *tr.* clothe in or as if in a mantle; cover; envelop. **2** *intr.* **a** (of the blood) suffuse the cheeks. **b** (of the face) glow with a blush.

mant·let var. of MANTELET.

man·tling /mántling/ *n.* *Heraldry* **1** ornamental drapery, etc. behind and around a shield. **2** a representation of this.

man-to-man *adv.* with candor; honestly.

man·tra /mántrə, maán-, mún-/ *n.* **1** a word or sound repeated to aid concentration in meditation, orig. in Hinduism and Buddhism. **2** a Vedic hymn.

man·u·al /mányōōəl/ *adj.* & *n.* ● *adj.* **1** of or done with the hands (*manual labor*). **2** (of a machine, etc.) worked by hand. ● *n.* **1 a** a book of instructions; a handbook. **b** any small book. **2** a nonelectric typewriter **3** an organ keyboard played only with the hands. ▷ ORGAN. □□ **man·u·al·ly** *adv.*.

man·u·fac·ture /mányəfákchər/ *n.* & *v.* ● *n.* **1 a** the making of articles, esp. in a factory, etc. **b** a branch of an industry (*woolen manufacture*). **2** esp. *derog.* the merely mechanical production of literature, etc. ● *v.tr.* **1** make (articles), esp. on an industrial scale. **2** invent or fabricate (evidence, etc.). **3** esp. *derog.* make or produce in a mechanical way. □□ **man·u·fac·tur·a·bil·i·ty** /-chərəbílitee/ *n.* **man·u·fac·tur·a·ble** *adj.* **man·u·fac·tur·er** *n.*

man·u·mit /mányəmít/ *v.tr.* (**manumitted, manumitting**) *hist.* set (a slave) free. □□ **man·u·mis·sion** /-míshən/ *n.*

ma·nure /mənŏŏr, -nyŏŏr/ *n.* & *v.* ● *n.* **1** animal dung used for fertilizing land. **2** any compost or artificial fertilizer. ● *v.tr.* (also *absol.*) apply manure to (land, etc.).

ma·nure spread·er *n.* a machine for spreading manure on fields. □□ **ma·nure spread·ing**

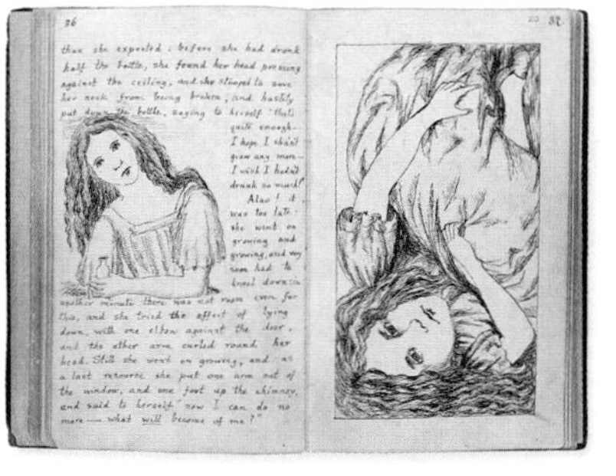

MANUSCRIPT OF *ALICE IN WONDERLAND* BY LEWIS CARROLL

man·u·script /mányəskript/ *n.* & *adj.* ● *n.* **1** ◀ a handwritten or typed text. **2** handwritten form. ● *adj.* written by hand.

Manx /mangks/ *adj.* & *n.* ● *adj.* of or relating to the Isle of Man. ● *n.* **1** the now extinct Celtic language formerly spoken in the Isle of Man. **2** (prec. by *the*; treated as *pl.*) the Manx people.

Manx cat *n.* a breed of tailless cat. ▷ CAT

Manx shear·wa·ter *n.* a brownish-black and white shearwater, *Puffinus puffinus*, of Atlantic and Mediterranean waters.

man·y /ménee/ *adj.* & *n.* ● *adj.* (**more** /mawr/; **most** /mōst/) great in number; numerous (*many times*). ● *n.* (as *pl.*) **1** a large number (*many went*). **2** (prec. by *the*) the multitude of esp. working people. □ **as many** the same number of (*six mistakes in as many lines*). **as many again** the same number additionally (*sixty here and as many again there*). **be too** (or **one too**) **many for** outwit, baffle. **a good** (or **great**) **many** a large number. **many's the time** often. **many a time** many times.

man·y-sid·ed *adj.* having many sides, aspects, interests, capabilities, etc. □□ **man·y-sid·ed·ness** *n.*

Mao·ism /mówizəm/ *n.* the Communist doctrines of Mao Zedong (d. 1976), Chinese statesman. □□ **Mao·ist** *n.* & *adj.*

Ma·o·ri /mówree/ *n.* & *adj.* ● *n.* (*pl.* same or **Maoris**) **1** a member of the Polynesian aboriginal people of New Zealand. **2** the language of the Maori. ● *adj.* of or concerning the Maori or their language.

map /map/ *n.* & *v.* ● *n.* **1 a** ▼ a usu. flat representation of the Earth's surface, or part of it, showing physical features, cities, etc. ▷ AZIMUTHAL PROJECTION, MERCATOR PROJECTION, RELIEF MAP. **b** a diagrammatic representation of a route, etc. (*drew a map of the journey*). **2** a two-dimensional representation of the stars, the heavens, etc. **3** a diagram showing the arrangement or components of a thing. **4** *sl.* the face. ● *v.tr.* (**mapped, mapping**) **1** represent (a country, etc.) on a map. **2** *Math.* associate each element of (a set) with one element of another set. □ **map out** arrange in detail; plan (a course of conduct, etc). **on the map** *colloq.* prominent, important. **wipe off the map** *colloq.* obliterate □□ **map·per** *n.*

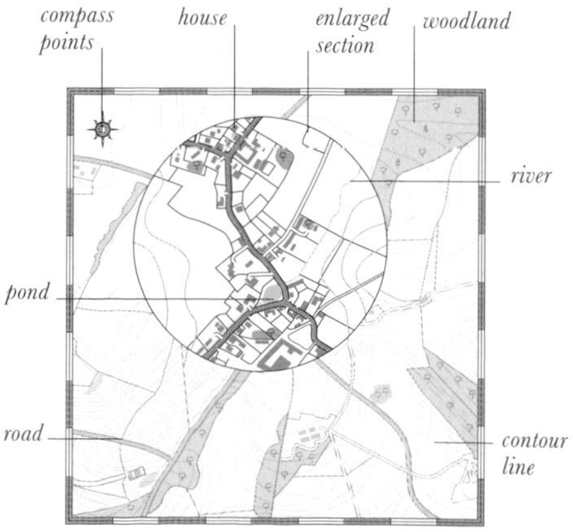
compass points
house
enlarged section
woodland
river
pond
road
contour line

MAP OF A VILLAGE AND SURROUNDING COUNTRYSIDE

M

ma·ple /máypəl/ *n.* **1** any tree or shrub of the genus *Acer*, grown for shade, ornament, wood, or its sugar. **2** the wood of the maple.

ma·ple leaf *n.* ▶ the leaf of the maple, used as an emblem of Canada.

MAPLE LEAF
(*Acer saccharinum*)

ma·ple sug·ar *n.* a sugar produced by evaporating the sap of the sugar maple, etc.

ma·ple syr·up *n.* a syrup produced from the sap of the sugar maple, etc.

ma·quette /məkét/ *n.* **1** a sculptor's small preliminary model in wax, clay, etc. **2** a preliminary sketch.

ma·quil·lage /mákeeyáazh/ *n.* **1** makeup; cosmetics. **2** the application of makeup.

Ma·quis /makée/ *n.* **1** the French resistance movement during the German occupation (1940–45). **2** a member of this.

Mar. *abbr.* March.

mar /maar/ *v.tr.* (**marred, marring**) **1** ruin. **2** impair the perfection of; spoil; disfigure.

mar·a·bou /márəboo/ *n.* (also **mar·a·bout**) **1** ▶ a large W. African stork, *Leptoptilos crumeniferus*. **2** a tuft of down from the wing or tail of the marabou used as a trimming for hats, etc.

MARABOU
(*Leptoptilos crumeniferus*)

ma·rac·a /məráakə/ *n.* a hollow clublike gourd or gourd-shaped container filled with beans, etc., and usu. shaken in pairs as a percussion instrument in Latin American music. ▷ ORCHESTRA, PERCUSSION

mar·a·schi·no /márəskéenō, -shée-/ *n.* (*pl.* **-os**) a strong, sweet liqueur made from a small black Dalmatian cherry.

mar·a·schi·no cher·ry *n.* a cherry preserved in or flavored with maraschino and used to decorate cocktails, desserts, etc.

ma·ras·mus /mərázməs/ *n.* a wasting away of the body. □□ **ma·ras·mic** *adj.*

mar·a·thon /márəthon/ *n.* **1** a long-distance running race, usu. of 26 miles 385 yards (42.195 km). **2** a long-lasting or difficult task, operation, etc.

ma·raud /məráwd/ *v.* **1** *intr.* **a** make a plundering raid. **b** pilfer systematically; plunder. **2** *tr.* plunder (a place). □□ **ma·raud·er** *n.*

mar·ble /máarbəl/ *n.* & *v.* ● *n.* **1** limestone in a metamorphic crystalline (or granular) state, and capable of taking a polish, used in sculpture and architecture. ▷ METAMORPHIC ROCKS. **2** (often *attrib.*) **a** anything made of marble (*a marble clock*). **b** anything resembling marble in hardness, coldness, durability, etc. (*her features were marble*). **3 a** a small ball of marble, glass, etc., used as a toy. **b** (in *pl.*; treated as *sing.*) a game using these. **4** (in *pl.*) *sl.* one's mental faculties (*he's lost his marbles*). **5** (in *pl.*) a collection of sculptures (*Roman marbles*). ● *v.tr.* **1** (esp. as **marbled** *adj.*) stain or color to look like variegated marble. **2** (as **marbled** *adj.*) (of meat) streaked with alternating layers of lean and fat.

mar·ble cake *n.* a cake with a streaked appearance, made of light and dark batter.

mar·bling /máarbling/ *n.* **1** coloring or marking like marble. **2** streaks of fat in lean meat.

marc /maark/ *n.* **1** the refuse of pressed grapes, etc. **2** a brandy made from this.

mar·ca·site /máarkəsīt/ *n.* **1** ▶ a yellowish crystalline iron sulfide mineral. **2** these bronze-yellow crystals used in jewelry.

marcasite crystals *chalk groundmass*

MARCASITE

mar·ca·to /maarkáatō/ *adv.* & *adj. Mus.* played with emphasis.

mar·cel /maarsél/ *n.* & *v.* ● *n.* (in full **marcel wave**) a deep wave in the hair. ● *v.tr.* (**marcelled, marcelling**) wave (hair) with a deep wave.

mar·ces·cent /maarsésənt/ *adj.* (of part of a plant) withering but not falling. □□ **mar·ces·cence** /-səns/ *n.*

March /maarch/ *n.* the third month of the year.

march[1] /maarch/ *v.* & *n.* ● *v.* **1** *intr.* (usu. foll. by *away, off, out,* etc.) walk in a military manner with a regular tread. **2** *tr.* (often foll. by *away, on, off,* etc.) cause to march or walk. **3** *intr.* **a** walk or proceed steadily, esp. across country. **b** continue unrelentingly (*time marches on*). **4** *intr.* take part in a protest march. ● *n.* **1 a** the act or an instance of marching. **b** the uniform step of troops, etc. (*a slow march*). **2 a** long difficult walk. **3** a procession as a demonstration. **4** (usu. foll. by *of*) progress or continuity (*the march of events*). **5 a** a piece of music composed to accompany a march. **b** a composition of similar character and form. □ **march on 1** advance toward (a military objective). **2** proceed. **on the march 1** marching. **2** in steady progress. □□ **march·er** *n.*

march[2] /maarch/ *n. hist.* **1** (usu. in *pl.*) a boundary; a frontier (esp. of the borderland between England and Scotland or Wales). **2** a tract of often disputed land between two countries.

march·er /máarchər/ *n.* an inhabitant of a march or border district.

march·ing or·ders *n.pl.* **1** *Mil.* the direction for troops to depart for war, etc. **2** a dismissal.

mar·chion·ess /máarshənés/ *n.* **1** the wife or widow of a marquess. **2** a woman holding the rank of marquess in her own right (cf. MARQUISE).

march past *n.* & *v.* ● *n.* the marching of troops past a saluting point at a review. ● *v.intr.* (of troops) carry out a march past.

Mar·di Gras /máardee gráa/ *n.* **1 a** the last day before Lent, celebrated in some places, as New Orleans; Shrove Tuesday. **b** merrymaking on this day. **2** the last day of a carnival, etc.

mare[1] /mair/ *n.* the female of any equine animal, esp. the horse.

ma·re[2] /máaray/ *n.* (*pl.* **maria** /máareeə/ or **mares**) **1** (in full **ma·re clau·sum** /klówsŏom/) *Law* the sea under the jurisdiction of a particular country. **2** (in full **ma·re li·be·rum** /léebərŏom/) *Law* the sea open to all nations. **3 a** any of a number of large dark flat areas on the surface of the Moon, once thought to be seas. **b** a similar area on Mars.

ma·rem·ma /mər-émə/ *n.* (*pl.* **maremme** /-mee/) low marshy land near a seashore.

mare's nest *n.* an illusory discovery.

mare's tail *n.* **1** a tall slender marsh plant, *Hippuris vulgaris.* **2** (in *pl.*) long straight streaks of cirrus cloud.

mar·ga·rine /máarjərin/ *n.* a butter substitute made from vegetable oils or animal fats with milk, etc.

mar·ga·ri·ta /maargəréetə/ *n.* a cocktail made with tequila, lime or lemon juice, and orange-flavored liqueur.

mar·gay /máargay/ *n.* a small wild S. American cat, *Felis wiedii.*

mar·gin /máarjin/ *n.* & *v.* ● *n.* **1** an edge or border. **2 a** the blank border on each side of the print on a page, etc. **b** a line or rule, as on paper, marking off a margin. **3** an amount (of time, money, etc.) by which a thing exceeds, falls short, etc. **4** the lower limit (*his effort fell below the margin*). **5** an amount deposited with a stockbroker by the customer when borrowing from the broker to purchase securities. **6** in banking, the difference between the current market value of a loan's collateral and the face value of the loan. ● *v.tr.* (**margined, margining**) provide with a margin or marginal notes.

mar·gin·al /máarjinəl/ *adj.* **1 a** of or written in a margin. **b** having marginal notes. **2 a** of or at the edge. **b** not significant or decisive (*of marginal interest*). **3** close to the limit, esp. of profitability. **4** (of the sea) adjacent to the shore of a state. **5** (of land) difficult to cultivate; unprofitable. **6** barely adequate; unprovided for. □□ **mar·gin·al·i·ty** /-nálitee/ *n.* **mar·gin·al·ly** *adv.*

mar·gin·al cost *n.* the cost added by making one extra copy, etc.

mar·gi·na·li·a /máarjináyleeə/ *n.pl.* marginal notes.

mar·gin·al·ize /máarjinəlīz/ *v.tr.* make or treat as insignificant. □□ **mar·gin·al·i·za·tion** *n.*

mar·gin·ate *v.* & *adj.* ● *v.tr.* /máarjinayt/ **1** = MARGINALIZE. **2** provide with a margin or border. ● *adj.* /máarjinət/ *Biol.* having a distinct margin or border. □□ **mar·gin·a·tion** /-náyshən/ *n.*

mar·gin of er·ror *n.* a usu. small difference allowed for miscalculation.

mar·gue·rite /máargəréet/ *n.* an oxeye daisy.

ma·ri·a *pl.* of MARE[2].

mar·i·ach·i /maareeáachee, mar-/ *n.* **1** a Mexican band of strolling street musicians. **2** the music played by such a band.

mar·i·gold /márigōld/ *n.* any plant of the genus *Tagetes* or *Calendula*, with bright yellow, orange, or maroon flowers. ▷ HERB

ma·ri·jua·na /máriwáanə/ *n.* (also **ma·ri·hua·na**) **1** the dried leaves, flowering tops, and stems of the hemp, used as a drug, often smoked in cigarettes. **2** the plant yielding these (cf. HEMP).

ma·rim·ba /mərímbə/ *n.* **1** a xylophone of Africa and Central America. **2** ◀ a modern orchestral instrument derived from this.

ma·ri·na /məréenə/ *n.* a specially designed harbor with moorings for yachts, etc.

ma·ri·nade /márináyd/ *n.* & *v.* ● *n.* **1** a mixture of wine, vinegar, oil, spices, etc., in which meat, fish, etc., is soaked before cooking. **2** meat, fish, etc., soaked in this liquid. ● *v.tr.* = MARINATE.

mallet

resonating metal tubes

MARIMBA

ma·ri·na·ra /marináarə/ *adj.* (of a pasta sauce) made with tomatoes, spices, etc., usu. without meat.

ma·ri·nate /márinayt/ *v.tr.* soak in a marinade. □□ **mar·i·na·tion** /-náyshən/ *n.*

ma·rine /məréen/ *adj.* & *n.* ● *adj.* **1** of, found in, or produced by the sea. **2 a** of or relating to shipping or naval matters. **b** for use at sea. ● *n.* **1** a country's shipping, fleet, or navy. **2 a** a member of the US Marine Corps. **b** a member of a body of troops trained to serve on land or sea. **3** a picture of a scene at sea.

mar·i·ner /márinər/ *n.* a seaman.

Mar·i·ol·a·try /máireeólətree/ *n. derog.* idolatrous worship of the Virgin Mary.

mar·i·on·ette /máreeənét/ *n.* ▼ a puppet worked by strings.

MARIONETTES

mar·i·tal /márital/ *adj.* of marriage or the relations between husband and wife. □□ **mar·i·tal·ly** *adv.*

mar·i·time /máritīm/ *adj.* **1** connected with the sea or seafaring. **2** living or found near the sea.

mar·jo·ram /máarjərəm/ *n.* an aromatic culinary herb of the genus *Origanum*. ▷ HERB

mark[1] /maark/ *n. & v.* ● *n.* **1** trace, sign, stain, etc., on a face, page, etc. **2** (esp. in *comb.*) **a** a written or printed symbol (*question mark*). **b** a number or letter denoting excellence, conduct, etc. (*got a good mark for effort*). **3** (usu. foll. by *of*) a sign or indication of quality, character, etc. (*as a mark of respect*). **4 a** a sign, seal, etc., used for distinction or identification. **b** a cross, etc., made in place of a signature by an illiterate person. **5 a** a target, object, goal, etc. (*missed the mark*). **b** a standard for attainment (*his work falls below the mark*). **6** a marker. **7** a runner's starting point in a race. ● *v.tr.* **1 a** make a mark on (a thing or person), esp. by writing, cutting, etc. **b** put an identifying mark, name, etc., on (*marked the tree with their initials*). **2 a** allot marks to (a student's work, etc.). **b** record (the points gained in games, etc.). **3** attach a price to (goods, etc.) (*marked the doll at $2*). **4** (often foll. by *by*) show or manifest (displeasure, etc.) (*marked his anger by leaving early*). **5** notice or observe (*she marked his agitation*). **6 a** characterize or be a feature of (*the day was marked by storms*). **b** celebrate (*marked the occasion with a toast*). **7** name or indicate by a sign or mark. **8** characterize (a person or a thing) as (*marked them as weak*). **9** (as **marked** *adj.*) having natural marks (*marked with silver spots*). **10** (of a graduated instrument) show, register (so many degrees, etc.). **11** castrate (a lamb). □ **beside** (or **off** or **wide of**) **the mark 1** irrelevant. **2** not accurate. **make one's mark** attain distinction. **mark down 1** mark (goods, etc.) at a lower price. **2** make a written note of. **3** choose (a person) as one's victim. **mark my words** heed my warning or prediction. **mark off** (often foll. by *from*) separate (one thing from another) by a boundary, etc. **mark out 1** plan a course of action, etc.). **2** destine (*marked out for success*). **3** trace out boundaries, etc. **mark time 1** *Mil.* march on the spot, without moving forward. **2** act routinely. **3** await an opportunity to advance. **mark up 1** mark (goods, etc.) at a higher price. **2** mark or correct (text, etc.). **off the mark 1** having made a start. **2** = *beside the mark*. **of mark** noteworthy. **on the mark** ready to start. **on your mark** (or **marks**) (as an instruction) get ready to start (esp. a race). **up to the mark** reaching the normal standard.

mark[2] /maark/ *n.* = DEUTSCHMARK.

mark·down /máarkdown/ *n.* a reduction in price.

marked /maarkt/ *adj.* **1** having a visible mark. **2** clearly noticeable (*a marked difference*). **3** (of playing cards) having distinctive marks to assist cheating. □□ **mark·ed·ly** /-kidlee/ *adv.* **mark·ed·ness** /-kidnis/ *n.*

marked man *n.* **1** a person whose conduct is watched with suspicion or hostility. **2** a person destined to succeed.

mark·er /máarkər/ *n.* **1** a stone, post, etc., used to mark a place reached, etc. **2** a person or thing that marks. **3** a felt-tipped pen with a broad tip.

mar·ket /máarkit/ *n. & v.* ● *n.* **1 a** the gathering of people for the purchase and sale of provisions, livestock, etc. **b** the time of this. **2** an open space or covered building used for this. **3** (often foll. by *for*) a demand for a commodity or service (*a ready market*). **4** a place or group providing such a demand. **5** conditions as regards, or opportunity for, buying or selling. **6** the rate of purchase and sale; market value (*the market fell*). **7** (prec. by *the*) the trade in a specified commodity (*the grain market*). ● *v.* **1** *tr.* sell. **2** *tr.* offer for sale. **3** *intr.* buy or sell goods in a market. □ **be in the market for** wish to buy. **be on** (or **come into**) **the market** be offered for sale. **put on the market** offer for sale. □□ **mar·ket·er** *n.*

mar·ket·a·ble /máarkitəbəl/ *adj.* able or fit to be sold. □□ **mar·ket·a·bil·i·ty** /-bílitee/ *n.*

mar·ket·eer /máarkiteér/ *n.* a marketer.

mar·ket·ing /máarkiting/ *n.* the activity or process involving research, promotion, sales, and distribution of a product or service.

mar·ket·place /máarkitplays/ *n.* **1** an open space where a market is held in a town. **2** the scene of actual dealings. **3** a forum or sphere for the exchange of ideas, etc.

mar·ket price *n.* the current price of a commodity, etc.

mar·ket re·search *n.* the study of consumers' needs and preferences.

mar·ket val·ue *n.* value as a salable thing (opp. BOOK VALUE).

mark·ing /máarking/ *n.* (usu. in *pl.*) **1** an identification mark, esp. a symbol on an aircraft. **2** the coloring of an animal's fur, feathers, skin, etc.

marks·man /máarksmən/ *n.* (*pl.* **-men**; *fem.* **-woman**, *pl.* **-women**) a person skilled in shooting, esp. with a pistol or rifle. □□ **marks·man·ship** *n.*

mark·up /máarkup/ *n.* the amount added to the cost of goods to cover overhead charges, etc.

marl /maarl/ *n. & v.* ● *n.* soil consisting of clay and lime, with fertilizing properties. ● *v.tr.* apply marl to. □□ **marl·y** *adj.*

mar·lin /máarlin/ *n.* ▼ any of various large marine fish of the genera *Makaira* and *Tetrapterus*, with a long upper jaw.

MARLIN: STRIPED MARLIN
(*Tetrapterus audax*)

mar·line /máarlin/ *n. Naut.* a light rope of two strands.

mar·lin·spike /máarlinspīk/ *n.* (also **mar·line·spike**) *Naut.* a pointed iron tool used to separate strands of rope or wire.

mar·ma·lade /máarmɔlayd/ *n.* a preserve of citrus fruit, usu. bitter oranges, made like jam.

mar·mo·re·al /maarmáwreeəl/ *adj. poet.* of or like marble. □□ **mar·mo·re·al·ly** *adv.*

mar·mo·set /máarmɔset, -zet/ *n.* ▶ any of several small tropical American monkeys of the family Callithricidae, having a long bushy tail.

MARMOSET:
COMMON MARMOSET
(*Callithrix jacchus*)

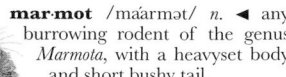

mar·mot /máarmɔt/ *n.* ◀ any burrowing rodent of the genus *Marmota*, with a heavyset body and short bushy tail.

MARMOT: BOBAK MARMOT
(*Marmota bobak*)

mar·o·cain /márɔkayn/ *n.* a dress fabric of ribbed crepe.

Mar·o·nite /márɔnīt/ *n.* a member of a sect of Syrian Christians living chiefly in Lebanon.

ma·roon[1] /mərōón/ *adj. & n.* ● *adj.* brownish-crimson. ● *n.* this color.

ma·roon[2] /mərōón/ *v.tr.* **1** leave (a person) isolated in a desolate place (esp. an island). **2** (of a person or a natural phenomenon) cause (a person) to be unable to leave a place.

marque /maark/ *n.* a make of a product, as a sports car (*the Porsche marque*).

mar·quee /maarkeé/ *n.* a rooflike projection over the entrance to a theater, hotel, etc.

mar·quess /máarkwis/ *n.* a British nobleman ranking between a duke and an earl (cf. MARQUIS). □□ **mar·quess·ate** /-kwisət/ *n.*

mar·que·try /máarkitree/ *n.* (also **mar·que·te·rie**) inlaid work in wood, ivory, etc.

mar·quis /máarkwis, -keé/ *n.* a nobleman ranking between a duke and a count (cf. MARQUESS). □□ **mar·quis·ate** /-kwisət/ *n.*

mar·quise /maarkeéz, -keé/ *n.* **1 a** the wife or widow of a marquis. **b** a woman holding the rank of marquis in her own right (cf. MARCHIONESS). **2 a** a finger ring set with a pointed oval cluster of gems. **b** (also **marquise cut**) an oval cut gem with many facets.

mar·qui·sette /máarkizét/ *n.* a fine light cotton, rayon, or silk fabric for net curtains, etc.

mar·ram /márəm/ *n.* ▼ a shore grass, *Ammophila arenaria*, that binds sand.

mar·riage /márij/ *n.* **1** the legal union of a man and a woman in order to live together and often to have children. **2** an act or ceremony establishing this union. **3** one particular union of this kind (*by a previous marriage*). **4** an intimate union (*the marriage of true minds*). **5** *Cards* the union of a king and queen of the same suit. □ **by marriage** as a result of a marriage (*related by marriage*). **in marriage** as husband or wife (*give in marriage; take in marriage*).

MARRAM
(*Ammophila arenaria*)

mar·riage·a·ble /márijəbəl/ *adj.* **1** fit for marriage, esp. old or rich enough to marry. **2** (of age) fit for marriage. □□ **mar·riage·a·bil·i·ty** /-bílitee/ *n.*

mar·riage of con·ven·ience *n.* a marriage concluded to achieve some practical purpose.

mar·ried /máreed/ *adj. & n.* ● *adj.* **1** united in marriage. **2** of or relating to marriage (*married name; married life*). ● *n.* (usu. in *pl.*) a married person (*young marrieds*).

mar·ron gla·cé /marṓn glaasáy/ *n.* (*pl.* **marrons glacés** *pronunc.* same) a chestnut preserved in and coated with sugar.

mar·row /márō/ *n.* **1** a soft fatty substance in the cavities of bones. **2** strength and vitality. **3** the essential part. □ **to the marrow** right through.

mar·row·bone /márōbṓn/ *n.* a bone containing edible marrow.

M

MARS

The fourth planet from the Sun, Mars is known as the red planet because of the iron-oxide dust that covers its surface. In its northern hemisphere are many vast plains formed of solidified lava. The southern hemisphere is pitted with craters and large impact basins. Olympus Mons is the largest extinct volcano in the solar system. The *Mariner 9* space probe discovered an enormous canyon, Valles Marineris, which dwarfs the Grand Canyon. The Martian atmosphere is thin, consisting mostly of carbon dioxide. Mars is orbited by two tiny moons, Phobos and Deimos.

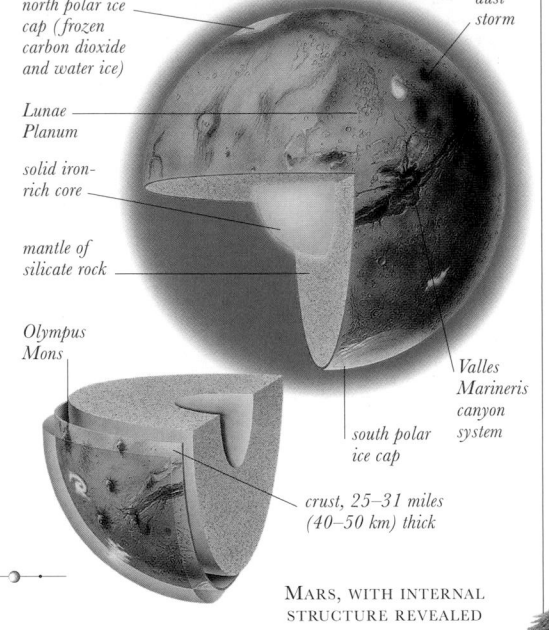

north polar ice cap (frozen carbon dioxide and water ice)

dust storm

Lunae Planum

solid iron-rich core

mantle of silicate rock

Olympus Mons

Valles Marineris canyon system

south polar ice cap

crust, 25–31 miles (40–50 km) thick

SOLAR SYSTEM

Earth

Sun

Mars

MARS, WITH INTERNAL STRUCTURE REVEALED

mar·ry[1] /máree/ v. (**-ies, -ied**) **1** tr. **a** take as one's spouse in marriage. **b** (of a priest, etc.) join or give in marriage. **c** (of a parent or guardian) give (a son, daughter, etc.) in marriage. **2** intr. enter into marriage. **3** tr. **a** unite intimately. **b** correlate (things) as a pair. □ **marry off** find a wife or husband for.

mar·ry[2] /máree/ int. archaic expressing surprise, asseveration, indignation, etc.

mar·ry·ing /máree-ing/ adj. likely or inclined to marry (not a marrying man).

Mars /maarz/ n. ▲ a reddish planet, fourth in order of distance from the Sun and next beyond the Earth. ▷ SOLAR SYSTEM

Mar·sa·la /maarsáalə/ n. a dark sweet fortified wine.

Mar·seil·laise /máarsayéz, máarsəláyz/ n. the national anthem of France.

marsh /maarsh/ n. **1** low land flooded in wet weather and usu. watery at all times. **2** (attrib.) of or inhabiting marshland. □□ **marsh·y** adj. (**marsh·i·er, marsh·i·est**). **marsh·i·ness** n.

mar·shal /máarshəl/ n. & v. ● n. **1** US an officer of a judicial district, similar to a sheriff. **2** US the head of a fire department. **3** a high-ranking officer in the armed forces of certain countries (air marshal; field marshal). **4** an officer arranging ceremonies, controlling procedure at races, etc. **5** US a court officer who assists a judge. ● v. **1** tr. arrange (soldiers, facts, one's thoughts, etc.) in due order. **2** tr. (often foll. by into, to) conduct (a person) ceremoniously. **3** tr. Heraldry combine (coats of arms). **4** intr. take up positions in due arrangement. □□ **mar·shal·er** n.

mar·shal·ship n.

marsh gas n. methane.

marsh·land /máarshland/ n. land consisting of marshes.

marsh·mal·low /máarshmélō, -málō/ n. a spongy confection made of sugar, albumen, gelatin, etc.

marsh mar·i·gold n. ◀ a golden-flowered ranunculaceous plant, *Caltha palustris*, growing in moist meadows, etc. Also called **cowslip**; **kingcup**.

MARSH MARIGOLD
(*Caltha palustris*)

mar·su·pi·al /maarsóopeeəl/ n. & adj. ● n. ▼ any mammal of the order Marsupialia, characterized by being carried and suckled in a pouch on the mother's belly. ● adj. **1** of or belonging to this order. **2** of or like a pouch (marsupial muscle).

mart /maart/ n. **1** a trade center. **2** an auction room. **3** a market. **b** a marketplace.

mar·ten /máart'n/ n. any weaselike carnivore of the genus *Martes*, having valuable fur. ▷ MUSTELID

mar·tens·ite /máart'nzīt/ n. the chief constituent of hardened steel.

mar·tial /máarshəl/ adj. **1** of or appropriate to warfare. **2** warlike; brave; fond of fighting. □□ **mar·tial·ly** adv.

martial arts n.pl. fighting sports such as judo and karate.

martial law n. military government, involving the suspension of ordinary law.

Mar·tian /máarshən/ adj. & n. ● adj. of the planet Mars. ● n. a hypothetical inhabitant of Mars.

mar·tin /máart'n/ n. any of several swallows of the family Hirundinidae, esp. the house martin and purple martin.

mar·ti·net /máart'nét/ n. a strict (esp. military or naval) disciplinarian.

mar·tin·gale /máart'ngayl/ n. ▼ a strap, or set of straps, fastened at one end to the noseband of a horse and at the other end to the girth, to prevent rearing, etc. ▷ SHOW JUMPING

noseband

neckstrap

rein

martingale

girth with martingale attached

MARTINGALE: RUNNING MARTINGALE

mar·ti·ni /maarteénee/ n. a cocktail made of gin and dry vermouth, often garnished with a green olive, lemon peel, etc.

mart·let /máartlit/ n. **1** Heraldry an imaginary foot-

MARSUPIAL

Marsupials are distinguished by the way their offspring develop. Following a brief gestation period, the female gives birth to small, extremely immature young, which make their way into a pouch (marsupium) on the outside of the mother's abdomen. There they attach themselves to a nipple and continue to grow and develop. Found mainly in Australasia, this mammal order contains some 250 species.

EXAMPLES OF MARSUPIALS

marsupium

joey

long hind legs and feet

RED KANGAROO
(*Macropus rufus*)

VIRGINIA OPOSSUM
(*Didelphis virginiana*)

KOALA
(*Phascolarctos cinereus*)

WOMBAT
(*Vombatidae ursinus*)

M

less bird borne as a charge. **2** *archaic* **a** a swift. **b** a house martin.

mar·tyr /máartər/ *n. & v.* ● *n.* **1 a** a person who is put to death for refusing to renounce a faith or belief. **b** a person who suffers for adhering to a principle, cause, etc. **2** a person who feigns or complains of suffering to gain sympathy. **3** (foll. by *to*) a constant sufferer from (an ailment). ● *v.tr.* **1** put to death as a martyr. **2** torment. □ **make a martyr of oneself** accept or pretend to accept unnecessary discomfort, etc.

mar·tyr·dom /máartərdəm/ *n.* **1** the sufferings and death of a martyr. **2** torment.

mar·tyr·ol·o·gy /máartəróləjee/ *n.* (*pl.* **-ies**) **1** a list or register of martyrs. **2** the history of martyrs. □□ **mar·tyr·o·log·i·cal** /-rəlójikəl/ *adj.* **mar·tyr·ol·o·gist** /-rólə-/ *n.*

mar·tyr·y /máartəree/ *n.* (*pl.* **-ies**) a shrine or church erected in honor of a martyr.

mar·vel /máarvəl/ *n. & v.* ● *n.* **1** a wonderful thing or person. **2** (often foll. by *of*) a wonderful example (*she's a marvel of patience*). ● *v.intr. literary* **1** (foll. by *at*, or *that* + clause) feel surprise or wonder. **2** (foll. by *how*, *why*, etc. + clause) wonder.

mar·vel·ous /máarvələs/ *adj.* **1** astonishing. **2** excellent. **3** extremely improbable. □□ **mar·vel·ous·ly** *adv.*

Marx·ism /máarksizəm/ *n.* the political and economic theories of Karl Marx (d. 1883), predicting the overthrow of capitalism and the eventual attainment of a classless society with the state controlling the means of production. □□ **Marx·ist** *n. & adj.*

mar·zi·pan /máarzipan/ *n. & v.* ● *n.* **1** a paste of ground almonds, sugar, etc., made up into small cakes, etc., or used to coat large cakes. **2** a piece of marzipan. ● *v.tr.* (**marzipanned**, **marzipanning**) cover with marzipan.

Ma·sai /maasí, maasí/ *n. & adj.* ● *n.* (*pl.* same or **Masais**) **1 a** a pastoral people of mainly Hamitic stock living in Kenya and Tanzania. **b** ▼ a member of this people. **2** the Nilotic language of the Masai. ● *adj.* of or relating to the Masai or their language.

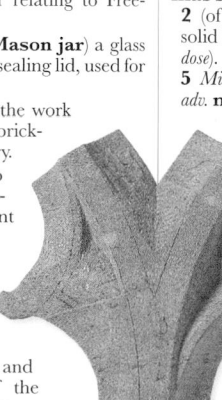

beaded necklace
elder's short staff
fly-swatting brush
traditional dress (rubeka) **MASAI** FAMILY *sandals* (namuka)

mas·car·a /maskárə/ *n.* a cosmetic for darkening the eyelashes. ▷ MAKEUP

mas·car·po·ne /maskáapóni/ *n.* a soft, mild Italian cream cheese.

mas·con /máskon/ *n. Astron.* a concentration of dense matter below the Moon's surface, producing a gravitational pull.

mas·cot /máskot/ *n.* a person, animal, or thing that is supposed to bring good luck.

mas·cu·line /máskyəlin/ *adj. & n.* ● *adj.* **1** of or characteristic of men. **2** manly; vigorous. **3** (of a woman) having qualities considered appropriate to a man. **4** *Gram.* of or denoting the gender proper to men's names. ● *n. Gram.* the masculine gender; a masculine word. □□ **mas·cu·lin·i·ty** /-línitee/ *n.*

ma·ser /máyzər/ *n.* a device using the stimulated emission of radiation by excited atoms to amplify or generate coherent monochromatic electromagnetic radiation in the microwave range (cf. LASER).

MASH /mash/ *abbr.* Mobile Army Surgical Hospital.

mash /mash/ *n. & v.* ● *n.* **1** a soft mixture. **2** a mixture of boiled grain, bran, etc., given warm to horses, etc. **3** a mixture of malt or other grain and hot water used in brewing, distilling, etc. **4** *Brit. colloq.* mashed potatoes. **5** a soft pulp made by crushing, mixing with water, etc. ● *v.tr.* **1** reduce (potatoes, etc.) to a uniform mass by crushing. **2** crush or pound to a pulp. **3** mix (malt) with hot water to form wort. □□ **mash·er** *n.*

mash·ie /máshee/ *n. Golf* former name of an iron used for lofting or for medium distances; five iron.

mask /mask/ *n. & v.* ● *n.* **1** ▶ a covering for all or part of the face worn as a disguise, for protection (e.g., by a fencer) or by a surgeon to prevent infection of a patient. ▷ FENCING **2** a respirator used to filter inhaled air or to supply gas for inhalation. **3** a likeness of a person's face, esp. one made by taking a mold from the face (*death mask*). **4** a disguise or pretense (*throw off the mask*). **5** the face or head of an animal, esp. a fox. **6** a cosmetic preparation spread on the face and left to dry before removal. ● *v.tr.* **1** cover (the face, etc.) with a mask. **2** disguise or conceal (a taste, one's feelings, etc.). **3** protect from a process. □□ **masked** /maskt/ *adj.* **mask·er** *n.*

mask·ing tape *n.* adhesive tape used in painting to cover areas on which paint is not wanted.

mas·och·ism /másəkizəm/ *n.* **1** a form of (esp. sexual) perversion characterized by gratification derived from one's own pain or humiliation (cf. SADISM). **2** *colloq.* the enjoyment of what appears to be painful or tiresome. □□ **mas·och·ist** *n.* **mas·och·is·tic** *adj.* **mas·och·is·ti·cal·ly** *adv.*

ma·son /máysən/ *n. & v.* ● *n.* **1** a person who builds with stone or brick. **2** (**Mason**) a Freemason. ● *v.tr.* build or strengthen with masonry.

Ma·son–Dix·on line /máysən-díksən/ *n.* the boundary between Maryland and Pennsylvania, taken as the northern limit of the slave-owning states before the abolition of slavery.

Ma·son·ic /məsónik/ *adj.* of or relating to Freemasons.

ma·son jar /máysən/ *n.* (also **Mason jar**) a glass jar with a wide mouth and tight-sealing lid, used for canning.

ma·son·ry /máysənree/ *n.* **1 a** the work of a mason. **b** ▶ stonework; brickwork. **2** (**Masonry**) Freemasonry.

Ma·so·rah /məsáwrə/ *n.* (also **Massorah**) a body of traditional information and comment on the text of the Hebrew Bible.

Mas·o·rete /másəreet/ *n.* (also **Massorete**) a Jewish scholar contributing to the Masorah. □□ **Mas·o·ret·ic** /-rétik/ *adj.*

masque /mask/ *n.* a dramatic and musical entertainment, esp. of the 16th and 17th c., originally with pantomime, later with metrical dialogue.

MASK: JAPANESE NOH MASK FROM EDO PERIOD

MASONRY: MEDIEVAL WINDOW STONEWORK

mas·quer·ade /máskəráyd/ *n. & v.* ● *n.* **1** a false show or pretense. **2** a masked ball. ● *v.intr.* (often foll. by *as*) appear in disguise; assume a false appearance. □□ **mas·quer·ad·er** *n.*

Mass. *abbr.* Massachusetts.

mass¹ /mas/ *n. & v.* ● *n.* **1** a body of matter of indefinite shape. **2** a dense aggregation of objects (*a mass of fibers*). **3** (in *sing.* or *pl.*; foll. by *of*) a large number or amount. **4** (usu. foll. by *of*) an unbroken expanse (of color, etc.). **5** (prec. by *a*; foll. by *of*) covered or abounding in (*was a mass of cuts and bruises*). **6** a main portion (of a painting, etc.) as perceived by the eye. **7** (prec. by *the*) **a** the majority. **b** (in *pl.*) the ordinary people. **8** *Physics* the quantity of matter a body contains. **9** (*attrib.*) relating to, done by, or affecting large numbers of people or things; large-scale (*mass audience; mass action; mass murder*). ● *v.tr. & intr.* **1** assemble into a mass or as one body (*the bands massed at dawn*). **2** *Mil.* (with ref. to troops) concentrate or be concentrated.

mass² /mas/ *n.* **1** (usu. **Mass**) the Eucharist, esp. in the Roman Catholic Church. **2** a celebration of this. **3** the liturgy used in the Mass. **4** a musical setting of parts of this.

Mas·sa·chu·set /masəchŏosət, -zət/ *n. & adj.* ● *n.* **1 a** a N. American people, no longer in existence as a separate people, who occupied eastern Massachusetts in colonial times. **b** a member of this people. **2** the language of this people. ● *adj.* of or relating to this people or their language.

mas·sa·cre /másəkər/ *n. & v.* ● *n.* **1** a general slaughter (of persons, occasionally of animals). **2** an utter defeat or destruction. ● *v.tr.* **1** make a massacre of. **2** murder (esp. a large number of people) cruelly or violently.

mas·sage /məsaázh, -saáj/ *n. & v.* ● *n.* **1** the rubbing, kneading, etc., of muscles and joints of the body with the hands for therapeutic benefit. **2** an instance of this. ● *v.tr.* **1** apply massage to. **2** manipulate (statistics) to give an acceptable result. □□ **mas·sag·er** *n.*

mas·sage par·lor *n.* **1** an establishment providing massage. **2** *euphem.* a brothel.

mas·sé /masáy/ *n. Billiards* a stroke made with the cue held nearly vertical.

mas·se·ter /maséétər/ *n.* either of two chewing muscles which run from the temporal bone to the lower jaw.

mas·seur /masór/ *n.* (*fem.* **masseuse** /masóz/) a person who provides massage professionally.

mas·sif /maséef, máseef/ *n.* a compact group of mountain heights.

mas·sive /másiv/ *adj.* **1** large and heavy or solid. **2** (of the features, head, etc.) relatively large; of solid build. **3** exceptionally large (*took a massive overdose*). **4** substantial; impressive (*a massive reputation*). **5** *Mineral.* not visibly crystalline. □□ **mas·sive·ly** *adv.* **mas·sive·ness** *n.*

mass-mar·ket *adj.* for wide distribution through a variety of retail outlets.

mass me·di·a *n.* = MEDIA¹ 2.

mass noun *n. Gram.* a noun that is not countable and cannot be used with the indefinite article or in the plural (e.g., *happiness*).

mass num·ber *n.* the total number of protons and neutrons in a nucleus.

Mas·so·rah var. of MASORAH.

Mas·so·rete var. of MASORETE.

mass pro·duc·tion *n.* the production of large quantities of a standardized article by a standardized mechanical process. □□ **mass-pro·duce** *v.tr.*

M

M

mast[1] /mast/ *n. & v.* ● *n.* **1** a long upright post of timber, iron, etc., set up from a ship's keel or deck, esp. to support sails. ▷ DINGHY, SAILBOAT. **2** a post or latticework upright for supporting a radio or television antenna. **3** a flagpole (*half-mast*). ● *v.tr.* furnish (a ship) with masts. □□ **mast·ed** *adj.* (also in *comb.*). **mas·ter** *n.* (also in *comb.*).

mast[2] /mast/ *n.* ◀ the fruit of the beech, oak, chestnut, and other forest trees, esp. as food for pigs.

mas·ta·ba /mástəbə/ *n.* **1** *Archaeol.* an ancient Egyptian tomb with sloping sides and a flat roof. **2** a bench, usu. of stone, attached to a house in Islamic countries.

mas·tec·to·my /mástéktə-mee/ *n.* (*pl.* **-ies**) *Surgery* the removal of breast tissue.

mas·ter /mástər/ *n., adj., & v.* ● *n.* **1 a** a person having control of persons or things. **b** an employer, esp. of a servant. **c** a male head of a household (*master of the house*). **d** the owner of a dog, horse, etc. **e** the owner of a slave. **f** *Naut.* the captain of a merchant ship. **g** *Hunting* the person in control of a pack of hounds, etc. **2** esp. *Brit.* a male teacher or tutor, esp. a schoolmaster. **3 a** the head of a private school, etc. **b** the presiding officer of a Masonic lodge, etc. **4** a person who has or gets the upper hand. **5** a person skilled in a particular trade and able to teach others (often *attrib.*: *master carpenter*). **6** a holder of a university degree orig. giving authority to teach in the university (*Master of Arts*). **7 a** a revered teacher in philosophy, etc. **b** (**the Master**) Christ. **8** a great artist. **9** *Chess*, etc., a player of proven ability at international level. **10** an original version (e.g., of a film or audio recording) from which copies can be made. **11** (**Master**) a title prefixed to the name of a boy not old enough to be called *Mr.* (*Master T. Jones; Master Tom*). **12** a machine or device directly controlling another (cf. SLAVE 4). ● *adj.* **1** commanding, superior (*a master spirit*). **2** main; principal (*master bedroom*). **3** controlling others (*master plan*). ● *v.tr.* **1** overcome; defeat. **2** reduce to subjection. **3** acquire complete knowledge of (a subject) or facility in using (an instrument, etc.). **4** rule as a master. □ **be master of 1** have at one's disposal. **2** know how to control. **be one's own master** be independent or free to do as one wishes. □□ **mas·ter·less** *adj.* **mas·ter·ship** /mástərship/ *n.*

mas·ter·ful /mástərfŏŏl/ *adj.* **1** imperious; domineering. **2** masterly. ¶ Normally used of a person, whereas *masterly* is used of achievements, abilities, etc. □□ **mas·ter·ful·ly** *adv.* **mas·ter·ful·ness** *n.*

mas·ter key *n.* a key that opens several locks, each of which also has its own key.

mas·ter·ly /mástərlee/ *adj.* worthy of a master; very skillful (*a masterly piece of work*). □□ **mas·ter·li·ness** *n.*

mas·ter·mind /mástərmīnd/ *n. & v.* ● *n.* **1 a** a person with an outstanding intellect. **b** such an intellect. **2** the person directing an intricate operation. ● *v.tr.* plan and direct (a scheme or enterprise).

mas·ter·piece /mástərpees/ *n.* **1** an outstanding piece of artistry or workmanship. **2** a person's best work.

mas·ter·stroke *n.* an outstandingly skillful act of policy, etc.

mas·ter switch *n.* a switch controlling the supply of electricity, etc., to an entire system.

mas·ter·work *n.* a masterpiece.

mas·ter·y /mástəree/ *n.* **1** dominion; sway. **2** masterly skill. **3** (often foll. by *of*) comprehensive knowledge or use of a subject or instrument. **4** (prec. by *the*) the upper hand.

MAST: BEECH MAST

nut

husk

mast·head /mást-hed/ *n. & v.* ● *n.* **1** the highest part of a ship's mast, esp. as a place of observation or punishment. **2 a** the title of a newspaper, etc., at the head of the front or editorial page. **b** the printed notice in a newspaper, magazine, etc., giving details of staff, ownership, etc. ● *v.tr.* **1** send (a sailor) to the masthead. **2** raise (a sail) to its position on the mast.

mas·tic /mástik/ *n.* **1** a gum or resin exuded from the bark of the mastic tree, used in making varnish. **2** (in full **mastic tree**) the evergreen tree, *Pistacia lentiscus*, yielding this. **3** a waterproof filler and sealant used in building. **4** a liquor flavored with mastic gum.

mas·ti·cate /mástikayt/ *v.tr.* grind or chew (food) with one's teeth. □□ **mas·ti·ca·tion** /-káyshən/ *n.* **mas·ti·ca·to·ry** /-kətáwree/ *adj.*

mas·tiff /mástif/ *n.* **1** ◀ a dog of a large strong breed with drooping ears and pendulous lips. **2** this breed of dog.

mas·ti·tis /mastítis/ *n.* an inflammation of the mammary gland in the breast or udder.

mas·to·don /mástədon/ *n.* a large extinct mammal of the genus *Mammut*, resembling the elephant. □□ **mas·to·don·tic** /-dóntik/ *adj.*

mas·toid /mástoyd/ *n.* **1** a conical prominence on the bone behind the ear, to which muscles are attached. ▷ EAR. **2** *colloq.* mastoiditis.

MASTIFF

mas·toid·i·tis /mástoydítis/ *n.* inflammation of the mastoid process.

mas·tur·bate /mástərbayt/ *v.intr. & tr.* arouse oneself sexually or cause (another person) to be aroused by manual stimulation of the genitals. □□ **mas·tur·ba·tion** /-báyshən/ *n.* **mas·tur·ba·tor** *n.* **mas·tur·ba·to·ry** /-tárbətawree/ *adj.*

mat[1] /mat/ *n. & v.* ● *n.* **1** a piece of coarse material for wiping shoes on, esp. a doormat. **2** a piece of cork, rubber, plastic, etc., to protect a surface from the heat or moisture of an object placed on it. **3** a piece of resilient material for landing on in gymnastics, wrestling, etc. **4** a piece of coarse fabric of plaited rushes, straw, etc., for lying on, packing furniture, etc. **5** a small rug. ● *v.* (**matted, matting**) **1 a** *tr.* (esp. as **matted** *adj.*) entangle in a thick mass (*matted hair*). **b** *intr.* become matted. **2** *tr.* cover or furnish with mats.

mat[2] var. of MATTE[1].

mat[3] /mat/ *n.* = MATRIX 1.

mat·a·dor /mátədawr/ *n.* ▼ a bullfighter whose task is to kill the bull.

matador

silk outfit with gold sequins (*traje de luces*)

scarlet cape (*muleta*)

barbed darts (*banderillas*)

fighting bull (*toro bravo*)

MATADOR AND BULL

match[1] /mach/ *n. & v.* ● *n.* **1** a contest or game in which persons or teams compete against each other. **2 a** a person able to contend with another as an equal (*meet one's match*). **b** a person equal to

another in some quality (*we shall never see his match*). **c** a person or thing exactly like or corresponding to another. **3** a marriage. **4** a person viewed in regard to his or her eligibility for marriage (*an excellent match*). ● *v.* **1 a** *tr.* be equal to or harmonious with (*the curtains match the wallpaper*). **b** *intr.* (often foll. by *with*) correspond; harmonize (*his socks do not match; does the ribbon match with your hat?*). **c** (as **matching** *adj.*) having correspondence in some essential respect (*matching curtains*). **2** *tr.* (foll. by *against, with*) place (a person, etc.) in conflict, contest, or competition with (another). **3** *tr.* find material, etc., that matches (another) (*can you match this silk?*). **4** *tr.* find a person or thing suitable for another (*matching unemployed workers to available jobs*). **5** *tr.* prove to be a match for. □ **make a match** bring about a marriage. **to match** corresponding in some essential respect with what has been mentioned (*yellow dress with gloves to match*). □□ **match·a·ble** *adj.*

match[2] /mach/ *n.* **1** a short thin piece of flammable material tipped with a composition that can be ignited by friction. **2** a piece of wick, cord, etc., designed to burn at a uniform rate, for firing a cannon, etc.

match·board /máchbawrd/ *n.* a board with a tongue cut along one edge and a groove along another, so as to fit with similar boards.

match·box /máchboks/ *n.* a box for holding matches.

match·less /máchlis/ *adj.* without an equal; incomparable. □□ **match·less·ly** *adv.*

match·lock /máchlok/ *n. hist.* **1** ▼ an old type of gun with a lock in which a match was placed for igniting the powder. **2** such a lock.

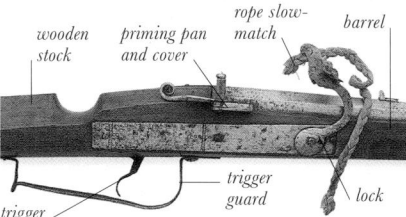

wooden stock   *priming pan and cover*   *rope slow-match*   *barrel*

trigger   *trigger guard*   *lock*

MATCHLOCK: 17TH-CENTURY GERMAN MATCHLOCK

match·mak·er /máchmaykər/ *n.* a person who tries to arrange an agreement or relationship between two parties, esp. a marriage partnership. □□ **match·mak·ing** *n.*

match point *n. Tennis*, etc. **1** the state of a game when one side needs only one more point to win the match. **2** this point.

match·stick /máchstik/ *n.* the stem of a match.

match·wood /máchwŏŏd/ *n.* **1** wood suitable for matches. **2** minute splinters.

mate[1] /mayt/ *n. & v.* ● *n.* **1** a friend or fellow worker. **2 a** each of a pair, esp. of animals, birds, or socks. **b** *colloq.* a partner in marriage. **c** (in *comb.*) a fellow member or joint occupant of (*teammate; roommate*). **3** *Naut.* an officer on a merchant ship subordinate to the master. **4** an assistant to a skilled worker (*plumber's mate*). ● *v.* (often foll. by *with*) **1 a** *tr.* bring (animals or birds) together for breeding. **b** *intr.* (of animals or birds) come together for breeding. **2 a** *tr.* join (persons) in marriage. **b** *intr.* (of persons) be joined in marriage. **3** *intr. Mech.* fit well. □□ **mate·less** *adj.*

mate[2] /mayt/ *n. & v.tr. Chess* = CHECK-MATE.

ma·té /máatay/ *n.* **1** an infusion of the leaves of a S. American shrub, *Ilex paraguayensis*. **2** this shrub, or its leaves. **3** a vessel in which these leaves are infused.

ma·te·ri·al /mətéereeəl/ n. & adj. ● n. **1** the matter from which a thing is made. **2** cloth; fabric. **3** (in pl.) things needed for an activity (*building materials; cleaning materials; writing materials*). **4** a person or thing of a specified kind or suitable for a purpose (*officer material*). **5** (in sing. or pl.) information, etc., to be used in writing a book, etc. **6** (in sing. or pl., often foll. by of) the elements or constituent parts of a substance. ● adj. **1** of matter; corporeal. **2** concerned with bodily comfort, etc. (*material well-being*). **3** (of conduct, points of view, etc.) not spiritual. **4** (often foll. by to) important; essential; relevant (*at the material time*). **5** concerned with the matter, not the form, of reasoning. □□ **ma·te·ri·al·i·ty** /-reeálitee/ n.

ma·te·ri·al·ism /mətéereeəlizəm/ n. **1** a tendency to prefer material possessions and physical comfort to spiritual values. **2** *Philos.* **a** the opinion that nothing exists but matter and its movements and modifications. **b** the doctrine that consciousness and will are wholly due to material agency. □□ **ma·te·ri·al·ist** n. **ma·te·ri·al·is·tic** /-lístik/ adj. **ma·te·ri·al·is·ti·cal·ly** /-lístiklee/ adv.

ma·te·ri·al·ize /mətéereeəlīz/ v. **1** intr. become actual fact. **2 a** tr. cause (a spirit) to appear in bodily form. **b** intr. (of a spirit) appear in this way. **3** intr. colloq. appear or be present when expected. **4** tr. represent or express in material form. □□ **ma·te·ri·al·i·za·tion** n.

ma·te·ri·al·ly /mətéereeəlee/ adv. **1** substantially; considerably. **2** in respect of matter.

ma·té·ri·el /mətéeree-él/ n. available means, esp. materials and equipment in warfare (opp. PERSONNEL).

ma·ter·nal /mətə́rnəl/ adj. **1** of or like a mother. **2** motherly. **3** related through the mother (*maternal uncle*). **4** of the mother in pregnancy and childbirth. □□ **ma·ter·nal·ism** n. **ma·ter·nal·ly** adv.

ma·ter·ni·ty /mətə́rnitee/ n. **1** motherhood. **2** motherliness. **3** (attrib.) **a** for women during and just after childbirth (*maternity hospital; maternity leave*). **b** suitable for a pregnant woman (*maternity dress; maternity wear*).

math /math/ n. US colloq. mathematics.

math·e·mat·i·cal /mathimátikəl/ adj. **1** of or relating to mathematics. **2** (of a proof, etc.) rigorously precise. □□ **math·e·mat·i·cal·ly** adv.

math·e·mat·ics /máthimátiks/ n.pl. **1** (also treated as sing.) the abstract science of number, quantity, and space studied in its own right (**pure mathematics**), or as applied to other disciplines such as physics, engineering, etc. (**applied mathematics**). **2** (as pl.) the use of mathematics in calculation, etc. □□ **math·e·ma·ti·cian** /-mətíshən/ n.

ma·ti·née /mat'náy/ n. (also **matinee**) an afternoon performance in a theater, etc.

ma·ti·née i·dol n. a handsome actor admired esp. by women.

mat·ins /mát'nz/ n. (also **mat·tins**) (as sing. or pl.) **1** a set prayer recited at daybreak or in the evening. **2** a service of morning prayer in churches of the Anglican communion.

ma·tri·arch /máytreeaark/ n. a woman who is the head of a family or tribe. □□ **ma·tri·ar·chal** /-áarkəl/ adj.

ma·tri·ar·chy /máytreeaarkee/ n. (pl. **-ies**) a form of social organization in which the mother is the head of the family and descent is reckoned through the female line.

ma·tri·ces pl. of MATRIX.

mat·ri·cide /mátrisīd, máy-/ n. **1** the killing of one's mother. **2** a person who does this. □□ **mat·ri·cid·al** adj.

ma·tric·u·late /mətríkyəlayt/ v. **1** intr. be enrolled at a college or university. **2** tr. admit (a student) to membership of a college or university. □□ **ma·tric·u·la·tion** /-láyshən/ n.

mat·ri·lin·e·al /mátrilíneeəl/ adj. of or based on kinship with the mother or the female line. □□ **mat·ri·lin·e·al·ly** adv.

mat·ri·mo·ny /mátrimōnee/ n. (pl. **-ies**) **1** the rite of marriage. **2** the state of being married. □□ **mat·ri·mo·ni·al** /-mṓneeəl/ adj. **mat·ri·mo·ni·al·ly** /-mṓneeəlee/ adv.

ma·trix /máytriks/ n. (pl. **matrices** /-triseez/ or **matrixes**) **1** a mold in which a thing is cast or shaped, such as a phonograph record, printing type, etc. **2** an environment or substance in which a thing is developed. **3** ▼ a rock in which gems, fossils, etc., are embedded. **4** *Math.* a rectangular array of elements in rows and columns that is treated as a single element. **5** *Biol.* the substance between cells or in which structures are embedded. **6** *Computing* a gridlike array of interconnected circuit elements.

emerald

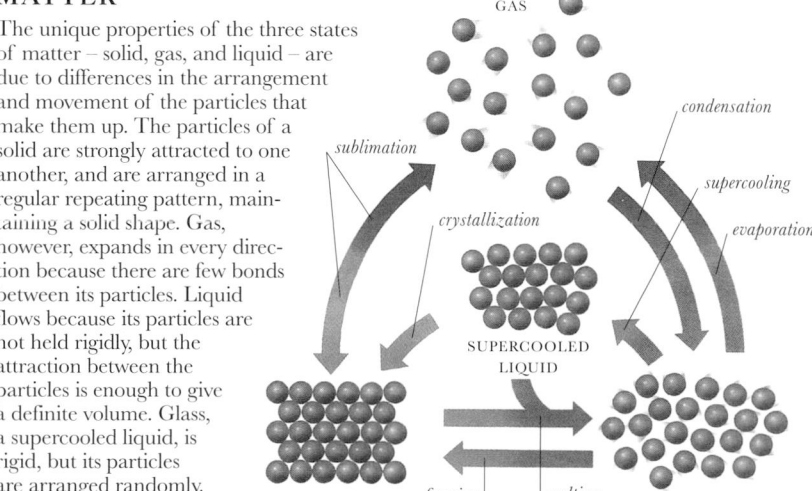

MATRIX: EMERALD
CRYSTAL IN MATRIX

calcite matrix

ma·tron /máytrən/ n. **1** a married woman, esp. a dignified and sober one. **2** a woman managing the domestic arrangements of a school, prison, etc. **3** *Brit.* a woman in charge of the nursing in a hospital. □□ **ma·tron·hood** n.

ma·tron·ly /máytrənlee/ adj. like or characteristic of a matron, esp. in respect of staidness or portliness.

ma·tron of hon·or n. a married woman attending the bride at a wedding.

matte[1] /mat/ adj., n., & v. (also **matt** or **mat**) ● adj. (of a color, surface, etc.) dull; without luster. ● n. **1** a border of dull gold around a framed picture. **2** (in full **matte paint**) paint formulated to give a dull flat finish (cf. GLOSS[1]). **3** the appearance of unburnished gold. ● v.tr. (**matted, matting**) **1** make (gilding, etc.) dull. **2** frost (glass).

matte[2] /mat/ n. *Cinematog.* a mask to obscure part of an image and allow another image to be superimposed, giving a combined effect.

mat·ter /mátər/ n. & v. ● n. **1 a** physical substance in general, as distinct from mind and spirit. **b** ▼ that which has mass and occupies space. **2** a particular substance (*coloring matter*). **3** (prec. by the; often foll. by with) the thing that is amiss (*what is the matter?*). **4** material for thought or expression. **5 a** the substance of a book, speech, etc., as distinct from its manner or form. **b** *Logic* the particular content of a proposition, as distinct from its form. **6** a thing or things of a specified kind (*printed matter; reading matter*). **7** an affair or situation being considered, esp. in a specified way (*a serious matter; a matter for concern*). **8** *Physiol.* **a** any substance in or discharged from the body (*fecal matter; gray matter*). **b** pus. **9** (foll. by of, for) what is or may be a good reason for (complaint, regret, etc.). **10** *Printing* the body of a printed work, as type or as printed sheets. ● v.intr. **1** (often foll. by to) be of importance; have significance (*it does not matter to me when it happened*). **2** secrete or discharge pus. □ **for that matter** (or **for the matter of that**) **1** as far as that is concerned. **2** and indeed also. **in the matter of** as regards. **a matter of 1** approximately (*for a matter of 40 years*). **2** a thing that relates to, depends on, or is determined by (*only a matter of time before they agree*). **no matter 1** (foll. by when, how, etc.) regardless of (*will do it no matter what the consequences*). **2** it is of no importance. **what is the matter with** surely there is no objection to. **what matter?** esp. *Brit.* that need not worry us.

mat·ter-of-fact n. & adj. ● n. **1** what belongs to the sphere of fact as distinct from opinion, etc. **2** *Law* the part of a judicial inquiry concerned with the truth of alleged facts. ● adj. (**matter-of-fact**) /mátərəfákt/ **1** unimaginative; prosaic. **2** unemotional. □ **as a matter of fact** in reality (esp. to correct a falsehood or misunderstanding). □□ **mat·ter-of-fact·ly** adv. **mat·ter-of-fact·ness** n.

mat·ter of form n. a mere routine.

mat·ter of life and death n. something of vital importance.

mat·ting /máting/ n. **1** fabric of hemp, bast, grass, etc., for mats (*coconut matting*). **2** in senses of MAT[1] v.

mat·tins var. of MATINS.

mat·tock /mátək/ n. ▶ an agricultural tool shaped like a pickax, with an adze and a chisel edge as the ends of the head.

mat·tress /mátris/ n. a fabric case stuffed with soft, firm, or springy material, or a similar case filled with air or water, used on or as a bed.

adze

chisel edge

MATTOCK

M

MATTER

The unique properties of the three states of matter – solid, gas, and liquid – are due to differences in the arrangement and movement of the particles that make them up. The particles of a solid are strongly attracted to one another, and are arranged in a regular repeating pattern, maintaining a solid shape. Gas, however, expands in every direction because there are few bonds between its particles. Liquid flows because its particles are not held rigidly, but the attraction between the particles is enough to give a definite volume. Glass, a supercooled liquid, is rigid, but its particles are arranged randomly.

GAS

sublimation

condensation

supercooling

evaporation

crystallization

SUPERCOOLED LIQUID

SOLID

freezing   *melting*

LIQUID

ARRANGEMENT OF PARTICLES IN DIFFERENT STATES OF MATTER

M

mat·u·rate /máchərayt/ *v.intr.* **1** *Med.* (of a boil, etc.) come to maturation. **2** mature.

mat·u·ra·tion /máchəráyshən/ *n.* **1** the act or an instance of maturing; the state of being matured. **2** the ripening of fruit. □□ **ma·tur·a·tive** /məchŏórətiv/ *adj.*

ma·ture /məchŏŏr, -tyŏŏr, -tŏŏr/ *adj. & v.* ● *adj.* (**maturer**, **maturest**) **1** with fully developed powers of body and mind; adult. **2** complete in natural development; ripe. **3** (of thought, intentions, etc.) duly careful and adequate. **4** (of a bond, etc.) due for payment. ● *v.* **1 a** *tr. & intr.* develop fully. **b** *tr. & intr.* ripen. **c** *intr.* come to maturity. **2** *tr.* perfect (a plan, etc.). **3** *intr.* (of a bond, etc.) become due for payment. □□ **ma·ture·ly** *adv.* **ma·tu·ri·ty** *n.*

ma·tu·ti·nal /mətŏŏt'n'l, -tyŏŏt-, máchŏŏtínəl/ *adj.* **1** of or occurring in the morning. **2** early.

mat·zo /máatsə/ *n.* (also **mat·zoh**; *pl.* **-os** or **-ohs** or **matzoth** /-sŏt/) **1** a wafer of unleavened bread for the Passover. **2** such bread collectively.

maud·lin /máwdlin/ *adj.* weakly or tearfully sentimental, esp. in a tearful and effusive stage of drunkenness.

maul /mawl/ *v.tr.* **1** beat and bruise. **2** handle roughly.

maul·stick /máwlstik/ *n.* (also **mahl·stick**) a light stick with a padded tip, used by a painter to support the working hand.

maun·der /máwndər/ *v.intr.* **1** talk in a dreamy or rambling manner. **2** move or act listlessly or idly.

maund·y /máwndee/ *n.* the ceremony of washing the feet of the poor, in commemoration of Jesus' washing of the disciples' feet at the Last Supper.

Maun·dy Thurs·day *n.* the Thursday before Easter.

mau·so·le·um /máwsəléeəm/ *n.* (*pl.* **mausoleums** or **mausolea**) a large and grand tomb.

mauve /mōv/ *adj. & n.* ● *adj.* pale purple. ● *n.* **1** this color. **2** a bright but delicate pale purple dye from coal-tar aniline. □□ **mauv·ish** *adj.*

ma·ven /máyvən/ *n.* (also **ma·vin**) *colloq.* an expert or connoisseur.

mav·er·ick /mávərik, mávrik/ *n.* **1** an unbranded calf or yearling. **2** an unorthodox or independent-minded person (for S.A. *Maverick*, Texas engineer and rancher d. 1870, who did not brand his cattle).

maw /maw/ *n.* **1 a** the stomach of an animal. **b** the jaws or throat of a voracious animal. **2** *colloq.* the stomach of a greedy person.

mawk·ish /máwkish/ *adj.* **1** sentimental in a feeble or sickly way. **2** having a faint sickly flavor. □□ **mawk·ish·ly** *adv.* **mawk·ish·ness** *n.*

max. *abbr.* maximum. □ **to the max** *sl.* to the utmost, to the fullest extent.

max·i /máksee/ *n.* (*pl.* **maxis**) *colloq.* a maxiskirt or other garment with a long skirt.

maxi- /máksee/ *comb. form* very large or long (*maxicoat, maxiskirt*).

max·il·la /maksílə/ *n.* (*pl.* **maxillae** /-lee/ or **maxillas**) **1** ▼ the jaw or jawbone, esp. the upper jaw in most vertebrates. ▷ SKELETON, SKULL. **2** the mouthpart of many arthropods used in chewing. □□ **max·il·lar·y** /máksəléree/ *adj.*

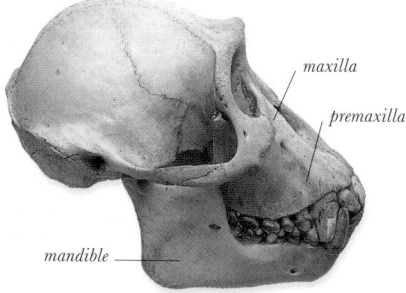

MAXILLA AND SKULL OF A CHIMPANZEE

maxilla

premaxilla

mandible

max·im /máksim/ *n.* a general truth or rule of conduct expressed in a sentence.

max·i·mal /máksiməl/ *adj.* being or relating to a maximum; the greatest possible in size, duration, etc. □□ **max·i·mal·ly** *adv.*

max·i·mal·ist /máksiməlist/ *n.* a person who rejects compromise and expects a full response to (esp. political) demands.

max·i·mize /máksimīz/ *v.tr.* increase or enhance to the utmost. □□ **max·i·mi·za·tion** *n.* **max·i·miz·er** *n.*

max·i·mum /máksiməm/ *n. & adj.* ● *n.* (*pl.* **maxima** /-mə/) the highest possible or attainable amount. ● *adj.* that is a maximum.

May /may/ *n.* the fifth month of the year.

may /may/ *v.aux.* (*3rd sing. present* may; *past* **might** /mīt/) **1** (often foll. by *well* for emphasis) expressing possibility (*it may be true; I may be wrong; you may well lose your way*). **2** expressing permission (*you may not go; may I come in?*). ¶ Both *can* and *may* are used to express permission; in more formal contexts *may* is usual since *can* also denotes capability (*can I move?* = am I physically able to move?; *may I move* = am I allowed to move?). **3** expressing a wish (*may he live to regret it*). **4** expressing uncertainty or irony in questions (*who may you be?; who are you, may I ask?*). **5** in purpose clauses and after *wish, fear*, etc. (*hope he may succeed*). □ **be that as it may** (or **that is as may be**) that may or may not be so.

ma·ya /máayə/ *n.* *Hinduism* a marvel or illusion, esp. in the phenomenal universe.

Ma·ya /máayə/ *n.* **1** (*pl.* same or **Mayas**) a member of an ancient native people of Central America. **2** the language of this people. □□ **Ma·yan** *adj. & n.*

may·ap·ple /máyapəl/ *n.* (also **man·drake**) an American herbaceous plant, *Podophyllum peltatum*, bearing a yellow egg-shaped fruit in May.

may·be /máybee/ *adv.* perhaps; possibly.

May Day *n.* May 1, esp. as a festival with dancing, or as an international holiday in honor of workers.

May·day /máyday/ *n.* an international radio-telephone distress signal used esp. by ships and aircraft.

may·flow·er /máyflowər/ *n.* **1** any of various flowers that bloom in May, esp. the trailing arbutus, *Epigaea repens*. **2** (*Mayflower*) the ship on which the Pilgrims traveled from England to N. America in 1620.

may·fly /máyflī/ *n.* (*pl.* **-flies**) **1** ► any insect of the order Ephemeroptera, living briefly in spring in the adult stage. **2** an imitation mayfly used by anglers.

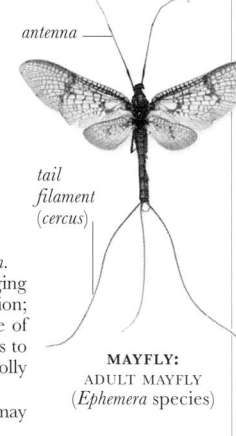

antenna

tail filament (cercus)

MAYFLY:
ADULT MAYFLY
(*Ephemera* species)

may·hap /máyháp/ *adv. archaic* perhaps; possibly.

may·hem /máyhem/ *n.* **1** violent or damaging action. **2** rowdy confusion; chaos. **3** *hist.* the crime of maiming a person so as to render him or her wholly defenseless.

mayn't /máyənt/ *contr.* may not.

may·on·naise /máyənáyz/ *n.* a thick creamy dressing made of egg yolks, oil, vinegar, etc.

may·or /máyər, mair/ *n.* the chief executive of a city or town. □□ **may·or·al** *adj.* **may·or·ship** *n.*

may·or·al·ty /máyərəltee, máir-/ *n.* (*pl.* **-ies**) **1** the office of mayor. **2** a mayor's period of office.

may·or·ess /máyəris, máir-/ *n.* **1** a woman holding the office of mayor. **2** the wife of a mayor.

may·pole /máypōl/ *n.* (also **Maypole**) a pole painted and decked with flowers and ribbons, for dancing around on May Day.

mayst /mayst/ *archaic 2nd sing. present* of MAY.

maz·a·rine /mázəreen/ *n. & adj.* a rich deep blue.

maze /mayz/ *n.* **1** ► a network of paths and hedges designed as a puzzle for those who try to penetrate it. **2** a complex network of paths or passages; a labyrinth. **3** a confused mass, etc. □□ **ma·zy** *adj.* (**ma·zi·er, ma·zi·est**)

MAZE

ma·zel tov /mázəl tof/ *int.* (among Jews) congratulations; good luck.

ma·zur·ka /məzúrkə/ *n.* **1** a usu. lively Polish dance in triple time. **2** the music for this.

MB *abbr. Computing* megabyte(s).

MBA *abbr.* Master of Business Administration.

MBE *abbr.* Member of the Order of the British Empire.

MC *abbr.* **1** master of ceremonies. **2** Marine Corps. **3** Medical Corps. **4** Member of Congress.

Mc·Car·thy·ism /məkáarthee-izəm/ *n.* the policy of hunting out suspected subversives or esp. Communists.

Mc·Coy /məkóy/ *n. colloq.* □ **the** (or **the real**) **McCoy** the real thing; the genuine article.

MD *abbr.* **1** Doctor of Medicine. **2** Maryland (in official postal use). **3** Managing Director. **4** muscular dystrophy.

Md *symb. Chem.* the element mendelevium.

Md. *abbr.* Maryland.

MDA *abbr.* methylene dioxymethamphetamine, an amphetamine-based drug that causes euphoric and hallucinatory effects, originally produced as an appetite suppressant (see ECSTASY 2).

ME *abbr.* **1** Maine (in official postal use). **2** Middle East. **3** middle English.

Me. *abbr.* Maine.

me[1] /mee/ *pron.* **1** *objective case* of I[2] (*he saw me*). **2** *colloq.* = I[2] (*it's me all right; is taller than me*). **3** *colloq.* myself; to or for myself (*I got me a gun*). **4** *colloq.* used in exclamations (*ah me!; dear me!; silly me!*). □ **me and mine** me and my relatives.

me[2] *var. of* MI.

me·a cul·pa /máyə kŏŏlpə, méeə kúlpə/ *n. & int.* ● *n.* an acknowledgment of one's fault or error. ● *int.* expressing such an acknowledgment.

mead /meed/ *n.* an alcoholic drink of fermented honey and water.

mead·ow /médō/ *n.* **1** a piece of grassland, esp. one used for hay. **2** a piece of low well-watered ground, esp. near a river. □□ **mead·ow·y** *adj.*

mead·ow·sweet /médōsweet/ *n.* **1** any of several rosaceous plants of the genus *Spiraea*, native to N. America. **2** ► a rosaceous plant, *Filipendula ulmaria*, common in meadows and damp places.

mea·ger /méegər/ *adj.* **1** lacking in amount or quality (*a meager salary*). **2** (of literary composition, ideas, etc.) lacking fullness; unsatisfying. **3** (of a person or animal) lean; thin. □□ **mea·ger·ly** *adv.* **mea·ger·ness** *n.*

meal[1] /meel/ *n.* **1** an occasion when food is eaten. **2** the food eaten on one occasion. □ **make a meal of 1** treat (a task, etc.) too laboriously or fussily. **2** consume as a meal.

meal[2] /meel/ *n.* **1** the edible part of a grain or pulse (usu. other than wheat) ground to powder. **2** any powdery substance made by grinding.

MEADOWSWEET
(*Filipendula ulmaria*)

meals on wheels *n.pl.* (usu. treated as *sing.*) a service by which meals are delivered to the elderly, invalids, etc.

meal tick·et *n.* **1** a ticket entitling one to a meal, esp. at a specified place with reduced cost. **2** a person or thing that is a source of food or income.

meal·time /méeltīm/ *n.* any of the usual times of eating.

meal·worm /méelwórm/ *n.* the larva of the meal beetle.

meal·y /méelee/ *adj.* (**mealier, mealiest**) **1 a** of or like meal; soft and powdery. **b** containing meal. **2** (of a complexion) pale. **3** (of a horse) spotty. **4** (in full **mealy-mouthed**) not outspoken; afraid to use plain expressions. □□ **meal·i·ness** *n.*

mean[1] /meen/ *v.tr.* (*past* and *past part.* **meant** /ment/) **1 a** (often foll. by *to* + infin.) have as one's purpose or intention; have in mind (*they really mean mischief*; *I didn't mean to break it*). **b** (foll. by *by*) have as a motive in explanation (*what do you mean by that?*). **2** (often in *passive*) design or destine for a purpose (*mean it to be used*; *is meant to be a gift*). **3** intend to convey or indicate or refer to (a particular thing or notion) (*I mean we cannot go*; *I mean Springfield in Ohio*). **4** entail, involve (*it means catching the early train*). **5** (often foll. by *that* + clause) portend; signify (*this means trouble*; *your refusal means that we must look elsewhere*). **6** (of a word) have as its explanation in the same language or its equivalent in another language. **7** (foll. by *to*) be of some specified importance to (a person) (*that means a lot to me*). □ **mean business** be in earnest. **mean it** not be joking or exaggerating. **mean to say** really admit (usu. in *interrog.*: *do you mean to say you have lost it?*). **mean well** (often foll. by *to, toward, by*) have good intentions.

mean[2] /meen/ *adj.* **1** niggardly; not generous. **2** ignoble; small-minded. **3** (of a person's capacity, understanding, etc.) inferior; poor. **4** (of housing) not imposing in appearance; shabby. **5 a** malicious; ill-tempered. **b** vicious or aggressive. **6** *colloq.* skillful; formidable (*is a mean fighter*). **7** *colloq.* ashamed (*feel mean*). □ **no mean** a very good (*that is no mean achievement*). □□ **mean·ly** *adv.* **mean·ness** *n.*

mean[3] /meen/ *n. & adj.* ● *n.* **1** a condition, quality, virtue, or course of action equally removed from two opposite (usu. unsatisfactory) extremes. **2** *Math.* **a** the term midway between the first and last terms of an arithmetical or geometrical, etc., progression (*2 and 8 have the arithmetic mean 5 and the geometric mean 4*). **b** average. ● *adj.* **1** (of a quantity) equally far from two extremes. **2** calculated as a mean.

me·an·der /meeándǝr/ *v. & n.* ● *v.intr.* **1** wander at random. **2** (of a stream) wind about. ● *n.* **1 a** a curve in a winding river, etc. ▷ RIVER. **b** a crooked or winding path or passage. **2** a circuitous journey. **3** an ornamental pattern of lines winding in and out; a fret. □□ **me·an·der·ing** *adj. & n.*

mean·ie /méenee/ *n.* (also **mean·y**) (*pl.* **-ies**) *colloq.* a mean, niggardly, or small-minded person.

mean·ing /méening/ *n. & adj.* ● *n.* **1** what is meant by a word, action, idea, etc. **2** significance. **3** importance. ● *adj.* expressive; significant (*a meaning glance*). □□ **mean·ing·ly** *adv.*

mean·ing·ful /méeningfool/ *adj.* **1** full of meaning; significant. **2** *Logic* able to be interpreted. □□ **mean·ing·ful·ly** *adv.* **mean·ing·ful·ness** *n.*

mean·ing·less /méeninglis/ *adj.* having no meaning or significance. □□ **mean·ing·less·ly** *adv.* **mean·ing·less·ness** *n.*

means /meenz/ *n.pl.* **1** (often treated as *sing.*) that by which a result is brought about (*a means of quick travel*). **2 a** money resources (*live beyond one's means*). **b** wealth (*a man of means*). □ **by all means** (or **all manner of means**) **1** certainly. **2** in every possible way. **3** at any cost. **by any means** in any way. **by means of** by the agency or instrumentality of (a thing or action). **by no means** (or **no manner of means**) not at all; certainly not.

mean sea lev·el *n.* the sea level halfway between the mean levels of high and low water.

meant *past* and *past part.* of MEAN[1].

mean·time /méentīm/ *adv. & n.* ● *adv.* = MEANWHILE. ● *n.* the intervening period (esp. *in the meantime*).

mean·while /méenwīl, -hwīl/ *adv. & n.* ● *adv.* **1** in the intervening period of time. **2** at the same time. ● *n.* the intervening period (esp. *in the meanwhile*).

mean·y var. of MEANIE.

mea·sles /méezǝlz/ *n.pl.* (also treated as *sing.*) **1** an acute infectious viral disease marked by red spots on the skin. **2** the spots of measles.

mea·sly /méezlee/ *adj.* (**measlier, measliest**) *colloq.* inferior; contemptibly meager.

meas·ur·a·ble /mézhǝrǝbǝl/ *adj.* that can be measured. □□ **meas·ur·a·bil·i·ty** /-bílitee/ *n.* **meas·ur·a·bly** *adv.*

meas·ure /mézhǝr/ *n. & v.* ● *n.* **1** a size or quantity found by measuring. **2** a system of measuring (*liquid measure*; *linear measure*). **3** a rod or tape, etc., for measuring. **4** a vessel of standard capacity for transferring or determining fixed quantities of liquids, etc. (*a pint measure*). **5 a** the degree, extent, or amount of a thing. **b** (foll. by *of*) some degree of (*there was a measure of wit in her remark*). **6** a unit of capacity, e.g., a bushel (*20 measures of wheat*). **7** a factor by which a person or thing is reckoned or evaluated (*their success is a measure of their determination*). **8** (usu. in *pl.*) suitable action to achieve some end (*took measures to ensure a good profit*). **9** a legislative act. **10** a quantity contained in another an exact number of times. **11** a prescribed extent or quantity. **12** a poetical rhythm; meter. **b** a metrical group of a dactyl or two iambs, trochees, spondees, etc. **13** *US Mus.* a bar or the time content of a bar. ● *v.* **1** *tr.* ascertain the extent or quantity of (a thing) by comparison with a fixed unit or with an object of known size. **2** *intr.* be of a specified size (*it measures six inches*). **3** *tr.* ascertain the size and proportion of (a person) for clothes. **4** *tr.* estimate (a quality, person's character, etc.) by some standard or rule. **5** *tr.* (often foll. by *off*) mark (a line, etc., of a given length). **6** *tr.* (foll. by *out*) distribute (a thing) in measured quantities. **7** *tr.* (foll. by *with, against*) bring (oneself or one's strength, etc.) into competition with. □ **beyond measure** excessively. **for good measure** as something beyond the minimum; as a finishing touch. **in a** (or **some**) **measure** partly. **measure up 1 a** determine the size, etc., of by measurement. **b** take comprehensive measurements. **2** (often foll. by *to*) have the necessary qualifications (for).

meas·ured /mézhǝrd/ *adj.* **1** rhythmical; regular in movement (*a measured tread*). **2** (of language) carefully considered.

meas·ure·less /mézhǝrlis/ *adj.* not measurable; infinite.

meas·ure·ment /mézhǝrmǝnt/ *n.* **1** the act or an instance of measuring. **2** an amount determined by measuring. **3** (in *pl.*) detailed dimensions.

meas·ur·ing cup *n.* a cup marked to measure its contents.

meat /meet/ *n.* **1** the flesh of animals (esp. mammals) as food. ▷ CUT. **2** (foll. by *of*) the essence or chief part of. **3** the edible part of fruits, nuts, eggs, shellfish, etc. □□ **meat·less** *adj.*

meat-and-po·ta·toes *adj.* essential; fundamental; basic.

meat·ball /méetbawl/ *n.* seasoned ground meat formed into a small round ball.

meat loaf *n.* seasoned ground meat molded into the shape of a loaf and baked.

meat·pack·ing /méetpaking/ *n.* the business of slaughtering animals and processing the meat for sale as food.

meat·space /méetspays/ *n. Computing* the physical world as opposed to cyberspace or another virtual environment.

me·a·tus /meeáytǝs/ *n.* (*pl.* same or **meatuses**) *Anat.* a channel or passage in the body or its opening.

meat·y /méetee/ *adj.* (**meatier, meatiest**) **1** full of meat; fleshy. **2** of or like meat. **3** full of substance. □□ **meat·i·ly** *adv.* **meat·i·ness** *n.*

Mec·ca /mékǝ/ *n.* **1** a place one aspires to visit. **2** the birthplace of a faith, policy, pursuit, etc.

me·chan·ic /mikánik/ *n.* a skilled worker, esp. one who makes or uses or repairs machinery.

me·chan·i·cal /mikánikǝl/ *adj.* **1** of or relating to machines or mechanisms. **2** working or produced by machinery. **3** (of a person or action) automatic; lacking originality. **4 a** (of an agency, principle, etc.) belonging to mechanics. **b** (of a theory, etc.) explaining phenomena by the assumption of mechanical action. **5** of or relating to mechanics as a science. □□ **me·chan·i·cal·ism** *n.* (in sense 4). **me·chan·i·cal·ly** *adv.* **me·chan·i·cal·ness** *n.*

me·chan·ics /mikániks/ *n.pl.* (usu. treated as *sing.*) **1** the branch of applied mathematics dealing with motion and tendencies to motion. **2** the science of machinery. **3** the method of construction or routine operation of a thing.

mech·an·ism /mékǝnizǝm/ *n.* **1** the structure or adaptation of parts of a machine. **2** a system of parts working together in or as a machine. **3** the mode of operation of a process. **4** *Art* mechanical execution; technique. **5** *Philos.* the doctrine that all natural phenomena, including life, allow mechanical explanation by physics and chemistry. □□ **mech·a·nis·tic** /mékǝnistik/ *adj.* **mech·a·nis·ti·cal·ly** /-nístiklee/ *adv.*

mech·a·nize /mékǝnīz/ *v.tr.* **1** give a mechanical character to. **2** introduce machines in. **3** *Mil.* equip with tanks, armored cars, etc. □□ **mech·a·ni·za·tion** *n.* **mech·a·niz·er** *n.*

mech·a·no·re·cep·tor /mékǝnōriséptǝr/ *n. Biol.* a sensory receptor that responds to mechanical stimuli such as touch or sound.

mech·a·tron·ics /mékǝtróniks/ *n.* the science of the combination of electronics and mechanics in developing new manufacturing techniques.

M.Ed. *abbr.* Master of Education.

med /med/ *adj. colloq.* medical (*med school*).

med·al /méd'l/ *n.* ▼ a piece of metal, usu. in the form of a disk, awarded as a distinction to a soldier, scholar, athlete, etc., for services rendered, for proficiency, etc.

Korean action bar

ribbon

Olympic Games symbol

United Nations symbol

UNITED NATIONS' KOREA medal

1996 OLYMPIAD GOLD MEDAL

MEDALS

med·al·ist /méd'list/ *n.* **1** a recipient of a (specified) medal (*gold medalist*). **2** an engraver or designer of medals.

me·dal·lion /midályǝn/ *n.* **1** a large medal. **2** a thing shaped like this, e.g., a decorative panel or tablet, portrait, etc.

Med·al of Free·dom *n.* (also **Presidential Medal of Freedom**) medal awarded by the US president for achievement in various fields.

Med·al of Hon·or *n.* (also **Congressional Medal of Honor**) the highest US military decoration, awarded by Congress for exceptional valor.

med·dle /méd'l/ *v.intr.* (often foll. by *with, in*) interfere in or busy oneself unduly with others' concerns. □□ **med·dler** *n.*

M

M

med·dle·some /méd'lsəm/ *adj.* fond of meddling; interfering.

me·di·a[1] /méedeeə/ *n. pl.* **1** *pl.* of MEDIUM. **2** (usu. prec. by *the*) the main means of mass communication (esp. newspapers and broadcasting) regarded collectively. ¶ Use as a mass noun with a singular verb is common (e.g., *the media is on our side*), but is generally disfavored (cf. DATA).

me·di·a[2] /méedeeə/ *n.* (*pl.* **mediae** /-dee-ée/) **1** *Phonet.* a voiced stop, e.g., *g*, *b*, *d*. **2** *Anat.* a middle layer of the wall of an artery or other vessel.

me·di·ae·val var. of MEDIEVAL.

me·di·al /méedeeəl/ *adj.* **1** situated in the middle. **2** of average size. □□ **me·di·al·ly** *adv.*

me·di·an /méedeeən/ *adj. & n.* ● *adj.* situated in the middle. ● *n.* **1** *Anat.* a median artery, vein, nerve, etc. **2** *Geom.* a straight line drawn from any vertex of a triangle to the middle of the opposite side. **3** *Math.* the middle value of a series of values arranged in order of size. **4** (also **median strip**) center divider separating opposing lanes on a divided highway.

me·di·ant /méedeeənt/ *n. Mus.* the third note of a diatonic scale of any key.

me·di·ate *v. & adj.* ● *v.* /méedeeayt/ **1** *intr.* (often foll. by *between*) intervene (between parties in a dispute) to produce agreement or reconciliation. **2** *tr.* be the medium for bringing about (a result) or for conveying (a gift, etc.). **3** *tr.* form a connecting link between. ● *adj.* /méedeeət/ **1** connected not directly but through some other person or thing. **2** involving an intermediate agency. □□ **me·di·a·tion** /-áyshən/ *n.* **me·di·a·tor** /méedeeaytər/ *n.* **me·di·a·to·ry** /méedeeətáwree/ *adj.*

med·ic /médik/ *n. colloq.* a medical practitioner or student.

med·i·ca·ble /médikəbəl/ *adj.* able to benefit from medical treatment.

Med·i·caid /médikayd/ *n.* a federal system of health insurance for those requiring financial assistance.

med·i·cal /médikəl/ *adj. & n.* ● *adj.* **1** of or relating to the science of medicine in general. **2** of or relating to conditions requiring medical and not surgical treatment (*medical ward*). ● *n. colloq.* = MEDICAL EXAMINATION. □□ **med·i·cal·ly** *adv.*

med·i·cal ex·am·i·na·tion *n.* an examination to determine a person's physical fitness.

med·i·cal ex·am·in·er *n.* a person, usu. a physician, employed by a city, county, etc., to conduct autopsies and determine the cause of death.

med·i·cal prac·ti·tion·er *n.* a physician or surgeon.

med·i·ca·ment /médikəmənt, midíkə-/ *n.* a substance used for medical treatment.

Med·i·care /médikair/ *n.* US federal government program for health insurance for persons esp. over 65 years of age.

med·i·cate /médikayt/ *v.tr.* **1** treat medically. **2** impregnate with a medicinal substance.

med·i·ca·tion /médikáyshən/ *n.* **1** a substance used for medical treatment. **2** treatment using drugs.

me·dic·i·nal /mədísinəl/ *adj. & n.* ● *adj.* (of a substance) having healing properties. ● *n.* a medicinal substance. □□ **me·dic·i·nal·ly** *adv.*

med·i·cine /médisin/ *n.* **1** the science or practice of the diagnosis, treatment, and prevention of disease, esp. as distinct from surgical methods. **2** ▼ any drug or preparation used for the treatment or prevention of disease, esp. one taken by mouth. **3** a spell, charm, or fetish which is thought to cure afflictions. □ **a dose** (or **taste**) **of one's own medicine** treatment such as one is accustomed to giving others. **take one's medicine** submit to something disagreeable.

med·i·cine ball *n.* a stuffed leather ball thrown and caught for exercise.

med·i·cine chest *n.* a box containing medicines, etc.

med·i·cine man *n.* a person believed to have magical powers of healing, esp. among Native Americans.

med·i·co /médikō/ *n.* (*pl.* **-os**) *colloq.* a medical practitioner or student.

me·di·e·val /méedee-ée·vəl, méd-, míd-/ *adj.* (also **me·di·ae·val**) **1** of, or in the style of, the Middle Ages. **2** *colloq.* old-fashioned. □□ **me·di·e·val·ism** *n.* **me·di·e·val·ist** *n.*

me·di·e·val Lat·in *n.* Latin of about AD 600–1500.

me·di·o·cre /méedeeókər/ *adj.* **1** of middling quality, neither good nor bad. **2** second-rate.

me·di·oc·ri·ty /méedeeókritee/ *n.* (*pl.* **-ies**) **1** the state of being mediocre. **2** a mediocre person or thing.

med·i·tate /méditayt/ *v.* **1** *intr.* **a** exercise the mind in (esp. religious) contemplation. **b** (usu. foll. by *on*, *upon*) focus on a subject in this manner. **2** *tr.* plan mentally. □□ **med·i·ta·tion** /-táyshən/ *n.* **med·i·ta·tor** *n.*

med·i·ta·tive /méditaytiv/ *adj.* **1** inclined to meditate. **2** indicative of meditation. □□ **med·i·ta·tive·ly** *adv.*

Med·i·ter·ra·ne·an /méditəráyneeən/ *n. & adj.* ● *n.* **1** a large landlocked sea bordered by S. Europe, SW Asia, and N. Africa. **2** a native of a country bordering on the Mediterranean Sea. ● *adj.* **1** of or characteristic of the Mediterranean or its surrounding region (*Mediterranean climate*; *Mediterranean cooking*). **2** (of a person) dark-complexioned and not tall.

me·di·um /méedeeəm/ *n. & adj.* ● *n.* (*pl.* **media** or **mediums**) **1** the middle quality, degree, etc., between extremes (*find a happy medium*). **2** the means by which something is communicated (*the medium of sound; the medium of television*). **3** the intervening substance through which impressions are conveyed to the senses, etc. (*light passing from one medium into another*). **4** *Biol.* the physical environment or conditions of growth, storage, or transport of a living organism (*the shape of a fish is ideal for its fluid medium; growing mold on the surface of a medium*). **5** a means of doing something (*the medium through which money is raised*). **6** the material or form used by an artist, composer, etc. **7** the liquid (e.g., oil or gel) with which pigments are mixed for use in painting. **8** (*pl.* **mediums**) a person claiming to communicate between the dead and the living. ● *adj.* **1** between two qualities, degrees, etc. **2** average; moderate (*of medium height*).

med·lar /médlər/ *n.* **1** ▶ a rosaceous tree, *Mespilus germanica*, bearing small brown apple-like fruits. **2** the fruit of this tree that is eaten when decayed.

med·ley /médlee/ *n.* (*pl.* **-eys**) **1** a varied mixture. **2** a collection of musical items from one work or various sources arranged as a continuous whole.

fruit

MEDLAR
(*Mespilus germanica*)

me·dul·la /midúlə/ *n.* **1** the inner region of certain organs or tissues. **2** the myelin layer of certain nerve fibers. **3** the soft internal tissue of plants. □□ **med·ul·lar·y** /méd'léree, mejə-, mədúləree/ *adj.*

me·dul·la ob·long·a·ta /midúlə óblonggáatə/ *n.* the continuation of the spinal cord within the skull, forming the lowest part of the brain stem. ▷ BRAIN STEM

me·du·sa /midóōsə, -zə, -dyōō-/ *n.* (*pl.* **medusae** /-see/ or **medu·sas**) **1** a jellyfish. **2** a free-swimming form of any coelenterate, having tentacles around the edge of a jellylike body.

meek /meek/ *adj.* **1** humble and submissive. **2** piously gentle in nature. □□ **meek·ly** *adv.* **meek·ness** *n.*

meer·kat /méerkat/ *n.* ▶ a small S. African mongoose, esp the suricate.

MEERKAT: GRAY
MEERKAT
(*Suricata suricatta*)

MEDICINE

Medicinal drugs are used for the prevention, treatment, and diagnosis of illness and can be taken in many forms. They are most commonly administered through ingestion, but can also be injected into a muscle, a vein, or under the skin. Inhalers deliver a drug through the lining of the nose or mouth to the lungs. Topical applications are applied to the surfaces of the body. Suppositories are inserted in the rectum or vagina, and droppers introduce drugs into the eye or the ear.

MEDICINAL APPLICATIONS

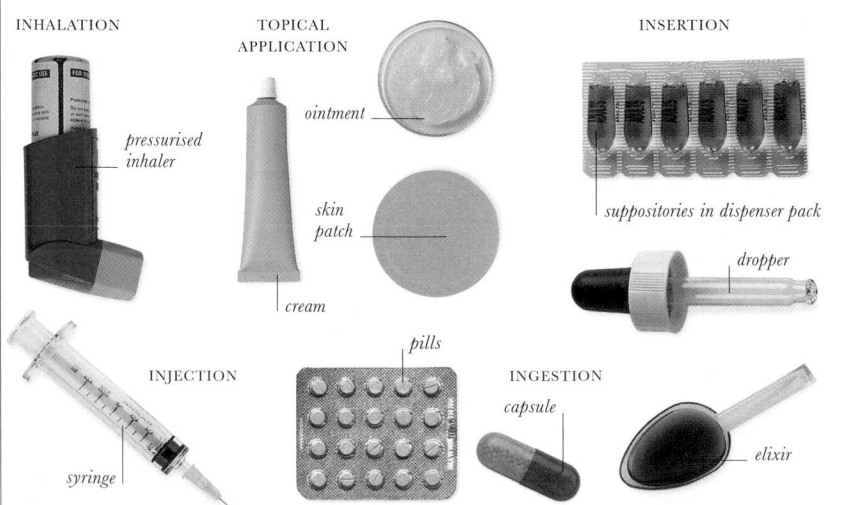

INHALATION

TOPICAL
APPLICATION

INSERTION

pressurised inhaler

ointment

skin patch

cream

suppositories in dispenser pack

dropper

INJECTION

pills

INGESTION

capsule

elixir

syringe

meer·schaum /meérshəm, -shawm/ *n.* **1** a soft white form of hydrated magnesium silicate, which resembles clay. **2** ▶ a tobacco pipe with the bowl made from this.

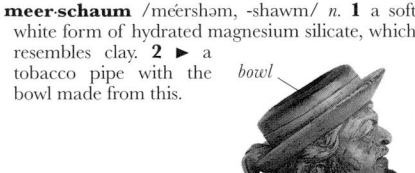

bowl

MEERSCHAUM: MID-19TH-CENTURY MEERSCHAUM PIPE

meet[1] /meet/ *v. & n.* ● *v.* (*past* and *past part.* **met** /met/) **1 a** *tr.* encounter (a person or persons) by accident or design; come face to face with. **b** *intr.* (of two or more people) come into each other's company by accident or design (*decided to meet on the bridge*). **2** *tr.* go to a place to be present at the arrival of (a person, train, etc.). **3 a** *tr.* come together or into contact with (*where the road meets the river*). **b** *intr.* come together or into contact (*where the sea and the sky meet*). **4 a** *tr.* make the acquaintance of (*delighted to meet you*). **b** *intr.* (of two or more people) make each other's acquaintance. **5** *intr. & tr.* come together or come into contact with for the purposes of conference, business, worship, etc. (*the committee meets every week; the union met management yesterday*). **6** *tr.* **a** deal with or answer (a demand, objection, etc.) (*met the original proposal with hostility*). **b** satisfy or conform with (proposals, deadlines, a person, etc.) (*agreed to meet the new terms*). **7** *tr.* pay (a bill, etc.); provide the funds required by (*meet the cost of the move*). **8** *tr. &* (foll. by *with*) *intr.* experience, encounter, or receive (success, disaster, a difficulty, etc.) (*met their death; met with many problems*). **9** *tr.* oppose in battle, contest, or confrontation. ● *n.* **1** the assembly of competitors for various sporting activities, as track, swimming, etc. **2** the assembly of riders and hounds for a hunt. □ **make ends meet** see END. **meet the eye** (or **the ear**) be visible (or audible). **meet a person's eye** check if another person is watching and look into his or her eyes in return. **meet a person halfway** make a compromise. **meet up** *colloq.* happen to meet. **meet with 1** see sense 8 of *v.* **2** receive (a reaction) (*met with the committee's approval*). **3** see sense 1a of *v.* **more than meets the eye** possessing hidden qualities or complications.

meet[2] /meet/ *adj. archaic* suitable; fit; proper.

meet·ing /meéting/ *n.* **1** in senses of MEET[1]. **2** an assembly of people, esp. the members of a society, committee, etc. **3** an assembly (esp. of Quakers) for worship. **4** the persons assembled (*address the meeting*).

meet·ing·house /meétinghows/ *n.* a place of worship, esp. of Quakers, etc.

meg·a /méga/ *adj. & adv. sl.* ● *adj.* **1** excellent. **2** enormous. ● *adv.* extremely.

mega- /méga/ *comb. form* **1** large. **2** denoting a factor of one million (10^6) in the metric system of measurement. ¶ Abbr.: **M**.

meg·a·buck /mégabuk/ *n. colloq.* **1** a million dollars. **2** (in *pl.*) great sums of money.

meg·a·byte /mégabīt/ *n. Computing* 1,048,576 (i.e., 2^{20}) bytes as a measure of data capacity, or loosely 1,000,000 bytes. ¶ Abbr.: **MB**.

meg·a·hertz /mégahərts/ *n.* one million hertz, esp. as a measure of frequency of radio transmissions. ¶ Abbr.: **MHz**.

meg·a·lith /mégalith/ *n. Archaeol.* a large stone, esp. as a monument or part of one.

meg·a·lith·ic /mégalithik/ *adj. Archaeol.* made of or marked by the use of large stones.

megalo- /mégalō/ *comb. form* great (*megalomania*).

meg·a·lo·ma·ni·a /mégalōmáyneeə/ *n.* **1** a mental disorder producing delusions of grandeur. **2** a passion for grandiose schemes. □□ **meg·a·lo·ma·ni·ac** *adj. & n.* **meg·a·lo·ma·ni·a·cal** /-mənîəkəl/ *adj.*

MEIOSIS

Before meiosis, a reproductive cell contains one set of chromosomes from each parent. First, the chromosomes duplicate, and matching chromosomes, each with two chromatids, pair up to form tetrads. The chromatids then break, exchange genetic material, and recombine. In Division I, the matching chromosomes separate, and two new cells are formed. In Division II, the chromatids of each chromosome separate, forming four daughter cells, each with half the genetic content of the original cell.

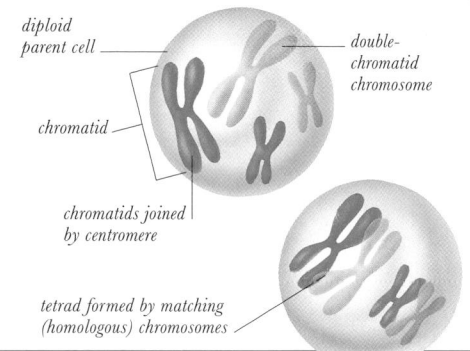

DEMONSTRATION OF MEIOTIC CELL DIVISION

recombined chromatids

single-chromatid chromosome

diploid parent cell

double-chromatid chromosome

chromatid

haploid daughter cell

chromatids joined by centromere

DIVISION I

tetrad formed by matching (homologous) chromosomes

DIVISION II

---

meg·a·lop·o·lis /mégalópəlis/ *n.* **1** a great city or its way of life. **2** an urban complex consisting of a city and its environs.

meg·a·lo·sau·rus /mégaləsawrəs/ *n.* ▼ a large flesh-eating dinosaur of the genus *Megalosaurus*, with stout hind legs and small fore-limbs.

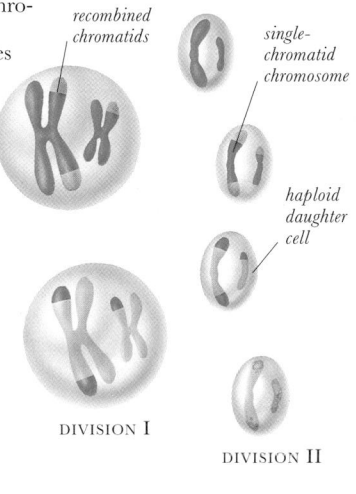

MEGALOSAURUS (*Megalosaurus* species)

meg·a·phone /mégafōn/ *n.* a large funnel-shaped device for amplifying the voice.

meg·a·star /mégastaar/ *n.* a very famous person, esp. in the world of entertainment.

meg·a·ton /mégatun/ *n.* a unit of explosive power equal to one million tons of TNT.

meg·a·volt /mégavōlt/ *n.* one million volts, esp. as a unit of electromotive force. ¶ Abbr.: **MV**.

meg·a·watt /mégawot/ *n.* one million watts, esp. as a measure of electrical power as generated by power stations. ¶ Abbr.: **MW**.

mei·o·sis /mīôsis/ *n.* **1** *Biol.* ▲ a type of cell division in reproductive cells (e.g,. egg or sperm) that results in daughter cells with half the chromosome number of the parent cell (cf. MITOSIS). **2** = LITOTES. □□ **mei·ot·ic** /mīótik/ *adj.*

mel·a·mine /mélameen/ *n.* **1** a white crystalline compound used in making thermosetting resins. **2** (in full **melamine resin**) a plastic made from melamine and used esp. for laminated coatings.

mel·an·cho·li·a /mélankóleeə/ *n.* a mental condition marked by depression and ill-founded fears.

mel·an·chol·y /mélankolee/ *n. & adj.* ● *n.* (*pl.* **-ies**) **1** a pensive sadness. **2 a** mental depression. **b** a habitual or constitutional tendency to this. **3** *hist.* one of the four humors; black bile (see HUMOR *n.* 4). ● *adj.* sad; gloomy; saddening; depressing; expressing sadness. □□ **mel·an·chol·ic** /-kólik/ *adj.*

Mel·a·ne·sian /mélaneézhən, -shən/ *n. & adj.* ● *n.* **1** a member of the dominant Negroid people of Melanesia, an island group in the W. Pacific. **2** the

---

language of this people. ● *adj.* of or relating to this people or their language.

mé·lange /maylónzh/ *n.* a mixture; a medley.

mel·a·nin /mélanin/ *n.* a dark pigment occurring in the hair, skin, and iris of the eye that is responsible for tanning of the skin when exposed to sunlight.

mel·a·no·ma /mélanômə/ *n.* a malignant tumor of melanin-forming cells, usu. in the skin.

Mel·ba toast /mélbə/ *n.* very thin crisp toast.

meld[1] /meld/ *v. & n.* ● *v. tr.* (also *absol.*) (in rummy, canasta, etc.) lay down or declare (one's cards) in order to score points. ● *n.* a completed set or run of cards in any of these games.

meld[2] /meld/ *v.tr. & intr.* merge; blend; combine.

me·lee /máyláy/ *n.* (also **mêlée**) **1** a confused fight, skirmish, or scuffle. **2** a muddle.

mel·i·lot /mélilot/ *n.* a leguminous plant of the genus *Melilotus*, with trifoliate leaves, small flowers, and a scent of hay when dried.

mel·lif·lu·ous /məliflōōəs/ *adj.* (of a voice or words) pleasing; musical; flowing. □□ **mel·lif·lu·ous·ly** *adv.*

mel·low /mélō/ *adj. & v.* ● *adj.* **1** (of sound, color, light) soft and rich; free from harshness. **2** (of character) softened or matured by age or experience. **3** genial; jovial. **4** partly intoxicated. **5** (of fruit) soft, sweet, and juicy. **6** (of wine) well-matured; smooth. **7** (of earth) rich; loamy. ● *v.tr. & intr.* make or become mellow. □ **mellow out** *sl.* relax. □□ **mel·low·ness** *n.*

me·lo·de·on /məlôdeeən/ *n.* (also **me·lo·di·on**) **1** a small organ popular in the 19th c., similar to the harmonium. **2** a small German accordion.

me·lod·ic /məlódik/ *adj.* **1** of or relating to melody. **2** having or producing melody. □□ **me·lod·i·cal·ly** *adv.*

me·lo·di·ous /məlôdeeəs/ *adj.* **1** of, producing, or having melody. **2** sweet-sounding. □□ **me·lo·di·ous·ly** *adv.* **me·lo·di·ous·ness** *n.*

mel·o·dra·ma /méladraámə, -dramə/ *n.* **1** a sensational dramatic piece with crude appeals to the emotions and usu. a happy ending. **2** the genre of drama of this type. **3** language, behavior, or an occurrence suggestive of this. □□ **me·lo·dra·mat·ic** /-drəmátik/ *adj.* **me·lo·dra·mat·i·cal·ly** /-drəmátiklee/ *adv.* **me·lo·dram·a·tize** /-drámətīz/ *v.tr.*

M

mel·o·dy /mélədee/ n. (pl. **-ies**) **1** an arrangement of single notes in a musically expressive succession. **2** the principal part in harmonized music. **3** a musical arrangement of words. **4** sweet music; tunefulness.

mel·on /mélən/ n. **1** the sweet fruit of various gourds. ▷ FRUIT. **2** the gourd producing this (honeydew melon; watermelon). **3** Zool. ▼ a mass of waxy material in the head of some toothed whales, thought to focus acoustic signals.

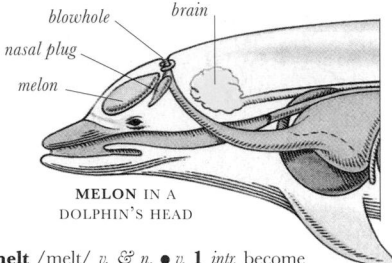

blowhole
brain
nasal plug
melon

MELON IN A
DOLPHIN'S HEAD

melt /melt/ v. & n. ● v. **1** intr. become liquefied by heat. **2** tr. change to a liquid condition by heat. **3** tr. (as **molten** adj.) (usu. of materials that require a great deal of heat to melt them) liquefied by heat (molten lava; molten lead). **4 a** intr. & tr. dissolve. **b** intr. (of food) be easily dissolved in the mouth. **5** intr. **a** (of a person, feelings, the heart, etc.) be softened as a result of pity, love, etc. **b** dissolve into tears. **6** tr. soften (a person, feelings, the heart, etc.) (a look to melt a heart of stone). **7** intr. (usu. foll. by into) change or merge imperceptibly into another form or state (night melted into dawn). **8** intr. (often foll. by away) (of a person) leave or disappear unobtrusively (melted into the background; melted away into the crowd). **9** intr. (usu. as **melting** adj.) (of sound) be soft and liquid (melting chords). ● n. **1** liquid metal, etc. **2** an amount melted at any one time. **3** the process or an instance of melting. □ **melt away** disappear or make disappear by liquefaction. **melt down 1** melt (esp. metal articles) in order to reuse the raw material. **2** become liquid and lose structure (cf. MELTDOWN). □□ **melt·er** n. **melt·ing·ly** adv.

melt·down /méltdown/ n. **1** the melting of (and consequent damage to) a structure, esp. the overheated core of a nuclear reactor. **2** a disastrous event, as a rapid fall in stock prices.

melt·ing point n. the temperature at which a solid will melt.

melt·ing pot n. **1** a pot in which metals, etc., are melted and mixed. **2** a place where races, theories, etc., are mixed, or an imaginary pool where ideas are mixed together.

mem·ber /mémbər/ n. **1** a person, animal or plant, etc., belonging to a society, team, taxonomic group, etc. **2** a person formally elected to take part in the proceedings of certain organizations (Member of Congress). **3** (also attrib.) a part or branch of a political body (member state; a member of the United Nations). **4** a constituent portion of a complex structure. **5** a part of a sentence, equation, group of figures, mathematical set, etc. **6 a** any part or organ of the body, esp. a limb. **b** = PENIS. □□ **mem·bered** adj. (also in comb.).

mem·ber·ship /mémbərship/ n. **1** being a member. **2** the number of members. **3** the body of members.

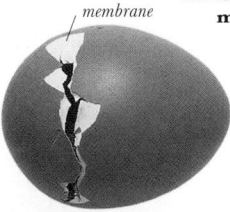

membrane

MEMBRANE LINING AN
EGGSHELL

mem·brane /mémbrayn/ n. **1** ◀ any type of pliable sheetlike structure acting as a boundary, lining, or partition in an organism. **2** a thin pliable sheet or skin. □□ **mem·bra·nous** /-brənəs/ adj.

meme /meem/ n. Biol. an element of behavior or culture passed on by imitation or other non-genetic means.

me·men·to /miméntō/ n. (pl. **-os** or **-oes**) an object kept as a reminder or a souvenir of a person or an event.

me·men·to mo·ri /məméntō máwree, -rī/ n. (pl. same) a warning or reminder of death (e.g., a skull).

mem·o /mémō/ n. (pl. **-os**) colloq. a memorandum.

mem·oir /mémwaar/ n. **1** a historical account or biography written from personal knowledge or special sources. **2** (in pl.) an autobiography. □□ **mem·oir·ist** n.

mem·o·ra·bil·i·a /mémərəbileeə, -bílyə/ n.pl. **1** souvenirs of memorable events.

mem·o·ra·ble /mémərəbəl/ adj. **1** worth remembering. **2** easily remembered. □□ **mem·o·ra·bil·i·ty** /-bílitee/ n. **mem·o·ra·bly** adv.

mem·o·ran·dum /mémərándəm/ n. (pl. **memo·randa** /-də/ or **memorandums**) **1** a note or record made for future use. **2** an informal written message, esp. in business, diplomacy, etc. **3** Law a document recording the terms of a contract or other legal details.

me·mo·ri·al /məmáwreeəl/ n. & adj. ● n. an object, institution, or custom established in memory of a person or event (the Albert Memorial). ● adj. intending to commemorate a person or thing (memorial service). □□ **me·mo·ri·al·ist** n.

Me·mo·ri·al Day n. holiday on which those who died in war are remembered, usu. the last Monday in May.

me·mo·ri·al·ize /məmáwreeəlīz/ v.tr. **1** commemorate. **2** address a memorial to.

mem·o·rize /mémərīz/ v.tr. commit to memory. □□ **mem·o·ri·za·tion** n.

mem·o·ry /mémoree/ n. (pl. **-ies**) **1** the faculty by which things are recalled to or kept in the mind. **2 a** this faculty in an individual (my memory is beginning to fail). **b** one's store of things remembered (buried deep in my memory). **3** a recollection or remembrance (the memory of better times). **4** the storage capacity of a computer or other electronic machinery. **5** the remembrance of a person or thing (his mother's memory haunted him). **6 a** the reputation of a dead person (his memory lives on). **b** in formulaic phrases used of a dead sovereign, etc. (of blessed memory). **7** the length of time over which the memory or memories of any given person or group extends (within living memory; within the memory of anyone still working here). **8** the act of remembering (a deed worthy of memory). □ **from memory** without verification in books, etc.

mem·o·ry lane n. (usu. prec. by down, along) an imaginary and sentimental journey into the past.

men pl. of MAN.

men·ace /ménis/ n. & v. ● n. **1** a threat. **2** a dangerous or obnoxious thing or person. **3** joc. a pest, a nuisance. ● v.tr. & intr. threaten. □□ **men·ac·ing** adj. **men·ac·ing·ly** adv.

mé·nage à trois /maynáazh aa trwáa/ n. (pl. **ménages à trois** pronunc. same) an arrangement in which three people live together, usu. a married couple and the lover of one of them.

me·nag·er·ie /mənájəree, -názh-/ n. a small zoo.

mend /mend/ v. & n. ● v. **1** tr. restore to a sound condition; repair. **2** intr. heal. **3** tr. improve (mend matters). **4** tr. add fuel to (a fire). ● n. a darn or repair in material, etc. (a mend in my shirt). □ **mend one's fences** make peace with a person. **mend one's ways** reform, improve one's habits. **on the mend** improving in health or condition. □□ **mend·er** n.

men·da·cious /mendáyshəs/ adj. lying, untruthful. □□ **men·da·cious·ly** adv. **men·dac·i·ty** /-dásitee/ n. (pl. **-ies**).

men·de·le·vi·um /méndəleéveeəm/ n. Chem. an artificially made transuranic radioactive metallic element. ¶ Symb.: **Md**.

Men·del·ism /méndəlizəm/ n. ▼ the theory of heredity based on the recurrence of certain inherited characteristics transmitted by genes. □□ **Men·de·li·an** /-deéleeən/ adj. & n.

men·di·cant /méndikənt/ adj. & n. ● adj. **1** begging. **2** (of a friar) living solely on alms. ● n. **1** a beggar. **2** a mendicant friar.

mend·ing /ménding/ n. **1** the action of a person who mends. **2** things, esp. clothes, to be mended.

men·folk /ménfōk/ n.pl. **1** men in general. **2** the men of one's family.

men·ha·den /menháyd'n/ n. (pl. same) any large herringlike fish of the genus Brevoortia, of the E. coast of N. America, yielding valuable oil and used for manure.

MENDELISM

Certain basic principles of genetics were established by the Austrian botanist Gregor Mendel, who found that the inheritance of characteristics follows predictable mathematical patterns. The expression of inherited characteristics depends on whether the genes are dominant (R) or recessive (r) in form. A recessive gene is expressed only if it is partnered by an identical recessive gene. If paired with a dominant gene the effect is masked, but it still forms part of the genetic information passed to the next generation.

DEMONSTRATION OF MENDELISM IN A PLANT

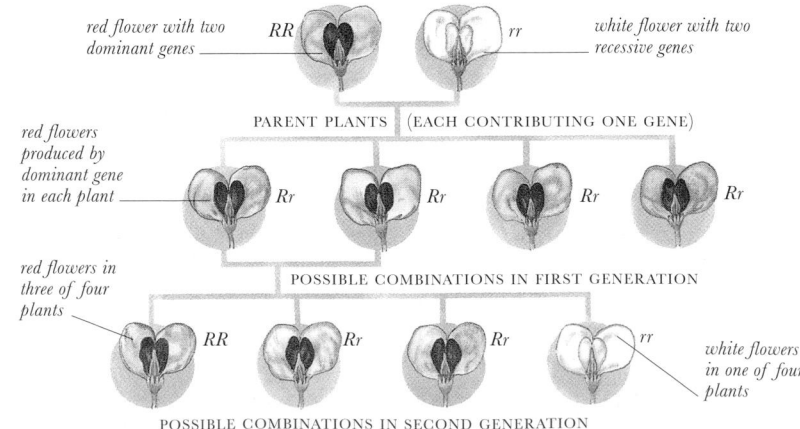

red flower with two dominant genes — RR   rr — white flower with two recessive genes

PARENT PLANTS (EACH CONTRIBUTING ONE GENE)

red flowers produced by dominant gene in each plant — Rr   Rr   Rr   Rr

POSSIBLE COMBINATIONS IN FIRST GENERATION

red flowers in three of four plants — RR   Rr   Rr   rr — white flowers in one of four plants

POSSIBLE COMBINATIONS IN SECOND GENERATION

M

men·hir /ménheer/ *n. Archaeol.* ► a tall upright usu. prehistoric monumental stone.

me·ni·al /méeneeəl/ *adj. & n.* ● *adj.* **1** (esp. of work) degrading, servile. **2** usu. *derog.* (of a servant) domestic. ● *n.* **1** a menial servant. **2** a servile person.

men·in·gi·tis /méninjítis/ *n.* an inflammation of the meninges due to infection by viruses or bacteria.

me·ninx /méeningks/ *n.* (*pl.* **meninges** /mənínjeez/) (usu. in *pl.*) ▼ any of the three membranes that line the skull and vertebral canal and enclose the brain and spinal cord. □□ **me·nin·ge·al** /minínjeeəl/ *adj.*

MENHIR: PREHISTORIC MENHIRS NEAR CARNAC, FRANCE

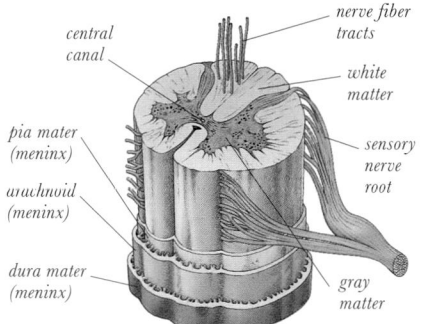

central canal
nerve fiber tracts
white matter
pia mater (meninx)
arachnoid (meninx)
dura mater (meninx)
sensory nerve root
gray matter

MENINX: SECTION THROUGH THE HUMAN SPINAL CORD SHOWING MENINGES

me·nis·cus /mənískəs/ *n.* (*pl.* **menisci** /-nísī/ or **meniscuses**) **1** *Physics* ▼ the curved upper surface of a liquid in a tube. **2** a lens that is convex on one side and concave on the other. **3** *Math.* a crescent-shaped figure. **4** *Anat.* a cartilaginous disk within a joint, esp. the knee. ▷ KNEE

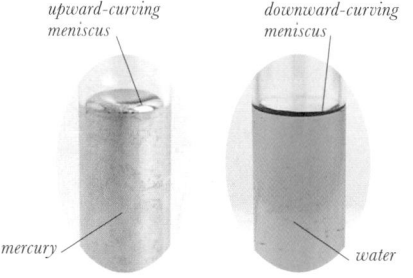

upward-curving meniscus
downward-curving meniscus
mercury
water

MENISCUS: MERCURY AND WATER MENISCI

me·nol·o·gy /minóləjee/ *n.* (*pl.* **-ies**) a calendar, esp. that of the Greek Church, with biographies of the saints.

Men·non·ite /ménənīt/ *n.* a member of a Protestant sect, emphasizing adult baptism and rejecting church organization, military service, and public office.

men·o·pause /ménəpawz/ *n.* **1** the ceasing of menstruation. **2** the period in a woman's life when this occurs. □□ **men·o·pau·sal** /-páwzəl/ *adj.*

me·nor·ah /mənáwrə, -nórə/ *n.* ► a candelabrum used in Jewish worship, originally one with seven branches, now often replicated as a nine-branched candelabrum used at Hanukkah.

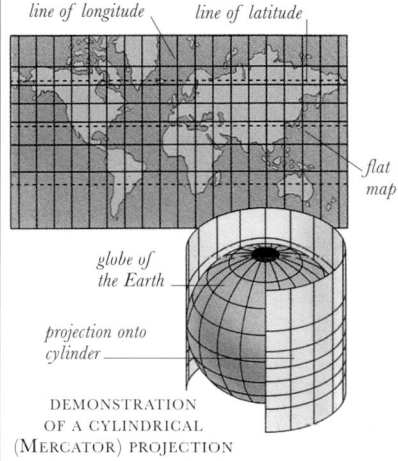

MENORAH

men·serv·ants see MANSERVANT.

men·ses /ménseez/ *n.pl.* **1** blood and other materials discharged from the uterus at menstruation. **2** the time of menstruation.

men's room *n.* a usu. public restroom for men.

men·stru·al /ménstrōŏəl/ *adj.* of or relating to the menses or menstruation.

men·stru·al cy·cle *n.* the process of ovulation and menstruation in female primates.

men·stru·ate /ménstrōŏ-ayt/ *v.intr.* undergo menstruation.

men·stru·a·tion /ménstrōŏ-áyshən/ *n.* the process of discharging blood and other materials from the uterus in sexually mature nonpregnant women at intervals of about one lunar month until the menopause.

men·su·ra·tion /ménshəráyshən, -sə-/ *n.* **1** measuring. **2** *Math.* the measuring of geometric magnitudes such as lengths of lines, areas of surfaces, and volumes of solids.

mens·wear /ménzwair/ *n.* clothes for men.

men·tal /mént'l/ *adj.* **1** of or in the mind. **2** done by the mind. **3** *colloq.* **a** insane. **b** crazy, wild, eccentric (*is mental about pop music*). □□ **men·tal·ly** *adv.*

men·tal age *n.* the degree of a person's mental development expressed as an age at which the same degree is attained by an average person.

men·tal cru·el·ty *n.* the infliction of suffering on another's mind, esp. *Law* as grounds for divorce.

men·tal ill·ness *n.* a disorder of the mind.

men·tal·i·ty /mentálitee/ *n.* (*pl.* **-ies**) **1** mental character or disposition. **2** kind or degree of intelligence. **3** what is in or of the mind.

men·ta·tion /mentáyshən/ *n.* **1** mental action. **2** state of mind.

men·thol /ménthawl/ *n.* a mint-tasting organic alcohol found in oil of peppermint, etc., used as a flavoring and to relieve local pain.

men·tho·lat·ed /ménthəlaytid/ *adj.* treated with or containing menthol.

men·tion /ménshən/ *v. & n.* ● *v.tr.* **1** refer to briefly. **2** specify by name. **3** reveal or disclose (*do not mention this to anyone*). ● *n.* a reference, esp. by name, to a person or thing. □ **don't mention it** said in polite dismissal of an apology or thanks. **make mention** (or **no mention**) **of** refer (or not refer) to. **not to mention** introducing a fact or thing of secondary or (as a rhetorical device) of primary importance. □□ **men·tion·a·ble** *adj.*

men·tor /méntawr/ *n.* an experienced and trusted adviser.

men·u /ményōō/ *n.* **1 a** a list of dishes available in a restaurant, etc. **b** a list of items to be served at a meal. **2** *Computing* a list of options showing the commands or facilities available.

men·u-driv·en *adj.* (of a program or computer) used by making selections from menus.

me·ow /mee-ów/ *n. & v.* ● *n.* the characteristic cry of a cat. ● *v.intr.* make this cry.

me·per·i·dine /məpérədeen/ *n.* a narcotic compound, $C_{15}H_{21}NO_2$, used as an analgesic, sedative, and antispasmodic.

me·phit·ic /-fítik/ *adj.* **1** foul-smelling. **2** (of a vapor, etc.) noxious, poisonous.

me·phi·tis /məfítis/ *n.* **1** a noxious emanation, esp. from the earth. **2** a foul-smelling or poisonous stench. □□ **me·phit·ic** /-fítik/ *adj.*

mer·can·tile /márkəntīl/ *adj.* **1** of trade, trading. **2** commercial. **3** mercenary, fond of bargaining.

MERCATOR PROJECTION

The most common type of world map was devised by the Dutch mapmaker Gerardus Mercator in 1569. In the projection on which the map is based, the Earth's sphere is "unwrapped" from a cylinder onto a flat rectangular surface, with the lines of longitude and latitude shown as a regular grid of straight lines. In a cylindrical projection such as this, the Earth's surface becomes visually more distorted toward the poles.

line of longitude
line of latitude
flat map
globe of the Earth
projection onto cylinder

DEMONSTRATION OF A CYLINDRICAL (MERCATOR) PROJECTION

mer·can·til·ism /márkəntilizəm/ *n.* an old economic theory that money is the only form of wealth. □□ **mer·can·til·ist** *n.*

mer·cap·tan /mərkáptən/ *n.* = THIOL.

Mer·ca·tor pro·jec·tion /mərkáytər/ *n.* (also **Mercator's projection**) ▲ a projection of a map of the world onto a cylinder so that all the parallels of latitude have the same length as the equator.

mer·ce·nar·y /mársəneree/ *adj. & n.* ● *adj.* primarily concerned with money or other reward (*mercenary motives*). ● *n.* (*pl.* **-ies**) a hired soldier in foreign service.

mer·cer·ize /mársərīz/ *v.tr.* treat (cotton fabric or thread) under tension with caustic alkali to give greater strength and impart luster.

mer·chan·dise /márchəndīz/ *n. & v.* ● *n.* goods for sale. ● *v.* **1** *intr.* trade, traffic. **2** *tr.* trade or traffic in. **3** *tr.* **a** promote the sale of (goods, etc.). **b** advertise, publicize (an idea or person). □□ **mer·chan·dis·er** *n.*

mer·chant /márchənt/ *n.* **1** a retail trader; dealer; storekeeper. **2** *colloq.* usu. *derog.* a person showing a partiality for a specified activity or practice (*speed merchant*).

mer·chant·a·ble /márchəntəbəl/ *adj.* salable; marketable.

mer·chant·man /márchəntmən/ *n.* (*pl.* **-men**) a ship conveying merchandise.

mer·chant ma·rine *n.* a nation's commercial shipping.

mer·chant ship = MERCHANTMAN.

mer·ci·ful /mársifŏŏl/ *adj.* having, showing, or feeling mercy.

mer·ci·ful·ly /mársifŏŏlee/ *adv.* **1** in a merciful manner. **2** (qualifying a whole sentence) fortunately (*mercifully, the sun came out*).

mer·ci·less /mársilis/ *adj.* **1** pitiless. **2** showing no mercy. □□ **mer·ci·less·ly** *adv.*

mer·cu·ri·al /mərkyŏŏreeəl/ *adj.* **1** (of a person) ready-witted, volatile. **2** of or containing mercury. □□ **mer·cu·ri·al·ly** *adv.*

M

mer·cu·ry /mɔ́rkyɔree/ *n.* **1** *Chem.* ◄ a silvery-white heavy liquid metallic element used in barometers, thermometers, and amalgams. ¶ Symb.: **Hg**. ▷ METAL, SPHYGMO-MANOMETER. **2** (**Mercury**) ▶ the planet nearest to the Sun. ▷ SOLAR SYSTEM. **3** any plant of the genus *Mercurialis*, esp. *M. perenne*. □□ **mer·cu·ric** /-kyŏorik/ *adj.*

mer·cy /mɔ́rsee/ *n. & int.* ● *n.* (*pl.* **-ies**) **1** compassion or forbearance shown to enemies or offenders in one's power. **2** the quality of compassion. **3** an act of mercy. **4** (*attrib.*) administered or performed out of mercy or pity for a suffering person (*mercy killing*). **5** something to be thankful for (*small mercies*). ● *int.* expressing surprise or fear. □ **at the mercy of 1** in the power of. **2** liable to danger or harm from. **have mercy on** (or **upon**) show mercy to.

mer·cy kill·ing *n.* = EUTHANASIA.

mercury

mere /meer/ *attrib.adj.* (**merest**) that is solely or no more or better than what is specified (*a mere boy; no mere theory*). □□ **mere·ly** *adv.*

mer·e·tri·cious /méritríshɔs/ *adj.* **1** showily but falsely attractive. **2** of or befitting a prostitute.

mer·gan·ser /mɔrgánsɔr/ *n.* diving fish-eating duck with a serrated hooked bill.

merge /mɔrj/ *vtr. & intr.* **1** (often foll. by *with*) **a** combine or be combined. **b** join or blend gradually. **2** lose or cause to lose character and identity in (something else).

merg·er /mɔ́rjɔr/ *n.* **1** the combining of two commercial companies, etc., into one. **2** a merging.

me·rid·i·an /mɔrídeeɔn/ *n. & adj.* ● *n.* **1** a circle passing through the celestial poles and zenith of any place on the Earth's surface. **2 a** a circle of constant longitude, passing through a given place and the terrestrial poles. **b** the corresponding line on a map. **3** prime; full splendor. ● *adj.* **1** of noon. **2** of the period of greatest splendor, vigor, etc.

me·rid·i·o·nal /mɔrídeeɔnɔl/ *adj. & n.* ● *adj.* **1** of or in the south (esp. of Europe). **2** of or relating to a meridian. ● *n.* an inhabitant of the south (esp. of France).

me·ringue /mɔráng/ *n.* a confection of sugar, egg whites, etc., browned by baking.

me·ri·no /mɔréenō/ *n.* (*pl.* **-os**) **1** (in full **merino sheep**) a variety of sheep with long fine wool. **2** a soft woolen or wool-and-cotton material like cashmere, orig. of merino wool. **3** a fine woolen yarn.

mer·i·stem /méristem/ *n. Bot.* a plant tissue consisting of actively dividing cells forming new tissue. □□ **mer·i·ste·mat·ic** /-stɔmátik/ *adj.*

mer·it /mérit/ *n. & v.* ● *n.* **1** the quality of deserving well. **2** excellence, worth. **3** (usu. in *pl.*) **a** a thing that entitles one to reward or gratitude. **b** esp. *Law* intrinsic rights and wrongs (*the merits of a case*). ● *v.tr.* deserve. □ **make a merit of** regard or represent (one's own conduct) as praiseworthy. **on its merits** with regard only to its intrinsic worth.

mer·i·toc·ra·cy /méritókrɔsee/ *n.* (*pl.* **-ies**) **1** government by persons selected competitively according to merit. **2** a group of persons selected in this way. **3** a society governed by meritocracy.

mer·i·to·ri·ous /méritáwreeɔs/ *adj.* **1** deserving reward, praise, or gratitude. **2** deserving commendation for thoroughness, etc.

mer·lin /mɔ́rlin/ *n.* a small European or N. American falcon, *Falco columbarius*.

mer·lon /mɔ́rlɔn/ *n.* the solid part of an embattled parapet between two embrasures.

mer·maid /mɔ́rmayd/ *n.* an imaginary sea creature, with the head and trunk of a woman and the tail of a fish.

MERCURY

Mercury is a small, rocky planet whose surface has been heavily cratered by meteorites. The surface also has many ridges, called rupes, that are believed to have formed as the core of the young planet cooled and shrank. Mercury orbits the Sun in 88 Earth days – faster than any other planet – but takes nearly 59 to spin on its axis. A day on Mercury (from sunrise to sunrise) takes 176 Earth days; in one day Mercury will orbit the Sun twice and spin three times on its axis. Surface temperature on the planet varies from 806°F (430°C) on the sunlit side to -338°F (-170°C) on the dark side.

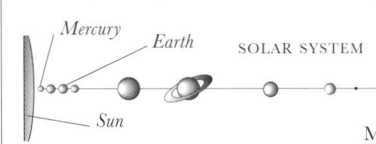

Mercury   Earth   SOLAR SYSTEM   Sun

thin crust of silicate rock · *Rubens crater* · *unmapped region* · *mantle of silicate rock* · *Vivaldi crater* · *Caloris Basin* · *atmosphere of minute amounts of helium and hydrogen* · *iron core* · *Renoir crater* · *Chekhov crater* · *Fram rupes* · *Discovery rupes*

MERCURY, WITH INTERNAL STRUCTURE REVEALED

---

mer·man /mɔ́rman/ *n.* (*pl.* **-men**) the male equivalent of a mermaid.

mer·ri·ment /mérimɔnt/ *n.* **1** exuberant enjoyment; being merry. **2** mirth, fun.

mer·ry /méree/ *adj.* (**merrier, merriest**) **1** joyous. **2** full of laughter or gaiety. □ **make merry 1** be festive; enjoy oneself. **2** (foll. by *over*) make fun of. □□ **mer·ri·ly** *adv.*

mer·ry-go-round /méreegōrownd/ *n.* **1** a revolving machine with wooden horses or other animals, etc., for riding on at an amusement park, etc. **2** a cycle of bustling activities.

mer·ry·mak·ing /méreemayking/ *n.* festivity, fun. □□ **mer·ry·mak·er** *n.*

me·sa /máysɔ/ *n.* an isolated flat-topped hill with steep sides. ▷ ERODE

mé·sal·li·ance /mayzáleeɔns, máyzalyaáns/ *n.* a marriage with a person of a lower social position.

mes·cal /méskal/ *n.* **1 a** maguey. **b** liquor obtained from this. **2** a peyote cactus.

mes·ca·line /méskɔleen, -lin/ *n.* (also **mes·ca·lin** /-lin/) a hallucinogenic alkaloid present in mescal.

Mes·dames *pl.* of MADAME.

Mes·de·moi·selles *pl.* of MADEMOISELLE.

me·sem·bry·an·the·mum /mizémbreeánthimɔm/ *n.* any of various succulent plants of the genus *Mesembryanthemum*, with colorful daisylike flowers.

mes·en·ceph·a·lon /mésɔnséfɔlon, méz-/ *n.* the part of the brain developing from the middle of the primitive or embryonic brain. Also called **midbrain**.

mes·en·ter·y /mésɔnteree, méz-/ *n.* (*pl.* **-ies**) a double layer of peritoneum attaching the abdominal organs to the posterior wall of the abdomen. □□ **mes·en·ter·ic** /-térik/ *adj.* **mes·en·ter·i·tis** /-rítis/ *n.*

mesh /mesh/ *n. & v.* ● *n.* **1** a network fabric or structure. **2** each of the open spaces between the strands of a net or sieve, etc. **3** (in *pl.*) **a** a network. **b** a snare. **4** (in *pl.*) *Physiol.* an interlaced structure. ● *v.intr.* **1** (often foll. by *with*) (of the teeth of a wheel) be engaged. **2** be harmonious.

me·si·al /méezeeɔl/ *adj. Anat.* of, in, or directed toward the middle line of a body. □□ **me·si·al·ly** *adv.*

mes·mer·ism /mézmɔrizɔm/ *n.* **1** *Psychol.* **a** a hypnotic state produced in a person by another's influence. **b** a doctrine concerning this. **c** an influence producing this. **2** fascination. □□ **mes·mer·ic** /mezmérik/ *adj.* **mes·mer·ist** *n.*

mes·mer·ize /mézmɔrīz/ *v.tr.* **1** *Psychol.* hypnotize; exercise mesmerism on. **2** fascinate, spellbind.

---

meso- /mésō, méz-/ *comb. form* middle, intermediate.

mes·o·blast /mésɔblast, méz-/ *n. Biol.* the middle germ layer of an embryo.

mes·o·derm /mésɔderm, méz-/ *n. Biol.* = MESOBLAST.

mes·o·lith·ic /mézɔlithik, més-/ *adj. Archaeol.* of or concerning the Stone Age between the Paleolithic and Neolithic periods.

mes·o·morph /mézɔmawrf, més-/ *n.* ▼ person with a compact and muscular body (cf. ECTOMORPH, ENDOMORPH). □□ **mes·o·mor·phic** /-máwrfik/ *adj.*

me·son /mézon, més-, méezon, -son/ *n. Physics* any of a class of elementary particles believed to participate in the forces that hold nucleons together in the atomic nucleus.

mes·o·phyll /mésɔfil, méz-/ *n.* the inner tissue of a leaf.

mes·o·phyte /mésɔfīt, méz-/ *n.* a plant needing only a moderate amount of water.

mes·o·sphere /mésɔsfeer, méz-/ *n.* the region of the atmosphere extending from the top of the stratosphere to an altitude of about 50 miles. ▷ ATMOSPHERE

MESOMORPH

Mesomorphs are one of the three basic body shapes, or "somatypes," identified by W. H. Sheldon in the 1950s. They have strong, muscular bodies, with wide shoulders and narrow hips. Endomorphs tend to be overweight, gaining weight in the abdominal region and with poorly developed muscle and bone. Ectomorphs, the third type, have tall, thin, lean physiques.

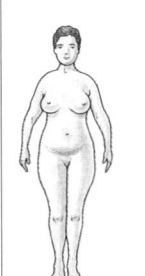 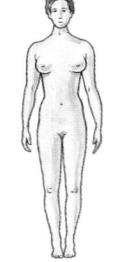 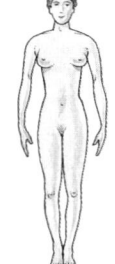

ENDOMORPH   MESOMORPH   ECTOMORPH

M

Mes·o·zo·ic /mésəzṓ-ik, méz-/ *adj. & n. Geol.* ● *adj.* of or relating to an era of geological time marked by the development of dinosaurs, and with evidence of the first mammals, birds, and flowering plants. ● *n.* this era (cf. CENOZOIC, PALEOZOIC).

mes·quite /meskéet/ *n.* **1** any N. American leguminous tree of the genus *Prosopis,* esp. *P. juliflora.* **2** the wood of the mesquite, as used in grilling food.

mess /mes/ *n. & v.* ● *n.* **1** a dirty or untidy state of things (*the room is a mess*). **2** a state of confusion, embarrassment, or trouble. **3** something causing a mess, e.g., spilled liquid, etc. **4** a domestic animal's excreta. **5 a** a company of persons who take meals together, esp. in the armed forces. **b** a place where such meals or recreation take place communally. **c** a meal taken there. **6** *derog.* a disagreeable concoction. **7** a portion of liquid or pulpy food. ● *v.* **1** *tr.* (often foll. by *up*) **a** make a mess of; dirty. **b** muddle; make into a state of confusion. **2** *intr.* (foll. by *with*) interfere with. **3** *intr.* take one's meals. **4** *intr. colloq.* defecate. □ **make a mess of** bungle. **mess about** (or **around**) **1** act desultorily. **2** *colloq.* make things awkward for; cause arbitrary inconvenience to. **3** philander. **4** associate, esp. for immoral purposes.

mes·sage /mésij/ *n.* **1** a communication sent by one person to another. **2** the central import or meaning of an artistic work, etc. □ **get the message** *colloq.* understand what is meant.

Mes·sei·gneurs *pl.* of MONSEIGNEUR.

mes·sen·ger /mésinjər/ *n.* **1** a person who carries a message. **2** a person employed to carry messages.

mes·sen·ger RNA *n.* a form of RNA carrying genetic information from DNA to a ribosome. ¶ Abbr.: **mRNA**.

mess hall *n.* a communal, esp. military, dining area.

Mes·si·ah /misíə/ *n.* **1** (also **messiah**) a liberator or would-be liberator of an oppressed people or country. **2 a** the promised deliverer of the Jews. **b** (usu. prec. by *the*) Christ regarded as this. □□ **Messi·ah·ship** *n.*

Mes·si·an·ic /méseeánik/ *adj.* **1** of the Messiah. **2** inspired by hope or belief in a Messiah. □□ **Messi·a·nism** /mesíənizəm/ *n.*

Mes·sieurs *pl.* of MONSIEUR.

mess kit *n.* a soldier's cooking and eating utensils.

mess·mate /mésmayt/ *n.* a person with whom one regularly takes meals, esp. in the armed forces.

Messrs. /mésərz/ *pl.* of MR.

mess·y /mésee/ *adj.* (**messier, messiest**) **1** untidy or dirty. **2** causing or accompanied by a mess. **3** difficult to deal with; full of awkward complications. □□ **mess·i·ly** *adv.* **mess·i·ness** *n.*

mes·ti·zo /mesteézō/ *n.* (*pl.* **-os**; *fem.* **mestiza** /-zə/, *pl.* **-as**) a Latin American of mixed race, esp. the offspring of a Spaniard and a Native American.

Met /met/ *n.* (in full **the Met**) *colloq.* the Metropolitan Opera House in New York.

met *past* and *past part.* of MEET[1].

met. /met/ *abbr.* **1** meteorology; meteorological. **2** metropolitan.

meta- /métə/ *comb. form* (usu. **met-** before a vowel or *h*) **1** denoting change of position or condition (*metabolism*). **2** denoting position: **a** behind. **b** after or beyond (*metaphysics; metacarpus*). **c** of a higher or second-order kind (*metalanguage*).

me·tab·o·lism /mətábəlizəm/ *n.* all the chemical processes that occur within a living organism, resulting in energy production (CATABOLISM) and growth (ANABOLISM). □□ **met·a·bol·ic** /métəbólik/ *adj.* **met·a·bol·i·cal·ly** /métəbóliklee/ *adv.*

me·tab·o·lite /mətábəlīt/ *n. Physiol.* a substance formed in or necessary for metabolism.

me·tab·o·lize /mətábəlīz/ *v.tr. & intr.* process or be processed by metabolism.

met·a·car·pus /métəkáarpəs/ *n.* (*pl.* **metacarpi** /-pī/) **1** the set of five bones of the hand that connects the wrist to the fingers. ▷ HAND, SKELETON. **2** this part of the hand. □□ **met·a·car·pal** *adj.*

METAL

Metals have been valued since early times for their hardness and strength, and for the ease with which they can be shaped; some are also prized for their beauty and rarity. Few occur in a pure native state: most have to be extracted by refining and smelting the ore minerals in which they occur. Some metals, such as aluminum, tin, and lead, are weaker and melt more easily than others. These are widely used in the production of alloys – metal mixtures that exploit the distinctive qualities of different metals.

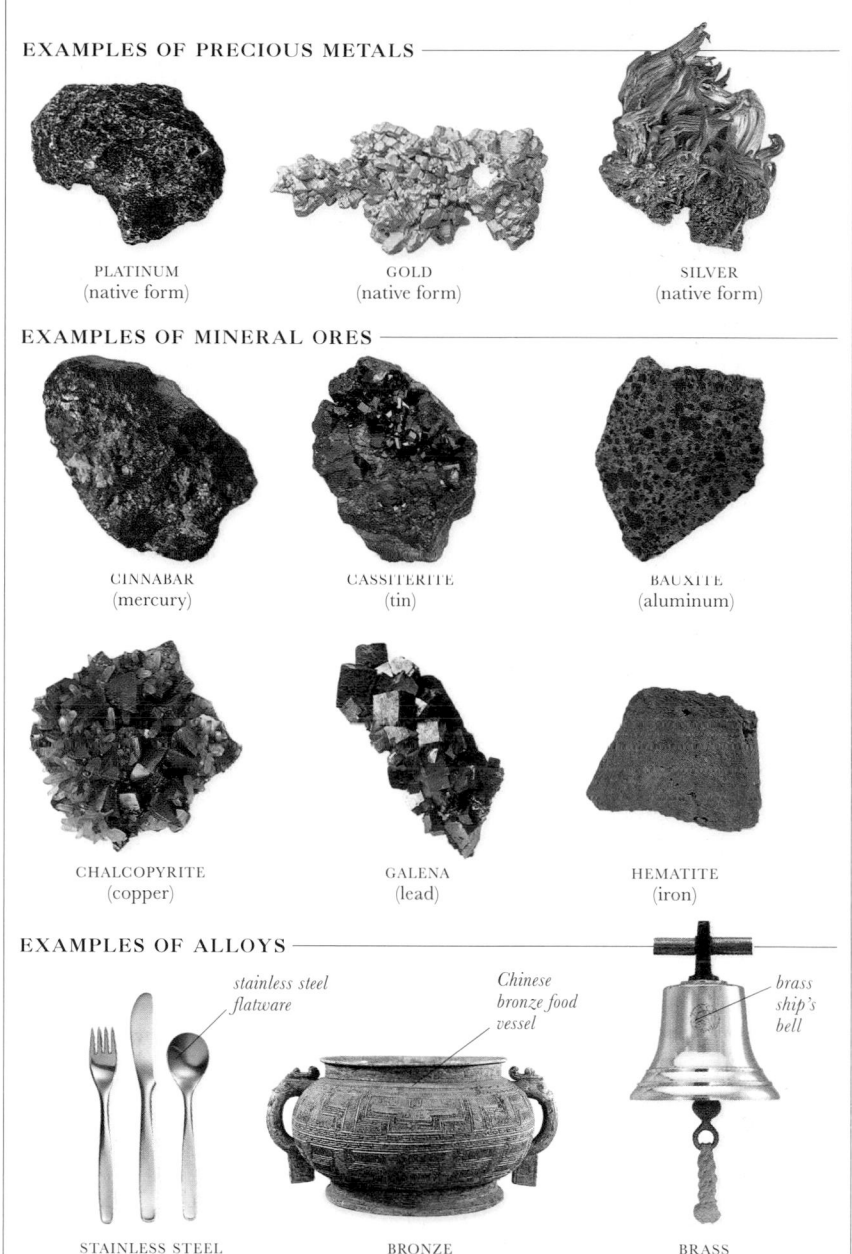

EXAMPLES OF PRECIOUS METALS

PLATINUM
(native form)

GOLD
(native form)

SILVER
(native form)

EXAMPLES OF MINERAL ORES

CINNABAR
(mercury)

CASSITERITE
(tin)

BAUXITE
(aluminum)

CHALCOPYRITE
(copper)

GALENA
(lead)

HEMATITE
(iron)

EXAMPLES OF ALLOYS

stainless steel flatware

Chinese bronze food vessel

brass ship's bell

STAINLESS STEEL
(iron, chromium, nickel, etc.)

BRONZE
(copper and tin)

BRASS
(copper and zinc)

M

---

met·a·cen·ter /métəsentər/ *n.* the point of intersection between a line (vertical in equilibrium) through the center of gravity of a floating body and a vertical line through the center of pressure after a slight angular displacement, which must be above the center of gravity to ensure stability. □□ **met·a·cen·tric** /-séntrik/ *adj.*

me·ta·da·ta /métədaytə/ *n.* a set of data that describes and gives information about other data.

met·a·gen·e·sis /métəjénisis/ *n.* the alternation of generations between sexual and asexual reproduction. □□ **met·a·ge·net·ic** /-jinétik/ *adj.*

met·al /mét'l/ *n., adj., & v.* ● *n.* **1 a** ▲ any of a class of chemical elements such as gold, silver, iron, and tin, usu. lustrous ductile solids and good conductors of heat and electricity and forming basic oxides. **b** an alloy of any of these. **2** material used for making glass, in a molten state. **3** (in *pl.*) the rails of a railroad line. ● *adj.* made of metal. ● *v.tr.* provide or fit with metal.

METAMORPHIC

Metamorphic rocks are formed by the application of heat and pressure to preexisting igneous, sedimentary, or earlier metamorphic rocks. The variations in metamorphic rock types are due to variations in the original rock type as well as the differing conditions to which the rocks were subjected. There are two main types of metamorphic rock. When rocks in a mountain-forming region are transformed by both heat and pressure, regional metamorphic rock, such as slate, schist, and gneiss, is formed. Contact metamorphism occurs in the area around an igneous intrusion, where rocks may be altered by direct heat alone; marble, for example, is formed by the application of heat to limestone. A third type of metamorphism – dynamic – occurs when movements at a fault in the Earth's crust force rock masses into contact with each other, producing a very fine-grained rock called mylonite.

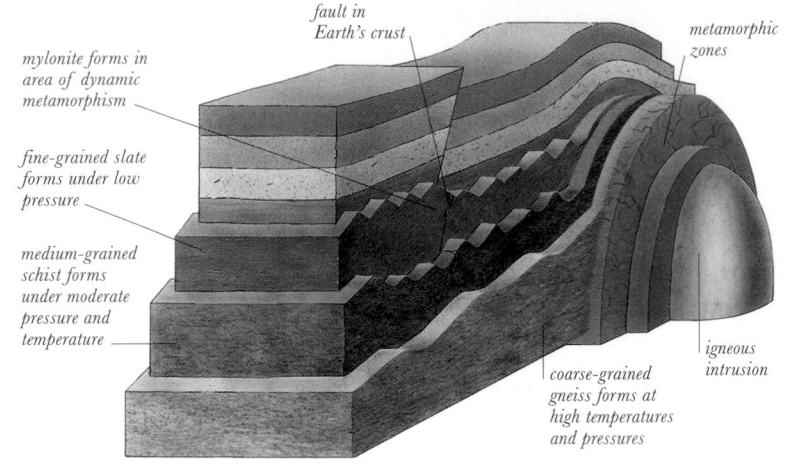

mylonite forms in area of dynamic metamorphism

fine-grained slate forms under low pressure

medium-grained schist forms under moderate pressure and temperature

fault in Earth's crust

metamorphic zones

igneous intrusion

coarse-grained gneiss forms at high temperatures and pressures

MODEL SHOWING THE FORMATION OF METAMORPHIC ROCKS

EXAMPLES OF METAMORPHIC ROCKS

REGIONAL METAMORPHIC ROCKS

SLATE   SCHIST   GNEISS

CONTACT METAMORPHIC ROCKS

METAQUARTZITE   MARBLE

DYNAMIC METAMORPHIC ROCK

MYLONITE

M

met·a·lan·guage /métəlanggwij/ *n*. **1** a form of language used to discuss a language. **2** a system of propositions about propositions.

met·al de·tec·tor *n*. an electronic device giving a signal when it locates metal.

met·al·ize /mét'līz/ *v.tr.* **1** render metallic. **2** coat with a thin layer of metal.

me·tal·lic /mətálik/ *adj*. **1** of, consisting of, or characteristic of metal or metals. **2** sounding sharp and ringing, like struck metal. **3** having the sheen or luster of metals. □□ **me·tal·li·cal·ly** *adv*.

met·al·lif·er·ous /mét'lifərəs/ *adj*. bearing or producing metal.

met·al·log·ra·phy /mét'lógrəfee/ *n*. the descriptive science of the structure and properties of metals. □□ **met·al·lo·graph·ic** /métaləgráfik/ *adj*. **met·al·lo·graph·i·cal** *adj*.

met·al·loid /mét'loyd/ *adj*. & *n*. ● *adj*. having the form or appearance of a metal. ● *n*. any element intermediate in properties between metals and nonmetals, e.g., boron, silicon, and germanium.

met·al·lur·gy /mét'lərjee/ *n*. the science concerned with the production, purification, and properties of metals and their application. □□ **met·al·lur·gic** /mét'lərjik/ *adj*. **met·al·lur·gi·cal** *adj*. **met·al·lur·gist** *n*.

met·al·work /mét'lwərk/ *n*. **1** the art of working in metal. **2** metal objects collectively. □□ **met·al·work·er** *n*.

met·a·mere /métəmeer/ *n*. *Zool*. each of several similar segments, that contain the same internal structures, of an animal body.

met·a·mer·ic /métəmérik/ *adj*. **1** *Chem*. having the same proportional composition and molecular weight, but different functional groups and chemical properties. **2** *Zool*. of or relating to metameres. □□ **met·a·mer** /métəmər/ *n*. **me·tam·er·ism** /metámərizəm/ *n*.

met·a·mor·phic /métəmáwrfik/ *adj*. **1** of or marked by metamorphosis. **2** *Geol*. ▲ (of rock) that

has undergone transformation by natural agencies such as heat and pressure. ▷ ROCK CYCLE. □□ **met·a·mor·phism** *n*.

met·a·mor·phose /métəmawrfōz/ *v.tr.* **1** change in form. **2** (foll. by *to, into*) **a** turn (into a new form). **b** change the nature of.

met·a·mor·pho·sis /métəmáwrfəsis/ *n*. (*pl*. **metamorphoses** /-seez/) **1** a change of form (by natural or supernatural means). **2** a changed form. **3** a change of character, conditions, etc. **4** *Zool*. ▼ the transformation between an immature form and an adult form, e.g., from a pupa to an insect or from a tadpole to a frog.

met·a·phase /métəfayz/ *n*. *Biol*. the stage of meiotic or mitotic cell division when the chromosomes become attached to the spindle fibers.

met·a·phor /métəfawr/ *n*. **1** the application of a name or descriptive term or phrase to an object or

action to which it is imaginatively but not literally applicable (e.g., *killing him with kindness*). **2** an instance of this. □□ **met·a·phor·ic** /-fáwrik, -fórik/ *adj*. **met·a·phor·i·cal** /-fáwrikəl, -fórikəl/ *adj*. **met·a·phor·i·cal·ly** /-fáwriklee, -fóriklee/ *adv*.

met·a·phrase /métəfrayz/ *n*. & *v*. ● *n*. a literal translation. ● *v.tr.* **1** translate; esp. literally. **2** put into other words. □□ **met·a·phras·tic** /-frástik/ *adj*.

met·a·phys·ic /métəfizik/ *n*. a system of metaphysics.

met·a·phys·i·cal /métəfizikəl/ *adj*. & *n*. ● *adj*. **1** of or relating to metaphysics. **2** based on abstract general reasoning. **3** excessively subtle or theoretical. **4** incorporeal; supernatural. **5** visionary. **6** (of poetry, esp. in the 17th c. in England) characterized by subtlety of thought and complex imagery. ● *n*. (**the Metaphysicals**) the metaphysical poets. □□ **met·a·phys·i·cal·ly** *adv*.

METAMORPHOSIS

Most invertebrates, as well as many fish and amphibians, start life as larvae. These look unlike their parents, often live in different habitats, and eat different food. They then undergo a total change of body form and appearance, called complete metamorphosis. A more gradual change in body shape, called incomplete metamorphosis, occurs in many insects. These hatch into miniature but immature versions of their parents and progress through a series of molts to adulthood.

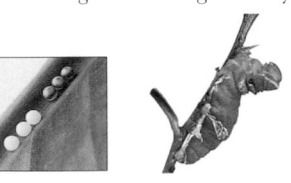

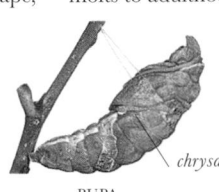

pupal case

butterfly

chrysalis

EGGS   LARVA   PUPA   MATURE BUTTERFLY

COMPLETE METAMORPHOSIS OF A BUTTERFLY

met·a·phys·ics /métəfiziks/ *n.pl.* (usu. treated as *sing.*) **1** the theoretical philosophy of being and knowing. **2** the philosophy of mind. **3** *colloq.* abstract talk; mere theory. □□ **met·a·phy·si·cian** /-zíshən/ *n.*

met·a·pla·sia /métəpláyzhə, -zeeə/ *n. Physiol.* an abnormal change in the nature of a tissue. □□ **met·a·plas·tic** /-plástik/ *adj.*

met·a·psy·chol·o·gy /métəsīkóləjee/ *n.* the study of the nature and functions of the mind beyond what can be studied experimentally. □□ **met·a·psy·cho·log·i·cal** /-kəlójikəl/ *adj.*

met·a·sta·ble /métəstáybəl/ *adj.* **1** (of a state of equilibrium) stable only under small disturbances. **2** passing to another state so slowly as to seem stable. □□ **met·a·sta·bil·i·ty** /-stəbílitee/ *n.*

me·tas·ta·sis /métástəsis/ *n.* (*pl.* **metastases** /-seez/) *Physiol.* **1** the transference of a disease, etc., from one part or organ to another. **2** the transformation of chemical compounds into others in the process of assimilation by an organism. □□ **me·tas·ta·size** *v.intr.* **met·a·stat·ic** /métəstátik/ *adj.*

met·a·tar·sus /métətáarsəs/ *n.* (*pl.* **metatarsi** /-sī/) **1** the part of the foot between the ankle and the toes. ▷ skeleton. **2** the set of bones in this. □□ **met·a·tar·sal** *adj.*

me·tath·e·sis /mitáthisis/ *n.* (*pl.* **metatheses** /-seez/) **1** *Gram.* the transposition of sounds or letters in a word. **2** *Chem.* the interchange of atoms or groups of atoms between two molecules. **3** an instance of either of these. □□ **met·a·thet·ic** /métəthétik/ *adj.* **met·a·thet·i·cal** /métəthétikəl/ *adj.*

mete /meet/ *v.tr.* **1** (usu. foll. by *out*) *literary* apportion or allot (a punishment or reward). **2** *poet.* or *Bibl.* measure.

me·tem·psy·cho·sis /mətémsīkósis, métəm-/ *n.* (*pl.* **-psychoses** /-seez/) **1** the supposed transmigration of the soul of a human being or animal at death into a new body of the same or a different species. **2** an instance of this. □□ **me·tem·psy·cho·sist** *n.*

me·te·or /méeteeər, -eeawr/ *n.* **1** a small body of matter from outer space that becomes incandescent as a result of friction with the Earth's atmosphere. **2** a streak of light emanating from a meteor.

me·te·or·ic /méetee-áwrik, -ór-/ *adj.* **1 a** of or relating to the atmosphere. **b** dependent on atmospheric conditions. **2** of meteors. **3** dazzling, transient (*meteoric rise to fame*). □□ **me·te·or·i·cal·ly** *adv.*

me·te·or·ite /méeteeərīt/ *n.* ▶ a fallen meteor, or fragment of natural rock or metal, that reaches the Earth's surface from outer space. □□ **me·te·or·it·ic** /-rítik/ *adj.*

me·te·or·o·graph /méeteeərəgraf/ *n.* an apparatus that records several meteorological phenomena at the same time.

me·te·or·oid /méeteeəróyd/ *n.* any small body, often the remnant of a comet, moving in the solar system that becomes visible as it passes through the Earth's atmosphere as a meteor. □□ **me·te·or·oid·al** /-róyd'l/ *adj.*

METEORITE

me·te·or·ol·o·gy /méeteeəróləjee/ *n.* **1** the study of the processes and phenomena of the atmosphere, esp. as a means of forecasting the weather. **2** the atmospheric character of a region. □□ **me·te·or·o·log·i·cal** /-rəlójikəl/ *adj.* **me·te·or·o·log·i·cal·ly** *adv.* **me·te·or·ol·o·gist** *n.*

me·te·or show·er *n.* a group of meteors appearing to come from one point in the sky.

me·ter[1] /méetər/ *n.* a metric unit and the base SI unit of linear measure, equal to about 39.4 inches. ¶ Abbr.: **m.** □□ **me·ter·age** /méetərij/ *n.*

me·ter[2] /méetər/ *n.* **1** any form of poetic rhythm, determined by the number and length of feet in a line. **b** a metrical group or measure. **2** the basic pulse and rhythm of a piece of music.

me·ter[3] /méetər/ *n. & v.*
● *n.* **1** ▶ an instrument that measures, esp. one for recording a quantity of gas, electricity, postage, etc. **2** = PARKING METER. ● *v.tr.* measure by means of a meter.

-meter /mitər, méetər/ *comb. form* **1** forming nouns denoting measuring instruments (*barometer*). **2** *Prosody* forming nouns denoting lines of poetry with a specified number of measures (*pentameter*).

meth·a·done /méthədōn/ *n.* a potent narcotic analgesic drug used to relieve severe pain, as a cough suppressant or as a morphine or heroin substitute.

METER: HOUSEPLANT LIGHT AND MOISTURE METER

light meter

moisture gauge

meth·am·phet·a·mine /méthamfétəmin, -meen/ *n.* an amphetamine derivative with quicker and longer action, used as a stimulant.

meth·ane /méthayn/ *n. Chem.* a colorless, odorless, flammable, gaseous hydrocarbon, the main constituent of natural gas. ¶ Chem. formula: CH_4.

meth·a·nol /méthənawl, -nol/ *n. Chem.* a colorless, volatile, flammable liquid, used as a solvent. ¶ Chem. formula: CH_3OH. Also called **methyl alcohol**.

me·thinks /mithíngks/ *v.intr.* (*past* **methought** /mitháwt/) *archaic* it seems to me.

meth·od /méthəd/ *n.* **1** a special form of procedure, esp. in any branch of mental activity. **2** orderliness. **3** the orderly arrangement of ideas. **4** a scheme of classification. **5** *Theatr.* a technique of acting based on the actor's thorough emotional identification with the character. □ **method in** (or **to**) **one's madness** sense in what appears to be foolish or strange behavior.

me·thod·i·cal /mithódikəl/ *adj.* (also **me·thod·ic**) characterized by method or order. □□ **me·thod·i·cal·ly** *adv.*

Meth·od·ist /méthədist/ *n.* **1** a member of any of several Protestant religious bodies (now united) originating in the 18th-c. evangelistic movement. **2** (**methodist**) a person who follows or advocates a particular method or system of procedure. □□ **Meth·od·ism** *n.*

meth·od·ize /méthədīz/ *v.tr.* **1** reduce to order. **2** arrange in an orderly manner. □□ **meth·od·iz·er** *n.*

meth·od·ol·o·gy /méthədóləjee/ *n.* (*pl.* **-ies**) **1** the science of method. **2** a body of methods used in a particular branch of activity. □□ **meth·od·o·log·i·cal** /-dəlójikəl/ *adj.* **meth·od·o·log·i·cal·ly** *adv.* **meth·od·ol·o·gist** *n.*

me·thought *past* of METHINKS.

meth·yl /méthil/ *n. Chem.* the univalent hydrocarbon radical CH_3, present in many organic compounds. □□ **me·thyl·ic** /methílik/ *adj.*

meth·yl al·co·hol *n.* = METHANOL.

meth·yl·ate /méthilayt/ *v.tr.* **1** mix or impregnate with methanol. **2** introduce a methyl group into (a molecule or compound). □□ **meth·yl·a·tion** /-láyshən/ *n.*

meth·yl ben·zene *n.* = TOLUENE.

me·tic·u·lous /mətíkyələs/ *adj.* **1** giving great or excessive attention to details. **2** very careful and precise. □□ **me·tic·u·lous·ly** *adv.* **me·tic·u·lous·ness** *n.*

mé·ti·er /métyáy/ *n.* (also **me·tier**) **1** one's trade, profession, or department of activity. **2** one's forte.

Me·ton·ic cy·cle /mitónik/ *n.* a period of 19 years (235 lunar months) covering all the changes of the

Moon's position relative to the Sun and the Earth.

me·ton·y·my /mitónimee/ *n.* the substitution of the name of an attribute or adjunct for that of the thing meant (e.g., *White House* for *president*, *the turf* for *horse racing*). □□ **met·o·nym** /métənim/ *n.* **met·o·nym·ic** /métənímik/ *adj.* **met·o·nym·i·cal** /métənímikəl/ *adj.*

met·ric /métrik/ *adj.* of or based on the meter.

met·ri·cal /métrikəl/ *adj.* **1** of, relating to, or composed in meter. **2** of or involving measurement. □□ **met·ri·cal·ly** *adv.*

met·ri·cate /métrikayt/ *v.intr. & tr.* change or adapt to a metric system of measurement. □□ **met·ri·ca·tion** /-káyshən/ *n.*

met·ric sys·tem *n.* the decimal measuring system with the meter, liter, and gram (or kilogram) as units of length, volume, and mass (see also SI).

met·ric ton *n.* (also **met·ric tonne**) 1,000 kilograms (2,205 lb.).

met·ro /métró/ *n.* (*pl.* **-os**) a subway system in a city, esp. Paris.

met·ro·nome /métrənōm/ *n. Mus.* an instrument marking time at a selected rate by giving a regular tick. □□ **met·ro·nom·ic** /-nómik/ *adj.*

met·ro·nym·ic /métrənímik/ *adj & n* ● *adj.* (of a name) derived from the name of a mother or female ancestor. ● *n.* a metronymic name.

me·trop·o·lis /mitrópəlis/ *n.* **1** the chief city of a country. **2** a metropolitan bishop's see. **3** a center of activity.

met·ro·pol·i·tan /métrəpólit'n/ *adj. & n.* ● *adj.* **1** of or relating to a metropolis, esp. as distinct from its environs (*metropolitan New York*). **2** belonging to, forming or forming part of, a mother country as distinct from its colonies, etc. (*metropolitan France*). **3** of an ecclesiastical metropolis. ● *n.* **1** (in full **metropolitan bishop**) a bishop having authority over the bishops of a province. **2** an inhabitant of a metropolis. □□ **me·tro·pol·i·tan·ate** *n.* (in sense 1 of *n.*). **met·ro·pol·i·tan·ism** *n.*

me·tror·rha·gi·a /méetrə-ráyjeeə, -jə/ *n.* abnormal bleeding from the womb.

met·tle /mét'l/ *n.* **1** the quality of a person's disposition or temperament (*a chance to show your mettle*). **2** natural ardor. **3** spirit, courage. □ **on one's mettle** incited to do one's best. □□ **met·tled** *adj.* (also in *comb.*). **met·tle·some** *adj.*

meu·nière /mónyáir/ *adj.* (esp. of fish) cooked or served in lightly browned butter with lemon juice and parsley (*sole meunière*).

MeV *abbr.* megaelectronvolt(s).

mew[1] /myoo/ *v. & n.* ● *v.intr.* (of a cat, gull, etc.) utter its characteristic cry. ● *n.* this sound, esp. of a cat.

mew[2] /myoo/ *n. & v.* ● *n.* a cage for hawks, esp. while molting. ● *v.tr.* **1** put (a hawk) in a cage. **2** (often foll. by *up*) shut up; confine.

mewl /myool/ *v.intr.* **1** cry feebly; whimper. **2** mew like a cat.

mews /myooz/ *n.* esp. *Brit.* a set of stables around an open yard, now often converted into dwellings.

Mex·i·can /méksikən/ *n. & adj.* ● *n.* **1 a** a native or national of Mexico, a country in southern N. America. **b** a person of Mexican descent. **2** a language spoken in Mexico, esp. Nahuatl. ● *adj.* **1** of or relating to Mexico or its people. **2** of Mexican descent.

me·ze /máyzay/ *n.* (also **mez·ze**) (in Turkish, Greek, and Middle Eastern cookery) a selection of hot and cold hors d'oeuvres.

me·zu·zah /mezóozə, -zōozáa/ *n.* (also **me·zu·za**; *pl.* **-s**; also **me·zu·zot** or **me·zu·zoth** /-zōozót/) a parchment inscribed with religious texts and attached in a case to the doorpost of a Jewish house as a sign of faith.

mez·za·lu·na /metzəlóonə/ *n.* a utensil for chopping herbs, vegetables, etc., with a semicircular blade and a handle at each end.

M

mez·za·nine /mézənéen/ n. **1** a low story between two others (usu. between the first and second floors). **2 a** the lowest balcony in a theater. **b** the first several rows of this balcony.

mez·za vo·ce /métsə vóchay/ adv. Mus. with less than the full strength of the voice or sound.

mez·zo /métsō/ adv. & n. Mus. ● adv. half, moderately. ● n. (in full **mezzo-soprano**) (pl. **-os**) **1 a** female singing voice between soprano and contralto. **b** a singer with this voice. **2** a part written for mezzo-soprano.

mez·zo-re·lie·vo /métsō-rileévō/ n. (also **mez·zo-ri·lie·vo** /-rilyáyvō/) (pl. **-os**) a raised surface in the form of half-relief, in which the figures project half their true proportions.

mez·zo·tint /métsōtint/ n. & v. ● n. **1** a method of printing or engraving in which the surface of a plate is roughened by scraping so that it produces tones and halftones. **2** a print produced by this process. ● v.tr. engrave in mezzotint. □□ **mez·zo·tint·er** n.

MF abbr. medium frequency.

mfg. abbr. manufacturing.

m.f.n. abbr. most favored nation.

mfr. abbr. **1** manufacture. **2** manufacturer.

Mg symb. Chem. the element magnesium.

mg abbr. milligram(s).

Mgr. abbr. **1** Manager. **2** Monseigneur. **3** Monsignor.

mho /mō/ n. (pl. **-os**) Electr. the reciprocal of an ohm, a former unit of conductance.

MHz abbr. megahertz.

MI abbr. **1** Michigan (in official postal use). **2** myocardial infarction.

mi /mee/ n. (also **me**) Mus. **1** the third tone of the diatonic scale. **2** the note E in the fixed solmization system.

mi. abbr. mile(s).

M.I.5 abbr. (in the UK) the department of Military Intelligence concerned with government security. ¶ Not in official use.

M.I.6 abbr. (in the UK) the department of Military Intelligence concerned with espionage. ¶ Not in official use.

MIA abbr. missing in action.

Mi·am·i /mīámee/ n. & adj. ● n. **1 a** a N. American people native to the midwestern United States. **b** a member of this people. **2** the language of this people. ● adj. of or relating to this people or their language.

mi·as·ma /mī-ázmə, mee-/ n. (pl. **miasmata** /-mətə/ or **miasmas**) archaic an infectious or noxious vapor. □□ **mi·as·mal**, **mi·as·mat·ic** /-mátik/ adj. **mi·as·mic** adj. **mi·as·mic·al·ly** adv.

Mic. abbr. Micah (Old Testament).

mi·ca /mīkə/ n. ▶ any of a group of silicate minerals with a layered structure, esp. muscovite. ▷ AGGREGATE. □□ **mi·ca·ceous** /-káyshəs/ adj.

MICA:
MUSCOVITE

mice pl. of MOUSE.

mi·celle /misél, mī-/ n. Chem. an aggregate of molecules in a colloidal solution, as occurs, e.g., when soap dissolves in water.

Mich. abbr. Michigan.

Mich·ael·mas /míkəlməs/ n. the feast of St. Michael, September 29.

Mich·ael·mas dai·sy n. ▶ an autumn-flowering aster.

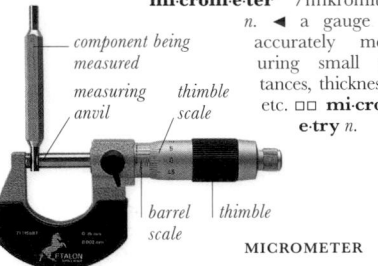

MICHAELMAS DAISY
(Aster novi-belgii)

Mick·ey Finn /míkee fin/ (often **Mickey**) n. sl. **1** a drink, adulterated with a narcotic or laxative. **2** the adulterant itself.

mi·cro /míkrō/ n. (pl. **-os**) colloq. **1** = MICROCOMPUTER. **2** = MICROPROCESSOR.

micro- /míkrō/ comb. form **1** small (microchip). **2** denoting a factor of one millionth (10^{-6}) (microgram).

mi·cro·a·nal·y·sis /míkrōənálisis/ n. quantitative analysis using a sample of a few milligrams.

mi·crobe /míkrōb/ n. a microorganism, esp. a pathogenic bacterium. □□ **mi·cro·bi·al** /-krōbeeəl/ adj. **mi·cro·bic** /-krōbik/ adj.

mi·cro·bi·ol·o·gy /míkrōbīóləjee/ n. the scientific study of microorganisms. □□ **mi·cro·bi·o·log·i·cal** /-bīəlójikəl/ adj. **mi·cro·bi·o·log·i·cal·ly** /-bīəlójiklee/ adv. **mi·cro·bi·ol·o·gist** n.

mi·cro·brew·ery /míkrōbróoəree/ n. a limited-production brewery, often selling only locally.

mi·cro·burst /míkrōbərst/ n. a particularly violent wind shear, esp. during a thunderstorm.

mi·cro·ceph·a·ly /míkrōséfəlee/ n. an abnormal smallness of the head in relation to the rest of the body. □□ **mi·cro·ceph·al·ic** /-sifálik/ adj. & n. **mi·cro·ceph·al·ous** /-séfələs/ adj.

mi·cro·chip /míkrōchip/ n. a small piece of semiconductor used to carry electronic circuits.

mi·cro·cir·cuit /míkrōsərkit/ n. an integrated circuit on a microchip. □□ **mi·cro·cir·cuit·ry** n.

mi·cro·cli·mate /míkrōklīmit/ n. ▼ the climate of a small local area, e.g., inside a greenhouse. □□ **mi·cro·cli·mat·ic** /-mátik/ adj. **mi·cro·cli·mat·i·cal·ly** /-mátiklee/ adv.

mi·cro·code /míkrōkōd/ n. **1** = MICROINSTRUCTION. **2** = MICROPROGRAM.

mi·cro·com·pu·ter /míkrōkəmpyóōtər/ n. a small computer that contains a microprocessor.

mi·cro·cop·y /míkrōkópee/ n. & v. ● n. (pl. **-ies**) a copy of printed matter that has been reduced by microphotography. ● v.tr. (**-ies**, **-ied**) make a microcopy of.

mi·cro·cosm /míkrəkozəm/ n. **1** (often foll. by of) a miniature representation. **2** mankind viewed as the epitome of the universe. **3** any community or complex unity viewed in this way. □□ **mi·cro·cos·mic** /-kózmik/ adj.

mi·cro·dot /míkrōdot/ n. a microphotograph reduced to the size of a period.

mi·cro·ec·o·nom·ics /míkrō-éekənómiks/ n. the branch of economics dealing with individual commodities, producers, etc. □□ **mi·cro·ec·o·nom·ic** adj.

mi·cro·e·lec·tron·ics /míkrō-ilektróniks/ n. the design, manufacture, and use of microchips and microcircuits. □□ **mi·cro·e·lec·tron·ic** adj.

mi·cro·fiche /míkrōfeesh/ n. (pl. same or **microfiches**) a flat rectangular piece of film bearing microphotographs of the pages of a printed text or document.

mi·cro·film /míkrōfilm/ n. & v. ● n. a length of film bearing microphotographs of documents, etc. ● v.tr. photograph (a document, etc.) on microfilm.

mi·cro·form /míkrōfawrm/ n. microphotographic reproduction of a manuscript, etc.

mi·cro·gram /míkrōgram/ n. one-millionth of a gram.

mi·cro·graph /míkrōgraf/ n. a photograph taken by means of a microscope.

mi·cro·in·struc·tion /míkrō-instrúkshən/ n. a machine-code instruction that effects a basic operation in a computer system.

mi·cro·man·age /míkrōmánij/ v.tr. control every part, no matter how detailed, of an enterprise or large organization.

mi·cro·mesh /míkrōmesh/ n. (often attrib.) material, esp. nylon, consisting of a very fine mesh.

mi·crom·e·ter[1] /mīkrómitər/ n. ◄ a gauge for accurately measuring small distances, thicknesses, etc. □□ **mi·crom·e·try** n.

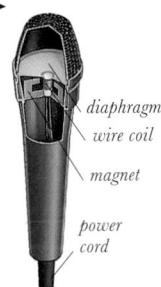

component being measured

measuring anvil

thimble scale

barrel scale

thimble

MICROMETER

mi·crom·e·ter[2] /míkrōméetər/ n. = MICRON.

mi·cro·min·i·a·tur·i·za·tion /míkrōmíneeəchərīzáyshən/ n. the manufacture of very small electronic devices by using integrated circuits.

mi·cron /míkron/ n. one-millionth of a meter. Also called **micrometer**.

Mi·cro·ne·sian /míkrənéezhən/ adj. & n. ● adj. of or relating to Micronesia, an island group in the W. Pacific. ● n. a native of Micronesia.

mi·cro·or·gan·ism /míkrō-áwrgənizəm/ n. any of various microscopic organisms, including algae, bacteria, fungi, protozoa, and viruses.

mi·cro·phone /míkrəfōn/ n. ▶ an instrument for converting sound waves into electrical energy variations that may be reconverted into sound after transmission by wire or radio or after recording. □□ **mi·cro·phon·ic** /-fónik/ adj.

mi·cro·pho·to·graph /míkrō-fṓtəgraf/ n. a photograph, of a document, etc., reduced to a very small size.

mi·cro·phyte /míkrōfīt/ n. a microscopic plant.

mi·cro·proc·es·sor /míkrō-prósesər/ n. an integrated circuit that contains all the functions of a central processing unit of a computer. ▷ COMPUTER

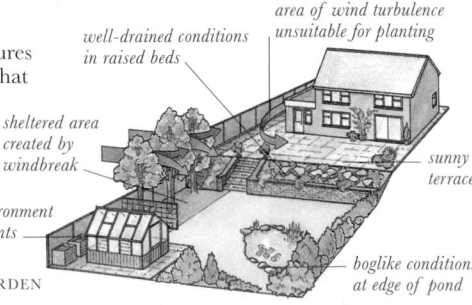

diaphragm
wire coil
magnet
power cord

MICROPHONE:
CUTAWAY VIEW OF
A MOVING COIL
MICROPHONE

mi·cro·pro·gram /míkrōprógram/ n. a microinstruction program that controls the functions of a central processing unit of a computer.

mi·cro·pyle /míkrōpīl/ n. Bot. a small opening in the surface of an ovule, through which pollen passes.

MICROCLIMATE

Naturally occurring topograpical features in an area can create a microclimate that differs greatly from the climate of the surrounding region. Features in a small area, such as a garden, can also be manipulated to create specific conditions. For example, beds can be sloped to face the sun.

MICROCLIMATES IN A GARDEN

area of wind turbulence unsuitable for planting

well-drained conditions in raised beds

sheltered area created by windbreak

protected environment for tender plants

sunny terrace

boglike conditions at edge of pond

M

mi·cro·scope /míkrəskōp/ *n.* ▶ an instrument magnifying small objects by means of a lens or lenses so as to reveal details invisible to the naked eye.

mi·cro·scop·ic /míkrəskópik/ *adj.* **1** so small as to be visible only with a microscope. **2** extremely small. **3** regarded in terms of small units. **4** of the microscope. □□ **mi·cro·scop·i·cal** *adj.* (in sense 4). **mi·cro·scop·i·cal·ly** *adv.*

mi·cros·co·py /mīkróskəpee/ *n.* the use of the microscope. □□ **mi·cros·co·pist** *n.*

mi·cro·sec·ond /míkrōsek-ənd/ *n.* one-millionth of a second.

mi·cro·some /míkrəsōm/ *n. Biol.* a small particle of organelle fragments obtained by centrifugation of homogenized cells.

mi·cro·spore /míkrəspawr/ *n.* the smaller of the two kinds of spore produced by some ferns.

mi·cro·struc·ture /míkrōstrúkchər/ *n.* (in a metal or other material) the arrangement of crystals, etc., that can be made visible and examined with a microscope.

mi·cro·sur·ger·y /míkrōsúrjəree/ *n.* intricate surgery performed using microscopes. □□ **mi·cro·sur·gi·cal** /-súrjikəl/ *adj.*

mi·cro·switch /míkrōswich/ *n.* a switch that can be operated rapidly by a small movement.

mi·cro·tome /míkrətōm/ *n.* an instrument for cutting extremely thin sections of material for examination under a microscope.

mi·cro·tone /míkrətōn/ *n. Mus.* an interval smaller than a semitone.

mi·cro·wave /míkrəwayv/ *n. & v.* ● *n.* **1** an electromagnetic wave with a wavelength in the range 0.001–0.3m ▷ ELECTROMAGNETIC RADIATION **2** (in full **microwave oven**) ▼ an oven that uses microwaves to cook or heat food. ● *v.tr.* cook in a microwave oven.

mic·tu·ri·tion /míkchəríshən/ *n. formal* or *Med.* urination.

MICROWAVE OVEN

In a microwave oven, high-frequency electromagnetic waves generated by a magnetron tube are bounced around the oven's metal-walled interior. The waves penetrate food, causing water, fat, and sugar molecules to vibrate, thus producing heat. Heat is transferred to the center of the food by conduction.

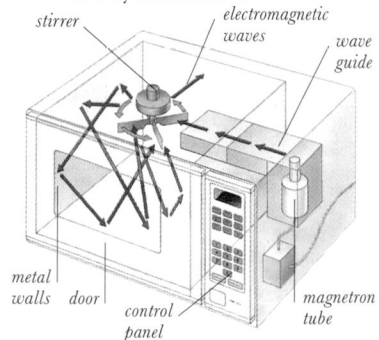

COMPONENTS OF A MICROWAVE OVEN

eyepiece
focusing knob
objective lens
specimen
glass slide
condenser lens
mirror to illuminate slide
light
base

MICROSCOPE: OPTICAL MICROSCOPE

---

mid¹ /mid/ *attrib.adj.* **1** (usu. in *comb.*) that is the middle of (*in midair*). **2** that is in the middle; medium, half.

mid² /mid/ *prep. poet.* = AMID.

mid·air /midáir/ *n.* a place or point in the air far removed from the ground or other solid surface.

Mi·das touch /mídəs túch/ *n.* the ability to make a lot of money out of anything one undertakes.

mid·brain /mídbrayn/ *n.* the part of the brain developing from the middle of the primitive or embryonic brain. ▷ BRAINSTEM

mid·day /míd-dáy/ *n.* the middle of the day; noon.

mid·den /míd'n/ *n.* **1** a dunghill. **2** a refuse heap.

mid·dle /míd'l/ *adj., n., & v.* ● *attrib.adj.* **1** at an equal distance from the extremities of a thing. **2** (of a member of a group) so placed as to have the same number of members on each side. **3** intermediate in rank, quality, etc. **4** average (*of middle height*). **5** (of a language) of the period between the old and modern forms. ● *n.* **1** (often foll. by *of*) the middle point or position or part. **2** a person's waist. ● *v.tr.* **1** place in the middle. **2** *Soccer* return (the ball) from the wing to the midfield. **3** *Naut.* fold in the middle. □ **in the middle of** (often foll. by *verbal noun*) in the process of; during.

mid·dle age *n.* the period between youth and old age, about 45 to 60. □□ **mid·dle-aged** *adj.*

Mid·dle Ag·es *n.pl.* (prec. by *the*) the period of European history from c.1000 to 1453.

Middle A·mer·i·ca *n.* **1** Mexico and Central America. **2** the middle class in the US, esp. as a conservative political force. **3** the US Middle West.

mid·dle·brow /míd'lbrow/ *adj. & n. colloq.* ● *adj.* claiming to be or regarded as only moderately intellectual. ● *n.* a middlebrow person.

mid·dle class *n.* the class of society between the upper and the lower, including professional and business workers and their families. □□ **mid·dle-class** *adj.*

mid·dle ear *n.* the cavity of the central part of the ear behind the eardrum. ▷ EAR

Mid·dle East *n.* (prec. by *the*) the area covered by countries from Egypt to Iran inclusive. □□ **Mid·dle East·ern** *adj.*

Mid·dle Eng·lish *n.* the English language from c.1150 to 1500.

mid·dle ground *n.* a neutral position between two opposing extremes.

mid·dle-in·come *attrib.adj.* of the wages earned by the middle class.

mid·dle·man /míd'lman/ *n.* (*pl.* **-men**) **1** any of the traders who handle a commodity between its producer and its consumer. **2** an intermediary.

mid·dle man·age·ment *n.* in business and industry, the mid-level positions in administration.

mid·dle name *n.* **1** a person's name placed after the first name and before the surname. **2** a person's most characteristic quality (*sobriety is my middle name*).

mid·dle-of-the-road *adj.* (of a person, course of action, etc.) moderate; avoiding extremes.

mid·dle school *n.* a school for children from about 10 to 13 years old (grades 5–8).

mid·dle·weight /míd'lwayt/ *n.* **1** a weight in certain sports intermediate between welterweight and light heavyweight. **2** a sportsman of this weight.

Mid·dle West *n.* = MIDWEST.

mid·dling /mídling/ *adj., n., & adv.* ● *adj.* **1 a** moderately good (esp. *fair to middling*). **b** second-rate. **2** (of goods) of the second of three grades. ● *adv.* **1** fairly or moderately (*middling good*). **2** *colloq.* fairly well (esp. in health). □□ **mid·dling·ly** *adv.*

Mid·east /mídéest/ *n.* MIDDLE EAST.

mid·field /mídféeld/ *n.* in certain sports, esp. football and soccer, the area of the field midway between the two goals. ▷ FOOTBALL. □□ **mid·field·er** *n.*

midge /mij/ *n.* **1** *colloq.* **a** a gnatlike insect. **b** a small person. **2 a** any dipterous nonbiting insect of the family Chironomidae. **b** any similar insect of the family Ceratopogonidae with piercing mouthparts.

mid·get /míjit/ *n.* **1** an extremely small person or thing. **2** (*attrib.*) very small.

mid·gut /mídgút/ *n.* the middle part of the alimentary canal, including the small intestine.

MIDI /mídee/ *n.* a system for using combinations of electronic equipment, esp. audio and computer equipment.

mi·di /mídee/ *n.* (*pl.* **midis**) a garment of medium length, usu. reaching to mid-calf.

mid·land /mídlənd/ *n. & adj.* ● *n.* **1** the middle part of a country. **2** the dialect of American English spoken in the east-central US, from southern New Jersey and northern Delaware west across the Appalachians and the Ohio and Mississippi river valleys. **3** (**the Midlands**) the inland counties of central England. ● *adj.* (also **Mid·land**) of or in the midland or Midlands. □□ **mid·land·er** *n.*

mid·life /mídlīf/ *n.* middle age.

mid·life cri·sis *n.* an emotional crisis of self-confidence that can occur in early middle age.

mid·line /mídlīn/ *n.* a median line, or plane of bilateral symmetry.

mid·night /mídnīt/ *n.* **1** the middle of the night; 12 o'clock at night. **2** intense darkness.

mid·night blue *n.* a very dark blue.

mid·night sun *n.* the Sun visible at midnight during the summer in polar regions.

mid·rib /mídrib/ *n.* ▶ the central rib of a leaf.

mid·riff /mídrif/ *n.* **1 a** the region of the front of the body between the thorax and abdomen. **b** the diaphragm. **2** a garment or part of a garment covering this area.

midrib

MIDRIB OF A BEECH LEAF

M

mid·ship /mídship/ *n.* the middle part of a ship or boat.

mid·ship·man /mídshipmən/ *n.* (*pl.* **-men**) **1** a cadet in the US Naval Academy. **2** *Brit.* a naval officer of rank between naval cadet and sublieutenant.

mid·ships /mídships/ *adv.* = AMIDSHIPS.

midst /midst/ *prep. & n.* ● *prep. poet.* amidst. ● *n.* middle (now only in phrases as below). □ **in the midst of** among; in the middle of. **in our** (or **your** or **their**) **midst** among us (or you or them).

mid·sum·mer /mídsúmər/ *n.* the period of or near the summer solstice.

mid·term /mídtərm/ *n.* the middle of a period of office, an academic term, or a pregnancy.

mid·town /mídtown/ *n.* the central part of a city between the downtown and uptown areas.

mid·way /mídwáy/ *n. & adv.* ● *n.* area for concessions and amusements at a carnival, fair, etc. ● *adv.* in or toward the middle of the distance between two points.

Mid·west /mídwést/ *n.* region of northern US states from Ohio west to the Rocky Mountains. □□ **Mid·west** *adj.* **Mid·western** *adj.*

mid·wife /mídwīf/ *n.* (*pl.* **-wives** /-wīvz/) **1** a person (usu. a woman) trained to assist women in childbirth. **2** a person who helps in producing or bringing something forth. □□ **mid·wife·ry** /-wífəree/ *n.*

mid·win·ter /mídwintər/ *n.* the period of or near the winter solstice.

mien /meen/ *n. literary* a person's look or bearing.

miff /mif/ *v. & n. colloq.* ● *v.tr.* (usu. in *passive*) put out of humor; offend. ● *n.* **1** a petty quarrel. **2** a huff.

might[1] /mīt/ *past* of MAY, used esp.: **1** in reported speech, expressing possibility (*said he might come*) or permission (*asked if I might leave*) (cf. MAY 1, 2). **2** expressing a possibility based on a condition not fulfilled (*if you'd looked you might have found it*). **3** expressing complaint that an obligation or expectation is not or has not been fulfilled (*they might have asked*). **4** expressing a request (*you might call in at the butcher's*). **5** *colloq.* **a** = MAY 1 (*it might be true*). **b** (in tentative questions) = MAY 2 (*might I have the pleasure of this dance?*). **c** = MAY 4 (*who might you be?*). □ **might as well** expressing that it is probably at least as desirable to do a thing as not to do it (*won't win but might as well try*).

might[2] /mīt/ *n.* **1** great bodily or mental strength. **2** power to enforce one's will (usu. in contrast with *right*). □ **with all one's might** to the utmost of one's power. **with might and main** see MAIN.

mightn't /mít'nt/ *contr.* might not.

might·y /mítee/ *adj. & adv.* ● *adj.* (**mightier**, **mightiest**) **1** powerful or strong, in body, mind, or influence. **2** massive, bulky. **3** *colloq.* great, considerable. ● *adv. colloq.* very (*a mighty difficult task*). □□ **might·i·ly** *adv.* **might·i·ness** *n.*

mi·gnon·ette /mínyənét/ *n.* **1 a** ▶ any of various plants of the genus *Reseda*, with racemes of fragrant greenish-white flowers. **b** the color of these. **2** a light, fine, narrow pillow lace.

mi·graine /mígrayn/ *n.* a recurrent throbbing headache that usually affects one side of the head, often accompanied by nausea and disturbance of vision.

mi·grant /mígrənt/ *adj. & n.* ● *adj.* that migrates. ● *n.* **1** a person who moves regularly, as for work. **2** an animal that changes habitats, as with the seasons.

mi·grate /mígrayt/ *v.intr.* **1** (of people) move from one place of abode to another, esp. in a different country. **2** (of a bird or fish) change its area of habitation with the seasons. **3** move under natural forces. □□ **mi·gra·tion** /-gráyshən/ *n.* **mi·gra·tion·al** /-gráyshənəl/ *adj.* **mi·gra·tor** *n.* **mi·gra·to·ry** /-grətáwree/ *adj.*

MIGNONETTE: WILD MIGNONETTE (*Reseda lutea*)

mih·rab /méeraab/ *n.* ▶ a niche or slab in a mosque, used to show the direction of Mecca.

mi·ka·do /mikaádō/ *n. (pl.* **-os**) *hist.* the emperor of Japan.

mike /mīk/ *n. colloq.* a microphone.

mil /mil/ *n.* one-thousandth of an inch, as a unit of measure for the diameter of wire, etc.

mi·la·dy /miláydee/ *n. (pl.* **-ies**) **1** an English noblewoman or great lady. **2** a form used in speaking of or to such a person.

mil·age var. of MILEAGE.

Mi·lan·ese /mílənéez/ *adj. & n.* ● *adj.* of or relating to Milan in N. Italy. ● *n. (pl.* same) a native of Milan.

milch /milch/ *adj.* (of a domestic mammal) giving or kept for milk.

milch cow *n.* = MILK COW.

mild /mīld/ *adj.* **1** (esp. of a person) gentle and conciliatory. **2** (of a rule, illness, etc.) moderate; not severe. **3** (of food, tobacco etc.) not sharp or strong in taste, etc. **4** tame, feeble, lacking energy or vivacity. □□ **mild·ish** *adj.* **mild·ness** *n.*

MIHRAB IN THE GREAT MOSQUE AT CORDOBA, SPAIN

---

mil·dew /míldoō, -dyoō/ *n. & v.* ● *n.* **1** a destructive growth of minute fungi on plants. **2** a similar growth on paper, leather, etc., exposed to damp. ● *v.tr. & intr.* taint or be tainted with mildew.

mild·ly /míldlee/ *adv.* in a mild fashion. □ **to put it mildly** as an understatement (implying the reality is more extreme).

mile /mīl/ *n.* **1** (also **stat·ute mile**) a unit of linear measure equal to 1,760 yards (approx. 1.609 kilometers). **2** (in *pl.*) *colloq.* a great distance or amount (*miles better*). **3** a race extending over a mile.

mile·age /mílij/ *n.* (also **mil·age**) **1 a** a number of miles traveled, used, etc. **b** the number of miles traveled by a vehicle per unit of fuel. **2** traveling expenses (per mile). **3** *colloq.* benefit, profit, advantage.

mile·post /mílpōst/ *n.* **1** a post or sign giving distance in miles, as along a highway. **2** a post one mile from the finish line of a race, etc.

mil·er /mílər/ *n. colloq.* a person or horse qualified or trained specially to run a mile.

mile·stone /mílstōn/ *n.* **1** a stone set up beside a road to mark a distance in miles. **2** a significant event or stage in a life, project, etc.

mil·foil /mílfoyl/ *n.* the common yarrow, *Achillea millefolium*, with small white flowers and finely divided leaves.

mi·lieu /milyő, méelyö/ *n. (pl.* **milieus** or **milieux** /-lyőz/) one's environment or social surroundings.

mil·i·tant /mílit'nt/ *adj. & n.* ● *adj.* **1** aggressively active, esp. in support of a (usu. political) cause. **2** engaged in warfare. ● *n.* **1** a militant person, esp. a political activist. **2** a person engaged in warfare. □□ **mil·i·tan·cy** *n.* **mil·i·tant·ly** *adv.*

mil·i·ta·rism /mílitərizəm/ *n.* **1** the spirit or tendencies of a professional soldier. **2** undue prevalence of the military spirit or ideals. □□ **mil·i·ta·rist** /-rist/ *n.* **mil·i·ta·ris·tic** /-rístik/ *adj.*

mil·i·ta·rist /mílitərist/ *n.* **1** a person dominated by militaristic ideas. **2** a student of military science.

mil·i·ta·rize /mílitərīz/ *v.tr.* **1** equip with military resources. **2** make military or warlike. **3** imbue with militarism. □□ **mil·i·ta·ri·za·tion** *n.*

mil·i·tar·y /mílitéree/ *adj. & n.* ● *adj.* of, relating to, or characteristic of soldiers or armed forces. ● *n.* (as *sing.* or *pl.*; prec. by *the*) members of the armed forces. □□ **mil·i·tar·i·ly** /-táirəlee/ *adv.*

mil·i·tar·y po·lice *n.* a corps responsible for police and disciplinary duties in the army.

mil·i·tate /mílitayt/ *v.intr.* (usu. foll. by *against*) (of facts or evidence) have force or effect.

mi·li·tia /milishə/ *n.* a military force, esp. one raised from the civil population and supplementing a regular army in an emergency. □□ **mi·li·tia·man** /-mən/ *n. (pl.* **-men**)

mi·li·tia·man /milishəmən/ *n. (pl.* **-men**) a member of a militia.

milk /milk/ *n. & v.* ● *n.* **1** an opaque white fluid secreted by female mammals for the nourishment of their young. **2** the milk of cows, goats, or sheep as food. **3** the milklike juice, e.g., in the coconut. **4** a milklike preparation of herbs, drugs, etc. ● *v.tr.* **1** draw milk from (a cow, etc.). **2 a** exploit (a person) esp. financially. **b** get all possible advantage from (a situation). **3** extract sap, venom, etc., from. **4** *sl.* tap (telegraph or telephone wires, etc.). □ **cry over spilled milk** lament an irremediable loss or error. **in milk** secreting milk. □□ **milk·er** *n.*

milk and hon·ey *n.* abundant means of prosperity.

---

milk choc·o·late *n.* chocolate made with milk.

milk cow *n.* a source of easy profit, esp. a person.

milk·maid /mílkmayd/ *n.* a girl or woman who milks cows or works in a dairy.

milk·man /mílkman/ *n. (pl.* **-men**) a person who sells or delivers milk.

milk of mag·ne·sia *n.* a white suspension of magnesium hydroxide usu. in water as an antacid or laxative.

milk run *n.* a routine expedition or service journey.

milk shake *n.* a drink of milk, flavoring, and usu. ice cream, mixed by shaking or blending.

milk·sop /mílksop/ *n.* a spiritless or meek person, esp. a man.

milk tooth *n.* a temporary tooth in young mammals.

milk·weed /mílkweed/ *n.* any of various wild plants with milky juice.

milk·wort /mílkwərt/ *n.* any plant of the genus *Polygala*, formerly supposed to increase women's milk.

milk·y /mílkee/ *adj.* (**milkier**, **milkiest**) **1** of, like, or mixed with milk. **2** ◄ (of a gem or liquid) cloudy; not clear. **3** effeminate; weakly amiable. □□ **milk·i·ness** *n.*

Milk·y Way *n.* ▶ a faint band of light emitted by countless stars encircling the heavens; the Galaxy. ▷ GALAXY

mill[1] /mil/ *n. & v.* ● *n.* **1 a** a building fitted with a mechanical apparatus for grinding grain. **b** ▼ such an apparatus. **2** an apparatus for grinding any solid substance to powder or pulp. **3 a** a building fitted with machinery for manufacturing processes, etc. (*cotton mill*). **b** such machinery. **4 a** a boxing match. **b** a fistfight. **5** a place that processes things or people in a mechanical way (*diploma mill*). ● *v.* **1** *tr.* grind (grain), produce (flour), or hull (seeds) in a mill. **2** *tr.* produce regular ribbed markings on the edge of (a coin). **3** *tr.* cut or shape (metal) with a rotating tool. **4** *intr.* (often foll. by *about, around*) (of people or animals) move in an aimless manner, esp. in a confused mass. **5** *tr.* thicken (cloth, etc.) by fulling. **6** *tr.* beat (chocolate, etc.) to froth. **7** *tr. sl.* beat, strike, fight. □ **go** (or **put**) **through the mill** undergo (or cause to undergo) intensive work or training, etc. □□ **mill·a·ble** *adj.*

MILKY QUARTZ

MILL: MODEL OF A GREEK MILL, *c.* 85 BC

grain to be milled — *milled flour* — *millstone* — *water supply* — *horizontal water wheel drives millstone*

mill[2] /mil/ *n.* one-thousandth of a US dollar.

mill·board /mílbawrd/ *n.* stout pasteboard for bookbinding, etc.

mille-feuille /meelfő_yə/ *n.* a rich confection of puff pastry split and filled with custard, cream, etc.

mil·le·nar·i·an /mílináreeən/ *adj. & n.* ● *adj.* **1** of or related to the millennium. **2** believing in the millennium. ● *n.* a person who believes in the millennium.

mil·le·nar·y /mílənéeree/ *n. & adj.* ● *n. (pl.* **-ies**) **1** a period of 1,000 years. **2** the festival of the 1,000th anniversary of a person or thing. **3** a person who believes in the millennium. ● *adj.* of or relating to millenary.

Milky Way

The Milky Way is made up of the combined light of many of the 200 billion stars and nebulae in our Galaxy. The Galaxy consists of a central bulge surrounded by a thin disk and a spheroidal halo. The central bulge contains mainly older red and yellow stars. Matter in the disk is aggregated into several spiral arms which contain young hot blue stars and nebulae. The oldest stars are situated in the sparsely populated halo. Our solar system is in one of the spiral arms (the Orion arm), about halfway out from the center, and from this position our view of the galactic center is completely obscured by dust clouds.

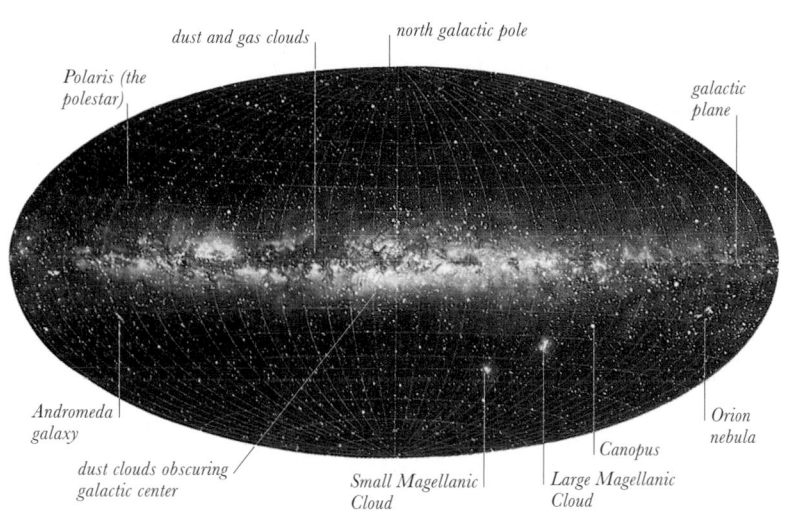

MAP OF THE GALAXY VIEWED FROM THE EARTH

- dust and gas clouds
- north galactic pole
- Polaris (the polestar)
- galactic plane
- Andromeda galaxy
- dust clouds obscuring galactic center
- Small Magellanic Cloud
- Canopus
- Large Magellanic Cloud
- Orion nebula

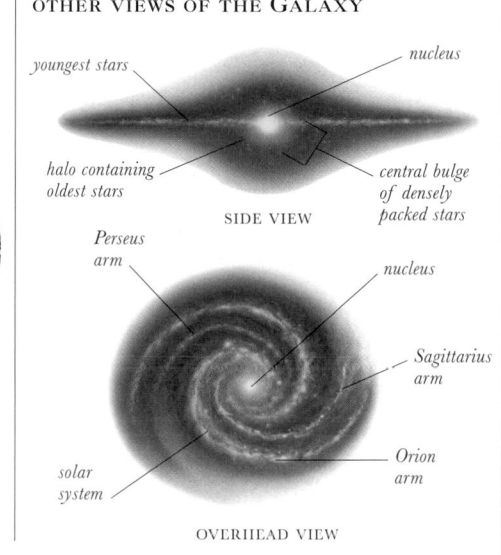

OTHER VIEWS OF THE GALAXY

SIDE VIEW
- youngest stars
- nucleus
- halo containing oldest stars
- central bulge of densely packed stars

OVERHEAD VIEW
- Perseus arm
- nucleus
- Sagittarius arm
- Orion arm
- solar system

mil·len·ni·um /miléneeəm/ n. (pl. **millennia** /-neeə/ or **millenniums**) 1 a period of 1,000 years. 2 Christ's prophesied reign in person on Earth, as mentioned in Revelation 20. 3 a period of happiness, and prosperity. □□ **mil·len·ni·al** adj. **mil·len·ni·al·ist** n. & adj.

mil·le·pede var. of MILLIPEDE.

mill·er /mílər/ n. 1 the proprietor or tenant of a mill. 2 a person who works or owns a mill.

mil·les·i·mal /milésiməl/ adj. & n. ● adj. 1 thousandth. 2 of or belonging to a thousandth. 3 of or dealing with thousandths. ● n. a thousandth part.

mil·let /mílit/ n. 1 any of various cereal plants, esp. Panicum miliaceum, bearing a large crop of small nutritious seeds. 2 the seed of this. ▷ GRAIN

milli- /mílee, -i, -ə/ comb. form a thousand, esp. denoting a factor of one thousandth. ¶ Abbr.: **m.**

mil·li·am·pere /mílleeámpir/ n. one-thousandth of an ampere, a measure for small electrical currents.

mil·li·ard /mílyərd, -yaard/ n. Brit. one thousand million. ¶ Now largely superseded by billion.

mil·li·bar /mílibaar/ n. one-thousandth of a bar, the cgs unit of atmospheric pressure equivalent to 100 pascals.

mil·li·gram /mílligram/ n. one-thousandth of a gram.

mil·li·li·ter /mílileetər/ n. one-thousandth of a liter (0.002 pint).

mil·li·me·ter /mílimeetər/ n. one-thousandth of a meter (0.039 in.).

mil·li·ner /mílinər/ n. a person who makes or sells women's hats. □□ **mil·li·ner·y** /-eree/ n.

mil·lion /mílyən/ n. & adj. ● n. (pl. same or (in sense 2) **millions**) (in sing. prec. by a or one) 1 a thousand thousand. 2 (in pl.) colloq. a very large number (millions of years). 3 (prec. by the) the bulk of the population. 4 (prec. by a) a million dollars. ● adj. that amount to a million. □□ **mil·lionth** adj. & n.

mil·lion·aire /mílyənáir/ n. (fem. **millionairess** /-ris/) 1 a person whose assets are worth at least one million dollars, pounds, etc. 2 a person of great wealth.

mil·li·pede /mílapeed/ n. (also **mil·le·pede**) ► any arthropod of the class Diplopoda, having a long segmented body with two pairs of legs on each segment.

mil·li·sec·ond /mílisekənd/ n. one-thousandth of a second.

mill·pond /mílpond/ n. a pool of water retained by a dam for the operation of a mill. □ **like a millpond** (of a stretch of water) very calm.

mill·race /mílrays/ n. a current of water that drives a mill wheel.

MILLIPEDE

mill·stone /mílstōn/ n. 1 each of two circular stones used for grinding grain. ▷ MILL. 2 a heavy burden or responsibility.

mill·wright /mílrīt/ n. a person who designs, builds, or operates a mill or milling machinery.

milt /milt/ n. 1 a sperm-filled reproductive gland of a male fish. 2 the sperm-filled secretion of this gland.

mime /mīm/ n. & v. ● n. 1 the theatrical technique of suggesting action, character, etc., by gesture and expression without using words. 2 a theatrical performance using this technique. 3 (also **mime art·ist**) a practitioner of mime. ● v. tr. (also absol.) convey (an idea or emotion) by gesture without words. □□ **mim·er** n.

mim·e·o·graph /mímeeəgraf/ n. & v. ● n. 1 (often attrib.) a duplicating machine that produces copies from a stencil. 2 a copy produced in this way. ● v.tr. reproduce (text or diagrams) by this process.

mi·me·sis /miméésis, mī-/ n. = MIMICRY 3.

mi·met·ic /mimétik/ adj. 1 relating to or habitually practicing imitation or mimicry. 2 Biol. of or exhibiting mimicry. □□ **mi·met·i·cal·ly** adv.

mim·ic /mímik/ v. & n. ● v.tr. (**mimicked, mimicking**) 1 imitate (a person, gesture, etc.) esp. to entertain or ridicule. 2 copy minutely or servilely. 3 (of a thing) resemble closely. ● n. a person skilled in imitation. ● adj. having an aptitude for mimicry; imitating; esp. for amusement. □□ **mim·ick·er** n.

mim·ic·ry /mímikree/ n. (pl. **-ies**) 1 the act or art of mimicking. 2 a thing that mimics another. 3 Biol. ▼ a close resemblance of an organism to another organism or an inanimate object, for example the hornet moth and giant hornet.

MIMICRY

Many examples exist in nature of harmless animals and plants that have developed the appearance or behavior of a dangerous species as a defense against predators. For example, the black and yellow banding on a hornet moth gives it a close resemblance to a giant hornet – a large wasp with a painful sting.

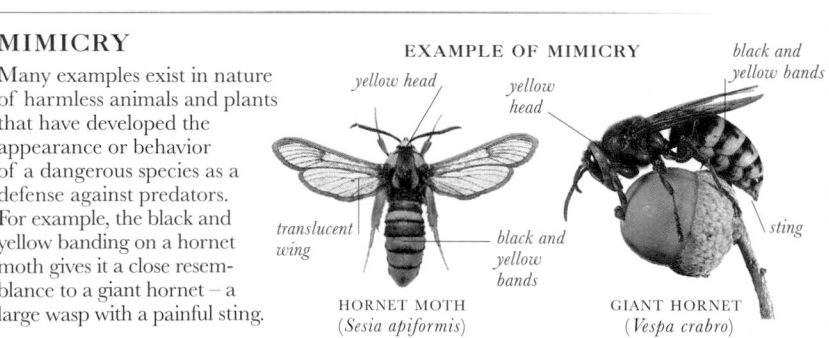

EXAMPLE OF MIMICRY
- yellow head
- yellow head
- black and yellow bands
- translucent wing
- black and yellow bands
- sting

HORNET MOTH (Sesia apiformis)

GIANT HORNET (Vespa crabro)

M

M

mi·mo·sa /mimósə, -zə/ *n.* **1** any leguminous shrub of the genus *Mimosa*, esp. *M. pudica*, having globular usu. yellow flowers. **2** any of various acacia plants with showy yellow flowers. **3** a cocktail of champagne and orange juice.

mim·u·lus /mímyələs/ *n.* any flowering plant of the genus *Mimulus*, including musk and the monkey flower.

Min /min/ *n.* any of the Chinese languages or dialects spoken in the Fukien province in SE China.

min. *abbr.* **1** minute(s). **2** minimum. **3** minim (fluid measure).

mi·na var. of MYNAH.

min·a·ret /mínərét/ *n.* a slender turret connected to a mosque and having a balcony from which the muezzin calls at hours of prayer. ▷ MOSQUE. □□ **min·a·ret·ed** *adj.*

min·a·to·ry /mínətáwree/ *adj.* threatening, menacing.

mince /mins/ *v.* **1** *tr.* cut up or grind into very small pieces. **2** *tr.* (usu. with *neg.*) restrain (one's words, etc.) within the bounds of politeness. **3** *intr.* (usu. as **mincing** *adj.*) speak or walk with an affected delicacy. □□ **minc·er** *n.* **minc·ing·ly** *adv.* (in sense 3 of *v.*).

mince·meat /mínsmeet/ *n.* a mixture of currants, raisins, sugar, apples, candied peel, spices, often suet, and sometimes meat. □ **make mincemeat of** utterly defeat (a person, argument, etc.).

mind /mīnd/ *n. & v.* ● *n.* **1 a** the seat of consciousness, thought, volition, and feeling. **b** attention, concentration (*my mind keeps wandering*). **2** the intellect; intellectual powers. **3** memory (*I can't call it to mind*). **4** one's opinion (*we're of the same mind*). **5** a way of thinking or feeling (*shocking to the Victorian mind*). **6** the focus of one's thoughts or desires (*put one's mind to it*). **7** the state of normal mental functioning (*lose one's mind*). **8** a person as embodying mental faculties (*a great mind*). ● *v.tr.* **1** (usu. with *neg.* or *interrog.*) object to (*I don't mind your being late*). **2 a** take care to (*mind you come on time*). **b** take care; be careful. **3** have charge of temporarily (*mind the house while I'm away*). **4** concern oneself with (*I try to mind my own business*). **5** give heed to (*mind the step*). **6** be obedient to (*mind what your mother says*). □ **be of two minds** be undecided. **be of a mind** (often foll. by *to* + infin.) be prepared or disposed. **come into a person's mind** be remembered. **come to mind** (of a thought, idea, etc.) suggest itself. **cross one's mind** happen to occur to one. **don't mind me** *iron.* do as you please. **do you mind!** *iron.* an expression of annoyance. **give a person a piece of one's mind** scold or reproach a person. **have a good** (or **half a**) **mind to** (often as a threat, usu. unfulfilled) feel tempted to. **have (it) in mind** intend. **have a mind of one's own** be capable of independent opinion. **have on one's mind** be troubled by the thought of. **in one's mind's eye** in one's imagination. **mind one's Ps & Qs** be careful in one's behavior. **mind the store** have charge of affairs temporarily. **mind you** an expression used to qualify a previous statement (*I found it quite quickly–mind you, it wasn't easy*). **never mind 1** an expression used to comfort or console. **2** (also **never you mind**) an expression used to evade a question. **3** disregard (*never mind the cost*). **open** (or **close**) **one's mind to** be receptive (or unreceptive) to (changes, new ideas, etc.). **out of one's mind** crazy. **put** (or **set**) **a person's mind at rest** reassure a person. **put a person** (or **thing**) **out of one's mind** deliberately forget. **read a person's mind** discern a person's thoughts. **to my mind** in my opinion.

mind-bend·ing *adj. colloq.* (esp. of a psychedelic drug) influencing or altering one's state of mind.

mind-blow·ing *adj. sl.* **1** confusing, shattering. **2** (esp. of drugs, etc.) inducing hallucinations.

mind-bog·gling *adj. colloq.* overwhelming, startling.

mind·ed /míndid/ *adj.* **1** (in *comb.*) **a** inclined to

think in some specified way (*fair-minded*). **b** having a specified kind of mind (*high-minded*). **c** interested in or enthusiastic about a specified thing (*car-minded*). **2** (usu. foll. by *to* + infin.) disposed or inclined (to an action).

mind·er /míndər/ *n.* a person whose job it is to attend to a person or thing.

mind-ex·pand·ing *adj.* causing heightened perceptions, as from psychedelic drugs.

mind·ful /míndfōōl/ *adj.* (often foll. by *of*) taking heed or care; being conscious. □□ **mind·ful·ly** *adv.*

mind·less /míndlis/ *adj.* **1** lacking intelligence; stupid. **2** not requiring thought or skill (*totally mindless work*). **3** (usu. foll. by *of*) heedless of (advice, etc.). □□ **mind·less·ly** *adv.* **mind·less·ness** *n.*

mind-read *v.tr.* (*past* and *past part.* **-read**) discern the thoughts of (another person). □□ **mind read·er** *n.*

mind·set /míndset/ *n.* **1** a mental attitude that can influence one's interpretation of events or situations. **2** an inclination or a fixed way of thinking.

mine[1] /mīn/ *poss.pron.* **1** the one or ones belonging to or associated with me (*it is mine, mine are over there*). **2** (*attrib.* before a vowel or following a noun) *archaic* = MY (*mine eyes have seen; child mine*). □ **of mine** of or belonging to me (*a friend of mine*).

mine[2] /mīn/ *n. & v.* ● *n.* **1** ▼ an excavation in the earth for extracting metal, coal, etc. **2** an abundant source (of information, etc.). **3** a receptacle filled with explosive and placed in the ground or in the water. **4** a subterranean gallery in which explosive is placed to blow up fortifications. ● *v.tr.* **1** obtain (coal, etc.) from a mine. **2** (also *absol.*, often foll. by *for*) dig in (the earth, etc.) for ore, etc. **3 a** dig or burrow in (usu. the earth). **b** delve into (an abundant source) for information, etc. **c** make (a passage, etc.) underground. **4** lay explosive mines under or in. **5** = UNDERMINE. □□ **min·ing** *n.*

mine·field /mínfeeld/ *n.* **1** an area planted with explosive mines. **2** a subject or situation presenting unseen hazards.

mine·lay·er /mínlayər/ *n.* a ship or aircraft for laying mines.

min·er /mínər/ *n.* **1** a person who works in a mine. **2** any burrowing insect or grub.

min·er·al /mínərəl/ *n. & adj.* ● *n.* **1** ▶ any of the species into which inorganic substances are classified. **2** a substance obtained by mining. ● *adj.* **1** of or containing a mineral or minerals. **2** obtained by mining.

min·er·a·lize /mínərəlīz/ *v.* **1** *v.tr. & intr.* change wholly or partly into a mineral. **2** *v.tr.* impregnate (water, etc.) with a mineral substance.

min·er·al·o·gy /mínəroləjee/ *n.* the scientific study of minerals. □□ **min·er·al·og·i·cal** /-rəlójikəl/ *adj.* **min·er·al·o·gist** *n.*

min·er·al oil *n. Pharm.* a colorless, odorless, oily liquid obtained from petroleum and used as a laxative, in manufacturing cosmetics, etc.

min·er·al wa·ter *n.* **1** water found in nature with some dissolved salts present. **2** an artificial imitation of this, esp. soda water.

min·e·stro·ne /ministrónee/ *n.* a soup containing vegetables, pasta, and beans.

mine·sweep·er /mínsweepər/ *n.* a ship for clearing away floating and submarine mines.

mine·work·er /mínwərkər/ *n.* a person who works in a mine.

Ming /ming/ *n.* **1** the dynasty ruling China 1368–1644. **2** ▶ Chinese porcelain made during the rule of this dynasty.

min·gle /mínggəl/ *v.* **1** *tr. & intr.* mix, blend. **2** *intr.* (often foll. by *with*) (of a person) move about, associate.

min·gy /mínjee/ *adj.* (**mingier**, **mingiest**) *colloq.* mean, stingy. □□ **min·gi·ly** *adv.*

min·i /mínee/ *n.* (*pl.* **minis**) *colloq.* a miniskirt, minidress, etc.

mini- /mínee/ *comb. form* miniature; minor of its kind.

min·i·a·ture /míneeəchər, mínichər/ *adj., n., & v.* ● *adj.* **1** much smaller than normal. **2** represented on a small scale. ● *n.* **1** any object reduced in size. **2** a small-scale minutely finished portrait. **3** this branch of painting. **4** a picture or decorated letters in an illuminated manuscript. ● *v.tr.* represent on a smaller scale. □ **in miniature**

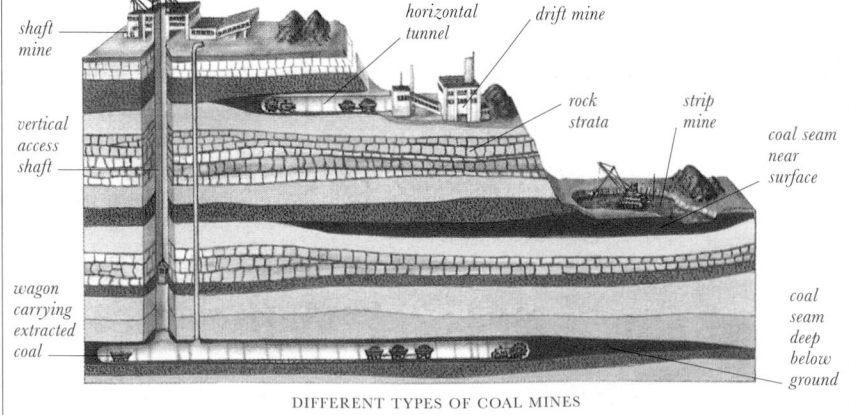

MING: 15TH-CENTURY MING FIGURINE

MINE

Mines allow the extraction of raw materials from the rocks and sediments of the Earth's interior. Ores, such as those containing gold, silver, iron, and tin, are recovered by blasting and boring rock in underground mines. Coal mines vary with the location of the seam being worked: the deepest are reached by a vertical shaft, whereas seams nearer the surface are mined via a horizontal tunnel, known as a drift mine. In a strip mine, coal just below the surface is reached by stripping away the covering layers of ground.

shaft mine   *horizontal tunnel*   *drift mine*   *vertical access shaft*   *rock strata*   *strip mine*   *coal seam near surface*   *wagon carrying extracted coal*   *coal seam deep below ground*

DIFFERENT TYPES OF COAL MINES

MINERAL

Minerals are solid, inorganic substances. A few minerals, such as gold, silver, carbon, copper, lead, mercury, and iron, are classified as elements, but the majority have a definite crystalline form and are classified according to their chemical composition.

Sulfides, for example, are compounds in which sulfur has combined with metallic and semimetallic elements; minerals called halides contain an element of the halogen group. Aggregates of minerals, fused together, form the rocks that make up the Earth's crust.

EXAMPLES OF MAIN MINERAL GROUPS

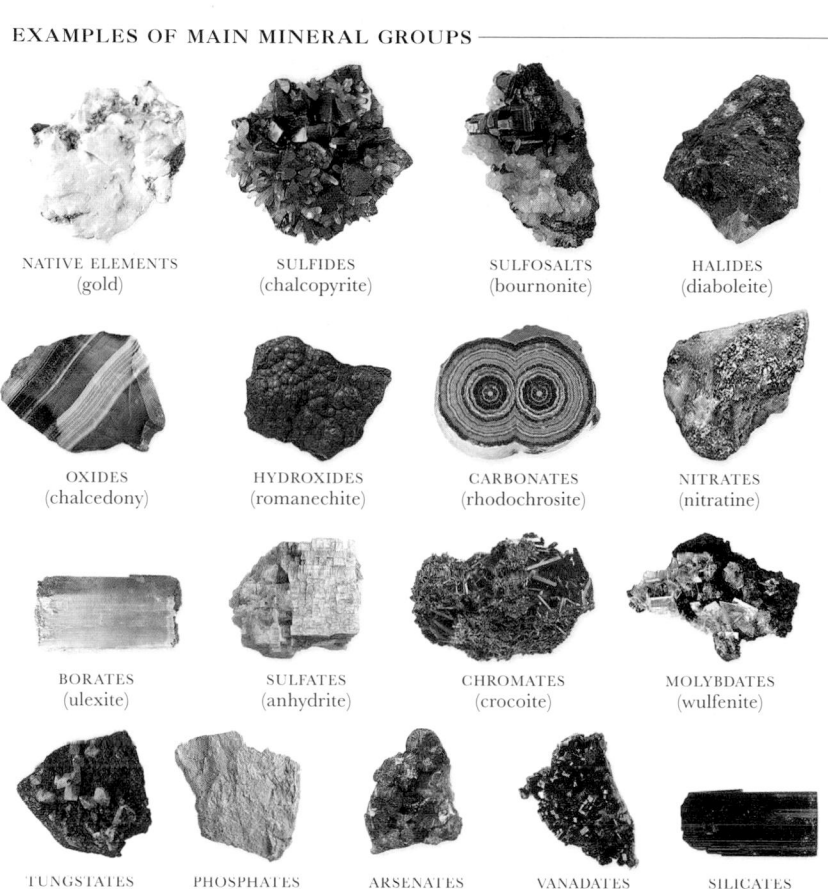

NATIVE ELEMENTS (gold)

SULFIDES (chalcopyrite)

SULFOSALTS (bournonite)

HALIDES (diaboleite)

OXIDES (chalcedony)

HYDROXIDES (romanechite)

CARBONATES (rhodochrosite)

NITRATES (nitratine)

BORATES (ulexite)

SULFATES (anhydrite)

CHROMATES (crocoite)

MOLYBDATES (wulfenite)

TUNGSTATES (scheelite)

PHOSPHATES (turquoise)

ARSENATES (clinoclase)

VANADATES (vanadinite)

SILICATES (tourmaline)

---

on a small scale. □□ **min·i·a·tur·ist** *n.* (in senses 2 and 3 of *n.*). **min·i·a·tur·iz·a·tion** *n.* **min·i·a·tur·ize** /mineeəchərīz, mínichə-/ *v.tr.*

min·i·bus /míneebus/ *n.* a small bus or van.

min·i·cab /míneekab/ *n. Brit.* a small car used as a taxi.

min·i·cam /míneekam/ *n.* a portable lightweight video camera.

min·i·com·put·er /míneekəmpyōtər/ *n.* a computer of medium power, more than a microcomputer but less than a mainframe.

min·i·disk /míneedisk/ *n.* ▼ a disk similar to a small CD but able to record sound or data as well as play it back.

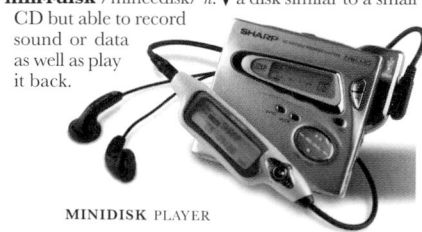

MINIDISK PLAYER

min·im /mínim/ *n.* **1** one-sixtieth of a fluid dram, about a drop. **2** an object or portion of the smallest size or importance. **3** a single downstroke of the pen.

min·i·mal /mínimal/ *adj.* **1** very minute or slight. **2** being or related to a minimum. **3** the least possible in size, duration, etc. **4** art, etc., characterized by the use of simple or primary forms or structures, etc. □□ **min·i·mal·ism** *n.* (in sense 4). **min·i·mal·ist** *n. & adj.* (in sense 4). **min·i·mal·ly** *adv.* (in senses 1–3).

min·i·max /míneemaks/ *n.* **1** *Math.* the lowest of a set of maximum values. **2** (usu. *attrib.*) **a** a strategy that minimizes the greatest risk to a participant in a game, etc. **b** the theory that in a game with two players, a player's smallest possible maximum loss is equal to the same player's greatest possible minimum gain.

min·i·mize /mínimīz/ *v.* **1** *tr.* reduce to, or estimate at, the smallest possible amount or degree. **2** *tr.* estimate or represent at less than the true value or importance. **3** *intr.* attain a minimum value. □□ **min·i·mi·za·tion** *n.*

min·i·mum /mínimǝm/ *n. & adj.* (*pl.* **minima** /-mǝ/) ● *n.* the least possible or attainable amount (*reduced to a minimum*). ● *adj.* that is a minimum.

min·i·mum wage *n.* the lowest wage permitted by law.

min·ion /mínyǝn/ *n. derog.* a servile agent of a powerful person.

min·i·se·ries /míneeseereez/ *n.* a short series of television programs on a common theme.

min·i·skirt /míneeskǝrt/ *n.* a very short skirt.

min·is·ter /mínistǝr/ *n. & v.* ● *n.* **1** a member of the clergy; a person authorized to officiate in religious worship. **2** a head of a government department (in some countries). **3** a diplomatic agent, usu. ranking below an ambassador. **4** (usu. foll. by *of*) a person employed in the execution of (a purpose, will, etc.) (*a minister of justice*). **5** (in full **minister general**) the superior of some religious orders. ● *v. intr.* (usu. foll. by *to*) render aid or service (to a person, cause, etc.). □□ **min·is·tra·ble** *adj.*

min·is·te·ri·al /mínisteêreeǝl/ *adj.* **1** of a minister of religion or a minister's office. **2** instrumental or subsidiary in achieving a purpose. **3** of a government minister. □□ **min·is·te·ri·al·ly** *adv.*

min·is·tra·tion /mínistráyshǝn/ *n.* **1** (usu. in *pl.*) aid or service. **2** ministering, esp. in religious matters. **3** (usu. foll. by *of*) the supplying (of help, justice, etc.). □□ **min·is·trant** /mínistrǝnt/ *adj. & n.* **min·is·tra·tive** /mínistráytiv/ *adj.*

min·is·try /mínistree/ *n.* (*pl.* **-ies**) **1 a** (prec. by *the*) the vocation or profession of a religious minister. **b** the office of a religious minister, etc. **c** the period of tenure of this. **2** (prec. by *the*) the body of ministers of a government or of a religion. **3 a** a government department headed by a minister. **b** the building which it occupies. **4** a period of government under one Prime Minister. **5** ministering, ministration.

min·i·van /míneevan/ *n.* a vehicle, smaller than a full-sized van, for passengers, cargo, etc. ▷ CAR

mink /mingk/ *n.* **1** ▼ either of two small semiaquatic stoatlike animals of the genus *Mustela*. **2** the thick brown fur of these. **3** a coat made of this.

MINK: NORTH AMERICAN MINK (*Mustela vison*)

min·ke /míngkǝ/ *n.* a baleen whale, *Balaenoptera acutorostrata*, with a pointed snout. ▷ CETACEAN

Minn. *abbr.* Minnesota.

min·ne·sing·er /mínisingǝr/ *n.* a German lyric poet and singer of the 12th–14th c.

min·now /mínō/ *n.* any of various small freshwater fish of the carp family.

Mi·no·an /minôǝn/ *adj. & n. Archaeol.* ● *adj.* of or relating to the Bronze Age civilization centered on Crete (*c.*3000–1100 BC). ● *n.* **1** an inhabitant of Minoan Crete or the Minoan world. **2** the language or scripts associated with the Minoans.

mi·nor /mínǝr/ *adj., n., & v.* ● *adj.* **1** lesser or comparatively small in size or importance. **2** *Mus.* **a** (of a scale) having intervals of a semitone between the second and third, fifth and sixth, and seventh and eighth degrees. **b** (of an interval) less by a semitone than a major interval. **c** (of a key) based on a minor scale. **3** pertaining to a student's secondary field of study. ● *n.* **1** a person under the legal age limit or majority. **2** *Mus.* a minor key, etc. **3** a student's subsidiary subject or course. ● *v.intr.* (foll. by *in*) study in as a subsidiary to a main subject. □ **in a minor key** (of novels, events, people's lives, etc.) understated, uneventful.

mi·nor·i·ty /mīnáwritee, -nór-/ *n.* (*pl.* **-ies**) **1** (often foll. by *of*) a smaller number or part, esp. within a political party or structure. **2** the number of votes cast for this (*a minority of two*). **3** the state of being supported by less than half of the body of opinion (*in the minority*). **4** a relatively small group of people differing from others in race, religion, language, etc. **5** (*attrib.*) relating to or done by the minority (*minority interests*). **6 a** the state of being under full legal age. **b** the period of this.

M

mi·nor·i·ty lead·er *n.* the leader of the minority political party in a legislature.

mi·nor league *n.* (in baseball, etc.) a league of professional clubs other than a major league.

Min·o·taur /mínɔtawr/ *n.* (in Greek mythology) a man with a bull's head, kept in a Cretan labyrinth and fed with human flesh.

min·ox·i·dil /mɔnóksɔdil/ *n.* a vasodilator drug taken orally to treat hypertension or applied topically to stimulate hair growth in certain types of baldness.

min·ster /mínstɔr/ *n.* **1** a large or important church. **2** the church of a monastery.

min·strel /mínstrɔl/ *n.* **1** a medieval singer or musician. **2** *hist.* a person who entertained patrons with singing, buffoonery, etc. **3** (usu. in *pl.*) a member of a band of public entertainers with blackened faces, etc., performing songs ostensibly of African-American origin. □□ **min·strel·sy** /mínstrɔlsee/ *n.* (*pl.* **-ies**).

mint[1] /mint/ *n.* **1** ◄ any aromatic plant of the genus *Mentha*. ▷ HERB. **2** a peppermint sweet or lozenge. □□ **mint·y** *adj.* (**mintier**, **mintiest**).

mint[2] /mint/ *n. & v.* ● *n.* **1** a place where money is coined, usu. under government authority. **2** a vast sum of money (*making a mint*). **3** a source of invention, etc. (*a mint of ideas*). ● *v.tr.* **1** make (coin) by stamping metal. **2** invent, coin (a word, etc.). □ **in mint condition** as new.

mint ju·lep *n.* a sweet iced alcoholic drink of bourbon flavored with mint.

MINT:
BOWLES' MINT
(*Mentha* × *villosa*)

min·u·end /mínyōō-énd/ *n.* *Math.* a quantity or number from which another is to be subtracted.

min·u·et /mínyōō-ét/ *n. & v.* ● *n.* **1** a slow stately dance for two in triple time. **2** *Mus.* the music for this, or music in the same rhythm and style. ● *v.intr.* (**minueted**, **minueting**) dance a minuet.

mi·nus /mínɔs/ *prep., adj., & n.* ● *prep.* **1** with the subtraction of (*7 minus 4 equals 3*). ¶ Symb.: −. **2** (of temperature) below zero (*minus 2°*). **3** *colloq.* lacking (*returned minus their dog*). ● *adj.* **1** *Math.* negative. **2** *Electronics* having a negative charge. ● *n.* **1** = MINUS SIGN. **2** *Math.* a negative quantity. **3** a disadvantage.

mi·nus·cule /mínɔskyōōl/ *n. & adj.* ● *n.* a lowercase letter. ● *adj.* **1** lowercase. **2** *colloq.* extremely small or unimportant.

mi·nus sign *n.* the symbol (−) indicating subtraction or a negative value.

min·ute[1] /mínit/ *n. & v.* ● *n.* **1** the sixtieth part of an hour. **2** a distance covered in one minute (*twenty minutes from the station*). **3 a** a moment (*expecting her any minute*). **b** (prec. by *this*) *colloq.* the present time (*what are you doing at this minute?*). **c** (foll. by clause) as soon as (*call me the minute you get back*). **4** the sixtieth part of an angular degree. **5** (in *pl.*) a brief summary of the proceedings at a meeting. **6** an official memorandum authorizing or recommending a course of action. ● *v.tr.* **1** record in the minutes. **2** send the minutes to (a person). □ **just** (or **wait**) **a minute 1** a request to wait for a short time. **2** as a prelude to a query or objection.

min·ute[2] /mīnōōt, -yōōt/ *adj.* (**minutest**) **1** very small. **2** trifling, petty. **3** (of an inquiry, inquirer, etc.) accurate, detailed, precise. □□ **mi·nute·ly** *adv.* **mi·nute·ness** *n.*

min·ute hand *n.* the hand on a watch or clock that indicates minutes. ▷ WATCH

min·ute·man /mínitman/ *n.* (*pl.* **-men**) **1** *US Hist.* (also **Minuteman**) an American militiaman of the Revolutionary War period (ready to march at a minute's notice). **2** a type of three-stage intercontinental ballistic missile.

min·ute steak *n.* a thin slice of steak to be cooked quickly.

mi·nu·ti·a /minōōsheeɔ, -shɔ, -nyōō-/ *n.* (*pl.* **-iae** /-shee-ee/) (usu. in *pl.*) a precise, trivial, or minor detail.

minx /mingks/ *n.* a pert, sly, or playful girl.

Mi·o·cene /míɔseen/ *adj. & n. Geol.* ● *adj.* of or relating to the fourth epoch of the Tertiary period. ● *n.* this epoch or system.

mi·o·sis /mīōsis/ *n.* (also **my·o·sis**) (*pl.* **-ses** /-seez/) excessive constriction of the pupil of the eye. □□ **mi·ot·ic** /mīótik/ *adj.*

mir·a·belle /mírɔbél/ *n.* **1 a** a European variety of plum tree, *Prunus insititia*, bearing small round yellow fruit. **b** ◄ a fruit from this tree. **2** a liqueur distilled from this fruit.

MIRABELLE
(*Prunus insititia*)

mir·a·cle /mírɔkɔl/ *n.* **1** an extraordinary event attributed to some supernatural agency. **2 a** any remarkable occurrence. **b** a remarkable development in some specified area (*an economic miracle*). **3** (usu. foll. by *of*) a remarkable specimen (*a miracle of ingenuity*).

mir·a·cle play *n.* a medieval play based on the Bible or the lives of the saints.

mi·rac·u·lous /mirákyɔlɔs/ *adj.* **1** of the nature of a miracle. **2** supernatural. **3** remarkable, surprising. □□ **mi·rac·u·lous·ly** *adv.*

mi·rage /miráazh/ *n.* **1** ▼ an optical illusion caused by atmospheric conditions, esp. the appearance of a sheet of water in a desert or on a hot road from the reflection of light. **2** an illusory thing.

mire /mīr/ *n. & v.* ● *n.* **1** a stretch of swampy ground. **2** mud, dirt. ● *v.* **1** *tr. & intr.* plunge or sink in a mire. **2** *tr.* involve in difficulties. □ **in the mire** in difficulties.

mirk var. of MURK.

mirk·y var. of MURKY.

mir·ror /mírɔr/ *n. & v.* ● *n.* **1** ▲ a polished surface, usu. of coated glass, which reflects an image. ▷ OBSERVATORY, PERISCOPE. **2** anything regarded as giving an accurate reflection or description of something else. ● *v.tr.* reflect as in a mirror.

mir·ror·ball /mírɔrbawl/ *n.* a revolving ball covered with small mirrored facets, used to provide lighting effects at discos.

mir·ror im·age *n.* an identical image, but with the structure reversed, as in a mirror.

mirth /mɔrth/ *n.* merriment, laughter. □□ **mirth·ful** *adj.* **mirth·ful·ly** *adv.* **mirth·less** *adj.* **mirth·less·ly** *adv.* **mirth·less·ness** *n.*

MIRROR

Incoming light rays from an object viewed in a mirror are reflected back at exactly the same, but reversed, angle. The brain, assuming that the reflected rays have reached the eye in a straight line, works backward along the light path and perceives an image behind the mirror.

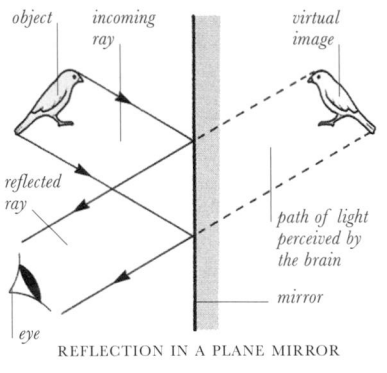

object   incoming ray   virtual image

reflected ray

path of light perceived by the brain

mirror

eye

REFLECTION IN A PLANE MIRROR

MIRV /mɔrv/ *abbr.* multiple independently targeted reentry vehicle (a type of missile).

MIS *abbr. Computing* management information system.

mis·ad·ven·ture /mísɔdvénchɔr/ *n.* **1** *Law* an accident without concomitant crime or negligence (*death by misadventure*). **2** bad luck. **3** a misfortune.

mis·a·lign /mísɔlín/ *v.tr.* give the wrong alignment to. □□ **mis·a·lign·ment** *n.*

mis·al·li·ance /mísɔlíɔns/ *n.* an unsuitable alliance, esp. an unsuitable marriage.

mis·an·thrope /mísɔnthrōp, míz-/ *n.* (also **mis·an·thro·pist** /mísánthrɔpist/) **1** a person who hates mankind. **2** a person who avoids human society. □□ **mis·an·throp·ic** /-thrópik/ *adj.* **mis·an·thro·py** /mísánthrɔpee/ *n.*

mis·ap·ply /mísɔplí/ *v.tr.* (**-ies**, **-ied**) apply (esp. funds) wrongly. □□ **mis·ap·pli·ca·tion** /mísaplikáyshɔn/ *n.*

mis·ap·pre·hend /mísaprihénd/ *v.tr.* misunderstand (words, a person). □□ **mis·ap·pre·hen·sion** /-hénshɔn/ *n.* **mis·ap·pre·hen·sive** *adj.*

mis·ap·pro·pri·ate /mísɔprōpreeayt/ *v.tr.* apply (usu. another's money) to one's own use, or to a wrong use. □□ **mis·ap·pro·pri·a·tion** /-áyshɔn/ *n.*

mis·be·got·ten /mísbigót'n/ *adj.* **1** illegitimate, bastard. **2** contemptible, disreputable.

mis·be·have /mísbiháyv/ *v.intr. & refl.* (of a person or machine) behave badly. □□ **mis·be·hav·ior** *n.*

misc. *abbr.* miscellaneous.

mis·cal·cu·late /mískálkyɔlayt/ *v.tr.* (also *absol.*) calculate (amounts, results, etc.) wrongly. □□ **mis·cal·cu·la·tion** /-láyshɔn/ *n.*

mis·car·riage /mískárij/ *n.* **1** a spontaneous abortion. **2** the failure (of a plan, letter, etc.) to reach completion or its destination.

mis·car·riage of jus·tice *n.* any failure of the judicial system to attain the ends of justice.

mis·car·ry /mískáree/ *v.intr.* (**-ies**, **-ied**) **1** (of a woman) have a miscarriage. **2** (of a letter, etc.) fail to reach its destination. **3** (of a business, plan, etc.) fail, be unsuccessful.

mis·cast /mískást/ *v.tr.* (*past* and *past part.* **-cast**) allot an unsuitable part to (an actor).

mis·ceg·e·na·tion /miséjináyshɔn, mísɔjɔ-/ *n.* the interbreeding of races, esp. of whites and nonwhites.

mis·cel·la·ne·ous /mísɔláyneeɔs/ *adj.* **1** of mixed

MIRAGE

A mirage occurs in hot places, such as a desert, when a layer of warm air above the ground is trapped by cooler air above. Light rays, which normally travel in straight lines, bend as they pass through the different temperatures, but eventually travel upward. The observer perceives the light rays as if they are traveling in a straight line from the object. The mirage is an inverted, virtual image of the object.

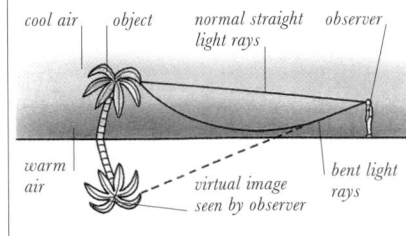

cool air   object   normal straight light rays   observer

warm air   virtual image seen by observer   bent light rays

PERCEPTION OF A MIRAGE

M

composition or character. **2** (foll. by *pl. noun*) of various kinds. **3** (of a person) many-sided. □□ **mis·cel·la·ne·ous·ly** *adv.*

mis·cel·la·ny /míssəlaynee/ *n.* (*pl.* **-ies**) **1** a mixture, a medley. **2** a book containing various literary compositions.

mis·chance /míscháns/ *n.* **1** bad luck. **2** an instance of this.

mis·chief /míschif/ *n.* **1** conduct that is troublesome, but not malicious, esp. in children. **2** pranks, scrapes (*get into mischief*). **3** playful malice; archness; satire (*eyes full of mischief*). **4** harm or injury caused by a person or thing. **5** a person or thing responsible for harm or annoyance (*that loose connection is the mischief*). **6** (prec. by *the*) the annoying part or aspect (*the mischief of it is that*, etc.).

mis·chie·vous /míschivəs/ *adj.* **1** (of a person) disposed to mischief. **2** (of conduct) playfully malicious. **3** (of a thing) harmful. □□ **mis·chie·vous·ly** *adv.* **mis·chie·vous·ness** *n.*

mis·ci·ble /mísibəl/ *adj.* (often foll. by *with*) capable of being mixed. □□ **mis·ci·bil·i·ty** /-bílitee/ *n.*

mis·con·ceive /mískənseev/ *v.* **1** *intr.* (often foll. by *of*) have a wrong idea or conception. **2** *tr.* (as **misconceived** *adj.*) badly planned, organized, etc. **3** *tr.* misunderstand (a word, person, etc.). □□ **mis·con·cep·tion** /-sépshən/ *n.*

mis·con·duct *n. & v.* /mískóndukt/ **1** improper or unprofessional behavior. **2** bad management. ● *v.* /mískəndúkt/ **1** *refl.* misbehave. **2** *tr.* mismanage.

mis·con·strue /mískənstrōō/ *v.tr.* (**-construes,** **-construed,** **-construing**) **1** interpret (a word, action, etc.) wrongly. **2** mistake the meaning of (a person). □□ **mis·con·struc·tion** /-strúkshən/ *n.*

mis·count /mískównt/ *v. & n.* ● *v.tr.* (also *absol.*) count wrongly. ● *n.* a wrong count.

mis·cre·ant /mískreeənt/ *n. & adj.* ● *n.* a wretch, a villain. ● *adj.* depraved, villainous.

mis·cue /mískyōō/ *n. & v.* ● *n.* (in billiards, etc.) the failure to strike the ball properly with the cue. ● *v.intr.* (**-cues, -cued, -cueing** or **-cuing**) make a miscue.

mis·date /misdáyt/ *v.tr.* date (an event, a letter, etc.) wrongly.

mis·deal /misdeel/ *v. & n.* ● *v.tr.* (also *absol.*) (*past* and *past part.* **-dealt** /-délt/) make a mistake in dealing (cards). ● *n.* **1** a mistake in dealing cards. **2** a misdealt hand.

mis·deed /misdeed/ *n.* an evil deed, a wrongdoing; a crime.

mis·de·mean·or /mísdimeenər/ *n.* **1** an offense, a misdeed. **2** *Law* an indictable offense, less heinous than a felony.

mis·di·ag·nose /misdíəgnōs, -nōz/ *v.tr.* diagnose incorrectly. □□ **mis·di·ag·no·sis** /-nósis/ *n.*

mis·di·al /misdíəl/ *v.tr.* (also *absol.*) dial (a telephone number, etc.) incorrectly.

mis·di·rect /mísdirékt, -dī-/ *v.tr.* **1** direct (a person, letter, blow, etc.) wrongly. **2** (of a judge) instruct (the jury) wrongly. □□ **mis·di·rec·tion** /-rékshən/ *n.*

mise-en-scène /meez oN sén/ ● *n.* **1** *Theatr.* the scenery and properties of a play. **2** the setting or surroundings of an event.

mi·ser /mízər/ *n.* **1** a person who hoards wealth and lives miserably. **2** an avaricious person.

mis·er·a·ble /mízərəbəl/ *adj.* **1** wretchedly unhappy or uncomfortable. **2** unworthy, inadequate (*a miserable hovel*); contemptible. **3** causing wretchedness or discomfort (*miserable weather*). stingy; mean. □□ **mis·er·a·ble·ness** *n.* **mis·er·a·bly** *adv.*

mis·er·i·cord /mízərikawrd, -mízér-/ *n.* **1** a shelving projection on the underside of a hinged seat in a choir stall serving (when the seat is turned up) to help support a person standing. **2** an apartment in a monastery in which some relaxations of discipline are permitted. **3** a dagger for dealing the death stroke.

mi·ser·ly /mízərlee/ *adj.* like a miser, niggardly. □□ **mi·ser·li·ness** *n.*

mis·er·y /mízəree/ *n.* (*pl.* **-ies**) **1** a wretched state of mind, or of outward circumstances. **2** a thing causing this. □ **put out of its**, etc., **misery 1** release (a person, animal, etc.) from suffering or suspense. **2** kill (an animal in pain).

mis·feas·ance /mísféezəns/ ● *n.* *Law* a transgression, esp. the wrongful exercise of lawful authority.

mis·fire /mísfír/ *v. & n.* ● *v.intr.* **1** (of a gun, motor engine, etc.) fail to go off or start or function regularly. **2** (of an action, etc.) fail to have the intended effect. ● *n.* a failure of function or intention.

mis·fit /mísfit/ *n.* **1** a person unsuited to a particular kind of environment, occupation, etc. **2** a garment, etc., that does not fit.

mis·for·tune /mísfáwrchən/ *n.* **1** bad luck. **2** an unfortunate condition or event.

mis·give /misgív/ ● *v.tr.* (*past* **-gave** /-gáyv/; *past part.* **-given** /-gívən/) (often foll. by *about, that*) (of a person's mind, heart, etc.) fill (a person) with suspicion or foreboding.

mis·giv·ing /misgíving/ *n.* (usu. in *pl.*) a feeling of mistrust or apprehension.

mis·gov·ern /misgúvərn/ *v.tr.* govern (a state, etc.) badly. □□ **mis·gov·ern·ment** *n.*

mis·guide /misgíd/ *v.tr.* **1** (as **misguided** *adj.*) mistaken in thought or action. **2** mislead, misdirect. □□ **mis·guid·ed·ly** *adv.* **mis·guid·ed·ness** *n.*

mis·han·dle /mis-hánd'l/ *v.tr.* **1** deal with incorrectly or ineffectively. **2** handle (a person or thing) roughly or rudely; ill-treat.

mis·hap /mís-háp/ *n.* an unlucky accident.

mis·hear /mis-heer/ *v.tr.* (*past* and *past part.* **-heard** /-hérd/) hear incorrectly or imperfectly.

mis·hit *v. & n.* ● *v.tr.* /mis-hít/ (**-hitting**; *past* and *past part.* **-hit**) hit (a ball, etc.) faultily. ● *n.* /mís-hít/ a faulty or bad hit.

mish·mash /míshmash, -maash/ *n.* a confused mixture.

Mish·nah /míshnə/ ● *n.* a collection of precepts forming the basis of the Talmud, and embodying Jewish oral law. □□ **Mish·na·ic** /-náyik/ *adj.*

mis·i·den·ti·fy /mísīdéntifī/ *v.tr.* (**-ies, -ied**) identify erroneously. □□ **mis·i·den·ti·fi·ca·tion** /-fikáyshən/ *n.*

mis·in·form /mísinfórm/ *v.tr.* give wrong information to; mislead. □□ **mis·in·for·ma·tion** /-fər máyshən/ *n.*

mis·in·ter·pret /mísintórprit/ *v.tr.* (**-interpreted, -interpreting**) **1** interpret wrongly. **2** draw a wrong inference from. □□ **mis·in·ter·pre·ta·tion** /-táyshən/ *n.*

mis·judge /misjúj/ *v.tr.* (also *absol.*) **1** judge wrongly. **2** have a wrong opinion of. □□ **mis·judg·ment** *n.*

mis·key /mískée/ *v.tr.* (**-keys, -keyed**) key (data) wrongly.

mis·lay /misláy/ *v.tr.* (*past* and *past part.* **-laid** /-láyd/) **1** unintentionally put (a thing) where it cannot readily be found. **2** *euphem.* lose.

mis·lead /misleed/ *v.tr.* (*past* and *past part.* **-led** /-léd/) **1** cause (a person) to go wrong, in conduct, belief, etc. **2** lead astray or in the wrong direction. □□ **mis·lead·ing** /misleeding/ *adj.* **mis·lead·ing·ly** *adv.*

mis·man·age /mismánij/ *v.tr.* manage badly or wrongly. □□ **mis·man·age·ment** *n.*

mis·match *v. & n.* ● *v.tr.* /mismách/ (usu. as **mismatched** *adj.*) match unsuitably or incorrectly, esp. in marriage. ● *n.* /mísmach/ a bad match.

mis·name /misnáym/ *v.tr.* = MISCALL.

mis·no·mer /misnómər/ *n.* **1** a name or term used wrongly. **2** the wrong use of a name or term.

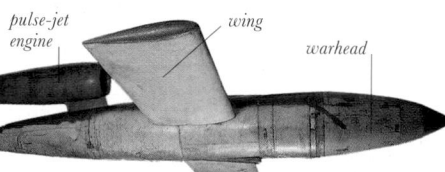

mi·so /meesō/ *n.* ◄ a paste made from fermented soy beans and barley or rice malt, used in Japanese cooking.

hatcho miso

genmai miso

MISO: SOYBEAN PASTE

mi·sog·a·my /misógəmee/ *n.* the hatred of marriage. □□ **mi·sog·a·mist** *n.*

mi·sog·y·ny /misójinee/ *n.* the hatred of women. □□ **mi·sog·y·nist** *n.* **mi·sog·y·nous** *adj.*

mis·pick·el /míspikəl/ *n. Mineral.* arsenical pyrite.

mis·place /mispláys/ *v.tr.* **1** put in the wrong place. **2** bestow (affections, confidence, etc.) on an inappropriate object. **3** time (words, actions, etc.) badly. □□ **mis·place·ment** *n.*

mis·print *n. & v.* ● *n.* /mísprint/ a mistake in printing. ● *v.tr.* /misprínt/ print wrongly.

mis·pro·nounce /míspronówns/ *v.tr.* pronounce (a word, etc.) wrongly. □□ **mis·pro·nun·ci·a·tion** /-nunseeáyshən/ *n.*

mis·quote /mískwót/ *v.tr.* quote wrongly. □□ **mis·quo·ta·tion** /-táyshən/ *n.*

mis·read /mísreed/ *v.tr.* (*past* and *past part.* **-read** /-réd/) read or interpret (text, a situation, etc.) wrongly.

mis·rep·re·sent /mísreprizént/ *v.tr.* represent wrongly; give a false or misleading account or idea of. □□ **mis·rep·re·sen·ta·tion** /-táyshən/ *n.* **mis·rep·re·sen·ta·tive** *adj.*

mis·rule /mísrōol/ *n. & v.* ● *n.* bad government; disorder. ● *v.tr.* govern badly.

Miss. *abbr.* Mississippi.

miss[1] /mis/ *v. & n.* ● *v.* **1** *tr.* (also *absol.*) fail to hit, reach, find, catch, etc. (an object or goal). **2** *tr.* fail to catch (a bus, train, etc.). **3** *tr.* fail to experience, see, or attend (an occurrence or event). **4** *tr.* fail to meet (a person); fail to keep (an appointment). **5** *tr.* fail to seize (an opportunity, etc.) (*I missed my chance*). **6** *tr.* fail to hear or understand (*I missed what you said*). **7** *tr.* **a** regret the loss or absence of (a person or thing) (*did you miss me?*). **b** notice the loss or absence of (an object) (*bound to miss the key if it isn't there*). **8** *tr.* avoid (*go early to miss the traffic*). **9** *tr.* = miss out. **10** *intr.* (of an engine, etc.) fail, misfire. ● *n.* **1** a failure to hit, reach, etc. **2** *colloq.* = miscarriage 1. □ **be missing** see MISSING *adj.* **miss the boat** (or **bus**) lose an opportunity. **miss fire** (of a gun) fail to go off or hit the mark (cf. MISFIRE). **miss out** (usu. foll. by *on*) *colloq.* fail to get or experience (*always misses out on the good times*). **not miss much** be alert. **not miss a trick** never fail to seize an opportunity, advantage, etc. □□ **miss·a·ble** *adj.*

miss[2] /mis/ *n.* **1** a girl or unmarried woman. **2** (**Miss**) **a** a respectful title of an unmarried woman or girl, or of a married woman retaining her maiden name for professional purposes (cf. **Ms.**). **b** the title of a beauty queen (*Miss World*). **3** usu. *derog.* or *joc.* a girl, esp. a schoolgirl. **4** the title used to address a young woman or girl.

mis·sal /mísəl/ *n. RC Ch., Anglican Ch.* **1** a book containing the texts used in the service of the Mass throughout the year. **2** a book of prayers.

mis·shap·en /mís-sháypən/ *adj.* ill-shaped, deformed, distorted. □□ **mis·shap·en·ness** *n.*

mis·sile /mísrōl/ *n.* **1** an object or weapon for throwing at a target or for discharge from a machine. **2** ▼ a weapon directed by remote control or automatically. □□ **mis·sile·ry** /-əlree/ *n.*

pulse-jet engine   *wing*

warhead

MISSILE: WORLD WAR II GERMAN V-1 FLYING BOMB

M

miss·ing /mísing/ *adj.* **1** not in its place; lost. **2** (of a person) not yet traced or confirmed as alive but not known to be dead. **3** not present.

miss·ing link *n.* **1** a thing lacking to complete a series. **2** a hypothetical intermediate type, esp. between humans and apes.

mis·sion /míshən/ *n.* **1 a** a particular task or goal assigned to a person or group. **b** a journey undertaken as part of this. **c** a person's vocation (*mission in life*). **2** a military or scientific operation or expedition for a particular purpose. **3** a body of persons sent, esp. to a foreign country, to conduct negotiations, etc. **4 a** a body sent to propagate a religious faith. **b** a field of missionary activity. **c** a missionary post or organization. **d** a place of worship attached to a mission. **5** a particular course or period of preaching, services, etc., undertaken by a parish or community.

mis·sion·ar·y /míshəneree/ *adj. & n.* ● *adj.* of, concerned with, or characteristic of, religious missions. ● *n.* (*pl.* **-ies**) a person doing missionary work.

mis·sion·er /míshənər/ *n.* **1** a missionary. **2** a person in charge of a religious mission.

mis·sis var. of MISSUS.

mis·sive /mísiv/ *n.* **1** *joc.* a letter. **2** an official letter.

Mis·sour·i /mizóoree, -zóorə/ *n. & adj.* ● *n.* **1** a N. American tribe native to the Missouri River valley. **2** a member of this people. ● *adj.* of or relating to this people.

mis·spell /mís-spél/ *v.tr.* spell wrongly.

mis·spell·ing /mís-spéling/ *n.* a wrong spelling.

mis·spend /mís-spénd/ *v.tr.* (*past* and *past part.* **-spent** /-spént/) (esp. as **misspent** *adj.*) spend amiss or wastefully.

mis·state /mís-stáyt/ *v.tr.* state wrongly or inaccurately. □□ **mis·state·ment** /-mənt/ *n.*

mis·sus /mísəz/ *n.* (also **mis·sis** /-siz/) *sl.* or *joc.* **1** a form of address to a woman. **2** a wife. □ **the missus** my or your wife.

miss·y /mísee/ *n.* (*pl.* **-ies**) an affectionate or derogatory form of address to a young girl.

mist /mist/ *n. & v.* ● *n.* **1 a** water vapor near the ground in minute droplets limiting visibility. **b** condensed vapor settling on a surface and obscuring glass, etc. **2** dimness or blurring of the sight caused by tears, etc. **3** a cloud of particles resembling mist. ● *v.tr. & intr.* (usu. foll. by *up, over*) cover or become covered with mist or as with mist.

mis·take /mistáyk/ *n. & v.* ● *n.* **1** an incorrect idea or opinion; a thing incorrectly done or thought. **2** an error of judgment. ● *v.tr.* (*past* **mistook** /-tóok/; *past part.* **mistaken** /-táykən/) **1** misunderstand the meaning or intention of (a person, a statement, etc.). **2** (foll. by *for*) wrongly take or identify (*mistook me for you*). **3** choose wrongly (*mistake one's vocation*). □ **and** (or **make**) **no mistake** *colloq.* undoubtedly. **by mistake** accidentally; in error. **there is no mistaking** one is sure to recognize (a person or thing). □□ **mis·tak·a·ble** *adj.*

mis·tak·en /mistáykən/ *adj.* **1** wrong in opinion or judgment. **2** based on or resulting from this (*mistaken loyalty; mistaken identity*). □□ **mis·tak·en·ly** *adv.*

mis·teach /mís-téech/ *v.tr.* (*past* and *past part.* **-taught** /-táwt/) teach wrongly or incorrectly.

mis·ter /místər/ *n.* **1** (**Mister**) respectful title for a man, usu. abbr. (as **Mr.**). **2** *sl.* or *joc.* sir; a form of address to a man (*Hey, mister!*). **3** a husband.

mis·time /mís-tím/ *v.tr.* say or do at the wrong time.

mis·tle·toe /mísəltō/ *n.* **1** ◀ a parasitic plant, *Viscum album*, growing on apple and other trees and bearing white glutinous berries in winter. **2** a similar plant, genus *Phoradendron*, native to N. America.

mis·took *past* of MISTAKE.

mis·tral /místrəl, mistráal/ *n.* a cold northerly wind of southern France.

MISTLETOE
(*Viscum album*)

mis·trans·late /místranzláyt, -trans-, mistránzlayt, -tráns-/ *v.tr.* translate incorrectly. □□ **mis·trans·la·tion** /-láyshən/ *n.*

mis·treat /místréet/ *v.tr.* treat badly. □□ **mis·treat·ment** *n.*

mis·tress /místris/ *n.* **1** a female head of a household. **2 a** a woman in authority over others. **b** the female owner of a pet. **3** a woman with power to control, etc. (often foll. by *of*: *mistress of the situation*). **4 a** a woman (other than his wife) with whom a married man has a sexual relationship. **b** *archaic* or *poet.* a woman loved and courted by a man.

mis·tri·al /mís-tríəl/ *n.* **1** a trial rendered invalid through some error in the proceedings. **2** a trial in which the jury cannot agree on a verdict.

mis·trust /mís-trúst/ *v. & n.* ● *v.tr.* **1** be suspicious of. **2** feel no confidence in (a person, oneself, one's powers, etc.). ● *n.* **1** suspicion. **2** lack of confidence.

mis·trust·ful /mís-trústfool/ *adj.* **1** (foll. by *of*) suspicious. **2** lacking confidence or trust. □□ **mis·trust·ful·ly** *adv.*

mist·y /místee/ *adj.* (**mistier, mistiest**) **1** of or covered with mist. **2** indistinct or dim in outline. **3** obscure, vague (*a misty idea*). □□ **mist·i·ly** *adv.* **mist·i·ness** *n.*

mis·type /mís-típ/ *v.tr.* type wrongly.

angled slit

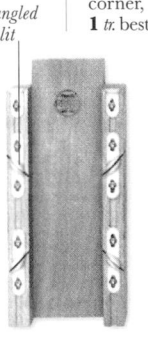

MITER BOX

mis·un·der·stand /mísundərstánd/ *v.tr.* (*past* and *past part.* **-understood** /-stóod/) **1** fail to understand correctly. **2** (usu. as **misunderstood** *adj.*) misinterpret the words or actions of (a person).

mis·un·der·stand·ing /mísundərstánding/ *n.* **1** a failure to understand correctly. **2** a slight disagreement or quarrel.

mis·use *v. & n.* ● *v.tr.* /mísyóoz/ **1** use wrongly; apply to the wrong purpose. **2** ill-treat. ● *n.* /mísyóos/ wrong or improper use or application.

MIT *abbr.* Massachusetts Institute of Technology.

mite[1] /mīt/ *n.* any small arachnid of the order Acari. ▷ ARACHNID

mite[2] /mīt/ *n. & adv.* ● *n.* **1** any small monetary unit. **2** a small object or person, esp. a child. **3** a modest contribution; the best one can do (*offered my mite of comfort*). ● *adv.* (usu. prec. by *a*) *colloq.* somewhat (*is a mite shy*).

mi·ter /mítər/ *n. & v.* ● *n.* ▶ **1** a tall deeply-cleft headdress worn by bishops and abbots, esp. as a symbol of office. **2** the joint of two pieces of wood or other material at an angle of 90°, such that the line of junction bisects this angle. **3** a diagonal join of two pieces of fabric that meet at a corner, made by folding. ● *v.* **1** *tr.* bestow the miter on. **2** *tr. & intr.* join with a miter. □□ **mi·tered** *adj.*

mi·ter box *n.* ◀ a frame with slits for guiding a saw in cutting miter joints.

mit·i·gate /mítgayt/ *v.tr.* make milder or less intense or severe. ¶ Often confused with *militate.* □□ **mit·i·ga·tion** /-gáyshən/ *n.* **mit·i·ga·to·ry** /-gətáwree/ *adj.*

mit·i·gat·ing cir·cum·stances *n.pl. Law* circumstances permitting greater leniency.

mi·to·chon·drion /mítəkóndreeən/ *n.* (*pl.* **mitochondria** /-dreeə/) *Biol.* an organelle found in most eukaryotic cells, containing enzymes for respiration and energy production.

mi·to·sis /mītósis/ *n. Biol.* ▼ a type of cell division that results in two daughter cells each having the same number and kind of chromosomes as the parent nucleus (cf. MEIOSIS). □□ **mi·tot·ic** /-tótik/ *adj.*

mi·tral /mítrəl/ *adj.* of or like a miter.

MITER:
BISHOP'S MITER

MITOSIS

Mitosis is a type of cell division that produces two new genetically identical cells. During prophase, the cell's genetic material (chromatin) tightens up to form chromosomes. The membrane around the nucleus begins to disintegrate, and a system of microtubules forms a structure called the spindle. This is complete by metaphase, when the chromosomes line up across the cell's center. During anaphase, the spindle microtubules contract, pulling the chromosomes apart so that each half (or chromatid) moves to opposite poles of the cell. During telophase, the spindle disappears and a new nuclear membrane forms around each group of chromosomes. The cell's plasma membrane then begins to constrict, eventually forming two new daughter cells.

DEMONSTRATION OF MITOTIC CELL DIVISION

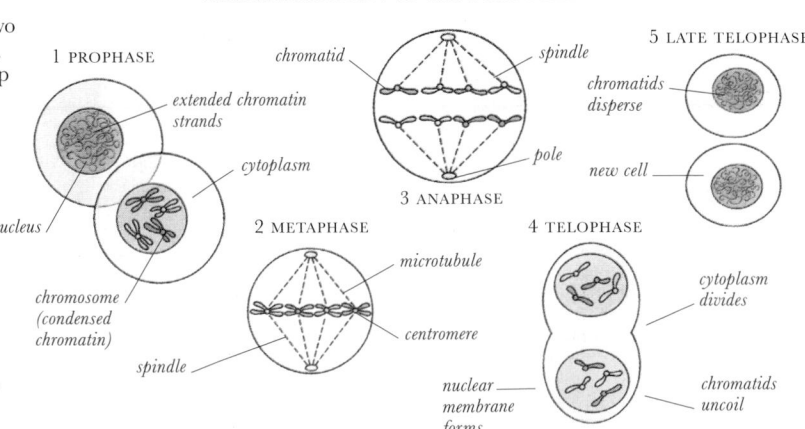

1 PROPHASE — chromatid — spindle — 5 LATE TELOPHASE — chromatids disperse — extended chromatin strands — cytoplasm — pole — new cell — 3 ANAPHASE — nucleus — 2 METAPHASE — 4 TELOPHASE — chromosome (condensed chromatin) — microtubule — centromere — cytoplasm divides — spindle — nuclear membrane forms — chromatids uncoil

mi·tral valve *n.* a two-cusped valve between the left atrium and the left ventricle of the heart.

mitt /mit/ *n.* **1** a baseball glove for catching the ball. **2** = MITTEN. **3** *sl.* a hand or fist. **4** a glove leaving the fingers and thumb-tip exposed.

mit·ten /mít'n/ *n.* a glove with two sections, one for the thumb and the other for all four fingers.

mitz·vah /mítsvə/ *n.* (*pl.* **mitzvoth** /-vōt/ or **mitzvahs**) in Judaism: **1** a precept or commandment. **2** a good deed done from religious duty.

mix /miks/ *v. & n.* ● *v.* **1** *tr.* combine or put together (two or more substances or things) so that they are diffused into each other. **2** *tr.* prepare (a compound, cocktail, etc.) by combining the ingredients. **3** *tr.* combine (an activity, etc.) with another simultaneously (*mix business and pleasure*). **4** *intr.* **a** join, be mixed, or combine, esp. readily (*oil and water will not mix*). **b** be compatible. **c** be sociable (*must learn to mix*). **5** *intr.* **a** (foll. by *with*) (of a person) be harmonious or sociable with; have regular dealings with. **b** (foll. by *in*) participate in. ● *n.* **1 a** the act or an instance of mixing; a mixture. **b** the proportion of materials, etc., in a mixture. **2** *colloq.* a group of persons of different types (*social mix*). **3** the ingredients prepared commercially for making a cake, etc., or for a process such as making concrete. **4** the merging of film pictures or sound. □ **be mixed up in** (or **with**) be involved in or with (esp. something undesirable). **mix in** be harmonious or sociable. **mix it** (usu. foll. by *up*) *colloq.* start fighting. **mix up 1** mix thoroughly. **2** confuse; mistake the identity of.

mixed /mikst/ *adj.* **1** of diverse qualities or elements. **2** containing persons from various backgrounds, both genders, etc.

mixed bag *n.* a diverse assortment of things or persons.

mixed bless·ing *n.* a thing having advantages and disadvantages.

mixed dou·bles *n.pl. Tennis* a doubles game with a man and a woman as partners on each side.

mixed feel·ings *n.pl.* a mixture of pleasure and dismay about something.

mixed mar·riage *n.* a marriage between persons of different races or religions.

mixed met·a·phor *n.* a combination of inconsistent metaphors (e.g., *this tower of strength will forge ahead*).

mixed-up *adj. colloq.* mentally or emotionally confused; socially ill-adjusted.

mix·er /míksər/ *n.* **1** ◄ a device for mixing foods, etc. or for processing other materials. **2** a person who manages socially in a specified way (*a good mixer*). **3** a (usu. soft) drink to be mixed with another. **4** *Broadcasting & Cinematog.* **a** a device for merging input signals to produce a combined output in the form of sound or pictures. **b** a person who operates this.

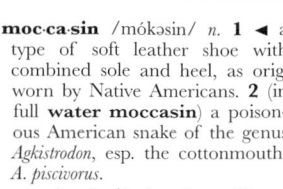

MIXER: HAND-HELD
FOOD MIXER

beater

mix·ture /míks-chər/ *n.* **1** the process of mixing or being mixed. **2** the result of mixing; something mixed; a combination. **3** *Chem.* the product of the random distribution of one substance through another without any chemical reaction taking place between the components, as distinct from a chemical compound. **4** ingredients mixed together to produce a substance, esp. a medicine (*cough mixture*). **5** a person regarded as a combination of qualities and attributes.

mix-up *n.* a confusion, misunderstanding, or mistake.

miz·zen /mízən/ *n.* (also **miz·en**) *Naut.* (in full **mizzen sail**) the lowest fore-and-aft sail of a fully rigged ship's mizzenmast.

miz·zen·mast /mízənmast/ *n. Naut.* the mast next aft of a ship's mainmast. ▷ RIGGING, SHIP

---

ml *abbr.* milliliter(s).

MLA *abbr.* Modern Language Association (of America).

MLD *abbr.* minimum lethal dose.

M.Litt. *abbr.* Master of Letters.

Mlle. *abbr.* (*pl.* **Mlles.**) Mademoiselle.

MM *abbr.* (as **MM.**) Messieurs.

mm *abbr.* millimeter(s).

Mme. *abbr.* (*pl.* **Mmes.**) Madame.

m.m.f. *abbr.* magnetomotive force.

MN *abbr.* Minnesota (in official postal use).

Mn *symb. Chem.* the element manganese.

mne·mon·ic /nimónik/ *adj. & n.* ● *adj.* of or designed to aid the memory. ● *n.* a mnemonic device. □□ **mne·mon·i·cal·ly** *adv.*

mne·mon·ics /nimóniks/ *n.pl.* (usu. treated as *sing.*) **1** the art of improving memory. **2** a system for this.

MO *abbr.* **1** Missouri (in official postal use). **2** money order.

Mo *symb. Chem.* the element molybdenum.

Mo. *abbr.* Missouri.

mo. *abbr.* month.

m.o. *abbr.* modus operandi.

mo·a /móə/ *n.* ◄ any extinct flightless New Zealand bird of the family Dinornithidae, resembling the ostrich.

moan /mōn/ *n. & v.* ● *n.* **1** a long murmur expressing suffering or passion. **2** a low plaintive sound of wind, etc. **3** a complaint; a grievance. ● *v.* **1** *intr.* make a moan or moans. **2** *intr. colloq.* complain or grumble. **3** *tr.* **a** utter with moans. **b** lament. □□ **moan·er** *n.*

moat /mōt/ *n. & v.* ● *n.* a deep defensive ditch around a castle, town, etc., usu. filled with water. ▷ CASTLE. ● *v.tr.* surround with or as with a moat.

mob /mob/ *n. & v.* ● *n.* **1** a disorderly crowd; a rabble. **2** (prec. by *the*) usu. *derog.* the populace. **3** *colloq.* a gang. **4** = MAFIA. ● *v.tr. & intr.* (**mobbed**, **mobbing**) **1** *tr.* **a** crowd around in order to attack or admire. **b** crowd into (a building). **2** *intr.* assemble in a mob.

MOA
(*Dinornis maximus*)

mob·cap /móbkap/ *n. hist.* ◄ a woman's large indoor cap covering all the hair, worn in the 18th and early 19th c.

mo·bile /móbəl, -beel, -bīl/ *adj. & n.* ● *adj.* **1** movable; able to move or flow easily. **2** (of the face etc.) readily changing its expression. **3** (of a business, library etc.) accommodated in a vehicle so as to serve various places. **4** (of a person) able to change his or her social status. ● *n.* /-béel/ a decorative structure hung so as to turn freely. □□ **mo·bil·i·ty** /mōbílitee/ *n.*

MOBCAP

mo·bile home *n.* a transportable structure usu. parked and used as a residence.

mo·bi·lize /móbilīz/ *v.* **1 a** *tr.* organize for service or action (esp. troops in time of war). **b** *intr.* be organized in this way. **2** *tr.* render movable; bring into circulation. □□ **mo·bi·li·za·tion** *n.*

Mö·bi·us strip /móbiəs, máy-, mó-/ *n. Math.* a one-sided surface formed by joining the ends of a rectangle after twisting one end through 180°.

mob·oc·ra·cy /mobókrəsee/ *n.* (*pl.* **-ies**) *colloq.* **1** rule by a mob. **2** a ruling mob.

mob rule *n.* rule imposed and enforced by a mob.

mob·ster /móbstər/ *n. sl.* a gangster.

MOCCASIN: NATIVE
AMERICAN BEADED
DEERSKIN MOCCASINS

moc·ca·sin /mókəsin/ *n.* **1** ◄ a type of soft leather shoe with combined sole and heel, as orig. worn by Native Americans. **2** (in full **water moccasin**) a poisonous American snake of the genus *Agkistrodon*, esp. the cottonmouth, *A. piscivorus*.

mo·cha /mókə/ *n.* **1** a coffee of fine quality. **2** a beverage or flavoring made with this. **3** a soft kind of sheepskin.

mo·chac·ci·no /mokəchéenō/ *n.* a cappuccino containing chocolate syrup or chocolate flavoring.

mock /mok/ *v. & adj.* ● *v.* **1 a** *tr.* ridicule; scoff at. **b** *intr.* (foll. by *at*) act with scorn or contempt for. **2** *tr.* mimic contemptuously. **3** *tr.* jeer, defy, or delude contemptuously. ● *attrib.adj.* sham, imitation (esp. without intention to deceive); pretended (*a mock battle; mock cream*). □□ **mock·er** *n.* **mock·ing·ly** *adv.*

mock·er·y /mókəree/ *n.* (*pl.* **-ies**) **1 a** a derision, ridicule. **b** a subject or occasion of this. **2** (often foll. by *of*) a counterfeit or absurdly inadequate representation.

mock·ing·bird /mókingbərd/ *n.* a bird, esp. the American songbird *Mimus polyglottos*, that mimics the notes of other birds.

mock or·ange *n.* ▶ a white-flowered heavy-scented shrub, *Philadelphus coronarius*.

mock tur·tle soup *n.* soup made from a calf's head, etc., to resemble turtle soup.

mock-up *n.* an experimental model or replica of a proposed structure, etc.

mod /mod/ *adj. colloq.* modern, esp. in style of dress.

MOCK ORANGE:
GOLDEN MOCK ORANGE
(*Philadelphus coronarius*
'Aureus')

mod·al /mód'l/ *adj.* **1** of or relating to mode or form as opposed to substance. **2** *Gram.* **a** of or denoting the mood of a verb. **b** (of an auxiliary verb, e.g., *would*) used to express the mood of another verb. **c** (of a particle) denoting manner. □□ **mod·al·ly** *adv.*

mo·dal·i·ty /mōdálitee/ *n.* (*pl.* **-ies**) (in *sing.* or *pl.*) **1** the state of being modal. **2** a prescribed method of procedure.

mode /mōd/ *n.* **1** a way or manner in which a thing is done. **2** a prevailing fashion or custom. **3** *Computing* a way of operating or using a system (*print mode*). **4** *Mus.* **a** each of the scale systems that result when the white notes of the piano are played consecutively over an octave (*Lydian mode*). **b** each of the two main modern scale systems, the major and minor (*minor mode*).

mod·el /mód'l/ *n. & v.* ● *n.* **1** a representation in three dimensions of an existing person or thing or of a proposed structure, esp. on a smaller scale (often *attrib.: a model train*). **2** a simplified (often mathematical) description of a system, etc., to assist calculations and predictions. **3** a figure in clay, wax, etc., to be reproduced in another material. **4** a particular design or style, esp. of a car. **5 a** an exemplary person or thing (*a model of self-discipline*). **b** (*attrib.*) ideal, exemplary (*a model student*). **6** a person employed to pose for an artist or photographer or to display clothes, etc., by wearing them. **7** a garment, etc., by a well-known designer, or a copy of this. ● *v.* **1** *tr.* **a** fashion or shape (a figure) in clay, wax, etc. **b** (foll. by *after, on,* etc.) form (a thing in imitation of). **2 a** *intr.* act or pose as a model. **b** *tr.* (of a person acting as a model) display (a garment). **3** *tr.* devise a (usu. mathematical) model of (a phenomenon, system, etc.). □□ **mod·el·er** *n.*

M

MODEM

A modem is a device that converts data from binary code – the string of ones and zeros that a computer reads and interprets – into an analog signal that can be transmitted over the telephone network. It forms the basis for the transmission of e-mail and faxes and access to the Internet. An internal modem occupies an expansion slot inside a computer; an external model plugs into a serial port on the outside of the computer.

server routes messages to addressees

service-provider's modem

monitor

telephone network

computer system

modem converts data

MODEM IN A MODERN COMMUNICATIONS SYSTEM

mo·dem /módem/ *n.* ▲ a device for modulation and demodulation, e.g., between a computer and a telephone line.

mod·er·ate *adj., n.,* & *v.* ● *adj.* /módərət/ **1** avoiding extremes; temperate in conduct or expression. **2** fairly or tolerably large or good. **3** (of the wind) of medium strength. **4** (of prices) fairly low. ● *n.* /módərət/ a person who holds moderate views, esp. in politics. ● *v.* /módərayt/ **1** *tr.* & *intr.* make or become less violent, intense, rigorous, etc. **2** *tr.* (also *absol.*) act as a moderator of or to. □□ **mod·er·ate·ly** /-rətlee/ *adv.*

mod·er·a·tion /módəráyshən/ *n.* **1** the process or an instance of moderating. **2** the quality of being moderate. □ **in moderation** in a moderate manner or degree.

mod·er·a·to /módəraátō/ *adj., adv.,* & *n. Mus.* ● *adj.* & *adv.* performed at a moderate pace. ● *n.* (*pl.* **-os**) a piece of music to be performed in this way.

mod·er·a·tor /módəraytər/ *n.* **1** an arbitrator or mediator. **2** a presiding officer. **3** *Eccl.* a Presbyterian minister presiding over an ecclesiastical body.

mod·ern /módərn/ *adj.* & *n.* ● *adj.* **1** of the present and recent times. **2** in current fashion; not antiquated. ● *n.* (usu. in *pl.*) a person living in modern times. □□ **mo·der·ni·ty** /-dérnitee/ *n.*

mod·ern Eng·lish *n.* English from about 1500 onward.

mod·ern·ism /módərnizəm/ *n.* **1 a** modern ideas or methods. **b** the tendency of religious belief to harmonize with modern ideas. **2** a modern term or expression. □□ **mod·ern·ist** *n.* **mod·ern·is·tic** /-nístik/ *adj.*

mod·ern·ize /módərnīz/ *v.* **1** *tr.* make modern; adapt to modern needs or habits. **2** *intr.* adopt modern ways or views. □□ **mod·ern·i·za·tion** /-záyshən/ *n.* **mod·ern·iz·er** *n.*

mod·est /módist/ *adj.* **1** having or expressing a humble or moderate estimate of one's own merits or achievements. **2** diffident, bashful, retiring. **3** decorous. **4** moderate or restrained in amount, extent, severity, etc. (*a modest sum*). **5** (of a thing) unpretentious in appearance, etc. □□ **mod·est·ly** *adv.*

mod·es·ty /módistee/ *n.* the quality of being modest.

mod·i·cum /módikəm/ *n.* (foll. by *of*) a small quantity.

mod·i·fi·ca·tion /módifikáyshən/ ● *n.* **1** the act or an instance of modifying or being modified. **2** a change made.

mod·i·fi·er /módifīər/ *n.* **1** a person or thing that modifies. **2** *Gram.* a word, esp. an adjective or noun used attributively, that qualifies the sense of another word (e.g., *good* and *family* in *a good family house*).

mod·i·fy /módifī/ *v.tr.* (**-ies, -ied**) **1** make less severe or extreme (*modify one's demands*). **2** make partial changes in; make different. **3** *Gram.* qualify or expand

the sense of (a word, etc.). □□ **mod·i·fi·ca·tion** /-fikáyshən/ *n.* **mod·i·fi·ca·to·ry** /-fikətáwree/ *adj.*

mod·ish /módish/ *adj.* fashionable. □□ **mod·ish·ly** *adv.* **mod·ish·ness** *n.*

mo·diste /mōdeést/ *n.* a milliner; a dressmaker.

mod·u·lar /mójələr/ *adj.* of or consisting of modules or moduli. □□ **mod·u·lar·i·ty** /-láritee/ *n.*

mod·u·late /mójəlayt/ *v.* **1** *tr.* **a** regulate or adjust. **b** moderate. **2** *tr.* adjust or vary the tone or pitch of (the speaking voice). **3** *tr.* alter the amplitude or frequency of (a wave) by a wave of a lower frequency to convey a signal. **4** *intr.* & *tr. Mus.* (often foll. by *from, to*) change or cause to change from one key to another. □□ **mod·u·la·tion** /-láyshən/ *n.* **mod·u·la·tor** *n.*

mod·ule /mójōōl/ *n.* **1** a standardized part or independent unit used in construction, esp. of furniture, a building, or an electronic system. **2** an independent unit of a spacecraft (*lunar module*). ▷ LUNAR MODULE, SPACECRAFT. **3** a unit or period of training or education. **4** a standard or unit of measurement.

mod·u·lus /mójələs/ *n.* (*pl.* **moduli** /-lī/) *Math.* **1 a** the magnitude of a real number without regard to its sign. **b** the positive square root of the sum of the squares of the real and imaginary parts of a complex number. **2** a constant factor or ratio.

mo·dus op·e·ran·di /módəs ópərándee, -dī/ *n.* (*pl.* **modi operandi** /módee, -dī/) **1** the particular way in which a person performs a task or action. **2** the way a thing operates.

mo·dus vi·ven·di /módəs vivéndee, -dī/ *n.* (*pl.* **modi vivendi** /módee, -dī/) **1** a way of living or coping. **2 a** an arrangement whereby those in dispute can carry on pending a settlement. **b** an arrangement between people who agree to differ.

mo·gul /mógəl/ *n.* **1** *colloq.* an important or influential person. **2** *hist.* (**Mogul**) (often **the Great Mogul**) any of the emperors of Delhi in the 16th–19th c.

mo·hair /móhair/ *n.* **1** the hair of the angora goat. **2** a yarn or fabric from this.

Mo·ham·med·an var. of MUHAMMADAN.

Mo·ha·ve var. of MOJAVE.

Mo·hawk /móhawk/ *n.* **1 a** a member of a Native American people of New York State. **b** the language of this people. **2** (of a hairstyle) with the head shaved except for a strip of hair from the middle of the forehead to the back of the neck, often worn in tall spikes.

Mo·he·gan /mōheégən/ *n.* & *adj.* ● *n.* a member of a Native American people of Connecticut. ● *adj.* of or relating to this people.

Mo·hi·can var. of MAHICAN.

mo·ho /móhō/ ● *n.* (*pl.* **-os**) *Geol.* a boundary of discontinuity separating the Earth's crust and mantle.

moi·dore /móydawr/ ● *n. hist.* a Portuguese gold coin, current in England in the 18th c.

moi·e·ty /móyətee/ *n.* (*pl.* **-ies**) *Law* or *literary* **1** a

half. **2** each of the two parts into which a thing is divided.

moil /moyl/ *v.* & *n. archaic* ● *v.intr.* drudge (esp. toil and moil). ● *n.* drudgery.

moire /mwaar, mawr/ *n.* (in full **moire antique**) watered fabric, now usu. silk.

moir·é /mwaaráy, máwray/ *adj.* & *n.* ● *adj.* **1** ▼ (of silk) watered. **2** (of metal) having a patterned appearance like watered silk. ● *n.* **1** this patterned appearance. **2** = MOIRE.

MOIRÉ RIBBON

moist /moyst/ *adj.* **1 a** slightly wet; damp. **b** (of the season, etc.) rainy. **2** (of a disease) marked by a discharge of matter, etc. □□ **moist·ness** *n.*

mois·ten /móysən/ *v.tr.* & *intr.* make or become moist.

mois·ture /móys-chər/ *n.* water or other liquid diffused in a small quantity as vapor, or within a solid, or condensed on a surface.

mois·tur·ize /móys-chərīz/ *v.tr.* make less dry (esp. the skin by use of a cosmetic). □□ **mois·tur·iz·er** *n.*

Mo·ja·ve /mōháavee/ *n.* & *adj.* (also **Mo·ha·ve**) ● *n.* **1 a** N. American people native to Arizona and California. **2** a member of this people. ● *adj.* of or relating to this people.

mo·jo /mójō/ *n.* chiefly *US* **1** a magic charm or spell. **2** supernatural power or luck.

mol /mōl/ *abbr.* = MOLE[4].

mo·lar[1] /mólər/ *adj.* & *n.* ● *adj.* (usu. of a mammal's back teeth) serving to grind. ● *n.* ▼ a molar tooth. ▷ DENTITION, PREMOLAR, TOOTH

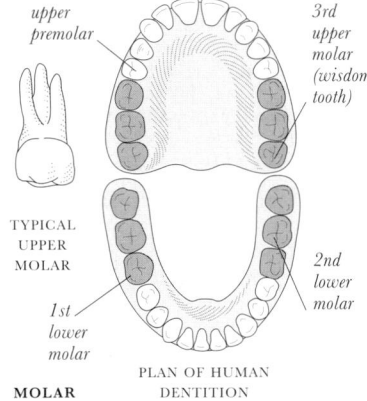

upper premolar

3rd upper molar (wisdom tooth)

TYPICAL UPPER MOLAR

1st lower molar

2nd lower molar

MOLAR

PLAN OF HUMAN DENTITION

mo·lar[2] /mólər/ *adj. Chem.* **1** of a mass of substance usu. per mole (*molar latent heat*). **2** (of a solution) containing one mole of solute per liter of solvent. □□ **mol·ar·i·ty** /məláritee/ *n.*

mo·las·ses /məlásiz/ *n.pl.* (treated as *sing.*) uncrystallized syrup extracted from raw sugar during refining.

mold[1] /mōld/ *n.* & *v.* ● *n.* **1** a hollow container into which molten metal, etc., is poured or soft material is pressed to harden into a required shape. **2 a** a metal or earthenware vessel used to give shape to cakes, gelatins, etc. **b** a dessert, etc., made in this way. **3** a form or shape, esp. of an animal body. **4** *Archit.* a molding or group of moldings. **5** a frame or template for producing moldings. **6** character or disposition (*in heroic mold*). ● *v.tr.* **1** make in a required shape or from certain ingredients (*was molded out of clay*). **2** give a shape to. **3** influence the formation or development of (*consultation helps to mold policies*). **4** (esp. of clothing) fit closely to (*the gloves molded his hands*). □□ **mold·er** *n.*

MOLECULE

A molecule is a discrete unit made from atoms joined by chemical bonds. All molecules of the same compound are identical. All water molecules, for example, consist of an atom of oxygen, chemically bound to two hydrogen atoms. Molecules may consist of just two atoms, or many thousands.

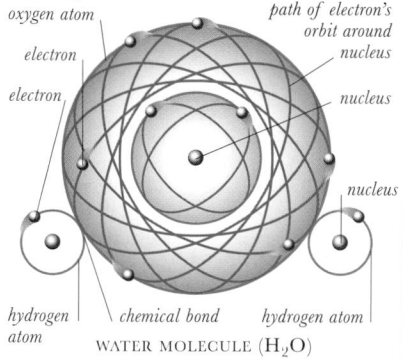

oxygen atom

electron

electron

path of electron's orbit around nucleus

nucleus

nucleus

hydrogen atom

chemical bond

hydrogen atom

WATER MOLECULE (H_2O)

mold[2] /mōld/ *n.* a woolly or furry growth of minute fungi occurring esp. in moist warm conditions.
▷ FUNGUS

mold[3] /mōld/ *n.* **1** loose earth. **2** the upper soil of cultivated land, esp. when rich in organic matter.

mold·er /mṓldər/ *v.intr.* **1** decay to dust; deteriorate.

mold·ing /mṓlding/ *n.* **1 a** an ornamentally shaped outline as an architectural feature. **b** a strip of material in wood or stone, etc., for use as molding. **2** similar material in wood or plastic, etc., used for other decorative purposes.

mold·y /mṓldee/ *adj.* (**-ier, -iest**) **1** covered with mold. **2** stale; out of date. **3** *colloq.* dull, miserable, boring.

mole[1] /mōl/ *n.* **1** any small burrowing insect-eating mammal of the family Talpidae, esp. *Talpa europaea*, with dark velvety fur and very small eyes. ▷ INSECTIVORE, NEST. **2** *colloq.* **a** a spy, within an organization, usu. dormant for a long period while attaining a position of trust. **b** a betrayer of confidential information.

mole[2] /mōl/ *n.* a small often slightly raised dark blemish on the skin caused by a high concentration of melanin.

mole[3] /mōl/ *n.* **1** a structure serving as a pier, breakwater, or causeway. **2** an artificial harbor.

mole[4] /mōl/ *n. Chem.* the SI unit of amount of substance equal to the quantity containing as many elementary units as there are atoms in 0.012 kg of carbon 12.

mo·lec·u·lar /məlékyələr/ *adj.* of, relating to, or consisting of molecules. □□ **mo·lec·u·lar·i·ty** /-láritee/ *n.*

mo·lec·u·lar bi·ol·o·gy *n.* the study of the structure and function of large molecules associated with living organisms.

mol·e·cule /mólikyool/ *n.* **1** *Chem.* ▲ the smallest fundamental unit (usu. a group of atoms) of a chemical compound that can take part in a chemical reaction. **2** (in general use) a small particle.

mole·hill /mṓlhil/ *n.* a small mound thrown up by a mole in burrowing. □ **make a mountain out of a molehill** exaggerate the importance of a minor difficulty.

mole·skin /mṓlskin/ *n.* **1** the skin of a mole used as fur. **2 a** a kind of cotton fustian with its surface shaved before dyeing. **b** (*in* pl.) clothes, esp. trousers, made of this.

mo·lest /məlést/ *v.tr.* **1** annoy or pester (a person) in a hostile or injurious way. **2** attack or interfere

with (a person), esp. sexually. □□ **mo·les·ta·tion** /mólestáyshən, mól-/ *n.* **mo·lest·er** *n.*

moll /mol/ *n. sl.* **1** a gangster's female companion. **2** a prostitute.

mol·li·fy /mólifī/ *v.tr.* (**-ies, -ied**) **1** appease, pacify. **2** reduce the severity of; soften. □□ **mol·li·fi·ca·tion** /-fikáyshən/ *n.*

mol·lusk /mólŭsk/ *n.* (also **mol·lusc**) ▼ any invertebrate of the phylum Mollusca, with a soft body and usu. a hard shell, including snails, cuttlefish, mussels, etc. □□ **mol·lus·kan** or **mol·lus·can** /məlúskən/ *n. & adj.*

mol·ly·cod·dle /móleekodəl/ *v. & n.* ● *v.tr.* coddle, pamper. ● *n.* an effeminate man or boy; a milksop.

Mo·loch /mṓlok, mólək/ ● *n.* **1 a** a Canaanite idol to whom children were sacrificed. **b** a tyrannical object of sacrifices. **2** (**moloch**) the spiny slow-moving grotesque Australian reptile, *Moloch horridus*.

Mo·lo·tov cock·tail /mólətáwf/ *n.* a crude incendiary device usu. consisting of a bottle filled with flammable liquid.

molt /mōlt/ *v. & n.* ● *v.* **1** *intr.* shed feathers, hair, a shell, etc., in the process of renewing plumage, a coat, etc. **2** *tr.* shed (feathers, hair, etc.). ● *n.* the act or an instance of molting (*is in molt once a year*).

mol·ten /mṓltən/ *adj.* melted, esp. made liquid by heat (*molten lava*).

mol·to /mṓltō/ *adv. Mus.* very (*molto sostenuto; allegro molto*).

moly /mṓlee/ ● *n.* (*pl.* **-ies**) **1** an alliaceous plant, *Allium moly*, with small yellow flowers. **2** a mythical herb with white flowers and black roots, endowed with magic properties.

mol·yb·den·ite /məlíbdinīt/ ● *n.* molybdenum disulfide as an ore.

mo·lyb·de·num /məlíbdinəm/ *n. Chem.* a silver-white brittle metallic transition element occurring naturally in molybdenite and used in steel to give strength and resistance to corrosion. ¶ Symb.: **Mo**.

mom /mom/ *n. colloq.* mother.

mom-and-pop *adj.* of or pertaining to a small retail business, as a grocery store, owned and operated by members of a family.

mo·ment /mṓmənt/ *n.* **1** a very brief portion of time; an instant. **2** a short period of time (*wait a moment*) (see also MINUTE[1] 3). **3** an exact or particular point of time (*at last the moment arrived*). **4** importance (*of no great moment*). **5** *Physics & Mech.*, etc. **a** the turning effect produced by a force acting at a distance on an object. **b** this effect expressed as the product of the force and the distance from its line of action to a point. □ **at the moment** at this time; now. **in a moment 1** very soon. **2** instantly. **man** (or **woman**, etc.) **of the moment** the one of importance at the time in question. **not for a** (or **one**) **moment** never; not at all.

mo·men·ta *pl.* of MOMENTUM.

mo·men·tar·i·ly /mṓməntairilee/ *adv.* **1** for a moment. **2 a** at any moment. **b** instantly.

mo·men·tar·y /mṓmənteree/ *adj.* **1** lasting only a moment. **2** short-lived; transitory.

mo·ment of truth *n.* a time of crisis or test (orig. the final sword thrust in a bullfight).

mo·men·tous /mōméntəs/ *adj.* having great importance. □□ **mo·men·tous·ly** *adv.* **mo·men·tous·ness** *n.*

M

MOLLUSK

With over 80,000 species, mollusks form the second largest phylum of animals on Earth, and range from tiny snails to giant squid. Most mollusks are aquatic, but some slugs and snails live on land. A typical mollusk has a soft body, protected by a shell. The shell is formed by a layer of tissue called the mantle. Most mollusks belong to one of four main groups – gastropods, bivalves, cephalopods, and chitons. Gastropods move with the help of a single suckerlike foot, which moves in a series of muscular waves.

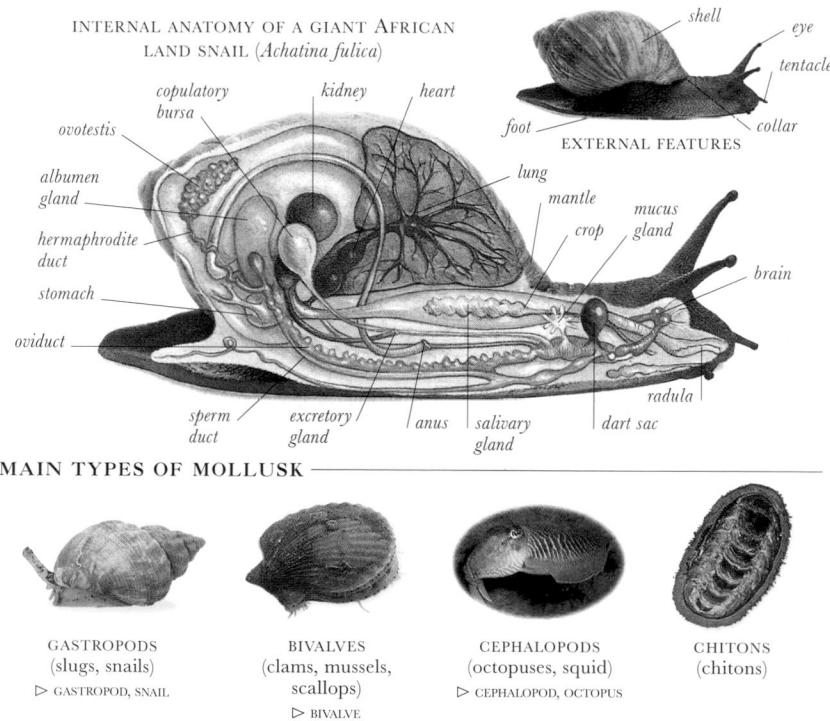

INTERNAL ANATOMY OF A GIANT AFRICAN LAND SNAIL (*Achatina fulica*)

copulatory bursa

ovotestis

albumen gland

hermaphrodite duct

stomach

oviduct

sperm duct

excretory gland

kidney

heart

anus

salivary gland

lung

mantle

crop

mucus gland

dart sac

brain

radula

shell

eye

tentacle

foot

collar

EXTERNAL FEATURES

MAIN TYPES OF MOLLUSK

GASTROPODS (slugs, snails)
▷ GASTROPOD, SNAIL

BIVALVES (clams, mussels, scallops)
▷ BIVALVE

CEPHALOPODS (octopuses, squid)
▷ CEPHALOPOD, OCTOPUS

CHITONS (chitons)

527

mo·men·tum /mōméntəm/ *n.* (*pl.* **momenta** /-tə/) **1** *Physics* the quantity of motion of a moving body, measured as a product of its mass and velocity. **2** the impetus gained by movement. **3** strength or continuity derived from an initial effort.

mom·ma /mómə/ *n.* var. of MAMMA[1].

mom·my /mómee/ *n.* (*pl.* **-ies**) *colloq.* mother.

mom·my track *n. N. Amer. colloq.* a career path for women who sacrifice some promotions and pay raises in order to devote more time to raising their children.

Mon. *abbr.* Monday.

mon·ad /mónad, mṓ-/ *n.* **1** the number one; a unit. **2** *Philos.* any ultimate unit of being (e.g., a soul, an atom, a person, God). **3** *Biol.* a simple organism, e.g., one assumed as the first in the genealogy of living beings. □□ **mo·nad·ic** /mənádik/ *adj.*

mon·a·del·phous /mónədélfəs/ *adj. Bot.* **1** (of stamens) having filaments united into one bundle. **2** (of a plant) with such stamens.

mo·nan·dry /mənándree/ *n.* **1** the custom of having only one husband at a time. **2** *Bot.* the state of having a single stamen. □□ **mo·nan·drous** *adj.*

mon·arch /mónərk, -aark/ *n.* **1** a sovereign with the title of king, queen, emperor, empress, or the equivalent. **2** a supreme ruler. **3** a powerful or preeminent person. **4** a large orange and black butterfly, *Danaus plexippus.* □□ **mo·nar·chic** /mənáarkik/ *adj.* **mo·nar·chi·cal** /mənáarkikəl/ *adj.*

mon·ar·chism /mónərkizəm/ *n.* the advocacy of or the principles of monarchy. □□ **mon·ar·chist** *n.*

mon·ar·chy /mónərkee/ *n.* (*pl.* **-ies**) **1** a form of government with a monarch at the head. **2** a nation with this. □□ **mo·nar·chi·al** /mónáarkeeəl/ *adj.*

mon·as·ter·y /mónəsteree/ *n.* (*pl.* **-ies**) ▼ the residence of a religious community, esp. of monks living in seclusion.

mo·nas·tic /mənástik/ *adj. & n.* ● *adj.* **1** of or relating to monasteries or the religious communities living in them. **2** resembling these or their way of life; solitary and celibate. ● *n.* a monk or other follower of a monastic rule. □□ **mo·nas·ti·cal·ly** *adv.* **mo·nas·ti·cism** /-tisizəm/ *n.*

mon·a·tom·ic /mónətómik/ *adj. Chem.* **1** (esp. of a molecule) consisting of one atom. **2** having one replaceable atom or radical.

mon·au·ral /mónáwrəl/ *adj.* **1** = MONOPHONIC. **2** of or involving one ear. □□ **mon·au·ral·ly** *adv.*

mon·a·zite /mónəzīt/ *n.* a phosphate mineral containing rare-earth elements and thorium.

Mon·day /múnday, -dee/ *n. & adv.* ● *n.* the second day of the week, following Sunday. ● *adv. colloq.* **1** on Monday. **2** (**Mondays**) on Mondays; each Monday.

Mon·el /mōnél/ *n.* (in full **Monel metal**) *propr.* a nickel-copper alloy with high tensile strength and resisting corrosion.

mon·e·ta·rism /mónitərizəm, mún-/ *n.* the theory or practice of controlling the supply of money as the chief method of stabilizing the economy.

mon·e·tar·ist /mónitərist, mún-/ *n. & adj.* ● *n.* an advocate of monetarism. ● *adj.* in accordance with the principles of monetarism.

mon·e·tar·y /móniteree, -mún/ *adj.* **1** of the currency in use. **2** of or consisting of money.

mon·e·tize /mónitīz, mún-/ *v.tr.* **1** give a fixed value as currency. **2** put (a metal) into circulation as money. □□ **mon·e·ti·za·tion** *n.*

mon·ey /múnee/ *n.* **1 a** a current medium of exchange in the form of coins and paper currency. **b** a particular form of this (*silver money*). **2** (*pl.* **-eys** or **-ies**) (in *pl.*) sums of money. **3 a** wealth. **b** a rich person or family (*has married into money*). **4 a** money as a resource (*time is money*). **b** profit, remuneration (*in it for the money*). □ **for my money** in my opinion or judgment; for my preference (*is too aggressive for my money*). □□ **mon·ey·less** *adj.*

mon·ey·bags /múneebagz/ *n.pl.* (treated as *sing.*) *colloq.* usu. *derog.* a wealthy person.

mon·eyed /múneed/ *adj.* **1** having much money; wealthy. **2** consisting of money (*moneyed assistance*).

mon·ey-grub·ber *n. colloq.* a person greedily intent on amassing money. □□ **mon·ey-grub·bing** *n. & adj.*

mon·ey·lend·er /múneelendər/ *n.* a person who lends money, esp. as a business, at interest. □□ **mon·ey·lend·ing** *n. & adj.*

mon·ey·mak·er /múneemaykər/ *n.* **1** a person who earns much money. **2** a thing, idea, etc., that produces much money. □□ **mon·ey·mak·ing** *n. & adj.*

mon·ey mar·ket *n. Stock Exch.* trade in short-term stocks, loans, etc.

mon·ey or·der *n.* an order for payment of a specified sum, issued by a bank or post office.

mon·ey's worth *n.* (prec. by *your, my, one's,* etc.) good value for one's money.

mon·ey·wort /múneewərt/ *n.* a trailing evergreen plant, *Lysimachia nummularia,* with round glossy leaves and yellow flowers.

mon·ger /múnggər, móng-/ *n.* (usu. in *comb.*) **1** esp. *Brit.* a dealer or trader (*fishmonger; ironmonger*). **2** usu. *derog.* a person who promotes or deals in something specified (*warmonger; scaremonger*).

Mon·gol /mónggəl, -gōl/ *adj. & n.* ● *adj.* **1** of or relating to the Asian people now inhabiting Mongolia in Central Asia. **2** resembling this people, esp. in appearance. ● *n.* a Mongolian.

Mon·go·li·an /monggṓleeən/ *n. & adj.* ● *n.* **1** a native or inhabitant of Mongolia. **2** the language of Mongolia. ● *adj.* of or relating to Mongolia or its people or language.

mon·gol·ism /mónggəlizəm/ *n.* often *offens.* = DOWN'S SYNDROME. ¶ The term *Down's syndrome* is now preferred.

Mon·gol·oid /mónggəloyd/ *adj. & n.* ● *adj.* **1** characteristic of the Mongolians, esp. in having a broad flat yellowish face. **2** (**mongoloid**) often *offens.* having the characteristic symptoms of Down's syndrome. ● *n.* a Mongoloid or mongoloid person.

mon·goose /mónggōos/ *n.* (*pl.* **mongooses**) ◄ any of various African or Asian flesh-eating civetlike mammals of the genus *Herpestes* and related genera.

MONGOOSE: BANDED MONGOOSE
(*Mungos mungo*)

mon·grel /múnggrəl, móng-/ *n. & adj.* ● *n.* **1** a dog of no definable type or breed. **2** any other animal or plant resulting from the crossing of different breeds or types. **3** *derog.* a person of mixed race. ● *adj.* of mixed origin, nature, or character.

'mongst *poet.* var. of AMONG.

mon·ies see MONEY 2.

mon·i·ker /mónikər/ *n.* (also **mon·ick·er**) *sl.* a name.

mon·ism /mónizəm, mṓ-/ *n.* **1** any theory denying the duality of matter and mind. **2** the doctrine that only one ultimate being exists. □□ **mon·ist** *n.* **mo·nis·tic** /-nístik/ *adj.*

mon·i·tor /mónitər/ *n. & v.* ● *n.* **1** any of various persons or devices for checking or warning about a situation, operation, etc. **2** a school pupil with disciplinary or other special duties. **3** ► a cathode-ray tube used as a television receiver or computer display device. ▷ COMPUTER, TOUCH SCREEN. **4** a person who listens to and reports on foreign broadcasts, etc. **5** a detector of radioactive contamination. **6** *Zool.* any tropical lizard of the genus *Varanus,* supposed to give warning of the approach of crocodiles. ▷ LIZARD. **7** a heavily armed shallow-draft warship. ● *v.tr.* **1** act as a monitor of. **2** maintain regular surveillance over. **3** regulate the strength of (a recorded or transmitted signal). □□ **mon·i·to·ri·al** /-táwreeəl/ *adj.*

monk /mungk/ *n.* a member of a religious community of men living under certain vows, esp. of poverty, chastity, and obedience. □□ **monk·ish** *adj.*

mon·key /múngkee/ *n. & v.* ● *n.* (*pl.* **-eys**) **1** any of various New World and Old World primates, esp. of the families Cebidae, Callithricidae, and Cercopithecidae. ▷ PRIMATE. **2** a mischievous person, esp. a child (*little monkey*). **3** (in full **monkey engine**) a machine hammer for pile driving, etc. ● *v.* (**-eys, -eyed**) **1** *tr.* mimic or mock. **2** *intr.* (often foll. by *with*) tamper or play mischievous tricks. **3** *intr.* (foll. by *around, about*) fool around. □ **have a monkey on one's back 1** *sl.* have a drug addiction. **2** have a persistent problem or hindrance. **make a monkey of** humiliate by making appear ridiculous.

mon·key busi·ness *n. colloq.* mischief.

mon·key·shine /múngkeeshīn/ *n.* (usu. in *pl.*) US *colloq.* = MONKEY BUSINESS.

mon·key suit *n. colloq.* formal attire, esp. a tuxedo.

mon·key wrench *n.* ▼ a wrench with an adjustable jaw.

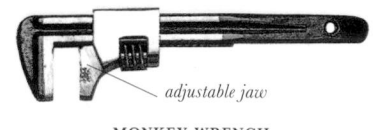

adjustable jaw

MONKEY WRENCH

MONASTERY

Most organized religions, especially the Christian and Buddhist traditions, have monasteries where monks, who have chosen to devote their lives to their religion, live apart from society. Monastic life is dominated by prayer, so the church is a central feature, but there are also rooms for eating, washing, sleeping, and studying as well as an infirmary. A garden, or farm, is another important feature, providing a means of sustenance and revenue for the religious community.

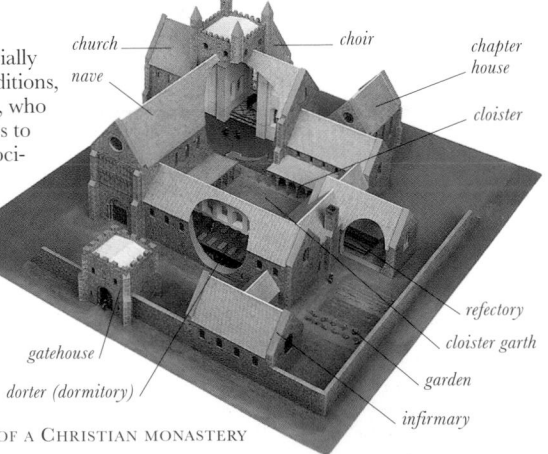

church   choir   chapter house
nave
cloister
refectory
cloister garth
gatehouse
garden
dorter (dormitory)
infirmary

MODEL OF A CHRISTIAN MONASTERY

M

MONITOR

A computer monitor is a very precise type of television screen that displays images created by the graphics card in a computer. The display area is divided into a grid of pixels (picture elements) of phosphor, a substance that glows when stimulated by electrons. Each pixel is made up of at least one set of three dots (one red, one blue, and one green). Electron beams, directed through a mask in the monitor, can vary the brightness of each dot to make any pixel produce any color. On-screen graphics are created by manipulating the colors of pixels and the number of pixels displayed.

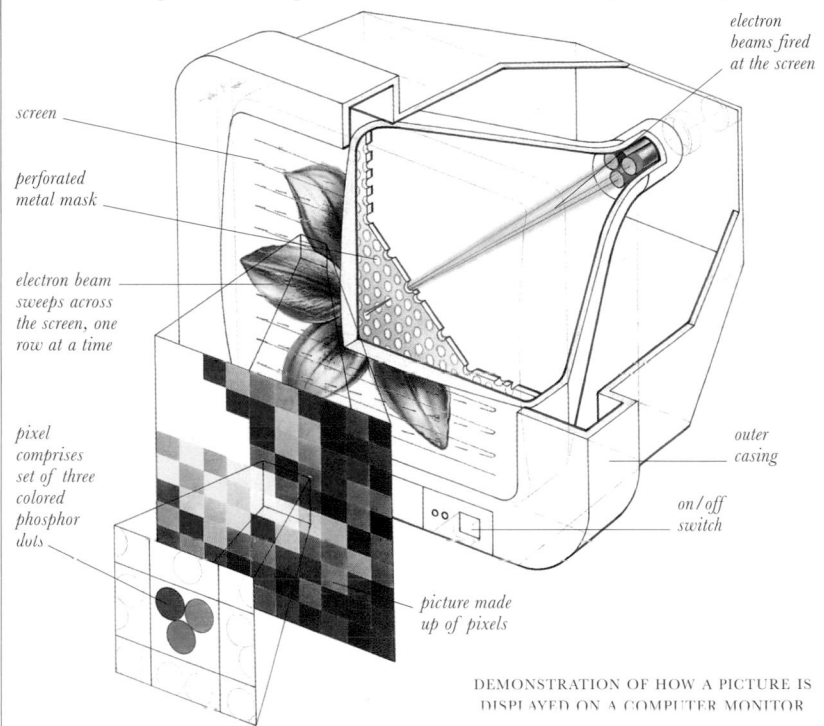

screen

perforated metal mask

electron beam sweeps across the screen, one row at a time

pixel comprises set of three colored phosphor dots

electron beams fired at the screen

outer casing

on/off switch

picture made up of pixels

DEMONSTRATION OF HOW A PICTURE IS DISPLAYED ON A COMPUTER MONITOR

---

monk·fish /múnkfish/ n. (pl. same) **1** an angler-fish, esp. *Lophius piscatorius*, often used as food. **2** a large cartilaginous fish, *Squatina squatina*, with a flattened body and large pectoral fins. Also called **angel shark**.

monk seal n. a seal with a dark back and pale underside, found in warm waters of the northern hemisphere.

monks·hood /múngks-hŏod/ n. Bot. ▶ a poisonous garden plant *Aconitum napellus*, with hood-shaped blue or purple flowers.

mon·o[1] /mónō/ n. colloq. infectious mononucleosis.

mon·o[2] /mónō/ adj. & n. colloq. ● adj. monophonic. ● n. (pl. -os) a monophonic record, reproduction, etc.

mono- /mónō/ comb. form (usu. **mon-** before a vowel) **1** one, alone, single. **2** Chem. (forming names of compounds) containing one atom or group of a specified kind.

mon·o·ac·id /mónōásid/ adj. Chem. (of a base) having one replaceable hydroxide ion.

mon·o·bas·ic /mónōbáysik/ adj. Chem. (of an acid) having one replaceable hydrogen atom.

mon·o·car·pic /mónōkáarpik/ adj. (also **mon·o·car·pous** /-káarpəs/) Bot. bearing fruit only once.

mon·o·caus·al /mónōkáwzəl/ adj. in terms of a sole cause.

mon·o·chro·mat·ic /mónəkrəmátik/ adj. **1** Physics (of light or other radiation) of a single wavelength

MONKSHOOD
(Aconitum napellus)

or frequency. **2** containing only one color. □□ **mon·o·chro·mat·i·cal·ly** adv.

mono·chro·ma·tism /mónōkrómətizəm/ n. complete color blindness in which all colors appear as shades of one color.

mon·o·chrome /mónəkrōm/ n. & adj. ● n. a photograph or picture done in one color or different tones of this, or in black and white only. ● adj. having or using only one color or in black and white only.

mon·o·cle /mónəkəl/ n. a single eyeglass.

mon·o·cline /mónōklīn/ n. Geol. a bend in rock strata that are otherwise uniformly dipping or horizontal. □□ **mon·o·cli·nal** /-klín'l/ adj.

mon·o·clin·ic /mónōklínik/ adj. (of a crystal) having one axial intersection oblique.

mon·o·cli·nous adj. Bot. (of a plant) having stamens and pistils in the same flower.

mo·no·clo·nal /mónōklónəl/ adj. forming a single clone; derived from a single individual or cell.

mo·no·clo·nal an·ti·bod·ies n.pl. antibodies produced artificially by a single clone and consisting of identical antibody molecules.

mon·o·coque /mónəkok/ n. Aeron. an aircraft or vehicle structure in which the chassis is integral with the body.

mon·o·cot /mónəkot, -kōt/ n. = MONOCOTYLEDON.

mon·o·cot·y·le·don /mónəkót'léed'n/ n. Bot. any flowering plant with a single cotyledon. ▷ ANGIO-SPERM, FLOWER. □□ **mon·o·cot·y·le·don·ous** adj.

mon·oc·ra·cy /mənókrəsee/ n. (pl. -ies) government by one person only. □□ **mon·o·crat·ic** /mónəkrátik/ adj.

mo·noc·u·lar /mənókyələr/ adj. with or for one eye.

mon·o·cul·ture /mónōkulchər/ n. the cultivation of a single crop.

mon·o·cy·cle /mónəsīkəl/ n. a one-wheeled vehicle, esp. a unicycle.

mon·o·cyte /mónəsīt/ n. Biol. a large type of leukocyte.

mon·o·dy /mónədee/ n. (pl. -ies) **1** an ode sung by a single actor in a Greek tragedy. **2** a poem lamenting a person's death. **3** Mus. a composition with only one melodic line. □□ **mo·nod·ic** /mənódik/ adj. **mon·o·dist** /mónə-/ n.

mo·noe·cious /məneéshəs/ adj. **1** Bot. with unisexual male and female organs on the same plant. **2** Zool. hermaphroditic.

mo·no·fil·a·ment /mónōfíləmənt/ n. **1** a single strand of man-made fiber. **2** a type of fishing line using this.

mo·nog·a·my /mənógəmee/ n. **1** the practice or state of being married to one person at a time. **2** Zool. the habit of having only one mate at a time. □□ **mo·nog·a·mist** n. **mo·nog·a·mous** adj. **mo·nog·a·mous·ly** adv.

mon·o·gen·e·sis /mónōjénisis/ n. (also **mon·og·en·y** /mənójinee/) **1** the theory of the development of all beings from a single cell. **2** the theory that mankind descended from one pair of ancestors. □□ **mon·o·gen·e·tic** /-jinétik/ adj.

mon·o·glot /mónōglot/ adj. & n. ● adj. using only one language. ● n. a monoglot person.

mon·o·gram /mónəgram/ n. two or more letters, esp. a person's initials, interwoven as a device. □□ **mon·o·grammed** adj.

mon·o·graph /mónógraf/ n. & v. ● n. a separate treatise on a single subject or an aspect of it. ● v.tr. write a monograph on. □□ **mon·o·graph·er** /mənógrəfər/ n. **mon·o·graph·ist** /mənəgráfist/ n. **mon·o·graph·ic** /mónəgráfik/ adj.

mon·o·hull /mónōhul/ n. a boat with a single hull.

mon·o·ki·ni /mónōkéenee/ n. a woman's bathing suit equivalent to the lower half of a bikini.

mon·o·lay·er /mónōlayər/ n. Chem. a layer only one molecule in thickness.

mon·o·lin·gual /mónōlínggwəl/ adj. speaking or using only one language.

mon·o·lith /mónəlith/ n. **1** a single block of stone, esp. shaped into a pillar or monument. **2** a person or thing like a monolith in being massive, immovable, or solidly uniform. **3** a large block of concrete. □□ **mon·o·lith·ic** /-líthik/ adj.

mon·o·logue /mónəlawg, -log/ n. **1 a** a scene in a drama in which a person speaks alone. **b** a dramatic composition for one performer. **2** a long speech by one person in a conversation, etc. □□ **mon·o·log·ic** /-lójik/ adj. **mon·o·log·i·cal** /-lójikəl/ adj. **mon·o·log·ist** /mənóləjist/ n. (also **-loguist**).

mon·o·ma·ni·a /mónəmáyneeə/ n. obsession of the mind by one idea or interest. □□ **mon·o·ma·ni·ac** n. & adj. **mon·o·ma·ni·a·cal** /-məníəkəl/ adj.

mon·o·mer /mónəmər/ n. Chem. **1** a molecule that can be bonded to other identical molecules to form a polymer. **2** a molecule or compound that can be polymerized. □□ **mon·o·mer·ic** /-mérik/ adj.

mon·o·mo·lec·u·lar /mónōmələkyələr/ adj. Chem. (of a layer) only one molecule in thickness.

mo·no·nu·cle·o·sis /mónōnōókleeósis, -nyōó-/ n. an abnormally high proportion of monocytes in the blood, esp. = infectious mononucleosis.

mon·o·pet·al·ous /mónəpét'ləs/ adj. Bot. having the corolla in one piece, or the petals united into a tube.

mon·o·phon·ic /mónəfónik/ adj. **1** (of sound reproduction) using only one channel of transmission (cf. STEREOPHONIC). **2** Mus. homophonic.

M

single wing · starboard elevator · nose-ring · seven-cylinder rotary engine · tailskid

MONOPLANE:
1912 BLACKBURN
MONOPLANE

mon·o·plane /mónōplayn/ *n.* ▲ an airplane with one set of wings (cf. BIPLANE). ▷ AIRCRAFT

mo·nop·o·list /mənópəlist/ *n.* a person who has or advocates a monopoly. □□ **mo·nop·o·lis·tic** /-lístik/ *adj.*

mo·nop·o·lize /mənópəlīz/ *v.tr.* **1** obtain exclusive possession or control of (a trade or commodity, etc.). **2** dominate or prevent others from sharing in (a conversation, person's attention, etc.). □□ **mo·nop·o·li·za·tion** *n.*

mo·nop·o·ly /mənópəlee/ *n.* (*pl.* **-ies**) **1 a** the exclusive possession or control of the trade in a commodity or service. **b** this conferred as a privilege by the government. **2 a** a commodity or service that is subject to a monopoly. **b** a company, etc., that possesses a monopoly. **3** (foll. by *on*) exclusive possession, control, or exercise.

mon·o·rail /mónōrayl/ *n.* ▼ a railway in which the track consists of a single rail, usu. elevated with the cars suspended from it.

MONORAIL IN WUPPERTAL, GERMANY

mon·o·sac·cha·ride /mónōsákərīd/ *n.* *Chem.* a sugar that cannot be hydrolyzed to give a simpler sugar, e.g., glucose.

mon·o·ski /mónōskee/ *n.* a single broad ski attached to both feet.

mon·o·so·di·um glu·ta·mate /mónəsódiəm glootəmayt/ *n.* *Chem.* a sodium salt of glutamic acid used to flavor food (cf. GLUTAMATE).

mon·o·syl·lab·ic /mónəsilábik/ *adj.* **1** (of a word) having one syllable. **2** (of a person or statement) using or expressed in monosyllables. □□ **mon·o·syl·lab·i·cal·ly** *adv.*

mon·o·syl·la·ble /mónəsiləbəl/ *n.* a word of one syllable. □ **in monosyllables** in simple direct words.

mon·o·the·ism /mónətheeizəm/ *n.* the doctrine that there is only one God. □□ **mon·o·the·ist** *n.* **mon·o·the·is·tic** /-ístik/ *adj.*

mon·o·tone /mónətōn/ *n. & adj.* ● *n.* **1** a sound or utterance continuing or repeated on one note without change of pitch. **2** sameness of style in writing. ● *adj.* without change of pitch.

mon·ot·o·nous /mənót'nəs/ *adj.* **1** lacking in variety; tedious through sameness. **2** (of a sound or utterance) without variation in tone or pitch. □□ **mo·not·o·nous·ly** *adv.*

mo·not·o·ny /mənót'nee/ *n.* **1** the state of being monotonous. **2** dull or tedious routine.

mon·o·treme /mónətreem/ *n.* any mammal of the order Monotremata, native to Australia and New Guinea, including the duckbill and spiny anteater, laying large yolky eggs through a common opening for urine, feces, etc. ▷ MAMMAL

mon·o·type /mónətīp/ *n.* **1** (**Mono·type**) *Printing Trademark* a typesetting machine that casts and sets up types in individual characters. **2** an impression on paper made from an inked design painted on glass or metal.

mon·o·va·lent /mónəváylənt/ *adj.* *Chem.* having a valence of one; univalent. □□ **mon·o·va·lence** /-ləns/ *n.* **mon·o·va·len·cy** *n.*

mon·ox·ide /mənóksīd/ *n.* *Chem.* an oxide containing one oxygen atom (*carbon monoxide*).

Mon·roe doc·trine /munrō/ *n.* the US policy of objecting to intervention by European powers in the affairs of the Western Hemisphere.

Mon·sei·gneur /máwⁿsenyór/ *n.* (*pl.* **Messeigneurs** /mésenyór/) a title given to an eminent French person, esp. a prince, cardinal, archbishop, or bishop.

Mon·sieur /məsyó/ *n.* (*pl.* **Messieurs** /mesyó/) **1** the title or form of address used of or to a French-speaking man, corresponding to Mr. or sir. **2** a Frenchman.

Mon·si·gnor /monseényər/ *n.* (*pl.* **Monsignors** or **Monsignori** /-nyáwree/) the title of various Roman Catholic prelates, officers of the papal court, etc.

mon·soon /monsoon, món-/ *n.* **1** a wind in S. Asia, esp. in the Indian Ocean, blowing from the southwest in summer (**wet monsoon**) and the northeast in winter (**dry monsoon**). **2** a rainy season accompanying a wet monsoon. **3** any other wind with periodic alternations.

mons pubis /monz pyóobis/ *n.* a rounded mass of fatty tissue lying over the joint of the pubic bones.

mon·ster /mónstər/ *n.* **1** an imaginary creature, usu. large and frightening, combining both human and animal features, such as a centaur. **2** an inhumanly cruel or wicked person. **3** a misshapen animal or plant. **4** a large hideous animal or thing (e.g., a building). **5** (*attrib.*) huge; extremely large of its kind.

mon·strance /mónstrəns/ *n.* *RC Ch.* a vessel in which the consecrated Host is displayed for veneration.

mon·stros·i·ty /monstrósitee/ *n.* (*pl.* **-ies**) **1** a huge or outrageous thing. **2** monstrousness. **3** = MONSTER 3.

mon·strous /mónstrəs/ *adj.* **1** like a monster; abnormally formed. **2** huge. **3 a** outrageously wrong or absurd. **b** atrocious. □□ **mon·strous·ly** *adv.* **mon·strous·ness** *n.*

Mont. *abbr.* Montana.

mon·tage /montáazh, mawⁿ-/ *n.* **1 a** a process of selecting, editing, and piecing together separate sections of movie or television film to form a continuous whole. **b** a sequence of such film as a section of a longer film. **2 a** the technique of producing a new composite whole from fragments of pictures, words, music, etc. **b** a composition produced in this way.

mon·tane /móntayn/ *adj.* of or inhabiting mountainous country.

month /munth/ *n.* **1** (in full **calendar month**) **a** each of usu. twelve periods into which a year is divided. **b** a period of time between the same dates in successive calendar months. **2** a period of 28 days or of four weeks. **3** = LUNAR MONTH.

month·ly /múnthlee/ *adj., adv., & n.* ● *adj.* done, produced, or occurring once a month. ● *adv.* once a month; from month to month. ● *n.* (*pl.* **-ies**) **1** a monthly periodical. **2** (in *pl.*) *colloq.* a menstrual period.

month of Sun·days *n.* a very long period.

mon·u·ment /mónyəmənt/ *n.* **1** anything enduring that serves to commemorate or make celebrated, esp. a structure or building. **2** a stone or other structure placed over a grave or in a church, etc., in memory of the dead. **3** an ancient building or site, etc., or been preserved. **4** (foll. by *of, to*) a typical or outstanding example (*a monument of indiscretion*). **5** a written record.

mon·u·men·tal /mónyəmént'l/ *adj.* **1 a** extremely great; stupendous (*a monumental achievement*). **b** (of a literary work) massive and permanent. **2** of or serving as a monument. **3** *colloq.* (as an intensifier) very great; calamitous (*a monumental blunder*). □□ **mon·u·men·tal·i·ty** /-tálitee/ *n.* **mon·u·men·tal·ly** *adv.*

MOON

The Moon is a natural satellite of the Earth and takes 27.3 days to travel around its orbit. Since the Moon takes the same time to rotate on its own axis, the surface seen from the Earth is always the same. The amount of the surface visible, however, varies according to how much of it is in sunlight; this produces the familiar lunar phases. The Moon is barren, with no atmosphere or liquid water, but polar craters are believed to contain small quantities of ice. Its dusty surface has been cratered by meteorites; some of the larger craters have filled with lava to form dark areas known as maria or mares (seas).

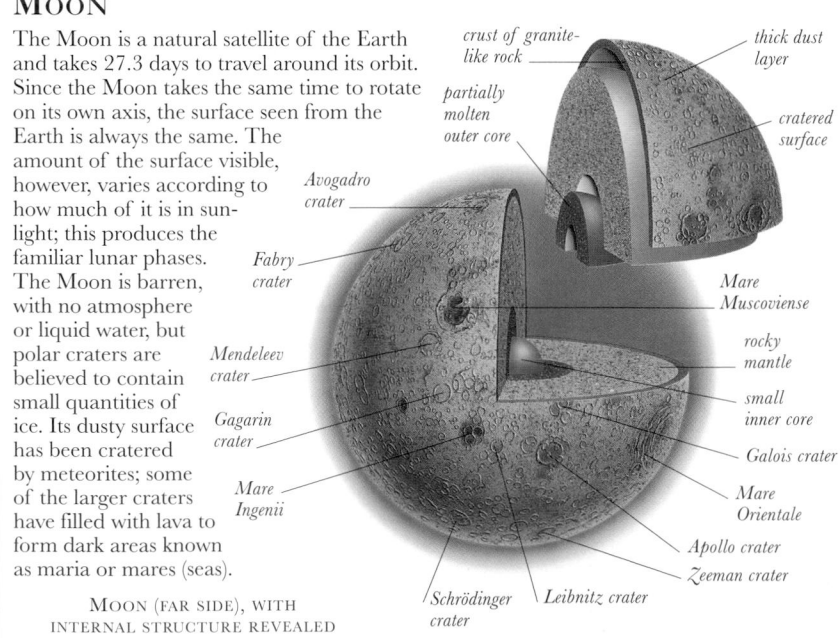

crust of granite-like rock · thick dust layer · partially molten outer core · cratered surface · Avogadro crater · Fabry crater · Mare Muscoviense · rocky mantle · Mendeleev crater · small inner core · Gagarin crater · Galois crater · Mare Ingenii · Mare Orientale · Apollo crater · Zeeman crater · Schrödinger crater · Leibnitz crater

MOON (FAR SIDE), WITH
INTERNAL STRUCTURE REVEALED

M

mon·u·men·tal·ize /mónyəmént'līz/ *v.tr.* commemorate by or as by a monument.

-mony /mōnee/ *suffix* forming nouns, esp. denoting an abstract state or quality (*acrimony; testimony*).

moo /mōō/ *v.* & *v.intr.* (**moos, mooed**) make the characteristic vocal sound of cattle. ● *n.* (*pl.* **moos**) this sound.

mooch /mōōch/ *v. colloq.* **1** borrow (an item, service, etc.) with no intention of making repayment. **2** beg. **3** steal. **4** sneak around; skulk. **5** *intr.* loiter or saunter desultorily. □□ **mooch·er** *n.*

mood[1] /mōōd/ *n.* **1** a state of mind or feeling. **2** (in *pl.*) fits of melancholy or bad temper. **3** (*attrib.*) inducing a particular mood (*mood music*). □ **in the** (or **no**) **mood** (foll. by *for*, or *to* + infin.) inclined (or disinclined) (*was in no mood to agree*).

mood[2] /mōōd/ *n.* **1** *Gram.* a form or set of forms of a verb serving to indicate whether it is to express fact, command, wish, etc. (*subjunctive mood*). **2** the distinction of meaning expressed by different moods.

mood·swing /mōōdswing/ *n.* a marked change in temperament, as from euphoria to depression.

mood·y /mōōdee/ *adj.* & *n.* ● *adj.* (**moodier, moodiest**) given to changes of mood; gloomy, sullen. ● *n. colloq.* a bad mood; a tantrum. □□ **mood·i·ly** *adv.* **mood·i·ness** *n.*

moon /mōōn/ *n.* & *v.* ● *n.* **1** (also **Moon**) a ◄ the natural satellite of the Earth, orbiting it monthly, illuminated by the Sun and reflecting some light to the Earth. ▷ ECLIPSE. **b** this regarded in terms of its waxing and waning in a particular month (*new Moon*). ▷ LUNAR MONTH. **c** the Moon when visible (*there is no moon tonight*). **2** a satellite of any planet. **3** (prec. by *the*) something desirable but unattainable (*promised them the moon*). **4** *poet.* a month. ● *v.* **1** *intr.* (often foll. by *about, around*, etc.) move or look listlessly. **2** *tr.* (foll. by *away*) spend (time) in a listless manner. **3** *intr.* (foll. by *over*) act aimlessly or inattentively from infatuation for (a person). **4** *tr. sl.* expose one's naked buttocks publicly as a joke, sign of disrespect, etc. □□ **moon·less** *adj.*

moon·beam /mōōnbeem/ *n.* a ray of moonlight.

moon-faced *adj.* having a round face.

moon·light /mōōnlīt/ *n.* & *v.* ● *n.* **1** the light of the Moon. **2** (*attrib.*) lighted by the Moon. ● *v.intr.* (**lighted**) *colloq.* have two paid occupations, esp. one by day and one by night. □□ **moon·light·er** *n.*

moon·lit /mōōnlit/ *adj.* lighted by the Moon.

moon·scape /mōōnskayp/ *n.* **1** the surface or landscape of the Moon. **2** an area resembling this; a wasteland.

moon·set /mōōnset/ *n.* **1** the setting of the Moon. **2** the time of this.

moon·shine /mōōnshīn/ *n.* **1** foolish or unrealistic talk or ideas. **2** *sl.* illicitly distilled or smuggled alcoholic liquor. **3** moonlight.

moon·shin·er /mōōnshīnər/ *n. sl.* an illicit distiller or smuggler of alcoholic liquor.

moon·shot /mōōnshot/ *n.* the launching of a spacecraft to the Moon.

moon·stone /mōōnstōn/ *n.* ► minerals in the Earth's crust of pearly appearance.

moon·struck /mōōnstruk/ *adj.* **1** mentally deranged. **2** romantically distracted.

moon·walk /mōōnwawk/ *v.intr.* move or dance in a way reminiscent of the weightless movement of walking on the moon.

moon·y /mōōnee/ *adj.* (**moonier, mooniest**) **1** listless; stupidly dreamy. **2** of or like the Moon.

Moor /mōōr/ *n.* a member of a Muslim people of mixed Berber and Arab descent, inhabiting NW Africa.

moor[1] /mōōr/ *n.* **1** a tract of open uncultivated upland, esp. when covered with heather. **2** a tract of ground preserved for shooting. **3** a marsh. □□ **moor·ish** *adj.* **moor·y** *adj.*

moor[2] /mōōr/ *v.* **1** *tr.* make fast (a boat, buoy, etc.) by attaching a cable, etc., to a fixed object. **2** *intr.* (of a boat) be moored. □□ **moor·age** *n.*

moor·hen /mōōrhen/ *n.* = GALLINULE 1.

moor·ing /mōōring/ *n.* **1 a** a fixed object to which a boat, buoy, etc., is moored. **b** (often in *pl.*) a place where a boat, etc., is moored. **2** (in *pl.*) a set of permanent anchors and chains laid down for ships to be moored to.

Moorish *adj.* ▼ of or relating to the Moors.

MOORISH PALACE
(THE ALHAMBRA, SPAIN)

moor·land /mōōrlənd/ *n.* an extensive area of moor.

moose /mōōs/ *n.* (*pl.* same) ► largest variety of N. American deer.

moot /mōōt/ *adj., v.,* & *n.* ● *adj.* (orig. the noun used *attrib.*) **1** debatable, undecided (*a moot point*). **2** *Law* having no practical significance. ● *v.tr.* raise (a question) for discussion. ● *n.* **1** *hist.* an assembly. **2** *Law* a discussion of a hypothetical case as an academic exercise.

mop /mop/ *n.* & *v.* ● *n.* **1** a wad or bundle of cotton or synthetic material fastened to the end of a stick, for cleaning floors, etc. **2** a similarly shaped implement for various purposes. **3** anything resembling a mop, esp. a thick mass of hair. **4** an act of mopping or being mopped (*gave it a mop*). ● *v.tr.* (**mopped, mopping**) **1** wipe or clean with or as with a mop. **2 a** wipe tears or sweat, etc., from (one's face or brow, etc.). **b** wipe away (tears, etc.). □ **mop up 1** wipe up with or as with a mop. **2** *colloq.* absorb (profits, etc.). **3** dispatch; make an end of. **4** *Mil.* **a** complete the occupation of (a district, etc.) by capturing or killing enemy troops left there. **b** capture or kill (stragglers).

mope /mōp/ *v.intr.* be gloomily depressed or listless; behave sulkily. □□ **mopy** *adj.* (**mopier, mopiest**)

mo·ped /mōped/ *n.* a low-power, lightweight motorized bicycle with pedals.

mop·head /mophed/ *n.* a person with thick matted hair.

mop·pet /mópit/ *n. colloq.* (esp. as a term of endearment) a baby or small child.

mo·quette /mōkét/ *n.* a thick pile or looped material used for carpets and upholstery.

mo·raine /məráyn/ *n.* an area covered by rocks and debris carried down and deposited by a glacier. ▷ GLACIER. □□ **mo·rain·ic** *adj.*

mor·al /máwrəl, mór-/ *adj.* & *n.* ● *adj.* **1 a** concerned with goodness or badness of human character or behavior, or with the distinction between right and wrong. **b** concerned with accepted rules and standards of human behavior. **2 a** conforming to accept-

ed standards of general conduct. **b** capable of moral action (*man is a moral agent*). **3** (of rights or duties, etc.) founded on moral law. **4 a** concerned with morals or ethics (*moral philosophy*). **b** (of a literary work, etc.) dealing with moral conduct. **5** concerned with or leading to a psychological effect associated with confidence in a right action (*moral courage; moral support; moral victory*). ● *n.* **1 a** a moral lesson of a fable, story, event, etc. **b** a moral maxim or principle. **2** (in *pl.*) moral behavior. □□ **mor·al·ly** *adv.*

mo·rale /mərál/ *n.* the mental attitude or bearing of a person or group, esp. as regards confidence, discipline, etc.

mor·al·ism /máwrəlizəm, mór-/ *n.* **1** a natural system of morality. **2** religion regarded as moral practice.

mor·al·ist /máwrəlist, mór-/ *n.* **1** a person who practices or teaches morality. **2** a person who follows a natural system of ethics. □□ **mor·al·is·tic** /-lístik/ *adj.*

mo·ral·i·ty /mərálitee/ *n.* (*pl.* **-ies**) **1** the degree of conformity of an idea, practice, etc., to moral principles. **2** right moral conduct. **3** a lesson in morals. **4** the science of morals. **5** a particular system of morals (*commercial morality*). **6** (in *pl.*) moral principles; points of ethics. **7** (in full **morality play**) *hist.* a kind of drama with personified abstract qualities as the main characters and inculcating a moral lesson, popular in the 16th c.

mor·al·ize /máwrəlīz, mór-/ *v.* **1** *intr.* (often foll. by *on*) indulge in moral reflection or talk. **2** *tr.* interpret morally; point the moral of. **3** *tr.* make moral or more moral. □□ **mor·al·o·i·za·tion** *n.* **mor·al·iz·er** *n.*

mo·rass /mərás/ *n.* **1** an entanglement; a disordered situation, esp. one impeding progress. **2** *literary* a bog or marsh.

mor·a·to·ri·um /máwrətáwreeəm/ *n.* (*pl.* **moratoriums** or **moratoria** /-reeə/) **1** (often foll. by *on*) a temporary prohibition or suspension (of an activity). **2 a** a legal authorization to debtors to postpone payment. **b** the period of this postponement.

Mo·ra·vi·an /məráyveeən/ *n.* & *adj.* ● *n.* **1** a native of Moravia, now part of the Czech Republic. **2** a member of a Protestant sect founded in Saxony by emigrants from Moravia, holding views derived from the Hussites and accepting the Bible as the only source of faith. ● *adj.* of or relating to Moravia or its people.

mo·ray /máwray/ *n.* ▼ any tropical eellike fish of the family Muraenidae, esp. *Muraena helena* found in Mediterranean waters.

MORAY EEL
(*Muraena* species)

mor·bid /máwrbid/ *adj.* **1 a** (of the mind, ideas, etc.) unwholesome. **b** given to morbid feelings. **2** *colloq.* melancholy. **3** *Med.* of the nature of or indicative of disease. □□ **mor·bid·i·ty** /-bíditee/ *n.* **mor·bid·ly** *adv.*

mor·bil·li /mawrbílī/ *n.pl.* **1** measles. **2** the spots characteristic of measles.

mor·dant /máwrd'nt/ *adj.* & *n.* ● *adj.* **1** (of sarcasm, etc.) caustic; biting. **2** pungent; smarting. **3** corrosive; cleansing. **4** (of a substance) serving to fix coloring matter or gold leaf on another substance. ● *n.* a mordant substance (in senses 3 and 4 of *adj.*). □□ **mor·dant·ly** *adv.*

mor·dent /máwrd'nt/ *n. Mus.* an ornament consisting of one rapid alternation of a written note with the note immediately below or above it.

more /mawr/ *adj., n.,* & *adv.* ● *adj.* **1** existing in a greater or additional quantity, amount, or degree

MOONSTONE: CAMEO
BROOCH OF BLUE
MOONSTONE

MOOSE
(*Alces alces*)

M

(*more problems than last time*; *bring some more water*). **2** greater in degree (*more's the pity*; *the more fool you*). ● *n.* a greater quantity, number, or amount (*more than three people*; *see more of it than meets the eye*). ● *adv.* **1** in a greater degree (*do it more carefully*). **2** to a greater extent (*people like to walk more these days*). **3** forming the comparative of adjectives and adverbs, esp. those of more than one syllable (*more absurd*; *more easily*). **4** again (*once more*; *never more*). **5** moreover. □ **more and more** in an increasing degree. **more like it** see LIKE[1]. **more of** to a greater extent (*more of a poet than a musician*). **more or less 1** in a greater or less degree. **2** approximately; as an estimate. **more so** of the same kind to a greater degree.

mo·rel /mərél/ *n.* an edible fungus of the genus *Morchella*, esp. *M. esculenta*, with ridged mushroom caps.

mo·rel·lo /mərélō/ *n.* (*pl.* **-os**) a sour kind of dark cherry.

more·o·ver /máwrṓvər/ *adv.* (introducing or accompanying a new statement) further, besides.

mo·res /máwrayz, -reez/ *n.pl.* customs or conventions regarded as characteristic of a community.

mor·ga·nat·ic /máwrgənátik/ *adj.* **1** (of a marriage) between a person of high rank and another of lower rank, the spouse and children having no claim to the possessions or title of the person of higher rank. **2** (of a wife) married in this way.

morgue /mawrg/ *n.* **1** a mortuary. **2** (in a newspaper office) a room or file of miscellaneous information, esp. for future obituaries.

mor·i·bund /máwribund, mór-/ *adj.* **1** at the point of death. **2** lacking vitality. **3** on the decline, stagnant.

Mor·mon /máwrmən/ *n.* a member of the Church of Jesus Christ of Latter-day Saints, a religion founded in 1830 by Joseph Smith on the basis of revelations in the Book of Mormon. □□ **Mor·mon·ism** *n.*

morn /mawrn/ *n. poet.* morning.

mor·nay /mawrnáy/ *n.* a cheese-flavored white sauce.

morn·ing /máwrning/ *n. & int.* ● *n.* **1** the early part of the day, from sunrise to noon (*this morning*; *during the morning*; *morning coffee*). **2** this time spent in a particular way (*had a busy morning*). **3** sunrise, daybreak. **4** a time compared with the morning, esp. the early part of one's life, etc. ● *int.* = good morning (see GOOD *adj.* 14). □ **in the morning 1** during or in the course of the morning. **2** *colloq.* tomorrow.

morn·ing glo·ry *n.* any of various twining plants of the genus *Ipomoea*, with trumpet-shaped flowers.

morn·ing sick·ness *n.* nausea felt in the morning in pregnancy.

morn·ing star *n.* a planet or bright star, usu. Venus, seen in the east before sunrise.

Mo·roc·can /mərókən/ *n. & adj.* ● *n.* **1** a native or national of Morocco in N. Africa. **2** a person of Moroccan descent. ● *adj.* of or relating to Morocco.

mo·roc·co /mərókō/ *n.* (*pl.* **-os**) **1** a fine flexible leather made from goatskins tanned with sumac. **2** an imitation of this in grained calf, etc.

mo·ron /máwron/ *n.* **1** *colloq.* a very stupid person. **2** an adult with a mental age of about 8–12. □□ **mo·ron·ic** /mərónik/ *adj.* **mo·ron·i·cal·ly** /məróniklee/ *adv.*

mo·rose /mərṓs/ *adj.* sullen and ill-tempered. □□ **mo·rose·ly** *adv.* **mo·rose·ness** *n.*

morph /mawrf/ *v.intr. Cinematog.* change form or appearance, as from person to animal, by computer-controlled special effects.

mor·pheme /máwrfeem/ *n. Linguistics* **1** a morphological element considered in respect of its functional relations in a linguistic system. **2** a meaningful morphological unit of a language that cannot be further divided (e.g., *in*, *come*, *-ing*, forming *incoming*). □□ **mor·phe·mic** /-féemik/ *adj.*

mor·phine /máwrfeen/ *n.* a narcotic drug obtained from opium and used to relieve pain.

morph·ing /máwrfing/ *n. Cinematog.* **1** a computer graphics technique whereby an image is transformed into another by a smooth progression. **2** the act or process of changing an image by this technique.

mor·pho·gen·e·sis /máwrfəjénisis/ *n. Biol.* the development of form in organisms. □□ **mor·pho·ge·net·ic** /-jinétik/ *adj.* **mor·pho·gen·ic** *adj.*

mor·phol·o·gy /mawrfóləjee/ *n.* the study of the forms of things, esp.: **1** *Biol.* the study of the forms of organisms. **2** *Philol.* **a** the study of the forms of words. **b** the system of forms in a language. □□ **mor·pho·log·i·cal** /mawrfəlójikəl/ *adj.* **mor·pho·log·i·cal·ly** /-fəlójiklee/ *adv.* **mor·phol·o·gist** *n.*

mor·ris dance /máwris, mór-/ *n.* a traditional English dance by groups of people in fancy costume, usu. as characters in legend, with ribbons and bells. □□ **mor·ris danc·er** *n.* **mor·ris danc·ing** *n.*

mor·row /máwrō, mór-/ *n.* (usu. prec. by *the*) *literary* **1** the following day. **2** the time following an event.

Morse /mawrs/ *n. & v.* ● *n.* (in full **Morse code**) ▾ a code in which letters are represented by combinations of long and short light or sound signals. ● *v.tr. & intr.* signal by Morse code.

mor·sel /máwrsəl/ *n.* a mouthful; a small piece (esp. of food).

mor·ta·del·la /mawrtədélə/ *n.* (*pl.* **mortadelle** /-déle/) a type of spiced pork sausage.

mor·tal /mawrt'l/ *adj. & n.* ● *adj.* **1 a** subject to death. **b** (of material or earthly existence) temporal, ephemeral. **2** (often foll. by *to*) causing death; fatal. **3** (of a battle) fought to the death. **4** associated with death (*mortal agony*). **5** (of an enemy) implacable. **6** (of pain, fear, an affront, etc.) intense, very serious. **7** *colloq.* **a** very great (*in a mortal hurry*). **b** long and tedious (*for two mortal hours*). **8** *colloq.* conceivable, imaginable (*every mortal thing*; *of no mortal use*). ● *n.* **1** a mortal being, esp. a human. **2** *joc.* a person described in some specified way (*a thirsty mortal*). □□ **mor·tal·ly** *adv.*

mor·tal·i·ty /mawrtálitee/ *n.* (*pl.* **-ies**) **1** the state of being subject to death. **2** loss of life on a large scale.

3 a the number of deaths in a given period, etc. **b** (in full **mortality rate**) a death rate.

mor·tal sin *n. Theol.* a sin that is regarded as depriving the soul of divine grace.

mor·tar /máwrtər/ *n. & v.* ● *n.* **1** a mixture of lime with cement, sand, and water, used in building to bond bricks or stones. **2** a short large-bore cannon for firing shells at high angles. **3** a contrivance for firing a lifeline or firework. **4** a vessel made of hard material, in which ingredients are pounded with a pestle. ▷ PESTLE. ● *v.tr.* **1** plaster or join with mortar. **2** attack or bombard with mortar shells.

mor·tar·board /máwrtərbawrd/ *n.* **1** an academic cap with a stiff, flat square top. **2** a flat board with a handle on the undersurface, for holding mortar in bricklaying, etc.

mort·gage /máwrgij/ *n. & v.* ● *n.* **1 a** a conveyance of property by a debtor to a creditor as security for a debt (esp. one incurred by the purchase of the property). **b** a deed effecting this. **2 a** a debt secured by a mortgage. **b** a loan resulting in such a debt. ● *v.tr.* **1** convey (a property) by mortgage. **2** (often foll. by *to*) pledge (oneself, one's powers, etc.).

mort·ga·gee /máwrgijée/ *n.* the creditor in a mortgage.

mort·ga·gor /máwrgijər/ *n.* (also **mort·ga·ger** /-jər/) the debtor in a mortgage.

mor·tice var. of MORTISE.

mor·ti·cian /mawrtíshən/ *n.* an undertaker.

mor·ti·fy /máwrtifī/ *v.* (**-ies**, **-ied**) **1** *tr.* **a** cause (a person) to feel shamed or humiliated. **b** wound (a person's feelings). **2** *tr.* bring (the body, the flesh, the passions, etc.) into subjection by self-denial or discipline. **3** *intr.* (of flesh) be affected by gangrene or necrosis. □□ **mor·ti·fi·ca·tion** /-fikáyshən/ *n.* **mor·ti·fy·ing** *adj.* **mor·ti·fy·ing·ly** *adv.*

mor·tise /máwrtis/ *n. & v.* (also **mor·tice**) ● *n.* **1** a hole in a framework designed to receive the end of another part, esp. a tenon. ● *v.tr.* **1** join securely, esp. by mortise and tenon. ▷ DOVETAIL. **2** cut a mortise in.

mor·tise lock *n.* ▾ a lock recessed into the frame of a door or window etc.

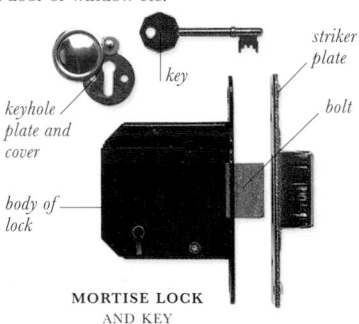

striker plate
key
keyhole plate and cover
bolt
body of lock

MORTISE LOCK
AND KEY

mor·tu·ar·y /máwrchōo-eree/ *n. & adj.* ● *n.* (*pl.* **-ies**) a room or building in which dead bodies may be kept until burial or cremation. ● *adj.* of or concerning death or burial.

Mo·sa·ic /mōzáyik/ *adj.* of or associated with Moses.

mo·sa·ic /mōzáyik/ *n. & v.* ● *n.* **1 a** a picture or pattern produced by an arrangement of small variously colored pieces of glass or stone, etc. **b** work of this kind as an art form. **2** a diversified thing. **3** an arrangement of photosensitive elements in a television camera. **4** (in full **mosaic disease**) a virus disease causing leaf-mottling in plants. **5** (*attrib.*) **a** of or like a mosaic. **b** diversified. ● *v.tr.* (**mosaicked**, **mosaicking**) **1** adorn with mosaics. **2** combine into or as into a mosaic. □□ **mo·sa·i·cist** /-záyisist/ *n.*

mo·sa·saur·us /mṓsəsáwrəs/ *n.* any large extinct marine reptile of the genus *Mosasaurus*, with a long slender body and flipperlike limbs.

Mo·selle /mōzél/ *n.* a light medium-dry white wine produced in the valley of the Moselle River in Germany.

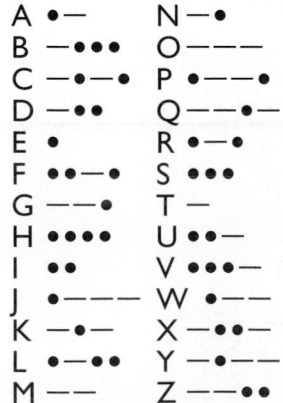

MORSE CODE

Devised by Samuel Morse, the Morse code was an integral part of the telegraph system he developed from 1832 onwards. Operators encoded a message by tapping a key to turn the electric current in the telegraph wires on and off. Letters of the alphabet were represented by combinations of dots and dashes, which were sent as long and short pulses of power. The Morse code fell out of use in the 1940s.

A	● ▬	N	▬ ●
B	▬ ● ● ●	O	▬ ▬ ▬
C	▬ ● ▬ ●	P	● ▬ ▬ ●
D	▬ ● ●	Q	▬ ▬ ● ▬
E	●	R	● ▬ ●
F	● ● ▬ ●	S	● ● ●
G	▬ ▬ ●	T	▬
H	● ● ● ●	U	● ● ▬
I	● ●	V	● ● ● ▬
J	● ▬ ▬ ▬	W	● ▬ ▬
K	▬ ● ▬	X	▬ ● ● ▬
L	● ▬ ● ●	Y	▬ ● ▬ ▬
M	▬ ▬	Z	▬ ▬ ● ●

THE ALPHABET IN MORSE CODE

mo·sey /mõzee/ *v.intr.* (**-eys**, **-eyed**) (often foll. by *along*) *sl.* walk in a leisurely manner.

Mos·lem var. of MUSLIM.

mosque /mosk/ *n.* ▼ a Muslim place of worship.

minaret

central dome

MOSQUE: THE BLUE MOSQUE, ISTANBUL, TURKEY

mos·qui·to /məskeétō/ *n.* (*pl.* **-oes** or **-os**) ► any of various slender biting insects, esp. of the genus *Culex*, *Anopheles*, or *Aedes*, the female of which punctures the skin of humans and other animal with a long proboscis to suck their blood and transmits diseases such as filariasis and malaria.

piercing stylet

MOSQUITO SUCKING BLOOD

moss /maws/ *n. & v.* ● *n.* any small cryptogamous plant of the class Musci, growing in dense clusters on the surface of the ground, in bogs, on trees, stones, etc. ▷ BRYOPHYTE. ● *v.tr.* cover with moss.

moss·y /máwsee/ *adj.* (**mossier**, **mossiest**) **1** covered in or resembling moss. **2** *sl.* antiquated, old-fashioned.

most /mōst/ *adj., n., & adv.* ● *adj.* **1** existing in the greatest quantity or degree (*see who can make the most noise*). **2** the majority of; nearly all of (*most people think so*). ● *n.* **1** the greatest quantity or number (*this is the most I can do*). **2** (**the most**) *sl.* the best of all. **3** the majority (*most of them are missing*). ● *adv.* **1** in the highest degree (*this is most interesting*; *what most annoys me*). **2** forming the superlative of adjectives and adverbs, esp. those of more than one syllable (*most certain*; *most easily*). **3** *colloq.* almost. □ **at most** no more or better than (*this is at most a makeshift*). **at the most 1** as the greatest amount. **2** not more than. **for the most part 1** as regards the greater part. **2** usually. **make the most of 1** employ to the best advantage. **2** represent at its best or worst.

-most /mōst/ *suffix* forming superlative adjectives and adverbs from prepositions and other words indicating relative position (*foremost*; *uttermost*).

most·ly /mõstlee/ *adv.* **1** as regards the greater part. **2** usually.

mot /mō/ *n.* (*pl.* **mots** *pronunc.* same) a witty saying.

mote /mōt/ *n.* a speck of dust.

mo·tel /mōtél/ *n.* a roadside hotel for motorists.

mo·tet /mōtét/ *n. Mus.* a short sacred choral composition.

moth /mawth, moth-/ *n.* **1** ► any usu. nocturnal insect of the order Lepidoptera excluding butterflies, having a stout body and without clubbed antennae. **2** any small lepidopterous insect of the family Tineidae breeding in cloth, etc., on which its larva feeds.

moth·ball /máwthbawl, móth-/ *n. & v.* ● *n.* a ball of naphthalene, etc., placed in stored clothes to keep away moths. ● *v.tr.* place in mothballs. □ **in mothballs** stored unused for a considerable time.

moth-eat·en *adj.* **1** damaged by moths. **2** timeworn.

moth·er /múthər/ *n. & v.* ● *n.* **1 a** a woman in relation to a child to whom she has given birth. **b** (in full **adoptive mother**) a woman who has continuous care of a child, esp. by adoption. **2** any female animal in relation to its offspring. **3** a quality or condition, etc., that gives rise to another (*necessity is the mother of invention*). **4** (in full **Mother Superior**) the head of a female religious community. **5** (*attrib.*) **a** designating an institution, etc., regarded as having maternal authority (*Mother Church*; *mother earth*). **b** designating the main ship, spacecraft, etc., in a convoy or mission (*the mother craft*). ● *v.tr.* **1** give birth to; be the mother of. **2** protect as a mother. **3** give rise to; be the source of. **4** acknowledge or profess oneself the mother of. □□ **moth·er·hood** /-hŏŏd/ *n.* **moth·er·less** *adj.*

moth·er·board /múthərbawrd/ *n.* a computer's main circuit board, into which other boards can be plugged or wired.

moth·er coun·try *n.* a country in relation to its colonies.

moth·er fig·ure *n.* an older woman who is regarded as a source of nurture, support, etc.

Moth·er Goose *n.* the fictitious author of a collection of nursery rhymes published in 1781.

moth·er-in-law *n.* (*pl.* **mothers-in-law**) the mother of one's husband or wife.

moth·er·land /múthərland/ *n.* one's native country.

moth·er lode *n. Mining* the main vein of a system.

moth·er·ly /múthərlee/ *adj.* **1** like or characteristic of a mother in affection, care, etc. **2** of or relating to a mother. □□ **moth·er·li·ness** *n.*

moth·er-of-pearl *n.* a smooth iridescent substance forming the inner layer of the shell of some mollusks. ▷ PEARL

Moth·er's Day *n.* the second Sunday in May, traditionally a day for honoring mothers.

moth·er's son *n. colloq.* a man (*every mother's son of you*).

Moth·er Su·pe·ri·or see MOTHER *n.* 4.

moth·er tongue *n.* **1** one's native language. **2** a language from which others have evolved.

moth·er wit *n.* native wit; common sense.

M

MOTH

The order Lepidoptera comprises at least 150,000 species of moth and 20,000 butterfly species. Although most moths are drab, some are brilliantly colored. They vary greatly in size, ranging in wingspan from $\frac{1}{12}$ to 12 in. (2 mm to 30 cm). Moths can often be distinguished by their feathered antennae, which lack the clubbed tips of butterflies' antennae. Most moths have a wing-coupling device consisting of bristles on the base of the hindwing that engage with a flap on the forewing.

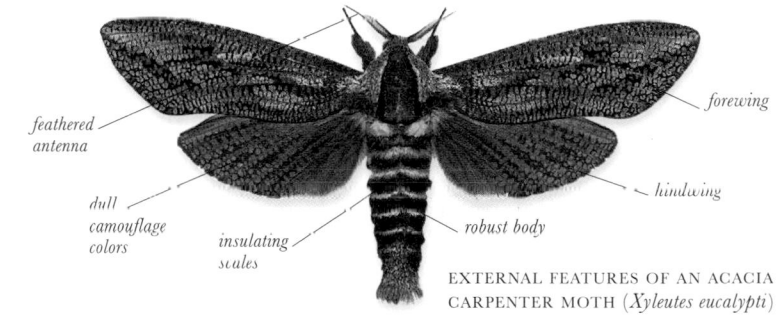

feathered antenna

forewing

dull camouflage colors

hindwing

insulating scales

robust body

EXTERNAL FEATURES OF AN ACACIA CARPENTER MOTH (*Xyleutes eucalypti*)

EXAMPLES OF OTHER MOTHS

DEATH'S HEAD HAWKMOTH (*Acherontia atropos*)

MAGPIE MOTH (*Abraxas grossulariata*)

GREAT TIGER MOTH (*Arctia caja*)

SILKWORM MOTH (*Bombyx mori*)

ATLAS MOTH (*Attacus atlas*)

SIX-SPOT BURNET (*Zygaena filipendulae*)

GOLDEN CLEARWING (*Albuna oberthuri*)

PINE EMPEROR (*Nudaurelia cytherea*)

SILVER "Y" MOTH (*Autographa gamma*)

MADAGASCAN SUNSET MOTH (*Chrysiridia madagascariensis*)

BEAUTIFUL TIGER (*Amphicallia bellatrix*)

PUSS MOTH (*Cerura vinula*)

MOTORCYCLE

One of the earliest attempts at creating a motorized bicycle, the Michaeux-Perreaux velocipede, was produced in France in 1869. A similar model was made at the same time by S. H. Roper in America. Both prototypes combined a wooden-framed bicycle and a small steam engine. Modern machines are infinitely more sophisticated, with internal-combustion engines ranging in size from 50 to over 1,000 cc. Designs are tailored to suit a wide range of uses, from competitive racing to touring and everyday use.

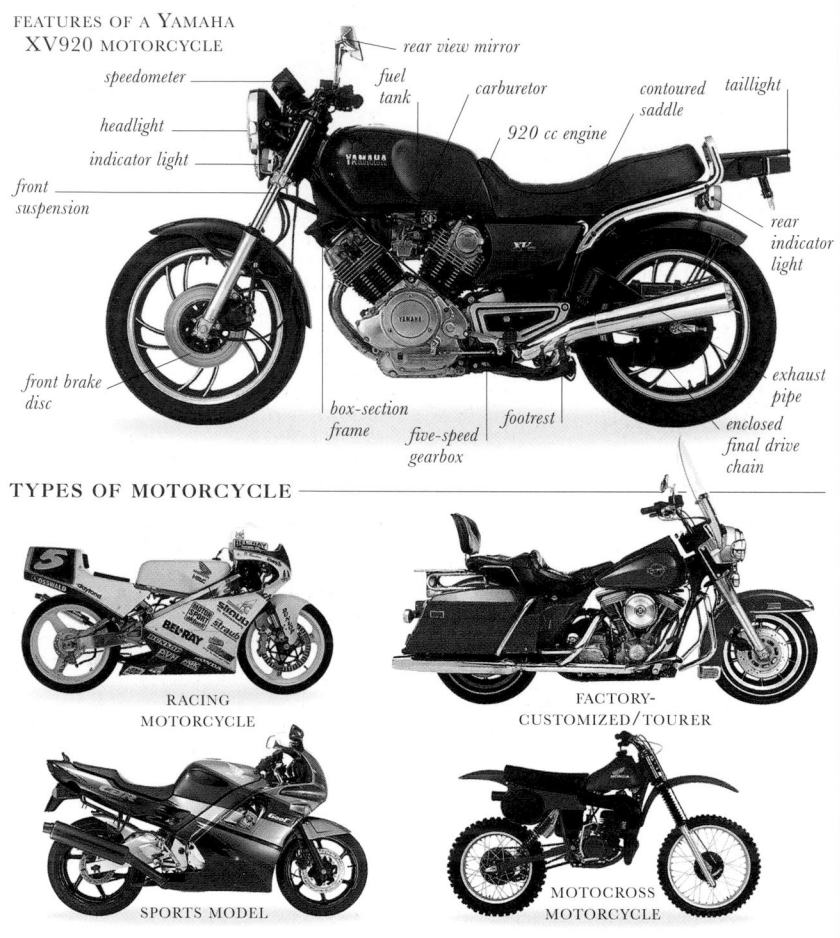

FEATURES OF A YAMAHA XV920 MOTORCYCLE

speedometer
rear view mirror
headlight
fuel tank
carburetor
contoured saddle
taillight
indicator light
920 cc engine
front suspension
rear indicator light
front brake disc
box-section frame
five-speed gearbox
footrest
exhaust pipe
enclosed final drive chain

TYPES OF MOTORCYCLE

RACING MOTORCYCLE

FACTORY-CUSTOMIZED/TOURER

SPORTS MODEL

MOTOCROSS MOTORCYCLE

M

---

moth·proof /máwthprōōf, móth-/ *adj. & v.* ● *adj.* (of clothes) treated so as to repel moths. ● *v.tr.* treat (clothes) in this way.

mo·tif /mōteéf/ *n.* **1** a distinctive feature or dominant idea in artistic or literary composition. **2** *Mus.* = FIGURE *n.* 10. **3** an ornament of lace, etc., sewn separately on a garment.

mo·tile /mōt'l, -tīl, -til/ *adj. Zool. & Bot.* capable of motion. □□ **mo·til·i·ty** /-tílitee/ *n.*

mo·tion /mṓshən/ *n. & v.* ● *n.* **1** the act or process of moving or of changing position. **2** a particular manner of moving the body in walking, etc. **3** a change of posture. **4** a gesture. **5** a formal proposal put to a committee, legislature, etc. **6** *Law* an application for a rule or order of court. **7** a piece of moving mechanism. ● *v.* (often foll. by *to* + infin.) **1** *tr.* direct (a person) by a sign or gesture. **2** *intr.* (often foll. by *to* a person) make a gesture directing (*motioned to me to leave*). □ **go through the motions 1** do something perfunctorily or superficially. **2** simulate an action by gestures. **in motion** moving; not at rest. **put** (or **set**) **in motion** set going or working. □□ **mo·tion·less** *adj.*

mo·tion pic·ture *n.* (often with hyphen) *attrib.*) a film or movie with the illusion of movement (see FILM *n.* 3).

mo·ti·vate /mṓtivayt/ *v.tr.* **1** supply a motive to; be the motive of. **2** cause (a person) to act in a particular way. **3** stimulate the interest of (a person in an activity). □□ **mo·ti·va·tion** /-váyshən/ *n.* **mo·ti·va·tion·al** /-váyshənəl/ *adj.*

mo·tive /mṓtiv/ *n., adj., & v.* ● *n.* **1** a factor or circumstance that induces a person to act in a particular way. **2** = MOTIF. ● *adj.* **1** tending to initiate movement. **2** concerned with movement. ● *v.tr.* = MOTIVATE. □□ **mo·tive·less** *adj.*

mot·ley /mótlee/ *adj. & n.* ● *adj.* (**motlier, motliest**) **1** diversified in color. **2** of varied character (*a motley crew*). ● *n.* **1** an incongruous mixture. **2** *hist.* the parti-colored costume of a jester.

mo·to·cross /mṓtōkraws, -kros/ *n.* cross-country racing on motorcycles. ▷ MOTORCYCLE

mo·tor /mṓtər/ *n. & adj.* ● *n.* **1** a thing that imparts motion. **2** a machine supplying motive power for a vehicle, etc., or for some other device with moving parts. ● *adj.* **1** giving, imparting, or producing motion. **2** driven by a motor. **3** of or for motor vehicles. **4** *Anat.* relating to muscular movement or the nerves activating it. ▷ PERIPHERAL NERVOUS SYSTEM

mo·tor·bike /mṓtərbīk/ *n.* **1** lightweight motorcyle. **2** motorized bicycle.

mo·tor·boat /mṓtərbōt/ *n. & v.* ● *n.* a motor-driven boat, esp. a recreational boat. ● *v.intr.* travel by motorboat.

mo·tor·cade /mṓtərkayd/ *n.* a procession of motor vehicles.

motor·car /mṓtərkaar/ *n.* esp. *Brit.* see CAR 1.

mo·tor·cy·cle /mṓtərsíkəl/ *n.* ◀ two-wheeled motor-driven road vehicle without pedal propulsion. ▷ OFF-ROAD. □□ **mo·tor·cy·clist** *n.*

mo·tor home *n.* a vehicle built on a truck frame that includes kitchen facilities, beds, etc. (see also TRAILER, MOBILE HOME).

mo·tor·ist /mṓtərist/ *n.* the driver or passenger of an automobile.

mo·tor·ize /mṓtərīz/ *v.tr.* **1** equip (troops, etc.) with motor transport. **2** provide with a motor for motor propulsion. □□ **mo·tor·i·za·tion** *n.*

mo·tor·man /mṓtərmən/ *n.* (*pl.* **-men**) the driver of a subway train, streetcar, etc.

mo·tor·mouth /mṓtərmówth/ *n. sl.* a person who talks incessantly and trivially.

mo·tor neu·ron dis·ease *n.* a progressive disease involving degeneration of the motor neurons and wasting of the muscles.

mo·tor pool *n.* a group of vehicles maintained by a government agency, military installation, etc., for use by personnel as needed.

mo·tor rac·ing *n.* ▶ the racing of motorized vehicles, esp. cars, as a sport.

mo·tor ve·hi·cle *n.* a road vehicle powered by an internal-combustion engine.

mo·tor·way /mṓtərwáy/ *n. Brit.* an expressway.

Mo·town /mṓtown/ *n.* a style of rhythm and blues music, popularized by Motown Records Corp.

motte /mot/ *n.* **1** a mound forming the site of a castle, camp, etc. ▷ BAILEY. **2** *SW US* (also **mott**) clump of trees; grove.

mot·tle /mót'l/ *v. & n.* ● *v.tr.* (esp. as **mottled** *adj.*) mark with spots or smears of color. ● *n.* **1** an irregular arrangement of spots or patches of color. **2** any of these spots or patches.

mot·to /mótō/ *n.* (*pl.* **-oes** or **-os**) **1** a maxim adopted as a rule of conduct. **2** a phrase or sentence accompanying a coat of arms. **3** a sentence inscribed on some object and expressing an appropriate sentiment. **4** quotation prefixed to a book or chapter.

moue /mōō/ *n.* = POUT *n.*

mouf·lon /mōōflon/ *n.* (also **mouf·flon**) a wild mountain sheep, *Ovis musimon*, of S. Europe.

mould *Brit.* var. of MOLD[1], MOLD[2], MOLD[3].

moult *Brit.* var. of MOLT.

mound /mownd/ *n. & v.* ● *n.* **1** a raised mass of earth, stones, or other compacted material. **2** a heap or pile. **3** a hillock. ● *v.tr.* **1** heap up in a mound or mounds. **2** enclose with mounds.

Mound Build·ers /mownd bíldərz/ *n.* prehistoric Native American peoples of the Mississippi River Valley who left behind earthworks and burial mounds.

mount[1] /mownt/ *v. & n.* ● *v.* **1** *tr.* ascend or climb. **2** *tr.* **a** get up on (an animal) to ride it. **b** set (a person) on horseback. **c** provide (a person) with a horse. **d** (as **mounted** *adj.*) serving on horseback (*mounted police*). **3** *tr.* go up or climb on to (a raised surface). **4** *intr.* **a** move upward. **b** (often foll. by *up*) increase, accumulate. **c** (of a feeling) become stronger or more intense (*excitement was mounting*). **d** (of the blood) rise into the cheeks. **5** *tr.* (esp. of a male animal) get on to (a female) to copulate. **6** *tr.* (often foll. by *on*) place (an object) on an elevated support. **7** *tr.* **a** set in or attach to a backing, setting, or other support. **b** attach (a picture, etc.) to a mount or frame. **c** fix (an object for viewing) on a microscope slide. **8** *tr.* **a** arrange (a play, exhibition, etc.) or present for public view or display. **b** take action to initiate (a program, campaign, etc.). **9** *tr.* prepare (specimens) for preservation. **10** *tr.* **a** bring into readiness for operation. **b** raise (guns)

MOTOR RACING

Motor racing involves many different types of four and two-wheeled vehicles competing on specially prepared tracks. Motor racing on four wheels includes Formula One, Indy car racing, rally driving, drag racing, and karting. In Formula One racing, drivers compete for points in a series of Grand Prix races on closed-circuit tracks around the world. Indy cars are similar to Formula One models, but racing takes place on large oval tracks and twisting road circuits – mainly in the United States.

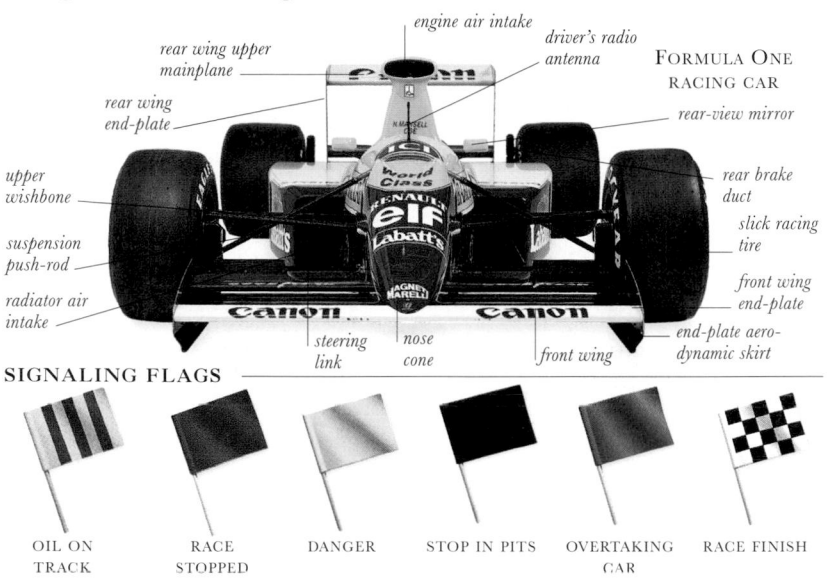

FORMULA ONE
RACING CAR

- rear wing upper mainplane
- engine air intake
- driver's radio antenna
- rear wing end-plate
- rear-view mirror
- upper wishbone
- rear brake duct
- suspension push-rod
- slick racing tire
- radiator air intake
- front wing end-plate
- steering link
- nose cone
- front wing
- end-plate aerodynamic skirt

SIGNALING FLAGS

| OIL ON TRACK | RACE STOPPED | DANGER | STOP IN PITS | OVERTAKING CAR | RACE FINISH |

into position on a fixed mounting. **11** *intr.* rise to a higher level of rank, power, etc. ● *n.* **1** a backing or setting on which a picture, etc., is set for display. **2** the margin surrounding a picture or photograph. **3 a** a horse available for riding. **b** an opportunity to ride a horse, esp. as a jockey. □□ **mount·a·ble** *adj.* **mount²** /mownt/ *n. archaic* (except before a name) mountain, hill (*Mount Everest; Mount of Olives*).

moun·tain /mównt'n/ *n.* **1** ▼ a large natural elevation of the Earth's surface rising abruptly from the surrounding level; a large or high and steep hill. **2** a large heap or pile; a huge quantity (*a mountain of work*). **3** a large surplus stock (*butter mountain*). □ **make a mountain out of a molehill** see MOLEHILL. **move mountains 1** achieve spectacular results. **2** make every possible effort.

moun·tain ash *n.* ▶ a tree, *Sorbus aucuparia*, with delicate pinnate leaves and scarlet berries. **2** any of several Australian eucalypts.

moun·tain bike *n.* a bicycle with a light sturdy frame, broad deep-treaded tires, and multiple gears, originally designed for riding on mountainous terrain. ▷ BICYCLE

MOUNTAIN ASH
(*Sorbus aucuparia*)

moun·tain·eer /mównt'neér/ *n. & v.* ● *n.* **1** a person skilled in mountain climbing. **2** a person living in an area of high mountains. ● *v.intr.* climb mountains as a sport. □□ **moun·tain·eer·ing** *n.*

moun·tain goat *n.* ▶ a white goatlike animal, *Oreamnos americanus*, of the Rocky Mountains, etc.

moun·tain li·on *n.* a puma.

moun·tain·ous /mównt'nəs/ *adj.* **1** having many mountains. **2** huge.

moun·tain range *n.* a line of mountains connected by high ground.

moun·tain sick·ness *n.* a sickness caused by the rarefaction of the air at great heights.

MOUNTAIN GOAT:
ROCKY MOUNTAIN GOAT
(*Oreamnos americanus*)

moun·tain·side /mównt'nsīd/ *n.* the slope of a mountain below the summit.

moun·tain time *n.* (also **Moun·tain Stand·ard Time**) the standard time of parts of Canada and the US in or near the Rocky Mountains.

moun·te·bank /mówntibángk/ *n.* **1** a swindler; a charlatan. **2** a clown. **3** *hist.* an itinerant quack appealing to an audience from a platform.

Moun·tie /mówntee/ *n. colloq.* a member of the Royal Canadian Mounted Police.

M

MOUNTAIN

Mountains are formed in three main ways, although each of the processes occurs as a result of the movement of the huge tectonic plates that make up the Earth's crust. Most mountains are folds, formed where plates push together, causing the rock to buckle upwards. A few are volcanoes, which often form along plate boundaries, and are built up by successive eruptions of lava and debris. Others are block mountains, formed when a block of land is uplifted between two faults as a result of compression or tension in the Earth's crust.

MOUNTAIN RANGES OF THE WORLD

- Alaska Range
- Appalachian Mountains
- Alps
- Caucasus
- Ural Mountains
- Tien Shan
- Rocky Mountains
- Himalaya-Karakoram-Hindu Kush
- West Sumatran Javan Range
- Central New Guinea Range
- Guiana Highlands
- Great Dividing Range
- Andes
- Ethiopian Highlands
- Brazilian Highlands
- Adamawa Highlands
- Transantarctic Mountains
- Drakensberg

MAIN MOUNTAIN TYPES

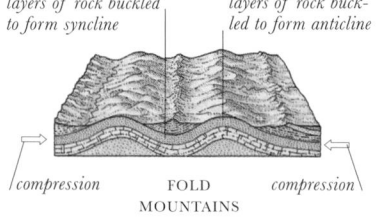

- layers of rock buckled to form syncline
- layers of rock buckled to form anticline
- compression
- FOLD MOUNTAINS
- compression

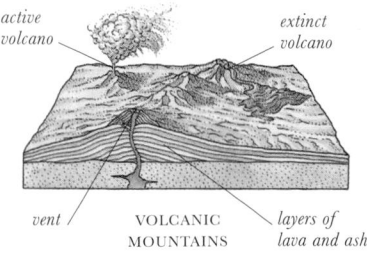

- active volcano
- extinct volcano
- vent
- VOLCANIC MOUNTAINS
- layers of lava and ash

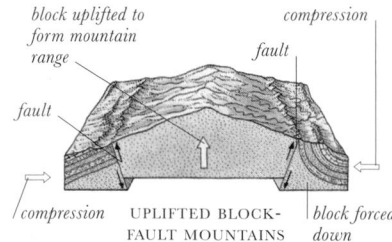

- block uplifted to form mountain range
- compression
- fault
- fault
- compression
- UPLIFTED BLOCK-FAULT MOUNTAINS
- block forced down

M

mourn /mawrn/ v. **1** tr. & (foll. by *for*) intr. feel or show deep sorrow or regret for (a dead person, a past event, etc.). **2** intr. show conventional signs of grief after a person's death.

mourn·er /mawrnər/ n. a person who mourns, esp. at a funeral.

mourn·ful /máwrnfŏŏl/ adj. **1** doleful, sad, sorrowing. **2** expressing or suggestive of mourning. □□ **mourn·ful·ly** adv. **mourn·ful·ness** n.

mourn·ing /mawrning/ n. **1** the expression of deep sorrow, esp. for a dead person, by the wearing of solemn dress. **2** the clothes worn in mourning. □ **in mourning** assuming the signs of mourning, esp. in dress.

mourn·ing dove n. ▶ an American dove with a plaintive note, *Zenaida macroura*.

mouse /mows/ n. & v. ● n. (*pl.* **mice** /mīs/) **1 a** any of various small rodents of the family Muridae, usu. having a pointed snout and relatively large ears and eyes. ▷ RODENT. **b** any of several similar rodents such as a small shrew or vole. **2** a timid or feeble person. **3** *Computing* ▼ a small handheld device that controls the cursor on a computer monitor. ▷ COMPUTER. **4** *sl.* a black eye. ● *v.intr.* (also /mowz/) **1** (esp. of a cat, owl, etc.) hunt for or catch mice. **2** (foll. by *about*) search industriously; prowl about as if searching. □□ **mouse·like** adj. & adv. **mous·er** n.

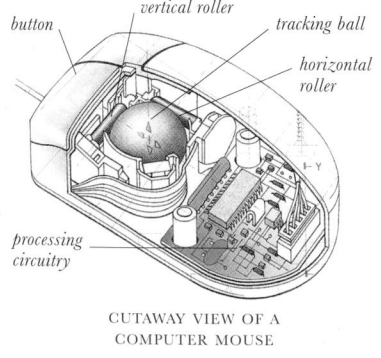

MORNING DOVE
(*Zenaida macroura*)

mouse·trap /mówstrap/ n. a spring trap with bait for catching and usu. killing mice.

mous·sa·ka /mōōsáaka, -saakáa/ n. (also **mou·sa·ka**) a Greek dish of ground meat, eggplant, etc., with a cheese sauce.

mousse /mōōs/ n. **1 a** a dessert of whipped cream, eggs, etc., usu. flavored with fruit or chocolate. **b** a meat or fish purée made with whipped cream, etc. **2** a preparation applied to the hair enabling it to be styled more easily. **3** a mixture of oil and seawater which forms a froth after an oil spill.

mousse·line /mōōsleen/ n. **1** a muslinlike fabric of silk, etc. **2** a sauce lightened by the addition of whipped cream or eggs.

mous·tache var. of MUSTACHE.

MOUSE

A mouse provides a means of pointing to items on a computer screen. The mouse is moved around on a flat surface until the cursor is in the desired position. By clicking a button, a signal is sent to the computer via the processor.

button   *vertical roller*   *tracking ball*

horizontal roller

processing circuitry

CUTAWAY VIEW OF A
COMPUTER MOUSE

mous·y /mówsee/ adj. (**mousier, mousiest**) **1** of or like a mouse. **2** (of a person) shy or timid; ineffectual. **3** of a nondescript shade of light brown, mid brown, or gray. □□ **mous·i·ly** adv. **mous·i·ness** n.

mouth n. & v. ● n. /mowth/ (*pl.* **mouths** /mowthz/) **1 a** an external opening in the head, through which most animals admit food and emit communicative sounds. ▷ DIGESTION. **b** (in humans and some animals) the cavity behind it containing the means of biting and chewing and the vocal organs. **2 a** the opening of a container such as a bag or sack. **b** the opening of a cave, volcano, etc. **c** the open end of a woodwind or brass instrument. **d** the muzzle of a gun. **3** the place where a river enters the sea. ▷ RIVER. **4** *colloq.* **a** talkativeness. **b** impudent talk; cheek. **5** an individual regarded as needing sustenance (*an extra mouth to feed*). ● v. /mowth/ **1** tr. & intr. utter or speak solemnly or with affectations. (*mouthing platitudes*). **2** tr. utter very distinctly. **3** intr. **a** move the lips silently. **b** grimace. **4** tr. take (food) in the mouth. **5** tr. touch with the mouth. **6** tr. train the mouth of (a horse). □ **keep one's mouth shut** *colloq.* not reveal a secret. **put words into a person's mouth** represent a person as having said something in a particular way. **take the words out of a person's mouth** say what another was about to say. □□ **mouthed** /mowthd/ adj. (also in *comb.*).

mouth·breed·er n. ▼ a fish which protects its eggs (and sometimes its young) by carrying them in its mouth.

young fish

MOUTHBREEDER:
BANDED YELLOW MOUTHBREEDER
(*Haplochromis* species)

mouth·ful /mówthfŏŏl/ n. (*pl.* **-fuls**) **1** a quantity, esp. of food, that fills the mouth. **2** a small quantity. **3** a long or complicated word or phrase. **4** *colloq.* something important said.

mouth·guard /mówthgaard/ n. ▶ a pad protecting an athlete's teeth and gums.

mouth or·gan n. = HARMONICA.

mouth·piece /mówthpees/ n. **1 a** the part of a musical instrument placed between or against the lips. ▷ BRASS. **b** the part of a telephone for speaking into. **2** a person who speaks for another or others.

mouth-to-mouth adj. (of resuscitation) in which a person breathes into a subject's lungs through the mouth.

mouth·wash /mówthwosh, -wawsh/ n. a liquid antiseptic, etc., for rinsing the mouth or gargling.

mouth·wa·ter·ing /mówthwawtəring/ adj. **1** (of food, etc.) having a delicious smell or appearance. **2** tempting; alluring.

mouth·y /mówthee/ adj. *colloq.* inclined to talk a lot, esp. in an impudent way.

mov·a·ble /mōōvəbəl/ adj. & n. (also **move·a·ble**) ● adj. **1** that can be moved. **2** *Law* (of property) of the nature of a chattel, as distinct from land or buildings. **3** (of a feast or festival) variable in date from year to year. ● n. **1** an article of furniture that may be removed from a house, as distinct from a fixture. **2** (in *pl.*) personal property. □□ **mov·a·bil·i·ty** /-bílitee/ n. **mov·a·bly** adv.

move /mōōv/ v. & n. ● v. **1** intr. & tr. change one's position or posture, or cause to do this. **2** tr. & intr. put or keep in motion. **3 a** intr. make a move in a board game. **b** tr. change the position of (a piece) in a board game. **4** intr. (often foll. by *about, away*, etc.) go from place to place. **5** intr. take action (*moved to reduce unemployment*). **6** intr. make progress (*the project is moving fast*). **7** intr. **a** change one's place of residence. **b** (of a business, etc.) change to new

premises (also *tr.*: *move offices*). **8** intr. (foll. by *in*) be socially active in (*moves in the best circles*). **9** tr. affect (a person) with emotion. **10** tr. **a** (foll. by *in*) stimulate (laughter, anger, etc., in a person). **b** (foll. by *to*) provoke (a person to laughter, etc.). **11** tr. (foll. by *to*, or *to* + infin.) prompt or incline (a person to a feeling or action). **12 a** tr. cause (the bowels) to be evacuated. **b** intr. (of the bowels) be evacuated. **13** tr. (often foll. by *that* + clause) propose in a meeting, etc. **14** intr. (foll. by *for*) make a formal request or application. **15** intr. (of merchandise) be sold. ● n. **1** the act or an instance of moving. **2** a change of house, business premises, etc. **3** an initiative. **4 a** the changing of the position of a piece in a board game. **b** a player's turn to do this. □ **get a move on** *colloq.* **1** hurry up. **2** make a start. **make a move** take action. **move along** (or **on**) change to a new position, esp. to avoid crowding, etc. **move in 1** take possession of a new house. **2** get into a position of influence, etc. **3** get into a position of readiness or proximity (for an offensive action, etc.). **move out 1** change one's place of residence. **2** leave a position, job, etc. **move over** (or **up**) adjust one's position to make room for another. **on the move 1** proceeding, progressing, advancing. **2** moving about. □□ **mov·er** n.

move·ment /mōōvmənt/ n. **1** the act or an instance of moving or being moved. **2 a** the moving parts of a mechanism (esp. a clock or watch). **b** a particular group of these. **3 a** a body of persons with a common object (*the peace movement*). **b** a campaign undertaken by such a body. **4** (usu. in *pl.*) a person's activities and whereabouts. **5** *Mus.* a principal division of a longer musical work. **6** the progressive development of a poem, story, etc. **7** motion of the bowels. **8 a** an activity in a market for some commodity. **b** a rise or fall in price. **9** a mental impulse. **10** a development of position by a military force or unit. **11** a prevailing tendency in the course of events or conditions; trend.

mov·er /mōōvər/ n. **1** a person or thing that moves. **2** a person or company that moves household goods, etc., from one location to another as a business. **3** the author of a fruitful idea.

mov·ie /mōōvee/ n. esp. *colloq.* **1** a motion picture. **2** (**the movies**) **a** the motion-picture industry or medium. **b** the showing of a movie (*going to the movies*).

mov·ie·dom /mōōveedəm/ n. the movie industry and its associated businesses, personnel, etc.

mov·ie house n. a theater that shows movies.

mov·ing /mōōving/ adj. **1** that moves or causes to move. **2** affecting with emotion. □□ **mov·ing·ly** adv. (in sense 2).

MOUTHGUARD

mov·ing van n. a large van used to move furniture, household goods, etc., from one house to another.

mow /mō/ v.tr. (*past part.* **mowed** or **mown**) **1** cut down (grass, hay, etc.) with a scythe or machine. **2** cut down the produce of (a field) or the grass, etc., of (a lawn) by mowing. □ **mow down** kill or destroy randomly or in great numbers. □□ **mow·er** n.

mox·a /móksə/ n. a downy substance from the dried leaves of *Artemisia moxa*, etc., burned on the skin in Eastern medicine as a counterirritant.

moxie /móksee/ n. *sl.* energy, courage, daring.

moz·za·rel·la /mótsərélə/ n. an Italian semisoft cheese.

MP abbr. **1 a** military police. **b** military policeman. **2** Member of Parliament.

mp abbr. mezzo piano.

m.p. abbr. melting point.

m.p.g. abbr. miles per gallon.

m.p.h. abbr. miles per hour.

MP3 n. a means of compressing a sound sequence into a very small file, used as a way of downloading audio files from the Internet.

Mr. /místər/ n. (*pl.* **Messrs.**) **1** the title of a man without a higher title (*Mr. Jones*). **2** a title prefixed to a designation of office, etc. (*Mr. President*).

MRI

Magnetic resonance imaging (MRI) is a medical diagnostic technique that provides high-quality cross-sectional or three-dimensional images of body structures and organs. During imaging, the patient lies inside a magnetic chamber, which causes the nuclei of hydrogen atoms in the body to line up. A pulse of radio waves is released, throwing the atoms out of alignment. As they realign, the atoms oscillate and resonate. The resonance is detected and analyzed by a computer to create an image.

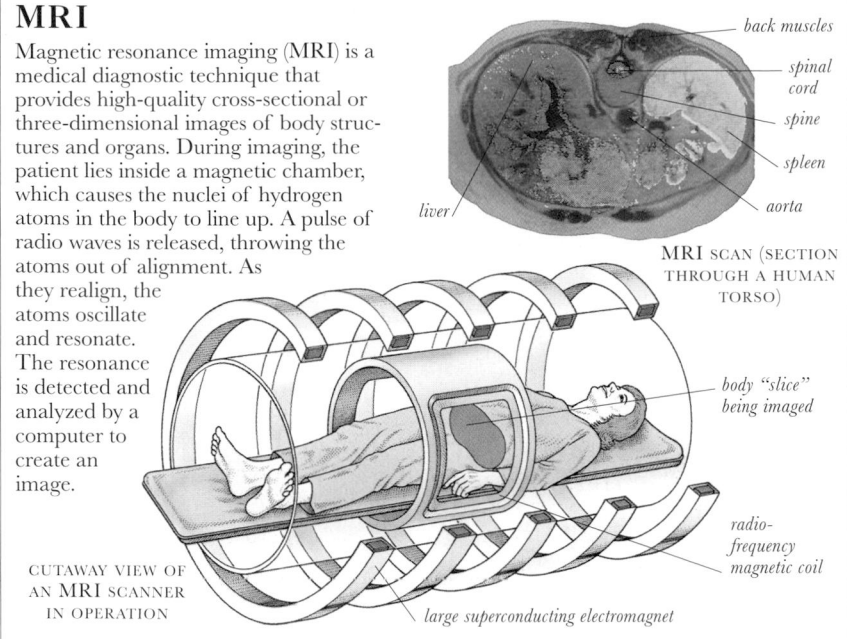

MRI SCAN (SECTION THROUGH A HUMAN TORSO)

back muscles
spinal cord
spine
spleen
aorta
liver

body "slice" being imaged
radio-frequency magnetic coil
large superconducting electromagnet

CUTAWAY VIEW OF AN MRI SCANNER IN OPERATION

MRI *abbr.* ▲ magnetic resonance imaging.

mRNA *abbr. Biol.* messenger RNA.

Mrs. /mísiz/ *n.* (*pl.* same or **Mesdames** /mɔydda̱am, -da̱m/) the title of a married woman without a higher title (*Mrs. Jones*).

MS *abbr.* **1** Mississippi (in official postal use). **2** Master of Science. **3** multiple sclerosis. **4** (also **ms.**) manuscript.

Ms. /miz/ *n.* form of address for a woman, used regardless of marital status.

M.Sc. *abbr.* Master of Science.

MS-DOS /émɛsdáws, -dòs/ *abbr. Trademark* a computer disk operating system developed by Microsoft Corp. for personal computers.

MSG *abbr.* monosodium glutamate.

Msgr. *abbr.* **1** Monseigneur. **2** Monsignor.

MSS *abbr.* (also **mss.**) manuscripts.

MST *abbr.* Mountain Standard Time.

MT *abbr.* **1** Montana (in official postal use). **2** Mountain Time.

Mt. *abbr.* **1** mount. **2** mountain.

MTB *abbr.* **1** *Brit.* motor torpedo boat. **2** mountain bike.

mu /myŏŏ, mŏŏ/ *n.* **1** the twelfth Greek letter (M, μ). **2** (m, as a symbol) = MICRO- 2.

much /much/ *adj., n., & adv.* ● *adj.* **1** existing or occurring in a great quantity (*not much rain*). **2** (prec. by *as, how, that,* etc.) with relative rather than distinctive sense (*I don't know how much money you want*). ● *n.* **1** a great quantity (*much of that is true*). **2** (prec. by *as, how, that,* etc.) with relative rather than distinctive sense (*we do not need that much*). **3** (usu. in *neg.*) a noteworthy or outstanding example (*not much of a party*). ● *adv.* **1 a** in a great degree (*is much the same*). **b** greatly (*they much regret the mistake*). **c** qualifying a comparative or superlative adjective (*much better*). **2** for a large part of one's time (*is much away from home*). □ **as much** the extent or quantity just specified (*I thought as much*). **a bit much** *colloq.* somewhat excessive or immoderate. **much as** even though (*much as I would like to*). **much less** see LESS. **not much** *colloq.* **1** *iron.* very much. **2** certainly not. **too much** *colloq.* an intolerable situation, etc. (*that really is too much*). **too much for 1** more than a match for. **2** beyond what is endurable by. □□ **much·ly** *adv. joc.*

mu·ci·lage /myŏŏsilij/ *n.* **1** a viscous substance obtained from plant seeds, etc., by maceration. **2** a solution of gum, glue, etc. □□ **mu·ci·lag·i·nous** /lájinəs/ *adj.*

muck /muk/ *n. & v.* ● *n.* **1** farmyard manure. **2** *colloq.* dirt or filth, anything disgusting. **3** *colloq.* a mess. ● *v.tr.* **1** (usu. foll. by *up*) *colloq.* bungle (a job). **2** (often foll. by *out*) remove muck from. **3** make dirty or untidy. **4** manure with muck. □ **make a muck of** *colloq.* bungle.

muck·rake /múkrayk/ *v.intr.* search out and reveal scandal, esp. among famous people. □□ **muck·rak·ing** *n.*

muck·y /múkee/ *adj.* (**muckier, muckiest**) **1** covered with muck. **2** dirty.

muco- /myŏŏkō/ *comb. form Biochem.* mucus, mucous.

mu·co·pol·y·sac·cha·ride /myŏŏkōpóleesákərīd/ *n. Biochem.* any of a group of polysaccharides whose molecules contain sugar residues and are often found as components of connective tissue.

mu·co·sa /myŏŏkősə/ *n.* (*pl.* **mucosae** /-see/) a mucous membrane.

mu·cous /myŏŏkəs/ *adj.* pertaining to or covered with mucus.

mu·cous mem·brane *n.* a mucus-secreting epithelial tissue lining many body cavities and tubular organs.

mu·cro /myŏŏkrō/ *n.* (*pl.* **mucrones** /-krőneez/) *Bot. & Zool.* a sharp-pointed part or organ. □□ **mu·cro·nate** /-krənat, -nayt/ *adj.*

mu·cus /myŏŏkəs/ *n.* **1** a slimy substance secreted by a mucous membrane. **2** a gummy substance found in all plants. **3** a slimy substance exuded by some animals, esp. fishes.

mud /mud/ *n.* **1** wet, soft, earthy matter. **2** hard ground from the drying of an area of this. **3** what is worthless or polluting. □ **as clear as mud** *colloq.* not at all clear. **fling** (or **sling** or **throw**) **mud** speak disparagingly or slanderously. **here's mud in your eye!** *colloq.* a drinking toast. **one's name is mud** one is unpopular or in disgrace.

mud bath *n.* **1** a bath in the mud of mineral springs, esp. to relieve rheumatism, etc. **2** a muddy scene or occasion.

mud·dle /múd'l/ *v. & n.* ● *v.* **1** *tr.* (often foll. by *up, together*) bring into disorder. **2** *tr.* bewilder, confuse. **3** *tr.* mismanage (an affair). **4** *tr.* crush and mix (the ingredients for a drink). **5** *intr.* (often foll. by *with*) busy oneself in a confused and ineffective way. ● *n.* **1** disorder. **2** a muddled condition. □ **make a muddle of 1** bring into disorder. **2** bungle. **muddle along** (or **on**) progress in a haphazard way. **muddle through** succeed by perseverance rather than skill or efficiency. **muddle up** confuse (two or more things). □□ **mud·dler** *n.*

mud·dle-head·ed *adj.* stupid, confused. □□ **mud·dle-head·ed·ness** *n.*

mud·dy /múdee/ *adj. & v.* ● *adj.* (**muddier, muddiest**) **1** like mud. **2** covered in or full of mud. **3** (of liquid) turbid. **4** mentally confused. **5** obscure. **6** (of light) dull. **7** (of color) impure. ● *v.tr.* (**-ies, -ied**) make muddy. □□ **mud·di·ly** *adv.*

mud·fish /múdfish/ *n.* any fish that burrows in mud, as the bowfin.

mud·flap /múdflap/ *n.* ▶ a flap hanging behind the wheel of a vehicle, to catch mud and stones, etc., thrown up from the road.

mud flat *n.* a stretch of muddy land left uncovered at low tide.

mud·guard /múdgaard/ *n.* a curved strip or cover over a wheel of a bicycle or motorcycle to reduce the amount of mud, etc., thrown up from the road.

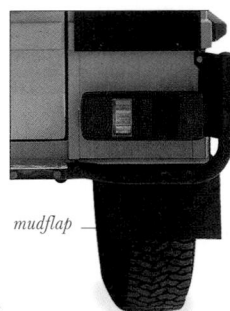

mudflap

MUDFLAP ON AN ALL-TERRAIN VEHICLE

mud pup·py *n.* a large nocturnal salamander, *Necturus maculosus,* of eastern US.

mud·stone /múdstōn/ *n.* a dark clay rock.

mues·li /mŏŏslee, myŏŏz-/ *n.* a breakfast food of crushed cereals, dried fruits, nuts, etc., eaten with milk.

mu·ez·zin /myŏŏ-ézin, mŏŏ-/ *n.* a Muslim crier who proclaims the hours of prayer.

muff[1] /muf/ *n.* a fur or other covering, usu. in the form of a tube with an opening at each end for the hands to be inserted for warmth.

muff[2] /muf/ *v. & n.* ● *v.tr.* **1** bungle. **2** fail to catch or receive (a ball, etc.). **3** blunder in (a theatrical part, etc.). ● *n.* a failure, esp. to catch a ball in baseball, etc.

muf·fin /múfin/ *n.* a small cake or quick bread made from batter or dough and baked in a muffin pan.

muf·fle /múfəl/ *v. & n.* ● *v.tr.* **1** (often foll. by *up*) wrap or cover for warmth. **2** cover or wrap up (a source of sound) to reduce its loudness. **3** (usu. as **muffled** *adj.*) stifle (an utterance). **4** prevent from speaking. ● *n.* **1** a receptacle in a furnace where substances may be heated without contact with combustion products. **2** a similar chamber in a kiln for baking painted pottery.

muf·fler /múflər/ *n.* **1** a wrap or scarf worn for warmth. **2** a noise-reducing device on a motor vehicle's exhaust system. **3** a mute.

muf·ti /múftee/ *n.* plain clothes worn by a person who also wears uniform (*in mufti*).

mug /mug/ *n. & v.* ● *n.* **1 a** a drinking vessel, usu. cylindrical and with a handle and used without a saucer. **b** its contents. **2** *sl.* the face or mouth of a person. **3** *sl.* a hoodlum or thug. ● *v.* (**mugged, mugging**) **1** *tr.* rob (a person) with violence, esp. in a public place. **2** *tr.* fight; thrash. **3** *tr.* strangle. **4** *intr. sl.* make faces, esp. before an audience, a camera, etc. □□ **mug·ger** *n.* (esp. in sense 1 of *v.*). **mug·ging** *n.* (in sense 1 of *v.*).

mug·gy /múgee/ *adj.* (**muggier, muggiest**) (of the weather, a day, etc.) oppressively damp and warm; humid. □□ **mug·gi·ness** *n.*

mug shot *n. sl.* a photograph of a face, esp. for official purposes.

mug·wort /múgwərt, -wawrt/ *n.* any of various plants of the genus *Artemisia,* esp. *A. vulgaris,* with silver-gray aromatic foliage.

M

mug·wump /múgwump/ *n.* **1** a great man; a boss. **2** a person who remains aloof, esp. from party politics.

Mu·ham·mad·an /məhámməd'n/ *n. & adj.* (also **Mo·ham·med·an**) = MUSLIM. ¶ A term not used or favored by Muslims, and often regarded as *offens.* □□ **Mu·ham·mad·an·ism** *n.*

mu·ja·hi·din /moōjaahidéen/ *n.pl.* (also **mu·ja·he·din, -deen**) guerrilla fighters in Islamic countries, esp. supporting Muslim fundamentalism.

muk·luk /múkluk/ *n. N. Amer.* a high, soft sealskin boot worn in the American Arctic.

mu·lat·to /moōláto, -laá-, myoō-/ *n. & adj.* ● *n.* (*pl.* **-oes** or **-os**) a person of mixed black and white parentage. ● *adj.* of the color of mulattoes; tawny.

mul·ber·ry /múlberee, -bəree/ *n.* (*pl.* **-ies**) **1** ▶ any deciduous tree of the genus *Morus*, grown, esp. for feeding silkworms or its fruit. **2** its dark-red or white berry. **3** a dark-red or purple color.

MULBERRY: BLACK MULBERRY (*Morus nigra*)
fruit

mulch /mulch/ *n. & v.* ● *n.* a mixture of straw, leaves, etc., spread around or over a plant to enrich or insulate the soil. ● *v.tr.* treat with mulch.

mulct /mulkt/ *v. & n.* ● *v.tr.* **1** extract money from by fine or taxation. **2 a** (often foll. by *of*) swindle. **b** obtain by swindling. ● *n.* a fine.

mule[1] /myoōl/ *n.* **1** ▶ the offspring of a male donkey and a female horse, or (in general use) of a female donkey and a male horse (cf. HINNY). **2** a stupid or obstinate person. **3** (often *attrib.*) a hybrid and usu. sterile plant or animal (*mule canary*). **4** (in full **spinning mule**) a kind of spinning machine producing yarn on spindles.

mule[2] /myoōl/ *n.* ▼ a light shoe or slipper without a back.

MULE

MULE: 19TH-CENTURY LEATHER MULES

mu·le·teer /myoōliteér/ *n.* a mule driver.

mul·ga /múlgə/ *n. Austral.* **1** a small spreading tree, *Acacia aneura*, which forms dense scrubby growth and yields brown and yellow timber. **2** the wood of this tree. **3** *colloq.* the outback.

mul·ish /myoōlish/ *adj.* **1** like a mule. **2** stubborn. □□ **mul·ish·ly** *adv.* **mul·ish·ness** *n.*

mull[1] /mul/ *v.tr. & intr.* (often foll. by *over*) ponder or consider.

mull[2] /mul/ *v.tr.* warm (wine or beer) with added spices, etc.

mull[3] /mul/ *n.* a thin, soft, plain muslin.

mul·lah /múlə, moōl-/ *n.* a Muslim learned in Islamic theology and sacred law.

mul·lein /múlin/ *n.* ▶ any herbaceous plant of the genus *Verbascum*, with woolly leaves and yellow flowers.

mul·let /múlit/ *n.* any fish of the family Mullidae (**red mullet**) or Mugilidae (**gray mullet**), usu. with a thick body and a large blunt-nosed head, commonly used as a food.

MULLEIN: DARK MULLEIN (*Verbascum nigrum*)

mul·li·ga·taw·ny /múligətáwnee/ *n.* a highly seasoned soup orig. from India.

mul·lion /múlyən/ *n.* (also **mun·nion** /mún-/) a vertical bar dividing the panes in a window (cf. TRANSOM). ▷ WINDOW. □□ **mul·lioned** *adj.*

multi- /múltee, -tī/ *comb. form* many; more than one.

mul·ti·ac·cess /múlteeákses, -tī-/ *n.* (often *attrib.*) the simultaneous connection to a computer of a number of terminals.

mul·ti·cel·lu·lar /múlteesélyələr, -tī-/ *adj. Biol.* having many cells.

mul·ti·chan·nel /múlteechánəl, -tī-/ *adj.* employing or possessing many communication or television channels.

mul·ti·col·or /múltikúlər/ *adj.* (also **mul·ti·col·ored**) of many colors.

mul·ti·cul·tur·al /múlteekúlchərəl/ *adj.* of or relating to or constituting several cultural or ethnic groups within a society. □□ **mul·ti·cul·tur·al·ism** *n.* **mul·ti·cul·tur·al·ly** *adv.*

mul·ti·di·men·sion·al /múlteediménshənəl, -dī-/ *adj.* of or involving more than three dimensions. □□ **mul·ti·di·men·sion·al·i·ty** /-nálitee/ *n.* **mul·ti·di·men·sion·al·ly** *adv.*

mul·ti·di·rec·tion·al /múlteediríkshənəl, -dī-, -tī-/ *adj.* of, involving, or operating in several directions.

mul·ti·fac·et·ed /múlteefásitid, -tī-/ *adj.* having several facets. ▷ FACET

mul·ti·far·i·ous /múltifáireeəs/ *adj.* **1** (foll. by pl. noun) many and various. **2** having great variety. □□ **mul·ti·far·i·ous·ness** *n.*

mul·ti·foil /múltifoyl/ *n. Archit.* an ornament consisting of more than five foils.

mul·ti·form /múltifawrm/ *n.* (usu. *attrib.*) **1** having many forms. **2** of many kinds. □□ **mul·ti·for·mi·ty** /-fáwrmitee/ *n.*

mul·ti·func·tion·al /múlteefúngkshənəl, -tī-/ *adj.* having or fulfilling several functions.

mul·ti·grade /múltigrayd/ *n.* (usu. *attrib.*) an engine oil, etc., meeting the requirements of several standard grades.

mul·ti·gym /múlteejim/ *n.* an apparatus on which a number of exercises can be performed.

mul·ti·lat·er·al /múltilátər-əl/ *adj.* **1 a** (of an agreement, etc.) in which three or more parties participate. **b** per-formed by more than two parties (*multilateral disarmament*). **2** having many sides. □□ **mul·ti·lat·er·al·ly** *adv.*

mul·ti·lin·gual /múlteelínggwəl, -tī-/ *adj.* in or using several languages. □□ **mul·ti·lin·gual·ly** *adv.*

mul·ti·me·di·a /múltiméedeeə/ *adj. & n.* ● *attrib. adj.* involving several media. ● *n.* the combined use of several media, such as film, print, sound, etc.

mul·ti·mil·lion /múlteemílyən, -tī-/ *attrib.adj.* costing or involving several million (dollars, pounds, etc.).

mul·ti·mil·lion·aire /múlteemílyənáir, -tī-/ *n.* a person with a fortune of several millions.

mul·ti·na·tion·al /múlteenáshənəl, -tī-/ *adj. & n.* ● *adj.* **1** (of a business organization) operating in several countries. **2** relating to or including several nationalities. ● *n.* a multinational company. □□ **mul·ti·na·tion·al·ly** *adv.*

mul·ti·par·tite /múltipáartīt/ *adj.* divided into many parts.

mul·ti·ple /múltipəl/ *adj. & n.* ● *adj.* **1** having several or many parts, elements, or individual components. **2** (foll. by pl. noun) many and various. **3** *Bot.* (of fruit) collective. ● *n.* a number that may be divided by another a certain number of times without a remainder (*56 is a multiple of 7*). □□ **mul·ti·ply** *adv.*

mul·ti·ple-choice *n.* (of a question in an examination) accompanied by several possible answers from which the correct one has to be chosen.

mul·ti·plex /múltipleks/ *adj., v., & n.* ● *adj.* **1** manifold; of many elements. **2** involving simultaneous transmission of several messages along a single channel of communication. ● *v.tr.* incorporate into a multiplex signal or system. ● *n.* a building that houses several movie theaters. □□ **mul·ti·plex·er** *n.* (also **mul·ti·plex·or**).

mul·ti·pli·cand /múltiplikánd/ *n.* a quantity to be multiplied by a multiplier.

mul·ti·pli·ca·tion /múltiplikáyshən/ *n.* **1** the arithmetical process of multiplying. **2** the act or an instance of multiplying. □□ **mul·ti·pli·ca·tive** /-plíkətiv/ *adj.*

mul·ti·pli·ca·tion sign *n.* the sign (×) to indicate that one quantity is to be multiplied by another.

mul·ti·pli·ca·tion ta·ble *n.* a list of multiples of a particular number, usu. from 1 to 12.

mul·ti·plic·i·ty /múltiplísitee/ *n.* (*pl.* **-ies**) **1** manifold variety. **2** (foll. by *of*) a great number.

mul·ti·pli·er /múltiplīər/ *n.* a quantity by which a given number is multiplied.

mul·ti·ply /múltiplī/ *v.* (**-ies, -ied**) **1** *tr.* (also *absol.*) obtain from (a number) another that is a specified number of times its value (*multiply 6 by 4 and you get 24*). **2** *intr.* increase in number esp. by procreation. **3** *tr.* produce a large number of (instances, etc.). **4** *tr.* **a** breed (animals). **b** propagate (plants).

mul·ti·po·lar /múltipólər/ *adj.* having many poles (see POLE[2]).

mul·ti·proc·es·sing /múlteeprósesing/ *n. Computing* processing by a number of processors sharing a common memory and common peripherals.

mul·ti·pro·gram·ming /múlteeprógraming/ *n. Computing* the execution of two or more independent programs concurrently.

mul·ti·pur·pose /múlteepárpəs, -tī-/ *n.* (*attrib.*) having several purposes.

mul·ti·ra·cial /múlteeráyshəl, -tī-/ *adj.* relating to or made up of many human races. □□ **mul·ti·ra·cial·ly** *adv.*

mul·ti·sto·ry /múltistáwree/ *n.* (*attrib.*) (of a building) having several stories.

mul·ti·tude /múltitoōd, -tyoōd/ *n.* **1** (often foll. by *of*) a great number. **2** a large gathering of people; a crowd. **3** (**the multitude**) the common people. **4** the state of being numerous.

mul·ti·tu·di·nous /múltitoōd'nəs, -tyoōd-/ *adj.* **1** very numerous. **2** consisting of many individuals or elements. **3** (of an ocean, etc.) vast. □□ **mul·ti·tu·di·nous·ly** *adv.*

mul·ti·us·er /múltiyoōzər/ *n.* (*attrib.*) (of a computer system) having a number of simultaneous users (cf. MULTI-ACCESS).

mul·ti·va·lent /múltiváylənt, multívə-/ *adj. Chem.* **1** having a valence of more than two. **2** having a variable valency. □□ **mul·ti·va·len·cy** *n.*

mul·ti·valve /múltivalv/ *n.* (*attrib.*) (of a shell, etc.) having several valves.

mul·ti·voc·al /multívəkəl/ *adj.* having many meanings.

mum[1] /mum/ *adj. colloq.* silent (*keep mum*). □ **mum's the word** say nothing.

mum[2] /mum/ *n.* = CHRYSANTHEMUM.

mum[3] /mum/ *n. esp. Brit.* = MOM.

mum·ble /múmbəl/ *v. & n.* **1** *intr. & tr.* speak or utter indistinctly. **2** *tr.* bite or chew with or as with toothless gums. ● *n.* an indistinct utterance. □□ **mum·bler** *n.*

mum·bo jum·bo /múmbōjúmbō/ *n.* (*pl.* **jumbos**) **1** meaningless or ignorant ritual. **2** language or action intended to mystify or confuse. **3** an object of senseless veneration.

mum·mer /múmər/ *n.* an actor in a traditional masked mime.

MUMMY

The ancient Egyptians developed a way of preserving the bodies of their dead, in the belief that this would ensure their eternal survival. The liver, lungs, and brain were first removed and stored in special jars. The heart, however, was left in place, so that it could be judged in the afterlife. The body was then covered with natron (a compound of sodium carbonate and sodium bicarbonate) to stop it from decaying, packed with dry material, and wrapped in bandages. Finally, the body was placed in a sarcophagus.

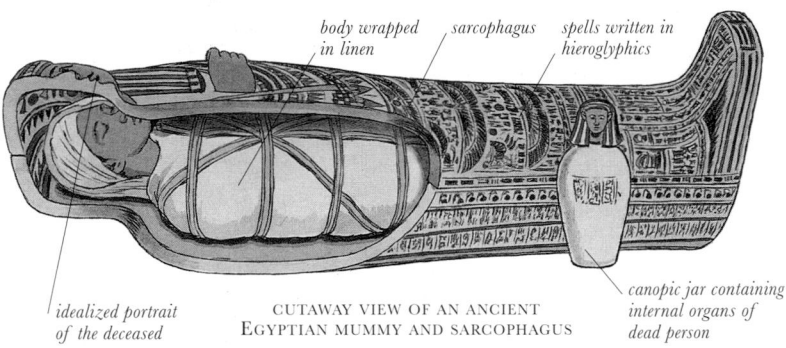

body wrapped in linen   *sarcophagus*   *spells written in hieroglyphics*

idealized portrait of the deceased

canopic jar containing internal organs of dead person

CUTAWAY VIEW OF AN ANCIENT EGYPTIAN MUMMY AND SARCOPHAGUS

mum·mer·y /múmóree/ *n.* (*pl.* **-ies**) **1** ridiculous (esp. religious) ceremonial. **2** a performance by mummers.

mum·mi·fy /múmifī/ *v.tr.* (**-ies**, **-ied**) **1** embalm and preserve (a body) in the form of a mummy (see MUMMY²). **2** (usu. as **mummified** *adj.*) shrivel or dry up (tissues, etc.). □□ **mum·mi·fi·ca·tion** /-fikáyshən/ *n.*

mum·my¹ /múmee/ *n.* (*pl.* **-ies**) esp. *Brit.* = MOMMY.

mum·my² /múmee/ *n.* (*pl.* **-ies**) **1** ▲ a body of a human being or animal embalmed for burial, esp. in ancient Egypt. **2** a dried-up body. **3** a rich brown pigment.

mumps /mumps/ *n.pl.* **1** (treated as *sing.*) a contagious and infectious viral disease with swelling of the parotid salivary glands in the face. **2** *Brit.* a fit of the sulks. □□ **mump·ish** *adj.*

munch /munch/ *v.tr.* eat steadily with a marked action of the jaws.

munch·ies /múncheez/ *n.pl. colloq.* **1** snack foods. **2** the urge to snack.

mun·dane /múndáyn/ *adj.* **1** dull, routine. **2** of this world; worldly. □□ **mun·dane·ly** *adv.* **mun·dan·i·ty** /-dánitee/ *n.* (*pl.* **-ies**).

mung /mung/ *n.* (in full **mung bean**) ◄ a leguminous plant of the genus *Phaseolus*, native to India and yielding a small bean used as food.

MUNG BEANS
(*Phaseolus aureus*)

mu·nic·i·pal /myōōnísipəl/ *adj.* of or concerning a municipality or its self-government. □□ **mu·nic·i·pal·ize** *v.tr.* **mu·nic·i·pal·ly** *adv.*

mu·nic·i·pal bond *n.* a bond issued by a city, county, state, etc., to finance public projects.

mu·nic·i·pal·i·ty /myōōnísipálitee/ *n.* (*pl.* **-ies**) **1** a town or district having local government. **2** the governing body of this area.

mu·nif·i·cent /myōōnífisənt/ *adj.* (of a giver or a gift) splendidly generous, bountiful. □□ **mu·nif·i·cence** *n.* /-səns/ **mu·nif·i·cent·ly** *adv.*

mu·ni·ment /myōōnimənt/ *n.* (usu. in *pl.*) **1** a document kept as evidence of rights or privileges, etc. **2** an archive.

mu·ni·tion /myōōníshən/ *n. & v.* ● *n.* (usu. in *pl.*) military weapons. ● *v.tr.* supply with munitions.

mun·nion var. of MULLION.

munt·jac /múntjak/ *n.* (also **munt·jak**) any small deer of the genus *Muntiacus*, native to SE Asia, the male having tusks and small antlers.

mu·on /myōō-on/ *n. Physics* an unstable elementary particle like an electron, but with a much greater mass.

mu·ral /myōōrəl/ *n. & adj.* ● *n.* ▼ a painting executed directly on a wall. ● *adj.* **1** of or like a wall. **2** on a wall.

MURAL: ANCIENT GREEK MURAL, KNOSSOS

mur·der /mórdər/ *n. & v.* ● *n.* **1** the unlawful premeditated killing of a human being by another (cf. MANSLAUGHTER). **2** *colloq.* an unpleasant, troublesome, or dangerous state of affairs (*it was murder here on Saturday*). ● *v.tr.* **1** kill (a human being) unlawfully, esp. wickedly and inhumanly. **2** *Law* kill (a human being) with a premeditated motive. **3** *colloq.* utterly defeat or spoil by a bad performance, mispronunciation, etc. (*murdered the soliloquy in the second act*). □ **cry bloody murder** *sl.* make an extravagant outcry. **get away with murder** *colloq.* do whatever one wishes and escape punishment. **murder will out** murder cannot remain undetected. □□ **mur·der·er** *n.* **mur·der·ess** *n.*

mur·der·ous /mórdərəs/ *adj.* **1** (of a person, weapon, action, etc.) capable of, intending, or involving murder or great harm. **2** *colloq.* extremely troublesome, unpleasant, or dangerous. □□ **mur·der·ous·ly** *adv.* **mur·der·ous·ness** *n.*

murex /myōōreks/ *n.* (*pl.* **murices** /-riseez/ or **murexes**) ► any gastropod mollusk of the genus *Murex* and related genera, yielding a purple dye.

mur·ine /myōōrīn/ *adj.* of or like a mouse or mice.

MUREX: SHELL OF TROSCHEL'S MUREX
(*Murex troscheli*)

murk /mərk/ *n. & adj.* (also **mirk**) ● *n.* **1** darkness, poor visibility. **2** air obscured by fog, etc. ● *adj. archaic* (of night, day, place, etc.) = MURKY.

murk·y /mórkee/ *adj.* (also **mirk·y**) (**-ier**, **-iest**) **1** dark, gloomy. **2** (of darkness) thick, dirty. **3** suspiciously obscure (*murky past*). □□ **murk·i·ly** *adv.* **murk·i·ness** *n.*

mur·mur /mórmər/ *n. & v.* ● *n.* **1** a subdued continuous sound, as made by waves, a brook, etc. **2** a softly spoken or nearly inarticulate utterance. **3** *Med.* a recurring sound heard in the auscultation of the heart and usu. indicating abnormality. **4** a subdued expression of discontent. ● *v.* **1** *intr.* make a subdued continuous sound. **2** *tr.* utter (words) in a low voice. **3** *intr.* (usu. foll. by *at, against*) complain in low tones, grumble. □□ **mur·mur·er** *n.* **mur·mur·ing·ly** *adv.* **mur·mur·ous** *adj.*

Mur·phy's Law /mórfeez/ *n. joc.* any of various maxims about the perverseness of things.

mur·rain /mórin/ *n.* **1** an infectious disease of cattle carried by parasites. **2** *archaic* a plague, esp. the potato blight during the Irish famine in the mid-19th c.

Mus.B. *abbr.* (also **Mus. Bac.**) Bachelor of Music.

mus·ca·del var. of MUSCATEL.

Mus·ca·det /múskəday/ *n.* **1** a white wine from the Loire region of France. **2** a variety of grape from which the wine is made.

mus·ca·dine /múskədin, -dīn/ *n.* a variety of grape with a musk flavor, used chiefly in wine making.

mus·ca·rine /múskərin/ *n.* a poisonous alkaloid from the fungus *Amanita muscaria*.

mus·cat /múskat, -kət/ *n.* **1** = MUSCATEL. **2** = MUSCADINE.

mus·ca·tel /múskətél/ *n.* (also **mus·ca·del** /-dél/) **1** a sweet fortified white wine made from muscadines. **2** a raisin from a muscadine grape.

mus·cle /músəl/ *n. & v.* ● *n.* **1** a fibrous tissue with the ability to contract, producing movement in or maintaining the position of an animal body. ▷ MUSCULATURE. **2** the part of an animal body that is composed of muscles. **3** physical power or strength. ● *v.intr.* (usu. foll. by *in*) *colloq.* force oneself on others; intrude by forceful means. □ **not move a muscle** be completely motionless. □□ **mus·cly** *adj.*

mus·cle-bound *adj.* with muscles stiff and inelastic through excessive exercise or training.

mus·cle man *n.* a man with highly developed muscles, esp. one employed as an intimidator.

mus·co·va·do /múskəváadō/ *n.* (*pl.* **-os**) an unrefined sugar made from the juice of sugar cane by evaporating it and draining off the molasses.

Mus·co·vite /múskəvīt/ *n. & adj.* ● *n.* **1** a native or citizen of Moscow. **2** *archaic* a Russian. ● *adj.* **1** of or relating to Moscow. **2** *archaic* of or relating to Russia.

mus·co·vite /múskəvīt/ *n.* a silver-gray form of mica with a sheetlike crystalline structure, used in the maufacture of electrical equipment, etc.

Mus·co·vy /múskəvee/ *n. archaic* Russia.

Muscovy duck a tropical American duck, *Cairina moschata*, having a small crest and red markings on its head.

mus·cu·lar /múskyələr/ *adj.* **1** of or affecting the muscles. **2** having well-developed muscles. □□ **mus·cu·lar·i·ty** /-láritee/ *n.* **mus·cu·lar·ly** *adv.*

mus·cu·lar dys·tro·phy *n.* a hereditary condition marked by progressive weakening and wasting of the muscles.

mus·cu·la·ture /músky ələchər/ *n.* ▼ the muscular system of a body or organ.

mus·cu·lo·skel·e·tal /məskyəlōskélət'l/ *adj.* of or involving both the muscles and the skeleton.

Mus.D. *abbr.* (also **Mus. Doc.**) Doctor of Music.

muse[1] /myo͞oz/ *n.* **1** (as **the Muses**) ► (in Greek and Roman mythology) nine goddesses who inspire poetry, music, drama, etc. **2** (usu. prec. by *the*) **a** a poet's inspiring goddess. **b** a poet's genius.

muse[2] /myo͞oz/ *v. literary* **1** *intr.* **a** (usu. foll. by *on, upon*) ponder, reflect. **b** (usu. foll. by *on*)

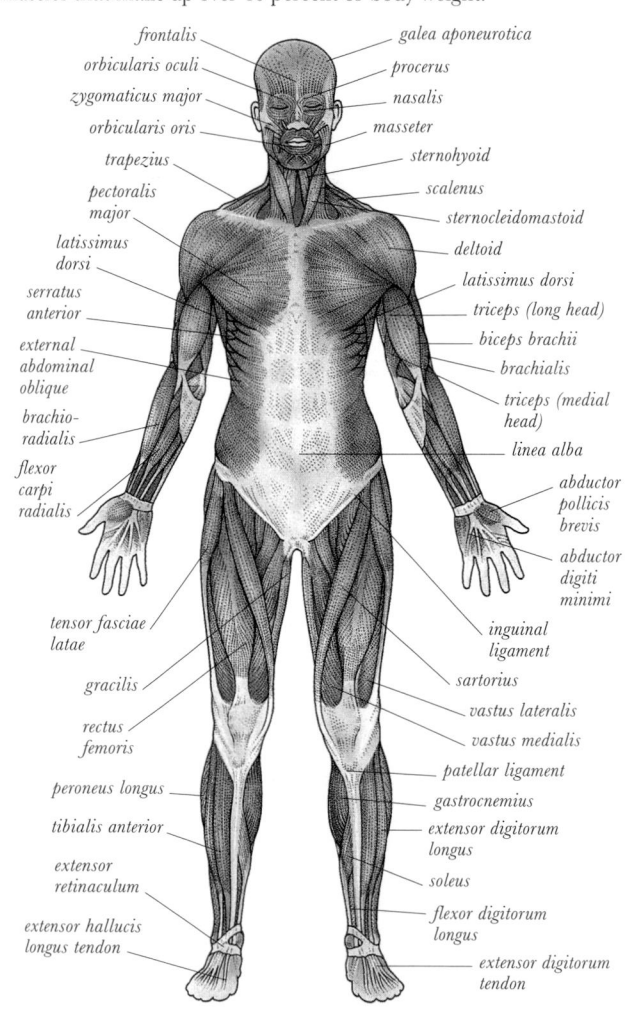

MUSE: DEPICTION OF THE GREEK MUSE TERPSICHORE

gaze meditatively (on a scene, etc.). **2** *tr.* say meditatively.

mu·se·um /myo͞ozéəm/ *n.* a building used for storing and exhibiting objects of historical, scientific, or cultural interest.

mu·se·um piece *n.* **1** a specimen of art, etc., fit for a museum. **2** *often derog.* an old-fashioned or quaint person or object.

mush[1] /mush/ *n.* **1** soft pulp. **2** feeble sentimentality. **3** a boiled cornmeal dish. **4** *sl.* the mouth; the face. □□ **mush·y** *adj.* (**mushier, mushiest**). **mush·i·ly** *adv.* **mush·i·ness** *n.*

mush[2] *v. & n.* ● *v.intr.* **1** (in *imper.*) used as a command to dogs pulling a sled to urge them forward. **2** go on

a journey across snow with a dogsled. ● *n.* a journey across snow with a dogsled.

mush·room /múshro͞om, -ro͝om/ *n. & v.* ● *n.* **1** ► the usu. edible, spore-producing body of various fungi, esp. *Agaricus campestris*, with a stem and domed cap. ▷ FUNGUS. **2** the pinkish-brown color of this. **3** any item resembling a mushroom in shape (*darning mushroom*). **4** (usu. *attrib.*) something that appears or develops suddenly or is ephemeral. ● *v.intr.* **1** appear or develop rapidly. **2** expand and flatten like a mushroom cap. **3** gather mushrooms.

mush·room cloud *n.* a cloud suggesting the shape of a mushroom, esp. from a nuclear explosion.

mu·sic /myo͞ozik/ *n.* **1** the art of combining vocal or instrumental sounds (or both) to produce beauty of form, harmony, and expression of emotion.

MUSCULATURE

All human movements depend on muscles, of which there are three types: skeletal, smooth, and cardiac. Only skeletal muscle (also known as voluntary muscle) is under our conscious control; the others work automatically and are described as "involuntary". Smooth muscle is found in the digestive system, bladder, and blood vessels, whereas cardiac muscle is found only in the heart. Muscles of all three kinds have in common the ability to be stretched, to contract, to be excited by a stimulus, and to return to their original size and shape. The skeletal muscular system consists of about 620 muscles that make up over 40 percent of body weight.

ENLARGED SECTION THROUGH A MUSCLE FASCICLE

fascicle (bundle of fibers)

blood vessel (capillary)

epimysium (muscle sheath)

perimysium

muscle fiber

muscle fibril

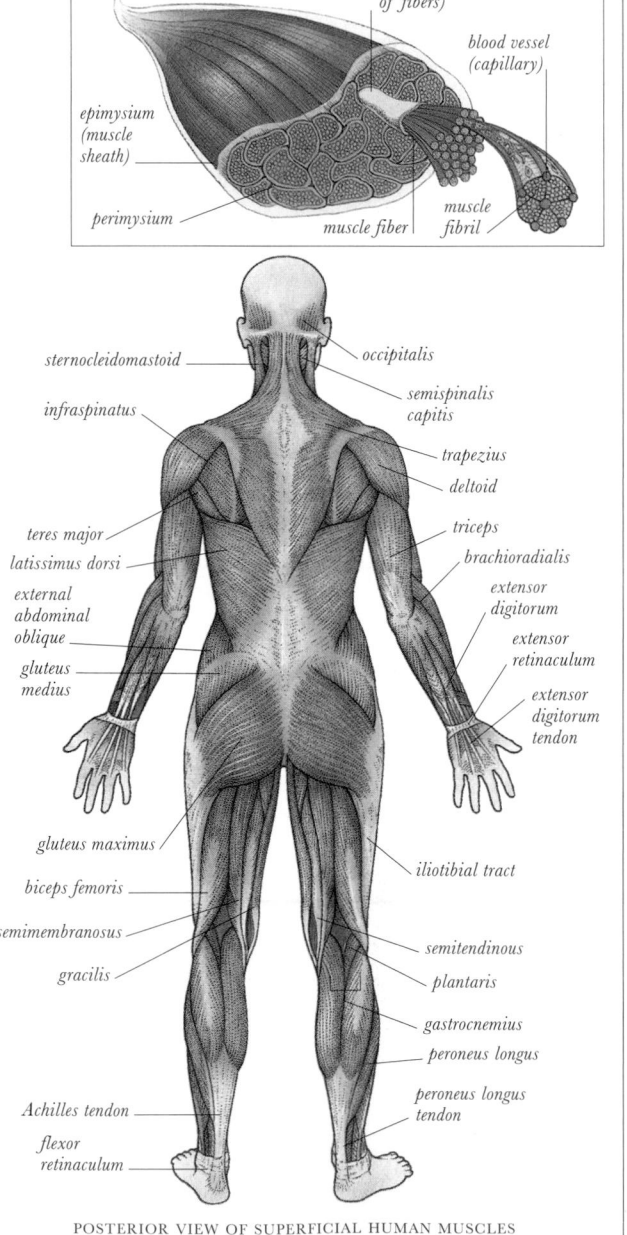

ANTERIOR VIEW OF SUPERFICIAL HUMAN MUSCLES

frontalis
orbicularis oculi
zygomaticus major
orbicularis oris
trapezius
pectoralis major
latissimus dorsi
serratus anterior
external abdominal oblique
brachio-radialis
flexor carpi radialis
tensor fasciae latae
gracilis
rectus femoris
peroneus longus
tibialis anterior
extensor retinaculum
extensor hallucis longus tendon

galea aponeurotica
procerus
nasalis
masseter
sternohyoid
scalenus
sternocleidomastoid
deltoid
latissimus dorsi
triceps (long head)
biceps brachii
brachialis
triceps (medial head)
linea alba
abductor pollicis brevis
abductor digiti minimi
inguinal ligament
sartorius
vastus lateralis
vastus medialis
patellar ligament
gastrocnemius
extensor digitorum longus
soleus
flexor digitorum longus
extensor digitorum tendon

POSTERIOR VIEW OF SUPERFICIAL HUMAN MUSCLES

sternocleidomastoid
infraspinatus
teres major
latissimus dorsi
external abdominal oblique
gluteus medius
gluteus maximus
biceps femoris
semimembranosus
gracilis
Achilles tendon
flexor retinaculum

occipitalis
semispinalis capitis
trapezius
deltoid
triceps
brachioradialis
extensor digitorum
extensor retinaculum
extensor digitorum tendon
iliotibial tract
semitendinous
plantaris
gastrocnemius
peroneus longus
peroneus longus tendon

M

2 the sounds so produced. **3** musical compositions. **4** the written or printed score of a musical composition. ▷ NOTATION. **5** certain pleasant sounds, e.g., birdsong, etc. □ **music to one's ears** something very pleasant to hear.

mu·si·cal /myo͞ozikəl/ *adj. & n.* ● *adj.* **1** of or relating to music. **2** (of sounds, a voice, etc.) melodious, harmonious. **3** fond of or skilled in music (*the musical one of the family*). **4** set to or accompanied by music. ● *n.* a movie or drama that features songs. □□ **mu·si·cal·i·ty** /-kálitee/ *n.* **mu·si·cal·ly** *adv.*

mu·si·cal chairs *n.pl.* **1** a party game in which the players compete in successive rounds for a decreasing number of chairs. **2** a series of changes or political maneuvering, etc., after the manner of the game.

mu·sic box *n.* a mechanical instrument playing a tune by causing a toothed cylinder to strike a comblike metal plate within a box.

mu·si·cian /myo͞ozíshən/ *n.* a person who plays a musical instrument, esp. professionally, or is otherwise musically gifted. □□ **mu·si·cian·ship** *n.*

mu·si·col·o·gy /myo͞ozikóləjee/ *n.* the study of music other than that directed to proficiency in performance or composition. □□ **mu·si·col·o·gist** *n.* **mu·si·co·log·i·cal** /-kəlójikəl/ *adj.*

mu·sic stand *n.* a rest or frame on which sheet music or a score is supported.

musk /musk/ *n.* **1** a strong-smelling reddish-brown substance produced by a gland in the male musk deer and used in perfumes. **2** the plant, *Mimulus moschatus*, with pale-green ovate leaves and yellow flowers. □□ **musk·y** *adj.* (**muskier, muskiest**). **musk·i·ness** *n.*

musk deer *n.* a small hornless Asian deer.

musk·kel·lunge /múskəlunj/ *n.* (also **mas·ki·nonge**) a large N. American pike.

mus·ket /múskit/ *n. hist.* a smoothbored light gun used by infantrymen. ▷ REDCOAT

mus·ket·eer /múskiteér/ *n. hist.* a soldier armed with a musket.

mus·ket·ry /múskitree/ *n.* **1** muskets, or soldiers armed with muskets, referred to collectively. **2** the knowledge of handling muskets.

musk·mel·on /múskmelən/ *n.* the common yellow or green melon, *Cucumis melo*, usu. with a raised network of markings on the skin.

musk ox *n.* a large goat-antelope, *Ovibos moschatus*, native to N. America, with a thick shaggy coat and small curved horns.

M

MUSHROOM

Like all fungi, mushrooms lack the green pigment chlorophyll, which plants use to make food. Instead, they absorb nutrients from decaying organic matter or from living plants and animals. The part that is visible above ground is, in fact, the fruiting body of the fungus. The main body consists of hyphal threads, which form a branching web known as the mycelium; this spreads through the substrate that the fungus has colonized, absorbing nutrients. Fruiting bodies vary in shape and color, but all are designed to spread the spores that enable a fungus to establish new colonies. Spores are produced on the underside of a mushroom and are released from flaps (gills) or hollows (pores). Many types of mushrooms are edible, and some are considered delicacies.

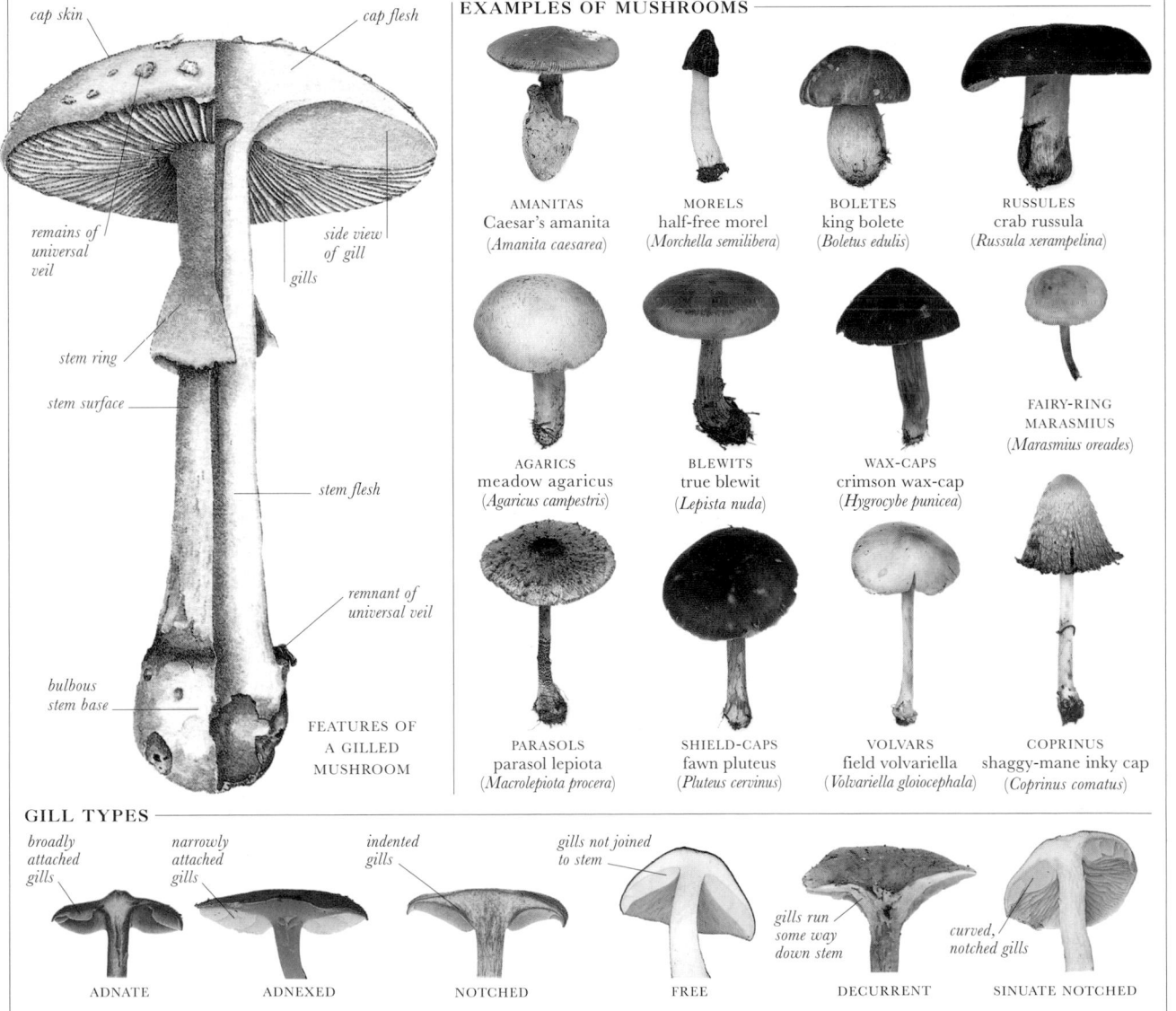

FEATURES OF A GILLED MUSHROOM

cap skin · cap flesh · remains of universal veil · side view of gill · gills · stem ring · stem surface · stem flesh · remnant of universal veil · bulbous stem base

EXAMPLES OF MUSHROOMS

AMANITAS
Caesar's amanita
(*Amanita caesarea*)

MORELS
half-free morel
(*Morchella semilibera*)

BOLETES
king bolete
(*Boletus edulis*)

RUSSULES
crab russula
(*Russula xerampelina*)

AGARICS
meadow agaricus
(*Agaricus campestris*)

BLEWITS
true blewit
(*Lepista nuda*)

WAX-CAPS
crimson wax-cap
(*Hygrocybe punicea*)

FAIRY-RING
MARASMIUS
(*Marasmius oreades*)

PARASOLS
parasol lepiota
(*Macrolepiota procera*)

SHIELD-CAPS
fawn pluteus
(*Pluteus cervinus*)

VOLVARS
field volvariella
(*Volvariella gloiocephala*)

COPRINUS
shaggy-mane inky cap
(*Coprinus comatus*)

GILL TYPES

broadly attached gills · narrowly attached gills · indented gills · gills not joined to stem · gills run some way down stem · curved, notched gills

ADNATE · ADNEXED · NOTCHED · FREE · DECURRENT · SINUATE NOTCHED

musk·rat /múskrat/ *n.* **1** a large aquatic rodent, *Ondatra zibethica*, native to N. America, with a musky smell. Also called **musquash**. **2** the fur of this.

Mus·lim /múzlim, mŏŏz-, mŏŏs-/ *n. & adj.* (also **Mos·lem** /mózləm/) ● *n.* a follower of the Islamic religion. ● *adj.* of or relating to the Muslims or their religion.

mus·lin /múzlin/ *n.* **1** a fine delicately woven cotton fabric. **2** cotton cloth in plain weave.

mus·quash /múskwosh/ *n.* = MUSKRAT.

muss /mus/ *v. & n. colloq.* ● *v.tr.* (often foll. by *up*) disarrange; throw into disorder. ● *n.* a state of confusion; untidiness, mess. □□ **muss·y** *adj.*

mus·sel /músəl/ *n.* **1** ◄ any bivalve mollusk of the genus *Mytilus*, living in seawater and often used for food. ▷ BIVALVE. **2** any similar freshwater mollusk of the genus *Margaritifer* or *Anodonta*, forming pearls.

MUSSEL
(*Mytilus* species)

must[1] /must/ *v. & n.* ● *v.aux.* (*3rd sing. present* **must**; *past* **had to** or in indirect speech **must**) (foll. by infin., or *absol.*) **1 a** be obliged to (*must we leave now?*). ¶ The negative (i.e., lack of obligation) is expressed by *not have to* or *need not*; *must not* denotes positive forbidding, as in *you must not smoke*. **b** in ironic questions (*must you slam the door?*). **2** be certain to (*they must have left by now*). **3** ought to (*it must be said that*). **4** expressing insistence (*I must ask you to leave*). **5** (foll. by *not* +infin.) **a** be forbidden to (*you must not smoke*). **b** ought not; need not (*you must not worry*). **c** expressing insistence that something should not be done (*they must not be told*). ● *n. colloq.* a thing that cannot or should not be missed (*if you go to London, St. Paul's is a must*). □ **I must say** often *iron.* I cannot refrain from saying (*a fine way to behave, I must say*).

must[2] /must/ *n.* grape juice before fermentation is complete.

must[3] /must/ *n.* mustiness, mold.

mus·tache /mústash, məstásh/ *n.* (also **moustache**) hair left to grow on a man's upper lip. □□ **mus·tached** *adj.*

mus·tang /mústang/ *n.* a small wild horse native to Mexico and California. ▷ HORSE

mus·tard /mústərd/ *n.* **1 a** any of various plants of the genus *Brassica*, with slender pods and yellow flowers. **b** any of various plants of the genus *Sinapis*, eaten at the seedling stage. **2** the seeds of these which are crushed, made into a paste, and used as a spicy condiment. ▷ SPICE. **3** the brownish-yellow color of this condiment. □ **cut the mustard** *sl.* to reach an expected level of performance.

mus·tard gas *n.* a colorless oily liquid whose vapor is a powerful irritant and causes blisters.

mus·te·lid /mústəlid/ *n. & adj.* ● *n.* ▼ a mammal of the family Mustelidae, including weasels, stoats, badgers, skunks, otters, martens, etc. ● *adj.* of or relating to this family.

mus·ter /mústər/ *v. & n.* ● *v.* **1** *tr.* collect (orig. soldiers) for inspection, to check numbers, etc. **2** *tr. & intr.* gather together. ● *n.* **1** the assembly of persons for inspection. **2** an assembly. □ **muster in** enroll (recruits). **muster out** discharge (soldiers, etc.). **muster up** collect or summon (courage, strength, etc.). **pass muster** be accepted as adequate.

must-have *n. & adj.* ● *n.* an essential or highly desirable item. ● *adj.* essential; highly desirable.

mustn't /músənt/ *contr.* must not.

mus·ty /mústee/ *adj.* (**mustier, mustiest**) **1** moldy. **2** of a moldy or stale smell or taste. **3** stale, antiquated (*musty old books*). □□ **mus·ti·ly** *adv.* **mus·ti·ness** *n.*

Mus·sul·man /músəlmən/ *n. & adj. archaic* ● *n.* (*pl.* **-mans** or **-men**) a Muslim. ● *adj.* of or concerning Muslims.

mu·ta·ble /myŏŏtəbəl/ *adj. literary* **1** liable to change. **2** fickle. □□ **mu·ta·bil·i·ty** /-bílitee/ *n.*

mu·ta·gen /myŏŏtəjən/ *n.* an agent promoting mutation, e.g., radiation. □□ **mu·ta·gen·ic** /-jénik/ *adj.* **mu·ta·gen·e·sis** /-jénisis/ *n.*

mu·tant /myŏŏt'nt/ *adj. & n.* ● *adj.* resulting from mutation. ● *n.* a mutant form.

mu·tate /myŏŏtáyt/ *v.intr. & tr.* undergo or cause to undergo mutation.

mu·ta·tion /myŏŏtáyshən/ *n.* **1** the process or an instance of change or alteration. **2** ▲ a genetic change which, when transmitted to offspring, gives rise to heritable variations. **3** a mutant. □□ **mu·ta·tion·al** *adj.* **mu·ta·tion·al·ly** *adv.*

mu·ta·tis mu·tan·dis /mŏŏtaátis mŏŏtaándis, myŏŏ-/ *adv.* (in comparing cases) making the necessary alterations.

mute /myŏŏt/ *adj., n., & v.* ● *adj.* **1** silent, refraining from speech. **2** not emitting articulate sound. **3** (of a person or animal) dumb. **4** not expressed in speech (*mute protest*). **5 a** (of a letter) not pronounced. **b** (of a consonant) plosive. ● *n.* **1** a dumb person (*a deaf mute*). **2** *Mus.* **a** a clamp for damping the resonance of the strings of a violin, etc. **b** ▼ a pad or cone for damping the sound of a wind instrument.

MUTATION

Mutations occur as a result of the chance alteration of a DNA molecule or by a change in the shape or number of chromosomes. If a mutation occurs in a sex cell it can be passed on from one generation to another. Although most mutations are damaging, and often impair survival, they are a source of variation in living things and allow evolution to take place. The mutant teasel shown here has curved, rather than straight spines on the seedhead.

straight spines

NORMAL TEASEL

curved spines

MUTANT TEASEL

MUSTELID

Mustelids are long-bodied mammalian carnivores. Most of the 65 species are terrestrial or arboreal, although some spend their time in water. They range in size from the least weasel, weighing less than 1 oz (28 g), to the sea otter, which can weigh up to 99 lb (45 kg). With their sharp teeth, acute senses, and agile bodies, they are highly effective hunters. Some species subsist on live prey, but others, such as badgers, eat carrion and a range of plant foods. Most mustelids mark their territories with a strong-smelling fluid, which is discharged from the anal glands.

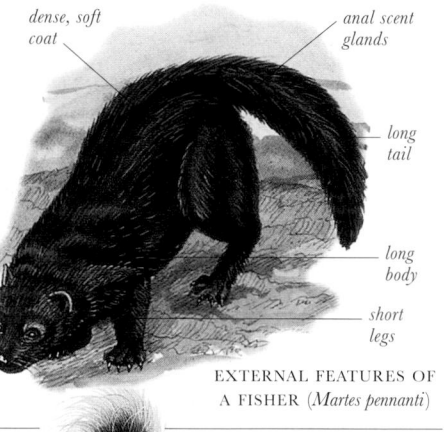

dense, soft coat

anal scent glands

long tail

long body

short legs

EXTERNAL FEATURES OF A FISHER (*Martes pennanti*)

EXAMPLES OF MUSTELIDS

PINE MARTEN
(*Martes martes*)

WOLVERINE
(*Gulo gulo*)

SPOTTED SKUNK
(*Spilogale putorius*)

POLECAT
(*Mustela putorius*)

WEASEL
(*Mustela nivalis*)

COMMON OTTER
(*Lutra lutra*)

STOAT
(*Mustela erminea*)

BADGER
(*Meles meles*)

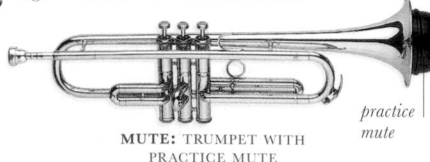

MUTE: TRUMPET WITH PRACTICE MUTE

practice mute

M

3 an unsounded consonant. **4** an actor whose part is in a dumb show. **5** a hired mourner. ● *v.tr.* **1** deaden, muffle, or soften the sound of (a thing, esp. a musical instrument). **2 a** tone down, make less intense. **b** (as **muted** *adj.*) (of colors, etc.) subdued (*a muted green*). □□ **mute·ly** *adv.* **mute·ness** *n.*

mute swan *n.* ► the common white swan, *Cygnus olor.* ▷ WATERFOWL

mu·ti·late /myōōt'layt/ *v.tr.* **1 a** deprive of a limb or organ. **b** destroy the use of (a limb or organ). **2** render (a book, etc.) imperfect by excision or some act of destruction. □□ **mu·ti·la·tion** /-láyshən/ *n.* **mu·ti·la·tor** *n.*

mu·ti·neer /myōōt'néer/ *n.* a person who mutinies.

mu·tin·ous /myōōt'nəs/ *adj.* rebellious; tending to mutiny. □□ **mu·tin·ous·ly** *adv.*

mu·ti·ny /myōōt'nee/ *n. & v.* ● *n.* (*pl.* **-ies**) an open revolt against constituted authority, esp. by soldiers or sailors against their officers. ● *v.intr.* (**-ies**, **-ied**) (often foll. by *against*) revolt; engage in mutiny. □□ **mu·ti·nous** /myōōt'nəs/ *adj.*

mutt /mut/ *n.* **1** a dog. **2** *sl.* an ignorant, stupid, or blundering person.

mut·ter /mútər/ *v. & n.* ● *v.* **1** *intr.* speak low in a barely audible manner. **2** *intr.* (often foll. by *against*, *at*) murmur or grumble about. **3** *tr.* utter (words, etc.) in a low tone. **4** *tr.* say in secret. ● *n.* **1** muttered words or sounds. **2** muttering. □□ **mut·ter·er** *n.*

mut·ton /mút'n/ *n.* **1** the flesh of sheep used for food. **2** *joc.* a sheep.

mut·ton·chops /mút'nchops/ *n.* side whiskers trimmed narrow at the temples and broad along the cheeks.

mu·tu·al /myōōchōōəl/ *adj.* **1** (of feelings, actions, etc.) experienced or done by each of two or more parties with reference to the other or others (*mutual affection*). **2** *colloq. disp.* common to two or more persons (*a mutual friend*). **3** standing in (a specified) relation to each other (*mutual beneficiaries*). □□ **mu·tu·al·ly** *adv.*

mu·tu·al fund *n.* an investment program funded by shareholders that trades in diversified holdings and is professionally managed.

mu·tu·al·ism /myōōchōōəlizəm/ *n.* **1** the doctrine that mutual dependence is necessary to social well-being. **2** mutually beneficial symbiosis. □□ **mu·tu·al·ist** *n. & adj.* **mu·tu·al·is·tic** /-lístik/ *adj.* **mu·tu·al·is·ti·cal·ly** /-listiklee/ *adv.*

mu·tule /myōōchool/ *n. Archit.* a block derived from wooden beam ends projecting under a Doric cornice.

muu·muu /myōōmōō/ *n.* a woman's loose brightly colored dress, as originally worn in Hawaii.

Mu·zak /myōōzak/ *n.* **1** *Trademark* a system of music transmission for playing in public places. **2** (**mu-zak**) recorded light background music.

muz·zle /múzəl/ *n. & v.* ● *n.* **1** the projecting part of an animal's face, including the nose and mouth. ▷ DOG. **2** ► a guard, usu. made of straps or wire, fitted over an animal's nose and mouth to stop it biting or feeding. **3** the open end of a firearm. ▷ GUN. ● *v.tr.* **1** put a muzzle on (an animal, etc.). **2** impose silence upon.

muz·zy /múzee/ *adj.* (**muzzier**, **muzziest**) **1** mentally hazy. **2** blurred. □□ **muz·zi·ly** *adv.* **muz·zi·ness** *n.*

MVP *abbr. Sports* most valuable player.

MW *abbr.* **1** megawatt(s). **2** medium wave.

mW *abbr.* milliwatt(s).

MUTE SWAN
(*Cygnus olor*)

MUZZLE ON A DOG

my /mī/ *poss.pron.* (*attrib.*) **1** of or belonging to me or myself (*my house*). **2** as a form of address in affectionate, sympathetic, contexts (*my dear boy*). **3** in various expressions of surprise (*my God!*; *oh my!*). **4** *colloq.* indicating the speaker's husband, wife, child, etc. (*my Johnny's ill again*).

my- *comb. form* var. of MYO-.

my·al·gi·a /mīáljə/ *n.* a pain in a muscle or group of muscles. □□ **my·al·gic** *adj.*

my·as·the·ni·a /mīəs-théeneeə/ *n.* a condition causing abnormal weakness of certain muscles.

my·as·the·ni·a gra·vis *n.* a disease characterized by fatigue and muscle weakness, caused by an autoimmune attack on acetylcholine receptors.

my·ce·li·um /mīséeleeəm/ *n.* (*pl.* **mycelia** /-leeə/) the vegetative part of a fungus, consisting of microscopic threadlike hyphae. □□ **my·ce·li·al** *adj.*

My·ce·nae·an /mísinéeən/ *adj. & n.* ● *adj. Archaeol.* ► of or relating to the late Bronze Age civilization in Greece (*c.*1580–1100 BC). ● *n.* an inhabitant of Mycenae or the Mycenaean world.

-mycin /mísin/ *comb. form* used to form the names of antibiotic compounds derived from fungi.

my·col·o·gy /mīkóləjee/ *n.* **1** the study of species of fungi. **2** the fungi of a particular region. □□ **my·co·log·i·cal** /-kəlójikəl/ *adj.* **my·col·o·gist** *n.*

my·co·sis /mīkósis/ *n.* any disease caused by a fungus, e.g., ringworm. □□ **my·cot·ic** /-kótik/ *adj.*

my·e·lin /mí-ilin/ *n.* a white substance which forms a sheath around certain nerve fibers. ▷ NERVOUS SYSTEM. □□ **my·e·li·na·tion** *n.*

my·e·li·tis /mī-ilítis/ *n.* inflammation of the spinal cord.

my·e·loid /mí iloyd/ *adj.* of or relating to bone marrow or the spinal cord.

my·e·lo·ma /mí ilómə/ *n.* (*pl.* **myelomas** or **myelomata** /-mətə/) a malignant tumor of the bone marrow.

My·lar /mílaar/ *n. Trademark* an extremely strong polyester film made in thin sheets and used for recording tapes, insulation, etc.

my·lo·don /mílədon/ *n.* an extinct gigantic ground sloth with cylindrical teeth.

my·nah /mínə/ *n.* (also **my·na**, **mi·na**) any of various SE Asian starlings, able to mimic the human voice.

myo- /mío/ *comb. form* (also **my-** before a vowel) muscle.

my·o·car·di·um /mīōkáardeeəm/ *n.* (*pl.* **myocardia** /-deeə/) the muscular tissue of the heart. ▷ HEART. □□ **my·o·car·di·al** *adj.*

my·o·car·di·al in·farc·tion *n.* a heart attack.

my·o·fib·ril /mīófíbril/ *n.* any of the elongated contractile threads found in striated muscle cells.

my·o·glo·bin /mīōglóbin/ *n.* an oxygen-carrying protein containing iron and found in muscle cells.

my·ol·o·gy /mīóləjee/ *n.* the study of the structure and function of muscles.

my·o·pi·a /mīópeeə/ *n.* **1** nearsightedness. ▷ SIGHT. **2** lack of imagination or intellectual insight. □□ **my·op·ic** /mīópik/ *adj.* **my·op·i·cal·ly** /mīópiklee/ *adv.*

my·o·sis var. of MIOSIS.

my·o·so·tis /míəsótis/ *n.* (also **my·o·sote** /míəsōt/) any plant of the genus *Myosotis* with blue, pink, or white flowers, esp. a forget-me-not.

MYCENAEAN CUP

myr·i·ad /míreeəd/ *n. & adj. literary* ● *n.* **1** an indefinitely great number. **2** ten thousand. ● *adj.* of an indefinitely great number.

myr·i·a·pod /míreeəpód/ *n. & adj.* ● *n.* any land-living arthropod of the group Myriapoda, with numerous leg-bearing segments. ● *adj.* of or relating to this group.

myr·mi·don /mə́rmid'n, -don/ *n.* **1** a hired ruffian. **2** a base servant.

myrrh /mər/ *n.* a gum resin from several trees of the genus *Commiphora* used, esp. in the Near East, in perfumery, incense, etc. □□ **myrrh·ic** *adj.* **myrrh·y** *adj.*

myr·tle /mə́rt'l/ *n.* **1** ► an evergreen shrub of the genus *Myrtus* with aromatic foliage and white flowers. **2** = PERIWINKLE.

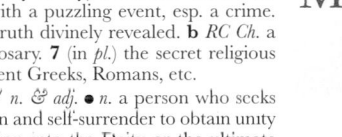

MYRTLE
(*Myrtus communis*)

my·self /mīsélf/ *pron.* **1** *emphat. form* of I[1] or ME[1] (*I saw it myself*). **2** *refl. form* of ME[1] (*able to dress myself*). **3** in my normal state of body and mind (*I'm not myself today*). **4** *poet.* = I[1]. □ **by myself** see by oneself (BY). **I myself** I for my part (*I myself am doubtful*).

mys·te·ri·ous /mistéereeəs/ *adj.* **1** full of or wrapped in mystery. **2** (of a person) delighting in mystery. □□ **mys·te·ri·ous·ly** *adv.* **mys·te·ri·ous·ness** *n.*

mys·ter·y /místəree/ *n.* (*pl.* **-ies**) **1** a secret, hidden, or inexplicable matter. **2** secrecy or obscurity (*wrapped in mystery*). **3** (*attrib.*) secret, undisclosed (*mystery guest*). **4** the practice of making a secret of (esp. unimportant) things (*engaged in mystery and intrigue*). **5** (in full **mystery story**) a fictional work dealing with a puzzling event, esp. a crime. **6 a** a religious truth divinely revealed. **b** *RC Ch.* a decade of the rosary. **7** (in *pl.*) the secret religious rites of the ancient Greeks, Romans, etc.

mys·tic /místik/ *n. & adj.* ● *n.* a person who seeks by contemplation and self-surrender to obtain unity with or absorption into the Deity or the ultimate reality, or who believes in the spiritual apprehension of truths that are beyond understanding. ● *adj.* **1** mysterious and awe-inspiring. **2** spiritually allegorical or symbolic. **3** occult, esoteric. **4** of hidden meaning. □□ **mys·ti·cism** /-tisizəm/ *n.*

mys·ti·cal /místikəl/ *adj.* of mystics or mysticism. □□ **mys·ti·cal·ly** *adv.*

mys·ti·fy /místifī/ *v.tr.* (**-ies**, **-ied**) **1** bewilder, confuse. **2** hoax, take advantage of the credulity of. **3** wrap up in mystery. □□ **mys·ti·fi·ca·tion** /-fikáyshən/ *n.*

mys·tique /mistéek/ *n.* **1** an atmosphere of mystery and veneration attending some activity or person. **2** any skill mystifying to the layman.

myth /mith/ *n.* **1** a traditional narrative usu. involving supernatural or imaginary persons and embodying popular ideas on natural or social phenomena, etc. **2** such narratives collectively. **3** a widely held but false notion. **4** a fictitious person, thing, or idea. **5** an allegory (*the Platonic myth*). □□ **myth·ic** *adj.* **myth·i·cal** *adj.* **myth·i·cal·ly** *adv.*

mytho- /míthō/ *comb. form* myth.

myth·o·gen·ic /míthōjénik/ *adj.* creating or capable of creating myths.

my·thol·o·gy /mithóləjee/ *n.* (*pl.* **-ies**) **1** a body of myths (*Greek mythology*). **2** the study of myths. □□ **my·thol·o·ger** *n.* **myth·o·log·i·cal** /-thəlójikəl/ *adj.* **myth·o·log·i·cal·ly** /-thəlójiklee/ *adv.* **my·thol·o·gist** *n.* **my·thol·o·gize** *v.tr & intr.*

myth·os /míthos/ *n.* (*pl.* **mythoi** /-thoy/) *literary* a myth.

myx·o·ma·to·sis /míksəmətósis/ *n.* an infectious usu. fatal viral disease in rabbits, causing swelling of the mucous membranes.

M

N

N¹ /en/ *n.* (also **n**) (*pl.* **Ns** or **N's**) **1** the fourteenth letter of the alphabet. **2** *Math.* (**n**) an indefinite number. □ **to the nth degree 1** *Math.* to any required power. **2** to the utmost.

N² *abbr.* (also **N.**) north; northern.

N³ *symb. Chem.* the element nitrogen.

n *abbr.* (also **n.**) **1** noun. **2** neuter. **3** north; northern.

'n *conj.* (also **'n'**) *colloq.* and.

Na *symb. Chem.* the element sodium.

N.A. *abbr.* North America.

n/a *abbr.* **1** not applicable. **2** not available.

NAACP /endəbəláyseepee/ *abbr.* National Association for the Advancement of Colored People.

nab /nab/ *v.tr.* (**nabbed**, **nabbing**) *sl.* **1** arrest; catch in wrongdoing. **2** seize; grab.

na·bob /náybob/ *n.* **1** *hist.* a Muslim official or governor under the Mughal empire. **2** (formerly) a conspicuously wealthy person.

na·cho /náachō/ *n.* (*pl.* **-os**) (usu. in *pl.*) a tortilla chip, usu. topped with melted cheese and spices, etc.

na·cre /náykər/ *n.* mother-of-pearl from any shelled mollusk. □□ **na·cre·ous** /náykreeəs/ *adj.*

na·da /náadə/ *pron. N. Amer. colloq.* nothing. [Spanish]

na·dir /náydər, -deer/ *n.* **1** the part of the celestial sphere directly below an observer (opp. ZENITH). **2** the lowest point in one's fortunes.

NAFTA /náftə/ *abbr.* North American Free Trade Agreement.

nag¹ /nag/ *v. & n.* ● *v.* (**nagged**, **nagging**) **1 a** *tr.* annoy or irritate (a person) with persistent fault-finding. **b** *intr.* (often foll. by *at*) find fault persistently. **2** *tr.* (of a pain) ache dully but persistently. **3** *tr.* worry or preoccupy (a person, the mind, etc.) (*his mistake nagged him*). ● *n.* a persistently nagging person. □□ **nag·ger** *n.* **nag·ging·ly** *adv.*

nag² /nag/ *n.* **1** *colloq.* a horse. **2** a small riding horse or pony.

Na·hua·tl /náawáat'l/ *n. & adj.* ● *n.* **1** a member of a group of peoples native to S. Mexico and Central America, including the Aztecs. **2** the language of these people. ● *adj.* of or concerning the Nahuatl peoples or language. □□ **Na·hua·tlan** *adj.*

nai·ad /níad/ *n.* (*pl.* **naiads** or **-des** /níədeez/) *Mythol.* a water nymph.

nail /nayl/ *n. & v.* ● *n.* **1** a small metal spike with a broadened flat head, driven in with a hammer to join things together or to serve as a peg, protection (cf. HOBNAIL), or decoration. **2** ▶ a horny covering on the upper surface of the tip of the finger or toe. ● *v.tr.* **1** fasten with a nail. **2 a** secure or get hold of (a person or thing). **b** expose (a lie or a liar). □ **nail one's colors to the mast** persist; refuse to give in. **nail down 1** bind (a person) to a promise, etc. **2** define precisely. **3** fasten (a thing) with nails. **nail in a person's coffin** something thought to increase the risk of death. **on the nail** (esp. of payment) without delay (*cash on the nail*). □□ **nailed** *adj.*

nail file *n.* a roughened metal or emery strip used for smoothing the nails.

nail pol·ish *n.* a varnish applied to the nails to color them or make them shiny.

na·ive /naa-éev/ *adj.* (also **na·ïve**) **1** artless; innocent. **2** foolishly credulous. □□ **na·ive·ly** *adv.*

na·ïve·té /naa-eevtáy, -éevtáy/ *n.* (also **naïveté**) **1** the state or quality of being naïve. **2** a naïve action.

na·ked /náykid/ *adj.* **1** without clothes; nude. **2** plain; exposed (*the naked truth; his naked soul*). **3** (of a light, flame, etc.) unprotected from the wind, etc. **4** defenseless. **5** (of landscape) barren; treeless. **6** (usu. foll. by *of*) devoid; without. **7** without leaves, hair, scales, shell, etc. **8** (of a sword, etc.) unsheathed.

na·ked eye *n.* (prec. by *the*) unassisted vision, e.g., without a telescope, microscope, etc.

nam·by-pam·by /námbeepámbee/ *adj. & n.* ● *adj.* **1** lacking vigor or drive. **2** insipidly pretty or sentimental. ● *n.* (*pl.* **-ies**) a namby-pamby person.

name /naym/ *n. & v.* ● *n.* **1** the word by which an individual person, animal, place, or thing is known. **2 a** a usu. abusive term used of a person, etc. (*called him names*). **b** a word denoting an object or class of objects, ideas, etc. (*what is the name of that kind of vase?*). **3** a famous person. **4** a reputation, esp. a good one (*has a name for honesty*). ● *v.tr.* **1** give a specified name to (*named the dog Spot*). **2** call (a person or thing) by the right name (*named the man in the photograph*). **3** mention; specify (*named her requirements*). **4** nominate, appoint, etc. (*was named the new chairman*). □ **have to one's name** possess. **in all but name** virtually. **in name** (or **name only**) as a mere formality (*is the leader in name only*). **in the name of** calling to witness (*in the name of goodness*). **make a name for oneself** become famous. **name after** (also **for**) call (a person) by the name of (a specified person) (*named him after his uncle Roger*). **name the day** arrange a date (esp. for a wedding). **name names** mention specific names, esp. in accusation. **name of the game** *colloq.* the purpose or essence of an action, etc. **put one's name down for 1** apply for. **2** promise to subscribe (a sum). **you name it** *colloq.* whatever you like. □□ **name·a·ble** *adj.*

name-call·ing *n.* abusive language.

name-check /náymchek/ *v.tr.* publicly mention the name of, esp. in acknowledgement or for publicity purposes.

name-drop·ping *n.* the familiar mention of famous people as a form of boasting. □□ **name-drop** *v.intr.* (**-dropped**, **-dropping**). **name-drop·per** *n.*

name·less /náymlis/ *adj.* **1** having no name or name inscription. **2** unnamed; anonymous (*our informant, who shall be nameless*). **3** too horrific to be named (*nameless vices*). □□ **name·less·ly** *adv.* **name·less·ness** *n.*

name·ly /náymlee/ *adv.* that is to say.

name·sake /náymsayk/ *n.* a person having the same name as another (*was her aunt's namesake*).

nan·a /nánə/ *n. colloq.* grandmother.

nan·dro·lone /nándrəlōn/ *n.* an anabolic steroid with tissue-building properties, used illegally to enhance performance in sports.

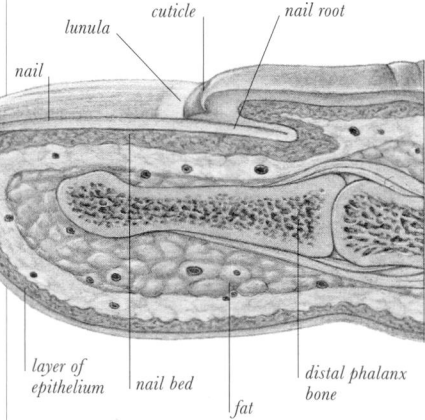

NAIL: CROSS SECTION OF A HUMAN FINGERTIP SHOWING THE NAIL

cuticle
nail root
lunula
nail
layer of epithelium
nail bed
fat
distal phalanx bone

nan·ny /nánee/ *n. & v.* ● *n.* (*pl.* **-ies**) a child's nursemaid. **2** (in full **nanny goat**) a female goat. ● *v.tr.* (**-ies**, **-ied**) be unduly protective toward.

nano- /nánō, náynō/ *comb. form* denoting a factor of 10^{-9} (*nanosecond*).

nan·om·e·ter /nánōmeetər/ *n.* one billionth of a meter. ¶ Abbr.: **nm**.

nan·o·sec·ond /nánōsekənd/ *n.* one billionth of a second. ¶ Abbr.: **ns**.

nap¹ /nap/ *v. & n.* ● *v.intr.* (**napped**, **napping**) sleep briefly. ● *n.* a short sleep (*took a nap*). □ **catch a person napping 1** find a person off guard. **2** detect in negligence.

nap² /nap/ *n.* the raised pile on textiles, esp. velvet.

nap³ /nap/ *n.* a form of whist in which players declare the number of tricks they expect to take.

na·palm /náypaam/ *n. & v.* ● *n.* a jellied substance used in incendiary bombs. ● *v.tr.* attack with napalm bombs.

nape /nayp/ *n.* the back of the neck.

naph·tha /náf-thə, náp-/ *n.* a flammable oil obtained by the dry distillation of organic substances such as coal, shale, or petroleum.

naph·tha·lene /náf-thəleen, náp-/ *n.* ▶ a white crystalline aromatic substance produced by the distillation of coal tar and used in mothballs and the manufacture of dyes, etc. □□ **naph·thal·ic** /-thálik/ *adj.*

nap·kin /nápkin/ *n.* (in full **table napkin**) a square piece of linen, paper, etc. used for wiping the lips, fingers, etc., at meals.

nap·kin ring *n.* a ring used to hold (and distinguish) a person's table napkin when not in use.

NAPHTHALENE

Na·po·le·on·ic /nəpōleeónik/ *adj.* of or relating to Napoleon I or his time.

narc /nark/ *n.* (also **nark**) *sl.* a federal agent or police officer who enforces the laws regarding illicit sale or use of drugs and narcotics.

nar·cis·sism /náarsisizəm/ *n. Psychol.* excessive or erotic interest in oneself, one's physical features, etc. □□ **nar·cis·sist** *n.* **nar·cis·sis·tic** *adj.* **nar·cis·sis·ti·cal·ly** *adv.*

nar·cis·sus /naarsísəs/ *n.* (*pl.* **narcissi** /-sī/ or **narcissuses**) ▼ any bulbous plant of the genus *Narcissus*, esp. *N. poeticus* bearing a heavily scented single flower.

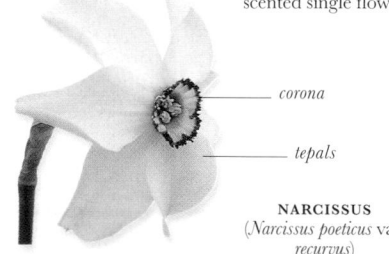

corona
tepals

NARCISSUS
(*Narcissus poeticus* var. *recurvus*)

nar·co·lep·sy /náarkəlepsee/ *n. Med.* a disease with fits of sleepiness and drowsiness. □□ **nar·co·lep·tic** /-léptik/ *adj. & n.*

nar·co·sis /naarkósis/ *n.* **1** *Med.* the working or effects of soporific narcotics. **2** a state of insensibility.

nar·cot·ic /naarkótik/ *adj. & n.* ● *adj.* **1** (of a substance) inducing drowsiness, sleep, insensibility. **2** (of a drug) affecting the mind. ● *n.* a narcotic substance, drug, or influence. □□ **nar·cot·i·cal·ly** *adv.* **nar·co·tism** /náarkətizəm/ *n.* **nar·co·tize** /náarkətīz/ *v.tr.*

nard /naard/ *n.* any of various plants yielding an aromatic balsam used by the ancients.

na·res /naireez/ *n.pl. Anat.* the nostrils. □□ **na·ri·al** *adj.*

Nar·ra·gan·sett /narəgánsət, -gánt-/ *n.* **1 a** a N. American people native to Rhode Island. **b** a member of this people. **2** the language of this people.

nar·rate /nárayt, naráyt/ *v.tr.* (also *absol.*) **1** give a continuous story or account of. **2** provide a spoken commentary or accompaniment for (a film, etc.). □□ **nar·rat·a·ble** *adj.* **nar·ra·tion** /-ráyshən/ *n.*

nar·ra·tive /nárətiv/ *n. & adj.* ● *n.* **1** a spoken or written account of connected events in order of happening. **2** the practice or art of narration. ● *adj.* in the form of, or concerned with, narration (*narrative verse*). □□ **nar·ra·tive·ly** *adv.*

nar·ra·tor /náraytər/ *n.* **1** an actor, announcer, etc., who delivers a commentary in a film, broadcast, etc. **2** a person who narrates.

nar·row /nárō/ *adj., n., & v.* ● *adj.* (**narrower**, **narrowest**) **1 a** of small width in proportion to length. **b** confined or confining (*within narrow bounds*). **2** of limited scope (*in the narrowest sense*). **3** with little margin (*a narrow escape*). ● *n.* **1** (usu. in *pl.*) the narrow part of a strait, river, etc. **2** a narrow pass. ● *v.* **1** *intr.* become narrow; diminish. **2** *tr.* make narrow; constrict. □□ **nar·row·ly** *adv.* **nar·row·ness** *n.*

nar·row gauge *n.* a railroad track that has a smaller gauge than the standard one.

nar·row-mind·ed /nárōmíndid/ *adj.* rigid or restricted in one's views; intolerant. □□ **nar·row-mind·ed·ly** *adv.* **nar·row-mind·ed·ness** *n.*

narthex /náartheks/ *n.* an antechamber in a church.

nar·whal /náarwəl/ *n.* ▼ an Arctic whale, *Monodon monoceros*, the male of which has a long spirally fluted tusk. Also called **beluga**.

NARWHAL
(*Monodon monoceros*)

nar·y /náiree/ *adj. colloq.* or *dial.* not any; no (*nary a one*).

NAS *abbr.* National Academy of Sciences.

NASA /násə/ *abbr.* National Aeronautics and Space Administration.

na·sal /náyzəl/ *adj. & n.* ● *adj.* **1** of, for, or relating to the nose. **2** *Phonet.* (of a sound) pronounced with the breath passing through the nose, e.g., *m*, *n*, *ng*, or French *en*. **3** (of the voice or speech) having an intonation caused by breathing through the nose. ● *n. Phonet.* a nasal sound. □□ **na·sal·i·ty** /-zálitee/ *n.* **na·sal·ize** *v.intr. & tr.* **na·sal·i·za·tion** *n.* **na·sal·ly** *adv.*

nas·cent /násənt, náy-/ *adj.* **1** in the act of being born. **2** just beginning to be; not yet mature. **3** *Chem.* just being formed and therefore unusually reactive (*nascent hydrogen*). □□ **nas·cen·cy** /násən-see, náy-/ *n.*

NASDAQ /názdak, nás-/ *abbr.* National Association of Securities Dealers Automated Quotations.

nas·tic /nástic/ *adj. Bot.* (of the movement of plant parts) not determined by an external stimulus.

nas·tur·tium /nəstərshəm/ *n.* **1** (in general use) a trailing plant, *Tropaeolum majus*, with rounded edible leaves and bright orange, yellow, or red flowers. **2** any cruciferous plant of the genus *Nasturtium*, including watercress.

nas·ty /nástee/ *adj. & n.* ● *adj.* (**nastier**, **nastiest**) **1 a** highly unpleasant. **b** annoying; objectionable

(*the car has a nasty habit of breaking down*). **2** difficult to negotiate; dangerous; serious (*a nasty fence; a nasty question; a nasty illness*). **3** (of a person or animal) ill-natured; spiteful; violent. **4** (of the weather) wet, stormy. ● *n.* (*pl.* **-ies**) *colloq.* a horror film, esp. one on video depicting cruelty or killing. □□ **nas·ti·ly** *adv.* **nas·ti·ness** *n.*

nat. *abbr.* **1** national. **2** natural.

na·tal /náytəl/ *adj.* of or from one's birth.

na·tal·i·ty /naytálitee, nə-/ *n.* (*pl.* **-ies**) birth rate.

Natch·ez /náchiz/ *n.* **1 a** a N. American people native to Mississippi. **b** a member of this people. **2** the language of this people.

na·tes /náyteez/ *n.pl. Anat.* the buttocks.

na·tion /náyshən/ *n.* **1** a community of people of mainly common descent, history, language, etc., forming a unified government or inhabiting a territory. **2** a tribe or confederation of tribes of Native Americans. □ **law of nations** *Law* international law. □□ **na·tion·hood** *n.*

na·tion·al /náshənəl/ *adj. & n.* ● *adj.* **1** of or common to a nation or the nation. **2** peculiar to or characteristic of a particular nation. ● *n.* a citizen of a specified country, usu. entitled to hold that country's passport (*French nationals*). □□ **na·tion·al·ly** *adv.*

na·tion·al an·them *n.* a song adopted by a nation, expressive of its identity, etc., and intended to inspire patriotism.

na·tion·al bank *n.* a bank chartered under the federal government.

na·tion·al debt *n.* the money owed by a country because of loans to it.

Na·tion·al Guard *n.* the primary reserve force partly maintained by the states of the United States but available for federal use.

na·tion·al·ism /náshənəlizəm/ *n.* **1 a** patriotic feeling, principles, etc. **b** an extreme form of this. **2** a policy of national independence. □□ **na·tion·al·ist** *n. & adj.* **na·tion·al·is·tic** *adj.* **na·tion·al·is·ti·cal·ly** *adv.*

na·tion·al·i·ty /náshənálitee/ *n.* (*pl.* **-ies**) **1 a** the status of belonging to a particular nation (*what is your nationality?; has Austrian nationality*). **b** a nation (*people of all nationalities*). **2** the condition of being national; distinctive national qualities. **3** an ethnic group forming a part of one or more political nations.

na·tion·al·ize /náshənəlīz/ *v.tr.* **1** take over (industry, land, etc.) from private ownership on behalf of the government. **2** make national. □□ **na·tion·al·i·za·tion** *n.*

na·tion·al park *n.* an area of natural beauty protected by the government for the use of the general public.

na·tion·wide /náyshənwíd/ *adj.* extending over the whole nation.

na·tive /náytiv/ *n. & adj.* ● *n.* **1 a** (usu. foll. by *of*) a person born in a specified place, or whose parents are domiciled in that place at the time of the birth (*a native of Chicago*). **b** a local inhabitant. **2** *offens.* a member of a nonwhite indigenous people, as regarded by the colonial settlers. **3** (usu. foll. by *of*) an indigenous animal or plant. ● *adj.* **1** (usu. foll. by *to*) belonging to a person or thing by nature; inherent; innate (*spoke with the facility native to him*). **2** of one's birth or birthplace (*native dress; native country*). **3** (usu. foll. by *to*) belonging to a specified place (*the anteater is native to S. America*). **4 a** (esp. of a non-European) born in a place. **b** of the natives of a place (*native customs*). □□ **na·tive·ly** *adv.* **na·tive·ness** *n.*

Na·tive A·mer·i·can *n.* a member of the aboriginal peoples of America or their descendants.

na·tiv·i·ty /nətivitee, nay-/ *n.* (*pl.* **-ies**) **1** (esp. the **Nativity**) **a** the birth of Christ. **b** the festival of Christ's birth; Christmas. **2** ▶ a picture of the Nativity. **3** birth. **4** the horoscope at a person's birth. **5** the birth of the Virgin Mary or St. John the Baptist.

NATO /náytō/ *abbr.* North Atlantic Treaty Organization.

nat·ter·jack /nátərjak/ *n.* ▼ a European toad, *Bufo calamita*, with a bright yellow stripe down its back, and moving by running, not hopping.

NATTERJACK
(*Bufo calamita*)

nat·ty /nátee/ *adj.* (**nattier**, **nattiest**) *colloq.* **1 a** smartly or neatly dressed. **b** spruce; smart (*a natty blouse*). **2** deft. □□ **nat·ti·ly** *adv.* **nat·ti·ness** *n.*

nat·u·ral /náchərəl/ *adj. & n.* ● *adj.* **1 a** existing in or caused by nature. **b** uncultivated (*existing in its natural state*). **2** in the course of nature (*died of natural causes*). **3** (of human nature, etc.) to be expected (*natural for her to be upset*). **4 a** (of a person or a person's behavior) unaffected, spontaneous. **b** (foll. by *to*) spontaneous; easy (*friendliness is natural to him*). **5 a** (of qualities, etc.) inherent (*a natural talent for music*). **b** (of a person) having such qualities (*a natural linguist*). **6** not disguised or altered by makeup, etc.). **7** lifelike. **8** likely by its or their nature to be such (*natural enemies*). **9 a** related by nature (*her natural son*). **b** illegitimate (*a natural child*). **10** *Mus.* (of a note) not sharpened or flattened (*B natural*). ● *n.* **1** *colloq.* (usu. foll. by *for*) a person or thing naturally suitable, adept etc. (*a natural for the championship*). **2** *Mus.* **a** a sign (♮) denoting a return to natural pitch after a sharp or a flat. ▷ NOTATION. **b** a natural note. □□ **nat·u·ral·ness** *n.*

nat·u·ral-born *adj.* having a character or position by birth.

nat·u·ral child·birth *n. Med.* childbirth with minimal medical or technological intervention.

nat·u·ral gas *n.* a flammable mainly methane gas found in the Earth's crust, not manufactured. ▷ GAS FIELD, OIL PLATFORM

nat·u·ral his·to·ry *n.* **1** the study of animals or plants. **2** the facts concerning the flora and fauna, etc., of a particular place or class (*a natural history of the Florida Keys*).

NATIVITY: 15TH-CENTURY NATIVITY BY FILIPPINO LIPPI

N

NATURALISM

Naturalist art and literature attempt to create an accurate representation of nature and character. This technique requires great attention to detail but does not exclude a concern for capturing the beauty of the subject.

The Gleaners (1857), JEAN-FRANÇOIS MILLET

nat·u·ral·ism /náchərəlizəm/ *n.* ▲ the theory or practice in art and literature of representing nature, character, etc. realistically and in great detail.

nat·u·ral·ist /náchərəlist/ *n.* **1** an expert in natural history. **2** a person who believes in or practices naturalism.

nat·u·ral·is·tic /náchərəlístik/ *adj.* **1** lifelike. **2** of or according to naturalism. **3** of natural history. □□ **nat·u·ral·is·ti·cal·ly** *adv.*

nat·ur·al·ize /náchərəlīz/ *v. tr.* **1** admit (a foreigner) to the citizenship of a country. **2** introduce (an animal, plant, etc.) into another region so that it flourishes in the wild. **3** adopt (a foreign word, custom, etc.). □□ **nat·ur·al·i·za·tion** *n.*

nat·u·ral law *n.* **1** *Philos.* unchanging moral principles common to all human beings. **2** a correct statement of an invariable sequence between specified conditions and a specified phenomenon.

nat·u·ral log·a·rithm *n.* a logarithm to the base *e* (2.71828 ...).

nat·u·ral·ly /náchərəlee, náchrə-/ *adv.* **1** in a natural manner. **2** as a natural result. **3** (qualifying a whole sentence) as might be expected; of course.

nat·u·ral num·bers *n.pl.* the integers 1, 2, 3, etc.

nat·u·ral re·sources *n.pl.* materials occurring in nature and capable of economic exploitation.

nat·u·ral sci·ence *n.* the sciences used in the study of the physical world, e.g., physics, chemistry, geology, biology, botany.

nat·u·ral se·lec·tion *n.* the Darwinian theory of the survival and propagation of organisms best adapted to their environment.

na·ture /náychər/ *n.* **1** a thing's or person's innate or essential qualities or character (*not in their nature to be cruel*). **2** (often **Nature**) **a** the physical power causing all the phenomena of the material world. **b** these phenomena, including plants, animals, landscape, etc. **3** a kind, sort, or class (*things of this nature*). **4** = HUMAN NATURE. **5 a** a specified element of human character (the rational nature; our animal nature). **b** a person of specified character (*even strong natures quail*). **6** the countryside, esp. when picturesque. **7** heredity as an influence on or determinant of personality. □ **by nature** innately. **from nature** *Art* using natural objects as models. **in** (or **of**) **the nature of** characteristically resembling or belonging to the class of (*the answer was in the nature of an excuse*).

na·tured /náychərd/ *adj.* (in comb.) having a specified disposition (*good-natured; ill-natured*).

na·tur·ism /náychərizəm/ *n.* **1** nudism. **2** naturalism in regard to religion. **3** the worship of natural objects. □□ **na·tur·ist** *n.*

na·tur·op·a·thy /náychərópəthee/ *n.* the treatment of disease, etc., without drugs, usu. involving diet, exercise, massage, etc. □□ **na·tur·o·path** /-əpáth/ *n.* **na·tur·o·path·ic** *adj.*

naught /nawt/ *n. & adj.* ● *n.* **1** *archaic* or *literary* nothing; nothingness. **2** zero; cipher. ● *adj.* (usu. *predic.*) *archaic* or *literary* worthless; useless. □ **come to naught** be ruined or baffled. **set at naught** disregard; despise.

naugh·ty /náwtee/ *adj.* (**naughtier, naughtiest**) **1** (esp. of children) disobedient; badly behaved. **2** *colloq. joc.* indecent. □□ **naugh·ti·ly** *adv.* **naugh·ti·ness** *n.*

nau·se·a /náwzeeə, -ᴢhə, -seeə, -shə/ *n.* **1** a feeling of sickness with an inclination to vomit. **2** loathing; revulsion.

nau·se·ate /náwzeeayt, -ᴢhee, -see, -shee/ *v.* **1** *tr.* affect with nausea; disgust (*was nauseated by the smell*). **2** *intr.* (usu. foll. by *at*) loathe food, an occupation, etc.; feel sick. □□ **nau·se·at·ing** *adj.* **nau·se·at·ing·ly** *adv.*

nau·seous /náwshəs, -zeeəs/ *adj.* **1** affected with nausea; sick. **2** causing nausea; offensive to the taste or smell. **3** disgusting; loathsome. □□ **nau·seous·ly** *adv.*

nau·ti·cal /náwtikəl/ *adj.* of or concerning sailors or navigation; naval; maritime. □□ **nau·ti·cal·ly** *adv.*

nau·ti·cal mile *n.* a unit of approx. 2,025 yards (1,852 meters). Also called **sea mile**.

nau·ti·lus /náwt'ləs/ *n.* (*pl.* **nautiluses** or **nautili** /-lī/) ◀ any cephalopod of the genus *Nautilus* with a light brittle spiral shell, esp. (**pearly nautilus**) one having a chambered shell with nacreous septa. ▷ SHELL

Nav·a·jo /návəhō, náa-/ *n.* (also **Nav·a·ho**) (*pl.* **-os**) **1** a member of a N. American people native to New Mexico and Arizona. **2** the language of this people.

na·val /náyvəl/ *adj.* **1** of, in, for, etc., the navy or a navy. **2** of or concerning ships (*a naval battle*).

na·val a·cad·e·my a college for training naval officers.

na·val ar·chi·tect *n.* a designer of ships.

na·val of·fi·cer an officer in a navy.

na·val stores all materials used in shipping.

nave¹ /nayv/ *n.* ▶ the central part of a church, usu. from the west door to the chancel and excluding the side aisles. ▷ CATHEDRAL

septum

buoyancy chambers

NAUTILUS: CROSS SECTION OF A NAUTILUS SHELL

nave² /nayv/ *n.* the hub of a wheel.

na·vel /náyvəl/ *n.* a depression in the center of the belly caused by the detachment of the umbilical cord.

nav·el or·ange *n.* a seedless orange with a navellike formation at the top. ▷ CITRUS FRUIT

nav·i·ga·ble /návigəbəl/ *adj.* (of a river, the sea, etc.) affording a passage for ships. □□ **nav·i·ga·bil·i·ty** *n.*

nav·i·gate /návigayt/ *v.* **1** *tr.* manage or direct the course of (a ship, aircraft, etc.). **2** *tr.* **a** sail on (a sea, river, etc.). **b** travel or fly through (the air). **3** *intr.* (of a passenger in a vehicle) assist the driver by map-reading, etc. **4** *intr.* sail a ship; sail in a ship.

nav·i·ga·tion /návigáyshən/ *n.* **1** the act of navigating. **2** any of several methods of determining a ship's or aircraft's position and course. □□ **nav·i·ga·tion·al** *adj.*

nav·i·ga·tor /návigaytər/ *n.* **1** a person skilled or engaged in navigation. **2** an explorer by sea.

na·vy /náyvee/ *n.* (*pl.* **-ies**) **1** (often **the Navy**) **a** the whole body of a nation's ships of war, including crews, maintenance systems, etc. **b** the officers, men, and women of a navy. **2** (in full **navy blue**) a dark-blue color.

na·vy bean *n.* a small white kidney bean, usu. dried for storage.

Na·vy Cross *n.* a US Navy decoration awarded for heroism.

na·vy yard *n.* a government shipyard where naval vessels are built, maintained, etc., and where naval supplies are stored.

na·wab /nəwaáb, -wáwb/ *n.* **1** the title of a distinguished Muslim in Pakistan. **2** *hist.* the title of a governor or nobleman in India.

nay /nay/ *adv. & n.* ● *adv.* **1** or rather; and more than that (*impressive, nay, magnificent*). **2** *archaic* = NO² *adv.* 1. ● *n.* **1** the word 'nay'. **2** a negative vote.

nay·say /náysay/ *v.* (*3rd sing. present* **-says**; *past* and *past part.* **-said**) **1** *intr.* utter a denial or refusal. **2** *tr.* refuse or contradict. □□ **nay·say·er** *n.*

Naz·a·rene /názəréen/ *n. & adj.* ● *n.* **1 a** (prec. by *the*) Christ. **b** (esp. in Jewish or Muslim use) a Christian. **2** a native or inhabitant of Nazareth. **3** a member of an early Jewish-Christian sect. ● *adj.* of or concerning Nazareth, Nazarenes, etc.

Na·zi /náatsee, nát-/ *n. & adj.* ● *n.* (*pl.* **Nazis**) **1** *hist.* a member of the German National Socialist party. **2** *derog.* a person holding extreme racist or authoritarian views or behaving brutally. ● *adj.* of or concerning the Nazis, Nazism, etc. □□ **Na·zi·dom** *n.* **Na·zi·fy** /-sifī/ *v.tr.* (**-ies, -ied**). **Na·zi·ism** /-see-izəm/ *n.* **Na·zism** /náatsizəm, nát-/ *n.*

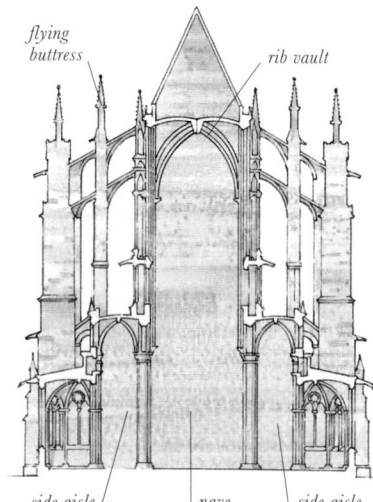

flying buttress

rib vault

side aisle   **nave**   **side aisle**

NAVE: CROSS SECTION OF A 13TH-CENTURY FRENCH CHURCH SHOWING THE NAVE

N

NB *abbr.* **1** New Brunswick. **2** nota bene.

Nb *symb. Chem.* the element niobium.

NBC *abbr.* National Broadcasting Company.

NC *abbr.* North Carolina (also in official postal use).

NCO *abbr.* noncommissioned officer.

ND *abbr.* North Dakota (in official postal use).

Nd *symb. Chem.* the element neodymium.

N.Dak. *abbr.* North Dakota.

NE *abbr.* **1** Nebraska (in official postal use). **2** northeast. **3** northeastern.

Ne *symb. Chem.* the element neon.

NEA *abbr.* National Education Association.

Ne·an·der·thal /neeándərthawl, -tawl, -taal/ *adj.* ► of or belonging to the type of human widely distributed in Paleolithic Europe, with a retreating forehead and massive brow ridges.

neap /neep/ *n.* (in full **neap tide**) a tide just after the first and third quarters of the Moon when there is least difference between high and low water. ▷ TIDE

retreating forehead

prominent brow ridge

NEANDERTHAL SKULL

Ne·a·pol·i·tan /néeəpólitən/ *n. & adj.* ● *n.* a native or citizen of Naples in Italy. ● *adj.* of or relating to Naples.

Ne·a·pol·i·tan ice cream *n.* ice cream made in layers of different colors and flavors, esp. vanilla, chocolate, and strawberry.

near /neer/ *adv., prep., adj., & v.* ● *adv.* **1** (often foll. by *to*) to or at a short distance in space or time; close by (*the time drew near; dropped near to them*). **2** closely (*as near as one can guess*). ● *prep.* (*compar. & superl.* also used) **1** to or at a short distance (in space, time, condition, or resemblance) from (*stood near the back; the sun is near setting*). **2** (in *comb.*) that is almost (*near-hysterical; a near-Communist*). ● *adj.* **1** close to, in place or time (*in the near future*). **2** closely related (*a near relation*). **3** (of a part of a vehicle, animal, or road) left (*the near foreleg*). **4** close; narrow (*a near escape*). **5** (of a road or way) direct. **6** niggardly; mean. ● *v.* **1** *tr.* approach; draw near to (*neared the harbor*). **2** *intr.* draw near (*could distinguish them as they neared*). □ **come** (or **go**) **near** (foll. by verbal noun, or *to* + verbal noun) almost succeed in (*came near to falling*). **go near** (foll. by *to* + infin.) narrowly fail. **near at hand 1** within easy reach. **2** in the immediate future. □□ **near·ish** *adj.* **near·ness** *n.*

near·by /néerbí/ *adj. & adv.* ● *adj.* situated in a near position (*a nearby hotel*). ● *adv.* close; not far away.

Near East *n.* the region comprising the countries of the eastern Mediterranean. □□ **Near East·ern** *adj.*

near·ly /néerlee/ *adv.* almost. □ **not nearly** nothing like (*not nearly enough*).

near miss *n.* **1** a bomb, etc., that is close to the target. **2** a situation in which a collision is narrowly avoided.

near·sight·ed /néersítid/ *adj.* having the inability to focus the eyes except on comparatively near objects. ▷ SIGHT. □□ **near·sight·ed·ly** *adv.* **near·sight·ed·ness** *n.*

neat /neet/ *adj.* **1** tidy and methodical. **2** elegantly simple in form. **3** (of language, style, etc.) brief, clear, and pointed. **4 a** cleverly executed (*a neat piece of work*). **b** deft; dexterous. **5** (of alcoholic liquor) undiluted. **6** *sl.* (as a general term of approval) pleasing, excellent. □□ **neat·ly** *adv.* **neat·ness** *n.*

neat·en /néet'n/ *v.tr.* make neat.

neath /neeth/ *prep. poet.* beneath.

Neb. *abbr.* Nebraska.

Nebr. *abbr.* Nebraska.

neb·u·la /nébyələ/ *n.* (*pl.* **nebulae** /-lee/ or **nebulas**) *Astron.* **1** ▼ a cloud of gas and dust, sometimes glowing and sometimes appearing as a dark silhouette against other glowing matter. **2** a bright area caused by a galaxy, or a large cloud of distant stars. ▷ STAR

neb·u·lar /nébyələr/ *adj.* of or relating to a nebula or nebulae.

neb·u·lous /nébyələs/ *adj.* **1** cloudlike. **2 a** formless; clouded. **b** hazy; indistinct; vague (*put forward a few nebulous ideas*). □□ **neb·u·los·i·ty** /-lósitee/ *n.* **neb·u·lous·ly** *adv.* **neb·u·lous·ness** *n.*

nec·es·sar·i·ly /nésəsérilee/ *adv.* as a necessary result; inevitably.

nec·es·sar·y /nésəseree/ *adj. & n.* ● *adj.* **1** requiring to be done, achieved, etc.; requisite; essential (*it is necessary to work; lacks the necessary documents*). **2** determined, existing, or happening by natural laws, predestination, etc., not by free will; inevitable (*a necessary evil*). ● *n.* (*pl.* **-ies**) (usu. in *pl.*) any of the basic requirements of life, such as food, warmth, etc. □ **the necessary** *colloq.* **1** money. **2** an action, item, etc., needed for a purpose (*they will do the necessary*).

ne·ces·si·tate /nisésitayt/ *v.tr.* make necessary (esp. as a result) (*will necessitate some sacrifice*).

ne·ces·si·tous /nisésitəs/ *adj.* poor; needy.

ne·ces·si·ty /nisésitee/ *n.* (*pl.* **-ies**) **1 a** an indispensable thing. **b** (usu. foll. by *of*) indispensability. **2** a state of things or circumstances enforcing a certain course (*there was a necessity to hurry*). **3** imperative need (*necessity is the mother of invention*). **4** want; poverty. □ **of necessity** unavoidably.

neck /nek/ *n. & v.* ● *n.* **1 a** ▼ the part of the body connecting the head to the shoulders. **b** the part of a shirt, dress, etc., around the neck. **2** something resembling a neck, such as the narrow part of a cavity or vessel, a channel isthmus, etc. **3** the part of a violin, etc., bearing the fingerboard. ▷ STRINGED. **4** the length of a horse's head and neck as a measure of its lead in a race. **5** the flesh of an animal's neck (*neck of lamb*). ● *v. intr. & tr. colloq.* kiss and caress amorously. □ **get it in the neck** *colloq.* **1** receive a severe reprimand. **2** suffer a severe blow. **neck and neck** running even in a race, etc. **up to one's neck** (often foll. by *in*) *colloq.* very deeply involved; very busy. □□ **necked** *adj.* (also in *comb.*). **neck·er** *n.* **neck·less** *adj.*

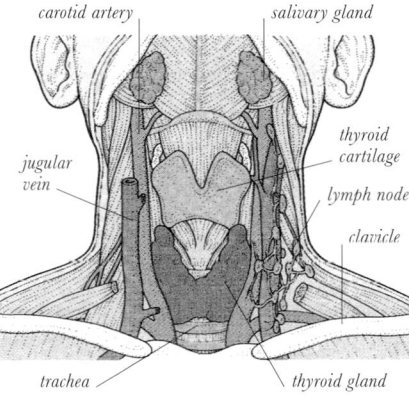

carotid artery   *salivary gland*

jugular vein   *thyroid cartilage*

lymph node

clavicle

trachea   *thyroid gland*

NECK: STRUCTURE OF THE
HUMAN NECK (FRONT VIEW)

neck·er·chief /nékərchif, -cheef/ *n.* a square of cloth worn around the neck.

neck·lace /nékləs/ *n.* a chain or string of beads, precious stones, links, etc., worn as an ornament around the neck.

neck·let /néklit/ *n.* **1** = NECKLACE. **2** a strip of fur worn around the neck.

neck·line /néklīn/ *n.* the edge or shape of the opening of a garment at the neck.

neck of the woods *n. colloq.* region; neighborhood.

neck·tie /néktī/ *n.* = TIE *n.* 2.

neck·tie par·ty /néktīpáartee/ *n. sl.* a lynching or hanging.

neck·wear /nékwair/ *n.* collars, ties, etc.

nec·ro·man·cy /nékrōmansee/ *n.* **1** the prediction of the future by supposed communication with the dead. **2** witchcraft. □□ **nec·ro·man·cer** *n.* **nec·ro·man·tic** /-mántik/ *adj.*

nec·ro·phil·i·a /nékrəfíleeə/ *n.* (also **nec·ro·phil·y** /nikrófilee/) a morbid and esp. erotic attraction to corpses. □□ **nec·ro·phile** /nékrəfīl/ *n.* **nec·ro·phil·i·ac** /-fíleeak/ *n.* **nec·ro·phil·ic** *adj.* **ne·croph·i·lism** /-krófilizəm/ *n.*

nec·rop·o·lis /nekrópəlis/ *n.* an ancient cemetery or burial place.

ne·cro·sis /nekrósis/ *n. Med. & Physiol.* the death of tissue caused by disease or injury, esp. gangrene or pulmonary tuberculosis. □□ **ne·crot·ic** /-krótik/ *adj.* **nec·ro·tize** /nékrətīz/ *v.intr.*

nec·tar /néktər/ *n.* **1** a sugary substance produced by plants and made into honey by bees. **2** (in Greek and Roman mythology) the drink of the gods. **3** a drink compared to this. □□ **nec·tar·if·er·ous** /-rífərəs/ *adj.* **nec·tar·ous** *adj.*

N

NEBULA

Nebulae are often called the birthplace of the stars. Dense regions of gas and dust contract and heat up under their own gravity, forming protostars. The rising heat can trigger a nuclear reaction, which creates a star.

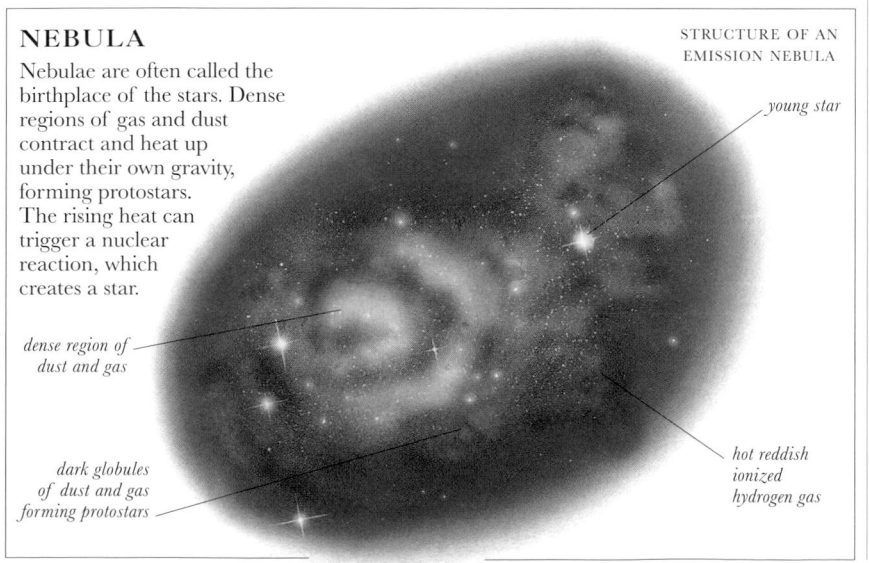

STRUCTURE OF AN
EMISSION NEBULA

young star

dense region of dust and gas

dark globules of dust and gas forming protostars

hot reddish ionized hydrogen gas

nec·tar·ine /néktəréen/ *n.* ▶ a variety of peach with a smooth skin.

née /nay/ *adj.* (also **nee**) (used in adding a married woman's maiden name after her surname) born (*Mrs. Ann Smith, née Jones*).

need /need/ *v. & n.* ● *v.tr.* **1** stand in want of; require. **2** (foll. by *to* + infin.; *3rd sing. present neg. or interrog.* **need** without *to*) be under the necessity or obligation (*it needs to be done carefully; need you ask?*). ● *n.* **1** a want or requirement (*my needs are few*). **2** circumstances requiring some course of action (*there is no need to worry*). **3** destitution; poverty. □ **at need** in time of need. **have need of** require; want. **in need** requiring help. **in need of** requiring. **need not have** did not need to (but did).

need·ful /néedfŏŏl/ *adj.* **1** requisite; necessary. **2** (prec. by *the*) **a** what is necessary. **b** *colloq.* money or action needed for a purpose. □□ **need·ful·ly** *adv.* **need·ful·ness** *n.*

nee·dle /néed'l/ *n. & v.* ● *n.* **1** **a** a very thin small piece of smooth steel, etc., pointed at one end and with a slit (eye) for thread at the other, used in sewing. ▷ SEWING MACHINE, STITCH. **b** a larger plastic, wooden, etc., slender stick without an eye, used in knitting. **2** a pointer on a dial. **3** any of several small thin pointed instruments, esp.: **a** a surgical instrument for stitching. **b** the end of a hypodermic syringe. **c** = STYLUS. **4** **a** an obelisk (*Cleopatra's Needle*). **b** a pointed rock or peak. **5** ▲ the leaf of a fir or pine tree. ▷ LEAF. ● *v.tr. colloq.* irritate; provoke (*the silence needled him*).

NEEDLES OF A PINE TREE

nee·dle·craft /néed'lkraft/ *n.* skill in needlework.

nee·dle in a hay·stack *n.* something almost impossible to find because it is concealed by so many other things, etc.

nee·dle·point /néed'lpoynt/ *n.* decorative needlework made with a needle.

need·less /néedlis/ *adj.* **1** unnecessary. **2** uncalled-for; gratuitous. □ **needless to say** of course; it goes without saying. □□ **need·less·ly** *adv.* **need·less·ness** *n.*

nee·dle·wom·an /néed'lwŏŏmən/ *n.* (*pl.* **-women**) **1** a seamstress. **2** a woman or girl with specified sewing skill (*a good needlewoman*).

nee·dle·work /néed'lwərk/ *n.* sewing or embroidery.

needs /needz/ *adv. archaic* (usu. prec. or foll. by *must*) of necessity.

need·y /néedee/ *adj.* (**needier**, **neediest**) **1** (of a person) poor; destitute. **2** (of circumstances) characterized by poverty. □□ **need·i·ness** *n.*

ne'er /nair/ *adv. poet.* = NEVER.

ne'er-do-well *n. & adj.* ● *n.* a good-for-nothing person. ● *adj.* good-for-nothing.

ne·far·i·ous /nifáireeəs/ *adj.* wicked. □□ **ne·far·i·ous·ly** *adv.* **ne·far·i·ous·ness** *n.*

neg. *abbr.* negative.

ne·gate /nigáyt/ *v.tr.* **1** nullify; invalidate. **2** assert the nonexistence of. **3** be the negation of. □□ **ne·ga·tor** *n.*

ne·ga·tion /nigáyshən/ *n.* **1** the absence or opposite of something actual or positive. **2 a** the act of denying. **b** an instance of this. **3** a contradiction, or denial. **4** a negative statement. **5** a negative or unreal thing. □□ **neg·a·to·ry** /négətáwree/ *adj.*

neg·a·tive /négətiv/ *adj., n., & v.* ● *adj.* **1** expressing or implying denial or refusal (*a negative vote; a negative answer*). **2** (of a person or attitude): lacking positive

attributes; apathetic; pessimistic. **3** marked by the absence of qualities (*a negative reaction; a negative result from the test*). **4** of the opposite nature to a thing regarded as positive (*debt is negative capital*). **5** *Algebra* (of a quantity) less than zero. **6** *Electr.* **a** of the kind of charge carried by electrons. **b** containing or producing such a charge. ● *n.* **1** a negative statement, reply, or word. **2** *Photog.* **a** ▼ an image with black and white reversed or colors replaced by complementary ones, from which positive pictures are obtained. **b** a developed film or plate bearing such an image. **3** (prec. by *the*) a position opposing the affirmative. ● *v.tr.* **1** refuse to accept or countenance; veto; reject. **2** disprove (an inference or hypothesis). **3** contradict (a statement). **4** neutralize (an effect). □□ **neg·a·tive·ly** *adv.* **neg·a·tive·ness** *n.* **neg·a·tiv·i·ty** /-tívitee/ *n.*

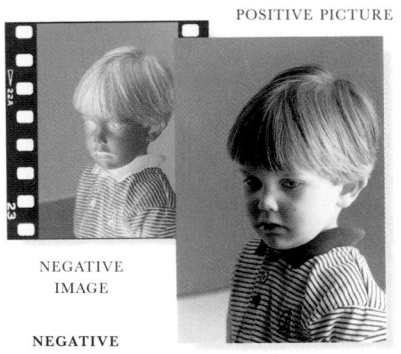

POSITIVE PICTURE

NEGATIVE IMAGE

NEGATIVE

neg·a·tive pole *n.* the south-seeking pole of a magnet. ▷ MAGNETIC FIELD

neg·a·tiv·ism /négətivizəm/ *n.* **1** a negative attitude; extreme skepticism, criticism, etc. **2** denial of accepted beliefs. □□ **neg·a·tiv·ist** *n.* **neg·a·tiv·is·tic** /-vístik/ *adj.*

ne·glect /niglékt/ *v. & n.* ● *v.tr.* **1** fail to care for or to do (*neglected their duty; neglected his children*). **2** (foll. by verbal noun, or *to* + infin.) overlook or forget the need to (*neglected to inform them*). **3** not pay attention to (*neglected the obvious warning*). ● *n.* **1** lack of caring; negligence (*the house suffered from neglect*). **2 a** the act of neglecting. **b** the state of being neglected (*the house fell into neglect*). **3** (usu. foll. by *of*) disregard. □□ **ne·glect·ful** *adj.* **ne·glect·ful·ly** *adv.*

neg·li·gee /néglizháy/ *n.* (also **negligée**, **négligé**) a woman's dressing gown made of sheer fabric.

neg·li·gence /néglijəns/ *n.* **1** a lack of proper care and attention. **2** an act of carelessness. □□ **neg·li·gent** /-jənt/ *adj.* **neg·li·gent·ly** *adv.*

neg·li·gi·ble /néglijibəl/ *adj.* not worth considering, trifling, insignificant. □□ **neg·li·gi·bil·i·ty** *n.* **neg·li·gi·bly** *adv.*

ne·go·tia·ble /nigóshəbəl, -sheeə-/ *adj.* **1** open to discussion. **2** able to be negotiated.

ne·go·ti·ate /nigósheeayt, -seeayt/ *v.* **1** *intr.* (usu. foll. by *with*) confer with others in order to reach a compromise or agreement. **2** *tr.* arrange (an affair) or bring about (a result) by negotiating (*negotiated a settlement*). **3** *tr.* find a way over, through, etc. (an obstacle, difficulty, etc.). **4** *tr.* **a** transfer (a check, etc.) to another for a consideration. **b** convert (a check, etc.) into cash. □□ **ne·go·ti·a·tion** /-áyshən/ *n.* **ne·go·ti·a·tor** *n.*

neg·ri·tude /néegritŏŏd, -tyŏŏd, nég-/ (also **Neg·ri·tude**) *n.* **1** the quality of being a Negro black person. **2** the affirmation or consciousness of the value of Negro black culture.

Ne·gro /néegrō/ *n. & adj.* ● *n.* (*pl.* **-oes**) a member of a dark-skinned race orig. native to Africa. ● *adj.* of or concerning Negroes (black people). ¶ The

term *black* or *African American* is usually preferred when referring to people.

Ne·groid /néegroyd/ *adj. & n.* ● *adj.* **1** (of features, etc.) characterizing a member of the Negro (black) race, esp. in having dark skin, tightly curled hair, and a broad flattish nose. **2** of or concerning Negroes (black people). ● *n.* a Negro (black person).

Ne·gus /néegəs/ *n. hist.* the title of the ruler of Ethiopia.

neigh /nay/ *n. & v.* ● *n.* the high whinnying sound of a horse. ● *v. intr.* make such a sound.

neigh·bor /náybər/ *n. & v.* ● *n.* **1** a person living next door to or near or nearest another. **2** a fellow human being. **3** a person or thing near or next to another. **4** (*attrib.*) neighboring. ● *v.* **1** *tr.* border on; adjoin. **2** *intr.* (often foll. by *on, upon*) border; adjoin. □□ **neigh·bor·ing** *adj.* **neigh·bor·less** *adj.* **neigh·bor·ship** *n.*

neigh·bor·hood /náybərhŏŏd/ *n.* **1** a district, esp. one forming a community within a town or city. **2** the people of a district. □ **in the neighborhood of** roughly; about (*paid in the neighborhood of $1000*).

neigh·bor·hood watch *n.* systematic local vigilance by householders to discourage crime, esp. against property.

neigh·bor·ly /náybərlee/ *adj.* friendly; kind. □□ **neigh·bor·li·ness** *n.*

nei·ther /néethər, nîth-/ *adj., pron., & adv.* ● *adj. & pron.* (foll. by sing. verb) not the one nor the other (of two things); not either (*neither of them knows; neither wish was granted*). ● *adv.* **1** not either; not on the one hand (foll. by *nor*, introducing the first of two or more things in the negative: *neither knowing nor caring; would neither come in nor go out*. **2** not either; also not (*if you do not, neither shall I*). **3** (with *neg.*) disp. either (*I don't know that neither*).

nek·ton /néktən/ *n. Zool.* any aquatic animal able to swim and move independently.

nel·lie /nélee/ *n.* a silly or effeminate person. □ **not on your nellie** *sl.* certainly not.

nel·son /nélsən/ *n.* a wrestling hold in which one arm is passed under the opponent's arm from behind and the hand is applied to the neck (**half nelson**), or both arms and hands are applied (**full nelson**).

nem·a·tode /némətōd/ *n.* any worm of the phylum Nematoda, with a slender unsegmented cylindrical shape. Also called **roundworm.**

nem. con. *abbr.* with no one dissenting.

nem·e·sis /némisis/ *n.* (*pl.* **nemeses** /-seez/) **1** retributive justice. **2 a** a downfall caused by this. **b** an agent of such a downfall.

neo- /née-ō/ *comb. form* **1** new; modern. **2** a new or revived form of.

ne·o·clas·si·cal /née-ōklásikəl/ *adj.* (also **ne·o·clas·sic** /-ik/) ▲ of or relating to a revival of a classical style in art. □□ **ne·o·clas·si·cism** /-sisizəm/ *n.* **ne·o·clas·si·cist** *n.*

ne·o·co·lo·ni·al·ism /née-ōkəlóneeəlizəm/ *n.* the use of economic, political, or other pressures to influence other countries, esp. former dependencies. □□ **ne·o·co·lo·ni·al·ist** *n. & adj.*

ne·o·dym·i·um /née-ədímeeəm/ *n. Chem.* a silvergray naturally occurring metallic element of the lanthanide series used in coloring glass, etc.

ne·o·lith·ic /née-əlíthik/ *adj.* of or relating to the later Stone Age.

ne·ol·o·gism /nee-óləjizəm/ *n.* **1** a new word or expression. **2** the coining or use of new words. □□ **ne·ol·o·gist** *n.* **ne·ol·o·gize** /-jīz/ *v.intr.*

ne·o·my·cin /née-ōmísin/ *n.* an antibiotic related to streptomycin.

ne·on /née-on/ *n. Chem.* an inert gaseous element giving an orange glow when electricity is passed through it (*neon sign*).

ne·o·nate /née-ənayt/ *n.* a newborn child. □□ **ne·o·na·tal** /-náyt'l/ *adj.*

ne·on tet·ra /nee-on tétrə/ *n.* a small brightly colored tropical freshwater fish, popular in aquariums.

N

NECTARINE (*Prunus persica* variety)

NEOCLASSICAL

In the late 18th and early 19th centuries, Europe became fascinated with the cultures of classical Greece and Rome. This interest was in part stimulated by the discovery and excavation of the remains of a number of ancient sites. Artists and architects were greatly influenced by the ancient civilizations and deliberately imitated their style, choosing symmetrical designs and classical motifs in rejection of the more frivolous rococo style. The movement spread from Europe to the US. Among the American classical revival buildings are the US Capitol by T. U. Walter and the University of Virginia by Thomas Jefferson.

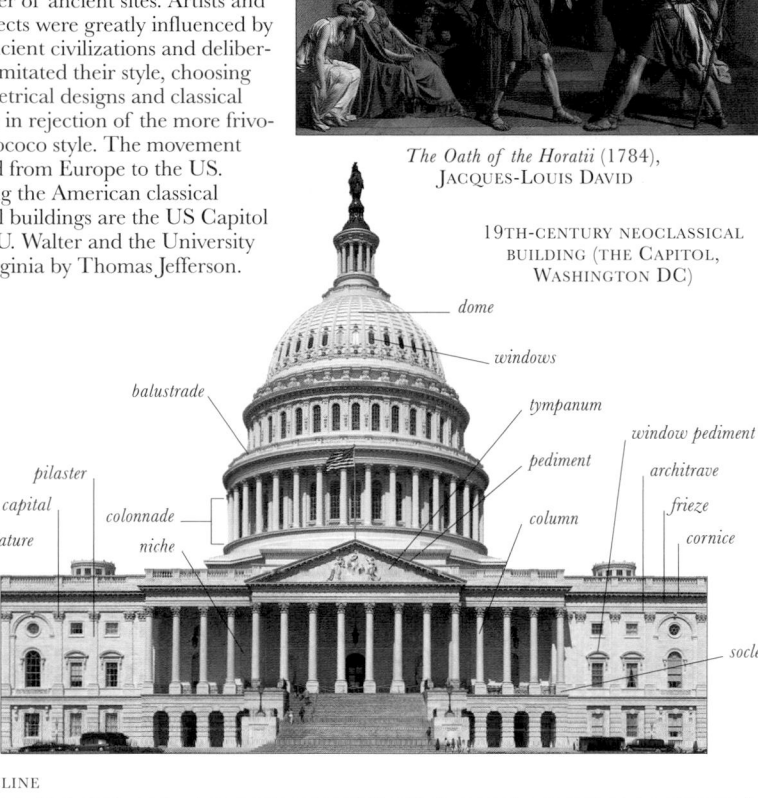

The Oath of the Horatii (1784),
JACQUES-LOUIS DAVID

19TH-CENTURY NEOCLASSICAL BUILDING (THE CAPITOL, WASHINGTON DC)

dome

windows

balustrade

tympanum

window pediment

pediment

pilaster

architrave

capital

colonnade

column

frieze

entablature

niche

cornice

socle

TIMELINE

| 1500 | 1550 | 1600 | 1650 | 1700 | 1750 | 1800 | 1850 | 1900 | 1950 | 2000 |

ne·o·phyte /nééəfīt/ *n.* **1** a new convert, esp. to a religious faith. **2** *RC Ch.* **a** a novice of a religious order. **b** a newly ordained priest. **3** a beginner; a novice.

ne·o·plasm /née-əplazəm/ *n.* a new and abnormal growth of tissue in some part of the body, esp. a tumor. □□ **ne·o·plas·tic** /-plástik/ *adj.*

ne·o·prene /née-əpreen/ *n.* a synthetic rubberlike polymer.

Nep·a·lese /népəleéz, -leés/ *adj. & n.* (*pl.* same) = NEPALI.

Ne·pal·i /nipáwlee/ *n. & adj.* ● *n.* (*pl.* same or **Nepalis**) **1 a** a native or national of Nepal in Central Asia. **b** a person of Nepali descent. **2** the language of Nepal. ● *adj.* of or relating to Nepal or its language or people.

neph·ew /néfyōō/ *n.* a son of one's brother or sister, or of one's brother-in-law or sister-in-law.

neph·rite /néfrīt/ ● *n.* ◄ a calcium magnesium silicate form of jade.

ne·phrit·ic /nəfrítik/ *adj.* **1** of or in the kidneys. **2** of or relating to nephritis.

ne·phri·tis /nefrítis/ *n.* inflammation of the kidneys. Also called **Bright's disease**.

NEPHRITE

ne plus ul·tra /náy plōōs ōōltraa, nē plus últrə/ *n.* **1** the furthest attainable point. **2** the culmination, acme, or perfection.

nep·o·tism /népətizəm/ *n.* favoritism shown to relatives in conferring offices or privileges. □□ **nep·o·tist** *n.* **nep·o·tis·tic** *adj.*

Nep·tune /néptōōn, -tyōōn/ *n.* ▼ a distant planet

of the solar system, eighth from the Sun, discovered in 1846 from mathematical computations. ▷ SOLAR SYSTEM

nep·tu·ni·um /neptōōneeəm, -tyōō-/ *n. Chem.* a radioactive transuranic metallic element produced when uranium atoms absorb bombarding neutrons.

nerd /nərd/ *n.* (also **nurd**) *sl.* **1** a foolish, feeble, or uninteresting person. **2** a person academically or intellectually talented but socially unskilled. □□ **nerd·y** *adj.*

ne·re·id /néereeid/ *n. Mythol.* a sea nymph.

ne·ro·li /nérəlee, néer-/ *n.* (in full **neroli oil**) an essential oil from the flowers of the Seville orange, used in perfumery.

nerv·ate /nérvayt/ *adj.* (of a leaf) having veins.

nerve /nərv/ *n. & v.* ● *n.* **1 a** a fiber or bundle of fibers that transmits impulses of sensation or motion between the brain or spinal cord and other parts of the body. ▷ NERVOUS SYSTEM, SKIN. **b** the material constituting these. **2 a** coolness in danger; bravery; assurance. **b** *colloq.* impudence; audacity (*they've got a nerve*). **3** (in *pl.*) nervousness; a condition of mental or physical stress (*need to calm my nerves*). **4** a rib of a leaf, esp. the midrib. ● *v.tr.* **1** (usu. *refl.*) brace (oneself) to face danger, suffering, etc. **2** give strength, vigor, or courage to. □ **get on a person's nerves** irritate or annoy a person. **have nerves of iron** (or **steel**) (of a person, etc.) be not easily upset or frightened. □□ **nerved** *adj.* (also in *comb.*).

nerve cell *n.* an elongated branched cell transmitting impulses in nerve tissue. ▷ NEURON

nerve cen·ter *n.* **1** a group of closely connected nerve cells associated in performing some function. **2** the center of control of an organization, etc.

nerve gas *n.* a poisonous gas affecting the nervous system.

nerve·less /nérvlis/ *adj.* **1** lacking vigor or spirit. **2** confident; not nervous. **3** *Anat. & Zool.* without nerves. □□ **nerve·less·ly** *adv.* **nerve·less·ness** *n.*

nerve-rack·ing *adj.* (also **nerve-wrack·ing**) stressful; frightening.

nerv·ine /nérvin/ *adj. & n.* ● *adj.* relieving nerve disorders. ● *n.* a nervine drug.

nervo- /nérvō/ *comb. form* (also **nerv-** before a vowel) a nerve or the nerves.

nerv·ous /nérvəs/ *adj.* **1** having delicate or disordered nerves. **2** timid or anxious. **3 a** excitable; highly strung; easily agitated. **b** resulting from this temperament (*nervous tension; a nervous headache*). **4** affecting or acting on the nerves. **5** (foll. by *about* + verbal noun) reluctant; afraid (*am nervous about meeting them*). □□ **nerv·ous·ly** *adv.* **nerv·ous·ness** *n.*

nerv·ous break·down *n.* a period of mental illness, usu. resulting from severe depression or anxiety.

N

NEPTUNE

The planet Neptune is believed to consist of a small solid core surrounded by a mixture of gases and liquids. It has four unstable rings and eight known moons.

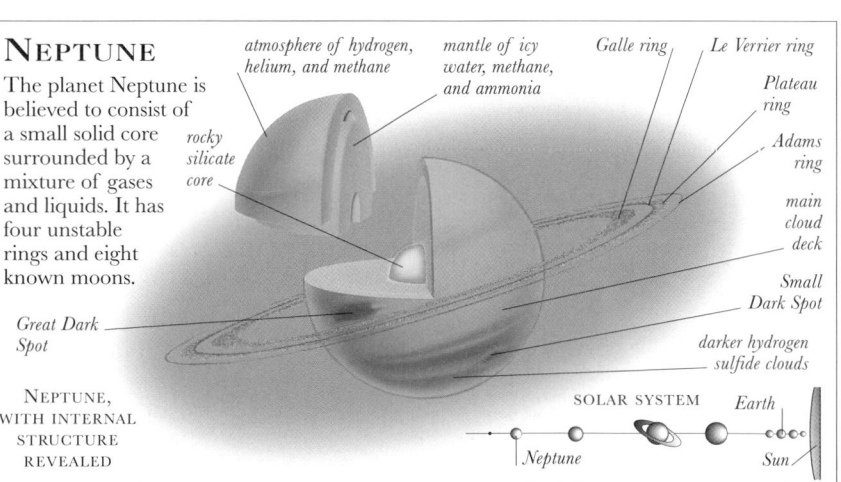

atmosphere of hydrogen, helium, and methane

mantle of icy water, methane, and ammonia

Galle ring

Le Verrier ring

Plateau ring

rocky silicate core

Adams ring

main cloud deck

Great Dark Spot

Small Dark Spot

darker hydrogen sulfide clouds

NEPTUNE, WITH INTERNAL STRUCTURE REVEALED

SOLAR SYSTEM

Earth

Neptune

Sun

nerv·ous sys·tem *n.* ▼ the body's network of specialized cells that transmit nerve impulses. ▷ AUTONOMIC NERVOUS SYSTEM, PERIPHERAL NERVOUS SYSTEM

nerv·ous wreck *n. colloq.* a person suffering from mental stress, exhaustion, etc.

ner·vure /nárvyər/ *n.* **1** each of the hollow tubes that form the framework of an insect's wing. **2** the principal vein of a leaf.

nerv·y /nárvee/ *adj.* (**nervier, nerviest**) **1** bold; impudent; pushy. **2** esp. *Brit.* nervous; easily excited or disturbed. **3** *archaic* sinewy; strong. □□ **nerv·i·ly** *adv.* **nerv·i·ness** *n.*

nes·cient /néshənt, -eeənt/ *adj. literary* (foll. by *of*) lacking knowledge; ignorant. □□ **nesc·ience** *n.*

ness /nes/ *n.* a headland or promontory.

nest /nest/ *n. & v.* ● *n.* **1** ▶ a structure or place where a bird lays eggs and shelters its young. **2** ▶ an animal's or insect's breeding place or lair. **3** a snug retreat or shelter. **4** (often foll. by *of*) a place fostering something undesirable (*a nest of vice*). **5** a brood or swarm. **6** a group or set of similar objects, often of different sizes and fitting together for storage (*a nest of tables*). ● *v.intr.* **1** use or build a nest. **2** collect wild birds' nests. **3** (of objects) fit together or one inside another. □□ **nest·ful** *n.* (*pl.* **-fuls**). **nest·ing** *n.* (in sense 2 of *v.*).

nest egg *n.* a sum of money saved for the future.

nes·tle /nésəl/ *v.* **1** *intr.* (often foll. by *down, in*, etc.) settle oneself comfortably. **2** *intr.* press oneself against another in affection, etc. **3** *tr.* (foll. by *in, into*, etc.) push (a head or shoulder, etc.) affectionately or snugly. **4** *intr.* lie half hidden.

nest·ling /nésling, nést-/ *n.* a bird that is too young to leave its nest.

net¹ /net/ *n. & v.* ● *n.* **1** an open-meshed fabric of cord, rope, etc.; a structure resembling this. **2** a piece of net used esp. to restrain, contain, or delimit, or to catch fish or other animals. ▷ SEINE, TRAWL. **3** a structure with net used in various games, esp. forming the goal in soccer, hockey, etc., and dividing the court in tennis, etc. ▷ BADMINTON. **4** a system or procedure for catching or entrapping a person or persons. **5** = NETWORK. ● *v.tr.* (**netted, netting**) **1 a** cover, confine, or catch with a net. **b** procure as with a net. **2** hit (a ball) into the net, esp. of a goal. **3** (usu. as **netted** *adj.*) mark with a netlike pattern. □□ **net·ful** *n.* (*pl.* **-fuls**).

net² /net/ *adj. & v.* ● *adj.* **1** (esp. of money) remaining after all necessary deductions, or free from deductions. **2** (of a price) to be paid in full; not reducible. **3** (of a weight) excluding that of the packaging, etc. **4** (of an effect, etc.) ultimate, effective. ● *v.tr.* (**netted, netting**) gain or yield (a sum) as net profit.

neth·er /néthər/ *adj. archaic* = LOWER¹. □□ **neth·er·most** *adj.*

Ne·ther·lan·der /néthərlandər/ *n.* **1** a native or national of the Netherlands. **2** a person of Dutch descent. □□ **Ne·ther·land·ish** *adj.*

neth·er re·gions *n.pl.* (also **world**) hell; the underworld.

net prof·it *n.* the effective profit; the actual gain after expenses have been paid.

ne·tsu·ke /nétsŏŏkee/ *n.* (*pl.* same or **netsukes**) (in Japan) ▶ a carved buttonlike ornament, esp. of ivory or wood.

net·ting /néting/ *n.* **1** netted fabric. **2** a piece of this.

net·tle /nét'l/ *n. & v.* ● *n.* **1** any plant of the genus *Urtica*, esp. *U. dioica*, with jagged leaves covered with stinging hairs. **2** a plant resembling this. ● *v.tr.* **1** irritate; annoy. **2** sting with nettles.

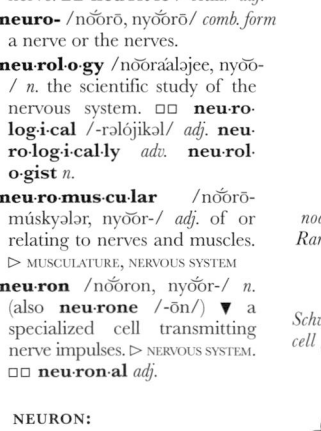

NETSUKE

net·work /nétwərk/ *n. & v.* ● *n.* **1** an arrangement of intersecting horizontal and vertical lines, like the structure of a net. **2** a complex system of railways, roads, canals, etc. **3** a group of people who exchange information, contacts, and experience for professional or social purposes. **4** a chain of interconnected computers, machines, or operations. **5** a system of connected electrical conductors. **6** a group of broadcasting stations connected for a simultaneous broadcast of a program. ● *v.* **1** *tr.* link (machines, esp. computers) to operate interactively. **2** *intr.* establish a network. **3** *Brit. tr.* broadcast on a network. **4** *intr.* be a member of a network (see sense 3 of *n.*).

net·work·er /nétwərkər/ *n. Computing* a member of a computer network who operates from home, from an external office, or from one of several computer terminals within an office.

neu·ral /nŏŏrəl, nyŏŏr-/ *adj.* of or relating to a nerve or the central nervous system. □□ **neu·ral·ly** *adv.*

neu·ral·gia /nŏŏráljə, nyŏŏ-/ *n.* an intense intermittent pain along the course of a nerve, esp. in the head or face. □□ **neu·ral·gic** *adj.*

neu·ral net·work *n.* (also **neu·ral net**) *Computing* a computer system modeled on the human brain and nervous system.

neur·as·the·ni·a /nŏŏrəstheéneeə, nyŏŏr-/ *n.* a general term for fatigue, anxiety, listlessness, etc. (not in medical use). □□ **neur·as·then·ic** /-thénik/ *adj. & n.*

neu·ri·tis /nŏŏrítis, nyŏŏ-/ *n.* inflammation of a nerve. □□ **neu·rit·ic** /-rítik/ *adj.*

neuro- /nŏŏrō, nyŏŏrō/ *comb. form* a nerve or the nerves.

neu·rol·o·gy /nŏŏráaləjee, nyŏŏ-/ *n.* the scientific study of the nervous system. □□ **neu·ro·log·i·cal** /-rəlójikəl/ *adj.* **neu·ro·log·i·cal·ly** *adv.* **neu·rol·o·gist** *n.*

neu·ro·mus·cu·lar /nŏŏrō-múskyələr, nyŏŏr-/ *adj.* of or relating to nerves and muscles. ▷ MUSCULATURE, NERVOUS SYSTEM

neu·ron /nŏŏron, nyŏŏr-/ *n.* (also **neu·rone** /-ōn/) ▼ a specialized cell transmitting nerve impulses. ▷ NERVOUS SYSTEM. □□ **neu·ron·al** *adj.*

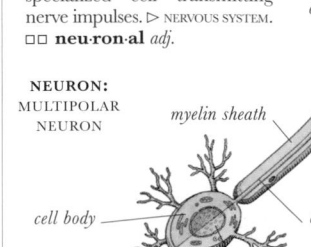

NERVOUS SYSTEM

The nervous system is a network of fibers and neurons controlling the actions and reactions of the body. The central nervous system (CNS) is composed of the brain and spinal cord, which receive and integrate signals relayed from the sense organs (such as the eyes, nose, and ears) via the peripheral nervous system. The latter includes the autonomic nervous system, which controls unconscious functions, such as heartbeat and breathing.

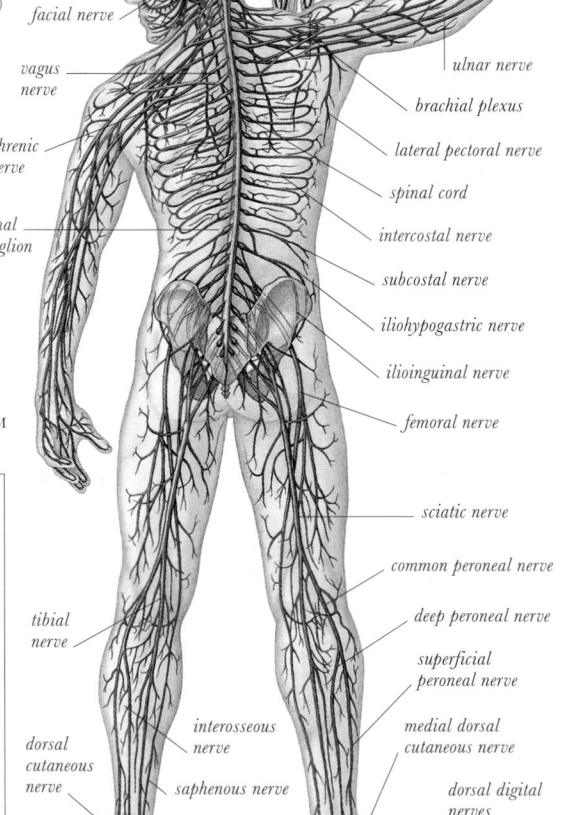

HUMAN
NERVOUS SYSTEM

cerebellum
brain
radial nerve
median nerve
optic nerve
facial nerve
vagus nerve
ulnar nerve
brachial plexus
phrenic nerve
lateral pectoral nerve
spinal cord
spinal ganglion
intercostal nerve
subcostal nerve
iliohypogastric nerve
ilioinguinal nerve
femoral nerve
sciatic nerve
common peroneal nerve
deep peroneal nerve
superficial peroneal nerve
tibial nerve
interosseous nerve
saphenous nerve
dorsal cutaneous nerve
medial dorsal cutaneous nerve
dorsal digital nerves
lateral plantar nerve
medial plantar nerve

SECTION THROUGH
A NERVE

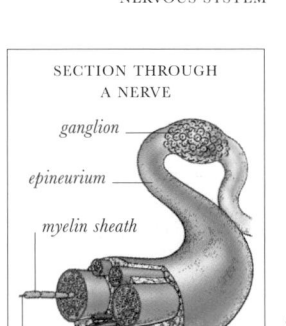

ganglion
epineurium
myelin sheath
axon
perineurium
fascicle (bundle)

N

synaptic knob

node of Ranvier

Schwann cell

myelin sheath

axon

cell body

dendrite

nucleus

NEURON:
MULTIPOLAR
NEURON

NEST

Many animals invest a lot of time and energy in building a nest. Construction may often involve complex techniques, such as grass weaving. It may also require a very specific building material, such as the "paper" made by wasps or the mixture of mud and saliva made by termites.

KESTREL NEST

MOLE NEST

TERMITE NEST (MOUND)

COMMUNAL WEAVERBIRD NESTS

WASP NEST

neu·ro·path /nŏŏrōpath, nyŏŏr-/ *n.* a person affected by nervous disease, or with an abnormally sensitive nervous system. □□ **neu·ro·path·ic** *adj.* **neu·rop·a·thy** /-rópəthee/ *n.*

neu·ro·pa·thol·o·gy /nŏŏrōpəthóləjee, nyŏŏr-/ *n.* the pathology of the nervous system. □□ **neu·ro·pa·thol·o·gist** *n.*

neu·ro·phys·i·ol·o·gy /nŏŏrōfizeeóləjee, nyŏŏr-/ *n.* the physiology of the nervous system. □□ **neu·ro·phys·i·o·log·i·cal** /-zeeəlójikəl/ *adj.* **neu·ro·phys·i·ol·o·gist** *n.*

neu·rop·ter·an /nŏŏróptərən, nyŏŏ-/ *n.* ▼ any insect of the order Neuroptera, including lacewings, having four finely veined membranous leaflike wings. ▷ INSECT. **neu·rop·ter·ous** *adj.*

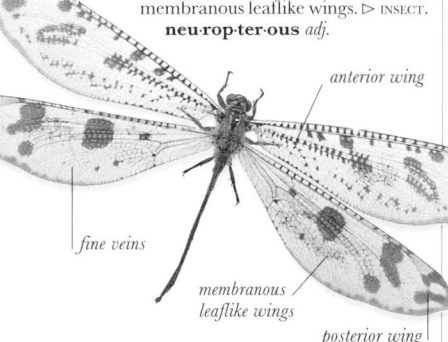

anterior wing

fine veins

membranous leaflike wings

posterior wing

NEUROPTERAN: ANT LION (*Palpares libelluloides*)

neu·ro·sis /nŏŏrṓsis, nyŏŏ-/ *n.* (*pl.* **neuroses** /-seez/) a mental illness characterized by irrational or depressive thought or behavior, caused by a disorder of the nervous system usu. without organic change.

neu·ro·sur·ger·y /nŏŏrōsɔ́rjəree, nyŏŏr-/ *n.* surgery performed on the nervous system, esp. the brain and spinal cord. **3** *colloq.* abnormally difficult. □□ **neu·ro·sur·geon** *n.* **neu·ro·sur·gi·cal** *adj.*

neu·rot·ic /nŏŏrótik, nyŏŏ-/ *adj.* & *n.* ● *adj.* **1** caused by or relating to neurosis. **2** (of a person) suffering from neurosis. **3** *colloq.* abnormally sensitive or obsessive. ● *n.* a neurotic person. □□ **neu·rot·i·cal·ly** *adv.* **neu·rot·i·cism** /-isizəm/ *n.*

neu·ro·trans·mit·ter /nŏŏrōtránsmitər, -tránz-, nyŏŏr-/ *n. Biochem.* a chemical substance released

from a nerve fiber that effects the transfer of an impulse to another nerve or muscle. ▷ SYNAPSE.

neu·ter /nŏŏtər, nyŏŏ-/ *adj., n., & v.* ● *adj.* **1** *Gram.* (of a noun, etc.) neither masculine nor feminine. **2** (of a plant) having neither pistils nor stamen. **3** (of an insect, animal, etc.) sexually undeveloped; castrated or spayed. ● *n.* **1** *Gram.* a neuter word. **2 a** a nonfertile insect, esp. a worker bee or ant. **b** a castrated animal. ● *v.tr.* castrate or spay.

neu·tral /nŏŏtrəl, nyŏŏ-/ *adj. & n.* ● *adj.* **1** not helping nor supporting either of two opposing sides; impartial. **2** belonging to a neutral party, nation, etc. (*neutral ships*). **3** indistinct; indeterminate. **4** (of a gear) in which the engine is disconnected from the driven parts. **5** (of colors) not strong nor positive; gray or beige. **6** *Chem.* neither acid nor alkaline. **7** *Electr.* neither positive nor negative. **8** *Biol.* sexually undeveloped. ● *n.* **1** a neutral nation, person, etc. **2** a neutral gear. □□ **neu·tral·i·ty** /-trálitee/ *n.* **neu·tral·ly** *adv.*

neu·tral·ism /nŏŏtrəlizəm, nyŏŏ-/ *n.* a policy of political neutrality. □□ **neu·tral·ist** *n.*

neu·tral·ize /nŏŏtrəlīz, nyŏŏ-/ *v.tr.* **1** make neutral. **2** counterbalance. **3** exempt or exclude (a place) from the sphere of hostilities. □□ **neu·tral·i·za·tion** *n.* **neu·tral·iz·er** *n.*

neu·tri·no /nŏŏtréenō, nyŏŏ-/ *n.* (*pl.* **-os**) any of a group of stable elementary particles with zero electric charge and probably zero mass, which travel at the speed of light.

neu·tron /nŏŏtron, nyŏŏ-/ *n.* an elementary particle of about the same mass as a proton but without an electric charge. ▷ ATOM, NUCLEUS

neu·tron bomb *n.* a bomb producing neutrons and little blast, causing damage to life but little destruction to property.

Nev. *abbr.* Nevada.

nev·er /névər/ *adv.* **1 a** at no time; on no occasion. **b** *colloq.* as an emphatic negative (*I never heard you come in*). **2** not at all (*never fear*). □ **never say die** see DIE[1]. **well I never!** expressing great surprise.

nev·er-end·ing *adj.* eternal; undying.

nev·er·more /névərmáwr/ *adv.* at no future time.

nev·er-nev·er land *n.* an imaginary utopian place.

nev·er·the·less /névərthəlés/ *adv.* in spite of that.

ne·vus /néevəs/ *n.* (*pl.* **nevi** /-vī/) **1** a birthmark in the form of a raised red patch on the skin. **2** = MOLE[2].

new /nŏŏ, nyŏŏ/ *adj. & adv.* ● *adj.* **1 a** of recent

origin or arrival. **b** made, discovered, acquired, or experienced recently or now for the first time. **2** in original condition; not worn or used. **3 a** renewed or reformed (*the new order*). **b** reinvigorated (*felt like a new person*). **4** different from a recent previous one (*has a new job*). **5** (often foll. by *to*) unfamiliar or strange (*a new sensation*). **6** (often foll. by *at*) (of a person) inexperienced (*am new at this business*). **7** (usu. prec. by *the*) often *derog.* **a** later; modern. **b** newfangled. **c** recently affected by social change (*the new rich*). **8** (often prec. by *the*) advanced in method or theory (*the new formula*). **9** (in place names) discovered or founded later than and named after (*New York*). ● *adv.* (usu. in *comb.*) **1** newly; recently (*new-baked*). **2** anew; afresh. □□ **new·ish** *adj.* **new·ness** *n.*

New Age *n.* a set of beliefs intended to replace traditional Western Culture, with alternative approaches to religion, medicine, the environment, music, etc.

new·born /nŏŏbawrn, nyŏŏ-/ *adj.* (of a child, etc.) recently born.

new·com·er /nŏŏkumər, nyŏŏ-/ *n.* **1** a person who has recently arrived. **2** a beginner in some activity.

new·el /nŏŏəl, nyŏŏ-/ *n.* **1** the supporting central post of winding stairs. **2** ▼ the top or bottom supporting post of a stair rail.

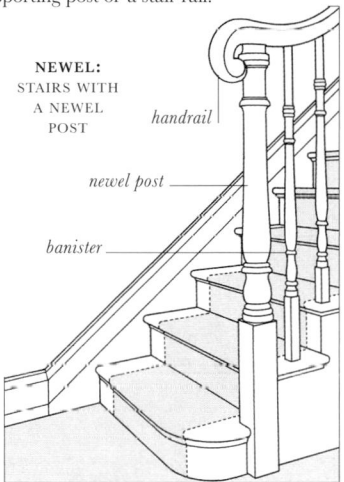

NEWEL: STAIRS WITH A NEWEL POST

handrail

newel post

banister

new·fan·gled /nŏŏfánggəld, nyŏŏ-/ *adj. derog.* different from what one is used to; objectionably new.

new·ly /nŏŏlee, nyŏŏ-/ *adv.* **1** recently (*a newly discovered country*). **2** afresh (*newly painted*). **3** in a different manner (*newly arranged*).

new·ly·wed /nŏŏleewed, nyŏŏ-/ *n.* a recently married person.

new moon *n.* **1** the Moon when first seen as a crescent after conjunction with the Sun. **2** the time of its appearance.

news /nŏŏz, nyŏŏz/ *n.pl.* (usu. treated as *sing.*) **1** information about important or interesting recent events, esp. when published or broadcast. **2** (prec. by *the*) a broadcast report of news. **3** newly received or noteworthy information. **4** (foll. by *to*) *colloq.* information not previously known (to a person) (*that's news to me*).

news·boy /nŏŏzboy, nyŏŏz-/ *n.* a boy who sells or delivers newspapers.

news·cast /nŏŏzkast, nyŏŏz-/ *n.* a broadcast of news reports.

news·cast·er /nŏŏzkastər, nyŏŏz-/ *n.* a person who reads the news broadcast on radio or television.

news flash /nŏŏzflash, nyŏŏz-/ *n.* a single item of important news, broadcast separately and often interrupting other programs.

news·girl /nŏŏzgərl, nyŏŏz-/ *n.* a girl who sells or delivers newspapers.

news·group /nŏŏzgrōŏp, nyŏŏ-/ *n.* a group of Internet users who exchange messages on a topic of mutual interest.

N

NEWT

Newts are amphibians that usually live on land for part of the year, returning to the water during the breeding season in spring. They have cylindrical bodies; four-toed feet; dry, not slippery, skin; and vertically compressed tails.

EXTERNAL FEATURES OF
A GREAT CRESTED NEWT
(*Triturus cristatus*)

cylindrical body

eye on top
of head

dry skin

crest

conspicuous
markings

vertically
compressed tail

four-toed
foot

EXAMPLES OF OTHER NEWTS

CALIFORNIA NEWT
(*Taricha torosa*)

MARBLED NEWT
(*Triturus marmoratus*)

FIRE-BELLIED NEWT
(*Cynops pyrrhogaster*)

MANDARIN NEWT
(*Tylototriton verrucosus*)

ITALIAN
CRESTED NEWT
(*Triturus carnifex*)

PALMATE NEWT
(*Triturus helveticus*)

ALPINE NEWT
(*Triturus alpestris*)

news·let·ter /nōōzletər, nyōōz-/ *n.* an informal printed report issued periodically to the members of a society, business, organization, etc.

news·man /nōōzman, -mən, nyōōz-/ *n.* (*pl.* **-men**) a journalist.

news·pa·per /nōōzpaypər, nyōōz-, nōōs-, nyōōs-/ *n.* **1** a printed publication (usu. daily or weekly) containing news, advertisements, correspondence, etc. **2** the sheets of paper forming this.

news·pa·per·man /nōōzpaypərman, -mən, nyōōz-, nōōs-, nyōōs-/ *n.* (*pl.* **-men**) a journalist.

new·speak /nōōspeek, nyōō-/ *n.* (also **New-speak**) ambiguous euphemistic language used esp. in political propaganda.

news·print /nōōzprint, nyōōz-/ *n.* a type of low-quality paper on which newspapers are printed.

news·read·er /nōōzreedər, nyōōz-/ *n. Brit.* = NEWSCASTER.

news·reel /nōōzreel, nyōōz-/ *n.* a short movie of recent events.

news·room /nōōzroom, nyōōz-/ *n.* a room in a newspaper or broadcasting office where news stories are prepared.

news·stand /nōōzstand, nyōōz-/ *n.* a stall for the sale of newspapers, etc.

news·wor·thy /nōōzwərthee, nyōōz-/ *adj.* topical. □□ **news·wor·thi·ness** *n.*

news·y /nōōzee, nyōō-/ *adj.* (**newsier, newsiest**) *colloq.* full of news.

newt /nōōt, nyōōt/ *n.* ◀ any of various small amphibians, esp. of the genus *Triturus*, having a well-developed tail.

New Tes·ta·ment *n.* the part of the Bible concerned with the life and teachings of Christ and his earliest followers.

new·ton /nōōt'n, nyōō-/ *n. Physics* the SI unit of force.

New·to·ni·an /nōōtóneeən, nyōō-/ *adj.* of or devised by Isaac Newton.

new wave *n.* **1** = a nontraditional trend or movement. **2** a style of rock music popular in the 1970s.

New World *n.* N. and S. America regarded collectively in relation to Europe.

New Year's Day *n.* January 1.

New Year's Eve *n.* December 31.

New York min·ute *n. US colloq.* a very short time; a moment.

New Zea·land·er /nōōzéeləndər, nyōō-/ *n.* **1** a native or national of New Zealand, an island group in the Pacific. **2** a person of New Zealand descent.

next /nekst/ *adj. & adv.* ● *adj.* **1** (often foll. by *to*) being or positioned or living nearest. **2** the nearest in order of time; the soonest encountered (*next Friday; ask the next person you see*). ● *adv.* **1** (often foll. by *to*) in the nearest place or degree (*came next to last*). **2** on the first or soonest occasion (*when we next meet*). □ **next to** almost (*next to nothing*).

next door *adv. & adj.* (as *adj.* often hyphenated) in or to the next house or room.

next of kin *n.* the closest living relative or relatives.

nex·us /néksəs/ *n.* (*pl.* same) **1** a connected group or series. **2** a connection.

Nez Per·cé /náy persáy/ *n.* (also **Nez Perce** /néz párs, nés pérs/) **1 a** a N. American people native to the northwestern US. **b** a member of this people. **2** the language of this people.

NFL *abbr.* National Football League.

Nfld. *abbr.* (also **NF**) Newfoundland.

NH *abbr.* New Hampshire (also in official postal use).

NI *abbr.* Northern Ireland.

Ni *symb. Chem.* the element nickel.

ni·a·cin /níəsin/ *n.* = NICO-TINIC ACID.

nib /nib/ *n.* **1** ▶ the point of a pen, which touches the writing surface. **2** (in *pl.*) shelled and crushed coffee or cocoa beans. **3** the point of a tool, etc.

nib·ble /níbəl/ *v. & n.* ● *v.* **1** *tr. &* (foll. by *at*) *intr.* **a** take small bites at. **b** eat in small amounts. **c** bite at gently. **2** *intr.* (foll. by *at*) show cautious interest in. ● *n.* **1** an instance of nibbling. **2** a very small amount of food. **3** *Computing* half a byte, i.e., 4 bits. □□ **nib·bler** *n.*

nib·lick /níblik/ *n. Golf* an iron with a large round heavy head, used esp. for playing out of bunkers.

nibs /nibz/ *n.* □ **his nibs** *colloq.* a mock title used to refer to a self-important man.

ni·cad /níkad/ *adj. & n.* ● *adj.* nickel and cadmium. ● *n.* a nickel and cadmium battery.

nice /nīs/ *adj.* **1** pleasant; satisfactory. **2** (of a person) kind; good-natured. **3** *iron.* bad or awkward (*a nice mess you've made*). **4** fine or subtle (*a nice distinction*). **5** fastidious; delicately sensitive. **6** scrupulous (*were not too nice about their methods*). **7** (foll. by an adj., often with *and*) satisfactory in terms of the

iridium tip

tine

slit

eye

wing

wing

heel

NIB OF A
FOUNTAIN PEN

N

quality described (*nice and warm*). □ **nice work** a task well done. □□ **nice·ly** *adv.* **nice·ness** *n.*

ni·ce·ty /nísitee/ *n.* (*pl.* **-ies**) **1** a subtle detail. **2** precision; accuracy. **3** subtle quality (*a point of great nicety*). **4** (in *pl.*) refinements. □ **to a nicety** with exactness.

niche /nich, neesh/ *n.* **1** a shallow recess, esp. in a wall to contain a statue, etc. ▷ FAÇADE. **2** a comfortable or suitable position in life or employment.

nick /nik/ *n. & v.* ● *n.* a small cut. ● *v.tr.* make a nick or nicks in. □ **in the nick of time** only just in time.

nick·el /níkəl/ *n. & v.* ● *n.* **1** *Chem.* a malleable ductile silver-white metallic element, used in magnetic alloys. **2** a five-cent coin. ● *v.tr.* (**nickeled, nickeling**) coat with nickel.

nick·el-and-dime *adj. & v.* ● *adj.* involving a small amount of money; trivial. ● *v.tr.* weaken (one's financial position) by continued small expenses, etc.

nick·el·o·de·on /níkəlṓdeeən/ *n. colloq.* **1** an early movie theater, esp. one with admission priced at 5 cents. **2** a jukebox.

nick·nack var. of KNICKKNACK.

nick·name /níknaym/ *n. & v.* ● *n.* a familiar name given to a person instead of or as well as the real name. ● *v.tr.* **1** give a nickname to. **2** call by a nickname.

nic·o·tine /níkəteen/ *n.* a colorless poisonous alkaloid present in tobacco.

nic·o·tin·ic ac·id /níkətinik/ *n.* a vitamin of the B complex. Also called **niacin**.

nic·ti·tate /níktitayt/ *v.intr.* blink or wink. □□ **nic·ti·ta·tion** /-táyshən/ *n.*

nic·ti·tat·ing mem·brane *n.* ▼ a clear membrane forming a third eyelid in amphibians, birds, and some other animals.

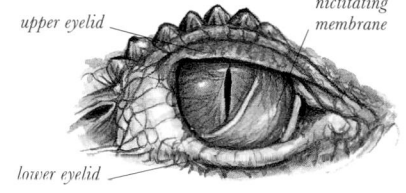

upper eyelid
nictitating membrane
lower eyelid

NICTITATING MEMBRANE
ON A CROCODILE EYE

niece /nees/ *n.* a daughter of one's brother or sister, or of one's brother-in-law or sister-in-law.

nif·ty /níftee/ *adj.* (**niftier, niftiest**) *colloq.* **1** clever. **2** stylish. □□ **nif·ti·ly** *adv.*

nig·gard /nígərd/ *n.* a mean or stingy person. □□ **nig·gard·ly** *adj. & adv.* **nig·gard·li·ness** *n.*

nig·ger /nígər/ *n.* **1** *offens.* a contemptuous term used of a black or dark-skinned person. **2** (in black English) a fellow black person. ¶ In sense 1, this term is considered a highly inflammatory expression of racial bigotry.

nig·gle /nígəl/ *v. & n.* ● *v.* **1** *intr.* be overattentive to details. **2** *intr.* find fault in a petty way. **3** *tr. colloq.* irritate. ● *n.* a trifling complaint.

nig·gling /nígling/ *adj.* **1** troublesome or irritating in a petty way. **2** petty.

nigh /nī/ *adv., prep., & adj. archaic* or *dial.* near. □ **nigh on** nearly; almost.

night /nīt/ *n.* **1** the period of darkness between one day and the next; the time from sunset to sunrise. **2** nightfall. **3** the darkness of night. **4** a night or evening appointed for some activity (*last night of the performance*).

night blind·ness *n.* = NYCTALOPIA.

night·cap /nítkap/ *n.* **1** *hist.* a cap worn in bed. **2** a hot or alcoholic drink taken at bedtime.

night·clothes /nítklōz, -klōthz/ *n.* clothes worn in bed.

night·club /nítklub/ *n.* a club that is open at night and provides refreshment and entertainment.

night·dress /nítdres/ *n.* = NIGHTGOWN.

night·fall /nítfawl/ *n.* the onset of night.

night·gown /nítgown/ *n.* **1** a woman's or child's loose garment worn in bed. **2** *hist.* a dressing gown.

night·ie /nítee/ *n. colloq.* a nightgown.

night·in·gale /nít'ngayl/ *n.* ▶ any small reddish-brown bird of the genus *Luscinia*, esp. *L. megarhynchos*, of which the male sings melodiously, esp. at night. ▷ SONGBIRD

night·jar /nítjaar/ *n.* any nocturnal bird of the family Caprimulgidae, having a characteristic harsh cry.

night·life /nítlīf/ *n.* entertainment available at night in a town.

night-light *n.* a dim light kept on in a bedroom at night.

night·long /nítlawng/ *adj. & adv.* ● *adj.* lasting all night. ● *adv.* throughout the night.

night·ly /nítlee/ *adj. & adv.* ● *adj.* **1** happening, done, or existing in the night. **2** recurring every night. ● *adv.* every night.

night·mare /nítmair/ *n.* **1** a frightening dream. **2** *colloq.* a very unpleasant experience. **3** a haunting fear. □□ **night·mar·ish** *adj.* **night·mar·ish·ly** *adv.*

night owl *n. colloq.* a person active at night.

night school *n.* an institution providing evening classes for those working by day.

night scope *n.* a night-vision telescope, used typically as the telescopic sight of a rifle.

night·shade /nítshayd/ *n.* ▶ any of various poisonous plants, esp. of the genus *Solanum*, including *S. nigrum* (**black nightshade**) with black berries, and *S. dulcamara* (**woody nightshade**) with red berries.

night shift *n.* a shift of workers employed during the night.

night·shirt /nítshərt/ *n.* a long shirt worn in bed.

night·spot /nítspot/ *n.* a nightclub.

night·stick /nítstik/ *n.* a policeman's club.

night·time /níttīm/ *n.* the time of darkness.

NIH *abbr.* National Institutes of Health.

ni·hil·ism /ní-ilizəm, née-/ *n.* **1** the rejection of all religious and moral principles. **2** a form of skepticism maintaining that nothing has a real existence. □□ **ni·hil·ist** *n.* **ni·hil·is·tic** *adj.*

nil /nil/ *n.* nothing; no number or amount (esp. *Brit.* as a score in games).

nim·ble /nímbəl/ *adj.* (**nimbler, nimblest**) quick and agile in movement, action, or thought. □□ **nim·ble·ness** *n.* **nim·bly** *adv.*

nim·bo·stra·tus /nímbōstráytəs, -strátəs/ *n.* (*pl.* **nimbostrati** /-tī/) *Meteorol.* a low dark-gray layer of cloud. ▷ CLOUD

nim·bus /nímbəs/ *n.* (*pl.* **nimbi** /-bī/ or **nimbuses**) **1** a halo. **2** *Meteorol.* a rain cloud. □□ **nim·bused** *adj.*

NIMBY /nímbee/ *abbr. colloq.* not in my backyard.

nin·com·poop /nínkəmpōōp/ *n.* a simpleton; a fool.

nine /nīn/ *n. & adj.* ● *n.* **1** one more than eight. **2** a symbol for this (9, ix, IX). **3** a size, etc., denoted by nine. **4** a set or team of nine. **5** nine o'clock. **6** a card with nine pips. ● *adj.* that amount to nine. □ **dressed to the nines** dressed very elaborately. **nine times out of ten** nearly always. **nine to five** a designation of typical office hours.

nine·fold /nínfōld/ *adj. & adv.* **1** nine times as much or as many. **2** consisting of nine parts.

nine·pin /nínpin/ *n.* **1** (in *pl.*; usu. treated as *sing.*) a game in which nine pins are set up at the end of an alley and bowled at in an attempt to knock them down. **2** a pin used in this game.

nine·teen /nínteén/ *n. & adj.* ● *n.* **1** one more than eighteen, nine more than ten. **2** the symbol for this (19, xix, XIX). **3** a size, etc., denoted by nineteen. ● *adj.* that amount to nineteen. □□ **nine·teenth** *adj. & n.*

nine·ty /níntee/ *n. & adj.* ● *n.* (*pl.* **-ies**) **1** the product of nine and ten. **2** a symbol for this (90, xc, XC). **3** (in *pl.*) the numbers from 90 to 99. ● *adj.* that amount to ninety. □□ **nine·ti·eth** *adj. & n.*

nin·ja /nínjə/ *n.* a person skilled in ninjutsu.

nin·jut·su /ninjōōtsōō/ *n.* one of the Japanese martial arts, characterized by stealthy movement and camouflage.

nin·ny /nínee/ *n.* (*pl.* **-ies**) a foolish or simple-minded person.

ninth /nīnth/ *n. & adj.* ● *n.* **1** the position in a sequence corresponding to the number 9 in the sequence 1–9. **2** something occupying this position. **3** each of nine equal parts of a thing. ● *adj.* that is the ninth. □□ **ninth·ly** *adv.*

ni·o·bi·um /nīṓbeeəm/ *n. Chem.* a rare gray-blue metallic element occurring naturally in several minerals and used in alloys for superconductors. Also called **columbium**. □□ **ni·o·bic** *adj.* **ni·o·bous** *adj.*

Nip /nip/ *n. sl. offens.* a Japanese person.

nip[1] /nip/ *v. & n.* ● *v.* (**nipped, nipping**) **1** *tr.* pinch, squeeze, or bite sharply. **2** *tr.* (often foll. by *off*) remove by pinching, etc. **3** *tr.* (of the frost, etc.) cause pain or harm to. ● *n.* **1 a** a pinch; a sharp squeeze. **b** a bite. **2** biting cold. □ **nip and tuck** neck and neck. **nip in the bud** suppress or destroy (esp. an idea) at an early stage. □□ **nip·ping** *adj.*

nip[2] /nip/ *n.* a small quantity of liquor.

nip·per /nípər/ *n.* **1** a person or thing that nips. **2** the claw of a crab, lobster, etc. **3** *Brit. colloq.* a young child. **4** (in *pl.*) any tool for gripping or cutting, e.g., forceps or pincers.

nip·ple /nípəl/ *n.* **1** a small projection in which the mammary ducts of either sex of mammals terminate and from which in females milk is secreted for the young. ▷ BREAST. **2** the mouthpiece of a feeding bottle or pacifier. **3** a device like a nipple in function, e.g., the tip of a grease gun. **4** a nipplelike protuberance. **5** a short section of pipe with a screw thread at each end for coupling.

nip·py /nípee/ *adj.* (**nippier, nippiest**) *colloq.* **1** esp. *Brit.* quick; nimble; active. **2** chilly; cold. □□ **nip·pi·ly** *adv.*

nir·va·na /nərváanə, neer-/ *n.* (in Buddhism) perfect bliss and release from karma, attained by the extinction of individuality.

ni·sei /néesay, neesáy/ (also **Ni·sei**) *n.* an American whose parents were immigrants from Japan.

Nis·sen hut /nísən/ *n.* a tunnel-shaped hut of corrugated iron with a cement floor.

nit /nit/ *n.* the egg or young form of a louse or other parasitic insect, esp. of human head lice or body lice.

ni·ter /nítər/ *n.* saltpeter; potassium nitrate.

NIGHTINGALE
(*Luscinia megarhynchos*)

berries
toothed leaves
star-shaped flowers

NIGHTSHADE: BLACK
NIGHTSHADE (*Solanum nigrum*)

N

553

N

NITROGEN CYCLE

All living things play a part in the nitrogen cycle. Bacteria have a double role: they can fix (combine) nitrogen with oxygen to form nitrates, which most living organisms can use, and they can break the nitrates down (denitrify them) into nitrogen and oxygen.

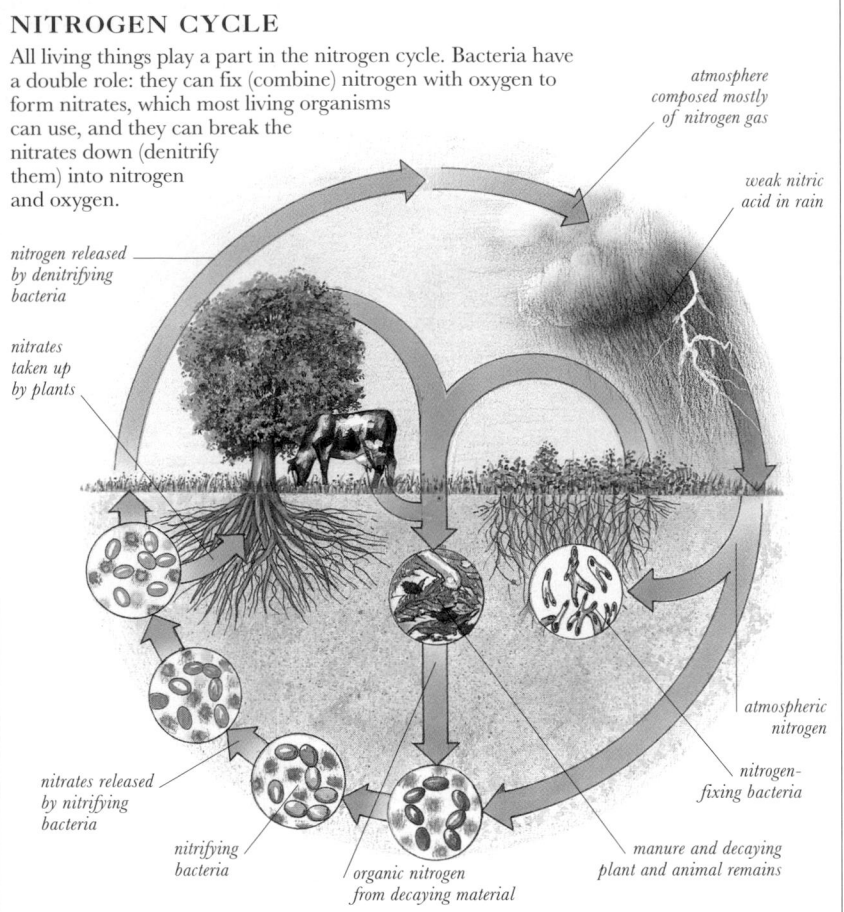

atmosphere composed mostly of nitrogen gas

weak nitric acid in rain

nitrogen released by denitrifying bacteria

nitrates taken up by plants

atmospheric nitrogen

nitrogen-fixing bacteria

nitrates released by nitrifying bacteria

nitrifying bacteria

organic nitrogen from decaying material

manure and decaying plant and animal remains

nit·pick /nítpik/ *v.intr. colloq.* find fault in a petty manner; criticize. □□ **nit·pick·er** *n.* **nit·pick·ing** *n.*

ni·trate /nítrayt/ *n. & v.* ● *n.* **1** any salt or ester of nitric acid. **2** potassium or sodium nitrate when used as a fertilizer. ● *v.tr. Chem.* treat, combine, or impregnate with nitric acid. □□ **ni·tra·tion** /-áyshən/ *n.*

ni·tric /nítrik/ *adj.* of or containing nitrogen, esp. in the quinquevalent state.

ni·tric ac·id *n.* a colorless corrosive poisonous liquid.

ni·tride /nítrīd/ *n. Chem.* a binary compound of nitrogen with a more electropositive element.

ni·tri·fy /nítrifī/ *v.tr.* (**-ies**, **-ied**) **1** impregnate with nitrogen. **2** convert (nitrogen, usu. in the form of ammonia) into nitrites or nitrates. ▷ NITROGEN CYCLE. □□ **ni·tri·fi·ca·tion** /-fikayshən/ *n.*

ni·trile /nítrīl/ *n. Chem.* an organic compound consisting of an alkyl radical bound to a cyanide radical.

ni·trite /nítrīt/ *n.* any salt or ester of nitrous acid.

nitro- /nítrō/ *comb. form* **1** of or containing nitric acid, niter, or nitrogen. **2** made with any of these. **3** of or containing the monovalent -NO_2 group.

ni·tro·ben·zene /nítrōbénzeen/ *n.* a yellow oily liquid made by the nitration of benzene and used to make aniline, etc.

ni·tro·cel·lu·lose /nítrōsélyələs/ *n.* a highly flammable material made by treating cellulose with concentrated nitric acid.

ni·tro·gen /nítrəjən/ *n. Chem.* a colorless, odorless gaseous element that forms four-fifths of the atmosphere and is an essential constituent of proteins and nucleic acids. ▷ NITROGEN CYCLE. □□ **ni·trog·e·nous** /-trójinəs/ *adj.*

ni·tro·gen cy·cle *n.* ▲ the interconversion of nitrogen and its compounds, usu. in the form of nitrates, in nature.

ni·tro·glyc·er·in /nítrōglísərin/ *n.* (also **ni·tro·glyc·er·ine**) an explosive yellow liquid made by reacting glycerol with concentrated sulfuric and nitric acids.

ni·trous /nítrəs/ *adj.* of, like, or impregnated with nitrogen.

ni·trous ox·ide *n.* a colorless gas used as an anesthetic (= laughing gas) and as an aerosol propellant.

nit·ty-grit·ty /níteegrítee/ *n. sl.* the realities or practical details of a matter.

nit·wit /nítwit/ *n. colloq.* a stupid person. □□ **nit·wit·ter·y** /-witəree/ *n.*

nix /niks/ *n. & v. sl.* ● *n.* **1** nothing. **2** a denial. ● *v.tr.* **1** cancel. **2** reject.

NJ *abbr.* New Jersey (also in official postal use).

NLRB *abbr.* National Labor Relations Board.

NM *abbr.* New Mexico (in official postal use).

N.Mex. *abbr.* New Mexico.

NMR *abbr.* (also **nmr**) nuclear magnetic resonance. ▷ MRI

No[1] *symb. Chem.* the element nobelium.

No[2] /nō/ *n.* (also **Noh**) traditional Japanese drama with dance and song.

No. *abbr.* **1** number. **2** North.

no[1] /nō/ *adj.* **1** not any (*there is no excuse*). **2** not a, quite other than (*is no fool*). **3** hardly any (*did it in no time*). **4** used elliptically as a notice, etc., to forbid, reject, or deplore the thing specified (*no parking*). □ **by no means** see MEANS. **no dice** see DICE. **no doubt** see DOUBT. **no end** see END. **no entry** (of a notice) prohibiting vehicles or persons from entering a road or place. **no joke** see JOKE. **no joy** see JOY *n.* 3. **no little** see LITTLE. **no man** no person,

nobody. **no small** see SMALL. **no sweat** *colloq.* no bother, no trouble. **no trumps** (or **trump**) *Bridge* a declaration or bid involving playing without a trump suit. **no way** *colloq.* **1** I will not agree, etc. **2** I it is impossible. □ **no wonder** see WONDER. **... or no ...** regardless of the ... (*rain or no rain, I shall go out*). **there is no ...ing** it is impossible to ... (*there is no accounting for taste*).

no[2] /nō/ *adv. & n.* ● *adv.* **1** equivalent to a negative sentence: the answer to your question is negative; your request will not be complied with; the statement made or conclusion arrived at is not correct or satisfactory; the negative statement made is correct. **2** (foll. by *compar.*) by no amount (*no better than before*). ● *n.* (*pl.* **noes**) **1** an utterance of the word *no*. **2** a denial or refusal. **3** a negative vote. □ **is no more** has died or ceased to exist. **no can do** *colloq.* I am unable to do it. **no less** (often foll. by *than*) **1** as much (*gave me $50, no less*). **2** as important (*no less a person than the president*). **3** *disp.* no fewer (*no less than ten people*). **no longer** not now or henceforth as formerly. **no more** *n.* nothing further. ● *adj.* not any more (*no more wine?*). ● *adv.* **1** no longer. **2** never again. **3** to no greater extent (*is no more an authority than I am*). **4** neither (*you did not come, and no more did he*). **no sooner ... than** see SOON. **not take no for an answer** persist in spite of refusals. **or no** or not (*pleasant or no, it is true*). **whether or no 1** in either case. **2** (as an indirect question) which of a case and its negative (*tell me whether or no*).

NOAA /nóə/ *abbr.* National Oceanic and Atmospheric Administration.

no-ac·count *adj.* unimportant, worthless.

No·ah's ark /nóəz/ *n.* **1 a** the ship in which (according to the Bible) Noah, his family, and the animals were saved. **b** an imitation of this as a child's toy. **2** a large or cumbrous or old-fashioned trunk or vehicle. **3** a bivalve mollusk, *Arca noae*, with a boat-shaped shell.

nob /nob/ *n. sl.* the head.

nob·ble /nóbəl/ *v.tr. Brit. sl.* **1** tamper with (a racehorse) to prevent its winning. **2** get hold of (money) dishonestly. **3** seize, grab. **4** try to influence (e.g., a judge) unfairly.

No·bel·ist /nóbélist/ *n.* a winner of a Nobel prize.

no·bel·i·um /nōbéeleeəm/ *n. Chem.* a radioactive transuranic metallic element.

No·bel prize /nóbél/ *n.* any of six international prizes awarded annually for physics, chemistry, physiology or medicine, literature, economics, and the promotion of peace.

no·bil·i·ty /nōbílitee/ *n.* (*pl.* **-ies**) **1** nobleness of character, mind, birth, or rank. **2** (prec. by *a*, *the*) a class of nobles, an aristocracy.

no·ble /nóbəl/ *adj. & n.* ● *adj.* (**nobler, noblest**) **1** belonging by rank, title, or birth to the aristocracy. **2** having lofty ideals; free from pettiness and meanness. **3** of imposing appearance. **4** excellent; admirable (*noble horse; noble cellar*). ● *n.* a nobleman or noblewoman. □□ **no·ble·ness** *n.* **no·bly** *adv.*

no·ble gas *n.* any one of a group of gaseous elements that almost never combine with other elements.

no·ble·man /nóbəlmən/ *n.* (*pl.* **-men**) a man of noble rank or birth; a peer.

no·blesse /nōblés/ *n.* the class of nobles (as of France, etc.). □ **noblesse oblige** /ōblée<u>zh</u>/ privilege entails responsibility.

no·ble·wom·an /nóbəlwōōmən/ *n.* (*pl.* **-women**) a woman of noble rank or birth.

no·bod·y /nóbodee, -budee, -bədee/ *pron. & n.* ● *pron.* no person. ● *n.* (*pl.* **-ies**) a person of no importance. □ **like nobody's business** see BUSINESS. **nobody's fool** see FOOL.

no-brain·er *n.* a problem, question, examination, etc., that requires very little thought.

nock /nok/ *n. & v.* ● *n.* **1** a notch at either end of a bow for holding the string. **2** a notch at the butt end of an arrow for receiving the bowstring. ● *v.tr.* set (an arrow) on the string.

noc·tam·bu·list /noktámbyəlist/ *n.* a sleepwalker. □□ **noc·tam·bu·lism** *n.*

noc·tule /nókchōol/ *n.* a large W. European bat, *Nyctalus noctula.* ▷ BAT

noc·tur·nal /noktərnəl/ *adj.* of or in the night; active by night. □□ **noc·tur·nal·ly** *adv.*

noc·turne /nóktərn/ *n.* **1** *Mus.* a short composition of a romantic nature, usu. for piano. **2** a picture of a night scene.

nod /nod/ *v. & n.* ● *v.* (**nodded, nodding**) **1** *intr.* incline one's head slightly and briefly in greeting, assent, or command. **2** *intr.* let one's head fall forward in drowsiness. **3** *tr.* incline (one's head). **4** *tr.* signify (assent, etc.) by a nod. **5** *intr.* (of flowers, plumes, etc.) bend downward and sway. **6** *intr.* make a mistake due to a momentary lack of alertness or attention. ● *n.* a nodding of the head. □ **get the nod** be chosen or approved. **nod off** *colloq.* fall asleep. **on the nod** *colloq.* with merely formal assent and no discussion.

nod·dle /nód'l/ *n. colloq.* the head.

nod·dy /nódee/ *n.* (*pl.* **-ies**) **1** a simpleton. **2** any of various tropical seabirds of the genus *Anous,* resembling terns.

node /nōd/ *n.* **1** *Bot.* **a** the part of a plant stem from which leaves emerge. **b** a knob on a root or branch. **2** *Anat.* a natural swelling in a part of the body. **3** *Astron.* either of two points at which a planet's orbit intersects the plane of the ecliptic or the celestial equator. **4** *Physics* a point of minimum disturbance in a standing wave system. **5** *Electr.* a point of zero current or voltage. **6** *Math.* a point at which a curve intersects itself. **7** a component in a computer network. □□ **nod·al** *adj.* **nod·i·cal** *adj.* (in sense 3).

nod·ule /nójōol/ *n.* **1** a small, rounded lump of anything. **2** a small tumor, node, or ganglion. □□ **nod·u·lar** /-jələr/ *adj.* **nod·u·lat·ed** /-jəlaytid/ *adj.* **nod·u·la·tion** /-jəláyshən/ *n.* **nod·u·lose** /-jolōs/ *adj.*

No·el /nō-él/ *n.* Christmas (esp. as a refrain in carols).

no-fault *adj.* (of insurance) valid regardless of the allocation of blame for an accident, etc.

no-frills *adj.* lacking ornament or embellishment.

nog /nog/ *n.* a small block or peg of wood.

nog·gin /nógin/ *n.* **1** a small mug. **2** a small measure, usu. ¼ pint, of liquor. **3** *sl.* the head.

nog·ging /nóging/ *n.* ▼ brickwork or timber braces in a timber frame.

NOGGING
IN A TIMBER-FRAMED
GERMAN HOUSE

timber frame

brick
nogging

no-go *adj.* impossible, hopeless.

no-good *adj.* useless.

Noh var. of No².

no-hit·ter *n. Baseball* a game in which a pitcher allows no hits.

no·how /nóhow/ *adv.* **1** in no way; by no means. **2** *dial.* out of order.

noise /noyz/ *n. & v.* ● *n.* **1** a sound, esp. a loud or unpleasant one. **2** a series of loud sounds; a confused sound of voices. **3** irregular fluctuations accompanying a transmitted signal but not relevant to it. **4** (in *pl.*) conventional remarks, or speechlike sounds without actual words (*made sympathetic noises*). ● *v. tr.* (usu. in *passive*) make public. □ **make a noise 1** (usu. foll. by *about*) talk or complain much. **2** attain notoriety.

noise·less /nóyzlis/ *adj.* **1** silent. **2** making no avoidable noise. □□ **noise·less·ly** *adv.* **noise·less·ness** *n.*

noise pol·lu·tion *n.* harmful or annoying noise.

noi·sette /nwaazét/ *n.* a small, lean, usu. round piece of meat, etc.

noi·some /nóysəm/ *adj. literary* **1** harmful, noxious. **2** evil-smelling. **3** objectionable, offensive. □□ **noi·some·ness** *n.*

nois·y /nóyzee/ *adj.* (**noisier, noisiest**) **1** full of noise. **2** making much noise. **3** clamorous; turbulent. **4** (of a color etc.) conspicuous. □□ **nois·i·ly** *adv.* **nois·i·ness** *n.*

no·mad /nómad/ *n.* **1** a member of a tribe roaming from place to place for pasture. **2** a wanderer. □□ **no·mad·ic** /-mádik/ *adj.* **no·mad·i·cal·ly** *adv.* **no·mad·ism** *n.*

no man's land *n.* **1** *Mil.* the space between two opposing armies. **2** an area not assigned to any owner. **3** an area not clearly belonging to any one subject, etc.

nom de guerre /nóm də gáir/ *n.* (*pl.* **noms de guerre** *pronunc.* same) an assumed name under which a person fights, plays, writes, etc.

nom de plume /nóm də plōom/ *n.* (*pl.* **noms de plume** *pronunc.* same) an assumed name under which a person writes.

no·men·cla·ture /nómənklaychər, nōménkləchər/ *n.* **1** a person's or community's system of names for things. **2** the terminology of a science, etc. **3** systematic naming. **4** a catalog. □□ **no·men·cla·tur·al** /-kláchərəl/ *adj.*

nom·i·nal /nóminəl/ *adj.* **1** existing in name only (*nominal ruler*). **2** (of a sum of money, etc.) virtually nothing. **3** of or in names (*nominal and essential distinctions*). **4** consisting of or giving the names (*nominal list of officers*). **5** of or like a noun. □□ **nom·i·nal·ly** *adv.*

nom·i·nal val·ue *n.* the face value (of a coin, shares, etc.).

nom·i·nate /nóminayt/ *v.tr.* **1** propose (a candidate) for election. **2** (of a board of six nominated and six elected members). **3** appoint (a date or place). **4** mention by name. **5** call by the name of. □□ **nom·i·na·tor** *n.*

nom·i·na·tion /nómináyshən/ *n.* **1** the act of nominating. **2** the right of nominating for an appointment (*have a nomination at your disposal*).

nom·i·na·tive /nóminətiv/ *n. & adj.* ● *n. Gram.* **1** the case of nouns, pronouns, and adjectives, expressing the subject of a verb. **2** a word in this case. ● *adj.* **1** *Gram.* of or in this case. **2** /-naytiv/ of nomination (as distinct from election).

nom·i·nee /nóminée/ *n.* **1** a person who is nominated for an office or as the recipient of a grant, etc. **2** *Commerce* a person in whose name a stock, etc., is registered.

non- /non/ *prefix* giving the negative sense of words with which it is combined, esp.: **1** not doing or having or involved with (*nonattendance*). **2 a** not of the kind described (*nonalcoholic*). **b** forming terms used adjectivally (*nonunion*). **3** a lack of (*nonaccess*). **4** (with adverbs) not in the way described (*nonaggressively*). **5** forming adjectives from verbs, meaning "that does not" or "that is not meant to (or to be)" (*nonskid*). **6** used to form a neutral negative sense when a form in *in-* or *un-* has a special sense or (usu. unfavorable) connotation (*noncontroversial*). ¶ The number of words that can be formed with this prefix is unlimited; con-

sequently only a selection, considered the most current or semantically noteworthy, can be given here.

nona- /nónə/ *comb. form* nine.

non·ab·stain·er /nónəbstáynər/ *n.* a person who does not abstain (esp. from alcohol).

non·ac·cept·ance /nónəkséptəns/ *n.* a lack of acceptance.

non·ad·dic·tive /nónədíktiv/ *adj.* (of a drug, habit, etc.) not causing addiction.

non·age /nónij, nō-/ *n.* **1** *hist.* the state of being under full legal age, minority. **2** a period of immaturity.

non·a·ge·nar·i·an /nónəjináireeən, nō-/ *n. & adj.* ● *n.* a person from 90 to 99 years old. ● *adj.* of this age.

non·ag·gres·sion /nónəgréshən/ *n.* restraint from aggression (often *attrib.:* nonaggression pact).

non·a·gon /nónəgon/ *n.* ▶ a plane figure with nine sides and angles.

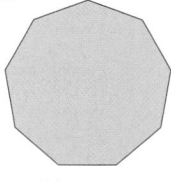

NONAGON

non·al·co·hol·ic /nónalkəhólik/ *adj.* (of a drink, etc.) not containing alcohol.

non·a·ligned /nónəlínd/ *adj.* (of nations, etc.) not aligned with another (esp. major) power. □□ **non·a·lign·ment** *n.*

non·al·ler·gic /nónələrjik/ *adj.* not causing allergy; not allergic.

non·ap·pear·ance /nónəpéerəns/ *n.* failure to appear or be present.

non·at·tached /nónətácht/ *adj.* that is not attached. ¶ Neutral in sense: see NON- 6, UNATTACHED.

non·at·ten·dance /nónəténdəns/ *n.* failure to attend.

non·at·trib·ut·a·ble /nónətríbyōotəbəl/ *adj.* that cannot or may not be attributed to a particular source, etc. □□ **non·at·trib·ut·a·bly** *adv.*

non·a·vail·a·bil·i·ty /nónəváyləbílitee/ *n.* a state of not being available.

non·be·liev·er /nónbiléévər/ *n.* a person who has no (esp. religious) faith.

non·bel·lig·er·ent /nónbəlíjərənt/ *adj. & n.* ● *adj.* not engaged in hostilities. ● *n.* a nonbelligerent nation, etc.

non·bi·o·log·i·cal /nónbīəlójikəl/ *adj.* not concerned with biology or living organisms.

non·black /nónblák/ *adj. & n.* ● *adj.* **1** (of a person) not black. **2** of or relating to nonblack people. ● *n.* a nonblack person.

non·cap·i·tal /nónkápit'l/ *adj.* (of an offense) not punishable by death.

non-Cath·o·lic /nónkáthəlik, -káthlik/ *adj. & n.* ● *adj.* not Roman Catholic. ● *n.* a non-Catholic person.

nonce /nons/ *n.* □ **for the nonce** for the time being; for the present occasion.

nonce word *n.* a word coined for one occasion.

non·cha·lant /nónshəláant/ *adj.* calm and casual. □□ **non·cha·lance** /-áans/ *n.* **non·cha·lant·ly** *adv.*

non-Chris·tian /nónkris-chən/ *adj. & n.* ● *adj.* not Christian. ● *n.* a non-Christian person.

non·cit·i·zen /nónsítizən/ *n.* a person who is not a citizen (of a particular nation, town, etc.).

non·cler·i·cal /nónklérikəl/ *adj.* not doing or involving clerical work.

non·com /nónkom/ *n. colloq.* a noncommissioned officer.

non·com·bat·ant /nónkəmbát'nt, -kómbət'nt/ *n.* a person not fighting in a war, esp. a civilian, army chaplain, etc.

non·com·mis·sioned /nónkəmíshənd/ *adj. Mil.* (of an officer) not holding a commission.

non·com·mit·tal /nónkəmít'l/ *adj.* avoiding commitment to a definite opinion or course of action. □□ **non·com·mit·tal·ly** *adv.*

N

non·com·mu·nist /nónkómyənist/ *adj. & n.* (also **non-Com·mu·nist** with ref. to a particular party) ● *adj.* not advocating or practicing communism. ● *n.* a noncommunist person.

non·com·pli·ance /nónkəmplíəns/ *n.* failure to comply; a lack of compliance.

non com·pos men·tis /nón kompəs méntis/ *adj.* (also **non com·pos**) not in one's right mind.

non·con·duc·tor /nónkəndúktər/ *n.* a substance that does not conduct heat or electricity. □□ **non·con·duct·ing** *adj.*

non·con·form·ist /nónkənfáwrmist/ *n.* **1** a person who does not conform to the doctrine or discipline of an established Church, esp. (**Nonconformist**) a member of a (usu. Protestant) sect dissenting from the Anglican Church. **2** a person who does not conform to a prevailing principle. □□ **non·con·form·ism** *n.* **Non·con·form·ism** *n.*

non·con·form·i·ty /nónkənfáwrmitee/ *n.* **1** a nonconformists as a body, esp. (**Nonconformity**) Protestants dissenting from the Anglican Church. **b** the principles or practice of nonconformists, esp. (**Nonconformity**) Protestant dissent. **2** (usu. foll. by *to*) failure to conform. **3** lack of correspondence between things.

non·con·ten·tious /nónkənténshəs/ *adj.* not contentious.

non·con·trib·u·to·ry /nónkəntríbyətawree/ *adj.* not contributing or (esp. of a pension plan) involving contributions.

non·con·tro·ver·sial /nónkóntrəvórshəl/ *adj.* not controversial. ¶ Neutral in sense: see NON- 6, UNCONTROVERSIAL.

non·co·op·er·a·tion /nónkō-ópəráyshən/ *n.* failure to cooperate.

non·de·liv·er·y /nóndilívəree/ *n.* failure to deliver.

non·de·nom·i·na·tion·al /nóndinómináyshənəl/ *adj.* not restricted as regards religious denomination.

non·de·script /nóndiskript/ *adj. & n.* ● *adj.* lacking distinctive characteristics; not easily classified. ● *n.* a nondescript person or thing.

non·de·struc·tive /nóndistrúktiv/ *adj.* that does not involve destruction.

non·drink·er /nóndríngkər/ *n.* a person who does not drink alcoholic liquor.

non·driv·er /nóndrívər/ *n.* a person who does not drive a motor vehicle.

none /nun/ *pron., adj., & adv.* ● *pron.* **1** (foll. by *of*) **a** not any of (*none of this concerns me; none of your impudence!*). **b** not any one of (*none of them has come*). ¶ The verb following *none* in this sense can be singular or plural according to the sense. **2 a** no persons (*none but fools have ever believed it*). **b** no person (*none can tell*). ● *adj.* (usu. with a preceding noun implied) **1** no; not any (*you have money and I have none*). **2** not to be counted in a specified class (*his understanding is none of the clearest*). ● *adv.* (foll. by *the* + compar., or *so, too*) not at all (*none the wiser*). □ **none other** (usu. foll. by *than*) no other person.

non·ef·fec·tive /nónifféktiv/ *adj.* that does not have an effect. ¶ Neutral in sense: see NON- 6, INEFFECTIVE.

non·en·ti·ty /nónéntitee/ *n.* (*pl.* **-ies**) **1** a person of no importance. **2 a** nonexistence. **b** a nonexistent thing.

nones /nōnz/ *n.pl.* in the ancient Roman calendar, the ninth day before the ides by inclusive reckoning, i.e., the 7th day of March, May, July, and October, and the 5th of other months.

non·es·sen·tial /nónisénshəl/ *adj.* not essential. ¶ Neutral in sense: see NON- 6, INESSENTIAL.

none·such /núnsuch/ *n.* (also **non·such**) a person or thing that is unrivaled, a paragon.

none·the·less /núnthəlés/ *adv.* nevertheless.

non-Eu·clid·e·an /nónyōōklídeeən/ *adj.* denying or going beyond Euclidean principles in geometry.

non·e·vent /nónivént/ *n.* an unimportant or anticlimactic occurrence.

non·ex·ist·ent /nónigzístənt/ *adj.* not existing. □□ **non·ex·ist·ence** /-təns/ *n.*

non·ex·plo·sive /nóniksplósiv/ *adj.* (of a substance) that does not explode.

non·fat·ten·ing /nónfát'ning/ *adj.* (of food) that does not fatten.

non·fer·rous /nónférəs/ *adj.* (of a metal) other than iron or steel.

non·fic·tion /nónfíkshən/ *n.* literary work other than fiction. □□ **non·fic·tion·al** *adj.*

non·flam·ma·ble /nónflámməbəl/ *adj.* not flammable.

non·ful·fill·ment /nónfŏŏlfílmənt/ *n.* failure to fulfill (an obligation).

non·func·tion·al /nónfúngkshənəl/ *adj.* not having a function.

non·gov·ern·men·tal /nón-guvərnmént'l/ *adj.* not belonging to or associated with a government.

non·hu·man /nónhyŏŏmən/ *adj. & n.* ● *adj.* (of a being) not human. ● *n.* a nonhuman being. ¶ Neutral in sense: see NON- 6, INHUMAN, UNHUMAN.

non·in·fec·tious /nóninfékshəs/ *adj.* (of a disease) not infectious.

non·in·ter·fer·ence /nónintərféerəns/ *n.* a lack of interference.

non·in·ter·ven·tion /nónintərvénshən/ *n.* the principle or practice of not becoming involved in others' affairs, esp. by one nation in regard to another.

non·i·ron /nóníərn/ *adj. Brit.* (of a fabric) that needs no ironing.

non·lin·e·ar /nónlíneeər/ *adj.* not linear, esp. with regard to dimension.

non·lit·er·ar·y /nónlítərəree/ *adj.* (of writing, etc.) not literary in character.

non·mag·net·ic /nónmagnétik/ *adj.* (of a substance) not magnetic.

non·mem·ber /nónmémbər/ *n.* a person who is not a member (of a particular association, club, etc.). □□ **non·mem·ber·ship** *n.*

non·met·al /nónmét'l/ *adj.* not made of metal. □□ **non·me·tal·lic** /-mətálik/ *adj.*

non·mil·i·tant /nónmílitənt/ *adj.* not militant.

non·mil·i·tar·y /nónmíliteree/ *adj.* not military; not involving armed forces.

non·nat·u·ral /nón-náchərəl/ *adj.* not involving natural means nor processes. ¶ Neutral in sense: see NON- 6, UNNATURAL.

non·ne·go·ti·a·ble /nón-nigóshəbəl, -sheeə-/ *adj.* that cannot be negotiated (esp. in financial senses).

non·nu·cle·ar /nón-nŏŏkleeər, -nyŏŏ-/ *adj.* **1** not involving nuclei nor nuclear energy. **2** (of a nation, etc.) not having nuclear weapons.

no-no *n. colloq.* a thing not possible or acceptable.

non·ob·serv·ance /nónəbzórvəns/ *n.* failure to observe (an agreement, etc.).

no-non·sense *adj.* serious, without flippancy.

non·op·er·a·tion·al /nónopəráyshənəl/ *adj.* **1** that does not operate. **2** out of order.

non·or·gan·ic /nóawrgánik/ *adj.* not organic. ¶ Neutral in sense: see NON- 6, INORGANIC.

non·pa·reil /nónpərél/ *adj. & n.* ● *adj.* unrivaled or unique. ● *n.* **1** such a person or thing. **2** a chocolate disk, decorated with sugar pellets.

non·par·tic·i·pat·ing /nónpaartísipayting/ *adj.* not taking part.

non·par·ti·san /nónpaartizən/ *adj.* not partisan.

non·par·ty /nónpáartee/ *adj.* independent of political parties.

non·pay·ment /nónpáymənt/ *n.* failure to pay; a lack of payment.

non·per·son /nónpórsən/ *n.* a person regarded as nonexistent or insignificant (cf. UNPERSON).

non·per·son·al /nónpórsənəl/ *adj.* not personal. ¶ Neutral in sense: see NON- 6, IMPERSONAL.

non·phys·i·cal /nónfizikəl/ *adj.* not physical. □□ **non·phys·i·cal·ly** *adv.*

non·play·ing /nónpláying/ *adj.* that does not play or take part (in a game, etc.).

non·plus /nonplús/ *v.tr.* (**nonplussed** or **non-plused, nonplussing** or **nonplusing**) completely perplex.

non·po·lit·i·cal /nónpəlítikəl/ *adj.* not political; not involved in politics.

non·po·rous /nónpáwrəs/ *adj.* (of a substance) not porous.

non·pro·duc·tive /nónprədúktiv/ *adj.* not productive. ¶ Neutral in sense: see NON- 6, UNPRODUCTIVE. □□ **non·pro·duc·tive·ly** *adv.*

non·pro·fes·sion·al /nónprəféshənəl/ *adj.* not professional (esp. in status). ¶ Neutral in sense: see NON- 6, UNPROFESSIONAL.

non·prof·it /nónprófit/ *adj.* not involving nor making a profit.

non·pro·lif·er·a·tion /nónprəlífəráyshən/ *n.* the prevention of an increase in something, esp. possession of nuclear weapons.

non·ra·cial /nónráyshəl/ *adj.* not involving race or racial factors.

non·res·i·dent /nónrézidənt/ *adj.* **1** not residing in a particular place. **2** (of a post) not requiring the holder to reside at the place of work. □□ **non·res·i·dence** /-dəns/ *n.* **non·res·i·den·tial** /-dénshəl/ *adj.*

non·re·sis·tance /nónrizístəns/ *n.* failure to resist; a lack of resistance.

non·re·turn·a·ble /nónritórnəbəl/ *adj.* that may or need or will not be returned.

non·rig·id /nónríjid/ *adj.* (esp. of materials) not rigid.

non·sci·en·tif·ic /nónsīəntifik/ *adj.* not involving science or scientific methods. ¶ Neutral in sense: see NON- 6, UNSCIENTIFIC. □□ **non·sci·en·tist** /-síəntist/ *n.*

non·sec·tar·i·an /nónsektáireeən/ *adj.* not sectarian.

non·sense /nónsens, -səns/ *n.* **1 a** (often as *int.*) absurd or meaningless words or ideas; foolish conduct. **b** an instance of this. **2** a scheme, etc., that one disapproves of. **3** (often *attrib.*) a form of literature meant to amuse by absurdity (*nonsense verse*). □□ **non·sen·si·cal** /-sénsikəl/ *adj.* **non·sen·si·cal·i·ty** /nónsensikálitee/ *n.* (*pl.* **-ies**). **non·sen·si·cal·ly** /-sénsiklee/ *adv.*

non se·qui·tur /non sékwitər/ *n.* a conclusion that does not logically follow from the premises.

non·sex·u·al /nónséksŏŏəl/ *adj.* not involving sex. □□ **non·sex·u·al·ly** *adv.*

non·skid /nónskíd/ *adj.* **1** that does not skid. **2** that inhibits skidding.

non·slip /nónslíp/ *adj.* **1** that does not slip. **2** that inhibits slipping.

non·smok·er /nónsmókər/ *n.* **1** a person who does not smoke. **2** a train compartment, etc., in which smoking is forbidden. □□ **non·smok·ing** *adj. & n.*

non·spe·cial·ist /nónspéshəlist/ *n.* a person who is not a specialist.

non·spe·cif·ic /nónspisifik/ *adj.* that cannot be specified.

non·stand·ard /nónstándərd/ *adj.* not standard.

non·start·er /nónstáartər/ *n.* **1** a person or animal that does not start in a race. **2** *colloq.* a person or thing that is unlikely to succeed or be effective.

non·stick /nónstík/ *adj.* **1** that does not stick. **2** that does not allow things to stick to it.

non·stop /nónstóp/ *adj. & adv.* ● *adj.* **1** (of a train, etc.) not stopping at intermediate places. **2** done without a stop or intermission. ● *adv.* without stopping or pausing.

non·such var. of NONESUCH.

non·swim·mer /nónswímər/ *n.* a person who cannot swim.

non·tech·ni·cal /nóntéknikəl/ *adj.* **1** not technical. **2** without technical knowledge.

non·tox·ic /nóntóksik/ *adj.* not toxic.

non·trans·fer·a·ble /nóntransfárəbəl/ *adj.* that may not be transferred.

non-U /nónyŏŏ/ *adj. esp. Brit. colloq.* not characteristic of the upper class.

non·u·ni·form /nónyŏŏnifawrm/ *adj.* not uniform.

N

NORMAN

From the late 10th to the late 12th centuries, the Norman style of architecture prevailed in Normandy and, from 1066 on, in most of England. The main characteristic features of this style were massive solid stonework, semicircular arches, arcades, pitched roofs, cylindrical or polygonal piers, and ribbed stone vaulting.

SECTION THROUGH
A FRENCH
NORMAN ABBEY

incline
loophole
round-arched window
series of jambs
series of colonettes
pitched roof
quadrant arch
colonette
round stilted arch
attached half column

semicircular transverse arch
vaulting shaft
massive stonework
Norman capital
compound polygonal pier
rounded arcade arch

TIMELINE

| 800 | 850 | 900 | 950 | 1000 | 1050 | 1100 | 1150 | 1200 | 1250 | 1300 |

---

non·un·ion /nónyŏŏnyən/ *adj.* **1** not belonging to a labor union. **2** not done or produced by members of a labor union.

non·ver·bal /nónvárbəl/ *adj.* not involving words. □□ **non·ver·bal·ly** *adv.*

non·vi·o·lence /nónvíələns/ *n.* the avoidance of violence, esp. as a principle. □□ **non·vi·o·lent** /-lənt/ *adj.*

non·vot·ing /nónvóting/ *adj.* not having or using a vote. □□ **non·vot·er** *n.*

non·white /nónhwīt, -wīt/ *adj. & n.* ● *adj.* **1** (of a person) not white. **2** of or relating to nonwhite people. ● *n.* a nonwhite person.

noo·dle[1] /nŏŏd'l/ *n.* a strip or ring of pasta.

noo·dle[2] /nŏŏd'l/ *n.* **1** a simpleton. **2** *sl.* the head.

nook /nŏŏk/ *n.* a corner or recess; a secluded place.

noon /nŏŏn/ *n.* **1** twelve o'clock in the day; midday. **2** the culminating point.

noon·day /nŏŏnday/ *n.* midday.

no one /nŏ wun/ *n.* no person; nobody.

noon·time /nŏŏntīm/ *n.* (also **noon·tide** /-tīd/) midday.

noose /nŏŏs/ *n. & v.* ● *n.* **1** a loop with a running knot, tightening as the rope or wire is pulled. **2** a snare or bond. ● *v.tr.* catch with or enclose in a noose, ensnare. □ **put one's head in a noose** bring about one's own downfall.

nope /nŏp/ *adv. colloq.* = NO[2] *adv.* 1.

nor /nawr, nər/ *conj.* **1** and not; and not either (*neither one thing nor the other, can neither read nor write*). **2** and no more; neither ("*I cannot go*" – "*Nor can I*").
□ **nor ... nor ...** *poet.* or *archaic* neither ... nor ...

nor' /nawr/ *n., adj., & adv.* (esp. in compounds) = NORTH (*nor'ward*).

Nor·dic /náwrdik/ *adj. & n.* ● *adj.* **1** of or relating to the tall blond Germanic people found in N. Europe, esp. in Scandinavia. **2** of or relating to Scandinavia or Finland. ● *n.* a Nordic person.

nor'·easter /noréestər/ *n.* a northeaster.

nor·ep·i·neph·rine /nawrəpənéfrin/ *n. Biochem.* an adrenal hormone which functions as a neurotransmitter and is also used as a drug to raise blood pressure.

Nor·folk jack·et /nawrfək/ *n.* a man's loose belted jacket, with box pleats.

norm /nawrm/ *n.* **1** a standard or pattern or type. **2** a standard quantity to be produced or amount of work to be done. **3** customary behavior, etc.

nor·mal /náwrməl/ *adj. & n.* ● *adj.* **1** conforming to a standard; regular; usual. **2** free from mental or emotional disorder. **3** *Geom.* (of a line) at right angles. ● *n.* **1 a** the normal value of a temperature, etc. **b** the usual state, level, etc. **2** *Geom.* a line at right angles. □□ **nor·mal·cy** *n.* **nor·mal·i·ty** /-málitee/ *n.*

nor·mal dis·tri·bu·tion *n. Statistics* a function that represents the distribution of many random variables as a symmetrical bell-shaped graph.

nor·mal·ize /náwrməlīz/ *v.* **1** *tr.* make normal. **2** *intr.* become normal. **3** *tr.* cause to conform. □□ **nor·mal·i·za·tion** *n.* **nor·mal·iz·er** *n.*

nor·mal·ly /náwrməlee/ *adv.* **1** in a normal manner. **2** usually.

Nor·man /náwrmən/ *n. & adj.* ● *n.* **1** a native or inhabitant of medieval Normandy (now part of France). **2** a descendant of the people of mixed Scandinavian and Frankish origin established there in the 10th c., who conquered England in 1066. **3** Norman French. ● *adj.* **1** of or relating to the Normans. **2** ◄ of or relating to the Norman style of architecture. □□ **Nor·man·esque** /-nésk/ *adj.* **Nor·man·ism** *n.* **Nor·man·ize** *v.tr. & intr.*

Nor·man Con·quest *n.* see CONQUEST.

nor·ma·tive /náwrmətiv/ *adj.* of or establishing a norm. □□ **nor·ma·tive·ly** *adv.* **nor·ma·tive·ness** *n.*

Norse /nawrs/ *n. & adj.* ● *n.* **1** the Norwegian language. **2** the Scandinavian language group. ● *adj.* of ancient Scandinavia, esp. Norway. □□ **Norse·man** *n.* (*pl.* **-men**).

north /nawrth/ *n., adj., & adv.* ● *n.* **1 a** the point of the horizon 90° counterclockwise from east. **b** the compass point corresponding to this. ▷ COMPASS. **c** the direction in which this lies. **2** (usu. **the North**) **a** the part of the world or a country or a town lying to the north. **b** the arctic. ● *adj.* **1** toward, at, near, or facing north. **2** coming from the north (*north wind*). ● *adv.* **1** toward, at, or near the north. **2** (foll. by *of*) further north than. □ **north and south** lengthwise along a line from north to south. **to the north** (often foll. by *of*) in a northerly direction.

North A·mer·i·can *adj. & n.* ● *adj.* of North America. ● *n.* a native or inhabitant of North America, esp. a citizen of the US or Canada.

north·bound /náwrthbownd/ *adj.* traveling or leading northward.

North Coun·try *n.* the geographical region including Alaska and the Canadian Yukon.

north·east /nawrthéest/ *n., adj., & adv.* ● *n.* **1** the point of the horizon midway between north and east. **2** the compass point corresponding to this. **3** the direction in which this lies. ● *adj.* of, toward, or coming from the northeast. ● *adv.* toward, at, or near the northeast.

north·east·er /nawrthéestər, náwréestər/ *n.* (also **nor'easter**) **1** a northeast wind. **2** a strong storm from the northeast, esp. in New England.

north·er·ly /náwrthərlee/ *adj., adv., & n.* ● *adj. & adv.* **1** in a northern position or direction. **2** (of wind) blowing from the north. ● *n.* (*pl.* **-ies**) (usu. in *pl.*) a wind blowing from the north.

north·ern /náwrthərn/ *adj.* **1** of or in the north. **2** toward the north. □□ **north·ern·most** *adj.*

north·ern·er /náwrthərnər/ *n.* a native or inhabitant of the north.

north·ern hem·i·sphere *n.* (also **North·ern Hem·i·sphere**) the half of the Earth north of the equator.

north·ern lights *n.pl.* the aurora borealis. ▷ AURORA

North·man /náwrthmən/ *n.* (*pl.* **-men**) a native of Scandinavia, esp. of Norway.

north-north·east *n.* the point or direction midway between north and northeast.

north-north·west *n.* the point or direction midway between north and northwest.

north pole *n.* (also **North Pole**) the northernmost point of the Earth's axis of rotation.

North Star *n.* the polestar.

north·ward /náwrthwərd/ *adj., adv., & n.* ● *adj. & adv.* (also **north·wards**) toward the north. ● *n.* a northward direction or region.

north·west /náwrthwést/ *n., adj., & adv.* ● *n.* **1** the point of the horizon midway between north and west. **2** the compass point corresponding to this. **3** the direction in which this lies. ● *adj.* of, toward, or coming from the northwest. ● *adv.* toward, at, or near the northwest.

north·west·er /náwrthwéstər, náwrthwés-/ *n.* (also **nor'wester**) a northwest wind.

Nor·we·gian /nawrwééjən/ *n. & adj.* ● *n.* **1 a** a native or national of Norway. **b** a person of Norwegian descent. **2** the language of Norway. ● *adj.* of or relating to Norway or its people or language.

N

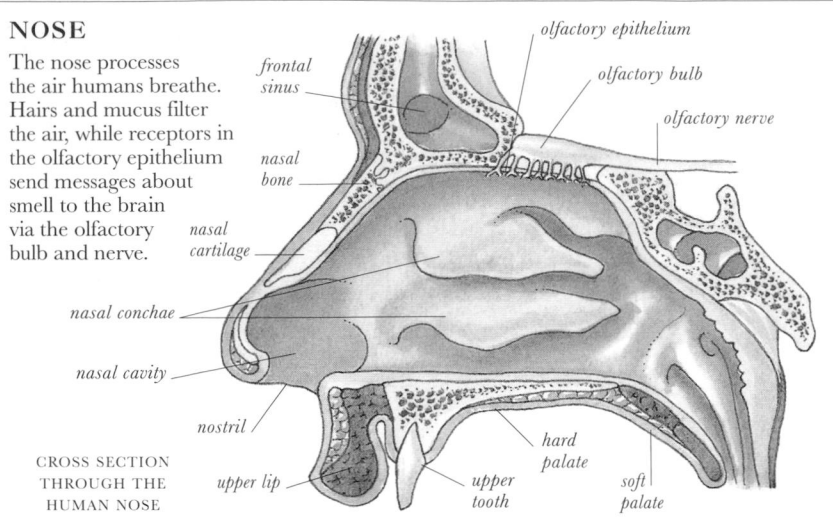

NOSE

The nose processes the air humans breathe. Hairs and mucus filter the air, while receptors in the olfactory epithelium send messages about smell to the brain via the olfactory bulb and nerve.

olfactory epithelium
olfactory bulb
olfactory nerve
frontal sinus
nasal bone
nasal cartilage
nasal conchae
nasal cavity
nostril
upper lip
upper tooth
hard palate
soft palate

CROSS SECTION THROUGH THE HUMAN NOSE

Nos. *abbr.* (also **nos.**) numbers.

nose /nōz/ *n. & v.* ● *n.* **1** ▲ an organ above the mouth of a human or animal, used for smelling and breathing. ▷ RESPIRATION. **2 a** the sense of smell (*dogs have a good nose*). **b** the ability to detect a particular thing (*a nose for scandal*). **3** the odor or perfume of wine, tea, etc. **4** the open end or nozzle of a tube, pipe, etc. **5** the front end or projecting part of a thing, e.g., of a car or aircraft. ● *v.* **1** *tr.* (often foll. by *out*) **a** perceive the smell of, discover by smell. **b** detect. **2** *tr.* thrust or rub one's nose against or into. **3** *intr.* (usu. foll. by *about*, *around*, etc.) pry or search. **4 a** *intr.* make one's way cautiously forward. **b** *tr.* make (one's or its way). □ **as plain as the nose on your face** easily seen. **by a nose** by a very narrow margin (*won the race by a nose*). **keep one's nose clean** *sl.* stay out of trouble. **keep one's nose to the grindstone** see GRINDSTONE. **on the nose** *sl.* precisely. **put a person's nose out of joint** *colloq.* disconcert or supplant a person. **turn up one's nose** (usu. foll. by *at*) *colloq.* show disdain. **under a person's nose** *colloq.* right before a person. **with one's nose in the air** haughtily. □□ **nosed** *adj.* (also in *comb.*).

nose-bag /nōzbag/ *n.* a bag containing fodder, hung on a horse's head.

nose-band /nōzband/ *n.* the lower band of a bridle, passing over the horse's nose. ▷ BRIDLE

nose-bleed /nōzbleed/ *n.* an instance of bleeding from the nose.

nose cone *n.* the cone-shaped nose of a rocket, etc. ▷ BALLISTIC MISSILE, ROCKET

nose-dive /nōzdīv/ *n. & v.* ● *n.* **1 a** steep downward plunge by an airplane. **2** a sudden plunge or drop. ● *v.intr.* make a nosedive.

no-see-um *n.* (also **no-see-em**) a small bloodsucking insect, esp. a midge of the family *Ceratopogonidae*.

nose flute *n.* ▶ a musical instrument blown with the nose.

nose-gay /nōzgay/ *n.* a bunch of flowers, esp. a sweet-scented posy.

nose job *n. sl.* surgery on the nose, esp. for cosmetic reasons.

nose-piece /nōzpees/ *n.* **1** = NOSEBAND. **2** the part of a helmet, etc., protecting the upper. **3** the part of a microscope to which the objective is attached. **4** the bridge on the frame of eyeglasses.

nose ring *n.* a ring fixed in the nose.

nos-ey var. of NOSY.

nosh /nosh/ *v. & n. sl.* ● *v.tr. & intr.* **1** eat or drink. **2** eat between meals. ● *n.* **1** food or drink. **2** a snack.

no-show *n.* a person who has reserved a seat, etc., but neither uses it nor cancels the reservation.

nos-ing /nōzing/ *n.* a rounded edge of a step, molding, etc., or a metal shield for it.

no-so-lo-gy /nōsóləjee/ *n.* the branch of medical science concerned with the classification of diseases.

nos-tal-gia /nostáljə, -jeeə, nə-/ *n.* **1** (often foll. by *for*) sentimental yearning for a period of the past. **2** regretful or wistful memory of an earlier time. □□ **nos-tal-gic** *adj.* **nos-tal-gi-cal-ly** *adv.*

nos-tril /nóstrəl/ *n.* either of two external openings of the nasal cavity in vertebrates that admit air to the lungs and smells to the olfactory nerves.

nos-trum /nóstrəm/ *n.* **1** a quack remedy, a patent medicine, esp. one prepared by the person recommending it. **2** a panacea scheme, esp. for political or social reform.

nos-y /nōzee/ *adj.* (also **nos-ey**) (**nosier**, **nosiest**) *colloq.* inquisitive, prying. □□ **nos-i-ly** *adv.* **nos-i-ness** *n.*

not /not/ *adv.* expressing negation, esp.: **1** (also **n't** joined to a preceding verb) following an auxiliary verb or *be* or (in a question) the subject of such a verb (*she isn't there*; *didn't you tell me?*). ¶ Use with other verbs is now *archaic* (*I know not*; *fear not*), except with participles and infinitives (*not knowing*, *I cannot say*; *we asked them not to come*). **2** used elliptically for a negative sentence or verb or phrase (*Is she coming? — I hope not*; *Do you want it? — Certainly not!*). **3** used to express the negative of other words (*not a single one was left*; *Are they pleased? — Not they*). □ **not at all** (in polite reply to thanks) there is no need for thanks. **not half** see HALF. **not least** notably. **not quite 1** almost (*am not quite there*). **2** noticeably not (*not quite proper*). **not that** (foll. by clause) it is not to be inferred that (*if he said so — not that he ever did — he lied*). **not a thing** nothing at all. **not very** see VERY.

no-ta be-ne /nōtə bénay/ *v.tr.* (as *imper.*) observe what follows, take notice (usu. drawing attention to a following qualification of what has preceded).

no-ta-bil-i-ty /nōtəbílitee/ *n.* (*pl.* **-ies**) **1** the state of being notable (*names of no historical notability*). **2** a prominent person.

no-ta-ble /nōtəbəl/ *adj. & n.* ● *adj.* worthy of note; remarkable. ● *n.* an eminent person. □□ **no-ta-bly** *adv.*

no-ta-rize /nōtərīz/ *v.tr.* certify (a document) as a notary.

no-ta-ry /nōtəree/ *n.* (*pl.* **-ies**) (in full **notary public**) a person authorized to

perform certain legal formalities, esp. to draw up or certify contracts, deeds, etc. □□ **no-tar-i-al** /nōtáireeəl/ *adj.*

no-tate /nōtayt/ *v.tr.* write in notation.

no-ta-tion /nōtáyshən/ *n.* **1 a** ▶ the representation of numbers, quantities, pitch and duration, etc., of musical notes, etc., by symbols. **b** any set of such symbols. **2** a set of symbols used to represent chess moves, dance steps, etc. **3 a** a note or annotation. **b** a record. □□ **no-ta-tion-al** *adj.*

notch /noch/ *n. & v.* ● *n.* **1** a V-shaped indentation on an edge or surface. **2** a nick made on a stick, etc., in order to keep count. **3** *colloq.* a step or degree (*move up a notch*). **4** a deep, narrow mountain pass. ● *v.tr.* **1** make notches in. **2** (foll. by *up*) record or score with or as with notches. **3** secure or insert by notches. □□ **notched** *adj.* **notch-er** *n.* **notch-y** *adj.* (**notchier**, **notchiest**).

note /nōt/ *n. & v.* ● *n.* **1** a brief record as an aid to memory (often in *pl.*: *make notes*; *spoke without notes*). **2** an observation, usu. unwritten, of experiences, etc. (*compare notes*). **3** a short letter. **4** a formal diplomatic or parliamentary communication. **5** a short annotation in a book, etc. **6 a** notice, attention (*worthy of note*). **b** eminence (*a person of note*). **7 a** a written sign representing the pitch and duration of a musical sound. ▷ NOTATION. **b** a single tone of definite pitch made by a musical instrument, the human voice, etc. **c** a key of a piano, etc. **8 a** a bird's song or call. **b** a single tone in this. **9** a quality or tone of speaking, expressing mood or attitude, etc. (*sound a note of warning*). ● *v.tr.* **1** give or draw attention to. **2** record as a thing to be remembered. **3** (in *passive*; often foll. by *for*) be famous or well known (for a quality, activity, etc.) (*were noted for their generosity*). □ **hit** (or **strike**) **the right note** act in exactly the right manner. **of note** distinguished (*a person of note*). **take note** (often foll. by *of*) pay attention (to). □□ **not-ed** *adj.* (in sense 3 of *v.*). **note-less** *adj.*

note-book com-pu-ter *n.* a lightweight computer that closes to notebook size for portability.

note-pa-per /nōtpaypər/ *n.* paper for writing notes.

note-wor-thy /nōtwərthee/ *adj.* worthy of attention. □□ **note-wor-thi-ness** *n.*

noth-ing /núthing/ *n. & adv.* ● *n.* **1** not anything (*nothing has been done*; *have nothing to do*). **2** no thing (often foll. by compl.: *I see nothing that I want*). **3** a person or thing of no importance (*was nothing to me*). **4** nonexistence; what does not exist. **5** (in calculations) no amount; naught (*a third of nothing is nothing*). ● *adv.* not at all, in no way (*is nothing like what we expected*). □ **be nothing to 1** not concern. **2** compare with. **be** (or **have**) **nothing to do with 1** have no connection with. **2** not be associated with. **for nothing 1** at no cost; without payment. **2** to no purpose. **have nothing on 1** be naked. **2** have no engagements. **nothing doing** *colloq.* **1 a** there is no prospect of success. **b** I refuse. **2** nothing is happening. **nothing** (or **not much**) **in it** (or **to it**) **1** unimportant. **2** simple to do. **3** no (or little) advantage to be seen in one possibility over another. **think nothing of it** do not apologize or feel bound to show gratitude.

noth-ing-ness /núthingnis/ *n.* **1** nonexistence; the nonexistent. **2** worthlessness, triviality.

no-tice /nótis/ *n. & v.* ● *n.* **1** attention; observation (*it escaped my notice*). **2** a displayed sheet, etc., bearing an announcement. **3 a** an intimation or warning, esp. a formal one (*give notice*; *at a moment's notice*). **b** (often foll. by *to* + infin.) a formal announcement or declaration of intention to end an agreement or leave employment at a specified time (*hand in one's notice*). **4** a short published review or comment about a new play, book, etc. ● *v.tr.* **1** (often foll. by *that*, *how*, etc., + clause) observe; take notice of. **2** remark upon. □ **at short** (or **a moment's**) **notice** with little warning. **take notice** (or **no notice**) show signs (or no signs) of interest. **take notice of 1** pay attention to. **2** act upon. **under notice** served with a formal notice.

nose-bleed *n.*

blow-hole
finger-hole

NOSE FLUTE:
FIJIAN BAMBOO NOSE FLUTE

NOTATION

Conventional musical notation is written on a five-line staff divided into bars. Notes indicate the duration and pitch of a sound; they can be arranged in order of pitch to form scales. Clefs fix the pitch of the notes; accidentals indicate brief changes in pitch. Rests specify the duration of a silence.

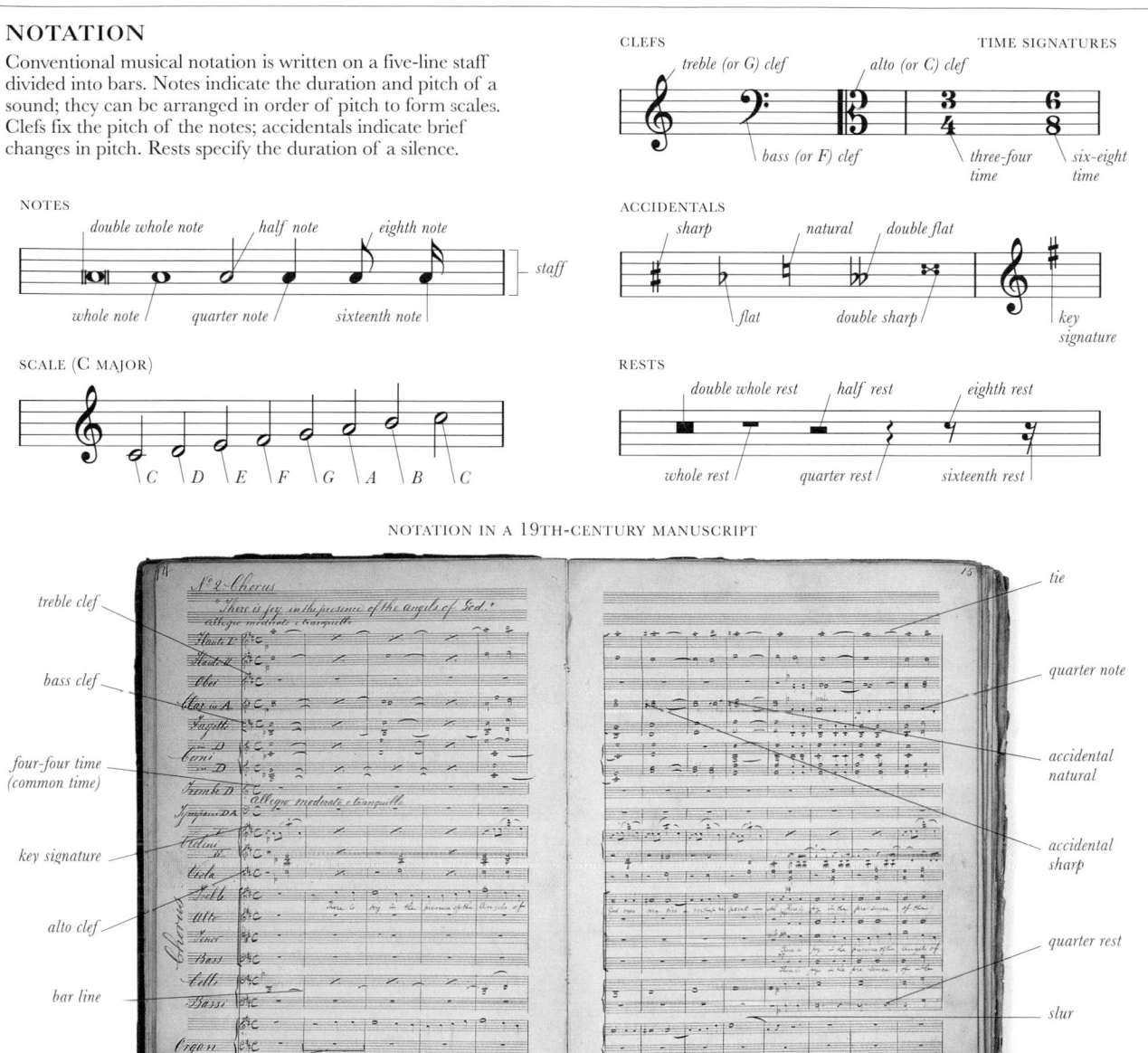

NOTATION IN A 19TH-CENTURY MANUSCRIPT

N

---

no·tice·a·ble /nótisəbəl/ *adj.* **1** easily seen or noticed; perceptible. **2** noteworthy. □□ **no·tice·a·bly** *adv.*

no·ti·fi·a·ble /nótifīəbəl/ *adj.* (of a disease) that must be reported to the health authorities.

no·ti·fy /nótifī/ *v.tr.* (**-ies, -ied**) **1** (often foll. by *of*, or *that* + clause) inform or give notice to (a person). **2** make known; announce or report (a thing). □□ **no·ti·fi·ca·tion** /-fikáyshən/ *n.*

no·tion /nóshən/ *n.* **1 a** a concept or idea (*it was an absurd notion*). **b** an opinion (*has the notion that people are honest*). **c** a vague view or understanding (*have no notion what you mean*). **2** an inclination or intention (*has no notion of conforming*). **3** (in *pl.*) small, useful articles.

no·tion·al /nóshənəl/ *adj.* hypothetical, imaginary. □□ **no·tion·al·ly** *adv.*

no·to·chord /nótəkawrd/ *n.* a cartilaginous skeletal rod supporting the body in all embryo and some adult chordate animals.

no·to·ri·ous /nōtáwreeəs/ *adj.* well-known, esp. unfavorably (*a notorious criminal*). □□ **no·to·ri·e·ty** /-təríətee/ *n.* **no·to·ri·ous·ly** *adv.*

not·with·stand·ing /nótwithstánding, -with-/ *prep., adv., & conj.* ● *prep.* in spite of (*notwithstanding your objections; this fact notwithstanding*). ● *adv.* nevertheless. ● *conj.* (usu. foll. by *that* + clause) although.

nou·gat /nóŏgət/ *n.* a chewy candy made from sugar or honey, nuts, egg white, and often fruit pieces.

nought var. of NAUGHT.

noun /nown/ *n. Gram.* a word (other than a pronoun) or group of words used to name or identify any of a class of persons, places, or things (**common noun**), or a particular one of these (**proper noun**).

nour·ish /nórish, núr-/ *v.tr.* **1 a** sustain with food. **b** promote the development of (the soil, etc.). **c** provide with intellectual or emotional sustenance. **2** cherish (a feeling, etc.).

nour·ish·ing /nórishing, núr-/ *adj.* (esp. of food) containing much nourishment. □□ **nour·ish·ing·ly** *adv.*

nour·ish·ment /nórishmənt, núr-/ *n.* sustenance, food.

nous /noŏs/ *n. Philos.* the mind or intellect.

nou·veau riche /noŏvō réesh/ *n.* (*pl.* **nouveaux riches** *pronunc.* same) a person who has recently acquired (usu. ostentatious) wealth.

nou·velle cui·sine /noŏvél kwizéen/ *n.* a modern style of cookery avoiding heaviness and emphasizing presentation.

Nov. *abbr.* November.

no·va /nóvə/ *n.* (*pl.* **novas** or **novae** /-vee/) a star showing a sudden large increase of brightness that then subsides.

nov·el[1] /nóvəl/ *n.* **1** a fictitious prose story of book length. **2** (prec. by *the*) this type of literature.

nov·el[2] /nóvəl/ *adj.* interestingly new and unusual.

nov·el·ette /nóvəlét/ *n.* a short novel.

nov·el·ist /nóvəlist/ *n.* a writer of novels. □□ **nov·el·is·tic** *adj.*

no·vel·la /nəvélə/ *n.* (*pl.* **novellas** or **novelle**) a short novel or narrative story; a tale.

nov·el·ty /nóvəltee/ *n.* (*pl.* **-ies**) **1 a** newness; new character. **b** originality. **2** a new or unusual thing or occurrence. **3** a small toy or decoration, etc., of novel design. **4** (*attrib.*) having novelty (*novelty toys*).

No·vem·ber /nōvémbər/ *n.* the eleventh month of the year.

no·ve·na /nōvéenə, nə-/ *n. RC Ch.* a devotion consisting of special prayers or services on nine successive days.

nov·ice /nóvis/ *n.* **1** a probationary member of a religious order, before the taking of vows. **2** a beginner. **3** an animal that has not won a major prize in a competition.

no·vi·ti·ate /nōvísheeət, -ayt/ *n.* (also **no·vi·ci·ate**) **1** the period of being a novice. **2** a religious novice. **3** novices' quarters.

No·vo·caine /nóvəkayn/ *n.* (also **novocaine**) *Trademark* a local anesthetic derived from benzoic acid.

now /now/ *adv., conj., & n.* ● *adv.* **1** at the present or mentioned time. **2** immediately (*I must go now*). **3** by this or that time (*it was now clear*). **4** under the present circumstances (*I cannot now agree*). **5** on this further occasion (*what do you want now?*). **6** in the immediate past (*just now*). **7** (without reference to time, giving various tones to a sentence) surely, I insist, I wonder, etc. (*now what do you mean by that?; oh come now!*). ● *conj.* (often foll. by *that* + clause) as a consequence of the fact (*now that I am older; now you mention it*). ● *n.* this time; the present (*should be there by now; has happened before now*). □ **as of now** from or at this time. **for now** until a later time (*goodbye for now*). **now and again** (or **then**) from time to time; intermittently. **now or never** an expression of urgency.

now·a·days /nówədayz/ *adv. & n.* ● *adv.* at the present time or age. ● *n.* the present time.

no·where /nóhwair, -wair/ *adv. & pron.* ● *adv.* in or to no place. ● *pron.* no place. □ **come from nowhere** be suddenly evident or successful. **get nowhere** make or cause to make no progress. **in the middle of nowhere** *colloq.* remote from urban life. **nowhere near** not nearly.

no·wheres·ville /nóhwairzvil/ *n. N. Amer. colloq.* a place or situation of no significance, promise, or interest.

no-win *adj.* of or designating a situation in which success is impossible.

nox·ious /nókshəs/ *adj.* harmful, unwholesome. □□ **nox·ious·ly** *adv.* **nox·ious·ness** *n.*

noz·zle /nózəl/ *n.* a spout on a hose, etc., from which a jet issues. ▷ AIRBRUSH, SPRAY GUN

NP *abbr.* **1** notary public. **2** nurse-practitioner.

Np *symb. Chem.* the element neptunium.

n.p. *abbr.* **1** new paragraph. **2** no place of publication.

NRC *abbr.* Nuclear Regulatory Commission.

NS *abbr.* **1** new style. **2** new series. **3** Nova Scotia.

NSA *abbr.* National Security Agency.

NSC *abbr.* National Security Council.

NSF *abbr.* National Science Foundation.

NSW *abbr.* New South Wales.

NT *abbr.* **1** New Testament. **2** Northern Territory (of Australia).

-n't /ənt/ *adv.* (in *comb.*) = NOT (usu. with *is, are, have, must,* and the auxiliary verbs *can, do, should, would*: *isn't; mustn't*).

nth see N[1].

nu /nōō, nyōō/ *n.* the thirteenth letter of the Greek alphabet (N, ν).

nu·ance /nōō-áans, nyōō-/ *n. & v.* ● *n.* a subtle difference in or shade of meaning, feeling, color, etc. ● *v.tr.* give a nuance or nuances to.

nub /nub/ *n.* **1** the point or gist (of a matter or story). **2** a small lump, esp. of coal. □□ **nub·by** *adj.*

nu·bile /nōōbīl, -bil, nyōō-/ *adj.* (of a woman) marriageable or sexually attractive. □□ **nu·bil·i·ty** /-bílitee/ *n.*

nu·buck /nōōbuk, nyōō-/ *n.* cowhide leather which has been rubbed on the flesh side to give a suede-like effect.

nu·cle·ar /nōōkleeər, nyōō-/ *adj.* **1** of, relating to, or constituting a nucleus. **2** using nuclear energy (*nuclear reactor*). **3** having nuclear weapons.

nu·cle·ar bomb *n.* a bomb involving the release of energy by nuclear fission or fusion or both.

nu·cle·ar dis·ar·ma·ment *n.* the gradual or total reduction by a nation of its nuclear weapons.

nu·cle·ar en·er·gy *n.* energy obtained by nuclear fission or fusion.

nu·cle·ar fam·i·ly *n.* a couple and their children, regarded as a basic social unit.

nu·cle·ar fis·sion *n.* ▼ a nuclear reaction in which a heavy nucleus splits spontaneously or on impact with another particle, with the release of energy.

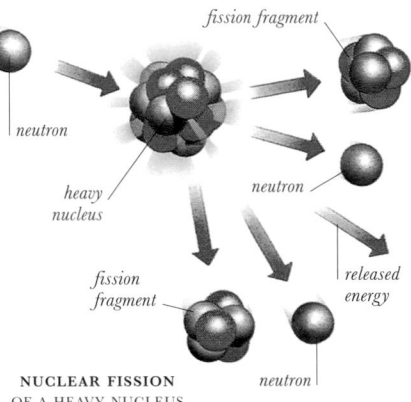

fission fragment

neutron

heavy nucleus

neutron

fission fragment

released energy

neutron

NUCLEAR FISSION
OF A HEAVY NUCLEUS

N

NUCLEAR POWER

Nuclear power is produced through controlled nuclear fission inside the core of a reactor. The heat created by the fission of the fuel (usually uranium) is taken away by a coolant and used to turn water into steam. The steam powers a turbine that runs an electricity generator.

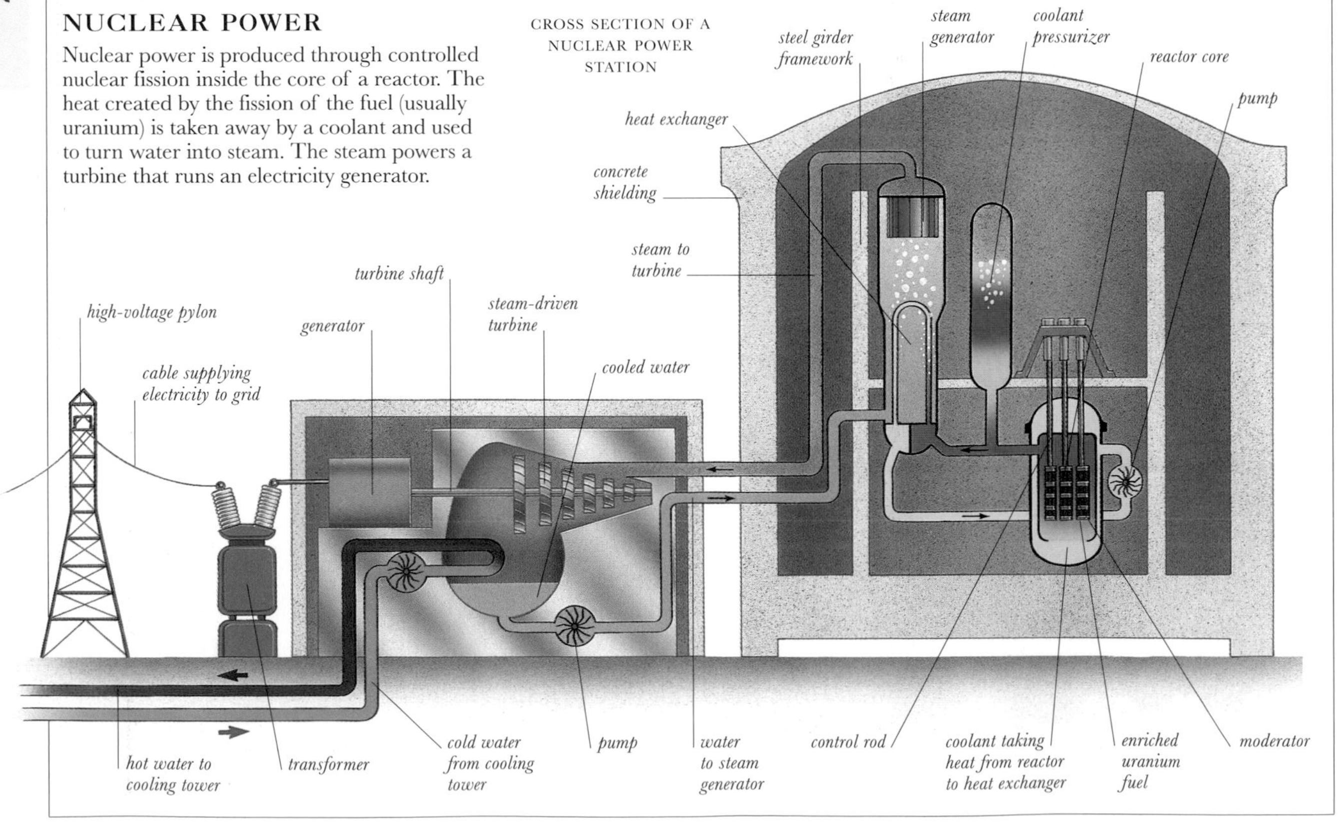

CROSS SECTION OF A NUCLEAR POWER STATION

steel girder framework

heat exchanger

concrete shielding

steam to turbine

steam generator

coolant pressurizer

reactor core

pump

high-voltage pylon

turbine shaft

generator

steam-driven turbine

cooled water

cable supplying electricity to grid

hot water to cooling tower

transformer

cold water from cooling tower

pump

water to steam generator

control rod

coolant taking heat from reactor to heat exchanger

enriched uranium fuel

moderator

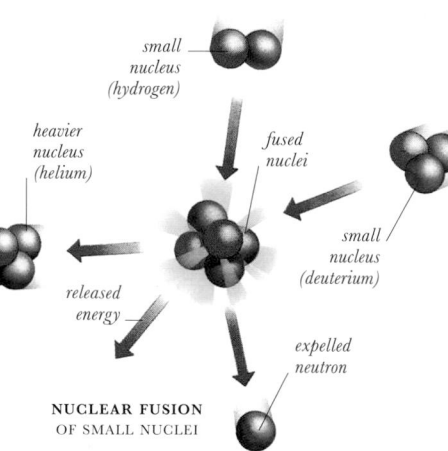

NUCLEAR FUSION
OF SMALL NUCLEI

nu·cle·ar fu·sion *n.* ▲ a nuclear reaction in which atomic nuclei of low atomic number fuse to form a heavier nucleus with the release of energy.

nu·cle·ar mag·net·ic res·o·nance *n.* the absorption of electromagnetic radiation by a nucleus having a magnetic moment when in an external magnetic field, used mainly as an analytical technique and in body imaging for diagnosis. ▷ MRI

nu·cle·ar med·i·cine *n. Med.* a specialty that uses radioactive materials for diagnosis and treatment.

nu·cle·ar phys·ics *n.* the physics of atomic nuclei and their interactions.

nu·cle·ar pow·er 1 ◀ power generated by a nuclear reactor. **2** a country that has nuclear weapons.

nu·cle·ar re·ac·tor *n.* a device in which a nuclear fission chain reaction is sustained and controlled in order to produce energy.

nu·cle·ar war·fare *n.* warfare in which nuclear weapons are used.

nu·cle·ar waste *n.* any radioactive waste material.

nu·cle·ase /nóōkleeayz, -ays, nyóō-/ *n.* an enzyme that catalyzes the breakdown of nucleic acids.

nu·cle·ate /nóōkleeayt, nyóō-/ *adj. & v.* ● *adj.* having a nucleus. ● *v.intr. & tr.* form or form into a nucleus. □□ **nu·cle·a·tion** /-áyshən/ *n.*

nu·cle·i *pl.* of NUCLEUS.

nu·cle·ic acid /nōōkléeik, -kláyik, nyóō-/ *n.* either of two complex organic molecules (DNA and RNA), consisting of many nucleotides linked in a long chain, and present in all living cells. ▷ DNA

nucleo- /nóōkleeō, nyóō-/ *comb. form* nucleus; nucleic acid (*nucleoprotein*).

nu·cle·o·lus /nōōkléeələs, nyóō-/ *n.* (*pl.* **nucleoli** /-lī/) a small dense spherical structure within a nondividing nucleus. □□ **nu·cle·o·lar** *adj.*

nu·cle·on /nóōkleeon, nyóō-/ *n. Physics* a proton or neutron.

nu·cle·o·side /nóōkleeəsīd, nyóō-/ *n. Biochem.* an organic compound consisting of a purine or pyrimidine base linked to a sugar, e.g., adenosine.

nu·cle·o·tide /nóōkleeətīd, nyóō-/ *n. Biochem.* an organic compound consisting of a nucleoside linked to a phosphate group.

nu·cle·us /nóōkleeəs/ *n.* (*pl.* **nuclei** /-lee-ī/) **1 a** the central part or thing around which others are collected. **b** the kernel of an aggregate or mass. **2** an initial part meant to receive additions. **3** *Astron.* the solid part of a comet's head. **4** *Physics* ▶ the central core of an atom. ▷ ATOM. **5** *Biol.* a large dense organelle of eukaryotic cells, containing the genetic material. ▷ ALGA

nude /nōōd, nyōōd/ *adj. & n.* ● *adj.* naked, unclothed. ● *n.* **1** a painting, sculpture, photograph, etc., of a nude human figure. **2** a nude person. **3** (prec. by *the*) **a** an unclothed state. **b** the representation of an undraped human figure as a genre in art.

nudge /nuj/ *v. & n.* ● *v.tr.* **1** prod gently with the elbow to attract attention. **2** push gently or gradually. **3** give a gentle reminder or encouragement to (a person). ● *n.* the act or an instance of nudging; a gentle push.

nud·ist /nóōdist, nyóō-/ *n.* a person who advocates or practices going unclothed. □□ **nud·ism** *n.*

nu·di·ty /nóōditee, nyóō-/ *n.* the state of being nude; nakedness.

nu·ga·to·ry /nóōgətáwree, nyóō-/ *adj.* **1** futile; trifling; worthless. **2** inoperative.

nug·get /núgit/ *n.* **1 a** ▶ a lump of gold, platinum, etc., as found in the earth. **b** a lump of anything compared to this. **2** something valuable for its size.

nui·sance /nóōsəns, nyóō-/ *n.* **1** a person, thing, or circumstance causing trouble or annoyance. **2** anything harmful to the community for which a legal remedy exists.

nuke /nōōk, nyōōk/ *n. & v. colloq.* ● *n.* a nuclear weapon. ● *v.tr. colloq.* bomb or destroy with nuclear weapons.

null /nul/ *adj.* **1** (esp. **null and void**) invalid. **2** nonexistent. **3** having the value zero. **4** *Computing* **a** empty (*null list*). **b** all the elements of which are zeros (*null matrix*). **5** without character or expression.

null·i·fy /núlifī/ *v.tr.* (**-ies, -ied**) make null; neutralize; invalidate; cancel. □□ **null·i·fi·ca·tion** /-fikáyshən/ *n.* **null·i·fi·er** *n.*

numb /num/ *adj. & v.* ● *adj.* (often foll. by *with*) deprived of feeling (*numb with cold*). ● *v.tr.* **1** make numb. **2** paralyze. □□ **numb·ly** *adv.* **numb·ness** *n.*

num·ber /númbər/ *n. & v.* ● *n.* **1 a** an arithmetical value representing a particular quantity. **b** a word, symbol, or figure representing this. **c** an arithmetical value showing position in a series (*registration number*). **2** (often foll. by *of*) the total count or aggregate (*the number of accidents has decreased*). **3 a** numerical reckoning (*the laws of number*). **b** (in *pl.*) arithmetic (*not good at numbers*). **4 a** (in *sing.* or *pl.*) a quantity or amount (*a large number of people*). **b** (in *pl.*) numerical preponderance (*force of numbers*). **5 a** a person or thing having a place in a series, esp. a single issue of a magazine, etc. **b** a song, dance, etc. **6** company, group (*among our number*). **7** *Gram.* **a** the classification of words by their singular or plural forms. **b** a particular such form. **8** *colloq.* a person or thing regarded familiarly (usu. qualified in some way: *an attractive little number*). ● *v.tr.* **1** include (*I number you among my friends*). **2** assign a number to. **3** amount to (a specified number). **4 a** count. **b** comprise (*numbering forty thousand men*). □ **one's days are numbered** one does not have long to live. **have a person's number** *colloq.* understand a person's real motives, character, etc. **one's number is up** *colloq.* one is finished or doomed to die. **without number** innumerable.

num·ber crunch·er *n. Computing & Math. sl.* a machine capable of complex calculations, etc. □□ **num·ber crunch·ing** *n.*

num·ber·less /númbərlis/ *adj.* innumerable.

num·ber one *n. & adj.* ● *n. colloq.* oneself (*take care of number one*). ● *adj.* most important (*the number-one priority*).

num·bers game *n.* an illegal lottery based on the occurrence of unpredictable numbers in the results of races, etc.

numb·skull var. of NUMSKULL.

nu·mer·al /nóōmərəl, nyóō-/ *n. & adj.* ● *n.* a word, figure, or group of figures denoting a number. ● *adj.* of or denoting a number.

nu·mer·ate /nóōmərət, nyóō-/ *adj.* acquainted with the basic principles of mathematics. □□ **nu·mer·a·cy** /-əsee/ *n.*

nu·mer·a·tion /nóōməráyshən, nyóō-/ *n.* **1** a method or process of numbering or computing. **2** the expression in words of a number written in figures.

nu·mer·a·tor /nóōməraytər, nyóō-/ *n.* the number above the line in a common fraction showing how many of the parts indicated by the denominator are taken (e.g., 2 in $^2/_3$).

nu·mer·i·cal /nōōmérikəl, nyóō-/ *adj.* (also **nu·mer·ic**) of or relating to a number or numbers. □□ **nu·mer·i·cal·ly** *adv.*

nu·mer·ol·o·gy /nóōməróləjee, nyóō-/ *n.* (*pl.* **-ies**) the study of the supposed occult significance of numbers. □□ **nu·mer·o·log·i·cal** /-rəlójikəl/ *adj.* **nu·mer·ol·o·gist** *n.*

nu·mer·ous /nóōmərəs, nyóō-/ *adj.* **1** (with *pl.*) great in number. **2** consisting of many. □□ **nu·mer·ous·ly** *adv.* **nu·mer·ous·ness** *n.*

nu·mi·nous /nóōminəs, nyóō-/ *adj.* having a strong spiritual or religious quality.

nu·mis·mat·ic /nóōmizmátik, nyóō-/ *adj.* of or relating to coins or medals. □□ **nu·mis·mat·i·cal·ly** *adv.*

nu·mis·mat·ics /nóōmizmátiks, nyóō-/ *n.pl.* (usu. treated as *sing.*) the study of coins or medals. □□ **nu·mis·ma·tist** /nóōmizmətist, nyóō-/ *n.*

num·skull /númskul/ *n.* (also **numb·skull**) a stupid or foolish person.

nun /nun/ *n.* a member of a community of women living apart under religious vows. □□ **nun·like** *adj.* **nun·nish** *adj.*

nun·a·tak /núnətak/ *n.* an isolated peak of rock projecting above a surface of inland ice or snow.

nun·ci·a·ture /núnsheeəchŏōr, -chər, nóōn-/ *n. RC Ch.* the office of a nuncio.

nun·ci·o /núnsheeō/ *n.* (*pl.* **-os**) *RC Ch.* a papal ambassador.

nun·ner·y /núnəree/ *n.* (*pl.* **-ies**) a convent.

nup·tial /núpshəl/ *adj. & n.* ● *adj.* of or relating to marriage or weddings. ● *n.* (usu. in *pl.*) a wedding.

nurd var. of NERD.

NUGGET:
GOLD NUGGET

N

NUCLEUS

A nucleus consists of particles called protons and neutrons, which are in turn made up of quarks held together by particles called gluons.

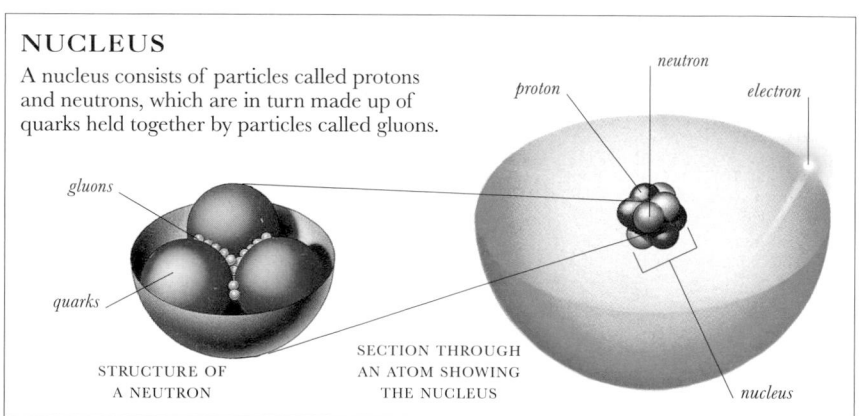

gluons

quarks

STRUCTURE OF
A NEUTRON

neutron

proton

electron

SECTION THROUGH
AN ATOM SHOWING
THE NUCLEUS

nucleus

NUT

In strict botanical terms, a nut is a dry fruit with a hard nonsplitting pericarp (shell) surrounding usually only one seed. In common usage, the term is widely applied to any dry fruit that has a hard shell surrounding an edible kernel.

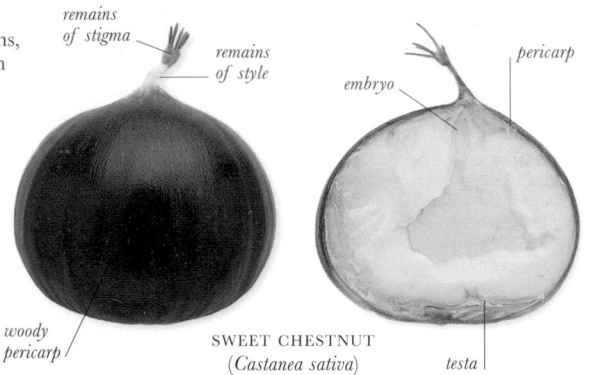

remains of stigma
remains of style
pericarp
embryo
woody pericarp
testa

SWEET CHESTNUT
(*Castanea sativa*)

EXAMPLES OF OTHER NUTS

HAZELNUT
(*Corylus avellana*)

WALNUT
(*Juglans nigra*)

ALMOND
(*Prunus dulcis*)

BRAZIL NUT
(*Bertholletia excelsa*)

nurse /nərs/ *n. & v.* ● *n.* **1** a person trained to care for the sick. **2** (formerly) a person employed to take charge of young children. ● *v.* **1 a** *intr.* work as a nurse. **b** *tr.* attend to (a sick person). **c** *tr.* give medical attention to (an illness or injury). **2** *tr. & intr.* feed or be fed at the breast. **3** *tr.* **a** foster; promote the development of (the arts, plants, etc.). **b** harbor (a grievance, etc.).

nurse·ling var. of NURSLING.

nurse·maid /nərsmayd/ *n.* **1** a woman in charge of a child or children. **2** a person who watches over or guides another carefully.

nurse-prac·ti·tion·er *n.* a registered nurse who has received training in diagnosing and treating illness.

nurs·er·y /nə́rsəree/ *n.* (*pl.* **-ies**) **1 a** a room or place equipped for young children. **b** a nursery where children are looked after during the working day. **2** a place where plants, etc., are reared for sale or transplantation.

nurs·er·y·man /nə́rsəreemən/ *n.* (*pl.* **-men**) an owner of or worker in a plant nursery.

nurs·er·y rhyme *n.* a simple traditional song or story in rhyme for children.

nurs·er·y school *n.* a school for children from the age of about three to five.

nurs·ing /nə́rsing/ *n.* **1** the practice or profession of caring for the sick as a nurse. **2** (*attrib.*) concerned with or suitable for nursing the sick or elderly, etc.

nurs·ling /nə́rsling/ *n.* (also **nurse·ling**) an infant that is being suckled.

nur·ture /nə́rchər/ *n. & v.* ● *n.* **1** the process of bringing up; fostering care. **2** nourishment. **3** sociological factors as a determinant of personality. ● *v.tr.* **1** bring up; rear. **2** nourish. □□ **nur·tur·er** *n.*

nut /nut/ *n.* **1 a** ▲ a fruit consisting of a hard or tough shell around an edible kernel. **b** this kernel. **2** a pod containing hard seeds. **3** a small usu. hexagonal flat piece of metal or other material with a threaded hole through it for screwing on the

end of a bolt to secure it. **4** *sl.* a person's head. **5** *sl.* **a** a crazy or eccentric person. **b** an obsessive enthusiast (*a health-food nut*). **6** (in *pl.*) coarse *sl.* the testicles. □ **off one's nut** *sl.* crazy. □□ **nut·like** *adj.*

nu·tant /nóot'nt, nyóo-/ *adj. Bot.* nodding, drooping.

nu·ta·tion /nōotáyshən, nyōo-/ *n.* the act or an instance of nodding.

nut·case /nútkays/ *n. sl.* a crazy or foolish person.

nut·crack·er /nútkrakər/ *n.* a device for cracking nuts.

nut·gall /nútgawl/ *n.* a gall found esp. on oak, often used as a dyestuff.

nut·hatch /nút-hach/ *n.* ◄ any small bird of the family Sittidae, climbing up and down tree trunks and feeding on nuts, insects, etc., esp. the Eurasian *Sitta europaea*.

nut·house /núthows/ *n. sl.* a mental home or hospital.

nut·meg /nútmeg/ *n.* **1** an evergreen E. Indian tree, *Myristica fragrans*, yielding a hard aromatic spheroidal seed. **2** the seed of this grated and used as a spice.

nu·tri·a /nóotreeə, nyóo-/ *n.* **1** an aquatic beaverlike rodent, *Myocastor coypus*, native to S. America. **2** its skin or fur.

nu·tri·ent /nóotree-ənt, nyóo-/ *n. & adj.* ● *n.* any substance that provides essential nourishment for the maintenance of life. ● *adj.* serving as or providing nourishment.

nu·tri·ment /nóotrimənt, nyóo-/ *n.* **1** nourishing food. **2** an intellectual or artistic, etc., nourishment or stimulus. □□ **nu·tri·men·tal** /-mént'l/ *adj.*

nu·tri·tion /nōotríshən, nyóo-/ *n.* **1 a** the process of providing or receiving nourishing substances.

NUTHATCH:
EURASIAN NUTHATCH
(*Sitta europaea*)

b food, nourishment. **2** the study of nutrients and nutrition. □□ **nu·tri·tion·al** *adj.* **nu·tri·tion·ist** *n.*

nu·tri·tious /nōotríshəs, nyóo-/ *adj.* efficient as food. □□ **nu·tri·tious·ly** *adv.*

nu·tri·tive /nóotritiv, nyóo-/ *adj.* **1** of or concerned in nutrition. **2** serving as nutritious food.

nuts /nuts/ *adj. & int.* ● *adj. sl.* mad, eccentric. ● *int. sl.* an expression of contempt (*nuts to you*). □ **be nuts about** *colloq.* be enthusiastic about or very fond of.

nuts and bolts *n.pl. colloq.* the practical details.

nut·shell /nútshel/ *n.* the hard exterior covering of a nut. □ **in a nutshell** in a few words.

nut·ter /nútər/ *n. Brit. sl.* a crazy or eccentric person.

nut·ty /nútee/ *adj.* (**nuttier, nuttiest**) **1 a** full of nuts. **b** tasting like nuts. **2** *sl.* = NUTS *adj.* □□ **nut·ti·ness** *n.*

nux vom·i·ca /nuks vómikə/ *n.* **1** ▼ an E. Indian tree, *Strychnos nux-vomica*, yielding a poisonous fruit. **2** the seeds of this tree, containing strychnine.

oval leaves
seeds

NUX VOMICA
(*Strychnos nux-vomica*)

nuz·zle /núzəl/ *v.* **1** *tr.* prod or rub gently with the nose. **2** *intr.* (foll. by *against, up to*) press the nose gently. **3** *tr.* (also *refl.*) nestle; lie snug.

NV *abbr.* Nevada (in official postal use).

NW *abbr.* **1** northwest. **2** northwestern.

NY *abbr.* New York (also in official postal use).

NYC *abbr.* New York City.

nyc·ta·lo·pi·a /níktəlṓpeeə/ *n.* inability to see in dim light. Also called **night blindness**.

ny·lon /nílon/ *n.* **1** any of various synthetic polyamide fibers having a proteinlike structure, with tough, lightweight, elastic properties, used in industry and for textiles, etc. ▷ ROPE. **2** a nylon fabric. **3** (in *pl.*) stockings made of nylon.

nymph /nimf/ *n.* **1** any of various mythological semidivine spirits regarded as maidens and associated with aspects of nature. **2** *poet.* a beautiful young woman. **3** ▼ an immature form of some insects. □□ **nymph·al** *adj.*

NYMPH:
DAMSELFLY NYMPH

nym·phet /nimfét/ *n.* an attractive and sexually mature young girl.

nym·pho /nímfō/ *n.* (*pl.* **-os**) *colloq.* a nymphomaniac.

nym·pho·ma·ni·a /nímfəmáyneeə/ *n.* excessive sexual desire in women. □□ **nym·pho·ma·ni·ac** *n. & adj.*

NYSE *abbr.* New York Stock Exchange.

NZ *abbr.* New Zealand.

N

O

O¹ /ō/ n. (also **o**) (pl. **Os** or **O's**) **1** the fifteenth letter of the alphabet. **2** (**0**) naught; zero (in a sequence of numerals, esp. when spoken). **3** a human blood type.

O² symb. Chem. the element oxygen.

O³ /ō/ int. **1** var. of OH¹. **2** prefixed to a name in the vocative (O God).

O' /ō, ə/ prefix of Irish patronymic names (O'Connor).

o' /ə/ prep. of, on (esp. in phrases: o'clock; will-o'-the-wisp).

-o /ō/ suffix forming usu. sl. or colloq. variants or derivatives (weirdo; wino).

oaf /ōf/ n. (pl. **oafs**) **1** an awkward lout. **2** a stupid person. □□ **oaf·ish** adj. **oaf·ish·ly** adv. **oaf·ish·ness** n.

oak /ōk/ n. **1** ▼ any tree of the genus Quercus usu. having lobed leaves and bearing acorns. ▷ DECIDUOUS. **2** the durable wood of this tree. ▷ WOOD. **3** (attrib.) made of oak (oak table). □□ **oak·en** adj.

acorn

OAK: WHITE OAK
(Quercus alba)

lobed leaf

oak gall n. (also **oak apple**) ◀ an applelike gall containing larvae of certain wasps, found on oak trees.

OAK GALL

oa·kum /ōkəm/ n. a loose fiber obtained by picking old rope to pieces and used esp. in caulking.

oar /awr/ n. **1** a pole with a blade used for rowing or steering a boat by leverage against the water. ▷ ROW. **2** a rower. □ **put** (or **stick**) **one's oar in** interfere; meddle. □□ **oared** adj. (also in comb.).

oar·lock /awrlok,/ n. ▶ a device on a boat's gunwale, esp. a pair of tholepins, serving as a fulcrum for an oar and keeping it in place.

oars·man /awrzmən/ n. (pl. **-men**; fem. **oars·woman**, pl. **-women**) a rower. □□ **oars·man·ship** n.

OAS abbr. Organization of American States.

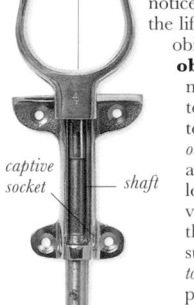

captive socket

shaft

OARLOCK

o·a·sis /ō-áysis/ n. (pl. **oases** /-seez/) **1** a fertile spot in a desert, where water is found. **2** an area or period of calm in the midst of turbulence.

oast /ōst/ n. a kiln for drying hops.

oast house n. esp. Brit. a building containing a kiln for drying hops.

oat /ōt/ n. **1 a** a cereal plant, Avena sativa, cultivated in cool climates. **b** (in pl.) the grain yielded by this, used as food. ▷ GRAIN. **2** any other cereal of the genus Avena, esp. the wild oat, A. fatua. □ **off one's oats** colloq. not hungry.

oath /ōth/ n. (pl. **oaths** /ōthz, ōths/) **1** a solemn declaration or undertaking (often naming God). **2** a statement or promise contained in an oath (oath of allegiance). **3** a profane utterance. □ **under oath** having sworn a solemn oath.

oat·meal /ōtmeel/ n. **1** meal made from ground oats used esp. in breakfast cereal, cookies, etc. **2** a grayish-fawn color flecked with brown.

OB abbr. **1 a** obstetric. **b** obstetrician. **c** obstetrics. **2** off Broadway.

ob. abbr. he or she died.

ob·bli·ga·to /óbligáatō/ n. (pl. **-os**) Mus. an accompaniment, usu. special and unusual in effect, forming an integral part of a composition.

ob·du·rate /óbdōrit, -dyōr-/ adj. **1** stubborn. **2** hardened against influence. □□ **ob·du·ra·cy** /-dōrəsee, -dyōr-/ n. **ob·du·rate·ly** adv.

OBE abbr. (in the UK) Officer (of the Order) of the British Empire.

o·be·di·ence /ōbeedeeəns/ n. **1** obeying as an act or quality. **2** submission to another's rule or authority.

o·be·di·ent /ōbeedeeənt/ adj. **1** obeying or ready to obey. **2** (often foll. by to) submissive to another's will. □□ **o·be·di·ent·ly** adv.

o·bei·sance /ōbáysəns, ōbee-/ n. **1** a bow, curtsy, or other respectful or submissive gesture (make an obeisance). **2** homage.

ob·e·li pl. of OBELUS.

ob·e·lisk /óbəlisk/ n. **1** ▶ a tapering, usu. four-sided stone pillar set up as a monument or landmark, etc. **2** = OBELUS.

ob·e·lus /óbələs/ n. (pl. **obeli** /-lī/) **1** a dagger-shaped reference mark in printed matter. **2** a mark (- or ÷) used in ancient manuscripts to mark a word.

o·bese /ōbees/ adj. very fat; corpulent. □□ **o·be·si·ty** n.

o·bey /ōbáy/ v. **1** tr. **a** carry out the command of. **b** carry out (a command). **2** intr. do what one is told to do. **3** tr. be actuated by (a force or impulse).

ob·fus·cate /óbfuskayt/ v.tr. **1** obscure or confuse (a mind, topic, etc.). **2** stupefy; bewilder. □□ **ob·fus·ca·tion** /-káyshən/ n. **ob·fus·ca·to·ry** /obfúskətawree/ adj.

o·bit /ōbít, óbit/ n. colloq. an obituary.

o·bit·u·ar·y /ōbíchōō-eree/ n. (pl. **-ies**) **1** a notice of a death or deaths. **2** an account of the life of a deceased person. **3** (attrib.) of an obituary. □□ **o·bit·u·ar·i·al** /-áireeəl/ adj.

ob·ject n. & v. ● n. /óbjikt, -jekt/ **1** a material thing that can be seen or touched. **2** (foll. by of) a person or thing to which action or feeling is directed (the object of attention). **3** a thing sought or aimed at. **4** Gram. a noun or its equivalent governed by an active transitive verb or by a preposition. **5** Philos. a thing external to the thinking mind or subject. ● v. /əbjékt/ **1** intr. (often foll. by to) express or feel opposition, disapproval, or reluctance. **2** tr. (foll. by that + clause) state as an objection. **3** tr. (foll. by to or that + clause) adduce (a quality or

fact) as contrary or damaging (to a case). □ **no object** not forming an important or restricting factor (money no object). □□ **ob·ject·less** /óbjiktlis/ adj. **ob·jec·tor** /əbjéktər/ n.

ob·jec·ti·fy /əbjéktifī/ v.tr. (**-ies**, **-ied**) **1** make objective. **2** present as an object of perception. □□ **ob·jec·ti·fi·ca·tion** /-fikáyshən/ n.

ob·jec·tion /əbjékshən/ n. **1** an expression of opposition or disapproval. **2** the act of objecting. **3** an adverse reason or statement.

ob·jec·tion·a·ble /əbjékshənəbəl/ adj. **1** open to objection. **2** unpleasant; offensive. □□ **ob·jec·tion·a·ble·ness** n. **ob·jec·tion·a·bly** adv.

ob·jec·tive /əbjéktiv/ adj. & n. ● adj. **1** external to the mind; real. **2** dealing with outward things or exhibiting facts uncolored by feelings or opinions. **3** Gram. (of a case or word) constructed as or appropriate to the object of a transitive verb or preposition. **4** aimed at (objective point). ● n. **1** something sought or aimed at. **2** Gram. the objective case. □□ **ob·jec·tive·ly** adv. **ob·jec·tiv·i·ty** /-tívitee/ n. **ob·jec·tiv·ize** v.tr.

ob·ject les·son n. a striking practical example of some principle.

ob·jet d'art /áwbzhay daár/ n. (pl. **objets d'art** pronunc. same) a small decorative object.

ob·jur·gate /óbjərgayt, objór-/ v.tr. literary chide or scold. □□ **ob·jur·ga·tion** /-gáyshən/ n.

ob·late¹ /óblayt/ n. a person dedicated to a monastic or religious life or work.

ob·late² /óblayt/ adj. Geom. (of a spheroid) flattened at the poles.

ob·la·tion /əbláyshon, ob-/ n. Relig. **1** a thing offered to a divine being. **2** the presentation of bread and wine to God in the Eucharist. □□ **ob·la·tion·al** adj. **ob·la·to·ry** /óblətáwree/ adj.

ob·li·gate /óbligayt/ v.tr. **1** (usu. in passive; foll. by to + infin.) bind (a person) legally or morally. **2** commit (assets) as security. □□ **ob·li·ga·tor** n.

ob·li·ga·tion /óbligáyshon/ n. **1** the constraining power of a law, precept, duty, contract, etc. **2** a duty; a burdensome task. **3** a binding agreement. **4 a** a kindness done or received (repay an obligation). **b** indebtedness for this (be under an obligation).

ob·li·ga·to·ry /əbligətawree/ adj. **1** legally or morally binding. **2** compulsory. **3** constituting an obligation. □□ **ob·li·ga·to·ri·ly** adv.

o·blige /əblíj/ v.tr. **1** (foll. by to + infin.) constrain; compel. **2** be binding on. **3 a** make indebted by conferring a favor. **b** (foll. by with, or by + verbal noun) gratify (oblige me by leaving). **4** (in passive; foll. by to) be indebted. □ **much obliged** an expression of thanks.

o·blig·ing /əblíjing/ adj. courteous; accommodating; ready to do (someone) a service or kindness. □□ **o·blig·ing·ly** adv.

o·blique /əbleék/ adj. **1 a** declining from the vertical or horizontal. **b** diverging from a straight line or course. **2** not going straight to the point; indirect. **3** Geom. inclined at other than a right angle. **4** Bot. (of a leaf) with unequal sides. **5** Gram. denoting any case other than the nominative or vocative. □□ **o·blique·ly** adv. **o·blique·ness** n. **o·bliq·ui·ty** /əblíkwitee/ n.

ob·lit·er·ate /əblítərayt/ v.tr. **1 a** blot out; efface; erase; destroy. **b** leave no clear traces of. **2** deface (a postage stamp, etc.) to prevent further use. □□ **ob·lit·er·a·tion** /-ráyshon/ n. **ob·lit·er·a·tive** /-rətiv/ adj. **ob·lit·er·a·tor** n.

ob·liv·i·on /əblíveeən/ n. the state of having or being forgotten.

ob·liv·i·ous /əblíveeəs/ adj. **1** (often foll. by of) forgetful; unmindful. **2** (foll. by to, of) unaware or unconscious of. □□ **ob·liv·i·ous·ly** adv. **ob·liv·i·ous·ness** n.

ob·long /óblawng/ adj. & n. ● adj. **1** rectangular with adjacent sides unequal. **2** greater in breadth than in height. ● n. an oblong figure or object.

ob·lo·quy /óbləkwee/ n. **1** the state of being generally ill spoken of. **2** abuse.

OBELISK: CLEOPATRA'S NEEDLE, ENGLAND

OBSERVATORY

Astronomers use observatories to study the movement, position, and physical composition of celestial bodies. Observatories are built where viewing conditions are best: on high ground, in low-population areas with stable air and little cloud cover. The two Keck telescopes on Mauna Kea in Hawaii are the largest in the world. Each telescope has 36 mirrors, each with a diameter of 33 ft (10 m).

EXPLODED CROSS SECTION OF AN ASTRONOMICAL OBSERVATORY

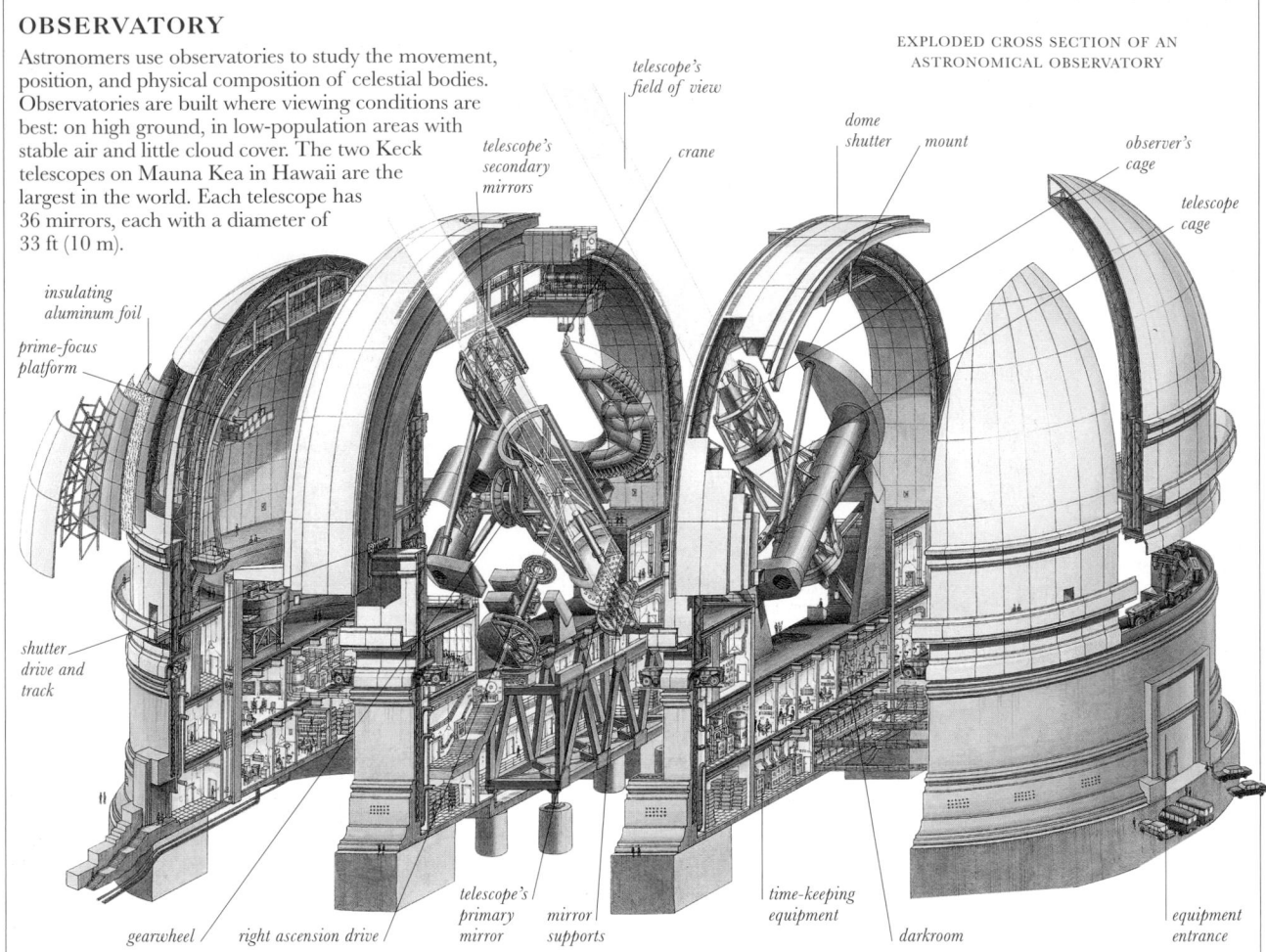

telescope's field of view

dome shutter

mount

observer's cage

telescope cage

crane

telescope's secondary mirrors

insulating aluminum foil

prime-focus platform

shutter drive and track

gearwheel

right ascension drive

telescope's primary mirror

mirror supports

time-keeping equipment

darkroom

equipment entrance

---

ob·nox·ious /əbnókshəs/ *adj.* extremely unpleasant. □□ **ob·nox·ious·ly** *adv.* **ob·nox·ious·ness** *n.*

o·boe /ṓbō/ *n.* a woodwind double-reed instrument of treble pitch and plaintive incisive tone. ▷ ORCHESTRA, WOODWIND. □□ **o·bo·ist** /ṓbō-ist/ *n.*

o·boe d'amour /dəmóor/ *n.* an oboe with a pear-shaped bell, pitched a minor third below a normal oboe, commonly used in baroque music.

ob·scene /əbséen/ *adj.* **1** offensively or repulsively indecent. **2** *colloq.* highly repugnant (*obscene wealth*). □□ **ob·scene·ly** *adv.*

ob·scen·i·ty /əbsénitee/ *n.* (*pl.* **-ies**) **1** the quality of being obscene. **2** an obscene action, word, etc.

ob·scu·rant·ism /əbskyŏorəntizəm, óbskyŏorán-/ *n.* opposition to knowledge and enlightenment. □□ **ob·scu·rant·ist** *n.*

ob·scure /əbskyŏor/ *adj. & v.* ● *adj.* **1** not clearly expressed nor easily understood. **2** unexplained. **3** dark; dim. **4** not clear. **5** not important or well known. ● *v.tr.* **1** make obscure. **2** dim the glory of. **3** conceal from sight. □□ **ob·scu·ra·tion** *n.* **ob·scure·ly** *adv.* **ob·scu·ri·ty** *n.*

ob·se·quies /óbsikweez/ *n.pl.* **1** funeral rites. **2** a funeral.

ob·se·qui·ous /əbséekweeəs/ *adj.* servilely obedient or attentive. □□ **ob·se·qui·ous·ly** *adv.* **ob·se·qui·ous·ness** *n.*

ob·serv·ance /əbzérvəns/ *n.* **1** the act or process of keeping or performing a law, duty, etc. **2** a customary rite.

ob·serv·ant /əbzérvənt/ *adj.* **1** acute or diligent in taking notice. **2** attentive in esp. religious observances (*an observant Jew*). □□ **ob·serv·ant·ly** *adv.*

ob·ser·va·tion /óbzərváyshən/ *n.* **1** the act or an instance of noticing. **2** the faculty of taking notice. **3** a remark or statement. **4 a** the accurate watching and noting of phenomena with regard to cause and effect or mutual relations. **b** the noting of the symptoms of a patient, the behavior of a suspect, etc. □ **under observation** being watched. □□ **ob·ser·va·tion·al** *adj.* **ob·ser·va·tion·al·ly** *adv.*

ob·ser·va·tion car *n.* esp. *US* a railroad car built so as to afford good views.

ob·serv·a·to·ry /əbzérvətawree/ *n.* (*pl.* **-ies**) ▲ a room or building equipped for the observation of natural, esp. astronomical or meteorological, phenomena.

OBSIDIAN

ob·serve /əbzérv/ *v.tr.* **1** (often foll. by *that* or *how* + clause) perceive; note. **2** watch carefully. **3 a** follow or adhere to (a law, principle, etc.). **b** keep or adhere to (an appointed time). **c** maintain (silence). **d** duly perform (a rite). **e** celebrate (an anniversary). **4** examine and note (phenomena). **5** (oftenfoll. by *that* + clause) say, esp. by way of comment. □□ **ob·serv·a·ble** *adj.* **ob·serv·a·bly** *adv.*

ob·serv·er /əbzérvər/ *n.* **1** a person who observes. **2** an interested spectator. **3** a person who attends a conference, etc., to note the proceedings but does not participate.

ob·sess /əbsés/ *v.tr. & intr.* (often in *passive*) preoccupy; fill the mind of (a person) continually. □□ **ob·ses·sive** *adj. & n.* **ob·ses·sive·ly** *adv.* **ob·ses·sive·ness** *n.*

ob·ses·sion /əbséshən/ *n.* **1** the state of being obsessed. **2** a persistent idea or thought dominating a person's mind. **3** a condition in which such ideas are present. □□ **ob·ses·sion·al** *adj.* **ob·ses·óo·sion·al·ly** *adv.*

ob·ses·sive-com·pul·sive *adj. Psychol.* relating to a disorder in which a person feels compelled to perform certain actions repeatedly to alleviate persistent fears or intrusive thoughts.

ob·sid·i·an /əbsídeeən/ *n.* ◀ a dark volcanic rock formed from rapidly chilled hardened lava. ▷ IGNEOUS

ob·so·les·cent /óbsəlésənt/ *adj.* becoming obsolete. □□ **ob·so·les·cence** /-səns/ *n.*

ob·so·lete /óbsəléet/ *adj.* **1** disused; antiquated. **2** *Biol.* rudimentary.

ob·sta·cle /óbstəkəl/ *n.* a person or thing that obstructs progress.

ob·stet·ric /əbstétrik, ob-/ *adj.* (also **ob·stet·ri·cal**) of or relating to childbirth and associated processes. □□ **ob·stet·ri·cal·ly** *adv.* **ob·ste·tri·cian** /-stətríshən/ *n.*

ob·stet·rics /əbstétriks, ob-/ *n.pl.* (usu. treated as *sing.*) the branch of medicine and surgery concerned with childbirth and midwifery.

ob·sti·nate /óbstinət/ *adj.* **1** stubborn; intractable.

O

2 firmly adhering to one's chosen course of action or opinion despite dissuasion. **3** not readily responding to treatment, etc. □□ **ob·sti·na·cy** *n.* **ob·sti·nate·ly** *adv.*

ob·strep·er·ous /əbstrépərəs/ *adj.* **1** turbulent; unruly. **2** noisy; vociferous. □□ **ob·strep·er·ous·ly** *adv.* **ob·strep·er·ous·ness** *n.*

ob·struct /əbstrúkt/ *v.tr.* **1** block up; make hard to pass. **2** impede.

ob·struc·tion /əbstrúkshən/ *n.* **1** the act of blocking. **2** an obstacle or blockage. **3** the retarding of progress by deliberate delays, esp. within a legislative assembly. **4** *Sports* the act of unlawfully obstructing another player. □□ **ob·struc·tion·ism** *n.* (in sense 3). **ob·struc·tion·ist** *n.* (in sense 3).

ob·struc·tive /əbstrúktiv/ *adj.* causing or intended to cause an obstruction. □□ **ob·struc·tive·ly** *adv.* **ob·struc·tive·ness** *n.*

ob·tain /əbtáyn/ *v.* **1** *tr.* acquire; secure. **2** *intr.* be prevalent or in vogue. □□ **ob·tain·a·ble** *adj.*

ob·trude /əbtróōd/ *v.* **1** *intr.* be or become obtrusive. **2** *tr.* (often foll. by *on*, *upon*) thrust forward (oneself, one's opinion, etc.) importunately.

ob·tru·sive /əbtróōsiv/ *adj.* **1** unpleasantly or unduly noticeable. **2** obtruding oneself. □□ **ob·tru·sive·ly** *adv.* **ob·tru·sive·ness** *n.*

ob·tuse /əbtóōs, -tyóōs/ *adj.* **1** slow to understand. **2** of blunt form. **3** (of an angle) more than 90° and less than 180°. ▷ TRIANGLE. □□ **ob·tuse·ly** *adv.* **ob·tuse·ness** *n.*

ob·verse /óbvərs/ *n.* **1 a** the side of a coin or medal bearing the head or principal design. **b** this design. **2** the front or top side of a thing. **3** the counterpart of a fact or truth. □□ **ob·verse·ly** *adv.*

ob·vi·ate /óbveeayt/ *v.tr.* get around or do away with (a need, inconvenience, etc.). □□ **ob·vi·a·tion** /-áyshən/ *n.*

ob·vi·ous /óbveeəs/ *adj.* easily seen or understood. □□ **ob·vi·ous·ly** *adv.* **ob·vi·ous·ness** *n.*

OC *abbr.* officer candidate.

oc·a·ri·na /ókəréenə/ *n.* ▼ a small egg-shaped ceramic or metal wind instrument.

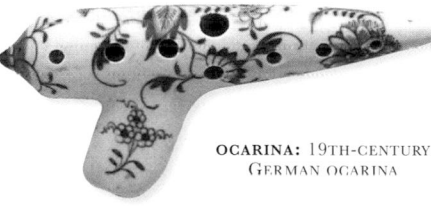

OCARINA: 19TH-CENTURY GERMAN OCARINA

Oc·cam's ra·zor /ókəmz ráyzər/ *n.* (also **Ock·ham's ra·zor**) the scientific principle that in explaining a thing no more assumptions should be made than are necessary.

oc·ca·sion /əkáyzhən/ *n. & v.* ● *n.* **1 a** a special or noteworthy event. **b** the time or occurrence of this. **2** (often foll. by *for*, or *to* + infin.) a reason or justification (*there is no occasion to be angry*). **3** a juncture suitable for doing something. **4** an immediate but subordinate cause (*the assassination was the occasion of the war*). ● *v.tr.* **1** be the occasion or cause of. **2** (foll. by *to* + infin.) cause (a person or thing to do something). □ **on occasion** now and then. **rise to the occasion** produce the necessary will, energy, etc., in unusually demanding circumstances.

oc·ca·sion·al /əkáyzhənəl/ *adj.* **1** happening irregularly and infrequently. **2 a** meant for or associated with a special occasion. **b** (of furniture, etc.) made for infrequent and varied use. □□ **oc·ca·sion·al·ly** *adv.*

Oc·ci·dent /óksidənt, -dent/ *n. poet. or rhet.* **1** (prec. by *the*) the West. **2** western Europe. **3** Europe, America, or both, as distinct from the Orient. **4** European, in contrast to Oriental, civilization.

oc·ci·den·tal /óksidént'l/ *adj. & n.* ● *adj.* **1** of the Occident. **2** western. **3** of Western nations. ● *n.* (**Occidental**) a native of the Occident.

oc·ci·put /óksiput/ *n.* the back of the head. ▷ SKULL. □□ **oc·cip·i·tal** /-sípit'l/ *adj.*

OCEAN

Approximately seventy percent of the Earth's surface is covered by oceans and seas. Due to the action of tides, wind, and currents (flows of water that may travel thousands of miles), the world's oceans are constantly moving. Oceans support a huge diversity of life, with most species found in water 0–655 ft (0–200 m) deep (the sunlit zone).

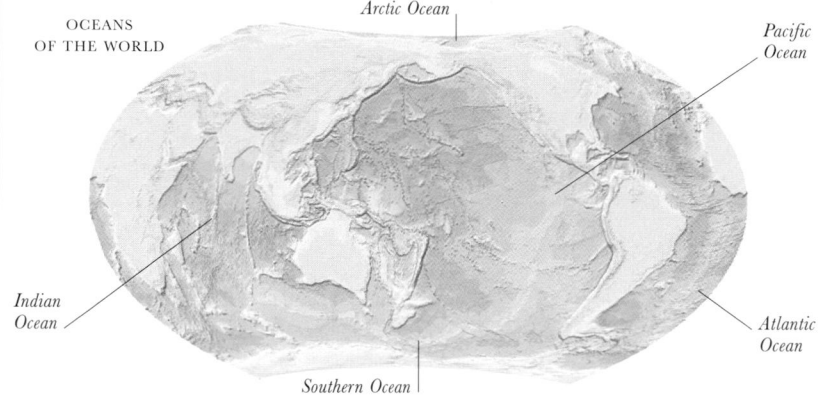

OCEANS OF THE WORLD

Arctic Ocean
Pacific Ocean
Indian Ocean
Atlantic Ocean
Southern Ocean

Oc·ci·tan /óksitan/ *n.* (also *attrib.*) the Provençal language. □□ **Oc·ci·tan·ian** /-táyneeən/ *n. & adj.*

oc·clude /əklóōd/ *v.tr.* **1** stop up or close. **2** *Chem.* absorb and retain (gases or impurities).

oc·clud·ed front *n. Meteorol.* a front resulting from occlusion. ▷ WEATHER CHART

oc·clu·sion /əklóōzhən/ *n.* **1** the act or process of occluding. **2** *Meteorol.* a phenomenon in which the cold front of a depression overtakes the warm front. □□ **oc·clu·sive** *adj.*

oc·cult /əkúlt, ókult/ *adj. & v.* ● *adj.* **1** involving the supernatural. **2** kept secret. **3** beyond the range of ordinary knowledge. ● *v.tr. Astron.* (of a concealing body) hide from view by passing in front; conceal by being in front. □ **the occult** occult phenomena generally. □□ **oc·cult·ism** *n.* **oc·cult·ist** *n.*

oc·cu·pant /ókyəpənt/ *n.* **1** a person who occupies, resides in, or is in a place. **2** a person holding property, esp. land, in actual possession. □□ **oc·cu·pan·cy** /-pənsee/ *n.* (*pl.* **-ies**).

oc·cu·pa·tion /ókyəp-áyshən/ *n.* **1** a means of passing one's time. **2** a person's temporary or regular employment. **3** the action, state, or period of occupying or being occupied.

oc·cu·pa·tion·al /ókyəpáy-shənəl/ *adj.* **1** of or in the nature of an occupation. **2** (of a disease, hazard, etc.) rendered more likely by one's occupation.

oc·cu·pa·tion·al ther·a·py *n.* mental or physical activity designed to assist recovery from disease or injury.

oc·cu·py /ókyəpī/ *v.tr.* (**-ies, -ied**) **1** reside in. **2** take up or fill (space or time or a place). **3** hold (a position or office). **4** take military possession of. **5** place oneself in (a building, etc.) forcibly or without authority. **6** (usu. in *passive*; often foll. by *in*, *with*) keep busy or engaged.

oc·cur /əkér/ *v.intr.* (**occurred, occurring**) **1** come into being as an event or process at some time; happen. **2** exist or be encountered in some place or conditions. **3** (foll. by *to*; usu. foll. by *that* + clause) come into the mind of, esp. as an unexpected or casual thought.

oc·cur·rence /əkórəns, əkúr-/ *n.* **1** an instance of occurring. **2** an event.

o·cean /óshən/ *n.* **1** ▲ a large expanse of sea, esp. each of the main areas called the Atlantic, Pacific, Indian, Arctic, and Antarctic Oceans. **2** (usu. prec. by *the*) the sea. **3** (often in *pl.*) a very large expanse or quantity of anything (*oceans of time*).

o·cea·nar·i·um /óshənáireeəm/ *n.* (*pl.* **oceanariums** or **-ria** /-reeə/) a large seawater aquarium for keeping sea animals.

o·cean·go·ing /óshən-góing/ *adj.* (of a ship) able to cross oceans.

o·cea·nog·ra·phy /óshənógrəfee/ *n.* the study of the oceans. □□ **o·cea·nog·ra·pher** *n.* **o·cea·no·graph·ic** /-nəgráfik/ *adj.*

oc·e·lot /ósilot, ósi-/ *n.* **1** ◀ a medium-sized feline, *Felis pardalis*, having a deep yellow or orange coat with black striped and spotted markings. **2** its fur.

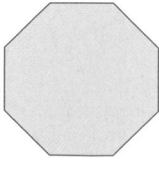

och /okh/ *int. Sc. & Ir.* expressing surprise or regret.

o·cher /ókər/ *n.* **1** a mineral of clay and ferric oxide, used as a pigment varying from light yellow to brown or red. **2** a pale brownish yellow. □□ **o·cher·ous** *adj.* **o·cher·y** *adj.*

Ock·ham's razor *n.* = Occam's razor.

o'·clock /əklók/ *adv.* of the clock (used to specify the hour) (*6 o'clock*).

OCR *abbr.* optical character recognition.

OCELOT (*Felis pardalis*)

OCS *abbr.* officer candidate school.

Oct. *abbr.* October.

oct. *abbr.* octavo.

oct- /okt/ *comb. form* assim. form of OCTA-, OCTO- before a vowel.

octa- /óktə/ *comb. form* (also **oct-** before a vowel) eight.

oc·tad /óktad/ *n.* a group of eight.

oc·ta·gon /óktəgon, -gən/ *n.* **1** ▶ a plane figure with eight sides and angles. **2** an object or building with this cross section. □□ **oc·tag·o·nal** /-tágənəl/ *adj.* **oc·tag·o·nal·ly** *adv.*

OCTAGON

oc·ta·he·dron /óktəheédrən/ n. (pl. **octahe-drons** or **octahedra** /-drə/) ▶ a solid figure contained by eight (esp. triangular) plane faces. □□ **oc·ta·he·dral** adj.

oc·tal /óktəl/ adj. reckoning or proceeding by eights (*octal scale*).

oc·tane /óktayn/ n. a colorless flammable hydrocarbon of the alkane series.

oc·tane num·ber n. (also **oc·tane rat·ing**) a figure indicating the antiknock properties of a fuel.

oc·ta·va·lent /óktəváylənt/ adj. Chem. having a valence of eight.

oc·tave /óktiv, -tayv/ n. 1 Mus. **a** a series of eight notes occupying the interval between (and including) two notes, one having twice or half the frequency of vibration of the other. **b** this interval. **c** each of the two notes at the extremes of this interval. **d** these two notes sounding together. 2 a group or stanza of eight lines.

oc·ta·vo /oktáyvō, oktáavō/ n. (pl. **-os**) 1 a size of book or page given by folding a standard sheet three times to form eight leaves. 2 a book or sheet of this size.

oc·ten·ni·al /ókténeeəl/ adj. 1 lasting eight years. 2 occurring every eight years.

oc·tet /oktét/ n. (also **oc·tette**) 1 Mus. **a** a composition for eight voices or instruments. **b** the performers of such a piece. 2 a group of eight. 3 the first eight lines of a sonnet.

octo- /óktō/ comb. form (also **oct-** before a vowel) eight.

Oc·to·ber /októbər/ n. the tenth month of the year.

oc·to·cen·te·na·ry /óktōsenténəree, -sént'neree/ n. & adj. ● n. (pl. **-ies**) 1 an eight-hundredth anniversary. 2 a celebration of this. ● adj. of or relating to an octocentenary.

oc·to·ge·nar·i·an /óktəjináireeən/ n. a person from 80 to 89 years old.

oc·to·pod /óktəpod/ n. any cephalopod of the order Octopoda, with eight arms.

oc·to·pus /óktəpəs/ n. (pl. **octopuses**) ▼ any cephalopod mollusk of the genus *Octopus* having eight suckered arms, a soft saclike body, and beaklike jaws. ▷ CEPHALOPOD

oc·tu·ple /óktəpəl, októo-, -tyóo-/ adj., n., & v. ● adj. eightfold. ● n. an eightfold amount. ● v.tr. & intr. multiply by eight.

oc·u·lar /ókyoolər/ adj. of or connected with the eyes or sight; visual.

oc·u·list /ókyəlist/ n. formerly 1 an ophthalmologist. 2 an optometrist. □□ **oc·u·lis·tic** /-lístik/ adj.

OD[1] abbr. doctor of optometry.

OD[2] /ōdeé/ n. & v. sl. ● n. an overdose, esp. of a narcotic drug. ● v.intr. (**OD's**, **OD'd**, **OD'ing**) take an overdose.

o·da·lisque /ódəlisk/ n. hist. an Eastern female slave or concubine, esp. in the Turkish sultan's seraglio.

odd /od/ adj. 1 strange; queer; remarkable. 2 casual; occasional (*odd jobs*; *odd moments*). 3 not normally noticed or considered (*in some odd corner*). 4 **a** (of numbers) not integrally divisible by two. **b** bearing such a number (*no parking on odd dates*). 5 left over when the rest have been distributed or divided into pairs (*have got an odd sock*). 6 detached from a set or series (*a few odd volumes*). 7 somewhat more than (*forty odd*). 8 by which a round number, given sum, etc., is exceeded (*we have 102 — what shall we do with the odd 2?*). □□ **odd·ly** adv. **odd·ness** n.

odd·ball /ódbawl/ n. colloq. 1 an odd person. 2 (attrib.) strange; bizarre.

Odd Fel·low /ód fellō/ n. a member of a fraternity similar to the Freemasons.

odd·i·ty /óditee/ n. (pl. **-ies**) 1 a strange person, thing, or occurrence. 2 a peculiar trait. 3 the state of being odd.

odd job n. a casual isolated piece of work.

odd man out n. 1 a person or thing differing from all the others in a group in some respect. 2 a method of selecting one of three or more persons, e.g., by tossing a coin.

odd·ment /ódmənt/ n. 1 something left over. 2 (in pl.) miscellaneous articles. 3 Printing matter other than the main text.

odds /odz/ n.pl. 1 the ratio between the amounts staked by the parties to a bet, based on the expected probability either way. 2 the chances or balance of probability in favor of or against some result (*the odds are against it*). 3 the balance of advantage (*the odds are in your favor*). 4 a difference giving an advantage (*makes no odds*). □ **at odds** (often foll. by *with*) in conflict or at variance. **take odds** offer a bet with odds unfavorable to the other bettor. **what's the odds?** colloq. what are the chances? (implying a slim likelihood).

odds and ends n.pl. miscellaneous articles or remnants.

odds-on n. a state when success is more likely than failure, esp. as indicated by the betting odds.

ode /ōd/ n. a lyric poem, usu. rhymed and in the form of an address, in varied or irregular meter.

o·di·ous /ódeeəs/ adj. hateful; repulsive. □□ **o·di·ous·ly** adv. **o·di·ous·ness** n.

o·di·um /ódeeəm/ n. a general or widespread dislike or reprobation.

ODOMETER: OVERHEAD VIEW OF
A MOTORCYCLE ODOMETER

cable-driven worm gear

distance counter

tenths wheel

faceplate

o·dom·e·ter /ōdómitər/ n. ▲ an instrument for measuring the distance traveled by a wheeled vehicle. □□ **o·dom·e·try** n.

o·dor /ódər/ n. 1 the property of a substance that has an effect on the nasal sense of smell. 2 a lasting quality or trace (*an odor of intolerance*). 3 regard; repute (*in bad odor*). □□ **o·dor·less** adj. (in sense 1).

o·dor·if·er·ous /ódərifərəs/ adj. diffusing a scent, esp. an agreeable one. □□ **o·dor·if·er·ous·ly** adv.

o·dor·ous /ódərəs/ adj. 1 having a scent. 2 = ODOR-IFEROUS. □□ **o·dor·ous·ly** adv.

od·ys·sey /ódisee/ n. (pl. **-eys**) a long adventurous journey. □□ **Od·ys·se·an** adj.

OECD abbr. Organization for Economic Cooperation and Development.

OED abbr. Oxford English Dictionary.

Oed·i·pus com·plex /édipəs, eédi-/ n. Psychol. (according to Freud, etc.) the complex of emotions aroused in a young (esp. male) child by a subconscious sexual desire for the parent of the opposite sex. □□ **Oed·i·pal** adj.

oe·nol·o·gy var. of ENOLOGY.

o'er /ōər/ adv. & prep. poet. = OVER.

oeu·vre /ővrə/ n. the works of an author, painter, composer, etc.

of /uv, ov, əv/ prep. connecting a noun (often a verbal noun) or pronoun with a preceding noun, adjective, adverb, or verb, expressing a wide range of relations broadly describable as follows: 1 origin, cause, or authorship (*paintings of Turner*; *people of Rome*). 2 the material or substance constituting a thing (*a house of cards*). 3 belonging, connection, or possession (*articles of clothing*; *the tip of the iceberg*). 4 identity or close relation (*the city of Rome*; *a fool of a man*). 5 removal, separation, or privation (*north of the city*; *got rid of them*). 6 reference, direction, or respect (*beware of the dog*; *very good of you*; *the selling of goods*). 7 objective relation (*love of music*). 8 partition, classification, or inclusion (*no more of that*; *part of the story*). 9 description, quality, or condition (*the hour of prayer*; *a girl of ten*). 10 time in relation to the following hour (*a quarter of three*). □ **be of** possess intrinsically (*is of great interest*). **of all** designating the (nominally) least likely example (*you of all people!*). **of all the nerve** an exclamation of indignation at a person's impudence, etc. **of an evening** (or **morning**, etc.) colloq. 1 on most evenings (or mornings, etc.). 2 at some time in the evenings (or mornings, etc.). **of late** recently. **of old** formerly; long ago.

off. abbr. 1 office. 2 officer.

off /awf, of/ adv., prep., & adj. ● adv. 1 at or to a distance (*drove off*; *is three miles off*). 2 out of position; not on or touching or attached (*has come off*; *take your coat off*). 3 so as to be rid of (*sleep it off*). 4 so as to break continuity; discontinued (*take a day off*). 5 to the end; entirely (*finish off*; *pay off*). 6 situated as

---

OCTOPUS

Unlike most other mollusks, the majority of octopuses have no shell (internal or external). They usually hide in rocky lairs by day and emerge to feed at night. The powerful suckers on an octopus's arms are used to hold captured prey (such as a crab). A poisonous secretion from the octopus's beak then paralyzes the trapped prey. When threatened, octopuses can change color to hide from, or confuse, attackers. Octopus species range in length from 2 in (5 cm) to around 30 ft (9 m).

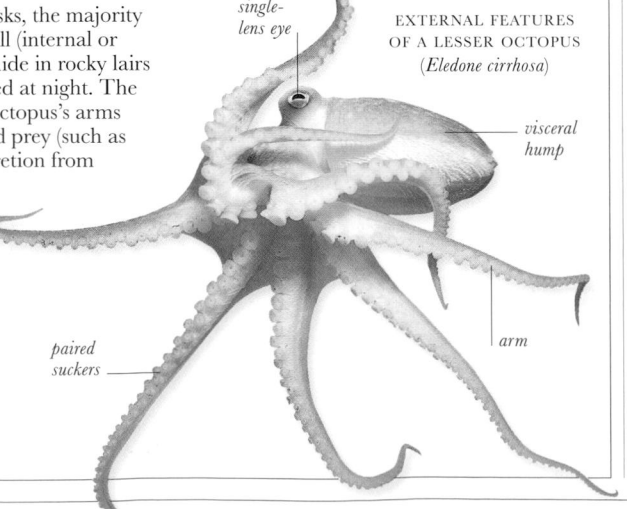

single-lens eye

EXTERNAL FEATURES
OF A LESSER OCTOPUS
(*Eledone cirrhosa*)

visceral hump

arm

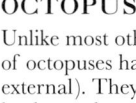

paired suckers

O

regards money, etc. (*is badly off*). ● *prep.* **1 a** from; away or down or up from (*fell off the chair*). **b** not on (*was already off the pitch*). **2 a** (temporarily) relieved of or abstaining from (*off duty*). **b** not attracted by for the time being (*off their food*). **c** not achieving or doing one's best in (*off one's game*). **3** using as a source or means of support (*live off the land*). **4** leading from (*a street off 1st Avenue*). **5** at a short distance to sea from (*sank off Cape Horn*). ● *adj.* **1** far; further (*the off side of the wall*). **2** (of a part of a vehicle, animal, or road) right (*the off front wheel*). □ **off and on** intermittently; now and then. **off guard** see GUARD. **off of** *sl. disp.* = OFF *prep.* (*picked it off of the floor*). **off the point** *adj.* irrelevant. *adv.* irrelevantly. **off the record** see RECORD.

of·fal /áwfəl, óf-/ *n.* **1** the less valuable edible parts of a carcass, esp. the entrails and internal organs. **2** refuse or waste stuff.

off·beat *adj. & n.* ● *adj.* /áwfbéet, óf-/ **1** not coinciding with the beat. **2** eccentric; unconventional. ● *n.* /ófbeet/ any of the unaccented beats in a bar.

off-cen·ter *adj.* not quite coinciding with a central position.

off-col·or *adj.* somewhat indecent.

off day *n.* a day when one is not at one's best.

of·fend /əfénd/ *v.* **1** *tr.* cause offense to. **2** *tr.* displease or anger. **3** *intr.* (often foll. by *against*) do wrong. □□ **of·fend·ed·ly** *adv.* **of·fend·er** *n.* **of·fend·ing** *adj.*

of·fense /əféns/ *n.* **1** an illegal act; a misdemeanor. **2** a wounding of the feelings (*no offense was meant*). **3** /áwfens, óf-/ the act of attacking or taking the offensive. **4** /áwfens, óf-/ *Sports* the team in possession of the ball, puck, etc.

of·fen·sive /əfénsiv/ *adj. & n.* ● *adj.* **1** giving or meant to give offense; insulting. **2** disgusting; repulsive. **3 a** aggressive; attacking. **b** (of a weapon) meant for use in attack. ● *n.* **1** an aggressive action or attitude. **2** an attack. **3** aggressive action in pursuit of a cause. □□ **of·fen·sive·ly** *adv.* **of·fen·sive·ness** *n.*

of·fer /áwfər, óf-/ *v. & n.* ● *v.* **1** *tr.* present for acceptance or refusal. **2** *intr.* (foll. by *to* + infin.) express readiness or show intention (*offered to take the children*). **3** *tr.* give an opportunity for. **4** *tr.* make available for sale. **5** *tr.* (of a thing) present to one's attention (*each day offers new opportunities*). **6** *tr.* present (a sacrifice, etc.) to a deity. **7** *intr.* occur (*as opportunity offers*). **8** *tr.* attempt, or try to show (violence, resistance, etc.). ● *n.* **1** an expression of readiness to do or give if desired, or to buy or sell (for a certain amount). **2** an amount offered. **3** a proposal (esp. of marriage). **4** a bid.

of·fer·ing /áwfəring, óf-/ *n.* **1** a contribution, esp. of money, to a church. **2** a thing offered as a sacrifice. **3** anything contributed or offered.

of·fer·to·ry /áwfərtáwree, óf-/ *n.* (*pl.* **-ies**) **1** *Eccl.* **a** the offering of the bread and wine at the Eucharist. **b** an anthem accompanying this. **2 a** the collection of money at a religious service. **b** the money collected.

off·hand /áwfhánd, óf-/ *adj. & adv.* ● *adj.* curt or casual in manner. ● *adv.* **1** in an offhand manner. **2** without preparation or premeditation. □□ **off·hand·ed** *adj.* **off·hand·ed·ly** *adv.* **off·hand·ed·ness** *n.*

of·fice /áwfis, óf-/ *n.* **1** a room or building used as a place of business, esp. for clerical or administrative work. **2** a room or department or building for a particular kind of business (*post office*). **3** the local center of a large business (*our Honolulu office*). **4** a position with duties attached to it. **5** tenure of an official position, esp. that of government (*hold office*). **6** a duty attaching to one's position; a task or function. **7** (usu. in *pl.*) a piece of kindness (esp. **through the good offices of**). **8** *Eccl.* **a** an authorized form of worship (*Office for the Dead*). **b** (in full **divine office**) the daily service of the Roman Catholic breviary (*say the office*).

of·fice hours *n.pl.* the hours during which business is normally conducted.

OFF-ROAD

Off-road motorcycles need special modifications such as long suspensions, which make the ride smoother and help keep the rear wheel on the ground. In four-wheeled off-road vehicles, power is usually transmitted to all four wheels, which improves traction.

OFF-ROAD COMPETITION MOTORCYCLE

of·fi·cer /áwfisər, óf-/ *n.* **1** a person holding a position of authority or trust, esp. one with a commission in the armed services. **2** a policeman or policewoman. **3** a holder of a post in a society (e.g., the president or secretary). **4** a holder of a public, civil, or ecclesiastical office.

of·fi·cial /əfíshəl/ *adj. & n.* ● *adj.* **1** of or relating to an office or its tenure or duties. **2** characteristic of officials and bureaucracy. **3** properly authorized. **4** employed in a public capacity. ● *n.* a person holding office or engaged in official duties. □□ **of·fi·cial·dom** *n.* **of·fi·cial·ism** *n.* **of·fi·cial·ly** *adv.*

of·fi·cial·ese /əfíshəléez/ *n. derog.* the formal precise language characteristic of official documents.

of·fi·ci·ant /əfíshənt/ *n.* a person who officiates at a religious ceremony.

of·fi·ci·ate /əfísheeáyt/ *v.intr.* **1** act in an official capacity, esp. on a particular occasion. **2** perform a divine service. □□ **of·fi·ci·a·tion** /-áyshən/ *n.* **of·fi·ci·a·tor** *n.*

of·fic·i·nal /əfísinəl/ *adj.* (of an herb or drug) used in medicine. □□ **of·fic·i·nal·ly** *adv.*

of·fi·cious /əfíshəs/ *adj.* **1** domineering. **2** intrusive in offering help, etc. **3** *Diplomacy* informal; unofficial. □□ **of·fi·cious·ly** *adv.* **of·fi·cious·ness** *n.*

off·ing /áwfing, óf-/ *n.* the more distant part of the sea in view. □ **in the offing** not far away; likely to appear or happen soon.

off-key *adj.* **1** out of tune. **2** not quite suitable or fitting.

off limits *adj.* out of bounds.

off-line *adj.* *Computing* (of a computer terminal or process) not directly controlled by or connected to a central processor.

off-load *v.tr.* = UNLOAD.

off-peak *adj.* used or for use at times other than those of greatest demand.

off·print /áwfprint, óf-/ *n.* a printed copy of an article, etc., originally forming part of a larger publication.

off-put·ting *adj.* disconcerting; repellent.

off-ramp /óframp/ *n. N. Amer.* an exit road from a main highway.

off-road *attrib.adj.* **1** away from the road; on rough terrain. **2** ▲ (of a vehicle, etc.) designed for rough terrain or for cross-country driving.

off-screen /áwfskréen, óf-/ *adj. & adv.* ● *adj.* not appearing on a movie, television, or computer screen. ● *adv.* **1** without use of a screen. **2** outside the view presented by a filmed scene.

off-sea·son *n.* a time when business, etc., is slack.

off·set *n. & v.* ● *n.* /áwfset, óf-/ **1** a side shoot from a plant serving for propagation. **2** an offshoot or scion. **3** a compensation. **4** *Archit.* a sloping ledge in a wall, etc. **5** a bend in a pipe, etc., to carry it past an obstacle. **6** (often *attrib.*) a method of printing in which ink is transferred from a plate or stone to a uniform rubber surface and from there to paper, etc. ▷ PRINTING. ● *v.tr.* /áwfsét, óf-/ (**-setting**; *past* and *past part.* **-set**) **1** counterbalance; compensate. **2** place out of line. **3** print by the offset process.

off·shoot /áwfshoot, óf-/ *n.* **1** a side shoot or branch. **2** something derivative.

off·shore /áwfsháwr, óf-/ *adj.* **1** at sea some distance from the shore. **2** (of the wind) blowing seaward. **3** made or registered abroad.

off·side /áwfsíd, óf-/ *adj. Sports* (of a player in a field game) in a position, that is not allowed if it affects play.

off·spring /áwfspring, of-/ *n.* (*pl.* same) **1** a person's child or children or descendant(s). **2** an animal's young or descendant(s). **3** a result.

off·stage /áwfstayj, óf-/ *adj. & adv. Theatr.* not on the stage and so not visible to the audience.

off-the-cuff *adj. colloq.* without preparation; extempore.

off-white *adj.* white with a gray or yellowish tinge.

oft /awft, oft/ *adv. archaic* or *literary* often (usu. in *comb.*: *oft-recurring*).

of·ten /áwfən, áwftən, óf-/ *adv.* (**oftener, oftenest**) **1 a** frequently. **b** at short intervals. **2** in many instances. □ **as often as not** in roughly half the instances.

of·ten·times /áwfəntīmz, óf-/ *adv.* (also **oft·times**) often.

off-the-rack *adj.* (of clothes) ready-made.

o·gee /ōjée, ójee/ *adj. & n. Archit.* ● *adj.* showing in section a double continuous S-shaped curve. ● *n.* an S-shaped line or molding.

o·give /ōjív, ójīv/ *n.* **1** a pointed arch. **2** one of the diagonal ribs of a vault. **3** an S-shaped line. □□ **o·gi·val** *adj.*

o·gle /ōgəl/ *v. & n.* ● *v.* **1** *tr.* eye amorously or lecherously. **2** *intr.* look amorously. ● *n.* an amorous or lecherous look.

o·gre /ōgər/ *n.* (*fem.* **ogress** /ógris/) **1** a human-eating giant in folklore, etc. **2** a terrifying person. □□ **o·gre·ish** *adj.* (also **o·grish**)

OH *abbr.* Ohio (in official postal use).

oh /ō/ *int.* (also **O**) expressing surprise, pain, etc. (*oh, what a mess*). □ **oh boy** expressing surprise, excitement, etc. **oh well** expressing resignation.

ohm /ōm/ *n. Electr.* the SI unit of resistance.

oho /ōhō/ *int.* expressing surprise or exultation.

OIL PLATFORM

Since most of the world's oil is trapped between layers of rock buried beneath the ocean floor, oil platforms are needed to exploit the valuable liquid. The oil rig is the part of the platform that actually drills the oil wells. The rig's motor turns the rotary table, which turns the drill string, a long shaft that may weigh hundreds of tons. The drill string is held by a tall support structure called the derrick. As a drill bit at the end of the drill string cuts deeper into the rock, sections of pipe are added one by one. When oil is struck, the shaft becomes a producing well. Retrieved oil is transported to shore by pipeline or tanker. Most oil platforms also recover natural gas, and if there is excess gas, it is burned off at the flare stack.

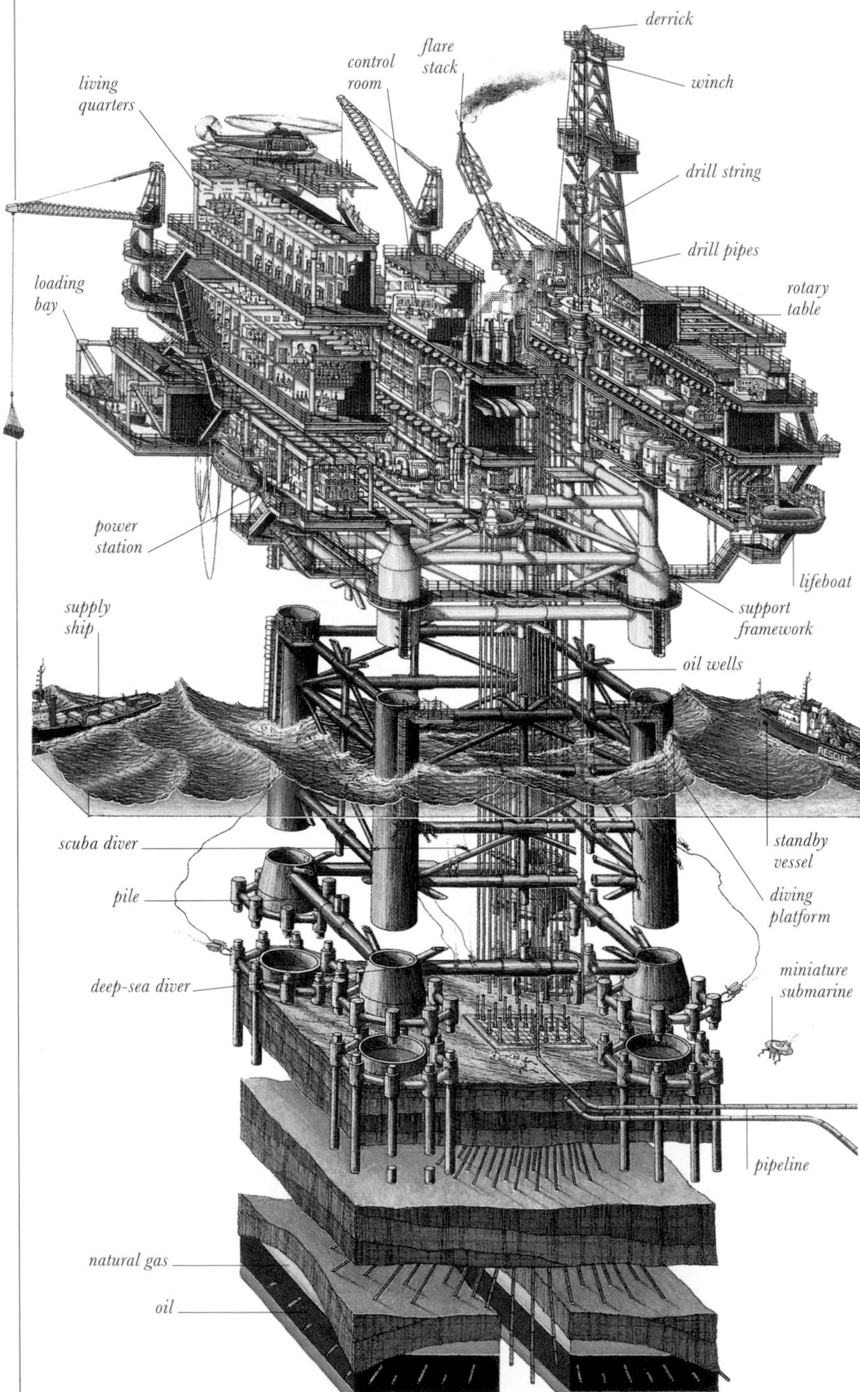

living quarters
control room
flare stack
derrick
winch
drill string
drill pipes
loading bay
rotary table
power station
lifeboat
supply ship
support framework
oil wells
scuba diver
standby vessel
pile
diving platform
deep-sea diver
miniature submarine
pipeline
natural gas
oil

EXPLODED CROSS SECTION OF A
NORTH SEA OIL PLATFORM

oil /oyl/ *n. & v.* ● *n.* **1** any of various thick, viscous, usu. flammable liquids insoluble in water but soluble in organic solvents. ▷ OIL PLATFORM. **2** petroleum. **3** using oil as fuel (*oil heater*). **4 a** (usu. in *pl.*) = OIL PAINT. **b** *colloq.* a picture painted in oil paints. **5** (in *pl.*) = OILSKIN. ● *v.* **1** *tr.* apply oil to; lubricate. **2** *tr.* impregnate or treat with oil (*oiled silk*). **3** *tr. & intr.* supply with or take on oil as fuel.

oil·can /óylkan/ *n.* a can with a long spout for oiling machinery.

oil·cloth /óylklawth, -kloth/ *n.* **1** a fabric waterproofed with oil. **2** an oilskin. **3** a canvas coated with linseed or other oil and used to cover a table or floor.

oil·er /óylər/ *n.* **1** an oilcan. **2** an oil tanker. **3 a** an oil well. **b** (in *pl.*) oilskin.

oil lamp *n.* a lamp using oil as fuel.

oil·man /óylmən/ *n.* (*pl.* **-men**) a person who deals in oil.

oil paint *n.* (also **oilcolor**) a mix of ground color pigment and oil.

oil paint·ing *n.* **1** the art of painting in oil paints. **2** a picture painted in oil paints.

oil plat·form *n.* ◄ a structure designed to stand on the seabed to provide a stable base above water for the drilling and regulation of oil wells.

oil rig *n.* esp. *Brit.* a structure with equipment for drilling an oil well. ▷ OIL PLATFORM

oil·seed /óylseed/ *n.* any of various seeds from crops yielding oil.

oil·skin /óylskin/ *n.* **1** cloth waterproofed with oil. **2 a** a garment made of this. **b** (in *pl.*) a suit made of this.

oil slick *n.* a smooth patch of oil, esp. one on the sea.

oil·stone /óylstōn/ *n.* a fine-grained flat stone used with oil for sharpening flat tools, e.g., chisels, planes, etc. (cf. WHETSTONE).

oil well *n.* a well from which petroleum is drawn. ▷ OIL PLATFORM

oil·y /óylee/ *adj.* (**oilier, oiliest**) **1** of, like, or containing much oil. **2** covered or soaked with oil. **3** fawning; insinuating; unctuous. □□ **oil·i·ness** *n.*

oink /oyngk/ *v.intr.* (of a pig) make its characteristic grunt.

oint·ment /óyntmənt/ *n.* a smooth greasy preparation for the skin. ▷ MEDICINE

O·jib·wa /ōjíbway/ *n. & adj.* ● *n.* **1 a** a N. American people native to Canada and the eastern and central northern United States. **b** a member of this people. **2** the language of this people. ● *adj.* of or relating to this people or their language. Also called **Chippewa**.

OK[1] /ōkáy/ *adj., adv., n., & v.* (also **o·kay**) *colloq.* ● *adj.* (often as *int.*) all right; satisfactory. ● *adv.* well; satisfactorily (*that worked out OK*). ● *n.* (*pl.* **OKs**) approval. ● *v.tr.* (**OK's, OK'd, OK'ing**) approve.

OK[2] *abbr.* Oklahoma (in official postal use).

o·ka·pi /ōkáapee/ *n.* (*pl.* same or **okapis**) ▼ a ruminant mammal, *Okapia johnstoni*, native to N. and NE Zaïre, with a head resembling that of a giraffe and a body resembling that of a zebra.

OKAPI
(*Okapia johnstoni*)

okay var. of OK[1].

o·key-doke /ókeedók/ adj. & adv. (also **o·key-do·key** /-dókee/) sl. = ok[1].

O·kie /ókee/ n. US colloq. **1** a person from Oklahoma. **2** derog. a migrant agricultural worker from Oklahoma who was forced to leave his or her farm during the depression of the 1930s.

Okla. abbr. Oklahoma.

o·kra /ókrə/ n. **1** a malvaceous African plant, Abelmoschus esculentus, yielding long ridged seedpods. **2** ▶ the seedpods eaten as a vegetable and used to thicken soups and stews. Also called **gumbo**.

OKRA
(Abelmoschus esculentus)

old /ōld/ adj. (**older, oldest**) (cf. ELDER, ELDEST). **1 a** advanced in age. **b** not young or near its beginning. **2** made long ago. **3** long in use. **4** worn or shabby from the passage of time. **5** having the characteristics of age (the child has an old face). **6** practiced; inveterate (an old offender). **7** belonging to the past; lingering on (old times). **8** dating from far back; long established or known (old as the hills; old friends). **9** (appended to a period of time) of age (is four years old; a four-year-old boy). **10** (of language) as used in former or earliest times. **11** colloq. as a term of affection or casual reference (good old Charlie). **12** the former or first of two or more similar things (our old house). □□ **old·ish** adj. **old·ness** n.

old age n. the later part of normal life.

old-boy net·work n. preferment in employment of those from a similar social background, esp. fellow alumni.

old coun·try n. (prec. by the) the native country of colonists, etc.

old·en /ōldən/ adj. archaic of old; of a former age.

Old Eng·lish n. the English language up to c.1150.

old-fash·ioned n. in a fashion or tastes no longer current.

Old Glo·ry n. the US national flag.

old guard n. the original or conservative members of a group.

old hand n. a person with much experience.

old hat n. adj. colloq. tediously familiar or out-of-date.

old·ie /óldee/ n. colloq. an old person or thing.

old la·dy n. colloq. **1** a mother. **2** a wife or girlfriend.

old maid n. **1** derog. an elderly unmarried woman. **2** a prim and fussy person. **3** a card game in which players try not to be left with an unpaired queen. □□ **old-maid·ish** adj.

old man n. colloq. **1** one's husband or father. **2** one's employer or other person in authority over one.

old man's beard n. ▶ a wild clematis, Clematis vitalba, with gray fluffy hairs around the seeds.

OLD MAN'S BEARD
SEED HEAD
(Clematis vitalba)

old mas·ter n. **1** a great artist of former times, esp. of the 13th–17th c. in Europe. **2** a painting by such a painter.

Old Nick n. colloq. the Devil.

old school n. **1** traditional attitudes. **2** people having such attitudes.

old·ster /óldstər/ n. an old person.

Old Tes·ta·ment n. the part of the Christian Bible containing the scriptures of the Hebrews.

old-time adj. belonging to former times.

old-tim·er n. a person with long experience or standing.

old wives' tale n. a foolish or unscientific belief.

Old World n. Europe, Asia, and Africa.

old-world adj. belonging to or associated with old times.

o·le·ag·i·nous /ōleeájinəs/ adj. **1** oily; greasy. **2** obsequious; ingratiating.

o·le·an·der /ōleeándər/ n. an evergreen poisonous shrub, Nerium oleander, native to the Mediterranean and bearing clusters of white, pink, or red flowers.

o·le·fin /ólifin/ n. (also **o·le·fine**) Chem = ALKENE.

oleo- /óleeō/ comb. form oil.

o·le·o·graph /óleeəgraf/ n. a print made to resemble an oil painting.

o·le·o·mar·ga·rine /óleeōmáarjərin/ n. **1** margarine made from vegetable oils. **2** a fatty substance extracted from beef fat and used in margarine.

ol·fac·tion /olfákshən, ōl-/ n. the capacity of smelling; the sense of smell.

ol·fac·to·ry /olfáktəree, ōl-/ adj. of or relating to the sense of smell. ▷ NOSE

ol·i·garch /óligaark, óli-/ n. a member of an oligarchy.

ol·i·gar·chy /óligaarkee, óli-/ n. (pl. **-ies**) **1** government by a small group of people. **2** a nation governed in this way. **3** the members of such a government. □□ **ol·i·gar·chic** /-gáarkik/ adj. **ol·i·gar·chi·cal** adj.

Ol·i·go·cene /óligəseen, óli-/ adj. & n. Geol. ● adj. of or relating to the third epoch of the Tertiary period, with evidence of the first primates. ● n. this epoch or system.

ol·ive /óliv/ n. & adj. ● n. **1** (in full **olive tree**) ▼ any evergreen tree of the genus Olea, having dark-green, lance-shaped leathery leaves with silvery undersides, esp. O. europaea of the Mediterranean, and O. africana native to S. Africa. **2** the small oval fruit of this, having a hard stone and bitter flesh, green when unripe and bluish-black when ripe. **3** (in full **olive-green**) the grayish-green color of an unripe olive. **4** the wood of the olive tree. ● adj. **1** colored like an unripe olive. **2** (of the complexion) yellowish-brown.

unripe fruit

OLIVE
(Olea europaea)

ol·ive branch n. **1** the branch of an olive tree as a symbol of peace. **2** a gesture of reconciliation or friendship.

ol·ive drab n. the dull olive color of US Army uniforms.

ol·ive oil n. an oil extracted from olives used esp. in cookery.

ol·i·vine /óliveen/ n. Mineral. a naturally occurring form of magnesium-iron silicate, usu. olive-green.

O·lym·pi·ad /ōlímpeead/ n. **1 a** a period of four years between Olympic games, used by the ancient Greeks in dating events. **b** a four-yearly celebration of the ancient Olympic Games. **2** a celebration of the modern Olympic Games. **3** a regular international contest in chess, etc.

O·lym·pi·an /əlímpeeən, ōlím-/ adj. & n. ● adj. **1 a** of or associated with Mount Olympus in NE Greece, traditionally the home of the Greek gods. **b** celestial. **2** (of manners, etc.) magnificent; condescending. **3** = OLYMPIC. ● n. **1** any of the gods regarded as living on Olympus. **2** a person of great attainments or of superhuman calm and detachment.

O·lym·pic /əlímpik, ōlim-/ adj. & n. ● adj. of ancient Olympia or the Olympic games. ● n.pl. (**the Olympics**) the Olympic games.

O·lym·pic games n.pl. **1** an ancient Greek festival held at Olympia every four years, with athletic, literary, and musical competitions. **2** a modern international revival of this as a sports festival usu. held every four years since 1896 in different venues.

O·ma·ha /ōməhaw, -haa/ n. & adj. ● n. **1 a** a N. American people native to Nebraska. **b** a member of this people. **2** the language of this people. ● adj. of or relating to this people or their language.

OMB abbr. Office of Management and Budget.

om·buds·man /ómbŏŏdzmən/ n. (pl. **-men**) an official appointed to investigate individuals' complaints against public authorities, etc.

o·me·ga /ōmáygə, ōmeegə, ōmégə/ n. **1** the last (24th) letter of the Greek alphabet (Ω, ω). **2** the last of a series; the final development.

om·e·lette /ómlit/ n. (also **om·e·let**) a dish of beaten eggs cooked in a frying pan and served plain or with a savory or sweet filling.

o·men /ómən/ n. **1** an occurrence or object regarded as portending good or evil. **2** prophetic significance (of good omen).

omertà /ōmairtáa/ n. a code of silence, esp. as practiced by the Mafia.

om·i·cron /ómikron, ómi-/ n. the fifteenth letter of the Greek alphabet (O, o).

om·i·nous /óminəs/ adj. **1** threatening; indicating disaster or difficulty. **2** of evil omen; inauspicious. **3** giving or being an omen. □□ **om·i·nous·ly** adv.

o·mis·sion /ōmíshən/ n. **1** the act or an instance of omitting. **2** something omitted.

o·mit /ōmít/ v.tr. (**omitted, omitting**) **1** leave out **2** leave undone. **3** (foll. by verbal noun or to + infin.) fail or neglect (omitted to say). □□ **o·mis·si·ble** /- mísəbəl/ adj.

omni- /ómnee/ comb. form **1** all; of all things. **2** in all ways or places.

om·ni·bus /ómnibəs/ n. & adj. ● n. **1** formal = BUS. **2** a volume containing several novels, etc., previously published separately. ● adj. **1** serving several purposes at once. **2** comprising several items.

om·ni·di·rec·tion·al /ómneedirékshən'l/ adj. (of an antenna, etc.) receiving or transmitting in all directions.

om·nip·o·tent /omnípət'nt/ adj. having absolute power. □□ **om·nip·o·tence** /-t'ns/ n.

om·ni·pres·ent /ómniprézənt/ adj. present everywhere at the same time. □□ **om·ni·pres·ence** /-zəns/ n.

om·nis·cient /omníshənt/ adj. knowing everything. □□ **om·nis·cience** /-shəns/ n.

om·ni·um gath·er·um /ómneeəm gáthərəm/ n. colloq. a miscellany.

om·niv·o·rous /omnívərəs/ adj. **1** feeding on many kinds of food, esp. on both plants and flesh. **2** making use of everything available. □□ **om·ni·vore** /ómnivawr/ n.

om·pha·los /ómfəlos/ n. Gk Antiq. **1** a conical stone (esp. that at Delphi) representing the navel of the earth. **2** a boss on a shield. **3** a center or hub.

on /on, awn/ prep., adv., & adj. ● prep. **1** (so as to be) supported by or attached to or covering or enclosing (sat on a chair; stuck on the wall; rings on her fingers; leaned on his elbow). **2** carried with; about the person (do you have a pen on you?). **3** (of time) exactly at; during; contemporaneously with (on May 29; on schedule; on Tuesday). **4** immediately after or before (I saw them on my return). **5** as a result of (on further examination I found this). **6** (so as to be) having membership, etc., of or residence at or in (on the board of directors; lives on the waterfront). **7** supported financially by (lives on $200 a week; on his wits). **8** close to; just by (a house on the sea; lives on the main road). **9** in the direction of. **10** so as to threaten (advanced on him; a punch on the nose). **11** having as an axis or pivot (turned on his heels). **12** having as a basis or motive (arrested on suspicion). **13** having as a standard, confirmation, or guarantee (had it on good

O

authority; *did it on purpose*). **14** concerning or about (*writes on finance*). **15** using or engaged with (*is on the pill; here on business*). **16** so as to affect (*walked out on her*). **17** at the expense of (*the drinks are on me*). **18** added to (*disaster on disaster*). **19** in a specified manner or style (*on the cheap; on the run*). • *adv.* **1** (so as to be) covering or in contact (*put your boots on*). **2** in the appropriate direction (*look on*). **3** further forward (*getting on in years; it happened later on*). **4** with continued movement (*went plodding on; keeps on complaining*). **5** in operation or activity (*the light is on; the chase was on*). **6** due to take place as planned (*is the party still on?*). **7** *colloq.* willing to participate or approve, or make a bet. **8** being shown or performed (*a good movie on tonight*). **9** on stage. **10** on duty. **11** forward (*head on*). • *adj.* *Baseball* positioned at a base as a runner. □ **be on to 1** realize the significance or intentions of. **2** get in touch with. **on and off** intermittently; now and then. **on and on** continually. **on time** punctual; punctually. **on to** to a position or state on or in contact with (cf. ONTO).

on·a·ger /ónəgər/ *n.* a wild ass, esp. *Equus hemionus* of central Asia.

o·nan·ism /ónənizəm/ *n.* **1** masturbation. **2** coitus interruptus. □□ **o·nan·ist** *n.* **o·nan·is·tic** /-nístik/ *adj.*

once /wuns/ *adv., conj., & n.* • *adv.* **1** on one occasion or for one time only (*have read it once*). **2** at some point in the past (*could once play chess*). **3** ever or at all (*if you once forget it*). **4** multiplied by one. • *conj.* as soon as (*once they have gone we can relax*). • *n.* one time or occasion (*just the once*). □ **all at once 1** suddenly. **2** all together. **at once 1** immediately. **2** simultaneously. **for once** on this (or that) occasion. **once again** (or **more**) another time. **once and for all** (or **once for all**) (done) in a final or conclusive manner. **once** (or **every once**) **in a while** from time to time. **once or twice** a few times. **once upon a time** at some vague time in the past. **once-o·ver** *n. colloq.* a rapid preliminary inspection.

onco- /óngkō/ *comb. form Med.* tumor.

on·co·gene /óngkəjeen/ *n.* a gene that can transform a cell into a tumor cell. □□ **on·co·gen·ic** /-jénik/ *adj.*

on·col·o·gy /ongkóləjee/ *n. Med.* the study of tumors.

on·com·ing /ónkuming, áwn-/ *adj.* approaching from the front.

one /wun/ *adj., n., & pron.* • *adj.* **1** single and integral in number. **2** (with a noun implied) a single person or thing of the kind expressed or implied (*one of the best*). **3 a** particular but undefined, esp. as contrasted with another (*that is one view*). **b** *colloq.* a noteworthy example of (*that is one difficult question*). **4** only such (*the one man who can do it*). **5** forming a unity (*one and undivided*). **6** the same (*of one opinion*). • *n.* **1** the lowest cardinal number. **2** unity; a unit (*one is half of two; came in ones and twos*). **3** a single thing or person or example (often referring to a noun previously expressed or implied: *the big dog and the small one*). **4** *colloq.* an alcoholic drink (*have a quick one; have one on me*). **5** a story or joke (*the one about the frog*). • *pron.* **1** a person of a specified kind (*loved ones; like one possessed*). **2** any person, as representing people in general (*one is bound to lose in the end*). **3** I, me (*one would like to help*). ¶ Often regarded as an affectation. □ **at one** in agreement. **for one** being one, even if the only one (*I for one do not believe it*). **for one thing** as a single consideration, ignoring others. **one another** each the other or others (as a formula of reciprocity: *love one another*). **one by one** singly, successively. **one day 1** on an unspecified day. **2** at some unspecified future date. **one or two** see OR[1]. **one up** (often foll. by *on*) *colloq.* having a particular advantage.

O·nei·da /ōnídə/ *n. & adj.* • *n.* **1 a** a N. American people native to New York state. **b** a member of this people. **2** the language of this people. • *adj.* of or relating to this people or their language.

one-armed ban·dit *n. colloq.* a slot machine worked by a long handle.

one-horse *adj.* **1** using a single horse. **2** *colloq.* small; poorly equipped.

one·ness /wún-nis/ *n.* **1** the fact or state of being one. **2** uniqueness. **3** agreement. **4** sameness.

one-lin·er *n. colloq.* a single brief sentence, often witty or apposite.

one-man *adj.* involving, done, or operated by only one person.

one-night stand *n.* **1** a single performance of a play, etc., in a place. **2** *colloq.* a sexual liaison lasting only one night.

one-on-one *adj.* **1** of a direct confrontation between two persons. **2** *Sports* playing directly against one opposing player.

one-piece *adj.* made as a single garment.

on·er·ous /ónərəs, ṓn-/ *adj.* **1** burdensome. **2** *Law* involving heavy obligations.

one·self /wunsélf/ *pron.* the reflexive and emphatic form of *one.*

one-shot *adj. colloq.*, chiefly *N. Amer.* **1** achieved with a single attempt or action. **2** done, produced, or occurring only once.

one-sid·ed *adj.* **1** favoring one side in a dispute. **2** having or occurring on one side only. **3** larger or more developed on one side. □□ **one-sid·ed·ly** *adv.* **one-sid·ed·ness** *n.*

one·time /wúntīm/ *adj. & adv.* former.

one-to-one *n.* with one member of one group corresponding to one of another.

one-track mind *n.* a mind preoccupied with one subject.

one-trick po·ny *n. colloq.* a person or thing with only one special feature, talent, etc.

one-two *n. colloq.* **1** *Boxing* the delivery of two punches in quick succession. **2** *Soccer*, etc. a series of reciprocal passes between two advancing players.

one-up·man·ship *n. colloq.* the art of maintaining a psychological advantage.

one-way *adj.* allowing movement or travel in one direction only.

on·go·ing /ón-gṓing, áwn-/ *adj.* **1** continuing. **2** in progress (*ongoing discussions*).

on·ion /únyən/ *n.* **1** a liliaceous plant, *Allium cepa*, having a short stem and bearing greenish-white flowers. **2** the bulb of this used in cooking, pickling, etc. □ **know one's onions** *colloq.* be fully knowledgeable. □□ **on·ion·y** *adj.*

on-line *adj. Computing* (of equipment or a process) directly controlled by or connected to a central processor.

on·look·er /ónlŏŏkər, áwn-/ *n.* a spectator. □□ **on·look·ing** *adj.*

on·ly /ónlee/ *adv., adj., & conj.* • *adv.* **1** solely; merely; exclusively. (*I only want to sit down; is only a child*). **2** no longer ago than (*saw them only yesterday*). **3** not until (*arrives only on Tuesday*). **4** with no better result than (*hurried home only to find her gone*). ¶ In informal English *only* is usually placed between the subject and verb regardless of what it refers to (e.g., *I only want to talk to you*); in more formal English it is often placed more exactly, esp. to avoid ambiguity (e.g., *I want to talk only to you*). In speech, intonation usually serves to clarify the sense. • *attrib.adj.* **1** existing alone of its or their kind (*their only son*). **2** best or alone worth knowing (*the only place to eat*). • *conj. colloq.* **1** except that (*I would go, only I feel ill*). **2** but then (as an extra consideration) (*he always makes promises, only he never keeps them*). □ **only too** extremely (*only too willing*).

on·o·mas·tic /ónəmástik/ *adj.* relating to names or nomenclature.

on·o·mas·tics /ónəmástiks/ *n.pl.* (treated as *sing.*) the study of the origin and formation of (esp. personal) proper names.

on·o·mat·o·poe·ia /ónəmátəpéeə, -máatə-/ *n.* **1** the formation of a word from a sound associated with what is named (e.g., *cuckoo, sizzle*). **2** the use of such words. □□ **on·o·mat·o·poe·ic** *adj.*

On·on·da·ga /aanəndáwgə, -da-, -daa-/ *n. & adj.* • *n.* **1 a** a N. American people native to New York state. **b** a member of these people. **2** the language of these people. • *adj.* of or relating to these people or their language.

on·rush /ónrush, áwn-/ *n.* an onward rush.

on-screen *adj. & adv.* **1** shown or appearing in a movie or on television. **2** making use of or performed with the aid of a video screen.

on·set /ónset, áwn-/ *n.* **1** an attack. **2** a beginning, esp. an energetic one.

on·shore /ónsháwr, áwn-/ *adj. & adv.* • *adj.* **1** on the shore. **2** (of the wind) blowing from the sea toward the land. • *adv.* ashore.

on·side /ónsíd, áwn-/ *adj.* (of a player in a field game) not offside.

on·slaught /ónslawt, áwn-/ *n.* a fierce attack.

on·stage /ónstáyj/ *Theatr. adj. & adv.* on the stage; visible to the audience.

Ont. *abbr.* Ontario.

on·to /óntoo, áwn-/ *prep. disp.* to a position or state on or in contact with (cf. on to). ¶ The form *onto* is still not fully accepted in the way that *into* is, although it is in wide use. It is, however, useful in distinguishing sense as between *we drove on to the beach* (i.e., in that direction) and *we drove onto the beach* (i.e., in contact with it).

on·to·gen·e·sis /óntəjénisis/ *n.* the origin and development of an individual. □□ **on·to·ge·net·ic** /-jinétik/ *adj.*

on·tog·e·ny /ontójənee/ *n.* = ONTOGENESIS.

on·tol·o·gy /ontóləjee/ *n.* the branch of metaphysics dealing with the nature of being. □□ **on·to·log·i·cal** /-təlójikəl/ *adj.* **on·to·log·i·cal·ly** *adv.*

o·nus /ónəs/ *n.* (*pl.* **onuses**) a burden, duty, or responsibility.

on·ward /ónwərd, áwn-/ *adv. & adj.* • *adv.* (also **on·wards**) **1** further on. **2** toward the front. **3** with advancing motion. • *adj.* directed onward.

on·yx /óniks/ *n.* ◄ a semiprecious variety of agate with colors in layers. ▷ GEM

oo·dles /óŏd'lz/ *n.pl. colloq.* a very great amount.

ooh /ŏŏ/ *int.* expressing surprise, delight, pain, etc.

o·o·lite /ṓəlīt/ *n.* a sedimentary rock, usu. limestone, consisting of rounded grains made up of concentric layers. □□ **o·o·lit·ic** /-lítik/ *adj.*

oom·pah /ŏŏmpaa/ *n. colloq.* the rhythmical sound of deep-toned brass instruments in a band.

oomph /ŏŏmf/ *n. sl.* **1** energy; enthusiasm. **2** attractiveness; esp. sexual appeal.

oops /ŏŏps, ŏŏps/ *int. colloq.* expressing surprise or apology.

ooze[1] /ŏŏz/ *v. & n.* • *v.* **1** *intr.* slowly trickle or seep out. **2** *tr.* exude (a feeling) liberally (*oozed sympathy*). • *n.* a sluggish flow. □□ **ooz·y** *adj.*

ooze[2] /ŏŏz/ *n.* **1** a deposit of wet mud or slime. **2** a bog or marsh. □□ **ooz·y** *adj.*

op. /op/ *abbr.* **1** *Mus.* opus. **2** operator.

o.p. *abbr.* out of print.

o·pac·i·ty /ōpásitee/ *n.* **1** the state of being opaque. **2** obscurity of meaning.

o·pal /ṓpəl/ *n.* ► a quartzlike form of hydrated silica, usu. white or colorless, sometimes showing changing colors, often used as a gemstone. ▷ GEM

o·pal·es·cent /ṓpəlésənt/ *adj.* showing changing colors like an opal. □□ **o·pal·es·cence** /-səns/ *n.*

o·pal·ine /ṓpəlin, -leen, -līn/ *adj.* opalescent.

ONYX

OPAL

o·paque /ōpáyk/ *adj.* (**opaquer**, **opaquest**) **1** not transmitting light. **2** impenetrable to sight. **3** not lucid. **4** dull-witted. □□ **o·paque·ly** *adv.* **o·paque·ness** *n.*

op art /op/ *n. colloq.* = OPTICAL ART.

op. cit. *abbr.* in the work already quoted.

OPEC /ópek/ *abbr.* Organization of Petroleum Exporting Countries.

o·pen /ópən/ *adj., v., & n.* ● *adj.* **1** not closed nor locked nor blocked up. **2 a** (of a room, field, or other area) having its door or gate in a position allowing access, or part of its confining boundary removed. **b** (of a container) not fastened nor sealed. **3** unenclosed; unconfined (*the open road; open views*). **4 a** uncovered; bare; exposed (*open drain; open wound*). **b** *Sports* (of a goal or other object of attack) unprotected; vulnerable. **5** undisguised; public; manifest (*open scandal; open hostilities*). **6** expanded, unfolded, or spread out (*had the map open on the table*). **7** (of a fabric) with gaps. **8 a** frank and communicative. **b** accessible to new ideas. **9 a** (of a race, competition, etc.) unrestricted as to who may compete. **b** (of a champion, scholar, etc.) having won such a contest. **10** (of government) conducted in an informative manner receptive to inquiry, criticism, etc., from the public. **11** (foll. by *to*) **a** willing to receive (*is open to offers*). **b** (of a choice, or opportunity) still available (*there are three courses open to us*). **c** likely to suffer from (*open to abuse*). **12 a** (of the mouth) with lips apart. **b** (of the ears or eyes) eagerly attentive. **13** *Mus.* **a** (of a string) allowed to vibrate along its whole length. **b** (of a pipe) unstopped at each end. **c** (of a note) sounded from an open string or pipe. **14** (of an electrical circuit) having a break in the conducting path. **15** (of the bowels) not constipated. **16** (of a return ticket) not restricted as to day of travel. **17** (of a boat) without a deck. ● *v.* **1** *tr. & intr.* make or become open or more open. **2 a** *tr.* change from a closed or fastened position so as to allow access (*opened the door; opened the box*). **b** *intr.* (of a door, lid, etc.) have its position changed to allow access (*the door opened slowly*). **3** *tr.* remove the fastening element of (a container) to get access to the contents (*opened the envelope*). **4** *intr.* (foll. by *into, on to*, etc.) (of a door, room, etc.) afford access as specified (*opened on to a large garden*). **5 a** *tr.* start or establish (a business, activity, etc.). **b** *intr.* start (*the session opens tomorrow; the story opens with a murder*). **c** *tr.* (of a counsel in a court of law) make a preliminary statement in (a case) before calling witnesses. **6** *tr.* **a** spread out or unfold (a map, newspaper, etc.). **b** (often *absol.*) refer to the contents of (a book). **7** *intr.* begin speaking, writing, etc. (*he opened with a warning*). **8** *intr.* (of a prospect) come into view. **9** *tr.* reveal (one's feelings, intentions, etc.). **10** *tr.* make (one's mind, heart, etc.) more sympathetic. **11** *tr.* ceremonially declare (a building, etc.) to be completed and in use. **12** *tr.* break up (ground) with a plow, etc. **13** *tr.* cause evacuation of (the bowels). ● *n.* **1** (prec. by *the*) **a** open space or country or air. **b** public notice; general attention (esp. *into the open*). **2** an open championship, competition, or scholarship. □ **be open with** speak frankly to. **open the door** to see DOOR. **open a person's eyes** see EYE. **open out 1** unfold. **2** develop; expand. **3** *Brit.* become communicative. **4** *Brit.* accelerate. **open up 1** unlock (premises). **2** make accessible. **3** reveal; bring to notice. **4** accelerate. **5** begin shooting or sounding. **6** become communicative. □□ **o·pen·ness** *n.*

o·pen air *n.* (usu. prec. by *the*) a free or unenclosed space outdoors. □□ **o·pen-air** *adj.* (*attrib.*)

o·pen-and-shut *adj.* straightforward and conclusive.

o·pen book *n.* a person who is easily understood.

o·pen·cast /ópənkast/ *adj. Brit.* (of a mine or mining) with removal of the surface layers and working from above, not from shafts. ▷ MINE

o·pen door *n.* free admission of foreign trade and immigrants. □□ **o·pen-door** *adj.*

o·pen-end·ed *adj.* having no predetermined limit or boundary.

o·pen·er /ópənər/ *n.* **1** a device for opening cans, bottles, etc. **2** *colloq.* the first item on a program, etc.

o·pen-faced *adj.* having a frank or ingenuous expression.

o·pen·hand·ed /ópənhandid/ *adj.* generous.

o·pen-heart·ed *adj.* frank and kindly. □□ **o·pen-heart·ed·ness** *n.*

o·pen-heart sur·ger·y *n.* surgery with the heart exposed and the blood made to bypass it. ▷ HEART

o·pen house *n.* **1** hospitality for all visitors. **2** time when real estate offered for sale is open to prospective buyers.

o·pen·ing /ópəning/ *n. & adj.* ● *n.* **1** an aperture or gap. **2** a beginning. **3** a favorable opportunity. **4** *Chess* a recognized sequence of moves at the beginning of a game. **5** a counsel's preliminary statement of a case in a court of law. ● *adj.* initial; first.

o·pen sea·son *n.* the season when restrictions on the hunting of game, etc., are lifted.

o·pen·ly /ópənlee/ *adv.* **1** frankly; honestly. **2** publicly; without concealment.

o·pen-mind·ed *adj.* accessible to new ideas; unprejudiced. □□ **o·pen-mind·ed·ly** *adv* **o·pen-mind·ed·ness** *n*

o·pen-mouthed *adj.* with the mouth open, esp. in surprise.

o·pen ques·tion *n.* a matter on which differences of opinion are legitimate.

o·pen·work /ópənwərk/ *n.* ▼ a pattern with intervening spaces in metal, lace, etc.

metal / openwork

OPENWORK: 9TH-CENTURY SCANDINAVIAN WEATHER VANE

op·er·a[1] /ópərə, óprə/ *n.* **1 a** a dramatic work set to music for singers and instrumentalists. **b** this as a genre. **2** a building for the performance of opera.

o·pe·ra[2] *pl.* of OPUS.

op·er·a·ble /ópərəbəl/ *adj.* **1** that can be operated. **2** suitable for treatment by surgical operation. □□ **op·er·a·bil·i·ty** /-bílitee/ *n.*

op·er·a glass·es *n.pl.* small binoculars for use at the opera or theater.

op·er·a hat *n.* a man's tall collapsible top hat.

op·er·a house *n.* a theater for the performance of opera.

op·er·and /ópərand/ *n. Math.* the quantity, etc., on which an operation is to be done.

op·er·ate /ópərayt/ *v.* **1** *tr.* manage; work; control; put or keep in a functional state. **2** *intr.* be in action; function. **3** *intr.* (often foll. by *on*) **a** perform a surgical operation. **b** conduct a military or naval action. **c** be active in business, etc., esp. dealing in stocks and shares. **4** *intr.* (foll. by *on*) influence or affect (feelings, etc.). **5** *tr.* bring about; accomplish.

op·er·at·ic /ópərátik/ *adj.* **1** of or relating to opera. **2** resembling or characteristic of opera. □□ **op·er·at·i·cal·ly** *adv*

op·er·at·ics /ópərátiks/ *n.pl.* the production and performance of operas.

op·er·at·ing sys·tem *n.* the basic software that enables the running of a computer program.

op·er·at·ing room *n.* a room equipped for surgical operations.

op·er·a·tion /ópəráyshən/ *n.* **1 a** the action or process or method of working or operating. **b** the scope or range of effectiveness of a thing's activity. **2** an active process (*the operation of breathing*). **3** a piece of work, esp. one in a series (often in *pl.*: *begin operations*). **4** an act of surgery performed on a patient. **5** a strategic movement of troops, ships, etc., for military action. **6** a financial transaction. **7** *Math.* the subjection of a number or quantity or function to a process affecting its value or form, e.g., multiplication, differentiation.

op·er·a·tion·al /ópəráyshənəl/ *adj.* **1 a** of or used for operations. **b** engaged or involved in operations. **2** able or ready to function. □□ **op·er·a·tion·al·ly** *adv.*

op·er·a·tive /ópərətiv, óprə-/ *adj. & n.* ● *adj.* **1** in operation; having effect. **2** having the principal relevance (*"may" is the operative word*). **3** of or by surgery. ● *n.* **1** a worker, esp. a skilled one. **2** an agent employed by a detective agency or secret service. □□ **op·er·a·tive·ly** *adv.* **op·er·a·tive·ness** *n.*

op·er·a·tor /ópəraytər/ *n.* **1** a person operating a machine, etc., esp. making connections of lines in a telephone exchange. **2** a person operating or engaging in business. **3** *colloq.* a person acting in a specified way (*a smooth operator*). **4** *Math.* a symbol or function denoting an operation (e.g., x, +).

op·er·et·ta /ópərétə/ *n.* **1** a one-act or short opera. **2** a light opera.

o·phid·i·an /ōfídeeən/ *n. & adj.* ● *n.* any reptile of the suborder Serpentes (formerly Ophidia). ● *adj.* **1** of or relating to this group. **2** snakelike.

oph·thal·mi·a /of-thálmeeə, op-/ *n.* an inflammation of the eye.

oph·thal·mic /of-thálmik, op-/ *adj.* of or relating to the eye and its diseases.

ophthalmo- /of-thálmō, op-/ *comb. form Optics* denoting the eye.

oph·thal·mol·o·gist /óf-thalmóləjist, -thə-, op /n,* a medical doctor who specializes in ophthalmology.

oph·thal·mol·o·gy /óf-thalmóləjee, -thə-, op-/ *n.* the scientific study of the eye. □□ **oph·thal·mo·log·i·cal** /-məlójikəl/ *adj.*

oph·thal·mo·scope /of-thálməskōp, op-/ *n.* ▶ an instrument for inspecting the retina and other parts of the eye.

o·pi·ate /ópeeət/ *adj. & n.* ● *adj.* **1** containing opium. **2** narcotic; soporific. ● *n.* **1** a drug containing opium, usu. to ease pain or induce sleep. **2** a thing which soothes or stupefies.

o·pine /ōpín/ *v.tr.* (often foll. by *that* + clause) hold or express as an opinion.

o·pin·ion /əpínyən/ *n.* **1** a belief or assessment based on grounds short of proof. **2** a view held as probable. **3** (often foll. by *on*) what one thinks about a particular topic (*my opinion on capital punishment*). **4** a formal statement of professional advice (*get a second opinion*). **5** an estimation (*had a low opinion of it*). □ **a matter of opinion** a disputable point.

o·pin·ion·at·ed /əpínyənaytid/ *adj.* conceitedly assertive in one's opinions.

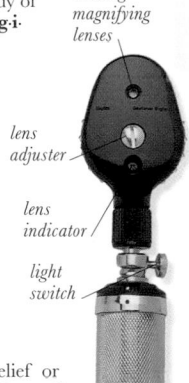

rotating magnifying lenses

lens adjuster

lens indicator

light switch

OPHTHALMOSCOPE

o·pi·um /ópeeəm/ *n.* **1** a reddish-brown heavy-scented addictive drug prepared from the juice of the opium poppy, used in medicine as an analgesic and narcotic. **2** anything regarded as soothing or stupefying.

OPOSSUM: VIRGINIA OPOSSUM
(*Didelphis virginiana*)

o·pos·sum /əpósəm/ *n.* ▲ any mainly tree-living marsupial of the family Didelphidae, native to America, having a prehensile tail. ▷ MARSUPIAL.

opp. *abbr.* opposite.

op·po·nent /əpṓnənt/ *n.* a person who opposes or belongs to an opposing side.

op·por·tune /ópərtōōn, -tyōōn/ *adj.* **1** (of a time) especially favorable or appropriate (*an opportune moment*). **2** (of an action or event) done or occurring at a favorable or useful time. □□ **op·por·tune·ly** *adv.* **op·por·tune·ness** *n.*

op·por·tun·ism /ópərtōōnizəm, -tyōō-/ *n.* the adaptation of policy or judgment to circumstances or opportunity, esp. regardless of principle. □□ **op·por·tun·ist** *n. & adj.* **op·por·tun·is·tic** *adj.* **op·por·tun·is·ti·cal·ly** *adv.*

op·por·tu·ni·ty /ópərtōōnitee, -tyōō-/ *n.* (*pl.* **-ies**) a good chance; a favorable occasion. □ **opportunity knocks** an opportunity occurs.

op·pos·a·ble /əpṓzəbəl/ *adj. Zool.* (of the thumb in primates) capable of facing and touching the other digits on the same hand.

op·pose /əpṓz/ *v.tr.* (often *absol.*) **1** set oneself against. **2** take part in a game, sport, etc., against (another competitor or team). **3** (foll. by *to*) place in opposition or contrast. □ **as opposed to** in contrast with.

op·po·site /ópəzit/ *adj., n., adv., & prep.* ● *adj.* **1** (often foll. by *to*) on the other or further side, facing or back to back. **2** (often foll. by *to, from*) **a** diametrically different. **b** being the other of a contrasted pair. **3** (of angles) between opposite sides of the intersection of two lines. ● *n.* an opposite thing or person or term. ● *adv.* in an opposite position (*the tree stands opposite*). ● *prep.* in a position opposite to (*opposite the house is a tree*). □□ **op·po·site·ly** *adv.* **op·po·site·ness** *n.*

op·po·site num·ber *n.* a person holding an equivalent position in another group or organization.

op·po·site sex *n.* women in relation to men or vice versa.

op·po·si·tion /ópəzíshən/ *n.* **1** resistance; antagonism. **2** the state of being hostile or in conflict. **3** contrast or antithesis. **4 a** a group of opponents. **b** (**the Opposition**) the principal political party opposed to that in office. **5** the act of opposing or placing opposite. □□ **op·po·si·tion·al** *adj.*

op·press /əprés/ *v.tr.* **1** keep in subservience by coercion. **2** govern or treat harshly or with cruel injustice. **3** weigh down (with cares). □□ **op·pres·sion** *n.* **op·pres·sor** *n.*

op·pres·sive /əprésiv/ *adj.* **1** harsh or cruel. **2** (of weather) close and sultry. □□ **op·pres·sive·ly** *adv.* **op·pres·sive·ness** *n.*

op·pro·bri·ous /əprṓbreeəs/ *adj.* (of language) severely scornful; abusive. □□ **op·pro·bri·ous·ly** *adv.*

op·pro·bri·um /əprṓbreeəm/ *n.* **1** disgrace. **2** a cause of this.

op·si·math /ópsimath/ *n. rare* a person who begins to learn or study only late in life.

opt /opt/ *v.intr.* (usu. foll. by *for, between*) exercise an option; make a choice. □ **opt out** (often foll. by *of*) choose not to participate (*opted out of the race*).

op·ta·tive /óptaytiv, óptətiv/ *adj. & n. Gram.* ● *adj.* expressing a wish. ● *n.* the optative mood.

op·tic /óptik/ *adj. & n.* ● *adj.* of or relating to the eye or vision (*optic nerve*). ● *n.* a lens, etc., in an optical instrument.

op·ti·cal /óptikəl/ *adj.* **1** of sight; visual. **2 a** of sight or light in relation to each other. **b** belonging to optics. **3** (esp. of a lens) constructed to assist sight. □□ **op·ti·cal·ly** *adv.*

op·ti·cal art *n.* a style of painting that gives the illusion of movement by the precise use of pattern and color.

op·ti·cal char·ac·ter rec·og·ni·tion *n.* the identification of printed characters using photoelectric devices.

op·ti·cal fi·ber *n.* ▼ thin glass fiber through which light can be transmitted.

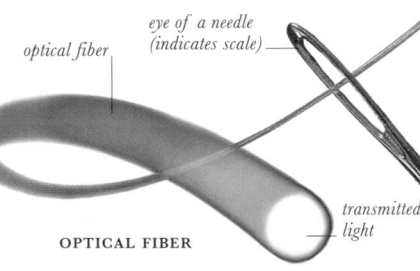

optical fiber

eye of a needle
(indicates scale)

transmitted light

OPTICAL FIBER

op·ti·cal il·lu·sion *n.* **1** a thing having an appearance so resembling something else as to deceive the eye. **2** a mental misapprehension caused by this.

op·ti·cian /óptíshən/ *n.* **1** a maker or seller of optical instruments. **2** a person trained in the detection and correction of poor eyesight (see OPHTHALMOLOGIST, OPTOMETRIST).

op·tic nerve *n.* ▼ each of the second pair of cranial nerves, transmitting impulses to the brain from the retina at the back of the eye. ▷ EYE.

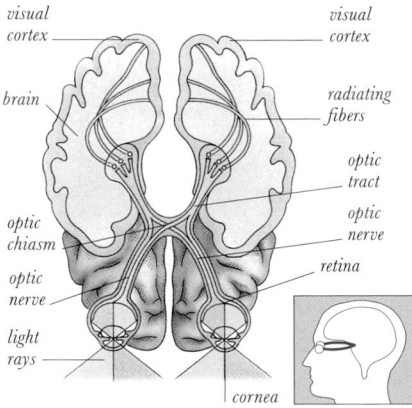

visual cortex
visual cortex
brain
radiating fibers
optic tract
optic nerve
optic chiasm
retina
optic nerve
light rays
cornea

OPTIC NERVE: PATH OF IMPULSES FROM RETINA TO BRAIN (VIEWED FROM UNDERNEATH)

op·tics /óptiks/ *n.pl.* (treated as *sing.*) the scientific study of sight and the behavior of light, or of other radiation or particles (*electron optics*).

op·ti·ma *pl.* of OPTIMUM.

op·ti·mal /óptiməl/ *adj.* best or most favorable. □□ **op·ti·mal·ly** *adv.*

op·ti·mism /óptimizəm/ *n.* **1** an inclination to hopefulness and confidence. **2** *Philos.* **a** the doctrine that this world is the best of all possible worlds. **b** the theory that good must ultimately prevail over evil. □□ **op·ti·mist** *n.* **op·ti·mis·tic** *adj.* **op·ti·mis·ti·cal·ly** *adv.*

op·ti·mize /óptimīz/ *v.* **1** *tr.* make the best or most effective use of (a situation, an opportunity, etc.). **2** *intr.* be an optimist. □□ **op·ti·mi·za·tion** *n.*

op·ti·mum /óptiməm/ *n. & adj.* ● *n.* (*pl.* **optima** /-mə/ or **optimums**) **1** the most favorable conditions. **2** the best possible compromise between opposing tendencies. ● *adj.* = OPTIMAL.

op·tion /ópshən/ *n.* **1** a thing that is or may be chosen. **2** freedom of choice. **3** *Stock Exch.*, etc. the right to buy, sell, etc., specified stocks, etc., at a specified price within a set time. □ **have no option but to** must. **keep** (or **leave**) **one's options open** not commit oneself.

op·tion·al /ópshənəl/ *adj.* not obligatory. □□ **op·tion·al·i·ty** /-álitee/ *n.* **op·tion·al·ly** *adv.*

op·tom·e·ter /optómitər/ *n.* an instrument for testing the refractive power and visual range of the eye. □□ **op·to·met·ric** /óptəmétrik/ *adj.*

op·tom·e·trist /optómitrist/ *n.* a person who practices optometry.

op·tom·e·try /optómitree/ *n.* the practice or profession of testing the eyes for defects in vision and prescribing corrective lenses or exercises.

op·u·lent /ópyələnt/ *adj.* **1** ostentatiously rich. **2** luxurious. **3** abundant; profuse. □□ **op·u·lence** /-ləns/ *n.* **op·u·lent·ly** *adv.*

o·pun·ti·a /ōpúnsheeə, -shə/ *n.* any cactus of the genus *Opuntia*, with jointed cylindrical or elliptical stems and barbed bristles. Also called **prickly pear**.

o·pus /ópəs/ *n.* (*pl.* **opera** /ópərə/ or **opuses**) **1** *Mus.* **a** a separate musical composition or set of compositions of any kind. **b** (also **op.**) used before a number given to a composer's work, usu. indicating the order of publication (*Beethoven, op. 15*). **2** any artistic work.

OR *abbr.* **1** Oregon (in official postal use). **2** operating room.

or /awr, ər/ *conj.* **1 a** introducing the second of two alternatives (*white or black*). **b** introducing all but the first, or only the last, of any number of alternatives (*white or gray or black; white, gray, or black*). **2** introducing a synonym or explanation of a preceding word, etc. (*suffered from vertigo or dizziness*). **3** introducing a significant afterthought (*he must know—or is he bluffing?*). **4** otherwise (*run or you'll be late*). □ **one or two** (or **two or three**, etc.) *colloq.* a few. **or else 1** otherwise (*do it now, or else you will have to do it tomorrow*). **2** *colloq.* expressing a warning or threat (*hand over the money or else*). **or rather** introducing a rephrasing or qualification of a preceding statement, etc. (*he was there, or rather I heard that he was*). **or so** approximately (*send me ten or so*).

or·a·cle /áwrəkəl, ór-/ *n.* **1 a** a place at which advice or prophecy was sought from the gods in classical antiquity. **b** the usu. ambiguous or obscure response given at an oracle. **c** a prophet or prophetess at an oracle. **2 a** a person or thing regarded as an infallible guide to future action, etc. **b** a saying, etc., regarded as infallible guidance.

o·rac·u·lar /awrák-yələr/ *adj.* **1** of or concerning an oracle. **2** (esp. of advice, etc.) mysterious. **3** prophetic.

o·ra·cy /áwrəsee/ *n.* the ability to express oneself fluently in speech.

o·ral /áwrəl/ *adj. & n.* ● *adj.* **1** spoken; not written (*the oral tradition*). **2** done or taken by the mouth (*oral contraceptive*). **3** of the mouth. **4** *n. colloq.* a spoken examination, test, etc. □□ **o·ral·ly** *adv.*

or·ange /áwrinj, ór-/ *n. & adj.* ● *n.* **1 a** a large roundish juicy citrus fruit with a bright reddish-yellow tough rind. ▷ CITRUS FRUIT. **b** any of various trees or shrubs of the genus *Citrus*, esp. *C. sinensis* or *C. aurantium*, bearing fragrant white flowers and yielding this fruit. **2** the reddish-yellow color of an orange. ● *adj.* orange-colored.

Or·ange·man /áwrinjmən, ór-/ *n.* (*pl.* **-men**) a member of a political society formed in 1795 to support Protestantism in Ireland.

or·ange·ry /áwrinjree, ór-/ *n.* (*pl.* **-ies**) a place where orange trees are cultivated.

o·rang·u·tan /awrángətán, əráng-/ *n.* (also **o·rang-ou·tang** /-táng/) a large red long-haired tree-living ape, *Pongo pygmaeus*, native to Borneo and Sumatra. ▷ PRIMATE.

o·rate /awráyt, áwrayt/ *v.intr. esp. joc.* or *derog.* make a speech or speak, esp. pompously or at length.

o·ra·tion /awráyshən, ōráy-/ *n.* a formal speech, etc., esp. when ceremonial.

or·a·tor /áwrətər, ór-/ *n.* **1** a person making a speech. **2** an eloquent public speaker.

or·a·to·ri·o /áwrətáwreeō, ór-/ *n.* (*pl.* **-os**) a semi-dramatic work for orchestra and voices, esp. on a sacred theme.

or·a·to·ry /áwrətawree, ór-/ *n.* (*pl.* **-ies**) **1** the art or practice of formal speaking, esp. in public. **2** a small chapel, esp. for private worship. □□ **or·a·tor·i·cal** /-táwrikəl/ *adj.*

orb /awrb/ *n.* **1** ◀ a globe surmounted by a cross, esp. carried by a sovereign at a coronation. **2** a sphere; a globe.

ORB:
17TH-CENTURY
ENGLISH ORB

or·bit /áwrbit/ *n. & v.* ● *n.* **1 a** ▶ the curved course of a planet, satellite, etc. **b** (prec. by *in*, *into*, *out of*, etc.) the state of motion in an orbit. **c** one complete passage around an orbited body. ▷ SOLAR SYSTEM. **2** the path of an electron around an atomic nucleus. ▷ ATOM. **3** a range or sphere of action. ● *v.* (**orbited**, **orbiting**) **1** *intr.* (of a satellite, etc.) go around in orbit. ▷ SPACECRAFT. **2** *tr.* move in orbit around.

or·bit·al /áwrbitəl/ *adj. Astron.* & *Physics* of an orbit

or·bit·al sand·er *n.* a sander having a circular and not oscillating motion.

orc /awrk/ *n.* a member of an imaginary race of ugly, aggressive, humanlike creatures.

or·ca /áwrkə/ *n.* the killer whale.

ORBIT

In space, smaller bodies (such as a satellite) orbit larger bodies (such as Earth) because of the gravitational pull exerted by the larger object. This is why the Earth orbits the Sun. Satellites orbiting the Earth perform tasks such as recording weather patterns.

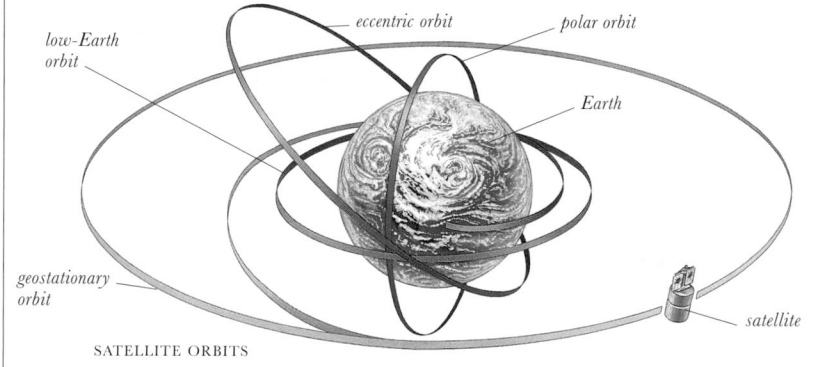

SATELLITE ORBITS

or·chard /áwrchərd/ *n.* a piece of land with fruit trees. □□ **or·char·dist** *n.*

or·chard·ing /áwrchərding/ *n.* the cultivation of fruit trees.

or·chard·man /áwrchərdmən/ *n.* (*pl.* **-men**) a fruit grower.

or·ches·tra /áwrkəstrə/ *n.* **1** ▼ a usu. large group of instrumentalists, esp. combining strings, wood-winds, brass, and percussion (*symphony orchestra*). ▷ AUDITORIUM, BRASS, PERCUSSION, STRINGED, WOODWIND. **2 a** (in full **orchestra pit**) the part of a theater, etc., where the orchestra plays, usu. in front of the stage and on a lower level. ▷ THEATER. **b** the main-floor seating area in a theater. **3** the semicircular space in front of an ancient Greek theater stage. □□ **or·ches·tral** /-késtrəl/ *adj.* **or·ches·tral·ly** *adv.*

ORCHESTRA

Orchestras as we know them today were first established in the 18th century and numbered 30–40 players. During the 19th century, instrument-making techniques improved markedly, and orchestra sizes increased. Today an average orchestra may contain 40–70 players. Each of the four sections in an orchestra has a different role. The strings, almost always the largest division, usually provide the melody. The woodwinds sometimes carry the tune, but more often give color and warmth to the overall sound. The brass instruments commonly add brightness and emphasis in dramatic passages, while the percussion section provides the orchestra's rhythmic backbone. The conductor dictates the tempo, volume, and balance of the piece.

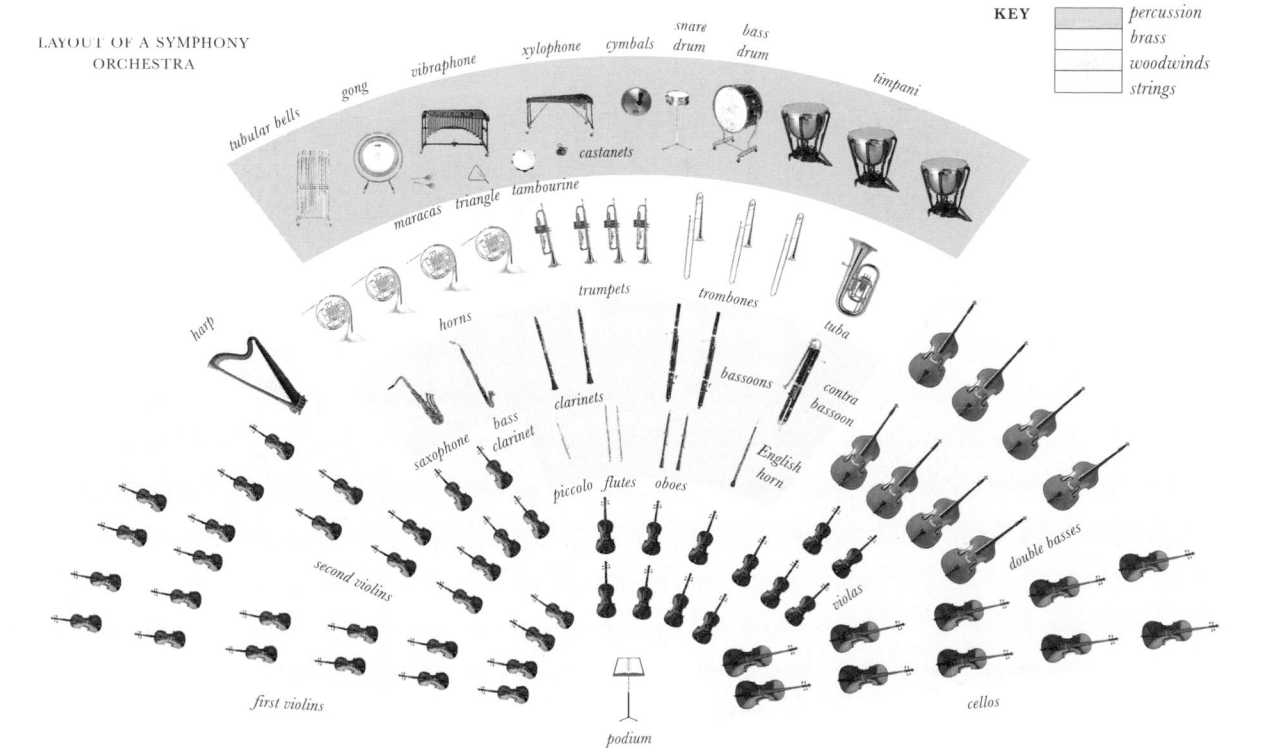

LAYOUT OF A SYMPHONY ORCHESTRA

KEY
percussion
brass
woodwinds
strings

or·ches·trate /áwrkəstrayt/ *v.tr.* **1** arrange, score, or compose for orchestral performance. **2** combine, arrange, or build up (elements of a situation, etc.) for maximum effect. □□ **or·ches·tra·tion** /-tráyshən/ *n.* **or·ches·tra·tor** *n.*

or·chid /áwrkid/ *n.* **1** ◀ any usu. epiphytic plant of the family Orchidaceae, bearing flowers in fantastic shapes and brilliant colors. ▷ EPIPHYTE. **2** a flower of any of these plants. □□ **or·chi·da·ceous** /-dáyshəs/ *adj.*

or·chi·tis /awrkítis/ *n.* inflammation of the testicles.

or·dain /awrdáyn/ *v.tr.* **1** confer holy orders on; appoint to the Christian ministry (*ordained him priest; ordained in 1970*). **2 a** (often foll. by *that* + clause) decree (*ordained that he should go*). **b** (of God, fate, etc.) destine; appoint (*has ordained us to die*). □□ **or·dain·er** *n.*

or·deal /awrdéel/ *n.* a painful or horrific experience; a severe trial.

or·der /áwrdər/ *n. & v.* ● *n.* **1 a** the condition in which every part, unit, etc., is in its right place. **b** a usu. specified sequence, succession, etc. (*alphabetical order*). **2** (in *sing.* or *pl.*) an authoritative command, instruction, etc. **3** a state of peaceful harmony under a constituted authority (*order was restored*). **4** a kind (*talents of a high order*). **5 a** a direction to a manufacturer, waiter, etc., to supply something. **b** the goods, etc., supplied. **6** the constitution or nature of the world, society, etc. (*the moral order; the order of things*). **7** *Biol.* a taxonomic rank below a class and above a family. **8** (esp. **Order**) a fraternity of monks and friars bound by a common rule of life (*the Franciscan order*). **9 a** any of the grades of the Christian ministry. **b** (in *pl.*) the status of a member of the clergy (*Anglican orders*). **10** any of the five classical styles of architecture (Doric, Ionic, Corinthian, Tuscan, and Composite) based on the proportions of columns, amount of decoration, etc. ▷ CORINTHIAN, DORIC, IONIC. **11** *Eccl.* the stated form of divine service (*the order of confirmation*). **12** the principles of procedure, decorum, etc., accepted by a meeting, legislative assembly, etc. **13** any of the nine grades of angelic beings (seraphim, cherubim, thrones, dominations, principalities, powers, virtues, archangels, angels). ● *v.tr.* **1** (usu. foll. by *to* + infin., or *that* + clause) command; prescribe (*ordered him to go*). **2** command or direct (a person) to a specified destination (*was ordered to Singapore*). **3** direct a manufacturer, waiter, etc., to supply something (*ordered a new suit*). **4** put in order; regulate (*ordered her affairs*). **5** (of God, fate, etc.) ordain (*fate ordered it otherwise*). **6** command (a thing) done or (a person) dealt with (*ordered him expelled*). □ **by order** according to the proper authority. **in bad** (or **good**, etc.) **order** not working (or working properly, etc.). **in order 1** one after another according to some principle. **2** ready for use. **3** according to the rules (of procedure at a meeting, etc.). **in order that** so that. **in order to** with a view to. **keep order** enforce orderly behavior. **of** (or **in** or **on**) **the order of 1** approximately. **2** having the order of magnitude specified by (*of the order of one in a million*). **on order** (of goods, etc.) ordered but not yet received. **order about 1** command officiously. **2** send here and there. **out of order 1** not working properly. **2** not according to the rules (of a meeting, organization, etc.). **3** not in proper sequence. **take orders 1** accept commissions. **2** accept and carry out commands.

or·der·ly /áwrd'rlee/ *adj. & n.* ● *adj.* **1** methodically arranged. **2** obedient to discipline; well-behaved.

ORCHID
(× *Odontocidium* cultivar)

sepal
fused style and stamen
petal
sepal
lip

● *n.* (*pl.* **-ies**) **1** a hospital attendant with nonmedical duties, esp. cleaning. **2** a soldier who carries orders for an officer, etc. □□ **or·der·li·ness** *n.*

or·der of the day *n.* **1** the prevailing state of things. **2** a principal topic of action or a procedure decided upon. **3** business set down for discussion.

or·di·nal /áwrd'nəl/ *n. & adj.* ● *n.* (in full **ordinal number**) a number defining a thing's position in a series, e.g., "first," "second," etc. ● *adj.* **1** of or relating to an ordinal number. **2** defining a thing's position in a series, etc.

or·di·nance /áwrd'nəns/ *n.* **1** a decree. **2** an enactment by a local authority. **3** a religious rite.

or·di·nand /áwrd'nənd/ *n. Eccl.* a candidate for ordination.

or·di·nar·y /áwrd'neree/ *adj. & n.* ● *adj.* **1** regular; normal; usual (*in the ordinary course of events*). **2** boring; commonplace (*an ordinary man*). ● *n.* (*pl.* **-ies**) **1** *RC Ch.* (usu. **Ordinary**) those parts of a service, esp. the mass, that do not vary from day to day. **2** a rule or book laying down the order of divine service. **3** an early type of bicycle with one large and one very small wheel. □□ **out of the ordinary** unusual. □□ **or·di·nar·i·ly** /-áirəlee/ *adv.* **or·di·nar·i·ness** *n.*

or·di·nar·y sea·man *n.* a sailor of the lowest rank.

or·di·nate /áwrd'nit/ *n. Math.* a straight line from any point drawn parallel to one coordinate axis and meeting the other, usually a coordinate measured parallel to the vertical.

ORE

A rock or mineral is considered an ore if the valuable commodity it contains (such as iron) can be profitably extracted. Some ores contain less than one percent of the precious material. Most ores form by sedimentary, magmatic, or hydrothermal processes.

EXAMPLES OF ORES

HEMATITE
(iron ore)

GOLD IN QUARTZ
(gold ore)

GALENA
(lead ore)

CINNABAR
(mercury ore)

BAUXITE
(aluminum ore)

ORGAN

Depressing a key or foot pedal on an organ sends compressed air into the pipes, which are arranged in scalelike ranks (rows). Each rank has a particular sound (e.g., diapason, flute, trumpet), and each individual pipe produces a single pitch. Each manual (keyboard) is a separate organ in itself, offering a variety of sound combinations and possibilities. Pistons are used to select contrasting mixtures and combinations of sounds, creating the full organ tone.

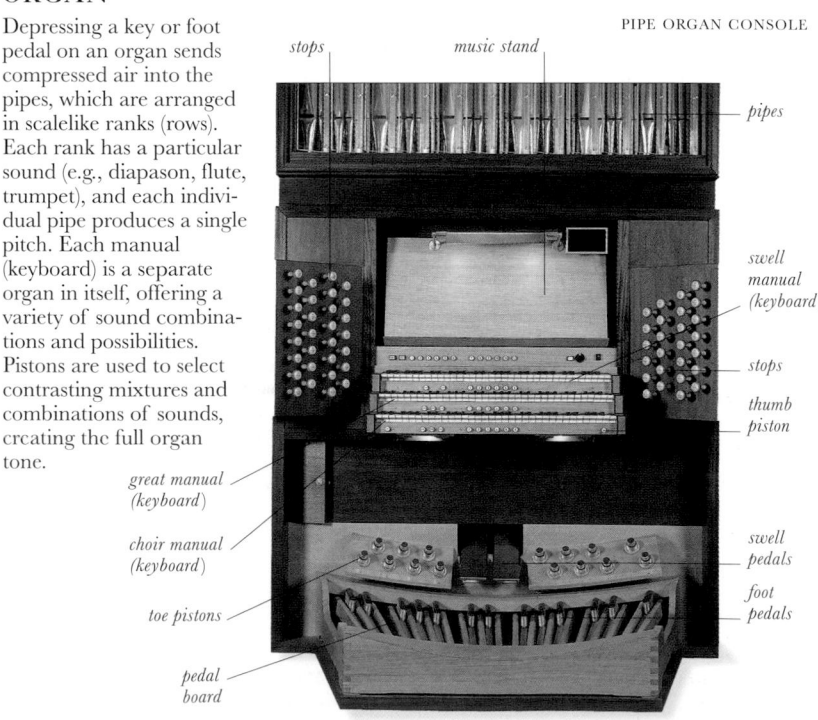

PIPE ORGAN CONSOLE

stops
music stand
pipes
swell manual (keyboard)
stops
thumb piston
great manual (keyboard)
choir manual (keyboard)
swell pedals
foot pedals
toe pistons
pedal board

or·di·na·tion /áwrd'náyshən/ *n.* the act of conferring holy orders, esp. on a priest or deacon.

ord·nance /áwrdnəns/ *n.* **1** mounted guns; cannon. **2** a branch of the armed forces dealing esp. with military stores and materials.

Or·do·vi·cian /áwrdəvíshən/ *adj. & n. Geol.* ● *adj.* of or relating to the second period of the Paleozoic era. ● *n.* this period or system.

or·dure /áwrjər, -dyŏŏr/ *n.* **1** excrement; dung. **2** obscenity; filth; foul language.

Ore. *abbr.* Oregon.

ore /awr/ *n.* ◀ a naturally occurring solid material from which metal or other valuable minerals may be extracted. ▷ METAL

Oreg. *abbr.* Oregon.

o·reg·a·no /ərégənō, awrég-/ *n.* an aromatic herb, *Origanum vulgare*, the leaves of which are used as a flavoring in cooking. Also called **wild marjoram** ▷ HERB.

or·gan /áwrgən/ *n.* **1 a** ◀ usu. large musical instrument having pipes supplied with air from bellows, sounded by keys (*pedal organ*). **b** a smaller instrument without pipes, producing similar sounds electronically. **c** a smaller keyboard wind instrument with metal reeds. **d** = BARREL ORGAN. **2 a** a usu. self-contained part of an organism having a special vital function (*vocal organs*). **b** esp. *joc.* the penis. **3** a medium of communication, esp. a newspaper, etc.

or·gan·dy /áwrgəndee/ *n.* (also **or·gan·die**) (*pl.* **-ies**) a fine translucent cotton muslin, usu. stiffened.

or·gan·elle /áwrgənél/ *n. Biol.* any of various organized or specialized structures that form part of a cell.

or·gan-grind·er *n.* the player of a barrel organ.

or·gan·ic /awrgánik/ *adj.* **1 a** *Physiol.* of or relating to a bodily organ or organs. **b** *Med.* (of a disease) affecting the structure of an organ. **2** (of a plant or animal) having organs or an organized physical structure. **3** produced or involving production without chemical fertilizers, pesticides, etc. **4** *Chem.* (of a compound, etc.) containing carbon (opp. INORGANIC). **5 a** structural; inherent. **b** constitutional; fundamental. **6** organized; systematic (*an organic whole*). □□ **or·gan·i·cal·ly** *adv.*

or·gan·ic chem·is·try *n.* the chemistry of carbon compounds. ▷ ALKANE, ALKENE, ALKYNE

or·gan·ism /áwrgənizəm/ *n.* **1** a living individual consisting of a single cell or of a group of interdependent parts. **2** an individual live plant or animal. **3** a whole with interdependent parts compared to a living being.

or·gan·ist /áwrgənist/ *n.* the player of an organ.

or·gan·i·za·tion /áwrgənizáyshən/ *n.* **1** the act of organizing. **2** an organized body, esp. a business, charity, etc. **3** systematic arrangement. □□ **or·gan·i·za·tion·al** *adj.* **or·gan·i·za·tion·al·ly** *adv.*

or·gan·ize /áwrgənīz/ *v.tr.* **1 a** give an orderly structure to. **b** make arrangements for (a person). **2** (often *absol.*) **a** enroll (new members) in a labor union, political party, etc. **b** form (a labor union or other political group). **3** (esp. as **organized** *adj.*) make organic; make into a living being or tissue.

or·gan·ized crime *n.* **1** an organization of people who carry out illegal activities for profit. **2** the people involved in this.

or·gan loft *n.* a gallery in a church or concert room for an organ.

or·gan·za /awrgánzə/ *n.* a thin stiff transparent silk or synthetic dress fabric.

or·gasm /áwrgazəm/ *n. & v.* ● *n.* the climax of sexual excitement. ● *v.intr.* experience a sexual orgasm. □□ **or·gas·mic** /-gázmik/ *adj.* **or·gas·mic·al·ly** *adv.*

or·gi·as·tic /áwrjeeástik/ *adj.* of or resembling an orgy. □□ **or·gi·as·tic·al·ly** *adv.*

or·gy /áwrjee/ *n.* (*pl.* **-ies**) **1** a wild drunken festivity, esp. one at which indiscriminate sexual activity takes place. **2** excessive indulgence in an activity.

o·ri·el /áwreeəl/ *n.* (in full **oriel window**) the projecting window of an upper story.

o·ri·ent *n. & v.* ● *n.* /áwreeənt/ (**the Orient**) **1** *poet.* the east. **2** the countries east of the Mediterranean, esp. E. Asia. ● *v.* /áwree-ent/ **1** *tr.* **a** place or exactly determine the position of with the aid of a compass. **b** (often foll. by *toward*) direct. **2** *tr.* place or build (a church, etc.) facing toward the East. **3** *intr.* turn eastward or in a specified direction. □ **orient oneself** determine how one stands in relation to one's surroundings.

o·ri·en·tal /áwree-éntəl/ *adj. & n.* ● *adj.* (often **Oriental**) **1** of or characteristic of Eastern civilization, etc. **2** of or concerning the East, esp. E. Asia. ● *n.* (esp. **Oriental**) a native of the Orient. □□ **o·ri·en·tal·ism** *n.* **o·ri·en·tal·ist** *n.* **o·ri·en·tal·ize** *v.intr. & tr.*

o·ri·en·tate /áwree-entayt/ *v.tr. & intr.* = ORIENT *v.*

o·ri·en·ta·tion /áwree-entáy-shən/ *n.* **1** the act of orienting. **2 a** a relative position. **b** a person's attitude or adjustment in relation to circumstances, esp. psychologically. **3** an introduction to a subject or situation; a briefing. □□ **o·ri·en·ta·tion·al** *adj.*

o·ri·en·ta·tion course *n.* a course giving information to newcomers to a university, etc.

o·ri·en·teer·ing /áwree-entééring/ *n.* a competitive sport in which runners cross open country with a map, compass, etc. □□ **o·ri·en·teer** *n. & v.intr.*

or·i·fice /áwrifis, ór-/ *n.* an opening, esp. a bodily aperture, etc.

o·ri·ga·mi /áwrigáámee/ *n.* ◀ the Japanese art of folding paper into decorative shapes and figures.

or·i·gan /áwrigən, ór-/ *n.* (also **origanum** /ərígənəm/) any plant of the genus *Origanum*, esp. oregano.

or·i·gin /áwrijin, ór-/ *n.* **1** a beginning or starting point; a derivation (*a word of Latin origin*). **2** (often in *pl.*) a person's ancestry (*what are his origins?*). **3** *Math* a fixed point from which coordinates are measured.

ORIGAMI: FIGURE OF A DOG

o·rig·i·nal /əríjinəl/ *adj. & n.* ● *adj.* **1** existing from the beginning; innate. **2** novel; inventive; creative (*has an original mind*). **3** serving as a pattern; not derivative or imitative; firsthand (*in the original Greek; has an original Rembrandt*). ● *n.* **1** an original model, picture, etc., from which another is copied or translated (*kept the copy and destroyed the original*). **2** an eccentric or unusual person. □□ **o·rig·i·nal·ly** *adv.*

o·rig·i·nal·i·ty /ərijinálitee/ *n.* (*pl.* **-ies**) **1** the power of creating or thinking creatively. **2** newness or freshness (*this vase has originality*).

o·rig·i·nal sin *n.* the innate depravity of all humankind held to be a consequence of the Fall of Adam.

o·rig·i·nate /əríjinayt/ *v.* **1** *tr.* cause to begin. **2** *intr.* (usu. foll. by *from, in, with*) have as an origin. □□ **o·rig·i·na·tion** /-náyshən/ *n.* **o·rig·i·na·tor** *n.*

O-ring /ó-ring/ *n.* a gasket in the form of a ring with a circular cross section.

o·ri·ole /áwreeōl/ *n.* **1** any Old World bird of the genus *Oriolus*, many of which have brightly colored plumage. **2** any New World bird of the genus *Icterus*, with similar coloration. ▷ SONGBIRD

O·ri·on /əríən/ *n.* ◀ a brilliant constellation on the celestial equator visible from most parts of the earth.

or·mo·lu /áwrməloo/ *n.* **1** (often *attrib.*) a gilded bronze or gold-colored alloy of copper, zinc, and tin. **2** articles made of or decorated with these.

or·na·ment *n. & v.* ● *n.* /áwrnə-mənt/ **1** a thing used or serving to adorn, esp. a small trinket, vase, figure, etc. **2** decoration added to embellish, esp. a building (*a tower rich in ornament*). ● *v.tr.* /áwrnəmənt/ adorn; beautify. □□ **or·na·men·ta·tion** /-táyshən/ *n.*

or·na·men·tal /áwrnəmént'l/ *adj. & n.* ● *adj.* serving as an ornament. ● *n.* a thing considered to be ornamental, esp. a cultivated plant. □□ **or·na·men·tal·ism** *n.*

or·nate /awrnáyt/ *adj.* **1** elaborately adorned. **2** (of literary style) convoluted; flowery. □□ **or·nate·ly** *adv.*

or·ner·y /áwrnəree/ *adj. colloq.* cantankerous.

or·ni·this·chi·an /awrnithískiən/ *adj. & n.* ● *adj.* of or relating to the order Ornithischia, including dinosaurs with a pelvic structure like that of birds. ● *n.* a dinosaur of this order. ▷ DINOSAUR

or·ni·thol·o·gy /áwrnithóləjee/ *n.* the scientific study of birds. □□ **or·ni·tho·log·i·cal** /-thəlójikəl/ *adj.* **or·ni·tho·log·i·cal·ly** *adv.* **or·ni·thol·o·gist** *n.*

o·ro·tund /áwrətund/ *adj.* **1** (of the voice or phrasing) full and round; imposing. **2** (of writing, style, expression, etc.) pompous; pretentious.

or·phan /áwrfən/ *n. & v.* ● *n.* (often *attrib.*) a child bereaved of both parents. ● *v.tr.* bereave (a child) of its parents. □□ **or·phan·hood** *n.*

or·phan·age /áwrfənij/ *n.* a home for orphans.

or·rer·y /áwrəree, ór-/ *n.* (*pl.* **-ies**) ▼ a clockwork model of the solar system.

ORION: FIGURE OF A HUNTER FORMED FROM THE STARS OF ORION

Betelgeuse · Bellatrix · Alnilam · Alnitak · Mintaka · Rigel · Saiph

ORRERY

English scientist Isaac Newton (1642–1727) proposed that the universe runs like a giant clockwork machine. An orrery (named after the Earl of Orrery, for whom one was built around 1712) is a clockwork model of the universe with a complex gearing system that enables each planet to complete its solar orbit correctly relative to the other planets.

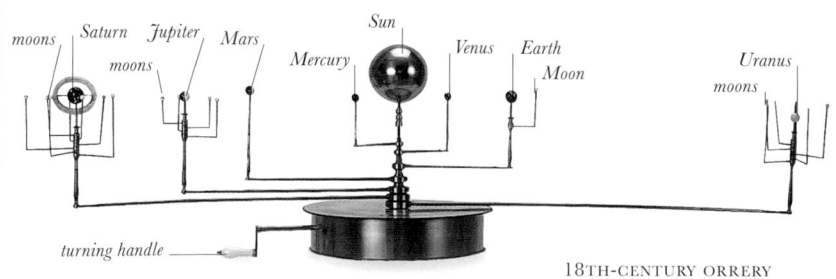

moons · Saturn · Jupiter · Mars · Sun · Mercury · Venus · Earth · Moon · Uranus · moons · moons · turning handle

18TH-CENTURY ORRERY

or·ris /áwris, ór-/ *n.* **1** any plant of the genus *Iris*, esp. *I. florentina*. **2** = ORRISROOT.

or·ris·root /áwrisrōōt, -rŏŏt, ór-/ *n.* the fragrant rootstock of the orris, used in perfumery and formerly in medicine.

ortho- /áwrthō/ *comb. form* **1** straight; rectangular; upright. **2** right; correct.

or·tho·don·tics /áwrthədóntiks/ *n.pl.* (treated as *sing.*) (also **or·tho·don·tia** /-dónshə/) the treatment of irregularities in the teeth and jaws. □□ **or·tho·don·tic** *adj.* **or·tho·don·tist** *n.*

or·tho·dox /áwrthədoks/ *adj.* **1** holding currently accepted opinions, esp. on religious doctrine, morals, etc. **2** (of religious doctrine, standards of morality, etc.) generally accepted as right or true; conventional. **3** (also **Orthodox**) (of Judaism) strictly keeping to traditional doctrine and ritual. □□ **or·tho·dox·ly** *adv.*

Or·tho·dox Church *n.* the Eastern Christian Church having the Patriarch of Constantinople as its head, and including the national churches of Russia, Romania, Greece, etc.

or·tho·dox·y /áwrthədoksee/ *n.* (*pl.* **-ies**) **1** the state of being orthodox. **2 a** the orthodox practice of Judaism. **b** the body of orthodox Jews. **3** esp. *Relig.* an authorized or generally accepted theory, doctrine, etc.

or·thog·o·nal /awrthógənəl/ *adj.* of or involving right angles.

or·thog·ra·phy /awrthógrəfee/ *n.* (*pl.* **-ies**) **1** correct spelling. **2** spelling with reference to its correctness (*dreadful orthography*). **3** the study or science of spelling. □□ **or·tho·graph·ic** /awrthəgráfik/ *adj.* **or·tho·graph·i·cal** *adj.* **or·tho·graph·i·cal·ly** *adv.*

or·tho·pe·dics /awrthəpeédiks/ *n.pl.* (treated as *sing.*) the branch of medicine dealing with the correction of deformities. □□ **or·tho·pe·dic** *adj.* **or·tho·pe·dist** *n.*

or·thop·ter·an /awrthóptərən/ *n.* ▶ any insect of the order Orthoptera, with straight narrow forewings, and hind legs modified for jumping, etc., including grasshoppers and crickets. □□ **or·thop·ter·ous** *adj.*

or·thop·tics /awrthóptiks/ *n. Med.* the study or treatment of irregularities of the eyes, esp. with reference to the eye muscles.

or·to·lan /áwrt'lən/ *n.* (in full **ortolan bunting**) *Zool.* a small European bird, *Emberiza hortulana*, eaten as a delicacy.

OS *abbr.* **1** old style. **2** ordinary seaman. **3** *oculus sinister* (left eye). **4** outsize. **5** out of stock.

Os *symb. Chem.* the element osmium.

O·sage /ōsáyj, ṓ-/ *n. & adj.* ● *n.* **1 a** a N. American people native to Missouri. **b** a member of this people. **2** the language of this people. ● *adj.* of or relating to this people or their language.

Os·car /óskər/ *n.* any of the statuettes awarded by the Academy of Motion Picture Arts and Sciences for excellence in motion-picture acting, directing, etc.

os·cil·late /ósilayt/ *v.* **1** *intr. & tr.* **a** swing back and forth like a pendulum. **b** move back and forth between points. **2** *intr.* vary between extremes of opinion, action, etc. **3** *intr. Physics* move with periodic regularity. **4** *intr. Electr.* (of a current) undergo high-frequency alternations as across a spark gap. □□ **os·cil·la·tion** /-áyshən/ *n.* **os·cil·la·tor** *n.* **os·cil·la·to·ry** /-ətáwree/ *adj.*

os·cil·lo·gram /əsíləgram/ *n.* a record obtained from an oscillograph.

os·cil·lo·graph /əsíləgraf/ *n.* a device for recording oscillations.

os·cil·lo·scope /əsíləskōp/ *n.* a device for viewing oscillations by a display on the screen of a cathode-ray tube.

os·ci·ta·tion /ósitáyshən/ *n. formal* **1** yawning; drowsiness. **2** inattention; negligence.

os·cu·lar /óskyələr/ *adj.* of or relating to the mouth.

ORTHOPTERAN

There are over 20,000 species in the order Orthoptera. These insects usually travel by jumping, even though many have wings.

Orthopterans communicate by stridulation: rubbing roughened areas of wings or legs together to produce a sound.

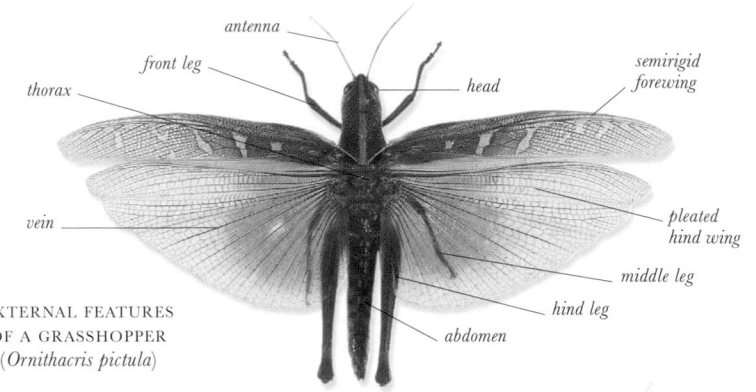

EXTERNAL FEATURES
OF A GRASSHOPPER
(*Ornithacris pictura*)

antenna · *front leg* · *thorax* · *head* · *semirigid forewing* · *vein* · *pleated hind wing* · *middle leg* · *hind leg* · *abdomen*

EXAMPLES OF OTHER ORTHOPTERANS

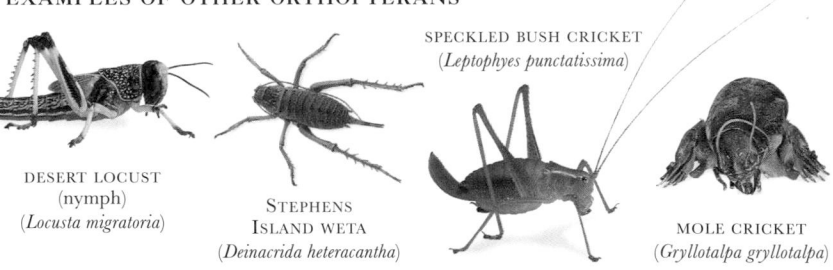

DESERT LOCUST
(nymph)
(*Locusta migratoria*)

STEPHENS
ISLAND WETA
(*Deinacrida heteracantha*)

SPECKLED BUSH CRICKET
(*Leptophyes punctatissima*)

MOLE CRICKET
(*Gryllotalpa gryllotalpa*)

---

os·cu·late /óskyəlayt/ *v.intr. & tr. joc.* kiss. □□ **os·cu·la·tion** /-láyshən/ *n.*

OSHA /óshə/ *abbr.* Occupational Safety and Health Administration.

o·sier /ṓzhər/ *n.* **1** any of various willows, esp. *Salix viminalis*, with long flexible shoots used in basketwork. **2** a shoot of a willow.

os·mic /ózmik/ *adj.* of or relating to odors or the sense of smell. □□ **os·mic·al·ly** *adv.*

os·mi·um /ózmeeəm/ *n. Chem.* a hard, bluish-white transition element, the heaviest known metal, used in certain alloys. ¶ symb.: **Os**.

os·mo·sis /ozmṓsis, os-/ *n.* **1** *Biochem.* the passage of a solvent through a semipermeable partition into a more concentrated solution. **2** any process by which something is acquired by absorption. □□ **os·mot·ic** /-mótik/ *adj.* **os·mot·i·cal·ly** /-mótikəlee/ *adv.*

os·prey /óspray, -pree/ *n.* (*pl.* **-eys**) ▼ a large bird of prey, *Pandion haliaetus*, with a brown back and white markings, feeding on fish. Also called **fish hawk**. ▷ RAPTOR

OSPREY
(*Pandion haliaetus*)

OSS *abbr.* Office of Strategic Services.

os·se·ous /óseeəs/ *adj.* **1** consisting of bone. **2** having a bony skeleton. **3** ossified.

os·si·cle /ósikəl/ *n.* **1** *Anat.* any small bone, esp. of the middle ear. ▷ EAR. **2** a small piece of bonelike substance.

os·si·fy /ósifī/ *v.tr. & intr.* (**-ies, -ied**) **1** turn into bone. **2** make or become rigid or unprogressive. □□ **os·si·fi·ca·tion** /-fikáyshən/ *n.*

os·so bu·co /áwsō bōōkō/ *n.* (also **osso bucco**) veal stewed in wine with vegetables.

os·su·ar·y /óshōōeree, ósyōō-/ *n.* (*pl.* **-ies**) **1** a receptacle for the bones of the dead; a charnel house; a bone urn. **2** a cave in which ancient bones are found.

os·ten·si·ble /osténsibəl/ *adj.* apparent but not necessarily real; professed (*his ostensible function was that of interpreter*). □□ **os·ten·si·bly** *adv.*

os·ten·sive /osténsiv/ *adj.* **1** directly demonstrative. **2** (of a definition) indicating by direct demonstration that which is signified by a term. □□ **os·ten·sive·ly** *adv.* **os·ten·sive·ness** *n.*

os·ten·ta·tion /óstentáyshən/ *n.* **1** a vulgar display of wealth. **2** showing off. □□ **os·ten·ta·tious** *adj.* **os·ten·ta·tious·ly** *adv.*

osteo- /ósteeō/ *comb. form* bone.

os·te·o·ar·thri·tis /ósteeōaarthrítis/ *n.* a degenerative disease of joint cartilage, esp. in the elderly. □□ **os·te·o·ar·thrit·ic** /-thrítik/ *adj.*

os·te·ol·o·gy /ósteeóləjee/ *n.* the study of the structure and function of the skeleton. □□ **os·te·o·log·i·cal** /-teeəlójikəl/ *adj.* **os·te·ol·o·gist** *n.*

os·te·o·my·e·li·tis /ósteeōmī-ilítis/ *n.* inflammation of the bone or of bone marrow, usu. due to infection.

os·te·op·a·thy /ósteeópəthee/ *n.* the treatment of disease through the manipulation of bones, esp. the spine. □□ **os·te·o·path** /ósteeəpath/ *n.* **os·te·o·path·ic** *adj.*

os·te·o·po·ro·sis /ósteeōpərósis/ *n.* a condition of brittle bones caused by loss of bony tissue, esp. as a result of hormonal changes, or deficiency of calcium or vitamin D.

os·ti·na·to /óstinaátō/ *n.* (*pl.* **-os**) (often *attrib.*) *Mus.* a persistent phrase or rhythm repeated through all or part of a piece.

ost·ler /óslər/ *n. Brit. hist.* a stableman at an inn.

os·tra·cize /óstrəsīz/ *v.tr.* exclude (a person) from a society, favor, common privileges, etc.; refuse to associate with. ▫▫ **os·tra·cism** /-sizəm/ *n.*

os·trich /óstrich, áw-/ *n.* **1** a large African swift-running flightless bird, *Struthio camelus*, with long legs and two toes on each foot. ▷ FLIGHTLESS. **2** a person who refuses to accept facts.

OT *abbr.* Old Testament.

OTB *abbr.* off-track betting.

OTC *abbr.* over-the-counter.

oth·er /ú<u>th</u>ər/ *adj., n.* or *pron., & adv.* ● *adj.* **1** not the same as one or some already mentioned or implied (*other people; use other means*). **2 a** additional (*a few other examples*). **b** alternative of two (*open your other eye*). **3** (prec. by *the*) that remains after all except the one in question have been considered, etc. (*must be in the other pocket; where are the other two?*). **4** (foll. by *than*) apart from (*any person other than you*). ● *n.* or *pron.* **1** an additional, different, or extra person, thing, example, etc. (*some others have come*) (see also ANOTHER, EACH OTHER). **2** (in *pl.*; prec. by *the*) the ones remaining (*where are the others?*). ● *adv.* (usu. foll. by *than*) *disp.* otherwise (*cannot react other than angrily*). ¶ In this sense *otherwise* is standard except in less formal use. ▫ **on the other hand** see HAND. **the other day** (or **night** or **week**, etc.) a few days, etc., ago (*heard from him the other day*). **someone** (or **something** or **somehow**, etc.) **or other** some unspecified person, manner, etc.

oth·er half *n. colloq.* one's wife or husband.

oth·er·ness /ú<u>th</u>ərnis/ *n.* **1** the state of being different. **2** a thing or existence other than the thing mentioned and the thinking subject.

oth·er·wise /ú<u>th</u>ərwīz/ *adv. & adj.* ● *adv.* **1** else; or else (*bring your umbrella, otherwise you will get wet*). **2** in other respects (*he is somewhat unkempt, but otherwise very suitable*). **3** (often foll. by *than*) in a different way (*could not have acted otherwise*). **4** as an alternative (*otherwise known as Jack*). ● *adj.* (*predic.*) in a different state (*the matter is quite otherwise*). ▫ **and** (or **or**) **otherwise** the negation or opposite (of a specified thing) (*the merits or otherwise of the proposal; experiences pleasant and otherwise*).

oth·er·world·ly /ú<u>th</u>ərwórldlee/ *adj.* **1** unworldly; impractical. **2** concerned with life after death, etc. ▫▫ **oth·er·world·li·ness** *n.*

o·ti·ose /ósheeōs, ótee-/ *adj.* serving no practical purpose; not required; functionless. ▫▫ **o·ti·ose·ly** *adv.* **o·ti·ose·ness** *n.*

o·ti·tis /ōtítis/ *n.* inflammation of the ear.

oto- /ótō/ *comb. form* ear.

o·tol·o·gy /ōtóləjee/ *n.* the study of the anatomy and diseases of the ear. ▫▫ **o·to·log·i·cal** /ótəlójikəl/ *adj.* **o·tol·o·gist** *n.*

o·to·scope /ótəskōp/ *n.* an apparatus for examining the eardrum and the passage leading to it from the ear. ▫▫ **o·to·scop·ic** /-skópik/ *adj.*

Ot·ta·wa /aátəwə, -waa, -waw/ *n. & adj.* ● *n.* **1 a** a N. American people native to Canada and the Great Lakes region. **b** a member of this people. **2** the language of this people. ● *adj.* of or relating to this people or their language.

ot·ter /ótər/ *n.* **1** ▶ any of several aquatic fish-eating mammals of the family Mustelidae, esp. of the genus *Lutra*, having strong claws and webbed feet. ▷ MUSTELID. **2** its fur or pelt.

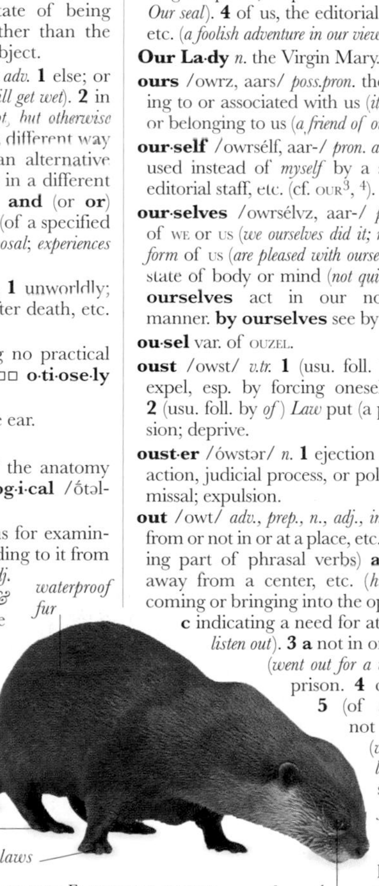
waterproof fur
strong tail
webbed feet
sharp claws
forward-facing eyes
OTTER: EUROPEAN OTTER (*Lutra lutra*)

Ot·to·man /ótəmən/ *adj. & n.* ● *adj. hist.* **1** concerning the dynasty of Osman or Othman I, the branch of the Turks to which he belonged, or the empire ruled by his descendants. **2** Turkish. ● *n.* (*pl.* **Ottomans**) an Ottoman person; a Turk.

ot·to·man /ótəmən/ *n.* (*pl.* **ottomans**) **1 a** an upholstered seat, usu. square and without a back or arms, sometimes a box with a padded top. **b** a footstool of similar design. **2** a heavy silken fabric with a mixture of cotton or wool.

ou·bli·ette /ōōblee-ét/ *n.* a secret dungeon with access only through a trapdoor.

ouch /owch/ *int.* expressing pain or annoyance.

ought /awt/ *v.aux.* (usu. foll. by *to* + infin.; present and past indicated by the following infin.) **1** expressing rightness (*we ought to love our neighbors*). **2** expressing shortcoming (*it ought to have been done long ago*). **3** expressing advisability (*you ought to go for your own good*). **4** expressing esp. strong probability (*he ought to be there by now*). ▫ **ought not** the negative form of *ought* (*he ought not to have stolen it*).

oughtn't /áwt'nt/ *contr.* ought not.

Oui·ja /wéejə, -jee/ *n.* (in full **Ouija board**) *Trademark* a board having letters or signs at its rim to which a planchette, movable pointer, or upturned glass points in answer to questions from attenders at a seance, etc.

ounce[1] /owns/ *n.* **1** a unit of weight of one-sixteenth of a pound avoirdupois (approx. 28 grams). **2** a small quantity.

ounce[2] /owns/ *n.* a large Asian feline, *Panthera uncia*, with leopardlike markings on a cream-colored coat. Also called **mountain panther**, **snow leopard**.

our /owr, aar/ *poss.pron.* (*attrib.*) **1** of or belonging to us or ourselves (*our house*). **2** of or belonging to all people (*our children's future*). **3** (esp. as **Our**) of Us the king or queen, emperor or empress, etc. (*given under Our seal*). **4** of us, the editorial staff of a newspaper, etc. (*a foolish adventure in our view*).

Our La·dy *n.* the Virgin Mary.

ours /owrz, aars/ *poss.pron.* the one or ones belonging to or associated with us (*it is ours*) ▫ **of ours** of or belonging to us (*a friend of ours*).

our·self /owrsélf, aar-/ *pron. archaic* a word formerly used instead of *myself* by a sovereign, newspaper editorial staff, etc. (cf. OUR[3], [4]).

our·selves /owrsélvz, aar-/ *pron.* **1 a** *emphat. form* of WE or US (*we ourselves did it; made it ourselves*). **b** *refl. form* of US (*are pleased with ourselves*). **2** in our normal state of body or mind (*not quite ourselves today*). ▫ **be ourselves** act in our normal unconstrained manner. **by ourselves** see by oneself.

ou·sel var. of OUZEL.

oust /owst/ *v.tr.* **1** (usu. foll. by *from*) drive out or expel, esp. by forcing oneself into the place of. **2** (usu. foll. by *of*) *Law* put (a person) out of possession; deprive.

oust·er /ówstər/ *n.* **1** ejection as a result of physical action, judicial process, or political upheaval. **2** dismissal; expulsion.

out /owt/ *adv., prep., n., adj., int., & v.* ● *adv.* **1** away from or not in or at a place, etc. (*keep him out*). **2** (forming part of phrasal verbs) **a** indicating dispersal away from a center, etc. (*hire out*). **b** indicating coming or bringing into the open (*send out; shine out*). **c** indicating a need for attentiveness (*watch out; listen out*). **3 a** not in one's house, office, etc. (*went out for a walk*). **b** no longer in prison. **4** completely (*tired out*). **5** (of a fire, candle, etc.) not burning. **6** in error (*was 3% out in my calculations*). **7** *colloq.* unconscious (*she was out for five minutes*). **8 a** (of a tooth) extracted. **b** (of a joint, etc.) dislocated. **9** (of a party, politician, etc.) not in office. **10** (of a jury) considering its verdict in secrecy. **11** (of workers) on strike. **12** (of a secret) revealed. **13** (of a flower) blooming; open. **14** (of a book) published. **15** (of a star) visible after dark. **16** unfashionable (*wide lapels are out*). **17** *Sports* (of a batter, baserunner, etc.) no longer taking part, having been tagged, struck out, etc. **18** not worth considering (*that idea is out*). **19** *colloq.* (prec. by *superl.*) known to exist (*the best game out*). **20** (of a stain, etc.) removed (*painted out the sign*). **21** (of time) not spent working (*took five minutes out*). **22** (of a rash, bruise, etc.) visible. **23** (of the tide) at the lowest point. **24** *Boxing* unable to rise from the floor (*out for the count*). **25** (in a radio conversation, etc.) transmission ends (*over and out*). ● *prep.* out of (*looked out the window*). ● *n.* **1** *colloq.* a way of escape; an excuse. **2** *Baseball* play in which a batter or baserunner is retired from an inning. ● *adj.* (of an island) away from the mainland. ● *int.* a peremptory dismissal, reproach, etc. (*out, you scoundrel!*). ● *v.* **1** *tr.* **a** put out. **b** *colloq.* eject forcibly. **2** *intr.* come or go out (*murder will out*). **3** *tr. Boxing* knock out. **4** *tr. colloq.* expose the homosexuality of (a prominent person). ▫ **out and about** (of a person, esp. after an illness) engaging in normal activity. **out and away** by far. **out for** having one's interest or effort directed to. **out of 1** from within (*came out of the house*). **2** not within (*I was never out of the city*). **3** from among (*nine people out of ten*). **4** beyond the range of (*is out of reach*). **5** without or so as to be without. **6** from (*get money out of him*). **7** owing to (*out of curiosity*). **8** by the use of (material) (*what did you make it out of?*). **9** at a specified distance from (*seven miles out of Topeka*). **10** beyond (*something out of the ordinary*). **11** *Racing* (of an animal, esp. a horse) born of. **come out of the closet** see CLOSET. **out of doors** see DOOR. **out of hand** see HAND. **out of it 1** not included. **2** *sl.* extremely drunk or otherwise disoriented. **out of order** see ORDER. **out of pocket** see POCKET. **out of the question** see QUESTION. **out of sorts** see SORT. **out of temper** see TEMPER. **out of this world** see WORLD. **out of the way** see WAY. **out to** keenly striving to do. **out to lunch** *colloq.* crazy; mad. **out with it** say what you are thinking.

out·act /ówtákt/ *v.tr.* surpass in acting or performing.

out·age /ówtij/ *n.* a period of time during which a power supply, etc., is not operating.

out-and-out *adj. & adv.* ● *adj.* thorough; surpassing. ● *adv.* throughly; surpassingly.

out-and-out·er *n.sl.* **1** a thorough or supreme person or thing. **2** an extremist.

out·back /ówtbak/ *n.* esp. *Austral.* the remote and usu. uninhabited inland districts. ▫▫ **out·back·er** *n.*

out·bal·ance /ówtbáləns/ *v.tr.* **1** count as more important than. **2** outweigh.

out·bid /ówtbíd/ *v.tr.* (**-bidding**; *past* and *past part.* **-bid**) **1** bid higher than (another person) at an auction. **2** surpass in exaggeration, etc.

out·board /ówtbawrd/ *adj., adv., & n.* ● *adj.* **1** (of a motor) portable and attachable to the outside of the stern of a boat. **2** (of a boat) having an outboard motor. ● *adj. & adv.* on, toward, or near the outside of esp. a ship, an aircraft, etc. ● *n.* **1** an outboard engine. **2** a boat with an outboard engine.

out·bound /ówtbownd/ *adj.* outward bound

out·brave /ówtbráyv/ *v.tr.* **1** outdo in bravery. **2** face defiantly.

out·break /ówtbrayk/ *n.* **1** a sudden eruption of war, disease, etc. **2** an outcrop.

out·breed·ing /ówtbreeding/ *n.* the theory or practice of breeding from animals not closely related. ▫▫ **out·breed** *v.intr. & tr.* (*past* and *past part.* **-bred**).

out·build·ing /ówtbilding/ *n.* a detached shed, barn, garage, etc., within the grounds of a main building.

out·burst /ówtbərst/ *n.* **1** an explosion of anger, etc., expressed in words. **2** an act or instance of bursting out. **3** an outcrop.

out·cast /ówtkast/ *n. & adj.* ● *n.* **1** a person cast out from or rejected by his or her home, country, society, etc. **2** a tramp or vagabond. ● *adj.* rejected; homeless; friendless.

O

out·caste *n. & v.* ● *n.* /ówtkast/ (also *attrib.*) **1** a person who has no caste, esp. in Hindu society. **2** a person who has lost his or her caste. ● *v.tr.* /ówtkast/ cause (a person) to lose his or her caste.

out·class /ówtklás/ *v.tr.* **1** belong to a higher class than. **2** defeat easily.

out·come /ówtkum/ *n.* a result; a visible effect.

out·crop /ówtkrop/ *n. & v.* ● *n.* **1 a** ▼ the emergence of a stratum, vein, or rock, at the surface. **b** a stratum, etc., emerging. **2** a noticeable manifestation or occurrence. ● *v.intr.* (**-cropped**, **-cropping**) appear as an outcrop; crop out.

out·cry /ówtkrī/ *n.* (*pl.* **-ies**) **1** the act or an instance of crying out. **2** an uproar. **3** a noisy or prolonged public protest.

out·dance /ówtdáns/ *v.tr.* surpass in dancing.

out·dat·ed /ówtdáytid/ *adj.* out of date; obsolete.

out·dis·tance /ówtdístəns/ *v.tr.* leave (a competitor) behind completely.

out·do /ówtdōō/ *v.tr.* (*3rd sing. present* **-does**; *past* **-did**; *past part.* **-done**) exceed or excel in doing or performance; surpass.

out·door /ówtdawr/ *adj.* done, existing, or used out of doors.

out·doors /owtdáwrz/ *adv. & n.* ● *adv.* out of doors. ● *n.* the open air.

out·doors·man /owtdɔ́rzmən, -dáwrz-/ *n.* a person who spends much time in outdoor activities, as fishing, camping, etc.

out·er /ówtər/ *adj.* **1** outside; external (*pierced the outer layer*). **2** farther from the center or inside. **3** objective or physical, not subjective nor psychical.

out·er·most /ówtərmōst/ *adj.* furthest from the inside; the most far out.

out·er space *n.* the universe beyond the Earth's atmosphere.

out·er·wear /ówtərwair/ *n.* clothes worn over other clothes, esp. for warmth, protection, etc.

out·face /ówtfáys/ *v.tr.* disconcert by staring or by a display of confidence.

out·fall /ówtfawl/ *n.* the mouth of a river, etc., where it empties into the sea, etc.

out·field /ówtfeeld/ *n.* **1** the outer part of a baseball field. ▷ BASEBALL. **2** outlying land. □□ **out·field·er** *n.*

out·fight /ówtfít/ *v.tr.* fight better than; beat in a fight.

out·fit /ówtfit/ *n. & v.* ● *n.* **1** a set of clothes worn or esp. designed to be worn together. **2** a complete set of equipment, etc., for a specific purpose. **3** *colloq.* a group of people regarded as a unit, etc. ● *v.tr.* (also *refl.*) (**-fitted**, **-fitting**) provide with an outfit, esp. of clothes.

out·fit·ter /ówtfitər/ *n.* **1** a business that supplies outdoor equipment, arranges tours, etc. **2** a supplier of men's clothing; a haberdasher.

out·flank /ówtflángk/ *v.tr.* **1 a** extend one's flank beyond that of (an enemy). **b** outmaneuver (an enemy) in this way. **2** get the better of (an opponent).

out·flow /ówtflō/ *n.* **1** an outward flow. **2** the amount that flows out.

out·fly /ówtflí/ *v.tr.* (**-flies**; *past* **-flew**; *past part.* **-flown**) **1** surpass in flying. **2** fly faster or farther than.

out·fox /ówtfóks/ *v.tr. colloq.* outwit.

out·gen·er·al /ówtjénərəl/ *v.tr.* **1** outdo in generalship. **2** get the better of by superior strategy or tactics.

out·go·ing *adj.* /ówtgóing/ **1** friendly; sociable; extrovert. **2** retiring from office. **3** going out or away.

out·grow /ówtgrṓ/ *v.tr.* (*past* **-grew**; *past part.*

-grown) **1** grow too big for (one's clothes). **2** leave behind (a childish habit, ailment, etc.) as one matures. **3** grow faster or taller than.

out·growth /ówtgrōth/ *n.* **1** something that grows out. **2** an offshoot; a natural product. **3** the process of growing out.

out·guess /ówtgés/ *v.tr.* guess correctly what is intended by (another person).

out·gun /ówtgún/ *v.tr.* (**-gunned**, **-gunning**) **1** surpass in military or other power or strength. **2** shoot better than.

out·house /ówt-hows/ *n.* **1** a building, esp. a shed, barn, etc., built next to or in the grounds of a house. **2** an outbuilding used as a toilet.

out·ing /ówting/ *n.* **1** a short holiday away from home, esp. of one day or part of a day; a pleasure trip; an excursion. **2** any brief journey from home. **3** an appearance in an athletic contest, race, etc. **4** *colloq.* the practice or policy of exposing the homosexuality of a prominent person.

out·jump /ówtjúmp/ *v.tr.* surpass in jumping.

out·land·er /ówtlandər/ *n.* a foreigner, alien, or stranger.

out·land·ish /owtlándish/ *adj.* **1** looking or sounding foreign. **2** bizarre; strange; unfamiliar. □□ **out·land·ish·ly** *adv.* **out·land·ish·ness** *n.*

out·last /ówtlást/ *v.tr.* last longer than (a person, thing, or duration).

out·law /ówtlaw/ *n. & v.* ● *n.* **1** a fugitive from the law. **2** *hist.* a person deprived of the protection of the law. ● *v.tr.* **1** declare an outlaw. **2** make illegal. □□ **out·law·ry** *n.*

out·lay /ówtlay/ *n.* what is spent on something.

out·let /ówtlet, -lit/ *n.* **1** a means of exit or escape. **2** (usu. foll. by *for*) a means of expression (*find an outlet for tension*). **3** an agency, distributor, or market for goods (*a new retail outlet*). **4** an electrical power receptacle.

out·line /ówtlīn/ *n. & v.* ● *n.* **1** a rough draft of a diagram, plan, etc. **2 a** a précis of a proposed novel, article, etc. **b** a verbal description of essential parts only. **3** a sketch containing only contour lines. **4** (in *sing.* or *pl.*) **a** lines enclosing or indicating an object (*the outline of a shape under the blankets*). **b** a contour. **c** an external boundary. **5** (in *pl.*) the main features or general principles (*the outlines of a plan*). ● *v.tr.* **1** draw or describe in outline. **2** mark the outline of. □ **in outline** sketched or represented as an outline.

out·live /ówtlív/ *v.tr.* **1** live longer than (another person). **2** live beyond (a specified date or time). **3** live through (an experience).

out·look /ówtlŏŏk/ *n.* **1** the prospect for the future (*the outlook is bleak*). **2** one's mental attitude (*narrow in their outlook*). **3** what is seen on looking out.

out·ly·ing /ówtlī-ing/ *adj.* situated far from a center; remote.

out·ma·neu·ver /ówtmənóŏvər/ *v.tr.* **1** use skill and cunning to secure an advantage over (a person). **2** outdo in maneuvering.

out·match /ówtmách/ *v.tr.* be more than a match for (an opponent, etc.).

out·mod·ed /ówtmódid/ *adj.* **1** no longer in fashion. **2** obsolete.

out·num·ber /ówtnúmbər/ *v.tr.* exceed in number.

out of date *adj.* (*attrib.* **out-of-date**) old fashioned; obsolete.

out-of-pock·et ex·pen·ses *n.pl.* the actual outlay of cash incurred.

out·pace /ówtpáys/ *v.tr.* **1** go faster than. **2** outdo in a contest.

out·pa·tient /ówtpayshənt/ *n.* a hospital patient whose treatment does not require overnight hospitalization.

out·per·form /ówtpərfáwrm/ *v.tr.* **1** perform better than. **2** surpass in a specified field or activity. □□ **out·per·for·mance** *n.*

out·place·ment /ówtplaysmənt/ *n.* the act or process of finding new employment for workers who have been dismissed.

out·play /ówtpláy/ *v.tr.* surpass in playing; play better than.

out·post /ówtpōst/ *n.* **1** a detachment set at a distance from the main body of an army, esp. to prevent surprise. **2** a distant branch or settlement. **3** the furthest territory of an empire.

out·pour·ing /ówtpawring/ *n.* **1** (usu. in *pl.*) a copious spoken or written expression of emotion. **2** what is poured out.

out·put /ówtpŏŏt/ *n. & v.* ● *n.* **1** the product of a process, esp. of manufacture, or of mental or artistic work. **2** the quantity or amount of this. **3** the printout, results, etc., supplied by a computer. **4** the power, etc., delivered by an apparatus. **5** a place where energy, information, etc., leaves a system. ● *v.tr.* (**-putting**; *past* and *past part.* **-put** or **-putted**) **1** put or send out. **2** (of a computer) supply (results, etc.).

out·rage /ówt-rayj/ *n. & v.* ● *n.* **1** an extreme or shocking violation of others' rights, sentiments, etc. **2** a gross offense. **3** fierce anger or resentment (*a feeling of outrage*). ● *v.tr.* **1** subject to outrage. **2** injure, insult, etc., flagrantly. **3** shock and anger.

out·ra·geous /owt-ráyjəs/ *adj.* **1** immoderate. **2** shocking. **3** grossly cruel. **4** immoral; offensive. □□ **out·ra·geous·ly** *adv.* **out·ra·geous·ness** *n.*

out·ran *past of* OUTRUN.

out·range /ówt-ráynj/ *v.tr.* (of a gun or its user) have a longer range than.

out·rank /ówt-rángk/ *v.tr.* **1** be superior in rank to. **2** take priority over.

ou·tré /ōōtráy/ *adj.* **1** outside the bounds of what is usual or proper. **2** eccentric or indecorous.

out·reach /ówtreech/ *n & v.* ● *n.* any organization's involvement with or influence in the community, esp. in the context of social welfare. ● *v.tr.* **1** reach further than. **2** surpass. **3** *poet.* stretch out (ones's arms, etc.).

out·ride /ówt-ríd/ *v.tr.* (*past* **-rode**; *past part.* **-ridden**) **1** ride better, faster, or further than. **2** (of a ship) come safely through (a storm, etc.).

out·rid·er /ówt-rídər/ *n.* **1** a mounted attendant riding ahead of, or with, a carriage, etc. **2** a motorcyclist acting as a guard in a similar manner. **3** a cowhand, etc., keeping cattle, etc., within bounds. □□ **out·rid·ing** *n.*

out·rig·ged /ówt-rigd/ *adj.* (of a boat, etc.) having outriggers.

out·rig·ger /ówt-rigər/ *n.* **1** a beam, spar, or framework, rigged out and projecting from or over a ship's side for various purposes. **2** a similar projecting beam, etc., in a building. **3** ◄ a log, etc., fixed parallel to a canoe to stabilize it. **4** a an iron bracket bearing an oarlock attached horizontally to a boat's side to increase the leverage of the oar. ▷ SCULL. **b** a boat fitted with these.

outcrop of harder, unweathered rocks

softer, weathered rocks

OUTCROP

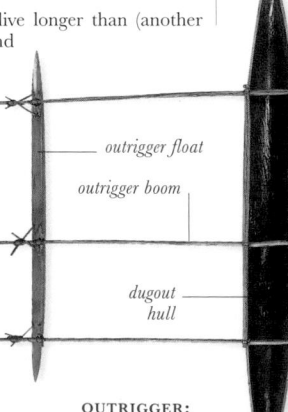

— outrigger float

outrigger boom

dugout hull

OUTRIGGER:
CANOE FITTED WITH
OUTRIGGER

out·right *adv. & adj.* ● *adv.* /owt-rít/ **1** altogether; entirely (*proved outright*). **2** not gradually, nor by degrees, nor by installments (*bought it outright*). **3** without reservation (*denied the charge outright*). ● *adj.* /ówt-rīt/ **1** downright; complete (*resentment turned to outright anger*). **2** undisputed; clear (*the outright winner*).

out·rode *past* of OUTRIDE.

out·run *v.tr.* /ówt-rún/ (**-running**; *past* **-ran**; *past part.* **-run**) **1 a** run faster or farther than. **b** escape from. **2** go beyond (a specified point or limit).

out·rush /ówt-rush/ *n.* **1** a rushing out. **2** a violent overflow.

out·sail /ówtsáyl/ *v.tr.* sail better or faster than.

out·sell /ówtsél/ *v.tr.* (*past* and *past part.* **-sold**) **1** sell more than. **2** be sold in greater quantities than.

out·set /ówtset/ *n.* the start; the beginning. □ **at** (or **from**) **the outset** at or from the beginning.

out·shine /ówtshín/ *v.tr.* (*past* and *past part.* **-shone**) shine brighter than; surpass in ability, excellence, etc.

out·shoot /ówtshóot/ *v.tr.* (*past* and *past part.* **-shot**) **1** shoot better or further than (another person). **2** attempt or score more goals, points, etc., than.

out·side *n., adj., adv., & prep.* ● *n.* /ówtsíd/ **1** the external side or surface (*painted blue on the outside*). **2** the outward aspect of a building, etc. **3** (also *attrib.*) all that is without (*learn about the outside world*). **4** a position on the outer side (*the gate opens from the outside*). **5** *colloq.* the highest computation (*it is a mile at the outside*). ● *adj.* /ówtsíd/ **1** of or on or nearer the outside. **2** not of or belonging to some circle or institution (*outside help*). **3** (of a chance, etc.) remote. **4** (of an estimate, etc.) the greatest or highest possible (*the outside price*). **5** *Baseball* (of a pitched ball) missing the strike zone by passing home plate on the side away from the batter. ● *adv.* /owtsíd/ **1** on or to the outside. **2** not within or enclosed or included. **3** *sl.* not in prison. ● *prep.* /ówtsíd/ (also *disp.* foll. by *of*) **1** to or at the exterior of (*meet me outside the post office*). **2** beyond the limits of (*outside the law*). □ **at the outside** (of an estimate, etc.) at the most. **get outside of** *sl.* eat or drink. **outside and in** outside and inside. **outside in** = INSIDE OUT.

out·side in·ter·est *n.* a hobby; an interest not connected with one's work or normal way of life.

out·sid·er /ówtsídər/ *n.* **1 a** a nonmember of some circle, party, etc. **b** an uninitiated person; a layman. **2** a competitor, applicant, etc., thought to have little chance of success.

out·size /ówtsíz/ *adj.* **1** unusually large. **2** (of garments, etc.) of an exceptionally large size.

out·skirts /ówtskərts/ *n.pl.* the outer border or fringe of a town, etc.

out·smart /ówtsmaárt/ *v.tr. colloq.* outwit; be cleverer than.

out·sold *past* and *past part.* of OUTSELL.

out·spend /ówtspénd/ *v.tr.* (*past* and *past part.* **-spent**) spend more than (one's resources or another person).

out·spo·ken /ówtspókən/ *adj.* frank in stating one's opinions. □□ **out·spo·ken·ly** *adv.* **out·spo·ken·ness** *n.*

out·spread /ówtspréd/ *adj. & v.* ● *adj.* spread out; fully extended or expanded. ● *v.tr. & intr.* (*past* and *past part.* **-spread**) spread out; expand.

out·stand·ing /ówtstánding/ *adj.* **1 a** conspicuous; eminent, esp. because of excellence. **b** (usu. foll. by *at, in*) remarkable in (a specified field). **2** (esp. of a debt) not yet settled (*$200 still outstanding*). □□ **out·stand·ing·ly** *adv.*

out·stare /ówtstáir/ *v.tr.* **1** outdo in staring. **2** abash by staring.

out·sta·tion /ówtstayshən/ *n.* a branch of a business in a remote area.

out·stay /ówtstáy/ *v.tr.* **1** stay beyond the limit of (one's welcome). **2** stay or endure longer than (another person, etc.).

out·step /ówtstép/ *v.tr.* (**-stepped, -stepping**) step outside or beyond.

out·stretch /ówtstréch/ *v.tr.* **1** (usu. as **outstretched** *adj.*) reach out or stretch out (esp. one's hands or arms). **2** reach or stretch further than.

out·strip /ówtstríp/ *v.tr.* (**-stripped, -stripping**) **1** pass in running, etc. **2** surpass in competition or relative progress or ability.

out·take /ówt-tayk/ *n.* a length of film or tape rejected in editing.

out·talk /ówt-táwk/ *v.tr.* outdo or overcome in talking.

out·think /ówt-thíngk/ *v.tr.* (*past* and *past part.* **-thought**) outdo in thinking.

out·thrust /ówt-thrúst/ *adj.* extended; projected (*with outthrust arms*).

out·turn /ówt-tərn/ *n.* **1** the quantity produced. **2** the result of a process or sequence of events.

out·vote /ówtvót/ *v.tr.* defeat by a majority of votes.

out·ward /ówt-word/ *adj., adv., & n.* ● *adj.* **1** situated on or directed toward the outside. **2** going out (*on the outward voyage*). **3** external; apparent; superficial (*in all outward respects*). ● *adv.* (also **outwards**) in an outward direction. ● *n.* the outward appearance of something. □□ **out·ward·ly** *adv.*

out·ward·ness /ówt-wordnis/ *n.* external existence; objectivity.

out·wards var. of OUTWARD *adv.*

out·wash /ówt-wosh, -wawsh/ *n.* ▼ the material carried from a glacier by meltwater and deposited beyond the moraine. ▷ GLACIER

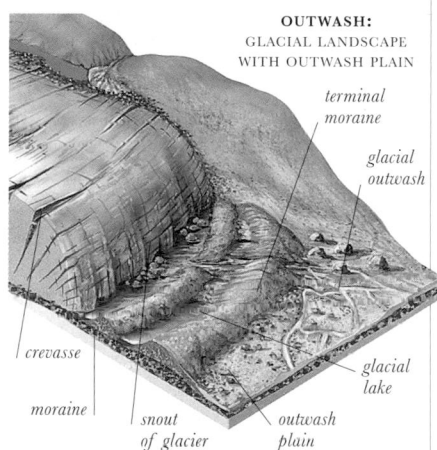

OUTWASH:
GLACIAL LANDSCAPE
WITH OUTWASH PLAIN

terminal moraine

glacial outwash

crevasse

moraine

snout of glacier

outwash plain

glacial lake

out·weigh /ówt-wáy/ *v.tr.* exceed in weight, value, importance, or influence.

out·wit /ówt-wít/ *v.tr.* (**-witted, -witting**) be too clever or crafty for; deceive by greater ingenuity.

out·with /ówt-wíth/ *prep. Sc.* outside; beyond.

out·work *v. & n.* ● *v.* /ówt-wórk/ work harder, faster, or longer than. ● *n.* /ówt-wərk/ an advanced or detached part of a fortification.

ou·zel /ōōzəl/ *n.* (also **ou·sel**) **1** = RING OUZEL. **2** (in full **water ouzel**) = DIPPER. **3** *archaic* a blackbird.

ou·zo /ōōzō/ *n.* (*pl.* **-os**) a Greek anise-flavored liqueur.

o·va *pl.* of OVUM.

o·val /ōvəl/ *adj. & n.* ● *adj.* **1** egg-shaped; ellipsoidal. **2** having the outline of an egg. ● *n.* **1** an egg-shaped or elliptical closed curve. **2** any object with an oval outline. **3** *Austral.* a field for Australian Rules football.

O·val Of·fice *n.* the office of the US president in the White House.

o·va·ry /ōvəree/ *n.* (*pl.* **-ies**) **1** ► each of the female reproductive organs in which ova are produced. ▷ ENDOCRINE, REPRODUCTIVE ORGANS. **2** the hollow base of the carpel of a flower, containing one or more ovules. ▷ FLOWER. □□ **o·var·i·an** /ōváireeən/ *adj.* **o·var·i·ec·to·my** /-ree-éktəmee/ *n.* (*pl.* **-ies**) (in sense 1). **o·var·i·ot·o·my** /-reeótəmee/ *n.* (*pl.* **-ies**) (in sense 1). **o·va·ri·tis** /-rítis/ *n.* (in sense 1).

o·vate /ōvayt/ *adj. Biol.* egg-shaped as a solid or in outline; oval.

o·va·tion /ōváyshən/ *n.* an enthusiastic reception, esp. spontaneous and sustained applause. □□ **o·va·tion·al** *adj.*

ov·en /úvən/ *n.* **1** an enclosed compartment of brick, stone, or metal for cooking food. **2** a chamber for heating or drying.

ov·en·proof /úvənproof/ *adj.* suitable for use in an oven; heat-resistant.

ov·en·ware /úvənwair/ *n.* dishes that can be used for cooking food in the oven.

o·ver /ōvər/ *adv., prep., & adj.* ● *adv.* expressing movement or position or state above or beyond something stated or implied: **1** outward and downward from a brink or from any erect position (*knocked the man over*). **2** so as to cover or touch a whole surface (*paint it over*). **3** so as to produce a fold, or reverse a position. **4 a** across a street or other space (*decided to cross over*). **b** for a visit, etc. (*invited them over last night*). **5** with transference or change from one hand or part to another (*handed them over*). **6** with motion above something (*climb over*). **7** from beginning to end with repetition or detailed concentration (*think it over*). **8** in excess (*left over*). **9** for a later time (*hold it over*). **10** at an end (*the crisis is over*). **11** (in full **over to you**) (as *int.*) (in radio conversations, etc.) said to indicate that it is the other person's turn to speak. ● *prep.* **1** above, in, or to a position higher than. **2** out and down from (*fell over the cliff*). **3** so as to cover (*a hat over his eyes*). **4** above and across (*a bridge over the Hudson*). **5** concerning; as a result of; while occupied with (*laughed over a good joke*). **6 a** in superiority of; in charge of (*a victory over the enemy*). **b** in preference to. **7** divided by. **8 a** throughout; covering (*a blush spread over his face*). **b** so as to deal with completely (*went over the plans*). **9 a** for the duration of (*stay over Saturday night*). **b** at any point during the course of (*I'll do it over the weekend*). **10** more than (*bids of over $50*). **11** transmitted by (*heard it over the radio*). **12** in comparison with (*gained 20% over last year*). **13** having recovered from (*am now over my cold*). ● *adj.* **1** upper; outer. **2** superior. **3** extra. □ **begin** (or **start**, etc.) **over** begin again. **get it over with** do or undergo something unpleasant, etc., so as to be rid of it. **not over** not very (*not over friendly*). **over again** once again. **over against** in an opposite situation to; adjacent to. **over and above** in addition to (*$100 over and above the asking price*). **over and over** so that the same thing comes up again and again. **over one's head** see HEAD. **over the hill** see HILL.

o·ver·a·bun·dant /ōvərəbúndənt/ *adj.* in excessive quantity. □□ **o·ver·a·bun·dance** *n.* **o·ver·a·bun·dant·ly** *adv.*

o·ver·a·chieve /ōvərəchéev/ *v.* **1** *intr.* do more than might be expected (esp. scholastically). **2** *tr.* achieve more than (an expected goal or objective, etc.). □□ **o·ver·a·chieve·ment** *n.* **o·ver·a·chiev·er** *n.*

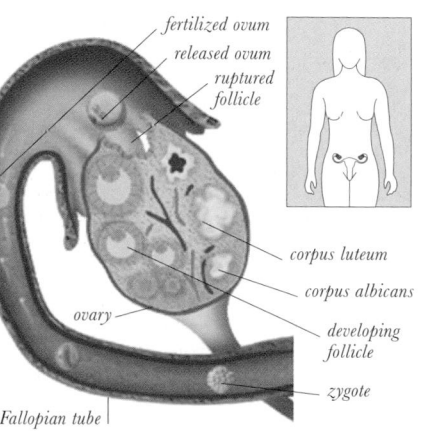

fertilized ovum
released ovum
ruptured follicle

corpus luteum
corpus albicans
developing follicle
zygote

ovary

Fallopian tube

OVARY: CROSS SECTION OF A HUMAN OVARY
AND FALLOPIAN TUBE

o·ver·act /ṓvərákt/ *v.tr. & intr.* act in an exaggerated manner.

o·ver·ac·tive /ṓvəráktiv/ *adj.* excessively active. □□ **o·ver·ac·tiv·i·ty** /-tívitee/ *n.*

o·ver·age¹ /ṓvəráyj/ *adj.* **1** having attained a certain age limit. **2** too old.

o·ver·age² /ṓvərij/ *n.* a surplus or excess, esp. an amount greater than estimated.

o·ver·all *adj., adv., & n.* ● *adj.* /ṓvərawl/ **1** from end to end (*overall length*). **2** inclusive of all (*overall cost*). ● *adv.* /ṓvəráwl/ taken as a whole (*overall, the performance was excellent*). ● *n.* /ṓvərawl/ (in *pl.*) protective trousers, dungarees, etc., usually with a bib, worn by workmen, etc. □□ **o·ver·alled** /ṓvərawld/ *adj.*

o·ver·am·bi·tious /ṓvərambíshəs/ *adj.* excessively ambitious. □□ **o·ver·am·bi·tion** *n.* **o·ver·am·bi·tious·ly** *adv.*

o·ver·anx·ious /ṓvərángkshəs/ *adj.* excessively anxious. □□ **o·ver·anx·i·e·ty** /-angzí-itee/ *n.* **o·ver·anx·ious·ly** *adv.*

o·ver·arch /ṓvəráarch/ *v.tr.* form an arch over.

o·ver·arch·ing /ṓvəráarching/ *adj.* **1** forming an arch. **2** dominating.

o·ver·arm /ṓvəraarm/ *adj. & adv.* **1** ▶ thrown with the hand above the shoulder (*an overarm tennis serve*). **2** *Swimming* with one or both arms lifted out of the water during a stroke.

o·ver·ate *past* of OVEREAT.

o·ver·awe /ṓvər-áw/ *v.tr.* **1** restrain by awe. **2** keep in awe.

o·ver·bal·ance /ṓvərbáləns/ *v.* **1** *tr.* outweigh. **2** *intr.* fall over; capsize.

o·ver·bear /ṓvərbáir/ *v.tr.* (*past* **-bore**; *past part.* **-borne**) **1** upset by force or emotional pressure. **2** put down or repress by power or authority.

o·ver·bear·ing /ṓvərbéring/ *adj.* **1** domineering; masterful. **2** overpowerful. □□ **o·ver·bear·ing·ly** *adv.* **o·ver·bear·ing·ness** *n.*

o·ver·bid *v. & n.* ● *v.tr.* /ṓvərbíd/ (**-bidding**; *past* and *past part.* **-bid**) **1** make a higher bid than. **2** (also *absol.*) *Bridge* **a** bid more on (one's hand) than warranted. **b** overcall. ● *n.* /ṓvərbid/ a bid that is higher than another, or higher than is justified. □□ **o·ver·bid·der** *n.*

o·ver·bite /ṓvərbīt/ *n.* a condition in which the teeth of the upper jaw project forward over those of the lower jaw.

o·ver·blouse /ṓvərblows, -blowz/ *n.* a garment like a blouse, but worn without tucking it into a skirt or slacks.

o·ver·blown /ṓvərblṓn/ *adj.* **1** excessively inflated or pretentious. **2** (of a flower or a woman's beauty, etc.) past its prime.

o·ver·board /ṓvərbáwrd/ *adv.* from a ship into the water (*fall overboard*). □ **go overboard 1** be highly enthusiastic. **2** behave immoderately. **throw overboard** discard.

o·ver·book /ṓvərbŏŏk/ *v.tr.* (also *absol.*) make too many bookings for (an aircraft, hotel, etc.).

o·ver·bore *past* of OVERBEAR.

o·ver·borne *past part.* of OVERBEAR.

o·ver·bur·den /ṓvərbárd'n/ *v.tr.* burden (a person, thing, etc.) to excess. □□ **o·ver·bur·den·some** *adj.*

o·ver·call *v. & n.* ● *v.tr.* /ṓvərkáwl/ (also *absol.*) *Bridge* make a higher bid than (a previous bid or opponent). ● *n.* /ṓvərkawl/ an act of overcalling.

o·ver·came *past* of OVERCOME.

o·ver·ca·pac·i·ty /ṓvərkəpásitee/ *n.* a state of saturation or an excess of productive capacity.

o·ver·cap·i·tal·ize /ṓvərkápit'līz/ *v.tr.* estimate the capital of (a company, etc.) too high.

o·ver·care·ful /ṓvərkáirfŏŏl/ *adj.* excessively careful. □□ **o·ver·care·ful·ly** *adv.*

o·ver·cast /ṓvərkást/ *adj. & v.* ● *adj.* **1** covered with cloud. **2** (in sewing) edged with stitching to prevent fraying. ▷ STITCH. ● *v.tr.* (*past* and *past part.* **-cast**) **1** cover (the sky, etc.) with clouds or darkness. **2** stitch over to prevent fraying.

o·ver·cau·tious /ṓvərkáwshəs/ *adj.* excessively cautious. □□ **o·ver·cau·tion** *n.* **o·ver·cau·tious·ly** *adv.* **o·ver·cau·tious·ness** *n.*

o·ver·charge /ṓvərcháarj/ *v.tr.* **1 a** charge too high a price to (a person) for (a thing). **b** charge (a specified sum) beyond the right price. **2** put too much charge into (a battery, etc.).

o·ver·coat /ṓvərkōt/ *n.* a heavy coat, esp. one worn over indoor clothes.

o·ver·come /ṓvərkúm/ *v.* (*past* **-came**; *past part.* **-come**) **1** *tr.* defeat. **2** *tr.* (as **overcome** *adj.*) **a** made helpless. **b** (usu. foll. by *with*, *by*) affected by (emotion, etc.). **3** *intr.* be victorious.

o·ver·com·pen·sate /ṓvərkómpensayt/ *v.* **1** *tr.* (usu. foll. by *for*) compensate excessively for (something). **2** *intr. Psychol.* strive for power, etc., in an exaggerated way, esp. to make amends for a grievance, handicap, etc. □□ **o·ver·com·pen·sa·tion** /-áyshən/ *n.* **o·ver·com·pen·sa·to·ry** /-kəmpénsitawree/ *adj.*

o·ver·con·fi·dent /ṓvərkónfidənt/ *adj.* excessively confident. □□ **o·ver·con·fi·dence** *n.* **o·ver·con·fi·dent·ly** *adv.*

o·ver·cook /ṓvərkŏŏk/ *v.tr.* cook too much or for too long. □□ **o·ver·cooked** *adj.*

o·ver·crit·i·cal /ṓvərkrítikəl/ *adj.* excessively critical; quick to find fault.

o·ver·crowd /ṓvərkrówd/ *v.tr.* fill (a space, object, etc.) beyond what is usual or comfortable. □□ **o·ver·crowd·ing** *n.*

o·ver·de·vel·op /ṓvərdivéləp/ *v.tr.* **1** develop too much. **2** *Photog.* treat with developer for too long.

o·ver·do /ṓvərdŏŏ/ *v.tr.* (*3rd sing. present* **-does**; *past* **-did**; *past part.* **-done**) **1** carry to excess (*I think you overdid the sarcasm*). **2** (esp. as **overdone** *adj.*) overcook. □ **overdo it** (or **things**) exhaust oneself.

o·ver·dose /ṓvərdōs/ *n. & v.* ● *n.* an excessive dose (of a drug, etc.). ● *v.* **1** *tr.* give an excessive dose of (a drug, etc.) to (a person). **2** *intr.* take an excessive dose of a drug. □□ **o·ver·dos·age** /ṓvərdósij/ *n.*

o·ver·draft /ṓvərdraft/ *n.* **1** a deficit in a bank account caused by drawing more money than is credited to it. **2** the amount of this.

o·ver·draw /ṓvərdráw/ *v.* (*past* **-drew**; *past part.* **-drawn**) **1** *tr.* **a** draw a sum of money in excess of the amount credited to (one's bank account). **b** (as **overdrawn** *adj.*) having overdrawn one's account. **2** *intr.* overdraw one's account.

o·ver·dress *v. & n.* ● *v.* /ṓvərdrés/ *intr.* dress with too much formality. ● *n.* /ṓvərdres/ a dress worn over another dress or a blouse, etc.

o·ver·drive /ṓvərdrīv/ *n.* **1 a** a mechanism in a motor vehicle providing a gear ratio higher than that of the usual gear. **b** an additional speed-increasing gear. **2** (usu. prec. by *in*, *into*) a state of high or excessive activity.

o·ver·dub /ṓvərdub/ *v. & n.* ● *v.tr.* record (additional sounds) on an existing recording. ● *n.* an instance of overdubbing.

o·ver·due /ṓvərdŏŏ, -dyŏŏ/ *adj.* **1** past the time when due or ready. **2** not yet paid, arrived, born, etc., although after the expected time.

o·ver·ea·ger /ṓvəréegər/ *adj.* excessively eager. □□ **o·ver·ea·ger·ly** *adv.* **o·ver·ea·ger·ness** *n.*

o·ver eas·y *adj. N. Amer.* (of an egg) fried on both sides, with the yolk remaining slightly liquid.

o·ver·eat /ṓvəréet/ *v.intr. & refl.* (*past* **-ate**; *past part.* **-eaten**) eat too much.

o·ver·e·lab·o·rate /ṓvərilábərət/ *adj.* excessively elaborate. □□ **o·ver·e·lab·o·rate·ly** *adv.*

o·ver·e·mo·tion·al /ṓvərimṓshənəl/ *adj.* excessively emotional. □□ **o·ver·e·mo·tion·al·ly** *adv.*

o·ver·em·pha·sis /ṓvərémfəsis/ *n.* excessive emphasis. □□ **o·ver·em·pha·size** /-fəsīz/ *v.tr. & intr.*

o·ver·en·thu·si·asm /ṓvərinthŏŏzeeazəm, -thyŏŏ-/ *n.* excessive enthusiasm. □□ **o·ver·en·thu·si·as·tic** /-zeeástik/ *adj.* **o·ver·en·thu·si·as·ti·cal·ly** *adv.*

o·ver·es·ti·mate *v. & n.* ● *v.tr.* /ṓvəréstimayt/ form too high an estimate of (a person, ability, cost, etc.). ● *n.* /ṓvəréstimit/ too high an estimate. □□ **o·ver·es·ti·ma·tion** /-áyshən/ *n.*

o·ver·ex·cite /ṓvəriksít/ *v.tr.* excite excessively. □□ **o·ver·ex·cite·ment** *n.*

o·ver·ex·er·cise /ṓvəréksərsīz/ *v. & n.* ● *v.* **1** *tr.* use (a part of the body, one's authority, etc.) too much. **2** *intr.* do too much exercise. ● *n.* excessive exercise.

o·ver·ex·ert /ṓvərigzárt/ *v.tr. & refl.* exert too much. □□ **o·ver·ex·er·tion** /-zérshən/ *n.*

o·ver·ex·pose /ṓvərikspṓz/ *v.tr.* (also *absol.*) **1** expose too much, esp. to the public eye. **2** *Photog.* expose (film) for too long a time. □□ **o·ver·ex·po·sure** /-spṓzhər/ *n.*

o·ver·ex·tend /ṓvəriksténd/ *v.tr.* **1** extend (a thing) too far. **2** (also *refl.*) take on (oneself) or impose on (another person) an excessive burden of work.

o·ver·fa·mil·iar /ṓvərfəmílyər/ *adj.* excessively familiar.

o·ver·fa·tigue /ṓvərfətéeg/ *n.* excessive fatigue.

o·ver·feed /ṓvərféed/ *v.tr.* (*past* and *past part.* **-fed**) feed excessively.

o·ver·fill /ṓvərfíl/ *v.tr. & intr.* fill to excess.

o·ver·fish /ṓvərfísh/ *v.tr.* deplete (a stream, etc.) by too much fishing.

o·ver·flow *v. & n.* ● *v.* /ṓvərflṓ/ **1** *tr.* **a** flow over (the brim, etc.). **b** flow over the brim or limits of. **2** *intr.* **a** (of a receptacle, etc.) be so full that the contents overflow it. **b** (of contents) overflow a container. **3** *tr.* (of a crowd, etc.) extend beyond the limits of (a room, etc.). **4** *tr.* flood (a surface or area). **5** *intr.* (foll. by *with*) be full of. ● *n.* /ṓvərflō/ (also *attrib.*) **1** what overflows or is superfluous (*mop up the overflow*). **2** an instance of overflowing. **3** (esp. in a bath or sink) an outlet for excess water, etc. **4** *Computing* the generation of a number having more digits than the assigned location.

o·ver·fly /ṓvərflī/ *v.tr.* (**-flies**; *past* **-flew**; *past part.* **-flown**) fly over or beyond (a place or territory). □□ **o·ver·flight** /ṓvərflīt/ *n.*

o·ver·fond /ṓvərfónd/ *adj.* (often foll. by *of*) having too great an affection or liking (for a person or thing). □□ **o·ver·fond·ly** *adv.* **o·ver·fond·ness** *n.*

o·ver·full /ṓvərfŏŏl/ *adj.* excessively full.

o·ver·gen·er·al·ize /ṓvərjénərəlīz/ *v.* **1** *intr.* draw general conclusions from inadequate data, etc. **2** *intr.* argue more widely than is justified by the available evidence, etc. **3** *tr.* draw an overgeneral conclusion from (data, etc.). □□ **o·ver·gen·er·al·i·za·tion** *n.*

o·ver·gen·er·ous /ṓvərjénərəs/ *adj.* excessively generous. □□ **o·ver·gen·er·ous·ly** *adv.*

o·ver·ground /ṓvərgrownd/ *adj.* **1** raised above the ground. **2** not underground.

o·ver·grow /ṓvərgrṓ/ *v.tr.* (*past* **-grew**; *past part.* **-grown**) **1** (as **overgrown** *adj.*) **a** abnormally large (*an overgrown eggplant*). **b** grown over with vegetation (*an overgrown pond*). **2** grow over, esp. so as to choke (*brambles have overgrown the pathway*). □□ **o·ver·growth** *n.*

o·ver·hand /ṓvərhand/ *adj. & adv.* (in tennis, baseball, etc.) thrown or played with the hand above the shoulder; overarm.

o·ver·hang *v. & n.* ● *v.* /ṓvərháng/ (*past* and *past part.* **-hung**) **1** *tr. & intr.* hang over. **2** *tr.* menace; threaten. ● *n.* /ṓvərhang/ **1** the overhanging part of a structure or rock formation. **2** the amount by which this projects.

o·ver·haul *v. & n.* ● *v.tr.* /ṓvərháwl/ **1 a** take to pieces in order to examine. **b** examine the condition of (and repair if necessary). **2** overtake. ● *n.* /ṓvərhawl/ a thorough examination, with repairs if necessary.

OVERARM TENNIS STROKE

o·ver·head *adv., adj., & n.* ● *adv.* /ṓvərhéd/ **1** above one's head. **2** in the sky or on the floor above. ● *adj.* /ṓvərhed/ **1** (of a driving mechanism, etc.) above the object driven. **2** (of expenses) arising from general operating costs, as distinct from particular business transactions. ● *n.* /ṓvərhed/ overhead expenses.

o·ver·head pro·jec·tor *n.* a device that projects an enlarged image of a transparency onto a surface above and behind the user.

o·ver·hear /ṓvərheér/ *v.tr.* (*past* and *past part.* **-heard**) (also *absol.*) hear as an eavesdropper or as an unperceived or unintentional listener.

o·ver·heat /ṓvərheét/ *v.* **1** *tr. & intr.* make or become too hot. **2** *tr.* (as **overheated** *adj.*) too passionate about a matter.

o·ver·in·dulge /ṓvərindúlj/ *v.tr. & intr.* indulge to excess. □□ **o·ver·in·dul·gence** *n.* **o·ver·in·dul·gent** *adj.*

o·ver·in·sure /ṓvərinshoŏr/ *v.tr.* insure (property, etc.) for more than its real value; insure excessively. □□ **o·ver·in·sur·ance** *n.*

o·ver·joyed /ṓvərjóyd/ *adj.* (often foll. by *at, to hear,* etc.) filled with great joy.

o·ver·kill /ṓvərkil/ *n.* **1** the amount by which capacity for destruction exceeds what is necessary for victory or annihilation. **2** excess; excessive behavior.

o·ver·lad·en /ṓvərláyd'n/ *adj.* bearing or carrying too large a load.

o·ver·laid *past* and *past part.* of OVERLAY[1].

o·ver·lain *past part.* of OVERLIE.

o·ver·land /ṓvərland, -lənd/ *adj. & adv.* also /ṓvərlánd/ **1** by land. **2** not by sea.

o·ver·lap *v. & n.* ● *v.* /ṓvərláp/ (**-lapped, -lapping**) **1** *tr.* (of part of an object) partly cover (another object). **2** *tr.* cover and extend beyond. **3** *intr.* (of two things) partly coincide. ● *n.* /ṓvərlap/ **1** an instance of overlapping. **2** the amount of this.

o·ver·lay[1] *v. & n.* ● *v.tr.* /ṓvərláy/ (*past* and *past part.* **-laid**) **1** lay over. **2** (foll. by *with*) cover the surface of (a thing) with (a coating, etc.). **3** overlie. ● *n.* /ṓvərlay/ a thing laid over another.

o·ver·lay[2] *past* of OVERLIE.

o·ver·leaf /ṓvərleéf/ *adv.* on the other side of the leaf (of a book).

o·ver·lie /ṓvərlí/ *v.tr.* (**-lying**; *past* **-lay**; *past part.* **-lain**) **1** lie on top of. **2** smother (a child, etc.) by lying on top.

o·ver·load *v. & n.* ● *v.tr.* /ṓvərlṓd/ force (a person, thing, etc.) beyond normal or reasonable capacity. ● *n.* /ṓvərlṓd/ an excessive quantity.

o·ver·look *v.tr.* /ṓvərloŏk/ **1** ignore or condone (an offense, etc.). **2** be higher than. **3** supervise; oversee. **4** bewitch with the evil eye. □□ **o·ver·look·er** *n.*

o·ver·lord /ṓvərlawrd/ *n.* a supreme lord. □□ **o·ver·lord·ship** *n.*

o·ver·ly /ṓvərlee/ *adv.* excessively; too.

o·ver·ly·ing *pres. part.* of OVERLIE.

o·ver·man *v.tr.* /ṓvərmán/ (**-manned, -manning**) provide with too large a crew, staff, etc.

o·ver·man·tel /ṓvərmant'l/ *n.* ornamental shelves, etc., over a mantelpiece.

o·ver·mas·ter /ṓvərmástər/ *v.tr.* master completely; conquer. □□ **o·ver·mas·ter·ing** *adj.* **o·ver·mas·ter·y** *n.*

o·ver·much /ṓvərmúch/ *adv. & adj.* ● *adv.* excessively. ● *adj.* excessive.

o·ver·nice /ṓvərnís/ *adj.* excessively fussy, etc. □□ **o·ver·nice·ness** *n.*

o·ver·night *adv. & adj.* ● *adv.* /ṓvərnít/ **1** for the duration of a night (*stay overnight*). **2** during the course of a night. **3** suddenly (*the situation changed overnight*). ● *adj.* /ṓvərnīt/ **1** for use overnight (*an overnight bag*). **2** done, etc., overnight (*an overnight stop*).

o·ver·night·er /ṓvərnítər/ *n.* **1** a person who stops at a place overnight. **2** an overnight bag.

o·ver·paid *past* and *past part.* of OVERPAY.

o·ver·par·tic·u·lar /ṓvərpərtíkyələr, -pətík-/ *adj.* excessively particular or fussy.

o·ver·pass /ṓvərpas/ *n.* a road or railroad line that passes over another by means of a bridge.

o·ver·pay /ṓvərpáy/ *v.tr.* (*past* and *past part.* **-paid**) recompense (a person, service, etc.) too highly. □□ **o·ver·pay·ment** *n.*

o·ver·play /ṓvərpláy/ *v.tr.* give undue importance to. □ **overplay one's hand 1** be unduly optimistic about one's capabilities. **2** spoil a good case by exaggerating its value.

o·ver·pop·u·lat·ed /ṓvərpópyəlaytid/ *adj.* having too large a population. □□ **o·ver·pop·u·la·tion** /-láyshən/ *n.*

o·ver·pow·er /ṓvərpówr/ *v.tr.* **1** reduce to submission. **2** make (a thing) ineffective by greater intensity. **3** (of heat, emotion, etc.) overwhelm. □□ **o·ver·pow·er·ing** *adj.* **o·ver·pow·er·ing·ly** *adv.*

o·ver·price /ṓvərprís/ *v.tr.* price (a thing) too highly.

o·ver·print *v. & n.* ● *v.tr.* /ṓvərprínt/ **1** print further matter on (a surface already printed, esp. a postage stamp). **2** print (further matter) in this way. ● *n.* /ṓvərprint/ the words, etc., overprinted.

o·ver·pro·duce /ṓvərprədoōs, -dyoōs/ *v.tr.* (usu. *absol.*) **1** produce more of (a commodity) than is wanted. **2** produce to an excessive degree. □□ **o·ver·pro·duc·tion** /-dúkshən/ *n.*

o·ver·pro·tec·tive /ṓvərprətéktiv/ *adj.* excessively protective.

o·ver·qual·i·fied /ṓvərkwólifīd/ *adj.* too highly qualified for a particular job.

o·ver·ran *past* of OVERRUN.

o·ver·rate /ṓvəráyt/ *v.tr.* assess too highly.

o·ver·reach /ṓvəreéch/ *v.tr.* circumvent; outwit. □ **overreach oneself 1** strain oneself by reaching too far. **2** defeat one's object by going too far.

o·ver·re·act /ṓvəreeákt/ *v.intr.* respond more forcibly, etc., than is justified. □□ **o·ver·re·ac·tion** /-ákshən/ *n.*

o·ver·re·fine /ṓvərifín/ *v.tr.* (also *absol.*) **1** refine too much. **2** make too subtle distinctions in (an argument, etc.)

o·ver·ride *v. & n.* ● *v.tr.* /ṓvəríd/ (*past* **-rode**, *past part.* **-ridden**) **1** (often as **overriding** *adj.*) have or claim precedence over (*an overriding consideration*). **2 a** intervene and make ineffective. **b** interrupt the action of (an automatic device), esp. to take manual control. **3 a** trample down or underfoot. **b** supersede arrogantly. ● *n.* /ṓvərīd/ **1** the action of suspending an automatic function. **2** a device for this.

o·ver·ripe /ṓvəríp/ *adj.* (esp. of fruit, etc.) past its best; excessively ripe.

o·ver·rode *past* of OVERRIDE.

o·ver·rule /ṓvəroōl/ *v.tr.* **1** set aside (a decision, etc.) by exercising a superior authority. **2** annul a decision by or reject a proposal of (a person) in this way.

o·ver·run *v. & n.* ● *v.tr.* /ṓvərún/ (**-running**; *past* **-ran**; *past part.* **-run**) **1** (of pests, weeds, etc.) swarm or spread over. **2** conquer or ravage (territory) by force. **3** (of time, expenditure, etc.) exceed (a fixed limit). **4** *Printing* carry over (a word, etc.) to the next line or page. ● *n.* /ṓvərun/ **1** an instance of overrunning. **2** the amount of this.

o·ver·saw *past* of OVERSEE.

o·ver·scru·pu·lous /ṓvərskroōpyələs/ *adj.* excessively particular.

o·ver·seas *adv. & adj.* ● *adv.* /ṓvərseéz/ abroad. ● *adj.* /ṓvərseez/ foreign; across or beyond the sea.

o·ver·see /ṓvərseé/ *v.tr.* (**-sees**; *past* **-saw**; *past part.* **-seen**) officially supervise. □□ **o·ver·seer** *n.*

o·ver·sell /ṓvərsél/ *v.tr.* (*past* and *past part.* **-sold**) (also *absol.*) **1** sell more of (a commodity, etc.) than one can deliver. **2** exaggerate the merits of.

o·ver·sen·si·tive /ṓvərsénsitiv/ *adj.* easily hurt or too quick to react. □□ **o·ver·sen·si·tive·ness** *n.* **o·ver·sen·si·tiv·i·ty** /-tívitee/ *n.*

o·ver·sew /ṓvərsṓ/ *v.tr.* (*past part.* **-sewn** or **-sewed**) sew with stitches that pass over an edge.

o·ver·sexed /ṓvərsékst/ *adj.* having unusually strong sexual desires.

o·ver·shad·ow /ṓvərshádō/ *v.tr.* **1** appear much more prominent or important than. **2** cast into the shade.

o·ver·shoe /ṓvərshoō/ *n.* a shoe of rubber, etc., worn over another as protection from wet, cold, etc.

o·ver·shoot *v. & n.* ● *v.tr.* /ṓvərshoōt/ (*past* and *past part.* **-shot**) **1** pass or send beyond (a target or limit). **2** (of an aircraft) fly beyond (the runway) when landing or taking off. ● *n.* /ṓvərshoōt/ **1** the act of overshooting. **2** the amount of this. □ **overshoot the mark** go beyond what is intended or proper.

o·ver·sight /ṓvərsīt/ *n.* **1** a failure to notice something. **2** an inadvertent mistake. **3** supervision.

o·ver·sim·pli·fy /ṓvərsímplifī/ *v.tr.* (**-ies, -ied**) (also *absol.*) distort (a problem, etc.) by stating it in too simple terms. □□ **o·ver·sim·pli·fi·ca·tion** *n.*

o·ver·size /ṓvərsīz/ *adj.* (also **-sized** /-sīzd/) of more than the usual size.

o·ver·skirt /ṓvərskərt/ *n.* an outer or second skirt.

o·ver·sleep /ṓvərsleép/ *v.intr. & refl.* (*past* and *past part.* **-slept**) continue sleeping beyond the intended time of waking.

o·ver·sold *past* and *past part.* of OVERSELL.

o·ver·so·lic·i·tous /ṓvərsəlísitəs/ *adj.* excessively worried, anxious, eager, etc. □□ **o·ver·so·lic·i·tude** /-sitoōd, -tyoōd/ *n.*

o·ver·spe·cial·ize /ṓvərspéshəlīz/ *v.intr.* concentrate too much on one aspect or area. □□ **o·ver·spe·cial·i·za·tion** *n.*

o·ver·spend /ṓvərspénd/ *v.* (*past* and *past part.* **-spent**) **1** *intr. & refl.* spend too much. **2** *tr.* spend more than (a specified amount).

o·ver·spill /ṓvərspil/ *n.* what is spilled over or overflows.

o·ver·spread /ṓvərspréd/ *v.tr.* (*past* and *past part.* **-spread**) **1** become spread or diffused over. **2** cover or occupy the surface of.

o·ver·staff /ṓvərstáf/ *v.tr.* provide with too large a staff.

o·ver·state /ṓvərstáyt/ *v.tr.* **1** state (esp. a case or argument) too strongly. **2** exaggerate. □□ **o·ver·state·ment** *n.*

o·ver·stay /ṓvərstáy/ *v.tr.* stay longer than (one's welcome, a time limit, etc.).

o·ver·steer /ṓvərsteér/ *v. & n.* ● *v.intr.* (of a motor vehicle) have a tendency to turn more sharply than was intended. ● *n.* this tendency.

o·ver·step /ṓvərstép/ *v.tr.* (**-stepped, -stepping**) **1** pass beyond (a boundary or mark). **2** violate (certain standards of behavior, etc.).

o·ver·stock /ṓvərstók/ *v. & n.* ● *v.tr.* stock excessively. ● *n.* stock that is in excess of need or demand.

o·ver·strain /ṓvərstráyn/ *v.tr.* strain too much.

o·ver·stress /ṓvərstrés/ *v.tr.* stress too much.

o·ver·stretch /ṓvərstréch/ *v.tr.* **1** stretch too much. **2** (esp. as **overstretched** *adj.*) make excessive demands on (resources, a person, etc.).

o·ver·strung /ṓvərstrúng/ *adj.* (of a person, disposition, etc.) intensely strained, highly strung.

o·ver·stuff /ṓvərstúf/ *v.tr.* **1** stuff more than is necessary. **2** (as **overstuffed** *adj.*) (of furniture) made soft and comfortable by thick upholstery.

o·ver·sub·scribe /ṓvərsəbskríb/ *v.tr.* (usu. as **oversubscribed** *adj.*) subscribe for more than the amount available of (*the offer was oversubscribed*).

o·ver·sub·tle /ṓvərsút'l/ *adj.* excessively subtle; not plain or clear.

o·ver·sup·ply /ṓvərsəplí/ *v. & n.* ● *v.tr.* (**-ies, -ied**) supply with too much. ● *n.* an excessive supply.

o·ver·sus·cep·ti·ble /ṓvərsəséptibəl/ *adj.* too susceptible or vulnerable.

o·vert /ōvért, ṓvərt/ *adj.* done openly. □□ **o·vert·ly** *adv.*

o·ver·take /ṓvərtáyk/ *v.tr.* (*past* **-took**; *past part.* **-taken**) **1** (of a misfortune, etc.) come suddenly upon.

o·ver·tax /ōvərtáks/ *v.tr.* **1** make excessive demands on (a person's strength, etc.). **2** tax too heavily.

o·ver-the-coun·ter *adj.* (of medicine) sold without a prescription.

o·ver-the-top *adj. Brit. colloq.* (esp. of behavior, etc.) outrageous, excessive.

o·ver·throw *v. & n.* ● *v.tr.* /ōvərthrō/ (*past* **-threw**; *past part.* **-thrown**) **1** remove forcibly from power. **2** put an end to (an institution, etc.). **3** conquer; overcome. **4** knock down; upset. **5** *Baseball* **a** (of a fielder) throw beyond the intended place. **b** (of a pitcher) throw too vigorously. ● *n.* /ōvərthrō/ a defeat or downfall.

o·ver·time /ōvərtīm/ *n. & adv.* ● *n.* **1** the time during which a person works at a job in addition to the regular hours. **2** payment for this. ● *adv.* in addition to regular hours.

o·ver·tire /ōvərtír/ *v.tr. & refl.* exhaust or wear out (esp. an invalid, etc.).

o·ver·tone /ōvərtōn/ *n.* **1** *Mus.* any of the tones above the lowest in a harmonic series. **2** a subtle or elusive quality or implication (*sinister overtones*).

o·ver·train /ōvərtráyn/ *v.tr. & intr.* subject to or undergo too much (esp. athletic) training with a consequent loss of proficiency.

o·ver·ture /ōvərchər, -chŏŏr/ *n.* **1** an orchestral piece opening an opera, etc. **2** a one-movement composition in this style. **3** (usu. in *pl.*) **a** an opening of negotiations. **b** a formal proposal or offer. **4** the beginning of a poem, etc.

o·ver·turn *v. & n.* ● *v.* /ōvərtúrn/ **1** *tr.* cause to turn over. **2** *tr.* reverse; invalidate. **3** *intr.* turn over. ● *n.* /ōvərtərn/ a subversion; an act of upsetting.

o·ver·use *v. & n.* ● *v.tr.* /ōvəryŏŏz/ use too much. ● *n.* /ōvəryŏŏs/ excessive use.

o·ver·val·ue /ōvərvályŏŏ/ *v.tr.* (**-values, -valued, -valuing**) value too highly.

o·ver·view /ōvərvyŏŏ/ *n.* a general survey.

o·ver·ween·ing /ōvərwéening/ *adj.* arrogant; presumptuous; conceited; self-confident. □□ **o·ver·ween·ing·ly** *adv.*

o·ver·weight *adj., n., & v.* ● *adj.* /ōvərwáyt/ beyond an allowed or suitable weight. ● *n.* /ōvərwayt/ excessive or extra weight; preponderance. ● *v.tr.* /ōvərwáyt/ (usu. foll. by *with*) load unduly.

o·ver·whelm /ōvərhwélm, -wélm/ *v.tr.* **1** overpower with emotion. **2** (usu. foll. by *with*) overpower with an excess of business, etc. **3** bring to sudden ruin or destruction. **4** bury or drown beneath a huge mass; submerge utterly.

o·ver·whelm·ing /ōvərhwélming, -wél-/ *adj.* irresistible by force of numbers, influence, amount, etc. □□ **o·ver·whelm·ing·ly** *adv.*

o·ver·wind /ōvərwínd/ *v.tr.* (*past* and *past part.* **-wound**) wind (a mechanism, esp. a watch) beyond the proper stopping point.

o·ver·win·ter /ōvərwíntər/ *v.* **1** *intr.* (usu. foll. by *at, in*) spend the winter. **2** *intr.* (of insects, fungi, etc.) live through the winter. **3** *tr.* keep (animals, plants, etc.) alive through the winter.

o·ver·work /ōvərwórk/ *v. & n.* ● *v.* **1** *intr.* work too hard. **2** *tr.* cause (another person) to work too hard. **3** *tr.* weary or exhaust with too much work. **4** *tr.* make excessive use of. ● *n.* excessive work.

o·ver·wound *past* and *past part.* of OVERWIND.

o·ver·write /ōvərít/ *v.* (*past* **-wrote**; *past part.* **-written**) **1** *tr.* write on top of (other writing). **2** *tr. Computing* destroy (data) in (a file, etc.) by entering new data. **3** *intr.* (esp. as **overwritten** *adj.*) write too elaborately.

o·ver·wrought /ōvəráwt/ *adj.* **1** overexcited; nervous; distraught. **2** overdone.

o·ver·zeal·ous /ōvərzéləs/ *adj.* too zealous in one's attitude, behavior, etc.

ovi- /ōvee/ *comb. form* egg; ovum.

o·vi·duct /ōvidukt/ *n.* the tube through which an ovum passes from the ovary. □□ **o·vi·duc·tal** /-dúktəl/ *adj.*

o·vi·form /ōvifawrm/ *adj.* egg-shaped.

o·vine /ōvīn/ *adj.* of or like sheep.

o·vip·a·rous /ōvípərəs/ *adj. Zool.* producing young by means of eggs expelled from the body before they are hatched. □□ **o·vi·par·i·ty** /-párítee/ *n.* **o·vip·a·rous·ly** *adv.*

o·vi·pos·i·tor /ōvipózitər/ *n.* ▼ a pointed tubular organ with which a female insect deposits her eggs.

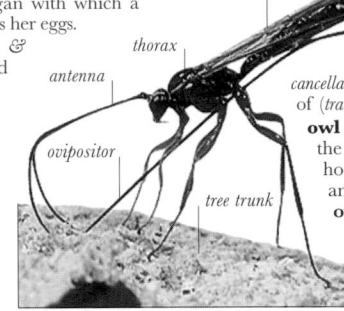

OVIPOSITOR: ICHNEUMON WASP
DEPOSITING EGGS

o·void /ōvoyd/ *adj. & n.* ● *adj.* **1** (of a solid or of a surface) egg-shaped. **2** oval, with one end more pointed than the other. ● *n.* an ovoid body or surface.

ov·u·late /ōvyəlayt, óvyə-/ *v.intr.* produce ova or ovules, or discharge them from the ovary. □□ **ov·u·la·tion** /-láyshən/ *n.* **ov·u·la·to·ry** /-lətawree/ *adj.*

ov·ule /áavyŏŏl, ōvyŏŏl/ *n.* the part of the ovary of seed plants that contains the germ cell; an unfertilized seed. ▷ FLOWER. □□ **ov·u·lar** *adj.*

o·vum /ōvəm/ *n.* (*pl.* **ova** /ōvə/) **1** a mature reproductive cell of female animals, produced by the ovary. ▷ OVARY. **2** the egg cell of plants.

ow /ow/ *int.* expressing sudden pain.

owe /ō/ *v.tr.* **1 a** be under obligation (to a person, etc.) to pay or repay (money, etc.) (*we owe you five dollars; owe more than I can pay for.* **b** (*absol.*, usu. foll. by *for*) be in debt (*still owe for my car*). **2** (often foll. by *to*) be under obligation to render (*owe grateful thanks to*). **3** (usu. foll. by *to*) be indebted to a person or thing for (*we owe to Newton the principle of gravitation*). □ **owe it to oneself** (often foll. by *to* + infin.) need (to do) something to protect one's own interests.

ow·ing /ō-ing/ *predic.adj.* **1** yet to be paid (*the balance owing*). **2** (foll. by *to*) **a** caused by; attributable to (*the cancellation was owing to ill health*). **b** (as *prep.*) because of (*trains are delayed owing to bad weather*).

owl /owl/ *n.* **1** ▼ any nocturnal bird of prey of the order Strigiformes, with large eyes and a hooked beak. **2** *colloq.* a person compared to an owl, esp. in looking wise. □□ **owl·ish** *adj.* **owl·ish·ly** *adv.* **owl·like** *adj.*

owl·et /ówlit/ *n.* a small or young owl.

own /ōn/ *adj. & v.* ● *adj.* (prec. by possessive) **1 a** belonging to oneself or itself (*saw it with my own eyes*). **b** individual; particular (*a charm all of its own*). **2** used to emphasize identity rather than possession (*cooks his own meals*). **3** (*absol.*) **a** private property (*is it your own?*). **b** kindred (*among my own*). ● *v.* **1 a** have as property. **2 a** *tr.* confess (*own their faults; owns he did not know*). **b** *intr.* (foll. by *to*) confess to (*owned to a prejudice*). **3** *tr.* acknowledge paternity, authorship, or possession of. □ **come into one's own 1** receive one's due. **2** achieve recognition. **get one's own back** (often foll. by *on*) *colloq.* get revenge. **hold one's own** maintain one's position. **of one's own** belonging to

---

OWL

There are about 130 owl species, most of which are nocturnal hunters. They have large, forward-facing eyes for long-range binocular vision, and hearing so acute they can locate prey in total darkness. Owls have no external ears, although some have tufts of feathers that look like ears. Instead, the broad facial disk gathers sound waves (like an external ear does) and directs them to the internal ear drum. Owls typically have fringed feathers that reduce air turbulence; this means quarry can be approached almost silently. Most owls have feathers covering their legs and feet, which also helps quieten their flight. An owl's diet consists mainly of small birds, insects, frogs, and rodents.

fringed flight feathers
alula
facial disk
tail feathers
large eyes
hooked beak
long, feathered legs
strong talons

EXTERNAL FEATURES
OF A BARN OWL
(*Tyto alba*)

EXAMPLES OF OTHER OWLS

TAWNY OWL
(*Strix aluco*)

SOUTHERN BOOBOOK
(*Ninox novaeseelandiae*)

SNOWY OWL
(*Nyctea scandiaca*)

EURASIAN EAGLE OWL
(*Bubo bubo*)

O

oneself alone. **on one's own 1** alone. **2** independently; without help. **own up** (often foll. by *to*) confess frankly. □□ **-owned** *adj.* (in *comb.*).

own·er /ṓnər/ *n.* **1** a person who owns something. **2** *sl.* the captain of a ship. □□ **own·er·ship** *n.*

own·er·oc·cu·pi·er *esp. Brit.* a person who owns the house, etc., he or she lives in.

ox /oks/ *n.* (*pl.* **oxen** /ṓksən/) **1** any bovine animal, esp. a large usu. horned domesticated ruminant used for draft, for supplying milk, and for eating as meat. ▷ RUMINANT. **2** a castrated male of a domesticated species of cattle, *Bos taurus*.

ox- var. of OXY-.

ox·al·ic ac·id /oksálik/ *n.* Chem. a very poisonous and sour acid found in sorrel and rhubarb leaves. □□ **ox·a·late** /ṓksəlayt/ *n.*

ox·a·lis /ṓksəlis, oksál-/ *n.* any plant of the genus *Oxalis*, with trifoliate leaves and white or pink flowers.

ox·bow /ṓksbō/ *n.* **1** a U-shaped collar of an ox yoke. **2 a** a loop formed by a horseshoe bend in a river. ▷ RIVER. **b** a lake formed when the river cuts across the narrow end of the loop. ▷ LAKE

ox·en *pl.* of OX.

ox·eye /ṓksī/ *n.* any plant of the genus *Heliopsis*, with dark-centered, daisylike flowers.

ox·eye daisy *n.* a daisy, *Leucanthemum vulgare*, having flowers with white petals and a yellow center.

Ox·fam /ṓksfam/ *abbr.* Oxford Committee for Famine Relief.

ox·ford /ṓksfərd/ *n.* **1** a low-heeled shoe that laces over the instep. **2** a fabric of cotton or a cotton blend made in a basket weave, used for shirts and sportswear.

ox·hide /ṓks-hīd/ *n.* **1** the hide of an ox. **2** leather made from this.

ox·i·dant /ṓksidənt/ *n.* an oxidizing agent. □□ **ox·i·da·tion** /-dáyshən/ *n.*

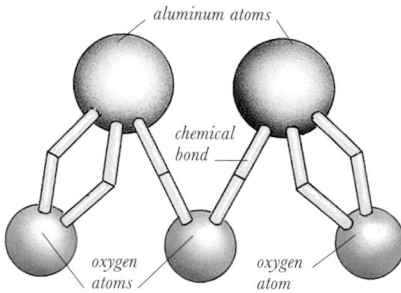

OXIDE: ALUMINUM OXIDE MOLECULE

(labels: *aluminum atoms*, *chemical bond*, *oxygen atoms*, *oxygen atom*)

ox·ide /ṓksīd/ *n.* ▲ a binary compound of oxygen.

ox·i·dize /ṓksidīz/ *v.tr. & intr.* **1** combine or cause to combine with oxygen. **2** cover (metal) or (of metal) become covered with a coating of oxide; make or become rusty. □□ **ox·i·diz·a·ble** *adj.* **ox·i·di·za·tion** *n.* **ox·i·diz·er** *n.*

ox·tail /ṓkstayl/ *n.* the tail of an ox, often used in making soup.

oxy- /ṓksee/ *comb. form* (also **ox-** /oks/) *Chem.* oxygen (*oxyacetylene*).

ox·y·a·cet·y·lene /ṓkseeəsét'leen/ *adj.* of or using a mixture of oxygen and acetylene, esp. in cutting or welding metals (*oxyacetylene burner*).

ox·y·gen /ṓksijən/ *n.* Chem. a colorless, tasteless, odorless gaseous element essential to plant and animal life. ¶ Symb.: **O**. □□ **ox·yg·e·nous** /oksíjinəs/ *adj.*

ox·y·gen·ate /ṓksijənayt/ *v.tr.* supply, treat, or mix with oxygen. □□ **ox·y·gen·a·tion** /-náyshən/ *n.*

ox·y·gen mask *n.* a mask placed over the nose and mouth to supply oxygen for breathing.

ox·y·gen tent *n.* a tentlike enclosure supplying a patient with air rich in oxygen.

ox·y·he·mo·glo·bin /ṓkseeheeməglṓbin/ *n. Biochem.*

a bright red complex formed when hemoglobin combines with oxygen.

ox·y·mo·ron /ṓkseemáwron/ *n. rhet.* a figure of speech in which apparently contradictory terms appear in conjunction (e.g., *faith unfaithful kept him falsely true*).

ox·y·to·cin /ṓksitṓsin/ *n.* **1** a hormone released by the pituitary gland that causes increased contraction of the womb during labor and stimulates the ejection of milk into the ducts of the breasts. **2** a synthetic form of this used to induce labor, etc.

o·yez /ṓ-yés, ṓ-yéz/ *int.* (also **o·yes**) uttered, usu. three times, by a public crier or a court officer to command silence and attention.

oys·ter /ṓystər/ *n.* **1** any of various bivalve mollusks of the family Ostreidae or Aviculidae. ▷ BIVALVE. **2** an oyster-shaped morsel of meat in a fowl's back. **3** something regarded as containing all that one desires (*the world is my oyster*).

oys·ter bed *n.* a part of the sea bottom where oysters breed or are bred.

oys·ter mush·room *n.* an edible fungus, *Pleurotus ostreatus*, which grows on trees.

oy vey /oy váy/ *int.* indicating dismay or grief (used mainly by Yiddish-speakers).

oz. *abbr.* ounce(s).

o·zone /ṓzon/ *n.* **1** *Chem.* a colorless unstable gas with a pungent odor and powerful oxidizing properties. **2** *colloq.* invigorating air at the seaside, etc. □□ **o·zon·ic** /ōzónik/ *adj.* **o·zon·ize** *v.tr.* **o·zon·i·za·tion** *n.* **o·zon·iz·er** *n.*

o·zone-friend·ly *adj.* (of manufactured articles) containing chemicals that are not destructive to the ozone layer.

o·zone hole *n.* an area of the ozone layer in which depletion has occurred.

o·zone lay·er *n.* a layer in the stratosphere that absorbs most of the sun's ultraviolet radiation. ▷ ATMOSPHERE

O

P

P[1] /pee/ *n.* (also **p**) (*pl.* **Ps** or **P's**) the sixteenth letter of the alphabet.

P[2] *abbr.* (also **P.**) (on road signs) parking.

P[3] *symb. Chem.* the element phosphorus.

p *abbr.* (also **p.**) **1** page. **2** piano (softly). **3** *Brit.* penny; pence.

PA *abbr.* **1** Pennsylvania (in official postal use). **2** public address (esp. **PA system**). **3** Press Association. **4** *Brit.* personal assistant.

Pa *symb. Chem.* the element protactinium.

pa /paa/ *n. colloq.* father.

p.a. *abbr.* per annum.

Pab·lum /páblǝm/ *n.* **1** *Trademark* a bland cereal food for infants. **2** (**pablum**) simplistic or unimaginative writing, speech, or ideas.

pab·u·lum /pábyǝlǝm/ *n.* **1** food; a nourishing substance. **2** insipid or bland ideas, writings, etc.

PAC /pak/ *abbr.* = POLITICAL ACTION COMMITTEE.

pace /pays/ *n. & v.* ● *n.* **1 a** a single step in walking or running. **b** the distance covered in this (about 30 in. or 75 cm). **c** the distance between two successive stationary positions of the same foot in walking. **2** speed in walking or running. **3** *Theatr. & Mus.* speed or tempo in theatrical or musical performance (*played with great pace*). **4** a rate of progression. **5 a** a manner of walking or running; a gait. **b** any of various gaits, esp. of a trained horse, etc. (*rode at an ambling pace*). ● *v.* **1** *intr.* **a** walk (esp. repeatedly or methodically) with a slow or regular pace (*pacing up and down*). **b** (of a horse) = AMBLE. **2** *tr.* traverse by pacing. **3** *tr.* set the pace for (a rider, runner, etc.). **4** *tr.* (often foll. by *out*) measure (a distance) by pacing. □ **keep pace** (often foll. by *with*) advance at an equal rate (as). **put a person through his** (or **her**) **paces** test a person's qualities in action, etc. **set the pace** determine the speed, esp. by leading. **stand** (or **stay**) **the pace** be able to keep up with others. □□ **paced** *adj.* **pac·er** *n.*

pace·mak·er /páysmaykǝr/ *n.* **1** ▼ a natural or artificial device for stimulating the heart muscle and determining the rate of its contractions. **2** a competitor who sets the pace in a race.

pace·set·ter /páys-setǝr/ *n.* a leader.

pach·y·derm /pákidǝrm/ *n.* any thick-skinned mammal, esp. an elephant or rhinoceros. ▷ ELEPHANT, RHINOCEROS. □□ **pach·y·der·ma·tous** /-dérmǝtǝs/ *adj.*

pa·cif·ic /pǝsífik/ *adj. & n.* ● *adj.* **1** characterized by or tending to peace; tranquil. **2** (**Pacific**) of or adjoining the Pacific. ● *n.* (**the Pacific**) the expanse of ocean between N. and S. America to the east and Asia to the west. ▷ OCEAN. □□ **pa·cif·i·cal·ly** *adv.*

Pa·cif·ic Time *n.* the standard time used in the Pacific region of Canada and the US.

pac·i·fi·er /pásifīǝr/ *n.* **1** a person or thing that pacifies. **2** a rubber or plastic nipple for a baby to suck on.

pac·i·fism /pásifizǝm/ *n.* the belief that war and violence are morally unjustified and that all disputes can be settled by peaceful means. □□ **pac·i·fist** *n. & adj.*

pac·i·fy /pásifī/ *v.tr.* (**-ies**, **-ied**) **1** appease (a person, anger, etc.). **2** bring peace to (a country, etc.) □□ **pac·i·fi·ca·to·ry** *adj.* **pac·i·fi·ca·tion** *n.*

pack[1] /pak/ *n. & v.* ● *n.* **1 a** a collection of things wrapped up or tied together for carrying. **b** = BACKPACK. **2** a set of items packaged for use or disposal together. **3** usu. *derog.* a lot or set (of similar things or persons) (*a pack of lies; a pack of thieves*). **4** a set of playing cards. **5 a** a group of hounds esp. for foxhunting. **b** a group of wild animals, esp. wolves, hunting together. **6** an organized group of Cub Scouts or Brownies. ● *v.* **1** *tr.* (often foll. by *up*) **a** fill (a suitcase, bag, etc.) with clothes and other items. **b** put (things) together in a bag or suitcase, esp. for traveling. **2** *intr.* come or put closely together; crowd or cram (*packed a lot into a few hours; passengers packed like sardines*). **3** *tr.* (in *passive*; often foll. by *with*) be filled (with); contain extensively (*the restaurant was packed; the book is packed with information*). **4** *tr.* fill (a hall, theater, etc.) with an audience, etc. **5** *tr.* cover (a thing) with something pressed tightly around. **6** *intr.* be suitable for packing. **7** *tr. colloq.* **a** carry (a gun, etc.). **b** be capable of delivering (a punch) with skill or force. □ **pack it in** *colloq.* end or stop it. **pack off** send (a person) away, esp. abruptly or promptly. **send packing** *colloq.* dismiss (a person) summarily. □□ **pack·a·ble** *adj.*

pack[2] /pak/ *v.tr.* select (a jury, etc.) or fill (a meeting) so as to secure a decision in one's favor.

pack·age /pákij/ *n. & v.* ● *n.* **1 a** a bundle of things packed. **b** a box, parcel, etc., in which things are packed. **2** (in full **package deal**) a set of proposals or items offered or agreed to as a whole. **3** *Computing* a piece of software suitable for various applications rather than one which is custom-built. **4** *colloq.* = PACKAGE TOUR. ● *v.tr.* make up into or enclose in a package. □□ **pack·ag·er** *n.*

pack·age store *n.* a retail store selling alcoholic beverages in sealed containers.

pack·age tour *n.* (also *Brit.* **package holiday**) a tour with all arrangements made at an inclusive price.

pack·ag·ing /pákijing/ *n.* material used to wrap or protect goods.

pack an·i·mal *n.* an animal used for carrying packs.

pack·er /pákǝr/ *n.* a person or thing that packs, esp. a dealer who processes and packs food for transportation and sale.

pack·et /pákit/ *n.* a small package.

pack·et switch·ing *n. Computing* data transmission in which a message is broken into parts and reassembled at the destination.

pack·horse /pák-hawrs/ *n.* a horse for carrying loads.

pack ice *n.* an area of large crowded pieces of floating ice in the sea.

pack·ing /páking/ *n.* material used as padding to pack esp. fragile articles.

pack rat *n.* **1** a bushy-tailed N. American wood rat that hoards various items in its nest. **2** a person who hoards unneeded things.

pact /pakt/ *n.* an agreement or a treaty.

pad[1] /pad/ *n. & v.* ● *n.* **1** a piece of soft material used to reduce friction or jarring, fill out hollows, hold or absorb liquid, etc. **2** a number of sheets of blank paper fastened together at one edge, for writing or drawing on. **3** ◀ the fleshy underpart of an animal's foot or of a human finger. **4** a soft guard for the limbs or joints protecting them from injury, esp. in sports. ▷ CRICKET. **5** a flat surface for helicopter takeoff or rocket launching. **6** *colloq.* an apartment or bedroom. **7** the floating leaf of a water lily. ● *v.tr.* (**padded, padding**) **1** provide with a pad or padding; stuff. **2 a** (foll. by *out*) lengthen or fill out (a book, etc.) with unnecessary material. **b** to increase fraudulently, as an expense account.

pad[2] /pad/ *v. & n.* ● *v.* (**padded, padding**) **1** *intr.* walk with a soft dull steady step. **2 a** *tr.* hike along (a road, etc.) on foot. **b** *intr.* travel on foot. ● *n.* the sound of soft steady steps.

pad·ded cell *n.* a room with padded walls in a mental hospital.

pad·ding /páding/ *n.* **1** soft material used to pad or stuff with. **2** ▼ material laid under a carpet as protection or support.

PACEMAKER

An artificial pacemaker is implanted in the human body when the natural pacemaker – a knot of tissue in the heart muscle that initiates the rhythmic heartbeat – does not function properly. It consists of a battery-powered generator that delivers short pulses of electricity to the heart to stimulate or regulate the heartbeat. The illustration below shows the position of a common pacemaker.

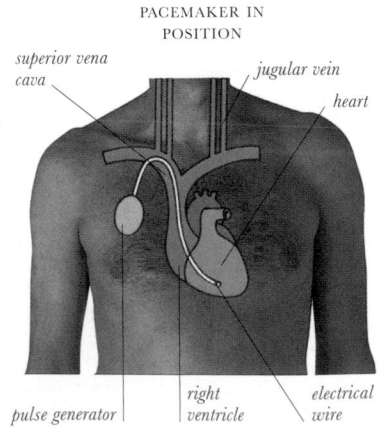

PACEMAKER IN POSITION

superior vena cava — *jugular vein* — *heart* — *pulse generator* — *right ventricle* — *electrical wire*

PAD OF A DOMESTIC CAT

claw — *dewclaw* — *toe pad* — *metacarpal pad*

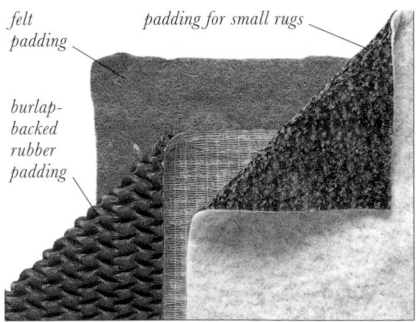

PADDING: TYPES OF CARPET PADDING

felt padding — *padding for small rugs* — *burlap-backed rubber padding*

pad·dle[1] /pád'l/ *n. & v.* ● *n.* **1** a short broad-bladed oar used without an oarlock. ▷ CANOE. **2** a paddle-shaped instrument. **3** *Zool.* a fin or flipper. **4** each of the boards fitted around the circumference of a paddle wheel or mill wheel. **5** esp. *Brit.* the action or a period of paddling. ● *v.* **1** *intr. & tr.* move on water or propel a boat by means of paddles. **2** *intr. & tr.* row gently. **3** *tr. colloq.* spank. □□ **pad·dler** *n.*

pad·dle[2] /pád'l/ *v. & n.* esp. *Brit.* ● *v.intr.* walk barefoot or dabble the feet or hands in shallow water. ● *n.* the action or a period of paddling. □□ **pad·dler** *n.*

pad·dle·ball /pád'lbawl/ *n.* a game played on an

P

PADDLEBOAT

The invention of the steam engine in the 18th century made paddleboats a viable alternative to ships propelled by sails. As the wheels of a paddleboat turn, their floats (boards) dip in the water and drive the boat. Paddlewheelers are suited to rivers and lakes but were superseded by the propeller on oceangoing vessels in the mid-19th century.

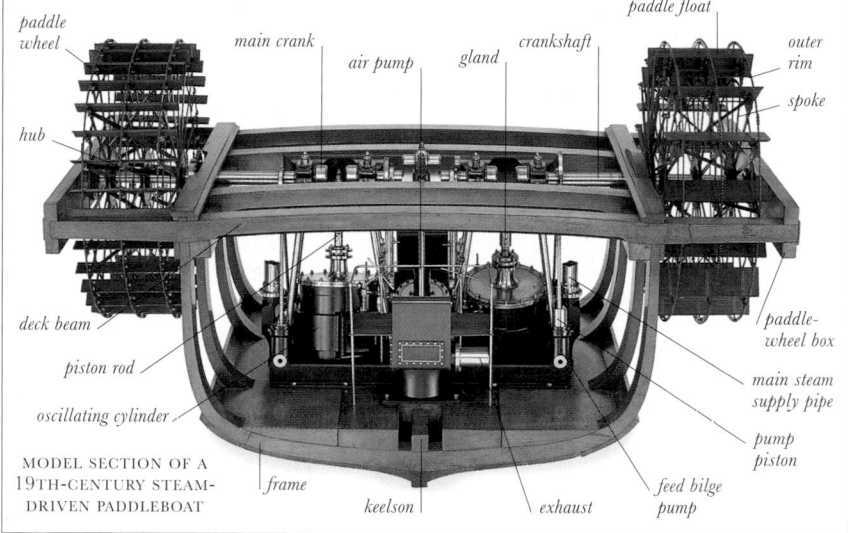

MODEL SECTION OF A 19TH-CENTURY STEAM-DRIVEN PADDLEBOAT

Labels: paddle wheel, main crank, air pump, gland, crankshaft, paddle float, outer rim, spoke, hub, deck beam, piston rod, oscillating cylinder, frame, keelson, exhaust, paddle-wheel box, main steam supply pipe, pump piston, feed bilge pump

---

enclosed court with short-handled perforated paddles and a ball similar to a tennis ball.

pad·dle·boat /pádlbōt/ *n.* ▲ a boat propelled by a paddle wheel.

pad·dle wheel *n.* a wheel for propelling a ship, with boards around the circumference so as to press backward against the water. ▷ PADDLEBOAT

pad·dock /pádək/ *n.* **1** a small field, esp. for keeping horses in. **2** an enclosure adjoining a racetrack where horses or cars are assembled before a race. ▷ RACETRACK. **3** *Austral. & NZ* a field; a plot of land.

pad·dy /pádee/ *n.* (*pl.* **-ies**) **1** a field where rice is grown. **2** rice before threshing or in the husk.

pad·lock /pádlok/ *n. & v.* ● *n.* a detachable lock hanging by a pivoted hook on the object fastened. ● *v.tr.* secure with a padlock.

pa·dre /páadray, -dree/ *n.* **1** a clergyman, esp. a priest. **2** a chaplain in any of the armed services.

pa·dro·ne /padrónay, -ni/ *n.* a patron or master, esp. a Mafia boss.

pae·an /péeən/ *n.* a song of praise or triumph.

paedo *Brit.* var. of PEDO-.

pa·el·la /pī-élə, paa-áyaa/ *n.* a Spanish dish of rice, saffron, chicken, seafood, etc., cooked and served in a large shallow pan.

pae·on /péeən/ *n.* a metrical foot of one long syllable and three short syllables in any order.

pa·gan /páygon/ *n. & adj.* ● *n.* **1** a person not subscribing to any of the main religions of the world. **2** a person following a polytheistic or pantheistic religion. ● *adj.* **1** of or relating to pagans. **2** identifying divinity or spirituality in nature; pantheistic. □□ **pa·gan·ish** *adj.* **pa·gan·ism** *n.* **pa·gan·ize** *v.tr. & intr.*

page[1] /payj/ *n. & v.* ● *n.* **1 a** a leaf of a book, periodical, etc. **b** each side of this. **c** what is written or printed on this. **2 a** an episode that might fill a page in written history, etc.; a record. **b** a memorable event. **3** *Computing* a section of computer memory of specified size, esp. one that can be readily transferred between main and auxiliary memories. ● *v.tr.* paginate.

page[2] /payj/ *n. & v.* ● *n.* **1** a person employed to run errands, attend to a door, etc. **2** a boy employed as a personal attendant of a bride, etc. **3** *hist.* a boy in training for knighthood and attached to a knight's service. ● *v.tr.* **1** (in hotels, airports, etc.) summon by making an announcement or by sending a messenger. **2** summon by means of a pager.

pag·eant /pájənt/ *n.* **1 a** an elaborate parade or spectacle. **b** a spectacular procession, or play performed in the open, illustrating historical events. **c** a tableau, etc., on a fixed stage or moving vehicle. **2** an empty or specious show.

pag·eant·ry /pájəntree/ *n.* (*pl.* **-ies**) **1** elaborate or sumptuous show or display. **2** an instance of this.

page boy *n.* **1** = PAGE[2] *n.* 2. **2** a hairstyle with the hair reaching to the shoulder and rolled under at the ends.

pag·er /páyjər/ *n.* a radio device with a beeper, activated from a central point to alert the person wearing it.

pag·i·nate /pájinayt/ *v.tr.* assign numbers to the pages of a book, etc. □□ **pag·i·na·tion** /-náyshən/ *n.*

pa·go·da /pəgódə/ *n.* **1** ▶ a Hindu or Buddhist temple or sacred building, esp. a many-tiered tower, in India and the Far East. **2** an ornamental imitation of this.

paid past and past part. of PAY[1].

pail /payl/ *n.* **1** a bucket. **2** an amount contained in this. □□ **pail·ful** *n.* (*pl.* **-fuls**).

pain /payn/ *n. & v.* ● *n.* **1 a** the range of unpleasant bodily sensations produced by illness or by harmful physical contact, etc. **b** a particular kind or instance of this (often in *pl.*: *suffering from stomach pains*). **2** mental suffering or distress. **3** (in *pl.*) careful effort; trouble taken (*take pains; got nothing for my pains*). **4** (also **pain in the**

PAGODA: MODEL OF A 9TH–10TH-CENTURY BURMESE PAGODA

---

neck, etc.) *colloq.* a troublesome person or thing; a nuisance. ● *v.tr.* **1** cause pain to. **2** (as **pained** *adj.*) expressing pain (*a pained expression*). □ **in pain** suffering pain. **on** (or **under**) **pain of** with (death, etc.) as the penalty.

pain·ful /páynfool/ *adj.* **1** causing bodily or mental pain or distress. **2** (esp. of part of the body) suffering pain. **3** causing trouble or difficulty; laborious (*a painful climb*). □□ **pain·ful·ly** *adv.* **pain·ful·ness** *n.*

pain·kil·ler /páynkilər/ *n.* a medicine or drug for alleviating pain. □□ **pain·kil·ling** *adj.*

pain·less /páynlis/ *adj.* not causing suffering or pain. □□ **pain·less·ly** *adv.* **pain·less·ness** *n.*

pain·stak·ing /páynztayking/ *adj.* careful, industrious, thorough. □□ **pain·stak·ing·ly** *adv.* **pain·stak·ing·ness** *n.*

paint /paynt/ *n. & v.* ● *n.* **1 a** a coloring matter, esp. in liquid form for imparting color to a surface. **b** this as a dried film or coating (*the paint peeled off*). **2** cosmetic makeup, esp. rouge or nail polish. **3** = PINTO. ● *v.tr.* **1 a** cover the surface of (a wall, object, etc.) with paint. **b** apply paint of a specified color to (*paint the door green*). **2** depict (an object, scene, etc.) with paint; produce (a picture) by painting. **3** describe vividly as if by painting (*paint a gloomy picture of the future*). **4 a** apply liquid or cosmetic to (the face, skin, etc.). **b** apply (a liquid to the skin, etc.). □ **paint out** efface with paint. **paint the town red** *colloq.* enjoy oneself flamboyantly; celebrate. □□ **paint·a·ble** *adj.*

paint·box /páyntboks/ *n.* a box holding dry paints for painting pictures.

paint·brush /páyntbrush/ *n.* a brush for applying paint.

paint·ed la·dy *n.* **1** ▼ an orange-red butterfly, esp. *Vanessa cardui*, with black and brown markings. **2** (also **painted woman**) = PROSTITUTE.

P

PAINTED LADY (*Vanessa cardui*)

paint·er[1] /páyntər/ *n.* a person who paints, esp. an artist or decorator.

paint·er[2] /páyntər/ *n.* a rope attached to the bow of a boat for tying it to a pier, dock, etc.

paint·er·ly /páyntərlee/ *adj.* **1 a** using paint well; artistic. **b** characteristic of a painter or paintings. **2** (of a painting) lacking clearly defined outlines.

paint·ing /páynting/ *n.* **1** the process or art of using paint. **2** a painted picture.

paint·work /páyntwərk/ *n.* **1** a painted surface or area in a building, etc. **2** the work of painting.

pair /pair/ *n. & v.* ● *n.* **1** a set of two persons or things used together or regarded as a unit (*a pair of gloves; a pair of eyes*). **2** an article (e.g., scissors, pants, or pajamas) consisting of two joined or corresponding parts not used separately. **3 a** a romantically involved couple. **b** a mated couple of animals. **4** two horses harnessed side by side (*a coach and pair*). **5** the second member of a pair in relation to the first (*cannot find its pair*). **6** two playing cards of the same denomination. **7** either or both of two members of a legislative assembly on opposite sides absenting themselves from voting by mutual arrangement. ● *v.tr. & intr.* **1** (often foll. by *off* or *up*) arrange or be arranged in couples. **2 a** join or be joined in marriage. **b** (of animals) mate. **3** form a legislative pair. □ **in pairs** in twos.

pai·sa /píːsáa/ *n.* (*pl.* **paise** /-sáy/) a coin and monetary unit of India, Pakistan, Nepal, and Bangladesh, equal to one hundredth of a rupee or taka.

Pais·ley /páyzlee/ *n.* (also **pais·ley**) (often *attrib.*) **1** ▼ a distinctive detailed pattern of curved feather-shaped figures. **2** a soft woolen garment or fabric having this pattern.

PAISLEY PATTERN ON SILK

Pai·ute /píyōōt/ *n.* (also **Pi·ute**) **1 a** a N. American people native to the southwestern US. **b** a member of this people. **2** the language of this people.

pa·ja·mas /pəjáaməz, -jám-/ *n.pl.* **1** a suit of loose pants and jacket for sleeping in. **2** loose pants tied at the waist, worn by both sexes in some Asian countries. **3** (**pajama**) (*attrib.*) designating parts of a suit of pajamas (*pajama top*; *pajama pants*; *pajama bottoms*).

Pak·i·sta·ni /pákistáanee, páakistáanee/ *n. & adj.* ● *n.* **1** a native or national of Pakistan. **2** a person of Pakistani descent. ● *adj.* of or relating to Pakistan.

pa·ko·ra /pəkáwrə/ *n.* a piece of cauliflower, carrot, or other vegetable, coated in seasoned batter and deep-fried.

pal /pal/ *n. & v.* ● *n. colloq.* a friend or comrade. ● *v.intr.* (**palled**, **palling**) (usu. foll. by *up*) associate; form a friendship.

pal·ace /pális/ *n.* **1 a** the official residence of a president or sovereign. **b** esp. *Brit.* the official residence of an archbishop or bishop. **2** a mansion; a spacious building.

pal·a·din /pálədin/ *n. hist.* **1** any of the twelve peers of Charlemagne's court, of whom the Count Palatine was the chief. **2** a knight errant; a champion.

palaeo- *comb. form Brit.* var. of PALEO-.

Pa·lae·o·zo·ic *Brit.* var. of PALEOZOIC.

pal·an·quin /pálənkéen/ *n.* (also **pal·an·keen**) (in India and Asia) a covered litter for one passenger.

pal·at·a·ble /pálətəbəl/ *adj.* **1** pleasant to taste. **2** (of an idea, suggestion, etc.) acceptable, satisfactory. □□ **pal·at·a·bil·i·ty** *n.* **pal·at·a·ble·ness** *n.* **pal·at·a·bly** *adv.*

pal·a·tal /pálət'l/ *adj. & n.* ● *adj.* **1** of the palate. **2** (of a sound) made by placing the surface of the tongue against the hard palate (e.g., *y* in *yes*). ● *n.* a palatal sound. □□ **pal·a·tal·ize** *v.tr.* **pal·a·tal·i·za·tion** *n.* **pal·a·tal·ly** *adv.*

pal·ate /pálət/ *n.* **1** a structure closing the upper part of the mouth cavity in vertebrates. **2** the sense of taste. **3** a mental taste or inclination; liking.

pa·la·tial /pəláyshəl/ *adj.* (of a building) like a palace, esp. spacious and magnificent. □□ **pa·la·tial·ly** *adv.*

pa·lat·i·nate /pəlát'nayt/ *n.* territory under the jurisdiction of a Count Palatine.

pal·a·tine /pálətīn/ *adj.* (also **Palatine**) *hist.* **1** (of

an official or feudal lord) having local authority that elsewhere belongs only to a sovereign (*Count Palatine*). **2** (of a territory) subject to this authority.

pa·lav·er /pəláavər, -láavər/ *n. & v.* ● *n.* **1** fuss and bother, esp. prolonged. **2** profuse or idle talk. **3** cajolery. **4** *colloq.* a prolonged or tiresome business. **5** esp. *hist.* a parley between European traders and Africans or other indigenous peoples. ● *v.* **1** *intr.* talk profusely. **2** *tr.* flatter, wheedle.

pale[1] /payl/ *adj. & v.* ● *adj.* **1** (of a person or complexion) diminished in coloration; of a whitish or ashen appearance. **2 a** (of a color) faint; not dark or deep. **b** faintly colored. **3** of faint luster; dim. **4** lacking intensity, vigor, or strength (*pale imitation*). ● *v.* **1** *intr. & tr.* grow or make pale. **2** *intr.* (often foll. by *before, beside*) become feeble in comparison (with). □□ **pale·ly** *adv.* **pale·ness** *n.* **pal·ish** *adj.*

pale[2] /payl/ *n.* **1** a pointed piece of wood for fencing, etc.; a stake. **2** a boundary or enclosed area. **3** *Heraldry* a vertical stripe in the middle of a shield. □ **beyond the pale** outside the bounds of acceptable behavior.

paled /payld/ *adj.* having palings.

pale·face /páylfays/ *n.* a white person.

paleo- /páyleeō/ *comb. form* ancient; old; of ancient (esp. prehistoric) times.

pa·le·o·bot·a·ny /páyleeōbót'nee/ *n.* (*Brit.* **palaeo·botany**) the study of fossil plants.

Pa·le·o·cene /páyleeəséen/ *adj. & n. Geol.* ● *adj.* of or relating to the earliest epoch of the Tertiary period with evidence of the emergence and development of mammals. ● *n.* this epoch or system.

pa·le·o·cli·ma·tol·o·gy /páyleeōklímətóləjee/ *n.* (*Brit.* **palaeoclimatology**) the study of the climate in geologically past times.

pa·le·o·ge·og·ra·phy /páyleeōjeeógrəfee/ *n.* (*Brit.* **palaeogeography**) the study of the geographical features at periods in the geological past.

pa·le·og·ra·phy /páyleeógrəfee/ *n.* (*Brit.* **palaeography**) the study of writing and documents from the past. □□ **pa·le·og·ra·pher** *n.* **pa·le·o·graph·ic** /-leeəgráfik/ *adj.* **pa·le·o·graph·i·cal** *adj.* **pa·le·o·graph·i·cal·ly** *adv.*

pa·le·o·lith·ic /páyleeəlíthik/ *adj.* (*Brit.* **palae·olithic**) *Archaeol.* of or relating to the early part of the Stone Age.

pa·le·on·tol·o·gy /páyleeontóləjee/ *n.* (*Brit.* **palae·ontology**) the study of life in the geological past. □□ **pa·le·on·to·log·i·cal** *adj.* **pa·le·on·tol·o·gist** *n.*

Pa·le·o·zo·ic /páyleeəzóik/ *adj. & n. Geol.* ● *adj.* of or relating to an era of geological time marked by the appearance of marine and terrestrial plants and animals, esp. invertebrates. ● *n.* this era (cf. CENOZOIC, MESOZOIC).

Pal·es·tin·i·an /pálistíneeən/ *adj. & n.* ● *adj.* of or relating to Palestine, a region (in ancient and modern times) and former British territory on the E. Mediterranean coast. ● *n.* **1** a native of Palestine in ancient or modern times. **2** an Arab, or a descendant of one, born or living in the area called Palestine.

pal·ette /pálit/ *n.* **1** ▼ a thin board or slab or other surface, usu. with a hole for the thumb, on which an artist holds and mixes colors. **2** the range of colors, etc., used by an artist.

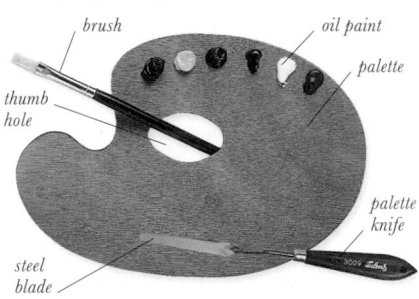

brush   *oil paint*
    palette
thumb hole
palette knife
steel blade

PALETTE WITH BRUSH AND PALETTE KNIFE

pal·frey /páwlfree/ *n.* (*pl.* **-eys**) *archaic* a horse for ordinary riding, esp. for women.

Pa·li /páalee/ *n.* an Indic language used in the canonical books of Buddhists.

pal·i·mo·ny /pálimōnee/ *n. colloq.* usu. court-ordered allowance made by one member of an unmarried couple to the other after separation.

pal·imp·sest /pálimpsest/ *n.* **1** a piece of writing material or manuscript on which the original writing has been erased to make room for other writing. **2** a place, etc., showing layers of history, etc. **3** a monumental brass turned and re-engraved on the reverse side.

pal·in·drome /pálindrōm/ *n.* a word or phrase that reads the same backward as forward (e.g., *rotator*, *nurses run*). □□ **pal·in·drom·ic** /-drómik, -drō-/ *adj.* **pa·lin·dro·mist** *n.*

PALLADIAN

Palladian is a neoclassical architectural style derived from the Renaissance buildings and writings of Andrea Palladio (1508–80). Palladio's Villa Rotonda (shown below) bears many of his hallmarks. The villa's design, both plan and elevation, is symmetrical, and centers on a domed room. Each of the four façades is identical and is dominated by huge columns and a pedimented temple porch, a favorite motif of Palladio.

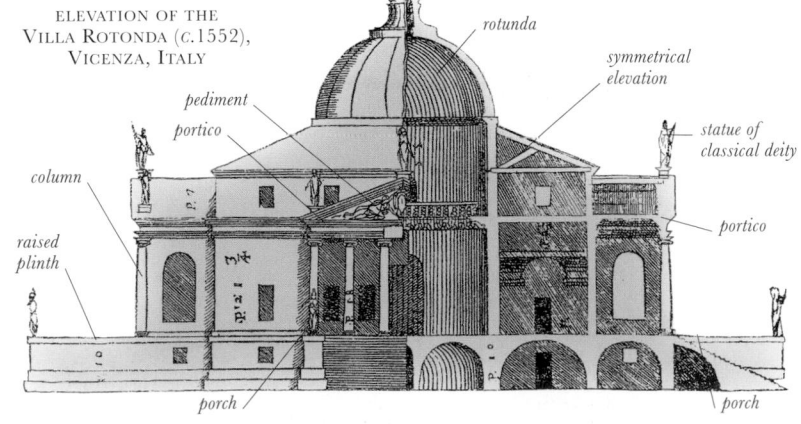

ELEVATION OF THE
VILLA ROTONDA (*c.*1552),
VICENZA, ITALY

rotunda
symmetrical elevation
statue of classical deity
pediment
portico
column
raised plinth
portico
porch
porch

pal·ing /páyling/ *n.* **1** a fence of pales. **2** a pale.

pal·i·sade /pálisáyd/ *n. & v.* ● *n.* **1 a** a fence of pales or iron railings. **b** a strong pointed wooden stake used in a close row for defense. **2** (in *pl.*) a line of high cliffs. ● *v.tr.* enclose or provide (a building or place) with a palisade.

pall¹ /pawl/ *n.* **1** a cloth spread over a coffin, hearse, or tomb. **2** a shoulder band with pendants, worn as an ecclesiastical vestment and sign of authority. **3** a dark covering (*a pall of darkness; a pall of smoke*).

pall² /pawl/ *v.* **1** *intr.* (often foll. by *on*) become uninteresting (to). **2** *tr.* satiate; cloy.

Pal·la·di·an /pəláydeeən/ *adj. Archit.* ▼ in the neoclassical style of Palladio. □□ **Pal·la·di·an·ism** *n.*

pal·la·di·um /pəláydeeəm/ *n. Chem.* a white ductile metallic element occurring naturally in various ores and used in chemistry as a catalyst and for making jewelry. ¶ Symb.: **Pd**.

pall·bear·er /páwlbairər/ *n.* a person helping to carry or officially escorting a coffin at a funeral.

pal·let¹ /pálit/ *n.* **1** a straw mattress. **2** a mean or makeshift bed.

pal·let² /pálit/ *n.* **1** a flat wooden blade with a handle, used in ceramics to shape clay. **2** = PALETTE. **3** a portable platform for transporting and storing loads. □□ **pal·let·ize** *v.tr.* (in sense 3).

pal·liasse /palyás/ *n.* a straw mattress.

pal·li·ate /páleeayt/ *v.tr.* **1** alleviate (disease) without curing it. **2** excuse; extenuate. □□ **pal·li·a·tion** /-áyshən/ *n.* **pal·li·a·tor** *n.*

pal·li·a·tive /páleeətiv/ *n. & adj.* ● *n.* anything used to alleviate pain, anxiety, etc. ● *adj.* serving to alleviate. □□ **pal·li·a·tive·ly** *adv.*

pal·lid /pálid/ *adj.* pale, esp. from illness. □□ **pal·lid·i·ty** /-líditee/ *n.* **pal·lid·ly** *adv.* **pal·lid·ness** *n.*

pal·lor /pálər/ *n.* pallidness; paleness.

pal·ly /pálee/ *adj.* (**pallier, palliest**) *colloq.* like a pal; friendly.

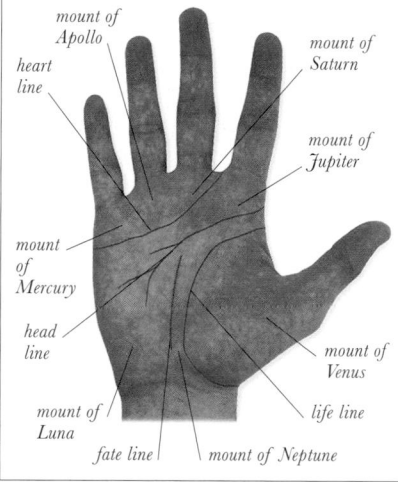

palm¹ /paam, paw(l)m/ *n.* **1** ◄ any usu. tropical tree of the family Palmae, with no branches and a mass of large pinnate or fan-shaped leaves at the top. **2 a** the leaf of this tree as a symbol of victory. **b** a military decoration shaped like a palm leaf. **3 a** supreme excellence. **b** a prize for this. **4** a branch of various trees used instead of a palm in non-tropical countries, esp. in celebrating Palm Sunday. □□ **pal·ma·ceous** /palmáyshəs, paa(l)-/ *adj.*

palm² /paam, paw(l)m/ *n. & v.* ● *n.* **1** the inner surface of the hand between the wrist and fingers. **2** the part of a glove, etc., that covers this. **3** the palmate part of an antler. ● *v.tr.* **1** conceal in the hand. **2** *Basketball* hold (the ball) in one hand. □ **in the palm of one's hand** under one's control or influence. **palm off 1** (often foll. by *on*) **a** impose or thrust fraudulently (on a person). **b** cause a person to accept unwillingly or unknowingly (*palmed my old typewriter off on him*). **2** (often foll. by *with*) cause (a person) to accept unwillingly or unknowingly (*palmed him off with my old typewriter*). □□ **palmar** /pálmər, páa(l)-/ *adj.* **palmed** *adj.* **palm·ful** *n.* (*pl.* **-fuls**).

PALM TREE
(Borassus flabellifer)

pal·mate /pálmayt, páal-, páamayt/ *adj.* **1** shaped like an open hand. **2** having lobes, etc., like spread fingers. ▷ LEAF

pal·mer·worm /páamərwərm/ *n.* a destructive hairy caterpillar of a moth, *Dichomeris ligulella*, of the eastern US.

palm·ette /palmét/ *n. Archaeol.* an ornament of radiating petals like a palm leaf.

PALMISTRY

Palmistry is the practice of interpreting character and telling fortunes by examining the lines and other features, such as mounts, on a person's palm. The four main lines are claimed to relate to vitality of life (life line), emotional security (heart line), intelligence (head line), and external influences that might affect one's life (fate line).

HAND FEATURES USED IN PALMISTRY

mount of Apollo
mount of Saturn
heart line
mount of Jupiter
mount of Saturn
mount of Mercury
mount of Venus
head line
mount of Luna
life line
fate line
mount of Neptune

pal·met·to /palmétō/ *n.* (*pl.* **-os**) **1** a small palm tree, e.g., any of various fan palms of the genus *Sabal*. **2** palm fronds used in weaving.

pal·mi·ped /pálmiped/ *adj. & n.* (also **palmipede** /-peed/) ● *adj.* a web-footed. ● *n.* a web-footed bird.

palm·is·try /páamistree/ *n.* ▲ supposed divination from lines and other features on the palm of the hand. □□ **palm·ist** *n.*

Palm Sun·day *n.* the Sunday before Easter, celebrating Christ's entry into Jerusalem.

palm·y /páamee/ *adj.* (**palmier, palmiest**) **1** of or like or abounding in palms. **2** triumphant; flourishing (*palmy days*).

pal·my·ra /palmírə/ *n.* an Asian palm, *Borassus flabellifer*, with fan-shaped leaves used for matting, etc.

pal·o·mi·no /páləméenō/ *n.* (*pl.* **-os**) ▼ a golden or tan-colored horse with a light-colored mane and tail, orig. bred in the southwestern US.

PALOMINO

pal·o·ver·de /pálōvárdee, -várd/ *n.* a thorny tree of the genus *Cercidium* having greenish bark and yellow flowers, found in the southwestern US.

palp /palp/ *n.* (also **palpus** /pálpəs/) (*pl.* **palps** or **palpi** /-pī/) a segmented sensory organ at the mouth of an arthropod; a feeler. ▷ SPIDER. □□ **pal·pal** *adj.*

pal·pa·ble /pálpəbəl/ *adj.* **1** that can be touched or felt. **2** readily perceived by the senses or mind. □□ **pal·pa·bil·i·ty** *n.* **pal·pa·bly** *adv.*

pal·pate /pálpayt/ *v.tr.* examine (esp. medically) by touch. □□ **pal·pa·tion** /-páyshən/ *n.*

pal·pi·tate /pálpitayt/ *v.intr.* **1** pulsate; throb. **2** tremble. □□ **pal·pi·tant** *adj.*

pal·pi·ta·tion /pálpitáyshən/ *n.* **1** throbbing; trembling. **2** (often in *pl.*) increased activity of the heart due to exertion, agitation, or disease.

pal·sy /páwlzee/ *n. & v.* ● *n.* (*pl.* **-ies**) **1** paralysis, esp. with involuntary tremors. **2 a** a condition of utter helplessness. **b** a cause of this. ● *v.tr.* (**-ies, -ied**) **1** affect with palsy. **2** render helpless.

pal·try /páwltree/ *adj.* (**paltrier, paltriest**) worthless; contemptible; trifling. □□ **pal·tri·ness** *n.*

pal·y·nol·o·gy /pálinóləjee/ *n.* the study of pollen, spores, etc., for rock dating and the study of past environments. □□ **pal·y·no·log·i·cal** /-nəlójikəl/ *adj.* **pal·y·nol·o·gist** *n.*

pam·pas /pámpəs/ *n.pl.* large treeless plains in S. America.

pam·pas grass *n.* ▼ a tall grass, *Cortaderia selloana*, from S. America, with silky flowering plumes.

PAMPAS GRASS (*Cortaderia selloana*)

pam·per /pámpər/ *v.tr.* **1** overindulge (a person, taste, etc.); cosset. **2** spoil (a person) with luxury. □□ **pam·per·er** *n.*

pam·pe·ro /pampáirō/ *n.* (*pl.* **-os**) a strong cold SW wind in S. America, blowing from the Andes to the Atlantic.

pam·phlet /pámflit/ *n. & v.* ● *n.* a small, usu. unbound booklet or leaflet. ● *v.tr.* (**pamphleted, pamphleting**) distribute pamphlets to.

pam·phlet·eer /pámfliteér/ *n. & v.* ● *n.* a writer of (esp. political) pamphlets. ● *v.intr.* write pamphlets.

pan¹ /pan/ *n. & v.* ● *n.* **1 a** a vessel of metal, earthenware, etc., usu. broad and shallow, used for cooking and other domestic purposes. **b** the contents of this. **2** a panlike vessel in which substances are heated, etc. **3** any similar shallow container such as the bowl of a pair of scales or that used for washing gravel, etc., to separate gold. **4** *Brit.* toilet bowl. **5** part of the lock that held the priming in old guns. **6** a hollow in the ground (*salt pan*). **7** a hard substratum of soil. **8** *sl.* the face. **9** a negative or unfavorable review. ● *v.* (**panned, panning**) **1** *tr. colloq.* criticize severely. **2 a** *tr.* (often foll. by *off, out*) wash (gold-bearing gravel) in a pan. **b** *intr.* search for gold by panning gravel. **c** *intr.* (foll. by *out*) (of gravel) yield gold. □ **pan out** (of an action, etc.) turn out well or in a specified way. □□ **pan·ful** *n.* (*pl.* **-fuls**).

pan² /pan/ *v. & n.* ● *v.* (**panned, panning**) **1** *tr.* swing (a video or movie camera) horizontally to give a panoramic effect or to follow a moving object. **2** *intr.* (of a video or movie camera) be moved in this way. ● *n.* a panning movement.

pan- /pan/ *comb. form* **1** all; the whole of. **2** relating to the whole or all the parts of a continent, racial group, religion, etc. (*pan-American; pan-African; pan-Hellenic; pan-Anglican*).

P

PANCREAS

In vertebrates, the pancreas gland is located behind the stomach and close to the duodenum. Part of the pancreas produces enzymes, which flow through the pancreatic duct into the duodenum to help digest foods. The pancreas also has groups of cells called islets, which produce two hormones: glucagon and insulin. These hormones, which play an important role in regulating blood sugar levels, pass directly into the bloodstream.

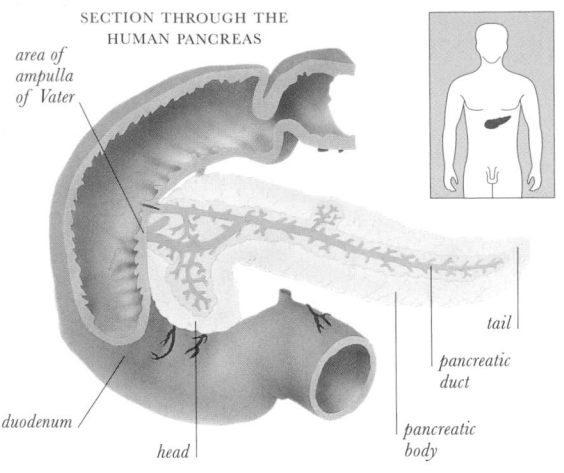

SECTION THROUGH THE HUMAN PANCREAS

area of ampulla of Vater

tail

pancreatic duct

duodenum

pancreatic body

head

pan·a·ce·a /pánəséeə/ n. a universal remedy. □□ **pan·a·ce·an** adj.

pa·nache /pənásh, -náash/ n. assertiveness or flamboyant confidence of style or manner.

pa·na·da /pənáadə/ n. a thick paste of milk and bread or flour, etc., used as a sauce base.

pan·a·ma /pánəmaa/ n. a hat of strawlike material made from the leaves of a palmlike tropical plant.

Pan·a·ma·ni·an /pánəmáyneeən/ n. & adj. ● n. 1 a native or national of the Republic of Panama in Central America. 2 a person of Panamanian descent. ● adj. of or relating to Panama.

pan·a·tel·la /pánətélə/ n. a long thin cigar.

pan·cake /pánkayk/ n. & v. ● n. 1 a thin flat cake of batter usu. fried and turned in a pan or on a griddle. 2 a flat cake of makeup, etc. ● v. 1 intr. make a pancake landing. 2 tr. cause (an aircraft) to pancake. □ **flat as a pancake** completely flat.

pan·chro·mat·ic /pánkrōmátik/ adj. Photog. (of film, etc.) sensitive to all visible colors of the spectrum.

pan·cre·as /pángkreeəs/ n. ▲ a gland near the stomach supplying the duodenum with digestive fluid and secreting insulin into the blood. ▷ DIGESTION, ENDOCRINE. □□ **pan·cre·at·ic** /-kreeátik/ adj. **pan·cre·a·ti·tis** /-kreeátítis/ n.

pan·cre·a·tin /pánkreeətən, páng-/ n. a digestive extract containing pancreatic enzymes, prepared from animal pancreases.

pan·da /pándə/ n. 1 (also **giant panda**) a large bearlike mammal, Ailuropoda melanoleuca, native to China and Tibet, having characteristic black and white markings. 2 (also **red panda**) ▼ a Himalayan raccoon-like mammal, Ailurus fulgens, with reddish-brown fur and a long bushy tail.

PANDA: RED PANDA
(Ailurus fulgens)

pan·dect /pándekt/ n. (usu. in pl.) 1 a complete body of laws. 2 hist. a compendium in 50 books of the Roman civil law made by order of Justinian in the 6th c.

pan·dem·ic /pandémik/ adj. & n. ● adj. 1 (of a disease) prevalent over a whole country or the world. 2 universal; widespread (a pandemic fear of nuclear weapons). ● n. a pandemic disease.

pan·de·mo·ni·um /pándimṓneeəm/ n. 1 uproar; utter confusion. 2 a scene of this.

pan·der /pándər/ v. & n. v.intr. (foll. by to) gratify or indulge a person, a desire or weakness, etc. ● n. (also **panderer**) 1 a go-between in illicit love affairs; a procurer. 2 a person who encourages licentiousness.

pan·dic·u·la·tion /pandikyəláyshən/ n. the act or process of stretching oneself.

pan·dit var. of PUNDIT 1.

Pan·do·ra's box /pandáwrəz/ n. a process that once activated will generate many unmanageable problems.

pane /payn/ n. 1 a single sheet of glass in a window or door. 2 a rectangular division of a checkered pattern, etc. 3 a sheet of postage stamps.

pan·e·gyr·ic /pánijírik, -jírik/ n. a laudatory discourse; a eulogy. □□ **pan·e·gyr·i·cal** adj.

pan·e·gy·rize /pánijiríz/ v.tr. speak or write in praise of; eulogize. □□ **pan·e·gyr·ist** /-jírist/ n.

pan·el /pánəl/ n. & v. ● n. 1 a a distinct, usu. rectangular, section of a surface (e.g., of a wall or door). b a control panel (see CONTROL n. 5). c = INSTRUMENT PANEL. 2 a strip of material as part of a garment. 3 a group of people gathered to form a team in a broadcast game, for a discussion, etc. 4 a list of available jurors; a jury. ● v.tr. (**paneled** or **panelled**, **paneling** or **panelling**) 1 fit or provide with panels. 2 cover or decorate with panels.

pan·el·ing /pánəling/ n. (also **pan·el·ling**) 1 paneled work. 2 wood for making panels.

pan·el·ist /pánəlist/ n. (also **pan·el·list**) a member of a panel (esp. in broadcasting).

pan·el truck n. a small enclosed delivery truck.

pang /pang/ n. (often in pl.) a sudden sharp pain or painful emotion.

pan·ga /pánggə/ n. a bladed African tool like a machete.

pan·go·lin /pánggəlin, panggṓ-/ n. ▶ any scaly anteater of the genus Manis, native to Asia and Africa, having a small head with elongated snout and tongue, and a tapering tail.

pan·han·dle /pánhand'l/ n. & v. ● n. a narrow strip of territory extending from one state into another. ● v.tr. & intr. colloq. beg for money in the street. □□ **pan·han·dler** n.

pan·ic /pánik/ n. & v. ● n. 1 a sudden uncontrollable fear or alarm. b (attrib.) characterized or caused by panic (panic buying). 2 infectious apprehension or fright esp. in commercial dealings. ● v.tr. & intr. (**panicked**, **panicking**) (often foll. by into) affect or be affected with panic (was panicked into buying). □□ **pan·ick·y** adj.

pan·ic but·ton n. a button for summoning help in an emergency.

pan·i·cle /pánikəl/ n. Bot. a loose branching cluster of flowers, as in oats. ▷ INFLORESCENCE. □□ **pan·i·cled** adj.

pan·ic-strick·en adj. (also **pan·ic-struck**) affected with panic; very apprehensive.

pa·ni·no /panéenō/ n. a sandwich made with a baguette or with crusty Italian bread.

pan·jan·drum /panjándrəm/ n. a person who has or claims to have great authority or power.

pan·nier /pányər/ n. 1 a basket, esp. one of a pair carried by a beast of burden. 2 each of a pair of bags or boxes on either side of the rear wheel of a bicycle or motorcycle.

pan·o·ply /pánəplee/ n. (pl. **-ies**) 1 a complete or magnificent array. 2 a complete suit of armor. □□ **pan·o·plied** adj.

pan·op·tic /panóptik/ adj. showing or seeing the whole at one view.

pan·o·ram·a /pánərámə, -ráà-/ n. 1 an unbroken view of a surrounding region. 2 a complete survey of a subject, sequence of events, etc. 3 a picture or photograph containing a wide view. □□ **pan·o·ram·ic** adj. **pan·o·ram·i·cal·ly** adv.

pan·pipes /pánpīps/ n.pl. ▼ a musical instrument orig. associated with the Greek rural god Pan, made of a series of short pipes graduated in length and fixed together with the mouthpieces in line.

PANPIPES

pan·sy /pánzee/ n. (pl. **-ies**) 1 any garden plant of the genus Viola, with flowers of various rich colors. 2 colloq. derog. a an effeminate man. b a male homosexual.

pant /pant/ v. & n. ● v. 1 intr. breathe with short quick breaths. 2 tr. (often foll. by out) utter breathlessly. 3 intr. (often foll. by for) yearn or crave. 4 intr. (of the heart, etc.) throb violently. ● n. 1 a panting breath. 2 a throb. □□ **pant·ing·ly** adv.

pan·ta·loon /pántəlṓn/ n. 1 (in pl.) hist. men's close-fitting trousers fastened below the calf or at the foot. 2 (**Pantaloon**) a character in Italian comedy wearing pantaloons.

pan·the·ism /pántheeizəm/ n. 1 the belief that God is identifiable with the forces of nature and with natural substances. 2 worship that admits or tolerates all gods. □□ **pan·the·ist** n. **pan·the·is·tic** adj. **pan·the·is·ti·cal** adj. **pan·the·is·ti·cal·ly** adv.

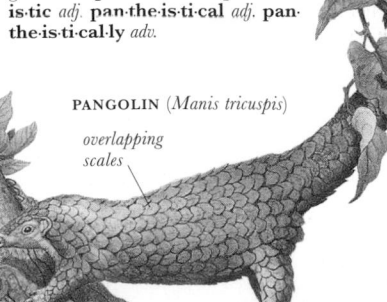

PANGOLIN (Manis tricuspis)

overlapping scales

PANTHEON

The term *pantheon* is often used to refer specifically to the Pantheon at Rome, which was built by the Roman emperor Hadrian (AD 76–138). Its huge hemispherical dome is a symbolic reference to the temple's dedication to all the gods in the universe.

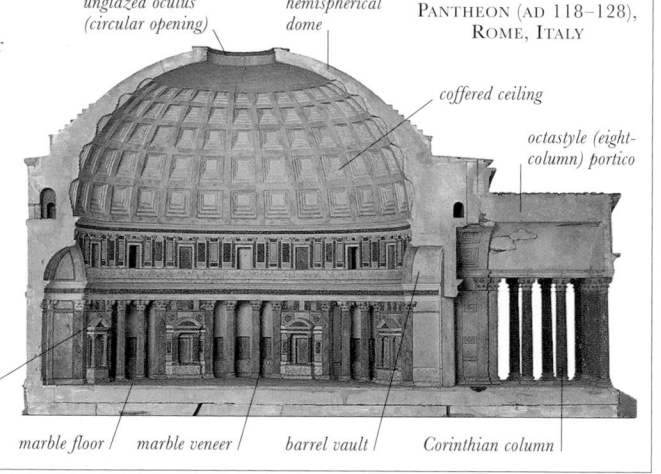

MODEL OF THE
PANTHEON (AD 118–128),
ROME, ITALY

unglazed oculus (circular opening) — *hemispherical dome* — *coffered ceiling* — *octastyle (eight-column) portico* — *pediment* — *marble floor* — *marble veneer* — *barrel vault* — *Corinthian column*

pan·the·on /pántheeon, -ən/ *n.* **1** a building in which illustrious dead are buried or have memorials. **2** the deities of a people collectively. **3** ▲ a temple dedicated to all the gods, esp. the circular one at Rome. **4** a group of esteemed persons.

pan·ther /pánthər/ *n.* **1** a leopard, esp. with black fur. **2** a cougar.

pant·ies /pánteez/ *n.pl. colloq.* short-legged or legless underpants worn by women and girls.

pan·tile /pántīl/ *n.* a roofing tile curved to form an S-shaped section, fitted to overlap.

panto- /pántō/ *comb. form* all; universal.

PANTOGRAPH ON AN
ELECTRIC LOCOMOTIVE

collector strip for electric current — *double-arm pantograph* — *locomotive*

pan·to·graph /pántəgraf/ *n.* **1** *Art & Painting* an instrument for copying a plan or drawing, etc., on a different scale by a system of jointed rods. **2** ◀ a jointed framework conveying a current to an electric vehicle from overhead wires. □□ **pan·to·graph·ic** *adj.*

pan·to·mime /pántəmīm/ *n.* **1** the use of gestures and facial expression to convey meaning without speech, esp. in drama and dance. **2** *Brit.* a theatrical entertainment based on a fairy tale, with music, topical jokes, etc., usu. produced around Christmas. **3** *colloq.* an absurd or outrageous piece of behavior.

pan·to·then·ic ac·id /pántəthénik/ *n.* a vitamin of the B complex, found in rice, bran, and many other foods, and essential for the oxidation of fats and carbohydrates.

pan·try /pántree/ *n.* (*pl.* **-ies**) **1** a small room or cupboard in which dishes, silverware, table linen, etc., are kept. **2** a small room or cupboard in which groceries, etc., are kept.

pants /pants/ *n.pl.* **1** an outer garment reaching from the waist usu. to the ankles, divided into two parts to cover the legs. **2** *Brit.* underpants. □ **bore** (or **scare**, etc.) **the pants off** *colloq.* bore, scare, etc., to an intolerable degree. **wear the pants** be the dominant partner in a marriage.

pant·suit /pántsoot/ *n.* (also **pants suit**) a woman's suit with pants and a jacket.

pan·ty hose /pánteehōz/ *n. pl. N. Amer.* women's thin nylon tights.

pan·ty·waist /pánteewayst/ *n. N. Amer. colloq.* a feeble or effeminate person.

pan·zer /pánzər, páants-/ *n.* **1** (in *pl.*) armored troops. **2** (*attrib.*) heavily armored (*panzer division*).

pap /pap/ *n.* **1 a** a soft or semiliquid food for infants or invalids. **b** a mash or pulp. **2** light or trivial reading matter; nonsense. □□ **pap·py** *adj.*

pa·pa /páapə, pəpáa/ *n.* father (esp. as a child's word).

pa·pa·cy /páypəsee/ *n.* (*pl.* **-ies**) **1** a pope's office or tenure. **2** the papal system.

Pap·a·go /páapəgō, pá-/ *n.* **1 a** a N. American people native to southwestern Arizona and adjoining parts of Mexico. **b** a member of this people. **2** the language of this people.

pa·pa·in /pəpáyin, -pī-in/ *n.* an enzyme obtained from unripe papaya, used to tenderize meat and as a food supplement to aid digestion.

pa·pal /páypəl/ *adj.* of or relating to a pope or to the papacy. □□ **pa·pal·ly** *adv.*

Pa·pal States *n.pl. hist.* the temporal dominions belonging to the Pope, esp. in central Italy.

pa·pa·raz·zo /páapəráatsō/ *n.* (*pl.* **paparazzi** /-see/) a freelance photographer who pursues celebrities to get photographs of them.

pa·paw var. of PAWPAW.

pa·pa·ya /pəpíə/ *n.* **1** ▼ an elongated melon-shaped fruit with edible orange flesh and small black seeds. **2** a tropical tree, *Carica papaya*, bearing this and producing a milky sap from which papain is obtained.

edible flesh — *seeds*

PAPAYA (*Carica papaya*)

pa·per /páypər/ *n. & v.* ● *n.* **1** ▼ a material manufactured in thin sheets from the pulp of wood or other fibrous substances, used for writing or drawing or printing on, or as wrapping material, etc. **2** (*attrib.*) **a** made of or using paper. **b** flimsy like paper. **3** = NEWSPAPER. **4 a** a document printed on paper. **b** (in *pl.*) documents attesting identity or credentials. **c** (in *pl.*) documents belonging to a person or relating to a matter. **5** *Commerce* **a** negotiable documents, e.g., bills of exchange. **b** (*attrib.*)

P

PAPER

Most paper is made from the pulped wood of trees. Logs (mostly softwood) are broken into pieces and treated with chemicals in a pulping machine, which converts the wood to a mass of fibers known as pulp. Wet wood pulp flows onto a papermaking machine. Water is sucked out, and the damp paper passes through rollers and cylinders that press and dry it. Recycled paper is made in the same way, using waste paper.

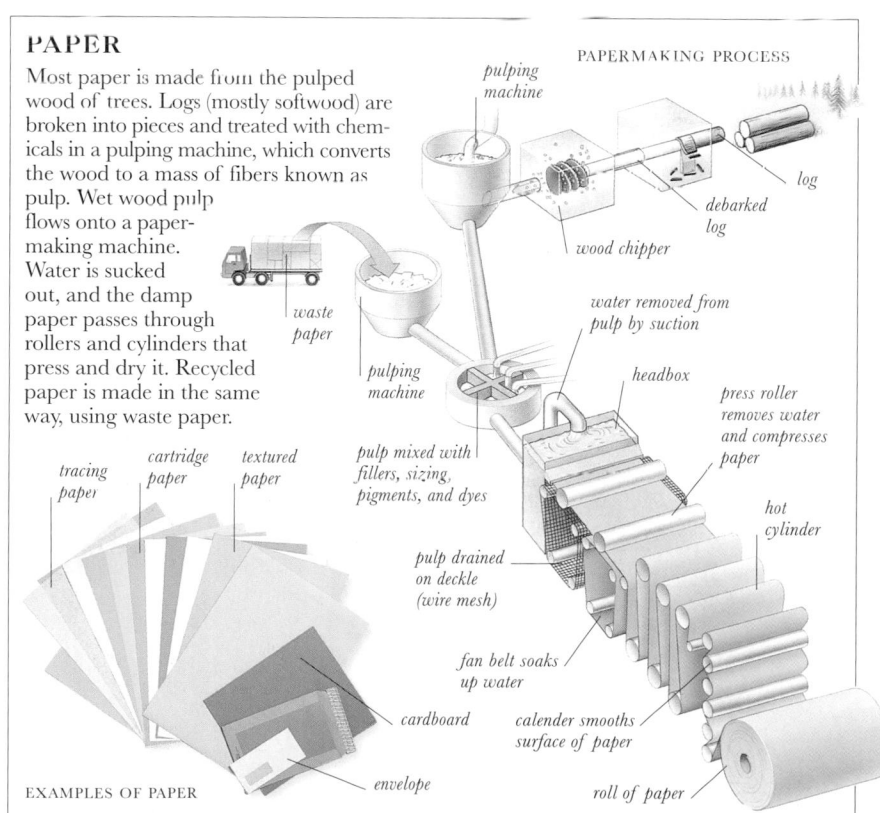

PAPERMAKING PROCESS

pulping machine — *log* — *debarked log* — *wood chipper* — *waste paper* — *pulping machine* — *water removed from pulp by suction* — *headbox* — *press roller removes water and compresses paper* — *pulp mixed with fillers, sizing, pigments, and dyes* — *hot cylinder* — *pulp drained on deckle (wire mesh)* — *fan belt soaks up water* — *calender smooths surface of paper* — *roll of paper*

tracing paper — *cartridge paper* — *textured paper* — *cardboard* — *envelope*

EXAMPLES OF PAPER

recorded on paper though not existing (*paper profits*). **6 a** a set of questions to be answered at one session in an examination. **b** the written answers to these. **7** = WALLPAPER. **8** an essay or dissertation, esp. one read to a learned society or published in a learned journal. **9** a piece of paper, esp. as a wrapper, etc. ● *v.tr.* **1** apply paper to, esp. decorate (a wall, etc.) with wallpaper. **2** (foll. by *over*) **a** cover (a hole or blemish) with paper. **b** disguise or try to hide (a fault, etc.). **3** distribute flyers, pamphlets, etc., as in a neighborhood. □ **on paper 1** in writing. **2** in theory; to judge from written or printed evidence. □□ **pa·per·er** *n.* **pa·per·less** *adj.*

pa·per·back /páypərbak/ (*US also* **paperbound**) *adj. & n.* ● *adj.* (of a book) bound in stiff paper. ● *n.* a paperback book.

pa·per·boy /páypərboy/ *n.* (*fem.* **pa·per·girl** /-gərl/) a boy or girl who delivers or sells newspapers.

pa·per clip *n.* a clip of bent wire or of plastic for holding several sheets of paper together.

pa·per mon·ey *n.* money in the form of bills.

pa·per route *n.* (*Brit.* **paper round**) **1** a job of regularly delivering newspapers. **2** a route taken doing this.

pa·per ti·ger *n.* an apparently threatening, but ineffectual, person or thing.

pa·per trail *n.* documentation of transactions, etc.

pa·per·weight /páypərwayt/ *n.* a small heavy object for keeping loose papers in place.

pa·per·work /páypərwork/ *n.* **1** routine clerical or administrative work. **2** documents, esp. for a particular purpose.

pa·per·y /páypəree/ *adj.* like paper in thinness or texture.

pa·pier mâ·ché /páypər məsháy, papyáy/ *n.* paper pulp used for molding into boxes, trays, etc.

pa·pil·i·o·na·ceous /pəpíleeənáyshəs/ *adj.* (of a plant) with a corolla shaped like a butterfly.

pa·pil·la /pəpílə/ *n.* (*pl.* **papillae** /-pílee/) **1** a small nipplelike protuberance in a part or organ of the body. **2** *Bot.* a small fleshy projection on a plant. □□ **pap·il·la·ry** *adj.* **pa·pil·late** /pápilayt/ *adj.* **pap·il·lose** /pápilōs/ *adj.*

pap·il·lo·ma /pápilómə/ *n.* (*pl.* **papillomas** or **papillomata** /-mətə/) a wartlike usu. benign tumor.

pap·il·lon /paapeeyóN, pá-/ *n.* **1** a toy dog of a breed with ears suggesting the form of a butterfly. **2** this breed.

pa·pist /páypist/ *n. & adj.* often *derog.* ● *n.* **1** a Roman Catholic. **2** *hist.* an advocate of papal supremacy. ● *adj.* of or relating to Roman Catholics. □□ **pa·pis·tic** *adj.* **pa·pis·ti·cal** *adj.* **pa·pist·ry** *n.*

pa·poose /papóos, pə-/ *n.* a young Native American child.

pap·pus /pápəs/ *n.* (*pl.* **pappi** /-pī/) a group of hairs on the fruit of thistles, dandelions, etc. □□ **pap·pose** *adj.*

pa·pri·ka /pəprēckə, páprikə/ *n.* **1** *Bot.* a red pepper. **2** a condiment made from it. ▷ SPICE

Pap smear /pap/ *n.* (*also* **Pap test**) a test for cervical cancer, etc., done by a cervical smear.

pap·u·la /pápyələ/ *n.* (*pl.* **papulae** /-lee/) (*also* **pap·ule** /pápyōol/) **1** a pimple. **2** a small fleshy projection on a plant. □□ **pap·u·lar** *adj.* **pap·u·lose** *adj.* **pap·u·lous** *adj.*

pa·py·rol·o·gy /pápiróləjee/ *n.* the study of ancient papyri. □□ **pa·py·ro·log·i·cal** /-rəlój·ikəl/ *adj.* **pa·py·rol·o·gist** *n.*

pa·py·rus /pəpírəs/ *n.* (*pl.* **pa·pyri** /-rī/) **1** ▶ an aquatic plant, *Cyperus papyrus*, with dark green stems topped with fluffy inflorescences. **2 a** a writing material prepared in ancient

Egypt from the pithy stem of this. **b** a document written on this.

par /paar/ *n. & v.* ● *n.* **1** the average or normal amount, degree, condition, etc. (*be up to par*). **2** equality; an equal status or footing (*on a par with*). **3** *Golf* the number of strokes a skilled player should normally require for a hole or course. **4** *Stock Exch.* the face value of stocks and shares, etc. (*at par*). **5** (in full **par of exchange**) the recognized value of one country's currency in terms of another's. ● *v.intr. Golf* to score par. □ **below par** less good than usual in health or other quality. **par for the course** *colloq.* what is normal or expected in any given circumstances.

par. *abbr.* (*also* **para.**) paragraph.

par·a /párə/ *n. colloq.* **1** a paratrooper. **2** a paraprofessional. **3** *Brit.* a paragraph.

par·a·a·min·o·ben·zo·ic ac·id /parə-əmēenōbenzóik/ *n. Biochem.* a yellow crystalline compound, often used in suntan lotions and sunscreens to absorb ultraviolet light. ¶ *Abbr.:* **PABA**.

par·a·ble /párəbəl/ *n.* **1** a narrative of imagined events used to illustrate a moral or spiritual lesson. **2** an allegory.

pa·rab·o·la /pərábələ/ *n.* ▶ an open plane curve formed by the intersection of a cone with a plane parallel to its side, resembling the path of a projectile under the action of gravity.

parabola

PARABOLA

par·a·bol·ic /párəbólik/ *adj.* **1** of or expressed in a parable. **2** of or like a parabola. □□ **par·a·bol·i·cal·ly** *adv.*

par·a·bol·i·cal /párəbólikəl/ *adj.* = PARABOLIC 1.

axis of symmetry

pa·rab·o·loid /pərábəloyd/ *n.* (in full **paraboloid of revolution**) ▶ a solid generated by the rotation of a parabola about its axis of symmetry. **2** a solid having two or more nonparallel parabolic cross sections. □□ **pa·rab·o·loi·dal** *adj.*

PARABOLOID

par·a·chute /párəshōōt/ *n. & v.* ● *n.* **1** a rectangular or umbrella-shaped canopy allowing a person or heavy object attached to it to descend slowly from a height, esp. from an aircraft, or to retard motion in other ways. **2** (*attrib.*) dropped or to be dropped by parachute (*parachute drop*). ● *v.tr. & intr.* convey or descend by parachute.

par·a·chut·ist /párəshōōtist/ *n.* **1** a person who uses a parachute. **2** (in *pl.*) parachute troops.

Par·a·clete /párəkleet/ *n.* the Holy Spirit as advocate or counselor.

pa·rade /pəráyd/ *n. & v.* ● *n.* **1 a** a formal or ceremonial muster of troops for inspection. **b** = PARADE GROUND. **2** a public procession. **3** ostentatious display (*made a parade of their wealth*). **4** *Brit.* a public square, promenade, or row of shops. ● *v.* **1** *intr.* assemble for parade. **2 a** *tr.* march through (streets, etc.) in procession. **b** *intr.* march ceremonially. **3** *tr.* display ostentatiously. □ **on parade 1** taking part in a parade. **2** on display. □□ **pa·rad·er** *n.*

pa·rade ground *n.* a place for the muster of troops.

par·a·did·dle /párədid'l/ *n.* a drum roll with alternate beating of sticks.

par·a·digm /párədīm/ *n.* **1** an example or pattern. **2** *Gram.* a representative set of the inflections of a noun, verb, etc. □□ **par·a·dig·mat·ic** /-digmátik/ *adj.* **par·a·dig·mat·i·cal·ly** *adv.*

par·a·dise /párədīs/ *n.* **1** (in some religions) heaven as the ultimate abode of the just. **2** a place or state of complete happiness. **3** (in full **earthly paradise**) the abode of Adam and Eve in the biblical account of the Creation; the garden of Eden. □□ **par·a·di·sa·i·cal** /-disáyikəl/ *adj.* **par·a·dis·al** /párədísəl/ *adj.* **par·a·di·si·a·cal** /-disíəkəl/ *adj.* **par·a·di·si·cal** /-disíkəl/ *adj.*

par·a·dox /párədoks/ *n.* **1 a** a seemingly absurd or contradictory statement, even if actually well-founded. **b** a self-contradictory or essentially absurd statement. **2** a person or thing conflicting with a preconceived notion of what is reasonable or possible. **3** a paradoxical quality or character.

par·a·dox·i·cal /párədóksikəl/ *adj.* **1** of or like or involving paradox. **2** fond of paradox. □□ **par·a·dox·i·cal·ly** *adv.*

par·af·fin /párəfin/ *n.* **1** (*also* **paraffin wax**) a waxy mixture of hydrocarbons used in candles, waterproofing, etc. **2** *Brit.* = KEROSENE. **3** *Chem.* = ALKANE.

par·a·go·ge /párəgójee/ *n.* the addition of a letter or syllable to a word in some contexts or as a language develops (e.g., *t* in *peasant*).

par·a·gon /párəgon, -gən/ *n.* **1 a** a model of excellence. **b** a supremely excellent person or thing. **2** (foll. by *of*) a model (of virtue, etc.). **3** a perfect diamond of 100 carats or more.

par·a·graph /párəgraf/ *n. & v.* ● *n.* **1** a distinct section of a piece of writing, beginning on a new usu. indented line. **2** a symbol (usu. ¶) used to mark a new paragraph, and also as a reference mark. **3** a short item in a newspaper, usu. of only one paragraph. ● *v.tr.* arrange (a piece of writing) in paragraphs. □□ **par·a·graph·ic** /-gráfik/ *adj.*

par·a·keet /párəkéet/ *n.* any of various small usu. long-tailed parrots.

par·a·lan·guage /párəlanggwij/ *n.* elements or factors in communication that are ancillary to language proper, e.g., intonation and gesture.

par·al·de·hyde /pəráldihīd/ *n.* a cyclic polymer of acetaldehyde, used as a narcotic and sedative.

par·a·le·gal /párəleegəl/ *adj. & n.* ● *adj.* of or relating to auxiliary aspects of the law. ● *n.* a person trained in subsidiary legal matters.

par·a·li·pom·e·na /párəlipóminə/ *n. pl.* (*also* **-leipomena** /-párəlī-/) **1** things omitted from a work and added as a supplement. **2** *Bibl.* the books of Chronicles in the Old Testament, containing particulars omitted from the books of Kings.

par·a·lip·sis /párəlípsis/ *n.* (*also* **-leipsis** /-lípsis/) (*pl.* **-ses** /-seez/) *Rhet.* **1** the device of giving emphasis by professing to say little or nothing of a subject, as in *not to mention their unpaid debts of several million dollars*. **2** an instance of this.

par·al·lax /párəlaks/ *n.* **1** ▲ the apparent difference in the position or direction of an object caused when the observer's position is changed. **2** the angular amount of this. □□ **par·al·lac·tic** /-láktik/ *adj.*

par·al·lel /párəlel/ *adj., n., & v.* ● *adj.* **1 a** (of lines or planes) side by side and having the same distance continuously between them. **b** (foll. by *to, with*) (of a line or plane) having this relation (to another). **2** (of circumstances, etc.) precisely similar, analogous, or corresponding. **3 a** (of processes, etc.) occurring or performed simultaneously. **b** *Computing* involving the simultaneous performance of operations. ● *n.* **1** a person or thing precisely analogous or equal to another. **2** a comparison (*drew a parallel between the two situations*). **3** (in full **parallel of latitude**) *Geog.* **a** each of the imaginary parallel circles of constant latitude on the Earth's surface. **b** a corresponding line on a map (*the 49th parallel*). **4** *Printing* two parallel lines (‖) used as a reference mark. ● *v.tr.* (**paralleled**, **paralleling**) **1** be parallel to; correspond to. **2** represent as similar; compare. **3** adduce as a parallel instance. □ **in parallel** (of electric circuits) arranged so as to join at common points at each end. □□ **par·al·lel·ism** *n.*

PAPYRUS (*Cyperus papyrus*)

PARALLAX

In astronomy, the term *parallax* refers to the apparent displacement of nearby stars against the background of more distant stars when viewed from opposite sides of the Earth's orbit. The greater the parallax, the nearer the star is to Earth. In the illustration shown here, star B has the greater shift and is closer to Earth than star A.

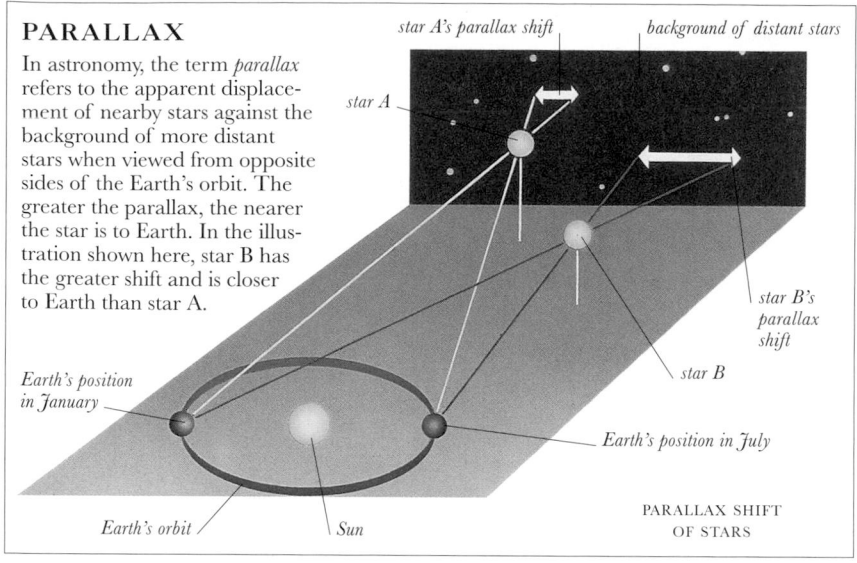

star A's parallax shift

background of distant stars

star A

star B's parallax shift

star B

Earth's position in January

Earth's position in July

Earth's orbit

Sun

PARALLAX SHIFT OF STARS

---

par·al·lel bars *n.pl.* a pair of parallel rails on posts for gymnastics.

par·al·lel·e·pi·ped /párəleləpípid, -pípid/ *n. Geom.* a solid body of which each face is a parallelogram.

par·al·lel·o·gram /párəléləgram/ *n. Geom.* ◄ a four-sided plane rectilinear figure with opposite sides parallel.

PARALLELOGRAM

par·a·log·ism /pəráləjizəm/ *n. Logic* **1** a fallacy. **2** illogical reasoning (esp. of which the reasoner is unconscious). □□ **pa·ral·o·gist** *n.*

pa·ral·y·sis /pərálisis/ *n.* (*pl.* **paralyses** /-seez/) **1** impairment or loss of esp. the motor function of the nerves. **2** a state of utter powerlessness.

par·a·lyt·ic /párəlitik/ *adj. & n.* ● *adj.* **1** affected by paralysis. **2** esp. *Brit. sl.* very drunk. ● *n.* a person affected by paralysis. □□ **par·a·lyt·i·cal·ly** *adv.*

par·a·lyze /párəlīz/ *v.tr.* (also *Brit.* **paralyse**) **1** affect with paralysis. **2** render powerless; cripple. □□ **par·a·ly·za·tion** *n.* **par·a·lyz·ing·ly** *adv.*

par·a·mag·net·ic /párəmagnétik/ *adj.* (of a body or substance) tending to become weakly magnetized so as to lie parallel to a magnetic field force. □□ **par·a·mag·net·ism** /-mágnitizəm/ *n.*

par·a·me·ci·um /párəmēéseeəm/ *n.* any freshwater protozoan of the genus *Paramecium*, of a characteristic slipper-like shape covered with cilia.

par·a·med·ic /párəmédik/ *n.* **1** a paramedical worker. **2** a person trained in emergency medical procedures.

par·a·med·i·cal /párəmédikəl/ *adj.* (of services, etc.) supplementing and supporting medical work.

par·am·e·ter /pərámitər/ *n.* **1** *Math.* a quantity constant in the case considered but varying in different cases. **2 a** an (esp. measurable or quantifiable) characteristic or feature. **b** (loosely) a constant element or factor, esp. serving as a limit or boundary. □□ **par·a·met·ric** /párəmétrik/ *adj.* **pa·ram·e·trize** *v.tr.*

par·a·mil·i·tar·y /párəmíliteree/ *adj.* organized similarly to a military force.

par·a·mount /párəmownt/ *adj.* **1** supreme; requiring first consideration; preeminent (*of paramount importance*). **2** in supreme authority. □□ **par·a·mount·cy** *n.* **par·a·mount·ly** *adv.*

par·a·mour /párəmoor/ *n.* an illicit lover, esp. of a married person.

pa·rang /párang/ *n.* a large heavy Malayan knife used for clearing vegetation, etc.

par·a·noi·a /párənóyə/ *n.* **1** a personality disorder esp. characterized by delusions of persecution and self importance. **2** an abnormal tendency to suspect and mistrust others. □□ **par·a·noi·ac** *adj. & n.* **par·a·noi·a·cal·ly** *adv.* **par·a·no·ic** /-nóyik, -nóik/ *adj.* **par·a·no·i·cal·ly** *adv.* **par·a·noid** /-noyd/ *adj. & n.*

par·a·nor·mal /párənórməl/ *adj.* beyond the scope of normal objective investigation or explanation. □□ **par·a·nor·mal·ly** *adv.*

par·a·pet /párəpit/ *n.* **1** a low wall at the edge of a roof, balcony, etc., or along the sides of a bridge. **2** a defense of earth or stone to conceal and protect troops. □□ **par·a·pet·ed** *adj.*

par·a·pher·na·lia /párəfərnáylyə/ *n.pl.* (also treated as *sing.*) miscellaneous belongings, items of equipment, accessories, etc.

par·a·phil·i·a /párəfileeə/ *n. Psychol.* a condition characterized by abnormal sexual desires involving extreme or dangerous activities.

par·a·phrase /párəfrayz/ *n. & v.* ● *n.* a free rendering or rewording of a passage. ● *v.tr.* express the meaning of (a passage) in other words. □□ **par·a·phras·tic** /-frástik/ *adj.*

par·a·ple·gi·a /párəpléejə/ *n.* paralysis of the legs and part or the whole of the trunk. □□ **par·a·ple·gic** *adj. & n.*

par·a·psy·chol·o·gy /párəsīkóləjee/ *n.* the study of mental phenomena outside the sphere of ordinary psychology (hypnosis, telepathy, etc.). □□ **par·a·psy·cho·log·i·cal** /-sīkəlójikəl/ *adj.* **par·a·psy·chol·o·gist** *n.*

par·a·quat /párəkwot/ *n.* a quick-acting herbicide, becoming inactive on contact with the soil.

par·a·site /párəsīt/ *n.* **1** ▼ an organism living in or on another and benefiting at the expense of the other. **2** a person who lives off or exploits another or others. □□ **par·a·sit·ic** /-sítik/ *adj.* **par·a·sit·i·cal** /-sítikəl/ *adj.* **par·a·sit·i·cal·ly** *adv.* **par·a·sit·i·cide** /-sítisīd/ *n.* **par·a·sit·ism** /-sitizəm/ *n.* **par·a·si·tol·o·gy** /-tóləjee/ *n.* **par·a·si·tol·o·gist** /-tóləjist/ *n.*

par·a·si·tize /párəsītīz/ *v.tr.* infest as a parasite. □□ **par·a·sit·i·za·tion** *n.*

par·a·sol /párəsawl, -sol/ *n.* **1** a light umbrella used to give shade from the sun. **2** (in full **parasol mushroom**) ▶ any of several fungi of the genus *Lepiota*, typically with a broad, scaly, shaggy domed cap.

par·a·sym·pa·thet·ic /párəsimpəthétik/ *adj. Anat.* relating to the part of the nervous system that consists of nerves leaving the lower end of the spinal cord and connecting with those in or near the viscera.

PARASOL MUSHROOM (*Lepiota aspera*)

P

PARASITE

Parasitic lifestyles are common in invertebrates, flowering plants, fungi, and single-celled organisms. Endoparasites live inside their hosts (a tapeworm, for example, uses hooks and suckers on its head to grip its host's intestine). Ectoparasites, such as lice, live on the surface of their hosts' bodies and often attach themselves by their claws or sharp mouthparts. Some parasitic plants live entirely within their hosts, but most – such as the dodder – invade their hosts' tissue through specially adapted roots or stems.

TYPES OF PARASITE

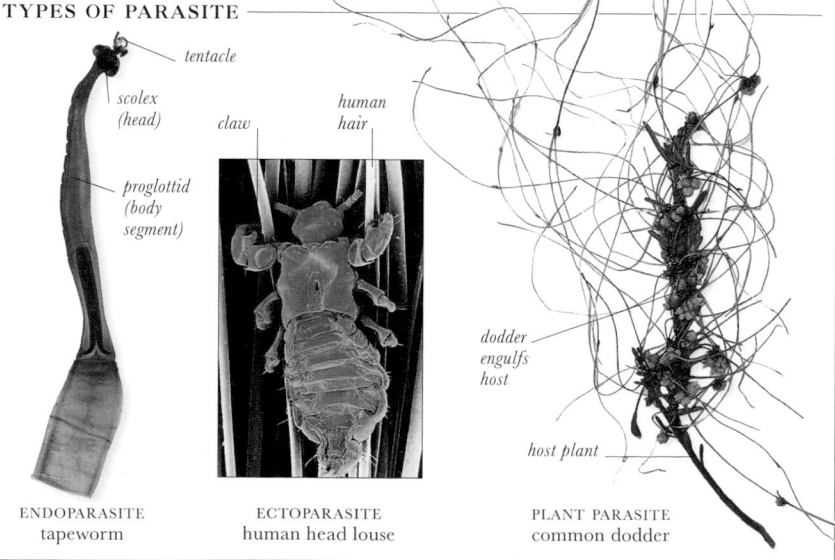

tentacle

scolex (head)

claw

human hair

proglottid (body segment)

dodder engulfs host

host plant

ENDOPARASITE
tapeworm

ECTOPARASITE
human head louse

PLANT PARASITE
common dodder

par·a·tax·is /párətáksis/ *n. Gram.* the placing of clauses, etc., one after another, without words to indicate coordination or subordination, e.g., *Tell me, how are you?* □□ **par·a·tac·tic** /-táktik/ *adj.* **par·a·tac·ti·cal·ly** *adv.*

par·a·thy·roid /párəthíroyd/ *n. & adj. Anat.* ● *n.* a gland next to the thyroid, secreting a hormone that regulates calcium levels in the body. ▷ ENDOCRINE. ● *adj.* of or associated with this gland.

par·a·troop /párətrōōp/ *n. (attrib.)* of or consisting of paratroops (*paratroop regiment*).

par·a·troop·er /párətrōōpər/ *n.* a member of a body of paratroops.

par·a·troops /párətrōōps/ *n.pl.* troops equipped to be dropped by parachute from aircraft.

par·a·ty·phoid /párətífoyd/ *n. & adj.* ● *n.* a fever resembling typhoid but caused by various different though related bacteria. ● *adj.* of, relating to, or caused by this fever.

par·boil /paárboyl/ *v.tr.* partly cook by boiling.

par·cel /paársəl/ *n. & v.* ● *n.* **1 a** goods, etc., wrapped up in a single package. **b** a bundle of things wrapped up, usu. in paper. **2** a piece of land, esp. as part of a larger lot. **3** a quantity dealt with in one commercial transaction. **4** a group or collection of things, people, etc. **5** part. ● *v.tr.* (**parceled, parceling** or **parcelled, parcelling**) **1** (foll. by *out*) divide into portions. **2** (foll. by *up*) wrap as a parcel. **3** cover (rope) with strips of canvas.

par·cel post *n.* **1** a mail service dealing with parcels. **2** a postage rate for parcels.

parch /paarch/ *v.* **1** *tr. & intr.* make or become hot and dry. **2** *tr.* roast (peas, grain, etc.) slightly.

parched /paarcht/ *adj.* **1** hot and dry; dried out with heat. **2** *colloq.* thirsty.

parch·ment /paárchmənt/ *n.* **1** an animal skin, esp. that of a sheep or goat, prepared as a writing or painting surface. ▷ SCROLL. **2** a manuscript written on this.

pard·ner /paárdnər/ *n. US dial. colloq.* a partner or comrade.

par·don /paárd'n/ *n., v., & int.* ● *n.* **1** the act of excusing or forgiving an offense, error, etc. **2** (in full **full pardon**, *Brit.* **free pardon**) a remission of the legal consequences of a crime or conviction. **3** *RC Ch.* an indulgence. ● *v.tr.* **1** release from the consequences of an offense, error, etc. **2** forgive or excuse a person for (an offense, etc.). **3** make (esp. courteous) allowances for; excuse. ● *int.* (also **pardon me** or **I beg your pardon**) **1** a formula of apology or disagreement. **2** a request to repeat something said. □□ **par·don·a·ble** *adj.* **par·don·a·bly** *adv.*

pare /pair/ *v.tr.* **1 a** trim (esp. fruit and vegetables) by cutting away the surface or edge. **b** (often foll. by *off, away*) cut off (the surface or edge). **2** (often foll. by *away, down*) diminish little by little. □□ **par·er** *n.*

par·e·gor·ic /párigáwrik, -gór-/ *n.* a camphorated tincture of opium used to reduce pain or relieve diarrhea.

pa·ren·chy·ma /pəréngkimə/ *n.* **1** *Anat.* the functional part of an organ as distinguished from the connective and supporting tissue. **2** *Bot.* the cellular material, usu. soft and succulent, found esp. in the softer parts of leaves, pulp of fruits, bark and pith of stems, etc. □□ **pa·ren·chy·mal** *adj.* **pa·ren·chym·a·tous** /-kímətəs/ *adj.*

par·ent /páirənt, pár-/ *n. & v.* ● *n.* **1** a person who has begotten or borne offspring; a father or mother. **2** a person who holds the position or exercises the functions of such a parent. **3** an ancestor. **4** an animal or plant from which others are derived. **5** a source or origin. **6** an initiating organization or enterprise. ● *v.tr.* (also *absol.*) be a parent of. □□ **pa·ren·tal** /pərént'l/ *adj.* **pa·ren·tal·ly** /pəréntəlee/ *adv.* **par·ent·hood** *n.*

par·ent·age /páirəntij, pár-/ *n.* lineage; descent from or through parents (*their parentage is unknown*).

par·ent com·pa·ny *n.* a company of which other companies are subsidiaries.

par·en·ter·al /pəréntərəl/ *adj. Med.* administered or occurring elsewhere than in the alimentary canal. □□ **par·en·ter·al·ly** *adv.*

pa·ren·the·sis /pərénthəsis/ *n. (pl.* **parentheses** /-seez/) **1 a** a word, clause, or sentence inserted as an explanation or afterthought into a passage which is grammatically complete without it, and usu. marked off by brackets or dashes or commas. **b** (in *pl.*) a pair of rounded brackets ( ) used for this. **2** an interlude or interval. □ **in parenthesis** as a parenthesis or afterthought.

pa·ren·the·size /pərénthəsīz/ *v.tr.* **1** (also *absol.*) insert as a parenthesis. **2** put into brackets or similar punctuation.

par·en·thet·ic /párənthétik/ *adj.* **1** of or by way of a parenthesis. **2** interposed. □□ **par·en·thet·i·cal** *adj.* **par·en·thet·i·cal·ly** *adv.*

par·ent·ing /páirənting, pár-/ *n.* the occupation or concerns of parents.

Par·ent-Teach·er As·so·ci·a·tion *n.* a local organization of parents and teachers for promoting closer relations and improving educational facilities at a school. ¶ Abbr.: **PTA**.

pa·re·sis /pəréesis, párisis/ *n. (pl.* **pareses** /-seez/) *Med.* partial paralysis. □□ **pa·re·tic** /pərétik/ *adj.*

pa·reve /páarəvə, paárvə/ *adj.* made without milk or meat and thus suitable for kosher use.

par ex·cel·lence /paár eksəlóns/ *adv.* as having special excellence; being the supreme example of its kind (*the short story par excellence*).

par·fait /paarfáy/ *n.* **1** a rich frozen custard of whipped cream, eggs, etc. **2** layers of ice cream, meringue, etc., served in a tall glass.

par·get /paárjit/ *v. & n.* ● *v.tr.* (**pargeted, pargeting**) **1** plaster (a wall, etc.) esp. with an ornamental pattern. **2** roughcast. ● *n.* **1** ▼ plaster applied in this way; ornamental plasterwork. **2** roughcast.

pargeting

DIEV·ET·MON·DROIT

PARGET: PARGETED ROYAL COAT OF ARMS ON A 17TH-CENTURY HOUSE

pa·ri·ah /pəríə/ *n.* **1** a social outcast. **2** *hist.* a member of a low caste or of no caste in S. India.

pa·ri·e·tal /pəríətəl/ *adj.* **1** *Anat.* of the wall of the body or any of its cavities. **2** *Bot.* of the wall of a hollow structure, etc. **3** relating to residence and visitation rules in a college dormitory.

par·i·mu·tu·el /párimyōōchōōəl/ *n.* **1** a form of betting in which those backing the first three places divide the losers' stakes (less the operator's commission). **2 a** a device showing the number and amount of bets staked on a race, to facilitate the division of the total among those backing the winner. **b** a system of betting based on this.

par·ing /páiring/ *n.* a strip or piece cut off.

par·ish /párish/ *n.* **1** an area having its own church and clergy. **2** a county in Louisiana. **3** *Brit.* (in full **civil parish**) a district constituted for purposes of local government. **4** the inhabitants of a parish.

par·ish·ion·er /pəríshənər/ *n.* an inhabitant or member of a parish.

Pa·ri·sian /pəréezhən, -rízhən, -rízeeən/ *adj. & n.* ● *adj.* of or relating to Paris in France. ● *n.* **1** a native or inhabitant of Paris. **2** the kind of French spoken in Paris.

par·i·ty[1] /páritee/ *n.* **1** equality or equal status, esp. as regards status or pay. **2** parallelism or analogy (*parity of reasoning*). **3** equivalence of one currency with another; being at par. **4 a** (of a number) the fact of being even or odd. **b** *Computing* mathematical parity used for error detection. **5** *Physics* (of a quantity) the fact of changing its sign or remaining unaltered under a given transformation of coordinates, etc.

par·i·ty[2] /páritee/ *n. Med.* **1** the fact or condition of having borne children. **2** the number of children previously borne.

park /paark/ *n. & v.* ● *n.* **1** a large public area in a town, used for recreation. **2** a large enclosed piece of ground, usu. with woodland and pasture, attached to a country house, etc. **3 a** a large area of land kept in its natural state for public recreational use. **b** esp. *Brit.* a large enclosed area of land used to accommodate wild animals in captivity (*wildlife park*). **4** esp. *Brit.* an area for motor vehicles, etc., to be left in (*car park*). **5** the gear position or function in an automatic transmission in which the gears are locked, preventing the vehicle's movement. **6** an area devoted to a specified purpose (*industrial park*). **7** a sports arena or stadium. ● *v.* **1** *tr.* (also *absol.*) leave (a vehicle) usu. temporarily, in a parking lot, by the side of the road, etc. **2** *tr. colloq.* deposit and leave, usu. temporarily. **3** *intr. sl.* engage in petting or kissing in a parked car. □ **park oneself** *colloq.* sit down.

par·ka /paárkə/ *n.* **1** ▶ a skin jacket with hood, worn by Eskimos. **2** a similar windproof fabric garment worn in cold weather.

hood

reindeer skin

mittens sewn into sleeves

fur trim

PARKA

park·ing lot *n.* an area for parking vehicles.

park·ing me·ter *n.* a coin-operated meter that receives payment for vehicles parked in the street and indicates the time available.

park·ing tick·et *n.* a notice, usu. attached to a vehicle, of a penalty imposed for parking illegally.

Par·kin·son·ism /paárkinsənizəm/ *n.* = PARKINSON'S DISEASE.

Par·kin·son's dis·ease /paárkinsənz/ *n.* a progressive disease of the nervous system with tremor, muscular rigidity, and emaciation. Also called **Parkinsonism**.

Par·kin·son's law /paárkinsənz/ *n.* the notion that work expands so as to fill the time available for its completion.

park·land /paárkland/ *n.* open grassland with clumps of trees, etc.

park·way /paárkway/ *n.* **1** an open landscaped highway. **2** *Brit.* a railroad station with extensive parking facilities.

par·lance /paárləns/ *n.* a particular way of speaking, esp. as regards choice of words, idiom, etc.

par·lay /paárlay/ *v. & n.* ● *v.tr.* **1** use (money won on a bet) as a further stake. **2** increase in value by or

P

as if by parlaying. ● *n.* **1** an act of parlaying. **2** a bet made by parlaying.

par·ley /paárlee/ *n. & v.* ● *n.* (*pl.* **-eys**) a conference for debating points in a dispute, esp. of terms for an armistice, etc. ● *v.intr.* (**-leys**, **-leyed**) (often foll. by *with*) hold a parley.

par·lia·ment /paárləmənt/ *n.* **1** (**Parliament**) **a** (in the UK) the highest legislature, consisting of the Sovereign, the House of Lords, and the House of Commons. **b** the members of this legislature for a particular period, esp. between one dissolution and the next. **2** a similar legislature in other nations.

par·lia·men·tar·i·an /paárləmentáireeən/ *n. & adj.* ● *n.* **1** a member of a parliament. **2** a person who is well-versed in parliamentary procedures. **3** *hist.* an adherent of Parliament in the English Civil War of the 17th c. ● *adj.* = PARLIAMENTARY.

par·lia·men·ta·ry /paárləméntəree, -tree/ *adj.* **1** of, relating to, or enacted by a parliament. **2** (of language) admissible in a parliament; polite.

par·lor /paárlər/ *n.* (*Brit.* **parlour**) **1** a sitting room in a private house. **2** a room in a hotel, club, etc., for the private use of residents. **3** a store providing specified goods or services (*beauty parlor*; *ice cream parlor*). **4** a room or building equipped for milking cows. **5** (*attrib.*) *derog.* denoting support for esp. political views by those who do not try to practice them (*parlor socialist*).

par·lor game *n.* an indoor game, esp. a word game.

par·lous /paárləs/ *adj. & adv.* ● *adj.* **1** dangerous or difficult. **2** *archaic* clever; cunning. ● *adv.* extremely. □□ **par·lous·ly** *adv.* **par·lous·ness** *n.*

Par·ma vi·o·let /paármə/ *n.* a variety of sweet violet with heavy scent and lavender-colored flowers.

Par·me·san /paármizaán, -zaán, -zən/ *n.* a kind of hard dry cheese made orig. at Parma and used esp. in grated form. ▷ CHEESE

par·mi·gia·na /paarmijaánə/ *adj.* cooked or served with Parmesan cheese.

pa·ro·chi·al /pərókeeəl/ *adj.* **1** of or concerning a parish. **2** (of affairs, views, etc.) merely local, narrow or restricted in scope. □□ **pa·ro·chi·al·ism** *n.* **pa·ro·chi·al·i·ty** /-álitee/ *n.* **pa·ro·chi·al·ly** *adv.*

pa·ro·chi·al school *n.* a private elementary or high school maintained by a religious organization, esp. the Roman Catholic Church.

par·o·dy /párədee/ *n. & v.* ● *n.* (*pl.* **-ies**) **1** a humorous exaggerated imitation of an author, literary work, style, etc. **2** a feeble imitation; a travesty. ● *v.tr.* (**-ies**, **-ied**) **1** compose a parody of. **2** mimic humorously. □□ **par·o·dic** /pəródik/ *adj.* **par·o·dist** *n.*

pa·rol /pərṓl/ *adj. & n. Law* ● *adj.* given orally. ● *n.* an oral declaration.

pa·role /pərṓl/ *n. & v.* ● *n.* **1 a** the release of a prisoner temporarily for a special purpose or completely before the fulfillment of a sentence, on the promise of good behavior. **b** such a promise. **2** a word of honor. ● *v.tr.* put (a prisoner) on parole. □ **on parole** released on the terms of parole. □□ **pa·rol·ee** /-leé/ *n.*

par·o·no·ma·si·a /páranōmázhə, -zheeə/ *n.* a pun.

pa·rot·id /pərótid/ *adj. & n.* ● *adj.* situated near the ear. ● *n.* (in full **parotid gland**) ▼ a salivary gland in front of the ear.

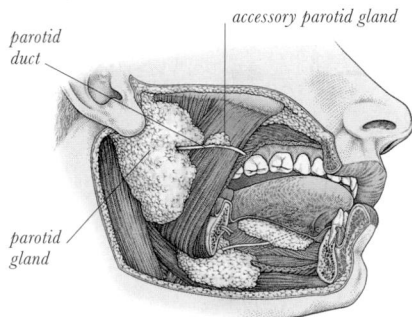

accessory parotid gland
parotid duct
parotid gland

PAROTID GLAND: HUMAN HEAD SHOWING
THE PAROTID GLAND

PARROT

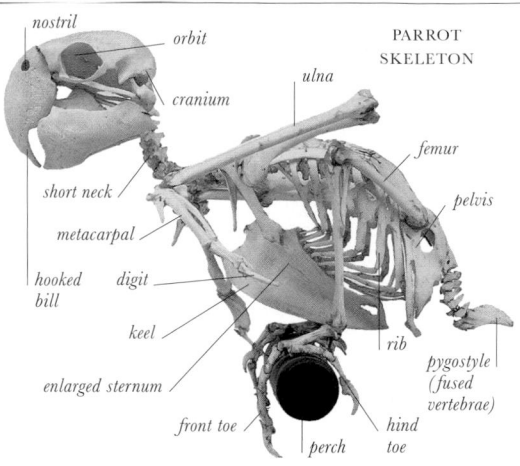

nostril   *orbit*   PARROT SKELETON

cranium   *ulna*

short neck   *femur*

metacarpal   *pelvis*

hooked bill   *digit*

keel   *rib*

enlarged sternum   *pygostyle (fused vertebrae)*

front toe   *hind toe*

perch

There are more than 300 species in the parrot family, including lorics, macaws, and lorikeets. They all share such common features as a relatively large head, hooked bill, and strong grasping feet with two toes in front and two behind, which aid in holding food and climbing. Most species are diurnal birds that live in trees, but a few are nocturnal or stay on the ground. Parrots often gather in flocks, within which they are commonly in pairs. Most species are monogamous, mating for years and sometimes for life.

EXAMPLES OF PARROTS

ECLECTUS PARROT
(*Eclectus roratus*)

CELESTIAL PARROTLET
(*Forpus coelestis*)

AFRICAN GRAY PARROT
(*Psittacus erithacus*)

GREEN-WINGED MACAW
(*Ara chloroptera*)

BLUE-CROWNED HANGING PARROT
(*Loriculus galgulus*)

GALAH
(*Eolophus roseicapillus*)

UMBRELLA COCKATOO
(*Cacatua alba*)

CHATTERING LORY
(*Lorius garrulus*)

RAINBOW LORIKEET
(*Trichoglossus haematodus*)

---

par·o·ti·tis /páratítis/ *n.* **1** inflammation of the parotid gland. **2** mumps.

-parous /pərəs/ *comb. form* bearing offspring of a specified number or kind (*multiparous*; *viviparous*).

par·ox·ysm /párəksizəm/ *n.* **1** (often foll. by *of*) a sudden attack or outburst (of rage, laughter, etc.). **2** a fit of disease. □□ **par·ox·ys·mal** /-sízməl/ *adj.*

par·pen /paárpən/ *n.* (also **per·pend**) a stone passing through a wall from side to side, with two smooth vertical faces.

par·quet /paárkáy/ *n.* **1** a flooring of wooden blocks arranged in a pattern. **2** the main-floor seating area of a theater.

par·quet·ry /paárkitree/ *n.* the use of wooden blocks to make floors or inlay for furniture.

parr /paar/ *n.* a young salmon with blue-gray fingerlike markings on its sides, younger than a smolt.

par·ri·cide /párisīd/ *n.* **1** the killing of a near relative, esp. of a parent. **2** an act of parricide. **3** a person who commits parricide. □□ **par·ri·cid·al** /-síd'l/ *adj.*

par·rot /párət/ *n. & v.* ● *n.* **1** ▲ any of various mainly tropical birds of the order Psittaciformes, with a short hooked bill, often having vivid plumage and able to mimic the human voice. **2** a person who mechanically repeats the words or actions of another. ● *v.tr.* (**parroted, parroting**) repeat mechanically.

par·rot·fish *n.* ▶ any fish of the family Scaridae, with a mouth like a parrot's bill and forming a protective mucous cocoon against predators.

PARROTFISH
(*Bolbometaon bicolor*)

P

par·ry /páree/ *v.* & *n.* • *v.tr.* (**-ies, -ied**) **1** avert or ward off (a weapon or attack), esp. with a countermove. **2** deal skillfully with (an awkward question, etc.). • *n.* (*pl.* **-ies**) an act of parrying.

parse /paars/ *v.tr.* **1** describe (a word in context) grammatically, stating its inflection, relation to the sentence, etc. **2** resolve (a sentence) into its component parts and describe them grammatically. □□ **pars·er** *n.* esp. *Computing.*

par·sec /paársek/ *n.* a unit of stellar distance, equal to about 3.25 light years (3.08 x 10^{16} meters), the distance at which the mean radius of the Earth's orbit subtends an angle of one second of arc.

par·si·mo·ny /paársimōnee/ *n.* **1** carefulness in the use of money or other resources. **2** stinginess. □□ **par·si·mo·ni·ous** /-mṓneeəs/ *adj.* **par·si·mo·ni·ous·ly** *adv.* **par·si·mo·ni·ous·ness** *n.*

pars·ley /paárslee/ *n.* a biennial herb, *Petroselinum crispum*, with white flowers and crinkly aromatic leaves, used for seasoning and garnishing food. ▷ HERB

pars·nip /paársnip/ *n.* **1** a biennial umbelliferous plant, *Pastinaca sativa*, with yellow flowers and a large pale yellow tapering root. **2** this root eaten as a vegetable.

par·son /paársən/ *n.* **1** a rector. **2** any (esp. Protestant) member of the clergy. □□ **par·son·i·cal** /-sónikəl/ *adj.*

par·son·age /paársənij/ *n.* a church house provided for a parson.

part /paart/ *n.*, *v.*, & *adv.* • *n.* **1** some but not all of a thing or number of things. **2** an essential member or constituent of anything (*part of the family*; *a large part of the job*). **3** a component of a machine, etc. (*spare parts*; *needs a new part*). **4 a** a portion of a human or animal body. **b** (in *pl.*) *colloq.* = PRIVATE PARTS. **5** a division of a book, broadcast serial, etc., esp. as much as is issued or broadcast at one time. **6** each of several equal portions of a whole (*the recipe has 3 parts sugar to 2 parts flour*). **7 a** a portion allotted; a share. **b** a person's share in an action or enterprise (*will have no part in it*). **c** one's duty (*was not my part to interfere*). **8 a** a character assigned to an actor on stage. **b** the words spoken by an actor on stage. **c** a copy of these. **9** *Mus.* a melody or other constituent of harmony assigned to a particular voice or instrument. **10** each of the sides in an agreement or dispute. **11** (in *pl.*) a region or district (*am not from these parts*). **12** (in *pl.*) abilities (*a man of many parts*). **13** a dividing line in combed hair. • *v.* **1** *tr.* & *intr.* divide or separate into parts (*the crowd parted to let them through*). **2** *intr.* **a** leave one another's company (*they parted the best of friends*). **b** (foll. by *from*) say goodbye to. **3** *tr.* cause to separate (*they fought hard and had to be parted*). **4** *intr.* (foll. by *with*) give up possession of; hand over. **5** *tr.* separate (the hair of the head on either side of the part) with a comb. • *adv.* to some extent; partly (*is part iron and part wood*; *a lie that is part truth*). □ **for one's part** as far as one is concerned. **in part** (or **parts**) to some extent; partly. **look the part** appear suitable for a role. **on the part of** on the behalf or initiative of (*no objection on my part*). **part and parcel** (usu. foll. by *of*) an essential part. **take part** (often foll. by *in*) assist or have a share (in). **take the part of 1** support; back up. **2** perform the role of. **three parts** three quarters.

par·take /paartáyk/ *v.intr.* (*past* **partook** /-tŏŏk/; *past part.* **partaken** /-táykən/) **1** (foll. by *of*, *in*) take a share or part. **2** (foll. by *of*) eat or drink. **3** (foll. by *of*) have some (of a quality, etc.) (*their manner partook of insolence*). □□ **par·tak·er** *n.*

par·terre /paartáir/ *n.* a level space in a garden occupied by flower beds arranged formally.

par·the·no·gen·e·sis /paárthinōjénisis/ *n.* *Biol.* reproduction by a female gamete without fertilization, esp. as a normal process in invertebrates and lower plants. □□ **par·the·no·ge·net·ic** /-jinétik/ *adj.* **par·the·no·ge·net·i·cal·ly** *adv.*

par·tial /paárshəl/ *adj.* & *n.* • *adj.* **1** not complete; forming only part (*a partial success*). **2** biased; unfair. **3** (foll. by *to*) having a liking for. • *n.* **1** *Mus.* any of the component tones of a complex tone. **2** a denture for replacing one or several, but not all, of the teeth. □□ **par·ti·al·i·ty** /-sheeálitee/ *n.* **par·tial·ly** *adv.* **par·tial·ness** *n.*

par·tic·i·pant /paartísipənt/ *n.* someone who or something that participates.

par·tic·i·pate /paartísipayt/ *v.intr.* **1** (often foll. by *in*) take a part or share (in). **2** *literary* or *formal* (foll. by *of*) have a certain quality (*the speech participated of wit*). □□ **par·tic·i·pa·tion** /-páyshən/ *n.* **par·tic·i·pa·tor** *n.* **par·tic·i·pa·to·ry** /-tísəpətáwree/ *adj.*

par·ti·ci·ple /paártisipəl/ *n.* *Gram.* a word formed from a verb (e.g., *going, gone, being, been*) and used in compound verb forms (e.g., *is going, has been*) or as an adjective (e.g., *working woman, burned toast*). □□ **par·ti·cip·i·al** /-sípeeəl/ *adj.* **par·ti·cip·i·al·ly** /-sípeeəlee/ *adv.*

par·ti·cle /paártikəl/ *n.* **1** a minute portion of matter. **2** the least possible amount (*not a particle of sense*). **3** *Gram.* **a** a minor part of speech, esp. a short indeclinable one. **b** a common prefix or suffix such as *in-*, *-ness*.

par·ti·cle·board /paártikəlbōrd, -bawrd/ *n.* a building material made in flat sheets from scrap wood bonded with adhesive.

par·ti-col·ored /paárteekúlərd/ *adj.* partly of one color, partly of another or others.

par·tic·u·lar /pərtíkyələr, pətík-/ *adj.* & *n.* • *adj.* **1** relating to or considered as one thing or person as distinct from others; individual (*in this particular instance*). **2** more than is usual; special (*took particular trouble*). **3** scrupulously exact; fastidious. **4** detailed (*a full and particular account*). **5** *Logic* (of a proposition) in which something is asserted of some but not all of a class (opp. UNIVERSAL *adj.* 2). • *n.* **1** a detail. **2** (in *pl.*) points of information; a detailed account. □ **in particular** especially.

par·tic·u·lar·i·ty /pərtíkyəláritee, pətík-/ *n.* **1** the quality of being individual or particular. **2** fullness or minuteness of detail in a description.

par·tic·u·lar·ize /pərtíkyələrīz, pətík-/ *v.tr.* (also *absol.*) **1** name specifically or one by one. **2** specify (items). □□ **par·tic·u·lar·i·za·tion** *n.*

par·tic·u·lar·ly /pərtíkyələrlee, pətík-/ *adv.* **1** especially; very. **2** specifically (*they particularly asked for you*). **3** in a particular or fastidious manner.

par·tic·u·late /pərtíkyəlayt, -lət, paar-/ *adj.* & *n.* • *adj.* in the form of separate particles. • *n.* matter in this form.

part·ing /paárting/ *n.* **1** a leave-taking or departure (often *attrib.*: *parting words*). **2** *Brit.* = PART *n.* 13. **3** a division; an act of separating.

par·ti·san /paártizən/ *n.* & *adj.* (also **par·ti·zan**) • *n.* **1** a strong, esp. unreasoning, supporter of a party, cause, etc. **2** *Mil.* a guerrilla in wartime. • *adj.* **1** of or characteristic of partisans. **2** loyal to a particular cause; biased. □□ **par·ti·san·ship** *n.*

par·ti·tion /paartíshən/ *n.* & *v.* • *n.* **1** division into parts, esp. *Polit.* of a country with separate areas of government. **2** a structure dividing a space into two parts, esp. a light interior wall. • *v.tr.* **1** divide into parts. **2** (foll. by *off*) separate (part of a room, etc.) with a partition. □□ **par·ti·tioned** *adj.* **par·ti·tion·er** *n.* **par·ti·tion·ist** *n.*

par·ti·zan var. of PARTISAN.

part·ly /paártlee/ *adv.* to some extent.

part·ner /paártnər/ *n.* & *v.* • *n.* **1** a person who shares or takes part with another or others, esp. in a business firm with shared risks and profits. **2** a companion in dancing. **3** a player (esp. one of two) on the same side in a game. **4** either member of a married couple, or of an unmarried couple living together. • *v.tr.* **1** be the partner of. **2** associate as partners. □□ **part·ner·less** *adj.*

part·ner·ship /paártnərship/ *n.* **1** the state of being a partner or partners. **2** a joint business. **3** a pair or group of partners.

part of speech *n.* each of the categories to which words are assigned in accordance with their grammatical and semantic functions (in English esp. noun, pronoun, adjective, adverb, verb, preposition, conjunction, and interjection).

partook *past* of PARTAKE.

par·tridge /paártrij/ *n.* (*pl.* same or **partridges**) **1** any game bird of the genus *Perdix*, esp. *P. perdix* of Europe and Asia. **2** any other of various similar birds of Europe or N. America, including the snow partridge, ruffed grouse, and bobwhite.

part-time *adj.* occupying or using only part of one's working time. □□ **part-tim·er** *n.*

par·tu·ri·tion /paártŏŏríshən, -tyŏŏ-, -chŏŏ-/ *n.* *Med.* the act of bringing forth young; childbirth.

par·ty /paártee/ *n.* & *v.* • *n.* (*pl.* **-ies**) **1** a social gathering, usu. of invited guests. **2** a body of persons engaged in an activity or traveling together (*fishing party*; *search party*). **3** a group of people united in a cause, opinion, etc., esp. an organized political group. **4** a person or persons forming one side in an agreement or dispute. **5** (foll. by *to*) *Law* an accessory (to an action). **6** *colloq.* a person. • *v.tr.* & *intr.* (**-ies, -ied**) entertain at or attend a party.

par·ty line *n.* **1** the policy adopted by a political party. **2** a telephone line shared by two or more subscribers.

par·ve·nu /paárvənōō/ *n.* & *adj.* • *n.* (*fem.* **parvenue**) **1** a person who has recently gained wealth or position. **2** an upstart. • *adj.* **1** associated with or characteristic of such a person. **2** upstart.

pas /paa/ *n.* (*pl.* same) a step in dancing, esp. in classical ballet.

pas·cal /paskál, paaskaál/ *n.* **1** a standard unit of pressure, equal to one newton per square meter. **2** (**Pascal** or **PASCAL**) *Computing* a programming language esp. used in education.

Pas·cal's tri·an·gle /paskəlz trīanggəl/ *n.* *Math.* ► a triangular array of numbers in which each number is the sum of the two numbers immediately above, and 1 is at the apex and at both ends of each row.

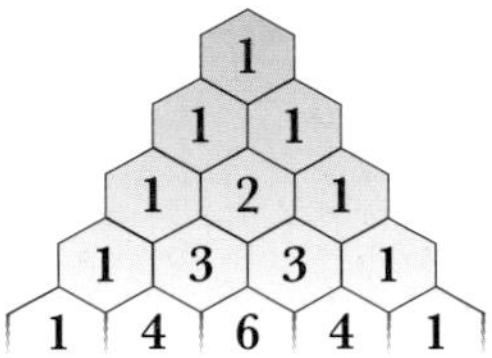

PASCAL'S TRIANGLE

pas·chal /páskəl/ *adj.* **1** of or relating to the Jewish Passover. **2** of or relating to Easter.

pas de deux /də dṓ/ *n.* a dance for two persons.

pa·sha /paáshə/ *n.* *hist.* the title (placed after the name) of a Turkish officer of high rank.

Pash·to /páshtō/ *n.* & *adj.* • *n.* the official language of Afghanistan, also spoken in areas of Pakistan. • *adj.* of or in this language.

pasque·flow·er /páskflowər/ *n.* a plant of the buttercup family with bell-shaped purple flowers.

pass[1] /pas/ *v.* & *n.* • *v.* (*past part.* **passed**) (see also PAST). **1** *intr.* (often foll. by *along, by, down, on*, etc.) move onward; proceed, esp. past some point of reference. **2** *tr.* **a** go past; leave (a thing, etc.) on one side or behind in proceeding. **b** overtake, esp. in a vehicle. **c** go across (a frontier, mountain range, etc.). **3** *intr.* & *tr.* be transferred or cause to be transferred from one person or place to another (*pass the butter*; *the estate passes to his son*). **4** *tr.* surpass; be too great for (*it passes my comprehension*). **5** *intr.* get through; effect a passage. **6** *intr.* **a** be accepted as adequate; go uncensured (*let the matter pass*). **b** (foll. by *as, for*) be accepted or currently known as. **7** *tr.* move; cause to go (*passed her hand over her face*; *passed a rope round it*). **8 a** *intr.* (of a candidate in an examination) be successful. **b** *tr.* be successful in (an examination). **c** *tr.* (of an examiner) judge the performance of (a candidate) to be satisfactory. **9 a** *tr.* (of a bill) be approved by (a parliamentary body or process). **b** *tr.* cause or allow (a bill) to proceed to further legislative processes. **c** *intr.* (of a bill or proposal) be approved. **10** *intr.* **a** occur; elapse (*the remark passed unnoticed*; *time passes slowly*). **b** happen; be done or said (*heard what passed between them*). **11 a** *intr.* circulate; be current. **b** *tr.* put into circulation (*was passing forged checks*). **12** *tr.* spend or use up (a certain time or period). **13** *tr.* (also *absol.*) *Sports* send (the ball) to another player of one's own team. **14** *intr.* forgo one's turn or chance in a game, etc. **15** *intr.* (foll. by *to, into*) change from one form (to another). **16** *intr.* come to an end. **17** *tr.* discharge from the body as or with excreta. **18** *tr.* (foll. by *on, upon*) **a** utter (criticism) about. **b** pronounce (a judicial sentence) on. **19** *intr.* (often foll. by *on, upon*) adjudicate. **20** *tr.* not declare or pay (a dividend). **21** *tr.* cause (troops, etc.) to go by, esp. ceremonially. ● *n.* **1** an act or instance of passing. **2** *Brit.* **a** success in an examination. **b** the status of a university degree without honors. **3** written permission to pass into or out of a place, or to be absent from quarters. **4** a ticket or permit giving free entry or access, etc. **5** *Sports* a transference of the ball to another player on the same side. **6** *Baseball* a base on balls. **7** a thrust in fencing. **8** an act of passing the hands over anything, as in conjuring or hypnotism. **9** a critical position (*has come to a fine pass*). □ **make a pass at** *colloq.* make amorous or sexual advances to. **pass around 1** distribute. **2** send or give to each of a number in turn. **pass away 1** *euphem.* die. **2** cease to exist; come to an end. **pass the buck** *US colloq.* deny or shift responsibility. **pass by 1** go past. **2** disregard; omit. **pass off 1** (of feelings, etc.) disappear gradually. **2** (of proceedings) be carried through (in a specified way). **3** (foll. by *as*) misrepresent (a person or thing) as something else. **pass on 1** proceed on one's way. **2** *euphem.* die. **3** transmit to the next person in a series. **pass out 1** become unconscious. **2** distribute. **pass over 1** omit, ignore, or disregard. **2** ignore the claims of (a person) to promotion or advancement. **3** *euphem.* die. **pass up** *colloq.* refuse or neglect (an opportunity, etc.). **pass water** urinate. □□ **pass·er** *n.*

pass² /pas/ *n.* **1** a narrow passage through mountains. **2** a navigable channel, esp. at the mouth of a river.

pass·a·ble /pásəbəl/ *adj.* **1** barely satisfactory; just adequate. **2** (of a road, pass, etc.) that can be passed. □□ **pass·a·ble·ness** *n.* **pass·a·bly** *adv.*

pas·sage /pásij/ *n.* **1** the process or means of passing; transit. **2** = PASSAGEWAY. **3** the liberty or right to pass through. **4 a** the right of conveyance as a passenger by sea or air. **b** a journey by sea or air. **5** a transition from one state to another. **6 a** a short extract from a book, etc. **b** a section of a piece of music. **c** a detail or section of a painting. **7** the passing of a bill, etc., into law. **8** (in *pl.*) an interchange of words, etc. **9** *Anat.* a duct, etc., in the body. □ **work one's passage** earn a right (orig. of passage) by working for it.

pas·sage·way /pásijway/ *n.* a narrow way for passing along, esp. with walls on either side; a corridor.

pas·sant /pásənt/ *adj. Heraldry* (of an animal) walking and looking to the dexter side, with three paws on the ground and the right forepaw raised.

pass·book /pásbo͝ok/ *n.* a book issued by a bank, etc., to an account holder for recording amounts deposited and withdrawn.

pass·é /pasáy/ *adj.* **1** behind the times; out-of-date. **2** past its prime.

pas·sen·ger /pásinjər/ *n.* **1** a traveler in or on a public or private conveyance (other than the driver, pilot, crew, etc.). **2** *colloq.* a member of a team, crew, etc., who does no effective work. **3** (*attrib.*) for the use of passengers (*passenger seat*).

passe-par·tout /páspaarto͞o/ *n.* **1** a master key. **2** a picture frame (esp. for mounted photographs) consisting of two pieces of glass or one piece of glass and a backing of cardboard, etc., stuck together at the edges with adhesive paper or tape. **3** adhesive tape or paper used for this.

pass·er·by /pásərbí/ *n.* (*pl.* **passersby**) a person who goes past, esp. by chance.

pas·ser·ine /pásərīn, -reen/ *n. & adj.* ● *n.* ▶ any perching bird of the order Passeriformes, having feet with three toes pointing forward and one pointing backward, including sparrows and most land birds. ▷ SONGBIRD. ● *adj.* **1** of or relating to this order. **2** of the size of a sparrow.

PASSERINE

The passerines, also known as the perching birds, are the largest bird order, containing approximately half of the world's birds. All passerines have four unwebbed toes – three facing forward, and a hind toe facing backward. When a passerine lands on a perch, its weight makes its leg tendons tighten and its toes clamp tightly shut. The passerines comprise two suborders. The oscines, also known as songbirds, can produce complex vocalizations, but the suboscine families have fairly limited vocal powers.

LOWER LEG OF A PASSERINE

lower leg tendon

hind toe faces backward

three toes face forward

perch

EXAMPLES OF PASSERINES

OSCINES

CACTUS WREN
(*Campylorhynchus brunneicapillus*)

WOOD WARBLER
(*Phylloscopus sibilatrix*)

SWALLOW
(*Hirundo rustica*)

KING BIRD-OF-PARADISE
(*Cicinnurus regius*)

EURASIAN JAY
(*Garrulus glandarius*)

RED-TUFTED SUNBIRD
(*Nectarinia johnstoni*)

AMERICAN ROBIN
(*Turdus migratorius*)

BLUE TIT
(*Parus caeruleus*)

SUBOSCINES

RUFOUS HORNERO
(*Furnarius rufus*)

SUPERB LYREBIRD
(*Menura novaehollandiae*)

P

pas·si·ble /pásibəl/ adj. capable of feeling or suffering. □□ **pas·si·bil·i·ty** n.

pas·sim /pásim/ adv. (of allusions or references in a published work) to be found at various places throughout the text.

pass·ing /pásing/ adj., adv., & n. ● adj. **1** in senses of PASS v. **2** transient; fleeting (a passing glance). **3** cursory; incidental (a passing reference). ● adv. exceedingly; very. ● n. **1** in senses of PASS v. **2** euphem. the death of a person (mourned his passing). □ **in passing 1** by the way. **2** in the course of speech, conversation, etc. □□ **pass·ing·ly** adv.

pas·sion /páshən/ n. **1** strong barely controllable emotion. **2** an outburst of anger (flew into a passion). **3 a** intense sexual love. **b** a person arousing this. **4** a strong enthusiasm (has a passion for football). **b** an object arousing this. **5** (**the Passion**) a Relig. the suffering of Christ during his last days. **b** a narrative of this from the Gospels. **c** a musical setting of any of these narratives. □□ **pas·sion·less** adj.

pas·sion·ate /páshənət/ adj. **1** dominated by or easily moved to strong feeling, esp. love or anger. **2** showing or caused by passion. □□ **pas·sion·ate·ly** adv. **pas·sion·ate·ness** n.

PASSIONFLOWER
(*Passiflora caerulea*)

pas·sion·flow·er /páshənflowr, -flowər/ n. ◄ any climbing plant of the genus *Passiflora*, with a flower that was supposed to suggest the instruments of the Crucifixion.

pas·sion play n. a miracle play representing Christ's Passion.

Pas·sion·tide /páshəntīd/ n. the last two weeks of Lent.

pas·sive /pásiv/ adj. **1** suffering action; acted upon. **2** offering no opposition; submissive. **3** not active; inert. **4** Gram. designating the voice in which the subject undergoes the action of the verb (e.g., in they were killed). **5** (of a debt) incurring no interest payment. **6** collecting or distributing the Sun's energy without use of machinery (passive solar heating). □□ **pas·sive·ly** adv. **pas·sive·ness** n. **pas·siv·i·ty** /-sívətee/ n.

pas·sive re·sist·ance n. a nonviolent refusal to cooperate.

pas·sive smok·ing n. the involuntary inhaling, esp. by a nonsmoker, of smoke from others' cigarettes, etc.

pass·key /páskee/ n. **1** a private key to a gate, etc., for special purposes. **2** a skeleton key or master key.

Pass·o·ver /pásōvər/ n. the Jewish spring festival commemorating the liberation of the Israelites from Egyptian bondage, held from the 14th to the 21st day of the seventh month of the Jewish year.

pass·port /páspawrt/ n. **1** an official document issued by a government certifying the holder's identity and citizenship, and entitling the holder to travel under its protection to and from foreign countries. **2** (foll. by to) a thing that ensures admission or attainment (a passport to success).

pass·word /pásword/ n. **1** a selected word or phrase securing recognition, admission, etc., when used by those to whom it is disclosed. **2** Computing a word or string of characters securing access to an account or file for those authorized.

past /past/ adj., n., prep., & adv. ● adj. **1** gone by in time and no longer existing (in past years; the time is past). **2** recently completed or gone by (the past month; for some time past). **3** relating to a former time (past president). **4** Gram. expressing a past action or state. ● n. **1** (prec. by the) **a** past time. **b** what has happened in past time (cannot undo the past). **2** a person's past life or career, esp. if discreditable (a

man with a past). **3** a past tense or form. ● prep. **1** beyond in time or place (is past two o'clock; ran past the house). **2** beyond the range, duration, or compass of (past belief; past endurance). ● adv. so as to pass by (hurried past). □ **not put it past a person** believe it possible of a person. **past it** colloq. incompetent or unusable through age.

pas·ta /paástə/ n. **1** ▼ a dried flour paste used in various shapes in cooking (e.g., lasagna, spaghetti). **2** a cooked dish made from this.

paste /payst/ n. & v. ● n. **1** any moist fairly stiff mixture, esp. of powder and liquid. **2** a dough of flour with fat, water, etc., used in baking. **3** an adhesive of flour, water, etc., esp. for sticking paper and other light materials. **4** an easily spread preparation of ground meat, fish, etc. **5** a hard vitreous composition used in making imitation gems. **6** a mixture of clay, water, etc., used in making ceramic ware, esp. porcelain. ● v.tr. **1** fasten or coat with paste. **2** sl. **a** beat soundly. **b** bomb or bombard heavily. □□ **past·ing** n. (esp. in sense 2 of v.).

paste·board /páystbawrd/ n. **1** a sheet of stiff material made by pasting together sheets of paper. **2** (attrib.) **a** flimsy; unsubstantial. **b** fake.

pas·tel /pastél/ n. **1** a crayon consisting of powdered pigments bound with a gum solution. **2** a work of art in pastel. **3** a light and subdued shade of a color. □□ **pas·tel·ist** or **pas·tel·list** n.

PASTA

Most pasta is made from durum wheat flour; because of its high gluten content, it makes a strong elastic dough. The flour is mixed with water, kneaded to form a thick paste, and then forced through perforated plates or dies that shape it into one of more than a hundred different forms. Pasta can be colored with spinach or beet juice.

EXAMPLES OF PASTA

LONG

CAPELLINI

TAGLIATELLE VERDE

FEDELI

SPAGHETTI

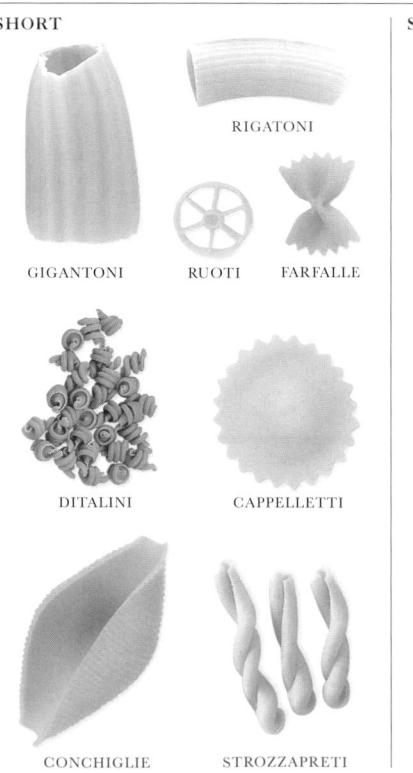

SHORT

RIGATONI

GIGANTONI

RUOTI

FARFALLE

DITALINI

CAPPELLETTI

CONCHIGLIE

STROZZAPRETI

STUFFED AND LAYERED

CANNELLONI

TORTELLINI VERDE

RAVIOLI

LASAGNE VERDE

P

pas·tern /pástərn/ n. **1** the part of a horse's foot between the fetlock and the hoof. ▷ HORSE. **2** a corresponding part in other animals.

pas·teur·ize /páschəriz, pástyə-/ v.tr. subject (milk, etc.) to the process of partial sterilization by heating. □□ **pas·teur·i·za·tion** /-záyshən/ n. **pas·teur·iz·er** n.

pas·tiche /pasteésh/ n. **1** a medley, esp. a picture or a musical composition, made up from or imitating various sources. **2** a literary or other work of art composed in the style of a well-known author.

pas·tille /pasteél, -til/ n. a small candy or medicated lozenge.

pas·time /pástīm/ n. **1** a pleasant recreation or hobby. **2** a sport or game.

past mas·ter n. **1** a person who is especially adept or expert in an activity, subject, etc. **2** a person who has been a master in a guild, lodge, etc.

pas·tor /pástər/ n. **1** a priest or minister in charge of a church or a congregation. **2** a person exercising spiritual guidance. □□ **pas·tor·ship** n.

pas·to·ral /pástərəl/ adj. & n. ● adj. **1** of, relating to, or associated with shepherds or flocks and herds. **2** (of land) used for pasture. **3** (of a poem, picture, etc.) portraying country life, usu. in a romantic or idealized form. **4** of or appropriate to a pastor. ● n. **1** a pastoral poem, play, picture, etc. **2** a letter from a pastor (esp. a bishop) to the clergy or people. □□ **pas·to·ral·ism** n. **pas·to·ral·i·ty** /-álitee/ n. **pas·to·ral·ly** adv.

pas·to·rale /pástəráal, -rál, -ráalee/ n. (pl. **pastorales** or **pastorali** /-lee/) **1** a slow instrumental composition in compound time, usu. with drone notes in the bass. **2** a simple musical play with a rural subject.

past per·fect n. Gram. = PLUPERFECT.

pas·tra·mi /pəstraámee/ n. seasoned smoked beef.

pas·try /páystree/ n. (pl. **-ies**) **1** a dough of flour, fat, and water baked and used as a base and covering for pies, etc. **2 a** food, wholly or partly of this. **b** a piece or item of this food.

pas·tur·age /páschərij/ n. **1** land for pasture. **2** the process of pasturing cattle, etc.

pas·ture /páschər/ n. & v. ● n. **1** land covered with grass, etc., suitable for grazing animals, esp. cattle or sheep. **2** herbage for animals. ● v. **1** tr. put (animals) to graze in a pasture. **2** intr. & tr. (of animals) graze.

past·y[1] /pástee/ n. esp. Brit. (pl. **-ies**) a pastry case with a sweet or savory filling, baked without a dish to shape it.

pas·ty[2] /páystee/ adj. (**pastier, pastiest**) **1** of or like or covered with paste. **2** unhealthily pale (esp. in complexion) (pasty-faced). □□ **past·i·ly** adv. **past·i·ness** n.

Pat. abbr. Patent.

pat[1] /pat/ v. & n. ● v. (**patted, patting**) **1** tr. strike gently with the hand or a flat surface. **2** tr. flatten or mold by patting. **3** tr. strike gently with the inner surface of the hand, esp. as a sign of affection, sympathy, or congratulation. **4** intr. beat lightly. ● n. **1** a light stroke or tap, esp. with the hand in affection, etc. **2** the sound made by this. **3** a small mass (esp. of butter) formed by patting. □ **pat on the back** a gesture of approval or congratulation. **pat a person on the back** congratulate a person.

pat[2] /pat/ adj. & adv. ● adj. **1** known thoroughly and ready for any occasion. **2** apposite or opportune, esp. unconvincingly so (gave a pat answer). ● adv. **1** in a pat manner. **2** appositely; opportunely. □ **have** (or **know**) **down pat** (Brit. **have off pat**) know or have memorized perfectly. **stand pat 1** stick stubbornly to one's opinion or decision. **2** Poker retain one's hand as dealt; not draw other cards. □□ **pat·ly** adv. **pat·ness** n.

patch /pach/ n. & v. ● n. **1** a piece of material or metal, etc., used to mend a hole or as reinforcement. **2** a pad worn to protect an injured eye. **3** a dressing, etc., put over a wound. **4** a large or irregular distinguishable area on a surface. **5** Brit. colloq. a period of time in terms of its characteristic quality (went through a bad patch). **6** a piece of ground. **7** a number of plants growing in one place (brier patch). **8** a scrap or remnant. **9** a temporary electrical connection. **10** a temporary correction in a computer program. **11** hist. a small disk, etc., of black silk attached to the face, worn esp. by women in the 17th–18th c. for adornment. **12** Mil. a piece of cloth on a uniform as the badge of a unit. ● v.tr. **1** (often foll. by up) repair with a patch or patches; put a patch or patches on. **2** (of material) serve as a patch to. **3** (often foll. by up) put together, esp. hastily or in a makeshift way. **4** (foll. by up) settle (a quarrel, etc.) esp. hastily or temporarily. □□ **patch·er** n.

patch·ou·li /pəchōólee, páchōōlee/ n. **1** ► a strongly scented E. Indian plant, Pogostemon cablin. **2** the perfume obtained from this.

patch test n. a test for allergy by applying to the skin patches containing allergenic substances.

patch·work /páchwərk/ n. **1** ▼ sewn work using small pieces of cloth with different designs, forming a pattern. **2** a thing composed of various small pieces or fragments.

PATCHOULI
(Pogostemon cablin)

PATCHWORK OF BROCADES AND VELVETS

patch·y /páchee/ adj. (**patchier, patchiest**) **1** uneven in quality. **2** having or existing in patches. □□ **patch·i·ly** adv. **patch·i·ness** n.

pate /payt/ n. colloq. or joc. **1** the top of the head **2** the head, esp. representing the seat of intellect.

pâte /paat/ n. the paste of which porcelain is made.

pâ·té /paatáy, pa-/ n. a rich paste or spread of finely chopped and spiced meat or fish, etc.

pâ·té de foie gras /də fwaa graá/ n. a paste of fatted goose liver.

pa·tel·la /pətélə/ n. (pl. **patellae** /-lee/) the kneecap. ▷ KNEE, SKELETON. □□ **pa·tel·lar** adj. **pa·tel·late** /-lət/ adj.

pat·ent /pát'nt/ n., adj., & v. ● n. **1** a government authority to an individual or organization conferring a right or title, esp. the sole right to make or use or sell some invention. **2** a document granting this authority. **3** an invention or process protected by it. ● adj. **1** /páyt'nt/ obvious; plain. **2** conferred or protected by patent. **3 a** made and marketed under a patent; proprietary. **b** to which one has a proprietary claim. **4** such as might be patented; ingenious; well-contrived. **5** (of an opening, etc.) allowing free passage. ● v.tr. obtain a patent for (an invention). □□ **pa·ten·cy** n. **pat·ent·a·ble** adj. **pat·ent·ee** n. **pat·ent·ly** /páyt'ntlee, pát-/ adv. (in sense 1 of adj.).

pat·ent leath·er n. glossy varnished leather.

pat·ent med·i·cine n. medicine made and marketed under a patent and available without prescription.

pat·ent of·fice n. an office from which patents are issued.

pa·ter·fa·mil·i·as /páytərfəmíleeas, páa-, pátər-/ n. the male head of a family or household.

pa·ter·nal /pətárnəl/ adj. **1** of or like or appropriate to a father. **2** fatherly. **3** related through the father. **4** (of a government, etc.) limiting freedom and responsibility by well-meaning regulations. □□ **pa·ter·nal·ly** adv.

pa·ter·nal·ism /pətárnəlizəm/ n. the policy of governing in a paternal way, or behaving paternally to one's associates or subordinates. □□ **pa·ter·nal·ist** n. **pa·ter·nal·is·tic** adj. **pa·ter·nal·is·ti·cal·ly** adv.

pa·ter·ni·ty /pətárnitee/ n. **1** fatherhood. **2** one's paternal origin.

pa·ter·ni·ty suit n. a lawsuit held to determine whether a certain man is the father of a certain child.

pa·ter·nos·ter /páytərnóstər, páa-, pátər-/ n. **1 a** the Lord's Prayer, esp. in Latin. **b** a rosary bead indicating that this is to be said. **2** an elevator consisting of a series of linked doorless compartments moving continuously on a circular belt.

path /path/ n. (pl. **paths** /paathz/) **1** a way or track laid or trodden down for walking. **2** the line along which a person or thing moves (flight path). **3** a course of action or conduct. **4** a sequence of movements or operations taken by a system. □□ **path·less** adj.

-path /path/ comb. form forming nouns denoting: **1** a practitioner of curative treatment (homeopath; osteopath). **2** a person who suffers from a disease (psychopath).

pa·thet·ic /pəthétik/ adj. **1** arousing pity or sadness or contempt. **2** colloq. miserably inadequate. **3** archaic of the emotions. □□ **pa·thet·i·cal·ly** adv.

path·find·er /páthfīndər/ n. **1** a person who explores new territory, investigates a new subject, etc. **2** an aircraft or its pilot sent ahead to locate and mark the target area for bombing.

path·name /páthnaym/ n. Computing a description of where an item is to be found in a hierarchy of directories.

patho- /páthō/ comb. form disease.

path·o·gen /páthəjən/ n. an agent causing disease. □□ **path·o·gen·ic** /-jenik/ adj. **pa·thog·e·nous** /-thójənəs/ adj.

path·o·gen·e·sis /páthəjénisis/ n. (also **pa·thog·e·ny** /pəthójənee/) the manner of development of a disease. □□ **path·o·ge·net·ic** /-jinétik/ adj.

path·o·log·i·cal /páthəlójikəl/ adj. **1** of pathology. **2** of or caused by a physical or mental disorder (a pathological fear of spiders). □□ **path·o·log·i·cal·ly** adv.

pa·thol·o·gy /pəthóləjee/ n. **1** the science of bodily diseases. **2** the symptoms of a disease. □□ **pa·thol·o·gist** n.

pa·thos /páythos, -thaws, -thōs/ n. a quality that evokes pity or sadness.

path·way /páthway/ n. **1** a path or its course. **2** Biochem., etc., a sequence of reactions undergone in a living organism.

-pathy /pəthee/ comb. form forming nouns denoting: **1** curative treatment (allopathy; homeopathy). **2** feeling (telepathy).

pa·tience /páyshəns/ n. **1** calm endurance of hardship, provocation, pain, delay, etc. **2** tolerant perseverance or forbearance. **3** the capacity for calm self-possessed waiting. **4** esp. Brit. = SOLITAIRE 4.

pa·tient /páyshənt/ adj. & n. ● adj. having or showing patience. ● n. a person receiving or registered to receive medical treatment. □□ **pa·tient·ly** adv.

pat·i·na /pətéenə, pát'nə/ *n.* (*pl.* **patinas**) **1** a film, usu. green, formed on the surface of old bronze. **2** a similar film on other surfaces. **3** a gloss produced by age on woodwork. □□ **pat·i·nat·ed** /pát'naytid/ *adj.* **pat·i·na·tion** *n.*

pa·ti·o /páteeō/ *n.* (*pl.* **-os**) **1** a paved usu. roofless area adjoining and belonging to a house. **2** an inner court open to the sky esp. in a Spanish or Spanish-American house.

pa·tis·se·rie /pətísəree, paateesrée/ *n.* **1** a shop where pastries are made and sold. **2** pastries collectively.

pat·ois /patwáa, pátwaa/ *n.* (*pl.* same, *pronunc.* /-waaz/) the dialect of the common people in a region, differing fundamentally from the literary language.

pa·tri·arch /páytreeaark/ *n.* **1** the male head of a family or tribe. **2** (often in *pl.*) *Bibl.* any of those regarded as fathers of the human race, esp. Adam and his descendants, including Noah; Abraham, Isaac, and Jacob; or the sons of Jacob, founders of the tribes of Israel. **3** *Eccl.* **a** the title of a chief bishop, esp. those presiding over the Churches of Antioch, Alexandria, Constantinople, and (formerly) Rome; now also the title of the heads of certain autocephalous Orthodox Churches. **b** (in the Roman Catholic Church) a bishop ranking next above primates and metropolitans, and immediately below the pope. **c** the head of a Uniate community. **d** a high dignitary of the Mormon church. **4 a** the founder of an order, science, etc. **b** a venerable old man. **c** the oldest member of a group. □□ **pa·tri·ar·chal** /-áarkəl/ *adj.* **pa·tri·ar·chal·ly** /-áarkəlee/ *adv.*

pa·tri·arch·ate /páytreeaarkət, -kayt/ *n.* **1** the office, see, or residence of an ecclesiastical patriarch. **2** the rank of a tribal patriarch.

pa·tri·arch·y /páytreeaarkee/ *n.* (*pl.* **-ies**) a system of society, government, etc., ruled by a man or men and with descent through the male line. □□ **pa·tri·arch·ism** *n.*

pa·tri·cian /pətríshən/ *n.* & *adj.* • *n.* **1** *hist.* a member of the ancient Roman nobility (cf. PLEBEIAN). **2** *hist.* a nobleman in some Italian republics. **3** an aristocrat. **4** a person of educated or refined tastes and upbringing. • *adj.* **1** noble; aristocratic; well-bred. **2** *hist.* of the ancient Roman nobility.

pa·tri·ci·ate /pətrísheeət, -ayt/ *n.* **1** a patrician order; an aristocracy. **2** the rank of patrician.

pat·ri·cide /pátrisīd/ *n.* = PARRICIDE (esp. with reference to the killing of one's father). □□ **pat·ri·cid·al** /-síd'l/ *adj.*

pat·ri·lin·e·al /pátrilíneeəl/ *adj.* of or relating to, or based on kinship with, the father or descent through the male line.

pat·ri·mo·ny /pátrimōnee/ *n.* (*pl.* **-ies**) **1** property inherited from one's father or ancestor. **2** a heritage. **3** the endowment of a church, etc. □□ **pat·ri·mo·ni·al** *adj.*

pa·tri·ot /páytreeət, -ot/ *n.* a person who is devoted to and ready to support or defend his or her country. □□ **pa·tri·ot·ic** /-reeótik/ *adj.* **pa·tri·ot·i·cal·ly** *adv.* **pa·tri·ot·ism** *n.*

pa·trol /pətrṓl/ *n.* & *v.* • *n.* **1** the act of walking or traveling around an area, esp. at regular intervals, in order to protect or supervise it. **2** one or more persons or vehicles assigned or sent out on patrol, esp. a detachment of guards, police, etc. **3 a** a detachment of troops sent out to reconnoiter. **b** such reconnaissance. **4** a routine operational voyage of a ship or aircraft. **5** a unit of Boy or Girl Scouts. • *v.* (**patrolled**, **patrolling**) **1** *tr.* carry out a patrol of. **2** *intr.* act as a patrol. □□ **pa·trol·ler** *n.*

pa·trol car *n.* a police car used in patrolling roads and streets.

pa·trol·man /pətrṓlmən/ *n.* (*pl.* **-men**) a police officer assigned to or patrolling a specific route.

pa·tron /páytrən/ *n.* (*fem.* **patroness**) **1** a person who gives financial or other support to a person, cause, work of art, etc., esp. one who buys works of art. **2** a usu. regular customer of a store, etc.

pa·tron·age /pátrənij/ *n.* **1** the support, promotion, or encouragement given by a patron. **2** a patronizing or condescending manner. **3 a** the power to appoint others to government jobs. **b** the distribution of such jobs. **4** a customer's support for a store, etc.

pa·tron·ize /páytrənīz, pát-/ *v.tr.* **1** treat condescendingly. **2** act as a patron toward (a person, cause, artist, etc.); support; encourage. **3** frequent (a store, etc.) as a customer. □□ **pa·tron·i·za·tion** *n.* **pa·tron·iz·er** *n.* **pa·tron·iz·ing** *adj.* **pa·tron·iz·ing·ly** *adv.*

pa·tron saint *n.* the protecting or guiding saint of a person, place, etc.

pat·ro·nym·ic /pátrənímik/ *n.* & *adj.* • *n.* a name derived from the name of a father or ancestor, e.g., *Johnson, O'Brien, Ivanovich.* • *adj.* (of a name) so derived.

pa·troon /pətrōon/ *n. hist.* a landowner with manorial privileges under the Dutch governments of New York and New Jersey.

pat·sy /pátsee/ *n.* (*pl.* **-ies**) *sl.* a person who is deceived, ridiculed, tricked, etc.

pat·ten /pát'n/ *n. hist.* ▼ a shoe or clog with a raised sole or set on an iron ring, for walking in mud, etc.

leather strap

wooden base

iron ring

PATTEN

pat·ter[1] /pátər/ *v.* & *n.* • *v.* **1** *intr.* make a rapid succession of taps, as of rain on a windowpane. **2** *intr.* run with quick short steps. **3** *tr.* cause (water, etc.) to patter. • *n.* a rapid succession of taps, short light steps, etc.

pat·ter[2] /pátər/ *n.* **1 a** the rapid speech used by a comedian or introduced into a song. **b** the words of a comic song. **2** the words used by a person selling or promoting a product; a sales pitch. **3** the special language or jargon of a profession, class, etc. **4** *colloq.* mere talk; chatter.

pat·tern /pátərn/ *n.* & *v.* • *n.* **1** a repeated decorative design on wallpaper, cloth, a carpet, etc. **2** a regular or logical form, order, or arrangement of parts (*behavior pattern; the pattern of one's daily life*). **3** a model or design, e.g., of a garment, from which copies can be made. **4** an example of excellence; an ideal; a model (*a pattern of elegance*). **5** the prescribed flight path for an airplane taking off or esp. landing at an airport. **6** a wooden or metal figure from which a mold is made for a casting. **7** a sample (of cloth, wallpaper, etc.). **8** the marks made by shots, bombs, etc. on a target or target area. • *v.tr.* **1** (usu. foll. by *after, on*) model (a thing) on a design, etc. **2** decorate with a pattern.

pat·ty /pátee/ *n.* (*pl.* **-ies**) **1** a small flat cake of ground meat, etc., sometimes breaded and fried. **2** esp. *Brit.* a little pie or pastry.

pat·ty·pan /páteepan/ *n.* **1** a flattish summer squash having a scalloped edge. **2** a pan for baking a patty.

pau·ci·ty /páwsitee/ *n.* smallness of number or quantity.

Pau·line /páwlīn, -leen/ *adj.* of or relating to St. Paul (*the Pauline epistles*).

paunch /pawnch/ *n.* **1** the belly or stomach, esp. when protruding. **2** a ruminant's first stomach; the rumen. □□ **paunch·y** *adj.* (**paunchier, paunchiest**). **paunch·i·ness** *n.*

pau·per /páwpər/ *n.* **1** a person without means; a beggar. **2** a person dependent on private or

government charity. □□ **pau·per·dom** /-pərdəm/ *n.* **pau·per·ism** /-rizəm/ *n.* **pau·per·ize** *v.tr.* **pau·per·i·za·tion** /-rīzáysh'n/ *n.*

pause /pawz/ *n.* & *v.* • *n.* **1** an interval of inaction, esp. when due to hesitation; a temporary stop. **2** a break in speaking or reading; a silence. **3** *Mus.* a fermata. • *v.* **1** *intr.* make a pause; wait. **2** *intr.* (usu. foll. by *upon*) linger over (a word, etc.). **3** *tr.* cause to hesitate or pause.

pave /payv/ *v.tr.* **1** cover (a street, floor, etc.) with paving, etc. **2** cover or strew (a floor, etc.) with anything (*paved with flowers*). □ **pave the way for** prepare for; facilitate. □□ **pav·er** *n.* **pav·ing** *n.*

pave·ment /páyvmənt/ *n.* **1** the hard, durable covering of a street, driveway, etc., as of asphalt or concrete. **2** esp. *Brit.* = SIDEWALK. **3** a roadway.

pa·vil·ion /pəvílyən/ *n.* **1** a usu. open building at a fairground, park, etc., used for exhibits, refreshments, etc. **2** a decorative building in a garden. **3** a tent, esp. a large one at a show, fair, etc. **4** a building used for entertainments. **5** a temporary stand at an exhibition. **6** a detached building that is part of a connected set of buildings, as at a hospital. **7** the part of a cut gemstone below the girdle.

Pav·lov·i·an /pavlṓvēən/ *adj.* of or relating to I. P. Pavlov, Russian physiologist d. 1936, or his work, esp. on conditioned reflexes.

paw /paw/ *n.* & *v.* • *n.* **1** a foot of an animal having claws or nails. **2** *colloq.* a person's hand. • *v.* **1** *tr.* strike or scrape with a paw or foot. **2** *intr.* scrape the ground with a paw or hoof. **3** *tr. colloq.* fondle awkwardly or indecently.

pawl /pawl/ *n.* & *v.* • *n.* **1** a lever with a catch for the teeth of a wheel or bar. **2** *Naut.* a short bar used to lock a capstan, windlass, etc., to prevent it from recoiling. • *v.tr.* secure (a capstan, etc.) with a pawl.

pawn[1] /pawn/ *n.* **1** *Chess* a piece of the smallest size and value. ▷ CHESS. **2** a person used by others for their own purposes.

pawn[2] /pawn/ *v.tr.* **1** deposit an object, esp. with a pawnbroker, as security for money lent. **2** pledge or wager (one's life, honor, word, etc.).

pawn·brok·er /páwnbrōkər/ *n.* a person who lends money at interest on the security of personal property pawned. □□ **pawn·brok·ing** *n.*

Paw·nee /pawnée, paa-/ *n.* **1 a** a N. American people native to Kansas and Nebraska. **b** a member of this people. **2** the language of this people.

pawn·shop /páwnshop/ *n.* a shop where pawnbroking is conducted.

paw·paw /páwpaw/ *n.* (also **pa·paw**) a N. American tree, *Asimina triloba*, with purple flowers and edible fruit.

pay /pay/ *v.*, *n.*, & *adj.* • *v.tr.* (*past* and *past part.* **paid** /payd/) **1** (also *absol.*) give (a person, etc.) what is due for services done, goods received, debts incurred, etc. (*paid him in full; I assure you I have paid*). **2 a** give (a usu. specified amount) for work done, a debt, a ransom, etc. (*they pay $6 an hour*). **b** (foll. by *to*) hand over the amount of (a debt, wages, recompense, etc.) to (*paid the money to the assistant*). **3 a** give, bestow, or express (attention, respect, a compliment, etc.) (*paid them no heed*). **b** make (a visit, a call, etc.) (*paid a visit to their uncle*). **4** (also *absol.*) (of a business, undertaking, attitude, etc.) be profitable or advantageous to (a person, etc.). **5** reward or punish (*can never pay you for what you have done for us; I shall pay you for that*). **6** (usu. as **paid** *adj.*) recompense (work, time, etc.) (*paid holiday*). **7** (usu. foll. by *out, away*) let out (a rope) by slackening it. • *n.* **1** wages; payment. • *adj.* **1** requiring payment (for a service, etc.). **2** requiring payment of a coin for use (*pay phone*) □ **pay back 1** repay. **2** punish or be revenged on. **pay for 1** hand over the price of. **2** bear the cost of. **3** suffer or be punished for (a fault, etc.). **pay in** pay (money) into a bank account. **pay off 1** dismiss (workers) with a final payment. **2** *colloq.* yield good results; succeed. **3** pay (a debt) in full. **4** (of a ship) turn to leeward through the movement of the helm. **pay out 1** spend; hand

P

out (money). **2** let out (a rope). **pay up** pay the full amount, or the full amount of. □□ **pay·ee** /payée/ n. **pay·er** n.

pay·a·ble /páyəbəl/ adj. **1** that must be paid; due (*payable in April*). **2** that may be paid. **3** (of a mine, etc.) profitable.

pay·back /páybak/ n. **1** a financial return; a reward. **2** the profit from an investment, etc., esp. one equal to the initial outlay.

pay·day /páyday/ n. a day on which salary or wages are paid.

pay dirt n. **1** *Mineral.* ground worth working for ore. **2** a financially promising situation.

pay·load /páylōd/ n. **1** the part of an aircraft's load from which revenue is derived, as paying passengers. **2 a** the explosive warhead carried by an aircraft or rocket. **b** the instruments, etc., carried by a spaceship. ▷ ROCKET

pay·mas·ter /páymastər/ n. **1** an official who pays troops, workers, etc. **2** a person, organization, etc., to whom another owes duty or loyalty because of payment given.

pay·ment /páymənt/ n. **1** the act or an instance of paying. **2** an amount paid. **3** reward; recompense.

pay·off /páyawf/ n. *sl.* **1** an act of payment. **2** a climax. **3** a final reckoning. **4** *colloq.* a bribe; bribery.

pay·o·la /payólə/ n. **1** a bribe offered in return for unofficial promotion of a product, etc., in the media. **2** the practice of such bribery.

pay phone n. a telephone usu. requiring a coin payment for use.

pay·roll /páyrōl/ n. a list of employees receiving regular pay.

Pb *symb. Chem.* the element lead.

PBS *abbr.* Public Broadcasting Service.

PBX *abbr.* private branch exchange (private telephone switchboard).

PC *abbr.* **1** personal computer. **2** political correctness; politically correct. **3** Peace Corps. **4** (in the UK) police constable.

p.c. *abbr.* **1** percent. **2** postcard.

PCB *abbr.* **1** *Computing* ▼ printed circuit board. **2** *Chem.* polychlorinated biphenyl, any of several toxic compounds containing two benzene molecules

in which hydrogens have been replaced by chlorine atoms, formed as waste in industrial processes.

PCP n. **1** *sl.* an illicit hallucinogenic drug, phencyclidine hydrochloride (*phenyl cyclohexyl piperidine*). **2** primary care physician.

pct. *abbr.* percent.

PD *abbr.* Police Department.

Pd *symb. Chem.* the element palladium.

pd. *abbr.* paid.

p.d.q. *abbr. colloq.* pretty damn quick.

PDT *abbr.* Pacific Daylight Time.

PE *abbr.* physical education.

pea /pee/ n. **1 a** a hardy climbing plant, *Pisum sativum*, with seeds growing in pods and used for food. ▷ VEGETABLE. **b** its seed. ▷ SEED. **2** any of several similar plants (*sweet pea; chickpea*).

peace /pees/ n. **1 a** quiet; tranquillity (*needs peace to work well*). **b** mental calm; serenity (*peace of mind*). **2 a** (often *attrib.*) freedom from or the cessation of war (*peace talks*). **b** (esp. **Peace**) a treaty of peace between two nations, etc., at war. **3** freedom from civil disorder. □ **at peace 1** in a state of friendliness. **2** serene. **3** *euphem.* dead. **keep the peace** prevent, or refrain from, strife. **make one's peace** become reconciled.

peace·a·ble /péesəbəl/ adj. **1** disposed to peace; unwarlike. **2** free from disturbance; peaceful. □□ **peace·a·ble·ness** n. **peace·a·bly** adv.

Peace Corps n. a federal governmental organization sending people to work as volunteers in developing countries.

peace·ful /péesfōol/ adj. **1** characterized by peace; tranquil. **2** not violating or infringing peace (*peaceful coexistence*). **3** belonging to a state of peace. □□ **peace·ful·ly** adv. **peace·ful·ness** n.

peace·mak·er /péesmaykər/ n. a person who brings about peace. □□ **peace·mak·ing** n. & adj.

peace·nik /péesnik/ n. *colloq.*, often *derog.* a member of a pacifist movement.

peace of·fer·ing n. **1** a propitiatory or conciliatory gift. **2** *Bibl.* an offering presented as a thanksgiving to God.

peace pipe n. a tobacco pipe smoked as a token of peace among some Native Americans.

peace·time /péestīm/ n. a period when a country is not at war.

peach[1] /peech/ n. **1 a** a round juicy fruit with downy cream or yellow skin flushed with red. ▷ FRUIT. **b** the tree, *Prunus persica*, bearing it. **2** the yellowish pink color of a peach. **3** *colloq.* a person or thing of superlative quality. □□ **peach·y** adj. (**peachier, peachiest**). **peach·i·ness** n.

peach[2] /peech/ v. **1** *intr.* (usu. foll. by *against, on*) *colloq.* turn informer; inform. **2** *tr.* inform against.

pea·cock /péekok/ n. **1** a male peafowl, having brilliant plumage and a tail (with eyelike markings) that can be expanded erect in display like a fan. **2** an ostentatious strutting person.

pea·cock butter·fly n. ◄ a butterfly, *Inachis io*, with eyelike markings on its wings.

pea·fowl /péefowl/ n. **1** a peacock or peahen. **2** a pheasant of the genus *Pavo*.

pea·hen /péehen/ n. a female peafowl.

peak[1] /peek/ n. & v. • n. **1** a projecting usu. pointed part, esp.: **a** the pointed top of a mountain. **b** a mountain with a peak. **c** a stiff brim at the front of a cap. **d** a pointed beard. **e** the narrow part of a ship's hold at the bow or stern. **f** *Naut.* the upper outer corner of a sail extended by a gaff. **2 a** the highest point in a curve (*on the peak of the wave*). **b** the time of greatest success (in a career, etc.). **c** the highest point on a graph, etc. • *v.intr.* reach the highest value, quality, etc. (*output peaked in September*). □□ **peaked** adj. **peak·i·ness** n.

peak[2] /peek/ v.intr. **1** waste away. **2** (as **peaked** /péekid/ adj.) pale; sickly.

peal /peel/ n. & v. • n. **1 a** the loud ringing of a bell or bells, esp. a series of changes. **b** a set of bells. **2** a loud repeated sound, esp. of thunder, laughter, etc. • v. **1** *intr.* sound forth in a peal. **2** *tr.* utter sonorously. **3** *tr.* ring (bells) in peals.

pea·nut /péenut/ n. **1** a leguminous plant, *Arachis hypogaea*, bearing pods that ripen underground and contain seeds used as food and yielding oil. **2** the seed of this plant. **3** (in *pl.*) *colloq.* a paltry or trivial thing or amount, esp. of money.

pea·nut brit·tle n. a confection made with peanuts and caramelized sugar.

pea·nut but·ter n. a paste of ground roasted peanuts.

pear /pair/ n. **1** a yellowish or brownish green fleshy fruit, tapering toward the stalk. **2** any of various trees of the genus *Pyrus* bearing it, esp. *P. communis*.

pear drop n. a small candy in the shape of a pear.

pearl /pərl/ n. **1 a** (often *attrib.*) ▼ a usu. white or bluish gray hard mass formed within the shell of a pearl oyster or other bivalve mollusk, highly prized as a gem for its luster (*pearl necklace*). ▷ GEM. **b** an imitation of this. **c** (in *pl.*) a necklace of pearls. **d** = MOTHER-OF-PEARL. (cf. SEED PEARL). **2** a precious thing; the finest example. **3** anything resembling a pearl, e.g., a dewdrop, tear, etc. □ **cast pearls before swine** offer a treasure to a person unable to appreciate it. □□ **pearl·er** n.

P

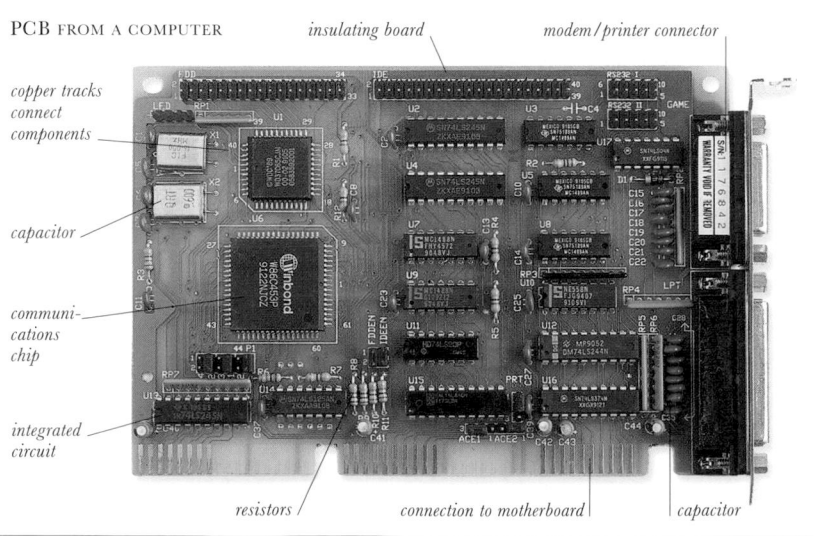

PCB

A PCB, or printed circuit board, is an electrical circuit used in most digital equipment, including computers. It is made by laying tracks of a conductor (such as copper) onto one or both sides of an insulating board.

Components, such as integrated circuits, resistors, and capacitors, can be soldered to the surface of the board or attached by inserting their connecting pins or wires into holes drilled in the board.

PCB FROM A COMPUTER — insulating board — modem/printer connector — copper tracks connect components — capacitor — communications chip — integrated circuit — resistors — connection to motherboard — capacitor

PEACOCK BUTTERFLY (*Inachis io*)

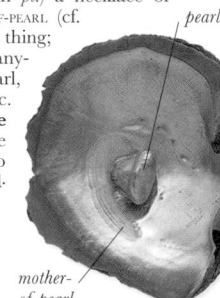

PEARL IN AN OYSTER SHELL — mother-of-pearl

pearl bar·ley *n.* barley reduced to small round grains by grinding.

pearl·es·cent /pərlésənt/ *adj.* having or producing the appearance of mother-of-pearl.

pearl·ite /pərlīt/ *n.* a ferrite and cementite mixture occurring in iron and carbon steel.

pearl·ized /pórlīzd/ *adj.* treated so as to resemble mother-of-pearl.

pearl on·ion *n.* a very small onion used in pickles.

pearl oys·ter *n.* any of various marine bivalve mollusks of the genus *Pinctada*, bearing pearls.

pearl·y /pórlee/ *adj.* (**pearlier, pearliest**) 1 resembling a pearl; lustrous. 2 containing pearls or mother-of-pearl. 3 adorned with pearls. □□ **pearl·i·ness** *n.*

Pearl·y Gates *n.pl. colloq.* the gates of Heaven.

peas·ant /pézənt/ *n.* 1 esp. *colloq.* a rural person; a rustic. 2 a a worker on the land, esp. a laborer or farmer. b *hist.* a member of an agricultural class dependent on subsistence farming. 3 *derog.* a boorish or unsophisticated person. □□ **peas·ant·ry** *n.* (*pl.* **-ies**). **peas·ant·y** *adj.*

pease /peez/ *n.pl. archaic* peas.

pea·shoot·er /péeshootər/ *n.* a small tube for blowing dried peas through as a toy.

peat /peet/ *n.* 1 vegetable matter decomposed in water and partly carbonized, used for fuel, in horticulture, etc. ▷ BOG, COAL. 2 a cut piece of this. □□ **peat·y** *adj.*

peat·bog /péetbawg, -bog/ *n.* a bog composed of peat.

peat·moss /péetmaws, -mos/ *n.* 1 a peatbog. 2 any of various mosses of the genus *Sphagnum*, which grow in damp conditions and form peat as they decay.

peb·ble /pébəl/ *n.* 1 a small smooth stone worn by the action of water. 2 a a type of colorless transparent rock crystal used for eyeglasses. b a lens of this. c (*attrib.*) *colloq.* (of a lens) very thick and convex. 3 an agate or other gem, esp. when found as a pebble in a stream, etc. 4 an irregular or grainy surface, as on paper, leather, etc. □□ **peb·bly** *adj.*

pec /pek/ *abbr.* pectoral (muscle).

pe·can /pikaán, -kán, péekan/ *n.* 1 ▶ a pinkish brown smooth nut with an edible kernel. 2 a hickory, *Carya illinoensis*, of the southern US, producing this.

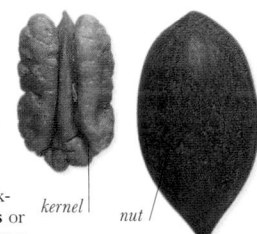

kernel   *nut*

PECAN (*Carya illinoensis*)

pec·ca·dil·lo /pékədílō/ *n.* (*pl.* **-oes** or **-os**) a trifling offense; a venial sin.

peck[1] /pek/ *v. & n.* ● *v.tr.* 1 strike or bite (something) with a beak. 2 kiss (esp. a person's cheek) hastily or perfunctorily. 3 a make (a hole) by pecking. b (foll. by *out, off*) remove or pluck out by pecking. 4 *colloq.* (also *absol.*) eat (food) listlessly; nibble at. 5 mark with short strokes. ● *n.* 1 a a stroke or bite with a beak. b a mark made by this. 2 a hasty or perfunctory kiss. □ **peck at** 1 eat (food) listlessly; nibble. 2 carp at; nag 3 strike (a thing) repeatedly with a beak.

peck[2] /pek/ *n.* 1 a measure of capacity for dry goods, equal to 2 gallons or 8 quarts. 2 a vessel used to contain this amount. □ **a peck of** a large number or amount of (troubles, dirt, etc.).

peck·ing or·der *n.* a social hierarchy, orig. as observed among hens.

pec·tin /péktin/ *n. Biochem.* any of various soluble gelatinous polysaccharides found in ripe fruits, etc., and used as a gelling agent in jams and jellies. □□ **pec·tic** *adj.*

pec·to·ral /péktərəl/ *adj. & n.* ● *adj.* 1 of or relating to the breast or chest; thoracic (*pectoral fin; pectoral muscle*). 2 worn on the chest (*pectoral cross*). ● *n.* 1 (esp. in *pl.*) a pectoral muscle. 2 a pectoral fin.

▷ FISH. 3 an ornamental breastplate esp. of a Jewish high priest.

pec·tose /péktōs/ *n. Biochem.* an insoluble polysaccharide derivative found in unripe fruits and converted into pectin by ripening, heating, etc.

pec·u·late /pékyəlayt/ *v.tr. & intr.* embezzle (money). □□ **pec·u·la·tion** /-láyshən/ *n.* **pec·u·la·tor** *n.*

pe·cu·liar /pikyōolyər/ *adj.* 1 strange; odd; unusual (*a peculiar flavor; is a little peculiar*). 2 a (usu. foll. by *to*) belonging exclusively (*a fashion peculiar to the time*). b belonging to the individual (*in their own peculiar way*). 3 particular; special (*a point of peculiar interest*).

pe·cu·li·ar·i·ty /pikyōoleeáritee/ *n.* (*pl.* **-ies**) 1 a idiosyncrasy; oddity. b an instance of this. 2 a characteristic or habit (*meanness is his peculiarity*). 3 the state of being peculiar.

pe·cu·liar·ly /pikyōolyərlee/ *adv.* 1 more than usually; especially (*peculiarly annoying*). 2 oddly. 3 as regards oneself alone; individually (*does not affect him peculiarly*).

pe·cu·ni·ar·y /pikyōonee-eree/ *adj.* 1 of, concerning, or consisting of, money (*pecuniary aid; pecuniary considerations*). 2 (of an offense) entailing a money penalty or fine. □□ **pe·cu·ni·ar·i·ly** *adv.*

ped·a·gogue /pédəgog, -gawg/ *n.* a schoolmaster or teacher, esp. a pedantic one. □□ **ped·a·gog·ic** /-gójik, -gójik/ *adj.* **ped·a·gog·i·cal** *adj.* **ped·a·gog·i·cal·ly** *adv.*

ped·a·gog·y /pédəgojee, -gojee/ *n.* the science of teaching. □□ **ped·a·gog·ics** /-gójiks, -gójiks/ *n.*

ped·al /péd'l/ *n. & v.* ● *n.* any of several types of foot-operated levers or controls for mechanisms, esp.: a either of a pair of levers for transmitting power to a bicycle or tricycle wheel, etc. ▷ BICYCLE. b any of the foot-operated controls in a motor vehicle. c any of the foot-operated keys of an organ used for playing notes, or for drawing out several stops at once, etc. ▷ ORGAN. d each of the foot-levers on a piano, etc., for making the tone fuller or softer. ▷ UPRIGHT. e each of the foot-levers on a harp for altering the pitch of the strings. ● *v.* (**pedaled** or **pedalled, pedaling** or **pedalling**) 1 *intr.* operate a cycle, organ, etc., by using the pedals. 2 *tr.* work (a bicycle, etc.) with the pedals.

ped·al push·er *n.* 1 (in *pl.*) women's calf-length pants. 2 *colloq.* a cyclist.

ped·ant /péd'nt/ *n.* 1 a person who insists on strict adherence to formal rules or literal meaning at the expense of a wider view. 2 a person who rates academic learning or technical knowledge above everything. 3 a person who is obsessed by a theory; a doctrinaire. □□ **pe·dan·tic** /pidántik/ *adj.* **pe·dan·ti·cal·ly** *adv.* **ped·ant·ize** *v.intr. & tr.* **ped·ant·ry** *n.* (*pl.* **-ies**).

ped·dle /péd'l/ *v.* 1 *tr.* a sell (goods), esp. in small quantities, as a peddler. b advocate or promote (ideas, a philosophy, a way of life, etc.). 2 *tr.* sell (drugs) illegally.

ped·dler /pédlər/ *n.* 1 a traveling seller of small items esp. carried in a pack, etc. 2 (usu. foll. by *of*) a dealer in gossip, influence, etc. 3 a person who sells drugs illegally. □□ **ped·dler·y** *n.*

ped·er·as·ty /pédərastee/ *n.* anal intercourse esp. between a man and a boy. □□ **ped·er·ast** *n.*

ped·es·tal /pédistəl/ *n. & v.* ● *n.* 1 ▶ a base supporting a column or pillar. 2 the stone, etc., base of a statue, etc. 3 either of

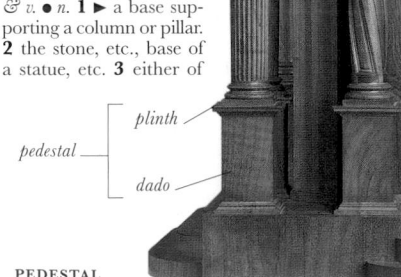

plinth

pedestal

dado

PEDESTAL

the two supports of a desk or table, usu. containing drawers. ● *v.tr.* (**pedestaled, pedestaling** or **pedestalled, pedestalling**) set or support on a pedestal. □ **put** (or **set**) **on a pedestal** regard as highly admirable, important, etc.; venerate.

pe·des·tri·an /pidéstreeən/ *n. & adj.* ● *n.* (often *attrib.*) a person who is walking, esp. in a town (*pedestrian crossing*). ● *adj.* prosaic; dull; uninspired. □□ **pe·des·tri·an·ism** *n.* **pe·des·tri·an·ize** *v.tr. & intr.* **pe·des·tri·an·i·za·tion** *n.*

pe·des·tri·an cross·ing *n.* a specified part of a road or street where pedestrians have right of way to cross.

pe·di·at·rics /péedeeátriks/ *n.pl.* (treated as *sing.*) the branch of medicine dealing with children and their diseases. □□ **pe·di·at·ric** *adj.* **pe·di·a·tri·cian** /-deeətríshən/ *n.*

ped·i·cab /pédikab/ *n.* = TRISHAW.

ped·i·cel /pédisəl/ *n.* (also **ped·i·cle** /pédikəl/) 1 a small (esp. subordinate) stalk-like structure in a plant or animal (cf. PEDUNCLE). 2 *Surgery* part of a graft left temporarily attached to its original site. □□ **ped·i·cel·late** /-sélət, -ayt/ *adj.* **pe·dic·u·late** /pidíkyələt, -layt/ *adj.*

pe·dic·u·lar /pidíkyələr/ *adj.* (also **pe·dic·u·lous** /-ləs/) infested with lice. □□ **pe·dic·u·lo·sis** /-lōsis/ *n.*

ped·i·cure /pédikyoor/ *n. & v.* ● *n.* 1 the care or treatment of the feet, esp. of the toenails. 2 a person practicing this, esp. professionally. ● *v.tr.* treat (the feet) by removing corns, etc.

ped·i·gree /pédigree/ *n.* 1 (often *attrib.*) a recorded line of descent of a person or esp. a pure-bred domestic or pet animal. 2 the derivation of a word. 3 a genealogical table. □□ **ped·i·greed** *adj.*

ped·i·ment /pédimənt/ *n.* 1 a ▼ the triangular front part of a building in Grecian style, surmounting esp. a portico of columns. ▷ FAÇADE. b a similar part of a building in Roman or Renaissance style. 2 *Geol.* a broad flattish rock surface at the foot of a mountain slope. □□ **ped·i·men·tal** /-mént'l/ *adj.* **ped·i·ment·ed** *adj.*

PEDIMENT

ped·lar var. of PEDDLER.

pedo- /pédō/ *comb. form* (*Brit.* **paedo-**) child.

pe·dol·o·gy /pidóləjee/ *n.* the scientific study of soil, esp. its formation, nature, and classification. □□ **pe·do·log·i·cal** /pédəlójikəl/ *adj.* **pe·dol·o·gist** *n.*

pe·dom·e·ter /pidómitər/ *n.* an instrument for estimating the distance traveled on foot by recording the number of steps taken.

pe·do·phile /péedəfīl, péd-/ *n.* a person who displays pedophilia.

pe·do·phil·i·a /péedəfíleeə, péd-/ *n.* sexual desire directed toward children.

pe·dun·cle /pedúngkəl, péedung-/ *n.* 1 *Bot.* the stalk of a flower, fruit, or cluster, esp. a main stalk bearing a solitary flower or subordinate stalks (cf. PEDICEL). ▷ INFLORESCENCE. 2 *Zool.* a stalk-like projection in an animal body. □□ **pe·dun·cu·lar** /-kyələr/ *adj.* **pe·dun·cu·late** /-kyələt/ *adj.*

pee /pee/ *v. & n. colloq.* or *coarse* ● *v.* (**pees, peed**) 1 *intr.* urinate. 2 *tr.* pass (urine, blood, etc.) from the bladder. ● *n.* 1 urination. 2 urine.

peek /peek/ *v. & n.* ● *v.intr.* (usu. foll. by *in, out, at*) look quickly or slyly; peep. ● *n.* a quick or sly look.

peek·a·boo /péekəbōo/ *adj. & n.* ● *adj.* 1 (of a garment, etc.) transparent or having a pattern of small holes. 2 (of a hairstyle) concealing one eye

P

with the bangs or a wave. ● *n.* game of hiding and suddenly reappearing, played with a young child.

peel[1] /peel/ *v. & n.* ● *v.* **1** *tr.* **a** strip the skin, rind, bark, wrapping, etc., from (a fruit, vegetable, tree, etc.). **b** (usu. foll. by *off*) strip (skin, peel, wrapping, etc.) from a fruit, etc. **2** *intr.* **a** (of a tree, an animal's or person's body, a painted surface, etc.) become bare of bark, skin, paint, etc. **b** (often foll. by *off*) (of bark, a person's skin, paint, etc.) flake off. **3** *intr.* (often foll. by *off*) *colloq.* (of a person) strip for exercise, etc. ● *n.* the outer covering of a fruit, vegetable, shrimp, etc.; rind. □ **peel off 1** veer away and detach oneself from a group of marchers, a formation of aircraft, etc. **2** *colloq.* strip off one's clothes. □□ **peel·er** *n.* (in sense 1 of *v.*).

peel[2] /peel/ *n.* a shovel, esp. a baker's shovel for bringing loaves, etc., into or out of an oven.

peel·ing /peeling/ *n.* a strip of the outer skin of a vegetable, fruit, etc. (*potato peelings*).

peen /peen/ *n.* ◄ the wedge-shaped or thin or curved end of a hammer head (opp. FACE *n.* 5a).

peen

PEEN:
HAMMER
WITH A
PEEN

peep[1] /peep/ *v. & n.* ● *v.intr.* **1** (usu. foll. by *at, in, out, into*) look through a narrow opening; look furtively. **2** (usu. foll. by *out*) **a** (of daylight, a flower beginning to bloom, etc.) come slowly into view; emerge. **b** (of a quality, etc.) show itself unconsciously. ● *n.* **1** a furtive or peering glance. **2** the first appearance (*at peep of day*).

peep[2] /peep/ *v. & n.* ● *v.intr.* make a shrill feeble sound as of young birds, mice, etc.; squeak; chirp. ● *n.* **1** such a sound; a cheep. **2** the slightest sound or utterance, esp. of protest, etc.

peep·hole /peephol/ *n.* a tiny hole in a solid door, fence, etc., to look through.

peep·ing Tom *n.* a furtive voyeur.

peer[1] /peer/ *v.intr.* **1** (usu. foll. by *into, at,* etc.) look keenly or with difficulty (*peered into the fog*). **2** appear; peep out.

peer[2] /peer/ *n.* **1** a person who is equal in ability, standing, rank, or value; a contemporary (*tried by a jury of his peers*). **2 a** (*fem.* **peeress**) a member of one of the degrees of the nobility in Britain, i.e. a duke, marquis, earl, viscount, or baron. **b** a noble of any country. □□ **peer·less** *adj.*

peer·age /peerij/ *n.* **1** peers as a class; the nobility. **2** the rank of peer or peeress (*was given a life peerage*). **3** a book containing a list of peers with their genealogy, etc.

peer group *n.* a group of people of the same age, status, interests, etc.

peeve /peev/ *v. & n. colloq.* ● *v.tr.* (usu. as **peeved** *adj.*) annoy; irritate. ● *n.* a cause of annoyance.

peev·ish /peevish/ *adj.* querulous; irritable. □□ **peev·ish·ly** *adv.* **peev·ish·ness** *n.*

peg /peg/ *n. & v.* ● *n.* **1 a** a usu. cylindrical pin or bolt of wood or metal, often tapered at one end, and used for holding esp. two things together. **b** such a peg attached to a wall, etc., and used for hanging garments, etc., on. **c** a peg driven into the ground and attached to a rope for holding up a tent. **d** a bung for stoppering a cask, etc. **e** each of several pegs used to tighten or loosen the strings of a violin, etc. ▷ STRINGED. **f** a small peg, matchstick, etc., stuck into holes in a board for calculating the scores at cribbage. **2** *Brit.* = CLOTHESPIN. ● *v.tr.* (**pegged, pegging**) **1** (usu. foll. by *down, in, out,* etc.) fix (a thing) with a peg. **2** *Econ.* **a** stabilize (prices, wages, exchange rates, etc.). **b** prevent the price of (stock, etc.) from falling or rising by freely buying or selling at a given price. □ **peg down** restrict (a person, etc.) to rules, a commitment, etc. **a round** (or **square**) **peg in a square** (or **round**) **hole** a misfit. **take a person down a peg or two** humble a person.

peg·board /pegbawrd/ *n.* a board having a regular pattern of small holes for pegs, used for commercial displays, games, etc.

peg·ma·tite /pégmətīt/ *n.* a coarsely crystalline type of granite.

peign·oir /paynwaar, pen-, páynwaar, pén-/ *n.* a woman's loose dressing gown.

pe·jo·ra·tive /pijáwrətiv, -jór-, péjəra-, pee-/ *adj. & n.* ● *adj.* (of a word, an expression, etc.) depreciatory. ● *n.* a depreciatory word. □□ **pe·jo·ra·tive·ly** *adv.*

pek·an /pékən/ = FISHER 1.

Pe·king duck *n.* a Chinese dish consisting of strips of roast duck served with shredded vegetables and a sweet sauce.

Pe·king·ese /péekineéz, -eés/ (also **Pe·kin·ese**) *n.* (*pl.* same) **1** a lapdog of a short-legged breed with long hair and a snub nose. ▷ DOG. **2** this breed.

pe·koe /péekó/ *n.* a superior kind of black tea.

pe·lag·ic /pilájik/ *adj.* **1** of or performed on the open sea (*pelagic whaling*). **2** (of marine life) belonging to the upper layers of the open sea.

pel·ar·go·ni·um /pélərgóneeəm/ *n.* any plant of the genus *Pelargonium*, with red, pink, or white flowers and fragrant leaves. Also called **geranium**.

pelf /pelf/ *n. derog.* or *joc.* money; wealth.

pel·ham /péləm/ *n.* a horse's bit combining a curb and a snaffle.

pel·i·can /pélikən/ *n.* ▼ any large gregarious water-fowl of the family Pelecanidae with a large bill and a pouch in the throat for storing fish.

pouch

PELICAN:
DALMATIAN PELICAN
(*Pelecanus crispus*)

pel·la·gra /pilágrə, -láygrə, -laá-/ *n.* a disease caused by deficiency of nicotinic acid, characterized by cracking of the skin and often resulting in insanity. □□ **pel·la·grous** *adj.*

pel·let /pélit/ *n. & v.* ● *n.* **1** a small compressed ball of paper, bread, etc. **2** a pill. **3 a** a small mass of bones, feathers, etc., regurgitated by a bird of prey. **b** a small hard piece of animal, usu. rodent, excreta. **4 a** a piece of small shot. **b** an imitation bullet for a toy gun. ● *v.tr.* (**pelleted, pelleting**) **1** make into a pellet or pellets. **2** hit with (esp. paper) pellets. □□ **pel·let·ize** *v.tr.*

pell-mell /pélmél/ *adv.* **1** headlong; recklessly (*rushed pell-mell out of the room*). **2** in disorder or confusion (*stuffed the papers together pell-mell*).

pel·lu·cid /pilōōsid/ *adj.* **1** (of water, light, etc.) transparent; clear. **2** (of style, speech, etc.) not confused; clear. **3** mentally clear. □□ **pel·lu·cid·i·ty** /-síditee/ *n.* **pel·lu·cid·ly** *adv.*

pelt[1] /pelt/ *v. & n.* ● *v.* **1** *tr.* (usu. foll. by *with*) **a** hurl many small missiles at. **b** hurl (something) at a person, etc. **c** assail (a person, etc.) with insults, abuse, etc. **2** *intr.* (usu. foll. by *down*) (of rain, etc.) fall quickly and torrentially. **3** *intr.* run fast.

pelt[2] /pelt/ *n.* **1** the undressed skin of a fur-bearing mammal. **2** the skin of a sheep, goat, etc., with short wool, or stripped ready for tanning. □□ **pelt·ry** *n.*

pel·vic /pélvik/ *adj.* of or relating to the pelvis.

pel·vic girdle *n.* the bony or cartilaginous structure in vertebrates to which the posterior limbs are attached.

pel·vis /pélvis/ *n.* (*pl.* **pelvises** or **pelves** /-veez/) **1** a basin-shaped cavity at the lower end of the torso of most vertebrates, formed from the innominate bones with the sacrum and other vertebrae.

▷ HIP JOINT, SKELETON. **2** the basin-like cavity of the kidney.

pem·mi·can /pémikən/ *n.* **1** a cake of dried pounded meat mixed with melted fat, orig. made by Native Americans. **2** beef so treated and flavored with dried fruit, etc., for use by Arctic travelers, etc.

Pen. *abbr.* Peninsula.

pen[1] /pen/ *n. & v.* ● *n.* **1** ▼ an instrument for writing or drawing with ink, orig. consisting of a shaft with a sharpened quill or metal nib, now more widely applied. ▷ CALLIGRAPHY. **2 a** (usu. prec. by *the*) the occupation of writing. **b** a style of writing. **3** *Zool.* the internal feather-shaped cartilaginous

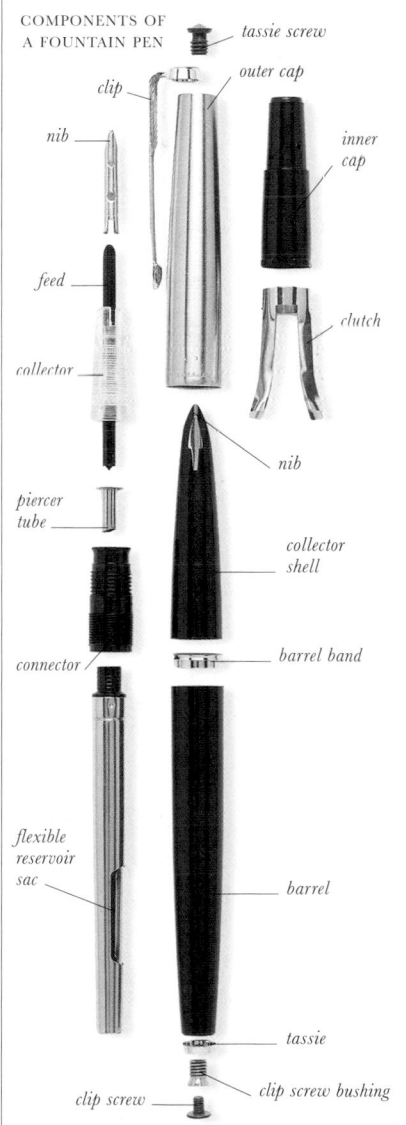

PEN

The basic components of a pen are a writing point, ink reservoir, and external housing. Types of writing points used include nibs (fountain pen), rotating ball (ballpoint pen), and felt or nylon point (felt-tip pen). Ink reservoirs are usually replaced when depleted, but some, like the one shown here, can be refilled.

COMPONENTS OF
A FOUNTAIN PEN

tassie screw
clip
outer cap
nib
inner cap
feed
clutch
collector
nib
piercer tube
collector shell
connector
barrel band
flexible reservoir sac
barrel
tassie
clip screw
clip screw bushing

P

P

shell of certain cuttlefish, esp. squid. ● *v.tr.* (**penned**, **penning**) **1** write. **2** compose and write. □ **put pen to paper** begin writing.

pen² /pen/ *n. & v.* ● *n.* **1** a small enclosure for cows, sheep, poultry, etc. **2** a place of confinement. **3** an enclosure for sheltering submarines. ● *v.tr.* (**penned**, **penning**) (often foll. by *in*, *up*) enclose or shut in a pen.

pen³ /pen/ *n.* a female swan.

pen⁴ /pen/ *n. sl.* = PENITENTIARY *n.* 1.

pe·nal /péenəl/ *adj.* **1 a** of or concerning punishment or its infliction (*penal laws; a penal sentence; a penal colony*). **b** (of an offense) punishable, esp. by law. **2** extremely severe (*penal taxation*). □□ **pe·nal·ly** *adv.*

pe·nal·ize /péenəlīz/ *v.tr.* **1** subject (a person) to a penalty or comparative disadvantage. **2** make or declare (an action) penal. □□ **pe·nal·i·za·tion** *n.*

pen·al·ty /pénəltee/ *n.* (*pl.* **-ies**) **1 a** a punishment, esp. a fine, for a breach of law, contract, etc. **b** a fine paid. **2** a disadvantage, loss, etc., esp. as a result of one's own actions. **3 a** a disadvantage imposed on a competitor or team in a game, etc., for a breach of the rules, etc. **b** (*attrib.*) awarded against a side incurring a penalty (*clipping penalty; penalty kick*). **4** *Bridge*, etc., points gained by opponents when a contract is not fulfilled. □ **under** (or **on**) **penalty of** under the threat of (*dismissal, etc.*).

pen·al·ty box *n. Ice Hockey* an area reserved for penalized players and some officials.

pen·ance /pénəns/ *n.* **1** an act of self-punishment as reparation for guilt. **2 a** (esp. in the RC and Orthodox Church) a sacrament including confession of and absolution for a sin. **b** a penalty imposed esp. by a priest, or undertaken voluntarily, for a sin. □ **do penance** perform a penance.

pe·na·tes /pináyteez, pináa-/ *n.pl.* (often **Pe·na·tes**) (in Roman mythology) the household gods, esp. of the storeroom.

pence *Brit. pl.* of PENNY.

pen·chant /pénchənt/ *n.* an inclination or liking (*has a penchant for old films*).

pen·cil /pénsil/ *n. & v.* ● *n.* **1** (often *attrib.*) **a** an instrument for writing or drawing, usu. consisting of a thin rod of graphite, etc., enclosed in a wooden cylinder (*a pencil sketch*). **b** a similar instrument with a metal or plastic cover and retractable lead. **c** a cosmetic in pencil form. **2** (*attrib.*) resembling a pencil in shape (*pencil skirt*). ● *v.tr.* (**penciled**, **penciling** or **pencilled**, **pencilling**) **1** tint or mark with or as if with a pencil. **2** (usu. foll. by *in*) **a** write, esp. tentatively or provisionally (*have penciled in the 29th for our meeting*). **b** (esp. as **penciled** *adj.*) fill (an area) with soft pencil strokes (*penciled in her eyebrows*). □□ **pen·cil·er** or *Brit.* **pen·cil·ler** *n.*

pen·cil push·er *n. colloq. derog.* a clerical worker or one who does considerable paperwork.

pend·ant /péndənt/ *n.* (also **pend·ent**) **1** ◀ a hanging jewel, etc., esp. one attached to a necklace, bracelet, etc. **2** a light fitting, ornament, etc., hanging from a ceiling.

necklace

link

crystal pendant

PENDANT

pend·ent /péndənt/ *adj.* (also **pend·ant**) **1 a** hanging. **b** overhanging. **2** undecided; pending. **3** *Gram.* (esp. of a sentence) incomplete; not having a finite verb (*pendent nominative*). □□ **pen·den·cy** *n.*

pend·ing /pénding/ *adj. & prep.* ● *predic.adj.* **1** awaiting decision or settlement; undecided (*a settlement was pending*). **2** about to come into existence (*patent pending*). ● *prep.* **1** during (*pending these negotiations*). **2** until (*pending his return*).

pen·drag·on /pendrágən/ *n. hist.* an ancient British or Welsh prince (often as a title).

pen·du·line /pénjəlīn, péndə-,**

-dyə-/ *adj.* **1** (of a nest) suspended. **2** (of a bird) of a kind that builds such a nest.

pen·du·lous /pénjələs, péndə-, -dyə-/ *adj.* **1** (of ears, breasts, flowers, bird's nests, etc.) hanging down; drooping and esp. swinging. **2** oscillating. □□ **pen·du·lous·ly** *adv.*

pen·du·lum /pénjələm, péndə-, -dyə-/ *n.* ▶ a weight suspended so as to swing freely, esp. a rod with a weighted end regulating the movement of a clock's works.

pen·e·trate /pénitrayt/ *v.* **1** *tr.* **a** find access into or through, esp. forcibly. **b** (usu. foll. by *with*) imbue (a person or thing) with; permeate. **2** *tr.* see into, find out, or discern (a person's mind, the truth, a meaning, etc.). **3** *tr.* see through (darkness, fog, etc.) (*could not penetrate the gloom*). **4** *intr.* be absorbed by the mind (*my hint did not penetrate*). **5** *tr.* (as **penetrating** *adj.*) **a** having or suggesting sensitivity or insight (*a penetrating remark*). **b** (of a voice, etc.) easily heard through or above other sounds; piercing. **c** (of a smell) sharp; pungent. **6** *tr.* (of a man) put the penis into the vagina of (a woman). **7** *intr.* (usu. foll. by *into, through, to*) make a way. □□ **pen·e·tra·ble** *adj.* **pen·e·tra·bil·i·ty** *n.* **pen·e·trant** *adj. & n.* **pen·e·trat·ing·ly** *adv.* **pen·e·tra·tion** *n.* **pen·e·tra·tive** /-trətiv/ *adj.* **pen·e·tra·tor** *n.*

pen·guin /pénggwin/ *n.* ▼ any flightless sea bird of the family Spheniscidae of the southern hemisphere, with black upperparts and white underparts, and wings developed into scaly flippers for swimming underwater.

pen·hold·er /pénhōldər/ *n.* **1** the esp. wooden shaft of a pen with a metal nib. **2** a rack for storing pens or nibs.

clock's mechanism

rod

pendulum controls clock's movement

falling weight drives clock's mechanism

PENDULUM OF A CLOCK

pen·i·cil·late /pénisílit, -ayt/ *adj. Biol.* **1** having or forming a small tuft or tufts. **2** marked with streaks as of a pencil or brush.

pen·i·cil·lin /pénisílin/ *n.* any of various antibiotics produced naturally by molds of the genus *Penicillium*, or synthetically, and able to prevent the growth of certain disease-causing bacteria.

pe·nile /péenīl, -nəl/ *adj.* of or concerning the penis.

pen·in·su·la /pəninsələ, -syələ/ *n.* a piece of land almost surrounded by water or projecting far into a sea or lake, etc. □□ **pen·in·su·lar** *adj.*

pe·nis /péenis/ *n.* (*pl.* **penises** or **penes** /-neez/) **1** the male organ of copulation and (in mammals) urination. ▷ REPRODUCTIVE ORGANS. **2** the male copulatory organ in lower vertebrates.

pen·i·tent /pénitənt/ *adj. & n.* ● *adj.* regretting and wishing to atone for sins, etc.; repentant. ● *n.* **1** a repentant sinner. **2** a person doing penance under the direction of a confessor. **3** (in *pl.*) various RC orders associated for mutual discipline, etc. □□ **pen·i·tence** *n.* **pen·i·tent·ly** *adv.*

pen·i·ten·tial /péniténshəl/ *adj.* of or concerning penitence or penance. □□ **pen·i·ten·tial·ly** *adv.*

pen·i·ten·tia·ry /péniténshəree/ *n. & adj.* ● *n.* (*pl.* **-ies**) **1** a reformatory prison, esp. a state or federal prison. **2** an office in the papal court deciding questions of penance, dispensations, etc. ● *adj.* **1** of or concerning penance. **2** of or concerning reformatory treatment. **3** (of an offense) making a culprit liable to a prison sentence.

pen·knife /pén-nīf/ *n.* a small folding knife, esp. for carrying in a pocket.

pen·light /pénlīt/ *n.* a pen-sized flashlight.

pen·man /pénmən/ *n.* (*pl.* **-men**) **1** a person who writes by hand with a specified skill (*a good penman*). **2** an author. □□ **penmanship** *n.*

Penn. *abbr.* (also **Penna.**) Pennsylvania.

pen name *n.* a literary pseudonym.

pen·nant /pénənt/ *n.* **1** *Naut.* a tapering flag, esp. that flown at the masthead of a vessel in commission. **2** = PENNON. **3 a** a flag denoting a sports championship, etc. **b** (by extension) a sports championship.

pen·ni·less /pénilis/ *adj.* having no money; destitute. □□ **pen·ni·less·ly** *adv.* **pen·ni·less·ness** *n.*

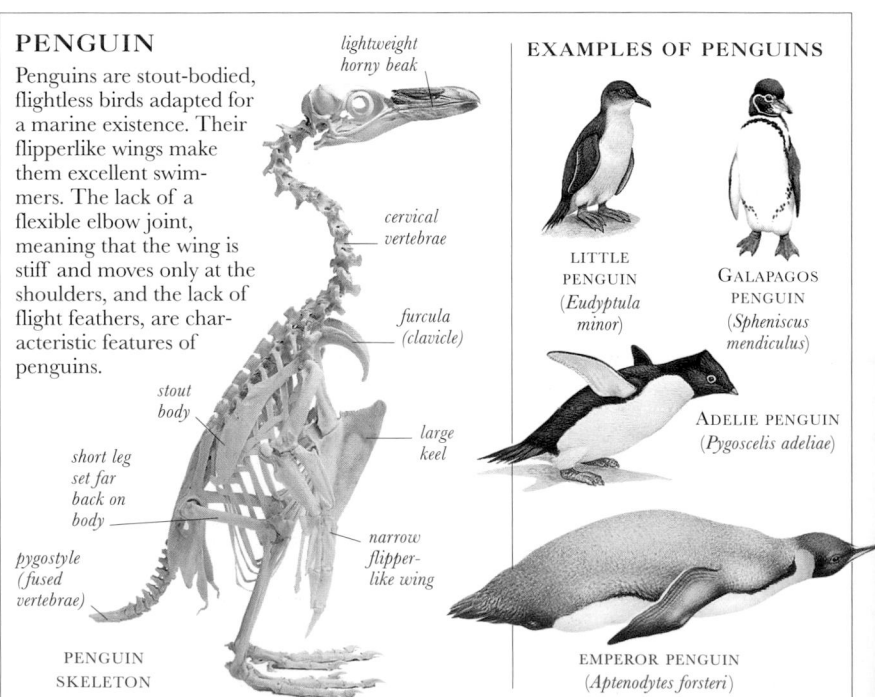

PENGUIN

Penguins are stout-bodied, flightless birds adapted for a marine existence. Their flipperlike wings make them excellent swimmers. The lack of a flexible elbow joint, meaning that the wing is stiff and moves only at the shoulders, and the lack of flight feathers, are characteristic features of penguins.

lightweight horny beak

cervical vertebrae

furcula (clavicle)

stout body

short leg set far back on body

pygostyle (fused vertebrae)

large keel

narrow flipperlike wing

PENGUIN SKELETON

EXAMPLES OF PENGUINS

LITTLE PENGUIN (*Eudyptula minor*)

GALAPAGOS PENGUIN (*Spheniscus mendiculus*)

ADELIE PENGUIN (*Pygoscelis adeliae*)

EMPEROR PENGUIN (*Aptenodytes forsteri*)

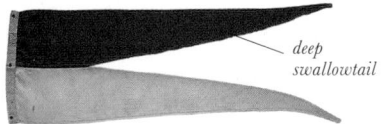

deep swallowtail

PENNON

pen·non /pénən/ *n.* ▲ a long narrow flag, triangular or swallow-tailed, esp. as the military ensign of lancer regiments. □□ **pen·noned** *adj.*

Penn·syl·va·ni·a Dutch /pénsilváynyə/ *n.* **1** a dialect of High German spoken by descendants of 17th–18th-c. German and Swiss immigrants to Pennsylvania, etc. **2** (as *pl.*) these settlers or their descendants.

Penn·syl·va·nian /pénseevárnyən/ *n. & adj.* ● *n.* **1** a native or inhabitant of Pennsylvania. **2** (prec. by *the*) *Geol.* the upper Carboniferous period or system in N. America. ● *adj.* **1** of or relating to Pennsylvania. **2** *Geol.* of or relating to the upper Carboniferous period or system in N. America.

pen·ny /pénee/ *n.* (*pl.* for separate coins **-ies**, *Brit.* for a sum of money **pence** /pens/) **1** (in the US, Canada, etc.) a one-cent coin. **2** a British coin and monetary unit equal to one hundredth of a pound. ¶ Abbr.: **p. 3** *hist.* a former British bronze coin and monetary unit equal to one two-hundred-and-fortieth of a pound. ¶ Abbr.: **d. 4** *Bibl.* a denarius. □ **like a bad penny** continually returning when unwanted. **pennies from heaven** unexpected benefits. **penny wise and pound foolish** frugal in small expenditures but wasteful of large amounts. **a pretty penny** a large sum of money.

pen·ny-pinch·ing *n. & adj.* ● *n.* frugality; cheapness. ● *adj.* frugal. □□ **pen·ny-pinch·er** *n.*

pen·ny·roy·al /péneeróyəl/ *n.* **1** a European creeping mint, *Mentha pulegium*, cultivated for its supposed medicinal properties. **2** an aromatic N. American plant, *Hedeoma pulegioides*.

pen·ny·weight /péneewayt/ *n.* a unit of weight, 24 grains or one twentieth of an ounce troy.

pen·ny whis·tle *n.* a tin pipe with six holes giving different notes.

pen·ny·wort /péneewərt, -wawrt/ *n.* any of several wild plants with rounded leaves, esp.: **1** (**wall pennywort**) *Umbilicus rupestris*, growing in crevices. **2** (**marsh** or **water pennywort**) *Hydrocotyle vulgaris*, growing in marshy places.

pen·ny·worth /péneewərth/ *n. esp. Brit.* (also **penn'orth** /pénərth/) **1** as much as can be bought for a penny. **2** a bargain of a specified kind (*a bad pennyworth*).

Pe·nob·scot /pənóbskot, -skət/ *n.* **1 a** a N. American people native to Maine. **b** a member of this people. **2** the language of this people.

pe·nol·o·gy /peenóləjee/ *n.* the study of the punishment of crime and of prison management. □□ **pe·no·log·i·cal** /-nəlójikəl/ *adj.* **pe·nol·o·gist** *n.*

pen pal *n. colloq.* a friend communicated with by letter only.

pen·sile /pénsil/ *adj.* **1** hanging down; pendulous. **2** (of a bird, etc.) building a pensile nest.

pen·sion[1] /pénshən/ *n. & v.* ● *n.* **1** a regular payment made by an employer, etc., after the retirement of an employee. **2** a similar payment made by a government to people above a specified age, to the disabled, etc. ● *v.tr.* grant a pension to. □ **pension off** dismiss with a pension. □□ **pen·sion·less** *adj.*

pen·sion[2] /paaNsyóN/ *n.* a European, esp. French, boardinghouse providing full or half board at a fixed rate.

pen·sion·a·ble /pénshənəbəl/ *adj.* **1** entitled to a pension. **2** (of a service, job, etc.) entitling an employee to a pension. □□ **pen·sion·a·bil·i·ty** *n.*

pen·sion·er /pénshənər/ *n.* a recipient of a pension, esp. a retirement pension.

pen·sive /pénsiv/ *adj.* **1** deep in thought. **2** sorrowfully thoughtful. □□ **pen·sive·ly** *adv.* **pen·sive·ness** *n.*

pen·ste·mon /pensteémən, pénstəmən/ *n.* (also **pent·ste·mon** /pentsteémən/) any American herbaceous plant of the genus *Penstemon*, with showy flowers and five stamens, one of which is sterile.

pen·stock /pénstok/ *n.* **1** a sluice; a floodgate. **2** a channel for conveying water to a waterwheel, etc.

pent /pent/ *adj.* (often foll. by *in*, *up*) closely confined; shut in (*pent-up feelings*).

penta- /péntə/ *comb. form* **1** five. **2** *Chem.* (forming the names of compounds) containing five atoms or groups of a specified kind (*pentachloride*; *pentoxide*).

pen·ta·cle /péntəkəl/ *n.* a figure used as a symbol, esp. in magic, e.g., a pentagram.

pen·ta·dac·tyl /péntədáktil/ *adj.* *Zool.* having five toes or fingers.

pen·ta·gon /péntəgon/ *n.* **1** ▶ a plane figure with five sides and angles. **2** (**the Pentagon**) **a** the pentagonal headquarters building of the US armed forces, located near Washington, D.C. **b** the US Department of Defense; the leaders of the US armed forces. □□ **pen·tag·o·nal** /-tágənəl/ *adj.*

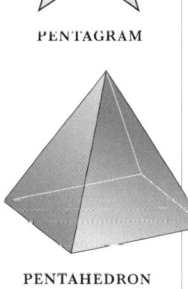

PENTAGON

pen·ta·gram /péntəgram/ *n.* ▶ a five-pointed star formed by extending the sides of a pentagon both ways until they intersect, formerly used as a mystic symbol.

PENTAGRAM

pen·ta·he·dron /péntəheédrən/ *n.* ▶ a solid figure with five faces. □□ **pen·ta·he·dral** *adj.*

pen·tam·e·ter /pentámitər/ *n.* **1** a verse of five feet, e.g., English iambic verse of ten syllables. **2** a form of Gk or Latin dactylic verse composed of two halves each of two feet and a long syllable, used in elegiac verse.

PENTAHEDRON

pen·tane /péntayn/ *n. Chem.* a hydrocarbon of the alkane series. ¶ Chem. formula: C_5H_{12}.

pen·tan·gle /péntanggəl/ *n.* = PENTAGRAM.

Pen·ta·teuch /péntətook, -tyook/ *n.* the first five books of the Old Testament, traditionally ascribed to Moses. □□ **pen·ta·teuch·al** *adj.*

pen·tath·lon /pentáthlən, -laan/ *n.* an athletic event comprising five different events for each competitor. □□ **pen·tath·lete** /-táthleet/ *n.*

pen·ta·ton·ic /péntətónik/ *adj. Mus.* **1** consisting of five notes. **2** relating to such a scale.

Pen·te·cost /péntikawst, -kost/ *n.* **1** a Christian holiday commemorating the descent of the Holy Spirit, fifty days after Easter. **2 a** the Jewish harvest festival, on the fiftieth day after the second day of Passover (Lev. 23: 15–16). **b** a synagogue ceremony on the anniversary of the giving of the Law on Mount Sinai.

Pen·te·cos·tal /péntikóst'l, -káwst'l/ *adj.* (also **pentecostal**) **1** of or relating to Pentecost. **2** of or designating Christian sects and individuals who emphasize the gifts of the Holy Spirit, are often fundamentalist in outlook, and express religious feelings by clapping, shouting, dancing, etc. ● *n.* a Pentecostalist. □□ **Pen·te·cos·tal·ism** *n.* **Pen·te·cos·tal·ist** *adj. & n.*

pent·house /pént-hows/ *n.* **1** a house or apartment on the roof or the top floor of a tall building. **2** a sloping roof, esp. of an outhouse built on to another building. **3** an awning; a canopy.

pen·to·bar·bi·tal /péntəbáarbitawl, -tal/ *n.* (also **pen·to·bar·bi·tone** /-tōn/) a narcotic and sedative barbiturate drug formerly used to relieve insomnia.

pen·tose /péntōs, -tōz/ *n. Biochem.* any monosaccharide containing five carbon atoms, including ribose.

Pen·to·thal /péntəthawl/ *n. Trademark* an intravenous anesthetic, thiopental sodium.

pent·ste·mon var. of PENSTEMON.

pen·tyl /péntil/ *n.* = AMYL.

pe·nult /pínúlt, peénult/ *n. & adj.* ● *n.* the next to the last (esp. syllable). ● *adj.* next to the last.

pe·nul·ti·mate /pínúltimət/ *adj. & n.* ● *adj.* next to the last. ● *n.* **1** the next to the last. **2** the next to the last syllable.

pe·num·bra /pinúmbrə/ *n.* (*pl.* **penumbrae** /-bree/ or **penumbras**) **1 a** the partly shaded region around the shadow of an opaque body, esp. that around the total shadow of the Moon or Earth in an eclipse. ▷ ECLIPSE. **b** the less dark outer part of a sunspot. **2** a partial shadow. □□ **pe·num·bral** *adj.*

pe·nu·ri·ous /pinōōreeəs, pinyŏŏr-/ *adj.* **1** poor; destitute. **2** stingy; grudging. **3** scanty. □□ **pe·nu·ri·ous·ly** *adv.* **pe·nu·ri·ous·ness** *n.*

pen·u·ry /pényəree/ *n.* (*pl.* **-ies**) **1** destitution; poverty. **2** a lack; scarcity.

pe·on /péeon, péeən/ *n.* **1** a Spanish American day laborer or farmworker. **2** an unskilled worker; drudge. **3** *hist.* a worker held in servitude in the southwestern US. □□ **pe·on·age** *n.*

pe·o·ny /péeənee/ *n.* (*pl.* **-ies**) ▶ any herbaceous plant of the genus *Paeonia*, with large globular red, pink, or white flowers, often double in cultivated varieties.

PEONY
(*Paeonia mascula*)

peo·ple /péepəl/ *n. & v.* ● *n.* **1** (usu. as *pl.*) **a** persons composing a community, tribe, race, nation, etc. (*the American people; a warlike people*). **b** a group of persons of a usu. specified kind (*the chosen people; these people here; right-thinking people*). **2** (prec. by *the*; treated as *pl.*) **a** the mass of people in a country, etc., not having special rank or position. **b** these considered as an electorate (*the people will reject it*). **3** parents or other relatives. **4 a** subjects, armed followers, a retinue, etc. **b** a congregation of a parish priest, etc. **5** persons in general (*people do not like rudeness*). ● *v.tr.* (usu. foll. by *with*) **1** fill with people, animals, etc.; populate. **2** (esp. as **peopled** *adj.*) inhabit; occupy; fill (*thickly peopled*).

pep /pep/ *n. & v. colloq.* ● *n.* vigor; go; spirit. ● *v.tr.* (**pepped**, **pepping**) (usu. foll. by *up*) fill with vigor.

pe·per·o·ni var. of PEPPERONI.

pep·per /pépər/ *n. & v.* ● *n.* **1 a** ◀ a hot aromatic condiment from the dried berries of certain plants used whole or ground. ▷ SPICE. **b** ◀ any climbing vine of the genus *Piper*, esp. *P. nigrum*, yielding these berries. **2** anything hot or pungent. **3 a** any plant of the genus *Capsicum*, esp. *C. annuum*. **b** the fruit of this used esp. as a vegetable or salad ingredient. **4** = CAYENNE. ● *v.tr.* **1** sprinkle or treat with or as if with pepper. **2 a** pelt with missiles. **b** hurl abuse, etc., at. **3** punish severely.

unripe fruit

black peppercorns

ground black pepper

PEPPER
(*Piper nigrum*)

P

pep·per·corn /pépərkawrn/ *n.* **1** the dried berry of *Piper nigrum* as a condiment. ▷ PEPPER. **2** *Brit.* (in full **peppercorn rent**) a nominal rent.

pep·per mill *n.* a device for grinding pepper by hand.

pep·per·mint /pépərmint/ *n.* **1 a** a mint plant, *Mentha piperita*, grown for the strong-flavored oil obtained from its leaves. **b** the oil from this. **2** a candy flavored with peppermint. □□ **pep·per·mint·y** *adj.*

pep·per·o·ni /pépərōnee/ *n.* (also **pep·er·o·ni**) beef and pork sausage seasoned with pepper.

pep·per spray *n.* an aerosol spray containing irritant oils derived from cayenne pepper, used as a disabling weapon.

pep·per·wort /pépərwərt, -wawrt/ *n.* any cruciferous plant of the genus *Lepidium*, esp. garden cress.

pep·per·y /pépəree/ *adj.* **1** of, like, or containing much pepper. **2** hot-tempered. **3** pungent; stinging. □□ **pep·per·i·ness** *n.*

pep pill *n.* a pill containing a stimulant drug.

pep·py /pépee/ *adj.* (**peppier**, **peppiest**) *colloq.* lively. □□ **pep·pi·ly** *adv.* **pep·pi·ness** *n.*

pep·sin /pépsin/ *n.* an enzyme contained in the gastric juice that hydrolyzes proteins.

pep talk *n.* a usu. short talk intended to enthuse, encourage, etc.

pep·tic /péptik/ *adj.* relating to digestion.

pep·tic ul·cer *n.* an ulcer in the stomach or duodenum.

pep·tide /péptīd/ *n. Biochem.* any of a group of organic compounds consisting of two or more amino acids bonded in sequence.

pep·tone /péptōn/ *n.* a protein fragment formed by hydrolysis in the process of digestion. □□ **pep·to·nize** /-tənīz/ *v.tr.*

Pe·quot /péekwot/ *n.* **1 a** a N. American people native to eastern Connecticut. **b** a member of this people. **2** the language of this people.

per /pər/ *prep. & adv.* ● *prep.* **1** for each; for every (*two cupcakes per child*; *five miles per hour*). **2** by means of; by; through (*per rail*). **3** (in full **as per**) in accordance with (*as per instructions*). ● *adv. colloq.* each; apiece. □ **as per usual** *colloq.* as usual.

per- /pər/ *prefix* **1** forming verbs, nouns, and adjectives meaning: **a** through; all over (*perforate*; *perforation*; *pervade*). **b** completely; very (*perfervid*; *perturb*). **c** to destruction; to the bad (*pervert*; *perdition*). **2** *Chem.* having the maximum of some element in combination, esp.: **a** in the names of binary compounds in *-ide* (*peroxide*). **b** in the names of oxides, acids, etc., in *-ic* (*perchloric*; *permanganic*). **c** in the names of salts of these acids (*perchlorate*; *permanganate*).

per·ad·ven·ture /pərədvénchər, pér-/ *adv. & n. archaic* or *joc.* ● *adv.* perhaps. ● *n.* uncertainty; doubt (*esp. beyond* or *without peradventure*).

per·am·bu·late /pərámbyəlayt/ *v.* **1** *tr.* walk through, over, or about (streets, the country, etc.). **2** *intr.* walk from place to place. **3** *tr.* **a** travel through and inspect (territory). **b** formally establish the boundaries of (a parish, etc.) by walking round them. □□ **per·am·bu·la·tion** /-láyshən/ *n.* **per·am·bu·la·to·ry** /-lətáwree/ *adj.*

per·am·bu·la·tor /pərámbyəláytər/ *n. Brit. formal* = PRAM.

per an·num /pər ánəm/ *adv.* for each year.

per·cale /pərkáyl/ *n.* a closely woven cotton fabric like calico.

per cap·i·ta /pər kápitə/ *adv. & adj.* (also **per ca·put** /kápŏŏt/) for each person.

per·ceive /pərséev/ *v.tr.* **1** apprehend, esp. through the sight; observe. **2** (usu. foll. by *that*, *how*, etc., + clause) apprehend with the mind; understand. **3** regard mentally in a specified manner (*perceives the universe as infinite*). □□ **per·ceiv·a·ble** *adj.* **per·ceiv·er** *n.*

per·cent /pərsént/ *adv. & n.* (also **per cent**) ● *adv.* in every hundred. ● *n.* **1** percentage. **2** one part in every hundred (*half a percent*). **3** (in *pl.*) *Brit.* public securities yielding interest of so much percent (*three percents*).

per·cent·age /pərséntij/ *n.* **1** a rate or proportion percent. **2** a proportion. **3** *colloq.* personal benefit or advantage.

per·cen·tile /pərséntīl/ *n. Statistics* one of 99 values of a variable dividing a population into 100 equal groups as regards the value of that variable.

per·cept /pérsept/ *n. Philos.* **1** an object of perception. **2** a mental concept resulting from perceiving, esp. by sight.

per·cep·ti·ble /pərséptibəl/ *adj.* capable of being perceived by the senses or intellect. □□ **per·cep·ti·bil·i·ty** /-bílitee/ *n.* **per·cep·ti·bly** *adv.*

per·cep·tion /pərsépshən/ *n.* **1 a** the faculty of perceiving. **b** an instance of this. **2** (often foll. by *of*) **a** the intuitive recognition of a truth, aesthetic quality, etc. **b** an instance of this (*a sudden perception of the true position*). **3** *Philos.* the ability of the mind to refer sensory information to an external object as its cause. □□ **per·cep·tion·al** *adj.* **per·cep·tu·al** /-chŏŏəl/ *adj.* **per·cep·tu·al·ly** *adv.*

per·cep·tive /pərséptiv/ *adj.* **1** capable of perceiving. **2** sensitive; discerning; observant (*a perceptive remark*). □□ **per·cep·tive·ly** *adv.* **per·cep·tive·ness** *n.* **per·cep·tiv·i·ty** /-séptivitee/ *n.*

perch¹ /pərch/ *n. & v.* ● *n.* **1** a usu. horizontal bar, branch, etc., used by a bird to rest on. **2** a usu. high or precarious place for a person or thing to rest on. **3** *esp. Brit.* a measure of length, esp. for land, of 5¹⁄₂ yards. Also called **rod**, **pole**. ● *v.intr. & tr.* (usu. foll. by *on*) settle or rest, or cause to settle or rest on or as if on a perch, etc. (*the bird perched on a branch*; *a town perched on a hill*).

perch² /pərch/ *n.* (*pl.* same or **perches**) **1** ▼ any spiny-finned freshwater edible fish of the genus *Perca*, esp. *P. flavescens* of N. America or *P. fluviatilis* of Europe. ▷ FISH. **2** any fish of several similar or related species.

PERCH (*Perca fluviatilis*)

per·chance /pərcháns/ *adv.* **1** by chance. **2** possibly; maybe.

perch·er /pórchər/ *n.* any bird with feet adapted for perching; a passerine.

per·cip·i·ent /pərsípeeənt/ *adj. & n.* ● *adj.* **1** able to perceive; conscious. **2** discerning; observant. ● *n.* a person who perceives, esp. something outside the range of the senses. □□ **per·cip·i·ence** *n.* **per·cip·i·ent·ly** *adv.*

per·co·late /pérkəlayt/ *v.* **1** *intr.* (often foll. by *through*) **a** (of liquid, etc.) filter or ooze gradually (esp. through a porous surface). **b** (of an idea, etc.) permeate gradually. **2** *tr.* prepare (coffee) by repeatedly passing boiling water through ground beans. **3** *tr.* ooze through; permeate. **4** *tr.* strain (a liquid, powder, etc.) through a fine mesh, etc. **5** *intr. colloq.* become livelier, more active, etc.) by walking round □□ **per·co·la·tion** /-láyshən/ *n.*

per·co·la·tor /pérkəlaytər/ *n.* a machine for making coffee by circulating boiling water through ground beans.

per·cuss /pərkús/ *v.tr. Med.* tap (a part of the body) gently with a finger or an instrument as part of a diagnosis.

per·cus·sion /pərkúshən/ *n.* **1** *Mus.* **a** (often *attrib.*) ► the playing of music by striking instruments with sticks, etc. (*a percussion band*). **b** the section of such instruments in an orchestra or band (*asked the percussion to stay behind*). ▷ ORCHESTRA. **2** *Med.* the act or an instance of percussing. **3** the forcible striking of one esp. solid body against another. □□ **per·cus·sion·ist** *n.* **per·cus·sive** *adj.* **per·cus·sive·ly** *adv.* **per·cus·sive·ness** *n.*

per·cus·sion cap *n.* a small amount of explosive powder contained in metal or paper and exploded by striking, used esp. in toy guns and formerly in some firearms.

per di·em /pər dée-em, díem/ *adv., adj., & n.* ● *adv. & adj.* for each day. ● *n.* an allowance or payment for each day.

per·di·tion /pərdíshən/ *n.* eternal death; damnation.

per·dur·a·ble /pərdŏŏrəbəl, -dyŏŏr-/ *adj. formal* permanent; eternal; durable. □□ **per·dur·a·bil·i·ty** /-bílitee/ *n.* **per·dur·a·bly** *adv.*

père /pair/ *n.* (added to a surname to distinguish a father from a son) the father; senior.

per·e·gri·nate /périgrinayt/ *v.intr.* travel; journey, esp. extensively or at leisure. □□ **per·e·gri·na·tion** /-náyshən/ *n.* **per·e·gri·na·tor** *n.*

per·e·grine /périgrin, -green/ *n.* (in full **peregrine falcon**) ► a widely distributed falcon, *Falco peregrinus*, much used for falconry.

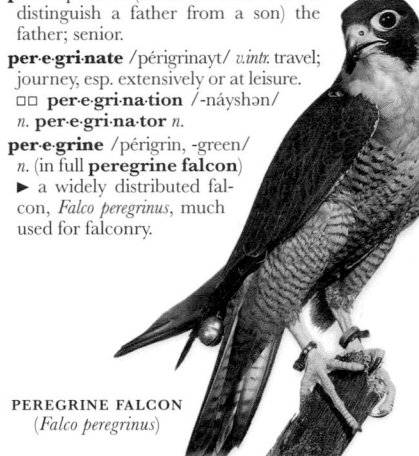

PEREGRINE FALCON
(*Falco peregrinus*)

per·emp·to·ry /pərémptəree/ *adj.* **1** (of a statement or command) admitting no denial or refusal. **2** (of a person, a person's manner, etc.) dogmatic; imperious; dictatorial. **3** *Law* not open to appeal or challenge; final. □□ **per·emp·to·ri·ly** *adv.* **per·emp·to·ri·ness** *n.*

per·en·ni·al /pəréneeəl/ *adj. & n.* ● *adj.* **1** lasting through a year or several years. **2** (of a plant) lasting several years. **3** lasting a long time or forever. **4** (of a stream) flowing through all seasons of the year. ● *n.* a perennial plant (*a herbaceous perennial*). □□ **per·en·ni·al·i·ty** /-neeálitee/ *n.* **per·en·ni·al·ly** *adv.*

pe·re·stroi·ka /pérestróykə/ *n. hist.* (in the former Soviet Union) the policy or practice of restructuring or reforming the economic and political system.

per·fect *adj., v., & n.* ● *adj.* /pérfikt/ **1** complete; not deficient. **2 a** faultless (*a perfect diamond*). **b** blameless in morals or behavior. **3 a** very satisfactory (*a perfect evening*). **b** (often foll. by *for*) most appropriate; suitable. **4** exact; precise (*a perfect circle*). **5** entire; unqualified (*a perfect stranger*). **6** *Math.* (of a number) equal to the sum of its divisors. **7** *Gram.* (of a tense) denoting a completed action or event in the past, formed in English with *have* or *has* and the past participle, as in *they have eaten*. **8** *Mus.* (of pitch) absolute. **9** (often foll. by *in*) thoroughly trained or skilled (*is perfect in geometry*). ● *v.tr.* /pərfékt/ **1** make perfect; improve. **2** carry through; complete. **3** complete (a sheet) by printing the other side. ● *n.* /pórfikt/ *Gram.* the perfect tense. □□ **per·fect·er** *n.* **per·fect·i·ble** *adj.* **per·fect·i·bil·i·ty** *n.* **per·fect·ness** *n.*

per·fec·ta /pərféktə/ *n.* a form of betting in which the first two places in a race must be predicted in the correct order.

per·fec·tion /pərfékshən/ *n.* **1** the act or process of making perfect. **2** the state of being perfect; faultlessness; excellence. **3** a perfect person, thing, or

PERCUSSION

Percussion instruments, played by being struck, shaken, scraped, or clashed together, are the oldest of the instrumental groups. Most percussion instruments, such as a snare drum, do not have a definite pitch and are used for rhythm and impact, and the distinctive timbre of their sound. Other percussion instruments, like tubular bells and timpani, are tuned to definite pitches and can play melody, harmony, and rhythms.

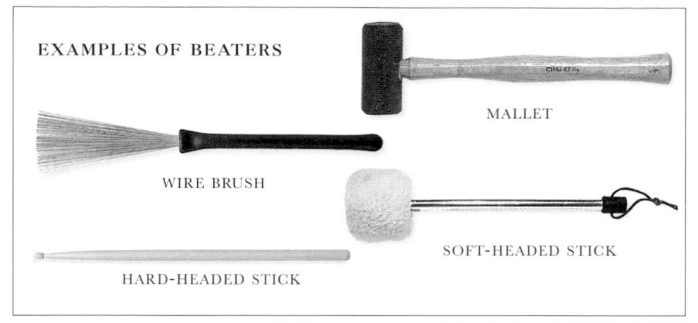

EXAMPLES OF BEATERS

MALLET

WIRE BRUSH

SOFT-HEADED STICK

HARD-HEADED STICK

UNTUNED INSTRUMENTS

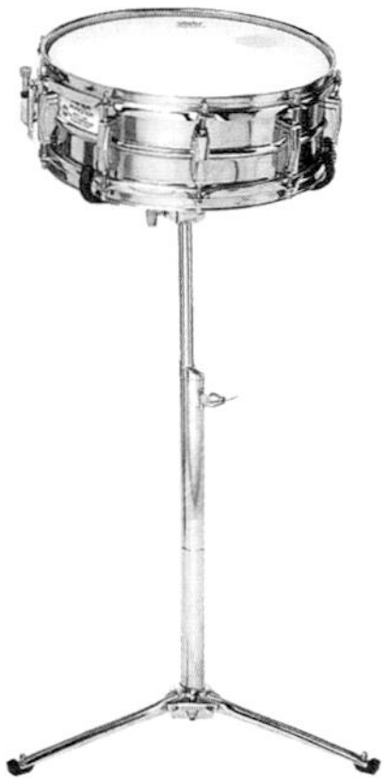

SNARE DRUM

CONGAS

BASS DRUM

TABLA

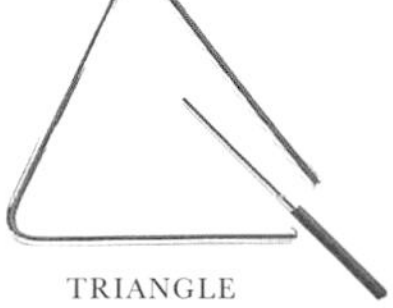

CLAVES

TRIANGLE

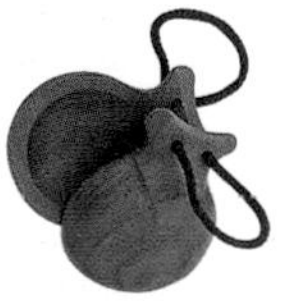

CASTANETS

TAMBOURINE

MARACAS

CYMBALS

TUNED INSTRUMENTS

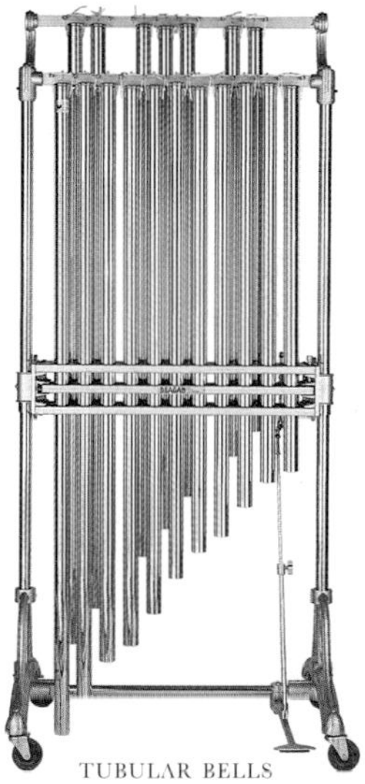

TUBULAR BELLS

KETTLEDRUM

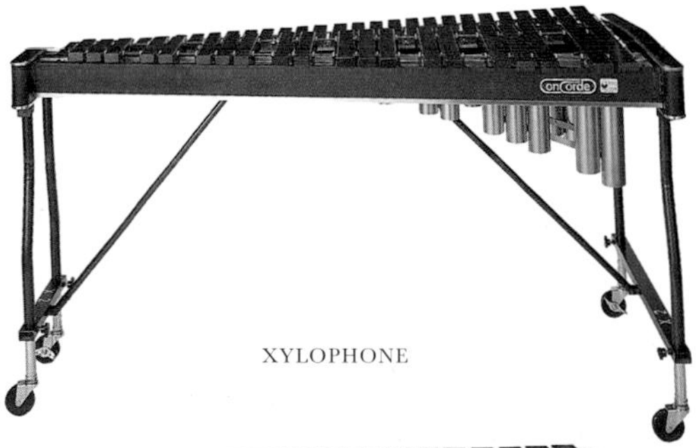

XYLOPHONE

VIBRAPHONE

P

example. **4** an accomplishment. **5** full development; completion.

per·fec·tion·ism /pərfékshənizəm/ *n.* **1** the uncompromising pursuit of excellence. **2** *Philos.* the belief that religious or moral perfection is attainable. □□ **per·fec·tion·ist** *n. & adj.*

per·fec·tive /pərféktiv/ *adj. & n. Gram.* ● *adj.* (of an aspect of a verb, etc.) expressing the completion of an action (opp. IMPERFECTIVE). ● *n.* the perfective aspect or form of a verb.

per·fect·ly /pérfiktlee/ *adv.* **1** completely; absolutely (*I understand you perfectly*). **2** quite; completely (*is perfectly capable of doing it*). **3** in a perfect way. **4** very (*you know perfectly well*).

per·fec·to /pərféktō/ *n.* (*pl.* **-os**) a large thick cigar pointed at each end.

perfect pitch *n.* = ABSOLUTE PITCH 1.

per·fi·dy /pérfidee/ *n.* breach of faith; treachery. □□ **per·fid·i·ous** /-fídeeəs/ *adj.* **per·fid·i·ous·ly** *adv.*

per·fo·rate *v. & adj.* ● *v.* /pérfərayt/ **1** *tr.* make a hole or holes through; pierce. **2** *tr.* make a row of small holes in (paper, etc.) so that a part may be torn off easily. **3** *tr.* make an opening into; pass into or extend through. **4** *intr.* (usu. foll. by *into*, *through*, etc.) penetrate. ● *adj.* /pérfərət/ perforated. □□ **per·fo·ra·tion** /-ráyshən/ *n.* **per·fo·ra·tive** /pórfərətiv/ *adj.* **per·fo·ra·tor** /pórfəraytər/ *n.*

per·force /pərfáwrs/ *adv. archaic* unavoidably; necessarily.

per·form /pərfáwrm/ *v.* **1** *tr.* (also *absol.*) carry into effect; be the agent of; do (a command, promise, task, etc.). **2** *tr.* (also *absol.*) go through; execute (a public function, play, piece of music, etc.). **3** *intr.* act in a play; play an instrument or sing, etc. (*likes performing*). **4** *intr.* operate; function. □□ **per·form·a·ble** *adj.* **per·form·a·bil·i·ty** *n.* **per·form·er** *n.* **per·form·ing** *adj.*

per·form·ance /pərfáwrməns/ *n.* **1** (usu. foll. by *of*) **a** the act or process of performing or carrying out. **b** the execution or fulfillment (of a duty, etc.). **2** a staging or production (of a drama, piece of music, etc.) (*the afternoon performance*). **3** a person's achievement under test conditions, etc. (*put up a good performance*). **4** *colloq.* a fuss; a scene; a public exhibition (*made such a performance about leaving*). **5 a** the capabilities of a machine, esp. a car or aircraft. **b** (*attrib.*) of high capability (*a performance car*).

per·for·ma·tive /pərfáwrmətiv/ *adj. & n.* ● *adj.* **1** of or relating to performance. **2** denoting an utterance that effects an action by being spoken or written (e.g., *I bet*, *I apologize*). ● *n.* a performative utterance.

per·form·ing arts /pərfáwrming/ *n.pl.* the arts, such as drama, music, and dance, that require performance for their realization.

per·fume /pórfyoōm/ *n. & v.* ● *n.* **1** a sweet smell. **2** fluid containing the essence of flowers, etc.; scent. ● *v.tr.* (also /pərfyoōm/) (usu. as **perfumed** *adj.*) impart a sweet scent to; impregnate with a sweet smell. □□ **per·fum·y** *adj.*

per·fum·er /pórfyoōmər/ *n.* a maker or seller of perfumes. □□ **per·fum·er·y** *n.* (*pl.* **-ies**)

per·func·to·ry /pərfúngktəree/ *adj.* **1 a** done merely for the sake of getting through a duty. **b** done in a cursory or careless manner. **2** superficial; mechanical. □□ **per·func·to·ri·ly** *adv.* **per·func·to·ri·ness** *n.*

per·go·la /pórgələ/ *n.* an arbor or covered walk, formed of growing plants trained over a trellis.

per·haps /pərháps/ *adv.* **1** it may be; possibly (*perhaps it is lost*). **2** introducing a polite request (*perhaps you would open the window?*).

peri- /péree/ *prefix* **1** around; about. **2** *Astron.* the point nearest to (*perigee*; *perihelion*).

per·i·anth /péreeánth/ *n.* the outer part of a flower. ▷ CORONA

per·i·car·di·um /périkáardeeəm/ *n.* (*pl.* **pericardia** /-deeə/) the membranous sac enclosing the heart. ▷ HEART. □□ **per·i·car·di·ac** /-deeak/ *adj.* **per·i·car·di·al** *adj.* **per·i·car·di·tis** /-dítis/ *n.*

per·i·carp /péri-kaarp/ *n.* ▶ the part of a fruit formed from the wall of the ripened ovary. ▷ NUT

PERICARP: CROSS SECTION OF A LITCHI SHOWING THE PERICARP

per·i·clase /périklays/ *n.* a pale mineral consisting of magnesia.

per·i·dot /péridot/ *n.* a green variety of olivine, used esp. as a semiprecious stone.

per·i·gee /périjee/ *n.* the point in an orbit where the orbiting body is nearest the center of the body it is orbiting. (opp. APOGEE). □□ **per·i·ge·an** /périjéeən/ *adj.*

per·i·gla·cial /périgláyshəl/ *adj.* of or relating to a region adjoining a glacier.

per·i·he·li·on /périhéelyən/ *n.* (*pl.* **perihelia** /-lyə/) the point of a planet's or comet's orbit nearest to the Sun's center.

per·il /péril/ *n. & v.* ● *n.* serious and immediate danger. ● *v.tr.* (**periled**, **periling** or **perilled**, **perilling**) threaten; endanger. □ **at one's peril** at one's own risk. **in peril of** with great risk to (*in peril of your life*).

per·il·ous /périləs/ *adj.* **1** full of risk; dangerous; hazardous. **2** exposed to imminent risk of destruction, etc. □□ **per·il·ous·ly** *adv.* **per·il·ous·ness** *n.*

per·i·lune /périloōn/ *n.* the point in a body's lunar orbit where it is closest to the Moon's center.

pe·rim·e·ter /pərímitər/ *n.* **1 a** the circumference or outline of a closed figure. **b** the length of this. **2 a** the outer boundary of an enclosed area. **b** a defended boundary. **3** an instrument for measuring a field of vision. □□ **per·i·met·ric** /périmétrik/ *adj.*

per·i·na·tal /pérináyt'l/ *adj.* of or relating to the time immediately before and after birth.

per·i·ne·um /périnéeəm/ *n.* the region of the body between the anus and the scrotum or vulva. □□ **per·i·ne·al** *adj.*

pe·ri·od /péereeəd/ *n. & adj.* ● *n.* **1** a length or portion of time (*periods of rain*). **2** a distinct portion of history, a person's life, etc. (*the Federal period*; *Picasso's Blue Period*). **3** *Geol.* a time forming part of a geological era (*the Quaternary period*). **4 a** an interval between recurrences of an astronomical or other phenomenon. **b** the time taken by a planet to rotate about its axis. **5** the time allowed for a lesson in school. **6** an occurrence of menstruation. **7 a** a complete sentence, esp. one consisting of several clauses. **b** (in *pl.*) rhetorical language. **8 a** a punctuation mark (.) used at the end of a sentence or an abbreviation. **b** used at the end of a sentence, etc., to indicate finality, absoluteness, etc. (*we want the best, period*). **9 a** a set of figures repeated in a recurring decimal. **b** the smallest interval over which a function takes the same value. **10** *Chem.* a sequence of elements between two noble gases forming a row in the periodic table. **11** *Music* a discrete division of a musical composition, containing two or more phrases and ending in a cadence. ● *adj.* belonging to or characteristic of some past period (*period furniture*). □ **of the period** of the era under discussion (*the custom of the period*).

pe·ri·o·date /pəríədayt/ *n. Chem.* a salt or ester of periodic acid.

pe·ri·od·ic /péereeódik/ *adj.* **1** appearing or occurring at regular intervals. **2** of or concerning the period of a celestial body (*periodic motion*). **3** (of diction, etc.) expressed in periods (see PERIOD *n.* 7a). □□ **pe·ri·o·dic·i·ty** /-reeədísitee/ *n.*

pe·ri·od·i·cal /péereeódikəl/ *n. & adj.* ● *n.* a newspaper, magazine, etc., issued at regular intervals, usu. monthly or weekly. ● *adj.* **1** published at regular intervals. **2** periodic; occasional. □□ **pe·ri·od·i·cal·ly** *adv.*

pe·ri·od·ic ta·ble *n.* an arrangement of elements in order of increasing atomic number and in which elements of similar chemical properties appear at regular intervals.

pe·ri·o·don·tics /péreeədóntiks/ *n.pl.* (treated as *sing.*) the branch of dentistry concerned with the structures surrounding and supporting the teeth. □□ **per·i·o·don·tal** *adj.* **per·i·o·don·tist** *n.*

pe·ri·o·don·tol·o·gy /péreeədontóləjee/ *n.* = PERIODONTICS.

per·i·od piece *n.* an object or work whose main interest lies in its historical, etc., associations.

per·i·pa·tet·ic /péripətétik/ *adj.* going from place to place; itinerant. □□ **per·i·pa·tet·i·cal·ly** *adv.* **per·i·pa·tet·i·cism** *n.*

pe·riph·er·al /pərífərəl/ *adj. & n.* ● *adj.* **1** of minor importance; marginal. **2** of the periphery; on the fringe. **3** *Anat.* near the surface of the body, with special reference to the circulation and nervous system. **4** (of equipment) used with a computer, etc.,

---

PERIPHERAL NERVOUS SYSTEM

The peripheral nervous system is a network of nerves that links the central nervous system (brain and spinal cord) and the rest of the body. It has three divisions: autonomic, sensory, and motor. Autonomic nerve fibers, which may join the autonomic nerve ganglia, regulate involuntary actions, such as heartbeat. Sensory nerve fibers receive external stimuli via sense receptors. Motor nerve fibers initiate the relaxation and contraction of the muscles.

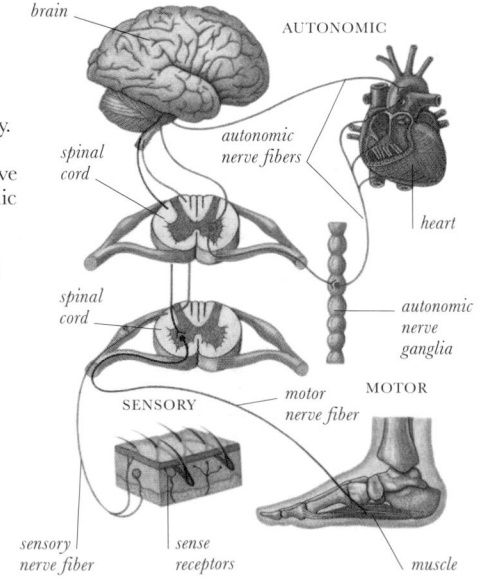

STRUCTURE OF THE
PERIPHERAL NERVOUS SYSTEM
IN THE HUMAN BODY

P

but not an integral part of it. ● *n.* a peripheral device or piece of equipment. □□ **pe·riph·er·al·ly** *adv.*

pe·riph·er·al ner·vous sys·tem *n. Anat.* ▼ the nervous system outside the brain and spinal cord. ▷ AUTONOMIC NERVOUS SYSTEM, NERVOUS SYSTEM

pe·riph·er·al vi·sion *n.* **1** area seen around the outside of one's field of vision. **2** ability to perceive in this area.

pe·riph·er·y /pərífəree/ *n.* (*pl.* **-ies**) **1** the boundary of an area or surface. **2** an outer or surrounding region (*built on the periphery of the old town*).

pe·riph·ra·sis /pərífrəsis/ *n.* (*pl.* **periphrases** /-seez/) **1** a roundabout way of speaking; circumlocution. **2** a roundabout phrase.

per·i·phras·tic /périfrástik/ *adj.* **1** of or involving periphrasis. **2** *Gram.* (of a case, tense, etc.) formed by combination of words rather than by inflection. □□ **per·i·phras·ti·cal·ly** *adv.*

pe·rip·ter·al /pəríptərəl/ *adj.* (of a temple) surrounded by a single row of columns.

per·i·scope /périskōp/ *n.* ▼ an apparatus with a tube and mirrors or prisms, by which an observer in a trench, submerged submarine, or at the rear of a crowd, etc., can see things otherwise out of sight. ▷ SUBMARINE. □□ **per·i·scop·ic** *adj.* **per·i·scop·i·cal·ly** *adv.*

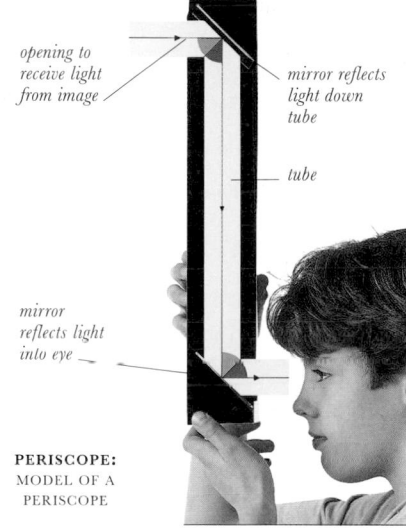

opening to receive light from image

mirror reflects light down tube

tube

mirror reflects light into eye

PERISCOPE:
MODEL OF A
PERISCOPE

per·ish /pérish/ *v.* **1** *intr.* be destroyed; suffer death or ruin (*a great part of his army perished of hunger and disease*). **2** *Brit.* **a** *intr.* (esp. of rubber, a rubber object, etc.) lose its normal qualities; deteriorate; rot. **b** *tr.* cause to rot or deteriorate. **3** *Brit. tr.* (in *passive*) suffer from cold or exposure (*we were perished standing outside*). □ **perish the thought** an exclamation of horror against an unwelcome idea. □□ **per·ish·less** *adj.*

per·ish·a·ble /périshəbəl/ *adj. & n.* ● *adj.* liable to perish; subject to decay. ● *n.* a thing, esp. a foodstuff, subject to speedy decay. □□ **per·ish·a·bil·i·ty** /-bílitee/ *n.* **per·ish·a·ble·ness** *n.*

per·i·sperm /périspərm/ *n.* a mass of nutritive material outside the embryo in some seeds.

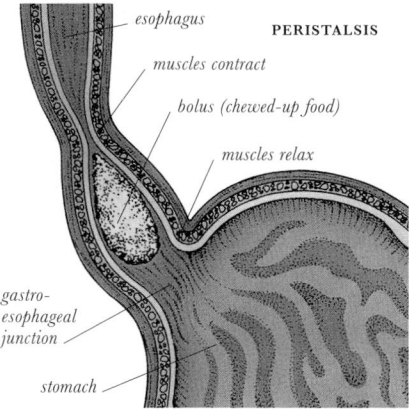

esophagus

PERISTALSIS

muscles contract

bolus (chewed-up food)

muscles relax

gastro-esophageal junction

stomach

per·i·stal·sis /péristáwlsis, -stál-/ *n.* ▲ an involuntary muscular wavelike movement by which the contents of the alimentary canal, etc., are propelled along. □□ **per·i·stal·tic** *adj.* **per·i·stal·ti·cal·ly** *adv.*

per·i·style /péristīl/ *n.* a row of columns surrounding a temple, court, cloister, etc.; a space surrounded by columns.

per·i·to·ne·um /périt'néeəm/ *n.* (*pl.* **peritoneums** or **peritonea** /-néeə/) the serous membrane lining the cavity of the abdomen. □□ **per·i·to·ne·al** *adj.*

per·i·to·ni·tis /périt'nítis/ *n.* an inflammatory disease of the peritoneum.

per·i·wig /périwig/ *n. esp. hist.* ► a wig. □□ **per·i·wigged** *adj.*

PERIWIG:
TWO-HORNED
PERIWIG

per·i·win·kle[1] /périwingkəl/ *n.* **1** ► any plant of the genus *Vinca*, esp. an evergreen trailing plant with blue or white flowers. **2** a tropical shrub, *Catharanthus roseus*, native to Madagascar.

per·i·win·kle[2] /périwingkəl/ *n.* any edible marine gastropod mollusk of the genus *Littorina*; a winkle.

per·jure /pórjər/ *v.refl. Law* **1** willfully tell an untruth when under oath. **2** (as **perjured** *adj.*) guilty of or involving perjury. □□ **per·jur·er** *n.*

PERIWINKLE
(*Vinca difformis*)

per·ju·ry /pórjəree/ *n.* (*pl.* **-ies**) *Law* **1** a breach of an oath, esp. the act of willfully telling an untruth when under oath. **2** the practice of this. □□ **per·ju·ri·ous** /-jŏoreeəs/ *adj.*

perk[1] /pərk/ *v. & adj.* ● *v.tr.* raise (one's head, etc.) briskly. ● *adj.* perky; pert. □ **perk up 1** recover confidence, courage, life, or zest. **2** restore confidence or courage or liveliness in (esp. another person). **3** freshen up.

perk[2] /pərk/ *n. colloq.* a perquisite.

perk[3] /pərk/ *v. colloq.* **1** *intr.* (of coffee) percolate; make a bubbling sound in the percolator. **2** *tr.* percolate (coffee).

perk·y /pórkee/ *adj.* (**perkier, perkiest**) **1** self-assertive; cocky; pert. **2** lively; cheerful. □□ **perk·i·ly** *adv.* **perk·i·ness** *n.*

per·lite /pórlīt/ *n.* (also **pearl·ite**) a glassy type of vermiculite, expandable to a solid form by heating, used for insulation, etc.

perm /pərm/ *n. & v.* ● *n.* a permanent wave. ● *v.tr.* give a permanent wave to (a person or a person's hair).

per·ma·frost /pórməfrawst, -frost/ *n.* subsoil that remains frozen throughout the year, as in polar regions. ▷ TUNDRA

per·ma·nent /pórmənənt/ *adj. & n.* ● *adj.* lasting, or intended to last or function, indefinitely (opp. TEMPORARY). ● *n.* = PERMANENT WAVE. □□ **per·ma·nence** *n.* **per·ma·nen·cy** *n.* **per·ma·nent·ize** *v.tr.* **per·ma·nent·ly** *adv.*

per·ma·nent press *n.* a process applied to a fabric to make it wrinkle-free.

per·ma·nent wave *n.* an artificial wave in the hair, intended to last for some time.

per·man·ga·nate /pərmánggənayt/ *n. Chem.* any salt of permanganic acid, esp. potassium permanganate.

per·man·gan·ic acid /pórmanggánik/ *n. Chem.* an acid containing heptavalent manganese.

per·me·a·bil·i·ty /pórmeeəbílitee/ *n.* **1** the state or quality of being permeable. **2** a quantity measuring the influence of a substance on the magnetic flux in the region it occupies.

per·me·a·ble /pórmeeəbəl/ *adj.* capable of being permeated.

per·me·ate /pórmeeayt/ *v.* **1** *tr.* penetrate throughout; pervade; saturate. **2** *intr.* (usu. foll. by *through, among,* etc.) diffuse itself. □□ **per·me·ance** *n.* **per·me·ant** *adj.* **per·me·a·tion** /-áyshən/ *n.* **per·me·a·tor** *n.*

Per·mi·an /pórmeeən/ *adj. & n. Geol.* ● *adj.* of or relating to the last period of the Paleozoic era with evidence of the development of reptiles and amphibians, and deposits of sandstone. ● *n.* this period or system.

per·mis·si·ble /pərmísibəl/ *adj.* allowable. □□ **per·mis·si·bil·i·ty** *n.* **per·mis·si·bly** *adv.*

per·mis·sion /pərmíshən/ *n.* (often foll. by *to* + infin.) consent; authorization.

per·mis·sive /pərmísiv/ *adj.* **1** tolerant; liberal, esp. in sexual matters (*the permissive society*). **2** giving permission. □□ **per·mis·sive·ly** *adv.* **per·mis·sive·ness** *n.*

per·mit *v. & n.* ● *v.* /pərmít/ (**permitted, permitting**) **1** *tr.* give permission or consent to; authorize (*permit me to say*). **2** **a** *tr.* allow as possible; give an opportunity to (*permit the traffic to flow again*). **b** *intr.* give an opportunity (*circumstances permitting*). **3** *intr.* (foll. by *of*) admit; allow for. ● *n.* /pórmit/ **1 a** a document giving permission to act in a specified way (*was granted a work permit*). **b** a document, etc., that allows entry into a specified zone. **2** permission. □□ **per·mit·tee** /pórmitee/ *n.* **per·mit·ter** *n.*

per·mu·tate /pórmyōotayt/ *v.tr.* change the order or arrangement of.

per·mu·ta·tion /pórmyōotáyshən/ *n.* **1** an ordered arrangement or grouping of a set of numbers, items, etc. **2** any combination or selection of a specified number of things from a larger group. □□ **per·mu·ta·tion·al** *adj.*

per·mute /pərmyōot/ *v.tr.* alter the sequence or arrangement of.

per·ni·cious /pərníshəs/ *adj.* destructive; ruinous; fatal. □□ **per·ni·cious·ly** *adv.* **per·ni·cious·ness** *n.*

per·ni·cious a·ne·mi·a *n.* a defective formation of red blood cells through a lack of vitamin B_{12} or folic acid.

per·o·rate /pérərayt/ *v.intr.* **1** sum up and conclude a speech. **2** speak at length.

per·o·ra·tion /pérəráyshən/ *n.* **1** the concluding part of a speech, forcefully summing up what has been said. **2** a long or overly rhetorical speech.

per·is·so·dac·tyl /pərísōdáktəl/ *adj. & n. Zool.* ● *adj.* ◄ of or relating to the order Perissodactyla of ungulate mammals with one main central toe, or a single toe, on each foot, including horses, rhinoceroses, and tapirs. ● *n.* an animal of this order. ▷ UNGULATE

single toe

PERISSODACTYL:
HORSE'S HOOF

P

per·ox·ide /pəróksīd/ *n. & v.* ● *n. Chem.* **1 a** = HYDROGEN PEROXIDE. **b** (often *attrib.*) a solution of hydrogen peroxide used to bleach the hair or as an antiseptic. **2** a compound of oxygen with another element containing the greatest possible proportion of oxygen. **3** any salt or ester of hydrogen peroxide. ● *v.tr.* bleach (the hair) with peroxide.

per·pend var. of PARPEN.

per·pen·dic·u·lar /pərpəndíkyələr/ *adj. & n.* ● *adj.* **1 a** at right angles to the plane of the horizon. **b** (usu. foll. by *to*) *Geom.* at right angles (to a given line, plane, or surface). **2** upright; vertical. **3** (of a slope, etc.) very steep. **4** (**Perpendicular**) *Archit.* ◀ of the third stage of English Gothic (15th–16th c.) with vertical tracery in large windows. **5** in a standing position. ● *n.* **1** a perpendicular line. **2** a plumb rule or a similar instrument. **3** (prec. by *the*) a perpendicular line or direction (*is out of the perpendicular*). □□ **per·pen·dic·u·lar·i·ty** /-dikyōōláritee/ *n.* **per·pen·dic·u·lar·ly** *adv.*

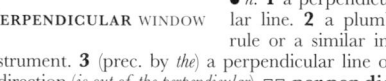
tracery

PERPENDICULAR WINDOW

per·pe·trate /pórpitrayt/ *v.tr.* commit or perform (a crime, blunder, or anything outrageous). □□ **per·pe·tra·tion** /-tráyshən/ *n.* **per·pe·tra·tor** *n.*

per·pet·u·al /pərpéchōōəl/ *adj.* **1** eternal; lasting forever or indefinitely. **2** continuous; uninterrupted. **3** *colloq.* frequent; much repeated (*perpetual interruptions*). **4** (of an office, etc.) held for life (*perpetual secretary*). □□ **per·pet·u·al·ism** *n.* **per·pet·u·al·ly** *adv.*

per·pet·u·al cal·en·dar *n.* a calendar that can be adjusted to show any combination of day, month, and year.

per·pet·u·al mo·tion *n.* the motion of a hypothetical machine which once set in motion would run forever unless subject to an external force or to wear.

per·pet·u·ate /pərpéchōō-ayt/ *v.tr.* **1** make perpetual. **2** preserve from oblivion. □□ **per·pet·u·ance** *n.* **per·pet·u·a·tion** /-áyshən/ *n.* **per·pet·u·a·tor** *n.*

per·pe·tu·i·ty /pórpitōō-itee, -tyōō-/ *n.* (*pl.* **-ies**) **1** the state or quality of being perpetual. **2** a perpetual annuity. **3** a perpetual possession or position. □ **in** (or **to** or **for**) **perpetuity** forever.

per·plex /pərpléks/ *v.tr.* **1** puzzle, bewilder, or disconcert (a person, a person's mind, etc.). **2** complicate or confuse (a matter). □□ **per·plex·ed·ly** /-pléksidlee/ *adv.* **per·plex·ing** *adj.* **per·plex·ing·ly** *adv.*

per·plex·i·ty /pərpléksitee/ *n.* (*pl.* **-ies**) **1** bewilderment; the state of being perplexed. **2** a thing which perplexes. **3** the state of being complicated.

per·qui·site /pórkwizit/ *n.* **1** an extra profit or allowance additional to a main income, etc. **2** a customary extra right or privilege. **3** an incidental benefit attached to employment, etc.

per·ry /péree/ *n.* (*pl.* **-ies**) a drink like cider, made from the fermented juice of pears.

per se /pər sáy/ *adv.* by or in itself; intrinsically.

per·se·cute /pórsikyōōt/ *v.tr.* **1** subject (a person, etc.) to hostility or ill-treatment, esp. on the grounds of political or religious belief. **2** harass; worry. **3** (often foll. by *with*) bombard (a person) with questions, etc. □□ **per·se·cu·tor** *n.* **per·se·cu·to·ry** *adj.*

per·se·cu·tion /pórsikyōóshən/ *n.* the act or an instance of persecuting; the state of being persecuted.

per·se·cu·tion com·plex *n.* (also **per·se·cu·tion ma·ni·a**) an irrational obsessive fear that others are scheming against one.

per·se·ver·ance /pórsiveérəns/ *n.* **1** the steadfast pursuit of an objective. **2** (often foll. by *in*) constant persistence (in a belief, etc.).

per·sev·er·ate /pərsévərayt/ *v.intr.* continue action, etc., for an unusually or excessively long time. □□ **per·sev·er·a·tion** /-ráyshən/ *n.*

per·se·vere /pórsiveér/ *v.intr.* (often foll. by *in, at, with*) continue steadfastly or determinedly; persist.

Per·sian /pérzhən, -shən/ *n. & adj.* ● *n.* **1 a** a native or inhabitant of ancient or modern Persia (now Iran). **b** a person of Persian descent. **2** the language of ancient Persia or modern Iran. ¶ With modern reference the preferred terms are *Iranian* and *Farsi.* **3** (in full **Persian cat**) **a** a cat of a breed with long silky hair and a thick tail. ▷ CAT. **b** this breed. ● *adj.* of or relating to Persia or its people or language.

Per·sian lamb *n.* the silky tightly curled fur of a young karakul, used in clothing.

per·si·flage /pórsiflaazh/ *n.* light raillery; banter.

per·sim·mon /pərsímən/ *n.* **1** any usu. tropical evergreen tree of the genus *Diospyros*, bearing edible tomatolike fruits. **2** ▶ the fruit of this.

per·sist /pərsíst/ *v.intr.* **1** (often foll. by *in*) continue firmly or obstinately (in an opinion or a course of action), esp. despite obstacles, remonstrance, etc. **2** (of an institution, custom, phenomenon, etc.) continue in existence; survive.

per·sis·tent /pərsístənt/ *adj.* **1** continuing obstinately; persisting. **2** enduring. **3** constantly repeated (*persistent nagging*). □□ **per·sis·tence** *n.* **per·sis·ten·cy** *n.* **per·sist·ent·ly** *adv.*

PERSIMMON
(*Diospyros virginiana*)

per·snick·et·y /pərsníkitee/ *adj. colloq.* **1** fastidious. **2** precise or overprecise. **3** requiring tact or careful handling.

per·son /pórsən/ *n.* **1** an individual human being (*a cheerful and forthright person*). **2** the living body of a human being (*hidden about your person*). **3** *Gram.* any of three classes of personal pronouns, verb forms, etc.: the person speaking (**first person**); the person spoken to (**second person**); the person spoken of (**third person**). **4** (in *comb.*) used to replace *-man* in words referring to either sex (*salesperson*). **5** (in Christianity) God as Father, Son, or Holy Ghost (*three persons in one God*). □ **in person** physically present.

per·so·na /pórsónə/ *n.* (*pl.* **personae** /-nee/) **1** an aspect of the personality as shown to or perceived by others (opp. ANIMA). **2** *Literary criticism* an author's assumed character in his or her writing.

per·son·a·ble /pórsənəbəl/ *adj.* pleasing in appearance and behavior. □□ **per·son·a·ble·ness** *n.* **per·son·a·bly** *adv.*

per·son·age /pórsənij/ *n.* **1** a person, esp. of rank or importance. **2** a character in a play, etc.

per·son·al /pórsənəl/ *adj.* **1** one's own; individual; private. **2** done or made in person (*made a personal appearance; my personal attention*). **3** directed to or concerning an individual (*a personal letter*). **4 a** referring (esp. in a hostile way) to an individual's private life or concerns (*making personal remarks; no need to be personal*). **b** close; intimate (*a personal friend*). **5** of the body and clothing (*personal hygiene; personal appearance*). **6** existing as a person, not as an abstraction or thing (*a personal God*). **7** *Gram.* of or denoting one of the three persons (*personal pronoun*).

per·son·al col·umn *n.* (also **per·son·als**) the part of a newspaper devoted to private advertisements or messages.

per·son·al com·pu·ter *n.* a computer designed for use by a single individual. ▷ COMPUTER

per·son·al i·den·ti·fi·ca·tion num·ber *n.* a number allocated to an individual, serving as a password esp. for an ATM, computer, etc. ¶ Abbr.: **PIN**.

per·son·al·i·ty /pórsənálitee/ *n.* (*pl.* **-ies**) **1** the distinctive character or qualities of a person, often as distinct from others (*an attractive personality*). **2** a famous person; a celebrity (*a TV personality*). **3** a person who stands out from others by virtue of his or her character (*is a real personality*).

per·son·al·ize /pórsənalīz/ *v.tr.* **1** make personal, esp. by marking with one's name, etc. **2** personify. □□ **per·son·al·i·za·tion** *n.*

per·son·al·ly /pórsənalee/ *adv.* **1** in person (*see to it personally*). **2** for one's own part (*speaking personally*). **3** in the form of a person (*a god existing personally*). **4** in a personal manner (*took the criticism personally*). **5** as a person; on a personal level.

per·son·al or·gan·iz·er *n.* **1** a loose-leaf notebook with sections for various kinds of information, including a diary, etc. **2** a handheld microcomputer serving the same purpose.

per·son·al pro·noun *n.* a pronoun replacing the subject, object, etc., of a clause, etc., e.g., *I, we, you, them, us.*

per·son·al prop·er·ty *n.* (also **personal estate**) *Law* all one's property except land and those interests in land that pass to one's heirs (cf. REAL[1] *adj.* 3).

per·son·al touch *n.* a characteristic or individual approach to a situation.

per·so·na non gra·ta /non gráatə, grátə/ *n.* a person not acceptable.

per·son·ate /pórsənayt/ *v.tr.* **1** play the part of (a character in a drama, etc.; another type of person). **2** pretend to be (another person), esp. for fraudulent purposes; impersonate. □□ **per·son·a·tion** /-náyshən/ *n.* **per·son·a·tor** *n.*

per·son·i·fi·ca·tion /pərsónifikáyshən/ *n.* **1** the act of personifying. **2** (foll. by *of*) a person or thing viewed as a striking example of (a quality, etc.) (*the personification of ugliness*).

per·son·i·fy /pərsónifī/ *v.tr.* (**-ies, -ied**) **1** attribute a personal nature to (an abstraction or thing). **2** symbolize (a quality, etc.) by a figure in human form. **3** (usu. as **personified** *adj.*) embody (a quality) in one's own person; exemplify typically (*has always been kindness personified*). □□ **per·son·i·fi·er** *n.*

per·son·nel /pórsənél/ *n.* a body of employees, persons involved in a public undertaking, armed forces, etc.

per·son·nel car·ri·er *n.* an armored vehicle for transporting troops, etc.

per·son-to-per·son *adj.* **1** between individuals. **2** (of a phone call) booked through the operator to a specified person.

per·spec·tive /pərspéktiv/ *n. & adj.* ● *n.* **1 a** ▶ the art of drawing solid objects on a two-dimensional surface so as to give the right impression of relative positions, size, etc. **b** a picture drawn in this way. **2** the apparent relation between visible objects as to position, distance, etc. **3** a mental view of the relative importance of things (*keep the right perspective*). **4** a geographical or imaginary prospect. ● *adj.* of or in perspective. □ **in perspective 1** drawn or viewed according to the rules of perspective. **2** correctly regarded in terms of relative importance. □□ **per·spec·tiv·al** *adj.* **per·spec·tive·ly** *adv.*

per·spi·ca·cious /pórspikáyshəs/ *adj.* having mental penetration or discernment. □□ **per·spi·ca·cious·ly** *adv.* **per·spi·ca·cious·ness** *n.* **per·spi·cac·i·ty** /-kásitee/ *n.*

per·spic·u·ous /pərspíkyōōəs/ *adj.* **1** easily understood; clearly expressed. **2** (of a person) expressing things clearly. □□ **per·spi·cu·i·ty** /pórspikyōō-tee/ *n.* **per·spic·u·ous·ly** *adv.* **per·spic·u·ous·ness** *n.*

per·spi·ra·tion /pórspiráyshən/ *n.* **1** = SWEAT. **2** sweating. □□ **per·spi·ra·to·ry** /pərspīrətawree, pórspirə-/ *adj.*

per·spire /pərspír/ *v.* **1** *intr.* sweat or exude perspiration, esp. as the result of heat, exercise, anxiety, etc. **2** *tr.* sweat or exude (fluid, etc.).

P

per·suade /pərswáyd/ *v.tr. & refl.* **1** (often foll. by *of*, or *that* + clause) cause (another person or oneself) to believe; convince (*persuaded them that it would be helpful*). **2 a** (often foll. by *to* + infin.) induce (another person or oneself) (*managed to persuade them at last*). **b** (foll. by *away from*, *down to*, etc.) lure, attract, entice, etc. (*persuaded them away from the pub*). □□ **per·suad·a·ble** *adj.* **per·suad·a·bil·i·ty** *n.* **per·sua·si·ble** *adj.*

per·suad·er /pərswáydər/ *n.* **1** a person who persuades. **2** *sl.* a gun or other weapon.

per·sua·sion /pərswáyzhən/ *n.* **1** persuading (*yielded to persuasion*). **2** persuasiveness (*use all your persuasion*). **3** a belief or conviction (*my private persuasion*). **4** a religious belief, or the group or sect holding it (*of a different persuasion*). **5** *colloq.* any group or party (*the male persuasion*).

per·sua·sive /pərswáysiv, -ziv/ *adj.* able to persuade. □□ **per·sua·sive·ly** *adv.* **per·sua·sive·ness** *n.*

pert /pərt/ *adj.* **1** saucy or impudent, esp. in speech or conduct. **2** (of clothes, etc.) neat and jaunty. □□ **pert·ly** *adv.* **pert·ness** *n.*

PERT *abbr.* program evaluation and review technique

pert. *abbr.* pertaining.

per·tain /pərtáyn/ *v.intr.* **1** (foll. by *to*) **a** relate or have reference to. **b** belong to as a part or appendage or accessory. **2** (usu. foll. by *to*) be appropriate to.

per·ti·na·cious /pərt'náyshəs/ *adj.* stubborn; persistent; obstinate (in a course of action, etc.).

□□ **per·ti·na·cious·ly** *adv.* **per·ti·na·cious·ness** *n.* **per·ti·nac·i·ty** /-násitee/ *n.*

per·ti·nent /pórt'nənt/ *adj.* **1** (often foll. by *to*) relevant to the matter in hand; apposite. **2** to the point. □□ **per·ti·nence** *n.* **per·ti·nen·cy** *n.* **per·ti·nent·ly** *adv.*

per·turb /pərtárb/ *v.tr.* **1** throw into confusion or disorder. **2** disturb mentally; agitate. □□ **per·turb·a·ble** *adj.* **per·tur·ba·tion** *n.* **per·tur·ba·tive** /pərtúrbətiv, pórtərbáytiv/ *adj.* **per·turb·ing·ly** *adv.*

per·tus·sis /pərtúsis/ *n.* whooping cough.

pe·ruse /pərōōz/ *v.tr.* **1** (also *absol.*) read or study, esp. thoroughly or carefully. **2** examine (a person's face, etc.) carefully. □□ **pe·rus·al** *n.* **pe·rus·er** *n.*

Pe·ru·vi·an /pərōōveeən/ *n. & adj.* ● *n.* **1** a native or national of Peru. **2** a person of Peruvian descent. ● *adj.* of or relating to Peru. □ **Peruvian bark** the bark of the cinchona tree.

per·vade /pərváyd/ *v.tr.* **1** spread throughout; permeate. **2** (of influences, etc.) become widespread among or in. **3** be rife among or through. □□ **per·va·sion** /-váyzhən/ *n.*

per·va·sive /pərváysiv, -ziv/ *adj.* **1** pervading. **2** able to pervade. □□ **per·va·sive·ly** *adv.* **per·va·sive·ness** *n.*

per·verse /pərvérs/ *adj.* **1** (of a person or action) deliberately or stubbornly departing from what is reasonable or required. **2** persistent in error. **3** wayward; intractable; peevish. **4** perverted; wicked. **5** (of a verdict, etc.) against the weight of evidence

or the judge's direction. □□ **per·verse·ly** *adv.* **per·verse·ness** *n.* **per·ver·si·ty** *n.* (*pl.* **-ies**).

per·ver·sion /pərvórzhən, -shən/ *n.* **1** an act of perverting; the state of being perverted. **2** a perverted form of an act or thing. **3 a** preference for an abnormal form of sexual activity. **b** such an activity.

per·vert *v. & n.* ● *v.tr.* /pərvórt/ **1** turn (a person or thing) aside from its proper use or nature. **2** misapply or misconstrue (words, etc.). **3** lead astray (a person, a person's mind, etc.) from right opinion or conduct, or esp. religious belief. **4** (as **perverted** *adj.*) showing perversion. ● *n.* /pórvərt/ **1** a perverted person. **2** a person showing sexual perversion. □□ **per·ver·sive** /-vórsiv/ *adj.* **per·vert·ed·ly** /-vórtidlee/ *adv.* **per·vert·er** /-vórtər/ *n.*

per·vi·ous /pórveeəs/ *adj.* **1** permeable. **2** (usu. foll. by *to*) **a** affording passage. **b** accessible (to reason, etc.). □□ **per·vi·ous·ness** *n.*

pe·se·ta /pəsáytə/ *n.* (until the introduction of the euro in 2002) the chief monetary unit of Spain, orig. a silver coin.

pes·ky /péskee/ *adj.* (**peskier, peskiest**) *colloq.* troublesome; annoying. □□ **pesk·i·ly** *adv.* **pesk·i·ness** *n.*

pe·so /páysō/ *n.* (*pl.* **-os**) **1** the chief monetary unit of several Latin American countries and of the Philippines. **2** a note or coin worth one peso.

pes·sa·ry /pésəree/ *n.* (*pl.* **-ies**) *Med.* **1** a device worn in the vagina to support the uterus or as a contraceptive. **2** a vaginal suppository.

PERSPECTIVE

In the early 15th century, Battista Alberti, a writer and architect, formulated a method of perspective construction that artists, like Paolo Uccello, could follow. In Alberti's system, the picture surface is imagined as an "open window" through which a painted world is seen. He showed how a perspectival construction can be created by using parallel lines, known as orthogonals, to represent visual rays that connect the viewer's eye to a spot in the distance. The spot on which all the rays converge is known as the vanishing point and is positioned opposite the spectator's viewpoint. The single viewpoint meant that the artist could now control and focus the way that the spectator looked at the picture.

PERSPECTIVE ANALYSIS OF UCCELLO'S
The Hunt in the Forest

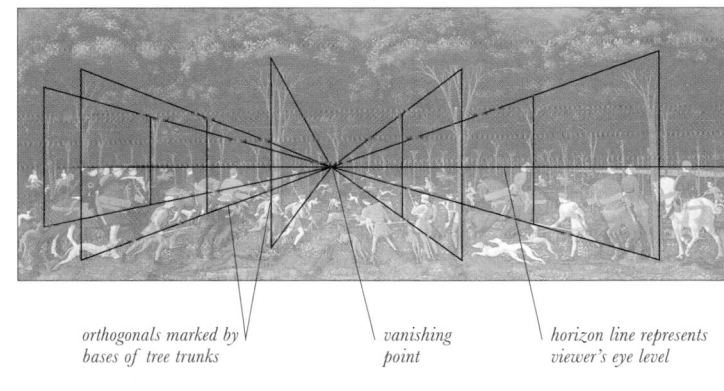

orthogonals marked by bases of tree trunks

vanishing point

horizon line represents viewer's eye level

The Hunt in the Forest (*c.*1460),
PAOLO UCCELLO

P

pes·si·mism /pésimizəm/ *n.* a tendency to take the worst view or expect the worst outcome. □□ **pes·si·mist** *n.* **pes·si·mis·tic** *adj.* **pes·si·mis·ti·cal·ly** *adv.*

pest /pest/ *n.* **1** a troublesome or annoying person or thing; a nuisance. **2** ◄ a destructive animal, esp. an insect which attacks crops, livestock, etc.

pes·ter /péstər/ *v.tr.* trouble or annoy, esp. with frequent or persistent requests. □□ **pes·ter·er** *n.*

pes·ti·cide /péstisīd/ *n.* a substance used for destroying insects or other organisms harmful to cultivated plants or to animals. □□ **pes·ti·cid·al** /-síd'l/ *adj.*

PEST: SOLOMON'S SEAL SAWFLY LARVAE ATTACKING A PLANT

pes·ti·lence /péstiləns/ *n.* **1** a fatal epidemic disease, esp. bubonic plague. **2** something evil or destructive.

pes·ti·lent /péstilənt/ *adj.* **1** destructive to life; deadly. **2** harmful or morally destructive. **3** *colloq.* troublesome; annoying. □□ **pes·ti·lent·ly** *adv.*

pes·ti·len·tial /péstilénshəl/ *adj.* **1** of or relating to pestilence. **2** dangerous; troublesome; pestilent. □□ **pes·ti·len·tial·ly** *adv.*

pes·tle /pésəl/ *n.* **1** ▼ a club-shaped instrument for pounding substances in a mortar. **2** an appliance for pounding, etc.

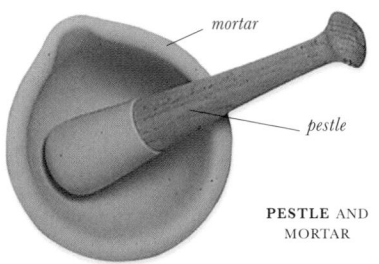

mortar

pestle

PESTLE AND MORTAR

pes·to /péstō/ *n.* a sauce made of fresh chopped basil, garlic, olive oil, and Parmesan cheese, used for pasta, fish, etc.

pet[1] /pet/ *n., adj., & v.* • *n.* **1** a domestic or tamed animal kept for pleasure or companionship. **2** a darling; a favorite (often as a term of endearment). • *attrib.adj.* **1** kept as a pet (*pet lamb*). **2** of or for pet animals (*pet food*). **3** often *joc.* favorite or particular (*pet aversion*). **4** expressing fondness or familiarity (*pet name*). • *v.tr.* (**petted, petting**) **1** treat as a pet. **2** (also *absol.*) fondle, esp. erotically. □□ **pet·ter** *n.*

pet[2] /pet/ *n.* a feeling of petty resentment or ill-humor (esp. *be in a pet*).

peta- /pétə/ *comb. form* denoting a factor of 10^{15}.

pet·al /pét'l/ *n.* each of the parts of the corolla of a flower. ▷ FLOWER. □□ **pet·al·ine** /-līn, -lin/ *adj.* **pet·alled** *adj.* (also in *comb.*). **pet·al·like** *adj.* **pet·al·oid** *adj.*

pe·tard /pitáard/ *n. hist.* **1** a small bomb used to blast down a door, etc. **2** a kind of firework. □ **hoist with** (or **by**) **one's own petard** affected oneself by one's schemes against others.

pe·ter[1] /péetər/ *v.intr.* (foll. by *out*) (orig. of a vein of ore, etc.) diminish; come to an end.

pe·ter[2] /péetər/ *n. sl.* **1** a prison cell. **2** a safe. **3** *coarse sl.* penis.

Pe·ter Pan /péetər pán/ *n.* a person who retains youthful features, or who is immature.

Pe·ter Prin·ci·ple /péetər/ *n. joc.* the principle that members of a hierarchy are promoted until they reach the level at which they are no longer competent.

pe·ter·sham /péetərshəm/ *n.* thick corded silk ribbon used for belts, etc.

pet·i·ole /péteeōl/ *n.* ► the slender stalk joining a leaf to a stem. □□ **pet·i·o·lar** *adj.* **pet·i·o·late** /pétiəláyt/ *adj.*

pet·it /pétee/ *adj.* esp. *Law* petty; small; of lesser importance.

pe·tit bour·geois /pétee boŏrzhwaa, boŏrzhwáa, pətée/ *n.* (*pl.* **petits bourgeois** *pronunc.* same) a member of the lower middle classes.

pe·tite /pətéet/ *adj. & n.* • *adj.* (of a woman) of small and dainty build. • *n.* a clothing size for petite women.

pe·tite bour·geoi·sie *n.* the lower middle classes.

pe·tit four /pétee fáwr/ *n.* (*pl.* **petits fours** /fórz/) a very small fancy frosted cake.

pe·ti·tion /pətíshən/ *n. & v.* • *n.* **1** a supplication or request. **2** a formal written request, esp. one signed by many people, appealing to authority in some cause. **3** *Law* an application to a court for a writ, etc. • *v.* **1** *tr.* make or address a petition to (*petition the court*). **2** *intr.* (often foll. by *for, to*) appeal earnestly or humbly. □□ **pe·ti·tion·a·ble** *adj.* **pe·ti·tion·ar·y** *adj.* **pe·ti·tion·er** *n.*

pe·tit ju·ry *n.* a jury of 12 persons who try the final issue of fact in civil or criminal cases and pronounce a verdict.

pe·tit mal /pétee máal, mál/ *n.* a mild form of epilepsy with only momentary loss of consciousness (cf. GRAND MAL).

pe·tit point /pétee póynt, pətée pwán/ *n.* **1** embroidery on canvas using small stitches. **2** tent stitch.

pet peeve *n. colloq.* something especially annoying to an individual.

Pe·trar·chan /pitráarkən/ *adj.* denoting a sonnet of the kind used by the Italian poet Petrarch (d. 1374), with an octave rhyming *abbaabba*, and a sestet usu. rhyming *cdcdcd* or *cdecde*.

pet·rel /pétrəl/ *n.* any of various seabirds of the family Procellariidae or Hydrobatidae, usu. flying far from land. ▷ SEABIRD

Pe·tri dish /péetree/ *n.* a shallow covered dish used for the culture of bacteria, etc.

pet·ri·fac·tion /pétrifákshən/ *n.* **1** the process of fossilization whereby organic matter is turned into a stony substance. **2** ▼ a petrified substance or mass. **3** a state of extreme fear or terror.

petrified nest

petrified egg

PETRIFACTION: PETRIFIED BIRD'S NEST

pet·ri·fy /pétrifī/ *v.* (**-ies, -ied**) **1** *tr.* (also as **petrified** *adj.*) paralyze with fear, astonishment, etc. **2** *tr.* change (organic matter) into a stony substance. **3** *intr.* become like stone.

petro- /pétrō/ *comb. form* **1** rock. **2** petroleum (*petrochemistry*).

pet·ro·chem·i·cal /pétrōkémikəl/ *n. & adj.* • *n.* a substance industrially obtained from petroleum or natural gas. • *adj.* of or relating to petrochemistry or petrochemicals.

pet·ro·chem·is·try /pétrōkémistree/ *n.* **1** the chemistry of rocks. **2** the chemistry of petroleum.

pet·ro·dol·lar /pétrōdolər/ *n.* a notional unit of currency earned by a petroleum-exporting country.

pet·ro·glyph /pétrəglif/ *n.* a rock carving, esp. a prehistoric one.

pe·trog·ra·phy /petrógrəfee/ *n.* the scientific description of the composition and formation of rocks. □□ **pe·trog·ra·pher** *n.* **pet·ro·graph·ic** /-rəgráfik/ *adj.* **pet·ro·graph·i·cal** *adj.*

pet·rol /pétrəl/ *n. Brit.* **1** refined petroleum used as a fuel in motor vehicles, aircraft, etc.; gasoline. **2** (*attrib.*) concerned with the supply of petrol (*petrol pump; petrol station*).

pet·ro·la·tum /pétrəláytəm/ *n.* petroleum jelly.

pe·tro·le·um /pətrōleeəm/ *n.* a hydrocarbon oil found in the upper strata of the Earth, refined for use as a fuel for heating and in internal-combustion engines, for lighting, dry cleaning, etc.

PETIOLE OF A COMMON MULBERRY LEAF

---

pH

The concentration of hydrogen ions in a solution is known as its pH. This value gives an indication of the acidity or alkalinity of a substance. The pH value can be determined by the use of indicators, such as universal indicator paper, which contain compounds that change color over a certain pH range. A pH value may fall anywhere on a scale from 0 (strongly acidic) to 14 (strongly alkaline), with a value of 7 representing neutrality.

SCALE OF pH VALUES

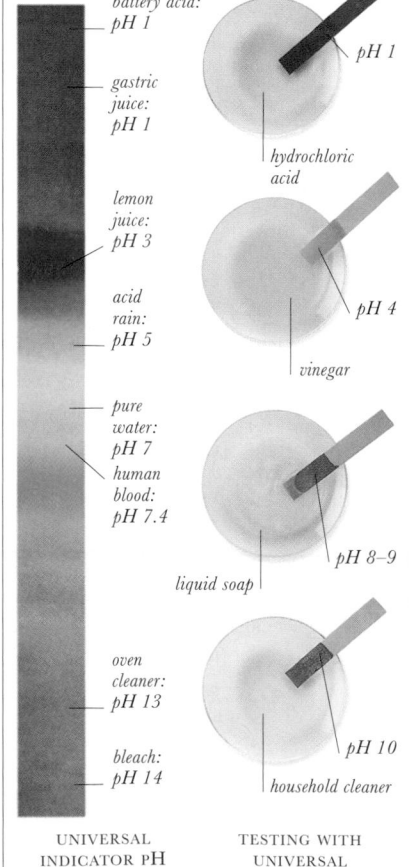

battery acid: pH 1

gastric juice: pH 1

lemon juice: pH 3

acid rain: pH 5

pure water: pH 7

human blood: pH 7.4

oven cleaner: pH 13

bleach: pH 14

pH 1

hydrochloric acid

pH 4

vinegar

pH 8–9

liquid soap

pH 10

household cleaner

UNIVERSAL INDICATOR pH COLOR CHART

TESTING WITH UNIVERSAL INDICATOR PAPER

P

pe·tro·le·um jel·ly *n.* a translucent solid mixture of hydrocarbons used as a lubricant, ointment, etc.

pe·trol·o·gy /petróləjee/ *n.* the study of the origin, structure, composition, etc., of rocks. □□ **pet·ro·log·ic** /pétrəlójik/ *adj.* **pet·ro·log·i·cal** *adj.* **pe·trol·o·gist** *n.*

pet·ti·coat /péteekôt/ *n.* **1** a woman's or girl's skirted undergarment hanging from the waist or shoulders. **2** often *derog. sl.* **a** a woman or girl. **b** (in *pl.*) the female sex. **3** (*attrib.*) often *derog.* feminine; associated with women (*petticoat pedantry*). □□ **pet·ti·coat·ed** *adj.* **pet·ti·coat·less** *adj.*

pet·ti·fog /péteefawg, -fog/ *v.intr.* (**pettifogged, pettifogging**) **1** practice legal deception or trickery. **2** quibble or wrangle about petty points.

pet·ti·fog·ger /péteefáwgər, -fóg-/ *n.* an inferior legal practitioner. □□ **pet·ti·fog·ger·y** *n.* **pet·ti·fog·ging** *adj.*

pet·tish /pétish/ *adj.* peevish, petulant; easily put out. □□ **pet·tish·ly** *adv.* **pet·tish·ness** *n.*

pet·ty /pétee/ *adj.* (**pettier, pettiest**) **1** unimportant; trivial. **2** mean; small-minded; contemptible. **3** minor; inferior; on a small scale (*petty princes*). **4** *Law* (of a crime) of lesser importance (*a shoplifter convicted of petty theft*). □□ **pet·ti·ly** *adv.* **pet·ti·ness** *n.*

pet·ty bour·geois = PETIT BOURGEOIS.

pet·ty bour·geoi·sie = PETITE BOURGEOISIE.

pet·ty cash *n.* money from or for small items of receipt or expenditure.

pet·ty of·fi·cer *n.* a naval NCO.

pet·u·lant /péchələnt/ *adj.* peevishly impatient or irritable (*a petulant child*). □□ **pet·u·lance** *n.* **pet·u·lant·ly** *adv.*

pe·tu·nia /pitoॅonyə, -tyoॅon-/ *n.* **1** ▶ any plant of the genus *Petunia* with white, purple, red, etc., funnel-shaped flowers. **2** a dark violet or purple color.

pew /pyoॅo/ *n. & v.* ● *n.* **1** (in a church) a long bench with a back; an enclosed compartment. **2** *Brit. colloq.* a seat (esp. *take a pew*). ● *v.tr.* furnish with pews. □□ **pew·age** *n.* **pew·less** *adj.*

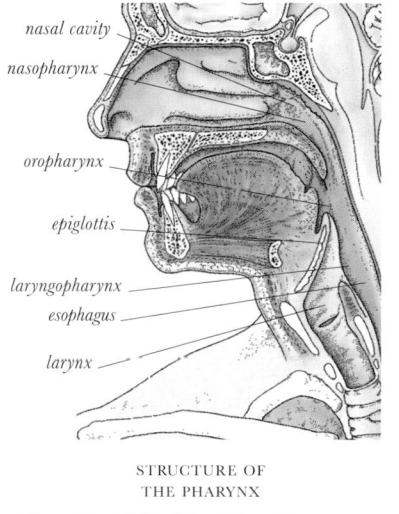

PETUNIA
CULTIVAR

pew·ter /pyoॅotər/ *n.* **1** a gray alloy of tin with lead, copper, antimony, or various other metals. **2** utensils made of this. □□ **pew·ter·er** *n.*

pe·yo·te /payótee/ *n.* **1** any Mexican cactus of the genus *Lophophora*, esp. *L. williamsii* having no spines and button-like tops when dried. **2** a hallucinogenic drug containing mescaline prepared from this.

Pfc. *abbr.* (also **PFC**) Private First Class.

pfen·nig /fénig, pféniKH/ *n.* (until the introduction of the euro in 2002) a small German coin, worth one hundredth of a mark.

pg. *abbr.* page.

PGA *abbr.* Professional Golfers' Association.

PG-13 *abbr.* (of a film) classified as suitable for children under age 13 subject to parental guidance.

pH /pée-áych/ *n. Chem.* ◀ a logarithm of the reciprocal of the hydrogen-ion concentration in moles per liter of a solution, giving a measure of its acidity or alkalinity.

pha·e·ton /fáyit'n, fáyt'n/ *n.* **1** a light open four-wheeled carriage, usu. drawn by a pair of horses. **2** a vintage touring car.

phage /fayj/ *n. Biol.* a kind of virus which acts as a parasite of bacteria, infecting them and reproducing inside them.

phag·o·cyte /fágəsīt/ *n.* ▼ a type of cell capable of engulfing and absorbing foreign matter, esp. a leukocyte ingesting bacteria in the body. □□ **phag·o·cyt·ic** /-sítik/ *adj.*

-phagous /fəgəs/ *comb. form* that eats (as specified) (*ichthyophagous*).

-phagy /fəjee/ *comb. form* the eating of (specified food) (*ichthyophagy*).

pha·lan·ge·al /fəlánjeeəl/ *adj. Anat.* of or relating to a phalanx.

pha·lan·ger /fəlánjər/ *n.* any of various marsupials of the family Phalangeridae, including cuscuses and possums.

pha·lanx /fá.langks/ *n.* (*pl.* **phalanxes** or **phalanges** /fəlánjeez/) **1** *Gk Antiq.* a line of battle, esp. a body of Macedonian infantry drawn up in close order. **2** a set of people, etc., forming a compact mass, or banded for a common purpose. **3** a bone of the finger or toe.

phal·li *pl.* of PHALLUS.

phal·lic /fálik/ *adj.* **1** of, relating to, or resembling a phallus. **2** *Psychol.* denoting the stage of male sexual development characterized by preoccupation with the genitals. □□ **phal·li·cal·ly** *adv.*

phal·lus /fáləs/ *n.* (*pl.* **phalli** /-lī/ or **phalluses**) **1** the (esp. erect) penis. **2** an image of this as a symbol of generative power in nature. □□ **phal·li·cism** /-lisīzəm/ *n.* **phal·lism** *n.*

phan·tasm /fántazəm/ *n.* **1** an illusion; a phantom. **2** (usu. foll. by *of*) an illusory likeness. **3** a supposed vision of an absent (living or dead) person. □□ **phan·tas·mal** /-tázm'l/ *adj.* **phan·tas·mic** /-tázmik/ *adj.*

phan·tas·ma·go·ri·a /fántazməgáwreeə/ *n.* **1** a shifting series of real or imaginary figures as seen in a dream. **2** an optical device for rapidly varying the size of images on a screen. □□ **phan·tas·ma·gor·ic** /-gáwrik, -gór-/ *adj.* **phan·tas·ma·gor·i·cal** *adj.*

phan·tom /fántəm/ *n. & adj.* ● *n.* **1** a ghost; an apparition; a specter. **2** a form without substance or

---

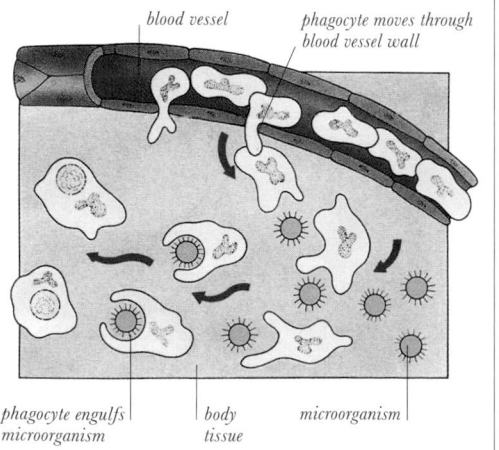

blood vessel

phagocyte moves through blood vessel wall

CROSS SECTION OF A HUMAN BLOOD VESSEL AND TISSUE

phagocyte engulfs microorganism

body tissue

microorganism

PHARYNX

The pharynx is a muscular passage lined with mucous membrane that extends from the nasal cavity to the esophagus. The upper part, the nasopharynx, connects to the ear via the Eustachian tube and acts as an air passage. The oropharynx, a passage for air and food, lies between the soft palate and the upper edge of the epiglottis. The laryngopharynx lies below the epiglottis and opens into both the larynx for breathing and the esophagus for swallowing.

nasal cavity

nasopharynx

oropharynx

epiglottis

laryngopharynx

esophagus

larynx

STRUCTURE OF
THE PHARYNX

reality; a mental illusion. **3** *Med.* a model of the whole or part of the body used to practice or demonstrate operative or therapeutic methods. ● *adj.* merely apparent; illusory.

Phar·aoh /fáirō, fárō, fáyrō/ *n.* **1** the ruler of ancient Egypt. **2** the title of this ruler. □□ **Phar·a·on·ic** /fáirayónik/ *adj.*

Phar·i·see /fárisee/ (also **phar·i·see**) *n.* **1** a member of an ancient Jewish sect, distinguished by strict observance of the traditional and written law. **2** a self-righteous person; a hypocrite. □□ **Phar·i·sa·ic** /fárisáyik/ *adj.* **Phar·i·sa·i·cal** /fárisáyikəl/ *adj.* **Phar·i·sa·ism** /fárisayizəm/ *n.*

phar·ma·ceu·ti·cal /fáarməsóॅotikəl/ *adj. & n.* ● *adj.* **1** of or engaged in pharmacy. **2** of the use or sale of medicinal drugs. ● *n.* a medicinal drug. □□ **phar·ma·ceu·ti·cal·ly** *adv.* **phar·ma·ceu·tics** *n.*

phar·ma·cist /fáarməsist/ *n.* a person qualified to prepare and dispense drugs.

phar·ma·col·o·gy /fáarməkóləjee/ *n.* the science of the action of drugs on the body. □□ **phar·ma·co·log·i·cal** *adj.* **phar·ma·co·log·i·cal·ly** *adv.* **phar·ma·col·o·gist** *n.*

phar·ma·co·poe·ia /fáarməkəpéeə/ *n.* **1** a book, esp. one officially published, containing a list of drugs with directions for use. **2** a stock of drugs. □□ **phar·ma·co·poe·ial** *adj.*

phar·ma·cy /fáarməsee/ *n.* (*pl.* **-ies**) **1** the preparation and the (esp. medicinal) dispensing of drugs. **2** a drugstore; a dispensary.

pharyngo- /fəriNGgō/ *comb. form* denoting the pharynx.

phar·ynx /fáriNGks/ *n.* (*pl.* **pharynges** /fərínjeez/) ▲ a cavity behind the nose and mouth, connecting them to the esophagus. □□ **pha·ryn·gal** /-ríNGgəl/ *adj.* **pha·ryn·ge·al** /fərínjeeəl, -jəl, fárinjéeəl/ *adj.*

P

phase /fayz/ *n. & v.* ● *n.* **1** a distinct period or stage in a process of change or development. **2** each of the aspects of the Moon or a planet, according to the amount of its illumination, esp. the new moon, the first quarter, the last quarter, and the full moon. **3** *Physics* a stage in a periodically recurring sequence, esp. of alternating electric currents or light vibrations. **4** a difficult or unhappy period, esp. in adolescence. **5** a genetic or seasonal variety of an animal's coloration, etc. **6** *Chem.* a distinct and homogeneous form of matter separated by its surface from other forms. ● *v.tr.* carry out (a program, etc.) in phases or stages. □ **phase in** (or **out**) bring gradually into (or out of) use. □□ **pha·sic** *adj.*

phat /fat/ *adj. black sl.* excellent.

phat·ic /fátik/ *adj.* (of speech, etc.) used to convey general sociability rather than to communicate a specific meaning, e.g., "How do you do?"

Ph.D. *abbr.* Doctor of Philosophy.

pheas·ant /fézənt/ *n.* ▶ any of several long-tailed game birds of the family Phasianidae, orig. from Asia. □□ **pheas·ant·ry** *n.* (*pl.* **-ies**).

PHEASANT: GOLDEN PHEASANT
(*Chrysolophus pictus*)

pheno- /féenō/ *comb. form* **1** *Chem.* derived from benzene (*phenol*; *phenyl*). **2** showing (*phenocryst*).

phe·no·bar·bi·tal /féenōbáarbitawl, -tal/ *n.* a narcotic and sedative barbiturate drug used esp. to treat epilepsy.

phe·nol /féenawl, -nol/ *n. Chem.* **1** the monohydroxyl derivative of benzene used in dilute form as an antiseptic and disinfectant. Also called **carbolic**. ¶ *Chem.* formula: C_6H_5OH. **2** any hydroxyl derivative of an aromatic hydrocarbon. □□ **phe·no·lic** /finólik/ *adj.*

phe·nol·phtha·lein /féenolftháyleen/ *n. Chem.* a white crystalline solid used in solution as an acid base indicator and medicinally as a laxative.

phe·nom·e·na *pl.* of PHENOMENON.

phe·nom·e·nal /finómənəl/ *adj.* **1** of the nature of a phenomenon. **2** extraordinary; remarkable; prodigious. **3** perceptible by, or perceptible only to, the senses. □□ **phe·nom·e·nal·ize** *v.tr.* **phe·nom·e·nal·ly** *adv.*

phe·nom·e·nal·ism /finómənəlizəm/ *n. Philos.* **1** the doctrine that human knowledge is confined to the appearances presented to the senses. **2** the doctrine that appearances are the foundation of all our knowledge. □□ **phe·nom·e·nal·ist** *n.* **phe·nom·e·nal·is·tic** *adj.*

phe·nom·e·non /finómənən/ *n.* (*pl.* **phenomena** /-nə/) **1** a fact or occurrence that appears or is perceived, esp. one of which the cause is in question. **2** a remarkable person or thing.

phe·no·type /féenōtīp/ *n. Biol.* a set of observable characteristics of an individual or group as determined by its genotype and environment. □□ **phe·no·typ·ic** /-típik/ *adj.* **phe·no·typ·i·cal** *adj.* **phe·no·typ·i·cal·ly** *adv.*

phen·yl /fénil, fée-/ *n. Chem.* the univalent radical formed from benzene by the removal of a hydrogen atom.

phen·yl·ke·to·nu·ri·a /fénilkéetōnóoreeə, -yóor, fée-/ *n.* an inherited inability to metabolize phenylalanine, ultimately leading to mental deficiency if untreated.

pher·o·mone /férəmōn/ *n.* a chemical substance secreted and released by an animal for detection and response by another usu. of the same species. □□ **pher·o·mo·nal** /-mōn'l/ *adj.*

phew /fyoō/ *int.* an expression of relief.

phi /fī/ *n.* the twenty-first letter of the Greek alphabet (Φ, φ).

phi·al /fíəl/ *n.* a small glass bottle, esp. for liquid medicine; vial.

Phil. *abbr.* **1** Philharmonic. **2** Philippines. **3** Philosophy.

phil- *comb. form* var. of PHILO-.

-phil *comb. form* var. of -PHILE.

phil·a·del·phus /filədélfəs/ *n.* any highly-scented deciduous flowering shrub of the genus *Philadelphus*, esp. the mock orange.

phi·lan·der /filándər/ *v.intr.* (often foll. by *with*) flirt or have casual affairs with women; womanize. □□ **phi·lan·der·er** *n.*

phil·an·thrope /filənthrōp/ *n.* = *philanthropist* (see PHILANTHROPY).

phil·an·throp·ic /filənthrópik/ *adj.* loving one's fellow people; benevolent. □□ **phil·an·throp·i·cal·ly** *adv.*

phi·lan·thro·py /filánthrəpee/ *n.* **1** a love of humankind. **2** practical benevolence, esp. charity on a large scale. □□ **phi·lan·thro·pism** *n.* **phi·lan·thro·pist** *n.* **phi·lan·thro·pize** *v.tr. & intr.*

phi·lat·e·ly /filát'lee/ *n.* the collection and study of postage stamps. □□ **phil·a·tel·ic** /filətélik/ *adj.* **phil·a·tel·i·cal·ly** *adv.* **phil·at·e·list** *n.*

-phile /fīl/ *comb. form* (also **-phil** /fil/) forming nouns and adjectives denoting fondness for what is specified (*bibliophile*; *Francophile*).

phil·har·mon·ic /filhaarmónik/ *adj.* **1** fond of music. **2** used characteristically in the names of orchestras, choirs, etc. (*New York Philharmonic Orchestra*).

-philia /fíleeə/ *comb. form* **1** denoting (esp. abnormal) fondness or love for what is specified (*necrophilia*). **2** denoting undue inclination (*hemophilia*). □□ **-philiac** /-leeak/ *comb. form* forming nouns and adjectives. **-philic** /-ik/ *comb. form* forming adjectives. **-philous** /-əs/ *comb. form* forming adjectives.

phi·lip·pic /filípik/ *n.* a bitter verbal attack or denunciation.

Phil·ip·pine /filipeen/ *adj.* of or relating to the Philippine Islands or their people; Filipino.

Phil·is·tine /filisteen, -stīn, filístin, -teen/ *n. & adj.* ● *n.* **1** a member of a people opposing the Israelites in ancient Palestine. **2** (usu. **philistine**) a person who is hostile or indifferent to culture, or one whose interests or tastes are commonplace or material. ● *adj.* hostile or indifferent to culture; commonplace; prosaic. □□ **phil·is·tin·ism** /filistinízəm/ *n.*

Phil·lips /filips/ *n.* (usu. *attrib.*) *Trademark* denoting a screw with a cross-shaped slot for turning, or a corresponding screwdriver.

philo- /fílō/ *comb. form* (also **phil-** before a vowel or *h*) denoting a liking for what is specified.

phi·lo·den·dron /filədéndrən/ *n.* (*pl.* **philodendrons** or **philodendra** /-drə/) ▶ any tropical American climbing plant of the genus *Philodendron*, with bright foliage.

phi·log·y·nist /filójənist/ *n.* a person who likes or admires women.

phi·lol·o·gy /filóləjee/ *n.* **1** the science of language, esp. in its historical and comparative aspects. **2** the love of learning and literature. □□ **phil·o·lo·gi·an** /-lələjeeən/ *n.* **phi·lol·o·gist** *n.* **phil·o·log·i·cal** /-lələjikal/ *adj.* **phil·o·log·i·cal·ly** /-ləlójiklee/ *adv.* **phi·lol·o·gize** *v.intr.*

phil·o·pro·gen·i·tive /filōprōjénitiv/ *adj.* **1** prolific. **2** loving one's offspring.

phi·los·o·pher /filósəfər/ *n.* **1** a person engaged or learned in philosophy or a branch of it. **2** a person who lives by philosophy. **3** a person who shows philosophic calmness in trying circumstances.

phil·o·soph·i·cal /filəsófikəl/ *adj.* (also **phil·o·soph·ic**) **1** of or according to philosophy. **2** skilled in or devoted to philosophy or learning; learned (*philosophical society*). **3** wise; serene; temperate. **4** calm in adverse circumstances. □□ **phil·o·soph·i·cal·ly** *adv.*

phi·los·o·phize /filósəfīz/ *v.* **1** *intr.* reason like a philosopher. **2** *intr.* moralize. **3** *intr.* speculate; theorize. **4** *tr.* render philosophic. □□ **phi·los·o·phiz·er** *n.*

phi·los·o·phy /filósəfee/ *n.* (*pl.* **-ies**) **1** the use of reason and argument in seeking truth and knowledge of reality, esp. of the causes and nature of things and of the principles governing existence, the material universe, perception of physical phenomena, and human behavior. **2 a** a particular system or set of beliefs reached by this. **b** a personal rule of life. **3** advanced learning in general (*doctor of philosophy*).

phil·ter /fíltər/ *n.* (also **phil·tre**) a drink supposed to excite sexual love in the drinker.

-phily /filee/ *comb. form* = -PHILIA.

phiz /fiz/ *n.* (also **phi·zog** /fízog/) *colloq.* **1** the face. **2** the expression on a face.

phle·bi·tis /flibítis/ *n.* inflammation of the walls of a vein. □□ **phle·bit·ic** /-bítik/ *adj.*

phle·bot·o·my /flibótəmee/ *n.* the surgical opening or puncture of a vein. □□ **phle·bot·o·mist** *n.* **phle·bot·o·mize** *v.tr.*

phlegm /flem/ *n.* **1** the thick viscous substance secreted by the mucous membranes of the respiratory passages, discharged by coughing. **2 a** coolness and calmness of disposition. **b** sluggishness or apathy (supposed to result from too much phlegm in the constitution). □□ **phlegm·y** *adj.*

phleg·mat·ic /flegmátik/ *adj.* stolidly calm; unexcitable; unemotional. □□ **phleg·mat·i·cal·ly** *adv.*

phlo·em /flōem/ *n. Bot.* the tissue conducting food material in plants (cf. XYLEM). ▷ STEM

phlo·gis·ton /flōjiston/ *n.* a substance formerly supposed to exist in all combustible bodies, and to be released in combustion.

phlox /floks/ *n.* any cultivated plant of the genus *Phlox*, with scented clusters of esp. white, blue, and red flowers.

-phobe /fōb/ *comb. form* forming nouns and adjectives denoting a person having a fear or dislike of what is specified (*xenophobe*).

pho·bi·a /fōbeeə/ *n.* an abnormal or morbid fear or aversion. □□ **pho·bic** *adj. & n.*

-phobia /fōbeeə/ *comb. form* forming abstract nouns denoting a fear or dislike of what is specified (*agoraphobia*; *xenophobia*). □□ **-phobic** *comb. form* forming adjectives.

phoe·be /féebee/ *n.* any American flycatcher of the genus *Sayornis*.

Phoe·ni·cian /fənéeshən, fəní-/ *n. & adj.* ● *n.* a member of a Semitic people of ancient Phoenicia in S. Syria or of its colonies. ● *adj.* of or relating to Phoenicia.

phoe·nix /féeniks/ *n.* **1** a mythical bird, the only one of its kind, that after living for five or six centuries in the Arabian desert, burned itself on a funeral pyre and rose from the ashes with renewed youth to live through another cycle. **2 a** a unique person or thing. **b** a person or thing having recovered, esp. seemingly miraculously, from a disaster.

phon /fon/ *n.* a unit of the perceived loudness of sounds.

pho·nate /fōnayt/ *v.intr.* utter a vocal sound. □□ **pho·na·tion** /-náyshən/ *n.* **pho·na·to·ry** /fōnətawree/ *adj.*

phone /fōn/ *n. & v.tr. & intr. colloq.* = TELEPHONE.

PHILODENDRON
(*Philodendron erubescens* 'Red Emerald')

P

-phone /fōn/ *comb. form* forming nouns and adjectives meaning: **1** an instrument using or connected with sound (*telephone*; *xylophone*). **2** a person who uses a specified language (*anglophone*).

pho·neme /fŏneem/ *n.* any of the units of sound in a specified language that distinguish one word from another (e.g., *p*, *b*, *d*, *t* as in pad, pat, bad, bat, in English). □□ **pho·ne·mic** /-neemik/ *adj.* **pho·ne·mics** /-neemiks/ *n.*

pho·net·ic /fənétik/ *adj.* **1** representing vocal sounds. **2** (of a system of spelling, etc.) having a direct correspondence between symbols and sounds. **3** of or relating to phonetics. □□ **pho·net·i·cal·ly** *adv.* **pho·net·i·cism** /-nétəsizəm/ *n.* **pho·net·i·cist** /-nétəsist/ *n.* **pho·net·i·cize** /-nétəsīz/ *v.tr.*

pho·net·ics /fənétiks/ *n.pl.* (usu. treated as *sing.*) **1** vocal sounds and their classification. **2** the study of these. □□ **pho·ne·ti·cian** /fŏnitíshən/ *n.*

pho·net·ist /fŏnitist/ *n.* an advocate of phonetic spelling.

phon·ic /fónik/ *adj. & n.* ● *adj.* of sound; acoustic; of vocal sounds. ● *n.* (in *pl.*) a method of teaching reading based on sounds. □□ **phon·i·cal·ly** *adv.*

phono- /fónō/ *comb. form* denoting sound.

pho·no·gram /fŏnəgram/ *n.* a symbol representing a spoken sound.

pho·no·graph /fónəgraf/ *n.* **1** an instrument that reproduces recorded sound by a stylus that is in contact with a rotating grooved disk. ¶ Now more usually called a RECORD PLAYER. **2** *Brit.* ▼ an early form of phonograph, usually called a gramophone, using cylinders and able to record as well as reproduce sound.

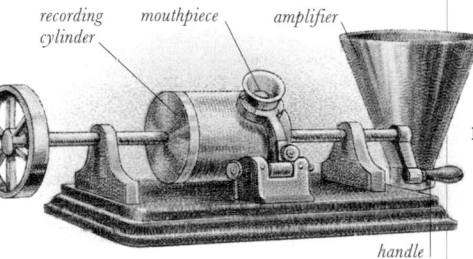

PHONOGRAPH DESIGNED BY
THOMAS EDISON (1877)

pho·nog·ra·phy /fənógrəfee/ *n.* **1** writing in esp. shorthand symbols, corresponding to the sounds of speech. **2** the recording of sounds by phonograph. □□ **pho·no·graph·ic** /fŏnəgráfik/ *adj.*

pho·nol·o·gy /fənóləjee/ *n.* the study of sounds in a language. □□ **pho·no·log·i·cal** /fŏnəlójikəl/ *adj.* **pho·no·log·i·cal·ly** *adv.* **pho·nol·o·gist** /fənólə-jist/ *n.*

pho·non /fónon/ *n. Physics* a quantum of sound or elastic vibrations.

pho·ny /fónee/ *adj. & n.* (also **pho·ney**) *colloq.* ● *adj.* (**phonier**, **phoniest**) **1** sham; counterfeit. **2** fictitious; fraudulent. ● *n.* (*pl.* **-ies** or **-eys**) a phony person or thing. □□ **pho·ni·ly** *adv.* **pho·ni·ness** *n.*

phoo·ey /fŏo-ee/ *int.* an expression of disgust or disbelief.

-phore /fawr/ *comb. form* forming nouns meaning 'bearer' (*ctenophore*; *semaphore*). □□ **-phorous** /fərəs/ *comb. form* forming adjectives.

phos·gene /fósjeen, fóz-/ *n.* a colorless poisonous gas (carbonyl chloride), formerly used in warfare. ¶ Chem. formula: $COCl_2$.

phos·pha·tase /fósfətays, -tayz/ *n. Biochem.* any enzyme that catalyzes the synthesis or hydrolysis of an organic phosphate.

phos·phate /fósfayt/ *n.* **1** any salt or ester of phosphoric acid, esp. used as a fertilizer. **2** a flavored effervescent drink containing a small amount of phosphate. □□ **phos·phat·ic** /-fátik/ *adj.*

phos·phide /fósfīd/ *n. Chem.* a binary compound of phosphorus with another element or group.

phos·phine /fósfeen/ *n. Chem.* a colorless ill-smelling gas, phosphorus trihydride. ¶ Chem. formula: PH_3. □□ **phos·phin·ic** /-fínik/ *adj.*

phos·phite /fósfīt/ *n. Chem.* any salt or ester of phosphorous acid.

phospho- /fósfō/ *comb. form* denoting phosphorus.

phos·pho·lip·id /fósfəlípid/ *n. Biochem.* any lipid consisting of a phosphate group and one or more fatty acids.

phos·phor /fósfər/ *n.* **1** = PHOSPHORUS. **2** a synthetic fluorescent or phosphorescent substance esp. used in cathode-ray tubes.

phos·pho·rate /fósfərayt/ *v.tr.* combine or impregnate with phosphorus.

phos·pho·res·cence /fósfərésəns/ *n.* **1** radiation similar to fluorescence but detectable after excitation ceases. **2** the emission of light without combustion or perceptible heat. □□ **phos·pho·resce** *v.intr.* **phos·pho·res·cent** *adj.*

phos·pho·rus /fósfərəs/ *n. Chem.* a nonmetallic element occurring naturally in various phosphate rocks and existing in allotropic forms, esp. as a poisonous whitish waxy substance burning slowly at ordinary temperatures and so appearing luminous in the dark, and a reddish form used in matches, fertilizers, etc. ¶ Symb.: **P**. □□ **phos·phor·ic** /-fórik/ *adj.* **phos·pho·rous** *adj.*

phot /fot, fōt/ *n.* a unit of illumination equal to one lumen per square centimeter.

pho·tic /fŏtik/ *adj.* **1** of or relating to light. **2** (of ocean layers) reached by sunlight.

pho·tism /fŏtizəm/ *n.* a hallucinatory sensation or vision of light.

pho·to /fŏtō/ *n. & v.* ● *n.* (*pl.* **-os**) = PHOTOGRAPH *n.* ● *v.tr.* (**-oes**, **-oed**) = PHOTOGRAPH *v.*

photo- /fŏtō/ *comb. form* denoting: **1** light (*photosensitive*). **2** photography (*photocomposition*).

pho·to·cell /fŏtōsel/ *n.* = PHOTOELECTRIC CELL.

pho·to·chem·is·try /fŏtōkémistree/ *n.* the study of the chemical effects of light. □□ **pho·to·chem·i·cal** *adj.*

pho·to·com·po·si·tion /fŏtōkómpəzishən/ *n. Printing* a typesetting process in which characters, etc., are projected onto a light-sensitive material such as photographic film.

pho·to·con·duc·tiv·i·ty /fŏtōkónduktívitee/ *n.* conductivity due to the action of light. □□ **pho·to·con·duc·tive** /-dúktiv/ *adj.* **pho·to·con·duc·tor** /-dúktər/ *n.*

pho·to·cop·i·er /fŏtōkópeeər/ *n.* ▼ a machine for producing photocopies.

pho·to·cop·y /fŏtōkópee/ *n. & v.* ● *n.* (*pl.* **-ies**) a photographic copy of printed or written material produced by a process involving the action of light on a specially prepared surface. ● *v.tr.* (**-ies**, **-ied**) make a photocopy of. □□ **pho·to·cop·i·a·ble** *adj.*

pho·to·di·ode /fŏtōdíōd/ *n.* a semiconductor diode responding electrically to illumination.

pho·to·e·lec·tric /fŏtōiléktrik/ *adj.* marked by or using emissions of electrons from substances exposed to light. □□ **pho·to·e·lec·tric·i·ty** /-trísitee/ *n.*

pho·to·e·lec·tric cell *n.* a device using this effect to generate current.

pho·to·e·lec·tron /fŏtōiléktron/ *n.* an electron emitted from an atom by interaction with a photon, esp. one emitted from a solid surface by the action of light.

pho·to·e·mis·sion /fŏtōimíshən/ *n.* the emission of electrons from a surface by the action of light incident on it. □□ **pho·to·e·mit·ter** *n.*

pho·to fin·ish *n.* a close finish of a race or contest, esp. one where the winner is only distinguishable on a photograph.

pho·to·fin·ish·ing /fŏtōfinishing/ *n.* the process of developing and printing photographic film.

pho·to·gen·ic /fŏtəjénik/ *adj.* **1** (esp. of a person) having an appearance that looks pleasing in photographs. **2** *Biol.* producing or emitting light. □□ **pho·to·gen·i·cal·ly** *adv.*

pho·to·graph /fŏtəgraf/ *n. & v.* ● *n.* a picture taken by means of the chemical action of light or other radiation on sensitive film. ● *v.tr.* (also *absol.*) take a photograph of (a person, etc.). □□ **pho·to·graph·a·ble** *adj.* **pho·tog·ra·pher** /fətógrəfər/ *n.*

pho·to·graph·ic /fŏtəgráfik/ *adj.* **1** of, used in, or produced by photography. **2** having the accuracy of a photograph (*photographic likeness*). □□ **pho·to·graph·i·cal·ly** *adv.*

pho·tog·ra·phy /fətógrəfee/ *n.* the taking and processing of photographs.

pho·to·gra·vure /fŏtōgrəvyŏor/ *n.* **1** an image produced from a photographic negative transferred to a metal plate and etched in. **2** this process.

pho·to·jour·nal·ism /fŏtōjərnəlizəm/ *n.* the art or practice of relating news by photographs, with or without an accompanying text, esp. in magazines, etc. □□ **pho·to·jour·nal·ist** *n.*

pho·to·li·thog·ra·phy /fŏtōlithógrəfee/ *n.* (*Brit.* also **pho·to·li·tho** /-lithō/) lithography using plates made photographically. □□ **pho·to·li·thog·ra·pher**

P

PHOTOCOPIER

At the heart of a photocopier is a charged photoconductive drum. The image to be copied is projected via a lens and mirrors onto the drum. Light from white areas of the image disperses the charge where it hits the drum. The drum is left with charged areas that correspond to the black parts of the document. These attract toner from a roller to form a copy of the document on the drum, which is then transferred to a sheet of paper.

INSIDE A BLACK AND
WHITE PHOTOCOPIER

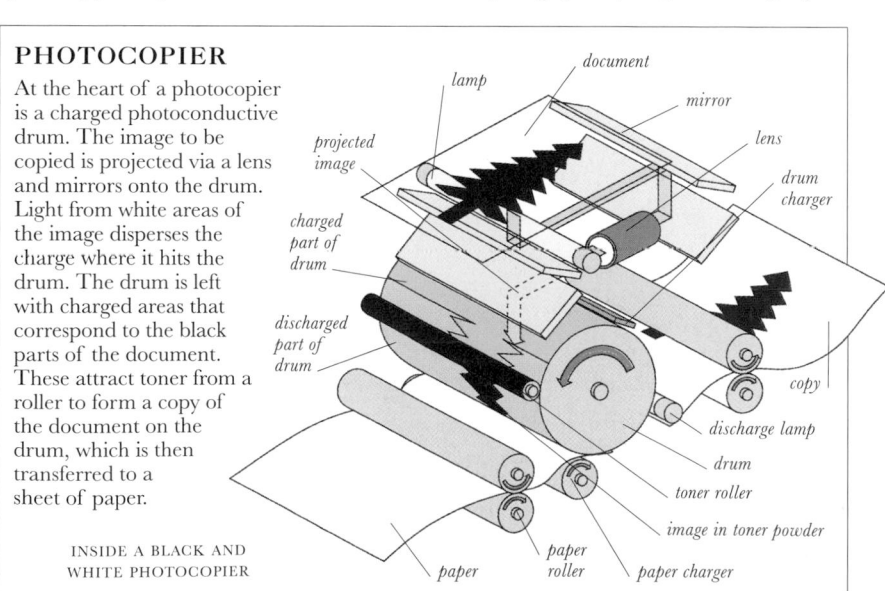

lamp · document · mirror · lens · drum charger · projected image · charged part of drum · discharged part of drum · copy · discharge lamp · drum · toner roller · image in toner powder · paper · paper roller · paper charger

n. **pho·to·lith·o·graph·ic** /-thəgráfik/ *adj.* **pho·to·lith·o·graph·i·cal·ly** *adv.*

pho·tom·e·ter /fōtómitər/ *n.* an instrument for measuring light. □□ **pho·to·met·ric** /fŏtōmétrik/ *adj.* **pho·tom·e·try** /-tómitree/ *n.*

pho·to·mi·cro·graph /fŏtōmíkrəgraf/ *n.* a photograph of an image produced by a microscope. □□ **pho·to·mi·crog·ra·phy** /-krógrəfee/ *n.*

pho·ton /fṓton/ *n.* **1** a quantum of electromagnetic radiation energy, proportional to the frequency of radiation. **2** a unit of luminous intensity as measured at the retina.

pho·to-off·set /fŏtō-áwfset, -óf-/ *n.* offset printing with plates made photographically.

pho·to op·por·tu·ni·ty *n.* (also **pho·to-op**) an occasion on which famous people pose for photographers by arrangement.

pho·to·pe·ri·od·ism /fŏtōpéereeədizəm/ *n.* the response of an organism to changes in the lengths of the daily periods of light.

pho·to·pho·bi·a /fŏtōfṓbeeə/ *n.* an abnormal fear of or aversion to light. □□ **pho·to·pho·bic** *adj.*

pho·to·re·cep·tor /fŏtōriséptər/ *n.* any living structure that responds to incident light.

pho·to·sen·si·tive /fŏtōsénsitiv/ *adj.* reacting chemically, electrically, etc., to light. □□ **pho·to·sen·si·tiv·i·ty** /-tívitee/ *n.*

pho·to·set·ting /fŏtōseting/ *n.* = PHOTOCOMPOSITION. □□ **pho·to·set** *v.tr.* (*past* and *past part.* **-set**). **pho·to·set·ter** *n.*

pho·to·sphere /fŏtəsfeer/ *n.* the luminous envelope of a star from which its light and heat radiate. □□ **pho·to·spher·ic** /-sférik/ *adj.*

Pho·to·stat /fŏtəstat/ *n.* & *v.* ● *n. Trademark* **1** a type of machine for making photocopies. **2** a copy made by this means. ● *v.tr.* (**photostat**) (**-statted, -statting**) make a Photostat of. □□ **pho·to·stat·ic** /-státik/ *adj.*

pho·to·syn·the·sis /fŏtōsínthisis/ *n.* ▼ the process in which the energy of sunlight is used by organisms, esp. green plants, to synthesize carbohydrates from carbon dioxide and water. □□ **pho·to·syn·the·size** *v.tr.* & *intr.* **pho·to·syn·thet·ic** /-thétik/ *adj.* **pho·to·syn·thet·i·cal·ly** *adv.*

pho·to·tran·sis·tor /fŏtōtranzístər/ *n.* a transistor that responds to incident light by generating and amplifying an electric current.

pho·tot·ro·pism /fətótrəpizəm, fŏtōtrṓpizəm/ *n.* ► the tendency of a plant, etc., to bend or turn toward or away from a source of light. □□ **pho·to·trop·ic** /-trópik/ *adj.*

pho·to·vol·ta·ic /fŏtōvoltáyik, -vōl-/ *adj.* relating to the production of electric current at the junction of two substances exposed to light.

phras·al /fráyzəl/ *adj. Gram.* consisting of a phrase.

phras·al verb *n.* an idiomatic phrase consisting of a verb and an adverb (e.g., *break down*), a verb and a preposition (e.g., *see to*), or a combination of both (e.g., *look down on*).

phrase /frayz/ *n.* & *v.* ● *n.* **1** a group of words forming a conceptual unit, but not a sentence. **2** an idiomatic or short pithy expression. **3** a manner or mode of expression (*a nice turn of phrase*). **4** *Mus.* a group of notes forming a distinct unit within a larger piece. ● *v.tr.* **1** express in words (*phrased the reply badly*). **2** (esp. when reading aloud or speaking) divide (sentences, etc.) into units so as to convey the meaning of the whole. **3** *Mus.* divide (music) into phrases, etc., in performance. □□ **phras·ing** *n.*

phrase book *n.* a book for tourists, etc., listing useful expressions with their equivalents in a foreign language.

phra·se·o·gram /fráyzeeəgrám/ *n.* a written symbol representing a phrase, esp. in shorthand.

phra·se·ol·o·gy /fráyzeeóləjee/ *n.* (*pl.* **-ies**) a particular or characteristic mode of expression. □□ **phra·se·o·log·i·cal** /-əlójikəl/ *adj.*

phreak·ing /fréeking/ *n. colloq.*, chiefly *N. Amer.* the action of hacking into telecommunications systems, esp. to obtain free calls.

phre·at·ic /freeátik/ *adj. Geol.* **1** (of water) situated underground in the zone of saturation; ground water. **2** (of a volcanic eruption or explosion) caused by the heating and expansion of underground water.

phre·net·ic /frənétik/ *adj.* (also **fre·net·ic**) **1** frantic. **2** fanatic. □□ **phre·net·i·cal·ly** *adv.*

phre·nol·o·gy /frinóləjee/ *n. hist.* the study of the shape and size of the cranium as a supposed indication of character and mental faculties. □□ **phren·o·log·i·cal** /-nəlójikəl/ *adj.* **phre·nol·o·gist** *n.*

PHOTOTROPISM

Phototropism in a plant is manifested by the growth of the roots or shoots toward or away from a source of light. Shoots show positive phototropism, detecting the source of light and orienting themselves to receive the maximum amount (as demonstrated here). Roots show negative phototropism by growing away from light.

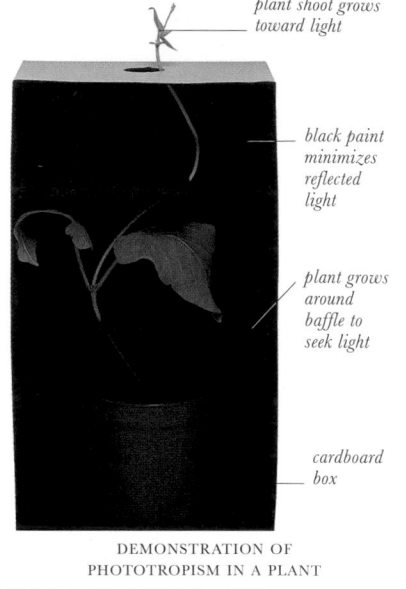

plant shoot grows toward light

black paint minimizes reflected light

plant grows around baffle to seek light

cardboard box

DEMONSTRATION OF
PHOTOTROPISM IN A PLANT

phthi·sis /thísis, tí-/ *n.* any progressive wasting disease, esp. pulmonary tuberculosis. □□ **phthis·ic** /tízik, thíz-/ *adj.* **phthis·i·cal** *adj.*

phy·co·my·cete /fíkōmíseet, -mīseét/ *n.* any of various fungi that typically resemble algae.

phy·la *pl.* of PHYLUM.

phy·lac·ter·y /filáktəree/ *n.* (*pl.* **-ies**) **1** a small leather box containing Hebrew texts on vellum, worn by Jewish men at morning prayer as a reminder to keep the law. **2** an amulet; a charm.

phy·lum /fíləm/ *n.* (*pl.* **phyla** /-lə/) *Biol.* a taxonomic rank below kingdom comprising a class or classes and subordinate taxa.

phys·ic /fízik/ *n.* & *v. archaic* ● *n.* medicinal drugs or medical treatment. ● *v.tr.* (**physicked, physicking**) dose with medicine.

phys·i·cal /fízikəl/ *adj.* & *n.* ● *adj.* **1** of or concerning the body (*physical exercise*; *physical education*). **2** of matter; material (*both mental and physical force*). **3 a** of, or according to, the laws of nature (*a physical impossibility*). **b** belonging to physics (*physical science*). **4** rough; violent. ● *n.* (in full **physical examination**) a medical examination to determine physical fitness. □□ **phys·i·cal·i·ty** /-kálitee/ *n.* **phys·i·cal·ly** *adv.* **phys·i·cal·ness** *n.*

phys·i·cal chem·is·try *n.* the application of physics to the study of chemical behavior.

phys·i·cal ed·u·ca·tion *n.* instruction in physical exercise, sports and games, esp. in schools. ¶ Abbr.: **PE** or **Phys. Ed.**

phys·i·cal ge·og·ra·phy *n.* geography dealing with natural features.

phys·i·cal sci·ence *n.* the sciences used in the study of inanimate natural objects, e.g., physics, chemistry, astronomy, etc.

phys·i·cal ther·a·py *n.* the treatment of disease, injury, deformity, etc., by physical methods including

P

PHOTOSYNTHESIS

Photosynthesis takes place in chloroplasts, the microscopic green organelles inside the cells of green plant tissue, especially leaves. During photosynthesis, a plant uses the energy in sunlight to carry out a chain of chemical reactions. It makes the food substance glucose, which is the energy source for the whole plant, from molecules of carbon dioxide and water. Oxygen is formed as a by-product. Photosynthesis is vital to life on Earth, since all animals are directly or indirectly dependent on plants for food.

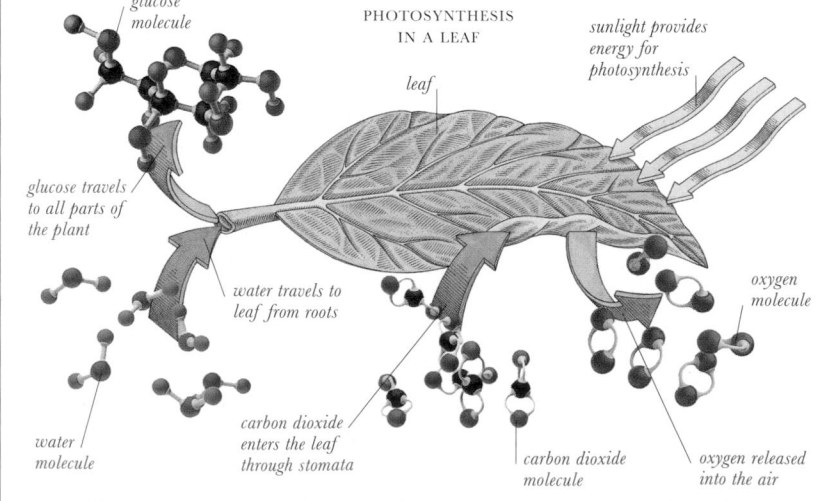

glucose molecule

PHOTOSYNTHESIS
IN A LEAF

sunlight provides energy for photosynthesis

leaf

glucose travels to all parts of the plant

water travels to leaf from roots

oxygen molecule

water molecule

carbon dioxide enters the leaf through stomata

carbon dioxide molecule

oxygen released into the air

manipulation, massage, infrared heat treatment, remedial exercise, etc., not by drugs. □□ **phys·i·cal ther·a·pist** n.

phy·si·cian /fizíshən/ n. **1 a** a person legally qualified to practice medicine and surgery. **b** a specialist in medical diagnosis and treatment. **c** any medical practitioner. **2** a healer (work is the best physician).

phys·i·cist /fízisist/ n. a person skilled or qualified in physics.

physico- /fízikō/ comb. form **1** physical (and). **2** of physics (and).

phys·i·co·chem·i·cal /fízikōkémikəl/ adj. relating to physics and chemistry or to physical chemistry.

phys·ics /fíziks/ n. the science dealing with the properties and interactions of matter and energy.

physio- /fízeeō/ comb. form nature; what is natural.

phys·i·og·no·my /fízeeógnəmee, -ónəmee/ n. (pl. **-ies**) **1 a** the cast or form of a person's features, expression, body, etc. **b** the art of supposedly judging character from facial characteristics, etc. **2** the external features of a landscape, etc. **3** a characteristic, esp. moral, aspect. □□ **phys·i·og·nom·ic** /-ognómik/ adj. **phys·i·og·nom·i·cal** adj. **phys·i·og·nom·i·cal·ly** adv. **phys·i·og·no·mist** n.

phys·i·o·log·i·cal /fízeeəlójikəl/ adj. (also **phys·i·o·log·ic**) of or concerning physiology. □□ **phys·i·o·log·i·cal·ly** adv.

phys·i·ol·o·gy /fízeeóləjee/ n. **1** the science of the functions of living organisms and their parts. **2** these functions. □□ **phys·i·ol·o·gist** n.

phys·i·o·ther·a·py /fízeeōthérəpee/ = PHYSICAL THERAPY.

phy·sique /fizéek/ n. the bodily structure, development, and organization of an individual (an athletic physique).

-phyte /fīt/ comb. form forming nouns denoting a vegetable or plantlike organism (saprophyte; zoophyte). □□ **-phytic** /fítik/ comb. form forming adjectives.

phyto- /fítō/ comb. form denoting a plant.

phy·to·chem·is·try /fítōkémistree/ n. the chemistry of plant products. □□ **phy·to·chem·i·cal** adj. **phy·to·chem·ist** n.

phy·to·chrome /fítəkrōm/ n. Biochem. a blue-green pigment found in many plants, and regulating various developmental processes according to the nature and timing of the light it absorbs.

phy·to·gen·e·sis /fítōjénisis/ n. (also **phy·tog·e·ny** /-tójinee/) the science of the origin or evolution of plants.

phy·to·plank·ton /fítōplángktən/ n. plankton consisting of plants.

phy·to·tox·ic /fítōtóksik/ adj. poisonous to plants.

phy·to·tox·in /fítōtóksin/ n. **1** any toxin derived from a plant. **2** a substance poisonous or injurious to plants, esp. one produced by a parasite.

pi /pī/ n. **1** the sixteenth letter of the Greek alphabet (Π, π). **2** (as π) the symbol of the ratio of the circumference of a circle to its diameter (approx. 3.14159).

pi·a ma·ter /píə máytər, péə/ n. Anat. the delicate innermost membrane enveloping the brain and spinal cord (see MENINX).

pi·a·nism /péeənizəm/ n. **1** the art or technique of piano playing. **2** the skill or style of a composer of piano music. □□ **pi·a·nis·tic** /-nístik/ adj. **pi·a·nis·ti·cal·ly** /-nístiklee/ adv.

pi·a·nis·si·mo /péeənísimō/ adj., adv., & n. Mus. ● adj. performed very softly. ● adv. very softly. ● n. (pl. **-os** or **pianissimi** /-mee/) a passage to be performed very softly.

pi·an·ist /péeənist, pee-án-/ n. the player of a piano.

pi·an·o¹ /peeánō, pyánō/ n. (pl. **-os**) ▼ a large musical instrument played by pressing down keys on a keyboard and causing hammers to strike metal strings, the vibration from which is stopped by dampers when the keys are released. ▷ UPRIGHT

pi·an·o² /pyaánō/ adj., adv., & n. ● adj. **1** Mus. performed softly. **2** subdued. ● adv. **1** Mus. softly. **2** in a subdued manner. ● n. (pl. **-os** or **piani** /-nee/) Mus. a piano passage.

Pi·an·o·la /péeənólə/ n. **1** Trademark a kind of automatic piano; a player piano. **2** (**pianola**) Bridge an easy hand needing no skill. **3** (**pianola**) an easy task.

pi·as·tre /peeástər/ n. (also **pi·as·ter**) a small coin and monetary unit of several Middle Eastern countries.

pi·az·za /pee-aatsə, -saa/ n. **1** a public square or marketplace, esp. in an Italian town. **2** /peeázə, -áazə/ dial. the veranda of a house.

pi·broch /péebrokh, -brawkh/ n. a series of esp. martial or funerary variations on a theme for the bagpipes.

pic /pik/ n. colloq. a picture, esp. a movie.

pi·ca /píkə/ n. Printing **1** a unit of type size (⅙ inch). **2** a size of letters in typewriting (10 per inch).

pi·ca·dor /píkədawr/ n. a mounted man with a lance who goads the bull in a bullfight.

pic·a·resque /píkərésk/ adj. (of a style of fiction) dealing with the episodic adventures of rogues, etc.

pic·a·yune /píkəyōōn/ n. & adj. ● n. **1** colloq. a small coin of little value, esp. a 5-cent piece. **2** an insignificant person or thing. ● adj. **1** of little value; trivial. **2** mean; contemptible; petty (the picayune squabbling of party politicians).

pic·ca·lil·li /píkəlilee/ n. (pl. **piccalillis**) a pickle of chopped vegetables, mustard, and hot spices.

pic·co·lo /píkəlō/ n. & adj. ● n. (pl. **-os**) **1** ▼ a small flute sounding an octave higher than the ordinary one. ▷ ORCHESTRA, WOODWIND. **2** its player. ● adj. (esp. of a musical instrument) smaller or having a higher range than usual (piccolo trumpet).

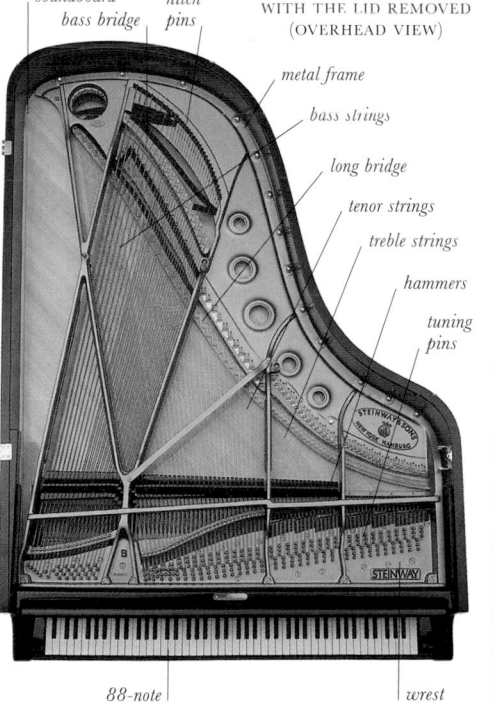

PICCOLO

blow hole
head joint
key
body joint
cylindrical metal tube

pick¹ /pik/ v. & n. ● v.tr. **1** (also absol.) choose carefully from a number of alternatives. **2** detach or pluck (a flower, fruit, etc.) from a stem, tree, etc. **3 a** probe (the teeth, nose, ears, a pimple, etc.) with the finger, an instrument, etc., to remove unwanted matter. **b** clear (a bone, carcass, etc.) of scraps of meat, etc. **4** (also absol.) (of a person) eat (food, a meal, etc.) in small bits; nibble without appetite. **5** (also absol.) pluck the strings of (a banjo, etc.). **6** remove stalks, etc., from (esp. soft fruit) before cooking. **7 a** select (a route or path) carefully over difficult terrain by foot. **b** place (one's steps, etc.) carefully. **8** pull apart. **9** (of a bird) take up (grains, etc.) in the beak. **10** open (a lock) with an instrument other than the proper key. ● n. **1** the act or an instance of picking. **2 a** a selection or choice. **b** the right to select (had first pick of the prizes). **3** (usu. foll. by of) the best (the pick of the bunch). □ **pick and choose** select carefully or fastidiously. **pick at 1** eat (food) without interest; nibble. **2** = pick on 1 (PICK¹). **pick a person's brains** extract ideas, information, etc., from a person for one's own use. **pick holes** (or **a hole**) **in 1** make holes in (material, etc.) by plucking, poking, etc. **2** find fault with (an idea, etc.). **pick off 1** pluck (leaves, etc.) off. **2** shoot (people, etc.) one by one without haste. **3** eliminate (opposition, etc.) singly. **4** Baseball put out a base runner caught off base. **pick on 1** find fault with; nag at. **2** select, as for special attention. **pick out 1** take from a larger number (picked him out from the others). **2** distinguish from surrounding objects or at a distance (can just pick out the church spire). **3** play (a tune) by ear on the piano, etc. **pick over** select the best from. **pick a quarrel** (or **fight**) start an argument or a fight deliberately. **pick up 1 a** grasp and raise (from the ground, etc.) (picked up his hat). **b** clean up; straighten up. **2** gain or acquire by chance or without effort (picked up a cold). **3 a** fetch (a person, animal, or thing) left in another person's charge. **b** stop for and take along with one, esp. in a vehicle (pick me up on the corner). **4** make the acquaintance of (a person)

P

PIANO

A piano frame is either vertical – as in the upright piano – or horizontal – as in the grand piano (shown here). Metal strings are stretched over the frame under great tension. Pressing a key makes a felt-tipped hammer strike a string, which vibrates. This causes the soundboard underneath the strings to resonate, making the piano's distinctive sound.

CONCERT GRAND PIANO (FRONT VIEW)

lid
wooden case
una corda (soft) pedal
sostenuto pedal
damper pedal

CONCERT GRAND PIANO WITH THE LID REMOVED (OVERHEAD VIEW)

soundboard
bass bridge
hitch pins
metal frame
bass strings
long bridge
tenor strings
treble strings
hammers
tuning pins
88-note keyboard
wrest plank

P

casually, esp. as a sexual overture. **5** (of one's health, the weather, stock prices, etc.) recover; prosper; improve. **6** (of an engine, etc.) recover speed; accelerate. **7** (of the police, etc.) take into custody; arrest. **8** detect by scrutiny or with a telescope, searchlight, radio, etc. (*picked up most of the mistakes*; *picked up a distress signal*). **9** (often foll. by *with*) form or renew a friendship. **10** accept the responsibility of paying (a bill, etc.). **11** (*refl.*) raise (oneself, etc.) after a fall, etc. **12** raise (the feet, etc.) clear of the ground. **take one's pick** make a choice. □□ **pick·a·ble** *adj.*

pick² /pik/ *n. & v.* ● *n.* **1** a long-handled tool having a usu. curved iron bar pointed at one or both ends, used for breaking up hard ground, masonry, etc. **2** *colloq.* a plectrum. **3** any instrument for picking, such as a toothpick. ● *v.tr.* **1** break the surface of (the ground, etc.) with or as if with a pick. **2** make (holes, etc.) in this way.

pick·a·back var. of PIGGYBACK.

pick·ax /píkaks/ *n. & v.* (also **pick·axe**) ● *n.* = PICK² *n.* 1. ● *v.* **1** *tr.* break (the ground, etc.) with a pickaxe. **2** *intr.* work with a pickax.

pick·er /píkər/ *n.* **1** a person or thing that picks. **2** (often in *comb.*) a person who gathers or collects (*grape-picker*; *rag-picker*).

pick·er·el /píkərəl/ *n.* (*pl.* same or **pickerels**) **1** any of various species of N. American pike of the genus *Esox.* **2** = WALLEYE.

pick·et /píkit/ *n. & v.* ● *n.* **1** a person or group of people outside a place of work, intending to persuade esp. workers not to enter during a strike, etc. **2** a pointed stake or peg driven into the ground to form a fence or palisade, to tether a horse, etc. **3** (also **pic·quet, pi·quet**) *Mil.* **a** a small body of troops or a single soldier sent out to watch for the enemy, held in readiness, etc. **b** a party of sentries. **c** an outpost. **d** a camp guard on police duty in a garrison town, etc. ● *v.* (**picketed, picketing**) **1 a** *tr. & intr.* station or act as a picket. **b** *tr.* beset or guard (a factory, workers, etc.) with a picket or pickets. **2** *tr.* secure with stakes. **3** *tr.* tether (an animal). □□ **pick·et·er** *n.*

pick·et line *n.* a boundary established by workers on strike, esp. at the entrance to the place of work, which others are asked not to cross.

pick·ings /píkingz/ *n.pl.* **1** perquisites; pilferings (*rich pickings*). **2** remaining scraps; gleanings.

pick·le /píkəl/ *n. & v.* ● *n.* **1 a** (often in *pl.*) vegetables, esp. cucumbers, preserved in brine, vinegar, mustard, etc., and used as a relish. **b** the brine, vinegar, etc., in which food is preserved. **2** *colloq.* a plight (*a fine pickle we are in!*). **3** *Brit. colloq.* a mischievous child. **4** an acid solution for cleaning metal, etc. ● *v.tr.* **1** preserve in pickle. **2** treat with pickle. **3** (as **pickled** *adj.*) *sl.* drunk.

pick·ler /píklər/ *n.* **1** a person who pickles vegetables, etc. **2** a vegetable suitable for pickling.

pick·lock /píklok/ *n.* **1** a person who picks locks. **2** an instrument for this.

pick·me-up *n.* **1** a restorative tonic, as for the nerves, etc. **2** a good experience, good news, etc., that cheers.

pick·pock·et /píkpokit/ *n.* a person who steals from the pockets of others.

pick·up /píkəp/ *n.* **1** *sl.* a person met casually, esp. for sexual purposes. **2** a small truck with an enclosed cab and open back. **3 a** the part of a record player carrying the stylus. **b** ▶ a device on a musical instrument which converts sound vibrations into electrical signals for amplification. **4 a** the act of picking up. **b** something picked up. **5** the capacity for acceleration. **6** = PICK-ME-UP.

pickups

pick·y /píkee/ *adj.* (**pickier, pickiest**) *colloq.* excessively fastidious; choosy. □□ **pick·i·ness** *n.*

pick-your-own *adj.* (usu. *attrib.*) (of commercially grown fruit and vegetables) dug or picked by the customer at the place of production.

pic·nic /píknik/ *n. & v.* ● *n.* **1** an outing or excursion including a packed meal eaten out of doors. **2** any meal eaten out of doors or without preparation, tables, chairs, etc. **3** (usu. with *neg.*) *colloq.* something agreeable or easily accomplished, etc. (*it was no picnic organizing the meeting*). ● *v.intr.* (**picnicked, picnicking**) take part in a picnic. □□ **pic·nick·er** *n.* **pic·nick·y** *adj. colloq.*

pico- /péekō, píkō/ *comb. form* denoting a factor of 10^{-12} (*picometer*).

pi·cot /peékō/ *n.* ▼ a small loop of twisted thread in a lace edging etc.

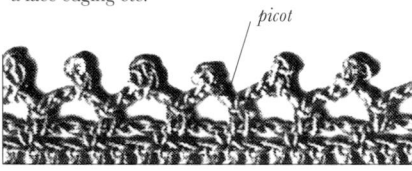

picot

PICOT

pic·o·tee /píkətee/ *n.* a type of carnation whose flowers have light petals with darker edges.

pic·quet var. of PICKET 3.

pic·to·graph /píktəgraf/ *n.* (also **pic·to·gram** /píktəgram/) **1 a** ▼ a pictorial symbol for a word or phrase. **b** an ancient record consisting of these. **2** a pictorial representation of statistics, etc., on a chart, graph, etc. □□ **pic·to·graph·ic** *adj.* **pic·tog·ra·phy** /-tógrəfee/ *n.*

HOUSE   PLATE   CHILD

NO   TO GIVE   TO GO

PICTOGRAPHS FROM CAMEROON *c.*1900

pic·to·ri·al /piktáwreeəl/ *adj. & n.* ● *adj.* **1** of or expressed in a picture or pictures. **2** illustrated. **3** picturesque. ● *n.* a journal, postage stamp, etc., with a picture or pictures as the main feature. □□ **pic·to·ri·al·ly** *adv.*

pic·ture /píkchər/ *n. & v.* ● *n.* **1 a** (often *attrib.*) a painting, drawing, photograph, etc., esp. as a work of art (*picture frame*). **b** a portrait, esp. a photograph, of a person. **c** a beautiful object (*her hat is a picture*). **2 a** a total visual or mental impression produced; a scene (*the picture looks bleak*). **b** a written or spoken description (*drew a vivid picture of moral decay*). **3 a** a movie. **b** (in *pl.*) a showing of movies at a movie theater (*went to the pictures*). **c** (in *pl.*) movies in general. **4** an image on a television screen. **5** *colloq.* **a** esp. *iron.* a person or thing exemplifying something (*he was the picture of innocence*). **b** a person or thing resembling another closely (*the picture of her aunt*). ● *v.tr.* **1** represent in a picture. **2** (also *refl.*; often foll. by *to*) imagine, esp. visually or vividly (*pictured it to herself*). **3** describe graphically. □ **get the picture** *colloq.* grasp the tendency or drift of circumstances, information, etc.

pic·tur·esque /píkchərésk/ *adj.* **1** (of landscape, etc.) beautiful or striking, as in a picture. **2** (of language, etc.) strikingly

graphic; vivid. □□ **pic·tur·esque·ly** *adv.* **pic·tur·esque·ness** *n.*

pic·ture tube *n.* the cathode-ray tube of a television set.

pic·ture win·dow *n.* a very large window consisting of one pane of glass.

pid·dle /píd'l/ *v. & n.* ● *v.intr.* **1** *colloq.* urinate (used esp. to or by children). **2** work or act in a trifling way. **3** (as **piddling** *adj.*) *colloq.* trivial; trifling. ● *n.* *colloq.* **1** urination. **2** urine (used esp. to or by children). □□ **pid·dler** *n.*

pidg·in /píjin/ *n.* a simplified language containing vocabulary from two or more languages, used for communication between people not having a common language.

pidg·in Eng·lish *n.* a pidgin in which the chief language is English, used orig. between Chinese and Europeans.

pie¹ /pī/ *n.* **1** a baked dish of fruit, meat, custard, etc., usu. with a top and base of pastry. **2** anything resembling a pie in form (*a mud pie*).

pie² /pī/ var. of PI.

pie·bald /píbawld/ *adj. & n.* ● *adj.* **1** (usu. of an animal, esp. a horse) having irregular patches of two colors, esp. black and white. **2** motley; mongrel. ● *n.* a piebald animal, esp. a horse.

piece /pees/ *n. & v.* ● *n.* **1 a** (often foll. by *of*) one of the distinct portions forming part of or broken off from a larger object; a bit; a part (*a piece of string*). **b** each of the parts of which a set or category is composed (*a five-piece band*; *a piece of furniture*). **2** a coin of specified value (*50-cent piece*). **3 a** a usu. short literary or musical composition or a picture. **b** a theatrical play. **4** an item, instance, or example (*a piece of news*). **5 a** any of the objects used to make moves in board games. **b** a chessman (strictly, other than a pawn). **6** a definite quantity in which a thing is sold. **7** (often foll. by *of*) an enclosed portion (of land, etc.). **8** *sl. derog.* a woman. **9** (foll. by *of*) *sl.* a financial share or investment in (*has a piece of the new production*). **10** *colloq.* a short distance. **11** *sl.* = PISTOL. ● *v.tr.* **1** (usu. foll. by *together*) form into a whole; put together; join (*finally pieced his story together*). **2** (usu. foll. by *out*) **a** eke out. **b** form (a theory, etc.) by combining parts, etc. **3** (usu. foll. by *up*) patch. **4** join (threads) in spinning. □ **break to pieces** break into fragments. **go to pieces** collapse emotionally; suffer a breakdown. **in one piece 1** unbroken. **2** unharmed. **in pieces** broken. **of a piece** (often foll. by *with*) uniform; consistent; in keeping. **a piece of the action** *sl.* a share of the profits; a share in the excitement. **a piece of one's mind** a sharp rebuke or lecture. **say one's piece** give one's opinion or make a prepared statement. **take to pieces 1** break up or dismantle. **2** criticize harshly. □□ **piec·er** *n.* (in sense 4 of *v.*).

piè·ce de ré·sis·tance /pyés də rayzéestons/ *n.* (*pl.* **pièces de résistance** *pronunc.* same) **1** the most important or remarkable item. **2** the most substantial dish at a meal.

piece·meal /peésmeel/ *adv. & adj.* ● *adv.* piece by piece; gradually. ● *adj.* partial; gradual; unsystematic.

piece of eight *n. hist.* a Spanish dollar, equivalent to 8 reals.

piece·work *n.* work paid for by the amount produced.

pie chart *n.* ▼ a circle divided into sections to represent relative quantities.

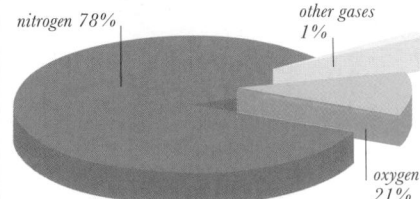

nitrogen 78%

other gases 1%

oxygen 21%

PIE CHART SHOWING THE RELATIVE CONSTITUENTS OF THE EARTH'S ATMOSPHERE

pie·crust /píkrust/ *n.* the baked pastry crust of a pie.

pied /pīd/ *adj.* particolored.

pied-à-terre /pyáydaatáir/ *n.* (*pl.* **pieds-à-terre** *pronunc.* same) a usu. small apartment, house, etc., kept for occasional use.

pied·mont /peédmont/ *n.* a gentle slope leading from the foot of mountains to a region of flat land.

Pied Pip·er *n.* a person enticing followers, esp. to their doom.

pier /peer/ *n.* **1 a** a structure of iron or wood raised on piles and leading out to sea, a lake, etc., used as a promenade and landing place. **b** a breakwater; a mole. **2 a** a support of an arch or of the span of a bridge; a pillar. **b** solid masonry between windows, etc.

pierce /peers/ *v.* **1** *tr.* **a** (of a sharp instrument, etc.) penetrate the surface of. **b** (often foll. by *with*) prick with a sharp instrument, esp. to make a hole in. **c** make (a hole, etc.) (*pierced a hole in the belt*). **d** (of cold, grief, etc.) affect keenly or sharply. **e** (of a light, glance, sound, etc.) penetrate keenly or sharply. **2** (as **piercing** *adj.*) (of a glance, intuition, high noise, bright light, etc.) keen, sharp, or unpleasantly penetrating. **3** *tr.* force (a way, etc.) through or into (something) (*pierced their way through the jungle*). **4** *intr.* (usu. foll. by *through, into*) penetrate. □□ **pierc·er** *n.* **pierc·ing·ly** *adv.*

pie·ro·gi /pərógee, pee-/ *n.* (also **pi·ro·gi**) (*pl.* **-gi** or **-gies**) small pastry envelopes filled with mashed potatoes, cabbage, or chopped meat.

pi·et·à /pyetaá/ *n.* a picture or sculpture of the Virgin Mary holding the dead body of Christ on her lap or in her arms.

pi·e·tism /píətizəm/ *n.* **1** pious sentiment. **2** an exaggerated or affected piety. □□ **pi·e·tist** *n.* **pi·e·tis·tic** *adj.* **pi·e·tis·ti·cal** *adj.*

pi·e·ty /pí-itee/ *n.* (*pl.* **-ies**) **1** the quality of being pious. **2** a pious act.

pi·e·zo·e·lec·tric·i·ty /pī-éezōilektrísitee, pee-áyzō-/ *n.* electric polarization in a substance resulting from the application of mechanical stress, esp. in certain crystals. □□ **pi·e·zo·e·lec·tric** /-iléktrik/ *adj.* **pi·e·zo·e·lec·tri·cal·ly** *adv.*

pif·fle /pífəl/ *n.* & *v. colloq.* ● *n.* nonsense; empty speech. ● *v.intr.* talk or act feebly; trifle. □□ **pif·fler** *n.*

pif·fling /pífling/ *adj. colloq.* trivial; worthless.

pig /pig/ *n.* & *v.* ● *n.* **1 a** any omnivorous hoofed bristly mammal of the family Suidae, esp. a domesticated kind, *Sus scrofa*. ▷ UNGULATE. **b** a young pig; a piglet. **c** (often in *comb.*) any similar animal (*guinea pig*). **2** the flesh of esp. a young or suckling pig as food (*roast pig*). **3** *colloq.* **a** a greedy, dirty, obstinate, sulky, or annoying person. **b** a person who eats too much or too fast. **c** an unpleasant, awkward, or difficult thing, task, etc. **4** an oblong mass of metal (esp. iron or lead) from a smelting furnace. **5** *sl. derog.* a policeman. **6** *sl. derog.* a sexist or racist person. ● *v.* (**pigged**, **pigging**) *tr.* **1** (also *absol.*) (of a sow) bring forth (piglets). **2** *colloq.* eat (food) greedily. □ **buy a pig in a poke** buy, accept, etc., something without knowing its value or esp. seeing it. **in a pig's eye** *colloq.* certainly not. **make a pig of oneself** overeat. **pig it** live in a disorderly, untidy, or filthy fashion. **pig out** (often foll. by *on*) *sl.* eat gluttonously. □□ **pig·gish** *adj.* **pig·gish·ly** *adv.* **pig·gish·ness** *n.* **pig·let** *n.* **pig·like** *adj.* **pig·ling** *n.*

pi·geon[1] /píjin/ *n.* **1** any of several large usu. gray and white birds of the family Columbidae, esp. *Columba livia*, often domesticated and bred and trained to carry messages, etc.; a dove (cf. ROCK PIGEON). **2** a person easily swindled; a simpleton. □□ **pi·geon·ry** *n.* (*pl.* **-ies**).

pi·geon[2] /píjin/ *n.* **1** = PIDGIN. **2** *colloq.* a particular concern, job, or business (*that's not my pigeon*).

pi·geon·hole /píjinhōl/ *n.* & *v.* ● *n.* **1** each of a set of compartments in a cabinet or on a wall for papers, letters, etc. **2** a small recess for a pigeon to nest in. ● *v.tr.* **1** deposit (a document) in a pigeonhole. **2** put (a matter) aside for future consideration or to forget it. **3** assign (a person or thing) to a preconceived category.

pi·geon-toed *adj.* (of a person) having the toes turned inward.

pig·ger·y /pígəree/ *n.* (*pl.* **-ies**) **1** a pig-breeding farm, etc. **2** = PIGSTY. **3** piggishness.

pig·gy /pígee/ *n.* & *adj.* ● *n.* (also **pig·gie**) *colloq.* a child's word for a pig or a piglet. ● *adj.* (**piggier**, **piggiest**) **1** like a pig. **2** (of features, etc.) like those of a pig (*little piggy eyes*).

pig·gy·back /pígeebak/ *n.* & *adv.* (also **pick·a·back** /píkəbak/) ● *n.* a ride on the back and shoulders of another person. ● *adv.* **1** on the back and shoulders of another person. **2 a** on the back or top of a larger object. **b** in addition to; along with.

pig·gy bank *n.* a pig-shaped box for coins.

pig·head·ed /píghédid/ *adj.* obstinate. □□ **pig·head·ed·ly** *adv.* **pig·head·ed·ness** *n.*

pig i·ron *n.* crude iron from a smelting furnace.

pig Lat·in *n.* a jargon based on alternation of English sounds (e.g., "igpay atinlay" for *pig Latin*).

pig·ment /pígmənt/ *n.* & *v.* ● *n.* **1** coloring matter used as paint or dye, usu. as an insoluble suspension ▷ FRESCO. **2** the natural coloring matter of animal or plant tissue, e.g., chlorophyll, hemoglobin. ● *v.tr.* color with or as if with pigment. □□ **pig·men·tar·y** /-mənteree/ *adj.* **pig·men·ta·tion** /-táyshən/ *n.*

pig·my var. of PYGMY.

pig·pen /pígpen/ *n.* = PIGSTY.

pig·skin /pigskin/ *n.* **1** the hide of a pig. **2** leather made from this. **3** a football.

pig·sty /pígstī/ *n.* (*pl.* **-ies**) **1** a pen or enclosure for a pig or pigs. **2** a filthy house, room, etc.

pig·tail /pígtayl/ *n.* **1** a braid or gathered hank of hair hanging from the back of the head, or either of a pair at the sides. **2** a thin twist of tobacco. □□ **pig·tailed** *adj.*

pig·weed /pígweed/ *n.* **1** any herb of the genus *Amaranthus*, grown for grain or fodder. **2** a herbaceous weed, *Chenopodium alba*, with mealy edible leaves.

pike[1] /pīk/ *n.* (*pl.* same) ▼ a large voracious freshwater fish, *Esox lucius*, with a long narrow snout and sharp teeth.

PIKE (*Esox lucius*)

pike[2] /pīk/ *n. hist.* an infantry weapon with a pointed steel or iron head on a long wooden shaft.

pike[3] /pīk/ *n.* a turnpike. □ **come down the pike** *colloq.* appear; occur.

pike[4] /pīk/ *n.* a jackknife position in diving or gymnastics.

pik·er /píkər/ *n.* a cautious, timid, or cheap person.

pike·staff /píkstaf/ *n.* **1** the wooden shaft of a pike. **2** a walking stick with a metal point. □ **plain as a pikestaff** quite plain or obvious (orig. *packstaff*, a smooth staff used by a peddler).

pi·laf /pilaáf, peélaaf/ *n.* (also **pi·laff**; **pi·law**, **pi·lau** /-láw, -lów/) a dish of spiced rice or wheat with meat, fish, vegetables, etc.

pi·las·ter /pilástər/ *n.* a rectangular column, esp. one projecting from a wall. ▷ FAÇADE. □□ **pi·las·tered** *adj.*

Pi·la·tes /piláateez/ *n.* a system of exercises using special apparatus, designed to improve physical strength, flexibility, and posture, and enhance mental awareness.

pil·chard /pílchərd/ *n.* a small marine fish, *Sardinia pilchardus*, of the herring family (see SARDINE).

pile[1] /pīl/ *n.* & *v.* ● *n.* **1** a heap of things laid or gathered upon one another (*a pile of leaves*). **2 a** a large imposing building (*a stately pile*). **b** a large group of tall buildings. **3** *colloq.* **a** a large quantity. **b** a large amount of money; a fortune (*made his pile*). **4 a** a series of plates of dissimilar metals laid one on another alternately to produce an electric current. **b** a nuclear reactor. Also called **atomic pile**. **5** a funeral pyre. ● *v.* **1** *tr.* **a** (often foll. by *up*, *on*) heap up (*piled the plates on the table*). **b** (foll. by *with*) load (*piled the bed with coats*). **2** *intr.* (usu. foll. by *in*, *into*, *on*, *out of*, etc.) crowd hurriedly or tightly. □ **pile it on** *colloq.* exaggerate. **pile up 1** accumulate; heap up. **2** *colloq.* run (a ship) aground or cause (a vehicle, etc.) to crash.

pile[2] /pīl/ *n.* & *v.* ● *n.* **1** a heavy beam driven vertically into the bed of a river, soft ground, etc., to support the foundations of a superstructure. ▷ OIL PLATFORM. **2** a pointed stake or post. ● *v.tr.* **1** provide with piles. **2** drive (piles) into the ground, etc.

pile[3] /pīl/ *n.* the soft projecting surface on velvet, plush, etc., or esp. on a carpet; nap.

pi·le·at·ed wood·peck·er /pílee-aytid/ *n.* a black-and-white N. American woodpecker, *Dryocopus pileatus*, with a red crest.

pile driv·er *n.* a machine for driving piles into the ground.

piles /pīlz/ *n.pl. colloq.* hemorrhoids.

pile·up /pīlup/ *n.* **1** a collision of (esp. several) motor vehicles. **2** any mass or pile resulting from accumulation.

pil·fer /pílfər/ *v.tr.* (also *absol.*) steal (objects) esp. in small quantities. □□ **pil·fer·age** /-fərij/ *n.* **pil·fer·er** *n.*

pil·grim /pílgrim/ *n.* **1** a person who journeys to a sacred place for religious reasons. **2** a person regarded as journeying through life, etc. **3** a traveler.

pil·grim·age /pílgrimij/ *n.* & *v.* ● *n.* **1** a pilgrim's journey (*go on a pilgrimage*). **2** life viewed as a journey. **3** any journey taken for nostalgic or sentimental reasons. ● *v.intr.* go on a pilgrimage.

Pil·grim Fa·thers *n.pl.* English Puritans who founded the colony of Plymouth, Massachusetts, in 1620.

Pil·i·pi·no /pilipeénō/ *n.* the national language of the Philippines.

pill /pil/ *n.* **1 a** solid medicine formed into a ball or a flat disk for swallowing whole. ▷ MEDICINE. **b** (usu. prec. by *the*) *colloq.* a contraceptive pill. **2** an unpleasant or painful necessity; a humiliation (*a bitter pill*; *must swallow the pill*). **3** *colloq.* or *joc.* a ball. **4** *sl.* a difficult or unpleasant person. □ **sweeten** (or **sugar**) **the pill** make an unpleasant necessity acceptable.

pil·lage /pílij/ *v.* & *n.* ● *v.tr.* (also *absol.*) plunder; sack (a place or a person). ● *n.* the act or an instance of pillaging, esp. in war. □□ **pil·lag·er** *n.*

pil·lar /pílər/ *n.* **1 a** a usu. slender vertical structure of wood, metal, or esp. stone used as a support for a roof, etc. **b** a similar structure used for ornament. **c** a post supporting a structure. **2** a person regarded as a mainstay or support (*a pillar of the faith*). **3** an upright mass of air, water, rock, etc. □ **from pillar to post** (driven, etc.) from one place to another; to and fro. □□ **pil·lared** *adj.* **pil·lar·et** *n.*

pill·box /pílboks/ *n.* **1** a small shallow cylindrical box for holding pills. **2** a hat of a similar shape. **3** *Mil.* a small partly underground enclosed concrete fort used as an outpost.

pil·lo·ry /píləree/ *n.* & *v.* ● *n.* (*pl.* **-ies**) *hist.* a wooden framework with holes for the head and hands, enabling the public to assault or ridicule a person so imprisoned. ● *v.tr.* (**-ies**, **-ied**) **1** expose (a person) to ridicule or public contempt. **2** *hist.* put in the pillory.

pil·low /pílō/ *n.* & *v.* ● *n.* **1** a usu. oblong support for the head, esp. in bed, with a cloth cover stuffed with feathers, down, foam rubber, etc. **2** any pillow-shaped block or support. ● *v.tr.* **1** rest (the

head, etc.) on or as if on a pillow (*pillowed his head on his arms*). **2** serve as a pillow for (*moss pillowed her head*). □□ **pil·low·y** *adj.*

pil·low·case /píllōkays/ *n.* a washable cotton, etc., cover for a pillow.

pil·low fight *n.* a mock fight with pillows, esp. by children.

pil·low·slip /píllōslip/ *n.* = PILLOWCASE.

pil·low talk *n.* romantic or intimate conversation in bed.

pill pop·per *n. colloq.* a person who takes pills freely; a drug addict.

pil·lule var. of PILULE.

pi·lot /pílət/ *n. & v.* ● *n.* **1** a person who operates the flying controls of an aircraft. **2** a person qualified to take charge of a ship entering or leaving a harbor. **3** (usu. *attrib.*) an experimental undertaking or test, esp. in advance of a larger one (*a pilot project*). **4** a guide; a leader. **5** = PILOT LIGHT. ● *v.tr.* (**piloted, piloting**) **1** act as a pilot on (a ship) or of (an aircraft). **2** conduct, lead, or initiate as a pilot (*piloted the new scheme*). □□ **pi·lot·age** *n.* **pi·lot·less** *adj.*

pi·lot fish *n.* a small fish, *Naucrates ductor*, said to act as a pilot leading a shark to food.

pi·lot·house /pílət-hows/ *n.* ▼ an enclosed area on a vessel for the helmsman, etc. ▷ FACTORY SHIP

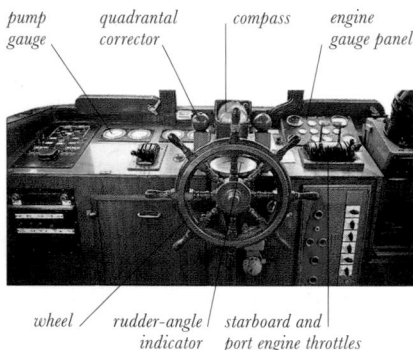

pump gauge / quadrantal corrector / compass / engine gauge panel

wheel / rudder-angle indicator / starboard and port engine throttles

PILOTHOUSE OF FIRE-FIGHTING BOAT

P

pi·lot light *n.* **1** a small gas burner kept alight to light another. **2** an electric indicator light or control light.

Pil·sner /pílznər, píls-/ *n.* (also **Pil·sen·er**) **1** a lager beer brewed or like that brewed at Pilsen (Plzeň) in the Czech Republic. **2** (usu. **pil·sner**) a tall tapered glass used for serving beer, etc.

pil·ule /pílyōōl/ *n.* (also **pil·lule**) a small pill. □□ **pil·u·lar** /-yələr/ **pil·u·lous** *adj.*

Pi·ma /péemə/ *n.* **1 a** a N. American people native to southern Arizona and adjoining parts of Mexico. **b** a member of this people. **2** the language of this people. □□ **Pi·man** *adj.*

pi·men·to /piméntō/ *n.* (*pl.* **-os**) **1** a small tropical tree, *Pimenta dioica*, native to Jamaica. **2** the unripe dried berries of this, usu. crushed for culinary use. Also called **allspice**. **3** = PIMIENTO.

pi·mien·to /piméntō, pímyéntō/ *n.* (*pl.* **-os**) **1** = SWEET PEPPER. **2** a sweet red pepper used as a garnish, esp. in olives.

pimp /pimp/ *n. & v.* ● *n.* a man who lives off the earnings of a prostitute or a brothel; a pander. ● *v.intr.* act as a pimp.

pim·per·nel /pímpərnel/ *n.* ▶ any plant of the genus *Anagallis*.

PIMPERNEL: BLUE PIMPERNEL (*Anagallis foemina*)

pimp·ing /pímping/ *adj.* **1** small or insignificant. **2** esp. *dial.* sickly.

pim·ple /pímpəl/ *n.* **1** a small hard inflamed spot on the skin. **2** anything resembling a pimple, esp. in relative size. □□ **pim·pled** *adj.* **pim·ply** *adj.*

PIN /pin/ *n.* personal identification number (as issued by a bank, etc., to validate electronic transactions).

pin /pin/ *n. & v.* ● *n.* **1 a** a small thin pointed piece of esp. steel wire with a round or flattened head used (esp. in sewing) for holding things in place, attaching one thing to another, etc. **b** any of several types of pin (*safety pin; hairpin*). **c** a small brooch (*diamond pin*). **d** a badge fastened with a pin. **2** a peg of wood or metal for various purposes, e.g., one of the slender rods making up part of an electrical connector. **3** something of small value (*don't care a pin*). **4** (in *pl.*) *colloq.* legs (*quick on his pins*). **5** *Med.* a steel rod used to join the ends of fractured bones while they heal. **6** *Chess* a position in which a piece is pinned to another. **7** *Golf* a stick with a flag placed in a hole to mark its position. ● *v.tr.* (**pinned, pinning**) **1 a** (often foll. by *to, up, together*) fasten with a pin or pins. **b** transfix with a pin, lance, etc. **2** (usu. foll. by *on*) fix (blame, responsibility, etc.) on a person, etc. **3** (often foll. by *against, on*, etc.) seize and hold fast. **4** *US* show affection for a woman by giving her a fraternity pin. □ **on pins and needles** in an agitated state of suspense. **pin down 1** (often foll. by *to*) bind (a person, etc.) to a promise, arrangement, etc. **2** force (a person) to declare his or her intentions. **3** restrict the actions or movement of (an enemy, etc.). **4** specify (a thing) precisely (*could not pin down his reason for leaving*). **5** hold (a person, etc.) down by force. **pin one's faith** (or **hopes**, etc.) **on** rely implicitly on.

pi·na co·la·da /péenə kəláədə/ *n.* (also **piña colada** /péenyə/) a drink made from pineapple juice, rum, and cream of coconut.

pin·a·fore /pínəfawr/ *n.* **1 a** *Brit.* an apron, esp. with a bib. **b** a woman's sleeveless, wraparound, washable covering for the clothes, tied at the back. **2** (in full **pinafore dress**) a collarless sleeveless dress worn over a blouse or sweater.

pi·ña·ta /peenyáátə/ *n.* a decorated container, often of papier mâché, filled with toys, candy, etc., that is used in a game in which it is suspended at a height and attempts are made to break it open with a stick while blindfolded.

pin·ball /pínbawl/ *n.* a game in which small metal balls are shot across a board and score points by striking pins with lights, etc.

pince-nez /pánsnáy, píns-/ *n.* (*pl.* same) a pair of eyeglasses with a nose-clip instead of earpieces.

pin·cers /pínsərz/ *n.pl.* **1** (also **pair of pin·cers**) a gripping tool resembling scissors but with blunt usu. concave jaws to hold a nail, etc., for extraction. **2** the front claws of lobsters and some other crustaceans.

pinch /pinch/ *v. & n.* ● *v.* **1** *tr.* **a** grip (esp. the skin of part of the body or of another person) tightly, esp. between finger and thumb. **b** (often *absol.*) (of a shoe, garment, etc.) constrict (the flesh) painfully. **2** *tr.* (of cold, hunger, etc.) grip (a person) painfully (*her face was pinched with cold*). **3** *tr. sl.* **a** steal; take without permission. **b** arrest (a person). **4** (as **pinched** *adj.*) (of the features) drawn, as with cold, hunger, worry, etc. **5 a** *tr.* (usu. foll. by *in, of, for*, etc.) stint (a person). **b** *intr.* be niggardly with money, food, etc. **6** *tr.* (usu. foll. by *out, back, down*) *Hort.* remove (leaves, buds, etc.) to encourage bushy growth. ● *n.* **1** the act or an instance of pinching, etc., the flesh. **2** an amount that can be taken up with fingers and thumb (*a pinch of snuff*). **3** the stress or pain caused by poverty, cold, hunger, etc. **4** *sl.* **a** an arrest. **b** a theft. □ **at** (or **in**) **a pinch** in an emergency; if necessary. **feel the pinch** experience the effects of poverty.

pinch·beck /pínchbek/ *n. & adj.* ● *n.* an alloy of copper and zinc resembling gold and used in cheap jewelry, etc. ● *adj.* **1** counterfeit; sham. **2** cheap; tawdry.

pinch-hit *v.intr.* **1** *Baseball* bat instead of another player. **2** fill in as a substitute, esp. at the last minute. □□ **pinch hit·ter** *n.*

pinch·pen·ny /pínchpenee/ *n.* (*pl.* **-ies**) (also *attrib.*) a miserly person.

pin·cush·ion /pínkŏŏshən/ *n.* a small cushion for holding pins.

pine[1] /pīn/ *n.* **1** ◀ any evergreen tree of the genus *Pinus* native to northern temperate regions, with needle-shaped leaves growing in clusters. **2** the soft timber of this. **3** (*attrib.*) made of pine. □□ **pin·er·y** *n.* (*pl.* **-ies**).

pine[2] /pīn/ *v.intr.* **1** (often foll. by *away*) decline or waste away, esp. from grief, disease, etc. **2** (usu. foll. by *for, after*, or *to* + infin.) long eagerly; yearn.

pin·e·al gland *n.* (also **pin·e·al bod·y**) a pea-sized conical mass of tissue behind the third ventricle of the brain, secreting a hormonelike substance in some mammals. ▷ ENDOCRINE

PINE: HIMALAYAN PINE (*Pinus wallichiana*)

pine·ap·ple /pínapəl/ *n.* **1** a tropical plant, *Ananas comosus*, with a spiral of sword-shaped leaves and a thick stem bearing a large fruit developed from many flowers. **2** the fruit of this, consisting of yellow flesh surrounded by a tough segmented skin and topped with a tuft of stiff leaves.

pine cone *n.* the cone-shaped fruit of the pine tree.

pine mar·ten *n.* ▶ a weasellike mammal, *Martes martes*, native to Europe and America, with a dark brown coat and white throat and stomach.

pine nut *n.* the edible seed of various pine trees.

pine·y var. of PINY.

pin·fold /pínfōld/ *n. & v.* ● *n.* **1** a pound for stray cattle, etc. **2** any place of confinement. ● *v.tr.* confine (cattle) in a pinfold.

ping /ping/ *n.* a single short high ringing sound.

ping·er /pínggər/ *n.* **1** a device that transmits pings at short intervals for purposes of detection or measurement, etc. **2** a device to ring a bell.

PINE MARTEN (*Martes martes*)

Ping-Pong /pingpong/ *n. Trademark* = TABLE TENNIS.

pin·head /pínhed/ *n.* **1** the flattened head of a pin. **2** a very small thing. **3** *colloq.* a stupid or foolish person.

pin·head·ed /pínhédid/ *adj. colloq.* stupid; foolish. □□ **pin·head·ed·ness** *n.*

pin·hole /pínhōl/ *n.* **1** a hole made by a pin. **2** a hole into which a peg fits.

pin·hole cam·er·a *n.* a camera with a pinhole aperture and no lens.

pin·ion[1] /pínyən/ *n. & v.* ● *n.* **1** the outer part of a bird's wing, usu. including the flight feathers. **2** *poet.* a wing; a flight feather. ● *v.tr.* **1** cut off the pinion of (a wing or bird) to prevent flight. **2 a** bind the arms of (a person). **b** (often foll. by *to*) bind (the arms, a person, etc.) esp. to a thing.

pin·ion[2] /pínyən/ *n.* **1** a small toothed gear engaging with a larger one. ▷ RACK-AND-PINION, RACK RAILWAY. **2** a toothed spindle engaging with a wheel.

PINK
(*Dianthus* 'Dad's Favorite')

pink[1] /pingk/ *n. & adj.* ● *n.* **1** a pale red color (*decorated in pink*). **2 a** ◄ any cultivated plant of the genus *Dianthus*, with sweet-smelling crimson, pink, white, etc., flowers. **b** the flower of this plant. **3** (prec. by *the*) the most perfect condition, etc. (*the pink of health*). **4** (also **hunting pink**) **a** a foxhunter's red coat. **b** the cloth for this. **c** a foxhunter. ● *adj.* **1** (often in *comb.*) of a pale red color of any of various shades (*rose pink; salmon pink*). **2** esp. *derog.* tending to socialism. □ **in the pink** *colloq.* in very good health. □□ **pink·ish** *adj.* **pink·ly** *adv.* **pink·ness** *n.* **pink·y** *adj.*

pink[2] /pingk/ *v.tr.* **1** pierce slightly with a sword, etc. **2** cut a scalloped or zigzag edge on.

pink-col·lar *adj.* (usu. *attrib.*) (of a profession, etc.) traditionally held by women (cf. WHITE-COLLAR, BLUE-COLLAR).

pink·eye /pingkī/ *n.* acute conjunctivitis.

pink·ie /pingkee/ *n.* (also **pink·y**) esp. *US & Sc.* the little finger.

pink·ing shears /pinking/ *n.pl.* (also **pinking scissors**) ▼ a dressmaker's serrated shears for cutting a zigzag edge.

pinked edge

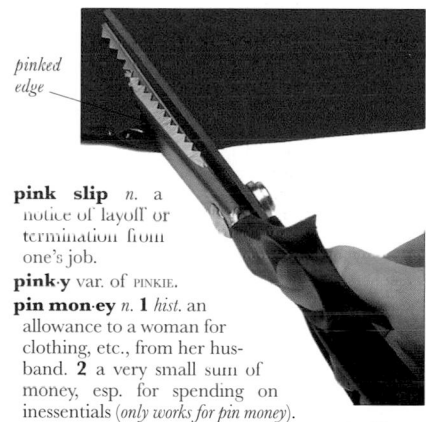

PINKING SHEARS

pink slip *n.* a notice of layoff or termination from one's job.

pink·y var. of PINKIE.

pin mon·ey *n.* **1** *hist.* an allowance to a woman for clothing, etc., from her husband. **2** a very small sum of money, esp. for spending on inessentials (*only works for pin money*).

pin·na /pínə/ *n.* (*pl.* **pinnae** /-nee/ or **pinnas**) **1** the auricle; the external part of the ear. ▷ EAR, ELEPHANT. **2** a primary division of a pinnate leaf. **3** a fin or finlike structure, feather, wing, etc.

pin·nace /pínis/ *n. Naut.* a warship's or other ship's small boat, usu. motor-driven, orig. schooner-rigged or eight-oared.

pin·na·cle /pínəkəl/ *n. & v.* ● *n.* **1** the culmination or climax (of endeavor, success, etc.). **2** a natural peak. **3** a small ornamental turret usu. ending in a pyramid or cone, crowning a buttress, roof, etc. ▷ CATHEDRAL. ● *v.tr.* **1** set on or as if on a pinnacle. **2** form the pinnacle of. **3** provide with pinnacles.

pin·nae *pl.* of PINNA.

pin·nate /pínayt/ *adj.* **1** (of a compound leaf) having leaflets arranged on either side of the stem, usu. in pairs opposite each other. ▷ LEAF. **2** having branches, tentacles, etc., on each side of an axis. □□ **pin·nat·ed** *adj.* **pin·nate·ly** *adv.* **pin·na·tion** /-náyshən/ *n.*

pin·ni·ped /piniped/ *adj. & n.* ● *adj.* ▲ denoting any aquatic mammal with limbs ending in fins. ▷ SEAL. ● *n.* a pinniped mammal.

pin·nule /pínyool/ *n.* **1** the secondary division of a pinnate leaf. **2** a part or organ like a small wing or fin. □□ **pin·nu·lar** *adj.*

PINNIPED

Pinniped mammals belong to the order Pinnipedia, which contains the two main groups of seals – true seals and eared seals – and the walrus, which is the sole member of its family. Highly adapted to an aquatic life, pinnipeds have limbs modified into flippers and streamlined bodies. All pinnipeds must emerge onto shores or ice to breed, typically gathering in large groups at traditional breeding sites, known as rookeries.

TYPES OF PINNIPED

EARED SEALS
California sea lion
(*Zalophus californianus*)

WALRUS
walrus
(*Odobenus rosmarus*)

TRUE SEALS
gray seal
(*Halichoerus grypus*)

PIN num·ber /pin/ *n.* personal identification number (as issued by a bank, etc., to validate electronic transactions).

pi·noch·le /péenokəl/ *n.* **1** a card game with a double pack of 48 cards (nine to ace only). **2** the combination of queen of spades and jack of diamonds in this game.

pi·no·le /pinōlee/ *n.* flour made from parched cornflour, esp. mixed with sweet flour made of mesquite beans, sugar, etc.

pi·ñon /peenyón, pinyən/ *n.* **1** a pine, *Pinus cembra*, bearing edible seeds. **2** the seed of this, a type of pine nut.

pin·point /pínpoynt/ *n. & v.* ● *n.* **1** the point of a pin. **2** something very small or sharp. **3** (*attrib.*) **a** very small. **b** precise; accurate. ● *v.tr.* locate with precision (*pinpointed the target*).

pin·prick /pínprik/ *n.* **1** a prick caused by a pin. **2** a trifling irritation.

pins and nee·dles *n.pl.* a tingling sensation in a limb recovering from numbness.

pin·stripe /pínstrīp/ *n.* **1** a very narrow stripe in cloth. **2** a fabric or garment with this.

pint /pīnt/ *n.* **1** a measure of capacity for liquids, etc., one eighth of a gallon or 16 fluid oz. (0.47 liter). **2** esp. *Brit.* **a** *colloq.* a pint of beer. **b** a pint of a liquid, esp. milk. **3** *Brit.* a measure of shellfish, being the amount containable in a pint mug (*bought a pint of whelks*).

pin·tail /píntayl/ *n.* a duck, esp. *Anas acuta*, or a grouse with a pointed tail.

pin·tle /pínt'l/ *n.* a pin or bolt, esp. one on which some other part turns.

pin·to /píntō/ *adj. & n.* ● *adj.* piebald. ● *n.* (*pl.* **-os**) ▼ a piebald horse.

brown and white markings

PINTO

pin·to bean *n.* a variety of bean with a mottled or spotted appearance, grown mainly in the southwestern US.

pint-sized *adj.* (also **pint-size**) *colloq.* very small, esp. of a person.

pin-up /pínup/ *n.* **1** a photograph of a movie star, etc., for display. **2** a person in such a photograph.

pin·wheel /pínhweel/ *n.* **1** a fireworks device that whirls and emits colored fire. **2** a child's toy consisting of a stick with vanes that twirl in the wind.

pin·worm /pínwərm/ *n.* a small parasitic nematode worm, *Enterobius vermicularis*, of which the female has a pointed tail.

pin·y /pínee/ *adj.* (also **pine·y**) of, like, or full of pines.

Pin·yin /pinyín/ *n.* a system of romanized spelling for transliterating Chinese.

pi·o·let /pɛɛláy/ *n.* a two-headed ice ax for mountaineering.

pi·o·neer /píənéer/ *n. & v.* ● *n.* **1** an initiator of a new enterprise, an inventor, etc. **2** an explorer or settler; a colonist. **3** *Mil.* a member of an infantry group preparing roads, terrain, etc., for the main body of troops. ● *v.* **1 a** *tr.* initiate or originate (an enterprise, etc.). **b** *intr.* act or prepare the way as a pioneer. **2** *tr Mil.* open up (a road, etc.) as a pioneer. **3** *tr.* go before, lead, or conduct (another person or persons).

pi·ous /píəs/ *adj.* **1** devout; religious. **2** hypocritically virtuous; sanctimonious. **3** dutiful. □□ **pi·ous·ly** *adv.* **pi·ous·ness** *n.*

pi·ous fraud *n.* a deception intended to benefit those deceived, esp. religiously.

pip[1] /pip/ *n. & v.* ● *n.* **1** the seed of an apple, pear, orange, grape, etc. ▷ SEED. **2** an extraordinary person or thing. ● *v.tr.* (**pipped**, **pipping**) remove the pips from (fruit, etc.). □□ **pip·less** *adj.*

pip[2] /pip/ *n. Brit.* a short high-pitched sound, usu. mechanically produced, esp. as a radio time signal.

pip[3] /pip/ *n.* **1** any of the spots on playing cards, dice, or dominos. **2** *Brit.* a star (1–3 according to rank) on the shoulder of an army officer's uniform. **3** a single blossom of a clustered head of flowers. **4** a diamond-shaped segment of the surface of a pineapple. **5** an image of an object on a radar screen.

pip[4] /pip/ *n.* **1** a disease of poultry, etc., causing thick mucus in the throat and white scale on the

P

tongue. **2** esp. *Brit. colloq.* a fit of disgust or bad temper (esp. *give one the pip*).

pip⁵ /pip/ *v.tr.* (**pipped, pipping**) *Brit. colloq.* **1** hit with a shot. **2** defeat. **3** blackball. □ **pip at the post** defeat at the last moment. **pip out** die.

pipe /pīp/ *n. & v.* ● *n.* **1** a tube of metal, plastic, wood, etc., used to convey water, gas, etc. **2 a** (also **tobacco pipe**) a narrow wooden or clay, etc., tube with a bowl at one end containing burning tobacco, etc., the smoke from which is drawn into the mouth. **b** the quantity of tobacco held by this (*smoked a pipe*). **c** a hookah. **3** *Mus.* **a** a wind instrument consisting of a single tube. **b** any of the tubes by which sound is produced in an organ. ▷ ORGAN. **c** (in *pl.*) = BAGPIPE(s). **d** (in *pl.*) a set of pipes joined together, e.g., panpipes. **4** a tubal organ, vessel, etc., in an animal's body. **5** a high note or song, esp. of a bird. **6** a cylindrical vein of ore. **7** a cavity in cast metal. **8 a** a boatswain's whistle. **b** the sounding of this. **9** a cask for wine, esp. as a measure of two hogsheads, usu. equivalent to 105 gallons (about 477 liters). **10** *colloq.* (also in *pl.*) the voice, esp. in singing. ● *v.tr.* **1** (also *absol.*) play (a tune, etc.) on a pipe or pipes. **2 a** convey (oil, water, gas, etc.) by pipes. **b** provide with pipes. **3** transmit (music, a radio program, etc.) by wire or cable. **4** (usu. foll. by *up, on, to,* etc.) *Naut.* **a** summon (a crew) to a meal, work, etc. **b** signal the arrival of (an officer, etc.) on board. **5** utter in a shrill voice; whistle. **6 a** arrange (icing, etc.) in decorative lines or twists on a cake, etc. **b** ornament (a cake, etc.) with piping. **7** trim (a dress, etc.) with piping. **8** lead or bring (a person, etc.) by the sound of a pipe. **9** propagate (pinks, etc.) by taking cuttings at the joint of a stem. □ **pipe away** give a signal for (a boat) to start. **pipe down 1** *colloq.* be quiet or less insistent. **2** *Naut.* dismiss from duty. **pipe up** begin to play, sing, speak, etc. **put that in your pipe and smoke it** *colloq.* a challenge to another to accept something frank or unwelcome. □□ **pipe·ful** *n.* (*pl.* **-fuls**) **pipe·less** *adj.* **pip·y** *adj.*

pipe bomb *n.* a homemade bomb made by sealing explosives inside a metal pipe.

pipe clay /pīp klay/ *n. & v.* ● *n.* a fine white clay used for making tobacco pipes, whitening leather, etc. ● *v.tr.* (**pipe-clay**) whiten (leather, etc.) with pipe clay.

pipe clean·er *n.* a piece of flexible wire covered with tufts or bristles, used for cleaning a tobacco pipe and in handicrafts.

pipe dream /pīp dreem/ *n.* an unattainable or fanciful hope or scheme.

pipe·fish /pīpfish/ *n.* (*pl.* usu. same) ▼ any of various long slender fish of the family Syngnathidae, with an elongated snout.

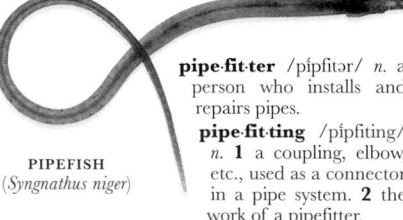

PIPEFISH
(*Syngnathus niger*)

pipe·fit·ter /pípfitər/ *n.* a person who installs and repairs pipes.

pipe·fit·ting /pípfiting/ *n.* **1** a coupling, elbow, etc., used as a connector in a pipe system. **2** the work of a pipefitter.

pipe·line /píplīn/ *n.* **1** a long, usu. underground, pipe for conveying esp. oil. ▷ OIL PLATFORM. **2** a channel supplying goods, information, etc. □ **in the pipeline** awaiting completion or processing.

pipe or·gan *n. Mus.* an organ using pipes instead of or as well as reeds. ▷ ORGAN

pip·er /pípər/ *n.* **1** a bagpipe player. **2** a person who plays a pipe, esp. an itinerant musician.

pipe·stem /pípstem/ *n.* **1** the stem of a tobacco pipe. **2** something very thin or slender, as an arm or leg.

pi·pette /pīpét/ *n. & v.* ● *n.* a slender tube for transferring or measuring small quantities of liquids esp. in chemistry. ● *v.tr.* transfer or measure (a liquid) using a pipette.

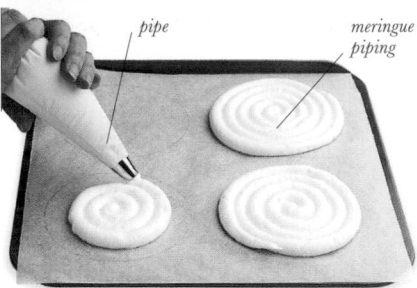

one's own benefit. **2** plunder. □□ **pi·rat·ic** /-rátik/ *adj.* **pi·rat·i·cal** *adj.* **pi·rat·i·cal·ly** *adv.*

pi·ro·gi /pərógee/ *n.* var. of PIEROGI.

pir·ou·ette /píroo-ét/ *n. & v.* ● *n.* a dancer's spin on one foot or the point of the toe. ● *v.intr.* perform a pirouette.

pis·ca·to·ri·al /pískətáwreeəl/ *adj.* = PISCATORY 1.

pis·ca·to·ry /pískətawree/ *adj.* **1** of or concerning fishermen or fishing. **2** addicted to fishing.

Pis·ces /píseez/ *n.* (*pl.* same) **1** ▼ a constellation, traditionally regarded as contained in the figure of fishes. **2 a** the twelfth sign of the zodiac (the Fishes). ▷ ZODIAC. **b** a person born when the Sun is in this sign. □□ **Pis·ce·an** /píseeən/ *n. & adj.*

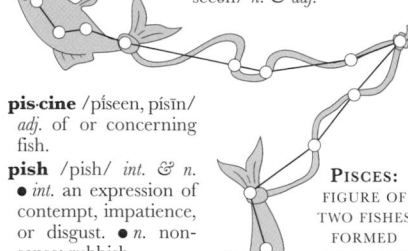

PISCES: FIGURE OF TWO FISHES FORMED FROM THE STARS OF PISCES

pis·cine /píseen, písīn/ *adj.* of or concerning fish.

pish /pish/ *int. & n.* ● *int.* an expression of contempt, impatience, or disgust; rubbish. ● *n.* nonsense; rubbish.

piss /pis/ *v. & n. coarse sl.* ¶ Usually considered a taboo word. ● *v.* **1** *intr.* urinate. **2** *tr.* a discharge (blood, etc.) when urinating. **b** wet with urine. **3** *tr.* (as **pissed** *adj.*) **a** esp. *Brit.* drunk. **b** angry; annoyed. ● *n.* **1** urine. **2** an act of urinating. □ **piss off 1** (often as **pissed off** *adj.*) annoy; depress. **2** *Brit.* go away.

pis·soir /peeswaár/ *n.* a public urinal, esp. in Europe.

pis·tach·i·o /pistásheeō, -staásheeō/ *n.* (*pl.* **-os**) **1** an evergreen tree, *Pistacia vera*, bearing small brownish green flowers and ovoid reddish fruit. **2** (in full **pistachio nut**) the edible pale green seed of this. **3** a pale green color.

piste /peest/ *n.* a ski run of compacted snow.

pis·til /pístil/ *n.* the female organs of a flower, comprising the stigma, style, and ovary. ▷ HERMAPHRODITE

pis·tol /pístəl/ *n. & v.* ● *n.* **1** ▼ a small hand-held firearm. ▷ GUN. **2** anything of a similar shape. ● *v.tr.* (**pistoled, pistoling** or **pistolled, pistolling**) shoot with a pistol.

PISTOL: WORLD WAR II JAPANESE AUTOMATIC PISTOL

pis·tol-whip *v.tr.* (**-whipped, -whipping**) beat with a pistol.

pis·ton /pístən/ *n.* **1** a disk or short cylinder fitting closely within a tube in which it moves up and down against a liquid or gas, used in an internal-combustion engine to impart motion, or in a pump to receive motion. ▷ PNEUMATIC, SHOCK ABSORBER. **2** a sliding valve in a trumpet, etc.

pis·ton ring *n.* a ring on a piston sealing the gap between the piston and the cylinder wall.

pis·ton rod *n.* a rod or crankshaft attached to a piston to drive a wheel or to impart motion.

PIPING: WHORLS OF MERINGUE PIPING

pip·ing /píping/ *n. & adj.* ● *n.* **1** the act or an instance of piping, esp. whistling or singing. **2** a thin pipelike fold used to edge hems or frills on clothing, seams on upholstery, etc. **3** ▲ ornamental lines of icing, potato, etc., on a cake or other dish. **4** lengths of pipe, or a system of pipes, esp. in domestic use. ● *adj.* (of a noise) high; whistling.

pip·ing hot *adj.* very or suitably hot (esp. as required of food, water, etc.).

pip·i·strelle /pípistrél/ *n.* any bat of the genus *Pipistrellus*, native to temperate regions and feeding on insects.

pip·it /pípit/ *n.* any of various birds of the family Motacillidae, esp. of the genus *Anthus*, found worldwide and having brown plumage often heavily streaked with a lighter color.

pip·pin /pípin/ *n.* **1 a** an apple grown from seed. **b** a red and yellow dessert apple. **2** *colloq.* an excellent person or thing; a beauty.

pip·squeak /pípskweek/ *n. colloq.* an insignificant or contemptible person or thing.

pi·quant /péekənt, -kaant, peekáant/ *adj.* **1** agreeably pungent, sharp, or appetizing. **2** pleasantly stimulating, or disquieting, to the mind. □□ **pi·quan·cy** *n.* **pi·quant·ly** *adv.*

pique /peek/ *v. & n.* ● *v.tr.* (**piques, piqued, piquing**) **1** wound the pride of; irritate. **2** arouse (curiosity, interest, etc.). **3** (*refl.*; usu. foll. by *on*) pride or congratulate oneself. ● *n.* ill-feeling; enmity; resentment (*in a fit of pique*).

pi·qué /peekáy/ *n.* a stiff ribbed cotton or other fabric.

pi·quet¹ /pikáy, -két/ *n.* a game for two players with a pack of 32 cards (seven to ace only).

pi·quet² var. of PICKET *n.* 3.

pi·ra·cy /pírəsee/ *n.* (*pl.* **-ies**) **1** the practice or an act of robbery of ships at sea. **2** a similar practice or act in other forms, esp. hijacking. **3** the infringement of copyright.

pi·ra·nha /piráanə, -ránə, -raányə, -rányə/ *n.* ▼ any of various freshwater predatory fish of the genera *Pygocentrus, Rooseveltiella,* or *Serrasalmus,* native to S. America and having sharp cutting teeth.

PIRANHA (*Serrasalmus niger*)

pi·rate /pírət/ *n. & v.* ● *n.* **1 a** a person who commits piracy. **b** a ship used by pirates. **2** a person who infringes another's copyright or other business rights; a plagiarist. **3** (often *attrib.*) a person, organization, etc., that broadcasts without official authorization. ● *v.tr.* **1** appropriate or reproduce (the work or ideas, etc., of another) without permission, for

P

pit[1] /pit/ n. & v. ● n. **1 a** a usu. large deep hole in the ground. **b** a hole made in digging for industrial purposes, esp. for coal (*chalk pit; gravel pit*). **c** a covered hole as a trap for esp. wild animals. **2 a** an indentation left after smallpox, acne, etc. **b** a hollow in a plant or animal body or on any surface. **3** the part of a theater in which the orchestra is situated. **4 a** (**the pit** or **bottomless pit**) hell. **b** (**the pits**) *sl.* a wretched or the worst imaginable place, situation, person, etc. **5 a** an area at the side of a track where racing cars are serviced and re-fueled. **b** a sunken area in a workshop floor for access to a car's underside. **6** the part of the floor of an exchange allotted to special trading (*wheat pit*). **7** = COCKPIT. **8** *Brit. sl.* a bed. ● *v.tr.* (**pitted, pitting**) **1** (usu. foll. by *against*) **a** set (one's wits, strength, etc.) in opposition or rivalry. **b** set (a cock, dog, etc.) to fight, orig. in a pit, against another. **2** (usu. as **pitted** *adj.*) make pits, esp. scars, in. □ **dig a pit for** try to ensnare.

pit[2] /pit/ n. & v. ● n. the stone of a fruit. ● *v.tr.* (**pitted, pitting**) remove pits from (fruit).

pi·ta /péetə/ n. (also **pit·ta**) a flat, hollow, unleavened bread that can be split and filled with salad, etc.

pit-a-pat /pítəpát/ *adv. & n.* (also **pit·ter-pat·ter** /pítərpátər/) ● *adv.* **1** with a sound like quick light steps. **2** with a faltering sound (*heart went pit-a-pat*). ● *n.* such a sound.

pit bull ter·ri·er n. ◀ a strong, compact breed of dog, usu. the American Staffordshire terrier.

PIT BULL TERRIER

pitch[1] /pich/ v. & n. ● v. **1** *tr.* (also *absol.*) erect and fix (a tent, camp, etc.). **2** *tr.* **a** throw; fling. **b** (in games) throw (an object) toward a mark. **3** *tr.* fix or plant (a thing) in a definite position. **4** *tr.* express in a particular style or at a particular level (*pitched his argument at the most basic level*). **5** *intr.* (often foll. by *against, into*, etc.) fall heavily, esp. headlong. **6** *intr.* (of a ship, aircraft, etc.) plunge in a longitudinal direction (cf. ROLL *v.* 8a). **7** *tr. Mus.* set at a particular pitch. **8** *intr.* (of a roof, etc.) slope downwards. ▷ ROOF. **9** *intr.* (often foll. by *about*) move with a vigorous jogging motion, as in a train, carriage, etc. **10** *Baseball* **a** *tr.* deliver (the ball) to the batter. **b** *intr.* play at the position of pitcher. ● *n.* **1** *Brit.* the area of play in a field game. **2** height, degree, intensity, etc. (*the pitch of despair*). **3 a** the steepness of a slope, esp. of a roof, stratum, etc. **b** the degree of such a pitch. **4** *Mus.* **a** that quality of a sound which is governed by the rate of vibrations producing it; the degree of highness or lowness of a tone. **b** = CONCERT PITCH 1. **5** the pitching motion of a ship, etc. **6** the delivery of a baseball by a pitcher. **7** *colloq.* a salesman's advertising or selling approach. □ **pitch in** *colloq.* **1** set to work vigorously. **2** assist; cooperate. **pitch into** *colloq.* **1** attack forcibly with blows, words, etc. **2** assail (food, work, etc.) vigorously.

pitch[2] /pich/ n. & v. ● n. **1** a sticky resinous black or dark brown substance obtained by distilling tar or turpentine, semiliquid when hot, hard when cold, and used for caulking the seams of ships, etc. **2** any of various bituminous substances including asphalt. ● *v.tr.* cover, coat, or smear with pitch.

pitch-black adj. (also **pitch-dark**) very or completely dark.

pitch·blende /píchblend/ n. a mineral form of uranium oxide occurring in pitchlike masses and yielding radium.

pitched bat·tle n. **1** a vigorous argument, etc. **2** *Mil.* a battle planned beforehand and fought on chosen ground.

pitch·er[1] /píchər/ n. **1** a large usu. earthenware or glass jug with a lip and a handle, for holding liquids.

2 a modified leaf in pitcher form. □□ **pitch·er·ful** n. (*pl.* **-fuls**).

pitch·er[2] /píchər/ n. **1** a person or thing that pitches. **2** *Baseball* a player who delivers the ball to the batter.

pitch·er plant n. ◀ any of various plants, esp. of the family Nepenthaceae or Sarraceniaceae, with pitcher leaves that can hold liquids, trap insects, etc.

nectar on rim attracts insects

partially digested insects

PITCHER PLANT: CROSS SECTION OF THE LEAF POUCH

pitch·fork /píchfawrk/ n. & v. ● n. a long-handled two-pronged fork for pitching hay, etc. ● *v.tr.* **1** throw with or as if with a pitchfork. **2** (usu. foll. by *into*) thrust (a person) forcibly into a position, office, etc.

pitch·man /píchmən/ n. **1** a salesperson who uses overly aggressive selling tactics. **2** a person who delivers commercial messages on radio or television.

pitch pine n. any of various pine trees, esp. *Pinus rigida* or *P. palustris*, yielding much resin.

pitch pipe n. *Mus.* a small pipe blown to set the pitch for singing or tuning.

pit·e·ous /píteeəs/ adj. deserving or causing pity; wretched. □□ **pit·e·ous·ly** adv. **pit·e·ous·ness** n.

pit·fall /pítfawl/ n. **1** an unsuspected snare, danger, or drawback. **2** a covered pit for trapping animals, etc.

pith /pith/ n. **1** spongy white tissue lining the rind of an orange, lemon, etc. **2** the essential part; the quintessence (*came to the pith of his argument*). **3** *Bot.* the spongy cellular tissue in the stems and branches of dicotyledonous plants. **4 a** physical strength; vigor. **b** force; energy. □□ **pith·less** adj.

pith hel·met n. ▶ a lightweight sun helmet made from the dried pith of the sola, etc.

pith·y /píthee/ adj. (**pithier, pithiest**) **1** (of style, speech, etc.) condensed, terse, and forceful. **2** of, like, or containing much pith. □□ **pith·i·ly** adv. **pith·i·ness** n.

PITH HELMET

pit·i·a·ble /píteeəbəl/ adj. **1** deserving or causing pity. **2** contemptible. □□ **pit·i·a·ble·ness** n. **pit·i·a·bly** adv.

pit·i·ful /pítifŏŏl/ adj. **1** causing pity. **2** contemptible. **3** *archaic* compassionate. □□ **pit·i·ful·ly** adv. **pit·i·ful·ness** n.

pit·i·less /pítilis/ adj. showing no pity. □□ **pit·i·less·ly** adv. **pit·i·less·ness** n.

pit·man /pítmən/ n. **1** (*pl.* **-men**) a person who works in a pit, as a miner. **2** (*pl.* **-mans**) a connecting rod in machinery.

pi·ton /péeton/ n. a peg or spike driven into a rock or crack to support a climber or a rope.

pit stop n. **1** a brief stop at the pit by a racing car for servicing or refueling. **2** *colloq.* **a** a stop, as during a long journey, for food, rest, etc. **b** the place where such a stop is made.

pit·tance /pít'ns/ n. **1** a scanty or meager allowance, remuneration, etc. (*paid him a mere pittance*). **2** a small number or amount.

pit·ter-pat·ter var. of PIT-A-PAT.

pit·tos·po·rum /pitóspərəm, pitōspáwrəm/ n. ▶ any evergreen shrub of the family Pittosporaceae, chiefly native to Australasia with many species having fragrant foliage.

PITTOSPORUM: JAPANESE PITTOSPORUM (*Pittosporum tobira*)

pi·tu·i·tar·y /pitŏō-iteree, -tyŏō-/ n. & adj. ● n. (*pl.* **-ies**) (also **pituitary gland** or **body**) a small ductless gland at the base of the brain secreting various hormones essential for growth and other bodily functions. ▷ BRAIN, ENDOCRINE. ● adj. of or relating to this gland.

pit·y /pítee/ n. & v. ● n. (*pl.* **-ies**) **1** sorrow and compassion aroused by another's condition (*felt pity for the child*). **2** something to be regretted; grounds for regret (*what a pity!*). ● *v.tr.* (**-ies, -ied**) feel (often contemptuous) pity for. □ **for pity's sake** an exclamation of urgent supplication, anger, etc. **more's the pity** so much the worse. **take pity on** feel or act compassionately toward. □□ **pit·y·ing** adj. **pit·y·ing·ly** adv.

Pi·ute /píŏŏt, píōōt/ n. = PAIUTE.

piv·ot /pívət/ n. & v. ● n. **1** a short shaft or pin on which something turns or oscillates. **2** a crucial or essential person, point, etc., in a scheme or enterprise. **3** *Mil.* the man or men about whom a body of troops wheels. ● v. (**pivoted, pivoting**) **1** *intr.* turn on or as if on a pivot. **2** *intr.* (foll. by *on, upon*) hinge on; depend on. **3** *tr.* provide with or attach by a pivot. □□ **piv·ot·a·ble** adj. **piv·ot·a·bil·i·ty** n. **piv·ot·al** adj.

pix[1] /piks/ n.pl. *colloq.* pictures, esp. photographs.

pix[2] var. of PYX.

pix·el /píksəl/ n. *Electronics* any of the minute areas of uniform illumination of which an image on a display screen is composed. ▷ MONITOR

pix·ie /píksee/ n. (also **pix·y**) (*pl.* **-ies**) a being like a fairy; an elf.

pix·i·lat·ed /píksilaytid/ adj. (also **pix·il·lat·ed**) **1** bewildered; crazy. **2** drunk.

piz·za /péetsə/ n. a flat round base of dough baked with a topping of tomatoes, cheese, onions, etc.

piz·zazz /pizáz/ n. (also **pi·zazz**) *sl.* verve; energy; liveliness; sparkle.

piz·ze·ri·a /péetsəréeə/ n. a place where pizzas are made or sold.

piz·zi·ca·to /pítsikáatō/ adv., adj., & n. *Mus.* ● adv. plucking the strings of a violin, etc., with the finger. ● adj. (of a note, passage, etc.) performed pizzicato. ● n. (*pl.* **pizzicatos** or **pizzicati** /-tee/) a note, passage, etc., played pizzicato.

pk. abbr. **1** park. **2** peak. **3** peck(s). **4** pack.

pkg. abbr. package.

pl. abbr. **1** plural. **2** place. **3** plate. **4** esp. *Mil.* platoon.

plac·a·ble /plákəbəl, pláy-/ adj. easily placated; mild; forgiving. □□ **plac·a·bil·i·ty** n. **plac·a·bly** adv.

plac·ard /plákaard, -kərd/ n. & v. ● n. a printed or handwritten poster, esp. for advertising. ● *v.tr.* **1** set up placards on (a wall, etc.). **2** advertise by placards. **3** display (a poster, etc.) as a placard.

pla·cate /pláykayt, plák-/ *v.tr.* pacify; conciliate. □□ **pla·cat·ing·ly** adv. **pla·ca·tion** /-áyshən/ n. **pla·ca·to·ry** /-kətawree/ adj.

place /plays/ n. & v. ● n. **1 a** a particular portion of space. **b** a portion of space occupied by a person or thing. **c** a proper or natural position (*he is out of his place; take your places*). **d** situation; circumstances (*put yourself in my place*). **2** a city, town, village, etc. (*was born in this place*). **3** a residence; a dwelling (*has a place in the country; come around to my place*). **4 a** a group of houses in a town, etc., esp. a square. **b** a country house with its surroundings. **5** a person's rank or status (*know their place; a place in history*). **6** a space, esp. a seat, for a person (*two places in the coach*). **7** a building or area for a specific purpose (*place*

P

of worship; fireplace). **8 a** a point reached in a book, etc. (*lost my place*). **b** a passage in a book. **9** a particular spot on a surface, esp. of the skin (*a sore place on his wrist*). **10 a** employment or office (*lost his place at the university*). **b** the duties or entitlements of office, etc. (*is his place to hire staff*). **11** a position as a member of a team, a student in a college, etc. **12** the second finishing position, esp. in a horse race. **13** the position of a number in a series indicated in decimal or similar notation (*calculated to 5 decimal places*). ● *v.tr.* **1** put (a thing, etc.) in a particular place or state; arrange. **2** identify, classify, or remember correctly (*cannot place him*). **3** assign to a particular place; locate. **4 a** appoint (a person, esp. a member of the clergy) to a post. **b** find a job, clerical post, etc., for. **c** (usu. foll. by *with*) consign to a person's care, etc. (*placed her with her aunt*). **5** assign rank, importance, or worth to (*place him among the best teachers*). **6 a** dispose of (goods) to a customer. **b** make (an order for goods, etc.). **7** (often foll. by *in, on,* etc.) have (confidence, etc.). **8** invest (money). **9** *tr.* as **placed** *adj.*) second in a race. □ **all over the place** in disorder; chaotic. **give place to** be replaced by. **go places** *colloq.* be successful. **in place** in the right position; suitable. **in place of** in exchange for; instead of. **in places** at some places or in some parts, but not others. **keep a person in his** (or **her**) **place** suppress a person's esp. social pretensions. **out of place 1** in the wrong position. **2** unsuitable. **put oneself in another's place** imagine oneself in another's position. **put a person in his** (or **her**) **place** deflate or humiliate a person. **take place** occur. **take one's place** go to one's correct position, be seated, etc. **take the place of** replace. □□ **place·less** *adj.* **place·ment** *n.*

pla·ce·bo /pləséébō/ *n.* (*pl.* **-os**) **1** a medicine, etc., prescribed more for psychological reasons than for any physiological effect. **2** an inactive substance used as a control in testing new drugs, etc.

place card *n.* a card marking a person's place at a table, etc.

place·kick /pláyskik/ *n. Football* a kick made with the ball held on the ground or on a tee.

place mat *n.* a small mat on a table underneath a person's plate.

place-name *n.* the name of a geographic location, as a city, town, hill, lake, etc.

pla·cen·ta /pləséntə/ *n.* (*pl.* **placentae** /-tee/ or **placentas**) a flattened organ in the uterus of pregnant mammals nourishing and maintaining the fetus through the umbilical cord and expelled after birth. ▷ FETUS, UMBILICAL CORD. □□ **pla·cen·tal** *adj.*

plac·er /plásər/ *n.* a deposit of sand, gravel, etc., in the bed of a stream, etc., containing valuable minerals in particles.

place set·ting *n.* a set of plates, silverware, etc., for one person at a meal.

plac·id /plásid/ *adj.* **1** (of a person) not easily aroused or disturbed; peaceful. **2** calm; serene. □□ **pla·cid·i·ty** /pləsíditee/ *n.* **plac·id·ly** *adv.*

plack·et /plákit/ *n.* **1** an opening or slit in a garment, for fastenings or access to a pocket. **2** the flap of fabric under this.

pla·gia·rism /pláyjərizəm/ *n.* **1** the act or an instance of plagiarizing. **2** something plagiarized. □□ **pla·gia·rist** *n.* **pla·gia·ris·tic** *adj.*

pla·gia·rize /pláyjərīz/ *v.tr.* (also *absol.*) **1** take and use (the thoughts, writings, inventions, etc., of another person) as one's own. **2** pass off the thoughts, etc., of (another person) as one's own. □□ **pla·gia·riz·er** *n.*

pla·gi·o·clase /pláyjeeōkláys/ *n.* a series of feldspar minerals forming glassy crystals.

plague /playg/ *n. & v.* ● *n.* **1** a deadly contagious disease spreading rapidly over a wide area. **2** (foll. by *of*) an unusual infestation of a pest, etc. (*a plague of frogs*). **3 a** great trouble. **b** an affliction, esp. as regarded as divine punishment. **4** *colloq.* a nuisance. ● *v.tr.* (**plagues, plagued, plaguing**) **1** affect with plague. **2** *colloq.* pester or harass continually. □□ **plague·some** *adj.*

white underside

upper side

PLAICE (*Pleuronectes platessa*)

plaice /plays/ *n.* (*pl.* same) **1** ▲ a European flatfish, *Pleuronectes platessa*, having a brown back with orange spots and a white underside, much used for food. **2** (in full **American plaice**) a N. Atlantic fish, *Hippoglossoides platessoides*.

plaid /plad/ *n.* **1 a** (often *attrib.*) tartan usu. woolen twilled cloth (*a plaid skirt*). **b** any cloth with a tartan pattern. **2** a long piece of plaid worn over the shoulder as part of Highland Scottish costume. □□ **plaid·ed** *adj.*

plain /playn/ *adj., adv., & n.* ● *adj.* **1** clear; evident (*is plain to see*). **2** readily understood; simple (*in plain words*). **3 a** (of food, sewing, decoration, etc.) uncomplicated; not elaborate; unembellished; simple. **b** without a decorative pattern. **4** (esp. of a woman or girl) not good-looking; homely. **5** outspoken; straightforward. **6** (of manners, dress, etc.) unsophisticated; homely (*a plain man*). **7** (of drawings, etc.) not colored. **8** not in code. ● *adv.* **1** clearly; unequivocally (*to speak plain, I don't approve*). **2** simply (*that is plain stupid*). ● *n.* **1** a level tract of esp. treeless country. **2** a basic knitting stitch made by putting the needle through the back of the stitch and passing the wool around the front of the needle (opp. PURL). ▷ KNITTING. □□ **plain·ly** *adv.* **plain·ness** /pláyn-nis/ *n.*

plain·clothes·man /playnklôzmən, klôthz-, -man/ *n.* a police officer who wears civilian clothes while on duty.

plains·man /pláynzmən/ *n.* (*pl.* **-men**) a person who lives on a plain, esp. in N. America.

plain·song /pláynsawng, -song/ *n.* unaccompanied church music sung in unison in medieval modes and in free rhythm corresponding to the accentuation of the words (cf. GREGORIAN CHANT).

plain-speak·ing *n.* blunt or candid expression of one's opinions etc.

plain-spo·ken *adj.* outspoken; blunt.

plaint /playnt/ *n.* **1** *Brit. Law* an accusation; a charge. **2** *literary* or *archaic* a complaint; a lamentation.

plain·tiff /pláyntif/ *n. Law* a person who brings a case against another into court (opp. DEFENDANT).

plain·tive /pláyntiv/ *adj.* **1** expressing sorrow; mournful. **2** mournful-sounding. □□ **plain·tive·ly** *adv.* **plain·tive·ness** *n.*

plait /playt, plat/ *n. & v.* ● *n.* **1** = BRAID 2. **2** = PLEAT. ● *v.tr.* = BRAID 1.

plan /plan/ *n. & v.* ● *n.* **1 a** a formulated and esp. detailed method by which a thing is to be done; a design or scheme. **b** an intention or proposed proceeding (*my plan was to distract them; plan of campaign*). **2** a drawing or diagram made by projection on a horizontal plane, esp. showing a building or one floor of a building (cf. ELEVATION). **3** a large-scale detailed map of a town or district. **4 a** a table, etc., indicating times, places, etc., of intended proceedings. **b** a scheme or arrangement (*prepared the seating plan*). **5** an imaginary plane perpendicular to the line of vision and containing the objects shown in a picture. ● *v.* (**planned, planning**) **1** *tr.* (often foll. by *that* + clause or *to* + infin.) arrange (a procedure, etc.) beforehand; form a plan (*planned to*

catch the evening ferry). **2 tr.** a design (a building, new town, etc.). **b** make a plan of (an existing building, an area, etc.). **3 tr.** (as **planned** *adj.*) in accordance with a plan (*his planned arrival*). **4** *intr.* make plans. □ **plan on** *colloq.* aim at doing; intend. □□ **plan·ning** *n.*

plan·chette /planshét/ *n.* a small usu. heart-shaped board on casters with a pencil that is supposedly caused to write spirit messages when a person's fingers rest lightly on it.

plane[1] /playn/ *n., adj., & v.* ● *n.* **1 a** a flat surface on which a straight line joining any two points on it would wholly lie. **b** an imaginary flat surface through or joining, etc., material objects. **2** a level surface. **3** *colloq.* = AIRPLANE. **4** a flat surface producing lift by the action of air or water over and under it (usu. in *comb.*: *hydroplane*). **5** (often foll. by *of*) a level of attainment, thought, knowledge, etc. **6** a flat thin object such as a tabletop. ● *adj.* **1** (of a surface, etc.) perfectly level. **2** (of an angle, figure, etc.) lying in a plane. ● *v.intr.* **1** (often foll. by *down*) travel or glide in an airplane. **2** (of a speedboat, etc.) skim over water. **3** soar.

plane[2] /playn/ *n. & v.* ● *n.* **1 ▼** a tool consisting of a wooden or metal block with a projecting steel blade, used to smooth a wooden surface by paring shavings from it. **2** a similar tool for smoothing metal. ● *v.tr.* **1** smooth (wood, metal, etc.) with a plane. **2** (often foll. by *away, down*) pare (irregularities) with a plane.

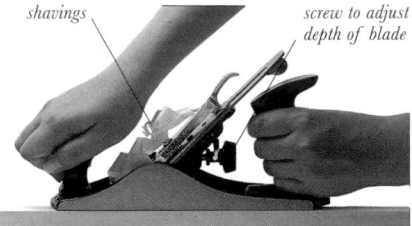

shavings

screw to adjust depth of blade

PLANE

plane[3] /playn/ *n.* (in full **plane tree**) any tree of the genus *Platanus*, often growing to great heights, with maplelike leaves and bark which peels in uneven patches.

plan·et /plánit/ *n.* **1 a** a celestial body moving in an elliptical orbit around a star. ▷ SOLAR SYSTEM. **b** the Earth. **2** esp. *Astrol. hist.* a celestial body distinguished from the fixed stars by having an apparent motion of its own (including the Moon and Sun), esp. with reference to its supposed influence on people and events. □□ **plan·e·tol·o·gy** /-tólǝjee/ *n.*

plan·e·tar·i·um /plánitáireeǝm/ *n.* (*pl.* **planetariums** or **planetaria** /-reeǝ/) **1** a domed building in which images of stars, planets, constellations, etc., are projected for public entertainment or education. **2** the device used for such projection. **3** = ORRERY.

plan·e·tar·y /plániteree/ *adj.* **1** of or like planets (*planetary influence*). **2** terrestrial; mundane. **3** wandering; erratic.

plan·e·tar·y neb·u·la *n.* **▼** a ring-shaped nebula formed by an expanding shell of gas around a star. ▷ NEBULA, STAR

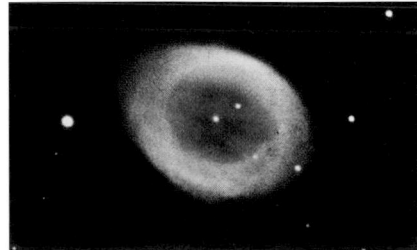

PLANETARY NEBULA IN THE CONSTELLATION LYRA

plan·et·oid /plánitoyd/ *n.* = ASTEROID 1.

plan·gent /plánjənt/ *adj.* **1** (of a sound) loud and reverberating. **2** (of a sound) plaintive; sad. □□ **plan·gen·cy** *n.*

pla·nim·e·ter /plənímitər/ *n.* an instrument for mechanically measuring the area of a plane figure. □□ **plan·i·met·ric** /plánimétrik/ *adj.* **plan·i·met·ri·cal** *adj.* **pla·nim·e·try** /-mətree/ *n.*

plan·i·sphere /plánisfeer/ *n.* a map formed by the projection of a sphere or part of a sphere on a plane, esp. to show the appearance of the heavens at a specific time or place. □□ **plan·i·spher·ic** /-sférik/ *adj.*

plank /plangk/ *n. & v.* ● *n.* **1** a long flat piece of timber used esp. in building, flooring, etc. **2** an item of a political or other program (cf. PLATFORM). ● *v.tr.* **1** provide, cover, or floor with planks. **2** cook and serve (fish, steak, etc.) on a plank. **3** (usu. foll. by *down*; also *absol.*) *colloq.* **a** put (a thing, person, etc.) down roughly or violently. **b** pay (money) on the spot or abruptly (*planked down $5*). □ **walk the plank** *hist.* (of a pirate's captive, etc.) be made to walk blindfold along a plank over the side of a ship to one's death in the sea.

plank·ing /plángking/ *n.* planks as flooring, etc.

plank·ton /plángktən/ *n.* the chiefly microscopic organisms drifting or floating in the sea or fresh water. □□ **plank·ton·ic** /-tónik/ *adj.*

plan·ner /plánər/ *n.* **1** a person who controls or plans the development of towns, designs buildings, etc. **2** a person who makes plans. **3** a list, table, booklet, etc., with information helpful in planning.

plan·o·con·cave /pláynōkónkayv, -kónkáyv/ *adj.* (of a lens, etc.) with one surface plane and the other concave.

plan·o·con·vex /pláynōkónveks, -konvéks/ *adj.* (of a lens, etc.) with one surface plane and the other convex.

plant /plant/ *n. & v.* ● *n.* **1 a** any living organism of the kingdom Plantae, usu. containing chlorophyll enabling it to live wholly on inorganic substances and lacking specialized sense organs and the power of voluntary movement. **b** a small organism of this kind, as distinguished from a shrub or tree. **2 a** machinery, fixtures, etc., used in industrial processes. **b** a factory. **c** buildings, fixtures, equipment, etc., of an institution. **3 a** *colloq.* something, esp. incriminating or compromising, positioned or concealed so as to be discovered later. **b** *sl.* a spy or detective; hidden police officers. ● *v.tr.* **1** place (a seed, bulb, or growing thing) in the ground so that it may take root and flourish. **2** (often foll. by *in*, *on*, etc.) put or fix in position. **3** deposit (young fish, spawn, oysters, etc.) in a river or lake. **4** station (a person, etc.), esp. as a spy or source of information. **5** *refl.* take up a position (*planted myself by the door*). **6** cause (an idea, etc.) to be established esp. in another person's mind. **7** deliver (a blow, kiss, etc.) with a deliberate aim. **8 a** *colloq.* position or conceal (something incriminating or compromising) for later discovery. **b** *sl.* post or infiltrate (a person) as a spy. **9 a** settle or people (a colony, etc.). **b** found or establish (a city, community, etc.). **10** bury. □ **plant out** transfer (a plant) from a pot or frame to the open ground; set out (seedlings) at intervals. □□ **plant·a·ble** *adj.* **plant·let** *n.* **plant·like** *adj.*

Plan·tag·e·net /plantájinit/ *adj. & n.* ● *adj.* of or relating to the kings of England from Henry II to Richard II (1154–1485). ● *n.* any of these kings.

plan·tain[1] /plántin/ ► any shrub of the genus *Plantago*, with broad flat leaves spread out close to the ground and seeds used as food for birds and as a mild laxative.

PLANTAIN: COMMON PLANTAIN
(*Plantago major*)

plan·tain[2] /plántin/ *n.* **1** a banana plant, *Musa paradisiaca*, widely grown for its fruit. **2** the starchy fruit of this containing less sugar than a banana and chiefly used in cooking.

plan·tar /plántər/ *adj.* of or relating to the sole of the foot.

plan·ta·tion /plantáyshən/ *n.* **1** an estate on which cotton, tobacco, etc., is cultivated esp. by resident (formerly slave) labor. **2** an area planted with trees, etc., for cultivation. **3** *hist.* a colony; colonization.

plant·er /plántər/ *n.* **1** a person who cultivates the soil. **2** the manager or occupier of a coffee, cotton, tobacco, etc., plantation. **3** a large container for decorative plants. **4** a machine for planting seeds, etc.

plan·ti·grade /plántigrayd/ *adj. & n.* ● *adj.* (of an animal) walking on the soles of its feet. ● *n.* a plantigrade animal, e.g., humans or bears.

plaque /plak/ *n.* **1** an ornamental tablet of metal, porcelain, etc., esp. affixed to a building in commemoration. **2** a deposit on teeth where bacteria proliferate. □□ **pla·quette** /plakét/ *n.*

plash[1] /plash/ *n. & v.* ● *n.* **1** a splash. **2 a** a marshy pool. **b** a puddle. ● *v.* **1** *tr. & intr.* splash. **2** *tr.* strike the surface of (water). □□ **plash·y** *adj.*

plash[2] /plash/ *v.tr.* esp. *Brit.* **1** bend down and interweave (branches, twigs, etc.) to form a hedge. **2** make or renew (a hedge) in this way.

plas·ma /plázmə/ *n.* (also **plasm** /plázəm/) **1** the colorless fluid part of blood, lymph, or milk, in which corpuscles or fat globules are suspended. ▷ BLOOD. **2** = PROTOPLASM. **3** a gas of positive ions and free electrons with an approximately equal positive and negative charge. □□ **plas·mic** *adj.*

plas·mo·di·um /plazmṓdeeəm/ ● *n.* (*pl.* **plas·modia** /-deeə/) **1** any parasitic protozoan of the genus *Plasmodium*, including those causing malaria in humans. **2** a form within the life cycle of various microorganisms, including slime molds, usu. consisting of a mass of naked protoplasm containing many nuclei. □□ **plas·mo·di·al** *adj.*

plas·ter /plástər/ *n. & v.* ● *n.* **1** a soft pliable mixture, esp. of lime putty with sand or Portland cement, etc., for spreading on walls, ceilings, etc., to form a smooth hard surface when dried. **2** *hist.* a curative or protective substance spread on a bandage, etc., and applied to the body (*mustard plaster*). ● *v.tr.* **1** cover (a wall, etc.) with plaster or a similar substance. **2** (often foll. by *with*) coat thickly or to excess; bedaub (*plastered the bread with jam; the wall was plastered with slogans*). **3** stick or apply (a thing) thickly like plaster (*plastered glue all over it*). **4** (often foll. by *down*) make (esp. hair) smooth with water, gel, etc.; fix flat. **5** (as **plastered** *adj.*) *sl.* drunk. **6** apply a medical plaster or plaster cast to. □□ **plas·ter·er** *n.* **plas·ter·y** *adj.*

plas·ter·board /plástərbawrd/ *n.* a type of board with a center filling of plaster, used to form or line the inner walls of houses, etc.

plas·ter cast *n.* **1** a bandage stiffened with plaster of Paris and applied to a broken limb, etc. **2** a statue or mold made of plaster.

PLASTER CAST
OF A FOSSIL

plas·ter of Par·is *n.* fine white plaster made of gypsum and used for making plaster casts. ▷ CORNICE

plas·ter saint *n. iron.* a person regarded as being without moral faults or human frailty.

plas·tic /plástik/ *n. & adj.* ● *n.* **1** ▲ any of a number of synthetic polymeric substances that can be given any required shape. **2** (*attrib.*) made of plastic (*plastic bag*); made of cheap materials. **3** = PLASTIC MONEY. ● *adj.* **1 a** capable of being molded; pliant; supple. **b** susceptible; impressionable. **c** artificial; unsincere. **2** molding or giving form to clay, wax, etc. **3** *Biol.* exhibiting an adaptability to environmental changes. **4** (esp. in philosophy) formative;

creative. □□ **plas·ti·cal·ly** *adv.* **plas·tic·i·ty** /-tísitee/ *n.* **plas·ti·cize** /-tisīz/ *v.tr.* **plas·ti·ci·za·tion** /-tisīzáyshən/ *n.* **plas·ti·ciz·er** *n.* **plas·tick·y** *adj.*

plas·tic ex·plo·sive *n.* a putty-like explosive capable of being molded by hand.

Plas·ti·cine /plástiseen/ *n. Trademark* a soft plastic material used, esp. by children, for modeling.

plas·tic mon·ey *n. colloq.* a credit card, charge card, or other plastic card that can be used in place of money.

plas·tic sur·geon *n.* a qualified practitioner of plastic surgery. □□ **plas·tic sur·ge·ry** *n.*

plas·tid /plástid/ *n.* any small organelle in the cytoplasm of a plant cell, containing pigment or food. ▷ DIATOM

plat du jour /pláá də zhoor/ *n.* a dish specially featured on a day's menu.

plate /playt/ *n. & v.* ● *n.* **1 a** a shallow vessel, usu. circular and of earthenware or china, from which food is eaten or served. **b** the contents of this (*ate a plate of sandwiches*). **2** a similar vessel usu. of metal or wood, used esp. for making a collection in a church, etc. **3** a main course of a meal, served on one plate. **4** food and service for one person (*a fundraiser with a $30 per plate dinner*). **5 a** (*collect.*) utensils of silver, gold, or other metal. **b** (*collect.*) objects of plated metal. **c** = PLATING. **6 a** a piece of metal with a name or inscription for affixing to a door, container, etc. **b** = LICENSE PLATE. **7** an illustration on special paper in a book. **8** a thin sheet of metal, glass, etc., coated with a sensitive film for photography. **9** a flat thin usu. rigid sheet of metal, etc., with an even surface and uniform thickness, often as part of a mechanism. **10 a** a smooth piece of metal, etc., for engraving. **b** an impression made from this. **11 a** a thin piece of plastic material, molded to the shape of the mouth and gums, to which artificial teeth or another orthodontic appliance are attached. **b** *colloq.*

PLASTIC

Plastics fall into two main classes according to the way they react to heat. Thermoplastics, such as polyethylene and Plexiglas, can be repeatedly softened and hardened by heating and cooling. Thermosetting plastics, such as epoxy resins and polyurethane, are soft but set hard after heating and cannot be softened by reheating. Some plastics are given added strength by reinforcing them with fibers. These are known as composites.

EXAMPLES OF PLASTICS

THERMOPLASTIC
(POLYETHYLENE BAG)

THERMOSETTING
PLASTIC (EPOXY
BIKE HELMET)

COMPOSITE
PLASTIC
(TENNIS RACKET)

P

a complete denture or orthodontic appliance. **12** *Geol.* each of several rigid sheets of rock thought to form the Earth's outer crust. ▷ PLATE TECTONICS. **13** *Biol.* a thin flat organic structure or formation. **14** a light shoe for a racehorse. **15** stereotype, electrotype, or plastic cast of a page of composed movable types, or a metal or plastic copy of filmset matter, from which sheets are printed. **16** *Baseball* a flat five-sided piece of whitened rubber at which the batter stands and by stepping on which a runner scores.

17 the anode of a vacuum tube. **18** a horizontal timber laid along the top of a wall to support the ends of joists or rafters. ● *v.tr.* **1** apply a thin coat esp. of silver, gold, or tin to (another metal). **2** cover (esp. a ship) with plates of metal, esp. for protection. **3** make a plate of (type, etc.) for printing. □ **on a plate** *colloq.* available with little trouble to the recipient. **on one's plate** for one to deal with or consider. □□ **plate·ful** *n.* (*pl.* **-fuls**). **plate·less** *adj.* **plat·er** *n.*

PLATE TECTONICS

The Earth's lithosphere is thought to consist of semirigid plates that move relative to each other on the underlying asthenosphere (a partly molten layer of the mantle). The movement of these tectonic plates may be caused by convection currents in the Earth's mantle. Mountain-forming, earth-quakes, and volcanoes occur mostly near plate boundaries, where the plates may be moving apart or together, or sliding past each other. The effect this movement has depends on whether the boundary is between two continental plates, two oceanic plates, or an oceanic and a continental plate.

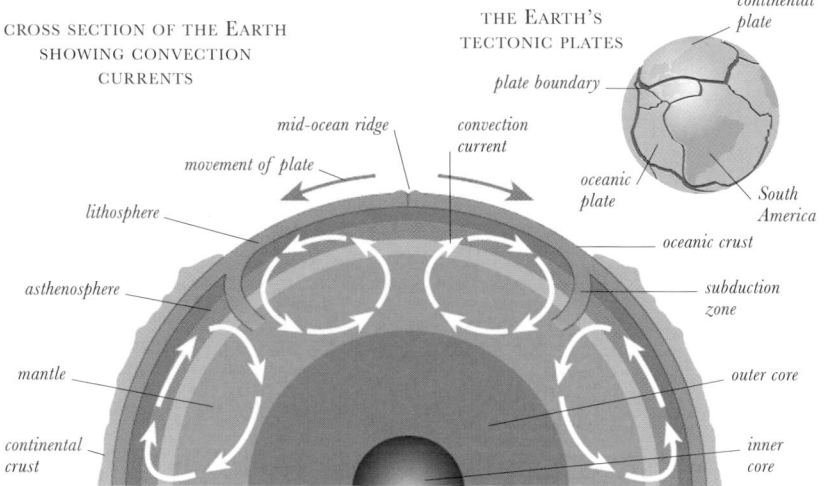

CROSS SECTION OF THE EARTH
SHOWING CONVECTION
CURRENTS

mid-ocean ridge
movement of plate
lithosphere
asthenosphere
mantle
continental
crust

THE EARTH'S
TECTONIC PLATES

continental
plate
plate boundary
convection
current
oceanic
plate
South
America

oceanic crust
subduction
zone
outer core
inner
core

EXAMPLES OF PLATE MOVEMENT

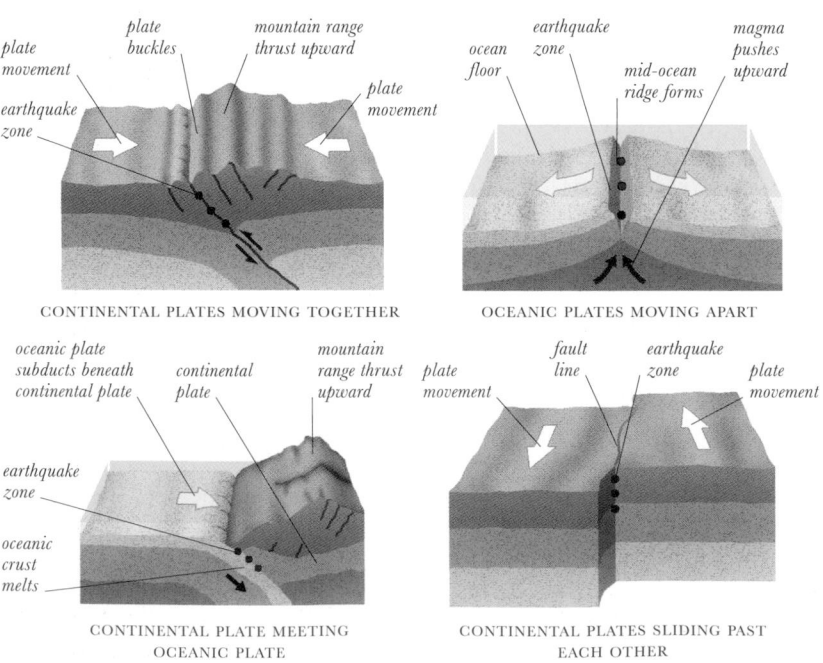

plate
movement
earthquake
zone
plate
buckles
mountain range
thrust upward
plate
movement

CONTINENTAL PLATES MOVING TOGETHER

ocean
floor
earthquake
zone
mid-ocean
ridge forms
magma
pushes
upward

OCEANIC PLATES MOVING APART

oceanic plate
subducts beneath
continental plate
continental
plate
mountain
range thrust
upward
earthquake
zone
oceanic
crust
melts

CONTINENTAL PLATE MEETING
OCEANIC PLATE

plate
movement
fault
line
earthquake
zone
plate
movement

CONTINENTAL PLATES SLIDING PAST
EACH OTHER

plate ar·mor *n.* armor of metal plates, for a man, ship, etc. ▷ ARMOR

pla·teau /platố/ *n. & v.* ● *n.* (*pl.* **plateaux** /-tôz/ or **plateaus**) **1** an area of fairly level high ground. **2** a state of little variation after an increase. ● *v.intr.* (**plateaus**, **plateaued**) (often foll. by *out*) reach a level or stable state after an increase.

plate glass *n.* thick fine-quality glass for storefront windows, etc., orig. cast in plates.

plate·let /pláytlit/ *n.* a small colorless disk of protoplasm found in blood and involved in clotting. ▷ BLOOD

plat·en /plát'n/ *n.* **1** a plate in a printing press which presses the paper against the type. **2** a cylindrical roller in a typewriter against which the paper is held.

plate tec·ton·ics *n.pl.* (usually treated as *sing.*) *Geol.* ◀ the study of the Earth's surface based on the concept of moving plates (see PLATE 12 *n.*) forming its structure. ▷ SEABED

plat·form /plátfawrm/ *n.* **1** a raised level surface; a natural or artificial terrace. **2** a raised surface from which a speaker addresses an audience. **3** a raised elongated structure along the side of a track in a railroad, subway station, etc. **4** the floor area at the entrance to a bus. **5** a thick sole of a shoe. **6** the declared policy of a political party.

plat·ing /pláyting/ *n.* **1** a coating of gold, silver, etc. **2** an act of plating.

pla·tin·ic /plətínik/ *adj.* of or containing (esp. tetravalent) platinum.

plat·i·nize /plát'nīz/ *v.tr.* coat with platinum. □□ **plat·i·ni·za·tion** *n.*

plat·i·noid /plát'noyd/ *n.* an alloy of copper, zinc, nickel, and tungsten.

plat·i·num /plát'nəm/ *n.* *Chem.* ▶ a ductile malleable silvery-white metallic element occurring naturally in nickel and copper ores, unaffected by simple acids and fusible only at a very high temperature, used in making jewelry and laboratory apparatus. ¶ Symb.: **Pt**.

plat·i·num black *n.* platinum in powder form like lampblack.

plat·i·num blonde *adj. & n.* ● *adj.* (also **platinum blond**) silvery-blond. ● *n.* a person with esp. bleached or dyed silvery-blond hair.

PLATINUM
NUGGET

plat·i·tude /plátitood, -tyood/ *n.* **1** a trite or commonplace remark, esp. one solemnly delivered. **2** the use of platitudes; dullness; insipidity. □□ **plat·i·tu·di·nize** /-tood'nīz, -tyoo-/ *v.intr.* **plat·i·tu·di·nous** /-toodənəs/ *adj.*

Pla·ton·ic /plətónik/ *adj.* **1** of or associated with the Greek philosopher Plato (d. 347 BC) or his ideas. **2** (**platonic**) (of love or friendship) purely spiritual; not sexual. **3** (**platonic**) confined to words or theory; not leading to action; harmless. □□ **Pla·ton·i·cal·ly** *adv.*

Pla·ton·ic sol·id (also **Pla·ton·ic bod·y**) *n.* any of the five regular solids (tetrahedron, cube, octahedron, dodecahedron, icosahedron).

Pla·to·nism /pláyt'nizəm/ *n.* the philosophy of Plato or his followers. □□ **Pla·to·nist** *n.*

pla·toon /plətoon/ *n.* **1** *Mil.* a subdivision of a company, a tactical unit commanded by a lieutenant and usu. divided into three sections. **2** a group of persons acting together.

plat·ter /plátər/ *n.* **1** a large flat dish or plate, esp. for food. **2** *colloq.* a phonograph record. □ **on a platter** = *on a plate* (see PLATE).

platy- /pláti, -tee/ *comb. form* broad; flat.

plat·y·hel·minth /plátihélminth/ *n.* any invertebrate of the phylum Platyhelminthes, including flatworms, flukes, and tapeworms.

P

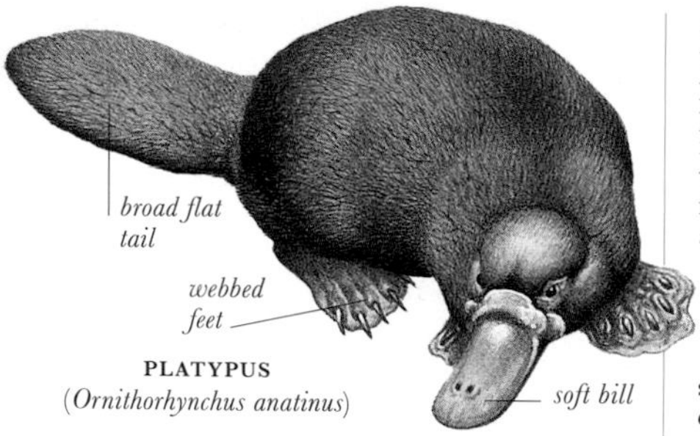

PLATYPUS
(*Ornithorhynchus anatinus*)

plat·y·pus /plátipəs/ *n.* ▲ an Australian aquatic egg-laying mammal, *Ornithorhynchus anatinus,* having a pliable ducklike bill, webbed feet, and sleek gray fur. Also called **duckbill**.

plau·dit /pláwdit/ *n.* (usu. in *pl.*) **1** a round of applause. **2** an emphatic expression of approval.

plau·si·ble /pláwzibəl/ *adj.* **1** (of an argument, statement, etc.) seeming reasonable or probable. **2** (of a person) persuasive but deceptive. ▫▫ **plau·si·bil·i·ty** /-bílitee/ *n.* **plau·si·bly** *adv.*

play /play/ *v.* & *n.* ● *v.* **1** *intr.* (often foll. by *with*) occupy or amuse oneself pleasantly with some recreation, game, exercise, etc. **2** *intr.* (foll. by *with*) act lightheartedly or flippantly (with feelings, etc.). **3** *tr.* **a** perform on or be able to perform on (a musical instrument). **b** perform (a piece of music, etc.). **c** cause (a record, record player, etc.) to produce sounds. **4 a** *intr.* (foll. by *in*) perform a role in (a drama, etc.). **b** *tr.* perform (a drama or role) on stage, or in a movie or broadcast. **c** *tr.* give a dramatic performance at (a particular theater or place). **5** *tr.* act in real life the part of (*play truant; play the fool*). **6** *tr.* (foll. by *on*) perform (a trick or joke, etc.) on (a person). **7** *tr.* (foll. by *for*) regard (a person) as (something specified) (*played me for a fool*). **8** *intr. colloq.* participate; cooperate; do what is wanted (*they won't play*). **9** *intr.* gamble. **10** *tr.* gamble on. **11** *tr.* **a** take part in (a game or recreation). **b** compete with (another player or team) in a game. **c** occupy (a specified position) in a team for a game. **d** (foll. by *in, on, at,* etc.) assign (a player) to a position. **12** *tr.* move (a piece) or display (a playing card) in one's turn in a game. **13** *tr.* (also *absol.*) strike or catch (a ball, etc.) or execute (a stroke) in a game. **14** *intr.* move about in a lively or unrestrained manner. **15** *intr.* (often foll. by *on*) touch gently. **16** *intr.* (often foll. by *at*) **a** engage in a half-hearted way (in an activity). **b** pretend to be. **17** *intr.* (of a court, field, etc.) be conducive to play as specified (*the greens are playing fast*). **18** *intr. colloq.* act or behave (as specified) (*play fair*). **19** *tr.* (foll. by *in, out,* etc.) accompany (a person) with music (*were played out with bagpipes*). ● *n.* **1** recreation, amusement, esp. as the spontaneous activity of children and young animals. **2 a** the playing of a game. **b** the action or manner of this. **c** the status of the ball, etc., in a game as being available to be played according to the rules (*in play; out of play*). **3** a dramatic piece for the stage, etc. **4** activity or operation (*are in full play; brought into play*). **5 a** freedom of movement. **b** space or scope for this. **6** brisk, light, or fitful movement. **7** gambling. **8** an action or maneuver, esp. in or as in a game. ▫ **at play** engaged in recreation. **in play** for amusement; not seriously. **make a play for** *colloq.* make a conspicuous attempt to acquire or attract. **play along** pretend to cooperate. **play around** (or **about**) **1** behave irresponsibly. **2** philander. **play back** play (sounds recently recorded), esp. to monitor recording quality, etc. **play ball** see BALL[1]. **play by ear 1** perform (music) previously heard without having or having seen a score. **2** (also **play it by ear**) proceed instinctively or step by step according to results and circumstances. **play one's cards right** (or **well**) make good use of opportunities; act shrewdly. **play down** minimize the importance of. **played out** exhausted of energy or usefulness. **play false** act, or treat a (person), deceitfully or treacherously. **play fast and loose** act unreliably; ignore one's obligations. **play for time** seek to gain time by delaying. **play into a person's hands** act so as unwittingly to give a person an advantage. **play it cool** *colloq.* **1** affect indifference. **2** be relaxed or unemotional. **play the market** speculate in stocks, etc. **play off** (usu. foll. by *against*) **1** oppose (one person against another), esp. for one's own advantage. **2** play an extra match to decide a draw or tie. **play on 1** continue to play. **2** take advantage of (a person's feelings, etc.). **play on words** a pun. **play possum** see POSSUM. **play safe** (or **for safety**) avoid risks. **play up** make the most of; emphasize. **play up to** flatter, esp. to win favor. **play with fire** take foolish risks. ▫▫ **play·a·ble** *adj.* **play·a·bil·i·ty** /pláyabílitee/ *n.*

pla·ya /plaáyə/ *n.* a flat dried-up area, esp. a desert basin from which water evaporates quickly.

play·act /pláyakt/ *v.* **1** *intr.* act in a play. **2** *intr.* behave affectedly or insincerely. **3** *tr.* act (a scene, part, etc.). ▫▫ **play·act·ing** *n.* **play·ac·tor** *n.*

play·back /pláybak/ *n.* an act or instance of replaying recorded audio or video from a tape, etc.

play·bill /pláybil/ *n.* **1** a poster announcing a theatrical performance. **2** a theater program.

play·book /pláybŏŏk/ *n. N. Amer.* a book containing a sports team's strategies and plays, esp. in football.

play·boy /pláyboy/ *n.* an irresponsible pleasure-seeking man, esp. a wealthy one.

play-by-play *adj.* & *n.* ● *adj.* pertaining to a description, esp. of a sports event, with continuous commentary. ● *n.* such a description.

play·er /pláyər/ *n.* **1 a** a person taking part in a sport or game. **b** a gambler. **2** a person playing a musical instrument. **3** a person who plays a part on the stage; an actor. **4** = RECORD PLAYER.

play·er pi·an·o *n.* a piano fitted with an apparatus enabling it to be played automatically.

play·fel·low /pláyfelō/ *n.* a playmate.

play·ful /pláyfŏŏl/ *adj.* **1** fond of games, etc. **2** done in fun. ▫▫ **play·ful·ly** *adv.* **play·ful·ness** *n.*

play·go·er /pláygōər/ *n.* a person who goes often to the theater.

play·ground /pláygrownd/ *n.* an outdoor area set aside for children to play.

play·group /pláygrōōp/ *n.* a group of preschool children who play regularly together at a particular place under supervision.

play·house /pláyhows/ *n.* **1** a theater. ▷ THEATER. **2** a toy house for children to play in.

play·ing card /pláying/ *n.* each of a set of usu. 52 rectangular pieces of card or other material with an identical pattern on one side and different values represented by numbers and symbols on the other, used to play various games.

play·ing field /pláying/ *n.* a field used for outdoor team games.

play·let /pláylit/ *n.* a short play or dramatic piece.

play·mate /pláymayt/ *n.* a child's companion in play.

play-off *n. Sports* a game played to break a tie.

play·pen /pláypen/ *n.* a portable enclosure for young children to play in.

play·thing /pláything/ *n.* **1** a toy or other thing to play with. **2** a person treated as a toy.

play·time /pláytīm/ *n.* time for play or recreation.

play·wright /pláyrīt/ *n.* a person who writes plays.

pla·za /plaázə/ *n.* **1** a marketplace or open square (esp. in a town). **2** a public area beside an expressway with facilities such as restaurants or service stations.

plc *Brit. abbr.* (also **PLC**) Public Limited Company.

plea /plee/ *n.* **1** an earnest appeal or entreaty. **2** *Law* a formal statement by or on behalf of a defendant. **3** an argument or excuse.

plea bar·gain *n.* (also **plea bar·gain·ing**) an arrangement between prosecutor and defendant whereby the defendant pleads guilty to a lesser charge in the expectation of leniency. ▫▫ **plea-bar·gain** *v.intr.*

plead /pleed/ *v.* (*past* and *past part.* **pleaded** or **pled** /pled/) **1** *intr.* (foll. by *with*) make an earnest appeal to. **2** *intr. Law* address a court of law as an advocate on behalf of a party. **3** *tr.* maintain (a cause) esp. in a court of law. **4** *tr. Law* declare to be one's state as regards guilt in or responsibility for a crime (*plead guilty; plead insanity*). **5** *tr.* offer or allege as an excuse (*pleaded forgetfulness*). **6** *intr.* make an appeal or entreaty. ▫ **plead** (or **take**) **the Fifth** refuse to incriminate oneself legally, in accordance with the Fifth Amendment to the Constitution. ▫▫ **plead·a·ble** *adj.* **plead·er** *n.* **plead·ing·ly** *adv.*

plead·ing /pléeding/ *n.* (usu. in *pl.*) a formal statement of the cause of an action or defense.

pleas·ant /plézənt/ *adj.* (**pleasanter, pleasantest**) pleasing to the mind, feelings, or senses. ▫▫ **pleas·ant·ly** *adv.* **pleas·ant·ness** *n.*

pleas·ant·ry /plézəntree/ *n.* (*pl.* **-ies**) **1** a pleasant or amusing remark, esp. made in casual conversation. **2** a humorous manner of speech. **3** jocularity.

please /pleez/ *v.* **1** *tr.* (also *absol.*) be agreeable to; make glad; give pleasure to. **2** *tr.* (in *passive*) **a** (foll. by *to* + infin.) be glad or willing to. **b** (often foll. by *about, at, with*) derive pleasure or satisfaction (from). **3** *tr.* (with *it* as subject; usu. foll. by *to* + infin.) be the inclination or wish of. **4** *intr.* think fit; have the will or desire (*take as many as you please*). **5** *tr.* used in polite requests (*come in, please*). ▫ **if you please** if you are willing, esp. *iron.* to indicate unreasonableness (*then, if you please, we had to pay*). **please oneself** do as one likes. ▫▫ **pleased** *adj.* **pleas·ing** *adj.* **pleas·ing·ly** *adv.*

pleas·ur·a·ble /plézhərəbəl/ *adj.* causing pleasure. ▫▫ **pleas·ur·a·ble·ness** *n.* **pleas·ur·a·bly** *adv.*

pleas·ure /plézhər/ *n.* & *v.* ● *n.* **1** a feeling of satisfaction or joy. **2** enjoyment. **3** a source of pleasure or gratification. **4** *formal* a person's will or desire (*what is your pleasure?*). **5** sensual gratification or enjoyment. **6** (*attrib.*) done or used for pleasure (*pleasure ground*). ● *v.* **1** *tr.* give (esp. sexual) pleasure to. **2** *intr.* (often foll. by *in*) take pleasure. ▫ **take pleasure in** like doing. **with pleasure** gladly.

pleat /pleet/ *n.* & *v.* ● *n.* a fold or crease, esp. a flattened fold in cloth doubled upon itself. ● *v.tr.* make a pleat or pleats in.

pleb /pleb/ *n. colloq.* usu. *derog.* an ordinary insignificant person. ▫▫ **pleb·by** *adj.*

plebe /pleeb/ *n.* a first-year student at a military academy.

ple·be·ian /plibéeən/ *n.* & *adj.* ● *n.* a commoner, esp. in ancient Rome. (cf. PATRICIAN). ● *adj.* **1** of low birth; of the common people. **2** uncultured. **3** coarse; ignoble. ▫▫ **ple·be·ian·ism** *n.*

pleb·i·scite /plébisīt, -sit/ *n.* **1** the direct vote of all the electors of a nation, etc., on an important public question, e.g., a change in the constitution. **2** the public expression of a community's opinion, with or without binding force. **3** *Rom.Hist.* a law enacted by the plebeians' assembly. ▫▫ **ple·bi·sci·ta·ry** /pləbísiteree, plebisít-/ *adj.*

plec·trum /pléktrəm/ *n.* (*pl.* **plectrums** or **plectra** /-trə/) a thin flat piece of plastic or horn, etc., held in the hand and used to pluck a string, esp. of a guitar.

pled *past* of PLEAD.

pledge /plej/ *n.* & *v.* ● *n.* **1** a solemn promise or undertaking. **2** a thing given as security for the fulfillment of a contract, the payment of a debt, etc., and liable to forfeiture in the event of failure. **3** a thing put in pawn. **4** a thing given as a token of love, favor, or something to come. **5** the drinking of a person's health; a toast. **6** a solemn undertaking to abstain from alcohol (*sign the pledge*). **7** a person who has promised to join a fraternity or sorority. ● *v.tr.* **1 a** deposit as security. **b** pawn. **2** promise solemnly by the pledge of (one's honor, word, etc.). **3** (often *refl.*) bind by a solemn promise. **4** drink to the health of. ▫ **pledge one's troth** see TROTH. ▫▫ **pledg·er** *n.* **pledg·or** *n.*

Ple·ia·des /plée·ədeez, pláy-/ *n.pl.* a cluster of six visible stars in the constellation Taurus, usu. known as the Seven Sisters after seven sisters in Greek mythology.

Pleis·to·cene /plístəseen/ *adj. & n. Geol.* ● *adj.* of or relating to the first epoch of the Quaternary period marked by great fluctuations in temperature with glacial periods followed by interglacial periods. ● *n.* this epoch or system. Also called **Ice Age**.

ple·na·ry /pléenəree, plén-/ *adj.* **1** entire; unqualified; absolute (*plenary indulgence*). **2** (of an assembly) to be attended by all members.

plen·i·po·ten·ti·a·ry /plénipəténshəree, -shee-eree/ *n. & adj.* ● *n.* (*pl.* **-ies**) a person (esp. a diplomat) invested with the full power of independent action. ● *adj.* **1** having this power. **2** (of power) absolute.

plen·i·tude /plénitood, -tyood/ *n.* **1** fullness; completeness. **2** abundance.

plen·te·ous /pléntees/ *adj.* plentiful. □□ **plen·te·ous·ly** *adv.* **plen·te·ous·ness** *n.*

plen·ti·ful /pléntifool/ *adj.* abundant; copious. □□ **plen·ti·ful·ly** *adv.* **plen·ti·ful·ness** *n.*

plen·ty /pléntee/ *n., adj., & adv.* ● *n.* **1** (often foll. by *of*) a great or sufficient quantity or number (*we have plenty*; *plenty of time*). **2** abundance (*in great plenty*). ● *adj. colloq.* existing in an ample quantity. ● *adv. colloq.* fully; entirely (*it is plenty large enough*).

ple·num /pléenəm, plénəm/ *n.* **1** a full assembly of people or a committee, etc. **2** *Physics* space filled with matter.

ple·o·nasm /pléeənazəm/ *n.* the use of more words than are needed to give the sense (e.g., *see with one's eyes*). □□ **ple·o·nas·tic** /-nástik/ *adj.* **ple·o·nas·ti·cal·ly** *adv.*

ple·si·o·sau·rus /pléeseeəsáwrəs/ *n.* (also **ple·si·o·saur** /-sawr/) any of a group of extinct marine reptiles with a broad flat body, short tail, long flexible neck, and large paddle-like limbs. ▷ ELASMOSAURUS

pleth·o·ra /pléthərə/ *n.* **1** an oversupply, glut, or excess. **2** *Med.* **a** an abnormal excess of red corpuscles in the blood. **b** an excess of any body fluid. □□ **ple·thor·ic** /plətháwrik, -thór-/ *adj.* **ple·thor·i·cal·ly** *adv.*

pleu·ra /plōrə/ *n.* (*pl.* **pleurae** /-ree/) each of a pair of serous membranes lining the thorax and enveloping the lungs in mammals. □□ **pleu·ral** *adj.*

pleu·ri·sy /plōrisee/ *n.* inflammation of the pleura, marked by pain in the chest or side, fever, etc. □□ **pleu·rit·ic** /-ritik/ *adj.*

pleuro- /plōrō/ *comb. form* **1** denoting the pleura. **2** denoting the side.

Plex·i·glas /pléksiglas/ *n. Trademark* tough, clear thermoplastic used instead of glass.

plex·us /pléksəs/ *n.* (*pl.* same or **plexuses**) *Anat.* a network of nerves or vessels (*gastric plexus*). □□ **plex·i·form** *adj.*

pli·a·ble /plíəbəl/ *adj.* **1** bending easily; supple. **2** yielding; compliant. □□ **pli·a·bil·i·ty** *n.* **pli·a·ble·ness** *n.* **pli·a·bly** *adv.*

pli·ant /plíənt/ *adj.* = PLIABLE 1. □□ **pli·an·cy** *n.* **pli·ant·ly** *adv.*

plié /plee-áy/ *n. Ballet* a bending of the knees with the feet on the ground.

pli·ers /plíərz/ *n.pl.* ◀ pincers with parallel flat usu. serrated surfaces for holding small objects, bending wire, etc.

plight[1] /plīt/ *n.* a condition or state, esp. an unfortunate one.

plight[2] /plīt/ *v.tr. archaic* **1** pledge or promise solemnly (one's faith, loyalty, etc.). **2** (foll. by *to*) engage, esp. in marriage. □ **plight one's troth** see TROTH.

plim·soll /plímsəl, -sōl/ *n.* (also **plim·sole**) *Brit.* a kind of sneaker with a canvas upper.

Plimsoll line /plímsəl, -sōl/ *n.* (also **Plimsoll mark**) a marking on a ship's side showing the limit of legal submersion under various conditions.

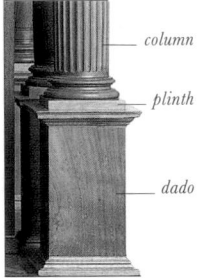

PLINTH

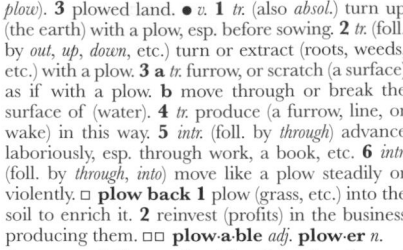

column

plinth

dado

plink /plingk/ *v.* **1** *intr.* emit a short, sharp, metallic ringing sound. **2** *tr. chiefly N. Amer.* shoot at (a target) casually.

plinth /plinth/ *n.* **1** ◀ the lower square slab at the base of a column. **2** a base supporting a vase or statue, etc.

Pli·o·cene /plíəseen/ *adj. & n. Geol.* ● *adj.* of or relating to the last epoch of the Tertiary period with evidence of the extinction of many mammals, and the development of hominids. ● *n.* this epoch or system.

PLO *abbr.* Palestine Liberation Organization.

plod /plod/ *v. & n.* ● *v.* (**plodded, plodding**) **1** *intr.* (often foll. by *along, on,* etc.) walk doggedly or laboriously; trudge. **2** *intr.* (often foll. by *at*) work slowly and steadily. **3** *tr.* tread or make (one's way) laboriously. ● *n.* the act or a spell of plodding. □□ **plod·der** *n.* **plod·ding·ly** *adv.*

-ploid /ployd/ *comb. form Biol.* forming adjectives denoting the number of sets of chromosomes in a cell (*diploid*; *polyploid*).

ploi·dy /plóydee/ *n.* the number of sets of chromosomes in a cell.

plonk var. of PLUNK.

plop /plop/ *n., v., & adv.* ● *n.* **1** a sound as of a smooth object dropping into water without a splash. **2** an act of falling with this sound. ● *v.* (**plopped, plopping**) *intr. & tr.* fall or drop with a plop. ● *adv.* with a plop.

plo·sion /plṓzhən/ *n. Phonet.* the sudden release of breath in the pronunciation of a stop consonant.

plo·sive /plṓsiv/ *adj. & n. Phonet.* ● *adj.* pronounced with a sudden release of breath. ● *n.* a plosive sound.

plot /plot/ *n. & v.* ● *n.* **1** a defined and usu. small piece of ground. **2** the interrelationship of the main events in a play, novel, movie, etc. **3** a conspiracy or secret plan, esp. to achieve an unlawful end. **4** a graph or diagram. **5** a graph showing the relation between two variables. ● *v.* (**plotted, plotting**) *tr.* **1** make a plan or map of (an existing object, a place or thing to be laid out, constructed, etc.). **2** (also *absol.*) plan or contrive secretly (a crime, conspiracy, etc.). **3** mark (a point or course, etc.) on a chart or diagram. **4 a** mark out or allocate (points) on a graph. **b** make (a curve, etc.) by marking out a number of points. □□ **plot·less** *adj.* **plot·less·ness** *n.* **plot·ter** *n.*

plough esp. *Brit.* var. of PLOW. □ **the Plough** *Brit.* = BIG DIPPER.

plov·er /plúvər, plṓ-/ *n.* any plump-breasted shorebird of the family Charadriidae, including the lapwing, sandpiper, etc.

plow /plow/ *n. & v.* (also *Brit.* **plough**) ● *n.* **1** ▼ an implement with a cutting blade fixed in a frame drawn by a tractor or by horses, for cutting furrows in the soil and turning it up. **2** an implement resembling this and having a comparable function (*snow-*

PLOW: 1940s TRACTOR-DRAWN PLOW

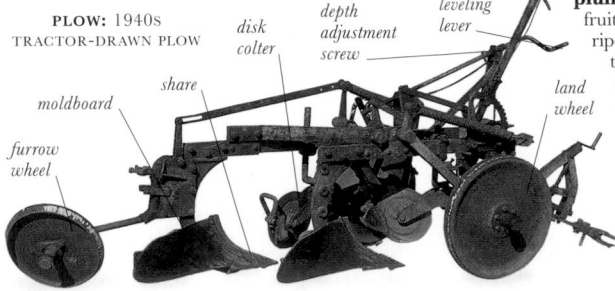

disk colter

depth adjustment screw

leveling lever

land wheel

share

moldboard

furrow wheel

plow). **3** plowed land. ● *v.* **1** *tr.* (also *absol.*) turn up (the earth) with a plow, esp. before sowing. **2** *tr.* (foll. by *out, up, down,* etc.) turn or extract (roots, weeds, etc.) with a plow. **3 a** *tr.* furrow, or scratch (a surface) as if with a plow. **b** move through or break the surface of (water). **4** *tr.* produce (a furrow, line, or wake) in this way. **5** *intr.* (foll. by *through*) advance laboriously, esp. through work, a book, etc. **6** *intr.* (foll. by *through, into*) move like a plow steadily or violently. □ **plow back 1** plow (grass, etc.) into the soil to enrich it. **2** reinvest (profits) in the business producing them. □□ **plow·a·ble** *adj.* **plow·er** *n.*

plow·man /plṓwmən/ *n.* (also *Brit.* **ploughman**) (*pl.* **-men**) a person who uses a plow.

plow·share /plṓwshair/ *n.* the cutting blade of a plow.

ploy /ploy/ *n. colloq.* a stratagem; a cunning maneuver to gain an advantage.

pluck /pluk/ *v. & n.* ● *v.* **1** *tr.* (often foll. by *out, off,* etc.) remove by picking or pulling out or away. **2** *tr.* strip (a bird) of feathers. **3** *tr.* pull at; twitch. **4** *intr.* (foll. by *at*) tug or snatch at. **5** *tr.* sound (the string of a musical instrument) with the finger or plectrum, etc. **6** *tr.* plunder. **7** *tr.* swindle. ● *n.* **1** courage; spirit. **2** an act of plucking; a twitch. □ **pluck up** summon up (one's courage, spirits, etc.). □□ **pluck·er** *n.* **pluck·less** *adj.*

pluck·y /plúkee/ *adj.* (**pluckier, pluckiest**) brave; spirited. □□ **pluck·i·ly** *adv.* **pluck·i·ness** *n.*

plug /plug/ *n. & v.* ● *n.* **1** a piece of solid material fitting tightly into a hole, used to fill a gap or cavity or act as a wedge or stopper. **2 a** a device of metal pins in an insulated casing fitting into holes in a socket for making an electrical connection, esp. between an appliance and a power supply. **b** *colloq.* an electric socket. **3** = SPARK PLUG. **4** *colloq.* a piece of (often free) publicity for an idea, product, etc. **5** ▼ a mass of solidified lava filling the neck of a volcano. **6** a cake or stick of tobacco; a piece of this for chewing. **7** = FIREPLUG. ● *v.* (**plugged, plugging**) **1** *tr.* (often foll. by *up*) stop up (a hole, etc.) with a plug. **2** *tr. sl.* shoot or hit (a person, etc.). **3** *tr. colloq.* seek to popularize (an idea, product, etc.) by constant recommendation. **4** *intr. colloq.* (often foll. by *at*) work steadily away (at). □ **plug away (at)** work steadily (at). **plug in** connect electrically by inserting a plug in a socket. **plug into** connect with, as by means of a plug. □□ **plug·ger** *n.*

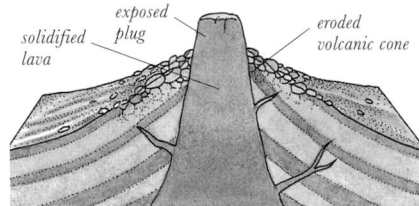

exposed plug

solidified lava

eroded volcanic cone

PLUG: EXPOSED VOLCANIC PLUG

plug-in *adj.* able to be connected by means of a plug.

plug·o·la /plugṓlə/ *n. colloq.* **1** a bribe offered in return for incidental or surreptitious promotion of a person or product, esp. on radio or television. **2** the practice of such bribery.

plum /plum/ *n.* **1 a** an oval fleshy fruit, usu. purple or yellow when ripe, with sweet pulp and a flattish pointed stone. **b** any deciduous tree of the genus *Prunus*, bearing this. **2** a reddish-purple color. **3** a dried grape or raisin used in cooking. **4** *colloq.* the best of a collection; something especially prized (often *attrib.: a plum job*).

plum·age /plṓomij/ *n.* a bird's feathers. □□ **plum·aged** *adj.* (usu. in *comb.*).

P

PLIERS

plumb

PLUMB AND LINE

plumb[1] /plum/ *n., adv., adj., & v.* ● *n.* ◄ a ball of lead or other heavy material, esp. one attached to the end of a line for finding the depth of water or determining the vertical on an upright surface. ● *adv.* **1** exactly (*plumb in the center*). **2** vertically. **3** *sl.* quite; utterly (*plumb crazy*). ● *adj.* vertical. ● *v.tr.* **1 a** measure the depth of (water) with a plumb. **b** determine (a depth). **2** test (an upright surface) to determine the vertical. **3** reach or experience in extremes (*plumb the depths of fear*). **4** learn in detail the facts about (a matter). □ **out of plumb** not vertical.

plumb[2] /plum/ *v.* **1** *tr.* provide (a building or room, etc.) with plumbing. **2** *tr.* (often foll. by *in*) fit as part of a plumbing system. **3** *intr.* work as a plumber.

plum·ba·go /plumbáygō/ *n.* (*pl.* **-os**) **1** = GRAPHITE. **2** ▼ any plant of the genus *Plumbago*, with gray or blue flowers.

PLUMBAGO
(*Plumbago auriculata*)

plum·be·ous /plúmbeeəs/ *adj.* **1** of or like lead. **2** lead-glazed.

plumb·er /plúmər/ *n.* a person who fits and repairs the apparatus of a water supply system.

plum·bic /plúmbik/ *adj.* **1** *Chem.* containing lead, esp. in its tetravalent form. **2** *Med.* due to the presence of lead. □□ **plum·bism** *n.* (in sense 2).

plumb·ing /plúming/ *n.* **1** the system or apparatus of water supply, heating, etc., in a building. **2** the work of a plumber. **3** *colloq.* any system of tubes, vessels, etc., that carry fluids.

plumb·less /plúmlis/ *adj.* (of a depth of water, etc.) that cannot be plumbed.

plumb line *n.* a line with a plumb attached. ▷ PLUMB

plum·bous /plúmbəs/ *n. Chem.* containing lead in its divalent form.

plume /plṓm/ *n. & v.* ● *n.* **1** a feather, esp. a large one used for ornament. **2** an ornament of feathers, etc., attached to a helmet or hat or worn in the hair. ▷ SHAKO. **3** something resembling this (*a plume of smoke*). **4** *Zool.* a feather-like part or formation. ● *v.* **1** *tr.* decorate or provide with a plume or plumes. **2** *refl.* (foll. by *on, upon*) pride (oneself on esp. something trivial). □□ **plume·less** *adj.* **plume·like** *adj.* **plum·er·y** *n.*

plum·met /plúmit/ *n. & v.* ● *n.* **1** a plumb or plumb line. **2** a sounding line. **3** a weight attached to a fishing line to keep the float upright. ● *v.intr.* (**plummeted**, **plummeting**) fall or plunge rapidly.

plum·my /plúmee/ *adj.* (**plummier, plummiest**) **1** abounding or rich in plums. **2** *colloq.* **a** (of a voice) sounding affectedly rich or deep in tone. **b** snobbish. **3** *colloq.* good; desirable.

plu·mose /plṓmōs/ *adj.* **1** feathered. **2** feather-like.

plump[1] /plump/ *adj. & v.* ● *adj.* (esp. of a person or animal or part of the body) having a full rounded shape; fleshy; filled out. ● *v.tr. & intr.* (often foll. by *up, out*) make or become plump; fatten. □□ **plump·ish** *adj.* **plump·ly** *adv.* **plump·ness** *n.* **plump·y** *adj.*

plump[2] /plump/ *v., n., adv., & adj.* ● *v.* **1** *intr. & tr.* (often foll. by *down*) drop or fall abruptly (*plumped down on the chair*). **2** *intr.* (foll. by *for*) decide definitely in favor of (one of two or more possibilities). **3** *tr.* (often foll. by *out*) utter abruptly; blurt out. ● *n.* an abrupt plunge; a heavy fall. ● *adv. colloq.* **1** with a sudden or heavy fall. **2** directly; bluntly (*I told him plump*). ● *adj. colloq.* direct; unqualified (*answered with a plump 'no'*).

plum·y /plṓmee/ *adj.* (**plumier, plumiest**) **1** plumelike; feathery. **2** adorned with plumes.

plun·der /plúndər/ *v. & n.* ● *v.tr.* **1** rob (a place or person) forcibly of goods, e.g., as in war. **2** rob systematically. **3** (also *absol.*) steal or embezzle (goods). ● *n.* **1** the violent or dishonest acquisition of property. **2** property acquired by plundering. **3** *colloq.* profit; gain. □□ **plun·der·er** *n.*

plunge /plunj/ *v. & n.* ● *v.* **1** (usu. foll. by *in, into*) **a** *tr.* thrust forcefully or abruptly. **b** *intr.* dive; propel oneself forcibly. **c** *intr. & tr.* enter or cause to enter a certain condition or embark on a certain course abruptly or impetuously (*the room was plunged into darkness*). **2** *tr.* immerse completely. **3** *intr.* **a** move suddenly and dramatically downward. **b** (foll. by *down, into*, etc.) move with a rush (*plunged down the stairs*). **c** diminish rapidly (*share prices have plunged*). ● *n.* a plunging action or movement; a dive. □ **take the plunge** *colloq.* commit oneself to a (usu. risky) course of action.

plung·er /plúnjər/ *n.* **1** a part of a mechanism that works with a plunging or thrusting movement. **2** a rubber cup on a handle for clearing blocked pipes by a plunging and sucking action.

plunk /plungk/ *n. & v.* ● *n.* **1** the sound made by the sharply plucked string of a stringed instrument. **2** a heavy blow or thud. ● *v.* **1** *intr. & tr.* sound or cause to sound with a plunk. **2** *tr.* hit abruptly. **3** *tr.* set down hurriedly or clumsily. **4** *tr.* (usu. foll. by *down*) set down firmly.

plu·per·fect /plṓpárfikt/ *adj. & n. Gram.* ● *adj.* (of a tense) denoting an action completed prior to some past point of time specified or implied, formed in English by *had* and the past participle, as: *he had gone by then.* ● *n.* the pluperfect tense.

plu·ral /plṓrəl/ *adj. & n.* ● *adj.* **1** more than one in number. **2** *Gram.* (of a word or form) denoting more than one, or (in languages with dual number) more than two. ● *n. Gram.* **1** a plural word or form. **2** the plural number. □□ **plu·ral·ly** *adv.*

plu·ral·ism /plṓrəlizəm/ *n.* **1** holding more than one office, esp. an ecclesiastical office or benefice, at a time. **2** a form of society in which the members of minority groups maintain their independent cultural traditions. □□ **plu·ral·ist** *n.* **plu·ral·is·tic** *adj.* **plu·ral·is·ti·cal·ly** *adv.*

plu·ral·i·ty /plṓrálitee/ *n.* (*pl.* **-ies**) **1** the state of being plural. **2** = PLURALISM 1. **3** a large or the greater number. **4** a majority that is not absolute.

plu·ral·ize /plṓrəlīz/ *v.* **1** *tr. & intr.* make or become plural. **2** *tr.* express in the plural. **3** *intr.* hold more than one ecclesiastical office or benefice.

pluri- /plṓree/ *comb. form* several.

plus /plus/ *prep., adj., n., & conj.* ● *prep.* **1** *Math.* with the addition of (*3 plus 4 equals 7*). ¶ Symbol: +. **2** (of temperature) above zero (*plus 2° C*). **3** *colloq.* with; having gained; newly possessing (*returned plus a new car*). ● *adj.* **1** (after a number) at least (*fifteen plus*). **2** (after a grade, etc.) somewhat better than (*C plus*). **3** *Math.* positive. **4** having a positive electrical charge. **5** (*attrib.*) additional; extra (*plus business*). ● *n.* **1** = PLUS SIGN. **2** *Math.* an additional or positive quantity. **3** an advantage (*experience is a definite plus*). ● *conj. colloq. disp.* also; and furthermore (*they arrived late, plus they were hungry*).

plus fours *n.* ► long wide men's knickers usu. worn for golf, etc.

plush /plush/ *n. & adj.* ● *n.* cloth of silk, cotton, etc., with a long soft nap. ● *adj.* **1** made of plush. **2** plushy. □□ **plush·ly** *adv.* **plush·ness** *n.*

plush·y /plúshee/ *adj.* (**plushier, plushiest**) *colloq.* stylish, luxurious. □□ **plush·i·ness** *n.*

plus sign *n.* the symbol +, indicating addition or a positive value.

plu·tarch·y /plṓtaarkee/ *n.* (*pl.* **-ies**) plutocracy.

Plu·to /plṓto/ *n.* ▼ the outermost known planet of the solar system. ▷ SOLAR SYSTEM

plus fours

PLUS FOURS

P

PLUTO

Pluto is the smallest planet in the solar system, and the outermost, except for the 20 years of its 248-year elliptical orbit when it passes inside the path of Neptune. It is a rocky planet, probably covered with ice and frozen methane, but little else is known about it. Pluto's only known moon, Charon, is large for a moon, at half the size of its parent planet.

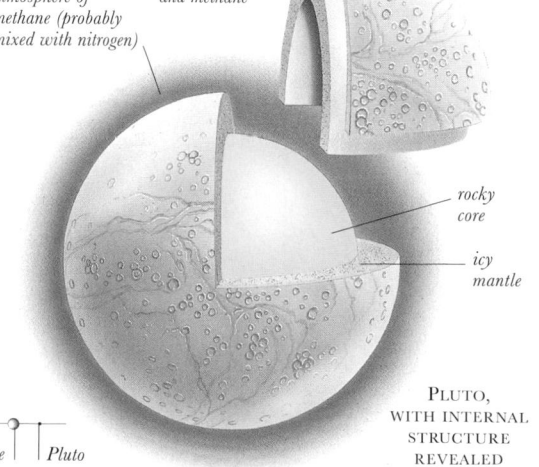

surface of ice and methane

atmosphere of methane (probably mixed with nitrogen)

rocky core

icy mantle

Earth

SOLAR SYSTEM

Sun

Neptune

Pluto

PLUTO, WITH INTERNAL STRUCTURE REVEALED

plu·toc·ra·cy /plō͞otókrəsee/ *n.* (*pl.* **-ies**) **1 a** govern ment by the wealthy. **b** a nation governed in this way. **2** a wealthy élite or ruling class. □□ **plu·to·crat·ic** /plō͞otəkrátik/ *adj.* **plu·to·crat·i·cal·ly** *adv.*

plu·to·crat /plō͞otəkrat/ *n.* **1** a member of a plutocracy or wealthy élite. **2** a wealthy and influential person.

Plu·to·ni·an /plō͞otṓneeən/ *adj.* **1** infernal. **2** of the infernal regions.

plu·ton·ic /plō͞otónik/ *adj.* **1** *Geol.* (of rock) formed as igneous rock by solidification below the surface of the Earth. **2** (**Plutonic**) = PLUTONIAN.

plu·to·ni·um /plō͞otṓneeəm/ *n. Chem.* a dense silvery radioactive metallic transuranic element of the actinide series, used in some nuclear reactors and weapons. ¶ Symb.: **Pu**.

plu·vi·al /plō͞oveeəl/ *adj. & n.* ● *adj.* **1** of rain; rainy. **2** *Geol.* caused by rain. ● *n.* a period of prolonged rainfall. □□ **plu·vi·ous** *adj.* (in sense 1).

ply[1] /plī/ *n.* (*pl.* **-ies**) **1** a thickness or layer of certain materials, esp. wood or cloth (*three-ply*). **2** a strand of yarn or rope, etc.

ply[2] /plī/ *v.* (**-ies, -ied**) **1** *tr.* use or wield vigorously (a tool, weapon, etc.). **2** *tr.* work steadily at (one's business or trade). **3** *tr.* (foll. by *with*) **a** supply (a person) continuously (with food, drink, etc.). **b** approach repeatedly (with questions, demands, etc.). **4 a** *intr.* (often foll. by *between*) (of a vehicle, etc.) travel regularly (to and fro between two points). **b** *tr.* work (a route) in this way. **5** *intr.* (of a

PNEUMATIC DRILL

A pneumatic drill is used to break up concrete and asphalt, often on roads. Compressed air forces the tool of the drill up and down in a four-stage cycle. In the stage shown here, compressed air enters a cylinder above a piston, forcing it down. The piston strikes the anvil, driving the tool into the road surface.

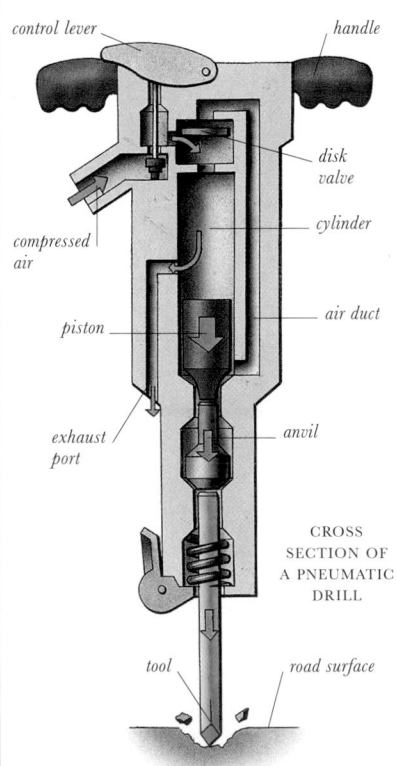

control lever · handle · disk valve · cylinder · compressed air · air duct · piston · anvil · exhaust port · tool · road surface

CROSS SECTION OF A PNEUMATIC DRILL

taxi driver, boatman, etc.) attend regularly for custom (*ply for trade*).

ply·wood /plíwŏŏd/ *n.* a strong thin board consisting of two or more layers glued and pressed together with the direction of the grain alternating.

PM *abbr.* **1** Postmaster. **2** postmortem. **3** Prime Minister.

Pm *symb. Chem.* the element promethium.

p.m. *abbr.* between noon and midnight.

PMS *abbr.* premenstrual syndrome.

pneu·mat·ic /nŏŏmátik, nyŏŏ-/ *adj.* **1** of or relating to air or wind. **2** containing or operated by compressed air. **3** connected with or containing air cavities, esp. in the bones of birds or in fish. □□ **pneu·mat·i·cal·ly** *adv.* **pneu·ma·tic·i·ty** /nŏŏmətísitee, nyŏŏ-/ *n.*

pneu·mat·ic drill *n.* ▼ a drill driven by compressed air, for breaking up a hard surface.

pneu·mat·ics /nŏŏmátiks, nyŏŏ-/ *n.pl.* (treated as *sing.*) the science of the mechanical properties of gases.

pneumo- /nŏŏmō, nyŏŏ-/ *comb. form* denoting the lungs.

pneu·mo·co·ni·o·sis /nŏŏmōkōneeṓsis, nyŏŏ-/ *n.* a lung disease caused by inhalation of dust or small particles.

pneu·mo·nia /nŏŏmṓnyə, nyŏŏ-/ *n.* a bacterial inflammation of one lung (**single pneumonia**) or both lungs (**double pneumonia**) causing the air sacs to fill with pus and become solid. □□ **pneu·mon·ic** /-mónik/ *adj.*

PO *abbr.* **1** Post Office. **2** postal order. **3** Petty Officer.

Po *symb. Chem.* the element polonium.

poach[1] /pōch/ *v.tr.* **1** cook (an egg) without its shell in or over boiling water. **2** cook (fish, etc.) by simmering in a small amount of liquid. □□ **poach·er** *n.*

poach[2] /pōch/ *v.* **1** *tr.* (also *absol.*) catch (game or fish) illegally. **2** *intr.* (often foll. by *on*) trespass or encroach (on another's property, ideas, etc.). **3** *tr.* appropriate illicitly or unfairly (a person, thing, idea, etc.). □□ **poach·er** *n.*

po·chard /pṓchərd/ *n.* any duck of the genus *Aythya*, esp. *A. ferina*, the male of which has a bright reddish-brown head and neck and a gray breast.

pock /pok/ *n.* (also **pock·mark**) **1** a small pus-filled spot on the skin, esp. caused by chickenpox or smallpox. **2** a mark resembling this. □□ **pock·y** *adj.*

pock·et /pókit/ *n. & v.* ● *n.* **1** a small bag sewn into or on clothing, for carrying small articles. **2** a pouchlike compartment in a suitcase, car door, etc. **3** one's financial resources (*it is beyond my pocket*). **4** an isolated group or area (*a few pockets of resistance remain*). **5 a** a cavity in the earth containing ore, esp. gold. **b** a cavity in rock, esp. filled with foreign matter. **6** a pouch at the corner or on the side of a billiard table into which balls are driven. ▷ POOL. **7** = AIR POCKET. **8** (*attrib.*) **a** of a suitable size and shape for carrying in a pocket. **b** smaller than the usual size. **9** the area of a baseball mitt or glove around the center of the palm. ● *v.tr.* (**pocketed, pocketing**) **1** put into one's pocket. **2** appropriate, esp. dishonestly. **3** confine in a pocket. **4** submit to (an injury or affront). **5** conceal or suppress (one's feelings). **6** *Billiards*, etc. drive (a ball) into a pocket. □ **in a person's pocket 1** under a person's control. **2** close to or intimate with a person. **out of pocket** (of an expense) paid for with one's own money, rather than from a particular fund or account. □□ **pock·et·a·ble** *adj.* **pock·et·less** *adj.* **pock·et·y** *adj.* (in sense 5 of *n.*).

pock·et·book /pókitbŏŏk/ *n.* **1** a notebook. **2** a booklike case for papers or money carried in a pocket. **3** a purse or handbag. **4** a paperback or other small book. **5** economic resources.

pock·et·ful /pókitfŏŏl/ *n.* (*pl.* **-fuls**) as much as a pocket will hold.

pock·et·knife *n.* a knife with a folding blade or blades, for carrying in the pocket.

pock·et mon·ey *n.* money for minor expenses.

pock·et ve·to *n.* executive veto of a legislative bill by allowing it to go unsigned.

pock·marked *adj.* bearing marks resembling or left by such spots.

pod /pod/ *n. & v.* ● *n.* **1** a long seed vessel, esp. of a leguminous plant, e.g., a pea. ▷ LEGUME. **2** the cocoon of a silkworm. **3** the case surrounding grasshopper eggs. **4** a narrow-necked eel net. **5** a compartment suspended under an aircraft for equipment, etc. ● *v.* (**podded, podding**) **1** *intr.* bear or form pods. **2** *tr.* remove (peas, etc.) from pods.

po·di·a·try /pədíətree/ *n. Med.* care and treatment of the foot. □□ **po·di·a·trist** *n.*

po·di·um /pṓdeeəm/ *n.* (*pl.* **podiums** or **podia** /-deeə/) **1** a continuous projecting base or pedestal around a room or house, etc. **2** a raised platform around the arena of an amphitheater. **3** a platform or rostrum.

po·em /pṓəm/ *n.* **1** a metrical composition, usu. concerned with feeling or imaginative description. **2** an elevated composition in verse or prose. **3** something with poetic qualities (*a poem in stone*).

po·e·sy /pṓəzee, -see/ *n. archaic* **1** poetry. **2** the art or composition of poetry.

po·et /pṓit/ *n.* (*fem.* **poetess** /pṓətis/) **1** a writer of poems. **2** a person possessing high powers of imagination or expression, etc.

po·et·as·ter /pṓətástər/ *n.* a paltry or inferior poet.

po·et·ic /pō-étik/ *adj.* (also **po·et·i·cal** /-tikəl/) **1 a** of or like poetry or poets. **b** written in verse. **2** elevated or sublime in expression. □ **po·et·i·cal·ly** *adv.*

po·et·i·cize /pō-étisīz/ *v.tr.* make (a theme) poetic.

po·et·ic jus·tice *n.* well-deserved unforeseen retribution or reward.

po·et·ic li·cense *n.* a writer's or artist's transgression of established rules for effect.

po·et·ics /pō-étiks/ *n.* **1** the art of writing poetry. **2** the study of poetry and its techniques.

po·et·ize /pṓətīz/ *v.* **1** *intr.* play the poet. **2** *intr.* compose poetry. **3** *tr.* treat poetically. **4** *tr.* celebrate in poetry.

po·et lau·re·ate *n.* a poet appointed to write poems for official state occasions.

po·et·ry /pṓətree/ *n.* **1** the art or work of a poet. **2** poems collectively. **3** a poetic or tenderly pleasing quality. **4** anything compared to poetry.

pogo stick /pṓgō/ *n.* a toy consisting of a spring-loaded stick with rests for the feet, for jumping around on.

po·grom /pṓgrəm, pəgrúm, -gróm/ *n.* an organized massacre (orig. of Jews in Russia).

poign·ant /póynyənt/ *adj.* **1** painfully sharp to the emotions or senses; deeply moving. **2** arousing sympathy. **3** sharp or pungent in taste or smell. **4** pleasantly piquant. □□ **poign·ance** *n.* **poign·an·cy** *n.* **poign·ant·ly** *adv.*

poi·ki·lo·therm /poykíləthərm, póykilə-/ *n.* an organism that regulates its body temperature by behavioral means, such as basking or burrowing; a cold-blooded organism (cf. HOMEOTHERM). □□ **poi·ki·lo·ther·mal** *adj.* **poi·ki·lo·ther·mi·a** /-thə́rmeeə/ *n.* **poi·ki·lo·ther·mic** *adj.* **poi·ki·lo·ther·my** *n.*

poin·set·ti·a /poynsēteeə, -sétə/ *n.* ▶ a shrub, *Euphorbia pulcherrima*, with large showy scarlet or cream-colored bracts that surround small yellow flowers.

bright red bract

POINSETTIA
(*Euphorbia pulcherrima*)

POINTILLISM

Pointillism was a technique used by certain Impressionists and developed by Georges Seurat and Paul Signac into a systematic approach to the use of color based on 19th-century scientific color theories. Dots or small dabs of pure, unmixed color are methodically applied on the canvas. When viewed from a distance, these dots are merged by the eye, creating more vibrant effects than if the same colors had been physically mixed together. Pointillism was adopted by the neo-Impressionists and was extensively used in early 20th-century art.

DETAIL FROM
Les Poseuses

image composed of tiny dots

Les Poseuses (*c*.1888),
GEORGES SEURAT

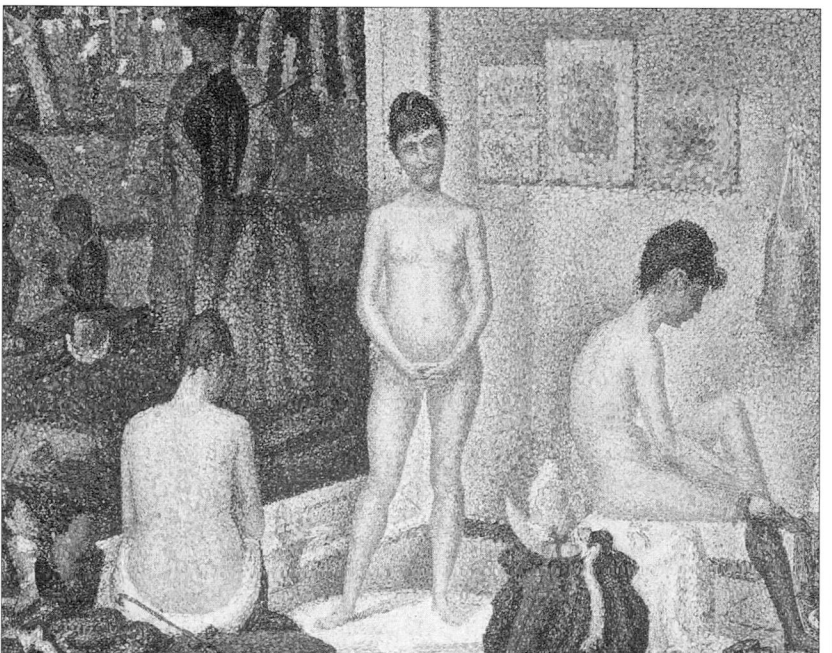

point /poynt/ *n. & v.* ● *n.* **1** the sharp or tapered end of a tool, weapon, pencil, etc. **2** a tip or extreme end. **3** that which in geometry has position but not magnitude, e.g., the intersection of two lines. **4** a particular place or position (*Bombay and points east; point of contact*). **5 a** a precise or particular moment (*at the point of death*). **b** the critical or decisive moment (*when it came to the point, he refused*). **6** a very small mark on a surface. **7** a dot or other punctuation mark, esp. = PERIOD 8 a. **8** = DECIMAL POINT. **9** a stage or degree in progress or increase (*abrupt to the point of rudeness; at that point we gave up*). **10** a level of temperature at which a change of state occurs (*freezing point*). **11** a single item; a detail or particular (*we differ on these points; it is a point of principle*). **12 a** a unit of scoring in games or of measuring value, etc. **b** an advantage or success in less quantifiable contexts such as an argument or discussion. **c** a unit of weight (2 mg) for diamonds. **d** a unit of varying value in quoting the price of stocks, etc. **e** a percentage point. **13 a** (usu. prec. by *the*) the significant or essential thing; what is actually intended or under discussion (*that was the point of the question*). **b** (usu. with *neg.* or *interrog.*; often foll. by *in*) sense or purpose; advantage or value (*saw no point in staying*). **c** (usu. prec. by *the*) a salient feature of a story, joke, remark, etc. (*don't see the point*). **14** a distinctive feature or characteristic (*it has its points; tact is not his good point*). **15 a** each of 32 directions marked at equal distances round a compass. **b** the

corresponding direction toward the horizon. **16** (usu. in *pl.*) each of a set of electrical contacts in the distributor of a motor vehicle. **17** the tip of the toe in ballet. **18** a promontory. **19** the prong of a deer's antler. **20** *Printing* a unit of measurement for type bodies (in the US and UK 0.351 mm, in Europe 0.376 mm). **21** *Mil.* a small leading party of an advanced guard, or the lead soldier's position in a patrol unit. ● *v.* **1** (usu. foll. by *to, at*) **a** *tr.* direct or aim (a finger, weapon, etc.). **b** *intr.* direct attention in a certain direction (*pointed to the house across the road*). **2** *intr.* (foll. by *at, toward*) **a** aim or be directed to. **b** tend toward. **3** *intr.* (foll. by *to*) indicate; be evidence of (*it all points to murder*). **4** *tr.* give point or force to (words or actions). **5** *tr.* fill in or repair the joints of (brickwork) with smoothly finished mortar or cement. **6** *tr.* **a** punctuate. **b** insert points in (written Hebrew, etc.). **7** *tr.* (also *absol.*) (of a dog) indicate the presence of (game) by acting as pointer. □ **at all points** in every part or respect. **at the point of** (often foll. by verbal noun) on the verge of; about to do (the action specified). **beside the point** irrelevant or irrelevantly. **have a point** be correct or effective in one's contention. **in point** apposite; relevant. **in point of fact** see FACT. **make** (or **prove**) **a** (or **one's**) **point** establish a proposition; prove one's contention. **make a point of** (often foll. by verbal noun) insist on; treat or regard as essential. **on** (or **upon**) **the point of** (foll. by verbal noun) about to do (the action specified).

point out (often foll. by *that* + clause) indicate; show; draw attention to. **point up** emphasize; show as important. **score points off** get the better of in an argument, etc. **to the point** relevant or relevantly. **up to a point** to some extent but not completely. **win on points** *Boxing* win by scoring more points, not by a knockout.

point-blank *adj. & adv.* ● *adj.* **1 a** (of a shot) aimed or fired horizontally at a range very close to the target. **b** (of a distance or range) very close. **2** (of a remark, question, etc.) blunt; direct. ● *adv.* **1** at very close range. **2** directly, bluntly.

point·ed /póyntid/ *adj.* **1** sharpened or tapering to a point. **2** (of a remark, etc.) having point; penetrating; cutting. **3** emphasized; made evident. □□ **point·ed·ly** *adv.* **point·ed·ness** *n.*

point·er /póyntər/ *n.* **1** a thing that points, e.g., the index hand of a gauge, etc. **2** a rod for pointing to features on a map, chart, etc. **3** *colloq.* a hint, clue, or indication. **4 a** a dog of a breed that on scenting game stands rigid looking toward it. ▷ DOG. **b** this breed.

poin·til·lism /pwántilizəm, póyn-/ *n. Art* ◀ a technique of impressionist painting using tiny dots of various pure colors, which become blended in the viewer's eye. □□ **poin·til·list** *n. & adj.* **poin·til·lis·tic** /-listik/ *adj.*

point·ing /póyntiŋ/ *n.* **1** cement or mortar filling the joints of brickwork. **2** facing produced by this. **3** the process of producing this.

point·less /póyntlis/ *adj.* **1** without a point. **2** lacking force, purpose, or meaning. **3** (in games) without a point scored. □□ **point·less·ly** *adv.* **point·less·ness** *n.*

point of no re·turn *n.* a point in a journey or enterprise at which it becomes essential or more practical to continue to the end.

point of or·der *n.* a query in a debate, etc., as to whether correct procedure is being followed.

point of view *n.* **1** a position from which a thing is viewed. **2** a particular way of considering a matter.

points·man /póyntsmən/ *n.* (*pl.* **-men**) *Brit.* **1** a railroad switchman. **2** a police officer or traffic warden on point-duty.

point·y /póyntee/ *adj.* (**pointier**, **pointiest**) having a noticeably sharp end; pointed.

poise /poyz/ *n. & v.* ● *n.* **1** composure or self-possession of manner. **2** equilibrium; a stable state. **3** carriage (of the head, etc.). ● *v.* **1** *tr.* balance; hold suspended or supported. **2** *tr.* carry (one's head, etc., in a specified way). **3** *intr.* be balanced; hover in the air, etc.

poised /poyzd/ *adj.* **1** composed; self-assured. **2** (often foll. by *for*, or *to* + infin.) ready for action.

poi·son /póyzən/ *n. & v.* ● *n.* **1** a substance that when introduced into or absorbed by a living organism causes death or injury, esp. one that kills by rapid action even in a small quantity. **2** *colloq.* a harmful influence or principle, etc. ● *v.tr.* **1** administer poison to (a person or animal). **2** kill or injure or infect with poison. **3** infect (air, water, etc.) with poison. **4** (esp. as **poisoned** *adj.*) treat (a weapon) with poison. **5** corrupt or pervert (a person or mind). **6** spoil or destroy (a person's pleasure, etc.). **7** render (land, etc.) foul and unfit for its purpose by a noxious application, etc. □□ **poi·son·er** *n.* **poi·son·ab** *adj.* **poi·son·ous·ly** *adv.*

poi·son i·vy *n.* ▶ a N. American climbing plant, *Rhus radicans*, secreting an irritant oil from its leaves.

poke[1] /pōk/ *v. & n.* ● *v.* **1** (foll. by *in, up, down,* etc.) **a** *tr.* thrust or push with the hand, point of a stick, etc. **b** *intr.* be thrust forward. **2** *intr.* (foll. by *at,* etc.) make thrusts with a stick, etc. **3** *tr.* thrust the end of a finger, etc., against. **4** *tr.* (foll. by *in*) produce (a hole, etc., in a thing) by poking. **5** *tr.* thrust forward, esp. obtru-

POISON IVY
(*Rhus radicans*)

sively. **6** *tr.* stir (a fire) with a poker. **7** *intr.* **a** (often foll. by *about, along, around*) move or act desultorily; putter. **b** (foll. by *about, into*) pry; search casually. ● *n.* **1** the act or an instance of poking. **2** a thrust or nudge. **3** a punch; a jab. □ **poke fun at** ridicule; tease. **poke** (or **stick**) **one's nose into** *colloq.* pry or intrude into (esp. a person's affairs).

poke² /pōk/ *n. dial.* a bag or sack. □ **buy a pig in a poke** see PIG.

pok·er¹ /pṓkər/ *n.* a stiff metal rod with a handle for stirring an open fire.

pok·er² /pṓkər/ *n.* a card game in which bluff is used as players bet on the value of their hands.

pok·er face *n.* **1** the impassive countenance appropriate to a poker player. **2** a person with this. □□ **pok·er-faced** *adj.*

poke·weed /pṓkweed/ *n.* a tall hardy American plant, *Phytolacca americana*, with spikes of cream flowers and purple berries that yield emetics and purgatives.

pok·ey /pṓkee/ *n. sl.* prison.

pok·y /pṓkee/ *adj.* (**pokier, pokiest**) **1** (of a room, etc.) small and cramped. **2** slow. □□ **pok·i·ly** *adv.* **pok·i·ness** *n.*

Po·lack /pṓlok, -lak/ *n. sl. offens.* a person of Polish origin.

po·lar /pṓlər/ *adj.* **1 a** of or near a pole of the Earth or a celestial body, or of the celestial sphere. **b** (of a species or variety) living in the north polar region. **2** having magnetic polarity. **3 a** (of a molecule) having a positive charge at one end and a negative charge at the other. **b** (of a compound) having electric charges. **4** *Geom.* of or relating to a pole. **5** directly opposite in character or tendency. **6** *colloq.* (esp. of weather) very cold. □□ **po·lar·ly** *adv.*

po·lar bear *n.* ▼ a white bear, *Ursus maritimus*, of the Arctic regions. ▷ BEAR

POLAR BEAR
(*Ursus maritimus*)

po·lar·im·e·ter /pṓlərímitər/ *n.* an instrument used to measure the polarization of light or the effect of a substance on the rotation of the plane of polarized light. □□ **po·lar·i·met·ric** /-métrik/ *adj.* **po·lar·im·e·try** *n.*

po·lar·i·ty /pōláritee/ *n.* (*pl.* **-ies**) **1** the tendency of a lodestone, magnetized bar, etc., to point with its extremities to the magnetic poles of the Earth. **2** the condition of having two poles with contrary qualities. **3** the state of having two opposite tendencies, opinions, etc. **4** the electrical condition of a body (positive or negative). **5** a magnetic attraction toward an object or person.

po·lar·ize /pṓlərīz/ *v.* **1** *tr.* ▲ restrict the vibrations of (a transverse wave, esp. light) to one direction. **2** *tr.* give magnetic or electric polarity to (a substance or body). **3** *tr.* reduce the voltage of (an electric cell) by the action of electrolysis products. **4** *tr. & intr.* divide into two groups of opposing opinion, etc. □□ **po·lar·iz·a·ble** *adj.* **po·lar·i·za·tion** *n.* **po·lar·iz·er** *n.*

Po·lar·oid /pṓləroyd/ *n. Trademark* **1** material in thin plastic sheets that produces a high degree of plane polarization in light passing through it. **2 a**

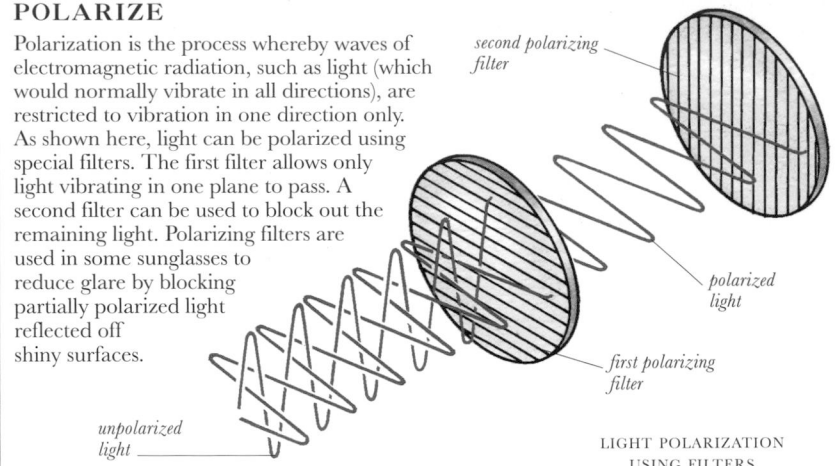

POLARIZE

Polarization is the process whereby waves of electromagnetic radiation, such as light (which would normally vibrate in all directions), are restricted to vibration in one direction only. As shown here, light can be polarized using special filters. The first filter allows only light vibrating in one plane to pass. A second filter can be used to block out the remaining light. Polarizing filters are used in some sunglasses to reduce glare by blocking partially polarized light reflected off shiny surfaces.

second polarizing filter

polarized light

first polarizing filter

unpolarized light

LIGHT POLARIZATION
USING FILTERS

type of camera with internal processing that produces a finished print rapidly after each exposure. **b** a print made with such a camera. **3** (in *pl.*) sunglasses with lenses made from Polaroid.

pol·der /pṓldər/ *n.* a piece of low-lying land reclaimed from the sea or a river, esp. in the Netherlands.

Pole /pōl/ *n.* **1** a native or national of Poland. **2** a person of Polish descent.

pole¹ /pōl/ *n. & v.* ● *n.* **1** a long slender rounded piece of wood or metal, esp. with the end placed in the ground as a support, etc. **2** a wooden shaft fitted to the front of a vehicle and attached to the yokes or collars of the draft animals. **3** = PERCH¹ 3. ● *v.tr.* **1** provide with poles. **2** push or propel (a small boat) with a pole.

pole² /pōl/ *n.* **1** (in full **north pole, south pole**) **a** each of the two points in the celestial sphere about which the stars appear to revolve. ▷ EQUATOR. **b** each of the extremities of the axis of rotation of the Earth or another body. **c** see MAGNETIC POLE. ¶ The spelling is *North Pole* and *South Pole* when used as geographical designations. **2** each of the two opposite points on the surface of a magnet at which magnetic forces are strongest. **3** each of two terminals (positive and negative) of an electric cell or battery, etc. **4** each of two opposed principles or ideas. **5** *Geom.* each of two points in which the axis of a circle cuts the surface of a sphere. □ **be poles apart** differ greatly, esp. in nature or opinion. □□ **pole·ward** *adj.* **pole·wards** *adj. & adv.*

pole·ax /pṓlaks/ *n. & v.* ● *n.* **1** a battleax. **2** a butcher's ax. ● *v.tr.* hit or kill with or as if with a poleax.

pole·cat /pṓlkat/ *n.* **1** *US* a skunk. **2** *Brit.* ▶ a small European brownish black flesh-eating mammal, *Mustela putorius*, of the weasel family.

po·lem·ic /pəlémik/ *n. & adj.* ● *n.* **1** a controversial discussion. **2** *Polit.* a verbal or written attack, esp. on a political opponent. ● *adj.* (also **po·lem·i·cal**) involving dispute; controversial. □□ **po·lem·i·cal·ly** *adv.* **po·lem·i·cist** /-misist/ *n.* **po·lem·i·cize** *v.tr.* **pol·e·mize** /pólimīz/ *v.tr.*

po·lem·ics /pəlémiks/ *n.pl.* the art or practice of controversial discussion.

po·len·ta /pəléntə, pō-/ *n.* mush made of cornmeal, etc.

pole·star /pṓlstar/ *n.* **1** *Astron.* a star in Ursa Minor now about 1° distant from the celestial north pole. ▷ LODESTAR. **2 a** a thing or principle serving as a guide. **b** a center of attraction.

pole vault *n. & v.* ● *n.* the sport of vaulting over a high bar with the aid of a long flexible pole held in the hands and giving extra spring. ● *v.intr.* (**pole-vault**) take part in this sport. □□ **pole-vault·er** *n.*

po·lice /pəlées/ *n. & v.* ● *n.* **1** (usu. prec. by *the*) the civil force of a government, responsible for maintaining public order. **2** (as *pl.*) the members of a police force (*several hundred police*). **3** a force with similar functions of enforcing regulations (*military police; transit police*). ● *v.tr.* **1** control (a country or area) by means of police. **2** provide with police. **3** keep order in; control; monitor.

po·lice dog *n.* a dog, esp. a German shepherd, used in police work.

po·lice·man /pəléesmən/ *n.* (*pl.* **-men**; *fem.* **policewoman**, *pl.* **-women**) a member of a police force.

po·lice of·fi·cer *n.* a policeman or policewoman.

po·lice state *n.* a totalitarian country controlled by political police supervising the citizens' activities.

po·lice sta·tion *n.* the office of a local police force.

pol·i·cy¹ /pólisee/ *n.* (*pl.* **-ies**) **1** a course or principle of action adopted or proposed by a government, party, business, or individual, etc. **2** prudent conduct; sagacity.

pol·i·cy² /pólisee/ *n.* (*pl.* **-ies**) **1** a contract of insurance. **2** a document containing this.

pol·i·cy·hold·er /póliseehōldər/ *n.* a person or body holding an insurance policy.

po·li·o /pṓleeō/ *n.* = POLIOMYELITIS.

po·li·o·my·e·li·tis /pṓleeōmí-ilítis/ *n. Med.* an infectious viral disease that affects the central nervous system and that can cause temporary or permanent paralysis.

Po·lish /pṓlish/ *adj. & n.* ● *adj.* **1** of or relating to Poland. **2** of the Poles or their language. ● *n.* the language of Poland.

pol·ish /pólish/ *v. & n.* ● *v.* **1** *tr. & intr.* make or become smooth or glossy, esp. by rubbing. **2** (esp. as **polished** *adj.*) refine or improve; add finishing touches to. ● *n.* **1** a substance used for polishing. **2** smoothness or glossiness produced by friction. **3** the act or an instance of polishing. **4** refinement or elegance of manner, conduct, etc. □ **polish off 1** finish (esp. food) quickly. **2** *colloq.* kill; murder. **polish up** revise or improve (a skill, etc.). □□ **pol·ish·a·ble** *adj.* **pol·ish·er** *n.*

POLECAT
(*Mustela putorius*)

po·lit·bu·ro /pólitbyŏŏrō, pəlít-/ *n.* (*pl.* **-os**) the principal policy-making committee of a Communist party, esp. in the former USSR.

po·lite /pəlít/ *adj.* (**politer**, **politest**) **1** having good manners; courteous. **2** cultivated; cultured. **3** refined; elegant (*polite letters*). □□ **po·lite·ly** *adv.* **po·lite·ness** *n.*

pol·i·tic /pólitik/ *adj. & v.* ● *adj.* **1** (of an action) judicious; expedient. **2** (of a person:) **a** prudent; sagacious. **b** scheming; sly. **3** political (now only in *body politic*). ● *v.intr.* (**politicked**, **politicking**) engage in politics. □□ **pol·i·tic·ly** *adv.*

po·lit·i·cal /pəlítikəl/ *adj.* **1 a** of or concerning government, or public affairs generally. **b** of, relating to, or engaged in politics. **c** belonging to or forming part of a civil administration. **2** having an organized form of society or government. **3** taking or belonging to a side in politics or in controversial matters. **4** relating to or affecting interests of status or authority in an organization rather than matters of principle (*a political decision*). □□ **po·lit·i·cal·ly** *adv.*

po·lit·i·cal ac·tion com·mit·tee *n.* a permanent organization that collects and distributes funds for political purposes. ¶ Abbr.: **PAC**.

po·lit·i·cal a·sy·lum *n.* protection given by a government to a political refugee.

po·lit·i·cal cor·rect·ness *n.* avoidance of forms of expression and action that exclude or marginalize sexual, racial, and cultural minorities; advocacy of this.

po·lit·i·cal·ly cor·rect *adj.* in conformance with political correctness.

po·lit·i·cal pris·on·er *n.* a person imprisoned for political beliefs or actions.

po·lit·i·cal sci·ence *n.* the study of systems of government. □□ **po·lit·i·cal sci·en·tist** *n.*

pol·i·ti·cian /pólitíshən/ *n.* **1** a person engaged in or concerned with politics, esp. as a practitioner. **2** a person skilled in politics. **3** *derog.* a person with self-interested political concerns.

po·lit·i·cize /pəlítisīz/ *v.* **1** *tr.* **a** give a political character to. **b** make politically aware. **2** *intr.* engage in or talk politics. □□ **po·lit·i·ci·za·tion** *n.*

po·lit·i·co /pəlítikō/ *n.* (*pl.* **-os**) *colloq.* a politician or political enthusiast.

politico- /pəlítikō/ *comb. form* **1** politically. **2** political and (*politico-social*)

pol·i·tics /pólitiks/ *n.pl.* **1** (treated as *sing.* or *pl.*) **a** the art and science of government. **b** public life and affairs as involving authority and government. **2** (usu. treated as *pl.*) **a** a particular set of ideas, principles, or commitments in politics (*what are their politics?*). **b** activities concerned with the acquisition or exercise of authority or government. **c** an organizational process or principle affecting authority, status, etc. (*the politics of the decision*).

pol·i·ty /pólitee/ *n.* (*pl.* **-ies**) **1** a form or process of civil government or constitution. **2** an organized society; a nation as a political entity.

pol·ka /pólkə, pókə/ *n. & v.* ● *n.* **1** a lively dance of Bohemian origin in duple time. **2** the music for this. ● *v.intr.* (**polkas**, **polkaed** /-kəd/ or **polka'd**, **polkaing** /-kəing/) dance the polka.

pol·ka dot *n.* a round dot as one of many forming a regular pattern on a textile fabric, etc.

poll /pōl/ *n. & v.* ● *n.* **1 a** the process of voting at an election. **b** the counting of votes at an election. **c** the result of voting. **d** the number of votes recorded (*a heavy poll*). **e** (also **polls**) place for voting. **2** an assessment of public opinion by questioning a representative sample, as for forecasting the results of voting, etc. **3 a** a human head. **b** the part of this on which hair grows (*flaxen poll*). **4** a hornless animal, esp. one of a breed of hornless cattle. ● *v.* **1** *tr.* **a** take the vote or votes of. **b** (in *passive*) have one's vote taken. **c** (of a candidate) receive (so many votes). **d** give (a vote). **2** *tr.* record the opinion of (a person or group) in an opinion poll. **3** *intr.* give one's vote. **4** *tr.* cut off the top of (a tree or plant), esp. make a pollard of. **5** *tr.* (esp. as **polled** *adj.*) cut the horns off (cattle). **6** *tr. Computing* check the status of (a computer system) at intervals. □□ **poll·ee** /pōleé/ *n.* (in sense 2 of *n.*). **poll·ster** *n.*

pol·lack /pólək/ *n.* (also **pol·lock**) a European marine fish, *Pollachius pollachius*, with a characteristic protruding lower jaw, used for food.

pol·lard /pólərd/ *n. & v.* ● *n.* **1** an animal that has lost or cast its horns; an ox, sheep, or goat of a hornless breed. **2** a tree whose branches have been cut off to encourage the growth of new young branches, esp. a riverside willow. **3 a** the bran sifted from flour. **b** a fine bran containing some flour. ● *v.tr.* make (a tree) a pollard.

pol·len /pólən/ *n.* ► the fine dustlike grains discharged from the male part of a flower containing the gamete that fertilizes the female ovule. ▷ POLLINATE

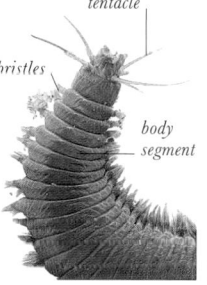

POLLEN: GRAIN OF PINE POLLEN (MAGNIFIED)

pol·len count *n.* an index of the amount of pollen in the air, published esp. for the benefit of those allergic to it.

pol·li·nate /pólinàyt/ *v.tr.* (also *absol.*) ▼ sprinkle (a stigma) with pollen. □□ **pol·li·na·tion** /-náyshən/ *n.* **pol·li·na·tor** *n.*

poll·ing booth *n.* a compartment in which a voter stands to mark a paper ballot or use a voting machine.

poll·ing place *n.* a building where voting takes place during an election.

pol·lin·ic /pólínik/ *adj.* of or relating to pollen.

pol·li·wog /póleewog/ *n.* (also **pollywog**) *dial.* a tadpole.

poll tax *n. hist.* a tax levied on every adult.

pol·lute /pəlóõt/ *v.tr.* **1** contaminate or defile (the environment). **2** make foul or filthy. **3** destroy the purity or sanctity of. □□ **pol·lu·tant** *adj. & n.* **pol·lut·er** *n.* **pol·lu·tion** *n.*

Pol·ly·an·na /póleeánə/ *n.* a cheerful optimist; an excessively cheerful person. □□ **Pol·ly·an·na·ish** *adj.* **Pol·ly·an·na·ism** *n.*

po·lo /pṓlō/ *n.* a game of Asian origin played on horseback with a long-handled mallet.

pol·o·naise /pólənáyz, pō-/ *n. & adj.* ● *n.* **1** a dance of Polish origin in triple time. **2** the music for this. **3** *hist.* a woman's dress consisting of a bodice and a draped skirt open from the waist downward to show an underskirt. ● *adj.* cooked in a Polish style.

POLLINATE

For a flower to be pollinated, pollen must be transferred from the male to the female part. The main pollen-carrying agents are wind and animals (mostly insects but also birds and bats). Animal pollinators carry the pollen on their bodies and are attracted to the flower by scent or by the sight of the petals.

sticky pollen attaches to bee

bee feeds on nectar

scented petal attracts insects

INSECT POLLINATION

---

po·lo·ni·um /pəlṓneeəm/ *n. Chem.* a rare radioactive metallic element, occurring naturally in uranium ores. ¶ Symb.: **Po**.

po·lo shirt *n.* a pullover shirt, usu. of knit fabric, with a rounded neckband or a turnover collar.

polo stick *n.* a mallet for playing polo.

pol·ter·geist /póltərgīst/ *n.* a noisy mischievous ghost, esp. one manifesting itself by physical damage.

pol·troon /poltróõn/ *n.* a spiritless coward. □□ **pol·troon·er·y** *n.*

pol·y /pólee/ *n.* (*pl.* **polys**) esp. *Brit. colloq.* polytechnic.

poly-[1] /pólee/ *comb. form* denoting many or much.

poly-[2] /pólee/ *comb. form Chem.* polymerized (*polyunsaturated*).

pol·y·am·ide /póleeámīd/ *n. Chem.* any of a class of condensation polymers produced from the interaction of an amino group of one molecule and a carboxylic acid group of another, and which includes many synthetic fibers such as nylon.

pol·y·an·dry /póleeandree/ *n.* polygamy in which a woman has more than one husband. □□ **pol·y·an·drous** /-ándrəs/ *adj.*

pol·y·an·thus /póleeánthəs/ *n.* (*pl.* **polyanthuses**) **1** a hybridized primrose, *Primula polyantha*. **2** a narcissus, *Narcissus tazetta*, with small white or yellow flowers.

pol·y·car·bon·ate /póleekáarbənayt/ *n.* any of a class of polymers in which the units are linked through a carbonate group, mainly used as molding materials.

pol·y·chaete /pólikeet/ *n.* ◄ any aquatic annelid worm of the class Polychaeta, including lugworms and ragworms, having numerous bristles on the fleshy lobes of each body segment. □□ **pol·y·chae·tan** /-kéet'n/ *adj.* **pol·y·chae·tous** /-kéetəs/ *adj.*

tentacle

bristles

body segment

POLYCHAETE: KING RAGWORM (*Nereis pelagica*)

pol·y·chro·mat·ic /póleekrōmátik/ *adj.* **1** many-colored. **2** (of radiation) containing more than one wavelength. □□ **pol·y·chro·ma·tism** /-krṓmətizəm/ *n.*

pol·y·chrome /póleekrōm/ *adj. & n.* ● *adj.* painted, printed, or decorated in many colors. ● *n.* **1** a work of art in several colors, esp. a colored statue. **2** varied coloring. □□ **pol·y·chro·mic** /-krṓmik/ *adj.* **pol·y·chro·mous** /-krṓməs/ *adj.* **pol·y·chro·my** *n.*

pol·y·crys·tal·line /póleekríst'lin, -līn, -leen/ *adj.* (of a solid substance) consisting of many crystalline parts at various orientations, e.g., a metal casting.

pol·y·dac·tyl /póleedáktil/ *adj. & n.* ● *adj.* (of a person or animal) having more than five fingers or toes on each hand or foot. ● *n.* a polydactyl animal.

pol·y·es·ter /pólee-éstər/ *n.* any of a group of condensation polymers used to form synthetic fibers or to make resins. ▷ ROPE

pol·y·eth·ene /pólee-étheen/ *n. Chem.* = POLYETHYLENE.

pol·y·eth·yl·ene /pólee-éthileen/ *n. Chem.* a tough light thermoplastic polymer of ethylene, usu. translucent and flexible or opaque and rigid, used for packaging and insulating materials. Also called **polyethene**, **polythene**.

po·lyg·a·mous /pəlígəməs/ *adj.* **1** having more than one wife or husband at the same time. **2** having more than one mate. **3** bearing some flowers with stamens only, some with pistils only, and some with both on the same or different plants. □□ **po·lyg·am·ic** /póligámik/ *adj.* **po·lyg·a·mist** /-gəmist/ *n.* **po·lyg·a·mous·ly** *adv.*

P

P

po·lyg·a·my /pəligəmee/ *n.* the practice of having more than one husband or wife at the same time. □□ **po·lyg·a·mic** /póligámik/ *adj.* **po·lyg·a·mist** /-gəmist/ *n.* **po·lyg·a·mous·ly** *adv.*

pol·y·glot /póleeglot/ *adj. & n.* ● *adj.* **1** knowing or using many languages. **2** (of a book, esp. the Bible) with the text translated into several languages. ● *n.* **1** a polyglot person. **2** a polyglot book, esp. a Bible.

pol·y·gon /póleegon/ *n.* a plane figure with many (usu. a minimum of three) sides and angles. □□ **po·lyg·o·nal** /pəligənəl/ *adj.*

poly·go·num /pəligənəm/ *n.* any plant of the genus *Polygonum*, with small bell-shaped flowers. Also called **knotgrass, knotweed**.

pol·y·graph /póleegraf/ *n.* a machine designed to detect and record changes in physiological characteristics (e.g., rates of pulse and breathing), used esp. as a lie-detector.

po·lyg·y·ny /pəlijinee/ *n.* polygamy in which a man has more than one wife. □□ **po·lyg·y·nous** /pəlijinəs/ *adj.*

pol·y·he·dron /póleehéedrən/ *n.* (*pl.* **polyhedra** /-drə/ or **polyhedrons**) a solid figure with many (usu. more than six) faces. □□ **pol·y·he·dral** *adj.* **pol·y·he·dric** *adj.*

pol·y·math /póleemath/ *n.* **1** a person of much or varied learning. **2** a great scholar. □□ **pol·y·math·ic** /-máthik/ *adj.* **po·lym·a·thy** /pəlímməthee/ *n.*

pol·y·mer /pólimər/ *n.* a compound composed of one or more large molecules that are formed from repeated units of smaller molecules. □□ **pol·y·mer·ic** /-mérik/ *adj.* **po·lym·er·ism** *n.* **po·lym·er·ize** *v.intr. & tr.* **po·lym·er·i·za·tion** *n.*

pol·y·morph·ism /poleemáwrfizəm/ *n.* the occurrence of something in several different forms.

Pol·y·ne·sian /pólinéezhən/ *adj. & n.* ● *adj.* of or relating to Polynesia, a group of Pacific islands including New Zealand, Hawaii, Samoa, etc. ● *n.* **1 a** a native of Polynesia. **b** a person of Polynesian descent. **2** the family of languages including Maori, Hawaiian, and Samoan.

pol·y·no·mi·al /pólinṓmeeəl/ *n. & adj. Math.* ● *n.* an expression of more than two algebraic terms, esp. the sum of several terms that contain different powers of the same variable(s). ● *adj.* of or being a polynomial.

po·lyn·ya /pəlínyə/ *n.* a stretch of open water surrounded by ice, esp. in the Arctic seas.

pol·yp /pólip/ *n.* **1** *Zool.* an individual cnidarian. **2** *Med.* a small usu. benign growth protruding from a mucous membrane. □□ **pol·yp·oid** /póleepoyd/ *adj.* **pol·yp·ous** /-pəs/ *adj.*

pol·y·pep·tide /póleepéptīd/ *n. Biochem.* a peptide formed by the combination of about ten or more amino acids.

pol·y·phone /póleefōn/ *n. Phonet.* a symbol or letter that represents several different sounds.

pol·y·phon·ic /póleefónik/ *adj.* **1** *Mus.* (of vocal music, etc.) in two or more relatively independent parts; contrapuntal. **2** *Phonet.* (of a letter, etc.) representing more than one sound. □□ **pol·y·phon·i·cal·ly** *adv.*

po·lyph·o·ny /pəlífənee/ *n.* (*pl.* **-ies**) **1** *Mus.* **a** polyphonic style in musical composition; counterpoint. **b** a composition written in this style. **2** *Philol.* the symbolization of different vocal sounds by the same letter or character. □□ **po·lyph·o·nous** *adj.*

pol·y·pro·pene /póleeprṓpeen/ *n.* = POLYPROPYLENE.

pol·y·pro·pyl·ene /póleeprṓpileen/ *n. Chem.* any of various polymers of propylene including thermoplastic materials used for films, fibers, or molding materials. ▷ ROPE. Also called **polypropene**.

pol·y·sac·cha·ride /póleesákərīd/ *n.* any of a group of carbohydrates whose molecules consist of long chains of monosaccharides.

pol·y·se·my /póleeséemee, pəlísəmee/ *n. Philol.* the existence of many meanings (of a word, etc.). □□ **pol·y·se·mic** /-séemik/ *adj.* **pol·y·se·mous** /-séeməs, -səməs/ *adj.*

pol·y·sty·rene /póleestíreen/ *n.* a thermoplastic polymer of styrene, usu. hard and colorless or expanded with a gas to produce a lightweight rigid white substance, used for insulation and in packaging.

pol·y·syl·lab·ic /póleesilábik/ *adj.* **1** (of a word) having many syllables. **2** characterized by the use of words of many syllables. □□ **pol·y·syl·lab·i·cal·ly** *adv.*

pol·y·syl·la·ble /póleesíləbəl/ *n.* a polysyllabic word.

pol·y·tech·nic /póleetéknik/ *n. & adj.* ● *n.* an institution of higher education offering courses in many esp. vocational or technical subjects. ● *adj.* dealing with or devoted to various vocational or technical subjects.

pol·y·tet·ra·fluor·o·eth·y·lene /pólitétrəflóoróōéthileen, -fláwr-/ *n. Chem.* a tough translucent polymer resistant to chemicals and used to coat cooking utensils, etc. ¶ Abbr.: **PTFE**.

pol·y·the·ism /póleethéeizəm/ *n.* the belief in or worship of more than one god. □□ **pol·y·the·ist** *n.* **pol·y·the·is·tic** *adj.*

pol·y·thene /póleetheen/ *n. Brit.* = POLYETHYLENE.

pol·y·un·sat·u·rat·ed /póleeunsáchəraytid/ *adj. Chem.* (of a compound, esp. a fat or oil molecule) containing several double or triple bonds and therefore capable of further reaction.

pol·y·u·re·thane /póleeyóorəthayn/ *n.* any polymer containing the urethane group, used in adhesives, paints, plastics, foams, etc.

pol·y·va·lent /póleeváylənt/ *adj. Chem.* having a valence of more than two, or several valencies. □□ **pol·y·va·lence** *n.*

pol·y·vi·nyl ace·tate /póleevínil/ *n. Chem.* a soft plastic polymer used in paints and adhesives. ¶ Abbr.: **PVA**.

pol·y·vi·nyl chlo·ride /póleevínil/ *n.* a tough transparent solid polymer of vinyl chloride, easily colored and used for a wide variety of products including pipes, flooring, etc. ¶ Abbr.: **PVC**.

po·made /pōmáyd, -máad/ *n. & v.* ● *n.* scented dressing for the hair and the skin of the head. ● *v.tr.* anoint with pomade.

po·man·der /pṓmandər, pōmán-/ *n.* **1** a ball of mixed aromatic substances placed in a cupboard, etc., or *hist.* carried in a box, bag, etc., as a protection against infection. **2** a (usu. spherical) container for this. **3** ◀ a spiced orange, etc., similarly used.

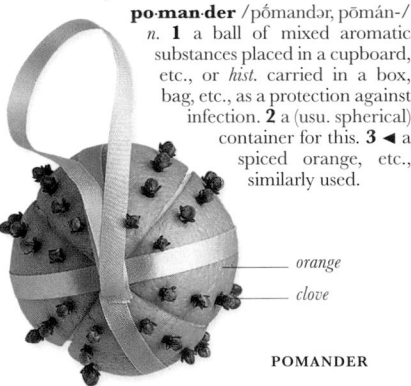

orange

clove

POMANDER

pome /pōm/ *n.* a firm-fleshed fruit in which the carpels from the central core enclose the seeds, e.g., the apple, pear, and quince. ▷ FRUIT. □□ **po·mif·er·ous** /pəmífərəs/ *adj.*

pome·gran·ate /pómigranit, pómgranit, púm-/ *n.* **1** ▶ an orange-sized fruit with a tough reddish outer skin and containing many seeds in a red pulp. **2** the tree bearing this fruit, *Punica granatum*, native to N. Africa and W. Asia.

seed

POMEGRANATE
(*Punica granatum*)

pom·e·lo /póməlō/ *n.* (*pl.* **-os**) **1** = SHADDOCK. **2** = GRAPEFRUIT.

Pom·er·a·ni·an /póməráyneeən/ *n.* a small dog with long silky hair, a pointed muzzle, and pricked ears.

pom·fret /pómfrit, púm-/ *n.* **1** any of various fish of the family Stromateidae of the Indian and Pacific Oceans. **2** a dark-colored deep-bodied marine fish, *Brama brama*, used as food.

pom·mel /púməl, póm-/ *n. & v.* ● *n.* **1** a knob, esp. at the end of a sword hilt. **2** the upward projecting front part of a saddle. ▷ SADDLE, SIDESADDLE. ● *v.tr.* (**pommeled, pommeling** or **pommelled, pommelling**) = PUMMEL.

pom·mel horse *n.* a vaulting horse fitted with a pair of curved handgrips.

pomp /pomp/ *n.* **1** a splendid display; splendor. **2** (often in *pl.*) vainglory (*the pomps and vanities of this wicked world*).

pom·pom /pómpom/ *n.* (also **pom·pon** /-pon/) **1** ▼ an ornamental ball or tuft of wool, silk, or ribbons, often worn on hats or clothing. **2** (often *attrib.*) (usu. **pompon**) a dahlia or chrysanthemum with small tightly-clustered petals.

pompom

POMPOM ON A FRENCH FUSILIER'S SHAKO

pomp·ous /pómpəs/ *adj.* **1** self-important, affectedly grand or solemn. **2** (of language) pretentious; unduly grand in style. □□ **pom·pos·i·ty** /pompósitee/ *n.* (*pl.* **-ies**). **pomp·ous·ly** *adv.* **pomp·ous·ness** *n.*

pon·ceau /ponsṓ/ *n. & adj.* ● *n.* a bright reddish-orange color. ● *adj.* of this color.

pon·cho /pónchō/ *n.* (*pl.* **-os**) **1** a S. American cloak made of a blanket-like piece of cloth with a slit in the middle for the head. ▷ GAUCHO. **2** a garment in this style, esp. one waterproof and worn as a raincoat. □□ **pon·choed** *adj.*

pond /pond/ *n. & v.* ● *n.* **1** a fairly small body of still water formed naturally or by hollowing or embanking. **2** *joc.* the sea. ● *v.* **1** *tr.* hold back; dam up (a stream, etc.). **2** *intr.* form a pond.

pon·der /póndər/ *v.* **1** *tr.* weigh mentally; think over; consider. **2** *intr.* (usu. foll. by *on, over*) think; muse.

pon·der·a·ble /póndərəbəl/ *adj.* having appreciable weight or significance. □□ **pon·der·a·bil·i·ty** /-bílitee/ *n.*

ponderation /póndəráyshən/ *n. literary* the act of an instance of considering or deliberating.

pon·der·o·sa /póndərṓsə/ *n.* **1** a N. American pine tree, *Pinus ponderosa*. **2** the timber of this tree.

pon·der·ous /póndərəs/ *adj.* **1** heavy; unwieldy. **2** laborious. **3** (of style, etc.) dull; tedious. □□ **pon·der·os·i·ty** /-rósitee/ *n.* **pon·der·ous·ly** *adv.* **pon·der·ous·ness** *n.*

pond life *n.* animals (esp. invertebrates) that live in ponds.

pond·weed /póndweed/ *n.* ▶ any of various aquatic plants, esp. of the genus *Potamogeton*, growing in still or running water.

pone /pōn/ *n. US dial.* **1** unleavened cornbread, esp. as made by Native Americans. **2** a fine light bread made with milk, eggs, etc. **3** a cake or loaf of this.

pong /pong/ *n. & v. Brit. colloq.* ● *n.* an unpleasant smell. ● *v.intr.* stink. □□ **pon·gy** /póngee/ *adj.* (**pongier, pongiest**).

pon·tiff /póntif/ *n. RC Ch.* (in full **sovereign** or **supreme pontiff**) the pope.

PONDWEED: CURLED PONDWEED (*Potamogeton crispus*)

POOL

Pool is played using a cue to hit a cue ball against a colored or striped ball, with the aim of causing it to fall into a pocket. The most popular form of pool is eight-ball, in which one player shoots only at colored balls, and the other player only at striped balls. After a player sinks an entire group, the 8-ball must be pocketed to end the game. Other forms include sinking balls in numerical order (rotation), and sinking a designated ball into a designated pocket (straight pool).

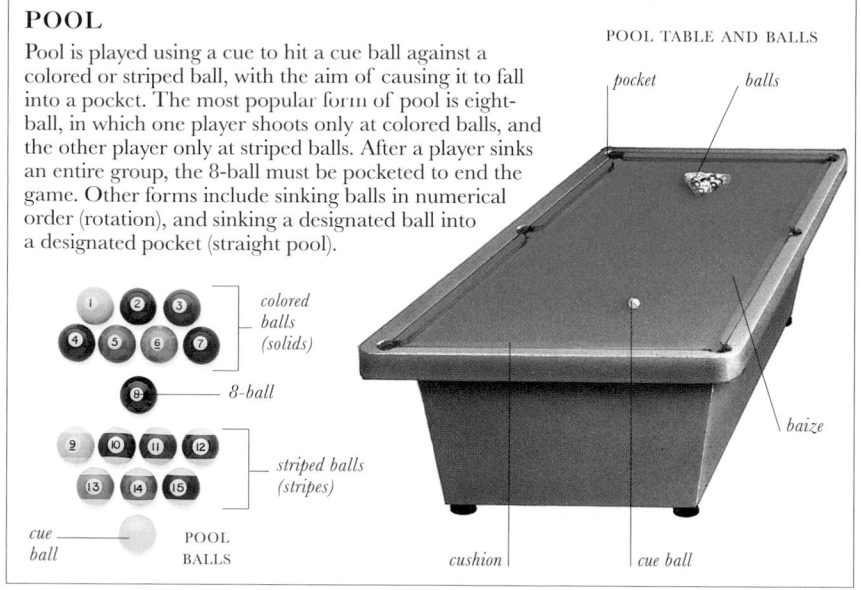

POOL TABLE AND BALLS

pocket · balls · baize · cushion · cue ball

colored balls (solids)

8-ball

striped balls (stripes)

cue ball · POOL BALLS

pon·tif·i·cal /pontífikǝl/ *adj. & n.* ● *adj.* **1** *RC Ch.* of or befitting a pontiff; papal. **2** pompously dogmatic; with an attitude of infallibility. ● *n.* **1** an office book containing rites to be performed by bishops. **2** (in *pl.*) the vestments and insignia of a bishop, cardinal, or abbot. □□ **pon·tif·i·cal·ly** *adv.*

pon·tif·i·cate *v. & n.* ● *v.intr.* /pontífikayt/ **1 a** play the pontiff; pretend to be infallible. **b** be pompously dogmatic. **2** *RC Ch.* officiate as bishop, esp. at mass. ● *n.* /pontífikǝt/ **1** the office of pontifex, bishop, or pope. **2** the period of this.

pon·toon¹ /pontóon/ *n.* **1** a flat-bottomed boat. **2 a** each of several boats, hollow metal cylinders, etc., used to support a temporary bridge. **b** a bridge so formed; a floating platform. **3** = CAISSON 1, 2. **4** a float for a seaplane.

pon·toon² /pontóon/ *n. Brit.* = BLACKJACK 1.

po·ny /pṓnee/ *n.* (*pl.* **-ies**) **1** a horse of any small breed. ▷ HORSE. **2** a small drinking glass. **3** (in *pl.*) *sl.* racehorses. **4** a literal translation of a foreign-language text, used by students.

po·ny ex·press *n.* (also **Pony Express**) *US Hist.* an express delivery system of the early 1860s that carried mail, etc., by relays of pony riders.

po·ny·tail /pṓneetayl/ *n.* a person's hair drawn back, tied, and hanging down like a pony's tail.

pooch /pooch/ *n. sl.* a dog.

poo·dle /pṓd'l/ *n.* **1 a** a dog of a breed with a curly coat that is usually clipped. ▷ DOG. **b** this breed. **2** *Brit.* a lackey or servile follower.

pooh /poo/ *int. & n.* (also **poo**) ● *int.* expressing impatience or contempt. ● *n. sl.* **1** excrement. **2** an act of defecation.

Pooh-Bah /pṓobaa/ *n.* (also **pooh-bah**) a holder of many offices at once.

pooh-pooh /pṓopṓo/ *v.tr.* express contempt for; ridicule; dismiss (an idea, etc.) scornfully.

pool¹ /pool/ *n. & v.* ● *n.* **1** a small body of still water, usu. of natural formation. **2** a small shallow body of any liquid. **3** = SWIMMING POOL. **4** a deep place in a river. ● *v.* **1** *tr.* form into a pool. **2** *intr.* (of blood) become static.

pool² /pool/ *n. & v.* ● *n.* **1 a** (often *attrib.*) a common supply of persons, vehicles, commodities, etc., for sharing by a group of people (*a typing pool; a car pool*). **b** a group of persons sharing duties, etc. **2 a** the collective amount of players' stakes in gambling, etc. **b** a receptacle for this. **3 a** a joint commercial venture, esp. an arrangement between competing parties to fix prices and share business to eliminate competition. **b** the common funding

for this. **4** ▲ any of several games similar to billiards played on a pool table with usu. 16 balls. **5** a group of contestants who compete against each other in a tournament for the right to advance to the next round. ● *v.tr.* **1** put (resources, etc.) into a common fund. **2** share (things) in common. **3** (of transport or organizations, etc.) share (traffic, receipts).

pool·room /pṓolroom, -room/ *n.* **1** a place for playing pool; pool hall. **2** a bookmaking establishment.

poop¹ /poop/ *n.* the stern of a ship; the aftermost and highest deck.

poop² /poop/ *v.tr.* (esp. as **pooped** *adj.*) *colloq.* exhaust; tire out.

poop³ /poop/ *n. sl.* up to date or inside information; the lowdown.

poop⁴ /poop/ *n. & v. sl.* ● *n.* excrement. ● *v.intr.* defecate.

poor /poor/ *adj.* **1** lacking adequate money or means to live comfortably. **2 a** (foll. by *in*) deficient in (a possession or quality) (*the poor in spirit*). **b** (of

soil, ore, etc.) unproductive. **3 a** scanty; inadequate (*a poor crop*). **b** less good than is usual or expected (*poor visibility; is a poor driver; in poor health*). **c** paltry; inferior (*poor condition; came a poor third*). **4 a** deserving pity or sympathy; unfortunate (*you poor thing*). **b** with reference to a dead person (*as my poor father used to say*). **5** spiritless; despicable (*is a poor creature*). **6** often *iron.* or *joc.* humble; insignificant (*in my poor opinion*). □ **take a poor view of** regard with disfavor or pessimism.

poor·house /poorhows/ *n. hist.* = WORKHOUSE 2.

poor·ly /poorlee/ *adv. & adj.* ● *adv.* **1** scantily; defectively. **2** with no great success. **3** meanly; contemptibly. ● *predic.adj.* unwell.

poor·ness /poornis/ *n.* **1** defectiveness. **2** the lack of some good quality or constituent.

poor white *n. offens.* a member of an underprivileged group of white people.

pop¹ /pop/ *n., v., & adv.* ● *n.* **1** a sudden sharp explosive sound as of a cork when drawn. **2** *colloq.* an effervescent soft drink. ● *v.* (**popped**, **popping**) **1** *intr. & tr.* make or cause to make a pop. **2** *intr. & tr.* (foll. by *in, out, up, down*, etc.) go, move, come, or put unexpectedly or in a quick or hasty manner (*pop out to the store; pop in for a visit; pop it on your head*). **3 a** *intr. & tr.* burst, making a popping sound. **b** *tr.* heat (popcorn, etc.) until it pops. **4** *intr.* (often foll. by *at*) *colloq.* fire a gun (at birds, etc.). ● *adv.* with the sound of a pop (*heard it go pop*). □ **pop off** *colloq.* **1** die. **2** quietly slip away (cf. sense 2 of *v.*). **pop the question** *colloq.* propose marriage.

pop² /pop/ *adj. & n. colloq.* ● *adj.* **1** in a popular or modern style. **2** performing popular music, etc. (*pop group; pop star*). ● *n.* **1** pop music. **2** a pop record or song (*top of the pops*).

pop³ /pop/ *n. esp. colloq.* father.

pop. *abbr.* population.

pop·a·dam var. of POPPADAM.

pop art *n.* ▼ art based on modern popular culture and the mass media, esp. as a critical comment on traditional fine art values.

pop·corn /pópkawrn/ *n.* **1** corn which bursts open when heated. **2** these kernels when popped.

pop cul·ture *n.* commercial culture based on popular taste.

P

POP ART

The term *pop art* was coined in the 1950s by the critic Lawrence Alloway. He used it to describe works by artists who employed popular imagery drawn from advertising, comic strips, film, and television. The materials and techniques long used by abstract and action painters – acrylic paints, stencils, silk screens, spray guns – were applied to figurative uses by pop artists. The leading pop artists include Roy Lichtenstein, Peter Blake, Richard Hamilton, and Andy Warhol.

Marilyn, ANDY WARHOL

TIMELINE

| 1500 | 1550 | 1600 | 1650 | 1700 | 1750 | 1800 | 1850 | 1900 | 1950 | 2000 |

pope /pōp/ *n.* **1** (as title usu. **Pope**) the head of the Roman Catholic Church. Also called **Bishop of Rome**. **2** the head of the Coptic Church and Orthodox patriarch of Alexandria. □□ **pope·dom** *n.* **pope·less** *adj.*

pop·er·y /pṓpəree/ *n. derog.* the papal system; the Roman Catholic Church.

pop·gun /pópgun/ *n.* **1** a child's toy gun which shoots a pellet, etc., by the compression of air with a piston. **2** *derog.* an inefficient firearm.

pop·in·jay /pópinjay/ *n.* **1** a fop; a conceited person; a coxcomb. **2 a** *archaic* a parrot. **b** *hist.* a figure of a parrot on a pole as a mark to shoot at.

pop·ish /pṓpish/ *adj. derog.* Roman Catholic. □□ **pop·ish·ly** *adv.*

pop·lar /póplər/ *n.* **1** any tree of the genus *Populus*, with a usu. rapidly growing trunk and tremulous leaves. **2** = TULIP TREE.

pop·lin /póplin/ *n.* a plain woven fabric usu. of cotton, with a corded surface.

pop·o·ver /pópōvər/ *n.* a light puffy hollow muffin made from an egg-rich batter.

pop·pa /pópə/ *n. colloq.* father (esp. as a child's word).

pop·pa·dam /pópədəm/ *n.* (also **pop·pa·dom, popadam**) *Ind.* a thin, crisp, spiced bread eaten with curry, etc.

pop·per /pópər/ *n.* **1 a** a person or thing that pops. **b** a device or machine for making popcorn. **2** *colloq.* a small vial of amyl nitrite used for inhalation. **3** *Brit. colloq.* a snap fastener.

pop·pet /pópit/ *n.* **1** (also **poppet valve**) *Engin.* a mushroom-shaped valve, lifted bodily from its seat rather than hinged. **2** (in full **poppet head**) the head of a lathe. **3** *Brit. colloq.* (esp. as a term of endearment) a small or dainty person.

pop·ple /pópəl/ *v.intr.* (of water) tumble or bubble, toss to and fro. □□ **pop·ply** *adj.*

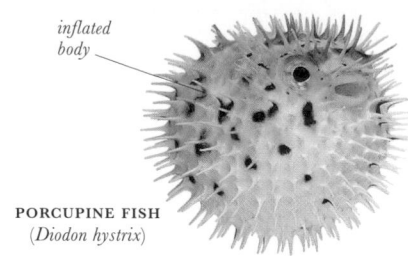

PORCUPINE FISH
(*Diodon hystrix*)

pop·py /pópee/ *n.* (*pl.* **-ies**) ◄ any plant of the genus *Papaver*, with showy often red flowers and a milky sap with narcotic properties.

seeds

poppy head

POPPY: OPIUM POPPY
(*Papaver somniferum*)

pop·py·cock /pópeekok/ *n. sl.* nonsense.

Pop·si·cle /pópsikəl/ *n. Trademark* a flavored ice confection on a stick.

pop·u·lace /pópyələs/ *n.* **1** the common people. **2** *derog.* the rabble.

pop·u·lar /pópyələr/ *adj.* **1** liked or admired by many people or by a specified group (*popular teachers; a popular hero*). **2 a** of or carried on by the general public (*popular meetings*). **b** prevalent among the general public (*popular discontent*). **3** adapted to the understanding, taste, or means of the people (*popular science; popular medicine*). □□ **pop·u·lar·ism** *n.* **pop·u·lar·i·ty** /-láritee/ *n.* **pop·u·lar·ly** *adv.*

pop·u·lar front *n.* a party or coalition representing left-wing elements.

pop·u·lar·ize /pópyələrīz/ *v.tr.* **1** make popular. **2** cause (a person, principle, etc.) to be generally known or liked. **3** present (a technical subject, specialized vocabulary, etc.) in a popular or readily understandable form. □□ **pop·u·lar·i·za·tion** /-rəzáyshən/ *n.* **pop·u·lar·iz·er** *n.*

pop·u·lar mu·sic *n.* songs, folk tunes, etc., appealing to popular tastes.

pop·u·late /pópyəlayt/ *v.tr.* **1** inhabit; form the population of (a town, country, etc.). **2** supply with inhabitants; people (*a densely populated district*).

pop·u·la·tion /pópyəláyshən/ *n.* **1 a** the inhabitants of a place, country, etc., referred to collectively. **b** any specified group within this (*the Polish population of Chicago*). **2** the total number of any of these (*a population of eight million; the seal population*). **3** the act or process of supplying with inhabitants (*the population of forest areas*). **4** *Statistics* any finite or infinite collection of items under consideration.

pop·u·la·tion ex·plo·sion *n.* a sudden large increase of population.

pop·u·list /pópyəlist/ *n. & adj.* ● *n.* a member or adherent of a political party seeking support mainly from the ordinary people. ● *adj.* of or relating to such a political party. □□ **pop·u·lism** *n.* **pop·u·lis·tic** /-listik/ *adj.*

Pop·u·list Par·ty *n.* a US political party formed in 1891 that advocated the interests of labor and farmers, free coinage of silver, a graduated income tax, and government control of monopolies.

pop·u·lous /pópyələs/ *adj.* thickly inhabited. □□ **pop·u·lous·ly** *adv.* **pop·u·lous·ness** *n.*

pop-up *adj.* **1** (of a toaster, etc.) operating so as to move the object (toast when ready, etc.) quickly upward. **2** (of a book, greeting card, etc.) containing three-dimensional figures, illustrations, etc., that rise up when the page is turned. **3** *Computing* (of a menu) able to be superimposed on the screen being worked on and suppressed rapidly.

por·bea·gle /páwrbeegəl/ *n.* a large shark, *Lamna nasus*, having a pointed snout.

por·ce·lain /páwrsəlin, páwrslin/ *n.* **1** a hard vitrified translucent ceramic. **2** objects made of this.

por·ce·lain clay *n.* kaolin.

porch /pawrch/ *n.* **1** a covered shelter for the entrance of a building. ▷ HOUSE. **2** a veranda. □□ **porched** *adj.*

por·cine /páwrsīn, -sin/ *adj.* of or like pigs.

por·ci·ni /pawrchéenee/ *n.* chiefly *N. Amer.* cepes.

por·cu·pine /páwrkyəpīn/ *n.* **1** any rodent of the family Hystricidae native to Africa, Asia, and SE Europe, or the family Erethizontidae native to America, having defensive spines or quills. ▷ RODENT. **2** (*attrib.*) denoting any of various animals or other organisms with spines.

por·cu·pine fish *n.* ▲ a marine fish, *Diodon hystrix*, covered with sharp spines and often distending itself into a spherical shape.

pore[1] /pawr/ *n. esp. Biol.* a minute opening in a surface through which gases, liquids, or fine solids may pass. ▷ SKIN

pore[2] /pawr/ *v.intr.* (foll. by *over*) **1** be absorbed in studying (a book, etc.). **2** meditate on, think intently about (a subject).

por·gy /páwrgee/ *n.* (*pl.* **-ies**) any usu. marine fish of the family Sparidae, used as food. Also called **sea bream**.

pork /pawrk/ *n.* **1** the (esp. unsalted) flesh of a pig, used as food. ▷ CUT. **2** = PORK BARREL.

pork bar·rel *n. US colloq.* government funds as a source of political benefit.

pork·er /páwrkər/ *n.* **1** a pig raised for food. **2** a young fattened pig.

pork·pie hat /páwrkpī/ *n.* a hat with a flat crown and a brim turned up all around.

pork·y /páwrkee/ *adj. & n.* ● *adj.* (**porkier, porkiest**) **1** *colloq.* fleshy; fat. **2** of or like pork. ● *n. Brit. rhyming sl.* a lie (short for *porky pie*).

porn /pawrn/ *n. colloq.* pornography.

por·no /páwrnō/ *n. & adj. colloq.* ● *n.* pornography. ● *adj.* pornographic.

por·nog·ra·phy /pawrnógrəfee/ *n.* **1** the explicit description or exhibition of sexual activity in literature, films, etc., intended to stimulate erotic rather than aesthetic or emotional feelings. **2** literature, etc., characterized by this. □□ **por·nog·ra·pher** *n.* **por·no·graph·ic** /-nəgráfik/ *adj.* **por·no·graph·i·cal·ly** *adv.*

po·rous /páwrəs/ *adj.* **1** full of pores. **2** letting through air, water, etc. **3** (of an argument, security system, etc.) leaky; admitting infiltration.

PORPOISE

The six species of porpoise are typically smaller than other cetaceans (whales and dolphins) and have blunt snouts without beaks. Porpoise teeth are spade-shaped, whereas those of the dolphin are conical.

well-defined dorsal fin

small rounded head

notched fluke

PORPOISE TOOTH   DOLPHIN TOOTH

blunt snout

EXTERNAL FEATURES OF A HARBOR PORPOISE
(*Phocoena phocoena*)

EXAMPLES OF OTHER PORPOISES

FINLESS PORPOISE
(*Neophocaena phocaenoides*)

SPECTACLED PORPOISE
(*Australophocaena dioptrica*)

P

PORT

A port is a protected body of water where ships take on and discharge passengers and goods. Large ports can deal with many types of vessels and have warehouses for storing goods and dry docks for repairing ships. Some ports can handle containers, which are loaded straight off ships and directly onto trains and trucks.

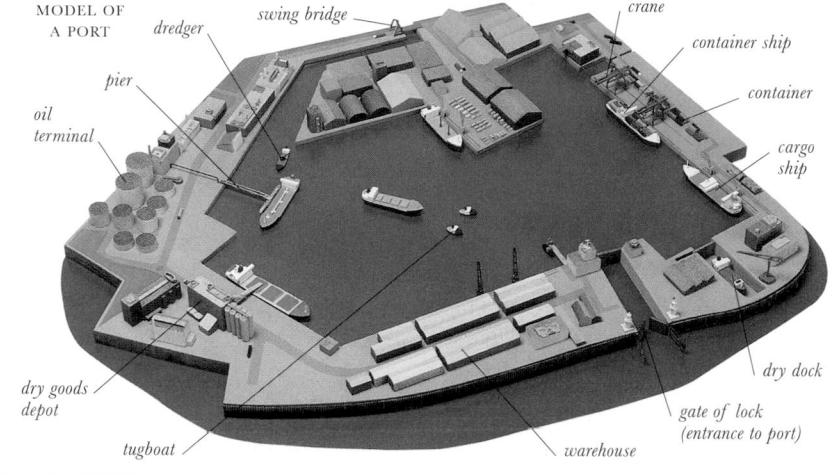

MODEL OF A PORT — swing bridge — dredger — crane — container ship — container — cargo ship — pier — oil terminal — dry goods depot — tugboat — warehouse — gate of lock (entrance to port) — dry dock

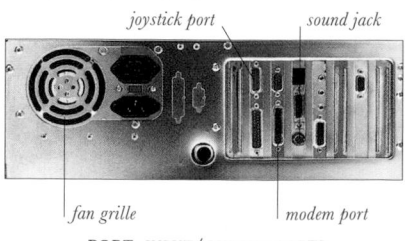

fan grille — modem port — joystick port — sound jack

PORT: INPUT/OUTPUT PORTS
ON THE BACK OF A COMPUTER

□□ **po·ros·i·ty** /porósitee/ *n.* **po·rous·ly** *adv.* **po·rous·ness** *n.*

por·phyr·i·a /pawrfíreeə/ *n.* any of a group of genetic disorders associated with abnormal metabolism of various pigments.

por·phy·ry /páwrfiree/ *n.* (*pl.* **-ies**) **1** a hard rock quarried in ancient Egypt, composed of crystals of white or red feldspar in a red matrix. **2** *Geol.* an igneous rock with large crystals scattered in a matrix of much smaller crystals. □□ **por·phy·rit·ic** /-rítik/ *adj.*

por·poise /páwrpəs/ *n.* ◀ any of various small toothed whales of the family Phocaenidae, esp. of the genus *Phocaena*, with a low triangular dorsal fin and a blunt rounded snout. ▷ CETACEAN

por·ridge /páwrij, pór / *n.* **1** a dish consisting of oatmeal or another cereal boiled in water or milk. **2** *Brit. sl.* imprisonment. □□ **por·ridg·y** *adj.*

por·rin·ger /páwrinjər, pór / *n.* a small bowl, often with a handle, for soup, stew, etc.

port[1] /pawrt/ *n.* **1** ▲ a harbor. **2** a place of refuge. **3** a town or place possessing a harbor, esp. one where customs officers are stationed.

port[2] /pawrt/ *n.* (in full **port wine**) a strong, sweet, dark red (occas. brown or white) fortified wine of Portugal.

port[3] /pawrt/ *n.* the left side (looking forward) of a ship, boat, or aircraft (cf. STARBOARD).

port[4] /pawrt/ *n.* **1 a** an opening in the side of a ship for entrance, loading, etc. **b** a porthole. **2** an aperture for the passage of steam, water, etc. **3** *Electr.* ▼ a socket or aperture in an electronic circuit, esp. in a computer network, where connections can be made with peripheral equipment. **4** an aperture in a wall, etc., for a gun to be fired through. **5** esp. *Sc.* a gate or gateway, esp. of a walled town.

port[5] /pawrt/ *v.tr. & n.* ● *v.tr. Mil.* carry (a rifle, or other weapon) diagonally across and close to the body with the barrel, etc., near the left shoulder (esp. *port arms!*). ● *n.* **1** *Mil.* this position. **2** external deportment; carriage; bearing.

port·a·ble /páwrtəbəl/ *adj. & n.* ● *adj.* easily movable; convenient for carrying (*portable TV*; *portable computer*). ● *n.* a portable object, e.g., a radio, typewriter, etc. (*decided to buy a portable*). □□ **port·a·bil·i·ty** *n.* **port·a·ble·ness** *n.* **port·a·bly** *adv.*

por·tage /páwrtij, -táazh/ *n. & v.* ● *n.* **1** the carrying of boats or goods between two navigable waters. **2** a place at which this is necessary. **3 a** the act or an instance of carrying or transporting. **b** the cost of this. ● *v.tr.* convey (a boat or goods) between navigable waters.

por·tal[1] /páwrt'l/ *n.* a doorway or gate, etc., esp. a large and elaborate one.

por·tal[2] /páwrt'l/ *adj.* of or relating to an aperture in an organ through which its associated vessels pass.

por·ta·men·to /páwrtəméntō/ *n.* (*pl.* **portamenti** /-tee/) *Mus.* **1** the act or an instance of gliding from one note to another in singing, playing the violin, etc. **2** piano playing in a manner intermediate between legato and staccato.

port·cul·lis /pawrtkúlis/ *n.* ▶ a strong heavy grating sliding up and down in vertical grooves, lowered to block a gateway in a fortress, etc. □□ **port·cul·lised** *adj.*

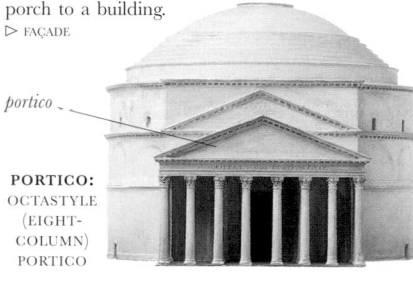

portcullis — wooden gates

PORTCULLIS

por·tend /pawrténd/ *v.tr.* **1** foreshadow as an omen. **2** give warning of.

por·tent /páwrtent/ *n.* **1** an omen, a sign of something to come, esp. something of a momentous or calamitous nature. **2** a prodigy; a marvelous thing.

por·ten·tous /pawrténtəs/ *adj.* **1** like or serving as a portent. **2** pompously solemn. □□ **por·ten·tous·ly** *adv.*

por·ter[1] /páwrtər/ *n.* **1 a** a person employed to carry luggage, etc., at an airport, hotel, etc. **b** a hospital employee who moves equipment, trolleys, etc. **2** a dark brown bitter beer brewed from charred or browned malt. **3** a sleeping-car attendant. **4** a cleaning person or maintenance worker, as in a hospital, etc. □□ **por·ter·age** *n.*

por·ter[2] /páwrtər/ *n. Brit.* a gatekeeper or doorkeeper, esp. of a large building.

por·ter·house steak /páwrtərhows/ *n.* a thick steak cut from the thick end of a sirloin.

port·fo·li·o /pawrtfóleeō/ *n.* (*pl.* **-os**) **1** a case for keeping loose sheets of paper, drawings, etc. **2** a range of investments held by a company, etc. **3** the office of a minister of state. **4** samples of an artist's work.

port·hole /páwrt-hōl/ *n.* an (esp. glassed-in) aperture in a ship's or aircraft's side for the admission of light.

por·ti·co /páwrtikō/ *n.* (*pl.* **-oes** or **-os**) ▼ a colonnade; a roof supported by columns at regular intervals usu. attached as a porch to a building.
▷ FAÇADE

portico

PORTICO:
OCTASTYLE
(EIGHT-COLUMN)
PORTICO

por·tion /páwrshən/ *n. & v.* ● *n.* **1** a part or share. **2** the amount of food allotted to one person. **3** a specified or limited quantity. **4** one's destiny or lot. **5** a dowry. ● *v.tr.* **1** divide (a thing) into portions. **2** (foll. by *out*) distribute. **3** give a dowry to. **4** (foll. by *to*) assign (a thing) to (a person). □□ **por·tion·less** *adj.* (in sense 5 of *n.*).

Port·land ce·ment /páwrtlənd/ *n.* a cement manufactured from chalk and clay that when hard resembles Portland stone in color.

Port·land stone /páwrtlənd/ *n.* a limestone from the Isle of Portland in Dorset, England, used in building.

port·ly /páwrtlee/ *adj.* (**portlier**, **portliest**) **1** corpulent; stout. **2** *archaic* of a stately appearance. □□ **port·li·ness** *n.*

port·man·teau /pawrtmántō, páwrtmantō/ *n.* (*pl.* **portmanteaus** or **portmanteaux** /-tōz, -tŏz/) a leather trunk for clothes, etc., opening into two equal parts.

port·man·teau word *n.* a word blending the sounds and combining the meanings of two others, e.g., *motel* from *motor* and *hotel*.

port of call *n.* a place where a ship or a person stops on a journey.

por·trait /páwrtrit, -trayt/ *n.* **1** a representation of a person or animal, esp. of the face, made by drawing, painting, photography, etc. **2** a verbal picture; a graphic description. **3** (in graphic design, etc.) a format in which the height of an illustration, etc., is greater than the width (cf. LANDSCAPE).

por·trait·ist /páwrtritist/ *n.* a person who takes or paints portraits.

por·trai·ture /páwrtrichər/ *n.* **1** the art of painting or taking portraits. **2** graphic description. **3** a portrait.

por·tray /pawrtráy/ *v.tr.* **1** represent (an object) by a painting, carving, etc; make a likeness of. **2** describe graphically. **3** represent dramatically. □□ **por·tray·a·ble** *adj.* **por·tray·al** *n.* **por·tray·er** *n.*

Por·tu·guese /páwrchəgeéz, -geés/ *n. & adj.* ● *n.* (*pl.* same) **1 a** a native or national of Portugal. **b** a person of Portuguese descent. **2** the language of Portugal. ● *adj.* of or relating to Portugal or its people or language.

P

PORTUGUESE MAN-OF-WAR
(*Physalia* species)

crest

tentacles

Por·tu·guese man-of-war *n.* ◀ a dangerous tropical or subtropical marine hydrozoan of the genus *Physalia* with a large crest and a poisonous sting.

POS *abbr.* point-of-sale.

pose[1] /pōz/ *v. & n.* ● *v.* **1** *intr.* assume a certain attitude of body, esp. when being photographed or being painted for a portrait. **2** *intr.* (foll. by *as*) set oneself up as or pretend to be (another person, etc.) (*posing as a celebrity*). **3** *intr.* behave affectedly in order to impress others. **4** *tr.* put forward or present (a question, etc.). **5** *tr.* place (an artist's model, etc.) in a certain attitude or position. ● *n.* **1** an attitude of body or mind. **2** an attitude or pretense, esp. one assumed for effect (*his generosity is a mere pose*).

pose[2] /pōz/ *v.tr.* puzzle (a person) with a question or problem.

pos·er /pōzər/ *n.* **1** a person who poses (see POSE[1] *v.* 3). **2** a puzzling question or problem.

po·seur /pōzǒr/ *n.* (*fem.* **poseuse** /pōzǒz/) a person who poses for effect or behaves affectedly.

posh /posh/ *adj. & adv. colloq.* ● *adj.* **1** elegant; stylish. **2** esp. *Brit.* of or associated with the upper classes (*spoke with a posh accent*). ● *adv.* esp. *Brit.* in a stylish or upper-class way (*talk posh*; *act posh*). □□ **posh·ly** *adv.* **posh·ness** *n.*

pos·it /pózit/ *v.tr.* (**posited**, **positing**) **1** assume as a fact; postulate. **2** put in place or position.

po·si·tion /pəzíshən/ *n. & v.* ● *n.* **1** a place occupied by a person or thing. **2** the way in which a thing or its parts are placed or arranged (*sitting in an uncomfortable position*). **3** the proper place (*in position*). **4** the state of being advantageously placed (*jockeying for position*). **5** a person's mental attitude; a way of looking at a question (*changed their position on nuclear disarmament*). **6** a person's situation in relation to others (*puts one in an awkward position*). **7** rank or status; high social standing. **8** paid employment. **9** a place where troops, etc., are posted for strategical purposes (*the position was stormed*). **10** a specific pose in ballet, etc. (*hold first position*). ● *v.tr.* place in position. □ **in a position to** enabled by circumstances, resources, information, etc., to (do, state, etc.). □□ **po·si·tion·al** *adj.* **po·si·tion·al·ly** *adv.* **po·si·tion·er** *n.*

pos·i·tive /pózitiv/ *adj. & n.* ● *adj.* **1** formally or explicitly stated; definite; unquestionable (*positive proof*). **2** (of a person) convinced, confident, or overconfident in his or her opinion (*positive that I was not there*). **3 a** absolute; not relative. **b** *Gram.* (of an adjective or adverb) expressing a simple quality without comparison (cf. COMPARATIVE, SUPERLATIVE). **4** *colloq.* downright; complete (*it would be a positive miracle*). **5 a** constructive; directional (*positive criticism*; *positive thinking*). **b** favorable; optimistic (*positive reaction*; *positive outlook*). **6** marked by the presence rather than absence of qualities or *Med.* symptoms (*the test was positive*). **7** esp. *Philos.* dealing only with matters of fact; practical (cf. POSITIVISM 1). **8** tending in a direction naturally or arbitrarily taken as that of increase or progress (*clockwise rotation is positive*). **9** greater than zero (*positive and negative integers*). **10** *Electr.* of, containing, or producing the kind of electrical charge produced by rubbing glass with silk; an absence of electrons. **11** (of a photographic image) showing lights and shades or colors true to the original (opp. NEGATIVE). ● *n.* a positive adjective, photograph, quantity, etc. □□ **pos·i·tive·ly** *adv.* **pos·i·tive·ness** *n.* **pos·i·tiv·i·ty** /pózitívitee/ *n.*

pos·i·tive feed·back *n.* **1** a constructive response to an experiment, questionnaire, etc. **2** *Electronics* the return of part of an output signal to the input, tending to increase the amplification, etc.

pos·i·tive sign *n.* = PLUS SIGN.

pos·i·tiv·ism /pózitivizəm/ *n.* **1** *Philos.* the philosophical system of Auguste Comte, recognizing only nonmetaphysical facts and observable phenomena, and rejecting metaphysics and theism. **2** a religious system founded on this. **3** = LOGICAL POSITIVISM. □□ **pos·i·tiv·ist** *n.* **pos·i·tiv·is·tic** *adj.* **pos·i·tiv·is·ti·cal·ly** /-vístiklee/ *adv.*

pos·i·tron /pózitron/ *n.* *Physics* ▼ an elementary particle with a positive charge equal to the negative charge of an electron and having the same mass as an electron.

poss. *abbr.* **1** possession. **2** possessive. **3** possible. **4** possibly.

pos·se /pósee/ *n.* **1** a strong force or company or assemblage. **2** (in full **posse comitatus** /kómitáytəs/) **a** a body of constables, enforcers of the law, etc. **b** a body of men summoned by a sheriff, etc., to enforce the law.

pos·sess /pəzés/ *v.tr.* **1** hold as property; own. **2** have a faculty, quality, etc. (*they possess a special value for us*). **3** (also *refl.*; foll. by *in*) maintain (oneself, one's soul, etc.) in a specified state (*possess oneself in patience*). **4 a** (of a demon, etc.) occupy; have power over (a person, etc.) (*possessed by the devil*). **b** (of an emotion, infatuation, etc.) dominate; be an obsession of (*possessed by fear*). **5** have sexual intercourse with (esp. a woman). □ **be possessed of** own; have. **possess oneself of** take or get for one's own. **what possessed you?** an expression of incredulity. □□ **pos·ses·sor** *n.* **pos·ses·so·ry** *adj.*

pos·ses·sion /pəzéshən/ *n.* **1** the act or state of possessing or being possessed. **2 a** the thing possessed. **b** a foreign territory subject to a state or ruler. **3** the act or state of actual holding or occupancy. **4** *Law* power or control similar to lawful ownership but which may exist separately from it (*prosecuted for possession of narcotic drugs*). **5** (in *pl.*) property, wealth, subject territory, etc. **6** *Sports* temporary control, in team sports, of the ball, puck, etc., by a particular player. □ **in possession 1** (of a person) possessing. **2** (of a thing) possessed. **in possession of 1** having in one's possession. **2** maintaining control over (*in possession of one's wits*). **in the possession of** held or owned by. **take possession** (often foll. by *of*) become the owner or possessor (of a thing). □□ **pos·ses·sion·less** *adj.*

pos·ses·sive /pəzésiv/ *adj. & n.* ● *adj.* **1** showing a desire to possess or retain what one already owns. **2** showing jealous and domineering tendencies toward another person. **3** *Gram.* indicating possession. ● *n.* (in full **possessive case**) *Gram.* the case of nouns and pronouns expressing possession. □□ **pos·ses·sive·ly** *adv.* **pos·ses·sive·ness** *n.*

pos·ses·sive pro·noun *n.* each of the pronouns indicating possession (*my*, *your*, *his*, *their*, etc.) or the corresponding absolute forms (*mine*, *yours*, *his*, *theirs*, etc.).

pos·si·bil·i·ty /pósibílitee/ *n.* (*pl.* **-ies**) **1** the state or fact of being possible, or an occurrence of this. **2** a thing that may exist or happen (*there are three possibilities*). **3** (usu. in *pl.*) the capability of being used, improved, etc.; the potential of an object or situation (esp. *have possibilities*).

pos·si·ble /pósibəl/ *adj. & n.* ● *adj.* **1** capable of existing or happening; that may be managed, achieved, etc. (*came as early as possible*; *did as much as possible*). **2** that is likely to happen, etc. (*few thought their victory possible*). **3** acceptable; potential (*a possible way of doing it*). ● *n.* **1** a possible candidate, member of a team, etc. **2** (prec. by *the*) whatever is likely, manageable, etc.

pos·si·bly /pósiblee/ *adv.* **1** perhaps. **2** in accordance with possibility (*cannot possibly refuse*).

pos·sum /pósəm/ *n.* **1** *colloq.* = OPOSSUM. **2** *Austral. & NZ colloq.* ▶ a phalanger resembling an American opossum. □ **play possum 1** pretend to be asleep or unconscious when threatened. **2** feign ignorance.

POSSUM:
HONEY POSSUM
(*Tarsipes spenserae*)

post- /pōst/ *prefix* after in time or order.

post[1] /pōst/ *n. & v.* ● *n.* **1** a long stout piece of timber or metal set upright in the ground, etc.: **a** to support something, esp. in building. **b** to mark a position, boundary, etc. **c** to carry notices. **2** a pole, etc., marking the start or finish of a race. **3** a metal pin, as on a pierced earring. ● *v.tr.* **1** (often foll. by *up*) **a** attach (a paper, etc.) in a prominent place; stick up (*post no bills*). **b** announce or advertise by placard or in a published text. **2** publish the name of (a ship, etc.) as overdue or missing. **3** placard (a wall, etc.) with handbills, etc. **4** achieve (a score in a game, etc.).

post[2] /pōst/ *n., v., & adv.* ● *n.* **1** esp. *Brit.* the official conveyance of packages, letters, etc.; the mail (*send it by post*). **2** esp. *Brit.* a single collection, dispatch, or delivery of the mail; the letters, etc., dispatched (*has the post arrived yet?*). **3** esp. *Brit.* a place where letters, etc., are dealt with; a post office or mailbox (*take it to the post*). **4** *hist.* **a** one of a series of couriers who carried mail on horseback between fixed stages. **b** a letter carrier; a mail cart. ● *v.* **1** *tr.* esp. *Brit.* put (a letter, etc.) in the mail. **2** *tr.* (esp. as **posted** *adj.*) supply a person with information (*keep me posted*). **3** *tr.* **a** enter (an item) in a ledger. **b** (often foll. by *up*) complete (a ledger) in this way. **c** carry (an entry) from an auxiliary book to a more formal one, or from one account to another. **4** *intr.* **a** travel with haste; hurry. **b** *hist.* travel with relays of horses. ● *adv.* express; with haste.

post[3] /pōst/ *n. & v.* ● *n.* **1** a place where a soldier is stationed or which he patrols. **2** a place of duty. **3 a** a position taken up by a body of soldiers. **b** a force occupying this. **c** a fort. **4** a situation; paid employment. **5** = TRADING POST. ● *v.tr.* **1** place or

POSITRON

A positron is the antiparticle of an electron and has a positive charge. Pairs of particles and their antiparticles can be created in particle accelerators. Shown here, a burst of energy produces a positron and an electron, which spiral in opposite directions due to their opposing charges.

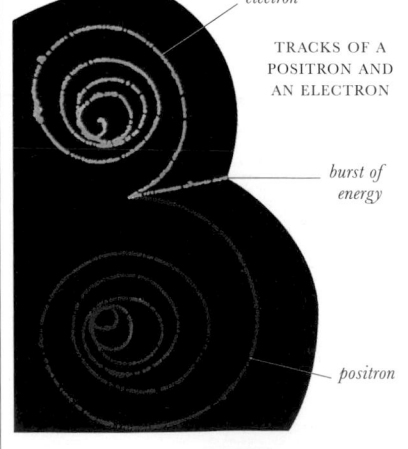

electron

TRACKS OF A POSITRON AND AN ELECTRON

burst of energy

positron

station (soldiers, an employee, etc.). **2** esp. *Brit.* appoint to a post or command.

post·age /pṓstij/ *n.* the amount charged for sending a letter, etc., by mail, usu. prepaid in the form of a stamp (*$5 for postage*).

pos·tage me·ter *n.* a machine for printing prepaid postage and a postmark.

pos·tage stamp *n.* an official stamp affixed to or imprinted on a letter, etc., indicating the amount of postage paid.

post·al /pṓst'l/ *adj.* **1** of the post office or mail. **2** by mail. □□ **post·al·ly** *adv.*

pos·tal code *n.* **1** = POSTCODE. **2** (in Canada) a mailing code similar to the US ZIP code.

post·bel·lum /pōstbélǝm/ *adj.* occurring or existing after a war, in particular the American Civil War.

post·card /pṓstkaard/ *n.* a card, often with a photograph on one side, for sending a short message by mail without an envelope.

post chaise *n. hist.* a fast carriage drawn by horses that were changed at regular intervals.

post·code /pṓstkōd/ *n. Brit., Austral., & NZ* a group of letters or letters and figures that are added to a mailing address to assist sorting.

post·co·i·tal /pōstkṓǝt'l/ *adj.* occurring or done after sexual intercourse. □□ **post·co·i·tal·ly** *adv.*

post·date *v. & n.* ● *v.tr.* /pōstdáyt/ affix or assign a date later than the actual one to (a document, event, etc.). ● *n.* /pṓstdayt/ such a date.

post·doc·tor·al /pōstdóktǝrǝl/ *adj.* (of research) undertaken after the completion of a doctorate.

post·er /pṓstǝr/ *n.* **1** a placard in a public place. **2** a large printed picture. **3** *Brit.* a billposter.

pos·te·ri·or /posteéreeǝr, pō-/ *adj. & n.* ● *adj.* **1** later, coming after in series, order, or time. **2** situated at the back. ● *n.* (in *sing.* or *pl.*) the buttocks. □□ **pos·te·ri·or·i·ty** /-áwritee, -ór-/ *n.* **pos·te·ri·or·ly** *adv.*

pos·ter·i·ty /postéritee/ *n.* **1** all succeeding generations. **2** the descendants of a person.

pos·tern /pṓstǝrn, pō-/ *n.* **1** a back door. **2** a side way or entrance.

post ex·change *n. Mil.* a store at a military base, etc. ¶ Abbr.: **PX.**

post horn *n. hist.* ▼ a valveless horn formerly used to announce the arrival of the mail.

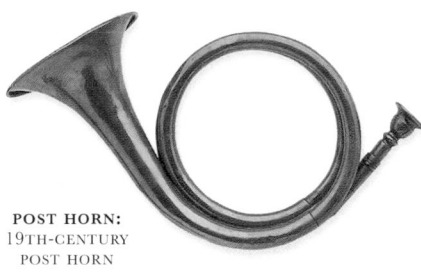

POST HORN:
19TH-CENTURY
POST HORN

post·grad·u·ate /pōstgrájōōǝt/ *adj. & n.* ● *adj.* **1** (of a course of study) carried on after taking a high school or college degree. **2** of or relating to students following this course of study (*postgraduate fees*). ● *n.* a postgraduate student.

post-haste *adv.* with great speed.

post·hu·mous /póschǝmǝs/ *adj.* **1** occurring after death. **2** (of a child) born after the death of its father. **3** (of a book, etc.) published after the author's death. □□ **post·hu·mous·ly** *adv.*

pos·til·ion /postílyǝn, pō-/ *n.* (also **pos·til·lion**) the rider on the near (left-hand side) horse drawing a coach, etc., when there is no coachman.

Post·im·pres·sion·ism /pṓstimpréshǝnizǝm/ *n.* ▲ artistic aims and methods developed as a reaction against impressionism and intending to express the individual artist's conception of the objects represented rather than the ordinary observer's view. □□ **Post·im·pres·sion·ist** *n. & adj.* **Post·im·pres·sion·is·tic** *adj.*

POSTIMPRESSIONISM

Postimpressionism is a term first used by British art critic Roger Fry in 1910 to describe the various styles of painting that flourished in France from 1880 to 1910. Generally, the word is used to cover the generation of artists who sought new forms of expression following the pictorial revolution brought about by Impressionism. Among the principal figures in this group were Paul Cezanne, Paul Gauguin, Georges Seurat, and Vincent van Gogh. Although their individual styles differed markedly, all these artists developed the Impressionist style far beyond the representational.

The Italian Woman (1888),
VINCENT VAN GOGH

TIMELINE

1500 1550 1600 1650 1700 1750 1800 1850 1900 1950 2000

---

post·in·dus·tri·al /pōstindústreeǝl/ *adj.* relating to or characteristic of a society or economy that no longer relies on heavy industry.

post·man /pṓstmǝn/ *n.* (*pl.* **-men**; *fem.* **post·woman**, *pl.* **-women**) a person who is employed to deliver and collect letters, etc.

post·mark /pṓstmaark/ *n. & v.* ● *n.* an official mark stamped on a letter, esp. one giving the place, date, etc., of sending or arrival, and serving to cancel the stamp. ● *v.tr.* mark (an envelope, etc.) with this.

post·mas·ter /pṓstmastǝr/ *n.* the person in charge of a post office.

post·mil·len·ni·al /pṓstmiléneeǝl/ *n.* following the millennium.

post·mis·tress /pṓstmistris/ *n.* a woman in charge of a post office.

post·mod·ern /pōstmódǝrn/ *adj.* ▼ (in literature, architecture, the arts, etc.) denoting a movement reacting against modern tendencies, esp. by drawing attention to former conventions. □□ **post·mod·ern·ism** *n.* **post·mod·ern·ist** *n. & adj.*

post·mor·tem /pōstmáwrtǝm/ *n., adv., & adj.* ● *n.* **1** (in full **postmortem examination**) an examination made after death, esp. to determine its cause. **2** *colloq.* a discussion analysing the course and result of a game, election, etc. ● *adv. & adj.* after death.

post·na·tal /pōstnáyt'l/ *adj.* characteristic of or relating to the period after childbirth.

post·nup·tial /pōstnúpshǝl/ *adj.* after marriage.

Post Office *n.* **1** the public department or corporation responsible for postal services and (in some countries) telecommunication. **2** (**post office**) a room or building where postal business is carried on.

post·paid /pṓstpáyd/ *adj.* on which postage has been paid.

P

POSTMODERN

Postmodernism is a late 20th-century term used in various disciplines to refer to a rejection of modernism's preoccupation with pure form and technique. Postmodern designers use an amalgam of style elements from the past, such as the classical and baroque, introducing ornament, color, and sculpture, often with ironic intent.

pediment

ornamental motif

classical column

columned gateway

PUMPING STATION (1989), LONDON, ENGLAND

TIMELINE

1500 1550 1600 1650 1700 1750 1800 1850 1900 1950 2000

post·par·tum /póstpáartəm/ *adj.* following parturition.

post·pone /pōstpṓn, pəspṓn/ *v.tr.* cause or arrange (an event, etc.) to take place at a later time. □□ **post·pon·a·ble** *adj.* **post·pone·ment** *n.* **post·pon·er** *n.*

post·po·si·tion /póstpəzíshən/ *n.* **1** a word or particle, esp. an enclitic, placed after the word it modifies, e.g., *-ward* in *homeward* and *at* in *the books we looked at.* **2** the use of a postposition. □□ **post·po·si·tion·al** *adj. & n.* **post·pos·i·tive** /póstpózitiv/ *adj. & n.* **post·pos·i·tive·ly** *adv.*

post·pran·di·al /póstprándeeəl/ *adj. formal* or *joc.* after dinner or lunch.

post·script /póstskript, pṓskript/ *n.* **1** an additional paragraph or remark, usu. at the end of a letter after the signature and introduced by 'PS.' **2** any additional information, action, etc.

pos·tu·lant /póschələnt/ *n.* a candidate, esp. for admission into a religious order.

pos·tu·late *v. & n.* ● *v.tr.* /póschəlayt/ **1** (often foll. by *that* + clause) assume as a necessary condition, esp. as a basis for reasoning; take for granted. **2** claim. **3** (in ecclesiastical law) nominate or elect to a higher rank. ● *n.* /póschələt/ **1** a thing postulated. **2** a fundamental prerequisite or condition. **3** *Math.* an assumption used as a basis for mathematical reasoning. □□ **pos·tu·la·tion** /-láyshən/ *n.* **pos·tu·la·tor** *n.*

pos·tu·la·tor /póschəlaytər/ *n.* **1** a person who postulates. **2** *RC Ch.* a person who presents a case for canonization or beatification.

pos·ture /póschər/ *n. & v.* ● *n.* **1** the relative position of parts, esp. of the body (*in a reclining posture*). **2** carriage or bearing (*improved by good posture and balance*). **3** a mental or spiritual attitude or condition. **4** the condition or state (of affairs, etc.) (*in more diplomatic postures*). ● *v.* **1** *intr.* assume a mental or physical attitude, esp. for effect (*inclined to strut and posture*). **2** *tr.* pose (a person). □□ **pos·tur·al** *adj.* **pos·tur·er** *n.*

post·war /póstwáwr/ *adj.* occurring or existing after a war (esp. the most recent major war).

po·sy /pṓzee/ *n.* (*pl.* **-ies**) a small bunch of flowers.

pot[1] /pot/ *n. & v.* ● *n.* **1** a vessel, usu. rounded, of ceramic ware or metal or glass for holding liquids or solids or for cooking in. **2** a coffeepot, flowerpot, teapot, etc. **3** a drinking vessel of pewter, etc. **4** the contents of a pot (*ate a whole pot of jam*). **5** the total amount of the bet in a game, etc. **6** *colloq.* a large sum (*pots of money*). **7** *Brit. sl.* a vessel given as a prize in an athletic contest, esp. a silver cup. **8** = POTBELLY 1. ● *v.tr.* (**potted**, **potting**) **1** place in a pot. **2** (usu. as **potted** *adj.*) preserve in a sealed pot (*potted shrimps*). **3** *Brit.* sit (a young child) on a chamber pot. **4** *Brit.* pocket (a ball) in billiards, etc. **5** shoot at, hit, or kill (an animal) with a potshot. **6** seize or secure. **7** *Brit.* abridge or epitomize (*in a potted version; potted wisdom*). □ **go to pot** *colloq.* deteriorate; be ruined. □□ **pot·ful** *n.* (*pl.* **-fuls**).

pot[2] /pot/ *n. sl.* marijuana.

po·ta·ble /pṓtəbəl/ *adj.* drinkable. □□ **po·ta·bil·i·ty** /-bílitee/ *n.*

po·tage /pōtáazh/ *n.* thick soup.

po·tam·ic /pətámik, pō-/ *adj.* of rivers. □□ **po·ta·mol·o·gy** /pótəmólijee/ *n.*

pot·ash /pótash/ *n.* an alkaline potassium compound, usu. potassium carbonate or hydroxide.

po·tas·si·um /pətáseeəm/ *n. Chem.* ◄ a soft silvery white metallic element occurring naturally in seawater and various minerals, an essential element for living organisms, and forming many useful compounds used industrially. ¶ Symb.: **K.** □□ **po·tas·sic** *adj.*

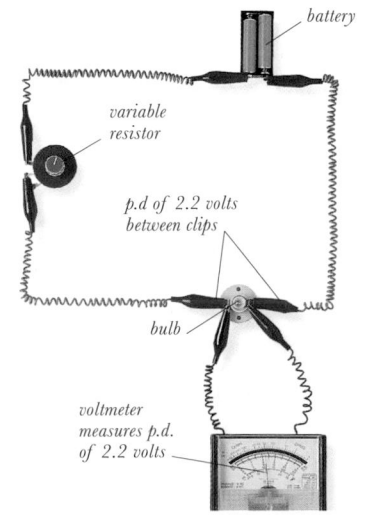

POTASSIUM:
PURE FORM

po·ta·tion /pōtáyshən/ *n.* **1** a drink. **2** the act or an instance of drinking. **3** (usu. in *pl.*) the act or an instance of tippling. □□ **po·ta·to·ry** /pṓtətawree/ *adj.*

po·ta·to /pətáytō/ *n.* (*pl.* **-oes**) **1** a starchy plant tuber that is cooked and used for food. **2** ▼ the plant, *Solanum tuberosum,* bearing this. **3** = SWEET POTATO.

flower

tuber (potato)

POTATO
(*Solanum tuberosum*)

root

po·ta·to chip *n.* a thin slice of potato deep-fried, eaten as a snack food.

pot-au-feu /páwtōfő/ *n.* **1** the traditional French dish of boiled meat and vegetables. **2** the soup or broth from it. **3** a large cooking pot of the kind common in France.

pot·bel·ly /pótbelee/ *n.* (*pl.* **-ies**) **1** a protruding

POTENTIAL DIFFERENCE

Electric potential is a measure of the energy of electrons or other charged particles. Current is the movement of electric charge between positions with different electric potentials. The potential difference (p.d.) between two points is measured in volts.

battery

variable resistor

p.d of 2.2 volts between clips

bulb

voltmeter measures p.d. of 2.2 volts

DEMONSTRATION OF POTENTIAL DIFFERENCE
IN AN ELECTRICAL CIRCUIT

stomach. **2** a person with this. **3** a small bulbous stove. □□ **pot·bel·lied** *adj.*

pot·boil·er /pótboylər/ *n.* **1** a work of literature or art done merely to make the writer or artist a living. **2** a writer or artist who does this.

pot-bound *adj.* (of a plant) having roots that fill the flowerpot, leaving no room to expand.

po·teen /pōtéen, pə-/ *n.* (also **po·theen** /-chéen/) *Ir.* alcohol made illicitly, usu. from potatoes.

po·tent /pṓt'nt/ *adj.* **1** powerful; strong. **2** (of a reason) cogent; forceful. **3** (of a male) capable of sexual erection or orgasm. **4** *literary* mighty. □□ **po·tence** *n.* **po·ten·cy** *n.* **po·tent·ly** *adv.*

po·ten·tate /pṓt'ntayt/ *n.* a monarch or ruler.

po·ten·tial /pəténshəl/ *adj. & n.* ● *adj.* capable of coming into being or action; latent. ● *n.* **1** the capacity for use or development; possibility (*achieved its highest potential*). **2** usable resources. **3** *Physics* the quantity determining the energy of mass in a gravitational field or of charge in an electric field. □□ **po·ten·ti·al·i·ty** /-sheeálitee/ *n.* **po·ten·tial·ize** *v.tr.* **po·ten·tial·ly** *adv.*

po·ten·tial dif·fer·ence *n.* ▼ the difference of electric potential between two points.

po·ten·tial en·er·gy *n.* a body's ability to do work by virtue of its position relative to others, stresses within itself, electric charge, etc.

po·ten·ti·ate /pəténsheeayt/ *v.tr.* **1** make more powerful, esp. increase the effectiveness of (a drug). **2** make possible.

po·ten·ti·om·e·ter /pəténsheeómitər/ *n.* ▼ an instrument for measuring or adjusting small electrical potentials. ▷ RESISTOR. □□ **po·ten·ti·o·met·ric** /-sheeəmétrik/ *adj.* **po·ten·ti·om·e·try** /-sheeómitree/ *n.*

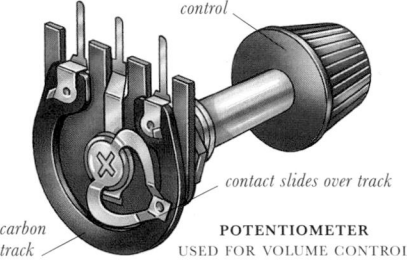

control

contact slides over track

carbon track

POTENTIOMETER
USED FOR VOLUME CONTROL

pot·head /pót-hed/ *n. sl.* a person who smokes marijuana frequently.

po·theen var. of POTEEN.

poth·er /póthər/ *n. & v.* ● *n.* a noise; commotion; fuss. ● *v.* **1** *tr.* fluster; worry. **2** *intr.* make a fuss.

pot·herb /pótərb, -hərb/ *n.* any herb grown in a kitchen garden or a pot.

pot·hole /pót-hōl/ *n. & v.* ● *n.* **1** *Geol.* a deep hole or system of caves and underground riverbeds formed by the erosion of rock esp. by the action of water. **2** a deep hole in the ground or a riverbed. **3** a hole in a road surface caused by wear, weather, or subsidence. ● *v.intr. Brit.* explore potholes. □□ **pot·holed** *adj.* **pot·hol·er** *n.* **pot·hol·ing** *n.*

po·tion /pṓshən/ *n.* a liquid medicine, drug, poison, etc.

pot·latch /pótlach/ *n.* (among Native Americans of the Pacific Northwest) a ceremonial festival of gift giving or destruction of the owner's property to display wealth.

pot·luck /pótluk/ *n.* **1** whatever (hospitality, food, etc.) is available. **2** a meal to which each guest brings a dish to share.

pot·pie /pótpī/ *n.* a pie of meat, vegetables, etc., with a crust baked in a pot or deep-dish pie plate.

pot·pour·ri /pṓpōōrée/ *n.* **1** a mixture of dried petals and spices used to perfume a room, etc. **2** a musical or literary medley.

pot roast *n.* a piece of meat cooked slowly in a covered dish. □□ **pot-roast** *v.tr.*

P

pot·sherd /pótshərd/ n. a broken piece of pottery, esp. one found on an archaeological site.

pot·shot /pótshot/ n. **1** a random shot. **2** a shot aimed at an animal, etc., within easy reach. **3** a shot at a game bird, etc., merely to provide a meal.

pot·tage /pótij/ n. archaic soup; stew.

pot·ter /pótər/ n. a maker of ceramic vessels.

pot·ter's field n. a burial place for paupers, strangers, etc.

pot·ter's wheel n. ◀ a horizontal revolving disk to carry clay for making pots.

POTTER'S WHEEL

wheel

pedal
turns wheel

pot·ter·y /pótəree/ n. (pl. **-ies**) **1** vessels, etc., made of fired clay. **2** a potter's work. **3** a potter's workshop.

pot·ting shed /póting/ n. a building in which plants are potted and tools, etc., are stored.

pot·ty[1] /pótee/ adj. (**pottier, pottiest**) Brit. sl. **1** foolish or crazy. **2** insignificant; trivial (esp. potty little). □□ **pot·ti·ness** n.

pot·ty[2] /pótee/ n. (pl. **-ies**) colloq. a small pot for toilet-training a child.

pouch /powch/ n. & v. ● n. **1** a small bag or detachable outside pocket. **2** a baggy area of skin underneath the eyes, etc. **3 a** a pocketlike receptacle in which marsupials carry their young during lactation. ▷ MARSUPIAL. **b** any of several similar structures in various animals, e.g., in the cheeks of rodents. **4** a soldier's ammunition bag. **5** a lockable bag for mail or dispatches. **6** Bot. a baglike cavity, esp. the seed vessel, in a plant. ● v.tr. put or make into a pouch. □□ **pouched** adj. **pouch·y** adj.

pouffe /poof/ n. (also **pouf**) a large firm cushion used as a low seat or footstool.

poult /pōlt/ n. a young domestic fowl, turkey, pheasant, etc.

poul·ter·er /pốltərər/ n. Brit. a dealer in poultry and usu. game.

poul·tice /pốltis/ n. & v. ● n. a soft medicated and usu. heated mass applied to the body and kept in place with muslin, etc., for relieving soreness and inflammation. ● v.tr. apply a poultice to.

poul·try /pốltree/ n. domestic fowls (ducks, geese, turkeys, chickens, etc.), as a source of food.

pounce /powns/ v. & n. ● v.intr. **1** spring or swoop, esp. as in capturing prey. **2** (often foll. by on, upon) **a** make a sudden attack. **b** seize eagerly upon an object, remark, etc. ● n. **1** the act or an instance of pouncing. **2** the claw or talon of a bird of prey. □□ **pounc·er** n.

pound[1] /pownd/ n. **1** a unit of weight equal to 16 oz. avoirdupois (0.4536 kg), or 12 oz. troy (0.3732 kg). **2** (in full **pound sterling**) (pl. same or **pounds**) the chief monetary unit of the UK and several other countries.

pound[2] /pownd/ v. & n. ● v. **1 tr. a** crush or beat with repeated heavy blows. **b** pummel, esp. with the fists. **c** grind to a powder or pulp. **2** intr. (foll. by at, on) deliver heavy blows or gunfire. **3** intr. (foll. by along, etc.) make one's way heavily or clumsily. **4** intr. (of the heart) beat heavily. ● n. a heavy blow

or thump; the sound of this. □ **pound out** produce with or as if with heavy blows. □□ **pound·er** n.

pound[3] /pownd/ n. **1** an enclosure where stray animals or officially removed vehicles are kept until redeemed. **2** a place of confinement.

pound·age /pówndij/ n. **1 a** a weight in pounds. **b** a person's weight, esp. that which is regarded as excess. **2** Brit. a commission or fee of so much per pound sterling or weight. **3** Brit. a percentage of the total earnings of a business, paid as wages.

pound cake n. a rich cake orig. containing a pound (or equal weights) of each chief ingredient.

pound·er /pówndər/ n. (usu. in comb.) **1** a thing or person weighing a specified number of pounds (a five-pounder). **2** a gun carrying a shell of a specified number of pounds. **3** a thing worth, or a person possessing, so many pounds sterling.

pound of flesh n. any legitimate but crippling demand.

pound sign n. **1** the sign #. **2** the sign £, representing a pound sterling.

pour /pawr/ v. **1** intr. & tr. (usu. foll. by down, out, over, etc.) flow or cause to flow esp. downwards in a stream or shower. **2** tr. dispense (a drink) by pouring. **3** intr. (of rain, or with it as subject) fall heavily. **4** intr. (usu. foll. by in, out, etc.) come or go in profusion or rapid succession (the crowd poured out; letters poured in). **5** tr. discharge or send freely (poured forth arrows). **6** tr. (often foll. by out) utter at length or in a rush (poured out their story; poured scorn on my attempts). □ **it never rains but it pours** misfortunes rarely come singly. **pour cold water on** see COLD. **pour oil on the waters** (or **on troubled waters**) calm a disagreement or disturbance, esp. with conciliatory words. □□ **pour·a·ble** adj. **pour·er** n.

pout /powt/ v. & n. ● v. **1** intr. **a** push the lips forward as an expression of displeasure or sulking. **b** (of the lips) be pushed forward. **2** tr. push (the lips) forward in pouting. ● n. **1** such an action or expression. **2** (**the pouts**) a fit of sulking. □□ **pout·er** n. **pout·ing·ly** adv. **pout·y** adj.

pout·er /pówtər/ n. **1** a person who pouts. **2** a kind of pigeon able to inflate its crop considerably.

pov·er·ty /póvərtee/ n. **1** the state of being poor; want of the necessities of life. **2** (often foll. by of, in) scarcity or lack. **3** inferiority; poorness; meanness. **4** Eccl. renunciation of the right to individual ownership of property esp. by a member of a religious order.

pov·er·ty line n. (also **poverty level**) the minimum income level, as defined by a government standard, needed to secure the necessities of life.

pov·er·ty-strick·en adj. extremely poor.

POW abbr. prisoner of war.

pow /pow/ int. expressing the sound of a blow or explosion.

pow·der /pówdər/ n. & v. ● n. **1** a substance in the form of fine dry particles. **2** a medicine or cosmetic in this form. **3** = GUNPOWDER. ● v.tr. **1 a** apply powder to. **b** sprinkle or decorate with or as with powder. **2** (esp. as **powdered** adj.) reduce to a fine powder (powdered milk). □ **keep one's powder dry** be cautious and alert. **take a powder** sl. depart quickly. □□ **pow·der·y** adj.

pow·der blue n. pale blue.

pow·der keg n. **1** a barrel of gunpowder. **2** a dangerous or volatile situation.

pow·der puff n. a soft pad for applying powder to the skin, esp. the face.

pow·der room n. a women's toilet in a public building.

pow·er /pówər/ n. & v. ● n. **1** the ability to do or act (has the power to change color). **2** a particular faculty of body or mind (lost the power of speech). **3 a** government, influence, or authority. **b** political or social ascendancy or control. **4** authorization; delegated authority (power of attorney; police powers). **5** (often foll. by over) personal ascendancy. **6** an influential person, group, or organization (the press is a power in the land). **7 a** military strength. **b** a nation having international influence, esp. based on military strength (the leading powers). **8** vigor; energy. **9** an active property or function (has a high heating power). **10** colloq. a large number or amount (has done me a power of good). **11** the capacity for exerting mechanical force or doing work (horsepower). **12** mechanical or electrical energy as distinct from hand labor (often attrib.: power tools; power steering). **13 a** a public supply of (esp. electrical) energy. **b** a particular source or form of energy (hydroelectric power). **14** a mechanical force applied, e.g., by means of a lever. **15** Physics the rate of energy output. **16** the product obtained when a number is multiplied by itself a certain number of times (2 to the power of 3 = 8). **17** the magnifying capacity of a lens. **18 a** a deity. **b** (in pl.) the sixth order of the ninefold celestial hierarchy. ● v.tr. **1** supply with mechanical or electrical energy. **2** (foll. by up, down) increase or decrease the power supplied to (a device); switch on or off. □ **in the power of** under the control of. **power behind the throne** a person who asserts authority or influence without having formal status. **the powers that be** those in authority. □□ **pow·ered** adj. (also in comb.).

pow·er·boat /pówərbōt/ n. ▼ a powerful motorboat. ▷ BOAT.

P

POWERBOAT

Powerboats are fitted with high-powered inboard or outboard engines and are used to race over courses. Offshore powerboats, which can reach speeds of over 100 m.p.h. (160 k.p.h.), race on ocean courses up to 160 miles (257 km) long. The driver steers using satellite navigation systems, while the throttle operator controls the trim and engine speed.

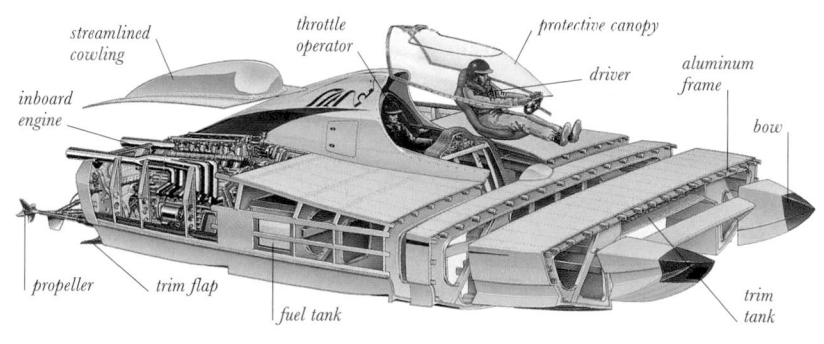

streamlined cowling

throttle operator

protective canopy

driver

aluminum frame

inboard engine

bow

propeller

trim flap

fuel tank

trim tank

EXPLODED VIEW OF AN OFFSHORE CATAMARAN POWERBOAT

pow·er brakes *n.pl.* automotive brakes in which engine power supplements that provided by the driver's pressure on the brake pedal.

pow·er fail·ure *n.* a temporary withdrawal or failure of an electric power supply.

pow·er·ful /pówərfŏŏl/ *adj.* **1** having much power or strength. **2** politically or socially influential. □□ **pow·er·ful·ly** *adv.* **pow·er·ful·ness** *n.*

pow·er·house /pówərhows/ *n.* **1** = POWER PLANT. **2** a person or thing of great energy.

pow·er·less /pówərlis/ *adj.* **1** without power or strength. **2** (often foll. by *to* + infin.) wholly unable (*powerless to help*). □□ **pow·er·less·ly** *adv.* **pow·er·less·ness** *n.*

pow·er line *n.* a conductor supplying electrical power, esp. one supported by pylons or poles.

pow·er of at·tor·ney *n.* the authority to act for another person in legal or financial matters.

pow·er plant *n.* **1** (also **power station**) ▼ a facility producing esp. electrical power. ▷ HYDROELECTRIC, NUCLEAR POWER. **2** a source of power, as an engine.

pow·er play *n.* **1** tactics involving the concentration of players at a particular point. **2** similar tactics in business, politics, etc., involving a concentration of resources, effort, etc. **3** *Ice Hockey* situation in which one team has an extra skater owing to a penalty on the opposing team.

pow·er-shar·ing *n.* a policy agreed between parties or within a coalition to share responsibility for decision making and political action.

pow·wow /pów-wow/ *n. & v.* ● *n.* a conference or meeting for discussion (orig. among Native Americans). ● *v.tr.* hold a powwow.

pox /poks/ *n.* **1** any virus disease producing a rash of pimples that become pus-filled and leave pockmarks on healing. **2** *colloq.* = SYPHILIS.

pp *abbr.* pianissimo.

pp. *abbr.* pages.

p.p.b. *abbr.* parts per billion.

ppd. *abbr.* **1** postpaid. **2** prepaid.

p.p.m. *abbr.* parts per million.

PPS *abbr.* **1** additional postscript. **2** *Brit.* Parliamentary Private Secretary.

PR *abbr.* **1** public relations. **2** Puerto Rico. **3** proportional representation.

Pr *symb. Chem.* the element praseodymium.

pr. *abbr.* pair.

prac·ti·ca·ble /práktikəbəl/ *adj.* **1** that can be done or used. **2** possible in practice. □□ **prac·ti·ca·bil·i·ty** /-bílitee/ *n.* **prac·ti·ca·ble·ness** *n.* **prac·ti·ca·bly** *adv.*

prac·ti·cal /práktikəl/ *adj. & n.* ● *adj.* **1** of or concerned with practice or use rather than theory. **2** suited to use or action; designed mainly to fulfill a function (*practical shoes*). **3** (of a person) inclined to action rather than speculation; able to make things function well. **4 a** that is such in effect though not nominally (*for all practical purposes*). **b** virtual (*in practical control*). **5** feasible; concerned with what is actually possible (*practical politics*). ● *n. Brit.* a practical examination or lesson. □□ **prac·ti·cal·i·ty** /-kálitee/ *n.* (*pl.* **-ies**). **prac·ti·cal·ness** *n.*

prac·ti·cal joke *n.* a humorous trick played on a person.

prac·ti·cal·ly /práktiklee/ *adv.* **1** virtually; almost (*practically nothing*). **2** in a practical way.

prac·tice /práktis/ *n. & v.* ● *n.* **1** habitual action or performance (*the practice of teaching*; *makes a practice of saving*). **2** a habit or custom (*has been my regular practice*). **3 a** repeated exercise in an activity requiring the development of skill (*to sing well needs much practice*). **b** a session of this (*time for target practice*). **4** action or execution as opposed to theory. **5** the professional work or business of a doctor, lawyer, etc. (*has a practice in town*). **6** an established method of legal procedure. **7** procedure generally, esp. of a specified kind (*bad practice*). ● *v.tr. & intr.* (also *Brit.* **practise**) **1** *tr.* perform habitually; carry out in action (*practice the same method*; *practice what you preach*). **2** *tr. &* (foll. by *in*, *on*) *intr.* do repeatedly as an exercise to improve a skill; exercise oneself in or on (an activity requiring skill) (*practice your reading*). **3** *tr.* (as **practiced** *adj.*) experienced, expert (*a practiced liar*). **4** *tr.* **a** pursue or be engaged in (a profession, religion, etc.). **b** (as **practicing** *adj.*) currently active or engaged in (a profession or activity) (*a practicing Christian*; *a practicing lawyer*). **5** *intr.* (foll. by *on*, *upon*) take advantage of; impose upon. **6** *intr. archaic* scheme; contrive (*when first we practice to deceive*). □ **in practice 1** when actually applied; in reality. **2** skillful because of recent exercise in a particular pursuit. **out of practice** lacking a former skill from lack of recent practice. **put into practice** actually apply (an idea, method, etc.). □□ **prac·tic·er** *n.*

prac·tise *Brit.* var. of PRACTICE *v.*

prac·ti·tion·er /praktíshənər/ *n.* a person practicing a profession, esp. medicine (*general practitioner*).

prae- /pree/ *prefix* = PRE- (esp. in words regarded as Latin or relating to Roman antiquity).

prae·ci·pe /préesipee, prés-/ *n.* **1** a writ demanding action or an explanation of inaction. **2** an order requesting a writ.

prae·si·di·um var. of PRESIDIUM.

prae·tor /préetər/ *n.* (also **pre·tor**) *Rom.Hist.* each of two ancient Roman magistrates ranking below consul. □□ **prae·to·ri·al** /-tóreeəl/ *adj.* **prae·tor·ship** *n.*

prae·to·ri·an /preetáwreeən/ *adj. & n.* (also **pre·to·ri·an**) *Rom.Hist.* ● *adj.* of or having the powers of a praetor. ● *n.* a man of praetorian rank.

prae·to·ri·an guard *n.* the bodyguard of the Roman emperor.

prag·mat·ic /pragmátik/ *adj.* **1** dealing with matters with regard to their practical requirements or consequences. **2** treating the facts of history with reference to their practical lessons. **3** *hist.* of or relating to the affairs of a state. **4** (also **prag·mat·i·cal**) **a** concerning pragmatism. **b** meddlesome. **c** dogmatic. □□ **prag·mat·i·cal·i·ty** /-tikálitee/ *n.* **prag·mat·i·cal·ly** *adv.*

prag·mat·ics /pragmátiks/ *n.pl.* (usu. treated as *sing.*) the branch of linguistics dealing with language in use.

prag·ma·tism /prágmətizəm/ *n.* **1** a pragmatic attitude or procedure. **2** a philosophy that evaluates assertions solely by their practical consequences and bearing on human interests. □□ **prag·ma·tist** *n.* **prag·ma·tis·tic** /-tístik/ *adj.*

prag·ma·tize /prágmətīz/ *v.tr.* **1** represent as real. **2** rationalize (a myth).

prai·rie /práiree/ *n.* a large area of usu. treeless grassland esp. in central N. America.

prai·rie dog *n.* ◀ any central or western N. American rodent of the genus *Cynomys*, living in burrows and making a barking sound.

prai·rie schoon·er *n.* a covered wagon used by the 19th-c. pioneers in crossing the prairies.

praise /prayz/ *v. & n.* ● *v.tr.* **1** express warm approval or admiration of. **2** glorify (God) in words. ● *n.* the act or an instance of praising; commendation (*won high praise*; *were loud in their praises*). □ **praise be!** an exclamation of pious gratitude. **sing the praises of** commend (a person) highly. □□ **praise·ful** *adj.* **prais·er** *n.*

PRAIRIE DOG
(*Cynomys ludovicianus*)

praise·wor·thy /práyzwərthee/ *adj.* worthy of praise; commendable. □□ **praise·wor·thi·ly** *adv.* **praise·wor·thi·ness** *n.*

pra·line /práaleen, práy-/ *n.* any of several candies made with almonds, pecans, or other nuts and sugar.

pram /pram/ *n. Brit.* a baby carriage.

prance /prans/ *v. & n.* ● *v.intr.* **1** (of a horse) raise the forelegs and spring from the hind legs. **2** (often foll. by *about*) walk or behave in an arrogant manner. ● *n.* **1** the act of prancing. **2** a prancing movement. □□ **pranc·er** *n.*

pran·di·al /prándeeəl/ *adj.* of a meal, usu. dinner.

prang /prang/ *v. & n. Brit. sl.* ● *v.tr.* **1** crash or damage (an aircraft or vehicle). **2** bomb (a target) successfully. ● *n.* the act or an instance of pranging.

prank /prangk/ *n.* a practical joke; a piece of mischief. □□ **prank·ful** *adj.* **prank·ish** *adj.* **prank·some** *adj.*

prank·ster /prángkstər/ *n.* a person fond of playing pranks.

prat /prat/ *n. Brit. sl.* **1** a silly or foolish person. **2** the buttocks.

POWER PLANT

Virtually all commercial electric energy is produced by power plants driven by steam from the burning of fossil fuels, by nuclear sources, or by waterpower. Inside a coal- or an oil-fired power plant, energy stored in fuel is released in a furnace. The heat is used to boil water into steam, which drives turbines linked to electricity generators. The electricity is distributed to consumers via a system of cables called a grid.

concrete tower for cooling water

boiler house

chimney

coal store

turbine house

connections to electricity grid

MODEL OF A
COAL-FIRED
POWER PLANT

P

prate /prayt/ v. & n. ● v. **1** intr. chatter; talk too much. **2** intr. talk foolishly or irrelevantly. **3** tr. tell or say in a prating manner. ● n. prating; idle talk. □□ **prat·er** n. **prat·ing** adj.

prat·fall /prátfawl/ n. sl. **1** a fall on the buttocks. **2** a humiliating failure.

prat·tle /prát'l/ v. & n. ● v.intr. & tr. chatter or say in a childish or inconsequential way. ● n. **1** childish chatter. **2** inconsequential talk. □□ **prat·tler** n. **prat·tling** adj.

prawn /prawn/ n. & v. ● n. ▼ any of various marine crustaceans, resembling a shrimp but usu. larger. ● v.intr. fish for prawns.

PRAWN

antenna

carapace

segmented abdomen

telson (tail fan)

prax·is /práksis/ n. **1** accepted practice or custom. **2** the practicing of an art or skill.

pray /pray/ v. (often foll. by *for* or *to* + infin. or *that* + clause) **1** intr. (often foll. by *to*) say prayers (to God, etc.); make devout supplication. **2 a** tr. entreat; beseech. **b** tr. & intr. ask earnestly (*prayed to be released*). **3** tr. (as *imper.*) old-fashioned please (*pray tell me*).

prayer¹ /prair/ n. **1 a** a solemn request or thanksgiving to God or an object of worship (*say a prayer*). **b** a formula or form of words used in praying (*the Lord's prayer*). **c** the act of praying (*be at prayer*). **d** a religious service consisting largely of prayers (*morning prayers*). **2 a** an entreaty to a person. **b** a thing entreated or prayed for. □ **not have a prayer** colloq. have no chance (of success, etc.).

prayer² /práyər/ n. a person who prays.

prayer book n. a book containing the forms of prayer in regular use.

prayer·ful /práirfŏŏl/ adj. **1** (of a person) given to praying; devout. **2** (of speech, actions, etc.) characterized by or expressive of prayer. □□ **prayer·ful·ly** adv. **prayer·ful·ness** n.

prayer rug (or **mat**) n. ◄ a small carpet knelt on by Muslims when praying.

PRAYER RUG:
19TH-CENTURY
OTTOMAN PRAYER RUG

prayer wheel n. ▶ a revolving cylindrical box inscribed with or containing prayers, used esp. by Tibetan Buddhists.

pray·ing man·tis n. a mantis, *Mantis religiosa*, that holds its forelegs in a position suggestive of hands folded in prayer, while waiting to pounce on its prey.

preach /preech/ v. **1 a** intr. deliver a sermon or religious address. **b** tr. deliver (a sermon); proclaim or expound. **2** intr. give moral advice in an obtrusive way. **3** tr. advocate or inculcate (a quality or practice, etc.).

mantra

PRAYER WHEEL
WITH MANTRA REVEALED

preach·er /préechər/ n. a person who preaches, esp. a minister of religion.

preach·i·fy /préechifì/ v.intr. (**-ies**, **-ied**) colloq. preach or moralize tediously.

preach·y /préechee/ adj. (**preachier**, **preachiest**) colloq. inclined to moralize. □□ **preach·i·ness** n.

pre·am·ble /prée-ámbəl/ n. **1** a preliminary statement or introduction. **2** the introductory part of a constitution, statute, or deed, etc.

pre·amp /prée-ámp/ n. = PREAMPLIFIER.

pre·am·pli·fi·er /prée-ámplifîər/ n. an electronic device that amplifies a very weak signal (e.g., from a microphone or pickup) and transmits it to a main amplifier. □□ **pre·am·pli·fied** adj.

pre·ar·range /prée-əráynj/ v.tr. arrange beforehand. □□ **pre·ar·range·ment** n.

pre·a·tom·ic /prée-ətómik/ adj. existing or occurring before the use of atomic weapons or energy.

preb·end /prébənd/ n. Eccl. **1** the stipend of a canon or member of a chapter. **2** a portion of land or tithe from which this is drawn. □□ **pre·ben·dal** /pribénd'l, prébən-/ adj.

preb·en·dar·y /prébəndèree/ n. (pl. **-ies**) **1** the holder of a prebend. **2** an honorary canon. □□ **preb·en·dar·y·ship** n.

pre·but·tal /pribútəl/ n. (in politics) a response formulated in anticipation of a criticism; a preemptive rebuttal.

Pre·cam·bri·an /prée-kámbreeən/ adj. & n. Geol. ● adj. of or relating to the earliest era of geological time from the formation of the Earth to the first forms of life. ● n. this era.

pre·can·cer /prée-kánsər, -kántsər-/ n. a precancerous state or condition.

pre·can·cer·ous /prée-kánsrəs, -kántsər-/ adj. having the tendency to develop into a cancer. □□ **pre·can·cer·ous·ly** adv.

pre·car·i·ous /prikáireeəs/ adj. **1** uncertain; dependent on chance (*makes a precarious living*). **2** insecure; perilous (*precarious health*). □□ **pre·car·i·ous·ly** adv. **pre·car·i·ous·ness** n.

pre·cast /préekást/ adj. (of concrete) cast in its final shape before positioning.

pre·ca·to·ry /prékətawree/ adj. relating to or expressing a wish or request.

pre·cau·tion /prikáwshən/ n. **1** an action taken beforehand to avoid risk or ensure a good result. **2** (in pl.) colloq. the use of contraceptives. **3** caution exercised beforehand; prudent forethought. □□ **pre·cau·tion·ar·y** adj.

pre·cede /priséed/ v.tr. **1 a** (often as **preceding** adj.) come or go before in time, order, importance, etc. (*preceding generations*). **b** walk, etc., in front of (*preceded by our guide*). **2** (foll. by *by*) cause to be preceded (*must precede this measure by milder ones*).

prec·e·dence /présidəns, priséed'ns/ n. (also **prec·e·den·cy**) **1** priority in time, order, or importance, etc. **2** the right to precede others on formal occasions. □ **take precedence** (often foll. by *over, of*) have priority (over).

prec·e·dent n. & adj. ● n. /présidənt/ a previous case or legal decision, etc., taken as a guide for subsequent cases or as a justification. ● adj. /priséed'nt, présidənt/ preceding in time, order, importance, etc. □□ **prec·e·dent·ly** /présidəntlee/ adv.

prec·e·dent·ed /présidentid/ adj. having or supported by a precedent.

pre·cent /prisént/ v. **1** intr. act as a precentor. **2** tr. lead the singing of (a psalm, etc.).

pre·cen·tor /priséntər/ n. **1** a person who leads the singing or (in a synagogue) the prayers of a congregation. **2** Brit. a minor canon who administers the musical life of a cathedral. □□ **pre·cen·tor·ship** n.

pre·cept /préesept/ n. **1** a command; a rule of conduct. **2 a** a moral instruction (*example is better than precept*). **b** a general or proverbial rule; a maxim. **3** Law a writ, order, or warrant. □□ **pre·cep·tive** /-séptiv/ adj.

pre·cep·tor /priséptər/ n. a teacher or instructor. □□ **pre·cep·to·ri·al** /prééseptawreeəl/ adj. **pre·cep·tor·ship** n. **pre·cep·tress** /-tris/ n.

pre·cess /preesés, préeses/ v. undergo or be subject to precession.

pre·ces·sion /priséshən/ n. ▼ the slow movement of the axis of a spinning body around another axis. □□ **pre·ces·sion·al** adj.

pre·ces·sion of the e·qui·nox·es n. **1** the slow retrograde motion of equinoctial points along the ecliptic. **2** the resulting earlier occurrence of equinoxes in each successive sidereal year.

pre-Chris·tian /prée-kríschən/ adj. before Christ or the advent of Christianity.

pre·cinct /préesingkt/ n. **1** an enclosed or specially designated area. **2** (in pl.) **a** the surrounding area or environs. **b** the boundaries. **3 a** a subdivision of a county, city, etc., for police or electoral purposes. **b** a police station in such a subdivision. **c** (in pl.) a neighborhood.

pre·cious /préshəs/ adj. & adv. ● adj. **1** of great value or worth. **2** beloved; much prized (*precious memories*). **3** affectedly refined, esp. in language or manner. **4** colloq. often iron. **a** considerable (*a precious lot you know about it*). **b** expressing contempt or disdain (*you can keep your precious flowers*). ● adv. colloq. extremely; very (*had precious little left*). □□ **pre·cious·ly** adv. **pre·cious·ness** n.

pre·cious met·als n.pl. gold, silver, and platinum.

pre·cious stone n. a piece of mineral having great value esp. as used in jewelry. ▷ GEM

prec·i·pice /présipis/ n. **1** a vertical or steep face of a rock, cliff, mountain, etc. **2** a dangerous situation.

pre·cip·i·tant /prisípit'nt/ adj. & n. ● adj. = PRECIPITATE. ● n. Chem. a substance that causes another substance to precipitate. □□ **pre·cip·i·tance** n. **pre·cip·i·tan·cy** n.

pre·cip·i·tate v., adj., & n. ● v.tr. /prisípitàyt/ **1** hasten the occurrence of; cause to occur prematurely. **2** (foll. by *into*) send rapidly into a certain state or condition (*were precipitated into war*). **3** throw down headlong. **4** Chem. cause (a substance) to be deposited in solid form from a solution. **5** Physics

PRECESSION

Although the Earth's axis is always tilted at an angle of 23.5°, the direction in space to which it points changes continuously, tracing out a circle every 25,800 years. This phenomenon is called precession.

circle of precession

Earth's axis

Earth

Earth's axis inclined at 23.5° from vertical

PRECESSION OF THE EARTH

P

a cause (dust, etc.) to be deposited from the air on a surface. **b** condense (vapor) into drops and so deposit it. ● *adj.* /prisípitət/ **1** headlong; violently hurried (*precipitate departure*). **2** (of a person or act) hasty; rash; inconsiderate. ● *n.* /prisípitət/ **1** *Chem.* a substance precipitated from a solution. **2** *Physics* moisture condensed from vapor by cooling and depositing, e.g., rain or dew. □□ **pre·cip·i·ta·ble** /-sípitəbəl/ *adj.* **pre·cip·i·ta·bil·i·ty** *n.* **pre·cip·i·tate·ly** /-sípitətlee/ *adv.* **pre·cip·i·tate·ness** /-sípitətnəs/ *n.* **pre·cip·i·ta·tor** *n.*

pre·cip·i·ta·tion /prisìpitáyshən/ *n.* **1** the act of precipitating or the process of being precipitated. **2** rash haste. **3 a** rain or snow, etc., falling to the ground. **b** a quantity of this.

pre·cip·i·tous /prisípitəs/ *adj.* **1 a** of or like a precipice. **b** dangerously steep. **2** = PRECIPITATE *adj.* □□ **pre·cip·i·tous·ly** *adv.* **pre·cip·i·tous·ness** *n.*

pré·cis /práysee/ *n. & v.* ● *n.* (*pl.* same /-seez/) a summary or abstract, esp. of a text or speech. ● *v.tr.* (**précises** /-seez/; **précised** /-seed/; **précising** /-seeing/) make a précis of.

pre·cise /prisís/ *adj.* **1 a** accurately expressed. **b** definite; exact. **2 a** punctilious; scrupulous in being exact, observing rules, etc. **b** often *derog.* rigid; fastidious. **3** identical; exact (*at that precise moment*). □□ **pre·cise·ness** *n.*

pre·cise·ly /prisíslee/ *adv.* **1** in a precise manner; exactly. **2** (as a reply) quite so; as you say.

pre·ci·sion /prisízhən/ *n.* **1** the condition of being precise; accuracy. **2** the degree of refinement in measurement, etc. **3** (*attrib.*) marked by or adapted for precision (*precision instruments*). □□ **pre·ci·sion·ism** *n.* **pre·ci·sion·ist** *n.*

pre·clin·i·cal /préeklínikəl/ *adj.* **1** of or relating to the first, chiefly theoretical, stage of a medical or dental education. **2** (of a stage in a disease) before symptoms can be identified.

pre·clude /priklóod/ *v.tr.* **1** (foll. by *from*) prevent; exclude (*precluded from taking part*). **2** make impossible; remove (*so as to preclude all doubt*). □□ **pre·clu·sion** /-klóozhən/ *n.* **pre·clu·sive** /-klóosiv/ *adj.*

pre·co·cious /prikóshəs/ *adj.* **1** (of a person, esp. a child) prematurely developed in some faculty or characteristic. **2** (of an action, etc.) indicating such development. **3** (of a plant) flowering or fruiting early. □□ **pre·co·cious·ly** *adv.* **pre·co·cious·ness** *n.* **pre·coc·i·ty** /-kósitee/ *n.*

pre·cog·ni·tion /préekogníshən/ *n.* (supposed) foreknowledge, esp. of a supernatural kind. □□ **pre·cog·ni·tive** /-kógnitiv/ *adj.*

pre·co·i·tal /préekóit'l, -kō-éet'l/ *adj.* preceding sexual intercourse. □□ **pre·co·i·tal·ly** *adv.*

pre·Co·lum·bi·an /préekəlúmbeeən/ *adj.* before the arrival in America of Columbus.

pre·con·ceive /préekənseév/ *v.tr.* (esp. as **preconceived** *adj.*) form (an idea or opinion, etc.) beforehand; anticipate in thought.

pre·con·cep·tion /préekənsépshən/ *n.* **1** a preconceived idea. **2** a prejudice.

pre·con·di·tion /préekəndíshən/ *n. & v.* ● *n.* a prior condition, that must be fulfilled before other things can be done. ● *v.tr.* bring into a required condition beforehand.

pre·cur·sor /prikúrsər, préekər-/ *n.* **1 a** a forerunner. **b** a person who precedes in office, etc. **2** a harbinger. **3** a substance from which another is formed by decay or chemical reaction, etc.

pre·cur·so·ry /prikúrsəree/ *adj.* (also **pre·cur·sive** /-siv/) **1** preliminary; introductory. **2** (foll. by *of*) serving as a harbinger of.

pred. *abbr.* predicate.

pre·da·cious /pridáyshəs/ *adj.* (also **pre·da·ceous**) **1** (of an animal) predatory. **2** relating to such animals (*predacious instincts*). □□ **pre·da·cious·ness** *n.* **pre·dac·i·ty** /-dásitee/ *n.*

pre·date /préedáyt/ *v.tr.* exist or occur at a date earlier than.

pre·da·tion /pridáyshən/ *n.* **1** (usu. in *pl.*) = DEPRE-

DATION. **2** *Zool.* the natural preying of one animal on others. ▷ FOOD CHAIN

pred·a·tor /prédətər/ *n.* **1** an animal naturally preying on others. **2** a predatory person, institution, etc.

pred·a·to·ry /prédətawree/ *adj.* **1** (of an animal) preying naturally upon others. **2** (of a nation, state, or individual) plundering or exploiting others. □□ **pred·a·to·ri·ly** *adv.* **pred·a·to·ri·ness** *n.*

pre·de·cease /préedisées/ *v. & n.* ● *v.tr.* die earlier than (another person). ● *n.* a death preceding that of another.

pred·e·ces·sor /prédisesər, prée-/ *n.* **1** a former holder of an office or position with respect to a later holder (*my immediate predecessor*). **2** an ancestor. **3** a thing to which another has succeeded (*the new plan will share the fate of its predecessor*).

pre·des·ti·na·tion /préedestináyshən/ *n.* *Theol.* (as a belief or doctrine) the divine foreordaining of all that will happen, esp. with regard to the salvation of some and not others.

pre·des·tine /préedéstin/ *v.tr.* **1** determine beforehand. **2** ordain in advance by divine will or as if by fate.

pre·de·ter·mine /préeditúrmin/ *v.tr.* **1** determine or decree beforehand. **2** predestine. □□ **pre·de·ter·min·a·ble** *adj.* **pre·de·ter·mi·nate** /-nət/ *adj.* **pre·de·ter·mi·na·tion** *n.*

pred·i·ca·ble /prédikəbəl/ *adj. & n.* ● *adj.* that may be predicated or affirmed. ● *n.* **1** a predicable thing. **2** (in *pl.*) *Logic* the five classes to which predicates belong: genus, species, difference, property, and accident. □□ **pred·i·ca·bil·i·ty** *n.*

pre·dic·a·ment /pridíkə·mənt/ *n.* **1** a difficult, unpleasant, or embarrassing situation. **2** *Philos.* a category in (esp. Aristotelian) logic.

pred·i·cant /prédikənt/ *adj. & n.* ● *adj. hist.* (of a religious order) engaged in preaching. ● *n. hist.* a predicant person, esp. a Dominican friar.

pred·i·cate *v. & n.* ● *v.tr.* /prédikayt/ **1** assert or affirm as true or existent. **2** (foll. by *on*) found or base (a statement, etc.) on. ● *n.* /-kət/ **1** *Gram.* what is said about the subject of a sentence, etc. (e.g., *went home* in *John went home*). **2** *Logic* **a** what is predicated. **b** what is affirmed or denied of the subject by means of the copula (e.g., *mortal* in *all men are mortal*). □□ **pred·i·ca·tion** /-káyshən/ *n.*

pred·i·ca·tive /prédikaytiv/ *adj.* **1** *Gram.* (of an adjective or noun) forming or contained in the predicate, as *old* in *the dog is old* (but not in *the old dog*) and *house* in *there is a large house* (opp. ATTRIBUTIVE). **2** that predicates. □□ **pred·i·ca·tive·ly** *adv.*

pre·dict /pridíkt/ *v.tr.* (often foll. by *that* + clause) make a statement about the future; foretell; prophesy. □□ **pre·dic·tive** *adj.* **pre·dic·tive·ly** *adv.* **pre·dic·tor** *n.*

pre·dict·a·ble /pridíktəbəl/ *adj.* that can be predicted or is to be expected. □□ **pre·dict·a·bil·i·ty** *n.* **pre·dict·a·bly** *adv.*

pre·dic·tion /pridíkshən/ *n.* **1** the art of predicting or the process of being predicted. **2** a thing predicted; a forecast.

pre·di·lec·tion /préd'lékshən, prée-/ *n.* (often foll. by *for*) a preference or special liking.

pre·dis·pose /préedispóz/ *v.tr.* **1** influence favorably in advance. **2** (foll. by *to*, or *to* + infin.) render liable or inclined beforehand. □□ **pre·dis·po·si·tion** /-pəzíshən/ *n.*

pre·dom·i·nant /pridómínənt/ *adj.* **1** predominating. **2** being the strongest or main element. □□ **pre·dom·i·nance** *n.* **pre·dom·i·nant·ly** *adv.*

pre·dom·i·nate /pridómínayt/ *v.intr.* **1** (foll. by *over*) have or exert control. **2** be superior. **3** be the strongest or main element; preponderate (*a garden in which dahlias predominate*).

pre·dom·i·nate·ly /pridómínətlee/ *adv.* = *predominantly* (see PREDOMINANT).

pre·e·clamp·si·a /préeiklámpseeə/ *n.* a condition of pregnancy characterized by high blood pressure and other symptoms associated with eclampsia. □□ **pre·e·clamp·tic** *adj.*

pre·em·bry·o /pree-émbreeō/ *n. Med.* a human embryo in the first fourteen days after fertilization. □□ **pre·em·bry·on·ic** /-breeónik/ *adj.*

pree·mie /préemee/ *n. colloq.* an infant born prematurely.

pre·em·i·nent /prée-éminənt/ *adj.* **1** surpassing others. **2** outstanding; distinguished in some quality. **3** principal; leading; predominant. □□ **pre·em·i·nence** *n.* **pre·em·i·nent·ly** *adv.*

pre·empt /pree-émpt/ *v.* **1** *tr.* **a** forestall. **b** acquire or appropriate in advance. **2** *tr.* prevent (an attack) by disabling the enemy. **3** *tr.* obtain by preemption. □□ **pre·emp·tor** *n.* **pre·emp·to·ry** *adj.*

pre·emp·tion /pree-émpshən/ *n.* **1 a** the purchase or appropriation by one person or party before the opportunity is offered to others. **b** the right to purchase (esp. public land) in this way. **2** prior appropriation or acquisition.

pre·emp·tive /pree-émptiv/ *adj.* **1** preempting; serving to preempt. **2** (of military action) intended to prevent attack by disabling the enemy (*a preemptive strike*). **3** *Bridge* (of a bid) intended to be high enough to discourage further bidding.

preen /preen/ *v.tr. & refl.* **1** ◀ (of a bird) straighten (the feathers or itself) with its beak. **2** (of a person) primp or admire (oneself, one's hair, clothes, etc.). **3** (often foll. by *on*) congratulate or pride (oneself). □□ **preen·er** *n.*

pre·ex·ist /préeigzíst/ *v.intr.* exist at an earlier time. □□ **pre·ex·ist·ence** *n.* **pre·ex·ist·ent** *adj.*

pref. *abbr.* **1** prefix. **2** preface **3 a** preference. **b** preferred.

pre·fab /préefáb/ *n. colloq.* a prefabricated building, esp. a small house.

pre·fab·ri·cate /préefábrikayt/ *v.tr.* **1** manufacture sections of (a building, etc.) prior to their assembly on a site. **2** produce in an artificially standardized way. □□ **pre·fab·ri·ca·tion** /-brikáyshən/ *n.*

PREEN: QUAKER PARROT PREENING ITS FEATHERS

pref·ace /préfəs/ *n. & v.* ● *n.* **1** an introduction to a book stating its subject, scope, etc. **2** the preliminary part of a speech. **3** *Eccl.* the introduction to the central part of a Eucharistic service. ● *v.tr.* **1** (foll. by *with*) introduce or begin (a speech or event) (*prefaced my remarks with a warning*). **2** provide (a book, etc.) with a preface. **3** (of an event, etc.) lead up to (another). □□ **pref·a·to·ri·al** /-fətáwreeəl/ *adj.* **pref·a·to·ry** /-fətawree/ *adj.*

pre·fect /préefekt/ *n.* **1** *Rom. Antiq.* a senior magistrate or military commander. **2** a student monitor, as in a private school. **3** the chief administrative officer of certain government departments, esp. in France. □□ **pre·fec·tor·al** /-féktərəl/ *adj.* **pre·fec·to·ri·al** /-táwreeəl/ *adj.*

pre·fec·ture /préefekchər/ *n.* **1** a district under the government of a prefect. **2** a prefect's office, tenure, or official residence. □□ **pre·fec·tur·al** /prifékchərəl/ *adj.*

pre·fer /prifúr/ *v.tr.* (**preferred, preferring**) **1** (often foll. by *to*, or *to* + infin.) choose; like better (*would prefer to stay; prefers coffee to tea*). **2** submit (information, an accusation, etc.) for consideration. **3** promote or advance (a person).

pref·er·a·ble /préfərəbəl, *disp.* prifér-/ *adj.* **1** to be preferred. **2** more desirable. □□ **pref·er·a·bly** *adv.*

pref·er·ence /préfərəns, préfrəns/ *n.* **1** the act or an instance of preferring or being preferred. **2** a thing preferred. **3** the favoring of one person, etc., before others. **4** *Law* a prior right, esp. to the

P

payment of debts. □ **in preference to** as a thing preferred over (another).

pref·er·en·tial /préfərénshəl/ *adj.* **1** of or involving preference (*preferential treatment*). **2** giving or receiving a favor. **3** (of voting) in which the voter puts candidates in order of preference. □□ **pref·er·en·tial·ly** *adv.*

pre·fer·ment /prifə́rmənt/ *n.* **1** act or state of being preferred. **2** promotion to office.

pre·ferred stock *n.* stock whose entitlement to dividend takes priority over that of common stock.

pre·fig·ure /preéfígyər/ *v.tr.* **1** represent beforehand by a figure or type. **2** imagine beforehand. □□ **pre·fig·u·ra·tion** *n.* **pre·fig·ur·a·tive** /-rətiv/ *adj.* **pre·fig·ure·ment** *n.*

pre·fix /preéfiks/ *n. & v.* ● *n.* **1** a verbal element placed at the beginning of a word to adjust or qualify its meaning (e.g., *ex-, non-, re-*) or (in some languages) as an inflectional formative. **2** a title placed before a name (e.g., *Mr.*). ● *v.tr.* (often foll. by *to*) **1** add as an introduction. **2** join (a word or element) as a prefix. □□ **pre·fix·a·tion** *n.* **pre·fix·ion** /-fíkshən/ *n.*

pre·flight /preéflīt/ *attrib.adj.* occurring or provided before an aircraft flight.

pre·form /preéfáwrm/ *v.tr.* form beforehand. □□ **pre·for·ma·tion** /-máyshən/ *n.*

pre·for·ma·tive /preéfáwrmətiv/ *adj. & n.* ● *adj.* **1** forming beforehand. **2** prefixed as the formative element of a word. ● *n.* a preformative syllable or letter.

pre·fron·tal /preéfrúnt'l/ *adj.* **1** in front of the frontal bone of the skull. **2** in the forepart of the frontal lobe of the brain.

pre·front·al lo·bo·to·my *n.* the surgical cutting of the nerve fibers that connect the frontal lobes with the rest of the brain, formerly used in psychosurgery.

pre·gla·cial /preégl, áyshəl/ *adj.* before a glacial period.

preg·nan·cy /prégnənsee/ *n.* (*pl.* **-ies**) the condition or an instance of being pregnant.

preg·nant /prégnənt/ *adj.* **1** (of a woman or female animal) having a child or young developing in the uterus. **2** full of meaning; significant or suggestive (*a pregnant pause*). **3** (esp. of a person's mind) imaginative; inventive. **4** (foll. by *with*) full of; abundant in (*pregnant with danger*). □□ **preg·nant·ly** *adv.* (in sense 2).

pre·heat /preéheét/ *v.tr.* heat beforehand.

pre·hen·sile /preéhénsəl, -sīl/ *adj. Zool.* ▶ (of a tail or limb) capable of grasping. ▷ DUGONG, SEA HORSE. □□ **pre·hen·sil·i·ty** /-sílitee/ *n.*

PREHENSILE:
BLACK SPIDER
MONKEY WITH
PREHENSILE TAIL

tail gripping branch

pre·his·tor·ic /preéhistáwrik, -stór-/ *adj.* **1** of or relating to the period before written records. **2** *colloq.* utterly out of date. □□ **pre·his·to·ri·an** /-stáwreeən, -stór-/ *n.* **pre·his·tor·i·cal·ly** *adv.* **pre·his·to·ry** /-hístəree/ *n.*

pre·ig·ni·tion /preéignishən/ *n.* the premature firing of the explosive mixture in an internal-combustion engine.

pre·judge /preéjúj/ *v.tr.* **1** form a premature judg-

---

ment on (a person, issue, etc.). **2** pass judgment on (a person) before a trial or proper inquiry. □□ **pre·judg·ment** *n.* **pre·ju·di·ca·tion** /-jóodikáyshən/ *n.*

prej·u·dice /préjədis/ *n. & v.* ● *n.* **1 a** a preconceived opinion. **b** (usu. foll. by *against, in favor of*) bias or partiality. **c** intolerance of or discrimination against a person or group, esp. on account of race, religion, or gender; bigotry (*racial prejudice*). **2** harm or injury that results or may result from some action or judgment (*to the prejudice of*). ● *v.tr.* **1** impair the validity or force of (a right, claim, statement, etc.). **2** (esp. as **prejudiced** *adj.*) cause (a person) to have a prejudice. □ **without prejudice** (often foll. by *to*) without detriment (to any existing right or claim).

prej·u·di·cial /préjədíshəl/ *adj.* causing prejudice; detrimental. □□ **prej·u·di·cial·ly** *adv.*

prel·a·cy /préləsee/ *n.* (*pl.* **-ies**) **1** church government by prelates. **2** (prec. by *the*) prelates collectively. **3** the office or rank of prelate.

pre·lap·sar·i·an /preélapsáireeən/ *adj. Theol.* before the Fall of Adam and Eve.

prel·ate /prélət/ *n.* a high ecclesiastical dignitary, e.g., a bishop, abbot, etc. □□ **pre·lat·ic** /prilátik/ *adj.* **pre·lat·i·cal** *adj.*

prel·a·ture /préləchər, -chŏŏr/ *n.* **1** the office of prelate. **2** (prec. by *the*) prelates collectively.

pre·lim /preélim, prilím/ *n. colloq.* preliminary.

pre·lim·i·nar·y /prilíminəree/ *adj., n., & adv.* ● *adj.* introductory; preparatory. ● *n.* (*pl.* **-ies**) (usu. in *pl.*) **1** a preliminary action or arrangement (*dispense with the preliminaries*). **2 a** a preliminary trial or contest. **b** a preliminary examination. ● *adv.* (foll. by *to*) preparatory to; in advance of. □□ **pre·lim·i·nar·i·ly** *adv.*

pre-loved /preelúvd/ *adj. colloq.* secondhand.

prel·ude /prélyood, práylood, preé-/ *n. & v.* ● *n.* (often foll. by *to*) **1** an action, event, or situation serving as an introduction. **2** the introductory part of a poem, etc. **3 a** an introductory piece of music, often preceding a fugue or forming the first piece of a suite or beginning an act of an opera. **b** a short piece of music of a similar type, esp. for the piano. ● *v.tr.* **1** serve as a prelude to. **2** introduce with a prelude. □□ **pre·lu·di·al** /prilóodeeəl/ *adj.*

pre·mar·i·tal /preémárit'l/ *adj.* existing or (esp. of sexual relations) occurring before marriage. □□ **pre·mar·i·tal·ly** *adv.*

pre·ma·ture /preémachŏŏr, -tyŏŏr, -tŏŏr/ *adj.* **1 a** occurring or done before the usual or proper time; too early (*a premature decision*). **b** too hasty (*must not be premature*). **2** (of a baby, esp. a viable one) born (esp. three or more weeks) before the end of the full term of gestation. □□ **pre·ma·ture·ly** *adv.* **pre·ma·ture·ness** *n.* **pre·ma·tu·ri·ty** /-chŏŏrətee/ *n.*

pre·med /preémd/ *n. colloq.* a premedical course of study or student.

pre·med·i·cal /preémédikəl/ *adj.* of or relating to preparation for a course of study in medicine.

pre·med·i·tate /preémédətayt/ *v.tr.* (often as **premeditated** *adj.*) plan (an action) beforehand (*premeditated murder*). □□ **pre·med·i·ta·tion** *n.*

pre·men·stru·al /preéménstrŏŏəl/ *adj.* of, occurring, or experienced before menstruation (*premenstrual tension*). □□ **pre·men·stru·al·ly** *adv.*

pre·men·stru·al syn·drome *n.* any of a complex of symptoms (including tension, fluid retention, etc.) experienced by some women in the days immediately preceding menstruation. ¶ Abbr.: **PMS.**

pre·mier /prəmeér, -myeér, preémeer/ *n. & adj.* ● *n.* a prime minister or other head of government

---

in certain countries. ● *adj.* **1** first in importance, order, or time. **2** of earliest creation; oldest. □□ **pre·mier·ship** *n.*

pre·miere /prəmeér, -myáir/ *n., adj., & v.* (also **première**) ● *n.* the first performance or showing of a play or movie. ● *adj.* = PREMIER *adj.* 1. ● *v.tr.* give a premiere of.

prem·ise /prémis/ *n. & v.* ● *n.* **1** *Logic* (also esp. *Brit.* **premiss**) a previous statement from which another is inferred. **2** (in *pl.*) **a** a house or building with its grounds and appurtenances. **b** *Law* houses, land, etc., previously specified in a document, etc. ● *v.* **1** *tr.* say or write by way of introduction. **2** *tr. & intr.* assert or assume as a premise. □ **on the premises** in the building, etc., concerned.

pre·mi·um /preémeeəm/ *n.* **1** an amount to be paid for a contract of insurance. **2 a** a sum added to interest, wages, etc.; a bonus. **b** a sum added to ordinary charges. **3** a reward or prize. **4** (*attrib.*) (of a commodity) of best quality and therefore more expensive. **5** an item offered free or cheaply as an incentive to buy, sample, or subscribe to something. □ **at a premium 1** highly valued; above the usual or nominal price. **2** scarce and in demand. **put a premium on 1** provide or act as an incentive to. **2** attach special value to.

pre·mo·lar /preémólər/ *adj. & n.* ● *adj.* in front of a molar tooth. ● *n.* ◀ (in an adult human) each of eight teeth situated in pairs between each of the four canine teeth and each first molar. ▷ DENTITION, TOOTH

pre·mo·ni·tion /prémənishən, preé-/ *n.* a forewarning; a presentiment. □□ **pre·mon·i·tor** /primónitər/ *n.* **pre·mon·i·to·ry** /primónitawree/ *adj.*

pre·na·tal /preénáyt'l/ *adj.* of or concerning the period before birth. □□ **pre·na·tal·ly** *adv.*

pren·tice /préntis/ *n. & v. archaic* ● *n.* = APPRENTICE. ● *v.tr.* (as **prenticed** *adj.*) apprenticed. □□ **pren·tice·ship** *n.*

pre·nup·tial /preénúpshəl, -chəl/ *adj.* existing or occurring before marriage.

pre·oc·cu·pa·tion /preéókyəpáyshən/ *n.* **1** the state of being preoccupied. **2** a thing that engrosses or dominates the mind.

pre·oc·cu·py /preé-ókyəpī/ *v.tr.* (**-ies**, **-ied**) **1** (of a thought, etc.) dominate or engross the mind of (a person) to the exclusion of other thoughts. **2** (as **preoccupied** *adj.*) otherwise engrossed; mentally distracted. **3** occupy beforehand.

pre·or·dain /preéawrdáyn/ *v.tr.* ordain or determine beforehand.

prep /prep/ *n. colloq.* **1 a** a student in a preparatory school. **b** a preparatory school. **2** *Brit.* **a** the preparation of school work by a pupil. **b** the period when this is done.

prep. *abbr.* preposition.

pre·pack·age /preépákij/ *v.tr.* (also **pre·pack** /-pák/) package (goods) on the site of production or before retail.

pre·paid *past* and *past part.* of PREPAY.

prep·a·ra·tion /prépəráyshən/ *n.* **1** the act or an instance of preparing; the process of being prepared. **2** (often in *pl.*) something done to make ready. **3** a specially prepared substance, esp. a food or medicine. **4** work done by students to prepare for a lesson. **5** *Mus.* the sounding of the discordant note in a chord in the preceding chord where it is not discordant, lessening the effect of the discord.

pre·par·a·tive /pripárətiv, -páir-/ *adj. & n.* ● *adj.* preparatory. ● *n.* a preparatory act. □□ **pre·par·a·tive·ly** *adv.*

upper premolars

upper premolars

lower premolars   *lower premolars*

PLAN OF HUMAN
DENTITION

INDIVIDUAL
PREMOLAR

PREMOLAR

P

P

pre·par·a·to·ry /pripárətawree, -páir-, prépərə-/ *adj. & adv.* ● *adj.* (often foll. by *to*) serving to prepare; introductory. ● *adv.* (often foll. by *to*) in a preparatory manner (*was packing preparatory to departure*). □□ **pre·par·a·to·ri·ly** *adv.*

pre·par·a·to·ry school *n.* a usu. private school preparing pupils for college.

pre·pare /pripáir/ *v.* **1** *tr.* make or get ready for use, consideration, etc. **2** *tr.* make ready or assemble (food, a meal, etc.) for eating. **3 a** *tr.* make (a person or oneself) ready or disposed in some way (*prepares students for university; prepared them for a shock*). **b** *intr.* put oneself or things in readiness; get ready (*prepare to jump*). **4** *tr.* make (a chemical product, etc.) by a regular process; manufacture. □ **be prepared** (often foll. by *for*, or *to* + infin.) be disposed or willing to. □□ **pre·par·er** *n.*

pre·par·ed·ness /pripáiridnis/ *n.* a state of readiness, esp. for war.

pre·pay /préepáy/ *v.tr.* (*past* and *past part.* **prepaid**) **1** pay (a charge) in advance. **2** pay postage on (a letter or package, etc.) before mailing. □□ **pre·pay·a·ble** *adj.* **pre·pay·ment** *n.*

pre·pense /pripéns/ *adj.* (usu. placed after noun) esp. *Law* deliberate; intentional (*malice prepense*). □□ **pre·pense·ly** *adv.*

pre·plan /préeplán/ *v.tr.* (**preplanned**, **preplanning**) plan in advance.

pre·pon·der·ant /pripóndərənt/ *adj.* surpassing in influence, power, number, or importance; predominant; preponderating. □□ **pre·pon·der·ance** *n.* **pre·pon·der·ant·ly** *adv.*

pre·pon·der·ate /pripóndərayt/ *v.intr.* (often foll. by *over*) **1 a** be greater in influence, quantity, or number. **b** predominate. **2 a** be of greater importance. **b** weigh more.

prep·o·si·tion /prépəzíshən/ *n. Gram.* a word governing (and usu. preceding) a noun or pronoun and expressing a relation to another word or element, as in: "the man *on* the platform," "came *after* dinner," "what did you do it *for?*". □□ **prep·o·si·tion·al** *adj.* **prep·o·si·tion·al·ly** *adv.*

pre·pos·i·tive /préepózitiv/ *adj. Gram.* (of a word, particle, etc.) that should be placed before or prefixed.

pre·pos·sess /préepəzés/ *v.tr.* **1** (usu. in *passive*) (of an idea, feeling, etc.) take possession of (a person); imbue. **2 a** prejudice (usu. favorably and spontaneously). **b** (as **prepossessing** *adj.*) attractive; appealing. □□ **pre·pos·ses·sion** /-zéshən/ *n.*

pre·pos·ter·ous /pripóstərəs/ *adj.* **1** utterly absurd; outrageous. **2** contrary to nature, reason, or common sense. □□ **pre·pos·ter·ous·ly** *adv.* **pre·pos·ter·ous·ness** *n.*

prep·py /prépee/ *n. & adj.* (also **prep·pie**) *US colloq.* ● *n.* (*pl.* **-ies**) a person attending an expensive private school or who strives to look like such a person. ● *adj.* (**preppier**, **preppiest**) **1** like a preppy. **2** neat and fashionable.

pre·pran·di·al /préeprándeeəl/ *adj. formal* or *joc.* before a meal, esp. dinner.

pre·proc·es·sor /preeprósesər/ *n.* a computer program that modifies data to conform with the input requirements of another program.

prep school /prep/ *n.* = PREPARATORY SCHOOL.

pre·pu·bes·cence /préepyoobésəns/ *n.* the time, esp. the last two or three years, before puberty. □□ **pre·pu·bes·cent** *adj.*

pre·pub·li·ca·tion /préepublikáyshən/ *adj. & n.* ● *attrib.adj.* produced or occurring before publication. ● *n.* publication in advance or beforehand.

pre·puce /préepyoos/ *n.* **1** = FORESKIN. **2** the fold of skin surrounding the clitoris. □□ **pre·pu·tial** /préepyoshəl/ *adj.*

pre·quel /préekwəl/ *n.* a story, movie, etc., whose events or concerns precede those of an existing work.

Pre-Raph·a·el·ite /préeráfeeəlīt/ *n. & adj.* ● *n.* ▼ a member of a group of English 19th-c. artists, including Holman Hunt, Millais, and D. G. Rossetti, emulating the work of Italian artists before the time of Raphael. ● *adj.* **1** of or relating to the Pre-Raphaelites. **2** (**pre-Raphaelite**) (esp. of a woman) like a type painted by a Pre-Raphaelite (e.g., with long thick curly auburn hair). □□ **pre·raph·a·el·it·ism** *n.*

pre·re·cord /préerikáwrd/ *v.tr.* record (esp. material for broadcasting) in advance.

pre·req·ui·site /préerékwizit/ *adj. & n.* ● *adj.* required as a precondition. ● *n.* a prerequisite thing.

pre·rog·a·tive /prirógətiv/ *n.* **1** a right or privilege exclusive to an individual or class. **2** (in full **royal prerogative**) *Brit.* the right of the sovereign, theoretically subject to no restriction.

Pres. *abbr.* President.

pres·age /présij/ *n. & v.* ● *n.* **1** an omen or portent. **2** a presentiment or foreboding. ● *v.tr.* (also /prisáyj/) **1** portend; foreshadow. **2** give warning of (an event, etc.) by natural means. **3** (of a person) predict or have a presentiment of. □□ **pres·age·ful** *adj.* **pres·ag·er** *n.*

pres·by·ter /prézbitər/ *n.* **1** an elder in the early Christian Church. **2** (in episcopal churches) a minister of the second order; a priest. **3** (in the Presbyterian Church) an elder. □□ **pres·byt·er·al** /-bítərəl/ *adj.* **pres·byt·er·ate** /-bítərət/ *n.* **pres·by·te·ri·al** /-téereeəl/ *adj.* **pres·byt·er·ship** *n.*

Pres·by·te·ri·an /prézbitéereeən/ *n. & adj.* ● *adj.* (of a church) governed by elders all of equal rank. ● *n.* **1** a member of a Presbyterian Church. **2** an adherent of the Presbyterian system. □□ **Pres·by·te·ri·an·ism** *n.*

pres·by·ter·y /prézbiteree/ *n.* (*pl.* **-ies**) **1** the eastern part of a chancel beyond the choir; the sanctuary. **2 a** a body of presbyters. **b** a district represented by this. **3** the house of a Roman Catholic priest.

pre·school /préeskool/ *adj.* of or relating to the time before a child is old enough to go to school. □□ **pre·school·er** *n.*

pre·scient /préshənt, -eeənt, pré-/ *adj.* having foreknowledge or foresight. □□ **pre·science** *n.* **pre·scient·ly** *adv.*

pre·scind /prisínd/ *v.* **1** *tr.* (foll. by *from*) cut off (a part from a whole), esp. prematurely or abruptly. **2** *intr.* (foll. by *from*) leave out of consideration. **3** withdraw or turn away in thought.

pre·scribe /priskríb/ *v.* **1** *tr.* **a** advise the use of (a medicine, etc.), esp. by an authorized prescription. **b** recommend, esp. as a benefit (*prescribed a change of scenery*). **2** *tr.* lay down or impose authoritatively. **3** *intr.* (foll. by *to*, *for*) assert a prescriptive right or claim. □□ **pre·scrib·er** *n.*

pre·script /préeskript/ *adj. & n.* ● *adj.* prescribed. ● *n.* an ordinance, law, or command.

pre·scrip·tion /priskrípshən/ *n.* **1** the act or an instance of prescribing. **2 a** a doctor's (usu. written) instruction for the preparation and use of a medicine. **b** a medicine prescribed.

pre·scrip·tive /priskríptiv/ *adj.* **1** prescribing. **2** *Linguistics* concerned with or laying down rules of usage. **3** based on prescription (*prescriptive right*). **4** prescribed by custom. □□ **pre·scrip·tive·ly** *adv.* **pre·scrip·tive·ness** *n.* **pre·scrip·tiv·ism** *n.* **pre·scrip·tiv·ist** *n. & adj.*

pre·se·lect /préesilékt/ *v.tr.* select in advance. □□ **pre·se·lec·tion** *n.*

pres·ence /prézəns/ *n.* **1 a** the state or condition of being present (*your presence is requested*). **b** existence; location (*the presence of a hospital nearby*). **2** a place where a person is (*was admitted to their presence*). **3 a** a person's appearance or bearing, esp. when imposing (*an august presence*). **b** a person's force of personality (esp. *have presence*). **4** a person or thing that is present (*there was a presence in the room*). □ **in the presence of** in front of; observed by.

pres·ence of mind *n.* ability to think, act constructively, etc., during a crisis.

pres·ent[1] /prézənt/ *adj. & n.* ● *adj.* **1** (usu. *predic.*) being in the place in question (*was present at the trial*). **2 a** now existing, occurring, or being such (*during the present season*). **b** now being considered or discussed, etc. (*in the present case*). **3** *Gram.* expressing an action, etc., now going on or habitually performed (*present participle*; *present tense*). ● *n.* (prec. by *the*) **1** the time now passing (*no time like the present*). **2** *Gram.* the present tense. □ **at present** now. **for the present 1** just now. **2** as far as the present is concerned. **present company excepted** excluding those who are here now.

pre·sent[2] /prizént/ *v. & n.* ● *v.tr.* **1** introduce, offer, or exhibit, esp. for public attention or consideration. **2 a** (with a thing as object, usu. foll. by *to*) offer, give, or award as a gift (to a person), esp. formally

PRE-RAPHAELITE

The Pre-Raphaelites, formed in 1848, were a coalition of British artists united in their distaste for formal academic art and the neoclassical style, which dominated the art of the early 19th century. The principal members of the movement were William Holman Hunt, John Everett Millais, and Dante Gabriel Rossetti. Despite individual differences, the members of the group shared certain characteristics of style, looking to the past for inspiration and dealing primarily with religious, historical, and literary subjects, in the spirit of Italian artists prior to Raphael (1483–1520). They painted directly from nature and tried to represent historical events exactly as they might have occurred.

Horatio Discovering the Madness of Ophelia (1864), DANTE GABRIEL ROSSETTI

TIMELINE

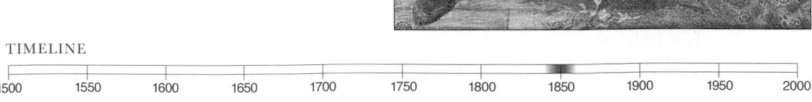

| 1500 | 1550 | 1600 | 1650 | 1700 | 1750 | 1800 | 1850 | 1900 | 1950 | 2000 |

or ceremonially. **b** (with a person as object, foll. by *with*) make available to; cause to have (*presented them with a new car; that presents us with a problem*). **3 a** (of a company, producer, etc.) put (a form of entertainment) before the public. **b** (of a performer, etc.) introduce or put before an audience. **4** introduce (a person) formally (*may I present my fiancé?*). **5** offer; give (compliments, etc.) (*may I present my card; present my regards to your family*). **6 a** (of a circumstance) reveal (some quality, etc.) (*this presents some difficulty*). **b** exhibit (an appearance, etc.) (*presented a tough exterior*). **7** (of an idea, etc.) offer or suggest itself. **8** deliver (a check, bill, etc.) for acceptance or payment. **9 a** (usu. foll. by *at*) aim (a weapon). **b** hold out (a weapon) in a position for aiming. **10** (*refl.* or *absol.*) *Med.* (of a patient or illness, etc.) come forward for or undergo initial medical examination. **11** (*absol.*) *Med.* (of a part of a fetus) be directed toward the cervix at the time of delivery. **12** (foll. by *to*) *Law* bring formally under notice; submit (an offense, complaint, etc.). • *n.* the position of presenting arms in salute. □ **present arms** hold a rifle, etc., vertically in front of the body as a salute. **present oneself 1** appear. **2** come forward for examination, etc. □□ **present·er** *n.* (in sense 3 of *v.*).

pres·ent[3] /prézənt/ *n.* a gift; a thing given or presented. □ **make a present of** give as a gift.

pre·sent·a·ble /prizéntəbəl/ *adj.* **1** of good appearance; fit to be presented to other people. **2** fit for presentation. □□ **pre·sent·a·bil·i·ty** /-bílitee/ *n.* **pre·sent·a·ble·ness** *n.* **pre·sent·a·bly** *adv.*

pres·en·ta·tion /prézəntáyshən, preezen-/ *n.* **1 a** the act or an instance of presenting; the process of being presented. **b** a thing presented. **2** the manner or quality of presenting. **3** a demonstration or display of materials, information, etc.; a lecture. **4** an exhibition or theatrical performance. **5** a formal introduction. **6** the position of the fetus in relation to the cervix at the time of delivery. □□ **pres·en·ta·tion·al** *adj.* **pres·en·ta·tion·al·ly** *adv.*

pres·ent-day *adj.* of this time; modern.

pres·en·tee /prézəntée, prizén-/ *n.* **1** the recipient of a present. **2** a person presented.

pre·sen·tient /preesénshənt, -shéeənt/ *adj.* (often foll. by *of*) having a presentiment.

pre·sen·ti·ment /prizéntimənt, -séntimənt/ *n.* a vague expectation; a foreboding (esp. of misfortune).

pres·ent·ly /prézəntlee/ *adv.* **1** soon; after a short time. **2** at the present time; now.

pre·sent·ment /prizéntmənt/ *n.* **1** an act or a manner of presenting. **2** the presenting of a bill, note, etc., esp. for payment. **3** the act of presenting information, esp. a statement on oath by a jury of a fact known to them.

pres·er·va·tion /prézərváyshən/ *n.* **1** the act of preserving or process of being preserved. **2** a state of being well or badly preserved (*in an excellent state of preservation*).

pres·er·va·tion·ist /prézərváyshənist/ *n.* a supporter or advocate of preservation, esp. of wildlife or historic buildings.

pre·serv·a·tive /prizérvətiv/ *n. & adj.* • *n.* ◀ a substance for preserving perishable foods, wood, etc. • *adj.* tending to preserve.

pre·serve /prizérv/ *v. & n.* • *v.tr.* **1 a** keep safe or free from harm, decay, etc. **b** keep alive (a name, memory, etc.). **2** maintain (a thing) in its existing state. **3** retain (a quality or condition). **4 a** treat or refrigerate (food)

PRESERVATIVE:
PICKLING SPICE

to prevent decomposition or fermentation. **b** prepare (fruit or vegetables) by boiling with sugar, canning, etc., for long-term storage. **5** keep (wildlife, a river, etc.) undisturbed for private use. • *n.* (in *sing.* or *pl.*) **1** preserved fruit; jam. **2** a place where

game or fish, etc., are preserved. **3** a sphere or area of activity regarded as a person's own. □□ **pre·serv·a·ble** *adj.* **pre·serv·er** *n.*

pre·set /preesét/ *v.tr.* (**-setting**; *past* and *past part.* **-set**) **1** set or fix (a device) in advance of its operation. **2** settle or decide beforehand.

pre·shrunk /preeshrúngk/ *adj.* (of a fabric or garment) treated so that it shrinks during manufacture and not in use.

pre·side /prizíd/ *v.intr.* **1** (often foll. by *at, over*) be in a position of authority, esp. as the chairperson or president. **2 a** exercise control or authority. **b** (foll. by *at*) play a featured instrument (*presided at the piano*).

pres·i·den·cy /prézidənsee/ *n.* (*pl.* **-ies**) **1** the office, term, or function of president. **2** the office of the President of the United States. **3** a Mormon administrative or governing body.

pres·i·dent /prézidənt/ *n.* **1** the elected head of a republican government. **2** the head of a college, university, company, society, etc. **3** a person in charge of a meeting, council, etc. □□ **pres·i·den·tial** /-dénshəl/ *adj.* **pres·i·den·tial·ly** *adv.* **pres·i·dent·ship** *n.*

pre·sid·i·um /prisídeeəm, -zídeeəm/ *n.* (also **prae·sid·i·um**) a standing executive committee in a Communist country, esp. *hist.* in the former USSR.

press[1] /pres/ *v. & n.* • *v.* **1** *tr.* apply steady force to (a thing in contact) (*pressed the two surfaces together*). **2** *tr.* **a** compress or apply pressure to a thing to flatten, shape, or smooth it, as by ironing (*got the curtains pressed*). **b** squeeze (a fruit, etc.) to extract its juice. **c** manufacture (a record, etc.) by molding under pressure. **3** *tr.* (foll. by *out of, from*, etc.) squeeze (juice, etc.). **4** *tr.* embrace or caress by squeezing (*pressed my hand*). **5** *intr.* (foll. by *on, against*, etc.) exert pressure. **6** *intr.* be urgent; demand immediate action (*time was pressing*). **7** *intr.* (foll. by *for*) make an insistent demand. **8** *intr.* (foll. by *up, round*, etc.) form a crowd. **9** *intr.* (foll. by *on, forward*, etc.) hasten insistently. **10** *tr.* (often in *passive*) (of an enemy, etc.) bear heavily on. **11** *tr.* (often foll. by *for*, or *to* + infin.) urge or entreat (*pressed me for an answer*). **12** *tr.* (foll. by *on, upon*) **a** put forward or urge (an opinion, claim, or course of action). **b** insist on the acceptance of (an offer, a gift, etc.). **13** *tr.* insist on (*did not press the point*). **14** *intr.* (foll. by *on*) produce a strong mental or moral impression; oppress; weigh heavily. • *n.* **1** the act or an instance of pressing. **2 a** ▼ a device for compressing, flattening, shaping, extracting juice, etc. (*wine press*). **b** a machine that applies pressure to a workpiece by means of a tool, in order to punch shapes, bend it, etc. **3** = PRINTING PRESS. **4** (prec. by *the*) **a** the art or practice of printing. **b** newspapers, journalists, etc., generally or collectively (*read it in the press; pursued by the press*). **5** a notice or piece of publicity in newspapers, etc. (*got a good press*). **6** (**Press**) **a** a printing house or establishment. **b** a publishing company (*Yale University Press*). **7 a** crowding. **b** a crowd (of people, etc.). **8** the pressure of affairs. **9** a large usu. shelved cupboard

PRESS FOR
EXTRACTING JUICE
FROM FRUIT

juice

for clothes, books, etc. □ **be pressed for** have barely enough (time, etc.). **go** (or **send**) **to press** go or send to be printed.

press[2] /pres/ *v.tr.* **1** *hist.* force to serve in the army or navy; impress. **2** bring into use as a makeshift (*was pressed into service*).

press a·gent *n.* a person employed to attend to advertising and press publicity.

press box *n.* a reporters' enclosure esp. at a sports event.

press con·fer·ence *n.* an interview given to journalists to make an announcement or answer questions.

press·ing /présing/ *adj. & n.* • *adj.* **1** urgent (*pressing business*). **2 a** urging strongly (*a pressing invitation*). **b** persistent; importunate (*since you are so pressing*). • *n.* **1** a thing made by pressing, esp. a record, compact disc, etc. **2** a series of these made at one time. **3** the act or an instance of pressing a thing, esp. a record or grapes, etc. (*all at one pressing*). □□ **press·ing·ly** *adv.*

pres·sure /préshər/ *n. & v.* • *n.* **1 a** ▲ the exertion of continuous force on or against a body by another in contact with it. **b** the force exerted. **c** the amount of this (expressed by the force on a unit

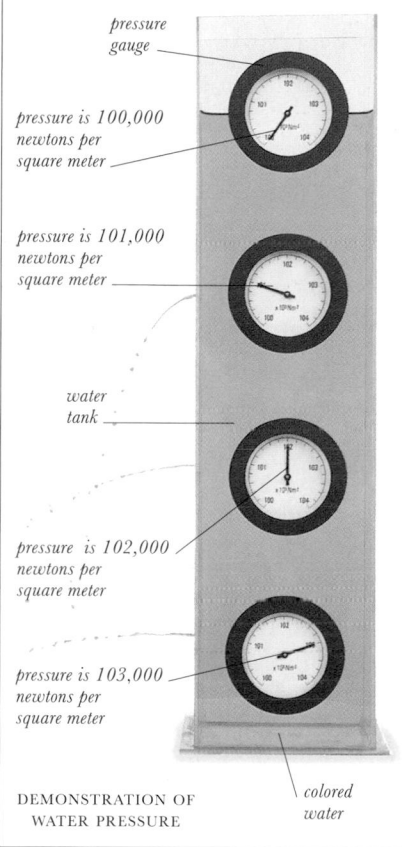

PRESSURE

Pressure may be exerted by solids, liquids, and gases, and is scientifically measured in newtons per square meter. In the experiment shown here, a liquid (water) in a tall tank exerts pressure on the sides of the tank. The water escapes more quickly from holes at the bottom of the tank than from holes at the top. This is because pressure exerted by the water is greatest at the bottom of the tank, due to the weight of the water above it.

pressure gauge

pressure is 100,000 newtons per square meter

pressure is 101,000 newtons per square meter

water tank

pressure is 102,000 newtons per square meter

pressure is 103,000 newtons per square meter

DEMONSTRATION OF
WATER PRESSURE

colored water

P

PRESSURE COOKER

Inside a sealed pressure cooker, air pressure is increased by heating water to produce steam. The higher pressure raises both the boiling point of the water and the temperature of the steam, so that food suspended inside cooks more quickly.

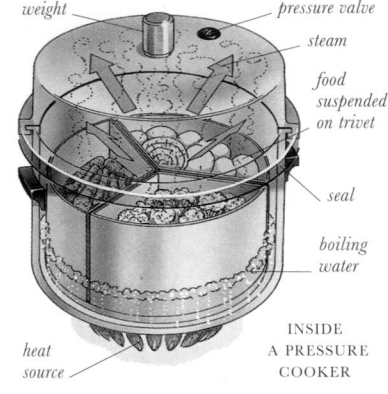

weight
pressure valve
steam
food suspended on trivet
seal
boiling water
heat source

INSIDE A PRESSURE COOKER

area) (*atmospheric pressure*). **2** urgency; the need to meet a deadline, etc. (*work under pressure*). **3** affliction or difficulty (*under financial pressure*). **4** constraining influence (*if pressure is brought to bear*). • *v.tr.* **1** apply pressure to. **2 a** coerce. **b** (often foll. by *into*) persuade (*was pressured into attending*).

pres·sure cook·er *n.* ▲ an airtight pot for cooking quickly under steam pressure. □□ **pres·sure-cook** *v.tr.*

pres·sure gauge *n.* a gauge showing the pressure of steam, etc.

pres·sure group *n.* a group or association formed to promote a particular interest or cause by influencing public policy.

pres·sure point *n.* **1** ▶ a point where an artery can be pressed against a bone to inhibit bleeding. **2** a point on the skin sensitive to pressure. **3** a target for political pressure or influence.

pres·sur·ize /préshərīz/ *v.tr.* **1** (esp. as **pressurized** *adj.*) maintain normal atmospheric pressure in (an aircraft cabin, etc.) at a high altitude. **2** raise to a high pressure. **3** pressure (a person). □□ **pres·sur·i·za·tion** *n.*

pres·ti·dig·i·ta·tor /préstidíjitaytər/ *n. formal* a magician. □□ **pres·ti·dig·i·ta·tion** /-táyshən/ *n.*

pres·tige /presteézh/ *n.* **1** respect, reputation, or influence derived from achievements, power, associations, etc. **2** (*attrib.*) having or conferring prestige. □□ **pres·tige·ful** *adj.*

pres·tig·ious /presteéjəs, -stíj-/ *adj.* having or showing prestige. □□ **pres·tig·ious·ly** *adv.* **pres·tig·ious·ness** *n.*

pres·tis·si·mo /prestísimō/ *adv. & n. Mus.* • *adv.* in a very quick tempo. • *n.* (*pl.* **-os**) a movement or passage played in this way.

pres·to /préstō/ *adv. & n.* • *adv.* **1** *Mus.* in quick tempo. **2** (in a magician's formula in performing a trick) quickly. • *n.* (*pl.* **-os**) *Mus.* a movement to be played in a quick tempo.

pre·stressed /préestrést/ *adj.* strengthened by stressing in advance, esp. of concrete by means of stretched rods or wires put in during manufacture.

pre·sum·a·bly /prizoomablee/ *adv.* as may reasonably be presumed.

pre·sume /prizoom/ *v.* **1** *tr.* (often foll. by *that* + clause) suppose to be true; take for granted. **2** *tr.* (often foll. by *to* + infin.) **a** take the liberty; be impudent enough (*presumed to question their authority*). **b** dare; venture (*may I presume to ask?*). **3** *intr.* be

presumptuous; take liberties. **4** *intr.* (foll. by *on, upon*) take advantage of or make unscrupulous use of (a person's good nature, etc.). □□ **pre·sum·a·ble** *adj.*

pre·sum·ing /prizooming/ *adj.* presumptuous. □□ **pre·sum·ing·ly** *adv.* **pre·sum·ing·ness** *n.*

pre·sump·tion /prizúmpshən/ *n.* **1** presumptuous behavior. **2 a** the act of presuming a thing to be true. **b** a thing that is presumed to be true. **3** a ground for presuming (*a strong presumption against their being guilty*). **4** *Law* an inference from known facts.

pre·sump·tive /prizúmptiv/ *adj.* **1** based on presumption or inference. **2** giving reasonable grounds for presumption (*presumptive evidence*). □□ **pre·sump·tive·ly** *adv.*

pre·sump·tu·ous /prizúmpchōōəs/ *adj.* unduly or overbearingly confident and presuming. □□ **pre·sump·tu·ous·ly** *adv.* **pre·sump·tu·ous·ness** *n.*

pre·sup·pose /préesəpóz/ *v.tr.* (often foll. by *that* + clause) **1** assume beforehand. **2** require as a precondition; imply. □□ **pre·sup·po·si·tion** /préesupəsíshən/ *n.*

prêt-à-port·er /pretəpáwrtay/ *n.* designer clothing sold ready-to-wear.

pre·tax /préetáks/ *adj.* (of income or profits) before the deduction of taxes.

pre·teen /préetéen/ *adj.* of or relating to a child just under the age of thirteen.

pre·tence esp. *Brit.* var. of PRETENSE.

pre·tend /priténd/ *v. & adj.* • *v.* **1** *tr.* claim or assert falsely so as to deceive (*pretended that they were foreigners*). **2 a** *tr.* imagine to oneself in play (*pretended to be monsters*) **b** *absol.* make pretense, esp. in imagination or play; make believe (*they're just pretending*). **3** *tr.* **a** profess, esp. falsely or extravagantly (*does not pretend to be a scholar*). **b** (as **pretended** *adj.*) falsely claim to be such (*a pretended friend*). **4** *intr.* (foll. by *to*) **a** lay claim to (a right or title, etc.). **b** profess to have (a quality, etc.). **5** *tr.* (foll. by *to*) aspire or presume; venture (*I cannot pretend to guess*). • *adj. colloq.* pretended; in pretense (*pretend money*).

pre·tend·er /priténdər/ *n.* **1** a person who claims a throne or title, etc. **2** a person who pretends.

pre·tense /préetens, priténs/ *n.* (also **pretence**) **1** pretending; make-believe. **2 a** a pretext or excuse (*on the slightest pretense*). **b** a false show of intentions or motives (*under the pretense of friendship; under false pretenses*). **3** (foll. by *to*) a claim, esp. a false or ambitious one (*has no pretense to any great talent*). **4 a** affectation; display. **b** pretentiousness; ostentation (*stripped of all pretense*).

pre·ten·sion /priténshən/ *n.* **1** (often foll. by *to*) **a** an assertion of a claim. **b** a justifiable claim (*has no pretensions to the name; has some pretensions to be included*). **2** pretentiousness.

pre·ten·tious /priténshəs/ *adj.* **1** making an excessive claim to great merit or importance. **2** ostentatious. □□ **pre·ten·tious·ly** *adv.* **pre·ten·tious·ness** *n.*

preter- /préetər/ *comb. form* more than.

pre·term /préetérm/ *adj.* born or occurring prematurely.

pre·ter·nat·u·ral /préetərnáchərəl/ *adj.* outside the ordinary course of nature; supernatural. □□ **pre·ter·nat·u·ral·ism** *n.* **pre·ter·nat·u·ral·ly** *adv.*

pre·text /préetekst/ *n.* **1** an ostensible or alleged reason or intention. **2** an excuse offered. □ **on** (or **under**) **the pretext** (foll. by *of*, or *that* + clause) professing as one's object or intention.

pretor var. of PRAETOR.

pre·tor·i·an var. of PRAETORIAN.

pret·ti·fy /prítifī/ *v.tr.* (**-ies, -ied**) make (a thing or person) pretty esp. in an affected way. □□ **pret·ti·fi·ca·tion** *n.* **pret·ti·fi·er** *n.*

pret·ty /prítee/ *adj., adv., n., & v.* • *adj.* (**prettier, prettiest**) **1** attractive in a delicate way without being truly beautiful or handsome (*a pretty child; a pretty dress; a pretty tune*). **2** fine or good of its kind (*a pretty wit*). **3** *iron.* considerable; fine (*a pretty penny; a pretty mess you have made*). • *adv. colloq.* fairly; moderately; considerably (*am pretty well; find it pretty difficult*). • *n.* (*pl.* **-ies**) a pretty person (esp. as a form of address to a child). • *v.tr.* (**-ies, -ied**) (often foll. by *up*) make pretty or attractive. □ **pretty much** (or **nearly** or **well**) *colloq.* almost; very nearly. **sitting pretty** *colloq.* in a favorable or advantageous position. □□ **pret·ti·ly** *adv.* **pret·ti·ness** *n.* **pret·ty·ish** *adj.*

PRESSURE POINT

Bleeding from a wound can be controlled by applying pressure directly to it or by applying pressure to certain points on the body (pressure points) where it is possible to press an artery against underlying bone. When the appropriate artery is pressed, the flow of blood from the heart to the injured part of the body is reduced.

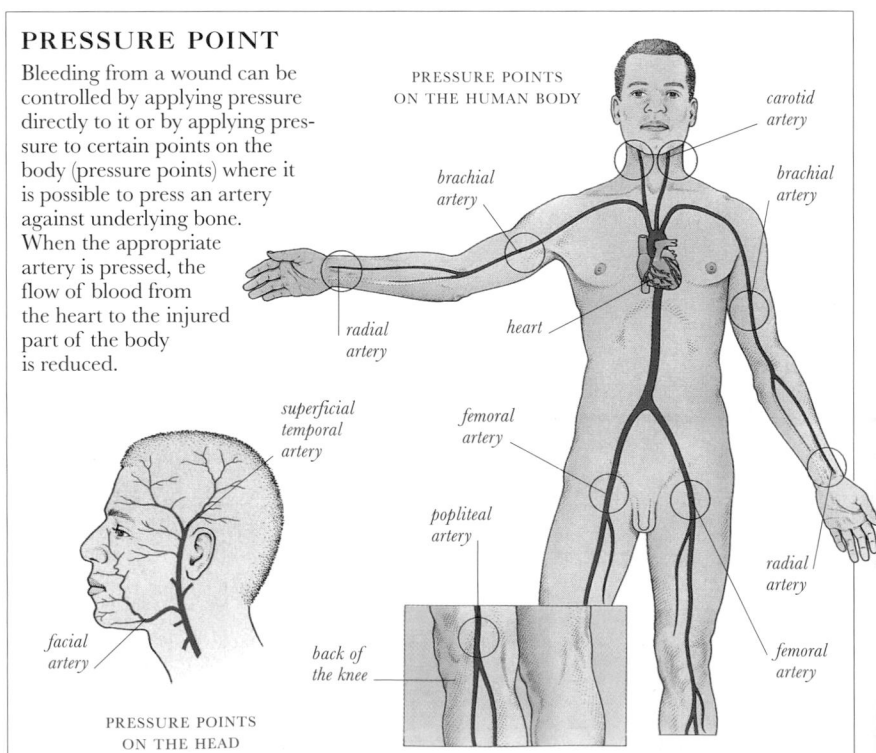

PRESSURE POINTS ON THE HUMAN BODY

carotid artery
brachial artery
brachial artery
radial artery
heart
femoral artery
femoral artery
radial artery

superficial temporal artery
facial artery
popliteal artery
back of the knee

PRESSURE POINTS ON THE HEAD

pret·zel /prétsəl/ *n.* ▶ a crisp or chewy knot-shaped or stick-shaped bread, usu. salted.

pre·vail /priváyl/ *v.intr.* **1** (often foll. by *against, over*) be victorious or gain mastery. **2** be the more usual or predominant. **3** exist or occur in general use or experience; be current. **4** (foll. by *on, upon*) persuade. **5** (as **prevailing** *adj.*) predominant; generally current or accepted (*prevailing opinion*). □□ **pre·vail·ing·ly** *adv.*

PRETZELS

pre·vail·ing wind *n.* the wind that most frequently occurs at a place.

prev·a·lent /prévələnt/ *adj.* **1** generally existing or occurring. **2** predominant. □□ **prev·a·lence** *n.* **prev·a·lent·ly** *adv.*

pre·var·i·cate /privárikayt/ *v.intr.* **1** speak or act evasively or misleadingly. **2** quibble; equivocate. □□ **pre·var·i·ca·tion** /-rikáyshən/ *n.* **pre·var·i·ca·tor** *n.*

pre·vent /privént/ *v.tr.* (often foll. by *from* + verbal noun) stop from happening or doing something; hinder; make impossible (*the weather prevented me from going*). □□ **pre·vent·a·ble** *adj.* (also **pre·vent·i·ble**) **pre·vent·a·bil·i·ty** *n.* **pre·vent·er** *n.* **pre·ven·tion** /-vénshən/ *n.*

pre·ven·ta·tive /privéntətiv/ *adj. & n.* = PREVENTIVE. □□ **pre·ven·ta·tive·ly** *adv.*

pre·ven·tive /privéntiv/ *adj. & n.* ● *adj.* serving to prevent, esp. preventing disease, breakdown, etc. (*preventive medicine; preventive maintenance*). ● *n.* a preventive agent, measure, drug, etc. □□ **pre·ven·tive·ly** *adv.*

pre·view /préevyoo/ *n. & v.* ● *n.* **1** the act of seeing in advance. **2 a** the showing of a movie, play, exhibition, etc., before it is seen by the general public. **b** (also **pre·vue**) an advance promotional sample of a movie; trailer. ● *v.tr.* see or show in advance.

pre·vi·ous /préevēəs/ *adj. & adv.* ● *adj.* **1** (often foll. by *to*) coming before in time or order. **2** done or acting hastily. ● *adv.* (foll. by *to*) before (*had called previous to writing*). □□ **pre·vi·ous·ly** *adv.* **pre·vi·ous·ness** *n.*

pre·vue var. of PREVIEW *n.* 2b.

pre·war /préewáwr/ *adj.* existing or occurring before a war (esp. the most recent major war).

prex /preks/ *n.* (also **prex·y**) *sl.* a president (esp. of a college).

prey /pray/ *n. & v.* ● *n.* **1** an animal that is hunted or killed by another for food. **2** (often foll. by *to*) a person or thing that is influenced by or vulnerable to (something undesirable) (*became a prey to morbid fears*). ● *v.intr.* (foll. by *on, upon*) **1** seek or take as prey. **2** make a victim of. **3** (of a disease, emotion, etc.) exert a harmful influence (*fear preyed on his mind*). □□ **prey·er** *n.*

pri·ap·ic /prīápik/ *adj.* phallic.

pri·a·pism /prīəpizəm/ *n.* **1** lewdness; licentiousness. **2** *Med.* persistent erection of the penis.

price /prīs/ *n. & v.* ● *n.* **1 a** the amount of money or goods for which a thing is bought or sold. **b** value or worth (*a pearl of great price; beyond price*). **2** what is or must be given, done, sacrificed, etc., to obtain or achieve something. **3** the odds in betting (*starting price*). **4** a sum of money offered or given as a reward, esp. for the capture or killing of a person. ● *v.tr.* **1** fix or find the price of (a thing for sale). **2** estimate the value of. □ **above** (or **beyond** or **without**) **price** so valuable that no price can be stated. **at any price** no matter what the cost, sacrifice, etc. (*peace at any price*). **at a price** at a high cost. **price oneself out of the market** lose to one's competitors by charging more than customers are willing to pay. **set a price on** declare the price of. **what price …?** (often foll. by verbal noun) *colloq.* **1** *iron.* the expected or much boasted … proves

disappointing (*what price your friendship now?*). **2** *Brit.* what is the chance of …? (*what price your finishing the course?*). □□ **priced** *adj.* (also in *comb.*). **pric·er** *n.*

price-fix·ing *n.* (also **price fixing**) the maintaining of prices at a certain level by agreement between competing sellers.

price·less /príslis/ *adj.* **1** invaluable; beyond price. **2** *colloq.* very amusing or absurd. □□ **price·less·ly** *adv.* **price·less·ness** *n.*

price tag *n.* **1** the label on an item showing its price. **2** the cost of an enterprise or undertaking.

price war *n.* fierce competition among traders cutting prices.

pric·ey /prísee/ *adj.* (also **pric·y**) (**pricier**, **priciest**) *colloq.* expensive. □□ **pric·i·ness** *n.*

prick /prik/ *v. & n.* ● *v.* **1** *tr.* pierce slightly; make a small hole in. **2** *tr.* (foll. by *off, out*) mark (esp. a pattern) with small holes or dots. **3** *tr.* trouble mentally (*my conscience is pricking me*). **4** *intr.* feel a pricking sensation. **5** *intr.* (foll. by *at, into, etc.*) make a thrust as if to prick. **6** *tr.* (foll. by *in, off, out*) plant (seedlings, etc.) in small holes pricked in the earth. ● *n.* **1** the act or an instance of pricking. **2** a small hole or mark made by pricking. **3** a pain caused as by pricking. **4** a mental pain (*felt the pricks of conscience*). **5** *coarse sl.* **a** the penis. **b** *derog.* (as a term of contempt) a contemptible or mean-spirited person. ¶ Usually considered a taboo use. □ **kick against the pricks** *Brit.* persist in futile resistance. **prick up one's ears 1** (of a dog, etc.) make the ears erect when on the alert. **2** (of a person) become suddenly attentive.

prick·er /príkər/ *n.* **1** one that pricks, as an animal or plant. **2** a small thorn or other sharp pointed outgrowth.

prick·le /príkəl/ *n. & v.* ● *n.* **1 a** a small thorn. **b** *Bot.* a thornlike process developed from the epidermis of a plant. **2** a hard pointed spine of a hedgehog, etc. **3** a prickling sensation. ● *v.tr. & intr.* affect or be affected with a sensation as of pricking.

prick·ly /príklee/ *adj.* (**pricklier**, **prickliest**) **1** (esp. in the names of plants and animals) having prickles. **2 a** (of a person) ready to take offense. **b** (of a topic, argument, etc.) full of contentious or complicated points; thorny. **3** tingling. □□ **prick·li·ness** *n.*

prick·ly heat *n.* an itchy inflammation of the skin, causing a tingling sensation and common in hot countries.

prick·ly pear *n.* **1** any cactus of the genus *Opuntia*, native to arid regions of America, bearing barbed bristles and large pear-shaped prickly fruits. **2** ▼ its fruit.

PRICKLY PEAR
(*Opuntia ficus-indica*)

prick·ly pop·py *n.* a tropical poppylike plant, *Argemone mexicana*, with prickly leaves and yellow flowers.

pric·y var. of PRICEY.

pride /prīd/ *n. & v.* ● *n.* **1 a** a feeling of elation or satisfaction at achievements, qualities, or possessions, etc., that do one credit. **b** an object of this feeling. **2** a high or overbearing opinion of one's worth or importance. **3** a proper sense of what befits one's position; self-respect. **4** a group or company (of animals, esp. lions). **5** the best condi-

tion; the prime. ● *v.refl.* (foll. by *on, upon*) be proud of. □ **my, his,** etc., **pride and joy** a thing of which one is very proud. **pride of the morning** a mist or shower at sunrise, supposedly indicating a fine day to come. **pride of place** the most important or prominent position. **take pride** (or **a pride**) **in 1** be proud of. **2** maintain in good condition or appearance. □□ **pride·ful** *adj.* **pride·ful·ly** *adv.* **pride·less** *adj.*

prie-dieu /preedyő/ *n.* (*pl.* **prie-dieux** *pronunc.* same) a kneeling desk for prayer.

priest /preest/ *n.* **1** an ordained minister of the Roman Catholic or Orthodox Church, or of the Anglican Church (above a deacon and below a bishop), authorized to perform certain rites and administer certain sacraments. **2** an official minister of a non-Christian religion. □□ **priest·less** *adj.* **priest·like** *adj.* **priest·ling** *n.*

priest·ess /préestis/ *n.* a female priest of a non-Christian religion.

priest·hood /préest-hood/ *n.* (usu. prec. by *the*) **1** the office or position of a priest. **2** priests in general.

priest·ly /préestlee/ *adj.* of or associated with priests. □□ **priest·li·ness** *n.*

prig /prig/ *n.* a self-righteously correct or moralistic person. □□ **prig·ger·y** *n.* **prig·gish** *adj.* **prig·gish·ly** *adv.* **prig·gish·ness** *n.*

prim /prim/ *adj. & v.* (**primmer**, **primmest**) **1** (of a person or manner) stiffly formal and precise. **2** (of a woman or girl) demure. **3** prudish. ● *v.tr.* (**primmed**, **primming**) **1** form (the face, lips, etc.) into a prim expression. **2** make prim. □□ **prim·ly** *adv.* **prim·ness** *n.*

pri·ma bal·ler·i·na /préemə/ *n.* the chief female dancer in a ballet or ballet company.

pri·ma·cy /prímosee/ *n.* (*pl.* **-ies**) **1** preeminence. **2** the office of an ecclesiastical primate.

pri·ma don·na /préemə/ *n.* (*pl.* **prima donnas**) **1** the chief female singer in an opera or opera company. **2** a temperamentally self-important person. □□ **pri·ma don·na·ish** *adj.*

pri·ma fa·cie /prímə fáyshee, -shee-ee, shə, préemə/ *adv. & adj.* ● *adv.* at first sight; from a first impression (*seems prima facie to be guilty*). ● *adj.* (of evidence) based on the first impression (*can see a prima facie reason for it*).

pri·mal /prímal/ *adj.* **1** primitive; primeval. **2** chief; fundamental. □□ **pri·mal·ly** *adv.*

pri·ma·ry /prímeree, -məree/ *adj. & n.* ● *adj.* **1 a** of the first importance; chief (*that is our primary concern*). **b** fundamental; basic. **2** earliest; original; first in a series. **3** of the first rank in a series; not derived (*the primary meaning of a word*). **4** designating any of the colors red, green, and blue, or for pigments red, blue, and yellow, from which all other colors can be obtained by mixing. ▷ COLOR. **5** (of a battery or cell) generating electricity by irreversible chemical reaction. **6** (of education) for young children, esp. below the age of 11. **7** (**Primary**) *Geol.* of the lowest series of strata. **8** *Biol.* belonging to the first stage of development. **9** (of an industry or source of production) concerned with obtaining or using raw materials. ● *n.* (*pl.* **-ies**) **1** a thing that is primary. **2** (in full **primary election**) a preliminary election to appoint delegates to a party convention or to select the candidates for a principal election. **3** (**Primary**) *Geol.* the Primary period. □□ **pri·ma·ri·ly** /prímérilee/ *adv.*

pri·ma·ry coil *n.* a coil to which current is supplied in a transformer.

pri·ma·ry feath·er *n.* a large flight feather of a bird's wing. ▷ FEATHER

pri·ma·ry in·dus·try *n.* an industry (such as mining, forestry, agriculture, etc.) that provides raw materials for conversion into commodities and products for the consumer.

pri·ma·ry school *n.* a school where young children are taught, esp. the first three elementary grades and kindergarten.

P

PRIMATE

Primates are mostly tree-dwelling animals with forward-pointing eyes, long arms, and gripping fingers. The majority have large brains and a high level of intelligence, and live in social groups. There are two sub-orders: anthropoids, the advanced primates, which include monkeys, apes, and humans; and prosimians, the primitive primates, which include lemurs, tarsiers, and lorises.

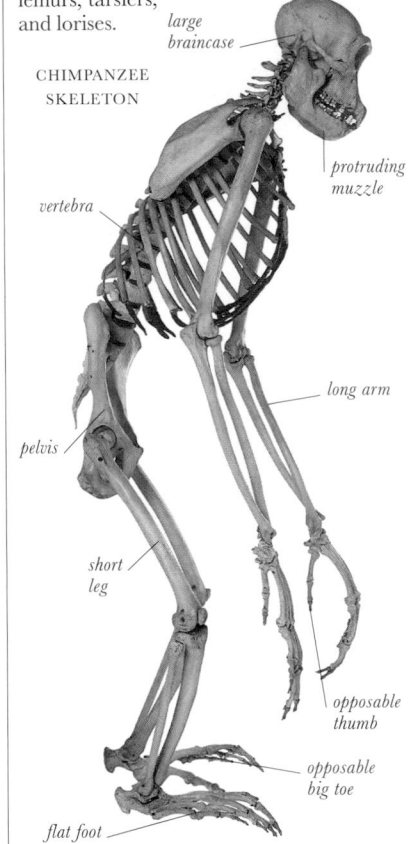

CHIMPANZEE SKELETON

large braincase

protruding muzzle

vertebra

long arm

pelvis

short leg

opposable thumb

opposable big toe

flat foot

TYPES OF PRIMATE

ANTHROPOIDS

PROBOSCIS MONKEY
(*Nasalis larvatus*)

RED HOWLER MONKEY
(*Alouatta seniculus*)

SPIDER MONKEY
(*Ateles geoffroyi*)

ORANGUTAN
(*Pongo pygmaeus*)

GORILLA
(*Gorilla gorilla*)

PROSIMIANS

AYE-AYE
(*Daubentonia madagascariensis*)

INDRI
(*Indri indri*)

---

pri·mate /prímayt/ *n.* **1** ▲ any animal of the order Primates, the highest order of mammals, including tarsiers, lemurs, apes, monkeys, and human beings. **2** an archbishop. □□ **pri·ma·tial** /-máyshəl/ *adj.* **pri·ma·tol·o·gy** /-mətóləjee/ *n.* (in sense 1).

pri·ma·ve·ra /préemɔvaíra/ *adj.* (of a pasta dish) made with spring vegetables.

prime[1] /prīm/ *adj. & n.* ● *adj.* **1** chief; most important (*the prime agent; the prime motive*). **2** (esp. of beef) first-rate; excellent. **3** primary; fundamental. **4** *Math.* **a** (of a number) divisible only by itself and 1 (e.g., 2, 3, 5, 7, 11). **b** (of numbers) having no common factor but 1. ● *n.* **1** the state of the highest perfection of something (*in the prime of life*). **2** the beginning or first age of anything. **3** a prime number. □□ **prime·ness** *n.*

prime[2] /prīm/ *v.tr.* **1** prepare (a thing) for use or action. **2** prepare (a gun) for firing or (an explosive) for detonation. **3 a** pour (liquid) into a pump to prepare it for working. **b** inject fuel into (the cylinder or carburetor of an internal-combustion engine). **4** prepare (wood, etc.) for painting by applying a substance that prevents paint from being absorbed. **5** equip (a person) with information, etc.

prime min·is·ter *n.* the head of an elected parliamentary government; the principal minister of a nation or sovereign.

prime mov·er *n.* **1** an initial source of motive power. **2** the author of a fruitful idea.

prim·er[1] /prímər/ *n.* **1** a substance used to prime wood, etc. ▷ UNDERCOAT. **2** a cap, cylinder, etc., used to ignite the powder of a cartridge, etc.

prim·er[2] /prímər, prímər/ *n.* **1** an elementary textbook for teaching children to read. **2** an introductory book.

prime rate *n.* the lowest rate at which money can be borrowed commercially.

prime time *n.* the time at which a radio or television audience is expected to consist of the greatest number of people.

pri·me·val /prīméevəl/ *adj.* **1** of or relating to the earliest age of the world. **2** ancient; primitive. □□ **pri·me·val·ly** *adv.*

prim·i·tive /prímitiv/ *adj. & n.* ● *adj.* **1** early; ancient; at an early stage of civilization (*primitive humans*). **2** undeveloped; crude; simple (*primitive methods*). **3** original; primary. **4** *Gram. & Philol.* (of words or language) radical; not derivative. **5** (of a color) primary. ● *n.* **1 a** a painter of the period before the Renaissance. **b** a modern imitator of such. **2 a** an untutored painter with a direct naïve style. **b** a picture by such a painter. □□ **prim·i·tive·ly** *adv.* **prim·i·tive·ness** *n.*

prim·i·tiv·ism /prímitivizəm/ *n.* **1** primitive behavior. **2** belief in the superiority of what is primitive. **3** the practice of primitive art. □□ **prim·i·tiv·ist** *n. & adj.*

pri·mo /préemō/ *n.* (*pl.* **-os**) **1** *Mus.* the leading or upper part in a duet, etc. **2** *colloq.* first-rate; excellent.

pri·mo·gen·i·tor /prímōjénitər/ *n.* **1** the earliest ancestor of a people, etc. **2** an ancestor.

pri·mo·gen·i·ture /prímōjénichər/ *n.* **1** the fact or condition of being the firstborn child. **2** (in full **right of primogeniture**) the right of succession belonging to the firstborn, esp. the feudal rule by which the whole real estate of an intestate passes to the eldest son.

pri·mor·di·al /prīmáwrdeeəl/ *adj.* **1** existing at or from the beginning; primeval. **2** original; fundamental. □□ **pri·mor·di·al·i·ty** /-mawrdeeálitee/ *n.* **pri·mor·di·al·ly** *adv.*

pri·mor·di·al soup *n.* a solution rich in organic compounds in which life on earth is supposed to have originated.

primp /primp/ *v.tr.* **1** make (the hair, one's clothes, etc.) neat or overly tidy. **2** *refl.* groom (oneself) painstakingly.

P

prim·rose /prímrōz/ *n.* **1 a** ▶ any plant of the genus *Primula*, esp. *P. vulgaris*, bearing pale yellow flowers. **b** the flower of this. **2** a pale yellow color.

prim·rose path *n.* the pursuit of pleasure, esp. with disastrous consequences.

prim·u·la /prímyələ/ *n.* any plant of the genus *Primula*, bearing

PRIMROSE
(*Primula vulgaris*)

primrose-like flowers in a wide variety of colors during the spring, including primroses, cowslips, and polyanthuses.

pri·mus in·ter pa·res /préemŏŏs íntər paáres, príməs intər páireez/ *n.* a first among equals; the senior or representative member of a group.

prince /prins/ *n.* (as a title usu. **Prince**) **1** a male member of a royal family other than a reigning king. **2** (in full **prince of the blood**) a son or grandson of a British monarch. **3** a ruler of a small nation, actually or nominally subject to a king or emperor. **4** (as an English rendering of foreign titles) a noble usu. ranking next below a duke. **5** (as a courtesy title in some connections) a duke, marquess, or earl. **6** (often foll. by *of*) the chief or greatest (*the prince of novelists*). □□ **prince·dom** *n.* **prince·like** *adj.* **prince·ship** *n.*

Prince Charm·ing *n.* an idealized young hero or lover.

prince·ly /prínslee/ *adj.* (**princelier, princeliest**) **1 a** of or worthy of a prince. **b** held by a prince. **2 a** sumptuous; generous; splendid. **b** (of a sum of money) substantial. □□ **prince·li·ness** *n.*

Prince of Dark·ness *n.* Satan.

Prince of Peace *n.* Christ.

Prince of Wales *n.* the heir apparent to the British throne, as a title conferred by the monarch.

prin·cess /prínses/ *n.* (as a title usu. **Princess**) **1** the wife of a prince. **2** a female member of a royal family other than a reigning queen. **3** (in full **princess of the blood**) a daughter or granddaughter of a British monarch. **4** a preeminent woman or thing personified as a woman.

prin·ci·pal /prínsipəl/ *adj. & n.* ● *adj.* **1** (usu. *attrib.*) first in rank or importance; chief (*the principal town of the district*). **2** main; leading (*a principal cause of my success*). **3** (of money) constituting the original sum invested or lent. ● *n.* **1** a head, ruler, or superior. **2** the head of an elementary, middle, or high school. **3** the leading performer in a concert, play, etc. **4** a capital sum as distinguished from interest or income. **5** a person for whom another acts as agent, etc. **6** (in the UK) a civil servant of the grade below Secretary. **7** the person actually responsible for a crime. **8** a person for whom another is surety. **9** *Mus.* the leading player in each section of an orchestra. □□ **prin·ci·pal·ship** *n.*

prin·ci·pal·i·ty /prínsipálitee/ *n.* (*pl.* **-ies**) **1** a nation ruled by a prince. **2** (in *pl.*) the fifth order of the ninefold celestial hierarchy.

prin·ci·pal·ly /prínsiplee/ *adv.* for the most part.

prin·ci·pal parts *n.pl. Gram.* the parts of a verb from which all other parts can be deduced.

prin·ci·ple /prínsipəl/ *n.* **1** a fundamental truth or law as the basis of reasoning or action (*arguing from first principles; moral principles*). **2 a** a personal code of conduct (*a person of high principle*). **b** (in *pl.*) such rules of conduct (*has no principles*). **3** a general law in physics, etc. (*the uncertainty principle*). **4** a law of nature forming the basis for the construction or working of a machine, etc. **5** a fundamental source; a primary element (*held water to be the first principle of all things*). **6** *Chem.* a constituent of a substance, esp. one giving rise to some quality, etc. □ **in principle** as regards fundamentals but not necessarily in detail. **on principle** on the basis of a moral attitude (*I refuse on principle*).

prin·ci·pled /prínsipəld/ *adj.* based on or having (esp. praiseworthy) principles of behavior.

print /print/ *n., v., & adj.* ● *n.* **1** an indentation or mark on a surface left by the pressure of a thing in contact with it (*fingerprint; footprint*). **2 a** printed lettering or writing (*large print*). **b** words in printed form. **c** a printed publication, esp. a newspaper. **d** the quantity of a book, etc., printed at one time. **e** the state of being printed. **3** a picture or design printed from a block or plate. **4 a** *Photog.* a picture produced on paper from a negative. **b** a copy of a motion picture suitable for showing. **5** a printed cotton fabric. ● *v.tr.* **1 a** produce or reproduce (a book, picture, etc.) by applying inked types, blocks, or plates, to paper, vellum, etc. **b** (of an author, publisher, or editor) cause (a book or manuscript, etc.) to be produced or reproduced in this way. **2** express or publish in print. **3 a** (often foll. by *on, in*) impress or stamp (a mark or figure on a surface). **b** (often foll. by *with*) impress or stamp (a soft surface, e.g., of butter or wax, with a seal, die, etc.). **4** (often *absol.*) write (words or letters) without joining, in imitation of typography. **5** (often foll. by *off, out*) *Photog.* produce (a picture) by the transmission of light through a negative. **6** (usu. foll. by *out*) (of a computer, etc.) produce output in printed form. **7** mark (a textile fabric) with a decorative design in colors. **8** (foll. by *on*) impress (an idea, scene, etc., on the mind or memory). **9** transfer (a colored or plain design) from paper, etc., to the unglazed or glazed surface of ceramic ware. ● *adj.* of, for, or concerning printed publications. □ **in print 1** (of a book, etc.) available from the publisher. **2** in printed form. **out of print** no longer available from the publisher. □□ **print·a·ble** *adj.* **print·a·bil·i·ty** /príntəbilitee/ *n.* **print·less** *adj.* (in sense 1 of *n.*).

print·ed cir·cuit *n.* an electric circuit with thin strips of conductive material on a flat insulating sheet, usu. made by a process like printing.

print·er /príntər/ *n.* **1** a person who prints books, magazines, advertising matter, etc. **2** the owner of a printing business. **3** a device that prints, esp. as part of a computer system.

print·er·y /príntəree/ *n.* (*pl.* **-ies**) a printer's works.

print·head /print-hed/ *n.* the component in a printer (see PRINTER 3) that assembles and prints the characters on the paper.

print·ing /prínting/ *n.* **1** ▼ the production of printed books, etc. **2** a single impression of a book. **3** printed letters or writing imitating them.

print·ing press *n.* a machine for printing from types or plates, etc. ▷ PRINTING

print·mak·er /príntmaykər/ *n.* a person who makes a print. □□ **print·mak·ing** *n.*

print·out /príntowt/ *n.* computer output in printed form.

print·works /príntwərks/ *n.* a factory where fabrics are printed.

pri·on /príon/ *n. Biol.* a submicroscopic protein particle believed to be the cause of certain brain diseases.

pri·or /príər/ *adj., adv., & n.* ● *adj.* **1** earlier. **2** (often foll. by *to*) coming before in time, order, or importance. ● *adv.* (foll. by *to*) before (*decided prior to their arrival*). ● *n.* **1** the superior officer of a religious

---

PRINTING

There are four basic printing processes – intaglio, lithographic, relief, and screen – each of which can be used by a printing press. In intaglio printing, a design is etched or engraved into a metal plate. In lithography, the printing image on the plate is made with a greasy medium that attracts ink. A relief printing plate has raised images. In screen printing, the printing surface is a mesh. Color printing uses four plates, each of which prints in black, cyan, magenta, or yellow ink to create a complete color image.

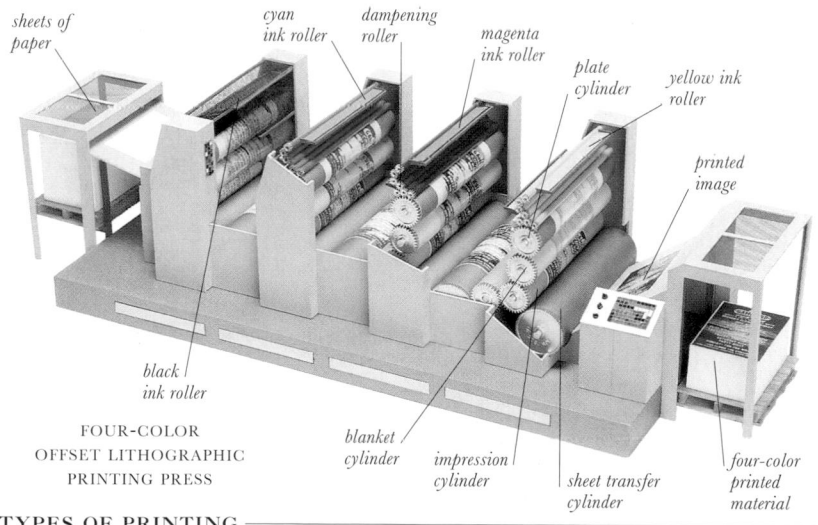

sheets of paper   *cyan ink roller*   *dampening roller*   *magenta ink roller*   *plate cylinder*   *yellow ink roller*   *printed image*

black ink roller

FOUR-COLOR
OFFSET LITHOGRAPHIC
PRINTING PRESS

blanket cylinder   *impression cylinder*   *sheet transfer cylinder*   *four-color printed material*

TYPES OF PRINTING

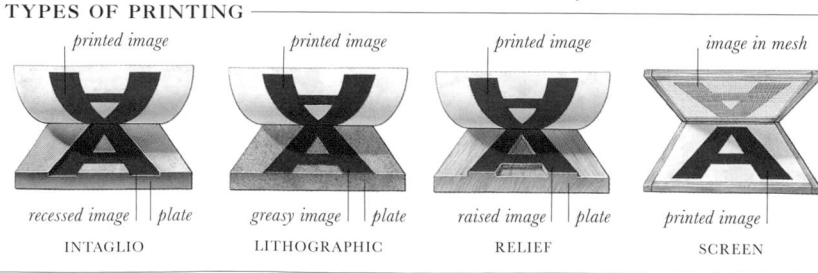

printed image	*printed image*	*printed image*	*image in mesh*
recessed image / *plate*	*greasy image* / *plate*	*raised image* / *plate*	*printed image*
INTAGLIO	LITHOGRAPHIC	RELIEF	SCREEN

P

house or order. **2** (in an abbey) the officer next under the abbot. □□ **pri·or·ate** /-rət/ *n.* **pri·or·ess** /príəris/ *n.* **pri·or·ship** *n.*

pri·or·i·ty /prīáwritee, -ór-/ *n.* (*pl.* **-ies**) **1** the fact or condition of being earlier or antecedent. **2** precedence in rank, etc. **3** an interest having prior claim to consideration. □□ **pri·or·i·tize** *v.tr.* **pri·or·i·ti·za·tion** *n.*

pri·or·y /príoree/ *n.* (*pl.* **-ies**) a monastery governed by a prior or a convent governed by a prioress.

prise esp. *Brit.* var. of PRIZE[2].

prism /prízəm/ *n.* **1** ▶ a solid geometric figure whose two ends are similar, equal, and parallel rectilinear figures, and whose sides are parallelograms. **2** a transparent body in this form, usu. triangular with refracting surfaces at an acute angle with each other, which separates white light into a spectrum of colors. □□ **pris·mal** /prízməl/ *adj.*

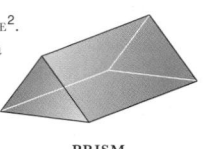

PRISM

pris·mat·ic /prizmátik/ *adj.* **1** of, like, or using a prism. **2 a** (of colors) distributed by or as if by a transparent prism. **b** (of light) displayed in the form of a spectrum. □□ **pris·mat·i·cal·ly** *adv.*

pris·on /prízən/ *n.* **1** a place in which a person is kept in captivity, esp. a building to which persons are legally committed while awaiting trial or for punishment; a jail. **2** custody; confinement (*in prison*). ● *v.tr. poet.* (**prisoned, prisoning**) put in prison.

pris·on camp *n.* **1** a camp for prisoners of war or political prisoners. **2** a minimum-security prison.

pris·on·er /príznər/ *n.* **1** a person kept in prison. **2** *Brit.* (in full **prisoner at the bar**) a person in custody on a criminal charge and on trial. **3** a person or thing confined by illness, another's grasp, etc. **4** (in full **prisoner of war**) a person who has been captured in war. □ **take prisoner** seize and hold as a prisoner.

pris·on·er of con·science *n.* a person imprisoned by a government for holding political or religious views it does not tolerate.

pris·sy /prísee/ *adj.* (**prissier, prissiest**) prim; prudish. □□ **pris·si·ly** *adv.* **pris·si·ness** *n.*

pris·tine /prísteen, pristéen/ *adj.* **1** in its original condition; unspoiled. **2** *disp.* spotless; fresh as if new. **3** ancient; primitive.

prith·ee /príthee/ *int. archaic* pray; please.

pri·va·cy /prívəsee/ *n.* **1 a** the state of being private and undisturbed. **b** a person's right to this. **2** freedom from intrusion or public attention. **3** avoidance of publicity.

pri·vate /prívət/ *adj. & n.* ● *adj.* **1** belonging to an individual; one's own; personal (*private property*). **2** confidential; not to be disclosed to others (*private talks*). **3** kept or removed from public knowledge or observation. **4 a** not open to the public. **b** for an individual's exclusive use (*private room*). **5** (of a place) secluded; affording privacy. **6** (of a person) not holding public office or an official position. **7** (of education) conducted outside the government system. **8** (of a person) retiring; reserved; unsociable. **9** (of a company) not having publicly traded shares. ● *n.* **1** a soldier with a rank below corporal. **2** (in *pl.*) *colloq.* the genitals. □ **in private** privately; in private company or life. □□ **pri·vate·ly** *adv.*

pri·vate de·tec·tive *n.* a usu. freelance detective employed privately, outside an official police force.

pri·vate en·ter·prise *n.* **1** a business or businesses not under government control. **2** individual initiative.

pri·va·teer /prívəteér/ *n.* **1** an armed vessel owned and officered by private individuals holding a government commission and authorized for war service. **2 a** a commander of such a vessel. **b** (in *pl.*) its crew. □□ **pri·va·teer·ing** *n.*

pri·vate eye *n. colloq.* a private detective.

pri·vate in·ves·ti·ga·tor *n.* private detective. ¶ Abbr.: **PI**.

pri·vate life *n.* life as a private person, not as an official, public performer, etc.

pri·vate parts *n.pl.* the genitals.

pri·vate prac·tice *n.* **1** *US* an independent practice, esp. of law, medicine, or counseling services. **2** *Brit.* medical practice that is not part of the National Health Service.

pri·vate school *n.* **1** *US* a school not supported mainly by the government. **2** *Brit.* a school supported wholly by the payment of fees.

pri·vate sec·re·ta·ry *n.* a secretary dealing with the personal and confidential concerns of a business executive.

pri·vate sec·tor *n.* the part of the economy free of direct government control.

pri·va·tion /prīváyshən/ *n.* **1** lack of the comforts or necessities of life (*suffered many privations*). **2** (often foll. by *of*) loss or absence (of a quality).

pri·va·tize /prívətīz/ *v.tr.* make private, esp. transfer (a business, etc.) to private as distinct from government control or ownership. □□ **pri·va·ti·za·tion** *n.*

priv·et /prívit/ *n.* ▼ any deciduous or evergreen shrub of the genus *Ligustrum*, esp. *L. vulgare* bearing small white flowers and black berries, and much used for hedges.

PRIVET: CHINESE PRIVET
(*Ligustrum sinense*)

priv·i·lege /prívilij, prívlij/ *n. & v.* ● *n.* **1 a** a right, advantage, or immunity, belonging to a person, class, or office. **b** the freedom of members of a legislative assembly when speaking at its meetings. **2** a special benefit or honor (*it is a privilege to meet you*). **3** a monopoly or patent granted to an individual, corporation, etc. **4** *Stock Exch.* an option to buy or sell. ● *v.tr.* **1** invest with a privilege. **2** (foll. by *to* + infin.) allow (a person) as a privilege (to do something). **3** (often foll. by *from*) exempt (a person from a liability, etc.).

priv·i·leged /prívilijd, prívlijd/ *adj.* **1 a** invested with or enjoying a certain privilege or privileges; honored; favored. **b** exempt from standard regulations or procedures. **c** powerful; affluent. **2** (of information, etc.) confidential; restricted.

priv·y /prívee/ *adj. & n.* ● *adj.* **1** (foll. by *to*) sharing in the secret of (a person's plans, etc.). **2** *archaic* hidden; secret. ● *n.* (*pl.* **-ies**) **1** a toilet, esp. an outhouse. **2** *Law* a person having a part or interest in any action, matter, or thing. □□ **priv·i·ly** *adv.*

prize[1] /prīz/ *n. & v.* ● *n.* **1** something that can be won in a competition, lottery, etc. **2** a reward given as a symbol of victory or superiority. **3** something striven for or worth striving for (*missed all the great prizes of life*). **4** (*attrib.*) **a** to which a prize is awarded (*a prize bull*). **b** supremely excellent or outstanding of its kind. ● *v.tr.* value highly (*a much prized possession*).

prize[2] /prīz/ *v. & n.* (also **prise**) ● *v.tr.* force open or out by leverage (*prized up the lid; prized the box open*). ● *n.* leverage; purchase.

prize·fight /prízfīt/ *n.* a boxing match fought for prize money. □□ **prize·fight·er** *n.*

prize mon·ey *n.* money offered as a prize.

prize·win·ner /prízwinər/ *n.* a winner of a prize. □□ **prize·win·ning** *adj.*

pro[1] /prō/ *n. & adj. colloq.* ● *n.* (*pl.* **pros**) a professional. ● *adj.* professional.

pro[2] /prō/ *adj., n., & prep.* ● *adj.* (of an argument or reason) for; in favor. ● *n.* (*pl.* **pros**) a reason or argument for or in favor. ● *prep.* in favor of.

pro·a /prṓə/ *n.* (also **prau, prah·u** /práə-ōō/) a Malay boat, esp. with a large triangular sail and a canoe-like outrigger.

pro·ac·tive /prō-áktiv/ *adj.* **1** (of a person, policy, etc.) creating or controlling a situation by taking the initiative. **2** of or relating to mental conditioning or a habit, etc., which has been learned. □□ **pro·ac·tive·ly** *adv.*

pro-am *adj.* involving professionals and amateurs.

prob. *abbr.* **1** probable. **2** probably. **3** problem.

prob·a·bi·lis·tic /probəbəlístik/ *adj.* based on or subject to probability.

prob·a·bil·i·ty /próbəbilitee/ *n.* (*pl.* **-ies**) **1** the state or condition of being probable. **2** the likelihood of something happening. **3** a probable or most probable event (*the probability is that they will come*). **4** *Math.* the extent to which an event is likely to occur, measured by the ratio of the favorable cases to the whole number of cases possible. □ **in all probability** most probably.

prob·a·ble /próbəbəl/ *adj. & n.* ● *adj.* **1** (often foll. by *that* + clause) that may be expected to happen or prove true; likely (*the probable explanation; it is probable that they forgot*). **2** statistically likely but not proven. ● *n.* a probable candidate, member of a team, etc. □□ **prob·a·bly** *adv.*

pro·bate /prṓbayt/ *n. & v.* ● *n.* **1** the official proving of a will. **2** a verified copy of a will. ● *v.tr.* **1** establish the validity of (a will). **2** to put (a criminal offender) on probation.

pro·ba·tion /prəbáyshən/ *n.* **1** *Law* a system of suspending the sentence of a criminal offender subject to a period of good behavior under supervision. **2** a process or period of testing the character or abilities of a person in a certain role, esp. of a new employee. □ **on probation** undergoing probation, esp. legal supervision. □□ **pro·ba·tion·al** *adj.* **pro·ba·tion·ar·y** *adj.*

pro·ba·tion·er /prōbáyshənər/ *n.* **1** a person on probation, e.g., a newly appointed nurse, teacher, etc. **2** a criminal offender on probation. □□ **pro·ba·tion·er·ship** *n.*

pro·ba·tion of·fi·cer *n.* an official supervising offenders on probation.

probe /prōb/ *n. & v.* ● *n.* **1** a penetrating investigation. **2** any small device, esp. an electrode, for measuring, testing, etc. **3** a blunt surgical instrument usu. of metal for exploring a wound, etc. **4** (in full **space probe**) an unmanned exploratory spacecraft transmitting information about its environment. ● *v.* **1** *tr.* examine or inquire into closely. **2** *tr.* explore (a wound or part of the body) with a probe. **3** *tr.* penetrate with or as with a sharp instrument, esp. in order to explore. **4** *intr.* make an investigation with or as with a probe (*the detective probed into her past life*). □□ **probe·a·ble** *adj.* **prob·er** *n.* **prob·ing·ly** *adv.*

pro·bi·ty /prṓbitee, prób-/ *n.* uprightness; honesty.

prob·lem /próbləm/ *n.* **1** a doubtful or difficult matter requiring a solution (*how to prevent it is a problem; the problem of ventilation*). **2** something hard to understand, accomplish, or deal with. **3** (*attrib.*) **a** causing problems; difficult to deal with (*problem child*). **b** (of a play, novel, etc.) in which a social or other problem is treated. **4 a** *Physics & Math.* an inquiry starting from given conditions to investigate or demonstrate a fact, result, or law. **b** *Geom.* a

P

proposition in which something has to be constructed (cf. THEOREM).

prob·lem·at·ic /prόbləmátik/ *adj.* (also **prob·lem·at·i·cal**) **1** difficult; posing a problem. **2** doubtful or questionable. ▫▫ **prob·lem·at·i·cal·ly** *adv.*

pro bo·no *adj.* pertaining to a service, esp. legal work, for which no fee is charged.

pro·bos·cis /prōbósis/ *n.* **1** the long flexible trunk or snout of some mammals, e.g., an elephant or tapir. ▷ ELEPHANT. **2** ▼ the elongated mouth parts of some insects. ▷ BUTTERFLY, HOUSEFLY. **3** the sucking organ in some worms. ▫▫ **pro·bos·cid·if·er·ous** /-sidífərəs/ *adj.* **pro·bos·cid·i·form** /-sídifawrm/ *adj.*

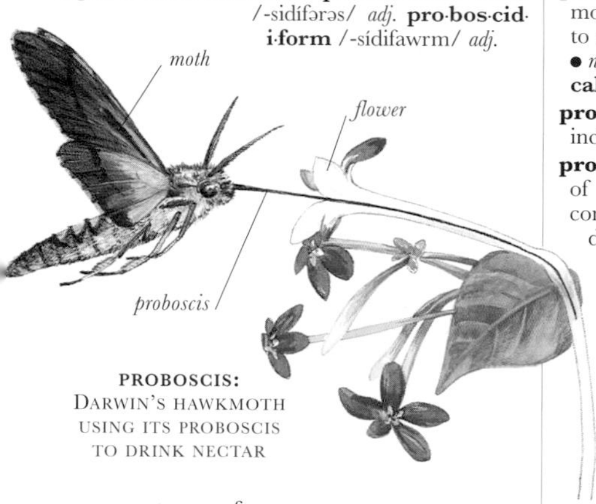

PROBOSCIS: DARWIN'S HAWKMOTH USING ITS PROBOSCIS TO DRINK NECTAR

pro·car·y·ote var. of PROKARYOTE.

pro·ce·dure /prəséejər/ *n.* **1** a way of proceeding, esp. a mode of conducting business or a legal action. **2** a mode of performing a task. **3** a series of actions conducted in a certain order or manner. **4** a proceeding. **5** *Computing* = SUBROUTINE. ▫▫ **pro·ce·dur·al** *adj.* **pro·ce·dur·al·ly** *adv.*

pro·ceed /prōséed, prə-/ *v.intr.* **1** (often foll. by *to*) go forward or on further; make one's way. **2** (often foll. by *with*, or *to* + infin.) continue; go on with an activity (*proceeded with their work; proceeded to tell the whole story*). **3** (of an action) be carried on or continued (*the case will now proceed*). **4** adopt a course of action (*how shall we proceed?*). **5** go on to say. **6** (foll. by *against*) start a lawsuit (against a person). **7** (often foll. by *from*) come forth or originate (*shouts proceeded from the bedroom*).

pro·ceed·ing /prōséeding, prə-/ *n.* **1** an action or piece of conduct. **2** (in *pl.*) (in full **legal proceedings**) a legal action; a lawsuit. **3** (in *pl.*) a published report of discussions or a conference. **4** (in *pl.*) business, actions, or events in progress (*the proceedings were enlivened by a dog running onto the field*).

pro·ceeds /prṓseedz/ *n.pl.* money produced by a transaction or other undertaking.

proc·ess[1] /próses, prṓ-/ *n.* & *v.* • *n.* **1** a course of action or proceeding, esp. a series of stages in manufacture or some other operation. **2** the progress or course of something (*in process of construction*). **3** a natural or involuntary operation or series of changes (*the process of growing old*). **4** a legal action; a summons or writ. **5** *Anat., Zool., & Bot.* a natural appendage or outgrowth on an organism. • *v.tr.* **1** handle or deal with by a particular process. **2** treat (food, esp. to prevent decay) (*processed cheese*). **3** *Computing* operate on (data) by means of a program. ▫▫ **proc·ess·a·ble** *adj.*

proc·ess[2] /prəsés/ *v.intr.* walk in procession.

pro·ces·sion /prəséshən/ *n.* **1** a number of people or vehicles, etc., moving forward in orderly succession, esp. at a ceremony, demonstration, or festivity. **2** the movement of such a group (*go in procession*). **3** a regular succession of things; a sequence. **4** *Theol.* the emanation of the Holy Spirit. ▫▫ **pro·ces·sion·ist** *n.*

pro·ces·sion·al /prəséshənəl/ *adj.* & *n.* • *adj.* **1** of processions. **2** used, carried, or sung in processions. • *n. Eccl.* a book of processional hymns, etc.

proc·es·sor /prósesər, prṓ-/ *n.* a machine that processes things, esp.: **1** = CENTRAL PROCESSOR. **2** = FOOD PROCESSOR.

pro-choice *adj.* in favor of the right to legal abortion.

pro·claim /prōkláym, prə-/ *v.tr.* **1** (often foll. by *that* + clause) announce or declare publicly or officially. **2** declare (a person) to be (a king, traitor, etc.). **3** reveal as being (*an accent that proclaims you a Southerner*). ▫▫ **pro·claim·er** *n.* **proc·la·ma·tion** /prókləmáyshən/ *n.* **pro·clam·a·to·ry** /-klámətawree/ *adj.*

pro·clit·ic /prōklítik/ *adj.* & *n. Gram.* • *adj.* (of a monosyllable) closely attached in pronunciation to a following word and having itself no accent. • *n.* such a word, e.g., *at* in *at home.* ▫▫ **pro·clit·i·cal·ly** *adv.*

pro·cliv·i·ty /prōklívitee/ *n.* (*pl.* **-ies**) a tendency or inclination.

pro·con·sul /prōkónsəl/ *n.* **1** *Rom.Hist.* a governor of a province, in the later republic usu. an ex-consul. **2** a governor of a modern colony, etc. **3** a deputy consul. ▫▫ **pro·con·su·lar** /-kónsələr/ *adj.* **pro·con·su·late** /-kónsələt/ *n.* **pro·con·sul·ship** *n.*

pro·cras·ti·nate /prōkrástinayt/ *v.* **1** *intr.* defer action; delay, esp. intentionally. **2** *tr.* defer or delay, esp. intentionally or habitually. ▫▫ **pro·cras·ti·na·tion** /-náyshən/ *n.* **pro·cras·ti·na·tive** /-nətiv/ *adj.* **pro·cras·ti·na·tor** *n.* **pro·cras·ti·na·to·ry** /-nətawree/ *adj.*

pro·cre·ate /prṓkreeayt/ *v.tr.* (often *absol.*) bring (offspring) into existence by the natural process of reproduction. ▫▫ **pro·cre·ant** /prṓkreeənt/ *adj.* **pro·cre·a·tive** *adj.* **pro·cre·a·tion** *n.* **pro·cre·a·tor** *n.*

proc·tol·o·gy /proktóləjee/ *n.* the branch of medicine concerned with the anus and rectum. ▫▫ **proc·to·log·i·cal** /-təlójikəl/ *adj.* **proc·tol·o·gist** *n.*

proc·tor /próktər/ *n.* **1** a supervisor of students in an examination, etc. **2** *Brit.* an officer (usu. one of two) at certain universities. **3** *Brit.Law* a person managing causes in a court (now chiefly ecclesiastical) that administers civil or canon law. ▫▫ **proc·to·ri·al** /-táwreeəl/ *adj.* **proc·tor·ship** *n.*

pro·cum·bent /prōkúmbənt/ *adj.* **1** lying on the face; prostrate. **2** *Bot.* growing along the ground.

proc·u·ra·tion /prókyŏŏráyshən/ *n.* **1** the action of procuring, obtaining, or bringing about. **2** the function or an authorized action of an attorney.

proc·u·ra·tor /prókyŏŏraytər/ *n.* **1** an agent or proxy, esp. one who has power of attorney. **2** *Rom.Hist.* a treasury officer in an imperial province. ▫▫ **proc·u·ra·to·ri·al** /-rətáwreeəl/ *adj.* **proc·u·ra·tor·ship** *n.*

pro·cure /prōkyŏŏr, prə-/ *v.tr.* **1** obtain, esp. by care or effort; acquire (*managed to procure a copy*). **2** bring about (*procured their dismissal*). **3** (also *absol.*) obtain (people) for prostitution. ▫▫ **pro·cur·a·ble** *adj.* **pro·cu·ral** *n.* **pro·cure·ment** *n.*

pro·cur·er /prōkyŏŏrər, prə-/ *n.* a person who obtains people for prostitution.

prod /prod/ *v.* & *n.* • *v.* (**prodded, prodding**) **1** *tr.* poke with the finger or a pointed object. **2** *tr.* stimulate or goad to action. **3** *intr.* (foll. by *at*) make a prodding motion. • *n.* **1** a poke or thrust. **2** a stimulus to action. **3** a pointed instrument. ▫▫ **prod·der** *n.*

prod·i·gal /pródigəl/ *adj.* & *n.* • *adj.* **1** recklessly wasteful. **2** (foll. by *of*) lavish. • *n.* **1** a prodigal person. **2** (in full **prodigal son**) a repentant wastrel, returned wanderer, etc. ▫▫ **prod·i·gal·i·ty** /-gálitee/ *n.* **prod·i·gal·ly** *adv.*

pro·di·gious /prədíjəs/ *adj.* **1** marvelous or amazing. **2** enormous. **3** abnormal. ▫▫ **pro·di·gious·ly** *adv.* **pro·di·gious·ness** *n.*

prod·i·gy /pródijee/ *n.* (*pl.* **-ies**) **1** a person endowed with exceptional qualities or abilities, esp. a precocious child. **2** a marvelous thing, esp. one out of the ordinary course of nature. **3** (foll. by *of*) a wonderful example (of a quality).

pro·duce *v.* & *n.* • *v.tr.* /prədŏŏs, -dyŏŏs/ **1** bring forward for consideration, inspection, or use (*will produce evidence*). **2** manufacture (goods) from raw materials, etc. **3** bear or yield (offspring, fruit, a harvest, etc.). **4** bring into existence. **5** cause or bring about (a reaction, sensation, etc.). **6** *Geom.* extend or continue (a line). **7** **a** bring (a play, performer, book, etc.) before the public. **b** supervise the production of (a movie, broadcast, etc.). • *n.* /pródŏŏs, -dyŏŏs, prṓ-/ **1** **a** what is produced, esp. agricultural products. **b** fruits and vegetables collectively. **2** (often foll. by *of*) a result (of labor, efforts, etc.). **3** a yield, esp. in the assay of ore. ▫▫ **pro·duc·i·ble** /-sib'l/ *adj.* **pro·duc·i·bil·i·ty** *n.*

pro·duc·er /prədŏŏsər, -dyŏŏ-/ *n.* **1** **a** *Econ.* a person who produces goods or commodities. **b** a person who or thing which produces something or someone. **2** **a** a person generally responsible for the production of a movie, play, or radio or television program (apart from the direction of the acting). **b** *Brit.* the director of a play or broadcast program.

prod·uct /pródukt/ *n.* **1** a thing or substance produced by natural process or manufacture. **2** a result (*the product of their labors*). **3** *Math.* a quantity obtained by multiplying quantities together.

pro·duc·tion /prədúkshən/ *n.* **1** the act or an instance of producing; the process of being produced. **2** the process of being manufactured, esp. in large quantities (*go into production*). **3** a total yield. **4** a thing produced, esp. a literary or artistic work, a movie, broadcast, play, etc. ▫▫ **pro·duc·tion·al** *adj.*

pro·duc·tive /prədúktiv/ *adj.* **1** of or engaged in the production of goods. **2** **a** producing much (*productive soil; a productive writer*). **b** (of the mind) inventive; creative. **3** *Econ.* producing commodities of exchangeable value (*productive labor*). **4** (foll. by *of*) producing or giving rise to (*productive of great annoyance*). ▫▫ **pro·duc·tive·ly** *adv.* **pro·duc·tive·ness** *n.*

pro·duc·tiv·i·ty /próduktívitee, prṓ-/ *n.* **1** the capacity to produce. **2** the quality or state of being productive. **3** the effectiveness of productive effort, esp. in industry. **4** production per unit of effort.

prod·uct place·ment *n.* a practice in which companies pay for their products to be featured in movies and television programs.

pro·em /prṓim/ *n.* a preface or preamble to a book or speech. ▫▫ **pro·e·mi·al** /prōéemeeəl/ *adj.*

Prof. *abbr.* Professor.

prof /prof/ *n. colloq.* a professor.

pro·fane /prōfáyn, prə-/ *adj.* **1** secular rather than religious. **2** **a** irreverent; blasphemous. **b** vulgar; obscene. **3** not initiated into religious rites or any esoteric knowledge. ▫▫ **pro·fane·ly** *adv.* **pro·fane·ness** *n.*

pro·fan·i·ty /prōfánitee, prə-/ *n.* (*pl.* **-ies**) **1** a profane act. **2** profane language; blasphemy.

pro·fess /prəfés, prō-/ *v.* **1** *tr.* claim openly to have (a quality or feeling). **2** *tr.* (foll. by *to* + infin.) pretend. **3** *tr.* (often foll. by *that* + clause; also *refl.*) declare (*profess ignorance; professed herself satisfied*). **4** *tr.* affirm one's faith in or allegiance to.

pro·fessed /prəfést, prō-/ *adj.* **1** self-acknowledged (*a professed Christian*). **2** alleged; ostensible. **3** claiming to be duly qualified. **4** (of a monk or nun) having taken the vows of a religious order. ▫▫ **pro·fess·ed·ly** /-fésidlee/ *adv.* (in senses 1, 2).

pro·fes·sion /prəféshən/ *n.* **1** a vocation or calling, esp. one that involves some branch of advanced learning or science (*the medical profession*). **2** a body of people engaged in a profession. **3** a declaration or avowal. **4** a declaration of belief in a religion. ▫ **the oldest profession** prostitution.

pro·fes·sion·al /prəféshənəl/ *adj.* & *n.* • *adj.* **1** of or belonging to or connected with a profession. **2** **a** having or showing the skill of a professional; competent. **b** worthy of a professional (*professional conduct*). **3** engaged in a specified activity as one's main paid occupation (cf. AMATEUR) (*a professional boxer*). **4** *derog.* engaged in a specified activity

P

regarded with disfavor (*a professional agitator*). ● *n.* a professional person. ▫▫ **pro·fes·sion·al·ly** *adv.*

pro·fes·sion·al·ism /prəféshənəlizəm/ *n.* the qualities or typical features of a profession or of professionals, esp. competence, skill, etc. ▫▫ **pro·fes·sion·al·ize** *v.tr.*

pro·fes·sor /prəfésər/ *n.* **1 a** (often as a title) a university academic of the highest rank. **b** a university teacher. **c** a teacher of some specific art, sport, or skill. **2** a person who professes a religion. ▫▫ **pro·fes·sor·ate** /-rət/ *n.* **pro·fes·so·ri·al** /prófisáwreeəl/ *adj.* **pro·fes·so·ri·al·ly** *adv.* **pro·fes·so·ri·ate** /-fisáwreeət/ *n.* **pro·fes·sor·ship** *n.*

prof·fer /prófər/ *v.* & *n.* ● *v.tr.* (esp. as **proffered** *adj.*) offer (a gift, services, a hand, etc.). ● *n.* an offer or proposal.

pro·fi·cient /prəfishənt/ *adj.* & *n.* ● *adj.* (often foll. by *in, at*) adept; expert. ● *n.* a person who is proficient. ▫▫ **pro·fi·cien·cy** /-shənsee/ *n.* **pro·fi·cient·ly** *adv.*

pro·file /prṓfīl/ *n.* & *v.* ● *n.* **1 a** an outline (esp. of a human face) as seen from one side. **b** a representation of this. **2 a** a short biographical or character sketch. **b** a report, esp. one written by a teacher on a pupil's academic and social progress. **3** *Statistics* a representation by a graph or chart of information (esp. on certain characteristics) recorded in a quantified form. **4** a characteristic personal manner or attitude. **5** a vertical cross section of a structure. **6** a flat outline piece of scenery on stage. ● *v.tr.* **1** represent in profile. **2** give a profile to. **3** write a profile about. ▫ **in profile** as seen from one side. **keep a low profile** remain inconspicuous. ▫▫ **pro·fil·er** *n.* **pro·fil·ist** *n.*

prof·it /prófit/ *n.* & *v.* ● *n.* **1** an advantage or benefit. **2** financial gain; excess of returns over expenditures. ● *v.* (**profited, profiting**) **1** *tr.* (also *absol.*) be beneficial to. **2** *intr.* obtain an advantage or benefit (*profited by the experience*). **3** *intr.* make a profit. ▫ **at a profit** with financial gain. ▫▫ **prof·it·less** *adj.*

prof·it·a·ble /prófitəbəl/ *adj.* **1** yielding profit; lucrative. **2** beneficial; useful. ▫▫ **prof·it·a·bil·i·ty** /-bilitee/ *n.* **prof·it·a·ble·ness** *n.* **prof·it·a·bly** *adv.*

prof·it·eer /prófitéer/ *v.* & *n.* ● *v.intr.* make or seek to make excessive profits, esp. illegally or in black market conditions. ● *n.* a person who profiteers.

P

pro·fit·er·ole /prəfitərōl/ *n.* a small hollow pastry usu. filled with cream and covered with chocolate sauce.

prof·it mar·gin *n.* the profit remaining in a business after costs have been deducted.

prof·it shar·ing *n* the sharing of profits esp. between employer and employees.

prof·li·gate /prófligət/ *adj.* & *n.* ● *adj.* **1** licentious; dissolute. **2** recklessly extravagant. ● *n.* a profligate person. ▫▫ **prof·li·ga·cy** /-gəsee/ *n.* **prof·li·gate·ly** *adv.*

pro for·ma /prō fáwrmə/ *adv., adj.,* & *n.* ● *adv.* & *adj.* as or being a matter of form; for the sake of form. ● *n.* (in full **pro-forma invoice**) an invoice sent in advance of goods supplied.

pro·found /prəfównd, prō-/ *adj.* (**profounder, profoundest**) **1 a** having or showing great knowledge or insight (*a profound treatise*). **b** demanding deep study or thought (*profound doctrines*). **2** (of a state or quality) deep; intense; unqualified (*a profound sleep*; *profound indifference*). **3** at or extending to a great depth (*profound crevasses*). **4** coming from a great depth (*a profound sigh*). **5** (of a disease) deep-seated. ▫▫ **pro·found·ly** *adv.* **pro·found·ness** *n.* **pro·fun·di·ty** /-fúnditee/ *n.* (*pl.* **-ies**).

pro·fuse /prəfyṓos, prō-/ *adj.* **1** (often foll. by *in, of*) lavish; extravagant (*was profuse in her generosity*). **2** (of a thing) exuberantly plentiful; abundant (*profuse bleeding*). ▫▫ **pro·fuse·ly** *adv.* **pro·fuse·ness** *n.* **pro·fu·sion** /-fyṓozhən/ *n.*

pro·gen·i·tive /prōjénitiv/ *adj.* capable of or connected with the production of offspring.

pro·gen·i·tor /prōjénitər/ *n.* **1** the ancestor of a person, animal, or plant. **2** a political or intellectual predecessor. **3** the origin of a copy. ▫▫ **pro·gen·i·to·ri·al** /-táwreeəl/ *adj.* **pro·gen·i·tor·ship** *n.*

prog·e·ny /prójinee/ *n.* **1** the offspring of a person or other organism. **2** a descendant or descendants. **3** an outcome or issue.

pro·ges·ter·one /prōjéstərōn/ *n.* a steroid hormone released by the corpus luteum which stimulates the preparation of the uterus for pregnancy.

pro·ges·to·gen /prōjéstəjin/ *n.* **1** any of a group of steroid hormones (including progesterone) that maintain pregnancy and prevent further ovulation during it. **2** a similar hormone produced synthetically.

prog·na·thous /prognáythəs, prógnəthəs/ *adj.* **1** having a projecting jaw. **2** (of a jaw) projecting. ▫▫ **prog·nath·ic** /prognáthik/ *adj.* **prog·na·thism** *n.*

prog·no·sis /prognṓsis/ *n.* (*pl.* **prognoses** /-seez/) **1** a forecast; a prognostication. **2** a forecast of the course of a disease.

prog·nos·tic /prognóstik/ *n.* & *adj.* ● *n.* **1** (often foll. by *of*) an advance indication or omen, esp. of the course of a disease, etc. **2** a prediction; a forecast. ● *adj.* foretelling; predictive (*prognostic of a good result*). ▫▫ **prog·nos·ti·cal·ly** *adv.*

prog·nos·ti·cate /prognóstikayt/ *v.tr.* **1** (often foll. by *that* + clause) foretell; foresee; prophesy. **2** (of a thing) betoken; indicate (future events, etc.). ▫▫ **prog·nos·ti·ca·ble** /-kəbəl/ *adj.* **prog·nos·ti·ca·tion** *n.* **prog·nos·ti·ca·tive** /-kətiv/ *adj.* **prog·nos·ti·ca·tor** *n.* **prog·nos·ti·ca·to·ry** /-kətawree/ *adj.*

pro·gram /prṓgram, -grəm/ *n.* & *v.* (*Brit.* **programme**) ● *n.* **1** a usu. printed list of a series of events, performers, etc., at a public function, etc. **2** a radio or television broadcast. **3** a plan of future events (*the program is dinner and an early night*). **4** a course or series of studies, lectures, etc.; a syllabus. **5** a series of coded instructions to control the operation of a computer or other machine. ● *v.tr.* (**programmed, programming**; also **programed, programing**) **1** make a program or definite plan of. **2** express (a problem) or instruct (a computer) by means of a program. ▫▫ **pro·gram·mable** *adj.* **pro·gram·ma·bil·i·ty** /-gramәbilitee/ *n.* **pro·gram·mat·ic** /-grəmátik/ *adj.* **pro·gram·mat·i·cal·ly** /-grəmátiklee/ *adv.* **pro·gram·mer, pro·gram·er** *n.*

pro·gress *n.* & *v.* ● *n.* /prógres/ **1** forward or onward movement toward a destination. **2** advance or development toward completion, betterment, etc.; improvement (*has made little progress this term*; *the progress of civilization*). **3** *Brit. archaic* a state journey or official tour, esp. by royalty. ● *v.* /prəgrés/ **1** *intr.* move or be moved forward or onward; continue (*the argument is progressing*). **2** /prəgrés/ *intr.* advance or develop toward completion, improvement, etc. (*science progresses*). **3** *tr.* cause (work, etc.) to make regular progress. ▫ **in progress** in the course of developing; going on.

pro·gres·sion /prəgréshən/ *n.* **1** the act or an instance of progressing (*a mode of progression*). **2** a succession; a series. **3** *Math.* a sequence of numbers related by some rule (see ARITHMETIC PROGRESSION, GEOMETRIC PROGRESSION). **4** *Mus.* passing from one note or chord to another. ▫▫ **pro·gres·sion·al** *adj.*

pro·gres·sive /prəgrésiv/ *adj.* & *n.* ● *adj.* **1** moving forward (*progressive motion*). **2** proceeding step-by-step; cumulative (*progressive drug use*). **3 a** (of a political party, government, etc.) favoring or implementing rapid progress or social reform. **b** modern; efficient (*this is a progressive company*). **4** (of disease, violence, etc.) increasing in severity or extent. **5** (of taxation) at rates increasing with the sum taxed. **6** (of a card game, dance, etc.) with periodic changes of partners. **7** *Gram.* (of an aspect) expressing an action in progress, e.g., *am writing, was writing*. **8** (of education) informal and without strict discipline, stressing individual needs. ● *n.* (also **Progressive**) an advocate of progressive political policies. ▫▫ **pro·gres·sive·ly** *adv.* **pro·gres·sive·ness** *n.* **pro·gres·siv·ism** *n.* **pro·gres·siv·ist** *n.* & *adj.*

prog·ress re·port *n.* an account of progress made.

pro·hib·it /prōhíbit/ *v.tr.* (**prohibited, prohibiting**) (often foll. by *from* + verbal noun) **1** formally forbid, esp. by authority. **2** prevent; make impossible (*his accident prohibits him from playing football*). ▫▫ **pro·hib·it·er** *n.* **pro·hib·i·tor** *n.*

pro·hi·bi·tion /prṓhibíshən, prṓibíshən/ *n.* **1** the act or an instance of forbidding; a state of being forbidden. **2** *Law* an edict or order that forbids. **3** (usu. **Prohibition**) the period (1920–33) in the US when the manufacture and sale of alcoholic beverages was prohibited by law. ▫▫ **pro·hi·bi·tion·ar·y** *adj.* **pro·hi·bi·tion·ist** *n.*

pro·hib·i·tive /prōhíbitiv/ *adj.* **1** prohibiting. **2** (of prices, taxes, etc.) so high as to prevent purchase, use, abuse, etc. (*published at a prohibitive price*). ▫▫ **pro·hib·i·tive·ly** *adv.* **pro·hib·i·tive·ness** *n.* **pro·hib·i·to·ry** *adj.*

pro·ject *n.* & *v.* ● *n.* /prójekt/ **1** a plan; a scheme. **2** a planned undertaking. **3** a usu. long-term task undertaken by a student or group of students to be submitted for grading. **4** (often *pl.) a housing development, esp.* for low-income residents. ● *v.* /prəjékt/ **1** *tr.* plan or contrive (a course of action, scheme, etc.). **2** *intr.* protrude; jut out. **3** *tr.* throw; cast; impel. **4** *tr.* extrapolate (results, etc.) to a future time; forecast (*I project that we will produce two million next year*). **5** *tr.* cause (light, shadow, images, etc.) to fall on a surface, screen, etc. **6** *tr.* cause (a sound, esp. the voice) to be heard at a distance. **7** *tr.* (often *refl.* or *absol.*) express or promote (oneself or an image) forcefully or effectively. **8** *tr. Geom.* **a** draw straight lines from a center or parallel lines through every point of (a given figure) to produce a corresponding figure on a surface or a line by intersecting it. **b** draw (such lines). **c** produce (such a corresponding figure). **9** *tr.* make a projection of (the Earth, sky, etc.). **10** *tr. Psychol.* **a** (also *absol.*) attribute (an emotion, etc.) to an external object or person, esp. unconsciously. **b** (*refl.*) project (oneself) into another's feelings, the future, etc.

pro·jec·tile /prəjéktəl, -tīl/ *n.* & *adj.* ● *n.* **1** a missile, esp. fired by a rocket. **2** a bullet, shell, etc., fired from a gun. **3** any object thrown as a weapon. ● *adj.* **1** capable of being projected by force, esp. from a gun. **2** projecting or impelling.

pro·jec·tion /prəjékshən/ *n.* **1** the act or an instance of projecting; the process of being projected. **2** a thing that projects or obtrudes. **3** the presentation of an image, etc., on a surface or screen. **4 a** a forecast or estimate based on present trends. **b** this process. **5 a** a mental image or preoccupation viewed as an objective reality. **b** the unconscious transfer of one's own impressions or feelings to external objects or persons. **6** *Geom.* the act or an instance of projecting a figure. **7** the representation on a plane surface of any part of the surface of the Earth or a celestial sphere (*Mercator projection*). ▷ AZIMUTHAL PROJECTION, MERCATOR PROJECTION. ▫▫ **pro·jec·tion·ist** *n.* (in sense 3).

pro·jec·tive /prəjéktiv/ *adj.* **1** *Geom.* **a** relating to or derived by projection. **b** (of a property of a figure) unchanged by projection. **2** *Psychol.* mentally projecting or projected (*a projective imagination*). ▫▫ **pro·jec·tive·ly** *adv.*

pro·jec·tor /prəjéktər/ *n.* **1 a** ► an apparatus containing a source of light and a system of lenses for projecting slides or movies onto a screen. **b** an apparatus for projecting rays of light. **2** a person who forms or promotes a project. **3** *archaic* a promoter of speculative companies.

pro·kar·y·ote /prōkáreeōt/ *n.* (also **procaryote**) an organism in which the chromosomes are not separated from the cytoplasm by a membrane; a bacterium (cf. EUKARYOTE). ▫▫ **pro·kar·y·o·tic** /-reeótik/ *adj.*

pro·lac·tin /prōláktin/ *n.* a hormone released from the anterior pituitary gland that stimulates milk production after childbirth.

pro·lapse /prōlaps/ *n. & v.* ● *n.* (also **pro·lap·sus** /-lápsəs/) **1** the forward or downward displacement of a part or organ. **2** the prolapsed part or organ, esp. the womb or rectum. ● *v.intr.* undergo prolapse.

prole /prōl/ *adj. & n. derog. colloq.* ● *adj.* proletarian. ● *n.* a proletarian.

pro·lep·sis /prōlépsis/ *n.* (*pl.* **prolepses** /-seez/) **1** the anticipation and answering of possible objections in rhetorical speech. **2** anticipation. **3** the representation of a thing as existing before it actually does or did so, as in *he was a dead man when he entered.* **4** *Gram.* the anticipatory use of adjectives, as in *paint the town red.* ○○ **pro·lep·tic** *adj.*

pro·le·tar·i·an /prōlitáireeən/ *adj. & n.* ● *adj.* of or concerning the proletariat. ● *n.* a member of the proletariat. ○○ **pro·le·tar·i·an·ism** *n.* **pro·le·tari·an·ize** *v.tr.*

pro·le·tar·i·at /prōlitáireeət/ *n.* (also **pro·le·tar·i·ate**) **1 a** *Econ.* wage earners collectively, esp. those without capital and dependent on selling their labor. **b** esp. *derog.* the lowest class of the community, esp. when considered as uncultured. **2** *Rom.Hist.* the lowest class of citizens.

pro-life /prōlíf/ *adj.* opposing abortion. ○○ **pro-lif·er** *n.*

pro·lif·er·ate /prəlífərayt/ *v.* **1** *intr.* reproduce; increase rapidly in numbers; grow by multiplication. **2** *tr.* produce (cells, etc.) rapidly. ○○ **pro·lif·er·a·tion** /-fəráyshən/ *n.* **pro·lif·er·a·tive** /-rətiv/ *adj.*

pro·lif·er·ous /prəlífərəs/ *adj.* **1** (of a plant) producing many leaf or flower buds; growing luxuriantly. **2** growing or multiplying by budding. **3** spreading by proliferation.

pro·lif·ic /prəlífik/ *adj.* **1** producing many offspring or much output. **2** (often foll. by *of*) abundantly productive. **3** (often foll. by *in*) abounding; copious. ○○ **pro·lif·i·ca·cy** *n.* **pro·lif·i·cal·ly** *adv.* **pro·lif·ic·ness** *n.*

pro·lix /prōliks, prōliks/ *adj.* (of speech, writing, etc.) lengthy; tedious. ○○ **pro·lix·i·ty** /-líksitee/ *n.* **pro·lix·ly** *adv.*

pro·logue /prōlawg, -log/ *n. & v.* (also **pro·log**) ● *n.* **1 a** a preliminary speech, poem, etc., esp. introducing a play (cf. EPILOGUE). **b** the actor speaking the prologue. **2** (usu. foll. by *to*) any act or event serving as an introduction. ● *v.tr.* (**prologues, prologued, prologuing**) introduce with or provide with a prologue.

pro·long /prəláwng, -lóng/ *v.tr.* **1** extend (an action, condition, etc.) in time or space. **2** lengthen the pronunciation of (a syllable, etc.). **3** (as **prolonged** *adj.*) lengthy, esp. tediously so. ○○ **pro·lon·ga·tion** *n.* **pro·long·ed·ly** /-idli/ *adv.* **pro·long·er** *n.*

prom /prom/ *n. colloq.* **1** a school or college formal dance. **2** anticipation. **3** = PROMENADE *n.* 4a.

prom·e·nade /prómənáyd, -naád/ *n. & v.* ● *n.* **1 a** walk, or sometimes a ride or drive, taken esp. for display, social intercourse, etc. **2** a school or university ball or dance. **3** a march of dancers in country dancing, etc. **4 a** *Brit.* a paved public walk along the sea front at a resort. **b** any paved public walk. ● *v.* **1** *intr.* make a promenade. **2** *tr.* lead (a person, etc.) about a place esp. for display. **3** *tr.* make a promenade through (a place).

prom·e·nade deck *n.* an upper deck on a passenger ship where passengers may promenade.

Pro·me·the·an /prəméetheeən/ *adj.* daring or inventive like Prometheus, who in Greek myth was punished for stealing fire from the gods and giving it to the human race.

pro·me·thi·um /prəméetheeəm/ *n. Chem.* a radioactive metallic element of the lanthanide series occurring in nuclear waste material. ¶ Symb.: **Pm.**

prom·i·nence /próminəns/ *n.* **1** the state of being prominent. **2** a prominent thing, esp. a jutting outcrop, mountain, etc.

prom·i·nent /próminənt/ *adj.* **1** jutting out; projecting. **2** conspicuous. **3** distinguished; important. ○○ **prom·i·nen·cy** *n.* **prom·i·nent·ly** *adv.*

pro·mis·cu·ous /prəmískyōōəs/ *adj.* **1 a** (of a person) having frequent and diverse sexual relationships, esp. transient ones. **b** (of sexual relationships) of this kind. **2** *colloq.* carelessly irregular; casual. ○○ **prom·is·cu·i·ty** /prómiskyōōitee/ *n.* **pro·mis·cu·ous·ly** *adv.* **pro·mis·cu·ous·ness** *n.*

prom·ise /prómis/ *n. & v.* ● *n.* **1** an assurance that one will or will not undertake a certain action, behavior, etc. (*a promise of help; gave a promise to be generous*). **2** a sign or signs of future achievements, good results, etc. (*a writer of great promise*). ● *v.tr.* **1** (usu. foll. by *to* + infin., or *that* + clause; also *absol.*) make (a person) a promise, esp. to do, give, or

procure (a thing) (*I promise you a fair hearing; cannot positively promise*). **2 a** afford expectations of (the discussions promise future problems; promises to be a good cook). **b** (foll. by *to* + infin.) seem likely to (*is promising to rain*). **3** *colloq.* assure; confirm (*I promise you, it will not be easy*). **4** (usu. in *passive*) esp. *archaic* betroth (*she is promised to another*). ○○ **prom·is·ee** /-séé/ *n.* esp. *Law* . **prom·is·er** *n.* **prom·is·or** *n.* esp. *Law*.

prom·ised land *n.* (prec. by *the*) **1** *Bibl.* Canaan. **2** any desired place, esp. heaven.

prom·is·ing /prómising/ *adj.* likely to turn out well; hopeful; full of promise (*a promising start*). ○○ **prom·is·ing·ly** *adv.*

prom·is·so·ry /prómisawree/ *adj.* **1** conveying or implying a promise. **2** (often foll. by *of*) full of promise.

prom·is·so·ry note *n.* a signed document containing a written promise to pay a stated sum to a specified person or the bearer at a specified date or on demand.

pro·mo /prómō/ *n. & adj. colloq.* ● *n.* (*pl.* **-os**) **1** publicity blurb or advertisement. **2** a trailer for a television program. ● *adj.* promotional.

prom·on·to·ry /prómantawree/ *n.* (*pl.* **-ies**) a point of high land jutting out into the sea, etc.; a headland.

pro·mote /prəmốt/ *v.tr.* **1** (often foll. by *to*) advance or raise (a person) to a higher office, rank, grade, etc. (*was promoted to captain*). **2** help forward; encourage; support actively (a cause, process, desired result, etc.) (*promoted women's suffrage*). **3** publicize and sell (a product). **4** attempt to ensure the passing of (a legislative act). **5** *Chess* raise (a pawn) to the rank of queen, etc., when it reaches the opponent's end of the board. ○○ **pro·mot·a·ble** *adj.* **pro·mot·a·bil·i·ty** *n.* **pro·mo·tion** /-móshən/ *n.* **pro·mo·tion·al** *adj.* **pro·mo·tive** *adj.*

pro·mot·er /prəmốtər/ *n.* **1** a person who promotes. **2** a person who finances, organizes, etc., a sporting event, theatrical production, etc. **3** a person who promotes the formation of a company, project, etc. **4** *Chem.* an additive that increases the activity of a catalyst.

prompt /prompt/ *adj., adv., v., & n.* ● *adj.* **1 a** acting with alacrity; ready. **b** made, done, etc., readily or at once (*a prompt reply*). **2 a** (of a payment) made quickly or immediately. **b** (of goods) for immediate delivery and payment. ● *adv.* punctually. ● *v.tr.* **1** (usu. foll. by *to*, or *to* + infin.) incite; urge (*prompted them to action*). **2 a** (also *absol.*) supply a forgotten word, sentence, etc., to (an actor, reciter, etc.). **b** assist (a hesitating speaker) with a suggestion. **3** give rise to; inspire (a feeling, thought, action, etc.). ● *n.* **1 a** an act of prompting. **b** a thing said to help the memory of an actor, etc. **c** = PROMPTER 2. **d** *Computing* an indication or sign on a computer screen to show that the system is waiting for input. **2** the time limit for the payment of an account, stated on a prompt note. ○○ **prompt·ing** *n.* **promp·ti·tude** *n.* **prompt·ly** *adv.* **prompt·ness** *n.*

prompt·er /prómptər/ *n.* **1** a person who prompts. **2** *Theatr.* a person seated out of sight of the audience who prompts the actors.

prom·ul·gate /prómʌlgayt/ *v.tr.* **1** make known to the public; disseminate; promote (a cause, etc.). **2** proclaim (a decree, news, etc.). ○○ **prom·ul·ga·tion** /-gáyshən/ *n.* **prom·ul·ga·tor** *n.*

prone /prōn/ *adj.* **1 a** lying face downward (cf. SUPINE). **b** lying flat; prostrate. **c** having the front part downwards, esp. the palm of the hand. **2** (usu. foll. by *to*, or *to* + infin.) disposed or liable, esp. to a bad action, condition, etc. (*is prone to bite his nails*). **3** (usu. in *comb.*) more than usually likely to suffer (*accident-prone*). ○○ **prone·ly** *adv.* **prone·ness** /prón-nis/ *n.*

prong /prong/ *n. & v.* ● *n.* each of two or more projecting pointed parts at the end of a fork, etc. ▷ TUNING FORK. ● *v.tr.* **1** pierce or stab with a fork. **2** turn up (soil) with a fork. ○○ **pronged** *adj.* (also in *comb.*).

P

PROJECTOR

Inside a film projector, light from a lamp is condensed into a strong beam. The beam shines through a rotating shutter and onto a moving strip of film. The shutter lets light through only when each picture on the film is in the right position. The images are flashed onto a screen in such rapid succession that the picture appears to be moving continuously.

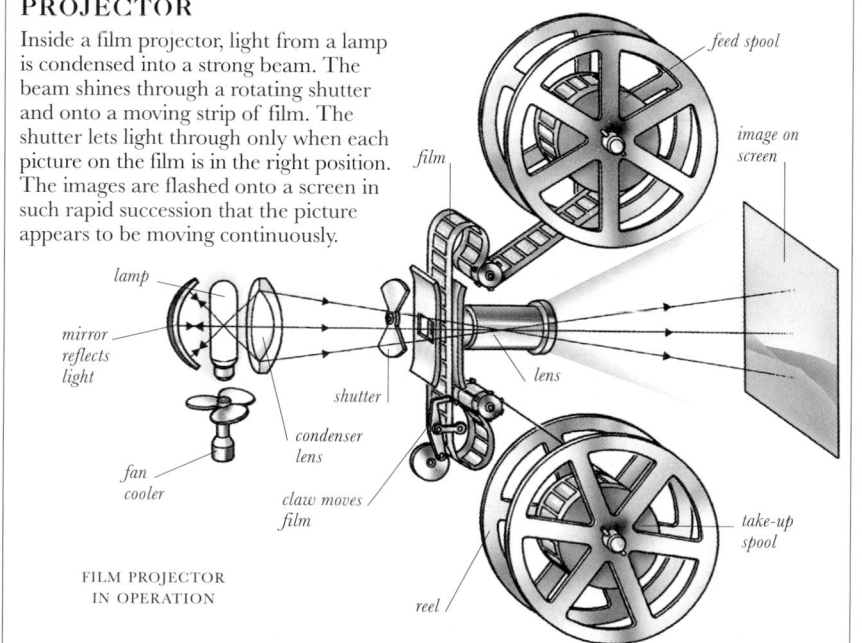

feed spool
image on screen
film
lamp
mirror reflects light
shutter
lens
condenser lens
fan cooler
claw moves film
take-up spool
reel

FILM PROJECTOR
IN OPERATION

pronghorn /prónghawrn/ *n.* ► a N. American deerlike ruminant, *Antilocapra americana*, the male of which has horns with forward-pointing prongs.

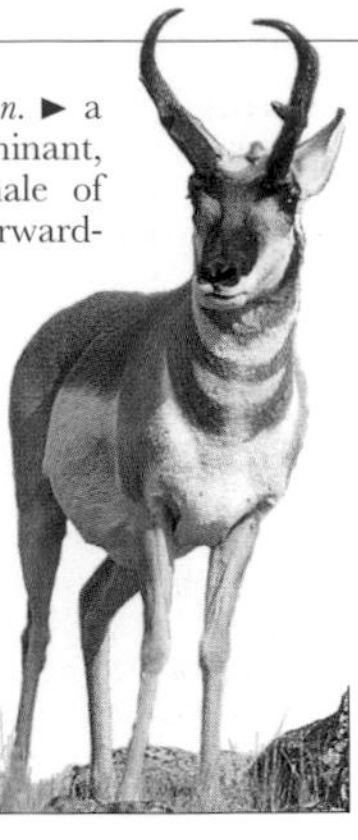

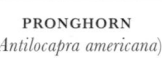

PRONGHORN
(*Antilocapra americana*)

pro·nom·i·nal /prōnómiəl/ *adj.* of, concerning, or being, a pronoun. ▫▫ **pro·nom·i·nal·ize** *v.tr.* **pro·nom·i·nal·ly** *adv.*

pro·noun /prṓnown/ *n.* a word used instead of and to indicate a noun already mentioned or known, esp. to avoid repetition (e.g., *we, their, this, ourselves*).

pro·nounce /prənówns/ *v.* **1** *tr.* (also *absol.*) utter or speak (words, sounds, etc.) in a certain way. **2** *tr.* **a** utter or deliver (a judgment, sentence, curse, etc.) formally or solemnly. **b** proclaim or announce officially (*I pronounce you husband and wife*). **3** *tr.* state or declare, as being one's opinion (*the apples were pronounced excellent*). **4** *intr.* (usu. foll. by *on, for, against, in favor of*) pass judgment; give one's opinion (*pronounced for the defendant*). ▫▫ **pro·nounce·a·ble** /-nównsəbəl/ *adj.* **pro·nounce·ment** *n.* **pro·nounc·er** *n.*

pro·nounced /prənównst/ *adj.* **1** (of a word, sound, etc.) uttered. **2** strongly marked; decided (*a pronounced flavor; a pronounced limp*). ▫▫ **pro·nounc·ed·ly** /-nównsidlee/ *adv.*

pron·to /prónto̅/ *adv. colloq.* promptly; quickly.

pro·nun·ci·a·tion /prənúnseeáyshən/ *n.* **1** the way in which a word is pronounced, esp. with reference to a standard. **2** the act or an instance of pronouncing. **3** a person's way of pronouncing words, etc.

proof /pro̅o̅f/ *n., adj., & v.* ● *n.* **1** facts, evidence, argument, etc., establishing or helping to establish a fact (*proof of their honesty*). **2** *Law* the spoken or written evidence in a trial. **3** a demonstration or act of proving (*not capable of proof; in proof of my assertion*). **4** a test or trial (*the proof of the pudding is in the eating*). **5** the standard of strength of distilled alcoholic spirits. **6** *Printing* a trial impression taken from type or film, used for making corrections before final printing. **7** the stages in the resolution of a mathematical or philosophical problem. **8** each of a limited number of impressions from an engraved plate. **9** a photographic print made for selection, etc. **10** a newly issued coin struck from a polished die esp. for collectors, etc. ● *adj.* **1** impervious to penetration, ill effects, etc. (*proof against the harshest weather*). **2** (in *comb.*) able to withstand damage or destruction by a specified agent (*soundproof; childproof*). **3** being of proof alcoholic strength. **4** (of armor) of tried strength. ● *v.tr.* **1** proofread **2** make (something) proof, esp. make (fabric) waterproof. **3** make a proof of (a printed work, engraving, etc.). ▫▫ **proof·less** *adj.*

P

proof-of-pur·chase *n.* a sales receipt, product label, etc., that serves as proof that a product has been purchased.

proof pos·i·tive *n.* absolutely certain proof.

proof·read /pro̅o̅freed/ *v.tr.* (*past* and *past part.* **-read** /-red/) read (esp. printer's proofs) and mark any errors. ▫▫ **proof·read·er** *n.* **proof·read·ing** *n.*

prop[1] /prop/ *n. & v.* ● *n.* **1** a rigid support, esp. one not an integral part of the thing supported. **2** a person who supplies support, assistance, comfort, etc. ▷ RUGBY. ● *v.tr.* (**propped**, **propping**) (often foll. by *against, up*, etc.) support with or as if with a prop (*propped him against the wall; propped it up with a brick*).

prop[2] /prop/ *n. Theatr. colloq.* **1** = PROPERTY 3. **2** (in *pl.*) a property man or mistress.

prop[3] /prop/ *n. colloq.* an aircraft propeller.

prop. *abbr.* **1** proper; properly. **2** property. **3** proprietary. **4** proprietor. **5** proposition.

prop·a·gan·da /própəgándə/ *n.* **1** an organized program of publicity, selected information, etc., used to propagate a doctrine, practice, etc. **2** usu. *derog.* the information, doctrines, etc., propagated in this way.

prop·a·gan·dist /própəgándist/ *n.* a member or agent of a propaganda organization; a person who spreads propaganda. ▫▫ **prop·a·gan·dism** *n.* **prop·a·gan·dis·tic** *adj.* **prop·a·gan·dis·ti·cal·ly** *adv.* **prop·a·gan·dize** *v.intr. & tr.*

prop·a·gate /própəgayt/ **1** *tr.* **a** breed specimens of (a plant, animal, etc.) by natural processes from the parent stock. **b** (*refl.* or *absol.*) (of a plant, animal, etc.) reproduce itself. **2 a** *tr.* disseminate; spread (a statement, belief, theory, etc.). **b** *intr.* grow more widespread or numerous; spread. **3** *tr.* hand down (a quality, etc.) from one generation to another. **4** *tr.* extend the operation of; transmit (a vibration, earthquake, etc.). ▫▫ **prop·a·ga·tion** /-gáyshən/ *n.* **prop·a·ga·tive** *adj.*

prop·a·ga·tor /própəgaytər/ *n.* **1** a person or thing that propagates. **2** ▼ a small box that can be heated, used for germinating seeds or raising seedlings.

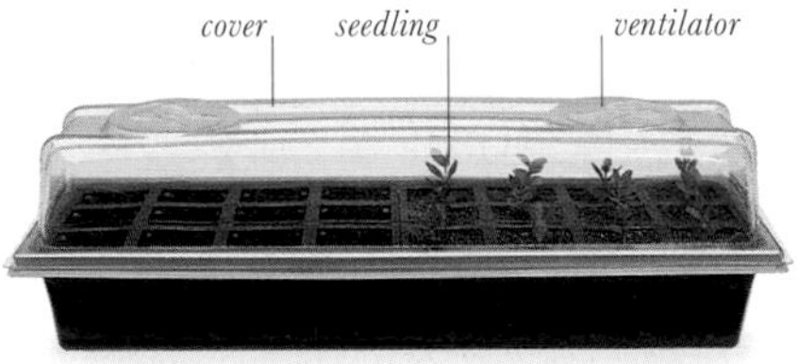

PROPAGATOR

pro·pane /prṓpayn/ *n.* a gaseous hydrocarbon of the alkane series used as bottled fuel. ▷ ALKANE. ¶ Chem. formula: C_3H_8.

pro·pel /prəpél/ *v.tr.* (**propelled**, **propelling**) **1** drive or push forward. **2** urge on; encourage.

pro·pel·lant /prəpélənt/ *n. & adj.* (also **pro·pel·lent**) ● *n.* **1** a thing that propels. **2** an explosive that fires bullets, etc., from a firearm. **3** a substance used as a reagent in a rocket engine, etc., to provide thrust. ● *adj.* propelling; capable of driving or pushing forward.

pro·pel·ler /prəpélər/ *n.* **1** a person or thing that propels. **2** a revolving shaft with blades, esp. for propelling a ship or aircraft (cf. SCREW *n.* 6). ▷ AIRCRAFT, SCREW PROPELLER

pro·pene /prṓpeen/ *n. Chem.* = PROPYLENE.

pro·pen·si·ty /prəpénsitee/ *n.* (*pl.* **-ies**) an inclination or tendency (*has a propensity for wandering*).

prop·er /própər/ *adj. & adv.* ● *adj.* **1 a** accurate; correct (*in the proper sense of the word; gave him the proper amount*). **b** fit; suitable; right (*at the proper time; do it the proper way*). **2** decent; respectable, esp. excessively so (*not quite proper*). **3** (usu. foll. by *to*) belonging or relating exclusively or distinctively; particular; special (*with the respect proper to them*). **4** (usu. placed after noun) strictly so called; real; genuine (*this is the crypt, not the cathedral proper*). **5** esp. *Brit. colloq.* thorough; complete (*had a proper row about it*). **6** (usu. placed after noun) *Heraldry* in the natural, not conventional, colors (*a peacock proper*). ● *adv. Brit. dial.* or *colloq.* (with reference to speech) in a genteel manner (*learn to talk proper*). ▫▫ **prop·er·ness** *n.*

prop·er frac·tion *n.* a fraction that is less than unity, with the numerator less than the denominator.

prop·er·ly /própərlee/ *adv.* **1** fittingly; suitably (*do it properly*). **2** accurately; correctly (*properly speaking*). **3** rightly (*he very properly refused*). **4** with decency; respectably (*behave properly*). **5** esp. *Brit. colloq.* thoroughly (*they were properly ashamed*).

prop·er noun *n.* (also **proper name**) *Gram.* a name used for an individual person, place, animal, country, title, etc., and spelled with a capital letter, e.g., Jane, London, Everest.

prop·er·tied /própərteed/ *adj.* having property, esp. land.

prop·er·ty /própərtee/ *n.* (*pl.* **-ies**) **1 a** something owned; a possession, esp. a house, land, etc. **b** *Law* the right to possession, use, etc. **c** possessions collectively, esp. real estate (*has money in property*). **2** an attribute, quality, or characteristic (*has the property of dissolving grease*). **3** a movable object used on a theater stage, in a movie, etc.

prop·er·ty tax *n.* a tax levied directly on property.

proph·e·cy /prófisee/ *n.* (*pl.* **-ies**) **1 a** a prophetic utterance, esp. Biblical. **b** a prediction of future events (*a prophecy of massive inflation*). **2** the faculty, function, or practice of prophesying (*the gift of prophecy*).

proph·e·sy /prófisī/ *v.* (**-ies, -ied**) **1** *tr.* (usu. foll. by *that, who*, etc.) foretell (an event, etc.). **2** *intr.* speak as a prophet; foretell future events. ▫▫ **proph·e·si·er** /-sīər/ *n.*

proph·et /prófit/ *n.* (*fem.* **prophetess** /-tis/) **1** a teacher or interpreter of the supposed will of God, esp. any of the Old Testament or Hebrew prophets. **2 a** a person who foretells events. **b** a person who advocates and speaks innovatively for a cause (*a prophet of the new order*). **3** (**the Prophet**) **a** Muhammad. **b** Joseph Smith, founder of the Mormons, or one of his successors. **c** (in *pl.*) the prophetic writings of the Old Testament. ▫▫ **proph·et·hood** *n.* **proph·et·ism** *n.* **proph·et·ship** *n.*

pro·phet·ic /prəfétik/ *adj.* **1** (often foll. by *of*) containing a prediction; predicting. **2** of or concerning a prophet. ▫▫ **pro·phet·i·cal** *adj.* **pro·phet·i·cal·ly** *adv.* **pro·phet·i·cism** /-sizəm/ *n.*

pro·phy·lac·tic /prṓfiláktik, próf-/ *adj. & n.* ● *adj.* tending to prevent disease. ● *n.* **1** a preventive medicine or course of action. **2** a condom.

pro·phy·lax·is /prṓfiláksis, próf-/ *n.* (*pl.* **prophylaxes** /-seez/) preventive treatment against disease.

pro·pin·qui·ty /prəpíngkwitee/ *n.* **1** nearness in space; proximity. **2** close kinship. **3** similarity.

pro·pi·ti·ate /prōpísheeayt/ *v.tr.* appease (an offended person, etc.). ▫▫ **pro·pi·ti·a·tor** *n.*

pro·pi·ti·a·tion /prōpísheeáyshən/ *n.* **1** appeasement. **2** *Bibl.* atonement, esp. Christ's.

pro·pi·ti·a·to·ry /prōpísheeətawree, -píshə-/ *adj.* serving or intended to propitiate (*a propitiatory smile*). ▫▫ **pro·pi·ti·a·to·ri·ly** *adv.*

pro·pi·tious /prəpíshəs/ *adj.* **1** (of an omen, etc.) favorable. **2** (often foll. by *for, to*) (of the weather, an occasion, etc.) suitable. **3** well-disposed (*the fates were propitious*). ▫▫ **pro·pi·tious·ly** *adv.* **pro·pi·tious·ness** *n.*

prop·jet /própjet/ *n.* a jet airplane powered by turboprops.

pro·po·nent /prəpṓnənt/ *n. & adj.* ● *n.* a person advocating a motion, theory, or proposal. ● *adj.* proposing or advocating a theory, etc.

pro·por·tion /prəpáwrshən/ *n. & v.* ● *n.* **1 a** a comparative part or share (*a large proportion of the profits*). **b** a comparative ratio (*the proportion of births to deaths*). **2** the correct or pleasing relation of things or parts of a thing (*the house has fine proportions; exaggerated out of all proportion*). **3** (in *pl.*) dimensions; size (*large proportions*). **4** *Math.* **a** an equality of ratios between two pairs of quantities, e.g., 3:5 and 9:15. **b** a set of such quantities. ● *v.tr.* (usu. foll. by *to*) make (a thing, etc.) proportionate (*must proportion the punishment to the crime*). ▫ **in proportion 1** by the same factor. **2** without exaggerating (importance, etc.) (*must get the facts in proportion*). ▫▫ **pro·por·tioned** *adj.* (also in *comb.*). **pro·por·tion·less** *adj.* **pro·por·tion·ment** *n.*

pro·por·tion·al /prəpáwrshənəl/ *adj.* in due proportion; comparable (*a proportional increase in the expense; resentment proportional to his injuries*). ▫▫ **pro·por·tion·al·i·ty** /-nálitee/ *n.* **pro·por·tion·al·ly** *adv.*

pro·por·tion·al re·pre·sen·ta·tion *n.* an electoral system in which all parties gain seats in proportion to the number of votes cast for them.

pro·por·tion·ate /prəpáwrshənət/ *adj.* = PROPORTIONAL. ▫▫ **pro·por·tion·ate·ly** *adv.*

pro·pos·al /prəpózəl/ *n.* **1 a** the act or an instance of proposing something. **b** a course of action, etc., so proposed (*the proposal was never carried out*). **2** an offer of marriage.

pro·pose /prəpóz/ *v.* **1** *tr.* (also *absol.*) put forward for consideration or as a plan. **2** *tr.* (usu. foll. by *to* + infin., or verbal noun) intend; purpose (*propose to open a restaurant*). **3** *intr.* (usu. foll. by *to*) make an offer of marriage. **4** *tr.* nominate (a person) as a member of a society, for an office, etc. **5** *tr.* offer (a person's health, a person, etc.) as a subject for a toast. □□ **pro·pos·er** *n.*

prop·o·si·tion /própəzíshən/ *n. & v.* ● *n.* **1** a statement or assertion. **2** a scheme proposed; a proposal. **3** *Logic* a statement consisting of subject and predicate that is subject to proof or disproof. **4** *colloq.* a problem, opponent, prospect, etc., that is to be dealt with (*a difficult proposition*). **5** *Math.* a formal statement of a theorem or problem, often including the demonstration. **6 a** an enterprise, etc., with regard to its likelihood of commercial, etc., success. **b** a person regarded similarly. **7** *colloq.* a sexual proposal. ● *v.tr. colloq.* make a proposal (esp. of sexual intercourse) to. □ **not a proposition** unlikely to succeed. □□ **prop·o·si·tion·al** *adj.*

pro·pound /prəpównd/ *v.tr.* offer for consideration; propose. □□ **pro·pound·er** *n.*

pro·pri·e·tar·y /prəpríəteree/ *adj.* **1 a** of, holding, or concerning property (*the proprietary classes*). **b** of or relating to a proprietor (*proprietary rights*). **2** held in private ownership.

pro·pri·e·tar·y name *n.* a name of a product, etc., registered by its owner as a trademark and not usable by another without permission.

pro·pri·e·tor /prəpríətər/ *n.* (*fem.* **proprietress**) **1** a holder of property. **2** the owner of a business, etc., esp. of a hotel. □□ **pro·pri·e·to·ri·al** /-táwreeəl/ *adj.* **pro·pri·e·to·ri·al·ly** /-táwreeəlee/ *adv.* **pro·pri·e·tor·ship** *n.*

pro·pri·e·ty /prəprí-itee/ *n.* (*pl.* **-ies**) **1** fitness; rightness (*doubt the propriety of refusing him*). **2** correctness of behavior or morals (*highest standards of propriety*). **3** (in *pl.*) the details or rules of correct conduct (*must observe the proprieties*).

pro·pul·sion /prəpúlshən/ *n.* **1** the act or an instance of driving or pushing forward. **2** an impelling influence. □□ **pro·pul·sive** /-púlsiv/ *adj.*

pro·pyl /própil/ *n. Chem.* the univalent radical of propane. ¶ *Chem.* formula: C_3H_7.

pro·pyl·ene /própəleen/ *n. Chem.* a gaseous hydrocarbon of the alkene series used in the manufacture of chemicals. ¶ *Chem.* formula: C_3H_6.

pro ra·ta /prō ráytə, ráátə/ *adj. & adv.* ● *adj.* proportional. ● *adv.* proportionally.

pro·rate /próráyt/ *v.tr.* allocate or distribute pro rata. □□ **pro·ra·tion** *n.*

pro·rogue /prōróg/ *v.* (**prorogues, prorogued, proroguing**) **1** *tr.* discontinue the meetings of (a parliament, etc.) without dissolving it. **2** *intr.* (of a parliament, etc.) be prorogued. □□ **pro·ro·ga·tion** /prórəgáyshən/ *n.*

pro·sa·ic /prōzáyik/ *adj.* like prose; lacking poetic beauty. **2** unromantic; dull; commonplace (*took a prosaic view of life*). □□ **pro·sa·i·cal·ly** *adv.* **pro·sa·ic·ness** *n.*

pros and cons *n.pl.* reasons or considerations for and against a proposition, etc.

pro·sce·ni·um /prəsseeneeəm/ *n.* (*pl.* **prosceniums** or **proscenia** /-neeə/) **1** the part of the stage in front of the drop or curtain, usu. with the enclosing arch. ▷ THEATER. **2** the stage of an ancient theater.

pro·sciut·to /prōshoōtō/ *n.* (*pl.* **-os**) specially cured ham, usu. sliced thin and used as an hors d'oeuvre.

pro·scribe /prəskríb/ *v.tr.* **1** banish; exile (*proscribed from the club*). **2** put (a person) outside the protection of the law. **3** reject or denounce (a practice, etc.) as dangerous, etc. □□ **pro·scrip·tion** /-skrípshən/ *n.* **pro·scrip·tive** /-skríptiv/ *adj.*

prose /prōz/ *n. & v.* ● *n.* **1** the ordinary form of the

written or spoken language (cf. POETRY, VERSE 1) (*Milton's prose works*). **2** a passage of prose, esp. for translation into a foreign language. **3** a tedious speech or conversation. ● *v.* **1** *intr.* (usu. foll. by *about, away*, etc.) talk tediously (*was prosing away about his dog*). **2** *tr.* turn (a poem, etc.) into prose. **3** *tr.* write prose. □□ **pros·er** *n.*

pros·e·cute /prósikyoōt/ *v.tr.* **1** (also *absol.*) **a** institute legal proceedings against (a person). **b** institute a prosecution with reference to (a claim, crime, etc.) (*decided not to prosecute*). **2** follow up; pursue (an inquiry, studies, etc.). **3** carry on (a trade, pursuit, etc.). □□ **pros·e·cut·a·ble** *adj.*

pros·e·cu·tion /prósikyoōshən/ *n.* **1 a** the institution and carrying on of a criminal charge in a court. **b** the carrying on of legal proceedings against a person. **c** the prosecuting party in a court case (*the prosecution denied this*). **2** the act or an instance of prosecuting (*met her in the prosecution of his hobby*).

pros·e·cu·tor /prósikyoōtər/ *n.* (also **pros·e·cut·ing at·tor·ney**) a person who prosecutes, esp. in a criminal court. □□ **pros·e·cu·to·ri·al** /-táwreeəl/ *adj.*

pros·e·lyte /prósilīt/ *n. & v.* **1** a person converted, esp. recently, from one opinion, creed, party, etc., to another. **2** a convert to Judaism. ● *v.tr.* = PROSELYTIZE. □□ **pros·e·lyt·ism** /-səlítizəm/ *n.*

pros·e·lyt·ize /prósilitīz/ *v.tr.* (also *absol.*) convert (a person or people) from one belief, etc., to another, esp. habitually. □□ **pros·e·lyt·iz·er** *n.*

pro·si·fy /prózifī/ *v.* (**-ies, -ied**) **1** *tr.* turn into prose. **2** *intr.* make prosaic. **3** *intr.* write prose.

pro·sim·i·an /prōsímeeən/ *Zool. n. & adj.* ● *n.* ▼ a primitive primate of the suborder Prosimii, which includes lemurs, lorises, galagos, and tarsiers. ▷ PRIMATE. ● *adj.* of or relating to this suborder.

PROSIMIAN:
GREATER BUSHBABY
(*Galago crassicaudatus*)

pros·o·dy /prósədee/ *n.* **1** the theory and practice of versification; the laws of meter. **2** the study of speech rhythms. □□ **pro·sod·ic** /prəsódik/ *adj.* **pros·o·dist** *n.*

pros·pect /próspekt/ *n. & v.* ● *n.* **1 a** (often in *pl.*) an expectation; esp. of success in a career, etc. (*his prospects were brilliant; offers a gloomy prospect; no prospect of success*). **b** something one has to look forward to (*don't relish the prospect of meeting him*). **2** an extensive view of landscape, etc. (*a striking prospect*). **3** a mental picture (*a new prospect in his mind*). **4 a** a place likely to yield mineral deposits. **b** a sample of ore for testing. **c** the resulting yield. **5** a possible or probable customer, subscriber, etc. ● *v.* **1** *intr.* (usu. foll. by *for*) **a** explore a region for gold, etc. **b** look out for or search for something. **2** *tr.* **a** explore (a region) for gold, etc. **b** work (a mine) experimentally. **c** (of a mine) promise (a specified yield). □ **in prospect 1** in sight; within view. **2** within the range of expectation, likely. □□ **pros·pect·less** *adj.* **pros·pec·tor** *n.*

pro·spec·tive /prəspéktiv/ *adj.* **1** concerned with or applying to the future (*implies a prospective obligation*) (cf. RETROSPECTIVE). **2** some day to be; expected; future (*prospective bridegroom*). □□ **pro·spec·tive·ly** *adv.* **pro·spec·tive·ness** *n.*

pro·spec·tus /prəspéktəs/ *n.* a printed document

advertising or describing a school, commercial enterprise, forthcoming book, etc.

pros·per /próspər/ *v.* **1** *intr.* succeed; thrive (*nothing he touches prospers*). **2** *tr.* make successful (*Heaven prosper him*).

pros·per·i·ty /prospéritee/ *n.* a state of being prosperous; wealth or success.

pros·per·ous /próspərəs/ *adj.* **1** successful; rich (*a prosperous merchant*). **2** flourishing; thriving (*a prosperous enterprise*). **3** auspicious (*a prosperous wind*). □□ **pros·per·ous·ly** *adv.* **pros·per·ous·ness** *n.*

pros·ta·glan·din /próstəglándin/ *n.* any of a group of hormonelike substances causing contraction of the muscles in mammalian (esp. uterine) tissues, etc.

pros·tate /próstayt/ *n.* (in full **prostate gland**) a gland surrounding the neck of the bladder in male mammals and releasing a fluid forming part of the semen. ▷ URINARY SYSTEM. □□ **pros·tat·ic** /-státik/ *adj.*

pros·the·sis /próstheesis/ *n.* (*pl.* **prostheses** /-seez/) an artificial part supplied to replace a missing body part, e.g., a false breast, leg, tooth, etc. □□ **pros·thet·ic** /-thétik/ *adj.* **pros·thet·i·cal·ly** *adv.*

pros·thet·ics /prosthétiks/ *n.pl.* (usu. treated as *sing.*) the branch of medicine or dentistry supplying and fitting prostheses.

pros·ti·tute /próstitoōt, -tyoōt/ *n. & v.* ● *n.* **1 a** a woman who engages in sexual activity for payment. **b** (usu. **male prostitute**) a man or boy who engages in sexual activity, esp. with homosexual men, for payment. **2** a person who debases himself or herself for personal gain. ● *v.tr.* **1** (esp. *refl.*) make a prostitute of (esp. oneself). **2 a** misuse (one's talents, skills, etc.) for money. **b** offer (oneself, one's honor, etc.) for unworthy ends, esp. for money. □□ **pros·ti·tu·tion** /-toōshən/ *n.* **pros·ti·tu·tor** *n.*

pros·trate /próstrayt/ *adj. & v.* ● *adj.* **1 a** lying face downwards, esp. in submission. **b** lying horizontally. **2** overcome, esp. by grief, exhaustion, etc. (*prostrate with self-pity*). **3** *Bot.* growing along the ground. ● *v.tr.* **1** lay (a person, etc.) flat on the ground. **2** (*refl.*) throw (oneself) down in submission, etc. **3** (of fatigue, illness, etc.) overcome, reduce to extreme physical weakness. □□ **pros·tra·tion** /prostráyshən/ *n.*

pros·y /prózee/ *adj.* (**prosier, prosiest**) tedious; commonplace; dull (*prosy talk*). □□ **pros·i·ly** *adv.* **pros·i·ness** *n.*

Prot. *abbr.* Protestant.

pro·tag·o·nist /prōtágənist/ *n.* **1** the chief person in a drama, story, etc. **2** the leading person in a contest, etc.; a principal performer. **3** (usu. foll. by *of, for*) *disp.* an advocate or champion of a cause, course of action, etc. (*a protagonist of women's rights*).

prot·a·sis /prótəsis/ *n.* (*pl.* **protases** /-seez/) the clause expressing the condition in a conditional sentence. □□ **pro·tat·ic** /prōtátik/ *adj.*

pro·te·a /prốteeə/ *n.* any shrub of the genus *Protea*, native to S. Africa, with conelike flower heads.

pro·te·an /prốteeən, -téeən/ *adj.* **1** variable; taking many forms. **2** (of an artist, writer, etc.) versatile.

pro·te·ase /prốteeays/ *n.* any enzyme able to hydrolyze proteins and peptides.

pro·tect /prətékt/ *v.tr.* **1** (often foll. by *from, against*) keep (a person, thing, etc.) safe; defend; guard (*goggles protected her eyes from dust; guards protected the military base*). **2** *Econ.* shield (domestic industry) from competition by imposing import duties on foreign goods. **3** cover; provide funds to meet (a bill, bank draft, etc.).

pro·tec·tion /prətékshən/ *n.* **1 a** the act or an instance of protecting. **b** the state of being protected; defense (*affords protection against the weather*). **c** a thing, person, or animal that provides protection (*bought a dog as protection*). **2** (also **pro·tec·tion·ism**) *Econ.* the theory or practice of protecting domestic industries. **3** *colloq.* **a** immunity from molestation obtained by payment to orga-

P

PROTOZOAN

Most protozoans live in damp environments. They can be found in water, in the films of moisture around soil grains, and sometimes in other organisms. The majority of protozoans are solitary, but some – such as *Vorticella* – form aggregations composed of many individuals.

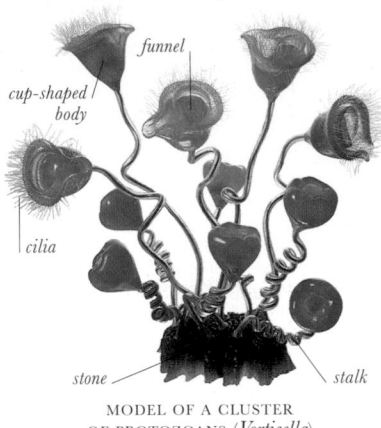

funnel

cup-shaped body

cilia

stone   *stalk*

MODEL OF A CLUSTER
OF PROTOZOANS (*Vorticella*)

P

nized criminals, etc., under threat of violence. **b** (in full **protection money**) payment, as bribes, made to police, etc., for overlooking criminal activities. **c** (in full **protection money**) the money so paid, esp. on a regular basis. **4** = SAFE-CONDUCT. □□ **pro·tec·tion·ist** *n.*

pro·tec·tive /prətéktiv/ *adj.* **1** protecting; intended or intending to protect. **2** (of a person) tending to protect in a possessive way. □□ **pro·tec·tive·ly** *adv.* **pro·tec·tive·ness** *n.*

pro·tec·tive cus·to·dy *n.* the detention of a person for his or her own protection.

pro·tec·tor /prətéktər/ *n.* (*fem.* **protectress** /-tris/) **1 a** a person who protects. **b** a guardian or patron. **2** *hist.* a regent in charge of a kingdom during the minority, absence, etc., of the sovereign. **3** (often in *comb.*) a thing or device that protects. □□ **pro·tec·tor·al** *adj.*

pro·tec·tor·ate /prətéktərət/ *n.* **1** a nation that is controlled and protected by another. **2** such a relation of one nation to another.

pro·té·gé /prótizhay, prótizháy/ *n.* (*fem.* **protégée** *pronunc.* same) a person under the protection, patronage, tutelage, etc., of another.

pro·tein /próteen/ *n.* any of a group of organic compounds composed of one or more chains of amino acids and forming an essential part of all living organisms. ▷ ALGA. □□ **pro·tein·a·ceous** /-teenáyshəs/ *adj.* **pro·tein·ic** /-téenik/ *adj.* **pro·tein·ous** /-téenəs/ *adj.*

pro tem /prō tém/ *adj. & adv. colloq.* = PRO TEMPORE.

pro tem·po·re /prō témpəree/ *adj. & adv.* for the time being.

pro·te·ol·y·sis /próteeólisis/ *n.* the splitting of proteins or peptides by the action of enzymes, esp. during the process of digestion. □□ **pro·te·o·lyt·ic** /-teeəlítik/ *adj.*

pro·test *n. & v.* ● *n.* /prótest/ **1** a statement of dissent or disapproval; a remonstrance (*made a protest*). **2** (often *attrib.*) a usu. public demonstration of objection to government, etc., policy (*marched in protest; protest demonstration*). **3** a solemn declaration. ● *v.* /prətést, prō-/ **1** *intr.* (usu. foll. by *against, at, about,* etc.) make a protest against an action, proposal, etc. **2** *tr.* (often foll. by *that* + clause; also *absol.*) affirm (one's innocence, etc.) solemnly, esp. in reply to an accusation. **3** *tr.* object to (a deci-

sion, etc.). □ **under protest** unwillingly. □□ **pro·test·er** *n.* **pro·test·ing·ly** *adv.* **pro·tes·tor** *n.*

Prot·es·tant /prótistənt/ *n. & adj.* ● *n.* a member or follower of any of the western Christian Churches that are separate from the Roman Catholic Church in accordance with the principles of the Reformation. ● *adj.* of or relating to any of the Protestant Churches or their members, etc. □□ **Prot·es·tant·ism** *n.* **Prot·es·tant·ize** *v.tr. & intr.*

prot·es·ta·tion /prótistáyshən, prōte-/ *n.* **1** a strong affirmation. **2** a protest.

proth·e·sis /próthisis/ *n.* (*pl.* **protheses** /-seez/) *Gram.* = PROSTHESIS 2. □□ **pro·thet·ic** /prəthétik/ *adj.*

pro·ti·um /próteeəm, -sheeəm/ *n.* the ordinary isotope of hydrogen as distinct from heavy hydrogen (cf. DEUTERIUM, TRITIUM). ▷ ISOTOPE.

proto- /prótō/ *comb. form* **1** original; primitive (*protoGermanic; protoSlavic*). **2** first; original (*protomartyr; protophyte*).

pro·to·col /prótəkawl, -kol/ *n. & v.* ● *n.* **1 a** official, esp. diplomatic, formality and etiquette observed on governmental or military occasions, etc. **b** the rules, formalities, etc., of any procedure, group, etc. **2** the original draft of a diplomatic document, esp. of the terms of a treaty agreed to in conference and signed by the parties. **3** a formal statement of a transaction. **4** the official formulae at the beginning and end of a charter, papal bull, etc. **5** a plan or record of experimental observation, medical treatment, etc. **6** *Computing* a set of rules governing the electronic transmission of data between computers. ● *v.* (**protocolled, protocolling**) **1** *intr.* draw up a protocol or protocols. **2** *tr.* record in a protocol.

pro·to·lan·guage /prótōlanggwij/ *n.* a language from which other languages are believed to have been derived.

pro·ton /próton/ *n. Physics* a stable elementary particle with a positive electric charge, equal in magnitude to that of an electron, and occurring in all atomic nuclei. ▷ ATOM. □□ **pro·ton·ic** /prətónik/ *adj.*

pro·to·plasm /prótəplazəm/ *n.* the material comprising the living part of a cell, consisting of a nucleus embedded in membrane-enclosed cytoplasm. □□ **pro·to·plas·mal** /-plazməl/ *adj.* **pro·to·plas·mat·ic** /-mátik/ *adj.* **pro·to·plas·mic** *adj.*

pro·to·plast /prótəplast/ *n.* the protoplasm of one cell. □□ **pro·to·plas·tic** *adj.*

pro·to·type /prótətīp/ *n.* **1** an original thing or person of which or whom copies, imitations, improved forms, representations, etc., are made. **2** a trial model or preliminary version of a vehicle, machine, etc. **3** a thing or person representative of a type; an exemplar. □□ **pro·to·typ·al** *adj.* **pro·to·typ·ic** /-típik/ *adj.* **pro·to·typ·i·cal** *adj.* **pro·to·typ·i·cal·ly** *adv.*

pro·to·zo·an /prótəzóən/ *n. & adj.* ● *n.* (also **pro·to·zo·on** /-zō-on/) (*pl.* **protozoa** /-zóə/ or **protozoans**) ▲ any usu. unicellular and microscopic organism of the subkingdom Protozoa, including amoebas and ciliates. ● *adj.* (also **pro·to·zo·ic** /-zō-ik/) of or relating to this phylum. □□ **pro·to·zo·al** *adj.*

pro·tract /prótrákt, prə-/ *v.tr.* **1 a** prolong or lengthen in space or esp. time (*protracted their stay for some weeks*). **b** (as **protracted** *adj.*) of excessive length or duration (*a protracted illness*). **2** draw (a plan, etc.) to scale. □□ **pro·tract·ed·ly** *adv.* **pro·tract·ed·ness** *n.*

pro·trac·tion /prōtrákshən, prə-/ *n.* **1** the act or an instance of protracting; the state of being protracted. **2** a drawing to scale.

pro·trac·tor /prōtráktər, prə-/ *n.* ▶ an instrument for measuring angles, usu. in the form of a graduated semicircle.

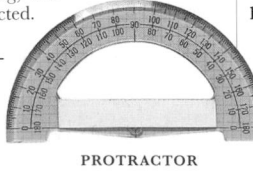

PROTRACTOR

pro·trude /prōtrood/ *v.* **1** *intr.* extend beyond or above a surface; project. **2** *tr.* thrust or cause to thrust forth. □□ **pro·trud·ent** *adj.* **pro·tru·si·ble** /-səbəl, -zə-/ *adj.* **pro·tru·sion** /-trōozhən/ *n.* **pro·tru·sive** *adj.*

pro·tu·ber·ant /prótōobərənt, -tyōo-, prə-/ *adj.* bulging out; prominent (*protuberant eyes*). □□ **pro·tu·ber·ance** *n.*

proud /prowd/ *adj.* **1** feeling greatly honored or pleased (*am proud to know him; proud of his friendship*). **2 a** (often foll. by *of*) valuing oneself, one's possessions, etc., highly, or esp. too highly; haughty; arrogant (*proud of his ancient name*). **b** (often in *comb.*) having a proper pride; satisfied (*proud of a job well done*). **3 a** (of an occasion, etc.) justly arousing pride (*a proud day for us; a proud sight*). **b** (of an action, etc.) showing pride (*a proud wave of the hand*). **4** (of a thing) imposing; splendid. **5** *Brit.* slightly projecting from a surface, etc. (*the nail stood proud of the plank*). **6** (of flesh) overgrown around a healing wound. □ **do proud** *colloq.* **1** treat (a person) with lavish generosity or honor (*they did us proud on our anniversary*). **2** (*refl.*) act honorably or worthily. □□ **proud·ly** *adv.* **proud·ness** *n.*

Prov. *abbr.* **1** Proverbs (Old Testament). **2** Province. **3** Pro·ven·çal.

prove /proov/ *v.* (*past part.* **proved** or **proven**) **1** *tr.* (often foll. by *that* + clause) demonstrate the truth of by evidence or argument. **2** *intr.* **a** (usu. foll. by *to* + infin.) be found (*it proved to be untrue*). **b** emerge incontrovertibly as (*will prove the winner*). **3** *tr. Math.* test the accuracy of (a calculation). **4** *tr.* establish the genuineness and validity of (a will). **5** *intr.* (of dough) rise in breadmaking. **6** *tr.* = PROOF 3. **7** *tr.* subject (a gun, etc.) to a testing process. □ **prove oneself** show one's abilities, courage, etc. □□ **prov·a·ble** *adj.* **prov·a·bil·i·ty** /proovəbílitee/ *n.* **prov·a·bly** *adv.*

prov·e·nance /próvinəns/ *n.* **1** the place of origin or history, esp. of a work of art, etc. **2** origin.

Pro·ven·çal /próvonsáal, próv-/ *adj. & n.* ● *adj.* **1** of or concerning the language, inhabitants, landscape, etc., of Provence, a former province of SE France. **2** (also **Pro·ven·çale**) cooked with garlic and tomato and usu. onions, olive oil, and herbs. ● *n.* **1** a native of Provence. **2** the language of Provence.

prov·en·der /próvindər/ *n.* **1** animal fodder. **2** *joc.* food for human beings.

prov·e·ni·ence /prəveenyəns, -veeneeəns/ *n.* = PROVENANCE.

prov·erb /próvərb/ *n.* **1** a short pithy saying in general use, held to embody a general truth. **2** a person or thing that is notorious (*he is a proverb for inaccuracy*). **3** (**Proverbs** or **Book of Proverbs**) a didactic poetic Old Testament book of maxims attributed to Solomon and others.

pro·ver·bi·al /prəvərbeeəl/ *adj.* **1** (esp. of a specific characteristic, etc.) as well-known as a proverb; notorious (*his proverbial honesty*). **2** of or referred to in a proverb (*the proverbial ill wind*). □□ **pro·ver·bi·al·i·ty** /-beeálitee/ *n.* **pro·ver·bi·al·ly** *adv.*

pro·vide /prəvíd/ *v.* **1** *tr.* supply; furnish (*provided them with food; provided food for them*). **2** *intr.* **a** (usu. foll. by *for, against*) make due preparation (*provided for any eventuality*). **b** (usu. foll. by *for*) prepare for the maintenance of a person, etc. **3** *tr.* (also *refl.*) equip with necessities. **4** *tr.* (usu. foll. by *that*) stipulate in a will, statute, etc.

pro·vid·ed /prəvídid/ *adj. & conj.* ● *adj.* supplied; furnished. ● *conj.* (often foll. by *that*) on the condition or understanding (that).

prov·i·dence /próvidəns/ *n.* **1** the protective care of God or nature. **2** (**Providence**) God in this aspect. **3** timely care or preparation; foresight; thrift.

prov·i·dent /próvidənt, -dent/ *adj.* having or showing foresight; thrifty. □□ **prov·i·dent·ly** *adv.*

prov·i·den·tial /próvidénshəl/ *adj.* **1** of or by

divine foresight or interposition. **2** opportune; lucky. □□ **prov·i·den·tial·ly** *adv.*

pro·vid·er /prəvídər/ *n.* **1** a person or thing that provides. **2** the breadwinner of a family, etc.

pro·vid·ing /prəvíding/ *conj.* = PROVIDED *conj.*

prov·ince /próvins/ *n.* **1** a principal administrative division of some countries. **2** (**the provinces**) the whole of a country outside major cities, esp. regarded as uncultured, unsophisticated, etc. **3** a sphere of action; business (*outside my province as a teacher*). **4** a branch of learning, etc. (*in the province of aesthetics*). **5** *Eccl.* a district under an archbishop or a metropolitan. **6** *Rom.Hist.* a territory outside Italy under a Roman governor.

pro·vin·cial /prəvínshəl/ *adj. & n.* ● *adj.* **1 a** of or concerning a province. **b** of or concerning the provinces. **2** unsophisticated or uncultured in manner, speech, opinion, etc. ● *n.* **1** an inhabitant of a province or the provinces. **2** an unsophisticated or uncultured person. **3** *Eccl.* the head or chief of a province or of a religious order in a province. □□ **pro·vin·ci·al·i·ty** /-sheeálitee/ *n.* **pro·vin·cial·ize** *v.tr.* **pro·vin·cial·ly** *adv.*

pro·vin·cial·ism /prəvínshəlizəm/ *n.* **1** provincial manners, fashion, mode of thought, etc., esp. regarded as restricting or narrow. **2** a word or phrase peculiar to a provincial region. **3** concern for one's local area rather than one's country. □□ **pro·vin·cial·ist** *n.*

pro·ving ground *n.* an area or situation in which a person or thing is tested or proved.

pro·vi·sion /prəvízhən/ *n. & v.* ● *n.* **1 a** the act or an instance of providing (*made no provision for his future*). **b** something provided (*a provision of bread*). **2** (in *pl.*) food, drink, etc., esp. for an expedition. **3 a** a legal or formal statement providing for something. **b** a clause of this. ● *v.tr.* supply (an expedition, etc.) with provisions. □□ **pro·vi·sion·er** *n.* **pro·vi·sion·less** *adj.* **pro·vi·sion·ment** *n.*

pro·vi·sion·al /prəvízhənəl/ *adj. & n.* ● *adj.* **1** providing for immediate needs only; temporary. **2** (**Provisional**) designating the unofficial wing of the Irish Republican Army (IRA), advocating terrorism. ● *n.* (**Provisional**) a member of the Provisional wing of the IRA. □□ **pro·vi·sion·al·i·ty** /-álitee/ *n.* **pro·vi·sion·al·ly** *adv.* **pro·vi·sion·al·ness** *n.*

pro·vi·so /prəvízō/ *n.* (*pl.* **-os**) **1** a stipulation. **2** a clause of stipulation or limitation in a document.

pro·vi·so·ry /prəvízəree/ *adj.* conditional; having a proviso. □□ **pro·vi·so·ri·ly** *adv.*

Pro·vo /próvō/ *n.* (*pl.* **-os**) *colloq.* a member of the Provisional IRA.

prov·o·ca·tion /próvəkáyshən/ *n.* **1** the act or an instance of provoking; a state of being provoked. **2** a cause of annoyance.

pro·voc·a·tive /prəvókətiv/ *adj. & n.* ● *adj.* **1** tending to provoke, esp. anger or sexual desire. **2** intentionally annoying. □□ **pro·voc·a·tive·ly** *adv.* **pro·voc·a·tive·ness** *n.*

pro·voke /prəvók/ *v.tr.* **1 a** (often foll. by *to*, or *to* + infin.) rouse or incite (*provoked him to fury*). **b** (often as **provoking** *adj.*) annoy; irritate; exasperate. **2** call forth; instigate (indignation, an inquiry, a storm, etc.). **3** (usu. foll. by *into* + verbal noun) irritate or stimulate (a person) (*the itch provoked him into scratching*). **4** tempt; allure. **5** cause; give rise to (*will provoke discussion*). □□ **pro·vok·a·ble** *adj.* **pro·vok·ing·ly** *adv.*

pro·vo·lo·ne /próvəlónee/ *n.* a medium hard Italian cheese, often with a mild smoked flavor.

pro·vost /próvōst, próvəst/ *n.* **1** a high administrative officer in a university. **2** *Brit.* the head of some colleges, esp. at Oxford or Cambridge. **3** *Eccl.* **a** the head of a chapter in a cathedral. **b** *hist.* the head of a religious community. **4** *Sc.* the head of a municipal corporation or burgh. **5** = PROVOST MARSHAL. □□ **pro·vost·ship** *n.*

pro·vost mar·shal /próvō/ *n.* **1** the head of military police within a military command, as on a

military base. **2** the master-at-arms of a ship in which a court-martial is to be held.

prow /prow/ *n.* **1** the bow of a ship adjoining the stem. ▷ TRIREME. **2** a pointed or projecting front part.

prow·ess /prówis/ *n.* **1** skill; expertise. **2** valor; gallantry.

prowl /prowl/ *v. & n.* ● *v.* **1** *tr.* roam (a place) in search or as if in search of prey, plunder, etc. **2** *intr.* (often foll. by *about*, *around*) move about like a hunter. ● *n.* the act or an instance of prowling. □ **on the prowl** in search of something, esp. sexual contact, etc. □□ **prowl·er** *n.*

prox·i·mal /próksiməl/ *adj.* situated toward the center of the body or point of attachment. □□ **prox·i·mal·ly** *adv.*

prox·im·i·ty /proksímitee/ *n.* nearness in space, time, etc. (*sat in close proximity to them*).

prox·y /próksee/ *n.* (*pl.* **-ies**) (also *attrib.*) **1** the authorization given to a substitute or deputy (*a proxy vote*; *was married by proxy*). **2** a person authorized to act as a substitute, etc. **3 a** a document giving the power to act as a proxy, esp. in voting. **b** a vote given by this.

prude /prood/ *n.* a person having or affecting an attitude of extreme propriety or modesty, esp. in sexual matters. □□ **prud·er·y** /proodəree/ *n.* (*pl.* **-ies**). **prud·ish** *adj.* **prud·ish·ly** *adv.* **prud·ish·ness** *n.*

pru·dent /prood'nt/ *adj.* **1** (of a person or conduct) careful to avoid undesirable consequences; circumspect. **2** discreet. □□ **pru·dence** *n.* **pru·dent·ly** *adv.*

pru·den·tial /proodénshəl/ *adj. & n.* ● *adj.* of, involving, or marked by prudence (*prudential motives*). ● *n.* (in *pl.*) **1** prudential considerations or matters. **2** minor administrative or financial matters. □□ **pru·den·tial·ism** *n.* **pru·den·tial·ist** *n.* **pru·den·tial·ly** *adv.*

prune¹ /proon/ *n.* **1** a dried plum. **2** *colloq.* a stupid or disliked person.

prune² /proon/ *v.tr.* **1 a** (often foll. by *down*) trim (a tree, etc.) by cutting away dead or overgrown branches, etc. **b** (usu. foll. by *off*, *away*) lop (branches, etc.) from a tree. **2** reduce (costs, etc.) (*must try to prune expenses*). □□ **prun·er** *n.*

pru·ri·ent /prooreeənt/ *adj.* **1** having an unhealthy obsession with sexual matters. **2** encouraging such an obsession. □□ **pru·ri·ence** *n.* **pru·ri·en·cy** *n.* **pru·ri·ent·ly** *adv.*

pru·ri·tus /proorítəs/ *n.* severe itching of the skin. □□ **pru·ri·tic** /-rítik/ *adj.*

Prus·sian /prúshən/ *adj. & n.* ● *adj.* of or relating to Prussia, a former German kingdom, or relating to its rigidly militaristic tradition. ● *n.* a native of Prussia.

pry¹ /prī/ *v.intr.* (**pries**, **pried**) **1** (usu. foll. by *into*) inquire presumptuously (into a person's private affairs, etc.). **2** (usu. foll. by *into*, *about*, etc.) look or peer inquisitively. □□ **pry·ing** *adj.* **pry·ing·ly** *adv.*

pry² /prī/ *v.tr.* (**pries**, **pried**) (often foll. by *out of*, *open*, etc.) = PRIZE².

PS *abbr.* **1** postscript. **2** *Brit.* Police Sergeant. **3** private secretary. **4** prompt side.

Ps. *abbr.* (*pl.* **Pss.**) Psalm, Psalms (Old Testament).

psalm /saam/ *n.* **1 a** (also **Psalm**) any of the sacred songs contained in the Book of Psalms. **b** (**the Psalms** or **the Book of Psalms**) the book of the Old Testament containing the Psalms. **2** a sacred song or hymn. □□ **psalm·ic** *adj.*

psalm·ist /sáamist/ *n.* **1** the author or composer of a psalm. **2** (**the Psalmist**) David or the author of any of the Psalms.

psal·mo·dy /sáamədee, sál-/ *n.* **1** the practice or art of singing psalms, hymns, etc., esp. in public worship. **2 a** the arrangement of psalms for singing. **b** the psalms so arranged. □□ **psal·mod·ic** /salmódik/ *adj.* **psal·mo·dist** *n.* **psal·mo·dize** *v.intr.*

psal·ter /sáwltər/ *n.* **1 a** the Book of Psalms. **b** a version of this (*the English Psalter*). **2** a copy of the Psalms, esp. for liturgical use.

psal·ter·y /sáwltəree/ *n.* (*pl.* **-ies**) an ancient and medieval instrument like a dulcimer but played by plucking the strings with the fingers or a plectrum.

p's and q's *n.pl.* □ **mind one's p's and q's 1** attend to one's own conduct and manners. **2** attend to one's own accuracy in work.

PSAT *abbr.* Preliminary Scholastic Assessment Test.

pse·phol·o·gy /sefóləjee/ *n.* the statistical study of elections, voting, etc. □□ **pse·pho·log·i·cal** /-əlójikəl/ *adj.* **pse·pho·log·i·cal·ly** *adv.* **pse·phol·o·gist** *n.*

pseud /sood/ *adj. & n. Brit. colloq.* ● *adj.* intellectually or socially pretentious; not genuine. ● *n.* such a person; a poseur.

pseud- var. of PSEUDO-.

pseud. *abbr.* pseudonym.

pseu·do /soodō/ *adj. & n.* ● *adj.* **1** sham; spurious. **2** insincere. ● *n. Brit.* (*pl.* **-os**) a pretentious or insincere person.

pseudo- /soodō/ *comb. form* (also **pseud-** before a vowel) **1** supposed or purporting to be but not really so; false; not genuine (*pseudointellectual*). **2** resembling or imitating (often in technical applications) (*pseudomalaria*).

pseu·do·carp /soodōkaarp/ *n.* a fruit formed from parts other than the ovary, e.g., the strawberry or fig.

pseu·do·nym /soodənim/ *n.* a fictitious name, esp. one assumed by an author.

pseu·don·y·mous /soodónimas/ *adj.* writing or written under a false name. □□ **pseu·do·nym·i·ty** /soodənímitee/ *n.* **pseu·don·y·mous·ly** *adv.*

pseu·do·pod /soodōpod/ *n.* = PSEUDOPODIUM.

pseu·do·po·di·um /soodōpódeeəm/ *n.* (*pl.* **pseu·dopodia** /-deeə/) ▼ (in amoeboid cells) a temporary protrusion of protoplasm for movement, feeding, etc.

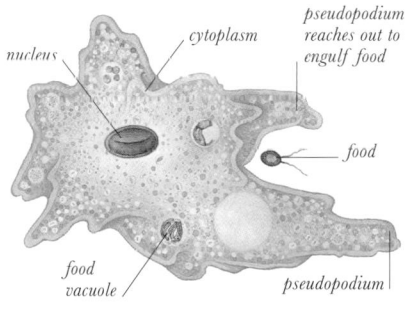

PSEUDOPODIA OF AN AMOEBA

psf. *abbr.* (also **p.s.f.**) pounds per square foot.

p.s.i. *abbr.* pounds per square inch.

psi /sī, psī/ *n.* **1** the twenty-third letter of the Greek alphabet (Ψ, ψ). **2** supposed parapsychological faculties, phenomena, etc., regarded collectively.

psit·ta·cine /sítəsīn/ *adj.* of or relating to parrots; parrot-like.

psit·ta·co·sis /sítəkósis/ *n.* a contagious viral disease of birds transmissible (esp. from parrots) to human beings as a form of pneumonia.

pso·ri·a·sis /sərīəsis/ *n.* a skin disease marked by red scaly patches. □□ **pso·ri·at·ic** /sáwreeátik/ *adj.*

psst /pst/ *int.* (also **pst**) a whispered exclamation seeking to attract a person's attention surreptitiously.

PST *abbr.* Pacific Standard Time.

psych /sīk/ *v.tr. colloq.* (also **psyche**) **1** (usu. foll. by *up*; often *refl.*) prepare (oneself or another person) mentally for an ordeal, etc. **2 a** (usu. foll. by *out*) analyze (a person's motivation, etc.) for one's own advantage (*can't psych him out*). **b** subject to psychoanalysis. **3** (often foll. by *out*) influence a person psychologically, esp. negatively; intimidate; frighten.

P

psy·che /síkee/ *n. & v.* ● *n.* **1** the soul; the spirit. **2** the mind. ● *v.* var. of PSYCH.

psych·e·de·lia /síkidéeleeə, -déelyə/ *n.pl.* **1** ▼ psychedelic articles, esp. posters, paintings, etc. **2** psychedelic drugs.

PSYCHEDELIA: 1960s PSYCHEDELIC POSTER

psych·e·del·ic /síkidélik/ *adj. & n.* ● *adj.* **1 a** expanding the mind's awareness, etc., esp. through the use of hallucinogenic drugs. **b** (of an experience) hallucinatory; bizarre. **c** (of a drug) producing hallucinations. **2** *colloq.* **a** producing an effect resembling that of a psychedelic drug; having vivid colors or designs, etc. **b** (of colors, patterns, etc.) bright, bold and often abstract. ● *n.* a hallucinogenic drug. □□ **psych·e·del·i·cal·ly** *adv.*

psy·chi·a·try /síkíətree/ *n.* the study and treatment of mental disease. □□ **psy·chi·at·ric** /-keeátrik/ *adj.* **psy·chi·at·ri·cal** *adj.* **psy·chi·at·ri·cal·ly** *adv.* **psy·chi·a·trist** /-kíətrist/ *n.*

psy·chic /síkik/ *adj. & n.* ● *adj.* **1 a** (of a person) considered to have occult powers, such as telepathy, clairvoyance, etc. **b** (of a faculty, phenomenon, etc.) inexplicable by natural laws. **2** of the soul or mind. ● *n.* a person considered to have psychic powers; a medium.

psy·chi·cal /síkikəl/ *adj.* **1** concerning psychic phenomena or faculties (*psychical research*). **2** of the soul or mind. □□ **psy·chi·cal·ly** *adv.* **psy·chi·cism** /-kisizəm/ *n.* **psy·chi·cist** /-kisist/ *n.*

psy·cho /síkō/ *n. & adj. colloq.* ● *n.* (*pl.* **-os**) a psychopath. ● *adj.* psychopathic.

psycho- /síkō/ *comb. form* relating to the mind or psychology.

psy·cho·ac·tive /síkō-áktiv/ *adj.* affecting the mind (*psychoactive drugs*).

psy·cho·a·nal·y·sis /síkōənálisis/ *n.* a therapeutic method of treating mental disorders by investigating the interaction of conscious and unconscious elements in the mind and bringing repressed fears and conflicts into the conscious mind. □□ **psy·cho·an·a·lyze** /-ánəlīz/ *v.tr.* **psy·cho·an·a·lyst** /-ánəlist/ *n.* **psy·cho·an·a·lyt·ic** /-anəlítik/ *adj.* **psy·cho·an·a·lyt·i·cal** *adj.* **psy·cho·an·a·lyt·i·cal·ly** *adv.*

psy·cho·bab·ble /síkōbabəl/ *n. colloq. derog.* jargon used in popular psychology. □□ **psy·cho·bab·bler** *n.*

psy·cho·dra·ma /síkōdraamə, -drámə/ *n.* **1** a form of psychotherapy in which patients act out events from their past. **2** a play or movie, etc., in which psychological elements are the main interest.

psy·cho·ki·ne·sis /síkōkineésis/ *n.* the movement of objects supposedly by mental effort without the action of natural forces.

psy·cho·lin·guis·tics /síkōlinggwístiks/ *n.pl.* (treated as *sing.*) the study of the psychological aspects of language and language acquisition. □□ **psy·cho·lin·guist** /-línggwist/ *n.* **psy·cho·lin·guis·tic** *adj.*

psy·cho·log·i·cal /síkəlójikəl/ *adj.* **1** of, relating to, or arising in the mind. **2** of or relating to psychology. **3** *colloq.* (of an ailment, etc.) having a basis in the mind; imaginary (*her cold is psychological*). □□ **psy·cho·log·i·cal·ly** *adv.*

psy·cho·log·i·cal war·fare *n.* a campaign directed at reducing an opponent's morale.

psy·chol·o·gy /síkóləjee/ *n.* (*pl.* **-ies**) **1** the scientific study of the human mind and its functions, esp. those affecting behavior in a given context. **2** a treatise on or theory of this. **3 a** the mental characteristics or attitude of a person or group. **b** the mental factors governing a situation or activity (*the psychology of crime*). □□ **psy·chol·o·gist** *n.* **psy·chol·o·gize** *v.tr. & intr.*

psy·cho·met·rics /síkōmétriks/ *n.pl.* (treated as *sing.*) the science of measuring mental capacities and processes.

psy·chom·e·try /síkómitree/ *n.* **1** the supposed divination of facts about events, people, etc., from inanimate objects associated with them. **2** the measurement of mental abilities. □□ **psy·cho·met·ric** /-kəmétrik/ *adj.* **psy·cho·met·ri·cal·ly** *adv.* **psy·chom·e·trist** *n.*

psy·cho·path /síkəpath/ *n.* **1** a person suffering from chronic mental disorder, esp. with abnormal or violent social behavior. **2** a mentally or emotionally unstable person. □□ **psy·cho·path·ic** /-páthik/ *adj.* **psy·cho·path·i·cal·ly** *adv.*

psy·cho·pa·thol·o·gy /síkōpathóləjee/ *n.* **1** the scientific study of mental disorders. **2** a mentally or behaviorally disordered state. □□ **psy·cho·path·o·log·i·cal** /-pathəlójikəl/ *adj.*

psy·chop·a·thy /síkópəthee/ *n.* psychopathic or psychologically abnormal behavior.

psy·cho·sex·u·al /síkōsékshōōəl/ *adj.* of or involving the psychological aspects of the sexual impulse. □□ **psy·cho·sex·u·al·ly** *adv.*

psy·cho·sis /síkósis/ *n.* (*pl.* **psychoses** /-seez/) a severe mental derangement, esp. when resulting in delusions and loss of or defective contact with external reality.

psy·cho·so·mat·ic /síkōsəmátik/ *adj.* **1** (of an illness, etc.) caused or aggravated by mental conflict, stress, etc. **2** of the mind and body together. □□ **psy·cho·so·mat·i·cal·ly** *adv.*

psy·cho·ther·a·py /síkōthérəpee/ *n.* the treatment of mental disorder by psychological means. □□ **psy·cho·ther·a·peu·tic** /-pyōōtik/ *adj.* **psy·cho·ther·a·pist** *n.*

psy·chot·ic /síkótik/ *adj. & n.* ● *adj.* of or characterized by a psychosis. ● *n.* a person suffering from a psychosis. □□ **psy·chot·i·cal·ly** *adv.*

psy·cho·tro·pic /síkōtrópik, -tróp-/ *n.* (of a drug) acting on the mind.

PT *abbr.* **1** physical therapy. **2** physical training.

Pt *symb. Chem.* the element platinum.

pt. *abbr.* **1** part. **2** pint. **3** point. **4** port.

PTA *abbr.* Parent-Teacher Association.

ptar·mi·gan /taármigən/ *n.* any of various grouses of the genus *Lagopus*, esp. *L. mutus*, with black or gray plumage in the summer and white in the winter.

PT boat *n.* a military patrol boat armed with torpedoes, etc.

ptero- /térō/ *comb. form* wing.

pter·o·dac·tyl /térədáktil/ *n.* a large extinct flying birdlike reptile with a long slender head and neck.

pter·o·pod /térəpod/ *n.* a marine gastropod having a modified foot with a pair of winglike lobes.

pter·o·saur /térəsawr/ *n.* any of a group of extinct flying reptiles with large bat-like wings, including pterodactyls.

PTO *abbr.* **1** Parent-Teacher Organization. **2** please turn over.

Ptol·e·ma·ic /tólimáyik/ *adj. hist.* **1** of or relating to Ptolemy, a 2nd-c. Alexandrian astronomer, or his theories. **2** of or relating to the Ptolemies, Macedonian rulers of Egypt from the death of Alexander the Great (323 BC) to the death of Cleopatra (30 BC).

Ptol·e·ma·ic sys·tem *n.* ▼ the theory that the Earth is the stationary center of the universe (cf. COPERNICAN SYSTEM).

pto·maine /tómayn/ *n.* any of various amine compounds, some toxic, in putrefying animal and vegetable matter.

P2P *abbr.* peer-to-peer, an Internet network that enables a group of users to access and copy files from each other's hard drives.

Pu *symb. Chem.* the element plutonium.

pub /pub/ *n. Brit. colloq.* a tavern or bar.

pub. *abbr.* (also **publ.**) **1** public. **2** publication. **3** published. **4** publisher. **5** publishing.

pu·ber·ty /pyōōbərtee/ *n.* the period during which adolescents reach sexual maturity and become capable of reproduction. □□ **pu·ber·tal** *adj.*

pu·bes[1] /pyōōbeez/ *n.* (*pl.* same) **1** the lower part of the abdomen at the front of the pelvis, covered with hair from puberty. **2** pubic hair.

pubes[2] *pl.* of PUBIS.

pu·bes·cence /pyōōbésəns/ *n.* the time when puberty begins. □□ **pu·bes·cent** *adj.*

pu·bic /pyōōbik/ *adj.* of or relating to the pubes or pubis.

pu·bis /pyōōbis/ *n.* (*pl.* **pubes** /-beez/) either of a pair of bones forming the two sides of the pelvis. ▷ SKELETON

pub·lic /públik/ *adj. & n.* ● *adj.* **1** of or concerning the people as a whole (*a public holiday; the public interest*). **2** open to or shared by all the people (*public library; public meeting*). **3** done or existing openly (*made his views public; a public protest*). **4 a** (of a service, funds, etc.) provided by or concerning local or central government (*public money; public records; public expenditure*). **b** (of a person) in government (*had a distinguished public career*). **5** well-known; famous (*a public figure*). **6** *Brit.* of, for, or acting for, a university (*public examination*). ● *n.* **1** (as *sing.* or *pl.*) the commu-

PTOLEMAIC SYSTEM

Ptolemy, a 2nd-century Egyptian astronomer, saw the Earth as the center of the universe, with the Sun, Moon, and the five known planets moving around it. This theory, known as the Ptolemaic or geocentric system, was universally accepted until the 16th century, when Nicolaus Copernicus, a Polish astronomer, proposed that the Sun was the center of the universe, a theory known as the heliocentric system.

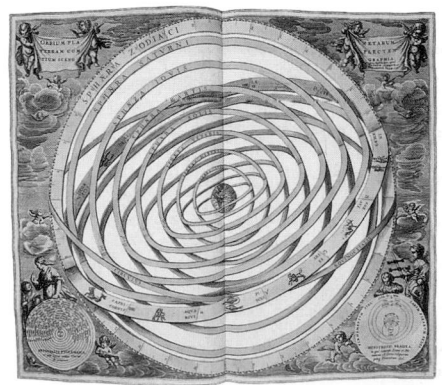

ILLUSTRATION OF THE PTOLEMAIC SYSTEM

P

nity in general, or members of the community. **2** a section of the community having a particular interest or some special connection (*the reading public*; *my public demands my loyalty*). □ **go public** become a public company or corporation. **in public** openly; publicly. **in the public domain** belonging to the public as a whole, esp. not subject to copyright. **in the public eye** famous or notorious. **make public** publicize; make known; publish. □□ **pub·lic·ly** *adv.*

pub·lic-ad·dress sys·tem *n.* loudspeakers, microphones, amplifiers, etc., used in addressing large audiences.

pub·li·can /públikən/ *n.* **1 a** *Brit.* the keeper of a public house. **b** *Austral.* the keeper of a hotel. **2** *Rom.Hist. & Bibl.* a tax collector.

pub·li·ca·tion /públikáyshən/ *n.* **1 a** the preparation and issuing of a book, newspaper, engraving, music, etc., to the public. **b** a book, etc., so issued. **2** the act or an instance of making something publicly known.

pub·lic de·fen·der *n.* an attorney who provides legal representation at public expense for defendants who cannot afford their own attorney.

pub·lic en·e·my *n.* a notorious wanted criminal.

pub·lic health *n.* the provision of adequate sanitation, drainage, etc., by government.

pub·li·cist /públisist/ *n.* **1** a publicity agent or public relations manager. **2** a journalist, esp. concerned with current affairs. □□ **pub·li·cism** *n.* **pub·li·cis·tic** /-sistik/ *adj.*

pub·lic·i·ty /publísitee/ *n.* **1 a** the professional exploitation of a product, person, etc., by advertising or popularizing. **b** material or information used for this. **2** public exposure; notoriety.

pub·lic·i·ty a·gent *n.* a person employed to produce or heighten public exposure.

pub·li·cize /públisīz/ *v.tr.* advertise; make publicly known.

pu·blic o·pin·ion *n.* views generally prevalent, esp. on moral questions.

pub·lic re·la·tions *n.pl.* the professional maintenance of a favorable public image, esp. by a company, famous person, etc.

pub·lic school *n.* **1** *US, Austral., & Sc.,* etc. a free, government-supported school. **2** *Brit.* a private tuition-paying secondary school, esp. for boarders.

pub·lic sec·tor *n.* that part of an economy, industry, etc., that is controlled by the government.

pub·lic serv·ant *n.* a government official.

pub·lic tel·e·vi·sion *n.* television funded by government appropriation and private donations rather than by advertising.

pub·lic u·til·i·ty *n.* an organization supplying water, gas, etc., to the community.

pub·lish /públish/ *v.tr.* **1** (also *absol.*) (of an author, publisher, etc.) prepare and issue (a book, newspaper, etc.) for public sale. **2** make generally known. **3** announce (an edict, etc.) formally; read (marriage banns). □□ **pub·lish·a·ble** *adj.*

pub·lish·er /públishər/ *n.* **1** a person or esp. a company that produces and distributes copies of a book, newspaper, etc., for sale. **2** the owner or chief executive of a publishing company. **3** a person or thing that publishes.

puce /pyoos/ *adj. & n.* dark red or purplish brown.

puck[1] /puk/ *n.* a rubber disk used in ice hockey. ▷ HOCKEY

puck[2] /puk/ *n.* **1** a mischievous or evil sprite. **2** a mischievous child. □□ **puck·ish** *adj.* **puck·ish·ly** *adv.* **puck·ish·ness** *n.* **puck·like** *adj.*

puck·er /púkər/ *v. & n.* ● *v.tr. & intr.* (often foll. by *up*) gather or cause to gather into wrinkles, folds, or bulges (*puckered her eyebrows*; *this seam is puckered up*). ● *n.* such a wrinkle, bulge, fold, etc. □ **puck·er up** *colloq.* get ready for a kiss. □□ **puck·er·y** *adj.*

pud /pood/ *n. Brit. colloq.* = PUDDING.

pud·ding /pooding/ *n.* **1 a** any of various dessert dishes, usu. containing flavoring, sugar, milk, etc.

PUEBLO

The Pueblo Indians of the American Southwest built settlements, known as pueblos, composed of rows of adjoining rooms, often many stories high. The largest, Pueblo Bonito (completed in about AD 1115), had over 800 rooms. Each pueblo contained several underground circular chambers – known as kivas – where ceremonies were held.

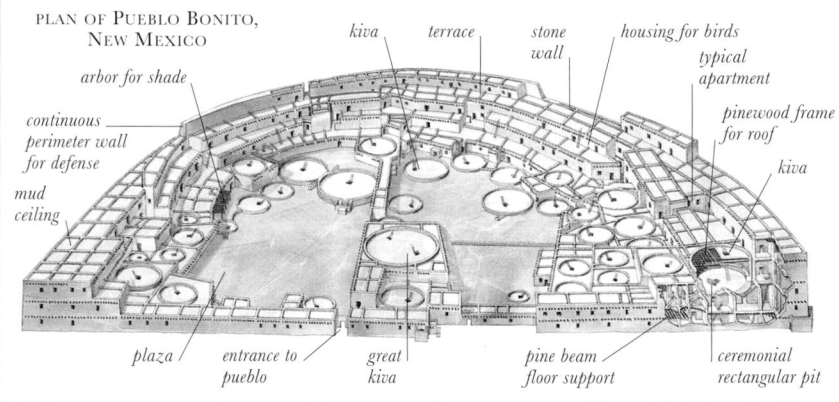

PLAN OF PUEBLO BONITO, NEW MEXICO

arbor for shade · continuous perimeter wall for defense · mud ceiling · kiva · terrace · stone wall · housing for birds · typical apartment · pinewood frame for roof · kiva · plaza · entrance to pueblo · great kiva · pine beam floor support · ceremonial rectangular pit

---

(*chocolate pudding*; *rice pudding*). **b** *Brit.* a savory dish containing flour, suet, etc. (*steak and kidney pudding*). **c** *Brit.* the dessert course of a meal. **d** the intestines of a pig, etc., stuffed with oatmeal, spices, blood, etc. **2** *colloq.* a person or thing resembling a pudding. □□ **pud·ding·like** *adj.*

pud·dle /púd'l/ *n. & v.* ● *n.* **1** a small pool, esp. of rainwater on a road, etc. **2** clay and sand mixed with water and used as a watertight covering for embankments, etc. **3** a circular patch of disturbed water made by the blade of an oar at each stroke. ● *v.* **1** *tr.* **a** knead (clay and sand) into puddle. **b** line (a canal, etc.) with puddle. **c** to coat the roots of (a plant) with mud to reduce water loss during transplantation. **2** *intr.* make puddle from clay, etc. **3** *tr.* stir (molten iron) to produce wrought iron by expelling carbon. **4** *intr.* **a** wade or wallow in mud or shallow water. **b** busy oneself in an untidy way. **5** *tr.* make (water, etc.) muddy. □□ **pud·dler** *n.* **pud·dly** *adj.*

pu·den·dum /pyoodéndəm/ *n.* (*pl.* **pudenda** /-də/) (usu. in *pl.*) the genitals, esp. of a woman. □□ **pu·den·dal** *adj.* **pu·dic** /pyoodik/ *adj.*

pudg·y /púje/ *adj.* (**pudgier**, **pudgiest**) *colloq.* (esp. of a person) plump; slightly overweight. □□ **pudge** *n.* **pudg·i·ly** *adv.* **pudg·i·ness** *n.*

pueb·lo /pwéblō/ *n.* (*pl.* **-os**) **1** (**Pueblo**) a member of a Native American people of the southwestern US. **2** ▲ a Native American settlement of the southwestern US, esp. one consisting of multi-storied adobe houses built by the Pueblo people.

pu·er·ile /pyoorril, pyoril, -rīl/ *adj.* **1** trivial; childish; immature. **2** of or like a child. □□ **pu·er·ile·ly** *adv.* **pu·er·il·i·ty** /-rílitee/ *n.* (*pl.* **-ies**)

pu·er·per·al /pyoo-érpərəl/ *adj.* of or caused by childbirth.

Pu·er·to Ri·can /pwértō réekən, páwrtə/ *n. & adj.* ● *n.* **1** a native of Puerto Rico, an island of the West Indies. **2** a person of Puerto Rican descent. ● *adj.* of or relating to Puerto Rico or its inhabitants.

puff /puf/ *n. & v.* ● *n.* **1 a** a short quick blast of breath or wind. **b** the sound of this; a similar sound. **c** a small quantity of vapor, smoke, etc., emitted in one blast; an inhalation or exhalation from a cigarette, pipe, etc. (*went up in a puff of smoke*; *took a puff from his cigarette*). **2** a light pastry containing jam, cream, etc. **3** a gathered mass of material in a dress, etc. (*puff sleeve*). **4** a protuberant roll of hair. **5 a** an extravagantly enthusiastic review of a book, etc., esp. in a newspaper. **b** an advertisement for goods, etc., esp. in a newspaper. **6** = POWDER PUFF. **7** an eiderdown. **8** *Brit. colloq.* one's life (*in all my puff*). ● *v.* **1** *intr.* emit a puff of air or breath; blow with short blasts. **2** *intr.* (usu. foll. by *away, out,* etc.) (of a person smoking, a steam engine, etc.) emit or move with puffs (*puffing away at his cigar*; *a train puffed out of the station*). **3** *tr.* esp. *Brit.* (usu. in *passive*; often foll. by *out*) put out of breath (*arrived somewhat puffed*; *completely puffed him out*). **4** *intr.* breathe hard; pant. **5** *tr.* utter pantingly ("*No more,*" *he puffed*). **6** *intr. & tr.* (usu. foll. by *up, out*) become or cause to become inflated; swell (*his eye was inflamed and puffed up*). **7** *tr.* (usu. foll. by *out, up, away*) blow or emit (dust, smoke, a light object, etc.) with a puff. **8** *tr.* smoke (a pipe, etc.) in puffs. **9** *tr.* (usu. as **puffed up** *adj.*) elate; make proud or boastful. **10** *tr.* advertise or promote (goods, a book, etc.) with exaggerated or false praise. □ **puff up** = sense 9 of *v.*

puff add·er *n.* a large venomous African viper, *Bitis arietans*, which inflates the upper part of its body and hisses when excited. ▷ SNAKE

puff·ball /púfbawl/ *n.* any fungus of the genus *Lycoperdon* and related genera producing a ball-shaped spore-bearing structure that releases its contents in a powdery cloud when broken. ▷ FUNGUS

puff·er /púfər/ *n.* **1** a person or thing that puffs. **2** any tropical fish of the family *Tetraodontidae*, able to inflate itself into a spherical form. Also called **globe fish.** □□ **puff·er·y** *n.*

puf·fin /púfin/ *n.* any of various seabirds of the family Alcidae native to the N. Atlantic and N. Pacific, esp. *Fratercula arctica*, having a large head with a brightly colored triangular bill and black and white plumage. ▷ SEABIRD

puff pas·try *n.* light flaky pastry.

puff·y /púfee/ *adj.* (**puffier**, **puffiest**) **1** swollen, esp. of the face, etc. **2** fat. **3** gusty. **4** short-winded. □□ **puff·i·ly** *adv.* **puff·i·ness** *n.*

pug[1] /pug/ *n.* (in full **pugdog**) **1** a dwarf breed of dog like a bulldog with a broad flat nose and deeply wrinkled face. **2** a dog of this breed. □□ **pug·gish** *adj.* **pug·gy** *adj.*

pug[2] /pug/ *n.* the footprint of an animal.

pu·gi·list /pyoojilist/ *n.* a boxer, esp. a professional. □□ **pu·gi·lism** *n.* **pu·gi·lis·tic** *adj.*

pug·na·cious /pugnáyshəs/ *adj.* quarrelsome; disposed to fight. □□ **pug·na·cious·ly** *adv.* **pug·na·cious·ness** *n.* **pug·nac·i·ty** /-násitee/ *n.*

pug nose *n.* a short squat or snub nose. □□ **pug-nosed** *adj.*

pu·is·sant /pwísənt, pyoo-ís-/ *adj. literary* or *archaic* having great power or influence; mighty. □□ **pu·is·sance** *n.* **puis·sant·ly** *adv.*

puke /pyook/ *v.tr. & intr. sl.* vomit. □□ **puk·ey** *adj.*

pul·chri·tude /púlkritood, -tyood/ *n. literary* beauty. □□ **pul·chri·tu·di·nous** /-toodinəs, -tyood-/ *adj.*

P

PULLEY

A simple pulley, with one pulley wheel, changes the direction of a force but not its size: a 1-kg mass weighing 10 newtons is lifted by a 10-newton force. Adding more pulley wheels increases the mechanical advantage – the ratio of the load overcome to the effort expended. A double pulley will lift a 1-kg mass with a 5-newton effort, because the load is shared between two ropes. A quadruple pulley will lift a 1-kg mass with a 2.5-newton effort because the load is shared among four ropes.

EXAMPLES OF PULLEYS

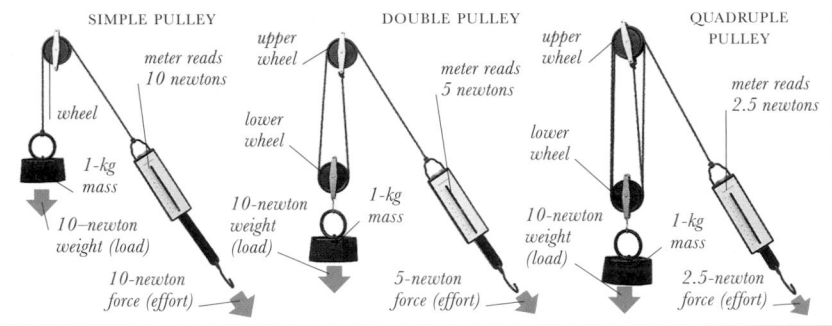

SIMPLE PULLEY   DOUBLE PULLEY   QUADRUPLE PULLEY

pule /pyool/ *v.intr.* cry querulously or weakly; whine; whimper.

Pu·litz·er prize /poolitsər, pyoo-/ *n.* each of a group of annual awards for achievements in American journalism, literature, and music.

pull /pool/ *v. & n.* ● *v.* **1** *tr.* exert force upon (a thing) tending to move it to oneself or the origin of the force (*stop pulling my hair*). **2** *tr.* cause to move in this way (*pulled it nearer; pulled me into the room*). **3** *intr.* exert a pulling force (*the horse pulls well; the engine will not pull*). **4** *tr.* extract (a cork or tooth) by pulling. **5** *tr.* damage (a muscle, etc.) by abnormal strain. **6 a** *tr.* move (a boat) by pulling on the oars. **b** *intr.* (of a boat, etc.) be caused to move, esp. in a specified direction. **7** *intr.* (often foll. by *up*) proceed with effort (*up a hill, etc.*). **8** *tr.* (foll. by *on*) bring out (a weapon) for use against (a person). **9 a** *tr.* check the speed of (a horse), esp. so as to make it lose the race. **b** *intr.* (of a horse) strain against the bit. **10** *tr.* attract or secure (custom or support). **11** *tr.* draw (liquor) from a barrel, etc. **12** *intr.* (foll. by *at*) tear or pluck at. **13** *intr.* (often foll. by *on, at*) inhale deeply; draw or suck (on a pipe, etc.). **14** *tr.* (often foll. by *up*) remove (a plant) by the root. **15** *tr.* **a** *Baseball* hit (a ball) to the left (for a right-handed batter) or to the right (for a left-handed batter). **b** *Golf* strike (the ball) widely to the left (or right for a left-handed swing). **16** *tr.* print (a proof, etc.). **17** *tr. colloq.* achieve or accomplish (esp. something illicit). **18** *tr.* to stretch repeatedly, as candy. ● *n.* **1** the act of pulling. **2** the force exerted by this. **3** a means of exerting influence; an advantage. **4** something that attracts or draws attention. **5** a deep draft of esp. liquor. **6** a prolonged effort, e.g., in going up a hill. **7** a handle, etc., for applying a pull. **8** a spell of rowing. **9** a printer's rough proof. **10** *Golf* a pulling stroke. **11** a suck at a cigarette. □ **pull apart** (or **to pieces**) = *take to pieces* (see PIECE). **pull away** withdraw; move away; move ahead. **pull back** retreat or cause to retreat. **pull down 1** demolish (esp. a building). **2** humiliate. **3** *colloq.* earn (a sum of money) as income, etc. **pull a fast one** see FAST[1]. **pull in 1 a** arrive, esp. at a destination. **b** to restrain; tighten. **2** (of a bus, train, etc.) arrive to take passengers. **3** earn or acquire. **4** *colloq.* arrest. **pull a person's leg** deceive a person playfully. **pull off 1** remove by pulling. **2** succeed in achieving or winning. **pull oneself together** recover control of oneself. **pull the other one** *colloq.* expressing disbelief (with ref. to *pull a person's leg*). **pull out 1** take out by pulling. **2** depart. **3** withdraw from an undertaking. **4** (of a bus, train, etc.) leave with its passengers. **5 a** (of a vehicle) move out from the side of the road, or from its normal position to overtake. **b** (of an airplane) resume level flight from a dive. **pull over** (of a vehicle) move to the side of or off the road. **pull the plug on** *colloq.* withdraw support. **pull one's punches** avoid using one's full force. **pull rank** take unfair advantage of one's seniority. **pull strings** exert (esp. clandestine) influence. **pull the strings** be the real actuator of what another does. **pull through** recover or cause to recover from an illness. **pull together** work in harmony. **pull up 1** stop or cause to stop moving. **2** pull out of the ground. **3** draw closer to or even with, as in a race. **4** check oneself. **pull one's weight** do one's fair share of work. □□ **pull·er** *n.*

pull-down *adj. Computing* (of a menu) appearing below a menu title when selected.

pul·let /poolit/ *n.* a young hen, esp. one less than one year old.

pul·ley /poolee/ *n.* (*pl.* **-eys**) **1** ▲ a grooved wheel or set of wheels for a rope, etc., to pass over, set in a block and used for changing the direction of a force. **2** a wheel or drum fixed on a shaft and turned by a belt, used esp. to increase speed or power. ▷ HOIST.

Pull·man /poolmən/ *n.* **1** a railroad car affording special comfort, esp. one with sleeping berths. **2** (in full **Pullman trunk** or **case**) a large suitcase.

pull·o·ver /poolōvər/ *n.* a knitted garment put on over the head and covering the top half of the body.

pull-tab *adj.* (of a can) having a ring or tab for pulling to break its seal.

pul·mo·nar·y /poolmǝneree, púl-/ *adj.* **1** of or relating to the lungs. ▷ CARDIOVASCULAR, HEART, RESPIRATION. **2** having lungs or lunglike organs. **3** affected with or susceptible to lung disease. □□ **pul·mo·nate** /-nayt, -nǝt/ *adj.*

pul·mon·ic /poolmónik, pul-/ *adj.* = PULMONARY 1.

pulp /pulp/ *n. & v.* ● *n.* **1** the soft fleshy part of fruit, etc. **2** any soft thick wet mass. **3** a soft shapeless mass derived from rags, wood, etc., used in papermaking. **4** (often *attrib.*) poor quality (often sensational) writing orig. printed on rough paper (*pulp fiction*). **5** vascular tissue filling the interior cavity and root canals of a tooth. **6** *Mining* pulverized ore mixed with water. ● *v.* **1** *tr.* reduce to pulp. **2** *tr.* withdraw (a publication) from the market, usu. recycling the paper. **3** *tr.* remove pulp from. **4** *intr.* become pulp. □□ **pulp·er** *n.* **pulp·less** *adj.* **pulp·y** *adj.* **pulp·i·ness** *n.*

pul·pit /poolpit, púl-/ *n.* a raised enclosed platform in a church, etc., from which the preacher delivers a sermon. ▷ CHURCH

pulp·wood /púlpwood/ *n.* timber suitable for making pulp.

pul·que /poolkay, poolkee, pool-/ *n.* a Mexican fermented drink made from the sap of the maguey.

pul·sar /púlsaar/ *n. Astron.* ▼ a cosmic source of regular and rapid pulses of radiation usu. at radio frequencies, e.g., a rotating neutron star.

pul·sate /púlsayt/ *v.intr.* **1** expand and contract rhythmically; throb. **2** vibrate; quiver; thrill. □□ **pul·sa·tion** /-sáyshən/ *n.* **pul·sa·tor** *n.* **pul·sa·to·ry** /púlsǝtawree/ *adj.*

pulse[1] /puls/ *n. & v.* ● *n.* **1 a** a rhythmical throbbing of the arteries as blood is propelled through them, esp. as felt in the wrists, temples, etc. **b** each successive beat of the arteries or heart. **c** (in full **pulse rate**) the number of such beats in a specified period of time, esp. one minute. **2** a throb or thrill of life or emotion. **3** a latent feeling. **4** a single vibration of sound, electric current, light, etc., esp. as a signal. **5** a musical beat. **6** any regular or recurrent rhythm, e.g., of the stroke of oars. ● *v.intr.* **1** pulsate. **2** (foll. by *out, in,* etc.) transmit, etc., by rhythmical beats. □□ **pulse·less** *adj.*

PULSAR

As neutron stars rotate, they emit beams of light and radio waves that, if they sweep past the Earth, are detected as pulses. This has led astronomers to call them pulsars (from *pulsating stars*). The fastest pulsars rotate at almost a thousand times per second. Over 400 are known to exist in our galaxy.

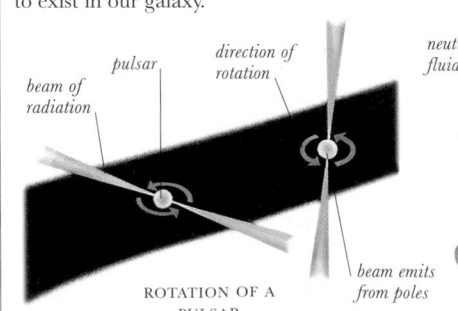

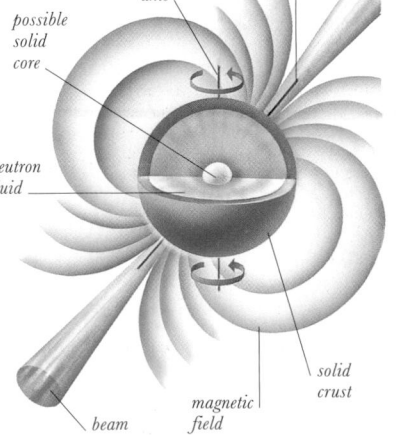

INTERNAL STRUCTURE OF A PULSAR

magnetic axis

rotational axis

possible solid core

neutron fluid

beam of radiation

pulsar

direction of rotation

beam emits from poles

ROTATION OF A PULSAR

magnetic field

beam

solid crust

P

PULSE

Pulses are derived from wild members of the pea family, such as the common and diverse *Phaseolus vulgaris*. Their seeds, a major source of protein, make a vital contribution to human diets where meat is scarce.

EXAMPLES OF PULSES

RED KIDNEY BEANS
(*Phaseolus vulgaris*)

PINTO BEANS
(*Phaseolus vulgaris*)

HARICOT BEANS
(*Phaseolus vulgaris*)

BROWN LENTILS
(*Lens esculenta*)

CHICKPEAS
(*Cicer arietinum*)

LIMA BEANS
(*Phaseolus lunatus*)

pulse[2] /puls/ *n.* (as *sing.* or *pl.*) **1** ▲ the edible seeds of various leguminous plants, e.g., chickpeas, lentils, beans, etc. **2** the plant or plants producing this.

pul·ver·ize /púlvərīz/ *v.* **1** *tr.* reduce to fine particles. **2** *intr.* be reduced to dust. **3** *tr. colloq.* **a** demolish. **b** defeat utterly. □□ **pul·ver·iz·a·ble** *adj.* **pul·ver·i·za·tion** *n.* **pul·ver·iz·er** *n.*

pu·ma /pyōōmə, pŏō-/ *n.* ▶ an American wild cat, *Felis concolor*, usu. with a plain tawny coat. Also called **mountain lion, panther, cougar.**

PUMA (*Felis concolor*)

pum·ice /púmis/ *n. & v.* ● *n.* (in full **pumice stone**) **1** ▶ a light porous volcanic rock often used as an abrasive in cleaning or polishing substances. **2** a piece of this used for removing callused skin, etc. ● *v.tr.* rub or clean with a pumice. □□ **pu·mi·ceous** /pyōōmíshəs/ *adj.*

pum·mel /púməl/ *v.tr.* (**pummeled** or **pummelled, pummeling** or **pummelling**) strike repeatedly, esp. with the fist.

pump[1] /pump/ *n. & v.* ● *n.* **1** ▶ a machine, usu. with rotary action or the reciprocal action of a piston, for raising or moving liquids, compressing gases, inflating tires, etc. **2** a physiological or electromagnetic process or mechanism having a similar purpose. **3** an instance of pumping; a stroke of a pump. ● *v.* **1** *tr.* (often foll.

PUMICE
STONE

by *in, out, into, up,* etc.) raise or remove (liquid, gas, etc.) with a pump. **2** *tr.* (often foll. by *up*) fill (a tire, etc.) with air. **3** *tr.* **a** remove (water, etc.) with a pump. **b** (foll. by *out*) remove liquid from (a place, well, etc.) with a pump. **4** *intr.* work a pump. **5** *tr.* (often foll. by *out*) cause to move, pour forth, etc., as if by pumping. **6** *tr.* question (a person) persistently to obtain information. **7** *tr.* **a** move vigorously up and down. **b** shake (a person's hand) effusively. **8** *tr.* (usu. foll. by *up*) arouse; excite. □ **pump iron** (also **pump up**) *colloq.* exercise with weights.

pump[2] /pump/ *n.* **1** a usu. medium-heeled slip-on women's dress shoe. **2** a slip-on men's patent leather shoe for formal wear.

pum·per·nick·el /púmpərnikəl/ *n.* German-style dark, coarse rye bread.

pump·kin /púmpkin, púng-/ *n.* **1** any of various plants of the genus *Cucurbita*, with large lobed leaves and tendrils. **2** the large rounded edible orange or yellow fruit of this.

pun /pun/ *n. & v.* ● *n.* the humorous use of a word to suggest different meanings, or of words of the same sound and different meanings. ● *v.intr.* (**punned, punning**) (foll. by *on*) make a pun or puns with (words). □□ **pun·ning·ly** *adv.*

pu·na /pōōnə, pŏō-/ *n.* **1** a high plateau in the Peruvian Andes. **2** = MOUNTAIN SICKNESS.

punch[1] /punch/ *v. & n.* ● *v.tr.* **1** strike bluntly, esp. with a closed fist. **2** prod or poke with a blunt object. **3 a** pierce a hole in (metal, paper, a ticket, etc.) as or with a punch. **b** pierce (a hole) by punching. **4** drive (cattle) by prodding with a stick, etc. ● *n.* **1** a blow with a fist. **2** the ability to deliver this. **3** *colloq.* vigor; momentum; effective force. □ **punch in** (or **out**) record the time of one's arrival at (or departure from) work by punching a time clock. □□ **punch·er** *n.*

punch[2] /punch/ *n.* **1** any of various devices or machines for punching holes in materials (e.g., paper, leather, metal, plaster). **2** a tool or machine for impressing a design or stamping a die on a material.

punch[3] /punch/ *n.* a drink of fruit juices, sometimes mixed with wine or liquor, served cold or hot.

punch bowl *n.* a bowl in which punch is mixed and served.

punch-drunk *adj.* stupefied from or as though from a series of heavy blows.

pun·cheon[1] /púnchən/ *n.* **1** a short post, esp. one supporting a roof in a coal mine. **2** = PUNCH[2]. **3** a heavy timber finished on one side only, used in flooring, etc.

pun·cheon[2] /púnchən/ *n.* a large cask for liquids, etc., holding from 72 to 120 gallons.

Pun·chi·nel·lo /púnchinélō/ *n.* (*pl.* **-os**) **1** the chief character in a traditional Italian puppet show. **2** a short stout person of comical appearance.

punch·ing bag *n.* a usu. suspended stuffed or inflated bag used for punching as a form of exercise or training.

punch line *n.* words giving the point of a joke or story.

punch·y /púnchee/ *adj.* (**punchier, punchiest**) **1** having punch or vigor; forceful. **2** = PUNCH-DRUNK. □□ **punch·i·ly** *adv.* **punch·i·ness** *n.*

punc·til·i·ous /pungktíleeəs/ *adj.* **1** attentive to formality or etiquette. **2** precise in behavior. □□ **punc·til·i·ous·ly** *adv.* **punc·til·i·ous·ness** *n.*

punc·tu·al /púngkchōōəl/ *adj.* **1** observant of the appointed time. **2** neither early nor late. **3** *Geom.* of a point. □□ **punc·tu·al·i·ty** /-álitee/ *n.* **punc·tu·al·ly** *adv.*

punc·tu·ate /púngkchōō-ayt/ *v.tr.* **1** insert punctuation marks in. **2** interrupt at intervals (*punctuated his tale with heavy sighs*). **3** emphasize.

punc·tu·a·tion /púngkchōō-áyshən/ *n.* **1** the system or arrangement of marks used to punctuate a written passage. **2** the practice or skill of punctuating.

punc·tu·a·tion mark *n.* any of the marks (e.g., period and comma) used in writing to separate sentences and phrases, etc., and to clarify meaning.

punc·ture /púngkchər/ *n. & v.* ● *n.* **1** a pierced hole, esp. the accidental piercing of a pneumatic tire. **2** a hole made in this way. ● *v.* **1** *tr.* make a puncture in. **2** *intr.* become punctured. **3** *tr.* prick or pierce. **4** *tr.* cause (hopes, confidence, etc.) to collapse; dash; deflate.

pun·dit /púndit/ *n.* **1** (also **pan·dit**) a Hindu learned in Sanskrit and in the philosophy, religion, and jurisprudence of India. **2** often *iron.* **a** a learned expert or teacher. **b** a critic. □□ **pun·dit·ry** *n.*

pun·gent /púnjənt/ *adj.* **1** having a sharp or strong taste or smell. **2** (of remarks) penetrating; biting; caustic. □□ **pun·gen·cy** *n.* **pun·gent·ly** *adv.*

pun·ish /púnish/ *v.tr.* **1** cause (an offender) to suffer for an offense. **2** inflict a penalty on (an offense). **3** *colloq.* inflict severe blows on (an opponent). **4 a** tax severely; subject to severe treatment. **b** abuse or treat improperly. □□ **pun·ish·a·ble** *adj.* **pun·ish·er** *n.* **pun·ish·ing** *adj.* (in sense 4a). **pun·ish·ing·ly** *adv.*

pun·ish·ment /púnishmənt/ *n.* **1** the act or an instance of punishing; the condition of being punished. **2** the loss or suffering inflicted in this. **3** *colloq.* severe treatment or suffering.

pu·ni·tive /pyōōnitiv/ *adj.* (also **pu·ni·to·ry** /-tawree/) **1** inflicting or intended to inflict punishment. **2** (of taxation, etc.) extremely severe. □□ **pu·ni·tive·ly** *adv.*

pu·ni·tive dam·ages *n.pl. Law* additional compensation awarded by a court to a plaintiff in a suit as punishment to the defendant.

Pun·ja·bi /pōōnjáabee/ *n. & adj.* ● *n.* (*pl.* **Punjabis**) **1** a native of the Punjab in India. **2** the language of this people. ● *adj.* of or relating to the Punjab.

punk /pungk/ *n. & adj.* ● *n.* **1 a** a worthless person or thing (often as a general term of abuse). **b** nonsense. **2 a** (in full **punk rock**) a loud fast-moving form of rock music with crude and aggressive effects. **b** (in full **punk rocker**) a devotee of this. **3** a hoodlum or ruffian. **4** a young male homosexual partner. **5** an inexperienced person; a novice. **6** soft crumbly wood used as tinder. **7** a spongy fungal substance, esp. as used as a fuse. ● *adj.* **1** worthless; poor in quality. **2** denoting punk rock and its associations. **3** (of wood) rotten; decayed. □□ **punk·y** *adj.*

punt[1] /punt/ *n. & v.* ● *n.* a long narrow flat-bottomed boat, square at both ends, used mainly

P

PUMP

The simplest pump is the lift pump, which is used for drawing water from under ground. During the intake stroke, an inlet valve opens, the cylinder volume is increased, and water is drawn in. Water above the plunger is lifted up and pours out of the spout.

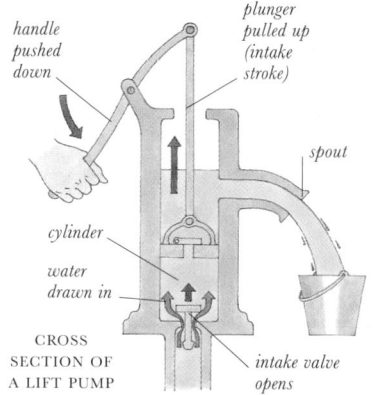

handle pushed down

plunger pulled up (intake stroke)

spout

cylinder

water drawn in

intake valve opens

CROSS SECTION OF A LIFT PUMP

on rivers and propelled by a long pole. ● v. **1** *tr.* propel (a punt) with a pole. **2** *intr. & tr.* travel or convey in a punt. □□ **punt·er** *n.*

punt[2] /punt/ *v. & n.* ● *v.tr.* kick (a ball, as in football or rugby) after it has dropped from the hands and before it reaches the ground. ● *n.* such a kick. □□ **punt·er** *n.*

punt[3] /punt/ *v. & n.* ● *v.intr.* **1** (in some card games) lay a stake against the bank. **2** *Brit. colloq.* **a** bet on a horse, etc. **b** speculate in shares, etc. ● *n.* **1** *esp. Brit.* a bet. **2** a point in faro. **3** a person who plays against the bank in faro.

punt[4] /poont/ *n.* (until the introduction of the euro in 2002) the chief monetary unit of the Republic of Ireland.

punt·er /púntər/ *n.* **1** one who punts, esp. one who punts a ball. **2** *Brit.* a person who gambles or lays a bet. **3** *Brit. colloq.* a customer or client; a member of an audience. **b** *colloq.* a participant in any activity; a person. **c** *sl.* a prostitute's client.

pu·ny /pyo͞onee/ *adj.* (**punier**, **puniest**) **1** undersized. **2** weak; feeble. **3** petty. □□ **pu·ni·ly** *adv.* **pu·ni·ness** *n.*

pup /pup/ *n. & v.* ● *n.* **1** a young dog. **2** a young wolf, rat, seal, etc. **3** *esp. Brit.* an unpleasant or arrogant young man. ● *v.tr.* (**pupped**, **pupping**) (also *absol.*) bring forth (pups). □ **in pup** (of a dog, wolf, etc.) pregnant.

pu·pa /pyo͞opə/ *n.* (*pl.* **pupae** /-pee/) ◀ an insect in the stage of development between larva and imago. ▷ METAMORPHOSIS. □□ **pu·pal** *adj.*

pu·pate /pyo͞opayt/ *v.intr.* become a pupa. □□ **pu·pa·tion** *n.*

pu·pil[1] /pyo͞opəl/ *n.* a person who is taught by another, esp. a student in relation to a teacher. □□ **pu·pil·age** *n.* (also **pu·pil·lage**). **pu·pil·lar·y** *adj.*

pu·pil[2] /pyo͞opəl/ *n.* the dark circular opening in the center of the iris of the eye, varying in size to regulate the passage of light to the retina. ▷ EYE. □□ **pu·pil·lar** *adj.* (also **pu·pil·ar**). **pu·pil·lar·y** *adj.* (also **pu·pil·ar·y**).

P

PUPA OF A FRUIT FLY MAGGOT

pup·pet /púpit/ *n.* **1** ▶ a small figure representing a human being or animal and moved by various means as entertainment. ▷ MARIONETTE. **2** a person whose actions are controlled by another. □□ **pup·pet·ry** *n.*

pup·pet·eer /púpiteér/ *n.* a person who works puppets.

pup·pet state *n.* a country that is nominally independent but actually under the control of another power.

pup·py /púpee/ *n.* (*pl.* **-ies**) **1** a young dog. **2** a conceited or arrogant young man. □□ **pup·py·hood** *n.* **pup·py·ish** *adj.*

pup·py love *n.* romantic attachment or affection between adolescents.

pup tent *n.* a small two-person tent, usu. made of two pieces fastened together.

pur·blind /púrblīnd/ *adj.* **1** partly blind. **2** obtuse; dim-witted. □□ **pur·blind·ness** *n.*

pur·chase /púrchis/ *v. & n.* ● *v.tr.* **1** acquire by payment; buy. **2** obtain or achieve at some cost. ● *n.* **1** the act or an instance of buying. **2** something bought. **3** *Law* the acquisition of property by one's personal action and not by inheritance. **4** a firm hold on a thing to move it or to prevent it from slip-

PUPPET: JAVANESE SHADOW PUPPET

eye

wing

leg

thin rod moves puppet

ping; leverage. □□ **pur·chas·a·ble** *adj.* **pur·chas·er** *n.*

pur·dah /púrdə/ *n. Ind.* **1** a system in certain Muslim and Hindu societies of screening women from strangers by means of a veil or curtain. **2** a curtain in a house, used for this purpose.

pure /pyo͞or/ *adj.* **1** unmixed; unadulterated (*pure white*; *pure alcohol*). **2** of unmixed origin or descent (*pure-blooded*). **3** chaste. **4** morally or sexually undefiled; not corrupt. **5** conforming absolutely to a standard of quality; faultless. **6** guiltless. **7** sincere. **8** mere; simple; nothing but; sheer (*it was pure malice*). **9** (of a sound) not discordant; perfectly in tune. **10** (of a subject of study) dealing with abstract concepts and not practical application. □□ **pure·ness** *n.*

pure·bred /pyo͞orbred/ *adj. & n.* ● *adj.* belonging to a recognized breed of unmixed lineage. ● *n.* a purebred animal.

pu·rée /pyo͞oráy, pyo͞oréé/ *n. & v.* ● *n.* a pulp of vegetables or fruit, etc., reduced to a smooth, creamy substance. ● *v.tr.* (**purées**, **puréed**) make a purée of.

pure·ly /pyo͞orlee/ *adv.* **1** in a pure manner. **2** merely; solely; exclusively.

pur·ga·tion /pərgáyshən/ *n.* **1** purification. **2** purging of the bowels. **3** spiritual cleansing, esp. (*RC Ch.*) of a soul in purgatory. **4** *hist.* the cleansing of oneself from accusation or suspicion by an oath or ordeal.

pur·ga·tive /púrgətiv/ *adj. & n.* ● *adj.* **1** serving to purify. **2** strongly laxative. ● *n.* **1** a purgative thing. **2** a laxative.

pur·ga·to·ry /púrgətawree/ *n. & adj.* ● *n.* (*pl.* **-ies**) **1** the condition or supposed place of spiritual cleansing, esp. (*RC Ch.*) of those dying in the grace of God but having to expiate venial sins, etc. **2** a place or state of temporary suffering or expiation. ● *adj.* purifying. □□ **pur·ga·to·ri·al** /-táwreeəl/ *adj.*

purge /pərj/ *v. & n.* ● *v.tr.* **1** (often foll. by *of, from*) make physically or spiritually clean. **2** remove by a cleansing or erasing (as of computer files) process. **3 a** rid (an organization, party, etc.) of persons regarded as undesirable. **b** remove (a person regarded as undesirable) from an organization, party, etc., often violently or by force. **4 a** empty (the bowels). **b** empty the bowels of. ● *n.* **1 a** the act or an instance of purging. **b** the removal, often in a forcible or violent manner, of people regarded as undesirable from an organization, party, etc. **2** a purgative. □□ **purg·er** *n.*

pu·ri·fy /pyo͞orifī/ *v.tr.* (**-ies**, **-ied**) **1** (often foll. by *of, from*) cleanse or make pure. **2** make ceremonially clean. **3** clear of extraneous elements. □□ **pu·ri·fi·ca·tion** /-fikáshən/ *n.* **pu·rif·i·ca·to·ry** /-rífəkətáwree/ *adj.* **pu·ri·fi·er** *n.*

Pu·rim /po͞orim, po͞oréém/ *n.* a Jewish spring festival commemorating the defeat of Haman's plot to massacre the Jews (Esth. 9).

pur·ist /pyo͞orist/ *n.* a stickler for or advocate of scrupulous purity, esp. in language or art. □□ **pur·ism** *n.* **pu·ris·tic** *adj.*

pu·ri·tan /pyo͞orit'n/ *n. & adj.* ● *n.* **1** (**Puritan**) *hist.* a member of a group of English Protestants who regarded the Reformation of the Church under Elizabeth as incomplete and sought to simplify and regulate forms of worship. **2** a purist member of any party. **3** a person practicing or affecting extreme strictness in religion or morals. ● *adj.* **1** *hist.* of or relating to the Puritans. **2** scrupulous and austere in religion or morals. □□ **pu·ri·tan·ism** *n.*

pu·ri·tan·i·cal /pyo͞oritánikəl/ *adj.* often *derog.* practicing or affecting strict religious or moral behavior. □□ **pu·ri·tan·i·cal·ly** *adv.*

pu·ri·ty /pyo͞oritee/ *n.* **1** pureness; cleanness. **2** freedom from physical or moral pollution.

purl /pərl/ *n. & v.* ● *n.* a knitting stitch made by putting the needle through the front of the previous stitch and passing the yarn around the back of the needle. ● *v.tr.* (also *absol.*) knit with a purl stitch.

pur·lieu /púrlyo͞o/ *n.* (*pl.* **purlieus**) **1** a person's bounds or limits. **2** a person's usual haunts. **3** (in *pl.*) the outskirts; an outlying region.

pur·lin /púrlin/ *n.* a horizontal beam along the length of a roof, resting on principals and supporting the common rafters or boards. ▷ ROOF

pur·loin /pərlóyn/ *v.tr. literary* steal; pilfer. □□ **pur·loin·er** *n.*

pur·ple /púrpəl/ *n., adj., & v.* ● *n.* **1** a color intermediate between red and blue. **2** a purple robe, esp. as the dress of an emperor or senior magistrate. **3** the scarlet official dress of a cardinal. **4** (*prec. by the*) a position of rank, authority, or privilege. ● *adj.* of a purple color. ● *v.tr. & intr.* make or become purple. □ **born in** (or **to**) **the purple** **1** born into a reigning family. **2** belonging to the most privileged class. □□ **pur·ple·ness** *n.* **pur·plish** *adj.* **pur·ply** *adj.*

Pur·ple Heart *n.* ◀ a US military decoration for those wounded in action.

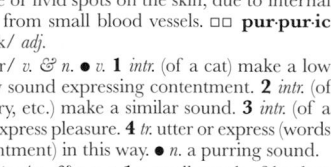

ribbon

PURPLE HEART

pur·ple pas·sage *n.* (also **purple prose** or **purple patch**) an overly ornate or elaborate passage, esp. in a literary composition.

pur·port *v. & n.* ● *v.tr.* /pərpáwrt/ **1** profess; be intended to seem. **2** (often foll. by *that* + clause) (of a document or speech) have as its meaning; state. ● *n.* /púrpawrt/ □□ **pur·port·ed·ly** /-páwrtidlee/ *adv.*

pur·pose /púrpəs/ *n. & v.* ● *n.* **1** an object to be attained; a thing intended. **2** the intention to act. **3** resolution; determination. **4** the reason for which something is done or made. ● *v.tr.* have as one's purpose; intend. □ **on purpose** intentionally.

pur·pose·ful /púrpəsfo͞ol/ *adj.* **1** having or indicating purpose. **2** intentional. **3** resolute. □□ **pur·pose·ful·ly** *adv.* **pur·pose·ful·ness** *n.*

pur·pose·less /púrpəslis/ *adj.* having no aim or plan. □□ **pur·pose·less·ly** *adv.* **pur·pose·less·ness** *n.*

pur·pose·ly /púrpəslee/ *adv.* intentionally.

pur·pos·ive /púrpəsiv, pərpó-/ *adj.* **1** having, serving, or done with a purpose. **2** resolute; purposeful. □□ **pur·pos·ive·ly** *adv.* **pur·pos·ive·ness** *n.*

pur·pur·a /púrpyo͞orə/ *n.* a disease characterized by purple or livid spots on the skin, due to internal bleeding from small blood vessels. □□ **pur·pur·ic** /-pyo͞orik/ *adj.*

purr /pər/ *v. & n.* ● *v.* **1** *intr.* (of a cat) make a low vibratory sound expressing contentment. **2** *intr.* (of machinery, etc.) make a similar sound. **3** *intr.* (of a person) express pleasure. **4** *tr.* utter or express (words or contentment) in this way. ● *n.* a purring sound.

purse /pərs/ *n. & v.* ● *n.* **1** a small pouch of leather, etc., for carrying money on the person. **2** a small bag for carrying personal effects, esp. one carried by a woman. **3** a receptacle resembling a purse in form or purpose. **4** money; funds. **5** a sum collected as a present or given as a prize in a contest. ● *v.* **1** *tr.* (often foll. by *up*) pucker or contract (the lips). **2** *intr.* become contracted and wrinkled. □ **hold the purse strings** have control of expenditure.

purs·er /púrsər/ *n.* an officer on a ship who keeps the accounts, esp. the head steward in a passenger vessel. □□ **purs·er·ship** *n.*

purs·lane /púrslayn/ *n.* ▶ any of various plants of the genus *Portulaca*, esp. *P. oleracea*, with green or golden leaves, used as a herb and salad vegetable.

PURSLANE
(*Portulaca oleracea*)

pur·su·ance /pərsóoəns/ *n.* (foll. by *of*) the carrying out or observance (of a plan, idea, etc.).

pur·su·ant /pərsóoənt/ *adj.* & *adv.* ● *adj.* pursuing. ● *adv.* (foll. by *to*) conforming to or in accordance with. □□ **pur·su·ant·ly** *adv.*

pur·sue /pərsóo/ *v.* (**pursues**, **pursued**, **pursuing**) **1** *tr.* follow with intent to overtake or capture or do harm to. **2** *tr.* continue or proceed along (a route or course of action). **3** *tr.* follow or engage in (study or other activity). **4** *tr.* proceed in compliance with (a plan, etc.). **5** *tr.* seek after; aim at. **6** *tr.* continue to investigate or discuss (a topic). **7** *tr.* seek the attention or acquaintance of (a person) persistently. **8** *tr.* (of misfortune, etc.) persistently assail. **9** *tr.* persistently attend; stick to. **10** *intr.* go in pursuit. □□ **pur·su·a·ble** *adj.* **pur·su·er** *n.*

pur·suit /pərsóot/ *n.* **1** the act or an instance of pursuing. **2** an occupation or activity pursued. □ **in pursuit of** pursuing.

pu·ru·lent /pyóorələnt, pyóoryə-/ *adj.* **1** consisting of or containing pus. **2** discharging pus. □□ **pu·ru·lence** *n.* **pu·ru·len·cy** *n.* **pu·ru·lent·ly** *adv.*

pur·vey /pərváy/ *v.* **1** *tr.* provide or supply (articles of food) as one's business. **2** *intr.* (often foll. by *for*) **a** make provision. **b** act as supplier. □□ **pur·vey·or** *n.*

pur·vey·ance /pərváyəns/ *n.* the act of purveying.

pur·view /pɔ́rvyoo/ *n.* **1** the scope or range of a document, scheme, etc. **2** the range of physical or mental vision.

pus /pus/ *n.* a thick yellowish or greenish liquid produced from infected tissue.

push /poosh/ *v.* & *n.* ● *v.* **1** *tr.* exert a force on (a thing) to move it away from oneself or from the origin of the force. **2** *tr.* cause to move in this direction. **3** *intr.* exert such a force (*do not push against the door*). **4** *tr.* press; depress (*push the button for service*). **5** *intr.* & *tr.* **a** thrust forward or upward. **b** project or cause to project (*pushes out new roots*). **6** *intr.* move forward by force or persistence. **7** *tr.* make (one's way) by pushing. **8** *intr.* exert oneself, esp. to surpass others. **9** *tr.* (often foll. by *to*, *into*, or *to* + infin.) urge or impel. **10** *tr.* tax the abilities or tolerance of; press (a person) hard. **11** *tr.* pursue (a claim, etc.). **12** *tr.* promote the use or sale or adoption of, e.g., by advertising. **13** *intr.* (foll. by *for*) demand persistently (*pushed hard for reform*). **14** *tr. colloq.* sell (a drug) illegally. **15** *tr. colloq.* to approach, esp. in age (*pushing thirty*). ● *n.* **1** the act or an instance of pushing; a shove or thrust. **2** the force exerted in this. **3** a vigorous effort. **4** a military attack in force. **5** enterprise; determination to succeed. **6** the use of influence to advance a person. **7** the pressure of affairs. **8** a crisis. □ **be pushed for** *colloq.* have very little of (esp. time). **if** (or **when**) **push comes to shove** when a problem must be faced; in a crisis. **push around** *colloq.* bully. **push one's luck 1** take undue risks. **2** act presumptuously. **push off 1 a** set off; depart. **b** push with an oar, etc., to get a boat out into a river, etc. **2** esp. *Brit.* (often in *imper.*) *colloq.* go away. **push through** get (a scheme, proposal, etc.) completed or accepted quickly.

push but·ton *n.* **1** a button to be pushed, esp. to operate an electrical device. **2** (*attrib.*) operated in this way.

push·er /pooshər/ *n.* **1** *colloq.* an illegal seller of drugs. **2** *colloq.* a pushing or pushy person.

push·ing /pooshing/ *adj.* **1** pushy; aggressively ambitious. **2** *colloq.* having nearly reached (a specified age). □□ **push·ing·ly** *adv.*

push·o·ver /pooshōvər/ *n. colloq.* **1** something that is easily done. **2** a person who can easily be overcome, persuaded, etc.

push-up *n.* an exercise in which the body, extended and prone, is raised upwards by pushing down with the hands until the arms are straight.

push·y /pooshee/ *adj.* (**pushier**, **pushiest**) *colloq.* **1** excessively self-assertive. **2** selfishly determined to succeed. □□ **push·i·ly** *adv.* **push·i·ness** *n.*

pu·sil·lan·i·mous /pyóosilánimǝs/ *adj.* lacking courage; timid. □□ **pu·sil·la·nim·i·ty** /-lənímitee/ *n.* **pu·sil·lan·i·mous·ly** *adv.*

puss /poos/ *n. colloq.* **1** a cat (esp. as a form of address). **2** a girl. **3** *Brit.* a hare.

pus·sy /poosee/ *n.* (*pl.* **-ies**) **1** (also **pus·sy·cat**) *colloq.* a cat. **2** *coarse sl.* the vulva. ¶ Usually considered a taboo use.

pus·sy·foot /pooseefoot/ *v.intr.* **1** move stealthily or warily. **2** act cautiously or noncommittally. □□ **pus·sy·foot·er** *n.*

pus·sy wil·low *n.* any of various willows, esp. *Salix discolor*, with furry catkins.

pus·tule /púschool/ *n.* a pimple containing pus. □□ **pus·tu·lar** *adj.* **pus·tu·lous** *adj.*

put[1] /poot/ *v.*, *n.*, & *adj.* ● *v.* (**putting**; *past* and *past part.* **put**) **1** *tr.* move to or cause to be in a specified place or position (*put it in your pocket*; *put the children to bed*). **2** *tr.* bring into a specified condition, relation, or state (*an accident put the car out of action*). **3** *tr.* **a** (often foll. by *on*) impose or assign (*where do you put the blame?*). **b** (foll. by *on*, *to*) impose or enforce the existence of (*put a stop to it*). **4** *tr.* **a** cause (a person) to go or be, habitually or temporarily (*put them at their ease*; *put them on the right track*). **b** *refl.* imagine (oneself) in a specified situation (*put yourself in my shoes*). **5** *tr.* (foll. by *for*) substitute (one thing for another). **6** *tr.* express (a thought or idea) in a specified way (*to put it mildly*). **7** *tr.* (foll. by *at*) estimate (an amount, etc., at a specified amount) (*put the cost at $50*). **8** *tr.* (foll. by *into*) express or translate in (words, or another language). **9** *tr.* (foll. by *into*) invest (money in an asset, e.g., land). **10** *tr.* (foll. by *on*) stake (money) on (a horse, etc.). **11** *tr.* (foll. by *to*) apply or devote to a use or purpose (*put it to good use*). **12** *tr.* (foll. by *to*) submit for consideration or attention (*let me put it to you another way*; *shall now put it to a vote*). **13** *tr.* (foll. by *to*) subject (a person) to (death, suffering, etc.). **14** *tr.* throw (esp. a shot or weight) as an athletic sport or exercise. ▷ SHOT PUT. **15** *tr.* (foll. by *to*) couple (an animal) with (another of the opposite sex) for breeding. **16** *intr.* (foll. by *back*, *off*, *out*, etc.) (of a ship, etc.) proceed or follow a course in a specified direction. ● *n.* **1** a throw of the shot or weight. **2** *Stock Exch.* the option of selling stock or a commodity at a fixed price at a given date. ● *adj.* stationary; fixed (*stay put*). □ **put about 1** spread (information, rumor, etc.). **2** *Naut.* turn around; put (a ship) on the opposite tack. **put across 1** make acceptable or effective. **2** express in an understandable way. **3** (often in **put it** (or **one**) **across**) achieve by deceit. **put aside 1** = *put by*. **2** set aside; ignore. **put away 1** put (a thing) back in the place where it is normally kept. **2** set (money, etc.) aside for future use. **3 a** confine or imprison. **b** commit to a mental institution. **4** consume (food and drink), esp. in large quantities. **5** put (an old or sick animal) to death. **put back 1** restore to its proper or former place. **2** change (a planned event) to a later date or time. **put a bold**, etc., **face on it** see FACE. **put by** lay (money, etc.) aside for future use. **put down 1** suppress by force or authority. **2** *colloq.* snub or humiliate. **3** record or enter in writing. **4** enter the name of (a person) on a list, esp. as a member or subscriber. **5** (foll. by *as*, *for*) account, reckon, or categorize. **6** (foll. by *to*) attribute (*put it down to bad planning*). **7** put (an old or sick animal) to death. **8** preserve or store (eggs, etc.) for future use. **9** pay (a specified sum) as a deposit. **10** put (a baby) to bed. **11** land (an aircraft). **12** stop to let (passengers) get off. **put one's finger on** identify, esp. a problem or difficulty. **put one's foot down** see FOOT. **put one's foot in it** see FOOT. **put forth 1** (of a plant) send out (buds or leaves). **2** *formal* submit or put into circulation. **put forward** suggest or propose. **put in 1 a** enter or submit (a claim, etc.). **b** (foll. by *for*) submit a claim for (a specified thing). **2** (foll. by *for*) be a candidate for (an appointment, election, etc.). **3** spend (time). **4** perform (a spell of work) as part of a whole. **5** interpose (a remark, blow, etc.). **6** insert as an addition. **put it to a person** (often foll. by *that* + clause) challenge a person to deny. **put off 1 a** postpone. **b** postpone an engagement with (a person). **2** (often foll. by *with*) evade (a person) with an excuse, etc. **3** hinder or dissuade. **put on 1** clothe oneself with. **2** cause (an electrical device, light, etc.) to function. **3** cause (esp. transport) to be available; provide. **4** stage (a play, show, etc.). **5 a** pretend to be affected by (an emotion). **b** assume; take on (a character or appearance). **c** (**put it on**) exaggerate one's feelings, etc. **6** increase one's weight by (a specified amount). **7** (foll. by *to*) make aware of or put in touch with (*put us on to their new accountant*). **8** *colloq.* tease; play a trick on. **put out 1 a** (often as **put out** *adj.*) disconcert or annoy. **b** (often *refl.*) inconvenience (*don't put yourself out*). **2** extinguish (a fire or light). **3** *Baseball* cause (a batter or runner) to be out. **4** dislocate (a joint). **5** exert (strength, etc.). **6** allocate (work) to be done off the premises. **7** blind (a person's eyes). **8** issue; publish. **9** *coarse sl.* engage in sexual intercourse. **put over 1** make acceptable or effective. **2** express in an understandable way. **3** postpone. **4** achieve by deceit. **put one over** (usu. foll. by *on*) get the better of; outsmart; trick. **put through 1** carry out or complete (a task or transaction). **2** (often foll. by *to*) connect (a person) by telephone to another. **put together 1** assemble (a whole) from parts. **2** combine (parts) to form a whole. **put under** render unconscious by anesthetic, etc. **put up 1** build or erect. **2** to can; preserve (food) for later use. **3** take or provide accommodation for (*friends put me up for the night*). **4** engage in (a fight, struggle, etc.) as a form of resistance. **5** present (a proposal). **6 a** present oneself for election. **b** propose for election. **7** provide (money) as a backer in an enterprise. **8** display (a notice). **9** publish (banns). **10** offer for sale or competition. **11** esp. *Brit.* raise (a price, etc.). **put upon** *colloq.* make unfair or excessive demands on; take advantage of (a person). **put a person up to** (usu. foll. by verbal noun) instigate a person in (*put them up to stealing the money*). **put up with** endure; tolerate; submit to. □□ **put·ter** *n.*

put[2] var. of PUTT.

pu·ta·tive /pyóotətiv/ *adj.* reputed; supposed (*his putative father*). □□ **pu·ta·tive·ly** *adv.*

put-down *n. colloq.* an act or instance of snubbing or humiliating (someone).

put-on *n. colloq.* a deception or hoax.

pu·tre·fy /pyóotrifī/ *v.* (**-ies**, **-ied**) **1** *intr.* & *tr.* become or make putrid; go bad. **2** *intr.* fester; suppurate. **3** *intr.* become morally corrupt. □□ **pu·tre·fa·cient** /-fáyshənt/ *adj.* **pu·tre·fac·tion** /-fákshən/ *n.* **pu·tre·fac·tive** /-fáktiv/ *adj.*

pu·tres·cent /pyootrésənt/ *adj.* **1** in the process of rotting. **2** of or accompanying this process. □□ **pu·tres·cence** *n.*

pu·trid /pyóotrid/ *adj.* **1** decomposed; rotten. **2** foul; noxious. **3** corrupt. **4** *sl.* of poor quality; contemptible; very unpleasant. □□ **pu·trid·i·ty** /-tríditee/ *n.* **pu·trid·ly** *adv.* **pu·trid·ness** *n.*

putsch /pooch/ *n.* an attempt at political revolution; a violent uprising.

putt /put/ *v.* & *n.* (also *Brit.* **put**) ● *v.tr.* (**putted**, **putting**) strike (a golf ball) gently to get it into or nearer to a hole on a putting green. ● *n.* a putting stroke.

puttee /putée, pútee/ *n.* **1** ◀ a long strip of cloth wound spirally around the leg from ankle to knee for protection and support. **2** *US* a leather legging.

PUTTEE

put·ter[1] /pútər/ *n.* **1** a golf club used in putting. ▷ GOLF. **2** a golfer who putts.

put·ter[2] /pútər/ *v.* (also *Brit.* **potter**) **1** *intr.* **a** (often foll. by *about*, *around*) work or occupy oneself in a desultory but pleasant manner (*likes puttering around in the garden*). **b** (often foll. by *at*, *in*) dabble in a subject or occupation. **2** *intr.* go slowly; dawdle;

P

loiter. **3** *tr.* (foll. by *away*) fritter away (one's time, etc.). □□ **put·ter·er** *n.*

put·ting green *n.* (in golf) the area of close-cropped grass around a hole. ▷ GOLF

put·to /pŏŏtō/ *n.* (*pl.* **putti** /-tee/) a representation of a naked child (esp. a cherub or a cupid) in (esp. Renaissance) art.

put·ty /pútee/ *n. & v.* ● *n.* (*pl.* **-ies**) **1** a cement made from whiting and raw linseed oil, used for fixing panes of glass, filling holes in woodwork, etc. **2** a fine white mortar of lime and water, used in pointing brickwork, etc. **3** a polishing powder usu. made from tin oxide, used in jewelry work. ● *v.tr.* (**-ies**, **-ied**) cover, fix, join, or fill up with putty. □ **putty in a person's hands** someone who is overcompliant, or easily influenced.

putz /puts/ *n. & v.* ● *n.* **1** *coarse sl.* the penis. **2** *sl.* a simple-minded foolish person. ● *v.intr. sl.* (usu. foll. by *around*) move (about) or occupy oneself in an aimless or idle manner.

puz·zle /púzəl/ *n. & v.* ● *n.* **1** a difficult or confusing problem; an enigma. **2** a problem or toy designed to test knowledge or ingenuity. ● *v.* **1** *tr.* confound or disconcert mentally. **2** *intr.* (usu. foll. by *over*, etc.) be perplexed (about). **3** *tr.* (usu. as **puzzling** *adj.*) require much thought to comprehend (*a puzzling situation*). **4** *tr.* (foll. by *out*) solve or understand by hard thought. □□ **puz·zle·ment** *n.* **puz·zling·ly** *adv.*

puz·zler /púzlər/ *n.* a difficult question or problem.

PVA *abbr.* polyvinyl acetate.

PVC *abbr.* polyvinyl chloride.

Pvt. *abbr.* private.

p.w. *abbr.* per week.

PX *abbr.* post exchange.

py·e·mi·a /pī-éemeeə/ *n.* blood poisoning caused by the spread of pus-forming bacteria in the bloodstream from a source of infection. □□ **py·e·mic** *adj.*

pyg·my /pígmee/ *n.* (also **pig·my**) (*pl.* **-ies**) **1** a member of a small people of equatorial Africa and parts of SE Asia. **2** a very small person, animal, or thing. **3** an insignificant person. **4** (*attrib.*) **a** of or relating to pygmies. **b** (of a person, animal, etc.) dwarf. □□ **pyg·mae·an** /pigméeən, pígmee-/ *adj.* (also **pyg·me·an**)

py·ja·mas esp. *Brit.* var. of PAJAMAS.

py·lon /pílon/ *n.* **1** a tall structure erected as a support (esp. for electric power cables) or boundary or decoration. **2** a gateway, esp. of an ancient Egyptian temple. **3** a structure marking a path for aircraft. **4** a structure supporting an aircraft engine.

py·lo·rus /pīláwrəs, pi-/ *n.* (*pl.* **pylori** /-rī/) *Anat.* the opening from the stomach into the duodenum. □□ **py·lor·ic** /-láwrik/ *adj.*

py·or·rhe·a /píəréeə/ *n.* **1** a disease of periodontal tissue causing shrinkage of the gums and loosening of the teeth. **2** any discharge of pus.

py·ra·can·tha /pírəkánthə/ *n.* ◀ any evergreen thorny shrub of the genus *Pyracantha*, having white flowers and bright red or yellow berries.

PYRACANTHA
(*Pyracantha rogersiana*)

pyr·a·mid /pírəmid/ *n.* **1 a** ▲ a monumental structure, usu. of stone, with a square base and sloping sides meeting centrally at an apex, esp. an ancient Egyptian royal tomb. **b** a similar structure, esp. a Mayan temple of this type. **2** a solid of this type with a base of three or more sides. **3** a pyramid-shaped thing or pile of things. □□ **py·ram·i·dal** /-rámid'l/ *adj.* **py·ram·**

P

PYRAMID

The Egyptian pyramids were funerary monuments built for the kings (also known as *pharaohs*) and their closest relatives. Classical Egyptian pyramids characteristically are one structure in a temple complex, comprising a valley temple at a short distance from the pyramid and connected by a causeway, and a mortuary temple situated adjacent to the pyramid.

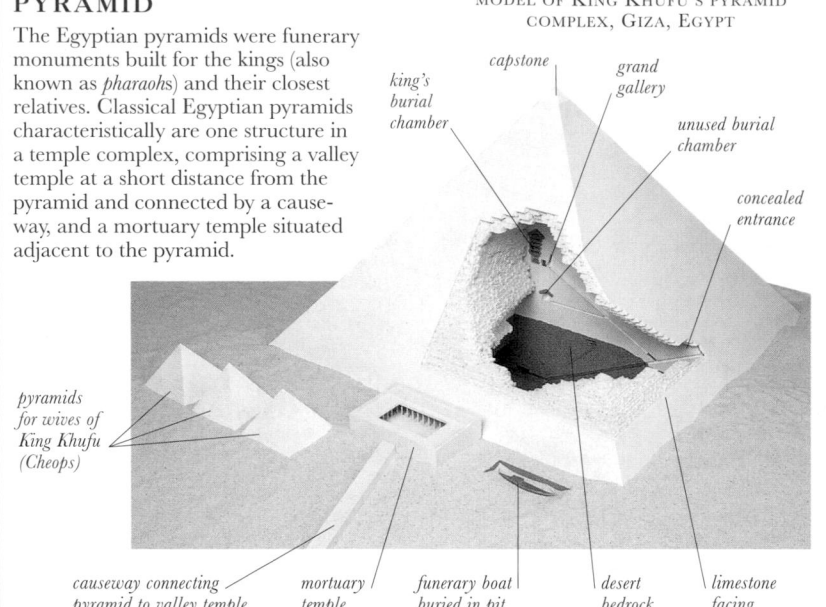

MODEL OF KING KHUFU'S PYRAMID COMPLEX, GIZA, EGYPT

king's burial chamber — capstone — grand gallery — unused burial chamber — concealed entrance

pyramids for wives of King Khufu (Cheops)

causeway connecting pyramid to valley temple — mortuary temple — funerary boat buried in pit — desert bedrock — limestone facing

---

i·dal·ly *adv.* **pyr·a·mid·ic** /-mídik/ *adj.* (also **pyr·a·mid·i·cal**). **pyr·a·mid·i·cal·ly** *adv.*

pyre /pīr/ *n.* a heap of combustible material, esp. a funeral pile for burning a corpse.

py·re·thrin /pīréethrin, -réth-/ *n.* any of several active constituents of pyrethrum flowers used in the manufacture of insecticides.

py·re·thrum /pīréethrəm, -réth-/ *n.* **1** any of several aromatic chrysanthemums of the genus *Chrysanthemum*. **2** an insecticide made from the dried flowers of these plants.

py·ret·ic /pīrétik/ *adj.* of, for, or producing fever.

Py·rex /píreks/ *n. Trademark* a hard heat-resistant type of glass, often used for cookware.

py·rex·i·a /pīrékseeə/ *n. Med.* = FEVER 1. □□ **py·rex·i·al** /-rékseeəl/. **py·rex·ic** **py·rex·i·cal** *adj.*

pyr·i·dox·ine /píridókseen, -sin/ *n.* a vitamin of the B complex found in yeast, and important in the body's use of unsaturated fatty acids. Also called **vitamin B$_6$**.

py·rite /pírīt/ *n.* = PYRITES.

py·rites /pīríteez, pírīts/ *n.* (in full **iron pyrites**) a yellow lustrous form of iron disulfide. ▷ FOOL'S GOLD. □□ **py·rit·ic** /-rítik/ *adj.* **py·ri·tif·er·ous** /-ritif-ərəs/ *adj.* **py·ri·tize** /píritīz/ *v.tr.* **py·ri·tous** /píritəs/ *adj.*

py·ro·gen·ic /pīrōjénik/ *adj.* (also **py·rog·e·nous** /pīrójinəs/) **1 a** producing heat, esp. in the body. **b** producing fever. **2** produced by combustion or volcanic processes.

py·ro·ma·ni·a /pīrōmáyneeə/ *n.* an obsessive desire to set fire to things. □□ **py·ro·ma·ni·ac** *n.*

py·rom·e·ter /pīrómitər/ *n.* an instrument for measuring high temperatures, esp. in furnaces and kilns. □□ **py·ro·met·ric** /-rəmétrik/ *adj.* **py·ro·met·ri·cal·ly** *adv.* **py·rom·e·try** /-rómitree/ *n.*

pyrope /pírōp/ *n.* a deep red variety of garnet.

py·ro·sis /pīrṓsis/ *n. Med.* a burning sensation in the lower part of the chest, combined with the return of gastric acid to the mouth. Also called **heartburn**.

py·ro·tech·nic /pírōtéknik/ *adj.* **1** of or relating to fireworks. **2** (of wit, etc.) brilliant or sensational. □□ **py·ro·tech·ni·cal** *adj.* **py·ro·tech·nist** *n.* **py·ro·tech·ny** *n.*

py·ro·tech·nics /pírōtékniks/ *n.pl.* **1** the art of making fireworks. **2** a display of fireworks. **3** any brilliant display.

py·rox·ene /pīrókseen/ *n.* any of a group of minerals commonly found as components of igneous rocks, composed of silicates of calcium, magnesium, and iron.

pyr·rhic[1] /pírik/ *adj.* (of a victory) won at too great a cost to be of use to the victor.

pyr·rhic[2] /pírik/ *n. & adj.* ● *n.* a metrical foot of two short or unaccented syllables. ● *adj.* written in or based on pyrrhics.

Py·thag·o·re·an /pīthágəréeən/ *adj. & n.* ● *adj.* of or relating to the Greek philosopher Pythagoras (6th c. BC) or his philosophy, esp. regarding the transmigration of souls. ● *n.* a follower of Pythagoras.

Py·thag·o·re·an the·o·rem /pīthágəréeən/ *n.* the theorem attributed to Pythagoras (see PYTHAGOREAN) that the square of the hypotenuse of a right triangle is equal to the sum of the squares of the other two sides.

py·thon /píthon, -thən/ *n.* ▼ any constricting snake of the family Pythonidae, esp. of the genus *Python*, found throughout the tropics in the Old World. ▷ EGG, SNAKE. □□ **py·thon·ic** /-thónik/ *adj.*

PYTHON:
RETICULATED
PYTHON
(*Python reticulatus*)

pyx /piks/ *n.* (also **pix**) **1** *Eccl.* the vessel in which the consecrated bread of the Eucharist is kept. **2** (also **pyx chest**) a box at a mint in which specimen gold and silver coins are deposited to be tested by weight and assayed.

Q /kyoo/ *n.* (also **q**) (*pl.* **Qs** or **Q's**) the seventeenth letter of the alphabet.

qa·di /káadi, káydi/ *n.* (also **kadi**) (*pl.* **-is**) a judge in a Muslim country.

qb *abbr.* quarterback.

QED *abbr.* QUOD ERAT DEMONSTRANDUM.

qi·gong /cheegóng/ *n.* a Chinese system of physical exercises and breathing control related to tai chi.

QM *abbr.* quartermaster.

qr. *abbr.* quarter(s).

qt. *abbr.* quart(s).

q.t. *n. colloq.* quiet (esp. *on the q.t.*).

Q-tip /kyóotip/ *n. Trademark* a swab consisting of a thin stick with cotton affixed to each end.

qty. *abbr.* quantity.

quack[1] /kwak/ *n. & v.* ● *n.* the harsh sound made by ducks. ● *v.intr.* utter this sound.

quack[2] /kwak/ *n.* **1 a** an unqualified person who dishonestly claims to have medical knowledge. **b** (*attrib.*) of or characteristic of unskilled medical practice (*quack cure*). **2** *Brit. sl.* a doctor. □□ **quack·er·y** *n.* **quack·ish** *adj.*

quad[1] /kwod/ *n. colloq.* a quadrangle.

quad[2] /kwod/ *n. colloq.* = QUADRUPLET 1.

quad[3] /kwod/ *n. Printing* a piece of blank metal type used in spacing.

quad[4] /kwod/ *adj.* quadraphonic.

quad bike *n.* ▼ a motorcycle with four large tires, for off-road use.

QUAD BIKE: 4 X 4 QUAD BIKE

quad·ra·ge·nar·i·an /kwódrəjináireeən/ *n. & adj.* ● *n.* a person from 40 to 49 years old. ● *adj.* of this age.

quad·ran·gle /kwódranggəl/ *n.* **1** a four-sided plane figure, esp. a square or rectangle. **2 a** a four-sided yard or courtyard, esp. enclosed by buildings, as in some colleges. **b** such a courtyard with the buildings around it. **3** the land area represented on one map sheet as published by the U.S. Geological Survey. □□ **quad·ran·gu·lar** /-ránggyələr/ *adj.*

quad·rant /kwódrənt/ *n.* **1** a quarter of a circle's circumference. **2** a plane figure enclosed by two radii of a circle at right angles and the arc cut off by them. ▷ CIRCLE. **3** a quarter of a sphere, etc. **4 a** a thing, esp. a graduated strip of metal, shaped like a quarter circle. **b** ► an instrument graduated (esp. through an arc of 90°) for taking angular measurements. □□ **quad·ran·tal** /-dránt'l/ *adj.*

quad·ra·phon·ic /kwódrəfónik/ *adj.* (also **quad·ro·phon·ic** or **quad·ri·phon·ic**) (of sound reproduction) using four transmission channels. □□ **quad·ra·phon·i·cal·ly** *adv.* **quad·ra·phon·ics** *n.pl.* **qua·draph·o·ny** /-rófənee/ *n.*

quad·rate *adj., n., & v.* ● *adj.* /kwódrət/ esp. *Anat. & Zool.* square or rectangular (*quadrate bone; quadrate muscle*). ● *n.* /kwódrət/ **1** a quadrate bone or muscle. **2** a rectangular object. ● *v.* /kwodráyt/ **1** *tr.* make square. **2** *intr. & tr.* (often foll. by *with*) conform or make conform.

quad·rat·ic /kwodrátik/ *adj. & n. Math.* ● *adj.* **1** involving the second and no higher power of an unknown quantity or variable (*quadratic equation*). **2** square. ● *n.* **1** a quadratic equation. **2** (in *pl.*) the branch of algebra dealing with these.

quad·ra·ture /kwódrəchər/ *n. Math.* the process of constructing a square with an area equal to that of a figure bounded by a curve, e.g., a circle.

quad·ren·ni·al /kwodréneeəl/ *adj.* **1** lasting four years. **2** recurring every four years. □□ **quad·ren·ni·al·ly** *adv.*

quadri- /kwódree/ (also **quadr-** or **quadru-**) *comb. form* denoting four.

quad·ric /kwódrik/ *adj. & n. Geom.* ● *adj.* (of a surface) described by an equation of the second degree. ● *n.* a quadric surface.

quad·ri·ceps /kwódriseps/ *n. Anat.* a four-part muscle at the front of the thigh.

quad·ri·lat·er·al /kwódrilátərəl/ *adj. & n.* ● *adj.* having four sides. ● *n.* a four-sided figure.

quad·rille[1] /kwodríl/ *n.* **1** a square dance containing usu. five parts. **2** the music for this.

quad·rille[2] /kwodríl/ *n.* a card game for four players with forty cards, fashionable in the 18th c.

quad·ril·lion /kwodrílyən/ *n.* (*pl.* same or **quad·rillions**) a thousand raised to the fifth (or esp. *Brit.* the eighth) power (10^{15} and 10^{24} respectively).

quad·ri·no·mi·al /kwódrinómeeəl/ *n. & adj. Math.* ● *n.* an expression of four algebraic terms. ● *adj.* of or being a quadrinomial.

quad·ri·ple·gi·a /kwódripléejeeə, -jə/ *n. Med.* paralysis of all four limbs. □□ **quad·ri·ple·gic** *adj. & n.*

quad·ri·va·lent /kwódriváylənt/ *adj. Chem.* having a valence of four.

quad·roon /kwodróon/ *n.* a person of one-quarter black ancestry.

quadro·phon·ic var. of QUADRAPHONIC.

quadru- var. of QUADRI-.

quad·ru·ped /kwódrəped/ *n. & adj.* ● *n.* a four-footed animal, esp. a four-footed mammal. ● *adj.* four-footed. □□ **quad·ru·pe·dal** /-róopid'l/ *adj.*

quad·ru·ple /kwodróopəl, -drúp-, kwódróopəl/ *adj., n., & v.* ● *adj.* **1** fourfold. **2 a** having four parts.

sight line
peephole
peephole
apex
degree scale
angle read where string crosses scale
plumb bob

QUADRANT:
MEASURING ALTITUDE
USING A QUADRANT

b involving four participants (*quadruple alliance*). **3** being four times as many or as much. **4** (of time in music) having four beats in a bar. ● *n.* a fourfold number or amount. ● *v.tr. & intr.* multiply by four; increase fourfold. □□ **quad·ru·ply** *adv.*

quad·ru·plet /kwodróoplit, -drúp-, kwódróoplit/ *n.* **1** each of four children born at one birth. **2** a set of four things working together. **3** *Mus.* a group of four notes to be performed in the time of three.

quad·ru·pli·cate *adj. & v.* ● *adj.* /kwodróoplikət/ **1** fourfold. **2** of which four copies are made. ● *v.tr.* /-kayt/ **1** multiply by four. **2** make four identical copies of. **3 in quadruplicate** in four identical copies. □□ **quad·ru·pli·ca·tion** /-káyshən/ *n.*

quad·ru·plic·i·ty /kwódróoplísitee/ *n.* the state of being fourfold.

quaff /kwof, kwaf, kwawf/ *v. literary* **1** *tr. & intr.* drink deeply. **2** *tr.* drain (a cup, etc.) in long drafts. □□ **quaff·a·ble** *adj.* **quaff·er** *n.*

quag·ga /kwágə/ *n.* ▼ an extinct zebralike mammal, *Equus quagga*, formerly native to S. Africa, with yellowish-brown stripes on the head, neck, and forebody.

quag·mire /kwágmīr, kwóg-/ *n.* **1** a soft boggy or marshy area that gives way underfoot. **2** a hazardous or awkward situation.

qua·hog /kwáwhawg, -hog, kwó-, kō-/ *n.* (also **qua·haug**) an edible clam, *Mercenaria* (formerly *Venus*) *mercinaria*, of the Atlantic coast of N. America.

QUAGGA
(*Equus quagga*)

quaich /kwaykh/ *n.* (also **quaigh**) *Sc.* a kind of drinking cup, usu. of wood and with two handles.

quail[1] /kwayl/ *n.* (*pl.* same or **quails**) **1** any small migratory Old World bird of the genus *Coturnix*, with a short tail and related to the partridge. **2** any small migratory New World bird of the genus *Colinus*, esp. the bobwhite.

quail[2] /kwayl/ *v.intr.* flinch; be apprehensive with fear.

quaint /kwaynt/ *adj.* **1** piquantly or attractively unfamiliar or old-fashioned. **2** unusual; odd. □□ **quaint·ly** *adv.* **quaint·ness** *n.*

quake /kwayk/ *v. & n.* ● *v.intr.* **1** shake; tremble. **2** (of a person) shake or shudder (*was quaking with fear*). ● *n.* **1** *colloq.* an earthquake. **2** an act of quaking. □□ **quak·y** *adj.* (**quakier**, **quakiest**).

Quak·er /kwáykər/ *n.* a member of the Society of Friends, a Christian movement devoted to peaceful principles and eschewing formal doctrine, sacraments, and ordained ministers. □□ **Quak·er·ish** *adj.* **Quak·er·ism** *n.*

quak·ing grass *n.* any grass of the genus *Briza*, having slender stalks and trembling in the wind. Also called **dodder-grass**.

qual·i·fi·ca·tion /kwólifikáyshən/ *n.* **1** the act or an instance of qualifying. **2** (often in *pl.*) a quality, skill, or accomplishment fitting a person for a position or purpose. **3 a** a circumstance, condition, etc., that modifies or limits (*the statement had many qualifications*). **b** a thing that detracts from completeness or absoluteness (*their relief had one qualification*). **4** a condition that must be fulfilled before a right can be acquired, etc. **5** an attribution of a quality (*the qualification of our policy as opportunist is unfair*). □□ **qual·i·fi·ca·to·ry** /-lífikətawree/ *adj.*

qual·i·fy /kwólifī/ *v.* (**-ies, -ied**) **1** *tr.* make competent or fit for a position or purpose. **2** *tr.* make legally entitled. **3** *intr.* (foll. by *for* or *as*) (of a person) satisfy the conditions or requirements for (a position, award, competition, etc.). **4** *tr.* add reservations to; modify or make less absolute (a statement or assertion). **5** *tr. Gram.* (of a word, esp. an adjective) attribute a quality to another word, esp. a noun. **6** *tr.* moderate; mitigate; make less severe or extreme. **7** *tr.* alter the strength or flavor of. **8** *tr.* (foll. by *as*) attribute a specified quality to; describe

Q

as (*the idea was qualified as absurd*). **9** *tr.* (as **qualifying** *adj.*) serving to determine those that qualify (*qualifying examination*). **10** (as **qualified** *adj.*) **a** having the qualifications necessary for a particular office or function. **b** dependent on other factors; not definite (*a qualified "yes"*). □□ **qual·i·fi·a·ble** *adj.* **qual·i·fi·er** *n.*

qual·i·ta·tive /kwólitaytiv/ *adj.* concerned with or depending on quality. □□ **qual·i·ta·tive·ly** *adv.*

qual·i·ty /kwólitee/ *n.* (*pl.* **-ies**) **1** the degree of excellence of a thing (*of good quality; poor in quality*). **2 a** general excellence (*their work has quality*). **b** (*attrib.*) of high quality (*a quality product*). **3** a distinctive attribute or faculty; a characteristic trait. **4** the relative nature or kind or character of a thing. **5** the distinctive timbre of a voice or sound. **6** *archaic* high social standing (*people of quality*).

qual·i·ty con·trol *n.* a system of maintaining standards in manufactured products by testing a sample of the output against the specification.

qualm /kwaam, kwawm/ *n.* **1** a misgiving; an uneasy doubt esp. about one's own conduct. **2** a momentary faint or sick feeling. □□ **qualm·ish** *adj.*

quan·da·ry /kwóndəree, -dree/ *n.* (*pl.* **-ies**) **1** a state of perplexity. **2** a difficult situation; a dilemma.

quanta *pl.* of QUANTUM.

quan·tal /kwónt'l/ *adj.* **1** composed of discrete units; varying in steps, not continuously. **2** of or relating to a quantum or quantum theory. □□ **quan·tal·ly** *adv.*

quan·tic /kwóntik/ *n.* *Math.* a rational integral homogeneous function of two or more variables.

quan·ti·fy /kwóntifī/ *v.tr.* (**-ies**, **-ied**) **1** determine the quantity of. **2** measure or express as a quantity. □□ **quan·ti·fi·a·ble** *adj.* **quan·ti·fi·a·bil·i·ty** *n.* **quan·ti·fi·ca·tion** /-fikáyshən/ *n.* **quan·ti·fi·er** *n.*

quan·ti·ta·tive /kwóntitaytiv/ *adj.* **1 a** concerned with quantity. **b** measured or measurable by quantity. **2** of or based on the quantity of syllables. □□ **quan·ti·ta·tive·ly** *adv.*

quan·ti·tive /kwóntitiv/ *adj.* = QUANTITATIVE. □□ **quan·ti·tive·ly** *adv.*

quan·ti·ty /kwóntitee/ *n.* (*pl.* **-ies**) **1** the property of things that is measurable. **2** the size or extent or weight or amount or number. **3** a specified or considerable portion or number or amount (*buys in quantity; the quantity of heat in a body*). **4** (in *pl.*) large amounts or numbers; an abundance (*quantities of food*). **5** *Math.* **a** a value, component, etc., that may be expressed in numbers. **b** the figure or symbol representing this.

quan·tize /kwóntīz/ *v.tr.* **1** form into quanta. **2** apply quantum mechanics to. □□ **quan·ti·za·tion** *n.*

quan·tum /kwóntəm/ *n.* (*pl.* **quanta** /-tə/) **1** *Physics* **a** a discrete quantity of energy proportional in magnitude to the frequency of radiation it represents. **b** an analogous discrete amount of any other physical quantity. **2 a** a required or allowed amount. **b** a share or portion.

quan·tum com·put·er *n.* a computer which makes use of the quantum states of subatomic particles to store information.

quan·tum jump *n.* (also **quantum leap**) **1** a sudden large increase or advance. **2** *Physics* an abrupt transition in an atom or molecule from one quantum state to another.

quan·tum me·chan·ics *n.pl.* (treated as *sing.*) *Physics* a system or theory using the assumption that energy exists in discrete units. Also called **quantum theory**.

quar·an·tine /kwáwrənteen, kwór-/ *n. & v.* ● *n.* **1** isolation imposed on persons or animals that have arrived from elsewhere or been exposed to, and might spread, infectious or contagious disease. **2** the period of this isolation. ● *v.tr.* impose such isolation on; put in quarantine.

quark[1] /kwawrk, kwaark/ *n.* *Physics* any of several postulated components of elementary particles. ▷ NUCLEUS

quark[2] /kwawrk, kwaark/ *n.* a type of European lowfat curd cheese.

QUARTZ

Quartz is one of the most common minerals. It can be found in sedimentary, igneous, and metamorphic rocks and in mineral veins with metal ores. Quartz faces are often striated, with twinned and distorted crystals. Its varied colors include white, gray, red, purple, pink, yellow, green, brown, and black, or it may be colorless. Semiprecious varieties of quartz include citrine and amethyst.

EXAMPLES OF QUARTZ

AMETHYST

CITRINE

ROCK CRYSTAL

ROSE QUARTZ

SMOKY QUARTZ

---

quar·rel /kwáwrəl, kwór-/ *n. & v.* ● *n.* **1** a usu. verbal contention or altercation between individuals or with others. **2** a rupture of friendly relations. **3** an occasion of complaint against a person, a person's actions, etc. ● *v.intr.* (**quarreled** or **quarrelled**, **quarreling** or **quarrelling**) **1** (often foll. by *with*) take exception; find fault. **2** fall out; have a dispute; break off friendly relations. □□ **quar·rel·er** *n.* **quar·rel·ler** *n.*

quar·rel·some /kwáwrəlsəm, kwór-/ *adj.* given to or characterized by quarreling. □□ **quar·rel·some·ly** *adv.* **quar·rel·some·ness** *n.*

quar·ry[1] /kwáwree, kwór-/ *n. & v.* ● *n.* (*pl.* **-ies**) **1** an excavation made by taking stone, etc., for building, etc. **2** a place from which stone, etc., may be extracted. **3** a source of information, knowledge, etc. ● *v.tr.* (**-ies**, **-ied**) extract (stone) from a quarry.

quar·ry[2] /kwáwree, kwór-/ *n.* (*pl.* **-ies**) **1** the object of pursuit by a bird of prey, hounds, hunters, etc. **2** an intended victim or prey.

quar·ry[3] /kwáwree, kwór-/ *n.* (*pl.* **-ies**) **1** (also **quarrel**) a diamond-shaped pane of glass as used in lattice windows. **2** (in full **quarry tile**) an unglazed floor tile.

quar·ry·man /kwáwreemən, kwór-/ *n.* a worker in a quarry.

quart /kwawrt/ *n.* **1** a liquid measure equal to a quarter of a gallon; two pints (.95 liter). **2** a vessel containing this amount. **3** a unit of dry measure, equivalent to one-thirty-second of a bushel (1.1 liter).

quar·tan /kwáwrt'n/ *adj.* (of a fever, etc.) recurring every fourth day.

quar·ter /kwáwrtər/ *n. & v.* ● *n.* **1** each of four equal parts into which a thing is or might be divided. **2** a period of three months. **3** a point of time 15 minutes before or after any hour. **4** a school term, usu. 10–12 weeks. **5 a** 25 cents. **b** a coin of this denomination. **6** a part of a town, esp. as occupied by a particular class or group (*residential quarter*). **7 a** a point of the compass. **b** a region at such a point. **8** the direction, district, or source of supply, etc. (*help from any quarter, came from all quarters*). **9** (in *pl.*) **a** lodgings; an abode. **b** *Mil.* the living accommodation of troops, etc. **10 a** one fourth of a lunar month. ▷ LUNAR MONTH. **b** the Moon's position between the first and second (**first quarter**) or third and fourth (**last quarter**) of these. **11 a** each of the four parts into which an animal's or bird's carcass is divided, each including a leg or wing. **b** (in *pl.*) *hist.* the four parts into which a traitor, etc., was cut after execution. **c** (in *pl.*) *Brit.* = HINDQUARTERS. **12** mercy offered or granted to an enemy in battle, etc., on condition of surrender. **13 a** *Brit.* a grain measure equivalent to 8 bushels. **b** one-fourth of a hundredweight (25 lb. or *Brit.* 28 lb.). **14** *Heraldry* **a** each of four divisions on a shield. **b** a charge occupying this, placed in chief. **15** either side of a ship abaft the beam. **16** *Sports* each of four equal periods into which a game is divided, as in football or basketball. ● *v.tr.* **1** divide into quarters. **2** *hist.* divide (the body of an executed person) in this way. **3 a** put (troops, etc.) into quarters. **b** station or lodge in a specified place. **4** (foll. by *on*) impose (a person) on another as a lodger. **5** cut (a log) into quarters, and these into planks so as to show the grain well. **6** range or traverse (the ground) in every direction. **7** *Heraldry* **a** place or bear (charges or coats of arms) on the four quarters of a shield's surface. ▷ QUARTERING. **b** add (another's coat) to one's hereditary arms. **c** (foll. by *with*) place in alternate quarters with. **d** divide (a shield) into four or more parts by vertical and horizontal lines.

quar·ter·back /kwáwrtərbak/ *n. & v.* *Football* ● *n.* a player who directs offensive play. ● *v.* **1** *intr.* play at this position. **2** *tr.* direct the action of, as a quarterback.

quar·ter·deck /kwáwrtərdek/ *n.* **1** part of a ship's upper deck near the stern, usu. reserved for officers. ▷ MAN-OF-WAR. **2** the officers of a ship or the navy.

quar·ter·fi·nal /kwáwrtərfīn'l/ *adj. & n.* *Sports* ● *adj.* relating to a match or round immediately preceding a semifinal. ● *n.* a quarterfinal match, round, or contest.

quar·ter·ing /kwáwrtəring/ *n.* **1** (in *pl.*) ▼ the coats of arms marshaled on a shield to denote the alliances of a family with others. **2** the provision of quarters for soldiers. **3** the act or an instance of dividing, esp. into four equal parts. **4** timber sawn into lengths, used for high-quality floorboards, etc.

quartered shield

QUARTERING: 15TH-CENTURY SPANISH DISH SHOWING QUARTERED COAT OF ARMS

Q

quar·ter·ly /kwáwrtərlee/ *adj., adv., & n.* ● *adj.* **1** produced, payable, or occurring once every quarter of a year. **2** (of a shield) quartered. ▷ QUARTERING. ● *adv.* **1** once every quarter of a year. **2** in the four, or in two diagonally opposite, quarters of a shield. ● *n.* (*pl.* **-ies**) a quarterly review or magazine.

quar·ter·mas·ter /kwáwrtərmastər/ *n.* **1** an army officer in charge of quartering, rations, etc. **2** a naval petty officer in charge of steering, signals, etc.

quar·ter note *n. Mus.* a note with a duration of one quarter of a whole note.

quar·ter·staff /kwáwrtərstaf/ *n. hist.* a stout pole 6–8 feet long, formerly used as a weapon.

quar·tet /kwawrtét/ *n.* (also **quar·tette**) **1** *Mus.* **a** a composition for four voices or instruments. **b** the performers of such a piece. **2** any group of four.

quar·to /kwáwrtō/ *n.* (*pl.* **-os**) *Printing* **1** the size given by folding a (usu. specified) sheet of paper twice. **2** a book consisting of sheets folded in this way. ¶ Abbr.: **4to.**

quartz /kwawrts/ *n.* ◀ a mineral form of silica that crystallizes as hexagonal prisms. ▷ AGGREGATE, ORE.

quartz watch *n.* ▼ a watch operated by vibrations of an electrically driven quartz crystal.

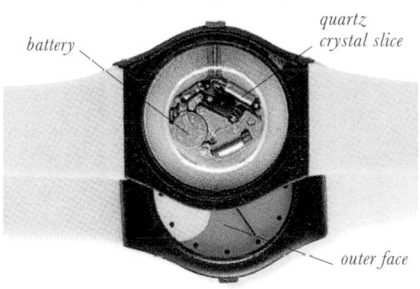

QUARTZ WATCH: INTERNAL MECHANISM AND OUTER FACE

battery   *quartz crystal slice*   *outer face*

quartz·ite /kwáwrtsīt/ *n.* a metamorphic rock consisting mainly of quartz.

qua·sar /kwáyzaar, -zər, -saar, -sər/ *n. Astron.* ▼ any of a class of starlike celestial objects having a spectrum with a large red shift.

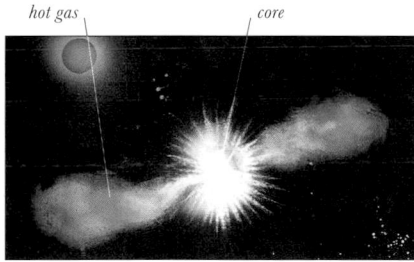

QUASAR: ARTIST'S IMPRESSION OF A QUASAR

hot gas   *core*

quash /kwosh/ *v.tr.* **1** annul; reject as not valid, esp. by a legal procedure. **2** suppress; crush (a rebellion, etc.).

quasi- /kwáyzī, kwáazee/ *comb. form* **1** seemingly; apparently but not really (*quasi-scientific*). **2** being partly or almost (*quasi-independent*).

quat·er·cen·ten·ar·y /kwótərsenténəree, -sént'neree/ *n. & adj.* ● *n.* (*pl.* **-ies**) **1** a four-hundredth anniversary. **2** a festival marking this. ● *adj.* of this anniversary.

quat·er·nar·y /kwótərneree, kwətárnəree/ *adj. & n.* **1** having four parts. **2** (**Quaternary**) *Geol.* of or relating to the most recent period in the Cenozoic era with evidence of many species of present-day plants and animals (cf. PLEISTOCENE, HOLOCENE). ● *n.* (*pl.* **-ies**) **1** a set of four things. **2** (**Quaternary**) *Geol.* the Quaternary period or system.

quat·rain /kwótrayn/ *n.* a stanza of four lines, usu. with alternate rhymes.

QUATTROCENTO

The term *quattrocento* is often used to describe the Italian Renaissance of the 15th century. New ideas flourished during this period. They included rules governing perspective, more naturalistic and expressive painting and sculpture, and a revival of themes from classical Italy. Key artists included Botticelli, Donatello, and Masaccio.

Crucifixion of Jesus Christ, a common 15th-century subject

Masaccio's patron, Lorenzo Lenzi

The Trinity (*c.*1427), MASACCIO

use of perspective gives three-dimensional effect

ancient Roman architectural styles

realistic, not idealized, figures of the Virgin and St. John

TIMELINE

| 1000 | 1050 | 1100 | 1150 | 1200 | 1250 | 1300 | 1350 | 1400 | 1450 | 1500 |

quat·re·foil /kátərfoyl, kátrə-/ *n.* ▶ a four-pointed or four-leafed figure, esp. as an ornament in architectural tracery, resembling a flower or clover leaf.

quat·tro·cen·to /kwátrōchéntō/ *n.* ▲ the style of Italian art of the 15th c. ▷ RENAISSANCE. □□ **quat·tro·cen·tist** *n.*

qua·ver /kwáyvər/ *v. & n.* ● *v.* **1** *intr.* **a** (esp. of a voice or musical sound) vibrate; shake; tremble. **b** use trills or shakes in singing. **2** *tr.* **a** sing (a note or song) with quavering. **b** (often foll. by *out*) say in a trembling voice. ● *n.* **1** *Mus.* = EIGHTH NOTE. **2** a trill in singing. **3** a tremble in speech. □□ **qua·ver·ing·ly** *adv.*

qua·ver·y /kwáyvəree/ *adj.* (of a voice, etc.) tremulous. □□ **qua·ver·i·ness** *n.*

quay /kee, kay/ *n.* a solid, stationary, artificial landing place lying alongside or projecting into water for loading and unloading ships. □□ **quay·age** *n.*

quay·side /kéesīd, káy-/ *n.* the land forming or near a quay.

Que. *abbr.* Quebec.

quea·sy /kwéezee/ *adj.* (**-ier**, **-iest**) **1 a** (of a person) feeling nausea. **b** (of a person's stomach) easily upset; weak of digestion. **2** (of the conscience, etc.) overscrupulous; tender. **3** (of a feeling, thought, etc.) uncomfortable; uneasy. □□ **quea·si·ly** *adv.* **quea·si·ness** *n.*

Quech·ua /kéchwa, -waa/ *n.* **1** a member of a central Peruvian native people. **2** a S. American native language widely spoken in Peru and neighboring countries. □□ **Quech·uan** *adj.*

queen /kween/ *n. & v.* ● *n.* **1** (as a title usu. **Queen**) a female sovereign, etc., esp. the hereditary ruler of an independent nation. **2** (in full **queen consort**) a king's wife. **3** a woman, country, or thing preeminent or supreme in a specified area or of its kind (*tennis queen; the queen of roses*). **4** the fertile female among ants, bees, etc. **5** the most powerful piece in chess. ▷ CHESS. **6** a playing card with a picture of a queen. ▷ FACE CARD. **7** *sl.* a male homosexual, esp. an effeminate one. **8 a** an honored female, e.g., the Virgin Mary (*Queen of Heaven*). **b** an

quatrefoil

QUATREFOIL DECORATION ON A MODEL OF A 12TH-CENTURY CATHEDRAL SPIRE

ancient goddess (*Venus, queen of love*). **9** a mock sovereign on some occasion (*beauty queen; queen of the May*). ● *v.* **1** *tr.* make (a woman) queen. **2** *tr. Chess* convert (a pawn) into a queen when it reaches the opponent's side of the board. **3** *intr.* to act like a queen, esp. to act imperiously or flamboyantly. □□ **queen·dom** *n.* **queen·hood** *n.* **queen·less** *adj.* **queen·like** *adj.* **queen·ship** *n.*

Queen Anne's lace *n.* a widely cultivated orig. Eurasian herb, *Daucus carota*, with a whitish taproot; wild carrot.

queen bee *n.* **1** the fertile female in a hive. **2** the chief or controlling woman in an organization or social group.

queen·ly /kwéenlee/ *adj.* (**queenlier**, **queenliest**) **1** fit for or appropriate to a queen. **2** majestic; queenlike. □□ **queen·li·ness** *n.*

queen post *n.* ▼ one of two upright timbers between the tie beam and principal rafters of a roof truss.

collar beam   *straight brace*

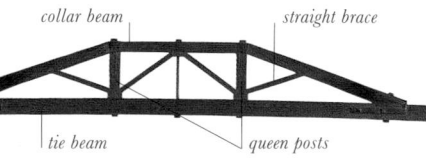

tie beam   *queen posts*

QUEEN POSTS IN A ROOF TRUSS

Queens·ber·ry Rules /kwéenzberee, -bəree/ *n.pl.* the standard rules, esp. of boxing.

Queen's Eng·lish *n.* (also **King's English**) the English language as correctly written or spoken in Britain.

queen-size *adj.* (also **queensized**) of an extra-large size, between full-size and king-size.

queer /kweer/ *adj., n., & v.* ● *adj.* **1** strange; odd; eccentric. **2** shady; suspect; of questionable character. **3 a** esp. *Brit.* slightly ill; giddy; faint. **b** *Brit. sl.* drunk. **4** *derog. sl.* homosexual. **5** *colloq.* (of a person or behavior) crazy; unbalanced; slightly mad. **6** *sl.* counterfeit. ● *n. derog. sl.* a homosexual. ● *v.tr. sl.* spoil; put out of order. □□ **queer·ish** *adj.* **queer·ly** *adv.* **queer·ness** *n.*

Q

quell /kwel/ *v.tr.* **1 a** crush or put down (a rebellion, etc.). **b** reduce (rebels, etc.) to submission. **2** suppress or alleviate (fear, anger, etc.). □□ **quell·er** *n.* (also in *comb.*).

quench /kwench/ *v.tr.* **1** satisfy (thirst) by drinking. **2** extinguish (a fire or light, etc.). **3** cool, esp. with water (heat, a heated thing). **4** esp. *Metallurgy* cool (a hot substance) in cold water, air, oil, etc. **5 a** stifle or suppress (desire, etc.). **b** *Physics & Electronics* inhibit or prevent (oscillation, luminescence, etc.) by counteractive means. □□ **quench·a·ble** *adj.* **quench·er** *n.* **quench·less** *adj.*

que·nelle /kənél/ *n.* a poached seasoned dumpling of minced fish or meat.

que·rist /kwéerist/ *n. literary* a person who asks questions; a questioner.

quern /kwərn/ *n.* **1** ▶ a hand mill for grinding grain. **2** a small hand mill for pepper, etc.

quer·u·lous /kwérələs, kwéryə-/ *adj.* complaining; peevish. □□ **quer·u·lous·ly** *adv.* **quer·u·lous·ness** *n.*

que·ry /kwéeree/ *n. & v.* ● *n.* (*pl.* **-ies**) **1** a question, esp. expressing doubt or objection. **2** a question mark, or the word *query* spoken or written to question accuracy or as a mark of interrogation. ● *v.tr.* (**-ies**, **-ied**) **1** (often foll. by *whether, if,* etc. + clause) ask or inquire. **2** call (a thing) in question in speech or writing. **3** dispute the accuracy of.

QUERN:
STONE QUERN
*c.*4000–2000 BC

sandstone grinder

quest /kwest/ *n.* **1** a search or the act of seeking. **2** the thing sought, esp. the object of a medieval knight's pursuit. □□ **quest·er** *n.* **quest·ing·ly** *adv.*

ques·tion /kwéschən/ *n. & v.* ● *n.* **1** a sentence worded or expressed so as to seek information. **2 a** doubt about or objection to a thing's truth, credibility, advisability, etc. (*allowed it without question*). **b** the raising of such doubt, etc. **3** a matter to be discussed or decided or voted on. **4** a problem requiring an answer or solution. **5** (foll. by *of*) a matter or concern depending on conditions (*it's a question of money*). ● *v.tr.* **1** ask questions of; interrogate. **2** subject (a person) to examination. **3** throw doubt upon; raise objections to. **4** seek information from the study of (phenomena, facts). □ **be a question of time** be certain to happen sooner or later. **beyond all question** undoubtedly. **call in** (or **into**) **question** make a matter of dispute; query. **come into question** be discussed; become of practical importance. **in question 1** that is being discussed or referred to (*the person in question*). **2** in dispute (*that was never in question*). **is not the question** is irrelevant. **out of the question** too impracticable, etc., to be worth discussing; impossible. **put the question** require supporters and opponents of a proposal to record their votes, divide a meeting. **without question** see *beyond all question* above. □□ **ques·tion·er** *n.* **ques·tion·ing·ly** *adv.* **ques·tion·less** *adj.*

ques·tion·a·ble /kwéschənəbəl/ *adj.* **1** doubtful as regards truth or quality. **2** not clearly in accordance with honesty, honor, wisdom, etc. □□ **ques·tion·a·bil·i·ty** /-əbílitee/ *n.* **ques·tion·a·ble·ness** *n.* **ques·tion·a·bly** *adv.*

ques·tion·ar·y /kwéschəneree/ *n.* (*pl.* **-ies**) = QUESTIONNAIRE.

ques·tion mark *n.* a punctuation mark (?) indicating a question.

ques·tion·naire /kwéschənáir/ *n.* **1** a formulated series of questions, esp. for statistical study. **2** a document containing these.

quet·zal /ketsáal, -sál/ *n.* **1** ▶ any of various brightly colored birds of the family Trogonidae, esp. the Central and S. American *Pharomachrus mocinno*, the male of which has long green tail coverts. **2** the chief monetary unit of Guatemala.

queue /kyōō/ *n. & v.* ● *n.* **1** esp. *Brit.* a line or sequence of persons, vehicles, etc., awaiting their turn to be attended to or to proceed. **2** a pigtail or braid of hair. **3** *Computing* a sequence of jobs or processes waiting to be acted upon. ● *v.intr.* (**queues, queued, queuing** or **queueing**) esp. *Brit.* (often foll. by *up*) (of persons, etc.) form a line; take one's place in a line.

quib·ble /kwíbəl/ *n. & v.* ● *n.* **1** a petty objection; a trivial point of criticism. **2** a play on words; a pun. **3** an evasion; an insubstantial argument which relies on an ambiguity, etc. ● *v.intr.* use quibbles. □□ **quib·bler** *n.* **quib·bling** *adj.* **quib·bling·ly** *adv.*

quiche /keesh/ *n.* an unsweetened custard pie with a savory filling.

quiche Lorraine /lawráyn/ *n.* a quiche made with cheese and ham or bacon.

quick /kwik/ *adj., adv., & n.* ● *adj.* **1** taking only a short time (*a quick worker; a quick visit*). **2 a** arriving after a short time; prompt (*quick action; quick results*). **b** (of an action, occurrence, etc.) sudden; hasty; abrupt. **3** with only a short interval (*in quick succession*). **4** lively; intelligent. **5 a** acute; alert (*has a quick ear*). **b** agile; nimble; energetic. **6** (of a temper) easily roused. **7** *archaic* living; alive (*the quick and the dead*). ● *adv.* **1** quickly; at a rapid rate. **2** (as *int.*) come, go, etc., quickly. ● *n.* **1** the soft flesh below the nails, or the skin, or a sore. **2** the seat of feeling or emotion (*cut to the quick*). □□ **quick·ly** *adv.* **quick·ness** *n.*

quick·en /kwíkən/ *v.* **1** *tr. & intr.* make or become quicker; accelerate. **2** *tr.* give life or vigor to; rouse; animate; stimulate. **3** *intr.* **a** (of a woman) reach a stage in pregnancy when movements of the fetus can be felt. **b** (of a fetus) begin to show signs of life. **4** *tr. archaic* kindle; make (a fire) burn brighter. **5** *intr.* come to life.

quick fix *n.* an expedient but inadequate repair or solution.

quick·ie /kwíkee/ *n. colloq.* **1** a thing done or made quickly or hastily. **2** a drink taken quickly. **3** a hasty act of sexual intercourse.

quick·lime /kwíklīm/ *n.* = LIME[1] *n.* 1.

quick march *n. Mil.* **1** a march in quick time. **2** the command to begin this.

quick·sand /kwíksand/ *n.* **1** loose wet sand that sucks in anything placed or falling into it. **2** a bed of this.

quick·sil·ver /kwíksilvər/ *n.* **1** mercury. **2** mobility of temperament or mood.

quick·step /kwíkstep/ *n. & v.* ● *n.* a fast foxtrot (cf. QUICK STEP). ● *v.intr.* (**-stepped, -stepping**) dance the quickstep.

quick step *n. Mil.* a step used in quick time (cf. QUICKSTEP).

quick stud·y *n.* one who learns rapidly.

quick-tem·pered *adj.* quick to lose one's temper; irascible.

quick-wit·ted /kwíkwítid/ *adj.* quick to grasp a situation, make repartee, etc. □□ **quick-wit·ted·ness** *n.*

QUETZAL
(*Pharomachrus mocinno*)

female
male

quid[1] /kwid/ *n.* (*pl.* same) *Brit. sl.* one pound sterling.

quid[2] /kwid/ *n.* a lump of tobacco for chewing.

quid·di·ty /kwíditee/ *n.* (*pl.* **-ies**) **1** *Philos.* the essence of a person or thing; what makes a thing what it is. **2** a quibble; a trivial objection.

quid pro quo /kwíd prō kwṓ/ *n.* **1** a thing given as compensation. **2** return made (for a gift, favor, etc.).

qui·es·cent /kwīésənt, kwee-/ *adj.* **1** motionless; inert. **2** silent; dormant. □□ **qui·es·cence** *n.* **qui·es·cen·cy** *n.* **qui·es·cent·ly** *adv.*

qui·et /kwíət/ *adj., n., & v.* ● *adj.* (**quieter, quietest**) **1** with little or no sound or motion. **2 a** of gentle or peaceful disposition. **b** shy; reticent; reserved. **3** (of a color, piece of clothing, etc.) unobtrusive; not showy. **4** not overt; private; disguised (*quiet resentment*). **5** undisturbed; uninterrupted; free or far from vigorous action (*a quiet time for prayer*). **6** informal; simple (*just a quiet wedding*). **7** enjoyed in quiet (*a quiet smoke*). **8** tranquil; not anxious or remorseful. ● *n.* **1** silence; stillness. **2** an undisturbed state; tranquillity. **3** a state of being free from urgent tasks or agitation (*a period of quiet*). **4** a peaceful state of affairs (*could do with some quiet*). ● *v.* **1** *tr.* soothe; make quiet. **2** *intr.* (often foll. by *down*) become quiet or calm. □ **be quiet** (esp. in *imper.*) cease talking, etc. **keep quiet 1** refrain from making a noise. **2** (often foll. by *about*) suppress or refrain from disclosing information, etc. **on the quiet** unobtrusively; secretly. □□ **qui·et·ly** *adv.* **qui·et·ness** *n.*

qui·et·en /kwíət'n/ *v.tr. & intr. Brit.* (often foll. by *down*) make or become quiet.

qui·et·ism /kwíətizəm/ *n.* **1** a passive attitude toward life, with devotional contemplation and abandonment of the will, as a form of religious mysticism. **2** the principle of nonresistance. □□ **qui·et·ist** *n. & adj.* **qui·et·is·tic** *adj.*

qui·e·tude /kwíitōōd, -tyōōd/ *n.* a state of quiet.

qui·e·tus /kwī-éetəs/ *n.* **1** something which quiets or represses. **2** discharge or release from life; death; final riddance.

quiff /kwif/ *n. Brit.* **1** a man's tuft of hair, brushed upward over the forehead. **2** a curl plastered down on the forehead.

quill /kwil/ *n.* **1** a large feather in a wing or tail. ▷ FEATHER. **2** the hollow stem of this. **3** (in full **quill pen**) ▼ a pen made of a quill. **4** (usu. in *pl.*) the spines of a porcupine. **5** a musical pipe made of a hollow stem.

QUILL PEN MADE FROM
A GOOSE FEATHER

quilt /kwilt/ *n. & v.* ● *n.* **1** ◀ a bedcovering made of padding enclosed between layers of cloth, etc., and kept in place by patterned stitching. **2** a bedspread of similar design (*patchwork quilt*). ● *v.tr.* **1** cover or line with padded material. **2** make or join together (pieces of cloth with padding between) after the manner of a quilt. **3** sew up (a coin, letter, etc.) between two layers of a garment, etc. □□ **quilt·er** *n.* **quilt·ing** *n.*

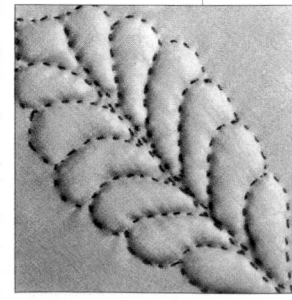

QUILT: DETAIL OF PADDED
(TRAPUNTO) QUILTING

Q

qui·na·ry /kwínəree/ *adj.* **1** of the number five. **2** having five parts.

quince /kwins/ *n.* **1** ▶ a hard acidic pear-shaped fruit used chiefly in preserves. **2** any shrub or small tree of the genus *Cydonia*, esp. *C. oblonga*, bearing this fruit.

quin·cen·ten·a·ry /kwinsenténəree, -sént'neree/ *n. & adj.* ● *n.* (*pl.* **-ies**) **1** a five-hundredth anniversary. **2** a festival marking this. ● *adj.* of this anniversary. □□ **quin·cen·ten·ni·al** /-téneeəl/ *adj. & n.*

quin·cunx /kwínkungks/ *n.* five objects set so that four are at the corners of a square or rectangle and the fifth is at its center, e.g., the five on dice or cards. □□ **quin·cun·cial** /-kúnshəl/ *adj.* **quin·cun·cial·ly** *adv.*

quin·ella /kwinélə/ *n.* a form of betting in which the bettor must select the first two place winners in a race, not necessarily in the correct order.

qui·nine /kwínīn, kwin-/ *n.* **1** ◀ an alkaloid found esp. in cinchona bark. **2** a bitter drug containing this, used as a tonic and to reduce fever.

quin·qua·ge·nar·i·an /kwíngkwəjináireeən/ *n. & adj.* ● *n.* a person from 50 to 59 years old. ● *adj.* of or relating to this age.

quinque- /kwíngkwee/ *comb. form* five.

quin·que·va·lent /kwíngkwəváylənt/ *adj.* having a valence of five.

quin·sy /kwínzee/ *n.* an inflammation of the throat, esp. an abscess in the region around the tonsils. □□ **quin·sied** *adj.*

quint /kwint/ *n.* **1** a sequence of five cards in the same suit in piquet, etc. **2** *colloq.* a quintuplet.

quin·tal /kwínt'l/ *n.* **1** a weight of about 100 lb. **2** (in the UK) a weight of 112 lb. (a hundredweight) **3** a weight of 100 kg.

quin·tan /kwínt'n/ *adj.* (of a fever, etc.) recurring every fifth day.

quinte /kaNt/ *n.* the fifth of eight parrying positions in fencing

quin·tes·sence /kwintésəns/ *n.* **1** the most essential part of any substance; a refined extract. **2** (usu. foll. by *of*) the purest and most perfect, or most typical, form, manifestation, or embodiment of some quality or class. □□ **quin·tes·sen·tial** /kwíntisénshəl/ *adj.* **quin·tes·sen·tial·ly** *adv.*

quin·tet /kwintét/ *n.* (also **quin·tette**) **1** *Mus.* **a** a composition for five voices or instruments. **b** the performers of such a piece. **2** any group of five.

quin·til·lion /kwintílyən/ *n.* (*pl.* same or **quintillions**) a thousand raised to the sixth (or esp. *Brit.* the tenth) power (10^{18} and 10^{30} respectively). □□ **quin·til·lionth** *adj. & n.*

quin·tu·ple /kwintŏopəl, -tyŏo-, -túpəl, kwíntəpəl/ *adj., n., & v.* ● *adj.* **1** fivefold; consisting of five parts. **2** involving five parties. ● *n.* a fivefold number or amount. ● *v.tr. & intr.* multiply by five; increase fivefold. □□ **quin·tu·ply** *adv.*

quin·tu·plet /kwintúplit, -tŏo-, -tyŏo-, kwíntə-/ *n.* **1** each of five children born at one birth. **2** a set of five things working together.

quip /kwip/ *n. & v.* ● *n.* **1** a clever saying; an epigram; a sarcastic remark, etc. **2** a quibble; an equivocation. ● *v.intr.* (**quipped, quipping**) make quips. □□ **quip·ster** *n.*

qui·pu /keepŏo, kwee-/ *n.* the ancient Peruvians' substitute for writing by variously knotting threads of various colors.

QUINCE
(*Cydonia oblonga*)

QUININE: BARK OF THE CINCHONA TREE CONTAINING QUININE

---

quire /kwīr/ *n.* **1** four sheets of paper, etc., folded to form eight leaves, as often in medieval manuscripts. **2** any collection of leaves one within another in a manuscript or book. **3** 25 (also 24) sheets of paper. □ **in quires** unbound; in sheets.

quirk /kwərk/ *n.* **1** a peculiarity of behavior. **2** a trick of fate; a freak. **3** a flourish in writing. □□ **quirk·ish** *adj.* **quirk·y** *adj.* (**quirkier, quirkiest**). **quirk·i·ly** *adv.* **quirk·i·ness** *n.*

quirt /kwərt/ *n.* a short-handled riding whip with a braided leather lash.

quis·ling /kwízling/ *n.* **1** a person cooperating with an occupying enemy; a collaborator or fifth columnist. **2** a traitor. □□ **quis·ling·ite** *adj. & n.*

quit /kwit/ *v. & adj.* ● *v.tr.* (**quitting**; *past* and *past part.* **quit** or **quitted**) **1** (also *absol.*) give up; let go; abandon (a task, etc.). **2** cease; stop (*quit grumbling*). **3 a** leave or depart from (a place, person, employment, etc.). **b** (*absol.*) (of a tenant) leave occupied premises (esp. *notice to quit*). **4** (*refl.*) acquit; behave (*quit oneself well*). ● *predic.adj.* (foll. by *of*) rid (*glad to be quit of the problem*). □ **quit hold of** loose. □□ **quit·ter** *n.*

quite /kwīt/ *adv.* **1** completely; entirely; wholly; to the utmost extent; in the fullest sense. **2** somewhat; rather; to some extent. **3** (often foll. by *so*) said to indicate agreement. **4** absolutely; definitely; very much. □ **quite another** (or **other**) very different (*that's quite another matter*). **quite a few** *colloq.* a fairly large number of. **quite something** a remarkable thing.

quits /kwits/ *predic.adj.* on even terms by retaliation or repayment (*then we'll be quits*). □ **call it** (or *Brit.* **cry**) **quits** acknowledge that things are now even; agree not to proceed further in a quarrel, etc.

quit·tance /kwít'ns/ *n.* **1** (foll. by *from*) a release. **2** an acknowledgment of payment; a receipt.

quit·ter /kwítər/ *n.* **1** a person who gives up easily. **2** a shirker.

quiv·er[1] /kwívər/ *v. & n.* ● *v.* **1** *intr.* tremble or vibrate with a slight rapid motion, esp.; **a** (usu. foll. by *with*) as the result of emotion (*quiver with anger*). **b** (usu. foll. by *in*) as the result of air currents, etc. (*quiver in the breeze*). **2** *tr.* (of a bird) make (its wings) quiver. ● *n.* a quivering motion or sound. □□ **quiv·er·ing·ly** *adv.* **quiv·er·y** *adj.*

quiv·er[2] /kwívər/ *n.* ▶ a case for holding arrows. ▷ ARCHERY. □ **have an arrow** (or **shaft**) **left in one's quiver** not be resourceless.

qui vive /kee véev/ *n.* □ **on the qui vive** on the alert; watching for something to happen.

quix·ot·ic /kwiksótik/ *adj.* **1** extravagantly and romantically chivalrous; regardless of material interests in comparison with honor or devotion. **2** visionary; pursuing lofty but unattainable ideals. **3** *derog.* ridiculously impractical; preposterous; foolhardy. □□ **quix·ot·i·cal·ly** *adv.* **quix·o·tism** /kwíksətizəm/ *n.* **quix·o·try** /kwíksətree/ *n.*

quiz /kwiz/ *n. & v.* ● *n.* (*pl.* **quizzes**) **1 a** a quick or informal test. **b** an interrogation, examination, or questionnaire. **2** (also **quiz show**) a test of knowledge, esp. between individuals or teams as a form of entertainment. ● *v.tr.* (**quizzed, quizzing**) examine by questioning.

quiz·zi·cal /kwízikəl/ *adj.* **1** expressing or done with mild or amused perplexity. **2** strange; comical. □□ **quiz·zi·cal·i·ty** /-kálitee/ *n.* **quiz·zi·cal·ly** *adv.* **quiz·zi·cal·ness** *n.*

quod erat demonstrandum /kwod érat démənstrándəm, éraat démōnstraándōōm/ (esp. at the conclusion of a proof, etc.) which was the thing to be proved. ¶ Abbr.: **QED**.

arrow

QUIVER

---

quod vide /kwod veéday, vídee/ which see (in cross-references, etc.). ¶ Abbr.: **q.v.**

quoin /koyn, kwoin/ *n.* **1** an external angle of a building. **2** a stone or brick forming an angle; a cornerstone. **3** *Printing* a wedge used for securing composed type. **4** a wedge for raising the level of a gun, keeping the barrel from rolling, etc. ● *v.tr.* secure or raise with quoins. □□ **quoin·ing** *n.*

quoit /koyt, kwoit/ *n. & v.* ● *n.* **1** a heavy flattish sharp-edged iron ring thrown to encircle an iron peg or to land as near as possible to the peg. **2** (in *pl.*) a game consisting of aiming and throwing these. **3** a ring of rope, rubber, etc., for use in a similar game. **4** *Brit.* **a** ▼ the flat stone of a dolmen. **b** the dolmen itself. ● *v.tr.* fling like a quoit.

quoit

support stone

QUOIT ON A PREHISTORIC DOLMEN, ENGLAND

quok·ka /kwókə/ *n.* a small Australian short-tailed wallaby, *Setonix brachyurus*.

quon·dam /kwóndəm, -dam/ *predic.adj.* that once was; sometime; former.

Quon·set hut /kwónsit/ *n. Trademark* a prefabricated metal building with a semicylindrical corrugated roof.

quo·rate /kwáwrət, -rayt/ *adj. Brit.* (of a meeting) attended by a quorum.

quo·rum /kwáwrəm/ *n.* the fixed minimum number of members that must be present to make the proceedings of an assembly or society legally valid.

quo·ta /kwốtə/ *n.* **1** the share that an individual person, group, or company is bound to contribute to or entitled to receive from a total. **2** a quantity of goods, etc., which under official controls must be manufactured, exported, imported, etc. **3** the number of immigrants allowed to enter a country annually, students allowed to enroll in a course, etc.

quot·a·ble /kwốtəbəl/ *adj.* worth, or suitable for, quoting. □□ **quot·a·bil·i·ty** *n.*

quo·ta·tion /kwōtáyshən/ *n.* **1** the act or an instance of quoting or being quoted. **2** a passage or remark quoted. **3** *Mus.* a short passage or tune taken from one piece of music to another. **4** *Stock Exch.* an amount stated as the current price of stocks or commodities. **5** a contractor's estimate.

quo·ta·tion mark *n.* each of a set of punctuation marks, single (' ') or double (" "), used to mark the beginning and end of a quoted passage, a book title, etc., or words regarded as slang or jargon.

quote /kwōt/ *v. & n.* ● *v.tr.* **1** cite or appeal to (an author, book, etc.) in confirmation of some view. **2** repeat a statement by (another person) or copy out a passage from (*don't*

Q

quote me). **3** (often *absol.*) **a** repeat or copy out (a passage) usu. with an indication that it is borrowed. **b** (foll. by *from*) cite (an author, book, etc.). **4** (foll. by *as*) cite (an author, etc.) as proof, evidence, etc. **5 a** enclose (words) in quotation marks. **b** (as *int.*) (in dictation, reading aloud, etc.) indicate the presence of opening quotation marks (*he said, quote, "I shall stay"*). **6** (often foll. by *at*) state the price of (a commodity, bet, etc.) (*quoted at 200 to 1*). **7** *Stock Exch.* regularly list the price of. ● *n. colloq.* **1** a passage quoted. **2 a** a price quoted. **b** a contractor's estimate. **3** (usu. in *pl.*) quotation marks.

quoth /kwōth/ *v.tr.* (only in 1st and 3rd person) *archaic* said.

quo·tid·i·an /kwotídeeən/ *adj. & n.* ● *adj.* **1** daily; of every day. **2** commonplace; trivial. ● *n.* (in full **quotidian fever**) a fever recurring every day.

quo·tient /kwṓshənt/ *n.* a result obtained by dividing one quantity by another.

Qur'·an var. of KORAN.

q.v. *abbr.* quod vide.

qwerty /kwə́rtee/ *attrib.adj.* ▸ denoting the standard keyboard on English-language typewriters, word processors, etc., with *q, w, e, r, t,* and *y* as the first keys on the top row of letters.

QWERTY KEYBOARD OF A
WORD PROCESSOR

Q

R

R¹ /aar/ *n.* (also **r**) (*pl.* **Rs** or **R's**) the eighteenth letter of the alphabet.

R² *abbr.* (also **R.**) **1** river. **2** *Brit. Regina* (*Elizabeth R*). **3** *Brit. Rex.* **4** (also ®) registered as a trademark. **5** *Chess* rook. **6** rand. **7** *Electr.* resistance. **8** radius. **9** roentgen. **10** (of movies) classified as prohibited to people under a certain age (as 17) unless accompanied by a parent or guardian.

r. *abbr.* (also **r**) **1** right. **2** recto. **3** run(s). **4** radius.

Ra *symb. Chem.* the element radium.

rab·bet /rábit/ *n. & v.* ● *n.* a step-shaped channel, etc., cut along the edge or face or projecting angle of a length of wood, etc. ▷ WINDOW. ● *v.tr.* **1** join or fix with a rabbet. **2** make a rabbet in.

rab·bi /rábī/ *n.* (*pl.* **rabbis**) **1** a Jewish scholar or teacher, esp. of the law. **2** a person appointed as a Jewish religious leader. □□ **rab·bin·ate** /rábinət/ *n.*

rab·bin·i·cal /rəbínikəl/ *adj.* of or relating to rabbis, or to Jewish law or teaching. □□ **rab·bin·i·cal·ly** *adv.*

rab·bit /rábit/ *n. & v.* ● *n.* **1** any of various burrowing gregarious plant-eating mammals of the family Leporidae, with long ears and a short tail. ▷ LAGOMORPH. **2** a hare. **3** the fur of the rabbit. ● *v.intr.* hunt rabbits. □□ **rab·bit·y** *adj.*

rab·bit ears *n.pl.* a television antenna consisting of two movable rods, usu. on top of the set.

rab·bit punch *n.* a short chop with the edge of the hand to the nape of the neck.

rab·bit's foot *n.* the foot of a rabbit, carried to bring luck.

rab·ble¹ /rábəl/ *n.* **1** a disorderly crowd; a mob. **2** a contemptible or inferior set of people. **3** (prec. by *the*) the lower or disorderly classes of the populace.

rab·ble² /rábəl/ *n.* an iron bar with a bent end for stirring molten metal, etc.

rab·ble-rous·er *n.* a person who stirs up a crowd of people in agitation for social or political change. □□ **rab·ble-rous·ing** *adj. & n.*

Rab·e·lai·si·an /rábəláyzeeən, -zhən/ *adj.* **1** of or like Rabelais or his writings. **2** marked by exuberant imagination and language, coarse humor, and satire.

rab·id /rábid/ *adj.* **1** furious; violent (*rabid hatred*). **2** unreasoning; headstrong; fanatical (*a rabid anarchist*). **3** affected with rabies; mad. **4** of or connected with rabies. □□ **rab·id·ly** *adv.* **rab·id·ness** *n.*

ra·bies /ráybeez/ *n.* a contagious and fatal viral disease, esp. of dogs, cats, raccoons, etc., transmissible to humans, etc., and causing madness and convulsions.

rac·coon /rakóōn/ *n.* (also **ra·coon**) **1** any furry N. American nocturnal mammal of the genus *Procyon*, with a bushy tail and masklike band across the eyes. **2** the fur of the raccoon.

race¹ /rays/ *n. & v.* ● *n.* **1** a contest of speed between runners, vehicles, etc. **2** (in *pl.*) a series of these for horses, dogs, etc., at a fixed time on a regular course. **3** a contest between persons to be first to achieve something. **4** a strong or rapid current flowing through a narrow channel in the sea or a river. **b** the channel of a stream, etc. (*a mill-race*). **5** each of two grooved rings in a ball bearing or roller bearing. ● *v.* **1** *intr.* take part in a race. **2** *tr.* have a race with. **3** *tr.* try to surpass in speed. **4** *intr.* (foll. by *with*) compete in speed with. **5** *tr.* cause (a horse, car, etc.) to race. **6 a** *intr.* go at full or (of an engine, etc.) excessive speed. **b** *tr.* cause (a person or thing) to do this (*raced the bill through*). **7** *intr.* (usu. as **racing** *adj.*) follow horse racing (*a racing man*). □ **out of the race** (of a person, etc., in contention for something) having no chance.

race² /rays/ *n.* **1** each of the major divisions of humankind, having distinct physical characteristics. **2** a nation, etc., regarded as of a distinct ethnic stock. **3** the fact or concept of division into races (*discrimination based on race*). **4** a genus, species, breed, or variety of animals, plants, or microorganisms. **5** a group of persons, animals, or plants connected by common descent. **6** any great division of living creatures (*the feathered race; the four-footed race*). **7** descent; kindred (*of noble race*). **8** a class of persons, etc., with some common feature (*the race of poets*).

race·course /ráyskawrs/ *n.* **1** = RACETRACK. **2** any path laid out for racing, esp. skiing, cross-country running, etc.

race·go·er /ráysgōər/ *n.* a person who frequents horse races.

race·horse /ráys-hors/ *n.* a horse bred or kept for racing.

ra·ceme /rayseém, rə-/ *n. Bot.* a flower cluster with the separate flowers attached by short equal stalks at equal distances along a central stem. ▷ INFLORESCENCE

rac·e·mose /rásimōs/ *adj.* **1** *Bot.* in the form of a raceme. **2** *Anat.* (of a gland, etc.) clustered.

rac·er /ráysər/ *n.* **1** a horse, yacht, bicycle, etc., of a kind used for racing. **2** a circular horizontal rail along which the traversing platform of a heavy gun moves. **3** a person or thing that races.

race re·la·tions *n.pl.* relations between members of different races, usu. in the same country.

race ri·ot *n.* an outbreak of violence due to racial antagonism.

race·track /ráystrak/ *n.* ▲ a usu. oval track for horse, dog, or automobile racing.

race·way /ráysway/ *n.* **1** a track or channel along which something runs, esp. *a* esp. *Brit.* a channel for water. **b** a groove in which ball bearings run. **c** a pipe or tubing enclosing electrical wires. **2 a** a track for trotting, pacing, or harness racing. **b** = RACETRACK.

ra·chis /ráykis/ *n.* (*pl.* **rachises** or **rachides** /rákideez, ráy-/) **1** *Bot.* **a** a stem of grass, etc., bearing flower stalks at short intervals. **b** the axis of a compound leaf or frond. **2** *Anat.* the vertebral column or the cord from which it develops. **3** *Zool.* a feather shaft, esp. the part bearing the barbs. □□ **rach·i·di·al** /rəkídeeəl/ *adj.*

ra·chi·tis /rəkítis/ *n.* rickets. □□ **ra·chit·ic** /-kítik/ *adj.*

ra·cial /ráyshəl/ *adj.* **1** of or concerning race. **2** on the grounds of or connected with difference in race. □□ **ra·cial·ly** *adv.*

ra·cial·ism /ráyshəlizəm/ *n.* = RACISM 1. □□ **ra·cial·ist** *n. & adj.*

rac·ism /ráysizəm/ *n.* **1 a** a belief in the superiority of a particular race; prejudice based on this. **b** antagonism toward other races, esp. as a result of this. **2** the theory that human abilities, etc., are determined by race. □□ **rac·ist** *n. & adj.*

rack¹ /rak/ *n. & v.* ● *n.* **1 a** a framework, usu. with rails, hooks, etc., for holding or storing things. **b** a frame for holding animal fodder. **2** a cogged or toothed bar or rail engaging with a wheel or pinion, etc. ▷ RACK-AND-PINION, RACK RAILWAY. **3 a** *hist.* an instrument of torture stretching the victim's joints by the turning of rollers to which the wrists and ankles were tied. ● *v.tr.* **1** (of disease or pain) inflict suffering on. **2** *hist.* torture (a person) on the rack. **3** place in or on a rack. **4** shake violently. **5** injure by straining. **6** exhaust (the land) by excessive use. □ **on the rack** in distress or under strain. **rack one's brains** make a great mental effort. **rack up** accumulate or achieve (a score, etc.).

rack² /rak/ *n.* destruction (esp. rack and ruin).

rack³ /rak/ *n.* a joint of lamb, etc., including the front ribs.

rack⁴ /rak/ *v.tr.* (often foll. by *off*) draw off (wine, etc.) from the lees.

rack⁵ /rak/ *n. & v.* ● *n.* driving clouds. ● *v.intr.* (of clouds) be driven before the wind.

rack⁶ /rak/ *n. & v.* ● *n.* a horse's gait between a trot and a canter. ● *v.intr.* progress in this way.

rack-and-pinion *attrib.adj.* ▼ (esp. of a steering system) using a rack-and-pinion.

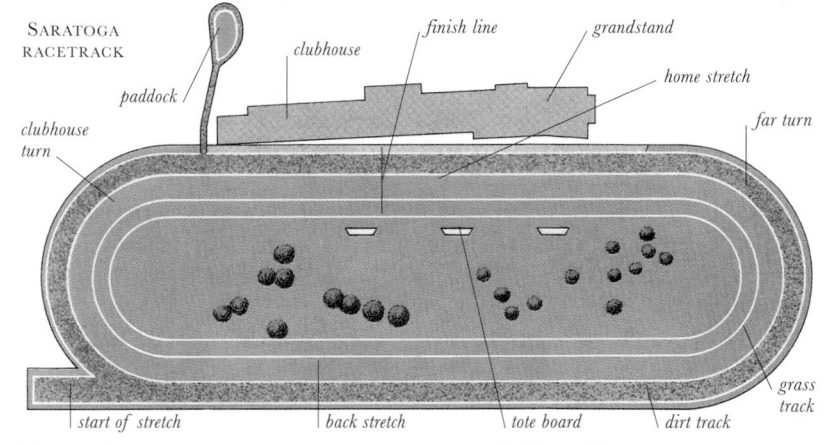

RACETRACK

While many early racetracks were adapted to the landscape, most modern tracks are oval and about 1 mile (1.6 km) long. Some are grassy; others have a dirt surface. They vary mainly in the distance to the first turn, the sharpness of the turns, and the type of soil.

SARATOGA RACETRACK

paddock · clubhouse · finish line · grandstand · home stretch · far turn · clubhouse turn · grass track

start of stretch · back stretch · tote board · dirt track

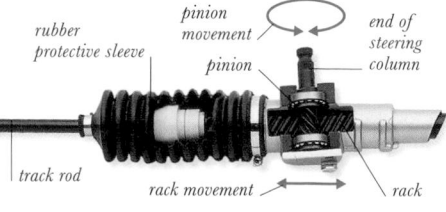

rubber protective sleeve · pinion movement · end of steering column · pinion · link to wheel · swiveling "ball joint" · track rod · rack movement · rack

RACK-AND-PINION
CAR STEERING SYSTEM (CUTAWAY VIEW)

RACK RAILWAY

Early trains needed a rack rail in order to climb steep slopes. As the pinion wheel turns, its teeth lock into slots in the rack, pulling the train up and preventing it from sliding back. Some mountain tracks still use rack rails.

EXPLODED VIEW OF A STEAM RACK LOCOMOTIVE

whistle pull chain

chimney

steam pipe

boiler

water tank

rack

pressure gauge

driver's cab

regulator

brake handwheel

coupling hook

rear buffer

bearing rail

driving axle

teeth

piston rod

water valve

crank

pinion wheel

flanged wheel

---

rack·et[1] /rákit/ *n.* (also **rac·quet**) **1** a hand-held implement with a round or oval frame strung with catgut, nylon, etc., used in tennis, squash, etc. **2** (in *pl.*) a ball game for two or four persons played with rackets in a plain four-walled court. **3** a snowshoe resembling a tennis racket.

rack·et[2] /rákit/ *n.* **1 a** a disturbance; a din. **b** social excitement; gaiety. **2** *sl.* **a** a scheme for obtaining money or attaining other ends by fraudulent and often violent means. **b** a dodge. **3** *colloq.* an activity; a way of life; a line of business. □□ **rack·et·y** *adj.*

rack·et·eer /rákitéer/ *n.* a person who operates a dishonest business. □□ **rack·et·eer·ing** *n.*

rack rail·way *n.* ▲ a railway with a cogged third rail designed to mesh with a cogwheel on a locomotive to prevent slippage on steep slopes.

ra·con /ráykon/ *n.* a radar beacon that can be identified and located by its response to a radar signal from a ship, etc.

rac·on·teur /rákontőr/ *n.* (*fem.* **raconteuse** /-tőz/) a teller of anecdotes.

ra·coon var. of RACCOON.

rac·quet var. of RACKET[1].

rac·quet·ball /rákətbawl/ *n.* a game played with rackets and a rubber ball on an enclosed, four-walled court.

rac·y /ráysee/ *adj.* (**racier, raciest**) **1** lively and vigorous in style. **2** risqué, suggestive. **3** having characteristic qualities in a high degree (*a racy flavor*). □□ **rac·i·ly** *adv.* **rac·i·ness** *n.*

rad[1] /rad/ *n.* (*pl.* same) radian.

rad[2] /rad/ *n. & adj.* • *n. sl.* a political radical. • *adj. sl.* wonderful; terrific.

rad[3] /rad/ *n. Physics* a unit of absorbed dose of ionizing radiation, corresponding to the absorption of 0.01 joule per kilogram of absorbing material.

ra·dar /ráydaar/ *n.* ▼ a system for detecting the presence, etc., of aircraft, ships, etc., by sending out pulses of high-frequency electromagnetic waves (acronym of *ra*dio *d*etecting *a*nd *r*anging).

rad·dle /rád'l/ *n. & v.* (also **rud·dle**) • *n.* red ocher (often used to mark sheep). • *v.tr.* **1** color with raddle or too much rouge. **2** (as **raddled** *adj.*) worn out; untidy; unkempt.

ra·di·al /ráydeeəl/ *adj. & n.* • *adj.* **1** of, concerning, or in rays. **2 a** arranged like rays or radii; having the position or direction of a radius. **b** having spokes or radiating lines. **c** acting or moving along lines diverging from a center. **3** *Anat.* relating to the radius (*radial artery*). **4** (of a vehicle tire) having the core fabric layers arranged radially and the tread strengthened. ▷ TIRE. • *n.* **1** *Anat.* the radial nerve or artery. **2** a radial tire. □□ **ra·di·al·ly** *adv.*

ra·di·al en·gine *n.* ▼ an engine having cylinders arranged along radii.

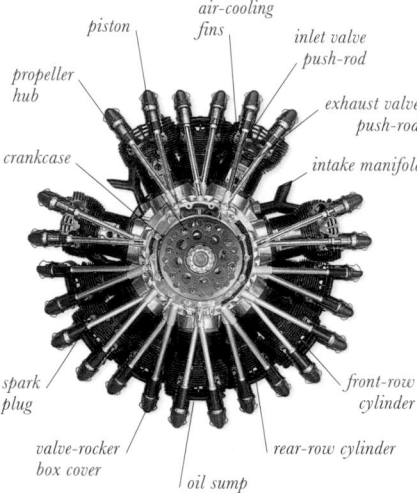

air-cooling fins

inlet valve push-rod

exhaust valve push-rod

intake manifold

piston

propeller hub

crankcase

spark plug

front-row cylinder

valve-rocker box cover

rear-row cylinder

oil sump

RADIAL ENGINE: EARLY 20TH-CENTURY 14-CYLINDER RADIAL ENGINE

ra·di·an /ráydeeən/ *n. Geom.* ▶ a unit of angle, equal to an angle at the center of a circle, the arc of which is equal in length to the radius.

ra·di·ant /ráydeeənt/ *adj. & n.* • *adj.* **1** emitting rays of light. **2** (of eyes or looks) beaming with joy or hope or love. **3** (of beauty) splendid or dazzling. **4** (of light) issuing in rays. **5** operating radially. **6** extending radially; radiating. • *n.* **1** the point or object from which light or heat radiates. **2** *Astron.* a radiant point. □□ **ra·di·ance** *n.* **ra·di·ant·ly** *adv.*

radian

radius

arc

RADIAN

ra·di·ant heat *n.* heat transmitted by radiation.

ra·di·ate *v. & adj.* • *v.* /ráydeeayt/ **1** *intr.* **a** emit rays of light, heat, etc. **b** (of light or heat) be emitted in rays. **2** *tr.* emit (light, heat, or sound) from a center. **3** *tr.* transmit or demonstrate (life, love, joy, etc.) (*radiates happiness*). **4** *intr. & tr.* diverge or cause to diverge or spread from a center. **5** *tr.* (as **radiated** *adj.*) with parts arranged in rays. • *adj.* /ráydeeət/ having divergent rays or parts radially arranged. □□ **ra·di·a·tive** /-ətiv/ *adj.*

ra·di·a·tion /ráydeeáyshən/ *n.* **1** the act or an instance of radiating; the process of being radiated. **2** *Physics* **a** the emission of energy as electromagnetic waves or as moving particles. ▷ ELECTROMAGNETIC RADIATION. **b** the energy transmitted in this way, esp. invisibly. **3** (in full **radiation therapy**) treatment of cancer and other diseases using radiation, such as X rays or ultraviolet light.

ra·di·a·tion sick·ness *n.* sickness caused by exposure to radiation, such as X rays or gamma rays.

ra·di·a·tor /ráydeeaytər/ *n.* **1** a person or thing

R

RADAR

Primary radar locates a target by measuring the time it takes for the echo of a pulse to return to the antenna, and by recording the direction it travels back from. In secondary radar, a transponder sends more detailed information in response to a pulse from a radar scanner.

weather radar in airplane nose

return pulses from onboard transponder

pulses from secondary radar scanner

pulses from antenna

reflected radar pulses

rotating secondary radar scanner

rotating primary radar antenna

AIRPLANE RADAR SYSTEMS

that radiates. **2 a** a device for heating a room, etc., consisting of a metal case through which hot water or steam circulates. **b** a usu. portable oil or electric heater resembling this. **3** an engine-cooling device in a motor vehicle or aircraft. ▷ AIRCRAFT, CAR

rad·i·cal /rádikəl/ *adj. & n.* ● *adj.* **1** of the root or roots; fundamental. **2** far-reaching; thorough (*radical change*). **3** advocating thorough reform; politically extreme. **4** forming the basis; primary (*the radical idea*). **5** *Math.* of the root of a number or quantity. **6** (of surgery, etc.) intended to be completely curative. **7** of the roots of words. **8** *US Hist.* seeking extreme anti-South action at the time of the Civil War. ● *n.* **1** a person holding radical views or belonging to a radical party. **2** *Chem.* **a** a free radical. **b** an element or atom or a group of these normally forming part of a compound and remaining unaltered during the compound's ordinary chemical changes. **3** the root of a word. **4** *Math.* a quantity forming or expressed as the root of another. □□ **rad·i·cal·ism** *n.* **rad·i·cal·ize** *v.tr. & intr.* **rad·i·cal·ly** *adv.* **rad·i·cal·ness** *n.*

rad·i·cal chic *n.* the fashionable affectation of radical left-wing views.

ra·dic·chi·o /rədéekeeō/ *n.* (*pl.* **-os**) a variety of chicory with dark red leaves.

ra·di·ces *pl.* of RADIX.

rad·i·cle /rádikəl/ *n.* **1** ▶ the part of a plant embryo that develops into the primary root. **2** a rootlike subdivision of a nerve or vein.

ra·di·i *pl.* of RADIUS.

ra·di·o /ráydeeō/ *n. & v.* ● *n.* (*pl.* **-os**) **1** (often *attrib.*) **a** the transmission and reception of sound messages, etc., by electromagnetic waves of radio frequency. ▷ ELECTROMAGNETIC RADIATION. **b** ▼ an apparatus for receiving, broadcasting, or transmitting radio signals. **c** a message sent or received by radio. **2 a** sound broadcasting in general (*prefers the radio*). **b** a broadcasting station, channel, or organization (*Armed Forces Radio*). ● *v.* (**-oed**) **1** *tr.* **a** send (a message) by radio. **b** send a message to (a person) by radio. **2** *intr.* communicate or broadcast by radio.

radio- /ráydeeō/ *comb. form* **1** denoting radio or broadcasting. **2 a** connected with radioactivity. **b** denoting artificially prepared radioisotopes of

elements (*radiocesium*). **3** connected with rays or radiation. **4** *Anat.* belonging to the radius in conjunction with some other part (*radiocarpal*).

ra·di·o·ac·tive /ráydeeō-áktiv/ *adj.* of or exhibiting radioactivity. □□ **ra·di·o·ac·tive·ly** *adv.*

ra·di·o·ac·tiv·i·ty /ráydeeō-aktívitee/ *n.* ▲ the spontaneous disintegration of atomic nuclei, with the emission of usu. penetrating radiation or particles.

ra·di·o as·tron·o·my *n.* the branch of astronomy concerned with the radio-frequency range of the electromagnetic spectrum.

ra·di·o·car·bon /ráydeeōkáarbən/ *n.* a radioactive isotope of carbon.

ra·di·o·car·bon dat·ing *n.* = CARBON DATING.

ra·di·o·el·e·ment /ráydeeō-élimənt/ *n.* a natural or artificial radioactive element or isotope.

ra·di·o fre·quen·cy *n.* (*pl.* **-ies**) the frequency band of telecommunication, ranging from 10^1 to 10^{11} or 10^{12} Hz.

ra·di·o·gen·ic /ráydeeōjénik/ *adj.* **1** produced by radioactivity. **2** suitable for broadcasting by radio. □□ **ra·di·o·gen·i·cal·ly** *adv.*

ra·di·o·gram /ráydeeōgram/ *n.* **1** a picture obtained by X rays, gamma rays, etc. **2** a radiotelegram.

ra·di·o·graph /ráydeeōgráf/ *n. & v.* ● *n.* **1** an instrument recording the intensity of radiation. **2** = RADIOGRAM 1. ● *v.tr.* obtain a picture of by X ray, gamma ray, etc. □□ **ra·di·og·ra·pher** /-deeógrəfər/ *n.* **ra·di·o·graph·ic** *adj.* **ra·di·o·graph·i·cal·ly** *adv.* **ra·di·og·ra·phy** /-deeógrəfee/ *n.*

ra·di·o·i·so·tope /ráydeeō-ísətōp/ *n.* a radioactive isotope. □□ **ra·di·o·i·so·top·ic** /-tópik/ *adj.*

ra·di·o·lar·i·an /ráydeeōláireeən/ *n.* any marine protozoan of the order Radiolaria, having a siliceous skeleton and radiating pseudopodia.

ra·di·ol·o·gy /ráydeeóləjee/ *n.* the scientific study of X rays and other high-energy radiation, esp. as used in medicine. □□ **ra·di·o·log·ic** /-deeəlójik/ *adj.* **ra·di·o·log·i·cal** /-deeəlójikəl/ *adj.* **ra·di·ol·o·gist** *n.*

ra·di·om·e·ter /ráydeeómitər/ *n.* an instrument for measuring the intensity or force of radiation. □□ **ra·di·o·met·ric** /-deeōmétrik/ *adj.* **ra·di·om·e·try** *n.*

ra·di·on·ics /ráydeeóniks/ *n.pl.* (usu. treated as *sing.*) the study and interpretation of radiation believed to be emitted from substances, esp. as a form of diagnosis.

ra·di·o·phon·ic /ráydeeōfónik/ *adj.* of or relating to synthetic sound, esp. music, produced electronically.

ra·di·os·co·py /ráydeeóskəpee/ *n.* the examination by X rays, etc., of objects opaque to light. □□ **ra·di·o·scop·ic** /-deeəskópik/ *adj.*

ra·di·o·sonde /ráydeeōsond/ *n.* a miniature radio transmitter broadcasting information about pressure, temperature, etc., from various levels of the atmosphere.

ra·di·o·tel·e·gram /ráydeeōtéligram/ *n.* a telegram sent by radio, usu. from a ship to land.

ra·di·o·te·leg·ra·phy /ráydeeōtilégrəfee/ *n.* telegraphy using radio transmission. □□ **ra·di·o·tel·e·graph** /-téligraaf/ *n.*

ra·di·o·te·leph·o·ny /ráydeeōtiléfənee/ *n.* telephony using radio transmission. □□ **ra·di·o·tel·e·phone** /-télifōn/ *n.*

ra·di·o tel·e·scope *n.* a directional aerial system for collecting and analyzing radiation in the radio-frequency range from stars, etc.

ra·di·o·tel·ex /ráydeeōtéleks/ *n.* a telex sent usu. from a ship to land.

ra·di·o·ther·a·py /ráydeeōthérəpee/ *n.* radiation therapy (see RADIATION 3). □□ **ra·di·o·ther·a·peu·tic** /-pyōōtik/ *adj.* **ra·di·o·ther·a·pist** *n.*

rad·ish /rádish/ *n.* **1** a cruciferous plant, *Raphanus sativus*, with a fleshy pungent root. **2** this root, eaten esp. raw in salads, etc. ▷ VEGETABLE

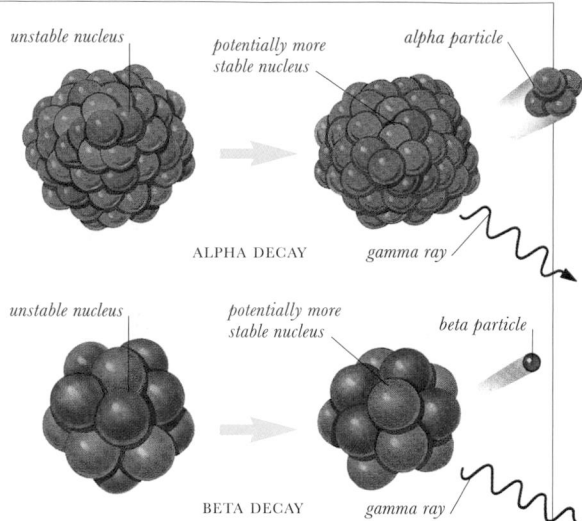

RADIOACTIVITY

A nucleus is composed of protons and neutrons. All the protons are positively charged and so repel one another. An equivalent nuclear force holds the nucleus together. If there is an imbalance between the two forces, the nucleus becomes unstable and decays, and charged particles are emitted. This process is called radioactivity. In alpha decay, an alpha particle (two neutrons and two protons) is released. In beta decay, a beta particle (a fast electron) is released. In both cases, gamma radiation may also be emitted.

unstable nucleus   *potentially more stable nucleus*   *alpha particle*

ALPHA DECAY   *gamma ray*

unstable nucleus   *potentially more stable nucleus*   *beta particle*

BETA DECAY   *gamma ray*

---

radicle

RADICLE EMERGING FROM A BROAD BEAN SEED

RADIO

Radios re-form radio waves: a diode or variable capacitor tunes in one of the many signals picked up by the antenna; diodes and capacitors turn the signal into a smooth direct current; a transistor amplifies the electrical signal and feeds it to a loudspeaker.

COMPONENTS OF A PORTABLE RADIO

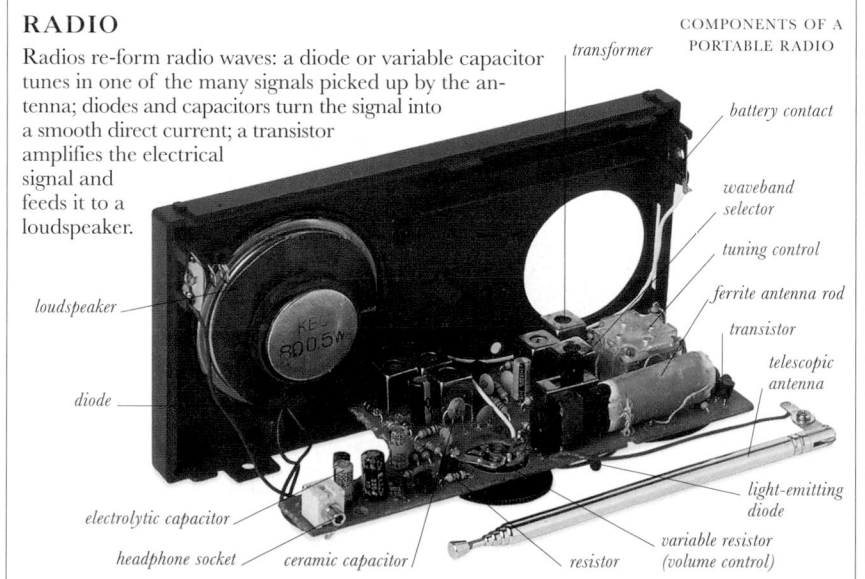

transformer
battery contact
waveband selector
tuning control
ferrite antenna rod
transistor
telescopic antenna
light-emitting diode
variable resistor (volume control)
resistor
ceramic capacitor
headphone socket
electrolytic capacitor
diode
loudspeaker

R

ra·di·um /ráydeeəm/ *n. Chem.* a radioactive metallic element orig. obtained from pitchblende, etc., used esp. in radiotherapy. ¶ Symb.: **Ra**.

ra·di·us /ráydeeəs/ *n. & v.* ● *n.* (*pl.* **radii** /-dee-ī/ or **radiuses**) **1** *Math.* **a** a straight line from the center to the circumference of a circle or sphere. **b** a radial line from the focus to any point of a curve. **c** the length of the radius of a circle, etc. **2** a usu. specified distance from a center in all directions. **3 a** ◄ the thicker and shorter of the two bones in the human forearm (cf. ULNA). ▷ SKELETON. **b** the corresponding bone in a vertebrate's foreleg or a bird's wing. **4** any of the five armlike structures of a starfish. **5 a** any of a set of lines diverging from a point like the radii of a circle. **b** an object of this kind, e.g., a spoke. ● *v.tr.* give a rounded form to (an edge, etc.).

radius

RADIUS (**1a**)

RADIUS (3a): HUMAN FOREARM SHOWING THE RADIUS

radius

ra·dix /ráydiks/ *n.* (*pl.* **radices** /-diseez/ or **radixes**) **1** *Math.* a number or symbol used as the basis of a numeration scale (e.g., ten in the decimal system). **2** (usu. foll. by *of*) a source or origin.

ra·dome /ráydōm/ *n.* a dome or other structure, transparent to radio waves, protecting radar equipment, esp. on the outer surface of an aircraft.

ra·don /ráydon/ *n. Chem.* a gaseous radioactive inert element arising from the disintegration of radium. ¶ Symb.: **Rn**.

RAF *abbr.* (in the UK) Royal Air Force.

raf·fi·a /ráfeeə/ *n.* (also **ra·phi·a**) **1** a palm tree, *Raphia ruffia*, native to Madagascar, having very long leaves. **2** ▼ the fiber from its leaves used for making hats, baskets, etc., and for tying plants, etc.

RAFFIA

R

raf·fi·nate /ráfinayt/ *n. Chem.* a refined liquid oil produced by solvent extraction of impurities.

raff·ish /ráfish/ *adj.* **1** disreputable; rakish. **2** tawdry. □□ **raff·ish·ly** *adv.* **raff·ish·ness** *n.*

raf·fle /ráfəl/ *n. & v.* ● *n.* a fund-raising lottery with goods as prizes. ● *v.tr.* (often foll. by *off*) dispose of by means of a raffle.

raft[1] /raft/ *n. & v.* ● *n.* **1** a flat floating structure of logs or other materials for conveying persons or things. **2** a lifeboat or small (often inflatable) boat, esp. for use in emergencies. **3** a floating accumulation of trees, ice, etc. ● *v.* **1** *tr.* transport as or on a raft. **2** *tr.* cross (water) on a raft. **3** *tr.* form into a raft. **4** *intr.* (often foll. by *across*) work a raft (across water, etc.).

raft[2] /raft/ *n. colloq.* **1** a large collection. **2** (foll. by *of*) a crowd.

raft·er[1] /ráftər/ *n.* each of the sloping beams forming the framework of a roof. ▷ ROOF. □□ **raft·ered** *adj.*

raft·er[2] /ráftər/ *n.* **1** a person who builds rafts. **2** a person who travels by raft.

rag[1] /rag/ *n.* **1 a** a torn, frayed, or worn piece of woven material. **b** one of the irregular scraps to which cloth, etc., is reduced by wear and tear. **2 a** (in *pl.*) old or worn clothes. **b** (usu. in *pl.*) *colloq.* a garment of any kind. **3** (*collect.*) scraps of cloth used as material for paper, stuffing, etc. **4** *derog.* **a** a newspaper. **b** a flag, handkerchief, curtain, etc. **5** (usu. with *neg.*) the smallest scrap of cloth, etc. (*not a rag to cover him*). **6** an odd scrap; an irregular piece. **7** a jagged projection, esp. on metal. □ **in rags 1** much torn. **2** in old torn clothes. **rags to riches** poverty to affluence.

rag[2] /rag/ *n. & v.* ● *n. Brit.* **1** a fund-raising program of stunts, parades, and entertainment organized by students. **2** *colloq.* a prank. **3 a** a rowdy celebration. **b** a noisy discordant scene. ● *v.* (**ragged**, **ragging**) **1** *tr.* tease; torment; play rough jokes on. **2** *tr.* scold; reprove severely. **3** *intr. Brit.* engage in rough play; be noisy and riotous.

rag[3] /rag/ *n.* **1** a large, coarse roofing slate. **2** any of various kinds of hard, coarse, sedimentary stone that break into thick slabs.

rag[4] /rag/ *n. Mus.* a ragtime composition or tune.

ra·ga /ráagə/ *n.* (also **rag** /raag/) *Ind. Mus.* **1** a pattern of notes used as a basis for improvisation. **2** a piece using a particular raga.

rag·a·muf·fin /rágəmufin/ *n.* a person in ragged dirty clothes, esp. a child.

rag·bag /rágbag/ *n.* **1** a bag in which scraps of fabric, etc., are kept for use. **2** a miscellaneous collection.

rag doll *n.* a stuffed doll made of cloth.

rage /rayj/ *n. & v.* ● *n.* **1** fierce or violent anger. **2** a fit of this (*flew into a rage*). **3** the violent action of a natural force (*the rage of a storm*). **4** (foll. by *for*) a vehement desire or passion. **b** a widespread temporary enthusiasm or fashion. **5** *poet.* poetic, prophetic, or martial enthusiasm or ardor. ● *v.tr.* **1** be full of anger. **2** (often foll. by *at*, *against*) speak furiously or madly; rave. **3** (of wind, fever, etc.) be violent; be at its height. □ **all the rage** popular; fashionable.

rag·ged /rágid/ *adj.* **1 a** (of clothes, etc.) torn; frayed. **b** (of a place) dilapidated. **2** rough; shaggy; hanging in tufts. **3** (of a person) in ragged clothes. **4** with a broken or jagged outline or surface. **5** faulty; imperfect. **6 a** lacking finish, smoothness, or uniformity (*ragged rhymes*). **b** (of a sound) harsh; discordant. **7** exhausted (esp. *be run ragged*). □□ **rag·ged·ly** *adv.* **rag·ged·ness** *n.* **rag·ged·y** *adj.*

rag·ged rob·in *n.* a pink-flowered campion, *Lychnis flos-cuculi*, with tattered petals.

rag·gle-tag·gle /rágəltagəl/ *adj.* (also **wraggle-taggle**) rambling; straggling.

rag·lan /ráglən/ *n.* (often *attrib.*) an overcoat without shoulder seams, the sleeves running up to the neck.

rag·lan sleeve *n.* a sleeve that runs up to the neck of a garment.

ra·gout /ragōō/ *n. & v.* ● *n.* meat in small pieces stewed with vegetables and highly seasoned. ● *v.tr.* cook (food) in this way.

rag·stone /rágstōn/ *n.* = RAG[3] 2.

rag·tag /rágtag/ *n. & adj.* ● *n.* (in full **ragtag and bobtail**) *derog.* the rabble or common people. ● *adj.* motley.

rag·time /rágtīm/ *n. & adj.* ● *n.* music characterized by a syncopated melodic line and regularly accented accompaniment, evolved by African-American musicians in the 1890s and played esp. on the piano. ● *adj. sl.* disorderly, disreputable, inferior (*a ragtime army*).

rag trade *n. colloq.* the business of designing, making, and selling clothes.

ra·gu·ly /rágəlee/ *adj. Heraldry* like a row of sawn-off branches.

rag·weed /rágweed/ *n.* any plant of the genus *Ambrosia*, esp. *A. trifida*, with allergenic pollen.

rag·wort /rágwərt, -wawrt/ *n.* ► any yellow-flowered, ragged-leaved plant of the genus *Senecio*.

rah /raa/ *int. colloq.* an expression of encouragement, approval, etc., esp. to a team or a player.

raid /rayd/ *n. & v.* ● *n.* **1** a rapid surprise attack, esp.: **a** in warfare. **b** to commit a crime or do harm. **2** a surprise attack by police, etc., to arrest suspected persons or seize illicit goods. **3** *Stock Exch.* an attempt to lower prices by the concerted selling of shares. **4** (foll. by *on*, *upon*) a forceful or insistent attempt to make a person or thing provide something. ● *v.tr.* **1** make a raid on (a person, place, or thing). **2** plunder; deplete. □□ **raid·er** *n.*

RAGWORT (*Senecio jacobaea*)

rail[1] /rayl/ *n. & v.* ● *n.* **1** a level or sloping bar or series of bars: **a** used to hang things on. **b** running along the top of a set of banisters. **c** forming part of a barrier. **2** ▼ a steel bar or continuous line of bars laid on the ground, usu. as one of a pair forming a railroad track. **3** (often *attrib.*) a railroad (*by rail*). **4** (in *pl.*) the inside boundary fence of a racecourse. **5** a horizontal piece in the frame of a paneled door, etc. ● *v.tr.* **1** furnish with a rail or rails. **2** (usu. foll. by *in*, *off*) enclose with rails. **3** convey (goods) by rail. □ **off the rails** disorganized; out of order; deranged. **over the rails** over the side of a ship. □□ **rail·less** *adj.*

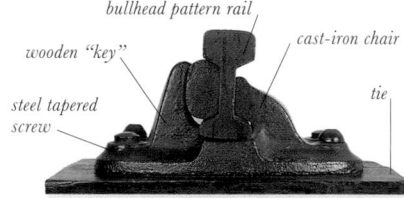

bullhead pattern rail

wooden "key"

cast-iron chair

steel tapered screw

tie

RAIL: CROSS SECTION OF A BULLHEAD RAIL

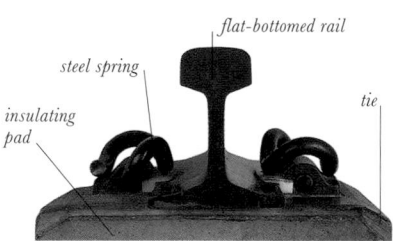

flat-bottomed rail

steel spring

insulating pad

tie

RAIL: CROSS SECTION OF A FLAT-BOTTOMED RAIL

rail[2] /rayl/ *v.intr.* (often foll. by *at*, *against*) complain using abusive language. □□ **rail·er** *n.* **rail·ing** *n. & adj.*

rail[3] /rayl/ *n.* any bird of the family Rallidae, often inhabiting marshes, esp. the Virginia rail and corn crake.

rail·car /ráylkaar/ *n.* **1** any railroad car. **2** a railroad vehicle consisting of a single powered car.

rail·head /ráylhed/ *n.* **1** the furthest point reached by a railroad under construction. **2** the point on a railroad at which road transport of goods begins.

rail·ing /ráyling/ *n.* **1** (usu. in *pl.*) a fence or barrier made of rails. **2** the material for these.

rail·ler·y /ráyləree/ *n.* (*pl.* **-ies**) **1** good-humored ridicule; rallying. **2** an instance of this.

rail·road /ráylrōd/ *n. & v.* ● *n.* **1** a track or set of

RAIN

Rain forms when warm air rises and cools, the water vapor in it condensing into small droplets. These droplets collide with one another, forming larger drops that fall as rain. At very low temperatures, the droplets are supercooled, often forming crystals. These grow into snowflakes, which melt into rain as they fall into warmer air.

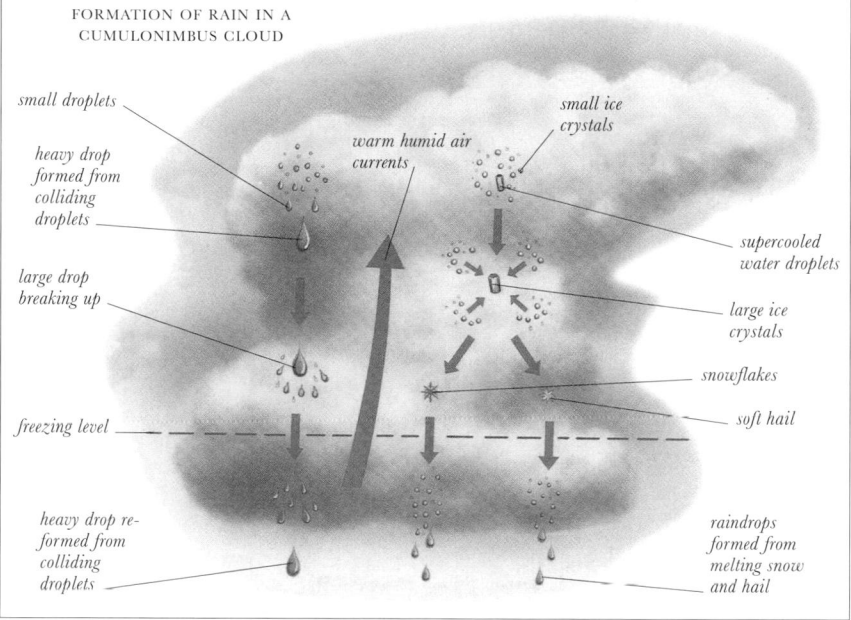

FORMATION OF RAIN IN A CUMULONIMBUS CLOUD

small droplets

heavy drop formed from colliding droplets

warm humid air currents

small ice crystals

supercooled water droplets

large drop breaking up

large ice crystals

snowflakes

freezing level

soft hail

heavy drop re-formed from colliding droplets

raindrops formed from melting snow and hail

tracks made of steel rails upon which goods trucks and passenger trains run. **2** such a system worked by a single company (*B & O Railroad*). **3** the organization ßand personnel required for its working. **4** a similar set of tracks for other vehicles, etc. ● *v.tr.* **1** (often foll. by *to, into, through*, etc.) rush or coerce (a person or thing) (*railroaded me into going too*). **2** send (a person) to prison by means of false evidence. **3** transport by railroad.

rail·way /ráylway/ *n.* esp. *Brit.* = RAILROAD.

rai·ment /ráymənt/ *n. archaic* clothing.

rain /rayn/ *n. & v.* ● *n.* **1 a ▲** the condensed moisture of the atmosphere falling visibly in separate drops. **b** the fall of such drops. **2** (in *pl.*) **a** rainfalls. **b** (prec. by *the*) the rainy season in tropical countries. **3 a** falling liquid or solid particles or objects. **b** the rainlike descent of these. **c** a large or overwhelming quantity (*a rain of congratulations*). ● *v.* **1** *intr.* (prec. by *it* as subject) rain falls (*if it rains*). **2 a** *intr.* fall in showers or like rain (*blows rain upon him*). **b** *tr.* (prec. by *it* as subject) send in large quantities (*it rained blood*). **3** *tr.* send down like rain;

lavishly bestow (*rained blows upon him*). **4** *intr.* (of the sky, etc.) send down rain. □ **rain cats and dogs** see CAT. **rain out** (esp. in *passive*) cause (an event, etc.) to be terminated or canceled because of rain. **rain or shine** whether it rains or not. □□ **rain·less** *adj.*

rain·bow /ráynbō/ *n. & adj.* ● *n.* **1 ▼** an arch of colors formed in the sky by reflection, twofold refraction, and dispersion of the Sun's rays in falling rain or in spray or mist. ▷ LIGHT, REFLECTION, REFRACTION. **2** a similar effect formed by the Moon's rays. ● *adj.* many-colored.

rain·bow trout *n.* a large trout, *Salmo gairdneri*, orig. of the Pacific coast of N. America.

rain check *n.* **1** a ticket given for later use when an outdoor event is interrupted or postponed by rain. **2** a promise that an offer will be maintained though deferred.

rain·coat /ráynkōt/ *n.* a waterproof or water-resistant coat.

rain date *n.* a date on which an event postponed by rain is held.

rain·drop /ráyndrop/ *n.* a single drop of rain.

rain·fall /ráynfawl/ *n.* **1** a fall of rain. **2** the quantity of rain falling within a given area in a given time.

rain for·est *n.* ▼ luxuriant tropical forest with heavy rainfall.

emergent layer

canopy layer

understory

liana

RAIN FOREST LAYERS

forest floor

R

rain gauge *n.* an instrument measuring rainfall.

rain·mak·ing /ráynmayking/ *n.* the action of attempting to increase rainfall by artificial means.

rain·proof /ráynprōof/ *adj.* (esp. of a building, garment, etc.) resistant to rainwater.

rain·storm /ráynstawrm/ *n.* a storm with heavy rain.

rain·wa·ter /ráynwawtər, -wotər/ *n.* water obtained from collected rain, as distinct from a well, etc.

rain·y /ráynee/ *adj.* (**rainier**, **rainiest**) **1** (of weather, a climate, day, region, etc.) in or on which rain is falling or much rain usually falls. **2** (of cloud, wind, etc.) laden with or bringing rain. □□ **rain·i·ly** *adv.* **rain·i·ness** *n.*

rain·y day *n.* a time of special need in the future.

raise /rayz/ *v. & n.* ● *v.tr.* **1** put or take into a higher position. **2** (often foll. by *up*) cause to rise or be vertical. **3** increase the amount or value or strength of. **4** (often foll. by *up*) construct or build up. **5** levy or collect or bring together. **6** cause to be heard or considered (*raise an objection*). **7** bring into being; arouse (*raise hopes*). **8** bring up; educate. **9** breed or grow (*raise one's own vegetables*). **10** promote to a higher rank. **11** (foll. by *to*) *Math.* multiply a quantity to a specified power. **12** cause (bread) to rise

RAINBOW

Sunlight is a mixture of colors, each with its own wavelength. As light enters a drop of water, each wavelength is refracted at a different angle. It is then reflected at the back of the droplet and refracts again as it exits. This splits the light into a spectrum that is visible as bands of color and forms a rainbow.

Sun

sunlight

refraction

reflection

refraction

raindrops

violet ray

red ray

observer's eye

green ray

FORMATION OF A RAINBOW

RAKE

Rakes can be used to level, clear, or break up ground. Garden rakes are general-purpose tools, spring-tined lawn rakes are suited to clearing light debris, and scarifying rakes aerate a lawn.

GARDEN RAKE

tine

SPRING-TINED LAWN RAKE

SCARIFYING RAKE

R

with yeast. **13** *Cards* **a** bet more than (another player). **b** increase (a stake). **c** *Bridge* make a bid contracting for more tricks in the same suit as (one's partner); increase (a bid) in this way. **14** abandon or force an enemy to abandon (a siege or blockade). **15** remove (a barrier or embargo). **16** cause (a ghost, etc.) to appear (opp. LAY[1] *v.* 6b). **17** *colloq.* find (a person, etc., wanted). **18** establish contact with (a person, etc.) by radio or telephone. ● *n.* **1** *Cards* an increase in a stake or bid (cf. sense 13 of *v.*). **2** an increase in salary. □ **raise Cain** see CAIN. **raise the devil** *colloq.* make a disturbance. **raise one's eyebrows** see EYEBROW. **raise from the dead** restore to life. **raise one's glass to** drink the health or good fortune of. **raise one's hand to** make as if to strike (a person). **raise one's hat** (often foll. by *to*) remove it momentarily as a gesture of courtesy or respect. **raise hell** *colloq.* make a disturbance. **raise one's voice** speak, esp. louder. □□ **rais·a·ble** *adj.*

rai·sin /ráyzən/ *n.* a partially dried grape. □□ **rai·sin·y** *adj.*

rai·son d'être /ráyzon détrə/ *n.* (*pl.* **raisons d'être** *pronunc.* same) the most important reason or purpose for a person's or thing's existence.

raj /raaj/ *n.* (prec. by *the*) *hist.* British sovereignty in India.

ra·ja /ráajə/ *n.* (also **ra·jah**) *hist.* **1** an Indian king or prince. **2** a petty dignitary or noble in India. **3** a Malay or Javanese chief.

---

rake[1] /rayk/ *n. & v.* ● *n.* **1 a** ◄ an implement consisting of a pole with a crossbar toothed like a comb at the end, or with several tines held together by a crosspiece, for drawing together hay, etc., or smoothing loose soil or gravel. **b** a wheeled implement for the same purpose. **2** a similar implement used for other purposes, e.g., by a croupier. ● *v.* **1** *tr.* (usu. foll. by *out, together, up*, etc.) collect or gather or remove with or as with a rake. **2** *tr.* make tidy or smooth with a rake. **3** *intr.* use a rake. **4** *tr. & intr.* search thoroughly; ransack. **5** *tr.* **a** direct gunfire along (a line) from end to end. **b** sweep with the eyes. **c** (of a window, etc.) have a commanding view of. **6** *tr.* scratch or scrape. □ **rake in** *colloq.* amass (profits, etc.). **rake it in** *colloq.* make much money. **rake up** (or **over**) revive the memory of (past quarrels, etc.). □□ **rak·er** *n.*

rake[2] /rayk/ *n.* a dissolute man of fashion.

rake[3] /rayk/ *v. & n.* ● *v.* **1** *tr. & intr.* set or be set at a sloping angle. **2** *intr.* **a** (of a mast or funnel) incline from the perpendicular toward the stern. **b** (of a ship or its bow or stern) project at the upper part of the bow or stern beyond the keel. ● *n.* **1** a raking position or build. **2** the amount by which a thing rakes. **3** the slope of the stage or the auditorium in a theater. **4** the slope of a seat back, etc. **5** the angle of the edge or face of a cutting tool.

ra·ki /rəkée, rákee/ *n.* a strong alcoholic spirit made in eastern Europe or the Middle East.

rak·ish[1] /ráykish/ *adj.* of or like a rake (see RAKE[2]); dashing; jaunty. □□ **rak·ish·ly** *adv.* **rak·ish·ness** *n.*

rak·ish[2] /ráykish/ *adj.* (of a ship) smart and fast looking, and therefore open to suspicion of piracy.

rale /raal/ *n.* an abnormal rattling sound heard in the auscultation of unhealthy lungs.

ral·len·tan·do /rálentándō, ráalentáandō/ *adv., adj., & n. Mus.* ● *adv. & adj.* with a gradual decrease of speed. ● *n.* (*pl.* **-os** or **rallentandi** /-dee/) a passage to be performed in this way.

ral·ly[1] /rálee/ *v. & n.* ● *v.* (**-ies, -ied**) **1** *tr. & intr.* (often foll. by *round, behind, to*) bring or come together as support or for concentrated action. **2** *tr. & intr.* bring or come together again after a rout or dispersion. **3 a** *intr.* renew a conflict. **b** *tr.* cause to do this. **4 a** *tr.* revive (courage, etc.) by an effort of will. **b** *tr.* rouse (a person or animal) to fresh energy. **c** *intr.* pull oneself together. **5** *intr.* recover after illness or prostration or fear. **6** *intr.* (of share prices, etc.) increase after a fall. ● *n.* (*pl.* **-ies**) **1** an act of reassembling forces or renewing conflict. **2** a recovery of energy after or in the middle of exhaustion or illness. **3** a mass meeting of supporters or persons having a common interest. **4** a competition for motor vehicles, usu. over public roads. **5** (in tennis, etc.) an extended exchange of strokes between players. □□ **ral·li·er** *n.*

ral·ly[2] /rálee/ *v.tr.* (**-ies, -ied**) subject to good-humored ridicule.

RAM /ram/ *abbr. Computing* random-access memory; internally stored software or data that is directly accessible, not requiring sequential search or reading. ▷ COMPUTER

ram /ram/ *n. & v.* ● *n.* **1** an uncastrated male sheep. **2** (**the Ram**) the zodiacal sign or constellation Aries. ▷ ARIES. **3** *hist.* **a** = BATTERING RAM. **b** a beak projecting from the bow of a battleship, for piercing the sides of other ships. **c** a battleship with such a beak. **4** the falling weight of a pile-driving machine. **5 a** a hydraulic water-raising or lifting machine. ▷ EXCAVATE. **b** the piston of a hydrostatic press. **c** the plunger of a force pump. ● *v.tr.* (**rammed, ramming**) **1** force or squeeze into place by pressure. **2** (usu. foll. by *down, in, into*) beat down or in by heavy blows. **3** (of a ship, etc.) strike violently; crash against. **4** (foll. by *against, at, on, into*) violently impel. □ **ram home** stress forcefully (a lesson, etc.). □□ **ram·mer** *n.*

Ram·a·dan /rámədan, ramədáan/ *n.* (also **Ram·a·dhan**) the ninth month of the Muslim year,

---

during which strict fasting is observed from sunrise to sunset.

ram·ble /rámbəl/ *v. & n.* ● *v.intr.* **1** walk for pleasure, with or without a definite route. **2** wander in discourse; talk or write disconnectedly. ● *n.* a walk taken for pleasure.

ram·bler /rámblər/ *n.* **1** a person who rambles. **2** a straggling or climbing rose.

ram·bling /rámbling/ *adj.* **1** peripatetic; wandering. **2** desultory; incoherent. **3** (of a house, etc.) irregularly arranged. **4** (of a plant) straggling. □□ **ram·bling·ly** *adv.*

ram·bunc·tious /rambúngkshəs/ *adj. colloq.* **1** uncontrollably exuberant. **2** unruly. □□ **ram·bunc·tious·ly** *adv.* **ram·bunc·tious·ness** *n.*

ram·bu·tan /rambóot'n/ *n.* **1** ► a red, plum-sized prickly fruit. **2** an East Indian tree, *Nephelium lappaceum*, that bears this.

ram·e·kin /rámikin/ *n.* (also **ram·e·quin**) **1** a small dish for baking and serving an individual portion of food. **2** food served in such a dish.

ram·i·fi·ca·tion /rámifikáyshən/ *n.* **1** the act or an instance of ramifying; the state of being ramified. **2** a subdivision of a complex structure or process comparable to a tree's branches. **3** a consequence, esp. when complex or unwelcome.

RAMBUTAN (*Nephelium lappaceum*)

edible flesh

ram·i·fy /rámifī/ *v.* (**-ies, -ied**) **1** *intr.* form branches or subdivisions or offshoots. **2** *tr.* (usu. in *passive*) cause to branch out; arrange in a branching manner.

ram·jet /rámjet/ *n.* a type of jet engine in which air is drawn in and compressed by the forward motion of the engine.

ram·mer see RAM.

ra·mose /rámōs, ráy-/ *adj.* branched; branching.

ramp /ramp/ *n. & v.* ● *n.* **1** a slope or inclined plane, esp. for joining two levels of ground, etc. **2** (in full **boarding ramp**) movable stairs for entering or leaving an aircraft. **3** an upward bend in a staircase railing. ● *v.* **1** *tr.* furnish or build with a ramp. **2** *intr.* **a** assume or be in a threatening posture. **b** (often foll. by *about*) storm; rage; rush. **3** *intr. Archit.* (of a wall) ascend or descend to a different level.

ram·page *v. & n.* ● *v.intr.* /rámpáyj/ **1** (often foll. by *about*) rush wildly or violently about. **2** rage; storm. ● *n.* /rámpayj/ wild or violent behavior. □ **on the rampage** rampaging. □□ **ram·pa·geous** *adj.* **ram·pag·er** *n.*

ramp·ant /rámpənt/ *adj.* **1** (placed after noun) *Heraldry* ▼ (of an animal) standing on its left hind foot with its forepaws in the air. **2** flourishing excessively (*rampant violence*). **3** violent or extravagant in action or opinion (*rampant theorists*). **4** rank; luxuriant. □□ **ramp·an·cy** *n.* **ramp·ant·ly** *adv.*

ram·part /rámpaart/ *n. & v.* ● *n.* **1 a** a defensive wall with a broad top and usu. a stone parapet. **b** a walkway on top of such a wall. **2** a defense or protection. ● *v.tr.* fortify or protect with or as with a rampart.

RAMPANT: SHIELD WITH BEAR RAMPANT

ram·rod /rámrod/ *n.* **1 ▶** a rod for ramming down the charge of a muzzleloading firearm. **2** a thing that is very straight or rigid.

ramming end

ram·shack·le /rámshakəl/ *adj.* (usu. of a house or vehicle) tumbledown; rickety.

ran *past* of RUN.

ranch /ranch/ *n. & v.* ● *n.* **1 a** a cattle-breeding establishment, esp. in the western US and Canada. **b** a farm where other animals are bred (*mink ranch*). **2** (in full **ranch house**) a single-story or split-level house. ● *v.intr.* farm on a ranch.

ranch·er /ránchər/ *n.* a person who farms on a ranch.

cleaning brush

ran·che·ro / rancháirō/ *n.* (*pl.* **-os**) a person who farms or works on a ranch, esp. in Mexico.

ran·cid /ránsid/ *adj.* smelling or tasting like rank stale fat. □□ **ran·cid·i·ty** /-síditee/ *n.*

ran·cor /rángkər/ *n.* inveterate bitterness; malignant hate. □□ **ran·cor·ous** *adj.* **ran·cor·ous·ly** *adv.*

RAMROD

rand[1] /rand, raant/ *n.* the chief monetary unit of South Africa.

rand[2] /rand/ *n.* a leveling strip of leather between the heel and sides of a shoe or boot.

R & B *abbr.* (also **R. & B.**) rhythm and blues.

R & D *abbr.* (also **R. & D.**) research and development.

ran·dom /rándəm/ *adj.* **1** made, done, etc., without method or conscious choice. **2** *Statistics* **a** with equal chances for each item. **b** given by a random process. **3** (of masonry) with stones of irregular size and shape. □ **at random** without aim or purpose or principle. □□ **ran·dom·ize** *v.tr.* **ran·dom·i·za·tion** *n.* **ran·dom·ly** *adv.* **ran·dom·ness** *n.*

ran·dom-ac·cess *adj. Computing* (of a memory or file) having all parts directly accessible, so that it need not be read sequentially.

R and R *abbr.* (also **R. and R.**) **1** rescue and resuscitation. **2** rest and recreation (or recuperation or relaxation). **3** rock and roll.

ra·nee var. of RANI.

rang *past* of RING[2].

range /raynj/ *n. & v.* ● *n.* **1 a** the region between limits of variation, esp. a scope of effective operation (*the whole range of politics*). **b** such limits. **c** a limited scale or series (*the range is about 10 degrees*). **d** a series representing variety or choice; a selection. **2** the area included in or concerned with something. **3 a** the distance attainable by a gun or projectile. **b** the distance between a gun or projectile and its objective. **4** a row, series, line, or tier, esp. of mountains or buildings. **5 a** an open or enclosed area with targets for shooting. **b** a testing ground for military equipment. **6** a cooking stove with one or more ovens and a set of burners on the top surface. **7** the area over which a thing, esp. a plant or animal, is distributed. **8** the distance that can be covered by a vehicle or aircraft without refueling. **9** the distance between a camera and the subject to be photographed. **10** the extent of time covered by a forecast, etc. **11 a** a large area of open land for grazing or hunting. **b** a tract over which one wanders. **12** lie; direction (*the range of the strata is east and west*). ● *v.* **1** *intr.* **a** reach; lie spread out; extend; vary between limits. **b** run in a line (*ranges north and south*). **2** *tr.* (usu. in *passive* or *refl.*) place or arrange in ranks or in a specified situation or order or company (*ranged their troops*). **3** *intr.* rove; wander (*ranged through the woods*). **4** *intr.* traverse in all directions (*ranging the woods*). **5** *intr.* **a** (often foll. by *with*) be level. **b** (foll. by *with, among*) rank (*ranges with the great writers*). **6** *intr.* **a** (of a gun) send a projectile over a specified distance (*ranges over a mile*). **b** (of a projectile)

cover a specified distance. **c** obtain the range of a target by adjustment after firing past it or short of it.

range find·er *n.* an instrument for estimating the distance of an object, esp. one to be shot at or photographed.

rang·er /ráynjər/ *n.* **1** a keeper of a national or royal park or forest. **2** a member of a body of armed men, esp.: **a** a mounted soldier. **b** a commando. **3** a wanderer. □□ **rang·er·ship** *n.*

rang·y /ráynjee/ *adj.* (**rangier**, **rangiest**) **1** (of a person) tall and slim. **2** hilly; mountainous.

ra·ni /ráanee/ *n.* (also **ra·nee**) *hist.* a raja's wife or widow; a Hindu queen.

rank[1] /rangk/ *n. & v.* ● *n.* **1 a** a position in a hierarchy; a grade of advancement. **b** a grade of dignity or achievement (*in the top rank of performers*). **c** high social position (*persons of rank*). **d** a place in a scale. **2** a row or line. **3** a single line of soldiers drawn up abreast. **4** order; array. **5** *Chess* a row of squares across the board (cf. FILE[2]). ● *v.* **1** *intr.* have rank or place (*ranks next to the chief of staff*). **2** *tr.* classify. **3** *tr.* arrange (esp. soldiers) in a rank or ranks. **4 a** *tr.* take precedence of (a person) in respect to rank. **b** *intr.* have the senior position among the members of a hierarchy, etc. □ **break rank** fail to remain in line. **close ranks** maintain solidarity. **keep rank** remain in line. **pull rank** use one's superior rank to gain advantage, coerce another, etc.

rank[2] /rangk/ *adj.* **1** too luxuriant; choked with or apt to produce weeds or excessive foliage. **2 a** foul-smelling; offensive. **b** loathsome; corrupt. **3** flagrant; virulent; gross; complete (*rank outsider*). □□ **rank·ly** *adv.* **rank·ness** *n.*

rank and file *n.* (usu. treated as *pl.*) ordinary undistinguished people.

rank·ing /rángking/ *n. & adj.* ● *n.* ordering by rank; classification. ● *adj.* having a high rank or position.

ran·kle /rángkəl/ *v.intr.* (of envy, disappointment, etc.) cause persistent annoyance or resentment.

ran·sack /ránsak/ *v.tr.* **1** pillage or plunder (a house, country, etc.). **2** thoroughly search (a place, a receptacle, a person's pockets, etc.). □□ **ran·sack·er** *n.*

ran·som /ránsəm/ *n. & v.* ● *n.* **1** a sum of money or other payment demanded or paid for the release of a prisoner. **2** the liberation of a prisoner in return for this. ● *v.tr.* **1** buy the freedom or restoration of; redeem. **2** hold to ransom. **3** release for a ransom.

rant /rant/ *v. & n.* ● *v.* **1** *intr.* use bombastic language. **2** *tr. & intr.* declaim; recite theatrically. **3** *tr. & intr.* preach noisily. **4** *intr.* (often foll. by *about, on*) speak vehemently or intemperately. ● *n.* **1** a piece of ranting; a tirade. **2** empty turgid talk. □□ **rant·er** *n.* **rant·ing·ly** *adv.*

ra·nun·cu·la·ceous /rənúngkyəláyshəs/ *adj.* of or relating to the family Ranunculaceae of flowering plants, including clematis and delphiniums.

ra·nun·cu·lus /rənúngkyələs/ *n.* (*pl.* **ranunculuses** or **ranunculi** /-lī/) any plant of the genus *Ranunculus*, esp. buttercups.

rap[1] /rap/ *n. & v.* ● *n.* **1** a smart, slight blow. **2** a knock; a sharp tapping sound. **3** *sl.* blame; censure; punishment. **4** *sl.* a conversation. **5 a** a rhyming monologue recited rhythmically to prerecorded music. **b** (in full **rap music**) a style of pop music with a pronounced beat and words recited rather than sung. ● *v.* (**rapped**, **rapping**) **1** *tr.* strike smartly. **2** *intr.* make a sharp tapping sound. **3** *tr.* criticize adversely. **4** *intr. sl.* talk. □ **beat the rap** escape punishment. **rap on** (or **over**) **the knuckles** ● *n.* a reprimand or reproof. ● *v.tr.* reprimand; reprove. **rap out** *Spiritualism* express (a message or word) by raps. **take the rap** suffer the consequences. □□ **rap·per** *n.*

rap[2] /rap/ *n.* a small amount, the least bit.

ra·pa·cious /rəpáyshəs/ *adj.* grasping; extortionate;

predatory. □□ **ra·pa·cious·ly** *adv.* **ra·pa·cious·ness** *n.* **ra·pac·i·ty** /rəpásitee/ *n.*

rape[1] /rayp/ *n. & v.* ● *n.* **1 a** the act of forcing another person to have sexual intercourse. **b** forcible sodomy. **2** (often foll. by *of*) violent assault; forcible interference; violation. **3** an instance of rape. ● *v.tr.* **1** commit rape on (a person, usu. a woman). **2** violate; assault; pillage.

rape[2] /rayp/ *n.* **▶** a plant, *Brassica napus*, grown as food for livestock and for its seed, from which oil is made. Also called **colza, cole**.

rape[3] /rayp/ *n.* **1** the refuse of grapes after wine making, used in making vinegar. **2** a vessel used in vinegar making.

rape·seed /ráypseed/ *n.* the seed of the rape plant.

ra·phia var. of RAFFIA.

ra·phide /ráyfīd/ *n.* a needle-shaped crystal of an irritant substance such as oxalic acid formed in a plant.

rap·id /rápid/ *adj. & n.* ● *adj.* **1** quick; swift. **2** acting or completed in a short time. **3** (of a slope) descending steeply. **4** *Photog.* fast. ● *n.* (usu. in *pl.*) a steep descent in a riverbed, with a swift current. □□ **ra·pid·i·ty** /rəpíditee/ *n.* **rap·id·ly** *adv.* **rap·id·ness** *n.*

RAPE (*Brassica napus*)

rap·id eye move·ment *n.* a type of jerky movement of the eyes during periods of dreaming.

rap·id-fire *adj. attrib.* fired, asked, etc., in quick succession.

ra·pi·er /ráypeeər, ráypyər/ *n.* **▼** a light slender sword used for thrusting. ▷ SWORD

RAPIER: 17TH-CENTURY PAPPENHEIMER RAPIER

rap·ine /rápin, -īn/ *n. rhet.* plundering; robbery.

rap·ist /ráypist/ *n.* a person who commits rape.

rap·pel /rapél/ *n. & v.* (**rappelled, rappelling**; or **rappeled, rappeling**) ● *n.* **▼** technique or act of controlled descent from a height, as a steep rockface, by using a doubled rope coiled around the body and fixed at a higher point, with which one slides downward gradually. ● *v.intr.* make a descent in this way.

R

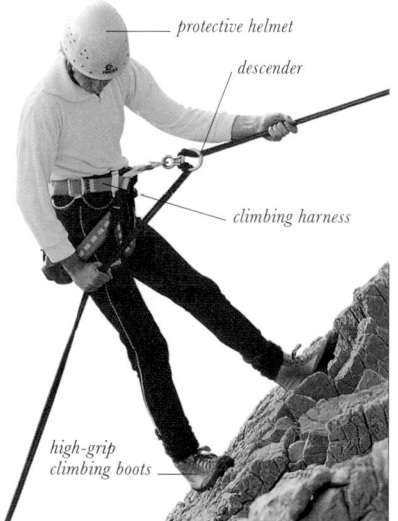

protective helmet

descender

climbing harness

high-grip climbing boots

RAPPEL: CLIMBER RAPPELLING

RAPTOR

The majority of raptors belong to the order Falconiformes; owls constitute a separate order, Strigiformes. Although some raptors, e.g., vultures, are carrion eaters, most are highly adapted to hunting live prey. Forward-facing eyes provide excellent binocular vision, powerful talons kill and grasp the quarry, and a sharp, hooked beak tears flesh.

long primary feathers

wide wingspan

forward-facing eyes

broad secondary feathers

powerful breast muscles

strong, hooked beak

tail feathers for steering, soaring, and braking

downy leg feathers

powerful talons

EXTERNAL FEATURES OF A
RED-TAILED HAWK
(*Buteo jamaicensis*)

TYPES OF RAPTOR

PANDIONINAE
(osprey)
▷ OSPREY

CATHARTIDAE
(New World vultures)
▷ VULTURE

STRIGIFORMES
(owls)
▷ OWL

ACCIPITRINAE
(eagles, buteos, hawks, kites, Old World vultures)
▷ EAGLE, HAWK, VULTURE

FALCONIDAE
(caracaras, falcons)
▷ FALCON

R

rap·port /rapáwr/ *n.* **1** relationship or communication, esp. when useful and harmonious (*in rapport with*; *establish a rapport*). **2** *Spiritualism* communication through a medium.

rap·proche·ment /raprōshmón/ *n.* the resumption of harmonious relations, esp. between nations.

rap·scal·lion /rapskályən/ *n.* *archaic* or *joc.* rascal; scamp; rogue.

rapt /rapt/ *adj.* **1** fully absorbed or intent. **2** carried away with joyous feeling or lofty thought. **3** carried away bodily. □□ **rapt·ly** *adv.* **rapt·ness** *n.*

rap·tor /ráptər/ *n.* ▲ any bird of prey, e.g., an owl, falcon, or eagle. □□ **rap·to·ri·al** /raptáwreeəl/ *adj. & n.*

rap·ture /rápchər/ *n.* **1 a** ecstatic delight; mental transport. **b** (in *pl.*) great pleasure or enthusiasm or the expression of it. **2** a mystical experience in which the soul gains a knowledge of divine things. □ **go into** (or **be in**) **raptures** be enthusiastic; talk enthusiastically. □□ **rap·tur·ous** *adj.* **rap·tur·ous·ly** *adv.* **rap·tur·ous·ness** *n.*

rare[1] /rair/ *adj.* (**rarer, rarest**) **1** seldom done or found or occurring; uncommon. **2** of less than the usual density (*the rare atmosphere of the mountaintops*). □□ **rare·ness** *n.*

rare[2] /rair/ *adj.* (**rarer, rarest**) (of meat) cooked lightly, so as to be still red inside.

rare·bit /ráirbit/ *n.* = WELSH RABBIT.

rare earth *n.* **1** a lanthanide element. **2** an oxide of such an element.

rar·ee-show /ráireeshō/ *n.* **1** a show or spectacle. **2** a show carried about in a box; a peep show.

rar·e·fy /ráirifī/ *v.* (**-ies, -ied**) (esp. as **rarefied** *adj.*) **1** *tr. & intr.* make or become less dense (*rarefied air*). **2** *tr.* refine (a person's nature, etc.). **3** *tr.* **a** make (an idea, etc.) subtle. **b** (as **rarefied** *adj.*) refined; subtle; elevated; exalted; select. □□ **rar·e·fac·tion** /-fákshən/ *n.* **rar·e·fac·tive** *adj.* **rar·e·fi·ca·tion** /-fikáyshən/ *n.*

rare·ly /ráirlee/ *adv.* **1** seldom; not often. **2** in an unusual degree; exceptionally. **3** exceptionally well.

rar·ing /ráiring/ *adj.* (foll. by *to* + infin.) *colloq.* enthusiastic, eager (*raring to go*).

rar·i·ty /ráiritee/ *n.* (*pl.* **-ies**) **1** rareness. **2** an uncommon thing, esp. one valued for being rare.

ras·cal /ráskəl/ *n.* often *joc.* a dishonest or mischievous person, esp. a child. □□ **ras·cal·i·ty** /-kálitee/ *n.* (*pl.* **-ies**). **ras·cal·ly** *adj.*

rash[1] /rash/ *adj.* reckless; impetuous; hasty. □□ **rash·ly** *adv.* **rash·ness** *n.*

rash[2] /rash/ *n.* **1** an eruption of the skin in spots or patches. **2** (usu. foll. by *of*) a sudden widespread phenomenon (*a rash of strikes*).

rash·er /ráshər/ *n.* a thin slice of bacon or ham.

rasp /rasp/ *n. & v.* ● *n.* **1** a coarse kind of file having separate teeth. **2** a rough grating sound. ● *v.* **1** *tr.* **a** scrape with a rasp. **b** scrape roughly. **c** (foll. by *off, away*) remove by scraping. **2 a** *intr.* make a grating sound. **b** *tr.* say gratingly or hoarsely. **3** *tr.* grate upon (a person or a person's feelings). □□ **rasp·ing·ly** *adv.* **rasp·y** *adj.*

rasp·ber·ry /rázberee/ *n.* (*pl.* **-ies**) **1 a** a bramble, *Rubus idaeus*, having usu. red berries. **b** this berry. **2** any of various red colors. **3** *colloq.* **a** a sound made with the lips expressing derision or disapproval (orig. *raspberry tart*, rhyming sl. = *fart*). **b** a show of strong disapproval (*got a raspberry from the audience*).

Ras·ta /ráastə, rást-/ *n. & adj. colloq.* = RASTAFARIAN.

Ras·ta·far·i·an /ráastəfáareeən, rástəfáir-/ *n. & adj.* ● *n.* a member of a sect of Jamaican origin regarding the former Emperor Haile Selassie of Ethiopia (d. 1975, entitled *Ras Tafari*) as God. ● *adj.* of or relating to this sect. □□ **Ras·ta·far·i·an·ism** *n.*

ras·ter /rástər/ *n.* a pattern of scanning lines for a cathode-ray tube picture.

rat /rat/ *n. & v.* ● *n.* **1 a** any of several rodents of the genus *Rattus*. ▷ RODENT. **b** any similar rodent (*muskrat*). **2** a deserter from a party, cause, etc. **3** *colloq.* an unpleasant person. **4** a worker who refuses to join a strike, or a strikebreaker. **5** (in *pl.*) *sl.* an exclamation of contempt, annoyance, etc. ● *v.intr.* (**ratted, ratting**) **1** (of a person or dog) hunt or kill rats. **2** *colloq.* desert a cause, party, etc. **3** *colloq.* (foll. by *on*) **a** betray; let down. **b** inform on.

rat·a·ble /ráytəbəl/ *adj.* (also **rate·a·ble**) able to be rated or estimated.

rat·a·fi·a /rátəféeə/ *n.* **1** a liqueur flavored with almonds or kernels of peach, apricot, or cherry. **2** a kind of cookie similarly flavored.

ra·tan var. of RATTAN.

rat·a·plan /rátəplán/ *n. & v.* ● *n.* a drumming sound. ● *v.* (**rataplanned, rataplanning**) **1** *tr.* play (a tune) on or as on a drum. **2** *intr.* make a rataplan.

rat-a-tat /rátətát/ *n.* (also **rat-a-tat-tat**) a rapping or knocking sound.

ra·ta·touille /rátətŏŏ-ee, ráataa-/ *n.* a vegetable dish made of stewed eggplant, onions, tomatoes, zucchini, and peppers.

ratch /rach/ *n.* **1** a ratchet. **2** a ratchet wheel.

ratch·et /ráchit/ *n. & v.* ● *n.* **1** a set of teeth on the edge of a bar or wheel in which a device engages to ensure motion in one direction only. **2** (in full **ratchet wheel**) a wheel with a rim so toothed. ● *v.* **1** *tr.* **a** provide with a ratchet. **b** make into a ratchet. **2** *tr. & intr.* move as under the control of a ratchet. □ **ratchet up** (or **down**) move steadily or by degrees (*health costs continue to ratchet up*).

rate[1] /rayt/ *n. & v.* ● *n.* **1** a stated numerical proportion between two sets of things (*at a rate of 50 miles* *per hour*) or as the basis of calculating an amount or value (*rate of taxation*). **2** a fixed or appropriate charge or cost or value; a measure of this (*postal rates*). **3** rapidity of movement or change (*a great rate*). **4** class or rank (*first-rate*). ● *v.* **1** *tr.* **a** estimate the worth or value of (*I do not rate him very highly*). **b** assign a value to (work, the power of a machine, etc.). **2** *tr.* consider; regard as. **3** *intr.* (foll. by *as*) rank or be rated. **4** *tr.* be worthy of, deserve. **at any rate** in any case; whatever happens. **at this** (or **that**) **rate** if this example is typical or this assumption is true.

rate² /rayt/ *v.tr.* scold angrily.

rate·a·ble var. of RATABLE.

rat·fink /rátfingk/ *n. sl.* = FINK.

rathe /rayth/ *adj. poet.* coming, blooming, etc., early in the year or day.

rath·er /ráthər/ *adv.* **1** by preference (*would rather not go*). **2** (usu. foll. by *than*) as a more likely alternative (*is stupid rather than honest*). **3** more precisely (*a book, or rather, a pamphlet*). **4** slightly; somewhat (*rather drunk*). □ **had rather** prefer to.

rat·i·fy /rátifī/ *v.tr.* (**-ies, -ied**) confirm or accept (an agreement made in one's name) by formal consent, signature, etc. □□ **rat·i·fi·a·ble** *adj.* **rat·i·fi·ca·tion** /-fikáyshən/ *n.* **rat·i·fi·er** *n.*

rat·ing¹ /ráyting/ *n.* **1** the act or an instance of placing in a rank or class or assigning a value to. **2** the estimated standing of a person as regards credit, etc. **3** *Naut.* a person's position or class on a ship's books. **4** the relative popularity of a broadcast program as determined by the estimated size of the audience. **5** *Naut.* any of the classes into which racing yachts are distributed by tonnage.

rat·ing² /ráyting/ *n.* an angry reprimand.

ra·tio /ráysheeō, ráyshō/ *n.* (*pl.* **-os**) the quantitative relation between two similar magnitudes determined by the number of times one contains the other integrally or fractionally (*the ratios 1:5 and 20:100 are the same*).

ra·ti·oc·i·nate /rásheeósinayt/ *v.intr. literary* go through logical processes of reasoning, esp. using syllogisms. □□ **ra·ti·oc·i·na·tion** /-ōsínáyshən, -ósináyshən/ *n.* **ra·ti·oc·i·na·tive** *adj.*

ra·tion /ráshən, ráy-/ *n. & v.* ● *n.* **1** a fixed official allowance of food, clothing, etc., in a time of shortage. **2** (foll. by *of*) a single portion of provisions, etc. **3** (usu. in *pl.*) a fixed daily allowance of food, esp. in the armed forces. **4** (in *pl.*) provisions. ● *v.tr.* **1** limit (persons or provisions) to a fixed ration. **2** (usu. foll. by *out*) distribute (food, etc.) in fixed quantities.

ra·tion·al /ráshənəl/ *adj.* **1** of or based on reasoning or reason. **2** able to think sensibly or logically. **3** endowed with reason or reasoning. **4** *Math.* (of a quantity or ratio) expressible as a ratio of whole numbers. □□ **ra·tion·al·i·ty** /-nálitee/ *n.* **ra·tion·al·ly** *adv.*

ra·tion·ale /ráshənál/ *n.* **1** (often foll. by *for*) the fundamental reason or logical basis of anything. **2** a reasoned exposition.

ra·tion·al·ism /ráshənəlizəm/ *n.* **1** *Philos.* the theory that reason is the foundation of certainty in knowledge (opp. *empiricism* (see EMPIRIC)), sensationalism). **2** *Theol.* the practice of treating reason as the ultimate authority in religion. **3** a belief in reason rather than religion as a guiding principle in life. □□ **ra·tion·al·ist** *n.* **ra·tion·al·is·tic** *adj.* **ra·tion·al·is·ti·cal·ly** *adv.*

ra·tion·al·ize /ráshənəlīz/ *v.* **1 a** *tr.* offer a rational but specious explanation of (one's behavior or attitude). **b** *intr.* explain one's behavior or attitude in this way. **2** *tr.* make logical and consistent. **3** *tr.* make (a business, etc.) more efficient by reorganizing it to reduce or eliminate waste of labor, time, and materials. **4** *tr.* (often foll. by *away*) explain or explain away rationally. **5** *tr. Math.* eliminate irrational quantities from (an equation, etc.) **6** *intr.* be

or act as a rationalist. □□ **ra·tion·al·i·za·tion** *n.* **ra·tion·al·iz·er** *n.*

rat·ite /rátīt/ *adj. & n.* ● *adj.* (of a bird) having a keelless breastbone, and unable to fly (opp. CARINATE). ● *n.* a flightless bird, e.g., an ostrich, emu, cassowary, or moa.

rat·line /rátlin/ *n.* (also **rat·lin**) (usu. in *pl.*) ▶ any of the small lines fastened across a sailing ship's shrouds like ladder rungs.

rat pack *n. colloq.* a group of journalists and photographers perceived as aggressive or relentless in their pursuit of stories.

rat race *n.* a fiercely competitive struggle for position, power, etc.

rats·bane /rátsbayn/ *n.* anything poisonous to rats, esp. a plant.

rat·tan /rətán/ *n.* (also **ra·tan**) **1** any East Indian climbing palm of the genus *Calamus*, etc., with long, thin, jointed pliable stems. **2** a piece of rattan stem used as a walking stick, etc.

rat·ter /rátər/ *n.* a dog or other animal that hunts rats.

rat·tle /rát'l/ *v. & n.* ● *v.* **1 a** *intr.* give out a rapid succession of short, sharp, hard sounds. **b** *tr.* make (a cup and saucer, window, etc.) do this. **c** *intr.* cause such sounds by shaking something. **2 a** *intr.* move with a rattling noise. **b** *intr.* ride or run briskly. **3 a** *tr.* (usu. foll. by *off*) say or recite rapidly. **b** *intr.* (usu. foll. by *on*) talk in a lively thoughtless way. **4** *tr. colloq.* disconcert; alarm. ● *n.* **1 a** rattling sound. **2** an instrument or plaything made to rattle. **3** the set of horny rings in a rattlesnake's tail. **4** a plant with seeds that rattle in their cases when ripe. **5** uproar; bustle; noisy gaiety, racket. **6 a** a noisy flow of words. **b** empty chatter; trivial talk. □ **rattle the saber** threaten war. □□ **rat·tly** *adj.*

rat·tler /rátlər/ *n.* **1** a thing that rattles, esp. an old or rickety vehicle. **2** *colloq.* a rattlesnake. **3** *colloq.* a fast freight train.

rat·tle·snake /rát'lsnayk/ *n.* ▼ any of various poisonous American snakes of the family Viperidae, esp. of the genus *Crotalus* or *Sistrurus*, with a rattling structure of horny rings in its tail. ▷ SNAKE

RATTLESNAKE: EASTERN DIAMONDBACK
RATTLESNAKE (*Crotalus adamanteus*)

rat·tle·trap /rát'ltrap/ *n. & adj. colloq.* ● *n.* a rickety old vehicle, etc. ● *adj.* rickety.

rat·tling /rátling/ *adj. & adv.* ● *adj.* **1** that rattles. **2** brisk; vigorous (*a rattling pace*). ● *adv.* remarkably (*a rattling good story*).

rat·ty /rátee/ *adj.* (**rattier, rattiest**) **1** relating to or infested with rats. **2** *colloq.* **a** shabby; wretched; nasty. **b** unkempt; seedy; dirty. □□ **rat·ti·ly** *adv.* **rat·ti·ness** *n.*

rau·cous /ráwkəs/ *adj.* harsh sounding; loud and hoarse. □□ **rau·cous·ly** *adv.* **rau·cous·ness** *n.*

RATLINES ON A 16TH-CENTURY WARSHIP

ratline · *shroud* · *ratline*

raun·chy /ráwnchee/ *adj.* (**raunchier, raunchiest**) *colloq.* **1** coarse; boisterous; sexually provocative. **2** slovenly; grubby. □□ **raun·chi·ly** *adv.* **raun·chi·ness** *n.*

rav·age /rávij/ *v. & n.* ● *v.tr. & intr.* devastate; plunder. ● *n.* **1** the act or an instance of ravaging; devastation; damage. **2** (usu. in *pl.*; foll. by *of*) destructive effect (*survived the ravages of winter*). □□ **rav·ag·er** *n.*

rave /rayv/ *v. & n.* ● *v.* **1** *intr.* talk wildly or furiously in or as in delirium. **2** *intr.* (usu. foll. by *about, of, over*) speak with rapturous admiration; go into raptures. **3** *tr.* bring into a specified state by raving (*raved himself hoarse*). **4** *tr.* utter with ravings (*raved their grief*). **5** *intr.* (of the sea, wind, etc.) howl; roar. ● *n.* **1** (usu. *attrib.*) *colloq.* a highly enthusiastic review (*a rave review*). **2** a dance party, often involving drug use.

rav·el /rávəl/ *v. & n.* ● *v.* **1** *tr. & intr.* entangle or become entangled. **2** *tr.* confuse or complicate (a question or problem). **3** *intr.* fray out. **4** *tr.* (often foll. by *out*) disentangle; unravel; distinguish the separate threads or subdivisions of. ● *n.* **1** a tangle or knot. **2** a complication. **3** a frayed or loose end.

ra·ven¹ /ráyvən/ *n. & adj.* ● *n.* a large glossy blue-black crow, *Corvus corax*, having a hoarse cry. ● *adj.* glossy black (*raven tresses*).

rav·en² /rávən/ *v.* **1** *intr.* **a** plunder. **b** (foll. by *after*) seek prey or booty. **c** (foll. by *about*) go plundering. **d** prowl for prey (*ravening beast*). **2** *tr.* devour voraciously. **b** (usu. foll. by *for*) have a ravenous appetite. **c** *intr.* (often foll. by *on*) feed voraciously.

rav·en·ous /rávənəs/ *adj.* **1** very hungry. **2** voracious. **3** rapacious. □□ **rav·en·ous·ly** *adv.*

rav·in /rávin/ *n. poet. or rhet.* **1** robbery; plundering. **2** the seizing and devouring of prey. **3** prey.

ra·vine /rəvéen/ *n.* a deep narrow gorge or cleft. □□ **ra·vined** *adj.*

rav·ing /ráyving/ *n., adj., & adv.* ● *n.* (usu. in *pl.*) wild or delirious talk. ● *adj.* **1** delirious; frenzied. **2** remarkable; intensive (*a raving beauty*) ● *adv.* intensively; wildly (*raving mad*).

ra·vi·o·li /ráveeōlee/ *n.* small pasta envelopes containing ground meat, etc. ▷ PASTA

rav·ish /rávish/ *v.tr.* **1** commit rape on (a person). **2** enrapture. □□ **rav·ish·er** *n.* **rav·ish·ment** *n.*

rav·ish·ing /rávishing/ *adj.* entrancing; delightful. □□ **rav·ish·ing·ly** *adv.*

raw /raw/ *adj. & n.* ● *adj.* **1** uncooked. **2** in the natural state; not processed or manufactured (*raw sewage*). **3** (of alcoholic spirit) undiluted. **4** (of statistics, etc.) not analyzed or processed. **5** inexperienced; untrained (*raw recruits*). **6 a** stripped of skin; having the flesh exposed. **b** sensitive to the touch from having the flesh exposed. **c** sensitive to emotional pain, etc. **7** (of the atmosphere, day, etc.) chilly and damp. **8 a** crude in artistic quality; lacking finish. **b** unmitigated; brutal. **9** (of the edge of cloth) without hem or selvage. **10** (of silk) as reeled from cocoons. **11** (of grain) unmalted. ● *n.* a raw place on a person's or horse's body. □ **in the raw 1** in its natural state without mitigation. **2** naked. □□ **raw·ly** *adv.* **raw·ness** *n.*

raw·boned /ráwbōnd/ *adj.* gaunt.

raw deal *n.* unfair treatment.

raw·hide /ráwhīd/ *n.* **1** untanned hide. **2** a rope or whip of this.

raw ma·te·ri·al *n.* that from which the process of manufacture makes products.

raw si·en·na *n.* ▶ a brownish-yellow ferruginous earth used as a pigment.

raw um·ber *n.* ▶ umber in its natural state, yellowish-brown in color.

RAW
SIENNA

RAW
UMBER

R

RAY

Rays are adapted to life on or near the sea-bed. Their flattened bodies allow them to lie on the ocean floor, often camouflaged and undetected. Their gills are on the underside of their bodies, but clean water is admitted to the gill chambers through a spiracle on the upper side, just behind the eye. Rays feed primarily on shellfish, crustaceans, and fish, which they hunt by scent. Mantas can have a wingspan of over 20 ft (6 m).

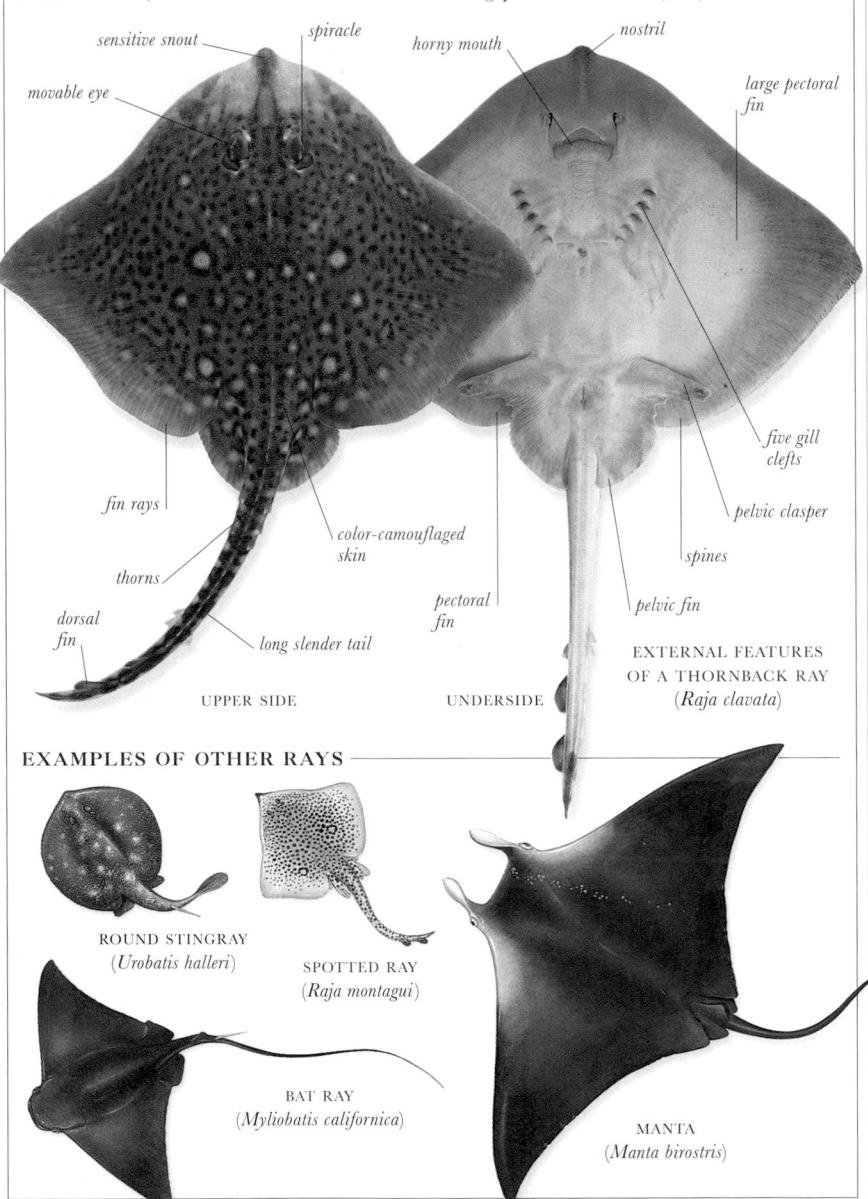

sensitive snout

spiracle

horny mouth

nostril

large pectoral fin

movable eye

fin rays

thorns

dorsal fin

color-camouflaged skin

long slender tail

pectoral fin

five gill clefts

pelvic clasper

spines

pelvic fin

UPPER SIDE

UNDERSIDE

EXTERNAL FEATURES OF A THORNBACK RAY
(*Raja clavata*)

EXAMPLES OF OTHER RAYS

ROUND STINGRAY
(*Urobatis halleri*)

SPOTTED RAY
(*Raja montagui*)

BAT RAY
(*Myliobatis californica*)

MANTA
(*Manta birostris*)

R

ray[1] /ray/ *n. & v.* ● *n.* **1** a single line or narrow beam of light from a small or distant source. **2** a straight line in which radiation travels to a given point. **3** (in *pl.*) radiation of a specified type (*gamma rays*; *X rays*). **4** a trace or beginning of an enlightening or cheering influence (*a ray of hope*). **5 a** any of a set of radiating lines or parts or things. **b** any of a set of straight lines passing through one point. **6** the marginal portion of a composite flower, e.g., a daisy. **7 a** a radial division of a starfish. **b** each of a set of bones, etc., supporting a fish's fin. ● *v.* **1** *intr.* (foll. by *forth*, *out*) (of light, thought, emotion, etc.) issue in or as if in rays. **2** *intr. & tr.* radiate. □□ **rayed** *adj.* **ray·less** *adj.*

ray[2] /ray/ *n.* ▲ a cartilaginous fish of the order Batoidea, with a broad flat body, winglike pectoral fins, and a long slender tail. ▷ FISH

Ray·naud's disease /raynoz/ *n.* a disease characterized by spasm of the arteries in the extremities, esp. the fingers.

ray·on /ráyon/ *n.* any of various textile fibers or fabrics made from cellulose.

raze /rayz/ *v.tr.* **1** completely destroy; tear down (esp. *raze to the ground*). **2** erase; scratch out (esp. in abstract senses).

ra·zor /ráyzər/ *n. & v.* ● *n.* an instrument with a sharp blade used in cutting hair, esp. from the skin. ● *v.tr.* **1** use a razor on. **2** shave; cut down close.

ra·zor·back /ráyzərbak/ *n.* an animal with a sharp ridged back, esp. a wild hog of the southern US.

ra·zor·bill /ráyzərbil/ *n.* a black and white auk, *Alca torda*, with a sharp-edged bill.

ra·zor clam *n.* ▶ any of various bivalve mollusks of the family Solenidae, with a thin, elongated shell. ▷ SHELL

ra·zor's edge *n.* **1** a keen edge. **2** a sharp mountain ridge. **3** a critical situation (*found themselves on the razor's edge*). **4** a sharp line of division.

ra·zor wire *n.* wire with sharpened projections, often coiled atop walls for security.

raz·zle-daz·zle /rázəldázəl/ *n.* (also **raz·zle**) *sl.* **1 a** excitement; bustle. **b** a spree. **2** extravagant publicity.

razz·ma·tazz /rázmətáz/ *n.* (also **raz·za·ma·tazz** /rázəmə-/) *colloq.* **1** = RAZZLE-DAZZLE. **2** insincere actions.

Rb *symb. Chem.* the element rubidium.

RC *abbr.* **1** Roman Catholic. **2** reinforced concrete.

RCAF *abbr.* Royal Canadian Air Force.

RCMP *abbr.* Royal Canadian Mounted Police.

RCN *abbr.* Royal Canadian Navy.

Rd. *abbr.* Road (in names).

RDA *abbr.* **1** recommended daily allowance. **2** recommended dietary allowance.

Re *symb. Chem.* the element rhenium.

re[1] /ray, ree/ *prep.* **1** in the matter of (as the first word in a heading). **2** *colloq.* about; concerning.

re[2] /ray/ *n. Mus.* **1** (in tonic sol-fa) the second note of a major scale. **2** the note D in the fixed-do system.

re- /ree, ri, re/ *prefix* **1** attachable to almost any verb or its derivative; meaning: **a** once more; afresh; anew (*readjust*; *renumber*). **b** back; with return to a previous state (*reassemble*; *reverse*). ¶ A hyphen is sometimes used when the word begins with *e* (*re-enact*), or to distinguish the compound from a more familiar one-word form (*re-form* = form again). **2** (also **red-** before a vowel, as in *redolent*) in verbs and verbal derivatives denoting: **a** in return; mutually (*react*; *resemble*). **b** opposition (*repel*; *resist*). **c** behind or after (*relic*; *remain*). **d** retirement or secrecy (*recluse*; *reticence*). **e** off; away; down (*recede*; *relegate*; *repress*). **f** frequentative or intensive force (*redouble*; *refine*; *resplendent*). **g** negative force (*recant*; *reveal*).

re·ab·sorb /réeəbsáwrb, -záwrb/ *v.tr.* absorb again. □□ **re·ab·sorp·tion** /-absáwrpshən, -zawrp-/ *n.*

re·ac·cus·tom /réeəkústəm/ *v.tr.* accustom again.

reach /reech/ *v. & n.* ● *v.* **1** *intr. & tr.* (often foll. by *out*) stretch out; extend. **2** *intr.* stretch out a limb, the hand, etc.; make a reaching motion or effort. **3** *intr.* (often foll. by *for*) make a motion or effort to touch or get hold of, or to attain (*reached for his pipe*). **4** *tr.* get as far as (*reached Lincoln at lunchtime*; *your letter reached me today*). **5** *tr.* get to or attain (a specified point) on a scale (*the temperature reached 90°*; *the number of applications reached 100*). **6** *intr.* (foll. by *to*) attain to; be adequate for (*my income will not reach to it*). **7** *tr.* succeed in achieving; attain (*have reached an agreement*). **8** *tr.* make contact with the hand, etc., or by telephone, etc. (*was out all day and could not be reached*). **9** *tr.* succeed in influencing or having the required effect on (*could not manage to reach their audience*). **10** *tr.* hand; pass (*reach that book for me*). **11** *tr.* take with an outstretched hand. **12** *intr. Naut.* sail with the wind abeam or abaft the beam. ● *n.* **1** the extent to which a hand, etc., can be reached out, influence exerted, motion carried out, or mental powers used. **2** an act of reaching out. **3** a continuous extent, esp. a stretch of river between two bends, or the part of a canal between locks. **4** *Naut.* a distance traversed in reaching. **5** a pole connecting the rear axle, as of a wagon, to the bolster or bar at the front. □ **out of reach** not able to be reached or attained. □□ **reach·a·ble** *adj.*

RAZOR CLAM
(*Ensis siliqua*)

re·ac·quaint /réeəkwáynt/ *v.tr. & refl.* (usu. foll. by *with*) make acquainted again. □□ **re·ac·quaint·ance** *n.*

re·act /reeákt/ *v.* **1** *intr.* (foll. by *to*) respond to a stimulus; undergo a change or show behavior due to some influence (*how did they react to the news?*). **2** *intr.* (often foll. by *against*) be actuated by repulsion to; tend in a reverse or contrary direction. **3** *intr.* (often foll. by *upon*) produce a reciprocal or responsive effect; act upon the agent (*they react upon each other*). **4** *intr.* (foll. by *with*) *Chem.* & *Physics* (of a substance or particle) be the cause of activity or interaction with another (*nitrous oxide reacts with the metal*). **5** *tr.* (foll. by *with*) *Chem.* cause (a substance) to react with another. **6** *intr. Mil.* make a counterattack. **7** *intr. Stock Exch.* (of shares) fall after rising.

re·ac·tant /reeáktənt/ *n. Chem.* a substance that takes part in, and undergoes change during, a reaction.

re·ac·tion /reeákshən/ *n.* **1** the act or an instance of reacting; a responsive or reciprocal action. **2 a** a responsive feeling (*what was your reaction to the news?*). **b** an immediate or first impression. **3** the occurrence of a condition after a period of its opposite. **4** a bodily response to an external stimulus. **5** a tendency to oppose change or to advocate return to a former system. **6** the interaction of substances undergoing chemical change. **7** propulsion by emitting a jet of particles, etc., in the direction opposite to that of the intended motion. □□ **re·ac·tion·ist** *n. & adj.*

re·ac·tion·ar·y /reeákshəneree/ *adj. & n.* ● *adj.* tending to oppose change and advocate return to a former system. ● *n.* (*pl.* **-ies**) a reactionary person.

re·ac·ti·vate /reeáktivayt/ *v.tr.* restore to a state of activity. □□ **re·ac·ti·va·tion** /-váyshən/ *n.*

re·ac·tive /reeáktiv/ *adj.* **1** showing reaction. **2** of or relating to reactance. □□ **re·ac·tiv·i·ty** /-tívitee/ *n.*

re·ac·tor /reeáktər/ *n.* **1** a person or thing that reacts. **2** (in full **nuclear reactor**) an apparatus or structure in which a controlled nuclear chain reaction releases energy. ▷ NUCLEAR POWER. **3** *Electr.* a component used to provide reactance, esp. an inductor. **4** an apparatus for the chemical reaction of substances. **5** *Med.* a person who has a reaction to a drug, etc.

read /reed/ *v. & n.* ● *v.* (*past* and *past part.* **read** /red/) **1** *tr.* (also *absol.*) reproduce mentally or (often foll. by *aloud*, *out*, *off*, etc.) vocally the written or printed words of (a book, author, etc.). **2** *tr.* convert or be able to convert into the intended words or meaning (written or other symbols or the things expressed in this way). **3** *tr.* interpret mentally. **4** *tr.* deduce or declare an interpretation of (*read the expression on my face*). **5** *tr.* (often foll. by *that* + clause) find (a thing) recorded or stated in print, etc. (*I read somewhere that you are leaving*). **6** *tr.* interpret (a statement or action) in a certain sense (*my silence is not to be read as consent*). **7** *tr.* (often foll. by *into*) assume as intended or deducible (*you read too much into my letter*). **8** *tr.* bring into a specified state by reading (*read myself to sleep*). **9** *tr.* (of a meter or other recording instrument) show (a specified figure, etc.) (*the thermometer reads 20°*). **10** *intr.* convey meaning in a specified manner when read (*it reads persuasively*). **11** *intr.* sound or affect a hearer or reader as specified when read (*the book reads like a parody*). **12** *intr.* carry out a course of study by reading (*is reading for the bar*). **13** *tr.* (as **read** /red/ *adj.*) versed in a subject by reading (*a well-read person*; *was widely read in law*). **14** *tr.* **a** (of a computer) copy or transfer (data). **b** (foll. by *in*, *out*) enter or extract (data) in an electronic storage device. **15** *tr.* **a** understand or interpret (a person) by hearing words or seeing signs, gestures, etc. **b** interpret (cards, a person's hand, etc.) as a fortune teller. **c** interpret (the sky) as an astrologer or meteorologist. **16** *tr. Printing* check the correctness of and emend (a proof). **17** *tr.* (of a text) give as the word or words probably used or intended by an author. ● *n. colloq.* a book, etc., as regards its readability (*is a really good read*). □ **read a person like a book** understand a person's motives, etc. **read between the lines** look for or find hidden meaning. **read lips** determine what is being said by a person who cannot be heard by studying the movements of the speaker's lips. **read out 1** read aloud. **2** expel from a political party, etc. **read up** make a special study of (a subject).

read·a·ble /réedəbəl/ *adj.* **1** able to be read; legible. **2** interesting or pleasant to read. □□ **read·a·bil·i·ty** /-bílitee/ *n.* **read·a·bly** *adv.*

re·a·dapt /réeədápt/ *v.intr. & tr.* become or cause to become adapted anew. □□ **re·ad·ap·ta·tion** /rée-adaptáyshən/ *n.*

re·ad·dress /réeədrés/ *v.tr.* **1** change the address of (a letter or parcel). **2** address (a problem, etc.) anew. **3** speak or write to anew.

read·er /réedər/ *n.* **1** a person who reads or is reading. **2** a book of extracts for learning. **3** a device for producing an image that can be read from microfilm, etc. **4** a publisher's employee who reports on submitted manuscripts. **5** a printer's proof-corrector. **6** a person appointed to read aloud, esp. parts of a service in a church.

read·er·ship /réedərship/ *n.* **1** the readers of a newspaper, etc. **2** the number or extent of these.

read·i·ly /réd'lee/ *adv.* **1** without showing reluctance; willingly. **2 a** without difficulty. **b** without delay.

read·ing /réeding/ *n.* **1 a** the act or an instance of reading (*the reading of the will*). **b** matter to be read (*have plenty of reading with me*). **c** the specified quality of this (*it made exciting reading*). **2** (in *comb.*) used for reading (*reading lamp*; *reading room*). **3** literary knowledge (*a person of wide reading*). **4** an entertainment at which a play, poems, etc., are read (*poetry reading*). **5** a figure, etc., shown by a recording instrument. **6** an interpretation or view taken (*what is your reading of the facts?*). **7** an interpretation made (of drama, music, etc.). **8** each of the successive occasions on which a bill must be presented to a legislature for acceptance. **9** the version of a text, or the particular wording, conjectured or given by an editor, etc.

re·ad·just /réeəjúst/ *v.tr.* adjust again or to a former state. □□ **re·ad·just·ment** *n.*

re·ad·mit /reeədmít/ *v.tr.* (**readmitted**, **readmitting**) admit again. □□ **re·ad·mis·sion** /-ədmíshən/ *n.*

read-on·ly *adj. Computing* (of a memory) able to be read at high speed but not capable of being changed by program instructions (cf. READ-WRITE).

re·a·dopt /réeədópt/ *v.tr.* adopt again. □□ **re·a·dop·tion** *n.*

read·out /réedowt/ *n.* **1** display of information, as on a gauge, etc. **2** the information displayed.

read-write *adj. Computing* capable of reading existing data and accepting alterations or further input (cf. READ-ONLY). ▷ HARD DISK

read·y /rédee/ *adj. & v.* ● *adj.* (**readier**, **readiest**) (usu. *predic.*) **1** with preparations complete (*dinner is ready*). **2** in a fit state (*are you ready to go?*). **3** willing, inclined, or resolved (*he is always ready to complain*; *I am ready for anything*). **4** within reach; easily secured (*a ready source of income*). **5** fit for immediate use (*was ready to hand*). **6** immediate; unqualified (*found ready acceptance*). **7** prompt (*is always ready with excuses*; *has a ready wit*). **8** (foll. by *to* + infin.) about to do something (*a bud just ready to burst*). **9** provided beforehand. ● *v.tr.* (**-ies**, **-ied**) make ready; prepare. □ **at the ready** ready for action. **make ready** prepare. **ready, steady** (or **get set**), **go** the usual formula for starting a race. □□ **read·i·ness** *n.*

read·y-made *adj.* **1** made in a standard size, not to measure. **2** already available; convenient (*a ready-made excuse*).

read·y mon·ey *n.* **1** available cash. **2** payment on the spot.

read·y-to-wear *adj.* made in a standard size, not to measure.

re·af·firm /réeəfə́rm/ *v.tr.* affirm again. □□ **re·af·fir·ma·tion** /-afərmáyshən/ *n.*

re·a·gent /ree-áyjənt/ *n. Chem.* **1** a substance used to cause a reaction, esp. to detect another substance. **2** a reactive substance or force.

re·al[1] /reel/ *adj. & adv.* ● *adj.* **1** actually existing as a thing or occurring in fact. **2** genuine; rightly so called; not artificial or merely apparent. **3** *Law* consisting of or relating to immovable property such as land or houses (*real estate*) (cf. PERSONAL PROPERTY). **4** appraised by purchasing power; adjusted for changes in the value of money (*real value*; *income in real terms*). **5** *Philos.* having an absolute and necessary and not merely contingent existence. **6** *Math.* (of a quantity) having no imaginary part (see IMAGINARY 2). **7** *Optics* (of an image, etc.) such that light actually passes through it. ● *adv. colloq.* really, very. □ **for real** *colloq.* as a serious concern; in earnest. □□ **re·al·ness** *n.*

re·al[2] /rayaál/ *n.* **1** the chief monetary unit of Brazil since 1994. **2** *hist.* a former coin and monetary unit of various Spanish-speaking countries.

re·al ale *Brit.* beer regarded as brewed in a traditional way, with secondary fermentation in the cask.

re·al es·tate *n.* property, esp. land and buildings.

re·a·lign /réeəlín/ *v.tr.* **1** align again. **2** regroup in politics, etc. □□ **re·a·lign·ment** *n.*

re·al·ism /réeəlizəm/ *n.* **1** the practice of regarding things in their true nature and dealing with them as they are. **2** fidelity to nature in representation; the showing of life, etc., as it is in fact. **3** *Philos.* **a** the doctrine that universals or abstract concepts have an objective existence. **b** the belief that matter as an object of perception has real existence. □□ **re·al·ist** *n.*

re·al·is·tic /réeəlístik/ *adj.* **1** regarding things as they are; following a policy of realism. **2** based on facts rather than ideals. □□ **re·al·is·ti·cal·ly** *adv.*

re·al·i·ty /reeálitee/ *n.* (*pl.* **-ies**) **1** what is real or existent or underlies appearances. **2** (foll. by *of*) the real nature of. **3** real existence; the state of being real. **4** resemblance to an original (*the model was impressive in its reality*). □ **in reality** in fact.

re·al·ize /réeəlīz/ *v.tr.* **1** (often foll. by *that* + clause) (also *absol.*) be fully aware of; conceive as real. **2** (also *absol.*) understand clearly. **3** present as real; make realistic; give apparent reality to (*the story was powerfully realized on stage*). **4** convert into actuality; achieve (*realized a childhood dream*). **5 a** convert into money. **b** acquire (profit). **c** be sold for (a specified price). □□ **re·al·iz·a·ble** *adj.* **re·al·i·za·tion** *n.* **re·al·iz·er** *n.*

re·al life *n.* that lived by actual people, as distinct from fiction, drama, etc.

re·al live (*attrib.*) often *joc.* actual; not pretended or simulated (a real live burglar).

re·al·lo·cate /rée-áləkayt/ *v.tr.* allocate again or differently. □□ **re·al·lo·ca·tion** /-káyshən/ *n.*

re·al·ly /réeəlee, réelee/ *adv.* **1** in reality. **2** positively; assuredly (*really useful*). **3** indeed; I assure you. **4** an expression of mild protest or surprise. **5** (in *interrog.*) is that so? (*They're musicians. — Really?*).

realm /relm/ *n.* **1** *formal* esp. *Law* a kingdom. **2** a sphere or domain (*the realm of imagination*).

re·al mon·ey *n.* **1** current coin or notes; cash. **2** large amount of money.

re·al·po·li·tik /rayaálpōlitéek/ *n.* politics based on realities and material needs, rather than on morals or ideals.

re·al ten·nis *n. Brit.* the original form of tennis played on an indoor court.

re·al time *n.* the actual time during which a process or event occurs. □□ **re·al-time** (*attrib. adj.*)

re·al-time (*attrib.*) *Computing* (of a system) in which the response time is of the order of milliseconds, e.g., in an airline booking system.

re·al·tor /réeəltər/ *n.* a real estate agent, esp. (**Realtor**) a member of the National Association of Realtors.

re·al·ty /réeəltee/ *n. Law* real estate (opp. PERSONALTY).

R

ream[1] /reem/ *n.* **1** twenty quires of paper. **2** (in *pl.*) a large quantity of paper or writing (*wrote reams about it*).

ream[2] /reem/ *v.tr.* **1** widen (a hole in metal, etc.) with a borer. **2** turn over the edge of (a cartridge case, etc.). **3** squeeze the juice from (fruit). ▫▫ **ream·er** *n.*

re·an·i·mate /reé-ánimayt/ *v.tr.* **1** restore to life. **2** restore to activity or liveliness. ▫▫ **re·an·i·ma·tion** /-máyshən/ *n.*

reap /reep/ *v.tr.* **1** cut or gather (a crop, esp. grain) as a harvest. **2** harvest the crop of (a field, etc.). **3** receive as the consequence of one's own or others' actions.

reap·er /reépər/ *n.* **1** a person who reaps. **2** a machine for reaping. ▫ **the reaper** (or **grim reaper**) death personified.

re·ap·pear /reéəpeér/ *v.intr.* appear again or as previously. ▫▫ **re·ap·pear·ance** *n.*

re·ap·ply /reéəplí/ *v.tr.* & *intr.* (**-ies**, **-ied**) apply again, esp. submit a further application (for a position, etc.). ▫▫ **re·ap·pli·ca·tion** /reé-aplikáyshən/ *n.*

re·ap·point /reéəpóynt/ *v.tr.* appoint again to a position previously held. ▫▫ **re·ap·point·ment** *n.*

re·ap·por·tion /reéəpáwrshən/ *v.tr.* apportion again or differently. ▫▫ **re·ap·por·tion·ment** *n.*

re·ap·praise /reéəpráyz/ *v.tr.* appraise or assess again. ▫▫ **re·ap·prais·al** *n.*

rear[1] /reer/ *n.* & *adj.* ● *n.* **1** the back part of anything. **2** the space behind, or position at the back of, anything (*a large house with a terrace at the rear*). **3** the hindmost part of an army or fleet. **4** *colloq.* the buttocks. ● *adj.* at the back. ▫ **bring up the rear** come last. **in the rear** behind; at the back.

rear[2] /reer/ *v.* **1** *tr.* **a** bring up and educate (children). **b** breed and care for (animals). **c** cultivate (crops). **2** *intr.* (of a horse, etc.) raise itself on its hind legs. **3** *tr.* **a** set upright. **b** build. **c** hold upward (*rear one's head*). **4** *intr.* extend to a great height. ▫▫ **rear·er** *n.*

rear ad·mi·ral *n.* a naval officer ranking below vice admiral.

rear guard *n.* **1** a body of troops detached to protect the rear, esp. in retreats. **2** a defensive or conservative element in an organization, etc.

rear·guard ac·tion *n.* **1** *Mil.* an engagement undertaken by a rear guard. **2** a defensive stand in argument, etc., esp. when losing.

re·arm /reé-áarm/ *v.tr.* (also *absol.*) arm again, esp. with improved weapons. ▫▫ **re·ar·ma·ment** *n.*

rear·most /reérmōst/ *adj.* furthest back.

re·ar·range /reéəráynj/ *v.tr.* arrange again in a different way. ▫▫ **re·ar·range·ment** *n.*

re·ar·rest /reéərést/ *v.* & *n.* ● *v.tr.* arrest again. ● *n.* an instance of rearresting or being rearrested.

rear·view mir·ror *n.* a mirror fixed inside the windshield of a motor vehicle enabling the driver to see traffic, etc., behind.

rear·ward /reérwərd/ *n.*, *adj.*, & *adv.* ● *n.* rear, esp. in prepositional phrases (*to the rearward of*; *in the rearward*). ● *adj.* to the rear. ● *adv.* (also **rear·wards**) toward the rear.

rea·son /reézən/ *n.* & *v.* ● *n.* **1** a motive, cause, or justification (*has good reasons for doing this*; *there is no reason to be angry*). **2** a fact adduced or serving as this (*I can give you my reasons*). **3** the intellectual faculty by which conclusions are drawn from premises. **4** sanity (*has lost his reason*). **5** *Logic* a premise of a syllogism, esp. a minor premise when given after the conclusion. **6** a faculty transcending the understanding and providing a priori principles; intuition. **7** sense; sensible conduct; what is right or practical or practicable; moderation. ● *v.* **1** *intr.* form or try to reach conclusions by connected thought. **2** *intr.* (foll. by *with*) use an argument (with a person) by way of persuasion. **3** *tr.* (foll. by *that* + clause) conclude or assert in argument. **4** *tr.* (foll. by *why*, *whether*, *what* + clause) discuss; ask oneself. **5** *tr.* (foll. by *into*, *out of*) persuade or move by argument (*I reasoned them out of their fears*). **6** *tr.* (foll. by *out*) think or work out (consequences, etc.). **7** *tr.* (often as **reasoned** *adj.*) express in logical or argumentative form. **8** *tr.* embody reason in (an amendment, etc.). ▫ **by reason of** owing to. **in** (or **within**) **reason** within the bounds of moderation. **it stands to reason** (often foll. by *that* + clause) it is evident or logical. **listen to reason** be persuaded to act sensibly. **see reason** acknowledge the force of an argument. **with reason** justifiably. ▫▫ **rea·son·er** *n.* **rea·son·ing** *n.*

rea·son·a·ble /reézənəbəl/ *adj.* **1** having sound judgment; moderate; ready to listen to reason. **2** not absurd. **3 a** not greatly less or more than might be expected. **b** inexpensive. **c** tolerable; fair. ▫▫ **rea·son·a·ble·ness** *n.* **rea·son·a·bly** *adv.*

re·as·sem·ble /reéəsémbəl/ *v.intr.* & *tr.* assemble again or into a former state. ▫▫ **re·as·sem·bly** *n.*

re·as·sert /reéəsə́rt/ *v.tr.* assert again. ▫▫ **re·as·ser·tion** /-sə́rshən/ *n.*

re·as·sess /reéəsés/ *v.tr.* assess again, esp. differently. ▫▫ **re·as·sess·ment** *n.*

re·as·sign /reéəsín/ *v.tr.* assign again or differently. ▫▫ **re·as·sign·ment** *n.*

re·as·sure /reéəshŏŏr/ *v.tr.* **1** restore confidence to; dispel the apprehensions of. **2** confirm in an opinion or impression. ▫▫ **re·as·sur·ance** *n.* **re·as·sur·ing** *adj.* **re·as·sur·ing·ly** *adv.*

re·at·tach /reéətách/ *v.tr.* attach again or in a former position. ▫▫ **re·at·tach·ment** *n.*

re·at·tempt /reéətémpt/ *v.tr.* attempt again, esp. after failure.

Ré·au·mur /ráyōmyŏŏr/ *adj.* expressed in or related to the scale of temperature at which water freezes at 0° and boils at 80° under standard conditions.

reave /reev/ *v.* (*past* and *past part.* **reaved** or **reft** /reft/) *archaic* **1** *tr.* **a** (foll. by *of*) forcibly deprive of. **b** (foll. by *away*, *from*) take by force or carry off. **2** *intr.* make raids; plunder = REIVE.

re·a·wak·en /reéəwáykən/ *v.tr.* & *intr.* awaken again.

re·bar·ba·tive /reebaárbətiv/ *adj. literary* repellent; unattractive.

re·bate[1] /reébayt/ *n.* & *v.* ● *n.* **1** a partial refund. **2** a deduction from a sum to be paid; a discount. ● *v.tr.* pay back as a rebate.

re·bate[2] /reébayt/ *n.* & *v.tr.* = RABBET.

re·bec /reébek/ *n.* (also **re·beck**) *Mus.* a medieval usu. three-stringed instrument played with a bow.

re·bel *n.*, *adj.*, & *v.* ● *n.* /rébəl/ **1** a person who fights against, resists, or refuses allegiance to, the established government. **2** a person or thing that resists authority or control. ● *adj.* /rébəl/ (*attrib.*) **1** rebellious. **2** of or concerning rebels. **3** in rebellion. ● *v.intr.* /ribél/ (**rebelled**, **rebelling**) (usu. foll. by *against*) **1** act as a rebel; revolt. **2** feel or display repugnance.

re·bel·lion /ribélyən/ *n.* open resistance to authority, esp. organized armed resistance to an established government.

re·bel·lious /ribélyəs/ *adj.* **1** tending to rebel. **2** in rebellion. **3** defying lawful authority. **4** (of a thing) unmanageable; refractory. ▫▫ **re·bel·lious·ly** *adv.* **re·bel·lious·ness** *n.*

re·bind /reébínd/ *v.tr.* (*past* and *past part.* **rebound**) bind (esp. a book) again or differently.

re·birth /reébə́rth/ *n.* **1** a new incarnation. **2** spiritual enlightenment. **3** a revival (*the rebirth of learning*). ▫▫ **re·born** /reébáwrn/ *adj.*

re·boot /reébŏŏt/ *v.tr.* (often *absol.*) *Computing* start (a system) again.

re·bore *v.* & *n.* ● *v.tr.* /reébáwr/ make a new boring in, esp. widen the bore of (the cylinder in an internal-combustion engine). ● *n.* /reébawr/ **1** the process of doing this. **2** a rebored engine.

re·bound[1] *v.* & *n.* ● *v.intr.* /ribównd/ **1** spring back after action or impact. **2** (foll. by *upon*) (of an action) have an adverse effect upon (the doer). ● *n.* /reébownd/ **1** the act or an instance of rebounding; recoil. **2** a reaction after a strong emotion. ▫ **on the rebound** while still recovering from an emotional shock, esp. rejection by a lover.

re·bound[2] /reébównd/ *past* and *past part.* of REBIND.

re·broad·cast /reébráwdkast/ *v.* & *n.* ● *v.tr.* (*past* **rebroadcast** or **rebroadcasted**; *past part.* **rebroadcast**) broadcast again. ● *n.* a repeat broadcast.

re·buff /ribúf/ *n.* & *v.* ● *n.* **1** a rejection of one who makes advances, proffers help or sympathy, shows interest, makes a request, etc. **2** a repulse; a snub. ● *v.tr.* give a rebuff to.

re·build /reébíld/ *v.tr.* (*past* and *past part.* **rebuilt**) build again or differently.

re·buke /ribyŏŏk/ *v.* & *n.* ● *v.tr.* reprove sharply; subject to protest or censure. ● *n.* **1** the act of rebuking. **2** the process of being rebuked. **3** a reproof.

re·bus /reébəs/ *n.* an enigmatic representation of a word (esp. a name), by pictures, etc., suggesting its parts.

re·but /ribút/ *v.tr.* (**rebutted**, **rebutting**) **1** refute or disprove (evidence or a charge). **2** force or turn back; check. ▫▫ **re·but·ta·ble** *adj.* **re·but·tal** *n.*

re·butt·er /ribútər/ *n.* **1** a refutation. **2** *Law* a defendant's reply to a plaintiff.

re·cal·ci·trant /rikálsitrənt/ *adj.* & *n.* ● *adj.* **1** obstinately disobedient. **2** objecting to restraint. ● *n.* a recalcitrant person. ▫▫ **re·cal·ci·trance** *n.* **re·cal·ci·trant·ly** *adv.*

re·cal·cu·late /reékálkyəlayt/ *v.tr.* calculate again. ▫▫ **re·cal·cu·la·tion** /-láyshən/ *n.*

re·ca·lesce /reékəlés/ *v.intr.* grow hot again (esp. of white-hot iron allowed to cool, whose temperature rises briefly at a certain point during cooling). ▫▫ **re·cal·es·cence** *n.*

re·call /rikáwl/ *v.* & *n.* ● *v.tr.* **1** summon to return from a place, a different occupation, inattention, etc. (*recall an ambassador*) **2** recollect; remember. **3** bring back to memory; serve as a reminder of. **4** revoke or annul (an action or decision). **5** cancel or suspend the appointment of (an official sent overseas, etc.). **6** revive; resuscitate. **7** take back (a gift). ● *n.* (also /reékawl/) **1** the act or an instance of recalling, esp. a summons to come back. **2** the act of remembering. **3** the ability to remember. **4** the possibility of recalling, esp. in the sense of revoking (*beyond recall*). **5** removal of an elected official from office. **6** a request from a manufacturer that consumers return a product for repair, replacement, etc. ▫▫ **re·call·a·ble** *adj.*

re·cant /rikánt/ *v.* **1** *tr.* withdraw and renounce (a former belief or statement) as erroneous or heretical. **2** *intr.* disavow a former opinion, esp. with a public confession of error. ▫▫ **re·can·ta·tion** /reékantáyshən/ *n.* **re·cant·er** *n.*

re·cap /reékap/ *v.* & *n. colloq.* ● *v.tr.* & *intr.* (**recapped**, **recapping**) recapitulate. ● *n.* recapitulation.

re·cap·i·tal·ize /reekápitəlīz/ *v.tr.* capitalize (shares, etc.) again. ▫▫ **re·cap·i·tal·iza·tion** *n.*

re·ca·pit·u·late /reékəpíchəlayt/ *v.tr.* **1** go briefly through again; summarize. **2** go over the main points or headings of. ▫▫ **re·ca·pit·u·la·to·ry** /-lətáwree/ *adj.*

re·ca·pit·u·la·tion /reékəpíchəláyshən/ *n.* **1** the act or an instance of recapitulating. **2** *Biol.* the reappearance in embryos of successive type-forms in the evolutionary line of development. **3** *Mus.* part of a movement, esp. in sonata form, in which themes from the exposition are restated.

re·cap·ture /reékápchər/ *v.* & *n.* ● *v.tr.* **1** capture again; recover by capture. **2** reexperience (a past emotion, etc.). ● *n.* the act or an instance of recapturing.

re·cast /reékást/ *v.* & *n.* ● *v.tr.* (*past* and *past part.* **recast**) **1** put into a new form. **2** improve the arrangement of. **3** change the cast of (a play, etc.). ● *n.* **1** the act or an instance of recasting. **2** a recast form.

re·cede /riseéd/ *v.intr.* **1** go or shrink back or further off. **2** be left at an increasing distance by an observer's motion. **3** slope backward (*a receding chin*). **4** decline in force or value. **5** (foll. by *from*) withdraw from (an engagement, opinion, etc.). **6** (of a man's hair) cease to grow at the front, sides, etc.

re·ceipt /riséet/ *n. & v.* ● *n.* **1** the act or an instance of receiving or being received into one's possession (*will pay on receipt of the goods*). **2** a written acknowledgment of this, esp. of the payment of money. **3** (usu. in *pl.*) an amount of money, etc., received. **4** *archaic* a recipe. ● *v.tr.* place a written or printed receipt on (a bill).

re·ceive /riséev/ *v.tr.* **1** take or accept (something offered or given) into one's hands or possession. **2** acquire; be provided with or given (*have received no news; will receive a small fee*). **3** accept delivery of (something sent). **4** have conferred or inflicted on one (*received many honors; received a heavy blow to the head*). **5 a** stand the force or weight of. **b** bear up against; encounter with opposition. **6** consent to hear (a confession or oath) or consider (a petition). **7** (also *absol.*) accept or have dealings with stolen property (knowing of the theft). **8** admit; consent or prove able to hold; provide accommodation for (*received many visitors*). **9** (of a receptacle) be able to hold (a specified amount or contents). **10** greet or welcome, esp. in a specified manner (*how did they receive your offer?*). **11** entertain as a guest, etc. **12** admit to membership of a society, organization, etc. **13** be marked more or less permanently with (an impression, etc.). **14** convert (broadcast signals) into sound or pictures. **15 a** *Tennis* be the player to whom the server serves (the ball). **b** *Football* be the player or team to whom the ball is kicked or thrown. **16** (often as **received** *adj.*) give credit to; accept as authoritative or true (*received opinion*). □ **be at** (or **on**) **the receiving end** *colloq.* bear the brunt of something unpleasant. □□ **re·ceiv·a·ble** *adj.*

re·ceiv·er /riséevər/ *n.* **1** a person or thing that receives. **2** ▼ the part of a machine or instrument that receives sound, signals, etc. (esp. the part of a telephone that contains the earpiece). **3** a radio or television receiving apparatus. **4** a person who receives stolen goods. **5** *Football* an offensive player eligible to catch a forward pass. **6** *Chem.* a vessel for collecting the products of distillation, chromatography, etc.

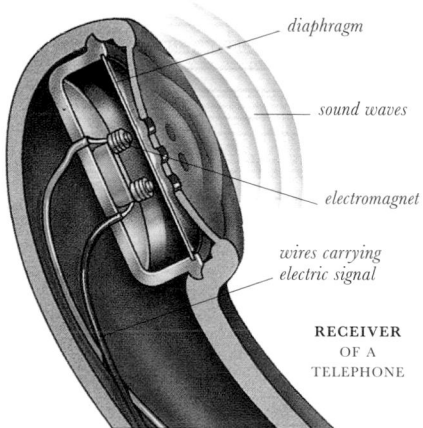

diaphragm

sound waves

electromagnet

wires carrying electric signal

RECEIVER
OF A
TELEPHONE

re·ceiv·er·ship /riséevərship/ *n.* the state of being dealt with by a receiver (esp. *in receivership*).

re·cen·sion /risénshən/ *n.* **1** the revision of a text. **2** a particular form or version of a text resulting from such revision.

re·cent /réesənt/ *adj. & n.* ● *adj.* **1** not long past; that happened, appeared, began to exist, or existed lately. **2** not long established; lately begun; modern. **3** (**Recent**) *Geol.* = HOLOCENE. ● *n.* (**Recent**) *Geol.* = HOLOCENE. □□ **re·cen·cy** *n.* **re·cent·ly** *adv.* **re·cent·ness** *n.*

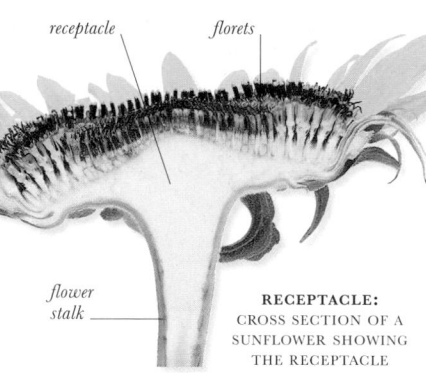

receptacle   *florets*

flower stalk

RECEPTACLE:
CROSS SECTION OF A
SUNFLOWER SHOWING
THE RECEPTACLE

re·cep·ta·cle /riséptəkəl/ *n.* **1** a containing vessel, place, or space. **2** *Bot.* **a** ▲ the common base of floral organs. **b** the part of a leaf or thallus in some algae where the reproductive organs are situated.

re·cep·tion /risépshən/ *n.* **1** the act or an instance of receiving or the process of being received, esp. of a person into a place or group. **2** the manner in which a person or thing is received (*got a cool reception*). **3** a social occasion for receiving guests, esp. after a wedding. **4** a formal or ceremonious welcome. **5** (also **reception desk**) a place where guests or clients, etc., report on arrival at a hotel, office, etc. **6 a** the receiving of broadcast signals. **b** the quality of this (*we have excellent reception*).

re·cep·tion·ist /risépshənist/ *n.* a person employed in a hotel, office, etc., to receive guests, clients, etc.

re·cep·tive /riséptiv/ *adj.* **1** able or quick to receive impressions or ideas. **2** concerned with receiving stimuli, etc. □□ **re·cep·tive·ly** *adv.* **re·cep·tive·ness** *n.* **re·cep·tiv·i·ty** /réeséptivitee/ *n.*

re·cep·tor /riséptər/ *n.* (often *attrib.*) *Biol.* **1** an organ able to respond to an external stimulus such as light, heat, or a drug, and transmit a signal to a sensory nerve. **2** a region of a cell, tissue, etc., that responds to a molecule or other substance.

re·cess /réeses, risés/ *n. & v.* ● *n.* **1** a space set back in a wall; a niche. **2** (often in *pl.*) a remote or secret place (*the innermost recesses*). **3** a temporary cessation from work, esp. of Congress, a court of law, or during a school day. **4** *Anat.* a fold or indentation in an organ. **5** *Geog.* a receding part of a mountain chain, etc. ● *v.* **1** *tr.* make a recess in. **2** *tr.* place in a recess. **3 a** *intr.* take a recess; adjourn. **b** *tr.* order a temporary cessation from the work of (a court, etc.).

re·ces·sion /riséshən/ *n.* **1** a temporary decline in economic activity or prosperity. **2** a receding or withdrawal from a place or point. **3** a receding part of an object; a recess. □□ **re·ces·sion·ar·y** *adj.*

re·ces·sion·al /riséshənəl/ *adj. & n.* ● *adj.* sung while the clergy and choir withdraw after a service. ● *n.* a recessional hymn.

re·ces·sive /risésiv/ *adj.* **1** tending to recede. **2** *Phonet.* (of an accent) falling near the beginning of a word. **3** *Genetics* (of an inherited characteristic) appearing in offspring only when not masked by a dominant characteristic. ▷ MENDELISM. □□ **re·ces·sive·ly** *adv.* **re·ces·sive·ness** *n.*

re·charge *v. & n.* ● *v.tr.* /réecháarj/ **1** charge again. **2** reload. ● *n.* /réecháarj/ **1** a renewed charge. **2** material, etc., used for this. □□ **re·charge·a·ble** *adj.*

re·check *v. & n.* ● *v.tr. & intr.* /réechék/ check again. ● *n.* /réechek/ a further check or inspection.

re·cher·ché /rəsháirshay/ *adj.* **1** carefully sought out; rare or exotic. **2** far-fetched.

re·chris·ten /réekrísən/ *v.tr.* **1** christen again. **2** give a new name to.

re·cid·i·vist /risídivist/ *n.* a person who relapses into crime. □□ **re·cid·i·vism** *n.*

rec·i·pe /résipee/ *n.* **1** a statement of the ingredients and procedure required for preparing cooked food. **2** an expedient; a device for achieving something. **3** a medical prescription.

re·cip·i·ent /risípeeənt/ *n. & adj.* ● *n.* a person who receives something. ● *adj.* **1** receiving. **2** receptive.

re·cip·ro·cal /risíprəkəl/ *adj. & n.* ● *adj.* **1** in return (*offered a reciprocal greeting*). **2** mutual (*their feelings are reciprocal*). **3** *Gram.* (of a pronoun) expressing mutual action or relation (as in *each other*). **4** inversely correspondent; complementary (*natural kindness matched by a reciprocal severity*). ● *n.* *Math.* an expression or function so related to another that their product is one ($\frac{1}{2}$ is the reciprocal of 2). □□ **re·cip·ro·cal·ly** *adv.*

re·cip·ro·cate /risíprəkayt/ *v.* **1** *tr.* return or requite (affection, etc.). **2** *intr.* (foll. by *with*) offer or give something in return (*reciprocated with an invitation to lunch*). **3** *tr.* give and receive mutually; interchange. **4 a** *intr.* (of a part of a machine) move backward and forward. **b** *tr.* cause to do this. □□ **re·cip·ro·ca·tion** /-káyshən/ *n.* **re·cip·ro·ca·tor** *n.*

rec·i·proc·i·ty /résiprósitee/ *n.* **1** the condition of being reciprocal. **2** mutual action. **3** give and take, esp. the interchange of privileges.

re·cir·cu·late /réesórkyəlayt/ *v.tr. & intr.* circulate again, esp. make available for reuse. □□ **re·cir·cu·la·tion** /-láyshən/ *n.*

re·cit·al /risít'l/ *n.* **1** the act or an instance of reciting or being recited. **2** the performance of a program of music by a solo instrumentalist or singer or by a small group. **3** (foll. by *of*) a detailed account of (connected things or facts); a narrative. □□ **re·cit·al·ist** *n.*

rec·i·ta·tion /résitáyshən/ *n.* **1** the act or an instance of reciting. **2** a thing recited.

rec·i·ta·tive /résitətéev/ *n.* **1** musical declamation of the kind usual in the narrative and dialogue parts of opera and oratorio. **2** the words or part given in this form.

re·cite /risít/ *v.* **1** *tr.* repeat aloud or declaim (a poem or passage) from memory. **2** *intr.* give a recitation. **3** *tr.* enumerate. □□ **re·cit·er** *n.*

reck /rek/ *v. archaic* or *poet.* (only in *neg.* or *interrog.*) **1** *tr.* (foll. by *of*) pay heed to; take account of; care about. **2** *tr.* pay heed to. **3** *intr.* (usu. with *it* as subject) be of importance (*it recks little*).

reck·less /réklis/ *adj.* disregarding the consequences or danger, etc.; rash. □□ **reck·less·ly** *adv.* **reck·less·ness** *n.*

reck·on /rékən/ *v.* **1** *tr.* count or compute by calculation. **2** *tr.* (foll. by *in*) count in or include in computation. **3** *tr.* (often foll. by *as* or *to be*) consider or regard (*reckon him wise; reckon them to be beyond hope*). **4** *tr.* **a** (foll. by *that* + clause) be of the considered opinion. **b** *colloq.* (foll. by *to* + infin.) expect (*reckons to finish by Friday*). **5** *intr.* make calculations; add up an account or sum. **6** *intr.* (foll. by *on, upon*) rely on, count on, or base plans on. **7** *intr.* (foll. by *with*) **a** take into account. **b** settle accounts with. **8** *US dial.* think; suppose (*I reckon I'll just stay home tonight*). □ **reckon up 1** count up; find the total of. **2** settle accounts. **to be reckoned with** of considerable importance; not to be ignored.

reck·on·ing /rékəning/ *n.* **1** the act or an instance of counting or calculating. **2** a consideration or opinion. **3 a** the settlement of an account. **b** an account.

re·claim /rikláym/ *v. & n.* ● *v.tr.* **1** seek the return of (one's property). **2** claim in return or as a rebate, etc. **3** bring under cultivation, esp. from a state of being under water. **4 a** win back or away from vice or error or a waste condition. **b** tame; civilize. ● *n.* the act or an instance of reclaiming; the process of being reclaimed. □□ **re·claim·a·ble** *adj.* **re·claim·er** *n.* **rec·la·ma·tion** /rékləmáyshən/ *n.*

re·clas·si·fy /réeklásifī/ *v.tr.* (-ies, -ied) classify again or differently. □□ **re·clas·si·fi·ca·tion** /-fikáyshən/ *n.*

rec·li·nate /réklinayt/ *adj. Bot.* bending downward.

re·cline /riklín/ *v.* **1** *intr.* assume or be in a horizontal or leaning position, esp. in resting. **2** *tr.* cause to recline or move from the vertical.

R

RECORD

Sound recording converts sound waves into electrical signals and stores them in a retrievable format. There are two main types of recordings: analog (records and tapes) and digital (such as CDs). On records, the signals are stored as a spiral groove; on tapes, they are recorded as varying levels of magnetism on two tracks. On CDs, the signals are transformed into binary numbers, represented by pits and spaces.

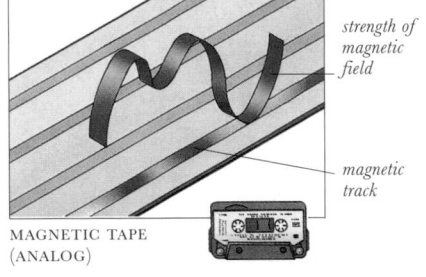

strength of magnetic field

magnetic track

MAGNETIC TAPE (ANALOG)

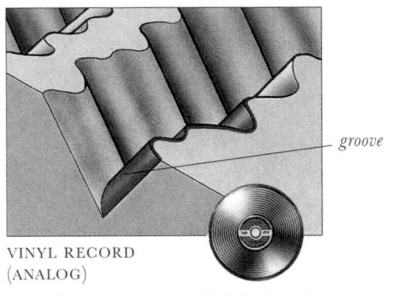

groove

VINYL RECORD (ANALOG)

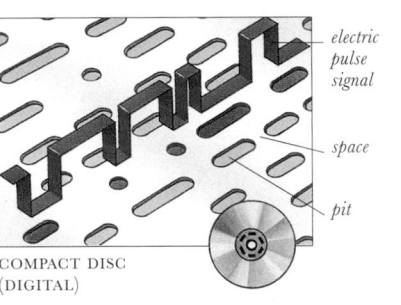

electric pulse signal

space

pit

COMPACT DISC (DIGITAL)

re·clin·er /riklínər/ *n.* **1** a comfortable chair for reclining in. **2** a person who reclines.

re·clothe /reeklṓth/ *v.tr.* clothe again or differently.

rec·luse /réklōōs, riklōōs/ *n. & adj.* ● *n.* a person given to or living in seclusion or isolation, esp. as a religious discipline. ● *adj.* favoring seclusion; solitary. □□ **re·clu·sion** /riklōōzhən/ *n.* **re·clu·sive** *adj.*

rec·og·ni·tion /rékəgníshən/ *n.* the act or an instance of recognizing or being recognized.

re·cog·ni·zance /rikógnizəns, -kónə-/ *n.* **1** a bond by which a person undertakes before a court, etc., to observe some condition, e.g., to appear when summoned. **2** a sum pledged as surety for this.

re·cog·ni·zant /rikógnizənt/ *adj.* (usu. foll. by *of*) **1** showing recognition (of a favor, etc.). **2** conscious or showing consciousness (of something).

rec·og·nize /rékəgnīz/ *v.tr.* **1** identify as already known. **2** realize or discover the nature of. **3** (foll. by *that*) realize or admit. **4** acknowledge the existence, validity, character, or claims of. **5** show appreciation of; reward. **6** (foll. by *as, for*) treat or acknowledge. **7** (of a chairperson, etc.) allow (a person) to speak in a debate, etc. □□ **rec·og·niz·a·ble** *adj.* **rec·og·niz·a·bil·i·ty** /-əbílitee/ *n.* **rec·og·niz·a·bly** *adv.* **rec·og·niz·er** *n.*

re·coil /rikóyl/ *v. & n.* ● *v.intr.* **1** suddenly move or spring back in fear, horror, or disgust. **2** shrink mentally in this way. **3** rebound after an impact. **4** (foll. by *on, upon*) have an adverse reactive effect on (the originator). **5** (of a gun) be driven backward by its discharge. **6** retreat under an enemy's attack. **7** *Physics* (of an atom, etc.) move backward by the conservation of momentum on emission of a particle. ● *n.* (also /réekoyl/) **1** the act or an instance of recoiling. **2** the sensation of recoiling.

rec·ol·lect /rékəlékt/ *v.tr.* **1** remember. **2** succeed in remembering; call to mind.

re·col·lect /reekəlékt/ *v.tr.* **1** collect again. **2** (*refl.*) recover control of (oneself).

rec·ol·lec·tion /rékəlékshən/ *n.* **1** the act or power of recollecting. **2** a thing recollected. **3 a** a person's memory (*to the best of my recollection*). **b** the time over which memory extends (*happened within my recollection*). □□ **rec·ol·lec·tive** *adj.*

re·col·o·nize /reekólənīz/ *v.tr.* colonize again. □□ **re·co·lo·ni·za·tion** *n.*

re·com·bi·na·tion /reekombináyshən/ *n. Biol.* the rearrangement, esp. by crossing over in chromosomes, of nucleic acid molecules forming a new sequence of the constituent nucleotides.

re·com·bine /reekəmbín/ *v.tr. & intr.* combine again or differently.

re·com·mence /reekəméns/ *v.tr. & intr.* begin again. □□ **re·com·mence·ment** *n.*

rec·om·mend /rékəménd/ *v.tr.* **1 a** suggest as fit for some purpose or use. **b** suggest (a person) as suitable for a particular position. **2** (often foll. by *that* + clause or *to* + infin.) advise as a course of action, etc. (*I recommend that you stay where you are*). **3** (of qualities, conduct, etc.) make acceptable or desirable. □□ **rec·om·mend·a·ble** *adj.* **rec·om·men·da·tion** *n.* **rec·om·mend·a·to·ry** /-dətawree/ *adj.*

rec·om·pense /rékəmpens/ *v. & n.* ● *v.tr.* **1** make amends to (a person) or for (a loss, etc.). **2** requite; reward or punish (a person or action). ● *n.* **1** a reward; requital. **2** retribution.

rec·on·cile /rékənsīl/ *v.tr.* **1** make friendly again after an estrangement. **2** (usu. in *refl.* or *passive*; foll. by *to*) make acquiescent or contentedly submissive to (something disagreeable or unwelcome) (*was reconciled to failure*). **3** settle (a quarrel, etc.). **4** harmonize; make compatible. □□ **rec·on·cil·a·ble** *adj.* **rec·on·cil·er** *n.* **rec·on·cil·i·a·tion** /-sileeáyshən/ *n.*

rec·on·dite /rékəndīt, rikón-/ *adj.* **1** (of a subject or knowledge) abstruse; out of the way; little known. **2** (of an author or style) dealing in abstruse knowledge or allusions; obscure.

re·con·di·tion /reekəndíshən/ *v.tr.* **1** overhaul; refit; renovate. **2** make usable again.

re·con·fig·ure /reekənfígyər/ *v.tr.* configure again or differently. □□ **re·con·fig·u·ra·tion** *n.*

re·con·firm /reekənfərm/ *v.tr.* confirm, establish, or ratify anew. □□ **re·con·fir·ma·tion** /-konfərmáyshən/ *n.*

re·con·nais·sance /rikónisəns/ *n.* **1** a survey of a region, esp. to locate an enemy or ascertain strategic features. **2** a preliminary survey.

re·con·nect /reekənékt/ *v.tr.* connect again. □□ **re·con·nec·tion** /-nékshən/ *n.*

re·con·noi·ter /reekənóytər, rékə-/ *v. & n.* ● *v.* **1** make a reconnaissance of. **2** *intr.* make a reconnaissance. ● *n.* a reconnaissance.

re·con·quer /reekóngkər/ *v.tr.* conquer again. □□ **re·con·quest** *n.*

re·con·sid·er /reekənsídər/ *v.tr. & intr.* consider again, esp. for a possible change of decision. □□ **re·con·sid·er·a·tion** *n.*

re·con·sti·tute /reekónstitōōt, -tyōōt/ *v.tr.* **1** recon-struct. **2** reorganize. **3** restore the previous constitution of (dried food, etc.) by adding water. □□ **re·con·sti·tu·tion** /-tōōshən/ *n.*

re·con·struct /reekənstrúkt/ *v.tr.* **1** build or form again. **2 a** form a mental or visual impression of (past events) by assembling the evidence for them. **b** reenact (a crime). **3** reorganize. □□ **re·con·struct·a·ble** *adj.* (also **re·con·struct·i·ble**). **re·con·struc·tion** /-strúkshən/ *n.* **re·con·struc·tive** *adj.* **re·con·struc·tor** *n.*

re·con·vene /reekənveén/ *v.tr. & intr.* convene again, esp. after a pause in proceedings.

re·con·vert /reekənvórt/ *v.tr.* convert back to a former state. □□ **re·con·ver·sion** /-vórzhən/ *n.*

re·cord *n. & v.* ● *n.* /rékərd/ **1 a** a piece of evidence or information constituting an account of something that has occurred, been said, etc. **b** a document preserving this. **2** the state of being set down or preserved in writing or some other permanent form (*is a matter of record*). **3 a** (in full **phonograph record**) a thin plastic disk carrying recorded sound in grooves on each surface, for reproduction by a record player. **b** a trace made on this or some other medium, e.g., magnetic tape. **4 a** an official report of the proceedings and judgment in a court of justice. **b** a copy of the pleadings, etc., constituting a case to be decided by a court. **5 a** the facts known about a person's past (*has an honorable record of service*). **b** a list of a person's previous criminal convictions. **6** the best performance (esp. in sport) or most remarkable event of its kind on record (often *attrib.*: *a record attempt*). **7** an object serving as a memorial; a portrait. **8** *Computing* a number of related items of information which are handled as a unit. ● *v.tr.* /rikáwrd/ **1** set down in writing or some other permanent form for later reference. **2** ◀ convert (sound, a broadcast, etc.) into permanent form for later reproduction. **3** establish or constitute a historical or other record of. □ **break** (or **beat**) **the record** outdo all previous performances, etc. **for the record** as an official statement, etc. **go on record** state one's opinion openly, so that it is recorded. **have a record** be known as a criminal. **a matter of record** a thing established as a fact by being recorded. **off the record** as an unofficial or confidential statement, etc. **on record** officially recorded; publicly known. **put** (or **get** or **set**, etc.) **the record straight** correct a misapprehension. □□ **re·cord·a·ble** *adj.*

re·cord·er /rikáwrdər/ *n.* **1** an apparatus for recording, esp. a tape recorder. **2 a** a keeper of records. **b** a person who makes an official record. **3** *Mus.* ◀ a woodwind instrument like a flute but blown through the end and having a more hollow tone. ▷ WOODWIND

re·cord·ing /rikáwrding/ *n.* **1** the process by which audio or video signals are recorded for later reproduction. **2** material or a program recorded.

re·cord·ist /rikáwrdist/ *n.* a person who records sound.

re·cord play·er *n.* an apparatus for reproducing sound from phonograph records.

re·count¹ /rikównt/ *v.tr.* **1** narrate. **2** tell in detail.

re·count² *v. & n.* ● *v.* /reé kównt/ *v.tr.* count again. ● *n.* /réekownt/ a recounting, esp. of votes in an election.

re·coup /rikōōp/ *v.tr.* **1** recover or regain (a loss). **2** compensate or reimburse for a loss. **3** *Law* deduct or keep back (part of a sum due). □ **recoup oneself** recover a loss. □□ **re·coup·a·ble** *adj.* **re·coup·ment** *n.*

re·course /reékawrs, rikáwrs/ *n.* **1** resorting to a possible source of help. **2** a person or thing resorted to. □ **have recourse to** turn to (a person or thing)

mouthpiece

finger holes

hollow shaft

RECORDER:
EARLY 18TH-CENTURY
SOPRANO RECORDER

R

for help. **without recourse** a formula used by the endorser of a bill, etc., to disclaim responsibility for payment.

re·cov·er /rikúvər/ v. **1** tr. regain possession or use or control of; reclaim. **2** intr. return to health or consciousness or to a normal state or position. **3** tr. obtain or secure (compensation, etc.) by legal process. **4** tr. retrieve or make up for (a loss, setback, etc.). **5** refl. regain composure or consciousness or control of one's limbs. **6** tr. retrieve (reusable substances) from industrial waste. □□ **re·cov·er·a·ble** adj. **re·cov·er·a·bil·i·ty** /-vərəbílitee/ n. **re·cov·er·er** n.

re-cov·er /réekúvər/ v.tr. **1** cover again. **2** provide (a chair, etc.) with a new cover.

re·cov·er·y /rikúvəree/ n. (pl. **-ies**) **1** the act or an instance of recovering; the process of being recovered. **2** Golf a stroke bringing the ball out of a bunker, etc.

rec·re·ant /rékreeənt/ adj. & n. literary ● adj. **1** craven; cowardly. **2** apostate. ● n. **1** a coward. **2** an apostate. □□ **rec·re·an·cy** n. **rec·re·ant·ly** adv.

re-cre·ate /réekree-áyt/ v.tr. create over again. □□ **re-cre·a·tion** n.

rec·re·a·tion /rékree-áyshən/ n. **1** the process or means of refreshing or entertaining oneself. **2** a pleasurable activity. □□ **rec·re·a·tion·al** adj. **rec·re·a·tion·al·ly** adv. **rec·re·a·tive** /rekreeáytiv/ adj.

re·crim·i·nate /rikrími nayt/ v.intr. make mutual or counter accusations. □□ **re·crim·i·na·tion** /-náyshən/ n. **re·crim·i·na·to·ry** /-nətawree/ adj.

re·cross /réekráws, -krós/ v.tr. & intr. cross or pass over again.

re·cru·desce /réekrōodés/ v.intr. (of a disease or difficulty, etc.) break out again. □□ **re·cru·des·cence** n. **re·cru·des·cent** adj.

re·cruit /rikróot/ n. & v. ● n. **1** a serviceman or servicewoman newly enlisted and not yet fully trained. **2** a new member of a society or organization. **3** a beginner. ● v. **1** tr. enlist (a person) as a recruit. **2** tr. form (an army, etc.) by enlisting recruits. **3** intr. get or seek recruits. **4** tr. replenish or reinvigorate (numbers, strength, etc.) □□ **re·cruit·er** n. **re·cruit·ment** n.

re·crys·tal·lize /réekrístəlīz/ v.tr. & intr. crystallize again. □□ **re·crys·tal·li·za·tion** n.

recta pl. of RECTUM.

rec·tal /réktəl/ adj. of or by means of the rectum. □□ **rec·tal·ly** adv.

rec·tan·gle /réktanggəl/ n. a plane figure with four straight sides and four right angles, esp. one with the adjacent sides unequal. □□ **rec·tan·gu·lar** /rektánggyələr/ adj. **rec·tan·gu·lar·i·ty** /-láritee/ n. **rec·tan·gu·lar·ly** adv.

rec·ti·fy /réktifī/ v.tr. (**-ies**, **-ied**) **1** adjust or make right; correct; amend. **2** purify or refine, esp. by repeated distillation. **3** find a straight line equal in length to (a curve). **4** convert (alternating current) to direct current. □□ **rec·ti·fi·a·ble** adj. **rec·ti·fi·ca·tion** /-fikáyshən/ n. **rec·ti·fi·er** /réktifīər/ n.

rec·ti·lin·e·ar /réktilíneeər/ adj. (also **rec·ti·lin·e·al** /-eeəl/) **1** bounded or characterized by straight lines. **2** in or forming a straight line. □□ **rec·ti·lin·e·ar·i·ty** /-neeáritee/ n. **rec·ti·lin·e·ar·ly** adv.

rec·ti·tude /réktitōod, -tyōod/ n. **1** moral uprightness. **2** righteousness. **3** correctness.

rec·to /réktō/ n. (pl. **-os**) **1** the right-hand page of an open book. **2** the front of a printed leaf of paper or manuscript (opp. VERSO).

rec·tor /réktər/ n. **1** (in the Church of England) the incumbent of a parish where all tithes formerly passed to the incumbent (cf. VICAR). **2** RC Ch., Episcopal Ch. a priest in charge of a parish or religious institution. **3** the head of some schools, universities, and colleges. □□ **rec·to·ri·al** /-táwreeəl/ adj. **rec·tor·ship** n.

rec·to·ry /réktəree/ n. (pl. **-ies**) **1** a rector's house. **2** (in the Church of England) a rector's benefice.

rec·trix /réktriks/ n. (pl. **rectrices** /-triseez/) a bird's strong tail feather that directs flight.

rec·tum /réktəm/ n. (pl. **rectums** or **recta** /-tə/) the final section of the large intestine, terminating at the anus. ▷ DIGESTION

rec·tus /réktəs/ n. (pl. **recti** /-tī/) Anat. a straight muscle.

re·cum·bent /rikúmbənt/ adj. lying down; reclining. □□ **re·cum·ben·cy** n. **re·cum·bent·ly** adv.

re·cu·per·ate /rikōopərayt/ v. **1** intr. recover from illness, exhaustion, loss, etc. **2** tr. regain (health, something lost, etc.). □□ **re·cu·per·a·ble** adj. **re·cu·per·a·tion** /-ráyshən/ n. **re·cu·per·a·tive** /-rətiv/ adj. **re·cu·per·a·tor** n.

re·cur /rikúr/ v.intr. (**recurred**, **recurring**) **1** occur again; be repeated. **2** (of a thought, etc.) come back to one's mind. **3** (foll. by to) go back in thought or speech.

re·cur·rent /rikúrənt, -kúr-/ adj. recurring; happening repeatedly. □□ **re·cur·rence** n. **re·cur·rent·ly** adv.

re·cur·sion /rikúrzhən/ n. the act or an instance of returning. □□ **re·cur·sive** adj.

re·curve /rikúrv/ v.tr. & intr. bend backward. □□ **re·curv·ate** /-vayt, -vət/ adj. **re·cur·va·ture** n.

re·cu·sant /rékyəzənt, rikyōo-/ n. & adj. ● n. a person who refuses submission to an authority or compliance with a regulation, esp. Brit.hist. a Roman Catholic who refused to attend services of the Church of England. ● adj. of or being a recusant. □□ **re·cu·sance** n. **re·cu·san·cy** n.

re·cy·cle /réesíkəl/ v.tr. convert (waste) to reusable material. □□ **re·cy·cla·ble** adj.

red /red/ adj. & n. ● adj. (**redder**, **reddest**) **1** of or near the color seen at the least-refracted end of the visible spectrum, of shades ranging from that of blood to pink or deep orange. **2** flushed in the face with shame, anger, etc. **3** (of the eyes) bloodshot or red-rimmed with weeping. **4** (of the hair) reddish-brown; tawny. **5** having to do with bloodshed, burning, violence, or revolution. **6** colloq. communist or socialist. **7** (**Red**) (formerly) Soviet, Russian (the Red Army). **8** (of wine) made from dark grapes and colored by their skins. ● n. **1** a red color or pigment. **2** red clothes or material. **3** colloq. a communist or socialist. **4 a** a red ball, piece, etc., in a game or sport. **b** the player using such pieces. **5** the debit side of an account. **6** a red light. □□ **red·dish** adj. **red·dy** adj. **red·ly** adv. **red·ness** n.

re·dact /ridákt/ v.tr. put into literary form; edit for publication. □□ **re·dac·tor** n.

re·dac·tion /ridákshən/ n. **1** preparation for publication. **2** revision; editing; rearrangement. **3** a new edition. □□ **re·dac·tion·al** adj.

red ad·mi·ral n. ▼ a butterfly, Vanessa atalanta, with red bands on each pair of wings.

UNDERSIDE

UPPER SIDE

RED ADMIRAL (Vanessa atalanta)

red a·lert n. **1** Mil. an alert sounded or given when an enemy attack appears imminent. **2** the signal for this.

red-blood·ed adj. virile; vigorous.

red·breast /rédbrest/ n. colloq. a robin.

red·cap /rédkap/ n. a baggage porter.

red car·pet n. privileged treatment of an eminent visitor.

red cell n. (also **red cor·pus·cle**) an erythrocyte.

red cent n. the lowest-value (orig. copper) coin; a trivial sum (not worth a red cent).

red·coat /rédkōt/ n. hist. ▼ a British soldier (so called from the scarlet uniform of most regiments).

cockade
shirt
scarlet coat
stock
musket
knapsack strap
bayonet
crossbelt
musket-lock brush
cartridge box
breeches
sling
stocking
butt

REDCOAT: PRIVATE OF THE BRITISH INFANTRY (c.1780)

Red Cross n. **1** an international organization (originally medical) bringing relief to victims of war or natural disaster. **2** the emblem of this organization.

red·den /réd'n/ v.tr. & intr. make or become red.

red·dle /réd'l/ n. red ocher; ruddle.

re·dec·o·rate /réedékərayt/ v.tr. decorate again or differently. □□ **re·dec·o·ra·tion** /-ráyshən/ n.

re·deem /rideém/ v.tr. **1** buy back; recover by expenditure of effort or by a stipulated payment. **2** make a single payment to discharge (a regular charge or obligation). **3** convert (tokens or bonds, etc.) into goods or cash. **4** (of God or Christ) deliver from sin and damnation. **5** be a compensating factor in. **6** (foll. by from) save from (a defect). **7** refl. save (oneself) from blame. **8** purchase the freedom of (a person). **9** save (a person's life) by ransom. **10** save or rescue or reclaim. **11** fulfill (a promise). □□ **re·deem·a·ble** adj.

re·deem·er /rideémər/ n. **1** a person who redeems. **2** (**the Redeemer**) Christ.

re·de·fine /réediffn/ v.tr. define again or differently. □□ **re·def·i·ni·tion** /-definíshən/ n.

re·demp·tion /ridémpshən/ n. **1** the act or an instance of redeeming; the process of being redeemed. **2** man's deliverance from sin and damnation. **3** a thing that redeems. □□ **re·demp·tive** adj.

re·de·ploy /réediplóy/ v.tr. send (troops, workers, etc.) to a new place or task. □□ **re·de·ploy·ment** n.

re·de·sign /réedizín/ v.tr. design again or differently.

re·de·vel·op /réedivéləp/ v.tr. develop anew (esp. an urban area). □□ **re·de·vel·op·er** n. **re·de·vel·op·ment** n.

red-eye n. **1** = RUDD. **2** late-night or overnight airline flight. **3** sl. cheap whiskey.

red-faced adj. embarrassed, ashamed.

red flag n. **1** the symbol of socialist revolution. **2** a warning of danger.

red gi·ant n. a relatively cool giant star. ▷ STAR

R

red·hand·ed *adv.* in or just after the act of committing a crime, doing wrong, etc.

red·head /rédhed/ *n.* a person with red hair.

red her·ring *n.* **1** dried smoked herring. **2** a misleading clue or distraction (so called from the practice of using the scent of red herring in training hounds).

red hot *n. & adj.* ● *n. colloq.* a hot dog. ● *adj.* (**red-hot**) **1** heated until red. **2** highly exciting. **3** (of news) fresh. **4** intensely excited. **5** enraged.

red-hot po·ker *n.* ▶ any plant of the genus *Kniphofia*, with spikes of usually red or yellow flowers.

re·di·al /réediəl, -díl/ *v.tr. & intr.* dial again.

redid *past of* REDO.

red·in·te·grate /ridíntigrayt/ *v.tr.* **1** restore to wholeness or unity. **2** renew or reestablish in a united or perfect state. □□ **red·in·te·gra·tion** /-gráyshən/ *n.* **red·in·te·gra·tive** /-grətiv/ *adj.*

re·di·rect /réedirékt, -dí-/ *v.tr.* direct again, esp. change the address of (a letter). □□ **re·di·rec·tion** *n.*

re·dis·cov·er /réediskúvər/ *v.tr.* discover again. □□ **re·dis·cov·er·y** *n.* (*pl.* **-ies**).

re·dis·tri·bute /réedistrí-byōot/ *v.tr.* distribute again or differently. □□ **re·dis·tri·bu·tion** /-byōoshən/ *n.* **re·dis·tri·bu·tive** /-tríbyōotiv/ *adj.*

re·di·vide /réediví́d/ *v.tr.* divide again or differently. □□ **re·di·vi·sion** /-vízhən/ *n.*

red·i·vi·vus /rédivívəs, -véevəs/ *adj.* (placed after noun) come back to life.

red lead *n.* a red form of lead oxide used as a pigment.

red-let·ter day *n.* a day that is pleasantly noteworthy or memorable.

red light *n.* **1** a signal to stop on a road, railroad, etc. **2** a warning or refusal.

red-light dis·trict *n.* a district containing many brothels.

red·line /rédlīn/ *v.tr. N. Amer. colloq.* **1** drive with (the car engine) at its maximum rpm. **2** refuse (a loan or insurance) to someone due to his or her area of residence.

red meat *n.* meat that is red when raw (e.g., beef or lamb).

red mul·let *n.* ▼ a marine fish, *Muletus surmuletus*, valued as food.

RED-HOT POKER
(*Kniphofia* 'Atlanta')

RED MULLET
(*Muletus surmuletus*)

red·neck /rédnek/ *n.* often *derog.* a working-class, politically conservative or reactionary white person, esp. in the rural southern US.

re·do /réedōo/ *v.tr.* (*3rd sing. present* **redoes**; *past* **redid**; *past part.* **redone**) **1** do again or differently. **2** redecorate.

red·o·lent /rédələnt/ *adj.* **1** (foll. by *of, with*) strongly reminiscent or suggestive or mentally associated. **2** fragrant. **3** having a strong smell. □□ **red·o·lence** *n.* **red·o·lent·ly** *adv.*

re·dou·ble /réedúbəl/ *v.* **1** *tr. & intr.* make or grow greater or more intense; intensify. **2** *intr. Bridge* double again a bid already doubled by an opponent.

re·doubt /ridówt/ *n. Mil.* an outwork or fieldwork usu. square or polygonal and without flanking defenses.

re·doubt·a·ble /ridówtəbəl/ *adj.* formidable, esp. as an opponent. □□ **re·doubt·a·bly** *adv.*

re·dound /ridównd/ *v.intr.* **1** (foll. by *to*) (of an action, etc.) make a great contribution to (one's credit or advantage, etc.). **2** (foll. by *upon, on*) come as the final result to; come back or recoil upon.

re·dox /réedoks/ *n. Chem.* (often *attrib.*) oxidation and reduction.

red pep·per *n.* **1** cayenne pepper. **2** the ripe fruit of the capsicum plant, *Capsicum annuum*.

re·draft /réedráft/ *v.tr.* draft (a document) again.

re·draw /réedráw/ *v.tr.* (*past* **redrew**; *past part.* **redrawn**) draw again or differently.

re·dress /ridrés/ *v. & n.* ● *v.tr.* **1** remedy or rectify (a wrong, etc.). **2** readjust; set straight again. ● *n.* (also /réedres/) reparation for a wrong. □ **redress the balance** restore equality. □□ **re·dress·a·ble** *adj.* **re·dress·al** *n.* **re·dress·er** *n.* (also **re·dres·sor**).

red·shank /rédshangk/ *n.* either of two sandpipers, *Tringa totanus* and *T. erythropus*, with bright red legs.

red·shift /rédshift/ *n. Astron.* the displacement of the spectrum to longer wavelengths in the light coming from distant galaxies, etc., in recession.

red·skin /rédskin/ *n. colloq. offens.* a Native American.

red squir·rel *n.* **1** a N. American squirrel, *Tamiasciurus hudsonicus*, with reddish fur. **2** ▼ a common Eurasian red squirrel, *Sciurus vulgaris*, with reddish fur.

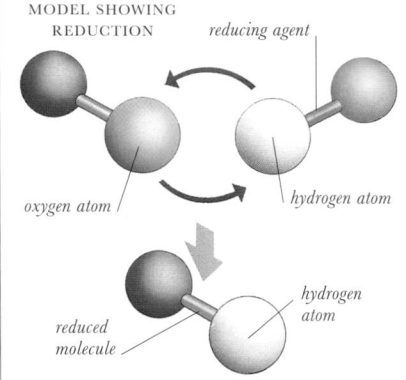

RED SQUIRREL
(*Sciurus vulgaris*)

red·start /rédstaart/ *n.* **1** any European red-tailed songbird of the genus *Phoenicurus*. **2** any of various similar American warblers of the family Parulidae.

red tape *n.* excessive bureaucracy or adherence to formalities.

re·duce /ridōos, -dyōos/ *v.* **1** *tr. & intr.* make or become smaller or less. **2** *tr.* (foll. by *to*) bring by force or necessity (to some undesirable state or action). **3** *tr.* convert to another (esp. simpler) form (*reduced it to a powder*). **4** *tr.* convert (a fraction) to the form with the lowest terms. **5** *tr.* (foll. by *to*) simplify or adapt by classification or analysis (*reduced to three issues*). **6** *tr.* make lower in status or rank. **7** *tr.* lower the price of. **8** *intr.* lessen one's weight or size. **9** *tr.* weaken (*is in a very reduced state*). **10** *tr.* impoverish. **11** *tr.* subdue; bring back to obedience. **12** *Chem. intr. & tr.* **a** combine or cause to combine with hydrogen. **b** undergo or cause to undergo addition of electrons. **13** *tr. Chem.* convert (oxide, etc.) to metal. **14** *tr.* **a** (in surgery) restore (a dislocated, etc., part) to its proper position. **b** remedy (a dislocation, etc.) in this way. **15** *tr. Photog.* make (a negative or print) less dense. **16** *tr. Cookery* boil off excess liquid from. □□ **re·duc·er** *n.* **re·duc·i·ble** *adj.* **re·duc·i·bil·i·ty** *n.*

REDUCE

In chemistry, a substance is reduced when it gains hydrogen during a chemical reaction. The substance providing the hydrogen is called the reducing agent. Oxidation, the gaining of oxygen, occurs simultaneously with reduction.

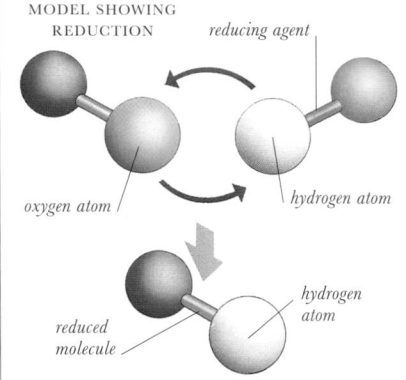

MODEL SHOWING
REDUCTION

reducing agent

oxygen atom

hydrogen atom

hydrogen atom

reduced molecule

re·duced cir·cum·stances *n.pl.* poverty after relative prosperity.

re·duc·ti·o ad ab·surd·um /ridúkteeō ad absórdəm/ *n.* a method of proving the falsity of a premise by showing that the logical consequence is absurd; an instance of this.

re·duc·tion /ridúkshən/ *n.* **1** the act or an instance of reducing; the process of being reduced. **2** an amount by which prices, etc., are reduced. **3** a reduced copy of a picture, etc. **4** an arrangement of an orchestral score for piano, etc. □□ **re·duc·tive** *adj.*

re·duc·tion·ism /ridúkshənizəm/ *n.* **1** the tendency to or principle of analyzing complex things into simple constituents. **2** often *derog.* the doctrine that a system can be fully understood in terms of its isolated parts. □□ **re·duc·tion·ist** *n.* **re·duc·tion·is·tic** /-nístik/ *adj.*

re·dun·dant /ridúndənt/ *adj.* **1** superfluous; not needed. **2** that can be omitted without any loss of significance. □□ **re·dun·dan·cy** *n.* (*pl.* **-ies**). **re·dun·dant·ly** *adv.*

re·du·pli·cate /ridōóplikayt, -dyōó-/ *v.tr.* **1** make double. **2** repeat. **3** repeat (a letter or syllable or word) exactly or with a slight change (e.g., hurly-burly, go-go). □□ **re·du·pli·ca·tion** /-káyshən/ *n.* **re·du·pli·ca·tive** /-kətiv/ *adj.*

re·dux /réeduks/ *adj.* revived; restored.

red·wing /rédwing/ *n.* a thrush, *Turdus iliacus*, with red underwings showing in flight.

red·wood /rédwōod/ *n.* **1** an exceptionally large Californian conifer, *Sequoia sempervirens*, yielding red wood. ▷ SEQUOIA. **2** any tree yielding red wood.

ree·bok var of RHEBOK.

re·ech·o /rée-ékō/ *v.intr. & tr.* (**-oes**, **-oed**) **1** echo. **2** echo repeatedly; resound.

reed /reed/ *n. & v.* ● *n.* **1 a** any of various water or marsh plants with a firm stem. **b** a tall straight stalk of this. **2** (*collect.*) reeds growing in a mass or used as material esp. for thatching. **3** a pipe of reed or straw. **4 a** the vibrating part of the mouthpiece of some wind instruments, made of reed or other material and producing the sound. ▷ WOODWIND. **b** (esp. in *pl.*) a reed instrument. **5** a weaver's comb-like implement for separating the threads of the warp and correctly positioning the weft.

reed·ed /réedid/ *adj.* **1** *Mus.* (of an instrument) having a vibrating reed. ▷ WOODWIND. **2** *Archit.* decorated with reeding.

R

reed·ing /réeding/ *n. Archit.* a small semicylindrical molding or ornamentation.

reed in·stru·ment *n.* a wind instrument with a single reed (e.g., clarinet) or double reed (e.g., oboe).

reed mace *n.* = CATTAIL.

re·ed·u·cate /rée-édjəkayt/ *v.tr.* educate again, esp. to change a person's views or beliefs. □□ **re·ed·u·ca·tion** /-káyshən/ *n.*

reed·y /réedee/ *adj.* (**reedier, reediest**) **1** full of reeds. **2** like a reed, esp. in weakness or slenderness. **3** (of a voice) not full. □□ **reed·i·ness** *n.*

reef[1] /reef/ *n.* **1** a ridge of rock or coral, etc., at or near the surface of the sea. **2** a lode of ore.

reef[2] /reef/ *n. & v. Naut.* • *n.* each of several strips across a sail, for taking it in or rolling it up to reduce the surface area in a high wind. • *v.tr.* **1** take in a reef or reefs of (a sail). **2** shorten (a topmast or a bowsprit).

reef·er /réefər/ *n.* **1** *sl.* a marijuana cigarette. **2** a thick close-fitting double-breasted jacket.

reek /reek/ *v. & n.* • *v.intr.* (often foll. by *of*) **1** smell strongly and unpleasantly. **2** have unpleasant or suspicious associations. **3** give off smoke or fumes. • *n.* a foul or stale smell.

reel /reel/ *n. & v.* • *n.* **1** a cylindrical device on which thread, film, etc., are wound. **2** a quantity of thread, etc., wound on a reel. **3** ▼ a device for winding a line as required, esp. in fishing. **4** a revolving part in various machines. **5 a** a lively folk or Scottish dance. **b** a piece of music for this. • *v.* **1** *tr.* wind on a reel. **2** *tr.* (foll. by *in, up*) draw (fish, etc.) in or up by the use of a reel. **3** *intr.* stand or walk or run unsteadily. **4** *intr.* be shaken mentally or physically. **5** *intr.* rock from side to side, or swing violently. **6** *intr.* dance a reel. □ **reel off** say or recite very rapidly and without apparent effort. □□ **reel·er** *n.*

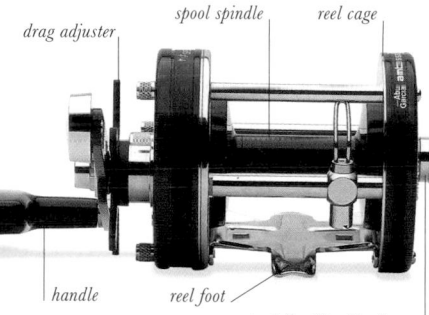

drag adjuster · spool spindle · reel cage · handle · reel foot · spool "endfloat" adjuster

REEL USED ON A FISHING ROD

re·el·ect /rée-ilékt/ *v.tr.* elect again, esp. to a further term of office. □□ **re·e·lec·tion** /-ilékshən/ *n.*

re·em·bark /rée-imbáark/ *v.intr. & tr.* go or put on board ship again. □□ **re·em·bar·ka·tion** *n.*

re·e·merge /rée-imórj/ *v.intr.* emerge again. □□ **re·e·mer·gence** *n.* **re·e·mer·gent** *adj.*

re·em·pha·size /rée-émfəsīz/ *v.tr.* place renewed emphasis on. □□ **re·em·pha·sis** /-émfəsis/ *n.*

re·em·ploy /rée-implóy/ *v.tr.* employ again. □□ **re·em·ploy·ment** *n.*

re·en·act /rée-inákt/ *v.tr.* act out (a past event). □□ **re·en·act·ment** *n.*

reen·gi·neer /ree-enjinéer/ *v.tr.* **1** redesign (a machine). **2** restructure (a company or its operations).

re·en·list /rée-inlist/ *v.intr.* enlist again, esp. in the armed services.

re·en·ter /rée-éntər/ *v.tr. & intr.* go back in. □□ **re·en·trance** /-éntrəns/ *n.*

re·en·trant /rée-éntrant/ *adj. & n.* • *adj.* **1** esp. *Fortification* (of an angle) pointing inward (opp. SALIENT). **2** *Geom.* reflex. • *n.* a reentrant angle.

re·en·try /rée-éntree/ *n.* (*pl.* **-ies**) **1** the act of entering again, esp. (of a spacecraft, etc.) reenter-

ing the Earth's atmosphere. **2** *Law* an act of retaking or repossession.

re·e·quip /rée-ikwíp/ *v.tr. & intr.* (**-equipped, -equipping**) provide with new equipment.

re·e·rect /rée-irékt/ *v.tr.* erect again.

re·es·tab·lish /rée-istáblish/ *v.tr.* establish again or anew. □□ **re·es·tab·lish·ment** *n.*

re·e·val·u·ate /rée-ivályōō-ayt/ *v.tr.* evaluate again or differently. □□ **re·e·val·u·a·tion** /-áyshən/ *n.*

reeve[1] /reev/ *n. hist.* **1** the chief administrator of a town or district. **2** any of various minor local officials.

reeve[2] /reev/ *v.tr.* (*past* **rove** /rōv/ or **reeved**) *Naut.* **1** (usu. foll. by *through*) thread (a rope or rod, etc.) through a ring or other aperture. **2** fasten (a rope or block) in this way.

reeve[3] /reev/ *n.* a female ruff (see RUFF[1] 4).

re·ex·am·ine /rée-igzámin/ *v.tr.* examine again or further (esp. a witness). □□ **re·ex·am·i·na·tion** /-náyshən/ *n.*

re·ex·port *v. & n.* • *v.tr.* /rée-ikspáwrt/ export again (esp. imported goods after further processing or manufacture)./ • *n.* /rée-ékspawrt/ **1** the process of reexporting. **2** something reexported. □□ **re·ex·por·ta·tion** *n.* **re·ex·por·ter** *n.*

ref /ref/ *n. colloq.* a referee in sports.

re·face /rée-fáys/ *v.tr.* put a new facing on (a building).

re·fash·ion /rée-fáshən/ *v.tr.* fashion again or differently.

re·fec·tion /rifékshən/ *n. literary* **1** refreshment by food or drink (*we took refection*). **2** a light meal.

re·fec·to·ry /riféktəree/ *n.* (*pl.* **-ies**) a room used for communal meals, esp. in a monastery or college. ▷ MONASTERY

re·fer /rifór/ *v.* (**referred, referring**) (usu. foll. by *to*) **1** *tr.* trace or ascribe (to a person or thing as a cause or source) (*referred their success to their popularity*). **2** *tr.* consider as belonging (to a certain date or place or class). **3** *tr.* send on or direct (a person, or a question for decision). **4** *intr.* make an appeal or have recourse to (*referred to his notes*). **5** *tr.* send (a person) to a medical specialist, etc. **6** *tr.* (foll. by *back to*) send (a proposal, etc.) back to (a lower body, court, etc.). **7** *intr.* (foll. by *to*) (of a person speaking) make an allusion or direct the hearer's attention (*decided not to refer to our other problems*). **8** *intr.* (foll. by *to*) (of a statement, etc.) have a particular relation; be directed (*this refers to last year*). **9** *tr.* (foll. by *to*) interpret (a statement) as being directed to (a particular context, etc.). **10** *tr.* fail (a candidate in an examination). □□ **re·fer·a·ble** /riférəbəl, réfər-/ *adj.*

ref·er·ee /réfərée/ *n. & v.* • *n.* **1** an umpire, esp. in sports, such as football, boxing, etc. **2** a person whose opinion or judgment is sought in a dispute, etc. • *v.* (**referees, refereed**) **1** *intr.* act as referee. **2** *tr.* be the referee of (a game).

ref·er·ence /réfərəns, réfrəns/ *n. & v.* • *n.* **1** the referring of a matter for decision or settlement or consideration to some authority. **2** the scope given to this authority. **3** (foll. by *to*) **a** a relation or respect or correspondence (*success has little reference to merit*). **b** an allusion (*made no reference to it*). **c** a direction to a book, etc., (or a passage in it) where information may be found. **d** a book or passage so cited. **4 a** the act of looking up a passage, etc., or looking in a book for information. **b** the act of referring to a person, etc., for information. **5 a** a written testimonial supporting an applicant for employment, etc. **b** a person giving this. • *v.tr.* provide (a book, etc.) with references to authorities. □ **with** (or **in**) **reference to** regarding; as regards. **without reference to** not taking account of. □□ **ref·er·en·tial** /réfərénshəl/ *adj.*

ref·er·ence book *n.* a book intended to be consulted for information on individual matters rather than read continuously.

ref·er·ence li·bra·ry *n.* (*pl.* **-ies**) a library in which the books are for consultation not loan.

ref·er·ence point *n.* a basis or standard for evaluation or comparison.

ref·er·en·dum /réfəréndəm/ *n.* (*pl.* **referendums**

or **referenda** /-də/) **1** the process of referring a political question to the electorate for a direct decision by general vote. **2** a vote taken by referendum.

ref·er·ent /réfərənt/ *n.* the idea or thing that a word, etc., symbolizes.

re·fer·ral /rifórəl/ *n.* the referring of an individual to an expert or specialist for advice, esp. the directing of a patient by a GP to a medical specialist.

re·fill *v. & n.* • *v.tr.* /réefil/ **1** fill again. **2** provide a new filling for. • *n.* /réefil/ **1** a new filling. **2** the material for this. □□ **re·fill·a·ble** *adj.*

re·fine /rifín/ *v.* **1** *tr.* free from impurities or defects. **2** *tr. & intr.* make or become more polished or elegant or cultured. **3** *tr. & intr.* make or become more subtle or delicate in feelings, etc. □□ **re·fin·a·ble** *adj.*

re·fined /rifínd/ *adj.* **1** characterized by polish or elegance or subtlety. **2** purified; clarified.

re·fine·ment /rifínmənt/ *n.* **1** the act of refining or the process of being refined. **2** fineness of feeling or taste. **3** polish or elegance in manner. **4** an added development or improvement (*a car with several refinements*). **5** a piece of subtle reasoning. **6** a fine distinction. **7** a subtle or ingenious example or display (*all the refinements of reasoning*).

re·fin·er /rifínər/ *n.* a person or firm whose business is to refine crude oil, metal, sugar, etc.

re·fin·er·y /rifínəree/ *n.* (*pl.* **-ies**) a place where oil, etc., is refined.

re·fit *v. & n.* • *v.tr. & intr.* /réefit/ (**refitted, refitting**) make or become fit or serviceable again (esp. of a ship undergoing renewal and repairs). • *n.* /réefit/ the act or an instance of refitting; the process of being refitted.

re·flate /réeflayt/ *v.tr.* cause reflation of (a currency or economy, etc.). □□ **re·fla·tion** /réefláyshən/ *n.* **re·fla·tion·ar·y** *adj.*

re·flect /riflékt/ *v.* **1** *tr.* **a** (of a surface or body) throw back (heat, light, etc.). **b** cause to rebound (*reflected light*). **2** *tr.* (of a mirror) show an image of; reproduce to the eye or mind. **3** *tr.* correspond in appearance or effect to (*their behavior reflects a wish to succeed*). **4** *tr.* **a** (of an action, result, etc.) show or bring (credit, discredit, etc.). **b** (*absol.*; usu. foll. by *on, upon*) bring discredit on. **5 a** *intr.* (often foll. by *on, upon*) meditate on. **b** *tr.* (foll. by *that, how,* etc., + *clause*) consider; remind oneself.

re·flec·tion /riflékshən/ *n.* **1** ▼ the act or an instance of reflecting; the process of being reflected. **2** a reflected light, heat, or color. **b** a reflected image. **3** reconsideration (*on reflection*). **4** (often foll. by *on*) discredit or a thing bringing discredit. **5** (often foll. by *on, upon*) an idea arising in the mind. **6** (usu. foll. by *of*) a consequence; evidence (*a reflection of how she feels*).

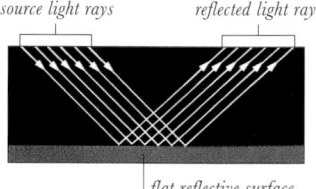

source light rays · reflected light rays · flat reflective surface

REFLECTION: LIGHT RAYS REFLECTED FROM A SMOOTH SURFACE

re·flec·tive /rifléktiv/ *adj.* **1** (of a surface, etc.) giving a reflection or image. **2** (of mental faculties) concerned in reflection or thought. **3** (of a person or mood, etc.) thoughtful; given to meditation. □□ **re·flec·tive·ly** *adv.* **re·flec·tive·ness** *n.*

re·flec·tor /rifléktər/ *n.* **1** a piece of glass or metal, etc., for reflecting light in a required direction, e.g., a red one on the back of a motor vehicle or bicycle. ▷ BICYCLE. **2 a** a telescope, etc., using a mirror to produce images. ▷ TELESCOPE. **b** the mirror itself.

R

re·flet /rəfláy/ *n.* luster or iridescence, esp. on pottery.

re·flex /réefleks/ *adj. & n.* ● *adj.* **1** (of an action) independent of the will, as an automatic response to the stimulation of a nerve (e.g., a sneeze). **2** (of an angle) exceeding 180°. **3** bent backward. **4** (of light) reflected. **5** (of a thought, etc.) introspective; directed back upon itself or its own operations. **6** (of an effect or influence) reactive; coming back upon its author or source. ● *n.* **1** a reflex action. **2** a sign or secondary manifestation (*law is a reflex of public opinion*). **3** reflected light or a reflected image. **4** a word formed by development from an earlier stage of a language. □□ **re·flex·ly** *adv.*

re·flex cam·er·a *n.* a camera with a ground-glass focusing screen on which the image is formed by a combination of lens and mirror.

re·flex·i·ble /rifléksibəl/ *adj.* capable of being reflected. □□ **re·flex·i·bil·i·ty** /-bílitee/ *n.*

re·flex·ive /rifléksiv/ *adj. & n. Gram.* ● *adj.* **1** (of a word or form) referring back to the subject of a sentence (e.g., *myself*). **2** (of a verb) having a reflexive pronoun as its object (as in *to wash oneself*). ● *n.* a reflexive word or form, esp. a pronoun. □□ **re·flex·ive·ly** *adv.* **re·flex·ive·ness** *n.* **re·flex·iv·i·ty** /-sívitee/ *n.*

re·flex·ol·o·gy /réefleksóləjee/ *n.* **1** ▼ a system of massage through reflex points on the feet, hands, and head, used to relieve tension and treat illness. **2** *Psychol.* the scientific study of reflexes. □□ **re·flex·ol·o·gist** *n.*

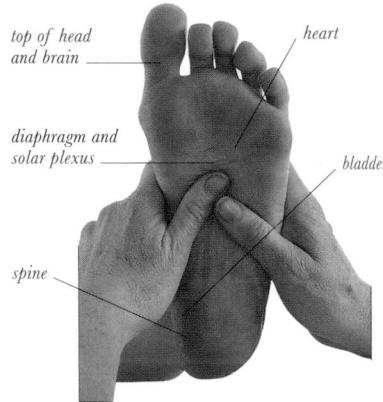

REFLEXOLOGY: REFLEX POINTS AND THE PARTS OF THE BODY THEY RELATE TO

top of head and brain

heart

diaphragm and solar plexus

bladder

spine

R

re·flu·ent /réflōōənt/ *adj.* flowing back (*refluent tide*). □□ **re·flu·ence** *n.*

re·flux /réefluks/ *n. & v.* ● *n.* **1** a backward flow. **2** *Chem.* a method of boiling a liquid so that any vapor is liquefied and returned to the boiler. ● *v.tr. & intr. Chem.* boil or be boiled under reflux.

re·fo·cus /réefṓkəs/ *v.tr.* (**refocused**, **refocusing** or **refocussed**, **refocussing**) adjust the focus of.

re·for·est /réefáwrist, fór-/ *v.tr.* replant (former forest land) with trees. □□ **re·for·est·a·tion** /-stáyshən/ *n.*

re·form /rifáwrm/ *v. & n.* ● *v.* **1** *tr. & intr.* make or become better by the removal of faults and errors. **2** *tr.* abolish or cure (an abuse or malpractice). **3** *tr.* correct (a legal document). ● *n.* **1** the removal of faults or abuses, esp. of a moral or political or social kind. **2** an improvement made or suggested. □□ **re·form·a·ble** *adj.*

re-form /réefáwrm/ *v.tr. & intr.* form again. □□ **re-for·ma·tion** /réefáwrmáyshən/ *n.*

re·for·mat /réefáwrmat/ *v.tr.* (**reformatted**, **reformatting**) format anew.

ref·or·ma·tion /réfərmáyshən/ *n.* **1** the act of reforming or process of being reformed, esp. a radical change for the better in political or religious or social affairs. **2** (**the Reformation**) *hist.* a 16th-c. movement for the reform of abuses in the Roman Church ending in the establishment of the Reformed and Protestant churches. □□ **Ref·or·ma·tion·al** *adj.*

re·for·ma·tion /réefawrmáyshən/ *n.* the process or an instance of forming or being formed again.

re·form·a·tive /rifáwrmətiv/ *adj.* tending or intended to produce reform.

re·form·a·to·ry /rifáwrmətawree/ *n. & adj.* ● *n.* (*pl.* **-ies**) = REFORM SCHOOL. ● *adj.* reformative.

re·form·er /rifáwrmər/ *n.* a person who advocates or brings about (esp. political or social) reform.

re·form·ism /rifáwrmizəm/ *n.* a policy of reform rather than abolition or revolution. □□ **re·form·ist** *n.*

re·form school *n.* an institution to which young offenders are sent to be reformed.

re·for·mu·late /réefáwrmyəlayt/ *v.tr.* formulate again or differently. □□ **re·for·mu·la·tion** /-láyshən/ *n.*

re·fract /rifrákt/ *v.tr.* **1** ▼ (of water, air, glass, etc.) deflect (a ray of light, etc.) at a certain angle when it enters obliquely from another medium. ▷ LIGHT. **2** determine the refractive condition of (the eye). □□ **re·frac·tion** /rifrákshən/ *n.* **re·frac·tive** /rifráktiv/ *adj.*

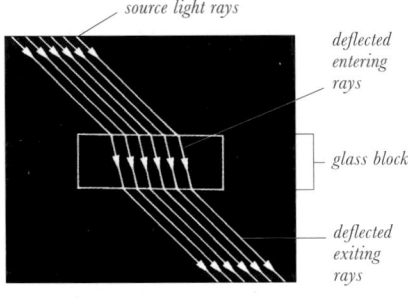

source light rays

deflected entering rays

glass block

deflected exiting rays

REFRACT: LIGHT RAYS REFRACTED BY A GLASS BLOCK

re·frac·tom·e·ter /reefraktómitər/ *n.* an instrument for measuring refraction. □□ **re·frac·to·met·ric** /-təmétrik/ *adj.* **re·frac·tom·e·try** *n.*

re·frac·tor /rifráktər/ *n.* **1** a refracting medium or lens. **2** a telescope using a lens to produce an image. ▷ TELESCOPE

re·frac·to·ry /rifráktəree/ *adj. & n.* ● *adj.* **1** stubborn; unmanageable, rebellious. **2 a** (of a wound, disease, etc.) not yielding to treatment. **b** (of a person, etc.) resistant to infection. **3** (of a substance) hard to fuse or work. ● *n.* (*pl.* **-ies**) a substance especially resistant to heat, corrosion, etc. □□ **re·frac·to·ri·ly** *adv.* **re·frac·to·ri·ness** *n.*

re·frain¹ /rifráyn/ *v.intr.* (foll. by *from*) avoid doing (an action); forbear; desist.

re·frain² /rifráyn/ *n.* **1** a recurring phrase or number of lines, esp. at the ends of stanzas. **2** the music accompanying this.

re·fran·gi·ble /rifránjibəl/ *adj.* that can be refracted. □□ **re·fran·gi·bil·i·ty** *n.*

re·freeze /réefréez/ *v.tr. & intr.* (*past* **refroze**; *past part.* **refrozen**) freeze again.

re·fresh /rifrésh/ *v.tr.* **1 a** (of food, rest, amusement, etc.) give fresh spirit or vigor to. **b** (esp. *refl.*) revive with food, rest, etc. (*refreshed myself with a short sleep*). **2** revive or stimulate (the memory), esp. by consulting the source of one's information. **3** make cool. **4** restore to a certain condition, esp. by provision of fresh supplies, equipment, etc.; replenish. **5** *Computing* **a** restore an image to the screen. **b** replace an image with one that displays more recent information.

re·fresh·er /rifréshər/ *n.* something that refreshes, esp. a drink.

re·fresh·er course *n.* a course reviewing or updating previous studies.

re·fresh·ing /rifréshing/ *adj.* **1** serving to refresh. **2** welcome or stimulating. □□ **re·fresh·ing·ly** *adv.*

re·fresh·ment /rifréshmənt/ *n.* **1** the act of refresh-ing or the process of being refreshed in mind or body. **2** (usu. in *pl.*) food or drink that refreshes. **3** something that refreshes or stimulates the mind.

re·fried beans *n.* (in Mexican cooking) pinto beans boiled and fried in advance and reheated when required.

re·frig·er·ant /rifríjərənt/ *n. & adj.* ● *n.* a substance used for refrigeration. ▷ REFRIGERATOR. ● *adj.* causing cooling or refrigeration.

re·frig·er·ate /rifríjərayt/ *v.* **1** *tr. & intr.* make or become cool or cold. **2** *tr.* subject (food, etc.) to cold in order to freeze or preserve it. □□ **re·frig·er·a·tion** /-ráyshən/ *n.*

re·frig·er·a·tor /rifríjəraytər/ *n.* ► a cabinet or room in which food, etc., is kept cold.

re·frig·er·a·to·ry /rifríjərətawree/ *adj.* serving to cool.

re·frin·gent /rifrínjənt/ *adj. Physics* refracting. □□ **re·frin·gence** *n.* **re·frin·gen·cy** *n.*

re·froze *past* of REFREEZE.

re·froz·en *past part.* of REFREEZE.

reft *past part.* of REAVE.

re·fu·el /réefyōōəl/ *v.* **1** *intr.* replenish a fuel supply. **2** *tr.* supply with more fuel.

ref·uge /réfyōōj/ *n.* **1** a shelter from pursuit or danger or trouble. **2** a person or place, etc., offering this. **3 a** a person, thing, or course resorted to in difficulties. **b** a pretext; an excuse. **4** a traffic island.

ref·u·gee /réfyōōjée/ *n.* a person taking refuge, esp. in a foreign country.

re·ful·gent /rifúljənt/ *adj. literary* shining; gloriously bright. □□ **re·ful·gence** *n.* **re·ful·gent·ly** *adv.*

re·fund¹ *v. & n.* ● *v.* /rifúnd/ *tr.* (also *absol.*) **1** pay back (money or expenses). **2** reimburse (a person). ● *n.* /réefund/ **1** an act of refunding. **2** a sum refunded; a repayment. □□ **re·fund·a·ble** *adj.*

re·fund² /réefúnd/ *v.tr.* fund (a debt, etc.) again.

re·fur·bish /rifárbish/ *v.tr.* **1** brighten up. **2** restore and redecorate. □□ **re·fur·bish·ment** *n.*

re·fur·nish /réefárnish/ *v.tr.* furnish again or differently.

re·fus·al /rifyōōzəl/ *n.* **1** the act or an instance of refusing; the state of being refused. **2** (in full **first refusal**) the right or privilege of deciding to take or leave a thing before it is offered to others.

re·fuse¹ /rifyōōz/ *v.* **1** *tr.* withhold acceptance of or consent to. **2** *tr.* (often foll. by *to* + infin.) indicate unwillingness (*I refuse to go*). **3** *tr.* (often with double object) not grant (a request) made by (a person) (*refused me a day off*). **4** *tr.* (also *absol.*) (of a horse) be unwilling to jump (a fence, etc.). □□ **re·fus·er** *n.*

ref·use² /réfyōōs/ *n.* rejected as worthless matter.

re·fuse·nik /rifyōōznik/ *n. hist.* a Jew refused permission to emigrate to Israel from the former Soviet Union.

re·fute /rifyōōt/ *v.tr.* **1** prove the falsity or error of (a statement, etc., or the person advancing it). **2** rebut or repel by argument. **3** *disp.* deny or contradict (without argument). ¶ Often confused in this sense with *repudiate*. □□ **re·fut·a·ble** *adj.* **re·fu·tal** *n.* **ref·u·ta·tion** /réfyōōtáyshən/ *n.* **re·fut·er** *n.*

reg /reg/ *n. colloq.* regulation.

re·gain /rigáyn/ *v.tr.* obtain possession or use of after loss.

re·gal /réegəl/ *adj.* **1** royal; of or by a monarch or monarchs. **2** fit for a monarch; magnificent. □□ **re·gal·i·ty** /rigálitee/ *n.* **re·gal·ly** *adv.*

re·gale /rigáyl/ *v.tr.* **1** entertain lavishly with feasting. **2** (foll. by *with*) entertain with (talk, etc.). **3** (of beauty, etc.) give delight to.

re·ga·li·a /rigáylyə/ *n.pl.* **1** the insignia of royalty used at coronations. **2** the insignia of an order or of civic dignity. **3** any distinctive or elaborate clothes, accoutrements, etc.; trappings; finery.

re·gal·ism /réegəlizəm/ *n.* the doctrine of a sovereign's ecclesiastical supremacy.

re·gard /rigáard/ *v. & n.* ● *v.tr.* **1** gaze on steadily (usu. in a specified way) (*regarded them suspiciously*).

REFRIGERATOR

In a refrigerator, a gas (refrigerant) is compressed (becoming warm) and then cools into a liquid in the condenser. When it reaches the evaporator, the pressure is released and the liquid expands into a cold gas that cools the air in the cabinet. The gas then returns to the compressor.

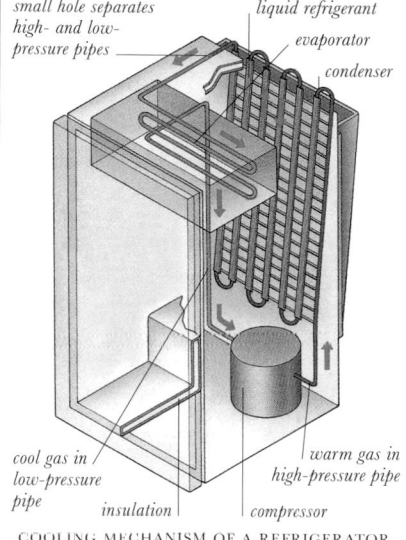

small hole separates high- and low-pressure pipes

liquid refrigerant

evaporator

condenser

cool gas in low-pressure pipe

warm gas in high-pressure pipe

insulation

compressor

COOLING MECHANISM OF A REFRIGERATOR

2 give heed to; take into account. **3** look upon or contemplate mentally in a specified way (*I regard it as an insult*). **4** (of a thing) have relation to; have some connection with. ● *n.* **1** a gaze; a steady or significant look. **2** (foll. by *to*, *for*) attention or care. **3** (foll. by *for*) esteem; kindly feeling; respectful opinion. **4 a** a point attended to (*in this regard*). **b** (usu. foll. by *to*) reference; connection, relevance. **5** (in *pl.*) an expression of friendliness in a letter, etc. (*sent my best regards*). □ **as regards** concerning; in respect of. **in** (or **with**) **regard to** as concerns; in respect of.

re·gard·ant /rigaárdʹnt/ *adj. Heraldry* (of a beast, etc.) looking backward.

re·gard·ful /rigaárdfŏŏl/ *adj.* (foll. by *of*) mindful of; paying attention to.

re·gard·ing /rigaárding/ *prep.* concerning; in respect of.

re·gard·less /rigaárdlis/ *adj. & adv.* ● *adj.* (foll. by *of*) without regard or consideration for. ● *adv.* without paying attention (*carried on regardless*). □□ **re·gard·less·ly** *adv.* **re·gard·less·ness** *n.*

re·gat·ta /rigaátə, -gátə/ *n.* a sporting event consisting of a series of boat or yacht races.

re·gen·cy /réejənsee/ *n.* (*pl.* **-ies**) **1** the office of regent. **2** a commission acting as regent. **3 a** the period of office of a regent or regency commission. **b** (**Regency**) a particular period of a regency, esp. (in Britain) from 1811 to 1820, and (in France) from 1715 to 1723.

re·gen·er·ate *v. & adj.* ● *v.* /rijénərayt/ **1** *tr. & intr.* bring or come into renewed existence; generate again. **2** *tr.* improve the moral condition of. **3** *tr.* impart new, more vigorous, and spiritually greater life to (a person or institution, etc.). **4** *intr.* reform oneself. **5** *tr.* invest with a new and higher spiritual nature. **6** *intr. & tr. Biol.* regrow or cause (new tissue) to regrow. ● *adj.* /rijénərət/ **1** spiritually born again. **2** reformed. □□ **re·gen·er·a·tion** /-jénəráyshən/ *n.* **re·gen·er·a·tive** /-rətiv/ *adj.* **re·gen·er·a·tive·ly** *adv.* **re·gen·er·a·tor** *n.*

re·gent /réejənt/ *n. & adj.* ● *n.* **1** a person appointed to administer a kingdom because the monarch is a minor or is absent or incapacitated. **2** a member of the governing body of a state university. ● *adj.* (placed after noun) acting as regent (*prince regent*).

reg·gae /régay/ *n.* a W. Indian style of music with a strongly accented subsidiary beat.

reg·i·cide /réjisīd/ *n.* **1** a person who kills or takes part in killing a king. **2** the act of killing a king. □□ **reg·i·cid·al** *adj.*

re·gild /réegíld/ *v.tr.* gild again, esp. to renew faded or worn gilding.

re·gime /rayzheém/ *n.* (also **régime**) **1 a** a method or system of government. **b** *derog.* a particular government. **2** a prevailing order or system of things. **3** the conditions under which a scientific or industrial process occurs. **4** = REGIMEN.

reg·i·men /réjimen/ *n.* esp. *Med.* a prescribed course of exercise, way of life, and diet.

reg·i·ment *n. & v.* ● *n.* /réjimənt/ **1 a** a permanent unit of an army usu. commanded by a colonel and divided into several companies or troops or batteries. **b** an operational unit of artillery, etc. **2** (usu. foll. by *of*) a large array or number. **3** *archaic* rule; government. ● *v.tr.* /réjiment/ **1** organize (esp. oppressively) in groups or according to a system. **2** form into a regiment or regiments. □□ **reg·i·men·ta·tion** *n.*

reg·i·men·tal /réjimént'l/ *adj. & n.* ● *adj.* of or relating to a regiment. ● *n.* (in *pl.*) military uniform, esp. of a particular regiment. □□ **reg·i·men·tal·ly** *adv.*

Re·gi·na /rijīnə/ *n. Brit. Law* the reigning queen (following a name or in the titles of lawsuits, e.g., *Regina v. Jones*, the Crown versus Jones).

re·gion /réejən/ *n.* **1** an area of land, or division of the Earth's surface, having definable boundaries or characteristics (*a mountainous region*). **2** an administrative district, esp. in Scotland. **3** a part of the body around or near some organ, etc. (*the lumbar region*). **4** a sphere or realm (*the region of metaphysics*). **5 a** a separate part of the world or universe. **b** a layer of the atmosphere or the sea according to its height or depth. □ **in the region of** approximately. □□ **re·gion·al** *adj.* **re·gion·al·ism** *n.* **re·gion·al·ist** *n. & adj.* **re·gion·al·ize** *v.tr.* **re·gion·al·ly** *adv.*

reg·is·ter /réjistər/ *n. & v.* ● *n.* **1** an official list, e.g., of births, marriages, and deaths; of shipping; of professionally qualified persons; or of qualified voters in a constituency. **2** a book in which items are recorded for reference. **3** a device recording speed, force, etc. **4** (in electronic devices) a location in a store of data. **5 a** the range of a voice or instrument. **b** a part of this range (*lower register*). **6** an adjustable plate for widening or narrowing an opening and regulating a draft, in a fire grate. **7 a** a set of organ pipes. ▷ ORGAN. **b** a sliding device controlling this. **8** = CASH REGISTER. ● *v.* **1** *tr.* set down (a name, fact, etc.) formally; record in writing. **2** *tr.* make a mental note of; notice. **3** *tr.* enter or cause to be entered in a particular register. **4** *tr.* entrust (a letter, etc.) to registered mail. **5** *intr. & refl.* put one's name on a register, esp. as an eligible voter or as a guest in a register kept by a hotel, etc. **6** *tr.* (of an instrument) record automatically; indicate. **7 a** *tr.* express (an emotion) facially or by gesture (*registered surprise*). **b** *intr.* (of an emotion) show in a person's face or gestures. **8** *intr.* make an impression on a person's mind (*did not register at all*). □□ **reg·is·tra·ble** *adj.*

reg·is·tered mail *n.* mail recorded at the post office and guaranteed against loss, damage, etc., during transmission.

reg·is·tered nurse *n.* a nurse with graduate training who has passed a state certification exam and is licensed to practice nursing.

reg·is·trar /réjistraár/ *n.* **1** an official responsible for keeping a register or official records. **2** the chief administrative officer in a university. □□ **reg·is·trar·ship** *n.*

reg·is·tra·tion /réjistráyshən/ *n.* **1** the act or an instance of registering; the process of being registered. **2** a certificate, etc., that attests to the registering (of a person, vehicle, etc.).

reg·is·try /réjistree/ *n.* (*pl.* **-ies**) **1** a place or office where registers or records are kept. **2** registration.

reg·nant /régnənt/ *adj.* **1** reigning (*queen regnant*). **2** (of things, qualities, etc.) predominant, prevalent.

reg·o·lith /régəlith/ *n. Geol.* unconsolidated solid material covering the bedrock of a planet.

re·gorge /rigáwrj/ *v.* **1** *tr.* bring up or expel again after swallowing. **2** *intr.* gush or flow back from a pit, channel, etc.

re·grade /réegráyd/ *v.tr.* grade again or differently.

re·gress *v. & n.* ● *v.* /rigrés/ **1** *intr.* move backward, esp. (in abstract senses) return to a former state. **2** *intr. & tr. Psychol.* return or cause to return mentally to a former stage of life. ● *n.* /réegres/ **1** the act or an instance of going back. **2** reasoning from effect to cause.

re·gres·sion /rigréshən/ *n.* **1** a backward movement, esp. a return to a former state. **2** a relapse or reversion. **3** *Psychol.* a return to an earlier stage of development.

re·gres·sive /rigrésiv/ *adj.* **1** regressing; characterized by regression. **2** (of a tax) proportionally greater on lower incomes. □□ **re·gres·sive·ly** *adv.* **re·gres·sive·ness** *n.*

re·gret /rigrét/ *v. & n.* ● *v.tr.* (**regretted, regretting**) **1** (often foll. by *that* + clause) feel or express sorrow or repentance or distress over (an action or loss, etc.). **2** (often foll. by *to* + infin. or *that* + clause) acknowledge with sorrow or remorse (*I regret to say*). ● *n.* **1** a feeling of sorrow, repentance, etc., over an action or loss, etc. **2** (often in *pl.*) an (esp. polite or formal) expression of disappointment or sorrow at an occurrence, inability to comply, etc. □ **give** (or **send**) **one's regrets** formally decline an invitation.

re·gret·ful /rigrétfŏŏl/ *adj.* feeling or showing regret. □□ **re·gret·ful·ly** *adv.* **re·gret·ful·ness** *n.*

re·gret·ta·ble /rigrétəbəl/ *adj.* (of events or conduct) undesirable; unwelcome; deserving censure. □□ **re·gret·ta·bly** *adv.*

re·group /réegrŏŏp/ *v.tr. & intr.* group or arrange again or differently. □□ **re·group·ment** *n.*

re·grow /réegrṓ/ *v.intr. & tr.* (*past* **regrew**; *past part.* **regrown**) grow again, esp. after an interval. □□ **re·growth** *n.*

reg·u·la·ble /régyələbəl/ *adj.* able to be regulated.

reg·u·lar /régyələr/ *adj. & n.* ● *adj.* **1** conforming to a rule or principle; systematic. **2 a** harmonious; symmetrical (*regular features*). **b** (of a surface, line, etc.) smooth; level; uniform. **3** acting or done or recurring uniformly or calculably in time or manner. **4** conforming to a standard of etiquette or procedure. **5** properly constituted or qualified; pursuing an occupation as one's main pursuit (*has no regular profession*). **6** *Gram.* (of a noun, verb, etc.) following the normal type of inflection. **7** *colloq.* complete; thorough; absolute (*a regular hero*). **8** *Geom.* **a** (of a figure) having all sides and all angles equal. **b** (of a solid) bounded by a number of equal figures. **9** *Eccl.* (placed before or after noun) **a** bound by religious rule. **b** belonging to a religious or monastic order (*canon regular*). **10** relating to or constituting a permanent professional body (*regular soldiers*). **11** (of a person) defecating or menstruating at predictable times. **12** *colloq.* likable; normal; reliable (esp. as *regular guy*). ● *n.* **1** a regular soldier. **2** *colloq.* a regular customer, visitor, etc. **3** *Eccl.* one of the regular clergy. **4** *colloq.* a person permanently employed. □ **keep regular hours** do the same thing, esp. going to bed and getting up, at the same time each day. □□ **reg·u·lar·i·ty** /-láritee/ *n.* **reg·u·lar·ize** *v.tr.* **reg·u·lar·i·za·tion** *n.* **reg·u·lar·ly** *adv.*

reg·u·late /régyəlayt/ *v.tr.* **1** control by rule. **2** subject to restrictions. **3** adapt to requirements. **4** alter the speed of (a machine or clock) so that it

R

may work accurately. □□ **reg·u·la·tive** /-lətiv/ *adj.* **reg·u·la·to·ry** /-lətáwree/ *adj.*

reg·u·la·tion /régyəláyshən/ *n.* **1** the act or an instance of regulating; the process of being regulated. **2** a prescribed rule. **3** (*attrib.*) **a** in accordance with regulations; of the correct type, etc. (*the regulation tie*). **b** *colloq.* usual (*the regulation soup*).

reg·u·lus /régyələs/ *n.* (*pl.* **reguluses** or **reguli** /-lī/) *Chem. archaic* a metallic form of a substance obtained by smelting or reduction. □□ **reg·u·line** /-līn/ *adj.*

re·gur·gi·tate /rigárjitayt/ *v.tr.* **1** bring (swallowed food) up again to the mouth. **2** cast or pour out again (*regurgitate facts*). □□ **re·gur·gi·ta·tion** /-táyshən/ *n.*

re·hab /réehab/ *n. colloq.* rehabilitation.

re·ha·bil·i·tate /réehəbílitayt/ *v.tr.* **1** restore to effectiveness or normal life by training, etc., esp. after imprisonment or illness. **2** restore to former privileges or reputation or a proper condition. □□ **re·ha·bil·i·ta·tion** /-táyshən/ *n.* **re·ha·bil·i·ta·tive** *adj.*

re·hang /réeháng/ *v.tr.* (*past* and *past part.* **rehung**) hang (esp. a picture or a curtain) again or differently.

re·hash *v.* & *n.* ● *v.tr.* /réehásh/ put (old material) into a new form without significant change or improvement. ● *n.* /réehash/ the act or an instance of rehashing.

re·hear /réeheer/ *v.tr.* (*past* and *past part.* **reheard** /réehérd/) hear again.

re·hears·al /rihársəl/ *n.* **1** the act or an instance of rehearsing. **2** a trial performance or practice of a play, recital, etc.

re·hearse /rihárs/ *v.* **1** *tr.* practice (a play, recital, etc.) for later public performance. **2** *intr.* hold a rehearsal. **3** *tr.* train (a person) by rehearsal. **4** *tr.* recite or say over. **5** *tr.* give a list of; enumerate. □□ **re·hears·er** *n.*

re·heat *v.* & *n.* ● *v.tr.* /réehéet/ heat again. ● *n.* /réeheet/ the process of using the hot exhaust to burn extra fuel in a jet engine and produce extra power. □□ **re·heat·er** *n.*

re·heel /réehéel/ *v.tr.* fit (a shoe) with a new heel.

re·ho·bo·am /réehəbóəm/ *n.* a wine bottle of about six times the standard size.

re·house /réehówz/ *v.tr.* provide with new housing.

re·hung *past* and *past part.* of REHANG.

re·hy·drate /réehīdráyt/ *v.* **1** *intr.* absorb water again after dehydration. **2** *tr.* add water to (esp. food) again to restore to a palatable state. □□ **re·hy·drat·a·ble** *adj.* **re·hy·dra·tion** /-dráyshən/ *n.*

Reich /rīkh/ *n.* the former German state, esp. the Third Reich.

re·i·fy /réeifī/ *v.tr.* (**-ies**, **-ied**) make (an abstract thing) more concrete or real. □□ **re·i·fi·ca·tion** /-fikáyshən/ *n.*

reign /rayn/ *v.* & *n.* ● *v.intr.* **1** hold royal office; be king or queen. **2** have power or predominance; prevail (*confusion reigns*). **3** (as **reigning** *adj.*) (of a champion, etc.) currently holding the title, etc. ● *n.* **1** sovereignty, rule. **2** the period during which a sovereign rules.

re·ig·nite /réeignít/ *v.tr.* & *intr.* ignite again.

reign of ter·ror *n.* a period of remorseless repression or bloodshed, esp. a period of the French Revolution 1793–94.

rei·ki /ráyki/ *n.* a healing technique based on the principle that the therapist can channel energy into the patient by means of touch, to activate the natural healing processes of the patient's body.

re·im·burse /réeimbárs/ *v.tr.* **1** repay (a person who has expended money). **2** repay (a person's expenses). □□ **re·im·burs·a·ble** *adj.* **re·im·burse·ment** *n.*

re·im·port *v.* & *n.* ● *v.tr.* /réeimpáwrt/ import (goods processed from exported materials). ● *n.* /réeimpawrt/ **1** the act or an instance of reimporting. **2** a reimported item. □□ **re·im·por·ta·tion** *n.*

re·im·pose /réeimpóz/ *v.tr.* impose again, esp. after a lapse. □□ **re·im·po·si·tion** /-pəzishən/ *n.*

rein /rayn/ *n.* & *v.* ● *n.* (in *sing.* or *pl.*) **1** a long narrow strap with each end attached to the bit, used to guide or check a horse, etc. ▷ HARNESS, SHOW JUMPING. **2** a similar device used to restrain a young child. **3** (a means of) control. ● *v.tr.* **1** check or manage with reins. **2** (foll. by *up*, *back*) pull up or back with reins. **3** (foll. by *in*) hold in as with reins; restrain. **4** govern; restrain; control. □ **draw rein** **1** stop one's horse. **2** pull up. **3** abandon an effort.

give free rein to remove constraints from; allow full scope to. **keep a tight rein on** allow little freedom to.

re·in·car·na·tion /réeinkaarnáyshən/ *n.* (in some beliefs) the rebirth of a soul in a new body. □□ **re·in·car·nate** /-káarnayt/ *v.tr.* **re·in·car·nate** /-káarnət/ *adj.*

re·in·cor·po·rate /réeinkáwrpərayt/ *v.tr.* incorporate afresh. □□ **re·in·cor·po·ra·tion** /-ráyshən/ *n.*

rein·deer /ráyndeer/ *n.* (*pl.* same or **reindeers**) ◀ a subarctic deer, *Rangifer tarandus*, of which both sexes have large antlers, used domestically for drawing sleds. ▷ DEER

re·in·fect /réeinfékt/ *v.tr.* infect again. □□ **re·in·fec·tion** /réeinfékshən/ *n.*

re·in·force /réeinfáwrs/ *v.tr.* strengthen or support, esp. with additional personnel or material or by an increase of numbers or quantity or size, etc. □□ **re·in·forc·er** *n.*

re·in·forced con·crete *n.* ▼ concrete with metal bars or wire, etc., embedded to increase its tensile strength.

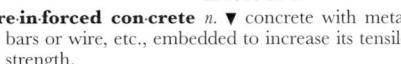

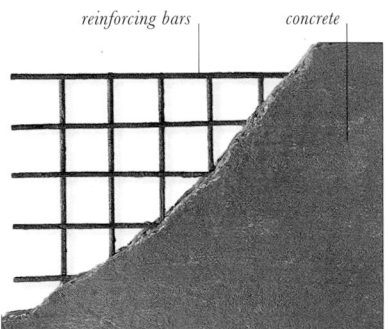

reinforcing bars　　　　concrete

REINFORCED CONCRETE

re·in·force·ment /réeinfáwrsmənt/ *n.* **1** the act or an instance of reinforcing; the process of being reinforced. **2** a thing that reinforces. **3** (in *pl.*) reinforcing personnel, etc.

re·in·sert /réeinsárt/ *v.tr.* insert again. □□ **re·in·ser·tion** /-sérshən/ *n.*

re·in·state /réeinstáyt/ *v.tr.* **1** replace in a former position. **2** restore (a person, etc.) to former privileges. □□ **re·in·state·ment** *n.*

re·in·sure /réeinshōór/ *v.tr.* & *intr.* insure again (esp. of an insurer securing the risk by transferring some or all of it to another insurer). □□ **re·in·sur·ance** *n.* **re·in·sur·er** *n.*

re·in·te·grate /rée-íntigrayt/ *v.tr.* **1** esp. *Brit.* = REDINTEGRATE. **2** integrate back into society. □□ **re·in·te·gra·tion** /-gráyshən/ *n.*

re·in·ter /réeintár/ *v.tr.* inter (a corpse) again. □□ **re·in·ter·ment** *n.*

re·in·ter·pret /réeintárprit/ *v.tr.* interpret again or differently. □□ **re·in·ter·pre·ta·tion** *n.*

re·in·tro·duce /réeintrədóos, -dyóos/ *v.tr.* introduce again. □□ **re·in·tro·duc·tion** /-dúkshən/ *n.*

re·in·vest /réeinvést/ *v.tr.* invest again (esp. money in other property, etc.). □□ **re·in·vest·ment** *n.*

re·in·vig·or·ate /réeinvígərayt/ *v.tr.* impart fresh vigor to. □□ **re·in·vig·or·a·tion** /-ráyshən/ *n.*

re·is·sue *v.* & *n.* ● *v.tr.* /rée-ishóo/ (**reissues**, **reissued**, **reissuing**) issue again or in a different form. ● *n.* /réeishoo/ a new issue, esp. of a previously published book.

REIT /reet/ *abbr.* real estate investment trust.

re·it·er·ate /rée-ítərayt/ *v.tr.* say or do again or repeatedly. □□ **re·it·er·a·tion** /-ráyshən/ *n.* **re·it·er·a·tive** /-raytiv, -rətiv/ *adj.*

reive /reev/ *v.intr.* esp. *Sc.* make raids; plunder. □□ **reiv·er** *n.*

re·ject *v.* & *n.* ● *v.tr.* /rijékt/ **1** put aside or send back as not to be used or done or complied with, etc. **2** refuse to accept or believe in. **3** rebuff or snub (a person). **4** (of a body or digestive system) cast up; vomit; evacuate. **5** *Med.* show an immune response to (a transplanted organ or tissue) so that it fails to survive. ● *n.* /réejekt/ a thing or person rejected as unfit or below standard. □□ **re·ject·a·ble** /rijéktəbəl/ *adj.* **re·ject·er** /rijéktər/ *n.* (also **re·jec·tor**). **re·jec·tion** /-jékshən/ *n.* **re·jec·tive** *adj.*

re·jig·ger /réejígər/ *v.tr.* rearrange or alter, esp. in an unethical way.

re·joice /rijóys/ *v.* **1** *intr.* feel great joy. **2** *intr.* (foll. by *that* + clause or *to* + infin.) be glad. **3** *intr.* (foll. by *in*, *at*) take delight. **4** *intr.* celebrate some event. **5** *tr.* cause joy to. □□ **re·joic·er** *n.* **re·joic·ing·ly** *adv.*

re·join[1] /réejóyn/ *v.* **1** *tr.* & *intr.* join together again; reunite. **2** *tr.* join (a companion, etc.) again.

re·join[2] /rijóyn/ *v.* **1** *tr.* say in answer; retort. **2** *intr.* *Law* reply to a charge or pleading in a lawsuit.

re·join·der /rijóyndər/ *n.* **1** what is said in reply. **2** a retort. **3** *Law* a reply by rejoining.

re·ju·ve·nate /rijóovinayt/ *v.tr.* make young or as if young again. □□ **re·ju·ve·na·tion** /-náyshən/ *n.* **re·ju·ve·na·tor** *n.*

re·ju·ve·nesce /rijóovinés/ *v.* **1** *intr.* become young again. **2** *Biol.* **a** *intr.* (of cells) gain fresh vitality. **b** impart fresh vitality to (cells). □□ **re·ju·ve·nes·cent** *adj.* **re·ju·ve·nes·cence** *n.*

re·kin·dle /réekind'l/ *v.tr.* & *intr.* kindle again.

-rel /rəl/ *suffix* with diminutive or derogatory force (*cockerel*; *scoundrel*).

rel. *abbr.* **1** relating. **2** relative. **3** released. **4** religion. **5** religious.

re·la·bel /réeláybəl/ *v.tr.* label (esp. a commodity) again or differently.

re·laid *past* and *past part.* of RELAY[2].

re·lapse /riláps/ *v.* & *n.* ● *v.intr.* (usu. foll. by *into*) fall back or sink again (into a worse state after an improvement). ● *n.* (also /réelaps/) the act or an instance of relapsing, esp. a deterioration in a patient's condition after a partial recovery. □□ **re·laps·er** *n.*

relapsing fever *n.* a bacterial infectious disease with recurrent periods of fever, caused by the bite of body lice or ticks infected with spirochaetes of the genus *Borrelia*.

re·late /riláyt/ *v.* **1** *tr.* narrate or recount (a story, etc.). **2** *tr.* (in *passive*; often foll. by *to*) be connected by blood or marriage. **3** *tr.* (usu. foll. by *to*, *with*) bring into relation (with one another); establish a connection between (*cannot relate your opinion to my own experience*). **4** *intr.* (foll. by *to*) have reference to; concern (*see only what relates to themselves*). **5** *intr.* (foll. by *to*) **a** bring oneself into relation to; **b** feel emotionally or sympathetically involved or connected; respond (*they relate well to one another*). □□ **re·lat·a·ble** *adj.*

re·lat·ed /riláytid/ *adj.* **1** connected by blood or marriage. **2** having (mutual) relation; associated; connected. □□ **re·lat·ed·ness** *n.*

REINDEER
(*Rangifer tarandus*)

R

RELATIVITY

According to Albert Einstein's general theory of relativity, astronomical bodies distort space-time, making it curve. This distortion creates gravitational fields: the larger the body and subsequent distortion, the greater the field produced. As other astronomical objects travel into the distortion, their paths are curved as the gravitational fields pull them in. Light is also curved in this way.

DEMONSTRATION OF THE DISTORTION OF SPACE-TIME

- path of passing comet
- Sun
- space-time distortion
- curved path of comet
- comet

re·lat·er /riláytər/ n. (also **re·la·tor**) a person who relates something, esp. a story; a narrator.

re·la·tion /riláyshən/ n. **1 a** what one person or thing has to do with another. **b** the way in which one person stands or is related to another. **c** the existence or effect of a connection, correspondence, contrast, or feeling prevailing between persons or things, esp. when qualified in some way (*bears no relation to the facts*). **2** a relative; a kinsman or kinswoman. **3** (in *pl.*) **a** (foll. by *with*) dealings (with others). **b** sexual intercourse. **4** = RELATIONSHIP. **5 a** narration (*his relation of the events*). **b** a narrative. **6** *Law* the laying of information. □ **in relation to** as regards.

re·la·tion·al /riláyshənəl/ adj. **1** of, belonging to, or characterized by relation. **2** having relation.

re·la·tion·ship /riláyshənship/ n. **1** the fact or state of being related. **2** *colloq.* a connection or association (*enjoyed a good working relationship*). **b** an emotional (esp. sexual) association between two people. **3** a condition or character due to being related. **4** kinship.

rel·a·tive /rélətiv/ adj. & n. ● adj. **1** considered or having significance in relation to something else (*relative velocity*). **2** (also foll. by *to*) existing or quantifiable only in terms of individual perception or consideration; not absolute nor independent (*truth is relative to your perspective; it's all relative, though, isn't it?*). **3** (foll. by *to*) proportioned to (something else) (*growth is relative to input*). **4** implying comparison or contextual relation ("*heat*" *is a relative word*). **5** compared one with another (*their relative advantages*). **6** having mutual relations; corresponding in some way; related to each other. **7** (foll. by *to*) having reference (*the facts relative to the issue*). **8** involving a different but corresponding idea (*the concepts of husband and wife are relative to each other*). **9** *Gram.* **a** (of a word, esp. a pronoun) referring to an expressed or implied antecedent and attaching a subordinate clause to it, e.g., *which*, *who*. **b** (of a clause) attached to an antecedent by a relative word. **10** *Mus.* (of major and minor keys) having the same key signature. **11** pertinent; relevant; related to the subject (*need more relative proof*). ● n. **1** a person connected by blood or marriage. **2** a species related to another by common origin. **3** *Gram.* a relative word, esp. a pronoun. □□ **rel·a·tiv·al** /-tívəl/ adj. (in sense 3 of n.). **rel·a·tive·ly** adv.

rel·a·tive hu·mid·i·ty n. the proportion of moisture to the value for saturation at the same temperature.

rel·a·tiv·ism /rélətivizəm/ n. the doctrine that knowledge is relative, not absolute. □□ **rel·a·tiv·ist** n.

rel·a·tiv·is·tic /rélətivístik/ adj. *Physics* (of phenomena, etc.) accurately described only by the theory of relativity. □□ **rel·a·tiv·is·ti·cal·ly** adv.

rel·a·tiv·i·ty /rélətívitee/ n. **1** the fact or state of being relative. **2** *Physics* **a** (**special theory of relativity** or **special relativity**) a theory based on the principle that all motion is relative and that light has constant velocity. **b** (**general theory of relativity** or **general relativity**) ▲ a theory extending this to gravitation and accelerated motion.

re·lax /riláks/ v. **1 a** *tr. & intr.* make or become less stiff or rigid. **b** *tr. & intr.* make or become loose or slack; diminish in force or tension (*relaxed my grip*). **c** *tr. & intr.* (also as *int.*) make or become less tense or anxious. **2** *tr. & intr.* make or become less formal or strict (*rules were relaxed*). **3** *tr.* reduce or abate (one's attention, efforts, etc.). **4** *intr.* cease work or effort. **5** *tr.* (as **relaxed** adj.) at ease; unperturbed.

re·lax·ant /riláksənt/ n. & adj. ● n. a drug, etc., that relaxes and reduces tension. ● adj. causing relaxation.

re·lax·a·tion /réelaksáyshən/ n. **1** the act of relaxing or state of being relaxed. **2** recreation. **3** a partial remission or relaxing of a penalty, duty, etc. **4** a lessening of severity, precision, etc.

re·lay[1] /réelay/ n. & v. ● n. **1** a fresh set of people or horses substituted for tired ones. **2** a gang of workers, supply of material, etc., deployed on the same basis (*operated in relays*). **3** = RELAY RACE. **4** a device activating changes in an electric circuit, etc., in response to other changes affecting itself. **5 a** a device to receive, reinforce, and transmit a message, broadcast, etc. **b** a relayed message or transmission. ● *v.tr.* (also /riláy/) **1** receive (a message, broadcast, etc.) and transmit it to others. **2 a** arrange in relays. **b** provide with or replace by relays.

re·lay[2] /réeláy/ *v.tr.* (*past* and *past part.* **relaid**) lay again or differently.

re·lay race n. a race between teams of which each member in turn covers part of the distance.

re·learn /réelórn/ *v.tr.* learn again.

re·lease /rilées/ v. & n. ● *v.tr.* **1** (often foll. by *from*) set free; liberate; unfasten. **2** allow to move from a fixed position. **3 a** make (information, a recording, etc.) publicly or generally available. **b** issue (a film, etc.) for general exhibition. **4** *Law* a remit (a debt). **b** surrender (a right). **c** make over (property or money) to another. ● n. **1** deliverance or liberation from a restriction, duty, or difficulty. **2** a handle or catch that releases part of a mechanism. **3** a document or item of information made available for publication (*press release*). **4 a** a film or record, etc., that is released. **b** the act or an instance of releasing or the process of being released in this way. **5** *Law* **a** the act of releasing (property, money, or a right) to another. **b** a document effecting this. □□ **re·leas·a·ble** adj. **re·leas·er** n. **re·leas·or** n. (in sense 4 of v.).

rel·e·gate /réligayt/ *v.tr.* **1** consign or dismiss to an inferior or less important position; demote. **2** transfer (a sports team) to a lower division of a league, etc. **3** banish. **4** (foll. by *to*) **a** transfer (a matter) for decision or implementation. **b** refer (a person) for information. □□ **rel·e·ga·tion** /-gáyshən/ n.

re·lent /rilént/ *v.intr.* **1** abandon a harsh intention. **2** yield to compassion. **3** relax one's severity; become less stern.

re·lent·less /riléntlis/ adj. **1** unrelenting. **2** oppressively constant. □□ **re·lent·less·ly** adv. **re·lent·less·ness** n.

rel·e·vant /rélivənt/ adj. (often foll. by *to*) bearing on or having reference to the matter in hand. □□ **rel·e·vance** n. **rel·e·van·cy** n. **rel·e·vant·ly** adv.

re·li·a·ble /rilíəbəl/ adj. **1** that may be relied on. **2** of sound and consistent character or quality. □□ **re·li·a·bil·i·ty** /-bílitee/ n. **re·li·a·bly** adv.

re·li·ance /rilíəns/ n. **1** (foll. by *in*, *on*) trust, confidence (*put full reliance in you*). **2** a thing relied upon. □□ **re·li·ant** adj.

rel·ic /rélik/ n. **1** an object interesting because of its age or association. **2** a part of a deceased holy person's body or belongings kept as an object of reverence. **3** a surviving custom or belief, etc., from a past age. **4** a memento or souvenir. **5** (in *pl.*) what has survived destruction or wasting or use. **6** (in *pl.*) the dead body or remains of a person.

rel·ict /rélikt/ n. **1** an object surviving in its primitive form. **2** an animal or plant known to have existed in the same form in previous geological ages.

re·lief /rilééf/ n. **1 a** the alleviation of or deliverance from pain, distress, anxiety, etc. **b** the feeling accompanying such deliverance. **2** a feature, etc., that diversifies monotony or relaxes tension. **3** assistance given to those in special need (*rent relief*). **4 a** the replacing of a person or persons on duty by another or others. **b** a person or persons replacing others in this way. **5 a** ▶ a method of molding or carving or stamping in which the design stands out from the surface, with projections proportioned and more (**high relief**) or less (**bas-relief** or **low relief**) closely approximating those of the objects depicted. ▷ PRINTING. **b** a piece of sculpture, etc., in relief. **c** a representation of relief given by an arrangement of line or color or shading. **6** vividness; distinctness (*brings the facts out in sharp relief*). **7** (foll. by *of*) the reinforcement (esp. the raising of a siege) of a place. **8** esp. *Law* the redress of a hardship or grievance.

RELIEF: ANCIENT GREEK BAS-RELIEF CARVING

re·lief map n. **1** ▶ a map indicating hills and valleys by shading, etc., rather than by contour lines alone. **2** a map model showing elevations and depressions, usu. on an exaggerated relative scale.

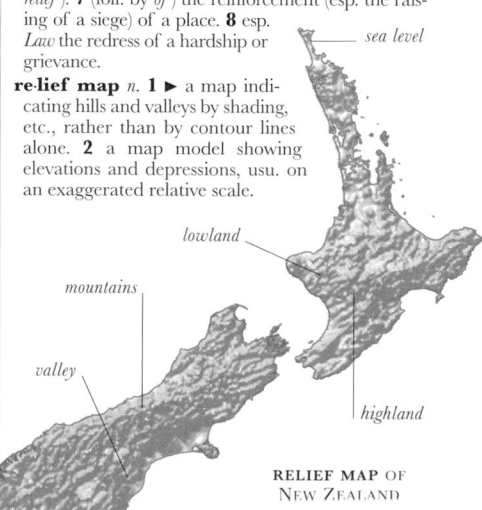

- sea level
- lowland
- mountains
- valley
- highland

RELIEF MAP OF NEW ZEALAND

R

re·lieve /rileév/ *v.tr.* **1** bring or provide aid or assistance to. **2** alleviate or reduce (pain, suffering, etc.). **3** mitigate the tedium or monotony of. **4** bring military support for (a besieged place). **5** release (a person) from a duty by acting as or providing a substitute. **6** (foll. by *of*) take (a burden or responsibility) away from (a person). **7** bring into relief; cause to appear solid or detached. □ **relieve oneself** urinate or defecate. □□ **re·liev·a·ble** *adj.* **re·liev·er** *n.*

re·lieved /rileévd/ *predic.adj.* freed from anxiety or distress (*am very relieved to hear it*). □□ **re·liev·ed·ly** *adv.*

re·lie·vo /rileévō/ *n.* (*pl.* **-os**) (also **ri·lie·vo** /reelyáyvō/ *n.* **-vi** /-vee/ /-vee/) = RELIEF 5.

re·light /réelít/ *v.tr.* (*past* and *past part.* **relighted** or **relit**) light (a fire, etc.) again.

re·li·gion /rilíjən/ *n.* **1** the belief in a superhuman controlling power, esp. in a personal God or gods entitled to obedience and worship. **2** the expression of this in worship. **3** a particular system of faith and worship. **4** life under monastic vows (*the way of religion*). **5** a thing that one is devoted to (*football is their religion*).

re·li·gion·ism /rilíjənizəm/ *n.* excessive religious zeal. □□ **re·li·gion·ist** *n.*

re·li·gi·ose /rilíjeeōs/ *adj.* excessively religious.

re·li·gi·os·i·ty /rilíjeeósitee/ *n.* the condition of being religious or religiose.

re·li·gious /rilíjəs/ *adj. & n.* ● *adj.* **1** devoted to religion; pious; devout. **2** of or concerned with religion. **3** of or belonging to a monastic order. **4** scrupulous; conscientious (*a religious attention to detail*). ● *n.* (*pl.* same) a person bound by monastic vows. □□ **re·li·gious·ly** *adv.* **re·li·gious·ness** *n.*

re·line /réelín/ *v.tr.* renew the lining of (a garment, etc.).

re·lin·quish /rilíngkwish/ *v.tr.* **1** surrender or resign (a right or possession). **2** give up or cease from (a habit, plan, belief, etc.). **3** relax hold of (an object held). □□ **re·lin·quish·ment** *n.*

rel·i·quar·y /rélikweree/ *n.* (*pl.* **-ies**) esp. *Relig.* ▶ a receptacle for relics.

re·liq·ui·ae /rilíkweeī, -ee/ *n.pl.* **1** remains. **2** *Geol.* fossil remains of animals or plants.

rel·ish /rélish/ *n. & v.* ● *n.* **1** (often foll. by *for*) **a** great liking or enjoyment. **b** keen or pleasurable longing (*had no relish for traveling*). **2 a** an appetizing flavor. **b** an attractive quality (*fishing loses its relish in winter*). **3** a condiment eaten with plainer food to add flavor. **4** (foll. by *of*) a distinctive taste or tinge. ● *v.tr.* **1 a** get pleasure out of; enjoy greatly. **b** anticipate with pleasure (*did not relish what lay before her*). **2** add relish to.

re·live /réelív/ *v.tr.* live (an experience, etc.) over again, esp. in the imagination.

re·load /réelṓd/ *v.tr.* (also *absol.*) load again.

re·lo·cate /reelṓkayt/ *v.* **1** *tr.* locate in a new place. **2** *tr. & intr.* move to a new place. □□ **re·lo·ca·tion** /-káyshən/ *n.*

re·luc·tant /rilúktənt/ *adj.* (often foll. by *to* + infin.) unwilling or disinclined (*most reluctant to agree*). □□ **re·luc·tance** *n.* **re·luc·tant·ly** *adv.*

re·ly /rilí/ *v.intr.* (**-ies**, **-ied**) (foll. by *on, upon*) **1** depend on with confidence or assurance (*am relying on your judgment*). **2** be dependent on (*relies on her for everything*).

REM /rem/ *abbr.* rapid eye movement.

rem /rem/ *n.* (*pl.* same) a unit of effective absorbed dose of ionizing radiation in human tissue.

re·made *past* and *past part.* of REMAKE.

re·main /rimáyn/ *v.intr.* **1 a** be left over after others or other parts have been removed or used or dealt with. **b** (of a period of time) be still to elapse.

2 be in the same place or condition during further time (*remained at home*). **3** continue to be (*remained calm*; *remains president*). **4** (as **remaining** *adj.*) left behind; not having been used or dealt with (*remaining supplies*).

re·main·der /rimáyndər/ *n. & v.* ● *n.* **1** a part remaining or left over. **2** remaining persons or things. **3** a number left after division or subtraction. **4** the copies of a book left unsold when demand has fallen. ● *v.tr.* dispose of (a remainder of books) at a reduced price.

re·mains /rimáynz/ *n.pl.* **1** what remains after other parts have been removed or used, etc. **2 a** traces of former animal or plant life (*fossil remains*). **b** relics of antiquity (*Roman remains*). **3** a person's body after death. **4** an author's (esp. unpublished) works left after death.

re·make *v. & n.* ● *v.tr.* /réemáyk/ (*past* and *past part.* **remade**) make again or differently. ● *n.* /réemayk/ a thing that has been remade, esp. a movie.

re·man /réemán/ *v.tr.* (**remanned**, **remanning**) **1** equip (troops, etc.) with new personnel. **2** make courageous again.

re·mand /rimánd/ *v. & n.* ● *v.tr.* **1** return (a prisoner) to custody, esp. to allow further inquiries. **2** return (a case) to a lower court for reconsideration. ● *n.* a recommittal to custody. □ **on remand** in custody pending trial.

rem·a·nent /rémənənt/ *adj.* **1** remaining; residual. **2** (of magnetism) remaining after the magnetizing field has been removed. □□ **rem·a·nence** *n.*

re·mark /rimaárk/ *v. & n.* ● *v.* **1** *tr.* (often foll. by *that* + clause) **a** say by way of comment. **b** take notice of; regard with attention. **2** *intr.* (usu. foll. by *on, upon*) make a comment. ● *n.* **1** a written or spoken comment; anything said. **2** the act of noticing or commenting (*worthy of remark*).

re·mark·a·ble /rimaárkəbəl/ *adj.* **1** worth notice; exceptional. **2** striking; conspicuous. □□ **re·mark·a·bly** *adv.*

re·mar·ry /réemáree/ *v.intr. & tr.* (**-ies**, **-ied**) marry again. □□ **re·mar·riage** *n.*

re·mas·ter /réemástər/ *v.tr.* make a new master of (a recording).

re·match /réemach/ *n.* a return match or game.

re·me·di·al /rimeédeeəl/ *adj.* **1** affording or intended as a remedy (*remedial therapy*). **2** (of teaching) for those in need of improvement in a particular discipline.

rem·e·dy /rémidee/ *n. & v.* ● *n.* (*pl.* **-ies**) (often foll. by *for, against*) **1** a medicine or treatment (for a disease, etc.). **2** a means of counteracting or removing anything undesirable. **3** redress; legal or other reparation. ● *v.tr.* (**-ies**, **-ied**) **1** rectify; make good. **2** heal; cure (a person, diseased part, etc.). □□ **re·me·di·a·ble** /rimeédeeəbəl/ *adj.*

re·mem·ber /rimémbər/ *v.tr.* **1** keep in the memory; not forget. **2 a** (also *absol.*) bring back into one's thoughts. **b** (often foll. by *to* + infin. or *that* + clause) have in mind (a duty, commitment, etc.) (*will you remember to lock the door?*). **3** think of or acknowledge (a person), esp. in making a gift, etc. **4** (foll. by *to*) convey greetings from (one person) to (another) (*remember me to your mother*). **5** mention (in prayer). □ **remember oneself** recover one's manners or intentions after a lapse.

re·mem·brance /rimémbrəns/ *n.* **1** the act of remembering or process of being remembered. **2** a memory or recollection. **3** a keepsake or souvenir. **4** (in *pl.*) greetings conveyed through a third person.

re·mex /réemeks/ *n.* (*pl.* **remiges** /rémijeez/) a primary or secondary feather in a bird's wing.

re·mind /rimínd/ *v.tr.* **1** (foll. by *of*) cause (a person) to think of. **2** (foll. by *to* + infin. or *that* + clause) cause (a person) to remember a commitment, etc.

re·mind·er /rimíndər/ *n.* **1 a** a thing that reminds, esp. a letter or bill. **b** a means of reminding; an aide-mémoire. **2** a memento or souvenir.

rem·i·nisce /réminís/ *v.intr.* (often foll. by *about*) indulge in reminiscence. □□ **rem·i·nis·cer** *n.*

rem·i·nis·cence /réminísəns/ *n.* **1** the act of remembering things past. **2 a** a past fact or experience that is remembered. **b** the process of narrating this. **3** (in *pl.*) a collection in literary form of incidents and experiences that a person remembers. **4** *Philos.* (esp. in Platonism) the theory of the recovery of things known to the soul in previous existences. **5** a characteristic of one thing reminding or suggestive of another.

rem·i·nis·cent /réminísənt/ *adj.* **1** (foll. by *of*) tending to remind one of or suggest. **2** concerned with reminiscence. **3** (of a person) given to reminiscing. □□ **rem·i·nis·cent·ly** *adv.*

re·mise /rimíz/ *v. & n. Fencing* ● *v.intr.* make a remise. ● *n.* a second thrust made after the first has failed.

re·miss /rimís/ *adj.* careless of duty; lax; negligent. □□ **re·miss·ness** *n.*

re·mis·si·ble /rimísibəl/ *adj.* that may be remitted.

re·mis·sion /rimíshən/ *n.* **1** (often foll. by *of*) forgiveness (of sins, etc.). **2** the remitting of a debt or penalty, etc. **3** a diminution of force, effect, or degree (esp. of disease or pain).

re·mit *v. & n.* ● *v.* /rimít/ (**remitted**, **remitting**) **1** *tr.* cancel or refrain from exacting or inflicting (a debt or punishment, etc.). **2** *intr. & tr.* abate or slacken; cease or cease from partly or entirely. **3** *tr.* send (money, etc.) in payment. **4** *tr.* cause to be conveyed by mail. **5** *tr.* **a** (foll. by *to*) refer (a matter for decision, etc.) to some authority. **b** *Law* send back (a case) to a lower court. **6** *tr.* **a** (often foll. by *to*) postpone or defer. **b** (foll. by *in, into*) send or put back into a previous state. **7** *tr. Theol.* pardon (sins, etc.). ● *n.* /réemit, rimít/ **1** the terms of reference of a committee, etc. **2** an item remitted for consideration. □□ **re·mit·ta·ble** /-mítəbəl/ *adj.*

re·mit·tance /rimít'ns/ *n.* **1** money sent, esp. by mail. **2** the act of sending money.

re·mit·tent /rimít'nt/ *adj.* (of a fever) that abates at intervals.

re·mix *v. & n.* ● *v.tr.* /réemíks/ mix again. ● *n.* /réemiks/ a sound recording that has been remixed.

rem·nant /rémnənt/ *n.* **1** a small remaining quantity. **2** a piece of cloth, etc., left when the greater part has been used or sold. **3** (foll. by *of*) a surviving trace (*a remnant of the empire*).

re·mod·el /réemód'l/ *v.tr.* **1** model again or differently. **2** reconstruct.

re·mold /réemṓld/ *v.tr.* **1** mold again; refashion. **2** reform the tread of (a tire).

re·mon·e·tize /réemónitīz, -mún-/ *v.tr.* restore a metal, etc.) to its former position as legal tender. □□ **re·mon·e·ti·za·tion** *n.*

re·mon·strance /rimónstrəns/ *n.* **1** the act or an instance of remonstrating. **2** an expostulation or protest.

re·mon·strate /rémonstrayt, rimón-/ *v.* **1** *intr.* (foll. by *with*) make a protest; argue forcibly (*remonstrated with them over the delays*). **2** *tr.* (often foll. by *that* + clause) urge protestingly. □□ **re·mon·stra·tion** /rémonstráyshən/ *n.*

re·mon·tant /rimóntənt/ *adj. & n.* ● *adj.* blooming more than once a year. ● *n.* a remontant rose.

re·mo·ra /rémərə/ *n.* a slender sea fish which attaches itself to large fish by means of a sucker on top of the head.

re·morse /rimáwrs/ *n.* **1** deep regret for a wrong committed. **2** compunction; a compassionate reluctance to inflict pain (esp. in *without remorse*).

re·morse·ful /rimáwrsfōol/ *adj.* filled with repentance. □□ **re·morse·ful·ly** *adv.*

re·morse·less /rimáwrslis/ *adj.* **1** without compassion or compunction. **2** relentless; unabating. □□ **re·morse·less·ly** *adv.* **re·morse·less·ness** *n.*

re·mort·gage /réemáwrgij/ *v. & n.* ● *v.tr.* (also

RELIQUARY: 12TH-CENTURY RELIQUARY CASKET

R

absol.) mortgage again; revise the terms of an existing mortgage on (a property). ● *n.* a different or altered mortgage.

re·mote /rimṓt/ *adj.* (**remoter, remotest**) **1** far away in place or time. **2** situated away from the main centers of population, society, etc. **3** distantly related (*a remote ancestor*). **4** slight; faint (esp. in *not the remotest chance, idea,* etc.). **5** (of a person) aloof; not friendly. **6** (foll. by *from*) widely different; separate by nature (*ideas remote from the subject*). □□ **re·mote·ly** *adv.* **re·mote·ness** *n.*

re·mote con·trol *n.* control of a machine or apparatus from a distance by means of signals transmitted from a radio or electronic device. □□ **re·mote-con·trolled** *adj.*

re·mount *v. & n.* ● *v.* /réemównt/ **1 a** *tr.* mount (a horse, etc.) again. **b** *intr.* get on horseback again. **2** *tr.* get on to or ascend (a ladder, hill, etc.) again. **3** *tr.* provide (a person) with a fresh horse, etc. **4** *tr.* put (a picture) on a fresh mount. ● *n.* /réemównt/ **1** a fresh horse for a rider. **2** a supply of fresh horses for a regiment.

re·mov·al /rimṓōvəl/ *n.* **1** the act or an instance of removing; the process of being removed. **2 a** dismissal from an office or post; deposition. **b** (an act of) murder.

re·move /rimṓōv/ *v. & n.* ● *v.* **1** *tr.* take off or away from the place or position occupied; detach (*remove the top carefully*). **2** *tr.* **a** move or take to another place; change the situation of (*will you remove the dishes?*). **b** get rid of; eliminate (*will remove all doubts*). **3** *tr.* cause to be no longer present or available; take away (*all privileges were removed*). **4** *tr.* (often foll. by *from*) dismiss (from office). **5** *tr. colloq.* kill; assassinate. **6** *tr.* (in *passive;* foll. by *from*) distant or remote in condition (*the country is not far removed from anarchy*). **7** *tr.* (as **removed** *adj.*) (esp. of cousins) separated by a specified number of steps of descent (*a first cousin twice removed* = a grandchild of a first cousin). **8** *formal* **a** *intr.* (usu. foll. by *from,* *to*) change one's home or place of residence. **b** *tr.* conduct the removal of. ● *n.* a stage in a gradation; a degree (*is several removes from what I expected*). □□ **re·mov·a·ble** *adj.* **re·mov·a·bil·i·ty** /mōōvəbílitee/ *n.* **re·mov·er** *n.* (esp. in sense 8b of *v.*).

re·mu·ner·ate /rimyōōnərayt/ *v.tr.* **1** reward; pay for services rendered. **2** serve as or provide recompense for (toil, etc.) or to (a person). □□ **re·mu·ner·a·tion** /-ráyshən/ *n.* **re·mu·ner·a·tive** /-rətiv, -raytiv/ *adj.*

Ren·ais·sance /rénəsáans, -záans, esp. *Brit.* rináysəns/ *n.* **1** ▲ the revival of art and literature in the 14th–16th c. **2** the period of this. **3** the culture and style of art, architecture, etc., developed during this era. **4** (**renaissance**) any similar revival.

re·nal /réenəl/ *adj.* of or concerning the kidneys.
▷ KIDNEY

re·name /réenáym/ *v.tr.* name again; give a new name to.

re·nas·cence /rinásəns, rináy-/ *n.* **1** rebirth; renewal. **2** = RENAISSANCE.

re·nas·cent /rinásənt, rináy-/ *adj.* springing up anew; being reborn.

ren·con·tre /renkóntər/ *n. archaic* = RENCOUNTER.

ren·coun·ter /renkówntər/ *n. & v.* ● *n.* **1** an encounter; a chance meeting. **2** a battle, skirmish, or duel. ● *v.tr.* encounter; meet by chance.

rend /rend/ *v.* (*past* and *past part.* **rent** /rent/) *archaic* or *rhet.* **1** *tr.* (foll. by *off, from, away,* etc.; also *absol.*) tear or wrench forcibly. **2** *tr. & intr.* divide in pieces or into factions (*a country rent by civil war*). **3** *tr.* cause emotional pain to (the heart, etc.). □ **rend the air** sound piercingly. **rend one's garments** (or **hair**) display extreme grief or rage.

ren·der /réndər/ *v.tr.* **1** cause to be or become (*rendered us helpless*). **2** give or pay (money, service, etc.), esp. in return or as a thing due (*render thanks; rendered good for evil*). **3** (often foll. by *to*) **a** give (assistance) (*rendered aid to the injured man*). **b** show

RENAISSANCE

The Renaissance saw an intellectual and artistic "rebirth" in Europe, built around an interest in naturalism and the revival of the art and literature of antiquity. Architects studied proportions and features of Roman buildings, while painters developed an interest in allegory, myth, history, and the technique of perspective.

The Birth of Venus (c.1486), SANDRO BOTTICELLI

PALAZZO STROZZI (1489), ITALY

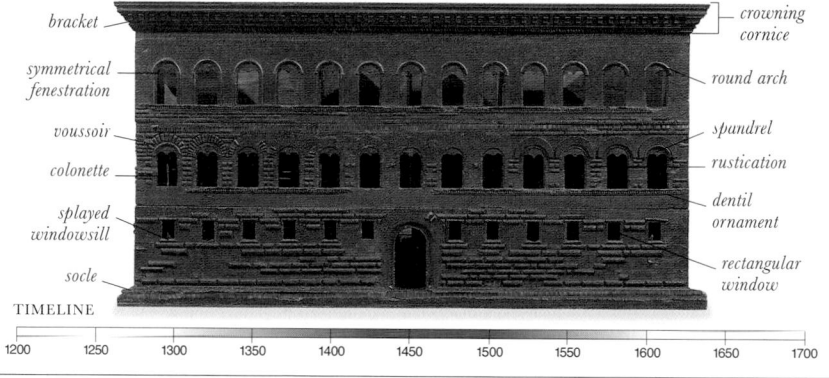

bracket — crowning cornice
symmetrical fenestration — round arch
voussoir — spandrel
colonette — rustication
splayed windowsill — dentil ornament
socle — rectangular window
TIMELINE

| 1200 | 1250 | 1300 | 1350 | 1400 | 1450 | 1500 | 1550 | 1600 | 1650 | 1700 |

(obedience, etc.). **c** do (a service, etc.). **4 a** submit; send in; present (an account, reason, etc.). **b** *Law* (of a judge or jury) deliver formally (a judgment or verdict). **5 a** represent or portray artistically, musically, etc. **b** act (a role); represent (a character, idea, etc.) (*the dramatist's conception was well rendered*). **c** *Mus.* perform; execute. **6** translate (*rendered the poem into French*). **7** (often foll. by *down*) melt down (fat, etc.) esp. to clarify; extract by melting. **8** cover (stone or brick) with a coat of plaster. **9** *archaic* give back; hand over; deliver; give up; surrender (*render unto Caesar the things that are Caesar's*). □□ **ren·der·er** *n.*

ren·der·ing /réndəring/ *n.* **1 a** the act or an instance of performing music, drama, etc.; an interpretation or performance (*an excellent rendering of the part*). **b** a translation. **2 a** the act or an instance of plastering stone, brick, etc. **b** this coating. **3** an act of giving, yielding, or surrendering.

ren·dez·vous /róndayvōō, -də-/ *n. & v.* ● *n.* (*pl.* same /-vōōz/) **1** an agreed or regular meeting place. **2** a meeting by arrangement. **3** a place appointed for assembling troops, ships, etc. ● *v.intr.* (**rendezvouses** /-vōōz/; **rendezvoused** /-vōōd/; **rendezvousing** /-vōōing/) meet at a rendezvous.

ren·di·tion /rendíshən/ *n.* (often foll. by *of*) **1** an interpretation or rendering of a dramatic role, piece of music, etc. **2** a visual representation.

ren·e·gade /rénigayd/ *n., adj., & v.* ● *n.* **1** a person who deserts a party or principles. **2** an apostate; a person who abandons one religion for another. ● *adj.* traitorous, heretical. ● *v.intr.* be a renegade.

re·nege /riníg, -nég, -néeg/ *v.* **1** *intr.* **a** go back on one's word; change one's mind; recant. **b** (foll. by *on*) go back on (a promise or undertaking or contract). **2** *tr.* deny; renounce; abandon (a person, faith, etc.). **3** *intr. Cards* revoke.

re·ne·go·ti·ate /réenigṓsheeayt/ *v.tr.* (also *absol.*) negotiate again or on different terms. □□ **re·ne·go·ti·a·ble** /-sheeəbəl, -shəbəl/ *adj.* **re·ne·go·ti·a·tion** /-sheeáyshən/ *n.*

re·new /rinṓō, -nyṓō/ *v.tr.* **1** revive; make new again; restore to the original state. **2** reinforce; resupply; replace. **3** repeat or reestablish; resume after an interruption (*renewed our acquaintance; a renewed attack*). **4** get, begin, make, say, give, etc., anew. **5** (also *absol.*) grant or be granted a continuation of (a license, subscription, lease, etc.). **6** recover (one's youth, strength, etc.). □□ **re·new·a·ble** *adj.* **re·new·al** *n.*

ren·i·form /rénifawrm, rée-/ *adj.* esp. *Med.* kidney-shaped.

ren·net /rénit/ *n.* **1** curdled milk found in the stomach of an unweaned calf, used in curdling milk for cheese, junket, etc. **2** a preparation made from the stomach membrane of a calf or from certain fungi, used for the same purpose.

ren·nin /rénin/ *n. Biochem.* an enzyme secreted into the stomach of unweaned mammals causing the clotting of milk.

re·nom·i·nate /réenóminayt/ *v.tr.* nominate for a further term of office. □□ **re·nom·i·na·tion** /-náyshən/ *n.*

re·nounce /rinówns/ *v.* **1** *tr.* consent formally to abandon (a claim, right, possession, etc.). **2** *tr.* repudiate; refuse to recognize any longer (*renouncing their father's authority*). **3** *tr.* **a** decline further association or disclaim relationship with (*renounced my former friends*). **b** withdraw from; discontinue; forsake. **4** *intr. Law* refuse or resign a right or position esp. as an heir or trustee. **5** *intr. Cards* follow with a card of another suit when having no card of the suit led (cf. REVOKE). □ **renounce the world** abandon society or material affairs. □□ **re·nounce·ment** *n.* **re·nounc·er** *n.*

ren·o·vate /rénəvayt/ *v.tr.* **1** restore to good condition; repair. **2** make new again. □□ **ren·o·va·tion** /-váyshən/ *n.* **ren·o·va·tor** *n.*

re·nown /rinówn/ *n.* fame; high distinction (*a city of great renown*).

re·nowned /rinównd/ *adj.* famous; celebrated.

rent[1] /rent/ *n. & v.* ● *n.* **1** a tenant's periodical payment to an owner for the use of land or premises. **2** payment for the use of a service, equipment, etc. ● *v.* **1** *tr.* (often foll. by *from*) take, occupy, or use at a rent (*rented a boat from the marina*). **2** *tr.* (often foll. by *out*) let or hire (a thing) for rent. **3** *intr.* (foll. by *for, at*) be let or hired out at a specified rate (*the room rents for $300 per month*). □ **for rent** available to be rented.

rent[2] /rent/ *n.* **1** a large tear in a garment, etc. **2** an opening in clouds, etc. **3** a cleft, fissure, or gorge.

rent[3] *past* and *past part.* of REND.

rent-a- *comb. form* often *joc.* denoting availability for hire (*rent-a-car*).

rent·a·ble /réntəbəl/ *adj.* **1** available or suitable for renting. **2** giving an adequate ratio of profit to capital. □□ **rent·a·bil·i·ty** /-bílitee/ *n.*

rent·al /rént'l/ *n.* **1** the amount paid or received as rent. **2** the act of renting. **3** an income from rents. **4** a rented house, etc.

rent·er /réntər/ *n.* a person who rents.

re·num·ber /réenúmbər/ *v.tr.* change the number or numbers given.

re·nun·ci·a·tion /rinúnseeáyshən/ *n.* **1** the act or an instance of renouncing. **2** self-denial. **3** a document expressing renunciation. □□ **re·nun·ci·ant** /rinúnseeənt/ *n. & adj.* **re·nun·ci·a·to·ry** /-seeə-táwree, -shətáwree/ *adj.*

re·oc·cu·py /réé-ókyəpī/ *v.tr.* (**-ies, -ied**) occupy again. □□ **re·oc·cu·pa·tion** /-páyshən/ *n.*

re·oc·cur /réé-ókúr/ *v.intr.* (**reoccurred, reoccurring**) occur again or habitually. □□ **re·oc·cur·rence** /-kúrəns/ *n.*

re·o·pen /rée-ópən/ *v.tr. & intr.* open again.

re·or·der /rée-áwrdər/ *v. & n.* ● *v.tr.* order again. ● *n.* a renewed or repeated order for goods.

re·or·gan·ize /rée-áwrgənīz/ *v.tr.* organize differently. □□ **re·or·gan·i·za·tion** /-záyshən/ *n.*

re·or·i·ent /rée-áwree-ent, -óree-ent/ *v.tr.* **1** give a new direction to (ideas, etc.); redirect (a thing). **2** help (a person) find his or her bearings again. **3** change the outlook of (a person). **4** (*refl.,* often foll. by *to*) adjust oneself to or come to terms with something.

re·or·i·en·tate /rée-áwreeəntayt, -óreeən-/ *v.tr.* = REORIENT. □□ **re·or·i·en·ta·tion** /-táyshən/ *n.*

Rep. *abbr.* **1** Representative (in Congress, state legislature, etc.). **2** Republican. **3** Republic.

rep[1] /rep/ *n. colloq.* a representative, esp. a salesperson.

rep[2] /rep/ *n. colloq.* **1** repertory. **2** a repertory theater or company.

rep[3] /rep/ *n.* (also **repp**) a textile fabric with a corded surface, used in curtains and upholstery.

re·pack /réepák/ *v.tr.* pack again.

re·pack·age /réepákij/ *v.tr.* **1** package again or differently. **2** present in a new form. □□ **re·pack·ag·ing** *n.*

re·pag·i·nate /réepájinayt/ *v.tr.* paginate again; renumber the pages of.

re·paid *past* and *past part.* of REPAY.

re·paint *v. & n.* ● *v.tr.* /réepáynt/ **1** paint again or differently. **2** restore the paint or coloring of. ● *n.* /réepaynt/ the act of repainting.

re·pair[1] /ripáir/ *v. & n.* ● *v.tr.* **1** restore to good condition after damage or wear. **2** renovate or mend by replacing or fixing parts or by compensating for loss or exhaustion. **3** set right or make amends for (loss, wrong, error, etc.). ● *n.* **1** the act or an instance of restoring to sound condition (*in need of repair; closed during repair*). **2** the result of this (*the repair is hardly visible*). **3** good or relative condition for working or using (*must be kept in repair; in good repair*). □□ **re·pair·a·ble** *adj.* **re·pair·er** *n.*

re·pair[2] /ripáir/ *v.intr.* (foll. by *to*) resort; have recourse; go often or in great numbers to or for a specific purpose (*repaired to Spain*).

re·pair·man /ripáirmən/ *n.* (*pl.* **-men**) a person who repairs machinery, etc.

re·pand /ripánd/ *adj. Bot.* with an undulating margin; wavy.

re·pap·er /réepáypər/ *v.tr.* paper (a wall, etc.) again.

rep·a·ra·ble /répərəbəl, ripáirəbəl/ *adj.* (of a loss, etc.) that can be made good.

rep·a·ra·tion /répəráyshən/ *n.* **1** the act or an instance of making amends. **2 a** compensation. **b** (esp. in *pl.*) compensation for war damage paid by the defeated nation, etc. **3** the act or an instance of repairing or being repaired.

rep·ar·tee /répaartée, -táy/ *n.* **1** the practice or faculty of making witty retorts. **2 a** a witty retort. **b** witty retorts collectively.

re·pass /réepás/ *v.tr. & intr.* pass again, esp. on the way back.

re·past /ripást/ *n.* **1** a meal, esp. of a specified kind (*a light repast*). **2** food and drink supplied for or eaten at a meal.

re·pa·tri·ate /réepáytreeayt/ *v. & n.* ● *v.* **1** *tr.* restore (a person) to his or her native land. **2** *intr.* return to one's own native land. ● *n.* a person who has been repatriated. □□ **re·pa·tri·a·tion** /-áyshən/ *n.*

re·pay /réepáy/ *v.* (*past* and *past part.* **repaid**) **1** *tr.* pay back (money). **2** *tr.* return (a blow, visit, etc.). **3** *tr.* make repayment to (a person). **4** *tr.* requite (a service, action, etc.) (*must repay their kindness; the book repays close study*). **6** *intr.* make repayment. □□ **re·pay·a·ble** *adj.* **re·pay·ment** *n.*

re·peal /ripéel/ *v. & n.* ● *v.tr.* revoke or annul (a law, act of Congress, etc.). ● *n.* the act or an instance of repealing.

re·peat /ripéet/ *v. & n.* ● *v.* **1** *tr.* say or do over again. **2** *tr.* recite, rehearse, report, or reproduce (something from memory) (*repeated a poem*). **3** *tr.* imitate (an action, etc.). **4 a** *intr.* recur; appear again (*a repeating pattern*). **b** *refl.* recur in the same or a similar form (*history repeats itself*). **5** *tr.* used for emphasis (*I am not, repeat not, going*). **6** *intr.* (of food) be tasted intermittently for some time after being swallowed as a result of belching or indigestion. **7** *intr.* (of a watch, etc.) strike the last quarter, etc., over again when required. **8** *intr.* (of a firearm) fire several shots without reloading. **9** *intr.* illegally vote more than once in an election. ● *n.* **1 a** the act or an instance of repeating. **b** a thing repeated (often *attrib.: repeat performance*). **2 a** repeated broadcast. **3** *Mus.* **a** a passage intended to be repeated. **b** a mark indicating this. **4** a pattern repeated in wallpaper, etc. **5** *Commerce* **a** a consignment similar to a previous one. **b** an order given for this; a reorder. □ **repeat oneself** say or do the same thing over again. □□ **re·peat·a·ble** *adj.* **re·peat·a·bil·i·ty** /-péetəbílitee/ *n.* **re·peat·ed·ly** *adv.*

re·peat·er /ripéetər/ *n.* **1** a person or thing that repeats. **2** a firearm that fires several shots without reloading. **3** a watch or clock that repeats its last strike when required. **4** a device for the automatic retransmission or amplification of an electrically transmitted message. **5** a signal lamp indicating the state of another that is invisible.

re·peat·ing dec·i·mal *n.* a decimal fraction in which the same figures repeat indefinitely.

re·pêch·age /répishaa*zh*/ *n.* (in rowing, etc.) an extra contest in which the runners-up in the eliminating heats compete for a place in the final.

re·pel /ripél/ *v.tr.* (**repelled, repelling**) **1** drive back; ward off; repulse. **2** refuse admission or approach or acceptance to (*repel an assailant*). **3** be repulsive or distasteful to. **4** resist mixing with or admitting (*oil repels water*). **5** (often *absol.*) ▶ (of a magnetic pole) push away from itself (*like poles repel*). □□ **re·pel·ler** *n.*

re·pel·lent /ripélənt/ *adj. & n.* ● *adj.* **1** that which repels. **2** disgusting; repulsive. ● *n.* a substance that repels esp. insects, etc. □□ **re·pel·lence** *n.* **re·pel·len·cy** *n.* **re·pel·lent·ly** *adv.*

re·pent[1] /ripént/ *v.* **1** *intr.* (often foll. by *of*) feel deep sorrow about one's actions, etc.; regret (one's wrong, omission, etc.); resolve not to continue (a wrongdoing, etc.). □□ **re·pent·ance** *n.* **re·pent·ant** *adj.* **re·pent·er** *n.*

re·pent[2] /réepent/ *adj. Bot.* creeping, esp. growing along the ground or just under the surface.

re·peo·ple /réepéepəl/ *v.tr.* people again; increase the population of.

re·per·cus·sion /réepərkúshən, répər-/ *n.* **1** (often foll. by *of*) an indirect effect or reaction following an event or action (*consider the repercussions of moving*). **2** the recoil after impact. **3** an echo.

rep·er·toire /répərtwaar/ *n.* **1** a stock of pieces, etc., that a company or a performer knows or is prepared to give. **2** a stock of regularly performed pieces, regularly used techniques, etc. (*went through his repertoire of excuses*).

rep·er·to·ry /répərtawree/ *n.* (*pl.* **-ies**) **1** = REPERTOIRE. **2** the theatrical performance of various plays for short periods by one company. **3 a** a repertory company. **b** repertory theaters regarded collectively. **4** a store or collection, esp. of information, instances, etc.

rep·e·tend /répitend/ *n.* **1** the recurring figures of a decimal. **2** the recurring word or phrase; a refrain.

ré·pé·ti·teur /répeetitőr/ *n.* **1** a tutor or coach of musicians, esp. opera singers. **2** a person who supervises ballet rehearsals, etc.

rep·e·ti·tion /répitíshən/ *n.* **1 a** the act or an instance of repeating or being repeated. **b** the thing repeated. **2** a copy. **3** a piece to be learned by heart. **4** the ability of a musical instrument to repeat a note quickly.

rep·e·ti·tious /répitíshəs/ *adj.* characterized by repetition, esp. when unnecessary or tiresome. □□ **rep·e·ti·tious·ly** *adv.* **rep·e·ti·tious·ness** *n.*

rep·e·ti·tive /ripétitiv/ *adj.* characterized by, or consisting of, repetition; monotonous. □□ **re·pet·i·tive·ly** *adv.* **re·pet·i·tive·ness** *n.*

rep·e·ti·tive strain in·ju·ry *n.* (*pl.* **-ies**) injury arising from the continued repeated use of particular muscles.

re·phrase /réefráyz/ *v.tr.* express in an alternative way.

re·pine /ripín/ *v.intr.* (often foll. by *at, against, for*) fret; be discontented.

re·pique /ripéek/ *n. & v.* ● *n.* (in piquet) the winning of 30 points on cards alone before beginning to play. ● *v.* (**repiques, repiqued, repiquing**) **1** *intr.* score repique. **2** *tr.* score repique against (another person).

re·place /ripláys/ *v.tr.* **1** put back in place. **2** take the place of; be substituted for. **3** find or provide a substitute for. **4** (often foll. by *with, by*) fill up the place of. **5** (in *passive,* often foll. by *by*) be succeeded or have one's place filled by another; be superseded. □□ **re·place·a·ble** *adj.* **re·plac·er** *n.*

re·place·ment /ripláysmənt/ *n.* **1** the act or an instance of replacing or being replaced. **2** a person or thing that takes the place of another.

re·plan /réeplán/ *v.tr.* (**replanned, replanning**) plan again or differently.

re·plant /réeplánt/ *v.tr.* **1** transfer (a plant, etc.) to a larger pot, a new site, etc. **2** plant (ground) again; provide with new plants.

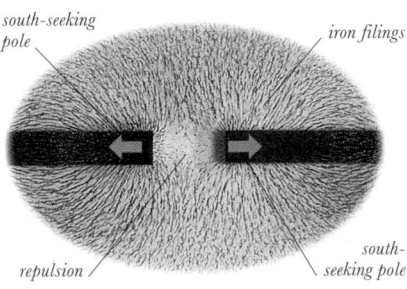

REPEL: DEMONSTRATION OF REPULSION BETWEEN MAGNETIC POLES

south-seeking pole   *iron filings*   *repulsion*   *south-seeking pole*

re·play *v.* & *n.* ● *v.tr.* /réepláy/ play (a match, recording, etc.) again. ● *n.* /réeplay/ the act or an instance of replaying a match, a recording, or a recorded incident in a game, etc.

re·plen·ish /riplénish/ *v.tr.* **1** (often foll. by *with*) fill up again. **2** renew (a supply, etc.). □□ **re·plen·ish·ment** *n.*

re·plete /ripléet/ *adj.* (often foll. by *with*) **1** filled or well-supplied. **2** gorged; sated. □□ **re·ple·tion** *n.*

re·plev·in /riplévən/ *n. Law* **1** the provisional restoration or recovery of distrained goods pending the outcome of trial and judgment. **2** a writ granting this. **3** the action arising from this process.

re·plev·y /riplévee/ *v.tr.* (**-ies, -ied**) *Law* recover by replevin.

rep·li·ca /réplikə/ *n.* **1** a duplicate of a work made by the original artist. **2 a** ◄ a facsimile; an exact copy. **b** (of a person) an exact likeness; a double. **3** a copy or model, esp. on a smaller scale.

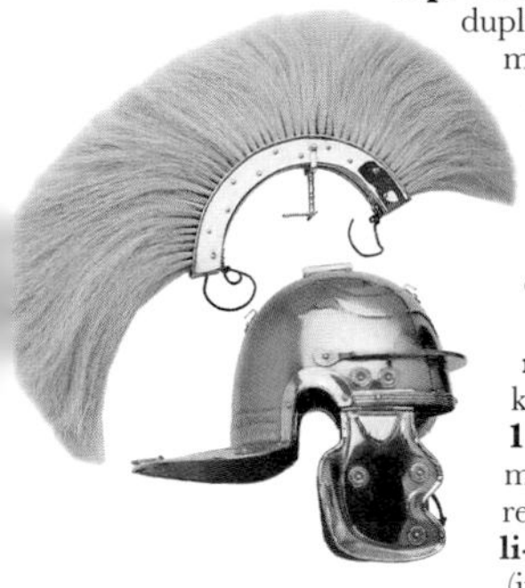

REPLICA OF AN ANCIENT ROMAN HELMET

rep·li·cate /réplikayt/ *v.* & *adj.* ● *v.tr.* **1** repeat (an experiment, etc.). **2** make a replica of. □□ **rep·li·ca·ble** /-kəbəl/ *adj.* (in sense 1). **rep·li·ca·bil·i·ty** /-bílitee/ *n.* (in sense 1). **rep·li·ca·tive** /-kətiv/ *adj.*

rep·li·ca·tion /réplikáyshən/ *n.* **1** a reply or response, esp. a reply to an answer. **2** *Law* the plaintiff's reply to the defendant's plea. **3 a** the act or an instance of copying. **b** a copy. **c** the process by which genetic material or a living organism gives rise to a copy of itself.

re·ply /riplí/ *v.* & *n.* ● *v.* (**-ies, -ied**) **1** *intr.* (often foll. by *to*) make an answer; respond in word or action. **2** *tr.* say in answer (*he replied, "Suit yourself"*). ● *n.* (*pl.* **-ies**) **1** the act of replying (*what did they say in reply?*). **2** what is replied; a response. **3** *Law* = REPLICATION.

re·ply-paid *adj.* (of an envelope, etc.) for which the addressee undertakes to pay postage.

re·po /réepō/ *N. Amer. colloq. n.* & *v.* ● *n.* a car or other item which has been repossessed. ● *v.tr.* (**repo's, repo'd**) repossess.

re·pop·u·late /reepópyəlayt/ *v.tr.* populate again or increase the population of. □□ **re·pop·u·la·tion** /-láyshən/ *n.*

re·port /ripáwrt/ *v.* & *n.* ● *v.* **1** *tr.* **a** bring back or give an account of. **b** state as fact or news; narrate or describe or repeat, esp. as an eyewitness or hearer, etc. **c** relate as spoken by another. **2** *tr.* make an official or formal statement about. **3** *tr.* (often foll. by *to*) name or specify (an offender or offense) (*will report you for insubordination*; *reported them to the police*). **4** *intr.* (often foll. by *to*) present oneself as having returned or arrived (*report to the manager on arrival*). **5** *tr.* (also *absol.*) take down word for word or summarize or write a description of for publication. **6** *intr.* make or draw up or send in a report. **7** *intr.* (often foll. by *to*) be responsible to (a superior, supervisor, etc.) (*reports directly to the managing director*). **8** *tr.* (often foll. by *out*) (of a committee, etc.) send back (a bill, etc.), with comments and recommendations, to a legislature, etc. **9** *intr.* (often foll. by *of*) give a report to convey that one is well, badly, etc., impressed (*reports well of the prospects*). **10** *intr.* (usu. foll. by *on*) investigate or scrutinize for a journalistic report; act as a reporter. ● *n.* **1** an account given or opinion formally expressed after investigation or consideration. **2** a description, summary, or reproduction of an event, speech or legal case, esp. for newspaper publication or broadcast. **3** common talk; rumor. **4** the way a person or thing is spoken of (*I hear a good report of you*). **5** a periodical statement on (esp. a student's) work, conduct, etc. **6** the sound of an explosion. □ **report back** deliver a report to the person, organization, etc., for whom one acts, etc. □□ **re·port·a·ble** *adj.* **re·port·ed·ly** *adv.*

re·port·age /ripáwrtij, répawrtáazh/ *n.* **1** the describing of events, esp. the reporting of news, etc., for the press and for broadcasting. **2** the typical style of this. **3** factual presentation in a book, etc.

re·port card *n.* an official report issued by a school showing a student's grades, progress, etc.

re·port·ed speech *n.* the speaker's words with the changes of person, tense, etc., usually in reports, e.g., *he said that he would go.*

re·port·er /ripáwrtər/ *n.* **1** a person employed to report news, etc., for newspapers or broadcasts. **2** a person who reports.

rep·or·to·ri·al /répawrtáwreeəl/ *adj.* **1** of newspaper reporters. **2** relating to or characteristic of a report. □□ **re·por·to·ri·al·ly** *adv.*

re·pose[1] /ripṓz/ *n.* & *v.* ● *n.* **1** the cessation of activity or excitement or toil. **2** sleep. **3** a peaceful or quiescent state; stillness; tranquillity. **4** *Art* a restful effect; harmonious combination. **5** composure or ease of manner. ● *v.* **1** *intr.* & *refl.* lie down in rest (*reposed on a sofa*). **2** *tr.* (often foll. by *on*) lay (one's head, etc.) to rest. **3** *intr.* (often foll. by *in, on*) lie, be lying or laid, esp. in sleep or death. **4** *tr.* give rest to; refresh with rest. **5** *intr.* (foll. by *on*) (of memory, etc.) dwell on. □□ **re·pose·ful** *adj.* **re·pose·ful·ly** *adv.*

re·pose[2] /ripṓz/ *v.tr.* (foll. by *in*) place (trust, etc.) in.

re·po·si·tion /réepəzíshən/ *v.* **1** *tr.* move or place in a different position. **2** *intr.* alter one's position.

re·pos·i·to·ry /ripózitawree/ *n.* (*pl.* **-ies**) **1** a place where things are stored or may be found, esp. a warehouse or museum. **2** a receptacle. **3** (often foll. by *of*) **a** a book, person, etc., regarded as a store of information, etc. **b** the recipient of confidences or secrets.

re·pos·sess /réepəzés/ *v.tr.* regain possession of (esp. property or goods on which repayment of a debt is in arrears). □□ **re·pos·ses·sion** *n.*

re·pot /réepót/ *v.tr.* (**repotted, repotting**) put (a plant) in another pot.

re·pous·sé /rəpōōsáy/ *adj.* & *n.* ● *adj.* hammered into relief from the reverse side. ● *n.* ornamental metalwork fashioned in this way.

repp var. of REP[3].

repped /rept/ *adj.* having a surface like rep.

rep·re·hend /réprihénd/ *v.tr.* rebuke; find fault with. □□ **rep·re·hen·sion** *n.*

rep·re·hen·si·ble /réprihénsibəl/ *adj.* deserving censure or rebuke; blameworthy. □□ **rep·re·hen·si·bil·i·ty** *n.* **rep·re·hen·si·bly** *adv.*

rep·re·sent /réprizént/ *v.tr.* **1** stand for or correspond to (*the comment does not represent all our views*). **2** (often in *passive*) be a specimen or example of (*all types of people were represented in the audience*). **3** act as an embodiment of; symbolize (*the eagle represents the United States*; *numbers are represented by letters*). **4** place a likeness of before the mind or senses. **5** serve or be meant as a likeness of. **6 a** state by way of expostulation or persuasion (*represented the rashness of it*). **b** (foll. by *to*) try to bring (the facts influencing conduct) home to (*represented the risks to his client*). **7 a** (often foll. by *as, to be*) describe or depict as; declare or make out (*represented them as martyrs*; *not what you represent it to be*). **b** (often *refl.*; usu. foll by *as*) portray; assume the guise of; pose as (*represents himself as an honest broker*). **8** (foll. by *that* + clause) allege. **9** show, or play the part of, on stage. **10** be a substitute or deputy for; be entitled to act or speak for (*the president was represented by the secretary of state*). **11** be elected as a member of Congress, a legislature, etc., by (*represents a rural constituency*). □□ **rep·re·sent·a·ble** *adj.*

rep·re·sen·ta·tion /réprizentáyshən/ *n.* **1** the act or an instance of representing or being represented. **2** a thing (esp. a painting, etc.) that represents another. **3** (esp. in *pl.*) a statement made by way of allegation or to convey opinion. □□ **rep·re·sen·ta·tion·al** /-shənəl/ *adj.*

rep·re·sen·ta·tion·ism /réprizentáyshənizəm/ *n.* the doctrine that perceived objects are only a representation of real external objects. □□ **rep·re·sen·ta·tion·ist** *n.*

rep·re·sen·ta·tive /réprizéntətiv/ *adj.* & *n.* ● *adj.* **1** typical of a class. **2** containing typical specimens of all or many classes (*a representative sample*). **3 a** consisting of elected deputies, etc. **b** based on representation by such deputies (*representative government*). **4** (foll. by *of*) serving as a portrayal or symbol of (*representative of their attitude to work*). **5** that presents or can present ideas to the mind (*imagination is a representative faculty*). ● *n.* **1** (foll. by *of*) a sample, specimen, or typical embodiment of. **2 a** the agent of a person or society. **b** a salesperson. **3** a delegate; a substitute. **4** a deputy in a representative assembly. □□ **rep·re·sen·ta·tive·ly** *adv.* **rep·re·sen·ta·tive·ness** *n.*

re·press /riprés/ *v.tr.* **1 a** keep under; quell. **b** suppress; prevent from sounding, rioting, or bursting out. **2** *Psychol.* actively exclude (an unwelcome thought) from conscious awareness. **3** (usu. as **repressed** *adj.*) subject (a person) to the suppression of his or her thoughts or impulses. □□ **re·press·i·ble** *adj.* **re·pres·sion** /-préshən/ *n.* **re·pres·sive** *adj.* **re·pres·sive·ly** *adv.* **re·pres·sive·ness** *n.* **re·pres·sor** *n.*

re·prieve /ripréev/ *v.* & *n.* ● *v.tr.* **1** remit, commute, or postpone the execution of (a condemned person). **2** give respite to. ● *n.* **1 a** the act or an instance of reprieving or being reprieved. **b** a warrant for this. **2** respite; a respite or temporary escape.

rep·ri·mand /réprimand/ *n.* & *v.* ● *n.* (often foll. by *for*) an official or sharp rebuke. ● *v.tr.* administer this to.

re·print *v.* & *n.* ● *v.tr.* /réeprínt/ print again. ● *n.* /réeprint/ **1** the act or an instance of reprinting a book, etc. **2** the book, etc., reprinted. **3** the quantity reprinted.

re·pris·al /riprízəl/ *n.* (an act of) retaliation.

re·prise /ripréez/ *n.* **1** a repeated passage in music. **2** a repeated item in a musical program.

re·pro /réeprō/ *n.* (*pl.* **-os**) (often *attrib.*) **1** a reproduction or copy. **2** (also **reproduction proof**) a proof, usu. on glossy paper, that can be used as photographic copy for a printing plate.

re·proach /riprṓch/ *v.* & *n.* ● *v.tr.* **1** express disapproval to (a person) for a fault, etc. **2** scold; rebuke; censure. ● *n.* **1** a rebuke or censure (*heaped reproaches on them*). **2** (often foll. by *to*) a thing that brings disgrace or discredit (*their behavior is a reproach to us all*). **3** a disgraced or discredited state (*live in reproach and ignominy*). □ **above** (or **beyond**) **reproach** perfect.

re·proach·ful /riprṓchfōōl/ *adj.* full of or expressing reproach. □□ **re·proach·ful·ly** *adv.*

rep·ro·bate /réprəbayt/ *n.*, *adj.*, & *v.* ● *n.* **1** an unprincipled person; a person of highly immoral character. **2** a person who is condemned by God. ● *adj.* **1** immoral. **2** hardened in sin. ● *v.tr.* **1** express or feel disapproval of; censure. **2** (of God) condemn; exclude from salvation. □□ **rep·ro·ba·tion** /-báyshən/ *n.*

re·pro·cess /réepróses, -prṓ-/ *v.tr.* process again or differently.

re·pro·duce /réeprədóōs, -dyóōs/ *v.* **1** *tr.* produce a copy or representation of. **2** *tr.* cause to be seen or heard, etc., again (*tried to reproduce the sound exactly*). **3** *intr.* produce further members of the same species by natural means. **4** *refl.* produce offspring (*reproduced itself several times*). **5** *intr.* give a specified quality or result when copied (*reproduces badly in black and white*). □□ **re·pro·duc·er** *n.* **re·pro·duc·i·ble** *adj.* **re·pro·duc·i·bil·i·ty** /-əbílitee/ *n.* **re·pro·duc·i·bly** *adv.*

re·pro·duc·tion /réeprədúkshən/ *n.* **1** the act or an instance of reproducing. **2** a copy of a work of art. **3** (*attrib.*) (of furniture, etc.) made in imitation of a certain style or of an earlier period. □□ **re·pro·duc·tive** *adj.* **re·pro·duc·tive·ly** *adv.*

R

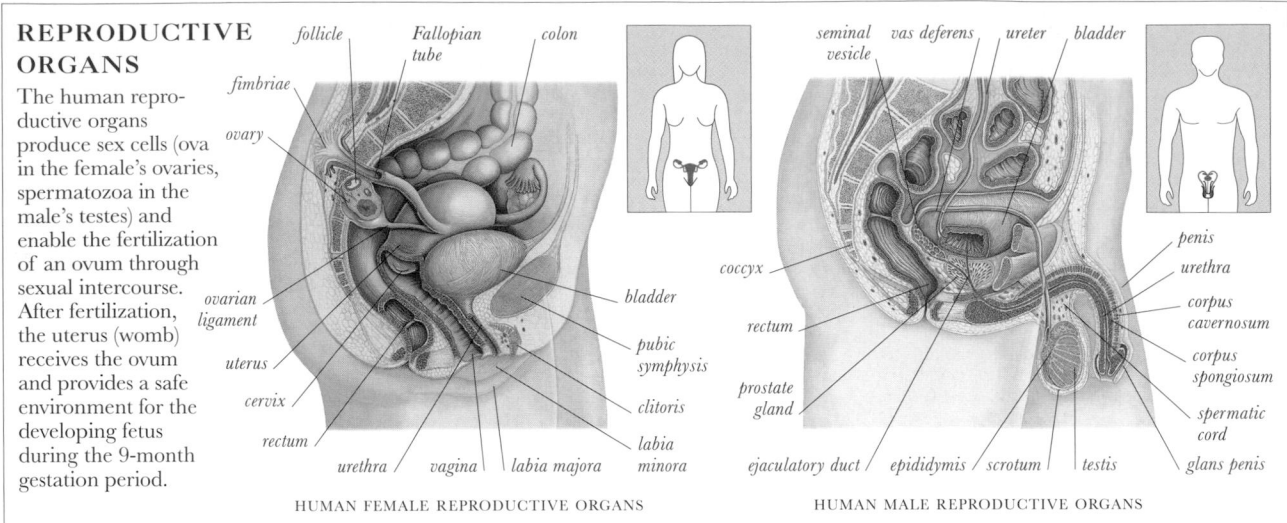

REPRODUCTIVE ORGANS

The human reproductive organs produce sex cells (ova in the female's ovaries, spermatozoa in the male's testes) and enable the fertilization of an ovum through sexual intercourse. After fertilization, the uterus (womb) receives the ovum and provides a safe environment for the developing fetus during the 9-month gestation period.

follicle   *Fallopian tube*   *colon*
fimbriae
ovary
ovarian ligament
uterus
cervix
rectum
urethra   *vagina*   *labia majora*
bladder
pubic symphysis
clitoris
labia minora

HUMAN FEMALE REPRODUCTIVE ORGANS

seminal vesicle   *vas deferens*   *ureter*   *bladder*
coccyx
rectum
prostate gland
ejaculatory duct   *epididymis*   *scrotum*   *testis*
penis
urethra
corpus cavernosum
corpus spongiosum
spermatic cord
glans penis

HUMAN MALE REPRODUCTIVE ORGANS

re·pro·duc·tive or·gans *n.pl.* ▲ the internal and external structures of a person, animal, or plant which are concerned with reproduction, especially sexual reproduction.

re·pro·gram /réeprógram/ *v.tr.* (**reprogrammed**, **reprogram·ming**) program (esp. a computer) again or differently. □□ **re·pro·gram·ma·ble** /-prógrəməbəl, -prógrám-/ *adj.*

re·prog·ra·phy /riprógrəfee/ *n.* the science and practice of copying documents by photography, xerography, etc. □□ **re·pro·graph·ic** /réeprəgráfik/ *adj.*

re·proof /riprooʹf/ *n.* **1** blame (*a glance of reproof*). **2** a rebuke.

re·prove /riprooʹv/ *v.tr.* rebuke. □□ **re·prov·ing·ly** *adv.*

rep·tant /réptənt/ *adj.* (of a plant or animal) creeping.

rep·tile /réptīl/ *n. & adj.* ● *n.* **1** ▶ any cold-blooded scaly animal of the class Reptilia, including snakes, lizards, crocodiles, turtles, tortoises, etc. **2** a mean, groveling, or repulsive person. ● *adj.* **1** (of an animal) creeping. **2** mean; groveling. □□ **rep·til·i·an** /-tíleeən, -tílyən/ *adj. & n.*

re·pub·lic /ripúblik/ *n.* **1** a nation in which supreme power is held by the people or their elected representatives or by an elected or nominated president, not by a monarch, etc. **2** a society with equality between its members (*the literary republic*).

re·pub·li·can /ripúblikən/ *adj. & n.* ● *adj.* **1** of or constituted as a republic. **2** characteristic of a republic. **3** advocating or supporting republican government. ● *n.* **1** a person advocating or supporting republican government. **2** (**Republican**) a member or supporter of the Republican party. **3** an advocate of a united Ireland. □□ **re·pub·li·can·ism** *n.*

Re·pub·li·can par·ty *n.* one of the two main US political parties, favoring a lesser degree of central power (cf. DEMOCRATIC PARTY).

re·pub·lish /réepúblish/ *v.tr.* (also *absol.*) publish again or in a new edition, etc. □□ **re·pub·li·ca·tion** /-likáyshən/ *n.*

re·pu·di·ate /ripyooʹdeeayt/ *v.tr.* **1 a** disown; disavow; reject. **b** refuse dealings with. **c** deny. **2** refuse to recognize or obey (authority or a treaty). **3** refuse to discharge (an obligation or debt). □□ **re·pu·di·a·tion** /-áyshən/ *n.*

re·pug·nance /ripúgnəns/ *n.* (also **re·pug·nan·cy**) **1** (usu. foll. by *to*, *against*) antipathy; aversion. **2** (usu. foll. by *of*, *between*, *to*, *with*) inconsistency or incompatibility of ideas, statements, etc.

re·pug·nant /ripúgnənt/ *adj.* **1** (often foll. by *to*) extremely distasteful. **2** (often foll. by *to*) contradictory. **3** (often foll. by *with*) incompatible.

re·pulse /ripúls/ *v. & n.* ● *v.tr.* **1** drive back by force of arms. **2 a** rebuff. **b** refuse. **3** be repulsive to; repel. **4** foil in controversy. ● *n.* **1** the act or an instance of repulsing or being repulsed. **2** a rebuff.

re·pul·sion /ripúlshən/ *n.* **1** aversion; disgust. **2** esp. *Physics* the force by which bodies tend to repel each other or increase their mutual distance (opp. ATTRACTION).

re·pul·sive /ripúlsiv/ *adj.* **1** causing aversion or loathing; disgusting. **2** *Physics* exerting repulsion. □□ **re·pul·sive·ly** *adv.* **re·pul·sive·ness** *n.*

re·pur·chase /réepórchis/ *v. & n.* ● *v.tr.* purchase again. ● *n.* the act or an instance of purchasing again.

rep·u·ta·ble /répyətəbəl/ *adj.* of good repute; respectable. □□ **rep·u·ta·bly** *adv.*

rep·u·ta·tion /répyətáyshən/ *n.* **1** what is generally said or believed about a person's or thing's character (*has a reputation for dishonesty*). **2** the state of being well thought of; distinction; respectability (*have my reputation to think of*). **3** (foll. by *of, for* + verbal noun) credit or discredit (*has the reputation of driving hard bargains*).

re·pute /ripyooʹt/ *n. & v.* ● *n.* reputation (*known by repute*). ● *v.tr.* **1** (as **reputed** *adj.*) (often foll. by *to* + infin.) be generally considered or reckoned (*is reputed to be the best*). **2** (as **reputed** *adj.*) passing as, but probably not (*his reputed father*). □□ **re·put·ed·ly** *adv.*

re·quest /rikwést/ *n. & v.* ● *n.* **1** the act or an instance of asking for something (*came at his request*). **2** a thing asked for. **3** the state of being sought after; demand (*in great request*). **4** a letter, etc., asking for a particular recording, etc., to be played on a radio program, often with a personal message. ● *v.tr.* **1** ask to be given or allowed or favored with (*request a hearing; requests your presence*). **2** (foll. by *to* + infin.) ask a person to do something (*requested her to answer*). **3** (foll. by *that* + clause) ask that. □ **by** (or **on**) **request** in response to an expressed wish. □□ **re·quest·er** *n.*

req·ui·em /rékweeəm, réekwee-/ *n.* **1** (**Requiem**) (also *attrib.*) *RC Ch., Anglican Ch.* a Mass for the repose of the souls of the dead. **2** *Mus.* the musical setting for this.

req·ui·es·cat /rékwee-éskat, -kaat/ *n.* a wish or prayer for the repose of a dead person.

re·quire /rikwír/ *v.tr.* **1** need; depend on for success or fulfillment (*the work requires much patience*). **2** lay down as an imperative (*did all that was required by law*). **3** command; instruct (a person, etc.). **4** order; insist on (an action or measure). **5** (often foll. by *of, from,* or *that* + clause) demand (of or from a person)

as a right. **6** wish to have (*is there anything else you require?*). □□ **re·quire·ment** *n.*

req·ui·site /rékwizit/ *adj. & n.* ● *adj.* required by circumstances; necessary to success, etc. ● *n.* (often foll. by *for*) a thing needed.

req·ui·si·tion /rékwizíshən/ *n. & v.* ● *n.* **1** an official order laying claim to the use of property or materials. **2** a formal written demand that some duty should be performed. **3** being called or put into service. ● *v.tr.* demand the use or supply of, esp. by requisition order. □□ **req·ui·si·tion·er** *n.*

re·quite /rikwít/ *v.tr.* **1** make return for (a service). **2** (often foll. by *with*) reward or avenge (a favor or injury). **3** (often foll. by *for*) make return to (a person). **4** (often foll. by *for, with*) repay with good or evil (*requite like for like; requite hate with love*). □□ **re·quit·al** *n.*

re·ran *past* of RERUN.

re·read /rée-réed/ *v. & n.* ● *v.tr.* (*past* and *past part.* **reread** /-réd/) read again. ● *n.* an instance of reading again. □□ **re·read·a·ble** *adj.*

rer·e·dos /rérədos, ríra-/ *n. Eccl.* ▼ an ornamental screen covering the wall at the back of an altar.
▷ CATHEDRAL.

REREDOS: INTERIOR OF A CHURCH SHOWING THE ALTAR AND REREDOS

R

re·re·lease /rée-rilées/ v. & n. ● v.tr. release (a recording, motion picture, etc.) again. ● n. a rereleased recording, motion picture, etc.

re·route /rée-róot, -rówt/ v.tr. send or carry by a different route.

re·run v. & n. ● v.tr. /rée-rún/ (**rerunning**; past **reran**; past part. **rerun**) run (a race, television program, etc.) again. ● n. /rée-run/ **1** the act or an instance of rerunning. **2** a television program, etc., shown again.

re·sale /réesáyl/ n. the sale of a thing previously bought. □□ **re·sal·a·ble** adj.

re·sched·ule /réeskéjool/ v.tr. alter the schedule of; replan.

re·scind /risínd/ v.tr. abrogate; revoke; cancel. □□ **re·scis·sion** /-sízhən/ n.

re·script /réeskript/ n. **1** a Roman emperor's written reply to an appeal for guidance, esp. on a legal point. **2** RC Ch. the Pope's decision on a question of doctrine or papal law. **3** an official edict or announcement. **4 a** the act or an instance of rewriting. **b** the thing rewritten.

res·cue /réskyoo/ v. & n. ● v.tr. (**rescues, rescued, rescuing**) **1** (often foll. by from) save or set free from danger or harm. **2** Law **a** unlawfully liberate (a person). **b** forcibly recover (property). ● n. the act or an instance of rescuing or being rescued; deliverance. □□ **res·cu·a·ble** adj. **res·cu·er** n.

re·seal /réeséel/ v.tr. seal again. □□ **re·seal·a·ble** adj.

re·search /risórch, réesərch/ n. & v. ● n. **1 a** the systematic investigation into and study of materials, sources, etc., in order to establish facts and reach new conclusions. **b** (usu. in pl.) an endeavor to discover new or collate old facts, etc., by the scientific study of a subject or by a course of critical investigation. **2** (attrib.) engaged in or intended for research. ● v. **1** tr. do research into or for. **2** intr. make researches. □□ **re·search·a·ble** adj. **re·search·er** n.

re·search and de·vel·op·ment n. (in industry, etc.) work directed toward the innovation, introduction, and improvement of products and processes.

re·seat /réeséet/ v.tr. **1** (also refl.) seat (oneself, a person, etc.) again. **2** provide with a fresh seat or seats.

re·sect /risékt/ v.tr. Surgery **1** cut out part of (a lung, etc.). **2** pare down (bone, cartilage, etc.). □□ **re·sec·tion** n. **re·sec·tion·al** adj. **re·sec·tion·ist** n.

re·se·lect /réesilékt/ v.tr. select again or differently. □□ **re·se·lec·tion** n.

re·sell /réesél/ v.tr. (past and past part. **resold**) sell (an object, etc.) after buying it.

re·sem·blance /rizémbləns/ n. (often foll. by to, between, of) a likeness or similarity. □□ **re·sem·blant** adj.

re·sem·ble /rizémbəl/ v.tr. be like; have a similarity to, or the same appearance as.

re·sent /rizént/ v.tr. show or feel indignation at; be aggrieved by.

re·sent·ful /rizéntfool/ adj. feeling resentment. □□ **re·sent·ful·ly** adv. **re·sent·ful·ness** n.

re·sent·ment /rizéntmənt/ n. (often foll. by at, of) indignant or bitter feelings; anger.

res·er·va·tion /rézərváyshən/ n. **1** the act or an instance of reserving or being reserved. **2** a booking (of a room, etc.). **3** the thing booked, e.g., a room in a hotel. **4** an express or tacit limitation or exception to an agreement, etc. **5** an area of land reserved for a particular group, as a tract designated by the federal government for use by Native Americans. **6 a** a right or interest retained in an estate being conveyed. **b** the clause reserving this.

re·serve /rizórv/ v. & n. ● v.tr. **1** postpone; put aside for a later occasion or special use. **2** order to be specially retained or allocated for a particular person or at a particular time. **3** retain or secure (reserve the right to). **4** postpone delivery of (judgment, etc.) (reserved my comments until the end).

REPTILE

Reptiles have waterproof skin covered in keratinous scales or shields, which enables them to survive in dry habitats. Most reptiles lay eggs. Unlike amphibians, they do not have a larval stage, and the young hatch as miniature forms of their parent. There are more than 6,000 species of reptile, over 95 percent of which belong to the order Squamata.

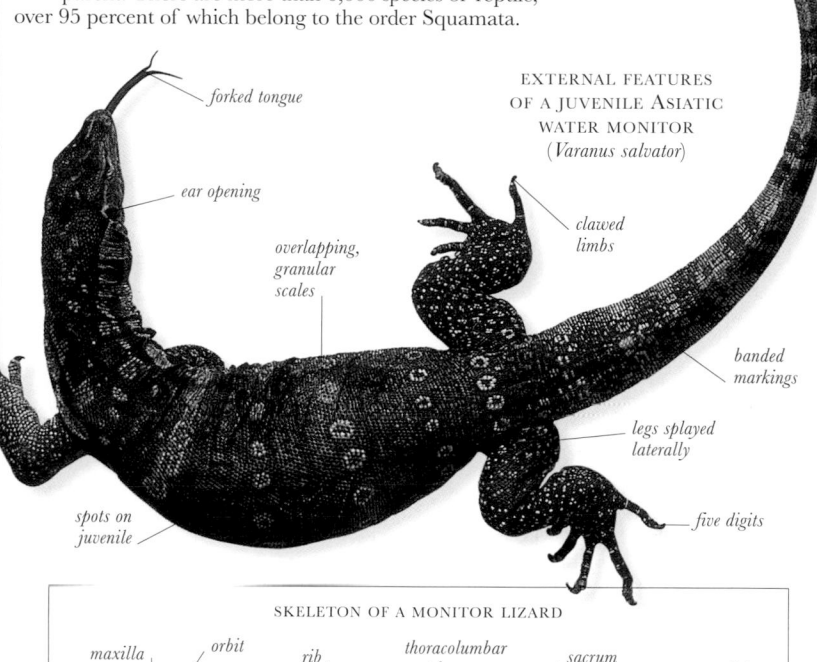

EXTERNAL FEATURES OF A JUVENILE ASIATIC WATER MONITOR (*Varanus salvator*)

well-developed muscular tail · forked tongue · ear opening · overlapping, granular scales · clawed limbs · banded markings · legs splayed laterally · five digits · spots on juvenile

SKELETON OF A MONITOR LIZARD

maxilla · orbit · rib · thoracolumbar vertebrae · sacrum · caudal vertebrae · mandible · scapula · ulna · tibia · radius · fibula

REPTILE ORDERS

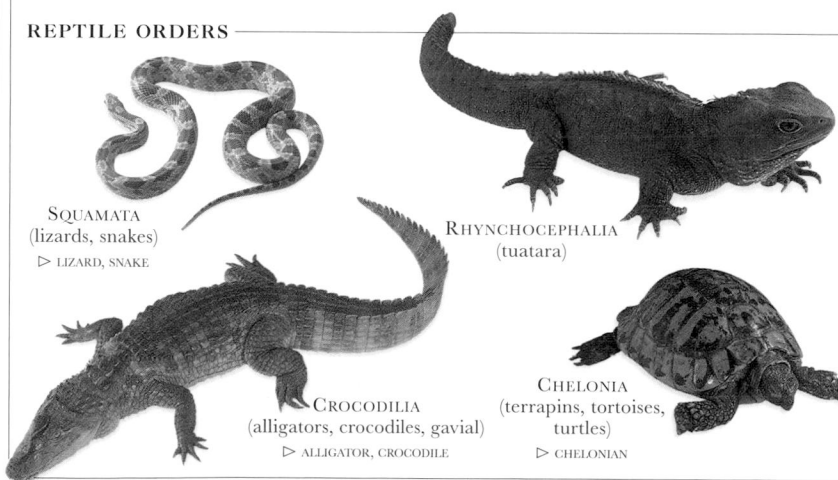

SQUAMATA (lizards, snakes)
▷ LIZARD, SNAKE

RHYNCHOCEPHALIA (tuatara)

CROCODILIA (alligators, crocodiles, gavial)
▷ ALLIGATOR, CROCODILE

CHELONIA (terrapins, tortoises, turtles)
▷ CHELONIAN

● n. **1** a thing reserved for future use; an extra stock or amount (energy reserves). **2** a limitation, qualification, or exception attached to something (without reserve). **3 a** self-restraint; reticence. **b** (in artistic or literary expression) absence from exaggeration or ill-proportioned effects. **4** a company's profit added to capital. **5** (in sing. or pl.) assets kept readily available as cash or at a central bank, or as gold or foreign exchange (reserve currency). **6** (in sing. or pl.) **a** troops withheld from action to reinforce or protect others. **b** forces in addition to the regular army, navy, air force, etc., but available in an emergency. **7** a member of the military reserve. **8** an extra player chosen to be a possible substitute on a team. **9** a place reserved for special use, esp. as a habitat for a native tribe or for wildlife. **10** the intentional suppression of the truth (exercised a certain amount of reserve). □ **in reserve** unused and available if required. □□ **re·serv·a·ble** adj. **re·serv·er** n.

R

re·serve /reesérv/ *v.tr. & intr.* serve again.

re·served /rizárvd/ *adj.* **1** reticent; slow to reveal emotion or opinions. **2 a** set apart; destined for some use or fate. **b** (often foll. by *for, to*) left by fate for; falling first or only to. □□ **re·serv·ed·ly** /-vidlee/ *adv.* **re·serv·ed·ness** *n.*

re·serv·ist /rizárvist/ *n.* a member of the reserve forces.

RESERVOIR

res·er·voir /rézərvwaar/ *n.* **1** ◄ a large natural or artificial lake used as a source of water supply. **2 a** any natural or artificial receptacle esp. for or of fluid. **b** a place where fluid, etc., collects. **3** a part of a machine, etc., holding fluid. **4** (usu. foll. by *of*) a supply esp. of information.

re·set /reesét/ *v.tr.* (**re·set·ting**; *past* and *past part.* **reset**) set again or differently (*set a broken bone*). □□ **re·set·ta·ble** *adj.*

re·set·tle /reesét'l/ *v.tr. & intr.* settle again. □□ **re·set·tle·ment** *n.*

re·shape /reesháyp/ *v.tr.* shape or form again or differently.

re·shuf·fle /reeshúfəl/ *v. & n.* ● *v.tr.* **1** shuffle (cards) again. **2** interchange the posts of (government ministers, etc.). ● *n.* the act or an instance of reshuffling.

re·side /rizíd/ *v.intr.* **1** (often foll. by *at, in, abroad*, etc.) (of a person) have one's home; dwell permanently. **2** (of power, a right, etc.) rest or be vested in. **3** (of an incumbent official) be in residence. **4** (foll. by *in*) (of a quality) be present or inherent in.

res·i·dence /rézidəns/ *n.* **1** the act or an instance of residing. **2 a** the place where a person resides. **b** a mansion; the official house of a government minister, etc. **c** a house, esp. one of considerable pretension (*returned to their Beverly Hills residence*). □ **in residence** dwelling at a specified place, esp. for the performance of duties or work.

res·i·den·cy /rézidənsee/ *n.* (*pl.* **-ies**) **1** = RESIDENCE 1, 2a. **2** a period of specialized medical training; the position of a resident. **3** *attrib.* based on or related to residence (*residency requirement for in-state tuition*).

res·i·dent /rézidənt/ *n. & adj.* ● *n.* **1** (often foll. by *of*) **a** a permanent inhabitant. **b** a bird belonging to a species that does not migrate. **2** a medical graduate engaged in specialized practice under supervision in a hospital. ● *adj.* **1** residing; in residence. **2 a** having quarters on the premises of one's work, etc. **b** working regularly in a particular place. **3** located in; inherent (*resident in the nerves*). **4** (of birds, etc.) nonmigratory.

res·i·den·tial /rézidénshəl/ *adj.* **1** suitable for or occupied by private houses (*residential area*). **2** used as a residence (*residential hotel*). **3** based on or connected with residence (*the residential qualification for voters*). □□ **res·i·den·tial·ly** *adv.*

res·i·den·ti·ar·y /rézidénshee-eree, -shəree/ *adj. & n.* ● *adj.* of, subject to, or requiring official residence. ● *n.* (*pl.* **-ies**) an ecclesiastic who must officially reside in a place.

res·i·du·a *pl.* of RESIDUUM.

re·sid·u·al /rizíj̄ooəl/ *adj. & n.* ● *adj.* **1** remaining; left as a residue or residuum. **2** *Math.* resulting from subtraction. ● *n.* **1** a quantity left over or *Math.* resulting from subtraction. **2** (usu. in *pl.*) a royalty paid to a writer, performer, etc. □□ **re·sid·u·al·ly** *adv.*

re·sid·u·ar·y /rizíj̄ooeree/ *adj.* **1** of the residue of an estate (*residuary bequest*). **2** of or being a residuum; residual; still remaining.

res·i·due /rézid̄oo, -dyoo/ *n.* **1** what is left over or remains; a remainder; the rest. **2** *Law* what remains of an estate after the payment of charges, debts, and bequests. **3** esp. *Chem.* a residuum.

re·sid·u·um /rizíj̄ooəm/ *n.* (*pl.* **residua** /-jóoə/) **1** *Chem.* ▶ a substance left after combustion or evaporation. **2** a remainder or residue.

re·sign /rizín/ *v.* **1** *intr.* **a** (often foll. by *from*) give up office, one's employment, etc. **b** (often foll. by *as*) retire (*resigned as chief executive*). **2** *tr.* give up (office, one's employment, etc.); surrender; hand over (a right, charge, task, etc.). **3** *tr.* give up (hope, etc.). **4** *refl.* (usu. foll. by *to*) **a** reconcile (oneself, one's mind, etc.) to the inevitable. **b** surrender (oneself to another's guidance). **5** *intr. Chess*, etc., discontinue play and admit defeat. □□ **re·sign·er** *n.*

res·ig·na·tion /rézignáyshən/ *n.* **1** the act or an instance of resigning, esp. from one's job or office. **2** the document, etc., conveying this intention. **3** the state of being resigned; the uncomplaining endurance of a sorrow or difficulty.

re·signed /rizínd/ *adj.* (often foll. by *to*) having resigned oneself; submissive, acquiescent. □□ **re·sign·ed·ly** /-zínidlee/ *adv.* **re·sign·ed·ness** *n.*

re·sil·i·ent /rizílyənt/ *adj.* **1** (of a substance, etc.) springing back; resuming its original shape after bending, compression, etc. **2** (of a person) readily recovering from shock, depression, etc.; buoyant. □□ **re·sil·i·ence** *n.* **re·sil·i·en·cy** *n.* **re·sil·i·ent·ly** *adv.*

res·in /rézin/ *n. & v.* ● *n.* **1** ▶ an adhesive flammable substance insoluble in water, secreted by some plants (cf. GUM[1]). **2** (in full **synthetic resin**) a solid or liquid organic compound made by polymerization, etc., and used in plastics, etc. ● *v.tr.* rub or treat with resin. □□ **res·in·ate** /-nayt/ *v.tr.* **res·in·oid** *adj. & n.* **res·in·ous** *adj.*

evaporating dish · *crystalline residuum*

tripod

Bunsen burner

RESIDUUM:
EXPERIMENT TO
PRODUCE A RESIDUUM
FROM A SOLUTION

RESIN SECRETED
FROM THE TRUNK
OF A SCOTS PINE

re·sist /rizíst/ *v.* **1** *tr.* withstand the action or effect of; repel. **2** *tr.* stop the course or progress of; prevent from reaching, penetrating, etc. **3** *tr.* abstain from (pleasure, temptation, etc.). **4** *tr.* try to impede; refuse to comply with (*resist arrest*). **5** offer opposition; refuse to comply. □ **cannot** (or **could not**, etc.) **resist 1** (foll. by verbal noun) feel strongly inclined to (*cannot resist teasing me*). **2** is certain to be attracted, etc., by (*can't resist chocolate*). □□ **re·sist·ant** *adj.* **re·sist·er** *n.* **re·sist·i·ble** *adj.*

re·sist·ance /rizístəns/ *n.* **1** the act or an instance of resisting; refusal to comply. **2** the power of resisting. **3** *Biol.* the ability to withstand adverse conditions. **4** the impeding or stopping effect exerted by one material thing on another. **5** *Physics* **a** the property of hindering the conduction of electricity, heat, etc. **b** the measure of this in a body. ¶ Symb.: R. **6** a resistor. **7** (in full **resistance movement**) a secret organization resisting authority, esp. in an occupied country.

re·sis·tive /rizístiv/ *adj.* **1** able to resist. **2** *Electr.* of or concerning resistance.

re·sis·tiv·i·ty /réezistívitee/ *n. Electr.* a measure of the resisting power of a specified material to the flow of an electric current.

re·sis·tor /rizístər/ *n. Electr.* ▼ a device having resistance to the passage of an electrical current. ▷ RADIO

re·sold *past* and *past part.* of RESELL.

re·sol·u·ble /rizólyəbəl/ *adj.* **1** that can be resolved. **2** (foll. by *into*) analyzable.

res·o·lute /rézəl̄oot/ *adj.* (of a person or a person's mind or action) determined; decided; firm of purpose. □□ **res·o·lute·ly** *adv.* **res·o·lute·ness** *n.*

res·o·lu·tion /rézəló̄oshən/ *n.* **1** a resolute temper or character; boldness and firmness of purpose. **2** a thing resolved on; an intention (*New Year's resolutions*). **3 a** a formal expression of opinion or intention by a legislative body or public meeting. **b** the formulation of this. **4** (usu. foll. by *of*) the act or an instance of solving doubt or a problem or question. **5 a** separation into components; decomposition. **b** the replacing of a single force, etc., by two or more jointly equivalent to it. **6** (foll. by *into*) analysis; conversion into another form. **7** *Mus.* causing discord to pass into concord. **8** *Physics*, etc., the smallest interval measurable by a scientific instrument; the resolving power.

re·sol·u·tive /rézəló̄otiv/ *adj. Med.* having the power or ability to dissolve.

RESISTOR

Resistors provide the electrical equivalent of friction. When current flows through a resistor, an opposing voltage is set up. This limits the current or produces a voltage proportional to it. Most resistors have a set resistance but some, such as potentiometers used as volume controls, are variable.

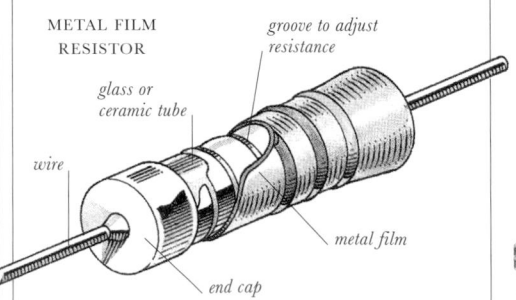

METAL FILM
RESISTOR

groove to adjust resistance

glass or ceramic tube

wire

metal film

end cap

EXAMPLES OF RESISTORS

LIGHT-DEPENDENT RESISTOR

THERMISTOR

PRE-SET
POTENTIOMETER

EIGHTH-WATT RESISTOR

HALF-WATT CARBON
RESISTOR

VARIABLE POTENTIOMETER

R

RESPIRATION

Human respiration relies on an involuntary muscle reflex that makes the diaphragm and external intercostal muscles contract. This increases the volume of the chest cavity, and the pressure inside it drops. Air rushes in through the nose, down the trachea, and into the lungs, where an exchange of oxygen and carbon dioxide takes place. As the muscles relax, the air with the waste (carbon dioxide) is forced back out of the lungs.

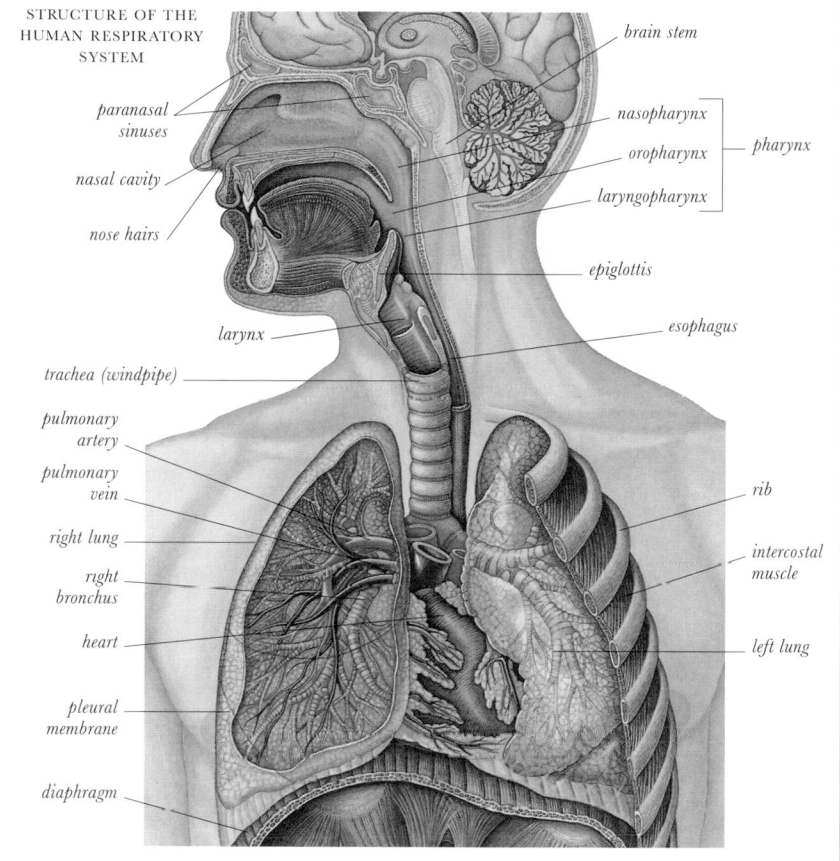

STRUCTURE OF THE HUMAN RESPIRATORY SYSTEM

brain stem

paranasal sinuses

nasopharynx

oropharynx — *pharynx*

laryngopharynx

nasal cavity

nose hairs

epiglottis

larynx

esophagus

trachea (windpipe)

pulmonary artery

pulmonary vein

right lung

rib

intercostal muscle

right bronchus

heart

left lung

pleural membrane

diaphragm

---

re·solve /rizólv/ *v. & n.* ● *v.* **1** *intr.* make up one's mind; decide firmly. **2** *tr.* (of circumstances, etc.) cause (a person) to do this (*events resolved him to leave*). **3** *tr.* (foll. by *that* + clause) (of an assembly or meeting) pass a resolution by vote. **4** *intr. & tr.* (often foll. by *into*) separate or cause to separate into constituent parts; analyze. **5** *tr.* (of optical or photographic equipment) separate or distinguish between closely adjacent objects. **6** *tr. & intr.* (foll. by *into*) convert or be converted. **7** *tr. & intr.* (foll. by *into*) reduce by mental analysis into. **8** *tr.* solve; clear up; settle (doubt, argument, etc.). **9** *tr. & intr. Mus.* convert or be converted into concord. ● *n.* **1 a** a firm mental decision or intention; a resolution. **b** a formal resolution by a legislative body or public meeting. **2** resoluteness; steadfastness. □□ **re·solv·a·ble** *adj.* **re·solv·a·bil·i·ty** /-zólvəbílitee/ *n.* **re·solv·er** *n.*

re·solved /rizólvd/ *adj.* resolute; determined. □□ **re·solv·ed·ly** /-zólvidlee/ *adv.* **re·solv·ed·ness** *n.*

re·sol·vent /rizólvənt/ *adj. & n.* esp. *Med.* ● *adj.* (of a drug, application, substance, etc.) effecting the resolution of a tumor, etc. ● *n.* such a drug, etc.

res·o·nant /rézənənt/ *adj.* **1** (of sound) echoing; resounding; continuing to sound; reinforced or prolonged by reflection or synchronous vibration. **2** (of a body, room, etc.) tending to reinforce or prolong sounds esp. by synchronous vibration. **3** (often foll. by *with*) (of a place) resounding. **4** of or relating to resonance. □□ **res·o·nance** /rézənəns/ *n.* **res·o·nant·ly** *adv.*

res·o·nate /rézənayt/ *v.intr.* produce or show resonance; resound. □□ **res·o·na·tor** /rézənaytər/ *n.*

re·sorb /risáwrb, -záwrb/ *v.tr.* absorb again. □□ **re·sorb·ence** *n.* **re·sorb·ent** *adj.*

re·sorp·tion /rizáwrpshən/ *n.* **1** the act or an instance of resorbing; the state of being resorbed. **2** the absorption of tissue within the body. □□ **re·sorp·tive** /-zórptiv/ *adj.*

re·sort /rizáwrt/ *n. & v.* ● *n.* **1** a place frequented esp. for vacations or for a specified purpose or quality. **2** a thing to which one has recourse; an expedient or measure (*a taxi was our best resort*). **3** a tendency to frequent or be frequented (*places of great resort*). ● *v.intr.* **1** (foll. by *to*) recourse to; use of (*to resort to violence*). **2** (foll. by *to*) turn to as an expedient. **3** (foll. by *to*) go often or in large numbers to. □ **in the** (or **as a**) **last resort** when all else has failed.

re-sort /rée-sáwrt/ *v.tr.* sort again or differently.

re·sound /rizównd/ *v.* **1** *intr.* (often foll. by *with*) (of a place) ring or echo. **2** *intr.* (of a voice, sound, etc.) produce echoes; go on sounding. **3** *intr.* **a** (of fame, etc.) be much talked of. **b** (foll. by *through*) produce a sensation (*resounded through Europe*). **4** *tr.* (often foll. by *of*) proclaim or repeat loudly (the praises) of a person or thing (*resounded the praises of Greece*). **5** *tr.* (of a place) reecho (a sound).

re·sound·ing /rizównding/ *adj.* **1** in senses of RESOUND. **2** unmistakable; emphatic (*was a resounding success*). □□ **re·sound·ing·ly** *adv.*

re·source /réesawrs, -zawrs, risáwrs, -záwrs/ *n.* **1** an expedient or device. **2** (usu. in *pl.*) **a** the means available to achieve an end, fulfill a function, etc. **b** a stock or supply that can be drawn on. **c** available assets. **3** (in *pl.*) a country's collective wealth or means of defense. **4 a** (often in *pl.*) skill in devising expedients (*a person of great resource*). **b** practical ingenuity; quick wit (*full of resource*). □ **one's own resources** one's own abilities, ingenuity, etc. □□ **re·source·ful** *adj.* **re·source·ful·ly** *adv.* **re·source·ful·ness** *n.* **re·source·less** *adj.* **re·source·less·ness** *n.*

re·spect /rispékt/ *n. & v.* ● *n.* **1** deferential esteem felt or shown toward a person or quality. **2 a** (foll. by *of, for*) heed or regard. **b** (foll. by *to*) attention to or consideration of (*without respect to the results*). **3** an aspect, detail, etc. (*except in this one respect*). **4** relation (*a morality that has no respect to religion*). **5** (in *pl.*) a person's polite messages or attentions (*give my respects to your mother*). ● *v.tr.* **1** regard with deference, esteem, or honor. **2 a** avoid interfering with, harming, degrading, insulting, injuring, or interrupting. **b** treat with consideration. **c** refrain from offending (a person, a person's feelings, etc.). □ **in respect that** because. **with all due respect** a mollifying formula preceding an expression of disagreement with another's views. **with respect to** in reference to, as concerns. □□ **re·spect·er** *n.*

re·spect·a·bil·i·ty /rispéktəbílitee/ *n.* **1** the state of being respectable. **2** those who are respectable.

re·spect·a·ble /rispéktəbəl/ *adj.* **1** deserving respect. **2 a** of good social standing. **b** characteristic of or associated with people of such status or character. **3 a** honest and decent in conduct. **b** characterized by (a sense of) convention or propriety; socially acceptable (*respectable behavior; a respectable publication*). **c** *derog.* highly conventional; prim. **4 a** commendable; meritorious (*an entirely respectable ambition*). **b** comparatively good or competent (*a respectable effort*). **5** reasonably good in condition or appearance. **6** appreciable in number, size, etc. **7** accepted or tolerated on account of prevalence (*materialism has become respectable again*). □□ **re·spect·a·bly** *adv.*

re·spect·ful /rispéktfŏŏl/ *adj.* showing deference. □□ **re·spect·ful·ly** *adv.* **re·spect·ful·ness** *n.*

re·spect·ing /rispékting/ *prep.* with reference or regard to; concerning.

re·spec·tive /rispéktiv/ *adj.* concerning or appropriate to each of several individually.

re·spec·tive·ly /rispéktivlee/ *adv.* for each separately or in turn, and in the order mentioned (*she and I gave $10 and $1, respectively*).

re·spell /réespél/ *v.tr.* spell again or differently, esp. phonetically.

res·pi·ra·ble /réspərəbəl, rispírə-/ *adj.* (of air, gas, etc.) able or fit to be breathed.

res·pi·rate /réspirayt/ *v.tr.* subject to artificial respiration.

res·pi·ra·tion /réspiráyshən/ *n.* **1 a** ▲ the act or an instance of breathing. **b** a breath. **2** *Biol.* in living organisms, the process involving the release of energy and carbon dioxide from the oxidation of complex organic substances.

res·pi·ra·tor /réspiraytər/ *n.* **1** an apparatus worn over the face to prevent poison gas, cold air, dust particles, etc., from being inhaled. **2** *Med.* an apparatus for maintaining artificial respiration.

re·spire /rispír/ *v.* **1** *intr.* breathe air. **2** *intr.* inhale and exhale air. **3** *intr.* (of a plant) carry out respiration. **4** *tr.* breathe (air, etc.). **5** *intr.* breathe again; take a breath. **6** *intr.* get rest or respite; recover hope or spirit. □□ **res·pi·ra·to·ry** /réspərətawree, rispírə-/ *adj.*

res·pite /réspit/ *n. & v.* ● *n.* **1** an interval of rest or relief. **2** a delay permitted before the discharge of an obligation or the suffering of a penalty. ● *v.tr.* **1** grant respite to; reprieve. **2** postpone the execution or exaction of (a sentence, obligation, etc.). **3** give temporary relief from (pain or care) or to (a sufferer).

R

re·splend·ent /rispléndənt/ *adj.* brilliant; dazzlingly or gloriously bright. □□ **re·splend·ence** *n.* **re·splend·en·cy** *n.* **re·splend·ent·ly** *adv.*

re·spond /rispónd/ *v.* **1** *intr.* answer; give a reply. **2** *intr.* act or behave in an answering or corresponding manner. **3** *intr.* (usu. foll. by *to*) show sensitivity to by behavior or change (*does not respond to kindness*). **4** *intr.* (of a congregation) make answers to a priest, etc. **5** *intr. Bridge* make a bid on the basis of a partner's preceding bid. **6** *tr.* say (something) in answer. □□ **re·spond·ence** *n.* **re·spond·er** *n.*

re·spond·ent /rispóndənt/ *n.* & *adj.* ● *n.* **1** a defendant, esp. in an appeal or divorce case. **2** a person who makes an answer or defends an argument, etc. ● *adj.* **1** giving answers. **2** (foll. by *to*) responsive. **3** in the position of defendant.

re·sponse /rispóns/ *n.* **1** an answer given in word or act; a reply. **2** a feeling, movement, change, etc., caused by a stimulus or influence. **3** (often in *pl.*) *Eccl.* any part of the liturgy said or sung in answer to the priest. **4** *Bridge* a bid made in responding.

re·spon·si·bil·i·ty /rispónsibílitee/ *n.* (*pl.* **-ies**) **1 a** (often foll. by *for*, *of*) the state or fact of being responsible. **b** the ability to act independently and make decisions (*a job with more responsibility*). **2** the person or thing for which one is responsible (*the food is my responsibility*). □ **on one's own responsibility** without authorization.

re·spon·si·ble /rispónsibəl/ *adj.* **1** (often foll. by *to*, *for*) liable to be called to account (to a person or for a thing). **2** morally accountable for one's actions; capable of rational conduct. **3** of good credit, position, or repute; respectable; evidently trustworthy. **4** (often foll. by *for*) being the primary cause (*a short circuit was responsible*). **5** (of a ruler or government) not autocratic. **6** involving responsibility (*a responsible job*). □□ **re·spon·si·ble·ness** *n.* **re·spon·si·bly** *adv.*

re·spon·sive /rispónsiv/ *adj.* **1** (often foll. by *to*) responding readily (to some influence). **2** sympathetic; impressionable. **3 a** answering. **b** by way of answer. **4** (of a liturgy, etc.) using responses. □□ **re·spon·sive·ly** *adv.* **re·spon·sive·ness** *n.*

re·spon·so·ry /rispónsəree/ *n.* (*pl.* **-ies**) an anthem said or sung by a soloist and choir after a lesson.

re·spray *v.* & *n.* ● *v.tr.* /reéspráy/ spray again (esp. to change the color of the paint on a vehicle, etc.). ● *n.* /reéspray/ the act or an instance of respraying.

rest[1] /rest/ *v.* & *n.* ● *v.* **1** *intr.* cease, abstain, or be relieved from exertion, action, etc. **2** *intr.* be still or asleep, esp. to refresh oneself. **3** *tr.* give relief or repose to (*a chair to rest my legs*). **4** *intr.* (foll. by *on*, *upon*, *against*) lie on; be supported by; be spread out on; be propped against. **5** *intr.* (foll. by *on*, *upon*) depend; be based; rely. **6** *intr.* (foll. by *on*, *upon*) (of a look) light upon or be steadily directed on. **7** *tr.* (foll. by *on*, *upon*) place for support or foundation. **8** *intr.* (of a problem or subject) be left without further investigation or discussion (*let the matter rest*). **9** *intr.* **a** lie in death. **b** (foll. by *in*) lie buried in (a churchyard, etc.). **10** *tr.* (as **rested** *adj.*) refreshed or reinvigorated by resting. **11** *intr.* conclude the calling of witnesses in a court case (*the prosecution rests*). **12** *intr.* (of land) lie fallow. **13** *intr.* (foll. by *in*) repose trust in (*am content to rest in God*). ● *n.* **1** repose or sleep, esp. in bed at night. **2** the cessation of exertion, worry, activity, etc. **3** a period of resting. **4** a support or prop for holding or steadying something. **5** *Mus.* **a** an interval of silence of a specified duration. **b** the sign denoting this. ▷ NOTATION. **6** a place of resting or abiding, esp. a lodging place or shelter for travelers. **7** a pause in elocution. **8** a caesura in verse. □ **at rest** not moving; not agitated or troubled; dead. **lay to rest** inter (a corpse). **rest one's case** conclude one's argument, etc. **rest** (or **God rest**) his (or **her**) **soul** may God grant his (or her) soul repose. **rest on one's laurels** see LAUREL. **rest up** rest oneself thoroughly. **set (or put) to (or at) rest** settle or relieve (a question, a person's mind, etc.).

rest[2] /rest/ *n.* & *v.* ● *n.* (prec. by *the*) the remaining part or parts; the others; the remainder of some quantity or number. ● *v.intr.* **1** remain in a specified state (*rest assured*). **2** (foll. by *with*) be left in the hands or charge of. □ **and all the rest** (or **the rest of it**) and all else that might be mentioned; et cetera. **for the rest** as regards anything else.

rest ar·e·a *n.* = REST STOP.

re·start *v.* & *n.* ● *v.tr.* & *intr.* /reéstaárt/ begin again. ● *n.* /reéstaart/ a new beginning.

re·state /reéstáyt/ *v.tr.* express again or differently, esp. more clearly or convincingly. □□ **re·state·ment** *n.*

res·tau·rant /réstərənt, -raant, réstraant/ *n.* public premises where meals or refreshments may be had.

res·tau·ra·teur /réstərətőr/ *n.* a restaurant owner or manager.

rest·ful /réstfŏŏl/ *adj.* **1** favorable to quiet or repose. **2** free from disturbing influences. **3** soothing. □□ **rest·ful·ly** *adv.* **rest·ful·ness** *n.*

rest home *n.* a place where old or frail people can be cared for.

res·ti·tu·tion /réstitőőshən, -tyőő-/ *n.* **1** (often foll. by *of*) the act or an instance of restoring a thing to its proper owner. **2** reparation for an injury (esp. *make restitution*). **3** esp. *Theol.* the restoration of a thing to its original state. **4** the resumption of an original shape or position because of elasticity. □□ **res·ti·tu·tive** /réstitőőtiv, -tyőő-/ *adj.*

res·tive /réstiv/ *adj.* **1** fidgety; restless. **2** (of a horse) refusing to advance. **3** (of a person) unmanageable; rejecting control. □□ **res·tive·ly** *adv.* **res·tive·ness** *n.*

rest·less /réstlis/ *adj.* **1** finding or affording no rest. **2** uneasy; agitated. **3** constantly in motion, fidgeting, etc. □□ **rest·less·ly** *adv.* **rest·less·ness** *n.*

re·stock /reéstók/ *v.tr.* (also *absol.*) stock again or differently.

res·to·ra·tion /réstəráyshən/ *n.* **1 a** the act or an instance of restoring or of being restored. **b** = RESTITUTION 1. **2** a model or drawing representing the supposed original form of an extinct animal, ruined building, etc. **3 a** the reestablishment of a monarch, etc. **b** the period of this. **4** (**Restoration**) *hist.* (prec. by *the*) the reestablishment of Charles II as king of England in 1660.

re·stor·a·tive /ristáwrətiv, -stór-/ *adj.* & *n.* ● *adj.* tending to restore health or strength. ● *n.* a restorative medicine, food, etc.

re·store /ristáwr/ *v.tr.* **1** bring back or attempt to bring back to the original state by rebuilding, repairing, etc. **2** bring back to health, etc.; cure. **3** give back to the original owner, etc. **4** reinstate; bring back to dignity or right. **5** replace; put back; bring back to a former condition. **6** make a representation of the supposed original state of (a ruin, extinct animal, etc.). **7** reinstate by conjecture (missing words in a text, missing pieces, etc.). □□ **re·stor·a·ble** *adj.* **re·stor·er** *n.*

re·strain /ristráyn/ *v.tr.* **1** (often *refl.*, usu. foll. by *from*) check or hold in; keep in check or under control or within bounds. **2** repress; keep down. **3** confine; imprison. □□ **re·strain·a·ble** *adj.* **re·strain·er** *n.*

re-strain /reéstráyn/ *v.tr.* strain again.

re·strain·ed·ly /ristráynidlee/ *adv.* with self-restraint.

re·straint /ristráynt/ *n.* **1** the act or an instance of restraining or being restrained. **2** a controlling agency or influence. **3 a** self-control; avoidance of excess or exaggeration. **b** austerity of literary expression. **4** reserve of manner. **5** confinement, esp. because of insanity. **6** something that restrains or holds in check. □ **in restraint of** in order to restrain.

re·strict /ristríkt/ *v.tr.* (often foll. by *to*, *within*) **1** confine; bound; limit. **2** subject to limitation. **3** withhold from general circulation or disclosure. □□ **re·strict·ed·ly** *adv.* **re·strict·ed·ness** *n.*

re·stric·tion /ristríkshən/ *n.* **1** the act or an instance of restricting; the state of being restricted. **2** a thing that restricts. **3** a limitation placed on action. □□ **re·stric·tion·ist** *adj.* & *n.*

re·stric·tive /ristríktiv/ *adj.* imposing restrictions. □□ **re·stric·tive·ly** *adv.* **re·stric·tive·ness** *n.*

re·string /reéstríng/ *v.tr.* (*past* and *past part.* **restrung**) **1** fit (a musical instrument) with new strings. **2** thread (beads, etc.) on a new string.

rest room *n.* a public toilet in a restaurant, store, office building, etc.

re·struc·ture /reéstrúkchər/ *v.tr.* give a new structure to; rebuild; rearrange.

rest stop *n.* an area along a highway for travelers to stop for rest, refreshment, etc.

re·style /reéstíl/ *v.tr.* **1** reshape; remake in a new style. **2** give a new designation to (a person or thing).

re·sult /rizúlt/ *n.* & *v.* ● *n.* **1** a consequence, issue, or outcome of something. **2** a satisfactory outcome (*gets results*). **3** a quantity, formula, etc., obtained by calculation. **4** (in *pl.*) a list of scores or winners, etc. ● *v.intr.* **1** (often foll. by *from*) arise as the actual consequence or follow as a logical consequence. **2** (often foll. by *in*) have a specified end or outcome (*resulted in a large profit*). □ **without result** in vain.

re·sult·ant /rizúlt'nt/ *adj.* resulting, esp. as the total outcome of more or less opposed forces.

re·sume /rizőőm/ *v.* & *n.* ● *v.* **1** *tr.* & *intr.* begin again or continue after an interruption. **2** *tr.* & *intr.* begin to speak, work, or use again; recommence. **3** *tr.* recover; reoccupy (*resume one's seat*). ● *n.* = RÉSUMÉ. □□ **re·sum·a·ble** *adj.*

ré·su·mé /rézőőmay/ *n.* (also **resumé**, **re·su·me**) **1** a summary. **2** a curriculum vitae.

re·sump·tion /rizúmpshən/ *n.* the act or an instance of resuming. □□ **re·sump·tive** *adj.*

re·su·pi·nate /risőőpinayt, -nət/ *adj.* (of a leaf, etc.) upside down.

re·sur·face /reésórfis/ *v.* **1** *tr.* lay a new surface on (a road, etc.). **2** *intr.* rise or arise again; turn up again.

re·sur·gent /risórjənt/ *adj.* **1** rising or arising again. **2** tending to rise again. □□ **re·sur·gence** *n.*

res·ur·rect /rézərékt/ *v.* **1** *tr.* & *intr.* raise or rise from the dead. **2** *tr. colloq.* revive the practice, use, or memory of.

res·ur·rec·tion /rézərékshən/ *n.* **1** the act or an instance of rising from the dead. **2** (**Resurrection**) **a** Christ's rising from the dead. **b** the rising of the dead at the Last Judgment. **3** a revival after disuse, inactivity, or decay. **4** exhumation. **5** restoration to vogue or memory. □□ **res·ur·rec·tion·al** *adj.*

re·sur·vey *v.* & *n.* ● *v.tr.* /reésərváy/ survey again; reconsider. ● *n.* /reésórvay/ the act or an instance of resurveying.

re·sus·ci·tate /risúsitayt/ *v.tr.* & *intr.* **1** revive from unconsciousness or apparent death. **2** return or restore to vogue, vigor, or vividness. □□ **re·sus·ci·ta·tion** /-táyshən/ *n.* **re·sus·ci·ta·tive** *adj.* **re·sus·ci·ta·tor** *n.*

ret /ret/ *v.* (also **rate** /rayt/) (**retted**, **retting**) **1** *tr.* soften (flax, hemp, etc.) by soaking or by exposure to moisture. **2** *intr.* (often as **retted** *adj.*) (of hay, etc.) be spoiled by wet or rot.

re·ta·ble /ritáybəl, reétay-, rétə-/ *n.* **1** a frame enclosing decorated panels above the back of an altar. **2** a shelf.

re·tail /reétayl/ *n.*, *adj.*, *adv.*, & *v.* ● *n.* the sale of goods in relatively small quantities to the public, and usu. not for resale (cf. WHOLESALE). ● *adj.* & *adv.* by retail; at a retail price. ● *v.* (also /ritáyl/) **1** *tr.* sell (goods) in retail trade. **2** *intr.* (often foll. by *at*, *for*) (of goods) be sold in this way (esp. for a specified price). **3** *tr.* recount; relate details of. □□ **re·tail·er** *n.*

re·tail ther·a·py *n. joc.* the practice of shopping in order to make oneself feel more cheerful.

re·tain /ritáyn/ *v.tr.* **1 a** keep possession of; not lose; continue to have. **b** not abolish, discard, nor alter. **2** keep in one's memory. **3 a** keep in place; hold fixed. **b** hold (water, etc.). **4** secure the services of (a person) with a preliminary payment. □□ **re·tain·a·ble** *adj.* **re·tain·a·bil·i·ty** /-taynəbílitee/ *n.* **re·tain·ment** *n.*

R

re·tain·er /ritáynər/ *n.* **1** a person or thing that retains. **2** *Law* a fee for retaining an attorney, etc. **3 a** *hist.* a dependent of a person of rank. **b** *joc.* a faithful friend or servant (esp. *old retainer*).

re·take *v. & n.* ● *v.tr.* /reétáyk/ (*past* **retook**; *past part.* **retaken**) **1** take again. **2** recapture. ● *n.* /reétayk/ **1 a** the act or an instance of retaking. **b** a thing retaken, e.g., an examination. **2 a** the act or an instance of filming a scene or recording music, etc., again. **b** the scene or recording obtained in this way.

re·tal·i·ate /ritálee·ayt/ *v.* **1** *intr.* repay an injury, insult, etc., in kind; attack in return; make reprisals. **2** *tr.* **a** (usu. foll. by *upon*) cast (an accusation) back upon a person. **b** repay (an injury or insult) in kind. □□ **re·tal·i·a·tion** /-áyshən/ *n.* **re·tal·i·a·tor** *n.* **re·tal·i·a·to·ry** /-táleeətáwree/ *adj.*

re·tard /ritáard/ *v. & n.* ● *v.tr.* **1** make slow or late. **2** delay the progress, development, arrival, or accomplishment of. ● *n.* **1** retardation. **2** /reétard/ *sl. derog.* a person with a mental handicap. □□ **re·tar·dant** *adj. & n.* **re·tar·da·tion** /reétaardáyshən/ *n.* **re·tar·da·to·ry** /-ətáwree/ *adj.* **re·tard·er** *n.* **re·tard·ment** *n.*

re·tard·ed /ritáardid/ *adj.* backward in mental or physical development.

retch /rech/ *v. & n.* ● *v.intr.* make a motion of vomiting esp. involuntarily and without effect. ● *n.* such a motion or the sound of it.

re·te /reétee/ *n.* (*pl.* **retia** /-teeə, -sheeə, -shə/) *Anat.* an elaborate network or plexus of blood vessels and nerve cells.

re·tell /reétél/ *v.tr.* (*past* and *past part.* **retold**) tell again or in a different version.

re·ten·tion /riténshən/ *n.* **1 a** the act or an instance of retaining; the state of being retained. **b** the ability to retain things experienced or learned; memory. **2** *Med.* the failure to evacuate urine or another secretion.

re·ten·tive /riténtiv/ *adj.* **1** (often foll. by *of*) tending to retain (moisture, etc.). **2** (of memory or a person) not forgetful. □□ **re·ten·tive·ly** *adv.* **re·ten·tive·ness** *n.*

re·tex·ture /reétékschər/ *v.tr.* treat (material, etc.) so as to restore its original texture.

re·think *v. & n.* ● *v.tr.* /reéthíngk/ (*past* and *past part.* **rethought**) think about (something) again, esp. with a view to making changes. ● *n.* /reéthingk/ a reassessment.

re·ti·a *pl.* of RETE.

re·ti·ar·i·us /reéshee·áireeəs/ *n.* (*pl.* **retiarii** /-áireeī, -áiree-ee/) a Roman gladiator using a net to trap his opponent.

ret·i·cence /rétisəns/ *n.* **1** the avoidance of saying all one knows or feels, or of saying more than is necessary. **2** a disposition to silence. **3** the act or instance of holding back some fact. **4** abstinence from overemphasis in art. □□ **ret·i·cent** *adj.* **ret·i·cent·ly** *adv.*

ret·i·cle /rétikəl/ *n.* a network of fine threads or lines in the focal plane of an optical instrument to help accurate observation.

re·tic·u·la *pl.* of RETICULUM.

re·tic·u·late *v. & adj.* ● *v.tr. & intr.* /ritikyəlayt/ **1** divide or be divided in fact or appearance into a network. **2** ◀ arrange or be arranged in small squares or with intersecting lines. ● *adj.* /-yələt, -layt/ reticulated. □□ **re·tic·u·la·tion** /-láyshən/ *n.*

RETICULATE
VEINS IN A LEAF

network of veins

drawstring

RETICULE:
19TH-CENTURY
EMBROIDERED
RETICULE

ret·i·cule /rétikyool/ *n. hist.* ◀ a woman's netted or other bag, esp. with a drawstring, carried or worn to serve the purpose of a pocket.

re·tic·u·lum /ritikyələm/ *n.* (*pl.* **reticula** /-lə/) **1** a netlike structure; a fine network, esp. of membranes, etc., in living organisms. **2** a ruminant's second stomach. □□ **re·tic·u·lar** *adj.* **re·tic·u·lose** *adj.*

re·tie /reétí/ *v.tr.* (**retying**) tie again.

re·ti·form /reétifawrm, réti-/ *adj.* netlike; reticulated.

ret·i·na /rét'nə/ *n.* (*pl.* **retinas**, **retinae** /-nee/) a layer at the back of the eyeball sensitive to light. ▷ EYE, OPTIC NERVE. □□ **ret·i·nal** *adj.*

ret·i·ni·tis /rét'nítis/ *n.* inflammation of the retina.

ret·i·nol /rét'nawl, -nol/ *n.* a vitamin found in green and yellow vegetables, egg yolk, and fish-liver oil, essential for growth and vision in dim light. Also called **vitamin A**.

ret·i·nue /rét'noo, -yoo/ *n.* a body of attendants accompanying an important person.

re·tire /ritír/ *v.* **1 a** *intr.* leave office or employment, esp. because of age. **b** *tr.* cause (a person) to retire from work. **2** *intr.* withdraw; go away; retreat. **3** *intr.* seek seclusion or shelter. **4** *intr.* go to bed. **5** *tr.* withdraw (troops). **6** *intr. & tr. Baseball* (of a batter or side) put out. □ **retire from the world** become a recluse. **retire into oneself** become uncommunicative or unsociable. □□ **re·tir·er** *n.*

re·tired /ritírd/ *adj.* **1** having retired from employment. **2** withdrawn from society or observation.

re·tire·ment /ritírmənt/ *n.* **1 a** the act or an instance of retiring. **b** the condition of having retired. **2 a** seclusion or privacy. **b** a secluded place. **3** income, esp. pension, on which a retired person lives.

re·tir·ing /ritíring/ *adj.* shy; fond of seclusion. □□ **re·tir·ing·ly** *adv.*

re·told *past* and *past part.* of RETELL.

re·took *past* of RETAKE.

re·tool /reétool/ *v.tr.* equip (a factory, etc.) with new tools.

re·tor·sion /ritáwrshən/ *n.* (also **re·tor·tion**) retaliation by one nation on another, as for unfair trade, etc.

re·tort[1] /ritáwrt/ *n. & v.* ● *n.* **1** an incisive or witty or angry reply. **2** the turning of a charge or argument against its originator. **3** a retaliation. ● *v.* **1 a** *tr.* say by way of a retort. **b** *intr.* make a retort. **2** *tr.* repay (an insult or attack) in kind. **3** *tr.* (often foll. by *on*, *upon*) return (mischief, a charge, sarcasm, etc.) to its originator. **4** *tr.* (often foll. by *against*) make (an argument) tell against its user. **5** *tr.* (as **retorted** *adj.*) recurved; twisted or bent backward.

re·tort[2] /ritáwrt, reétawrt/ *n. & v.* ● *n.* **1** ▶ a vessel usu. of glass with a long curved neck used in distilling liquids. **2** a vessel for heating mercury for purification, coal to generate gas, or iron and carbon to make steel. ● *v.tr.* purify (mercury) by heating in a retort.

RETORT: EARLY GLASS
RETORT ON A FURNACE

neck

furnace

re·tor·tion /ritáwrshən/ *n.* **1** the act or an instance of bending back; the condition of being bent back. **2** = RETORSION.

re·touch /reétúch/ *v. & n.* ● *v.tr.* improve or repair (a composition, picture, etc.) by fresh touches or alterations. ● *n.* the act or an instance of retouching. □□ **re·touch·er** *n.*

re·trace /reetráys/ *v.tr.* **1** go back over (one's steps, etc.). **2** trace back to a source or beginning. **3** recall the course of in one's memory.

re·tract /ritrákt/ *v.* **1** *tr.* (also *absol.*) withdraw (a statement or undertaking). **2 a** *tr. & intr.* (esp. with ref. to part of the body) draw or be drawn back or in. **b** *tr.* draw (an undercarriage, etc.) into the body of an aircraft. □□ **re·tract·a·ble** *adj.* **re·trac·tion** *n.* **re·trac·tive** *adj.*

re·trac·tile /ritráktil, -tīl/ *adj.* capable of being retracted. □□ **re·trac·til·i·ty** /-tílitee/ *n.*

re·trac·tor /ritráktər/ *n.* **1** a muscle used for retracting. **2** a device for retracting.

re·train /reétráyn/ *v.tr. & intr.* train again or further, esp. for new work.

re·tral /reétrəl, rét-/ *adj. Biol.* posterior; at the back.

re·trans·late /reétranzláyt, -trans-, reetránzlayt, -tráns-/ *v.tr.* translate again, esp. back into the original language. □□ **re·trans·la·tion** *n.*

re·trans·mit /reétranzmít, -trans-/ *v.tr.* (**retransmitted**, **retransmitting**) transmit (esp. radio signals or broadcast programs) back again or to a further distance. □□ **re·trans·mis·sion** /-míshən/ *n.*

re·tread *v. & n.* ● *v.tr.* /reétréd/ (*past* **retrod**; *past part.* **retrodden**) **1** tread (a path, etc.) again. **2** put a fresh tread on (a tire). ● *n.* /reétred/ a retreaded tire.

re·treat /ritreét/ *v. & n.* ● *v.* **1 a** *intr.* (esp. of military forces) go back, retire; relinquish a position. **b** *tr.* cause to retreat; move back. **2** *intr.* (esp. of features) recede. ● *n.* **1 a** the act or an instance of retreating. **b** *Mil.* a signal for this. **2** withdrawal into privacy or security. **3** a place of shelter or seclusion. **4** a period of seclusion for prayer and meditation. **5** *Mil.* a bugle call at sunset. **6** a place for the reception of the elderly or others in need of care.

re·trench /ritrénch/ *v.* **1 a** *tr.* reduce the amount of (costs). **b** *intr.* cut down expenses; introduce economies. **2** *tr.* shorten or abridge. □□ **re·trench·ment** *n.*

re·tri·al /reétríəl/ *n.* a second or further (judicial) trial.

ret·ri·bu·tion /rétribyóoshən/ *n.* requital usu. for evil done; vengeance. □□ **re·trib·u·tive** /ritríbyətiv/ *adj.* **re·trib·u·to·ry** /ritríbyətawree/ *adj.*

re·trieve /ritreév/ *v. & n.* ● *v.tr.* **1 a** regain possession of. **b** recover by investigation or effort of memory. **2 a** recall to mind. **b** obtain (information stored in a computer, etc.). **3** (of a dog) find and bring in (killed or wounded game, etc.). **4** (foll. by *from*) rescue (esp. from a bad state). **5** restore to a flourishing state; revive. **6** repair or set right (*managed to retrieve the situation*). ● *n.* the possibility of recovery (*beyond retrieve*). □□ **re·triev·a·ble** *adj.* **re·triev·al** *n.*

re·triev·er /ritreévər/ *n.* **1 a** a dog of a breed used for retrieving game. ▷ DOG. **b** this breed. **2** a person who retrieves something.

ret·ro /rétrō/ *adj. & n. sl.* ● *adj.* **1** reviving or harking back to the past. **2** retroactive. ● *n.* (*pl.* **-os**) a retro fashion or style.

retro- /rétrō/ *comb. form* **1** denoting action back or in return (*retroact*; *retroflex*). **2** *Anat. & Med.* denoting location behind.

ret·ro·act /rétrō-ákt/ *v.intr.* **1** operate in a backward direction. **2** have a retrospective effect. **3** react. □□ **ret·ro·ac·tion** *n.*

ret·ro·ac·tive /rétrō-áktiv/ *adj.* (esp. of legislation) having retrospective effect. □□ **ret·ro·ac·tive·ly** *adv.* **ret·ro·ac·tiv·i·ty** /-tívitee/ *n.*

ret·ro·cede /rétrōseéd/ *v.* **1** *intr.* move back; recede. **2** *tr.* cede back again. □□ **ret·ro·ced·ence** *n.* **ret·ro·ced·ent** *adj.* **ret·ro·ces·sion** /-séshən/ *n.* **ret·ro·ces·sive** /-sésiv/ *adj.*

R

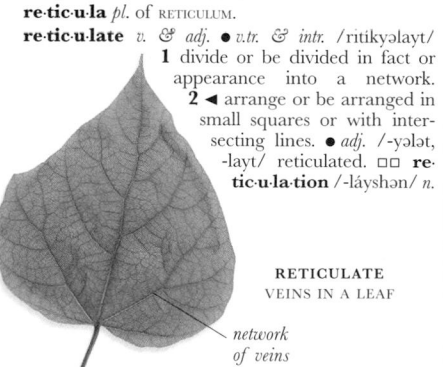

ret·ro·choir /rétrōkwīr/ *n.* the part of a cathedral or large church behind the high altar.

re·trod *past* of RETREAD.

re·trod·den *past part.* of RETREAD.

ret·ro·fit /rétrōfit/ *v.tr.* (**-fitted, -fitting**) modify (machinery, vehicles, etc.) to incorporate changes and developments introduced after manufacture.

ret·ro·flex /rétrəfleks/ *adj.* (also **ret·ro·flexed**) **1** *Anat., Med., & Bot.* turned backward. **2** *Phonet.* pronounced with the tip of the tongue curled up toward the hard palate. □□ **ret·ro·flex·ion** /-flékshən/ *n.*

ret·ro·grade /rétrəgrayd/ *adj., n., & v.* ● *adj.* **1** directed backward; retreating. **2** reverting esp. to an inferior state; declining. **3** inverse; reversed (*in retrograde order*). **4** *Astron.* in or showing retrogradation. ● *n.* a degenerate person. ● *v.intr.* **1** move backward; recede; retire. **2** decline; revert. □□ **ret·ro·grade·ly** *adv.*

ret·ro·gra·da·tion /rétrōgrədáyshən/ *n. Astron.* **1** the apparent backward motion of a planet in the zodiac. **2** the apparent motion of a celestial body from east to west. **3** backward movement of the lunar nodes on the ecliptic.

ret·ro·gress /rétrəgrés/ *v.intr.* **1** go back; move backward. **2** deteriorate. □□ **ret·ro·gres·sion** /-gréshən/ *n.* **ret·ro·gres·sive** /-grésiv/ *adj.*

ret·ro·ject /rétrōjekt/ *v.tr.* throw back (usu. opp. PROJECT).

ret·ro-rock·et /rétrō-rokit/ *n.* an auxiliary rocket for slowing down a spacecraft, etc.

ret·ro·spect /rétrəspekt/ *n.* **1** (foll. by *to*) regard or reference to precedent or authority, or to previous conditions. **2** a survey of past time or events. □ **in retrospect** when looked back on.

ret·ro·spec·tion /rétrəspékshən/ *n.* **1** the action of looking back esp. into the past. **2** an indulgence or engagement in retrospect.

ret·ro·spec·tive /rétrəspéktiv/ *adj. & n.* ● *adj.* **1** looking back on or dealing with the past. **2** (of an exhibition, recital, etc.) showing an artist's development over his or her lifetime. **3** (of a view) lying to the rear. ● *n.* a retrospective exhibition, recital, etc. □□ **ret·ro·spec·tive·ly** *adv.*

ret·ro·ster·nal /rétrōstə́rnəl/ *adj. Anat. & Med.* behind the breastbone.

re·trous·sé /rətrōōsáy/ *adj.* (of the nose) turned up at the tip.

ret·ro·vert /rétrōvərt/ *v.tr.* **1** turn backward. **2** *Med.* (as **retroverted** *adj.*) (of the womb) having a backward inclination. □□ **ret·ro·ver·sion** /-və́rzhən, -shən/ *n.*

ret·ro·vi·rus /rétrōvīrəs/ *n. Biol.* any of a group of RNA viruses that form DNA during the replication of their RNA.

re·try /réetrí/ *v.tr.* (**-ies, -ied**) try (a defendant or lawsuit) a second or further time.

ret·si·na /retséenə/ *n.* a Greek wine flavored with resin.

re·tune /réetōōn, -tyōōn/ *v.tr.* **1** tune (a musical instrument) again or differently. **2** tune (a radio, etc.) to a different frequency.

re·turf /réetə́rf/ *v.tr.* provide with new turf.

re·turn /ritə́rn/ *v. & n.* ● *v.* **1** *intr.* come or go back. **2** *tr.* bring or put or send back. **3** *tr.* pay back or reciprocate; give in response. **4** *tr.* yield (a profit). **5** *tr.* say in reply; retort. **6** *tr.* (in tennis, etc.) hit or send (the ball) back after receiving it. **7** *tr.* state or mention or describe officially, esp. in answer to a writ or formal demand. **8** *tr.* elect, esp. reelect, to political office, etc. **9** *tr. Cards* **a** lead (a suit) previously led or bid by a partner. **b** lead (a suit or card) after taking a trick. **10** *tr. Archit.* continue (a wall, etc.) in a changed direction, esp. at right angles. ● *n.* **1** the act or an instance of coming or going back. **2 a** the act or an instance of giving or sending or putting or paying back. **b** a thing given or sent back. **3** a key on a computer or typewriter to start a new line. **4** (in *sing.* or *pl.*) **a** the proceeds or profit of an undertaking. **b** the acquisition of these. **5** a

formal report or statement compiled or submitted by order (*an income-tax return*). **6** (in full **return match** or **game**) a second match, etc., between the same opponents. **7** a response or reply. **8** (in *pl.*) a report on votes counted in an election (*early returns from the third district*). **9** *Archit.* a part receding from the line of the front, e.g., the side of a house or of a window opening. □ **in return** as an exchange or reciprocal action. **many happy returns (of the day)** a greeting on a birthday, etc. □□ **re·turn·er** *n.*

re·turn·a·ble /ritə́rnəbəl/ *adj. & n.* ● *adj.* **1** intended to be returned, as an empty beverage container. **2** required by law to be returned, as a court writ. ● *n.* an empty beverage container, especially a bottle or can, that can be returned for a refund of the deposit paid at purchase.

re·turn·ee /ritə́rnéé/ *n.* a person who returns home from abroad, esp. after war service.

re·tuse /ritōōs, -tyōōs/ *adj.* esp. *Bot.* having a broad end with a central depression.

re·ty·ing *pres. part.* of RETIE.

re·type /réetíp/ *v.tr.* type again, esp. to correct errors.

re·u·ni·fy /réeyōōnifí/ *v.tr.* (**-ies, -ied**) restore (esp. separated territories) to a political unity. □□ **re·u·ni·fi·ca·tion** /-fikáyshən/ *n.*

re·un·ion /réeyōōnyən/ *n.* **1 a** the act or an instance of reuniting. **b** the condition of being reunited. **2** a social gathering esp. of people formerly associated.

re·u·nite /réeyōōnít/ *v.tr. & intr.* bring or come back together.

re·up·hol·ster /réeəphṓlstər, -əpṓl-/ *v.tr.* upholster anew. □□ **re·up·hol·ster·y** *n.*

re·use *v. & n.* ● *v.tr.* /réeyōōz/ use again or more than once. ● *n.* /réeyōōs/ a second or further use. □□ **re·us·a·ble** /-yōōzəbəl/ *adj.*

re·u·ti·lize /réeyōōt'līz/ *v.tr.* utilize again or for a different purpose. □□ **re·u·ti·li·za·tion** /-záyshən/ *n.*

Rev. *abbr.* **1** Reverend. **2** Revelation (New Testament).

rev /rev/ *n. & v. colloq.* ● *n.* (in *pl.*) the number of revolutions of an engine per minute. ● *v.* (**revved, revving**) **1** *intr.* (of an engine) revolve; turn over. **2** *tr.* (also *absol.*; often foll. by *up*) cause (an engine) to run quickly.

re·val·ue /réevályōō/ *v.tr.* (**revalues, revaluing**) *Econ.* give a different value to, esp. give a higher value to, (a currency) in relation to other currencies or gold (opp. DEVALUE). □□ **re·val·u·a·tion** /-vályōōáyshən/ *n.*

re·vamp /réevámp/ *v.tr.* **1** renovate; revise; improve. **2** patch up.

re·vanch·ism /rivánchizəm/ *n. Polit.* a policy of seeking to retaliate, esp. to recover lost territory. □□ **re·vanch·ist** *n. & adj.*

re·veal[1] /rivéel/ *v.tr.* **1** display or show; allow to appear. **2** (often as **revealing** *adj.*) disclose; divulge; betray. **3** *tr.* (in *refl.* or *passive*) come to sight or knowledge. **4** *Relig.* (esp. of God) make known by inspiration or supernatural means. □□ **re·veal·a·ble** *adj.* **re·veal·er** *n.* **re·veal·ing·ly** *adv.*

re·veal[2] /rivéel/ *n.* an internal side surface of an opening or recess, esp. of a doorway or a window aperture.

re·veil·le /révəlee/ *n.* a military wake-up signal.

rev·el /révəl/ *v. & n.* ● *v.* (**reveled, reveling** or **revelled, revelling**) **1** *intr.* have a good time; be extravagantly festive. **2** *intr.* (foll. by *in*) take keen delight in. **3** *tr.* (foll. by *away*) throw away (money or time) in revelry. ● *n.* (in *sing.* or *pl.*) the act or an instance of reveling. □□ **rev·el·er** *n.* **rev·el·ry** *n.* (*pl.* **-ies**)

rev·e·la·tion /révəláyshən/ *n.* **1 a** the act or an instance of revealing, esp. the supposed disclosure of knowledge to humankind by a divine or supernatural agency. **b** knowledge disclosed in this way. **2** a striking disclosure. **3** (**Revelation** or *colloq.*

Revelations) (in full **the Revelation of St. John the Divine**) the last book of the New Testament. □□ **rev·e·la·tion·al** *adj.*

rev·e·la·tion·ist /révəláyshənist/ *n.* a believer in divine revelation.

re·vel·a·to·ry /révələtawree, rəvélə-/ *adj.* serving to reveal, esp. something significant.

rev·e·nant /révənənt/ *n.* a person who has returned, esp. supposedly from the dead.

re·venge /rivénj/ *n. & v.* ● *n.* **1** retaliation for an offense or injury. **2** an act of retaliation. **3** the desire for this; a vindictive feeling. **4** (in games) a chance to win after an earlier defeat. ● *v.* **1** *tr.* (in *refl.* or *passive*; often foll. by *on, upon*) inflict retaliation for an offense. **2** *tr.* take revenge for (an offense). **3** *tr.* avenge (a person). **4** *intr.* take revenge. □□ **re·veng·er** *n.*

re·venge·ful /rivénjfŏŏl/ *adj.* eager for revenge. □□ **re·venge·ful·ly** *adv.*

rev·e·nue /révənōō, -nyōō/ *n.* **1 a** income, esp. of a large amount, from any source. **b** (in *pl.*) items constituting this. **2** a government's annual income from which public expenses are met. **3** the department of the civil service collecting this.

re·verb /rivə́rb, réevərb/ *n. & v. & intr.* reverberate. ● *n. Mus. colloq.* **1** reverberation. **2** a device to produce this.

re·ver·ber·ate /rivə́rbərayt/ *v.* **1 a** *intr.* (of sound, light, or heat) be returned or echoed repeatedly. **b** *tr.* return (a sound, etc.) in this way. **2** *intr.* (of a rumor, etc.) be heard much or repeatedly. □□ **re·ver·ber·ant** *adj.* **re·ver·ber·ant·ly** *adv.* **re·ver·ber·a·tion** /-ráyshən/ *n.* **re·ver·ber·a·tive** /-rətiv/ *adj.* **re·ver·ber·a·tor** *n.* **re·ver·ber·a·to·ry** /-rətawree/ *adj.*

re·vere /rivéer/ *v.tr.* hold in deep and usu. affectionate or religious respect; venerate.

rev·er·ence /révərəns, révrəns/ *n. & v.* ● *n.* **1 a** the act of revering or the state of being revered. **b** the capacity for revering. **2** (**Reverence**) a title used of or to some members of the clergy. ● *v.tr.* regard or treat with reverence.

rev·er·end /révərənd, révrənd/ *adj. & n.* ● *adj.* (as the title of a clergyman) deserving reverence. ● *n. colloq.* a clergyman.

rev·er·ent /révərənt, révrənt/ *adj.* feeling or showing reverence. □□ **rev·er·ent·ly** *adv.*

rev·er·en·tial /révərénshəl/ *adj.* of the nature of, due to, or characterized by reverence. □□ **rev·er·en·tial·ly** *adv.*

rev·er·ie /révəree/ *n.* **1** a state of abstracted musing (*was lost in a reverie*). **2** *archaic* a fantastic notion or theory; a delusion. **3** *Mus.* an instrumental piece suggesting a dreamy or musing state.

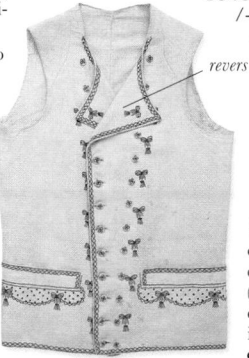

revers

REVERS ON A DRESS WAISTCOAT

re·vers /rivéer/ *n.* (*pl.* same /-véerz/) **1** ◄ the turned-back edge of a garment revealing the undersurface. **2** the material on this surface.

re·verse /rivə́rs/ *v., adj., & n.* ● *v.* **1** *tr.* turn the other way around or up or inside out. **2** *tr.* change to the opposite character or effect. **3** *intr. & tr.* travel or cause to travel backward. **4** *tr.* make (an engine, etc.) work in a contrary direction. **5** *tr.* revoke or annul (a decree, act, etc.). **6** *intr.* (of a dancer, esp. in a waltz) revolve in the opposite direction. ● *adj.* **1** placed or turned in an opposite direction or position. **2** opposite or contrary in character or order; inverted. ● *n.* **1** the opposite or contrary. **2** the contrary of the usual manner. **3** an occurrence of misfortune; a disaster, esp. a defeat. **4** reverse gear or motion. **5** the reverse side of something. **6 a** the side of a coin or medal, etc., bearing the secondary design. **b** this design (cf. OBVERSE). **7** the verso of a book leaf.

R

□ **reverse arms** hold a rifle with the butt upward. **reverse the charges** make the recipient of a telephone call responsible for payment. □□ **re·ver·sal** *n.* **re·verse·ly** *adv.* **re·vers·er** *n.* **re·vers·i·ble** *adj.* **re·vers·i·bil·i·ty** *n.* **re·vers·i·bly** *adv.*

reverse en·gi·neer·ing *n.* the reproduction of another manufacturer's product after detailed examination of its construction or composition.

re·ver·sion /rivárzhən/ *n.* **1 a** the legal right (esp. of the original owner, or his or her heirs) to possess or succeed to property on the death of the present possessor. **b** property to which a person has such a right. **2** *Biol.* a return to ancestral type. **3** a return to a previous state, habit, etc. **4** a sum payable on a person's death, esp. by way of life insurance. □□ **re·ver·sion·al** *adj.* **re·ver·sion·ar·y** *adj.*

re·vert /rivárt/ *v.* **1** *intr.* (foll. by *to*) return to a former state, practice, opinion, etc. **2** *intr.* (of property, an office, etc.) return by reversion. **3** *intr.* fall back into a wild state. **4** *tr.* turn (one's eyes or steps) back. □□ **re·vert·er** *n.* (in sense 2). **re·vert·i·ble** *adj.* (in sense 2).

re·vet /rivét/ *v.tr.* (**revetted, revetting**) face (a rampart, wall, etc.) with masonry, esp. in fortification.

re·vet·ment /rivétmənt/ *n.* a retaining wall or facing.

re·view /rivyōō/ *n. & v.* ● *n.* **1** a general survey or assessment of a subject or thing. **2** a retrospect or survey of the past. **3** revision or reconsideration (*is under review*). **4** a display and formal inspection of troops, etc. **5** a published account or criticism of a book, play, etc. **6** a periodical publication with critical articles on current events, the arts, etc. **7** a second view. ● *v.tr.* **1** survey or look back on. **2** reconsider or revise. **3** hold a review of (troops, etc.). **4** write a review of (a book, play, etc.). **5** view again. □□ **re·view·a·ble** *adj.* **re·view·er** *n.*

re·vile /rivíl/ *v.tr.* criticize abusively. □□ **re·vile·ment** *n.* **re·vil·er** *n.*

re·vise /rivíz/ *v. & n.* ● *v.tr.* **1** examine or reexamine and improve or amend (esp. written or printed matter). **2** consider and alter (an opinion, etc.). ● *n. Printing* a proof sheet including corrections made in an earlier proof. □□ **re·vis·a·ble** *adj.* **re·vis·al** *n.* **re·vis·er** *n.*

Re·vised Stand·ard Ver·sion *n.* a revision in 1946–52 of the Authorized Version of the Bible.

Re·vised Ver·sion *n.* a revision in 1881–85 of the Authorized Version of the Bible.

re·vi·sion /rivízhən/ *n.* **1** the act or an instance of revising; the process of being revised. **2** a revised edition or form. □□ **re·vi·sion·ar·y** *adj.*

re·vi·sion·ism /rivízhənizəm/ *n.* often *derog.* **1** a policy of revision or modification, esp. of Marxism. **2** any departure from or modification of accepted doctrine, theory, view of history, etc. □□ **re·vi·sion·ist** *n. & adj.*

re·vi·tal·ize /réevítˈlīz/ *v.tr.* imbue with new life and vitality. □□ **re·vi·tal·i·za·tion** /-záyshən/ *n.*

re·viv·al /rivívəl/ *n.* **1** the act or an instance of reviving; the process of being revived. **2** a new production of an old play, etc. **3** a revived use of an old practice, custom, etc. **4 a** a reawakening of religious fervor. **b** one or a series of evangelistic meetings to promote this. **5** restoration to bodily or mental vigor or to life or consciousness.

re·viv·al·ism /rivívəlizəm/ *n.* belief in or the promotion of a revival, esp. of religious fervor. □□ **re·viv·al·ist** *n.* **re·viv·al·is·tic** /-lístik/ *adj.*

re·vive /rivív/ *v.intr. & tr.* **1** come or bring back to consciousness or life or strength. **2** come or bring back to existence, use, notice, etc. □□ **re·viv·a·ble** *adj.* **re·viv·er** /rivívər/ *n.*

re·viv·i·fy /rivívifí/ *v.tr.* (**-ies, -ied**) restore to animation, activity, vigor, or life. □□ **re·viv·i·fi·ca·tion** /-fikáyshən/ *n.*

re·voke /rivók/ *v.* **1** *tr.* rescind, withdraw, or cancel.

2 *intr. Cards* fail to follow suit when able to do so. □□ **re·vo·ca·ble** /révəkəbəl/ *adj.* **rev·o·ca·tion** /révəkáyshən/ *n.* **re·vo·ca·to·ry** /révəkətawree/ *adj.* **re·vok·er** *n.*

re·volt /rivólt/ *v. & n.* ● *v.* **1** *intr.* **a** rise in rebellion. **b** (as **revolted** *adj.*) having revolted. **2 a** *tr.* (often in *passive*) affect with strong disgust; nauseate. **b** *intr.* (often foll. by *at, against*) feel strong disgust. ● *n.* **1** an act of rebelling. **2** a state of insurrection. **3** a sense of loathing. **4** a mood of protest or defiance.

re·volt·ing /rivólting/ *adj.* disgusting; horrible. □□ **re·volt·ing·ly** *adv.*

rev·o·lu·tion /révəlōōshən/ *n.* **1 a** the forcible overthrow of a government or social order. **b** (in Marxism) the replacement of one ruling class by another; the class struggle that is expected to lead to political change and the triumph of communism. **2** any fundamental change or reversal of conditions. **3** the act or an instance of revolving. **4 a** a motion in orbit or a circular course or around an axis or center; rotation. **b** the single completion of an orbit or rotation. **c** the time taken for this. **5** a cyclic recurrence. □□ **rev·o·lu·tion·ism** *n.* **rev·o·lu·tion·ist** *n.*

rev·o·lu·tion·ar·y /révəlōōshəneree/ *adj. & n.* ● *adj.* **1** involving great and often violent change or innovation. **2** of or causing political revolution. **3** (**Revolutionary**) of or relating to a particular revolution, esp. the American Revolution. ● *n.* (*pl.* **-ies**) an instigator or supporter of political revolution.

rev·o·lu·tion·ize /révəlōōshəníz/ *v.tr.* introduce fundamental change to.

re·volve /rivólv/ *v.* **1** *intr.* & *tr.* turn or cause to turn around, esp. on an axis; rotate. **2** *intr.* move in a circular orbit. **3** *tr.* ponder (a problem, etc.) in the mind.

re·volv·er /rivólvər/ *n.* ▼ a pistol with revolving chambers enabling several shots to be fired without reloading. ▷ GUN

REVOLVER:
COLT SINGLE-ACTION ARMY
REVOLVER

hammer — *revolving cylinder* — *barrel* — *single-action lock* — *ejector tube* — *sight* — *trigger* — *stock*

re·volv·ing cred·it *n.* credit that is automatically renewed as debts are paid off.

re·volv·ing door *n.* a door with usu. four partitions turning around a central axis.

re·vue /rivyōō/ *n.* a theatrical entertainment of a series of short usu. satirical sketches and songs.

re·vul·sion /rivúlshən/ *n.* **1** abhorrence; a sense of loathing. **2** a sudden violent change of feeling. **3** a sudden reaction in taste, fortune, trade, etc. **4** *Med.* counterirritation; the treatment of one disordered organ, etc., by acting upon another.

re·vul·sive /rivúlsiv/ *adj. & n. Med.* ● *adj.* producing revulsion. ● *n.* a revulsive substance.

re·ward /riwáwrd/ *n. & v.* ● *n.* **1 a** a return or recompense for service or merit. **b** requital for good or evil; retribution. **2** a sum offered for the detection of a criminal, the restoration of lost property, etc. ● *v.tr.* give a reward to (a person) or for (a service, etc.).

re·ward·ing /riwáwrding/ *adj.* (of an activity, etc.) well worth doing; providing satisfaction. □□ **re·ward·ing·ly** *adv.*

re·wash /réewásh, -wósh/ *v.tr.* wash again.

re·weigh /réewáy/ *v.tr.* weigh again.

re·wind /réewínd/ *v. & n.* ● *v.tr.* (*past* and *past part.*

rewound) wind (a film or tape, etc.) back to the beginning. ● *n.* **1** function on a tape deck, camera, etc., to rewind (tape, film, etc.). **2** the button that activates this function. □□ **re·wind·er** *n.*

re·wire /réewír/ *v.tr.* provide (a building, etc.) with new wiring. □□ **re·wir·a·ble** *adj.*

re·word /réewárd/ *v.tr.* change the wording of.

re·work /réewárk/ *v.tr.* revise; refashion; remake.

re·wound *past* and *past part.* of REWIND.

re·write *v. & n.* ● *v.tr.* /réerít/ (*past* **rewrote**; *past part.* **rewritten**) write again or differently. ● *n.* /réerīt/ **1** the act or an instance of rewriting. **2** a thing rewritten.

Rex /reks/ *n.* the reigning king (following a name or in the titles of lawsuits, e.g., *Rex v. Jones*, the Crown versus Jones).

Reye's syn·drome /ríz, ráz/ *n. Med.* an acute, often fatal brain disease of children that usually follows a viral infection such as influenza or chicken pox and that is associated with the use of aspirin.

Reyn·ard /ráynərd, -naard, rénərd/ *n.* a fox (esp. as a proper name in stories).

Rf *symb. Chem.* the element rutherfordium.

r.f. *abbr.* (also **RF**) radio frequency.

RFD *abbr.* rural free delivery.

Rh[1] *symb. Chem.* the element rhodium.

Rh[2] see RH FACTOR.

r.h. *abbr.* right hand.

rhab·do·man·cy /rábdəmansee/ *n.* the use of a divining rod, esp. for discovering subterranean water or mineral ore.

Rhad·a·man·thine /rádəmánthin, -thīn/ *adj.* stern and incorruptible in judgment.

rhap·sode /rápsōd/ *n.* a reciter of epic poems, esp. of Homer in ancient Greece.

rhap·so·dize /rápsədīz/ *v.intr.* talk or write rhapsodies.

rhap·so·dy /rápsədee/ *n.* (*pl.* **-ies**) **1** an enthusiastic, ecstatic, or extravagant utterance or composition. **2** *Mus.* a piece of music in one extended movement, usu. emotional in character. □□ **rhap·sod·ic** /rapsódik/ *adj.* **rhap·sod·i·cal** *adj.* **rhap·so·dist** /rápsədist/ *n.*

rhe·a /réeə/ *n.* ▼ any of several S. American flightless birds of the family Rheidae, like but smaller than an ostrich.

RHEA:
GREATER RHEA
(*Rhea americana*)

rhe·bok /réebok/ *n.* (also **reebok**) a small S. African antelope, *Pelea capreolus*, with sharp horns.

rhe·ni·um /réeneeəm/ *n. Chem.* a rare metallic element of the manganese group, occurring naturally in molybdenum ores and used in the manufacture of superconducting alloys. ¶ Symb.: **Re**.

rhe·ol·o·gy /reeóləjee/ *n.* the science dealing with the flow and deformation of matter. □□ **rhe·o·log·i·cal** /-əlójikəl/ *adj.* **rhe·ol·o·gist** *n.*

R

RHEOSTAT

In a rheostat, a current enters one terminal and flows through the resistance wire. On reaching the sliding contact, it is diverted along the bar. The more wire it travels through, the higher the resistance.

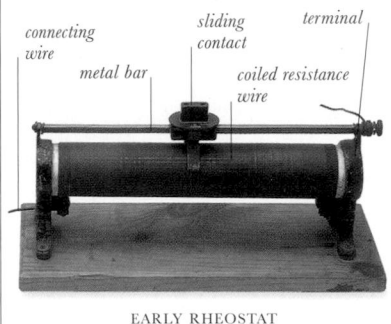

connecting wire
sliding contact
terminal
metal bar
coiled resistance wire

EARLY RHEOSTAT

rhe·o·stat /réeəstat/ n. Electr. ▲ an instrument used to control a current by varying the resistance. □□ **rhe·o·stat·ic** /-státik/ adj.

rhe·sus /réesəs/ n. (in full **rhesus monkey**) a small monkey, *Macaca mulatta*, common in N. India.

rhe·sus fac·tor n. = Rh FACTOR.

rhe·tor /réetər/ n. 1 an ancient Greek or Roman teacher or professor of rhetoric. 2 usu. derog. an orator.

rhet·o·ric /rétərik/ n. 1 the art of effective or persuasive speaking or writing. 2 language designed to persuade or impress (often with an implication of exaggeration, etc.).

rhe·tor·i·cal /ritáwrikəl, -tór-/ adj. 1 a expressed with a view to persuasive or impressive effect; artificial or extravagant in language. b (of a question) assuming a preferred answer. 2 of the nature of rhetoric. 3 a of or relating to the art of rhetoric. b given to rhetoric; oratorical. □□ **rhe·tor·i·cal·ly** adv.

rhe·tor·i·cal ques·tion n. a question asked not for information but to produce an effect, e.g., *who cares?* for *nobody cares.*

rhet·o·ri·cian /rétərishən/ n. 1 an orator. 2 a teacher of or expert in rhetoric. 3 a rhetorical speaker or writer.

rheum /room/ n. a watery discharge from a mucous membrane, esp. of the eyes or nose. □□ **rheum·y** adj.

rheu·mat·ic /roomátik/ adj. & n. ● adj. 1 of, relating to, or suffering from rheumatism. 2 producing or produced by rheumatism. ● n. a person suffering from rheumatism. □□ **rheu·mat·i·cal·ly** adv. **rheu·mat·ick·y** adj. colloq.

rheu·mat·ic fe·ver n. a noninfectious fever with inflammation and pain in the joints.

rheu·ma·tism /róōmətizəm/ n. any disease marked by inflammation and pain in the joints, muscles, or fibrous tissue, esp. rheumatoid arthritis.

rheu·ma·toid /róōmətoyd/ adj. having the character of rheumatism.

rheu·ma·toid ar·thri·tis n. a chronic progressive disease causing inflammation and stiffening of the joints.

rheu·ma·tol·o·gy /róōmətóləjee/ n. the study of rheumatic diseases. □□ **rheu·ma·to·log·i·cal** /-təlójikəl/ adj. **rheu·ma·tol·o·gist** n.

Rh factor Physiol. an antigen occurring on the red blood cells of most humans and some other primates.

rhi·nal /rínəl/ adj. Anat. of a nostril or the nose.

rhine·stone /rínston/ n. an imitation diamond.

rhi·ni·tis /rīnítis/ n. inflammation of the mucous membrane of the nose.

rhi·no /rínō/ n. (pl. same or **-os**) colloq. a rhinoceros.

rhino- /rínō/ comb. form Anat. the nose.

rhi·noc·er·os /rīnósərəs/ n. (pl. same or **rhinoceroses**) ▼ any of various large thick-skinned plant-eating ungulates of the family Rhinocerotidae, with usu. one horn. ▷ UNGULATE

rhi·no·plas·ty /rínōplastee/ n. plastic surgery of the nose. □□ **rhi·no·plas·tic** adj.

rhi·zoid /rízoyd/ adj. & n. Bot. ● adj. rootlike. ● n. a root hair or filament in mosses, ferns, etc.

rhi·zome /rízōm/ n. ▶ an underground rootlike stem bearing both roots and shoots.

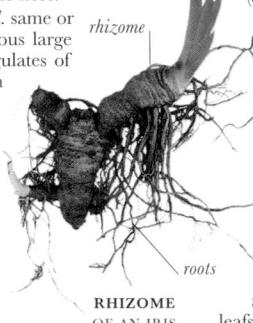

shoot
rhizome
roots

RHIZOME OF AN IRIS

rho /rō/ n. the seventeenth letter of the Greek alphabet (Ρ,ρ).

Rhode Is·land Red /rōd/ n. an orig. American breed of domestic fowl with brownish-red plumage.

rho·di·um /rṓdeeəm/ n. Chem. a hard white metallic element of the platinum group, used in making alloys and plating jewelry. ¶ Symb.: **Rh**.

rho·do·den·dron /rṓdədéndrən/ n. ▶ any evergreen shrub of the genus *Rhododendron*, with large clusters of trumpet-shaped flowers.

rho·dop·sin /rōdópsin/ n. a light-sensitive pigment in the retina. Also called **visual purple**.

rho·do·ra /rədáwrə/ N. American pink-flowered shrub, *Rhodora canadense*.

rhomb /rom/ n. = RHOMBUS. □□ **rhom·bic** adj.

rhom·bi pl. of RHOMBUS.

rhom·bo·he·dron /rómbə-heédrən/ n. (pl. **-hedrons** or **-hedra** /-drə/) 1 ▶ a solid bounded by six equal rhombuses. 2 a crystal in this form. □□ **rhom·bo·he·dral** adj.

rhom·boid /rómboyd/ adj. & n. ● adj. (also **rhom·boi·dal** /-bóyd'l/) having or nearly having the shape of a rhombus. ● n. a quadrilateral of which only the opposite sides and angles are equal.

rhom·boi·de·us /rombóydeeəs/ n. (pl. **rhomboidei** /-dee-ī/) Anat. a muscle connecting the scapula to the vertebrae.

rhom·bus /rómbəs/ n. (pl. **rhom·buses** or **rhombi** /-bī/) Geom. a parallelogram with oblique angles and equal sides.

rhu·barb /róōbaarb/ n. 1 a any of various plants of the genus *Rheum*, esp. *R. rhaponticum*, producing long fleshy dark-red leafstalks that are cooked and used as food. b the leafstalks of this. 2 a a root of a Chinese and Tibetan plant of the genus *Rheum*. b a purgative made from this. 3 sl. nonsense. 4 sl. a heated dispute.

rhumb /rum/ n. Naut. 1 any of the 32 points of the compass. 2 the angle between two successive compass points. 3 (in full **rhumb line**) a a line cutting all meridians at the same angle. b the line followed by a ship sailing in a fixed direction.

rhum·ba var. of RUMBA.

rhyme /rīm/ n. & v. ● n. 1 identity of sound between words or the endings of words, esp. in verse. 2 (in sing or pl.) verse having rhymes. 3 a the use of rhyme. b a poem having rhymes. 4 a word providing a rhyme. ● v. 1 intr. a (of words or lines) produce a rhyme. b (foll. by with) act as a rhyme (with another). 2 intr. make or write rhymes. 3 tr. put or make (a story, etc.) into rhyme. 4 tr. (foll. by with) treat (a word) as rhyming with another. □ **rhyme or reason** sense; logic. □□ **rhyme·less** adj. **rhym·er** n. **rhyme·ster** /rímstər/ n. a writer of (esp. simple) rhymes.

rhythm /ríthəm/ n. 1 a measured flow of words and phrases in verse or prose determined by various relations of long and short or accented and unaccented syllables. 2 the aspect of musical composition concerned with periodical accent and the duration of notes. 3 Physiol. movement with a regular succession of strong and weak elements. 4 a regularly recurring sequence of events. 5 Art a harmonious correlation of parts. □□ **rhythm·less** adj.

RHODODENDRON (*Rhododendron yakushimanum*)

RHOMBOHEDRON

R

RHINOCEROS

There are five species of rhinoceros, two from Africa and three from Asia. They have poor eyesight, but compensate with a highly developed sense of smell and acute hearing. Rhinoceroses are solitary and fiercely territorial animals with a lifespan of up to 40 years.

thick hairless skin
shieldlike skin folds
mobile pinnae
single horn
three digits

EXTERNAL FEATURES OF AN INDIAN RHINOCEROS (*Rhinoceros unicornis*)

OTHER SPECIES OF RHINOCEROS

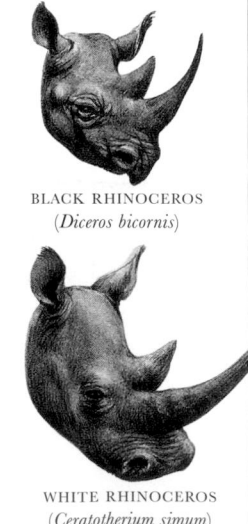

BLACK RHINOCEROS (*Diceros bicornis*)

WHITE RHINOCEROS (*Ceratotherium simum*)

rhythm and blues *n.* popular music with a blues theme and a strong rhythm.

rhyth·mic /ríthmik/ *adj.* (also **rhyth·mi·cal**) **1** relating to or characterized by rhythm. **2** regularly occurring. □□ **rhyth·mi·cal·ly** *adv.* **rhyth·mic·i·ty** /rithmísitee/ *n.*

rhythm meth·od *n.* birth control by avoiding sexual intercourse when ovulation is likely to occur.

RI *abbr.* Rhode Island (also in official postal use).

ri·a /rééə/ *n. Geog.* a long narrow inlet formed by the partial submergence of a river valley.

rib /rib/ *n. & v.* ● *n.* **1** each of the curved bones articulated in pairs to the spine and protecting the thoracic cavity and its organs. ▷ SKELETON. **2** a joint of meat from this part of an animal. ▷ CUT. **3** a ridge or long, raised piece often of stronger or thicker material across a surface or through a structure serving to support or strengthen it. **4** ▼ any of a ship's transverse curved timbers forming the framework of the hull. **5** *Knitting* a combination of plain and purl stitches producing a ribbed somewhat elastic fabric. **6** each of the hinged rods supporting the fabric of an umbrella. **7** a vein of a leaf or an insect's wing. **8** *Aeron.* a structural member in an airfoil. ● *v.tr.* (**ribbed, ribbing**) **1** provide with ribs; act as the ribs of. **2** *colloq.* make fun of; tease. **3** mark with ridges. □□ **rib·less** *adj.*

knighthead

riband

rib

keel

sternpost

RIB: HULL FRAMEWORK OF A COAL SHIP SHOWING RIBS

rib·ald /ríbəld/ *adj. & n.* ● *adj.* (of language or its user) coarsely or disrespectfully humorous. ● *n.* a user of ribald language.

rib·ald·ry /ríbəldree/ *n.* ribald talk or behavior.

rib·and /ríbənd/ *n.* a ribbon.

rib·bed /ribd/ *adj.* having ribs or riblike markings.

rib·bing /ríbing/ *n.* **1** ribs or a riblike structure. **2** *colloq.* the act or an instance of teasing.

rib·bon /ríbən/ *n.* **1 a** a narrow strip or band of fabric, used esp. for trimming or decoration. **b** material in this form. **2** a ribbon of a special color, etc., worn to indicate some honor or membership of a sports team, etc. **3** a long, narrow strip of anything, e.g., impregnated material forming the inking agent in a typewriter. **4** (in *pl.*) ragged strips (*torn to ribbons*). □□ **rib·boned** *adj.*

rib cage *n.* the wall of bones formed by the ribs around the chest. ▷ STERNUM

ri·bo·fla·vin /ríbōfláyvin/ *n.* a vitamin of the B complex, found in liver, milk, and eggs, essential for energy production. Also called **vitamin B₂**.

ri·bo·nu·cle·ic ac·id /ríbənōōkléeik, -kláyik, -nyōō-/ *n.* a nucleic acid present in living cells, esp. in ribosomes where it is involved in protein synthesis. ¶ Abbr.: **RNA**.

ri·bose /ríbōs/ *n.* a sugar found in many nucleosides and in several vitamins and enzymes.

ri·bo·some /ríbəsōm/ *n. Biochem.* each of the minute particles consisting of RNA and associated proteins found in the cytoplasm of living cells, concerned with the synthesis of proteins. ▷ BACTERIUM, CELL. □□ **ri·bo·so·mal** *adj.*

rice /rīs/ *n. & v.* ● *n.* **1** a swamp grass, *Oryza sativa*, cultivated in marshes, esp. in Asia. **2** the grains of this, used as cereal food. ● *v.tr.* sieve (cooked potatoes, etc.) into thin strings. □□ **ric·er** *n.*

rich /rich/ *adj. & n.* ● *adj.* **1** having much wealth. **2** (often foll. by *in, with*) splendid; costly; elaborate. **3** valuable (*rich offerings*). **4** copious; abundant; ample. **5** (often foll. by *in, with*) (of soil or a region, etc.) abounding in natural resources or means of production; fertile. **6** (of food or diet) containing much fat or spice, etc. **7** (of the mixture in an internal-combustion engine) containing a high proportion of fuel. **8** (of color or sound or smell) mellow and deep; strong and full. **9 a** (of an incident or assertion, etc.) ludicrous. **b** (of humor) earthy. ● *n.* (**the rich**) (used with a *pl. v.*) wealthy persons, collectively. □□ **rich·en** *v.intr. & tr.* **rich·ness** *n.*

rich·es /ríchiz/ *n.pl.* abundant means; valuable possessions.

rich·ly /ríchlee/ *adv.* **1** in a rich way. **2** fully; thoroughly.

Rich·ter scale /ríktər/ *n.* a scale of 0 to 10 for representing the strength of an earthquake.

rick /rik/ *n. & v.* ● *n.* (also **hayrick**) ► a stack of hay, wheat, etc., built into a regular shape and usu. thatched. ● *v.tr.* form into a rick or ricks.

rick·ets /ríkits/ *n.* (treated as *sing.* or *pl.*) a disease of children with softening of the bones (esp. the spine) and bowlegs, caused by a deficiency of vitamin D.

rick·et·y /ríkitee/ *adj.* **1 a** insecure or shaky in construction. **b** feeble. **2 a** suffering from rickets. **b** resembling or of the nature of rickets. □□ **rick·et·i·ness** *n.*

rick·rack /ríkrak/ *n.* ► a zigzag braided trimming for garments.

rick·sha /ríkshaw/ *n.* (also **rick·shaw**) a light two-wheeled hooded vehicle drawn by one or more persons.

ri·co·chet /ríkōshay, rikəsháy/ *n. & v.* ● *n.* **1** the action of esp. a shell or bullet in rebounding off a surface. **2** a hit made after this. ● *v.intr.* (**rico·cheted** /-shayd/; **ricocheting** /-shaying/) (of a projectile) rebound one or more times from a surface.

ri·cot·ta /rikótə, -káwtaa/ *n.* a soft Italian cheese.

ric·tus /ríktəs/ *n. Anat. & Zool.* the expanse or gape of a mouth or beak. □□ **ric·tal** *adj.*

rid /rid/ *v.tr.* (**ridding**; *past* and *past part.* **rid** or *archaic* **ridded**) (foll. by *of*) make (a person or place) free of something unwanted. □ **be** (or **get**) **rid of** be freed or relieved of (something unwanted); dispose of.

rid·dance /rídəns/ *n.* the act of getting rid of something. □ **good riddance** welcome relief from an unwanted person or thing.

rid·den *past part.* of RIDE.

rid·dle¹ /ríd'l/ *n. & v.* ● *n.* **1** a question or statement testing ingenuity in divining its answer or meaning. **2** a puzzling fact or thing or person. ● *v.* **1** *intr.* speak in or propound riddles. **2** *tr.* solve or explain (a riddle). □□ **rid·dler** *n.*

rid·dle² /ríd'l/ *n. & v.* ● *v.tr.* (usu. foll. by *with*) **1** make many holes in, esp. with gunshot. **2** (in *passive*) permeate (*riddled with errors*). **3** pass through a riddle. ● *n.* a coarse sieve.

rid·dling /rídling/ *adj.* expressed in riddles; puzzling. □□ **rid·dling·ly** *adv.*

ride /rīd/ *v. & n.* ● *v.* (*past* **rode** /rōd/; *past part.* **ridden** /ríd'n/) **1** *tr.* travel or be carried on (a bicycle, etc.) or in (a vehicle). **2** *intr.* (often foll. by *on, in*) travel or be conveyed (on a bicycle or in a vehicle). **3** *tr.* sit on and control or be carried by (a horse, etc.). **4** *intr.* (often foll. by *on*) be carried (on a horse, etc.). **5** *tr.* be carried or supported by (*the ship rides the waves*). **6** *tr.* **a** traverse on horseback, etc. (*rode the prairie*). **b** compete or take part in on horseback, etc. (*rode a good race*). **7** *intr.* **a** lie at anchor; float buoyantly. **b** (of the Moon) seem to float. **8** *intr.* (foll. by *in, on*) rest in or on while moving. **9** *tr.* yield to (a blow) so as to reduce its impact. **10** *tr.* give a ride to; cause to ride (*rode the child on his back*). **11** *tr.* (of a rider) cause (a horse, etc.) to move forward (*rode their horses at the fence*). **12** *tr.* **a** (in *passive*; foll. by *by, with*) be dominated by; be infested with (*was ridden with guilt*). **b** (as **ridden** *adj.*) infested or afflicted (usu. in *comb.*: *a rat-ridden cellar*). **13** *intr.* (of a thing normally level or even) project or overlap. **14** *tr. colloq.* mount (a sexual partner) in copulation. **15** *tr.* annoy or seek to annoy. ● *n.* **1** an act or period of travel in a vehicle. **2** a spell of riding on a horse, bicycle, etc. **3** the quality of sensations when riding (*gives a bumpy ride*). □ **let a thing ride** leave it alone; let it take its natural course. **ride again** reappear, esp. unexpectedly and reinvigorated. **ride down** overtake or trample on horseback. **ride high** be elated or successful. **ride out** come safely through (a storm, etc., or a danger or difficulty). **ride roughshod over** see ROUGHSHOD. **ride shotgun 1** *hist.* carry a shotgun while riding on top of a stage coach as a guard. **2** guard or keep watch (over someone or something), esp. in transit. **3** ride in the front passenger seat of a vehicle. **ride up** (of a garment, carpet, etc.) work or move out of its proper position. **take for a ride 1** *colloq.* hoax or deceive. **2** *sl.* abduct in order to murder. □□ **rid·a·ble** *adj.*

rid·er /rídər/ *n.* **1** a person who rides (esp. a horse). **2 a** an additional clause amending or supplementing a document. **b** an addition or amendment to a legislative bill. **c** a corollary. **3** *Math.* a problem arising as a corollary of a theorem, etc. **4** a piece in a machine, etc., that surmounts or bridges or works on or over others. □□ **rid·er·less** *adj.*

ridge /rij/ *n. & v.* ● *n.* **1** the line of the junction of two surfaces sloping upward toward each other (*the ridge of a roof*). ▷ ROOF. **2** a long, narrow hilltop, mountain range, or watershed. **3** any narrow elevation across a surface. **4** *Meteorol.* an elongated region of high barometric pressure. **5** *Agriculture* a raised strip of arable land, usu. one of a set separated by furrows. **6** *Hort.* a raised hotbed for melons, etc. ● *v.* **1** *tr.* mark with ridges. **2** *tr. Agriculture* break up (land) into ridges. **3** *tr. Hort.* plant (cucumbers, etc.) in ridges. **4** *tr. & intr.* gather into ridges. □□ **ridg·y** *adj.*

ridge·pole /ríjpōl/ *n.* **1** the horizontal pole of a long tent. **2** a beam along the ridge of a roof.

rid·i·cule /rídikyōol/ *n. & v.* ● *n.* subjection to derision or mockery. ● *v.tr.* make fun of; subject to ridicule; laugh at.

ri·dic·u·lous /ridíkyələs/ *adj.* **1** deserving or inviting ridicule. **2** unreasonable; absurd. □□ **ri·dic·u·lous·ly** *adv.* **ri·dic·u·lous·ness** *n.*

rid·ing¹ /ríding/ *n.* **1** in senses of RIDE *v.* **2** the practice or skill of riders of horses.

ri·ding² /ríding/ *n.* **1** each of three former administrative divisions (**East Riding, North Riding, West Riding**) of Yorkshire, England. **2** an electoral division of Canada.

rife /rīf/ *predic.adj.* **1** of common occurrence; widespread. **2** (foll. by *with*) abounding in; teeming with. □□ **rife·ness** *n.*

thatched top

RICK OF HAY

RICKRACK

R

riff /rif/ *n. & v.* ● *n.* a short repeated phrase in jazz, etc. ● *v.intr.* play riffs.

rif·fle /rífəl/ *v. & n.* ● *v.* **1** *tr.* **a** a turn (pages) in quick succession. **b** shuffle (playing cards), esp. by flexing and combining the two halves of a pack. **2** *intr.* (often foll. by *through*) leaf quickly (through pages). ● *n.* **1** the act or an instance of riffling. **2** (in gold panning) a groove or slat set in a trough or sluice to catch gold particles. **3 a** a shallow part of a stream where the water flows brokenly. **b** a patch of waves or ripples on water.

riff-raff /rífraf/ *n.* rabble; disreputable or undesirable persons.

ri·fle[1] /rífəl/ *n. & v.* ● *n.* **1** a gun with a long, rifled barrel, esp. one fired from shoulder level. ▷ GUN. **2** (in *pl.*) riflemen. ● *v.tr.* make spiral grooves in (a gun or its barrel or bore) to make a bullet spin.

ri·fle[2] /rífəl/ *v.tr. &* (foll. by *through*) intr. **1** search and rob, esp. of all that can be found. **2** carry off as booty.

ri·fle·man /rífəlmən/ *n.* (*pl.* **-men**) **1** a soldier armed with a rifle. **2** a person skilled in shooting a rifle.

ri·fle range *n.* a place for rifle practice.

ri·fling /rífling/ *n.* ▼ the arrangement of grooves on the inside of a gun's barrel.

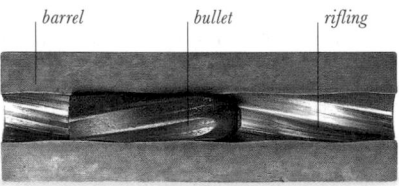

barrel   *bullet*   *rifling*

RIFLING: CROSS SECTION OF A GUN BARREL SHOWING RIFLING

rift /rift/ *n. & v.* ● *n.* **1 a** a crack or split in an object. **b** an opening in a cloud, etc. **2** a cleft or fissure in earth or rock. **3** a breach in friendly relations. ● *v.tr.* tear or burst apart. □□ **rift·less** *adj.*

rift val·ley *n.* ▼ a steep-sided valley formed by subsidence of the Earth's crust between nearly parallel faults.

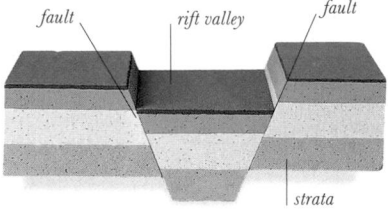

fault   *rift valley*   *fault*

strata

RIFT VALLEY: MODEL OF THE EARTH'S CRUST SHOWING A RIFT VALLEY

R

rig[1] /rig/ *v. & n.* ● *v.tr.* (**rig·ged, rigging**) **1 a** provide (a sailing ship) with sails, rigging, etc. **b** prepare ready for sailing. **2** (often foll. by *out, up*) fit with clothes or other equipment. **3** (foll. by *up*) set up hastily or as a makeshift. **4** assemble and adjust the parts of (an aircraft). ● *n.* **1** the arrangement of masts, sails, rigging, etc., of a sailing ship. **2** equipment for a special purpose, e.g., a radio transmitter. **3** a truck, esp. a tractor-trailer. □□ **rigged** *adj.* (also in *comb.*).

rig[2] /rig/ *v. & n.* ● *v.tr.* (**rigged, rigging**) manage or conduct fraudulently. ● *n.* **1** a trick or dodge. **2** a way of swindling. □ **rig the market** cause an artificial rise or fall in prices.

rig·a·doon /rígədoon/ *n.* **1** a lively dance in duple or quadruple time for two persons. **2** the music for this.

rig·ger /rígər/ *n.* **1** a person who rigs or who arranges rigging. **2** (of a rowboat) = OUTRIGGER 4a. **3** a ship rigged in a specified way. **4** a worker on an oil rig.

RIGGING

There are two types of rigging on a ship: standing rigging consists of the stays (ropes, wires, and chains) that fix the mast and yards in place; running rigging includes blocks, tackle, halyards, and sheets, which are used to hoist, lower, or trim the sails.

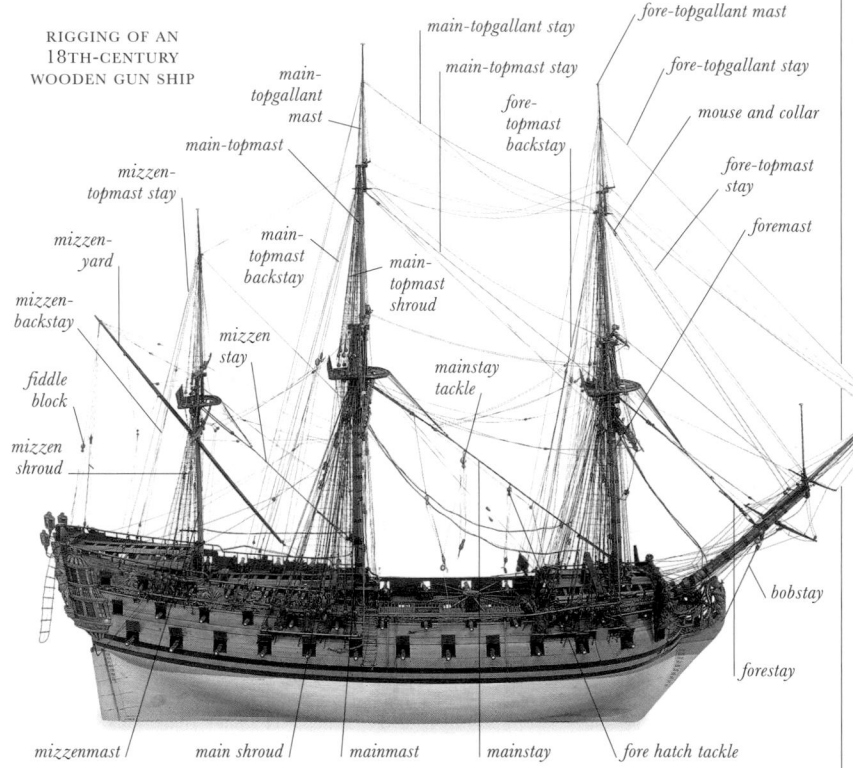

RIGGING OF AN 18TH-CENTURY WOODEN GUN SHIP

main-topgallant stay
fore-topgallant mast
main-topmast stay
fore-topgallant stay
main-topgallant mast
mouse and collar
main-topmast
fore-topmast backstay
fore-topmast stay
mizzen-topmast stay
main-topmast backstay
foremast
mizzen-yard
main-topmast shroud
mizzen-backstay
mizzen stay
mainstay tackle
fiddle block
mizzen shroud
bobstay
forestay
mizzenmast   *main shroud*   *mainmast*   *mainstay*   *fore hatch tackle*

rig·ging /ríging/ *n.* **1** ▲ a ship's ropes, etc., supporting and controlling the sails. ▷ SHIP. **2** the ropes and wires supporting the structure of an airship or biplane.

right /rīt/ *adj., n., v., adv., & int.* ● *adj.* **1** (of conduct, etc.) just; morally or socially correct (*do the right thing*). **2** true; correct (*the right time*). **3** less wrong or not wrong (*which is the right way?*). **4** more or most suitable or preferable (*the right person for the job*). **5** in a sound or normal condition (*the engine doesn't sound right*). **6 a** on or toward the side of the human body that corresponds to the position of east if one regards oneself as facing north. **b** on or toward that part of an object that is analogous to a person's right side or (with opposite sense) that is nearer to a spectator's right hand. **7** (of a side of fabric, etc.) meant for display or use (*turn it right side up*). ● *n.* **1** that which is morally or socially correct or just; fair treatment (often in *pl.*: *the rights and wrongs of the case*). **2** (often foll. by *to*, or *to* + infin.) a justification or fair claim (*has no right to speak like that*). **3** a thing one may legally or morally claim; authority to act (*human rights*). **4** the right-hand part or region or direction. **5** *Boxing* **a** the right hand. **b** a blow with this. **6** (often **Right**) *Polit.* **a** a group or section favoring conservatism. **b** such conservatives collectively. **7** the side of a stage which is to the right of a person facing the audience. **8** (esp. in marching) the right foot. **9** the right wing of an army. ● *v.tr.* **1** (often *refl.*) restore to a proper or straight or vertical position. **2 a** correct (mistakes, etc.); set in order. **b** avenge (a wrong or a wronged person); make reparation for or to. **c** vindicate; justify; rehabilitate. ● *adv.* **1** straight (*go right on*). **2** *colloq.* immediately; without delay (*do it right now*). **3 a** (foll. by *to, around, through*, etc.) all the way (*right to the bottom*). **b** (foll. by *off, out*, etc.) completely (*am right out of butter*). **4** exactly; quite (*right in the middle*). **5** justly; properly; correctly; truly; satisfactorily (*not holding it right*). **6** on or to the right side. **7** *archaic* very; to the full (*dined right royally*). ● *int. colloq.* expressing agreement or assent. □ **as right as rain** perfectly sound and healthy. **at right angles** placed to form a right angle. **by right** (or **rights**) if right were done. **do right by** act dutifully toward (a person). **in one's own right** through one's own position or effort, etc. **in the right** having justice or truth on one's side. **in one's right mind** sane; competent to think and act. **of** (or **as of**) **right** having legal or moral, etc., entitlement. **on the right side of 1** in the favor of (a person, etc.). **2** somewhat less than (a specified age). **put** (or **set**) **right 1** restore to order, health, etc. **2** correct the mistaken impression, etc., of (a person). **put** (or **set**) **to rights** make correct or well ordered. **right and left** (or **right, left, and center**) on all sides. **right away** (or **off**) immediately. **right on!** *colloq.* an expression of strong approval or encouragement. **right you are!** *colloq.* an exclamation of assent. **within one's rights** not exceeding one's authority or entitlement. □□ **right·er** *n.* **right·ish** *adj.* **right·less** *adj.* **right·ness** *n.*

right an·gle *n.* an angle of 90°, made by lines meeting with equal angles on either side. □□ **right-an·gled** *adj.*

right arm *n.* one's most reliable helper.

right·eous /ríchəs/ *adj.* **1** (of a person or conduct) morally right; virtuous; law-abiding. **2** *sl.* perfectly wonderful; fine and genuine (*she executed some righteous ski jumps*). □□ **right·eous·ly** *adv.* **right·eous·ness** *n.*

right·ful /rítfŏol/ *adj.* **1 a** (of a person) legitimately entitled to (a position, etc.). **b** of status or property, etc.) that one is entitled to. **2** (of an action, etc.) equitable; fair. □□ **right·ful·ly** *adv.* **right·ful·ness** *n.*

right-hand *adj.* **1** on or toward the right side of a person or thing. **2** done with the right hand. **3** (of a screw) = RIGHT-HANDED 4b.

right-hand·ed *adj.* **1** using the right hand by preference as more serviceable than the left. **2** (of a tool, etc.) made to be used with the right hand. **3** (of a blow) struck with the right hand. **4 a** turning to the right; toward the right. **b** (of a screw) advanced by turning to the right (clockwise).

right-hand man *n.* (*pl.* **men**) an indispensable or chief assistant.

right·ism /rítizəm/ *n. Polit.* the principles or policy of the right. □□ **right·ist** *n. & adj.*

right·ly /rítlee/ *adv.* justly; properly; correctly; justifiably.

right-mind·ed *adj.* having sound views and principles.

right·most /rítmōst/ *adj.* furthest to the right.

right of way *n.* **1** a right established by usage to pass over another's ground. **2** a path subject to such a right. **3** the right of one vehicle to proceed before another.

right·size /rítsīz/ *v.tr.* chiefly *US* convert to an appropriate or optimum size, in particular shed staff from (an organization).

right-think·ing *adj.* = RIGHT-MINDED.

right-to-die *adj.* pertaining to the avoidance of using artificial life support in case of severe illness or injury.

right-to-life *adj.* pertaining to the movement opposing abortion.

right-to-work *adj.* pertaining to legislation outlawing obligatory union membership.

right·ward /rítwərd/ *adv. & adj.* ● *adv.* (also **right·wards** /-wərdz/) toward the right. ● *adj.* going toward or facing the right.

right whale *n.* ▼ any large-headed whale of the family Balaenidae, rich in whalebone and easily captured. ▷ WHALE

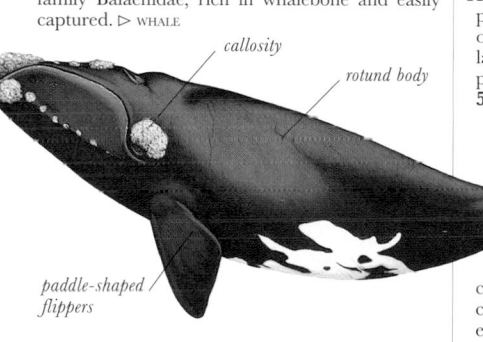

callosity

rotund body

paddle-shaped flippers

RIGHT WHALE: SOUTHERN RIGHT WHALE
(*Eubalaena australis*)

right wing *n.* **1** the right side of a soccer, etc., team on the field. ▷ RUGBY. **2** the conservative section of a political party or system. □□ **right-wing** *adj.* **right-wing·er** *n.*

rig·id /ríjid/ *adj.* **1** not flexible; that cannot be bent. **2** (of a person, conduct, etc.) **a** inflexible (*a rigid disciplinarian*). **b** strict; punctilious. □□ **ri·gid·i·ty** /rəjíditee/ *n.* **rig·id·ly** *adv.* **rig·id·ness** *n.*

ri·gid·i·fy /ríjidifī/ *v.tr. & intr.* (**-ies**, **-ied**) make or become rigid.

rig·ma·role /rígmərōl/ (also **rig·a·mo·role** /rígə-/) *n.* **1** a lengthy and complicated procedure. **2** a rambling or meaningless account or tale.

rig·or[1] /rígər/ *n. Med.* **1** a sudden feeling of cold with shivering accompanied by a rise in temperature. **2** rigidity of the body caused by shock or poisoning, etc.

rig·or[2] /rígər/ *n.* **1 a** severity; strictness; harshness. **b** (often in *pl.*) severity of weather or climate; extremity of cold. **c** (in *pl.*) harsh measures or conditions. **2** logical exactitude. **3** strict enforcement of rules, etc. (*the utmost rigor of the law*). **4** austerity of life; puritanical discipline.

rig·or mor·tis /rígər máwrtis/ *n.* stiffening of the body after death.

rig·or·ous /rígərəs/ *adj.* **1** characterized by or showing rigor; strict, severe. **2** strictly exact or accurate. **3** (of the weather) cold, severe. □□ **rig·or·ous·ly** *adv.* **rig·or·ous·ness** *n.*

rile /rīl/ *v.tr. colloq.* **1** anger; irritate. **2** make (water) turbulent or muddy.

Ri·ley /rílee/ *n.* □ **the life of Riley** *colloq.* a carefree existence.

rilievo var. of RELIEVO.

rill /ril/ *n.* **1** a small stream. **2** a shallow channel cut in the surface of soil or rocks by running water. **3** (also **rille**) *Astron.* a cleft or narrow valley on the Moon's surface.

rim /rim/ *n. & v.* ● *n.* **1 a** a raised edge or border. **b** a margin or verge, esp. of something circular. **2** the part of a pair of spectacles surrounding the lenses. **3** the outer edge of a wheel, on which the tire is fitted. **4** a boundary line (*the rim of the horizon*). ● *v.tr.* (**rimmed**, **rimming**) **1 a** provide with a rim. **b** be a rim for or to. **2** edge; border. □□ **rim·less** *adj.* **rimmed** *adj.* (also in *comb.*).

rime[1] /rīm/ *n. & v.* ● *n.* **1** frost, esp. formed from cloud or fog. **2** *poet.* hoarfrost. ● *v.tr.* cover with rime. □□ **rim·y** /rímee/ *adj.* (**rimier**, **rimiest**)

rime[2] *archaic* var. of RHYME.

rind /rīnd/ *n. & v.* ● *n.* **1** the tough outer layer or covering of fruit, cheese, bacon, etc. **2** the bark of a tree or plant. ● *v.tr.* strip the bark from. □□ **rind·ed** *adj.* (also in *comb.*). **rind·less** *adj.*

rin·der·pest /ríndərpest/ *n.* a virulent infectious disease of ruminants (esp. cattle).

ring[1] /ring/ *n. & v.* ● *n.* **1** a circular band, usu. of precious metal, worn on a finger. **2** a circular band of any material. **3** the rim of a cylindrical or circular object, or a line or band around it. **4** a mark or part having the form of a circular band (*smoke rings*). **5** = ANNUAL RING. **6 a** an enclosure for a circus performance, betting at races, the showing of cattle, etc. **b** (prec. by *the*) bookmakers collectively. **c** a roped enclosure for boxing or wrestling. **7 a** a group of people or things arranged in a circle. **b** such an arrangement. **8** a combination of traders, bookmakers, spies, politicians, etc., acting together usu. illicitly for profit, etc. **9** a circular or spiral course. **10** *Astron.* **a** a thin band or disk of particles, etc., around a planet. **b** a halo around the Moon. **11** *Archaeol.* a circular prehistoric earthwork usu. of a bank and ditch. **12** *Chem.* a group of atoms each bonded to two others in a closed sequence. ● *v.tr.* **1** make or draw a circle around. **2** (often foll. by *around*, *about*, *in*) encircle or hem in (game or cattle). **3** put a ring through the nose of (a pig, bull, etc.). **4** cut (fruit, vegetables, etc.) into rings. □ **run** (or **make**) **rings around** *colloq.* outclass or outwit (another person). □□ **ringed** *adj.* (also in *comb.*). **ring·less** *adj.*

ring[2] /ring/ *v. & n.* ● *v.* (*past* **rang** /rang/; *past part.* **rung** /rung/) **1** *intr.* (often foll. by *out*, etc.) give a clear resonant or vibrating sound or as of a bell (*a shot rang out*). **2** *tr.* **a** make (esp. a bell) ring. **b** (*absol.*) call for service or attention by ringing a bell. **3** *tr.* (also *absol.*; often foll. by *up*) esp. *Brit.* call by telephone. **4** *intr.* (usu. foll. by *with*, *to*) (of a place) resound or be permeated with a sound, or an attribute (*the theater rang with applause*). **5** *intr.* (of the ears) be filled with a sensation of ringing. **6** *tr.* **a** sound (a peal, etc.) on bells. **b** (of a bell) sound (the hour, etc.). **7** *tr.* (foll. by *in*, *out*) usher in or out with bell-ringing (*rang out the Old Year*). **8** *intr.* (of sentiments, etc.) convey a specified impression (*words rang hollow*). ● *n.* **1** a ringing sound or tone. **2 a** the act of ringing a bell. **b** the sound caused by this. **3** *colloq.* a telephone call. **4** a specified feeling conveyed by an utterance (*had a melancholy ring*). **5** a set of, esp. church, bells. □ **ring back** esp. *Brit.* make a return telephone call to. **ring a bell** see BELL. **ring down** (or **up**) **the curtain 1** *Theatr.* cause the curtain to be lowered or raised. **2** (foll. by *on*) mark the end or the beginning of (an enterprise, etc.). **ring in one's ears** (or **heart**, etc.) linger in the memory. **ring true** (or **false**) convey an impression of truth or falsehood. **ring up** record (an amount, etc.) on a cash register. □□ **ringed** *adj.* (also in *comb.*). **ring·er** *n.* **ring·ing** *adj.* **ring·ing·ly** *adv.*

ring bind·er *n.* a loose-leaf binder with ring-shaped clasps that can be opened to pass through holes in the paper.

ringed plov·er *n.* ◀ either of two small plovers, *Charadrius hiaticula* and *C. dubius.*

RINGED PLOVER (*Charadrius hiaticula*)

ring·er /ríngər/ *n. sl.* **1 a** an athlete or horse entered in a competition by fraudulent means, esp. as a substitute. **b** a person's double, esp. an impostor. **2** a person who rings, esp. a bell ringer. □ **be a ringer** (or **dead ringer**) **for** resemble (a person) exactly.

ring fin·ger *n.* the finger next to the little finger, esp. of the left hand, on which the wedding ring is usu. worn.

ring·lead·er /ríngleedər/ *n.* a leading instigator in an illicit or illegal activity.

ring·let /rínglit/ *n.* **1** a curly lock of hair, esp. a long one. **2** a butterfly, *Aphantopus hyperantus*, with spots on its wings. **3** *Astron.* one of the thin rings within the major rings of Saturn. □□ **ring·let·ed** *adj.*

ring·mas·ter /ríngmastər/ *n.* the person directing a circus performance.

ring ou·zel *n.* a thrush, *Turdus torquatus*, with a white crescent across its breast.

ring·side /ríngsīd/ *n.* (often *attrib.*) **1** the area immediately beside a boxing ring or circus ring, etc. **2** an advantageous position from which to observe or monitor something. □□ **ring·sid·er** *n.*

ring·ster /ríngstər/ *n.* a person who participates in a political or commercial ring (see RING[1] n. 8).

ring·worm /ríngwərm/ *n.* any of various fungous infections of the skin causing circular inflamed patches, esp. on the scalp.

rink /ringk/ *n.* **1** an area of natural or artificial ice for skating or playing ice hockey, etc. **2** an enclosed area for roller-skating. **3** a building containing either of these. **4** a strip of the green used for playing a match of lawn bowling. **5** a team in lawn bowling or curling.

rinse /rins/ *v. & n.* ● *v.tr.* (often foll. by *through*, *out*) **1** wash with clean water. **2** apply liquid to. **3** wash lightly. **4** put (clothes, etc.) through clean water to remove soap or detergent. **5** (foll. by *out*, *away*) clear (impurities) by rinsing. **6** treat (hair) with a rinse. ● *n.* **1** the act or an instance of rinsing (*give it a rinse*). **2** a solution for cleansing the mouth. **3** a dye for the temporary tinting of hair (*a blue rinse*). □□ **rins·er** *n.*

ri·ot /ríot/ *n. & v.* ● *n.* **1 a** a disturbance of the peace by a crowd; an occurrence of public disorder. **b** (*attrib.*) involved in suppressing riots (*riot police; riot shield*). **2** uncontrolled revelry; noisy behavior. **3** (foll. by *of*) a lavish display or enjoyment (*a riot of color and sound; a riot of emotion*). **4** *colloq.* a very amusing thing or person. ● *v.intr.* **1** make or engage in a riot. **2** live wantonly; revel. □ **read the Riot Act** put a firm stop to insubordination, etc.; give a severe warning. **run riot 1** throw off all restraint. **2** (of plants) grow or spread uncontrolled. □□ **ri·ot·er** *n.*

ri·ot·ous /ríotəs/ *adj.* **1** marked by or involving rioting. **2** characterized by wanton conduct. **3** wildly profuse. □□ **ri·ot·ous·ly** *adv.* **ri·ot·ous·ness** *n.*

R

RIVER

At its source, a river is usually steep, eroding downward to cut deep valleys and gorges. Rapids and waterfalls may form where the river flows from hard to softer rock. As it looses its steep gradient, the river slows down and deposits silt; sideways erosion increases and the river begins to meander, forming a flood-plain. Strong erosion in tight meanders can cut off sections, forming oxbow lakes.

source

waterfall

gorge

entrenched meander

interconnected channels

lake

river terrace

levee

beginning of floodplain

natural bridge

oxbow lake

sediment deposited on seabed

river mouth

lake

TYPICAL FEATURES OF A RIVER FROM SOURCE TO MOUTH

R

RIP *abbr.* may he or she or they rest in peace.

rip[1] /rip/ *v. & n.* • *v.tr. & intr.* (**ripped, ripping**) **1** *tr.* tear or cut (a thing) quickly or forcibly away or apart. **2** *tr.* **a** make (a hole, etc.) by ripping. **b** make a long tear or cut in. **3** *intr.* come violently apart. **4** *intr.* rush along. • *n.* **1** a long tear or cut. **2** an act of ripping. □ **let rip** *colloq.* **1** act or proceed without restraint. **2** speak violently. **3** not check the speed of or interfere with (a person or thing). **rip into** attack (a person) verbally.

rip[2] /rip/ *n.* **1** a dissolute person. **2** a rascal. **3** a worthless horse.

ri·par·i·an /rīpáireeən/ *adj. & n.* esp. *Law* • *adj.* of or on a riverbank. • *n.* an owner of property on a riverbank.

rip cord *n.* a cord for releasing a parachute from its pack.

ripe /rīp/ *adj.* **1** (of grain, cheese, etc.) ready to be reaped or picked or eaten. **2** mature; fully developed. **3** (of a person's age) advanced. **4** (often foll. by *for*) fit or ready (*when the time is ripe*). **5** (of the complexion, etc.) red and full like ripe fruit. □□ **ripe·ly** *adv.* **ripe·ness** *n.*

rip·en /rípən/ *v.tr. & intr.* make or become ripe.

ri·pie·no /ripyáynō/ *n.* (*pl.* **-os** or **ripieni** /-nee/) *Mus.* a body of accompanying instruments in baroque concerto music.

rip-off *n. & v. colloq.* • *n.* **1** a fraud or swindle. **2** financial exploitation. • *v.tr.* (**rip off**) defraud; steal.

ri·poste /rīpóst/ *n. & v.* • *n.* **1** a quick sharp reply or retort. **2** a quick return thrust in fencing. • *v.intr.* deliver a riposte.

rip·per /rípər/ *n.* **1** a person or thing that rips. **2** a murderer who rips the victims' bodies.

rip·ple /rípəl/ *n. & v.* • *n.* **1** a ruffling of the water's surface; a small wave or series of waves. **2 a** a gentle lively sound that rises and falls, e.g., of applause. **b** a brief wave of emotion, excitement, etc. (*the new recruit caused a ripple of interest in the company*). **3** a wavy appearance in hair, material, etc. **4** *Electr.* a slight variation in the strength of a current, etc. **5** ice cream with added syrup giving a

colored ripple effect (*raspberry ripple*). **6** a riffle in a stream. • *v.* **1 a** *intr.* form ripples; flow in ripples. **b** *tr.* cause to do this. **2** *intr.* show or sound like ripples. □□ **rip·ply** *adj.*

rip·rap /ríprap/ *n.* a collection of loose stone as a foundation for a structure.

rip-roar·ing /ríprawring/ *adj.* **1** wildly noisy or boisterous. **2** excellent, first-rate. □□ **rip-roar·ing·ly** *adv.*

rip·saw /rípsaw/ *n.* a coarse saw for sawing wood along the grain.

rip·snort·er /rípsnawrtər/ *n. colloq.* an energetic, remarkable, or excellent person or thing. □□ **rip·snort·ing** *adj.* **rip·snort·ing·ly** *adv.*

rise /rīz/ *v. & n.* • *v.intr.* (*past* **rose** /rōz/; *past part.* **risen** /rízən/) **1** come or go up. **2** grow, project, expand, or incline upward; become higher. **3** appear above the horizon. **4 a** get up from lying or sitting or kneeling. **b** get out of bed, esp. in the morning. **5** become erect. **6** reach a higher position or level or amount (*the flood has risen*). **7** develop greater intensity, strength, volume, or pitch (*their voices rose*). **8** make progress; reach a higher social position (*rose from the ranks*). **9 a** come to the surface of liquid. **b** (of a person) react to provocation (*rise to the bait*). **10** become or be visible above the surroundings, etc. **11 a** (of buildings, etc.) undergo construction from the foundations (*office buildings were rising all around*). **b** (of a tree, etc.) grow to a (usu. specified) height. **12** come to life again (*rise from the ashes*). **13** (of dough) swell by the action of yeast, etc. **14** (often foll. by *up*) rebel (*rise in arms*). **15** originate (*the river rises in the mountains*). **16** (of wind) start to blow. **17** (of a person's spirits) become cheerful. **18** (of a barometer) show a higher atmospheric pressure. **19** (of a horse) rear (*rose on its hind legs*). **20** (of a bump, blister, etc.) form. • *n.* **1** an act or manner or amount of rising. **2** an upward slope or hill or movement (*the house stood on a rise*). **3** an increase in sound or pitch. **4** an increase in amount, extent, etc. (*a rise in unemployment*). **5** an increase in status or power. **6** social, commercial, or political advancement. **7** the movement of fish to the surface. **8** origin. **9 a** the vertical height of a

step, arch, etc. **b** = RISER 2. □ **get** (or **take**) **a rise out of** *colloq.* provoke an emotional reaction from (a person), esp. by teasing. **on the rise** on the increase. **rise above 1** be superior to (petty feelings, etc.). **2** show dignity or strength in the face of (difficulty, poor conditions, etc.). **rise and shine** (usu. as *imper.*) *colloq.* get out of bed; wake up. **rise in the world** attain a higher social position. **rise to** develop powers equal to (an occasion).

ris·er /rízər/ *n.* **1** a person who rises, esp. from bed (*an early riser*). **2** a vertical section between the treads of a staircase. **3** a vertical pipe for the flow of liquid or gas.

rish·i /ríshee/ *n.* (*pl.* **rishis**) a Hindu sage or saint.

ris·i·ble /rízibəl/ *adj.* **1** laughable; ludicrous. **2** inclined to laugh. □□ **ris·i·bil·i·ty** *n.* **ris·i·bly** *adv.*

ris·ing /rízing/ *adj. & n.* • *adj.* **1** going up; getting higher. **2** increasing (*rising costs*). **3** advancing to maturity or high standing (*the rising generation; a rising young lawyer*). **4** approaching a higher level, grade, etc. (*rising seniors*) or a specified age (*the rising fives*). **5** (of ground) sloping upward. • *n.* a revolt or insurrection.

risk /risk/ *n. & v.* • *n.* **1** a chance or possibility of danger, loss, injury, etc. (*a health risk*). **2** a person or thing causing a risk or regarded in relation to risk (*is a poor risk*). • *v.tr.* **1** expose to risk. **2** accept the chance of (*risk getting wet*). **3** venture on. □ **at risk** exposed to danger. **at one's** (**own**) **risk** accepting responsibility or liability. **at the risk of** with the possibility of (an adverse consequence). **put at risk** expose to danger. **risk one's neck** put one's own life in danger. **run a** (or **the**) **risk** (often foll. by *of*) expose oneself to danger or loss, etc. **take** (or **run**) **a risk** chance the possibility of danger, etc.

risk·y /rískee/ *adj.* (**riskier, riskiest**) involving risk. □□ **risk·i·ly** *adv.* **risk·i·ness** *n.*

ri·sot·to /risáwtō, -sótō, -záwtō/ *n.* (*pl.* **-os**) an Italian dish of rice cooked in stock with meat, onions, etc.

ris·qué /riskáy/ *adj.* (of a story, etc.) slightly indecent.

ris·sole /risól, rísōl/ *n.* a pastry filled with a mixture of meat or fish and spices, usu. deep-fried.

ri·tar·dan·do /réetardándō/ *adv. & n. Mus.* (*pl.* **-os** or **ritardandi** /-dee/) = RALLENTANDO.

rite /rīt/ *n.* **1** a religious or solemn observance or act (*burial rites*). **2** an action or procedure required or usual in this. **3** a body of customary observances characteristic of a church or a part of it (*the Latin rite*).

ri·te·nu·to /réetənōōtō/ *adv. & n. Mus.* • *adv.* with immediate reduction of speed. • *n.* (*pl.* **-os** or **ritenuti** /-tee/) a passage played in this way.

rite of pas·sage *n.* (often in *pl.*) a ritual or event marking a stage of a person's advance through life, e.g., marriage.

ri·tor·nel·lo /réetawrnélō/ *n. Mus.* (*pl.* **-os** or **ritornelli** /-lee/) a short instrumental refrain, interlude, etc., in a vocal work.

rit·u·al /ríchōōəl/ *n. & adj.* • *n.* **1** a prescribed order of performing rites. **2** a procedure regularly followed. • *adj.* of or done as a ritual or rites. □□ **rit·u·al·ize** *v.tr. & intr.* **rit·u·al·i·za·tion** *n.* **rit·u·al·ly** *adv.*

rit·u·al·ism /ríchōōəlizəm/ *n.* the regular or excessive practice of ritual. □□ **rit·u·al·ist** *n.* **rit·u·al·is·tic** *adj.* **rit·u·al·is·ti·cal·ly** *adv.*

ritz·y /rítsee/ *adj.* (**ritzier, ritziest**) *colloq.* **1** high-class; luxurious. **2** ostentatiously smart. □□ **ritz·i·ly** *adv.* **ritz·i·ness** *n.*

ri·val /rívəl/ *n. & v.* • *n.* **1** a person competing with another for the same objective. **2** a person or thing that equals another in quality. **3** (*attrib.*) being a rival or rivals (*a rival firm*). • *v.tr.* **1** be the rival of or comparable to. **2** seem or claim to be as good as.

ri·val·ry /rívəlree/ *n.* (*pl.* **-ies**) the state or an instance of being rivals; competition.

rive /rīv/ *v.* (*past* **rived**; *past part.* **riven** /rívən/) *archaic or poet.* **1** *tr.* split or tear apart violently. **2 a** *tr.* split (wood or stone). **b** *intr.* be split.

riv·er /rívər/ *n.* **1** ◄ a copious natural stream of water flowing in a channel to the sea or a lake, etc. **2** a copious flow (*rivers of blood*). **3** (*attrib.*) (in the names of animals, plants, etc.) living in or associated with the river. □ **sell down the river** *colloq.* betray or let down. □□ **riv·ered** *adj.* (also in *comb.*).

riv·er·ine /rívərīn, -reen/ *adj.* of or on a river or riverbank; riparian.

riv·er·side /rívərsīd/ *n.* the ground along a riverbank.

riv·et /rívit/ *n. & v.* ● *n.* a nail or bolt for holding together metal plates, etc., its headless end being beaten out or pressed down when in place. ● *v.tr.* **1 a** join or fasten with rivets. **b** beat out or press down the end of (a nail or bolt). **c** fix; make immovable. **2 a** (foll. by *on, upon*) direct intently (one's eyes or attention, etc.). **b** (esp. as **riveting** *adj.*) engross (a person or the attention). □□ **riv·et·er** *n.*

riv·i·er·a /rìveeáirə/ *n.* (often **Riv·i·er·a**) a coastal region with a subtropical climate, vegetation, etc., esp. that of SE France and NW Italy.

ri·vière /reevyáir/ *n.* a gem necklace, esp. of more than one string.

riv·u·let /rívyəlit/ *n.* a small stream.

RN *abbr.* **1** registered nurse. **2** (in the UK) Royal Navy.

Rn *symb. Chem.* the element radon.

RNA *abbr.* ribonucleic acid.

roach[1] /rōch/ *n.* (*pl.* same) ▼ a small freshwater fish, esp. *Rutilus rutilus*, allied to the carp.

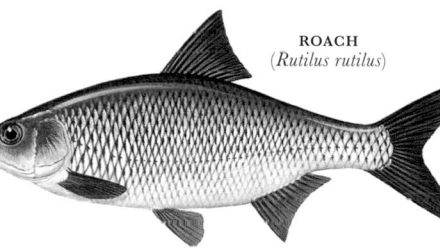

ROACH
(*Rutilus rutilus*)

roach[2] /rōch/ *n.* **1** *colloq.* a cockroach. **2** *sl.* the butt of a marijuana cigarette.

roach[3] /rōch/ *n. Naut.* an upward curve in the foot of a sail.

road[1] /rōd/ *n.* **1 a** a path or way with a specially prepared surface, used by vehicles, pedestrians, etc. **b** the part of this used by vehicles (*don't step in the road*). **2 a** one's way or route. **b** a method or means of accomplishing something. **3** an underground passage in a mine. **4** a railroad. **5** (usu. in *pl.*) a partly sheltered piece of water near the shore in which ships can ride at anchor. □ **by road** using transport along roads. **one for the road** *colloq.* a final (esp. alcoholic) drink before departure. **on the road** traveling, esp. as a firm's representative, itinerant performer, or vagrant. **the road to** the way of getting to or achieving (*the road to Miami; the road to ruin*). **take the road** set out. □□ **road·less** *adj.*

road[2] /rōd/ *v.tr.* (also *absol.*) (of a dog) follow and pursue (a game bird) by the scent of its trail.

road·bed /rōdbed/ *n.* **1** the foundation structure of a railroad. **2** the material laid down to form a road. **3** the part of a road on which vehicles travel.

road·block /rōdblok/ *n.* a barrier on a road set up to stop and examine traffic.

road hog *n. colloq.* a reckless or inconsiderate motorist.

road·house /rōdhows/ *n.* an inn or club on a major road.

road·ie /rōdee/ *n. colloq.* an assistant employed by a touring band of musicians to erect and maintain equipment.

road kill *n.* chiefly *N. Amer.* **1** animals killed on the road by a vehicle. **2** a killing of an animal on the road by a vehicle.

road man·ag·er *n.* the organizer and supervisor of a musicians' tour.

road·run·ner /rōdrunər/ *n.* ▼ a bird of Mexican and US deserts, *Geococcyx californianus*, related to the cuckoo, known as a poor flier but a fast runner.

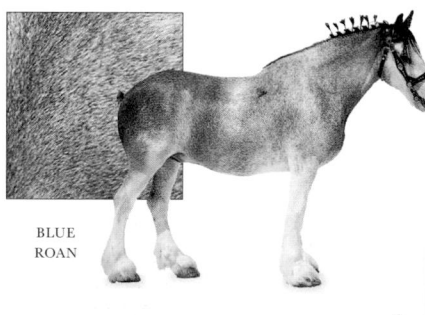

ROADRUNNER:
GREATER ROADRUNNER
(*Geococcyx californianus*)

road show *n.* **1** a performance given by a touring company, esp. a group of pop musicians. **2** a radio or television program done on location.

road·side /rōdsīd/ *n.* the strip of land beside a road.

road sign *n.* a sign giving information or instructions to road users.

road·stead /rōdsted/ *n.* = ROAD[1] 5.

road·ster /rōdstər/ *n.* **1** an open car without rear seats. **2** a horse or bicycle for use on the road.

road test *n.* a test of the performance of a vehicle on the road.

road·way /rōdway/ *n.* **1** a road. **2** = ROAD[1] 1b. **3** the part of a bridge or railroad used for traffic.

road·work /rōdwərk/ *n.* **1** the construction or repair of roads. **2** athletic exercise or training involving running on roads.

road·wor·thy /rōdwərthee/ *adj.* fit to be used on the road. □□ **road·wor·thi·ness** *n.*

roam /rōm/ *v. & n.* ● *v.* **1** *intr.* ramble; wander. **2** *tr.* travel unsystematically over, through, or about. ● *n.* an act of roaming; a ramble. □□ **roam·er** *n.*

roan[1] /rōn/ *adj. & n.* ● *adj.* ▼ (of an animal, esp. a horse or cow) having a coat of which the prevailing color is thickly interspersed with hairs of another color, esp. bay or sorrel or chestnut mixed with white or gray. ● *n.* a roan animal. □ **blue roan** *adj.* black mixed with white. **red roan** *adj.* bay mixed with white or gray. **strawberry roan** *adj.* chestnut mixed with white or gray.

BLUE
ROAN

STRAWBERRY
ROAN

ROAN: EXAMPLES OF ROAN HORSES

roan[2] /rōn/ *n.* soft sheepskin leather used in bookbinding as a substitute for morocco.

roar /rawr/ *n. & v.* ● *n.* **1** a loud, deep, hoarse sound, as made by a lion, thunder, a loud engine, or a person in pain, rage, or excitement. **2** a loud laugh. ● *v.* **1** *intr.* utter or make a roar. **b** utter loud laughter. **c** (of a horse) make a loud noise in breathing as a symptom of disease. **2** *intr.* travel in a vehicle at high speed, esp. with the engine roaring. **3** *tr.* (often foll. by *out*) say, sing, or utter (words, an oath, etc.) in a loud tone. □□ **roar·er** *n.*

roar·ing /ráwring/ *adj.* in senses of ROAR *v.* □ **roaring drunk** very drunk and noisy. □□ **roar·ing·ly** *adv.*

roar·ing for·ties *n.pl.* (prec. by *the*) stormy ocean tracts between lat. 40° and 50° S.

roar·ing twen·ties *n.pl.* the decade of the 1920s (with ref. to its postwar buoyancy).

roast /rōst/ *v., adj., & n.* ● *v.* **1** *tr.* **a** cook (food, esp. meat) in an oven or by exposure to open heat. **b** heat (coffee beans) before grinding. **2** *tr.* heat (the ore of metal) in a furnace. **3** *tr.* **a** expose (a torture victim) to fire or great heat. **b** *tr. & refl.* expose (oneself or part of oneself) to warmth. **4** *tr.* criticize severely; denounce. **5** *intr.* undergo roasting. ● *attrib adj.* (of meat or a potato, chestnut, etc.) roasted. ● *n.* **1 a** roast meat. **b** a dish of this. **c** a piece of meat for roasting. **2** the process of roasting. **3** a party where roasted food is eaten. **4** a banquet to honor a person at which the honoree is subjected to good-natured ridicule.

roast·er /rōstər/ *n.* **1** a person or thing that roasts. **2 a** an oven or dish for roasting food in. **b** an ore-roasting furnace. **c** a coffee-roasting apparatus. **3** something fit for roasting, e.g., a fowl, a potato, etc.

roast·ing /rōsting/ *adj. & n.* ● *adj.* very hot. ● *n.* **1** in senses of ROAST *v.* **2** a severe criticism or denunciation.

rob /rob/ *v.tr.* (**robbed, robbing**) (often foll. by *of*) **1** take unlawfully from, esp. by force or threat of force (*robbed the safe; robbed her of her jewels*). **2** deprive of what is due or normal (*was robbed of my sleep*). **3** (*absol.*) commit robbery. **4** *colloq.* cheat; swindle. □ **rob Peter to pay Paul** take away from one to give to another; discharge one debt by incurring another.

rob·ber /róbər/ *n.* a person who commits robbery.

rob·ber ba·ron *n.* **1** a plundering feudal lord. **2** an unscrupulous plutocrat.

rob·ber·y /róbəree/ *n.* (*pl.* **-ies**) **1 a** the act or process of robbing, esp. with force or threat of force. **b** an instance of this. **2** excessive financial demand or cost (*set us back $20—it was sheer robbery*).

robe /rōb/ *n. & v.* ● *n.* **1** a long, loose outer garment. **2** a loose, usu. belted garment worn over nightwear, while resting, or after bathing. **3** a baby's outer garment, esp. at a christening. **4** (often in *pl.*) a long outer garment worn as an indication of the wearer's rank, office, profession, etc.; a gown or vestment. **5** a blanket or wrap of fur. ● *v.* **1** *tr.* clothe (a person) in a robe; dress. **2** *intr.* put on one's robes or vestments.

rob·in /róbin/ *n.* **1** a red-breasted thrush, *Turdus migratorius*. **2** (also **robin redbreast**) a small brown European bird, *Erithacus rubecula*, the adult of which has a red throat and breast. **3** a bird similar in appearance, etc., to either of these.

Rob·in Hood *n.* (with ref. to the legend of the medieval forest outlaw) a person who acts illegally or unfavorably toward the rich for the benefit of the poor.

ro·bin·i·a /rəbíneeə/ *n.* any N. American tree or shrub of the genus *Robinia*, e.g., a locust tree or false acacia.

rob·o·rant /róbərənt/ *adj. & n. Med.* ● *adj.* strengthening. ● *n.* a strengthening drug.

R

wrist joint · *telescopic arm* · *elbow joint* · *motor to activate arm*

rotating joint · *sliding joint* · *rotating joint* · *gripper*

SENSOR-INTEGRATED
INDUSTRIAL ROBOT

motor to activate elbow

shoulder

pneumatic control hoses

ROBOT

Robots are computer-controlled machines, programmed to sense and react to aspects of their environment. They are frequently used where working conditions are unsuitable for humans. As well as working at a constant rate, robots can handle dangerous substances without fear of contamination and can be built to function in extreme environments, such as outer space or deep under water. The design of the most common factory robots is based on the human arm, with swivels replacing joints and grippers fitted with sensors as "hands."

swiveling base

motor

ro·bot /rṓbot/ *n.* **1** a machine with a human appearance or functioning like a human. **2** ▲ a machine capable of carrying out a complex series of actions automatically. **3** a person who works mechanically and efficiently but insensitively. □□ **ro·bot·ic** /-bótik/ *adj.* **ro·bot·ize** *v.tr.*

ro·bot·ics /rōbótiks/ *n.pl.* (usu. treated as *sing.*) the study of robots; the art or science of their design and operation.

ro·bust /rōbúst/ *adj.* (**robuster**, **robustest**) **1** (of a person, animal, or thing) strong and sturdy, esp. in physique or construction. **2** (of exercise, discipline, etc.) vigorous; requiring strength. **3** (of intellect or mental attitude) straightforward; not given to or confused by subtleties. **4** (of a statement, reply, etc.) bold; firm; unyielding. **5** (of wine, etc.) full-bodied. □□ **ro·bust·ly** *adv.* **ro·bust·ness** *n.*

roc /rok/ *n.* a gigantic bird of Eastern legend.

ro·caille /rōkī/ *n.* **1** an 18th-c. style of ornamentation based on rock and shell motifs. **2** a rococo style.

ro·cam·bole /rókəmbōl/ *n.* an alliaceous plant, *Allium scorodoprasum*, with a garliclike bulb used for seasoning.

roche mou·ton·née /ráwsh mōōtwnáy/ *n. Geol.* a small, bare outcrop of rock shaped by glacial erosion

roch·et /róchit/ *n.* a vestment resembling a surplice, used chiefly by bishops and abbots.

rock[1] /rok/ *n.* **1 a** the hard material of the Earth's crust, exposed on the surface or underlying the soil. **b** a similar material on other planets. **2** *Geol.* any natural material, hard or soft (e.g., clay), consisting of one or more minerals. **3 a** a mass of rock projecting and forming a hill, cliff, reef, etc. **b** (**the Rock**) Gibraltar. **4** a large detached stone. **5** a stone of any size. **6** a firm and dependable support or protection. **7** (in *pl.*) *sl.* money. **8** *sl.* a precious stone, esp. a diamond. **9** *sl.* a solid form of cocaine. **10** (in *pl.*) *coarse sl.* the testicles. □ **between a rock and a hard place** forced to choose between two unpleasant or difficult alternatives. **get one's rocks off** *coarse sl.* **1** achieve sexual satisfaction. **2** obtain enjoyment. **on the rocks** *colloq.* **1** short of money. **2** broken down. **3** (of a drink) served over ice cubes. □□ **rock·less** *adj.* **rock·let** *n.* **rock·like** *adj.*

rock[2] /rok/ *v. & n.* ● *v.* **1** *tr.* move gently to and fro in or as if in a cradle; set or maintain such motion (*rock him to sleep*; *the ship was rocked by the waves*). **2** *intr.* be or continue in such motion (*sat rocking in his chair*). **3 a** *intr.* sway from side to side; shake; oscillate; reel. **b** *tr.* cause to do this (*an earthquake rocked the house*). **4** *tr.* distress; perturb. **5** *intr.* dance to or play rock music. ● *n.* **1** a rocking movement. **2** a spell of rocking. **3 a** = ROCK AND ROLL. **b** any of a variety of types of modern popular music with a rocking or swinging beat, derived from rock and roll. □ **rock the boat** *colloq.* disturb the equilibrium of a situation.

rock·a·bil·ly /rókəbilee/ *n.* a type of popular music combining elements of rock and roll and hillbilly music.

rock and roll *n.* (also **rock 'n' roll**) a type of popular dance music originating in the 1950s, characterized by a heavy beat and simple melodies, often with a blues element. □□ **rock and rol·ler** *n.* (also **rock 'n' roller**).

rock-bot·tom *adj.* (of prices, etc.) the very lowest. □□ **rock bot·tom** *n.*

rock·bound /rókbównd/ *adj.* (of a coast) rocky and inaccessible.

rock can·dy *n.* sugar crystallized in large masses onto a string or stick, eaten as candy.

rock climb·ing *n.* ▼ the sport of climbing rock faces, esp. with the aid of ropes, etc.

rock crys·tal *n.* transparent colorless quartz usu. in hexagonal prisms. ▷ CRYSTAL, GEM, QUARTZ

rock cy·cle *n.* ► a cycle of geological processes involving intrusion of igneous rock, uplift, erosion, transportation, deposition as sedimentary rock, metamorphism, remelting, and further igneous intrusion.

rock dove *n.* a wild dove, *Columbia livia*, frequenting rocks; the supposed ancestor of the domestic pigeon.

rock·er /rókər/ *n.* **1** a person or thing that rocks. **2** a curved bar or similar support, on which something can rock. **3** a rocking chair. **4 a** a young devotee of rock music, characteristically associated with leather clothing and motorcycles. **b** a performer of rock music. **5** an ice skate with a highly curved blade. **6** a switch constructed on a pivot mechanism operating between the "on" and "off" positions. **7** any rocking device forming part of a mechanism. □ **off one's rocker** *sl.* crazy.

rock·er·y /rókəree/ *n.* (*pl.* **-ies**) a rock garden.

R

ROCK CLIMBING

The sport of rock climbing involves specialized safety equipment. Ropes stretch slightly to absorb the shock of a fall; anchors such as friends and nuts secure ropes and runners to the rock face; carabiners are secure coupling links; belay devices allow the climber to control the rope in the event of a fall; and descenders help safe rappelling. On a two-man climb (shown right), the first climber (leader) climbs to the first stage (pitch), putting in anchors on the way. The second follows the same route, collecting the equipment as he climbs.

BASIC EQUIPMENT

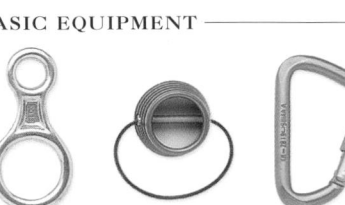

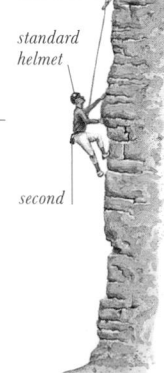

leader

anchor

SINGLE-PITCH CLIMB

runner

standard helmet

second

DESCENDER   BELAY DEVICE   SCREWGATE CARABINER   FRIEND   NUT

ROCK CYCLE

All types of rocks are constantly being generated and transformed. Igneous rock forms when magma rises from the Earth's mantle, cooling and solidifying below or above the surface. Crustal movements can thrust rock to the surface or bury it deeper. Below ground, any rock subjected to significant heat and pressure may turn into metamorphic rock or be remelted. At the surface, rocks are eventually eroded by wind, water, or ice. Compression and cementation of the eroded particles form sedimentary rock, which may be uplifted and eroded once again, metamorphosed, or remelted.

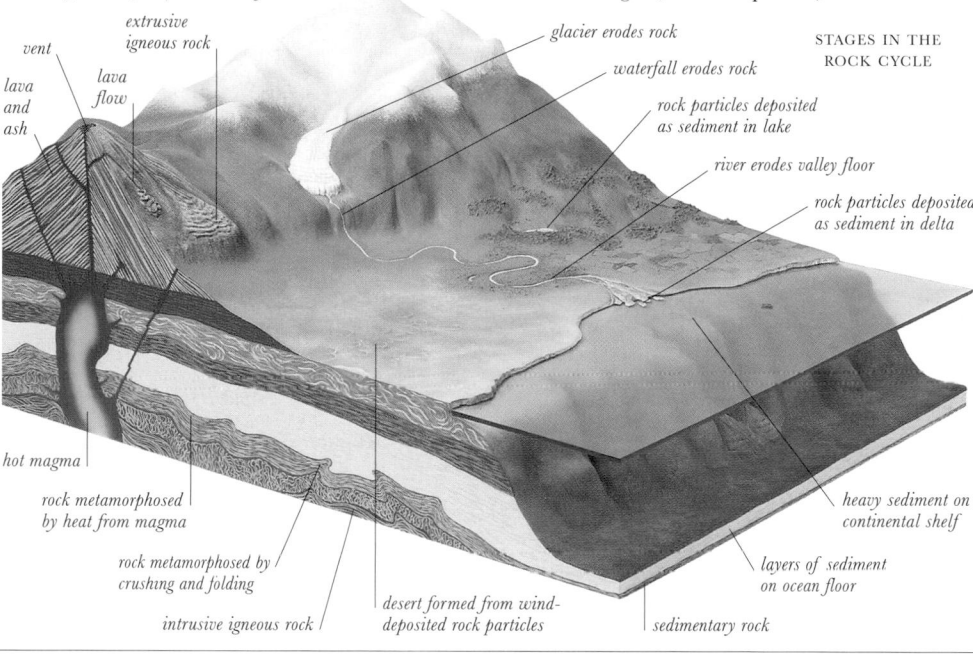

vent
extrusive igneous rock
lava and ash
lava flow
hot magma
rock metamorphosed by heat from magma
rock metamorphosed by crushing and folding
intrusive igneous rock
desert formed from wind-deposited rock particles
glacier erodes rock
waterfall erodes rock
rock particles deposited as sediment in lake
river erodes valley floor
rock particles deposited as sediment in delta
heavy sediment on continental shelf
layers of sediment on ocean floor
sedimentary rock

STAGES IN THE ROCK CYCLE

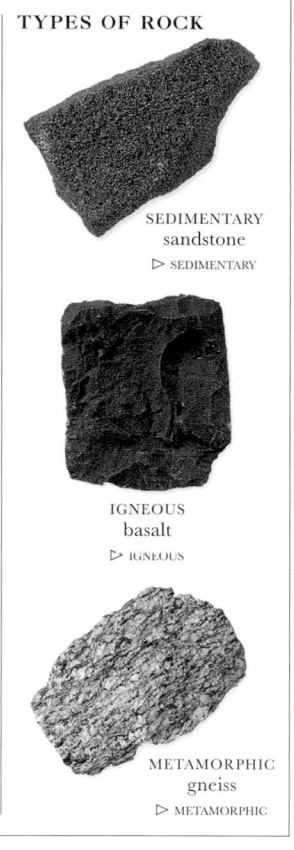

TYPES OF ROCK

SEDIMENTARY
sandstone
▷ SEDIMENTARY

IGNEOUS
basalt
▷ IGNEOUS

METAMORPHIC
gneiss
▷ METAMORPHIC

---

rock·et[1] /rókit/ *n. & v.* ● *n.* **1** a cylindrical projectile that can be propelled to a great height or distance by combustion of its contents. **2** an engine using a similar principle but not dependent on air intake for its operation. **3** ▶ a rocket-propelled missile, spacecraft, etc. ▷ SPACECRAFT. ● *v.* **1** *tr.* bombard with rockets. **2** *intr.* **a** move rapidly upward or away. **b** increase rapidly (*prices rocketed*).

nose cone
upper payload
lower payload
upper engine
liquid oxygen tank
fuel line
solid fuel booster
liquid helium
Vulcain engine
vehicle equipment bay
igniter
propellant-filled segment
steel casing
exhaust duct

ROCKET:
ARIANE SPACE ROCKET

rock·et[2] /rókit/ *n.* **1** (also **sweet rocket**) any of various fast-growing plants, esp. of the genus *Hesperis* or *Sisymbrium*. **2** a cruciferous annual plant, *Eruca sativa*, grown for salad.

rock·et·ry /rókitree/ *n.* the science or practice of rocket propulsion.

rock·fall /rókfawl/ *n.* **1** a descent of loose rocks. **2** a mass of fallen rock.

rock gar·den *n.* a garden in which interesting stones and rocks are a chief feature.

rock·hop·per /rók-hopər/ *n.* a small penguin, *Eudyptes crestatus*, with a crest of feathers on the forehead.

rock·ing chair *n.* a chair mounted on rockers or springs for gently rocking in.

rock·ing horse *n.* a model of a horse on rockers or springs for a child to rock on.

rock 'n' roll var. of ROCK AND ROLL.

rock pool *n.* a pool of water among rocks.

rock·rose /rókrōz/ *n.* ▶ any plant of the genus *Cistus*, *Helianthum*, etc., with rose-like flowers.

rock salt *n.* common salt as a solid mineral.

rock·shaft /rókshaft/ *n.* a shaft that oscillates about an axis without making complete revolutions.

rock·y[1] /rókee/ *adj. & n.* ● *adj.* (**rockier**, **rockiest**) **1** of or like rock. **2** full of or abounding in rock or rocks (*a rocky shore*). **3 a** firm as a rock; determined; steadfast. **b** unfeeling; cold; hard. ● *n.* (**the Rockies**) the Rocky Mountains in western N. America. □□ **rock·i·ness** *n.*

rock·y[2] /rókee/ *adj.* (**rockier**, **rockiest**) *colloq.* unsteady; tottering. □□ **rock·i·ly** *adv.* **rock·i·ness** *n.*

ro·co·co /rəkókō/ *adj. & n.* ● *adj.* **1** ▶ of a late baroque style of decoration prevalent in 18th-c. continental Europe, with asymmetrical patterns. **2** (of literature, music, architecture, and the decorative arts) highly ornamented; florid. ● *n.* the rococo style.

ROCKROSE:
GUM CISTUS
(*Cistus ladanifer*)

rod /rod/ *n.* **1** a slender straight bar, esp. of wood or metal. **2** this as a symbol of office. **3 a** a stick or bundle of twigs used in caning or flogging. **b** (prec. by *the*) the use of this; punishment; chastisement. **4 a** = FISHING ROD. **b** an angler using a rod. **5 a** a slender straight round stick growing as a shoot on a tree. **b** this when cut. **6** (as a measure) a perch or square perch (see PERCH[1]). **7** *sl.* = HOT ROD. **8** *sl.* a pistol or revolver. **9** *Anat.* any of numerous rod-shaped structures in the eye, detecting dim light. □□ **rod·less** *adj.* **rod·let** *n.* **rod·like** *adj.*

rode[1] *past* of RIDE.

rode[2] /rōd/ *v.intr.* (of wildfowl) fly landward in the evening.

R

ROCOCO: 18TH-CENTURY BAVARIAN ROCOCO CHURCH

ro·dent /ród'nt/ n. & adj. ● n. ▼ any mammal of the order Rodentia with strong incisors and no canine teeth, e.g., rat, mouse, squirrel, beaver, porcupine. ● adj. **1** of the order Rodentia. **2** gnawing (esp. Med. of slow-growing ulcers). □□ **ro·den·tial** /-dénshəl/ adj.

ro·den·ti·cide /rədéntisīd/ n. a poison used to kill rodents.

ro·de·o /ródiō, rōdáyō/ n. (pl. **-os**) **1** ▶ an exhibition or entertainment involving cowboys' skills in handling animals. **2** an exhibition of other skills, e.g., in motorcycling. **3 a** a roundup of cattle on a ranch for branding, etc. **b** an enclosure for this.

rod·o·mon·tade /ródəmontáyd, -táad, ródə-/ n., adj., & v. ● n. **1** boastful or bragging talk or behav-

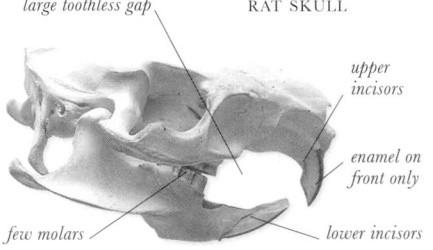

rope used as handhold

bare back

RODEO RIDER

ior. **2** an instance of this. ● adj. boastful or bragging. ● v.intr. brag; talk boastfully.

roe[1] /rō/ n. **1** (also **hard roe**) the mass of eggs in a female fish's ovary. **2** (also **soft roe**) the milt of a male fish. □□ **roed** adj. (also in comb.).

roe[2] /rō/ n. (pl. same or **roes**) (also **roe deer**) a small European and Asian deer, Capreolus capreolus.

roe·buck /róbuk/ n. (pl. same or **roebucks**) a male roe deer.

roent·gen /réntgən, -jən, rúnt-/ n. (also **röntgen**) a unit of ionizing radiation.

roent·gen·og·ra·phy /réntgənógrəfee, -jə-, rúnt-/ n. photography using X rays.

roent·gen·ol·o·gy /réntgənóləjee, -jə-, rúnt-/ n. = RADIOLOGY.

ro·ga·tion /rōgáyshən/ n. (usu. in pl.) Eccl. a solemn supplication consisting of the litany of the saints chanted on the three days before Ascension Day. □□ **ro·ga·tion·al** adj.

rog·er /rójər/ int. **1** your message has been received and understood (used in radio communication, etc.). **2** sl. I agree.

rogue /rōg/ n. & v. ● n. **1** a dishonest or unprincipled person. **2** joc. a mischievous person, esp. a child. **3** (usu. attrib.) **a** a wild animal driven away or living apart from the herd and of fierce temper (rogue elephant). **b** a stray, irresponsible, or undisciplined person or thing (rogue trader). **4** an inferior or defective specimen among many acceptable ones. ● v.tr. remove rogues (sense 4 of n.) from.

ro·guer·y /rógəree/ n. (pl. **-ies**) conduct or an action characteristic of rogues.

rogues' gal·ler·y n. a collection of photographs of known criminals, etc., used for identification of suspects.

ro·guish /rógish/ adj. **1** playfully mischievous. **2** characteristic of rogues. □□ **ro·guish·ly** adv. **ro·guish·ness** n.

roist·er /róystər/ v.intr. (esp. as **roistering** adj.) revel noisily; be uproarious. □□ **roist·er·er** n. **roist·er·ing** n. **roist·er·ous** adj.

role /rōl/ n. (also **rôle**) **1** an actor's part in a play, motion picture, etc. **2** a person's or thing's characteristic or expected function.

role mod·el n. a person looked to by others as an example in a particular role.

role-play·ing n. an exercise in which participants act the part of another character, used in psychotherapy, language teaching, etc.

roll /rōl/ v. & n. ● v. **1 a** intr. move or go in some direction by turning over and over on an axis. **b** tr. cause to do this (rolled the barrel into the cellar). **2** tr. make revolve between two surfaces (rolled the clay between his palms). **3 a** intr. (foll. by along, by, etc.) move or advance on or (of time, etc.) as if on wheels, etc. (the years rolled by). **b** tr. cause to do this (rolled the dessert cart to our table). **c** intr. (of a person) be conveyed in a vehicle (rolled by on his tractor). **4 a** tr. turn over and over on itself to form a more or less cylindrical or spherical shape (rolled a newspaper). **b** tr. make by forming material into a cylinder or ball (rolled a cigarette). **c** tr. accumulate into a mass (rolled the dough into a ball). **d** intr. (foll. by into) make a specified shape of itself (the caterpillar rolled into a ball). **5** tr. flatten or form by passing a roller, etc., over or by passing between rollers (roll pastry). **6** intr. & tr. change or cause to change direction by rotatory movement (his eyes rolled). **7** intr. **a** wallow, turn about in a fluid or a loose medium (the dog rolled in the dust). **b** (of a horse, etc.) lie on its back and kick about, esp. in an attempt to dislodge its rider. **8** intr. **a** (of a moving ship, aircraft, or vehicle) sway to and fro on an axis parallel to the direction of motion. **b** walk with an unsteady swaying gait (they rolled out of the bar). **9 a** intr. undulate; show or go with an undulating surface or motion (rolling hills). **b** tr. carry or propel with such motion (the river rolls its waters to the sea). **10 a** intr. (of machinery) start functioning or moving (the cameras rolled). **b** tr. cause (machinery) to do this. **11** intr. & tr. sound or utter with a vibratory or trilling effect (he rolls his rs). **12** sl. **a** tr. overturn (a car, etc.). **b** intr. (of a car, etc.) overturn. **13** tr. throw (dice). **14** tr. sl. rob (esp. a helpless victim). ● n. **1** a rolling motion or gait; undulation (the roll of the hills). **2 a** a spell of rolling (a roll in the mud). **b** a gymnastic exercise in which the body is rolled into a tucked position and turned in a forward or backward circle. **c** (esp. **a roll in the hay**) colloq. an act of sexual intercourse or erotic fondling. **3** the continuous rhythmic sound of thunder or a drum. **4** Aeron. a complete revolution of an aircraft about its longitudinal axis. **5** a cylinder formed by turning flexible material over and over on itself without folding (a roll of carpet). **6 a** a small

---

RODENT

Rodents constitute the largest order of mammals, with up to 2,000 species. There are three suborders: Sciuromorpha (squirrellike), Myomorpha (mouselike), and Cavimorpha (cavylike). All rodents have only one pair of incisors in each jaw. These incisors grow constantly, but are worn down and kept sharp by continual gnawing.

large toothless gap

RAT SKULL

upper incisors

enamel on front only

few molars

lower incisors

TYPES OF RODENT

SCIUROMORPHA

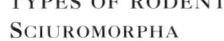

GRAY SQUIRREL
(*Sciurus carolinensis*)

CHIPMUNK
(*Eutamias* species)

BEAVER (*Castor fiber*)

MYOMORPHA

YELLOW-NECKED WOODMOUSE
(*Apodemus flavicollis*)

HAMSTER
(*Mesocricetus auratus*)

BROWN RAT (*Rattus norvegicus*)

PALLID GERBIL
(*Gerbillus* species)

CAVIMORPHA

CAPYBARA (*Hydrochoerus hydrochaeris*)

NAKED MOLE RAT
(*Heterocephalus glaber*)

MALAYAN PORCUPINE
(*Hystrix brachyura*)

GUINEA PIG
(*Cavia porcellus*)

R

portion of bread individually baked. **b** this with a specified filling (*ham roll*). **7** a more or less cylindrical or semicylindrical straight or curved mass of something (*rolls of fat*). **8 a** an official list or register. **b** the total numbers on this (*the schools' rolls have fallen*). **c** a document, esp. an official record, in scroll form. **9** a cylinder or roller, esp. to shape metal in a rolling mill. **10** *colloq.* money, esp. as bills rolled together. □ **be rolling in** *colloq.* have plenty of (esp. money). **on a roll** *sl.* experiencing a bout of success or progress; engaged in a period of intense activity. **roll back** cause (esp. prices) to decrease. **rolled into one** combined in one person or thing. **roll in 1** arrive in great numbers or quantity. **2** wallow; luxuriate in. **rolling drunk** swaying or staggering from drunkenness. **roll on** *v.tr.* put on or apply by rolling. **roll out** unroll; spread out. **roll over 1** *Econ.* finance the repayment of (maturing stock, etc.) by an issue of new stock. **2** reinvest funds in a similar financial instrument (*we decided to roll over the CDs*). **roll up 1** *colloq.* arrive in a vehicle; appear on the scene. **2** make into or form a roll. **roll with the punches** withstand adversity, difficulties, etc. **roll up one's sleeves** see SLEEVE. □□ **roll·a·ble** *adj.*

roll bar *n.* an overhead metal bar strengthening the frame of a vehicle (esp. in racing) and protecting the occupants if the vehicle overturns. ▷ INDY CAR

roll call *n.* a process of calling out a list of names to establish who is present.

rolled gold *n.* gold in the form of a thin coating applied to a baser metal by rolling.

roll·er /rṓlər/ *n.* **1 a** a hard revolving cylinder for smoothing the ground, spreading ink or paint, crushing or stamping, rolling up cloth on, etc., used alone or as a rotating part of a machine. ▷ PRINTING. **b** a cylinder for diminishing friction when moving a heavy object. **2** a small cylinder on which hair is rolled for setting. **3** a long, swelling wave. **4** (also **roller bandage**) a long surgical bandage rolled up for convenient application.

roll·er bear·ing *n.* ▼ a bearing like a ball bearing but with small cylinders instead of balls.

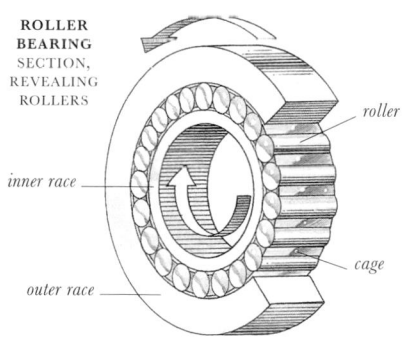

ROLLER BEARING SECTION, REVEALING ROLLERS

roller
inner race
cage
outer race

Roll·er·blade /rṓlərblayd/ *n. & v.* ● *n. Trademark* (usu. *pl.*) roller skates with wheels arranged in a straight line, used like ice skates; in-line skates. ● *v.intr.* (**rollerblade**) use Rollerblades.

roll·er coast·er *n.* an amusement ride consisting of an elevated track with open-car trains that rise and plunge steeply.

rol·lick /rólik/ *v. & n.* ● *v.intr.* (esp. as **rollicking** *adj.*) be jovial or exuberant. ● *n.* **1** exuberant gaiety. **2** a spree or escapade.

roll·ing pin *n.* a cylinder for rolling out pastry, dough, etc.

roll·ing stock *n.* **1** the locomotives, cars, or other vehicles, used on a railroad. **2** the road vehicles of a company.

roll·ing stone *n.* a person who is unwilling to settle for long in one place.

roll-on *attrib.adj.* (of a deodorant, etc.) applied by means of a rotating ball in the neck of the container.

---

roll·o·ver /rṓlōvər/ *n.* **1** *Econ.* the extension or transfer of a debt or other financial relationship. **2** *colloq.* the overturning of a vehicle, etc.

rolltop desk *n.* ▼ a desk with a flexible cover sliding in curved grooves.

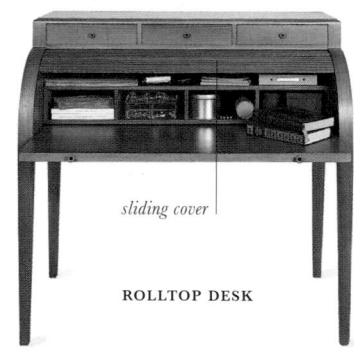

sliding cover

ROLLTOP DESK

ro·ly-po·ly /rṓleepṓlee/ *adj.* pudgy; plump.

ROM /rom/ *abbr. Computing* read-only memory.

ro·maine /rōmáyn/ *n.* a cos lettuce.

ro·ma·ji /rṓməjee/ *n.* a system of romanized spelling used to transliterate Japanese.

Ro·man /rṓmən/ *adj. & n.* ● *adj.* **1** of ancient Rome or its territory or people. **2** of medieval or modern Rome. **3** = ROMAN CATHOLIC. **4** of a kind ascribed to the early Romans (*Roman virtue*). **5** surviving from a period of Roman rule (*Roman road*). **6** (**roman**) (of type) of a plain upright kind used in ordinary print. **7** (of the alphabet, etc.) based on the ancient Roman system with letters A–Z. ● *n.* **1 a** a citizen of the ancient Roman Republic or Empire. **b** a soldier of the Roman Empire. **2** a citizen of modern Rome. **3** = ROMAN CATHOLIC. **4** (**roman**) roman type. **5** (in *pl.*) the Christians of ancient Rome.

ro·man à clef /rōmáänaakláy/ *n.* (*pl.* **romans à clef** *pronunc.* same) a novel in which real persons or events appear with invented names.

Ro·man can·dle *n.* a firework discharging a series of flaming colored balls.

Ro·man Cath·o·lic /rṓmən/ *adj. & n.* ● *adj.* of the

---

part of the Christian Church acknowledging the pope as its head. ● *n.* a member of this Church. □□ **Ro·man Cath·ol·i·cism** *n.*

ro·mance /rōmáns/ *n., adj., & v.* ● *n.* (also *disp.* /rṓmans/) **1** an atmosphere or tendency characterized by a sense of remoteness from or idealization of everyday life. **2 a** a prevailing sense of wonder or mystery surrounding the mutual attraction in a love affair. **b** sentimental or idealized love. **c** a love affair. **3 a** a literary genre with romantic love or highly imaginative unrealistic episodes forming the central theme. **b** a work of this genre. **4** a medieval tale of some hero of chivalry. **5 a** exaggeration or picturesque falsehood. **b** an instance of this. **6** (**Romance**) the languages descended from Latin. **7** *Mus.* a short informal piece. ● *adj.* (**Romance**) of any of the languages descended from Latin. ● *v.* **1** *intr.* exaggerate or distort the truth. **2** *tr.* court; woo.

ro·manc·er /rōmánsər/ *n.* **1** a writer of romances. **2** a liar who resorts to fantasy.

Ro·man Em·pire *n. hist.* that established by Augustus in 27 BC and divided by Theodosius in AD 395 into the Western or Latin and Eastern or Greek Empire.

Ro·man·esque /rṓmənésk/ *n. & adj.* ● *n.* ▼ a style of architecture prevalent in Europe *c.* 900–1200, with massive vaulting and round arches. ● *adj.* of the Romanesque style of architecture.

ro·man-fleuve /rṓmoɴflœ́v/ *n.* (*pl.* **romans-fleuves** *pronunc.* same) **1** a novel featuring the leisurely description of the lives of members of a family, etc. **2** a sequence of self-contained novels.

Ro·ma·ni·an /rōmáyneeən/ *n. & adj.* (also **Ru·ma·ni·an** /roo-/) ● *n.* **1 a** a native or national of Romania in E. Europe. **b** a person of Romanian descent. **2** the language of Romania. ● *adj.* of or relating to Romania or its people or language.

Ro·man·ic /rōmánik/ *n. & adj.* ● *n.* = ROMANCE *n.* 6. ● *adj.* **1 a** of or relating to Romance. **b** Romance-speaking. **2** descended from the ancient Romans or inheriting aspects of their social or political life.

Ro·man·ist /rṓmənist/ *n.* **1** a student of Roman history or law or of the Romance languages. **2 a** a supporter of Roman Catholicism. **b** a Roman Catholic.

ROMANESQUE

While the main inspiration for Romanesque architecture was classical Rome, the ornamentation of the Byzantine and Islamic worlds was also a strong influence, especially in the Mediterranean. The style's wide distribution led to local variation, but common features were large vaults, round arches, and massive stonework.

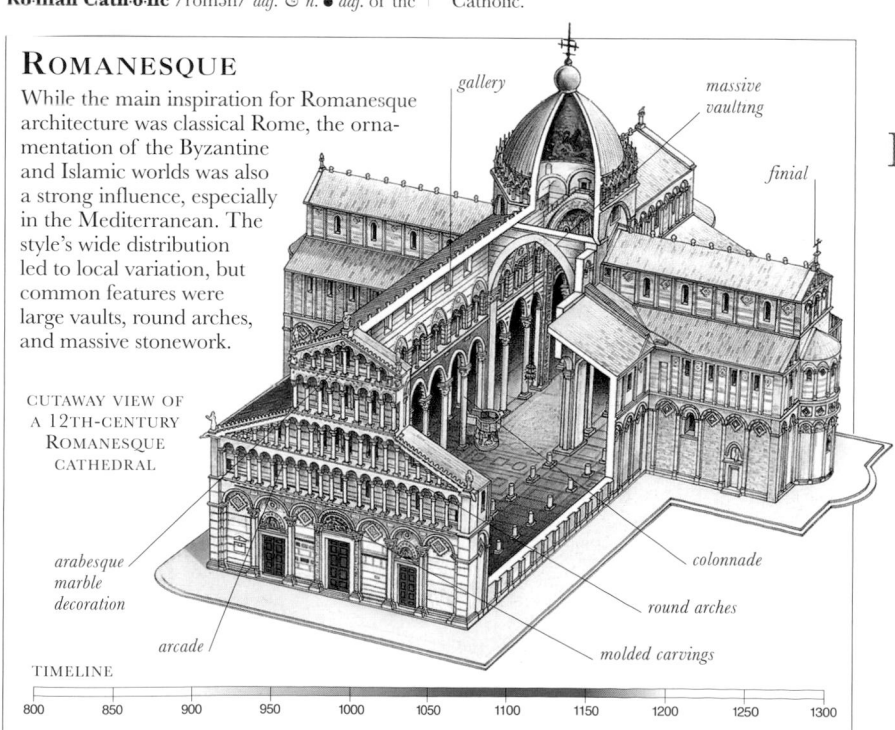

gallery
massive vaulting
finial

CUTAWAY VIEW OF A 12TH-CENTURY ROMANESQUE CATHEDRAL

arabesque marble decoration
arcade
colonnade
round arches
molded carvings

TIMELINE

| 800 | 850 | 900 | 950 | 1000 | 1050 | 1100 | 1150 | 1200 | 1250 | 1300 |

R

ro·man·ize /rṓmənīz/ *v.tr.* **1** make Roman or Roman Catholic in character. **2** put into the Roman alphabet or into roman type. □□ **ro·man·i·za·tion** *n.*

Ro·man nu·mer·al *n.* any of the Roman letters representing numbers: I = 1, V = 5, X = 10, L = 50, C = 100, D = 500, M = 1000.

Romano- /rōmáánō/ *comb. form* Roman; Roman and (*Romano-British*).

ro·man·tic /rōmántik/ *adj. & n.* ● *adj.* **1** of, characterized by, or suggestive of an idealized, sentimental, or fantastic view of reality (*a romantic picture; a romantic setting*). **2** inclined toward or suggestive of romance in love (*a romantic woman; a romantic evening*). **3** (of a person) imaginative; visionary; idealistic. **4 a** (of style in art, music, etc.) concerned more with feeling and emotion than with form and aesthetic qualities. **b** (also **Romantic**) of or relating to the 18th–19th-c. romantic movement or style in the European arts. ● *n.* **1** a romantic person. **2** a romanticist. □□ **ro·man·ti·cal·ly** *adv.*

ro·man·ti·cism /rōmántisizəm/ *n.* (also **Romanticism**) adherence to a romantic style in art, music, etc.

ro·man·ti·cist /rōmántisist/ *n.* (also **Romanticist**) a writer or artist of the romantic school.

ro·man·ti·cize /rōmántisīz/ *v.* **1** *tr.* describe or portray in a romantic fashion. **2** *intr.* indulge in romantic thoughts. □□ **ro·man·ti·ci·za·tion** *n.*

Rom·a·ny /rómənee, rṓ-/ *n. & adj.* ● *n.* (*pl.* **-ies**) **1** a Gypsy. **2** the language of the Gypsies. ● *adj.* **1** of or concerning Gypsies. **2** of the Romany language.

Ro·me·o /rṓmeeō/ *n.* an attractive, passionate male seducer or lover.

romp /romp/ *v. & n.* ● *v.intr.* **1** play about roughly and energetically. **2** (foll. by *along, past,* etc.) *colloq.* proceed without effort. ● *n.* a spell of romping.

romp·ers /rómpərz/ *n.pl.* a young child's one-piece outer garment.

ronde /rond/ *n.* **1** a dance in which the dancers move in a circle. **2** a course of talk, activity, etc.

ron·deau /róndō, rondṓ/ *n.* (*pl.* **rondeaux** *pronunc.* same or /-dōz/) a poem of ten or thirteen lines with only two rhymes throughout and with the opening words used twice as a refrain.

ron·del /rónd'l, rondél/ *n.* a rondeau, esp. one of special form.

ron·do /róndō/ *n.* (*pl.* **-os**) *Mus.* a form with a recurring leading theme.

rönt·gen var. of ROENTGEN.

rood /rōod/ *n.* **1** a crucifix, esp. one raised on a screen or beam at the entrance to the chancel. **2** a quarter of an acre.

rood screen *n.* ▼ a wooden or stone carved screen separating nave and chancel. ▷ CHURCH

ROOD SCREEN IN A 12TH-CENTURY CATHEDRAL, WALES

ROOF

Most roofs are sloped (pitched) and consist of a wooden frame and some form of covering, such as tiles, slates, thatch, or tin. The inclined part of the frame is formed by rafters. To prevent sagging or bowing, the rafters need to be supported by curved or diagonal beams (braces) or horizontal beams (purlins), which together form strong trusses.

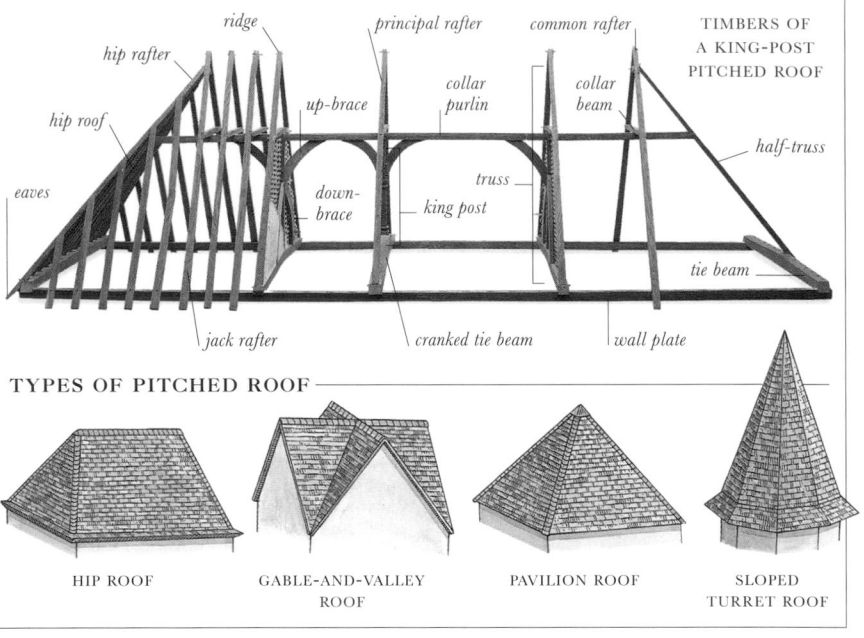

ridge — *principal rafter* — *common rafter* — TIMBERS OF A KING-POST PITCHED ROOF
hip rafter — *collar purlin* — *collar beam*
hip roof — *up-brace* — *half-truss*
eaves — *truss*
down-brace — *king post*
jack rafter — *cranked tie beam* — *wall plate*
tie beam

TYPES OF PITCHED ROOF

HIP ROOF   GABLE-AND-VALLEY ROOF   PAVILION ROOF   SLOPED TURRET ROOF

roof /rōof, rŏŏf/ *n. & v.* ● *n.* (*pl.* **roofs** or *disp.* **rooves** /rōovz, rŏŏvz/) **1 a** ▲ the upper covering of a building, usu. supported by its walls. **b** the top of a covered vehicle. **c** the top inner surface of an oven, refrigerator, etc. **2** the overhead rock in a cave or mine, etc. ▷ CAVE. **3** the branches or the sky, etc., overhead. **4** (of prices, etc.) the upper limit or ceiling. ● *v.tr.* **1** (often foll. by *in, over*) cover with or as with a roof. **2** be the roof of. □ **go through the roof** *colloq.* (of prices, etc.) reach extreme or unexpected heights. **hit** (or **go through** or **raise**) **the roof** *colloq.* become very angry. **raise the roof 1** create a noisy racket. **2** protest noisily. **under one roof** in the same building. **under a person's roof** in a person's house (esp. with ref. to hospitality). □□ **roofed** *adj.* (also in *comb.*). **roof·less** *adj.*

roof·er /rŏŏfər, rōof-/ *n.* a person who constructs or repairs roofs.

roof gar·den *n.* **1** a garden on the flat roof of a building. **2** a rooftop restaurant.

roof·ing /rŏŏfing, rōof-/ *n.* **1** material for constructing a roof. **2** the process of constructing a roof or roofs.

roof of the mouth *n.* the palate.

roof rack *n.* a framework for luggage, etc. on the roof of a vehicle.

roof·top /rŏŏftop, rōof-/ *n.* **1** the outer surface of a roof. **2** (esp. in *pl.*) the level of a roof.

roof·tree /rŏŏftree, rōof-/ *n.* a roof's ridgepole.

rook[1] /rŏŏk/ *n. & v.* ● *n.* **1** a black European and Asiatic bird, *Corvus frugilegus,* of the crow family, nesting in colonies. **2** a sharper, esp. at dice or cards; a person who lives off inexperienced gamblers, etc. ● *v.tr.* **1** charge (a customer) extortionately. **2** win money from (a person) at cards, etc., esp. by swindling.

rook[2] /rŏŏk/ *n.* ▶ a chess piece with its top in the shape of a battlement; castle. ▷ CHESS

ROOK

rook·er·y /rŏŏkəree/ *n.* (*pl.* **-ies**) **1 a** a colony of rooks. **b** a clump of trees having rooks' nests. **2** a colony of seabirds (esp. penguins) or seals.

rook·ie /rŏŏkee/ *n. sl.* **1** a new recruit. **2** a member of a sports team in his or her first season.

room /rōom, rŏŏm/ *n. & v.* ● *n.* **1 a** space that is or might be occupied by something; capaciousness or ability to accommodate contents (*it takes up too much room; there is plenty of room; we have no room here for idlers*). **b** space in or on (*shelf room*). **2 a** a part of a building enclosed by walls, floor, and ceiling. **b** (in *pl.*) apartments, etc. **c** persons present in a room (*the room fell silent*). **3** (in *comb.*) a room or area for a specified purpose (*reading room*). **4** (foll. by *for,* or *to* + *infin.*) opportunity or scope (*room to improve things; no room for dispute*). ● *v.intr.* have a room or rooms; lodge; board. □ **make room** (often foll. by *for*) clear a space (for a person or thing) by removal of others; make way; yield place. **not** (or **no**) **room to swing a cat** a very confined space. □□ **-roomed** *adj.* (in *comb.*). **room·ful** *n.* (*pl.* **-fuls**).

room·er /rōomər, rŏŏ-/ *n.* a renter of a room in another's house.

room·ie /rōomee, rŏŏm-/ *n. colloq.* a roommate.

room·ing house *n.* a house with rented rooms for lodging.

room·mate /rōom-mayt, rŏŏm-/ *n.* a person occupying the same room, apartment, etc., as another.

room serv·ice *n.* (in a hotel, etc.) service of food or drink taken to a guest's room.

room·y /rōomee, rŏŏ-/ *adj.* (**roomier, roomiest**) having much room; spacious. □□ **room·i·ness** *n.*

roost /rōost/ *n. & v.* ● *n.* **1** a support on which a bird perches, esp. a place where birds regularly settle to sleep. **2** a place offering temporary sleeping accommodation. ● *v.* **1** *intr.* **a** (of a bird) settle for rest or sleep. **b** (of a person) stay for the night. **2** *tr.* provide with a sleeping place. □ **come home to roost** (of a scheme, etc.) recoil unfavorably upon the originator. **rule the roost** hold a position of control; be in charge (esp. of others).

ROOT

A plant's root system anchors it in the ground and enables it to absorb water and nutrients from the soil. The surface area of the root system is increased by millions of microscopic projections called root hairs. These grow just behind the tip of each root.

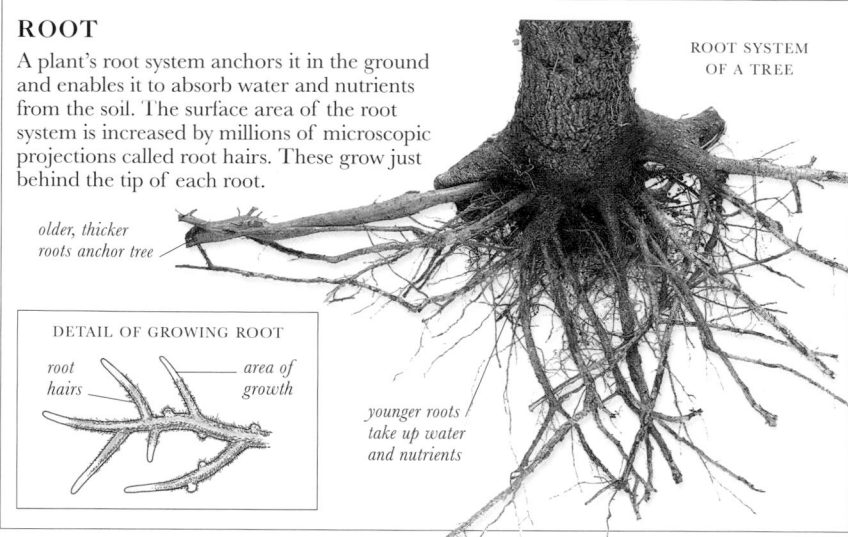

ROOT SYSTEM OF A TREE

older, thicker roots anchor tree

DETAIL OF GROWING ROOT

root hairs   *area of growth*

younger roots take up water and nutrients

---

roost·er /ro͞ostər/ *n.* a male domestic fowl.

root[1] /ro͞ot, ro͝ot/ *n. & v.* ● *n.* **1 a** ▲ the part of a plant normally below the ground, attaching it to the earth and conveying nourishment to it from the soil. ▷ SUCCULENT. **b** (in *pl.*) such a part divided into branches or fibers. **c** the corresponding organ of an epiphyte; the part attaching ivy to its support. **d** the permanent underground stock of a plant. **e** any small plant with a root for transplanting. **2 a** any plant, e.g., a turnip or carrot, with an edible root. ▷ VEGETABLE. **b** such a root. **3** (in *pl.*) the sources of or reasons for one's long-standing emotional attachment to a place, community, etc. **4 a** the embedded part of a bodily organ or structure, e.g., hair, tooth, nail, etc. ▷ NAIL, TOOTH. **b** the part of a thing attaching it to a greater whole. **c** (in *pl.*) the base of a mountain, etc. **5 a** the basic cause, source, or origin (*love of money is the root of all evil*; *has its roots in the distant past*). **b** (*attrib.*) (of an idea, etc.) from which the rest originated. **6** the basis of something, its means of continuance or growth (*has its root(s) in selfishness*; *has no root in the nature of things*). **7** the essential substance or nature of something (*get to the root of things*). **8** *Math.* **a** a number or quantity that when multiplied by itself a usu. specified number of times gives a specified number or quantity (*the cube root of eight is two*). **b** a square root. **c** a value of an unknown quantity satisfying a given equation. **9** *Philol.* any ultimate unanalyzable element of language; a basis on which words are made by the addition of prefixes or suffixes or by other modification. **10** *Mus.* the fundamental note of a chord. **11** *Bibl.* a scion, an offshoot (*there shall be a root of Jesse*). ● *v.* **1 a** *intr.* take root or grow roots. **b** *tr.* cause to do this (*take care to root them firmly*). **2 a** *tr.* fix firmly; establish (*fear rooted him to the spot*). **b** (as **rooted** *adj.*) firmly established (*her affection was deeply rooted*). **3** *tr.* (usu. foll. by *out, up*) drag or dig up by the roots. □ **put down roots 1** begin to draw nourishment from the soil. **2** become settled or established. **root and branch** thorough(ly), radical(ly). **root out** find and get rid of. **strike at the root** (or **roots**) **of** set about destroying. **take root 1** begin to grow and draw nourishment from the soil. **2** become fixed or established. □□ **root·ed·ness** *n.* **root·less** *adj.* **root·let** *n.* **root·like** *adj.* **root·y** *adj.*

root[2] /ro͞ot, ro͝ot/ *v.* **1 a** *intr.* turn up the ground with the snout, beak, etc., in search of food. **b** *tr.* (foll. by *up*) turn up (the ground) by rooting. **2 a** *intr.* (foll. by *around, in*, etc.) rummage. **b** *tr.* (foll. by *out* or *up*) find or extract by rummaging. **3** *intr.* (foll. by *for*) *sl.* encourage by applause or support. □□ **root·er** *n.* (in sense 3).

root beer *n.* a carbonated drink made from an extract of roots.

root ca·nal *n. Dentistry* surgery to remove the diseased nerve of a tooth.

root·in'-toot·in' /ro͞otntoot͞on/ *adj. N. Amer. colloq.* boisterous, noisy, or lively.

root·stock /ro͞otstok, ro͝ot-/ *n.* **1** a rhizome. **2** a plant into which a graft is inserted. **3** a primary form from which offshoots have arisen.

rooves see ROOF.

rope /rōp/ *n. & v.* ● *n.* **1 a** ▼ stout cord made by twisting together strands of hemp, sisal, flax, cotton, nylon, wire, or similar material. **b** a piece of this. **c** a lasso. **2** (foll. by *of*) a quantity of onions, garlic bulbs, pearls, etc., strung together. **3** (in *pl.*, prec. by *the*) **a** the conditions in some sphere of action (*know the ropes*; *show a person the ropes*). **b** the ropes enclosing a boxing or wrestling ring, etc. **4** (prec. by *the*) **a** a noose or halter for hanging a person. **b** execution by hanging. ● *v.* **1** *tr.* fasten, secure, or catch with rope. **2** *tr.* (usu. foll. by *off, in*) enclose (a space) with rope. **3** *Mountaineering* **a** *tr.* connect (a party) with a rope; attach (a person) to a rope. **b** (*absol.*) put on a rope. **c** *intr.* (foll. by *down, up*) climb down or up using a rope. □ **give a person plenty of rope** (or **enough rope to hang himself** or **herself**) give a person enough freedom of action to bring about his or her own downfall. **on the rope** *Mountaineering* roped together. **on the ropes 1** *Boxing* forced against the ropes by the opponent's attack. **2** near defeat. **rope in** persuade to take part. **rope into** persuade to take part in (*was roped into doing the laundry*). **rope ladder** two long ropes connected by short cross-pieces, used as a ladder.

rop·ing /rōping/ *n.* a set or arrangement of ropes.

rop·y /rōpee/ *adj.* (also **rop·ey**) (**ropier**, **ropiest**) **1** forming viscous or gelatinous threads. **2** like a rope.

roque /rōk/ *n.* croquet played on a hard court surrounded by a bank.

Roque·fort /rōkfərt/ *n. Trademark* **1** a soft blue cheese made from sheep's milk. ▷ CHEESE. **2** a salad dressing made of this.

ror·qual /rawrkwəl/ *n.* any of various whales of the family Balaenopteridae, esp. *Balaenoptera musculus*, having a dorsal fin. Also called **finback**, **fin whale**. ▷ FIN WHALE.

Ror·schach test /rawrshaak/ *n. Psychol.* a type of personality test in which a standard set of inkblot designs is presented one by one to the subject, who is asked to describe what they suggest or resemble.

ro·sa·ceous /rōzáyshəs/ *adj. Bot.* of the large plant family Rosaceae, which includes the rose.

ro·sa·ri·an /rəzáireeən/ *n.* a person who cultivates roses, esp. professionally.

ro·sar·i·um /rəzáireeəm/ *n.* a rose garden.

ro·sa·ry /rōzəree/ *n.* (*pl.* **-ies**) **1** *RC Ch.* **a** a form of devotion in which prayers are said while counting them on a special string of beads. **b** ▶ a string of 55 (or 165) beads for keeping count in this. ▷ HABIT. **c** a book containing this devotion. **2** a similar string of beads used in other religions. **3** a rose garden or rose bed.

beads

ROSARY

crucifix

R

ROPE

Although there are variations, there are two main constructions of rope: three-strand and braided. Together with the construction, the material used to make a rope determines durability, strength, and flexibility. Natural materials are increasingly giving way to synthetic ones, resulting in stronger, lighter, and more reliable ropes.

three strands twisted together

THREE-STRAND (LAID) ROPE

mantle of braided nylon fibers

core of three-strand cords

BRAIDED ROPE

nylon filaments

EXAMPLES OF ROPE MATERIALS

NATURAL

SISAL   COTTON   HEMP   COIR

SYNTHETIC

BRAIDED POLYESTER   NYLON BRAIDED   STAPLE-SPUN POLYPROPYLENE

ROSE

There are approximately 150 species of roses. Cross-breeding, selection, and hybridization have led to the development of many thousands of cultivars from these species. They are valued mainly for the scent and color of their flowers, although some are also grown for the ornamental value of their fruit (hips). Cultivars can be divided into Old Garden and Modern roses, and these into the well-recognized subgroups shown below.

EXAMPLES OF SPECIES ROSES

Rosa eglanteria

Rosa rugosa

Rosa moschata

OLD GARDEN ROSES

BOURBON
(*Rosa* 'Variegata di Bologna')

HYBRID PERPETUAL
(*Rosa* 'Baron Girod de l'Ain')

DAMASK
(*Rosa* 'Ispahan')

NOISETTE
(*Rosa* 'Alister Stella Gray')

ALBA
(*Rosa* 'Great Maiden's Blush')

SEMPERVIRENS
(*Rosa* 'Félicité Perpétue')

CHINA
(*Rosa* 'Perle d'Or')

CENTIFOLIA
(*Rosa* 'Tour de Malakoff')

TEA
(*Rosa* 'Duchesse de Brabant')

SCOTS
(*Rosa* 'Grandiflora')

MOSS
(*Rosa* 'Henri Martin')

PORTLAND
(*Rosa* 'Marchesa Boccella')

GALLICA
(*Rosa* 'Charles de Mills')

BOURSALT
(*Rosa* 'Mme. de Sancy de Parabère')

MODERN ROSES

FLORIBUNDA
(*Rosa* 'Arthur Bell')

MINIATURE SHRUB
(*Rosa* 'Blue Peter')

RAMBLER
(*Rosa* 'Wedding Day')

SHRUB
(*Rosa* 'Abraham Darby')

MINIATURE
(*Rosa* 'Gentle Touch')

CLIMBER
(*Rosa* 'Climbing Iceberg')

POLYANTHA
(*Rosa* 'Ballerina')

RUGOSA
(*Rosa* 'Yellow Dagmar Hastrup')

HYBRID TEA
(*Rosa* 'Cherry Brandy')

MINIATURE CLIMBER
(*Rosa* 'Laura Ford')

GROUNDCOVER
(*Rosa* 'Hertfordshire')

R

rose[1] /rōz/ *n., adj., & v.* ● *n.* **1** ◀ any prickly bush or shrub of the genus *Rosa*, bearing usu. fragrant flowers generally of a red, pink, yellow, or white color. **2** this flower. **3** any flowering plant resembling this (*rose of Sharon; rockrose*). **4 a** a light crimson color; pink. **b** (usu. in *pl.*) a rosy complexion (*roses in her cheeks*). **5 a** a representation of the flower in heraldry or decoration (esp. as the national emblem of England). **b** a rose-shaped design. **6** the sprinkling nozzle of a watering can or hose. **7** an ornamental through which the shaft of a doorknob passes. **8 a** a rose diamond. **b** a rose window. **9** (in *pl.*) used in various phrases to express favorable circumstances, ease, success, etc. (*roses all the way; everything's roses*). **10** an excellent person or thing, esp. a beautiful woman (*English rose; rose between two thorns*). ● *adj.* = ROSE-COLORED 1. ● *v.tr.* (esp. as **rosed** *adj.*) make (one's face, cheeks, etc.) rosy. □ **see** (or **look**) **through rose-colored** (or **-tinted**) **glasses** regard (circumstances, etc.) with unfounded favor or optimism. □□ **rose·like** *adj.*

rose[2] *past of* RISE.

ro·sé /rōzáy/ *n.* any light pink wine.

ro·se·ate /rōzeeət, -ayt/ *adj.* **1** = ROSE-COLORED. **2** having a partly pink plumage.

rose·bay /rōzbay/ *n.* an oleander or rhododendron.

rose·bud /rōzbud/ *n.* a bud of a rose.

rose-col·ored *adj.* **1** of a light crimson color; pink. **2** optimistic; cheerful (*takes rose-colored views*).

rose ge·ra·ni·um *n.* a pink-flowered, sweet-scented geranium, *Pelargonium graveolus*.

rose·mar·y /rōzmairee, -məree/ *n.* an evergreen fragrant shrub, *Rosmarinus officinalis*, with leaves used as a culinary herb, in perfumery, etc., and taken as an emblem of remembrance. ▷ HERB

    ro·se·o·la /rōzeeólə, rōzéeələ/ *n.* **1** a rosy rash in measles and similar diseases. **2** a mild febrile disease of infants.

    ro·sette /rōzét/ *n.* **1** ◀ a rose-shaped ornament made usu. of ribbon and worn esp. as the badge of a contest official, etc., or as an award or the symbol of an award in a competition. **2** *Archit.* **a** a carved or molded ornament resembling or representing a rose. **b** a rose window. **3** an object or design resembling a rose. **4** *Biol.* **a** a roselike cluster of parts. **b** markings resembling a rose. □□ **ro·set·ted** *adj.*

    rose wa·ter *n.* perfume made from roses.

ROSETTES

    rose win·dow *n.* ▼ a circular window, usu. with roselike or spokelike tracery.

rose·wood /rōzwood/ *n.* any of several fragrant close-grained woods used in making furniture.

Rosh Ha·sha·nah /ráwsh həsháwnə, -sháá-, haashaanaá, rósh/ *n.* (also **Rosh Ha·sha·na**) the Jewish New Year.

Ro·si·cru·cian /rōzikróoshən/ *n. & adj.* ● *n.* a member of a secret 17th- and 18th-century society devoted to the study of metaphysical, mystical, and alchemical lore. ● *adj.* relating to the Rosicrucians.

ros·in /rózin/ *n. & v.* ● *n.* resin, esp. the solid residue after distillation of oil of turpentine from crude turpentine. ● *v.tr.* (**rosined, rosining**) rub (esp. the bow of a violin, etc.) with rosin.

ROSE WINDOWS IN NOTRE DAME CATHEDRAL, FRANCE

ROTATION

The systematic rotation of crops helps prevent pests and diseases from building up and, by varying the demands made on the soil, avoids exhaustion. Each phase is beneficial in a different way. Legumes (e.g., clover) fix nitrogen into the soil, preparing it for more demanding cereal or root crops. Digging up the soil to plant and harvest root crops uproots weeds. Leaving the land in pasture rests and naturally fertilizes the soil.

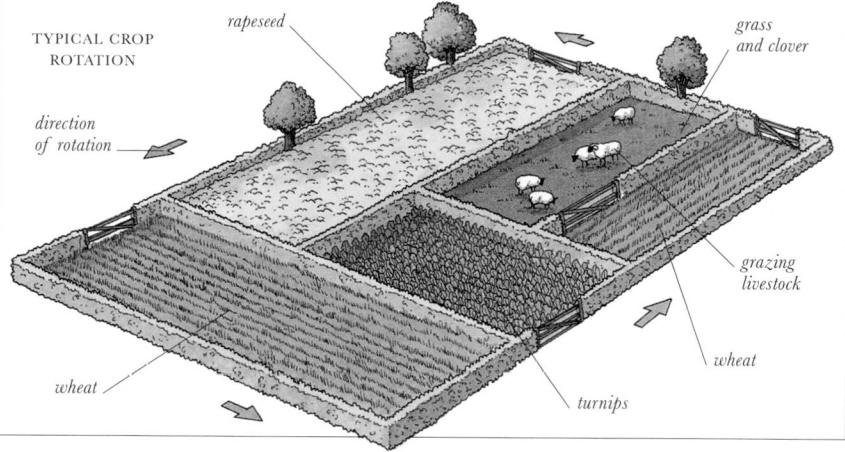

TYPICAL CROP ROTATION

rapeseed

grass and clover

direction of rotation

grazing livestock

wheat

wheat

turnips

ros·ter /róstər/ *n. & v.* ● *n.* **1** a list or plan showing turns of duty or leave for individuals or groups, esp. of a military force. **2** *Sports* a list of players, esp. one showing batting order in baseball. ● *v.tr.* place on a roster.

ros·tra *pl. of* ROSTRUM.

ros·trum /róstrəm/ *n.* (*pl.* **rostra** /-strə/ or **rostrums**) **1 a** a platform for public speaking. **b** a conductor's platform facing the orchestra. **c** a similar platform for other purposes. **2** *Zool. & Bot.* a beaklike projection.

ros·y /rózee/ *adj.* (**rosier, rosiest**) **1** colored like a pink or red rose (esp. of the complexion as indicating good health, or of a blush, wine, the sky, etc.). **2** optimistic; hopeful (*a rosy future; a rosy attitude to life*). □□ **ros·i·ly** *adv.* **ros·i·ness** *n.*

rot /rot/ *v., n., & int.* ● *v.* (**rotted, rotting**) **1** *intr.* **a** (of animal or vegetable matter) lose its original form by the chemical action of bacteria, fungi, etc.; decay. **b** (foll. by *off, away*) crumble or drop from a stem, etc., through decomposition. **2** *intr.* **a** (of society, institutions, etc.) gradually perish from lack of activity or use. **b** (of a prisoner, etc.) waste away (*left to rot in prison*); (of a person) languish. **3** *tr.* cause to rot; make rotten. ● *n.* **1** the process or state of rotting. **2** *sl.* nonsense. **3** (often prec. by *the*) a virulent liver disease of sheep. ● *int.* expressing incredulity or ridicule.

ro·ta /rótə/ *n.* **1** esp. *Brit.* a list of persons acting, or duties to be done, in rotation. **2** (**Rota**) *RC Ch.* the supreme ecclesiastical and secular court.

Ro·tar·i·an /rōtáireeən/ *n. & adj.* ● *n.* a member of a Rotary club. ● *adj.* of Rotarians or Rotary club.

ro·ta·ry /rótəree/ *adj. & n.* ● *adj.* acting by rotation (*rotary drill; rotary pump*). ● *n.* (*pl.* **-ies**) **1** a rotary machine. **2** a traffic circle. **3** (**Rotary**) (in full **Rotary International**) a worldwide charitable society of business people, orig. named from members entertaining in rotation.

Ro·ta·ry Club *n.* a local branch of Rotary.

ro·tate /rótayt/ *v.* **1** *intr. & tr.* move around an axis or center, revolve. **2 a** *tr.* take or arrange in rotation. **b** *intr.* act or take place in rotation

(*the chairmanship will rotate*). □□ **ro·tat·a·ble** *adj.* **ro·ta·tive** /rótaytiv/ *adj.* **ro·ta·to·ry** /rótətawree/ *adj.*

ro·ta·tion /rōtáyshən/ *n.* **1** the act or an instance of rotating or being rotated. **2** a recurrence; a recurrent series or period; a regular succession of various members of a group in office, etc. **3** ▲ a system of growing different crops in regular order to avoid exhausting the soil. □□ **ro·ta·tion·al** *adj.* **ro·ta·tion·al·ly** *adv.*

ro·ta·tor /rótaytər/ *n.* **1** a machine or device for causing something to rotate. **2** *Anat.* a muscle that rotates a limb, etc. **3** a revolving apparatus or part.

ROTC /rótsee/ *abbr.* Reserve Officers Training Corps.

rote /rōt/ *n.* (usu. prec. by *by*) mechanical or habitual repetition.

rote·none /rốt'nōn/ *n.* a toxic crystalline substance obtained from the roots of derris and other plants, used as an insecticide.

rot·gut /rótgut/ *n.* inferior whiskey.

ro·ti·fer /rótifər/ *n.* any minute aquatic animal of the phylum Rotifera, with rotatory organs used in swimming and feeding.

ro·tis·ser·ie /rōtísəree/ *n.* a cooking appliance with a rotating spit for roasting and barbecuing meat.

ro·to·gra·vure /rótəgrəvyōor/ *n.* **1** a printing system using a rotary press with intaglio cylinders, usu. running at high speed. **2** a sheet, etc., printed with this system.

ro·tor /rótər/ *n.* **1** a rotary part of a machine, esp. in the distributor of an internal combustion engine. ▷ DISTRIBUTOR. **2** a set of radiating airfoils around a hub on a helicopter, providing lift when rotated. ▷ HELICOPTER

ro·to·till·er /rótətilər/ *n.* a machine with a rotating blade for breaking up or tilling the soil. □□ **ro·to·till** *v.tr.*

rot·ten /rót'n/ *adj.* (**rottener, rottenest**) **1** rotting or rotted; falling to pieces or liable to break or tear from age or use. **2 a** morally or politically corrupt. **b** despicable; contemptible. **3** *sl.* **a** disagreeable; unpleasant (*had a rotten time*). **b** (of a plan, etc.) ill-advised, unsatisfactory (*a rotten idea*). **c** disagreeably ill (*feel rotten today*). □□ **rot·ten·ness** *n.*

rot·ten·stone /rot'nstōn/ *n.* decomposed siliceous limestone used as a powder for polishing metals.

R

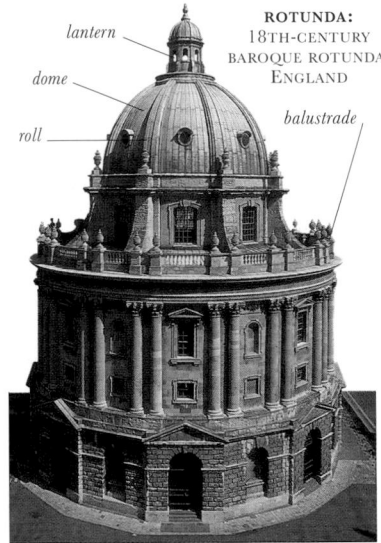

ROTTWEILLER

Rott·wei·ler /rótwīlər/ *n*. **1** ▲ a dog of a tall black-and-tan breed. **2** this breed.

ro·tund /rōtúnd/ *adj*. **1 a** circular; round. **b** (of a person) plump, pudgy. **2** (of speech, literary style, etc.) sonorous, grandiloquent. □□ **ro·tun·di·ty** *n*. **ro·tund·ly** *adv*.

ro·tun·da /rōtúndə/ *n*. **1** ▼ a building with a circular ground plan, esp. one with a dome. **2** a circular hall or room.

lantern
dome
roll
balustrade

ROTUNDA: 18TH-CENTURY BAROQUE ROTUNDA, ENGLAND

R

rou·ble var. of RUBLE.

rou·é /roō-áy/ *n*. a debauchee, esp. an elderly one.

rouge /roōzh/ *n. & v*. ● *n*. **1** a red powder or cream used for coloring the cheeks. **2** powdered ferric oxide, etc., as a polishing agent. ● *v*. **1** *tr*. color with rouge. **2** *intr*. **a** apply rouge to one's cheeks. **b** become red; blush.

rough /ruf/ *adj., adv., n., & v*. ● *adj*. **1 a** having an uneven or irregular surface, not smooth or level or polished. **b** *Tennis* applied to the side of a racket from which the twisted gut projects. **2** (of ground, country, etc.) having many bumps, obstacles, etc. **3 a** hairy; shaggy. **b** (of cloth) coarse in texture. **4 a** (of a person or behavior) not mild nor quiet nor gentle; boisterous; unrestrained (*rough manners; rough play*). **b** (of language, etc.) coarse; indelicate. **c** (of wine, etc.) sharp or harsh in taste. **d** (of a sound, the voice, etc.) harsh; discordant; gruff; hoarse. **5** (of the sea, weather, etc.) violent; stormy. **6** disorderly; riotous (*a rough part of town*). **7** harsh; insensitive (*rough words; rough treatment*). **8 a** unpleasant; severe; demanding (*had a rough time*). **b** (foll. by *on*) hard or unfair toward. **9** lacking finish, elaboration, comfort, etc. (*rough accommodations; a rough welcome*). **10** incomplete; rudimentary (*a rough attempt*). **11** inexact; approximate; preliminary (*a rough estimate; a rough sketch*). ● *adv*. in a rough manner (*play rough*). ● *n*. **1** (usu. prec. by *the*) a hard part or aspect of life; hardship (*take the rough with the smooth*). **2** rough ground (*over rough and smooth*). **3** *Golf* rough

ground off the fairway between tee and green. **4** an unfinished or provisional or natural state (*have written it in rough; shaped from the rough*). ● *v.tr*. **1** (foll. by *up*) ruffle (feathers, hair, etc.) by rubbing against the grain. **2 a** (foll. by *out*) shape or plan roughly. **b** (foll. by *in*) sketch roughly. **3** give the first shaping to (a gun, lens, etc.). □ **rough it** do without basic comforts. **rough up** *sl*. attack violently. □□ **rough·ness** *n*.

rough·age /rúfij/ *n*. **1** coarse material with a high fiber content, the part of food that stimulates digestion. **2** coarse fodder.

rough-and-read·y *adj*. crude but effective; not elaborate or over-particular.

rough-and-tum·ble *adj. & n*. ● *adj*. irregular; scrambling; disorderly. ● *n*. a haphazard fight; a scuffle.

rough·cast /rúfkast/ *n., adj., & v*. ● *n*. plaster of lime and gravel, used on outside walls. ● *adj*. **1** (of a wall, etc.) coated with roughcast. **2** (of a plan, etc.) roughly formed; preliminary. ● *v.tr*. (*past* and *past part*. **-cast**) **1** coat (a wall) with roughcast. **2** prepare (a plan, essay, etc.) in outline.

rough dia·mond *n*. **1** ▶ an uncut diamond. **2** (also **diamond in the rough**) a person of good nature but rough manners.

rough draft *n*. a first or original draft (of a story, report, document, etc.).

rough·en /rúfən/ *v.tr. & intr*. make or become rough.

rough-hewn *adj*. uncouth; unrefined.

rough·house /rúfhows/ *n. & v. sl*. ● *n*. a disturbance or row; boisterous play. ● *v*. **1** *tr*. handle (a person) roughly. **2** *intr*. make a disturbance; act violently.

rough·ly /rúflee/ *adv*. **1** in a rough manner. **2** approximately (*roughly 20 people attended*). □ **roughly speaking** in an approximate sense (*it is, roughly speaking, a square*).

rough·neck /rúfnek/ *n. colloq*. **1** a rough or rowdy person. **2** a worker on a drill rig.

rough pas·sage *n*. **1** a crossing over rough sea. **2** a difficult time or experience.

rough·rid·er /rúfrīdər/ *n*. **1** a person who breaks in or can ride unbroken horses. **2** (**Rough Rider**) a member of the cavalry unit in which Theodore Roosevelt fought during the Spanish-American War.

rough·shod /rúfshod/ *adj*. (of a horse) having shoes with nail heads projecting to prevent slipping. □ **ride roughshod over** treat inconsiderately or arrogantly.

rou·lade /roōláad/ *n*. **1** a dish cooked or served in the shape of a roll, esp. a rolled piece of meat with a filling. **2** *Mus*. a florid passage of runs, etc., in solo vocal music, usu. sung to one syllable.

rou·leau /roōló/ *n*. (*pl*. **rouleaux** or **rouleaus** /-lōz/) **1** a cylindrical packet of coins. **2** a coil or roll of ribbon, etc., esp. as trimming.

rou·lette /roōlét/ *n*. a gambling game using a table in which a ball is dropped on to a revolving wheel with numbered compartments.

round /rownd/ *adj., n., adv., prep., & v*. ● *adj*. **1** shaped like a circle, sphere, or cylinder; having

ROUGH DIAMOND

a convex or circular outline or surface; curved; not angular. **2** done with or involving circular motion. **3 a** entire; continuous; complete (*a round dozen*). **b** (of a sum of money) considerable. **4** candid; outspoken; (of a statement, etc.) categorical; unmistakable. **5** (usu. *attrib*.) (of a number) expressed for convenience or as an estimate in fewer significant numerals or with a fraction removed (*spent $297.32, or in round figures $300*). **6 a** (of a style) flowing. **b** (of a voice) not harsh. ● *n*. **1** a round object or form. **2 a** a revolving motion; a circular or recurring course (*the Earth in its yearly round*). **b** a regular recurring series of activities or functions (*one's daily round; a continuous round of pleasure*). **c** a recurring succession or series of meetings for discussion, etc. (*a new round of talks on disarmament*). **3** a route or sequence by which people or things are regularly supervised or inspected (*a watchman's round; a doctor's rounds*). **4** an allowance of something distributed or measured out, esp.: **a** a single provision of drinks, etc., to each member of a group. **b** ammunition to fire one shot; the act of firing this. **5** a thick disk of beef cut from the haunch as a joint. **6** each of a set or series, a sequence of actions by each member of a group in turn, esp. **a** one spell of play in a game, etc. **b** one stage in a competition. **7** *Golf* the playing of all the holes in a course once. **8** *Archery* a fixed number of arrows shot from a fixed distance. **9** (**the round**) a form of sculpture in which the figure stands clear of any ground (cf. RELIEF 5a). **10** *Mus*. a canon for three or more unaccompanied voices singing at the same pitch or in octaves. **11** a rung of a ladder. **12** (foll. by *of*) the circumference, bounds, or extent of (*in all the round of Nature*). ● *adv*. = AROUND *adv*. 5–12. ● *prep*. = AROUND *prep*. 5–12. ● *v*. **1 a** *tr*. give a round shape to. **b** *intr*. assume a round shape. **2** *tr*. pass around (a corner, cape, etc.). **3** *tr*. express (a number) in a less exact but more convenient form (also foll. by *down* when the number is decreased and *up* when it is increased). **4** *tr*. pronounce (a vowel) with rounded lips. □ **in the round 1** with all features shown; all things considered. **2** *Theatr*. with the audience around at least three sides of the stage. **3** (of sculpture) with all sides shown. **make the round of** go around. **make one's rounds** take a customary route for inspection, etc. **make the rounds** (of news, etc.) be passed on from person to person, etc. **round about 1** all around; on all sides (of). **2** with a change to an opposite position. **3** approximately (*cost round about $50*). **round and round** several times around. **round down** see sense 3 of *v*. **round off** (or **out**) **1** bring to a complete or symmetrical or well-ordered state. **2** blunt the corners or angles of. **round peg in a square hole** = square peg in a round hole (see PEG). **round up** collect or bring together (see also sense 3 of *v*.). □□ **round·ish** *adj*. **round·ness** *n*.

round·a·bout /równdə-bowt/ *n. & adj*. ● *n*. **1** *Brit*. = TRAFFIC CIRCLE. **2** *Brit*. = MERRY-GO-ROUND 1. ● *adj*. circuitous.

roun·del /równd'l/ *n*. **1** a small disk, esp. a decorative medallion. **2** a poem, esp. a modified rondeau of eleven lines in three stanzas.

roun·de·lay /równdilay/ *n*. a short simple song with a refrain.

Round·head /równdhed/ *n. hist*. ◀ a member of the Parliamentary party in the English Civil War.

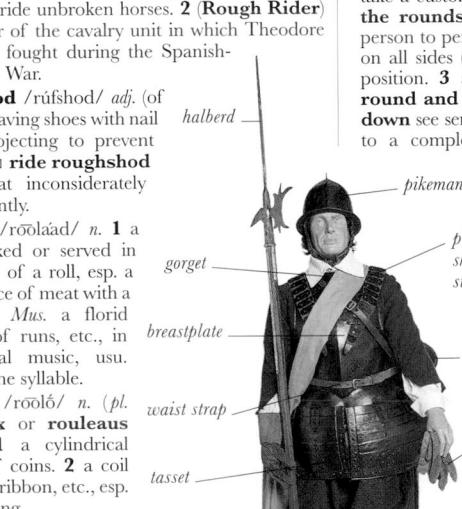

halberd
pikeman's pot
plated shoulder strap
gorget
breastplate
knapsack
waist strap
glove
tasset
sash
breeches
linen stockings
garter sash

ROUNDHEAD: SERGEANT OF PIKES

ROW

Rowing can be functional or recreational. As a sport, it includes two main types of competition: regattas and head-of-the-river races. Regattas are competition events held on a straight stretch of water divided into lanes; international regattas are held over 1¼ miles (2,000 m). In head-of-the-river races, boats set off at intervals and are timed over the course. Rowing crews may include a coxswain (cox), who coordinates the rhythm of the strokes and steers. In coxless crews, the rower at the front steers using a foot-operated rudder, while the one at the back (the stroke) sets the rhythm. Racing boats use a sliding seat, while recreational rowboats have a fixed seat.

COXLESS FOUR

angle of blade
line of shoulder
line of chest

STROKE CYCLE WITH A FIXED SEAT

oars forward   catch   pull through   finish   feather   square   oars forward

narrow competition boat

oar

bow (front rower)

oarlock

stroke

rudder indicator   blade

---

round·house /równdhows/ *n.* **1** a repair shed for railroad locomotives, built around a turntable. **2** *sl.* **a** a blow given with a wide sweep of the arm. **b** *Baseball* a pitch made with a sweeping sidearm motion.

round·ly /równdlee/ *adv.* **1** bluntly; severely (*was roundly criticized; told them roundly that he refused*). **2** in a thoroughgoing manner (*go roundly to work*). **3** in a circular way (*swells out roundly*).

round rob·in *n.* **1** a petition, esp. with signatures written in a circle to conceal the order of writing. **2** a tournament in which each competitor plays in turn against every other.

round-shoul·dered *adj.* with shoulders bent forward so that the back is rounded.

rounds·man /równdzmən/ *n.* (*pl.* **-men**) a police officer in charge of a patrol.

Round Ta·ble *n.* (in allusion to that at which King Arthur and his knights sat so that none should have precedence) **1** an international charitable association that holds discussions, debates, etc., and undertakes community service. **2** (**round table**) an assembly for discussion, esp. at a conference (often *attrib.*: *round-table talks*).

round trip *n.* a trip to one or more places and back again.

round·up /równdup/ *n.* **1** a systematic rounding up of people or things. **2** a summary; a résumé of facts or events.

round·worm /równdwərm/ *n.* a worm, esp. a nematode, with a rounded body.

rouse /rowz/ *v.* **1 a** *tr.* (often foll. by *from, out of*) bring out of sleep; wake. **b** *intr.* (often foll. by *up*) cease to sleep; wake up. **2** (often foll. by *up*) **a** *tr.* stir up; make active or excited (*roused them from their complacency; was roused to protest*). **b** *intr.* become active. **3** *tr.* provoke to anger (*is terrible when roused*). **4** *tr.* evoke (feelings). **5** *tr.* startle (game) from a lair or cover. □□ **rous·er** *n.*

rous·ing /rówzing/ *adj.* **1** exciting; stirring (*a rousing cheer; a rousing song*). **2** (of a fire) blazing strongly. □□ **rous·ing·ly** *adv.*

roust /rowst/ *v.tr.* **1** (often foll. by *up, out*) **a** rouse; stir up. **b** root out. **2** *sl.* jostle; harass; rough up.

roust·a·bout /rówstəbowt/ *n.* **1** a laborer in an oil field. **2** an unskilled or casual laborer. **3** a dock laborer or deckhand. **4** a circus laborer.

rout¹ /rowt/ *n. & v.* • *n.* **1 a** a disorderly retreat of defeated troops. **b** a heavy defeat. **2 a** an assemblage or company, esp. of revelers or rioters. **b** *Law* an assemblage of three or more persons who have made a move toward committing an illegal act. **3** riot; tumult; disturbance; clamor; fuss. • *v.tr.* cause to retreat in disorder; defeat. □ **put to rout** defeat; cause to retreat in disorder.

rout² /rowt/ *v.* **1** *intr. & tr.* = ROOT². **2** *tr.* cut a groove, or any pattern not extending to the edges, in (a wooden or metal surface). □ **rout out** force or fetch out of bed or from a house or a hiding place.

route /root, rowt/ *n. & v.* • *n.* **1** a way or course taken in getting from a starting point to a destination. **2** a round traveled in delivering, selling, or collecting goods. • *v.tr.* send or forward or direct to be sent by a particular route.

rout·er /rówtər/ *n.* any of various tools used in routing, including a two-handled plane used in carpentry, esp. a power machine for routing, etc.

rou·tine /rooteén/ *n. & adj.* • *n.* **1** a regular course or procedure, an unvarying performance of certain acts. **2** a set sequence in a dance, comedy act, etc. **3** *Computing* a sequence of instructions for performing a task. • *adj.* **1** performed as part of a routine (*routine duties*). **2** of a customary or standard kind. □□ **rou·tine·ly** *adv.*

rou·tin·ize /rooteéniz, root'niz/ *v.tr.* subject to a routine; make into a matter of routine. □□ **rou·tin·i·za·tion** *n.*

roux /roo/ *n.* (*pl.* same) a cooked mixture of fat and flour used in making sauces, etc.

rove¹ /rōv/ *v. & n.* • *v.* **1** *intr.* wander without a settled destination; roam; ramble. **2** *intr.* (of eyes) look in changing directions. **3** *tr.* wander over or through. • *n.* an act of roving (*on the rove*).

rove² *past* of REEVE².

rove³ /rōv/ *n. & v.* • *n.* a sliver of cotton, wool, etc., drawn out and slightly twisted. • *v.tr.* form into roves.

rove⁴ /rōv/ *n.* a small metal plate or ring for a rivet to pass through and be clenched over, esp. in boat building.

rov·er¹ /rōvər/ *n.* **1** a roving person; a wanderer. **2** *Croquet* a ball that has passed through all the wickets but has not yet struck the last peg.

rov·er² /rōvər/ *n.* a pirate.

rov·er³ /rōvər/ *n.* a person or machine that makes roves of fiber.

rov·ing eye *n.* a tendency to ogle or toward infidelity.

row¹ /rō/ *n.* **1** a number of persons or things in a more or less straight line. **2** a line of seats across a theater, etc. (*in the front row*). **3** a street with a continuous line of houses along one or each side. **4** a line of plants in a field or garden. **5** a horizontal line of entries in a table, etc. □ **a hard** (or **tough**) **row to hoe** a difficult task. **in a row 1** forming a row. **2** *colloq.* in succession (*two Sundays in a row*).

row² /rō/ *v. & n.* • *v.* **1** *tr.* ▲ propel (a boat) with oars. **2** *tr.* convey (a passenger) in a boat in this way. **3** *intr.* propel a boat in this way. **4** *tr.* make (a stroke) or achieve (a rate of striking) in rowing. **5** *tr.* compete (in a race) by rowing. **6** *tr.* row a race with. • *n.* **1** a spell of rowing. **2** an excursion in a rowboat. □ **row out** exhaust by rowing (*the crew were completely rowed out at the finish*). □□ **row·er** *n.*

row³ /row/ *n. & v. colloq.* • *n.* **1** a loud noise or commotion. **2** a fierce quarrel or dispute. **3 a** a severe reprimand. **b** the condition of being reprimanded (*shall get into a row*). • *v.* **1** *intr.* make or engage in a row. **2** *tr.* reprimand. □ **make** (or **kick up**) **a row 1** raise a noise. **2** make a vigorous protest.

row·an /rôən, rów-/ *n.* **1** the mountain ash. **2** a similar tree, *Sorbus americana*, native to N. America. **3** (also **row·an·ber·ry**) the scarlet berry of either of these trees.

row·boat /rôbot/ *n.* a small boat propelled by oars. ▷ ROW

row·dy /rówdee/ *adj. & n.* • *adj.* (**rowdier, rowdiest**) noisy and disorderly. • *n.* (*pl.* **-ies**) a rowdy person. □□ **row·di·ly** *adv.* **row·di·ness** *n.* **row·dy·ism** *n.*

row·el /rówəl/ *n. & v.* • *n.* ▼ a spiked revolving disk at the end of a spur. • *v.tr.* urge with a rowel.

rowel   heel grip

ROWEL ON A SOUTH AMERICAN BRASS SPUR

row·en /rôən/ *n.* (in *sing.* or *pl.*) a season's second growth of hay or grass; an aftermath.

row·ing ma·chine *n.* a device for exercising the muscles used in rowing.

R

roy·al /róyəl/ *adj. & n.* ● *adj.* **1** of or suited to or worthy of a king or queen. **2** in the service or under the patronage of a king or queen. **3** belonging to the king or queen (*the royal hands*). **4** majestic; splendid. **5** of exceptional size or quality; first-rate (*gave us royal entertainment*). ● *n. colloq.* a member of the royal family. □□ **roy·al·ly** *adv.*

roy·al blue *n.* a deep vivid blue.

roy·al fam·i·ly *n.* (*pl.* **-ies**) the family to which a sovereign belongs.

roy·al flush *n.* the highest straight flush in poker, including ace, king, queen, jack, and ten all in the same suit.

roy·al·ist /róyəlist/ *n.* **1 a** a supporter of monarchy. **b** *hist.* a supporter of the royal side in the English Civil War. **2** *hist.* a loyalist in the American Revolution. □□ **roy·al·ism** *n.*

roy·al jel·ly *n.* a substance secreted by honeybee workers and fed by them to future queen bees.

roy·al·ty /róyəltee/ *n.* (*pl.* **-ies**) **1** the office or dignity or power of a king or queen. **2 a** royal persons. **b** a member of a royal family. **3** a sum paid to a patentee for the use of a patent or to an author, etc., for each copy of a book, etc., sold or for each public performance of a work. **4 a** a royal right (now esp. over minerals) granted by the sovereign. **b** a payment made by a producer of minerals, oil, or natural gas to the owner of the site or of the mineral rights over it.

r.p.m. *abbr.* revolutions per minute.

RR *abbr.* **1** railroad. **2** rural route.

RSV *abbr.* Revised Standard Version (of the Bible).

RSVP *abbr.* (in an invitation, etc.) please answer [*répondez s'il vous plaît*].

rt. *abbr.* right.

rte. *abbr.* route.

Rt. Hon. *abbr.* Right Honorable.

Rt. Revd. *abbr.* (also **Rt. Rev.**) Right Reverend.

Ru *symb. Chem.* the element ruthenium.

rub /rub/ *v. & n.* ● *v.* (**rubbed**, **rubbing**) **1** *tr.* move one's hand or another object with firm pressure over the surface of. **2** *tr.* (usu. foll. by *against, in, on, over*) apply (one's hand, etc.) in this way. **3** *tr.* clean or polish or make dry or bare by rubbing. **4** *tr.* (often foll. by *over*) apply (polish, ointment, etc.) by rubbing. **5** *tr.* (foll. by *in, into, through*) use rubbing to make (a substance) go into or through something. **6** *tr.* (often foll. by *together*) move or slide (objects) against each other. **7** *tr.* (foll. by *against, on*) move with contact or friction. **8** *tr.* chafe or make sore by rubbing. **9** *intr.* (of cloth, skin, etc.) become frayed or worn or sore or bare with friction. **10** *tr.* reproduce the design of (a sepulchral brass or stone, etc.) by rubbing paper laid on it with heelball or colored chalk, etc. **11** *tr.* (foll. by *to*) reduce to powder, etc., by rubbing. ● *n.* **1** a spell or an instance of rubbing (*give it a rub*). **2** an impediment or difficulty (*there's the rub*). **rub elbows with** associate or come into contact with. **rub it in** (or **rub a person's nose in it**) emphasize or repeat an embarrassing fact, etc. **rub noses** rub one's nose against another's in greeting. **rub off** (usu. foll. by *on*) be transferred by contact; be transmitted (*some of his attitudes have rubbed off on me*). **rub out 1** erase with an eraser. **2** *sl.* kill. **rub shoulders with** = *rub elbows with*. **rub the wrong way** irritate or repel as by stroking a cat against the lie of its fur.

ru·ba·to /rōōbáatō/ *adj. & n. Mus.* ● *n.* (*pl.* **-os** or **rubati** /-tee/) the temporary disregarding of strict tempo. ● *adj.* performed with a flexible tempo.

rub·ber¹ /rúbər/ *n.* **1** a tough elastic substance made from the latex of plants or synthetically. **2** esp. *Brit.* a piece of this or another substance for erasing pencil or ink marks. **3** *colloq.* a condom. **4** (in *pl.*) galoshes. **5 a** an implement used for rubbing. **b** part of a machine operating by rubbing. □□ **rub·ber·y** *adj.* **rub·ber·i·ness** *n.*

rub·ber² /rúbər/ *n.* **1** a match of three or five successive games between the same sides or persons at whist, bridge, tennis, etc. **2** (prec. by *the*) **a** the act of winning two games in a rubber. **b** a third game when each side has won one.

rub·ber band *n.* a loop of rubber for holding papers, etc., together.

rub·ber·ize /rúbəriz/ *v.tr.* treat or coat with rubber.

rub·ber·neck /rúbərnek/ *n. & v. colloq.* ● *n.* a person who stares inquisitively or stupidly. ● *v.intr.* act in this way.

rub·ber plant *n.* **1** an evergreen plant, *Ficus elastica*, often cultivated as a houseplant. **2** (also **rubber tree**) any of various tropical trees yielding latex, esp. *Hevea brasiliensis*.

rub·ber stamp *n.* **1** a device for inking and imprinting on a surface. **2 a** a person who mechanically agrees to others' actions. **b** an indication of such agreement. □□ **rub·ber-stamp** *v.tr.*

rub·bing /rúbing/ *n.* **1** in senses of RUB *v.* **2** an impression or copy made by rubbing (see RUB *v.* 10).

rub·bing al·co·hol *n.* an isopropyl alcohol solution for external application.

rub·bish /rúbish/ *n. esp. Brit.* **1** waste material; refuse; litter. **2** worthless material or articles; junk. **3** (often as *int.*) nonsense. □□ **rub·bish·y** *adj.*

rub·ble /rúbəl/ *n.* **1** rough fragments of stone or brick, etc. **2** pieces of undressed stone used, esp. as fill, for walls. **3** *Geol.* loose angular stones, etc., as the covering of some rocks. **4** water-worn stones. □□ **rub·bly** *adj.*

rube /rōōb/ *n. colloq.* a country bumpkin.

Rube Gold·berg /rōōb góldbərg/ *adj.* unnecessarily or comically complex in design.

ru·bel·la /rōōbélə/ *n. Med.* an acute infectious viral disease with a red rash; German measles.

ru·be·o·la /rōōbeeōlə, -bééələ/ *n. Med.* measles.

Ru·bi·con /rōōbikon/ *n.* a boundary which once crossed signifies irrevocable commitment; a point of no return.

ru·bi·cund /rōōbikund/ *adj.* (of a face, complexion, or person) ruddy; high-colored.

ru·bid·i·um /rōōbídeeəm/ *n. Chem.* a soft silvery element occurring naturally in various minerals and as the radioactive isotope rubidium-87. ¶ Symb.: **Rb**.

ru·bi·fy /rōōbifi/ *v.tr.* (**-ies**, **-ied**) **1** make red. **2** *Med.* (of a counterirritant) stimulate (the skin, etc.) to redness. □□ **ru·be·fa·cient** /-fáyshənt/ *adj. & n.* **ru·be·fac·tion** /-fákshən/ *n.*

ru·big·i·nous /rōōbíjinəs/ *adj. formal* rust-colored.

ru·ble /rōōbəl/ *n.* (also **rou·ble**) the chief monetary unit of Russia, the USSR (*hist.*), and some other former republics of the USSR.

ru·bric /rōōbrik/ *n.* **1** a direction for the conduct of divine service in a liturgical book. **2** a heading or passage in red or special lettering. **3** explanatory words. **4** an established custom.

ru·bri·cate /rōōbrikayt/ *v.tr.* **1** mark with red; print or write in red. **2** provide with rubrics. □□ **ru·bri·ca·tion** /-káyshən/ *n.* **ru·bri·ca·tor** *n.*

ru·by /rōōbee/ *n. & adj.* ● *n.* (*pl.* **-ies**) **1** ◀ a rare precious stone consisting of corundum with a color varying from deep crimson or purple to pale rose. ▷ GEM. **2** a glowing, purple-tinged red color. ● *adj.* of this color.

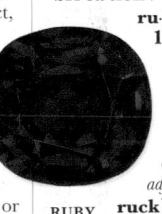

RUBY

ruche /rōōsh/ *n.* a frill or gathering of lace, etc., as a trimming. □□ **ruched** *adj.* **ruch·ing** *n.*

ruck¹ /ruk/ *n.* **1** (prec. by *the*) the main body of competitors not likely to overtake the leaders. **2** an undistinguished crowd of persons or things.

ruck² /ruk/ *v. & n.* ● *v.tr. & intr.* (often foll. by *up*) make or become creased or wrinkled. ● *n.* a crease or wrinkle.

ruck·sack /rúksak, rŏŏk-/ *n.* = BACKPACK *n.*

ruck·us /rúkəs/ *n.* a fracas or commotion.

ruc·tion /rúkshən/ *n. colloq.* **1** a disturbance or tumult. **2** (in *pl.*) unpleasant arguments or reactions.

tiller

rudder

RUDDER
ON A SAILING
DINGHY

rud·der /rúdər/ *n.* **1 a** ◀ a flat piece hinged vertically to the stern of a ship for steering. ▷ MAN-OF-WAR. **b** a vertical airfoil pivoted from the horizontal stabilizer of an aircraft, for controlling its horizontal movement. ▷ AIRCRAFT. □□ **rud·der·less** *adj.*

rud·dle var. of RADDLE.

rud·dy /rúdee/ *adj. & v.* ● *adj.* (**ruddier**, **ruddiest**) **1 a** (of a person or complexion) freshly or healthily red. **b** (of health, youth, etc.) marked by this. **2** reddish. ● *v.tr. & intr.* (**-ies**, **-ied**) make or grow ruddy. □□ **rud·di·ness** *n.*

rude /rōōd/ *adj.* **1** impolite or offensive. **2** roughly made or done (*a rude shelter*). **3** primitive or uneducated (*rude simplicity*). **4** abrupt; sudden; startling (*a rude awakening*). **5** *colloq.* indecent; lewd (*a rude joke*). □ **be rude to** speak impolitely to; insult. □□ **rude·ly** *adv.* **rude·ness** *n.* **ru·der·y** *n.*

ru·der·al /rōōdərəl/ *adj. & n.* ● *adj.* (of a plant) growing on or in rubbish or rubble. ● *n.* a ruderal plant.

ru·di·ment /rōōdimənt/ *n.* **1** (in *pl.*) the elements or first principles of a subject. **2** (in *pl.*) an imperfect beginning of something undeveloped or yet to develop. **3** a part or organ imperfectly developed as being vestigial or having no function (e.g., the breast in males).

ru·di·men·ta·ry /rōōdiméntəree/ *adj.* **1** involving basic principles; fundamental. **2** incompletely developed; vestigial. ▷ EMBRYO

rue¹ /rōō/ *v.tr.* (**rues**, **rued**, **ruing**) repent of; wish to be undone or nonexistent (esp. *rue the day*).

rue² /rōō/ *n.* a perennial evergreen shrub, *Ruta graveolens*, with bitter strong-scented leaves.

rue·ful /rōōfŏŏl/ *adj.* expressing sorrow, genuine or humorously affected. □□ **rue·ful·ly** *adv.* **rue·ful·ness** *n.*

ru·fes·cent /rōōfésənt/ *adj. Zool., etc.* reddish. □□ **ru·fes·cence** *n.*

ruff¹ /ruf/ *n.* **1** ▶ a projecting starched frill worn around the neck, esp. in the 16th c. **2** a projecting or conspicuously colored ring of feathers or hair around a bird's or animal's neck. **3** a domestic pigeon. **4** (*fem.* **reeve** /reev/) a wading bird, *Philomachus pugnax*, of which the male has a ruff and ear tufts in the breeding season.

ruff² /ruf/ *v. & n.* ● *v.intr. & tr.* trump at cards. ● *n.* an act of ruffing.

RUFF: LATE
16TH-CENTURY RUFF

ruf·fi·an /rúfeeən/ *n.* a violent, lawless person. □□ **ruf·fi·an·ism** *n.* **ruf·fi·an·ly** *adv.*

ruf·fle /rúfəl/ *v. & n.* ● *v.* **1** *tr.* disturb the smoothness or tranquillity of. **2** *tr.* upset the calmness of (a person). **3** *tr.* gather (lace, etc.) into a ruffle. **4** *tr.* (often foll. by *up*) (of a bird) erect (its feathers) in anger, display, etc. **5** *intr.* undergo ruffling. **6** *intr.* lose smoothness or calmness. ● *n.* **1** an ornamental frill of lace, etc., worn at the opening of a garment esp. around the wrist, breast, or neck. **2** perturbation; bustle. **3** a rippling effect on water. **4** the ruff of a bird, etc. (see RUFF¹ 2).

ru·fous /rōōfəs/ *adj.* (esp. of animals) reddish-brown.

R

RUGBY

Rugby is played with two teams of 15 players. Points are scored by placing the ball over the goal line (a try) or kicking it over the goal crossbar. One of the ways to restart play is with a scrum – an arrangement of 8 players from each team into which the ball is thrown.

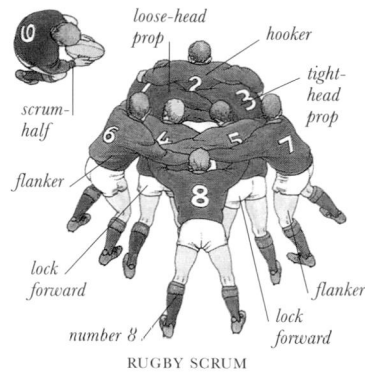

scrum-half, loose-head prop, hooker, tight-head prop, flanker, lock forward, lock forward, flanker, number 8

RUGBY SCRUM

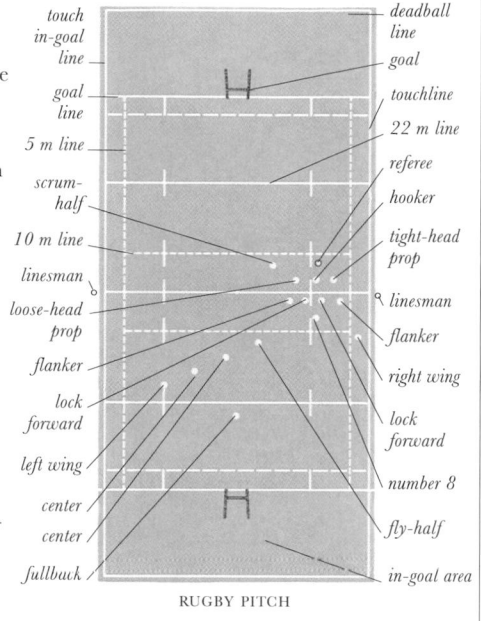

touch in-goal line, goal line, 5 m line, scrum-half, 10 m line, linesman, loose-head prop, flanker, lock forward, left wing, center, center, fullback

deadball line, goal, touchline, 22 m line, referee, hooker, tight-head prop, linesman, flanker, right wing, lock forward, number 8, fly-half, in-goal area

RUGBY PITCH

---

rug /rug/ n. a floor covering of shaggy material or thick pile. □ **pull the rug (out) from under** deprive of support; weaken; unsettle.

rug·by /rúgbee/ n. (also **Rugby football**) ▲ a team game played with an oval ball that may be kicked, carried, and passed from hand to hand.

rug·ged /rúgid/ adj. **1** (of ground or terrain) having a rough uneven surface. **2** (of features) strongly marked; irregular in outline. **3 a** unpolished; lacking refinement (*rugged grandeur*). **b** harsh in sound. **c** austere; unbending (*rugged honesty*). **d** involving hardship (*a rugged life*). **4** (esp. of a machine) robust; sturdy. □□ **rug·ged·ly** adv. **rug·ged·ness** n.

ru·gose /rōōgos/ adj. esp. *Biol.* wrinkled; corrugated. □□ **ru·gose·ly** adv. **ru·gos·i·ty** /-gósitee/ n.

ru·in /rōōin/ n. & v. ● n. **1** a destroyed or wrecked state. **2** a person's or thing's downfall or elimination (*the ruin of my hopes*). **3 a** a complete loss of one's property or position (*bring to ruin*). **b** a person who has suffered ruin. **4** (in *sing.* or *pl.*) the remains of a building, etc., that has suffered ruin (*an old ruin; ancient ruins*). **5** a cause of ruin (*will be the ruin of us*). ● v. **1** tr. **a** bring to ruin (*your extravagance has ruined me*). **b** utterly impair or wreck (*the rain ruined my hat*). **2** tr. (esp. as **ruined** adj.) reduce to ruins. □ **in ruins 1** in a state of ruin. **2** completely wrecked (*their hopes were in ruins*).

ru·in·a·tion /rōōináyshən/ n. **1** the act of bringing to ruin. **2** the act of ruining or the state of being ruined.

ru·in·ous /rōōinəs/ adj. **1** bringing ruin; disastrous (*at ruinous expense*). **2** dilapidated. □□ **ru·in·ous·ly** adv.

rule /rōōl/ n. & v. ● n. **1** a principle to which an action conforms or is required to conform. **2** a prevailing custom or standard; the normal state of things. **3** government or dominion (*under British rule; the rule of law*). **4** a graduated straight measure used in carpentry, etc.; a ruler. **5** *Printing* **a** a thin strip of metal for separating headings, columns, etc. **b** a thin line or dash. **6** a code of discipline of a religious order. **7** *Law* an order made by a judge or court with reference to a particular case only. ● v. **1** tr. keep under control. **2** tr. & (often foll. by *over*) intr. have sovereign control of (*rules over a vast kingdom*). **3** tr. (often foll. by *that* + clause) pronounce authoritatively (*was ruled out of order*). **4** tr. **a** make parallel lines across (paper). **b** make (a straight line) with a ruler, etc. **5** tr. (in *passive*; foll. by *by*) consent to follow (advice, etc.); be guided by. □ **as a rule** usually. **by rule** in a regulation manner; mechani-

cally. **rule out** exclude; pronounce irrelevant or ineligible. **rule the roost** be in control.

rule of thumb n. a rule for general guidance, based on experience or practice rather than theory.

rul·er /rōōlər/ n. **1** a person exercising government

or dominion. **2** a straight usu. graduated strip or cylinder of wood, metal, etc., used to draw lines or measure distance. □□ **rul·er·ship** n.

rul·ing /rōōling/ n. & adj. ● n. an authoritative decision or announcement. ● adj. dominant; prevailing; currently in force (*ruling prices*).

rum /rum/ n. **1** a spirit distilled from sugarcane residues or molasses. **2** *colloq.* intoxicating liquor.

Ru·ma·ni·an var. of ROMANIAN.

rum·ba /rúmbə, rōōm-/ n. & v. (also **rhum·ba**) ● n. **1** Cuban dance. **2 a** a ballroom dance imitative of this. **b** the music for it. ● v.tr. (**rumbas**, **rumbaed** /-bəd/, **rumbaing** /-bə-ing/) dance the rumba.

rum·ble /rúmbəl/ v. & n. ● v. **1** intr. make a continuous deep resonant sound as of distant thunder. **2** intr. (foll. by *along, by, past*, etc.) move with a rumbling noise. **3** intr. engage in a street fight, esp. as part of a gang. **4** tr. (often foll. by *out*) utter or say with a rumbling sound. ● n. **1** a rumbling sound. **2** *sl.* a street fight between gangs.

ru·men /rōōmen/ n. (*pl.* **rumina** /-minə/ or **rumens**) the first stomach of a ruminant, in which food, esp. cellulose, is partly digested by bacteria.

ru·mi·nant /rōōminənt/ n. & adj. ● n. ▼ an animal that chews the cud. ● adj. **1** of or belonging to ruminants. **2** contemplative; given to or engaged in meditation.

ru·mi·nate /rōōminayt/ v. **1** tr. & (foll. by *over, on,* etc.) intr. meditate, ponder. **2** intr. (of ruminants) chew the cud. □□ **ru·mi·na·tion** /-náyshən/ n. **ru·mi·na·tive** /-nətiv/ adj. **ru·mi·na·tive·ly** adv.

rum·mage /rúmij/ v. & n. ● v. **1** tr. & (foll. by *in, through, among*) intr. search, esp. unsystematically. **2** tr. (foll. by *out, up*) find among other things **3** tr. (foll. by

---

RUMINANT

Ruminants are even-toed mammals that have three- or four-chambered stomachs, and perform rumination. Fibrous food material (cud) from the largest chamber (rumen) is formed into masses in the reticulum, and then regurgitated and rechewed. When it returns to the rumen, it is digested further before entering the other chambers.

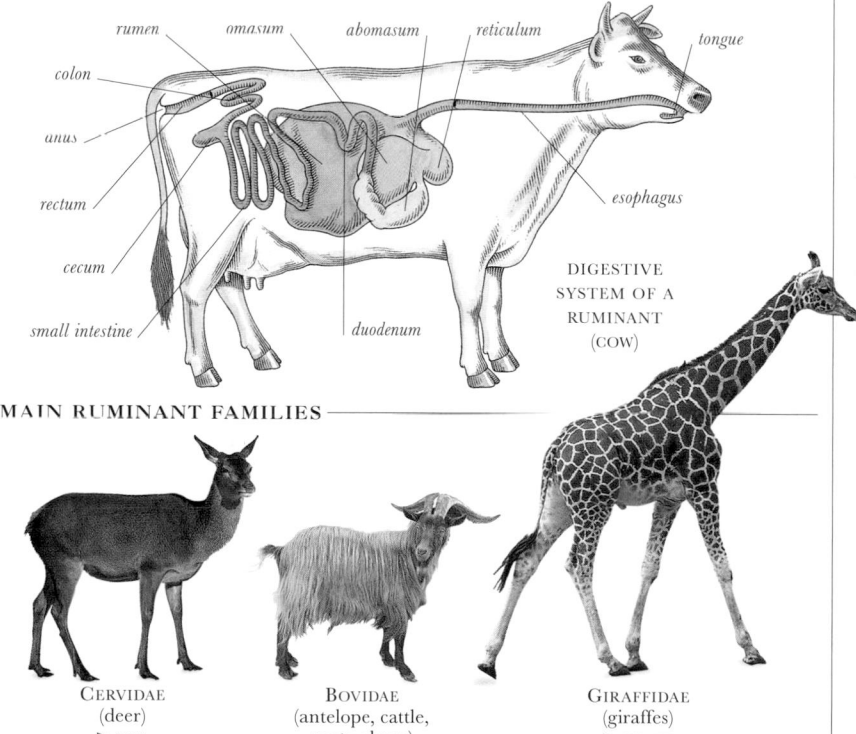

rumen, omasum, abomasum, reticulum, tongue, colon, anus, esophagus, rectum, cecum, small intestine, duodenum

DIGESTIVE SYSTEM OF A RUMINANT (COW)

MAIN RUMINANT FAMILIES

CERVIDAE (deer) ▷ DEER

BOVIDAE (antelope, cattle, goats, sheep)

GIRAFFIDAE (giraffes) ▷ GIRAFFE

R

about) disarrange; make untidy in searching. • *n.* **1** an instance of rummaging. **2** things found by rummaging; a miscellaneous accumulation.

rum·mage sale *n.* a sale of miscellaneous usu. secondhand articles, esp. for charity.

rum·my[1] /rúmee/ *n.* any of various card games in which the players try to form sets and sequences of cards.

rum·my[2] /rúmee/ *n. sl.* a drunkard or sot.

ru·mor /rōōmər/ *n.* & *v.* • *n.* **1** general talk or hearsay of doubtful accuracy. **2** (often foll. by *of*, or *that* + clause) a current but unverified statement or assertion (*heard a rumor that you are leaving*). • *v.tr.* (usu. in *passive*) report by way of rumor (*it is rumored that you are leaving*; *you are rumored to be leaving*).

rump /rump/ *n.* **1** the hind part of a mammal, esp. the buttocks. **2** a small or contemptible remnant.

rum·ple /rúmpəl/ *v.tr.* & *intr.* make or become creased or ruffled.

rum·pus /rúmpəs/ *n. colloq.* a disturbance, brawl, row, or uproar.

rum·pus room *n.* a room, usu. in the basement of a house, for games and play.

run /run/ *v.* & *n.* • *v.* (**running**; *past* **ran** /ran/; *past part.* **run**) **1** *intr.* go with quick steps on alternate feet, never having both or all feet on the ground at the same time. **2** *intr.* flee; abscond. **3** *intr.* go or travel hurriedly, briefly, etc. **4** *intr.* **a** advance by or as by rolling or on wheels, or smoothly or easily. **b** be in action or operation (*left the engine running*). **5** *intr.* be current or operative (*the lease runs for 99 years*). **6** *intr.* travel or be traveling on its route (*the train is running late*). **7** *intr.* (of a play, exhibition, etc.) be staged or presented (*is now running at the Apollo*). **8** *intr.* extend; have a course or order or tendency (*the road runs by the coast*; *prices are running high*). **9 a** *intr.* compete in a race. **b** *intr.* finish a race in a specified position. **c** *tr.* compete in (a race). **10** *intr.* (often foll. by *for*) seek election (*ran for president*). **11 a** *intr.* (of a liquid, etc.) flow; drip. **b** *tr.* flow with. **12** *tr.* **a** cause (water, etc.) to flow. **b** fill (a bath) with water. **13** *intr.* spread rapidly or beyond the proper place (*ink ran over the table*; *a shiver ran down my spine*). **14** *tr.* traverse (a course, race, or distance). **15** *tr.* perform (an errand). **16** *tr.* publish (an article, etc.) in a newspaper or magazine. **17 a** *tr.* cause to operate. **b** *intr.* (of a mechanism or component, etc.) move or work freely. **18** *tr.* direct or manage (a business, etc.). **19** *tr.* take (a person) for a journey in a vehicle (*shall I run you to the post office?*). **20** *tr.* cause to run or go in a specified way (*ran the car into a tree*). **21** *tr.* enter (a horse, etc.) for a race. **22** *tr.* smuggle (guns, etc.). **23** *tr.* chase or hunt. **24** *tr.* allow (an account) to accumulate for a time before paying. **25** *intr.* (of a color in a fabric) spread from the dyed parts. **26 a** *intr.* (of a thought, the eye, the memory, etc.) pass in a transitory or cursory way (*ideas ran through my mind*). **b** *tr.* cause (one's eye) to look cursorily (*ran my eye down the page*). **c** *tr.* pass (a hand, etc.) rapidly over (*ran his fingers down her spine*). **27** *intr.* (of hosiery) unravel along a line from the point of a snag. **28** *intr.* (of a candle) gutter. **29** *intr.* (of the eyes or nose) exude liquid matter. **30** *tr.* sew (fabric) loosely or hastily with running stitches; baste. **31** *tr.* turn (cattle, etc.) out to graze. • *n.* **1** an act or spell of running. **2** a short excursion. **3** a distance traveled. **4** a general tendency. **5** a rapid motion. **6** a regular route. **7 a** a continuous or long stretch or spell or course (*a 50-foot run of wiring*; *had a run of bad luck*). **b** a series or sequence, esp. of cards in a specified suit. **8** (often foll. by *on*) **a** a high general demand (for a commodity, currency, etc.) (*a run on the dollar*). **b** a sudden demand for repayment by a large number of customers (of a bank). **9** a quantity produced in one period of production (*a print run*). **10** a general or average type or class (*not typical of the general run*). **11 a** *Baseball* a point scored by a base runner upon touching home plate safely. **b** *Cricket* a point scored by the batsmen each running to the other's wicket, or an equivalent point awarded for some other reason. **12** (foll. by *of*) free use of or access to (*had the run of the house*). **13 a** an animal's regular track. **b** an enclosure for domestic animals or fowls. **c** a range of pasture. **14** a line of unraveled stitches, esp. from the point of a snag (in hosiery). **15** *Mus.* a rapid scale passage. **16** a class or line of goods. **17** a batch or drove of animals born or reared together. **18** a shoal of fish in motion. **19 a** a single journey, esp. by an aircraft. **b** (of an aircraft) a flight on a straight and even course at a constant speed before or while dropping bombs. **c** an offensive military operation. **20** a slope used for skiing or tobogganing, etc. **21** (**the runs**) *colloq.* an attack of diarrhea. □ **at a** (or **the**) **run** running. **on the run 1** escaping; running away. **2** hurrying about. **run about 1** bustle; hurry from one person or place to another. **2** (esp. of children) play without restraint. **run across 1** happen to meet. **2** (foll. by *to*) make a brief journey or a flying visit (to a place). **run afoul of** collide or become entangled with (another vessel, etc.). **run after 1** pursue with attentions; seek the society of. **2** give much time to (a pursuit, etc.). **3** pursue at a run. **run against** oppose, as in an election. **run along** *colloq.* depart. **run around 1** deceive or evade repeatedly. **2** (often foll. by *with*) *sl.* engage in sexual relations. **run at** attack by charging or rushing. **run away 1** flee; abscond. **2** elope. **3** (of a horse) bolt. **run away with 1** carry off. **2** win easily. **3** accept (a notion) hastily. **4** (of expense, etc.) consume (money, etc.). **5** (of a horse) bolt with (a rider, a carriage or its occupants). **run a blockade** see BLOCKADE. **run down 1** knock down. **2** reduce the strength or numbers of. **3** (of an unwound clock, etc.) stop. **4** (of a person or a person's health) become feeble from overwork or underfeeding. **5** discover after a search. **6** disparage (*his father always ran him down*). **run dry** cease to flow. **run for it** seek safety by fleeing. **a run** (or **a good run**) **for one's money 1** vigorous competition. **2** pleasure derived from an activity. **run the gauntlet** see GAUNTLET[2]. **run a person hard** (or **close**) press a person severely in a race or competition, or in comparative merit. **run high 1** (of the sea) have a strong current with a high tide. **2** (of feelings) be strong. **run in 1** *colloq.* arrest. **2** (of a combatant) rush to close quarters. **3** incur (a debt). **run in the family** (of a trait) be common in a family. **run into 1** collide with. **2** encounter. **3** reach as many as (a specified figure). **4** fall into (a practice, absurdity, etc.). **5** be continuous or coalesce with. **run into the ground** *colloq.* bring (a person, etc.) to exhaustion, etc. **run its course** follow its natural progress. **run low** (or **short**) become depleted; have too little (*our money ran short*; *we ran short of gas*). **run off 1** flee. **2** produce (copies, etc.) on a machine. **3** decide (a race or other contest) after a series of heats or in the event of a tie. **4** flow or cause to flow away. **5** write or recite fluently. **6** digress suddenly. **run off at the mouth** *sl.* talk incessantly. **run off one's feet** very busy. **run on 1** (of written characters) be joined together. **2** continue in operation. **3** elapse. **4** speak volubly. **5** talk incessantly. **6** *Printing* continue on the same line as the preceding matter. **run out 1** come to an end. **2** (foll. by *of*) exhaust one's stock of. **3** escape from a containing vessel. **4** expel; drive out (*they ran him out of town*). **run out on** *colloq.* desert (a person). **run over 1** overflow. **2** study or repeat quickly. **3** (of a vehicle or its driver) pass over; knock down or crush. **4** touch (the notes of a piano, etc.) in quick succession. **5** (often foll. by *to*) go quickly by a brief journey or for a quick visit. **run ragged** exhaust (a person). **run rings around** see RING[1]. **run riot** see RIOT. **run a** (or **the**) **risk** see RISK. **run the show** *colloq.* dominate in an undertaking, etc. **run a temperature** be feverish. **run through 1** examine or rehearse briefly. **2** peruse. **3** deal successively with. **4** consume (an estate, etc.) by reckless or quick spending. **5** traverse. **6** pervade. **7** pierce with a sword, etc. **8** draw a line through (written words). **run to 1** have the money or ability for. **2** reach (an amount or number). **3** (of a person) show a tendency to (*runs to fat*). **4 a** be enough for (some expense or undertaking). **b** have the resources or capacity for. **5** fall into (ruin). **run to earth** (or **ground**) **1** *Hunting* chase to its lair. **2** discover after a long search. **run to meet** anticipate (one's troubles, etc.). **run to seed** see SEED. **run up 1** accumulate (a debt, etc.) quickly. **2** build or make hurriedly. **3** raise (a flag). **4** grow quickly. **5** rise in price. **6** (foll. by *to*) amount to. **7** force (a rival bidder) to bid higher. **8** add up (a column of figures). **9** (foll. by *to*) go quickly by a brief journey or for a quick visit. **run up against** meet with (a difficulty or difficulties). **run upon** (of a person's thoughts, etc.) be engrossed by; dwell upon. **run wild** grow or stray unchecked or undisciplined or untrained. □□ **run·na·ble** *adj.*

run·a·bout /rúnəbowt/ *n.* a light car, boat, or aircraft.

run·a·round /rúnərownd/ *n.* (esp. in phr. *give a person the runaround*) deceit or evasion.

run·a·way /rúnəway/ *n.* **1** a fugitive. **2** an animal or vehicle that is running out of control. **3** (*attrib.*) **a** that is running away or out of control (*runaway inflation*; *had a runaway success*). **b** done or performed after running away (*a runaway wedding*).

run·ci·ble spoon /rúnsibəl/ *n.* a fork curved like a spoon, with three broad prongs.

run·ci·nate /rúnsinayt, -nət/ *adj. Bot.* (of a leaf) saw-toothed, with lobes pointing toward the base.

run·down /rúndown/ *n.* **1** *Baseball* a play in which a base runner is caught between two bases and is chased by fielders who try to tag the runner out. **2** a summary or brief analysis.

run-down *adj.* **1** decayed after prosperity. **2** enfeebled through overwork, etc.

rune /rōōn/ *n.* **1** any of the letters of the earliest Germanic alphabet used by Scandinavians and Anglo-Saxons from about the 3rd c. **2** ▼ a similar mark of mysterious or magic significance. **3** a Finnish poem or a division of it. □□ **ru·nic** *adj.*

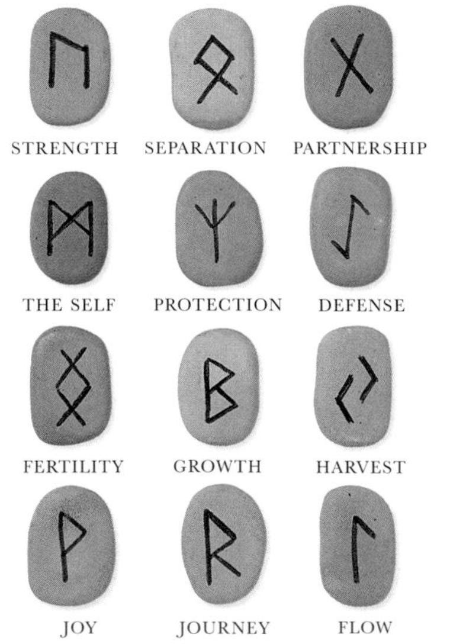
STRENGTH
SEPARATION
PARTNERSHIP
THE SELF
PROTECTION
DEFENSE
FERTILITY
GROWTH
HARVEST
JOY
JOURNEY
FLOW

RUNES WRITTEN ON PEBBLES USED FOR DIVINATION

rung[1] /rung/ *n.* **1** each of the horizontal supports of a ladder. **2** a strengthening crosspiece in a chair, etc.

rung[2] *past part.* of RING[2].

run-in *n.* **1** the approach to an action or event. **2** a quarrel.

run·let /rúnlit/ *n.* a small stream.

run·nel /rúnəl/ *n.* **1** a brook. **2** a gutter.

run·ner /rúnər/ *n.* **1** a person, horse, etc. that runs, esp. in a race. **2 a** a creeping plant stem that can take root. **b** a twining plant. **3** a rod or groove or blade on which a thing slides. **4** a sliding ring on a

R

rod, etc. **5** a messenger, scout, collector, or agent for a bank, etc. **6** a running bird. **7** a smuggler. **8** a revolving millstone. **9** each of the long pieces on the underside of a sled, etc., that forms the contact in sliding. ▷ SLED. **10** a roller for moving a heavy article. **11** a long, narrow ornamental cloth or rug.

run·ner-up *n.* (*pl.* **runners-up** or **runner-ups**) the competitor or team taking second place.

run·ning /rúning/ *n. & adj.* ● *n.* **1** the action of runners in a race, etc. **2** the way a race, etc., proceeds. **3** management; control; operation ● *adj.* **1** continuing on an essentially continuous basis though changing in detail (*a running battle*). **2** consecutive (*three days running*). **3** done with a run (*a running jump*). □ **in** (or **out of**) **the running** (of a competitor) with a good (or poor) chance of winning. **make** (or **take up**) **the running** take the lead; set the pace.

run·ning board *n.* ▼ a footboard on either side of a vehicle.

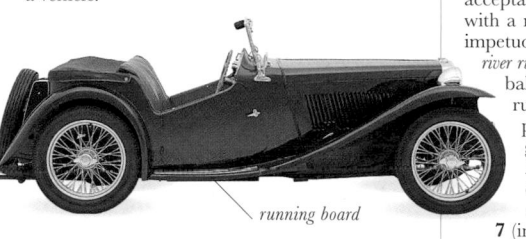

RUNNING BOARD ON A 1940S
MG TC MIDGET

run·ning com·men·ta·ry *n.* an oral description of events as they occur.

run·ning dog *n. colloq.* a servile follower, esp. of a political system.

run·ning light *n.* any of the navigational lights displayed by a ship, aircraft, etc., during hours of darkness.

run·ning mate *n.* **1** a candidate for a secondary position in an election. **2** a horse entered in a race in order to set the pace for another horse from the same stable which is intended to win.

run·ning stitch *n.* **1** a line of small nonoverlapping stitches for gathering, etc. ▷ STITCH. **2** one of these stitches.

run·ny /rúnee/ *adj.* (**runnier**, **runniest**) **1** tending to run or flow. **2** excessively fluid.

run·off /rúnawf/ *n.* **1** an additional competition, election, race, etc., after a tie. **2** an amount of rainfall that is carried off an area by streams and rivers.

run-of-the-mill *adj.* ordinary; undistinguished.

runt /runt/ *n.* **1** a small piglet, puppy, etc., esp. the smallest in a litter. **2** a weakling; an undersized person. □□ **runt·y** *adj.*

run-through *n.* **1** a rehearsal. **2** a brief survey.

run·way /rúnway/ *n.* **1** a specially prepared surface along which aircraft take off and land. **2** a trail to an animals' watering place. **3** an incline down which logs are slid. **4** a narrow walkway extending out from a stage into an auditorium. **5** a passageway along which football players, etc., run to enter the field.

ru·pee /roopée, roopee/ *n.* the chief monetary unit of India, Pakistan, Sri Lanka, Nepal, Mauritius, and the Seychelles.

rup·ture /rúpchər/ *n. & v.* ● *n.* **1** the act or an instance of breaking; a breach. **2** a breach of harmonious relations. **3** *Med.* an abdominal hernia. ● *v.* **1** *tr.* break or burst (a cell or membrane, etc.). **2** *tr.* sever (a connection). **3** *intr.* undergo a rupture. **4** *tr. & intr.* affect with or suffer a hernia.

ru·ral /roorəl/ *adj.* **1** in, of, or suggesting the country (opp. URBAN) (*in rural seclusion; a rural constituency*). **2** often *derog.* characteristic of country people; rustic; plain; simple. □□ **ru·ral·ism** *n.* **ru·ral·ist** *n.* **ru·ral·i·ty** /-rálitee/ *n.* **ru·ral·ize** *v.* **ru·ral·ly** *adv.*

ru·ral free de·liv·er·y *n.* (also **rural delivery service**) postal delivery to mailboxes in rural areas.

Ru·ri·ta·ni·an /roorītáyneeən/ *adj.* relating to or characteristic of romantic adventure or its setting.

ruse /rooz/ *n.* a stratagem or trick.

rush[1] /rush/ *v. & n.* ● *v.* **1** *intr.* go, move, or act precipitately or with great speed. **2** *tr.* move or transport with great haste (*was rushed to the hospital*). **3** *intr.* (foll. by *at*) **a** move suddenly toward. **b** begin impetuously. **4** *tr.* perform or deal with hurriedly (*don't rush your dinner; the bill was rushed through Congress*). **5** *tr.* force (a person) to act hastily. **6** *tr.* attack or capture by sudden assault. **7** *tr.* pay attentions to (a person) with a view to securing acceptance of a proposal. **8** *tr.* pass (an obstacle) with a rapid dash. **9** *intr.* flow, fall, spread, or roll impetuously or fast (*felt the blood rush to my face; the river rushes past*). **10** *tr. & intr. Football* advance the ball in a running play or plays. ● *n.* **1** an act of rushing; a violent advance or attack. **2** a period of great activity. **3** (*attrib.*) done with great haste or speed (*a rush job*). **4** a sudden migration of large numbers. **5** a surge of emotion, excitement, etc. **6** (foll. by *on, for*) a sudden, strong demand for a commodity. **7** (in *pl.*) *colloq.* the first prints of a film. **8** *Football* **a** the act of carrying the ball. **b** an attempt by a defensive player or players to reach the passer or kicker.

rush[2] /rush/ *n.* **1** ▶ any marsh or waterside plant of the family Juncaceae, with naked slender tapering pith-filled stems used for making chair bottoms and plaiting baskets, etc. **2** a stem of this. **3** (*collect.*) rushes as a material. □□ **rush·like** *adj.* **rush·y** *adj.*

rush hour *n.* a time each day when traffic is at its heaviest.

rusk /rusk/ *n.* a slice of bread rebaked usu. as a light biscuit, esp. as food for babies.

rus·set /rúsit/ *adj. & n.* ● *adj.* **1** a reddish-brown. ● *n.* **1** a reddish-brown color. **2** a kind of rough-skinned, russet-colored apple. **3** a baking potato, esp. one from Idaho.

Rus·sian /rúshən/ *n. & adj.* ● *n.* **1 a** a native or national of Russia or the former Soviet Union. **b** a person of Russian descent. **2** the language of Russia and the official language of the former Soviet Union. ● *adj.* **1** of or relating to Russia. **2** of or in Russian. □□ **Rus·sian·ize** *v.tr.* **Rus·sian·ness** *n.*

Rus·sian doll *n.* each of a set of brightly painted hollow wooden dolls that fit inside each other.

Rus·sian rou·lette *n.* **1** an act of daring in which one squeezes the trigger of a revolver held to one's head with one chamber loaded, having first spun the chamber. **2** a potentially dangerous enterprise.

Rus·si·fy /rúsifī/ *v.tr.* (**-ies**, **-ied**) make Russian in character. □□ **Rus·si·fi·ca·tion** *n.*

Russ·ki /rúskee, roos-, roos-/ *n.* (also **Russ·ky**) (*pl.* **Russkis** or **-ies**) often *offens.* a Russian or (formerly) a Soviet citizen.

Russo- /rúsō/ *comb. form* Russian; Russian and (*Russo-Japanese*).

rust /rust/ *n. & v.* ● *n.* **1 a** a reddish or yellowish-

RUSH:
WOODRUSH
(*Luzula*
species)

brown coating formed on iron or steel by oxidation, esp. as a result of moisture. **b** a similar coating on other metals. **2** any of various plant diseases with rust-colored spots caused by fungi of the order Uredinales. **3** an impaired state due to disuse or inactivity. ● *v.* **1** *tr. & intr.* affect or be affected with rust; undergo oxidation. **2** *intr.* lose quality or efficiency by disuse or inactivity. □□ **rust·less** *adj.*

rus·tic /rústik/ *adj. & n.* ● *adj.* **1** having the characteristics of or associations with the country or country life. **2** unsophisticated. **3** of rude workmanship. **4** made of untrimmed branches or rough lumber (*a rustic bench*). **5** (of lettering) freely formed. **6** *Archit.* with rough-hewn or roughened surface or with sunk joints. ● *n.* a person from or living in the country, esp. a simple, unsophisticated one. □□ **rus·tic·i·ty** /-tísitee/ *n.*

rus·ti·cate /rústikayt/ *v.intr.* retire to or live in the country. □□ **rus·ti·ca·tion** /-káyshən/ *n.*

rus·tle /rúsəl/ *v. & n.* ● *v.* **1** *intr. & tr.* make or cause to make a gentle sound as of dry leaves blown in a breeze. **2** *intr.* (often foll. by *along*, etc.) move with a rustling sound. **3** *tr.* (also *absol.*) steal (cattle or horses). **4** *intr. colloq.* hustle. ● *n.* a rustling sound or movement. □ **rustle up** *colloq.* produce quickly when needed. □□ **rus·tler** *n.* (esp. in sense 3 of *v.*).

rust·proof /rústproof/ *adj. & v.* ● *adj.* (of a metal) not susceptible to corrosion by rust. ● *v.tr.* make rustproof.

rust·y /rústee/ *adj.* (**rustier**, **rustiest**) **1** rusted or affected by rust. **2** stiff with age or disuse. **3** (of knowledge, etc.) impaired by neglect (*my French is a bit rusty*). **4** rust-colored. **5** (of black clothes) discolored by age. **6** (of a voice) croaking or creaking. □□ **rust·i·ly** *adv.* **rust·i·ness** *n.*

rut[1] /rut/ *n. & v.* ● *n.* **1** a deep track made by the passage of wheels. **2** an established mode of practice or procedure. ● *v.tr.* (**rutted**, **rutting**) mark with ruts. □ **in a rut** following a fixed pattern of behavior that is difficult to change. □□ **rut·ty** *adj.*

rut[2] /rut/ *n. & v.* ● *n.* the periodic sexual excitement of a male deer, goat, sheep, etc. ● *v.intr.* (**rutted**, **rutting**) be affected with rut. □□ **rut·tish** *adj.*

ru·ta·ba·ga /rootəbáygə/ *n.* a large yellow-fleshed turnip, *Brassica napus*, orig. from Sweden. Also called **swede**.

ru·the·ni·um /rootheeneeəm/ *n. Chem.* a rare hard white metallic transition element, occurring naturally in platinum ores, and used as a chemical catalyst and in certain alloys. ¶ Symb.: **Ru**.

ruth·er·for·di·um /rútherfáwrdeeəm/ *n. Chem.* an artificially made transuranic metallic element produced by bombarding an isotope of Californium. ¶ Symb.: **Rf**.

ruth·less /roothlis/ *adj.* having no pity nor compassion. □□ **ruth·less·ly** *adv.* **ruth·less·ness** *n.*

RV *abbr.* **1** Revised Version (of the Bible). **2** recreational vehicle.

rye /rī/ *n.* **1 a** a cereal plant, *Secale cereale*, with spikes bearing florets which yield wheatlike grains. **b** ▶ the grain of this used for bread and fodder. **2** (in full **rye whiskey**) whiskey distilled from fermented rye.

rye·grass /rígras/ *n.* any forage or lawn grass of the genus *Lolium*, esp. *L. perenne*.

RYE
(*Secale cereale*)

R

S

S[1] /es/ n. (also **s**) (pl. **Ss** or **S's** /ésiz/) **1** the nineteenth letter of the alphabet. **2** an S-shaped object or curve.

S[2] abbr. (also **S.**) **1** Saint. **2** siemens. **3** south, southern.

S[3] symb. Chem. the element sulfur.

s. abbr. **1** second(s). **2** shilling(s). **3** singular. **4** son.

-s' /s; z after a vowel sound or voiced consonant/ suffix denoting the possessive case of plural nouns and sometimes of singular nouns ending in s (the boys' shoes; Charles' book).

-s[1] /s; z after a vowel sound or voiced consonant, e.g., ways, bags/ suffix denoting the plurals of nouns (cf. -ES[1]).

-s[2] /s; z after a vowel sound or voiced consonant, e.g., ties, begs/ suffix forming the 3rd person sing. present of verbs.

-s[3] /s; z after a vowel sound or voiced consonant, e.g., besides/ suffix **1** forming adverbs (afterwards; besides; mornings). **2** forming possessive pronouns (hers; ours).

SA abbr. **1** Salvation Army. **2 a** South Africa. **b** South America. **c** South Australia. **3** hist. Sturmabteilung (the paramilitary force of the Nazi party).

sab·a·dil·la /sábədílə, -déeə/ n. **1** a Mexican plant, Schoenocaulon officinale, with seeds yielding veratrine. **2** a preparation of these seeds, used in medicine and agriculture.

Sab·ba·tar·i·an /sábətáireeən/ n. & adj. ● n. **1** a strict Sabbath-keeping Jew. **2** a Christian who favors observing Sunday strictly as the Sabbath. **3** a Christian who observes Saturday as the Sabbath. ● adj. relating to or holding the tenets of Sabbatarians. □□ **Sab·ba·tar·i·an·ism** n.

Sab·bath /sábəth/ n. (in full **Sabbath day**) a day of rest and religious observance kept by Christians on Sunday, Jews on Saturday, and Muslims on Friday.

sab·bat·i·cal /səbátikəl/ adj. & n. ● adj. **1** of or appropriate to the Sabbath. **2** (of leave) granted at intervals to a university teacher for study or travel. ● n. a period of sabbatical leave.

sa·ber /sáybər/ n. & v. ● n. **1** a cavalry sword with a curved blade. **2** a cavalry soldier and horse. **3** ▶ a light fencing sword with a tapering blade. ▷ FENCING. ● v.tr. cut down or wound with a saber.

sa·ber rat·tling n. a display or threat of military force.

sa·ber-toothed ti·ger n. (also **saber-toothed cat**) ▼ an extinct mammal of the cat family with long curved upper canine teeth.

SABER-TOOTHED TIGER
(*Smilodon* species)

Sa·bi·an /sáybeeən/ adj. & n. ● adj. of a sect classed in the Koran with Muslims, Jews, and Christians, as believers in the true God. ● n. a member of this sect.

Sa·bine /sáybīn/ adj. & n. ● adj. of or relating to a people of the central Apennines in ancient Italy. ● n. a member of this people.

sa·ble[1] /sáybəl/ n. **1 a** ▼ a small, brown-furred, flesh-eating mammal, Martes zibellina, of N. Europe and parts of N. Asia, related to the marten. **b** its skin or fur. **2** a fine paintbrush made of sable fur.

SABLE (*Martes zibellina*)

sa·ble[2] /sáybəl/ n. & adj. ● n. **1** esp. poet. black. **2** (in pl.) mourning garments. **3** (in full **sable antelope**) a large stout-horned African antelope, Hippotragus niger, the males of which are mostly black in old age. ● adj. esp. poet. dark, gloomy.

sab·ot /sabṓ, sábṓ/ n. **1** a kind of simple shoe hollowed out from a block of wood. **2** a wooden-soled shoe.

sab·o·tage /sábətaazh/ n. & v. ● n. deliberate damage to productive capacity. ● v.tr. **1** commit sabotage on. **2** destroy; spoil (sabotaged my plans).

sab·o·teur /sábətȫr/ n. a person who commits sabotage.

sa·bra /saábrə/ n. a Jew born in Israel.

SAC /sak/ Strategic Air Command.

Sac /sak, sawk/ n. SAUK.

sac /sak/ n. a baglike cavity, enclosed by a membrane, in an animal or plant.

sac·cha·ride /sákərīd/ n. Chem. = SUGAR n. 2.

sac·cha·rim·e·ter /sákərímitər/ n. any optical instrument that uses polarized light to measure the sugar content of a solution.

sac·cha·rin /sákərin/ n. a substance used as a substitute for sugar.

sac·cha·rine /sákərin, -reen, -rīn/ adj. **1** sugary. **2** of, containing, or like sugar. **3** unpleasantly overpolite, sentimental, etc.

saccharo- /sákərō/ comb. form sugar; sugar and.

sac·char·o·me·ter /sákərómitər/ n. any instrument, esp. a hydrometer, for measuring the sugar content of a solution.

sac·char·ose /sákərōs/ n. sucrose.

sac·ci·form /sáksifawrm/ adj. sac-shaped.

sac·cule /sákyōōl/ n. a small sac or cyst. □□ **sac·cu·lar** adj.

sac·er·do·tal /sásərdṓtəl, sák-/ adj. of priests or the priestly office; priestly. □□ **sac·er·do·tal·ism** n.

sa·chem /sáychəm/ n. the supreme leader of some Native American tribes.

sa·chet /sasháy/ n. **1** a small bag or packet containing a small portion of a substance, esp. shampoo. **2** a small perfumed bag. **3 a** dry perfume for laying among clothes, etc. **b** a packet of this.

sack[1] /sak/ n. & v. ● n. **1 a** a large, strong bag, for storing or conveying goods. **b** (usu. foll. by of) this with its contents (a sack of potatoes). **c** a quantity contained in a sack. **2** (prec. by the) colloq. dismissal from employment. **3** (prec. by the) sl. bed. **4** a woman's short, loose dress with a sacklike appearance. **5** a man's or woman's loose-hanging coat not shaped to the back. ● v.tr. **1** put into a sack. **2** colloq. dismiss from employment. □□ **sack·ful** n. (pl. **-fuls**). **sack·like** adj.

sack[2] /sak/ v. & n. ● v.tr. **1** plunder and destroy (a captured town, etc.). **2** steal valuables from (a place). ● n. the sacking of a captured place.

sack[3] /sak/ n. hist. a white wine formerly imported into Britain from Spain and the Canary Islands (sherry sack).

sack·but /sákbut/ n. an early form of trombone.

sack·cloth /sák-klawth, -kloth/ n. **1** a coarse fabric of flax or hemp. **2** clothing made of this, formerly worn as a penance (esp. sackcloth and ashes).

sack·ing /sáking/ n. material for making sacks; sackcloth.

sack race n. a race between competitors in sacks up to the waist or neck.

sa·cra pl. of SACRUM.

sa·cral /sáykrəl, sa-/ adj. **1** Anat. of or relating to the sacrum. **2** Anthropol. of or for sacred rites.

sac·ra·ment /sákrəmənt/ n. **1** a religious ceremony or act of the Christian churches regarded as an outward and visible sign of inward and spiritual grace, baptism, and the Eucharist. **2** a thing of mysterious and sacred significance; a sacred influence, symbol, etc. **3** (also **Blessed** or **Holy Sacrament**) (prec. by the) **a** the Eucharist. **b** the consecrated elements, esp. the bread or Host.

sac·ra·men·tal /sákrəmént'l/ adj. & n. ● adj. **1** of or of the nature of a sacrament. **2** (of a doctrine, etc.) attaching great importance to the sacraments. ● n. an observance analogous to but not reckoned among the sacraments, e.g., the use of holy water. □□ **sac·ra·men·tal·ly** adv.

sa·crar·i·um /səkráireeəm/ n. (pl. **sacraria** /-reeə/) **1** the sanctuary of a church. **2** RC Ch. a basin for use in the sacristy. **3** Rom. Antiq. a shrine; the room (in a house) containing the penates.

sa·cred /sáykrid/ adj. **1 a** (often foll. by to) exclusively dedicated or appropriated (to a god or to some religious purpose). **b** made holy by religious association. **c** connected with religion (sacred music). **2 a** safeguarded or required by religion, reverence, or tradition. **b** sacrosanct. **3** (of writings, etc.) embodying the laws or doctrines of a religion. □□ **sa·cred·ly** adv. **sa·cred·ness** n.

sa·cred cow n. colloq. an idea or institution unreasonably held to be above criticism (with ref. to the Hindus' respect for the cow as a holy animal).

sac·ri·fice /sákrifīs/ n. & v. ● n. **1 a** the act of giving up something valued for the sake of something else more important or worthy. **b** a thing given up in this way. **c** the loss entailed in this. **2 a** the slaughter of an animal or person or the surrender of a possession as an offering to a deity. **b** an animal, person, or thing offered in this way. **3** an act of prayer, thanksgiving, or penitence as propitiation. **4** (in games) a loss incurred deliberately to avoid a greater loss or to obtain a compensating advantage. ● v.tr. **1** give up (a thing) as a sacrifice. **2** (foll. by to) devote or give over to. **3** (also absol.) offer or kill as a sacrifice. □□ **sac·ri·fi·cial** /-físhəl/ adj. **sac·ri·fi·cial·ly** /-físhəlee/ adv.

sac·ri·lege /sákrilij/ n. the violation or misuse of what is regarded as sacred. □□ **sac·ri·le·gious** /-líjəs/ adj. **sac·ri·le·gious·ly** adv.

sac·ris·tan /sákristən/ n. a person in charge of a sacristy and its contents.

sac·ris·ty /sákristee/ n. (pl. **-ies**) a room in a church where the vestments, sacred vessels, etc., are kept and the celebrant can prepare for a service. ▷ CATHEDRAL

sacro- /sákrō, sáy-/ comb. form denoting the sacrum (sacroiliac).

sac·ro·il·i·ac /sákrōíleeak, sákrō-/ adj. relating to the juncture of the sacrum and the ilium bones of the pelvis.

sac·ro·sanct /sákrōsangkt/ adj. (of a person, place, law, etc.) most sacred; inviolable. □□ **sac·ro·sanc·ti·ty** /-sángktitee/ n.

sac·rum /sáykrəm, sák-/ n. (pl. **sacra** /-krə/ or **sacrums**) Anat. a triangular bone formed from fused vertebrae and situated between the two hipbones of the pelvis. ▷ SKELETON, SPINE

SAD abbr. seasonal affective disorder.

SABER:
FENCING SABER

S

sad /sad/ *adj.* (**sadder, saddest**) **1** unhappy. **2** causing or suggesting sorrow (*a sad story*). **3** regrettable. **4** shameful; deplorable (*a sad state*). □□ **sad·ly** *adv.* **sad·ness** *n.*

sad·den /sád'n/ *v.tr. & intr.* make or become sad.

sad·dle /sád'l/ *n. & v.* ● *n.* **1** ▼ a seat of leather, etc., fastened on a horse, etc., for riding. ▷ SIDESADDLE. **2** a seat for the rider of a bicycle, etc. ▷ BICYCLE. **3** a cut of meat consisting of the two loins. **4** a ridge rising to a summit at each end. **5** the part of a draft horse's harness to which the shafts are attached. **6** a part of an animal's back resembling a saddle in shape or marking. ● *v.tr.* **1** put a saddle on (a horse, etc.). **2 a** (foll. by *with*) burden (a person) with a task, responsibility, etc. **b** (foll. by *on, upon*) impose (a burden) on a person. □ **in the saddle 1** mounted. **2** in office or control. □□ **sad·dle·less** *adj.*

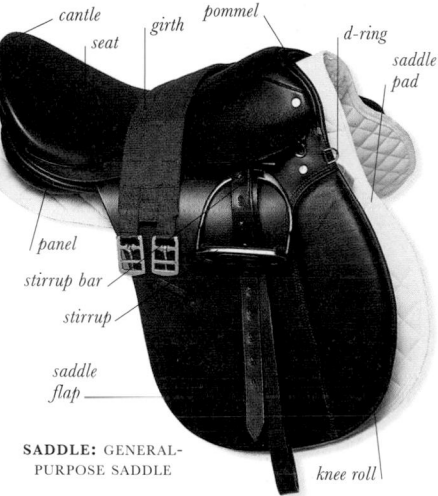

cantle · seat · girth · pommel · d-ring · saddle pad · panel · stirrup bar · stirrup · saddle flap · knee roll

SADDLE: GENERAL-PURPOSE SADDLE

sad·dle·back /sád'lbak/ *n.* **1** *Archit.* a tower-roof with two opposite gables. **2** a hill with a concave upper outline. **3** a black pig with a white band across the back. **4** any of various birds with a saddlelike marking, esp. a New Zealand bird, *Philesturnus carunculatus*. □□ **sad·dle·backed** *adj.*

sad·dle·bag /sád'lbag/ *n.* **1** each of a pair of bags laid across a horse, etc., behind the saddle. **2** a bag attached behind the saddle of a bicycle.

sad·dle·bow /sád'lbō/ *n.* the arched front or rear of a saddle.

sad·dle·cloth /sád'lklawth/ *n.* a cloth laid on a horse's back under the saddle.

sad·dler /sádlər/ *n.* a dealer in saddles and other equipment for horses.

sad·dler·y /sádləree/ *n.* (*pl.* **-ies**) **1** the saddles and other equipment of a saddler. **2** a saddler's business or premises.

sad·dle shoes *n.pl.* laced shoes with yokes that contrast in color with the rest of the upper.

sad·dle sore *n.* a chafe from riding on a saddle.

sad·dle stitch *n.* a stitch of thread or a wire staple passed through the center of a magazine or booklet.

sad·dle·tree /sád'ltree/ *n.* the frame of a saddle.

Sad·du·cee /sájəsee, sádyə-/ *n.* a member of a Jewish sect or party of the time of Christ that denied the resurrection of the dead, the existence of spirits, and the obligation of the traditional oral law. □□ **Sad·du·ce·an** /-séeən/ *adj.*

sa·dhu /sáadōō/ *n.* (in India) a holy man, sage, or ascetic.

sa·dism /sáydizəm, sád-/ *n.* **1** a form of sexual perversion characterized by the enjoyment of inflicting pain or suffering on others (cf. MASOCHISM). **2** *colloq.* the enjoyment of cruelty to others. □□ **sa·dist** *n.* **sa·dis·tic** /sədístik/ *adj.* **sa·dis·ti·cal·ly** *adv.*

sa·do·mas·o·chism /sáydōmásəkizəm, sádō-/ *n.* the combination of sadism and masochism in

one person. □□ **sa·do·mas·o·chist** *n.* **sa·do·mas·o·chis·tic** /-kístik/ *adj.*

sad sack *n. colloq.* a very inept person, esp. a soldier.

sa·fa·ri /səfáaree/ *n.* (*pl.* **safaris**) **1** a hunting or scientific expedition, esp. in E. Africa (*go on safari*). **2** a sightseeing trip to see African animals in their natural habitat.

sa·fa·ri park *n.* an enclosed area where lions, etc., are kept in the open and through which visitors may drive.

safe /sayf/ *adj. & n.* ● *adj.* **1 a** free of danger or injury. **b** (often foll. by *from*) out of or not exposed to danger (*safe from their enemies*). **2** affording security or not involving danger or risk (*put it in a safe place*). **3** reliable; certain (*a safe catch; a safe method; is safe to win*). **4** prevented from escaping or doing harm (*have got him safe*). **5** (also **safe and sound**) uninjured; with no harm done. **6** cautious and unenterprising. ● *n.* a strong, lockable cabinet, etc., for valuables. □ **on the safe side** with a margin of security against risks. □□ **safe·ly** *adv.* **safe·ness** *n.*

safe-con·duct *n.* **1** a privilege of immunity from arrest or harm, esp. on a particular occasion. **2** a document securing this.

safe-de·pos·it box *n.* a secured box (esp. in a bank vault) for storing valuables.

safe·guard /sáyfgaard/ *n. & v.* ● *n.* **1** a proviso, stipulation, quality, or circumstance that tends to prevent something undesirable. **2** a safe conduct. ● *v.tr.* guard or protect (rights, etc.) by a precaution or stipulation.

safe house *n.* a place of refuge or rendezvous for criminals, etc.

safe·keep·ing /sáyfkeeping/ *n.* preservation in a safe place.

safe sex *n.* sexual activity in which precautions are taken to reduce the risk of spreading sexually transmitted diseases.

safe·ty /sáyftee/ *n.* (*pl.* **-ies**) **1** the condition of being safe; freedom from danger or risks. **2** (*attrib.*) **a** designating any of various devices for preventing injury from machinery (*safety bar; safety lock*). **b** designating items of protective clothing (*safety helmet*).

safe·ty belt *n.* **1** = SEAT BELT. **2** a belt or strap securing a person to prevent injury.

safe·ty-de·pos·it box *n.* = SAFE-DEPOSIT BOX.

safe·ty glass *n.* glass that will not splinter when broken. ▷ CAR

safe·ty har·ness *n.* ▼ a system of belts or restraints to hold a person to prevent falling or injury.

gear loop · buckle · padded waist belt · leg loop · belay loop

SAFETY HARNESS: ROCK CLIMBER'S SIT HARNESS

safe·ty match *n.* a match igniting only on a specially prepared surface.

safe·ty net *n.* **1** a net placed to catch an acrobat, etc., in case of a fall. **2** a safeguard against hazard or adversity.

safe·ty pin *n.* a pin with a point that is held in a guard when closed.

safe·ty ra·zor *n.* a razor with a guard to reduce the risk of cutting the skin.

safe·ty valve *n.* **1** (in a steam boiler) a valve opening automatically to relieve excessive pressure. **2** a means of giving harmless vent to excitement, etc.

saf·flow·er /sáflowr/ *n.* **1 a** a thistlelike plant, *Carthamus tinctorius*, yielding a red dye. **b** its dried petals. **2** a dye made from these.

saf·ra·nine /sáfrəneen, -nin/ *n.* (also **saf·ra·nin** /-nin/) any of a large group of mainly red dyes used in biological staining, etc.

saf·fron /sáfrən/ *n. & adj.* ● *n.* **1** ▶ a bright yellow-orange food coloring and flavoring made from the dried stigmas of the crocus, *Crocus sativus*. ▷ SPICE. **2** the color of this. ● *adj.* saffron-colored.

SAFFRON: STIGMAS OF SAFFRON CROCUS (*Crocus sativus*)

sag /sag/ *v. & n.* ● *v.intr.* (**sagged, sagging**) **1** sink or subside, esp. unevenly. **2** have a downward bulge or curve in the middle. **3** fall in price. ● *n.* **1 a** the amount that a rope, etc., sags. **b** the distance from the middle of its curve to a straight line between its supports. **2** a sinking condition; subsidence. **3** a fall in price. □□ **sag·gy** *adj.*

sa·ga /sáagə/ *n.* **1** a long story of heroic achievement, esp. a medieval Icelandic or Norwegian prose narrative. **2** a series of connected books giving the history of a family, etc. **3** a long, involved story.

sa·ga·cious /səgáyshəs/ *adj.* **1** mentally penetrating; having practical wisdom. **2** acute-minded; shrewd. **3** (of a saying, plan, etc.) showing wisdom. □□ **sa·ga·cious·ly** *adv.* **sa·gac·i·ty** /səgásitee/ *n.*

sag·a·more /ságəmawr/ *n.* = SACHEM.

sage[1] /sayj/ *n.* **1** an aromatic herb, *Salvia officinalis*, with dull grayish-green leaves. **2** its leaves used in cooking. ▷ HERB

sage[2] /sayj/ *n. & adj.* ● *n.* **1** often *iron.* a wise person. **2** any of the ancients traditionally regarded as the wisest of their time. ● *adj.* **1** wise, esp. from experience. **2** of or indicating wisdom. **3** often *iron.* wise-looking. □□ **sage·ly** *adv.*

sage·brush /sáyjbrush/ *n.* **1** ▶ a growth of shrubby aromatic plants of the genus *Artemisia*, found in some semiarid regions of western N. America. **2** this plant.

sag·it·tal /sájit'l/ *adj. Anat.* **1** of or relating to the suture between the parietal bones of the skull. **2** in the same plane as this, or in a parallel plane.

Sag·it·tar·i·us /sájitáireeəs/ *n.* **1** ▼ a constellation, traditionally regarded as contained in the figure of an archer. **2 a** the ninth sign of the zodiac (the Archer). ▷ ZODIAC. **b** a person born when the Sun is in this sign. □□ **Sag·it·tar·i·an** *adj. & n.*

SAGEBRUSH (*Artemisia tridentata*)

S

SAGITTARIUS: FIGURE FORMED FROM THE STARS OF SAGITTARIUS

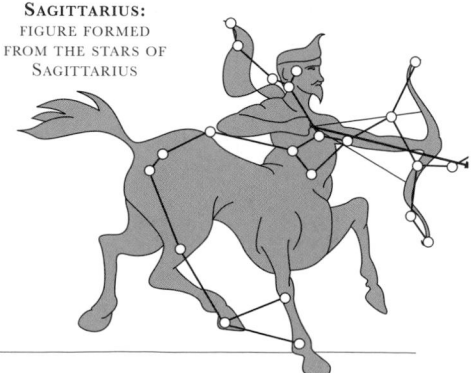

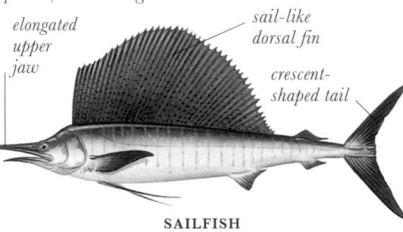

**SAGITTATE
LEAF**

sag·it·tate /sájitayt/ *adj. Bot. & Zool.* ◀ shaped like an arrowhead.

sa·go /sáygō/ *n. (pl. -os)* **1** a kind of starch, made from the powdered pith of the sago palm and used in puddings, etc. **2** (in full **sago palm**) any of several tropical palms and cycads, esp. *Cycas circinalis* and *Metroxylon sagu*, from which sago is made.

sa·gua·ro /səgwarŏ, səwarŏ/ *n.* (*pl.* **-os**) a giant cactus, *Carnegiea gigantea*, of the SW United States and Mexico.

sa·hib /saab, sáahib/ *n.* **1** *hist.* (in India) a form of address, often placed after the name, to European men. **2** *colloq.* a gentleman (*pukka sahib*).

said *past* and *past part.* of SAY.

sail /sayl/ *n. & v.* ● *n.* **1** a piece of material extended on rigging to catch the wind and propel a boat or ship. ▷ SAILBOAT, SHIP. **2** a ship's sails collectively. **3 a** a voyage or excursion in a sailing ship. **b** a voyage of specified duration. **4** a ship, esp. as discerned from its sails. **5** a wind-catching apparatus attached to the arm of a windmill. ● *v.* **1** *intr.* travel on water by the use of sails or engine power. **2** *tr.* **a** navigate (a ship, etc.). **b** travel on (a sea). **3** *tr.* set (a toy boat) afloat. **4** *intr.* glide or move smoothly or in a stately manner. **5** *intr. colloq.* succeed easily (*sailed through the exams*). □ **sail close to** (or **near**) **the wind 1** sail as nearly against the wind as possible. **2** come close to indecency or dishonesty. **take in sail** furl the sail or sails of a vessel. **under sail** with sails set. □□ **sail·a·ble** *adj.* **sailed** *adj.* (also in *comb.*). **sail·less** *adj.*

sail·board /sáylbawrd/ *n.* a board with a mast and sail, used in windsurfing. ▷ WINDSURFING. □□ **sail·board·er** *n.* **sail·board·ing** *n.*

sail·boat /sáylbōt/ *n.* ▼ a boat driven by sails. ▷ BOAT

sail·cloth /sáylklawth, -kloth/ *n.* **1** canvas for sails, upholstery, tents, etc. **2** a canvaslike dress material.

sail·er /sáylər/ *n.* a ship of specified sailing power (*a good sailer*).

sail·fish /sáylfish/ *n.* ▼ any fish of the genus *Istiophorus*, with a large dorsal fin.

elongated upper jaw　*sail-like dorsal fin*　*crescent-shaped tail*

SAILFISH
(*Istiophorus platypterus*)

sail·or /sáylər/ *n.* **1** a seaman or mariner, esp. one below the rank of officer. **2** a person considered as liable or not liable to seasickness (*a good sailor*). □□ **sail·or·ing** *n.* **sail·or·less** *adj.* **sail·or·ly** *adj.*

sail·plane /sáylplayn/ *n.* a glider designed for sustained flight.

sain·foin /sáynfoyn, sán-/ *n.* a leguminous plant, *Onobrychis viciifolia*, grown for fodder and having pink flowers.

saint /saynt/ *n. & v.* ● *n.* (*abbr.* **St.** or **S.**; *pl.* **Sts.** or **SS.**) **1** a holy or (in some churches) a canonized person regarded as having a place in heaven. **2** (**Saint** or **St.**) the title of a saint or archangel, hence the name of a church, etc. (*St. Paul's*) or (often with the loss of the apostrophe) the name of a town, etc. (*St. Andrews*). **3** a very virtuous person (*would try the patience of a saint*). **4** a member of the company of heaven (*with all the angels and saints*). ● *v.tr.* **1** canonize; admit to the calendar of saints. **2** call or regard as a saint. **3** (as **sainted** *adj.*) sacred; of a saintly life. □□ **saint·hood** *n.* **saint·like** *adj.*

St. Ber·nard /bərnaárd/ *n.* (in full **St. Bernard dog**) **1** a very large dog of a breed orig. kept to rescue travelers by the monks of the Hospice on the Great St. Bernard pass in the Alps. **2** this breed.

St. El·mo's fire /élmōz/ *n.* ▶ a luminous electrical discharge sometimes seen on a ship or aircraft during a storm.

St. John's-wort /jónzwərt/ *n.* any yellow-flowered plant of the genus *Hypericum*, esp. *H. androsaemum*.

ST. ELMO'S FIRE

saint·ly /sáyntlee/ *adj.* (**saintlier, saintliest**) very virtuous. □□ **saint·li·ness** *n.*

saint·pau·lia /səntpáwleeə/ *n.* the African violet.

St. Vi·tus's dance /vítəsiz, vítəs/ *n.* = SYDENHAM'S CHOREA.

saith /seth, sáyith *archaic* 3rd *sing. present* of SAY.

saithe /sayth/ *n. Sc.* a codlike fish, *Pollachius virens*, with skin that soils fingers like wet coal. Also called **coalfish, coley, pollock.**

sake[1] /sayk/ *n.* □ **for Christ's** (or **God's** or **goodness'** or **Heaven's** or **Pete's**) **sake** an expression of urgency, impatience, etc. **for old times' sake** in memory of former times. **for the sake of** (or **for a person's sake**) **1** out of consideration for; in the interest of (*for my own sake as well as yours*). **2** in order to please, get, or keep (*for the sake of uniformity*).

sake[2] /saakee, -ke/ *n.* a Japanese alcoholic drink made from rice.

sa·ker /sáykər/ *n.* **1** a large falcon, *Falco cherrug*, used in falconry, esp. the larger female bird. **2** *hist.* an old form of cannon.

sa·ki /saakee/ *n.* (*pl.* **sakis**) any monkey of the genus *Pithecia* or *Chiropotes*, native to S. America, having coarse fur and a long nonprehensile tail.

sal /sál/ *n. Pharm.* salt.

sa·laam /səláam/ *n. & v.* ● *n.* **1** the esp. Islamic salutation denoting 'peace.' **2** (in India) an obeisance consisting of a low bow of the head and body with the right palm on the forehead. **3** (in *pl.*) respectful compliments. ● *v.* **1** *tr.* make a salaam to (a person). **2** *intr.* make a salaam.

sal·a·ble /sáyləbəl/ *adj.* (also **sale·a·ble**) fit to be sold. □□ **sal·a·bil·i·ty** /-bílitee/ *n.*

sa·la·cious /səláyshəs/ *adj.* **1** lustful; lecherous. **2** (of writings, pictures, talk, etc.) tending to cause sexual desire. □□ **sa·la·cious·ly** *adv.* **sa·la·cious·ness** *n.*

sal·ad /sáləd/ *n.* **1** a cold dish of various mixtures of raw or cooked vegetables, usu. seasoned with oil, vinegar, etc. **2** a vegetable or herb suitable for eating raw.

sal·ad days *n.pl.* a period of youthful inexperience.

sal·ad dress·ing *n.* a mixture of oil, vinegar, etc., used in a salad.

sal·a·man·der /sáləmandər/ *n.* **1** *Zool.* ▶ any tailed newtlike amphibian of the order Urodela, esp. the genus *Salamandra*, once thought able to endure fire. **2** a mythical lizardlike creature credited with this property. **3** a metal plate heated and placed over food to brown it. □□ **sal·a·man·drine** /-mándrin/ *adj.*

sa·la·mi /səláamee/ *n.* (*pl.* **salamis**) a highly seasoned orig. Italian sausage.

sal am·mo·ni·ac /sál əmóneeak/ *n.* ammonium chloride, a white crystalline salt.

sa·lar·i·at /səláireeət/ *n.* the salaried class.

S

SAILBOAT

The first recorded sailboat was used in the Nile Valley, Egypt, about 8,000 years ago. Sailboats have been widely used ever since – for pleasure, for competition, and for transporting goods and people. Boat sizes range from one-person dinghies to ocean-going yachts, which may have crews of 12 or more.

19TH-CENTURY TWO-MASTED SCHOONER

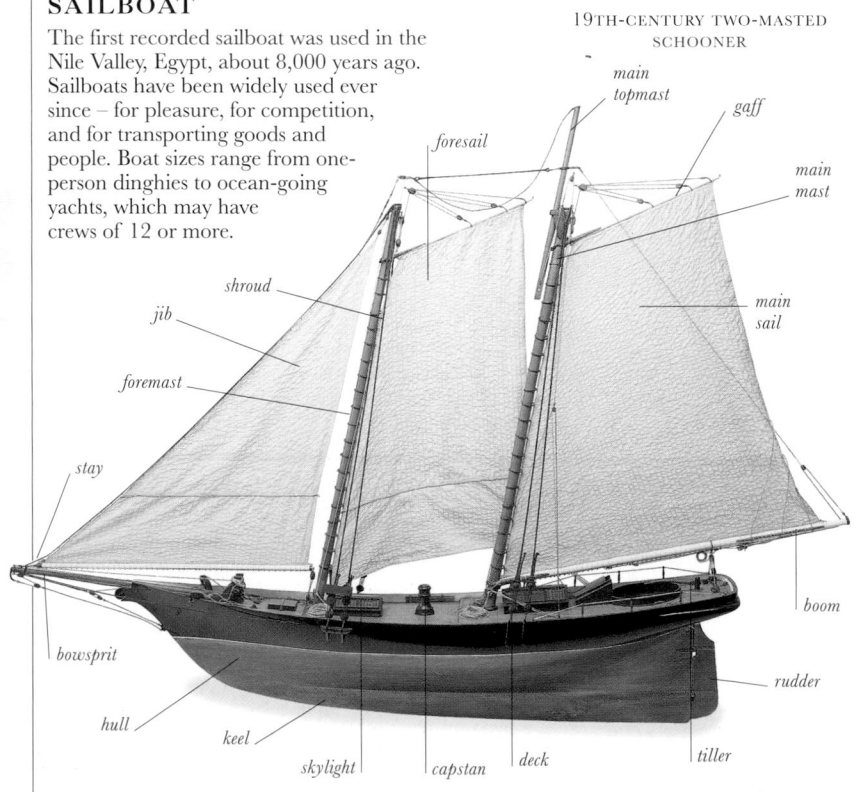

main topmast　*gaff*　*main mast*　*main sail*　*foresail*　*shroud*　*jib*　*foremast*　*stay*　*bowsprit*　*hull*　*keel*　*skylight*　*capstan*　*deck*　*tiller*　*rudder*　*boom*

sal·a·ry /sáləree/ *n. & v.* ● *n.* (*pl.* **-ies**) a fixed regular payment, usu. monthly or quarterly, made by an employer to an employee, esp. a white-collar worker (cf. WAGE *n.* 1). ● *v.tr.* (**-ies, -ied**) (usu. as **salaried** *adj.*) pay a salary to.

sale /sayl/ *n.* **1** the exchange of a commodity for money, etc.; an act of selling. **2** the amount sold (*the sales were enormous*). **3** the rapid disposal of goods at reduced prices for a period. **4 a** an event at which goods are sold. **b** a public auction. □ **for** (or **up for**) **sale** offered for purchase. **on sale** available for purchase, esp. at a reduced price.

sale·a·ble var. of SALABLE.

sal·ep /sáləp/ *n.* a starchy preparation of the dried tubers of various orchids, used in cooking and formerly medicinally.

sale·room /sáylrŏom, -rŏom/ *n.* esp. *Brit.* a salesroom.

sales·clerk /sáylzklərk/ *n.* a salesperson in a retail store.

sales·girl /sáylzgərl/ *n.* a saleswoman.

Sa·le·si·an /səleezhən, -shən/ *n. & adj.* ● *n.* a member of an educational religious order within the RC Church. ● *adj.* of or relating to this order.

sales·la·dy /sáylzlaydee/ *n.* (*pl.* **-ies**) a saleswoman.

sales·man /sáylzmən/ *n.* (*pl.* **-men**; *fem.* **saleswoman,** *pl.* **-women**) a person employed to sell goods or services in a store or on a route, etc.

sales·man·ship /sáylzmənship/ *n.* **1** skill in selling. **2** the techniques used in selling.

sales·per·son /sáylzpersən/ *n.* a salesman or saleswoman.

sales·room /sáylzrŏom, -rŏom/ *n.* a room for the display and purchase of items, esp. at an auction.

sales talk *n.* persuasive talk to promote the sale of goods or the acceptance of an idea, etc.

sales tax *n.* a tax on sales or on the receipts from sales.

Sa·li·an /sáyleeən, -yən/ *adj. & n.* ● *adj.* of or relating to the Salii, a 4th-c. Frankish people living near the Ijssel River, from which the Merovingians were descended. ● *n.* a member of this people.

sa·li·cet /sálisit/ *n.* an organ stop like a salicional but one octave higher.

sa·li·cin /sálisin/ *n.* (also **sa·li·cine** /-seen/) a bitter crystalline glucoside with analgesic properties, obtained from poplar and willow bark.

sa·li·cion·al /səlíshənəl/ *n.* an organ stop with a soft reedy tone like that of a willow pipe.

sal·i·cyl·ic ac·id /sálisílik/ *n.* a bitter chemical used as a fungicide and in the manufacture of aspirin and dyestuffs. □□ **sa·lic·y·late** /səlísilayt/ *n.*

sa·li·ent /sáylyənt/ *adj. & n.* ● *adj.* **1** prominent; conspicuous. **2** (of an angle, esp. in fortification) pointing outward. ● *n.* a salient angle or part of a work in fortification; an outward bulge in a line of military attack or defense. □□ **sa·li·ence** *n.* **sa·li·en·cy** *n.* **sa·li·ent·ly** *adv.*

sa·lif·er·ous /səlífərəs/ *adj. Geol.* (of rock, etc.) containing much salt.

sa·li·na /səlíənə, -lée-/ *n.* a salt lake.

sa·line /sáyleen, -lín/ *adj. & n.* ● *adj.* **1** (of natural waters, springs, etc.) impregnated with or containing salt or salts. **2** tasting of salt. **3** of chemical salts. **4** of the nature of a salt. **5** (of medicine) containing a salt or salts of alkaline metal or magnesium. ● *n.* **1** a saline substance. **2** a solution of salt in water. □□ **sa·lin·i·ty** /səlínitee/ *n.* **sal·i·ni·za·tion** /sálinizáyshən/ *n.* **sal·i·nom·e·ter** /sálinómitər/ *n.*

sa·li·va /səlívə/ *n.* liquid secreted into the mouth by glands to provide moisture and facilitate chewing and swallowing. ▷ DIGESTION. □□ **sal·i·var·y** /sáliveree/ *adj.*

sal·i·vate /sálivayt/ *v. intr.* secrete or discharge saliva esp. in excess or in greedy anticipation. □□ **sal·i·va·tion** /-váyshən/ *n.*

Salk vac·cine /sawlk/ *n.* a vaccine developed against polio.

SALAMANDER

Salamanders have small, regenerative limbs, a well-developed tail, webbed feet, and thin, rubbery skin. They are predominantly terrestrial and breathe through their skin as well as their lungs. Salamanders generally prefer damp, dark habitats, such as under logs or rocks. Salamander species range in length from 1 in. (2.5 cm) to around 6 ft (1.8 m).

EXAMPLES OF OTHER SALAMANDERS

eye　*head*

warning coloration

four-fingered forelimb

costal (rib) groove

EUROPEAN FIRE SALAMANDER
(*Salamandra salamandra*)

NORTH AMERICAN TIGER SALAMANDER
(*Ambystoma tigrinum*)

cylindrical tail

EXTERNAL FEATURES OF A SPOTTED SALAMANDER
(*Ambystoma maculatum*)

sal·let /sálit/ *n.* (also **sal·ade** /səláad/) *hist.* a light helmet with an outward-curving rear part.

sal·low /sálō/ *adj.* (**sallower, sallowest**) (of the skin or complexion, or of a person) of a sickly yellow or pale brown. □□ **sal·low·ness** *n.*

sal·ly /sálee/ *n. & v.* (*pl.* **-ies**) ● *n.* **1** a sudden charge from a fortification upon its besiegers. **2** an excursion. **3** a witticism; a piece of banter; a lively remark. **4** a sudden start into activity; an outburst. ● *v.ntr.* (**-ies, -ied**) **1** (usu. foll. by *out, forth*) go for a walk, set out on a journey, etc. **2** (usu. foll. by *out*) make a military sally.

Sal·ly Lunn /sálee lún/ *n.* a sweet, light teacake.

sal·ma·gun·di /sálməgúndee/ *n.* (*pl.* **salmagundis**) **1** a dish of chopped meat, anchovies, eggs, onions, and seasoning. **2** a miscellaneous collection or mixture.

Sal·ma·naz·ar /sálmənázər/ *n.* a wine bottle of about 12 times the standard size.

sal·mi /sálmee/ *n.* (*pl.* **salmis**) a ragout of partly roasted gamebirds.

salm·on /sámən/ *n. & adj.* ● *n.* (*pl.* same or (esp. of types) **salmons**) **1** ▼ any anadromous fish of the family Salmonidae, esp. of the genus *Salmo*, much prized for its (often smoked) pink flesh. **2** *Austral. & NZ* the barramundi or a similar fish. ● *adj.* salmon pink. □□ **sal·mo·noid** *adj. & n.* (in sense 1). **sal·mon·y** *adj.*

SALMON: ATLANTIC SALMON
(*Salmo salar*)

sal·mo·nel·la /sálmənélə/ *n.* (*pl.* **salmonellae** /-lee/) **1** any bacterium of the genus *Salmonella*, esp. any of various types causing food poisoning. **2** food poisoning caused by infection with salmonellae. □□ **sal·mo·nel·lo·sis** /-lōsis/ *n.*

sa·lon /səlón, saláwn/ *n.* **1** the reception room of a large or fashionable house. **2** a room or establishment where a hairdresser, beautician, etc., conducts business. **3** *hist.* a meeting of eminent people in the reception room of a lady of fashion.

sa·loon /səlŏon/ *n.* **1** a drinking establishment; a bar. **2** a public room on a ship. **3** a large public room used for a specified purpose (*billiard saloon*).

sa·loon keep·er *n.* a bartender or manager or owner of a bar.

sa·lo·pettes /sálōpéts/ *n.* padded or fleecy trousers with a high waist and shoulder straps, worn for skiing.

sal·pin·gec·to·my /sálpinjéktəmee/ *n.* (*pl.* **-ies**) *Med.* the surgical removal of the Fallopian tubes.

sal·pin·gi·tis /sálpinjítis/ *n. Med.* inflammation of the Fallopian tubes.

sal·sa /sáalsə/ *n.* **1** a kind of dance music of Latin American origin, incorporating jazz and rock elements. **2** a dance performed to this music. **3** a spicy sauce made from tomatoes, chilies, onions, etc., often served as a dip.

sal·si·fy /sálsifee, -fī/ *n.* (*pl.* **-ies**) **1** a European plant, *Tragopogon porrifolius*, with long cylindrical fleshy roots. **2** this root used as a vegetable.

SALT /sawlt/ *abbr.* Strategic Arms Limitation Talks (or Treaty).

salt /sawlt/ *n., adj., & v.* ● *n.* **1** (also **common salt**) sodium chloride; the substance that gives seawater its characteristic taste, got in crystalline form by mining or by the evaporation of seawater, and used for seasoning or preserving food, or for other purposes. **2** a chemical compound formed from the reaction of an acid with a base, with all or part of the hydrogen of the acid replaced by a metal or metallike radical. **3** piquancy; wit (*added salt to the conversation*). **4** (in *sing.* or *pl.*) **a** a substance resembling salt in taste, form, etc. (*bath salts; smelling salts*). **b** (esp. in *pl.*) this type of substance used as a laxative. **5** (also **old salt**) an experienced sailor. ● *adj.* **1** impregnated with, containing, or tasting of salt; cured or preserved or seasoned with salt. **2** (of a plant) growing in the sea or in salt marshes. **3** (of tears, etc.) bitter. **4** (of wit) pungent. ● *v.tr.* **1** cure or preserve with salt or brine. **2** season with salt. **3** make (a narrative, etc.) piquant. **4** sprinkle (the

S

ground, etc.) with salt. **5** treat with a solution of salt or mixture of salts. □ **salt away** (or **down**) *sl.* lay away money, etc.; save. **salt a mine** *sl.* introduce extraneous ore, material, etc., to make the source seem rich. **the salt of the earth** a person or people of great worthiness, reliability, honesty, etc. (Matt. 5:13). **take with a grain of salt** regard as exaggerated; be incredulous about. **worth one's salt** efficient; capable. □□ **salt·ish** *adj.* **salt·less** *adj.* **salt·ness** *n.*

salt-and-pep·per *adj.* with light and dark colors mixed together.

sal·ta·rel·lo /sáltərélō, sáwl-/ *n.* (*pl.* **-os** or **saltar·elli** /-lee/) an Italian and Spanish dance for one or two persons, with sudden skips.

sal·ta·tion /saltáyshən, sawl-/ *n.* **1** the act or an instance of leaping or dancing; a jump. **2** a sudden transition or movement. □□ **sal·ta·to·ry** /sáltətawree, -sáwl-/ *adj.* **sal·ta·to·ri·al** /-tətáwreeəl/ *adj.*

salt·bush /sáwltbŏŏsh/ *n.* an edible plant, *Atriplex hortensis*, with red, yellow, or green leaves sometimes used as a substitute for spinach or sorrel. Also called **orache**.

salt·cel·lar /sáwltselər/ *n.* a vessel holding salt for table use.

salt·er /sáwltər/ *n.* a manufacturer or dealer in salt.

sal·ti·grade /sáltigrayd, sáwl-/ *adj. & n. Zool.* ● *adj.* (of arthropods) moving by leaping or jumping. ● *n.* a saltigrade arthropod, e.g., a jumping spider, beach flea, etc.

sal·tine /sawltéen/ *n.* a lightly salted, square, flat cracker.

sal·tire /sáwlteer, -tīr, sál-/ *n. Heraldry* ◄ an ordinary formed by a bend and a bend sinister crossing like a St. Andrew's cross.

salt lake *n.* a lake of salt water.

salt lick *n.* **1** a place where animals go to lick salt from the ground. **2** this salt.

SALTIRE

salt marsh *n.* a marsh, esp. one flooded by the tide, often used as a pasture or for collecting water for salt making.

salt mine *n.* a mine yielding rock salt.

salt pan *n.* a vessel, or a depression near the sea, used for getting salt by evaporation.

salt·pe·ter /sáwltpéetər/ *n.* potassium nitrate, a white crystalline salty substance used in preserving meat and as a constituent of gunpowder.

salt·shak·er /sáwltshaykər/ *n.* a container of salt for sprinkling on food.

salt·wa·ter /sáwltwawtər/ *adj.* of or living in the sea.

salt wa·ter *n.* **1** sea water. **2** *sl.* tears.

salt·works /sáwltwərks/ *n.* a place where salt is produced.

salt·wort /sáwltwərt, -wawrt/ *n.* any plant of the genus *Salsola*; glasswort.

salt·y /sáwltee/ *adj.* (**saltier, saltiest**) **1** tasting of, containing, or preserved with salt. **2** racy, risqué. □□ **salt·i·ness** *n.*

sa·lu·bri·ous /səlŏŏbreeəs/ *adj.* **1** health-giving; healthy. **2** (of surroundings, etc.) pleasant; agreeable. □□ **sa·lu·bri·ous·ly** *adv.* **sa·lu·bri·ous·ness** *n.* **sa·lu·bri·ty** *n.*

sa·lu·ki /səlŏŏkee/ *n.* (*pl.* **salukis**) ▼ a tall, slender dog of a silky-coated breed.

SALUKI

sal·u·tar·y /sályəteree/ *adj.* producing good effects; beneficial.

sal·u·ta·tion /sályətáyshən/ *n.* **1** a sign or expression of greeting or recognition of another's arrival or departure. **2** (usu. in *pl.*) words spoken or written to inquire about another's health or well-being.

sa·lu·ta·to·ry /səlŏŏtətawree/ *adj.* of salutation.

sa·lute /səlŏŏt/ *n. & v.* ● *n.* **1** a gesture of respect, homage, or courteous recognition. **2 a** *Mil. & Naut.* a prescribed or specified movement of the hand or of weapons or flags as a sign of respect or recognition. **b** (prec. by *the*) the attitude taken by an individual soldier, sailor, policeman, etc., in saluting. **3** the discharge of a gun or guns as a ceremonial sign of respect or celebration. ● *v.* **1 a** *tr.* make a salute to. **b** *intr.* perform a salute. **2** *tr.* greet; make a salutation to. **3** *tr.* (foll. by *with*) receive or greet with (a smile, etc.). □ **take the salute 1** (of the highest officer present) acknowledge it by gesture as meant for him. **2** receive ceremonial salutes by members of a procession.

sal·vage /sálvij/ *n. & v.* ● *n.* **1** the rescue of a ship, its cargo, or other property, from loss at sea, destruction by fire, etc. **2** the property, etc., saved in this way. **3 a** the saving and utilization of waste paper, scrap material, etc. **b** the materials salvaged. ● *v.tr.* **1** save from a wreck, fire, etc. **2** retrieve or preserve in adverse circumstances (*tried to salvage some dignity*). □□ **sal·vage·a·ble** *adj.* **sal·vag·er** *n.*

sal·va·tion /salváyshən/ *n.* **1** the act of saving or being saved. **2** deliverance from sin and its consequences and admission to heaven. **3** a religious conversion. **4** a person or thing that saves (*was the salvation of*). □□ **sal·va·tion·ism** *n.* **sal·va·tion·ist** *n.* (both nouns esp. with ref. to the Salvation Army).

Sal·va·tion Ar·my *n.* a worldwide evangelical group organized on quasi-military lines for the revival of Christianity and helping the poor.

salve[1] /sav, saav/ *n. & v.* ● *n.* **1** a healing ointment. **2** a thing that is soothing or consoling for wounded feelings, an uneasy conscience, etc. ● *v.tr.* soothe (pride, self-love, conscience, etc.).

salve[2] /salv/ *v.tr.* **1** save (a ship or its cargo) from loss at sea. **2** save (property) from fire. □□ **salv·a·ble** *adj.*

sal·ver /sálvər/ *n.* a tray usu. of gold, silver, brass, or electroplate, on which drinks, letters, etc., are offered.

Sal·ve Re·gi·na /sáalvay rəjéenə/ *n.* **1** a Roman Catholic hymn or prayer said or sung to the Virgin Mary. **2** the music for this.

sal·vi·a /sálveeə/ *n.* ► any plant of the genus *Salvia*, esp. *S. splendens* with red or blue flowers.

sal·vo /sálvō/ *n.* (*pl.* **-oes** or **-os**) **1** the simultaneous firing of artillery or other guns. **2** a number of bombs released from aircraft at the same moment. **3** a round of applause.

sal vo·la·ti·le /sál vōlát'lee/ *n.* ammonium carbonate, esp. in the form of a flavored solution in alcohol used as smelling salts.

SALVIA: SCARLET SAGE (*Salvia splendens*)

sal·vor /sálvər/ *n.* a person or ship making or assisting in salvage.

SAM *abbr.* surface-to-air missile.

sa·ma·dhi /səmáadee/ *n. Buddhism & Hinduism* **1** a state of concentration induced by meditation. **2** a state into which a perfected holy man is said to pass at his apparent death.

sam·a·ra /sámərə, səmáirə, səmáa-/ *n. Bot.* a winged seed from the sycamore, ash, etc.

Sa·mar·i·tan /səmárit'n/ *n. & adj.* ● *n.* **1** (in full **good Samaritan**) a charitable or helpful person (with ref. to Luke 10:33, etc.). **2** a native of Samaria in West Jordan. ● *adj.* of Samaria or the Samaritans. □□ **Sa·mar·i·tan·ism** *n.*

sa·mar·i·um /səmáireeəm/ *n. Chem.* a soft, silvery metallic element of the lanthanide series, occurring naturally in the mineral monazite, etc., and used in making ferromagnetic alloys.

sam·ba /sámbə, sáam-/ *n. & v.* ● *n.* **1** a Brazilian dance of African origin. **2** a ballroom dance imitative of this. **3** the music for this. ● *v.intr.* (**sambas, sambaed** /-bəd/, **sambaing** /-bə-ing/) dance the samba.

sam·bar /sámbər, sáam-/ *n.* (also **sam·ba, samb·har**) either of two large deer, *Cervus unicolor* or *C. equinus*, native to S. Asia.

Sam Browne /sam brówn/ *n.* (in full **Sam Browne belt**) an army officer's belt and the shoulder strap supporting it.

sam·bu·ca /sambŏŏkə/ *n.* an Italian aniseed-flavored liqueur.

same /saym/ *adj., pron., & adv.* ● *adj.* **1** identical; not different; unchanged (*everyone was looking in the same direction; the same car was used in another crime*). **2** (usu. prec. by *this, these, that, those*) previously alluded to; just mentioned (*this same man was later my husband*). ● *pron.* (prec. by *the*) **1** the same person or thing (*the others asked for the same*). **2** *Law* or *archaic* the person or thing just mentioned (*detected the youth breaking in and apprehended the same*). ● *adv.* (usu. prec. by *the*) similarly; in the same way (*we all feel the same; I want to go, the same as you do*). □ **all** (or **just**) **the same** in spite of changed conditions, adverse circumstances, etc. (*but you should offer, all the same*). **at the same time 1** simultaneously. **2** notwithstanding. **be all** (or **just**) **the same to** an expression of indifference or impartiality (*it's all the same to me what we do*). **by the same token** see TOKEN. **same here** *colloq.* the same applies to me. **the same to you!** may you do, have, find, etc., the same thing. □□ **same·ness** *n.*

sam·i·sen /sámisen/ *n.* a long three-stringed Japanese guitar, played with a plectrum.

sam·ite /sámit, sáy-/ *n. hist.* a rich medieval dress fabric of silk sometimes interwoven with gold.

sam·iz·dat /sáamizdaat, səmyizdáat/ *n.* a system of clandestine publication of banned literature in the former USSR.

Sam·nite /sámnīt/ *n. & adj.* ● *n.* **1** a member of a people of ancient Italy often at war with republican Rome. **2** the language of this people. ● *adj.* of this people or their language.

Sa·mo·an /səmóən/ *n. & adj.* ● *n.* **1** a native of Samoa, a group of islands in the Pacific. **2** the language of this people. ● *adj.* of or relating to Samoa or its people or language.

sam·o·var /sáməvaar/ *n.* ▼ a Russian urn for making tea, with an internal heating tube to keep water at boiling point.

Sam·o·yed /sáməyed, səmóyed/ *n.* **1** a member of a people of northern Siberia. **2** the language of this people. **3** (also **samoyed**) **a** a dog of a white Arctic breed. **b** this breed.

Sam·o·yed·ic /sámə-yédik/ *n. & adj.* ● *n.* the language of the Samoyeds. ● *adj.* of or relating to the Samoyeds.

samp /samp/ *n.* **1** coarsely ground corn. **2** porridge made of this.

chimney

carrying handle

water container

air vents

spigot

SAMOVAR

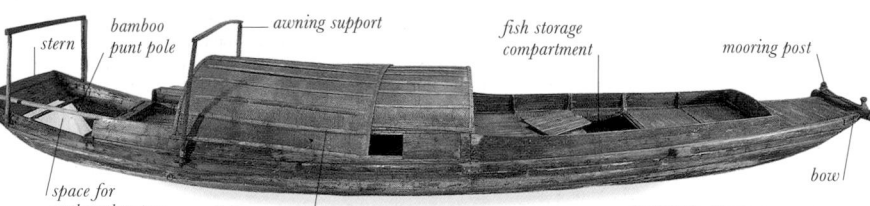

SAMPAN: CHINESE SAMPAN

stern · bamboo punt pole · awning support · fish storage compartment · mooring post · bow · space for outboard motors · sliding canopy

sam·pan /sámpan/ *n.* ▲ a small boat used in the Far East.

sam·phire /sámfīr/ *n.* **1** an umbelliferous maritime rock plant, *Crithmum maritimum*, with aromatic fleshy leaves used in pickles. **2** the glasswort.

sam·ple /sámpəl/ *n. & v.* ● *n.* **1** (also *attrib.*) a small part intended to show what the whole is like. **2** a small amount of fabric, food, or other commodity, given to a prospective customer. **3** a specimen, esp. one taken for scientific testing. **4** an illustrative or typical example. ● *v.tr.* **1** take or give samples of. **2** try the qualities of. **3** get a representative experience of.

sam·pler[1] /sámplər/ *n.* a piece of embroidery worked in various stitches as a specimen of proficiency (often displayed on a wall, etc.).

sam·pler[2] /sámplər/ *n.* **1** a person who samples. **2** a collection of representative items, etc.

sam·pling /sámpling/ *n.* a technique in electronic music involving digitally encoding a piece of sound and reusing it as part of a composition or recording.

sam·sa·ra /səmsáarə/ *n. Ind. Philos.* the endless cycle of death and rebirth to which life in the material world is bound. □□ **sam·sa·ric** *adj.*

sam·ska·ra /səmskáarə/ *n. Ind. Philos.* **1** a purificatory ceremony or rite marking an event in one's life. **2** a mental impression, instinct, or memory.

Sam·son /sámsən/ *n.* a person of great strength.

sam·u·rai /sámōōrī, sáa-/ *n.* (*pl.* same) **1** ▶ a Japanese army officer. **2** *hist.* a military retainer; a member of a military caste in Japan.

san·a·tive /sánətiv/ *adj.* **1** healing; curative. **2** of or tending to physical or moral health.

san·a·to·ri·um /sánətáwreeəm/ *n.* (*pl.* **sanatoriums** or **sanatoria** /-reeə/) an establishment for the treatment of invalids, esp. of convalescents and the chronically sick.

sanc·ti·fy /sángktifī/ *v.tr.* (**-ies, -ied**) **1** consecrate; set apart as holy. **2** free from sin. **3** make legitimate or binding by religious sanction; justify. **4** make productive of or conducive to holiness. □□ **sanc·ti·fi·ca·tion** /-fikáyshən/ *n.* **sanc·ti·fi·er** *n.*

sanc·ti·mo·ni·ous /sángktimṓneeəs/ *adj.* making a show of sanctity or piety. □□ **sanc·ti·mo·ni·ous·ly** *adv.* **sanc·ti·mo·ni·ous·ness** *n.* **sanc·ti·mo·ny** /sángktimṓnee/ *n.*

sanc·tion /sángkshən/ *n. & v.* ● *n.* **1** approval or encouragement given to an action, etc., by custom or tradition; express permission **2** confirmation of a law, etc. **3 a** a penalty for disobeying a law or rule, or a reward for obeying it. **b** a clause containing this. **4** *Ethics* a consideration operating to enforce obedience to any rule of conduct. **5** (esp. in *pl.*) esp. economic action by a nation to coerce another to conform to an international agreement or norms of conduct. ● *v.tr.* **1** authorize or agree to (an action, etc.). **2** ratify; make binding. □□ **sanc·tion·a·ble** *adj.*

sanc·ti·tude /sángktitōōd, -tyōōd/ *n. archaic* saintliness.

SAMURAI: 19TH-CENTURY SAMURAI ARMOR

sanc·ti·ty /sángktitee/ *n.* (*pl.* **-ies**) **1** holiness of life; saintliness. **2** sacredness. **3** inviolability. **4** (in *pl.*) sacred obligations, feelings, etc.

sanc·tu·ar·y /sángkchōōəree/ *n.* (*pl.* **-ies**) **1** a holy place. **2 a** the holiest part of a temple, etc. **b** the part of the chancel containing the high altar. **3** a place of refuge for birds, wild animals, etc. **4** a place of refuge. **5 a** immunity from arrest. **b** the right to offer this. **6** *hist.* a sacred place where a fugitive from the law or a debtor was secured by medieval church law against arrest or violence. □ **take sanctuary** resort to a place of refuge.

sanc·tum /sángktəm/ *n.* (*pl.* **sanctums**) **1** a holy place. **2** *colloq.* a person's private room, study, or den.

Sanc·tus /sángktəs, sáangktōōs/ *n.* (also **sanctus**) **1** the prayer or hymn beginning "Holy, holy, holy" said or sung at the end of the Eucharistic preface. **2** the music for this.

sand /sand/ *n. & v.* ● *n.* **1** a loose granular substance resulting from the wearing down of esp. siliceous rocks and found on the seashore, riverbeds, deserts, etc. **2** (in *pl.*) grains of sand. **3** (in *pl.*) an expanse or tracts of sand. **4** a light yellow-brown color like that of sand. **5** (in *pl.*) a sandbank. ● *v.tr.* **1** smooth with sandpaper or sand. **2** sprinkle or overlay with sand. □ **the sands are running out** the allotted time is nearly at an end. □□ **sand·er** *n.* **sand·like** *adj.*

san·dal[1] /sánd'l/ *n.* a light shoe with an openwork upper or no upper, attached to the foot usu. by straps.

san·dal[2] /sánd'l/ *n.* = SANDALWOOD.

san·dal tree *n.* any tree yielding sandalwood, esp. the white sandalwood.

san·dal·wood /sánd'lwŏŏd/ *n.* **1** the scented wood of a sandal tree. **2** a perfume derived from this.

san·da·rac /sándərak/ *n.* (also **san·da·rach**) the gummy resin of a N. African conifer, *Tetraclinis articulata*, used in making varnish.

sand·bag /sándbag/ *n. & v.* ● *n.* a bag filled with sand for use: **1** for making temporary defenses or for the protection of a building, etc., against blast and splinters or floodwaters. **2** as ballast esp. for a boat or balloon. **3** as a weapon to inflict a heavy blow without leaving a mark. **4** to stop a draft from a window or door. ● *v.tr.* (**-bagged, -bagging**) **1** barricade or defend. **2** place sandbags against (a window, chink, etc.). **3** fell with a blow from a sandbag. **4** coerce by harsh means. □□ **sand·bag·ger** *n.*

sand·bank /sándbangk/ *n.* a deposit of sand forming a shallow place in the sea.

sand·bar /sándbaar/ *n.* a sandbank at the mouth of a river or on the coast.

sand·blast /sándblast/ *v. & n.* ● *v.tr.* roughen, treat, or clean with a jet of sand driven by compressed steam or air. ● *n.* this jet. □□ **sand·blast·er** *n.*

sand·box /sándboks/ *n.* **1** a box of sand, esp. for children to play in.

sand·cas·tle /sándkasəl/ *n.* a shape like a castle made in sand, usu. by a child.

sand dol·lar *n.* any of various round, flat sea urchins, esp. of the order Clypeasteroida.

sand dune *n.* (also **sand hill**) a mound of sand formed by the wind.

san·dhi /sándee, sáan-/ *n. Gram.* the process whereby the form of a word changes as a result of its position in an utterance (e.g., the change from *a* to *an* before a vowel).

sand·hog /sándhawg, -hog/ *n.* a person who works underwater laying foundations, making tunnels, etc.

San·di·ni·sta /sandinéestə/ *n.* a member of a left-wing Nicaraguan political organization, in power from 1979 until 1990.

san·di·ver /sándivər/ *n.* liquid scum formed in glassmaking.

sand·lot /sándlot/ *n.* a piece of unoccupied sandy land used for children's games.

sand·man /sándman/ *n.* the personification of tiredness causing children's eyes to smart toward bedtime.

sand·pa·per /sándpaypər/ *n. & v.* ● *n.* paper with sand or another abrasive stuck to it for smoothing or polishing. ● *v.tr.* smooth with sandpaper.

sand·pi·per /sándpīpər/ *n.* any of various wading shore birds of the family Scolopacidae.

sand·pit /sándpit/ *n.* a pit from which sand is excavated.

sand·stone /sándstōn/ *n.* ▶ a sedimentary rock of consolidated sand. ▷ ROCK CYCLE, SEDIMENT

SANDSTONE

sand·storm /sándstawrm/ *n.* a desert storm of wind with clouds of sand.

sand·wich /sándwich, sán-/ *n. & v.* ● *n.* two or more slices of bread with a filling of meat, cheese, etc., between them. ● *v.tr.* **1** put (a thing, statement, etc.) between two of another character. **2** squeeze in between others (*sat sandwiched in the middle*).

sand·worm /sándwərm/ *n.* ▶ a carnivorous marine polychaete worm of the family Nereidae.

sand·y /sándee/ *adj.* (**sandier, sandiest**) **1** having the texture of sand. **2** having much sand. **3 a** (of hair) yellowish-red. **b** (of a person) having sandy hair. □□ **sand·i·ness** *n.* **sand·y·ish** *adj.*

SANDWORM

sane /sayn/ *adj.* **1** of sound mind; not mad. **2** (of views, etc.) moderate; sensible. □□ **sane·ly** *adv.* **sane·ness** *n.*

sang *past* of SING.

san·ga·ree /sánggəree/ *n.* **1** a cold drink of wine diluted and spiced. **2** sangria.

sang-froid /saanfrwáa/ *n.* composure, coolness, etc., in danger or under agitating circumstances.

san·gri·a /sanggreeə/ *n.* a sweet Spanish drink of iced red wine with lemonade, fruit, spices, etc.

san·guin·ar·y /sángwəneree/ *adj.* involving or causing much bloodshed.

san·guine /sánggwin/ *adj.* **1** optimistic; confident. **2** (of the complexion) florid; ruddy. □□ **san·guine·ly** *adv.* **san·guine·ness** *n.* (both in sense 1).

San·hed·rin /sanhédrin, -hée-, saan-/ *n.* (also **San·hed·rim** /-drim/) the highest court of justice and the supreme council in ancient Jerusalem.

san·i·cle /sánikəl/ *n.* any umbelliferous plant of the genus *Sanicula*, esp. *S. europaea*, formerly believed to have healing properties.

san·i·tar·i·um /sánitáireeəm/ *n.* (*pl.* **sanitariums** or **sanitaria** /-reeə/) **1** an establishment for the restoration of health; sanatorium. **2** a health resort.

san·i·tar·y /sániteree/ *adj.* **1** of the conditions that affect health. **2** hygienic. □□ **san·i·tar·i·an** /-áireeən/ *n. & adj.* **san·i·tar·i·ly** *adv.*

san·i·tar·y en·gi·neer *n.* a person dealing with systems needed to maintain public health.

S

san·i·tar·y nap·kin *n.* an absorbent pad used during menstruation.

san·i·ta·tion /sánitáyshən/ *n.* **1** sanitary conditions. **2** the maintenance or improving of these. **3** the disposal of sewage and refuse from houses, etc.

san·i·tize /sánitīz/ *v.tr.* **1** make sanitary. **2** render (information, etc.) more acceptable by removing improper or disturbing material. □□ **san·i·tiz·er** *n.*

san·i·ty /sánitee/ *n.* **1 a** the state of being sane. **b** mental health. **2** the tendency to avoid extreme views.

sans /sanz, sоɴ/ *prep.* archaic or joc. without.

San·skrit /sánskrit/ *n. & adj.* ● *n.* the ancient and sacred language of the Hindus in India. ● *adj.* of or in this language. □□ **San·skrit·ic** /-skrítik/ *adj.* **San·skrit·ist** *n.*

sans ser·if /sansérif/ *n. & adj.* (also **san·ser·if**) *Printing* ● *n.* a form of type without serifs. ▷ TYPE. ● *adj.* without serifs.

San·ta Claus /sántə klawz/ *n.* (also *colloq.* **Santa**) a legendary person said to bring children presents on the night before Christmas.

sap[1] /sap/ *n. & v.* ● *n.* **1** the vital juice circulating in plants. **2** vigor; vitality. **3** = SAPWOOD. ● *v.tr.* (**sapped, sapping**) drain or dry (wood) of sap. □□ **sap·ful** *adj.* **sap·less** *adj.*

sap[2] /sap/ *n. & v.* ● *n.* a tunnel or trench to conceal assailants' approach to a fortified place. ● *v.* (**sapped, sapping**) **1** *intr.* **a** dig a sap or saps. **b** approach by a sap. **2** *tr.* undermine; make insecure by removing the foundations. **3** *tr.* weaken or destroy insidiously.

sap[3] /sap/ *n. sl.* a foolish person.

sap·id /sápid/ *adj. literary* **1** having flavor; palatable; not insipid. **2** (of talk, writing, etc.) not vapid or uninteresting.

sa·pi·ent /sáypeeənt/ *adj. literary* **1** wise. **2** aping wisdom. □□ **sa·pi·ence** *n.* **sa·pi·ent·ly** *adv.*

sap·ling /sápling/ *n.* **1** a young tree. **2** a youth. **3** a greyhound in its first year.

sap·o·dil·la /sápədílə, -deeyə/ *n.* a large evergreen tropical American tree, *Manilkara zapota*, with sap from which chicle is obtained.

sa·pon·i·fy /səpónifī/ *v.* (-**ies, -ied**) **1** *tr.* turn (fat or oil) into soap by reaction with an alkali. **2** *tr.* convert (an ester) to an acid and alcohol. **3** *intr.* become saponified. □□ **sa·pon·i·fi·a·ble** *adj.* **sa·pon·i·fi·ca·tion** /-fikáyshən/ *n.*

sap·o·nin /sápənin/ *n.* any of a group of plant glycosides, esp. those derived from the bark of the tree *Quillaja saponaria*, that foam when shaken with water and are used in detergents and fire extinguishers.

sa·por /sáypər, -pawr/ *n.* **1** a quality perceptible by taste, e.g., sweetness. **2** the distinctive taste of a substance. **3** the sensation of taste.

sap·pan·wood /sápanwood, -pán-/ *n.* (also **sap·an·wood**) the heartwood of an E. Indian tree, *Caesalpinia sappan*, formerly used as a source of red dye.

sap·per /sápər/ *n.* **1** a person who digs saps. **2** a military demolitions expert.

Sap·phic /sáfik/ *adj. & n.* ● *adj.* **1** of or relating to Sappho, poetess of Lesbos *c.*600 BC, or her poetry. **2** lesbian. ● *n.* (in *pl.*) (**sapphics**) verse in a meter associated with Sappho.

sap·phire /sáfīr/ *n. & adj.* ● *n.* **1** ◄ a transparent blue precious stone consisting of corundum. ▷ GEM. **2** precious transparent corundum of any color. **3** the bright blue of a sapphire. ● *adj.* of sapphire blue. □□ **sap·phir·ine** /sáfirīn, -rin, -reen/ *adj.*

sap·py /sápee/ *adj.* (**sappier, sappiest**) **1** full of sap. **2** young and vigorous. **3** overly emotional. □□ **sap·pi·ly** *adv.* **sap·pi·ness** *n.*

sapro- /sáprō/ *comb. form Biol.* rotten, putrefying.

SAPPHIRE

sap·ro·gen·ic /sáprəjénik/ *adj.* causing or produced by putrefaction.

sa·proph·a·gous /saprófəgəs/ *adj.* feeding on decaying matter.

sap·ro·phyte /sáprəfīt/ *n.* ► any plant or microorganism living on dead or decayed organic matter. □□ **sap·ro·phyt·ic** /-fítik/ *adj.*

sap·wood /sápwood/ *n.* the soft outer layers of recently formed wood between the heartwood and the bark. ▷ WOOD

SAPROPHYTE: HONEY MUSHROOM ON DEAD WOOD

sar·a·band /sárəband/ *n.* **1** a stately Spanish dance. **2** music for this or in its rhythm, usu. in triple time often with a long note on the second beat of the bar.

Sar·a·cen /sárəsən/ *n. & adj. hist.* ● *n.* **1** an Arab or Muslim at the time of the Crusades. **2** a nomad of the Syrian and Arabian desert. ● *adj.* of the Saracens. □□ **Sar·a·cen·ic** /sárəsénik/ *adj.*

sar·casm /saárkazəm/ *n.* **1** a bitter or wounding remark. **2** language consisting of such remarks. **3** the use of this. □□ **sar·cas·tic** /-kástik/ *adj.* **sar·cas·ti·cal·ly** *adv.*

sarce·net /saársənit/ *n.* (also **sarse·net**) a fine, soft, silk material used esp. for linings.

sar·co·ma /saarkṓmə/ *n.* (*pl.* **sarcomas** or **sarco·mata** /-mətə/) a malignant tumor of connective tissue. □□ **sar·co·ma·to·sis** /-mətṓsis/ *n.* **sar·co·ma·tous** *adj.*

sar·coph·a·gus /saarkófəgəs/ *n.* (*pl.* **sarcophagi** /-gī, -jī/) a stone coffin.

sar·cous /saárkəs/ *adj.* consisting of flesh or muscle.

sard /saard/ *n.* a yellow or orange-red cornelian.

sar·dine /saardeén/ *n.* a young pilchard or similar young or small herringlike marine fish. ● **like sar·dines** crowded close together (as sardines are in tins).

sar·di·us /saárdeeəs/ *n. Bibl.*, etc., a precious stone.

sar·don·ic /saardónik/ *adj.* **1** grimly jocular. **2** (of laughter, etc.) bitterly mocking or cynical. □□ **sar·don·i·cal·ly** *adv.* **sar·don·i·cism** /-nisizəm/ *n.*

sar·don·yx /saardóniks, saárd'n-/ *n.* ◄ onyx in which white layers alternate with sard. ▷ GEM

sa·ree var. of SARI.

sar·gas·so /saargásō/ *n.* (also **sar·gas·sum**) (*pl.* **-os** or **-oes** or **sar·gassa**) any seaweed of the genus *Sargassum*, with berrylike air vessels, found floating in island-like masses.

sarge /saarj/ *n. sl.* sergeant.

sa·ri /saáree/ *n.* (also **sa·ree**) (*pl.* **saris** or **sarees**) a length of cotton or silk draped around the body, traditionally worn as a main garment by women of India.

SARDONYX

sar·men·tose /saárməntōs/ *adj.* (also **sar·men·tous** /-méntəs/) *Bot.* having long, thin trailing shoots.

sa·rong /səráwng, -róng/ *n.* **1** a Malay and Javanese garment consisting of a long strip of cloth worn by both sexes tucked around the waist or under the armpits. **2** a woman's garment resembling this.

sar·sa·pa·ril·la /sáspərílə, saárs-/ *n.* **1** a preparation of the dried roots of various plants, used to flavor some drinks and medicines and formerly as a tonic. **2** any of the plants yielding this.

sar·sen /saársən/ *n. Geol.* a sandstone boulder carried by ice during a glacial period.

sarse·net var. of SARCENET.

sar·to·ri·al /saartáwreeəl/ *adj.* **1** of a tailor or tailoring. **2** of men's clothes. □□ **sar·to·ri·al·ly** *adv.*

sar·to·ri·us /saartáwreeəs/ *n. Anat.* the long, narrow muscle running across the front of each thigh.

Sar·um use /sáirəm/ *n. Eccl.* the order of divine service used in the diocese of Salisbury before the Reformation.

s.a.s.e. *abbr.* self-addressed stamped envelope.

sash[1] /sash/ *n.* a strip or loop of cloth worn over one shoulder or around the waist. □□ **sashed** *adj.*

sash[2] /sash/ *n.* a frame holding the glass in a window and usu. made to slide up and down in the grooves of a window aperture. ▷ SASH WINDOW. □□ **sashed** *adj.*

sa·shay /sasháy/ *v.intr. colloq.* walk ostentatiously, casually, or diagonally.

sa·shi·mi /saashéemee/ *n.* a Japanese dish of garnished raw fish in thin slices.

sash win·dow *n.* ▼ a window with one or two sashes of which one or each can be slid vertically over the other to make an opening.

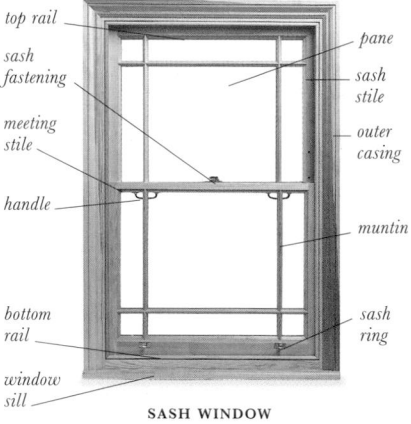

SASH WINDOW

Sask. *abbr.* Saskatchewan.

Sas·quatch /sáskwoch, -kwach/ *n.* a supposed yeti-like animal of NW America. Also called **Bigfoot**.

sass /sas/ *n. & v. colloq.* ● *n.* impudence; disrespectful mannerism or speech. ● *v.tr.* be impudent to.

sas·sa·fras /sásəfras/ *n.* **1** ► a small tree, *Sassafras albidum*, native to N. America, with aromatic leaves and bark. **2** a preparation of oil extracted from the leaves or bark of this tree, used medicinally or in perfumery.

Sas·sa·ni·an /sasáyneeən/ *n. & adj.* (also **Sas·sa·nid** /sásənid/) ● *n.* a member of a Persian dynasty ruling 211–651. ● *adj.* of or relating to this dynasty.

sas·sy /sásee/ *adj.* (**sassier, sassiest**) *colloq.* = SAUCY. □□ **sas·si·ly** *adv.* **sas·si·ness** *n.*

sas·tru·gi /sastrṓogee/ *n.pl.* wavelike irregularities on the surface of hard polar snow, caused by winds.

SAT *abbr. Trademark* Scholastic Assessment Test.

Sat. *abbr.* Saturday.

sat past and past part. of SIT.

Sa·tan /sáyt'n/ *n.* the Devil; Lucifer.

sa·tan·ic /sətánik, say-/ *adj.* **1** of, like, or befitting Satan. **2** diabolical; hellish. □□ **sa·tan·i·cal·ly** *adv.*

Sa·tan·ism /sáyt'nizəm/ *n.* **1** the worship of Satan. **2** the pursuit of evil for its own sake. □□ **Sa·tan·ist** *n.* **Sa·tan·ize** *v.tr.*

SASSAFRAS (*Sassafras albidum*)

three-lobed leaf

root bark

Sa·tan·ol·o·gy /sáyt'nólɵjee/ *n.* **1** beliefs concerning the Devil. **2** a history or collection of these.

sa·tay /saátay/ *n.* (also **sa·tai**, **saté**) an Indonesian and Malaysian dish consisting of small pieces of meat grilled on a skewer and usu. served with spiced peanut sauce.

satch·el /sáchɵl/ *n.* a small bag usu. of leather and hung from the shoulder with a strap, for carrying books, etc., esp. to and from school.

sate /sayt/ *v.tr.* **1** gratify to the full. **2** cloy; surfeit (*sated with pleasure*).

sa·teen /sateén/ *n.* cotton fabric woven like satin with a glossy surface.

sat·el·lite /sát'līt/ *n. & adj.* ● *n.* **1** a celestial body orbiting the earth or another planet. ▷ ORBIT. **2** ▼ an artificial body placed in orbit around the Earth or another planet. **3** a follower; a hanger-on. **4** an underling; a member of an important person's staff or retinue. ● *adj.* transmitted by satellite (*satellite communications; satellite television*).

sat·el·lite dish *n.* ◄ a dish-shaped antenna for receiving broadcasting signals transmitted by satellite.

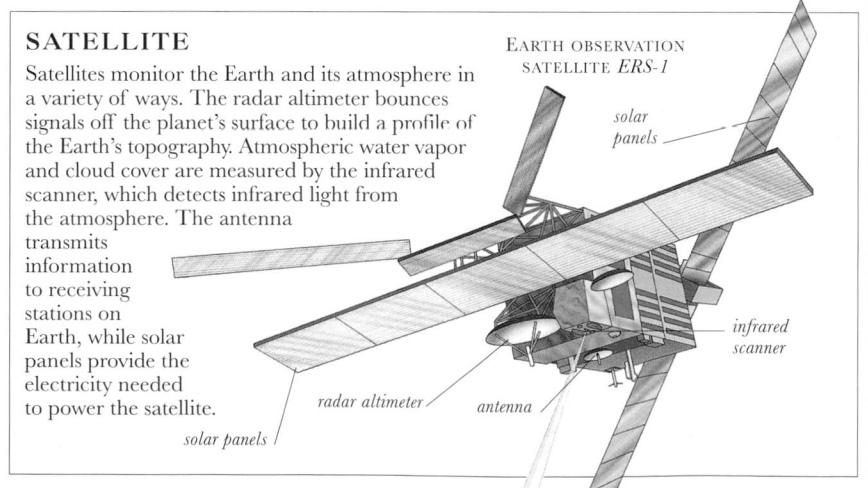

SATELLITE DISH:
HOME TELEVISION
SATELLITE DISH

mounting bracket
reflector
horn with weather shield
low-noise block

sa·ti var. of SUTTEE.

sa·ti·ate /sáysheeayt/ *adj. & v.* ● *adj. archaic* satiated. ● *v.tr.* = SATE. □□ **sa·tia·ble** /-shɵbɵl/ *adj. archaic*. **sa·ti·a·tion** /-áyshɵn/ *n.*

sa·ti·e·ty /sɵtí-itee/ *n.* **1** the state of being glutted or satiated. **2** the feeling of having too much of something. **3** (foll. by *of*) a cloyed dislike of. □ **to satiety** to an extent beyond what is desired.

sat·in /sát'n/ *n. & adj.* ● *n.* a fabric of silk or various synthetic fibers, with a glossy surface on one side. ● *adj.* smooth as satin □□ **sat·in·ized** *adj.* **sat·in·y** *adj.*

sat·i·net /sát'nét/ *n.* (also **sat·i·nette**) a satinlike fabric made partly or wholly of cotton or synthetic fiber.

sat·in fin·ish *n.* **1** a polish given to silver, etc., with a metallic brush. **2** any effect resembling satin in texture produced on materials in various ways.

sat·in stitch *n.* a long, straight embroidery stitch, giving the appearance of satin.

sat·in·wood /sát'nwŏŏd/ *n.* **1 a** (in full **Ceylon satinwood**) a tree, *Chloroxylon swietenia*, native to central and southern India and Sri Lanka. **b** (in full **West Indian satinwood**) a tree, *Fagara flava*, native to the West Indies, Bermuda, and southern Florida. **2** the yellow, glossy wood of these trees.

sat·ire /sátīr/ *n.* **1** the use of ridicule, irony, sarcasm, etc., to expose folly or vice or to lampoon an individual. **2** a work using satire. **3** this branch of literature.

sa·tir·ic /sɵtírik/ *adj.* **1** of satire or satires. **2** containing satire (*wrote a satiric review*). **3** writing satire (*a satiric poet*).

sa·tir·i·cal /sɵtírikɵl/ *adj.* **1** = SATIRIC. **2** given to the use of satire in speech or writing or to cynical observation of others; sarcastic; humorously critical. □□ **sa·tir·i·cal·ly** *adv.*

sat·i·rist /sátɵrist/ *n.* **1** a writer of satires. **2** a satirical person.

sat·i·rize /sátɵrīz/ *v.tr.* **1** assail or ridicule with satire. **2** write a satire upon. **3** describe satirically. □□ **sat·i·ri·za·tion** *n.*

sat·is·fac·tion /sátisfákshɵn/ *n.* **1** the act or an instance of satisfying; the state of being satisfied (*heard this with great satisfaction*). **2** a thing that satisfies desire or gratifies feeling (*is a great satisfaction to me*). **3** a thing that settles an obligation or pays a debt. **4** (foll. by *for*) atonement (*demanded satisfaction*). □ **to one's satisfaction** so that one is satisfied.

sat·is·fac·to·ry /sátisfáktɵree/ *adj.* **1** adequate; giving satisfaction (*was a satisfactory pupil*). **2** satisfying expectations or needs; leaving no room for complaint (*a satisfactory result*). □□ **sat·is·fac·to·ri·ly** *adv.* **sat·is·fac·to·ri·ness** *n.*

sat·is·fy /sátisfī/ *v.* (**-ies**, **-ied**) **1** *tr.* **a** meet the expectations or desires of; comply with (a demand) **b** be accepted by (a person, his or her taste) as adequate; be equal to (a preconception, etc.). **2** *tr.* put an end to (an appetite or want) by supplying what was required. **3** *tr.* rid (a person) of an appetite or want in a similar way. **4** *intr.* give satisfaction; leave nothing to be desired. **5** *tr.* pay (a debt or creditor). **6** *tr.* adequately meet, fulfill, or comply with (conditions, obligations, etc.) (*has satisfied all the legal conditions*). **7** *tr.* provide with adequate information or proof; convince (*satisfied the others that they were right; satisfy the court of their innocence*). **8** *tr. Math.* (of a quantity) make (an equation) true. **9** *tr.* (in *passive*) **a** (foll. by *with*) contented or pleased with. **b** (foll. by *to*) demand no more than or consider it enough to do. □□ **sat·is·fy·ing** *adj.* **sat·is·fy·ing·ly** *adv.*

sa·to·ri /sɵtáwree/ *n. Buddhism* sudden enlightenment.

sa·trap /sátrap, sáy/ *n.* **1** a provincial governor in the ancient Persian empire. **2** a subordinate ruler, colonial governor, etc.

sat·su·ma /satsŏŏmɵ, sátsŏŏmɵ/ *n.* **1** a variety of tangerine orig. grown in Japan. ▷ CITRUS FRUIT. **2** (**Satsuma**) (in full **Satsuma ware**) cream-colored Japanese pottery.

sat·u·rate /sáchɵrayt/ *v.tr.* **1** fill with moisture; soak thoroughly. **2** fill to capacity. **3** cause (a substance) to absorb, hold, or combine with the greatest possible amount of another substance, or of moisture, magnetism, electricity, etc. **4** supply (a market) beyond the point at which the demand for a product is satisfied. **5** (foll. by *with*, *in*) imbue with or steep in (learning, tradition, prejudice, etc.). **6** overwhelm by concentrated bombing. **7** (as **saturated** *adj.*) **a** (of color) full; rich; free from an admixture of white. **b** (of fat molecules) containing the greatest number of hydrogen atoms. □□ **sat·u·ra·ble** /-rɵbɵl/ *adj.*

sat·u·ra·tion /sáchɵráyshɵn/ *n.* the act or an instance of saturating; the state of being saturated.

sat·u·ra·tion point *n.* the stage beyond which no more can be absorbed or accepted.

Sat·ur·day /sátɵrday, -dee/ *n. & adv.* ● *n.* the seventh day of the week, following Friday. ● *adv. colloq.* **1** on Saturday. **2** (**Saturdays**) on Saturdays; each Saturday.

Sat·urn /sátɵrn/ *n.* **1 a** ▲ the sixth planet from the Sun, with a system of broad flat rings circling it, and the most distant of the five planets known in the ancient world. ▷ SOLAR SYSTEM. **b** *Astrol.* Saturn as a supposed astrological influence on those born under its sign, characterized by coldness and gloominess. **2** *Alchemy* the metal lead. □□ **Sat·ur·ni·an** /satárneeɵn/ *adj.*

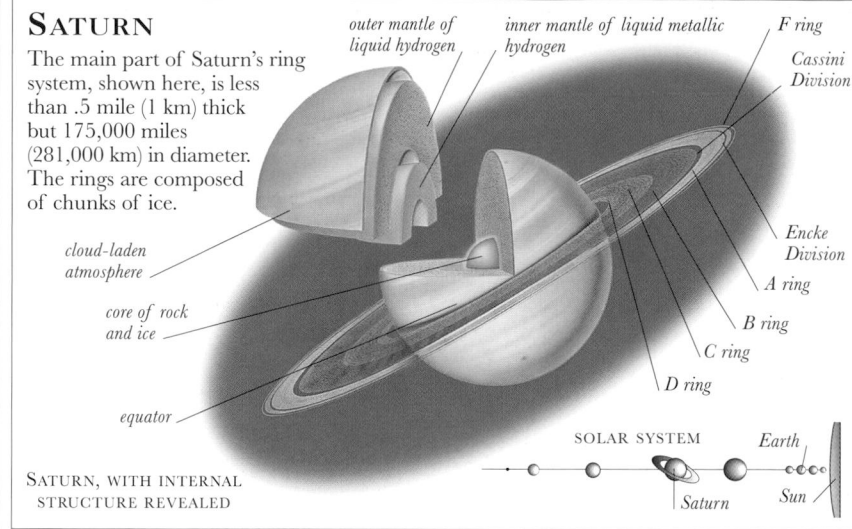

SATURN

The main part of Saturn's ring system, shown here, is less than .5 mile (1 km) thick but 175,000 miles (281,000 km) in diameter. The rings are composed of chunks of ice.

outer mantle of liquid hydrogen
inner mantle of liquid metallic hydrogen
F ring
Cassini Division
Encke Division
A ring
B ring
C ring
D ring
cloud-laden atmosphere
core of rock and ice
equator

SOLAR SYSTEM
Earth
Saturn
Sun

SATURN, WITH INTERNAL
STRUCTURE REVEALED

SATELLITE

Satellites monitor the Earth and its atmosphere in a variety of ways. The radar altimeter bounces signals off the planet's surface to build a profile of the Earth's topography. Atmospheric water vapor and cloud cover are measured by the infrared scanner, which detects infrared light from the atmosphere. The antenna transmits information to receiving stations on Earth, while solar panels provide the electricity needed to power the satellite.

EARTH OBSERVATION
SATELLITE *ERS-1*

solar panels
infrared scanner
radar altimeter
antenna
solar panels

S

sat·ur·na·li·a /sátərnáyleeə/ n. (pl. same or **saturnalias**) **1** (usu. **Saturnalia**) Rom.Hist. the festival of Saturn in December, characterized by unrestrained merrymaking. **2** (as sing. or pl.) a scene of wild revelry. □□ **sat·ur·na·li·an** adj.

sat·ur·nine /sátərnīn/ adj. **1** of a sluggish gloomy temperament. **2** (of looks, etc.) dark and brooding.

sat·ya·gra·ha /sutyáagrəhə/ n. Ind. **1** hist. a policy of passive resistance to British rule advocated by Gandhi. **2** passive resistance as a policy.

sa·tyr /sáytər, sát-/ n. **1** ◀ (in Greek mythology) one of a class of Greek woodland gods with a horse's ears and tail, or (in Roman representations) with a goat's ears, tail, legs, and budding horns. **2** a lustful or sensual man.

sa·ty·ri·a·sis /sáytiríəsis, sát-/ n. Med. excessive sexual desire in men.

sat·y·rid /sáytərid, sát-, sətírid/ n. any butterfly of the family Satyridae, with distinctive eyelike markings on the wings.

sauce /saws/ n. & v. ● n. **1** any of various liquid or semisolid preparations taken as a relish with food; the liquid constituent of a dish (mint sauce; tomato sauce; chicken in a lemon sauce). **2** something adding piquancy or excitement. **3** esp. Brit. colloq. impudence; impertinence. **4** stewed fruit, etc., eaten as dessert or used as a garnish. ● v.tr. **1** colloq. be impudent to. **2** archaic **a** season with sauce or condiments. **b** add excitement to. □□ **sauce·less** adj.

SATYR: GREEK GOD PAN

sauce·boat /sáwsbōt/ n. a small dish used for serving sauces, etc.

sauce·pan /sáwspan/ n. a cooking pan, usu. round with a lid and a long handle at the side, used for boiling, stewing, etc., on top of a stove. □□ **sauce·pan·ful** n. (pl. **-fuls**).

sau·cer /sáwsər/ n. **1** a shallow circular dish used for standing a cup on. **2** any similar dish used to stand a plant pot, etc., on. □□ **sau·cer·ful** n. (pl. **-fuls**). **sau·cer·less** adj.

sau·cy /sáwsee/ adj. (**saucier**, **sauciest**) **1** impudent. **2** colloq. smart-looking (a saucy hat). **3** colloq. smutty; suggestive. □□ **sau·ci·ly** adv. **sau·ci·ness** n.

Sau·di /sówdee, sáw-/ n. & adj. (also **Sau·di A·ra·bi·an**) ● n. (pl. **Saudis**) **1 a** a native or national of Saudi Arabia. **b** a person of Saudi descent. **2** a member of the dynasty founded by King Saud. ● adj. of or relating to Saudi Arabia or the Saudi dynasty.

sau·er·kraut /sówərkrowt/ n. a German dish of chopped pickled cabbage.

sau·ger /sáwgər/ n. a small N. American pike perch.

Sauk /sawk/ n. (also **Sac**) **1 a** a N. American people native to Wisconsin. **b** a member of this people. **2** the language of this people.

sau·na /sáwnə, sow-/ n. **1** a Finnish-style steam bath. **2** a building used for this.

saun·ter /sáwntər/ v. & n. ● v.intr. **1** walk slowly; stroll. **2** proceed without hurry or effort. ● n. **1** a leisurely ramble. **2** a slow gait. □□ **saun·ter·er** n.

sau·ri·an /sáwreeən/ adj. of or like a lizard.

sau·ro·pod /sáwrōpod/ n. any of a group of plant-eating dinosaurs with a long neck and tail, and four thick limbs. ▷ DINOSAUR

sau·ry /sáwree/ n. (pl. **-ies**) a long-beaked marine fish, Scomberesox saurus, of temperate waters.

sau·sage /sáwsij/ n. **1 a** ground pork, beef, or other meat seasoned and often mixed with other ingredients, encased in cylindrical form in a skin, for cooking and eating hot or cold. **b** a length of this. **2** a sausage-shaped object.

sau·té /sōtáy, saw-/ adj., n., & v. ● adj. quickly browned in a little hot fat. ● n. food cooked in this way. ● v.tr. (**sautéed** or **sautéd**) cook in this way.

Sau·ternes /sōtérn, saw-/ n. a sweet white wine from Sauternes in the Bordeaux region of France.

sav·age /sávij/ adj., n., & v. ● adj. **1** fierce; cruel (savage persecution; a savage blow). **2** wild; primitive (savage tribes; a savage animal). **3** colloq. angry; bad-tempered (in a savage mood). ● n. **1** Anthropol. derog. a member of a primitive tribe. **2** a cruel or barbarous person. ● v.tr. **1** (esp. of a dog, wolf, etc.) attack and bite or trample. **2** (of a critic, etc.) attack fiercely. □□ **sav·age·ly** adv. **sav·age·ness** n. **sav·age·ry** n. (pl. **-ies**).

sa·van·na /səvánə/ n. (also **sa·van·nah**) ▼ a grassy plain in tropical and subtropical regions, with few or no trees.

SAVANNA: SERENGETI PLAIN, TANZANIA

sa·vant /saváant, sávənt/ n. (fem. **savante**) a learned person.

sa·vate /səváat/ n. a form of boxing in which feet and fists are used.

save¹ /sayv/ v. & n. ● v. **1** tr. rescue, preserve, protect, or deliver from danger, harm, discredit, etc. (saved my life; saved me from drowning). **2** tr. keep for future use (saved up $150 for a new bike; likes to save plastic bags). **3** tr. (often refl.) **a** relieve (another person or oneself) from spending (money, time, trouble, etc.) (saved myself $50; a word processor saves time). **b** obviate the need or likelihood of (soaking saves scrubbing). **4** tr. preserve from damnation; convert (saved her soul). **5** tr. & refl. husband or preserve (one's strength, health, etc.) (saving himself for the last lap; save your energy). **6** intr. save money for future use. **7** tr. **a** avoid losing (a game, match, etc.). **b** prevent an opponent from scoring (a goal, etc.). **c** stop (a ball, etc.) from entering the goal. ● n. Ice hockey, soccer, etc. the act of preventing an opponent's scoring, etc. □ **save appearances** present a prosperous, respectable, etc., appearance. **save face** see FACE. **save one's breath** not waste time speaking to no effect. **save the day** find or provide a solution to difficulty or disaster. **save one's skin** (or **neck** or **bacon**) avoid loss, injury, or death; escape from danger. □□ **sav·a·ble** adj. (also **save·a·ble**).

save² /sayv/ prep. & conj. archaic or poet. ● prep. except; but (all save him). ● conj. (often foll. by for) unless; but; except (happy save for one want; is well save that he has a cold).

sav·er /sáyvər/ n. **1** a person who saves, esp. money. **2** (often in comb.) a device for economical use (of time, etc.) (found the short cut a time-saver).

sav·in /sávin/ n. (also **sav·ine**) **1** a bushy juniper, Juniperus sabina, usu. spreading horizontally, and yielding oil formerly used in the treatment of amenorrhea. **2** = red cedar.

sav·ing /sáyving/ adj., n., & prep. ● adj. (often in comb.) making economical use of (labor-saving). ● n. **1** anything that is saved. **2** an economy (a saving in expenses). **3** (usu. in pl.) money saved. ● prep. **1** except

(all saving that one). **2** without offense to (saving your presence).

saving grace n. **1** the redeeming grace of God. **2** a redeeming quality.

savings ac·count n. a bank account that earns interest and from which withdrawals are usu. made in person.

savings and loan as·so·ci·a·tion n. an institution, usu. owned by depositors and regulated by state or federal government, that accepts funds for savings accounts and lends funds for mortgages.

savings bank n. a bank receiving deposits at interest and returning the profits to the depositors.

sav·ior /sáyvyər/ n. (esp. Brit. **saviour**) **1** a person who saves from danger, destruction, etc. (the savior of the nation). **2** (**Savior**) (prec. by the, our) Christ.

sa·voir faire /sávwaar fáir/ n. the ability to act suitably in any situation; tact.

sa·voir vi·vre /véevrə/ n. knowledge of the world and the ways of society; ability to conduct oneself well; sophistication.

sa·vor /sáyvər/ n. & v. ● n. **1** a characteristic taste, flavor, etc. **2** a quality suggestive of or containing a small amount of another. **3** archaic a characteristic smell. ● v. **1** tr. appreciate and enjoy the taste of (food). **b** enjoy or appreciate (an experience, etc.). **2** intr. (foll. by of) **a** suggest by taste, smell, etc. (savors of mushrooms). **b** imply or suggest a specified quality (savors of impertinence). □□ **sa·vor·less** adj.

sa·vor·y¹ /sáyvəree/ n. (pl. **-ies**) ▶ any herb of the genus Satureja, esp. S. hortensis and S. montana, used in cooking.

sa·vor·y² /sáyvəree/ adj. **1** having an appetizing taste or smell. **2** (of food) salty or piquant, not sweet (a savory omelette). **3** pleasant; acceptable. □□ **sa·vor·i·ly** adv. **sa·vor·i·ness** n.

SAVORY: SUMMER SAVORY (Satureja hortensis)

sa·voy /səvóy/ n. ◀ a hardy variety of cabbage with wrinkled leaves.

Sa·voy·ard /səvóyaard, sávoyaárd/ adj. & n. ● n. a native of Savoy in SE France. ● adj. of or relating to Savoy or its people, etc.

sav·vy /sávee/ v., n., & adj. sl. ● v.intr. & tr. (**-ies**, **-ied**) know. ● n. knowingness; shrewdness; understanding. ● adj. (**savvier**, **savviest**) knowing; wise.

SAVOY (Brassica oleracea cultivar)

saw¹ /saw/ n. & v. ● n. **1** ▶ a hand tool having a toothed blade used to cut esp. wood with a to-and-fro movement. **2** any of several power-driven devices with a toothed rotating disk or moving band, for cutting. **3** Zool., etc., a serrated organ or part. ● v. (past part. **sawed** or **sawn** /sawn/) **1** tr. **a** cut (wood, etc.) with a saw. **b** make (boards, etc.) with a saw. **2** intr. use a saw. **3 a** intr. move to and fro with a motion as of a saw or person sawing (sawing away on his violin). **b** tr. divide (the air, etc.) with gesticulations. □□ **saw·like** adj.

saw² past of SEE¹.

saw³ /saw/ n. a proverb; a maxim (that's just an old saw).

saw·bones /sáwbōnz/ n. sl. a doctor or surgeon.

saw·buck /sáwbuk/ n. sl. a $10 bill.

saw·dust /sáwdust/ n. powdery particles of wood produced in sawing.

saw-edged adj. with a jagged edge like a saw.

sawed-off adj. (also **sawn-off**) **1** (of a gun) having part of the barrel sawed off to make it easier to handle and give a wider field of fire. **2** colloq. (of a person) short.

SAW

Saws were probably first used in the Bronze Age. Today they make up one of the most versatile classes of cutting tools used in the home and in industry. Saws are designed to perform specific tasks: for example, coping saws have a short, narrow blade for cutting elaborate shapes in thin wood; hacksaws have fine teeth for cutting harder substances such as metal.

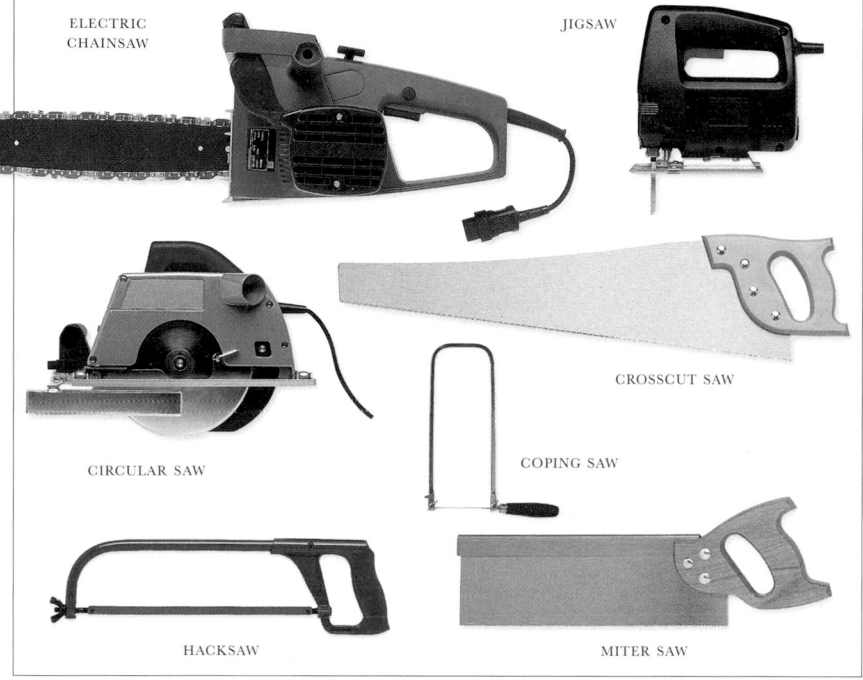

ELECTRIC CHAINSAW

JIGSAW

CIRCULAR SAW

CROSSCUT SAW

COPING SAW

HACKSAW

MITER SAW

saw·fish /sáwfish/ *n.* ▼ any large marine fish of the family Pristidae, with a toothed flat snout used as a weapon

SAWFISH: SMALLTOOTH SAWFISH (*Pristis pectinata*)

asymmetric tail

large pectoral fin

saw·fly /sáwflī/ *n.* (*pl.* **-flies**) any insect of the superfamily Tenthredinoidea, with a serrated ovipositor, the larvae of which are injurious to plants.

saw·horse /sáwhawrs/ *n.* a rack supporting wood for sawing.

saw·mill /sáwmil/ *n.* a factory in which wood is sawed mechanically into planks or boards.

sawn *past part.* of SAW[1].

saw·tooth /sáwtooth/ *adj.* (also **saw·toothed** /-tootht/) shaped like the teeth of a saw with one steep and one slanting side.

saw-whet owl *n.* a small N. American owl, *Aegolius acadicus*, noted for its harsh cry.

saw·yer /sáwyər/ *n.* a person who saws lumber professionally.

sax /saks/ *n. colloq.* **1** a saxophone. **2** esp. *Brit.* a saxophone player. □□ **sax·ist** *n.*

sax·a·tile /sáksətil, -tīl/ *adj.* living or growing on or among rocks.

sax·horn /sáks-hawrn/ *n.* any of a series of different-sized brass wind instruments with valves and a funnel-shaped mouthpiece, used mainly in military and brass bands.

sax·i·frage /sáksifrij, -frayj/ *n.* any plant of the genus *Saxifraga*, growing on rocky or stony ground and usu. bearing small white, yellow, or red flowers.

Sax·on /sáksən/ *n. & adj.* ● *n.* **1** *hist.* **a** a member of the Germanic people that conquered parts of England in 5th–6th c. **b** (usu. **Old Saxon**) the language of the Saxons. **2** = ANGLO-SAXON. ● *adj.* **1** *hist.* of or concerning the Saxons. **2** belonging to or originating from the Saxon language or Old English. □□ **Sax·on·ize** /-nīz/ *v.tr. & intr.*

sax·o·phone /sáksəfōn/ *n.* ◄ a keyed brass reed instrument in several sizes and registers, used esp. in jazz and dance music. ▷ ORCHESTRA, WOODWIND. □□ **sax·o·phon·ic** /-fónik/ *adj.* **sax·o·phon·ist** /-sófonist, -səfōnist/ *n.*

SAXOPHONE: TENOR SAXOPHONE

octave key

mouthpiece with single reed

main body

octave key

thumb holder

key rod

key

bell brace

flared bell

say /say/ *v. & n.* ● *v.* (*3rd sing. present* **says** /sez/; *past and past part.* **said** /sed/) **1** *tr.* a utter (specified words) in a speaking voice; remark (*said "Damn!"; said that he was satisfied*). **b** express (*that was well said; cannot say what I feel*). **2** *tr.* **a** state; promise or prophesy (*says that there will be war*). **b** have specified wording; indicate (*says here that he was killed; the clock says ten to six*). **3** *tr.* (in *passive;* usu. foll. by *to* + *infin.*) be asserted or described (*is said to be 93 years old*). **4** *tr.* (foll. by *to* + *infin.*) *colloq.* tell a person to do something (*he said to bring the car*). **5** *tr.* convey (information) (*spoke for an hour but said little*). **6** *tr.* put forward as an argument or excuse (*much to be said in favor of it; what have you to say for yourself?*). **7** *tr.* (often *absol.*) form and give an opinion or decision as to (*who did it I cannot say; please say which you prefer*). **8** *tr.* select, assume, or take as an example or as near enough (*shall we say this one?; paid, say, $20*). **9** *tr.* **a** speak the words of (prayers, Mass, a grace, etc.). **b** repeat (a lesson, etc.); recite (*can't say his tables*). **10** *tr. Art*, etc. convey (inner meaning or intention) (*what is the director saying in this film?*). **11** *tr.* (**the said**) *Law* or *joc.* the previously mentioned (*the said witness*). **12** *intr.* (as *int.*) an exclamation of surprise, to attract attention, etc. ● *n.* **1 a** an opportunity for stating one's opinion, etc. (*let him have his say*). **b** a stated opinion. **2** a share in a decision (*had no say in the matter*). □ **how say you?** *Law* how do you find? (addressed to the jury requesting its verdict). **I,** etc., **cannot** (or **could not**) **say** I, etc., do not know. **I'll say** *colloq.* yes indeed. **I say** *Brit.* an exclamation expressing surprise. **it is said** the rumor is that. **not to say** or possibly even (*his language was rude, not to say offensive*). **said he** (or **I**, etc.) *colloq.* or *poet.* he, etc., said. **say for oneself** say by way of conversation, etc. **say much** (or **something**) **for** indicate the high quality of. **say no** refuse or disagree. **says you!** *colloq.* I disagree. **say when** *colloq.* indicate when enough drink or food has been given. **say the word 1** indicate that you agree or give permission. **2** give the order, etc. **say yes** agree. **that is to say 1** in other words, more explicitly. **2** or at least. **they say** it is rumored. **to say nothing of** = not to mention (see MENTION). **what do** (or **would**) **you say to…?** would you like…? **when all is said and done** after all; in the long run. **you can say that again!** (or **you said it!**) *colloq.* I agree emphatically. **you don't say so** *colloq.* an expression of amazement or disbelief. □□ **say·a·ble** *adj.* **say·er** *n.*

say·ing /sáying/ *n.* **1** the act or an instance of saying. **2** a maxim, proverb, etc. □ **as the saying goes** (or **is**) an expression used in introducing a proverb, cliché, etc. **go without saying** be too well known or obvious to need mention. **there is no saying** it is impossible to know.

say-so *n.* **1** the power of decision. **2** mere assertion (*cannot proceed merely on his say-so*).

Sb *symb. Chem.* the element antimony.

SBA *abbr.* Small Business Administration.

SBN *abbr.* Standard Book Number (cf. ISBN).

SC *abbr.* South Carolina (also in official postal use).

Sc *symb. Chem.* the element scandium.

sc. *abbr.* scilicet.

s.c. *abbr.* small capitals.

scab /skab/ *n. & v.* ● *n.* **1** a dry rough crust formed over a cut, sore, etc., in healing. **2** (often *attrib.*) *colloq. derog.* a person who refuses to strike or join a trade union, or who tries to break a strike by working. **3** a skin disease, esp. in animals. **4** a fungus plant disease causing scablike roughness. **5** a dislikeable person. ● *v.intr.* (**scabbed**, **scabbing**) **1** act as a scab. **2** (of a wound, etc.) form a scab; heal over. □□ **scabbed** *adj.* **scab·by** *adj.* (**scabbier**, **scabbiest**). **scab·bi·ness** *n.* **scab·like** *adj.*

scab·bard /skábərd/ *n.* **1** *hist.* ▶ a sheath for a sword, bayonet, etc. **2** a sheath for a revolver, etc.

sca·bies /skáybeez/ *n.* a contagious skin disease causing severe itching.

sca·bi·ous /skáybeeəs/ *n.* any plant of the genus *Scabiosa*, *Knautia*, etc., with pink, white, or esp. blue pincushion-shaped flowers.

SCABBARD: 19TH-CENTURY INDIAN SWORD SCABBARD

S

scab·rous /skábrəs, skáy-/ *adj.* **1** having a rough surface; bearing short stiff hairs, scales, etc. **2** (of a subject, situation, etc.) requiring tactful treatment. **3 a** indecent; salacious. **b** behaving licentiously. □□ **scab·rous·ly** *adv.* **scab·rous·ness** *n.*

scad /skad/ *n.* any fish of the family Carangidae native to tropical and subtropical seas, usu. having an elongated body and very large spiky scales.

scads /skadz/ *n.pl. colloq.* large quantities.

scaf·fold /skáfəld, -fōld/ *n. & v.* **1** *hist.* a platform used for the execution of criminals. **2** = SCAFFOLDING. **3** (prec. by *the*) death by execution. ● *v.tr.* attach scaffolding to (a building). □□ **scaf·fold·er** *n.*

scaf·fold·ing /skáfəlding, -fōlding/ *n.* **1** a temporary structure formed of poles, planks, etc., erected by workers and used by them while building or repairing a house, etc. **2** materials used for this.

scagl·io·la /skalyólə/ *n.* imitation stone or plaster mixed with glue.

scal·a·ble /skáyləbəl/ *adj.* **1** capable of being scaled or climbed. **2** *Computing* capable of being used in a range of sizes. □□ **scal·a·bil·i·ty** /-bílitee/ *n.*

scal·ar /skáylər/ *adj. & n. Math. & Physics* ● *adj.* (of a quantity) having only magnitude, not direction. ● *n.* a scalar quantity (cf. VECTOR).

scal·a·wag /skáləwag/ *n.* (also **scal·ly·wag**) **1** a scamp; a rascal. **2** *US hist.* a white Southerner who supported Reconstructionists usu. for personal profit.

scald[1] /skawld/ *v. & n.* ● *v.tr.* **1** burn (the skin, etc.) with hot liquid or steam. **2** heat (esp. milk) to near boiling point. **3** (usu. foll. by *out*) clean (a pan, etc.) by rinsing with boiling water. ● *n.* a burn, etc., caused by scalding.

scald[2] var. of SKALD.

scale[1] /skayl/ *n. & v.* ● *n.* **1** each of the small, thin, overlapping plates protecting the skin of fish and reptiles. ▷ FISH, REPTILE. **2** something resembling a fish scale, esp. a flake of skin. **3** a thick, white deposit formed in a kettle, boiler, etc., by the action of heat on water. **4** plaque formed on teeth. ● *v.* **1** *tr.* remove scale or scales from (fish, etc.). **2** *tr.* remove plaque from (teeth) by scraping. **3** *intr.* (of skin, etc.) form, come off in, or drop, scales. □ **scales fall from a person's eyes** a person is no longer deceived (cf. Acts 9:18). □□ **scaled** *adj.* (also in *comb.*). **scale·less** *adj.* **scal·er** *n.*

scale[2] /skayl/ *n.* **1 a** (often in *pl.*) ▼ a weighing machine or device (*bathroom scales*). **b** (also **scale·pan**) each of the dishes on a simple scale balance. **2** (**the Scales**) the zodiacal sign or constellation Libra. ▷ LIBRA. □ **throw into the scale** cause to be a factor in a contest, debate, etc. **tip** (or **turn**) **the scales 1** (usu. foll. by *at*) outweigh the opposite scalepan (at a specified weight); weigh. **2** (of a motive, circumstance, etc.) be decisive.

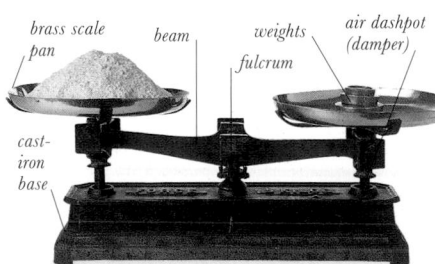

SCALE: TRADITIONAL KITCHEN SCALE

brass scale pan — *beam* — *weights* — *air dashpot (damper)* — *fulcrum* — *cast-iron base*

scale[3] /skayl/ *n. & v.* ● *n.* **1** a series of degrees; a graded classification system (*high on the social scale; seven points on the Richter scale*). **2 a** (often *attrib.*) *Geog. & Archit.* a ratio of size in a map, model, picture, etc. (*on a scale of one inch to the mile; a scale model*). **b** relative dimensions or degree (*generosity on a grand scale*). **3** *Mus.* an arrangement of all the notes in any system of music in ascending or descending order. ▷ NOTATION. **4 a** a set of marks on a line used in measuring, reducing, enlarging, etc. **b** a rule de-

termining the distances between these. **c** a piece of metal, apparatus, etc., on which these are marked. **5** (in full **scale of notation**) *Math.* the ratio between units in a numerical system (*decimal scale*). ● *v.* **1** *tr.* **a** climb (a wall, height, etc.) esp. with a ladder. **b** climb (the social scale, heights of ambition, etc.). **2** *tr.* represent in proportional dimensions; reduce to a common scale. **3** *intr.* (of quantities, etc.) have a common scale; be commensurable. □ **in scale** (of drawing, etc.) in proportion to the surroundings, etc. **scale down** make smaller in proportion; reduce in size. **scale up** make larger in proportion; increase in size. **to scale** with a uniform reduction or enlargement. □□ **scal·er** *n.*

scale in·sect *n.* any of various insects, esp. of the family Coccidae, clinging to plants and secreting a shieldlike scale as covering.

sca·lene /skáyleen/ *adj.* (esp. of a triangle) having sides unequal in length.

sca·le·nus /skəléenəs/ *n.* (*pl.* **scaleni** /-nī/) any of several muscles extending from the neck to the first and second ribs.

scal·lion /skályən/ *n.* a shallot or spring onion; any long-necked onion with a small bulb.

scal·lop /skáləp, skól-/ *n. & v.* (also **scol·lop** /skól-/) ● *n.* **1** ▶ any of various bivalve mollusks of the family Pectinidae, esp. of the genus *Chlamys* or *Pecten*, much prized as food. ▷ BIVALVE. **2** (in full **scallop shell**) a single valve from the shell of a scallop, often used for cooking or serving food. **3** (in *pl.*) an ornamental edging cut in material in imitation of a scallop edge. ● *v.tr.* (**scalloped, scalloping**) **1** cook in a scallop. **2** ornament (an edge or material) with scallops or scalloping. □□ **scal·lop·er** *n.* **scal·lop·ing** *n.* (in sense 3 of *n.*).

SCALLOP
(*Chlamys* species)

sensory tentacles — *paired shell valves*

scal·ly·wag var. of SCALAWAG.

scalp /skalp/ *n. & v.* ● *n.* **1** the skin covering the top of the head, with the hair, etc., attached. ▷ HEAD. **2** *hist.* the scalp of an enemy cut or torn away as a trophy by a Native American. ● *v.tr.* **1** *hist.* take the scalp of (an enemy). **2** defeat; humiliate. **3** *colloq.* resell (shares, tickets, etc.) at a high or quick profit. □□ **scalp·er** *n.* **scalp·less** *adj.*

scal·pel /skálpəl/ *n.* ▶ a surgeon's small sharp knife.

disposable blade — *grip*

SCALPEL

scal·y /skáylee/ *adj.* (**scalier, scaliest**) covered in scales. □□ **scal·i·ness** *n.*

scam /skam/ *n. sl.* a trick or swindle; a fraud.

scam·mo·ny /skámənee/ *n.* (*pl.* **-ies**) an Asian plant, *Convolvulus scammonia*, bearing white or pink flowers, the dried roots of which are used as a purgative.

scamp[1] /skamp/ *n. colloq.* a rascal; a rogue. □□ **scamp·ish** *adj.*

scamp[2] /skamp/ *v.tr.* do (work, etc.) in a perfunctory or inadequate way.

scam·per /skámpər/ *v. & n.* ● *v.intr.* (usu. foll. by *about, through*) run and skip impulsively or playfully. ● *n.* the act or an instance of scampering.

scam·pi /skámpee/ *n.pl.* **1** large shrimp. **2** (often treated as *sing.*) a dish of these sautéd in garlic butter.

scan /skan/ *v. & n.* ● *v.* (**scanned, scanning**) **1** *tr.* look at intently or quickly (*scanned the horizon; scanned the speech for errors*). **2** *intr.* (of a verse, etc.) be metrically correct (*this line doesn't scan*). **3** *tr.* **a** examine all parts of (a surface,

etc.) to detect radioactivity, etc. **b** cause (a particular region) to be traversed by a radar, etc., beam. **4** *tr.* resolve (a picture) into its elements of light and shade in a prearranged pattern for the purposes, esp. of television transmission. **5** *tr.* test the meter of (a line of verse, etc.) by reading with the emphasis on its rhythm, or by examining the number of feet, etc. **6** *tr.* make a scan of (the body or part of it). ● *n.* **1** the act or an instance of scanning. **2** an image obtained by scanning or with a scanner. □□ **scan·na·ble** *adj.*

scan·dal /skánd'l/ *n.* **1** a thing or a person causing public outrage or indignation. **2** the outrage, etc., so caused. **3** malicious gossip or backbiting. □□ **scan·dal·ous** *adj.* **scan·dal·ous·ly** *adv.* **scan·dal·ous·ness** *n.*

scan·dal·ize /skándəlīz/ *v.tr.* offend the moral feelings, sensibilities, etc., of.

scan·dal·mon·ger /skánd'lmonggər, -monggər/ *n.* a person who spreads malicious scandal.

scan·dal sheet *n. derog.* a newspaper, etc., giving prominence to esp. malicious gossip.

Scan·di·na·vi·an /skándináyveeən/ *n. & adj.* ● *n.* **1 a** a native or inhabitant of Scandinavia (Denmark, Norway, Sweden, and sometimes Finland and Iceland). **b** a person of Scandinavian descent. **2** the family of languages of Scandinavia. ● *adj.* of or relating to Scandinavia or its people or languages.

scan·di·um /skándeeəm/ *n. Chem.* a rare, soft, silver-white metallic element occurring naturally in lanthanide ores.

scan·na·ble see SCAN.

scan·ner /skánər/ *n.* **1 a** a device for scanning or systematically examining something. ▷ RADAR. **b** a device for monitoring several radio frequencies, police or emergency frequencies. **2** a machine for measuring the intensity of radiation, ultrasound reflections, etc., from the body as a diagnostic aid. ▷ MRI

scan·sion /skánshən/ *n.* **1** the metrical scanning of verse. **2** the way a verse, etc., scans.

scant /skant/ *adj.* barely sufficient; deficient (*scant regard for the truth*). □□ **scant·ly** *adv.* **scant·ness** *n.*

scant·ling /skántling/ *n.* **1 a** a timber beam of small cross section. **b** a size to which a stone or timber is to be cut. **2** a set of standard dimensions for parts of a structure, esp. in shipbuilding. **3** (usu. foll. by *of*) *archaic* **a** a specimen or sample. **b** one's necessary supply; a modicum or small amount.

scant·y /skántee/ *adj.* (**scantier, scantiest**) **1** of small extent or amount. **2** barely sufficient. □□ **scant·i·ly** *adv.* **scant·i·ness** *n.*

-scape /skayp/ *comb. form* forming nouns denoting a view or a representation of a view (*seascape*).

scape·goat /skáypgōt/ *n. & v.* ● *n.* a person bearing the blame for the sins, shortcomings, etc., of others. ● *v.tr.* make a scapegoat of. □□ **scape·goat·er** *n.*

scape·grace /skáypgrays/ *n.* a rascal; a scamp, esp. a young person or child.

scap·u·la /skápyələ/ *n.* (*pl.* **scapulae** /-lee/ or **scap·ulas**) ▶ the shoulder blade.

scap·u·lar /skápyələr/ *adj. & n.* ● *adj.* of or relating to the shoulder or shoulder blade. ● *n.* a monastic short cloak.

scar[1] /skaar/ *n. & v.* **1** a usu. permanent mark on the skin left after the healing of a wound, burn, or sore. **2** the lasting effect of grief, etc., on a person. **3** a mark left by damage, etc. (*the table bore many scars*). **4** a mark left on the stem, etc., of a plant by the fall of a leaf, etc. ● *v.* (**scarred, scarring**) **1** *tr.*

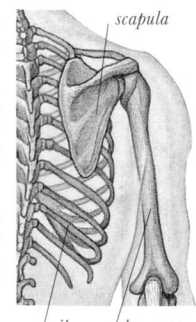

scapula — *ribcage* — *humerus*

SCAPULA:
HUMAN SKELETON
SHOWING
THE SCAPULA

S

(esp. as **scarred** *adj.*) mark with a scar or scars (*scarred for life*). **2** *intr.* heal over; form a scar. **3** *tr.* form a scar on. □□ **scar·less** *adj.*

scar[2] /skaar/ *n.* a steep craggy outcrop of a mountain or cliff.

scar·ab /skárəb/ *n.* **1** the sacred dung beetle of ancient Egypt. **2** ▶ an ancient Egyptian gem cut in the form of a beetle and engraved with symbols on its flat side.

hieroglyphics on flat side

beetle shape

SCARAB: ANCIENT EGYPTIAN SCARAB

scar·a·bae·id /skárəbéeid/ *n.* any beetle of the family Scarabaeidae, including the dung beetle, cockchafer, etc.

scar·a·mouch /skárəmoֹosh/ *n. archaic* a boastful coward; a braggart.

scarce /skairs/ *adj. & adv.* ● *adj.* **1** (usu. *predic.*) (esp. of food, money, etc.) insufficient for the demand. **2** hard to find; rare. ● *adv. archaic* or *literary* scarcely. □ **make oneself scarce** *colloq.* keep out of the way; surreptitiously disappear. □□ **scarce·ness** *n.*

scarce·ly /skáirslee/ *adv.* **1** hardly; only just (*I scarcely know her*). **2** surely not (*he can scarcely have said so*). **3** a mild or apologetic or ironical substitute for "not" (*I scarcely expected to be insulted*).

scar·ci·ty /skársitee/ *n.* (*pl.* **-ies**) (often foll. by *of*) a lack or inadequacy.

scare /skair/ *v. & n.* ● *v.* **1** *tr.* frighten, esp. suddenly (*his expression scared us*) **2** *tr.* (as **scared** *adj.*) (usu. foll. by *of*, or *to* + infin.) frightened; terrified (*scared of his own shadow*). **3** *tr.* (usu. foll. by *away*, *off*, *up*, etc.) drive away by frightening. **4** *intr.* become scared (*they don't scare easily*). ● *n.* **1** a sudden attack of fright (*gave me a scare*). **2** a general, esp. baseless, fear of war, invasion, epidemic, etc. (*a measles scare*). □ **scare up** (or **out**) **1** frighten (game, etc.) out of cover. **2** *colloq.* manage to find (*see if we can scare up a meal*) □□ **scar·er** *n.*

scare·crow /skáirkrō/ *n.* **1** a human figure dressed in old clothes and set up in a field to scare birds away. **2** *colloq.* a badly dressed, grotesque-looking, or very thin person.

scared·y-cat /skáirdeekat/ *n. colloq.* a timid person.

scare·head /skáirhed/ *n.* a shockingly large or sensational newspaper headline.

scare·mon·ger /skáirmunggər, -monggər/ *n.* a person who spreads frightening reports or rumors. □□ **scare·mon·ger·ing** *n.*

scarf[1] /skaarf/ *n.* (*pl.* **scarfs** or **scarves** /skaarvz/) a square, triangular, or esp. long narrow strip of material worn around the neck, over the shoulders, or tied around the head for warmth or ornament. □□ **scarfed** *adj.*

scarf[2] /skaarf/ *v. & n.* ● *v.tr.* join the ends of (pieces of esp. lumber, metal, or leather) by beveling or notching them to fit and then bolting, brazing, or sewing them together. ● *n.* a joint made by scarfing.

scarf[3] /skaarf/ *v.tr. & intr.* (often foll. by *up* or *down*) eat, esp. quickly, voraciously, greedily, etc.

scarf·pin /skáarfpin/ *n.* = TIEPIN.

scar·i·fi·er /skárifīər, skáir-/ *n.* **1** a thing or person that scarifies. **2** a machine with prongs for loosening soil without turning it. ▷ RAKE. **3** a spiked road-breaking machine.

scar·i·fy[1] /skárifī, skáir-/ *v.tr.* (**-ies**, **-ied**) **1 a** make superficial incisions in. **b** cut off skin from. **2** hurt by severe criticism, etc. **3** loosen (soil) with a scarifier. □□ **scar·i·fi·ca·tion** /-fikáyshən/ *n.*

scar·i·fy[2] /skáirifī/ *v.tr. & intr.* (**-ies**, **-ied**) *colloq.* scare; terrify.

scar·i·ous /skáireeəs/ *adj.* (of a part of a plant, etc.) having a dry membranous appearance; thin and brittle.

scar·la·ti·na /skáarlətéenə/ *n.* = SCARLET FEVER.

scar·let /skáarlit/ *n. & adj.* ● *n.* **1** a brilliant red color tinged with orange. **2** clothes or material of this color (*dressed in scarlet*). ● *adj.* of a scarlet color.

scar·let fe·ver *n.* an infectious bacterial fever, affecting esp. children, with a scarlet rash.

scar·let pim·per·nel *n.* ▶ a small annual wild plant, *Anagallis arvensis*, with small, esp. scarlet, flowers closing in rainy or cloudy weather: also called **poor man's weather-glass**.

scar·let wom·an *n. derog.* a notoriously promiscuous woman; a prostitute.

scar·oid /skároyd, skáir-/ *n. & adj.* ● *n.* any colorful marine fish of the family Scaridae, native to tropical and temperate seas, including the scarus. ● *adj.* of or relating to this family.

SCARLET PIMPERNEL (*Anagallis arvensis*)

scarp /skaarp/ *n. & v.* ● *n.* **1** the inner wall or slope of a ditch in a fortification. **2** a steep slope. ● *v.tr.* make (a slope) perpendicular or steep.

scar·us /skáirəs/ *n.* any fish of the genus *Scarus*, with brightly colored scales, and teeth fused to form a parrotlike beak used for eating coral. Also called **parrot fish**.

scarves *pl.* of SCARF[1].

scar·y /skáiree/ *adj.* (**scarier**, **scariest**) *colloq.* frightening. □□ **scar·i·ly** *adv.*

scat[1] /skat/ *v. & int. colloq.* ● *v.intr.* (**scatted**, **scatting**) depart quickly. ● *int.* go!

scat[2] /skat/ *n. & v.* ● *n.* improvised jazz singing using sounds imitating instruments, instead of words. ● *v.intr.* (**scatted**, **scatting**) sing scat.

scathe /skayth/ *v. & n.* ● *v.tr.* **1** *poet.* injure esp. by blasting or withering. **2** (as **scathing** *adj.*) witheringly scornful (*scathing sarcasm*). ● *n.* (usu. with *neg.*) *archaic* harm; injury (*without scathe*). □□ **scathe·less** *predic.adj.* **scath·ing·ly** *adv.*

sca·tol·o·gy /skatóləjee, skə-/ *n.* **1** a morbid interest in excrement. **2** a preoccupation with obscene literature, esp. that concerned with the excretory functions. **3** such literature. □□ **scat·o·log·i·cal** /-təlójikəl/ *adj.*

scat·oph·a·gous /skatófəgəs/ *adj.* feeding on dung.

scat·ter /skátər/ *v. & n.* ● *v.* **1** *tr.* **a** throw here and there (*scattered gravel on the road*). **b** cover by scattering (*scattered the road with gravel*). **2** *tr. & intr.* **a** move or cause to move in flight, etc. (*scattered to safety at the sound*). **b** disperse or cause (hopes, clouds, etc.) to disperse. **3** *tr.* (as **scattered** *adj.*) not clustered together; wide apart (*scattered villages*). **4** *tr. Physics* deflect or diffuse (light, particles, etc.). **5 a** *intr.* (of esp. a shotgun) fire a charge of shot diffusely. **b** *tr.* fire (a charge) in this way. ● *n.* **1** the act or an instance of scattering. **2** a small amount scattered. **3** the extent of distribution of esp. shot, etc. □□ **scat·ter·er** *n.*

scat·ter·brain /skátərbrayn/ *n.* a person given to silly or disorganized thought with lack of concentration. □□ **scat·ter·brained** *adj.*

scat·ter·shot /skátərshot/ *n. & adj.* firing at random.

scaup /skawp/ *n.* any diving duck of the genus *Aythya*.

scaur var. of SCAR[2].

scav·enge /skávinj/ *v.* **1** *tr. & intr.* (usu. foll. by *for*) search for and collect (discarded items). **2** *tr.* remove unwanted products from (an internal-combustion engine cylinder, etc.). **3** *intr.* feed on carrion.

scav·en·ger /skávinjər/ *n.* **1** a person who seeks and collects discarded items. **2** an animal feeding on carrion. □□ **sca·ven·ger·y** *n.*

Sc.D. *abbr.* Doctor of Science.

sce·na /sháynaa/ *n. Mus.* **1** a dramatic solo, usu. including recitative. **2** a scene or part of an opera.

sce·nar·i·o /sináreeō, -naáreeō/ *n.* (*pl.* **-os**) **1** an outline of the plot of a play, film, etc., with details of the scenes, situations, etc. **2** a postulated sequence of future events. □□ **sce·nar·ist** *n.* (in sense 1).

scene /seen/ *n.* **1** a place in which events in real life, drama, or fiction occur; the locality of an event, etc. (*the scene was set in India*; *the scene of the disaster*). **2 a** an incident in real life, fiction, etc. (*distressing scenes occurred*). **b** a description or representation of an incident, etc. (*scenes of clerical life*). **3** a public incident displaying emotion, temper, etc. (*made a scene in the restaurant*). **4 a a** continuous portion of a play in a fixed setting and usu. without a change of personnel; a subdivision of an act. **b** a similar section of a film, book, etc. **5 a** any of the pieces of scenery used in a play. **b** these collectively. **6** a landscape or a view (*a desolate scene*). **7** *colloq.* **a** an area of action or interest (*not my scene*). **b** a way of life; a milieu (*well-known on the jazz scene*). □ **behind the scenes 1** *Theatr.* among the actors, scenery, etc., offstage. **2** unknown to the public; secret(ly). **come on the scene** arrive. **quit the scene** die; leave. **set the scene 1** describe the location of events. **2** give preliminary information.

scen·er·y /séenəree/ *n.* **1** the general appearance of the natural features of a landscape, esp. when picturesque. **2** *Theatr.* the painted representations of landscape, rooms, etc., used as the background in a play, etc.

scene·shift·er /séenshiftər/ *n.* a person who moves scenery in a theater. □□ **scene·shift·ing** *n.*

sce·nic /séenik/ *adj.* **1** a picturesque; impressive or beautiful (*took the scenic route*). **b** of or concerning natural scenery (*hills are the main scenic feature*). **2** (of a picture, etc.) representing an incident. □□ **sce·ni·cal·ly** *adv.*

scent /sent/ *n. & v.* ● *n.* **1** a distinctive, esp. pleasant, smell. **2 a** a scent trail left by an animal perceptible to hounds, etc. **b** clues, etc., that can be followed like a scent trail (*lost the scent in Paris*). **c** the power of detecting or distinguishing smells, etc., or of discovering things (*some dogs have little scent*; *the scent for talent*). ● *v.* **1** *tr.* **a** discern by scent (*the dog scented game*). **b** sense the presence of (*scent treachery*). **2** *tr.* make fragrant or foul-smelling. **3** *tr.* (as **scented** *adj.*) having esp. a pleasant smell (*scented soap*). □ **on the scent** having a clue. **put** (or **throw**) **off the scent** deceive by false clues, etc. **scent out** discover by smelling or searching. □□ **scent·less** *adj.*

scent gland *n.* (also **scent or·gan**) a gland in some animals secreting musk, civet, etc.

scep·ter /séptər/ *n.* ▶ a staff borne esp. at a coronation as a symbol of sovereignty. □□ **scep·tered** *adj.*

scep·tic *Brit.* var. of SKEPTIC.

scha·den·freu·de /sháad'nfroydə/ *n.* the malicious enjoyment of another's misfortunes.

schap·pe /sháapə/ *n.* fabric or yarn made from waste silk.

sched·ule /skéjo͞ol, -o͞ol/ *n. & v.* ● *n.* **1 a a** list or plan of intended events, times, etc. **b** a plan of work (*not on my schedule for next week*). **2** a list of rates or prices. **3** a timetable. **4** a tabulated inventory. ● *v.tr.* **1** include in a schedule. **2** make a schedule of. □□ **sched·ul·er** *n.*

scheel·ite /shéelīt/ *n. Mineral.* calcium tungstate in its mineral crystalline form.

sche·ma /skéemə/ *n.* (*pl.* **schemata** /-mətə/ or **schemas**) **1** a synopsis, outline, or diagram. **2** a proposed arrangement.

sche·mat·ic /skimátik, skee-/ *adj. & n.* ● *adj.* **1** of or concerning a scheme or schema. **2** representing objects by symbols, etc. ● *n.* a schematic diagram, esp. of an electronic circuit. □□ **sche·mat·i·cal·ly** *adv.*

sche·ma·tism /skéemətizəm/ *n.* a schematic arrangement or presentation.

SCEPTER: PRUSSIAN SCEPTER

S

sche·ma·tize /skéemətīz/ *v.tr.* **1** put in a schematic form; arrange. **2** represent by a scheme or schema. □□ **sche·ma·ti·za·tion** *n.*

scheme /skeem/ *n. & v.* ● *n.* **1 a** a systematic plan or arrangement. **b** a proposed or operational systematic arrangement (*a color scheme*). **2** an artful or deceitful plot. ● *v.* **1** *intr.* (often foll. by *for*, or *to* + infin.) plan esp. secretly or deceitfully. **2** *tr.* plan to bring about, esp. artfully or deceitfully (*schemed their downfall*). □□ **schem·er** *n.*

schem·ing /skéeming/ *adj.* cunning or deceitful. □□ **schem·ing·ly** *adv.*

sche·moz·zle var. of SHEMOZZLE.

scher·zan·do /skairtsaándō/ *adv., adj., & n. Mus.* ● *adv. & adj.* in a playful manner. ● *n.* (*pl.* **scher·zandos** or **scherzandi** /-dee/) a passage played in this way.

scher·zo /skáirtsō/ *n.* (*pl.* **-os**) *Mus.* a vigorous, light, or playful composition, usu. as a movement in a symphony, sonata, etc.

schil·ling /shíling/ *n.* (until the introduction of the euro in 2002) the chief monetary unit of Austria.

schip·per·ke /skípərkee, ship-/ *n.* **1** a small, black, tailless dog of a breed with a ruff of fur around its neck. **2** this breed.

schism /sízəm, skíz-/ *n.* **1** the division of a group into opposing sections or parties. **2** any of the sections so formed.

schis·mat·ic /sizmátik, skiz-/ *adj. & n.* (also **schis·mat·i·cal**) ● *adj.* inclining to, concerning, or guilty of, schism. ● *n.* **1** a holder of schismatic opinions. **2** a member of a schismatic faction or a seceded branch of a church. □□ **schis·mat·i·cal·ly** *adv.*

schist /shist/ *n.* ▶ a foliated metamorphic rock composed of layers of different minerals and splitting into thin irregular plates. □□ **schis·tose** *adj.*

schis·to·some /shístəsōm/ *n.* = BILHARZIA.

schiz·an·thus /skizánthəs/ *n.* any plant of the genus *Schizanthus*, with showy flowers in various colors, and finely divided leaves.

SCHIST

schiz·o /skítsō/ *adj. & n. colloq.* ● *adj.* schizophrenic. ● *n.* (*pl.* **-os**) a schizophrenic.

schi·zo·carp /skízəkaarp, skítsə-/ *n. Bot.* any of a group of dry fruits that split into single-seeded parts when ripe. □□ **schizocarpic** /-kaárpik/ *adj.* **schizocarpous** /-kaárpəs/ *adj.*

schiz·oid /skítsoyd/ *adj. & n.* ● *adj.* (of a person or personality, etc.) tending to schizophrenia, but usu. without delusions. ● *n.* a schizoid person.

schiz·o·phre·ni·a /skítsəfréeneeə, -fréneeə/ *n.* a mental disease involving a breakdown in the relation between thoughts, feelings, and actions and withdrawal from reality into fantasy and delusion. □□ **schiz·o·phren·ic** /-frénik/ *adj. & n.*

schiz·o·thym·i·a /skítsōthímeeə, skíz-/ *n. Psychol.* an introvert condition with a tendency to schizophrenia. □□ **schiz·o·thym·ic** *adj.*

schle·miel /shləméel/ *n. colloq.* a foolish or unlucky person.

schlep /shlep/ *v. & n.* (also **schlepp**) *colloq.* ● *v.* (**schlepped, schlepping**) **1** *tr.* carry; drag. **2** *intr.* go or work tediously or effortfully. ● *n.* a person or thing that is tedious, awkward, or slow.

schlock /shlok/ *n. colloq.* inferior goods; trash.

schmaltz /shmaalts/ *n. colloq.* sentimentality, esp. in music, drama, etc. □□ **schmaltz·y** *adj.* (**schmaltzier, schmaltziest**).

schmooze /shmōoz/ *colloq., chiefly N. Amer. v. & n.* ● *v.* **1** *intr.* chat; gossip. **2** *tr.* chat to (someone) in order to gain an advantage. ● *n.* an intimate conversation.

schmuck /shmuk/ *n. sl.* a foolish or contemptible person.

schnapps /shnaaps, shnaps/ *n.* any of various spirits drunk in N. Europe.

schnau·zer /shnówzər, shnówtsər/ *n.* **1** a dog of a German breed with a close wiry coat and heavy whiskers around the muzzle. **2** this breed.

schnit·zel /shnítsəl/ *n.* a cutlet of veal.

schol·ar /skólər/ *n.* **1** a learned person, esp. in language, literature, etc.; an academic. **2** the holder of a scholarship. **3** a person with specified academic ability (*a poor scholar*). □□ **schol·ar·ly** *adj.* **schol·ar·li·ness** *n.*

schol·ar·ship /skólərship/ *n.* **1 a** academic achievement; learning of a high level. **b** the methods and standards characteristic of a good scholar (*shows great scholarship*). **2** payment from the funds of a school, university, local government, etc., to maintain a student in full-time education, awarded on the basis of scholarly achievement.

scho·las·tic /skəlástik/ *adj.* of or concerning universities, schools, education, etc. □□ **scho·las·ti·cal·ly** *adv.* **scho·las·ti·cism** /-tisizəm/ *n.*

scho·li·ast /skóleeast/ *n. hist.* an ancient or medieval scholar, esp. a grammarian, who annotated ancient literary texts. □□ **scho·li·as·tic** *adj.*

scho·li·um /skóleeəm/ *n.* (*pl.* **scho·li·a** /-leeə/) a marginal note or explanatory comment, esp. by an ancient grammarian on a classical text.

school[1] /skool/ *n. & v.* ● *n.* **1 a** an institution for educating or giving instruction at any level including college or university. **b** (*attrib.*) associated with or for use in school (*a school bag; school dinners*). **2 a** the buildings used by such an institution. **b** the pupils, staff, etc., of a school. **c** the time during which teaching is done, or the teaching itself (*no school today*). **3** a university department or faculty (*the history school*). **4 a** the disciples, imitators, or followers of a philosopher, artist, etc. **b** a group of artists, etc., whose works share distinctive characteristics. **c** a group of people sharing a cause, principle, method, etc. (*school of thought*). **5** *colloq.* instructive or disciplinary circumstances, occupation, etc. (*the school of adversity; learned in a hard school*). ● *v.tr.* **1** send to school; provide for the education of. **2** (often foll. by *to*) discipline; train. **3** (as **schooled** *adj.*) (foll. by *in*) educated or trained (*schooled in humility*). □ **go to school 1** begin one's education. **2** attend lessons. **leave school** finish one's education. **of the old school** according to former and esp. better tradition.

school[2] /skool/ *n. & v.* ● *n.* (often foll. by *of*) a shoal of fish, porpoises, whales, etc. ● *v.intr.* form schools.

school·a·ble /skóoləbəl/ *adj.* liable by age, etc., to compulsory education.

school age *n.* the age range in which children normally attend school.

school board *n.* a board or authority for local education.

school·boy /skóolboy/ *n.* a boy attending school.

school·child /skóolchīld/ *n.* a child attending school.

school days *n.pl.* the time of being at school, esp. in retrospect.

school·fel·low /skóolfelō/ *n. esp. Brit.* = SCHOOLMATE.

school·girl /skóolgərl/ *n.* a girl attending school.

school·house /skóolhows/ *n.* a building used as a school.

school·ing /skóoling/ *n.* **1** education, esp. at school. **2** training or discipline, esp. of an animal.

school·man /skóolmən/ *n.* (*pl.* **-men**) **1** *hist.* a teacher in a medieval European university. **2** *RC Ch. hist.* a theologian seeking to deal with religious doctrines by the rules of Aristotelian logic. **3** a person involved in academic pursuits.

school·marm /skóolmaarm/ *n. colloq.* (also **schoolma'am** /-maam/) a female schoolteacher. □□ **school·marm·ish** *adj.*

school·mas·ter /skóolmastər/ *n.* a male teacher. □□ **school·mas·ter·ly** *adj.*

school·mas·ter·ing /skóolmastəring/ *n.* teaching as a profession.

school·mate /skóolmayt/ *n.* a past or esp. present member of the same school.

school·mis·tress /skóolmistris/ *n.* a head or assistant female teacher.

school·mis·tress·y /skóolmistrisee/ *adj. colloq.* prim and fussy.

school of hard knocks *n.* experience gained from hard work, tough circumstances, etc.

school·room /skóolroom, -room/ *n.* a room used for lessons in a school.

school·teach·er /skóolteechər/ *n.* a person who teaches in a school. □□ **school·teach·ing** *n.*

school·time /skóoltīm/ *n.* **1** lesson time at school or at home. **2** school days.

school year *n.* = ACADEMIC YEAR.

schoon·er /skóonər/ *n.* **1** ▼ a fore-and-aft rigged ship with two or more masts, the foremast being smaller than the other masts. ▷ SAILBOAT. **2** a tall beer glass. **3** *US hist.* = PRAIRIE SCHOONER.

SCHOONER: 19TH-CENTURY FORE-AND-AFT SCHOONER

main gaff topsail
main-sail
main mast
fore topmast staysail
foresail
fore staysail
foremast
jib

schot·tische /shótish, shoteésh/ *n.* **1** a kind of slow polka. **2** the music for this.

Schott·ky ef·fect /shótkee/ *n. Electronics* the increase in thermionic emission from a solid surface due to the presence of an external electric field.

Schrö·ding·er e·qua·tion /shródingər, shráy-/ *n. Physics* a differential equation used in quantum mechanics for the wave function of a particle.

schuss /shōos/ *n. & v.* ● *n.* a straight downhill run on skis. ● *v.intr.* make a schuss.

schwa /schwaa/ *n.* (also **sheva** /shəva/) *Phonet.* **1** the indistinct unstressed vowel sound as in *a moment ago*. **2** the symbol /ə/ representing this in the International Phonetic Alphabet.

sci·am·a·chy /sīáməkee/ *n. formal* **1** fighting with shadows. **2** imaginary or futile combat.

sci·at·ic /sīátik/ *adj.* **1** of the hip. **2** of or affecting the sciatic nerve. **3** suffering from or liable to sciatica. □□ **sci·at·i·cal·ly** *adv.*

sci·at·i·ca /sīátikə/ *n.* neuralgia of the hip and thigh; a pain in the sciatic nerve.

sci·at·ic nerve *n.* the largest nerve in the body, running from the pelvis to the thigh. ▷ NERVOUS SYSTEM

sci·ence /síəns/ *n.* **1** a branch of knowledge involving the systematized observation of and experiment with phenomena (see also NATURAL SCIENCE). **2 a** systematic and formulated knowledge, esp. of a specified type or on a specified subject (*political science*). **b** the pursuit or principles of this.

sci·ence fic·tion *n.* fiction based on imagined future scientific discoveries or environmental changes, frequently dealing with space travel, life on other planets, etc.

sci·ence park *n.* an area devoted to scientific research or the development of science-based industries.

S

sci·en·ter /sīéntər/ *adv. Law* intentionally; knowingly.

sci·en·tif·ic /sīəntífik/ *adj.* **1 a** (of an investigation, etc.) according to rules laid down in exact science for performing observations and testing the soundness of conclusions. **b** systematic; accurate. **2** used in, engaged in, or relating to (esp. natural) science (*scientific discoveries*). □□ **sci·en·tif·i·cal·ly** *adv.*

sci·en·tism /sīəntizəm/ *n.* **1 a** a method or doctrine regarded as characteristic of scientists. **b** the use or practice of this. **2** often *derog.* an excessive belief in or application of scientific method. □□ **sci·en·tis·tic** /-tístik/ *adj.*

sci·en·tist /sīəntist/ *n.* a person with expert knowledge of a (usu. physical or natural) science.

Sci·en·tol·o·gy /sīəntólajee/ *n.* a religious system based on self-improvement and promotion through grades of esp. self-knowledge. □□ **Sci·en·tol·o·gist** *n.*

sci-fi /sīfī/ *n.* (often *attrib.*) *colloq.* science fiction.

scil·i·cet /skéeliket, síliset/ *adv.* that is to say; namely (introducing a word to be supplied or an explanation of an ambiguity).

scil·la /sílə/ *n.* any liliaceous plant of the genus *Scilla*, related to the bluebell, usu. bearing small blue star-shaped or bell-shaped flowers and having long, glossy, straplike leaves.

scim·i·tar /símitər, -taar/ *n.* an Oriental curved sword usu. broadening toward the point.

scin·ti·gram /síntigram/ *n.* an image of an internal part of the body, produced by scintigraphy.

scin·tig·ra·phy /síntígrəfee/ *n.* the use of a radioisotope and a scintillation counter to get an image or record of a bodily organ, etc.

scin·til·la /síntilə/ *n.* **1** a trace. **2** a spark.

scin·til·late /síntilayt/ *v.intr.* **1** (esp. as **scintillating** *adj.*) talk cleverly or wittily; be brilliant. **2** sparkle; twinkle. □□ **scin·til·lant** *adj.* **scin·til·lat·ing·ly** *adv.*

scin·til·la·tion /síntiláyshən/ *n.* **1** the process of scintillating. **2** the twinkling of a star. **3** a flash produced in a material by an ionizing particle, etc.

sci·on /sīən/ *n.* **1** (also **cion**) a shoot of a plant, etc., esp. one cut for grafting or planting. **2** a descendant; a younger member of (esp. a noble) family.

sci·roc·co var. of SIROCCO.

scis·sile /sísil, -īl/ *adj.* able to be cut or divided.

scis·sion /sízhən, sísh-/ *n.* **1** the act or an instance of cutting; the state of being cut. **2** a division or split.

scis·sor /sízər/ *v.tr.* **1** (usu. foll. by *off, up, into,* etc.) cut with scissors. **2** (usu. foll. by *out*) clip out (a newspaper cutting, etc.).

scis·sors /sízərz/ *n.pl.* **1** (also **pair of scissors** *sing.*) an instrument for cutting fabric, paper, hair, etc., having two pivoted blades with finger and thumb holes in the handles, operating by closing on the material to be cut. **2** (treated as *sing.*) a hold in wrestling in which the opponent's body or esp. head is gripped between the legs. □□ **scis·sor·wise** *adv.*

scle·ra /skléerə/ *n.* the white of the eye; a white membrane coating the eyeball. ▷ EYE. □□ **scle·ral** *adj.* **scle·ri·tis** /skleerítis/ *n.* **scle·rot·o·my** /-rótəmee/ *n.* (*pl.* **-ies**).

scle·ren·chy·ma /skleeréngkimə/ *n.* the woody tissue found in a plant, formed from lignified cells and usu. providing support.

scle·roid /skléeroyd/ *adj. Bot. & Zool.* having a hard texture; hardened.

scle·ro·ma /skleerṓmə/ *n.* (*pl.* **scleromata** /-mətə/) an abnormal patch of hardened skin or mucous membrane.

scle·rom·e·ter /skleerómitər/ *n.* an instrument for determining the hardness of materials.

scle·ro·phyll /skléerəfil/ *n.* any woody plant with leathery leaves retaining water. □□ **scle·ro·phyll·ous** /-rófiləs/ *adj.*

scle·rosed /skleerṓst, -rṓzd/ *adj.* affected by sclerosis.

scle·ro·sis /skleerṓsis/ *n.* **1** an abnormal hardening of body tissue. **2** (in full **multiple** or **disseminated sclerosis**) a chronic and progressive

disease of the nervous system resulting in symptoms including paralysis and speech defects.

scle·rot·ic /sklərótik/ *adj. & n.* ● *adj.* **1** of or having sclerosis. **2** of or relating to the sclera. ● *n.* = SCLERA. □□ **scle·ro·ti·tis** /-rətītis/ *n.*

scoff¹ /skof/ *v. & n.* ● *v.intr.* (usu. foll. by *at*) speak derisively, esp. of serious subjects; mock. ● *n.* mocking words; a taunt. □□ **scoff·er** *n.* **scoff·ing·ly** *adv.*

scoff² /skof/ *v. & n. colloq.* ● *v.tr. & intr.* eat greedily. ● *n.* food; a meal.

scold /skōld/ *v. & n.* ● *v.* **1** *tr.* rebuke (esp. a child). **2** *intr.* find fault noisily; complain. ● *n. archaic* a nagging or grumbling woman. □□ **scold·er** *n.* **scold·ing** *n.*

sco·li·o·sis /skōlee+sis, skól-/ *n.* an abnormal lateral curvature of the spine.

scol·lop var. of SCALLOP.

sco·lo·pen·dri·um /skóləpéndreeəm/ *n.* any of various ferns, esp. hart's tongue.

scom·ber /skómbər/ *n.* any marine fish of the family Scombridae, including mackerels, tunas, and bonitos. □□ **scom·brid** *n.* **scom·broid** *adj. & n.*

sconce¹ /skons/ *n.* **1** a flat candlestick with a handle. **2** ▶ a bracket candlestick to hang on a wall.

sconce² /skons/ *n.* **1** a small fort or earthwork usu. defending a ford, pass, etc. **2** *archaic* a shelter or screen.

scone /skon, skōn/ *n.* a small sweet or savory cake of flour, shortening, and milk, baked quickly in an oven.

scoop /skōōp/ *n. & v.* ● *n.* **1** any of various objects resembling a spoon, esp.: **a** a short-handled deep shovel used for transferring grain, sugar, coal, coins, etc. **b** the excavating part of a digging machine, etc. **c** an instrument used for serving portions of mashed potato, ice cream, etc. **2** a quantity taken up by a scoop. **3** a movement of or resembling scooping. **4** a piece of news published by a newspaper, etc., ahead of its rivals. **5** a large profit made quickly or by anticipating one's competitors. ● *v.tr.* **1** (usu. foll. by *out*) hollow out with or as if with a scoop. **2** (usu. foll. by *up*) lift with or as if with a scoop. **3** forestall (a rival newspaper, etc.) with a scoop. **4** secure (a large profit, etc.), esp. suddenly. □□ **scoop·er** *n.* **scoop·ful** *n.* (*pl.* **-fuls**).

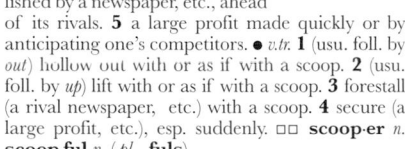

SCONCE:
SHAKER TIN
SCONCE

scoop neck *n.* the rounded low-cut neck of a garment.

scoot /skōōt/ *v. & n. colloq.* ● *v.intr.* run or dart away, esp. quickly. ● *n.* the act or an instance of scooting.

scoot·er /skṓōtər/ *n. & v.* ● *n.* **1** a child's toy consisting of a footboard mounted on two wheels and a long steering handle. **2** (in full **motor scooter**) a light two-wheeled open motor vehicle with a shieldlike protective front. ● *v.intr.* travel or ride on a scooter. □□ **scoot·er·ist** *n.*

scope¹ /skōp/ *n.* **1** the extent to which it is possible to range; the opportunity for action, etc. (*this is beyond the scope of our research*). **2** the sweep or reach of mental activity, observation, or outlook (*an intellect limited in its scope*).

scope² /skōp/ *n. colloq.* a telescope, microscope, or other device ending in *-scope*.

-scope /skōp/ *comb. form* forming nouns denoting: **1** a device looked at or through (*telescope*). **2** an instrument for observing or showing (*gyroscope*). □□ **-scopic** /skópik/ *comb. form* forming adjectives.

sco·pol·a·mine /skəpóləmeen, -min/ *n.* = HYOSCINE.

-scopy /skəpee/ *comb. form* indicating viewing or observation, usu. with an instrument ending in *-scope* (*microscopy*).

scor·bu·tic /skawrbyōōtik/ *adj. & n.* ● *adj.* relating to, resembling, or affected with scurvy. ● *n.* a person affected with scurvy.

scorch /skawrch/ *v. & n.* ● *v.* **1** *tr.* **a** burn the surface of with flame or heat so as to discolor, parch, injure, or hurt. **b** affect with the sensation of burning. **2** *intr.* become discolored, etc., with heat. **3** (as **scorching** *adj.*) *colloq.* **a** (of the weather) very hot. **b** (of criticism, etc.) stringent; harsh. ● *n.* a mark made by scorching. □□ **scorch·ing·ly** *adv.*

scorched earth pol·i·cy *n.* the burning of crops, etc., and the removing or destroying of anything that might be of use to an occupying enemy force.

score /skawr/ *n. & v.* ● *n.* **1 a** the number of points, goals, runs, etc., made by a player, side, etc., in some games. **b** the total number of points, etc., at the end of a game (*the score was five to one*). **c** the act of gaining, esp. a goal. **2** (*pl.* same or **scores**) twenty or a set of twenty. **3** (in *pl.*) a great many (*scores of people arrived*). **4 a** a reason or motive (*rejected on the score of absurdity*). **b** topic; subject (*no worries on that score*). **5** *Mus.* **a** a usu. printed copy of a composition. **b** the music composed for a film or play, esp. for a musical. **6** *colloq.* the state of affairs (*asked what the score was*). **7** a notch, line, etc., cut or scratched into a surface. ● *v.* **1** *tr.* **a** win or gain (a goal, run, points, or success, etc.). **b** count for a score of (points in a game, etc.) (*a bull's-eye scores the most points*). **c** make a record of (a point, etc.). **2** *intr.* **a** make a score in a game. **b** keep the tally of points, runs, etc., in a game. **3** *tr.* mark with notches, incisions, lines, etc.; slash (*scored his name on the desk*). **4** *intr.* secure an advantage (*that is where he scores*). **5** *tr. Mus.* **a** orchestrate (a piece of music). **b** (usu. foll. by *for*) arrange for an instrument or instruments. **6** *intr. sl.* **a** obtain drugs illegally. **b** make a sexual conquest. □ **keep score** (or **the score**) register the score as it is made. **know the score** *colloq.* be aware of the essential facts. **on that score** so far as that is concerned. **score off** (or **score points off**) esp *Brit. colloq.* humiliate, esp. verbally in repartee, etc. **score out** draw a line through (words, etc.). **score points with** make a favorable impression on. □□ **scor·er** *n.* **scor·ing** *n. Mus.*

score·board /skáwrbawrd/ *n.* a large board for publicly displaying the score in a game or match.

score·card /skáwrkaard/ *n.* a card prepared for entering scores on and usu. for indicating players by name, number, etc.

sco·ri·a /skáwreeə/ *n.* (*pl.* **scoriae** /-ree-ee/) **1** cellular lava, or fragments of it. **2** the slag or dross of metal. □□ **sco·ri·a·ceous** /-reeáyshəs/ *adj.*

scorn /skawrn/ *n. & v.* ● *n.* **1** disdain; contempt. **2** an object of contempt, etc. ● *v.tr.* **1** hold in contempt. **2** (often foll. by *to* + infin.) abstain from or refuse to do as unworthy. □□ **scorn·er** *n.*

scorn·ful /skáwrnfŏŏl/ *adj.* (often foll. by *of*) full of scorn; contemptuous. □□ **scorn·ful·ly** *adv.* **scorn·ful·ness** *n.*

Scor·pi·o /skáwrpeeō/ *n.* (*pl.* **-os**) **1** ▼ a constellation, traditionally regarded as contained in the figure of a scorpion. **2 a** the eighth sign of the zodiac (the Scorpion). ▷ ZODIAC. **b** a person born when the Sun is in this sign. □□ **Scor·pi·an** *adj. & n.*

S

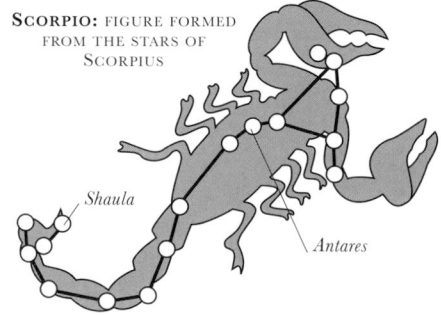

SCORPIO: FIGURE FORMED
FROM THE STARS OF
SCORPIUS

Shaula

Antares

scor·pi·oid /skáwrpeeoyd/ *adj.* & *n.* ● *adj.* **1** *Zool.* of, relating to, or resembling a scorpion; of the scorpion order. **2** *Bot.* (of an inflorescence) curled up at the end, and uncurling as the flowers develop. ● *n.* this type of inflorescence.

scor·pi·on /skáwrpeeən/ *n.* **1** ▼ an arachnid of the order Scorpionida, with lobsterlike pincers and a jointed tail that can be bent over to inflict a poisoned sting. **2** (**the Scorpion**) the zodiacal sign or constellation Scorpio.

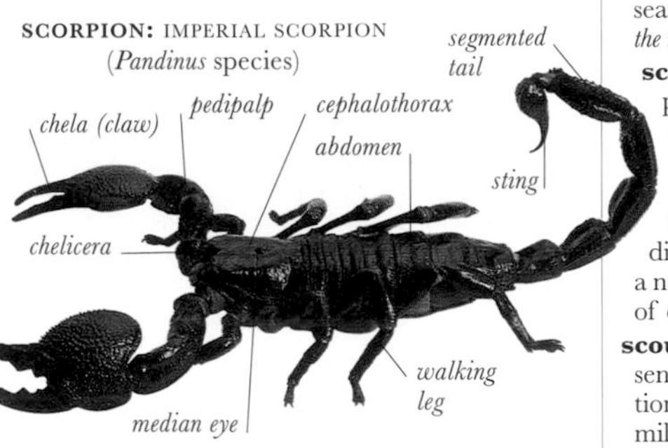

segmented tail
pedipalp
cephalothorax
chela (claw)
abdomen
sting
chelicera
walking leg
median eye

SCORPION: IMPERIAL SCORPION (*Pandinus* species)

scor·zo·ne·ra /skáwrzənéérə/ *n.* **1** a composite plant, *Scorzonera hispanica*, with long, tapering purple-brown roots. **2** the root used as a vegetable.

Scot /skot/ *n.* **1 a** a native of Scotland. **b** a person of Scottish descent. **2** *hist.* a member of a Gaelic people that migrated from Ireland to Scotland around the 6th c.

scot /skot/ *n. hist.* a payment corresponding to a modern tax, rate, etc.

Scotch /skoch/ *adj.* & *n.* ● *adj.* var. of SCOTTISH or SCOTS. ● *n.* **1** var. of SCOTTISH or SCOTS. **2** Scotch whiskey. ¶ *Scots* or *Scottish* is generally preferred in Scotland, except in the special compounds given below.

scotch /skoch/ *v.tr.* **1** put an end to; frustrate. **2** *archaic* wound without killing.

Scotch·man /skóchmən/ *n.* (*pl.* **-men**; *fem.* **Scotchwoman**, *pl.* **-women**) = SCOTSMAN. ¶ *Scotsman*, etc., are generally preferred in Scotland.

Scotch broth *n.* a soup made from beef or mutton with pearl barley, etc.

Scotch whis·key *n.* whiskey distilled in Scotland, esp. from malted barley.

scot-free *adj.* unharmed; unpunished; safe.

Scot·i·cism var. of SCOTTICISM.

Scot·i·cize var. of SCOTTICIZE.

Scot·land Yard /skótlənd/ *n.* **1** the headquarters of the London Metropolitan Police. **2** its Criminal Investigation Department.

S

sco·to·ma /skətṓmə/ *n.* (*pl.* **scotomata** /-mətə/) a partial loss of vision or blind spot in an otherwise normal visual field.

Scots /skots/ *adj.* & *n.* esp. *Sc.* ● *adj.* **1** = SCOTTISH *adj.* **2** in the dialect, accent, etc., of (esp. Lowlands) Scotland. ● *n.* **1** = SCOTTISH *n.* **2** the form of English spoken in (esp. Lowlands) Scotland.

Scots·man /skótsmən/ *n.* (*pl.* **-men**; *fem.* **Scots·woman**, *pl.* **-women**) **1** a native of Scotland. **2** a person of Scottish descent.

Scots pine *n.* a pine tree, *Pinus sylvestris*, native to Europe and much planted for its wood. ▷ CONIFER

Scot·ti·cism /skótisizəm/ *n.* (also **Scot·i·cism**) a Scottish phrase, word, or idiom.

Scot·ti·cize /skótisīz/ *v.* (also **Scot·i·cize**) **1** *tr.* imbue with or model on Scottish ways, etc. **2** *intr.* imitate the Scottish in idiom or habits.

Scot·tie /skótee/ *n. colloq.* **1** (also **Scottie dog**) a Scottish terrier. **2** a Scot.

Scot·tish /skótish/ *adj.* & *n.* ● *adj.* of or relating to Scotland or its inhabitants. ● *n.* (prec. by *the*; treated as *pl.*) the people of Scotland (see also SCOTS). ▫▫ **Scot·tish·ness** *n.*

Scot·tish ter·ri·er *n.* a small terrier of a rough-haired short-legged breed.

scoun·drel /skówndrəl/ *n.* an unscrupulous villain; a rogue. ▫▫ **scoun·drel·ism** *n.* **scoun·drel·ly** *adj.*

scour[1] /skowr/ *v.* & *n.* ● *v.tr.* **1 a** cleanse or brighten by rubbing, esp. with soap, chemicals, sand, etc. **b** (usu. foll. by *away*, *off*, etc.) clear (rust, stains, reputation, etc.) by rubbing, hard work, etc. (*scoured the slur from his name*). **2** clear out (a pipe, channel, etc.) by flushing through. ● *n.* the act or an instance of scouring. ▫▫ **scour·er** *n.*

scour[2] /skowr/ *v. tr.* hasten over (an area, etc.) searching thoroughly (*scoured the streets for him; scoured the newspaper*).

scourge /skərj/ *n.* & *v.* ● *n.* **1** a whip used for punishment, esp. of people. **2** a person or thing seen as punishing, esp. on a large scale (*Genghis Khan, the scourge of Asia*). ● *v.tr.* **1** whip. **2** punish; oppress. ▫▫ **scourg·er** *n.*

Scouse /skows/ *n.* & *adj. colloq.* ● *n.* **1** the dialect of Liverpool. **2** (also **Scous·er** /skówsə/) a native of Liverpool. **3** (**scouse**) = LOBSCOUSE. ● *adj.* of or relating to Liverpool.

scout /skowt/ *n.* & *v.* ● *n.* **1** a person, esp. a soldier, sent out to get information about the enemy's position, strength, etc. **2** the act of seeking (esp. military) information (*on the scout*). **3** = TALENT SCOUT. **4** (**Scout**) a Boy Scout or Girl Scout. **5** a ship or aircraft designed for reconnoitering, esp. a small fast aircraft. ● *v.* **1** *intr.* act as a scout. **2** *intr.* (foll. by *about*, *around*) make a search. **3** *tr.* (often foll. by *out*) *colloq.* explore to get information about (territory, etc.). ▫▫ **scout·er** *n.* **scout·ing** *n.*

Scout·er /skówtər/ *n.* an adult member of the Boy Scouts.

scout·mas·ter /skówtmastər/ *n.* a person in charge of a group of Scouts.

scow /skow/ *n.* a flat-bottomed boat used as a lighter, etc.

scowl /skowl/ *n.* & *v.* ● *n.* a severe frown producing a sullen, bad-tempered, or threatening look on a person's face. ● *v.intr.* make a scowl. ▫▫ **scowl·er** *n.*

scrab·ble /skrábəl/ *v.* & *n.* ● *v.intr.* (often foll. by *about*, *at*) scratch or grope to find or hold on to something. ● *n.* **1** an act of scrabbling. **2** (**Scrabble**) *Trademark* a game in which players build up words from letter blocks on a board.

scrag·gly /skráglee/ *adj.* sparse and irregular.

scrag·gy /skrágee/ *adj.* (**scraggier**, **scraggiest**) thin and bony. ▫▫ **scrag·gi·ly** *adv.* **scrag·gi·ness** *n.*

scram /skram/ *v.intr.* (**scrammed**, **scramming**) (esp. in *imper.*) *colloq.* go away.

scram·ble /skrámbəl/ *v.* & *n.* ● *v.* **1** *intr.* make one's way over rough ground, rocks, etc., by clambering, crawling, etc. **2** *intr.* (foll. by *for*, *at*) struggle with competitors (for a thing or share of it). **3** *intr.* move with difficulty or awkwardly. **4** *tr.* **a** mix together indiscriminately. **b** jumble or muddle. **5** *tr.* cook (eggs) by heating them when broken and well mixed, often with butter, milk, etc. **6** *tr.* change the speech frequency of (a broadcast transmission or telephone conversation) so as to make it unintelligible without a corresponding decoding device. **7** *intr.* (of fighter aircraft or their pilots) take off quickly in an emergency or for action. ● *n.* **1** an act of scrambling. **2** a difficult climb or walk. **3** (foll. by *for*) an eager struggle or competition. **4** an emergency takeoff by fighter aircraft.

scram·bler /skrámblər/ *n.* a device for scrambling telephone conversations.

scrap[1] /skrap/ *n.* & *v.* ● *n.* **1** a small detached piece; a fragment or remnant. **2** rubbish or waste material. **3** discarded metal for reprocessing (often *attrib.*: *scrap metal*). **4** (with *neg.*) the smallest piece or amount (*not a scrap of food left*). **5** (in *pl.*) **a** odds and ends. **b** bits of uneaten food. ● *v.tr.* (**scrapped**, **scrapping**) discard as useless.

scrap[2] /skrap/ *n.* & *v. colloq.* ● *n.* a fight or rough quarrel. ● *v.tr.* (**scrapped**, **scrapping**) (often foll. by *with*) have a scrap. ▫▫ **scrap·per** *n.*

scrap·book /skrápbŏŏk/ *n.* a book of blank pages for sticking cuttings, drawings, etc., in.

scrape /skrayp/ *v.* & *n.* ● *v.* **1** *tr.* **a** move a hard or sharp edge across (a surface), esp. to make something smooth. **b** apply (a hard or sharp edge) in this way. **2** *tr.* (foll. by *away*, *off*, etc.) remove (a stain, projection, etc.) by scraping. **3** *tr.* **a** rub (a surface) harshly against another. **b** scratch or damage by scraping. **4** *tr.* make (a hollow) by scraping. **5 a** *tr.* draw or move with a sound of, or resembling, scraping. **b** *intr.* emit or produce such a sound. **c** *tr.* produce such a sound from. **6** *intr.* (often foll. by *along*, *by*, *through*, etc.) move or pass along while almost touching close or surrounding features, obstacles, etc. (*the car scraped through the narrow lane*). **7** *tr.* just manage to achieve (a living, an examination pass, etc.). **8** *intr.* (often foll. by *by*, *through*) **a** barely manage. **b** pass an examination, etc., with difficulty. **9** *tr.* (foll. by *together*, *up*) contrive to bring or provide; amass with difficulty. **10** *intr.* be economical. **11** *intr.* draw back a foot in making a clumsy bow. ● *n.* **1** the act or sound of scraping. **2** a scraped place (on the skin, etc.). **3** the scraping of a foot in bowing. **4** *colloq.* an awkward predicament, esp. resulting from an escapade. ▫ **scrape acquaintance with esp.** *Brit.* contrive to get to know (a person). **scrape the barrel** *colloq.* be reduced to one's last resources.

scrap·er /skráypər/ *n.* a device used for scraping, esp. for removing dirt, etc., from a surface.

scra·per·board /skráypərbawrd/ *n.* = SCRATCHBOARD.

scrap heap *n.* **1** a pile of scrap materials. **2** a state of uselessness.

scrap·ie /skráypee, skráp-/ *n.* a viral disease of sheep involving the central nervous system and characterized by lack of coordination causing affected animals to rub against trees, etc., for support.

scrap·ing /skráyping/ *n.* **1** in senses of SCRAPE. **2** (esp. in *pl.*) a fragment produced by this.

scrap·py /skrápee/ *adj.* (**scrappier**, **scrappiest**) **1** consisting of scraps. **2** incomplete; carelessly arranged or put together. ▫▫ **scrap·pi·ly** *adv.* **scrap·pi·ness** *n.*

scrap·yard /skrápyaard/ *n.* a place where (esp. metal) scrap is collected.

scratch /skrach/ *v.*, *n.*, & *adj.* ● *v.* **1** *tr.* score or mark the surface of with a sharp or pointed object. **2** *tr.* make a long, narrow superficial wound in (the skin). **3** *tr.* (also *absol.*) scrape without marking, esp. with the hand to relieve itching. **4** *tr.* make or form by scratching. **5** *tr.* (foll. by *together*, *up*, etc.) obtain (a thing) by scratching or with difficulty. **6** *tr.* (foll. by *out*, *off*, *through*) cancel or strike (out) with a pencil, etc. **7** *tr.* (also *absol.*) withdraw (a competitor, candidate, etc.) from a race or competition. **8** *intr.* (often foll. by *about*, *around*, etc.) **a** scratch the ground, etc., in search. **b** look around haphazardly (*they were scratching about for evidence*). ● *n.* **1** a mark or wound made by scratching. **2** a sound of scratching. **3** a spell of scratching oneself. ● *attrib.adj.* **1** collected by chance. **2** collected or made from whatever is available (*a scratch crew*). **3** with no handicap given (*a scratch race*). ▫ **from scratch 1** from the beginning. **2** without help or advantage. **scratch along** make a living, etc., with difficulty. **scratch one's head** be perplexed. **scratch the surface** deal with a matter only superficially. **up to scratch** up to the required standard. ▫▫ **scratch·er** *n.*

scratch·board /skráchbawrd/ *n.* cardboard or board with a blackened surface which can be scraped off for making white-line drawings.

scratch pad *n.* **1** a pad of paper for scribbling. **2** *Computing* a small fast memory for the temporary storage of data.

scratch·y /skráchee/ *adj.* (**scratchier**, **scratchiest**) **1** tending to make scratches or a scratching noise. **2** (esp. of a garment) tending to cause itchiness. **3** (of a drawing, etc.) done carelessly. ▫▫ **scratch·i·ly** *adv.* **scratch·i·ness** *n.*

scrawl /skrawl/ *v.* & *n.* ● *v.* **1** *tr.* & *intr.* write in a hurried untidy way. **2** *tr.* (foll. by *out*) cross out by scrawling over. ● *n.* **1** a piece of hurried writing. **2** a scrawled note. ▫▫ **scrawl·y** *adj.*

scrawn·y /skráwnee/ adj. (**scrawnier**, **scrawniest**) lean; scraggy. □□ **scrawn·i·ness** n.

scream /skreem/ n. & v. ● n. **1** a loud, high-pitched, piercing cry expressing fear, pain, extreme fright, etc. **2** colloq. an irresistibly funny occurrence or person. ● v. **1** intr. emit a scream. **2** tr. speak or sing (words, etc.) in a screaming tone. **3** intr. make or move with a shrill sound like a scream. **4** intr. be blatantly obvious or conspicuous.

scream·er /skreemər/ n. **1** a person or thing that screams. **2** colloq. a sensational headline.

scree /skree/ n. small loose stones. ▷ ERODE

screech /skreech/ n. & v. ● n. a harsh, high-pitched scream. ● v.tr. & intr. utter with or make a screech. □□ **screech·er** n. **screech·y** adj. (**screechier**, **screechiest**).

screech owl n. any owl that screeches instead of hooting.

screed /skreed/ n. **1** a long usu. tiresome piece of writing or speech. **2** a leveled layer of material (e.g., concrete) applied to a floor or other surface.

screen /skreen/ n. & v. ● n. **1** a fixed or movable upright partition for separating, concealing, or sheltering from drafts or excessive heat or light. **2** a thing used as a shelter, esp. from observation. **3 a** a measure adopted for concealment. **b** the protection afforded by this (under the screen of night). **4 a** a blank usu. white or silver surface on which a photographic image is projected. **b** (prec. by the) the motion-picture industry. **5** the surface of a cathode-ray tube or similar electronic device, esp. of a television, computer monitor, etc., on which images appear. ▷ MONITOR, TELEVISION. **6** = WINDSCREEN. **7** a frame with fine wire netting to keep out flies, mosquitoes, etc. **8** a large sieve or riddle, esp. for sorting grain, coal, etc., into sizes. **9** a system of checking for the presence or absence of a disease, ability, attribute, etc. **10** Printing a transparent, finely ruled plate or film used in half-tone reproduction. ▷ PRINTING. ● v.tr. **1** (often foll. by from) **a** afford shelter to; hide. **b** protect from detection, censure, etc. **2** (foll. by off) hide behind a screen. **3 a** show (a film, etc.). **b** broadcast (a television program). **4** prevent from causing, or protect from, electrical interference. **5 a** test (a person or group) for the presence or absence of a disease. **b** check on (a person) for the presence or absence of a quality, esp. reliability or loyalty. **6** pass (grain, coal, etc.) through a screen. □□ **screen·a·ble** adj. **screen·er** n. **screen·ing** n.

screen·play /skreenplay/ n. the script of a motion picture etc., with acting instructions, scene directions, etc.

screen print·ing n. a process like stenciling with ink forced through a prepared sheet of fine material (orig. silk).

screen·sav·er /skreensayvər/ n. Computing a program which replaces an unchanging screen display with a moving image to prevent damage to the phosphor.

screen test n. an audition for a part in a motion picture.

screen·writ·er /skreenrītər/ n. a person who writes a screenplay.

screw /skroo/ n. & v. ● n. **1** a thin cylinder or cone with a spiral ridge or thread running around the outside (**male screw**) or the inside (**female screw**). **2** (in full **wood screw**) a metal male screw with a slotted head and a sharp point. **3** (in full **screw bolt**) a metal male screw with a blunt end on which a nut is threaded to bolt things together. **4** a wooden or metal straight screw used to exert pressure. **5** (in sing. or pl.) an instrument of torture acting in this way. **6** (in full **screw propeller**) ▶ a form of propeller with twisted blades acting like a screw on the water or air. **7** one turn of a screw. **8** sl. a prison warden or guard. **9** coarse sl. **a** an act of sexual intercourse.

b a partner in this. ¶ Usually considered a taboo use. ● v. **1** tr. fasten or tighten with a screw or screws. **2** tr. turn (a screw). **3** intr. twist or turn around like a screw. **4** tr. **a** put psychological, etc., pressure on to achieve an end. **b** oppress. **5** tr. (foll. by out of) extort (consent, money, etc.) from (a person). **6** tr. (also absol.) coarse sl. have sexual intercourse with. ¶ Usually considered a taboo use. **7** intr. (of a rolling ball, or of a person, etc.) take a curling course. □ **have one's head screwed on the right way** colloq. have common sense. **have a screw loose** colloq. be slightly crazy. **put the screws on** colloq. exert pressure on, esp. to extort or intimidate. **screw up 1** contract or contort (one's face, etc.). **2** contract and crush into a tight mass (a piece of paper, etc.). **3** summon up (one's courage, etc.). **4** cause to fail or go wrong. □□ **screw·a·ble** adj. **screw·er** n.

screw·ball /skroobawl/ n. & adj. sl. ● n. **1** Baseball a pitch thrown with spin opposite that of a curveball. **2** a crazy or eccentric person. ● adj. crazy.

screw·driv·er /skroodrīvər/ n. a tool with a shaped tip to fit into the head of a screw to turn it.

screwed /skrood/ adj. **1** twisted. **2** sl. ruined.

screw top n. a cap or lid that can be screwed on to a bottle, jar, etc.

screw-up n. sl. a bungle, muddle, or mess.

screw·y /skroo-ee/ adj. (**screwier**, **screwiest**) sl. **1** crazy or eccentric. **2** absurd. □□ **screw·i·ness** n.

scrib·ble /skríbəl/ v. & n. ● v. **1** tr. & intr. write carelessly or hurriedly. **2** intr. often derog. be an author or writer. **3** intr. & tr. draw carelessly or meaninglessly. ● n. **1** a scrawl. **2** a hasty note, etc. **3** careless handwriting. □□ **scrib·bler** n. **scrib·bly** adj.

scribe /skrīb/ n. & v. ● n. **1** a person who writes out documents, esp. an ancient or medieval copyist of manuscripts. **2** Bibl. an ancient Jewish record keeper or professional theologian and jurist. **3** (in full **scribe awl**) a pointed instrument for making marks on wood, bricks, etc. **4** colloq. a writer, esp. a journalist. ● v.tr. mark (wood, etc.) with a scribe (see sense 3 of n.). □□ **scrib·al** adj. **scrib·er** n.

scrim /skrim/ n. open-weave fabric for lining or upholstery, etc.

scrim·mage /skrímij/ n. & v. ● n. **1** a struggle; a brawl. **2** Football a single play from the snap of the ball till the ball is dead. ● v. intr. engage in a scrimmage. □□ **scrim·mag·er** n.

scrimp /skrimp/ v.intr. be thrifty or parsimonious; economize (I have scrimped and saved to give you a good education). □□ **scrimp·y** adj.

scrim·shaw /skrímshaw/ v. & n. ● v.tr. (also absol.) adorn (shells, ivory, etc.) with carved or colored designs (as sailors' pastime at sea). ● n. work or a piece of work of this kind.

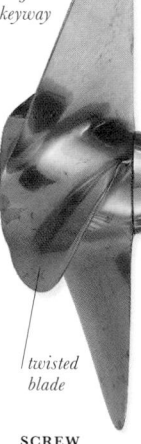

shaft

keyway

boss

twisted blade

SCREW PROPELLER

scrip /skrip/ n. **1** a provisional certificate of money subscribed to a bank, etc., entitling the holder to dividends. **2** (collect.) such certificates. **3** an extra share or shares instead of a dividend.

script /skript/ n. & v. ● n. **1** handwriting as distinct from print; written characters. **2** type imitating handwriting. **3** an alphabet or system of writing. **4** the text of a play, film, or broadcast. **5** an examinee's set of written answers. ● v.tr. write a script for (a motion picture, etc.).

scrip·to·ri·um /skriptáwreeəm/ n. (pl. **scriptoria** /-reeə/ or **scriptoriums**) a room set apart for writing, esp. in a monastery. □□ **scrip·to·ri·al** adj.

scrip·tur·al /skrípchərəl/ adj. **1** of or relating to a scripture, esp. the Bible. **2** having the authority of a scripture. □□ **scrip·tur·al·ly** adv.

scrip·ture /skrípchər/ n. **1** sacred writings. **2** (**Scripture** or **the Scriptures**) the Bible as a collection of sacred writings in Christianity.

script·writ·er /skriptrītər/ n. a person who writes a script for a motion picture, broadcast, etc. □□ **script·writ·ing** n.

scrive·ner /skrívnər, skrívnər/ n. hist. **1** a drafter of documents. **2** a notary.

scrod /skrod/ n. a young cod or haddock, esp. as food.

scrof·u·la /skrófyələ/ n. archaic a disease with glandular swellings, prob. a form of tuberculosis. □□ **scrof·u·lous** adj.

scroll /skrōl/ n. & v. ● n. **1** ▼ a roll of parchment or paper esp. with writing on it. **2** a book in the ancient roll form. **3** an ornamental design or carving imitating a roll of parchment. ● v. **1** tr. (often foll. by down, up) move (a display on a computer screen) in order to view new material. **2** tr. inscribe in or like a scroll. **3** intr. curl up like paper.

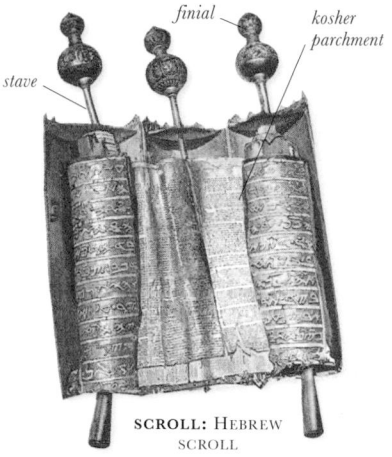

finial

kosher parchment

stave

SCROLL: HEBREW SCROLL

scroll·bar /skrōlbaar/ n. a long thin section at the edge of a computer display by which material can be scrolled using a mouse.

scrolled /skrōld/ adj. having a scroll ornament.

scroll·work /skrōlwərk/ n. decoration of spiral lines, esp. as cut by a scroll saw.

Scrooge /skrooj/ n. a mean or miserly person.

scro·tum /skrótəm/ n. (pl. **scrota** /-tə/ or **scrotums**) a pouch of skin containing the testicles. ▷ REPRODUCTIVE ORGANS. □□ **scro·tal** adj.

scrounge /skrownj/ v. & n. colloq. ● v. **1** tr. (also absol.) obtain (things) illicitly or by cadging. **2** intr. search about to find something at no cost. ● n. an act of scrounging. □ **on the scrounge** engaged in scrounging. □□ **scroung·er** n.

scrub¹ /skrub/ v. & n. ● v. (**scrubbed**, **scrubbing**) **1** tr. rub hard so as to clean, esp. with a hard brush. **2** intr. use a brush in this way. **3** intr. (often foll. by up) (of a surgeon, etc.) thoroughly clean the hands and arms by scrubbing, before operating. **4** tr. colloq. scrap or cancel. ● n. the act or an instance of scrubbing; the process of being scrubbed.

scrub² /skrub/ n. **1 a** vegetation consisting mainly of brushwood or stunted forest growth. **b** an area of land covered with this. **2** an animal of inferior breed or physique (often attrib.: scrub horse). **3** a small or dwarf variety (often attrib.: scrub pine). □□ **scrub·by** adj.

scrub·ber /skrúbər/ n. an apparatus using water or a solution for purifying gases, etc.

scruff /skruf/ n. the back of the neck (esp. scruff of the neck).

scruff·y /skrúfee/ adj. (**scruffier**, **scruffiest**) colloq. shabby; slovenly; untidy. □□ **scruff·i·ly** adv. **scruff·i·ness** n.

scrum /skrum/ n. **1** Rugby an arrangement of the forwards of each team in two opposing groups, each with arms interlocked and heads down, with the ball thrown in between them to restart play. ▷ RUGBY. **2** Brit. colloq. a milling crowd. □ **scrum**

S

SCUBA DIVING

When breathing underwater, a scuba diver draws compressed air from a tank worn on the back. On top of the tank is the regulator first-stage, which reduces the air pressure to just above that of the surrounding water. The air then travels down a tube to the regulator second-stage (which includes the mouthpiece). This part of the apparatus lowers the air pressure to exactly that of the external water, making the air safe to breathe.

SCUBA DIVERS

mask
regulator second-stage
buoyancy compensator
buoyancy compensator mouthpiece
octopus rig

regulator first-stage
protective mesh
air tank
wetsuit
instrument console

half a halfback who puts the ball into the scrum. ▷ RUGBY

scrum·mage /skrúmij/ n. Rugby = SCRUM 1.

scrum·my /skrúmee/ adj. Brit. colloq. excellent; enjoyable; delicious.

scrump·tious /skrúmpshəs/ adj. colloq. **1** delicious. **2** pleasing; delightful. □□ **scrump·tious·ly** adv. **scrump·tious·ness** n.

scrunch /skrunch/ v. & n. • v.tr. & intr. **1** (usu. foll. by up) make or become crushed or crumpled. **2** make or cause to make a crunching sound. • n. the act or an instance of scrunching.

scrunch·ie /skrúnchee/ n. a hair band of elastic enclosed by crumpled fabric, used for ponytails, etc.

scru·ple /skróopəl/ n. & v. • n. **1** (in sing. or pl.) regard to the morality or propriety of an action. **2** a feeling of doubt or hesitation caused by this. • v.intr. **1** (foll. by to + infin.; usu. with neg.) be reluctant because of scruples (did not scruple to stop their allowance). **2** feel or be influenced by scruples.

scru·pu·lous /skróopyələs/ adj. **1** conscientious or thorough even in small matters. **2** careful to avoid doing wrong. **3** punctilious; overattentive to details. □□ **scru·pu·los·i·ty** /-lósitee/ n. **scru·pu·lous·ly** adv. **scru·pu·lous·ness** n.

scru·ti·nize /skróot'nīz/ v.tr. look closely at; examine with close scrutiny. □□ **scru·ti·niz·er** n.

scru·ti·ny /skróot'nee/ n. (pl. **-ies**) **1** a critical gaze. **2** a close investigation or examination of details. **3** an official examination of ballot papers to check their validity or accuracy of counting.

scry /skrī/ v.intr. (**-ies**, **-ied**) divine by crystal gazing. □□ **scry·er** n.

scu·ba /skóobə/ n. (pl. **scubas**) gear that provides an air supply from a portable tank for swimming underwater (acronym for self-contained underwater breathing apparatus).

scu·ba div·ing n. ▲ swimming underwater using a scuba, esp. as a sport. □□ **scu·ba dive** v.intr. **scu·ba div·er** n.

scud /skud/ v. & n. • v.intr. (**scudded, scudding**) **1** fly or run straight, fast, and lightly. **2** Naut. run before the wind. • n. **1** a spell of scudding. **2** a scudding motion. **3** vapory driving clouds. **4** a driving shower; a gust. **5** wind-blown spray. **6** (**Scud**) a type of long-range surface-to-surface guided missile originally developed in the former Soviet Union.

scuff /skuf/ v. & n. • v. **1** tr. graze or brush against. **2** tr. mark or wear down (shoes) in this way. **3** intr. walk with dragging feet. • n. a mark of scuffing.

scuf·fle /skúfəl/ n. & v. • n. a confused struggle or disorderly fight at close quarters. • v.intr. engage in a scuffle.

scul·dug·ger·y var. of SKULDUGGERY.

scull /skul/ n. & v. • n. **1** either of a pair of small oars used by a single rower. ▷ ROW. **2** an oar placed over the stern of a boat to propel it, usu. by a twisting motion. **3** ► a small boat propelled with a scull or a pair of sculls. ▷ ROWBOAT. **4** (in pl.) a race between boats with single pairs of oars. • v.tr. propel (a boat) with sculls.

scul·ler /skúlər/ n. **1** a user of sculls. **2** a boat intended for sculling.

scul·ler·y /skúləree/ n. (pl. **-ies**) a small kitchen or room at the back of a house for washing dishes, etc.

scul·lion /skúlyən/ n. archaic **1** a cook's boy. **2** a person who washes dishes.

scul·pin /skúlpin/ n. any of numerous fish of the family Cottidae, native to nontropical regions, having large spiny heads.

sculpt /skulpt/ v.tr. & intr. (also **sculp**) sculpture.

sculp·tor /skúlptər/ n. (fem. **sculptress** /-tris/) an artist who makes sculptures.

sculp·ture /skúlpchər/ n. & v. • n. **1** the art of making forms, often representational, in the round or in relief by chiseling, carving, modeling, casting, etc. **2** a work or works of sculpture. • v. **1** tr. represent in or adorn with sculpture. **2** intr. practice sculpture. □□ **sculp·tur·al** adj. **sculp·tur·al·ly** adv. **sculp·tur·esque** adj.

scum /skum/ n. & v. • n. **1** a layer of dirt, froth, etc., forming at the top of liquid. **2** (foll. by of) the most worthless part of something. **3** colloq. a worthless person or group. • v. (**scummed, scumming**) **1** tr. remove scum from. **2** tr. be or form a scum on. □□ **scum·my** adj. (**scummier, scummiest**).

scum·bag /skúmbag/ n. sl. a worthless despicable person.

scum·ble /skúmbəl/ v. & n. • v.tr. **1** modify (a painting) by applying a thin opaque coat of paint to give a softer or duller effect. **2** modify (a drawing) similarly with light penciling, etc. • n. **1** material used in scumbling. **2** the effect produced by scumbling.

scun·ner /skúnər/ v. & n. Sc. • v.intr. & tr. feel disgust; nauseate. • n. **1** a strong dislike (esp. take a scunner at or against). **2** an object of loathing.

scup /skup/ n. an E. American fish, Stenostomus chrysops, a kind of porgy.

scup·per /skúpər/ n. a hole at the edge of a boat's deck to allow water to run off.

scurf /skərf/ n. **1** flakes on the surface of the skin, cast off as fresh skin develops below; dandruff. **2** any scaly matter on a surface. □□ **scurf·y** adj.

scur·ril·ous /skóriləs, skúr-/ adj. **1** (of a person or language) grossly or indecently abusive. **2** given to or expressed with low humor. □□ **scur·ril·i·ty** /-rilitee/ n. (pl. **-ies**). **scur·ril·ous·ly** adv. **scur·ril·ous·ness** n.

scur·ry /skóree, skúree/ v. & n. • v.intr. (**-ies, -ied**) run or move hurriedly, esp. with short quick steps; scamper. • n. (pl. **-ies**) **1** the act or sound of scurrying. **2** a flurry of rain or snow.

scur·vy /skúrvee/ n. & adj. • n. a disease caused by a deficiency of vitamin C. • adj. (**scurvier, scurviest**) dishonorable; contemptible. □□ **scur·vied** adj. **scur·vi·ly** adv.

scut /skut/ n. a short tail, esp. of a hare, rabbit, or deer.

scu·ta pl. of SCUTUM.

scu·tage /skyóotij/ n. hist. money paid by a feudal landowner instead of personal service.

scutch /skuch/ v.tr. dress (fibrous material, esp. retted flax) by beating. □□ **scutch·er** n.

scutch·eon /skúchən/ n. **1** = ESCUTCHEON. **2** an ornamented brass, etc., plate around or over a keyhole. **3** a plate for a name or inscription.

scute /skyoot/ n. Zool. = SCUTUM.

scu·tel·lum /skyootéləm/ n. (pl. **scutella** /-lə/) Bot. & Zool. a scale, plate, or any shieldlike formation on a plant, insect, bird, etc., esp. one of the horny scales on a bird's foot. □□ **scu·tel·late** /skyootélit, skyootəlayt/ adj. **scu·tel·la·tion** /skyootəláyshən/ n.

scut·tle[1] /skút'l/ n. a receptacle for carrying and holding a small supply of coal.

scut·tle[2] /skút'l/ v. & n. • v.intr. **1** scurry; hurry along. **2** run away. • n. **1** a hurried gait. **2** a precipitate flight.

scut·tle[3] /skút'l/ n. & v. • n. a hole with a lid in a ship's deck or side. • v.tr. let water into (a ship) to sink it.

scut·tle·butt /skút'lbut/ n. **1** a water cask on the deck of a ship, for drinking from. **2** colloq. rumor; gossip.

scu·tum /skyóotəm/ n. (pl. **scuta** /-tə/) each of the shieldlike plates or scales forming the bony covering of a crocodile, sturgeon, turtle, armadillo, etc. □□ **scu·tal** adj. **scu·tate** adj.

scuzz·y /skúzee/ adj. sl. abhorrent or disgusting.

Scyl·la and Cha·ryb·dis /sílə ənd kərĭbdis/ n.pl. two dangers such that avoidance of one increases the risk from the other.

scy·pho·zo·an /sífəzóən/ n. & adj. • n. any marine jellyfish of the class Scyphozoa, with tentacles bearing stinging cells. ▷ CNIDARIAN. • adj. of or relating to this class.

scy·phus /sífəs/ n. (pl. **scyphi** /-fī/) **1** Gk Antiq. a footless drinking cup with two handles below the level of the rim. **2** Bot. a cup-shaped part as in a narcissus flower or in lichens. □□ **scy·phose** adj.

SCULL:
SINGLE SCULL (WITH DECKING REMOVED) AND OARS

bowball
bowpost
diagonal deck support
internal frame
breakwater
hatch
sliding seat
slide track
outrigger
gate
keel
stretcher
blade
sculls (oars)

S

SEABED

The seabed consists of a number of distinctive geologic features. Mid-ocean ridges (underwater mountain ranges) form when tectonic plates pull apart and magma rises to fill the space. Seamounts are underwater volcanoes; when flat-topped, they are known as guyots. Deep-sea trenches form when one tectonic plate is forced under another (subduction).

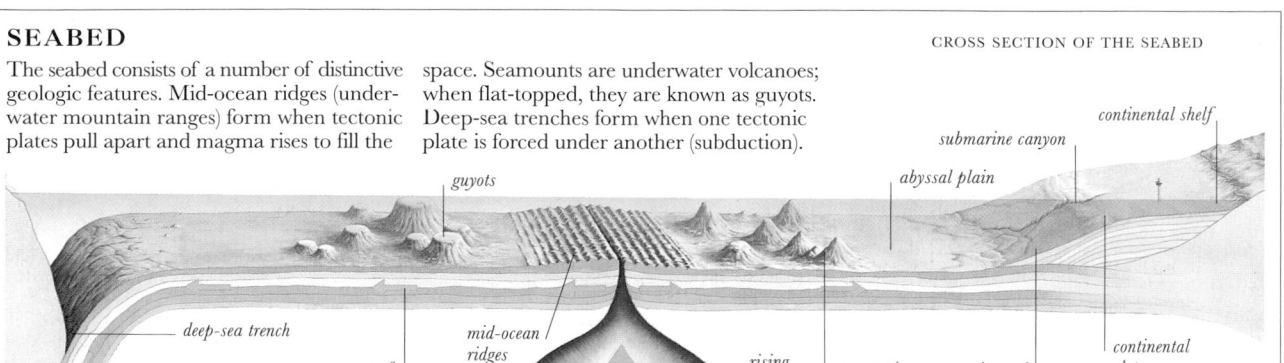

CROSS SECTION OF THE SEABED

continental shelf · submarine canyon · abyssal plain · guyots · deep-sea trench · subducted tectonic plate · movement of tectonic plate · mid-ocean ridges · rising magma · seamount · continental rise · continental slope

scythe /sīth/ *n. & v.* ● *n.* ◄ a mowing and reaping implement with a long curved blade swung over the ground by a long pole with two short handles projecting from it. ● *v.tr.* cut with a scythe.

Scyth·i·an /sítheeən, -thee-/ *adj. & n.* ● *adj.* of or relating to ancient Scythia, a region north of the Black Sea. ● *n.* **1** an inhabitant of Scythia. **2** the language of this region.

SD *abbr.* South Dakota (in official postal use).

S.Dak. *abbr.* South Dakota.

SDI *abbr.* strategic defense initiative.

SE *abbr.* **1** southeast. **2** southeastern. **3** Standard English.

Se *symb. Chem.* the element selenium.

sea /see/ *n.* **1** the expanse of salt water that covers most of the Earth's surface. **2** any part of this. **3** a particular (usu. named) tract of salt water partly or wholly enclosed by land (*the North Sea*). **4** a large inland lake (*the Sea of Galilee*). **5** the waves of the sea, esp. with reference to their local motion or state (*a choppy sea*). **6** (foll. by *of*) a vast quantity or expanse (*a sea of faces*). **7** (*attrib.*) living or used in, on, or near the sea (often prefixed to the name of a marine animal, plant, etc., having a superficial resemblance to what it is named after) (*sea lettuce*). □ **at sea 1** in a ship on the sea. **2** (also **all at sea**) perplexed; confused. **by sea** in a ship or ships. **go to sea** become a sailor. **on the sea 1** in a ship at sea. **2** situated on the coast. **put** (or **put out**) **to sea** leave land or port.

sea an·chor *n.* a device such as a heavy bag dragged in the water to retard the drifting of a ship.

sea a·nem·o·ne *n.* any of various coelenterates of the order Actiniaria bearing a ring of tentacles around the mouth. ▷ CNIDARIAN, SYMBIOSIS

sea bass *n.* any of various marine fishes like the bass, esp. *Centropristis striatus*.

sea·bed /séebed/ *n.* ▲ the ground under the sea; the ocean floor.

sea·bird /séebərd/ *n.* ► a bird frequenting the sea or the land near the sea.

sea·board /séebawrd/ *n.* **1** the seashore or coastal region. **2** the line of a coast.

sea·bor·gi·um /seebáwrgeeəm/ *n.* an artificially produced chemical element, atomic number 106. ¶ Symb.: **Sg**.

sea·borne /séebawrn/ *adj.* transported by sea.

sea bream *n.* = porgy.

sea change *n.* a notable or unexpected transformation.

sea·cock /séekok/ *n.* a valve below a ship's waterline for letting water in or out.

sea·coast /séekōst/ *n.* the land adjacent to the sea.

sea cow *n.* **1** a sirenian. **2** a walrus

sea cu·cum·ber *n.*
► a holothurian, esp. a bêche-de-mer.

sea dog *n.* an old or experienced sailor.

sea ea·gle *n.* any fish-eating eagle esp. of the genus *Haliaëtus*.

sea·far·er /séefairər/ *n.* **1** a sailor. **2** a traveler by sea.

sea·far·ing /séefairing/ *adj. & n.* traveling by sea, esp. regularly.

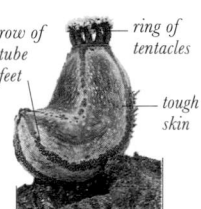

row of tube feet · ring of tentacles · tough skin

SEA CUCUMBER
(*Stichopus chloronotus*)

sea·food /séefōod/ *n.* edible sea fish or shellfish.

sea·front /séefrənt/ *n.* the part of a coastal town directly facing the sea.

sea·girt /séegərt/ *adj. literary* surrounded by sea.

sea·go·ing /séegōing/ *adj.* **1** (of ships) fit for crossing the sea. **2** (of a person) seafaring.

sea goose·ber·ry *n.* any marine animal of the phylum Ctenophora, with an ovoid body bearing numerous cilia.

sea green *adj.* bluish green (as of the sea).

sea·gull /séegul/ *n.* = GULL[1].

sea hare *n.* any of the various marine mollusks of the order Anaspidea, having an internal shell and long extensions from its foot.

SCYTHE: EARLY 20TH-CENTURY ENGLISH SCYTHE

SEABIRD

Birds living near the sea have special adaptations, including waterproof feathers, webbed feet, and facial glands that dispose of excess salt. Seabirds hunt prey in a variety of ways: surface feeders such as albatrosses grab food while flying near the ocean's surface; aerial divers such as gannets plummet into the water from a height; surface divers such as puffins swim on the surface and plunge underwater to feed. Almost all seabirds nest in colonies, often on cliffs and other places innaccessible to predators.

WANDERING ALBATROSS
(*Diomedea exulans*)

KELP GULL
(*Larus dominicanus*)

NORTHERN GANNET
(*Sula bassana*)

MAGNIFICENT FRIGATE BIRD
(*Fregata magnificens*)

ARCTIC TERN
(*Sterna paradisea*)

GIANT PETREL
(*Macronectes giganteus*)

ATLANTIC PUFFIN
(*Fratercula arctica*)

S

SEAL

True seals (shown below), as opposed to sea lions and fur seals, have no external ear flap (pinna). When underwater, these seals use their webbed hind flippers for propulsion and their front flippers to steer. They can stay underwater for more than 30 minutes, surviving on oxygen stored in the blood. Weddell seals can dive to depths of 1,950 ft (600 m).

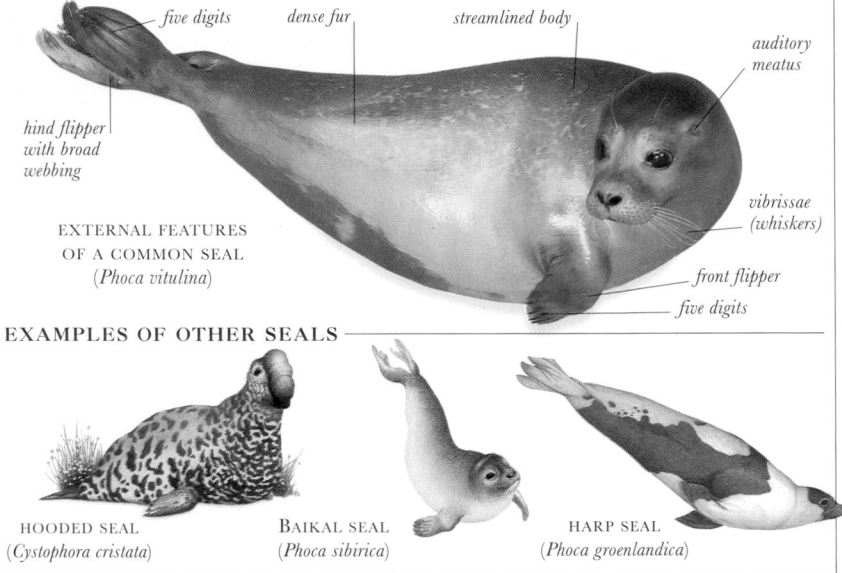

five digits   *dense fur*   *streamlined body*   *auditory meatus*

hind flipper with broad webbing

EXTERNAL FEATURES
OF A COMMON SEAL
(*Phoca vitulina*)

vibrissae (whiskers)

front flipper

five digits

EXAMPLES OF OTHER SEALS

HOODED SEAL
(*Cystophora cristata*)

BAIKAL SEAL
(*Phoca sibirica*)

HARP SEAL
(*Phoca groenlandica*)

sea hol·ly *n.* a spiny-leaved blue-flowered evergreen plant, *Eryngium maritimum*.

sea horse *n.* **1** ▶ any of various small upright marine fish of the family Syngnathidae, having a body suggestive of the head and neck of a horse. **2** a mythical creature with a horse's head and fish's tail.

sea is·land cot·ton *n.* a fine-quality long-stapled cotton grown on islands off the southern US.

seal[1] /seel/ *n. & v.* ● *n.* **1** a piece of wax, lead, paper, etc., with a stamped design, attached to a document as a guarantee of authenticity. **2** a similar material attached to a receptacle, envelope, etc., affording security by having to be broken to allow access to the contents. **3** an engraved piece of metal, gemstone, etc., for stamping a design on a seal. **4 a** a substance or device used to close an aperture or act as a fastening. **b** an amount of water standing in the trap of a drain to prevent foul air from rising. **5** an act or gesture or event regarded as a confirmation or guarantee (*gave her seal of approval to the venture*). **6** a significant or prophetic mark (*has the seal of death on his face*). **7** a decorative adhesive stamp. ● *v.tr.* **1** close securely or hermetically. **2** stamp or fasten with a seal. **3** fix a seal to. **4** certify as correct with a seal or stamp. **5** (often foll. by *up*) confine or fasten securely. **6** settle or decide (*their fate is sealed*). **7** (foll. by *off*) put barriers around (an area) to prevent entry and exit. **8** apply a nonporous coating to (a surface) to make it impervious. □ **one's lips are sealed** one is obliged to keep a secret. **set one's seal to** (or **on**) authorize or confirm. □□ **seal·a·ble** *adj.*

SEA HORSE
(*Hippocampus* species)

tubular snout

reduced fin

prehensile tail

seal[2] /seel/ *n. & v.* ● *n.* ▲ any fish-eating amphibious sea mammal of the family Phocidae or Otariidae, with flippers and webbed feet. ▷ PINNIPED. ● *v.intr.* hunt for seals.

seal·ant /séelənt/ *n.* material for sealing, esp. to make something airtight or watertight.

sea legs *n.pl.* the ability to keep one's balance and avoid seasickness when at sea.

seal·er /séelər/ *n.* a ship or person engaged in hunting seals.

sea lev·el *n.* the mean level of the sea's surface, used in reckoning the height of hills, etc., and as a barometric standard.

sea lil·y *n.* any of various sessile echinoderms, esp. of the class Crinoidea, with long jointed stalks and feather like arms for trapping food.

seal·ing wax *n.* a mixture of shellac and rosin with turpentine and pigment, softened by heating and used to make seals.

sea li·on *n.* any large, eared seal of the Pacific, esp. of the genus *Zalophus* or *Otaria*. ▷ PINNIPED

seal·skin /séelskin/ *n.* **1** the skin or prepared fur of a seal. **2** (often *attrib.*) a garment made from this.

Sea·ly·ham /séeleehəm, esp. *Brit.* -leeəm/ *n.* (in full **Sealyham terrier**) **1** ▼ a terrier of a wire-haired, short-legged breed. **2** this breed.

SEALYHAM TERRIER

seam /seem/ *n. & v.* ● *n.* **1** a line where two edges join, esp. of two pieces of cloth, etc., turned back and stitched together, or of boards fitted edge to edge. **2** a fissure between parallel edges. **3** a wrinkle or scar. **4** a stratum of coal, etc. ● *v.tr.* **1** join with a seam. **2** (esp. as **seamed** *adj.*) mark or score with or as with a seam. □□ **seam·er** *n.* **seam·less** *adj.*

sea·man /séemən/ *n.* (*pl.* **-men**) **1** a sailor, esp. one below the rank of officer. **2** a person regarded in terms of skill in navigation (*a poor seaman*). □□ **sea·man·like** *adj.* **sea·man·ly** *adj.*

sea·man·ship /séemənship/ *n.* skill in managing a ship or boat.

sea mile *n.* = NAUTICAL MILE.

seam·stress /séemstris/ *n.* (also **semp·stress** /semp-/) a woman who sews, esp. professionally.

seam·y /séemee/ *adj.* (**seamier**, **seamiest**) **1** marked with or showing seams. **2** unpleasant; disreputable (esp. *the seamy side*). □□ **seam·i·ness** *n.*

Sean·ad /shánəth/ *n.* the upper house of Parliament in the Republic of Ireland.

se·ance /sáyons/ *n.* (also **séance**) a meeting at which spiritualists attempt to make contact with the dead.

sea ot·ter *n.* a Pacific otter, *Enhydra lutris*.

sea·plane /séeplayn/ *n.* an aircraft designed to take off from and land and float on water.

sea·port /séepawrt/ *n.* a town with a harbor for seagoing ships.

sea·quake /séekwayk/ *n.* an earthquake under the sea.

sear /seer/ *v. & adj.* ● *v.tr.* **1 a** scorch, esp. with a hot iron; cauterize. **b** (as **searing** *adj.*) burning (*searing pain*). **2** cause pain or great anguish to. **3** brown (meat) quickly at a high temperature so that it will retain its juices in cooking. ● *adj.* var. of SERE[1].

search /sərch/ *v. & n.* ● *v.* **1** *tr.* look through or go over thoroughly to find something. **2** *tr.* examine or feel over (a person) to find anything concealed. **3** *tr.* **a** probe or penetrate into. **b** examine (one's mind, etc.) thoroughly. **4** *intr.* (often foll. by *for*) make a search or investigation. **5** *intr.* (as **searching** *adj.*) of an examination) thorough. **6** *tr.* (foll. by *out*) look probingly for. ● *n.* **1** an act of searching. **2** an investigation. □ **in search of** trying to find. **search me!** *colloq.* I do not know. □□ **search·a·ble** *adj.* **search·er** *n.* **search·ing·ly** *adv.*

search en·gine *n. Computing* software for the retrieval of data from a database or network.

search·light /sárchlīt/ *n.* **1** a powerful outdoor electric light with a concentrated beam that can be turned in any direction. **2** the light or beam from this.

search par·ty *n.* a group of people organized to look for a lost person or thing.

search war·rant *n.* an official authorization to enter and search a building.

sea salt *n.* salt produced by evaporating seawater.

sea·scape /séeskayp/ *n.* a picture or view of the sea.

sea ser·pent *n.* (also **sea snake**) **1** a snake of the family Hydrophidae, living in the sea. **2** an enormous legendary serpentlike sea monster.

sea·shell /séeshel/ *n.* the shell of a saltwater mollusk.

sea·shore /séeshawr/ *n.* land close to or bordering on the sea.

sea·sick /séesik/ *adj.* suffering from sickness or nausea from the motion of a ship at sea. □□ **sea·sick·ness** *n.*

sea·side /séesīd/ *n.* the seacoast, esp. as a holiday resort.

sea·son /séezən/ *n. & v.* ● *n.* **1** ▲ each of the four divisions of the year (spring, summer, autumn, and winter). **2** a time of year characterized by climatic or other features (*the dry season*). **3 a** the time of year when a plant is flowering, etc. **b** the time of year when an animal breeds or is hunted. **4** a proper or suitable time. **5** a time when something is plentiful or active or in vogue. **6** the time of year regularly devoted to an activity (*the football season*). ● *v.* **1** *tr.* flavor (food) with salt, herbs, etc. **2** *tr.* moderate or temper. **3** *tr.* temper or moderate. **4** *tr. & intr.* **a** make or become suitable, esp. by exposure to the air or weather. **b** make or become experienced or accustomed (*seasoned soldiers*). □ **in season 1** (of

S

SEASON

In relation to the Sun, the Earth spins on a tilted axis. Thus, as the Earth orbits the Sun over the course of a year, the Earth's two hemispheres are alternately nearer to, then farther from, the Sun's warmth. This produces four distinct weather phases, called seasons. If the Earth's axis were perpendicular to the Sun, there would be no change of seasons.

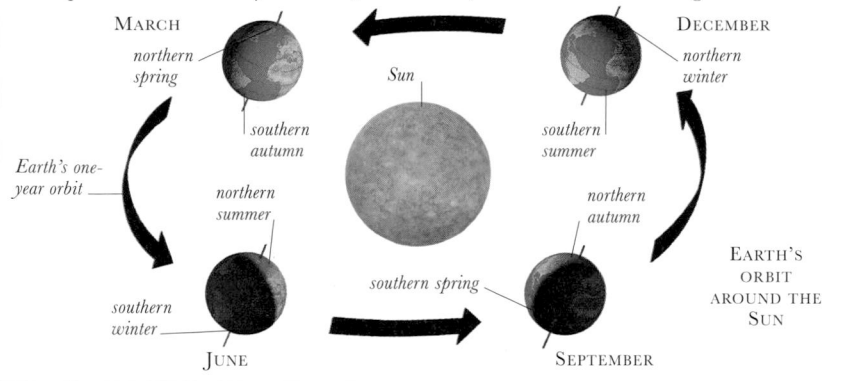

MARCH

northern spring

southern autumn

Sun

DECEMBER

northern winter

southern summer

Earth's one-year orbit

northern summer

northern autumn

southern winter

JUNE

southern spring

SEPTEMBER

EARTH'S ORBIT AROUND THE SUN

foodstuff) available in plenty and in good condition. **2** (of an animal) in heat.

sea·son·a·ble /séezənəbəl/ *adj.* **1** suitable to or usual in the season. **2** opportune. **3** meeting the needs of the occasion. □□ **sea·son·a·ble·ness** *n.* **sea·son·a·bly** *adv.*

sea·son·al /séezənəl/ *adj.* of, depending on, or varying with the season. □□ **sea·son·al·i·ty** /-nálitee/ *n.* **sea·son·al·ly** *adv.*

sea·son·ing /séezəning/ *n.* condiments added to food.

sea·son tick·et *n.* a ticket entitling the holder to any number of journeys, admittances, etc., in a given period.

seat /seet/ *n. & v.* ● *n.* **1** a thing made or used for sitting on. **2** the buttocks. **3** the part of a garment covering the buttocks. **4** the part of a chair, etc., on which the sitter's weight directly rests. **5** a place for one person in a theater, etc. **6** *Polit.* the right to occupy a seat, esp. as a member of Congress, etc. **7** the part of a machine that supports or guides another part. **8** a site or location of something specified (*a seat of learning*). **9** a country mansion. **10** the manner of sitting on a horse, etc. ● *v.tr.* **1** cause to sit. **2** provide sitting accommodation for. **3** (as **seated** *adj.*) sitting. □ **be seated** sit down. **by the seat of one's pants** *colloq.* by instinct rather than logic or knowledge. **take a** (or **one's**) **seat** sit down. □□ **seat·less** *adj.*

seat belt *n.* a belt securing a person in the seat of a car, aircraft, etc.

seat·ing /séeting/ *n.* **1** seats collectively. **2** sitting accommodation.

SEATO /séetō/ *abbr.* Southeast Asia Treaty Organization.

poisonous spines

SEA URCHIN
(*Sterechinus neumayer*)

sea ur·chin *n.* ◀ a small marine echinoderm of the class Echinoidea, with a spherical or flattened spiny shell.

sea·wall /séewawl/ *n.* a wall erected to prevent encroachment by the sea.

sea·ward /séewərd/ *adv., adj., & n.* ● *adv.* (also **sea·wards** /-wərdz/) toward the sea. ● *adj.* going or facing toward the sea. ● *n.* such a direction or position.

sea·wa·ter /séewawtər/ *n.* water in or taken from the sea.

sea·way /séeway/ *n.* **1** an inland waterway open to seagoing ships. **2** a ship's progress. **3** a ship's path across the sea.

sea·weed /séeweed/ *n.* ▼ any of various algae growing in the sea or on the rocks on a shore.

sea·wor·thy /séewərthee/ *adj.* (of a ship) fit to put to sea. □□ **sea·wor·thi·ness** *n.*

se·ba·ceous /sibáyshəs/ *adj.* fatty; of or relating to tallow or fat. ▷ SKIN

seb·or·rhe·a /sébəreeə/ *n.* excessive discharge of sebum from the sebaceous glands. □□ **seb·or·rhe·ic** *adj.*

se·bum /séebəm/ *n.* the oily secretion of the sebaceous glands. ▷ SKIN, FOLLICLE

Sec. *abbr.* secretary.

sec[1] *abbr.* secant.

sec[2] /sek/ *n. colloq.* (in phrases) a second (of time).

sec[3] /sek/ *adj.* (of wine) dry.

sec. *abbr.* second(s).

se·cant /séekant, -kənt/ *adj. & n. Math.* ● *adj.* cutting (*secant line*). ● *n.* **1** a line cutting a curve at one or more points. **2** the ratio of the hypotenuse to the shorter side adjacent to an acute angle (in a right triangle).

sec·co /sékō/ *n.* the technique of painting on dry plaster with pigments mixed in water.

se·cede /siséed/ *v.intr.* (usu. foll. by *from*) withdraw formally from membership of a political federation or a religious body. □□ **se·ced·er** *n.*

se·ces·sion /siséshən/ *n.* **1** the act or an instance of seceding. **2** (**Secession**) *hist.* the withdrawal of eleven southern states from the US Union in 1860–61, leading to the Civil War. □□ **se·ces·sion·al** *adj.* **se·ces·sion·ism** *n.* **se·ces·sion·ist** *n.*

se·clude /siklóod/ *v.tr.* (also *refl.*) **1** keep (a person or place) retired or away from company. **2** (esp. as **secluded** *adj.*) hide or screen from view.

se·clu·sion /siklóozhən/ *n.* **1** a secluded state; retirement; privacy. **2** a secluded place. □□ **se·clu·sion·ist** *n.* **se·clu·sive** /-klóosiv/ *adj.*

sec·ond[1] /sékənd/ *n., adj., & v.* ● *n.* **1** the position in a sequence corresponding to that of the number 2 in the sequence 1–2. **2** something occupying this position. **3** the second person, etc., in a race or competition. **4** another person or thing in addition to one previously mentioned (*the officer was then joined by a second*). **5** (in *pl.*) goods of a second or inferior quality. **6** (in *pl.*) *colloq.* **a** a second helping of food at a meal. **b** the second course of a meal. **7** an attendant assisting a combatant in a duel, etc. **8** esp. *Brit.* **a** a place in the second class of an examination. **b** a person having this. ● *adj.* **1** that is the second; next after first. **2** additional; further (*ate a second cupcake*). **3** subordinate; inferior. **4** *Mus.* performing a lower or subordinate part (*second violins*). **5** such as to be comparable to (*a second Callas*). ● *v.tr.* **1** supplement; support. **2** formally support or endorse (a nomination or resolution, etc., or its proposer). □ **at second hand** by hearsay, not direct observation, etc. **in the second place** as a second consideration, etc. **second to none** surpassed by no other.

sec·ond[2] /sékənd/ *n.* **1** a sixtieth of a minute of time or angular distance. **2** *colloq.* a very short time (*wait a second*).

sec·ond·ar·y /sékənderee/ *adj. & n.* ● *adj.* **1** coming after or next below what is primary. **2** derived from or depending on or supplementing what is primary. **3** (of education, a school, etc.) for those who have had primary education, usu. from 11 to 18 years. ● *n.* (*pl.* **-ies**) a secondary thing. □□ **sec·ond·ar·i·ly** *adv.* **sec·ond·ar·i·ness** *n.*

S

SEAWEED

Like all plants, seaweeds need sunlight to survive and so are found mostly in shallow waters around reefs or near the shore. They are divided into three groups according to color. Brown seaweeds are tough, slippery plants that can grow to over 195 ft (60 m) long. Green seaweeds often have thin, delicate fronds. Red seaweeds are found at the greatest depths – up to 720 ft (220 m) below the surface.

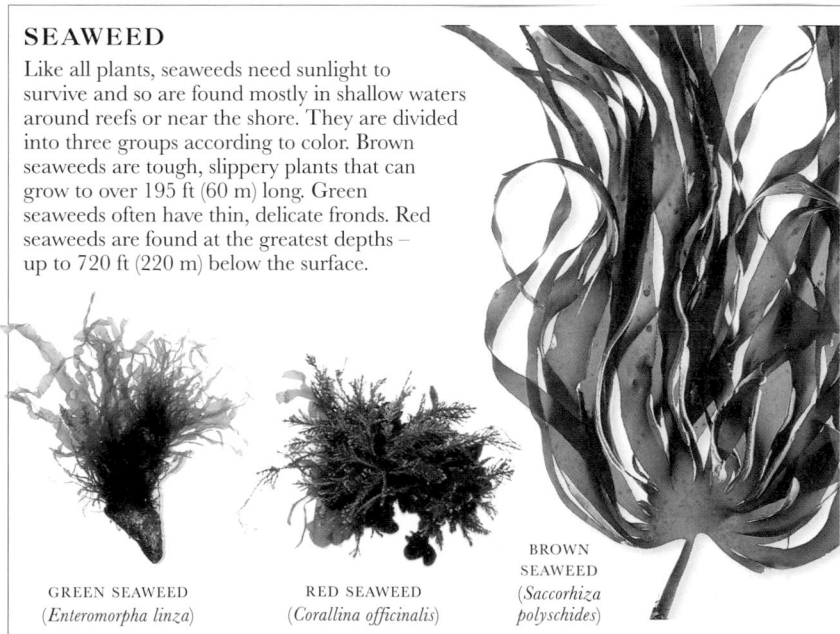

GREEN SEAWEED
(*Enteromorpha linza*)

RED SEAWEED
(*Corallina officinalis*)

BROWN SEAWEED
(*Saccorhiza polyschides*)

secondary colors

primary colors

SECONDARY COLORS
FORMED BY OVERLAPPING
PRIMARY PIGMENTS

sec·ond·ar·y col·or *n.* ◄ the result of mixing two primary colors. ▷ COLOR

sec·ond best *n.* a less adequate or desirable alternative. □□ **sec·ond-best** *adj.*

sec·ond class *n.* the second-best group or category, esp. of hotel or train accommodation or of postal services. □□ **sec·ond-class** *adj. & adv.*

Sec·ond Com·ing *n. Theol.* the second advent of Christ on Earth.

sec·ond cous·in *n.* a child of one's parent's first cousin.

sec·ond-de·gree *adj. Med.* denoting burns that cause blistering but not permanent scars.

se·conde /səkónd/ *n. Fencing* the second of eight parrying positions.

sec·ond-gen·er·a·tion *adj.* denoting the offspring of a first generation, esp. of immigrants.

sec·ond-guess *v.tr. colloq.* **1** anticipate or predict by guesswork. **2** judge or criticize with hindsight.

sec·ond·hand /sékəndhánd/ *adj. & adv.* ● *adj.* **1 a** (of goods) having had a previous owner. **b** (of a store, etc.) where such goods can be bought. **2** (of information, etc.) accepted on another's authority and not from original investigation. ● *adv.* **1** on a secondhand basis. **2** at second hand; not directly.

sec·ond hand *n.* a hand in some watches and clocks, recording seconds. ▷ WATCH

sec·ond in com·mand *n.* the officer next in rank to the commanding or chief officer.

sec·ond lieu·ten·ant *n.* in the US, the lowest-ranked commissioned officer of the army, air force, or marines.

sec·ond·ly /sékəndlee/ *adv.* **1** furthermore. **2** as a second item.

sec·ond na·ture *n.* (often foll. by *to*) an acquired tendency that has become instinctive (*is second nature to him*).

se·con·do /sikóndō/ *n.* (*pl.* **secondi** /-dee/) *Mus.* the second or lower part in a duet, etc.

sec·ond-rate *adj.* of mediocre quality; inferior.

sec·ond sight *n.* the supposed power of being able to perceive future or distant events.

sec·ond string *n.* an alternative available in case of need.

sec·ond thoughts *n.pl.* a new opinion or resolution reached after further consideration.

sec·ond wind *n.* **1** recovery of the power of normal breathing during exercise after initial breathlessness. **2** renewed energy to continue an effort.

se·cre·cy /séekrisee/ *n.* **1** the keeping of secrets as a fact, habit, or faculty. **2** a state in which all information is withheld (*was done in great secrecy*). □ **sworn to secrecy** having promised to keep a secret.

se·cret /séekrit/ *adj. & n.* ● *adj.* **1** kept or meant to be kept private, unknown, or hidden. **2** acting or operating secretly. **3** fond of, prone to, or able to preserve secrecy. **4** (of a place) completely secluded. ● *n.* **1** a thing kept or meant to be kept secret. **2** a thing known only to a few. **3** a mystery. **4** a valid but not commonly known method (*what's their secret?*). □ **in secret** secretly. **in** (or **in on**) **the secret** among the number of those who know it. **keep a secret** not reveal it. □□ **se·cret·ly** *adv.*

se·cret a·gent *n.* a spy acting for a country.

sec·re·tar·i·at /sékritáireeət/ *n.* **1** a permanent administrative office or department, esp. a governmental one. **2** its members or premises.

sec·re·tar·y /sékriteree/ *n.* (*pl.* **-ies**) **1** a person employed to assist with correspondence, keep records, make appointments, etc. **2** an official

appointed by a society, etc., to conduct its correspondence, keep its records, etc. **3** (in the UK) the principal assistant of a government minister, ambassador, etc. □□ **sec·re·tar·i·al** /-táireeəl/ *adj.* **se·cre·tar·y·ship** *n.*

se·cre·tar·y bird *n.* ► a long-legged, snake-eating African bird, *Sagittarius serpentarius*, with a crest likened to a quill pen stuck over a writer's ear.

sec·re·tar·y-gen·er·al *n.* the principal administrator of certain organizations, as the United Nations.

sec·re·tar·y of state *n.* **1** (in the US) the chief government official responsible for foreign affairs. **2** (in the UK) the head of a major government department.

se·cret bal·lot *n.* a ballot in which votes are cast in secret.

se·crete[1] /sikréet/ *v.tr. Biol.* (of a cell, organ, etc.) produce by secretion. □□ **se·cre·tor** *n.* **se·cre·to·ry** /séekrətáwree/ *adj.*

se·crete[2] /sikréet/ *v.tr.* conceal; put into hiding.

se·cre·tion /sikréeshən/ *n.* **1** *Biol.* **a** a process by which substances are produced and discharged from a cell for a function in the organism or for excretion. **b** the secreted substance. **2** the act or an instance of concealing.

se·cre·tive /séekritiv, sikrée-/ *adj.* inclined to make or keep secrets; uncommunicative. □□ **se·cre·tive·ly** *adv.* **se·cre·tive·ness** *n.*

se·cret po·lice *n.* a police force operating in secret for political purposes.

se·cret serv·ice *n.* **1** a government department concerned with espionage. **2** (**Secret Service**) a branch of the US Treasury Department charged with apprehending counterfeiters and protecting the president and certain other officials and their families.

se·cret so·ci·e·ty *n.* a society whose members are sworn to secrecy about it.

sect /sekt/ *n.* **1 a** a body of people subscribing to religious doctrines usu. different from those of an established church from which they have separated. **b** a religious denomination. **2** the followers of a particular philosopher or philosophy, or school of thought in politics, etc.

sec·tar·i·an /sektáireeən/ *adj. & n.* ● *adj.* **1** of or concerning a sect. **2** bigoted or narrow-minded in following the doctrines of one's sect. ● *n.* **1** a member of a sect. **2** a bigot. □□ **sec·tar·i·an·ism** *n.* **sec·tar·i·an·ize** *v.tr.*

sec·tion /sékshən/ *n. & v.* ● *n.* **1** a part cut off or separated from something. **2** each of the parts into which a thing is divided (actually or conceptually) or divisible or out of which a structure can be fitted together. **3** a group or subdivision of a larger body of people (*the wind section*). **4** a subdivision of a book, document, etc. **5** a one square mile of land. **b** a particular district of a town (*residential section*). **6** a subdivision of an army platoon. **7** esp. *Surgery* a separation by cutting. **8** *Biol.* ► a thin slice of tissue, etc., cut off for microscopic examination. **9 a** the cutting of a solid by or along a plane. **b** the resulting figure or the area of this. ● *v.tr.* **1** arrange in or divide into sections. **2** *Biol.* cut into thin slices for microscopic examination.

sec·tion·al /sékshənəl/ *adj.* **1 a** relating to a section, esp. of a community. **b** partisan. **2** made in sections. **3** local rather than general. □□ **sec·tion·al·ism** *n.* **sec·tion·al·ist** *n. & adj.* **sec·tion·al·ize** *v.tr.* **sec·tion·al·ly** *adv.*

sec·tor /séktər/ *n.* **1** a distinct part or branch of an enterprise, or of society, the economy, etc. **2** *Mil.* a subdivision of an area for military operations,

controlled by one commander or headquarters. **3** the plane figure enclosed by two radii of a circle, ellipse, etc., and the arc between them. ▷ CIRCLE. □□ **sec·tor·al** *adj.*

sec·u·lar /sékyələr/ *adj. & n.* ● *adj.* **1** concerned with the affairs of this world; not spiritual nor sacred. **2** (of education, etc.) not concerned with religion nor religious belief. **3 a** not ecclesiastical nor monastic. **b** (of clergy) not bound by a religious rule. **4** occurring once in an age or century. ● *n.* a secular priest. □□ **sec·u·lar·ism** *n.* **sec·u·lar·ist** *n.* **sec·u·lar·i·ty** /-láirətee/ *n.* **sec·u·lar·ize** *v.tr.* **sec·u·lar·i·za·tion** *n.* **sec·u·lar·ly** *adv.*

se·cure /sikyŏŏr/ *adj. & v.* ● *adj.* **1** untroubled by danger or fear. **2** safe against attack. **3** certain not to fail (*the plan is secure*). **4** fixed or fastened so as not to give way or get loose or be lost (*made the door secure*). **5 a** (foll. by *of*) certain to achieve (*secure of victory*). **b** (foll. by *against, from*) protected (*secure against attack*). ● *v.tr.* **1** make secure or safe; fortify. **2** fasten, close, or confine securely. **3** succeed in obtaining (*secured front seats*). **4** guarantee against loss (*a loan secured by property*). □□ **se·cur·a·ble** *adj.* **se·cure·ly** *adv.* **se·cure·ment** *n.*

se·cu·ri·ty /sikyŏŏritee/ *n.* (*pl.* **-ies**) **1** a secure condition or feeling. **2** a thing that guards or guarantees. **3 a** the safety of a nation, company, etc., against espionage, theft, or other danger. **b** an organization for ensuring this. **4** a thing deposited or pledged as a guarantee of an undertaking or a loan, to be forfeited in case of default. **5** (often in *pl.*) a certificate attesting credit or the ownership of stock, bonds, etc. □ **on security of** using as a guarantee.

se·cu·ri·ty blan·ket *n.* **1** an official sanction on information in the interest of security. **2** a blanket or other familiar object given as a comfort to a child.

Se·cu·ri·ty Coun·cil *n.* a permanent body of the United Nations seeking to maintain peace and security.

se·cu·ri·ty guard *n.* a person employed to protect the security of buildings, vehicles, etc.

se·cu·ri·ty risk *n.* a person whose presence may threaten security.

se·dan /sidán/ *n.* **1** (in full **sedan chair**) an enclosed chair for conveying one person, carried between horizontal poles by two porters. **2** an enclosed automobile for four or more people. ▷ CAR

se·date[1] /sidáyt/ *adj.* tranquil and dignified; equable; serious. □□ **se·date·ly** *adv.* **se·date·ness** *n.*

se·date[2] /sidáyt/ *v.tr.* put under sedation.

se·da·tion /sidáyshən/ *n.* a state of rest or sleep, esp. produced by a sedative drug.

sed·a·tive /sédətiv/ *n. & adj.* ● *n.* a drug, influence, etc., that tends to calm or soothe. ● *adj.* calming; soothing; inducing sleep.

sed·en·tar·y /séd'nteree/ *adj.* **1** sitting (*a sedentary posture*). **2** (of work, etc.) characterized by much sitting and little physical exercise. **3** (of a person) spending much time seated. □□ **sed·en·tar·i·ly** /-táirəlee/ *adv.* **sed·en·tar·i·ness** *n.*

sedge /sej/ *n.* **1** ► any grasslike plant of the genus *Carex* with triangular stems, usu. growing in wet areas. **2** an expanse of this plant. □□ **sedg·y** *adj.*

SECRETARY BIRD
(*Sagittarius serpentarius*)

SECTION: MICROGRAPH
OF A ROOT SECTION

SEDGE: GREAT
POND SEDGE
(*Carex riparia*)

S

SEDIMENT

Rock fragments that result from weathering may be transported by glacial movement, wind, waves, or currents. This debris is deposited at a new location (like the seabed) as a sediment. Over millions of years, the sediments are compacted and cemented to form sedimentary rocks such as sandstone. Some sedimentary rocks, such as coal or limestone, contain the remains of dead organisms.

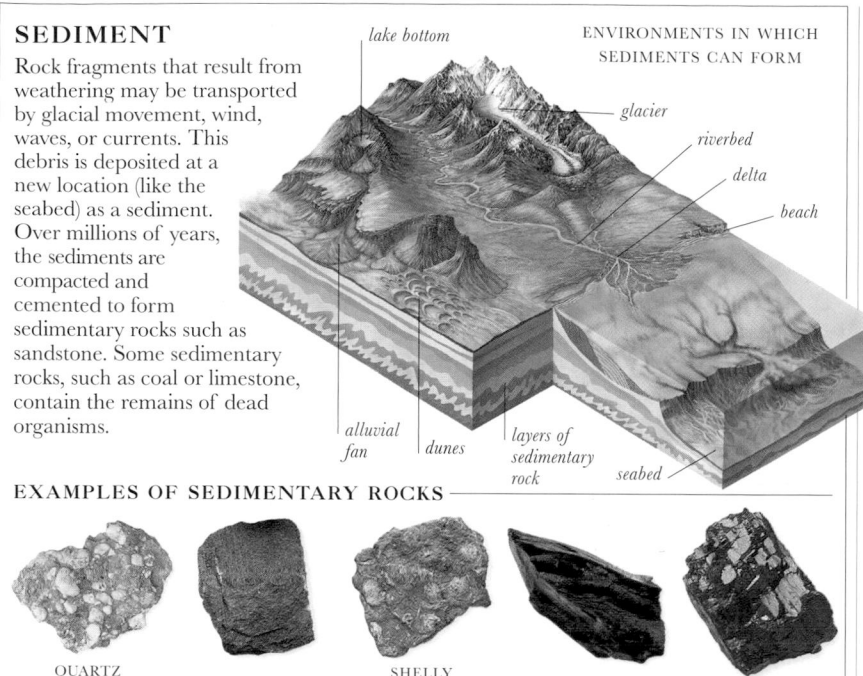

ENVIRONMENTS IN WHICH SEDIMENTS CAN FORM

lake bottom

glacier

riverbed

delta

beach

alluvial fan

dunes

layers of sedimentary rock

seabed

EXAMPLES OF SEDIMENTARY ROCKS

QUARTZ CONGLOMERATE   SANDSTONE   SHELLY LIMESTONE   OIL SHALE   COAL

---

sed·i·ment /sédimənt/ *n.* **1** matter that settles to the bottom of a liquid. **2** *Geol.* ▲ matter that is carried by water or wind and deposited on the surface of the land. ▷ ROCK CYCLE. □□ **sed·i·men·ta·ry** /-méntəree/ *adj.* **sed·i·men·ta·tion** /-táyshən/ *n.*

se·di·tion /sidíshən/ *n.* **1** conduct or speech inciting to rebellion. **2** agitation against the authority of a government. □□ **se·di·tious** *adj.* **se·di·tious·ly** *adv.*

se·duce /sidóōs, -dyóōs/ *v.tr.* **1** tempt or entice into sexual activity. **2** lead astray; tempt. □□ **se·duc·er** *n.* **se·duc·i·ble** *adj.*

se·duc·tion /sidúkshən/ *n.* **1** the act or an instance of seducing; the process of being seduced. **2** something that tempts or allures.

se·duc·tive /sidúktiv/ *adj.* tending to seduce; alluring; enticing. □□ **se·duc·tive·ly** *adv.* **se·duc·tive·ness** *n.*

se·duc·tress /sidúktris/ *n.* a female seducer.

sed·u·lous /séjələs/ *adj.* **1** persevering; diligent; assiduous. **2** (of an action, etc.) deliberately and consciously continued. □□ **se·du·li·ty** /sidóōlitee, -dyóō-/ *n.* **sed·u·lous·ly** *adv.* **sed·u·lous·ness** *n.*

se·dum /séedəm/ *n.* any plant of the genus *Sedum*, with fleshy leaves and star-shaped yellow, pink, or white flowers, e.g., stonecrop.

see[1] /see/ *v.* (*past* **saw** /saw/; *past part.* **seen** /seen/) **1** *tr.* discern by use of the eyes; observe. **2** *intr.* have or use the power of discerning objects with the eyes (*sees best at night*). **3** *tr.* discern mentally; understand (*I see what you mean*). **4** *tr.* watch; be a spectator of (a game, etc.). **5** *tr.* ascertain or establish by inquiry or research or reflection (*see if the door is open*). **6** *tr.* consider; deduce from observation (*I see you are a brave man*). **7** *tr.* contemplate; foresee mentally (*we saw that no good would come of it*). **8** *tr.* look at for information (usu. in *imper.*: *see page 15*). **9** *tr.* meet or be near and recognize (*I saw your mother in town*). **10** *tr.* **a** meet socially (*sees her sister most weeks*). **b** meet regularly as a boyfriend or girlfriend (*is still seeing that tall man*). **11** *tr.* give an interview to (*the doctor will see you now*). **12** *tr.* visit to consult (*went to see the doctor*). **13** *tr.* find, esp. from a visual source (*I see the match has been canceled*). **14** *intr.* reflect; wait until one knows more (*we shall have to see*). **15** *tr.* interpret (*I see things differently now*). **16** *tr.* experience (*I never thought I would see

this day*). **17** *tr.* recognize as acceptable; foresee (*do you see your daughter marrying this man?*). **18** *tr.* observe without interfering (*stood by and saw them squander my money*). **19** *tr.* find attractive (*can't think what she sees in him*). **20** *tr.* (usu. foll. by *to*, or *that* + infin.) ensure; attend to (*shall see to your request*) (cf. see to it). **21** *tr.* escort or conduct (to a place, etc.) (*saw them home*). **22** *tr.* be a witness of (an event, etc.) (*see the New Year in*). **23** *tr.* supervise (an action, etc.) (*stay and see the doors locked*). **24** *tr.* **a** (in gambling, esp. poker) equal (a bet). **b** equal the bet of (a player), esp. to see the player's cards. □ **as far as I can see** to the best of my understanding or belief. **as I see it** in my opinion. **do you see?** do you understand? **has seen better days** has declined from former prosperity, good condition, etc. **I see** I understand (referring to an explanation, etc.). **let me see** an appeal for time to think before speaking, etc. **see about** attend to. **see after 1** take care of. **2** = see through. **see eye to eye** see EYE. **see fit** see FIT[1]. **see into** investigate. **see life** gain experience of the world, often by enjoying oneself. **see the light 1** realize one's mistakes, etc. **2** suddenly see the way to proceed. **3** undergo religious conversion. **see the light of day** (usu. with *neg.*) come into existence. **see off 1** be present at the departure of (a person). **see out 1** accompany out of a building, etc. **2** finish (a project, etc.) completely. **see reason** see REASON. **see red** become suddenly enraged. **see service** see SERVICE. **see stars** *colloq.* see lights before one's eyes as a result of a blow on the head. **see things** have hallucinations or false imaginings. **see through 1** not be deceived by; detect the true nature of. **2** penetrate visually. **see a person through** support a person during a difficult time. **see a thing through** persist with it until it is completed. **see to it** (foll. by *that* + clause) ensure (*see to it that I am not disturbed*) (cf. sense 20 of *v.*). **see one's way clear to** feel able or entitled to. **see you** (or **see you later**) *colloq.* an expression on parting. **we shall see 1** let us await the outcome. **2** a formula for declining to act at once. **will see about it** a formula for declining to act at once. **you see 1** you understand. **2** you will understand when I explain. □□ **see·a·ble** *adj.*

see[2] /see/ *n.* **1** the area under the authority of a bishop or archbishop; a diocese. **2** the office or jurisdiction of a bishop or archbishop.

seed /seed/ *n. & v.* ● *n.* **1 a** ▼ a flowering plant's unit of reproduction (esp. in the form of grain) capable of developing into another such plant. **b** seeds collectively, esp. as collected for sowing (*kept for

---

SEED

A seed contains an embryonic plant together with a store of food, and is surrounded by a protective outer covering, or testa. In cereal grains, the food is stored primarily in a tissue called the endosperm. In many other seeds, such as beans, it is held in fleshy seed leaves called cotyledons. In flowering plants, seeds develop inside fruits, which help the seeds to disperse. Conifer seeds form on the surface of cone scales.

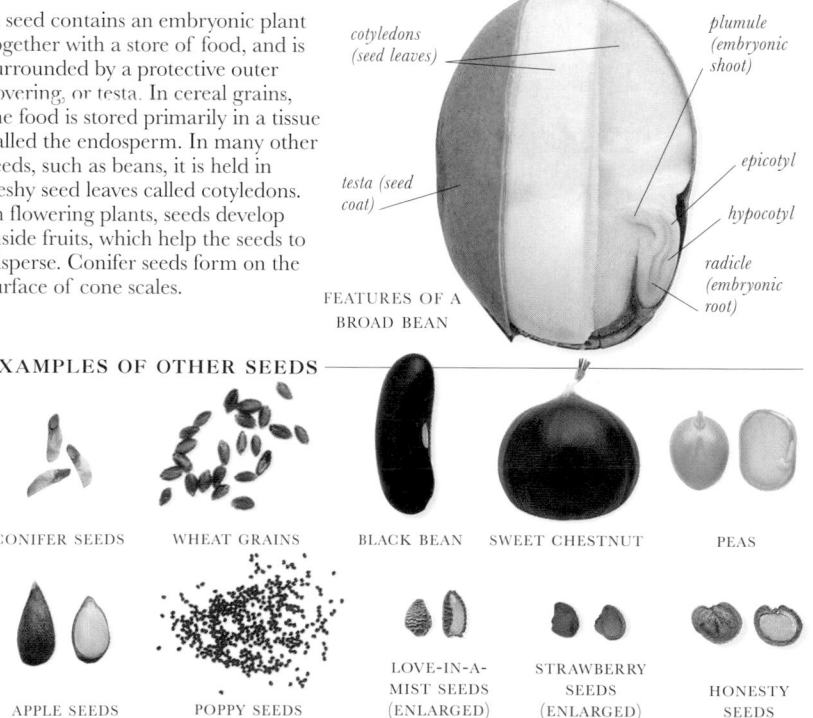

cotyledons (seed leaves)

plumule (embryonic shoot)

testa (seed coat)

epicotyl

hypocotyl

radicle (embryonic root)

FEATURES OF A BROAD BEAN

EXAMPLES OF OTHER SEEDS

CONIFER SEEDS   WHEAT GRAINS   BLACK BEAN   SWEET CHESTNUT   PEAS

APPLE SEEDS   POPPY SEEDS   LOVE-IN-A-MIST SEEDS (ENLARGED)   STRAWBERRY SEEDS (ENLARGED)   HONESTY SEEDS

S

seed). **2 a** semen. **b** milt. **3** (foll. by *of*) prime cause; beginning (*seeds of doubt*). **4** *archaic* offspring; descendants (*the seed of Abraham*). **5** *Sports* a seeded player. ● *v.* **1** *tr.* **a** place seeds in. **b** sprinkle with or as with seed. **2** *intr.* sow seeds. **3** *intr.* produce or drop seed. **4** *tr.* remove seeds from (fruit, etc.). **5** *tr.* place a crystal or crystalline substance in (a solution, etc.) to cause crystallization or condensation. **6** *tr. Sports* **a** assign to (a strong competitor in a knockout competition) a position in an ordered list so that strong competitors do not meet each other in early rounds. **b** arrange (the order of play) in this way. **7** *intr.* go to seed. □ **go** (or **run**) **to seed 1** cease flowering as seed develops. **2** become degenerate, unkempt, ineffective, etc. □□ **seed·less** *adj.*

seed·bed /séedbed/ *n.* **1** a bed of fine soil in which to sow seeds. **2** a place of development.

seed·cake /séedkayk/ *n.* cake containing whole seeds of sesame or caraway.

seed·er /séedər/ *n.* **1** a person or thing that seeds. **2** a machine for sowing seed.

seed·ling /séedling/ *n.* a young plant, esp. one raised from seed and not from a cutting, etc. ▷ GERMINATE

seed mon·ey *n.* money allocated to initiate a project.

seed pearl *n.* a very small pearl.

seed po·ta·to *n.* a potato kept for seed.

seeds·man /séedzmən/ *n.* (*pl.* **-men**) a dealer in seeds.

seed·time /séedtīm/ *n.* the sowing season.

seed·y /séedee/ *adj.* (**seedier, seediest**) **1** full of seed. **2** going to seed. **3** shabby looking; in worn clothes. **4** *colloq.* unwell. □□ **seed·i·ly** *adv.* **seed·i·ness** *n.*

see·ing /séeing/ *conj.* (usu. foll. by *that* + clause) considering that; inasmuch as; because (*seeing that you do not know it yourself*).

seek /seek/ *v.* (*past* and *past part.* **sought** /sawt/) **1 a** *tr.* make a search or inquiry for. **b** *intr.* (foll. by *for, after*) make a search or inquiry. **2** *tr.* **a** try or want to find or get. **b** ask for; request (*seeks my aid*). **3** *tr.* (foll. by *to* + infin.) endeavor or try. **4** *tr.* make for or resort to (*sought his bed; sought a fortune-teller*). **5** *tr. archaic* aim at; attempt. □ **seek out 1** search for and find. **2** single out for companionship, etc. □□ **seek·er** *n.* (also in *comb.*).

seem /seem/ *v.intr.* **1** give the impression or sensation of being. **2** (foll. by *to* + infin.) appear or be perceived or ascertained (*they seem to have left*). □ **can't seem to** *colloq.* seem unable to. **do not seem to** *colloq.* somehow do not (*I do not seem to like him*). **it seems** (or **would seem**) (often foll. by *that* + clause) it appears to be true or the fact (in a hesitant, guarded, or ironical statement).

seem·ing[1] /séeming/ *adj.* **1** apparent but perhaps not real. **2** apparent only; ostensible. □□ **seem·ing·ly** *adv.*

seem·ing[2] /séeming/ *n. literary* **1** appearance; aspect. **2** deceptive appearance.

seem·ly /séemlee/ *adj.* (**seemlier, seemliest**) conforming to propriety or good taste; decorous; suitable. □□ **seem·li·ness** *n.*

seen *past part.* of SEE[1].

seep /seep/ *v.intr.* ooze out; percolate slowly.

seep·age /séepij/ *n.* **1** the act of seeping. **2** the quantity that seeps out.

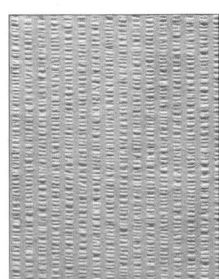
SEERSUCKER

seer /séeər, seer/ *n.* **1** a person who sees. **2** a prophet.

seer·suck·er /séersukər/ *n.* ◄ material of cotton, etc., with a puckered surface.

see·saw /séesaw/ *n., v., adj., & adv.* ● *n.* **1 a** a device consisting of a long plank balanced on a central support for children to sit on at each end and move up and down by push-

ing the ground with their feet. **b** a game played on this. **2** an up-and-down or to-and-fro motion. **3** a contest in which the advantage repeatedly changes from one side to the other. ● *v.intr.* **1** play on a seesaw. **2** move up and down as on a seesaw. **3** vacillate in policy, emotion, etc. ● *adj. & adv.* with up-and-down or backward-and-forward motion (*seesaw motion*).

seethe /seeth/ *v.* **1** *intr.* boil; bubble over. **2** *intr.* be very agitated, esp. with anger. □□ **seeth·ing·ly** *adv.*

see-through *adj.* (esp. of clothing) translucent.

seg·ment /ségmənt/ *n. & v.* ● *n.* **1** each of several parts into which a thing is or can be divided or marked off. **2** *Geom.* a part of a figure cut off by a line or plane intersecting it. ▷ CIRCLE. **3** *Zool.* each of the longitudinal sections of the body of certain animals (e.g., worms). ● *v.* (usu. -mént / *intr. & tr.* divide into segments. □□ **seg·men·tal** /-mént'l/ *adj.* **seg·men·tal·ly** /-mént'lee/ *adv.* **seg·men·ta·ry** /ségməntairee/ *adj.* **seg·men·ta·tion** /-táyshən/ *n.*

se·go /séegō/ *n.* (*pl.* **-os**) (in full **sego lily**) a N. American plant, *Calochortus nuttallii*, with green and white bell-shaped flowers.

seg·re·gate /ségrigayt/ *v.* **1** *tr.* put apart from the rest; isolate. **2** *tr.* enforce racial segregation on (persons) or in (a community, etc.). **3** *intr.* separate from a mass and collect together.

seg·re·ga·tion /ségrigáyshən/ *n.* **1** enforced separation of racial groups in a community, etc. **2** the act or an instance of segregating; the state of being segregated. □□ **seg·re·ga·tion·al** *adj.* **seg·re·ga·tion·ist** *n. & adj.*

se·gue /séegway/ *v. & n. esp. Mus.* ● *v.intr.* (**segues, segued, segueing**) (usu. foll. by *into*) go on without a pause. ● *n.* an uninterrupted transition from one song or melody to another.

sei /say/ *n.* a small rorqual, *Balaenoptera borealis*.

sei·cen·to /saychéntō/ *n.* the style of Italian art and literature of the 17th c. □□ **sei·cen·tist** *n.* **sei·cen·to·ist** *n.*

seiche /saysh/ *n.* a fluctuation in the water level of a lake, etc., usu. caused by changes in barometric pressure.

Seid·litz pow·ders /sédlits/ *n.* a laxative medicine of two powders mixed separately with water and then poured together to effervesce.

seif /seef, sayf/ *n.* (in full **seif dune**) a sand dune in the form of a long narrow ridge.

sei·gneur /saynyőr/ *n.* (also **seign·ior** /sáynyáwr/) a feudal lord; the lord of a manor. □□ **sei·gneu·ri·al** *adj.* **seign·ior·i·al** /-nyáwreeəl/ *adj.*

seine /sayn/ *n. & v.* ● *n.* ▼ a fishing net for encircling fish, with floats at the top and weights at the bottom edge, and usu. hauled ashore. ● *v.intr. & tr.* fish or catch with a seine. □□ **sein·er** *n.*

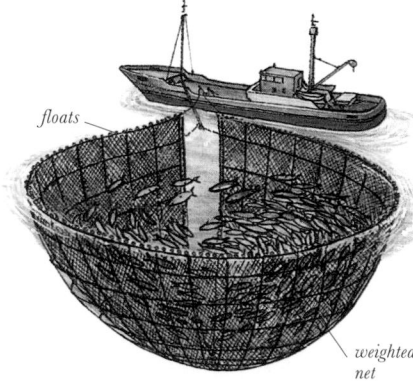
SEINE: PURSE SEINE

seise var. of SEIZE[9].

seis·mic /sízmik/ *adj.* of or relating to an earthquake or earthquakes. ▷ EARTHQUAKE. □□ **seis·mal** *adj.* **seis·mi·cal** *adj.* **seis·mi·cal·ly** *adv.*

seismo- /sízmō/ *comb. form* earthquake.

seis·mo·gram /sízməgram/ *n.* a record given by a seismograph. ▷ SEISMOGRAPH

seis·mo·graph /sízməgraf/ *n.* ▼ an instrument that records the force, direction, etc., of earthquakes. □□ **seis·mo·graph·ic** *adj.* **seis·mo·graph·i·cal** *adj.*

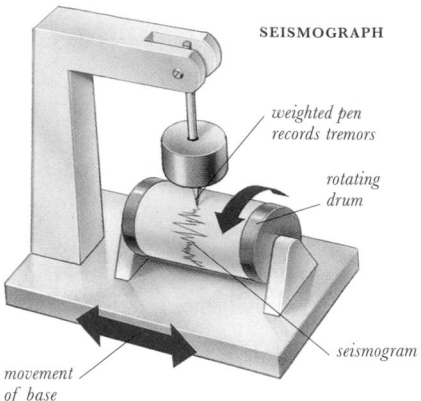

SEISMOGRAPH

weighted pen records tremors

rotating drum

seismogram

movement of base

seis·mol·o·gy /sízmóləjee/ *n.* the scientific study and recording of earthquakes and related phenomena. □□ **seis·mo·log·i·cal** /-məlójikəl/ *adj.* **seis·mo·log·i·cal·ly** /-lójiklee/ *adv.* **seis·mol·o·gist** *n.*

seize /seez/ *v.* **1** *tr.* take hold of forcibly or suddenly. **2** *tr.* take possession of forcibly (*seized power*). **3** *tr.* take possession of by warrant or legal right. **4** *tr.* affect suddenly (*panic seized us*). **5** *tr.* take advantage of (an opportunity). **6** *tr.* comprehend quickly or clearly. **7** *intr.* (usu. foll. by *on, upon*) **a** take hold forcibly or suddenly. **b** take advantage eagerly (*seized on a pretext*). **8** *intr.* (usu. foll. by *up*) (of a moving part in a machine) become jammed. **9** *tr.* (also **seise**) (usu. foll. by *of*) *Law* put in possession of. **10** *tr. Naut.* ▲ fasten or attach by binding with turns of yarn, etc. □ **seized** (or **seised**) **of 1** possessing legally. **2** aware or informed of. □□ **seiz·a·ble** *adj.* **seiz·er** *n.*

sei·zure /séezhər/ *n.* **1** the act or an instance of seizing; the state of being seized. **2** a sudden attack of apoplexy, etc.; a stroke.

Sekt /zekt/ *n.* a German sparkling white wine.

se·la·chi·an /siláykeeən/ *n. & adj.* ● *n.* any fish of the subclass Selachii, including sharks and dogfish. ● *adj.* of or relating to this subclass.

sel·dom /séldəm/ *adv. & adj.* ● *adv.* rarely; not often. ● *adj.* rare; uncommon.

se·lect /silékt/ *v. & adj.* ● *v.tr.* choose, esp. as the best or most suitable. ● *adj.* **1** chosen for excellence or suitability; choice. **2** (of a society, etc.) exclusive; cautious in admitting members. □□ **se·lect·a·ble** *adj.* **se·lect·ness** *n.*

se·lect com·mit·tee *n.* a small committee appointed by a legislative body, etc., for a special purpose.

se·lect·ee /síliktée/ *n.* one drafted for service in the armed forces.

se·lec·tion /silékshən/ *n.* **1** the act or an instance of selecting. **2** a selected person or thing. **3** things from which a choice may be made. **4** *Biol.* the process in which environmental and genetic influences determine which types of organism thrive better than others, regarded as a factor in evolution. □□ **se·lec·tion·al** *adj.* **se·lec·tion·al·ly** *adv.*

SEIZE caption: **SEIZE:** NAUTICAL BLOCK HELD IN A SEIZED ROPE LOOP

flat seizing · *block* · *rope loop*

S

se·lec·tive /siléktiv/ *adj.* **1** using or characterized by selection. **2** able to select. □□ **se·lec·tive·ly** *adv.* **se·lec·tive·ness** *n.* **se·lec·tiv·i·ty** /siléktívitee, sél-, séel-/ *n.*

se·lec·tive serv·ice *n.* service in the armed forces under conscription.

se·lec·tor /siléktər/ *n.* **1** a person who selects, esp. a representative team in a sport. **2** a device that selects, esp. a device in a vehicle that selects the required gear.

se·le·ni·um /sileéneeəm/ *n.* *Chem.* a nonmetallic element occurring naturally in various metallic sulfide ores.

sel·e·nog·ra·phy /sélinógrəfee/ *n.* the study or mapping of the Moon. □□ **sel·e·nog·ra·pher** *n.* **se·le·no·graph·ic** /-nəgráfik/ *adj.*

sel·e·nol·o·gy /sélenóləjee/ *n.* the scientific study of the Moon. □□ **sel·e·nol·o·gist** *n.*

self /self/ *n. & adj.* ● *n.* (*pl.* **selves** /selvz/) **1** a person's or thing's own individuality or essence (*his true self*). **2** a person or thing as the object of introspection or reflexive action (*the consciousness of self*). **3 a** one's own interests or pleasure. **b** concentration on these. **4** *Commerce* or *colloq.* myself, yourself, himself, etc. (*check drawn to self*). **5** used in phrases equivalent to *myself, yourself, himself,* etc. (*your good selves*). ● *adj.* **1** of the same color as the rest or throughout. **2** (of a flower) of the natural wild color. **3** (of color) uniform, the same throughout. □ **one's better self** one's nobler impulses. **one's former** (or **old**) **self** as one formerly was.

self- /self/ *comb. form* expressing reflexive action: **1** of or directed toward oneself or itself (*self-respect; self-cleaning*). **2** by oneself or itself, esp. without external agency (*self-evident*). **3** on, in, for, or relating to oneself or itself (*self-confident*).

self-a·base·ment /sélfəbáysmənt/ *n.* the abasement of oneself; self-humiliation.

self-ab·ne·ga·tion /sélfábnigáyshən/ *n.* self-sacrifice.

self-ab·sorp·tion /sélfəbsáwrpshən, -záwrp-/ *n.* absorption in oneself. □□ **self-ab·sorbed** /-sáwrbd, -záwrbd/ *adj.*

self-a·buse /sélfəbyóoz/ *n.* **1** the reviling or abuse of oneself. **2** masturbation.

self-ac·cu·sa·tion /sélfákyóozáyshən/ *n.* the accusing of oneself. □□ **self-ac·cu·sa·to·ry** /-əkyóozətáwree/ *adj.*

self-act·ing /sélfákting/ *adj.* acting without external influence or control.

self-ad·dressed /sélfədrèst/ *adj.* (of an envelope, etc.) having one's own address on for return communication.

self-ad·he·sive /sélfədheésiv/ *adj.* (of an envelope, label, etc.) adhesive, esp. without being moistened.

self-ad·just·ing /sélfəjústing/ *adj.* (of machinery, etc.) adjusting itself. □□ **self-ad·just·ment** *n.*

self-ad·mi·ra·tion /sélfádməráyshən/ *n.* the admiration of oneself; pride; conceit.

self-ad·vance·ment /sélfədvánsmənt/ *n.* the advancement of oneself.

self-ad·ver·tise·ment /sélfádvərtízmənt, -ədvér-tiz-/ *n.* the advertising or promotion of oneself. □□ **self-ad·ver·tis·er** /-ádvərtīzər/ *n.*

self-af·fir·ma·tion /sélfáfərmáyshən/ *n.* *Psychol.* the recognition and assertion of the existence of the conscious self.

self-ag·gran·dize·ment /sélfəgrándizmənt/ *n.* the act or process of enriching oneself or making oneself powerful. □□ **self-ag·gran·diz·ing** /-grándīzing/ *adj.*

self-a·nal·y·sis /sélfənálisis/ *n.* *Psychol.* the analysis of oneself, one's motives, character, etc. □□ **self-an·a·lyz·ing** /-ánəlīzing/ *adj.*

self-ap·point·ed /sélfəpóyntid/ *adj.* designated so by oneself; not authorized by another (*a self-appointed guardian*).

self-ap·pre·ci·a·tion /sélfəprèesheeáyshən/ *n.* a good opinion of oneself; conceit.

self-ap·pro·ba·tion /sélfáprəbáyshən/ *n.* = SELF-APPRECIATION.

self-ap·prov·al /sélfəprōʹvəl/ *n.* = SELF-APPRECIATION.

self-as·sem·bly /sélfəsémblee/ *n.* (often *attrib.*) construction (of furniture, etc.) from materials sold in kit form.

self-as·ser·tion /sélfəsórshən/ *n.* the aggressive promotion of oneself, one's views, etc. □□ **self-as·ser·tive** *adj.* **self-as·ser·tive·ness** *n.*

self-as·sess·ment *n.* assessment of oneself or one's performance in relation to an objective standard.

self-as·sur·ance /sélfəshōʹrəns/ *n.* confidence in one's own abilities, etc. □□ **self-as·sured** *adj.* **self-as·sur·ed·ly** *adv.*

self-a·ware /sélfəwáir/ *adj.* conscious of one's character, feelings, motives, etc. □□ **self-a·ware·ness** *n.*

self-be·tray·al /sélfbitráyəl/ *n.* the inadvertent revelation of one's true thoughts, etc.

self-bind·er /sélfbíndər/ *n.* a reaping machine with an automatic mechanism for binding the sheaves.

self-born /sélfbáwrn/ *adj.* produced by itself or oneself; not made externally.

self-cen·sor·ship /sélfsénsərship/ *n.* the censoring of oneself.

self-cen·tered /sélfséntərd/ *adj.* preoccupied with one's own personality or affairs. □□ **self-cen·tered·ly** *adv.* **self-cen·tered·ness** *n.*

self-clean·ing /sélfkleéning/ *adj.* (esp. of an oven) cleaning itself when heated, etc.

self-clos·ing /sélfklōʹzing/ *adj.* (of a door, etc.) closing automatically.

self-cock·ing /sélfkóking/ *adj.* (of a gun) with the hammer raised by the trigger, not by hand.

self-col·lect·ed /sélfkəléktid/ *adj.* composed; serene; self-assured.

self-col·ored /sélfkúlərd/ *adj.* **1 a** having the same color throughout (*buttons and belt are self-colored*). **b** (of material) natural; undyed. **2** (of a flower) **a** ▶ of uniform color. **b** having its color unchanged by cultivation or hybridization.

self-com·mand /sélfkəmánd/ *n.* = SELF-CONTROL.

self-con·ceit /sélfkənseét/ *n.* = SELF-SATISFACTION. □□ **self-con·ceit·ed** *adj.*

self-con·dem·na·tion /sélfkóndem-náyshən/ *n.* **1** the blaming of oneself. **2** the inadvertent revelation of one's own sin, crime, etc.

self-con·fessed /sélfkənfést/ *adj.* openly admitting oneself to be (*a self-confessed thief*).

self-con·fi·dence /sélfkónfidəns/ *n.* = SELF-ASSURANCE. □□ **self-con·fi·dent** *adj.* **self-con·fi·dent·ly** *adv.*

self-con·grat·u·la·tion /sélfkəngráchəláyshən, -gráj-, -kəng-/ *n.* = SELF-SATISFACTION. □□ **self-con·grat·u·la·to·ry** /-kəngrátyōʹlətáwree/ *adj.*

self-con·scious /sélfkónshəs/ *adj.* **1** socially inept through embarrassment or shyness. **2** *Philos.* having knowledge of one's own existence; self-contemplating. □□ **self-con·scious·ly** *adv.* **self-con·scious·ness** *n.*

self-con·sis·tent /sélfkənsístənt/ *adj.* (of parts of the same whole, etc.) consistent; not conflicting. □□ **self-con·sis·ten·cy** *n.*

self-con·sti·tut·ed /sélfkónstitōōtid -tyōō-/ *adj.* (of a person, group, etc.) assuming a function without authorization or right; self-appointed.

self-con·tained /sélfkəntáynd/ *adj.* (of a person) uncommunicative; independent. □□ **self-con·tain·ment** *n.*

self-con·tempt /sélfkəntémpt/ *n.* contempt for oneself. □□ **self-con·temp·tu·ous** *adj.*

self-con·tent /sélfkəntént/ *n.* satisfaction with oneself, one's life, achievements, etc. □□ **self-con·tent·ed** *adj.*

self-con·tra·dic·tion /sélfkóntrədíkshən/ *n.* internal inconsistency. □□ **self-con·tra·dic·to·ry** *adj.*

self-con·trol /sélfkəntrōl/ *n.* the power of controlling one's external reactions, emotions, etc.; equanimity. □□ **self-con·trolled** *adj.*

self-cor·rect·ing /sélfkərékting/ *adj.* correcting itself without external help.

self-cre·at·ed /sélfkreeáytid/ *adj.* created by oneself or itself. □□ **self-cre·a·tion** /-áyshən/ *n.*

self-crit·i·cal /sélfkrítikəl/ *adj.* critical of oneself, one's abilities, etc. □□ **self-crit·i·cism** /-tisizəm/ *n.*

self-de·cep·tion /sélfdisépshən/ *n.* deceiving oneself esp. concerning one's true feelings, etc. □□ **self-de·ceit** /-diseét/ *n.* **self-de·ceiv·er** /-diseévər/ *n.* **self-de·ceiv·ing** /-diseéving/ *adj.* **self-de·cep·tive** *adj.*

self-de·feat·ing /sélfdifeéting/ *adj.* (of an attempt, action, etc.) doomed to failure because of internal inconsistencies, etc.

self-de·fense /sélfdifèns/ *n.* **1** an aggressive act, speech, etc., intended as defense (*had to hit him in self-defense*). **2** (usu. **the noble art of self-defense**) boxing. □□ **self-de·fen·sive** *adj.*

self-de·lu·sion /sélfdilōʹzhən/ *n.* the act or an instance of deluding oneself.

self-de·ni·al /sélfdinīəl/ *n.* the negation of one's interests, needs, or wishes; self-control. □□ **self-de·ny·ing** *adj.*

self-dep·re·ca·tion /sélfdéprikáyshən/ *n.* the act of disparaging or belittling oneself. □□ **self-dep·re·cat·ing** /-kayting/ *adj.* **self-dep·re·cat·ing·ly** *adv.*

self-de·stroy·ing /sélfdistróying/ *adj.* destroying oneself or itself.

self-de·struct /sélfdistrúkt/ *v. & adj.* ● *v.intr.* (of a spacecraft, bomb, etc.) explode or disintegrate automatically, esp. when preset to do so. ● *attrib.adj.* enabling a thing to self-destruct (*a self-destruct device*).

self-de·struc·tion /sélfdistrúkshən/ *n.* **1** the process or an act of destroying oneself or itself. **2** the process or an act of self-destructing. □□ **self-de·struc·tive** *adj.* **self-de·struc·tive·ly** *adv.*

self-de·ter·mi·na·tion /sélfditórminàyshən/ *n.* **1** a nation's right to determine its own allegiance, government, etc. **2** the ability to act with free will, as opposed to fatalism, etc. □□ **self-de·ter·mined** /-tórmind/ *adj.* **self-de·ter·min·ing** /-tórmining/ *adj.*

self-de·vel·op·ment /sélfdivéləp-mənt/ *n.* the development of one's abilities, etc.

SELF-COLORED DAHLIA

self-dis·ci·pline /sélfdísiplin/ *n.* the act of or ability to apply oneself, control one's feelings, etc.; self-control. □□ **self-dis·ci·plined** *adj.*

self-dis·cov·er·y /sélfdiskúvəree/ *n.* the process of acquiring insight into oneself, one's character, desires, etc.

self-dis·gust /sélfdisgúst/ *n.* disgust with oneself.

self-doubt /sélfdówt/ *n.* lack of confidence in oneself, one's abilities, etc.

self-ed·u·cat·ed /sélféjəkaytid/ *adj.* educated by oneself by reading, etc., without formal instruction. □□ **self-ed·u·ca·tion** /-káyshən/ *n.*

self-ef·fac·ing /sélfifáysing/ *adj.* retiring; modest; timid. □□ **self-ef·face·ment** *n.* **self-ef·fac·ing·ly** *adv.*

self-em·ployed /sélfimplóyd/ *adj.* working for oneself, as a freelance or owner of a business, etc.; not employed by an employer. □□ **self-em·ploy·ment** *n.*

self-es·teem /sélfisteém/ *n.* **1** a good opinion of oneself; self-confidence. **2** an unduly high regard for oneself; conceit.

self-ev·i·dent /sélfévidənt/ *adj.* obvious; without the need of evidence or further explanation. □□ **self-ev·i·dence** *n.* **self-ev·i·dent·ly** *adv.*

S

self·ex·am·i·na·tion /sélfigzámináyshən/ *n.* **1** the study of one's own conduct, reasons, etc. **2** the examining of one's body for signs of illness, etc.

self·ex·e·cut·ing /sélféksikyo͞oting/ *adj. Law* (of a law, legal clause, etc.) not needing legislation, etc., to be enforced; automatic.

self·ex·ist·ent /sélfigzístənt/ *adj.* existing without prior cause; independent.

self·ex·plan·a·to·ry /sélfiksplánətawree/ *adj.* not needing explanation.

self·ex·pres·sion /sélfikspréshən/ *n.* the expression of one's feelings, thoughts, etc., esp. in writing, painting, music, etc. □□ **self·ex·pres·sive** *adj.*

self·feed·er /sélf-fēedər/ *n.* **1** a furnace, machine, etc., that renews its own fuel or material automatically. **2** a device for supplying food to farm animals automatically. □□ **self·feed·ing** *adj.*

self·fer·tile /sélf-fərt'l/ *adj.* (of a plant, etc.) self-fertilizing. □□ **self·fer·til·i·ty** /-tilitee/ *n.*

self·fer·ti·li·za·tion /sélf-fərt'lizáyshən/ *n.* the fertilization of plants by their own pollen, not from others. □□ **self·fer·ti·lized** /-fərt'līzd/ *adj.* **self·fer·ti·liz·ing** /-fərt'līzing/ *adj.*

self·fi·nanc·ing /sélf-fínansing, -fənán-/ *adj.* that finances itself, esp. (of a project or undertaking) that pays for its own implementation or continuation. □□ **self·fi·nance** *v.tr.*

self·for·get·ful /sélf-fərgétfŏŏl/ *adj.* unselfish. □□ **self·for·get·ful·ness** *n.*

self·ful·fill·ing /sélf-fŏŏlfiling/ *adj.* (of a prophecy, forecast, etc.) bound to come true as a result of actions brought about by its being made.

self·ful·fill·ment /sélf-fŏŏlfilmənt/ *n.* the fulfillment of one's own hopes and ambitions.

self·gen·er·at·ing /sélfjénərayting/ *adj.* generated by itself or oneself.

self·glo·ri·fi·ca·tion /sélfgláwrifikáyshən/ *n.* the proclamation of oneself, one's abilities, etc.; self-satisfaction.

self·gov·ern·ment /sélfgúvərnmənt/ *n.* **1** (esp. of a former colony, etc.) government by its own people. **2** = SELF-CONTROL. □□ **self·gov·erned** *adj.*

self·grat·i·fi·ca·tion /sélfgrátifikáyshən/ *n.* **1** gratification or pleasing of oneself. **2** self-indulgence; dissipation. **3** masturbation. □□ **self·grat·i·fy·ing** *adj.*

self·hate /sélfháyt/ *n.* = SELF-HATRED.

self·ha·tred /sélfháytrid/ *n.* hatred of oneself, esp. of one's actual self when contrasted with one's imagined self.

self·heal /sélfhéel/ *n.* any of several plants, esp. *Prunella vulgaris*, believed to have healing properties.

self·help /sélfhélp/ *n.* **1** the theory that individuals should provide for their own support and improvement in society. **2** the act or faculty of providing for or improving oneself.

self·hood /sélfhŏŏd/ *n.* personality; separate and conscious existence.

self·im·age /sélfímij/ *n.* one's own idea or picture of oneself.

self·im·por·tance /sélfimpáwrt'ns/ *n.* a high opinion of oneself; pompousness. □□ **self·im·por·tant** *adj.* **self·im·por·tant·ly** *adv.*

self·im·posed /sélfimpốzd/ *adj.* (of a task or condition, etc.) imposed on and by oneself, not externally (*self-imposed exile*).

self·im·prove·ment /sélfimprŏ́ŏvmənt/ *n.* the improvement of one's own position or disposition by one's own efforts.

self·in·duced /sélfindŏ́ŏst, -dyŏ́ŏst/ *adj.* induced by oneself or itself.

self·in·duct·ance /sélfindúktəns/ *n. Electr.* the property of an electric circuit that causes an electromotive force to be generated in it by a change in the current flowing through it.

self·in·duc·tion /sélfindúkshən/ *n. Electr.* the production of an electromotive force in a circuit when the current in that circuit is varied. □□ **self·in·duc·tive** *adj.*

self·in·dul·gent /sélfindúljənt/ *adj.* indulging oneself in pleasure, idleness, etc. □□ **self·in·dul·gence** *n.* **self·in·dul·gent·ly** *adv.*

self·in·flict·ed /sélfinfliktid/ *adj.* inflicted by and on oneself.

self·in·ter·est /sélfintrist, -tərist/ *n.* one's personal interest or advantage. □□ **self·in·ter·est·ed** *adj.*

self·ish /sélfish/ *adj.* **1** concerned chiefly with one's own personal profit or pleasure; actuated by self-interest. **2** (of a motive, etc.) appealing to self-interest. □□ **self·ish·ly** *adv.* **self·ish·ness** *n.*

self·jus·ti·fi·ca·tion /sélfjústifikáyshən/ *n.* the justification of one's actions.

self·knowl·edge /sélfnólij/ *n.* the understanding of one's motives, etc.

self·less /sélflis/ *adj.* disregarding oneself or one's own interests; unselfish. □□ **self·less·ly** *adv.* **self·less·ness** *n.*

self·load·ing /sélflṓding/ *adj.* (esp. of a gun) loading itself. □□ **self·load·er** *n.*

self·lock·ing /sélflóking/ *adj.* locking itself.

self·love /sélflúv/ *n.* **1** selfishness; self-indulgence. **2** *Philos.* regard for one's own well-being and happiness.

self·made /sélfmáyd/ *adj.* **1** rich by one's own effort. **2** made by oneself.

self·mate /sélfmayt/ *n. Chess* checkmate in which a player forces the opponent to achieve checkmate.

self·mock·ing /sélfmóking/ *adj.* mocking oneself or itself.

self·mo·tion /sélfmṓshən/ *n.* motion caused by oneself or itself, not externally. □□ **self·mov·ing** /-mṓoving/ *adj.*

self·mo·ti·vat·ed /sélfmṓtivaytid/ *adj.* acting on one's own initiative without any external pressure. □□ **self·mo·ti·va·tion** /-váyshən/ *n.*

self·mur·der /sélfmərdər/ *n.* = SUICIDE. □□ **self·mur·der·er** *n.*

self·ne·glect /sélfniglékt/ *n.* neglect of oneself.

self·ness /sélfnis/ *n.* **1** individuality; personality; essence. **2** selfishness or self-regard.

self·o·pin·ion·at·ed /sélfəpínyənaytid/ *adj.* **1** stubbornly adhering to one's own opinions. **2** arrogant. □□ **self·o·pin·ion** *n.*

self·per·pet·u·at·ing /sélfpərpécho͞o-ayting/ *adj.* perpetuating itself or oneself without external agency. □□ **self·per·pet·u·a·tion** /-áyshən/ *n.*

self·pit·y /sélfpítee/ *n.* extreme sorrow for one's own troubles, etc. □□ **self·pit·y·ing** *adj.* **self·pit·y·ing·ly** *adv.*

self·pol·li·na·tion /sélfpólináyshən/ *n.* the pollination of a flower by pollen from the same plant. □□ **self·pol·li·nat·ed** *adj.* **self·pol·li·nat·ing** *adj.* **self·pol·li·na·tor** *n.*

self·por·trait /sélfpáwrtrit/ *n.* ▶ a portrait or description of an artist, writer, etc., by himself or herself.

self·pos·sessed /sélfpəz-ést/ *adj.* habitually exercising self-control; composed. □□ **self·pos·ses·sion** /-zéshən/ *n.*

self·praise /sélfpráyz/ *n.* boasting; self-glorification.

self·pres·er·va·tion /sélf-prézərváyshən/ *n.* **1** the preservation of one's own life, safety, etc. **2** this as a basic instinct of human beings and animals.

self·pro·claimed /sélfprə-kláymd/ *adj.* proclaimed by oneself or itself to be such.

self·prop·a·gat·ing /sélf-própəgayting/ *adj.* able to propagate itself.

self·pro·pelled /sélfprəpéld/

adj. (esp. of a motor vehicle, etc.) moving or able to move without external propulsion. □□ **self·pro·pel·ling** *adj.*

self·pro·tec·tion /sélfprətékshən/ *n.* protecting oneself or itself. □□ **self·pro·tec·tive** *adj.*

self·re·al·i·za·tion /sélfréeəlizáyshən/ *n.* **1** the development of one's faculties, abilities, etc. **2** this as an ethical principle.

self·re·cord·ing /sélfrikáwrding/ *adj.* (of a scientific instrument, etc.) automatically recording its measurements.

self·re·gard /sélfrigaárd/ *n.* **1** a proper regard for oneself. **2 a** selfishness. **b** conceit.

self·reg·is·ter·ing /sélfréjistəring/ *adj.* (of a scientific instrument, etc.) automatically registering its measurements.

self·reg·u·lat·ing /sélfrégyəlayting/ *adj.* regulating oneself or itself without intervention. □□ **self·reg·u·la·tion** /-láyshən/ *n.* **self·reg·u·la·to·ry** /-lətawree/ *adj.*

self·re·li·ance /sélfrilíəns/ *n.* reliance on one's own resources, etc.; independence. □□ **self·re·li·ant** *adj.* **self·re·li·ant·ly** *adv.*

self·re·new·al /sélfrinŏ́ŏəl, -nyŏ́ŏ-/ *n.* the act of renewing oneself or itself.

self·re·proach /sélfripróch/ *n.* reproach or blame directed at oneself. □□ **self·re·proach·ful** *adj.*

self·re·spect /sélfrispékt/ *n.* respect for oneself. □□ **self·re·spect·ing** *adj.*

self·re·straint /sélfristráynt/ *n.* = SELF-CONTROL. □□ **self·re·strained** *adj.*

self·re·veal·ing /sélfrivéeling/ *adj.* revealing one's character, motives, etc., esp. inadvertently. □□ **self·rev·e·la·tion** /-révəláyshən/ *n.*

self·right·eous /sélfríchəs/ *adj.* excessively conscious of or insistent on one's rectitude, correctness, etc. □□ **self·right·eous·ly** *adv.* **self·right·eous·ness** *n.*

self·right·ing /sélfríting/ *adj.* (of a boat) righting itself when capsized.

self·ris·ing /sélfrízing/ *adj.* (of flour) having a raising agent already added.

self·rule /sélfrŏ́ŏl/ *n.* = SELF-GOVERNMENT 1.

self·sac·ri·fice /sélfsákrifīs/ *n.* the negation of one's own interests, wishes, etc., in favor of those of others. □□ **self·sac·ri·fic·ing** *adj.*

self·same /sélfsaym/ *attrib.adj.* (prec. by *the*) the very same.

self·sat·is·fac·tion /sélfsátisfákshən/ *n.* excessive and unwarranted satisfaction with oneself; complacency. □□ **self·sat·is·fied** /-sátisfīd/ *adj.*

self·seal·ing /sélfséeling/ *adj.* **1** (of a tire, fuel tank, etc.) automatically able to seal small punctures. **2** (of an envelope) self-adhesive.

self·seek·ing /sélfséeking/ *adj. & n.* seeking one's own welfare before that of others. □□ **self·seek·er** *n.*

self·se·lec·tion /sélfsilékshən/ *n.* the act of selecting oneself or itself. □□ **self·se·lect·ing** *adj.*

self·serv·ice /sélfsə́rvis/ *adj. & n.* ● *adj.* (often *attrib.*) **1** (of a store, restaurant, gas station, etc.) where customers serve themselves and pay at a checkout, etc. **2** (of a machine) serving goods after the insertion of coins. ● *n. colloq.* a self-service store, gas station, etc.

self·serv·ing /sélfsə́rving/ *adj.* = SELF-SEEKING.

self·sown /sélfsṓn/ *adj.* grown from seed scattered naturally.

self·start·er /sélfstaártər/ *n.* **1** an electric appliance for starting a motor vehicle engine without the use of a crank. **2** an ambitious person who needs no external motivation.

SELF-PORTRAIT BY
VINCENT VAN GOGH (1887)

S

self-ster·ile /sélfstéril, -īl/ *adj. Biol.* not being self-fertile. □□ **self-ste·ril·i·ty** /-stərílitee/ *n.*

self-styled /sélfstíld/ *adj.* called so by oneself (*a self-styled artist*).

self-suf·fi·cient /sélfsəfíshənt/ *adj.* **1 a** needing nothing; independent. **b** able to supply one's needs from one's own resources. **2** content with one's own opinion; arrogant. □□ **self-suf·fi·cien·cy** *n.* **self-suf·fi·cient·ly** *adv.*

self-sup·port·ing /sélfsəpáwrting/ *adj.* **1** capable of maintaining oneself or itself financially. **2** staying up without external aid. □□ **self-sup·port** *n.*

self-sur·ren·der /sélfsəréndər/ *n.* the surrender of oneself or one's will, etc., to an influence, emotion, or other person.

self-sus·tain·ing /sélfsəstáyning/ *adj.* sustaining oneself or itself. □□ **self-sus·tained** *adj.*

self-tapping *adj.* ◄ (of a screw) able to cut its own thread.

self-taught /sélftáwt/ *adj.* educated or trained by oneself, not externally.

self-tor·ture /sélftáwrchər/ *n.* the inflicting of pain, esp. mental, on oneself.

self-willed /sélfwíld/ *adj.* obstinately pursuing one's own wishes. □□ **self-will** *n.*

self-wind·ing /sélfwínding/ *adj.* (of a watch, etc.) having an automatic winding apparatus.

self-worth /sélfwórth/ *n.* = SELF-ESTEEM.

non-tapered edge

SELF-TAPPING SCREW

Sel·juk /séljōok/ *n. & adj.* ● *n.* a member of any of the Turkish dynasties (11th–13th c.) of central and western Asia preceding Ottoman rule. ● *adj.* of or relating to the Seljuks. □□ **Sel·juk·i·an** /-jōokeeən/ *adj. & n.*

sell /sel/ *v. & n.* ● *v.* (*past* and *past part.* **sold** /sōld/) **1** *tr.* make over or dispose of in exchange for money. **2** *tr.* keep a stock of for sale or be a dealer in (*do you sell candles?*). **3** *intr.* (of goods) be purchased (*these are selling well*). **4** *intr.* (foll. by *at, for*) have a specified price (*sells at $5*). **5** *tr.* betray for money or other reward (*sell one's country*). **6** *tr.* offer dishonorably for money or other consideration; make a matter of corrupt bargaining (*sell justice; sell one's honor*). **7** *tr.* **a** advertise or publish the merits of. **b** inspire with a desire to buy or acquire or agree to something. **8** *tr.* cause to be sold (*the author's name alone will sell many copies*). ● *n. colloq.* **1** a manner of selling (*soft sell*). **2** a deception or disappointment. □ **sell off** sell the remainder of (goods) at reduced prices. **sell out 1** sell (all or some of one's stock, shares, etc.). **2** betray. **sell short** disparage; underestimate. **sold on** *colloq.* enthusiastic about. □□ **sell·a·ble** *adj.*

sell-by date *n.* the latest recommended date of sale.

sell·er /sélər/ *n.* **1** a person who sells. **2** a commodity that sells well or badly.

sell·er's mar·ket *n.* (also **sellers' market**) an economic position in which goods are scarce and expensive.

sell·ing point *n.* an advantageous feature.

sell·out /sélowt/ *n.* **1** a commercial success, esp. the selling of all tickets for a show. **2** a betrayal.

selt·zer /séltsər/ *n.* (in full **selzer water**) **1** medicinal mineral water from Nieder-Selters in Germany. **2** an artificial substitute for this; soda water.

sel·vage /sélvij/ *n.* (also **sel·vedge**) **1** an edging that prevents cloth from unraveling. **2** a border of different material or finish intended to be removed or hidden.

selves *pl.* of SELF.

se·man·teme /simánteem/ *n. Linguistics* a fundamental element expressing an image or idea.

se·man·tic /simántik/ *adj.* relating to meaning in language. □□ **se·man·ti·cal·ly** *adv.*

se·man·tics /simántiks/ *n.pl.* (usu. treated as *sing.*) the branch of linguistics concerned with meaning. □□ **se·man·ti·cist** /-tisist/ *n.*

sem·a·phore /séməfawr/ *n. & v.* ● *n.* **1** *Mil.*, etc. ▼ a system of sending messages by holding the arms or two flags in certain positions according to an alphabetic code. **2** a signaling apparatus consisting of a post with a movable arm or arms, lanterns, etc. ▷ SIGNAL. ● *v.intr. & tr.* signal or send by semaphore. □□ **sem·a·phor·ic** *adj.* **sem·a·phor·i·cal·ly** /-fáwr-iklee/ *adv.*

se·ma·si·ol·o·gy /simáyseeóləjee/ *n.* semantics. □□ **se·ma·si·o·log·i·cal** /-seeəlójikəl/ *adj.*

se·ma·tic /simátik/ *adj. Zool.* (of coloring, markings, etc.) significant; serving to warn off enemies or attract attention.

sem·blance /sémbləns/ *n.* **1** the outward or superficial appearance of something (*put on a semblance of anger*). **2** resemblance.

sem·é /səmáy/ *adj.* (also **sem·ée**) *Heraldry* covered with small bearings of indefinite number (e.g., stars, fleurs-de-lis) arranged all over the field.

sem·eme /sémeem, seé-/ *n. Linguistics* the unit of meaning carried by a morpheme.

se·men /séemən/ *n.* the reproductive fluid of male animals.

se·mes·ter /siméstər/ *n.* **1** half of the academic year in an educational institution, usu. an 18-week period. **2** a half-year course or term in (esp. German) universities.

sem·i /sémī, sémee/ *n.* (*pl.* **semis**) *colloq.* **1** a semi-trailer. **2** a semifinal.

semi- /sémee, sémī/ *prefix* **1** half (*semicircle*). **2** partly (*semiofficial; semidetached*). **3** almost (*a semismile*). **4** occurring or appearing twice in a specified period (*semiannual*).

sem·i·an·nu·al /sémeeányōoəl, sémī-/ *adj.* occurring, published, etc., twice a year. □□ **sem·i·an·nu·al·ly** *adv.*

sem·i·au·to·mat·ic /sémeeáwtəmátik, sémī-/ *adj.* **1** partially automatic. **2** (of a firearm) having a mechanism for continuous loading but not for continuous firing.

sem·i·base·ment /sémeebáysmənt, sémī-/ *n.* a story partly below ground level.

sem·i·bold /sémeebốld, sémī-/ *adj. Printing* printed in a type darker than normal but not as dark as bold.

sem·i·breve /sémeebrev, -breev, sémī-/ *n. esp. Brit. Mus.* = WHOLE NOTE.

sem·i·cir·cle /sémeesərkəl, sémī-/ *n.* **1** half of a circle or of its circumference. ▷ CIRCLE. **2** an object, or arrangement of objects, forming a semicircle.

sem·i·cir·cu·lar /sémeesórkyələr, sémī-/ *adj.* **1** forming or shaped like a semicircle. **2** arranged as or in a semicircle.

sem·i·civ·i·lized /sémeesívilīzd, sémī-/ *adj.* partially civilized.

sem·i·co·lon /sémikốlən/ *n.* a punctuation mark (;) of intermediate value between a comma and a period.

sem·i·con·duct·ing /sémeekəndúkting, sémī-/ *adj.* having the properties of a semiconductor.

sem·i·con·duc·tor /sémeekəndúktər, sémī-/ *n.* a solid substance that is a nonconductor when pure

---

SEMAPHORE

Semaphore may have originated with the ancient Greeks and Romans, who used flags to signal over short distances. The invention of the telescope around 1600 increased the range of semaphore systems, and until the early 1900s semaphore was widely used by navies as a means of communication between ships. Even with today's sophisticated technology, ships sailing close to each other still occasionally use semaphore. The system can be used to express letters or numbers: the signals for the first nine letters of the alphabet double for the numbers one to nine ("J" is zero) when preceded by the "numbers follow" signal. Messages can be sent at a rate of around 25 words a minute.

THE SEMAPHORE ALPHABET

READY   A   B   C   D   E   F   G   H   I   J   K   L   M   N   O   P   Q   R   S   T   U   V   W   X   Y   Z

S

or at a low temperature but has a conductivity between that of insulators and that of most metals when containing a suitable impurity or at a higher temperature.

sem·i·con·scious /sémeekónshəs, sémī-/ *adj.* partly or imperfectly conscious.

sem·i·cyl·in·der /sémeesílindər, sémī-/ *n.* half of a cylinder cut longitudinally. □□ **sem·i·cy·lin·dri·cal** /-líndrikəl/ *adj.*

sem·i·de·tached /sémeeditácht, sémī-/ *adj. & n.* ● *adj.* (of a house) joined to another by a common wall on one side only. ● *n.* a semidetached house.

sem·i·di·am·e·ter /sémeedíámitər, sémī-/ *n.* half of a diameter; radius.

sem·i·doc·u·men·ta·ry /sémeedókyəméntəree, sémī-/ *adj. & n.* ● *adj.* (of a motion picture) having a factual background and a fictitious story. ● *n.* (*pl.* **-ies**) a semidocumentary motion picture.

sem·i·fi·nal /sémeefínəl, sémī-/ *n.* a match or round immediately preceding the final.

sem·i·fi·nal·ist /sémeefínəlist, sémī-/ *n.* a competitor in a semifinal.

sem·i·fin·ished /sémeefinisht, sémī-/ *adj.* prepared for the final stage of manufacture.

sem·i·fit·ted /sémeefitid, sémī-/ *adj.* (of a garment) shaped to the body but not closely fitted.

sem·i·flu·id /sémeefloóoid, sémī-/ *adj. & n.* ● *adj.* of a consistency between solid and liquid. ● *n.* a semifluid substance.

sem·i·in·va·lid /sémee-ínvəlid, sémī-/ *n.* a person somewhat enfeebled or partially disabled.

sem·i·liq·uid /sémeelíkwid, sémī-/ *adj. & n.* = SEMIFLUID.

sem·i·lu·nar /sémeelóonər, sémī-/ *adj.* shaped like a half moon or crescent.

sem·i·met·al /sémeemét'l, sémī-/ *n.* a substance with some of the properties of metals.

sem·i·month·ly /sémeemúnthlee, sémī-/ *adj. & adv.* ● *adj.* occurring, published, etc., twice a month. ● *adv.* twice a month.

sem·i·nal /séminəl/ *adj.* **1** of or relating to seed, semen, or reproduction. **2** (of ideas, etc.) providing the basis for future development. □□ **sem·i·nal·ly** *adv.*

sem·i·nar /séminaar/ *n.* **1** a small class at a university, etc., for discussion and research. **2** a short intensive course of study. **3** a conference of specialists.

sem·i·nar·y /sémineree/ *n.* (*pl.* **-ies**) **1** a training college for priests, rabbis, etc. **2** a place of education. □□ **sem·i·nar·i·an** /-náireeən/ *n.* **sem·i·na·rist** *n.*

sem·i·nif·er·ous /sémeenífərəs, sémī-/ *adj.* **1** bearing seed. **2** conveying semen.

Sem·i·nole /séminōl/ *n.* **1 a** a N. American people native to Florida. **b** a member of this people. **2** the language of this people.

sem·i·of·fi·cial /sémeeəfíshəl/ *adj.* **1** partly official. **2** (of communications) made by an official with the stipulation that the source should not be revealed. □□ **sem·i·of·fi·cial·ly** *adv.*

se·mi·ol·o·gy /séemeeóləjee, sémee-/ *n.* (also **se·mei·ol·o·gy**) = SEMIOTICS. □□ **se·mi·o·log·i·cal** /-meeəlójikəl/ *adj.* **se·mi·ol·o·gist** *n.*

sem·i·o·paque /sémeeōpáyk, sémī-/ *adj.* not fully transparent.

se·mi·ot·ics /séemeeótiks, sémee-/ *n.* (also **se·mei·ot·ics**) the study of signs and symbols in various fields, esp. language. □□ **se·mi·ot·ic** *adj.* **se·mi·ot·i·cal** *adj.* **se·mi·ot·i·cal·ly** *adv.* **se·mi·o·ti·cian** /-tíshən/ *n.*

sem·i·per·ma·nent /sémeepármənənt, sémī-/ *adj.* rather less than permanent.

sem·i·per·me·a·ble /sémeepármeeəbəl, sémī-/ *adj.* (of a membrane, etc.) allowing small molecules, but not large ones, to pass through.

sem·i·pre·cious /sémeepréshəs, sémī-/ *adj.* less valuable than a precious stone.

sem·i·pro /sémeeprő, sémī-/ *adj. & n.* (*pl.* **-os**) *colloq.* = SEMIPROFESSIONAL.

sem·i·pro·fes·sion·al /sémeeprəféshənəl, sémī-/ *adj. & n.* ● *adj.* **1** receiving payment for an activity but not relying on it for a living. **2** involving semiprofessionals. ● *n.* a semiprofessional musician, sportsman, etc.

sem·i·skilled /sémeeskíld, sémī-/ *adj.* (of work or a worker) having or needing some training but less than for a skilled worker.

sem·i·skimmed /sémeeskímd, sémī-/ *adj.* (of milk) from which some cream has been skimmed.

sem·i·sol·id /sémeesólid, sémī-/ *adj.* viscous; semifluid.

sem·i·sweet /sémeeswéet, sémī-/ *adj.* slightly sweetened.

sem·i·syn·thet·ic /sémeesinthétik, sémī-/ *adj. Chem.* (of a substance) that is prepared synthetically but derives from a naturally occurring material.

Sem·ite /sémīt/ *n.* a member of any of the peoples supposed to be descended from Shem, son of Noah (Gen. 10:21 ff.), including the Jews, Arabs, Assyrians, and Phoenicians. □□ **Sem·i·tism** /sémitizəm/ *n.* **Sem·i·tize** /-tīz/ *v.tr.* **Sem·i·ti·za·tion** *n.*

Se·mit·ic /simítik/ *adj.* **1** of or relating to the Semites, esp. the Jews. **2** of or relating to the languages of the family including Hebrew and Arabic.

sem·i·tone /sémeetōn, sémī-/ *n. Mus.* the smallest interval used in classical European music; a half step.

sem·i·trail·er /sémeetráylər, sémī-/ *n.* a trailer having wheels at the back but supported at the front by a towing vehicle.

sem·i·trans·par·ent /sémeetránzpárənt, sémī-, -páir/ *adj.* partially or imperfectly transparent.

sem·i·vow·el /sémeevowəl/ *n.* **1** a sound intermediate between a vowel and a consonant (e.g., *w, y*). **2** a letter representing this.

sem·i·week·ly /sémeeweéklee, sémī-/ *adj. & adv.* ● *adj.* occurring, published, etc., twice a week. ● *adv.* twice a week.

sem·o·li·na /séməleénə/ *n.* **1** the hard grains left after the milling of flour, used in puddings, etc., and in pasta. **2** a pudding, etc., made of this.

sem·pi·ter·nal /sémpitárnəl/ *adj. rhet.* eternal; everlasting. □□ **sem·pi·ter·nal·ly** *adv.* **sem·pi·ter·ni·ty** *n.*

sem·pli·ce /sémplichay/ *adv. Mus.* in a simple style of performance.

sem·pre /sémpray/ *adv. Mus.* throughout; always (*sempre forte*).

semp·stress var. of SEAMSTRESS.

Sem·tex /sémteks/ *n. Trademark* a highly malleable, odorless plastic explosive.

sen. *abbr.* **1 a** a senator. **b** senate. **2** senior.

sen·ar·i·us /sináireeəs/ *n.* (*pl.* **senarii** /-ee-ī/) *Prosody* a verse of six feet, esp. an iambic trimeter.

sen·a·ry /séenəree, sén-/ *adj.* of six; by sixes.

sen·ate /sénit/ *n.* **1** a legislative body, esp. the upper and smaller assembly in the US, France, and other countries, in the states of the US, etc. **2** the governing body of a university or college. **3** *Rom.Hist.* the state council of the republic and empire.

sen·a·tor /sénətər/ *n.* **1** a member of a senate. **2** (in Scotland) a Lord of Session. □□ **sen·a·to·ri·al** /-táwreeəl/ *adj.* **sen·a·tor·ship** *n.*

send /send/ *v.* (*past* and *past part.* **sent** /sent/) **1** *tr.* **a** order or cause to go or be conveyed (*send a message to headquarters; sent me a book*). **b** propel; cause to move (*send a bullet; sent him flying*). **c** cause to go or become (*send into raptures; send to sleep*). **d** dismiss with or without force (*sent her away; sent him about his business*). **2** *intr.* send a message or letter (*he sent to warn me*). **3** *tr.* (of God, providence, etc.) grant or bestow or inflict; bring about (*send rain; send a judgment*). **4** *tr. sl.* put into ecstasy. □ **send away for** send an order to a dealer for (goods). **send for** **1** summon. **2** order by mail. **send in** **1** cause to go in. **2** submit (an entry, etc.) for a competition, etc. **send off** **1** get (a letter, parcel, etc.) dispatched. **2** attend the

departure of (a person) as a sign of respect, etc. **3** *Sports* (of a referee) order (a player) to leave the field. **send on** transmit to a further destination or in advance of one's own arrival. **send a person to Coventry** refuse to deal with a person. **send up** **1** cause to go up. **2** transmit to a higher authority. **3** *colloq.* satirize or ridicule, esp. by mimicking. **4** sentence to imprisonment. **send word** send information. □□ **send·er** *n.*

send-off *n.* a demonstration of goodwill, etc., at the departure of a person, the start of a project, etc.

send-up *n. colloq.* a satire or parody.

Sen·e·ca /séniká/ *n.* **1 a** a N. American people native to western New York. **b** a member of this people. **2** the language of this people. □□ **Sen·e·can** *adj.*

se·nesce /sinés/ *v.intr.* grow old. □□ **se·nes·cence** *n.* **se·nes·cent** *adj.*

sen·e·schal /sénishəl/ *n.* the steward or majordomo of a medieval estate.

se·nhor /saynáwr/ *n.* a title used of or to a Portuguese or Brazilian man.

se·nho·ra /saynáwrə/ *n.* a title used of or to a Portuguese or a Brazilian married woman.

se·nho·ri·ta /sáynyəréetə/ *n.* a title used of or to a Portuguese or Brazilian unmarried woman.

se·nile /séenīl/ *adj.* **1** of or characteristic of old age (*senile decay*). **2** having the weaknesses or diseases of old age. □□ **se·nil·i·ty** /sinílitee/ *n.*

se·nile de·men·tia *n.* a severe form of mental deterioration in old age, characterized by loss of memory and disorientation.

sen·ior /séenyər/ *adj. & n.* ● *adj.* **1** more or most advanced in age or standing. **2** of high or highest position. **3** (placed after a person's name) senior to another of the same name. **4** of the final year at a university, high school, etc. ● *n.* **1** a person of advanced age or long service, etc. **2** one's elder, or one's superior in length of service, membership, etc. (*is my senior*). **3** a senior student. □□ **sen·ior·i·ty** /séenyáwritee, -yor-/ *n.*

sen·ior cit·i·zen *n.* an elderly person, esp. a retiree.

sen·ior of·fi·cer *n.* an officer to whom a junior is responsible.

sen·na /sénə/ *n.* **1** ▼ a cassia tree. **2** a laxative prepared from the dried pod of this.

sen·night /sénīt/ *n. archaic* a week.

sen·nit /sénit/ *n.* **1** *hist.* plaited straw, palm leaves, etc., used for making hats. **2** *Naut.* braided cordage made in flat or round or square form from 3 to 9 cords.

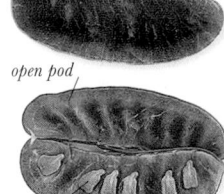

se·ñor /senyáwr/ *n.* (*pl.* **señores** /-rez/) a title used of or to a Spanish-speaking man.

se·ño·ra /senyáwrə/ *n.* a title used of or to a Spanish-speaking married woman.

SENNA: DRIED PODS OF THE CASSIA TREE (*Cassia senna*)

se·ño·ri·ta /sényəréetə/ *n.* a title used of or to a Spanish-speaking unmarried woman.

sen·sate /sénsayt/ *adj.* perceived by the senses.

sen·sa·tion /sensáyshən/ *n.* **1** the consciousness of perceiving or seeming to perceive some state or condition of one's body or its parts or senses; an instance of such consciousness (*lost all sensation in my left arm; had a sensation of giddiness*). **2 a** a stirring of emotions or intense interest esp. among a large group of people (*the news caused a sensation*). **b** a person, event, etc., causing such interest.

sen·sa·tion·al /sensáyshənəl/ *adj.* **1** causing great public excitement, etc. **2** of or causing sensation. □□ **sen·sa·tion·al·ize** *v.tr.* **sen·sa·tion·al·ly** *adv.*

sen·sa·tion·al·ism /sensáyshənəlizəm/ *n.* the use of or interest in the sensational. □□ **sen·sa·tion·al·ist** *n. & adj.* **sen·sa·tion·al·is·tic** /-listik/ *adj.*

S

sense /sens/ *n.* & *v.* ● *n.* **1 a** any of the special bodily faculties by which sensation is roused (*has keen senses; has a dull sense of smell*). **b** sensitiveness of all or any of these. **2** the ability to perceive or feel. **3** (foll. by *of*) consciousness (*sense of having done well; sense of one's own importance*). **4 a** quick or accurate appreciation, understanding, or instinct regarding a specified matter (*sense of the ridiculous; road sense*). **b** the habit of basing one's conduct on such instinct. **5** practical wisdom or judgment; common sense (*has plenty of sense; what is the sense of talking like that?*). **6 a** a meaning; the way in which a word, etc., is to be understood (*the sense of the word is clear; I mean that in the literal sense*). **b** intelligibility or coherence. **7** the prevailing opinion among a number of people. **8** (in *pl.*) a person's sanity or normal state of mind. ● *v.tr.* **1** perceive by a sense or senses. **2** be vaguely aware of. **3** realize. **4** (of a machine, etc.) detect. **5** understand. □ **bring a person to his** or **her senses 1** cure a person of folly. **2** restore a person to consciousness. **come to one's senses 1** regain consciousness. **2** become sensible after acting foolishly. **in a** (or **one**) **sense** if the statement is understood in a particular way (*what you say is true in a sense*). **in one's senses** sane. **make sense** be intelligible or practicable. **make sense of** show or find the meaning of. **out of one's senses** in or into a state of madness (*is out of her senses; frightened him out of his senses*). **take leave of one's senses** go mad.

sense·less /sénslis/ *adj.* **1** unconscious. **2** wildly foolish. **3** without meaning or purpose. **4** incapable of sensation. □□ **sense·less·ly** *adv.* **sense·less·ness** *n.*

sense of di·rec·tion *n.* the ability to know without guidance the direction in which one is or should be moving.

sen·si·bil·i·ty /sénsibílitee/ *n.* (*pl.* **-ies**) **1 a** openness to emotional impressions; susceptibility (*sensibility to kindness*). **b** an exceptional degree of this (*sense and sensibility*). **2** (in *pl.*) emotional capacities or feelings.

sen·si·ble /sénsibəl/ *adj.* **1** having or showing wisdom or common sense. **2 a** perceptible by the senses (*sensible phenomena*). **b** great enough to be perceived (*a sensible difference*). **3** (of clothing, etc.) practical. **4** (foll. by *of*) aware; not unmindful (*was sensible of his peril*). □□ **sen·si·ble·ness** *n.* **sen·si·bly** *adv.*

sen·si·tive /sénsitiv/ *adj.* & *n.* ● *adj.* **1** very open to or acutely affected by external stimuli or mental impressions. **2** easily offended or emotionally hurt. **3** (of an instrument, etc.) responsive to or recording slight changes. **4 a** (of photographic materials) prepared so as to respond rapidly to the action of light. **b** (of any material) responsive to external action. **5** (of a topic, etc.) subject to restriction of discussion to prevent embarrassment, ensure security, etc. □□ **sen·si·tive·ly** *adv.* **sen·si·tive·ness** *n.*

sen·si·tive plant *n.* **1** ▼ a plant whose leaves curve downward and leaflets fold together when touched, esp. mimosa. **2** a sensitive person.

SENSITIVE PLANT
(*Mimosa pudica*)

sen·si·tiv·i·ty /sénsitívitee/ *n.* the quality or degree of being sensitive.

sen·si·tize /sénsitīz/ *v.tr.* **1** make sensitive. **2** *Photog.* make sensitive to light. **3** make (an organism, etc.) abnormally sensitive to a foreign substance. □□ **sen·si·ti·za·tion** *n.* **sen·si·tiz·er** *n.*

sen·si·tom·e·ter /sénsitómitər/ *n. Photog.* a device for measuring sensitivity to light.

sen·sor /sénsər/ *n.* a device giving a signal for the detection or measurement of a physical property to which it responds.

sen·so·ri·um /sensáwreeəm/ *n.* (*pl.* **senso·ria** /-reeə/ or **sensoriums**) **1** the seat of sensation; the brain, brain and spinal cord, or gray matter of these. **2** *Biol.* the whole sensory apparatus including the nerve system. □□ **sen·so·ri·al** *adj.* **sen·so·ri·al·ly** *adv.*

sen·so·ry /sénsəree/ *adj.* of sensation or the senses. □□ **sen·so·ri·ly** *adv.*

sen·su·al /sénshooəl/ *adj.* **1 a** of or depending on the senses only and not on the intellect or spirit (*sensual pleasures*). **b** given to the pursuit of sensual pleasures or the gratification of the appetites; self-indulgent sexually or in regard to food and drink. **c** indicative of a sensual nature (*sensual lips*). **2** of sense or sensation; sensory. □□ **sen·su·al·ist** *n.* **sen·su·al·ize** *v.tr.* **sen·su·al·ly** *adv.*

sen·su·al·i·ty /sénshoo-álitee/ *n.* gratification of the senses, self-indulgence.

sen·sum /sénsəm/ *n.* (*pl.* **sensa** /-sə/) *Philos.* a sense-datum.

sen·su·ous /sénshooəs/ *adj.* **1** of or derived from or affecting the senses, esp. aesthetically rather than sensually; aesthetically pleasing. **2** readily affected by the senses. □□ **sen·su·ous·ly** *adv.* **sen·su·ous·ness** *n.*

sent past and past part. of SEND.

sen·tence /séntəns/ *n.* & *v.* ● *n.* **1 a** a set of words complete in itself as the expression of a thought, containing or implying a subject and predicate, and conveying a statement, question, exclamation, or command. **b** a piece of writing or speech between two full stops or equivalent pauses, often including several grammatical sentences (e.g., *I went; he came*). **2 a** a decision of a court of law, esp. the punishment allotted to a person convicted in a criminal trial. **b** the declaration of this. ● *v.tr.* **1** declare the sentence of (a convicted criminal, etc.). **2** (foll. by *to*) declare (such a person) to be condemned to a specified punishment. □ **under sentence of** having been condemned to (*under sentence of death*).

sen·ten·tial /senténshəl/ *adj. Gram.* & *Logic* of a sentence.

sen·ten·tious /senténshəs/ *adj.* **1** fond of pompous moralizing. **2** affectedly formal. **3** aphoristic; pithy; given to the use of maxims. □□ **sen·ten·tious·ly** *adv.* **sen·ten·tious·ness** *n.*

sen·tient /sénshənt/ *adj.* having the power of perception by the senses. □□ **sen·tience** *n.* **sen·tient·ly** *adv.*

sen·ti·ment /séntimənt/ *n.* **1** a mental feeling (*the sentiment of pity*). **2** the sum of what one feels on some subject. **3** an opinion as distinguished from the words meant to convey it (*the sentiment is good though the words are injudicious*). **4** the tendency to be swayed by feeling rather than by reason. **5 a** mawkish tenderness. **b** the display of this. **6** an emotional feeling conveyed in literature or art.

sen·ti·men·tal /séntimént'l/ *adj.* **1** of or characterized by sentiment. **2** showing or affected by emotion rather than reason. **3** appealing to sentiment. □□ **sen·ti·men·tal·ism** *n.* **sen·ti·men·tal·ist** *n.* **sen·ti·men·tal·i·ty** /-tálitee/ *n.* **sen·ti·men·tal·ize** *v.intr.* & *tr.* **sen·ti·men·tal·i·za·tion** *n.* **sen·ti·men·tal·ly** *adv.*

sen·ti·men·tal val·ue *n.* the value of a thing to a particular person because of its associations.

sen·ti·nel /séntinəl/ *n.* a sentry or lookout.

sen·try /séntree/ *n.* (*pl.* **-ies**) a soldier, etc., stationed to keep guard.

sen·try box *n.* ▶ a wooden cabin intended to shelter a standing sentry.

SENTRY BOX AND GUARD,
BUCKINGHAM PALACE,
ENGLAND

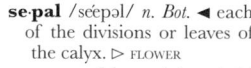

se·pal /séepəl/ *n. Bot.* ◀ each of the divisions or leaves of the calyx. ▷ FLOWER

sep·a·ra·ble /sépərəbəl/ *adj.* able to be separated. □□ **sep·a·ra·bil·i·ty** *n.* **sep·a·ra·bly** *adv.*

sep·a·rate *adj., n.,* & *v.* ● *adj.* /sépərət, séprət/ forming a unit that is apart or by itself; physically disconnected, distinct, or individual (*living in separate rooms; the two questions are essentially separate*). ● *n.* /sépərət, séprət/ **1** (in *pl.*) separate articles of clothing suitable for wearing together in various combinations. **2** an offprint. ● *v.* /sépərayt/ **1** *tr.* make separate; sever. **2** *tr.* prevent union or contact of. **3** *intr.* go different ways. **4** *intr.* cease to live together as a married couple. **5** *intr.* (foll. by *from*) secede. **6** *tr.* **a** divide or sort (milk, ore, fruit, light, etc.) into constituent parts or sizes. **b** extract or remove (an ingredient, waste product, etc.) by such a process for use or rejection. □□ **sep·a·rate·ly** *adv.* **sep·a·rate·ness** *n.*

sep·a·ra·tion /sépəráyshən/ *n.* **1** the act or an instance of separating; the state of being separated. **2** (in full **judicial separation** or **legal separation**) an arrangement by which a husband and wife remain married but live apart.

sep·a·ra·tion or·der *n.* a court order for judicial separation.

sep·a·ra·tist /sépərətist, séprə-/ *n.* a person who favors separation, esp. for political or ecclesiastical independence. □□ **sep·a·ra·tism** *n.*

sep·a·ra·tor /sépəraytər/ *n.* a machine for separating, e.g., cream from milk.

Se·phar·di /sifaárdee/ *n.* (*pl.* **Sephardim** /-dim/) a Jew of Spanish or Portuguese descent (cf. ASHKENAZI). □□ **Se·phar·dic** *adj.*

se·pi·a /séepeeə/ *n.* **1** a dark reddish-brown color. **2 a** a brown pigment prepared from a black fluid secreted by cuttlefish, used in monochrome drawing and in watercolors. **b** ▼ a brown tint used in photography. **3** a drawing done in sepia. **4** the fluid secreted by cuttlefish.

SEPIA PHOTOGRAPH

se·poy /séepoy/ *n. hist.* a native Indian soldier under European, esp. British, discipline.

sep·sis /sépsis/ *n.* **1** the state of being septic. **2** blood poisoning.

Sept. *abbr.* **1** September. **2** Septuagint.

sept /sept/ *n.* a clan, esp. in Ireland.

sept- var. of SEPTI-.

sep·tate /séptayt/ *adj. Bot., Zool.,* & *Anat.* having a septum or septa; partitioned. □□ **sep·ta·tion** /-táyshən/ *n.*

sept·cen·te·na·ry /séptsenténəree/ *n.* & *adj.* ● *n.* (*pl.* **-ies**) **1** a seven-hundredth anniversary. **2** a festival marking this. ● *adj.* of or concerning a septcentenary.

Sep·tem·ber /septémbər/ *n.* the ninth month of the year.

sep·ten·ni·al /septéneeəl/ *adj.* **1** lasting for seven years. **2** recurring every seven years.

sep·ten·ni·um /septéneeəm/ *n.* (*pl.* **septenniums** or **septennia** /-neeə/) a period of seven years.

sep·tet /septét/ *n.* (also **sep·tette**) **1** *Mus.* **a** a composition for seven performers. **b** the performers of such a composition. **2** any group of seven.

sept·foil /sétfoyl/ *n.* a seven-lobed ornamental figure.

septi- /séptee/ *comb. form* (also **sept-** before a vowel) seven.

sep·tic /séptik/ *adj.* contaminated; putrefying. □□ **sep·ti·cal·ly** *adv.* **sep·tic·i·ty** /-tísitee/ *n.*

sep·tic tank *n.* a tank in which the organic matter in sewage is disintegrated through bacterial activity.

sep·ti·ce·mi·a /séptiseémeeə/ *n.* blood poisoning. □□ **sep·ti·ce·mic** *adj.*

sep·ti·mal /séptiməl/ *adj.* of the number seven.

sep·time /sépteem/ *n. Fencing* the seventh of the eight parrying positions.

sep·tu·a·ge·nar·i·an /séptchooəjináreeən, -tōō-, -tyōō-/ *n. & adj.* ● *n.* a person from 70 to 79 years old. ● *adj.* of this age.

Sep·tu·a·ges·i·ma /séptooəjésimə, -choo-, -tyoo-/ *n.* (in full **Septuagesima Sunday**) the Sunday before Sexagesima.

Sep·tu·a·gint /séptooəjint, -tyōō-/ *n.* a Greek version of the Old Testament including the Apocrypha.

sep·tum /séptəm/ *n.* (*pl.* **septa** /-tə/) *Anat., Bot., & Zool.* a partition such as that between the nostrils or the chambers of a poppy fruit or of a shell. ▷ HEART

sep·tu·ple /septōōpəl, -tyōō-, -túpəl, séptoopəl/ *adj., n., & v.* ● *adj.* **1** sevenfold; having seven parts. **2** being seven times as many or as much. ● *n.* a sevenfold number or amount. ● *v.tr. & intr.* multiply by seven.

sep·tup·let /septúplit, -tōō-, -tyōō-/ *n.* **1** one of seven children born at one birth. **2** *Mus.* a group of seven notes to be played in the time of four or six.

se·pul·chral /sipúlkrəl/ *adj.* **1** of a tomb or interment (*sepulchral mound*). **2** suggestive of the tomb; gloomy (*sepulchral look*). □□ **se·pul·chral·ly** *adv.*

se·pul·cher /sépəlkər/ *n. & v.* (also **sep·ul·chre**) ● *n.* ▼ a tomb esp. cut in rock or built of stone or brick. ● *v.tr.* **1** lay in a sepulcher. **2** serve as a sepulcher for.

SEPULCHER:
ETRUSCAN TOMB, ITALY

sep·ul·ture /sépəlchər/ *n. literary* the act or an instance of burying or putting in the grave.

seq. *abbr.* (*pl.* **seqq.**) the following.

se·qua·cious /sikwáyshəs/ *adj.* **1** (of reasoning or a reasoner) not inconsequent; coherent. **2** *archaic* inclined to follow; lacking independence or originality; servile. □□ **se·qua·cious·ly** *adv.* **se·qua·ci·ty** /sikwásitee/ *n.*

se·quel /séekwəl/ *n.* **1** what follows (esp. as a result). **2** a novel, motion picture, etc., that continues the story of an earlier one.

se·que·la /sikwélə/ *n.* (*pl.* **sequelae** /-ee/) *Med.* (esp. in *pl.*) a morbid condition or symptom following a disease.

se·quence /séekwəns/ *n. & v.* ● *n.* **1** succession; coming after or next. **2** order of succession (*in historical sequence*). **3** a set of things belonging next to one another on some principle of order. **4** a part of a motion picture dealing with one scene or topic. ● *v.tr.* arrange in a definite order.

se·quenc·er /séekwənsər/ *n.* a programmable device for storing sequences of musical notes, chords, etc., and transmitting them when required to an electronic musical instrument.

se·quent /séekwənt/ *adj.* **1** following as a sequence or consequence. **2** consecutive. □□ **se·quent·ly** *adv.*

se·quen·tial /sikwénshəl/ *adj.* forming a sequence or consequence. □□ **se·quen·ti·al·i·ty** /-sheeálitee/ *n.* **se·quen·tial·ly** *adv.*

se·ques·ter /sikwéstər/ *v.tr.* **1** (esp. as **sequestered** *adj.*) seclude; isolate; set apart (*a sequestered jury*). **2** = SEQUESTRATE.

se·ques·trate /sikwéstrayt/ *v.tr.* **1** confiscate; appropriate. **2** *Law* take temporary possession of (a debtor's estate, etc.). □□ **se·ques·tra·ble** /-trəbəl/ *adj.* **se·ques·tra·tion** /séekwistráyshən/ *n.* **se·ques·tra·tor** /séekwistraytər/ *n.*

se·quin /séekwin/ *n.* ◀ a circular spangle for attaching to clothing as an ornament. □□ **se·quined** *adj.* (also **se·quinned**).

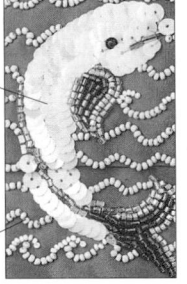

sequins

beads

SEQUIN AND BEAD
DESIGN ON A PURSE

se·quoi·a /sikwóyə/ *n.* ▶ one of two Californian evergreen coniferous trees with reddish bark and of very great height.

se·ra *pl.* of SERUM.

se·rac /serák/ *n.* one of the tower-shaped masses into which a glacier is divided at steep points by crevasses crossing it.

se·rag·li·o /sərályō, raál-/ *n.* (*pl.* **-os**) **1** a harem. **2** *hist.* a Turkish palace.

se·ra·i /serí/ *n.* a caravansary.

se·ra·pe /səraápee/ *n.* a shawl or blanket worn as a cloak by Spanish Americans.

ser·aph /sérəf/ *n.* (*pl.* **seraphim** /-fim/ or **seraphs**) an angelic being, one of the highest order of the ninefold celestial hierarchy.

se·raph·ic /sərafik/ *adj.* **1** of or like the seraphim. **2** ecstatically adoring, fervent, or serene. □□ **se·raph·i·cal·ly** *adv.*

Serb /sərb/ *n. & adj.* ● *n.* **1** a native of Serbia in the former Yugoslavia. **2** a person of Serbian descent. ● *adj.* = SERBIAN.

Ser·bi·an /sárbeeən/ *n. & adj.* ● *n.* **1** the dialect of the Serbs. **2** = SERB. ● *adj.* of or relating to the Serbs or their dialect.

Serbo- /sárbō/ *comb. form* Serbian.

Ser·bo-Cro·at /sárbōkrôat/ *n. & adj.* (also **Ser·bo-Cro·a·tian** /-krō-áyshən/) ● *n.* the main official language of the former Yugoslavia, combining Serbian and Croatian dialects. ● *adj.* of or relating to this language.

sere[1] /seer/ *adj.* (also **sear**) *literary* (esp. of a plant, etc.) withered; dried up.

sere[2] /seer/ *n. Ecol.* a sequence of animal or plant communities.

sere[3] /seer/ *n.* a catch of a gunlock holding the hammer at half or full cock.

se·rein /sərán/ *n.* a fine rain falling in tropical climates from a cloudless sky.

ser·e·nade /sérənáyd/ *n. & v.* ● *n.* a piece of music sung or played at night, esp. by a lover under his lady's window. ● *v.tr.* sing or play a serenade to. □□ **ser·e·nad·er** *n.*

ser·e·na·ta /sérənaátə/ *n. Mus.* **1** a cantata with a pastoral subject. **2** a simple form of suite for orchestra or wind band.

ser·en·dip·i·ty /sérəndípitee/ *n.* the faculty of making happy and unexpected discoveries by accident. □□ **ser·en·dip·i·tous** *adj.* **ser·en·dip·i·tous·ly** *adv.*

se·rene /sireén/ *adj. & n.* ● *adj.* (**serener, serenest**) **1 a** (of the sky, etc.) clear and calm. **b** (of the sea, etc.) unruffled. **2** placid; tranquil. □□ **se·rene·ly** *adv.* **se·rene·ness** *n.*

se·ren·i·ty /sirénitee/ *n.* (*pl.* **-ies**) tranquillity; being serene.

serf /sərf/ *n.* **1** *hist.* a laborer not allowed to leave the land on which he worked; a villein. **2** an oppressed person; a drudge. □□ **serf·dom** *n.*

serge /sərj/ *n.* a durable twilled worsted, etc., fabric.

ser·geant /saárjənt/ *n.* **1** a noncommissioned army, marine, or air force officer next below warrant officer. **2** a police officer ranking below captain.

ser·geant ma·jor *n. Mil.* the highest-ranking noncommissioned officer.

se·ri·al /séereeəl/ *n. & adj.* ● *n.* **1** a story, play, etc., that is published, broadcast, or shown in regular installments. **2** a periodical. ● *adj.* **1** of or in or forming a series. **2** (of a story, etc.) in the form of a serial. **3** *Mus.* using transformations of a fixed series of notes. □□ **se·ri·al·i·ty** /-reeálitee/ *n.* **se·ri·al·ly** *adv.*

se·ri·al·ist /séereeəlist/ *n.* a composer or advocate of serial music. □□ **se·ri·al·ism** *n.*

se·ri·al·ize /séereeəlīz/ *v.tr.* **1** publish or produce in installments. **2** arrange in a series. **3** *Mus.* compose according to a serial technique. □□ **se·ri·al·i·za·tion** *n.*

se·ri·al kill·er *n.* a person who murders continually with no apparent motive.

se·ri·al num·ber *n.* a number showing the position of an item in a series. ▷ BANKNOTE

se·ri·ate *adj. & v.* ● *adj.* /séereeət/ in the form of a series; in orderly sequence. ● *v.tr.* /séereeayt/ arrange in a seriate manner. □□ **se·ri·a·tion** /-reeáyshən/ *n.*

se·ri·cul·ture /sérikulchər/ *n.* **1** silkworm breeding. **2** the production of raw silk. □□ **se·ri·cul·tur·al** *adj.* **se·ri·cul·tur·ist** *n.*

se·ri·e·ma /séree-éemə/ *n.* (also **car·i·a·ma** /káreeaámə/) *Zool.* any S. American bird of the family Cariamidae, having a long neck and legs and a crest above the bill.

se·ries /séereez/ *n.* (*pl.* same) **1** a number of things of which each is similar to the preceding or in which each successive pair are similarly related; a succession, row, or set. **2** a set of successive games between the same teams. **3** a set of programs with the same actors, etc., or on related subjects but each complete in itself. **4** a set of lectures by the same speaker or on the same subject. **5 a** a set of successive issues of a periodical, of articles on one subject or by one writer, etc., esp. when numbered separately from a preceding or following set (*second series*). **b** a set of independent books in a common format or under a common title or supervised by a common general editor. **6** *Geol.* a set of strata with a common characteristic. **7** *Mus.* = TONE ROW. **8** *Electr.* **a** a set of circuits or components arranged so that the current passes through each successively. **b** a set of batteries, etc., having the positive electrode of each connected with the negative electrode of the next. □ **in series 1** in ordered succession. **2** *Electr.* (of a set of circuits or components) arranged so that the current passes through each successively.

SEQUOIA: GIANT
SEQUOIA
(*Sequoia sempervirens*)

S

ser·if /sérif/ *n.* ▶ a slight projection finishing off a stroke of a letter as in T contrasted with T (cf. SANS SERIF). ▷ TYPE. □□ **ser·iffed** *adj.*

SERIF LETTER

se·rig·ra·phy /sərígrəfee/ *n.* the art or process of printing designs by means of a silk screen. □□ **ser·i·graph** /sérigraf/ *n.* **se·rig·ra·pher** /sərígrəfər/ *n.*

ser·in /sérin/ *n.* any small yellow Mediterranean finch of the genus *Serinus,* esp. the wild canary *S. serinus.*

se·ri·o·com·ic /séeree-ōkómik/ *adj.* combining the serious and the comic; jocular in intention but simulating seriousness or vice versa. □□ **se·ri·o·com·i·cal·ly** *adv.*

se·ri·ous /séereeəs/ *adj.* **1** thoughtful; earnest; not reckless nor given to trifling (*a serious young person*). **2** important (*a serious matter*). **3** not slight or negligible (*a serious injury*). **4** sincere; not ironic nor joking (*are you serious?*). **5** (of music and literature) not merely for amusement. **6** not perfunctory (*serious thought*). **7** not to be trifled with (*a serious opponent*). □□ **se·ri·ous·ness** *n.*

se·ri·ous·ly /séereeəslee/ *adv.* **1** in a serious manner (esp. introducing a sentence, implying that irony, etc., is now to cease). **2** to a serious extent. **3** *colloq.* (as an intensifier) very; really; substantially (*seriously rich*).

ser·mon /sórmən/ *n.* **1** a spoken or written discourse on a religious or moral subject, esp. a discourse based on a text or passage of Scripture and delivered in a service by way of religious instruction or exhortation. **2** a piece of admonition, a lecture. **3** a moral reflection suggested by natural objects, etc. (*sermons in stones*).

ser·mon·ette /sórmənét/ *n.* a short sermon.

ser·mon·ize /sórmənīz/ *v.* **1** *tr.* deliver a moral lecture to. **2** *intr.* deliver a moral lecture. □□ **ser·mon·iz·er** *n.*

se·rol·o·gy /seeróləjee/ *n.* the scientific study of blood sera and their effects. □□ **se·ro·log·i·cal** /-rəlójikəl/ *adj.* **se·rol·o·gist** *n.*

ser·o·tine /sérətin, -tīn/ *n.* a chestnut-colored European bat, *Eptesicus serotinus.*

ser·o·to·nin /sérət+nin/ *n. Biol.* a compound present in blood serum, which constricts the blood vessels and acts as a neurotransmitter.

se·rous /séerəs/ *adj.* of or like or producing serum; watery. □□ **se·ros·i·ty** /-rósitee/ *n.*

ser·pent /sórpənt/ *n.* **1** usu. *literary* **a** a snake, esp. of a large kind. **b** a scaly limbless reptile. **2** a sly or treacherous person, esp. one who exploits a position of trust to betray it. **3** *Mus.* ▶ an old bass wind instrument made from leather-covered wood, roughly in the form of an S. **4** (**the Serpent**) *Bibl.* Satan.

ser·pen·tine /sórpəntīn/ *adj. & n.* ● *adj.* **1** of or like a serpent. **2** coiling; sinuous; meandering. **3** cunning; subtle; treacherous. ● *n.* ◀ a soft rock mainly of hydrated magnesium silicate, usu. dark green and sometimes mottled or spotted like a serpent's skin.

ser·pen·tine verse *n.* a metrical line beginning and ending with the same word.

SERPENTINE

ser·pig·i·nous /sərpíjinəs/ *adj.* (of a skin disease, etc.) creeping from one part to another.

ser·ra /sérə/ *n.* (*pl.* **serrae** /-ree/) a serrated organ, structure, or edge.

ser·ra·dil·la /sérədilə/ *n.* (*pl.* **serradillae** /-lee/) a clover, *Ornithopus sativus,* grown as fodder.

ser·ran /sérən/ *n.* any marine fish of the family Serranidae.

ser·rate *v. & adj.* ● *v.tr.* /seráyt/ (usu. as **serrated** *adj.*) provide with a sawlike edge. ● *adj.* /séráyt/ esp. *Anat., Bot., & Zool.* ▶ notched like a saw. □□ **ser·ra·tion** /-ráyshən/ *n.*

ser·ried /séreed/ *adj.* (of ranks of soldiers, etc.) pressed together; without gaps.

se·rum /séerəm/ *n.* (*pl.* **sera** /-rə/ or **serums**) **1 a** an amber-colored liquid that separates from a clot when blood coagulates. **b** whey. **2** *Med.* blood serum (usu. from a nonhuman mammal) as an antitoxin or therapeutic agent, esp. in inoculation. **3** a watery fluid in animal bodies.

serv·ant /sórvənt/ *n.* **1** a person who has undertaken to carry out the orders of an individual or corporate employer, esp. a person employed in a house on domestic duties. **2** a devoted follower (*a servant of Jesus Christ*).

serve /sórv/ *v. & n.* ● *v.* **1** *tr.* do a service for (a person, community, etc.). **2** *tr.* (also *absol.*) be a servant to. **3** *intr.* carry out duties (*served on six committees*). **4** *intr.* **a** (foll. by *in*) be employed in (an organization, esp. the armed forces, or a place, esp. a foreign country). **b** be a member of the armed forces. **5 a** *tr.* be useful to or serviceable for; meet the needs of; do what is required for (*serve a purpose*). **b** *intr.* perform a function (*a sofa serving as a bed*). **c** *intr.* (foll. by *to* + infin.) avail; suffice (*served only to postpone the inevitable*). **6** *tr.* go through a due period of (office, apprenticeship, a prison sentence, etc.). **7** *tr.* set out or present (food) for those about to eat it (*dinner was then served*). **8** *intr.* act as a waiter. **9** *tr.* **a** attend to (a customer in a store). **b** (foll. by *with*) supply with (goods) (*served the town with gas*). **10** *tr.* treat or act toward (a person) in a specified way (*has served me shamefully*). **11** *tr.* **a** (often foll. by *on*) deliver (a writ, etc.) to the person concerned in a legally formal manner. **b** (foll. by *with*) deliver a writ, etc., to (a person) in this way (*served her with a summons*). **12** *tr. Tennis,* etc. **a** (also *absol.*) deliver (a ball, etc.) to begin or resume play. **b** produce (a fault, etc.) by doing this. **13** *tr. Mil.* keep (a gun, battery, etc.) firing. **14** *tr.* (of an animal, esp. a stallion, etc., hired for the purpose) copulate with (a female). **15** *tr.* distribute (*served out the ammunition*). **16** *tr.* render obedience to (a deity, etc.). ● *n.* **1** *Tennis,* etc. the act or an instance of serving. **2** a manner of serving. **3** a person's turn to serve. □ **it will serve** it will be adequate. **serve one's needs** (or **need**) be adequate. **serve the purpose of** take the place of; be used as. **serve a person right** be a person's deserved punishment or misfortune. **serve one's time 1** esp. *Brit.* hold office for the normal period. **2** (also **serve time**) undergo imprisonment, apprenticeship, etc. **serve one's** (or **the**) **turn** be adequate. **serve up** offer for acceptance.

serv·er /sórvər/ *n.* **1** a person who serves. **2** *Eccl.* a person assisting the celebrant at a service, esp. the Eucharist.

serv·ice¹ /sórvis/ *n. & v.* ● *n.* **1** the act of helping or doing work for another or for a community, etc. **2** work done in this way. **3** assistance or benefit given to someone. **4** the provision or system of supplying a public need, e.g., transport. **5 a** the fact or status of being a servant. **b** employment or a position as a servant. **6** a state or period of employment doing work for an individual or organization (*resigned after 15 years'*

SERRATE: SHARK'S TOOTH WITH A SERRATED EDGE

serrated edge

service). **7 a** a public department or organization (*civil service*). **b** employment in this. **8** (in *pl.*) the armed forces. **9** (*attrib.*) of the kind issued to the armed forces (*a service revolver*). **10 a** a ceremony of worship according to prescribed forms. **b** a form of liturgy for this. **11 a** the provision of what is necessary for the installation and maintenance of a machine, etc., or operation. **b** a periodic routine maintenance of a motor vehicle, etc. **12** assistance or advice given to customers after the sale of goods. **13 a** the act or process of serving food, drinks, etc. **b** an extra charge nominally made for this. **14** a set of dishes, etc., used for serving meals (*a dinner service*). **15** *Tennis,* etc. **a** the act or an instance of serving; a person's turn to serve. ● *v.tr.* **1** provide service or services for, esp. maintain. **2** maintain or repair (a car, machine, etc.). **3** pay interest on (a debt). **4** supply with a service. □ **at a person's service** ready to serve or assist a person. **be of service** be available to assist. **in service 1** employed as a servant. **2** available for use. **on active service** serving in the armed forces in wartime. **out of service** not available for use. **see service 1** have experience of service, esp. in the armed forces. **2** (of a thing) be much used.

serv·ice² /sórvis/ *n.* (in full **service tree**) a European tree of the genus *Sorbus,* esp. *S. domestica* with toothed leaves, cream-colored flowers, and small round or pear-shaped fruit eaten when overripe.

serv·ice·a·ble /sórvisəbəl/ *adj.* **1** useful or usable. **2** able to render service. **4** suited for ordinary use rather than ornamental. □□ **serv·ice·a·bil·i·ty** *n.* **serv·ice·a·ble·ness** *n.* **serv·ice·a·bly** *adv.*

serv·ice ar·e·a *n.* **1** an area beside a major road for the supply of gasoline, refreshments, etc. **2** the area served by a broadcasting station.

serv·ice charge *n.* an additional charge for service in a restaurant, hotel, etc.

serv·ice in·dus·try *n.* one providing services not goods.

serv·ice·man /sórvismən/ *n.* (*pl.* **-men**) **1** a man serving in the armed forces. **2** a man providing service or maintenance.

serv·ice road *n.* a road parallel to a main road, serving houses, stores, etc.

serv·ice sta·tion *n.* an establishment beside a road selling gasoline and oil, etc., to motorists and often able to carry out maintenance.

serv·ice·wom·an /sórviswŏŏmən/ *n.* (*pl.* **-women**) a woman serving in the armed forces.

ser·vi·ette /sórvee-ét/ *n.* esp. *Brit.* a napkin for use at table.

ser·vile /sórvīl/ *adj.* **1** of or being or like a slave or slaves. **2** slavish; fawning; completely dependent. □□ **ser·vile·ly** *adv.* **ser·vil·i·ty** /-vílitee/ *n.*

serv·ing /sórving/ *n.* a quantity of food served to one person.

ser·vi·tor /sórvitər/ *n. archaic* **1** a servant. **2** an attendant. □□ **ser·vi·tor·ship** *n.*

ser·vi·tude /sórvitōōd, -tyōōd/ *n.* **1** slavery. **2** subjection (esp. involuntary).

ser·vo /sórvō/ *n.* (*pl.* **-os**) **1** (in full **servomechanism**) a powered mechanism producing motion or forces at a higher level of energy than the input level. **2** (in full **servomotor**) the motive element in a servomechanism. **3** (in *comb.*) of or involving a servomechanism (*servo-assisted*).

ses·a·me /sésəmee/ *n. Bot.* **1** an E. Indian herbaceous plant, *Sesamum indicum,* whose seeds yield an edible oil. **2** ▶ its seeds. □ **open sesame** a means of achieving what is normally unattainable.

S

black sesame seeds

white sesame seeds

SESAME SEEDS (*Sesamum indicum*)

SERPENT: 19TH-CENTURY FRENCH SERPENT

mouthpiece

key

left-hand fingerholes

key

bell

right-hand fingerholes

sesqui- /séskwee/ *comb. form* denoting one and a half.

ses·qui·cen·ten·ar·y /séskwisenténəree/ *n.* (*pl.* **-ies**) = SESQUICENTENNIAL.

ses·qui·cen·ten·ni·al /séskwisenténeeəl/ *n.* & *adj.* • *n.* a one-hundred-and-fiftieth anniversary. • *adj.* of or relating to a sesquicentennial.

ses·sile /sésīl, -əl/ *adj.* **1** *Bot.* & *Zool.* (of a flower, eye, etc.) attached directly by its base without a stalk or peduncle. **2** fixed in one position; immobile.

ses·sion /séshən/ *n.* **1** the process of assembly of a deliberative or judicial body to conduct its business. **2** a single meeting for this purpose. **3** a period during which such meetings are regularly held. **4 a** an academic year. **b** the period during which a school, etc., has classes. **5** a period devoted to an activity (*poker session*). **6** the governing body of a Presbyterian church. □ **in session** assembled for business; not on vacation. □□ **ses·sion·al** *adj.*

ses·terce /séstərs/ *n.* (also **ses·ter·tius** /sestə́rshəs/) (*pl.* **sesterces** /séstərseez/ or **sestertii** /-stə́rshee-ī/) an ancient Roman coin and monetary unit equal to one quarter of a denarius.

ses·tet /sestét/ *n.* the last six lines of a sonnet.

ses·ti·na /sesteénə/ *n.* a form of rhymed or unrhymed poem with six stanzas of six lines and a final triplet, all stanzas having the same six words at the line ends in six different sequences.

set[1] /set/ *v.* (**setting**; *past* and *past part.* **set**) **1** *tr.* put, lay, or stand (a thing) in a certain position or location (*set it upright*). **2** *tr.* (foll. by *to*) apply (one thing) to (another) (*set pen to paper*). **3** *tr.* **a** fix ready or in position. **b** dispose suitably for use, action, or display. **4** *tr.* **a** adjust the hands of (a clock or watch) to show the right time. **b** adjust (an alarm clock) to sound at the required time. **5** *tr.* **a** fix, arrange, or mount. **b** insert (a jewel) in a ring, etc. **6** *tr.* make (a device) ready to operate. **7** *tr.* lay (a table) for a meal. **8** *tr.* arrange (the hair) while damp. **9** *tr.* (foll. by *with*) ornament or provide (a surface, esp. a precious item) (*gold set with gems*). **10** *tr.* cause to be (*set things in motion*). **11** *intr.* & *tr.* harden or solidify (*the jelly is set*). **12** *intr.* (of the Sun, Moon, etc.) appear to move toward and below the Earth's horizon (as the Earth rotates). **13** *tr.* represent (a scene, etc.) as happening in a certain time or place. **14** *tr.* **a** (foll. by *to* + infin.) cause or instruct (a person) to perform a specified activity (*set them to work*). **b** (foll. by pres. part.) start (a person or thing) doing something (*set the ball rolling*). **15** *tr.* present or impose as work to be done or a matter to be dealt with (*set them an essay*). **16** *tr.* exhibit as a type or model (*set a good example*). **17** *tr.* initiate; take the lead in (*set the pace*). **18** *tr.* establish (a record, etc.). **19** *tr.* determine or decide (*the itinerary is set*). **20** *tr.* appoint or establish (*set them in authority*). **21** *tr.* join, attach, or fasten. **22** *tr.* **a** put parts of (a broken bone, etc.) into the correct position for healing. **b** deal with (a fracture or dislocation) in this way. **23** *tr.* (in full **set to music**) provide (words, etc.) with music for singing. **24** *tr.* (often foll. by *up*) *Printing* **a** arrange or produce (type or film, etc.) as required. **b** arrange the type or film, etc., for (a book, etc.). **25** *intr.* (of a tide, etc.) have a certain motion or direction. **26** *intr.* (of a face) assume a hard expression. **27** *tr.* **a** cause (a hen) to sit on eggs. **b** place (eggs) for a hen to sit on. **28** *tr.* put (a seed, etc.) in the ground to grow. **29** *tr.* give the teeth of (a saw) an alternate outward inclination. **30** *tr.* start (a fire). **31** *intr.* (of eyes, etc.) become motionless. **32** *intr.* feel or show a certain tendency (*opinion is setting against it*). **33** *intr.* **a** (of a blossom) form into fruit. **b** (of fruit) develop from a blossom. **c** (of a tree) develop fruit. **34** *intr.* (of a hunting dog) take a rigid attitude indicating the presence of game. □ **set about** begin or take steps toward. **set a person** (or **thing**) **against** (**another**) **1** consider or reckon (a person or thing) as a compensation for. **2** cause to oppose. **set apart** separate; reserve; differentiate. **set aside** see ASIDE. **set back 1** place further back in place or time. **2** impede or reverse the progress of. **3** *colloq.* cost (a person) a specified amount. **set by** save for future use. **set down 1** record in writing. **2** land an aircraft. **3** (foll. by *to*) attribute to. **4** (foll. by *as*) explain or describe to oneself as. **set eyes on** see EYE. **set one's face against** see FACE. **set foot on** (or **in**) see FOOT. **set forth 1** begin a journey. **2** make known; expound. **set forward** begin to advance. **set free** release. **set one's hand to** see HAND. **set one's heart** (or **hopes**) **on** want or hope for eagerly. **set in 1** (of weather, etc.) begin; become established. **2** insert (esp. a sleeve, etc., into a garment). **set a person's mind at rest** see MIND. **set much by** consider to be of much value. **set off 1** begin a journey. **2** detonate (a bomb, etc.). **3** initiate; stimulate. **4** cause (a person) to start laughing, talking, etc. **5** serve as an adornment to; enhance. **6** (foll. by *against*) use as a compensating item. **set on** (or **upon**) **1** attack violently. **2** cause or urge to attack. **set out 1** begin a journey. **2** (foll. by *to* + infin.) aim or intend. **3** demonstrate, arrange, or exhibit. **4** mark out. **5** declare. **set the pace** determine the rate of speed, proficiency, etc. for others to follow. **set sail 1** hoist the sails. **2** begin a voyage. **set the scene** see SCENE. **set the stage** see STAGE. **set store by** (or **on**) see STORE. **set one's teeth 1** clench them. **2** summon one's resolve. **set to** begin vigorously, esp. fighting, arguing, or eating. **set up 1** place in position or view. **2** organize or start (a business, etc.). **3** establish in some capacity. **4** supply the needs of. **5** begin making (a loud sound). **6** cause or make arrangements for (a condition or situation). **7** prepare (a task, etc., for another). **8** restore or enhance the health of (a person). **9** establish (a record). **10** propound (a theory). **11** *colloq.* put (a person) in a dangerous position. **set oneself up as** make pretensions to being.

set[2] /set/ *n.* **1** a number of things or persons that belong together or resemble one another or are usually found together. **2** a collection or group. **3** a section of society consorting together or having similar interests, etc. **4** a collection of implements, etc., needed for a specified purpose (*croquet set*; *tea set*). **5** a radio or television receiver. **6** (in tennis, etc.) a group of games counting as a unit toward a match for the player or side that wins a defined number or proportion of the games. **7** *Math.* & *Logic* a collection of distinct entities forming a unit. **8** a group of pupils or students having the same average ability. **9 a** a slip, shoot, bulb, etc., for planting. **b** a young fruit just set. **10 a** a habitual posture or conformation; the way the head, etc., is carried or a dress, etc., flows. **b** (also **dead set**) a setter's pointing in the presence of game. **11** the way, drift, or tendency (of public opinion, etc.) (*the set of public feeling is against it*). **12** the way in which a machine, device, etc., is set or adjusted. **13** a setting, stage furniture, etc., for a play or motion picture, etc. **14** a sequence of songs or pieces performed in jazz or popular music. **15** the setting of the hair when damp. **16** (also **sett**) a badger's burrow. **17** (also **sett**) a granite paving block. **18** a number of people making up a square dance.

set[3] /set/ *adj.* **1** in senses of SET[1]. **2** prescribed or determined in advance. **3** fixed; unchanging; unmoving. **4** (of a phrase or speech, etc.) having invariable or predetermined wording. **5** prepared for action. **6** (foll. by *on, upon*) determined to acquire or achieve, etc. **7** (of a book, etc.) specified for reading in preparation for an examination.

se·ta /seétə/ *n.* (*pl.* **setae** /-tee/) *Bot.* & *Zool.* stiff hair; bristle. □□ **se·ta·ceous** /-táyshəs/ *adj.*

set·back /sétbak/ *n.* **1** a reversal or arrest of progress. **2** a relapse.

SETI /sétee/ *abbr.* search for extraterrestrial intelligence.

set·off /sétawf/ *n.* **1** a thing set off against another. **2** a thing of which the amount or effect may be deducted from that of another or opposite tendency. **3** a counterbalance. **4** a counterclaim. **5** *Printing* = OFFSET 6.

set point *n.* *Tennis*, etc. **1** the state of a game when one side needs only one more point to win the set. **2** this point.

set screw *n.* a screw for adjusting or clamping parts of a machine.

set square *n.* ◄ a right-angled triangular plate for drawing lines, esp at 90°, 45°, 60°, or 30°.

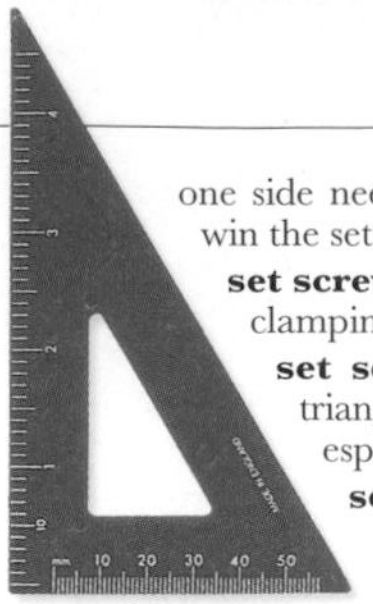

SET SQUARE

sett var. of SET[2] 16, 17.

set·tee /seteé/ *n.* a seat (usu. upholstered), with a back and usu. arms, for more than one person.

set·ter /sétər/ *n.* **1** ▼ a dog of a large, long-haired breed trained to stand rigid when scenting game. **2** a person or thing that sets.

SETTER: IRISH SETTER

set the·o·ry *n.* the branch of mathematics concerned with the manipulation of sets.

set·ting /séting/ *n.* **1** the position or manner in which a thing is set. **2** the immediate surroundings (of a house, etc.). **3** the surroundings of any object regarded as its framework. **4** the place and time, etc., of a drama, etc. **5** a frame in which a jewel is set. **6** the music to which words are set. **7** a set of cutlery and other accessories for one person at a table. **8** the way in which or level at which a machine is set to operate.

set·tle[1] /sét'l/ *v.* **1** *tr.* & *intr.* (often foll. by *down*) establish or become established in a more or less permanent abode or way of life. **2** *intr.* & *tr.* (often foll. by *down*) **a** cease or cause to cease from wandering, disturbance, movement, etc. **b** adopt a regular or secure style of life. **c** (foll. by *to*) apply oneself (*settled down to writing letters*). **3 a** *intr.* sit or come down to stay for some time. **b** *tr.* cause to do this. **4** *tr.* & *intr.* bring to or attain fixity, certainty, composure, or quietness. **5** *tr.* determine or decide or agree upon. **6** *tr.* **a** resolve (a dispute, etc.). **b** deal with (a matter) finally. **7** *tr.* terminate (a lawsuit) by mutual agreement. **8** *intr.* **a** (foll. by *for*) accept or agree to (esp. an alternative not one's first choice). **b** (foll. by *on*) decide on. **9** *tr.* (also *absol.*) pay (a debt, an account, etc.). **10** *intr.* (as **settled** *adj.*) not likely to change for a time (*settled weather*). **11** *tr.* **a** aid the digestion of (food). **b** remedy the disordered state of (nerves, etc.). **12** *tr.* **a** colonize. **b** establish colonists in. **13** *intr.* subside; fall to the bottom or on to a surface (*the dust will settle*). □ **settle one's affairs** make any necessary arrangements (e.g., write a will) when death is near. **settle in** become established in a place. **settle up 1** (also *absol.*) pay (an account, etc.). **2** finally arrange (a matter). **settle with 1** pay all or part of an amount due to (a creditor). **2** get revenge on. □□ **set·tle·a·ble** *adj.*

set·tle[2] /sét'l/ *n.* a bench with a high back and arms and often with a box fitted below the seat.

set·tle·ment /sét'lmənt/ *n.* **1** the act of settling. **2 a** the colonization of a region. **b** a place or area occupied by settlers. **c** a small village. **3 a** a political or financial, etc., agreement. **b** an arrangement ending a dispute. **4 a** the terms on which property is given to a person. **b** a deed stating these. **c** the amount or property given. **5** subsidence of a wall, house, soil, etc.

set·tler /sétlər/ *n.* a person who goes to settle in a new country or place.

set·tlor /sétlər/ *n.* *Law* a person who makes a settlement, esp. of a property.

set-to *n.* (*pl.* **-tos**) *colloq.* a fight or argument.

SEWING MACHINE

Producing a stitch on a sewing machine requires thread from two sources: the needle and the bobbin (a small reel beneath the needle plate). As the needle pushes through the fabric, the needle's thread forms a loop that is grabbed by the bobbin hook, a circular catch surrounding the bobbin. The bobbin hook then spins, taking the loop around the bobbin. As the needle moves upward, the loop tightens and pulls the bobbin thread to form a stitch.

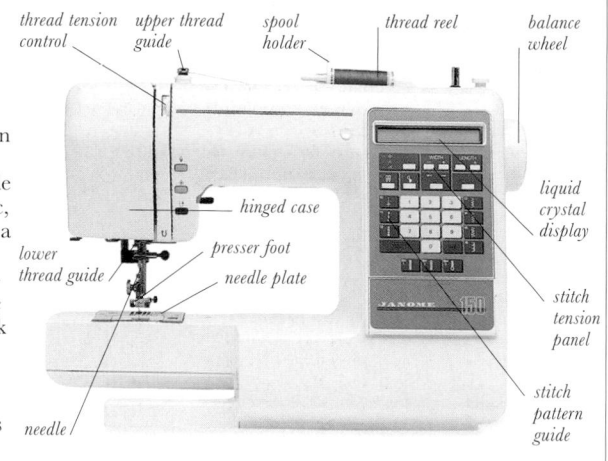

thread tension control · upper thread guide · spool holder · thread reel · balance wheel · hinged case · liquid crystal display · lower thread guide · presser foot · needle plate · stitch tension panel · stitch pattern guide · needle

ELECTRIC SEWING MACHINE

---

set·up /setup/ *n.* **1** an arrangement or organization. **2** the manner of this. **3** *colloq.* a trick or conspiracy, esp. to make an innocent person appear guilty.

sev·en /sévən/ *n. & adj.* ● *n.* **1** one more than six. **2** a symbol for this (7, vii, VII). **3** a size, etc., denoted by seven. **4** a set or team of seven individuals. **5** the time of seven o'clock. **6** a card with seven pips. ● *adj.* that amount to seven.

sev·en dead·ly sins *n.pl.* the sins of pride, covetousness, lust, anger, gluttony, envy, and sloth.

sev·en·fold /sévənfōld/ *adj. & adv.* **1** seven times as much or as many. **2** consisting of seven parts.

sev·en seas *n.pl.* the oceans of the world: the Arctic, Antarctic, N. Pacific, S. Pacific, N. Atlantic, S. Atlantic, and Indian Oceans.

sev·en·teen /sévəntéen/ *n. & adj.* ● *n.* **1** one more than sixteen. **2** a symbol for this (17, xvii, XVII). **3** a size, etc., denoted by seventeen. ● *adj.* that amount to seventeen. □□ **sev·en·teenth** *adj. & n.*

sev·enth /sévənth/ *n. & adj.* ● *n.* **1** the position in a sequence corresponding to the number 7 in the sequence 1–7. **2** something occupying this position. **3** one of seven equal parts of a thing. **4** *Mus.* **a** an interval or chord spanning seven consecutive notes in the diatonic scale. **b** a note separated from another by this interval. ● *adj.* that is the seventh. □□ **sev·enth·ly** *adv.*

sev·en·ty /sévəntee/ *n. & adj.* ● *n.* (*pl.* **-ies**) **1** the product of seven and ten. **2** a symbol for this (70, lxx, LXX). **3** (in *pl.*) the numbers from 70 to 79, esp. the years of a century or of a person's life. ● *adj.* that amount to seventy. □□ **sev·en·ti·eth** *adj. & n.* **sev·en·ty·fold** *adj. & adv.*

sev·en-year itch *n.* a supposed tendency to infidelity after seven years of marriage.

sev·er /sévər/ *v.* **1** *tr. & intr.* (often foll. by *from*) divide, break, or make separate, esp. by cutting. **2** *tr. & intr.* break off or away (*severed our friendship*). **3** *tr.* end the employment contract of (a person). □□ **sev·er·a·ble** *adj.*

sev·er·al /sévrəl/ *adj. & n.* ● *adj. & n.* more than two but not many. ● *adj.* separate or respective; distinct (*all went their several ways*). □□ **sev·er·al·ly** *adv.*

sev·er·al·ty /sévrəltee/ *n.* **1** separateness. **2** the individual or unshared tenure of an estate, etc.

sev·er·ance /sévərəns, sévrəns/ *n.* **1** the act or an instance of severing. **2** a severed state.

sev·er·ance pay *n.* an amount paid to an employee on the early termination of a contract.

se·vere /sivéer/ *adj.* **1** rigorous, strict, and harsh in attitude or treatment (*a severe critic*). **2** serious; critical (*a severe shortage*). **3** vehement or forceful (*a severe storm*). **4** extreme (in an unpleasant quality) (*a severe*

winter). **5** exacting (*severe competition*). **6** plain in style (*severe dress*). □□ **se·vere·ly** *adv.* **se·ver·i·ty** /-véritee/ *n.*

Se·ville or·ange /səvil/ *n.* a bitter orange used for marmalade.

sew /sō/ *v.tr.* (*past part.* **sewn** /sōn/ or **sewed**) **1** (also *absol.*) fasten, join, etc., by making stitches with a needle and thread or a sewing machine. ▷ STITCH. **2** make (a garment, etc.) by sewing. **3** (often foll. by *on, in,* etc.) attach by sewing. □ **sew up 1** join or enclose by sewing. **2** *colloq.* (esp. in *passive*) satisfactorily arrange or finish dealing with (a project, etc.). □□ **sew·er** *n.*

sew·age /sṓij/ (also **sew·er·age** /sṓwərij/) *n.* waste matter conveyed in sewers.

sew·er /sṓor/ *n.* a conduit, usu. underground, for carrying off sewage.

sew·er·age /sṓōərij/ *n.* **1** a system of or drainage by sewers. **2** = SEWAGE.

sew·ing /sṓing/ *n.* a piece of material or work to be sewn.

sew·ing ma·chine /sṓing/ *n.* ▲ a machine for sewing or stitching.

sewn *past part.* of SEW.

sex /seks/ *n., adj., & v.* ● *n.* **1** either of the main divisions (male and female) into which living things are placed on the basis of their reproductive functions. **2** the fact of belonging to one of these. **3** males or females collectively. **4** sexual desires, etc., or their manifestation. **5** *colloq.* sexual intercourse. ● *adj.* **1** of or relating to sex (*sex education*). **2** arising from a difference or consciousness of sex (*sex urge*). ● *v.tr.* **1** determine the sex of. **2** (as **sexed** *adj.*) **a** having a sexual appetite (*highly sexed*). **b** having sexual characteristics.

sex·a·ge·nar·i·an /séksəjináireeən/ *n. & adj.* ● *n.* a person from 60 to 69 years old. ● *adj.* of this age.

Sex·a·ges·i·ma /séksəjésimə/ *n.* the Sunday before Quinquagesima.

sex·a·ges·i·mal /séksəjésiməl/ *adj. & n.* ● *adj.* **1** of sixtieths. **2** of sixty. **3** reckoning or reckoned by sixtieths. ● *n.* (in full **sexagesimal fraction**) a fraction with a denominator equal to a power of 60 as in the divisions of the degree and hour. □□ **sex·a·ges·i·mal·ly** *adv.*

sex ap·peal *n.* sexual attractiveness.

sex·cen·ten·ar·y /séksenténəree/ *n. & adj.* ● *n.* (*pl.* **-ies**) **1** a six-hundredth anniversary. **2** a celebration of this. ● *adj.* **1** of or relating to a sexcentenary. **2** occurring every six hundred years.

sex chro·mo·some *n.* a chromosome concerned in determining the sex of an organism.

sex hor·mone *n.* a hormone affecting sexual development or behavior.

sex·ism /séksizəm/ *n.* prejudice or discrimination, esp. against women, on the grounds of sex. □□ **sex·ist** *adj. & n.*

sex·less /sékslis/ *adj.* **1** *Biol.* neither male nor female. **2** lacking in sexual desire or attractiveness. □□ **sex·less·ly** *adv.* **sex·less·ness** *n.*

sex life *n.* a person's activity related to sexual instincts.

sex ob·ject *n.* a person regarded mainly in terms of sexual attractiveness.

sex·ol·o·gy /seksóləjee/ *n.* the study of sexual life or relationships, esp. in human beings. □□ **sex·o·log·i·cal** /séksəlójikəl/ *adj.* **sex·ol·o·gist** *n.*

sex·ploi·ta·tion /séksploytáyshən/ *n. colloq.* the exploitation of sex, esp. commercially.

sex·pot /sékspot/ *n. colloq.* a sexy person (esp. a woman).

sex sym·bol *n.* a person widely noted for sex appeal.

sext /sekst/ *n. Eccl.* **1** the canonical hour of prayer appointed for the sixth daytime hour (i.e., noon). **2** the office of sext.

sex·tant /sékstənt/ *n.* ▼ an instrument with a graduated arc of 60° used in navigation and surveying for measuring the angular distance of objects by means of mirrors.

S

SEXTANT

Sextants are commonly used to measure the angle between the Earth's horizon and a celestial body. The image of a star (for example) is reflected from the index mirror onto the horizon mirror and into the telescope. Next, the index arm is adjusted until the horizon and the star's image align. The angle between the horizon and the star can then be read on the arc. After a series of calculations, the sextant user's latitude and longitude can be worked out.

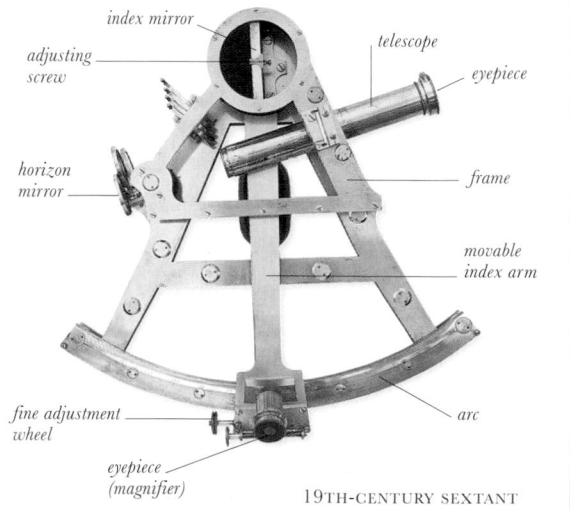

index mirror · telescope · adjusting screw · eyepiece · horizon mirror · frame · movable index arm · fine adjustment wheel · arc · eyepiece (magnifier)

19TH-CENTURY SEXTANT

sex·tet /sekstét/ *n.* (also **sex·tette**) **1** *Mus.* a composition for six voices or instruments. **2** the performers of such a piece. **3** any group of six.

sex·til·lion /sekstílyən/ *n.* (*pl.* same or **sextillions**) a thousand raised to the seventh (or formerly, esp. *Brit.,* the twelfth) power (10^{21} and 10^{36}, respectively). □□ **sex·til·lionth**

sex·to /sékstō/ *n.* (*pl.* **-os**) **1** a size of book or page in which each leaf is one-sixth that of a printing sheet. **2** a book or sheet of this size.

sex·ton /sékstən/ *n.* a person who looks after a church and churchyard, often acting as bell ringer and gravedigger.

sex·tu·ple /sekstóōpəl, -tyóō-, -túpəl, sékstóōpəl/ *adj., n.,* & *v.* ● *adj.* **1** sixfold. **2** having six parts. **3** being six times as many or much. ● *n.* a sixfold number or amount. ● *v.tr.* & *intr.* multiply by six; increase sixfold. □□ **sex·tu·ply** *adv.*

sex·tu·plet /sekstúplit, -tóō-, -tyóō-, sékstóō-, tyóō-/ *n.* each of six children born at one birth.

sex·u·al /sékshóōəl/ *adj.* **1** of or relating to sex, or to the sexes or the relations between them. **2** *Biol.* having a sex. □□ **sex·u·al·i·ty** /-álitee/ *n.* **sex·u·al·ly** *adv.*

sex·u·al in·ter·course *n.* the insertion of a man's erect penis into a woman's vagina, usu. followed by the ejaculation of semen.

sex work·er *n.* *euphem.* a prostitute.

sex·y /séksee/ *adj.* (**sexier, sexiest**) **1** sexually attractive or stimulating. **2** sexually aroused. **3** concerned with sex. **4** *sl.* exciting; appealing. □□ **sex·i·ly** *adv.* **sex·i·ness** *n.*

sez /sez/ *sl.* says (*sez you*).

SF *abbr.* science fiction.

sf *abbr. Mus.* sforzando.

sfor·zan·do /sfawrtsaándō/ *adj., adv.,* & *n.* (also **sfor·za·to** /-saátō/) ● *adj.* & *adv. Mus.* with sudden emphasis. ● *n.* (*pl.* **-os** or **sforzandi** /-dee/) **1** a note or group of notes especially emphasized. **2** an increase in emphasis and loudness.

sfu·ma·to /sfóōmaátō/ *n. Painting* the technique of allowing tones and colors to shade gradually into one another.

sfz *abbr. Mus.* sforzando.

SG *abbr.* **1** senior grade. **2** *Law* solicitor general. **3** specific gravity.

sgd. *abbr.* signed.

Sgt. (also **SGT**) *abbr.* Sergeant.

sh *int.* calling for silence.

shab·by /shábee/ *adj.* (**shabbier, shabbiest**) **1** in bad repair or condition; faded and worn. **2** dressed in old or worn clothes. **3** of poor quality. **4** dishonorable (*a shabby trick*). □□ **shab·bi·ly** *adv.* **shab·bi·ness** *n.*

shack /shak/ *n.* & *v.* ● *n.* a roughly built hut. ● *v.intr.* (foll. by *up*) *sl.* cohabit, esp. as lovers.

shack·le /shákəl/ *n.* & *v.* ● *n.* **1** ◄ a metal loop or link, closed by a bolt, to connect chains, etc. **2** a fetter enclosing the ankle or wrist. **3** (usu. in *pl.*) a restraint or impediment. ● *v.tr.* fetter; impede; restrain.

shad /shad/ *n.* (*pl.* same or **shads**) *Zool.* any deep-bodied edible marine fish of the genus *Alosa,* spawning in fresh water.

shad·dock /shádək/ *n. Bot.* **1** the largest citrus fruit, with a thick yellow skin and bitter pulp. Also called **pomelo.** ▷ CITRUS FRUIT. **2** the tree, *Citrus grandis,* bearing these.

shade /shayd/ *n.* & *v.* ● *n.* **1** comparative darkness (and usu. coolness) caused by shelter from direct light and heat. **2** a place or area sheltered from the sun. **3** a darker part of a picture, etc. **4** a color, esp. as distinguished from one nearly like it. **5** a slight amount (*a shade better*). **6** a screen excluding or moderating light. **7** an eye shield. **8** (in *pl.*) *colloq.* sunglasses. **9** a slightly differing variety (*all shades of*

opinion). **10** *literary* **a** a ghost. **b** (in *pl.*) Hades. **11** (in *pl.*; foll. by *of*) suggesting reminiscence (*shades of Dr Johnson!*). ● *v.* **1** *tr.* screen from light. **2** *tr.* cover, moderate, or exclude the light of. **3** *tr.* darken, esp. with parallel pencil lines to represent shadow, etc. **4** *intr.* & *tr.* (often foll. by *away, off, into*) pass or change by degrees. □ **put in the shade** appear superior to. □□ **shade·less** *adj.*

shad·ing /sháyding/ *n.* **1** the representation of light and shade, e.g., by penciled lines, on a map or drawing. **2** the graduation of tones from light to dark to create a sense of depth.

sha·doof /shədóof/ *n.* ▼ a pole with a bucket and counterbalance used esp. in Egypt for raising water.

SHADOOF USED TO RAISE WATER
FROM A RIVER IN EGYPT

shad·ow /shádō/ *n.* & *v.* ● *n.* **1** shade or a patch of shade. **2** a dark figure projected by a body intercepting rays of light. **3** an inseparable companion. **4** a person secretly following another. **5** the slightest trace. **6** a weak or insubstantial remnant. **7** the shaded part of a picture. **8** a substance used to color the eyelids. **9** gloom or sadness. ● *v.tr.* **1** cast a shadow over. **2** secretly follow and watch the movements of. □□ **shad·ow·er** *n.* **shad·ow·less** *adj.*

shad·ow·box /shádōboks/ *v. intr.* box against an imaginary opponent as a form of training.

shad·ow·graph /shádōgraf/ *n.* **1** an X-ray or radiogram. **2** a picture formed by a shadow cast on a lighted surface. **3** an image formed by light refracted differently by different densities of a fluid.

shad·ow e·con·o·my *n.* illicit economic activity existing alongside a country's official economy, e.g. black market transactions and undeclared work.

shad·ow·y /shádōee/ *adj.* **1** like or having a shadow. **2** full of shadows. **3** vague; indistinct. □□ **shad·ow·i·ness** *n.*

shad·y /sháydee/ *adj.* (**shadier, shadiest**) **1** giving shade. **2** situated in shade. **3** disreputable. □□ **shad·i·ly** *adv.* **shad·i·ness** *n.*

shaft /shaft/ *n.* & *v.* ● *n.* **1 a** an arrow or spear. **b** the long slender stem of these. **2** a remark intended to hurt or provoke (*shafts of wit*). **3** (foll. by *of*) **a** a ray (of light). **b** a bolt (of lightning). **4** the stem or handle of a tool, etc. **5** a column, esp. between the base and capital. **6** a long narrow space, usu. vertical, for an elevator, ventilation, etc. **7** a long and narrow part supporting or connecting or driving a part or parts of greater thickness, etc. **8** each of the pair of poles between which a horse is harnessed to a vehicle. ▷ TRACE. **9** *Mech.* a large axle or revolving bar transferring force by belts or cogs.

10 *colloq.* harsh or unfair treatment. ● *v.tr. colloq.* treat unfairly.

shag[1] /shag/ *n.* **1** a rough growth or mass of hair, etc. **2** a coarse kind of cut tobacco. **3** ► a cormorant, esp. the crested cormorant, *Phalacrocorax aristotelis.* **4 a** a thick, shaggy carpet pile. **b** the carpet itself.

shag[2] /shag/ *v.tr.* (**shagged, shagging**) *Baseball* catch and return (fly balls) during practice.

shag·gy /shágee/ *adj.* (**shaggier, shaggiest**) **1** hairy; rough-haired. **2** unkempt. **3** (of the hair) coarse and abundant. □□ **shag·gi·ly** *adv.* **shag·gi·ness** *n.*

SHAG: IMPERIAL SHAG
(*Phalacrocorax atriceps*)

shag·gy-dog sto·ry *n.* a long rambling story amusing only by being inconsequential.

sha·green /shəgréen/ *n.* **1** a kind of untanned leather with a rough, granulated surface. **2** a sharkskin rough with natural denticles.

shah /shaa/ *n. hist.* a title of the former monarch of Iran. □□ **shah·dom** *n.*

shake /shayk/ *v.* & *n.* ● *v.* (*past* **shook** /shŏok/; *past part.* **shaken** /sháykən/) **1** *tr.* & *intr.* move forcefully or quickly up and down or to and fro. **2 a** *intr.* tremble or vibrate markedly. **b** *tr.* cause to do this. **3** *tr.* **a** agitate or shock. **b** *colloq.* upset the composure of. **4** *tr.* weaken or impair (*shook his confidence*). **5** *intr.* make tremulous sounds (*his voice shook with emotion*). **6** *tr.* make a threatening gesture with (one's fist, etc.). **7** *intr. colloq.* shake hands. **8** *tr. colloq.* = shake off. ● *n.* **1** the act of shaking. **2** a jerk or shock. **3** (in *pl.*; prec. by *the*) a fit of or tendency to trembling. **4** = MILK SHAKE. □ **in two shakes (of a lamb's tail)** very quickly. **no great shakes** *colloq.* not very good or significant. **shake a person by the hand** = shake hands. **shake down 1** settle or cause to fall by shaking. **2** settle down. **3** get into harmony with circumstances, surroundings, etc. **4** *sl.* extort money from. **shake the dust off one's feet** depart indignantly or disdainfully. **shake hands** (often foll. by *with*) clasp right hands at meeting or parting, in reconciliation or congratulation, or over a concluded bargain. **shake one's head** move one's head from side to side in refusal, denial, disapproval, or concern. **shake in one's shoes** tremble with apprehension. **shake a leg** make a start. **shake off 1** get rid of (something unwanted). **2** manage to evade (a person). **shake up 1** disturb or make uncomfortable. **2** rouse from lethargy. □□ **shak·a·ble** *adj.* (also **shake·a·ble**).

shake·down /sháykdown/ *n.* **1** a makeshift bed. **2** *sl.* a swindle.

shak·en *past part.* of SHAKE.

shake·out /sháykowt/ *n.* **1** a rapid devaluation of securities, etc., sold in a stock exchange, etc. **2** a decline in the number of companies, services, etc., esp. as a result of competitive pressures.

shak·er /sháykər/ *n.* & *adj.* ● *n.* **1** a person or thing that shakes. **2** a container for shaking together the ingredients of cocktails, etc. **3** (**Shaker**) a member of an American religious sect living very simply in celibate mixed communities. ● *adj.* ◄ used to describe a simple, wholesome style of furniture made by Shakers.

SHAKER FURNITURE (WALL-MOUNTED
CABINET AND BOXES)

shackle

shackle
pin
(bolt)

SHACKLE

S

Shake·spear·e·an /shaykspéereeən/ *adj. & n.* (also **Shake·spear·i·an**) ● *adj.* **1** of or relating to William Shakespeare, English dramatist d. 1616. **2** in the style of Shakespeare. ● *n.* a student of Shakespeare's works, etc.

shake-up *n.* an upheaval or drastic reorganization.

shak·o /sháykō/ *n.* (*pl.* **-os**) ▼ a cylindrical peaked military hat with a plume.

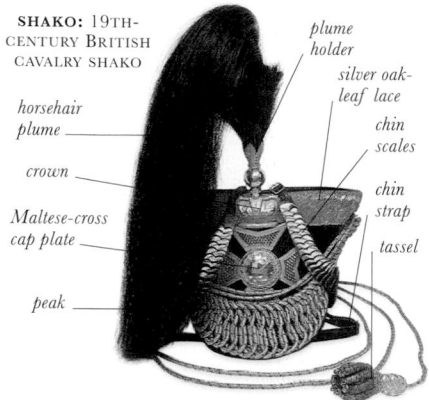

SHAKO: 19TH-CENTURY BRITISH CAVALRY SHAKO

plume holder

silver oak-leaf lace

chin scales

chin strap

tassel

horsehair plume

crown

Maltese-cross cap plate

peak

Shak·ta /sháaktə/ *n.* (also **Sak·ta**) a member of a Hindu sect worshiping the Shakti.

Shak·ti /shúkti/ *n.* (also **Sak·ti**) (in Hinduism) the female principle, esp. when personified as the wife of a god.

shak·u·ha·chi /sháakōōháachee/ *n.* (*pl.* **shakuhachis**) ◄ a Japanese bamboo flute.

notch

shak·y /sháykee/ *adj.* (**shakier, shakiest**) **1** unsteady; apt to shake; trembling. **2** unsound; infirm (*a shaky hand*). **3** unreliable; wavering (*a shaky promise; got off to a shaky start*). □□ **shak·i·ly** *adv.* **shak·i·ness** *n.*

shale /shayl/ *n.* ▶ soft, finely stratified rock that splits easily, consisting of consolidated mud or clay. □□ **shal·y** *adj.* ▷ SEDIMENT

fingerhole

shale oil *n.* oil obtained from bituminous shale.

shall /shal, shəl/ *v.aux.* (*3rd sing. present* **shall**; *archaic 2nd sing. present* **shalt** as below; *past* **should** /shŏŏd, shəd/ (foll. by *infin.* without *to*, or *absol.*; present and past only in use) **1** (in the 1st person) expressing the future tense (*I shall return soon*) or (with *shall* stressed) emphatic intention (*I shall have a party*). **2** (in the 2nd and 3rd persons) expressing a strong assertion or command rather than a wish (cf. WILL.[1]) (*you shall not catch me again; they shall go to the party*). ¶ For the other persons in senses 1, 2 see WILL.[1]. **3** expressing a command or duty (*thou shalt not steal; they shall obey*). **4** (in 2nd-person questions) expressing an inquiry, esp. to avoid the form of a request (cf. WILL.[1]) (*shall you go to France?*). □ **shall I?** do you want me to?

SHAKUHACHI

shal·lot /shálət, shəlót/ *n.* ▶ an onionlike plant, *Allium ascalonicum*, with a cluster of small bulbs.

shal·low /shálō/ *adj. & n.* ● *adj.* **1** of little depth. **2** superficial; trivial (*a shallow*

SHALLOT
BULB
(*Allium ascalonicum*)

mind). ● *n.* (often in *pl.*) a shallow place. □□ **shal·low·ly** *adv.* **shal·low·ness** *n.*

sha·lom /shaalóm/ *n. & int.* a Jewish salutation at meeting or parting.

shalt /shalt/ *archaic 2nd person sing.* of SHALL.

sham /sham/ *v., n., & adj.* ● *v.* (**shammed, shamming**) **1** *intr.* feign; pretend. **2** *tr.* **a** pretend to be. **b** simulate. ● *n.* **1** imposture; pretense. **2** a person or thing pretending to be what he or she or it is not. ● *adj.* pretended; counterfeit. □□ **sham·mer** *n.*

sha·man /sháamən, sháy-/ *n.* ▶ a witch doctor or priest claiming to communicate with and receive healing powers from gods, etc. □□ **sha·man·ism** *n.* **sha·man·ist** *n. & adj.* **sha·man·is·tic** /-nístik/ *adj.*

sham·ble /shámbəl/ *v. & n.* ● *v.intr.* walk or run with a shuffling or awkward gait. ● *n.* a shambling gait.

sham·bles /shámbəlz/ *n.pl.* (usu. treated as *sing.*) **1** *colloq.* a mess or muddle (*the room was a shambles*). **2** a butcher's slaughterhouse. **3** a scene of carnage.

shame /shaym/ *n. & v.* ● *n.* **1** a feeling of distress or humiliation caused by consciousness of the guilt or folly of oneself or an associate. **2** a capacity for experiencing this feeling (*has no shame*). **3** a state of disgrace, discredit, or intense regret. **4 a** a person or thing that brings disgrace, etc. **b** a thing or action that is wrong or regrettable. ● *v.tr.* **1** bring shame on; make ashamed. **2** (foll. by *into, out of*) force by shame. □ **for shame!** a reproof to a person for not showing shame. **put to shame** humiliate by revealing superior qualities, etc. **shame on you!** you should be ashamed. **what a shame!** how unfortunate!

shame·faced /sháymfayst/ *adj.* **1** showing shame. **2** bashful; diffident. □□ **shame·fac·ed·ly** /-fáystlee, fáysidlee/ *adv.* **shame·fac·ed·ness** *n.*

shame·ful /sháymfŏŏl/ *adj.* **1** that causes or is worthy of shame. **2** disgraceful; scandalous. □□ **shame·ful·ly** *adv.* **shame·ful·ness** *n.*

shame·less /sháymlis/ *adj.* **1** having or showing no sense of shame. **2** impudent. □□ **shame·less·ly** *adv.* **shame·less·ness** *n.*

sham·my /shámee/ *n.* (*pl.* **-ies**) (in full **shammy leather**) *colloq.* = CHAMOIS 2.

sham·poo /shampŏŏ/ *n. & v.* ● *n.* **1** liquid or cream used to lather and wash the hair. **2** a similar substance for washing a car or carpet, etc. **3** an act or instance of cleaning with shampoo. ● *v.tr.* (**shampoos, shampooed**) wash with shampoo.

sham·rock /shámrok/ *n.* any of various plants with trifoliate leaves, esp. *Trifolium repens* or *Medicago lupulina*, used as the national emblem of Ireland.

sha·mus /sháymɔs/ *n. sl.* a detective.

shan·dy /shándee/ *n.* (*pl.* **-ies**) a mixture of beer with lemonade.

shang·hai /shanghí/ *v.tr.* (**shanghais, shanghaied, shanghaiing**) **1** force (a person) to be a sailor on a ship by using drugs or other trickery. **2** *colloq.* put into detention or an awkward situation by trickery.

Shan·gri-la /shánggrilaá/ *n.* an imaginary paradise on earth.

shank /shangk/ *n.* **1 a** the leg. **b** the lower part of the leg; the leg from knee to ankle. **c** the shinbone. **2** the lower part of an animal's foreleg, esp. as a cut of meat. **3 a** shaft or stem. **4 a** the long narrow part of a tool, etc., joining the handle of it to the working end. **b** the stem of a key, spoon,

anchor, etc. **c** the straight part of a nail or fishhook. **5** the narrow middle of the sole of a shoe. □□ **shanked** *adj.* (also in *comb.*).

shanks's mare (or **pony**) *n.* one's own legs as a means of conveyance.

shanny /shánee/ *n.* (*pl.* **-ies**) a long-bodied, olive-green European marine fish, *Blennius pholis*.

shan't /shant/ *contr.* shall not.

shan·tung /shantúng/ *n.* soft undressed Chinese silk, usu. undyed.

shan·ty[1] /shántee/ *n.* (*pl.* **-ies**) **1** a hut or cabin. **2** a crudely built shack.

shan·ty[2] /shántee/ *n.* (*pl.* **-ies**) var. of CHANTEY.

shan·ty town *n.* a poor or depressed area of a town, consisting of shanties.

SHAPE /shayp/ *abbr.* Supreme Headquarters Allied Powers Europe.

shape /shayp/ *n. & v.* ● *n.* **1** the total effect produced by the outlines of a thing. **2** the external form or appearance of a person or thing. **3** a specific form or guise. **4** a description or sort or way (*not on offer in any shape or form*). **5** a definite or proper arrangement (*get our ideas into shape*). **6 a** condition, as qualified in some way (*in good shape*). **b** (when unqualified) good condition (*back in shape*). **7** a person or thing seen indistinctly or in the imagination (*a shape emerged from the mist*). **8** a mold or pattern. **9** a piece of material, paper, etc., made or cut in a particular form. ● *v.* **1** *tr.* give a certain shape or form to; fashion. **2** *tr.* (foll. by *to*) adapt or make conform. **3** *intr.* give signs of a future shape or development. **4** *tr.* frame mentally. **5** *intr.* assume or develop into a shape. **6** *tr.* direct (one's life, course, etc.). □ **lick** (or **knock**) **into shape** make presentable or efficient. **shape up 1** take a (specified) form. **2** show promise; make good progress. **shape up well** be promising. □□ **shap·a·ble** *adj.* (also **shape·a·ble**). **shaped** *adj.* (also in *comb.*). **shap·er** *n.*

shape·less /sháyplis/ *adj.* lacking definite or attractive shape. □□ **shape·less·ly** *adv.* **shape·less·ness** *n.*

shape·ly /sháyplee/ *adj.* (**shapelier, shapeliest**) **1** well formed or proportioned. **2** of elegant or pleasing shape or appearance. □□ **shape·li·ness** *n.*

shard /shaard/ *n.* **1** a broken piece of pottery or glass, etc. **2** = POTSHERD. **3** a fragment of volcanic rock.

share[1] /shair/ *n. & v.* ● *n.* **1** a portion that a person receives from or gives to a common amount. **2 a** a part contributed by an individual to an enterprise or commitment. **b** a part received by an individual from this (*got a large share of the credit*). **3** any of the equal parts into which a company's capital is divided entitling its owner to a proportion of the profits. ● *v.* **1** *tr.* get or have or give a share of. **2** *tr.* use or benefit from jointly with others. **3** *intr.* have a share; be a sharer (*shall I share with you?*). **4** *intr.* (foll. by *in*) participate. □ **share and share alike** have an equal division. □□ **share·a·ble** *adj.* (also **shar·a·ble**). **shar·er** *n.*

share[2] /shair/ *n.* = PLOWSHARE.

share·crop·per /sháirkropər/ *n.* a tenant farmer who gives a part of each crop as rent. □□ **share·crop** *v.tr. & intr.* (**-cropped, -cropping**).

share·hold·er /sháirhōldər/ *n.* an owner of shares in a company.

share·ware /sháirwair/ *n. Computing* software that is developed for sharing free of charge with other computer users rather than for sale.

sha·ri·ah /shaareé-aa/ *n.* the Muslim code of religious law.

sha·rif /shəreéf/ *n.* (also **she·reef, she·rif**) **1** a descendant of Muhammad through his daughter Fatima, entitled to wear a green turban or veil. **2** a Muslim leader.

SHAMAN: NATIVE AMERICAN SHAMAN'S CARVING OF A SPIRIT

SHALE:
OIL SHALE

S

SHARK

Sharks can be classified by the way in which they capture prey. Filter feeders, such as the whale shark, strain plankton with meshlike filters in their gills. Bottom dwellers, such as the wobbegong, use flat back teeth to grind crustaceans found on the seabed. Pursuit feeders, such as the great white shark, commonly eat smaller fish and have sharp teeth for tearing flesh. Sharks have adaptations that help them hunt, including ampullae of Lorenzini (sensory pores that detect electrical signals) and a lateral line (a series of pressure-sensitive organs down both sides of the head and body that detect the movement of prey).

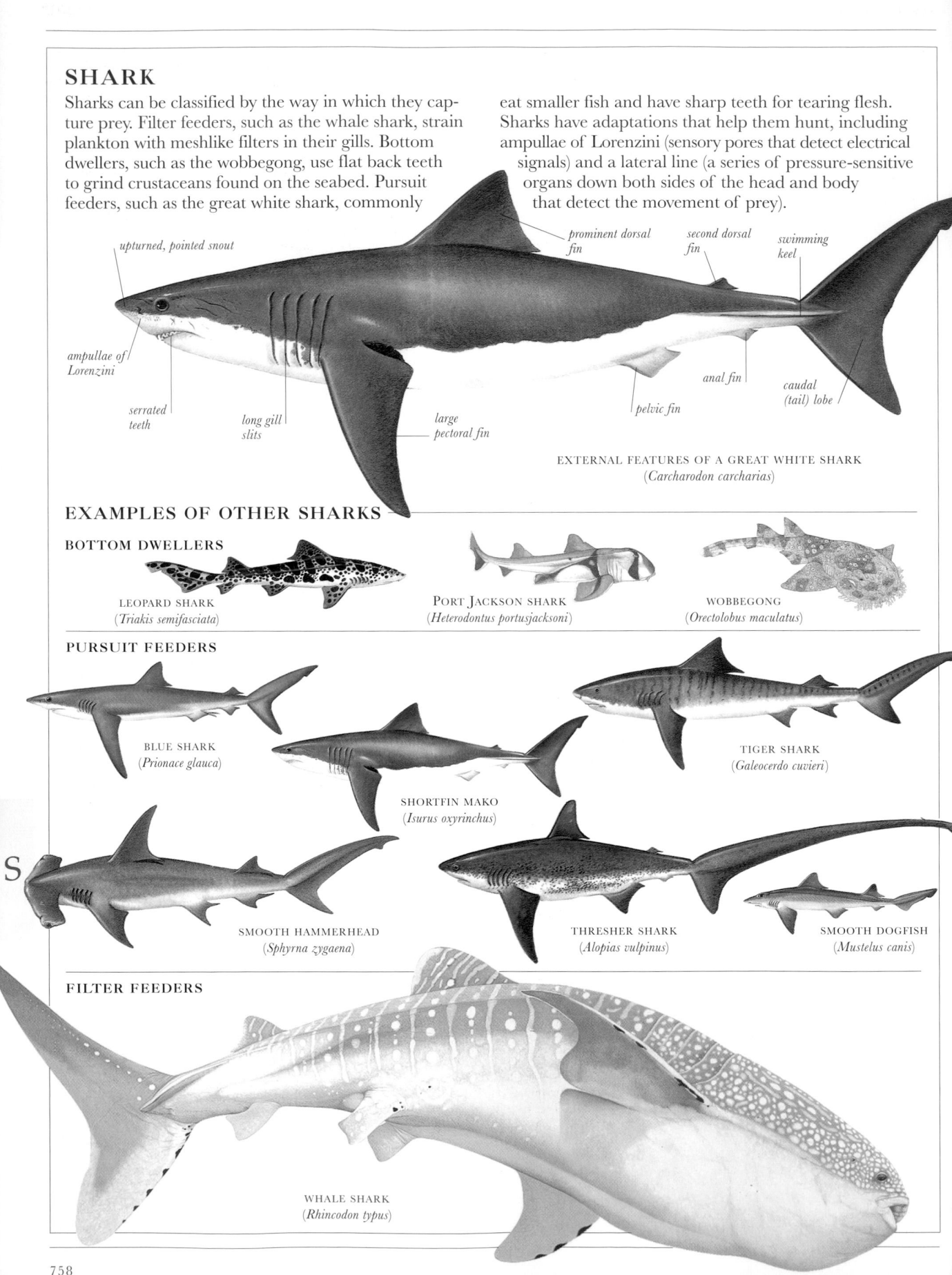

prominent dorsal fin

second dorsal fin

swimming keel

upturned, pointed snout

ampullae of Lorenzini

serrated teeth

long gill slits

large pectoral fin

pelvic fin

anal fin

caudal (tail) lobe

EXTERNAL FEATURES OF A GREAT WHITE SHARK
(*Carcharodon carcharias*)

EXAMPLES OF OTHER SHARKS

BOTTOM DWELLERS

LEOPARD SHARK
(*Triakis semifasciata*)

PORT JACKSON SHARK
(*Heterodontus portusjacksoni*)

WOBBEGONG
(*Orectolobus maculatus*)

PURSUIT FEEDERS

BLUE SHARK
(*Prionace glauca*)

TIGER SHARK
(*Galeocerdo cuvieri*)

SHORTFIN MAKO
(*Isurus oxyrinchus*)

SMOOTH HAMMERHEAD
(*Sphyrna zygaena*)

THRESHER SHARK
(*Alopias vulpinus*)

SMOOTH DOGFISH
(*Mustelus canis*)

FILTER FEEDERS

WHALE SHARK
(*Rhincodon typus*)

S

shark[1] /shaark/ *n.* ◄ any of various large, usu. voracious marine fish with a long body and prominent dorsal fin. ▷ CARTILAGINOUS FISH, ELASMOBRANCH, FISH

shark[2] /shaark/ *n. colloq.* a person who unscrupulously exploits others.

shark·skin /sha´arkskin/ *n.* **1** the skin of a shark. **2** a smooth, dull-surfaced fabric.

sharp /shaarp/ *adj., n., & adv.* ● *adj.* **1** having an edge or point able to cut or pierce. **2** tapering to a point or edge. **3** abrupt; steep; angular (*a sharp turn*). **4** well-defined. **5 a** intense (*has a sharp temper*). **b** (of food, etc.) pungent; keen (*a sharp appetite*). **c** (of a frost) severe; hard. **6** (of a voice or sound) shrill and piercing. **7** (of sand, etc.) composed of angular grains. **8** (of words, etc.) harsh or acrimonious. **9** (of a person) acute; quick to perceive or comprehend. **10** quick to take advantage; unscrupulous; dishonest. **11** vigorous or brisk. **12** *Mus.* **a** above the normal pitch. **b** (of a key) having a sharp or sharps in the signature. **c** (**C**, **F**, etc., **sharp**) a semitone higher than C, F, etc. ▷ NOTATION. **13** *colloq.* stylish or flashy with regard to dress. ● *n.* **1** *Mus.* **a** a note raised a semitone above natural pitch. **b** the sign (♯) indicating this. ▷ NOTATION. **2** *colloq.* a swindler or cheat. **3** a fine sewing needle. ● *adv.* **1** punctually (*at nine o'clock sharp*). **2** suddenly (*pulled up sharp*). **3** at a sharp angle. **4** *Mus.* above the true pitch (*sings sharp*). □□ **sharp·ly** *adv.* **sharp·ness** *n.*

sharp·en /sha´arpən/ *v.tr. & intr.* make or become sharp. □□ **sharp·en·er** *n.*

sharp·er /sha´arpər/ *n.* a swindler, esp. at cards.

sharp·ish /sha´arpish/ *adj. & adv. colloq.* ● *adj.* fairly sharp. ● *adv.* **1** fairly sharply. **2** quite quickly.

sharp-shinned hawk /sha´arpshind/ *n.* a N. American hawk, *Accipiter striatus*, with slender legs and a barred breast.

sharp·shoot·er /sha´arpsho͞otər/ *n.* a skilled marksman. □□ **sharp·shoot·ing** *n. & adj.*

sharp-wit·ted *adj.* keenly perceptive or intelligent.

shat·ter /sha´tər/ *v.* **1** *tr. & intr.* break suddenly in pieces. **2** *tr.* severely damage or utterly destroy. **3** *tr.* greatly upset or discompose. **4** *tr.* (usu. as **shattered** *adj.*) exhaust. □□ **shat·ter·er** *n.* **shat·ter·ing** *adj.* **shat·ter·ing·ly** *adv.* **shat·ter·proof** *adj.*

shave /shayv/ *v. & n.* ● *v.tr.* (*past part.* **shaved** or (as *adj.*) **shaven**) **1** remove (bristles or hair) from the face, etc., with a razor. **2** (also *absol.*) remove bristles or hair with a razor from (a part of the body). **3 a** reduce by a small amount. **b** take (a small amount) away from. **4** cut thin slices from the surface of (wood, etc.) to shape it. **5** pass close to without touching. ● *n.* **1** an act of shaving or the process of being shaved. **2** a close approach without contact. **3** a narrow miss or escape.

shav·er /sha´yvər/ *n.* **1** a person or thing that shaves. **2** an electric razor. **3** *colloq.* a young lad.

Sha·vi·an /sha´yveeən/ *adj. & n.* ● *adj.* of or in the manner of G. B. Shaw, Irish-born dramatist, d. 1950, or his ideas. ● *n.* an admirer of Shaw.

shav·ing /sha´yving/ *n.* **1** a thin strip cut off the surface of wood, etc. **2** (*attrib.*) used in shaving the face (*shaving cream*).

Sha·vu·oth /shəvo͞oˈəs, shaˈavo͞o-áwt/ *n.* (also **Sha·vu·ot**) the Jewish Pentecost.

shawl /shawl/ *n.* a piece of fabric, usu. rectangular and folded into a triangle, worn over the shoulders or head or wrapped around a baby. □□ **shawled** *adj.*

shawm /shawm/ *n. Mus.* a medieval double-reed wind instrument with a sharp penetrating tone.

Shaw·nee /shawnee, shaa-/ *n.* **1 a** a N. American people native to the central Ohio valley. **b** a member of this people. **2** the language of this people.

she /shee/ *pron. & n.* ● *pron.* (*obj.* **her**; *poss.* **her**; *pl.* **they**) **1** the woman or girl or female animal previously named or in question. **2** a thing regarded as female, e.g., a vehicle or ship. ● *n.* **1** a female; a woman. **2** (*in comb.*) female (*she-goat*).

s/he *pron.* a written representation of "he or she" used to indicate both sexes.

shea /shee, shay/ *n.* a W. African tree, *Vitellaria paradoxa*, bearing nuts containing a large amount of fat.

shea butter *n.* a butter made from the fat of shea nuts.

sheaf /sheef/ *n. & v.* ● *n.* (*pl.* **sheaves** /sheevz/) ► a group of things laid lengthways together, esp. a bundle of grain stalks or papers. ● *v.tr.* make into sheaves.

SHEAF OF WHEAT

shear /sheer/ *v. & n.* ● *v.* (*past* **sheared**, *archaic* **shore** /shor/; *past part.* **shorn** /shorn/ or **sheared**) **1** *tr.* cut with scissors or shears, etc. **2** *tr.* remove or take off by cutting. **3** *tr.* clip the wool off (a sheep, etc.). **4** *tr.* (foll. by *of*) **a** strip bare. **b** deprive. **5** *tr. & intr.* (often foll. by *off*) distort or be distorted, or break, from a structural strain. ● *n.* **1** *Mech. & Geol.* a strain produced by pressure in the structure of a substance. **2** (*in pl.*) (also **pair of shears** *sing.*) ◄ a large clipping or cutting instrument shaped like scissors for use in gardens, etc. □□ **shear·er** *n.*

SHEARS

shear·wa·ter /sheer´wawtər, -wotər/ *n.* ► any long-winged seabird of the genus *Puffinus*, usu. flying near the surface of the water.

sheat·fish /sheet´fish/ *n.* (*pl.* same or **sheat·fishes**) a large freshwater catfish, *Silurus glanis*, native to European waters.

sheath /sheeth/ *n.* (*pl.* **sheaths** /sheethz, sheeths/) **1** a close-fitting cover, esp. for the blade of a knife or sword. **2** a condom. **3** *Bot., Anat., & Zool.* an enclosing case or tissue. **4** the protective covering around an electric cable. **5** a woman's close-fitting dress. □□ **sheath·less** *adj.*

sheathe /sheeth/ *v.tr.* **1** put into a sheath. **2** encase; protect with a sheath.

sheath·ing /shee´thing/ *n.* a protective casing or covering.

sheath knife *n.* a daggerlike knife carried in a sheath.

sheave[1] /sheev/ *v.tr.* make into sheaves.

sheave[2] /sheev/ *n.* a grooved wheel in a pulley block, etc., for a rope to run on.

sheaves *pl.* of SHEAF.

she·bang /shibáng/ *n. sl.* a matter or affair (esp. *the whole shebang*).

she·been /shibe´en/ *n. esp. Ir.* an unlicensed house selling alcoholic liquor.

shed[1] /shed/ *n.* **1** a one-story structure usu. of wood for storage or shelter for animals, etc., or as a workshop. **2** a large roofed structure with one side open, for storing or maintaining machinery, etc.

shed[2] /shed/ *v.tr.* (**shedding**; *past* and *past part.* **shed**) **1** let or cause to fall off (*trees shed their leaves*). **2** take off (clothes). **3** reduce (an electrical power load) by disconnection, etc. **4** cause to fall or flow (*shed blood; shed tears*). **5** disperse; diffuse; radiate (*shed light*). □ **shed light on** see LIGHT[1].

she'd /sheed/ *contr.* **1** she had. **2** she would.

she-dev·il *n.* a malicious or spiteful woman.

sheen /sheen/ *n.* **1** a gloss or luster. **2** radiance; brightness. □□ **sheen·y** *adj.*

sheep /sheep/ *n.* (*pl.* same) **1** any ruminant mammal of the genus *Ovis* with a thick woolly coat, esp. kept in flocks for its wool or meat, and noted for its timidity. **2** a bashful, timid, or silly person.

3 (usu. in *pl.*) **a** a member of a minister's congregation. **b** a parishioner. □□ **sheep·like** *adj.*

sheep·dog /sheep´dawg, -dog/ *n.* **1** a dog trained to guard and herd sheep. **2** a dog of various breeds suitable for this.

sheep·fold /sheep´fold/ *n.* an enclosure for penning sheep.

sheep·ish /shee´pish/ *adj.* **1** bashful; shy; reticent. **2** embarrassed through shame. □□ **sheep·ish·ly** *adv.* **sheep·ish·ness** *n.*

sheep·shank /sheep´shangk/ *n.* ► a knot used to shorten a rope temporarily. ▷ KNOT

sheep·skin /sheep´skin/ *n.* **1** a garment or rug of sheep's skin with the wool on. **2** leather from a sheep's skin used in bookbinding.

SHEEPSHANK

sheer[1] /sheer/ *adj. & adv.* ● *adj.* **1** no more or less than; mere (*sheer luck; sheer determination*). **2** (of a cliff or ascent, etc.) perpendicular; very steep. **3** (of a textile) diaphanous. ● *adv.* **1** directly; outright. **2** perpendicularly. □□ **sheer·ly** *adv.* **sheer·ness** *n.*

sheer[2] /sheer/ *v.intr.* **1** esp. *Naut.* swerve or change course. **2** (foll. by *away, off*) go away, esp. from a person or topic one dislikes or fears.

sheer[3] /sheer/ *n.* the upward slope of a ship's lines toward the bow and stern.

sheer·legs /sheer´legz/ *n.pl.* (treated as *sing.*) a hoisting apparatus made from poles joined at or near the top and separated at the bottom for masting ships, installing engines, etc.

sheet[1] /sheet/ *n. & v.* ● *n.* **1** a large rectangular piece of cotton or other fabric, used esp. in pairs as inner bedclothes. **2 a** a broad usu. thin flat piece of material (e.g., paper or metal). **b** (*attrib.*) made in sheets (*sheet iron*). **3** a wide continuous surface or expanse of water, ice, flame, falling rain, etc. **4** a set of unseparated postage stamps. **5** *derog.* a newspaper. **6** a complete piece of paper of the size in which it was made, for printing and folding as part of a book. ● *v.* **1** *tr.* provide or cover with sheets. **2** *tr.* form into sheets. **3** *intr.* (of rain, etc.) fall in sheets.

sheet[2] /sheet/ *n.* a rope or chain attached to the lower corner of a sail for securing or controlling it.

sheet·ing /shee´ting/ *n.* fabric for making bed linen.

sheet light·ning *n.* lightning with its brightness diffused by reflection.

sheet met·al *n.* metal formed into thin sheets by rolling, hammering, etc.

sheet mu·sic *n.* music published in cut or folded sheets, not bound.

sheikh /sheek, shayk/ *n.* (also **sheik**, **shaikh**) **1** a chief or head of an Arab tribe, family, or village. **2** a Muslim leader. □□ **sheikh·dom** *n.*

shei·la /shee´lə/ *n. Austral. & NZ sl.* a girl or young woman.

shek·el /shék´əl/ *n.* **1** the chief monetary unit of modern Israel. **2** *hist.* a silver coin and unit of weight used in ancient Israel and the Middle East. **3** (in *pl.*) *colloq.* money; riches.

shel·duck /shél´duk/ *n.* (*pl.* same or **shelducks**; *masc.* **sheldrake**, *pl.* same or **sheldrakes**) ► any bright-plumaged coastal wild duck of the genus *Tadorna*, esp. *T. tadorna*.

shelf /shelf/ *n.* (*pl.* **shelves** /shelvz/) **1 a** a thin flat piece of wood or metal, etc., projecting from a wall, or as part of a unit, used to support books, etc. **b** a flat-topped recess in a wall, etc., used for supporting objects. **2 a** a projecting horizontal ledge in a cliff face, etc. **b** a reef or sandbank. □ **on the**

SHELDUCK
(*Tadorna tadorna*)

SHELL

A mollusk's shell consists of layers of a hard mineral (calcium carbonate) laid down within a framework of protein. It is produced by a soft tissue called the mantle, which surrounds the animal's internal organs. Some terrestrial mollusks have shells, but the greatest variation in shell size and shape appears in marine species. The two main groups are gastropods and bivalves, while tusk shells, chitons, and cephalopods form minor groups. Gastropods usually have a spiral shell, typically with a right-hand coil. Bivalves' shells have paired valves connected by a hinge.

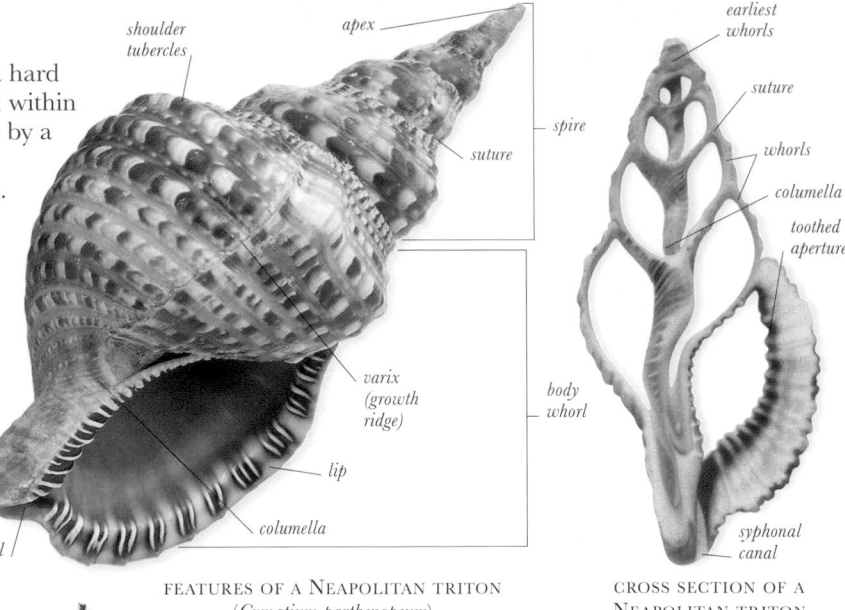

FEATURES OF A NEAPOLITAN TRITON
(*Cymatium parthenopeum*)

CROSS SECTION OF A NEAPOLITAN TRITON

EXAMPLES OF SHELLS

GASTROPODS

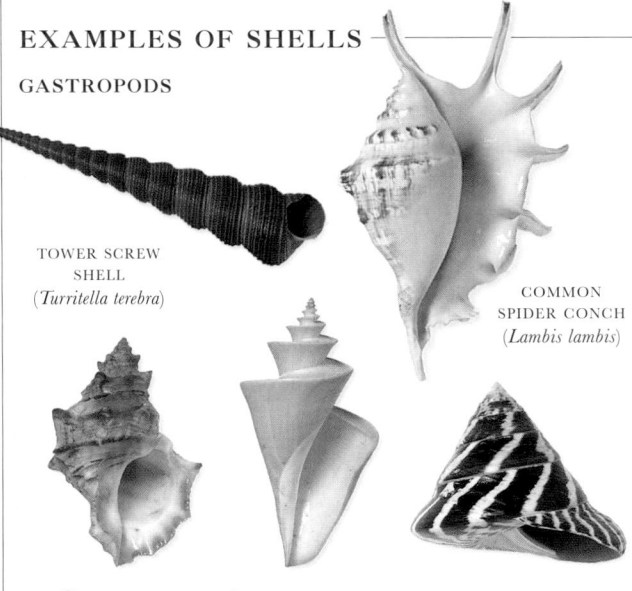

TOWER SCREW SHELL
(*Turritella terebra*)

COMMON SPIDER CONCH
(*Lambis lambis*)

CALIFORNIA FROG SHELL
(*Crossata californica*)

JAPANESE WONDER SHELL
(*Thatcheria mirabilis*)

COMMERCIAL TROCHUS
(*Trochus niloticus*)

WIDE-MOUTHED PURPURA
(*Purpura patula*)

WEST INDIAN WORM SHELL
(*Vermicularia spirata*)

FLEA-BITE CONE
(*Conus pulicarius*)

STRAWBERRY DRUPE
(*Drupa rubusidaeus*)

COMMON EGG COWRIE
(*Ovula ovum*)

FOOL'S CAP
(*Capulus ungaricus*)

BIVALVES

COCKSCOMB OYSTER
(*Lopha cristagalli*)

GIANT RAZOR SHELL
(*Ensis siliqua*)

SPECKLED TELLIN
(*Tellina listeri*)

FAN MUSSEL
(*Pinna rudis*)

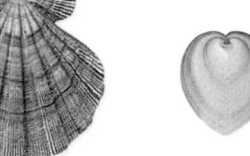

DOG COCKLE
(*Glycymeris glycymeris*)

LION'S PAW
(*Lyropecten nodosus*)

TRUE HEART COCKLE
(*Corculum cardissa*)

TUSK SHELLS

ELEPHANT TUSK
(*Dentalium elephantinum*)

CHITONS

BUTTERFLY CHITON
(*Chaetopleura papilio*)

CEPHALOPODS

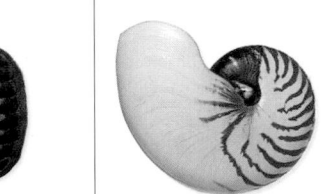

PEARLY NAUTILUS
(*Nautilus pompilius*)

S

shelf 1 (of a woman) past the age when she might expect to be married. **2** (esp. of a retired person) no longer active or of use. □□ **shelved** /shelvd/ *adj.* **shelf·ful** *n.* (*pl.* **-fuls**). **shelf·like** *adj.*

shelf life *n.* the amount of time for which a stored item remains usable.

shell /shel/ *n. & v.* ● *n.* **1 a** ◄ the hard outer case of many marine mollusks. ▷ MOLLUSK. **b** the hard but fragile outer covering of an egg. ▷ EGG. **c** the usu. hard outer case of a nut kernel, seed, etc. **d** the carapace of a tortoise, turtle, etc. **e** the elytron or cocoon, etc., of many insects, etc. **2 a** an explosive projectile or bomb for use in a big gun or mortar. **b** a hollow container for fireworks, explosives, cartridges, etc. **c** a cartridge. **3** a mere semblance or outer form without substance. **4** any of several things resembling a shell in being an outer case, esp.: **a** a light racing boat. **b** a hollow pastry case. **c** the metal framework of a vehicle body, etc. **d** the walls of an unfinished or gutted building, ship, etc. ● *v.tr.* **1** remove the shell or pod from. **2** bombard with shells. □ **come out of one's shell** cease to be shy. **shell out** *colloq.* **1** pay (money). **2** hand over (a required sum). □□ **shelled** *adj.* **shell·less** *adj.* **shell·like** *adj.* **shell·proof** *adj.* (in sense 2a of *n.*). **shell·y** *adj.*

she'll /sheel, shil/ *contr.* she will; she shall.

shel·lac /shəlák/ *n. & v.* ● *n.* lac resin melted into thin flakes and used for making varnish (cf. LAC). ● *v.tr.* (**shellacked, shellacking**) **1** varnish with shellac. **2** *sl.* defeat or thrash soundly.

shell·back /shélbak/ *n. sl.* an old sailor.

shell·fish /shélfish/ *n.* **1** an aquatic shelled mollusk, e.g., an oyster, mussel, etc. **2** a crustacean, e.g., a crab, shrimp, etc.

shell pink *n.* a delicate pale pink.

shell shock *n.* a nervous breakdown resulting from exposure to battle. □□ **shell-shocked** *adj.*

shell·work /shélwərk/ *n.* ornamentation consisting of shells cemented onto wood, etc.

shel·ter /shéltər/ *n. & v.* ● *n.* **1** anything serving as a shield or protection from danger, bad weather, etc. **2 a** a place of refuge provided esp. for the homeless. **b** an animal sanctuary. **3** a sheltered condition; protection (*took shelter under a tree*). ● *v.* **1** *tr.* act or serve as shelter to; protect; conceal; defend (*sheltered them from the storm; a sheltered upbringing*). **2** *intr. & refl.* find refuge; take cover (*sheltered under a tree; sheltered themselves behind the wall*). □□ **shel·ter·er** *n.* **shel·ter·less** *adj.*

shelve¹ /shelv/ *v.tr.* **1** put (books, etc.) on a shelf. **2 a** abandon or defer (a plan, etc.). **b** remove (a person) from active work, etc. **3** fit (a cupboard, etc.) with shelves. □□ **shelv·er** *n.* **shelv·ing** *n.*

shelve² /shelv/ *v.intr.* (of ground, etc.) slope (*land shelved away to the horizon*).

shelves *pl.* of SHELF.

she·moz·zle /shimózəl/ *n.* (also **sche·moz·zle**) *sl.* **1** a commotion. **2** a muddle.

she·nan·i·gan /shinánigən/ *n.* (esp. in *pl.*) *colloq.* **1** high-spirited behavior; nonsense. **2** trickery; dubious maneuvers.

She·ol /shée-ōl/ *n.* the Hebrew underworld abode of the dead.

shep·herd /shépərd/ *n. & v.* ● *n.* **1** (*fem.* **shepherdess** /shépərdis/) a person employed to tend sheep. **2** a member of the clergy, etc., who guides a congregation. ● *v.tr.* **1 a** tend (sheep, etc.). **b** guide (followers, etc.). **2** marshal or drive (a crowd, etc.).

sher·ard·ize /shérərdīz/ *v.tr.* coat (iron or steel) with zinc by heating in contact with zinc dust.

Sher·a·ton /shérət'n/ *n.* (often *attrib.*) a style of furniture introduced in England *c.*1790, with delicate and graceful forms.

sher·bet /shárbət/ *n.* **1** a fruit-flavored ice confec-

tion. **2** a cooling drink of sweet, diluted fruit juices, used esp. in the Middle East.

sherd /shərd/ *n.* = POTSHERD.

sher·iff /shérif/ *n.* an elected officer in a county, responsible for keeping the peace.

Sher·pa /shárpə/ *n.* (*pl.* same or **Sherpas**) **1** a Himalayan people living on the borders of Nepal and Tibet. **2** a member of this people.

sher·ry /shéree/ *n.* (*pl.* **-ies**) **1** a fortified wine orig. from S. Spain. **2** a glass of this.

she's /sheez/ *contr.* **1** she is. **2** she has.

Shet·land·er /shétləndər/ *n.* a native of the Shetland Islands, NNE of the mainland of Scotland.

Shet·land po·ny *n.* ◄ a pony of a small, hardy, rough-coated breed.

Shet·land sheep·dog *n.* a small dog of a collielike breed.

Shet·land wool *n.* a fine, loosely twisted wool from Shetland sheep.

she·va var. of SCHWA.

shew *archaic* var. of SHOW.

shew·bread /shóbred/ *n.* twelve loaves that were displayed in a Jewish temple and renewed each Sabbath.

Shi·a /shéeə/ *n.* one of the two main branches of Islam, esp. in Iran, that rejects the first three Sunni caliphs and regards Ali as Muhammad's first successor (cf. SUNNI).

shi·at·su /shiátsoo/ *n.* a kind of therapy of Japanese origin, in which pressure is applied with the fingers to certain points of the body.

shib·bo·leth /shíbələth/ *n.* a doctrine, phrase, etc., held to be true by a party or sect.

shield /sheeld/ *n. & v.* ● *n.* **1 a** esp. *hist.* ► a piece of armor carried on the arm or in the hand to deflect blows from the head or body ▷ QUARTERING. **b** a thing serving to protect (*insurance is a shield against disaster*). **2** a thing resembling a shield, esp.: **a** a trophy in the form of a shield. **b** a protective plate or screen in machinery, etc. **c** a shieldlike part of an animal, esp. a shell. **d** a similar part of a plant. ● *v.tr.* protect or screen.

shier *compar.* of SHY¹.

shiest *superl.* of SHY¹.

shift /shift/ *v. & n.* ● *v.* **1** *intr. & tr.* change or move or cause to change or move from one position to another. **2 a** *tr.* change (gear) in a vehicle. **b** *intr.* change gear. **3** *intr.* (of cargo) get shaken out of place. ● *n.* **1 a** the act of shifting. **b** the substitution of one thing for another. **2 a** a relay of workers (*the night shift*). **b** the time for which they work (*an eight-hour shift*). **3** a device or stratagem. **4 a** a woman's straight unwaisted dress. **b** *archaic* a loose-fitting undergarment. **5** a displacement of spectral lines (*red shift*). **6** a key on a keyboard used to switch between lowercase and uppercase, etc. **7 a** a gear lever in a motor vehicle. **b** a mechanism for this. □ **shift for oneself** rely on one's own efforts. **shift one's ground** take up a new position in an argument, etc. □□ **shift·a·ble** *adj.* **shift·er** *n.*

shift·less /shíftlis/ *adj.* lacking resourcefulness. □□ **shift·less·ly** *adv.* **shift·less·ness** *n.*

shift·y /shíftee/ *adj. colloq.* (**shiftier, shiftiest**) evasive; deceitful. □□ **shift·i·ly** *adv.* **shift·i·ness** *n.*

shih tzu /shée dzōo, shéetsōo/ *n.* (*pl.* **shih tzus** or same) **1** a dog of a breed with long silky hair and short legs. **2** this breed.

Shi·ite /shée-īt/ *n. & adj.* ● *n.* an adherent of the Shia branch of Islam. ● *adj.* of or relating to Shia. □□ **Shi·ism** /shée-izəm/ *n.*

shik·sa /shíksə/ *n.* often *offens.* (used by Jews) a gentile girl or woman.

shill /shil/ *n.* a person employed to decoy or entice others into buying, gambling, etc.

shil·le·lagh /shiláylee, -lə/ *n.* a thick stick of blackthorn or oak used in Ireland esp. as a weapon.

shil·ling /shíling/ *n.* **1** *hist.* a former British coin and monetary unit worth one-twentieth of a pound. **2** a monetary unit in Kenya, Tanzania, and Uganda.

shil·ly-shal·ly /shíleeshálee/ *v., adj., & n.* ● *v.intr.* (**-ies, -ied**) be undecided; vacillate. ● *adj.* vacillating. ● *n.* indecision; vacillation. □□ **shil·ly-shal·ly·er** *n.* (also **-shallier**).

shim /shim/ *n. & v.* ● *n.* a thin strip of material used in machinery, etc., to make parts fit. ● *v.tr.* (**shimmed, shimming**) fit or fill up with a shim.

shim·mer /shímər/ *v. & n.* ● *v.intr.* shine with a tremulous or faint diffused light. ● *n.* such a light. □□ **shim·mer·ing·ly** *adv.* **shim·mer·y** *adj.*

shim·my /shímee/ *n. & v.* ● *n.* (*pl.* **-ies**) *hist.* a kind of ragtime dance in which the whole body is shaken. ● *v.intr.* (**-ies, -ied**) **1** *hist.* dance a shimmy. **2** move in a similar manner.

shin /shin/ *n. & v.* ● *n.* **1** the front of the leg below the knee. **2** a cut of beef from the lower foreleg. ● *v.tr. &* (usu. foll. by *up, down*) *intr.* (**shinned, shinning**) climb quickly by clinging with the arms and legs.

shin·bone /shínbōn/ *n.* = TIBIA.

shin·dig /shíndig/ *n. colloq.* **1** a festive, esp. noisy, party. **2** = SHINDY 1.

shin·dy /shíndee/ *n.* (*pl.* **-ies**) *colloq.* **1** a brawl, disturbance, or noise (*kicked up a shindy*). **2** = SHINDIG 1.

shine /shīn/ *v. & n.* ● *v.* (*past* and *past part.* **shone** /shon/ or **shined**) **1** *intr.* emit or reflect light; be bright (*the lamp was shining; his face shone with gratitude*). **2** *intr.* (of the Sun, a star, etc.) be visible. **3** *tr.* cause (a lamp, etc.) to shine. **4** *tr.* (*past* and *past part.* **shined**) polish (*shined his shoes*). **5** *intr.* be brilliant; excel (*does not shine in conversation*). ● *n.* **1** brightness, esp. reflected. **2** a high polish. **3** the act of shining, esp. shoes. □ **shine up to** seek to ingratiate oneself with. **take the shine out of 1** spoil the brilliance or newness of. **2** throw into the shade by surpassing. **take a shine to** *colloq.* take a fancy to. □□ **shin·ing·ly** *adv.*

shin·er /shínər/ *n.* **1** a thing that shines. **2** *colloq.* a black eye.

shin·gle¹ /shínggəl/ *n.* (in *sing.* or *pl.*) small rounded pebbles, esp. on a seashore. □□ **shin·gly** *adj.*

shin·gle² /shínggəl/ *n. & v.* ● *n.* **1** a rectangular wooden tile used on roofs, spires, or esp. walls. **2** *archaic* shingled hair. **b** the act of shingling hair. **3** a small signboard, esp. of a doctor, lawyer, etc. ● *v.tr.* **1** roof or clad with shingles. **2** *archaic* cut (a woman's) hair very short.

shin·gles /shínggəlz/ *n.pl.* (usu. treated as *sing.*) an acute painful viral inflammation of the nerve ganglia, with a skin eruption often forming a girdle around the middle of the body.

shin·ny /shínee/ *v.intr.* (**-ies, -ied**) (usu. foll. by *up, down*) *colloq.* shin (up or down a tree, etc.).

Shi·no·la /shīnṓlə/ *n. US Trademark* a brand of boot polish. **not know shit from Shinola** *coarse sl.* be ignorant or innocent.

Shin·to /shíntō/ *n.* the official religion of Japan incorporating the worship of ancestors and nature spirits. □□ **Shin·to·ism** *n.* **Shin·to·ist** *n.*

shin·y /shínee/ *adj.* (**shinier, shiniest**) reflecting light because very smooth, clean, or polished. □□ **shin·i·ly** *adv.* **shin·i·ness** *n.*

SHETLAND PONY

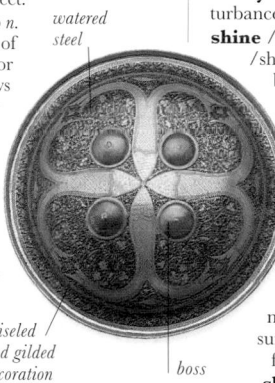

watered steel

chiseled and gilded decoration

boss

SHIELD: 19TH-CENTURY INDIAN SHIELD

S

ship /ship/ *n. & v.* ● *n.* **1** ▼ **a** any large seagoing vessel. **b** a sailing vessel with a bowsprit and three, four, or five square-rigged masts. **2** an aircraft. **3** a spaceship. **4** *colloq.* a boat, esp. a racing boat. ● *v.* (**shipped**, **shipping**) **1** *tr.* put, take, or send away on board ship. **2** *tr.* **a** take in (water) over the side of a ship, boat, etc. **b** take (oars) from the oarlocks and lay them inside a boat. **c** fix (a rudder, etc.) in its place. **d** step (a mast). **3** *intr.* **a** embark. **b** (of a sailor) take service on a ship (*shipped for Africa*). **4** *tr.* deliver (goods) to a forwarding agent for conveyance. □ **ship off 1** send or transport by ship. **2** *colloq.* send (a person) away. **take ship** embark. **when a person's ship comes in** when a person's fortune is made. □□ **ship·less** *adj.*

-ship /ship/ *suffix* forming nouns denoting: **1** a quality or condition (*friendship*; *hardship*). **2** status, office, or honor (*authorship*; *lordship*). **3** a tenure of office (*chairmanship*). **4** a skill in a certain capacity (*workmanship*). **5** the collective individuals of a group (*membership*).

ship·board /shípbawrd/ *n.* (usu. *attrib.*) used or occurring on board a ship (*a shipboard romance*). □ **on shipboard** on board ship.

ship·build·er /shípbildər/ *n.* a person, company, etc., that constructs ships. □□ **ship·build·ing** *n.*

ship·lap /shíplap/ *v. & n.* ● *v.tr.* fit (boards) together for cladding, etc., so that each overlaps the one below. ● *n.* such cladding.

ship·load /shíplōd/ *n.* a quantity of goods forming a cargo.

ship·mas·ter /shípmastər/ *n.* a ship's captain.

ship·mate /shípmayt/ *n.* a fellow member of a ship's crew.

ship·ment /shípmənt/ *n.* **1** an amount of goods shipped. **2** the act of shipping goods, etc.

ship of the des·ert *n.* the camel.

ship·own·er /shípōnər/ *n.* a person owning a ship or ships or shares in ships.

ship·per /shípər/ *n.* a person or company that sends or receives goods by ship, or by land or air.

ship·ping /shíping/ *n.* **1** the act or an instance of shipping goods, etc. **2** ships.

ship·shape /shípshayp/ *adv. & predic.adj.* in good order; trim and neat.

ship·way /shípway/ *n.* a slope on which a ship is built and down which it slides to be launched.

ship·worm /shípwərm/ *n.* = TEREDO.

ship·wreck /shíprek/ *n. & v.* ● *n.* **1 a** the destruction of a ship by a storm, foundering, etc. **b** a ship so destroyed. **2** (often foll. by *of*) the destruction of hopes, dreams, etc. ● *v.* **1** *tr.* inflict shipwreck on. **2** *intr.* suffer shipwreck.

ship·wright /shíprīt/ *n.* **1** a shipbuilder. **2** a ship's carpenter.

ship·yard /shípyaard/ *n.* a place where ships are built, repaired, etc.

shirk /shərk/ *v.tr.* (also *absol.*) avoid; get out of (duty, work, responsibility, fighting, etc.). □□ **shirk·er** *n.*

shirr /shər/ *n. & v.* ● *n.* **1** two or more rows of esp. elastic gathered threads in a garment, etc., forming smocking. **2** elastic webbing. ● *v.tr.* **1** gather (material) with parallel threads. **2** bake (eggs) without shells. □□ **shirr·ing** *n.*

shirt /shərt/ *n.* **1** an upper-body garment of cotton, etc., having a collar, sleeves, and buttons down the front. **2 a** an undershirt. **b** a T-shirt. □ **keep one's shirt on** *colloq.* keep one's temper. **lose one's shirt** lose all that one has. **the shirt off one's back** *colloq.* one's last remaining possessions. □□ **shirt·ed** *adj.* **shirt·ing** *n.* **shirt·less** *adj.*

shirt·dress /shártdress/ *n.* = SHIRTWAIST.

shirt·front /shártfrunt/ *n.* the breast of a shirt, esp. of a stiffened evening shirt.

shirt·sleeve /shártsleev/ *n.* (usu. in *pl.*) the sleeve of a shirt. □ **in shirtsleeves** wearing a shirt with no jacket, etc., over it.

shirt·tail /shárttayl/ *n.* the lower curved part of a shirt below the waist.

shirt·waist /shártwayst/ *n.* a woman's blouse resembling a shirt.

shish ke·bab /shísh kibób/ *n.* a dish of pieces of marinated meat and vegetables cooked and served on skewers.

shit /shit/ *v., n., & int. coarse sl.* ¶ Usually considered a taboo word. ● *v.* (**shitting**; *past* and *past part.* **shit** or **shat**) *intr. & tr.* expel feces from the body or cause (feces, etc.) to be expelled. ● *n.* **1** an act of defecating. **2** feces. **3** a contemptible person. **4** nonsense. **5** an intoxicating drug, esp. cannabis. ● *int.* an exclamation of disgust, anger, etc.

shit-hot *adj. coarse sl.* excellent.

shit·ty /shítee/ *adj.* (**shittier**, **shittiest**) *coarse sl.* **1** disgusting; contemptible. **2** covered with excrement.

shiv·er[1] /shívər/ *v. & n.* ● *v.intr.* **1** tremble with cold, fear, etc. **2** suffer a quick trembling movement of the body. ● *n.* **1** a momentary shivering movement.

SHIP

Throughout history, ships have been used to transport goods and people around the world. In wartime they are used in both defense and attack. From the 15th to the mid-19th century, sailing ships like the one shown here were widely used for exploration and trading. By the 1880s their dominance was ended by the rise of steamships. Today, ships are mainly turbine or diesel powered. They include ocean liners, some of which can accommodate over 1,000 passengers; warships such as frigates and aircraft carriers; cargo-carrying container ships; and supertankers, which can carry over 300,000 tons of oil.

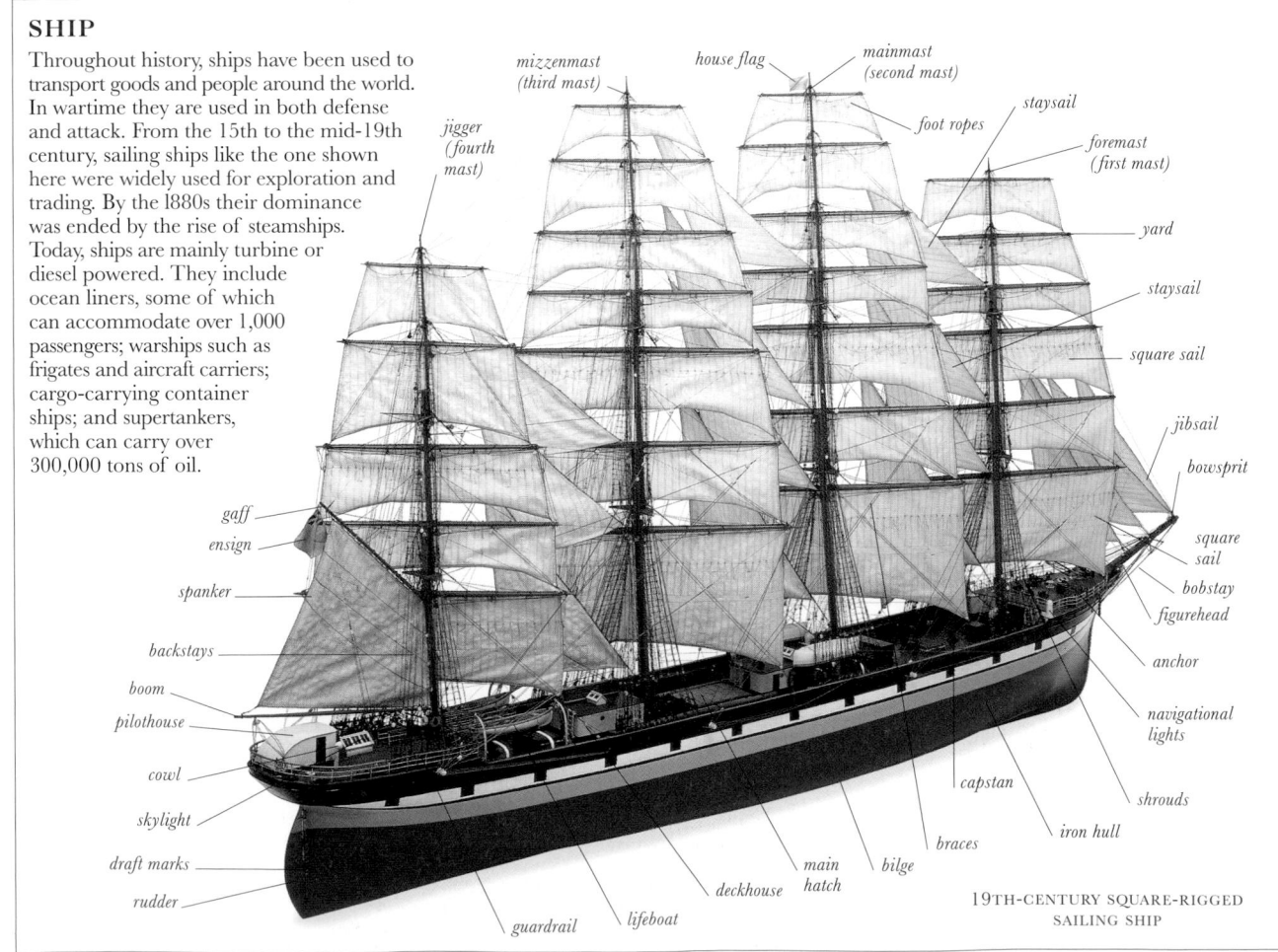

mizzenmast (third mast) · house flag · mainmast (second mast) · jigger (fourth mast) · foot ropes · staysail · foremast (first mast) · yard · staysail · square sail · jibsail · bowsprit · square sail · bobstay · figurehead · anchor · navigational lights · shrouds · iron hull · braces · capstan · bilge · main hatch · deckhouse · lifeboat · guardrail · rudder · draft marks · skylight · cowl · pilothouse · boom · backstays · spanker · ensign · gaff

19TH-CENTURY SQUARE-RIGGED SAILING SHIP

S

2 (in *pl.*) an attack of shivering, esp. from fear or horror (*got the shivers in the dark*). □□ **shiv·er·ing·ly** *adv.* **shiv·er·y** *adj.*

shiv·er[2] /shívər/ *n. & v.* ● *n.* (esp. in *pl.*) each of the small pieces into which esp. glass is shattered when broken; a splinter. ● *v.tr. & intr.* break into shivers. □ **shiver my timbers** a reputed pirate's curse.

Sho·ah /shṓwə/ *n.* (in Jewish use) the Holocaust.

shoal[1] /shōl/ *n. & v.* ● *n.* **1** a great number of fish swimming together. **2** a multitude; a crowd (*shoals of letters*). ● *v.intr.* (of fish) form shoals.

shoal[2] /shōl/ *n., v., & adj.* ● *n.* **1 a** an area of shallow water. **b** a submerged sandbank visible at low water. **2** (esp. in *pl.*) hidden danger. ● *v.intr.* (of water) get shallower. ● *adj. archaic* (of water) shallow. □□ **shoal·y** *adj.*

shoat /shōt/ *n.* a young pig, esp. newly weaned.

shock[1] /shok/ *n. & v.* ● *n.* **1** a violent collision, impact, tremor, etc. **2** a sudden and disturbing effect on the emotions, physical reactions, etc. (*the news was a great shock*). **3** an acute state of prostration following a wound, pain, etc. (*died of shock*). **4** the effect of a sudden discharge of electricity on a person or animal, usually with stimulation of the nerves and contraction of the muscles. ● *v.* **1** *tr.* affect with shock; horrify; outrage. **2** *tr.* (esp. in *passive*) affect with an electric or pathological shock. **3** *intr.* experience shock (*I don't shock easily*). □□ **shock·a·ble** *adj.* **shock·a·bil·i·ty** *n.*

shock[2] /shok/ *n.* a group of sheaves of grain stood up with their heads together in a field.

shock[3] /shok/ *n.* an unkempt or shaggy mass of hair.

shock ab·sorb·er *n.* ▶ a device on a vehicle, etc., for absorbing shocks, vibrations, etc. ▷ CAR

shock·er /shókər/ *n. colloq.* **1** a shocking person or thing. **2** *hist.* a sordid or sensational novel, etc.

shock·ing /shóking/ *adj. & adv.* ● *adj.* causing indignation or disgust. ● *adv. colloq.* shockingly (*shocking bad manners*). □□ **shock·ing·ly** *adv.* **shock·ing·ness** *n.*

shock·ing pink *n.* a vibrant shade of pink.

shock·proof /shók-prōōf/ *adj.* resistant to the effects of (esp. physical) shock.

shock ther·a·py *n.* (also **shock treat·ment**) *Psychol.* a method of treating depressive patients by means of electric shock or drugs inducing coma and convulsions.

shock troops *n.pl.* troops specially trained for assault.

shock wave *n.* ▼ a sharp change of pressure in a narrow region traveling through air, etc., caused by explosion or by a body moving faster than sound.

upper mount (chassis attachment)
outer tube
fluid reservoir
piston rod
small chamber
hydraulic cylinder
piston
spring
securing nut
large chamber
inner tube
control valve
spring
lower mount

SHOCK ABSORBER:
CUTAWAY VIEW OF A CAR'S
SHOCK ABSORBER

shock wave
plane flying faster than its sound waves
sound waves
shock wave

SHOCK WAVE PRODUCED BY A
SUPERSONIC AIRCRAFT

shod *past* and *past part.* of SHOE.

shod·dy /shódee/ *adj. & n.* ● *adj.* (**shoddier, shoddiest**) **1** poorly made. **2** counterfeit. ● *n.* (*pl.* **-ies**) **1 a** an inferior cloth made partly from the shredded fiber of old woolen cloth. **b** such fiber. **2** any thing of shoddy quality. □□ **shod·di·ly** *adv.* **shod·di·ness** *n.*

shoe /shōō/ *n. & v.* ● *n.* **1** ▼ either of a pair of protective foot coverings of leather, plastic, etc., having a sturdy sole and not reaching above the ankle. **2** a metal rim nailed to the hoof of a horse, etc. **3** anything resembling a shoe in shape or use, esp.: **a** a drag for a wheel. **b** = BRAKE SHOE. **c** a socket. ● *v.tr.* (**shoes, shoeing**; *past* and *past part.* **shod** /shod/) **1** fit (esp. a horse, etc.) with a shoe or shoes. **2** (as **shod** *adj.*) (in *comb.*) having shoes, etc., of a specified kind (*dry-shod; roughshod*). □ **be in a person's shoes** be in his or her situation, difficulty, etc. □□ **shoe·less** *adj.*

SHOE: CROSS
SECTION OF A
LEATHER SHOE

tongue
heel grip
cuff
vamp
wing cap
insole
welt
bottom filler
outsole
lining
steel shank
heel
seat lift

shoe·bill /shōōbil/ *n.* an African storklike bird, *Balaeniceps rex*, with a large flattened bill for catching aquatic prey.

shoe·black /shōōblak/ *n. esp. Brit.* = BOOTBLACK.

shoe·box /shōōboks/ *n.* **1** a box for packing shoes. **2** a very small space.

shoe·horn /shōōhawrn/ *n.* a curved piece of horn, metal, etc., for easing the heel into a shoe.

shoe·lace /shōōlays/ *n.* a cord for lacing up shoes.

shoe·mak·er /shōōmaykər/ *n.* a maker of boots and shoes. □□ **shoe·mak·ing** *n.*

shoe·shine /shōōshīn/ *n.* a polish given to shoes.

shoe·string /shōōstring/ *n.* **1** a shoelace. **2** *colloq.* a small esp. inadequate amount of money (*living on a shoestring*). **3** (*attrib.*) barely adequate.

shoe tree *n.* a shaped block for keeping a shoe in shape.

sho·far /shōfər, shawfar/ *n.* (*pl.* **shofroth** /shṓfrōt/) a ram's-horn trumpet used by Jews in religious ceremonies and as an ancient battle signal.

sho·gun /shṓgən, -gun/ *n. hist.* any of a succession of Japanese hereditary commanders in chief and virtual rulers before 1868. □□ **sho·gun·ate** /-nət, -nayt/ *n.*

shone *past* and *past part.* of SHINE.

shoo /shōō/ *int. & v.* ● *int.* an exclamation used to frighten away birds, children, etc. ● *v.* (**shoos, shooed**) *tr.* (usu. foll. by *away*) drive (birds, etc.) away by saying "shoo!"

shoo-in *n.* something easy or certain to succeed (*she's a shoo-in to win the election*).

shook[1] /shŏŏk/ *past* of SHAKE. *predic.adj. colloq.* (foll. by *up*) emotionally or physically disturbed.

shook[2] /shŏŏk/ *n.* a set of staves and headings for a cask, ready for fitting together.

shoot /shōōt/ *v., n., & int.* ● *v.* (*past* and *past part.* **shot** /shot/) *tr.* **1 a** cause (a gun, bow, etc.) to fire. **b** discharge (a bullet, arrow, etc.) from a gun, bow, etc. **c** kill or wound with a bullet, arrow, etc., from a gun, bow, etc. **2** *intr.* discharge a gun, etc. (*shoots well*). **3** *tr.* send out, discharge, propel, etc., esp. swiftly (*shot out the contents; shot a glance at his neighbor*). **4** *intr.* come or go swiftly or vigorously. **5** *intr.* **a** (of a plant, etc.) put forth buds, etc. **b** (of a bud, etc.) appear. **6** *intr.* hunt game, etc., with a gun. **7** *tr.* film or photograph. **8** *tr.* (also *absol.*) Basketball, etc. **a** score (a goal). **b** take a shot at (the goal). **9** *tr.* (of a boat) sweep swiftly down or under (a bridge, rapids, falls, etc.). **10** *tr.* move (a door bolt) to fasten or unfasten a door, etc. **11** *tr.* (often foll. by *up*) *sl.* inject esp. oneself with (a drug). **12** *tr. colloq.* **a** play

a game of (craps, pool, etc.). **b** throw (a die or dice). **13** *tr. Golf colloq.* make (a specified score) for a round or hole. **14** *tr. colloq.* pass (traffic lights at red). ● *n.* **1** the act of shooting. **2 a** a young branch or sucker. **b** the new growth of a plant. **3** = CHUTE[1]. ● *int. colloq. euphem.* an exclamation of disgust, anger, etc. (see SHIT). □ **shoot ahead** come quickly to the front of competitors, etc. **shoot down 1** kill by shooting. **2** cause (an aircraft, its pilot, etc.) to crash by shooting. **3** argue effectively against. **shoot it out** *sl.* engage in a decisive gun battle. **shoot one's mouth off** *sl.* talk too much or indiscreetly. **shoot up 1** grow rapidly. **2** rise suddenly. **3** terrorize (a district) by indiscriminate shooting. □□ **shoot·a·ble** *adj.*

shoot·er /shōōtər/ *n.* **1** a person or thing that shoots. **2 a** (in *comb.*) a gun or other device for shooting (*peashooter; six-shooter*). **b** *sl.* a pistol, gun. **3** a player who shoots or is able to shoot a goal in basketball, etc.

shoot·ing /shōōting/ *n. & v.* ● *n.* **1** the act of shooting. **2 a** the right of shooting over an area of land. **b** an estate, etc., rented to shoot over. ● *adj.* moving, growing, etc., quickly.

shoot·ing gal·ler·y *n.* a place used for shooting at targets with rifles, etc.

shoot·ing range *n.* a ground with butts for rifle practice.

shoot·ing star *n.* a small meteor moving rapidly and burning up on entering the Earth's atmosphere.

shoo·tist /shōōtist/ *n. N. Amer. colloq.* a person who shoots, esp. a marksman.

shoot-out *n. colloq.* a decisive gun battle.

shop /shop/ *n. & v.* ● *n.* **1** a building, room, etc., for the retail sale of goods or services (*dress shop; beauty shop*). **2** a place in which manufacture or repairing is done (*metal shop*). **3** a profession, trade, business, etc., esp. as a subject of conversation (*talk shop*). **4** *colloq.* the place where one works. ● *v.* (**shopped, shopping**) *intr.* go to a shop or shops to buy goods. □ **set up shop** establish oneself in business, etc. **shop around** look for the best bargain.

shop·keep·er /shópkeepər/ *n.* the owner and manager of a store. □□ **shop·keep·ing** *n.*

shop·lift·er /shópliftər/ *n.* a person who steals goods while appearing to shop. □□ **shop·lift** *v.tr. & intr.* **shop·lift·ing** *n.*

shop·per /shópər/ *n.* a person who makes purchases in a store.

shop·ping /shóping/ *n.* **1** (often *attrib.*) the purchase of goods, etc. (*shopping expedition*). **2** goods purchased (*put the shopping on the table*).

shop·ping cen·ter *n.* an area or complex of stores.

shop stew·ard *n.* a person elected by workers in a factory, etc., to represent them in dealings with management.

shop·worn /shópwawrn/ *adj.* **1** faded by display in a shop. **2** (of an idea, etc.) no longer fresh or new.

shor·an /sháwran/ *n.* a system of aircraft navigation using the return of two radar signals by two ground stations (acronym of *short-range navigation*).

shore[1] /shawr/ *n.* **1** the land that adjoins the sea or a large body of water. **2** (usu. in *pl.*) a country; a seacoast (*often visits these shores*). □□ **shore·less** *adj.* **shore·ward** *adj.* **shore·wards** *adv.*

shore[2] /shawr/ *v. & n.* ● *v.tr.* support with or as if with a shore or shores. ● *n.* a prop or beam set against a ship, wall, tree, etc., as a support. □□ **shor·ing** *n.*

shore[3] see SHEAR.

shore leave *n. Naut.* **1** permission to go ashore. **2** a period of time ashore.

shore·line /sháwrlīn/ *n.* the line along which a stretch of water meets the shore.

S

shore·weed /sháwrweed/ *n.* a stoloniferous plant, *Littorella uniflora*, growing in shallow water.

shorn *past part.* of SHEAR.

short /shawrt/ *adj.*, *adv.*, *n.*, & *v.* ● *adj.* **1 a** measuring little; not long from end to end (*a short distance*). **b** not long in duration (*a short time ago*). **c** seeming less than the stated amount (*a few short years of happiness*). **2** not tall (*a short square tower*). **3 a** (usu. foll. by *of*, *on*) having a partial or total lack; deficient (*short of spoons*; *short on sense*). **b** not far-reaching; acting or being near at hand (*within short range*). **4 a** concise; brief (*kept his speech short*). **b** curt; uncivil (*was short with her*). **5** (of the memory) unable to remember distant events. **6** *Phonet.* & *Prosody* of a vowel or syllable: **a** having the lesser of the two recognized durations. **b** (of a vowel) having a sound other than that called long (cf. LONG[1] *adj.* 8). **7** (of pastry) crumbling. **8** esp. *Stock Exch.* (of stocks, a stockbroker, crops, etc.) sold or selling when the amount is not in hand, with reliance on getting the deficit in time for delivery. ● *adv.* **1** before the natural or expected time or place (*pulled up short*; *cut short the celebrations*). **2** rudely (*spoke to him short*). ● *n.* **1** a short circuit. **2** a short movie. **3** *Stock Exch.* **a** a person who sells short. **b** (in *pl.*) short-dated stocks. ● *v.tr.* & *intr.* short-circuit. □ **be caught short** be put at a disadvantage. **bring up** (or **pull up**) **short** check or pause abruptly. **come short of** fail to reach or amount to. **for short** as a short name (*Tom for short*). **get** (or **have**) **by the short hairs** *colloq.* be in complete control of (a person). **in short order** immediately. **in the short run** over a short period of time. **in short supply** scarce. **in the short term = in the short run**. **make short work of** accomplish, dispose of, destroy, etc., quickly. **short and sweet** esp. *iron.* brief and pleasant. **short for** an abbreviation for (*"Bob" is short for "Robert"*). **short of 1** see sense 3a of *adj.* **2** less than (*nothing short of a miracle*). **3** distant from (*two miles short of home*). **4** except (*did everything short of destroying it*). **short of breath** panting, short-winded. **short on** *colloq.* see sense 3a of *adj.* □□ **short·ish** *adj.* **short·ness** *n.*

short·age /sháwrtij/ *n.* (often foll. by *of*) a deficiency; an amount lacking.

short·bread /sháwrtbred/ *n.* a crisp, rich, crumbly type of cookie made with butter, flour, and sugar.

short·cake /sháwrtkayk/ *n.* **1** = SHORTBREAD. **2** a cake made of short pastry and filled with fruit and cream.

short·change /sháwrtcháynj/ *v.tr.* cheat by giving insufficient money as change.

short cir·cuit *n.* an electric circuit through small resistance, esp. instead of the resistance of a normal circuit. □□ **short-cir·cuit** *v.*

short·com·ing /sháwrtkuming/ *n.* failure to come up to a standard; a defect.

short cut *n.* **1** a route shortening the distance traveled. **2** a quick way of accomplishing something.

short·en /sháwrt'n/ *v.* **1** *intr.* & *tr.* become or make shorter or short. **2** *tr. Naut.* reduce the amount of (sail spread).

short end of the stick *n.* the less or least favorable of the lot (*his younger brother always got the short end of the stick*).

short·en·ing /sháwrt'ning, sháwrtning/ *n.* fat used for making pastry, etc.

short·fall /sháwrtfawl/ *n.* a deficit below what was expected.

short fuse *n. colloq.* a quick temper.

short·hand /sháwrt-hand/ *n.* (often *attrib.*) a method of rapid writing in abbreviations and symbols. **2** an abbreviated or symbolic mode of expression.

short·hand·ed /shawrt-hánded/ *adj.* undermanned or understaffed.

short haul *n.* **1** the transport of goods over a short distance. **2** a short-term effort.

short·horn /sháwrt-horn/ *n.* an animal of a breed of cattle with short horns.

short·list /sháwrtlist/ *n.* a selective list of candidates from which a final choice is made. □□ **short·list** *v.tr.*

short-lived *adj.* ephemeral.

short·ly /sháwrtlee/ *adv.* **1** (often foll. by *before*, *after*) before long; soon (*will arrive shortly*; *arrived shortly after him*). **2** in a few words; briefly. **3** curtly.

short-or·der *adj.* **a** prepared quickly, esp. simple restaurant fare. **b** pertaining to one who provides this (*a short-order cook*).

short-range *adj.* **1** having a short range. **2** relating to a fairly immediate future time (*short-range possibilities*).

shorts /shawrts/ *n.pl.* **1** pants reaching to the knees or higher. **2** underpants.

short shrift *n.* curt treatment.

short·sight·ed /sháwrtsítid/ *adj.* **1** esp. *Brit.* = NEARSIGHTED. ▷ SIGHT. **2** lacking imagination or foresight. □□ **short·sight·ed·ly** *adv.* **short·sight·ed·ness** *n.*

short-sleeved *adj.* with sleeves not reaching below the elbow.

short·stop /sháwrtstop/ *n.* a baseball fielder between second and third base. ▷ BASEBALL

short sto·ry *n.* a story with a fully developed theme but shorter than a novel.

short tem·per *n.* self-control soon or easily lost. □□ **short-tem·pered** *adj.*

short-term *adj.* occurring in or relating to a short period of time.

short ton *n.* see TON.

short·wave /sháwrtwáyv/ *n.* a radio wave of frequency greater than 3 MHz.

short-wind·ed *adj.* **1** quickly exhausted of breath. **2** incapable of sustained effort.

short·y /sháwrtee/ *n.* (also **short·ie**) (*pl.* **-ies**) *colloq.* **1** a person shorter than average. **2** a short garment.

Sho·sho·ne /shəshṓn, -shṓnee/ *n.* (also **Sho·sho·ni**) **1 a** a N. American people native to the western US. **b** a member of this people. **2** the language of this people. □□ **Sho·sho·ne·an** *adj.*

shot[1] /shot/ *n.* **1** the act of firing a gun, etc. **2** an attempt to hit by shooting or throwing, etc (*took a shot at him*). **3 a** a single nonexplosive missile for a gun, etc. **b** (*pl.* same or **shots**) a small lead pellet used in quantity in a single charge or cartridge in a shotgun. ▷ SHOTGUN. **c** (as *pl.*) these collectively. **4 a** a photograph. **b** a film sequence photographed continuously by one camera. **5 a** a stroke or kick in a ball game. **b** *colloq.* an attempt to guess or do something (*let her have a shot at it*). **6** *colloq.* a person having a specified skill with a gun, etc. (*is not a good shot*). **7** a heavy ball thrown by a shot-putter. ▷ SHOT PUT. **8** the launch of a space rocket. **9** the range, reach, or distance to or at which a thing will carry or act. **10** a remark aimed at a person. **11** *colloq.* **a** a drink of esp. liquor. **b** an injection of a drug, vaccine, etc. □ **like a shot** *colloq.* without hesitation; willingly. **shot in the arm** *colloq.* stimulus or encouragement. **shot in the dark** a mere guess.

shot[2] /shot/ *past* and *past part.* of SHOOT. *adj.* **1** (of colored material) woven so as to show different colors at different angles. **2** *colloq.* **a** exhausted; finished. **b** drunk. □ **shot through** permeated or suffused.

shot·gun /shótgun/ *n.* ▼ a smoothbore gun for firing small shot at short range.

shot·gun mar·riage *n.* (also **shot·gun wed·ding**) *colloq.* an enforced or hurried wedding, esp. because of the bride's pregnancy.

shot put *n.* ▼ an athletic contest in which a shot is thrown. □□ **shot-put·ter** *n.*

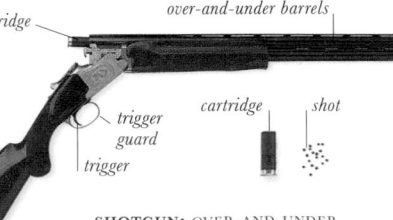

SHOT PUT: ATHLETE HEAVING A SHOT

should /shood/ *v.aux.* (*3rd sing.* **should**) *past* of SHALL, used esp.: **1** in reported speech, esp. with the reported element in the 1st person (*I said I should be home by evening*). ¶ Cf. WOULD. **2 a** to express a duty, obligation, or likelihood (*I should tell you*; *you should have been more careful*). **b** (in the 1st person) to express a tentative suggestion (*I should like to say something*). **3 a** expressing the conditional mood in the 1st person (cf. WOULD) (*I should have been killed if I had gone*). **b** forming a conditional protasis clause (*if you should see him*; *should they arrive, tell them where to go*). **4** expressing purpose (*in order that we should not worry*).

shoul·der /shṓldər/ *n.* & *v.* ● *n.* **1 a** the part of the body at which the arm, foreleg, or wing is attached. ▷ JOINT. **b** (in full **shoulder joint**) the end of the upper arm joining with the clavicle and scapula. **c** either of the two projections below the neck from which the arms hang. **2** the upper foreleg and shoulder blade of a pig, lamb, etc., when butchered. **3** (often in *pl.*) **a** the upper part of the back and arms. **b** this part of the body regarded as capable of bearing a burden or blame, providing comfort, etc. (*needs a shoulder to cry on*). **4** a strip of land next to a paved road. **5** a part of a garment covering the shoulder. **6** a part of anything resembling a shoulder in form or function, as in a bottle, mountain, tool, etc. ● *v.* **1 a** *tr.* push with the shoulder; jostle. **b** *intr.* make one's way by jostling (*shouldered through the crowd*). **2** *tr.* take (a burden, etc.) on one's shoulders (*shouldered the family's problems*). □ **put** (or **set**) **one's shoulder to the wheel** make an effort. **shoulder arms** hold a rifle with the barrel against the shoulder and the butt in the hand. **shoulder to shoulder 1** side by side. **2** with closed ranks or united effort. □□ **shoul·dered** *adj.* (also in *comb.*).

shoul·der blade *n. Anat.* either of the large flat bones of the upper back.

shouldn't /shood'nt/ *contr.* should not.

shout /showt/ *v.* & *n.* ● *v.* **1** *intr.* make a loud cry or vocal sound (*shouted for attention*). **2** *tr.* say or express loudly (*shouted that the coast was clear*). ● *n.* a loud cry expressing joy, etc., or calling attention. □ **all over but the shouting** *colloq.* the contest is virtually decided. **shout at** speak loudly to, etc. **shout down** reduce to silence by shouting. **shout for** call for by shouting. □□ **shout·er** *n.*

shove /shuv/ *v.* & *n.* ● *v.* **1** *tr.* (also *absol.*) push vigorously (*shoved him out of the way*). **2** *intr.* (usu. foll. by *along*, *past*, *through*, etc.) make one's way by pushing (*shoved through the crowd*). **3** *tr. colloq.* put somewhere (*shoved it in the drawer*). ● *n.* an act of shoving or of prompting a person into action. □ **shove off 1** start from the shore in a boat. **2** *sl.* depart; go away.

shov·el /shúvəl/ *n.* & *v.* ● *n.* **1 a** a spadelike tool for shifting quantities of coal, earth, etc., esp. having the sides curved upward. **b** the amount contained in a shovel. **2** a machine or part of a machine

over-and-under barrels

cartridge

cartridge   *shot*

trigger guard

trigger

stock

SHOTGUN: OVER-AND-UNDER SHOTGUN AND CARTRIDGE

S

having a similar form or function. ● *v.tr.* **1** shift or clear (coal, etc.) with or as if with a shovel. **2** *colloq.* move in large quantities or roughly (*shoveled peas into his mouth*). □□ **shov·el·ful** *n.* (*pl.* **-fuls**).

shov·el·er /shúvələr, shúvlər/ *n.* **1** a person or thing that shovels. **2** ▼ a duck, *Anas clypeata*, with a broad shovellike beak. ▷ DUCK

SHOVELER: NORTHERN SHOVELER
(*Anas clypeata*)

shov·el·head /shúvəlhed/ *n.* a shark, *Sphyrna tiburo*, like the hammerhead but smaller. Also called **bonnethead**.

show /shō/ *v. & n.* ● *v.* (*past part.* **shown** /shōn/ or **showed**) **1** *intr. & tr.* be, or allow or cause to be, visible (*the buds are beginning to show; white shows the dirt*). **2** *tr.* offer, exhibit, or produce (a thing) for scrutiny, etc. (*show your tickets please*). **3** *tr.* indicate (one's feelings) by one's behavior, etc. (*showed mercy to him*). **4** *intr.* (of feelings, etc.) be manifest (*his dislike shows*). **5** *tr.* **a** point out; prove (*has shown it to be false; showed that he knew the answer*). **b** (usu. foll. by *how to* + *infin.*) cause (a person) to understand or be capable of doing (*showed them how to knit*). **6** *tr.* (*refl.*) exhibit oneself as being (*showed herself to be fair*). **7** *tr. & intr.* (with ref. to a movie) be presented or cause to be presented. **8** *tr.* exhibit in a show. **9** *tr.* conduct or lead (*showed them to their rooms*). **10** *intr.* = SHOW UP 3

(*waited but he didn't show*). ● *n.* **1** the act of showing. **2 a** a spectacle, display, exhibition, etc. (*a fine show of blossom*). **b** a collection of things, etc., shown for public entertainment or in competition (*dog show; flower show*). **3 a** a play, etc., esp. a musical. **b** an entertainment program on television, etc. **c** any public entertainment or performance. **4 a** an outward appearance or display (*a show of strength*). **b** empty appearance; mere display (*did it for show; that's all show*). **5** esp. *Brit. colloq.* an opportunity of acting, defending oneself, etc. (*made a good show of it*). **6** *Med.* a discharge of blood, etc., from the vagina at the onset of childbirth. □ **give the show** (or **whole show**) **away** demonstrate the inadequacies or reveal the truth. **good** (or **bad** or **poor**) **show**! esp. *Brit. colloq.* **1** that was well (or badly) done. **2** that was lucky (or unlucky). **nothing to show for** no visible result of (effort, etc.). **on show** being exhibited. **show oneself** be seen in public. **show one's cards** = **show one's hand**. **show a clean pair of heels** *colloq.* retreat speedily; run away. **show one's colors** make one's opinion clear. **show a person the door** dismiss or eject a person. **show one's face** make an appearance. **show fight** be persistent or belligerent. **show forth** *archaic* exhibit; expound. **show one's hand 1** disclose one's plans. **2** reveal one's cards. **show a leg** *Brit. colloq.* get out of bed. **show off 1** display to advantage. **2** *colloq.* act pretentiously; display one's wealth, knowledge, etc. **show around** take (a person) to places of interest. **show one's teeth** esp. *Brit.* reveal one's strength. **show through 1** be visible although supposedly concealed. **2** (of real feelings, etc.) be revealed inadvertently. **show up 1** make or be conspicuous or clearly visible. **2** expose (a fraud, impostor, inferiority, etc.). **3** *colloq.* appear; arrive. **4** *colloq.* embarrass or humiliate (*don't show me up*

by wearing jeans). **show the way 1** indicate what has to be done, etc., by attempting it first. **2** show others which way to go, etc. **show willing** esp. *Brit.* display a willingness to help, etc.

show·biz /shóbiz/ *n. colloq.* = SHOW BUSINESS.

show·boat /shóbōt/ *n.* a river steamer on which theatrical performances are given.

show busi·ness *n. colloq.* the theatrical profession.

show·case /shókays/ *n. & v.* ● *n.* **1** a glass case used for exhibiting goods, etc. **2** a place or medium for presenting to general attention. ● *v.tr.* display in or as if in a showcase.

show·down /shódown/ *n.* **1** a final test or confrontation; a decisive situation. **2** the laying down face up of the players' cards in poker.

show·er /showr/ *n. & v.* ● *n.* **1** a brief fall of rain, hail, sleet, or snow. **2 a** a brisk flurry of arrows, bullets, dust, sparks, etc. **b** a flurry of gifts, praise, etc. **3** (in full **shower bath**) **a** a cubicle, bath, etc. in which one stands under a spray of water. **b** the apparatus, etc., used for this. **c** the act of bathing in a shower. **4** a party for giving presents to a prospective bride, etc. ● *v.* **1** *tr.* discharge (water, missiles, etc.) in a shower. **2** *intr.* use a shower bath. **3** *tr.* (usu. foll. by *on, upon*) lavishly bestow (gifts, etc.). **4** *intr.* descend in a shower (*it showered on and off all day*). □□ **show·er·y** *adj.*

show·er·proof /shówrproof/ *adj. & v.* ● *adj.* resistant to light rain. ● *v.tr.* render showerproof.

show·girl /shógərl/ *n.* an actress who sings and dances in musicals, etc.

show·ing /shóing/ *n.* **1** the act or an instance of showing. **2** a usu. specified quality of performance (*a poor showing*). **3** the presentation of a case.

show jump·ing *n.* ▼ the sport of riding horses over a course of fences and other obstacles, with penalty points for errors.

SHOW JUMPING

Although equestrian events were recorded at the Olympic Games of 642 BC, the first show-jumping contests were not staged until the early 1900s. A horse and rider in a show-jumping competition must negotiate a set course that includes fences and water hazards. Faults are incurred when the horse or rider falls, when a jump is refused, or when an obstacle is knocked down. Jumping fences in the wrong order results in elimination. Depending on the type of competition, the winning horse and rider have either the fewest faults or the quickest time. Most fences consist of planks or poles supported by wooden stands called standards or wings. To prevent injury, parts of these fences collapse on impact.

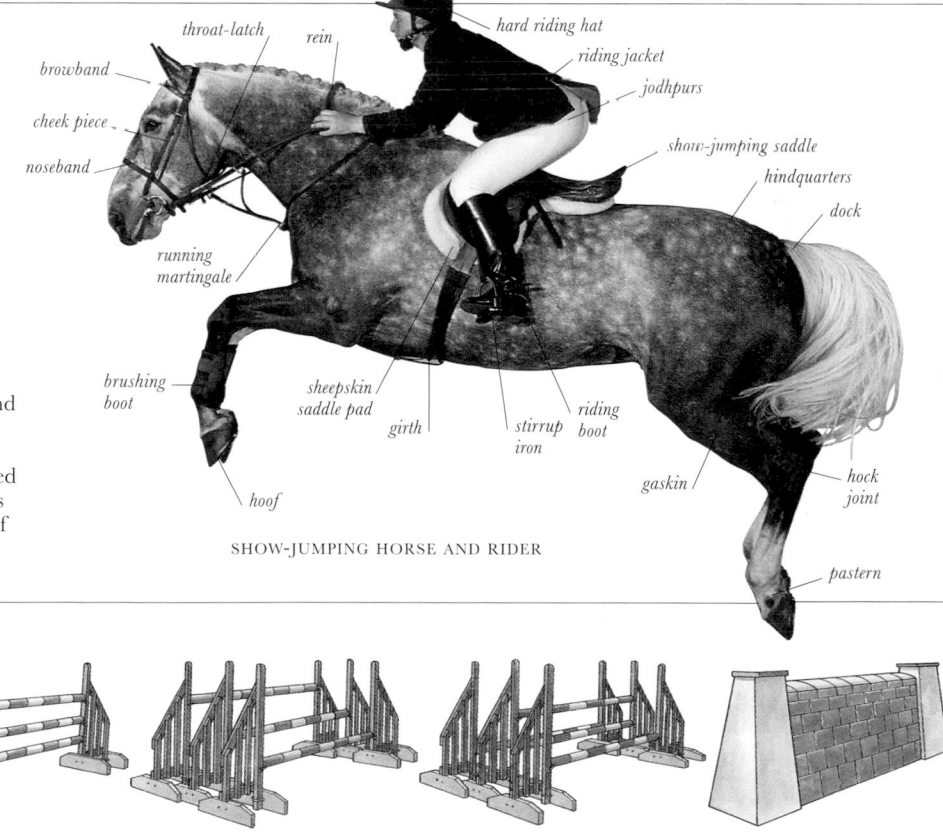

throat-latch · rein · hard riding hat · browband · riding jacket · jodhpurs · cheek piece · noseband · show-jumping saddle · hindquarters · dock · running martingale · brushing boot · sheepskin saddle pad · girth · stirrup iron · riding boot · gaskin · hock joint · hoof · pastern

SHOW-JUMPING HORSE AND RIDER

SHOW-JUMPING FENCES

UPRIGHT PLANKS   UPRIGHT POLES   TRIPLE BAR (STAIRCASE)   HOG'S-BACK   WALL

S

show·man /shṓmən/ *n.* (*pl.* **-men**) **1** the proprietor or manager of a circus, etc. **2** a person skilled in self-advertisement or publicity. □□ **show·man·ship** *n.*

show-off *n. colloq.* a person who shows off.

show of force *n.* proof that one is prepared to use force.

show of hands *n.* raised hands indicating a vote for or against.

shown *past part.* of SHOW.

show·piece /shṓpees/ *n.* **1** an item of work presented for exhibition or display. **2** an outstanding example or specimen.

show·place /shṓplays/ *n.* a house, etc., that tourists go to see.

show·room /shṓroom, -rŏŏm/ *n.* a room in a factory, office building, etc., used to display goods for sale.

show·stop·per /shṓstopər/ *n. colloq.* an act receiving prolonged applause.

show·y /shṓee/ *adj.* (**showier**, **showiest**) **1** brilliant; gaudy, esp. vulgarly so. **2** striking. □□ **show·i·ly** *adv.* **show·i·ness** *n.*

shrank *past* of SHRINK.

shrap·nel /shrápnəl/ *n.* **1** fragments of a bomb, etc., thrown out by an explosion. **2** a shell containing pieces of metal timed to burst short of impact.

shred /shred/ *n. & v.* ● *n.* **1** a scrap, fragment, or strip. **2** the least amount; remnant (*not a shred of evidence*). ● *v.tr.* (**shredded**, **shredding**) tear or cut into shreds. □ **tear to shreds** completely refute (an argument, etc.).

shred·der /shrédər/ *n.* **1** a machine used to reduce documents to shreds. **2** any device used for shredding.

shrew /shroo/ *n.* **1** ▼ any small, usu. insect-eating, mouselike mammal of the family Soricidae, with a long pointed snout. **2** a bad-tempered or scolding woman. □□ **shrew·ish** *adj.* (in sense 2). **shrew·ish·ly** *adv.* **shrew·ish·ness** *n.*

SHREW: COMMON SHREW
(*Sorex araneus*)

shrewd /shrood/ *adj.* **1** showing astute powers of judgment; clever and judicious. **2** (of a face, etc.) shrewd-looking. □□ **shrewd·ly** *adv.* **shrewd·ness** *n.*

shriek /shreek/ *v. & n.* ● *v.* **1** *intr.* **a** utter a shrill screeching sound or words. **b** (foll. by *of*) provide a clear or blatant indication of. **2** *tr.* **a** utter by shrieking (*shrieked his name*). **b** indicate clearly or blatantly. ● *n.* a high-pitched piercing cry or sound. □ **shriek out** say in shrill tones. **shriek with laughter** laugh uncontrollably. □□ **shriek·er** *n.*

shriev·al /shréevəl/ *adj.* of or relating to a sheriff.

shriev·al·ty /shréevəltee/ *n.* (*pl.* **-ies**) **1** a sheriff's office or jurisdiction. **2** the tenure of this.

shrift /shrift/ *n. archaic* **1** confession to a priest. **2** confession and absolution. □ **short shrift 1** curt treatment. **2** *archaic* little time between condemnation and execution or punishment.

shrike /shrīk/ *n.* any bird of the family Laniidae that impales its prey of small birds and insects on thorns.

shrill /shril/ *adj. & v.* ● *adj.* **1** piercing and high-pitched in sound. **2** *derog.* (esp. of a protester) sharp; unrestrained; unreasoning. ● *v.* **1** *intr.* (of a cry, etc.)

sound shrilly. **2** *tr.* (of a person, etc.) utter (a song, complaint, etc.) shrilly. □□ **shril·ly** *adv.* **shrill·ness** *n.*

shrimp /shrimp/ *n. & v.* ● *n.* **1** (*pl.* same or **shrimps**) ▼ any of various small (esp. marine) edible crustaceans, with ten legs, gray-green when alive and pink when cooked. **2** *colloq.* a very small slight person. ● *v.intr.* go catching shrimps. □□ **shrimp·er** *n.*

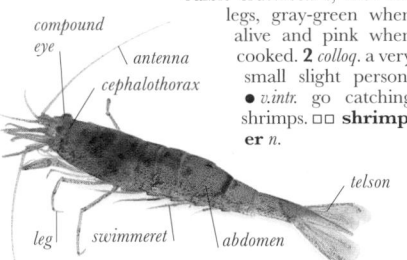

compound eye — *antenna*

cephalothorax

telson

leg — *swimmeret* — *abdomen*

SHRIMP: COMMON SHRIMP
(*Crangon crangon*)

shrine /shrīn/ *n. & v.* ● *n.* **1** esp. *RC Ch.* **a** a chapel, altar, etc., sacred to a saint, relic, etc. **b** the tomb of a saint, etc. **c** a casket, esp. containing sacred relics; a reliquary. **d** a niche containing a holy statue, etc. **2** a place associated with or containing memorabilia of a particular person, event, etc. **3** ▼ a Shinto place of worship. ● *v.tr. poet.* enshrine.

SHRINE: 19TH-CENTURY SHINTO
SHRINE, JAPAN

shrink /shringk/ *v. & n.* ● *v.* (*past* **shrank** /shrangk/; *past part.* **shrunk** /shrungk/ or (esp. as *adj.*) **shrunken** /shrúngkən/) **1** *tr. & intr.* make or become smaller; contract, esp. by the action of moisture, heat, or cold. **2** *intr.* (usu. foll. by *from*) **a** retire; recoil; flinch; cower (*shrank from her touch*). **b** be averse from doing (*shrinks from meeting them*). **3** (as **shrunken** *adj.*) (esp. of a person, etc.) having grown smaller esp. because of age, illness, etc. ● *n.* **1** the act of shrinking. **2** *sl.* a psychiatrist. □ **shrink into oneself** become withdrawn. □□ **shrink·a·ble** *adj.* **shrink·er** *n.* **shrink·ing·ly** *adv.* **shrink·proof** *adj.*

shrink·age /shríngkij/ *n.* **1 a** the process of shrinking. **b** the degree of shrinking. **2** an allowance made for the reduction in takings due to wastage, etc.

shrink·ing vi·o·let *n.* an exaggeratedly shy person.

shrink-re·sis·tant *adj.* (of textiles, etc.) resistant to shrinkage when wet, etc.

shrink-wrap *v. & n.* ● *v.tr.* (**-wrapped**, **-wrapping**) enclose (an article) in (esp. transparent) film that shrinks tightly on to it. ● *n.* plastic film used to shrink-wrap.

shrive /shrīv/ *v.tr.* (*past* **shrove** /shrōv/; *past part.* **shriven** /shrívən/) *Eccl. archaic* **1** (of a priest) hear the confession of, assign penance to, and absolve. **2** (*refl.*) (of a penitent) submit oneself to a priest for confession, etc.

shriv·el /shrívəl/ *v.tr. & intr.* wither into a wrinkled or dried-up state.

shriv·en *past part.* of SHRIVE.

shroud /shrowd/ *n. & v.* ● *n.* **1** a sheetlike garment for wrapping a corpse for burial. **2** anything that conceals like a shroud (*a shroud of mystery*). **3** (in *pl.*) *Naut.* a set of ropes supporting the mast or topmast. ▷ DINGHY, RIGGING. ● *v.tr.* **1** clothe (a body) for burial. **2** cover, conceal, or disguise (*shrouded in mist*). □□ **shroud·less** *adj.*

shrove *past* of SHRIVE.

Shrove·tide /shrṓvtīd/ *n.* Shrove Tuesday and the two days preceding it when it was formerly customary to be shriven.

Shrove Tues·day /shrōv/ *n.* the day before Ash Wednesday.

shrub[1] /shrub/ *n.* a woody plant smaller than a tree and having a very short stem with branches near the ground. □□ **shrub·by** *adj.*

shrub[2] /shrub/ *n.* a cordial made of sweetened fruit juice and spirits, esp. rum.

shrub·ber·y /shrúbəree/ *n.* (*pl.* **-ies**) an area planted with shrubs.

shrug /shrug/ *v. & n.* ● *v.* (**shrugged**, **shrugging**) **1** *intr.* slightly and momentarily raise the shoulders to express indifference, helplessness, etc. **2** *tr.* **a** raise (the shoulders) in this way. **b** shrug the shoulders to express (indifference, etc.). ● *n.* the act of shrugging. □ **shrug off** dismiss as unimportant, etc., by or as if by shrugging.

shrunk (also **shrunk·en**) *past part.* of SHRINK.

shtick /shtik/ *n. sl.* a theatrical routine, gimmick, etc.

shuck /shuk/ *n. & v.* ● *n.* **1** a husk or pod. **2** the shell of an oyster or clam. **3** (in *pl.*) *colloq.* an expression of contempt or self-deprecation in response to praise. ● *v.tr.* **1** remove the shucks of. **2** remove (*shucked his coat*). □□ **shuck·er** *n.*

shud·der /shúdər/ *v. & n.* ● *v.intr.* **1** shiver esp. convulsively from fear, cold, repugnance, etc. **2** feel strong repugnance, etc. (*shudder to think*). **3** (of a machine, etc.) vibrate or quiver. ● *n.* **1** the act or an instance of shuddering. **2** (in *pl.*; prec. by *the*) *colloq.* a state of shuddering. □□ **shud·der·ing·ly** *adv.* **shud·der·y** *adj.*

shuf·fle /shúfəl/ *v. & n.* ● *v.* **1** *tr. & intr.* move with a scraping, sliding, or dragging motion. **2** *tr.* **a** (also *absol.*) rearrange (a deck of cards) by sliding them over each other quickly. **b** rearrange; intermingle (*shuffled the documents*). **3** *tr.* (usu. foll. by *on*, *off*, *into*) assume or remove esp. clumsily or evasively (*shuffled on his clothes*; *shuffled off responsibility*). **4** *intr.* **a** equivocate; prevaricate. **b** continually shift one's position. ● *n.* **1** a shuffling movement. **2** the act of shuffling cards. **3** a change of relative positions. **4** a quick alternation of the position of the feet in dancing. □□ **shuf·fler** *n.*

shuf·fle·board /shúfəlbawrd/ *n.* a game played by pushing disks with the hand or esp. with a long-handled cue over a marked surface.

shun /shun/ *v.tr.* (**shunned**, **shunning**) avoid (*shuns human company*).

shunt /shunt/ *v. & n.* ● *v.* **1** *intr. & tr.* diverge or cause (a train) to be diverted onto a siding. **2** divert (a decision, etc.) on to another person, etc. ● *n.* **1** the act of shunting on to a siding. **2** *Electr.* a conductor joining two points of a circuit, through which more or less of a current may be diverted. □□ **shunt·er** *n.*

shush /shŏŏsh, shush/ *int. & v.* ● *int.* = HUSH *int.* ● *v.* **1** *intr.* **a** call for silence by saying *shush.* **b** be silent (*they shushed at once*). **2** *tr.* make or attempt to make silent.

shut /shut/ *v.* (**shutting**; *past* and *past part.* **shut**) **1** *tr.* **a** move (a door, lid, lips, etc.) into position so as to block an aperture. **b** close or seal (a room, window, box, etc.) by moving a door, etc. (*shut the box*). **2** *intr.* become or be capable of being closed or sealed (*the door shut with a bang*). **3** *intr. & tr.* esp. *Brit.* become or make (a store, etc.) closed for trade. **4** *tr.*

S

bring (a book, hand, etc.) into a folded-up or contracted state. **5** *tr.* (usu. foll. by *in, out*) keep (a person, sound, etc.) in or out of a room, etc., by shutting a door, etc. (*shut out the noise*). **6** *tr.* (usu. foll. by *in*) catch (a finger, dress, etc.) by shutting something on it (*shut her finger in the door*). □ **be** (or **get**) **shut of** *sl.* be (or get) rid of. **shut the door on** refuse to consider; make impossible. **shut down 1** stop (a factory, etc.) from operating. **2** (of a factory, etc.) stop operating. **shut one's eyes** (or **ears** or **heart** or **mind**) **to** pretend not, or refuse, to see (or hear or feel sympathy for or think about). **shut in** (of hills, houses, etc.) encircle, prevent access, etc., to or escape from (*shut in on three sides*). **shut off 1** stop the flow of (water, gas, etc.) by shutting a valve. **2** separate from society, etc. **shut out 1** exclude. **2** screen from view. **3** prevent (a possibility, etc.). **4** block from the mind. **shut up 1** close all doors and windows of; bolt and bar. **2** imprison (a person). **3** close (a box, etc.) securely. **4** *colloq.* reduce to silence by rebuke, etc. **5** put (a thing) away in a box, etc. **6** (esp. in *imper.*) *colloq.* stop talking.

shut·down /shútdown/ *n.* the closure of a factory, etc.

shut-eye *n. colloq.* sleep.

shut-in *n.* a person confined to home, bed, etc., due to infirmity, etc.

shut·off /shútawf/ *n.* **1** something used for stopping an operation. **2** a cessation of flow, supply, or activity.

shut·out /shútowt/ *n.* **1** a competition or game in which the losing side fails to score. **2** a preemptive bid in bridge.

shut·ter /shútər/ *n. & v.* ● *n.* **1** a person or thing that shuts. **2 a** each of a pair or set of panels fixed inside or outside a window for security or privacy or to keep the light in or out. **b** a structure of slats on rollers used for the same purpose. **3** a device that exposes the film in a photographic camera. ▷ CAMERA. ● *v.tr.* **1** put up the shutters of. **2** provide with shutters. □ **put up the shutters 1** cease business for the day. **2** cease business, etc., permanently. □□ **shut·ter·less** *adj.*

shut·ter·bug /shútərbəg/ *n. colloq.* an amateur photographer who takes many pictures.

shut·tle /shút'l/ *n. & v.* ● *n.* **1 a** a bobbin used for carrying the weft thread across between the warp threads in weaving. ▷ WEAVE. **b** a bobbin carrying the lower thread in a sewing machine. **2** a train, bus, etc., going to and fro over a short route continuously. **3** = SHUTTLECOCK. **4** = SPACE SHUTTLE. ● *v. & tr.* move or cause to move back and forth like a shuttle. **2** *intr.* travel in a shuttle.

shut·tle·cock /shút'lkok/ *n.* **1** ▶ a cork with a ring of feathers, or a similar device of plastic, used instead of a ball in badminton. ▷ BADMINTON. **2** a thing passed repeatedly back and forth.

goose feathers

cork base

SHUTTLECOCK

shut·tle di·plo·ma·cy *n.* negotiations conducted by a mediator who travels successively to several countries.

shut·tle serv·ice *n.* a train or bus, etc., service operating back and forth over a short route.

shy[1] /shī/ *adj., v., & n.* ● *adj.* (**shyer**, **shyest**) **1 a** diffident or uneasy in company. **b** (of an animal, bird, etc.) easily startled. **2** (foll. by *of*) avoiding; wary of (*shy of his aunt*). **3** (in *comb.*) showing fear of or distaste for (*work-shy*). ● *v.intr.* (**shies, shied**) **1** (usu. foll. by *at*) (esp. of a horse) start suddenly aside in fright. **2** (usu. foll. by *away from, at*) avoid accepting or becoming involved in (a proposal, etc.) in alarm. ● *n.* a sudden startled movement. □□ **shy·ly** *adv.* **shy·ness** *n.*

shy[2] /shī/ *v. & n.* ● *v.tr.* (**shies, shied**) (also *absol.*) fling or throw (a stone, etc.). ● *n.* (*pl.* **shies**) the act or an instance of shying. □□ **shy·er** *n.*

shy·ster /shístər/ *n. colloq.* a lawyer who uses unscrupulous methods.

SI *abbr.* the international system of units of measurement (F *Système International*).

Si *symb. Chem.* the element silicon.

si /see/ *n. Mus.* = TI.

si·a·logue /sīáləgawg, -gog/ *n. & adj.* ● *n.* a medicine inducing the flow of saliva. ● *adj.* inducing such a flow.

si·a·mang /seeˈəmang/ *n.* a large black gibbon, *Hylobates syndactylus*, native to Sumatra and the Malay peninsula.

Si·a·mese /sīəmeez/ *n. & adj.* ● *n.* (*pl.* same) **1 a** a native of Siam (now Thailand) in SE Asia. **b** the language of Siam. **2** (in full **Siamese cat**) ▶ a cat of a cream-colored short-haired breed with blue eyes. ▷ CAT. ● *adj.* of or concerning Siam, its people, or language.

Si·a·mese twins *n.pl.* **1** twins joined at any part of the body. **2** any closely associated pair.

sib /sib/ *n. & adj.* ● *n.* **1** a brother or sister. **2** a relative. **3** a group of people one recognizes as relatives.

Si·be·ri·an /sībéereeən/ *n. & adj.* ● *n.* **1** a native of Siberia in the northeastern part of the Russian Federation. **2** a person of Siberian descent. ● *adj.* of or relating to Siberia.

sib·i·lant /síbilənt/ *adj. & n.* ● *adj.* **1** (of a letter or set of letters, as *s, sh*) sounded with a hiss. **2** hissing. ● *n.* a sibilant letter or letters. □□ **sib·i·lance** *n.*

sib·i·late /síbilayt/ *v.tr. & intr.* pronounce with or utter a hissing sound. □□ **sib·i·la·tion** /-láyshən/ *n.*

sib·ling /síbling/ *n.* each of two or more children having one or both parents in common.

sib·ship /síbship/ *n.* **1** the state of belonging to a sib or the same sib. **2** a group of children having the same two parents.

sib·yl /síbil/ *n.* a prophetess, fortune-teller, or witch.

sib·yl·line /síbilīn, -leen/ *adj.* **1** of or from a sibyl. **2** oracular; prophetic.

sic[1] /sik/ *v.tr.* (**sicced, siccing**; also **sicked** /sikt/, **sicking**) (usu. in *imper.*) (esp. to a dog) set upon (a rat, etc.).

sic[2] /sik, seek/ *adv.* (usu. in brackets) used, spelled, etc., as written (confirming, or calling attention to, the form of quoted or copied words).

sic·ca·tive /síkətiv/ *n. & adj.* ● *n.* a substance causing drying, esp. mixed with oil paint, etc., for quick drying. ● *adj.* having such properties.

Si·cil·ian /sisílyən/ *n. & adj.* ● *n.* **1** a native of Sicily, an island off the S. coast of Italy. **2** a person of Sicilian descent. **3** the Italian dialect of Sicily. ● *adj.* of or relating to Sicily.

sick /sik/ *adj.* **1** (often in *comb.*) vomiting or tending to vomit (*I think I'm going to be sick*; *seasick*). **2** ill; affected by illness (*has been sick for a week*; *a sick man*; *sick with measles*). **3 a** (often foll. by *at*) esp. mentally perturbed (*the product of a sick mind*). **b** (often foll. by *for*, or in *comb.*) pining; longing (*lovesick*). **4** (often foll. by *of*) *colloq.* a disgusted; surfeited (*sick of chocolates*). **b** angry, esp. because of surfeit (*sick of being teased*). **5** *colloq.* (of humor, etc.) jeering at misfortune, illness, etc. (*sick joke*). □ **look sick** *colloq.* be unimpressive or embarrassed. **sick at** (or **to**) **one's stomach** vomiting or tending to vomit. **take sick** *colloq.* be taken ill. □□ **sick·ish** *adj.*

sick·bay /síkbay/ *n.* **1** part of a ship used as a hospital. **2** any room for sick people.

sick·bed /síkbed/ *n.* **1** an invalid's bed. **2** the state of being an invalid.

sick·en /síkən/ *v.* **1** *tr.* affect with disgust. **2** *intr.* (often foll. by *at*, or to + infin.) feel nausea or disgust (*he sickened at the sight*). **3** (as **sickening** *adj.*) **a** loath-

---

some; disgusting. **b** *colloq.* very annoying. □□ **sick·en·ing·ly** *adv.*

sick·en·er *n.* **1** something causing nausea, disgust, or severe disappointment. **2** a red toadstool of the genus *Russula*, esp. the poisonous *R. emetica*.

sick·le /síkəl/ *n.* ▶ a short-handled farming tool with a semicircular blade, used for cutting grain, lopping, or trimming.

sick leave *n.* leave of absence granted because of illness.

sick·le cell *n.* a sickle-shaped blood cell, esp. as found in a type of severe hereditary anemia.

sick·ly /síklee/ *adj.* (**sicklier, sickliest**) **1 a** of weak health. **b** (of a person's complexion, etc.) languid, faint, or pale. **c** (of light or color) faint; feeble. **2** causing ill health (*a sickly climate*). **3** (of a book, etc.) sentimental or mawkish. **4** inducing or connected with nausea (*a sickly taste*). □□ **sick·li·ness** *n.*

sick·ness /síknis/ *n.* **1** the state of being ill; disease. **2** a specified disease (*sleeping sickness*). **3** vomiting or a tendency to vomit.

sick·o /síkō/ *n.* a person who is mentally deranged or morally debased.

sick pay *n.* pay given to an employee, etc., on sick leave.

sick·room /síkroom, -room/ *n.* **1** a room occupied by a sick person. **2** a room adapted for sick people.

sid·al·ce·a /sidálseeə/ *n.* any mallowlike plant of the genus *Sidalcea*, bearing racemes of white, pink, or purple flowers.

side /sīd/ *n. & v.* ● *n.* **1 a** each of the more or less flat surfaces bounding an object (*this side up*). **b** a more or less vertical inner or outer plane or surface (*a mountainside*). **c** such a vertical lateral surface or plane as distinct from the top or bottom, front or back, or ends (*at the side of the house*). **2 a** the half of a person or animal that is on the right or the left, esp. of the torso (*pain in his right side*). **b** the left or right half of a specified part of a thing, area, etc. (*put the box on that side*). **c** (often in *comb.*) a position next to a person or thing (*graveside*). **d** a specified direction relating to a person or thing (*came from all sides*). **e** half of a butchered carcass (*a side of bacon*). **3 a** either surface of a thing regarded as having two surfaces. **b** the amount of writing needed to fill one side of a sheet of paper (*write three sides*). **4** any of several aspects of a question, character, etc. (*look on the bright side*). **5 a** each of two sets of opponents in war, politics, games, etc. (*the side that bats first*). **b** a cause or philosophical position, etc., regarded as being in conflict with another (*on the side of right*). **6 a** a part or region near the edge and remote from the center. **b** (*attrib.*) a subordinate, peripheral, or detached part (*a side road*). **7 a** each of the bounding lines of a plane rectilinear figure (*a hexagon has six sides*). **b** each of two quantities stated to be equal in an equation. **8** a position nearer or farther than, or right or left of, a dividing line (*on this side of the Alps*). **9** a line of hereditary descent through the father or the mother. ● *v.intr.* (usu. foll. by *with*) take part or be on the same side as a disputant, etc. (*sided with his father*). □ **by the side of 1** close to. **2** compared with. **from side to side 1** right across. **2** alternately each way from a central line. **on one side 1** not in the main or central position. **2** aside (*took him on one side*). **on the . . . side** fairly; somewhat (qualifying an adjective: *on the high side*). **on the side 1** as a sideline; in addition to one's regular work, etc. **2** secretly or illicitly. **3** as a side dish. **side by side** standing close together, esp. for

SICKLE:
19TH-CENTURY
SICKLE

SIAMESE CAT

S

mutual support. **take sides** support one or other cause, etc. □□ **side·less** *adj.*

side arms *n.pl.* swords, bayonets, or pistols.

side·band /sídband/ *n.* a range of frequencies near the carrier frequency of a radio wave, concerned in modulation.

side·bar /sídbaar/ *n.* **1** a short news article, printed alongside a major news story, that contains related incidental information. **2** *Law* discussion or consultation between a trial judge and counsel that the jury is not permitted to hear.

side bet *n.* a bet between opponents, esp. in card games, over and above the ordinary stakes.

side·board /sídbawrd/ *n.* a table or esp. a flat-topped cupboard at the side of a dining room for supporting and containing dishes, table linen, etc.

side·burns /sídbornz/ *n.pl. colloq.* hair grown by a man down the sides of his face; side-whiskers.

side·car /sídkaar/ *n.* ▼ a small car for a passenger or passengers attached to the side of a motorcycle.

SIDECAR: 1960S MOTORCYCLE WITH SIDECAR

sidelight · windshield · links · mud guard · bumper · coupling

sid·ed /sídid/ *adj.* **1** having sides. **2** (in *comb.*) having a specified side or sides (*one-sided*). □□ **-sid·ed·ly** *adv.* **sid·ed·ness** *n.* (also in *comb.*).

side dish *n.* an extra dish subsidiary to the main course.

side drum *n.* a snare drum (*see* SNARE *n.* 5). ▷ PERCUSSION, SNARE

side ef·fect *n.* a secondary, usu. undesirable, effect.

side·hill /sídhil/ *n.* a hillside.

side·kick /sídkik/ *n. colloq.* a close associate.

side·light /sídlīt/ *n.* **1** a light from the side. **2** incidental information, etc. **3** esp. *Brit.* a light at the side of the front of a motor vehicle. ▷ SIDECAR. **4** *Naut.* the red port or green starboard light on a ship under way.

side·line /sídlīn/ *n. & v.* • *n.* **1** work, etc., done in addition to one's main activity. **2** (usu. in *pl.*) **a** a line bounding the side of a football field, etc. ▷ TENNIS. **b** the space next to these where spectators, etc., sit. • *v.tr.* remove (a player) from a team through injury, suspension, etc. □ **on** (or **from**) **the sidelines** in (or from) a position removed from the main action.

side·long /sídlawng, -long/ *adj. & adv.* • *adj.* inclining to one side; oblique (*a sidelong glance*). • *adv.* obliquely (*moved sidelong*).

si·de·re·al /sīdéereeəl/ *adj.* of or concerning the constellations or fixed stars.

si·de·re·al day *n.* the time between successive meridional transits of a star or esp. of the first point of Aries, about four minutes shorter than the solar day.

sid·er·ite /sídərīt/ *n.* **1** a mineral form of ferrous carbonate. **2** a meteorite consisting mainly of nickel and iron.

side road *n.* a minor or subsidiary road, esp. diverging from a main road.

sid·er·o·stat /sídərəstat/ *n.* an instrument used for keeping the image of a celestial body in a fixed position.

side·sad·dle /sídsad'l/ *n. & adv.* • *n.* ▶ a saddle for a woman rider having supports for both feet on the same side of the horse. • *adv.* sitting in this position on a horse.

side·show /sídshō/ *n.* **1** a minor show or attraction in an exhibition or entertainment. **2** a minor incident or issue.

side·slip /sídslip/ *n. & v.* • *n.* **1 a** skid. **2** *Aeron.* a sideways movement instead of forward. • *v.intr.* **1** skid. **2** *Aeron.* move sideways instead of forward.

side·split·ting /sídspliting/ *adj.* causing violent laughter.

side·step /sídstep/ *n. & v.* • *n.* a step taken sideways. • *v.tr.* (**-stepped**, **-stepping**) **1** esp. *Football* avoid (esp. a tackle) by stepping sideways. **2** evade. □□ **side·step·per** *n.*

side street *n.* a minor or subsidiary street.

side·stroke /sídstrōk/ *n.* **1** a stroke toward or from a side. **2** an incidental action. **3** a swimming stroke in which the swimmer lies on his or her side.

side·swipe /sídswīp/ *n. & v.* • *n.* **1** a glancing blow along the side. **2** incidental criticism, etc. • *v.tr.* hit with or as if with a sideswipe.

side·track /sídtrak/ *n. & v.* • *n.* a railroad siding. • *v.tr.* **1** turn into a siding. **2 a** postpone, evade, or divert treatment or consideration of. **b** divert (a person) from considering, etc.

side trip *n.* a minor excursion during a voyage or trip.

side·walk /sídwawk/ *n.* a usu. paved pedestrian path at the side of a road.

side·wall /sídwawl/ *n.* **1** the part of a tire between the tread and the wheel rim. **2** a wall that forms the side of a structure.

side·ward /sídwərd/ *adj. & adv.* • *adj.* = SIDEWAYS. • *adv.* (also **side·wards** /-wərdz/) = SIDEWAYS.

side·ways /sídwayz/ *adv. & adj.* • *adv.* **1** to or from a side (*moved sideways*). **2** with one side facing forward (*sat sideways*). • *adj.* to or from a side (*a sideways movement*). □□ **side·wise** *adv. & adj.*

side·wind·er /sídwīndər/ *n.* **1** a desert rattlesnake, *Crotalus cerastes*, native to N. America, moving with a lateral motion. **2** a sideways blow.

sid·ing /síding/ *n.* **1** a short track at the side of and opening on to a railroad line, used for switching trains. **2** material for the outside of a building, e.g., clapboards, shingles, etc.

si·dle /síd'l/ *v. & n.* • *v.intr.* (usu. foll. by *along*, *up*) walk in a timid, furtive, stealthy, or cringing manner. • *n.* the act of sidling.

SIDS /sids/ *abbr.* sudden infant death syndrome; crib death.

siege /seej/ *n.* **1 a** a military operation to compel the surrender of a fortified place by surrounding it and cutting off supplies, etc. **b** a similar operation by police, etc., to force the surrender of an armed person. **c** the period during which a siege lasts. **2** a persistent attack or campaign of persuasion. □ **lay siege to** esp. *Mil.* conduct the siege of. **raise the siege of** abandon or cause the abandonment of an attempt to take (a place) by siege.

sie·mens /séemənz/ *n. Electr.* the SI unit of conductance.

si·en·na /seeénə/ *n.* **1** a kind of earth used as a pigment in paint. **2** its color of yellowish-brown (**raw sienna**) or reddish-brown (**burnt sienna**). ▷ RAW SIENNA

si·er·ra /seeérə/ *n.* a long jagged mountain chain, esp. in Spain.

si·es·ta /seeéstə/ *n.* an afternoon sleep or rest esp. in hot countries.

sieve /siv/ *n. & v.* • *n.* a utensil having a perforated or meshed bottom for separating solids or coarse

fixed head (top pommel) · leaping head (lower pommel) · suede seat · nearside flap · safe · nearside single stirrup

SIDESADDLE

material from liquids or fine particles, or for reducing a soft solid to a fine pulp. • *v.tr.* **1** put through or sift with a sieve. **2** examine (evidence, etc.) to select or separate. □□ **sieve·like** *adj.*

sift /sift/ *v.* **1** *tr.* sieve (material) into finer and coarser parts. **2** *tr.* (usu. foll. by *from*, *out*) separate (finer or coarser parts) from material. **3** *tr.* sprinkle (esp. sugar) from a perforated container. **4** *tr.* examine (evidence, facts, etc.). □ **sift through** examine by sifting. □□ **sift·er** *n.* (also in *comb.*).

sigh /sī/ *v. & n.* • *v.* **1** *intr.* emit a long, deep, audible breath expressive of sadness, weariness, relief, etc. **2** *intr.* (foll. by *for*) yearn for (a lost person or thing). **3** *intr.* (of the wind, etc.) make a sound like sighing. • *n.* **1** the act or an instance of sighing. **2** a sound made in sighing (*a sigh of relief*).

sight /sīt/ *n. & v.* • *n.* **1 a** ▶ the faculty of seeing with the eyes (*lost his sight*). ▷ EYE. **b** the act or an instance of seeing; the state of being seen. **2** a thing seen; a display, show, or spectacle (*not a pretty sight*; *a beautiful sight*). **3** a way of considering a thing (*in my sight he can do no wrong*). **4** a range of space within which a person, etc., can see or an object can be seen (*he's out of sight*; *they are just coming into sight*). **5** (usu. in *pl.*) noteworthy features of a town, area, etc. (*went to see the sights*). **6 a** a device on a gun or optical instrument used for assisting the precise aim or observation. ▷ GUN. **b** the aim or observation so gained (*got a sight of him*). **7** *colloq.* a person or thing having a ridiculous, repulsive, or disheveled appearance (*looked a perfect sight*). **8** *colloq.* a great quantity (*a sight better than he was*). • *v.tr.* **1** get sight of, esp. by approaching (*they sighted land*). **2** observe the presence of (esp. aircraft, animals, etc.) (*sighted buffalo*). **3** take observations of (a star, etc.) with an instrument. **4** aim (a gun, etc.) with sights. □ **at first sight** on first glimpse or impression. **at** (or **on**) **sight** as soon as a person or a thing has been seen. **catch** (or **lose**) **sight of** begin (or cease) to see or be aware of. **get a sight of** glimpse. **have lost sight of** no longer know the whereabouts of. **in sight 1** visible. **2** near at hand (*salvation is in sight*). **in** (or **within**) **sight of** so as to see or be seen from. **lower one's sights** become less ambitious. **out of my sight!** go at once! **out of sight 1** not visible. **2** *colloq.* excellent; delightful. **set one's sights on** aim at (*set her sights on a directorship*). **sight unseen** without previous inspection. □□ **sight·er** *n.*

sight·ed /sítid/ *adj.* **1** capable of seeing; not blind. **2** (in *comb.*) having a specified kind of sight (*far-sighted*).

sight·less /sítlis/ *adj.* **1** blind. **2** *poet.* invisible. □□ **sight·less·ly** *adv.* **sight·less·ness** *n.*

sight line *n.* a hypothetical line from a person's eye to what is seen.

sight·ly /sítlee/ *adj.* attractive to the sight; not unsightly. □□ **sight·li·ness** *n.*

sight-read *v.tr.* (*past* and *past part.* **-read** /-red/) read and perform (music) at sight. □□ **sight reader** *n.*

sight·se·er /sítseeər/ *n.* a person who visits places of interest; a tourist. □□ **sight·see** *v.intr. & tr.* **sight·see·ing** *n.*

sight·wor·thy /sítwurthee/ *adj.* worth seeing.

sig·il·late /síjilət/ *adj.* **1** (of pottery) having impressed patterns. **2** *Bot.* having seallike marks.

sig·ma /sígmə/ *n.* the eighteenth letter of the Greek alphabet (Σ, σ, or, when final, ς).

sig·mate /sígmət, -mayt/ *adj.* **1** sigma-shaped. **2** S shaped.

sig·moid /sígmoyd/ *adj. & n.* • *adj.* **1** curved like the uncial sigma (C); crescent-shaped. **2** S-shaped. • *n.* (in full **sigmoid flexure**) *Anat.* the curved part of the intestine between the colon and the rectum.

S

SIGHT

When the eye sees an object, incoming light rays are focused onto the retina by the cornea and lens, forming an inverted image. The retina then transmits signals to the brain's visual cortex, where the image is reinverted and interpreted. One cause of nearsightedness (myopia) is an elongated eyeball, in which the focus falls short of the retina. If the eyeball is shortened, the focus is behind the retina, causing farsightedness (hyperopia).

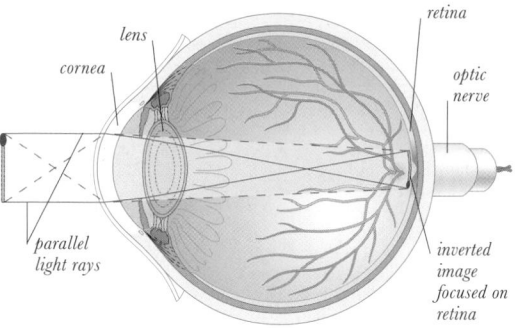

DEMONSTRATION OF HOW THE HUMAN EYE SEES AN IMAGE

COMMON SIGHT PROBLEMS

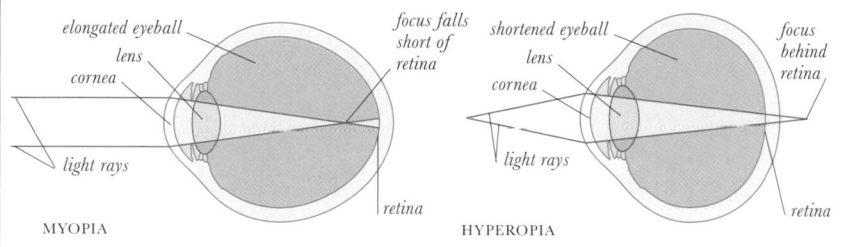

MYOPIA   HYPEROPIA

---

sign /sīn/ *n. & v.* ● *n.* **1 a** a thing indicating or suggesting a quality or state, etc.; a thing perceived as indicating a future state or occurrence (*violence is a sign of weakness; shows all the signs of decay*). **b** a miracle evidencing supernatural power; a portent (*did signs and wonders*). **2 a** a mark, symbol, or device used to represent something or to distinguish the thing on which it is put (*marked the jar with a sign*). **b** a technical symbol used in algebra, music, etc. (*a minus sign*) **3** a gesture or action used to convey information, an order, request, etc. (*conveyed by signs*). **4** a publicly displayed board, etc., giving information; a signboard or signpost. **5** a password (*advanced and gave the sign*). **6** any of the twelve divisions of the zodiac, named from constellations formerly situated in them (*the sign of Cancer*). ● *v.* **1** *tr.* (also *absol.*) write (one's name, initials, etc.) on a document, etc., indicating that one has authorized it. **b** write one's name, etc., on (a document) as authorization. **2** *intr. & tr.* communicate by gesture (*signed to me to come*). **3** *tr. & intr.* engage or be engaged by signing a contract, etc. (see also sign on, sign up). **4** *tr.* mark with a sign (esp. with the sign of the cross in baptism). □ **sign away** convey (one's right, property, etc.) by signing a deed, etc. **sign for** acknowledge receipt of by signing. **sign off** end work, broadcasting, a letter, etc., esp. by writing or speaking one's name. **sign on 1** agree to a contract, employment, etc. **2** begin work, broadcasting, etc. **3** employ (a person). **sign up 1** engage or employ (a person). **2** enlist in the armed forces. **3 a** commit (another person or oneself) by signing, etc. (*signed you up for dinner*). **b** enroll (*signed up for evening classes*). □□ **sign·a·ble** *adj.* **sign·er** *n.*

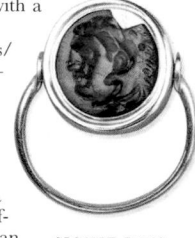

raised arm

actuating lever system

warning arm

tubular steel post

ladder

SIGNAL: MID-20TH-CENTURY SEMAPHORE SIGNAL

sig·nal¹ /signəl/ *n. & v.* ● *n.* **1 a** a usu. prearranged sign conveying information, guidance, etc., esp. at a distance (*waved as a signal to begin*). **b** a message made up of such signs (*signals made with flags*). **2** an immediate occasion for or cause of movement, action, etc. (*the uprising was a signal for repression*). **3** *Electr.* **a** an electrical impulse or impulses or radio waves transmitted. **b** a sequence of these **4** ◄ a light, semaphore, etc., on a railroad giving instructions or warnings to train engineers, etc. ● *v.* **1** *intr.* make signals. **2** *tr.* **a** (often foll. by *to* + infin.) make signals to; direct. **b** transmit (an order, information, etc.) by signal; announce (*signaled her agreement; signaled that the town had been taken*). □□ **sig·nal·er** or **sig·nal·ler** *n.*

sig·nal² /signəl/ *adj.* remarkably good or bad (*a signal victory*). □□ **sig·nal·ly** *adv.*

sig·nal·ize /signəlīz/ *v.tr.* **1** make noteworthy or remarkable. **2** indicate.

sig·nal·man /signəlmən/ *n.* (*pl.* **-men**) **1** a railroad employee responsible for operating signals. **2** a person who displays or receives naval, etc., signals.

sig·na·ry /signəree/ *n.* (*pl.* **-ies**) a list of signs constituting the syllabic or alphabetic symbols of a language.

sig·na·to·ry /signətawree/ *n. & adj.* ● *n.* (*pl.* **-ies**) a party or esp. a nation that has signed an agreement or esp. a treaty. ● *adj.* having signed such an agreement, etc.

sig·na·ture /signəchər/ *n.* **1 a** a person's name, initials, or mark used in signing a letter, document, etc. **b** the act of signing a document, etc. **2** *archaic* a distinctive action, characteristic, etc. **3** *Mus.* **a** = KEY SIGNATURE. **b** = TIME SIGNATURE. **4** *Printing* **a** a letter or figure placed at the foot of one or more pages of each sheet of a book as a guide for binding. **b** such a sheet after folding. **5** written directions given to a patient as part of a medical prescription.

sign·board /sīnbawrd/ *n.* a board with a name or symbol, etc., displayed outside a store or hotel.

sig·net /signit/ *n.* **1** a seal used instead of or with a signature as authentication. **2** (prec. by *the*) the royal seal formerly used for special purposes in England and Scotland, and in Scotland later as the seal of the Court of Session.

sig·net ring *n.* ► a ring with a seal set in it.

sig·nif·i·cance /signifikəns/ *n.* **1** importance (*of no significance*). **2** a concealed or real meaning (*what is the significance*). **3** the state of being significant. **4** *Statistics* the extent to which a result deviates from a hypothesis such that the difference is due to more than errors in sampling.

SIGNET RING

sig·nif·i·cant /signifikənt/ *adj.* **1** having a meaning. **2** having an unstated or secret meaning; (*refused it with a significant gesture*). **3** noteworthy; important (*a significant figure in history*). □□ **sig·nif·i·cant·ly** *adv.*

sig·nif·i·cant oth·er *n.* a person who is very important in one's life, esp. a spouse or lover.

sig·ni·fi·ca·tion /signifikáyshən/ *n.* **1** the act of signifying. **2** (usu. foll. by *of*) exact meaning or sense, esp. of a word or phrase.

sig·nif·i·ca·tive /signifikaytiv/ *adj.* **1** (esp. of a symbol, etc.) signifying. **2** having a meaning. **3** (usu. foll. by *of*) serving as a sign or evidence.

sig·ni·fy /signifī/ *v.* (**-ies, -ied**) **1** *tr.* be a sign of (*a yawn signifies boredom*). **2** *tr.* mean ("*Dr*" *signifies "doctor"*). **3** *tr.* make known (*signified their agreement*). **4** *intr.* matter (*it signifies little*). □□ **sig·ni·fi·er** *n.*

sign lan·guage *n.* a system of communication by hand gestures, used esp. by the hearing impaired.

sign of the cross *n.* a Christian sign made in blessing or prayer, by tracing a cross from the forehead to the chest and to each shoulder, or in the air.

sign of the times *n.* a portent, etc., showing a likely trend.

si·gnor /seenyáwr/ *n.* (*pl.* **signori** /-nyóree/) a title used of or to an Italian man.

si·gno·ra /seenyáwrə/ *n.* a title used of or to an Italian married woman.

si·gno·ri·na /seenyəreenə/ *n.* a title used of or to an Italian unmarried woman.

sign·post /sínpost/ *n. & v.* ● *n.* **1** a post erected at a crossroads with arms indicating the direction to various places. **2** a means of guidance. ● *v.tr.* provide with a signpost or signposts.

si·ka /seekə/ *n.* a small forest-dwelling deer, *Cervus nippon*, native to Japan.

Sikh /seek/ *n.* a member of an Indian monotheistic faith founded in the 16th c.

Sikh·ism /seekizəm/ *n.* the religious tenets of the Sikhs.

si·lage /sílij/ *n. & v.* ● *n.* **1** storage in a silo. **2** green fodder that has been stored in a silo. ● *v.tr.* put into a silo. ▷ SILO

sild /silt/ *n.* a small immature herring, esp. one caught in N. European seas.

si·lence /síləns/ *n. & v.* ● *n.* **1** absence of sound. **2** abstinence from speech or noise. **3** the avoidance of mentioning a thing, betraying a secret, etc. **4** oblivion; the state of not being mentioned. ● *v.tr.* make silent, esp. by coercion or superior argument. □ **in silence** without speech or other sound. **reduce** (or **put**) **to silence** refute in argument.

si·lenc·er /sílənsər/ *n.* any of various devices for reducing the noise emitted by a gun, etc. ▷ STEN GUN

si·lent /sílənt/ *adj.* **1** not speaking; not making or accompanied by any sound. **2** (of a letter) written but not pronounced, e.g., *b* in *doubt*. **3** (of a person) speaking little. **4** saying or recording nothing on some subject (*the records are silent on the incident*). □□ **si·lent·ly** *adv.*

si·lent ma·jor·i·ty *n.* those of moderate opinions who rarely assert them.

si·lent part·ner *n.* a partner not sharing in the actual work of a firm.

si·le·nus /síléenəs/ *n.* (*pl.* **sileni** /-nī/) (in Greek mythology) a bearded old man like a satyr, sometimes with the tail and legs of a horse.

S

si·lex /síleks/ *n.* a kind of glass made of fused quartz.

sil·hou·ette /silŏo-ét/ *n. & v.* ● *n.* **1** a representation of a person or thing showing the outline only, usu. done in solid black on white or cut from paper. **2** the dark shadow or outline of a person or thing against a lighter background. ● *v.tr.* represent or (usu. in *passive*) show in silhouette.

sil·i·ca /sílikə/ *n.* silicon dioxide, occurring as quartz, etc., and as a principal constituent of sandstone and other rocks. □□ **si·li·ceous** /-líshəs/ *adj.* (also **si·li·cious**). **si·lic·ic** /-lísik/ *adj.* **si·lic·i·fy** /-lisifí/ *v.tr. & intr.* (**-ies, -ied**). **si·lic·i·fi·ca·tion** /-fikáyshən/ *n.*

sil·i·ca gel *n.* hydrated silica in a hard granular form used as a desiccant.

sil·i·cate /sílikayt, -kət/ *n.* any of the many insoluble compounds of a metal combined with silicon and oxygen. ▷ MINERAL

sil·i·con /sílikən, -kon/ *n. Chem.* ◀ a nonmetallic element occurring widely in silica and silicates.

sil·i·con chip *n.* a silicon microchip.

sil·i·cone /sílikōn/ *n.* any of the many polymeric organic compounds of silicon and oxygen with high resistance to cold, heat, water, and electricity.

Sil·i·con Val·ley *n.* an area in California with a high concentration of electronics industries.

SILICON CRYSTAL USED FOR MAKING MICROCHIPS

sil·i·co·sis /sílikṓsis/ *n.* lung fibrosis caused by the inhalation of dust containing silica.

si·lique /sileék/ *the* long, narrow seedpod of a cruciferous plant. □□ **sil·i·quose** /sílikwōs/ *adj.* **sil·i·quous** /-kwəs/ *adj.*

silk /silk/ *n.* **1** a fine, strong, soft lustrous fiber produced by silkworms. **2** a similar fiber spun by some spiders, etc. **3 a** thread or cloth made from silk fiber. **b** a thread or fabric resembling silk. **4** (in *pl.*) kinds of silk cloth or garments made from it, esp. as worn by a jockey. ▷ JOCKEY **5** (*attrib.*) made of silk (*silk blouse*). □□ **silk·like** *adj.*

silk·en /sílkən/ *adj.* **1** made of silk. **2** wearing silk. **3** soft or lustrous as silk. **4** (of a person's manner, etc.) suave or insinuating.

silk-screen print·ing *n.* = SCREEN PRINTING.

silk·worm /sílkwərm/ *n.* ▼ the caterpillar of the moth *Bombyx mori*, which spins its cocoon of silk.

S

SILKWORM: CHINESE SILKWORM (*Bombyx mori*)

silkworm

beginnings of a silk cocoon

silk·y /sílkee/ *adj.* (**silkier, silkiest**) **1** like silk in smoothness, softness, or luster. **2** (of a person's manner, etc.) suave; insinuating. □□ **silk·i·ly** *adv.* **silk·i·ness** *n.*

sill /sil/ *n.* **1** a shelf or slab of stone, wood, or metal at the foot of a window or doorway. **2** a horizontal timber at the bottom of a dock or lock entrance, against which the gates close.

sil·la·bub var. of SYLLABUB.

sil·li·man·ite /sílimənīt/ *n.* an aluminum silicate occurring in orthorhombic crystals or fibrous masses.

sil·ly /sílee/ *adj. & n.* ● *adj.* (**sillier, silliest**) **1** lacking sense; foolish. **2** weak-minded. ● *n.* (*pl.* **-ies**) *colloq.* a foolish person. □□ **sil·li·ly** *adv.* **sil·li·ness** *n.*

si·lo /sílō/ *n. & v.* ● *n.* (*pl.* **-os**) **1** a pit or airtight structure in which green crops are pressed and kept for fodder. **2** ▼ a tower for the storage of grain, etc. **3** an underground chamber in which a guided missile is kept. ● *v.tr.* (**-oes, -oed**) make silage of.

silo

SILO: GRAIN SILO ATTACHED TO A BARN

silt /silt/ *n. & v.* ● *n.* sediment in a channel, harbor, etc. ● *v.tr. & intr.* (often foll. by *up*) choke with silt. □□ **sil·ta·tion** /-táyshən/ *n.* **silt·y** *adj.*

silt·stone /síltstōn/ *n.* rock of consolidated silt.

Si·lu·ri·an /silŏoreeən, sī-/ *adj. & n. Geol.* ● *adj.* of or relating to the third period of the Paleozoic era. ● *n.* this period or system.

sil·va /sílvə/ *n.* (also **syl·va**) (*pl.* **sylvae** /-vee/ or **sylvas**) **1** the trees of a region, epoch, or environment. **2** a treatise on or a list of such trees.

sil·van var. of SYLVAN.

sil·ver /sílvər/ *n., adj., & v.* ● *n. Chem.* **1** ▶ a grayish-white, lustrous, malleable, ductile, precious metallic element. **2** the color of silver. **3** silver or cupronickel coins. **4** silver vessels or implements, esp. cutlery. **5** = SILVER MEDAL. ● *adj.* **1** made wholly or chiefly of silver. **2** colored like silver. ● *v.* **1** *tr.* coat or plate with silver. **2** *tr.* provide (mirror glass) with a backing of tin amalgam, etc. **3** *tr.* (of the moon or a white light) give a silvery appearance to. **4 a** *tr.* turn (the hair) gray or white. **b** *intr.* (of the hair) turn gray or white.

SILVER: TYPICAL NATIVE SILVER

sil·ver birch *n.* ◀ a common European birch, *Betula pendula*, with silver-colored bark.

sil·ver·fish /sílvərfish/ *n.* (*pl.* same) any small silvery wingless insect of the order Thysanura, esp. *Lepisma saccharina* in houses and other buildings.

sil·ver lin·ing *n.* a consolation or hopeful feature in misfortune.

sil·ver med·al *n.* a medal of silver, usu. awarded as second prize.

sil·ver plate *n.* vessels, spoons, etc., of copper, etc., plated with silver.

SILVER BIRCH BARK (*Betula pendula*)

sil·ver screen *n.* (usu. prec. by *the*) motion pictures collectively.

sil·ver·smith /sílvərsmith/ *n.* a worker in silver. □□ **sil·ver·smith·ing** *n.*

sil·ver spoon *n.* a sign of future prosperity.

Sil·ver Star *n. US Mil.* a decoration awarded for gallantry in action.

sil·ver tongue *n.* eloquence.

sil·ver·ware /sílvərwair/ *n.* articles made of or coated with silver.

sil·ver·weed /sílvərweed/ *n.* a plant with silvery leaves, esp. a potentilla, *Potentilla anserina*, with silver-colored leaves.

sil·ver·y /sílvəree/ *adj.* **1** like silver in color or appearance. **2** having a clear, gentle, ringing sound. **3** (of the hair) white and lustrous. □□ **sil·ver·i·ness** *n.*

sil·vi·cul·ture /sílvikulchər/ *n.* (also **syl·vi·cul·ture**) the growing and tending of trees as a branch of forestry. □□ **sil·vi·cul·tur·al** /-kúlchərəl/ *adj.* **sil·vi·cul·tur·ist** /-kúlchərist/

sim·i·an /símeeən/ *adj. & n.* ● *adj.* **1** of or concerning the anthropoid apes. **2** like an ape or monkey (*a simian walk*). ● *n.* an ape or monkey.

sim·i·lar /símilər/ *adj.* **1** like; alike. **2** (often foll. by *to*) having a resemblance. **3** of the same kind, nature, or amount. **4** *Geom.* shaped alike. □□ **sim·i·lar·i·ty** /-láritee/ *n.* (*pl.* **-ies**). **sim·i·lar·ly** *adv.*

sim·i·le /símilee/ *n.* **1** a figure of speech involving the comparison of one thing with another of a different kind (e.g., *as brave as a lion*). **2** the use of such comparison.

si·mil·i·tude /símilitōod, -tyōod/ *n.* **1** the likeness, guise, or outward appearance of a thing or person. **2** a comparison or the expression of a comparison.

sim·mer /símər/ *v. & n.* ● *v.* **1** *intr. & tr.* be or keep bubbling or boiling gently. **2** *intr.* be in a state of suppressed anger or excitement. ● *n.* a simmering condition. □ **simmer down** become calm or less agitated.

sim·on-pure /símənpyŏor/ *adj.* real; genuine.

si·mo·ny /símənee, sím-/ *n.* the buying or selling of ecclesiastical privileges. □□ **si·mo·ni·ac** /-mṓneeak/ *adj. & n.* **si·mo·ni·a·cal** /-níəkəl/ *adj.*

si·moom /simṓom/ *n.* (also **si·moon** /-mōōn/) a hot, dry, dust-laden wind blowing at intervals esp. in the Arabian desert.

simp /simp/ *n. colloq.* a simpleton.

sim·pa·ti·co /simpátikō/ *adj.* congenial; likable.

sim·per /símpər/ *v. & n.* ● *v. intr.* smile in a silly or affected way. ● *n.* such a smile. □□ **sim·per·ing·ly** *adv.*

sim·ple /símpəl/ *adj.* **1** easily understood or done; presenting no difficulty (*a simple explanation; a simple task*). **2** not complicated or elaborate; without luxury or sophistication. **3** not compound; consisting of or involving only one element or operation, etc. **4** absolute; unqualified (*the simple truth; a simple majority*). **5** foolish or ignorant; gullible (*am not so simple as to agree to that*). **6** plain in appearance or manner; unsophisticated; ingenuous; artless. **7** of low rank; humble; insignificant (*simple people*). **8** *Bot.* **a** consisting of one part. **b** (of fruit) formed from one pistil. □□ **sim·ple·ness** *n.*

sim·ple eye *n.* ▼ an eye of an insect, having only one lens.

simple eyes

compound eye

segmented antenna

SIMPLE EYE: WASP'S HEAD SHOWING SIMPLE EYES

sim·ple frac·ture *n.* a fracture of the bone only, without a skin wound.

sim·ple in·ter·est *n.* interest payable on a capital sum only.

sim·ple·mind·ed /símpəlmíndid/ *adj.* **1** natural; unsophisticated. **2** feeble-minded. □□ **sim·ple·mind·ed·ly** *adv.* **sim·ple·mind·ed·ness** *n.*

SIMULATOR

Simulators are employed widely by military forces and the transportation industry, particularly to train pilots. They are also used to instruct aircraft engineers and for entertainment. In flight simulators, powerful hydraulic actuators re-create the forces experienced when flying, while computer graphics simulate the view from the cockpit window.

equipment bay · access door · display device · FLIGHT SIMULATOR COCKPIT · control cable · ventilation duct · control wire · hydraulic actuator · hydraulic hose

EXTERNAL VIEW OF A FLIGHT SIMULATOR

sim·ple sen·tence n. a sentence with a single subject and predicate.

sim·ple·ton /símpəltən/ n. a foolish, gullible, or halfwitted person.

sim·plex /símpleks/ adj. **1** simple; not compounded. **2** Computing (of a circuit) allowing transmission of signals in one direction only.

sim·plic·i·ty /simplísitee/ n. the fact or condition of being simple.

sim·pli·fy /símplifī/ v.tr. (-ies, -ied) make easy or easier to do or understand. □□ **sim·pli·fi·ca·tion** /-fikáyshən/ n.

sim·plis·tic /simplístik/ adj. **1** excessively or affectedly simple. **2** oversimplified so as to conceal or distort difficulties. □□ **sim·plis·ti·cal·ly** adv.

sim·ply /símplee/ adv. **1** in a simple manner. **2** absolutely; without doubt (simply astonishing). **3** merely (was simply trying to please).

sim·u·la·crum /símyəláykrəm, -lák-/ n. (pl. **simu·lacra** /-krə/) **1** an image of something. **2** an unsatisfactory imitation or substitute.

sim·u·late /símyəlayt/ v.tr. **1** pretend to have, feel, or be. **2** imitate or counterfeit. **3 a** imitate the conditions of (a situation, etc.), e.g., for training. **b** produce a computer model of. **4** (as **simulated** adj.) made to resemble the real thing (simulated fur). □□ **sim·u·la·tion** /-láyshən/ n.

sim·u·la·tor /símyəlaytər/ n. **1** a person or thing that simulates. **2** ▲ a device designed to simulate the operations of a complex system, used esp. in training.

si·mul·cast /síməlkast, sím-/ n. simultaneous transmission of the same program, as on radio and television.

si·mul·ta·ne·ous /síməltáyneeəs, sím-/ adj. occurring or operating at the same time. □□ **si·mul·ta·ne·i·ty** /-tənáyitee/ n. **si·mul·ta·ne·ous·ly** adv.

sin¹ /sin/ n. & v. ● n. **1 a** the breaking of divine or moral law, esp. by a conscious act. **b** such an act. **2** an offense against good taste or propriety, etc. ● v. (**sinned, sinning**) **1** intr. commit a sin. **2** intr. (foll. by against) offend. **3** tr. archaic commit (a sin). □ **as sin** colloq. extremely (ugly as sin). **for one's sins** joc. as a judgment on one for something done. **live in sin** colloq. live together without being married. □□ **sin·less** adj. **sin·less·ly** adv. **sin·less·ness** n.

sin² /sīn/ abbr. sine.

si·nan·thro·pus /sīnánthrəpəs, si-, sínanthrópəs, sín-/ n. an apelike human of the extinct genus Sinanthropus.

since /sins/ prep., conj., & adv. ● prep. throughout, or at a point in, the period between (a specified time, event, etc.) and the time present or being considered (going on since June; the greatest since Beethoven). ● conj. **1** during or in the time after (what have you been doing since we met?). **2** for the reason that; inasmuch as (since you are drunk I will drive). **3** (ellipt.) as being (more useful, since better designed). ● adv. **1** from that time or event until now or the time being considered (have not seen them since). **2** ago (happened many years since).

sin·cere /sinséer/ adj. (**sincerer, sincerest**) **1** free from pretense or deceit. **2** genuine; honest; frank. □□ **sin·cere·ness** n. **sin·cer·i·ty** /-séritee/ n.

sin·cere·ly /sinséerlee/ adv. in a sincere manner. □ **sincerely yours** a formula for ending an informal letter.

sin·ci·put /sínsipoot/ n. Anat. the front of the skull from the forehead to the crown. □□ **sin·cip·i·tal** /-sipitəl/ adj.

sine /sīn/ n. Math. the trigonometric function that is equal to the ratio of the side opposite a given angle (in a right triangle) to the hypotenuse.

si·ne·cure /sínikyoor, sín-/ n. a position that requires little or no work but usu. yields profit or honor. □□ **si·ne·cur·ism** n. **si·ne·cur·ist** n.

sine curve n. (also **sine wave**) a curve representing periodic oscillations of constant amplitude, as given by a graph of the value of the sine plotted as a function of angle.

si·ne di·e /sínee dí-ee, sínay deé-ay/ adv. (of business adjourned indefinitely) with no appointed date.

si·ne qua non /sínay kwaa nón/ n. an indispensable condition or qualification.

sin·ew /sínyoo/ n. **1** tough fibrous tissue uniting muscle to bone. **2** (in pl.) physical strength. **3** (in pl.) the strength or framework of a structure, system, etc. □□ **sin·ew·y** adj.

sin·fo·ni·a /sínfənéeə/ n. Mus. **1** a symphony. **2** (in Baroque music) an orchestral piece used as an introduction to an opera, cantata, or suite. **3** (**Sinfonia**; usu. in names) a symphony orchestra.

sin·fo·niet·ta /sínfənyétə/ n. Mus. **1** a short or simple symphony. **2** (**Sinfonietta**; usu. in names) a small symphony orchestra.

sin·ful /sínfool/ adj. **1** (of a person) committing sin, esp. habitually. **2** (of an act) involving or characterized by sin. □□ **sin·ful·ly** adv. **sin·ful·ness** n.

sing /sing/ v. & n. ● v. (past **sang** /sang/; past part. **sung** /sung/) **1** intr. utter musical sounds with the voice, esp. words with a set tune. **2** tr. utter or produce by singing. **3** intr. (of the wind, a kettle, etc.) make melodious or humming, or whistling sounds. **4** intr. (of the ears) be affected as with a buzzing sound. **5** intr. sl. turn informer; confess. ● n. **1** an act or spell of singing. **2** a meeting for amateur singing. □ **sing out** call out loudly. **sing the praises of** see PRAISE. **sing up** sing more loudly. □□ **sing·a·ble** adj. **sing·er** n. **sing·ing·ly** adv.

sing. abbr. singular.

sing·a·long n. **1** a tune, etc., to which one can sing in accompaniment. **2** a gathering at which such tunes, etc., are sung.

singe /sinj/ v. & n. ● v. (**singeing**) **1** tr. & intr. burn superficially or lightly. **2** tr. burn the bristles or down off (the carcass of a pig or fowl) to prepare it for cooking. ● n. a superficial burn.

Singh /sing/ n. **1** a title adopted by the warrior castes of N. India. **2** a surname adopted by male Sikhs.

Sin·gha·lese var. of SINHALESE.

sin·gle /sínggəl/ adj., n., & v. ● adj. **1** one only; not double or multiple. **2** united or undivided. **3 a** designed or suitable for one person (single room). **b** used or done by one person, etc. **4** one by itself (a single tree). **5** regarded separately (every single thing). **6** not married. **7** (with neg. or interrog.) even one (did not see a single person). **8** (of a flower) having only one circle of petals. ● n. **1** a single thing, or item in a series. **2** a recording with one piece of music, etc., on each side. **3** Baseball a hit that allows the batter to reach first base safely. **4** (usu. in pl.) a game, esp. tennis, with one player on each side. **5** an unmarried person (young singles). **6** sl. a one-dollar bill. ● v. **1** tr. (foll. by out) choose as an example or as distinguishable or to serve some purpose. **2** intr. Baseball hit a single. □□ **sin·gle·ness** n. **sin·gly** adv.

sin·gle-breast·ed adj. (of a coat, etc.) having only one set of buttons and buttonholes, not over lapping.

sin·gle file n. a line of people or things arranged one behind another.

sin·gle-hand·ed adv. & adj. ● adv. **1** without help from another. **2** with one hand. ● adj. **1** done, etc., single-handed. **2** for one hand. □□ **sin·gle-hand·ed·ly** adv.

sin·gle-lens re·flex adj. denoting a reflex camera in which a single lens serves the film and the viewfinder.

sin·gle malt n. whisky that has not been blended with any other malt.

sin·gle-mind·ed adj. having or intent on only one purpose.

sin·gle par·ent n. a person bringing up a child or children without a partner.

sin·gles bar n. a bar for single people seeking company.

sin·glet /síngglit/ n. a sleeveless athletic shirt.

sin·gle·ton /sínggəltən/ n. **1** Cards one card only of a suit, esp. as dealt to a player. **2 a** a single person or thing. **b** an only child.

sin·gle·tree /sínggəltree/ n. = WHIFFLETREE.

sing·song /síngsawng, -song/ adj., n., & v. ● adj. uttered with a monotonous rhythm or cadence. ● n. a singsong manner. ● v.intr. & tr. (past and past part. **singsonged**) speak or recite in a singsong manner.

sin·gu·lar /sínggyələr/ adj. & n. ● adj. **1** unique; much beyond the average. **2** eccentric or strange. **3** Gram. (of a word or form) denoting or referring to a single person or thing. **4** single; individual. ● n. Gram. **1** a singular word or form. **2** the singular number. □□ **sin·gu·lar·ly** adv.

sin·gu·lar·i·ty /sínggyəláritee/ n. (pl. **-ies**) **1** the state or condition of being singular. **2** an odd trait or peculiarity.

sin·gu·lar·ize /sínggyələrīz/ v.tr. **1** distinguish. **2** make singular. □□ **sin·gu·lar·i·za·tion** n.

sinh /sinch, sínaych/ abbr. Math. hyperbolic sine.

Sin·ha·lese /sínhəleéz, sínə-/ n. & adj. (also **Sin·gha·lese** /sínggə-/) ● n. (pl. same) **1** a member of a people originally from N. India and now forming the majority of the population of Sri Lanka. **2** an Indic language spoken by this people. ● adj. of or relating to this people or language.

sin·is·ter /sínistər/ adj. **1** suggestive of evil; looking villainous. **2** wicked or criminal (a sinister motive). **3** of evil omen. **4** Heraldry on the left-hand side of a shield, etc. (i.e., to the observer's right). □□ **sin·is·ter·ly** adv. **sin·is·ter·ness** n.

sin·is·tral /sínistrəl/ adj. & n. ● adj. **1** left-handed. **2** of or on the left. **3** (of a flatfish) with the left side uppermost. **4** (of a spiral shell) with whorls rising to the left and not (as usually) to the right. ● *n.* a left-handed person. ☐☐ **sin·is·tral·i·ty** /-trálitee/ *n.* **sin·is·tral·ly** *adv.*

sin·is·trorse /sínistrawrs/ *adj.* rising toward the left, esp. of the spiral stem of a plant.

sink /singk/ *v. & n.* (*past* **sank** /sangk/ or **sunk** /sungk/; *past part.* **sunk** or **sunken**) **1** *intr.* fall or come slowly downward. **2** *intr.* disappear below the horizon (*the sun is sinking*). **3** *intr.* **a** go or penetrate below the surface esp. of a liquid. **b** (of a ship) go to the bottom of the sea. **4** *intr.* settle comfortably (*sank into a chair*). **5** *intr.* **a** gradually lose strength or value or quality, etc. (*my heart sank*). **b** (of the voice) descend in pitch or volume. **c** (of a sick person) approach death. **6** *tr.* send (a ship) to the bottom of the sea, etc. **7** *tr.* cause or allow to sink or penetrate (*sank its teeth into my leg*). **8** *tr.* cause the failure of (a plan, etc.), or the discomfiture of (a person). **9** *tr.* dig (a well) or bore (a shaft). **10** *tr.* engrave (a die) or inlay (a design). **11** *tr.* **a** invest (money) (*sunk a large sum into the business*). **b** lose (money) by investment. **12** *tr.* **a** cause (a ball) to enter a pocket in billiards, a hole at golf, etc. **b** achieve this by (a stroke). **13** *intr.* (of a price, etc.) become lower. **14** *intr.* (of a storm or river) subside. **15** *intr.* (of ground) slope down, or reach a lower level by subsidence. **16** *intr.* (foll. by *on, upon*) (of darkness) descend (on a place). **17** *tr.* lower the level of. **18** *tr.* (usu. in *passive*; foll. by *in*) absorb; hold the attention of (*sunk in thought*). ● *n.* **1** a fixed basin with a water supply and outflow pipe. **2** a place where foul liquid collects. **3** a place of vice or corruption. **4** a pool or marsh in which a river's water disappears by evaporation or percolation. **5** *Physics* a body or process used to absorb or dissipate heat. ☐ **sink in 1** penetrate or make its way in. **2** become gradually comprehended (*paused to let the words sink in*). **sink or swim** even at the risk of complete failure. ☐☐ **sink·a·ble** *adj.* **sink·age** *n.*

sink·er /síngkər/ *n.* **1** ◀ a weight used to sink a fishing line or sounding line. **2** *Baseball* (in full **sinkerball**) a pitch thrown so that it curves sharply downward.

sink·hole /síngkhōl/ *n. Geol.* a cavity in limestone, etc., into which a stream, etc., disappears.

sink·ing feel·ing *n.* a bodily sensation caused by hunger or apprehension.

sink·ing fund *n.* money set aside for the gradual repayment of a debt.

SINKER: DISK WEIGHT USED FOR FISHING

sin·ner /sínər/ *n.* a person who sins, esp. habitually.

sin·net var. of SENNIT.

Sinn Fein /shin fáyn/ *n.* a political movement and party seeking a united republican Ireland, often linked to the IRA. ☐☐ **Sinn Fein·er** *n.*

Sino- /sínō/ *comb. form* Chinese; Chinese and (*Sino-American*).

si·no·logue /sínəlawg, -log, sín-/ *n.* an expert in sinology; sinologist.

si·nol·o·gy /sīnóləjee, sin-/ *n.* the study of Chinese language, history, customs, etc. ☐☐ **si·no·log·i·cal** /-nəlójikəl/ *adj.* **si·nol·o·gist** *n.*

sin·ter /síntər/ *n. & v.* ● *n.* **1** ▶ a siliceous or calcareous rock formed by deposition from springs. **2** a substance formed by sintering. ● *v.intr. & tr.* coalesce or cause to coalesce from powder into solid by heating.

sin·u·ate /sínyŏōət, -ayt/ *adj. esp. Bot.* wavy-edged; with distinct inward and outward bends along the edge.

sin·u·os·i·ty /sínyŏō-ósitee/ *n.* (*pl.* **-ies**) the state of being sinuous.

sin·u·ous /sínyŏōəs/ *adj.* with many curves; undulating. ☐☐ **sin·u·ous·ly** *adv.* **sin·u·ous·ness** *n.*

SINTER: TRAVERTINE

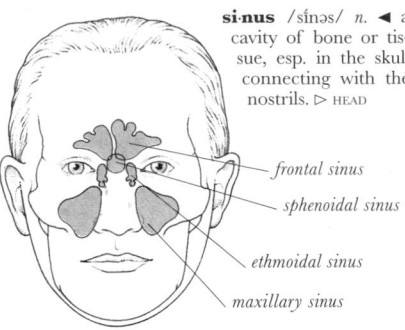

SINUS: LOCATION OF SINUSES

si·nus /sínəs/ *n.* ◀ a cavity of bone or tissue, esp. in the skull connecting with the nostrils. ▷ HEAD

frontal sinus
sphenoidal sinus
ethmoidal sinus
maxillary sinus

si·nus·i·tis /sínəsítis/ *n.* inflammation of a nasal sinus.

si·nus·oid /sínəsoyd/ *n.* **1** a curve having the form of a sine wave. **2** a small irregular-shaped blood vessel, esp. found in the liver. ☐☐ **si·nus·oi·dal** /-sóyd'l/ *adj.*

-sion /shən, zhən/ *suffix* forming nouns (see -ION) from Latin participial stems in -*s*- (*mansion; mission; persuasion*).

Si·on var. of ZION.

Sioux /sŏō/ *n. & adj.* ● *n.* (*pl.* same) **1** a member of a group of native N. American peoples. **2** the language of this group. ● *adj.* of or relating to this people or language.

sip /sip/ *v. & n.* ● *v.tr. & intr.* (**sipped, sipping**) drink in one or more small amounts or by spoonfuls. ● *n.* **1** a small mouthful of liquid (*a sip of brandy*). **2** the act of taking this. ☐☐ **sip·per** *n.*

si·phon /sífən/ *n. & v.* (also **sy·phon**) ● *n.* **1** ▶ a pipe or tube shaped like an inverted V or U with unequal legs to convey a liquid from a container to a lower level by atmospheric pressure. **2** (in full **siphon bottle**) an aerated-water bottle from which liquid is forced out through a tube by the pressure of gas. ● *v.tr. & intr.* (often foll. by *off*) **1** conduct or flow through a siphon. **2** divert or set aside (funds, etc.).

si·phon·o·phore /sīfónəfawr/ *n.* any usu. translucent marine hydrozoan of the order Siphonophora, e.g., the Portuguese man-of-war.

sip·pet /sípit/ *n.* **1** a small piece of bread, etc., soaked in liquid. **2** a piece of toast or fried bread as a garnish. **3** a fragment.

sir /sər/ *n.* **1** a polite form of address or mode of reference to a man. **2** (**Sir**) a titular prefix to the forename of a knight or baronet.

sir·dar /sárdaar/ *n. Ind.*, etc. **1** a person of high political or military rank. **2** a Sikh.

sire /sīr/ *n. & v.* ● *n.* **1** the male parent of an animal, esp. a stallion. **2** *archaic* a respectful form of address, esp. to a king. **3** *archaic poet.* a father or male ancestor. ● *v.tr.* (esp. of a stallion) beget.

si·ren /sírən/ *n.* **1 a** a device for making a loud prolonged signal or warning sound, esp. by revolving a perforated disk over a jet of compressed air or steam. **b** the sound made by this. **2** (in Greek mythology) each of a number of women or winged creatures whose singing lured unwary sailors onto rocks. **3 a** a temptress. **b** a tempting pursuit, etc.

si·re·ni·an /sīréeneeən/ *adj. & n.* ● *adj.* of the order Sirenia of large aquatic plant-eating mammals. ● *n.* any mammal of this order.

siphon tube
difference in liquid levels

SIPHON: DEMONSTRATION OF THE ACTION OF A SIPHON

sir·loin /sárloyn/ *n.* the upper and choicer part of a loin of beef.

si·roc·co /sirókō/ *n.* (also **sci·roc·co**) (*pl.* **-os**) **1** a Saharan simoom reaching the northern shores of the Mediterranean. **2** a warm rainy wind in S. Europe.

sir·rah /sírə/ *n. archaic* = SIR (as a form of address).

sir·ree /sirée/ *int. colloq.* as an emphatic, esp. after *yes* or *no*.

sir·up var. of SYRUP.

sis /sis/ *n. colloq.* a sister.

si·sal /sísəl/ *n.* **1** a Mexican plant, *Agave sisalana*, with large fleshy leaves. **2** the fiber made from this plant, used for cordage, ropes, etc. ▷ ROPE

sis·kin /sískin/ *n.* ▶ a dark-streaked, yellowish-green songbird, *Carduelis spinus*.

sis·sy /sísee/ *n. & adj. colloq.* ● *n.* (*pl.* **-ies**) an effeminate or cowardly person. ● *adj.* (**sissier, sissiest**) effeminate; cowardly. ☐☐ **sis·si·fied** *adj.* **sis·si·ness** *n.* **sis·sy·ish** *adj.*

SISKIN (*Carduelis spinus*)

sis·ter /sístər/ *n.* **1** a woman or girl in relation to sons and other daughters of her parents. **2 a** a close female friend or associate. **b** a female fellow member of a trade union, class, sect, or the human race. **3** a member of a female religious order. **4** (*attrib.*) of the same type or design or origin, etc. (*sister ship*). ☐☐ **sis·ter·less** *adj.* **sis·ter·ly** *adj.* **sis·ter·li·ness** *n.*

sis·ter·hood /sístərhŏŏd/ *n.* **1 a** the relationship between sisters. **b** sisterly friendliness; mutual support. **2 a** a society or association of women, esp. when bound by monastic vows or devoting themselves to religious or charitable work or the feminist cause. **b** its members collectively.

sis·ter-in-law *n.* (*pl.* **sisters-in-law**) **1** the sister of one's wife or husband. **2** the wife of one's brother. **3** the wife of one's brother-in-law.

Sis·tine /sísteen, sistéen/ *adj.* of any of the Popes called Sixtus, esp. Sixtus IV. ☐ **Sistine Chapel** a chapel in the Vatican, with frescoes by Michelangelo and other painters.

sis·trum /sístrəm/ *n.* (*pl.* **sistra** /-trə/) a jingling metal instrument used by the ancient Egyptians esp. in the worship of Isis.

Sis·y·phe·an /sísifée-ən/ *adj.* (of toil) endless and fruitless like that of Sisyphus in Greek mythology (whose task in Hades was to push uphill a stone that at once rolled down again).

sit /sit/ *v.* (**sitting**; *past* and *past part.* **sat** /sat/) **1** *intr.* adopt or be in a position in which the body is supported more or less upright by the buttocks resting on the ground or a raised seat, etc., with the thighs usu. horizontal. **2** *tr.* cause to sit; place in a sitting position. **3** *intr.* **a** (of a bird) perch. **b** (of an animal) rest with the hind legs bent and the body close to the ground. **4** *intr.* (of a bird) remain on its nest to hatch its eggs. **5** *intr.* **a** be engaged in an occupation in which the sitting position is usual. **b** (of a committee, legislative body, etc.) be engaged in business. **c** (of an individual) hold some office or position (*sat as a magistrate*). **6** *intr.* (usu. foll. by *for*) pose in a sitting position (for a portrait). **7** *intr.* (followed by *for*) *Brit.* be a member of Parliament for (a constituency). **8** *intr.* be in a more or less permanent position or condition (esp. of inactivity or being out of use or out of place). **9** *intr.* (of clothes, etc.) fit or hang in a certain way. **10** *tr.* keep or have one's seat on (a horse, etc.). **11** *intr.* act as a babysitter. **12** *intr.* (often foll. by *before*) (of an army) take a position outside a city, etc., to besiege it. ☐ **be sitting pretty** be comfort-

S

ably or advantageously placed. **make a person sit up** *colloq.* surprise or interest a person. **sit at a person's feet** be a person's pupil. **sit back** relax one's efforts. **sit by** look on without interfering. **sit down 1** sit after standing. **2** cause to sit. **sit in 1** occupy a place as a protest. **2** (foll. by *for*) take the place of. **3** (foll. by *on*) be present as a guest or observer at (a meeting, etc.). **sit in judgment** assume the right of judging others; be censorious. **sit on 1** be a member of (a committee, etc.). **2** hold a session or inquiry concerning. **3** *colloq.* delay action about (*the government has been sitting on the report*). **4** *colloq.* repress or rebuke or snub (*felt rather sat on*). **sit on the fence** see FENCE. **sit on one's hands 1** take no action. **2** refuse to applaud. **sit out 1** take no part in (a dance, etc.). **2** stay till the end of (esp. an ordeal). **sit tight** *colloq.* **1** remain firmly in one's place. **2** not be shaken off or move away or yield to distractions. **sit up 1** rise from a lying to a sitting position. **2** sit firmly upright. **3** go to bed later. **4** *colloq.* become interested or aroused, etc.

si·tar /sitáar, sítaar/ *n.* ◀ a long-necked E. Indian lute with movable frets. ▷ STRINGED. □□ **si·tar·ist** /sitáarist/ *n.*

sit·com /sítkom/ *n. colloq.* a situation comedy.

sit-down *adj.* (of a meal) eaten sitting at a table.

sit-down strike *n.* a strike in which workers refuse to leave their place of work.

site /sīt/ *n. & v.* ● *n.* **1** the ground chosen or used for a town or building. **2** a place where some activity is or has been conducted (*camping site; launching site*). ● *v.tr.* **1** locate or place. **2** provide with a site.

sit-in *n.* a protest involving sitting in.

Sit·ka /sítkə/ *n.* (in full **Sitka spruce**) a fast-growing spruce, *Picea sitchensis*, native to N. America and yielding timber.

sit·ter /sítər/ *n.* **1** a baby-sitter or nanny. **2** a sitting hen. **3** a person who sits, esp. for a portrait.

tuning peg

inlaid finger-board

arched metal fret

bridge

sound box

end pins

SITAR

sit·ting /síting/ *n. & adj.* ● *n.* **1** a continuous period of being seated, esp. engaged in an activity (*finished the book in one sitting*). **2** a time during which an assembly is engaged in business. **3** a session in which a meal is served (*dinner will be served in two sittings*). **4** a clutch of eggs. ● *adj.* **1** having sat down. **2** (of an animal or bird) not running or flying. **3** (of a hen) engaged in hatching. □ **sitting pretty** see PRETTY.

sit·ting duck *n.* (also **sit·ting tar·get**) *colloq.* a vulnerable person or thing.

sit·ting room *n.* esp. *Brit.* a room in a house for relaxed sitting in.

sit·u·ate *v. & adj.* ● *v.tr.* /síchoo-ayt/ (usu. in *passive*) **1** put in a certain position or circumstances (*is situated at the top of a hill; how are you situated at the moment?*). **2** establish or indicate the place of; put in a context. ● *adj.* /síchooət/ *Law* or *archaic* situated.

sit·u·a·tion /síchoo-áyshən/ *n.* **1** a place and its surroundings (*the house stands in a fine situation*). **2** a set of circumstances; a position in which one finds oneself; a state of affairs (*came out of a difficult situation with credit*). **3** an employee's position or job. **4** a critical point or complication in a drama. □□ **sit·u·a·tion·al** *adj.*

sit·u·a·tion com·e·dy *n.* a comedy in which the humor derives from the situations the characters are placed in.

sit-up *n.* a physical exercise in which a person sits up without raising the legs from the ground.

sitz bath /sítsbath, zíts-/ *n.* a usu. portable bath in which a person sits.

Si·va /séevə, shéevə/ *n.* (also **Shi·va** /shéevə/) a Hindu deity associated with the powers of repro-duction and dissolution, regarded by some as the supreme being and by others as a member of the triad. □□ **Si·va·ism** *n.* **Si·va·ite** *n. & adj.*

six /siks/ *n. & adj.* ● *n.* **1** one more than five. **2** a symbol for this (6, vi, VI). **3** a size, etc., denoted by six. **4** a set or team of six indi-viduals. **5** the time of six o'clock. **6** a card, etc., with six pips. ● *adj.* that amount to six. □ **at sixes and sevens** in confusion or disagreement. **six of one and half a dozen of another** a situation of little real difference between the alternatives.

six·ain /síksayn/ *n.* a six-line stanza.

six·fold /síksfōld/ *adj. & adv.* **1** six times as much or as many. **2** consisting of six parts.

six-gun *n.* = SIX-SHOOTER.

six-pack *n.* six cans or bottles, as of beer, a soft drink, etc., packaged and sold as a unit.

six-shoot·er *n.* a revolver with six chambers. ▷ REVOLVER

six·teen /síksteen/ *n. & adj.* ● *n.* **1** one more than fifteen. **2** a symbol for this (16, xvi, XVI). **3** a size, etc., denoted by sixteen. ● *adj.* that amount to sixteen. □□ **six·teenth** *adj. & n.*

six·teen·mo /siksteenmō/ *n.* (*pl.* **-os**) sextodecimo.

six·teenth note *n. Mus.* a note having a time value of a sixteenth of a whole note and represented by a large dot with a two-hooked stem. ▷ NOTATION

sixth /siksth/ *n. & adj.* ● *n.* **1** the position in a sequence corresponding to that of the number 6 in the sequence 1–6. **2** something occupying this posi-tion. **3** any of six equal parts of a thing. **4** *Mus.* **a** an interval or chord spanning six consecutive notes in the diatonic scale (e.g., C to A). **b** a note separated from another by this interval. ● *adj.* that is the sixth. □□ **sixth·ly** *adv.*

sixth sense *n.* **1** a supposed faculty giving intuitive or extrasensory knowledge. **2** such knowledge.

six·ty /síkstee/ *n. & adj.* ● *n.* (*pl.* **-ies**) **1** the product of six and ten. **2** a symbol for this (60, lx, LX). **3** (in *pl.*) the numbers from 60 to 69, esp. the years of a century or of a person's life. **4** a set of sixty persons or things. ● *adj.* that amount to sixty. □□ **six·ti·eth** *adj. & n.* **six·ty·fold** *adj. & adv.*

six·ty-four thou·sand dol·lar ques·tion *n.* (also **sixty-four dollar question**) a difficult and crucial question (from the top prize in a broadcast quiz show).

six·ty-nine *n. sl.* sexual activity between two people involving mutual oral stimulation of the genitals.

siz·a·ble /sízəbəl/ *adj.* (also **size·a·ble**) large or fairly large. □□ **siz·a·bly** *adv.*

size[1] /sīz/ *n. & v.* ● *n.* **1** the relative bigness or extent of a thing; dimensions (*is of vast size; size matters less than quality*). **2** each of the classes into which things otherwise similar are divided accord-ing to size (*is made in several sizes; is three sizes too big*). ● *v.tr.* sort in sizes or according to size. □ **of a size** having the same size. **of some size** fairly large. **the size of** as big as. **the size of it** *colloq.* a true account of the matter (*that is the size of it*). **size up 1** estimate the size of. **2** *colloq.* form a judgment of. □□ **sized** *adj.* (also in *comb.*). **siz·er** *n.*

size[2] /sīz/ *n. & v.* ● *n.* a gelatinous solution used in stiffening textiles, preparing plastered walls for decoration, etc. ● *v.tr.* glaze or stiffen or treat with size.

size·a·ble var. of SIZABLE.

size·ism /sízizəm/ *n.* prejudice or discrimination on the grounds of a person's size.

siz·zle /sízəl/ *v. & n.* ● *v.intr.* **1** make a sputtering or hissing sound as of frying. **2** *colloq.* be in a state of great heat or excitement or marked effectiveness. ● *n.* a sizzling sound. □□ **siz·zler** *n.* **siz·zling** *adj. & adv.* (*sizzling hot*).

SJ *abbr.* Society of Jesus.

sjam·bok /shámbok/ *n. & v.* ● *n.* (in S. Africa) a rhinoceros-hide whip. ● *v.tr.* flog with a sjambok.

skald /skawld/ *n.* (also **scald**) (in ancient Scandi-navia) a composer and reciter of poems honoring heroes and their deeds. □□ **skald·ic** *adj.*

skat /skat/ *n.* a three-handed card game with bidding.

skate[1] /skayt/ *n. & v.* ● *n.* **1** ◀ each of a pair of steel blades (or of boots with blades attached) for gliding on ice. ▷ HOCKEY. **2** (in full **roller skate**) each of a pair of metal frames with small wheels, fitted to shoes for riding on a hard surface. **3** a device on which a heavy object moves. ● *v.* **1 a** *intr.* move on skates. **b** *tr.* perform (a specified fig-ure) on skates. **2** *intr.* (foll. by *over*) refer fleetingly to; disre-gard. □ **skate on thin ice** *colloq.* behave rashly; risk dan-ger, esp. by dealing with a sub-ject needing tactful treatment. □□ **skat·er** *n.*

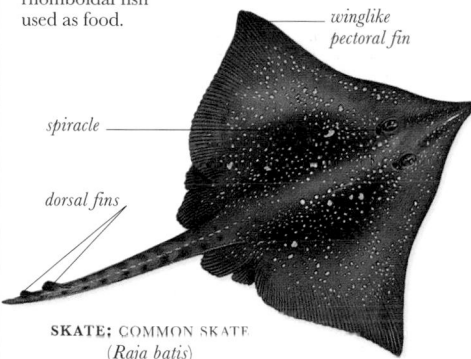

ankle support

boot

safety heel tip *blade*

SKATE: ICE HOCKEY SKATE

skate[2] /skayt/ *n.* (*pl.* same or **skates**) ▼ any ray of the family Rajidae, esp. *Raja batis*, a large, flat, rhomboidal fish used as food.

winglike pectoral fin

spiracle

dorsal fins

SKATE; COMMON SKATE
(*Raja batis*)

skate[3] /skayt/ *n. sl.* a contemptible or dishonest person (esp. *cheapskate*).

skate·board /skáytbawrd/ *n. & v.* ● *n.* ▼ a short narrow board on roller-skate wheels for riding on while standing. ● *v.intr.* ride on a skateboard. □□ **skate·board·er** *n.*

board *truck*

SKATEBOARD

skat·ing rink *n.* a piece of ice artificially made, or a floor used, for skating.

skean /skeen, skéeən/ *n. hist.* a Gaelic dagger formerly used in Ireland and Scotland.

skean-dhu /skeen-dóo/ *n.* a dagger worn in the stocking as part of Highland costume.

ske·dad·dle /skidád'l/ *v. & n.* ● *v.intr. colloq.* run away; depart quickly; flee. ● *n.* a hurried departure or flight.

skeet /skeet/ *n.* a shooting sport in which a clay target is thrown from a trap to simulate the flight of a bird.

skee·ter[1] /skéetər/ *n. US dial., Austral. sl.* a mosquito.

skee·ter[2] var. of SKITTER.

skeg /skeg/ *n.* **1** a fin underneath the rear of a surf-board. **2** the after part of a vessel's keel or a projec-tion from it.

skein /skayn/ *n.* **1** a loosely coiled bundle of yarn or thread. **2** a flock of wild geese, etc., in flight. **3** a tangle or confusion.

S

skel·e·ton /skélit'n/ *n.* **1** ▼ a hard framework of bones, cartilage, shell, woody fiber, etc., supporting or containing the body of an animal or plant. **2** the supporting framework or structure of a thing. **3** a very thin person or animal. **4** the remaining part of anything after its life or usefulness is gone. **5** an outline sketch. **6** (*attrib.*) having only the essential or minimum number of persons, parts, etc. (*skeleton staff*). □□ **skel·e·tal** *adj.* **skel·e·tal·ly** *adv.* **skel·e·ton·ize** *v.tr.*

skel·e·ton in the clos·et *n.* a discreditable or embarrassing fact kept secret.

skel·e·ton key *n.* a key designed to fit many locks.

skell /skel/ *n. US colloq.* (in New York) a tramp or homeless person.

skep /skep/ *n.* **1 a** a wooden or wicker basket of any of various forms. **b** the quantity contained in this. **2** ▶ a straw or wicker beehive.

skep·sis /sképsis/ *n.* (*Brit.* **scep·sis**) **1** philosophic doubt. **2** skeptical philosophy.

skep·tic /sképtik/ *n. & adj.* ● *n.* **1** a person inclined to doubt all accepted opinions. **2** a person who doubts the truth of religions. ● *adj.* = SKEPTICAL. □□ **skep·ti·cism** /-tisizəm/ *n.*

skep·ti·cal /sképtikəl/ *adj.* inclined to question the truth or

SKEP

soundness of accepted ideas, facts, etc. □□ **skep·ti·cal·ly** *adv.*

sketch /skech/ *n. & v.* ● *n.* **1** a rough, slight, merely outlined, or unfinished drawing or painting, often made to assist in making a more finished picture. **2** a brief account; a rough draft or general outline. **3** a very short play, usu. humorous and limited to one scene. **4** a short descriptive piece of writing. ● *v.* **1** *tr.* make or give a sketch of. **2** *intr.* draw sketches (*went out sketching*). **3** *tr.* (often foll. by *in*, *out*) indicate briefly or in outline. □□ **sketch·er** *n.*

sketch·book /skéchbook/ *n.* a book or pad of drawing paper for doing sketches on.

sketch·y /skéchee/ *adj.* (**sketchier**, **sketchiest**) **1** giving only a rough outline, like a sketch. **2** *colloq.* unsubstantial or imperfect esp. through haste. □□ **sketch·i·ly** *adv.* **sketch·i·ness** *n.*

skeu·o·morph /skyóoəmawrf/ *n.* **1** an object or feature copying the design of a similar artifact in another material. **2** an ornamental design resulting from the nature of the material used or the method of working it. □□ **skeu·o·mor·phic** /-máwrfik/ *adj.*

skew /skyoo/ *adj., n., & v.* ● *adj.* oblique; slanting; set askew. ● *v.* **1** *tr.* make skew. **2** *tr.* distort. **3** *intr.* move obliquely. **4** *intr.* twist. □ **on the skew** askew. □□ **skew·ness** *n.*

skew·back /skyóobak/ *n.* the sloping face of the abutment on which an extremity of an arch rests.

skew·bald /skyóobawld/ *adj. & n.* ● *adj.* ▼ (of an animal) with irregular patches of white and another color (properly not black). ● *n.* a skewbald animal.

SKEWBALD PONY

skew·er /skyóoər/ *n. & v.* ● *n.* a long pin designed for holding meat compactly together while cooking. ● *v.tr.* **1** fasten together or pierce with or as with a skewer. **2** criticize sharply.

ski /skee/ *n. & v.* ● *n.* (*pl.* **skis** or **ski**) **1** ▲ each of a pair of long narrow pieces of wood, etc., usu. pointed and turned up at the front, fastened under the feet for traveling over snow. **2** a similar device under a vehicle or aircraft. **3** = WATER SKI. **4** (*attrib.*) for wear when skiing (*ski boots*). ● *v.* (**skis**, **skied** /skeed/; **skiing**) **1** *intr.* ▲ travel on skis. **2** *tr.* ski at (a place). □□ **ski·a·ble** *adj.*

ski·a·gra·phy /skīágrəfee/ *n.* (also *Brit.* **sci·a·gra·phy**) the art of shading in drawing, etc. □□ **ski·a·gram** /skíəgram/ *n.* **ski·a·graph** /skíəgraf/ *n. & v.tr.* **ski·a·graph·ic** /-gráfik/ *adj.*

ski·bob /skéebob/ *n. & v.* ● *n.* a machine like a bicycle with skis instead of wheels. ● *v.intr.* (**-bobbed**, **-bobbing**) ride a skibob. □□ **ski·bob·ber** *n.*

skid /skid/ *v. & n.* ● *v.* (**skidded**, **skidding**) **1** *intr.* (of a vehicle, a wheel, or a driver) slide on slippery ground, esp. sideways or obliquely. **2** *tr.* cause (a vehicle, etc.) to skid. **3** *intr.* slip; slide. ● *n.* **1** the act or an instance of skidding. **2** a piece of wood, etc., serving as a support, ship's fender, inclined plane, etc. **3** a braking device, esp. a wooden or metal shoe preventing a wheel from revolving or used as a drag. **4** a runner beneath an aircraft for use when landing. □ **hit the skids** *colloq.* enter a rapid decline or deterioration. **on the skids** *colloq.* about to be discarded or defeated. **put the skids under**

SKELETON

The human skeleton supports the body, protects the internal organs, and provides anchorage for the muscles. It consists of bones and connective tissue called cartilage. An individual bone is about five times stronger than a steel bar of similar weight, and the many joints in a skeleton allow a wide range of movement. The human skeleton contains 206 bones (about half of which are in the hands and feet) and consists of two main groups: the axial skeleton (skull, vertebral column, and ribcage) and the appendicular skeleton (the bones of the arms and legs). To allow for childbirth, the female pelvic cavity is shallower and wider than the male cavity.

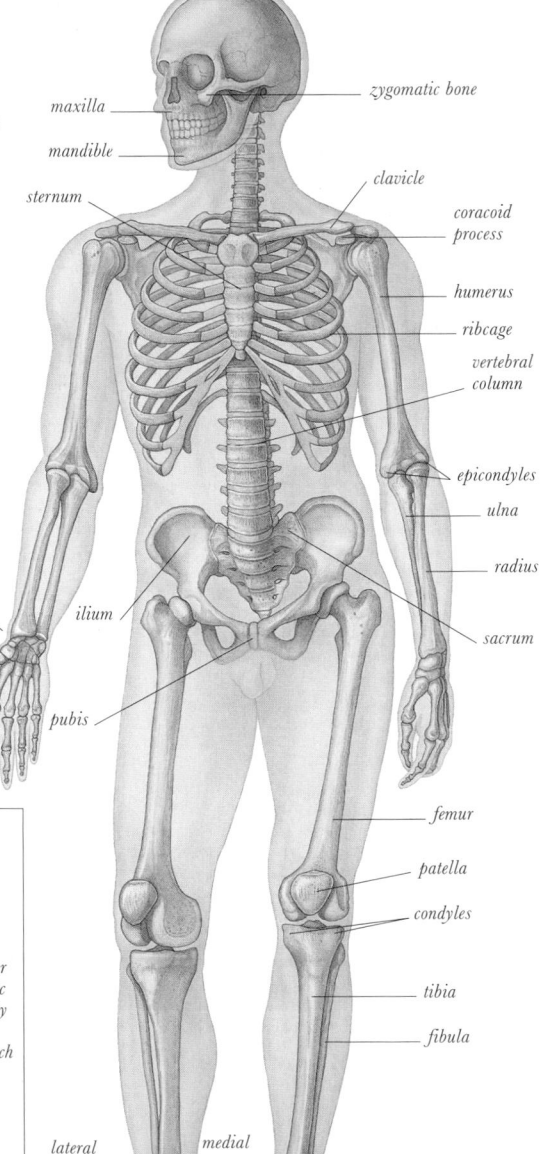

cranium
zygomatic bone
maxilla
mandible
clavicle
sternum
coracoid process
humerus
ribcage
vertebral column
epicondyles
ulna
radius
carpals
metacarpals
phalanges
ilium
sacrum
pubis

SKELETON OF A HUMAN MALE

femur
patella
condyles
tibia
fibula
lateral malleolus
medial malleolus
navicular
talus
tarsals
cuneiform bones
meta-tarsals
calcaneus
phalanges

SEXUAL DIFFERENCES IN THE PELVIS

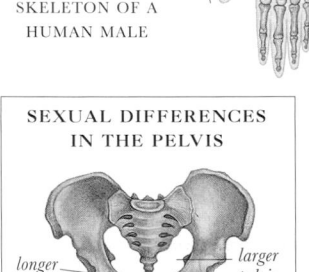

longer superior pubic ramus
larger pelvic cavity
wider subpubic arch

FEMALE PELVIS

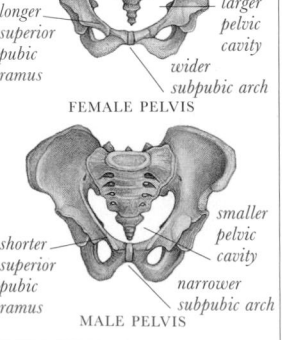

shorter superior pubic ramus
smaller pelvic cavity
narrower subpubic arch

MALE PELVIS

S

SKI

There are four types of competitive skiing: Alpine (downhill and slalom), Nordic (cross-country and ski jumping), freestyle (moguls and aerials), and biathlon (cross-country with rifle shooting). The skis, which are usually made of synthetic materials, vary in length and weight according to use. Slalom skis, for example, are shorter to aid maneuverability, while cross-country skis are light and narrow, with a toe fastening that allows the heel to move up and down with each stride. Downhill ski boots support the ankles and guarantee that the skier is leaning forward at the correct angle. Safety bindings fasten the boot to the ski but release under pressure. Ski poles assist with balance and turning.

wind- and waterproof jacket

ski pole

basket

safety binding

ski boot

afterbody of ski

forebody of ski

DOWNHILL SKIER

colloq. **1** hasten the downfall or failure of. **2** cause to hasten.

skid·doo /skidoō/ *v.intr.* (also **skid·oo**) (**-oos**, **-ooed**) *sl.* go away; depart.

skid row *n. colloq.* a part of a town frequented by vagrants, alcoholics, etc.

ski·er /skēˈər/ *n.* a person who skis.

skiff /skif/ *n.* a light rowboat or scull.

skif·fle /skifəl/ *n.* a kind of folk music played by a small group, mainly with a rhythmic accompaniment to a singing guitarist, etc.

ski jump *n.* **1** a steep slope leveling off before a sharp drop to allow a skier to leap through the air. **2** a jump made from this. □□ **ski jump·er** *n.* **ski jump·ing** *n.*

ski lift *n.* ◀ a device for carrying skiers up a slope, usu. on seats hung from an overhead cable.

pole to overhead cable

SKI LIFT

skill /skil/ *n.* expertness; practiced ability; facility in an action.

skilled /skild/ *adj.* **1** skillful. **2** (of a worker) highly trained or experienced. **3** (of work) requiring skill or special training.

skil·let /skilit/ *n.* a frying pan.

skill·ful /skilfoōl/ *adj.* having or showing skill. □□ **skill·ful·ly** *adv.* **skill·ful·ness** *n.*

skim /skim/ *v. & n.* ● *v.* (**skimmed**, **skimming**) **1** *tr.* **a** take scum or cream or a floating layer from the surface of (a liquid). **b** take (cream, etc.) from the surface of a liquid. **2** *tr.* **a** keep touching lightly or nearly touching (a surface) in passing over. **b** deal with or treat (a subject) superficially. **3** *intr.* **a** go lightly over a surface, glide along in the air. **b** (foll. by *over*) = sense 2b of *v.* **4** *tr.* **a** read superficially; look over cursorily. **b** *intr.* (usu. foll. by *through*) read or look over cursorily. ● *n.* **1** the act of skimming. **2** a thin covering on a liquid (*skim of ice*).

skim·mer /skimər/ *n.* **1** a device for skimming liquids. ▷ UTENSIL. **2** a person who skims. **3** a flat hat, esp. a broad-brimmed straw hat.

skim·mi·a /skimēə/ *n.* any evergreen shrub of the genus *Skimmia*, native to E. Asia, with red berries.

skim milk *n.* milk from which the cream has been skimmed.

ski·mo·bile /skēˈmōbeel/ *n.* = SNOWMOBILE.

skimp /skimp/ *v., adj., & n.* ● *v.* **1** *tr.* supply (a person, etc.) meagerly with food, money, etc. **2** *tr.* use a meager or insufficient amount of; stint (material, expenses, etc.). **3** *intr.* be parsimonious.

skimp·y /skimpee/ *adj.* (**skimpier**, **skimpiest**) meager; not ample or sufficient. □□ **skimp·i·ly** *adv.* **skimp·i·ness** *n.*

skin /skin/ *n. & v.* ● *n.* **1** ▼ the flexible covering of a body. **2 a** the skin of a flayed animal with or without the hair, etc. **b** a material prepared from skins, esp. of smaller animals. **3** a person's skin with reference to its color or complexion (*has a fair skin*). **4** an outer layer or covering, esp. the coating of a plant, fruit, or sausage. **5** a filmlike skin on the surface of a liquid, etc. **6** a container for liquid, made of an animal's skin. **7 a** the planking or plating of a ship or boat, inside or outside the ribs. **b** the outer covering of any craft or vehicle, esp. an aircraft or spacecraft. ● *v.* (**skinned**, **skinning**) **1** *tr.* remove the skin from. **2 a** *tr.* cover (a sore, etc.) with or as with skin. **b** *intr.* (of a wound, etc.) become covered with new skin. **3** *tr. sl.* swindle. □ **by** (or **with**) **the**

skin of one's teeth by a very narrow margin. **get under a person's skin** *colloq.* interest or annoy a person intensely. **have a thick** (or **thin**) **skin** be insensitive (or sensitive) to criticism, etc. **no skin off one's nose** *colloq.* a matter of indifference or even benefit to one. **to the skin** through all one's clothing (*soaked to the skin*). □□ **skin·less** *adj.* **skinned** *adj.* (also in *comb.*).

skin-deep *adj.* (of a wound, or of an emotion, an impression, beauty, etc.) superficial; not deep or lasting.

skin div·er *n.* a person who swims underwater without a diving suit, usu. with a mask, snorkel, flippers, etc. □□ **skin div·ing** *n.*

skin flick *n. sl.* an explicitly pornographic film.

skin·flint /skinflint/ *n.* a miserly person.

skin fric·tion *n.* friction at the surface of a solid and a fluid in relative motion.

skin·ful /skinfoōl/ *n.* (*pl.* **-fuls**) *colloq.* enough liquor to make one drunk.

skin graft *n.* **1** the surgical transplanting of skin. **2** a piece of skin transferred in this way.

skin·head /skinhed/ *n.* **1** a youth with close-cropped hair, esp. one of an aggressive gang. **2** a U.S. Marine recruit.

skink /skingk/ *n.* any small lizard of the family Scincidae.

skin·ner /skinər/ *n.* **1** a person who skins animals or prepares skins. **2** a dealer in skins; a furrier. **3** *Austral. Racing sl.* a result very profitable to bookmakers.

skin·ny /skinee/ *adj.* (**skinnier**, **skinniest**) **1** thin or emaciated. **2** (of clothing) tight-fitting. **3** made of or like skin. □□ **skin·ni·ness** *n.*

skin·ny-dip·ping *n. colloq.* swimming in the nude.

skin·tight /skintīt/ *adj.* (of a garment) very close-fitting.

skip[1] /skip/ *v. & n.* ● *v.* (**skipped**, **skipping**) **1** *intr.* **a** move along lightly, esp. by taking two steps with each foot in turn. **b** jump lightly from the ground, esp. so as to clear a jump rope. **c** gambol; caper; frisk. **2** *intr.* move quickly from one point, subject, or occupation to another. **3** *tr.* (also *absol.*) omit in dealing with a series or in reading (*skip every tenth row; always skips the small print*). **4** *tr. colloq.* not participate in. **5** *tr. colloq.* depart quickly from; leave hurriedly. ● *n.* **1** a skipping movement or action. **2** *Computing* the action of passing over part of a sequence of data or instructions. □ **skip it** *sl.* **1** abandon a topic, etc. **2** make off; disappear. **skip rope** play or exercise with a jump rope.

SKIN

Skin is the human body's largest organ. It protects internal organs, keeps body fluids in, helps regulate body temperature, and is sensitive to external stimuli. It has two main parts: the epidermis, a protective covering with an external layer of dead cells, and the dermis, which contains living structures such as nerve endings.

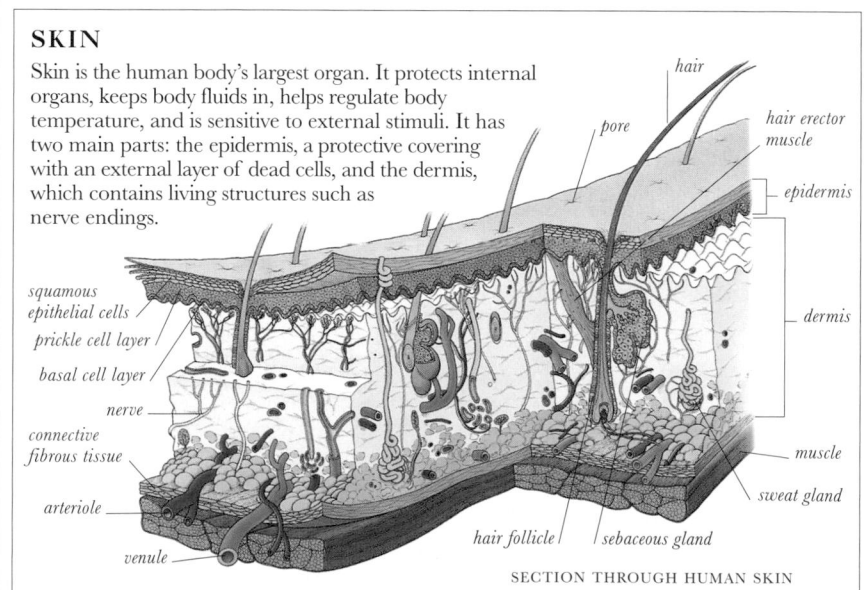

hair

pore

hair erector muscle

epidermis

dermis

muscle

sweat gland

sebaceous gland

hair follicle

venule

arteriole

connective fibrous tissue

nerve

basal cell layer

prickle cell layer

squamous epithelial cells

SECTION THROUGH HUMAN SKIN

S

skip² /skip/ *n.* **1** a cage, bucket, etc., in which workers or materials are lowered and raised in mines and quarries. **2** = SKEP.

skip·jack /skípjak/ *n.* (in full **skipjack tuna**) ▼ a small striped Pacific tuna, *Euthynnus pelamis*, used as food.

SKIPJACK TUNA
(*Euthynnus pelamis*)

ski·plane /skéeplayn/ *n.* an airplane having its undercarriage fitted with skis for landing on snow or ice.

skip·per /skípər/ *n. & v.* ● *n.* **1** a sea captain, esp. the master of a small trading or fishing vessel. **2** the captain of an aircraft. **3** the captain of a side in games. ● *v.tr.* act as captain of.

skip·pet /skípit/ *n.* a small, round wooden box to enclose and protect a seal attached to a document.

skirl /skərl/ *n. & v.* ● *n.* the shrill sound characteristic of bagpipes. ● *v.intr.* make a skirl.

skir·mish /skə́rmish/ *n. & v.* ● *n.* **1** a piece of irregular or unpremeditated fighting, esp. between small or outlying parts of armies or fleets; a slight engagement. **2** a short argument, etc. ● *v.intr.* engage in a skirmish. □□ **skir·mish·er** *n.*

skirr /skər/ *v.intr.* move rapidly, esp. with a whirring sound.

skirt /skərt/ *n. & v.* ● *n.* **1** a woman's outer garment hanging from the waist. **2** the part of a coat, etc., that hangs below the waist. **3** a hanging part around the base of a hovercraft. ▷ HOVERCRAFT. **4** (in *sing.* or *pl.*) an edge, border, or extreme part. **5** (in full **skirt of beef**, etc.) the diaphragm and other membranes as food. ● *v.tr.* **1** go along or around or past the edge of. **2** be situated along. **3** avoid dealing with (an issue, etc.). □□ **skirt·ed** *adj.* (also in *comb.*).

skirt·ing /skə́rting/ *n.* **1** fabric suitable for skirt making. **2** a border or edge.

ski run *n.* a slope prepared for skiing.

skit /skit/ *n.* (often foll. by *on*) a light, usu. short, piece of satire or burlesque.

skit·ter /skítər/ *v.intr.* (also **skee·ter** /skéetər/) **1** (usu. foll. by *along, across*) move lightly or hastily. **2** (usu. foll. by *about, off*) hurry about; dart off. **3** fish by drawing bait jerkily across the surface of the water.

skit·ter·y /skítəree/ *adj.* skittish; restless.

skit·tish /skítish/ *adj.* **1** lively; playful. **2** (of a horse, etc.) nervous; inclined to shy; fidgety. □□ **skit·tish·ly** *adv.* **skit·tish·ness** *n.*

skit·tle /skít'l/ *n.* a pin used in the game of skittles.

skive /skīv/ *v. & n.* ● *v.tr.* split or pare (hides, leather, etc.). ● *n. sl.* **1** an instance of shirking. **2** an easy option. □□ **skiv·er** *n.*

skiv·vy /skívee/ *n.* (*pl.* **-ies**) **1** (in *pl.*) underwear of T-shirt and shorts. **2** a thin high-necked long-sleeved garment.

skoal /skōl/ *n.* used as a toast in drinking.

sku·a /skyóoə/ *n.* ◀ any of several predatory seabirds of the genus *Catharacta*.

SKUA: GREAT SKUA
(*Catharacta skua*)

S

skul·dug·ger·y /skuldúgəree/ *n.* (also **scul·dug·ger·y**, **skull·dug·ger·y**) trickery; unscrupulous behavior.

skulk /skulk/ *v.intr.* **1** move stealthily, lurk, or keep oneself concealed. **2** stay or sneak away in time of danger. □□ **skulk·er** *n.*

skull /skul/ *n.* **1** the bony case of the brain of a vertebrate. **2 a** ▼ the part of the skeleton corresponding to the head. ▷ HEAD. **b** this with the skin and soft internal parts removed. **3** the head as the seat of intelligence. □□ **skulled** *adj.* (also in *comb.*).

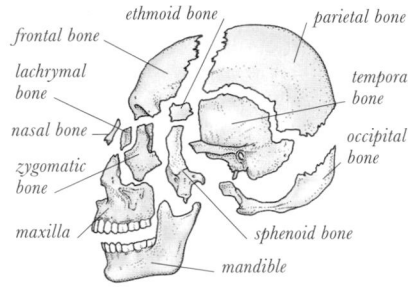

ethmoid bone   parietal bone
frontal bone
lachrymal bone   temporal bone
nasal bone   occipital bone
zygomatic bone
maxilla   sphenoid bone
mandible

SKULL: EXPLODED VIEW OF THE HUMAN SKULL

skull and cross·bones *n.* ◀ a representation of a skull with two thighbones crossed below it as an emblem of piracy or death.

skull·cap /skúlkap/ *n.* **1** a small, close-fitting, peakless cap. **2** the top part of the skull. ▷ HEAD

skunk /skungk/ *n.* **1** ▶ any of various cat-sized flesh-eating mammals of the family Mustelidae, esp. *Mephitis mephitis*, having a distinctive black and white striped fur and able to emit a powerful stench from a liquid secreted by its anal glands as a defense. ▷ MUSTELID. **2** *colloq.* a contemptible person.

skunk cab·bage *n.* one of two N. American herbaceous plants, esp. *Symplocarpus foetidus*, with an offensive-smelling spathe.

sky /skī/ *n. & v.* ● *n.* (*pl.* **skies**) (in *sing.* or *pl.*) **1** the region of the atmosphere and outer space seen from the earth. **2** the weather or climate evidenced by this. ● *v.tr.* (**skies**, **skied**) **1** *Baseball*, etc. hit (a ball) high into the air. **2** hang (a picture) high on a wall. □ **to the skies** without reserve (*praised to the skies*). **under the open sky** out of doors. □□ **sky·ey** *adj.* **sky·less** *adj.*

sky blue *n.* a bright, clear blue.

sky-blue pink *n.* an imaginary color.

sky·box /skíboks/ *n.* an elevated enclosure in a sports stadium containing plush seating, food services, and other amenities.

sky·cap /skíkap/ *n.* a person who carries baggage for passengers at airports.

sky·div·ing /skídīving/ *n.* the sport of performing acrobatic maneuvers under free fall with a parachute. □□ **sky·div·er** *n.*

sky-high *adv. & adj.* very high.

sky·jack /skíjak/ *v.tr.* hijack (an aircraft). □□ **sky·jack·er** *n.*

sky·lark /skílaark/ *n. & v.* ● *n.* a lark, *Alauda arvensis*, of Eurasia and N. Africa, that sings while hovering in flight. ● *v.intr.* play tricks; frolic.

sky·light /skílīt/ *n.* a window set in the plane of a roof or ceiling. ▷ SHIP

sky·line /skílīn/ *n.* the outline of hills, buildings, etc., defined against the sky.

sky pi·lot *n. sl.* a clergyman.

sky·rock·et /skírokkit/ *n. & v.* ● *n.* a rocket exploding high in the air. ● *v.intr.* (esp. of prices, etc.) rise very rapidly.

sky·sail /skísayl, -səl/ *n.* a light sail above the royal in a square-rigged ship.

sky·scape /skískayp/ *n.* **1** a picture chiefly representing the sky. **2** a view of the sky.

sky·scrap·er /skískraypər/ *n.* a very tall building of many stories.

Skye ter·ri·er /skí téreeər/ *n.* a small, long-bodied, short-legged, long-haired, slate- or fawn-colored variety of Scottish terrier.

sky·ward /skíwərd/ *adv. & adj.* ● *adv.* (also **sky·wards** /-wərdz/) toward the sky. ● *adj.* moving skyward.

sky·watch /skíwoch/ *n.* the activity of watching the sky for aircraft, etc.

sky·way /skíway/ *n.* **1** a route used by aircraft. **2** a covered overhead walkway between buildings.

sky·writ·ing /skírīting/ *n.* legible smoke trails made by an airplane, esp. for advertising.

slab /slab/ *n.* **1** a flat, broad, fairly thick, usu. square or rectangular piece of solid material, esp. stone. **2** a large flat piece of cake, chocolate, etc. **3** (of lumber) an outer piece sawn from a log.

slack¹ /slak/ *adj., n., v., & adv.* ● *adj.* **1** not taut. **2** inactive or sluggish. **3** negligent or remiss (*discipline was slack*). **4** (of tide, etc.) neither ebbing nor flowing. **5** (of trade or business or a market) with little happening. **6** loose. ● *n.* **1** the slack part of a rope (*haul in the slack*). **2** a slack time in trade, etc. **3** *colloq.* a spell of inactivity or laziness. **4** (in *pl.*) full-length loosely cut trousers for informal wear. ● *v.* **1** *tr. & intr.* slacken. **2** *tr.* loosen (rope, etc.). □ **slack off 1** loosen. **2** lose or cause to lose vigor. **slack up** reduce the speed of a train, etc., before stopping. **take up the slack** use up a surplus or make up a deficiency. □□ **slack·ly** *adv.* **slack·ness** *n.*

slack² /slak/ *n.* coal dust or small pieces of coal.

slack·en /slákən/ *v.tr. & intr.* make or become slack. □ **slacken off** = *slack off* (see SLACK¹).

slack·er /slákər/ *n.* a shirker; an indolent person.

slag /slag/ *n. & v.* ● *n.* vitreous refuse left after ore has been smelted. ▷ BLAST FURNACE. ● *v.* (**slagged**, **slagging**) **1** *intr.* form slag. **2** cohere into a mass like slag.

slag heap *n.* a hill of refuse from a mine, etc.

slain *past part.* of SLAY¹.

slainte /sláanchə/ *int.* a Gaelic toast: good health!

slake /slayk/ *v.tr.* **1** assuage or satisfy (thirst, revenge, etc.). **2** disintegrate (quicklime) by chemical combination with water.

sla·lom /sláaləm/ *n.* **1** ▼ a ski race down a zigzag course defined by artificial obstacles. **2** an obstacle race in canoes or cars or on skateboards or water skis.

SKUNK: STRIPED SKUNK
(*Mephitis mephitis*)

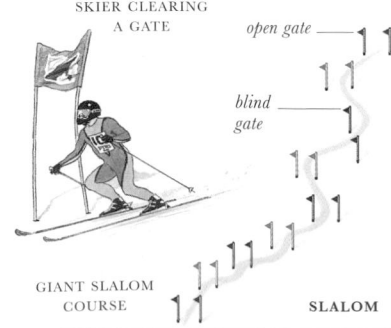

SKIER CLEARING A GATE
open gate
blind gate
GIANT SLALOM COURSE   SLALOM

SKULL AND CROSSBONES ON A POISON WARNING SIGN

slam[1] /slam/ *v. & n.* ● *v.* (**slammed, slamming**) **1** *tr. & intr.* shut forcefully and loudly. **2** *tr.* put down (an object) with a similar sound. **3** *intr.* move violently (*he slammed out of the room*). **4** *tr. & intr.* put or come into sudden action (*slam the brakes on*). **5** *tr. sl.* criticize severely. **6** *tr. sl.* hit. **7** *tr. sl.* gain an easy victory over. ● *n.* **1** a sound of or as of a slammed door. **2** the shutting of a door, etc., with a loud bang. **3** (usu. prec. by *the*) *sl.* prison.

slam[2] /slam/ *n. Cards* the winning of every trick in a game.

slam dunk ▼ *n. Basketball* a shot in which a player thrusts the ball down through the basket. □□ **slam-dunk** *v.tr.*

slam·mer /slámər/ *n.* (usu. prec. by *the*) *sl.* prison.

slan·der /slándər/ *n. & v.* ● *n.* **1** a malicious, false, and injurious statement spoken about a person. **2** the uttering of such statements. **3** *Law* false oral defamation. ● *v.tr.* utter slander about. □□ **slan·der·er** *n.* **slan·der·ous** *adj.*

SLAM DUNK

slang /slang/ *n. & v.* ● *n.* words, phrases, and uses that are regarded as very informal and are often restricted to special contexts or are peculiar to a specified profession, class, etc. (*racing slang*; *schoolboy slang*). ● *v.* **1** *tr.* use abusive language to. **2** *intr.* use such language.

slang·y /slángee/ *adj.* (**slangier, slangiest**) **1** of the character of slang. **2** fond of using slang. □□ **slang·i·ly** *adv.*

slant /slant/ *v., n., & adj.* ● *v.* **1** *intr.* slope; lie or go obliquely. **2** *tr.* cause to do this. **3** *tr.* (often as **slanted** ● *adj.*) present (information) from a particular angle, esp. in a biased or unfair way. ● *n.* **1** a slope. **2** a point of view, esp. a biased one. ● *adj.* sloping; oblique. □ **on a** (or **the**) **slant** aslant.

slant·wise /slántwīz/ (also **slantways** /slántwayz/) *adv.* aslant.

slap /slap/ *v., n., & adv.* ● *v.* (**slapped, slapping**) **1** *tr. & intr.* strike with the palm of the hand or a flat object, or so as to make a similar noise. **2** *tr.* lay forcefully (*slapped the money on the table*). **3** *tr.* put hastily or carelessly (*slap some paint on the walls*). **4** *tr.* (often foll. by *down*) *colloq.* reprimand or snub. ● *n.* **1** a blow with the palm of the hand or a flat object. **2** a slapping sound. ● *adv.* suddenly; fully; directly (*ran slap into him*). □ **slap in the face** a rebuff or affront. **slap on the back** *n.* congratulations. *v.tr.* congratulate. **slap on the wrist** *n. colloq.* a mild reprimand or rebuke. *v.tr. colloq.* reprimand.

slap·dash /slápdash/ *adj. & adv.* ● *adj.* hasty and careless. ● *adv.* in a slapdash manner.

slap·hap·py /sláp-hápee/ *adj. colloq.* **1** cheerfully casual. **2** punch-drunk.

slap·jack /sláp jak/ *n.* **1** a card game in which face-up jacks are slapped by the players' open hands. **2** a kind of pancake cooked on a griddle.

slap shot *n. Ice Hockey* a powerful shot made with a full swing of the stick.

slap·stick /slápstik/ *n.* boisterous knockabout comedy.

slash /slash/ *v. & n.* ● *v.* **1** *intr.* make a sweeping or random cut or cuts with a knife, sword, whip, etc. **2** *tr.* make such a cut or cuts at. **3** *tr.* make a long narrow gash or gashes in. **4** *tr.* reduce (prices, etc.) drastically. **5** *tr.* censure vigorously. **6** *tr.* make (one's way) by slashing. **7** *tr.* **a** lash (a person, etc.) with a whip. **b** crack (a whip). ● *n.* **1 a** a slashing cut or stroke. **b** a wound or slit made by this. **2** an oblique stroke. **3** debris resulting from the felling or destruction of trees. □□ **slash·er** *n.*

slash-and-burn *adj.* (of cultivation) in which vegetation is cut down, allowed to dry, and then burned off before seeds are planted.

slashed /slasht/ *adj.* ◄ (of a sleeve, etc.) having slits to show a lining or puffing of other material.

SLASHED
SLEEVES OF A 15TH-
CENTURY DRESS

slat /slat/ *n.* a thin narrow piece of wood or plastic or metal, esp. used in an overlapping series as in a fence or Venetian blind.

slate /slayt/ *n., v., & adj.* ● *n.* **1** ► a fine-grained, gray, green, or bluish-purple metamorphic rock easily split into flat smooth plates. ▷ META-MORPHIC. **2** a piece of such a plate used as roofing material. **3** a piece of such a plate used for writing on, usu. framed in wood. **4** the color of slate. **5** a list of nominees for office, etc. ● *v.tr.* **1** cover with slates esp. as roofing. **2** make arrangements for (an event, etc.). **3** nominate for office, etc. ● *adj.* made of slate. □ **wipe the slate clean** forgive or cancel the record of past offenses. □□ **slat·ing** *n.* **slat·y** *adj.*

SLATE

slat·er /sláytər/ *n.* **1** a person who slates roofs, etc. **2** a woodlouse or similar crustacean.

slath·er /sláthər/ *n. & v.* ● *n.* (usu. in *pl.*) *colloq.* a large amount. ● *v.tr. colloq.* **1** spread thickly. **2** squander.

slat·ted /slátid/ *adj.* having slats.

slat·tern /slátərn/ *n.* a slovenly woman. □□ **slat·tern·ly** *adj.*

slaugh·ter /sláwtər/ *n. & v.* ● *n.* **1** the killing of an animal or animals for food. **2** the killing of many persons or animals at once or continuously; carnage; massacre. ● *v.tr.* **1** kill (people) in a ruthless manner or on a great scale. **2** kill for food; butcher. **3** *colloq.* defeat utterly. □□ **slaugh·ter·er** *n.*

slaugh·ter·house /sláwtərhows/ *n.* **1** a place for the slaughter of animals as food. **2** a place of carnage.

Slav /slaav/ *n. & adj.* ● *n.* a member of a group of peoples in Central and Eastern Europe speaking Slavic languages. ● *adj.* **1** of or relating to the Slavs. **2** Slavic.

slave /slayv/ *n. & v.* ● *n.* **1** a person who is the legal property of another or others and is bound to absolute obedience; a human chattel. **2** a drudge; a person working very hard. **3** (foll. by *of, to*) a helpless victim of some dominating influence (*slave of fashion*; *slave to duty*). **4** a machine, or part of one, directly controlled by another. ▷ HYDRAULIC. ● *v.* **1** *intr.* (often foll. by *at, over*) work very hard. **2** *tr.* (foll. by *to*) subject (a device) to control by another.

slave brace·let *n.* a bangle or chain of gold, etc., worn around the ankle.

slave driv·er *n.* **1** an overseer of slaves. **2** a person who works others hard. □□ **slave-drive** *v.tr.*

slav·er[1] /sláyvər/ *n. hist.* a ship or person engaged in the slave trade.

slav·er[2] /slávər/ *n. & v.* ● *n.* **1** saliva running from the mouth. **2 a** fulsome flattery. **b** drivel; nonsense. ● *v.intr.* **1** let saliva run from the mouth; dribble. **2** (foll. by *over*) show excessive sentimentality over, or desire for.

slav·er·y /sláyvəree, sláyvree/ *n.* **1** the condition of a slave. **2** exhausting labor; drudgery. **3** the custom of having slaves.

slave ship *n. hist.* a ship transporting slaves, esp. from Africa.

slave trade *n. hist.* the procuring, transporting, and selling of human beings, esp. African blacks, as slaves. □□ **slave trad·er** *n.*

Slav·ic /sláavik/ *adj. & n.* ● *adj.* **1** of or relating to the group of Indo-European languages including Russian, Polish, and Czech. **2** of or relating to the Slavs. ● *n.* the Slavic language group.

slav·ish /sláyvish/ *adj.* **1** of, like, or as of slaves. **2** showing no attempt at originality or development. **3** abject; servile; base. □□ **slav·ish·ly** *adv.*

Sla·von·ic /sləvónik/ *adj. & n.* = SLAVIC.

slaw /slaw/ *n.* coleslaw.

slay /slay/ *v.tr.* (*past* **slew** /sloo/; *past part.* **slain** /slayn/) **1** *literary* or *joc.* kill. **2** *sl.* overwhelm with delight; convulse with laughter. □□ **slay·er** *n.*

SLBM *abbr.* **1** submarine-launched ballistic missile. **2** sea-launched ballistic missile.

sleaze /sleez/ *n. & v. colloq.* ● *n.* **1** sleaziness. **2** a person of low moral standards. ● *v.intr.* move in a sleazy fashion.

slea·zy /sléezee/ *adj.* (**sleazier, sleaziest**) **1** squalid; tawdry. **2** slatternly. **3** (of textiles, etc.) flimsy. □□ **slea·zi·ly** *adv.* **slea·zi·ness** *n.*

sled /sled/ *n. & v.* ● *n.* **1** ▼ a vehicle on runners for conveying loads or passengers esp. over snow, drawn by horses, dogs, or reindeer or pulled by one or more persons. **2** a toboggan. ● *v.intr.* (**sledded, sledding**) ride on a sled.

snow shovel   SLED   *canvas cover*

iron-topped wooden runner   *supply cases*

sledge[1] /slej/ *n. & v.* ● *n.* a heavy sled, esp. one drawn by draft animals. ● *v.intr. & tr.* travel or convey by sledge.

sledge[2] /slej/ *n.* = SLEDGEHAMMER.

sledge·ham·mer /sléjhamər/ *n.* **1** a large heavy hammer used to break stone, etc. **2** (*attrib.*) heavy or powerful (*a sledgehammer blow*).

sleek /sleek/ *adj. & v.* ● *adj.* **1** (of hair, fur, or skin, or an animal or person with such hair, etc.) smooth and glossy. **2** looking well-fed and comfortable. **3** ingratiating. **4** (of a thing) smooth and polished. ● *v.tr.* make sleek. □□ **sleek·ly** *adv.* **sleek·ness** *n.* **sleek·y** *adj.*

sleep /sleep/ *n. & v.* ● *n.* **1** a condition of body and mind that normally recurs for several hours every night, in which the nervous system is inactive, the eyes closed, the postural muscles relaxed, and consciousness practically suspended. **2** a period of sleep (*shall try to get a sleep*). **3** a state like sleep, such as rest, quiet, or death. **4** the prolonged inert condition of hibernating animals. **5** a substance found in the corners of the eyes after sleep. ● *v.* (*past and past part.* **slept** /slept/) **1** *intr.* **a** be in a state of sleep. **b** fall asleep. **2** *intr.* (foll. by *at, in, etc.*) spend the night. **3** *tr.* provide sleeping accommodation for (*the house sleeps six*). **4** *intr.* (foll. by *with, together*) have sexual intercourse, esp. in bed. **5** *intr.* (foll. by *on, over*) not decide (a question) until the next day. **6** *intr.* (foll. by *through*) fail to be woken by. **7** *intr.* be inactive or dormant. **8** *intr.* be dead; lie in the grave. □ **go to sleep 1** enter a state of sleep. **2** (of a limb) become numbed by pressure. **in one's sleep** while asleep. **put to sleep 1** anesthetize. **2** kill (an animal) painlessly. **sleep around** *colloq.* be sexually promiscuous. **sleep in 1** remain asleep later than usual in the morning. **2** sleep by night at one's place of work. **sleep out** sleep by night out of doors, or not at one's place of work.

sleep·er /sléepər/ *n.* **1** a person or animal that sleeps. **2** a wooden or concrete beam laid horizontally as a support, esp. for railroad track. ▷ RAIL. **3 a** a sleeping car. **b** a berth in this. **4** a ring worn in a pierced ear to keep the hole from closing. **5** a thing that is suddenly successful after being

S

undistinguished. **6** a spy who remains inactive while establishing a secure position.

sleep·ing bag *n.* a lined or padded bag to sleep in.

sleep·ing car *n.* a railroad car provided with beds or berths.

sleep·ing pill *n.* a pill to induce sleep.

sleep·ing sick·ness *n.* any of several tropical diseases with extreme lethargy.

sleep·less /sléeplis/ *adj.* **1** characterized by lack of sleep. **2** unable to sleep. **3** continually active or moving. □□ **sleep·less·ly** *adv.* **sleep·less·ness** *n.*

sleep·o·ver /sléepōvər/ *n.* chiefly *N. Amer.* an occasion of spending the night away from home.

sleep·walk /sléepwawk/ *v.intr.* walk or perform other actions while asleep. □□ **sleep·walk·er** *n.*

sleep·y /sléepee/ *adj.* (**sleepier, sleepiest**) **1** drowsy; about to fall asleep. **2** lacking activity (*a sleepy little town*). **3** habitually indolent, unobservant, etc. □□ **sleep·i·ly** *adv.* **sleep·i·ness** *n.*

sleep·y·head /sléepeehed/ *n.* a sleepy or inattentive person.

sleet /sleet/ *n.* & *v.* ● *n.* **1** a mixture of snow and rain falling together. **2** hail or snow melting as it falls. **3** a thin coating of ice. ● *v.intr.* (prec. by *it* as subject) sleet falls (*if it sleets*). □□ **sleet·y** *adj.*

sleeve /sleev/ *n.* **1** the part of a garment that wholly or partly covers an arm. **2** the cover of a phonograph record. **3** a tube enclosing a rod or smaller tube. **4** a wind sock. □ **roll up one's sleeves** prepare to fight or work. **up one's sleeve** in reserve. □□ **sleeved** *adj.* (also in *comb.*). **sleeve·less** *adj.*

sleev·ing /sléeving/ *n.* tubular covering for electric cable, etc.

sleigh /slay/ *n.* & *v.* ● *n.* a sled, esp. one for riding on. ● *v.intr.* travel on a sleigh.

sleigh bell *n.* any of a number of tinkling bells attached to the harness of a sleigh-horse, etc.

sleight /slīt/ *n. archaic* **1** a deceptive trick or device or movement. **2** dexterity. **3** cunning.

sleight of hand *n.* **1** manual dexterity, esp. in conjuring or fencing. **2** skilful deception.

slen·der /sléndər/ *adj.* (**slenderer, slenderest**) **1 a** of small girth or breadth (*a slender pillar*). **b** gracefully thin (*a slender waist*). **2** slight; meager; inadequate (*slender hopes; slender resources*). □□ **slen·der·ly** *adv.* **slen·der·ness** *n.*

slen·der·ize /sléndərīz/ *v.* **1** *tr.* make slender. **2** *intr.* make oneself slender; slim.

slept *past* and *past part.* of SLEEP.

sleuth /slooth/ *n.* & *v. colloq.* ● *n.* a detective. ● *v.* **1** *intr.* act as a detective. **2** *tr.* investigate.

sleuth·hound /slóothhownd/ *n.* **1** a bloodhound. **2** *colloq.* a detective.

slew¹ /sloo/ *v.* & *n.* (also **slue**) ● *v.tr.* & *intr.* (often foll. by *around*) turn or slide violently or uncontrollably. ● *n.* such a change of position.

slew² *past* of SLAY¹.

slew³ /sloo/ *n. colloq.* a large number or quantity.

sley /slay/ *n.* (also **slay**) a weaver's reed.

slice /slīs/ *n.* & *v.* ● *n.* **1** a thin, broad piece or wedge cut off or out esp. from meat or bread or a cake, pie, or large fruit. **2** a share; a part taken or allotted or gained (*a slice of the profits*). **3** an implement with a broad flat blade for serving fish, etc. **4** *Golf* & *Tennis* a slicing stroke. ● *v.* **1** *tr.* (often foll. by *up*) cut into slices. **2** *tr.* (foll. by *off*) cut (a piece) off. **3** *intr.* (foll. by *into, through*) cut with or like a knife. **4** *tr.* (also *absol.*) **a** *Golf* strike (the ball) so that it deviates away from the striker. **b** (in other sports) propel (the ball) forward at an angle. **5** *tr.* go through (air, etc.) with a cutting motion. □□ **slice·a·ble** *adj.* **slic·er** *n.* (also in *comb.*).

slice of life *n.* a realistic representation of everyday experience.

slick /slik/ *adj., n., & v.* ● *adj. colloq.* **1 a** (of a person or action) skillful or efficient (*a slick performance*). **b** superficially or pretentiously smooth and dexterous. **c** glib. **2 a** sleek; smooth. **b** slippery. ● *n.* **1 a** smooth patch of oil, etc., esp. on the sea. **2** *Motor Racing* a smooth tire. **3** *colloq.* a glossy magazine. **4** *sl.* a slick person. ● *v.tr. colloq.* **1** make sleek or smart. **2** (usu. foll. by *down*) flatten (one's hair, etc.). □□ **slick·ly** *adv.* **slick·ness** *n.*

slick·er /slíkər/ *n.* **1** *colloq.* **a** a plausible rogue. **b** a smart and sophisticated city dweller (cf. CITY SLICKER). **2** a raincoat of smooth material.

slide /slīd/ *v.* & *n.* ● *v.* (*past* and *past part.* **slid** /slid/) **1 a** *intr.* move along a smooth surface with continuous contact on the same part of the thing moving. **b** *tr.* cause to do this (*slide the drawer into place*). **2** *intr.* move quietly; glide; go smoothly along. **3** *intr.* pass gradually or imperceptibly. **4** *intr.* glide over ice on one or both feet without skates (under gravity or with momentum gotten by running). **5** *intr.* (foll. by *over*) barely touch upon (a delicate subject, etc.). **6** *intr.* & *tr.* (often foll. by *into*) move or cause to move quietly or unobtrusively (*slid his hand into mine*). **7** *intr.* take its own course (*let it slide*). **8** *intr.* decline (*shares slid to a new low*). ● *n.* **1 a** the act of sliding. **b** a rapid decline. **2** an inclined plane down which children, goods, etc., slide; a chute. **3 a** a track made by or for sliding, esp. on ice. **b** a slope prepared with snow or ice for tobogganing. **4** a part of a machine or instrument that slides, esp. a slide valve. ▷ BRASS, HARMONICA. **5 a** a thing slid into place, esp. a piece of glass holding an object for a microscope. **b** ◄ a mounted transparency usu. placed in a projector for viewing on a screen. **6** a part or parts of a machine on or between which a sliding part works. □□ **slide·a·ble** *adj.* **slid·er** *n.*

SLIDES

slide rule *n.* ▼ a ruler with a sliding central strip, graduated logarithmically for making rapid calculations, esp. multiplication and division.

SLIDE RULE   *sliding central strip*

slide valve *n.* a sliding piece that opens and closes an aperture by sliding across it.

slid·ing door *n.* a door drawn across an aperture on a slide, not turning on hinges.

slid·ing scale *n.* a scale of fees, taxes, wages, etc., that varies as a whole in accordance with variation of some standard.

slid·ing seat *n.* a seat able to slide to and fro on runners, etc., esp. in a racing scull to adjust the length of a stroke.

slight /slīt/ *adj., v., & n.* ● *adj.* **1 a** of little significance (*a slight cold*). **b** barely perceptible (*a slight smell of gas*). **c** not much or great; inadequate (*paid him slight attention*). **2** slender; frail-looking. **3** (in *superl.*, with *neg.* or *interrog.*) any whatever (*paid not the slightest attention*). ● *v.tr.* insult (a person) by treating them without respect or attention. ● *n.* an insult. □□ **slight·ing·ly** *adv.* **slight·ish** *adj.* **slight·ly** *adv.* **slight·ness** *n.*

sli·ly var. of SLYLY (see SLY).

slim /slim/ *adj.* & *v.* ● *adj.* (**slimmer, slimmest**) **1 a** of small girth or thickness. **b** gracefully thin. **c** not fat nor overweight. **2** small, insufficient (*a slim chance of success*). ● *v.* (**slimmed, slimming**) **1** *intr.* esp. *Brit.* make oneself slimmer by dieting, exercise, etc. **2** *tr.* make slim or slimmer. □□ **slim·ly** *adv.* **slim·mer** *n.* **slim·ming** *n.* & *adj.* **slim·ness** *n.*

slime /slīm/ *n.* & *v.* ● *n.* an unpleasant moist, soft, slippery substance. ● *v.tr.* cover with slime.

slime·ball /slímbawl/ *n. colloq.* a repulsive or despicable person.

slim·line /slímlīn/ *adj.* of slender design.

slim·y /slímee/ *adj.* (**slimier, slimiest**) **1** of the consistency of slime. **2** covered, smeared with, or full of slime. **3** disgustingly dishonest, meek, or flattering. **4** slippery; hard to hold. □□ **slim·i·ly** *adv.* **slim·i·ness** *n.*

sling¹ /sling/ *n.* & *v.* ● *n.* **1** a strap, belt, etc., used to support or raise a hanging weight, e.g., a rifle, a ship's boat, or goods being transferred. **2** a bandage looped around the neck to support an injured arm. **3** ▶ a strap or string used with the hand to give impetus to a small missile, esp. a stone. ● *v.tr.* (*past* and *past part.* **slung** /slung/) **1** (also *absol.*) hurl (a stone, etc.) from a sling. **2** *colloq.* throw. **3** suspend with a sling; allow to swing suspended; arrange so as to be supported from above; hoist or transfer with a sling.

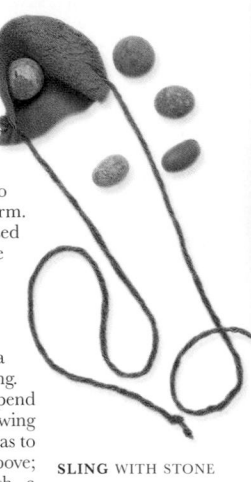

SLING WITH STONE MISSILES

sling² /sling/ *n.* a sweetened drink of liquor (esp. gin) and water.

sling·back *n.* ▼ a shoe held in place by a strap above the heel.

SLING-BACK

sling·er /slíngər/ *n.* a person who slings, esp. the user of a sling.

sling·shot /slíngshot/ *n.* a forked stick, etc., with elastic for shooting stones.

slink¹ /slingk/ *v.intr.* (*past* and *past part.* **slunk** /slungk/) (often foll. by *off, away, by*) move in a stealthy or guilty or sneaking manner.

slink² /slingk/ *v.* & *n.* ● *v.tr.* (also *absol.*) (of an animal) produce (young) prematurely. ● *n.* **1** an animal, esp. a calf, so born. **2** its flesh.

slink·y /slíngkee/ *adj.* (**slinkier, slinkiest**) **1** stealthy. **2** (of a garment) close-fitting and flowing; sinuous. **3** gracefully slender. □□ **slink·i·ly** *adv.* **slink·i·ness** *n.*

slip¹ /slip/ *v.* & *n.* ● *v.* (**slipped, slipping**) **1** *intr.* slide unintentionally esp. for a short distance; lose one's footing or balance or place by unintended sliding. **2** *intr.* go or move with a sliding motion (*slipped into her nightgown*). **3** *intr.* escape restraint or capture by being slippery or hard to hold or by not being grasped (*the eel slipped through his fingers*). **4** *intr.* make one's or its way unobserved or quietly or quickly. **5** *intr.* **a** make a careless or casual mistake. **b** fall below the normal standard. **6** *tr.* insert or transfer stealthily or casually or with a sliding motion (*slipped a coin into his hand*). **7** *tr.* **a** release from restraint (*slipped the greyhounds from the leash*). **b** release (the clutch of a motor vehicle) for a moment. **8** *tr.* move (a stitch) to the other needle without knitting it. **9** *tr.* (foll. by *on, off*) pull (a garment) hastily on or off. **10** *tr.* escape from (*the dog slipped its collar*). ● *n.* **1** the act or an instance of slipping. **2** an accidental or slight error. **3** a loose covering or garment, esp. pillowcase. **4 a** a reduction in the movement of a pulley, etc., due to slipping of the belt. **b** a reduction in the distance traveled by a ship or aircraft arising from the nature of the medium in which its propeller revolves. **5** (in *sing.* or

S

pl.) an inclined structure on which ships are built or repaired. □ **give a person the slip** escape from or evade him or her. **let slip 1** release accidentally or deliberately. **2** miss (an opportunity). **3** utter inadvertently. **slip away** depart without leave-taking, etc. **slip off** depart without leave-taking, etc. **slip up** *colloq.* make a mistake.

slip² /slip/ *n.* **1** a small piece of paper esp. for writing on. **2** a cutting taken from a plant for grafting or planting.

slip³ /slip/ *n.* clay in a creamy mixture with water, used mainly for decorating earthenware.

slip·case /slípcays/ *n.* a close-fitting case for a book.

slip·cov·er /slípkəvər/ *n.* **1** a removable covering for usu. upholstered furniture. **2** a jacket or slipcase for a book.

slip·knot /slípnot/ *n.* **1** ◄ a knot that can be undone by a pull. **2** a running knot.

slip of the tongue *n.* a small mistake in which something is said (or written) unintentionally.

slip-on *adj. & n.* ● *adj.* (of shoes or clothes) that can be easily slipped on and off. ● *n.* a slip-on shoe or garment.

slip·o·ver /slípōvər/ *adj. & n.* ● *adj.* (of a garment) to be slipped on over the head. ● *n.* a garment thus put on.

slip·page /slípij/ *n.* **1** the act or an instance of slipping. **2 a** a decline, esp. in popularity or value. **b** failure to meet a deadline or fulfill a promise; delay.

slipped disk *n.* a disk between vertebrae that has become displaced and causes lumbar pain.

slip·per /slípər/ *n.* **1** a light, loose, comfortable indoor shoe. **2** a light slip-on shoe for dancing, etc. □□ **slip·pered** *adj.*

slip·per·wort /slípərwərt, -wawrt/ *n.* calceolaria.

slip·per·y /slípəree/ *adj.* **1** difficult to hold firmly because of smoothness, wetness, or elusive motion. **2** (of a surface) difficult to stand on, causing slips by its smoothness or muddiness. **3** unreliable; shifty. **4** (of a subject) requiring tactful handling. □□ **slip·per·i·ly** *adv.* **slip·per·i·ness** *n.*

slip·per·y elm *n.* **1** the N. American red elm, *Ulmus rubra*. **2** ◄ the medicinal inner bark of this.

slip·py /slípee/ *adj.* (**slippier, slippiest**) *colloq.* slippery. □□ **slip·pi·ness** *n.*

slip·shod /slípshod/ *adj.* **1** careless; unsystematic; loose in arrangement. **2** slovenly. **3** having shoes down at the heel.

slip stitch *n.* **1** a loose stitch joining layers of fabric and not visible externally. **2** a stitch moved to the other needle without being knitted. ▷ STITCH. □□ **slip-stitch** *v.tr.*

slip·stream /slípstreem/ *n. & v.* ● *n.* **1** a current of air or water driven back by a revolving propeller or a moving vehicle. **2** an assisting force regarded as drawing something along behind something else. ● *v.tr.* **1** follow closely behind (another vehicle). **2** pass after traveling in another's slipstream.

slip-up /slípəp/ *n.* a mistake; a blunder.

slip·way /slípway/ *n.* a slip for building ships or landing boats.

slit /slit/ *n. & v.* ● *n.* **1** a long, straight, narrow incision. **2** a long, narrow opening comparable to a cut. ● *v.tr.* (**slitting**; *past* and *past part.* **slit**) **1** make a slit in; cut or tear lengthwise. **2** cut into strips.

slith·er /slíthər/ *v. & n.* ● *v.intr.* slide unsteadily; go with an irregular slipping motion. ● *n.* an instance of slithering. □□ **slith·er·y** *adj.*

slit·ty /slítee/ *adj.* (**slittier, slittiest**) (of the eyes) long and narrow.

sliv·er /slívər/ *n. & v.* ● *n.* **1** a long, thin piece cut or split off. **2** a piece of wood torn from a tree or from lumber. **3** a splinter, esp. from an exploded shell. ● *v.tr. & intr.* **1** break off as a sliver. **2** break up into slivers. **3** form into slivers.

sliv·o·vitz /slívəvits/ *n.* a plum brandy made esp. in Romania and the former Yugoslavia.

slob /slob/ *n. colloq.* a stupid, coarse, or fat person. □□ **slob·bish** *adj.*

slob·ber /slóbər/ *v. & n.* ● *v.intr.* **1** slaver. **2** (foll. by *over*) show excessive sentiment. ● *n.* saliva running from the mouth; slaver. □□ **slob·ber·y** *adj.*

sloe /slō/ *n.* **1** = BLACKTHORN 1. **2** ◄ its small bluish-black fruit with a sour taste.

sloe-eyed *adj.* **1** having bluish-black eyes. **2** slant-eyed.

sloe gin *n.* a liqueur of sloes steeped in gin.

slog /slog/ *v. & n.* ● *v.* (**slogged, slogging**) **1** *intr. & tr.* hit hard and usu. wildly, esp. in boxing or at cricket. **2** *intr.* (often foll. by *away, on*) walk or work doggedly. ● *n.* **1** a hard random hit. **2** a hard steady work or walking. **b** a spell of this. □□ **slog·ger** *n.*

fruit

SLOE (*Prunus spinosa*)

slo·gan /slógən/ *n.* **1** a short catchy phrase used in advertising, etc. **2** a party cry; a watchword or motto.

sloop /slōōp/ *n.* a small, one-masted, fore-and-aft-rigged vessel with mainsail and jib.

slop¹ /slop/ *v. & n.* ● *v.* (**slopped, slopping**) **1** (often foll. by *over*) **a** *intr.* spill or flow over the edge of a vessel. **b** *tr.* allow to do this. **2** *tr.* make (the floor, clothes, etc.) wet or messy by slopping. **3** *intr.* (usu. foll. by *over*) gush; be effusive or maudlin. ● *n.* **1** a quantity of liquid spilled or splashed. **2** weakly sentimental language. **3** (in *pl.*) waste liquid. **4** (in *sing.* or *pl.*) unappetizing weak liquid food.

slop² /slop/ *n.* **1** a worker's loose outer garment. **2** (in *pl.*) esp. *Brit.* ready-made or cheap clothing. **3** (in *pl.*) clothes and bedding supplied to sailors in the navy. **4** (in *pl.*) *archaic* wide baggy trousers esp. as worn by sailors.

slope /slōp/ *n. & v.* ● *n.* **1** an inclined position or direction. **2** a piece of rising or falling ground. **3 a a** difference in level between the two ends or sides of a thing (*a slope of 5 yards*). **b** the rate at which this increases with distance, etc. **4** a place for skiing on the side of a hill or mountain. **5** (prec. by *the*) the position of a rifle when sloped. ● *v.* **1** *intr.* have or take a slope; slant. **2** *intr. & tr.* place or arrange or make in or at a slope. □ **slope arms** place one's rifle in a sloping position against one's shoulder.

slop·py /slópee/ *adj.* (**sloppier, sloppiest**) **1 a** (of the ground) wet with rain; full of puddles. **b** (of food, etc.) watery and disagreeable. **c** (of a floor, table, etc.) wet with slops, having water, etc., spilled on it. **2** careless; not thorough. **3** (of a garment) ill-fitting or untidy. **4** (of sentiment or talk) weakly emotional. □□ **slop·pi·ly** *adv.* **slop·pi·ness** *n.*

slosh /slosh/ *v. & n.* ● *v.* **1** *intr.* (often foll. by *about*) splash or flounder about; move with a splashing sound. **2** *tr. colloq.* **a** pour (liquid) clumsily. **b** pour liquid on. ● *n.* **1** slush. **2** an instance of splashing. **b** the sound of this. **3** a quantity of liquid.

sloshed /slosht/ *adj. sl.* drunk.

slosh·y /slóshee/ *adj.* (**sloshier, sloshiest**) **1** slushy. **2** sloppy; sentimental.

slot¹ /slot/ *n. & v.* ● *n.* **1** a slit or other aperture in a machine, etc., for something (esp. a coin) to be inserted. **2** a slit, groove, channel, or long aperture into which something fits. **3** an allotted place in a scheme or schedule. ● *v.* (**slotted, slotting**) **1** *tr. &*

intr. place or be placed into or as if into a slot. **2** *tr.* provide with a slot or slots.

slot² /slot/ *n.* **1** the track of a deer, etc., esp. as shown by footprints. **2** a deer's foot.

sloth /slawth, slōth/ *n.* **1** laziness or indolence. **2** ▶ any slow-moving nocturnal mammal of the family Bradypodidae or Megalonychidae of S. America, having long limbs and hooked claws for hanging upside down from branches of trees. ▷ EDENTATE

large, hooked claws

SLOTH: TWO-
TOED SLOTH
(*Choloepus didactylus*)

downward-pointing fur

sloth·ful /sláwthfōōl, slōth-/ *adj.* lazy. □□ **sloth·ful·ly** *adv.* **sloth·ful·ness** *n.*

slot ma·chine *n.* a machine worked by the insertion of a coin, esp. a gambling machine operated by a pulled handle.

slouch /slowch/ *v. & n.* ● *v.* **1** *intr.* stand or move or sit in a drooping, ungainly fashion. **2** *tr.* bend one side of the brim of (a hat) downward. **3** *intr.* hang down loosely. ● *n.* **1** a slouching posture or movement. **2** a downward bend of a hat brim. **3** *sl.* an incompetent or slovenly worker or operator or performance (*he's no slouch*). □□ **slouch·y** *adj.* (**slouchier, slouchiest**).

slough¹ /slow/ *n.* **1** a swamp; a miry place; a quagmire. **2** a marshy pond, backwater. □□ **slough·y** *adj.*

slough² /sluf/ *n. & v.* ● *n.* **1** a part that an animal casts or molts, esp. a snake's cast skin. **2** dead tissue that drops off from living flesh, etc. ● *v.* **1** *tr.* ◄ cast off as a slough. **2** *intr.* (often foll. by *off*) drop off as a slough. **3** *intr.* cast off a slough. **4** *intr.* (often foll. by *away, down*) (of soil, rock, etc.) slide into a hole or depression. □□ **slough·y** *adj.*

sloughed skin

SLOUGH: SNAKE
CASTING OFF ITS SKIN

Slo·vak /slóvaak, -vak/ *n. & adj.* ● *n.* **1** a member of a Slavic people inhabiting Slovakia in central Europe. **2** the West Slavic language of this people. ● *adj.* of or relating to this people or language.

slov·en /slúvən/ *n.* a person who is habitually untidy or careless.

Slo·vene /slóveen, sləveén/ (also **Slo·ve·ni·an** /-véeneeən/) *n. & adj.* ● *n.* **1** a member of a Slavic people in Slovenia in the former Yugoslavia. **2** the language of this people. ● *adj.* of or relating to Slovenia or its people or language.

slov·en·ly /slúvənlee/ *adj. & adv.* ● *adj.* careless and untidy; unmethodical. ● *adv.* in a slovenly manner. □□ **slov·en·li·ness** *n.*

slow /slō/ *adj., adv., & v.* ● *adj.* **1 a** taking a relatively long time to do a thing or cover a distance (also foll. by *of*: *slow of speech*). **b** acting or moving or done without speed. **2** gradual (*slow growth*). **3** not producing, allowing, or conducive to speed (*in the slow lane*). **4** (of a clock, etc.) showing a time earlier than is the case. **5** (of a person) not understanding readily; not learning easily. **6** dull; uninteresting;

S

tedious. **7** sluggish (*business is slow*). **8** (of a fire or oven) giving little heat. **9** *Photog.* **a** (of a film) needing long exposure. **b** (of a lens) having a small aperture. **10 a** reluctant; tardy (*not slow to defend himself*). **b** not hasty or easily moved (*slow to take offense*). ● *adv.* **1** at a slow pace; slowly. **2** (in *comb.*) (*slow-moving traffic*). ● *v.* (usu. foll. by *down, up*) **1** *intr.* & *tr.* reduce one's speed or the speed of (a vehicle, etc.). **2** *intr.* reduce one's pace of life; live or work less intensely. ▫▫ **slow·ish** *adj.* **slow·ly** *adv.* **slow·ness** *n.*

slow·down /slṓdown/ *n.* the action of slowing down, as in productivity.

slow mo·tion *n.* **1** the operation or speed of a film using slower projection or more rapid exposure so that actions, etc., appear much slower than usual. **2** the simulation of this in real action.

slow·poke /slṓpōk/ *n.* **1** a slow or lazy person. **2** a dull-witted person.

slow-wit·ted *adj.* stupid.

slow·worm /slṓwərm/ *n.* a small European legless lizard, *Anguis fragilis*, giving birth to live young. Also called **blindworm**.

SLR *abbr.* **1** *Photog.* single-lens reflex. **2** self-loading rifle.

slub[1] /slub/ *n.* & *adj.* ● *n.* **1** a lump or thick place in yarn or thread. **2** fabric woven from thread, etc., with slubs. ● *adj.* (of material, etc.) with an irregular appearance caused by uneven thickness of the warp.

slub[2] /slub/ *n.* & *v.* ● *n.* wool slightly twisted in preparation for spinning. ● *v.tr.* (**slubbed**, **slubbing**) twist (wool) in this way.

sludge /sluj/ *n.* **1** thick, greasy mud. **2** muddy or slushy sediment. **3** sewage. **4** *Mech.* an accumulation of dirty oil, esp. in the sump of an internal-combustion engine. ▫▫ **sludg·y** *adj.*

slue var. of SLEW[1].

slug[1] /slug/ *n.* **1** a small shell-less mollusk of the class Gastropoda, usu. destructive to plants. ▷ GASTROPOD. **2 a** a bullet esp. of irregular shape. **b** a missile for an airgun. **3** a shot of liquor.

slug[2] /slug/ *v.* & *n.* ● *v.tr.* (**slugged**, **slugging**) strike with a hard blow. ● *n.* a hard blow. ▫ **slug it out 1** fight it out. **2** endure; stick it out. ▫▫ **slug·ger** *n.*

slug·a·bed /slúgəbed/ *n. archaic* a lazy person who lies late in bed.

slug·gard /slúgərd/ *n.* a lazy, sluggish person. ▫▫ **slug·gard·ly** *adj.*

slug·gish /slúgish/ *adj.* inert; inactive. ▫▫ **slug·gish·ly** *adv.* **slug·gish·ness** *n.*

sluice /slo͞os/ *n.* & *v.* ● *n.* **1** (also **sluice gate**, **sluice valve**) a sliding gate or other contrivance for controlling the volume or flow of water. **2** a sluiceway, esp. one for washing ore. **3** a place for rinsing. **4** the act or an instance of rinsing. **5** the water above or below or issuing through a floodgate. ● *v.* **1** *tr.* provide or wash with a sluice or sluices. **2** *tr.* rinse, throw water freely upon. **3** *tr.* (foll. by *out, away*) wash out or away with a flow of water. **4** *tr.* flood with water from a sluice. **5** *intr.* (of water) rush out from a sluice, or as if from a sluice.

S

sluice·way /slo͞osway/ *n.* an artificial channel in which the flow of water is controlled by a sluice.

slum /slum/ *n.* & *v.* ● *n.* **1** an overcrowded and squalid back street, district, etc., usu. in a city. **2** a house or building unfit for human habitation. ● *v.intr.* (**slummed**, **slumming**) **1** live in slumlike conditions. **2** go about the slums through curiosity or for charitable purposes. ▫ **slum it** *colloq.* put up with conditions less comfortable than usual. ▫▫ **slum·my** *adj.* (**slummier**, **slummiest**). **slum·mi·ness** *n.*

slum·ber /slúmbər/ *v.* & *n. poet. rhet.* ● *v.intr.* **1** sleep, esp. in a specified manner. **2** be idle, drowsy, or inactive. ● *n.* a sleep, esp. of a specified kind (*fell into a fitful slumber*). ▫▫ **slum·ber·er** *n.* **slum·ber·ous** *adj.* **slum·brous** *adj.*

slum·lord /slúmlawrd/ *n.* the landlord of substandard housing, esp. one who fails to maintain the property while charging high rents.

slump /slump/ *n.* & *v.* ● *n.* **1** a sudden severe or prolonged fall in prices or values of commodities or securities. **2** a sharp or sudden decline in trade business. **3** a lessening of interest in a subject or undertaking. ● *v.intr.* **1** undergo a slump; fail; fall in price. **2** sit or fall heavily or limply. **3** lean or subside.

slung *past* and *past part.* of SLING[1].

slunk *past* and *past part.* of SLINK[1].

slur /slər/ *v.* & *n.* ● *v.* (**slurred**, **slurring**) **1** *tr.* & *intr.* pronounce or write indistinctly so that the sounds or letters run into one another. **2** *tr. Mus.* **a** perform (notes) legato. **b** mark (notes) with a slur. ▷ NOTATION. **3** *tr.* put a slur on (a person or a person's character). **4** *tr.* (usu. foll. by *over*) pass over (a fact, fault, etc.) lightly. ● *n.* **1** an imputation of wrongdoing; stigma (*a slur on my reputation*). **2** the act or an instance of slurring. **3** *Mus.* a curved line to show that two or more notes are to be sung to one syllable or played or sung legato.

slurp /slərp/ *v.* & *n.* ● *v.tr.* eat or drink noisily. ● *n.* the sound of this; a slurping gulp.

slur·ry /slúree/ *n.* (*pl.* **-ies**) **1** a semiliquid mixture of fine particles and water. **2** thin liquid cement. **3** a fluid form of manure.

slush /slush/ *n.* **1** watery mud or thawing snow. **2** silly sentiment.

slush·y /slúshee/ *adj.* (**slushier**, **slushiest**) like slush; watery. ▫▫ **slush·i·ness** *n.*

slut /slut/ *n. derog.* a slovenly woman. ▫▫ **slut·tish** *adj.* **slut·tish·ness** *n.*

sly /slī/ *adj.* (**slier**, **sliest** or **slyer**, **slyest**) **1** cunning; wily. **2 a** (of a person) practicing secrecy or stealth. **b** (of an action, etc.) done, etc., in secret. **3** hypocritical; ironic. **4** knowing; arch; insinuating. ▫ **on the sly** privately; covertly. ▫▫ **sly·ly** *adv.* (also **sli·ly**). **sly·ness** *n.*

sly·boots /slībo͞ots/ *n. colloq.* a sly person.

sly dog *n. colloq.* a person who is discreet about mistakes or pleasures.

slype /slīp/ *n.* a covered way or passage between a cathedral, etc., transept and the chapter house or deanery.

Sm *symb. Chem.* the element samarium.

SM *abbr.* **1** sadomasochism. **2** sergeant major.

smack[1] /smak/ *n.*, *v.*, & *adv.* ● *n.* **1** a sharp slap or blow esp. with the palm of the hand or a flat object. **2** a hard hit in baseball, etc. **3** a loud kiss. **4** a loud, sharp sound. ● *v.* **1** *tr.* strike with the open hand, etc. **2** *tr.* part (one's lips) noisily in eager anticipation or enjoyment of food. **3** *tr.* crack (a whip). **4** *tr.* & *intr.* move, hit, etc., with a smack. ● *adv. colloq.* **1** with a smack. **2** suddenly; violently (*landed smack on my desk*). **3** exactly (*hit it smack in the center*). ▫ **have a smack at** *colloq.* make an attempt at. **a smack in the eye** (or **face**) *colloq.* a rebuff.

smack[2] /smak/ *v.* & *n.* (foll. by *of*) ● *v.intr.* **1** have a flavor of (*smacked of garlic*). **2** suggest the effects of (*it smacks of nepotism*). ● *n.* **1** a taste that suggests the presence of something. **2** (in a person's character, etc.) a barely discernible quality (*just a smack of superciliousness*).

smack[3] /smak/ *n.* a single-masted sailboat for coasting or fishing.

smack[4] /smak/ *n. sl.* a hard drug, esp. heroin.

smack·er /smákər/ *n. sl.* **1** a loud kiss. **2** a resounding blow. **3** (usu. in *pl.*) *sl.* a dollar.

small /smawl/ *adj.*, *n.*, & *adv.* ● *adj.* **1** not large or big. **2** slender; thin. **3** not great in importance, amount, number, strength, or power. **4** trifling (*a small token*). **5** insignificant; unimportant (*a small matter*). **6** consisting of small particles (*small gravel*). **7** doing something on a small scale (*a small farmer*). **8** socially undistinguished. **9** petty; paltry (*a small spiteful nature*). **10** young; not fully developed (*a small child*). ● *n.* the slenderest part of something (esp. **small of the back**). ● *adv.* into small pieces (*chop it small*). ▫ **in a small way** unambitiously; on a small scale. **no small** considerable (*no small excitement*). **small potatoes** an insignificant person or thing. **small wonder** not very surprising. ▫▫ **small·ish** *adj.* **small·ness** *n.*

small arms *n.pl.* portable firearms, esp. rifles, pistols, light machine guns, etc.

small-claims court *n.* a local court in which claims for small amounts can be heard and decided quickly without legal representation.

small fry *n.pl.* **1** young children or the young of various species. **2** small or insignificant things or people.

small in·tes·tine *n.* the duodenum, jejunum, and ileum collectively. ▷ DIGESTION, INTESTINE

small-mind·ed /smáwlmíndid/ *adj.* petty; of rigid opinions or narrow outlook. ▫▫ **small-mind·ed·ly** *adv.* **small-mind·ed·ness** *n.*

small·pox /smáwlpoks/ *n. hist.* an acute contagious viral disease, with fever and pustules, usu. leaving permanent scars.

small print *n.* **1** printed matter in small type. **2** inconspicuous and usu. unfavorable limitations, etc., in a contract.

small-scale *adj.* made or occurring in small amounts or to a lesser degree.

small·sword /smáwlsáwrd/ *n.* a light, tapering thrusting sword, esp. *hist.* for dueling.

small talk *n.* light social conversation.

small-time *adj. colloq.* unimportant or petty.

small-town *adj.* relating to or characteristic of a small town; unsophisticated; provincial.

smalt /smawlt/ *n.* **1** glass colored blue with cobalt. **2** a pigment made by pulverizing this.

smarm·y /smaármee/ *adj.* (**smarmier**, **smarmiest**) ingratiating; flattering; obsequious. ▫▫ **smarm·i·ly** *adv.* **smarm·i·ness** *n.*

smart /smaart/ *adj.*, *v.*, *n.*, & *adv.* ● *adj.* **1 a** clever; ingenious; quickwitted (*a smart answer*). **b** keen in bargaining. **c** (of transactions, etc.) unscrupulous to the point of dishonesty. **2** well-groomed; bright and fresh in appearance (*a smart suit*). **3** in good repair; showing bright colors, etc. (*a smart red bicycle*). **4** stylish; fashionable; prominent in society (*the smart set*). **5** brisk (*set a smart pace*). **6** painfully severe; sharp; vigorous (*a smart blow*). ● *v.intr.* **1** feel or give acute pain or distress (*my eye smarts*). **2** (of an insult, grievance, etc.) rankle. **3** (foll. by *for*) suffer the consequences of (*you will smart for this*). ● *n.* a bodily or mental sharp pain; a stinging sensation. ● *adv.* smartly; in a smart manner. ▫▫ **smart·ing·ly** *adv.* **smart·ly** *adv.* **smart·ness** *n.*

smart al·eck /álik/ *n.* (also **alec**) *colloq.* a person displaying ostentatious or smug cleverness. ▫▫ **smart-al·eck·y** *adj.*

smart-ass *n. sl.* = SMART ALECK.

smart bomb *n.* a bomb that can be guided directly to its target by use of radio waves, television, or lasers.

smart·en /smaárt'n/ *v.tr.* & *intr.* (usu. foll. by *up*) make or become smart.

smart·y /smaártee/ *n.* (*pl.* **-ies**) *colloq.* a know-it-all; a smart aleck.

smart·y-pants *n.* = SMARTY.

smash /smash/ *v.*, *n.*, & *adv.* ● *v.* **1** *tr.* & *intr.* (often foll. by *up*) **a** break into pieces. **b** bring or come to sudden or complete destruction, defeat, or disaster. **2** *tr.* (foll. by *into, through*) move with great force and impact. **3** *tr.* & *intr.* (foll. by *in*) break in with a crushing blow (*smashed in the window*). **4** *tr.* (in tennis, squash, etc.) hit (a ball, etc.) with great force, esp. downward. **5** *tr.* (as **smashed** *adj.*) *sl.* intoxicated. ● *n.* **1** the act of smashing; a violent fall, collision, or disaster. **2** the sound of this. **3** (in full **smash hit**) a very successful play, song, performer, etc. **4** a stroke in tennis, squash, etc., in which the ball is hit, esp. downward with great force. **5** a violent blow with a fist, etc. ● *adv.* with a smash (*fell smash on the floor*).

smash·er /smáshər/ *n.* a person or thing that smashes.

smash·ing /smáshing/ *adj. colloq.* excellent; wonderful. ▫▫ **smash·ing·ly** *adv.*

smash·up /smáshəp/ *n. colloq.* a violent collision, esp. of motor vehicles.

smat·ter /smátər/ *n.* (also **smat·ter·ing**) a slight superficial knowledge.

smear /smeer/ *v. & n.* ● *v.tr.* **1** daub or mark with a greasy or sticky substance or with something that stains. **2** blot; smudge (writing, artwork, etc.). **3** defame the character of; slander publicly. ● *n.* **1** the act or an instance of smearing. **2** *Med.* **a** material smeared on a microscopic slide, etc., for examination. **b** a specimen of this. ▫▫ **smear·er** *n.* **smear·y** *adj.*

smeg·ma /smégmə/ *n.* a sebaceous secretion in the folds of the skin, esp. of the foreskin. ▫▫ **smeg·matic** /-mátik/ *adj.*

smell /smel/ *n. & v.* ● *n.* **1** the faculty of perceiving odors or scents (*has a fine sense of smell*). **2** the quality in substances that is perceived by this (*the smell of thyme; this rose has no scent*). **3** an unpleasant odor. **4** the act of inhaling to ascertain smell. ● *v.* (*past* and *past part.* **smelled** or **smelt** /smelt/) **1** *tr.* perceive the smell of; examine by smell. **2** *intr.* emit odor. **3** *intr.* seem by smell to be (*smells sour*). **4** *intr.* (foll. by *of*) **a** be redolent of (*smells of fish*). **b** be suggestive of (*smells of dishonesty*). **5** *intr.* stink; be rank. **6** *tr.* perceive as if by smell; detect (*smell a bargain; smell blood*). **7** *intr.* have or use a sense of smell. **8** *intr.* (foll. by *about*) sniff or search about. **9** *intr.* (foll. by *at*) inhale the smell of. ▫ **smell out** detect by smell; find out by investigation. **smell a rat** begin to suspect trickery, etc. ▫▫ **smell·a·ble** *adj.* **smell·er** *n.* **smell-less** *adj.*

smell·ing salts *n.pl.* ammonium carbonate mixed with scent to be sniffed as a restorative in faintness, etc.

smell·y /smélee/ *adj.* (**smellier**, **smelliest**) having a strong smell. ▫▫ **smell·i·ness** *n.*

smelt[1] /smelt/ *v.tr.* **1** separate metal from (ore) by melting. **2** extract or refine (metal) in this way. ▫▫ **smelt·er** *n.* **smelt·er·y** *n.* (*pl.* **-ies**).

smelt[2] *past* and *past part.* of SMELL.

smelt[3] /smelt/ *n.* (*pl.* same or **smelts**) any small green and silver fish of the genus *Osmerus*, etc., allied to salmon and used as food.

smew /smyōō/ *n.* a small merganser, *Mergus albellus.*

smid·gen /smíjən/ *n.* (also **smid·gin**) *colloq.* a small bit or amount.

smi·lax /smílaks/ *n.* **1** any climbing shrub of the genus *Smilax*, the roots of some species of which yield sarsaparilla. **2** a climbing kind of asparagus, *Asparagus medeoloides*, used decoratively by florists.

smile /smīl/ *v. & n.* ● *v.* **1** *intr.* relax the features into a pleased or kind or gently skeptical expression, usu. with the corners of the mouth turned up. **2** *tr.* express by smiling (*smiled their consent*). **3** *tr.* give (a smile) of a specified kind (*smiled a sardonic smile*). **4** *intr.* (foll. by *on*, *upon*) adopt a favorable attitude toward (*fortune smiled on me*). **5** *intr.* (foll. by *at*) **a** show indifference to (*smiled at my feeble attempts*). **b** favor; smile on. ● *n.* **1** the act of smiling. **2** a smiling expression. ▫▫ **smil·er** *n.* **smil·ey** *adj.* **smil·ing·ly** *adv.*

smirch /smərch/ *v. & n.* ● *v.tr.* mark, soil, or smear (a thing, a person's reputation, etc.). ● *n.* **1** a spot or stain. **2** a blot (on one's character, etc.).

smirk /smərk/ *n. & v.* ● *n.* an affected, conceited, or silly smile. ● *v.intr.* put on or wear a smirk. ▫▫ **smirk·er** *n.* **smirk·ing·ly** *adv.* **smirk·y** *adj.*

smit /smit/ *archaic past part.* of SMITE.

smite /smīt/ *v.tr.* (*past* **smote** /smōt/; *past part.* **smitten** /smít'n/) *archaic* or *literary* **1** strike or hit. **2** chastise; defeat. **3** (in *passive*) **a** have a sudden strong effect on (*smitten by his conscience*). **b** infatuate; fascinate (*smitten by her beauty*). ▫▫ **smit·er** *n.*

smith /smith/ *n. & v.* ● *n.* **1** (esp. in *comb.*) a worker in metal (*goldsmith*). **2** a blacksmith. **3** a craftsman (*wordsmith*). ● *v.tr.* make or treat by forging.

smith·er·eens /smíthəreénz/ *n.pl.* (also **smith·ers** /smíthərz/) small fragments.

smith·er·y /smíthəree/ *n.* (*pl.* **-ies**) **1** a smith's work. **2** (esp. in naval dockyards) a smithy.

smith·y /smíthee/ *n.* (*pl.* **-ies**) a blacksmith's workshop; a forge.

smit·ten *past part.* of SMITE.

smock /smok/ *n. & v.* ● *n.* **1** a loose shirtlike garment with the upper part closely gathered in smocking. **2** a loose overall. ● *v.tr.* adorn with smocking.

smock·ing /smóking/ *n.* ► an ornamental effect on cloth made by gathering the material tightly into pleats, often with stitches in a decorative pattern.

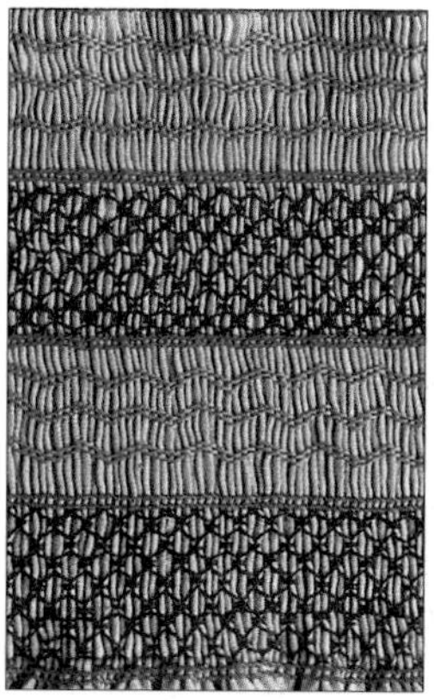

SMOCKING

smog /smog, smawg/ *n.* fog intensified by smoke. ▫▫ **smog·gy** *adj.* (**smoggier**, **smoggiest**).

smoke /smōk/ *n. & v.* ● *n.* **1** a visible suspension of carbon, etc., in air, emitted from a burning substance. **2** an act or period of smoking tobacco. **3** *colloq.* a cigarette or cigar (*got a smoke?*). ● *v.* **1** *intr.* **a** emit smoke or visible vapor. **b** (of a lamp, etc.) burn badly with the emission of smoke. **c** (of a chimney or fire) discharge smoke into the room. **2 a** *intr.* inhale and exhale the smoke of a cigarette. **b** *intr.* do this habitually. **c** *tr.* use (a cigarette, etc.) in this way. **3** *tr.* darken or preserve by the action of smoke (*smoked salmon*). ▫ **go up in smoke** *colloq.* **1** be destroyed by fire. **2** (of a plan, etc.) come to nothing. **smoke out 1** drive out by means of smoke. **2** drive out of hiding or secrecy, etc. ▫▫ **smok·a·ble** *adj.* (also **smoke·a·ble**).

smoke·less /smṓklis/ *adj.* having or producing little or no smoke.

smok·er /smṓkər/ *n.* **1** a person or thing that smokes, esp. a person who habitually smokes tobacco. **2** a compartment on a train, in which smoking is allowed. **3** an informal social gathering of men.

smoke·house /smṓkhows/ *n.* a shed or room for smoking fish or meat.

smoke screen *n.* **1** a cloud of smoke diffused to conceal (esp. military) operations. **2** a device or ruse for disguising one's activities.

smoke·stack /smṓkstak/ *n.* **1** a chimney or funnel for discharging the smoke of a locomotive or steamer. ▷ STEAM ENGINE. **2** a tall chimney.

smok·ing /smṓking/ *n. & adj.* ● *n.* the act of inhaling and exhaling from a cigarette, cigar, etc. ● *adj.* giving off smoke.

smok·ing gun *n.* something that serves as indisputable proof, esp. of a crime.

smok·y /smṓkee/ *adj.* (also **smokey**) (**smokier**, **smokiest**) **1** emitting, veiled or filled with, or obscured by, smoke (*smoky fire; smoky room*). **2** stained with or colored like smoke (*smoky glass*). **3** having the taste or flavor of smoked food (*smoky bacon*). ▫▫ **smok·i·ly** *adv.* **smok·i·ness** *n.*

smol·der /smṓldər/ *v. & n.* ● *v.intr.* **1** burn slowly with smoke but without a flame. **2** (of emotions, etc.) exist in a suppressed or concealed state. **3** (of a person) show silent anger, hatred, etc. ● *n.* a smoldering or slow-burning fire.

smolt /smōlt/ *n.* a young salmon migrating to the sea for the first time.

smooch /smōōch/ *n. & v. colloq.* ● *n.* a spell of kissing and caressing. ● *v.intr.* engage in a smooch. ▫▫ **smooch·er** *n.* **smooch·y** *adj.* (**smoochier**, **smoochiest**).

smooth /smōōth/ *adj., v., n., & adv.* ● *adj.* **1** having a relatively even and regular surface; free from perceptible projections, lumps, indentations, and roughness. **2** not wrinkled, pitted, scored, or hairy. **3** that can be traversed without check. **4** (of liquids) of even consistency; without lumps. **5** (of the sea, etc.) without waves or undulations. **6** (of a journey, progress, etc.) untroubled by difficulties or adverse conditions. **7** having an easy flow or correct rhythm (*smooth breathing*). **8 a** not harsh in sound or taste. **b** (of wine, etc.) not astringent. **9** (of a person, his or her manner, etc.) suave, conciliatory, flattering (*a smooth talker*). **10** (of movement, etc.) not suddenly varying; not jerky. ● *v.* **1** *tr. & intr.* (often foll. by *out*, *down*) make or become smooth. **2** (often foll. by *out*, *over*) **a** *tr.* reduce or get rid of (differences, faults, difficulties, etc.) in fact or appearance. **b** *intr.* (of difficulties, etc.) diminish. **3** *tr.* modify (a graph, curve, etc.) so as to lessen irregularities. **4** *tr.* free from impediments or discomfort (*smooth the way*). ● *n.* **1** a smoothing touch or stroke. **2** the easy part of life (*take the rough with the smooth*). ● *adv.* smoothly (*true love never did run smooth*). ▫▫ **smooth·a·ble** *adj.* **smooth·er** *n.* **smooth·ish** *adj.* **smooth·ly** *adv.* **smooth·ness** *n.*

smooth·ie /smōōthee/ *n. colloq.* a person who is smooth (see SMOOTH *adj.* 9).

smooth mus·cle *n.* a muscle without striations, usu. occurring in hollow organs and performing involuntary functions.

smooth talk *n. colloq.* bland specious language. ▫▫ **smooth-talk** *v.tr.*

smooth-tongued *adj.* insincerely flattering.

smor·gas·bord /smáwrgəsbawrd/ *n.* a buffet offering a variety of hot and cold meats, salads, hors d'oeuvres, etc.

smor·zan·do /smawrtsaándō/ *adj., adv., & n. Mus.* ● *adj. & adv.* dying away. ● *n.* (*pl.* **-os** or **smorzandi** /-dee/) a smorzando passage.

smote *past* of SMITE.

smoth·er /smúthər/ *v. & n.* ● *v.* **1** *tr.* suffocate; stifle. **2** *tr.* (foll. by *with*) overwhelm with (kisses, kindness, etc.). **3** *tr.* (foll. by *in*, *with*) cover entirely in or with (*smothered in mayonnaise*). **4** *tr.* extinguish or deaden (a fire or flame) by covering it. **5** *intr.* **a** die of suffocation. **b** have difficulty breathing. **6** *tr.* (often foll. by *up*) keep from notice or publicity. **7** *tr.* defeat rapidly or utterly. ● *n.* **1** a cloud of dust or smoke. **2** obscurity caused by this.

smudge[1] /smuj/ *n. & v.* ● *n.* **1** a blurred or smeared line or mark. **2** a stain or blot on a person's character, etc. ● *v.* **1** *tr.* make a smudge on. **2** *intr.* become smeared or blurred (*smudges easily*). **3** *tr.* smear or blur the lines of (writing, etc.) (*smudge the outline*). **4** *tr.* defile, sully, stain, or disgrace (a person's name, etc.).

smudge[2] /smuj/ *n.* an outdoor fire with dense smoke made to keep off insects, protect plants against frost, etc. ▫ **smudge pot** a container holding burning material that produces a smudge.

smudg·y /smújee/ *adj.* (**smudgier**, **smudgiest**) **1** smudged. **2** likely to produce smudges. ▫▫ **smudg·i·ly** *adv.* **smudg·i·ness** *n.*

smug /smug/ *adj.* (**smugger**, **smuggest**) self-satisfied. ▫▫ **smug·ly** *adv.* **smug·ness** *n.*

smug·gle /smúgəl/ *v.tr.* **1** (also *absol.*) import or export (goods) illegally, esp. without payment of customs duties. **2** (foll. by *in*, *out*) convey secretly. **3** (foll. by *away*) put into concealment. ▫▫ **smug·gler** *n.* **smug·gling** *n.*

smut /smut/ *n. & v.* ● *n.* **1** a small flake of soot, etc. **2** a spot or smudge made by this. **3** obscene or lascivious talk, pictures, or stories. **4** a fungal disease of cereals. ● *v.* (**smutted**, **smutting**) **1** *tr.* mark with smuts. **2** *tr.* infect (a plant) with smut. **3** *intr.* (of a plant) contract smut. ▫▫ **smut·ty** *adj.* (**smuttier**, **smuttiest**) (esp. in sense 3 of *n.*). **smut·ti·ly** *adv.* **smut·ti·ness** *n.*

Sn *symb. Chem.* the element tin.

snack /snak/ *n. & v.* ● *n.* **1** a light, casual, or hurried meal. **2** a small amount of food eaten between meals. ● *v.intr.* eat a snack.

snack bar *n.* a place where snacks are sold.

SNAKE

There are around 2,700 snake species, most of which belong to the four main families set out below. All snakes are carnivorous vertebrates, with jaws that can dislocate to swallow relatively large animals whole. Constrictor snakes, such as pythons and boas, kill their prey by squeezing; venomous snakes like the coral snake inject their victims with poison from their fangs. Other snakes simply crush prey in their jaws. Although snakes have no ears, they can detect vibrations, and their tongues are sensitive to smell, taste, and touch.

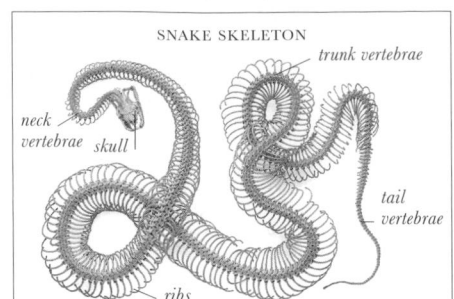

SNAKE SKELETON

neck vertebrae   skull   trunk vertebrae   tail vertebrae   ribs

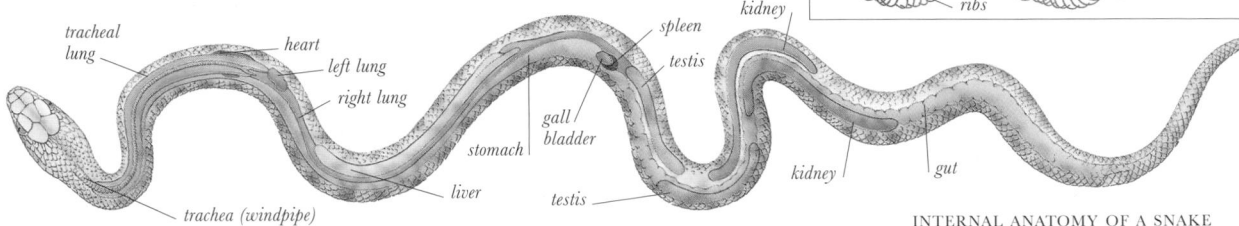

tracheal lung   heart   left lung   right lung   spleen   testis   kidney   stomach   gall bladder   liver   testis   kidney   gut   trachea (windpipe)

INTERNAL ANATOMY OF A SNAKE

EXAMPLES OF SNAKES

FAMILY BOIDAE

BOA CONSTRICTOR
(*Boa constrictor*)

INDIAN PYTHON
(*Python molurus*)

ANACONDA
(*Eunectes murinus*)

FAMILY COLUBRIDAE

FLYING TREE SNAKE
(*Chrysopelea pelias*)

CORN SNAKE
(*Elaphe guttata*)

CALIFORNIA KING SNAKE
(*Lampropeltis getulus*)

VINE SNAKE
(*Oxybelis fulgidus*)

FAMILY VIPERIDAE

WESTERN DIAMONDBACK RATTLESNAKE
(*Crotalus atrox*)

FAMILY ELAPIDAE

BLACK-NECKED COBRA
(*Naja nigricollis*)

PUFF-ADDER
(*Bitis arietans*)

CORAL SNAKE
(*Micrurus nigrocinctus*)

S

snaf·fle /snáfəl/ *n.* (in full **snaffle bit**) a simple bridle bit without a curb.

sna·fu /snafóo/ *adj. & n. sl.* ● *adj.* in utter confusion or chaos. ● *n.* this state.

snag /snag/ *n. & v.* ● *n.* **1** an unexpected or hidden obstacle or drawback. **2** a jagged or projecting point or broken stump. **3** a tear in material, etc. ● *v.tr.* (**snagged, snagging**) **1** catch or tear on a snag. **2** clear (land, a waterway, a tree trunk, etc.) of snags. □□ **snagged** *adj.* **snag·gy** *adj.*

snag·gle·tooth /snágəl/ *n.* (*pl.* **snaggleteeth**) an irregular or projecting tooth. □□ **snag·gle·toothed** *adj.*

snail /snayl/ *n.* any slow-moving mollusk with a spiral shell. ▷ GASTROPOD, MOLLUSK. □□ **snail·like** *adj.*

snail mail *n. colloq.* regular mail as opposed to email.

snail's pace *n.* a very slow movement.

snake /snayk/ *n. & v.* ● *n.* **1 a** ◀ any long, limbless reptile of the suborder Ophidia, including boas, pythons, cobras, and vipers. **b** a limbless lizard or amphibian. **2** (also **snake in the grass**) a treacherous person or secret enemy. ● *v.intr.* move or twist like a snake. □□ **snake·like** *adj.*

snake·bird /snáykbərd/ *n.* a fish-eating bird, *Anhinga anhinga*, with a long slender neck.

snake charm·er *n.* a person appearing to make snakes move by music, etc.

snake oil *n.* any of various concoctions sold as medicine but without medicinal value.

snake pit *n.* **1** a pit containing snakes. **2** a scene of vicious behavior. **3** a mental hospital in which inhumane treatment is known or suspect.

snake·root /snáykrŏot, -rŏot/ *n.* any of various N. American plants, esp. *Cimicifuga racemosa*, with roots reputed to contain an antidote to snake's poison.

snak·y /snáykee/ *adj.* **1** like a snake in appearance; long and sinuous. **2** showing coldness, venom, or guile. □□ **snak·i·ly** *adv.* **snak·i·ness** *n.*

snap /snap/ *v., n., adv., & adj.* ● *v.* (**snapped, snapping**) **1** *intr. & tr.* break suddenly or with a snap. **2** *intr. & tr.* emit or cause to emit a sudden sharp sound or crack. **3** *intr. & tr.* open or close with a snapping sound (*snapped shut*). **4 a** *intr.* (often foll. by *at*) speak irritably or spitefully (*did not mean to snap at you*). **b** *tr.* say irritably or spitefully. **5** *intr.* (often foll. by *at*) (esp. of a dog, etc.) make a sudden audible bite. **6** *tr. & intr.* move quickly (*snap into action*). **7** *tr.* take a snapshot of. **8** *tr. Football* put (the ball) into play on the ground by a quick backward movement. ● *n.* **1** an act or sound of snapping. **2** a crisp cookie (*gingersnap*). **3** a snapshot. **4** (in full **cold snap**) a sudden brief spell of cold weather. **5** crispness of style; zest; dash; spring. **6** *sl.* an easy task (*it was a snap*). **7** (also **snap fas·ten·er**) a two-piece device that snaps together, used esp. on garments, etc. (e.g., instead of buttons). **8** *Football* the beginning of a play, when the ball is passed quickly back. ● *adv.* with the sound of a snap (*heard it go snap*). ● *adj.* done or taken on the spur of the moment (*snap decision*). □ **snap one's fingers 1** make an audible fillip, esp. in rhythm to music, etc. **2** (often foll. by *at*) defy; show contempt for. **snap off** break off or bite off. **snap out** say irritably. **snap out of** *sl.* get rid of (an attitude, habit, etc.) by a sudden effort; recover (*snap out of a bad mood*). **snap up 1** accept (an offer) quickly or eagerly. **2** pick up or catch hastily or smartly (*the new copies of the book were snapped up in one day*).

snap·drag·on /snápdragən/ *n.* ◀ a plant of the genus *Antirrhinum*, esp. *Antirrhinum majus*, with a bag-shaped flower like a dragon's mouth.

SNAPDRAGON
(*Antirrhinum majus*)

snap·per /snápər/ *n.* **1** a person or thing that snaps. **2** any of several fish of the family Lutjanidae, used as food.

snap·ping tur·tle *n.* ▶ any large American freshwater turtle of the family Chelydridae which seizes prey with a snap of its jaws.

snap·pish /snápish/ *adj.* **1** (of a person's manner) curt; ill-tempered. **2** (of a dog, etc.) inclined to snap. □□ **snap·pish·ly** *adv.* **snap·pish·ness** *n.*

snap·py /snápee/ *adj.* (**snappier, snappiest**) *colloq.* **1** brisk; full of zest. **2** neat and elegant (*a snappy dresser*). **3** snappish. □ **make it snappy** be quick about it. □□ **snap·pi·ly** *adv.* **snap·pi·ness** *n.*

snap·shot /snápshot/ *n.* a casual photograph taken with a hand-held camera.

snare /snair/ *n. & v.* ● *n.* **1** a trap for catching birds or animals, esp. with a noose of wire or cord. **2** a thing that acts as a temptation. **3** a device for tempting an enemy, etc., to expose himself or herself to danger, failure, loss, capture, defeat, etc. **4** (in *sing.* or *pl.*) *Mus.* twisted strings of gut, hide, or wire stretched across the lower head of a snare drum to produce a rattling sound. **5** (in full **snare drum**) ▼ a small, double-headed drum fitted with snares, usu. played in a jazz or military band. ▷ DRUM SET, ORCHESTRA. ● *v.tr.* **1** catch in a snare. **2** trap with a snare. □□ **snar·er** *n.* (also in *comb.*).

snare
mounting

lug

snare
release lever

sticks

snare

damper

drumhead

SNARE DRUM
(VIEWED FROM BELOW)

snarf /snaarf/ *v.tr. colloq.*, chiefly *N. Amer.* consume quickly or greedily.

snark /snaark/ *n.* a fabulous animal, orig. the subject of a nonsense poem.

snarl¹ /snaarl/ *v. & n.* ● *v.* **1** *intr.* (of a dog) make an angry growl with bared teeth. **2** *intr.* (of a person) speak cynically; make bad-tempered complaints. **3** *tr.* (often foll. by *out*) **a** utter in a snarling tone. **b** express (discontent, etc.) by snarling. ● *n.* the act or sound of snarling. □□ **snarl·er** *n.* **snarl·ing·ly** *adv.* **snarl·y** *adj.* (**snarlier, snarliest**)

snarl² /snaarl/ *v. & n.* ● *v.* **1** *tr.* (often foll. by *up*) entangle; hamper the movement of. **2** *intr.* (often foll. by *up*) become entangled. ● *n.* a knot or tangle.

snarl-up *n. colloq.* a traffic jam; a muddle; a mistake.

snatch /snach/ *v. & n.* ● *v.tr.* **1** seize quickly, eagerly, or unexpectedly. **2** steal (a wallet, etc.). **3** secure with difficulty (*snatched an hour's rest*). **4** (foll. by *away, from*) take away or from, esp. suddenly (*snatched away my hand*). **5** (foll. by *from*) rescue narrowly. **6** (foll. by *at*) **a** try to seize by stretching or grasping suddenly. **b** take (an offer, etc.) eagerly. ● *n.* **1** an act of snatching (*made a snatch at it*). **2** a fragment of a song or talk, etc. **3** *sl.* a kidnapping. □□ **snatch·er** *n.* (esp. in sense 3 of *v.*). **snatch·y** *adj.*

snaz·zy /snázee/ *adj.* (**snazzier, snazziest**) *sl.* smart or attractive, esp. in an ostentatious way. □□ **snaz·zi·ly** *adv.* **snaz·zi·ness** *n.*

sneak /sneek/ *v., n., & adj.* ● *v.* **1** *intr. & tr.* (foll. by *in, out, past, away,* etc.) go or convey furtively; slink. **2** *tr. sl.* steal unobserved. **3** *intr.* (as **sneaking** *adj.*) **a** furtive; undisclosed (*a sneaking affection for him*). **b** persistent in one's mind (*a sneaking feeling*). ● *n.* a mean-spirited, cowardly, underhanded person. ● *adj.* acting or done without warning; secret. □□ **sneak·ing·ly** *adv.*

sneak·er /sneekər/ *n.* each of a pair of rubber-soled canvas, etc., shoes.

sneak thief *n.* a thief who steals without breaking in.

sneak·y /sneekee/ *adj.* (**sneakier, sneakiest**) given to or characterized by sneaking; furtive; mean. □□ **sneak·i·ly** *adv.* **sneak·i·ness** *n.*

sneer /sneer/ *n. & v.* ● *n.* a derisive smile or remark. ● *v.* **1** *intr.* (often foll. by *at*) smile derisively. **2** *tr.* say sneeringly. **3** *intr.* (often foll. by *at*) speak derisively. □□ **sneer·er** *n.* **sneer·ing·ly** *adv.*

sneeze /sneez/ *n. & v.* ● *n.* **1** a sudden involuntary expulsion of air from the nose and mouth caused by irritation of the nostrils. **2** the sound of this. ● *v.intr.* make a sneeze. □ **not to be sneezed at** *colloq.* not contemptible; considerable. □□ **sneez·er** *n.* **sneez·y** *adj.*

sneeze·wort /sneezwərt, -wawrt/ *n.* ▶ a kind of yarrow, *Achillea ptarmica*, whose dried leaves are used to induce sneezing.

Snell's law /snelz/ *n. Physics* the law that the ratio of the sines of the angles of incidence and refraction of a wave are constant when it passes between two given media.

snib /snib/ *v. & n., Sc. & Ir.* ● *v.tr.* (**snibbed, snibbing**) bolt, fasten, or lock (a door, etc.). ● *n.* a lock, catch, or fastening for a door or window.

SNEEZEWORT
(*Achillea ptarmica*)

snick /snik/ *v. & n.* ● *v.tr.* **1** cut a small notch in. **2** make a small incision in. **3** *Cricket* deflect (the ball) slightly with the bat. ● *n.* **1** a small notch or cut. **2** *Cricket* a slight deflection of the ball by the bat.

snick·er /sníkər/ *v. & n.* ● *v.intr.* **1** = SNIGGER *v.* **2** whinny; neigh. ● *n.* **1** = SNIGGER *n.* **2** a whinny, a neigh.

snide /snīd/ *adj. & n.* ● *adj.* **1** sneering; slyly derogatory. **2** counterfeit. **3** underhanded. ● *n.* a snide person or remark. □□ **snide·ly** *adv.* **snide·ness** *n.*

sniff /snif/ *v. & n.* ● *v.* **1** *intr.* draw up air audibly through the nose. **2** *tr.* (often foll. by *up*) draw in through the nose. **3** *tr.* draw in the scent of (food, flowers, etc.) through the nose. ● *n.* **1** an act or sound of sniffing. **2** the amount of air, etc., sniffed up. □ **sniff at 1** try the smell of. **2** show contempt for. **sniff out** detect; discover by investigation. □□ **sniff·ing·ly** *adv.*

sniff·er /snífər/ *n.* **1** a person who sniffs, esp. one who sniffs a drug or toxic substances (often in *comb.*: *glue-sniffer*). **2** *sl.* the nose. **3** *colloq.* any device for detecting gas, radiation, etc.

sniff·er dog *n. colloq.* a dog trained to sniff out drugs or explosives.

snif·fle /snífəl/ *v. & n.* ● *v.intr.* sniff slightly or repeatedly. ● *n.* **1** the act of sniffling. **2** (in *sing.* or *pl.*) a cold in the head causing a running nose and sniffling. □□ **snif·fler** *n.*

snif·fy /snífee/ *adj. colloq.* (**sniffier, sniffiest**) **1** inclined to sniff. **2** disdainful. □□ **sniff·i·ly** *adv.* **sniff·i·ness** *n.*

snif·ter /sníftər/ *n.* **1** *sl.* a small drink of alcohol. **2** a balloon glass for brandy.

SNAPPING TURTLE
(*Chelydra serpentina*)

beak

S

snig·ger /snígər/ *n. & v.* ● *n.* a half-suppressed secretive laugh. ● *v.intr.* utter such a laugh. □□ **snig·ger·er** *n.* **snig·ger·ing·ly** *adv.*

snig·gle /snígəl/ *v.intr.* fish (for eels) by pushing bait into a hole.

snip /snip/ *v. & n.* ● *v.tr.* (**snipped, snipping**) (also *absol.*) cut with scissors or shears, esp. in small, quick strokes. ● *n.* **1** an act of snipping. **2** a piece of material, etc., snipped off. **3** *sl.* something easily achieved. **4** (in *pl.*) hand shears for metal cutting. □□ **snip·ping** *n.*

snipe /snīp/ *n. & v.* ● *n.* (*pl.* same or **snipes**) ◀ any of various wading birds frequenting marshes, with a long, straight bill. ● *v.* **1** *intr.* fire shots from hiding, usu. at long range. **2** *intr.* (foll. by *at*) make a sly critical attack on a person. □□ **snip·er** *n.*

snip·pet /snípit/ *n.* **1** a small piece cut off. **2** (usu. in *pl.*; often foll. by *of*) **a** a scrap or fragment of information, knowledge, etc. **b** a short extract from a newspaper, book, magazine, etc. □□ **snip·pet·y** *adj.*

snip·py /snípee/ *adj.* (**snippier, snippiest**) *colloq.* faultfinding; snappish; sharp. □□ **snip·pi·ly** *adv.* **snip·pi·ness** *n.*

snit /snit/ *n.* a rage; a sulk (esp. in a *snit*).

snitch /snich/ *v. & n. sl.* ● *v.* **1** *tr.* steal. **2** *intr.* (often foll. by *on*) inform on a person. ● *n.* an informer.

sniv·el /snívəl/ *v. & n.* ● *v.intr.* **1** weep with sniffling. **2** run at the nose. **3** show tearful sentiment. ● *n.* **1** running mucus. **2** hypocritical talk. □□ **sniv·el·er** *n.* **sniv·el·ing** *adj.* **sniv·el·ing·ly** *adv.*

snob /snob/ *n.* **1** a person with an exaggerated respect for social position or wealth and who despises socially inferior connections. **2** a person who behaves with servility to social superiors. **3** a person who despises others whose (usu. specified) tastes or attainments are considered inferior (*an intellectual snob*). □□ **snob·ber·y** *n.* (*pl.* **-ies**). **snob·bish** *adj.* **snob·bish·ly** *adv.* **snob·bish·ness** *n.* **snob·by** *adj.* (**snobbier, snobbiest**).

snood /snood/ *n.* **1** an ornamental hairnet usu. worn at the back of the head. **2** a ring of woolen, etc., material worn as a hood. **3** a short line attaching a hook to a main line in sea fishing.

snook[1] /snook, snŏok/ *n. sl.* a contemptuous gesture with the thumb to the nose and the fingers spread out.

snook[2] /snook, snŏok/ *n.* ▼ any fish of the genus *Centropomus*, esp., *C. undecimalis*.

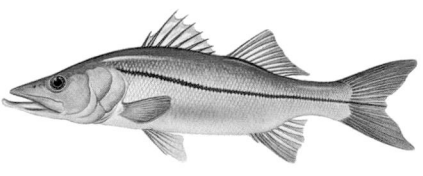

SNIPE: COMMON SNIPE
(*Gallinago gallinago*)

SNOOK
(*Centropomus undecimalis*)

snook·er /snŏokər, snook-/ *n. & v.* ● *n.* **1** ▲ a game similar to pool in which the players use a cue ball (white) to pocket the other balls (15 red and 6 colored) in a set order. **2** a position in this game in which a direct shot at a permitted ball is impossible. ● *v.tr.* **1** (also *refl.*) subject (oneself or another player) to a snooker. **2** (esp. as **snookered** *adj.*) *sl.* defeat, thwart.

snoop /snoop/ *v. & n. colloq.* ● *v.intr.* **1** pry into matters one need not be concerned with. **2** (often foll. by *about, around*) investigate in order to find out about transgressions of the law, etc. ● *n.* **1** an act of snooping. **2** a person who snoops; a detective. □□ **snoop·er** *n.* **snoop·y** *adj.*

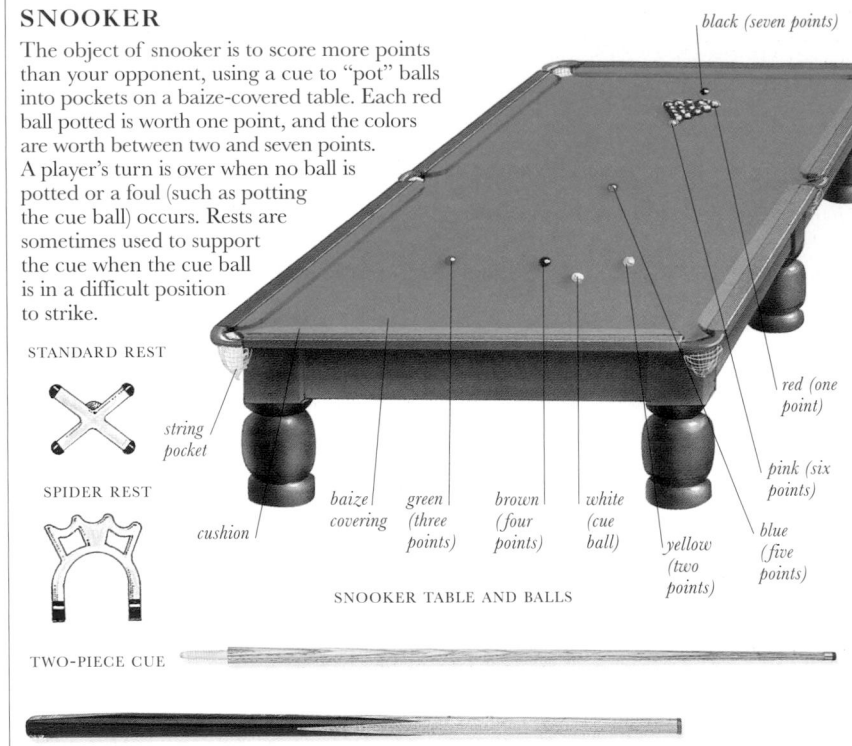

SNOOKER

The object of snooker is to score more points than your opponent, using a cue to "pot" balls into pockets on a baize-covered table. Each red ball potted is worth one point, and the colors are worth between two and seven points. A player's turn is over when no ball is potted or a foul (such as potting the cue ball) occurs. Rests are sometimes used to support the cue when the cue ball is in a difficult position to strike.

STANDARD REST

SPIDER REST

black (seven points)

red (one point)

pink (six points)

blue (five points)

yellow (two points)

white (cue ball)

brown (four points)

green (three points)

baize covering

cushion

string pocket

SNOOKER TABLE AND BALLS

TWO-PIECE CUE

snoop·er·scope /snŏopərskōp/ *n.* a device which converts infrared radiation into a visible image, esp. used for seeing in the dark.

snoot /snoot/ *n. sl.* the nose.

snoot·y /snŏotee/ *adj.* (**snootier, snootiest**) *colloq.* supercilious; conceited. □□ **snoot·i·ly** *adv.* **snoot·i·ness** *n.*

snooze /snŏoz/ *n. & v. colloq.* ● *n.* a short sleep, esp. in the daytime. ● *v.intr.* take a snooze. □□ **snooz·er** *n.* **snooz·y** *adj.* (**snooz·i·er, snooz·i·est**).

snore /snawr/ *n. & v.* ● *n.* a snorting or grunting sound in breathing during sleep. ● *v.intr.* make this sound. □□ **snor·er** *n.* **snor·ing·ly** *adv.*

snor·kel /snáwrkəl/ *n. & v.* ● *n.* **1** ▶ a breathing tube for an underwater swimmer. **2** a device for supplying air to a submerged submarine. ● *v.intr.* use a snorkel. □□ **snor·kel·er** *n.*

snort /snawrt/ *n. & v.* ● *n.* **1** an explosive sound made by the sudden forcing of breath through the nose, esp. expressing indignation or incredulity. **2** a similar sound made by an engine, etc. **3** *colloq.* a small drink of liquor. **4** *sl.* an inhaled dose of a (usu. illegal) powdered drug. ● *v.* **1** *intr.* make a snort. **2** *tr.* (also *absol.*) *sl.* inhale (esp. cocaine or heroin).

mask

snorkel

purge valve

SNORKEL

snot /snot/ *n. sl.* **1** nasal mucus. **2** a term of contempt for a person.

snot·ty /snótee/ *adj.* (**snottier, snottiest**) *sl.* **1** foul or running with nasal mucus. **2** contemptible. **3** supercilious; conceited. □□ **snot·ti·ly** *adv.* **snot·ti·ness** *n.*

snout /snowt/ *n.* **1** the projecting nose and mouth of an animal. **2** *derog.* a person's nose. **3** the pointed front of a thing; a nozzle. □□ **snout·ed** *adj.* (also in *comb.*). **snout·y** *adj.*

snow /snō/ *n. & v.* ● *n.* **1** atmospheric vapor frozen into ice crystals and falling to earth in light white flakes. **2** a fall of this, or a layer of it on the ground. **3** a thing resembling snow in whiteness or texture. **4** a mass of flickering white spots on a television or radar screen, caused by interference or a poor signal. **5** *sl.* cocaine. ● *v.* **1** *intr.* (prec. by *it* as subject) snow falls (*it is snowing*). **2** *tr.* (foll. by *in, over, up,* etc.) block with large quantities of snow. **3** *tr. & intr.* sprinkle or scatter or fall as or like snow. **4** *intr.* come in large numbers or quantities. □ **be snowed under** be overwhelmed, esp. with work. □□ **snow·less** *adj.* **snow·like** *adj.*

snow·ball /snóbawl/ *n. & v.* ● *n.* **1** snow pressed together into a ball, esp. for throwing in play. **2** anything that grows or increases rapidly like a snowball rolled on snow. ● *v.* **1** *intr. & tr.* throw or pelt with snowballs. **2** *intr.* increase rapidly.

snow·ber·ry /snóberee/ *n.* (*pl.* **-ies**) any shrub of the genus *Symphoricarpos*, with white berries.

snow·bird /snóbərd/ *n.* **1** a bird, such as the junco, commonly seen in snowy regions. **2** *colloq.* a person who moves from a cold climate to a warmer climate during the winter.

snow-blind *adj.* temporarily blinded by the glare of light reflected by large expanses of snow. □□ **snow blind·ness** *n.*

snow·blink /snóblingk/ *n.* the reflection in the sky of snow or ice fields.

snow·board /snóbawrd/ *n.* ▶ a flat board similar to a wide ski, ridden over snow in an upright or surfing position. □□ **snow·board·er** *n.*

boot

tail

binding

tip

SNOWBOARD AND SNOWBOARDER

S

snow·bound /snṓbownd/ *adj.* prevented by snow from going out or traveling.

snow·cap /snṓkap/ *n.* **1** the tip of a mountain when covered with snow. **2** a white-crowned hummingbird, *Microchera albocoronata*, native to Central America. □□ **snow·capped** *adj.*

snow·drift /snṓdrift/ *n.* a bank of snow heaped up by the action of the wind.

snow·drop /snṓdrop/ *n.* ◀ a bulbous plant, *Galanthus nivalis*, with white drooping flowers in the early spring.

SNOWDROP
(*Galanthus nivalis*)

snow·fall /snṓfawl/ *n.* **1** a fall of snow. **2** *Meteorol.* the amount of snow that falls on one occasion or on a given area within a given time.

snow·field /snṓfeeld/ *n.* a permanent white expanse of snow in mountainous or polar regions.

snow·flake /snṓflayk/ *n.* each of the small collections of crystals in which snow falls.

snow goose *n.* a white Arctic goose, *Anser caerulescens*, with black-tipped wings.

snow job *n. sl.* an attempt at flattery or deception.

snow leop·ard *n.* = OUNCE².

snow·man /snṓman/ *n.* (*pl.* **-men**) a figure resembling a man, made of compressed snow.

snow·mo·bile /snṓməbeel, -mō-/ *n.* ▼ a motor vehicle, esp. with runners or revolving treads, for traveling over snow.

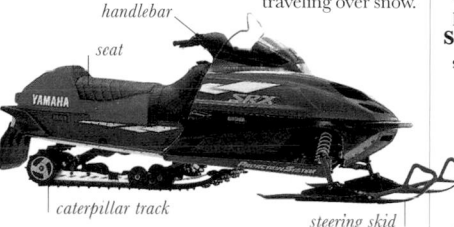

handlebar
seat
YAMAHA
caterpillar track   steering skid
SNOWMOBILE

snow·plow /snṓplow/ *n.* a device, or a vehicle equipped with one, for clearing roads of thick snow.

snow·shoe /snṓshoo/ *n.* ◀ a flat device like a racket attached to a boot for walking on snow without sinking in.

snow·slide /snṓslīd/ *n.* an avalanche of snow.

snow·storm /snṓstawrm/ *n.* a heavy fall of snow, esp. with a high wind.

snow-white *adj.* pure white.

snow·y /snṓee/ *adj.* (**snowier, snowiest**) **1** of or like snow. **2** (of the weather, etc.) with much snow.

snow·y owl *n.* a large white owl, *Nyctea scandiaca*, native to the Arctic.

SNOWSHOE

Snr. *abbr. esp. Brit.* senior.

snub /snub/ *v., n., & adj.* ● *v.tr.* (**snubbed, snubbing**) rebuff or humiliate with sharp words or a marked lack of cordiality. ● *n.* an act of snubbing; a rebuff. ● *adj.* short and blunt in shape.

snub nose *n.* a short turned-up nose. **snub-nosed** *adj.* having a snub nose.

snuff¹ /snuf/ *n. & v.* ● *n.* the charred part of a candlewick. ● *v.tr.* trim the snuff from (a candle). □ **snuff out 1** extinguish by snuffing. **2** kill; put an end to.

snuff² /snuf/ *n. & v.* ● *n.* powdered tobacco or medicine taken by sniffing it up the nostrils. ● *v.intr.* take snuff. □ **snuff-colored** dark yellowish-brown. **up to snuff** *colloq.* up to standard.

snuff·box /snúfboks/ *n.* ◀ a small usu. ornamental box for holding snuff.

SNUFFBOX: 18TH-CENTURY SNUFFBOX

snuff·er /snúfər/ *n.* **1** ▶ a small hollow cone with a handle used to extinguish a candle. **2** (in *pl.*) an implement like scissors used to extinguish a candle or trim its wick.

snuf·fle /snúfəl/ *v. & n.* ● *v.* **1** *intr.* make sniffing sounds. **2 a** *intr.* speak nasally, whiningly, or like one with a cold. **b** *tr.* say in this way. **3** *intr.* breathe noisily as through a partially blocked nose. **4** *intr.* sniff. ● *n.* **1** a snuffling sound. **2** (in *pl.*) a partial blockage of the nose causing snuffling. **3** a sniff. □□ **snuf·fler** *n.* **snuf·fly** *adj.*

snuff·y¹ /snúfee/ *adj.* (**snuffier, snuffiest**) **1** annoyed. **2** irritable. **3** supercilious or contemptuous.

snuff·y² /snúfee/ *adj.* like snuff in color or substance.

snug /snug/ *adj.* (**snugger, snuggest**) **1 a** cozy, comfortable; sheltered; well enclosed or placed or arranged. **b** cozily protected from the weather or cold. **c** close-fitting. **2** (of an income, etc.) allowing comfort and comparative ease. □□ **snug·ly** *adv.* **snug·ness** *n.*

snug·gle /snúgəl/ *v.intr. & tr.* (usu. foll. by *down, up, together*) settle or draw into a warm comfortable position.

So. *abbr.* South.

so¹ /sō/ *adv. & conj.* ● *adv.* **1** (often foll. by *that* + clause) to such an extent, or to the extent implied (*why are you so angry?; they were so pleased that they gave us a bonus*). **2** (with *neg.*) to the extent to which … is or does, etc., or to the extent implied (*was not so late as I expected; am not so eager as you*). **3** (foll. by *that* or *as* + clause) to the degree or in the manner implied (*so expensive that few can afford it; so small as to be invisible*). **4** (adding emphasis) to that extent (*I want to leave and so does she*). **5** to a great degree (*I am so glad*). **6** (with verbs of state) in the way described (*am not very fond of it but may become so*). **7** (with verb of saying or thinking, etc.) as previously mentioned or described (*I think so; so he said*). ● *conj.* **1** with the result that (*there was none left, so we had to go without*). **2** in order that (*came home early so that I could see you*). **3** and then; as the next step (*so then the car broke down*). **4 a** (introducing a question) then; after that (*so what did you tell them?*). **b** (*absol.*) = *so what?* □ **and so on** (or **forth**) **1** and others of the same kind. **2** and in other similar ways. **so as** (foll. by *to* + infin.) in order to (*did it so as to get it finished*). **so be it** an expression of acceptance or resignation. **so far** see FAR. **so far as** see FAR. **so far so good** see FAR. **so long!** *colloq.* good-bye until we meet again. **so long as** see LONG¹. **so much 1** a certain amount (of). **2** a great deal of (*so much nonsense*). **3** (with *neg.*) **a** less than; to a lesser extent (*not so much forgotten as ignored*). **b** not even (*didn't give me so much as a penny*). **so much for** that is all that need be done or said about. **so to say** (or **speak**) an expression of reserve or apology for an exaggeration, etc. **so what?** *colloq.* why should that be considered significant?

so² var. of SOL.

soak /sōk/ *v. & n.* ● *v.* **1** *tr. & intr.* make or become thoroughly wet through saturation with or in liquid. **2** *tr.* (of rain, etc.) drench. **3** *tr.* (foll. by *in, up*) **a** absorb (liquid). **b** acquire (knowledge, etc.) copiously. **4** *refl.* (often foll. by *in*) steep (oneself) in a subject of study, etc. **5** *intr.* (foll. by *into, through*) (of liquid) make its way or penetrate by saturation. **6** *tr. colloq.* extract money from by an extortionate charge, taxation, etc. (*soak the rich*). **7** *intr. colloq.* drink persistently; booze. **8** *tr.* (as **soaked** *adj.*) very drunk. ● *n.* **1** the act of soaking or the state of being soaked. **2** a drinking bout. **3** *colloq.* a hard drinker. □□ **soak·age** *n.* **soak·ing** *n. & adj.*

so-and-so /sṓəndsō/ *n.* (*pl.* **so-and-sos**) **1** a particular person or thing not needing to be specified (*told me to do so-and-so*). **2** *colloq.* a person disliked or regarded with disfavor (*the so-and-so left me behind*).

soap /sōp/ *n. & v.* ● *n.* **1** a cleansing agent which when rubbed in water yields a lather used in washing. **2** *colloq.* = SOAP OPERA. ● *v.tr.* **1** apply soap to. **2** scrub with soap.

soap·ber·ry /sṓpberee/ *n.* (*pl.* **-ies**) any of various tropical American shrubs, esp. of the genus *Sapindus*, with fruits yielding saponin.

soap·box /sṓpboks/ *n.* **1** a box for holding soap. **2** a makeshift stand for a public speaker.

soap op·er·a *n.* a broadcast drama, usu. serialized in many episodes, dealing with sentimental or melodramatic domestic themes (so called because orig. sponsored in the US by soap manufacturers).

soap·stone /sṓpstōn/ *n.* ▼ a soft, easily carved rock consisting largely of talc. Also called **steatite**.

SNUFFER

SOAPSTONE: VIKING FORGE STONE MADE OF SOAPSTONE

soap·suds /sṓpsudz/ *n.pl.* = SUDS 1

soap·wort /sṓpwərt, -wawrt/ *n.* ▶ a European plant, *Saponaria officinalis*, with pink or white flowers and leaves that yield a soapy substance.

soap·y /sṓpee/ *adj.* (**soapier, soapiest**) **1** of or like soap. **2** containing or smeared with soap. **3** (of a person or manner) unctuous or flattering.

soar /sawr/ *v.intr.* **1** fly or rise high. **2** reach a high level or standard (*prices soared*). **3** maintain height in the air without flapping the wings or using power. □□ **soar·ing·ly** *adv.*

S.O.B. *abbr. sl.* (also **SOB**) = SON OF A BITCH.

sob /sob/ *v. & n.* ● *v.* (**sobbed, sobbing**) **1** *intr.* draw breath in convulsive gasps usu. with weeping under mental distress or physical exhaustion. **2** *tr.* (usu. foll. by *out*) utter with sobs. **3** *tr.* bring (oneself) to a specified state by sobbing (*sobbed themselves to sleep*). ● *n.* a convulsive drawing of breath, esp. in weeping. □□ **sob·bing·ly** *adv.*

SOAPWORT
(*Saponaria officinalis*)

so·ber /sṓbər/ *adj. & v.* ● *adj.* (**soberer, soberest**) **1** not affected by alcohol. **2** not given to excessive drinking of alcohol. **3** moderate; well-balanced; tranquil; sedate. **4** not fanciful or exaggerated (*the sober truth*). **5** (of a color, etc.) quiet and inconspicuous. ● *v.tr. & intr.* (often foll. by *down, up*) make or become sober or less wild, reckless, enthusiastic, visionary, etc. (*a sobering thought*). □ **as sober as a judge** completely sober. □□ **so·ber·ing·ly** *adv.* **so·ber·ly** *adv.*

S

so·bri·e·ty /səbrī́-itee/ n. the state of being sober.

so·bri·quet /sṓbrikay, -ket/ n. (also **sou·bri·quet** /sṓo-/) **1** a nickname. **2** an assumed name.

sob sis·ter n. a journalist who writes or edits sentimental stories.

sob sto·ry n. a story or explanation appealing mainly to the emotions.

Soc. abbr. **1** Socialist. **2** Society.

soc·age /sókij/ n. (also **soc·cage**) a feudal tenure of land involving payment of rent or other nonmilitary service.

so-called adj. commonly known as, often incorrectly.

soc·cer /sókər/ n. a game played by two teams of eleven players with a round ball that cannot be touched with the hands during play except by the goalkeepers. ▷ FOOTBALL

so·cia·ble /sṓshəbəl/ adj. **1** fitted for or liking the society of other people; ready and willing to talk and act with others. **2** (of a person's manner or behavior, etc.) friendly. **3** (of a meeting, etc.) not stiff or formal. □□ **so·cia·bil·i·ty** /-bílitee/ n. **so·cia·bly** adv.

so·cial /sṓshəl/ adj. & n. ● adj. **1** of or relating to society or its organization. **2** concerned with the mutual relations of human beings or of classes of human beings. **3** living in organized communities; unfitted for a solitary life (a human is a social animal). **4 a** needing companionship; gregarious; interdependent. **b** cooperative; practicing the division of labor. **5 a** (of insects) living together in organized communities. **b** (of birds) nesting near each other in communities. ● n. a social gathering. □□ **so·ci·al·i·ty** /sṓsheeálitee/ n. **so·cial·ly** adv.

so·cial climb·er n. derog. a person anxious to gain a higher social status.

so·cial con·tract n. (also **so·cial com·pact**) an agreement to cooperate for social benefits, e.g., by sacrificing some individual freedom for government protection.

so·cial dis·ease n. a venereal disease.

so·cial·ism /sṓshəlizəm/ n. **1** a political and economic theory which advocates that the community as a whole should own and control the means of production, distribution, and exchange. **2** policy based on this theory. □□ **so·cial·ist** n. & adj. **so·cial·is·tic** adj.

so·cial·ite /sṓshəlīt/ n. a person prominent in fashionable society.

so·cial·ize /sṓshəlīz/ v. **1** intr. act in a sociable manner. **2** tr. make social. **3** tr. organize on socialistic principles. □□ **so·cial·i·za·tion** n.

so·cial or·der n. the network of human relationships in society.

so·cial sci·ence n. **1** the scientific study of human society and social relationships. **2** a branch of this (e.g., politics or economics). □□ **so·cial sci·en·tist** n.

so·cial se·cu·ri·ty n. (usu. **So·cial Se·cu·ri·ty**) a US government program of assistance to the elderly, disabled, etc., funded by mandatory contributions from employers and employees.

so·cial serv·ic·es n.pl. services provided by the government for the community, esp. education, health, and housing.

so·cial work n. work of benefit to those in need of help or welfare, esp. done by specially trained personnel. □□ **so·cial work·er** n.

so·ci·e·ty /səsī́ətee/ n. (pl. **-ies**) **1** the sum of human conditions and activity regarded as a whole functioning interdependently. **2** a social community (all societies must have firm laws). **3 a** a social mode of life. **b** the customs and organization of an ordered community. **4** Ecol. a plant community. **5 a** the socially advantaged or prominent members of a community (society would not approve). **b** this, or a part of it, qualified in some way (is not done in polite society). **6** participation in hospitality; other people's homes or company (avoids society). **7** companionship; company (avoids the society of such people). **8** an association of persons united by a common aim or interest (formed a music society). □□ **so·ci·e·tal** adj. (esp. in sense 1).

So·ci·e·ty of Friends n. see QUAKER.

So·ci·e·ty of Je·sus n. see JESUIT.

socio- /sṓseeō, sṓsheeō/ comb. form **1** of society (and). **2** of or relating to sociology (and).

so·ci·o·bi·ol·o·gy /sṓseeōbīóləjee, sṓsheeō-/ n. the scientific study of the biological aspects of social behavior. □□ **so·ci·o·bi·o·log·i·cal** /-bīəlójikəl/ adj. **so·ci·o·bi·ol·o·gist** n.

so·ci·o·cul·tur·al /sṓseeōkúlchərəl, sṓsheeō-/ adj. combining social and cultural factors. □□ **so·ci·o·cul·tur·al·ly** adv.

so·ci·o·ec·o·nom·ic /sṓseeōékənómik, -éekə-, sṓsheeō-/ adj. relating to the interaction of social and economic factors. □□ **so·ci·o·ec·o·nom·i·cal·ly** adv.

so·ci·o·lin·guis·tic /sṓseeōlinggwístik, sṓsheeō-/ adj. relating to or concerned with language in its social aspects. □□ **so·ci·o·lin·guist** n. **so·ci·o·lin·guis·ti·cal·ly** adv.

so·ci·o·lin·guis·tics /sṓseeōlinggwístiks, sṓsheeō-/ n. the study of language in relation to social factors.

so·ci·ol·o·gy /sṓseeóləjee, sṓshee-/ n. **1** the study of the development, structure, and functioning of human society. **2** the study of social problems. □□ **so·ci·o·log·i·cal** /-əlójikəl/ adj. **so·ci·o·log·i·cal·ly** adv.

so·ci·om·e·try /sṓseeómitree, sṓshee-/ n. the study of relationships within a group of people. □□ **so·ci·o·met·ric** /-əmétrik/ adj. **so·ci·o·met·ri·cal·ly** adv. **so·ci·om·e·trist** n.

so·ci·o·path /sṓseeōpáth, sṓshee-/ n. Psychol. a person who is asocial or antisocial and who lacks a social conscience, as a psychopath. □□ **so·ci·o·path·ic** adj.

sock[1] /sok/ n. (pl. **socks** or colloq. **sox** /soks/) a short knitted covering for the foot. □ **put a sock in it** sl. be quiet.

sock[2] /sok/ v. & n. colloq. ● v.tr. hit forcefully. ● n. a hard blow. □ **sock it to** attack or address (a person) vigorously.

sock·et /sókit/ n. **1** a natural or artificial hollow for something to fit into or stand firm or revolve in. **2** Electr. a device receiving a plug, lightbulb, etc., to make a connection.

sock·eye /sókī/ n. ▼ a blue-backed salmon of Alaska, etc., Oncorhynchus nerka.

SOCKEYE
(Oncorhynchus nerka)

sock·ing /sóking/ adv. & adj. Brit. ● adv. colloq. exceedingly; very (a socking great diamond ring). ● adj. sl. confounded.

so·cle /sókəl/ n. Archit. a plain low block or plinth serving as a support for a column, urn, statue, etc., or as the foundation of a wall.

So·crat·ic /səkrátik, sō-/ adj. of or relating to the Greek philosopher Socrates (d. 399 BC) or his philosophy, esp. the method associated with him of seeking the truth by a series of questions and answers.

So·crat·ic i·ro·ny n. a pose of ignorance assumed in order to entice others into making statements that can then be challenged.

sod /sod/ n. **1** turf or a piece of turf. **2** the surface of the ground. □ **under the sod** in the grave.

so·da /sṓdə/ n. **1** any of various compounds of sodium in common use, e.g., washing soda, baking soda. **2** (in full **soda water**) water made effervescent by impregnation with carbon dioxide under pressure. **3** (also **soda pop**) a sweet effervescent soft drink.

so·da foun·tain n. **1** a device supplying soda. **2** a store or counter equipped with this. **3** a store or counter for preparing and serving sodas, sundaes, and ice cream.

so·dal·i·ty /sōdálitee/ n. (pl. **-ies**) a confraternity or association, esp. a Roman Catholic devotional or charitable group.

sod·den /sódən/ adj. **1** saturated; soaked through. **2** rendered stupid or dull, etc., with drunkenness. □□ **sod·den·ly** adv.

so·di·um /sṓdeeəm/ n. Chem. a soft silver-white reactive metallic element, occurring naturally in soda, salt, etc., that is important in industry and is an essential element in living organisms. □□ **so·dic** adj.

so·di·um bi·car·bon·ate n. a white soluble powder used in the manufacture of fire extinguishers and effervescent drinks.

so·di·um chlo·ride n. a colorless crystalline compound occurring naturally in sea water and halite; common salt.

so·di·um hy·drox·ide n. a deliquescent compound which is strongly alkaline.

so·di·um-va·por lamp n. (or **sodium lamp**) ► a lamp using an electrical discharge in sodium vapor and giving a yellow light.

Sod·om /sódəm/ n. a wicked or depraved place.

sod·om·ite /sódəmīt/ n. a person who practices sodomy.

sod·om·y /sódəmee/ n. sexual intercourse involving anal or oral copulation. □□ **sod·om·ize** v.tr.

so·ev·er /sō-évər/ adv. literary of any kind; to any extent (how great soever it may be).

-soever /sō-évər/ comb. form (added to relative pronouns, adverbs, and adjectives) of any kind; to any extent (whatsoever; howsoever).

so·fa /sṓfə/ n. a long upholstered seat with a back and arms.

so·fa bed n. a sofa that can be converted into a temporary bed.

sof·fit /sófit/ n. the underside of an architrave, arch, balcony, etc.

soft /sawft, soft/ adj. & adv. ● adj. **1** (of a substance, material, etc.) lacking hardness or firmness; yielding to pressure; easily cut. **2** (of cloth, etc.) having a smooth surface or texture; not rough or coarse. **3** (of air, etc.) mellow; mild; balmy; not noticeably cold or hot. **4** (of water) free from mineral salts and therefore good for lathering. **5** (of a light or color, etc.) not brilliant or glaring. **6** (of a voice or sounds) gentle and pleasing. **7** Phonet. **a** (of a consonant) sibilant or palatal (as c in ice, g in age). **b** voiced or unaspirated. **8** (of an outline, etc.) not sharply defined. **9** (of an action or manner, etc.) gentle; conciliatory; complimentary; amorous. **10** (of the heart or feelings, etc.) compassionate; sympathetic. **11** (of a person) **a** feeble; lenient; silly; sentimental. **b** weak; not robust. **12** colloq. (of a job, etc.) easy. **13** (of drugs) mild; not likely to cause addiction. **14** (of radiation) having little penetrating power. **15** (also **soft-core**) (of pornography) suggestive or erotic but not explicit. **16** Stock Exch. (of currency, prices, etc.) likely to fall in value. **17** Polit. moderate; willing to compromise (the soft left). ● adv. softly (play soft). □ **be soft on** colloq. **1** be lenient toward. **2** be infatuated with. **have a soft spot for** be fond of or affectionate toward (a person). □□ **soft·ish** adj. **soft·ness** n.

SODIUM-VAPOR LAMP

cap
electrode supports
inner envelope
outer envelope
sodium vapor

S

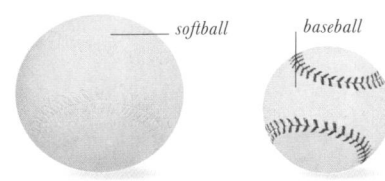

SOFTBALL AND BASEBALL

soft·ball /sáwftbawl, sóft-/ *n.* **1 ▲** a ball like a baseball but larger. **2** a modified form of baseball using this.

soft-boiled *adj.* (of an egg) lightly boiled with the yolk soft or liquid.

soft-cen·tered *adj.* (of a person) softhearted; sentimental.

soft·cov·er /sáwftcɔvər/ *adj. & n.* ● *adj.* (of a book) bound in flexible covers. ● *n.* a softcover book.

soft drink *n.* a nonalcoholic drink.

soft·en /sáwfən, sófən/ *v.* **1** *tr. & intr.* make or become soft or softer. **2** *tr.* **a** reduce the strength of (defenses) by preliminary attack. **b** reduce the resistance of (a person). □□ **soft·en·er** *n.*

soft fo·cus *n. Photog.* the slight deliberate blurring of a picture.

soft-head·ed *adj.* feebleminded. □□ **soft-head·ed·ness** *n.*

soft-heart·ed /sáwft-háartid, sóft-/ *adj.* tender; compassionate; □□ **soft-heart·ed·ness** *n.*

soft·ie var. of SOFTY.

soft·ly /sáwftlee, sóft-/ *adv.* in a soft, gentle, or quiet manner. □ **softly softly** (of an approach or strategy) cautious; discreet and cunning.

soft pal·ate *n.* the rear part of the palate. ▷ HEAD

soft ped·al *n.* a pedal on a piano that makes the tone softer. ▷ UPRIGHT. □□ **soft-ped·al** *v.tr.*

soft sell *n.* restrained or subtly persuasive salesmanship. □□ **soft-sell** *v.tr.* (*past* and *past part.* **-sold**)

soft soap *n.* **1** a semifluid soap. **2** *colloq.* persuasive flattery. □□ **soft-soap** *v.tr.*

soft-spo·ken *adj.* speaking with a gentle voice.

soft touch *n. colloq.* a gullible person, esp. over money.

soft·ware /sáwftwair, sóft-/ *n.* the programs and other operating information used by a computer.

soft·wood /sáwftwŏŏd, sóft-/ *n.* the wood of pine, spruce, or other conifers. ▷ WOOD

soft·y /sáwftee, sóftee/ *n.* (also **soft·ie**; *pl.* **-ies**) *colloq.* a weak or softhearted person.

sog·gy /sógee/ *adj.* (**soggier**, **soggiest**) sodden; saturated; dank. □□ **sog·gi·ly** *adv.* **sog·gi·ness** *n.*

soi-dis·ant /swaádeezón/ *adj.* self-styled.

soi·gné /swaanyáy/ *adj.* (*fem.* **soignée** *pronunc.* same) well-groomed.

soil¹ /soyl/ *n.* **1 ◄** the upper layer of earth in which plants grow. **2** ground belonging to a nation; territory. □□ **soil·less** *adj.*

soil² /soyl/ *v. & n.* ● *v.tr.* **1** make dirty; smear or stain (*soiled linen*). **2** tarnish; defile; bring discredit to. ● *n.* **1** a dirty mark. **2** filth; refuse.

soi·rée /swaaráy/ *n.* an evening party for conversation or music.

so·journ /sójərn/ *n. & v.* ● *n.* a temporary stay. ● *v.intr.* stay temporarily. □□ **so·journ·er** *n.*

soke /sōk/ *n. Brit. hist.* **1** a right of local jurisdiction. **2** a district under a particular jurisdiction.

Sol /sol/ *n.* (in Roman mythology) the Sun, esp. as a personification.

sol¹ /sōl/ *n.* (also **so** /sō/) *Mus.* **1** (in tonic sol-fa) the fifth note of a major scale. **2** the note G in the fixed do system.

sol² /sol/ *n. Chem.* a liquid suspension of a colloid.

sol·ace /sóləs/ *n. & v.* ● *n.* comfort in distress, disappointment, or tedium. ● *v.tr.* give solace to.

so·lan /sólən/ *n.* (in full **solan goose**) a gannet.

sol·a·na·ceous /sólənáyshəs/ *adj.* of or relating to the plant family Solanaceae, including potatoes, nightshades, and tobacco.

so·lar /sólər/ *adj.* of, relating to, or reckoned by the sun (*solar eclipse; solar time*).

so·lar bat·ter·y *n.* a battery composed of solar cells.

so·lar cell *n.* **▲** a device converting solar radiation into electricity. SUN

so·lar flare *n.* a brief eruption of intense high-energy radiation from the sun's surface. ▷ SUN

so·lar·i·um /səláireeəm/ *n.* (*pl.* **solaria** /-reeə/) a room equipped with sunlamps or fitted with extensive areas of glass for exposure to the Sun.

so·lar·ize /sólərīz/ *v.intr. & tr. Photog.* undergo or cause to undergo change in the relative darkness of parts of an image by long exposure. □□ **so·lar·i·za·tion** *n.*

so·lar pan·el *n.* **▼** a panel designed to absorb the sun's rays as a source of energy for operating electricity or heating. ▷ HOUSE, SATELLITE, SPACECRAFT

SOLAR CELL

A solar cell is made of two layers of semiconductor material. Sunlight striking a solar cell causes electrons in the bottom layer to leave their atoms. Other electrons then move, or migrate, into vacant positions. However, these electrons must pass through an external circuit to reach the top layer, creating a useful current.

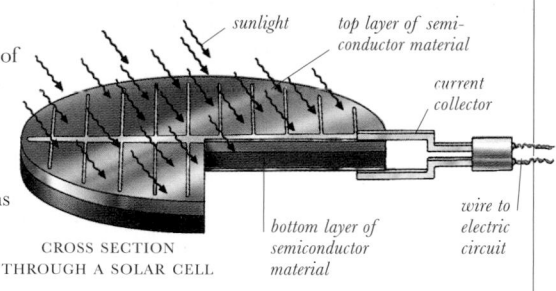

CROSS SECTION THROUGH A SOLAR CELL

SOIL

Soil is an ecosystem made up of rotting plants, animals, and weathered rock. Various horizontal layers (horizons) are discernible, including: humus, the topmost layer of rotting organic matter; topsoil, which is rich in minerals and humus; subsoil, which has less humus but many minerals (leached from above); a layer of rock fragments with little organic content; and bedrock, the underlying solid rock.

O horizon (humus)
A horizon (topsoil)
B horizon (subsoil)
C horizon (rock fragments)
D horizon (bedrock)
root system

SECTION THROUGH SOIL, SHOWING FIVE HORIZONS

TYPES OF SOIL

CHALK   PEAT   CLAY   SANDY   SILT

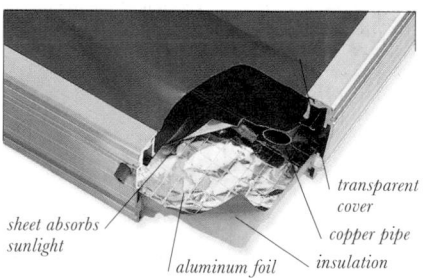

transparent cover
copper pipe
insulation
sheet absorbs sunlight
aluminum foil

SOLAR PANEL: INTERNAL STRUCTURE

S

SOLAR SYSTEM

The solar system, which is more than 7.5 billion miles (12 billion km) across, consists of nine planets; 61 known moons; vast numbers of comets, asteroids, and meteoroids; and inter-planetary gas and dust. The latest theories suggest that the solar system began 4.6 billion years ago as a spinning cloud of gas and dust that condensed to create the Sun. The rocky planets (Mercury, Venus, Earth, and Mars) formed from leftover material nearest the Sun, while in the colder outer reaches, the gas giants (Jupiter, Saturn, Uranus, and Neptune) developed from ice, gas, and dust. The smallest planet – Pluto is neither gas giant nor rocky planet; it is composed of rock and ice. The planets all orbit the Sun, following elliptical paths that are on roughly the same plane. Pluto's orbit is not only the most eccentric (elongated), but also the most tilted (17°).

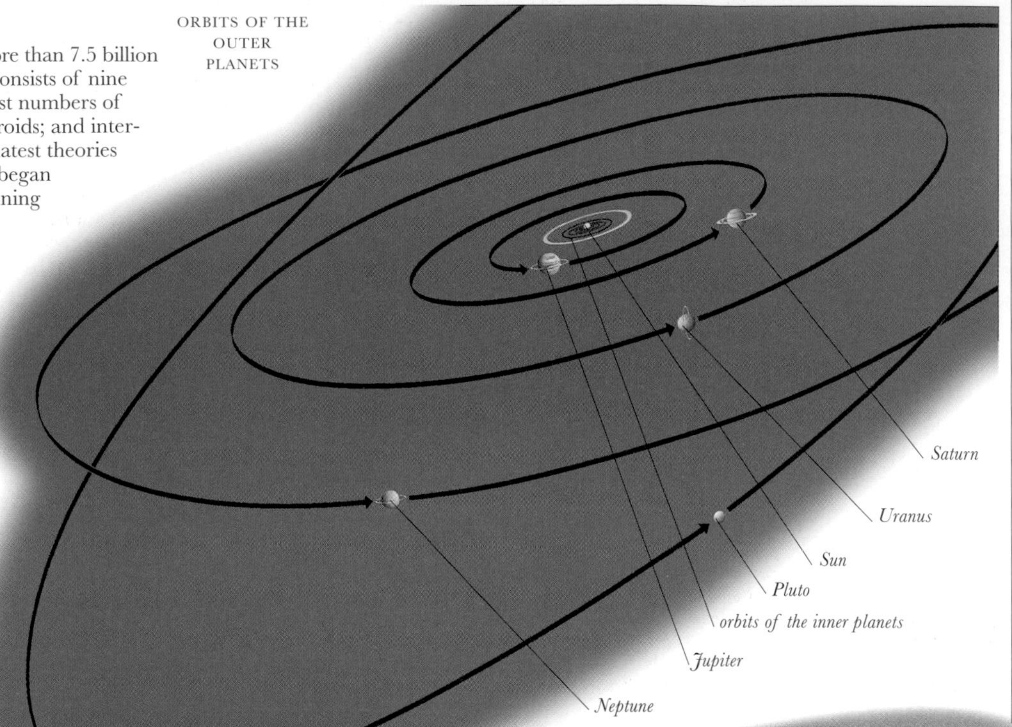

ORBITS OF THE OUTER PLANETS

Saturn

Uranus

Sun

Pluto

orbits of the inner planets

Jupiter

Neptune

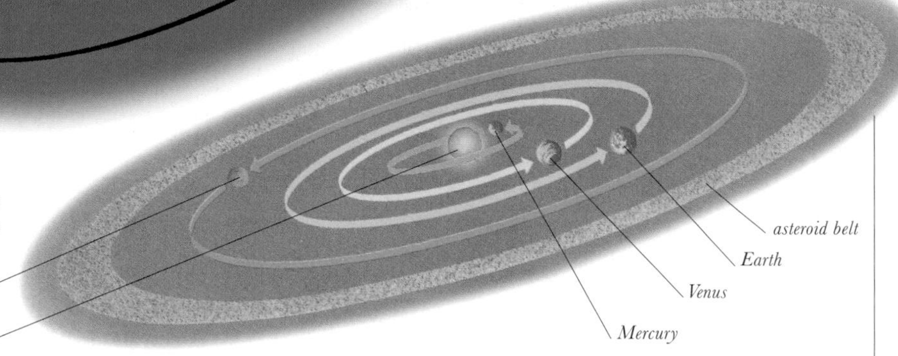

ORBITS OF THE INNER PLANETS

asteroid belt

Earth

Venus

Mercury

Mars

Sun

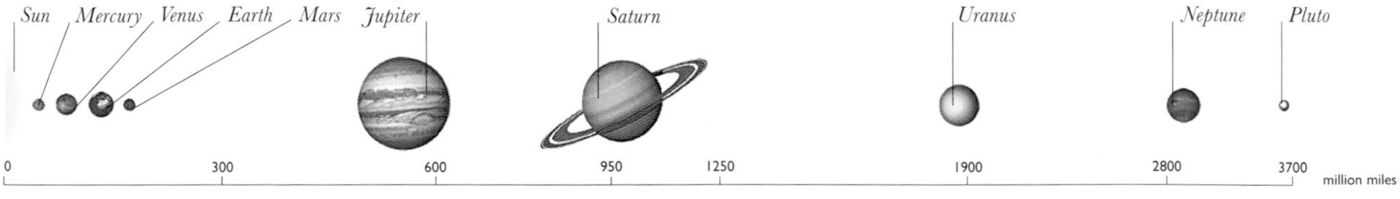

ORDER OF THE PLANETS AND DISTANCE FROM THE SUN

Sun   Mercury   Venus   Earth   Mars   Jupiter   Saturn   Uranus   Neptune   Pluto

| 0 | 300 | 600 | 950 | 1250 | 1900 | 2800 | 3700 |

million miles

S

---

so·lar plex·us *n.* a complex of nerves at the pit of the stomach.

so·lar sys·tem *n.* ▲ the Sun and the celestial bodies whose motion it governs. ▷ ORRERY

so·la·ti·um /səláysheeəm/ *n.* (*pl.* **solatia** /-sheeə/) a thing given as a compensation or consolation.

sold *past* and *past part.* of SELL.

sol·der /sódər/ *n. & v.* ● *n.* a fusible alloy used to join less fusible metals or wires, etc. ● *v.tr.* join with solder. □□ **sol·der·a·ble** *n.*

sol·dier /sóljər/ *n. & v.* ● *n.* **1** a person serving in an army. **2** (in full **common soldier**) an enlisted person in an army. **3** a military commander of specified ability (*a great soldier*). ● *v.intr.* serve as a soldier (*was off soldiering*). ● **soldier on** *colloq.* persevere doggedly. □□ **sol·dier·ly** *adj.*

sol·dier of for·tune *n.* a mercenary.

sol·dier·y /sóljəree/ *n.* (*pl.* **-ies**) **1** soldiers, esp. of a specified character. **2** a group of soldiers.

sole[1] /sōl/ *n. & v.* ● *n.* **1** the undersurface of the foot. **2** the part of a shoe, sock, etc., corresponding to this (esp. excluding the heel). **3** the lower surface or base of a plow, golf club head, etc. ● *v.tr.* provide (a shoe, etc.) with a sole. □□ **-soled** *adj.* (in *comb.*).

sole[2] /sōl/ *n.* ▼ any flatfish of the family Soleidae, esp. *Solea solea*, used as food.

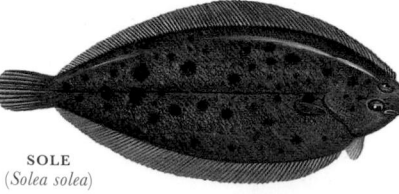

SOLE
(*Solea solea*)

sole[3] /sōl/ *adj.* (*attrib.*) one and only; single; exclusive (*the sole reason; has the sole right*). □□ **sole·ly** *adv.*

sol·e·cism /sólisizəm/ *n.* **1** a mistake of grammar or idiom. **2** a piece of bad manners or incorrect behavior.

sol·emn /sóləm/ *adj.* **1** serious and dignified (*a solemn occasion*). **2** formal; accompanied by ceremony (*a solemn oath*). **3** mysteriously impressive. **4** serious or cheerless in manner (*looks rather solemn*). **5** full of importance; weighty (*a solemn warning*). **6** grave; sober; deliberate (*a solemn promise*). □□ **sol·emn·ly** *adv.*

so·lem·ni·ty /səlémnitee/ *n.* (*pl.* **-ies**) **1** the state of being solemn; a solemn character or feeling; solemn behavior. **2** a rite or celebration; a piece of ceremony.

sol·em·nize /sóləmnīz/ *v.tr.* **1** duly perform (a ceremony, esp. of marriage). **2** celebrate (a festival, etc.). **3** make solemn. □□ **sol·em·ni·za·tion** *n.*

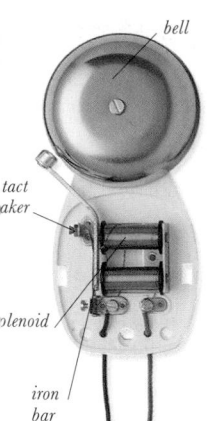

SOLENOID: DOORBELL
MECHANISM USING
A SOLENOID

so·le·noid /sólənoyd, sól-/ *n.* ◀ a cylindrical coil of wire acting as a magnet when carrying electric current. □□ **so·le·noi·dal** /-nóyd'l/ *adj.*

sol-fa /sólfaa/ *n.* = SOLMIZATION (cf. TONIC SOL-FA).

sol·fa·ta·ra /sólfətaárə/ *n.* a volcanic vent emitting only sulfurous and other vapors.

sol·feg·gi·o /solféjeeō/ *n.* (*pl.* **solfeggi** /-jee/) (also **solfège**) *Mus.* 1 an exercise in singing using sol-fa syllables. 2 solmization.

so·li *pl.* of SOLO.

so·lic·it /səlísit/ *v.* (**solicited**, **soliciting**) 1 *tr.* & (foll. by *for*) *intr.* ask repeatedly or earnestly for (business, etc.). 2 *tr.* make a request to (a person). 3 *tr.* accost (a person) and offer one's services as a prostitute. □□ **so·lic·i·ta·tion** *n.*

so·lic·i·tor /səlísitər/ *n.* 1 a person who solicits. 2 a canvasser. 3 the chief law officer of a city, county, etc.

so·lic·i·tous /səlísitəs/ *adj.* 1 showing interest or concern. 2 (foll. by *to* + infin.) eager; anxious. **so·lic·i·tous·ly** *adv.*

so·lic·i·tude /səlísitōōd, -tyōōd/ *n.* 1 the state of being solicitous; solicitous behavior. 2 anxiety or concern.

sol·id /sólid/ *adj.* & *n.* ● *adj.* (**solider**, **solidest**) 1 firm and stable in shape; not liquid or fluid (*solid food; water becomes solid at 32°F*) ▷ MATTER. 2 of one material throughout, not hollow (*a solid sphere*). 3 of the same substance throughout (*solid silver*). 4 of strong material or construction or build; not flimsy or slender, etc. 5 a having three dimensions. b concerned with solids (*solid geometry*). 6 a sound and reliable (*solid arguments*). b dependable (*a solid Republican*). 7 sound but without any special flair (*a solid piece of work*). 8 financially sound. 9 (of time) uninterrupted (*spend four solid hours on it*). 10 a unanimous; undivided (*support has been pretty solid so far*). b (foll. by *for*) united in favor of. ● *n.* 1 a solid substance or body. 2 (in *pl.*) solid food. 3 *Geom.* a body or magnitude having three dimensions. □□ **sol·id·ly** *adv.* **sol·id·ness** *n.*

sol·i·dar·i·ty /sólidáritee/ *n.* 1 unity of feeling or action. 2 mutual dependence.

sol·i·di *pl.* of SOLIDUS.

so·lid·i·fy /səlídifī/ *v.tr.* & *intr.* (**-ies**, **-ied**) make or become solid. □□ **so·lid·i·fi·ca·tion** /-fikáyshən/ *n.*

so·lid·i·ty /səlíditee/ *n.* the state of being solid; firmness.

sol·id-state *adj.* using the electronic properties of solids (e.g., a semiconductor) to replace those of vacuum tubes, etc.

sol·i·dus /sólidəs/ *n.* (*pl.* **solidi** /-dī/) an oblique stroke (/) used in writing fractions (³/₄), to separate other figures and letters, or to denote alternatives (*and/or*) and ratios (*miles/day*).

so·lil·o·quy /səlíləkwee/ *n.* (*pl.* **-ies**) 1 the act of talking when alone or regardless of any hearers, esp. in drama. 2 part of a play involving this. □□ **so·lil·o·quize** *v.intr.*

sol·i·ped /sóliped/ *adj.* & *n.* ● *adj.* (of an animal) solid-hoofed. ● *n.* a solid-hoofed animal.

sol·ip·sism /sólipsizəm/ *n. Philos.* the view that the self is all that exists or can be known. □□ **sol·ip·sist** *n.* **sol·ip·sis·tic** *adj.*

sol·i·taire /sólitáir/ *n.* 1 ▶ a diamond or other gem set by itself. 2 a ring having a single gem. 3 any of several card games for one player.

titanite gem

SOLITAIRE

sol·i·tar·y /sóliteree/ *adj.* & *n.* ● *adj.* 1 living alone; not gregarious; lonely (*a solitary existence*). 2 (of a place) secluded. 3 single or sole. 4 (of an insect) not living in communities. 5 *Bot.* growing singly; not in a cluster. ● *n.* (*pl.* **-ies**) 1 a recluse or anchorite. 2 *colloq.* = SOLITARY CONFINEMENT. □□ **sol·i·tar·i·ly** *adv.* **sol·i·tar·i·ness** *n.*

sol·i·tar·y con·fine·ment *n.* isolation of a prisoner in a separate cell.

sol·i·tude /sólitōōd, -tyōōd/ *n.* 1 the state of being solitary. 2 a lonely place.

sol·mi·za·tion /sólmizáyshən/ *n. Mus.* a system of associating each note of a scale with a particular syllable, now usu. *do re mi fa sol la ti*, with do as C in the fixed-do system and as the keynote in the tonic sol-fa system.

so·lo /sólō/ *n., v.,* & *adv.* ● *n.* (*pl.* **-os**) 1 (*pl.* **-os** or **soli** /-lee/) a vocal or instrumental piece or passage, or a dance, performed by one person with or without accompaniment. b (*attrib.*) performed or performing as a solo (*solo passage; solo violin*). 2 a an unaccompanied flight by a pilot in an aircraft. b anything done by one person unaccompanied. c (*attrib.*) unaccompanied. 3 (in full **solo whist**) a card game like whist in which one player may oppose the others. ● *v.* (**-oes**, **-oed**) 1 *intr.* perform a solo. 2 *tr.* perform or achieve as a solo. ● *adv.* unaccompanied; alone (*flew solo for the first time*).

so·lo·ist /sólōist/ *n.* a performer of a solo, esp. in music.

Sol·o·mon /sóləmən/ *n.* a very wise person. □□ **Sol·o·mon·ic** /sóləmónik/ *adj.*

sol·stice /sólstis, sól-, sáwl-/ *n.* either of the two times in the year, the summer solstice and the winter solstice, when the Sun reaches its highest or lowest point in the sky at noon, marked by the longest and shortest days. □□ **sol·sti·tial** /-stíshəl/ *adj.*

sol·u·bi·lize /sólyəbilīz/ ● *v.tr.* make soluble or more soluble. □□ **sol·u·bi·li·za·tion** /-lizáyshən/ *n.*

sol·u·ble /sólyəbəl/ *adj.* 1 that can be dissolved, esp. in water. 2 that can be solved. □□ **sol·u·bil·i·ty** /-bílitee/ *n.*

so·lus /sóləs/ *predic.adj.* (*fem.* **sola** /-lə/) (esp. in a stage direction) alone; unaccompanied.

sol·ute /sólyōōt, sólōōt/ *n.* a dissolved substance.

so·lu·tion /səlōōshən/ *n.* 1 the act or a means of solving a problem or difficulty. 2 a the conversion of a solid or gas into a liquid by mixture with a liquid. b the state resulting from this (*held in solution*). 3 the act of dissolving or the state of being dissolved. 4 the act of separating or breaking.

sol·vate /sólvayt/ *v.intr.* & *tr.* enter or cause to enter combination with a solvent. □□ **sol·va·tion** /-váyshən/ *n.*

solve /solv/ *v.tr.* find an answer to, or an action or course that removes or effectively deals with (a problem or difficulty). □□ **solv·a·ble** *adj.* **solv·er** *n.*

sol·vent /sólvənt/ *adj.* & *n.* ● *adj.* 1 able to dissolve or form a solution with something. 2 having enough money to meet one's liabilities. ● *n.* a solvent liquid, etc. □□ **sol·ven·cy** *n.* (in sense 2).

so·ma /sómə/ *n.* 1 *Biol.* the parts of an organism other than the reproductive cells. 2 the body as distinct from the soul, mind, or psyche.

So·ma·li /sōmaálee, sə-/ *n.* & *adj.* ● *n.* 1 (*pl.* same or **Somalis**) a member of a Hamitic Muslim people of Somalia in NE Africa. 2 the Cushitic language of this people. ● *adj.* of or relating to this people or language. □□ **So·ma·li·an** *adj.*

so·mat·ic /sōmátik, sə-/ *adj.* of or relating to the body, esp. as distinct from the mind. □□ **so·mat·i·cal·ly** *adv.*

somato- /sōmátō-, sómətō-/ *comb. form* human body.

so·mat·o·gen·ic /sōmátōjénik, sómə-/ *adj.* originating in the body.

so·ma·tol·o·gy /sōmətóləjee/ *n.* the study of the physical characteristics of living bodies.

so·ma·to·ton·ic /sōmátōtónik, sómə-/ *adj.* like a mesomorph in temperament, with predominantly physical interests.

so·mat·o·tro·phin /sōmátətrófin, sómə-/ (also **so·mat·o·tro·pin**) *n.* a growth hormone secreted by the pituitary gland.

so·mat·o·type /sōmátətīp, sómətə-/ *n.* physique expressed in relation to various extreme types.

som·ber /sómbər/ *adj.* (also **som·bre**) 1 dark; gloomy. 2 oppressively solemn or sober. 3 dismal, foreboding (*a somber prospect*). □□ **som·ber·ly** *adv.* **som·ber·ness** *n.*

som·bre·ro /sombráirō/ *n.* (*pl.* **-os**) ◀ a broad-brimmed hat worn esp. in Mexico and the southwest US.

SOMBRERO

some /sum/ *adj., pron.,* & *adv.* ● *adj.* 1 an unspecified amount or number of (*some water; some apples*). 2 that is unknown or unnamed (*will return some day; to some extent*). 3 denoting an approximate number (*waited some twenty minutes*). 4 a considerable amount or number of (*went to some trouble*). 5 (usu. stressed) a at least a small amount of (*do have some consideration*). b such to a certain extent (*that is some help*). c *colloq.* notably such (*I call that some story*). ● *pron.* some people or things; some number or amount (*I have some already; would you like some more?*). ● *adv. colloq.* to some extent (*we talked some; do it some more*).

-some¹ /səm/ *suffix* forming adjectives meaning: 1 adapted to; productive of (*cuddlesome; fearsome*). 2 characterized by being (*fulsome; lithesome*). 3 apt to (*tiresome; meddlesome*).

-some² /səm/ *suffix* forming nouns from numerals, meaning 'a group of (so many)' (*foursome*).

-some³ /sōm/ *comb. form* denoting a portion of a body, esp. of a cell (*chromosome; ribosome*).

some·bod·y /súmbodee, -budee, -bədee/ *pron.* & *n.* ● *pron.* some person. ● *n.* (*pl.* **-ies**) a person of importance (*is really somebody now*).

some·day /súmday/ *adv.* at some time in the future.

some·how /súmhow/ *adv.* 1 for some reason or other (*somehow I never liked them*). 2 in some unspecified or unknown way (*he somehow dropped behind*). 3 no matter how (*must get it finished somehow*).

some·one /súmwun/ *n.* & *pron.* = SOMEBODY.

some·place /súmplays/ *adv. colloq.* = SOMEWHERE.

som·er·sault /súmərsawlt/ *n.* & *v.* (also **sum·mer·sault**) ● *n.* an acrobatic movement in which a person turns head over heels in the air or on the ground and lands on the feet. ● *v.intr.* perform a somersault.

some·thing /súmthing/ *n.* & *pron.* 1 a some unspecified or unknown thing (*have something to tell you; something has happened*). b (in full **something or other**) as a substitute for an unknown or forgotten description (*a student of something or other*). 2 a known or understood but unexpressed quantity, quality, or extent (*there is something about it I do not like; is something of a fool*). 3 *colloq.* an important or notable person or thing (*the party was quite something*). □ **or something** or some unspecified alternative possibility (*must have run away or something*). **see something of** encounter (a person) occasionally. **something else** *colloq.* something exceptional. **something of** to some extent; in some sense (*he was something of an expert*).

some·time /súmtīm/ *adv.* & *adj.* ● *adv.* 1 at some unspecified time. 2 formerly. ● *attrib.adj.* former (*the sometime mayor*).

some·times /súmtīmz/ *adv.* occasionally.

S

SONGBIRD

Songbirds form the largest subgroup of the passerines (perching birds). They are characterized by their highly developed song, which is generated in the syrinx, a voice box with thin walls that vibrate to create complex sounds. During the breeding season, male songbirds use their song to deter competing males from their territory and to attract females (who usually do not sing). The song is recognized only by members of the same species and is ignored by other birds.

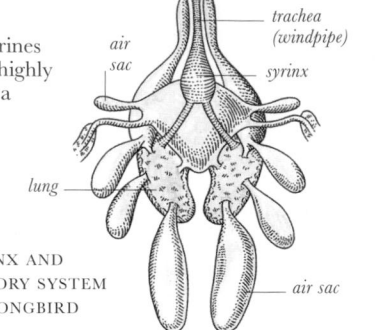

SYRINX AND
RESPIRATORY SYSTEM
OF A SONGBIRD

EXAMPLES OF SONGBIRDS

GOULDIAN FINCH
(*Chloebia gouldiae*)

SONG THRUSH
(*Turdus philomelos*)

NIGHTINGALE
(*Luscinia megarhynchos*)

BALTIMORE ORIOLE
(*Icterus galbula*)

some·what /súmhwut, -hwot, -hwət, -wut, -wot, -wət/ *adv.* to some extent (*behavior that was somewhat strange; answered somewhat hastily*).

some·when /súmhwen, -wen/ *adv. colloq.* at some time.

some·where /súmhwair, -wair/ *adv. & pron.* ● *adv.* in or to some place. ● *pron.* some unspecified place. □ **get somewhere** *colloq.* achieve success. **somewhere about** approximately.

so·mite /sómīt/ *n.* each body division of a metamerically segmented animal. □□ **so·mit·ic** /sómítik/ *adj.*

som·me·lier /sumɔlyáy, saw-/ *n.* a wine steward.

som·nam·bu·lism /somnámbyɔlizəm/ *n.* **1** sleep-walking. **2** a condition of the brain inducing this. □□ **som·nam·bu·lant** *adj.* **som·nam·bu·list** *n.* **som·nam·bu·lis·tic** *adj.* **som·nam·bu·lis·ti·cal·ly** *adv.*

som·nif·er·ous /somnífərəs/ *adj.* inducing sleep; soporific.

som·no·lent /sómnələnt/ *adj.* **1** sleepy; drowsy. **2** inducing drowsiness. □□ **som·no·lence** *n.* **som·no·lent·ly** *adv.*

son /sun/ *n.* **1** a boy or man in relation to either or both of his parents. **2 a** a male descendant. **b** (foll. by *of*) a male member of a family, nation, etc. **3** a person regarded as inheriting an occupation, quality, etc., or associated with a particular attribute (*sons of freedom; sons of the soil*). **4** (in full **my son**) a form of address, esp. to a boy. **5** (**the Son**) (in Christian belief) the second person of the Trinity. □□ **son·ship** *n.*

so·nant /sónɔnt/ *adj. & n. Phonet.* ● *adj.* (of a sound) voiced and syllabic. ● *n.* a voiced sound, esp. other than a vowel and capable of forming a syllable, e.g., *l, m, n, ng, r.* □□ **so·nan·cy** *n.*

so·nar /sónaar/ *n.* **1** a system for the underwater detection of objects by reflected sound. ▷ ECHO-LOCATION. **2** an apparatus for this.

so·na·ta /sɔnáátə/ *n.* a composition for one instrument or two usu. in several movements.

son·a·ti·na /sónəteénə/ *n.* a simple or short sonata.

sonde /sond/ *n.* a device sent up to obtain information about atmospheric conditions.

sone /sōn/ *n.* a unit of subjective loudness, equal to 40 phons.

son et lu·mi·ère /sáwn ay loomyair/ *n.* an entertainment by night at a historic monument, building, etc., using lighting effects and recorded sound to give a dramatic narrative of its history.

song /sawng, song/ *n.* **1** a short poem or other set of words set to music or meant to be sung. **2** singing or vocal music (*burst into song*). **3** a musical composition suggestive of a song. **4** the musical cry of some birds. □ **for a song** *colloq.* very cheaply.

song and dance *n. colloq.* a fuss or commotion.

song·bird /sáwngbərd, sóng-/ *n.* ▲ a bird with a musical call. ▷ PASSERINE

song·book /sáwngbook, sóng-/ *n.* a collection of songs with music.

song·smith /sáwngsmith, sóng-/ *n.* a writer of songs.

song·ster /sáwngstər, sóng-/ *n.* (*fem.* **songstress** /-stris/) **1** a singer. **2** a songbird. **3** a poet.

song thrush *n.* a thrush, *Turdus philomelos,* of Europe and W. Asia, with a song partly mimicked from other birds.

song·writ·er /sáwng-rītər, sóng-/ *n.* a writer of songs or the music for them.

son·ic /sónik/ *adj.* of or relating to or using sound or sound waves. □□ **son·i·cal·ly** *adv.*

son·ic bar·ri·er *n.* = SOUND BARRIER.

son·ic boom *n.* a loud explosive noise caused by the shock wave from an aircraft when it passes the speed of sound.

son-in-law *n.* (*pl.* **sons-in-law**) the husband of one's daughter.

son·net /sónit/ *n.* a poem of 14 lines using any of a number of formal rhyme schemes, in English usu. having ten syllables per line.

son·net·eer /sónitéer/ *n.* a writer of sonnets.

son·ny /súnee/ *n. colloq.* a familiar form of address to a young boy.

so·no·buoy /sónəboo-ee, -boy/ *n.* a buoy for detecting underwater sounds and transmitting them by radio.

son of a bitch *n. coarse sl.* a general term of contempt.

son of a gun *n. colloq.* a jocular or affectionate form of address or reference.

son·o·gram /sónəgram/ *n. Med.* an image of internal organs or structures produced by ultrasound waves, used for diagnostic purposes.

so·nom·e·ter /sənómitər/ *n.* **1** an instrument for measuring the vibration frequency of a string, etc. **2** an audiometer.

so·no·rous /sónərəs, sənáwrəs/ *adj.* **1** having a loud, full, or deep sound. **2** (of a speech, style, etc.) grand. □□ **so·nor·i·ty** /sənáwritee/ *n.* **so·no·rous·ly** *adv.*

son·sy /sónsee/ *adj.* (also **son·sie**) (**sonsier, sonsiest**) *Sc.* **1** plump; buxom. **2** of a cheerful disposition. **3** bringing good fortune.

sook /sook/ *n. Austral. & NZ sl.* **1** *derog.* a timid bashful person; a coward or sissy. **2** a hand-reared calf.

soon /soon/ *adv.* **1** after no long interval of time (*shall soon know the result*). **2** relatively early (*must you go so soon?*). **3** (prec. by *how*) early (*how soon will it be ready?*). **4** readily or willingly (in expressing choice or preference: *which would you sooner do?; would as soon stay behind*). □ **as** (or **so**) **soon as** at the moment that; not later than; as early as (*came as soon as I heard about it; disappears as soon as it's time to pay*). **no sooner ... than** at the very moment that (*we no sooner arrived than the rain stopped*). **sooner or later** at some future time. □□ **soon·ish** *adv.*

soot /soot/ *n. & v.* ● *n.* a black substance rising in fine flakes in smoke and deposited on the sides of a chimney, etc. ● *v.tr.* cover with soot.

sooth /sooth/ *n. archaic* truth; fact. □ **in sooth** really; truly.

soothe /sooth/ *v.tr.* **1** calm (a person or feelings). **2** soften or mitigate (pain). □□ **sooth·er** *n.* **sooth·ing** *adj.* **sooth·ing·ly** *adv.*

sooth·say·er /soothsayər/ *n.* a diviner or seer.

soot·y /sootee/ *adj.* (**sootier, sootiest**) **1** covered with soot. **2** black or brownish black.

sop /sop/ *n. & v.* ● *n.* **1** a piece of bread, etc., dipped in gravy, etc. **2** a thing done to pacify or bribe. ● *v.* (**sopped, sopping**) **1** *intr.* be drenched (*came home sopping*). **2** *tr.* (foll. by *up*) absorb (liquid) in a towel, etc. **3** *tr.* wet thoroughly.

soph. /sof/ *abbr.* sophomore.

soph·ism /sófizəm/ *n.* a false argument, esp. one intended to deceive.

soph·ist /sófist/ *n.* one who reasons with clever but fallacious arguments. □□ **so·phis·tic** /-fistik/ *adj.* **so·phis·ti·cal** *adj.*

so·phis·ti·cate *v., adj., & n.* ● *v.* /səfistikayt/ **1** make (a person, etc.) educated, cultured, or refined. **2** *tr.* make (equipment or techniques, etc.) highly developed or complex. **3** *tr.* deprive (a person or thing) of its natural simplicity. ● *adj.* /səfistikət/ sophisticated. ● *n.* /səfistikət/ a sophisticated person. □□ **so·phis·ti·ca·tion** /-káyshən/ *n.*

so·phis·ti·cat·ed /səfistikaytid/ *adj.* **1** (of a person) educated and refined. **2** (of a thing, idea, etc.) highly developed and complex. □□ **so·phis·ti·cat·ed·ly** *adv.*

soph·ist·ry /sófistree/ *n.* (*pl.* **-ies**) **1** the use of sophisms. **2** a sophism.

soph·o·more /sófəmawr, sófmawr/ *n.* a second-year college or high school student.

soph·o·mor·ic /sofəmáwrik, -mór-/ *adj.* **1** of or relating to a sophomore. **2** overconfident and pretentious but immature and lacking judgment.

sop·o·rif·ic /sópərífik/ *adj. & n.* ● *adj.* tending to produce sleep. ● *n.* a soporific drug or influence. □□ **sop·o·rif·i·cal·ly** *adv.*

sop·ping /sóping/ *adj.* (also **sop·ping wet**) soaked with liquid; wet through.

sop·py /sópee/ *adj.* (**soppier, soppiest**) *colloq.* **a** silly or foolish in a feeble or self-indulgent way.

b mawkishly sentimental. **2** soaked with water. □□ **sop·pi·ly** *adv.* **sop·pi·ness** *n.*

so·pra·ni·no /sópranéenō/ *n.* (*pl.* **-os**) *Mus.* an instrument higher than soprano, esp. a recorder or saxophone.

so·pran·o /səpránō, -práa-/ *n. & adj.* ● *n.* (*pl.* **-os** or **soprani** /-nee/) **1 a** the highest singing voice. **b** a female or boy singer with this voice. **c** a part written for it. **2** an instrument of a high or the highest pitch in its family. ● *adj.* of or relating to such a voice, part or instrument.

so·ra /sáwrə/ *n.* (in full **sora rail**) a bird, *Porzana carolina*, frequenting N. American marshes.

sor·be·fa·ci·ent /sáwrbifáyshənt/ *adj. & n. Med.* ● *adj.* causing absorption. ● *n.* a sorbefacient drug, etc.

sor·bet /sawrbáy, sáwrbit/ *n.* **1** a frozen confection of water, sugar, and usu. fruit flavoring. **2** = SHERBET 1.

sor·cer·er /sáwrsərər/ *n.* (*fem.* **sorceress** /-ris/) a magician or wizard. □□ **sor·cer·ous** *adj.* **sor·cer·y** *n.* (*pl.* **-ies**).

sor·did /sáwrdid/ *adj.* **1** dirty or squalid. **2** ignoble; mercenary. **3** avaricious or niggardly. □□ **sor·did·ly** *adv.* **sor·did·ness** *n.*

sor·di·no /sawrdéenō/ *n.* (*pl.* **sordini** /-nee/) *Mus.* a mute for a bowed or wind instrument.

sore /sawr/ *adj., n., & adv.* ● *adj.* **1** (of a part of the body) painful from injury or disease (*a sore arm*). **2** suffering pain. **3** angry or vexed. **4** *archaic* grievous or severe (*in sore need*). ● *n.* **1** a sore place on the body. **2** a source of distress (*reopen old sores*). ● *adv. archaic* grievously; severely. □□ **sore·ness** *n.*

sore·head /sáwrhed/ *n.* a touchy or disgruntled person.

sore·ly /sáwrlee/ *adv.* **1** extremely; badly (*am sorely tempted; sorely in need of repair*). **2** severely (*am sorely vexed*).

sore point *n.* a subject causing distress or annoyance.

sor·ghum /sáwrgəm/ *n.* any tropical cereal grass of the genus *Sorghum*.

so·ri *pl.* of SORUS.

So·rop·ti·mist /səróptimist/ *n.* a member of an international association of clubs for professional and business women.

so·ror·i·ty /səráwritee, -rór-/ *n.* (*pl.* **-ies**) a female students' society in a university or college, usu. for social purposes.

so·ro·sis /sərósis/ *n.* (*pl.* **soroses** /-seez/) *Bot.* a fleshy compound fruit, e.g., a pineapple or mulberry.

sorp·tion /sáwrpshən/ *n.* absorption or adsorption happening jointly or separately.

sor·rel[1] /sáwrəl, sór-/ *n.* any acid leaved herb of the genus *Rumex*, used in salads and for flavoring.

sor·rel[2] /sáwrəl, sór-/ *adj. & n.* ● *adj.* of a light reddish-brown color. ● *n.* **1** this color. **2** ▼ a sorrel animal, esp. a horse.

SORREL HORSE

sor·row /sáwrō, sór-/ *n. & v.* ● *n.* **1** mental distress caused by loss or disappointment, etc. **2** a cause of sorrow. **3** lamentation. ● *v.intr.* **1** feel sorrow. **2** mourn. □□ **sor·row·ing** *adj.*

sor·row·ful /sáwrōfŏŏl, sór-/ *adj.* **1** feeling or show-

---

ing sorrow. **2** distressing; lamentable. □□ **sor·row·ful·ly** *adv.*

sor·ry /sáwree, sór-/ *adj.* (**sorrier, sorriest**) **1** (*predic.*) regretful or penitent (*were sorry for what they had done; am sorry that you have to go*). **2** (*predic.*; foll. by *for*) feeling pity or sympathy for. **3** as an expression of apology. **4** wretched (*a sorry sight*). □ **sorry for oneself** dejected. □□ **sor·ri·ness** *n.*

sort /sawrt/ *n. & v.* ● *n.* **1** a group of things, etc., with common attributes; a class or kind. **2** (foll. by *of*) roughly of the kind specified (*is some sort of doctor*). **3** *colloq.* a person of a specified kind (*a good sort*). **4** *Printing* a letter or piece in a font of type. **5** *Computing* the arrangement of data in a prescribed sequence. ● *v.tr.* arrange systematically or according to type, class, etc. □ **after a sort** after a fashion. **in some sort** to a certain extent. **of a sort** (or **of sorts**) *colloq.* not fully deserving the name (*a holiday of sorts*). **out of sorts 1** slightly unwell. **2** irritable. **sort of** *colloq.* to some extent (*I sort of expected it*). **sort out 1** separate into sorts. **2** select from a miscellaneous group. **3** disentangle or put into order. **4** resolve (a problem or difficulty). **5** *colloq.* deal with or reprimand. □□ **sort·er** *n.* **sort·ing** *n.*

sort·ie /sáwrtee, sawrtée/ *n. & v.* ● *n.* **1** a sally, esp. from a besieged garrison. **2** an operational flight by a single military aircraft. ● *v.intr.* (**sorties, sortied, sortieing**) make a sortie; sally.

sor·ti·lege /sáwrt'lij/ *n.* divination by lots.

so·rus /sáwrəs/ *n.* (*pl.* **sori** /-rī/) *Bot.* a heap or cluster, esp. of spore cases on the underside of a fern leaf, or in a fungus or lichen.

SOS /ésō-és/ *n.* (*pl.* **SOSs**) **1** an international code signal of extreme distress. **2** an urgent appeal for help.

so-so /sósó/ *adj. & adv.* ● *adj.* (usu. *predic.*) indifferent. ● *adv.* indifferently.

sos·te·nu·to /sóstənŏŏtō/ *adv., adj., & n. Mus.* ● *adv. & adj.* in a sustained or prolonged manner. ● *n.* (*pl.* **-os**) a passage to be played in this way.

sot /sot/ *n.* a habitual drunkard. □□ **sot·tish** *adj.*

sot·to vo·ce /sótō vŏchee, sáwt-tō váwche/ *adv.* in an undertone or aside.

sou /sŏŏ/ *n.* **1** *hist.* a former French coin of low value. **2** (usu. with *neg.*) *colloq.* a very small amount of money (*hasn't a sou*).

sou·brette /sŏŏbrét/ *n.* a coquettish maidservant or similar female character in a comedy.

sou·bri·quet var. of SOBRIQUET.

sou·chong /sŏŏchóng, -shóng/ *n.* a fine variety of black tea.

souf·fle /sŏŏfəl/ *n. Med.* a low murmur heard in the auscultation of various organs, etc.

souf·flé /sŏŏfláy/ *n. & adj.* ● *n.* a light dish usu. made with flavored egg yolks added to stiffly beaten egg whites and baked (*cheese soufflé*). ● *adj.* light and frothy (*omelette soufflé*).

sough /sow, suf/ *v. & n.* ● *v.intr.* make a moaning, whistling, or rushing sound as of the wind in trees, etc. ● *n.* this sound.

sought *past* and *past part.* of SEEK.

sought-af·ter *adj.* much in demand; generally desired or courted.

souk /sŏŏk/ *n.* (also **suk, sukh**) a marketplace in Arab countries.

soul /sōl/ *n.* **1** the spiritual or immaterial part of a human being, often regarded as immortal. **2** the moral or emotional or intellectual nature of a person. **3** the personification or pattern of something (*the very soul of discretion*). **4** an individual (*not a soul in sight*). **5** a person regarded as the animating or essential part of something (*the life and soul of the party*). **6** emotional or intellectual energy or intensity, esp. as revealed in a work of art (*pictures that lack soul*). **7** African-American culture, music, ethnic pride, etc. □ **upon my soul** an exclamation of surprise. □□ **-souled** *adj.* (in *comb.*).

---

soul food *n.* traditional African-American cooking, which originated in the South.

soul·ful /sólfŏŏl/ *adj.* **1** having or expressing or evoking deep feeling. **2** *colloq.* overly emotional. □□ **soul·ful·ly** *adv.* **soul·ful·ness** *n.*

soul·less /sól-lis/ *adj.* **1** lacking sensitivity. **2** undistinguished or uninteresting. □□ **soul·less·ly** *adv.* **soul·less·ness** *n.*

soul mate *n.* a person ideally suited to another.

soul mu·sic *n.* a kind of music incorporating elements of rhythm and blues and gospel music, popularized by African Americans.

soul-search·ing *n. & adj.* ● *n.* the examination of one's emotions and motives. ● *adj.* characterized by this.

sound[1] /sownd/ *n. & v.* ● *n.* **1** a sensation caused in the ear by the vibration of the surrounding air or other medium. **2** vibrations causing this sensation. **3** what is or may be heard. **4** an idea or impression conveyed by words (*don't like the sound of that*). **5** mere words. **6** (in full **musical sound**) sound produced by continuous and regular vibrations. **7** any of a series of articulate utterances (*vowel and consonant sounds*). **8** music, speech, etc., accompanying a movie or other visual presentation. **9** (often *attrib.*) broadcasting by radio as distinct from television. ● *v.* **1** *intr. & tr.* emit or cause to emit sound. **2** *tr.* utter or pronounce (*sound a note of alarm*). **3** *intr.* convey an impression when heard (*you sound worried*). **4** *tr.* give an audible signal for (an alarm, etc.). **5** *tr.* test (the lungs, etc.) by noting the sound produced. **6** *tr.* cause to resound; make known (*sound their praises*). □ **sound off** talk loudly or express one's opinions forcefully. □□ **sound·less** *adj.* **sound·less·ly** *adv.* **sound·less·ness** *n.*

sound[2] /sownd/ *adj. & adv.* ● *adj.* **1** healthy; not diseased or injured. **2** (of an opinion or policy, etc.) correct; well-founded; judicious. **3** financially secure (*a sound investment*). **4** undisturbed (*a sound sleep*). ● *adv.* soundly (*sound asleep*). □□ **sound·ly** *adv.* **sound·ness** *n.*

sound[3] /sownd/ *v.tr.* **1** test the depth or quality of the bottom of (the sea or a river, etc.). **2** (often foll. by *out*) inquire (esp. cautiously or discreetly) into the opinions or feelings of (a person). □□ **sound·er** *n.*

sound[4] /sownd/ *n.* **1** a narrow passage of water. **2** an arm of the sea.

sound bar·ri·er *n.* the high resistance of air to objects moving at speeds near that of sound.

sound bite *n.* a short extract from a recorded interview, chosen for its pungency or appropriateness.

sound·board /sówndbawrd/ *n.* a thin sheet of wood over which the strings of a piano, etc., pass to increase the sound produced.

sound ef·fect *n.* a sound other than speech or music made artificially for use in a play, movie, etc.

sound·ing[1] /sównding/ *n.* **1 a** the action or process of measuring the depth of water, now usu. by means of echo. **b** an instance of this (*took a sounding*). **2** (in *pl.*) cautious investigation (*made soundings as to his suitability*).

sound·ing[2] /sównding/ *adj.* giving forth (esp. loud or resonant) sound (*sounding brass*).

sound·ing board *n.* **1** a canopy over a pulpit, etc., to direct sound toward the congregation. **2** a means of causing opinions, etc., to be more widely known (*used his students as a sounding board*).

sound·proof /sówndprŏŏf/ *adj. & v.* ● *adj.* impervious to sound. ● *v.tr.* make soundproof.

sound·track /sówndtrak/ *n.* **1** the recorded sound element of a movie. **2** this recorded on the edge of a film in optical or magnetic form.

sound wave *n.* a wave of compression and rarefaction, by which sound is propagated in an elastic medium, e.g., air. ▷ DOPPLER EFFECT

soup /sŏŏp/ *n. & v.* ● *n.* a liquid dish made by boiling meat, fish, or vegetables, etc., in stock or water. ● *v.tr.* (usu. foll. by *up*) *colloq.* **1** increase the power and efficiency of (an engine). **2** increase the power or impact of (writing, music, etc.). □ **in the soup** *colloq.* in difficulties.

soup·çon /sŏopsáwn, sŏopsón/ *n.* a very small quantity; a dash.

soup kitch·en *n.* a place dispensing soup, etc., to the poor.

soup·spoon /sŏopspŏon/ *n.* a spoon, usu. with a large rounded bowl, for eating soup.

soup·y /sŏopee/ *adj.* (**soupier**, **soupiest**) **1** resembling soup. **2** *colloq.* sentimental; mawkish. □□ **soup·i·ly** *adv.* **soup·i·ness** *n.*

sour /sowr/ *adj., n., & v.* ● *adj.* **1** having an acid taste like lemon or vinegar, esp. because of unripeness (*sour apples*). **2 a** (of food, esp. milk or bread) bad because of fermentation. **b** smelling or tasting rancid or unpleasant. **3** (of a person, temper, etc.) harsh; bitter. **4** (of a thing) unpleasant; distasteful. ● *n.* a drink with lemon or lime juice (*whiskey sour*). ● *v.tr. & intr.* make or become sour (*soured the cream; soured by misfortune*). □ **go** (or **turn**) **sour** **1** (of food, etc.) become sour. **2** turn out badly (*the job went sour on him*). **3** lose one's enthusiasm. □□ **sour·ish** *adj.* **sour·ly** *adv.* **sour·ness** *n.*

source /sawrs/ *n. & v.* ● *n.* **1** a spring or fountainhead from which a stream issues. **2** a place, person, or thing from which something originates (*the source of all our troubles*). **3** a person or document, etc., providing evidence (*reliable sources of information*. **4** a body emitting radiation, etc. ● *v.tr.* obtain (esp. components) from a specified source. □ **at source** at the point of origin or issue.

source·book /sáwrsbŏok/ *n.* a collection of documentary sources for the study of a subject.

sour cream *n.* cream deliberately fermented by adding bacteria.

sour·dough /sówrdō/ *n.* fermenting dough, esp. that left over from a previous baking, used as leaven.

sour grapes *n.pl.* resentful disparagement of something one cannot personally acquire.

sour·puss /sówrpŏos/ *n. colloq.* an ill-tempered person.

sour·sop /sówrsop/ *n.* **1** a W. Indian evergreen tree, *Annona muricata*. **2** the large succulent fruit of this tree.

sou·sa·phone /sŏozəfōn/ *n.* ▼ a large brass bass wind instrument encircling the player's body. ▷ BRASS. □□ **sou·sa·phon·ist** *n.*

bell

mouthpiece

valves

SOUSAPHONE

souse /sows/ *v. & n.* ● *v.* **1** *tr.* put (pickles, fish, etc.) in brine. **2** *tr. & intr.* plunge into liquid. **3** *tr.* (as **soused** *adj.*) *colloq.* drunk. ● *n.* **1 a** pickling brine made with salt. **b** food, esp. a pig's head, etc., in pickle. **2** a dip, plunge, or drenching in water. **3** *colloq.* **a** a drinking bout. **b** a drunkard.

sou·tane /sŏotáan/ *n.* *RC Ch., Anglican Ch.* a cassock worn by a priest.

sou·ter·rain /sŏotərayn/ *n.* esp. *Archaeol.* an underground chamber or passage.

south /sowth/ *n., adj., & adv.* ● *n.* **1** the point of the horizon 90° clockwise from east. **2** the compass point corresponding to this. ▷ COMPASS. **3** the direction in which this lies. **4** (usu. **the South**) **a** the part of the world or a country or a town lying to the south. **b** the southern states of the US. ● *adj.* **1** toward, at, near, or facing the south (*a south wall; south country*). **2** coming

from the south (*south wind*). ● *adv.* **1** toward, at, or near the south (*they traveled south*). **2** (foll. by *of*) further south than. □ **to the south** (often foll. by *of*) in a southerly direction.

South Af·ri·can *adj. & n.* ● *adj.* of or relating to the republic of South Africa. ● *n.* **1** a native or inhabitant of South Africa. **2** a person of South African descent.

South A·mer·i·can *adj. & n.* ● *adj.* of or relating to South America. ● *n.* a native or inhabitant of South America.

south·bound /sówthbownd/ *adj.* traveling or leading southward.

South·down /sówthdown/ *n.* **1** a sheep of a breed raised esp. for mutton, orig. in England. **2** this breed.

south·east *n., adj. & adv.* ● *n.* **1** the point of the horizon midway between south and east. **2** the compass point corresponding to this. **3** the direction in which this lies. ● *adj.* of, toward, or coming from the southeast. ● *adv.* toward, at, or near the southeast. □□ **south·east·er·ly** *adj., adv.* **south·east·ern** *adj., adv.*

south·east·er /sówthéestər, sou-éestər/ *n.* a southeast wind.

south·er /sówthər/ *n.* a south wind.

south·er·ly /súthərlee/ *adj., adv., & n.* ● *adj. & adv.* **1** in a southern position or direction. **2** (of a wind) blowing from the south. ● *n.* (*pl.* **-ies**) a southerly wind.

south·ern /súthərn/ *adj.* **1** of or in the south; inhabiting the south. **2** lying or directed toward the south. □□ **south·ern·most** *adj.*

South·ern Cross *n.* a southern constellation in the shape of a cross.

south·ern·er /súthərnər/ *n.* a native or inhabitant of the south.

south·ern hem·i·sphere (also **South·ern Hem·i·sphere**) *n.* the half of the Earth below the equator.

south·ern lights *n.pl.* the aurora australis.

south·ern·wood /súthərnwŏod/ *n.* a bushy kind of wormwood, *Artemisia abrotanum*.

south·ing /sówthing/ *n.* **1** a southern movement. **2** *Naut.* the distance traveled or measured southward. **3** *Astron.* the angular distance of a star, etc., south of the celestial equator.

south·paw /sówthpaw/ *n. & adj. colloq.* ● *n.* a left-handed person, esp. a left-handed pitcher in baseball. ● *adj.* left-handed.

south pole see POLE[2].

South Sea *n.* the southern Pacific Ocean.

south·ward /sówthwərd/ *adj., adv., & n.* ● *adj. & adv.* (also **south·wards**) toward the south. ● *n.* a southward direction or region.

south·west *n., adj., & adv.* ● *n.* **1** the point of the horizon midway between south and west. **2** the compass point corresponding to this. **3** the direction in which this lies. ● *adj.* of, toward, or coming from the southwest. ● *adv.* toward, at, or near the southwest. □□ **south·west·er·ly** *adj., adv.* **south·west·ern** *adj., adv*

south·west·er /sówthwéstər, sow-wéstər/ *n.* a southwest wind.

sou·ve·nir /sŏovənéer/ *n.* (often foll. by *of*) a memento of an occasion, etc.

souv·la·ki /sŏovláakee/ *n.* (*pl.* **souvlakia** /-keeə/) a Greek dish of pieces of meat (usu. lamb) grilled on a skewer.

sou'·west·er /sow-wéstər/ *n.* **1** = SOUTHWESTER. **2** a waterproof hat with a broad flap covering the neck.

sov. /sov/ *abbr. Brit.* sovereign.

sov·er·eign /sóvrin/ *n. & adj.* ● *n.* **1** a supreme ruler, esp. a monarch. **2** *Brit. hist.* a gold coin nominally worth £1. ● *adj.* **1 a** supreme (*sovereign power*). **b** unmitigated (*sovereign contempt*). **2** excellent; effective (*a sovereign remedy*). **3** possessing independent national power (*a sovereign state*). **4** royal (*our sovereign lord*). □□ **sov·er·eign·ly** *adv.* **sov·er·eign·ty** *n.* (*pl.* **-ies**).

so·vi·et /sóveeət, sóv-/ *n. & adj. hist.* ● *n.* **1** an

elected local, district, or national council in the former USSR. **2** (**Soviet**) a citizen of the former USSR. **3** a revolutionary council of workers, peasants, etc., before 1917. ● *adj.* of or concerning the former USSR. □□ **So·vi·et·ize** *v.tr.* **So·vi·et·i·za·tion** *n.*

so·vi·et·ol·o·gist /sóveeətóləjist, sóv-/ *n.* a person who studies the former Soviet Union.

sow[1] /sō/ *v.tr.* (*past* **sowed** /sōd/; *past part.* **sown** /sōn/ or **sowed**) **1** (also *absol.*) **a** scatter or put (seed) on or in the earth. **b** (often foll. by *with*) plant (a field, etc.) with seed. **2** initiate; arouse (*sowed doubt in her mind*). **3** (foll. by *with*) cover thickly with. □ **sow the seeds of** implant (an idea, etc.). □□ **sow·er** *n.* **sow·ing** *n.*

sow[2] /sow/ *n.* **1** a female adult pig, esp. after farrowing. **2** a female guinea pig. **3** the female of some other species.

sow·bread /sówbred/ *n.* a tuberous plant, *Cyclamen hederifolium*, with solitary nodding flowers.

sown *past part.* of SOW[1].

sow this·tle /sów thisəl/ *n.* any plant of the genus *Sonchus* with thistle-like leaves and milky juice.

sox *colloq. pl.* of SOCK[1].

soy /soy/ *n.* (also **soy·a** /sóyə/) (in full **soy sauce**) a sauce made esp. in Asia from pickled soybeans.

black soy·beans

soy·bean /sóybeen/ *n.* (also **soya bean**) **1** a leguminous plant, *Glycine max*, orig. of SE Asia, cultivated for the edible oil and flour it yields, and used as a replacement for animal protein in certain foods. **2** the seed of this.

soz·zled /sózəld/ *adj. colloq.* very drunk.

spa /spaa/ *n.* **1** a curative mineral spring. **2** a place or resort with this. **3** a hot tub, esp. one with a whirlpool device.

yellow soybeans

SOYBEANS
(Glycine max)

space /spays/ *n. & v.* ● *n.* **1 a a** continuous unlimited area or expanse which may or may not contain objects, etc. **b** an interval between one, two, or three dimensional points or objects (*a space of 10 feet*). **c** an empty area; room (*clear a space in the corner; occupies too much space*). **2** a large unoccupied region (*the wide open spaces*). **3** = OUTER SPACE. **4** an interval of time (*in the space of an hour*). **5** the amount of paper used in writing, etc. (*hadn't the space to discuss it*). **6** a blank between printed, typed, or written words, etc. **7** *Mus.* each of the blanks between the lines of a staff. ● *v.tr.* **1** set or arrange at intervals. **2** put spaces between (esp. words, lines, etc., in printing, typing, or writing). **3** (as **spaced** *adj.*) (often foll. by *out*) *sl.* in a state of euphoria, esp. from taking drugs. □□ **spac·er** *n.* **spac·ing** *n.* (esp. in sense 2 of *v.*).

space age *n.* the era when space travel has become possible.

space bar *n.* a long key on a keyboard for making a space between words, etc.

space ca·det *n. sl.* a person who appears absent-minded or removed from reality.

space·craft /spáyskraft/ *n.* ► a vehicle used for traveling in space.

space·flight *n.* a journey through space.

space heat·er *n.* a heater, usu. electric, that warms a limited space, as a room.

space·man /spáysman/ *n.* (*pl.* **-men**; *fem.* **space·woman**, *pl.* **-women**) a traveler in outer space; an astronaut.

space probe *n.* = PROBE *n.* 4.

space·ship /spáys-ship/ *n.* a spacecraft, esp. one controlled by its crew.

space shut·tle *n.* a rocket for repeated use carrying people and cargo between the Earth and space. ▷ SPACECRAFT

space sta·tion *n.* an artificial satellite used as a base for operations in space.

S

SPACECRAFT

Spacecraft have been used to collect data from around the solar system since 1959. Some craft, such as Giotto, fly by their target and record information as they pass. Others, like the Galileo space probe, go into orbit around a planet. Sometimes a spacecraft may send a "lander" to a planet in order to obtain detailed information. In 1969, Apollo 11 became the first crewed spacecraft to land on the Moon. The first reusable spacecraft, the space shuttle, was launched 12 years later. Spacecraft employ a variety of specialized components, including thrusters, which make directional corrections, and solar panels, which convert sunlight into electricity used to power on-board systems.

MAIN TYPES OF SPACECRAFT

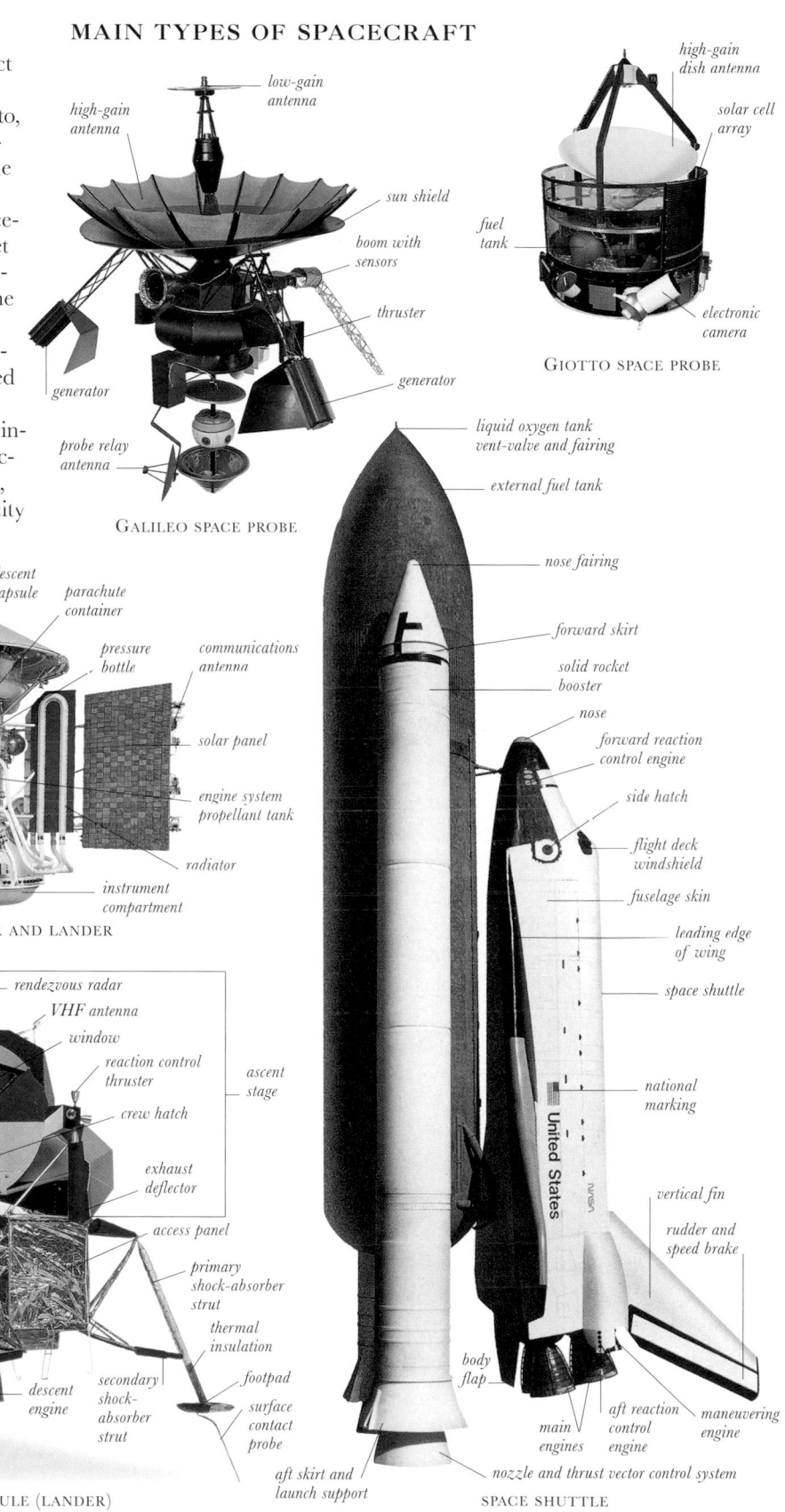

low-gain antenna
high-gain antenna
sun shield
boom with sensors
thruster
generator
generator
probe relay antenna

GALILEO SPACE PROBE

high-gain dish antenna
solar cell array
fuel tank
electronic camera

GIOTTO SPACE PROBE

research apparatus antenna
heat shield
descent capsule
parachute container
pressure bottle
communications antenna
high-gain parabolic antenna
solar panel
low-gain antenna
magnetometer
engine system propellant tank
automatic navigation system
radiator
astro-orientation sensor
instrument compartment

MARS 3 ORBITER AND LANDER

window
upper hatch
rendezvous radar
steerable antenna
VHF antenna
window
reaction control thruster
tracking light
ascent stage
crew hatch
reaction control thruster
exhaust deflector
entrance/exit platform
access panel
descent stage
primary shock-absorber strut
thermal insulation
thermal insulation
ladder
footpad
forward landing leg
descent engine
secondary shock-absorber strut
surface contact probe

APOLLO 16 LUNAR MODULE (LANDER)

liquid oxygen tank vent-valve and fairing
external fuel tank
nose fairing
forward skirt
solid rocket booster
nose
forward reaction control engine
side hatch
flight deck windshield
fuselage skin
leading edge of wing
space shuttle
national marking
vertical fin
rudder and speed brake
body flap
maneuvering engine
main engines
aft reaction control engine
aft skirt and launch support
nozzle and thrust vector control system

SPACE SHUTTLE

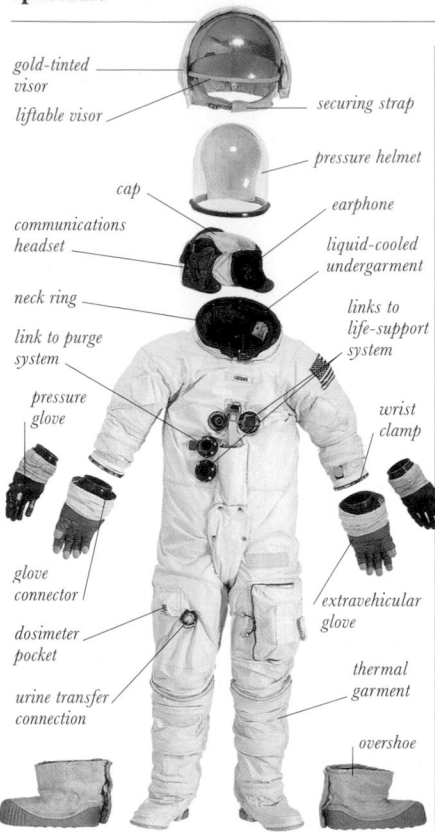

gold-tinted visor

liftable visor

securing strap

cap

pressure helmet

communications headset

earphone

liquid-cooled undergarment

neck ring

links to life-support system

link to purge system

pressure glove

wrist clamp

glove connector

extravehicular glove

dosimeter pocket

thermal garment

urine transfer connection

overshoe

SPACESUIT WORN ON APOLLO 9 MISSION

space·suit /spáys-soot, -syoot/ *n.* ▲ a garment designed to allow an astronaut to survive in space.

space-time *n.* (also **space-time con·tin·u·um**) the fusion of the concepts of space and time, esp. as a four-dimensional continuum.

spa·cey /spáysee/ *adj.* (also **spacy**) *sl.* seemingly out of touch with reality; disoriented; dazed.

spa·cial var. of SPATIAL.

spa·cious /spáyshəs/ *adj.* having ample space; covering a large area; roomy. □□ **spa·cious·ly** *adv.* **spa·cious·ness** *n.*

spade[1] /spayd/ *n. & v.* ● *n.* **1** a tool used for digging or cutting the ground, etc., with a sharp-edged metal blade and a long handle. **2** a tool of a similar shape for various purposes. ● *v.tr.* dig over (ground) with a spade. □ **call a spade a spade** speak plainly or bluntly. □□ **spade·ful** *n.* (*pl.* **-fuls**).

spade[2] /spayd/ *n.* **1 a** a playing card of a suit denoted by black inverted heart-shaped figures with small stalks. **b** (in *pl.*) this suit. **2** *sl. offens.* an African-American. □ **in spades** *sl.* to a high degree; with great force.

spade·work /spáydwərk/ *n.* hard or routine preparatory work.

spa·dix /spáydiks/ *n.* (*pl.* **spadices** /-seez/) *Bot.* a spike of flowers closely arranged around a fleshy axis and usu. enclosed in a spathe. □□ **spa·di·ceous** /-dishəs/ *adj.*

spae /spay/ *v.intr. & tr.* Sc. foretell; prophesy.

spa·ghet·ti /spəgétee/ *n.* pasta made in solid strings, between macaroni and vermicelli in thickness. ▷ PASTA

spa·ghet·ti squash *n.* a type of squash whose flesh forms spaghettilike strands when cooked.

spa·ghet·ti west·ern *n.* a movie about the American West made cheaply in Italy.

spake /spayk/ *archaic past* of SPEAK.

spall /spawl/ *n. & v.* ● *n.* a splinter or chip, esp. of rock. ● *v.intr. & tr.* break up or cause (ore) to break up in preparation for sorting.

spal·la·tion /spawláyshən/ *n. Physics* the breakup of a bombarded nucleus into several parts.

spal·peen /spalpéen/ *n. Ir.* **1** a rascal; a villain. **2** a youngster.

Spam /spam/ *n. Trademark* a canned meat product made mainly from ham.

span[1] /span/ *n. & v.* ● *n.* **1** the full extent from end to end in space or time (*the span of a bridge; the whole span of history*). **2** each arch or part of a bridge between piers or supports. ▷ ARCH. **3** the maximum lateral extent of an airplane, its wing, a bird's wing, etc. **4 a** the maximum distance between the tips of the thumb and little finger. **b** this as a measurement, equal to 9 inches. ● *v.* (**spanned, spanning**) **1** *tr.* **a** (of a bridge, arch, etc.) stretch from side to side of; extend across (*the bridge spanned the river*). **b** (of a builder, etc.) bridge (a river, etc.). **2** *tr.* extend across (space or a period of time, etc.).

span[2] see SPICK-AND-SPAN.

span[3] /span/ *archaic past* of SPIN.

span·dex /spándeks/ *n. Trademark* a type of stretchy polyurethane fabric.

span·drel /spándril/ *n. Archit.* **1** the almost triangular space between one side of the outer curve of an arch, a wall, and the ceiling or framework. **2** the space between the shoulders of adjoining arches and the ceiling or molding above.

spang /spang/ *adv. colloq.* exactly; completely (*spang in the middle*).

span·gle /spánggəl/ *n. & v.* ● *n.* a small thin piece of glittering material esp. used in quantity to ornament a dress, etc.; a sequin. ● *v.tr.* (esp. as **spangled** *adj.*) cover with or as with spangles (*spangled costume*). □□ **span·gly** /spángglee/ *adj.*

Span·iard /spányərd/ *n.* **a** a native or inhabitant of Spain in southern Europe. **b** a person of Spanish descent.

span·iel /spányəl/ *n.* **1 a** a dog of any of various breeds with a long silky coat and drooping ears. **b** any of these breeds. **2** an obsequious or fawning person.

Span·ish /spánish/ *adj. & n.* ● *adj.* of or relating to Spain or its people or language. ● *n.* **1** the language of Spain and Spanish America. **2** (prec. by *the*; treated as *pl.*) the people of Spain.

Span·ish A·mer·i·ca *n.* those parts of America orig. settled by Spaniards, including Central and South America and part of the West Indies.

Span·ish Main *n. hist.* the NE coast of South America between the Orinoco River and Panama, and adjoining parts of the Caribbean Sea.

Span·ish moss *n.* a plant, *Tillandsia usneoides*, common in the southern US, with grayish-green fronds that hang from the branches of trees.

spank /spangk/ *v. & n.* ● *v.* **1** *tr.* slap, esp. on the buttocks. **2** *intr.* (of a horse, etc.) move briskly, esp. between a trot and a gallop. ● *n.* a slap, esp. on the buttocks.

spank·er /spángkər/ *n.* **1** a person or thing that spanks. **2** *Naut.* a fore-and-aft sail set on the after side of the mizzenmast. ▷ SHIP

spank·ing /spángking/ *adj., adv., & n.* ● *adj.* **1** (esp. of a horse) moving swiftly; lively; brisk. **2** *colloq.* striking; excellent. ● *adv. colloq.* very; exceedingly (*spanking clean*). ● *n.* the act or an instance of slapping, esp. on the buttocks as a punishment for children.

span·ner /spánər/ *n.* the crossbrace of a bridge, etc.

spar[1] /spaar/ *n.* **1** a stout pole esp. used for the mast, yard, etc., of a ship. **2** the main longitudinal beam of an airplane wing.

spar[2] /spaar/ *v. & n.* ● *v.intr.* (**sparred**,

sparring) **1** (often foll. by *at*) make the motions of boxing without landing heavy blows. **2** engage in argument. ● *n.* **1** a sparring motion. **2** a boxing match.

spar[3] /spaar/ *n.* any crystalline, easily cleavable, and non-lustrous mineral, e.g. calcite or fluorspar. □□ **spar·ry** *adj.*

spare /spair/ *adj., n., & v.* ● *adj.* **1 a** not required for ordinary use; extra (*spare cash; spare time*). **b** reserved for emergency or occasional use (*the spare room*). **2** lean; thin. **3** scanty; frugal (*a spare diet; a spare prose style*). ● *n.* **1** a spare part; a duplicate. **2** *Bowling* the knocking down of all the pins with the first two balls. ● *v.* **1** *tr.* afford to give or do without; dispense with (*cannot spare him just now*). **2** *tr.* **a** abstain from killing, hurting, wounding, etc. (*spared his feelings; spared her life*). **b** abstain from inflicting or causing (*spare me this talk; spare my blushes*). **3** *tr.* be frugal or grudging of (*no expense spared*). □ **not spare oneself** exert one's utmost efforts. **to spare** left over; additional (*an hour to spare*). □□ **spare·ly** *adv.* **spare·ness** *n.*

spare·ribs /spáir-ríbs/ *n.pl.* closely trimmed ribs of esp. pork.

spare tire *n.* **1** an extra tire carried in a motor vehicle for emergencies. **2** *colloq.* a roll of fat round the waist.

sparge /spaarj/ *v.tr.* moisten by sprinkling, esp. in brewing. □□ **sparg·er** *n.*

spar·ing /spáiring/ *adj.* **1** economical. **2** restrained; limited. □□ **spar·ing·ly** *adv.*

spark /spaark/ *n. & v.* ● *n.* **1** a fiery particle thrown off from a fire, or remaining lit in ashes, or produced by a flint, match, etc. **2** (often foll. by *of*) a particle of a quality, etc. (*not a spark of life; a spark of interest*). **3** *Electr.* **a** a light produced by a sudden disruptive discharge through the air, etc. **b** such a discharge serving to ignite the explosive mixture in an internal-combustion engine. **4 a** a flash of wit, etc. **b** anything causing interest, excitement, etc. ● *v.* **1** *intr.* emit sparks of fire or electricity. **2** *tr.* (often foll. by *off*) stir into activity. **3** *intr. Electr.* produce sparks at the point where a circuit is interrupted. □□ **spark·less** *adj.* **spark·y** *adj.*

spar·kle /spáarkəl/ *v. & n.* ● *v.intr.* **1 a** emit or seem to emit sparks; glitter (*her eyes sparkled*). **b** be witty; scintillate (*sparkling repartee*). **2** (of wine, etc.) effervesce (cf. STILL[1] *adj.* 4). ● *n.* a gleam or spark. □□ **spark·ly** *adj.*

spar·kler /spáarklər/ *n.* **1** a person or thing that sparkles. **2** a handheld sparkling firework. **3** *colloq.* a diamond or other gem.

spark plug *n.* ◀ a device for firing the explosive mixture in an internal-combustion engine. ▷ INTERNAL-COMBUSTION ENGINE

high-tension connector

porcelain insulator

metal body

spark gap

SPARK PLUG

spar·ling /spáarling/ *n.* a European smelt, *Osmerus eperlanus*.

spar·oid /spároyd/ *n. & adj.* ● *n.* any marine fish of the family Sparidae, e.g. a porgy. ● *adj.* of or concerning the family Sparidae.

spar·ring part·ner *n.* **1** a boxer employed to engage in sparring with another as training. **2** a person with whom one enjoys arguing.

spar·row /spáro/ *n.* **1** any small brownish gray bird of the genus *Passer*, esp. the house sparrow and tree sparrow. **2** any of various birds of similar appearance such as the hedge sparrow.

spar·row·grass /spárōgras/ *n. dial.* or *colloq.* asparagus.

spar·row·hawk /spárōhawk/ *n.* ◀ a small hawk, *Accipiter nisus*, that preys on small birds.

SPARROWHAWK
WITH PREY
(*Accipiter nisus*)

sparse /spaars/ *adj.* **1** thinly dispersed or scattered; not dense (*sparse population*; *sparse graying hair*). **2** austere; meager. □□ **sparse·ly** *adv.* **sparse·ness** *n.* **spar·si·ty** *n.*

Spar·tan /spáart'n/ *adj. & n.* ● *adj.* **1** of or relating to Sparta in ancient Greece. **2 a** possessing courage, endurance, and stern frugality. **b** (of a regime, conditions, etc.) lacking comfort. ● *n.* a citizen of Sparta.

spar·ti·na /spaarteénə/ *n.* any grass of the genus *Spartina* growing in wet or marshy ground.

spasm /spázəm/ *n.* **1** a sudden involuntary muscular contraction. **2** a sudden convulsive movement or emotion, etc. **3** (usu. foll. by *of*) *colloq.* a brief spell of an activity.

spas·mod·ic /spazmódik/ *adj.* **1** of, caused by, or subject to, a spasm or spasms (*a spasmodic jerk*). **2** occurring or done by fits and starts (*spasmodic efforts*). □□ **spas·mod·i·cal·ly** *adv.*

spas·tic /spástik/ *adj. & n.* ● *adj.* **1** *Med.* suffering from spasms of the muscles. **2** *sl. offens.* weak; feeble. **3** spasmodic. ● *n. Med. offens.* a person suffering from cerebral palsy. □□ **spas·tic·i·ty** /-tísitee/ *n.*

spat[1] *past and past part.* of SPIT[1].

spat[2] /spat/ *n.* (usu. in *pl.*) *hist.* a short gaiter protecting the shoe from mud, etc.

spat[3] /spat/ *n. & v. colloq.* ● *n.* a petty quarrel ● *v.intr.* (**spatted, spatting**) quarrel pettily.

spat[4] /spat/ *n. & v.* ● *n.* the spawn of shellfish, esp. the oyster. ● *v.* (**spatted, spatting**) **1** *intr.* (of an oyster) spawn. **2** *tr.* shed (spawn).

spatch·cock /spáchkok/ *n. & v.* ● *n.* a chicken or esp. game bird split open and grilled. ● *v.tr.* treat (poultry) in this way.

spate /spayt/ *n.* **1** a river flood (*the river is in spate*). **2** a large amount.

spathe /spayth/ *n. Bot.* ▶ a large bract or pair of bracts enveloping a spadix.

spath·ic /spáthik/ ● *adj.* (of a mineral) like spar (see SPAR[3]), esp. in cleavage.

spa·tial /spáyshəl/ *adj.* (also **spa·cial**) of or concerning space (*spatial extent*). □□ **spa·ti·al·i·ty** /-sheeálitee/ *n.* **spa·tial·ize** *v.tr.* **spa·tial·ly** *adv.*

spa·ti·o·tem·po·ral /spáysheeō témpərəl/ *adj. Physics & Philos.* belonging to both space and time or to space-time. □□ **spa·ti·o·tem·po·ral·ly** *adv.*

spat·ter /spátər/ *v. & n.* ● *v.* **1** *tr.* **a** (often foll. by *with*) splash (a person, etc.). **b** scatter or splash (liquid, mud, etc.) here and there. **2** *intr.* (of rain, etc.) fall here and there. ● *n.* (usu. foll. by *of*) a splash (*a spatter of mud*).

spat·ter·dash /spátərdash/ *n.* **1** (usu. in *pl.*) *hist.* a cloth or other legging to protect the stockings, etc., from mud, etc. **2** = ROUGHCAST.

spat·u·la /spáchələ/ *n.* a broad-bladed flat implement used for spreading, lifting, stirring, mixing (food), etc. ▷ UTENSIL.

spat·u·late /spáchələt/ *adj.* **1** spatula-shaped. **2** (esp. of a leaf) having a broad rounded end.

spav·in /spávin/ *n.* a disease of a horse's hock with a hard bony tumor. □□ **spav·ined** *adj.*

female frog

male frog

spawn (eggs)

spawn /spawn/ *v. & n.* ● *v.* **1 a** *tr.* (also *absol.*) (of a fish, frog, mollusk, or crustacean) produce (eggs). **b** *intr.* be produced as eggs or young. **2** *tr.* produce or generate, esp. in large numbers. ● *n.* **1** ◀ the eggs of fish, frogs, etc. **2** a white fibrous matter from which fungi are produced. □□ **spawn·er** *n.*

spadix (flower cluster)

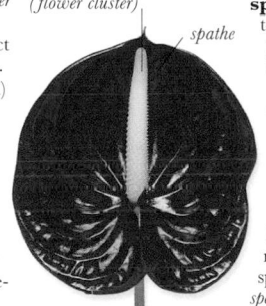

spathe

SPATHE AND **FLOWER OF** *Anthurium andreanum*

spay /spay/ *v.tr.* sterilize (a female animal) by removing the ovaries.

SPCA *abbr.* Society for the Prevention of Cruelty to Animals.

speak /speek/ *v.* (*past* **spoke** /spōk/; *past part.* **spoken** /spṓkən/) **1** *intr.* make articulate verbal utterances in an ordinary (not singing) voice. **2** *tr.* **a** utter (words). **b** make known or communicate (one's opinion, the truth, etc.) in this way. **3** *intr.* **a** (foll. by *to, with*) hold a conversation. **b** (foll. by *of*) mention in writing, etc. **c** (foll. by *for*) articulate the feelings of (another person, etc.) in speech or writing (*speaks for our generation*). **4** *intr.* (foll. by *to*) **a** address (a person, etc.). **b** speak in confirmation of or with reference to (*spoke to the resolution*). **c** *colloq.* reprove (*spoke to them about their lateness*). **5** *intr.* make a speech before an audience, etc. **6** *tr.* use or be able to use (a specified language) (*cannot speak French*). □ **not** (or **nothing**) **to speak of** practically not (or nothing). **speak for itself** need no supporting evidence. **speak for oneself 1** give one's own opinions. **2** not presume to speak for others. **speak one's mind** speak bluntly or frankly. **speak out** speak loudly or freely; give one's opinion. **speak up** = *speak out*. **speak volumes** (of a fact, etc.) be very significant. **speak volumes for** be abundant evidence of. □□ **speak·a·ble** *adj.*

speak·eas·y /speékeezee/ *n.* (*pl.* **-ies**) an illicit liquor store or drinking club during Prohibition in the US.

speak·er /speékər/ *n.* **1** a person who speaks, esp. in public. **2** a person who speaks a specified language (esp. in *comb.*: *a French speaker*). **3** (**Speaker**) the presiding officer in a legislative assembly. **4** = LOUDSPEAKER. □□ **speak·er·ship** *n.*

speak·er·phone /speékərfōn/ *n.* a telephone equipped with a microphone and loudspeaker, allowing it to be used without picking up the handset.

speak·ing /speéking/ *n. & adj.* ● *n.* the act or an instance of uttering words, etc. ● *adj.* **1** that speaks; capable of articulate speech. **2** (of a portrait) lifelike (*a speaking likeness*). **3** (in *comb.*) speaking a specified language (*French-speaking*). **4** with a reference or from a point of view specified (*roughly speaking*; *professionally speaking*). □ **on speaking terms** (foll. by *with*) **1** slightly acquainted. **2** on friendly terms.

spear /speer/ *n. & v.* ● *n.* **1** a thrusting or throwing weapon with a pointed usu. steel tip and a long shaft. **2** a similar barbed instrument used for catching fish, etc. **3** a pointed stem of asparagus, etc. ● *v.tr.* pierce or strike with or as if with a spear.

spear gun *n.* a gun used to propel a spear in underwater fishing.

spear·head /speérhed/ *n. & v.* ● *n.* **1** the point of a spear. **2** an individual or group chosen to lead a thrust or attack. ● *v.tr.* act as the spearhead of (an attack, etc.).

spear·man /speérmən/ *n.* (*pl.* **-men**) *archaic* a person, esp. a soldier, who uses a spear.

spear·mint /speérmint/ *n.* a common garden mint, *Mentha spicata*, used in cooking and to flavor chewing gum.

spear·wort /speérwərt, -wawrt/ *n.* an aquatic plant, *Ranunculus lingua*, with thick hollow stems, long narrow spear-shaped leaves, and yellow flowers.

spec[1] /spek/ *n.* □ **on spec** *colloq.* in the hope of success.

spec[2] /spek/ *n. colloq.* a detailed working description; a specification.

spe·cial /spéshəl/ *adj. & n.* ● *adj.* **1 a** particularly good; exceptional. **b** peculiar; specific; not general. **2** for a particular purpose (*sent on a special assignment*). **3** in which a person specializes (*statistics is his special field*). **4** denoting education for children with particular needs, e.g., the handicapped. ● *n.* a special person or thing, e.g., a special train, edition of a newspaper, dish on a menu, etc. □□ **spe·cial·ly** *adv.* **spe·cial·ness** *n.*

spe·cial de·liv·er·y *n.* a delivery of mail in advance of the regular delivery.

spe·cial ef·fects *n.pl.* movie or television illusions created by props, or camera work, or generated by computer.

Spe·cial Forc·es *n.pl.* US Army personnel specially trained in guerrilla warfare.

spe·cial in·ter·est (**group**) *n.* an organization, corporation, etc., that seeks advantage, usu. by lobbying for favorable legislation.

spe·cial·ist /spéshəlist/ *n.* (usu. foll. by *in*) **1** a person who is trained in a particular branch of a profession, esp. medicine. **2** a person who especially or exclusively studies a subject or a particular branch of a subject. □□ **spe·cial·ism** *n.*

spe·cial·i·ty /spésheeálitee/ *n.* (*pl.* **-ies**) *Brit.* = SPECIALTY.

spe·cial·ize /spéshəlīz/ *v.* **1** *intr.* (often foll. by *in*) **a** be or become a specialist (*specializes in optics*). **b** devote oneself to an area of interest, skill, etc. (*specializes in insulting people*). **2** *Biol.* **a** *tr.* (esp. in *passive*) adapt or set apart (an organ, etc.) for a particular purpose. **b** *intr.* (of an organ, etc.) become adapted, etc., in this way. **3** *tr.* make specific. □□ **spe·cial·i·za·tion** *n.*

Spe·cial O·lym·pics *n.pl.* a program modeled on the Olympics that features sports competitions for physically and mentally handicapped persons.

spe·cial·ty /spéshəltee/ *n.* (*pl.* **-ies**) a special pursuit, product, operation, etc., to which a company or a person gives special attention.

spe·ci·a·tion /speésheeáyshən, spées-/ *n. Biol.* the formation of a new species in evolution.

spe·cie /speéshee, -see/ *n.* coin money as opposed to paper money.

spe·cies /speésheez, -seez/ *n.* (*pl.* same) **1** a class of things having some characteristics in common. **2** *Biol.* a category of living organisms consisting of similar individuals capable of exchanging genes or interbreeding. **3** a kind or sort.

spe·cif·ic /spisifik/ *adj. & n.* ● *adj.* **1** clearly defined; definite (*has no specific name*; *told me so in specific terms*). **2** relating to a particular subject; peculiar (*a style specific to that*). ● *n.* a specific aspect or factor (*shall we discuss specifics?*). □□ **spe·cif·i·cal·ly** *adv.* **spe·ci·fic·i·ty** *n.*

spec·i·fi·ca·tion /spésifikáyshən/ *n.* **1** the act or an instance of specifying. **2** (esp. in *pl.*) a detailed description of the construction, workmanship, materials, etc., of work done or to be done.

spe·cif·ic grav·i·ty *n.* the ratio of the density of a substance to the density of a standard, as water for a liquid and air for a gas.

spec·i·fy /spésifī/ *v.tr.* (**-ies, -ied**) **1** (also *absol.*) name or mention expressly (*specified the type he needed*). **2** (usu. foll. by *that* + clause) name as a condition (*specified that he must be paid at once*). **3** include in specifications (*a French window was not specified*). □□ **spec·i·fi·a·ble** /-fīəbəl/ *adj.* **spec·i·fi·er** *n.*

spec·i·men /spésimən/ *n.* **1** an individual or part taken as an example of a class or whole, esp. when used for investigation or scientific examination. **2** *Med.* a sample of urine for testing. **3** *colloq.* a person of a specified sort.

spe·ci·ol·o·gy /speéseeóləjee/ *n.* the scientific study of species or of their origins, etc. □□ **spe·ci·o·log·i·cal** /-seeəlójikəl/ *adj.*

spe·cious /speéshəs/ *adj.* **1** superficially plausible but actually wrong (*a specious argument*). **2** misleadingly attractive in appearance. □□ **spe·cious·ly** *adv.* **spe·cious·ness** *n.*

speck /spek/ *n. & v.* ● *n.* **1** a small spot or stain. **2** (foll. by *of*) a particle (*speck of dirt*). ● *v.tr.* (esp. as **specked** *adj.*) mark with specks. □□ **speck·less** *adj.*

S

SPECKLED
SNIPE'S EGG

speck·le /spékəl/ n. & v. ● n. ◀ a small spot, mark, or stain, esp. in quantity on the skin, a bird's egg, etc. ● v.tr. (esp. as **speckled** adj.) mark with speckles.

specs /speks/ n.pl. colloq. a pair of eyeglasses.

spec·ta·cle /spéktəkəl/ n. 1 a public show, ceremony, etc. 2 anything attracting public attention (a charming spectacle; a disgusting spectacle). □ **make a spectacle of oneself** make oneself an object of ridicule.

spec·ta·cled /spéktəkəld/ adj. 1 wearing spectacles. 2 (of an animal) having facial markings resembling spectacles.

spec·ta·cles /spéktəkəlz/ n.pl. old-fashioned or joc. eyeglasses.

spec·tac·u·lar /spektákyələr/ adj. & n. ● adj. 1 of or like a public show; striking. 2 strikingly large or obvious (a spectacular increase in output). ● n. an event intended to be spectacular, esp. a musical. □□ **spec·tac·u·lar·ly** adv.

spec·tate /spéktayt/ v.intr. be a spectator, esp. at a sporting event.

spec·ta·tor /spéktaytər/ n. a person who looks on at a show, game, incident, etc. □□ **spec·ta·to·ri·al** /-tətáwreeəl/ adj.

spec·ta·tor sport n. a sport attracting spectators rather than participants.

spec·ter /spéktər/ n. 1 a ghost. 2 a haunting presentiment or preoccupation (the specter of war).

spec·tra pl. of SPECTRUM.

spec·tral /spéktrəl/ adj. 1 a of or relating to specters. b ghostlike. 2 of or concerning spectra or the spectrum (spectral colors). □□ **spec·tral·ly** adv.

spectro- /spéktrō/ comb. form a spectrum.

spec·tro·gram /spéktrəgram/ n. a record obtained with a spectrograph.

spec·tro·graph /spéktrəgraf/ n. an apparatus for photographing or otherwise recording spectra. □□ **spec·tro·graph·ic** adj. **spec·tro·graph·i·cal·ly** adv. **spec·trog·ra·phy** /spektrógrəfee/ n.

spec·trom·e·ter /spektrómitər/ n. an instrument used for the measurement of observed spectra. □□ **spec·tro·met·ric** /spéktrəmétrik/ adj. **spec·trom·e·try** n.

spec·tro·scope /spéktrəskōp/ n. an instrument for producing and recording spectra for examination. □□ **spec·tro·scop·ic** /-skópik/ adj. **spec·tro·scop·ist** /-tróskəpist/ n. **spec·tros·co·py** /-trós-kəpee/ n.

spec·trum /spéktrəm/ n. (pl. **spectra** /-trə/) 1 the band of colors, as seen in a rainbow, etc. ▷ LIGHT. 2 the entire range of wavelengths of electromagnetic radiation. ▷ ELECTROMAGNETIC RADIATION. 3 an image or distribution of parts of electromagnetic radiation arranged in a progressive series according to wavelength. 4 a similar image or distribution of energy, mass, etc., arranged according to frequency, charge, etc. 5 the entire range or a wide range of anything arranged by degree or quality, etc.

spec·u·la pl. of SPECULUM.

spec·u·lar /spékyələr/ adj. 1 of or having the nature of a speculum. 2 reflecting.

spec·u·late /spékyəlayt/ v. 1 intr. (usu. foll. by on, upon, about) form a theory or conjecture, esp. without a firm factual basis. 2 tr. (foll. by that, how, etc., + clause) conjecture; consider (speculated how he might achieve it). 3 intr. invest in stocks, etc., in the hope of gain but with the possibility of loss. □□ **spec·u·la·tor** n.

spec·u·la·tion /spékyəláyshən/ n. 1 the act of speculating; a conjecture. 2 a a speculative investment or enterprise. b the practice of business speculating.

spec·u·la·tive /spékyələtiv, -lay-/ adj. 1 of, based on, or inclined to speculation. 2 (of a business investment) involving the risk of loss. □□ **spec·u·la·tive·ly** adv.

spec·u·lum /spékyələm/ n. (pl. **specula** /-lə/) 1 Surgery an instrument for dilating the cavities of the human body for inspection. 2 a mirror, usu. of polished metal, esp. in a reflecting telescope.

sped past and past part. of SPEED.

speech /speech/ n. 1 the faculty or act of speaking. 2 a usu. formal address or discourse delivered to an audience or assembly. 3 a manner of speaking (a man of blunt speech). 4 the language of a nation, region, group, etc. □□ **speech·ful** adj.

speech·i·fy /speechifī/ v.intr. (-ies, -ied) joc. or derog. make boring or long speeches. □□ **speech·i·fi·er** n.

speech·less /speechlis/ adj. 1 temporarily unable to speak because of emotion, etc. (speechless with rage). 2 mute. □□ **speech·less·ly** adv. **speech·less·ness** n.

speech ther·a·py n. treatment to improve defective speech. □□ **speech ther·a·pist** n.

speed /speed/ n. & v. ● n. 1 rapidity of movement (at full speed). 2 a rate of progress or motion over a distance in time. 3 an arrangement of gears yielding a specific ratio in a bicycle or automobile transmission. 4 Photog. a the sensitivity of film to light. b the light-gathering power of a lens. c the duration of an exposure. 5 sl. an amphetamine drug, esp. methamphetamine. ● v. (past and past part. **sped** /sped/) 1 intr. go fast. 2 (past and past part. **speeded**) intr. (of a motorist, etc.) travel at an illegal or dangerous speed. 3 tr. send fast or on its way (speed an arrow from the bow). 4 intr. & tr. archaic be or make prosperous or successful (God speed you!). □ **speed up** move or work at greater speed. □□ **speed·er** n.

speed·ball /speedbawl/ n. sl. a mixture of cocaine with heroin or morphine.

speed·boat /speedbōt/ n. a motor boat designed for high speed.

speed bump n. a transverse ridge in the road to control the speed of vehicles.

speed lim·it n. the maximum speed at which a road vehicle may legally be driven in a particular area, etc.

speed·om·e·ter /spidómitər/ n. an instrument on a motor vehicle, etc., indicating its speed to the driver.

speed·way /speedway/ n. 1 a a track used for automobile racing. b a highway for high-speed travel. 2 a motorcycle racing. b a stadium used for this.

speed·well /speedwel/ n. ▶ any small herb of the genus Veronica, with a creeping or ascending stem and tiny blue or pink flowers.

speed·y /speedee/ adj. (**speedier**, **speediest**) 1 moving quickly. 2 done without delay (a speedy answer). □□ **speed·i·ly** adv. **speed·i·ness** n.

speiss /spīs/ n. a compound of arsenic, iron, etc., formed in smelting certain lead ores.

spe·le·ol·o·gy /speeleeólajee/ n. 1 the scientific study of caves. 2 the exploration of caves. □□ **spe·le·o·log·i·cal** /-leeəlójikəl/ adj. **spe·le·ol·o·gist** n.

spell[1] /spel/ v.tr. (past and past part. **spelled**) 1 (also absol.) write or name the letters that form (a word) in correct sequence. 2 a (of letters) make up or form (a word). b (of circumstances, a scheme, etc.) result in; involve (spell ruin). □ **spell out** 1 make out (words) letter by letter. 2 explain in detail (spelled out what the change would mean).

spell[2] /spel/ n. 1 a form of words used as a magical charm or incantation. 2 an attraction or fascination exercised by a person, activity, quality, etc. □ **under a spell** mastered by or as if by a spell.

spell[3] /spel/ n. 1 a short or fairly short period (a cold spell in April). 2 a turn of work (a spell of woodwork).

spell·bind /spélbīnd/ v.tr. (past and past part. **spellbound**) 1 bind with or as if with a spell; entrance. 2 (as **spellbound** adj.) entranced or fascinated,

SPEEDWELL:
GERMANDER
SPEEDWELL
(Veronica
chamaedrys)

esp. by a speaker, activity, quality, etc. □□ **spell·bind·er** n. **spell·bind·ing·ly** adv.

spell·er /spélər/ n. a person who spells in a specified way (a poor speller).

spel·li·can var. of SPILLIKIN.

spell·ing /spéling/ n. 1 the process or activity of writing or naming the letters of a word, etc. 2 the way a word is spelled. 3 the ability to spell (his spelling is weak).

spell·ing bee n. a spelling competition.

spelt /spelt/ n. a species of wheat, Triticum aestivum.

spel·ter /spéltər/ n. impure zinc, esp. for commercial purposes.

spe·lunk·er /spilúngkər, speelung-/ n. a person who explores caves, esp. as a hobby. □□ **spe·lunk·ing** n.

spen·cer /spénsər/ n. a short close-fitting jacket.

spend /spend/ v.tr. (past and past part. **spent** /spent/) 1 (usu. foll. by on) a (also absol.) pay out (money) in making a purchase, etc. b pay out (money) for a particular person's benefit or for the improvement of a thing (had to spend $200 on the car). 2 a use or consume (time or energy). b (also refl.) use up; exhaust. 3 tr. (as **spent** adj.) having lost its original force or strength (the storm is spent; spent bullets). □□ **spend·a·ble** adj. **spend·er** n.

spend·thrift /spéndthrift/ n. & adj. ● n. an extravagant person; a prodigal. ● adj. extravagant; prodigal.

spent past and past part. of SPEND.

sperm /spərm/ n. (pl. same or **sperms**) 1 = SPERMATOZOON. 2 the male reproductive fluid containing spermatozoa; semen.

sper·ma·cet·i /spárməsétee/ n. a white waxy substance produced by the sperm whale to aid buoyancy, and used in the manufacture of candles, ointments, etc. □□ **sper·ma·cet·ic** adj.

sper·mat·ic /spərmátik/ adj. of or relating to sperm.

sper·ma·tic cord n. a bundle of nerves, ducts, and blood vessels passing to the testicles. ▷ REPRODUCTIVE ORGANS

sper·ma·tid /spármətid/ n. Biol. an immature male sex cell formed from a spermatocyte and which may develop into a spermatozoon. □□ **sper·ma·ti·dal** /-tíd'l/ adj.

spermato- /spərmátō, spármətō/ comb. form Biol. a sperm or seed.

sper·mat·o·cyte /spərmátəsīt, spármətō-/ n. a cell produced from a spermatogonium and which may divide by meiosis into spermatids.

sper·mat·o·gen·e·sis /spərmátəjénisis, spármətə-/ n. the production or development of mature spermatozoa. □□ **sper·mat·o·ge·net·ic** /-jinétik/ adj.

sper·mat·o·go·ni·um /spərmátəgóneeəm, spármə-/ n. (pl. **spermatogonia** /-neeə/) a cell produced at an early stage in the formation of spermatozoa, from which spermatocytes develop.

sper·mat·o·phore /spərmátə-fawr, spármə-/ n. an albuminous capsule containing spermatozoa found in various invertebrates. □□ **sper·mat·o·pho·ric** /-fáw-rik, -fór-/ adj.

sper·mat·o·phyte /spərmátəfīt, spármə-/ n. any seed-bearing plant.

sper·ma·to·zoid /spərmátəzóid, spármə-/ n. the mature motile male sex cell of some plants.

sper·ma·to·zo·on /spərmátəzóon, -ən, spármə-/ n. (pl. **spermato·zoa** /-zóə/) ▶ the mature motile sex cell in animals. □□ **sper·ma·to·zo·al** adj. **sper·ma·to·zo·an** adj.

sper·mi·cide /spármisīd/ n. a substance able to kill spermatozoa. □□ **sper·mi·cid·al** /-síd'l/ adj.

spermo- /spármō/ comb. form = SPERMATO-.

SPERMATOZOON

acrosome

head

neck

mid-
piece

flagellum
(tail)

S

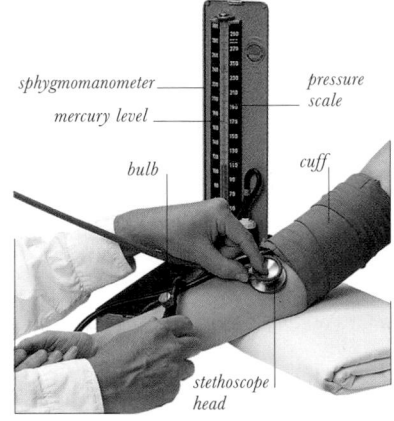

SPERM WHALE
(*Physeter macrocephalus*)

sperm whale *n.* ▲ a large whale, *Physeter macrocephalus*, hunted for spermaceti and ambergris. ▷ CETACEAN, WHALE

spew /spyōō/ *v.* (also **spue**) **1** *tr. & intr.* vomit. **2** (often foll. by *out*) **a** *tr.* expel (contents) rapidly and forcibly. **b** *intr.* (of contents) be expelled in this way. □□ **spew·er** *n.*

SPF *abbr.* sun protection factor.

sphag·num /sfágnəm/ *n.* (*pl.* **sphagna** /-nə/) (in full **sphagnum moss**) any moss of the genus *Sphagnum*, growing in bogs and used as fertilizer, etc.

spheno- /sféenō/ *comb. form* wedge-shaped.

sphere /sfeer/ *n.* **1** ◀ a solid figure, or its surface, with every point on its surface equidistant from its center. **2** an object having this shape; a ball or globe. **3** *hist.* each of a series of revolving concentrically arranged spherical shells in which celestial bodies were formerly thought to be set in a fixed relationship. **4 a** a field of action, influence, or existence. **b** a (usu. specified) stratum of society or social class. □ **music** (or **harmony**) **of the spheres** the natural harmonic tones supposedly produced by the movement of the celestial spheres (see sense 3) or the bodies fixed in them. □□ **spher·al** *adj.*

SPHERE

sphere of in·flu·ence *n.* the claimed or recognized area of a nation's interests, an individual's control, etc.

spher·ic /sféerik, sfér-/ *adj.* = SPHERICAL. □□ **spher·ic·i·ty** /-rísitee/ *n.*

spher·i·cal /sféerikəl, sfér-/ *adj.* **1** shaped like a sphere. **2** of or relating to the properties of spheres (*spherical geometry*). □□ **spher·i·cal·ly** *adv.*

sphe·roid /sféeroyd/ *n.* a spherelike but not perfectly spherical body. □□ **sphe·roi·dal** /-óyd'l/ *adj.* **sphe·roi·dic·i·ty** /-dísitee/ *n.*

sphe·rom·e·ter /sfeerómitər/ *n.* an instrument for finding the radius of a sphere and for the exact measurement of the thickness of small bodies.

spher·ule /sféerōol, -yōol, sfér-/ *n.* a small sphere. □□ **spher·u·lar** *adj.*

sphe·ru·lite /sféeryəlīt, sféerə-, sfér-/ *n.* a vitreous globule as a constituent of volcanic rocks. □□ **sphe·ru·li·tic** /-lítik/ *adj.*

sphinc·ter /sfíngktər/ *n.* *Anat.* a ring of muscle surrounding and serving to guard or close an opening or tube, esp. the anus. □□ **sphinc·ter·al** *adj.* **sphinc·ter·ic** /-térik/ *adj.*

sphin·gid /sfínggid/ *n.* any hawk moth of the family Sphingidae.

sphinx /sfingks/ *n.* **1** (**Sphinx**) (in Greek mythology) the winged monster of Thebes, having a woman's head and a lion's body, whose riddle Oedipus guessed. **2** *Antiq.* **a** any of several ancient Egyptian stone figures having a lion's body and a human or animal head. **b** (**the Sphinx**) the stone figure of a sphinx near the Pyramids at Giza. **3** an enigmatic or inscrutable person

sphygmo- /sfígmō/ *comb. form Physiol.* a pulse or pulsation.

sphyg·mo·ma·nom·e·ter /sfígmōmənómitər/ *n.* ▼ an instrument for measuring blood pressure. □□ **sphyg·mo·man·o·met·ric** /-nəmétrik/ *adj.*

sphygmomanometer — *pressure scale* — *mercury level* — *bulb* — *cuff* — *stethoscope head*

SPHYGMOMANOMETER BEING USED TO MEASURE BLOOD PRESSURE

spice /spīs/ *n. & v.* ● *n.* **1** ▼ an aromatic or pungent vegetable substance used to flavor food, e.g., cloves, pepper, or mace. **2** spices collectively (*a dealer in spice*). **3** an interesting or piquant quality. ● *v.tr.* **1** flavor with spice. **2** add an interesting or piquant quality to (*a book spiced with humor*).

SPICE

In the past, spices were often used to mask the taste of an unpalatable meal and were usually so expensive that only the wealthy could afford them. Today, spices are a common feature of everyday meals and can be divided into three groups. Hot spices, such as pepper, stimulate the palate and increase perspiration. Fragrant spices, such as mace, add a pungent, sweet taste and can be used in a variety of dishes. Coloring spices, such as turmeric, give meals a distinctive, often vibrant, hue.

COLORING SPICES

powder — PAPRIKA

dried stigmas — SAFFRON

powder — *root* — TURMERIC

HOT SPICES

powder — CAYENNE
powder — PEPPER

seeds — *peppercorns* — MUSTARD

seeds — *powder* — *flakes* — CHILI

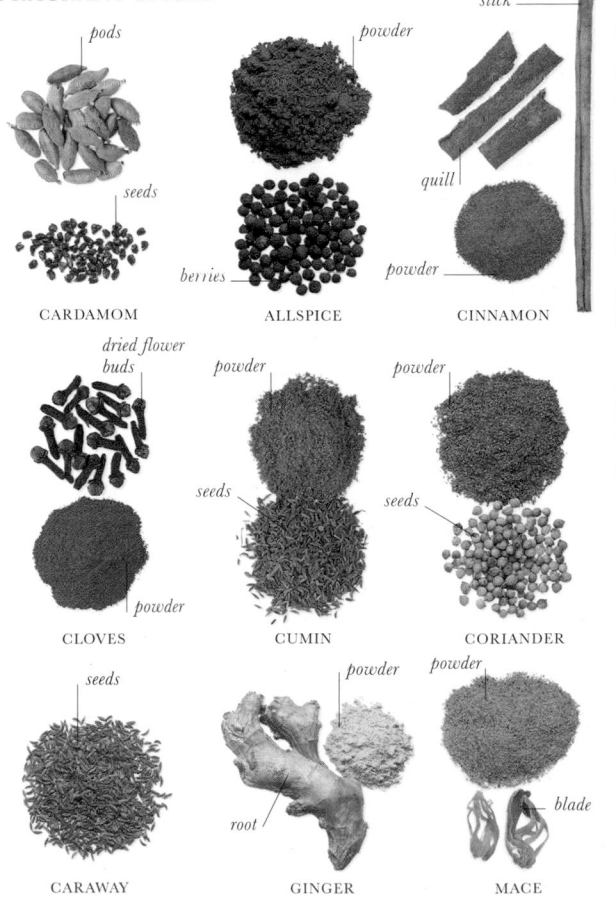

FRAGRANT SPICES

stick

pods — *seeds* — *berries* — CARDAMOM

powder — ALLSPICE

quill — *powder* — CINNAMON

dried flower buds — *powder* — CLOVES

powder — *seeds* — *powder* — CUMIN

powder — *seeds* — CORIANDER

seeds — CARAWAY

root — *powder* — GINGER

powder — *blade* — MACE

S

797

SPIDER

There are 40,000 known species of spiders, most of which can be divided into the suborders Mygalomorphae (spiders with fangs that bite downward) and Araneomorphae (spiders with fangs that bite sideways). Spiders' victims are either ensnared in a web (made of silk produced by the spider's spinnerets), or pounced on. Captured prey is injected with paralyzing venom from the spider's fangs, which are connected to poison glands.

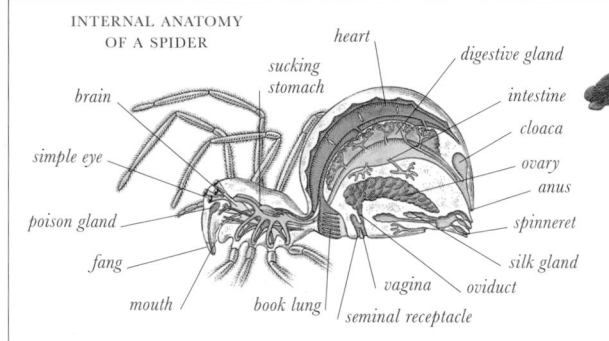

INTERNAL ANATOMY
OF A SPIDER

brain
sucking stomach
heart
digestive gland
intestine
cloaca
ovary
anus
spinneret
silk gland
oviduct
seminal receptacle
book lung
vagina
mouth
fang
poison gland
simple eye

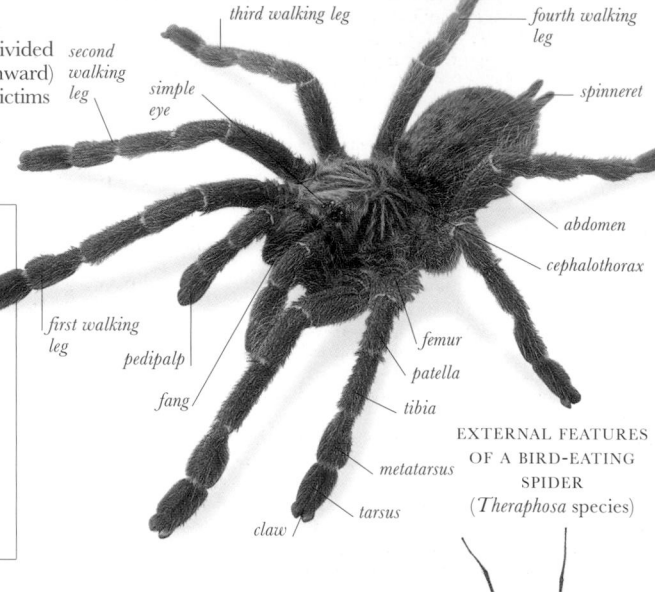

second walking leg
simple eye
third walking leg
fourth walking leg
spinneret
abdomen
cephalothorax
first walking leg
pedipalp
fang
femur
patella
tibia
metatarsus
tarsus
claw

EXTERNAL FEATURES
OF A BIRD-EATING
SPIDER
(*Theraphosa* species)

EXAMPLES OF OTHER SPIDERS

MYGALOMORPHAE

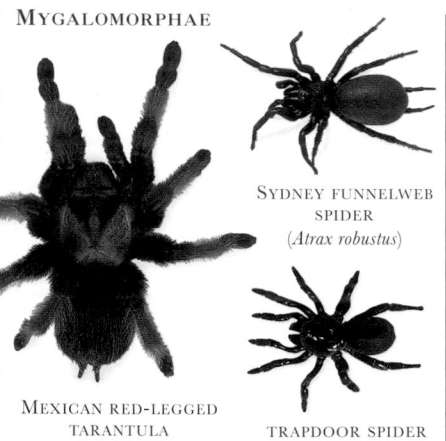

SYDNEY FUNNELWEB
SPIDER
(*Atrax robustus*)

MEXICAN RED-LEGGED
TARANTULA
(*Euathlus emilia*)

TRAPDOOR SPIDER
(*Ummidia* species)

ARANEOMORPHAE

JUMPING SPIDER
(*Plexippus paykulli*)

DADDY LONGLEGS SPIDER
(*Pholcus phalangioides*)

HOUSE SPIDER
(*Tegenaria gigantea*)

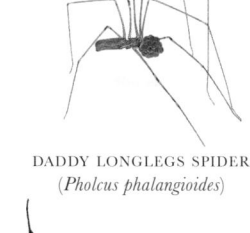

ORB SPIDER
(*Nuctenea umbratica*)

BLACK WIDOW
SPIDER
(*Latrodectus mactans*)

GIANT CRAB SPIDER
(*Olios* species)

WOLF SPIDER
(*Lycosa* species)

S

spice·bush /spísbŏŏsh/ ● *n.* any aromatic shrub of the genus *Lindera* or *Calycanthus*, native to America.

spick-and-span /spík ənd spán/ (also **spic-and-span**) *adj.* **1** fresh and new. **2** neat and clean.

spic·y /spísee/ *adj.* (**spicier, spiciest**) **1** of, flavored with, or fragrant with spice. **2** piquant; pungent; sensational (*a spicy story*). □□ **spic·i·ly** *adv.* **spic·i·ness** *n.*

spi·der /spídər/ *n. & v.* ● *n.* **1 a** ▲ any eight-legged arthropod of the order Araneae with a round unsegmented body, many of which spin webs for the capture of insects as food. **b** any of various similar or related arachnids. **2** any object comparable to a spider, esp. as having numerous legs or radiating spokes. ● *v.* **1** *intr.* move in a scuttling manner suggestive of a spider. **2** *tr.* cause to move or appear in this way. □□ **spi·der·ish** *adj.*

spi·der crab *n.* any of various crabs of the family Majidae with a pear-shaped body and long thin legs. ▷ CRAB

spi·der mon·key *n.* ◄ any S. American monkey of the genus *Ateles*, with long limbs and a prehensile tail. ▷ PRIMATE

spi·der·wort /spídərwərt, -wawrt/ *n.* ► any plant of the genus *Tradescantia*, esp. *T. virginiana*, having flowers with long hairy stamens.

spi·der·y /spídəree/ *adj.* elongated and thin (*spidery handwriting*).

spie·gel·ei·sen /spéé-gəlízən/ *n.* an alloy of iron and manganese, used in steel making.

spiel /speel, shpeel/ *n. & v. sl.* ● *n.* a glib speech or story, esp. a salesman's patter. ● *v.* **1** *intr.* speak glibly. **2** *tr.* reel off (patter, etc.). □□ **spiel·er** *n.*

spiff /spif/ *v. tr. colloq.* (usu. foll. by *up*) remodel; refurbish; make neat or clean.

spiff·ing /spífing/ *adj. Brit. archaic sl.* **1** excellent. **2** smart; handsome.

spiff·y /spífee/ *adj.* (**spiffier, spiffiest**) *sl.* stylish; smart. □□ **spiff·i·ly** *adv.*

spif·li·cate /spíflikayt/ *v.tr.* (also **spif·fli·cate**) esp. *Brit. joc.* **1** destroy. **2** beat (in a fight, etc.).

SPIDER MONKEY:
BLACK-HANDED
SPIDER MONKEY
(*Ateles geoffroyi*)

SPIDERWORT
(*Tradescantia* × *andersoniana*
'Blue and Gold')

spig·ot /spígət/ *n.* **1** a small peg or plug, esp. for insertion into the vent of a cask. **2 a** a faucet. **b** a device for controlling the flow of liquid in a faucet.

spike[1] /spīk/ *n. & v.* ● *n.* **1 a** a sharp point. **b** a pointed piece of metal, esp. the top of an iron railing, etc. **2 a** any of several metal points set into the sole of a running shoe to prevent slipping. **b** (in *pl.*) running shoes with spikes. **3** = SPINDLE *n.* 4. ● *v.tr.* **1 a** fasten or provide with spikes. **b** fix on or pierce with spikes. **2** (of a newspaper editor, etc.) reject (a story), esp. by filing it on a spindle. **3** *colloq.* **a** lace (a drink) with alcohol, a drug, etc. **b** contaminate (a substance) with something added. **4** *hist.* plug up the vent of (a gun) with a spike.

spike[2] /spīk/ *n. Bot.* a flower cluster formed of many flower heads attached closely on a long stem. ▷ INFLORESCENCE. □□ **spike·let** *n.*

spike·nard /spíknaard/ *n.* **1** an E. Indian plant, *Nardostachys grandiflora*. **2** *hist.* a costly perfumed ointment made from this.

spik·y /spíkee/ *adj.* (**spikier, spikiest**) **1** like a spike; having many spikes. **2** *colloq.* easily offended; prickly. □□ **spik·i·ly** *adv.* **spik·i·ness** *n.*

spile /spīl/ *n. & v.* ● *n.* **1** a wooden peg or spigot. **2** a large timber or pile for driving into the ground. **3** a small spout for tapping the sap from a sugar maple, etc. ● *v.tr.* tap (a cask, etc.) with a spile in order to draw off liquid.

spill[1] /spil/ *v. & n.* ● *v.* (*past* and *past part.* **spilled** or **spilt**) **1** *intr. & tr.* fall or run or cause (a liquid, powder, etc.) to fall or run out of a vessel, esp. unintentionally. **2 a** *tr.* throw from a vehicle, saddle, etc. **b** *intr.* (esp. of a crowd) tumble out quickly from a place, etc. **3** *tr. sl.* disclose (information, etc.). ● *n.* **1 a** the act or an instance of spilling or being spilled. **b** a quantity spilled. **2** a tumble or fall, esp. from a horse, etc. (*had a nasty spill*). □ **spill the beans** *colloq.* divulge information. **spill blood** be guilty of bloodshed. **spill the blood of** kill or injure (a person). **spill over 1** overflow. **2** (of a surplus population) be forced to move. □□ **spill·age** /spílij/ *n.* **spill·er** *n.*

spill[2] /spil/ *n.* a thin strip of wood, folded or twisted paper, etc., used for lighting a fire, candles, a pipe, etc.

spil·li·kin /spílikin/ *n.* (also **spel·li·can** /spélikən/) **1** a jackstraw. **2** (in *pl.*) a game of jackstraws.

spill·o·ver /spílōvər/ *n.* **1 a** the process or an instance of spilling over. **b** a thing that spills over. **2** a consequence, repercussion, or by-product.

spill·way /spílway/ *n.* a passage for surplus water from a dam.

spilt *past* and *past part.* of SPILL[1].

spin /spin/ *v. & n.* ● *v.* (**spinning**; *past* and *past part.* **spun** /spun/) **1** *intr. & tr.* turn or cause (a person or thing) to turn or whirl around quickly. **2** *tr.* (also *absol.*) **a** draw out and twist (wool, cotton, etc.) into threads. **b** make (yarn) in this way. **3** *tr.* (of a spider, silkworm, etc.) make (a web, a cocoon, etc.) by extruding a fine viscous thread. **4** *tr.* tell or write (a story, etc.) (*spins a good tale*). **5** *tr.* impart spin to (a ball). **6** *intr.* (of a person's head, etc.) be dizzy through excitement, astonishment, etc. **7** *tr.* (as **spun** *adj.*) converted into threads (*spun sugar*) **8** *tr.* toss (a coin). ● *n.* **1** a spinning motion. **2** an aircraft's diving descent combined with rotation. **3 a** a revolving motion through the air, esp. in a ball struck aslant. **b** *Baseball* a twisting motion given to the ball in pitching. **4** *colloq.* a brief drive in a motor vehicle, etc., esp. for pleasure. **5** emphasis; interpretation. □ **spin off** throw off by centrifugal force in spinning. **spin out 1** prolong (a discussion, etc.). **2** make (a story, money, etc.) last as long as possible. **3** consume (time, etc.) by discussion or in an occupation, etc.).

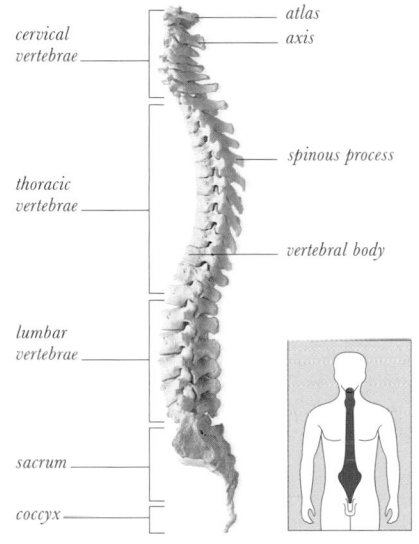

SPINAL CORD: CROSS SECTION OF THE HUMAN SPINAL CORD

(labels: *skull*, *cerebrum*, *cerebellum*, *vertebra*, *spinal cord*, *filum terminale*, *sacrum*)

spi·na bif·i·da /spínə bífidə/ *n.* a congenital defect of the spine, in which part of the spinal cord and its meninges are exposed through a gap in the backbone.

spin·ach /spínich, -nij/ *n.* **1** a green garden vegetable, *Spinacia oleracea*, with succulent leaves. **2** the leaves of this plant used as food. ▷ VEGETABLE. □□ **spin·ach·y** *adj.*

spi·nal /spín'l/ *adj.* of or relating to the spine (*spinal curvature; spinal disease*). □□ **spi·nal·ly** *adv.*

spi·nal col·umn *n.* the spine.

spi·nal cord *n.* ◀ a cylindrical structure of the central nervous system enclosed in the spine. ▷ HEAD, NERVOUS SYSTEM, PERIPHERAL NERVOUS SYSTEM

spin·dle /spínd'l/ *n.* **1 a** a pin in a spinning wheel used for twisting and winding the thread. **b** a small bar with tapered ends used for the same purpose in hand spinning. **c** a pin bearing the bobbin of a spinning machine. **2** a pin or axis that revolves or on which something revolves. **3** a turned piece of wood used as a banister, chair leg, etc. **4 a** a pointed metal rod standing on a base and used for filing news items, etc., esp. when rejected for publication. **b** a similar spike used for bills, etc.

spin·dly /spíndlee/ *adj.* (**spindlier**, **spindliest**) long or tall and thin.

spin doc·tor *n.* a political pundit employed to promote a favorable interpretation of developments to the media.

spin·drift /spíndrift/ *n.* spray blown along the surface of the sea.

spine /spīn/ *n.* **1** ▼ a series of vertebrae extending from the skull to the small of the back; the backbone. ▷ SKELETON, VERTEBRA. **2** *Zool. & Bot.* any hard pointed process or structure. ▷ SEA URCHIN, SUCCULENT. **3** a sharp ridge or projection, esp. of a mountain range or slope. **4** a central feature, main support, or source of strength. **5** the part of a book's jacket or cover that encloses the fastened edges of the pages. □□ **spined** *adj.*

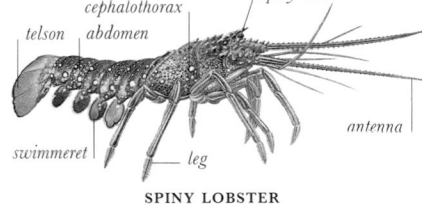

(labels: *cervical vertebrae*, *atlas*, *axis*, *thoracic vertebrae*, *spinous process*, *vertebral body*, *lumbar vertebrae*, *sacrum*, *coccyx*)

SPINE OF A HUMAN

spine chill·er *n.* a frightening story, movie, etc. □□ **spine-chill·ing** *adj.*

spi·nel /spinél/ *n.* **1** any of a group of hard crystalline minerals of various colors, consisting chiefly of oxides of magnesium and aluminum. **2** any substance of similar composition or properties.

spi·nel ru·by *n.* a deep red variety of spinel used as a gem.

spine·less /spínlis/ *adj.* **1 a** having no spine; invertebrate. **b** (of a fish) having no spines. **2** (of a person) weak and purposeless. □□ **spine·less·ly** *adv.* **spine·less·ness** *n.*

spin·et /spínit, spinét/ *n. Mus. hist.* ▼ a small harpsichord with oblique strings.

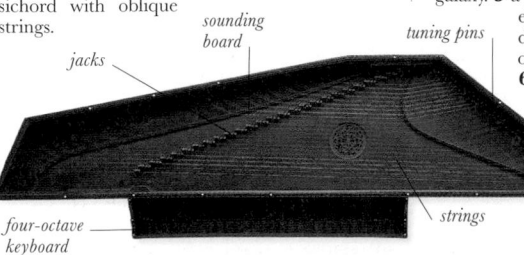

(labels: *jacks*, *sounding board*, *tuning pins*, *four-octave keyboard*, *strings*)

SPINET: 16TH-CENTURY ITALIAN SPINET

spine-ting·ling *adj.* thrilling; pleasurably exciting.

spi·ni·fex /spínifeks/ *n.* any Australian grass of the genus *Spinifex*, with coarse, spiny leaves.

spin·na·ker /spínəkər/ *n.* a large triangular sail carried opposite the mainsail of a racing yacht running before the wind.

spin·ner /spínər/ *n.* **1** a person or thing that spins. **2** *Cricket* **a** a spin bowler. **b** a spun ball. **3 a** a real or artificial fly for esp. trout fishing. **b** revolving bait. **4** a manufacturer or merchant engaged in (esp. cotton) spinning.

spin·ner·et /spínəret/ *n.* **1** the spinning organ in a spider, etc. ▷ SPIDER. **2** a device for forming filaments of synthetic fiber.

spin·ney /spínee/ *n.* (*pl.* **-eys**) *Brit.* a small wood; a thicket.

spin·ning /spíning/ *n.* the act or an instance of spinning.

spin·ning jen·ny *n. hist.* a machine for spinning with more than one spindle at a time.

spin·ning wheel *n.* a household machine for spinning yarn or thread with a spindle driven by a wheel attached to a crank or treadle.

spin-off *n.* an incidental result or results, esp. as a side benefit from industrial technology.

spi·nose /spínōs/ *adj.* (also **spi·nous** /-nəs/) *Bot.* (of a plant) having many spines.

spin·ster /spínstər/ *n.* **1** an unmarried woman. **2** a woman, esp. elderly, thought unlikely to marry. □□ **spin·ster·hood** *n.* **spin·ster·ish** *adj.*

spin·thar·i·scope /spinthárisk̄op/ *n.* an instrument with a fluorescent screen showing the incidence of alpha particles by flashes.

spi·nule /spínyōol/ *n. Bot. & Zool.* a small spine. □□ **spi·nu·lose** *adj.* **spi·nu·lous** *adj.*

spin·y /spínee/ *adj.* (**spinier**, **spiniest**) **1** full of spines; prickly. **2** perplexing; troublesome. □□ **spin·i·ness** *n.*

spin·y lob·ster *n.* ▼ any of various large edible crustaceans of the family Palinuridae, esp. *Palinuris vulgaris*, with a spiny shell and no large anterior claws.

(labels: *cephalothorax*, *spiny shell*, *telson*, *abdomen*, *swimmeret*, *leg*, *antenna*)

SPINY LOBSTER (*Palinurus vulgaris*)

spi·ra·cle /spírəkəl/ *n.* (also **spi·ra·cu·lum** /spírákyələm/) (*pl.* **spiracles** or **spiracula** /-rákyələ/) an external respiratory opening in insects, whales, and some fish. □□ **spi·ra·cu·lar** /-rákyələr/ *adj.*

spi·rae·a var. of SPIREA.

spi·ral /spírəl/ *adj., n., & v.* ● *adj.* **1** winding about a center in an enlarging or decreasing continuous circular motion, either on a flat plane or rising in a cone; coiled. **2** winding continuously along or as if along a cylinder, like the thread of a screw. ● *n.* **1** a plane or three-dimensional spiral curve. **2** a spiral spring. **3** a spiral formation in a shell, etc. **4** a spiral galaxy. **5** a progressive rise or fall of prices, wages, etc., each responding to an upward or downward stimulus provided by the other (*a spiral of rising prices and wages*). **6** *Football.* a kick or pass in which the ball rotates on its long axis while in the air. ● *v.* (**spiraled** or **spiralled**, **spiraling** or **spiralling**) **1** *intr.* move in a spiral course, esp. upward or downward. **2** *tr.* make spiral. **3** *intr. esp. Econ.* (of prices, wages, etc.) rise or fall, esp. rapidly. □□ **spi·ral·ly** *adv.*

S

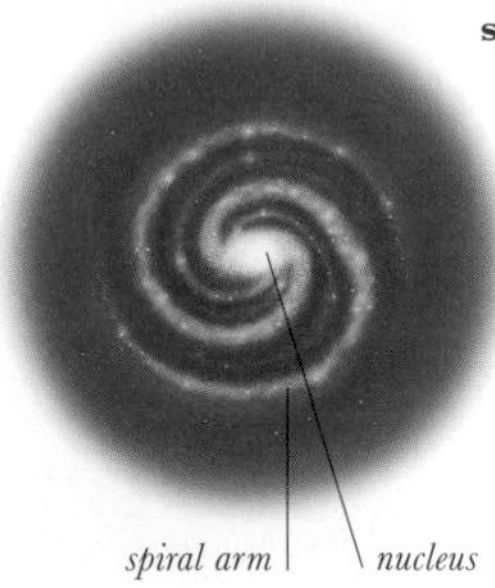

SPIRAL GALAXY

spi·ral gal·axy *n.* ◀ a galaxy in which the matter is concentrated mainly in one or more spiral arms. ▷ GALAXY

spi·rant /spírənt/ *adj.* & *n. Phonet.* ● *adj.* (of a consonant) uttered with a continuous expulsion of breath, esp. fricative. ● *n.* such a consonant.

spire /spīr/ *n.* & *v.* ● *n.* **1** a tapering cone- or pyramid-shaped structure built esp. on a church tower. ▷ CATHEDRAL. **2** any tapering thing, e.g., the spike of a flower. ● *v.tr.* provide with a spire. ▫▫ **spir·y** /spíree/ *adj.*

spi·re·a /spīréeə/ *n.* (also **spi·rae·a**) any rosaceous shrub of the genus *Spiraea*, with clusters of small white or pink flowers.

spi·ril·lum /spīríləm/ *n.* (*pl.* **spirilla** /-lə/) **1** any bacterium of the genus *Spirillum*, characterized by a rigid spiral structure. **2** any bacterium with a similar shape.

spir·it /spírit/ *n.* & *v.* ● *n.* **1 a** the vital animating essence of a person or animal (*broken in spirit*). **b** the soul. **2 a** a rational or intelligent being without a material body. **b** a supernatural being. **3** a prevailing mental or moral condition or attitude (*took it in the wrong spirit*). **4 a** (in *pl.*) strong distilled liquor, e.g., brandy, whiskey, gin, rum. **b** a distilled volatile liquid (*wood spirits*). **c** purified alcohol (*methylated spirits*). **d** a solution of a volatile principle in alcohol (*spirits of ammonia*). **5 a** a person's mental nature, usu. specified (*an unbending spirit*). **b** a person viewed as possessing these (*is an ardent spirit*). **c** courage; energy; vivacity (*played with spirit*). **6** the real meaning as opposed to lip service or verbal expression (*the spirit of the law*). ● *v.tr.* (**spirited**, **spiriting**) (usu. foll. by *away*, *off*, etc.) convey rapidly and secretly by or as if by spirits. ▫ **in spirit** inwardly (*will be with you in spirit*).

spir·it·ed /spíritid/ *adj.* **1** full of spirit; animated or courageous (*a spirited attack*). **2** having a spirit or spirits of a specified kind (*high spirited*). ▫▫ **spir·it·ed·ly** *adv.* **spir·it·ed·ness** *n.*

spir·it·less /spíritlis/ *adj.* lacking courage, vigor, or vivacity. ▫▫ **spir·it·less·ly** *adv.* **spir·it·less·ness** *n.*

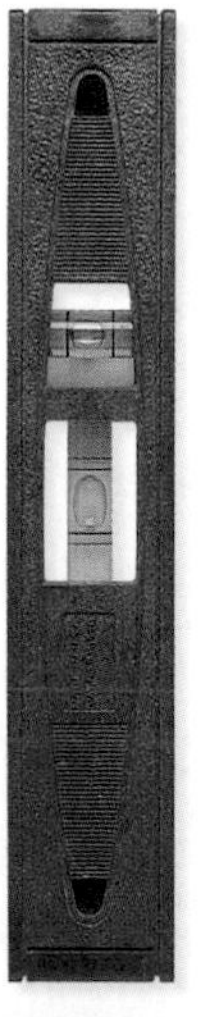
SPIRIT LEVEL

spir·it lev·el *n.* ◀ a sealed glass tube nearly filled with alcohol, containing an air bubble whose position is used to test horizontal and vertical directions.

spir·it·u·al /spírichōōəl/ *adj.* & *n.* ● *adj.* **1** of or concerning the spirit as opposed to matter. **2** concerned with sacred or religious things (*spiritual songs*). **3** (of the mind, etc.) refined; sensitive. **4** concerned with the spirit, etc., not with external reality (*his spiritual home*). ● *n.* a religious song derived from the musical traditions of African-American people in the southern US. ▫▫ **spir·it·u·al·i·ty** /-chōōálitee/ *n.* **spir·it·u·al·ly** *adv.* **spir·it·u·al·ness** *n.*

spir·it·u·al·ism /spírichōōəlizəm/ *n.* **1** the belief that the spirits of the dead can communicate with the living, esp. through mediums. **2** the practice of this. ▫▫ **spir·it·u·al·ist** *n.* **spir·it·u·al·is·tic** *adj.*

spir·it·u·al·ize /spírichōōəlīz/ *v.tr.* **1** make (a person or a person's thoughts, etc.) spiritual; elevate. **2** attach a spiritual as opposed to a literal meaning to. ▫▫ **spir·it·u·al·i·za·tion** *n.*

spir·it·u·ous /spírichōōəs/ *adj.* **1** containing much alcohol. **2** distilled, as whiskey, rum, etc. (*spirituous liquor*).

S

spiro-[1] /spírō/ *comb. form* a coil.

spiro-[2] /spírō/ *comb. form* breath.

spi·ro·chete /spírōkeet/ *n.* (also **spi·ro·chaete**) any of various flexible spiral-shaped bacteria.

spi·ro·graph /spírəgraf/ *n.* an instrument for recording breathing movements. ▫▫ **spi·ro·graph·ic** *adj.* **spi·ro·graph·i·cal·ly** *adv.*

spi·ro·gy·ra /spírōjírə/ *n.* any freshwater alga of the genus *Spirogyra*, with cells containing spiral bands of chlorophyll.

spi·rom·e·ter /spīrómitər/ *n.* an instrument for measuring the air capacity of the lungs.

spirt var. of SPURT.

spit[1] /spit/ *v.* & *n.* ● *v.* (**spitting**; *past* and *past part.* **spat** /spat/ or **spit**) **1** *intr.* **a** eject saliva from the mouth. **b** do this as a sign of hatred or contempt (*spat at him*). **2** *tr.* (usu. foll. by *out*) **a** eject from the mouth (*spat the meat out*). **b** utter vehemently (*"Damn you!" he spat*). **3** *intr.* (of a fire, pan, etc.) send out sparks, hot fat, etc. **4** *intr.* (of rain) fall lightly (*it's only spitting*). **5** *intr.* (esp. of a cat) make a spitting or hissing noise in anger or hostility. ● *n.* **1** spittle. **2** the act or an instance of spitting. ▫ **the spit of** *colloq.* the exact double of. **spit it out** *colloq.* say what is on one's mind. **spit up** regurgitate; vomit. ▫▫ **spit·ter** *n.*

spit[2] /spit/ *n.* & *v.* ● *n.* **1** a slender rod on which meat is skewered before being roasted on a fire, etc. **2 a** a small point of land projecting into the sea. ▷ LONGSHORE DRIFT. **b** a long narrow underwater bank. ● *v.tr.* (**spitted**, **spitting**) **1** thrust a spit through (meat, etc.). **2** pierce with a sword, etc. ▫▫ **spit·ty** *adj.*

spit and pol·ish *n.* **1** the cleaning and polishing duties of a soldier, etc. **2** exaggerated neatness and smartness.

spit·ball /spítbawl/ *n.* & *v.* ● *n.* **1** a ball of chewed paper, etc., used as a missile. **2** a baseball moistened by the pitcher to affect its flight. ● *v.intr.* throw out suggestions for discussion. ▫▫ **spit·ball·er** *n.*

spit curl *n.* a tight curl usu. pressed against the forehead, cheek, or temple.

spite /spīt/ *n.* & *v.* ● *n.* **1** ill will; malice toward a person. **2** a grudge. ● *v.tr.* thwart; mortify; annoy (*does it to spite me*). ▫ **in spite of** notwithstanding. **in spite of oneself** though one would rather have done otherwise.

spite·ful /spítfōōl/ *adj.* motivated by spite. ▫▫ **spite·ful·ly** *adv.* **spite·ful·ness** *n.*

spit·fire /spítfīr/ *n.* a person with a fiery temper.

spit·ting dis·tance *n.* a very short distance.

spit·ting im·age *n.* (foll. by *of*) *colloq.* the exact double of (another person or thing).

spit·tle /spít'l/ *n.* saliva, esp. as ejected from the mouth.

spit·toon /spitōōn/ *n.* a metal or earthenware pot with esp. a funnel shaped top, used for spitting into.

spitz /spits/ *n.* **1** any of a stocky type of dog with a pointed muzzle and a tail curved over the back, as a Pomeranian, Samoyed, etc. **2** this breed.

spiv /spiv/ *n. Brit. colloq.* a man, often characterized by flashy dress, who makes a living by illicit or unscrupulous dealings. ▫▫ **spiv·vish** *adj.* **spiv·vy** *adj.*

splash /splash/ *v.* & *n.* ● *v.* **1** *intr.* & *tr.* spatter or cause (liquid) to spatter in small drops. **2** *tr.* cause (a person) to be spattered with liquid, etc. **3** *intr.* **a** (of a person) cause liquid to spatter (*was splashing about*). **b** (usu. foll. by *across*, *along*, etc.) move while spattering liquid, etc. **c** step, fall, or plunge, etc., into a liquid, etc., so as to cause a splash. **4** *tr.* display (news) prominently. **5** *tr.* decorate with scattered color. ● *n.* **1** the act or an instance of splashing. **2 a** a quantity of liquid splashed. **b** the resulting noise. **3** a spot of dirt, etc., splashed on to a thing. **4** a prominent news feature, etc. **5** a daub or patch of color. **6** *colloq.* a small quantity of liquid, esp. of soda water, etc., to dilute liquor. ▫ **make a splash** attract much attention, esp. by extravagance. ▫▫ **splash·y** *adj.* (**splashier**, **splashiest**).

splash·down /spláshdown/ *n.* the landing of a spacecraft in the sea.

splat[1] /splat/ *n.* a flat piece of thin wood in the center of a chair back.

splat[2] /splat/ *n.*, *adv.*, & *v. colloq.* ● *n.* a sharp cracking or slapping sound. ● *adv.* with a splat (*fell splat into the puddle*). ● *v.intr.* & *tr.* (**splatted**, **splatting**) fall or hit with a splat.

splat·ter /splátər/ *v.* & *n.* ● *v.* **1** *tr.* & *intr.* splash esp. with a continuous noisy action. **2** *tr.* (often foll. by *with*) make wet or dirty by splashing. ● *n.* a noisy splashing sound.

splay /splay/ *v.*, *n.*, & *adj.* ● *v.* **1** *tr.* (usu. foll. by *out*) spread (the feet, etc.) out. **2** *intr.* (of an aperture or its sides) diverge in shape or position. **3** *tr.* construct (a window, aperture, etc.) so that it diverges or is wider at one side of the wall than the other. ● *n.* a surface making an oblique angle with another. ● *adj.* **1** wide and flat. **2** turned outward.

splay·foot /spláyfōōt/ *n.* a broad flat foot turned outward. ▫▫ **splay·foot·ed** *adj.*

spleen /spleen/ *n.* **1** an abdominal organ involved in maintaining the proper condition of blood in most vertebrates. ▷ LYMPHATIC SYSTEM. **2** lowness of spirits; ill temper, spite (from the earlier belief that the spleen was the seat of such feelings) (*vented their spleen*). ▫▫ **spleen·y** *adj.*

spleen·wort /spléenwərt, -wawrt/ *n.* any fern of the genus *Asplenium*, formerly used as a remedy for disorders of the spleen.

splen- /spleen/ *comb. form Anat.* the spleen.

splen·dent /spléndənt/ *adj. formal* **1** shining; lustrous. **2** illustrious.

splen·did /spléndid/ *adj.* **1** magnificent; gorgeous; brilliant. **2** dignified; impressive (*splendid isolation*). **3** excellent; fine (*a splendid chance*). ▫▫ **splen·did·ly** *adv.* **splen·did·ness** *n.*

splen·dif·er·ous /splendífərəs/ *adj. colloq.* or *joc.* splendid.

splen·dor /spléndər/ *n.* **1** dazzling brightness. **2** magnificence; grandeur.

splen·ec·to·my /splinéktəmee/ *n.* (*pl.* **-ies**) the surgical excision of the spleen.

sple·net·ic /splinétik/ *adj.* **1** ill-tempered. **2** of or concerning the spleen. ▫▫ **sple·net·i·cal·ly** *adv.*

splen·ic /splénik/ *adj.* of or in the spleen. ▫▫ **splen·oid** /spléenoyd/ *adj.*

splen·i·tis /spleenítis/ *n.* inflammation of the spleen.

sple·ni·us /spléeneeəs/ *n.* (*pl.* **splenii** /-nee-ī/) *Anat.* either section of muscle on each side of the neck and back serving to draw back the head. ▫▫ **sple·ni·al** *adj.*

sple·nol·o·gy /spleenóləjee/ *n.* the scientific study of the spleen.

sple·no·meg·a·ly /spléenəmégəlee/ *n.* a pathological enlargement of the spleen.

sple·not·o·my /spleenótəmee/ *n.* (*pl.* **-ies**) a surgical incision into or dissection of the spleen.

splice /splīs/ *v.* & *n.* ● *v.tr.* **1** join the ends of (ropes) by interweaving strands. **2** join (pieces of timber, film, etc.) in an overlapping position. **3** (esp. as **spliced** *adj.*) *colloq.* join in marriage. ● *n.* ▶ a joint consisting of two ropes, pieces of wood, film, etc., made by splicing. ▫ **splice the main brace** *Naut. hist.* issue an extra tot of rum. ▫▫ **splic·er** *n.*

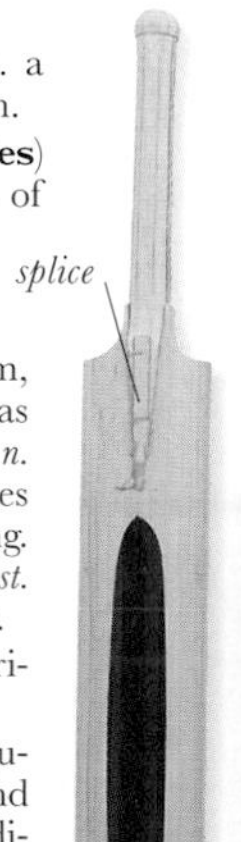

SPLICE: CRICKET BAT WITH HANDLE SPLICED TO BLADE

spliff /splif/ *n.* (also **splif**) *sl.* a marijuana cigarette.

spline /splīn/ *n.* & *v.* ● *n.* **1** a rectangular key fitting into grooves in the hub and shaft of a wheel and allowing longitudinal play. **2** a slat. ● *v.tr.* fit with a spline (sense 1).

splint /splint/ *n.* & *v.* ● *n.* **1 a** a strip of rigid material used for holding a broken bone, etc., when set. **b** a strip of esp. wood used in basketwork, etc. **2** a thin strip of wood, etc., used to light a fire, pipe, etc. ● *v.tr.* secure with a splint or splints.

splin·ter /splíntər/ v. & n. • v.tr. & intr. break into fragments. • n. a small thin sharp-edged piece broken off from wood, stone, etc. □□ **splin·ter·y** adj.

splin·ter group n. (also **splin·ter par·ty**) a group or party that has broken away from a larger one.

split /split/ v. & n. (**splitting**; past and past part. **split**) **1 a** intr. & tr. break or cause to break forcibly into parts, esp. with the grain or into halves. **b** intr. & tr. (often foll. by up) divide into parts (split into groups). **c** tr. Stock Exch. divide into two or more shares for each share owned. **2** tr. & intr. (often foll. by off, away) remove or be removed by breaking, separating, or dividing (split away from the group). **3** intr. & tr. (usu. foll. by up) separate esp. through discord. **b** (foll. by with) quarrel or cease association with (another person, etc.). **4** tr. cause the fission of (an atom). **5** intr. & tr. sl. leave, esp. suddenly. **6** intr. **a** (as **splitting** adj.) (of a headache) very painful; acute. **b** (of the head) suffer great pain from a headache, noise, etc. • n. **1** the act or an instance of splitting; the state of being split. **2** a fissure, crack, cleft, etc. **3** a separation into parties; a schism. **4** (in pl.) the athletic feat of leaping in the air or sitting down with the legs at right angles to the body in front and behind, or at the sides with the trunk facing forward. **5 a** half a bottle of mineral water. **b** half a glass of liquor. **6** colloq. a division of money, esp. the proceeds of crime. □ **split the difference** take the average of two proposed amounts. **split hairs** make insignificant distinctions. **split one's sides** be convulsed with laughter. **split the ticket** (or **one's vote**) vote for candidates of more than one party in an election. **split the vote** (of a candidate or minority party) attract votes from another so that both are defeated by a rival. □□ **split·ter** n.

split in·fin·i·tive n. a phrase consisting of an infinitive with an adverb, etc., inserted between to and the verb, e.g., seems to really like it.

split-lev·el adj. (of a building) having a room or rooms a fraction of a story higher than other parts.

split pea n. a dried pea split in half for cooking.

split per·son·al·i·ty n. the alteration or dissociation of personality occurring in some mental illnesses, esp. schizophrenia and hysteria.

split ring n. a small steel ring with two spiral turns, such as a key ring.

split screen n. a screen on which two or more separate images are displayed.

split sec·ond n. a very brief moment of time.

split shift n. a shift comprising two or more separate periods of duty.

splosh /splosh/ v. & n. colloq. • v.tr. & intr. move with a splashing sound. • n. **1** a splashing sound. **2** a splash of water, etc.

splotch /sploch/ n. & v.tr. colloq. • n. a daub, blot, or smear. • v.tr. make a large, esp. irregular, spot or patch on. □□ **splotch·y** adj.

splurge /splərj/ n. & v. colloq. • n. **1** an ostentatious display. **2** an instance of great extravagance. • v.intr. (usu. foll. by on) spend large sums of money.

splut·ter /splútər/ v. & n. **1** intr. **a** speak in a hurried, vehement, or choking manner. **b** emit spitting sounds. **2** tr. **a** speak or utter rapidly or incoherently. **b** emit (food, sparks, etc.) with a spitting sound. • n. spluttering speech. □□ **splut·ter·er** n. **splut·ter·ing·ly** adv.

Spode /spōd/ • n. a type of fine pottery or porcelain.

spoil /spoyl/ v. & n. • v. (past and past part. **spoiled** **1** tr. **a** damage; diminish the value of (spoiled by the rain). **b** reduce a person's enjoyment, etc., of (the news spoiled his dinner). **2** tr. injure the character of (a child, pet, etc.) by excessive indulgence. **3** intr. (of food) go bad; decay. **b** (usu. in neg) (of a joke, secret, etc.) become stale through long keeping. **4** tr. render (a ballot) invalid by improper marking. • n. **1** (usu. in pl.) **a** plunder taken from an enemy in war, or seized by force. **b** profit or advantage gained by succeeding to public office, high position, etc. **2** earth, etc., thrown up in excavating, dredging, etc. □ **be spoiling for** aggressively seek (a fight, etc.).

spoil·age /spóylij/ n. **1** paper spoiled in printing. **2** the spoiling of food, etc., by decay.

spoil·er /spóylər/ n. **1** a person or thing that spoils. **2 a** a device on an aircraft to retard its speed by interrupting the air flow. **b** a similar device on a vehicle to improve road-holding at speed.

spoils·man /spóylzmən/ • n. (pl. **-men**) esp. Polit. **1** an advocate of the spoils system. **2** a person who seeks to profit by it.

spoil·sport /spóylspawrt/ n. a person who spoils others' pleasure.

spoils sys·tem n. the practice of giving public office to the adherents of a successful party.

spoke[1] /spōk/ n. & v. • n. **1** each of the bars running from the hub to the rim of a wheel. ▷ BICYCLE. **2** a rung of a ladder. • v.tr. **1** provide with spokes. **2** obstruct (a wheel, etc.) by thrusting a spoke in. □□ **spoke·wise** adv.

spoke[2] past of SPEAK.

spo·ken /spókən/ past part. of SPEAK. • adj. (in comb.) speaking in a specified way (smooth-spoken; well-spoken). □ **spoken for** claimed; requisitioned.

spoke·shave /spókshayv/ n. ▼ a blade set between two handles, used for shaping spokes and other esp. curved work.

adjusting screw   blade

handle   handle

SPOKESHAVE

spokes·man /spóksmən/ n. (pl. **-men**; fem. **spokes·woman**, pl. **-women**) **1** a person who speaks on behalf of others, esp. in the course of public relations. **2** a person deputed to express the views of a group, etc.

spokes·per·son /spókspərsən/ n. (pl. **-persons** or **-people**) a spokesman or spokeswoman.

spo·li·a·tion /spólceáyshən/ n. **1** plunder or pillage, esp. of neutral vessels in war. **2** extortion.

spon·dee /spóndee/ n. Prosody a foot consisting of two long (or stressed) syllables.

spon·dy·li·tis /spóndəlítis/ • n. inflammation of the vertebrae.

sponge /spunj/ n. & v. • n. **1** any aquatic animal of the phylum Porifera, with pores in its body wall and a rigid internal skeleton. **2 a** ▶ the skeleton of a sponge, esp. the soft light elastic absorbent kind used in bathing, etc. **b** a piece of porous rubber or plastic, etc., used similarly. **3** a thing of spongelike absorbency or consistency, e.g., a sponge cake, porous metal, etc. **4** = SPONGER. **5** cleaning with or as with a sponge (gave the stove a quick sponge). • v. **1** tr. wipe or clean with a sponge. **2** tr. (also absol.; often foll. by down, over) sluice water over (the body, a car, etc.). **3** tr. (often foll. by out, away, etc.) wipe off or efface (writing, etc.) with or as with a sponge. **4** tr. (often foll. by up) absorb with or as with a sponge. **5** intr. (often foll. by on, off) live as a parasite; be dependent upon (another person). **6** tr. obtain (drink, etc.) by sponging. **7** intr. gather sponges. **8** tr. apply paint with a sponge to (walls, furniture, etc.). □□ **sponge·a·ble** adj. **sponge·like** adj. **spon·gi·form** adj. (esp. in senses 1, 2).

SPONGE: SKELETON OF A SPONGE (*Spongia officinalis*)

sponge cake n. a very light cake with a spongelike consistency.

spong·er /spúnjər/ n. a person who contrives to live at another's expense.

sponge rub·ber n. liquid rubber latex processed into a spongelike substance.

spon·gy /spúnjee/ adj. (**spongier**, **spongiest**) like

a sponge, esp. in being porous, compressible, elastic, or absorbent. □□ **spon·gi·ly** adv. **spon·gi·ness** n.

spon·sion /spónshən/ n. **1** being a surety for another. **2** a pledge or promise made on behalf of the government by an agent not authorized to do so.

spon·son /spónsən/ n. **1** a projection from the side of a warship or tank to enable a gun to be trained forward and aft. **2** a short subsidiary wing to stabilize a seaplane. **3** a triangular platform supporting the wheel on a paddle-steamer. **4** a flotation chamber along the gunwale of a canoe.

spon·sor /spónsər/ n. & v. • n. **1** a person who supports an activity done for charity by pledging money in advance. **2 a** a person or organization that promotes or supports an artistic or sporting activity, etc. **b** a business organization that promotes a broadcast program in return for advertising time. **3** an organization lending support to an election candidate. **4** a person who introduces a proposal for legislation. **5** a godparent at baptism or esp. a person who presents a candidate for confirmation. **6** a person who makes himself or herself responsible for another. • v.tr. be a sponsor for. □□ **spon·so·ri·al** /sponsáwreeəl/ adj. **spon·sor·ship** n.

spon·ta·ne·ous /spontáyneeəs/ adj. **1** acting or done or occurring without external cause. **2** without external incitement (made a spontaneous offer of his services). **3** (of bodily movement, literary style, etc.) gracefully natural and unconstrained. **4** (of sudden movement, etc.) involuntary; not due to conscious volition. **5** growing naturally without cultivation. □□ **spon·ta·ne·i·ty** /spóntənéeitee, -náyitee/ n. **spon·ta·ne·ous·ly** adv. **spon·ta·ne·ous·ness** n.

spon·ta·ne·ous com·bus·tion n. the ignition of a substance from heat engendered within itself.

spon·ta·ne·ous gen·er·a·tion n. the supposed production of living from nonliving matter as inferred from the appearance of life (due in fact to bacteria, etc.) in some infusions.

spoof /spoof/ n. & v. colloq. • n. **1** a parody. **2** a hoax or swindle. • v.tr. **1** parody. **2** hoax; swindle. □□ **spoof·er** n. **spoof·er·y** n.

spook /spook/ n. & v. • n. **1** colloq. a ghost. **2** sl. a spy. • v. sl. **1** tr. frighten; unnerve, alarm. **2** intr. take fright; become alarmed.

spook·y /spookee/ adj. (**spookier**, **spookiest**) **1** colloq. ghostly; eerie. **2** sl. nervous. □□ **spook·i·ly** adv. **spook·i·ness** n.

spool /spool/ n. & v. • n. **1 a** a reel for winding magnetic tape, etc., on. **b** a reel for winding thread or wire on. **c** a quantity of tape, etc., wound on a spool. **2** the revolving cylinder of an angler's reel. ▷ REEL. • v.tr. wind on a spool.

spoon /spoon/ n. & v. • n. **1 a** a utensil consisting of an oval or round bowl and a handle for conveying food (esp. liquid) to the mouth, for stirring, etc. **b** a spoonful, esp. of sugar. **2** a spoon shaped thing, esp.: **a** (in full **spoon-bait**) a bright revolving piece of metal used as a lure in fishing. **b** an oar with a broad curved blade. • v. **1** tr. (often foll. by up, out) take (liquid, etc.) with a spoon. **2** intr. colloq. behave in an amorous way, esp. foolishly. □ **born with a silver spoon in one's mouth** born into affluence. □□ **spoon·er** n. (esp. in sense 2 of v.). **spoon·ful** n. (pl. **-fuls**).

spoon·bill /spoonbil/ n. **1** ▶ any large wading bird of the subfamily Plataleiae, having a bill with a very broad flat tip. **2** a shoveler duck.

SPOONBILL: EURASIAN SPOONBILL (*Platalea leucorodia*)

S

spoon·er·ism /spo͞onərizəm/ *n.* a transposition, usu. accidental, of the initial letters, etc., of two or more words, e.g., *you have hissed the mystery lectures.*

spoon·feed /spo͞onfeed/ *v.tr.* (*past* and *past part.* **-fed**) **1** feed (a baby, etc.) with a spoon. **2** provide help, information, etc., to (a person) without requiring any effort on the recipient's part.

spoon·y /spo͞onee/ *adj. & n. colloq. archaic* ● *adj.* (**spoonier, spooniest**) **1** (often foll. by *on*) sentimental; amorous. **2** foolish; silly. ● *n.* (*pl.* **-ies**) a simpleton. □□ **spoon·i·ly** *adv.* **spoon·i·ness** *n.*

spoor /spo͞or/ *n. & v.* ● *n.* the track or scent of an animal. ● *v.tr. & intr.* follow by the spoor.

spo·rad·ic /spərádik, spaw-/ *adj.* occurring only here and there or occasionally; scattered. □□ **spo·rad·i·cal·ly** *adv.*

spor·an·gi·um /spəránjeeəm/ *n.* (*pl.* **sporangia** /-jeeə/) *Bot.* a receptacle in which spores are found. □□ **spor·an·gi·al** *adj.*

spore /spawr/ *n.* ◄ a specialized reproductive cell of many plants and microorganisms.

sporo- /spáwrō/ *comb. form Biol.* a spore.

spor·o·gen·e·sis /spáwr-əjénisis/ *n.* the process of spore formation.

spor·og·en·ous /spəróji-nəs/ *adj.* producing spores.

spor·o·phyte /spáwrə-fīt/ *n.* a spore-producing form of plant with alternating sexual and asexual generations. □□ **spor·o·phyt·ic** /-fítik/ *adj.* **spor·o·phyt·i·cal·ly** *adv.*

SPORE: MICROGRAPH OF A MOSS SPORE (*Funaria hygrometrica*)

spor·ran /spáwrən, spór-/ *n.* a pouch worn in front of the kilt.

sport /spawrt/ *n. & v.* ● *n.* **1 a** a game or competitive activity, esp. an outdoor one involving physical exertion. **b** such activities collectively. **2** amusement; fun. **3** *colloq.* **a** a fair or generous person. **b** a person behaving in a specified way, esp. regarding games, rules, etc. (*a bad sport at tennis*). **c** a form of address, esp. between males. **4** *Biol.* an animal or plant deviating from the normal type. **5** a plaything or laughingstock (*the sport of Fortune*). ● *v.* **1** *intr.* divert oneself; take part in a pastime. **2** *tr.* wear, exhibit, or produce, esp. ostentatiously. **3** *intr. Biol.* become or produce a sport. □ **in sport** jestingly. **make sport of** make fun of; ridicule. □□ **sport·er** *n.*

sport·ing /spáwrting/ *adj.* **1** interested in sports (*a sporting man*). **2** sportsmanlike; generous (*a sporting offer*). **3** concerned with sports (*sporting news*). □□ **sport·ing·ly** *adv.*

sport·ive /spáwrtiv/ *adj.* playful. □□ **sport·ive·ly** *adv.* **spor·tive·ness** *n.*

sports car *n.* a usu. open, low-built fast car. ▷ CAR

sports·cast /spáwrtskast/ *n.* a broadcast of a sports event or information about sports. □□ **sports·cast·er** *n.*

sports coat *n.* (also **sports jacket**) a man's jacket for informal wear.

sports·man /spáwrtsmən/ *n.* (*pl.* **-men**; *fem.* **sportswoman**, *pl.* **-women**) **1** a person who takes part in sports, esp. professionally. **2** a person who behaves fairly and generously. □□ **sports·man·like** *adj.* **sports·man·ly** *adj.* **sports·man·ship** *n.*

sports·wear /spáwrtswair/ *n.* clothes worn for sports or for casual use.

sport u·til·i·ty ve·hi·cle *n.* a high-performance passenger vehicle with a light-truck chassis and four-wheel drive. ▷ CAR. ¶ Abbr.: **SUV**

sport·y /spáwrtee/ *adj.* (**sportier, sportiest**) *colloq.* **1** fond of sports. **2** rakish; showy. □□ **sport·i·ly** *adv.* **sport·i·ness** *n.*

spor·ule /spáwryo͞ol/ *n.* a small spore or a single spore. □□ **spor·u·lar** *adj.*

spot /spot/ *n. & v.* ● *n.* **1 a** a small part of the sur-face of a thing distinguished by color, texture, etc., usu. round. **b** a small mark or stain. **c** a pimple. **d** a small shape used in various numbers to distinguish playing cards in a suit, etc. **e** a moral blemish or stain. **2 a** a particular place; a definite locality (*on this precise spot*). **b** a place used for a particular activity (often in *comb.*: *nightspot*). **c** (prec. by *the*) *Soccer* the place from which a penalty kick is taken. **3** a particular part of one's body or aspect of one's character. **4 a** *colloq.* one's esp. regular position in an organization, program, etc. **b** a place or position in a show (*did the spot before intermission*). **5** = SPOTLIGHT. **6** (usu. *attrib.*) money paid or goods delivered immediately after a sale (*spot cash*). ● *v.* (**spotted, spotting**) **1** *tr.* **a** *colloq.* single out beforehand (the winner of a race, etc.). **b** *colloq.* recognize the identity, nationality, etc., of. **c** watch for and take note of (trains, talent, etc.). **d** *colloq.* catch sight of. **e** *Mil.* locate (an enemy's position), esp. from the air. **2 a** *tr. & intr.* mark or become marked with spots. **b** *tr.* stain; soil (a person's character, etc.). **3** *intr.* rain slightly (*it was spotting with rain*). □ **on the spot 1** at the scene of an action or event. **2** *colloq.* in a position such that response or action is required. **3** then and there. **put on the spot** *sl.* make to feel uncomfortable, awkward, etc.

spot check *n.* a test made on the spot or on a randomly selected subject. □□ **spot-check** *v.tr.*

spot·less /spótlis/ *adj.* immaculate. □□ **spot·less·ly** *adv.* **spot·less·ness** *n.*

spot·light /spótlīt/ *n. & v.* ● *n.* **1** a beam of light directed on a small area. **2** a lamp projecting this. **3** full attention or publicity. ● *v.tr.* (*past* and *past part.* **-lighted** or **-lit**) **1** direct a spotlight on. **2** draw attention to.

spot·ted /spótid/ *adj.* marked or decorated with spots. □□ **spot·ted·ness** *n.*

spot·ter /spótər/ *n.* **1** (often in *comb.*) a person who spots people or things (*train spotter*). **2** an aviator or aircraft employed in locating enemy positions, etc.

spot·ty /spótee/ *adj.* (**spottier, spottiest**) **1** marked with spots. **2** patchy; irregular. □□ **spot·ti·ly** *adv.* **spot·ti·ness** *n.*

spot weld *v.tr.* weld (two surfaces) together in a series of discrete points. □□ **spot weld·ing** *n.*

spouse /spows, spowz/ *n.* a husband or wife.

spout /spowt/ *n. & v.* ● *n.* **1 a** a projecting tube or lip through which a liquid, etc., is poured from a teapot, kettle, etc., or issues from a fountain, pump, etc. **b** a sloping trough down which a thing may be shot into a receptacle. **2** a jet or column of liquid, grain, etc. **3** (in full **spout hole**) a whale's blowhole. ● *v.tr. & intr.* **1** discharge or issue forcibly in a jet. **2** utter (verses, etc.) or speak in a declamatory manner. □□ **spout·er** *n.*

sprain /sprayn/ *v. & n.* ● *v.tr.* wrench (an ankle, wrist, etc.) violently so as to cause pain and swelling but not dislocation. ● *n.* **1** such a wrench. **2** the resulting inflammation and swelling.

sprang *past* of SPRING.

sprat /sprat/ *n.* **1** a small European herringlike fish, *Sprattus sprattus*, much used as food. **2** a similar fish, e.g., a sand eel or a young herring. □□ **sprat·ting** *n.*

sprawl /sprawl/ *v. & n.* ● *v.* **1 a** *intr.* sit or lie or fall with limbs flung out or in an ungainly way. **b** *tr.* spread (one's limbs) in this way. **2** *intr.* (of handwriting, a plant, a town, etc.) be of irregular or straggling form. ● *n.* **1** a sprawling movement or attitude. **2** a straggling group or mass. **3** the straggling expansion of an urban or industrial area. □□ **sprawl·ing·ly** *adv.*

spray¹ /spray/ *n. & v.* ● *n.* **1** water or other liquid flying in small drops from the force of the wind or waves, the action of an atomizer, etc. **2** a liquid preparation to be applied in this form with an atomizer, etc., esp. for medical purposes. **3** an instrument for such application. ● *v.tr.* (also *absol.*) **1** throw (liquid) in the form of spray. **2** sprinkle (an object) with small drops or particles. **3** (*absol.*) (of a tomcat) mark its environment with the smell of its urine. □□ **spray·a·ble** *adj.* **spray·er** *n.*

spray² /spray/ *n.* **1** a sprig of flowers or leaves, or a branch of a tree with branchlets or flowers. **2** an ornament in a similar form (*a spray of diamonds*).

spray gun *n.* ▼ a gunlike device for spraying paint, etc.

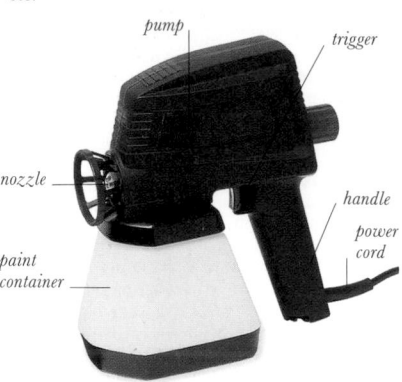

SPRAY GUN
(labels: *pump*, *trigger*, *nozzle*, *handle*, *power cord*, *paint container*)

spray paint *v.tr.* paint by means of a spray.

spread /spred/ *v. & n.* ● *v.* (*past* and *past part.* **spread**) **1** *tr.* (often foll. by *out*) **a** open or extend the surface of. **b** cause to cover a larger surface (*spread butter on bread*). **c** display to the eye or the mind (*the view spread before us*). **2** *intr.* (often foll. by *out*) have a wide or specified or increasing extent (*spreading trees*). **3** *intr. & tr.* become or make widely known, felt, etc. (*rumors are spreading*). **4** *tr.* **a** cover the surface of. **b** lay (a table). ● *n.* **1** the act or an instance of spreading. **2** diffusion (*spread of learning*). **3** breadth; compass (*arches of equal spread*). **4** an aircraft's wingspan. **5** the difference between two rates, prices, etc. **6** *colloq.* an elaborate meal. **7** a food paste for spreading on bread, etc. **8** a bedspread. **9** printed matter spread across more than one column. **10** a ranch with extensive land. □ **spread one's wings** see WING. □□ **spread·a·ble** *adj.* **spread·er** *n.*

spread bet·ting *n.* a form of betting in which money is won or lost according to the degree by which the score or result of a sports event varies from the spread of expected values quoted by the bookmaker.

spread ea·gle *n.* **1** ▼ a representation of an eagle with legs and wings extended as an emblem. **2** *hist.* a person secured with arms and legs spread out, esp. to be flogged.

SPREAD EAGLE: EMBLEM OF THE FRENCH 105TH REGIMENT

spread-ea·gle *v. & adj.* ● *v.* **1** *tr.* (usu. as **spread-eagled** *adj.*) place (a person) with arms and legs spread out. **2** *tr.* defeat utterly. **3** *tr.* spread out. ● *adj.* bombastic, esp. noisily patriotic.

S

spread·sheet /sprédsheet/ *n.* a computer program allowing manipulation and flexible retrieval of esp. tabulated numerical data.

spree /spree/ *n. & v. colloq.* • *n.* **1** a lively extravagant outing (*shopping spree*). **2** a bout of fun or drinking, etc. • *v.intr.* (**sprees**, **spreed**) have a spree. □ **on a spree** engaged in a spree.

sprig[1] /sprig/ *n. & v.* • *n.* **1** a small branch or shoot. **2** an ornament resembling this, esp. on fabric. • *v.tr.* (**sprigged**, **sprigging**) ornament with sprigs (*sprigged muslin*).

sprig[2] /sprig/ *n.* a small tapering headless tack.

spright·ly /sprítlee/ *adj.* (**sprightlier**, **sprightli-est**) vivacious; lively; brisk. □□ **spright·li·ness** *n.*

spring /spring/ *v. & n.* • *v.* (*past* **sprang** /sprang/ *also* **sprung** /sprung/; *past part.* **sprung**) **1** *intr.* jump; move rapidly or suddenly. **2** *intr.* move rapidly as from a constrained position or by the action of a spring. **3** *intr.* (usu. foll. by *from*) originate or arise. **4** *intr.* (usu. foll. by *up*) appear, esp. suddenly (*a breeze sprang up*). **5** *tr.* cause to act suddenly, esp. by means of a spring (*spring a trap*). **6** *tr.* (often foll. by *on*) produce suddenly or unexpectedly (*loves to spring surprises*). **7** *tr. sl.* contrive the escape or release of. **8** *tr.* rouse (game) from earth or covert. **9** *intr.* become warped or split. **10** *tr.* (usu. as **sprung** *adj.*) provide (a motor vehicle, etc.) with springs. • *n.* **1** a jump. **2** a backward movement from a constrained position. **3** ability to spring back strongly. **4** a resilient device usu. of bent or coiled metal used esp. to drive clockwork or for cushioning in furniture or vehicles. **5 a** the season in which vegetation begins to appear; the first season of the year. ▷ SEASON. **b** *Astron.* the period from the vernal equinox to the summer solstice. **c** (often foll. by *of*) the early stage of life, etc. **d** = SPRING TIDE. **6** a place where water, oil, etc., wells up from the earth; the basin or flow so formed. **7** the motive for or origin of an action, custom, etc. (*the springs of human action*). □ **spring a leak** develop a leak (orig. *Naut.*, from timbers springing out of position). □□ **spring·less** *adj* **spring·like** *adj.*

spring bal·ance *n.* ◀ a balance that measures weight by the tension of a spring.

spring·board /springbawrd/ *n.* **1** a springy board giving impetus in leaping, diving, etc. **2** a source of impetus in any activity.

spring·bok /springbok/ *n.* **1** a southern African gazelle, *Antidorcas marsupialis*, with the ability to run with high springing jumps. **2** (**Springbok**) a South African, esp. one who has played in international sporting competitions.

eye

scale

spring inside

hook

ring

weight

SPRING BALANCE

spring chick·en *n.* **1** a young fowl for eating (orig. available only in spring). **2** (esp. with *neg.*) a young person (*she's no spring chicken*).

spring·er /springər/ *n.* **1** a person or thing that springs. **2** ▼ a small spaniel of a breed used to spring game.

SPRINGER: ENGLISH SPRINGER SPANIEL

spring fe·ver *n.* a restless or lethargic feeling sometimes associated with spring.

spring-load·ed *adj.* containing a compressed or stretched spring pressing one part against another (*a switchblade with a spring-loaded clip*).

spring on·ion *n.* esp. *Brit.* an onion taken from the ground before the bulb has formed, and eaten raw.

spring roll *n.* an Asian snack consisting of a pancake filled with vegetables, etc., and fried.

spring·tail /springtayl/ *n.* ▶ any wingless insect of the order Collembola, leaping by means of a spring-like caudal part.

spring·tide /springtīd/ *n. poet.* = SPRINGTIME.

spring tide *n.* a tide just after new and full Moon when there is the greatest difference between high and low water. ▷ TIDES

spring·time /springtīm/ *n.* **1** the season of spring. **2** a time compared to this.

spring wa·ter *n.* water from a spring, as opposed to river or rain water.

spring·y /springee/ *adj.* (**springier**, **springiest**) **1** springing back quickly when squeezed or stretched. **2** (of movements) as of a springy substance. □□ **spring·i·ly** *adv.* **spring·i·ness** *n.*

sprin·kle /springkəl/ *v. & n.* • *v.tr.* **1** scatter (liquid, ashes, crumbs, etc.) in small drops or particles. **2** (often foll. by *with*) subject (the ground or an object) to sprinkling with liquid, etc. **3** (of liquid, etc.) fall on in this way. **4** distribute in small amounts. • *n.* (usu. foll. by *of*) **1** a light shower. **2** = SPRINKLING. **3** (in *pl.*) candy particles used as a topping on ice cream.

sprin·kler /springklər/ *n.* a device for sprinkling water on a lawn or to extinguish fires.

sprin·kling /springkling/ *n.* a small thinly distributed number or amount.

sprint /sprint/ *v. & n.* • *v.* **1** *intr.* run a short distance at full speed. **2** *tr.* run (a specified distance) in this way. • *n.* **1** such a run. **2** a short spell of maximum effort in cycling, swimming, auto racing, etc. □□ **sprint·er** *n.*

sprit /sprit/ *n.* a small spar reaching diagonally from the mast to the upper outer corner of the sail.

sprite /sprīt/ *n.* an elf, fairy, or goblin.

sprit·sail /spritsəl, -sayl/ *n.* **1** a sail extended by a sprit. **2** *hist.* a sail extended by a yard set under the bowsprit.

spritz /sprits/ *v. & n.* • *v.tr.* sprinkle, squirt, or spray. • *n.* the act or an instance of spritzing.

spritz·er /spritsər/ *n.* a mixture of wine and soda water.

sprock·et /spró-kit/ *n.* **1** each of several teeth on a wheel engaging with the links of a chain, e.g., on a bicycle, or with holes in film or tape or paper. ▷ DERAILLEUR. **2** (also **sprock·et wheel**) ▲ a wheel with sprockets.

roller chain

sprocket wheel

sprocket

SPROCKET WHEEL AND CHAIN OF A BICYCLE

sprout /sprowt/ *v. & n.* • *v.* **1** *tr.* put forth; produce (shoots, hair, etc.) (*he had sprouted a mustache*). **2** *intr.* begin to grow; put forth shoots. **3** *intr.* spring up, grow to a height. • *n.* **1** a shoot of a plant. **2** = BRUSSELS SPROUT.

spruce[1] /sproos/ *adj. & v.* • *adj.* neat in dress and appearance; trim; neat and fashionable. • *v.tr. & intr.* (also *refl.*; usu. foll. by *up*) make or become neat and fashionable. □□ **spruce·ly** *adv.* **spruce·ness** *n.*

spruce[2] /sproos/ *n.* **1** ▶ any coniferous tree of the genus *Picea*, with dense foliage growing in a conical shape. **2** the wood of this tree.

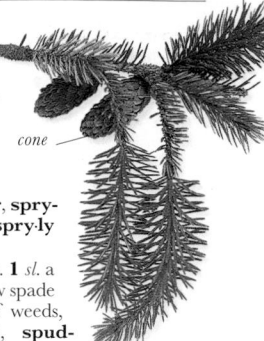

cone

needlelike leaves

SPRUCE (*Picea sitchensis*)

sprung see SPRING.

spry /sprī/ *adj.* (**spryer**, **spryest**) active; lively. □□ **spry·ly** *adv.* **spry·ness** *n.*

spud /spud/ *n. & v.* • *n.* **1** *sl.* a potato. **2** a small narrow spade for cutting the roots of weeds, etc. • *v.tr.* (**spudded**, **spudding**) **1** (foll. by *up*, *out*) remove (weeds) with a spud. **2** (also *absol.*; often foll. by *in*) make the initial drilling for (an oil well).

spue var. of SPEW.

spu·man·te /spōōmáantee, -tay/ *n.* a sweet white Italian sparkling wine.

spume /spyoom/ *n. & v.intr.* froth; foam. □□ **spu·mous** *adj.* **spum·y** *adj.*

spu·mo·ni /spōōmốnee/ *n.* an ice-cream dessert of different colors and flavors, usu. layered, with nuts and candied fruits.

spun *past* and *past part.* of SPIN.

spunk /spungk/ *n.* **1** touchwood. **2** *colloq.* courage; spirit.

spunk·y /spúngkee/ *adj.* (**spunkier**, **spunkiest**) *colloq.* spirited. □□ **spunk·i·ly** *adv.*

spur /spər/ *n. & v.* • *n.* **1** ▶ a device with a small spike or a spiked wheel worn on a rider's heel for urging a horse forward. **2** a stimulus or incentive. **3** a spur-shaped thing, esp.: **a** a projection from a mountain. **b** a branch road or railway. **c** a hard projection on a cock's leg. • *v.* (**spurred**, **spurring**) **1** *tr.* prick (a horse) with spurs. **2** *tr.* **a** (often foll. by *on*) incite (a person). **b** stimulate (interest, etc.). **3** *intr.* (often foll. by *on*, *forward*) ride a horse hard. **4** *tr.* (esp. as **spurred** *adj.*) provide with spurs. □ **on the spur of the moment** on a momentary impulse. □□ **spur·less** *adj.*

spiked wheel

SPUR: AMERICAN HAND-FORGED SPUR

spurge /spərj/ *n.* any plant of the genus *Euphorbia*, exuding an acrid juice.

spu·ri·ous /spyŏ̄ōreeəs/ *adj.* **1** not genuine; not being what it purports to be (*a spurious excuse*). **2** having an outward similarity of form or function only. **3** (of offspring) illegitimate. □□ **spu·ri·ous·ly** *adv.* **spu·ri·ous·ness** *n.*

spurn /spərn/ *v.tr.* **1** reject with disdain; treat with contempt. **2** repel or thrust back with one's foot.

spur-of-the-mo·ment *adj.* unpremeditated.

spur·ry /spóree, spúree/ *n.* (also **spur·rey**) (*pl.* **-ies** or **-eys**) a slender plant of the genus *Spergula*, esp. the corn spurry, a white-flowered weed in fields, etc.

spurt /spərt/ *v. & n.* • *v.* **1** (also **spirt**) **a** *intr.* gush out in a jet or stream. **b** *tr.* cause (liquid, etc.) to do this. **2** *intr.* make a sudden effort. • *n.* **1** (also **spirt**) a sudden gushing out; a jet. **2** a short sudden effort or increase of pace, esp. in racing.

sput·nik /spŏ̄ŏtnik, spút-/ *n.* ▶ each of a series of Russian artificial satellites that was launched from 1957.

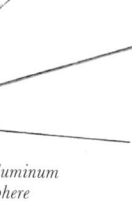

aluminum sphere

antenna

SPUTNIK

S

sput·ter /spútər/ v. & n. ● v. **1** intr. emit spitting sounds, esp. when being heated. **2** intr. (often foll. by *at*) speak in a hurried or vehement fashion. **3** tr. emit with a spitting sound. **4** tr. speak or utter rapidly or incoherently. ● n. a sputtering sound, esp. sputtering speech. □□ **sput·ter·er** n.

spu·tum /spyoőotəm/ n. (pl. **sputa** /-tə/) **1** saliva; spittle. **2** a mixture of saliva and mucus expectorated from the respiratory tract, usu. a sign of disease.

spy /spī/ n. & v. ● n. (pl. **spies**) **1** a person who secretly collects and reports information on the activities, etc., of an enemy, competitor, etc. **2** a person who keeps watch on others, esp. furtively. ● v. (**spies**, **spied**) **1** tr. discern or make out, esp. by careful observation. **2** intr. (often foll. by *on*) act as a spy; keep a close and secret watch. **3** intr. (often foll. by *into*) pry. □ **spy out** explore or discover, esp. secretly.

spy·glass /spíglas/ n. a small telescope.

spy·hole /spíhōl/ n. a peephole.

sq. abbr. square.

squab /skwob/ n. & adj. ● n. **1** a short fat person. **2** a young, esp. unfledged, pigeon or other bird. **3** a stuffed cushion. **4** a sofa. ● adj. squat.

squab·ble /skwóbəl/ n. & v. ● n. a petty or noisy quarrel. ● v.intr. engage in a squabble. □□ **squab·bler** n.

squab·by /skwóbee/ adj. (**squabbier**, **squabbiest**) short and fat; squat.

squad /skwod/ n. **1** a small group of people sharing a task, etc. **2** Mil. a small number of soldiers assembled for drill, etc. **3** Sports a group of players forming a team. **4** (often in comb.) a specialized unit within a police force (drug squad).

squad car n. a police car having a radio link with headquarters.

squad·ron /skwódrən/ n. **1** an organized body of persons. **2** a principal division of a cavalry regiment or armored formation, consisting of two troops. **3** a detachment of warships employed on a particular duty. **4** a unit of the US Air Force with two or more flights.

squal·id /skwólid/ adj. **1** repulsively dirty. **2** degraded or poor in appearance. **3** wretched; sordid. □□ **squa·lid·i·ty** n. /-líditee/ **squal·id·ly** adv. **squal·id·ness** n.

squall /skwawl/ n. & v. ● n. **1** a sudden or violent gust or storm of wind, esp. with rain or snow or sleet. **2** a discordant cry; a scream. **3** (esp. in pl.) trouble; difficulty. ● v. **1** intr. utter a squall; scream. **2** tr. utter in a screaming or discordant voice. □□ **squall·y** adj.

squal·or /skwólər/ n. the state of being filthy or squalid.

squa·ma /skwáymə/ n. (pl. **squamae** /-mee/) **1** a scale on an animal or plant. **2** a thin scalelike plate of bone. **3** a scalelike feather. □□ **squa·mate** /-mayt/ adj. **squa·mose** adj. **squa·mous** adj. **squa·mule** n.

squan·der /skwóndər/ v.tr. spend wastefully. □□ **squan·der·er** n.

square /skwair/ n., adj., adv., & v. ● n. **1** an equilateral rectangle. **2 a** an object of this shape or approximately this shape. **b** a small square area on a game board. **c** a square scarf. **3 a** an open (usu. four-sided) area surrounded by buildings. **b** an open area at the meeting of streets. **c** an area within barracks, etc., for drill. **d** a block of buildings bounded by four streets. **4** the product of a number multiplied by itself (81 is the square of 9). **5** an L-shaped or T-shaped instrument for obtaining or testing right angles. **6** sl. a conventional or old-fashioned person. **7** a square arrangement of letters, figures, etc. **8** a body of infantry drawn up in rectangular form. ● adj. **1** having the shape of a square. **2** having or in the form of a right angle (table with square corners). **3** angular and not round (a square jaw).

4 designating a unit of measure equal to the area of a square whose side is one of the unit specified (square meter). **5** (often foll. by with) **a** level; parallel. **b** on a proper footing; even. **6** (usu. foll. by to) at right angles. **7** having the breadth more nearly equal to the height than is usual (a man of square frame). **8** properly arranged; settled (get things square). **9** (also **all square**) **a** not in debt; with no money owed. **b** having equal scores. **c** (of scores) equal. **10** fair and honest. **11** uncompromising; direct. (a square refusal). **12** sl. conventional or old-fashioned. ● adv. **1** squarely (sat square on her seat). **2** fairly; honestly (play square). ● v. **1** tr. make square or rectangular; give a rectangular cross-section to (timber, etc.). **2** tr. multiply (a number) by itself (3 squared is 9). **3** tr. & intr. (usu. foll. by to, with) make or be suitable or consistent (the results do not square with your conclusions). **4** tr. mark out in squares. **5** tr. settle or pay (a bill, etc.). **6** tr. place (one's shoulders, etc.) squarely facing forward. **7** tr. colloq. **a** pay or bribe. **b** secure the acquiescence, etc., of (a person) in this way. **8** tr. (also absol.) make the scores of (a match, etc.) all square. □ **back to square one** colloq. back to the starting point with no progress made. **get square with** pay or compound with (a creditor). **on the square** adj. colloq. honest; fair. ● adv. colloq. honestly; fairly. **out of square** not at right angles. **square peg in a round hole** see PEG. **square up** settle an account, etc. **square up to 1** move toward (a person) in a fighting attitude. **2** face and tackle (a difficulty, etc.) resolutely. □□ **square·ly** adv. **square·ness** n. **squar·ish** adj.

square brack·ets n.pl. brackets of the form [ ].

square dance n. a dance with usu. four couples facing inward from four sides.

square deal n. a fair bargain; fair treatment.

square knot n. ▶ a double knot made symmetrically to hold securely and cast off easily. ▷ KNOT

square meal n. a substantial and satisfying meal.

square meas·ure n. measure expressed in square units.

square num·ber n. the square of an integer e.g., 1, 4, 9, 16.

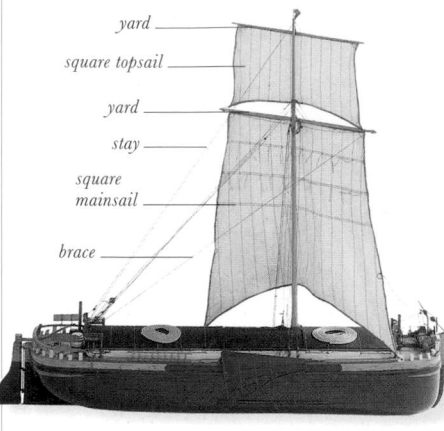

SQUARE-RIGGED 19TH-CENTURY ENGLISH BARGE

square-rigged adj. ▼ with the principal sails at right angles to the length of the ship and extended by horizontal yards slung to the mast by the middle (opp. fore-and-aft rigged (see FORE AND AFT). ▷ SHIP

yard
square topsail
yard
stay
square mainsail
brace

square root n. the number that multiplied by itself gives a specified number (3 is the square root of 9).

square sail n. a four-cornered sail extended on a yard slung to the mast by the middle.

square shoot·er n. a person who is honest, fair, and straightforward.

square-shoul·dered adj. with broad and not sloping shoulders (cf. ROUND-SHOULDERED).

squar·rose /skwáirōs, skwór-/ adj. Bot. & Zool. rough with scalelike projections.

squash[1] /skwosh/ v. & n. ● v. **1** tr. crush or squeeze flat or into pulp. **2** intr. (often foll. by into) make one's way by squeezing. **3** tr. pack tight; crowd. **4** tr. **a** silence (a person) with a crushing retort, etc. **b** dismiss (a proposal, etc.). **c** quash (a rebellion). ● n. **1** a crowd; a crowded assembly. **2** a sound of or as of something being squashed, or of a soft body falling. **3** ▼ a game played with rackets and a small ball against the walls of a closed court. **4** a squashed thing or mass. **5** Brit. a drink made of diluted crushed fruit, etc. □□ **squash·y** adj. (**squashier**, **squashiest**). **squash·i·ly** adv. **squash·i·ness** n.

SQUARE KNOT

SQUASH

Squash players take turns hitting a rubber ball against the front of a four-walled court. The ball is allowed to bounce on the floor only once but may rebound off any of the walls. It is in play when below the out-of-court lines and above the board. To serve, a player stands with part of one foot in the service box and hits the ball above the cut line. The ball must then bounce beyond the short line on the opponent's side of the half-court line.

INTERNATIONAL SQUASH COURT

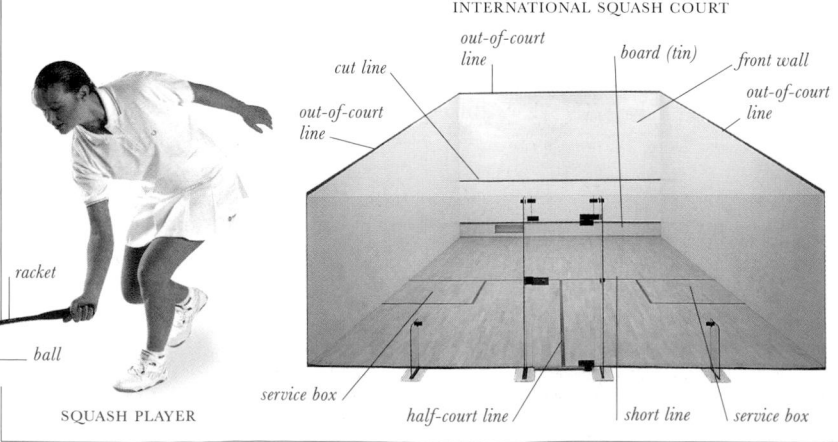

out-of-court line
cut line
board (tin)
front wall
out-of-court line
racket
ball
SQUASH PLAYER
service box
half-court line
short line
service box

S

SQUASH: ACORN
SQUASH
(*Cucurbita pepo*)

squash² /skwosh/ *n.* (*pl.* same or **squashes**) **1** ◄ any of various gourdlike trailing plants of the genus *Cucurbita*, whose fruits may be used as a vegetable. **2** the fruit of these cooked and eaten.

squat /skwot/ *v., adj., & n.* ● *v.* (**squatted, squatting**) **1** *intr.* **a** crouch with the buttocks resting on the backs of the heels. **b** sit on the ground, etc., with the knees drawn up and the heels close to or touching the hams. **2** *intr. colloq.* sit down. **3 a** *intr.* act as a squatter. **b** *tr.* occupy (a building) as a squatter. **4** *intr.* (of an animal) crouch close to the ground. ● *adj.* (**squatter, squattest**) **1** (of a person, etc.) dumpy. **2** in a squatting posture. ● *n.* **1** a squatting posture. **2 a** a place occupied by a squatter or squatters. **b** being a squatter. □□ **squat·ness** *n.*

squat·ter /skwótər/ *n.* **1** a person who takes unauthorized possession of unoccupied premises. **2** a person who settles on new, esp. public, land without title. **3** a person who squats.

squaw /skwaw/ *n.* often *offens.* a Native American woman or wife.

squawk /skwawk/ *n. & v.* ● *n.* **1** a loud harsh cry, esp. of a bird. **2** a complaint. ● *v.tr. & intr.* utter with or make a squawk. □□ **squawk·er** *n.*

squeak /skweek/ *n. & v.* ● *n.* **1 a** a short shrill cry as of a mouse. **b** a slight high-pitched sound as of an unoiled hinge. **2** (also **narrow squeak**) a narrow escape; a success barely attained. ● *v.* **1** *intr.* make a squeak. **2** *tr.* utter shrilly. **3** *intr.* (foll. by *by, through*) *colloq.* pass narrowly. **4** *intr. sl.* turn informer.

squeak·er /skweékər/ *n.* **1** a person or thing that squeaks. **2** a young bird, esp. a pigeon. **3** *colloq.* a close contest.

squeak·y /skweékee/ *adj.* (**squeakier, squeakiest**) making a squeaking sound. □□ **squeak·i·ly** *adv.* **squeak·i·ness** *n.*

squeak·y clean *adj.* **1** completely clean. **2** above criticism; beyond reproach.

squeal /skweel/ *n. & v.* ● *n.* a prolonged shrill sound, esp. a cry of a child or a pig. ● *v.* **1** *intr.* make a squeal. **2** *tr.* utter with a squeal. **3** *intr. sl.* turn informer. **4** *intr. sl.* protest loudly or excitedly. □□ **squeal·er** *n.*

squeam·ish /skweémish/ *adj.* **1** easily nauseated or disgusted. **2** fastidious. □□ **squeam·ish·ly** *adv.* **squeam·ish·ness** *n.*

squee·gee /skweéjee/ *n. & v.* ● *n.* a rubber-edged implement often set on a long handle and used for cleaning windows, etc. ● *v.tr.* (**squeegees, squeegeed**) treat with a squeegee.

squeeze /skweez/ *v. & n.* ● *v.* **1** *tr.* **a** exert pressure on from opposite or all sides, esp. in order to extract moisture or reduce size. **b** compress with one's hand or between two bodies. **c** reduce the size of or alter the shape of by squeezing. **2** *tr.* (often foll. by *out*) extract (moisture) by squeezing. **3 a** *tr.* force into or through a small or narrow space. **b** *intr.* make one's way by squeezing. **c** *tr.* make (one's way) by squeezing. **4** *tr.* **a** harass by exactions; extort money, etc., from. **b** bring pressure to bear on. **c** (usu. foll. by *out of*) obtain (money, etc.) by extortion, entreaty, etc. **5** *tr.* press as a sign of sympathy, etc. **6** *tr.* (often foll. by *out*) produce with effort. ● *n.* **1** an instance of squeezing. **2 a** a close embrace. **b** *sl.* a girlfriend or boyfriend. **3** a crush. **4** a small quantity produced by squeezing (*a squeeze of lemon*). **5** *Econ.* a restriction on borrowing, investment, etc., in a financial crisis. **6** *Baseball* bunting a ball to the infield to enable a runner on third base to start for home as soon as the ball is pitched. □ **put the squeeze on** *colloq.* coerce or pressure (a person). □□ **squeez·a·ble** *adj.* **squeez·er** *n.*

squeeze box *n. colloq.* an accordion or concertina.

squelch /skwelch/ *v. & n.* ● *v.* **1** *intr.* **a** make a sucking sound as of treading in thick mud. **b** move with a squelching sound. **2** *tr.* **a** disconcert; silence. **b** stamp on; put an end to. ● *n.* an instance of squelching. □□ **squelch·y** *adj.*

squib /skwib/ *n.* **1** a small firework burning with a hissing sound and usu. with a final explosion. **2** a short satirical composition; a lampoon.

squid /skwid/ *n.* ▼ any of various ten-armed cephalopods, esp. of the genus *Loligo* and other related genera, used as bait or food. ▷ CEPHALOPOD

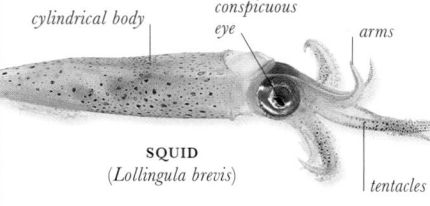

SQUID
(*Lollingula brevis*)

conspicuous
eye
cylindrical body
arms
tentacles

squif·fed /skwift/ *adj. sl.* = SQUIFFY.

squif·fy /skwífee/ *adj.* (**squiffier, squiffiest**) esp. *Brit. sl.* slightly drunk.

squig·gle /skwígəl/ *n. & v.* ● *n.* a short curly line, esp. in handwriting or doodling. ● *v.* **1** *tr.* write in a squiggly manner. **2** *intr.* wriggle. □□ **squig·gly** *adj.*

squill /skwil/ *n.* **1** ► any bulbous plant of the genus *Scilla*. **2** a seashore plant, *Urginea maritima*, having bulbs used in diuretic and purgative preparations.

squinch /skwinch/ *n.* a straight or arched structure across an interior angle of a square tower to carry a superstructure, e.g., a dome.

squint /skwint/ *v., n., & adj.* ● *v.* **1** *intr.* have the eyes turned in different directions; have a squint. **2** *intr.* (often foll. by *at*) look obliquely or with half-closed eyes. **3** *tr.* close (one's eyes) quickly; hold (one's eyes) half shut. ● *n.* **1** = STRABISMUS. **2** a stealthy or sidelong glance. **3** *colloq.* a glance or look (*had a squint at it*). **4** an oblique opening through the wall of a church affording a view of the altar. ● *adj.* **1** squinting. **2** looking different ways. □□ **squint·y** *adj.*

squire /skwīr/ *n. & v.* ● *n.* **1** a country gentleman, esp. the chief landowner in a district. **2** *hist.* a knight's attendant. ● *v.tr.* (of a man) attend upon or escort (a woman). □□ **squire·ling** *n.* **squire·ly** *adj.* **squire·ship** *n.*

squire·ar·chy /skwíraarkee/ *n.* (also **squir·ar·chy**) (*pl.* **-ies**) landowners collectively, esp. as a class having political or social influence.

squirl /skwərl/ *n. colloq.* a flourish or twirl, esp. in handwriting.

squirm /skwərm/ *v. & n.* ● *v.intr.* **1** wriggle; writhe. **2** show or feel embarrassment or discomfiture. ● *n.* a squirming movement. □□ **squirm·er** *n.* **squirm·y** *adj.* (**squirmier, squirmiest**).

squir·rel /skwə́rəl, skwúr-/ *n. & v.* ● *n.* **1** any rodent of the family Sciuridae, often of arboreal habits, with a bushy tail. ▷ RODENT. **2** the fur of this animal. **3** a person who hoards objects, food, etc. ● *v.* (**squirreled** or **squirrelled, squirreling** or **squirrelling**) *tr.* (often foll. by *away*) hoard (objects, food, time, etc.)

squir·rel·ly /skwə́rəlee, skwúr-/ *adj.* **1** like a squirrel. **2** nervous.

squir·rel-mon·key *n.* ► a small yellow-haired monkey, *Saimiri sciureus*, native to S. America.

SQUILL: SIBERIAN SQUILL
(*Scilla siberica*)

squirt /skwərt/ *v. & n.* ● *v.* **1** *tr.* eject (liquid or powder) in a jet as from a syringe. **2** *intr.* (of liquid or powder) be discharged in this way. **3** *tr.* splash with liquid or powder ejected by squirting. ● *n.* **1 a** a jet of water, etc. **b** a small quantity produced by squirting. **2** a syringe. **3** *colloq.* an insignificant but presumptuous person. □□ **squirt·er** *n.*

squish /skwish/ *n. & v.* ● *n.* a slight squelching sound. ● *v.* **1** *intr.* move with a squish. **2** *tr. colloq.* squash; squeeze. □□ **squish·y** *adj.* (**squishier, squishiest**)

squitch /skwich/ *n.* couch grass.

squiz /skwiz/ *n. Austral. & NZ sl.* a look or glance.

Sr *symb. Chem.* the element strontium.

Sr. *abbr.* **1** Senior. **2** Señor. **3** Signor. **4** *Eccl.* Sister.

Sri Lan·kan /shree lángkən, sree/ *n. & adj.* ● *n.* **1** a native or inhabitant of Sri Lanka (formerly Ceylon), an island in the Indian Ocean. **2** a person of Sri Lankan descent. ● *adj.* of or relating to Sri Lanka or its people.

SRO *abbr.* standing room only.

SS *abbr.* **1** steamship. **2** Saints. **3** *hist.* Nazi special police force.

SSA *abbr.* Social Security Administration.

SSE *abbr.* south-southeast.

SST *abbr.* supersonic transport.

SSW *abbr.* south-southwest.

St. *abbr.* **1** Street. **2** Saint.

st. *abbr.* **1** stanza. **2** state. **3** statute. **4** stone (in weight).

sta. *abbr.* station.

stab /stab/ *v. & n.* ● *v.* (**stabbed, stabbing**) **1** *tr.* pierce or wound with a pointed tool or weapon. **2** *intr.* (often foll. by *at*) aim a blow with such a weapon. **3** *intr.* cause a sensation like being stabbed (*stabbing pain*). **4** *tr.* hurt or distress (a person, feelings, conscience, etc.). ● *n.* **1 a** an instance of stabbing. **b** a blow or thrust made with a knife, etc. **2** a wound made in this way. **3** a sharply painful physical or mental sensation. **4** *colloq.* an attempt; a try. □ **stab in the back** *n.* a treacherous or slandrous attack. ● *v.tr.* slander or betray. □□ **stab·ber** *n.*

sta·bile /stáybeel, -bil/ *n.* a rigid, freestanding abstract sculpture or structure of wire, sheet metal, etc.

sta·bil·i·ty /stəbílitee/ *n.* the quality or state of being stable.

sta·bi·lize /stáybilīz/ *v.tr. & intr.* make or become stable. □□ **sta·bi·li·za·tion** *n.*

sta·bi·liz·er /stáybilīzər/ *n.* a device or substance used to keep something stable, esp.: **1** a gyroscope device to prevent rolling of a ship. **2** the horizontal airfoil in the tail assembly of an aircraft.

sta·ble¹ /stáybəl/ *adj.* (**stabler, stablest**) **1** firmly fixed or established; not easily adjusted, destroyed, or altered (*a stable structure; a stable government*). **2 a** firm; resolute; not wavering or fickle (*a stable and steadfast friend*). **b** sane; sensible. **3** *Chem.* (of a compound) not readily decomposing. **4** *Physics* (of an isotope) not subject to radioactive decay. □□ **sta·bly** *adv.*

sta·ble² /stáybəl/ *n. & v.* ● *n.* **1** a building for keeping horses. **2** an establishment where racehorses are kept and trained. **3** the racehorses of a particular stable. **4** persons, products, etc., having a common origin or affiliation. **5** such an origin or affiliation. ● *v.tr.* put or keep (a horse) in a stable. □□ **sta·ble·ful** *n.* (*pl.* **-fuls**)

sta·ble·man /stáybəlmən/ *n.* (*pl.* **-men**; *fem.* **stablewoman**, *pl.* **-women**) a person employed in a stable.

SQUIRREL-MONKEY
(*Saimiri sciureus*)

S

sta·bling /stáybling/ *n.* accommodation for horses.

stab·lish /stáblish/ *v.tr. archaic* fix firmly; establish; set up.

stac·ca·to /stəkaatō/ *adv., adj., & n. esp. Mus.* ● *adv. & adj.* with each sound or note sharply detached or separated from the others. ● *n.* (*pl.* **-os**) **1** a staccato passage in music, etc. **2** staccato delivery or presentation.

stack /stak/ *n. & v.* ● *n.* **1** a pile or heap, esp. in orderly arrangement. **2** a circular or rectangular pile of hay, straw, etc., or of grain in sheaf, often with a sloping thatched top. **3** *colloq.* a large quantity. **4 a** a number of chimneys in a group. **b** = SMOKESTACK. **c** a tall factory chimney. **5** a stacked group of aircraft. **6** (also **stacks**) a part of a library where books are compactly stored. **7** *Computing* a set of storage locations which store data in such a way that the most recently stored item is the first to be retrieved. ● *v.tr.* **1** pile in a stack. **2 a** arrange (cards) secretly for cheating. **b** manipulate (circumstances, etc.) to one's advantage. **3** cause (aircraft) to fly round the same point at different levels while waiting to land at an airport. □ **stack up** *colloq.* present oneself; measure up. □□ **stack·a·ble** *adj.* **stack·er** *n.*

stac·te /stáktee/ *n.* a sweet spice used by the ancient Jews in making incense.

stad·dle /stádəl/ *n.* a platform or framework supporting a rick, etc.

sta·di·um /stáydeeəm/ *n.* (*pl.* **stadiums**) an athletic or sports arena with tiers of seats for spectators.

stadt·hold·er /staádhōldər, staát-/ *n.* (also **stad·hold·er**) *hist.* **1** the chief magistrate of the United Provinces of the Netherlands. **2** the viceroy or governor of a province or town in the Netherlands. □□ **stadt·hold·er·ship** *n.*

staff /staf/ *n. & v.* ● *n.* **1 a** a stick or pole for use in walking or climbing or as a weapon. **b** a stick or pole as a sign of office or authority. **c** a flagstaff. **2 a** a body of persons employed in a business, etc. (*editorial staff of a newspaper*). **b** those in authority within an organization, esp. the teachers in a school. **c** *Mil.*, etc., a body of officers assisting an officer in high command and concerned with an army, regiment, fleet, or air force as a whole (*general staff*). **3** (*pl.* **staffs** or **staves** /stayvz/) *Mus.* a set of usu. five parallel lines on or between which notes are placed to indicate their pitch. ▷ NOTATION. ● *v.tr.* provide (an institution, etc.) with staff. □□ **staffed** *adj.* (also in *comb.*).

staf·fage /stəfaazh/ *n.* accessory items in a painting, esp. figures or animals in a landscape picture.

staff·er /stáfər/ *n.* a member of a staff, esp. of a newspaper.

S

stag /stag/ *n., adj., & v.* ● *n.* **1** an adult male deer, esp. one with a set of antlers. **2** a man who attends a social gathering unaccompanied by a woman. ● *adj.* **1** for men only, as a party. **2** intended for men only, esp. pornographic material. **3** unaccompanied by a date. ● *v.tr.* (**stagged**, **stagging**) to attend a gathering unaccompanied.

stag bee·tle *n.* ▶ any beetle of the family Lucanidae, the male of which has large branched mandibles resembling a stag's antlers. ▷ BEETLE

stage /stayj/ *n. & v.* ● *n.* **1** a point or period in a process or development (*is in the larval stage*). **2 a** a raised floor or platform, esp. one on which plays, etc., are performed. ▷ AUDITORIUM, THEATER. **b** (prec. by *the*) the theatrical profession. **c** the scene of action. **d** = LANDING STAGE. **3 a** a regular stopping place on a route. **b** the distance between two stopping places. **4** a section of a rocket with a separate engine. ● *v.tr.* **1** present (a play, etc.) on stage. **2** arrange the occurrence of (*staged a demonstration*). □ **go on the stage** become an actor. **hold the stage** dominate a conversation, etc. **set the stage for** prepare the way for; provide the basis for.

antlerlike jaws

STAG BEETLE
(*Lucanus cervus*)

stage·craft /stáyjkraft/ *n.* skill or experience in writing or staging plays.

stage door *n.* an actors' and workers' entrance from the street to a theater behind the stage.

stage fright *n.* nervousness on facing an audience, esp. for the first time.

stage·hand /stáyjhand/ *n.* a person handling scenery, etc., during a performance on stage.

stage name *n.* a name assumed for professional purposes by an actor.

stage-struck *adj.* filled with an inordinate desire to go on the stage.

stag·ey var. of STAGY.

stag·fla·tion /stagfláyshən/ *n. Econ.* a state of inflation without a corresponding increase of demand and employment.

stag·ger /stágər/ *v. & n.* ● *v.* **1 a** *intr.* walk unsteadily; totter. **b** *tr.* cause to totter (*was staggered by the blow*). **2 a** *tr.* shock; confuse. **b** *intr.* waver in purpose. **3** *tr.* arrange (events, hours of work, etc.) so that they do not coincide. **4** *tr.* arrange (objects) so that they are not in line. ● *n.* **1** a tottering movement. **2** (in *pl.*) **a** a disease of the brain and spinal cord, esp. in horses and cattle, causing staggering. **b** giddiness. **3** an overhanging or zigzag arrangement of like parts in a structure, etc. □□ **stag·ger·er** *n.*

stag·ger·ing /stágəring/ *adj.* **1** astonishing; bewildering. **2** that staggers. □□ **stag·ger·ing·ly** *adv.*

stag·hound /stághownd/ *n.* any large dog of a breed used for hunting deer by sight or scent.

stag·ing /stáyjing/ *n.* **1** the presentation of a play, etc. **2** a platform or support or scaffolding, esp. temporary.

stag·ing ar·e·a *n.* an intermediate assembly point for troops, etc., in transit.

stag·nant /stágnənt/ *adj.* **1** (of liquid) motionless, having no current. **2** showing no activity, dull, sluggish. □□ **stag·nan·cy** *n.* **stag·nant·ly** *adv.*

stag·nate /stágnayt/ *v.intr.* be stagnant. □□ **stag·na·tion** /-náy-shən/ *n.*

stag·y /stáyjee/ *adj.* (also **stag·ey**) (**stagier**, **stagiest**) theatrical; artificial; exaggerated. □□ **stag·i·ly** *adv.* **stag·i·ness** *n.*

staid /stayd/ *adj.* of quiet and steady character; sedate. □□ **staid·ly** *adv.* **staid·ness** *n.*

stain /stayn/ *v. & n.* ● *v.* **1** *tr. & intr.* discolor or be discolored by the action of liquid sinking in. **2** *tr.* spoil; damage (a reputation, character, etc.). **3** *tr.*

STAGECOACH: 19TH-CENTURY AMERICAN STAGECOACH

stage·coach /stáyjkōch/ *n. hist.* ▼ a large enclosed horse-drawn coach running regularly by stages between two places.

color (wood, glass, etc.) by a process other than painting or covering the surface. **4** *tr.* impregnate (a specimen) for microscopic examination with coloring matter that makes the structure visible. ● *n.* **1** a discoloration, a spot or mark caused esp. by foreign matter and not easily removed. **2 a** a blot or blemish. **b** damage to a reputation, etc. (*a stain on one's character*). **3** a substance used in staining. □□ **stain·a·ble** *adj.* **stain·er** *n.*

stained glass *n.* ◀ dyed or colored glass, esp. in a lead framework in a window (also (with hyphen) *attrib.*: *stained-glass window*).

stain·less /stáynlis/ *adj.* **1** (esp. of a reputation) without stains. **2** not liable to stain.

stain·less steel *n.* chrome steel not liable to rust or tarnish under ordinary conditions.

stair /stair/ *n.* **1** each of a set of fixed steps. **2** (usu. in *pl.*) a set of steps.

stair·case /stáirkays/ *n.* **1** a flight of stairs and the supporting structure. **2** a part of a building containing a staircase.

stair·head /stáirhed/ *n.* a level space at the top of stairs.

stair rod *n.* a rod for securing a carpet against the base of the riser.

stair·way /stáirway/ *n.* **1** a flight of stairs; a staircase. **2** the way up this.

stair·well /stáirwel/ *n.* the shaft in which a staircase is built.

STAINED-GLASS WINDOW, AUGSBURG CATHEDRAL, GERMANY

stake[1] /stayk/ *n. & v.* ● *n.* **1** a stout stick or post sharpened at one end and driven into the ground as a support, boundary mark, etc. **2** *hist.* **a** the post to which a person was tied to be burned alive. **b** (prec. by *the*) death by burning as a punishment (*condemned to the stake*). ● *v.tr.* **1** fasten or support with a stake or stakes. **2** (foll. by *off, out*) mark off (an area) with stakes. **3** state or establish (a claim). □ **stake out** *colloq.* **1** place under surveillance. **2** place (a person) to maintain surveillance.

stake[2] /stayk/ *n. & v.* ● *n.* **1** a sum of money, etc., wagered on an event, esp. deposited with a stakeholder. **2** (often foll. by *in*) an interest or concern, esp. financial. **3** (in *pl.*) **a** money offered as a prize, esp. in a horse race. **b** such a race (*maiden stakes*; *trial stakes*). ● *v.tr.* wager (*staked $5 on the next race*). □ **at stake 1** risked; to be won or lost (*life itself is at stake*). **2** at issue; in question.

stake·hold·er /stáyk-hōldər/ *n.* an independent party with whom each of those who make a wager deposits the money, etc., wagered.

stake·out /stáykowt/ *n. colloq.* a period of surveillance.

Sta·kha·nov·ite /stəkaánəvīt/ *n.* a worker (esp. in

the former USSR) who increases output to an exceptional extent, and so gains special awards.

sta·lac·tite /stəláktīt, stáləkt-/ *n.* a deposit of calcium carbonate having the shape of a large icicle, formed by the trickling of water from the roof of a cave. ▷ CAVE. □□ **sta·lac·tic** /-láktik/ *adj.* **stal·ac·tit·ic** /-títik/ *adj.*

sta·lag /stáalaag, stálag/ *n. hist.* a German prison camp, esp. for noncommissioned officers and privates.

sta·lag·mite /stəlágmīt, stáləg-/ *n.* a deposit of calcium carbonate formed by the dripping of water into the shape of a large inverted icicle rising from the floor of a cave, etc., often uniting with a stalactite. ▷ CAVE. □□ **stal·ag·mit·ic** /-mítik/ *adj.*

stale[1] /stayl/ *adj. & v.* ● *adj.* (**staler**, **stalest**) **1 a** not fresh; not quite new (*stale bread*). **b** musty, insipid, or otherwise the worse for age or use. **2** trite or unoriginal (*a stale joke*). **3** (of an athlete or other performer) having ability impaired by excessive exertion or practice. ● *v.tr. & intr.* make or become stale. □□ **stale·ness** *n.*

stale[2] /stayl/ *n. & v.* ● *n.* the urine of horses and cattle. ● *v.intr.* (esp. of horses and cattle) urinate.

stale·mate /stáylmayt/ *n. & v.* ● *n.* **1** *Chess* a position counting as a draw, in which a player is not in check but cannot move except into check. **2** a deadlock or drawn contest. ● *v.tr.* **1** *Chess* bring (a player) to a stalemate. **2** bring to a standstill.

Sta·lin·ism /staálinizəm/ *n.* **1** the policies followed by Stalin in the government of the former USSR, esp. centralization, totalitarianism, and the pursuit of socialism. **2** any rigid centralized authoritarian form of socialism. □□ **Sta·lin·ist** *n.*

stalk[1] /stawk/ *n.* **1** the main stem of a herbaceous plant. **2** the slender attachment or support of a leaf, flower, fruit, etc. **3** a similar support for an organ, etc., in an animal. **4** a slender support or linking shaft in a machine, object, etc., e.g., the stem of a wineglass. □□ **stalked** *adj.* (also in *comb.*). **stalk·less** *adj.* **stalk·like** *adj.* **stalk·y** *adj.*

stalk[2] /stawk/ *v. & n.* ● *v.* **1** *tr.* pursue or approach (game or an enemy) stealthily. **2** *intr.* stride, walk in a stately or haughty manner. ● *n.* **1** the stalking of game. **2** an imposing gait. □□ **stalk·er** *n.* (also in *comb.*).

stall[1] /stawl/ *n. & v.* ● *n.* **1** a trader's stand or booth in a market, etc. **2 a** a stable or cowhouse. **b** a compartment for one animal in this. **3** a fixed seat in the choir or chancel of a church, more or less enclosed at the back and sides and often canopied. **4 a** a compartment for one person in a shower, toilet, etc. **b** a compartment for one horse at the start of a race. **5 a** the stalling of an engine or aircraft. **b** the condition resulting from this. **6** a receptacle for one object. ● *v.* **1 a** *intr.* (of a motor vehicle or its engine) stop because of an overload on the engine or an inadequate supply of fuel to it. **b** *intr.* (of an aircraft) reach a condition where the speed is too low to allow effective operation of the controls. **c** *tr.* cause (an engine or vehicle or aircraft) to stall. **2** *tr.* put or keep (cattle, etc.) in a stall or stalls.

stall[2] /stawl/ *v.* **1** *intr.* play for time when being questioned, etc. **2** *tr.* delay; obstruct.

stal·lion /stályən/ *n.* an uncastrated adult male horse, esp. for breeding.

stal·wart /stáwlwərt/ *adj. & n.* ● *adj.* **1** strongly built. **2** resolute; determined (*stalwart supporters*). ● *n.* a stalwart person, esp. a loyal uncompromising partisan. □□ **stal·wart·ly** *adv.*

sta·men /stáymən/ *n.* the male fertilizing organ of a flowering plant, including the anther containing pollen. ▷ FLOWER. □□ **stam·i·nif·er·ous** /stáminífərəs/ *adj.*

stam·i·na /stáminə/ *n.* the ability to endure prolonged physical or mental strain.

stam·in·ate /stáminət, -nayt/ *adj.* (of a plant) having stamens, esp. stamens but not pistils.

stam·mer /stámər/ *v. & n.* ● *v.* **1** *intr.* speak with halting articulation, esp. with pauses or rapid repetitions of the same syllable. **2** *tr.* (often foll. by *out*) utter (words) in this way. ● *n.* **1** a tendency to stammer. **2** an instance of stammering. □□ **stam·mer·er** *n.* **stam·mer·ing·ly** *adv.*

stamp /stamp/ *v. & n.* ● *v.* **1 a** *tr.* bring down (one's foot) heavily on the ground, etc. **b** *tr.* crush, flatten, or bring into a specified state in this way (*stamped down the earth around the plant*). **c** *intr.* walk with heavy steps. **2** *tr.* **a** impress (a pattern, mark, etc.) on metal, paper, etc., with a die or similar instrument of metal, wood, rubber, etc. **b** impress (a surface) with a pattern, etc., in this way. **3** *tr.* affix a postage or other stamp to (an envelope or document). **4** *tr.* assign a specific character to; characterize (*stamps the story an invention*). ● *n.* **1** an instrument for stamping a pattern or mark. **2 a** a mark or pattern made by this. **b** the impression of an official mark required to be made on deeds, bills of exchange, etc., as evidence of payment of tax. **3** a small adhesive piece of paper indicating that a price, fee, or tax has been paid, esp. a postage stamp. **4** a mark impressed on or label, etc., affixed to a commodity as evidence of quality, etc. **5 a** a heavy downward blow with the foot. **b** the sound of this. **6** a characteristic mark or impression (*bears the stamp of genius*). □ **stamp on 1** impress (an idea, etc.) on (the memory, etc.). **2** suppress. **stamp out 1** produce by cutting out with a die, etc. **2** put an end to; destroy. □□ **stamp·er** *n.*

stam·pede /stampeéd/ *n. & v.* ● *n.* **1** a sudden flight and scattering of a number of horses, cattle, etc. **2** a sudden flight or hurried movement of people due to interest or panic. **3** the spontaneous response of many persons to a common impulse. **4** *W. US & Canada* a festival combining a rodeo and other events and competitions. ● *v.* **1** *intr.* take part in a stampede. **2** *tr.* cause to do this. **3** *tr.* cause to act hurriedly. □□ **stam·ped·er** *n.*

stamp·ing ground *n.* a favorite haunt or place of action.

stance /stans/ *n.* **1** an attitude or position of the body, esp. when hitting a ball, etc. **2** a standpoint; an attitude of mind.

stanch[1] /stawnch, stanch, staanch/ *v.tr.* (also **staunch**) **1** restrain the flow of (esp. blood). **2** restrain the flow from (esp. a wound).

stanch[2] var. of STAUNCH[1].

stan·chion /stánshən, -chən/ *n.* **1** a post or pillar; an upright support. **2** an upright bar, pair of bars, or frame for confining cattle in a stall.

stand /stand/ *v. & n.* ● *v.* (*past* and *past part.* **stood** /stŏŏd/) **1** *intr.* have or take or maintain an upright position, esp. on the feet or a base. **2** *intr.* be situated or located. **3** *intr.* be of a specified height (*stands six foot three*). **4** *intr.* be in a specified condition (*stands accused*; *the thermometer stood at 90°*). **5** *tr.* place or set in an upright or specified position (*stood it against the wall*). **6** *intr.* **a** move to and remain in a specified position (*stand aside*). **b** take a specified attitude (*stand aloof*). **7** *intr.* maintain a position; avoid falling or moving or being moved. **8** *intr.* assume a stationary position; cease to move. **9** *intr.* remain valid or unaltered; hold good. **10** *intr. Naut.* hold a specified course (*stand in for the shore*). **11** *tr.* endure; tolerate (*cannot stand the pain*; *how can you stand him?*). **12** *tr.* provide for another or others at one's own expense (*stood him a drink*). **13** *intr.* act in a specified capacity (*stood proxy*). **14** *tr.* undergo (trial). ● *n.* **1** a cessation from motion or progress. **2 a** a halt made for the purpose of resistance. **b** resistance to attack or compulsion (esp. *make a stand*). **3 a** a position taken up (*took his stand near the door*). **b** an attitude adopted. **4** a rack, set of shelves, table, etc., on or in which things may be placed. **5** a small open-fronted structure for a trader outdoors or in a market, etc. **6** a standing place for vehicles. **7 a** a raised structure for persons to sit or stand on. **b** a witness box. **8** *Theatr.* each halt made on a tour to give one or more performances. **9** a group of growing plants (*stand of trees*). □ **as it stands 1** in its present condition; unaltered. **2** in the present circumstances. **it stands to reason** see REASON. **stand alone** be unequaled. **stand and deliver!** *hist.* a highwayman's order to hand over valuables, etc. **stand back 1** take up a position further from the front. **2** withdraw psychologically in order to take an objective view. **stand by 1** stand nearby (*will not stand by and see him ill-treated*). **2** uphold; support. **3** adhere to; abide by (terms or promises). **4** *Naut.* stand ready to take hold of or operate (an anchor, etc.). **stand a chance** see CHANCE. **stand corrected** accept correction. **stand down** withdraw from a team, witness box, or similar position. **stand for 1** represent; signify (*"US" stands for "United States"*; *democracy stands for a great deal more than that*). **2** (often with *neg.*) *colloq.* endure, tolerate. **stand one's ground** maintain one's position, not yield. **stand in** (usu. foll. by *for*) deputize; act in place of another. **stand in good stead** see STEAD. **stand off** move or keep away; keep one's distance. **stand on** insist on; observe scrupulously (*stand on ceremony*; *stand on one's dignity*). **stand on one's own (two) feet** be self-reliant or independent. **stand out 1** be prominent or conspicuous or outstanding. **2** (usu. foll. by *against*, *for*) persist in opposition or support or endurance. **stand over 1** stand close to (a person) to watch, control, threaten, etc. **2** be postponed, be left for later settlement, etc. **stand pat** see PAT[2]. **stand to 1** *Mil.* stand ready for an attack (esp. before dawn or after dark). **2** be likely or certain to (*stands to lose everything*). **stand up 1 a** rise to one's feet from a sitting or other position. **b** come to or remain in or place in a standing position. **2** (of an argument, etc.) be valid. **3** *colloq.* fail to keep an appointment with. **stand up for** support; side with; maintain (a person or cause). **stand upon** = *stand on*. **stand up to 1** meet or face (an opponent) courageously. **2** be resistant to the harmful effects of (wear, use, etc.). **stand well** (usu. foll. by *with*) be on good terms or in good repute. **take one's stand on** base one's argument, etc., on; rely on.

stand-a·lone *adj.* (of a computer) operating independently of a network or other system.

stand·ard /stándərd/ *n. & adj.* ● *n.* **1** an object or quality or measure serving as a basis or example or principle to which others conform or should conform or by which others are judged (*by present-day standards*). **2 a** the degree of excellence, etc., required for a particular purpose (*not up to standard*). **b** average quality (*of a low standard*). **3** the ordinary procedure, or quality or design of a product, without added or novel features. **4** ▼ a distinctive flag, esp. the flag of a cavalry regiment as distinct from the *colors* of an infantry regiment. **5 a** an upright support. **b** an upright water or gas pipe. **6 a** a tree or shrub that grows on an erect stem of full height and stands alone without support. **b** a shrub grafted on an upright stem and trained in tree form (*standard rose*). **7** a thing recognized as a model for imitation, etc. **8** a tune or song of established popularity. ● *adj.* **1** serving or used as a standard (*a standard size*). **2** of a normal or prescribed quality or size, etc. **3** having recognized and permanent value (*the standard book on the subject*). **4** (of language) conforming to established educated usage (*Standard English*).

STANDARD: 17TH-CENTURY NORWEGIAN CAVALRY STANDARD

STAR

Stars are created from clouds of gas and dust called nebulae. Regions of higher density inside these clouds collapse under the force of gravity to form protostars. A protostar becomes a main sequence star (like our Sun) when nuclear reactions – hydrogen atoms fusing and forming helium – begin in the star's core. Low-mass and high-mass stars then develop differently. When all the hydrogen in a low-mass star's core has been used, the star expands and its surface cools.

It is then called a red giant and begins to "burn" helium. When an aging red giant blows its outer layer of gas into space, it becomes a planetary nebula. As its core dims and cools, the star becomes first a white dwarf then eventually a black dwarf (when the star stops shining). High-mass stars develop from main sequence stars more quickly, becoming red supergiants. These explode into supernovas, their cores collapsing to form neutron stars or, if sufficiently massive, black holes.

LIFE CYCLE OF A STAR

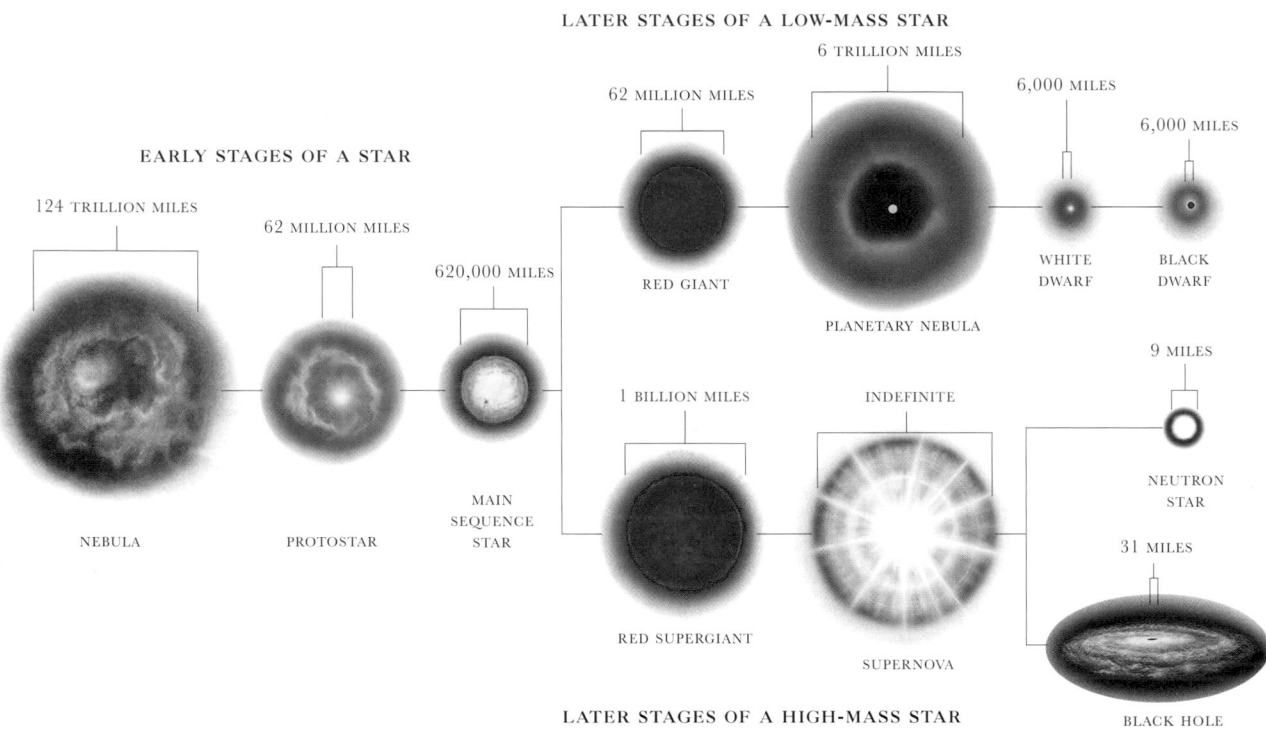

LATER STAGES OF A LOW-MASS STAR

EARLY STAGES OF A STAR

124 TRILLION MILES

62 MILLION MILES

620,000 MILES

62 MILLION MILES

6 TRILLION MILES

6,000 MILES

6,000 MILES

NEBULA   PROTOSTAR   MAIN SEQUENCE STAR

RED GIANT

PLANETARY NEBULA

WHITE DWARF   BLACK DWARF

1 BILLION MILES   INDEFINITE   9 MILLES

RED SUPERGIANT   SUPERNOVA

NEUTRON STAR

31 MILES

BLACK HOLE

LATER STAGES OF A HIGH-MASS STAR

RELATIVE STAR SIZES

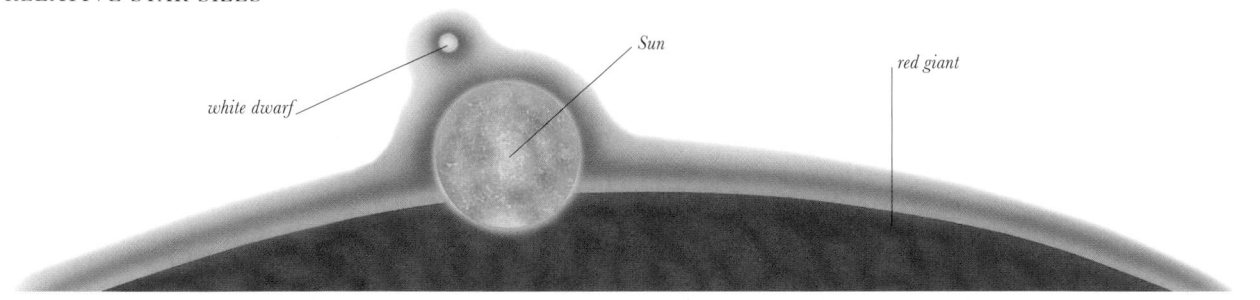

white dwarf   *Sun*   *red giant*

---

stand·ard-bear·er *n.* **1** a soldier who carries a standard. **2** a prominent leader in a cause.

Stan·dard·bred /stándərdbred/ *n.* **1** a horse of an American breed able to attain a specified speed, developed esp. for harness racing. **2** this breed. ▷ HORSE

stan·dard de·vi·a·tion *n. Statistics* a quantity calculated to indicate the extent of deviation for a group as a whole.

stand·ard·ize /stándərdīz/ *v.tr.* cause to conform to a standard. □□ **stand·ard·iz·a·ble** *adj.* **stand·ard·i·za·tion** *n.* **stand·ard·iz·er** *n.*

stand·ard of liv·ing *n.* the degree of material comfort available to a person or class or community.

stand·ard time *n.* a uniform time for places in approximately the same longitude.

stand·by /stándbī/ *n. & adj.* ● *n.* (*pl.* **standbys**) **1** a person or thing ready if needed in an emergency, etc. **2** readiness for duty (*on standby*). ● *adj.* **1** ready for immediate use. **2** (of air travel) not booked in advance but allocated on the basis of earliest availability.

stand·ee /standeé/ *n. colloq.* a person who stands, esp. when all seats are occupied.

stand-in *n.* a deputy or substitute, esp. for an actor when the latter's acting ability is not needed.

stand·ing /stánding/ *n. & adj.* ● *n.* **1** esteem or repute, esp. high; status; position (*people of high standing; is of no standing*). **2** duration (*a dispute of long standing*). **3** length of service, membership, etc. ● *adj.* **1** that stands; upright. **2 a** established; permanent (*a standing rule*). **b** not made, raised, etc.,

for the occasion (*a standing army*). **3** (of a jump, start, race, etc.) performed from rest or from a standing position. **4** (of water) stagnant. **5** (of grain) unreaped. □ **leave a person standing** make far more rapid progress than he or she.

stand·ing com·mit·tee *n.* a committee that is permanent during the existence of the appointing body.

stand·ing joke *n.* an object of permanent ridicule.

stand·off·ish /stándáwfish, -óf-/ *adj.* cold or distant in manner. □□ **stand·off·ish·ly** *adv.* **stand·off·ish·ness** *n.*

stand·out /stándowt/ *n.* a remarkable person or thing.

stand·pipe /stándpīp/ *n.* a vertical pipe extending

S

from a water supply, esp. one connecting a temporary faucet to the main water supply.

stand·point /stándpoynt/ *n.* **1** the position from which a thing is viewed. **2** a mental attitude.

stand·still /stándstil/ *n.* a stoppage; an inability to proceed.

stand-up *attrib.adj.* **1** (of a meal) eaten standing. **2** (of a fight) violent, thorough, or fair and square. **3** (of a collar) upright, not turned down. **4** (of a comedian) performing by standing before an audience and telling jokes.

stan·hope /stánhōp/ *n.* a light open carriage for one with two or four wheels.

stank *past of* STINK.

stan·nic /stánik/ *adj. Chem.* of or relating to tetravalent tin (*stannic acid; stannic chloride*).

stan·nous /stánəs/ *adj. Chem.* of or relating to bivalent tin (*stannous salts; stannous chloride*).

stan·za /stánzə/ *n.* the basic metrical unit in a poem or verse consisting of a recurring group of lines. □□ **stan·za'd** *adj.* (also **stan·zaed**) (also in *comb.*). **stan·za·ic** /-záyik/ *adj.*

sta·pe·li·a /stəpéeleeə/ *n.* ▶ any S. African plant of the genus *Stapelia*, with flowers having an unpleasant smell.

sta·pes /stáypeez/ *n.* (*pl.* same) a small stirrup-shaped bone in the ear of a mammal.

staph·y·lo·coc·cus /stáfiləkókəs/ *n.* (*pl.* **staphylococci** /-kóksī, kókī/) any bacterium of the genus *Staphylococcus*, occurring in grapelike clusters, and sometimes causing pus formation usu. in the skin and mucous membranes of animals. □□ **staph·y·lo·coc·cal** *adj.*

sta·ple[1] /stáypəl/ *n. & v.* ● *n.* a U-shaped metal bar or piece of wire with pointed ends for driving through and clinching papers, netting, electric wire, etc. ● *v.tr.* provide or fasten with a staple. □□ **sta·pler** *n.*

sta·ple[2] /stáypəl/ *n., adj., & v.* ● *n.* **1** a main item of trade or production. **2** the chief element or a main component, e.g., of a diet. **3** a raw material. **4** the fiber of cotton or wool, etc., as determining its quality (*cotton of fine staple*). ● *adj.* **1** main or principal (*staple commodities*). **2** important as a product or an export.

sta·ple gun *n.* a handheld device for driving in staples.

star /staar/ *n. & v.* ● *n.* **1** a celestial body appearing as a luminous point in the night sky. **2** (in full **fixed star**) such a body so far from the Earth as to appear motionless (cf. PLANET, COMET). **3** ◀ a large naturally gaseous body such as the Sun. ▷ SUN. **4** a celestial body regarded as influencing a person's fortunes, etc. (*born under a lucky star*). **5** a thing resembling a star in shape or appearance. **6** a star-shaped mark. **7** a figure or object with radiating points esp. as a mark of rank or excellence. **8 a** a famous or brilliant person; the principal or most prominent performer in a play, movie, etc. (*the star of the show*). **b** (*attrib.*) outstanding; particularly brilliant (*star pupil*). ● *v.* (**starred**, **starring**) **1 a** *tr.* (of a movie, etc.) feature as a principal performer. **b** *intr.* (of a performer) be featured in a movie, etc. **2** (esp. as **starred** *adj.*) **a** mark, set, or adorn with a star or stars. **b** put an asterisk or star beside (a name, an

item in a list, etc.). □□ **star·dom** *n.* **star·less** *adj.* **star·like** *adj.*

star an·ise /staar ánis/ *n.* a small star-shaped fruit with an aniseed flavor, used in Asian cookery.

star ap·ple *n.* an edible, purple, applelike fruit (with a starlike cross section) of a tropical evergreen tree, *chrysophyllum cainito*.

star·board /staarbərd/ *n. & v. Naut. & Aeron.* ● *n.* the right-hand side (looking forward) of a ship, boat, or aircraft (cf. PORT[3]). ● *v.tr.* (also *absol.*) turn (the helm) to starboard.

star·burst *n.* **1 a** a pattern of radiating lines or rays around a central object, light source, etc. **b** an explosion or a lens attachment producing this effect. **2** *Astron.* a period of intense activity, apparently star formation, in certain galaxies.

starch /staarch/ *n. & v.* ● *n.* **1** an odorless, tasteless carbohydrate which is obtained chiefly from cereals and potatoes, forming an important constituent of the human diet. **2** a preparation of this for stiffening fabric. **3** stiffness of manner. ● *v.tr.* stiffen (clothing) with starch. □□ **starch·er** *n.* **starch·y** /staarchee/ *adj.* (**starchier, starchiest**) **1 a** of or like starch. **b** containing much starch. **2** (of a person) overly formal. □□ **starch·i·ly** *adv.* **starch·i·ness** *n.*

star-crossed *adj. archaic* ill-fated.

star·dust /staardəst/ *n.* **1** a twinkling mass. **2** a multitude of stars resembling dust.

stare /stair/ *v. & n.* ● *v.* **1** *intr.* (usu. foll. by *at*) look fixedly with eyes open, esp. as the result of curiosity, surprise, etc. **2** *intr.* (of eyes) be wide open and fixed. **3** *tr.* (foll. by *into*) reduce (a person) to a specified condition by staring (*stared me into silence*). ● *n.* a staring gaze. □□ **stare down** (or **out**) outstare. **stare a person in the face** be obvious. □□ **star·er** *n.*

star·fish /staarfish/ *n.* (*pl.* usu. same) ◀ an echinoderm of the class Asteroidea with five or more radiating arms. ▷ ECHINODERM

star fruit = CARAMBOLA

star·gaze /staargayz/ *v.intr.* **1** gaze at or study the stars. **2** gaze intently.

star·gaz·er /staargayzər/ *n. colloq.* an astronomer or astrologer.

stark /staark/ *adj. & adv.* ● *adj.* **1** desolate; bare (*a stark landscape*). **2** brutally simple. (*in stark contrast; the stark reality*). **3** downright; sheer (*stark madness*). ● *adv.* completely (*stark naked*). □□ **stark·ly** *adv.* **stark·ness** *n.*

Stark effect /staark/ *n. Physics* the splitting of a spectrum line into several components by the application of an electric field.

stark·ers /staarkərz/ *adj. Brit. sl.* stark naked.

star·let /staarlit/ *n.* **1** a promising young performer, esp. a woman. **2** a little star.

star·light /staarlīt/ *n.* **1** the light of the stars (*walked home by starlight*). **2** (*attrib.*) = STARLIT (*a starlight night*).

star·ling /staarling/ *n.* ▶ a small gregarious partly migratory bird, *Sturnus vulgaris*, with blackish-brown speckled iridescent plumage, chiefly inhabiting cultivated areas. ▷ PREEN

star·lit /staarlit/ *adj.* **1** lighted by stars. **2** with stars visible.

star of Beth·le·hem *n.* any of various plants with star-like flowers, esp. *Ornithogalum umbellatum*, with white star-shaped flowers striped with green on the outside.

Star of Da·vid *n.* ▶ a figure consisting of two interlaced equilateral triangles used as a Jewish and Israeli symbol.

star route *n.* a rural mail delivery route served by private contractors.

star·ry /staaree/ *adj.* (**starrier, starriest**) **1** covered with stars. **2** resembling a star. □□ **star·ri·ly** *adv.* **star·ri·ness** *n.*

star·ry-eyed *adj. colloq.* **1** visionary; enthusiastic but impractical. **2** euphoric.

Stars and Bars *n.* the flag of the Confederate States of the US.

Stars and Stripes *n.* ▼ the national flag of the US.

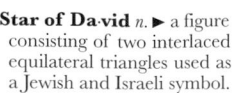
*symbol of
Elephantine Jews*

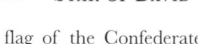
STAR OF DAVID

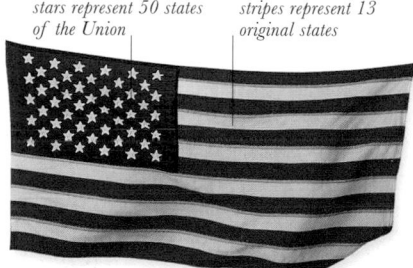

*stars represent 50 states
of the Union*   *stripes represent 13
original states*

STARS AND STRIPES

star sap·phire *n.* ▶ a cabochon sapphire reflecting a starlike image due to its regular internal structure.

star shell *n.* an explosive projectile designed to burst in the air and light up the enemy's position.

star-span·gled *adj.* (esp. of the US national flag) covered or glittering with stars.

star-stud·ded *adj.* containing or covered with many stars, esp. featuring many famous performers.

STAR SAPPHIRE

START /staart/ *abbr* Strategic Arms Reduction Treaty (or Talks).

start /staart/ *v. & n.* ● *v.* **1** *tr. & intr.* begin; commence. **2** *tr.* set (proceedings, an event, etc.) in motion (*start the meeting; started a fire*). **3** *intr.* (often foll. by *on*) make a beginning (*started on a new project*). **4** *intr.* (foll. by *after, for*) set oneself in motion or action ("*wait!*" he shouted, and started after her). **5** *intr.* set out; begin a journey, etc. **6** (often foll. by *up*) **a** *intr.* (of a machine) begin operating. **b** *tr.* cause (a machine, etc.) to begin operating. **7** *tr.* **a** cause or enable (a person) to make a beginning (with something) (*started me in business with $10,000*). **b** (foll. by pres. part.) cause (a person) to begin (doing something) (*the smoke started me coughing*). **8** *tr.* (often foll. by *up*) found or establish; originate. **9** *intr.* (foll. by *at, with*) have as the first of a series of items, e.g., in a meal (*we started with soup*). **10** *tr.* give a signal to (competitors) to start in a race. **11** *tr.* (often foll. by *up, from,* etc.) make a sudden movement from surprise, pain, etc. (*started at the sound of my voice*). **12** *intr.* (foll. by *out, up, from,* etc.) spring out, up, etc. (*started up from the chair*). **13** *tr.* conceive (a baby). **14** *tr.* rouse (game, etc.) from its lair. **15** *intr.* (of boards, etc.) spring from their proper position; give way. ● *n.* **1** a beginning of an event, action, journey, etc. (*missed the start; an early start tomorrow*). **2** the place from which a race, etc., begins. **3** an advantage given at the beginning of a race, etc. (*a 15-second start*). **4** an advantageous initial position in life, business, etc. (*a good start in*

S (large marginal letter)

STARLING
(*Sturnus vulgaris*)

STAPELIA: CARRION FLOWER
(*Stapelia gigantea*)

arm — *madreporite*

anus

STARFISH:
SCARLET STARFISH
(*Henricia sanguinolenta*)

S

life). **5** a sudden jerking movement of surprise, pain, alarm, etc. (*you gave me a start*). **6** an intermittent or spasmodic effort or movement (esp. *in* or *by fits and starts*). □ **for a start** *colloq.* as a beginning; in the first place. **start in** *colloq.* **1** begin. **2** (foll. by *on*) make a beginning on. **start off 1** begin; commence (*started off on a lengthy monologue*). **2** begin to move (*it's time we started off*). **start out 1** begin a journey. **2** *colloq.* (foll. by *to* + infin.) proceed as intending (to do something). **start over** begin again. **start up** arise; occur. **to start with 1** in the first place; before anything else is considered. **2** at the beginning.

start·er /staártər/ *n.* **1** a person or thing that starts. **2** an esp. automatic device for starting the engine of a motor vehicle, etc. **3** a person giving the signal for the start of a race. **4** a horse or competitor starting in a race. **5** *Baseball* **a** the pitcher who pitches first in a game. **b** a pitcher who normally starts games. □ **for starters** *sl.* to start with. **under starter's orders** (of racehorses, etc.) in a position to start a race and awaiting the starting signal.

start·ing block *n.* /staárting/ ▼ a shaped rigid block for bracing the feet of a runner at the start of a race.

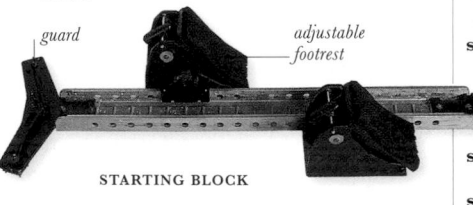

guard   *adjustable footrest*

STARTING BLOCK

start·ing gate *n.* a movable barrier for securing a fair start in horse races.

start·ing pis·tol *n.* ► a pistol used to give the signal for the start of a race.

start·ing point *n.* the point from which a journey, process, argument, etc., begins.

start·ing post *n.* the post from which competitors start in a race.

start·ing price *n.* the odds ruling at the start of a horse race.

STARTING PISTOL

start·ing stall *n.* a compartment for one horse at the start of a race.

star·tle /staárt'l/ *v.tr.* give a shock or surprise to; cause (a person, etc.) to start with surprise or sudden alarm. □□ **star·tler** *n.*

star·tling /staártling/ *adj.* **1** surprising. **2** alarming. □□ **star·tling·ly** *adv.*

starve /staarv/ *v.* **1** *intr.* die of hunger; suffer from malnourishment. **2** *tr.* cause to die of hunger or suffer from lack of food. **3** *intr. colloq.* (esp. as **starved** or **starving** *adj.*) feel very hungry (*I'm starving*). **4** *intr.* **a** suffer from mental or spiritual want. **b** (foll. by *for*) feel a strong craving for (sympathy, amusement, knowledge, etc.). **5** *tr.* **a** (foll. by *for, of*) deprive of; keep scantily supplied with (*starved for affection*). **b** cause to suffer from mental or spiritual want. **6** *tr.* **a** (foll. by *into*) compel by starving (*starved into submission*). **b** (foll. by *out*) compel to surrender, etc., by starving (*starved them out*). **7** *intr. archaic* or *dial.* perish with or suffer from cold. □□ **star·va·tion** /-váyshən/ *n.*

starve·ling /staárvling/ *n. & adj. archaic* ● *n.* a starving or ill-fed person or animal. ● *adj.* starving.

star·wort /staárwərt, -wawrt/ *n.* a plant of the genus *Stellaria* with starlike flowers.

Star Wars *n. colloq.* the strategic defense initiative of the US, begun in 1984.

stash /stash/ *v. & n. colloq.* ● *v.tr.* (often foll. by *away*) **1** conceal; put in a safe or hidden place. **2** hoard; stow. ● *n.* **1** a hiding place. **2** a thing hidden.

sta·sis /stáysis, stásis/ *n.* (*pl.* **stases** /-seez/) **1** inactivity; stagnation; a state of equilibrium. **2** a stoppage of circulation of any of the body fluids.

-stasis /stásis, stáysis/ *comb. form* (*pl.* **-stases** /-seez/) *Physiol.* forming nouns denoting a slowing or stopping (*hemostasis*). □□ **-static** *comb. form* forming adjectives.

-stat /stat/ *comb. form* forming nouns with ref. to keeping fixed or stationary (*rheostat*).

stat. *abbr.* **1** at once. **2** statistics. **3** statute.

state /stayt/ *n. & v.* ● *n.* **1** the existing condition or position of a person or thing (*in a bad state of repair; in a precarious state of health*). **2** *colloq.* **a** an excited, anxious, or agitated mental condition (esp. *in a state*). **b** an untidy condition. **3 a** an organized political community under one government; a commonwealth; a nation. **b** such a community forming part of a federal republic, esp. the United States of America. **c** (**the States**) the US. **4** (*attrib.*) **a** of, for, or concerned with the state (*state documents*). **b** reserved for or done on occasions of ceremony (*state apartments; state visit*). **5** (also **State**) civil government (*church and state; Secretary of State*). **6 a** pomp; rank; dignity (*as befits their state*). **b** imposing display; ceremony; splendor (*arrived in state*). ● *v.tr.* **1** express, formally or clearly, in speech or writing (*have stated my opinion*). **2** fix; specify (*at stated intervals*). □ **in state** with all due ceremony. **of state** concerning politics or government. □□ **stat·a·ble** *adj.* **state·hood** *n.*

state·craft /stáytkraft/ *n.* the art of conducting affairs of state.

State De·part·ment *n.* the federal government department concerned with foreign affairs.

state·hood /stáythŏod/ *n.* the condition or status of being a state, esp. a state of the United States.

state house *n.* the building where the legislature of a state meets.

state·less /stáytlis/ *adj.* **1** (*of a person*) having no nationality or citizenship. **2** without a state. □□ **state·less·ness** *n.*

state·ly /stáytlee/ *adj.* (**statelier, stateliest**) dignified; imposing; grand. □□ **state·li·ness** *n.*

state·ly home *n. Brit.* a large magnificent house, esp. one open to the public.

state·ment /stáytmənt/ *n.* **1** the act or an instance of stating or being stated; expression in words. **2** a thing stated; a declaration (*that statement is unfounded*). **3** a formal account of facts, esp. to the police or in a court of law (*make a statement*). **4** a record of transactions in a bank account, etc. **5** a formal notification of an amount due.

state of the art *n. & adj.* ● *n.* the current stage of development of a practical or technological subject. ● *adj.* (usu. **state-of-the-art**) (*attrib.*) using the latest techniques or equipment (*state-of-the-art weaponry*).

sta·ter /stáytər/ *n.* an ancient Greek gold or silver coin.

state·room /stáytrōŏm, -rŏŏm/ *n.* **1** a private compartment in a passenger ship or train. **2** a state apartment in a palace, hotel, etc.

state's ev·i·dence *n. Law* evidence for the prosecution given by a participant in or accomplice to the crime at issue.

state·side /stáytsīd/ *adj. colloq.* of, in, or toward the United States.

states·man /stáytsmən/ *n.* (*pl.* **-men**; *fem.* **stateswoman**, *pl.* **-women**) **1** a person skilled in affairs of state, esp. one taking an active part in politics. **2** a distinguished and capable politician. □□ **states·man·like** *adj.* **states·man·ly** *adj.* **states·man·ship** *n.*

state so·cial·ism *n.* a system of state control of industries and services.

states' rights *n.pl.* the rights and powers not assumed by the federal government of the United States but reserved to its individual states.

state u·ni·ver·si·ty *n.* a university managed by the public authorities of a state.

state·wide /stáytwīd/ *adj.* so as to include or cover a whole state.

stat·ic /státik/ *adj. & n.* ● *adj.* **1** stationary; not acting or changing. **2** *Physics* **a** concerned with bodies at rest or forces in equilibrium (opp. DYNAMIC). **b** acting as weight but not moving (*static pressure*). **c** of statics. ● *n.* **1** static electricity. **2** electrical disturbances in the atmosphere or the interference with telecommunications caused by this.

stat·i·cal /státikəl/ *adj.* = STATIC. □□ **stat·i·cal·ly** *adv.*

stat·ice /státisee, státis/ *n.* **1** sea lavender. **2** sea pink.

stat·ic e·lec·tric·i·ty *n.* ▼ electricity not flowing as a current but produced by friction.

STATIC ELECTRICITY

The buildup of charged particles in one location is called static electricity. When, for example, a plastic rod is rubbed against a sweater, the rod picks up electrons (the negatively charged particles in an atom) from the sweater and becomes charged with static electricity. Touching the rod to the top of an electroscope, as shown below, causes the electricity to discharge: electrons flow down the central strip. Because like charges repel, the rod's electrons and the gold leaf's electrons move apart, causing the gold leaf to rise.

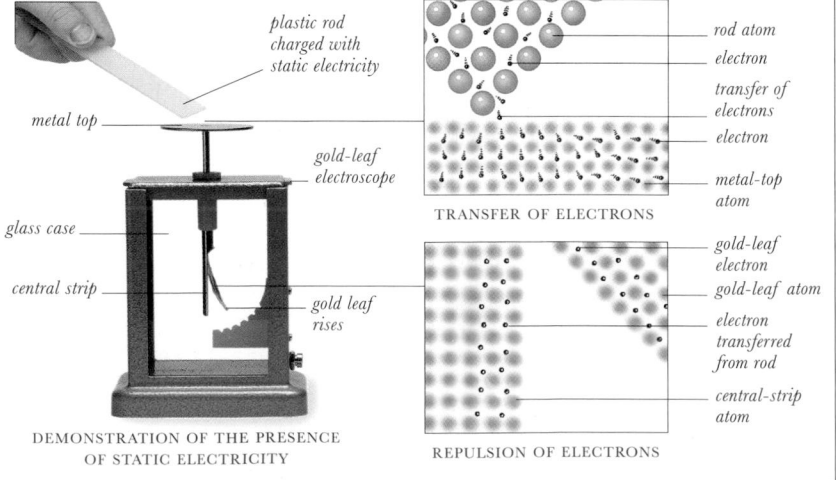

plastic rod charged with static electricity

metal top

gold-leaf electroscope

glass case

central strip

gold leaf rises

DEMONSTRATION OF THE PRESENCE
OF STATIC ELECTRICITY

rod atom
electron
transfer of electrons
electron
metal-top atom

TRANSFER OF ELECTRONS

gold-leaf electron
gold-leaf atom
electron transferred from rod
central-strip atom

REPULSION OF ELECTRONS

stat·ics /státiks/ *n.pl.* (usu. treated as *sing.*) **1** the science of bodies at rest or of forces in equilibrium (cf. DYNAMICS). **2** = STATIC.

sta·tion /stáyshən/ *n. & v.* ● *n.* **1 a** a regular stopping place on a railroad line. **b** these buildings (see also BUS STATION). **2** a place or building, etc., where a person or thing stands or is placed, esp. habitually or for a definite purpose. **3** a designated point or establishment where a particular service or activity is based or organized (*police station*; *polling station*). **4** an establishment involved in radio or television broadcasting. **5** a military or naval base. **6** position in life; rank or status (*ideas above your station*). ● *v.tr.* **1** assign a station to. **2** put in position.

sta·tion·ar·y /stáyshəneree/ *adj.* **1** not moving (*a stationary car*). **2** not meant to be moved; not portable (*stationary troops*; *stationary engine*). **3** not changing in magnitude, number, quality, efficiency, etc. (*stationary temperature*). **4** (*of a planet*) having no apparent motion in longitude. □□ **sta·tion·ar·i·ness** *n.*

sta·tion break *n.* a pause between or within broadcast programs for an announcement of the identity of the station transmitting them.

sta·tion·er /stáyshənər/ *n.* a person who sells writing materials, etc.

sta·tion·er·y /stáyshəneree/ *n.* writing materials such as paper, pens, etc.

sta·tion·mas·ter /stáyshənmastər/ *n.* the official in charge of a railroad station.

sta·tion of the cross *n.pl. RC Ch., Anglican Ch.* each of a series of usu. 14 images or pictures, representing the events in Christ's passion.

sta·tion wag·on *n.* a car with passenger seating and storage or extra seating area in the rear, accessible by a rear door. ▷ CAR

stat·ism /stáytizəm/ *n.* centralized government administration and control of social and economic affairs.

stat·ist /státist, stáytist/ *n.* **1** a statistician. **2** a supporter of statism.

sta·tis·tic /stətístik/ *n. & adj.* ● *n.* a statistical fact. ● *adj.* = STATISTICAL.

sta·tis·ti·cal /stətístikəl/ *adj.* of or relating to statistics. □□ **sta·tis·ti·cal·ly** *adv.*

sta·tis·tics /stətístiks/ *n.pl.* **1** (usu. treated as *sing.*) the science of collecting and analyzing numerical data. **2** any systematic collection or presentation of such facts. □□ **stat·is·ti·cian** /statistíshən/ *n.*

sta·tor /stáytər/ *n. Electr.* the stationary part of a machine, esp. of an electric motor or generator.

sta·to·scope /státəskōp/ *n.* an aneroid barometer used to show minute variations of pressure, esp. to indicate the altitude of an aircraft.

stat·u·ar·y /stáchōōeree/ *adj. & n.* ● *adj.* of or for statues (*statuary art*). ● *n.* (*pl.* **-ies**) **1** statues collectively. **2** the art of making statues.

stat·ue /stáchōō/ *n.* a sculptured, cast, carved, or molded figure of a person or animal, esp. life-size or larger (cf. STATUETTE). □□ **stat·ued** *adj.*

stat·u·esque /stáchōō-ésk/ *adj.* like, or having the dignity or beauty of, a statue. □□ **stat·u·esque·ly** *adv.*

stat·u·ette /stáchōō-ét/ *n.* a small statue; a statue less than life-size.

stat·ure /stáchər/ *n.* **1** the height of a (human) body. **2** a degree of eminence, social standing, or advancement. □□ **stat·ured** *adj.* (also in *comb.*).

sta·tus /stáytəs, stát-/ *n.* **1** rank; social position; relation to others; relative importance. **2** a superior social, etc., position. **3** the state of affairs (*let me know if the status changes*).

sta·tus quo /stáytəs kwṓ, státəs/ *n.* the existing state of affairs.

sta·tus sym·bol *n.* a possession, etc., taken to indicate a person's high status.

stat·ute /stáchōōt/ *n.* **1** a written law passed by a legislative body. **2** a rule of a corporation, founder, etc., intended to be permanent.

stat·ute mile *n.* see MILE[1].

stat·ute of lim·i·ta·tions *n.* a statute that sets a time limit during which legal action can be taken.

stat·u·to·ry /stáchətawree/ *adj.* required, permitted, or enacted by statute. □□ **stat·u·to·ri·ly** *adv.*

stat·u·to·ry rape *n.* the offense of sexual intercourse with a minor.

staunch[1] /stawnch, staanch/ *adj.* (also **stanch**) **1** trustworthy; loyal. **2** (of a ship, joint, etc.) strong, watertight, airtight, etc. □□ **staunch·ly** *adv.* **staunch·ness** *n.*

staunch[2] var. of STANCH[1].

stave /stayv/ *n. & v.* ● *n.* **1** ► each of the curved pieces of wood forming the sides of a cask, barrel, etc. **2** = STAFF[1] *n.* 3. **3** a stanza or verse. **4** the rung of a ladder. ● *v.tr.* (*past* and *past part.* **stove** /stōv/ or **staved**) **1** break a hole in. **2** crush or knock out of shape. **3** fit or furnish (a cask, etc.) with staves. □ **stave in** crush by forcing inward. **stave off** avert or defer (danger or misfortune).

STAVE OF A WINE BARREL

staves *pl.* of STAFF[1] *n.* 3.

staves·a·cre /stáyvzaykər/ *n.* a larkspur, *Delphinium staphisagria*, yielding seeds used as poison for vermin.

stay[1] /stay/ *v. & n.* ● *v.* **1** *intr.* continue to be in the same place or condition; not depart or change (*stay here until I come back*). **2** *intr.* (often foll. by *at, in, with*) have temporary residence as a visitor, etc. (*stayed with them for Christmas*). **3** *tr. archaic* or *literary* stop or check (progress, the inroads of a disease, etc.). **4** *tr.* postpone (judgment, decision, execution, etc.). **5 a** *intr.* show endurance. **b** *tr.* show endurance to the end of (a race, etc.). **6** *intr.* (foll. by *for, to*) wait long enough to share or join in an activity, etc. (*stay to supper*; *stay for the video*). ● *n.* **1 a** the act or an instance of staying or dwelling in one place. **b** the duration of this (*just a ten-minute stay*; *a long stay in London*). **2** a suspension or postponement of a sentence, judgment, etc. (*was granted a stay of execution*). **3** a prop or support. **4** (in *pl.*) *hist.* a corset esp. with whalebone, etc., stiffening, and laced. □ **has come** (or **is here**) **to stay** *colloq.* must be regarded as permanent. **stay the course** pursue a course of action or endure a struggle, etc., to the end. **stay in** remain indoors or at home, esp. in school after hours as a punishment. **stay the night** remain until the next day. **stay put** remain where it is placed or where one is. **stay up** not go to bed (until late at night). □□ **stay·er** *n.*

stay[2] /stay/ *n. & v.* ● *n.* **1** *Naut.* a rope or guy supporting a mast, spar, flagstaff, etc. ▷ RIGGING, SHIP. **2** a tie-piece in an aircraft, etc. ● *v.tr.* **1** support (a mast, etc.) by stays. **2** put (a ship) on another tack.

stay·ing pow·er *n.* endurance; stamina.

stay·sail /stáysayl, stáysəl/ *n.* a triangular fore-and-aft sail extended on a stay. ▷ SCHOONER, SHIP

STD *abbr.* **1** Doctor of Sacred Theology. **2** sexually transmitted disease.

std. *abbr.* standard.

stead /sted/ *n.* □ **in a person's** (or **thing's**) **stead** as a substitute; instead of him or her or it. **stand a person in good stead** be advantageous to him or her.

stead·fast /stédfast/ *adj.* constant; firm. □□ **stead·fast·ly** *adv.* **stead·fast·ness** *n.*

stead·y /stédee/ *adj., v., adv., int., & n.* ● *adj.* (**steadier, steadiest**) **1** firmly fixed or supported or standing or balanced; not tottering, rocking, or wavering. **2** done or operating or happening in a uniform and regular manner (*a steady pace*; *a steady increase*). **3 a** constant in mind or conduct; not changeable. **b** persistent. **4** (of a person) serious and dependable in behavior; of industrious and temperate habits; safe; cautious. **5** regular; established (*a steady girlfriend*). **6** accurately directed; not faltering; controlled (*a steady hand*; *a steady eye*; *steady nerves*). **7** (of a ship) on course and upright. ● *v.tr. & intr.* (**-ies, -ied**) make or become steady (*steady the boat*). ● *adv.* steadily (*hold it steady*). ● *int.* as a command or warning to take care. ● *n.* (*pl.* **-ies**) *colloq.* a regular boyfriend or girlfriend. □ **go steady** (often foll. by *with*) *colloq.* have as a regular boyfriend or girlfriend. **steady down** become steady. **steady-going** staid; sober. □□ **stead·i·er** *n.* **stead·i·ly** *adv.* **stead·i·ness** *n.*

stead·y state *n.* an unvarying condition, esp. in a physical process, e.g., of the universe having no beginning and no end.

steak /stayk/ *n.* **1** a thick slice of meat (esp. beef) or fish, often cut for grilling, frying, etc. **2** beef cut for stewing or braising. ▷ CUT

steak house *n.* a restaurant specializing in serving beefsteaks.

steak knife *n.* a table knife with a serrated steel blade for cutting steak.

steal /steel/ *v. & n.* ● *v.* (*past* **stole** /stōl/; *past part.* **stolen** /stṓlən/) **1** *tr.* (also *absol.*) **a** take (another person's property) illegally. **b** take (property, etc.) without right or permission, esp. in secret with the intention of not returning it. **2** *tr.* obtain surreptitiously or by surprise (*stole a kiss*). **3** *tr.* **a** gain insidiously or artfully. **b** (often foll. by *away*) win or get possession of (a person's affections, etc.), esp. insidiously (*stole her heart away*). **4** *intr.* **a** move, esp. silently or stealthily (*stole out of the room*). **b** (of a sound, etc.) become gradually perceptible. **5** *tr.* **a** (in various sports) gain (a run, the ball, etc.) surreptitiously or by luck. **b** *Baseball* run to (a base) while the pitcher is in the act of delivery. ● *n.* **1** *colloq.* the act or an instance of stealing or theft. **2** *colloq.* an unexpectedly easy task or good bargain. □ **steal a march on** get an advantage over by surreptitious means; anticipate. **steal the show** outshine other performers, esp. unexpectedly. **steal a person's thunder** use another person's words, ideas, etc., without permission and without giving credit. □□ **steal·er** *n.* (also in *comb.*).

stealth /stelth/ *n. & adj.* ● *n.* secrecy; a secret procedure. ● *adj.* of an aircraft design intended to avoid detection by radar. ▷ BOMBER. □ **by stealth** surreptitiously.

stealth·y /stélthee/ *adj.* (**stealthier, stealthiest**) **1** done with stealth; proceeding imperceptibly. **2** acting or moving with stealth. □□ **stealth·i·ly** *adv.* **stealth·i·ness** *n.*

steam /steem/ *n. & v.* ● *n.* **1 a** the gas into which water is changed by boiling. **b** a mist of liquid particles of water produced by the condensation of this gas. **2** any similar vapor. **3 a** energy or power provided by a steam engine or other machine. **b** *colloq.* power or energy generally. ● *v.* **1** *tr.* **a** cook (food) in steam. **b** soften or make pliable (lumber, etc.) or otherwise treat with steam. **2** *intr.* give off steam or other vapor, esp. visibly. **3** *intr.* **a** move under steam power (*the ship steamed down the river*). **b** (foll. by *ahead, away*, etc.) *colloq.* proceed or travel fast or with vigor. **4** *tr. & intr.* (usu. foll. by *up*) **a** cover or become covered with condensed steam. **b** (as **steamed up** *adj.*) *colloq.* angry or excited. **5** *tr.* (foll. by *open*, etc.) apply steam to the adhesive of (a sealed envelope) to get it open. □ **get up steam** **1** generate enough power to work a steam engine. **2** work oneself into an energetic or angry state. **let off steam** relieve one's pent up feelings or energy. **run out of steam** lose one's impetus or energy. **under one's own steam** without assistance; unaided.

steam age *n.* the era when trains were pulled by steam locomotives.

steam bath *n.* a room, etc., filled with steam for bathing in.

steam·boat /steémbōt/ *n.* a boat propelled by a steam engine.

S

STEAM ENGINE

To power a steam locomotive, coal is burned in a firebox, producing hot gases (mainly carbon dioxide and carbon monoxide). These gases then heat water in a boiler to produce steam. When the steam reaches a high pressure, it is fed into cylinders and expands, forcing pistons back and forth. The pistons turn the locomotive's wheels (via a rod and crank).

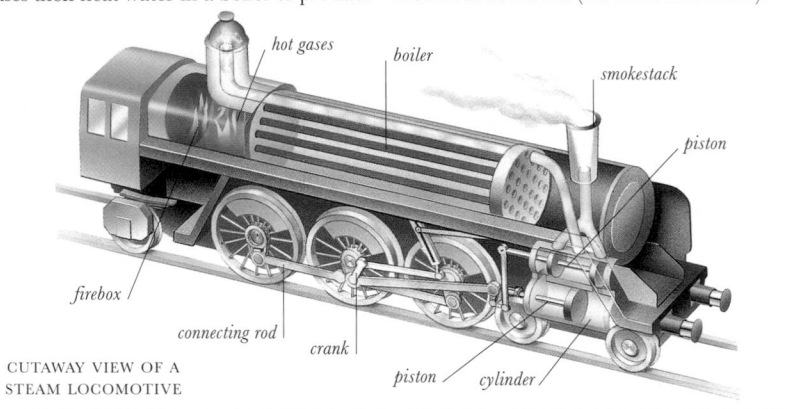

hot gases   *boiler*   *smokestack*   *piston*

firebox   *connecting rod*   *crank*   *piston*   *cylinder*

CUTAWAY VIEW OF A
STEAM LOCOMOTIVE

steam en·gine *n.* **1** an engine which uses the expansion or rapid condensation of steam to generate power. **2** ▲ a locomotive powered by this.

steam·er /stéemər/ *n.* **1** a person or thing that steams. **2** a vessel propelled by steam, esp. a ship. **3** a vessel in which things are cooked by steam.

steam i·ron *n.* an electric iron that emits steam from holes in its flat surface, to improve its ironing ability.

steam·roll·er /stéemrōlər/ *n. & v.* ● *n.* **1** a heavy slow-moving vehicle with a roller, used to flatten new-made roads. **2** a crushing power or force. ● *v.tr.* **1** crush forcibly or indiscriminately. **2** (foll. by *through*) force (a measure, etc.) through a legislature by overriding opposition.

steam·ship /stéemship/ *n.* a ship propelled by a steam engine.

steam shov·el *n.* an excavator powered by steam.

steam train *n.* a train driven by a steam engine.
▷ TRAIN

steam tur·bine *n.* ▼ a turbine in which a high-velocity jet of steam rotates a bladed disk or drum.

steam·y /stéemee/ *adj.* (**steamier**, **steamiest**) **1** like or full of steam. **2** *colloq.* erotic; salacious. □□ **steam·i·ly** *adv.*

ste·ar·ic /stéerik, steeárik/ *adj.* derived from stearin. □□ **ste·a·rate** /-rayt/ *n.*

ste·ar·ic ac·id *n.* a solid saturated fatty acid obtained from animal or vegetable fats.

ste·a·rin /stéerin/ *n.* **1** a glyceryl ester of stearic acid. **2** a mixture of fatty acids used in candle making.

ste·a·tite /stéeətīt/ *n.* a soapstone or other impure form of talc.

ste·at·o·py·gi·a /stéeátəpíjeeə, stéeətə-/ *n.* an excess of fat on the buttocks. □□ **ste·at·o·py·gous** /-pígəs, -tópigəs/ *adj.*

steed /steed/ *n. archaic or poet.* a horse, esp. a fast powerful one.

steel /steel/ *n., adj., & v.* ● *n.* **1** any of various alloys of iron and carbon with other elements, much used for making tools, weapons, etc. **2** strength; firmness (*nerves of steel*). **3** a rod of steel on which knives are sharpened. ▷ UTENSIL. **4** (not in *pl.*) *literary* a sword, lance, etc. (*foemen worthy of their steel*). ● *adj.* **1** made of steel. **2** like steel. ● *v.tr. & refl.* harden or make resolute (*steeled myself for a shock*).

steel band *n.* a group of usu. W. Indian musicians with percussion instruments made from oil drums.

steel engraving *v.* the process of engraving on or an impression taken from a steel-coated copper plate.

steel·head /stéelhed/ *n.* a large N. American rainbow trout.

steel wool *n.* ▶ an abrasive substance consisting of a mass of fine steel shavings.

steel·work /stéelwərk/ *n.* articles of steel.

steel·works /stéelwərks/ *n.pl.* (usu. treated as *sing.*) a place where steel is manufactured. □□ **steel·work·er** *n.*

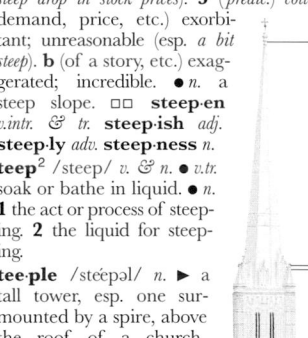

STEEL WOOL

steel·y /stéelee/ *adj.* (**steelier**, **steeliest**) **1** of, or hard as, steel. **2** severe; ruthless (*steely composure; steely-eyed glance*). □□ **steel·i·ness** *n.*

steel·yard /stéelyaard/ *n.* a kind of balance with a short arm to take the item to be weighed and a long graduated arm along which a weight is moved until it balances.

steen·bok /stéenbok, stáyn-/ *n.* an African dwarf antelope, *Raphicerus campestris*.

steep[1] /steep/ *adj. & n.* ● *adj.* **1** sloping sharply (*a steep hill; steep stairs*). **2** (of a rise or fall) rapid (*a steep drop in stock prices*). **3** (*predic.*) *colloq.* **a** (of a demand, price, etc.) exorbitant; unreasonable (esp. *a bit steep*). **b** (of a story, etc.) exaggerated; incredible. ● *n.* a steep slope. □□ **steep·en** *v.intr. & tr.* **steep·ish** *adj.* **steep·ly** *adv.* **steep·ness** *n.*

steep[2] /steep/ *v. & n.* ● *v.tr.* soak or bathe in liquid. ● *n.* **1** the act or process of steeping. **2** the liquid for steeping.

stee·ple /stéepəl/ *n.* ▶ a tall tower, esp. one surmounted by a spire, above the roof of a church. □□ **stee·pled** *adj.*

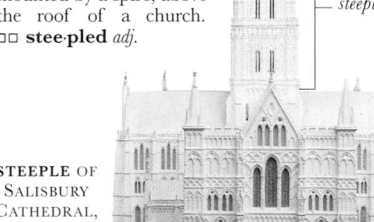

spire

steeple

STEEPLE OF
SALISBURY
CATHEDRAL,
ENGLAND

stee·ple·chase /stéepəlchays/ *n.* **1** a horse race (orig. with a steeple as the goal) across the countryside or on a racetrack with ditches, hedges, etc., to jump. **2** a cross-country foot race. □□ **stee·ple·chas·er** *n.* **stee·ple·chas·ing** *n.*

stee·ple·jack /stéepəljak/ *n.* a person who climbs tall chimneys, steeples, etc., to do repairs, etc.

steer[1] /steer/ *v.* **1** *tr.* **a** guide (a vehicle, aircraft, etc.) by a wheel, etc. **b** guide (a vessel) by a rudder or helm. **2** *intr.* guide a vessel or vehicle in a specified direction (*tried to steer left*). **3** *tr.* direct (one's course). **4** *intr.* direct one's course in a specified direction (*steered for the railroad station*). **5** *tr.* guide the movement or trend of (*steered them into the garden; steered the conversation away from that subject*). □ **steer clear of**

STEAM TURBINE

Steam turbines provide most of the world's power. To operate a turbine, high-pressure steam is directed onto moving metal blades connected to a central shaft. Fixed blades with slanting slots make sure that the steam hits the moving blades at the correct angle. As the steam expands, the blades spin, causing the turbine shaft to rotate. This turning shaft can be used to drive many devices, including an electric generator or a ship's propeller.

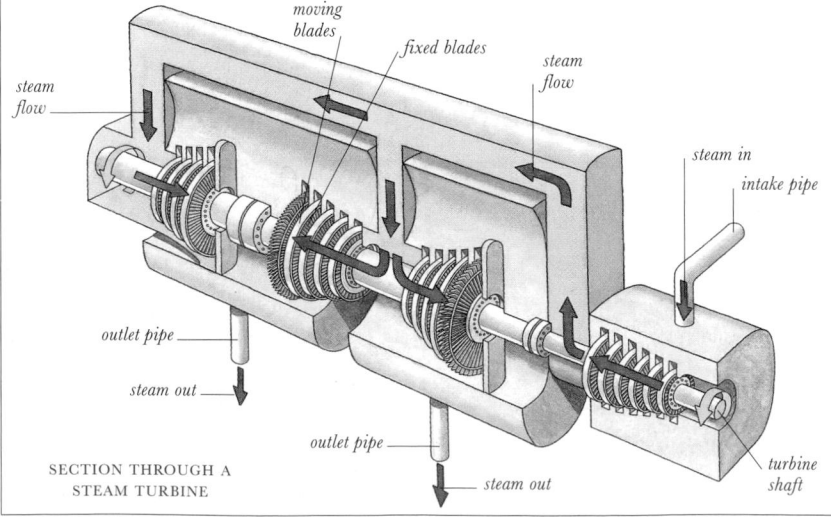

moving blades   *fixed blades*   *steam flow*

steam flow

steam in

intake pipe

outlet pipe

steam out

outlet pipe

steam out

turbine shaft

SECTION THROUGH A
STEAM TURBINE

take care to avoid. □□ **steer·a·ble** *adj.* **steer·er** *n.* **steer·ing** *n.* (esp. in senses 1, 2 of *v.*).

steer[2] /steer/ *n.* a young male bovine animal castrated before sexual maturity, esp. one raised for beef.

steer·age /steérij/ *n.* **1** the act of steering. **2** the effect of the helm on the ship. **3** the part of a ship allotted to passengers traveling at the cheapest rate. **4** *hist.* (in a warship) quarters assigned to midshipmen, etc., just forward of the wardroom.

steer·ing col·umn *n.* the shaft or column which connects the steering wheel, handlebars, etc., of a vehicle to the rest of the steering mechanism.

steer·ing com·mit·tee *n.* a committee deciding the order of business, or priorities and the general course of operations.

steer·ing wheel *n.* a wheel by which a vehicle, etc., is steered.

steers·man /steérzmən/ *n.* (*pl.* **-men**) a helmsman.

steeve /steev/ *n. Naut.* the angle of the bowsprit in relation to the horizontal.

steg·o·sau·rus /stégəsáwrəs/ *n.* ▼ any of a group of plant-eating dinosaurs with a double row of large bony plates along the spine. ▷ DINOSAUR

STEGOSAURUS (*Kentrosaurus* species)

stein /stīn/ *n.* a large earthenware, pewter, etc., mug, esp. for beer.

stein·bock /stínbok/ *n.* **1** an ibex native to the Alps. **2** = STEENBOK.

ste·la /steélə/ *n.* (*pl.* **stelae** /-lee/) *Archaeol.* an upright slab or pillar usu. with an inscription and sculpture, esp. as a gravestone.

ste·le /steel, steélee/ *n.* **1** *Bot.* the axial cylinder of vascular tissue in the stem and roots of most plants. **2** *Archaeol.* = STELA. □□ **stelar** *adj.*

stel·lar /stélər/ *adj.* **1** of or relating to a star or stars. **2** having the quality of a star entertainer or performer; leading; outstanding.

stel·late /stélayt/ *adj.* (also **stel·lat·ed** /stélaytid/) **1** arranged like a star; radiating. **2** *Bot.* (of leaves) surrounding the stem in a whorl.

stel·lu·lar /stélyələr/ *adj.* shaped like, or set with, small stars.

stem[1] /stem/ *n. & v.* ● *n.* **1** ▼ the main body or stalk of a plant or shrub, usu. rising into light, but occasionally subterranean. **2** the stalk supporting a fruit, flower, or leaf, and attaching it to a larger branch, twig, or stalk. **3** a stem-shaped part of an object: **a** the slender part of a wineglass between the body and the foot. **b** the tube of a tobacco pipe. **c** a vertical stroke in a letter or musical note. **d** the winding shaft of a watch. **4** *Gram.* the root or main part of a noun, verb, etc., to which inflections are added. **5** *Naut.* the main upright timber or metal piece at the bow of a ship (*from stem to stern*). ● *v.* (**stemmed**, **stemming**) **1** *intr.* (foll. by *from*) spring or originate from (*stems from a desire to win*). **2** *tr.* remove the stem or stems from (fruit, tobacco, etc.). **3** *tr.* (of a vessel, etc.) hold its own or make headway against (the tide, etc.). □□ **stem·less** *adj.* **stemmed** *adj.* (also in *comb.*).

stem[2] /stem/ *v.tr.* (**stemmed**, **stemming**) **1** check or stop. **2** dam up (a stream, etc.).

stem·ma /stémə/ *n.* (*pl.* **stemmata** /stémətə/) **1** a family tree; a pedigree. **2** the line of descent, e.g., of variant texts of a work. **3** *Zool.* a simple eye; a facet of a compound eye.

stem·ware /stémwair/ *n.* glasses with stems.

stench /stench/ *n.* an offensive or foul smell.

stench trap *n.* a trap in a sewer, etc., to prevent the upward passage of gas.

sten·cil /sténsil/ *n. & v.* ● *n.* **1** ▼ a thin sheet of plastic, metal, card, etc., in which a pattern or lettering is cut, used to produce a corresponding pattern on the surface beneath it by applying ink, paint, etc. **2** the pattern, lettering, etc., produced by a stencil. ● *v.tr.* (**stenciled** or **stencilled**, **stenciling** or **stencilling**) **1** produce (a pattern) with a stencil. **2** decorate or mark (a surface) in this way.

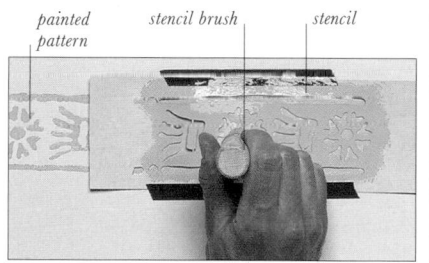

painted pattern   *stencil brush*   *stencil*

STENCIL

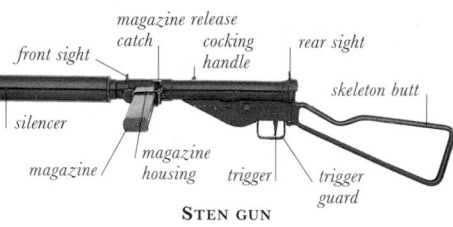

magazine release catch   *cocking handle*   *rear sight*
front sight   *skeleton butt*
silencer
magazine   *magazine housing*   *trigger*   *trigger guard*

STEN GUN

Sten gun /sten/ *n.* ▲ a type of lightweight submachine gun.

steno /sténō/ *n.* (*pl.* **-os**) *colloq.* a stenographer.

ste·nog·ra·phy /stənógrəfee/ *n.* shorthand or the art of writing this. □□ **ste·nog·ra·pher** *n.* **sten·o·graph·ic** /sténəgráfik/ *adj.*

ste·no·sis /stinósis/ *n. Med.* the abnormal narrowing of a passage in the body. □□ **ste·not·ic** /-nótik/ *adj.*

ste·no·type /sténətīp/ *n.* **1** a machine like a typewriter for recording speech in syllables or phonemes. **2** a symbol or the symbols used in this process. □□ **ste·no·typ·ist** *n.*

Sten·tor /sténtər/ *n.* (also **stentor**) a person with a powerful voice.

sten·to·ri·an /stentáwreeən/ *adj.* (of a voice or something uttered) loud and powerful.

step /step/ *n. & v.* ● *n.* **1 a** the complete movement of one leg in walking or running (*step forward*). **b** the distance covered by this. **2** a unit of movement in dancing. **3** a measure taken, esp. one of several in a course of action (*took steps to prevent it; considered it a wise step*). **4 a** a surface on which a foot is placed on ascending or descending a stair. **b** the rung of a ladder. **c** a platform, etc., in a vehicle provided for stepping up or down. **5** a short distance (*only a step from my door*). **6** the sound or mark made by a foot in walking, etc. (*heard a step on the stairs*). **7** the manner of walking, etc., as seen or heard (*know her by her step*). **8 a** a degree in the scale of promotion, advancement, or precedence. **b** one of a series of fixed points on a payscale, etc. ● *v.* (**stepped**, **stepping**) **1** *intr.* lift and set down one's foot or alternate feet in walking. **2** *intr.* come or go in a specified direction by stepping. **3** *intr.* make progress in a specified way (*stepped into a new job*). **4** *tr.* (foll. by *off*, *out*) measure (distance) by stepping. **5** *tr.* perform (a dance). □ **step down 1** resign. **2** *Electr.* decrease (voltage) using a transformer. **step in 1** enter a room, house, etc. **2 a** intervene. **b** act as a substitute. **step on it** (or **on the gas**) *colloq.* **1** accelerate a motor vehicle. **2** hurry up. **step out 1** leave a room, house, etc. **2** be active socially. **3** take large steps. **step up 1** increase; intensify (*must step up production*). **2** *Electr.* increase (voltage) using a transformer. **turn one's steps** go in a specified direction. □□ **stepped** *adj.* **step·wise** *adv. & adj.*

step- /step/ *comb. form* denoting a relationship resulting from a remarriage.

step aer·o·bics *n.* an exercise regimen using a step-climbing motion.

step·broth·er /stépbruthər/ *n.* a son of a stepparent by a marriage other than with one's father or mother.

step-by-step *adv.* gradually; cautiously.

step·child /stépchīld/ *n.* (*pl.* **-children**) a child of one's husband or wife by a previous marriage.

step·daugh·ter /stépdawtər/ *n.* a female stepchild.

step·fa·ther /stépfaathər/ *n.* a male stepparent.

steph·a·no·tis /stéfənótis/ *n.* any climbing tropical plant of the genus *Stephanotis*, cultivated for its fragrant waxy usu. white flowers.

step·lad·der /stépladər/ *n.* a short ladder with flat steps and a folding support.

step·moth·er /stépmuthər/ *n.* a female stepparent.

step·par·ent /stép-pairənt/ *n.* a mother's or father's later husband or wife.

steppe /step/ *n.* a level grassy unforested plain, esp. in SE Europe and Siberia.

S

STEM

The stem is a plant's support structure, bearing its leaves, buds, and flowers. It also forms part of a plant's transport system. Xylem tissue carries minerals and water from the roots to the rest of the plant, while phloem tissue conveys nutrients produced in the leaves. There are two types of stem: herbaceous (nonwoody) stems, which die at the end of each growing season; and woody stems, which develop continuously, adding a ring consisting of secondary xylem and secondary phloem every growing season.

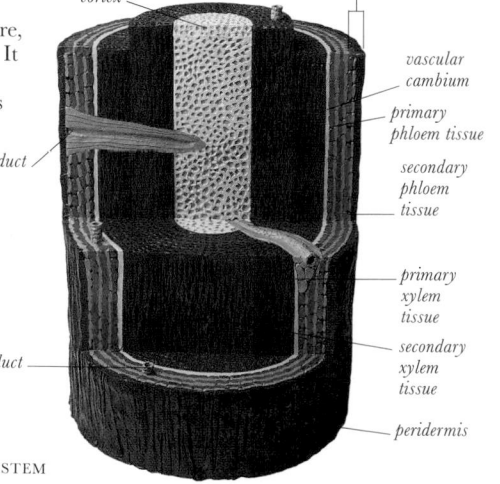

cortex   *bark*
vascular cambium
primary phloem tissue
resin duct
secondary phloem tissue
primary xylem tissue
resin duct
secondary xylem tissue
peridermis

SECTION THROUGH A WOODY (PINE) STEM

step·ping-stone *n.* **1** a raised stone in a stream, muddy place, etc., to help in crossing. **2** a means or stage of progress to an end.

step·sis·ter /stépsistər/ *n.* a daughter of a stepparent by a marriage other than with one's father or mother.

step·son /stépsun/ *n.* a male stepchild.

step stool *n.* a stool with usu. folding steps used to reach high shelves, etc.

-ster /stər/ *suffix* denoting a person engaged in or associated with a particular activity or thing (*gangster; youngster*).

ste·rad·i·an /stəráydeeən/ *n.* a solid angle equal to the angle at the center of a sphere subtended by a part of the surface equal in area to the square of the radius. ¶ Abbr.: **sr**.

ster·co·ra·ceous /stərkəráyshəs/ *adj.* **1** consisting of or resembling dung or feces. **2** living in dung.

stere /steer/ *n.* a unit of volume equal to one cubic meter.

ster·e·o /stéreeō, steéreeō/ *n. & adj.* ● *n.* (*pl.* **-os**) **1 a** a stereophonic record player, tape recorder, etc. **b** = *stereophony* (see STEREOPHONIC). **2** = STEREOSCOPE. ● *adj.* **1** = STEREOPHONIC. **2** = *stereoscopic* (see STEREOSCOPE).

stereo- /stéreeō, steéreeō/ *comb. form* solid; having three dimensions.

ster·e·o·bate /stéreeəbayt, steéreeə-/ *n. Archit.* a solid mass of masonry as a foundation for a building.

ster·e·o·chem·is·try /stéreeōkémstree, steéreeō-/ *n.* the branch of chemistry dealing with the three-dimensional arrangement of atoms in molecules.

ster·e·og·ra·phy /stéreeógrəfee, steéree-/ *n.* the art of depicting solid bodies in a plane.

ster·e·o·i·so·mer /stéreeō-ísəmər, steéreeō-/ *n. Chem.* any of two or more compounds differing only in their spatial arrangement of atoms.

ster·e·om·e·try /stéreeómitree, steéree-/ *n.* the measurement of solid bodies.

ster·e·o·phon·ic /stéreeōfónik, steéreeō-/ *adj.* (of sound reproduction) using two or more channels so that the sound has the effect of being distributed and of coming from more than one source. □□ **ster·e·o·phon·i·cal·ly** *adv.* **ster·e·oph·o·ny** /-reeófənee/ *n.*

ster·e·o·scope /stéreeəskōp, steéreeə-/ *n.* a device by which two photographs of the same object taken at slightly different angles are viewed together, giving an impression of depth and solidity as in ordinary human vision. □□ **ster·e·o·scop·ic** /-skópik/ *adj.* **ster·e·o·scop·i·cal·ly** *adv.* **ster·e·os·co·py** /-reeóskəpee/ *n.*

ster·e·o·type /stéreeətīp, steéree-/ *n. & v.* ● *n.* **1 a** a person or thing that conforms to an unjustifiably fixed mental picture. **b** such an impression or attitude. **2** a printing plate cast from a mold of composed type. ● *v.tr.* **1** (esp. as **stereotyped** *adj.*) standardize; cause to conform to a type. **2 a** print from a stereotype. **b** make a stereotype of. □□ **ster·e·o·typ·ic** /-típik/ *adj.* **ster·e·o·typ·i·cal** *adj.* **ster·e·o·typ·i·cal·ly** *adv.* **ster·e·o·typ·y** *n.*

ster·ic /stérik, steér-/ *adj. Chem.* relating to the spatial arrangement of atoms in a molecule. □ **steric hindrance** the inhibiting of a chemical reaction by the obstruction of reacting atoms.

ster·ile /stérəl, -īl/ *adj.* **1** not able to produce seeds or fruit or (of an animal) young; barren. **2** unfruitful; unproductive (*sterile discussions*). **3** free from living microorganisms, etc. **4** lacking originality or emotive force; mentally barren. □□ **ste·ril·i·ty** /stərílitee/ *n.*

ster·i·lize /stérilīz/ *v.tr.* **1** make sterile. **2** deprive of the power of reproduction. □□ **ster·i·liz·a·ble** *adj.* **ster·i·li·za·tion** *n.* **ster·i·liz·er** *n.*

ster·let /stárlit/ *n.* a small sturgeon, *Acipenser ruthenus*, found in the Caspian Sea area and yielding fine caviar.

ster·ling /stárling/ *adj. & n.* ● *adj.* **1** of or in British money (*pound sterling*). **2** (of a coin or precious metal) genuine; of standard value or purity. **3** (of a person or qualities, etc.) of solid worth; genuine; reliable (*sterling work*). ● *n.* British money (*paid in sterling*).

ster·ling sil·ver *n.* a mixture of 92.5 % silver and 7.5 % copper.

stern[1] /stərn/ *adj.* severe; enforcing discipline. □□ **stern·ly** *adv.* **stern·ness** *n.*

stern[2] /stərn/ *n.* **1** the rear part of a ship or boat. **2** any rear part. □□ **stern·ward** *adj. & adv.* **stern·wards** *adv.*

ster·nal /stárnəl/ *adj.* of or relating to the sternum.

ster·num /stárnəm/ *n.* (*pl.* **sternums** or **sterna** /-nə/) ◄ the breastbone.
▷ SKELETON

ster·nu·ta·tion /stárnyətáyshən/ *n. Med.* or *joc.* a sneeze or attack of sneezing.

ster·nu·ta·tor /stárnyətaytər/ *n.* a substance, esp. poison gas, that causes nasal irritation, violent coughing, etc. □□ **ster·nu·ta·to·ry** /-nyōōtətawree/ *adj. & n.* (*pl.* **-ies**).

stern·way /stárnway/ *n. Naut.* a backward motion or impetus of a ship.

ste·roid /steéroyd, stér-/ *n. Biochem.* any of a group of organic compounds with a characteristic structure of four rings of carbon atoms, including many hormones, alkaloids, and vitamins. □□ **ste·roi·dal** /-róyd'l/ *adj.*

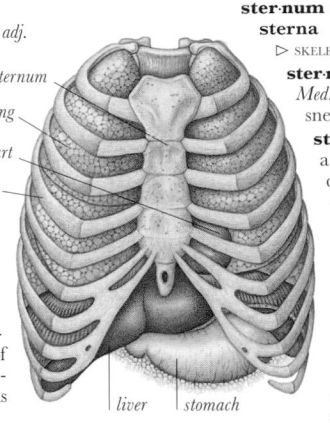

STERNUM: HUMAN RIB CAGE SHOWING THE STERNUM

ste·rol /steérawl, -ol, stér-/ *n. Chem.* any of a group of naturally occurring steroid alcohols.

ster·to·rous /stártərəs/ *adj.* (of breathing) labored and noisy. □□ **ster·to·rous·ly** *adv.*

stet /stet/ *v.* (**stetted, stetting**) **1** *intr.* (written on a proof) ignore or cancel the correction or alteration. **2** *tr.* cancel the correction of.

steth·o·scope /stéthəskōp/ *n.* ► an instrument used in listening to the action of the heart, lungs, etc., usu. consisting of a circular piece placed against the chest, with tubes leading to earpieces. ▷ SPHYGMOMANOMETER

Stet·son /stétsən/ *n. Trademark* a felt hat with a very wide brim and a high crown.

ste·ve·dore /steévədawr/ *n.* a person employed in loading and unloading ships.

Ste·ven·graph /steévəngraf/ *n.* a colorful woven silk picture.

stew /stoo, styoo/ *v. & n.* ● *v.* **1** *tr. & intr.* cook by long simmering in a closed pot with liquid. **2** *intr. colloq.* be oppressed by heat or humidity. **3** *intr. colloq.* **a** suffer prolonged embarrassment, anxiety, etc. **b** (foll. by *over*) fret or be anxious. **4** *tr.* (as **stewed** *adj.*) *colloq.* drunk. ● *n.* **1** a dish of stewed meat, etc. **2** *colloq.* an agitated or angry state (*be in a stew*). □ **stew in one's own juice** be left to suffer the consequences of one's own actions.

stew·ard /stóoərd, styóo-/ *n. & v.* ● *n.* **1** a passengers' attendant on a ship or aircraft or train. **2** an official appointed to keep order or supervise arrangements at a meeting or show or demonstration, etc. **3** = SHOP STEWARD. **4** a person responsible for supplies of food, etc., for a college or club, etc. **5** a person employed to manage another's property.

● *v.tr.* act as a steward of (*will steward the meeting*). □□ **stew·ard·ship** *n.*

stew·ard·ess /stóoərdis, styóo-/ *n.* a female steward, esp. on a ship or aircraft.

stg. *abbr.* sterling.

stick[1] /stik/ *n.* **1 a** a short slender length of wood broken or cut from a tree. **b** this trimmed for use as a support or weapon. **2** a thin rod or spike of wood, etc., for a particular purpose. **3** an implement used to propel the ball in hockey or polo, etc. ▷ HOCKEY. **4** a gearshift lever, esp. in a motor vehicle. **5** the lever controlling the ailerons and elevators in an airplane. **6** a conductor's baton. **7 a** a slender piece of celery, dynamite, deodorant, etc. **b** a number of bombs or paratroops released rapidly from aircraft. **8** punishment, esp. by beating. **9** esp. *Brit. colloq.* adverse criticism (*took a lot of stick*). **10** *colloq.* a piece of wood as part of a house or furniture (*a few sticks of furniture*). **11** *colloq.* a person, esp. one who is dull (*a funny old stick*). **12** (in *pl.*; prec. by *the*) *colloq.* remote rural areas; the country (*a dusty town out in the sticks*).

stick[2] /stik/ *v.* (*past* and *past part.* **stuck** /stuk/) **1** *tr.* (foll. by *in, into, through*) insert or thrust (a thing or its point) (*stuck a finger in my eye; stick a pin through it*). **2** *tr.* insert a pointed thing into; stab. **3** *tr. & intr.* (foll. by *in, into, on*, etc.) **a** fix or be fixed on a pointed thing. **b** fix or be fixed by or as by a pointed end. **4** *tr. & intr.* fix or become or remain fixed by or as by adhesive, etc. (*stick a label on it; the label won't stick*). **5** *intr.* endure; make a continued impression (*the scene stuck in my mind; the name stuck*). **6** *intr.* lose or be deprived of the power of motion or action through adhesion or jamming or other impediment. **7** *colloq.* **a** *tr.* put in a specified position or place, esp. quickly or haphazardly (*stick them down anywhere*). **b** *intr.* remain in a place (*stuck indoors*). **8** *colloq.* **a** *intr.* (of an accusation, etc.) be convincing or regarded as valid (*could not make the charges stick*). **b** *tr.* (foll. by *on*) place the blame for (a thing) on (a person). **9** *tr. Brit. colloq.* endure; tolerate (*could not stick it any longer*). **10** *tr.* (foll. by *at*) *colloq.* persevere with. □ **be stuck for** be at a loss for or in need of. **be stuck on** *colloq.* be infatuated with. **be stuck with** *colloq.* be unable to get rid of or escape from; be permanently involved with. **get stuck in** (or **into**) *sl.* begin in earnest. **stick around** *colloq.* linger; remain at the same place. **stick at it** *colloq.* persevere. **stick at nothing** allow nothing, esp. no scruples, to deter one. **stick by** (or **with**) stay loyal or close to. **stick 'em up!** *colloq.* hands up! **stick fast** adhere or become firmly fixed or trapped in a position or place. **stick in one's throat** be against one's principles. **stick it out** *colloq.* put up with or persevere with a burden, etc., to the end. **stick one's neck** (or **chin**) **out** expose oneself to censure, etc., by acting or speaking boldly. **stick out** protrude or cause to protrude or project (*stuck his tongue out; stick out your chest*). **stick out for** persist in demanding. **stick out a mile** (or **like a sore thumb**) *colloq.* be very obvious or incongruous. **stick to 1** remain close to or fixed on or to. **2** remain faithful to. **3** keep to (a subject, etc.) (*stick to the point*). **stick to a person's fingers** *colloq.* (of money) be embezzled by a person. **stick together** *colloq.* remain united or mutually loyal. **stick to one's guns** see GUN. **stick to it** persevere. **stick up 1** be or make erect or protruding upward. **2** fasten to an upright surface. **3** *colloq.* rob or threaten with a gun. **stick up for** support or defend. **stick with** *colloq.* remain in touch with or faithful to; persevere with. □□ **stick·a·bil·i·ty** /stikəbílitee/ *n.*

stick·ball /stíkbawl/ *n.* a form of baseball played with a stick or broom handle and a rubber ball.

stick·er /stíkər/ *n.* **1** an adhesive label or notice, etc. **2** a person or thing that sticks. **3** a persistent person.

stick·er price *n.* the full price of a new item, esp. the price listed on a sticker attached to a new automobile.

STETHOSCOPE

earpiece

hollow tube

bell

diaphragm

sternum

lung

heart

rib

liver

stomach

S

stick·er shock *n. colloq.* surprise at a higher-than-expected retail price.

stick·ing plas·ter *n. Brit.* an adhesive bandage for wounds, etc.

stick·ing point *n.* the limit of progress, agreement, etc.

stick in·sect *n.* ◄ any usu. wingless female insect of the family Phasmidae with a twiglike body.

STICK INSECT:
GIANT SPINY
STICK INSECT
(*Acrophylla titan*)

antenna

spiny abdomen

flattened, leaflike legs

real leaf

stick-in-the-mud *n. colloq.* an unprogressive or old-fashioned person.

stick·le·back /stíkəlbak/ *n.* ► any small fish of the family Gasterosteidae with sharp spines along the back.

stick·ler /stíklər/ *n.* (foll. by *for*) a person who insists on something.

stick·pin /stíkpin/ *n.* an ornamental tiepin.

stick shift *n.* a manual automotive transmission with a shift lever on the vehicle's floor or steering column.

stick-up *n. colloq.* an armed robbery.

stick·y /stíkee/ *adj.* (**stickier**, **stickiest**) **1** tending or intended to stick or adhere. **2** glutinous; viscous. **3** humid. **4** *colloq.* awkward or uncooperative; intransigent (*was very sticky about giving me leave*). **5** *colloq.* difficult; awkward (*a sticky problem*). □□ **stick·i·ly** *adv.* **stick·i·ness** *n.*

stiff /stif/ *adj. & n.* ● *adj.* **1** rigid; not flexible. **2** hard to bend or move or turn, etc. **3** hard to cope with; needing strength or effort (*a stiff test; a stiff climb*). **4** severe or strong (*a stiff breeze; a stiff penalty*). **5** formal; constrained. **6** (of a muscle or limb, etc., or a person affected by these) aching when used, owing to previous exertion, injury, etc. **7** (of an alcoholic or medicinal drink) strong. **8** (*predic.*) *colloq.* to an extreme degree (*bored stiff; scared stiff*). **9** (foll. by *with*) *colloq.* abounding in (*a place stiff with*

spines

STICKLEBACK: THREE-SPINED
STICKLEBACK
(*Gasterosteus aculeatus*)

tourists). ● *n. sl.* a corpse. □□ **stiff·ish** *adj.* **stiff·ly** *adv.* **stiff·ness** *n.*

stiff·en /stífən/ *v.tr. & intr.* make or become stiff. □□ **stiff·en·er** *n.* **stiff·en·ing** *n.*

stiff-necked *adj.* obstinate or haughty.

stiff up·per lip *n.* determination; fortitude.

sti·fle /stífəl/ *v.* **1** *tr.* smother; suppress. **2** *intr. & tr.* experience or cause to experience constraint of breathing. **3** *tr.* kill by suffocating. □□ **sti·fling·ly** *adv.*

stig·ma /stígmə/ *n.* (*pl.* **stigmas** or esp. in sense 4 **stigmata** /-mətə, -máátə/) **1** a mark or sign of disgrace or discredit. **2** (foll. by *of*) a distinguishing mark or characteristic. **3** the part of a pistil that receives the pollen in pollination. ▷ FLOWER. **4** (in *pl.*) *Eccl.* (in Christian belief) marks corresponding to those left on Christ's body by the Crucifixion, said to have appeared on the bodies of St. Francis of Assisi and others.

stig·mat·ic /stigmátik/ *adj. & n.* ● *adj.* **1** of or relating to a stigma or stigmas. **2** = ANASTIGMATIC. ● *n. Eccl.* a person bearing stigmata. □□ **stigmatically** *adv.*

stig·ma·tist /stígmətist/ *n. Eccl.* = STIGMATIC *n.*

stig·ma·tize /stígmətīz/ *v.tr.* describe as unworthy or disgraceful. □□ **stig·ma·ti·za·tion** *n.*

stilb /stilb/ *n.* a unit of luminance equal to one candela per square centimeter.

stil·bene /stílbeen/ *n. Chem.* an aromatic hydrocarbon forming phosphorescent crystals.

stil·bes·trol /stilbéstrawl, -rol/ *n.* (*Brit.* **stil·boes·trol**) a powerful synthetic estrogen derived from stilbene.

stile /stīl/ *n.* an arrangement of steps allowing people but not animals to climb over a fence or wall.

sti·let·to /stilétō/ *n.* (*pl.* **-os**) **1** a short dagger. **2** a pointed instrument for making eyelets, etc. **3** (in full **stiletto heel**) **a** a long tapering heel of a shoe. **b** a shoe with such a heel.

still¹ /stil/ *adj., n., adv., & v.* ● *adj.* **1** not or hardly moving. **2** with little or no sound; calm and tranquil (*a still evening*). **3** (of sounds) hushed; stilled. **4** (of a drink) not effervescent. ● *n.* **1** deep silence (*in the still of the night*). **2** an ordinary static photograph (as opposed to a motion picture), esp. a single shot from a movie. ● *adv.* **1** without moving (*stand still*). **2** even now or at a particular time (*they still did not understand; why are you still here?*). **3** nevertheless. **4** (with *compar.*, etc.) even; yet; increasingly (*still*

greater efforts; still another explanation). ● *v.tr. & intr.* make or become still. □□ **still·ness** *n.*

still² /stil/ *n.* ▼ an apparatus for distilling alcohol, etc.

still·age /stílij/ *n.* a bench, frame, etc., for keeping articles off the floor while draining, drying, waiting to be packed, etc.

still·birth /stílbərth/ *n.* the birth of a dead child.

still·born /stílbawrn/ *adj.* **1** born dead. **2** (of an idea, plan, etc.) abortive.

still life *n.* (*pl.* **still lifes**) a painting or drawing of inanimate objects such as fruit or flowers.

Still·son /stílsən/ *n.* (in full **Stillson wrench**) a large wrench with jaws that tighten as pressure is increased. ▷ WRENCH

still·y /stílee/ *adv. & adj.* ● *adv.* in a still manner. ● *adj. poet.* still; quiet.

stilt /stilt/ *n.* **1** either of a pair of poles with supports for the feet enabling the user to walk at a distance above the ground. **2** ▼ each of a set of piles or posts supporting a building, etc. **3** any wading bird of the genus *Himantopus* with long legs.

STILT HOUSE, THAILAND

stilt·ed /stíltid/ *adj.* **1** (of a literary style, etc.) stiff and unnatural; bombastic. **2** standing on stilts. **3** *Archit.* (of an arch) with pieces of upright masonry between the imposts and other stones. □□ **stilt·ed·ly** *adv.* **stilt·ed·ness** *n.*

Stil·ton /stílt'n/ *n. Trademark* a kind of strong rich cheese, often with blue veins, orig. sold in Stilton in eastern England. ▷ CHEESE

stim·u·lant /stímyələnt/ *adj. & n.* ● *adj.* that stimulates, esp. bodily or mental activity. ● *n.* **1** a stimulant substance, esp. a drug or a caffeinated beverage. **2** a stimulating influence.

stim·u·late /stímyəlayt/ *v.tr.* **1** apply or act as a stimulus to. **2** animate; excite; arouse. **3** be a stimulant to. □□ **stim·u·lat·ing** *adj.* **sti·m·u·la·tion** /-láyshən/ *n.* **stim·u·la·tive** *adj.* **stim·u·la·tor** *n.*

stim·u·lus /stímyələs/ *n.* (*pl.* **stimuli** /-lī/) **1** a thing that rouses to activity or energy. **2** a stimulating or rousing effect. **3** a thing that evokes a specific functional reaction in an organ or tissue.

sti·my var. of STYMIE.

sting /sting/ *n. & v.* ● *n.* **1** a sharp often poisonous wounding organ of an insect, nettle, etc. **2 a** the act of inflicting a wound with this. **b** the wound itself or the pain caused by it. **3** a wounding or painful quality or effect (*the sting of hunger; stings of remorse*). **4** pungency; sharpness; vigor (*a sting in the voice*). **5** *sl.* a swindle or robbery. ● *v.* (*past* and *past part.* **stung** /stung/) **1 a** *tr.* wound or pierce with a sting. **b** *intr.* be able to sting. **2** *intr. & tr.* feel or cause to feel a tingling physical or sharp mental pain. **3** *tr.* (foll. by *into*) incite by a strong or painful mental effect (*was stung into replying*). **4** *tr. sl.* swindle or charge exorbitantly. □ **sting in the tail** unexpected pain or difficulty at the end. □□ **sting·ing·ly** *adv.* **sting·less** *adj.*

sting·a·ree /stíngərée/ ● *n. US & Austral.* = STINGRAY.

sting·er /stíngər/ *n.* **1** a stinging insect, nettle, etc. **2** a sharp painful blow.

STILL

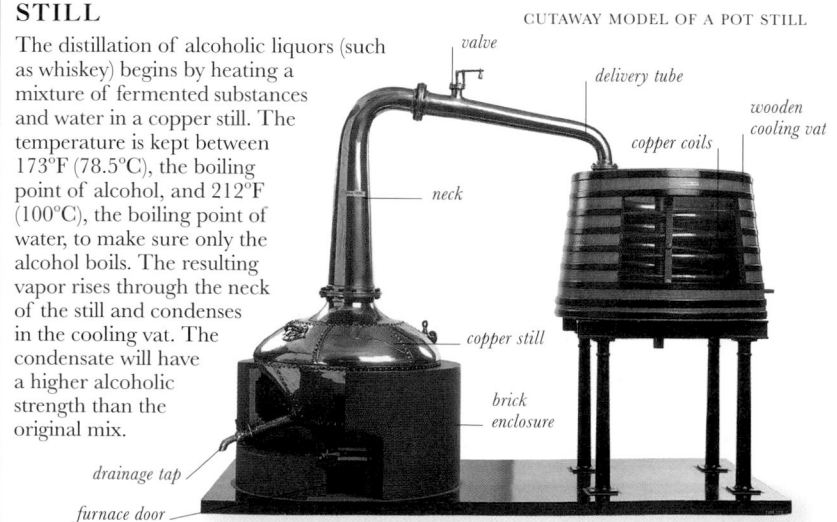

The distillation of alcoholic liquors (such as whiskey) begins by heating a mixture of fermented substances and water in a copper still. The temperature is kept between 173°F (78.5°C), the boiling point of alcohol, and 212°F (100°C), the boiling point of water, to make sure only the alcohol boils. The resulting vapor rises through the neck of the still and condenses in the cooling vat. The condensate will have a higher alcoholic strength than the original mix.

CUTAWAY MODEL OF A POT STILL

valve

delivery tube

wooden cooling vat

copper coils

neck

copper still

brick enclosure

drainage tap

furnace door

sting·ray
/stíngray/ *n.* ▶ any of various broad flatfish, esp. of the family Dasyatidae, having a long poisonous serrated spine at the base of its tail. ▷ RAY

— tail
— poisonous spine
— pelvic fin
— pectoral fin

STINGRAY
(*Dasyatis* species)

stin·gy /stínjee/ *adj.* (**stingier, stingiest**) ungenerous; mean. □□ **stin·gi·ly** *adv.* **stin·gi·ness** *n.*

stink /stingk/ *v. & n.* ● *v.* (*past* **stank** /stangk/ or **stunk** /stungk/; *past part.* **stunk**) **1** *intr.* emit a strong offensive smell. **2** *tr.* (often foll. by *out*) fill (a place) with a stink. **3** *tr.* (foll. by *out*, etc.) drive (a person) out, etc., by a stink. **4** *intr. colloq.* be or seem very unpleasant, contemptible, or scandalous. **5** *intr.* (foll. by *of*) *colloq.* have plenty of (esp. money). ● *n.* **1** a strong or offensive smell; a stench. **2** *colloq.* an outcry or fuss (*the affair caused quite a stink*).

— foul-smelling spore mass

stink·er /stíngkər/ *n.* **1** a person or thing that stinks. **2** *sl.* an objectionable person or thing. **3** *sl.* a difficult task.

stink·horn /stíngk-hawrn/ *n.* ◀ any foul-smelling fungus of the order Phallales.

stink·ing /stíngking/ *adj. & adv.* ● *adj.* **1** that stinks. **2** *sl.* very objectionable. ● *adv. sl.* extremely and usu. objectionably (*stinking rich*). □□ **stink·ing·ly** *adv.*

stink·o /stíngkō/ ● *adj. sl.* drunk.

stink·pot /stíngkpot/ ● *n. sl.* **1** a term of contempt for a person. **2** a vehicle or boat that emits foul exhaust fumes.

STINKHORN:
SHAMELESS STINKHORN
(*Phallus impudicus*)

stink·weed /stíngkweed/ ● *n.* any of several foul-smelling plants.

stink·wood /stíngkwŏŏd/ ● *n.* an African tree, *Ocotea bullata*, with foul-smelling timber.

stint /stint/ *v. & n.* ● *v.* **1** *tr.* supply (food or aid, etc.) in an ungenerous amount or grudgingly. **2** (often *refl.*) supply (a person, etc.) in this way. ● *n.* **1** a limitation of supply or effort (*without stint*). **2** a fixed or allotted amount of work (*do one's stint*). **3** a small sandpiper, esp. a dunlin.

stipe /stīp/ ● *n. Bot. & Zool.* a stalk or stem, esp. the support of a carpel, the stalk of a frond, the stem of a fungus, or an eyestalk. □□ **stip·i·form** *adj.*

stip·i·tate /stípitayt/ *adj.* **stip·i·ti·form** /stipíti-form/ *adj.*

sti·pel /stípəl/ *n. Bot.* a secondary stipule at the base of the leaflets of a compound leaf. □□ **sti·pellate** /stīpélayt/ *adj.*

sti·pend /stípend/ *n.* a fixed regular allowance or salary.

sti·pen·di·ar·y /stīpéndee-eree/ *adj. & n.* ● *adj.* **1** receiving a stipend. **2** working for pay. ● *n.* (*pl.* **-ies**) a person receiving a stipend.

stipes /stípeez/ *n.* (*pl.* **stipites** /stípiteez/) = STIPE.

stip·ple /stípəl/ *v. & n.* ● *v.* **1** *tr. & intr.* draw or paint with dots instead of lines. **2** *tr.* roughen the surface of (paint, cement, etc.). ● *n.* **1** the process or technique of stippling. **2** the effect of stippling. □□ **stip·pler** *n.* **stip·pling** *n.*

stip·u·late /stípyəlayt/ *v.tr.* **1** specify as part of a bargain or agreement. **2** (foll. by *for*) insist upon as an essential condition. **3** (as **stipulated** *adj.*) laid down in the terms of an agreement. □□ **stip·u·la·tion** /-láyshən/ *n.*

stip·ule /stípyŏŏl/ *n.* a small leaflike appendage to a leaf, usu. at the base of a leaf stem. □□ **stip·u·lar** *adj.*

stir[1] /stər/ *v. & n.* ● *v.* (**stirred, stirring**) **1** *tr.* move a spoon or other implement around and around in (a liquid, etc.) to mix the ingredients. **2 a** *tr.* cause to move, esp. slightly (*a breeze stirred the lake*). **b** *intr.* be or begin to be in motion (*not a creature was stirring*). **c** *refl.* rouse (oneself). **3** *intr.* rise from sleep (*is still not stirring*). **4** *intr.* (foll. by *out of*) leave; go out of. **5** *tr.* arouse or inspire or excite (the emotions, etc., or a person) (*was stirred to anger*; *it stirred the imagination*). ● *n.* **1** an act of stirring (*give it a good stir*). **2** commotion or excitement (*caused quite a stir*). **3** the slightest movement (*not a stir*). □ **stir the blood** inspire enthusiasm, etc. **stir in** mix (an added ingredient) with a substance by stirring. **stir up** **1** mix thoroughly by stirring. **2** incite (trouble, etc.) (*loved stirring things up*). **3** excite; arouse (*stirred up their curiosity*).

stir[2] /stər/ *n. sl.* a prison (esp. *in stir*).

stir-craz·y *adj.* deranged from long imprisonment.

stir-fry /stárfrī/ *v. & n.* ● *v.tr.* (**-ies, -ied**) fry rapidly while stirring. ● *n.* a dish consisting of stir-fried meat, vegetables, etc.

stirps /stərps/ *n.* (*pl.* **stirpes** /-peez/) **1** *Biol.* a classificatory group. **2** *Law* **a** a branch of a family. **b** its progenitor.

STITCH

Sewing stitches have a variety of uses, including creating a seam (when two or more pieces of material are joined by a line of stitches), finishing a raw edge, making a buttonhole, or producing a hem (a cloth's edge that has been turned under and then sewn down). Handstitches are often used to sew areas a machine cannot easily reach. Machine stitches perform the same functions as handstitches but are created much more quickly. Some stitches have decorative and practical uses. The zigzag stitch, for example, can be used as decoration on dress shirts, or as an edging stitch (to prevent fraying). Stitches are also utilized in embroidery, crocheting, and knitting.

HAND SEWING STITCHES

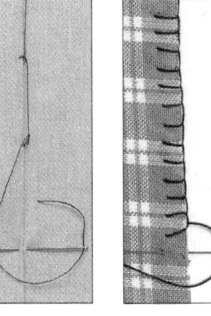
LOCK STITCH

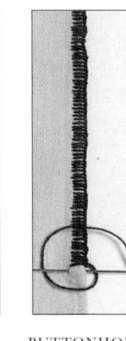
BLANKET STITCH

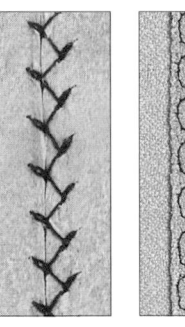
BUTTONHOLE STITCH

MACHINE STITCHES

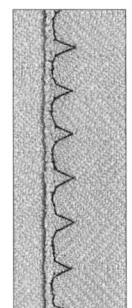
FEATHER STITCH

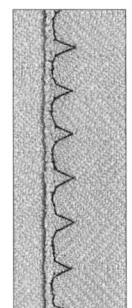
BLIND HEM STITCH

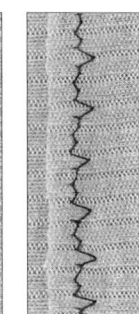
ZIGZAG BLIND HEM STITCH

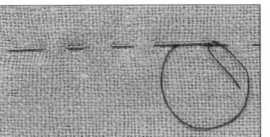
RUNNING STITCH

BACKSTITCH

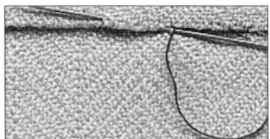
SLIPSTITCH

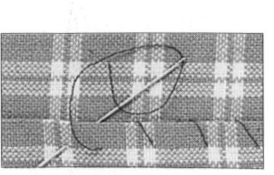
SLANTING HEMSTITCH

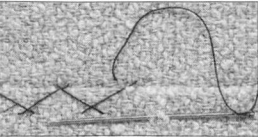
CATCH STITCH

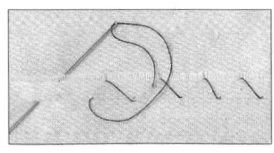
OVERCAST STITCH

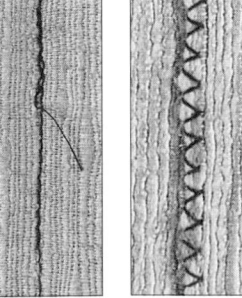
STRAIGHT STITCH

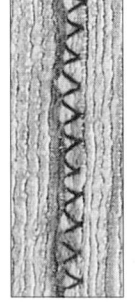
ZIGZAG STITCH

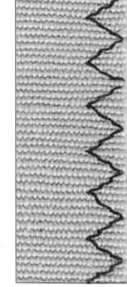
THREE-STEP ZIGZAG STITCH

S

stir·rer /stárər/ *n.* **1** a thing or a person that stirs; **2** *Brit. colloq.* a troublemaker; an agitator.

stir·ring /stáring/ *adj.* **1** stimulating; exciting; arousing. **2** actively occupied.

stir·rup /stárəp, stír-/ *n.* **1** each of a pair of devices attached to each side of a horse's saddle, in the form of a loop with a flat base to support the rider's foot. ▷ SADDLE, SHOW JUMPING. **2** (*attrib.*) having the shape of a stirrup. **3** (in full **stirrup bone**) = STAPES.

stitch /stich/ *n. & v.* ● *n.* **1 a** ▼ (in sewing or knitting, etc.) a single pass of a needle or the thread or loop, etc., resulting from this. ▷ KNITTING. **b** a particular method of sewing or knitting, etc. (*am learning a new stitch*). **2** (usu. in *pl.*) *Surgery* each of the loops of material used in sewing up a wound. **3** the least bit of clothing (*hadn't a stitch on*). **4** an acute pain in the side of the body induced by running, etc. ● *v.tr.* **1** sew; make stitches (in). **2** join or close with stitches. **in stitches** *colloq.* laughing uncontrollably. **stitch up** join or mend by sewing or stitching. □□ **stitch·er** *n.* **stitch·er·y** *n.*

stitch in time *n.* a timely remedy.

stitch·wort /stíchwərt, -wawrt/ *n.* any plant of the genus *Stellaria*, esp. *S. media* with an erect stem and white starry flowers, once thought to cure a stitch in the side.

sti·ver /stívər/ *n.* the smallest quantity or amount (*don't care a stiver*).

sto·a /stóə/ *n.* (*pl.* **stoas**) **1** a portico or roofed colonnade in ancient Greek architecture. **2** (**the Stoa**) the Stoic school of philosophy.

stoat /stōt/ *n.* a carnivorous mammal, *Mustela erminea*, of the weasel family, having brown fur in the summer turning mainly white in the winter. ▷ MUSTELID

sto·chas·tic /stōkástik/ *adj.* **1** determined by a random distribution of probabilities. **2** (of a process) characterized by a sequence of random variables. **3** governed by the laws of probability. □□ **sto·chas·ti·cal·ly** *adv.*

stock /stok/ *n., adj., & v.* ● *n.* **1** a store of goods, etc., ready for sale or distribution, etc. **2** a supply or quantity of anything for use (*lay in winter stocks of fuel; a great stock of information*). **3** equipment or raw material for manufacture or trade, etc. (*rolling stock; paper stock*). **4** farm animals or equipment; livestock. **5 a** the capital of a business. **b** shares in this. **6** one's reputation or popularity (*his stock is rising*). **7 a** money lent to a government at fixed interest. **b** the right to receive such interest. **8** a line of ancestry (*comes from German stock*). **9** liquid made by stewing bones, vegetables, etc., as a basis for soup, gravy, etc. **10** ▶ any of various fragrant-flowered cruciferous plants of the genus *Matthiola* or *Malcolmia*. **11** a plant into which a graft is inserted. **12** the main trunk of a tree. **13** (in *pl.*) *hist.* a wooden frame with holes for the feet in which offenders were locked as a public punishment. **14** = STOCK COMPANY. **15** (in *pl.*) the supports for a ship during building. **16** a band of material worn around the neck, esp. in horseback riding or below a clerical collar. ▷ REDCOAT. **17** hard solid brick pressed in a mold. ● *adj.* **1** kept in stock and so regularly available (*stock sizes*). **2** hackneyed; conventional (*a stock answer*). ● *v.tr.* **1** have or keep (goods) in stock. **2 a** provide (a store or a farm, etc.) with goods, equipment, or livestock. **b** fill with items needed (*shelves well-stocked with books*). □ **in stock** available immediately for sale, etc. **on the stocks** in construction or preparation. **out of stock** not immediately available for sale. **stock up 1** provide with or get stocks or supplies. **2** (foll. by *with, on*) get in or gather a stock of (food, fuel, etc.). **take stock 1** make an invent-

STOCK: VIRGINIA STOCK
(*Malcolmia maritima*)

ory of one's stock. **2** (often foll. by *of*) make a review or estimate of (a situation, etc.). □□ **stock·er** *n.*

stock·ade /stokáyd/ *n. & v.* ● *n.* **1** a line or enclosure of upright stakes. **2** a military prison. ● *v.tr.* fortify with a stockade.

stock·breed·er /stókbreedər/ *n.* a farmer who raises livestock. □□ **stock·breed·ing** *n.*

stock·brok·er /stókbrōkər/ *n.* = BROKER 2. □□ **stock·brok·er·age** *n.* **stock·brok·ing** *n.*

stock car *n.* **1** a specially modified production car for use in racing. **2** a railroad boxcar for transporting livestock.

stock com·pa·ny *n.* a repertory company performing mainly at a particular theater.

stock ex·change *n.* **1** a place where stocks and shares are bought and sold. **2** the dealers working there.

stock·fish /stókfish/ *n.* cod or a similar fish split and dried in the open air without salt.

stock·hold·er /stók-hōldər/ *n.* an owner of stocks or shares. □□ **stock·hold·ing** *n.*

stock·i·nette /stókinét/ *n.* (also **stock·i·net**) an elastic knitted material.

stock·ing /stóking/ *n.* **1 a** either of a pair of long separate coverings for the legs and feet, usu. closely woven. **b** = SOCK[1]. **2** any close-fitting garment resembling a stocking (*bodystocking*). **3** a differently colored, usu. white, lower part of the leg of a horse, etc. □ **in one's stocking** (or **stockinged**) **feet** without shoes. □□ **stock·inged** *adj.* (also in *comb.*).

stock·ing cap *n.* a knitted usu. conical cap.

stock·ing stuff·er *n.* a small present suitable for a Christmas stocking.

stock-in-trade *n.* **1** goods kept on sale by a retailer, dealer, etc. **2** all the requisites of a trade or profession. **3** a ready supply of characteristic phrases, attitudes, etc.

stock·job·ber /stókjobər/ *n.* = JOBBER 1b.

stock·list /stóklist/ *n. Brit.* a regular publication stating a dealer's stock of goods with current prices, etc.

stock·man /stókmən/ *n.* (*pl.* **-men**) **1** an owner of livestock. **2** a person in charge of a stock of goods in a warehouse, etc.

stock mar·ket *n.* **1** = STOCK EXCHANGE. **2** transactions that take place on this.

stock·pile /stókpīl/ *n. & v.* ● *n.* an accumulated stock of goods, materials, weapons, etc., held in reserve. ● *v.tr.* accumulate a stockpile of.

stock·pot /stókpot/ *n.* a pot for cooking stock for soup, etc.

stock·room /stókroom, -room/ *n.* a room for storing goods in stock.

stock-still *adv.* without moving.

stock·tak·ing /stóktayking/ *n.* **1** the process of making an inventory of stock in a warehouse, etc. **2** a review of one's position and resources.

stock·y /stókee/ *adj.* (**stockier, stockiest**) short and strongly built. □□ **stock·i·ly** *adv.*

stock·yard /stókyaard/ *n.* an enclosure for the sorting or temporary keeping of cattle.

stodge /stoj/ *n.* esp. *Brit. colloq.* **1** food, esp. of a thick heavy kind. **2** an unimaginative person or idea.

stodg·y /stójee/ *adj.* (**stodgier, stodgiest**) **1** dull and uninteresting. **2** (of a literary style, etc.) turgid and dull. **3** esp. *Brit.* (of food) heavy and indigestible. □□ **stodg·i·ness** *n.*

stoep /stoop/ *n. S.Afr.* a terraced veranda in front of a house.

sto·gy /stógee/ *n.* (also **sto·gie**) (*pl.* **-ies**) a long narrow roughly-made cigar.

Sto·ic /stóik/ *n. & adj.* ● *n.* **1** a member of the ancient Greek school of philosophy founded by Zeno *c.*308 BC, which sought virtue as the greatest

good and taught control of one's feelings. **2** (**stoic**) a stoical person. ● *adj.* **1** of or like the Stoics. **2** (**stoic**) = STOICAL.

sto·i·cal /stóikəl/ *adj.* showing great self-control in adversity. □□ **sto·i·cal·ly** *adv.*

stoi·chi·om·e·try /stóykeeómitree/ *n. Chem.* **1** the fixed numerical relationship between the relative quantities of substances in a reaction or compound. **2** the determination or measurement of these quantities. □□ **stoi·chi·o·met·ric** /-keeəmétrik/ *adj.*

Sto·i·cism /stóisizəm/ *n.* **1** the philosophy of the Stoics. **2** (**stoicism**) a stoical attitude.

stoke /stōk/ *v.* (often foll. by *up*) **1 a** *tr.* feed and tend (a fire or furnace, etc.). **b** *intr.* act as a stoker. **2** *intr. colloq.* consume food, esp. steadily and in large quantities.

stoke·hold /stók-hōld/ *n.* a compartment in a steamship, containing its boilers and furnace.

stoke·hole /stók-hōl/ *n.* a space for stokers in front of a furnace.

stok·er /stókər/ *n.* a person who tends to the furnace on a steamship.

STOL *abbr. Aeron.* short take-off and landing.

stole[1] /stōl/ *n.* **1** a woman's long garment like a scarf, worn around the shoulders. **2** a strip of silk, etc., worn over the shoulders as a vestment by a priest. ▷ VESTMENT

stole[2] *past* of STEAL.

sto·len *past part.* of STEAL.

stol·id /stólid/ *adj.* **1** lacking or concealing emotion or animation. **2** not easily excited or moved. □□ **sto·lid·i·ty** /-líditee/ *n.* **stol·id·ly** *adv.* **stol·id·ness** *n.*

sto·lon /stólon/ *n.* **1** *Bot.* a horizontal stem or branch that takes root at points along its length, forming new plants. **2** *Zool.* a branched stemlike structure in some invertebrates such as corals. □□ **stolonate** /-nayt/ *adj.* **sto·lon·i·fer·ous** /-nífərəs/ *adj.*

sto·ma /stómə/ *n.* (*pl.* **stomas** or **stomata** /-mətə/) **1** *Bot.* a minute pore in the epidermis of a leaf. **2** *Surgery* an artificial orifice made in the stomach.

stom·ach /stúmək/ *n. & v.* ● *n.* **1 a** ▼ the internal organ in which the first part of digestion occurs. ▷ DIGESTION. **b** any of several such organs in animals, esp. ruminants, in which there are four. **2 a** the belly, abdomen, or lower front of the body (*pit of the stomach*). **b** a protuberant belly (*what a stomach he has got!*). **3** (usu. foll. by *for*) **a** an appetite. **b** liking, readiness, or inclination (for controversy, conflict, danger, or an undertaking) (*had no stomach for the fight*). ● *v.tr.* **1** find sufficiently palatable to swallow or keep down. **2** submit to or endure (an affront, etc.) (usu. with *neg.: cannot stomach it*).

S

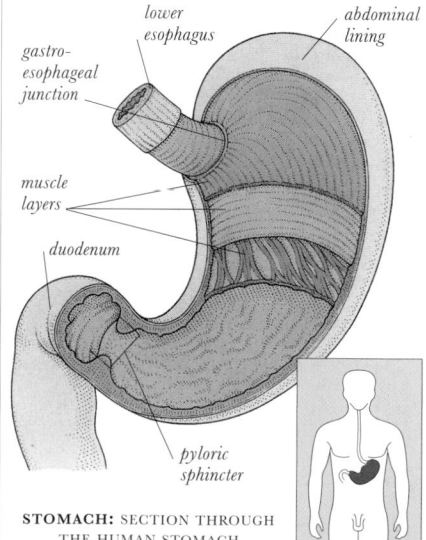

STOMACH: SECTION THROUGH
THE HUMAN STOMACH

lower esophagus

abdominal lining

gastro-esophageal junction

muscle layers

duodenum

pyloric sphincter

stom·ach·ache *n.* a pain in the abdomen or bowels.

stom·ach·er /stúmakər/ *n. hist.* **1** a front piece of a woman's dress covering the breast and pit of the stomach, often jeweled or embroidered. **2** an ornament worn on the front of a bodice.

stom·ach·ic /stəmákik/ *adj. & v.* ● *adj.* **1** of or relating to the stomach. **2** promoting the appetite or assisting digestion. ● *n.* a medicine or stimulant for the stomach.

sto·ma·ta *pl.* of STOMA.

sto·ma·ti·tis /stómətítis/ *n. Med.* inflammation of the mucous membrane of the mouth.

sto·ma·tol·o·gy /stómətólajee/ *n.* the scientific study of the mouth or its diseases. □□ **sto·mat·o·log·i·cal** /-təlójikəl/ *adj.* **sto·mat·ol·o·gist** *n.*

stomp /stomp/ *v. & n.* ● *v.intr.* tread or stamp heavily. ● *n.* a lively jazz dance with heavy stamping. □□ **stomp·er** *n.*

stone /stōn/ *n. & v.* ● *n.* **1 a** solid nonmetallic mineral matter, of which rock is made. **b** a piece of this, esp. a small piece. **2** *Building* **a** = LIMESTONE (*Portland stone*). **b** = SANDSTONE. **3** *Mineral.* = PRECIOUS STONE. **4** a stony meteorite; an aerolite. **5** (often in *comb.*) a piece of stone of a definite shape or for a particular purpose (*tombstone*; *stepping-stone*). **6 a** a thing resembling stone in hardness or form, e.g., the hard case of the kernel in some fruits. **b** *Med.* (often in *pl.*) a hard concretion in the body esp. in the kidney or gallbladder (*gallstones*). **7** (*attrib.*) **b** of the color of stone. ● *v.tr.* **1** pelt with stones. **2** remove the stones from (fruit). **3** face or pave, etc. with stone. **4** sharpen, polish etc., by rubbing with or against a stone. □ **cast** (or **throw**) **stones** (or **the first stone**) make aspersions on a person's character, etc. **leave no stone unturned** try all possible means to achieve a goal. **stone cold** completely cold. **stone cold sober** completely sober. **a stone's throw** a short distance. □□ **stoned** *adj.* (also in *comb.*). **stone·less** *adj.* **ston·er** *n.* **stone·like** *adj.*

Stone Age *n.* a prehistoric period when weapons and tools were made of stone.

stone·chat /stónchat/ *n.* ◄ any small brown bird of the thrush family with black and white markings, esp. *Saxicola torquata*, with a call like stones being knocked together.

stone·crop /stónkrop/ *n.* ► any succulent plant of the genus *Sedum*, usu. having yellow or white flowers and growing among rocks or in walls.

STONECHAT
(*Saxicola torquata*)

stone·cut·ter /stónkutər/ *n.* a person or machine that cuts or carves stone.

stoned /stōnd/ *adj. sl.* under the influence of alcohol or drugs.

stone-deaf *adj.* completely deaf.

stone·fish /stónfish/ *n.* (*pl.* same) a venomous tropical fish, *Synanceia verrucosa*, with poison glands underlying its erect dorsal spines. Also called **devilfish**.

stone·fly /stónflī/ *n.* (*pl.* **-flies**) any insect of the order Plecoptera, with aquatic larvae found under stones.

stone fruit *n.* a fruit with flesh enclosing a stone.

stone-ground /stón-grownd/ *adj.* (of grain) ground with millstones.

stone·hatch /stónhach/ *n.* a ringed plover.

stone·ma·son /stónmaysən/ *n.* a person who cuts, prepares, and builds with stone. □□ **stone·ma·son·ry** *n.*

stone·wall /stónwawl/ *v. tr. & intr.* obstruct (discussion or investigation) or be obstructive with evasive answers or denials, etc. □□ **stone·wall·ing** *n.*

STONECROP
(*Sedum sediforme*)

stone·ware /stónwair/ *n.* ceramic ware that is impermeable and partly vitrified but opaque.

stone·washed /stónwawsht, -wosht/ *adj.* (of a garment or fabric, esp. denim) washed with abrasives to produce a worn or faded appearance.

stone·work /stónwərk/ *n.* **1** masonry. **2** the parts of a building made of stone.

stone·wort /stónwort, -wawrt/ *n.* any plant of the genus *Chara*, related to green algae, often encrusted with a chalky deposit.

ston·y /stónee/ *adj.* (**stonier, stoniest**) **1** full of or covered with stones (*stony soil*; *a stony road*). **2 a** hard; rigid. **b** cold; unfeeling; obdurate; uncompromising (*a stony stare*; *a stony silence*). □□ **ston·i·ly** *adv.* **ston·i·ness** *n.*

stood *past* and *past part.* of STAND.

stooge /stōōj/ *n. & v. colloq.* ● *n.* **1** a butt or foil, esp. for a comedian. **2** an assistant or subordinate, esp. for routine or unpleasant work. **3** a compliant person; a puppet. ● *v.intr.* (foll. by *for*) act as a stooge for.

stool /stōōl/ *n. & v.* ● *n.* **1** a single seat without a back or arms, typically resting on three or four legs or on a single pedestal. **2** = FOOTSTOOL. **3** = FECES. **4** the root or stump of a tree or plant from which the shoots spring. ● *v.intr.* (of a plant) throw up shoots from the root. □ **fall between two stools** fail from vacillation between two courses, etc.

stool·ie /stōōlee/ *n. sl.* a person acting as a stool pigeon.

stool pi·geon *n.* **1** a person acting as a decoy. **2** a police informer.

stoop[1] /stōōp/ *v. & n.* ● *v.* **1** *tr.* bend (one's head or body) forward and downward. **2** *intr.* carry one's head and shoulders bowed forward. **3** *intr.* (foll. by *to* + infin.) deign or condescend. **4** *intr.* (foll. by *to*) descend or lower oneself to (some conduct) (*has stooped to crime*). ● *n.* a stooping posture.

stoop[2] /stōōp/ *n.* a porch or small veranda or set of steps in front of a house.

stoop[3] var. of STOUP.

stop /stop/ *v. & n.* ● *v.* (**stopped, stopping**) **1** *tr.* **a** put an end to (motion, etc.); completely check the progress or motion of. **b** effectively hinder or prevent (*stopped them playing so loudly*). **c** discontinue (an action or sequence of actions) (*stopped playing*; *stopped my visits*). **2** *intr.* come to an end (*supplies suddenly stopped*). **3** *intr.* cease from motion or speaking or action. **4** *tr.* cause to cease action; defeat. **5** *tr. sl.* receive (a blow, etc.). **6** *intr.* esp. *Brit.* stay for a short time. **7** *tr.* (often foll. by *up*) block or close up (a hole or leak, etc.). **8** *tr.* not permit or supply as usual (*shall stop their wages*). **9** *tr.* (in full **stop payment of** or **on**) instruct a bank to withhold payment on (a check). **10** *tr.* obtain the required pitch from (the string of a violin, etc.) by pressing at the appropriate point with the finger. **11** *tr. Boxing* **a** parry (a blow). **b** knock out (an opponent). **12** *tr.* pinch back (a plant). ● *n.* **1** the act or an instance of stopping; the state of being stopped (*put a stop to*). **2** a place designated for a bus or train, etc., to stop. **3** a device for stopping motion at a particular point. **4** a change of pitch effected by stopping a string. **5 a** (in an organ) a row of pipes of one character. ▷ ORGAN. **b** a knob, etc., operating these. **6 a** the effective diameter of a lens. **b** a device for reducing this. **c** a unit of change of relative aperture or exposure. **7** (of sound) = PLOSIVE. □ **put a stop to** cause to end, esp. abruptly. **stop at nothing** be ruthless. **stop by** (also *absol.*) call at (a place). **stop dead** (or **short**) cease abruptly. **stop down** *Photog.* reduce the aperture of (a lens) with a diaphragm. **stop one's ears 1** put one's fingers in one's ears to

avoid hearing. **2** refuse to listen. **stop off** (or **over**) break one's journey.

stop-and-go *n.* alternate stopping and restarting, esp. in traffic.

stop·bank /stópbangk/ *n. Austral. & NZ* an embankment built to prevent river flooding.

stop·cock /stópkok/ *n.* an externally operated valve regulating the flow of a liquid or gas through a pipe, etc.

stope /stōp/ *n.* a steplike part of a mine where ore, etc., is being extracted.

stop·gap /stópgap/ *n.* (often *attrib.*) a temporary substitute.

stop light *n.* a red traffic light.

stop-off /stópawf, -of/ *n.* = STOPOVER.

stop·o·ver /stópōvər/ *n.* a break in one's journey.

stop·page /stópij/ *n.* **1** the condition of being blocked or stopped. **2** a stopping (of pay). **3** a stopping or interruption of work in a factory, etc.

stop·per /stópər/ *n. & v.* ● *n.* **1** a plug for closing a bottle, etc. **2** a person or thing that stops something. ● *v.tr.* close with a stopper. □ **put a stopper on 1** put an end to (a thing). **2** keep (a person) quiet.

stop·ple /stópəl/ *n. & v.* ● *n.* a stopper or plug. ● *v.tr.* close with a stopple.

stop·watch /stópwoch/ *n.* ► a watch with a mechanism for recording elapsed time, used to time races, etc.

stor·age /stáwrij/ *n.* **1 a** the storing of goods, etc. **b** a particular method of storing or the space available for it. **2** the cost of storing. **3** the electronic retention of data in a computer, etc.

lap reset   mode   start/stop
button   button   button

*liquid/
crystal
display*

STOPWATCH

stor·age bat·ter·y *n.* (also **storage cell**) a battery (or cell) for storing electricity.

stor·ax /stáwraks/ *n.* **1 a** a fragrant resin, obtained from the tree *Styrax officinalis* and formerly used in perfume. **b** this tree. **2** (in full **Levant** or liquid storax) a balsam obtained from the tree *Liquidambar orientalis*.

store /stawr/ *n. & v.* ● *n.* **1** a quantity of something kept available for use. **2** (in *pl.*) **a** articles for a particular purpose accumulated for use (*naval stores*). **b** a supply of these or the place where they are kept. **3 a** = DEPARTMENT STORE. **b** a retail outlet or shop. **c** a shop selling basic necessities (*general store*). ● *v.tr.* **1** put (furniture, etc.) in storage. **2** (often foll. by *up*, *away*) accumulate (provisions, energy, electricity, etc.) for future use. **3** stock or provide with something useful (*a mind stored with facts*). **4** enter or retain (data) for retrieval. □ **in store 1** kept in readiness. **2** coming in the future. **3** (foll. by *for*) destined or intended. **set** (or **lay** or **put**) **store by** (or **on**) consider important or valuable; esteem. □□ **stor·a·ble** *adj.* **stor·er** *n.*

store·front /stáwrfrunt/ *n.* **1** the side of a store facing the street. **2** a room at the front of a store.

store·house /stáwrhows/ *n.* a place where things are stored.

store·keep·er /stáwrkeepər/ *n.* the owner or manager of a store.

store·man /stáwrmən/ *n.* (*pl.* **-men**) *Brit.* a person responsible for stored goods.

store·room /stáwr-rōōm, -rŏŏm/ *n.* a room in which items are stored.

storey *Brit.* var. of STORY[2].

sto·ried /stáwreed/ *adj. literary* celebrated in or associated with stories.

stork /stawrk/ *n.* any long-legged large wading bird of the family Ciconiidae, esp. *Ciconia ciconia* with white plumage, black wingtips, a long reddish beak, and red feet, nesting esp. on tall buildings.

storm /stawrm/ n. & v. ● n. 1 a violent disturbance of the atmosphere with strong winds and usu. with thunder and rain or snow, etc. 2 a violent disturbance of the established order in human affairs. 3 (foll. by of) a a violent shower of missiles or blows. b an outbreak of applause, indignation, hisses, etc. (they were greeted by a storm of abuse). 4 a a direct assault by troops on a fortified place. b the capture of a place by such an assault. ● v. 1 intr. (often foll. by at, away) talk violently; rage; bluster. 2 intr. (usu. foll. by in, out of, etc.) move violently or angrily (stormed out of the meeting). 3 tr. attack or capture by storm. 4 intr. (of wind, rain, etc.) rage; be violent. □ **take by storm 1** capture by direct assault. **2** rapidly captivate (a person, audience, etc.). □□ **storm·proof** adj.

storm·bound /stáwrmbownd/ adj. prevented by storms from leaving port.

storm door n. an additional outer door for protection in bad weather or winter.

storm pet·rel n. any of several small, black and white seabirds of the family Hydrobatidae.

storm sail n. a sail of smaller size and stouter canvas than the corresponding one used in ordinary weather.

storm sig·nal n. a device warning of an approaching storm.

storm troop·er n. 1 hist. a member of the Nazi political militia. 2 a member of the shock troops.

storm troops n.pl. = SHOCK TROOPS.

storm win·dow n. an additional outer window used like a storm door.

storm·y /stáwrmee/ adj. (**stormier, stormiest**) 1 characterized by or affected by storms. 2 (of a wind, etc.) violent; raging. 3 full of angry feeling or outbursts (a stormy relationship). □□ **storm·i·ly** adv. **storm·i·ness** n.

storm·y pet·rel n. = STORM PETREL.

sto·ry[1] /stáwree/ n. (pl. **-ies**) 1 an account of imaginary or past events. 2 the past course of the life of a person or institution, etc. 3 (in full **story line**) the plot of a novel or play, etc. 4 facts or experiences that deserve narration. 5 colloq. a lie. 6 a narrative or descriptive item of news. □ **the old** (or **same old**) **story** the familiar or predictable course of events. **the story goes** it is said. **to cut** (or **make**) **a long story short** a formula excusing the omission of details.

sto·ry[2] /stáwree/ n. (pl. **-ies**) 1 any of the parts into which a building is divided horizontally; the whole of the rooms having a continuous floor. 2 a thing forming a horizontal division.

sto·ry·board /stáwreebawrd/ n. a displayed sequence of pictures, etc., outlining the plan of a movie, television advertisement, etc.

sto·ry·book /stáwreebook/ n. 1 a book of stories for children. 2 (attrib.) unreal, romantic (a storybook ending).

sto·ry·tell·er /stáwreetelər/ n. 1 a person who tells or writes stories. 2 colloq. a liar. □□ **sto·ry·tell·ing** n. & adj.

stoup /stoop/ n. (also **stoop**) 1 a basin for holy water. 2 archaic a beaker.

stout /stowt/ adj. & n. ● adj. 1 somewhat fat; corpulent. 2 of considerable thickness or strength (a stout stick). 3 brave; vigorous (a stout fellow; stout resistance). ● n. a strong dark beer brewed with roasted malt or barley. □□ **stout·ish** adj. **stout·ly** adv. **stout·ness** n.

stout·heart·ed /stówt-haártəd/ adj. courageous; resolute; brave. □□ **stout·heart·ed·ly** adv. **stout·heart·ed·ness** n.

stove[1] /stōv/ n. a closed apparatus burning fuel or electricity for heating or cooking.

stove[2] past and past part. of STAVE v.

stove·pipe /stóvpīp/ n. a pipe conducting smoke and gases from a stove to a chimney.

stove·pipe hat n. colloq. a tall silk hat.

stow /stō/ v.tr. 1 pack (goods, etc.) tidily and compactly. 2 Naut. place (a cargo or provisions) in its proper place and order. 3 fill (a receptacle) with articles compactly arranged. 4 (usu. in imper.) sl. abstain from (stow the noise!). □ **stow away 1** place (a thing) where it will not cause an obstruction. **2** be a stowaway on a ship, etc.

stow·age /stóij/ n. 1 the act or an instance of stowing. 2 a place for this.

stow·a·way /stóəway/ n. a person who hides on board a ship or aircraft, etc., to get free passage.

STP abbr. standard temperature and pressure.

str. abbr. 1 strait. 2 stroke (of an oar).

stra·bis·mus /strəbízməs/ n. Med. the condition of one or both eyes not correctly aligned in direction; a squint. □□ **stra·bis·mal** adj. **stra·bis·mic** adj.

strad·dle /strád'l/ v. & n. ● v. 1 tr. a sit or stand across (a thing) with the legs wide apart. b be situated across or on both sides of (the town straddles the border). 2 tr. part (one's legs) widely. 3 tr. drop shots or bombs short of and beyond (a target). ● n. the act or an instance of straddling. □□ **strad·dler** n.

Strad·i·var·i·us /strádiváireeəs/ n. a violin or other stringed instrument made by Antonio Stradivari of Cremona (d. 1737) or his followers.

strafe /strayf/ v. & n. ● v.tr. 1 bombard; harass with gunfire. 2 abuse. ● n. an act of strafing.

strag·gle /strágəl/ v. & n. ● v.intr. 1 lack compactness or tidiness. 2 be dispersed or sporadic. 3 trail behind others in a march or race, etc. 4 (of a plant, beard, etc.) grow long and loose. ● n. a group of straggling or scattered persons or things. □□ **strag·gler** n. **strag·gly** adj. (**stragglier, straggliest**)

straight /strayt/ adj., n., & adv. ● adj. 1 extending uniformly in the same direction; without a curve or bend, etc. 2 successive; uninterrupted (three straight wins). 3 in proper order or place or condition; duly arranged (is the picture straight?; put things straight). 4 honest; candid; not evasive. 5 (of thinking, etc.) logical; unemotional. 6 (of drama, etc.) serious as opposed to popular or comic; employing conventional techniques. 7 a unmodified. b (of a drink) undiluted. 8 colloq. a (of a person, etc.) conventional or respectable. b heterosexual. 9 (of a person's back) not bowed. 10 (of the hair) not curly or wavy. 11 (of a knee) not bent. 12 (of a garment) not flared. 13 coming direct from its source. 14 (of an aim, blow, or course) going direct to the mark. ● n. 1 the straight part of something, esp. a racetrack. ▷ RACETRACK 2 a straight condition. 3 a sequence of five cards in poker. 4 colloq. a a conventional person. b a heterosexual. ● adv. 1 in a straight line; direct (came straight from Paris; I told them straight). 2 in the right direction; with a good aim (shoot straight). 3 correctly (can't see straight). □ **go straight** live an honest life after being a criminal. **the straight and narrow** morally correct behavior. **straight away** at once; immediately. **straight from the shoulder 1** (of a blow) well delivered. **2** (of a verbal attack) frank or direct. **straight off** colloq. without hesitation. **straight up** colloq. **1** truthfully; honestly. **2** without admixture or dilution. □□ **straight·ish** adj. **straight·ly** adv. **straight·ness** n.

straight·a·way /stráytəway/ adj. & n. ● adj. 1 (of a course, etc.) straight. 2 straightforward. ● n. a straight course, track, road, etc.

straight·edge /stráytej/ n. a bar with one edge accurately straight, used for testing.

straight·en /stráyt'n/ v.tr. & intr. 1 (often foll. by out) make or become straight. 2 (foll. by up) stand erect after bending. □□ **straight·en·er** n.

straight face n. an intentionally expressionless or serious face, esp. avoiding a show of amusement. □□ **straight-faced** adj.

straight·for·ward /stráytfáwrwərd/ adj. 1 honest or frank. 2 (of a task, etc.) uncomplicated. □□ **straight·for·ward·ly** adv. **straight·for·ward·ness** n.

straight·jacket var. of STRAITJACKET.

straight·laced var. of STRAITLACED.

straight man n. a comedian's stooge.

straight-out adj. 1 uncompromising. 2 straightforward; genuine.

straight ra·zor n. a razor with a straight blade that is hinged to a handle into which it can be folded.

straight·way /stráytway/ adv. archaic = straight away.

strain[1] /strayn/ v. & n. ● v. 1 tr. & intr. make or become taut or tense. 2 tr. exercise (oneself, one's senses, a thing, etc.) intensely or excessively. 3 a intr. make an intensive effort. b (foll. by after) strive intensely for. 4 intr. (foll. by at) tug; pull. 5 intr. hold out with difficulty under pressure (straining under the load). 6 tr. distort from the true intention or meaning. 7 tr. overtask or injure by overuse or excessive demands (strain a muscle; strained their loyalty). 8 a tr. clear (a liquid) of solid matter by passing it through a sieve, etc. b tr. (foll. by out) filter (solids) out from a liquid. 9 tr. use (one's ears, eyes, voice, etc.) to the best of one's power. ● n. 1 a the act or an instance of straining. b the force exerted in this. 2 an injury caused by straining a muscle, etc. 3 a a severe demand on physical strength or resources. b the exertion needed to meet this (is suffering from strain). 4 (in sing. or pl.) a snatch or spell of music or poetry. 5 a tone or tendency in speech or writing (more in the same strain). □ **strain oneself 1** injure oneself by effort. **2** make undue efforts.

strain[2] /strayn/ n. 1 a breed or stock of animals, plants, etc. 2 a moral tendency as part of a person's character (a strain of aggression).

strained /straynd/ adj. 1 constrained; forced; artificial. 2 (of a relationship) mutually distrustful or tense. 3 (of an interpretation) involving an unreasonable assumption; far-fetched; labored.

strain·er /stráynər/ n. a device for straining liquids, vegetables, etc.

strait /strayt/ n. 1 (in sing. or pl.) ▼ a narrow passage of water connecting two large bodies of water. 2 (usu. in pl.) difficulty, trouble, or distress (usu. in dire or desperate straits).

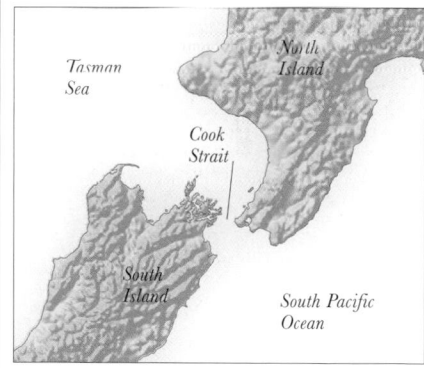

STRAIT: MAP SHOWING THE STRAIT BETWEEN NORTH AND SOUTH ISLANDS, NEW ZEALAND

strait·en /stráyt'n/ v.tr. 1 restrict in range or scope. 2 (as **straitened** adj.) (esp. of circumstances) characterized by poverty.

strait·jack·et /stráytjakit/ n. & v. (also **straight-jacket**) ● n. 1 a strong garment with long arms for confining the arms of a violent prisoner, mental patient, etc. 2 restrictive measures. ● v.tr. (**-jacketed, -jacketing**) 1 restrain with a straitjacket. 2 severely restrict.

strait·laced /stráytláyst/ adj. (also **straight·laced**) severely virtuous.

strake /strayk/ n. 1 a continuous line of planking or plates from the stem to the stern of a ship. 2 a section of the iron rim of a wheel.

stra·mo·ni·um /strəmóneeəm/ n. 1 datura. 2 the dried leaves of this plant used in the treatment of asthma.

strand[1] /strand/ v. & n. ● v.tr. 1 run aground. 2 (as **stranded** adj.) in difficulties, esp. without money

S

or means of transport. **3** *Baseball* leave (a runner) on base at the end of an inning. ● *n. poet.* the margin of a sea, lake, or river.

strand² /strand/ *n.* **1** each of the threads or wires twisted around each other to make a rope or cable. **2 a** a single thread or strip of fiber. **b** a constituent filament. **3** an element or strain in any composite whole.

strange /straynj/ *adj.* **1** unusual; peculiar. **2** unfamiliar; alien (*lost in a strange land*). **3** (foll. by *to*) unaccustomed. **4** not at ease; out of one's element. □ **feel strange** be unwell. □□ **strange·ly** *adv.*

strange·ness /stráynjnis/ *n.* **1** the state or fact of being strange or unfamiliar. **2** *Physics* a property of certain elementary particles that is conserved in strong interactions.

stran·ger /stráynjər/ *n.* **1** a person who does not know or is not known in a particular place or company. **2** (often foll. by *to*) a person one does not know (*was a complete stranger to me*). **3** (foll. by *to*) a person entirely unaccustomed to (a feeling, experience, etc.) (*no stranger to controversy*).

stran·gle /stránggəl/ *v.tr.* **1** squeeze the windpipe or neck of, esp. so as to kill. **2** hamper or suppress (a movement, impulse, cry, etc.). □□ **stran·gler** *n.*

stran·gle·hold /stránggəlhōld/ *n.* **1** a wrestling hold that throttles an opponent. **2** a deadly grip. **3** complete and exclusive control.

stran·gles /stránggəlz/ *n.pl.* (usu. treated as *sing.*) an infectious streptococcal fever, esp. affecting the respiratory tract, in a horse, donkey, etc.

stran·gu·late /stránggyəlayt/ *v.tr. Surgery* **1** prevent circulation through (a vein, intestine, etc.) by compression. **2** remove (a tumor, etc.) by binding with a cord.

stran·gu·la·tion /stránggyəláyshən/ *n.* **1** the act of strangling or the state of being strangled. **2** the act of strangulating.

stran·gu·ry /stránggyəree/ *n.* a condition in which the urine is passed painfully and in drops. □□ **stran·gu·ri·ous** /-gyŏōreeəs/ *adj.*

strap /strap/ *n. & v.* ● *n.* **1** a strip of leather or other flexible material, often with a buckle or other fastening for holding things together, etc. **2** a thing like this for keeping a garment in place. **3** a loop for grasping to steady oneself in a moving vehicle. ● *v.tr.* (**strapped, strapping**) **1** (often foll. by *down, up*, etc.) secure or bind with a strap. **2** beat with a strap. **3** (esp. as **strapped** *adj.*) *colloq.* subject to a shortage. □□ **strap·py** *adj.*

strap·hang·er /stráp-hangər/ *n. sl.* a standing passenger in a bus or subway, esp. a regular commuter. □□ **strap·hang** *v.intr.*

strap·less /stráplis/ *adj.* (of a garment) without straps, esp. shoulder straps.

strap·line /stráplīn/ *n.* a subheading or caption in a newspaper or magazine.

strap·pa·do /strəpáydō, -páʌ-/ *n.* (*pl.* **-os**) *hist.* **1** a form of torture in which the victim is raised from the ground by a rope and made to fall from a height almost to the ground then stopped with a jerk. **2** an application of this. **3** the instrument used.

strap·ping /stráping/ *adj.* (esp. of a person) large and sturdy.

stra·ta *pl.* of STRATUM.

strat·a·gem /strátəjəm/ *n.* **1** a cunning plan or scheme, esp. for deceiving an enemy. **2** trickery.

stra·tal see STRATUM.

stra·te·gic /strətéejik/ *adj.* **1** of or serving strategy (*strategic considerations; strategic move*). **2** (of materials) essential in fighting a war. **3** (of bombing or weapons) done or for use against an enemy's home territory as a longer-term military objective (opp. TACTICAL). □□ **stra·te·gi·cal** *adj.* **stra·te·gi·cal·ly** *adv.* **stra·te·gics** *n.pl.* (usu. treated as *sing.*).

stra·te·gic de·fense in·i·ti·a·tive *n.* a proposed US system of defense against nuclear weapons using satellites. ¶ Abbr.: **SDI**

strat·e·gy /strátijee/ *n.* (*pl.* **-ies**) **1** the art of war. **2 a** the art of moving troops, ships, aircraft, etc.,

into favorable positions (cf. TACTICS). **b** an instance of this or a plan formed according to it. **3** a plan of action or policy in business or politics, etc. (*economic strategy*). □□ **strat·e·gist** *n.*

strath /strath/ *n. Sc.* a broad mountain valley.

strath·spey /strathspáy/ *n.* **1** a slow Scottish dance. **2** the music for this.

stra·ti *pl.* of STRATUS.

strat·i·cu·late /strətíkyələt/ *adj. Geol.* (of rock formations) arranged in thin strata.

strat·i·fy /strátifī/ *v.tr.* (**-ies, -ied**) **1** (esp. as **stratified** *adj.*) arrange in strata. **2** construct in layers, social grades, etc. □□ **strat·i·fi·ca·tion** /-fikáyshən/ *n.*

stra·tig·ra·phy /strətígrəfee/ *n. Geol. & Archaeol.* **1** the order and relative position of strata. **2** the study of this as a means of historical interpretation. □□ **strat·i·graph·ic** /strátigráfik/ *adj.* **strat·i·graph·i·cal** *adj.*

strato- /strátō/ *comb. form* stratus.

stra·to·cir·rus /strátōsírəs/ *n.* clouds combining stratus and cirrus features.

stra·toc·ra·cy /strətókrəsee/ *n.* (*pl.* **-ies**) **1** a military government. **2** domination by soldiers.

stra·to·cu·mu·lus /strátōkyŏōmyələs/ *n.* clouds combining cumulus and stratus features.

strat·o·pause /strátōpawz/ *n.* the interface between the stratosphere and the ionosphere.

strat·o·sphere /strátəsfeer/ *n.* a layer of atmospheric air above the troposphere extending to about 30 miles above the Earth's surface. ▷ ATMOSPHERE. □□ **strat·o·spher·ic** /-féerik, -férik/ *adj.*

stra·tum /stráytəm, strát-/ *n.* (*pl.* **strata** /-tə/) **1** esp. *Geol.* or *Archaeol.* ▼ a layer or set of successive layers of any deposited substance. **2** an atmospheric layer. **3** a layer of tissue, etc. **4** a social grade, class, etc. (*the various strata of society*). □□ **stra·tal** *adj.*

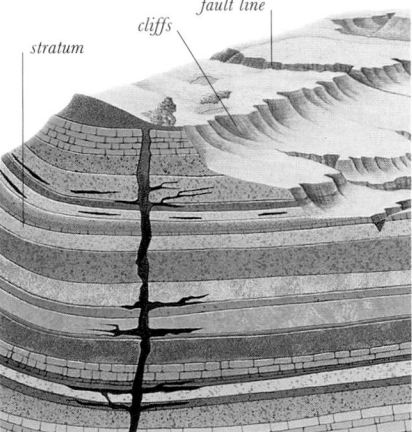

STRATUM: SECTION THROUGH THE GRAND CANYON, SHOWING STRATA

stra·tus /stráytəs, strát-/ *n.* a continuous horizontal sheet of cloud. ▷ CLOUD

straw /straw/ *n.* **1** dry cut stalks of grain for use as fodder or for thatching, packing, etc. **2** a single stalk of straw. **3** a thin tube for sucking a drink from a glass, etc. **4** the pale yellow color of straw. **5** a straw hat. □ **catch** (or **grasp**) **at straws** resort to an utterly inadequate expedient in desperation. □□ **straw·y** *adj.*

straw·ber·ry /stráwberee/ *n.* (*pl.* **-ies**) **1 a** any plant of the genus *Fragaria*, esp. any of various cultivated varieties, with white flowers and runners. **b** the pulpy red edible fruit of this, having a seed-studded surface. ▷ FRUIT, SEED. **2** a deep pinkish-red color.

straw·ber·ry blond *n.* **1** reddish blond hair. **2** a person with such hair.

straw·ber·ry mark *n.* a soft reddish birthmark.

straw vote *n.* (also **straw poll**) an unofficial ballot as a test of opinion.

stray /stray/ *v., n., & adj.* ● *v.intr.* **1** wander from the right place; become separated from one's companions. **2** deviate morally. **3** (as **strayed** *adj.*) that has gone astray. ● *n.* a person or thing that has strayed, esp. a domestic animal. ● *adj.* **1** strayed or lost. **2** found or occurring occasionally (*a stray customer or two; hit by a stray bullet*).

streak /streek/ *n. & v.* ● *n.* **1** a long thin usu. irregular line or band, esp. distinguished by color. **2** a strain or element in a person's character (*streak of mischief*). **3** a spell or series (*a winning streak*). ● *v.* **1** *tr.* mark with streaks. **2** *intr.* move very rapidly. **3** *intr. colloq.* run naked in a public place as a stunt. □□ **streak·er** *n.* **streak·ing** *n.*

streak·y /stréekee/ *adj.* (**streakier, streakiest**) full of streaks. □□ **streak·i·ly** *adv.* **streak·i·ness** *n.*

stream /streem/ *n. & v.* ● *n.* **1** a flowing body of water, esp. a small river. **2 a** the flow of a fluid or of a mass of people (*a stream of lava*). **b** (in *sing.* or *pl.*) a large quantity of something that flows or moves along. **3** a current or direction in which things are moving or tending (*against the stream*). ● *v.* **1** *intr.* flow or move as a stream. **2** *intr.* run with liquid (*my eyes were streaming*). **3** *intr.* (of a banner or hair, etc.) float or wave in the wind. **4** *tr.* emit a stream of (blood, etc.). □ **on stream** (of a factory, etc.) in operation.

stream·er /stréemər/ *n.* **1** a long narrow flag. **2** a long narrow strip of ribbon or paper, esp. in a coil that unrolls when thrown. **3** a banner headline.

stream·line /stréemlīn/ *v.tr.* **1** give (a vehicle, etc.) the form which presents the least resistance to motion. **2** make (an organization, process, etc.) simple or more efficient or better organized. **3** (as **streamlined** *adj.*) **a** ▼ having a smooth, slender, or elongated form. **b** having a simplified and more efficient structure or organization.

STREAMLINE: TESTING A CAR'S STREAMLINED SHAPE IN A WIND TUNNEL

stream of con·scious·ness *n.* **1** *Psychol.* a person's thoughts and conscious reactions to events perceived as a continuous flow. **2** a literary style depicting events in such a flow in the mind of a character.

street /street/ *n.* **1** a public road in a city, town, or village. **2** this with the houses or other buildings on each side. □ **on the streets 1** living by prostitution. **2** homeless. □□ **street·ed** *adj.* (also in *comb.*).

street A·rab often *offens.* **1** a homeless child. **2** an urchin.

street·car /stréetkaar/ *n.* a commuter vehicle that operates on rails in city streets.

street smarts *n. colloq.* social awareness gained from hard experience.

street val·ue *n.* the value of drugs sold illicitly.

street·walk·er /stréetwawkər/ *n.* a prostitute seeking customers in the street. □□ **street·walk·ing** *n. & adj.*

street·wise /stréetwīz/ *adj.* familiar with the ways of modern urban life.

stre·litz·i·a /strelitzeeə/ *n.* a southern African plant of the genus *Strelitzia*, with showy irregular flowers having a long projecting tongue.

strength /strengkth, strength, strenth/ *n.* **1** the state of being strong; the degree or respect in which a person or thing is strong. **2 a** a person or thing affording support. **b** an attribute making for strength of character (*patience is your great strength*). **3** the number of persons present. **4** a full complement (*below strength*). ▫ **from strength** from a strong position. **from strength to strength** with ever-increasing success. **in strength** in large numbers. **on the strength of** on the basis of. **the strength of** the essence or main features of. ▫▫ **strength·less** *adj.*

strength·en /stréngkthən, strén-/ *v.tr. & intr.* make or become stronger. ▫ **strengthen a person's hand** (or **hands**) encourage a person to vigorous action. ▫▫ **strength·en·er** *n.*

stren·u·ous /strényōōəs/ *adj.* **1** requiring or using great effort. **2** energetic or unrelaxing. ▫▫ **stren·u·ous·ly** *adv.* **stren·u·ous·ness** *n.*

strep /strep/ *n. colloq.* = STREPTOCOCCUS.

strep throat *n. colloq.* an acute sore throat caused by hemolytic streptococci and characterized by fever and inflammation.

strep·to·coc·cus /stréptəkókəs/ *n.* (*pl.* **streptococci** /-kóksī, -kókī/) any bacterium of the genus *Streptococcus*, usu. occurring in chains, some of which cause infectious diseases. ▫▫ **strep·to·coc·cal** *adj.*

strep·to·my·cin /stréptəmísin/ *n.* an antibiotic produced by the bacterium *Streptomyces griseus*, effective against many disease-producing bacteria.

stress /stres/ *n. & v.* ● *n.* **1 a** a pressure or tension exerted on a material object. **b** a quantity measuring this. **2 a** demand on physical or mental energy. **b** distress caused by this (*suffering from stress*). **3 a** emphasis (*the stress was on the need for success*). **b** accentuation; emphasis laid on a syllable or word. **c** an accent, esp. the principal one in a word (*the stress is on the first syllable*). ● *v.tr.* **1** lay stress on; emphasize. **2** subject to mechanical or physical or mental stress. ▫ **lay stress on** indicate as important. ▫▫ **stress·less** *adj.*

stress·ful /strésfōōl/ *adj.* causing stress; mentally tiring (*had a stressful day*). ▫▫ **stress·ful·ly** *adv.* **stress·ful·ness** *n.*

stretch /strech/ *v. & n.* ● *v.* **1** *tr. & intr.* draw or be drawn or admit of being drawn out into greater length or size. **2** *tr. & intr.* make or become taut. **3** *tr. & intr.* place or lie at full length or spread out (*with a canopy stretched over them*). **4** *tr.* **a** extend (an arm, leg, etc.). **b** (often *refl.*) thrust out (one's limbs) and tighten (one's muscles) after being relaxed. **5** *intr.* have a specified length or extension; extend (*farmland stretches for many miles*). **6** *tr.* strain or exert extremely or excessively; exaggerate (*stretch the truth*). **7** *tr.* (as **stretched** *adj.*) elongated or extended. ● *n.* **1** a continuous extent or expanse or period (*a stretch of open road*). **2** the act of stretching. **3** (*attrib.*) able to stretch; elastic (*stretch fabric*). **4 a** *colloq.* a period of imprisonment. **b** a period of service. ▫ **at full stretch** working to capacity. **at a stretch 1** in one continuous period. **2** with much effort. **stretch one's legs** exercise oneself by walking. **stretch out 1** *tr.* extend (a hand or foot, etc.). **2** *intr. & tr.* last for a longer period; prolong. **3** *tr.* make (money, etc.) last for a sufficient time. **stretch a point** agree to something not normally allowed. ▫▫ **stretch·a·ble** *adj.* **stretch·a·bil·i·ty** /stréchəbílitee/ *n.* **stretch·y** *adj.* **stretch·i·ness** *n.*

stretch·er /stréchər/ *n. & v.* ● *n.* **1** a framework of two poles with canvas, etc., between, for carrying injured, sick, or dead persons in a lying position. **2** a brick or stone laid with its long side along the face of a wall. ▷ BRICK. **3** a rod or bar as a tie between chair legs, etc. **4** a board in a boat against which a rower presses the feet. **5** ► a wooden frame over which a canvas is stretched ready for painting. ● *v.tr.* (often foll. by *off*) convey (a sick or injured person) on a stretcher.

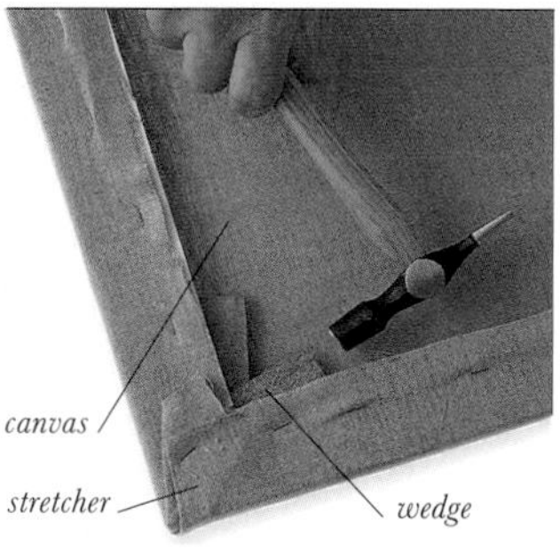

STRETCHER WITH CANVAS FITTED

stretch marks *n.pl.* marks on the skin resulting from a gain of weight, or on the abdomen after pregnancy.

stret·to /strétō/ *adv. Mus.* in quicker time.

strew /strōō/ *v.tr.* (*past part.* **strewn** or **strewed**) **1** scatter or spread about over a surface. **2** (usu. foll. by *with*) spread (a surface) with scattered things. ▫▫ **strew·er** *n.*

stri·a /stríə/ *n.* (*pl.* **-ae** /stríee/) *Anat., Zool., Bot., & Geol.* a linear mark on a surface. **2** a slight ridge, furrow, or score.

stri·ate *adj. & v. Anat., Zool., Bot., & Geol.* ● *adj.* /stríət/ (also **stri·at·ed** /stríaytid/) marked with striae. ● *v.tr.* /stríayt/ mark with striae. ▫▫ **stri·a·tion** /strīáyshən/ *n.*

strick·en /stríkən/ *adj.* **1** affected or overcome with illness or misfortune, etc. (*stricken with measles; grief-stricken*). **2** (often foll. by *from*, etc.) *Law* deleted. ▫ **stricken in years** *archaic* enfeebled by age.

strick·le /stríkəl/ *n.* **1** a rod used in strike measure. **2** a whetting tool.

strict /strikt/ *adj.* **1** precisely limited or defined (*lives in strict seclusion*). **2** requiring complete compliance or exact performance (*gave strict orders*). ▫▫ **strict·ness** *n.*

strict·ly /stríktlee/ *adv.* **1** in a strict manner. **2** (also **strict·ly speak·ing**) applying words in their strict sense (*he is, strictly, an absconder*). **3** *colloq.* definitely.

stric·ture /strikchər/ *n.* (usu. in *pl.*; often foll. by *upon, on*) a critical or censorious remark. ▫▫ **stric·tured** *adj.*

stride /strīd/ *v. & n.* ● *v.* (*past* **strode** /strōd/; *past part.* **stridden** /stríd'n/) **1** *intr. & tr.* walk with long firm steps. **2** *tr.* cross with one step. **3** *tr.* bestride; straddle. ● *n.* **1 a** a single long step. **b** the length of this. **2** a person's gait as determined by the length of stride. **3** (usu. in *pl.*) progress (*has made great strides*). **4** a settled rate of progress (*get into one's stride*). ▫ **take in one's stride 1** clear (an obstacle) without changing one's gait to jump. **2** manage without difficulty. ▫▫ **strid·er** *n.*

stri·dent /stríd'nt/ *adj.* loud and harsh. ▫▫ **stri·den·cy** *n.* **stri·dent·ly** *adv.*

strid·u·late /stríjəlayt/ *v.intr.* (of the cicada and grasshopper) make a shrill sound by rubbing the legs or wing cases together. ▫▫ **strid·u·la·tion** /-láyshən/ *n.*

strife /strīf/ *n.* conflict; struggle between opposed persons or things.

stri·gil /stríjil/ *n.* **1** *Gk & Rom. Antiq.* a skin scraper used by bathers after exercise. **2** a structure on the leg of an insect used to clean its antennae, etc.

stri·gose /strígōs/ *adj.* **1** (of leaves, etc.) having short stiff hairs or scales. **2** (of an insect, etc.) streaked, striped, or ridged.

strike /strīk/ *v. & n.* ● *v.* (*past* **struck** /struk/; *past part.* **struck** or *archaic* **stricken** /stríkən/) **1 a** *tr.* subject to an impact. **b** *tr.* deliver (a blow) or inflict a blow on. **2** *tr.* come or bring sharply into contact with. **3** *tr.* propel with a blow. **4** *intr.* (foll. by *at*) try to hit. **5** *tr.* cause to penetrate (*struck terror into him*). **6** *tr.* ignite (a match) or produce (sparks, etc.) by rubbing. **7** *tr.* make (a coin) by stamping. **8** *tr.* produce (a musical note) by striking. **9 a** *tr.* (also *absol.*) (of a clock) indicate (the time) by the sounding of a chime, etc. **b** *intr.* (of time) be indicated in this way. **10** *tr.* **a** attack or affect suddenly (*was struck with sudden terror*). **b** (of a disease) afflict. **11** *tr.* cause to become suddenly (*was struck dumb*). **12** *tr.* reach or achieve (*strike a balance*). **13** *tr.* agree on (a bargain). **14** *tr.* assume (an attitude) suddenly and dramatically. **15** *tr.* find (oil, etc.) by drilling. **16** come to the attention of or appear to (*it strikes me as silly; an idea suddenly struck me*). **17** *intr.* (of employees) cease work as a protest. **18** *tr.* lower or take down (a flag, tent, etc.). ● *n.* **1** the act of striking. **2 a** the organized refusal by employees to work until some grievance is remedied. **b** a similar refusal to participate. **3** a sudden find or success (*a lucky strike*). **4** an attack, esp. from the air. **5** *Baseball* a pitched ball counted against a batter, either for failure to hit it into fair territory or because it passes through the strike zone. **6** the act of knocking down all the pins with the first ball in bowling. ▫ **on strike** taking part in an industrial strike. **strike back** strike or attack in return. **strike down 1** knock down. **2** afflict (*struck down by a virus*). **strike home 1** deal an effective blow. **2** have an intended effect (*my words struck home*). **strike it rich** *colloq.* find a source of abundance or success. **strike a light** produce a light by striking a match. **strike lucky** esp. *Brit.* have a lucky success. **strike off 1** remove with a stroke. **2** delete (a name, etc.) from a list. **strike out 1** hit out. **2** act vigorously. **3** delete (an item or name, etc.). **4** set off or begin (*struck out eastward*). **5** use the arms and legs in swimming. **6** *Baseball* **a** dismiss (a batter) by means of three strikes. **b** be dismissed in this way. **strike through** delete (a word, etc.) with a stroke of one's pen. **strike up 1** start (an acquaintance, conversation, etc.) esp. casually. **2** (also *absol.*) begin playing (a tune, etc.). **strike upon 1** have (an idea, etc.) luckily occur to one. **2** (of light) illuminate. **strike while the iron is hot** act promptly at a good opportunity. ▫▫ **strik·a·ble** *adj.*

strike·bound /stríkbownd/ *adj.* immobilized or closed by a strike.

strike·break·er /stríkbraykər/ *n.* a person working in place of others who are on strike. ▫▫ **strike·break** *v.intr.*

strike·out /stríkowt/ *n. Baseball* an out charged against a batter who has three strikes and credited to the pitcher.

strik·er /stríkər/ *n.* **1** a person or thing that strikes. **2** an employee on strike. **3** *Sports* the player who is to strike, or who is to be the next to strike, the ball. **4** *Soccer* an attacking player positioned well forward in order to score goals. ▷ FOOTBALL

strike zone *n. Baseball* an area between a batter's knees and armpits and over home plate through which a pitch must pass in order to be called a strike.

strik·ing /stríking/ *adj.* impressive; attracting attention. ▫ **within striking distance** near enough to hit or to achieve. ▫▫ **strik·ing·ly** *adv.* **strik·ing·ness** *n.*

Strine /strīn/ *n.* **1** a comic transliteration of Australian speech, e.g., *Emma Chissitt* = 'How much is it?'. **2** (esp. uneducated) Australian English.

string /string/ *n. & v.* ● *n.* **1** twine or narrow cord. **2** a piece of this or of similar material used for tying or holding together, pulling, etc. **3** a length of catgut or wire, etc., on a musical instrument, producing a note by vibration. ▷ STRINGED. **4 a** (in *pl.*) the stringed instruments in an orchestra, etc. **b** (*attrib.*) relating to or consisting of stringed instruments (*string quartet*). **5** (in *pl.*) an awkward condition or complication (*the offer has no strings*). **6** a set of things strung together; a series or line of persons or things (*a string of beads*). **7** a tough piece connecting the two halves of a peapod, etc. **8** a piece of catgut, etc., interwoven with others to form the head of a tennis, etc., racket. ● *v.tr.* (*past* and *past part.* **strung** /strung/) **1** supply with a string or strings. **2** tie with string. **3** thread (beads, etc.) on a string. **4** arrange in or as a string. **5** remove the strings from (a bean, etc.). ▫ **on a string** under one's control. **string along** *colloq.* **1** deceive, esp. by appearing to comply with (a person). **2** (often foll. by *with*) keep company (with). **string out** extend; prolong (esp. unduly). **string up 1** hang up on strings, etc. **2** kill by hanging. ▫▫ **string·less** *adj.* **string·like** *adj.*

string bass *n. Mus.* a double bass.

string bean *n.* any of various beans eaten in their fibrous pods, esp. runner beans or snap beans.

string·board /stríngbawrd/ *n.* a supporting timber or skirting in which the ends of a staircase steps are set.

STRINGED

Most stringed instruments are characterized by a set of stretched strings attached to a hollow body, which amplifies the strings' vibrations. To produce these vibrations, a string can be plucked, as is a guitar; bowed, as is a cello; or struck, as is a piano. The thinner and shorter the string, the higher the note it will produce. Larger instruments are capable of creating lower notes: a double bass, for example, with its sizable body and long strings, can generate much deeper sounds than a violin.

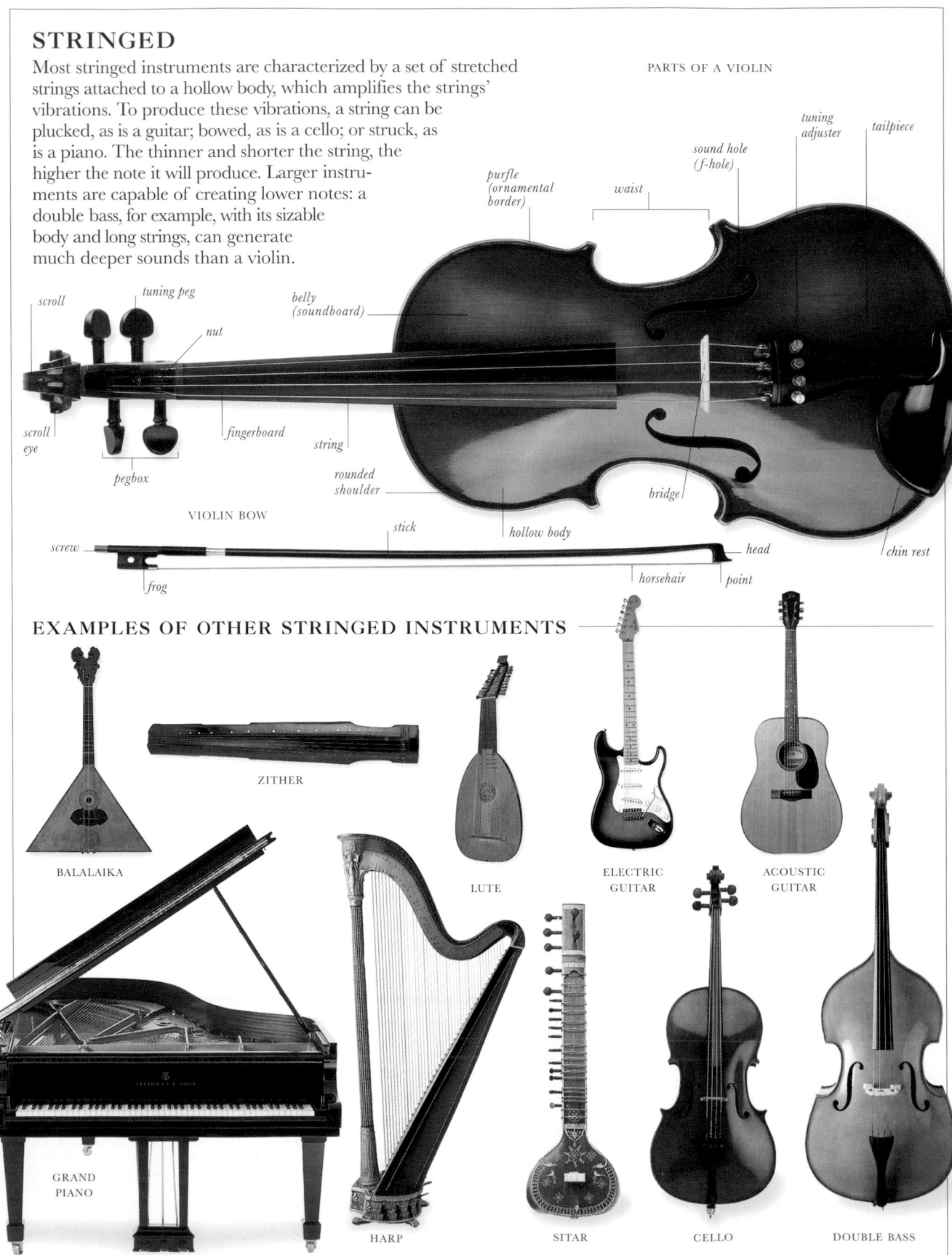

PARTS OF A VIOLIN

tuning adjuster

tailpiece

sound hole (f-hole)

purfle (ornamental border)

waist

scroll

tuning peg

belly (soundboard)

nut

scroll eye

fingerboard

string

pegbox

rounded shoulder

bridge

hollow body

chin rest

VIOLIN BOW

screw

stick

head

frog

horsehair

point

EXAMPLES OF OTHER STRINGED INSTRUMENTS

BALALAIKA

ZITHER

LUTE

ELECTRIC GUITAR

ACOUSTIC GUITAR

GRAND PIANO

HARP

SITAR

CELLO

DOUBLE BASS

S

stringed /stringd/ *adj.* ◄ (of musical instruments) having strings (also in *comb.*: *twelve-stringed guitar*). ▷ ORCHESTRA

strin·gen·do /strinjéndō/ *adj.* & *adv. Mus.* with increasing speed.

strin·gent /strínjənt/ *adj.* (of rules, etc.) strict; precise; requiring exact performance. ◻◻ **strin·gen·cy** *n.* **strin·gent·ly** *adv.*

string·er /stríngər/ *n.* **1** a longitudinal structural member in a framework, esp. of a ship or aircraft. **2** *colloq.* a newspaper correspondent not on the regular staff.

string·halt /strínghawlt/ *n.* spasmodic movement of a horse's hind leg.

string·y /strínge e/ *adj.* (**stringier**, **stringiest**) **1** (of food, etc.) fibrous; tough. **2** of or like string. **3** (of a person) tall and thin. ◻◻ **string·i·ly** *adv.* **string·i·ness** *n.*

strip[1] /strip/ *v.* & *n.* ● *v.* (**stripped**, **stripping**) **1** *tr.* (often foll. by *of*) remove the clothes or covering from (a person or thing). **2** *intr.* (often foll. by *off*) undress oneself. **3** *tr.* (often foll. by *of*) deprive (a person) of property or titles. **4** *tr.* leave bare of accessories or fittings. **5** *tr.* remove bark and branches from (a tree). **6** *tr.* (often foll. by *down*) remove the accessory fittings of or take apart (a machine, etc.) to inspect or adjust it. **7** *tr.* tear the thread from (a screw). **8** *tr.* tear the teeth from (a gearwheel). **9** *tr.* remove (paint) or remove paint from (a surface) with solvent. **10** *tr.* (often foll. by *from*) pull or tear (a covering or property, etc.) off (*stripped the masks from their faces*). **11** *intr.* (of a screw) lose its thread. ● *n.* an act of stripping, esp. of undressing in striptease.

strip[2] /strip/ *n.* **1** a long narrow piece (*a strip of land*). **2** (in full **strip cartoon**) = COMIC STRIP.

strip club *n.* a club at which striptease performances are given.

stripe /strīp/ *n.* **1** a long narrow band or strip differing in color or texture from the surface on either side of it (*black with a red stripe*). **2** *Mil.* a chevron, etc., denoting military rank. **3** a category of character, opinion, etc. (*a man of that stripe*). **4** (usu. in *pl.*) *archaic* a blow with a scourge or lash.

striped /strīpt/ *adj.* marked with stripes.

striped bass *n.* a fish, *Morone saxatilis*, with dark stripes along its sides, used for food and game along the N. American coasts.

strip·ling /strípling/ *n.* a youth not yet fully grown.

strip mine *n.* a mine worked by removing the material that overlies the ore, etc. ▷ MINE. ◻◻ **strip-mine** *v.tr.* & *intr.*

strip·per /strípər/ *n.* **1** a person or thing that strips something. **2** a device or solvent for removing paint, etc. **3** a striptease performer.

strip pok·er *n.* a form of poker in which a player with a losing hand takes off an item of clothing as a forfeit.

strip search *n.* a search of a person involving the removal of all clothes. ◻◻ **strip-search** *v.tr.*

strip·tease /strípteez/ *n.* & *v.* ● *n.* an entertainment in which the performer gradually undresses before the audience. ● *v.intr.* perform a striptease.

strip·y /strípee/ *adj.* (**stripier**, **stripiest**) striped; having many stripes.

strive /strīv/ *v.intr.* (*past* **strove** /strōv/; *past part.* **striven** /strívən/) **1** (often foll. by *for*, or *to* + infin.) try hard. **2** (often foll. by *with*, *against*) struggle. ◻◻ **striv·er** *n.*

strobe /strōb/ *n. colloq.* **1** a stroboscope. **2** a stroboscopic lamp.

stro·bi·la /strōbílə/ *n.* (*pl.* **strobilae** /-lee/) **1** the segmented part of the body of a tapeworm. **2** a sessile polyplike form which divides horizontally to produce jellyfish larvae.

stro·bi·lus /strṓbiləs/ *n.* (*pl.* **strobili** /-lī/) *Bot.* **1** the cone of a pine, etc. **2** the layered flower of the hop.

stro·bo·scope /strṓbəskōp/ *n.* **1** *Physics* an instrument for determining speeds of rotation, etc., by shining a bright light at intervals so that a rotating object appears stationary. **2** a lamp made to flash intermittently, esp. for this purpose. ◻◻ **stro·bo·scop·ic** /-skópik/ *adj.*

strode *past* of STRIDE.

stro·ga·noff /stráwgənawf, strṓ-/ *adj.* (of meat) cut into strips and cooked in a sour cream sauce (*beef stroganoff*).

stroke /strōk/ *n.* & *v.* ● *n.* **1** the act of striking; a blow or hit (*with a single stroke*; *a stroke of lightning*). **2** a sudden disabling attack or loss of consciousness caused by an interruption in the flow of blood to the brain, esp. through thrombosis. **3 a** an action or movement, esp. as one of a series. **b** the slightest such action (*has not done a stroke of work*). **4** the whole of the motion (of a wing, oar, etc.) until the starting position is regained. **5** (in rowing) the mode or action of moving the oar (*row a fast stroke*). ▷ ROW. **6** the whole motion (of a piston) in either direction. **7** *Golf* the action of hitting (or hitting at) a ball with a club, as a unit of scoring. **8** a mode of moving the arms and legs in swimming. **9** a specially successful or skillful effort (*a stroke of diplomacy*). **10 a** a mark made by the movement in one direction of a pen or pencil or paintbrush. **b** a similar mark printed. **11** a detail contributing to the general effect in a description. **12** the sound made by a striking clock. **13** (in full **stroke oar**) the oar or oarsman nearest the stern, setting the time of the stroke. **14** the act or a spell of stroking. ● *v.tr.* **1** pass one's hand gently along the surface of (hair or fur, etc.). **2** act as the stroke of (a boat or crew). ◻ **at a stroke** by a single action. **off one's stroke** not performing as well as usual. **on the stroke** punctually.

stroke of luck *n.* (also **stroke of good luck**) an unforeseen opportune occurrence.

stroll /strōl/ *v.* & *n.* ● *v.intr.* saunter or walk in a leisurely way. ● *n.* a short leisurely walk (*go for a stroll*).

stroll·er /strṓlər/ *n.* **1** a person who strolls. **2** a folding chair on wheels, for pushing a child in.

stroll·ing play·ers *n.pl.* actors, etc., going from place to place to give performances.

stro·ma /strṓmə/ *n.* (*pl.* **stromata** /-mətə/) *Biol.* **1** the framework of an organ or cell. **2** a fungous tissue containing spore-producing bodies. ◻◻ **stro·mat·ic** /-mátik/ *adj.*

strong /strawng, strong/ *adj.* & *adv.* ● *adj.* (**stronger** /stráwnggər, stróng-/; **strongest** /stráwnggist, stróng-/) **1** having the power of resistance; not easily damaged or overcome (*strong material*; *strong faith*). **2** (of a patient) restored to health. **3** (of a market) having steadily high or rising prices. **4** capable of exerting great force or of doing much. **5** forceful or powerful in effect (*a strong wind*; *a strong protest*). **6** decided or firmly held (*a strong suspicion*; *strong views*). **7** (of an argument, etc.) convincing or striking. **8** powerfully affecting the senses or emotions (*a strong light*; *strong acting*). **9** powerful in terms of size or numbers or quality (*a strong army*). **10** capable of doing much when united (*a strong combination*). **11** formidable; likely to succeed (*a strong candidate*). **12** (of a solution or drink, etc.) containing a large proportion of a substance in water or another solvent (*strong tea*). **13** (of a group) having a specified number (*200 strong*). **14** (of a voice) loud or penetrating. **15** (of food or its flavor) pungent. **16** (of a measure) drastic. **17** *Gram.* in Germanic languages: **a** (of a verb) forming inflections by change of vowel within the stem rather than by the addition of a suffix (e.g., *swim*, *swam*). **b** (of a noun or adjective) belonging to a declension in which the stem originally ended otherwise than in *-n*. ● *adv.* strongly (*the tide is running strong*). ◻ **come on strong** act aggressively, flamboyantly, etc. **going strong** *colloq.* continuing action vigorously; in good health. ◻◻ **strong·ish** *adj.* **strong·ly** *adv.*

strong-arm *adj.* using force (*strong-arm tactics*).

strong·box /stráwngboks, stróng-/ *n.* a strongly made small chest for valuables.

strong·hold /stráwnghōld, stróng-/ *n.* **1** a fortified place. **2** a secure refuge. **3** a center of support for a cause, etc.

strong lan·guage *n.* forceful language; swearing.

strong·room /stráwngrōōm, -rŏŏm, stróng-/ *n.* a room designed to protect valuables against fire and theft.

strong suit *n.* **1** a suit at cards in which one can take tricks. **2** a thing at which one excels.

stron·ti·a /strónshə/ *n. Chem.* strontium oxide.

stron·ti·um /strónteeəm/ *n. Chem.* a soft silver white metallic element occurring naturally in various minerals.

stron·ti·um 90 *n.* a radioactive isotope of strontium concentrated selectively in bones and teeth when taken into the body.

stron·ti·um ox·ide *n.* a white compound used in the manufacture of fireworks.

strop /strop/ *n.* & *v.* ● *n.* a device, esp. a strip of leather, for sharpening razors. ● *v.tr.* (**stropped**, **stropping**) sharpen on or with a strop.

stroph·an·thin /strəfánthin/ *n.* a white crystalline poisonous glucoside extracted from various tropical plants of the genus *Strophanthus* and used as a heart medication.

strophe /strṓfee/ *n.* **1 a** a turn in dancing made by an ancient Greek chorus. **b** lines recited during this. **c** the first section of an ancient Greek choral ode or of one division of it. **2** a group of lines forming a section of a lyric poem. ◻◻ **stro·phic** *adj.*

strop·py /strópee/ *adj.* (**stroppier**, **stroppiest**) *Brit. colloq.* bad-tempered; awkward to deal with. ◻◻ **strop·pi·ly** *adv.* **strop·pi·ness** *n.*

strove *past* of STRIVE.

strow /strō/ *v.tr.* (*past part.* **strown** /strōn/ or **strowed**) *archaic* = STREW.

struck *past* and *past part.* of STRIKE.

struc·tur·al /strúkchərəl/ *adj.* of, concerning, or having a structure. ◻◻ **struc·tur·al·ly** *adv.*

struc·tur·al·ism /strúkchərəlizəm/ *n.* **1** the doctrine that structure rather than function is important. **2** structural linguistics. **3** structural psychology. ◻◻ **struc·tur·al·ist** *n.* & *adj.*

struc·ture /strúkchər/ *n.* & *v.* ● *n.* **1 a** a whole constructed unit, esp. a building. **b** the way in which a building, etc., is constructed (*has a flimsy structure*). **2** a set of interconnecting parts of any complex thing (*the structure of a sentence*; *a new wages structure*). ● *v.tr.* give structure to; organize; frame. ◻◻ **struc·tured** *adj.* (also in *comb.*). **struc·ture·less** *adj.*

stru·del /strṓōd'l/ *n.* a confection of thin pastry rolled up around a filling and baked (*apple strudel*).

strug·gle /strúgəl/ *v.* & *n.* ● *v.intr.* **1** make forceful or violent efforts to get free of restraint or constriction. **2** (often foll. by *for*, or *to* + infin.) make violent or determined efforts under difficulties (*struggled to get the words out*). **3** (foll. by *with*, *against*) contend; fight strenuously. **4** make one's way with difficulty (*struggled to my feet*). **5** (esp. as **struggling** *adj.*) have difficulty in gaining recognition or a living (*a struggling artist*). ● *n.* **1** the act or a spell of struggling. **2** a hard or confused contest. **3** a determined effort under difficulties. ◻◻ **strug·gler** *n.*

strum /strum/ *v.* & *n.* ● *v.tr.* (**strummed**, **strumming**) **1** play on (a stringed or keyboard instrument), esp. carelessly or unskillfully. **2** play (a tune, etc.) in this way. ● *n.* the sound made by strumming. ◻◻ **strum·mer** *n.*

stru·ma /strṓōmə/ *n.* (*pl.* **strumae** /-mee/) **1** *Med.* **a** = SCROFULA. **b** = GOITER. **2** *Bot.* a cushionlike swelling of an organ. ◻◻ **stru·mose** *adj.* **stru·mous** *adj.*

strum·pet /strúmpit/ *n. archaic* or *rhet.* a prostitute.

strung *past* and *past part.* of STRING. ◻ **strung out** *sl.* **1 a** debilitated from long drug use. **b** agitated or incoherent from using drugs. **2** exhausted physically or emotionally.

S

strut /strut/ *n. & v.* ● *n.* **1** a bar forming part of a framework and designed to resist compression. **2** a strutting gait. ● *v.* (**strutted, strutting**) **1** *intr.* walk with a pompous or affected stiff erect gait. **2** *tr.* brace with a strut or struts. □□ **strut·ter** *n.* **strut·ting·ly** *adv.*

stru·thi·ous /strōōtheeəs/ *adj.* of or like an ostrich.

strych·nine /stríknīn, -nin, -neen/ *n.* a vegetable alkaloid obtained from plants of the genus *Strychnos* (esp. nux vomica), bitter and highly poisonous. □□ **strych·nic** *adj.*

Sts. *abbr.* Saints.

Stu·art /stōōərt, styōō-/ *adj. & n.* ● *adj.* of or relating to the royal family ruling Scotland 1371–1714 and England 1603–1649 and 1660–1714. ● *n.* a member of this family.

stub /stub/ *n. & v.* ● *n.* **1** the remnant of a pencil, cigarette, etc., after use. **2** part of a check, receipt, etc., retained as a record. **3** a stunted tail, etc. ● *v.tr.* (**stubbed, stubbing**) **1** strike (one's toe) against something. **2** (usu. foll. by *out*) extinguish (a lighted cigarette) by pressing the lighted end against something.

stub-ax·le *n.* an axle supporting only one wheel of a pair.

stub·ble /stúbəl/ *n.* **1** the cut stalks of cereal plants left sticking up after the harvest. **2 a** cropped hair or a cropped beard. **b** a short growth of unshaven hair. □□ **stub·bled** *adj.* **stub·bly** *adj.*

stub·born /stúbərn/ *adj.* **1** unreasonably obstinate. **2** unyielding; obdurate; inflexible. **3** refractory; intractable. □□ **stub·born·ly** *adv.* **stub·born·ness** *n.*

stub·by /stúbee/ *adj.* (**stubbier, stubbiest**) short and thick. □□ **stub·bi·ness** *n.*

stuc·co /stúkō/ *n. & v.* ● *n.* (*pl.* **-oes**) ▶ plaster or cement used for coating wall surfaces or molding into architectural decorations. ● *v.tr.* (**-oes, -oed**) coat with stucco.

stuck *past and past part.* of STICK[2].

stuck-up *adj. colloq.* affectedly superior and aloof; snobbish.

stud[1] /stud/ *n. & v.* ● *n.* **1** a large-headed nail or knob, projecting from a surface esp. for ornament. **2** a double button esp. for use with two buttonholes in a shirt front. **3** a small object projecting slightly from a road surface as a marker, etc. **4** a rivet or crosspiece in each link of a chain cable. ● *v.tr.* (**studded, studding**) **1** set with or as with studs. **2** (as **studded** *adj.*) (foll. by *with*) thickly set or strewn (*studded with diamonds*). **3** be scattered over or about (a surface).

stud[2] /stud/ *n.* **1 a** a number of horses kept for breeding, etc. **b** a place where these are kept. **2** (in full **stud horse**) a stallion. **3** *colloq.* a young man (esp. one noted for sexual prowess). **4** (in full **stud poker**) a form of poker with betting after the dealing of successive rounds of cards face up. □ **at stud** (of a male horse) publicly available for breeding on payment of a fee.

stud·book /stúdbŏŏk/ *n.* a book containing the pedigrees of horses.

stud·ding /stúding/ *n.* the woodwork of a lath-and-plaster or plasterboard wall.

stud·ding sail /stúdingsayl, stúnsəl/ *n.* a sail set on a small extra yard and boom beyond the leech of a square sail in light winds.

stu·dent /stōōd'nt, styōō-/ *n.* **1** a person who is studying, esp. at university or another place of higher education. **2** (*attrib.*) studying in order to become (*a student nurse*). **3** a person of studious habits.

stu·dent driv·er *n.* a person who is learning to drive a motor vehicle and has not yet passed a driving test.

stud farm *n.* a place where horses are bred.

stu·di·o /stōōdeeō, styōō-/ *n.* (*pl.* **-os**) **1** the workroom of a painter or photographer, etc. **2** a place

STUCCO: DECORATIVE MOLDED STUCCO

where movies or recordings are made or where television or radio programs are made or produced.

stu·di·o a·part·ment *n.* an apartment having only one main room, a kitchenette, and bath.

stu·di·o couch *n.* a couch that can be converted into a bed.

stu·di·ous /stōōdeeəs, styōō-/ *adj.* **1** devoted to or assiduous in study or reading. **2** deliberate; painstaking (*with studious care*). **3** (foll. by *to* + infin. or *in* + verbal noun) showing care or attention. □□ **stu·di·ous·ly** *adv.* **stu·di·ous·ness** *n.*

stud·y /stúdee/ *n. & v.* ● *n.* (*pl.* **-ies**) **1** the devotion of time and attention to acquiring information or knowledge, esp. from books. **2** (in *pl.*) the pursuit of academic knowledge (*continued their studies abroad*). **3** a room used for reading, writing, etc. **4** a piece of work, esp. a drawing, done for practice or as an experiment (*a study of a head*). **5** the portrayal in literature or another art form of an aspect of behavior or character, etc. **6** a musical composition designed to develop a player's skill. **7** a thing worth observing closely (*your face was a study*). **8** a thing that has been or deserves to be investigated. ● *v.* (**-ies, -ied**) **1** *tr.* make a study of; investigate or examine (a subject) (*study law*). **2** *intr.* (often foll. by *for*) apply oneself to study. **3** (as **studied** *adj.*) deliberate; intentional; affected (*with studied politeness*). □ **make a study of** investigate carefully. □□ **stud·ied·ly** *adv.* **stud·ied·ness** *n.*

stuff /stuf/ *n. & v.* ● *n.* **1** the material that a thing is made of; material that may be used for some purpose. **2** a substance or things or belongings of an indeterminate kind (*there's a lot of stuff about it in the newspapers*). **3** a particular knowledge or activity (*know one's stuff*). **4** valueless matter; trash (*take that stuff away*). **5** (prec. by *the*) **a** *colloq.* an available supply of something, esp. alcohol or drugs. **b** *sl.* money. ● *v.* **1** *tr.* pack (a receptacle) tightly. **2** *tr.* (foll. by *in, into*) force or cram (a thing). **3** *tr.* fill out the skin of (an animal or bird, etc.) with material to restore the original shape. **4** *tr.* fill (poultry, etc.) with a mixture, as of rice or seasoned bread crumbs, esp. before cooking. **5 a** *tr. & refl.* fill (a person or oneself) with food. **b** *tr. & intr.* eat greedily. **6** *tr.* push, esp. hastily or clumsily (*stuffed the note behind the cushion*). **7** *tr.* (usu. in *passive*; foll. by *up*) block up (a person's nose, etc.). **8** *tr. sl.* (esp. as an expression of contemptuous dismissal) dispose of as unwanted (*you can stuff the job*). □ **do one's stuff** *colloq.* do what one has to.

stuff it *sl.* an expression of rejection or disdain. **that's the stuff** *colloq.* that is what is wanted. □□ **stuff·er** *n.* (also in *comb.*).

stuffed shirt *n. colloq.* a pompous person.

stuff·ing /stúfing/ *n.* **1** padding used to stuff cushions, etc. **2** a mixture used to stuff poultry, etc., esp. before cooking. □ **knock** (or **take**) **the stuffing out of** *colloq.* beat soundly; defeat.

stuff·y /stúfee/ *adj.* (**stuffier, stuffiest**) **1** (of a room or the atmosphere in it) lacking fresh air or ventilation. **2** dull or uninteresting. **3** (of a person) dull and conventional. □□ **stuff·i·ly** *adv.* **stuff·i·ness** *n.*

stul·ti·fy /stúltifī/ *v.tr.* (**-ies, -ied**) make ineffective, useless, or futile, esp. as a result of tedious routine (*stultifying boredom*). □□ **stul·ti·fi·ca·tion** /-fikáyshən/ *n.*

stum /stum/ *n. & v.* ● *n.* unfermented grape juice; must. ● *v.tr.* (**stummed, stumming**) **1** prevent from fermenting, or secure (wine) against further fermentation in a cask, by the use of sulfur, etc. **2** add stum to renew the fermentation of wine.

stum·ble /stúmbəl/ *v. & n.* ● *v.intr.* **1** lurch forward or have a partial fall from catching or striking or misplacing one's foot. **2** (often foll. by *along*) walk with repeated stumbles. **3** make a mistake or repeated mistakes in speaking, etc. **4** (foll. by *on, upon, across*) find or encounter by chance. ● *n.* an act of stumbling.

stum·ble·bum /stúmbəlbum/ *n. colloq.* a clumsy or inept person.

stum·bling block *n.* an obstacle or circumstance causing difficulty or hesitation.

stump /stump/ *n. & v.* ● *n.* **1** the projecting remnant of a cut or fallen tree. **2** the similar remnant of anything else (e.g., a branch or limb) cut off or worn down. **3** (in *pl.*) *joc.* the legs. ● *v.* **1** *tr.* (of a question, etc.) be too hard for; puzzle. **2** *tr.* (as **stumped** *adj.*) at a loss; baffled. **3** *intr.* walk stiffly or noisily. **4** *tr.* (also *absol.*) traverse (a district) making political speeches. □ **on the stump** *colloq.* engaged in political speechmaking or agitation. **up a stump** in difficulties.

stump·er /stúmpər/ *n. colloq.* a puzzling question.

stump·y /stúmpee/ *adj.* (**stumpier, stumpiest**) short and thick.

stun /stun/ *v.tr.* (**stunned, stunning**) **1** knock senseless. **2** bewilder or shock.

stung *past and past part.* of STING.

stunk *past and past part.* of STINK.

stun·ner /stúnər/ *n. colloq.* a stunning person or thing.

stun·ning /stúning/ *adj. colloq.* extremely impressive or attractive. □□ **stun·ning·ly** *adv.*

stunt[1] /stunt/ *v.tr.* retard the growth or development of. □□ **stunt·ed·ness** *n.*

stunt[2] /stunt/ *n.* **1** something unusual done to attract attention. **2** a trick or daring maneuver.

stunt man *n.* (also **stunt wom·an**) a man (or woman) employed to take an actor's place in performing dangerous stunts.

stu·pa /stōōpə/ *n.* ▶ a round usu. domed building erected as a Buddhist shrine.

ringed spire

bell-shaped dome

entrance to relic chamber

moldings

STUPA: WAT PHRA SI SANPHET, THAILAND

stu·pe·fy /stōōpifī, styōō-/ *v.tr.* (**-ies, -ied**) **1** make stupid or insensible. **2** stun with astonishment. □□ **stu·pe·fa·cient** /-fáyshənt/ *adj. & n.* **stu·pe·fac·tion** /-fákshən/ *n.* **stu·pe·fy·ing** *adj.* **stu·pe·fy·ing·ly** *adv.*

stu·pen·dous /stōōpéndəs, styōō-/ *adj.* amazing or prodigious, esp. in size or degree. □□ **stu·pen·dous·ly** *adv.* **stu·pen·dous·ness** *n.*

stu·pid /stōōpid, styōō-/ *adj.* (**stupider, stupidest**) **1** unintelligent; foolish (*a stupid fellow*). **2** typical of stupid persons (*put it in a stupid place*). **3** uninteresting or boring. **4** in a state of stupor or lethargy. **5** obtuse; lacking in sensibility. □□ **stu·pid·i·ty** /-píditee/ *n.* (*pl.* **-ies**). **stu·pid·ly** *adv.*

stu·por /stōōpər, styōō-/ *n.* a dazed or amazed state. □□ **stu·por·ous** *adj.*

stur·dy /stárdee/ *adj.* (**sturdier, sturdiest**) **1** robust; strongly built. **2** vigorous and determined (*sturdy resistance*). □□ **stur·di·ly** *adv.* **stur·di·ness** *n.*

stur·geon /stárjən/ *n.* ▼ any large sharklike fish of the family Acipenseridae, etc., used as food and a source of caviar and isinglass.

narrow snout

platelike scales

STURGEON: ATLANTIC STURGEON (*Acipenser sturio*)

S

Sturm und Drang /shtŏŏrm ŏŏnt dráng/ *n.* a literary and artistic movement in Germany in the late 18th c., characterized by the expression of emotional unrest and strong feeling.

stut·ter /stútər/ *v. & n.* ● *v.* **1** *intr.* stammer, esp. by involuntarily repeating the first consonants of words. **2** *tr.* utter (words) in this way. ● *n.* **1** the act or habit of stuttering. **2** an instance of stuttering. □□ **stut·ter·er** *n.*

sty[1] /stī/ *n.* (*pl.* **sties**) **1** a pen or enclosure for pigs. **2** a filthy room or dwelling. **3** a place of debauchery.

sty[2] /stī/ *n.* (also **stye**) (*pl.* **sties** or **styes**) an inflamed swelling on the edge of an eyelid.

Styg·i·an /stíjeeən/ *adj.* **1** (in Greek mythology) of or relating to the Styx, a river in Hades. **2** *literary* dark; gloomy; indistinct.

style /stīl/ *n. & v.* ● *n.* **1** a kind or sort, esp. in regard to appearance and form (*an elegant style of house*). **2** a manner of writing or speaking or performing (*written in a florid style; started off in fine style*). **3** the distinctive manner of a person or school or period. **4** the correct way of designating a person or thing. **5** a superior quality or manner (*do it in style*). **6** a particular make, shape, or pattern (*in all sizes and styles*). **7** *Bot.* the narrow extension of the ovary supporting the stigma. ▷ FLOWER. ● *v.tr.* **1** design or make, etc., in a particular style. **2** designate in a specified way. □□ **style·less** *adj.* **styl·er** *n.*

sty·let /stílit/ *n.* **1** a slender pointed instrument; a stiletto. **2** *Med.* the stiffening wire of a catheter; a probe.

sty·li *pl.* of STYLUS.

styl·ish /stílish/ *adj.* **1** fashionable; elegant. **2** having a superior quality, manner, etc. □□ **styl·ish·ly** *adv.* **styl·ish·ness** *n.*

styl·ist /stílist/ *n.* **1 a** a designer of fashionable styles, etc. **b** a hairdresser. **2 a** a writer noted for or aspiring to good literary style. **b** (in sports or music) a person who performs with style.

sty·lis·tic /stīlístik/ *adj.* of or concerning esp. literary style. □□ **sty·lis·ti·cal·ly** *adv.*

sty·lis·tics /stīlístiks/ *n.* the study of literary style.

styl·ite /stílīt/ *n. Eccl. hist.* an ancient or medieval ascetic living on top of a pillar.

styl·ize /stílīz/ *v.tr.* (esp. as **stylized** *adj.*) paint, draw, etc., (a subject) in a conventional nonrealistic style. □□ **styl·i·za·tion** *n.*

sty·lo·bate /stíləbayt/ *n. Archit.* a continuous base supporting a row of columns.

sty·lo·graph /stíləgraf/ *n.* a kind of fountain pen having a point instead of a split nib. □□ **sty·lo·graph·ic** *adj.*

sty·loid /stíloyd/ *adj. & n.* ● *adj.* resembling a stylus or pen. ● *n.* (in full **styloid process**) a spine of bone, esp. that projecting from the base of the temporal bone.

sty·lus /stíləs/ *n.* (*pl.* **-li** /-lī/ or **-luses**) **1 ►** a hard point following a groove in a phonograph record and transmitting the recorded sound for reproduction. **2** a similar point producing such a groove when recording sound.

sty·mie /stímee/ *n. & v.* (also **sti·my**) ● *n.* (*pl.* **-ies**) **1** *Golf* a situation where an opponent's ball lies between the player and the hole (*lay a stymie*). **2** a difficult situation. ● *v.tr.* (**stymies**, **stymied**, **stymying** or **stymieing**) **1** obstruct; thwart. **2** *Golf* block with a stymie.

styp·tic /stíptik/ *adj. & n.* ● *adj.* that checks bleeding. ● *n.* a styptic substance.

styp·tic pen·cil *n.* a pencil-shaped wand containing a styptic substance used to check bleeding from minor cuts.

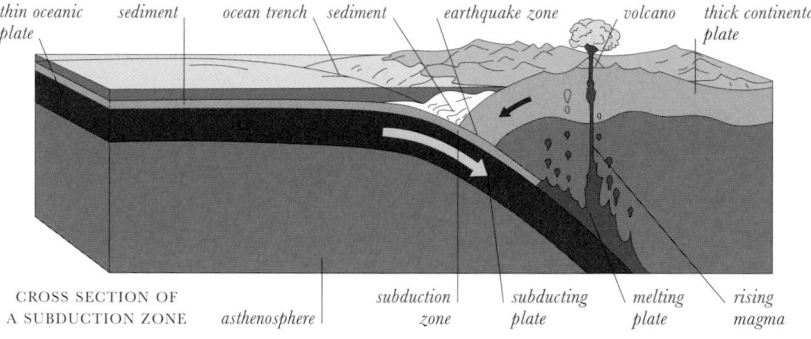

STYLUS: MICROGRAPH OF THE TIP OF A STYLUS IN A RECORD GROOVE

record groove   stylus tip

SUBDUCTION

Subduction usually occurs when a thin oceanic plate collides with a thick continental plate, forcing the oceanic plate into the asthenosphere and forming an ocean trench in the process. Magma, which forms as the heat of the asthenosphere melts the subducted plate, rises through the shattered edge of the overlying plate and may erupt as a volcano. Subduction may also occur at the point where two continental plates meet.

thin oceanic plate   sediment   ocean trench   sediment   earthquake zone   volcano   thick continental plate

CROSS SECTION OF A SUBDUCTION ZONE   *asthenosphere   subduction zone   subducting plate   melting plate   rising magma*

sty·rax /stíraks/ *n.* **1** storax resin. **2** any tree or shrub of the genus *Styrax*, e.g., the storax tree.

sty·rene /stíreen/ *n. Chem.* a liquid hydrocarbon easily polymerized and used in making plastics, etc.

Sty·ro·foam /stírəfōm/ *n. Trademark* a brand of expanded polystyrene.

su·a·ble /sóōəbəl/ *adj.* capable of being sued. □□ **su·a·bil·i·ty** /-bílitee/ *n.*

sua·sion /swáyzhən/ *n. formal* persuasion as opposed to force (*moral suasion*).

SUV *abbr.* sport utility vehicle.

suave /swaav/ *adj.* smooth; polite; sophisticated. □□ **suave·ly** *adv.* **suave·ness** *n.* **suav·i·ty** /-vitee/ *n.* (*pl.* **-ies**).

sub /sub/ *n. & v. colloq.* ● *n.* **1** a submarine. **2** a subscription. **3** a substitute. ● *v.intr.* (**subbed**, **subbing**) (usu. foll. by *for*) act as a substitute.

sub- /sub, səb/ *prefix* (also **suc-** before *c*, **suf-** before *f*, **sug-** before *g*, **sup-** before *p*, **sur-** before *r*, **sus-** before *c*, *p*, *t*) **1** at or to or from a lower position (*subordinate; submerge; subtract; subsoil*). **2** secondary or inferior in rank or position (*subclass; subcommittee; subtotal*). **3** somewhat; nearly; more or less (*subacid; subarctic*). **4** (forming verbs) denoting secondary action (*subdivide; sublet*). **5** denoting support (*subvention*). **6** *Chem.* (of a salt) basic (*subacetate*).

sub·ab·dom·i·nal /súbabdóminəl/ *adj.* below the abdomen.

sub·ac·id /súbásid/ *adj.* moderately acid or tart.

sub·a·cute /súbəkyóōt/ *adj. Med.* (of a condition) between acute and chronic.

sub·a·gen·cy /súbáyjənsee/ *n.* (*pl.* **-ies**) a secondary or subordinate agency. □□ **sub·a·gent** *n.*

sub·al·pine /súbálpīn/ *adj.* of or situated in the higher slopes of mountains just below the timberline.

sub·al·tern /subáwltərn/ *n. & adj.* ● *n. Brit. Mil.* an officer below the rank of captain, esp. a second lieutenant. ● *adj.* **1** of inferior rank. **2** /súbəltərn/ *Logic* (of a proposition) particular; not universal.

sub·a·quat·ic /súbəkwátik, -əkwótik/ *adj.* **1** of more or less aquatic habits or kind. **2** underwater.

sub·a·que·ous /súbáykweeəs, -ák-/ *adj.* existing or taking place under water.

sub·a·tom·ic /súbətómik/ *adj.* occurring in or smaller than an atom.

sub·au·di·tion /súbawdíshən/ *n.* **1** the act of mentally supplying an omitted word or words in speech. **2** the act or process of understanding the unexpressed; reading between the lines.

sub·ax·il·la·ry /súbáksilleree/ *adj.* **1** *Bot.* in or growing beneath the axil. **2** beneath the armpit.

sub·cat·e·go·ry /súbkátigawree/ *n.* (*pl.* **-ies**) a secondary or subordinate category. □□ **sub·cat·e·go·rize** *v.tr.* **sub·cat·e·gor·i·za·tion** *n.*

sub·cau·dal /súbkáwdəl/ *adj.* of or concerning the region under the tail or the back part of the body.

sub·class /súbklas/ *n.* **1** a secondary or subordinate class. **2** *Biol.* a taxonomic category below a class.

sub·clause /súbklawz/ *n.* **1** esp. *Law* a subsidiary section of a clause. **2** *Gram.* a subordinate clause.

sub·cla·vi·an /súbkláyveeən/ *adj. & n.* ● *adj.* (of an artery, etc.) lying or extending under the collar bone. ● *n.* such an artery.

sub·clin·i·cal /súbklínikəl/ *adj. Med.* (of a disease) not yet presenting definite symptoms.

sub·com·mit·tee /súbkəmitee/ *n.* a secondary committee.

sub·com·pact /səbkómpakt/ *n. & adj.* a car that is smaller than a compact.

sub·con·scious /súbkónshəs/ *adj. & n.* ● *adj.* of or concerning the part of the mind which is not fully conscious but influences actions, etc. ● *n.* this part of the mind. □□ **sub·con·scious·ly** *adv.* **sub·con·scious·ness** *n.*

sub·con·ti·nent /súbkóntinənt/ *n.* **1** a large land mass, smaller than a continent. **2** a large geographically or politically independent part of a continent. □□ **sub·con·ti·nen·tal** /-nént'l/ *adj.*

sub·con·tract *v.* ● *v.* /súbkəntrákt/ **1** *tr.* employ a firm, etc., to do (work) as part of a larger project. **2** *intr.* make or carry out a subcontract. ● *n.* /súbkóntrakt/ a secondary contract. □□ **sub·con·trac·tor** /-kóntraktər/ *n.*

sub·con·tra·ry /súbkóntreree/ *adj. & n. Logic* ● *adj.* (of a proposition) incapable of being false at the same time as another. ● *n.* (*pl.* **-ies**) such a proposition.

sub·cu·ta·ne·ous /súbkyōōtáyneeəs/ *adj.* under the skin.

sub·cul·ture /súbkulchər/ *n.* a cultural group within a larger culture. □□ **sub·cul·tur·al** /-kúlchərəl/ *adj.*

sub·di·vide /súbdivíd/ *v.tr. & intr.* divide again after a first division.

sub·di·vi·sion /súbdivízhən/ *n.* **1** the act of subdividing. **2** a secondary or subordinate division. **3** an area of land divided into plots for sale.

sub·dom·i·nant /súbdóminənt/ *n. Mus.* the fourth note of the diatonic scale of any key.

sub·duc·tion /súbdúkshən/ *n. Geol.* ▲ the sideways and downward movement of the edge of a plate of the Earth's crust into the mantle beneath another plate (*subduction zone*). ▷ PLATE TECTONICS, TRENCH

S

sub·due /səbdoo, -dyoo/ v.tr. (**subdues**, **subdued**, **subduing**) **1** conquer, subjugate, or tame. **2** (as **subdued** adj.) softened; lacking in intensity; toned down (*subdued light; in a subdued mood*). □□ **sub·du·a·ble** adj. **sub·du·er** n.

sub·ed·i·tor /súbéditər/ n. Brit. **1** an assistant editor. **2** a person who edits material for printing in a book, newspaper, etc. □□ **sub·ed·it** v.tr. (**-edited**, **-editing**).

sub·e·rect /súbirékt/ adj. (of an animal, plant, etc.) almost erect.

su·be·re·ous /soobéereeəs/ adj. (also **su·ber·ic** /soobérik/, **su·ber·ose** /sooberōs/) **1** of or concerning cork. **2** corky.

sub·fam·i·ly /súbfamilee/ n. (pl. **-ies**) **1** Biol. a taxonomic category below a family. **2** any subdivision of a group.

sub·floor /súbflawr/ (also **sub·floor·ing** /sub·floor·ing/) n. a foundation for a floor in a building.

sub·form /súbfawrm/ n. a subordinate or secondary form.

sub·fusc /súbfusk/ adj. formal dull; dusky; gloomy.

sub·ge·nus /súbjéenəs/ n. (pl. **subgenera** /-jénərə/) Biol. a taxonomic category below a genus. □□ **sub·ge·ner·ic** /-jinérik/ adj.

sub·gla·ci·al /súbgláyshəl/ adj. next to or at the bottom of a glacier.

sub·group /súbgroop/ n. Math., etc., a subset of a group.

sub·head /súbhed/ n. (also **sub·head·ing**) **1** a subordinate heading or title. **2** a subordinate division in a classification.

sub·hu·man /súbhyóomən/ adj. **1** (of an animal) closely related to humans. **2** (of behavior, intelligence, etc.) less than human.

subj. abbr. **1** subject. **2** subjective. **3** subjunctive.

sub·ja·cent /súbjáysənt/ adj. underlying; situated below.

sub·ject n., adj., adv., & v. ● n. /súbjikt/ **1 a** a matter, theme, etc., to be discussed, described, represented, etc. **b** (foll. by *for*) a person, circumstance, etc., giving rise to specified feeling, action, etc. (*a subject for congratulation*). **2** a field of study (*his best subject is geography*). **3** Gram. a noun or its equivalent about which a sentence is predicated and with which the verb agrees. **4 a** any person except a monarch living under a government (*the ruler and his subjects*). **b** any person owing obedience to another. **5** Mus. a theme of a fugue or sonata; a leading phrase or motif. **6** a person of specified tendencies (*a hysterical subject*). ● adj. /súbjikt/ **1** owing obedience to a government, colonizing power, force, etc.; in subjection. **2** (foll. by *to*) liable, exposed, or prone to (*is subject to infection*). **3** (foll. by *to*) conditional upon (*the arrangement is subject to your approval*). ● adv. /súbjikt/ (foll. by *to*) conditionally upon (*subject to your consent, I propose to try again*). ● v.tr. /səbjékt/ **1** (foll. by *to*) make liable; expose (*subjected us to hours of waiting*). **2** (usu. foll. by *to*) subdue (a nation, person, etc.) to one's control, etc. □□ **sub·jec·tion** /səbjékshən/ n. **sub·ject·less** /súbjiktlis/ adj.

sub·jec·tive /səbjéktiv/ adj. & n. ● adj. **1** (of art, literature, written history, a person's views, etc.) proceeding from personal idiosyncrasy or individuality; not impartial or literal. **2** Gram. of or concerning the subject. ● n. Gram. nominative. □□ **sub·jec·tive·ly** adv. **sub·jec·tiv·i·ty** /subjektívitee/ n.

sub·jec·tiv·ism /səbjéktivizəm/ n. Philos. the doctrine that knowledge is merely subjective and that there is no external or objective truth. □□ **sub·jec·tiv·ist** n.

sub·join /súbjóyn/ v.tr. add (an illustration, anecdote, etc.) at the end.

sub·joint /súbjoynt/ n. a secondary joint (in an insect's leg, etc.).

sub ju·di·ce /sub joodisee, soob yoodikay/ adj. Law under judicial consideration and therefore prohibited from public discussion elsewhere.

sub·ju·gate /súbjəgayt/ v.tr. bring into subjection; vanquish. □□ **sub·ju·ga·tion** /-gáyshən/ n.

sub·junc·tive /səbjúngktiv/ adj. & n. Gram. ● adj. (of a mood) denoting what is imagined or wished or possible (e.g., *if I were you; God help you; be that as it may*). ● n. **1** the subjunctive mood. **2** a verb in this mood.

sub·king·dom /súbkingdəm/ n. Biol. a taxonomic category below a kingdom.

sub·lease n. & v. ● n. /súblees/ a lease of a property by a tenant to a subtenant. ● v.tr. /súblées/ lease (a property) to a subtenant.

sub·les·see /súblesée/ n. a person who holds a sublease.

sub·les·sor /súblesáwr/ n. a person who grants a sublease.

sub·let n. & v. ● n. /súblet/ = SUBLEASE n. ● v.tr. /súblét/ (**-letting**; past and past part. **-let**) = SUBLEASE v.

sub·lieu·ten·ant /súblooténənt/ n. Brit. a naval officer ranking immediately below lieutenant.

sub·li·mate v., adj., & n. ● v. /súblimayt/ **1** tr. & intr. divert (the energy of a primitive impulse, esp. sexual) into a culturally more acceptable activity. **2** tr. & intr. Chem. convert (a substance) from the solid state directly to its vapor by heat, and usu. allow it to solidify again. ▷ MATTER. **3** tr. refine; purify; idealize. ● adj. /súblimət, -mayt/ **1** Chem. (of a substance) sublimated. **2** purified; refined. ● n. /súblimət/ Chem. a sublimated substance. □□ **sub·li·ma·tion** /-máyshən/ n.

sub·lime /səblím/ adj. & v. ● adj. (**sublimer**, **sublimest**) **1** of the most exalted or noble kind; awe inspiring (*sublime genius*). **2** (of indifference, impudence, etc.) arrogantly unruffled; extreme. ● v. **1** tr. & intr. Chem. = SUBLIMATE v. 2. **2** tr. purify or elevate by or as if by sublimation; make sublime. **3** intr. become pure by or as if by sublimation. □□ **sub·lime·ly** adv. **sub·lim·i·ty** /-límitee/ n.

sub·lim·i·nal /səblíminəl/ adj. Psychol. (of a stimulus, etc.) below the threshold of sensation or consciousness. □□ **sub·lim·i·nal·ly** adv.

sub·lim·i·nal ad·ver·tis·ing n. the use of subliminal images in advertising on television, etc., to influence the viewer at an unconscious level.

sub·lin·gual /súblínggwəl/ adj. under the tongue.

sub·lit·tor·al /súblítərəl/ adj. **1** (of plants, animals, deposits, etc.) living or found on the seashore just below the low tide line. **2** of or concerning the seashore.

sub·lu·nar·y /súbloonéree, subloonəree/ adj. **1** beneath the Moon. **2** Astron. **a** within the Moon's orbit. **b** subject to the Moon's influence. **3** of this world.

sub·ma·chine gun /súbməsheen/ n. a hand-held lightweight machine gun. ▷ GUN

sub·mar·gi·nal /súbmaárjinəl/ adj. **1** esp. Econ. not reaching minimum requirements. **2** (of land) that cannot be farmed profitably.

sub·ma·rine /súbməréen/ n. & adj. ● n. **1** ▼ a vessel, esp. a warship, capable of operating under water. **2** = SUBMARINE SANDWICH. ● adj. existing, occurring, done, or used under the surface of the sea (*submarine cable*). □□ **sub·ma·rin·er** /-maréenər, səbmárinər/ n.

sub·ma·rine sand·wich n. a large sandwich usu. consisting of a halved roll, meat, cheese, lettuce, tomato, etc.

sub·max·il·la·ry /submáksileree/ adj. beneath the lower jaw.

SUBMARINE

To remain submerged for extended periods, a submarine must have a hull strong enough to resist the high water pressure. Upright partitions called bulkheads divide the vessel into compartments, which can be sealed off in the event of a leak. Submarines have engines for surface and underwater use; these run on either nuclear power or a combination of electric and diesel motors.

When a submarine dives, valves are opened in ballast tanks located on each side of the hull. Water enters the tanks, and the extra weight causes the craft to submerge. To surface, water is ejected from the tanks. Today, there are two main types of military submarine: patrol submarines, which attack enemy vessels; and missile submarines, which carry long-range nuclear missiles.

S

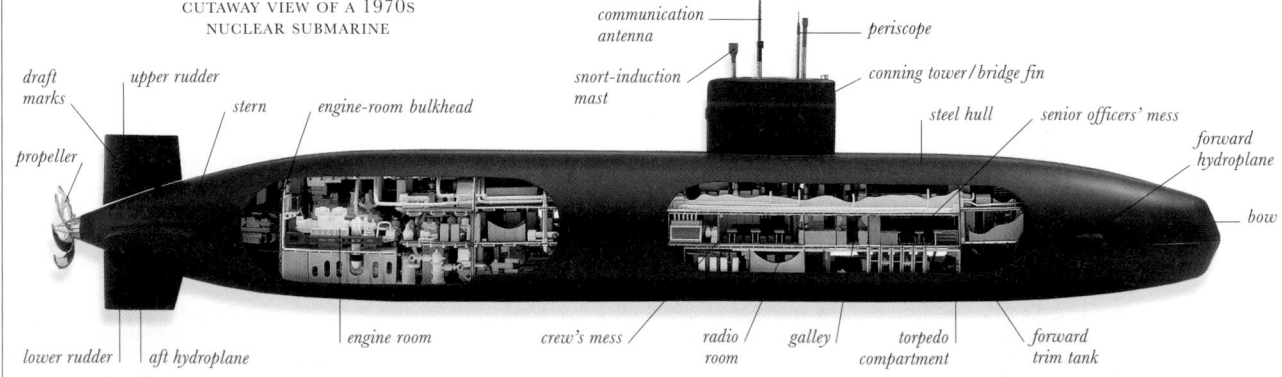

CUTAWAY VIEW OF A 1970s NUCLEAR SUBMARINE

draft marks • upper rudder • stern • engine-room bulkhead • communication antenna • periscope • conning tower/bridge fin • snort-induction mast • steel hull • senior officers' mess • forward hydroplane • propeller • forward hydroplane • bow • lower rudder • aft hydroplane • engine room • crew's mess • radio room • galley • torpedo compartment • forward trim tank

SUBMERSIBLE

Submersibles are designed to operate at great depths, sometimes over 2.5 miles (4 km) beneath the ocean's surface. The umbilical cable, which is attached to a vessel on the surface, provides power, control signals, and video lines. Submersibles have a variety of functions, including marine research, the repair of ocean pipelines, salvage, and the exploration of undersea wrecks. External mechanical arms and sensors, such as video cameras, are fitted to help with these specialized tasks.

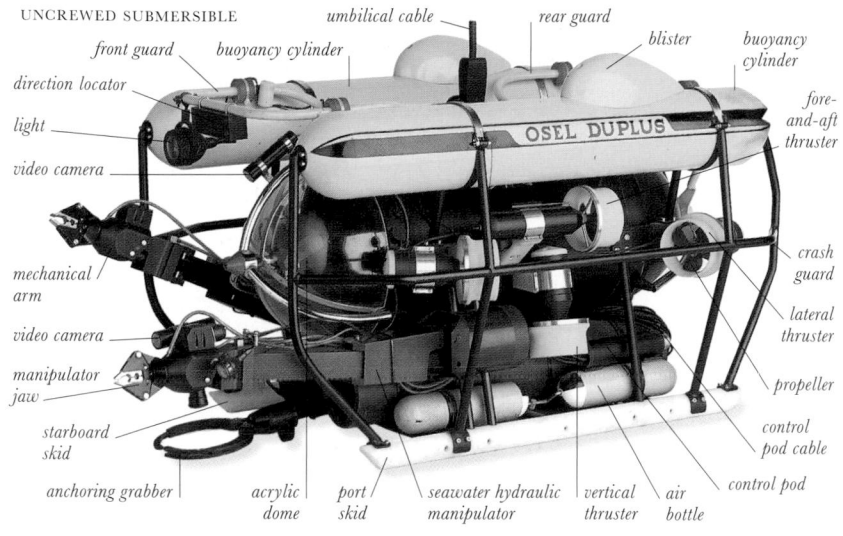

UNCREWED SUBMERSIBLE

front guard · buoyancy cylinder · umbilical cable · rear guard · blister · buoyancy cylinder · direction locator · light · video camera · mechanical arm · video camera · manipulator jaw · starboard skid · anchoring grabber · acrylic dome · port skid · seawater hydraulic manipulator · vertical thruster · air bottle · control pod · control pod cable · propeller · lateral thruster · crash guard · fore- and-aft thruster · OSEL DUPLUS

---

sub·me·di·ant /súbmeédeeənt/ *n. Mus.* the sixth note of the diatonic scale of any key.

sub·merge /səbmérj/ *v.* **1** *tr.* **a** place under water; flood. **b** inundate with work, problems, etc. **2** *intr.* dive below the surface of water. □□ **submergence** *n.* **sub·mer·sion** /-márzhən, -shən/ *n.*

sub·mers·i·ble /səbmársibəl/ *n. & adj.* ● *n.* ▲ a submarine operating under water for short periods. ● *adj.* capable of being submerged.

sub·mi·cro·scop·ic /súbmíkrəskópik/ *adj.* too small to be seen by an ordinary microscope.

sub·min·i·a·ture /súbmíneeəchər, -chŏŏr/ *adj.* **1** of greatly reduced size. **2** (of a camera) very small and using 16-mm film.

sub·mis·sion /səbmíshən/ *n.* **1 a** the act of submitting. **b** anything that is submitted. **2** humility; meekness; obedience (*showed great submission of spirit*). **3** *Law* a theory, etc., submitted by a lawyer to a judge or jury. **4** (in wrestling) the surrender of a participant yielding to the pain of a hold.

sub·mis·sive /səbmísiv/ *adj.* **1** humble; obedient. **2** yielding to power or authority; willing to submit. □□ **sub·mis·sive·ly** *adv.* **sub·mis·sive·ness** *n.*

sub·mit /səbmít/ *v.* (**submitted, submitting**) **1** (usu. foll. by *to*) **a** *intr.* cease resistance; yield (*had to submit to defeat; will never submit*). **b** *refl.* surrender (oneself) to the control of another, etc. **2** *tr.* present for consideration or decision. **3** *tr.* (usu. foll. by *to*) subject (a person or thing) to a process, treatment, etc. (*submitted it to the flames*). **4** *tr.* esp. *Law* urge or represent esp. deferentially (*that, I submit, is a misrepresentation*). □□ **sub·mit·ter** *n.*

sub·mul·ti·ple /súbmúltipəl/ *n. & adj.* ● *n.* a number that can be divided exactly into a specified number. ● *adj.* being such a number.

sub·nor·mal /súbnáwrməl/ *adj.* **1** (esp. as regards intelligence) below normal. **2** less than normal. □□ **sub·nor·mal·i·ty** /-málitee/ *n.*

sub·nu·cle·ar /súbnŏŏkleeər, -nyŏŏ-/ *adj. Physics* occurring in or smaller than an atomic nucleus.

sub·oc·u·lar /súbókyələr/ *adj.* situated below or under the eyes.

sub·or·bit·al /súbáwrbit'l/ *adj.* **1** situated below the orbit of the eye. **2** (of a spaceship, etc.) not completing a full orbit of the Earth.

sub·or·der /súbawrdər/ *n.* a taxonomic category below an order.

sub·or·di·nar·y /súbáwrd'neree/ *n.* (*pl.* **-ies**) *Heraldry* a device or bearing that is common but less so than ordinaries.

sub·or·di·nate *adj., n., & v.* ● *adj.* /səbáwrd'nət/ (usu. foll. by *to*) of inferior importance or rank; secondary; subservient. ● *n.* /səbáwrd'nət/ a person working under another. ● *v.tr.* /səbáwrd'nayt/ (usu. foll. by *to*) **1** make subordinate; treat or regard as of minor importance. **2** make subservient. □□ **sub·or·di·na·tion** /-náyshən/ *n.*

sub·or·di·nate clause *n.* a clause serving as an adjective, adverb, or noun in a main sentence because of its position or a preceding conjunction.

sub·orn /səbáwrn/ *v.tr.* induce by bribery, etc., to commit perjury or any other unlawful act.

sub·ox·ide /súbóksīd/ *n. Chem.* an oxide containing the smallest proportion of oxygen.

sub·phy·lum /súbfíləm/ *n.* (*pl.* **subphyla** /-lə/) *Biol.* a taxonomic category below a phylum.

sub·plot /súbplot/ *n.* a subordinate plot in a play, etc.

sub·poe·na /səpéenə/ *n. & v.* ● *n.* a writ ordering a person to appear in court. ● *v.tr.* (*past* and *past part.* **subpoenaed** or **subpoena'd**) serve a subpoena on.

sub·re·gion /súbréejən/ *n.* a division of a region, esp. with regard to natural life. □□ **sub·re·gion·al** /-réejənəl/ *adj.*

sub·rep·tion /səbrépshən/ *n. formal* the obtaining of a thing by surprise or misrepresentation.

sub·ro·ga·tion /súbrəgáyshən/ *n. Law* the substitution of one party for another as creditor, with the transfer of rights and duties. □□ **sub·ro·gate** /súbrəgayt/ *v.tr.*

sub ro·sa /sub rózə/ *adj. & adv.* in secrecy or confidence.

sub·rou·tine /súbrŏŏteen/ *n. Computing* a routine designed to perform a frequently used operation within a program.

sub·scribe /səbskríb/ *v.* **1** *tr.* & *intr.* (usu. foll. by *to*, *for*) contribute (a specified sum) or make or promise a contribution to a fund, project, charity, etc., esp. regularly. **2** *intr.* (usu. foll. by *to*) express one's agreement with an opinion, resolution, etc. (*cannot subscribe to that*).

sub·scrib·er /səbskríbər/ *n.* **1** a person who subscribes. **2** a person paying for the renting of a telephone line, television cable connection, etc.

sub·script /súbskript/ *adj. & n.* ● *adj.* written or printed below the line. ● *n.* a subscript number or symbol.

sub·scrip·tion /səbskrípshən/ *n.* **1 a** the act or an instance of subscribing. **b** money subscribed. **2 a** an agreement to take and pay for usu. a specified number of issues of a newspaper, magazine, etc. **b** the money paid by this.

sub·sec·tion /súbseksħən/ *n.* a division of a section.

sub·se·quent /súbsikwənt/ *adj.* (usu. foll. by *to*) following a specified event, etc., in time, esp. as a consequence. □□ **sub·se·quent·ly** *adv.*

sub·serve /səbsérv/ *v.tr.* serve as a means of furthering (a purpose, etc.).

sub·ser·vi·ent /səbsárveeənt/ *adj.* **1** cringing; obsequious. **2** (usu. foll. by *to*) instrumental. **3** (usu. foll. by *to*) subordinate. □□ **sub·ser·vi·ence** *n.* **sub·ser·vi·en·cy** *n.*

sub·set /súbset/ *n.* **1** a secondary part of a set. **2** *Math.* a set all the elements of which are contained in another set.

sub·shrub /súbshrub/ *n.* a low-growing or small shrub.

sub·side /səbsíd/ *v.intr.* **1** become tranquil; abate (*excitement subsided*). **2** (of water, suspended matter, etc.) sink. **3** (of the ground) cave in; sink. **4** (of a building, ship, etc.) sink lower in the ground or water. **5** (of a swelling, etc.) become less. **6** usu. *joc.* (of a person) sink into a sitting, kneeling, or lying posture. □□ **sub·sid·ence** /-síd'ns, súbsid'ns/ *n.*

sub·sid·i·ar·i·ty /səbsídeeáritee/ *n.* (*pl.* **-ies**) **1** the quality of being subsidiary. **2** the principle that a central authority should perform only tasks which cannot be performed effectively at a local level.

sub·sid·i·ar·y /səbsídee-aire/ *adj. & n.* ● *adj.* **1** serving to assist or supplement. **2** (of a company) controlled by another. ● *n.* (*pl.* **-ies**) **1** a subsidiary thing or person. **2** a subsidiary company.

sub·si·dize /súbsidīz/ *v.tr.* **1** pay a subsidy to. **2** reduce the cost of by subsidy (*subsidized lunches*). □□ **sub·si·di·za·tion** *n.*

sub·si·dy /súbsidee/ *n.* (*pl.* **-ies**) **1** money granted by the government or a public body, etc., to keep down the price of commodities, etc. (*housing subsidy*). **2** money granted to a charity or other undertaking held to be in the public interest. **3** any grant of money.

sub·sist /səbsíst/ *v.intr.* **1** (often foll. by *on*) keep oneself alive (*subsists on vegetables*). **2** remain in being; exist. **3** (foll. by *in*) be attributable to (*its excellence subsists in its freshness*). □□ **sub·sist·ent** *n.*

sub·sist·ence /səbsístəns/ *n.* **1** the state or an instance of subsisting. **2 a** the means of supporting life; a livelihood. **b** a minimal level of existence or the income providing this (*a bare subsistence*).

sub·sist·ence farm·ing *n.* farming which directly supports the farmer's household without producing a significant surplus for trade.

sub·soil /súbsoyl/ *n.* soil lying immediately under the surface soil. ▷ soil.

sub·son·ic /súbsónik/ *adj.* relating to speeds less than that of sound.

sub·spe·cies /súbspeesheez, -seez/ *n.* (*pl.* same) *Biol.* a taxonomic category below a species, usu. a fairly permanent geographically isolated variety. □□ **sub·spe·cif·ic** /-spəsífik/ *adj.*

subst. *abbr.* **1** substantive. **2** substitute.

sub·stance /súbstəns/ *n.* **1 a** the essential material forming a thing (*the substance was transparent*). **b** a particular kind of material having uniform properties (*this substance is salt*). **2 a** reality; solidity (*ghosts*

S

have no substance). **b** seriousness or steadiness of character (*there is no substance in him*). **3** addictive drugs or alcohol, etc. (*problems of substance abuse*). **4** the theme or subject of a work of art, argument, etc. (*prefer the substance to the style*). **5** the real meaning or essence of a thing. **6** wealth and possessions. □ **in substance** generally; apart from details.

sub·stand·ard /súbstándərd/ *adj.* **1** of less than the required or normal quality or size; inferior. **2** (of language) not conforming to standard usage.

sub·stan·tial /səbstánshəl/ *adj.* **1 a** of real importance or validity (*made a substantial contribution*). **b** of large size or amount (*awarded substantial damages*). **2** of solid material or structure (*a man of substantial build; a substantial house*). **3** commercially successful. **4** true in large part (*substantial truth*). **5** having substance. □□ **sub·stan·ti·al·i·ty** /-sheeálitee/ *n.* **sub·stan·tial·ly** *adv.*

sub·stan·tial·ism /səbstánshəlizəm/ *n. Philos.* the doctrine that behind phenomena there are substantial realities. □□ **sub·stan·tial·ist** *n.*

sub·stan·tial·ize /səbstánshəlīz/ *v.tr. & intr.* invest with or acquire substance or actual existence.

sub·stan·ti·ate /səbstánsheeayt/ *v.tr.* prove the truth of (a charge, statement, claim, etc.); give good grounds for. □□ **sub·stan·ti·a·tion** /-áyshən/ *n.*

sub·stan·tive /súbstəntiv/ *adj. & n.* ● *adj.* (also /səbstántiv)/ **1** having separate and independent existence. **2** *Gram.* expressing existence. **3** *Mil.* (of a rank, etc.) permanent, not acting or temporary. ● *n. Gram.* = NOUN. □□ **sub·stan·ti·val** /-tívəl/ *adj.* **sub·stan·tive·ly** *adv.*

sub·stan·tive verb *n.* the verb 'to be'.

sub·sta·tion /súbstayshən/ *n.* a subordinate station, esp. one reducing the high voltage of electric power transmission to that suitable for supply to consumers.

sub·stit·u·ent /səbstíchōōənt/ *adj. & n. Chem.* ● *adj.* (of a group of atoms) replacing another atom or group in a compound. ● *n.* such a group.

sub·sti·tute /súbstitōōt, -tyōōt/ *n. & v.* ● *n.* **1** (also *attrib.*) a person or thing acting or serving in place of another. **2** an artificial alternative to a natural substance (*butter substitute*). ● *v.* **1** *intr. & tr.* act or cause to act as a substitute; put or serve in exchange (*substituted for her mother*). **2** *tr.* (usu. foll. by *by*, *with*) *colloq.* replace (a person or thing) with another. □□ **sub·sti·tut·a·ble** *adj.* **sub·sti·tut·a·bil·i·ty** *n.* **sub·sti·tu·tion** /-tōōshən, -tyōō-/ *n.* **sub·sti·tu·tive** *adj.*

sub·strate /súbstrayt/ *n.* **1** = SUBSTRATUM. **2** a surface to be painted, printed, etc., on. **3** *Biol.* **a** the substance upon which an enzyme acts. **b** the surface or material on which any particular organism grows.

S

sub·stra·tum /súbstraytəm, -strát-/ *n.* (*pl.* **substrata** /-tə/) **1** an underlying layer or substance. **2** a layer of rock or soil beneath the surface. **3** a basis.

sub·struc·ture /súbstrukchər/ *n.* an underlying or supporting structure.

sub·sume /səbsōōm, -syōōm/ *v.tr.* (usu. foll. by *under*) include (an instance, idea, category, etc.) in a rule, class, category, etc. □□ **sub·sump·tion** /-súmpshən/ *n.*

sub·ten·ant /súbténənt/ *n.* a person who leases a property from a tenant. □□ **sub·ten·an·cy** *n.*

sub·tend /səbténd/ *v.tr.* **1** (usu. foll. by *at*) (of a line, arc, figure, etc.) form (an angle) at a particular point when its extremities are joined at that point. **2** (of an angle or chord) have bounding lines or points that meet or coincide with those of (a line or arc).

sub·ter·fuge /súbtərfyōōj/ *n.* **1 a** an attempt to avoid blame or defeat, esp. by lying or deceit. **b** a statement, etc., resorted to for such a purpose. **2** this as a practice or policy.

sub·ter·mi·nal /súbtérminəl/ *adj.* nearly at the end.

sub·ter·ra·ne·an /súbtəráyneeən/ *adj.* **1** existing, occurring, or done under the Earth's surface. **2** secret; underground; concealed.

sub·text /súbtekst/ *n.* an underlying theme.

sub·til·ize /sút'līz/ *v.* **1** *tr.* **a** make subtle. **b** elevate; refine. **2** *intr.* (usu. foll. by *upon*) argue or reason subtly. □□ **sub·til·i·za·tion** *n.*

sub·ti·tle /súbtīt'l/ *n. & v.* ● *n.* **1** a secondary or additional title of a book, etc. **2** a caption at the bottom of a movie, etc., esp. translating dialogue. ● *v.tr.* provide with subtitles.

sub·tle /sút'l/ *adj.* (**subtler**, **subtlest**) **1** evasive or mysterious; hard to grasp (*subtle charm*). **2** (of scent, color, etc.) faint; delicate (*subtle perfume*). **3 a** capable of making fine distinctions; perceptive (*subtle intellect; subtle senses*). **b** ingenious (*a subtle device*). □□ **sub·tle·ness** *n.* **sub·tly** *adv.*

sub·tle·ty /sút'ltee/ *n.* (*pl.* **-ies**) **1** the quality of being subtle. **2** a fine distinction; an instance of hair-splitting.

sub·ton·ic /súbtónik/ *n. Mus.* the note below the tonic, the seventh note of the diatonic scale of any key.

sub·to·tal /súbtōt'l/ *n.* the total of one part of a group of figures to be added.

sub·tract /səbtrákt/ *v.tr.* deduct (a part, quantity, or number) from another. □□ **sub·trac·tion** /-trákshən/ *n.* **sub·trac·tive** *adj.*

sub·tract·or /səbtráktər/ *n. Electronics* a circuit or device that produces an output dependent on the difference of two inputs.

sub·tra·hend /súbtrəhend/ *n. Math.* a quantity or number to be subtracted.

sub·trop·ics /súbtrópiks/ *n.pl.* the regions adjacent to the tropics. □□ **sub·trop·i·cal** *adj.*

su·bu·late /súbyələt/ *adj. Bot. & Zool.* slender and tapering.

sub·urb /súbərb/ *n.* an outlying district of a city, esp. residential.

sub·ur·ban /səbárbən/ *adj.* **1** of or characteristic of suburbs. **2** *derog.* provincial or naïve. □□ **sub·ur·ban·ite** *n.* **sub·ur·ban·ize** *v.tr.* **sub·ur·ban·i·za·tion** *n.*

sub·ur·bi·a /səbárbeeə/ *n.* often *derog.* the suburbs, their inhabitants, and their way of life.

sub·ven·tion /səbvénshən/ *n.* a grant of money from a government, etc.

sub·ver·sive /səbvársiv/ *adj. & n.* ● *adj.* seeking to subvert (esp. a government). ● *n.* a subversive person. □□ **sub·ver·sion** /-várzhən, -shən/ *n.* **sub·ver·sive·ly** *adv.* **sub·ver·sive·ness** *n.*

sub·vert /səbvárt/ *v.tr.* esp. *Polit.* overturn, overthrow, or upset (religion, government, morality, etc.). □□ **sub·vert·er** *n.*

sub·way /súbway/ *n.* **1** an underground railroad. **2 a** a tunnel beneath a road, etc., for pedestrians. **b** an underground passage for pipes, cables, etc.

sub·ze·ro /súbzéérō/ *adj.* (esp. of temperature) lower than zero.

suc- /suk, sək/ *prefix* assim. form of SUB- before *c*.

suc·ceed /səkséed/ *v.* **1** *intr.* **a** have success (*succeeded in his ambition*). **b** (of a plan, etc.) be successful. **2 a** *tr.* follow in order; come immediately after (*night succeeded day*). **b** *intr.* (foll. by *to*) come next; be subsequent. **3** *intr.* (often foll. by *to*) come by an inheritance, office, title, or property (*succeeded to the throne*). **4** *tr.* take over an office, property, inheritance, etc., from (*succeeded his father*).

suc·cen·tor /səkséntər/ *n. Eccl.* a precentor's deputy in some cathedrals. □□ **suc·cen·tor·ship** *n.*

suc·cess /səksés/ *n.* **1** the accomplishment of an aim; a favorable outcome (*their efforts met with success*). **2** the attainment of wealth, fame, or position (*spoiled by success*). **3** a thing or person that turns out well.

suc·cès de scan·dale /sōōksáy də skondáal/ *n.* a book, play, etc., having great success because of its scandalous nature or associations.

suc·cess·ful /səksésfōōl/ *adj.* having success; prosperous. □□ **suc·cess·ful·ly** *adv.* **suc·cess·ful·ness** *n.*

suc·ces·sion /səkséshən/ *n.* **1 a** the process of following in order; succeeding. **b** a series of things or people in succession. **2 a** the right of succeeding to a throne, an office, inheritance, etc. **b** the act or process of so succeeding. **c** those having such a right. □ **in succession** one after another. **in succession to** as the successor of. □□ **suc·ces·sion·al** *adj.*

suc·ces·sive /səksésiv/ *adj.* following one after another; consecutive. □□ **suc·ces·sive·ly** *adv.*

suc·ces·sor /səksésər/ *n.* a person or thing that succeeds another.

suc·cinct /səksíngkt/ *adj.* briefly expressed; terse; concise. □□ **suc·cinct·ly** *adv.* **suc·cinct·ness** *n.*

suc·cin·ic a·cid /suksínik/ *n. Chem.* a crystalline dibasic acid derived from amber, etc. □□ **suc·cin·ate** /súksinayt/ *n.*

suc·cor /súkər/ *n. & v.* ● *n.* aid; assistance, esp. in time of need. ● *v.tr.* assist or aid (esp. a person in danger or distress).

suc·co·ry /súkəree/ *n.* = CHICORY 1.

suc·co·tash /súkətash/ *n.* a dish of green corn and beans boiled together.

Suc·coth /sōōkəs, sōōkōt/ *n.* (also **Suk·koth**) the Jewish autumn thanksgiving festival commemorating the sheltering in the wilderness.

suc·cu·bus /súkyəbəs/ *n.* (*pl.* **succubi** /-bī/) a female demon believed to have sexual intercourse with sleeping men.

suc·cu·lent /súkyələnt/ *adj. & n.* ● *adj.* **1** juicy; palatable. **2** *colloq.* desirable. **3** *Bot.* (of a plant, its leaves, or stems) thick and fleshy. ● *n. Bot.* ► a succulent plant. □□ **suc·cu·lence** *n.* **suc·cu·lent·ly** *adv.*

suc·cumb /səkúm/ *v.intr.* (usu. foll. by *to*) **1** be forced to give way; be overcome (*succumbed to temptation*). **2** be overcome by death (*succumbed to his injuries*).

such /such/ *adj. & pron.* ● *adj.* **1** (often foll. by *as*) of the kind or degree in question or under consideration (*such a person*). **2** (usu. foll. by *as to* + infin. or *that* + clause) so great; in such high degree (*not such a fool as to believe them*). **3** of a more than normal kind or degree (*we had such an enjoyable evening*). **4** of the kind or degree already indicated, or implied by the context (*there are no such things*). ● *pron.* **1** the thing or action in question or referred to (*such were his words*). **2 a** *Commerce* or *colloq.* the aforesaid thing or things (*those without tickets should purchase such*). **b** similar things; suchlike (*brought sandwiches and such*). □ **as such** as being what has been indicated or named (*there is no theater as such*). **such and such** ● *adj.* of a particular kind but not needing to be specified. ● *n.* a person or thing of this kind. **such and such a person** someone; so-and-so. **such as 1** of a kind that (*a person such as we all admire*). **2** for example (*insects, such as moths and bees*). **3** those who (*such as don't need help*). **such as it is** despite its shortcomings (*you are welcome to it, such as it is*). **such a one 1** (usu. foll. by *as*) such a person or such a thing. **2** *archaic* some person or thing unspecified.

such·like /súchlīk/ *adj. & n. colloq.* ● *adj.* of such a kind. ● *n.* things, people, etc., of such a kind.

suck /suk/ *v. & n.* ● *v.* **1** *tr.* draw (a fluid) into the mouth by making a partial vacuum. **2** *tr.* (also *absol.*) **a** draw milk or other fluid from or through (the breast, etc., or a container). **b** extract juice from (a fruit) by sucking. **3** *tr.* **a** draw sustenance, knowledge, or advantage from (a book, etc.). **b** imbibe or gain (knowledge, advantage, etc.) as if by sucking. **4** *tr.* roll the tongue around (a candy, teeth, one's thumb, etc.). **5** *intr.* make a sucking action or sound (*sucking at his pipe*). **6** *intr. sl.* be very unpleasant, contemptible, or unfair. ● *n.* the act or an instance of sucking. □ **give suck** *archaic* (of a mother, dam, etc.) suckle. **suck dry 1** exhaust the contents of by sucking. **2** exhaust (a person's sympathy, resources, etc.) as if by sucking. **suck in 1** absorb. **2** involve (a person) in an activity, etc., esp. against his or her will. **suck up 1** (often foll. by *to*) *colloq.* behave obsequiously, esp. for one's own advantage. **2** absorb.

suck·er /súkər/ *n. & v.* ● *n.* **1 a** a person or thing that sucks. **b** a sucking pig, newborn whale, etc. **2** *sl.* **a** a gullible person. **b** (foll. by *for*) a person especially susceptible to. **3 a** a rubber cup, etc., that adheres by suction. **b** an organ enabling an organism to cling by suction. ▷ OCTOPUS. **4** *Bot.* a shoot springing from the

SUCCULENT

Succulents live in harsh environments, usually where water is scarce. Their distinctive appearance is due to fleshy water-storing tissue, which expands when moisture is plentiful and contracts during droughts. Succulents generally show one of two growth forms. In leaf succulents, the leaves act as water-storage organs and are small but plump. In stem succulents, the stem is swollen, and the leaves are reduced or absent. Most cacti are stem succulents.

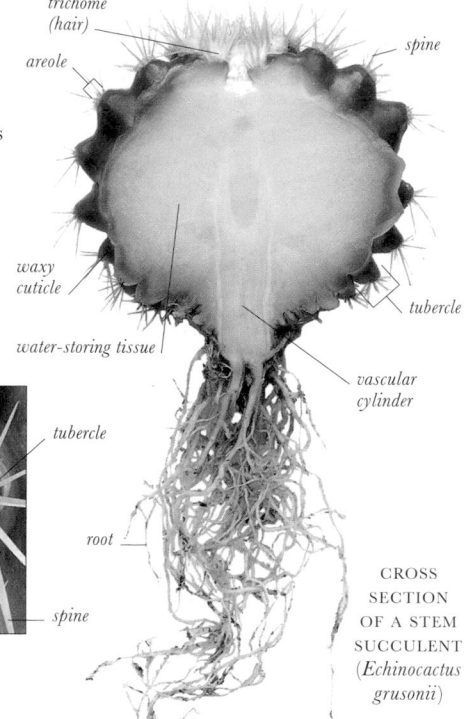

trichome (hair)

areole

spine

waxy cuticle

water-storing tissue

tubercle

vascular cylinder

CROSS SECTION OF A STEM SUCCULENT (*Echinocactus grusonii*)

tubercle

root

spine

areole

STEM SURFACE ENLARGED

EXAMPLES OF OTHER SUCCULENTS

LEAF SUCCULENTS

HAWORTHIA
(*Haworthia coarctata*)

COCOON PLANT
(*Senecio haworthii*)

LIVING STONE
(*Lithops salicola*)

STEM SUCCULENTS

BASEBALL EUPHORBIA
(*Euphorbia obesa*)

CLARETCUP CACTUS
(*Echinocereus triglochidiatus*)

REBUTIA
(*Rebutia canigueralii*)

---

rooted part of a stem, from the root at a distance from the main stem, from an axil, or from a branch. **5** *colloq.* a lollipop. ● *v. Bot.* **1** *tr.* remove suckers from. **2** *intr.* produce suckers. **3** *tr. sl.* cheat; fool.

suck·er punch *n. & v.* ● *n.* an unexpected punch or blow. ● *v.tr.* (**suck·er-punch**) hit with a sucker punch.

suck·ing /súking/ *adj.* not yet weaned.

suck·le /súkəl/ *v.* **1** *tr.* **a** feed (young) from the breast or udder. **b** nourish (*suckled his talent*). **2** *intr.* feed by sucking the breast, etc. □□ **suck·ler** *n.*

suck·ling /súkling/ *n.* an unweaned child or animal.

su·crose /sóōkrōs/ *n. Chem.* sugar; a disaccharide obtained from sugar cane, sugar beet, etc.

suc·tion /súkshən/ *n.* **1** the act of sucking. **2 a** the production of a partial vacuum by the removal of air, etc., in order to force in liquid, etc., or procure adhesion. **b** the force produced by this process.

suc·tor·i·al /suktáwreeəl/ *adj. Zool.* **1** adapted for or capable of sucking. **2** having a sucker for feeding or adhering. □□ **suc·tor·i·an** *n.*

Su·da·nese /sóōdəneez/ *adj. & n.* ● *adj.* of or relating to Sudan, a republic in NE Africa, or the Sudan region south of the Sahara. ● *n.* (*pl.* same) **1** a native, national, or inhabitant of Sudan. **2** a person of Sudanese descent.

su·da·to·ri·um /sóōdətáwreeəm/ *n.* (*pl.* **sudatoria** /-reeə/) esp. Rom. Antiq. **1** a hot air or steam bath. **2** a room where such a bath is taken.

sud·den /súd'n/ *adj.* occurring or done unexpectedly or without warning; abrupt; hurried (*a sudden storm; a sudden departure*). □ **all of a sudden** suddenly. □□ **sud·den·ly** *adv.* **sud·den·ness** *n.*

sud·den death *n. colloq.* a decision in a tied game, etc., dependent on one move, card, toss of a coin, etc.

sud·den in·fant death syn·drome *n. Med.* the death of a seemingly healthy infant from an unknown cause; crib death.

su·dor·if·ic /sóōdərífik/ *adj. & n.* ● *adj.* causing sweating. ● *n.* a sudorific drug.

suds /sudz/ *n. & v.* ● *n.pl.* **1** froth of soap and water. **2** *colloq.* beer. ● *v.* **1** *intr.* form suds. **2** *tr.* lather, cover, or wash in soapy water. □□ **suds·y** *adj.*

sue /sóō/ *v.* (**sues, sued, suing**) **1** *tr.* (also *absol.*) *Law* institute legal proceedings against (a person). **2** *intr. Law* make application to a court of law for redress. **3** *intr.* make entreaty to a person for a favor.

suede /swayd/ *n.* (often *attrib.*) **1** leather with the flesh side rubbed to make a velvety nap. **2** (also **suede cloth**) a woven fabric resembling suede.

su·et /sóō-it/ *n.* the hard white fat on the kidneys or loins of beef, etc., used in cooking, etc. □□ **su·et·y** *adj.*

suf- /suf, səf/ *prefix* assim. form of sub- before *f*.

suf·fer /súfər/ *v.* **1** *intr.* undergo pain, grief, etc. (*suffers acutely*). **2** *tr.* undergo, experience, or be subjected to (pain, loss, defeat, etc.) (*suffered banishment*). **3** *tr.* tolerate (*does not suffer fools gladly*). **4** *intr.* undergo martyrdom. **5** *tr.* (foll. by *to* + infin.) *archaic* allow. □□ **suf·fer·er** *n.* **suf·fer·ing** *n.*

suf·fer·ance /súfərəns, súfrəns/ *n.* tacit consent. □ **on sufferance** with toleration implied by lack of consent or objection.

suf·fice /səfís/ *v.* **1** *intr.* be enough or adequate (*that will suffice for our purpose*). **2** *tr.* satisfy (*six sufficed him*). □ **suffice it to say** I shall content myself with saying.

suf·fi·cien·cy /səfíshənsee/ *n.* (*pl.* **-ies**) an adequate amount or adequate resources.

suf·fi·cient /səfíshənt/ *adj.* sufficing; adequate; enough (*is sufficient for a family; didn't have sufficient funds*). □□ **suf·fi·cient·ly** *adv.*

suf·fix /súfiks/ *n. & v.* ● *n.* **1** a verbal element added at the end of a word to form a derivative (e.g., *-ation, -fy, -ing, -itis*). **2** *Math.* = subscript. ● *v.tr.* (also /səfíks/) append, esp. as a suffix. □□ **suf·fix·a·tion** *n.*

suf·fo·cate /súfəkayt/ *v.* **1** *tr.* choke or kill by stopping breathing. **2** *tr.* (often foll. by *by, with*) produce a choking or breathless sensation in. **3** *intr.* be or feel suffocated or breathless. □□ **suf·fo·cat·ing** *adj.* **suf·fo·cat·ing·ly** *adv.* **suf·fo·ca·tion** /-káyshən/ *n.*

S

Suf·folk /súfək/ *n.* **1** a sheep of a black-faced breed raised for food. **2** this breed.

suf·fra·gan /súfrəgən/ *n.* (in full **suffragan bishop** or **bishop suffragan**) **1** a bishop appointed to help a diocesan bishop in the administration of a diocese. **2** a bishop in relation to his archbishop or metropolitan.

suf·frage /súfrij/ *n.* the right to vote in political elections (*full adult suffrage*).

suf·fra·gette /súfrəjét/ *n. hist.* a woman seeking the right to vote through organized protest.

suf·fra·gist /súfrəjist/ *n.* esp. *hist.* a person who advocates the extension of suffrage, esp. to women. □□ **suf·fra·gism** *n.*

suf·fuse /səfyóoz/ *v.tr.* **1** (of color, moisture, etc.) spread from within to color or moisten (*a blush suffused her cheeks*). **2** cover with color, etc. □□ **suf·fu·sion** /-fyóozhən/ *n.*

Su·fi /sóofee/ *n.* (*pl.* **Sufis**) a Muslim mystic. □□ **Su·fic** *adj.* **Su·fism** *n.*

sug- /sug, səg/ *prefix* assim. form of SUB- before *g.*

sug·ar /shóogər/ *n. & v.* ● *n.* **1** a sweet crystalline substance obtained from various plants, esp. the sugar cane and sugar beet, used in cooking, confectionery, brewing, etc. **2** *Chem.* any of a group of soluble usu. sweet-tasting crystalline carbohydrates, e.g., glucose. **3** *colloq.* darling; dear (used as a term of address). **4** sweet words; flattery. **5** anything comparable to sugar encasing a pill in reconciling a person to what is unpalatable. ● *v.tr.* **1** sweeten with sugar. **2** make (one's words, meaning, etc.) more pleasant or welcome. **3** coat with sugar (*sugared almond*). □ **sugar the pill** see PILL. □□ **sug·ar·less** *adj.*

sug·ar beet *n.* a beet, *Beta vulgaris*, from which sugar is extracted.

sug·ar cane *n.* ◄ any perennial tropical grass of the genus *Saccharum*, esp. *S. officinarum*, with tall stout jointed stems from which sugar is made.

sug·ar-coat *v.tr.* **1** enclose (food) in sugar. **2** make superficially attractive. □□ **sug·ar-coat·ed** *adj.*

sug·ar dad·dy *n.* (*pl.* **-ies**) *sl.* an older man who lavishes gifts on a younger partner.

sug·ar ma·ple *n.* ► any of various trees, esp. *Acer saccharum*, from the sap of which sugar is made.

sug·ar·plum /shóogərplum/ *n. archaic* a small round candy of flavored boiled sugar.

SUGAR CANE (*Saccharum officinarum*)

sug·ar·y /shóogəree/ *adj.* **1** containing or resembling sugar. **2** excessively sweet or sentimental. **3** falsely sweet (*sugary compliments*). □□ **sug·ar·i·ness** *n.*

sug·gest /səgjést, səjést/ *v.tr.* **1** propose (a theory, plan, or hypothesis) (*suggested to them that they should wait*). **2 a** cause (an idea, memory, association, etc.) to present itself. **b** hint at (*his behavior suggests guilt*). □ **suggest itself** (of an idea, etc.) come into the mind.

sug·gest·i·ble /səgjéstəbəl, səjés-/ *adj.* **1** capable of being suggested. **2** open to suggestion; easily swayed. □□ **sug·gest·i·bil·i·ty** *n.*

sug·ges·tion /səgjéschən, səjés-/ *n.* **1** the act of suggesting. **2** a theory, plan, etc., suggested (*made a helpful suggestion*). **3** a slight trace (*a suggestion of garlic*). **4** *Psychol.* **a** the insinuation of a belief, etc., into the mind. **b** such a belief, etc.

sug·ges·tive /səgjéstiv, səjés-/ *adj.* **1** (usu. foll. by *of*) conveying a suggestion. **2** (esp. of a remark, etc.)

indecent; improper. □□ **sug·ges·tive·ly** *adv.* **sug·ges·tive·ness** *n.*

su·i·cid·al /sóoisíd'l/ *adj.* **1** inclined to commit suicide. **2** of or concerning suicide. **3** self-destructive; fatally or disastrously rash. □□ **su·i·cid·al·ly** *adv.*

su·i·cide /sóoisíd/ *n. & v.* ● *n.* **1 a** the intentional killing of oneself. **b** a person who commits suicide. **2** a self-destructive action or course (*political suicide*). ● *v.intr.* commit suicide.

su·i ge·ne·ris /sóo-ī jénəris, sóo-ee, sóo-ee gén-/ *adj.* of its own kind; unique.

su·i jur·is /sóo-ī jóoris, sóo-ee, sóo-ee yóoris / ● *adj. Law* of age; independent.

suint /swint/ *n.* the natural grease in sheep's wool.

suit /sóot/ *n. & v.* ● *n.* **1 a** ► a set of outer clothes of matching material for men, consisting of a jacket, trousers, and sometimes a vest. **b** a similar set of clothes for women, usu. having a skirt instead of trousers. **c** (esp. in *comb.*) a set of clothes for a special occasion, occupation, etc. (*playsuit; swimsuit*). **2** any of the four sets (spades, hearts, diamonds, clubs) into which a pack of cards is divided. **3** (in full **suit at law**) a lawsuit (*criminal suit*). **4 a** a petition, esp. to a person in authority. **b** the process of courting a woman (*paid suit to her*). **5** (usu. foll. by *of*) a set of sails, armor, etc. ● *v.tr.* **1** go well with (a person's figure, features, etc.). **2** (also *absol.*) meet the demands or requirements of (*does not suit all tastes*). **3** make fitting or appropriate (*suited his style to his audience*). **4** (as **suited** *adj.*) appropriate; well-fitted. □ **suit oneself 1** do as one chooses. **2** find some thing that satisfies one.

SUIT: TWO-PIECE SUIT

silk lining
notched lapel
collar
sleeve
breast pocket
cuff
cuff buttons
hip flap pocket
three-button front fastening
waistband
hemmed trousers

suit·a·ble /sóotəbəl/ *adj.* (usu. foll. by *to, for*) well fitted for the purpose; appropriate. □□ **suit·a·bil·i·ty** *n.* **suit·a·ble·ness** *n.* **suit·a·bly** *adv.*

suit·case /sóotkays/ *n.* a usu. oblong case for carrying clothes, etc., having a handle and often a flat hinged lid. □□ **suit·case·ful** *n.* (*pl.* **-fuls**)

suite /sweet/ *n.* **1** a set of things belonging together, esp.: **a** a set of rooms in a hotel, etc. **b** furniture intended for the same room and of the same design. **2** *Mus.* **a** a set of instrumental compositions to be played in succession. **b** a set of selected pieces from an opera, etc., to be played as one instrumental work. **3** a set of people in attendance.

SUGAR MAPLE (*Acer saccharum*)

suit·ing /sóoting/ *n.* cloth used for making suits.

suit·or /sóotər/ *n.* **1** a man seeking to marry a specified woman; a wooer. **2** a plaintiff or petitioner in a lawsuit.

suk (also **sukh**) var. of SOUK.

su·ki·ya·ki /sóokeeyáakee, skeeyáá-/ *n.* a Japanese dish of sliced meat simmered with vegetables and sauce.

Suk·koth var. of SUCCOTH.

sul·cate /súlkayt/ *adj.* grooved; fluted; channeled.

sul·cus /súlkəs/ *n.* (*pl.* **sulci** /-sī/) *Anat.* a groove or furrow, esp. on the surface of the brain.

sul·fa /súlfə/ *n.* any drug derived from sulfanilamide (often *attrib.*: *sulfa drug*).

sul·fam·ic acid /sulfámik/ *n.* a strong acid used in weedkiller, an amide of sulfuric acid. □□ **sul·fa·mate** /súlfəmayt/ *n.*

sul·fa·nil·a·mide /súlfəníləmīd/ *n.* a colorless sulfonamide drug with anti-bacterial properties.

sul·fate /súlfayt/ *n.* a salt or ester of sulfuric acid.

sul·fide /súlfīd/ *n. Chem.* a binary compound of sulfur.

sul·fite /súlfīt/ *n. Chem.* a salt or ester of sulfurous acid.

sul·fon·a·mide /sulfónəmīd/ *n.* a substance derived from an amide of a sulfonic acid, able to prevent the multiplication of some pathogenic bacteria.

sul·fon·ate /súlfənayt/ *n. & v. Chem.* ● *n.* a salt or ester of sulfonic acid. ● *v.tr.* convert into a sulfonate by reaction with sulfuric acid.

sul·fone /súlfōn/ *n.* an organic compound containing the SO_2 group united directly to two carbon atoms. □□ **sul·fon·ic** /-fónik/ *adj.*

sul·fur /súlfər/ *n.* **1 a** ► a pale yellow nonmetallic element having crystalline and amorphous forms, burning with a blue flame and a suffocating smell. **b** (*attrib.*) like or containing sulfur. **2** the material of which hellfire and lightning were believed to consist. **3** any yellow butterfly of the family Pieridae. **4** a pale greenish yellow color. □□ **sul·fur·y** *adj.*

SULFUR CRYSTALS

sul·fur·ate /súlfyərayt, -fə-/ *v.tr.* impregnate, fumigate, or treat with sulfur, esp. in bleaching. □□ **sul·fu·ra·tion** /-ráyshən/ *n.* **sul·fur·a·tor** *n.*

sul·fur di·ox·ide *n.* a colorless pungent gas formed by burning sulfur in air and used as a food preservative. ▷ ACID RAIN

sul·fu·re·ous /sulfyóoreeəs/ *adj.* **1** of, like, or suggesting sulfur. **2** sulfur-colored; yellow.

sul·fu·ric /sulfyóorik/ *adj. Chem.* containing sexivalent sulfur.

sul·fu·ric ac·id *n.* a dense, oily, colorless, highly acid and corrosive fluid.

sul·fu·rize /súlfyərīz, -fə-/ *v.tr.* = SULFURATE. □□ **sul·fu·ri·za·tion** *n.*

sul·fur·ous /súlfərəs, -fyoor-/ *adj.* **1** relating to or suggestive of sulfur, esp. in color. **2** *Chem.* containing quadrivalent sulfur.

sul·fur·ous ac·id *n.* an unstable weak acid used as a reducing and bleaching acid.

sulk /sulk/ *v. & n.* ● *v.intr.* be sulky. ● *n.* (also in *pl.*, prec. by *the*) a period of sullen, esp. resentful, silence (*having a sulk; got the sulks*). □□ **sulk·er** *n.*

sulk·y /súlkee/ *n. & adj.* ● *n.* (*pl.* **-ies**) a light two-wheeled horse-drawn vehicle for one, esp. in harness racing. ▷ TROTTING. ● *adj.* (**sulkier, sulkiest**) sullen, morose, or silent, esp. from resentment or ill temper. □□ **sulk·i·ly** *adv.* **sulk·i·ness** *n.*

sul·len /súlən/ *adj.* **1** morose; resentful; sulky. **2 a** (of a thing) slow moving. **b** dismal (*a sullen sky*). □□ **sul·len·ly** *adv.* **sul·len·ness** *n.*

sul·ly /súlee/ *v.tr.* (**-ies, -ied**) **1** disgrace or tarnish (a person's reputation, etc.). **2** *poet.* dirty; soil.

sul·tan /súlt'n/ *n.* a Muslim sovereign. □□ **sul·tan·ate** /-nayt/ *n.*

sul·tan·a /sultánə, -táanə/ *n.* **1 a** a seedless raisin used in cakes, etc. **b** the small, pale yellow grape producing this. **2** the mother, wife, concubine, or daughter of a sultan.

sul·try /súltree/ *adj.* (**sultrier, sultriest**) **1** (of the atmosphere or the weather) hot or oppressive. **2** (of a person, character, etc.) passionate; sensual. □□ **sul·tri·ly** *adv.* **sul·tri·ness** *n.*

sum /sum/ *n. & v.* ● *n.* **1** the total amount resulting from the addition of two or more items, etc. **2** a particular amount of money. **3 a** an arithmetical problem. **b** (esp. *pl.*) esp. *Brit. colloq.* arithmetic work (*good at sums*). ● *v.tr.* (**summed, summing**) find the sum of. □ **in sum** in brief. **sum up 1** (esp. of a judge) recapitulate or review the evidence in a case, etc. **2** form or express an idea of the character of (a person, etc.). **3** collect into or express as a total.

su·mac /sŏŏmak, shŏŏ–/ *n.* (also **su·mach**) **1** ▼ any shrub or tree of the genus *Rhus*, having reddish cone-shaped fruits used as a spice in cooking. **2** the dried and ground leaves of this used in tanning and dyeing.

fruit cluster

SUMAC:
STAG HORN SUMAC
(*Rhus typhina*)

Su·me·ri·an /sŏŏméereeən, –mér–/ *adj. & n.* ● *adj.* of or relating to the early and non-Semitic element in the civilization of ancient Babylonia. ● *n.* **1** a member of the early non-Semitic people of ancient Babylonia. **2** the Sumerian language.

sum·ma /sŏŏmə, súmə/ *n.* (*pl.* **summae** /–mee/) a summary of what is known of a subject.

sum·ma cum lau·de /sŏŏmə kŏŏm lówday, –də, –dee/ *adv. & adj.* (of a degree, diploma, etc.) of the highest standard; with the highest distinction.

sum·ma·rize /súmərīz/ *v.tr.* make or be a summary of; sum up. □□ **sum·ma·rist** *n.* **sum·ma·riz·a·ble** *adj.* **sum·ma·ri·za·tion** *n.* **sum·ma·riz·er** *n.*

sum·ma·ry /súməree/ *n. & adj.* ● *n.* (*pl.* **-ies**) a brief account. ● *adj.* **1** dispensing with needless details or formalities; brief (*a summary account*). **2** *Law* without the customary legal formalities (*summary justice*). □□ **sum·mar·i·ly** /səmáirilee/ *adv.* **sum·mar·i·ness** *n.*

sum·ma·tion /səmáyshən/ *n.* **1** the finding of a total or sum; an addition. **2** a summing-up. □□ **sum·ma·tion·al** *adj.*

sum·mer /súmər/ *n. & v.* ● *n.* **1** the warmest season of the year. ▷ SEASON. **2** *Astron.* the period from the summer solstice to the autumnal equinox. **3** the hot weather typical of summer. **4** (often foll. by *of*) the mature stage of life; the height of achievement, etc. **5** (esp. in *pl.*) *poet.* a year (esp. of a person's age) (*a child of ten summers*). **6** (*attrib.*) characteristic of or suitable for summer. ● *v.intr.* (usu. foll. by *at, in*) pass the summer. □□ **sum·mer·less** *adj.* **sum·mer·y** *adj.*

sum·mer·sault var. of SOMERSAULT.

sum·mer sol·stice *n.* the time at which the Sun is farthest north from the equator, about June 21 in the northern hemisphere.

sum·mer squash *n.* any of various cultivated squashes whose fruit is used as a vegetable. ▷ VEGETABLE

sum·mer·time /súmərtīm/ *n.* the season or period of summer.

sum·ming-up *n.* **1** a review of evidence and a direction given by a judge to a jury. **2** a recapitulation of the main points of an argument, case, etc.

sum·mit /súmit/ *n.* **1** the highest point, esp. of a mountain. **2** the highest degree of power, ambition, etc. **3** (in full **summit meeting, talks**, etc.) a discussion, esp. on disarmament, etc., between heads of government.

sum·mon /súmən/ *v.tr.* **1** call upon to appear, esp.

as a defendant or witness in a court of law. **2** (usu. foll. by *to* + infin.) call upon (*summoned her to assist*). **3** call together for a meeting or some other purpose. □□ **sum·mon·a·ble** *adj.* **sum·mon·er** *n.*

sum·mons /súmənz/ *n. & v.* ● *n.* (*pl.* **summonses**) **1** an authoritative or urgent call to attend on some occasion or do something. **2 a** a call to appear before a judge or magistrate. **b** the writ containing such a summons. ● *v.tr.* esp. *Law* serve with a summons.

sum·mum bo·num /sŏŏməm bónəm/ *n.* the highest good, esp. as the end or determining principle in an ethical system.

su·mo /sŏŏmō/ *n.* (*pl.* **-os**) **1** ▶ a style of Japanese wrestling in which a participant is defeated by touching the ground with any part of the body except the soles of the feet or by moving outside the marked area. **2** a sumo wrestler.

sump /sump/ *n.* **1** a pit, well, hole, etc., in which superfluous liquid collects in mines, machines, etc. **2** a cesspool.

sump·tu·ar·y /súmpchŏŏeree/ *adj.* **1** regulating expenditure. **2** (of a law or edict, etc.) limiting private expenditure in the interests of the government.

sump·tu·ous /súmpchŏŏəs/ *adj.* rich; lavish; costly (*a sumptuous setting*). □□ **sump·tu·os·i·ty** /–ósitee/ *n.* **sump·tu·ous·ly** *adv.* **sump·tu·ous·ness** *n.*

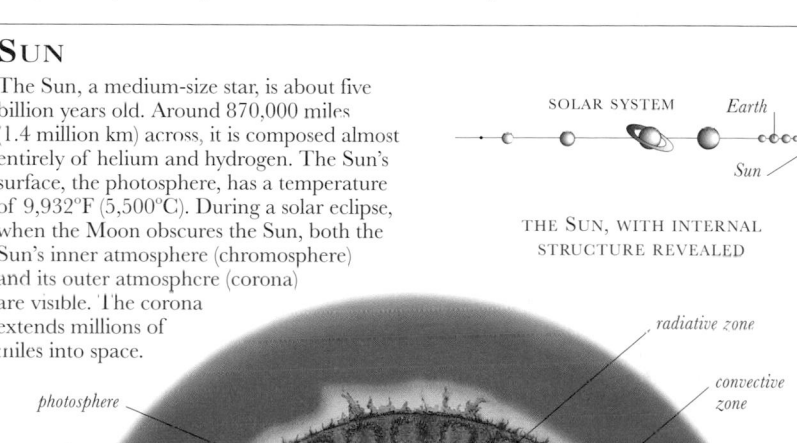

SUMO WRESTLERS

Sun. *abbr.* Sunday.

sun /sun/ *n. & v.* ● *n.* (also **Sun**) **1 a** ▼ the star around which the Earth orbits and from which it receives light and warmth. ▷ SOLAR SYSTEM. **b** any similar star in the universe with or without planets. **2** the light or warmth received from the Sun (*keep out the sun*). ● *v.* (**sunned, sunning**) **1** ● *refl.* bask in the sun. **2** *tr.* expose to the sun. □ **under the sun** anywhere in the world. □□ **sun·less** *adj.*

sun·bathe /súnbayth/ *v.intr.* bask in the sun.

sun·beam /súnbeem/ *n.* a ray of sunlight.

sun·belt /súnbelt/ *n.* a strip of territory receiving a high amount of sunshine.

sun·bird /súnbərd/ *n.* any small brightly plumaged Old World bird of the family Nectariniidae, resembling a hummingbird.

sun·block /súnblok/ *n.* a cream or lotion for protecting the skin from the sun.

sun·burn /súnbərn/ *n. & v.* ● *n.* reddening and inflammation of the skin caused by overexposure to the sun. ● *v.intr.* **1** suffer from sunburn. **2** (as **sunburned** or **sunburnt** *adj.*) suffering from sunburn.

Sun

The Sun, a medium-size star, is about five billion years old. Around 870,000 miles (1.4 million km) across, it is composed almost entirely of helium and hydrogen. The Sun's surface, the photosphere, has a temperature of 9,932°F (5,500°C). During a solar eclipse, when the Moon obscures the Sun, both the Sun's inner atmosphere (chromosphere) and its outer atmosphere (corona) are visible. The corona extends millions of miles into space.

SOLAR SYSTEM   *Earth*

Sun

THE SUN, WITH INTERNAL
STRUCTURE REVEALED

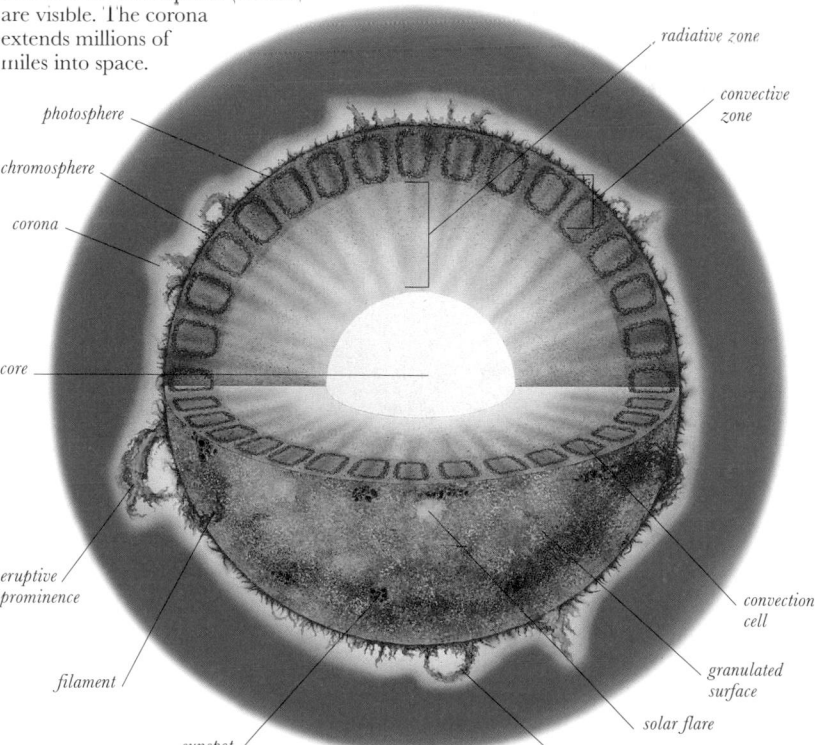

radiative zone

convective zone

photosphere

chromosphere

corona

core

eruptive prominence

filament

sunspot

convection cell

granulated surface

solar flare

looped gas prominence

S

SUNBURST: SYMBOL OF THE RISEN CHRIST, SIENA CATHEDRAL, ITALY

SUNDEW: FLY CAPTURED IN SUNDEW LEAF (*Drosera* species)

curled leaf

trapped fly

sticky hairs

sun·burst /súnbərst/ *n.* **1** ◀ something resembling the Sun and its rays, esp.: **a** a brooch, etc. **b** a firework. **2** the Sun shining suddenly from behind clouds.

sun·dae /súnday, -dee/ *n.* a dish of ice cream with fruit, nuts, syrup, etc.

Sun·day /súnday, -dee/ *n. & adv.* ● *n.* **1** the first day of the week, a Christian holiday and day of worship. **2** a newspaper published on a Sunday. ● *adv. colloq.* **1** on Sunday. **2** (**Sundays**) on Sundays; each Sunday.

Sun·day school *n.* a school for the religious instruction of children on Sundays.

sun·der /súndər/ *v.tr. & intr. archaic* separate; sever. □ **in sunder** apart.

sun·dew /súndōo, -dyōo/ *n.* ◀ any small insect-consuming bog plant of the family Droseraceae, esp. of the genus *Drosera*, with hairs secreting drops of moisture.

sun·di·al /súndīəl/ *n.* ▶ an instrument showing the time by the shadow of a pointer cast by the sun onto a graduated disk.

sun·down /súndown/ *n.* sunset.

sun·down·er /súndownər/ *n.* **1** *Austral.* a tramp who arrives at a sheep station, etc., in the evening for food and shelter too late to do any work. **2** *Brit. colloq.* an alcoholic drink taken at sunset.

sun·dress /súndres/ *n.* a dress without sleeves and with a low neck.

sun·dry /súndree/ *adj. & n.* ● *adj.* various; several (*sundry items*). ● *n.* (*pl.* **-ies**) (in *pl.*) items or oddments not mentioned individually.

sun·fast /súnfast/ *adj.* (of dye) not subject to fading by sunlight.

sun·fish /súnfish/ *n.* any of various almost spherical fish, esp. a large ocean fish, *Mola mola*.

sun·flow·er /súnflowr/ *n.* ▶ any tall plant of the genus *Helianthus*, esp. *H. annuus*, with very large, showy, golden-rayed flowers, grown also for its seeds which yield an edible oil.

sung *past part.* of SING.

sun·glass·es /súnglasiz/ *n.pl.* glasses tinted to protect the eyes from sunlight or glare.

sunk *past* and *past part.* of SINK.

sunk·en /súngkən/ *adj.* **1** that has been sunk. **2** beneath the surface; submerged. **3** (of the eyes, cheeks, etc.) hollow; depressed.

sun lamp *n.* **1** a lamp giving ultraviolet rays for an artificial suntan, therapy, etc. **2** *Cinematog.* a large lamp with a parabolic reflector used in filmmaking.

sun·light /súnlīt/ *n.* light from the Sun. □□ **sun·lit** *adj.*

sun·lit /súnlit/ *adj.* illuminated by sunlight.

sunn /sun/ *n.* (in full **sunn hemp**) an E. Indian hemplike fiber.

Sun·na /sóönə/ *n.* a traditional portion of Muslim law based on Muhammad's words or acts, accepted by Muslims as authoritative.

Sun·ni /sóönee/ *n. & adj.* ● *n.* (*pl.* same or **Sunnis**) **1** one of the two main branches of Islam, regarding the Sunna as equal in authority to the Koran (cf. SHIA). **2** an adherent of this branch of Islam. ● *adj.* of or relating to Sunni.

sun·ny /súnee/ *adj.* (**sunnier, sunniest**) **1 a** bright with sunlight. **b** exposed to or warmed by the sun. **2** cheery in temperament. □□ **sun·ni·ly** *adv.* **sun·ni·ness** *n.*

sun·ny·side up /súneesīd/ *adj.* (of an egg) fried on one side and served.

sun·rise /súnrīz/ *n.* **1** the Sun's rising at dawn. **2** the colored sky associated with this. **3** the time at which sunrise occurs.

sun·rise in·dus·try *n.* any newly established industry regarded as signaling prosperity.

sun·roof /súnrōof/ *n.* a section of an automobile roof that can be slid open.

sun·set /súnset/ *n.* **1** the Sun's setting in the evening. **2** the colored sky associated with this. **3** the time at which sunset occurs.

sun·shade /súnshayd/ *n.* **1** a parasol. **2** an awning.

sun·shine /súnshīn/ *n.* **1 a** the light of the Sun. **b** an area lit by the Sun. **2** good weather. **3** cheerfulness. □□ **sun·shin·y** *adj.*

sun·spot /súnspot/ *n.* one of the dark patches observed on the Sun's surface. ▷ SUN

sun·star /súnstaar/ *n.* any starfish of the genus *Solaster*, with many rays.

sun·stroke /súnstrōk/ *n.* acute prostration or collapse from the excessive heat of the sun.

sun·tan /súntan/ *n. & v.* ● *n.* the brownish coloring of skin caused by exposure to the Sun. ● *v.intr.* (**-tanned, -tanning**) color the skin with a suntan.

sun·trap /súntrap/ *n. Brit.* a place sheltered from the wind and suitable for catching the sunshine.

sun·up /súnup/ *n.* sunrise.

sup[1] /sup/ *v. & n.* ● *v.tr.* (**supped, supping**) **1** take (soup, tea, etc.) by sips or spoonfuls. **2** esp. *No. of Engl. colloq.* drink (alcohol). ● *n.* a sip of liquid.

sup[2] /sup/ *v.intr.* (**supped, supping**) (usu. foll. by *off, on*) *archaic* take supper.

sup- /sup, səp/ *prefix* assim. form of SUB- before *p*.

su·per /sóöpər/ *adj. & n.* ● *adj.* (also **su·per·du·per** /-dóöpər/) *colloq.* (also as *int.*) exceptional; splendid. ● *n. colloq.* **1** *Theatr.* a supernumerary actor. **2** a superintendent. **3** superphosphate. **4** an extra, unwanted, or unimportant person.

super- /sóöpər/ *prefix* forming nouns, adjectives, and verbs, meaning: **1** above, beyond, or over (*superstructure; superimpose*). **2** to a great or extreme degree (*superabundant*). **3** extra good or large of its kind (*supertanker*). **4** of a higher kind (*superclass*).

su·per·a·ble /sóöpərəbəl/ *adj.* able to be overcome.

su·per·a·bound /sóöpərəbównd/ *v.intr.* be very or too abundant.

su·per·a·bun·dant /sóöpərəbúndənt/ *adj.* abounding beyond what is normal or right. □□ **su·per·a·bun·dance** *n.* **su·per·a·bun·dant·ly** *adv.*

su·per·add /sóöpərád/ *v.tr.* add over and above. □□ **su·per·ad·di·tion** /-ədíshən/ *n.*

su·per·al·tar /sóöpərawltər/ *n. Eccl.* a portable slab of stone consecrated for use on an unconsecrated altar, etc.

su·per·an·nu·ate /sóöpərányōoayt/ *v.tr.* **1** retire (a person) with a pension. **2** dismiss or discard as too old. **3** (as **superannuated** *adj.*) too old. □□ **su·per·an·nu·a·ble** *adj.*

su·per·an·nu·a·tion /sóöpərányōo-áyshən/ *n.* a pension paid to a retired person.

su·perb /sóöpórb/ *adj.* **1** of the most impressive, splendid, or majestic kind. **2** *colloq.* excellent; fine. □□ **su·perb·ly** *adv.* **su·perb·ness** *n.*

su·per·bug /sóöpərbug/ *n.* a bacterium, insect, etc. regarded as having enhanced qualities, esp. of resistance to antibiotics or pesticides.

su·per·cal·en·der /sóöpərkálindər/ *v.tr.* give a highly glazed finish to (paper) by extra calendering.

su·per·car·go /sóöpərkaargō/ *n.* (*pl.* **-oes**) an officer in a merchant ship managing sales, etc., of cargo.

su·per·ce·les·ti·al /sóöpərsiléschəl/ *adj.* **1** above the heavens. **2** more than heavenly.

su·per·charge /sóöpərchaarj/ *v.tr.* **1** (usu. foll. by *with*) charge (the atmosphere, etc.) with energy, emotion, etc. **2** use a supercharger on.

su·per·charg·er /sóöpərchaarjər/ *n.* a device supplying air or fuel to an internal-combustion engine at above normal pressure to increase efficiency.

su·per·cil·i·ar·y /sóöpərsílee-eree/ *adj. Anat.* of or concerning the eyebrow; over the eye.

su·per·cil·i·ous /sóöpərsíleeəs/ *adj.* assuming an air of contemptuous indifference or superiority. □□ **su·per·cil·i·ous·ly** *adv.* **su·per·cil·i·ous·ness** *n.*

su·per·class /sóöpərklas/ *n.* a taxonomic category between class and phylum.

su·per·col·um·nar /sóöpərkəlúmnər/ *adj. Archit.* having one order or set of columns above another. □□ **su·per·col·um·ni·a·tion** /-neeáyshən/ *n.*

su·per·com·put·er /sóöpərkəmpyóötər/ *n.* a powerful computer capable of dealing with complex problems. □□ **su·per·com·put·ing** *n.*

su·per·con·duc·tiv·i·ty /sóöpərkónduktívitee/ *n. Physics* ▶ the property of zero electrical resistance in some substances at very low absolute temperatures. □□ **su·per·con·duct·ing** /-kəndúkting/ *adj.* **su·per·con·duc·tive** *adj.*

su·per·con·duc·tor /sóöpərkəndúktər/ *n. Physics* a substance having superconductivity. ▷ SUPERCONDUCTIVITY

su·per·con·scious /sóöpərkónshəs/ *adj.* transcending human consciousness. □□ **su·per·con·scious·ly** *adv.* **su·per·con·scious·ness** *n.*

su·per·cool /sóöpərkóöl/ *v. & adj.* ● *v. Chem.* **1** cool (a liquid) below its freezing point without solidification or crystallization. ▷ MATTER. **2** *intr.* (of a liquid) be cooled in this way.

su·per·crit·i·cal /sóöpərkrítikəl/ *adj. Physics* of more than critical mass, etc.

su·per·du·per var. of SUPER *adj.*

su·per·e·go /sóöpəreégō, -égō/ *n.* (*pl.* **-os**) *Psychol.* the part of the mind that acts as a conscience and responds to social rules.

su·per·el·e·va·tion /sóöpərélivayshən/ *n.* the amount by which the outer edge of a curve on a road or railroad is above the inner edge.

su·per·em·i·nent /sóöpəréminənt/ *adj.* supremely eminent, exalted, or remarkable. □□ **su·per·em·i·nence** *n.* **su·per·em·i·nent·ly** *adv.*

su·per·er·o·ga·tion /sóöpərérəgáyshən/ *n.* performance of more than duty requires. □□ **su·per·er·og·a·to·ry** /-írógətawree/ *adj.*

su·per·ex·cel·lent /sóöpəréksələnt/ *adj.* very or supremely excellent. □□ **su·per·ex·cel·lence** *n.* **su·per·ex·cel·lent·ly** *adv.*

su·per·fam·i·ly /sóöpərfamilee/ *n.* (*pl.* **-ies**) a taxonomic category between family and order.

su·per·fat·ted /sóöpərfátid/ *adj.* (of soap) containing extra fat.

su·per·fi·cial /sóöpərfíshəl/ *adj.* **1** of or on the surface; lacking depth. **2** swift or cursory. **3** apparent but not real (*a superficial resemblance*). **4** (esp. of a person) having no depth of character or knowledge.

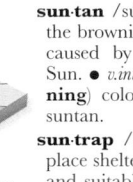

gnomon

12 noon

shadow

hour mark *marks the time*

SUNDIAL

SUNFLOWER (*Helianthus annuus*)

SUPERCONDUCTIVITY

A metal cooled to just above absolute zero (-459.67°F/-273.15°C) loses its electrical resistance and therefore carries current more efficiently. Materials cooled in this way are called superconductors and are used in electrical cables and scientific equipment.

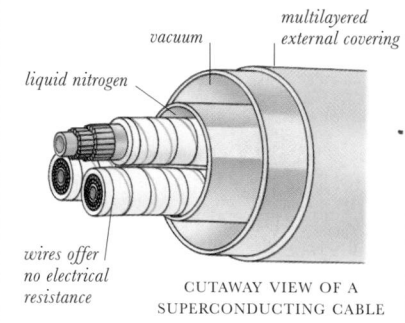

multilayered external covering

vacuum

liquid nitrogen

wires offer no electrical resistance

CUTAWAY VIEW OF A SUPERCONDUCTING CABLE

□□ **su·per·fi·ci·al·i·ty** /-sheeálitee/ *n.* (*pl.* **-ics**). **su·per·fi·cial·ly** *adv.*

su·per·fi·ci·es /sóopərfisheez, -fishee-eez/ *n.* (*pl.* same) *Geom.* a surface.

su·per·fine /sóopərfín/ *adj.* **1** *Commerce* of high quality. **2** pretending great refinement.

su·per·flu·i·ty /sóopərflóoitee/ *n.* (*pl.* **-ies**) **1** the state of being superfluous. **2** a superfluous amount or thing.

su·per·flu·ous /sóopərflóoəs/ *adj.* more than enough; redundant; needless. □□ **su·per·flu·ous·ly** *adv.* **su·per·flu·ous·ness** *n.*

su·per·gi·ant /sóopərjīənt/ *n.* a star of very great luminosity and size.

su·per·glue /sóopərgloo/ *n.* any of various adhesives with an exceptional bonding capability.

su·per·grass /sóopərgras/ *n. Brit. colloq.* a police informer who implicates a large number of people.

su·per·heat /sóopərheet/ *v.tr. Physics* **1** heat (a liquid) above its boiling point without vaporization. **2** heat (a vapor) above its boiling point. □□ **su·per·heat·er** *n.*

su·per·het /sóopərhét/ *n. colloq.* = SUPERHETERODYNE.

su·per·het·er·o·dyne /sóopərhétərōdīn/ *adj. & n.* ● *adj.* denoting or characteristic of a system of radio reception in which a local variable oscillator is tuned to beat at a constant ultrasonic frequency with carrier wave frequencies, making it unnecessary to vary the amplifier tuning and securing greater selectivity. ● *n.* a superheterodyne receiver.

su·per·high·way /sóopərhíway/ *n.* a multilane main road for fast traffic.

su·per·hu·man /sóopərhyóomən/ *adj.* **1** beyond normal human capability. **2** higher than man. □□ **su·per·hu·man·ly** *adv.*

su·per·hu·mer·al /sóopərhyóomərəl/ *n. Eccl.* a vestment worn over the shoulders, e.g., an amice, ephod, or pallium.

su·per·im·pose /sóopərimpóz/ *v.tr.* (usu. foll. by *on*) lay (a thing) on something else. □□ **su·per·im·po·si·tion** /-pəzíshən/ *n.*

su·per·in·cum·bent /sóopərinkúmbənt/ *adj.* lying on something else.

su·per·in·duce /sóopərindóos, -dyóos/ *v.tr.* introduce or induce in addition.

su·per·in·tend /sóopərinténd/ *v.tr. & intr.* supervise and inspect. □□ **su·per·in·tend·ence** *n.* **su·per·in·tend·en·cy** *n.*

su·per·in·tend·ent /sóopərinténdənt/ *n. & adj.* ● *n.* **1 a** a person who superintends. **b** a director of an institution, etc. **2** a high-ranking official, often the chief of a police department. **3** the caretaker of a building. ● *adj.* superintending.

su·pe·ri·or /sóopéereeər/ *adj. & n.* ● *adj.* **1** in a higher position; of higher rank. **2 a** above average in quality, etc. (*superior leather*). **b** supercilious (*a superior air*). **3** (often foll. by *to*) **a** better or greater in some respect. **b** above yielding, making concessions, etc. (*superior to bribery*). **4** *Printing* (of figures or letters) placed above the line. ● *n.* **1** a person superior to another in rank, character, etc. **2** (*fem.* **superioress** /-ris/) *Eccl.* the head of a monastery or other religious institution (*Mother Superior*). **3** *Printing* a superior letter or figure. □□ **su·pe·ri·or·ly** *adv.*

su·pe·ri·or·i·ty /sóopéeree-áwritee, -ór-/ *n.* the state of being superior.

su·pe·ri·or·i·ty com·plex *n. Psychol.* an undue conviction of one's own superiority to others.

su·per·ja·cent /sóopərjáysənt/ *adj.* overlying; superincumbent.

su·per·la·tive /sóopárlətiv/ *adj. & n.* ● *adj.* **1** of the highest quality or degree (*superlative wisdom*). **2** *Gram.* (of an adjective or adverb) expressing the highest or a very high degree of a quality (e.g., *bravest, most fiercely*). ● *n.* **1** *Gram.* **a** the superlative expression or form of an adjective or adverb. **b** a word in the superlative. **2** something embodying excellence. **3** an exaggerated or excessive statement, comment, etc. □□ **su·per·la·tive·ly** *adv.* **su·per·la·tive·ness** *n.*

su·per·lu·na·ry /sóopərlóonəree/ *adj.* **1** situated beyond the Moon. **2** celestial.

su·per·man /sóopərman/ *n.* (*pl.* **-men**) **1** esp. *Philos.* the ideal superior man of the future. **2** *colloq.* a man of exceptional strength or ability.

su·per·mar·ket /sóopərmaarkit/ *n.* a large self-service store selling foods, household goods, etc.

su·per·mun·dane /sóopərmundáyn/ *adj.* superior to earthly things.

su·per·nal /sóopárnəl/ *adj.* esp. *poet.* **1** heavenly; divine. **2** of or concerning the sky. **3** lofty. □□ **su·per·nal·ly** *adv.*

su·per·na·tant /sóopərnáyt'nt/ *adj. & n.* esp. *Chem.* ● *adj.* floating on the surface of a liquid. ● *n.* a supernatant substance.

su·per·nat·u·ral /sóopərnáchərəl/ *adj. & n.* ● *adj.* attributed to or thought to reveal some force above the laws of nature, magical; mystical. ● *n.* (prec. by *the*) supernatural, occult, or magical forces, effects, etc. □□ **su·per·nat·u·ral·ism** *n* **su·per·nat·u·ral·ly** *adv.* **su·per·nat·u·ral·ness** *n.*

su·per·nor·mal /sóopərnáwrməl/ *adj.* beyond what is normal or natural. □□ **su·per·nor·mal·i·ty** /-málitee/ *n.*

su·per·no·va /sóopərnóvə/ *n.* (*pl.* **-novae** /-vee/ or **-novas**) *Astron.* a star that suddenly increases very greatly in brightness because of an explosion ejecting most of its mass. ▷ STAR

su·per·nu·mer·ar·y /sóopərnóoməreree, -nyóo-/ *adj. & n.* ● *adj.* **1** in excess of the normal number. **2** engaged for extra work. **3** (of an actor) appearing on stage but not speaking. ● *n.* (*pl.* **-ies**) **1** an extra or unwanted person or thing. **2** a person engaged for extra work.

su·per·or·der /sóopərawrdər/ *n. Biol.* a taxonomic category between order and class.

su·per·or·di·nate /sóopəráwrd'nət/ *adj.* (usu. foll. by *to*) of superior importance or rank.

su·per·phos·phate /sóopərfósfayt/ *n.* a fertilizer made by treating phosphate rock with sulfuric or phosphoric acid.

su·per·phys·i·cal /sóopərfízikəl/ *adj.* **1** unexplainable by physical causes; supernatural. **2** beyond what is physical.

su·per·pose /sóopərpóz/ *v.tr.* (usu. foll. by *on*) esp. *Geom.* place (a thing or a geometric figure) on or above something else, esp. so as to coincide. □□ **su·per·po·si·tion** /-pəzíshən/ *n.*

su·per·pow·er /sóopərpowr/ *n.* a nation of supreme power and influence, esp. the US and the former USSR.

su·per·sat·u·rate /sóopəsáchərayt/ *v.tr.* add to (esp. a solution) beyond saturation point. □□ **su·per·sat·u·ra·tion** /-ráyshən/ *n.*

su·per·scribe /sóopərskríb/ *v.tr.* **1** write (an inscription) at the top of or on the outside of a document, etc. **2** write an inscription over or on (a thing). □□ **su·per·scrip·tion** /-skrípshən/ *n.*

su·per·script /sóopərskript/ *adj. & n.* ● *adj.* written or printed above. ● *n.* a superscript number or symbol.

su·per·sede /sóopərseéd/ *v.tr.* **1 a** adopt or appoint another person or thing in place of. **b** set aside; cease to employ. **2** (of a person or thing) take the place of. □□ **su·per·ses·sion** /-séshən/ *n.*

su·per·son·ic /sóopərsónik/ *adj.* designating or having a speed greater than that of sound. □□ **su·per·son·i·cal·ly** *adv.*

su·per·son·ics /sóopərsóniks/ *n.pl.* (treated as *sing.*) = ULTRASONICS.

su·per·star /sóopərstaar/ *n.* an extremely famous movie star, athlete, etc. □□ **su·per·star·dom** *n.*

su·per·sti·tion /sóopərstíshən/ *n.* **1** credulity regarding the supernatural. **2** an irrational fear of the unknown. **3** misdirected reverence. **4** a practice, opinion, or religion based on these tendencies. **5** a widely held but unjustified idea. □□ **su·per·sti·tious** *adj.* **su·per·sti·tious·ly** *adv.* **su·per·sti·tious·ness** *n.*

su·per·store /sóopərstawr/ *n.* a very large store selling a wide range of goods.

su·per·stra·tum /sóopərstraytəm, -strat-/ *n.* (*pl.* **-strata** /-tə/) an overlying stratum.

su·per·struc·ture /sóopərstrukchər/ *n.* **1** the part of a building above its foundations. **2** a structure built on top of something else. **3** a concept or idea based on others. □□ **su·per·struc·tur·al** *adj.*

su·per·sub·tle /sóopərsút'l/ *adj.* extremely or excessively subtle. □□ **su·per·sub·tle·ty** *n.*

su·per·tank·er /sóopərtangkər/ *n.* a very large tanker ship.

su·per·ter·res·tri·al /sóopərtəréstreeəl/ *adj.* **1** in or belonging to a region above the Earth. **2** celestial.

su·per·ti·tle var. of SURTITLE.

su·per·ton·ic /sóopərtónik/ *n. Mus.* the note above the tonic, the second note of the diatonic scale of any key.

su·per·vene /sóopərveén/ *v.intr.* occur as an interruption in or a change. □□ **su·per·ven·ient** *adj.* **su·per·ven·tion** /-vénshən/ *n.*

su·per·vise /sóopərvíz/ *v.tr.* superintend; oversee. □□ **su·per·vi·sion** /-vízhən/ *n.* **su·per·vi·sor** *n.* **su·per·vi·so·ry** *adj.*

su·per·wom·an /sóopərwoomən/ *n.* (*pl.* **-women**) *colloq.* a woman of exceptional strength or ability.

su·pi·nate /sóopinayt/ *v.tr.* put (a hand or foreleg, etc.) into a supine position. □□ **su·pi·na·tion** /-náyshən/ *n.*

su·pi·na·tor /sóopinaytər/ *n. Anat.* a muscle in the forearm effecting supination.

su·pine *adj.* /sóopín/ **1** lying face upwards (cf. PRONE). **2** inert; indolent. □□ **su·pine·ly** /-pínlee/ *adv.* **su·pine·ness** *n.*

sup·per /súpər/ *n.* a light evening meal. □ **sing for one's supper** do something in return for a benefit.

sup·plant /səplánt/ *v.tr.* dispossess and take the place of, esp. by underhand means. □□ **sup·plant·er** *n.*

sup·ple /súpəl/ *adj.* (**suppler, supplest**) flexible; pliant. □□ **sup·ple·ness** *n.*

sup·ple·jack /súpəljak/ *n.* any of various strong twining tropical shrubs, esp. *Berchemia scandens*.

sup·ple·ment *n. & v.* ● *n.* /súplimənt/ **1** a thing or part added to remedy deficiencies (*dietary supplement*). **2** a part added to a book, etc., to provide further information. **3** a separate section, esp. a color magazine, added to a newspaper or periodical. ● *v.tr.* also /súplimént/ provide a supplement for. □□ **sup·ple·men·tal** /-mént'l/ *adj.* **sup·ple·men·tal·ly** *adv.* **sup·ple·men·ta·tion** /-mentáyshən/ *n.*

sup·ple·men·ta·ry /súpliméntəree/ *adj.* forming or serving as a supplement; additional. □□ **sup·ple·men·tar·i·ly** *adv.*

S

sup·ple·tion /səpléeshən/ *n.* the act or an instance of supplementing, esp. *Linguistics* the occurrence of unrelated forms to supply gaps in conjugation (e.g., *went* as the past of *go*). □□ **sup·ple·tive** *adj.*

sup·pli·ant /súpleeənt/ *adj. & n.* ● *adj.* 1 supplicating. 2 expressing supplication. ● *n.* a supplicating person. □□ **sup·pli·ant·ly** *adv.*

sup·pli·cate /súplikayt/ *v.* 1 *tr.* petition humbly to (a person) or for (a thing). 2 *intr.* (foll. by *to, for*) make a petition. □□ **sup·pli·cant** *adj. & n.* **sup·pli·ca·tion** /-áyshən/ *n.* **sup·pli·ca·to·ry** *adj.*

sup·ply[1] /səplí/ *v. & n.* ● *v.tr.* (**-ies, -ied**) 1 provide or furnish (a thing needed). 2 (often foll. by *with*) provide (a person, etc., with a thing needed). 3 meet or make up for (a deficiency or need, etc.). 4 fill (a vacancy, etc.) as a substitute. ● *n.* (*pl.* **-ies**) 1 the act or an instance of providing what is needed. 2 a stock, amount, etc., of something provided or obtainable. 3 (in *pl.*) the provisions and equipment for an army, expedition, etc. 4 (often *attrib.*) a person, esp. a schoolteacher, acting as a temporary substitute for another. □ **in short supply** available in limited quantities. □□ **sup·pli·er** *n.*

sup·ply[2] /súplee/ *adv.* (also **sup·ple·ly** /súpəlee/) in a supple manner.

sup·ply and de·mand *n. Econ.* quantities available and required as factors regulating the price of commodities.

sup·ply-side *adj. Econ.* denoting a policy of low taxation and other incentives to produce goods and invest.

sup·port /səpáwrt/ *v. & n.* ● *v.tr.* 1 carry all or part of the weight of. 2 keep from falling or sinking or failing. 3 provide with a home and the necessities of life. 4 enable to last out; give strength to. 5 tend to substantiate or corroborate (a statement, theory, etc.). 6 back up; second. 7 speak in favor of (a resolution, etc.). 8 be actively interested in (a particular team or sport). 9 take a part that is secondary to (a principal actor, etc.). 10 endure; tolerate (*can no longer support the noise*). ● *n.* 1 the act of supporting. 2 a person or thing that supports. □ **in support of** in order to support. □□ **sup·port·a·ble** *adj.* **sup·port·a·bil·i·ty** *n.* **sup·port·a·bly** *adv.* **sup·port·ing·ly** *adv.*

sup·port·er /səpáwrtər/ *n.* a person or thing that supports, esp. a person supporting a team, sport, political candidate, etc.

sup·port·ive /səpáwrtiv/ *adj.* providing support or encouragement. □□ **sup·port·ive·ly** *adv.* **sup·port·ive·ness** *n.*

sup·pose /səpóz/ *v.tr.* (often foll. by *that* + clause) 1 assume, esp. in default of knowledge; be inclined to think. 2 take as a possibility or hypothesis (*let us suppose you are right*). 3 (in *imper.*) as a formula of proposal (*suppose we go to the party*). 4 (of a theory or result, etc.) require as a condition (*design supposes a creator*). 5 in the circumstances that; if (*supposing we stay*). 6 (as **supposed** *adj.*) generally accepted as being so (*his supposed brother*). 7 (in *passive*; foll. by *to* + infin.) **a** be expected or required (*was supposed to write to you*). **b** (with *neg.*) not have to; not be allowed to. □ **I suppose so** an expression of hesitant agreement. □□ **sup·pos·a·ble** *adj.*

sup·pos·ed·ly /səpózidlee/ *adv.* as is generally supposed.

sup·po·si·tion /súpəzíshən/ *n.* 1 a fact or idea, etc., supposed. 2 the act or an instance of supposing. □□ **sup·po·si·tion·al** *adj.*

sup·po·si·tious /súpəzíshəs/ *adj.* hypothetical; assumed.

sup·pos·i·ti·tious /səpózitíshəs/ *adj.* spurious; substituted for the real.

sup·pos·i·to·ry /səpózitawree/ *n.* (*pl.* **-ies**) a medical preparation in the form of a cone, cylinder, etc., to be inserted into the rectum or vagina to melt. ▷ MEDICINE

sup·press /səprés/ *v.tr.* 1 end the activity or existence of, esp. forcibly. 2 prevent (information, feelings, etc.) from being seen, heard, or known. 3 **a** partly or wholly eliminate (electrical interfer-

ence, etc.). **b** equip (a device) to reduce such interference due to it. □□ **sup·press·i·ble** *adj.* **sup·pres·sion** *n.* **sup·pres·sive** *adj.* **sup·pres·sor** *n.*

sup·pres·sant /səprésənt/ *n.* a suppressing or restraining agent, esp. a drug that suppresses the appetite.

sup·pu·rate /súpyərayt/ *v.intr.* 1 form pus. 2 fester. □□ **sup·pu·ra·tion** /-ráyshən/ *n.* **sup·pu·ra·tive** /-rətiv/ *adj.*

su·pra /sooprə/ *adv.* above or earlier on (in a book, etc.).

supra- /sooprə/ *prefix* 1 above. 2 beyond; transcending (*supranational*).

su·pra·max·il·lary /sooprəmáksileree/ *adj.* of or relating to the upper jaw.

su·pra·mun·dane /sooprəmundáyn/ *adj.* above or superior to the world.

su·pra·na·tion·al /sooprənáshənəl/ *adj.* transcending national limits. □□ **su·pra·na·tion·al·ism** *n.* **su·pra·na·tion·al·i·ty** /-nálitee/ *n.*

su·pra·or·bit·al /sooprəáwrbit'l/ *adj.* situated above the orbit of the eye.

su·pra·re·nal /sooprəréenəl/ *adj.* situated above the kidneys.

su·prem·a·cist /sooprémɔsist/ *n. & adj.* ● *n.* an advocate of the supremacy of a particular group. ● *adj.* advocating such supremacy. □□ **su·prem·a·cism** *n.*

su·prem·a·cy /sooprémɔsee/ *n.* (*pl.* **-ies**) the state of being supreme.

su·preme /soopréem/ *adj.* 1 highest in authority or rank. 2 greatest; most important. 3 (of a penalty or sacrifice, etc.) involving death. □□ **su·preme·ly** *adv.*

Su·preme Be·ing *n.* a name for God.

Su·preme Court *n.* the highest judicial court in a nation, etc.

su·pre·mo /soopréemō/ *n. Brit.* (*pl.* **-os**) 1 a supreme leader or ruler. 2 a person in overall charge.

suprv. *abbr.* supervisor.

Supt. *abbr.* Superintendent.

su·ra /soorə/ *n.* (also **sur·ah**) a chapter or section of the Koran.

su·rah /soorə/ *n.* a soft twilled silk for scarves, etc.

su·ral /sooɔrɔl/ *adj.* of or relating to the calf of the leg (*sural artery*).

sur·cease /sɔrsees, sɔrseés/ *n. & v. literary* ● *n.* a cessation. ● *v.intr. & tr.* cease.

sur·charge *n. & v.* ● *n.* /sɔrchaarj/ 1 an additional charge or payment. 2 a mark printed on a postage stamp changing its value. 3 an additional or excessive load. ● *v.tr.* /sɔrchaarj, -cháarj/ 1 exact a surcharge from. 2 exact (a sum) as a surcharge. 3 mark (a postage stamp) with a surcharge. 4 overload. 5 fill to excess.

sur·cin·gle /sɔrsinggɔl/ *n.* a band round a horse's body usu. to keep a pack, etc., in place.

sur·coat /sɔrkōt/ *n.* 1 *hist.* a loose robe worn over armor. 2 a similar sleeveless garment worn as part of the insignia of an order of knighthood. 3 *hist.* an outer coat of rich material.

sur·cu·lose /sɔrkyɔlōs/ *adj. Bot.* producing suckers.

surd /sɔrd/ *adj. & n.* ● *adj.* 1 *Math.* (of a number) irrational. 2 *Phonet.* (of a sound) uttered with the breath and not the voice (e.g., *f, k, p, s, t*). ● *n.* 1 *Math.* a surd number, esp. the root of an integer. 2 *Phonet.* a surd sound.

sure /shoor/ *adj. & adv.* ● *adj.* 1 having or seeming to have adequate reason for a belief or assertion. 2 (often foll. by *of*, or *that* + clause) convinced. 3 (foll. by *of*) having confident anticipation or satisfactory knowledge of. 4 reliable or unfailing (*one sure way to find out*). 5 (foll. by *to* + infin.) certain. 6 undoubtedly true or truthful. ● *adv. colloq.* certainly. □ **be sure** (in *imper.* or *infin.*; foll. by *that* + clause or *to* + infin.) take care to; not fail to. **for**

sure *colloq.* without doubt. **make sure** 1 make or become certain. 2 (foll. by *of*) establish the truth or ensure the existence or happening of. **sure enough** *colloq.* 1 in fact; certainly. 2 with near certainty. **sure thing** *n.* a certainty. *int. colloq.* certainly. **to be sure** 1 it is undeniable or admitted. 2 it must be admitted. □□ **sure·ness** *n.*

sure-fire *adj. colloq.* certain to succeed.

sure-foot·ed *adj.* never stumbling or making a mistake. □□ **sure-foot·ed·ly** *adv.* **sure-foot·ed·ness** *n.*

sure·ly /shoorlee/ *adv.* 1 with certainty (*slowly but surely*). 2 as an appeal to reason (*surely that can't be right*). 3 securely (*the goat plants its feet surely*).

sure·ty /shooritee/ *n.* (*pl.* **-ies**) 1 a person who takes responsibility for another's performance of an undertaking, e.g., to appear in court, or payment of a debt. 2 a certainty. □ **stand surety** become a surety. □□ **sure·ty·ship** *n.*

surf /sɔrf/ *n. & v.* ● *n.* 1 the swell of the sea breaking on the shore or reefs. 2 the foam produced by this. ● *v.intr.* ride the surf, with or as with a surfboard. □□ **surf·er** *n.* **surf·y** *adj.*

sur·face /sɔrfis/ *n. & v.* ● *n.* 1 **a** the outside of a material body. **b** the area of this. 2 any of the limits terminating a solid. 3 the upper boundary of a liquid or of the ground, etc. 4 the outward aspect of anything. 5 *Geom.* a set of points that has length and breadth but no thickness. 6 (*attrib.*) **a** of or on the surface. **b** superficial (*surface politeness*). ● *v.* 1 *tr.* give the required surface to (a road, paper, etc.). 2 *intr. & tr.* rise or bring to the surface. 3 *intr.* become visible or known. 4 *intr. colloq.* wake up. □ **come to the surface** become perceptible after being hidden. □□ **sur·faced** *adj.* (usu. in *comb.*). **sur·fac·er** *n.*

sur·face mail *n.* mail carried over land and by sea, and not by air.

sur·face ten·sion *n.* ◀ the tension of the surface film of a liquid, tending to minimize its surface area.

sur·fac·tant /sɔrfáktɔnt/ *n.* a substance which reduces surface tension.

surf·board /sɔrfbawrd/ *n.* ▶ a long narrow board used in surfing.

surf cast·ing *n.* fishing by casting a line into the sea from the shore.

sur·feit /sɔrfit/ *n. & v.* ● *n.* 1 an excess, esp. in eating or drinking. 2 a feeling of disgust resulting from this. ● *v.* (**surfeited, surfeiting**) 1 *tr.* overfeed. 2 *intr.* overeat. 3 *intr. & tr.* (foll. by *with*) be or cause to be wearied through excess.

sur·fi·cial /sɔrfishɔl/ *adj. Geol.* of or relating to the Earth's surface. □□ **sur·fi·cial·ly** *adv.*

surg. *abbr.* 1 surgeon. 2 surgery. 3 surgical.

surge /sɔrj/ *n. & v.* ● *n.* 1 a sudden or impetuous onset (*a surge of anger*). 2 the swell of the waves at sea. 3 a heavy forward or upward motion. 4 a rapid increase in price, activity, etc. 5 a sudden marked increase in voltage of an electric current. ● *v.intr.* 1 (of waves, etc.) rise and fall or move heavily forward. 2 (of a crowd, etc.) move suddenly and powerfully forward. 3 (of an electric current, etc.) increase suddenly.

sur·geon /súrjɔn/ *n.* 1 a medical practitioner qualified to practice surgery. 2 a medical officer in a navy or army or military hospital.

sur·geon gen·er·al *n.* (*pl.* **surgeons general**) the

surface film   *paper clip*

SURFACE TENSION
DEMONSTRATED
BY A PAPER CLIP
FLOATING ON
WATER

SURFBOARD

S

SURREALISM

Surrealism was influenced by the ideas of Freud and sought to express the imagination as shown in dreams, unshackled by reason or convention. This idea was given literary voice almost exclusively in France, by such writers as Jean Cocteau. In art, the movement spread throughout Europe. Artists such as Salvador Dali used disturbing, dreamlike symbols. Others, like Max Ernst, juxtaposed incongruous images, depicted in a realistic style.

The Sublime Moment (1938), SALVADOR DALI

TIMELINE

| 1500 | 1550 | 1600 | 1650 | 1700 | 1750 | 1800 | 1850 | 1900 | 1950 | 2000 |

head of a public health service or of an army, etc., medical service.

sur·ger·y /súrjəree/ n. (pl. **-ies**) the branch of medicine concerned with treatment of injuries or disorders of the body by incision, manipulation or alteration of organs, etc., with the hands or with instruments.

sur·gi·cal /sárjikəl/ adj. **1** of or relating to or done by surgeons or surgery. **2** resulting from surgery. **3 a** used in surgery. **b** worn to correct a deformity, etc. **4** extremely precise. □□ **sur·gi·cal·ly** adv.

su·ri·cate /sŏŏrikayt/ n. a South African burrowing mongoose, *Suricata suricatta*, with gray and black stripes. ▷ MEERKAT

sur·ly /sárlee/ adj. (**surlier, surliest**) bad-tempered and unfriendly; churlish. □□ **sur·li·ly** adv. **sur·li·ness** n.

sur·mise /sərmíz/ n. & v. ● n. a conjecture. ● v. **1** tr. (often foll. by *that* + clause) infer doubtfully; make a surmise about. **2** tr. suspect the existence of. **3** intr. make a guess.

sur·mount /sərmównt/ v.tr. overcome or get over (a difficulty or obstacle). **2** (usu. in *passive*) cap or crown. □□ **sur·mount·a·ble** adj.

sur·mul·let /sərmúlit, sórmul-/ n. the red mullet.

sur·name /sárnaym/ n. & v. ● n. a hereditary name common to members of a family (*her surname is "Johnson"*). ● v.tr. **1** give a surname to. **2** give (a person a surname). **3** (as **surnamed** adj.) having as a family name.

sur·pass /sərpás/ v.tr. **1** be greater or better than. **2** (as **surpassing** adj.) preeminent. □□ **sur·pass·ing·ly** adv.

sur·plice /sárplis/ n. a loose white linen vestment worn over a cassock by clergy and choristers. ▷ VESTMENT. □□ **sur·pliced** adj.

sur·plus /sárpləs, -plus/ n. & adj. ● n. **1** an amount left over. **2 a** an excess of revenue over expenditure. **b** the excess value of a company's assets over the face value of its stock. ● adj. exceeding what is needed or used.

sur·prise /sərpríz/ n. & v. ● n. **1** an unexpected or astonishing event or circumstance. **2** the emotion caused by this. **3** the act of catching a person, etc., unawares, or the process of being caught unawares. **4** (*attrib.*) unexpected (*a surprise visit*). ● v.tr. **1** affect with surprise; turn out contrary to the expectations of. **2** (usu. in *passive*; foll. by *at*) shock (*I am surprised at you*). **3** capture or attack by surprise. **4** come upon (a person) unawares (*surprised him taking a cookie*). **5** (foll. by *into*) startle (a person) by surprise into an action, etc. □ **take by surprise** affect with surprise, esp. by an unexpected encounter or statement. □□ **sur·pris·ed·ly** /-prízidlee/ adv. **sur·pris·ing** adj. **sur·pris·ing·ly** adv. **sur·pris·ing·ness** n.

sur·ra /sŏŏrə/ n. a febrile disease transmitted by bites of flies and affecting horses and cattle in the tropics.

sur·re·al /səréeəl/ adj. **1** having the qualities of surrealism. **2** strange; bizarre. □□ **sur·re·al·i·ty** /-ree-álitee/ n. **sur·re·al·ly** adv.

sur·re·al·ism /səréeəlizəm/ n. ▲ a 20th-c. movement in art and literature aiming at expressing the subconscious mind, e.g., by the irrational juxtaposition of images. □□ **sur·re·al·ist** n. & adj. **sur·re·al·is·tic** adj. **sur·re·al·is·ti·cal·ly** adv.

sur·ren·der /səréndər/ v. & n. ● v. **1** tr. hand over; relinquish possession of, give into another's power or control. **2** intr. **a** accept an enemy's demand for submission. **b** give oneself up; submit. **3** intr. & refl. (foll. by *to*) give oneself over to a habit, emotion, influence, etc. **4** tr. give up rights under (a life-insurance policy) in return for a smaller sum received immediately. ● n. the act or an instance of surrendering.

sur·rep·ti·tious /sárəptíshəs/ adj. **1** covert; kept secret. **2** done by stealth; clandestine. □□ **sur·rep·ti·tious·ly** adv. **sur·rep·ti·tious·ness** n.

sur·rey /sáree, súree/ n. (pl. **surreys**) a light four-wheeled carriage with two seats facing forward.

sur·ro·gate /sárəgət, -gayt, súr-/ n. a substitute, esp. for a person in a specific role or office. □□ **sur·ro·ga·cy** n. **sur·ro·gate·ship** n.

sur·ro·gate moth·er n. **1** a person acting the role of mother. **2** a woman who bears a child on behalf of another woman, usu. from her own egg fertilized by the other woman's partner.

sur·round /sərównd/ v. & n. ● v.tr. **1** come or be all around; encircle; enclose. **2** (in *passive*; foll. by *by, with*) have on all sides. ● n. an area or substance surrounding something. □□ **sur·round·ing** adj.

sur·round·ings /sərówndingz/ n.pl. the things in the neighborhood of, or the conditions affecting, a person or thing.

sur·tax /sártaks/ n. & v. ● n. an additional tax, esp. levied on incomes above a certain level. ● v.tr. impose a surtax on.

sur·ti·tle /sórtīt'l/ n. (esp. in opera) each of a sequence of captions projected above the stage, translating the text being sung.

sur·veil·lance /sərváyləns/ n. close observation, esp. of a suspected person.

sur·vey v. & n. ● v.tr. /sərváy/ **1** take or present a general view of. **2** examine the condition of (a building, etc.). **3** determine the boundaries, ownership, etc., of (a district, etc.). ● n. /sárvay/ **1** a general view or consideration of something. **2 a** the act of surveying opinions, etc. **b** the result or findings of this. **3** an inspection or investigation. **4** a map or plan made by surveying an area.

sur·vey·or /sərváyər/ n. **1** a person who surveys land and buildings, esp. professionally. **2** a person who carries out surveys.

sur·viv·al /sərvívəl/ n. **1** the process or an instance of surviving. **2** a person, thing, or practice that has remained from a former time. □ **survival of the fittest** the process or result of natural selection.

sur·viv·al·ism /sərvívəlizəm/ n. the practicing of outdoor survival skills as a sport or hobby. □□ **sur·viv·al·ist** adj. & n.

sur·viv·al kit n. emergency rations, etc., esp. carried by military personnel, etc.

sur·vive /sərvív/ v. **1** intr. continue to live or exist. **2** tr. live or exist longer than. **3** tr. remain alive after or continue to exist in spite of (a danger, accident, etc.).

sur·vi·vor /sərvívər/ n. a person who survives or has survived.

sus- /sus, səs/ prefix assim. form of SUB- before c, p, t.

sus·cep·ti·bil·i·ty /səséptibílitee/ n. (pl. **-ies**) **1** the state of being susceptible. **2** (in pl.) a person's sensitive feelings.

sus·cep·ti·ble /səséptibəl/ adj. **1** impressionable; sensitive; easily moved by emotion. **2** (*predic.*) **a** (foll. by *to*) liable or vulnerable to (*susceptible to pain*). **b** (foll. by *of*) admitting of (*facts not susceptible of proof*). □□ **sus·cep·ti·bly** adv.

sus·cep·tive /səséptiv/ adj. **1** concerned with the receiving of emotional impressions or ideas. **2** receptive.

su·shi /sŏŏshee/ n. ► a Japanese dish of balls of cold rice flavored and garnished, esp. with raw fish or shellfish.

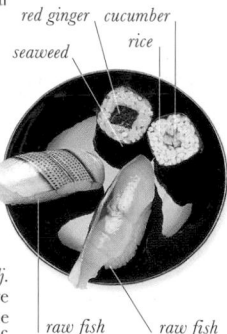

red ginger   cucumber   rice   seaweed   raw fish   raw fish

SUSHI

sus·lik /súslik/ n. an E. European and Asian ground squirrel, *Citellus citellus*.

sus·pect v., n., & adj. ● v.tr. /səspékt/ **1** have an impression of the existence or presence of. **2** (foll. by *to be*) believe

S

tentatively, without clear ground. **3** (foll. by *that* + clause) be inclined to think. **4** (often foll. by *of*) be inclined to mentally accuse (*suspect him of complicity*). **5** doubt the genuineness or truth of. ● *n.* /súspekt/ a suspected person. ● *adj.* /súspekt/ subject to or deserving suspicion or distrust.

sus·pend /səspénd/ *v.tr.* **1** hang up. **2** keep inoperative or undecided for a time. **3** bar temporarily from a school, function, office, etc. **4** (as **suspended** *adj.*) (of solid particles or a body in a fluid medium) sustained somewhere between top and bottom.

sus·pend·ed an·i·ma·tion *n.* a temporary cessation of the vital functions without death.

sus·pend·er /səspéndər/ *n.* (in *pl.*) straps worn across the shoulders and supporting trousers.

sus·pense /səspéns/ *n.* a state of anxious uncertainty or expectation. □ **keep in suspense** delay informing (a person) of urgent information. □□ **sus·pense·ful** *adj.*

sus·pen·sion /səspénshən/ *n.* **1** the act of suspending. **2** the means by which a vehicle is supported on its axles. ▷ CAR, OFF-ROAD. **3** a substance consisting of particles suspended in a medium.

sus·pen·sion bridge *n.* ▶ a bridge with a roadway suspended from cables supported by structures at each end. ▷ BRIDGE

sus·pen·sive /səspénsiv/ *adj.* **1** having the power or tendency to suspend or postpone. **2** causing suspense. □□ **sus·pen·sive·ly** *adv.* **sus·pen·sive·ness** *n.*

sus·pen·so·ry /səspénsəree/ *adj.* (of a ligament, muscle, bandage, etc.) holding an organ, etc., suspended.

sus·pi·cion /səspíshən/ *n.* **1** the feeling or thought of a person who suspects. **2** the act of suspecting. **3** (foll. by *of*) a slight trace of. □ **above suspicion** too obviously good, etc., to be suspected. **under suspicion** suspected.

sus·pi·cious /səspíshəs/ *adj.* **1** prone to or feeling suspicion. **2** indicating suspicion. **3** inviting suspicion. □□ **sus·pi·cious·ly** *adv.* **sus·pi·cious·ness** *n.*

suss /sus/ *v. & n.* (also **sus**) esp. *Brit. sl.* ● *v.tr.* (**sussed, sussing**) **1** suspect of a crime. **2** (usu. foll. by *out*) **a** investigate; inspect. **b** work out; grasp (*he had the market sussed*). ● *n.* **1** a suspect. **2** a suspicion; suspicious behavior. □ **on suss** on suspicion (of having committed a crime).

Sus·sex /súsiks/ *n.* **1** a speckled or red domestic chicken of an English breed. **2** this breed.

sus·tain /səstáyn/ *v.tr.* **1** support, bear the weight of, esp. for a long period. **2** encourage; support. **3** (of food) give nourishment to. **4** endure; stand. **5** undergo or suffer (defeat etc.). **6** (of a court, etc.) uphold (an objection, etc.). **7** substantiate (a statement or charge). **8** maintain or keep (a sound, effort, etc.) going continuously. **9** continue to represent (a part, character, etc.) adequately. □□ **sus·tain·a·ble** *adj.* **sus·tain·ed·ly** /-stáynidlee/ *adv.* **sus·tain·er** *n.* **sus·tain·ment** *n.*

sus·te·nance /sústinəns/ *n.* **1 a** nourishment; food. **b** the process of nourishing. **2** a means of support; a livelihood.

sus·ten·ta·tion /sústəntáyshən/ *n. formal* **1** the support of life. **2** maintenance.

sus·ur·ra·tion /sŏŏsəráyshən/ *n.* (also **sus·ur·rus** /sŏŏsárəs/) *literary* a sound of whispering or rustling.

Su·tra /sŏŏtrə/ *n.* **1** an aphorism or set of aphorisms in Hindu literature. **2** a narrative part of Buddhist scripture. **3** Jainist scripture.

sut·tee /sutée, sútee/ *n.* (also **sa·ti**) (*pl.* **suttees** or **satis**) esp. *hist.* **1** the Hindu practice of a widow immolating herself on her husband's funeral pyre. **2** a widow who undergoes or has undergone this.

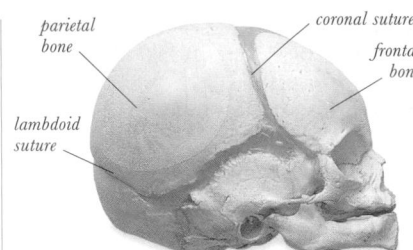

SUTURE: SKULL OF A HUMAN FETUS SHOWING SUTURES

parietal bone · coronal suture · frontal bone · lambdoid suture

su·ture /sŏŏchər/ *n. & v.* ● *n.* **1** *Surgery* **a** the joining of the edges of a wound or incision by stitching. **b** the thread or wire used for this. **2** ▲ the seamlike junction of two bones, esp. in the skull. ● *v.tr. Surgery* stitch up with a suture. □□ **su·tur·al** *adj.* **su·tured** *adj.*

SUV *abbr.* sport utility vehicle.

su·ze·rain /sŏŏzərən, -rayn/ *n.* **1** a feudal overlord. **2** a sovereign state having some control over another state that is internally autonomous. □□ **su·ze·rain·ty** *n.*

s.v. *abbr.* (in a reference) under the word or heading given.

svelte /svelt/ *adj.* slender; graceful.

sw *abbr.* (also **SW**) **1** southwest. **2** southwestern. **3** switch. **4** short wave.

swab /swob/ *n. & v.* (also **swob**) ● *n.* **1** a mop or other absorbent device for cleaning or mopping up. **2 a** an absorbent pad used in surgery. **b** a specimen of a possibly morbid secretion taken with a swab for examination. ● *v.tr.* (**swabbed, swabbing**) **1** clean with a swab. **2** (foll. by *up*) absorb (moisture) with a swab.

swad·dle /swód'l/ *v.tr.* swathe (esp. an infant) in garments or bandages, etc.

swag /swag/ *n. & v.* ● *n.* **1** *sl.* **a** the booty carried off by burglars, etc. **b** illicit gains. **2 a** ▼ an ornamental festoon of flowers, etc. **b** a carved, etc., representation of this. **c** drapery of similar appearance. ● *v.* (**swagged, swagging**) **1** *tr.* arrange (a curtain, etc.) in swags. **2** *intr.* **a** hang heavily. **b** sway from side to side. **3** *tr.* cause to sway or sag.

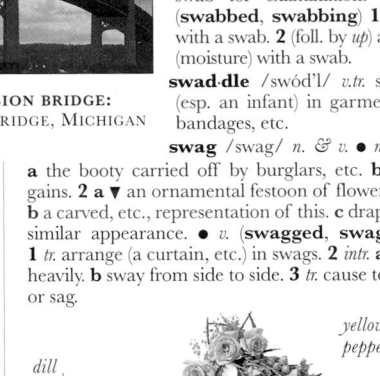

SUSPENSION BRIDGE: MACKINAC BRIDGE, MICHIGAN

SWAG OF FLOWERS, FOLIAGE, AND FRUIT

yellow pepper · dill · mimosa · rosemary leaves · rose

swage /swayj/ *n. & v.* ● *n.* a die or stamp for shaping wrought iron, etc., by hammering or pressure. ● *v.tr.* shape with a swage.

swage block *n.* a block with various perforations, grooves, etc., for shaping metal.

swag·ger /swágər/ *v. & n.* ● *v.intr.* **1** walk arrogantly or self-importantly. **2** behave arrogantly; be domineering. ● *n.* **1** a swaggering gait or manner. **2** swaggering behavior. **3** a dashing or confident air

or way of doing something. □□ **swag·ger·er** *n.* **swag·ger·ing·ly** *adv.*

swag·ger stick *n.* a short cane carried by a military officer.

Swa·hi·li /swaahéelee/ *n.* (*pl.* same) **1** a member of a Bantu people of Zanzibar and adjacent coasts. **2** their language, widely spoken in E. Africa.

swain /swayn/ *n.* **1** *archaic* a country youth. **2** *poet.* a young male lover or suitor.

swal·low¹ /swólō/ *v. & n.* ● *v.* **1** *tr.* cause or allow (food, etc.) to pass down the throat. **2** *intr.* perform the muscular movement of the esophagus required to do this. **3** *tr.* **a** accept meekly. **b** accept credulously. **4** *tr.* resist the expression of (*swallow one's pride*). **5** *tr.* articulate (words, etc.) indistinctly. **6** *tr.* (often foll. by *up*) engulf or absorb; exhaust. ● *n.* **1** the act of swallowing. **2** an amount swallowed in one action.

swal·low² /swólō/ *n.* any of various migratory swift-flying insect-eating birds of the family Hirundinidae, with a forked tail and long pointed wings. ▷ PASSERINE

swal·low·tail /swólōtayl/ *n.* **1** a deeply forked tail. **2** anything resembling this shape. **3** ▶ any butterfly of the family Papilionidae with wings extended at the back to this shape. □□ **swal·low-tailed** *adj.*

SWALLOWTAIL: GIANT SWALLOWTAIL (*Papilio cresphontes*)

swam *past* of SWIM.

swa·mi /swáamee/ *n.* (*pl.* **swamis**) a Hindu male religious teacher.

swamp /swaamp/ *n. & v.* ● *n.* a piece of waterlogged ground. ● *v.* **1 a** *tr.* overwhelm or soak with water. **b** *intr.* become swamped. **2** *tr.* overwhelm with an excess or large amount of something. □□ **swamp·y** *adj.* (**swampier, swampiest**).

swan /swon/ *n.* a large water bird of the genus *Cygnus*, etc., having a long flexible neck, webbed feet, and in most species white plumage. ▷ WATERFOWL

swan dive *n.* a dive with the arms outspread until close to the water.

swank /swangk/ *n., v., & adj. colloq.* ● *n.* ostentation; swagger; bluff. ● *v.intr.* behave with swank; show off. ● *adj.* = SWANKY.

swank·y /swángkee/ *adj.* (**swankier, swankiest**) **1** ostentatiously smart or showy. **2** (of a person) boastful. □□ **swank·i·ly** *adv.*

swan·ner·y /swónəree/ *n.* (*pl.* **-ies**) a place where swans are bred.

swans·down /swónzdown/ *n.* **1** the fine down of a swan, used in trimming clothing, etc. **2** a kind of thick cotton cloth with a soft nap on one side.

swan song *n.* a person's last work or act before death or retirement, etc.

swap /swop/ *v. & n.* (also **swop**) ● *v.tr. & intr.* (**swapped, swapping**) exchange (one thing for another). ● *n.* **1** an act of swapping. **2** a thing suitable for swapping. □□ **swap·per** *n.*

sward /swawrd/ *n. literary* **1** an expanse of short grass. **2** turf. □□ **sward·ed** *adj.*

swarf /swawrf/ *n.* **1** fine chips or filings of stone, metal, etc. **2** wax, etc., removed in cutting a phonograph record.

swarm¹ /swawrm/ *n. & v.* ● *n.* **1** a cluster of bees leaving the hive with the queen to establish a new colony. **2** a large number of insects or birds moving in a cluster. **3** a large group of people, esp. moving over or filling a large area. **4** (in *pl.*; foll. by *of*) great numbers. ● *v.intr.* **1** move in or form a swarm. **2** (foll. by *with*) (of a place) be overrun, crowded, or infested.

swarm² /swawrm/ *v.intr.* (foll. by *up*) & *tr.* climb (a rope or tree, etc.), esp. in a rush, by clasping or clinging with the hands and knees, etc.

S

swarth·y /swáwrthee/ *adj.* (**swarthier, swarthiest**) dark-complexioned. □□ **swarth·i·ly** *adv.* **swarth·i·ness** *n.*

swash /swosh/ *v. & n.* ● *v.* **1** *intr.* (of water, etc.) wash about; make the sound of washing or rising and falling. **2** *tr. archaic* strike violently. **3** *intr. archaic* swagger. ● *n.* the motion or sound of swashing water.

swash·buck·ler /swóshbuklər/ *n.* **1** a swaggering bully or ruffian. **2** a dashing or daring adventurer, esp. in a novel, movie, etc. □□ **swash·buck·ling** *adj. & n.*

swas·ti·ka /swóstikə/ *n.* **1** ▼ an ancient symbol formed by an equal-armed cross with each arm continued at a right angle. **2** ▼ this with clockwise continuations as the symbol of Nazi Germany.

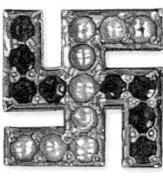

SWASTIKA (1)   SWASTIKA (2)

swat /swot/ *v. & n.* ● *v.tr.* (**swatted, swatting**) **1** crush (a fly, etc.) with a sharp blow. **2** hit hard. ● *n.* **1** a swatting blow. **2** a homerun in baseball.

swatch /swoch/ *n.* **1** ▶ a sample, esp. of cloth. **2** a collection of samples.

swath /swoth, swawth/ *n.* (also **swathe** /swoth, swayth/) (*pl.* **swaths** /swoths, swawths/ or **swathes** /swothz, swaythz/) **1** a ridge of grass or grain lying after being cut. **2** a space left clear after the passage of a mower. **3** a broad strip.

swathe /swoth, swayth/ *v. & n.* ● *v.tr.* bind or enclose in bandages or garments, etc. ● *n.* a bandage or wrapping.

SWATCHES OF WOVEN FABRIC

swat·ter /swótər/ *n.* an implement for swatting flies.

sway /sway/ *v. & n.* ● *v.* **1** *intr. & tr.* lean or cause to lean unsteadily in different directions alternately. **2** *intr.* oscillate irregularly; waver. **3** *tr.* **a** control the motion or direction of. **b** have influence or rule over. ● *n.* **1** rule, influence, or government (*hold sway*). **2** a swaying motion or position.

swear /swair/ *v.* (*past* **swore** /swor/; *past part.* **sworn** /sworn/) **1** *tr.* **a** (often foll. by *to* + infin. or *that* + clause) state or promise solemnly or on oath. **b** take (an oath). **2** *tr. colloq.* say emphatically. **3** *tr.* cause to take an oath (*swore them to secrecy*). **4** *intr.* (often foll. by *at*) use profane or indecent language. **5** *tr.* (often foll. by *against*) make a sworn affirmation of (*swear treason against*). **6** *intr.* (foll. by *by*) **a** appeal to as a witness in taking an oath (*swear by Almighty God*). **b** *colloq.* have or express great confidence in (*swears by yoga*). **7** *intr.* (foll. by *to*; usu. in *neg.*) admit the certainty of (*could not swear to it*). □ **swear in** induct into office, etc., by administering an oath. **swear off** *colloq.* promise to abstain from (drink, etc.). □□ **swear·er** *n.*

sweat /swet/ *n. & v.* ● *n.* **1** moisture exuded through the pores of the skin, esp. from heat or nervousness. **2** a state or period of sweating. **3** *colloq.* a state of anxiety (*in a sweat about it*). **4** *colloq.* **a** drudgery; effort. **b** a laborious task or undertaking. **5** condensed moisture on a surface. ● *v.* (*past* and *past part.* **sweat** or **sweated**) **1** *intr.* exude sweat. **2** *intr.* be terrified, suffering, etc. **3** *intr.* (of a wall, etc.) exhibit surface moisture. **4** *intr.* drudge; toil. **5** *tr.* heat (meat or vegetables) slowly in fat or water to extract the juices. **6** *tr.* emit (blood, gum, etc.) like sweat. **7** *tr.* make (a horse, athlete, etc.) sweat by exercise. **8** *tr.* (as **sweat** *adj.*) (of goods, workers, or labor) produced by or subjected to long hours under poor conditions. □ **by the sweat of one's brow** by one's own hard work. **no sweat** *colloq.* there is no need to worry. **sweat blood** *colloq.* **1** work strenuously. **2** be extremely anxious. **sweat it out** *colloq.* endure a difficult experience to the end.

sweat·band /swétband/ *n.* a band of absorbent material inside a hat or around a wrist, etc., to soak up sweat.

sweat·er /swétər/ *n.* a knitted jersey, pullover, or cardigan.

sweat gland *n. Anat.* a spiral tubular gland below the skin secreting sweat. ▷ HAIR, SKIN

sweat·pants /swétpants/ *n.pl.* loose pants of absorbent cotton material worn for exercise, etc.

sweat·shirt /swétshərt/ *n.* a sleeved cotton pullover of absorbent material, as worn by athletes before and after exercise.

sweat·shop /swétshop/ *n.* a shop where employees work under poor conditions and for low wages.

sweat·suit /swétsoot/ *n.* a suit of a sweatshirt and pants for exercise, etc.

sweat·y /swétee/ *adj.* (**sweatier, sweatiest**) **1** sweating; covered with sweat. **2** causing sweat. □□ **sweat·i·ly** *adv.* **sweat·i·ness** *n.*

Swede /sweed/ *n.* **1** a native or national of Sweden. **2** a person of Swedish descent.

Swed·ish /sweédish/ *adj. & n.* ● *adj.* of or relating to Sweden or its people or language. ● *n.* the language of Sweden.

sweep /sweep/ *v. & n.* ● *v.* (*past* and *past part.* **swept** /swept/) **1** *tr.* clean or clear (a room or area, etc.) with or as with a broom. **2** *intr.* (often foll. by *up*) clean a room, etc., in this way. **3** *tr.* (often foll. by *up*) collect or remove (dirt or litter, etc.) by sweeping. **4** *tr.* (foll. by *aside, away*, etc.) **a** push with or as with a broom. **b** dismiss or reject abruptly. **5** *tr.* (foll. by *along, down*, etc.) carry or drive along with force. **6** *tr.* (foll. by *off, away*, etc.) remove or clear forcefully. **7** *tr.* traverse swiftly or lightly. **8** *tr.* impart a sweeping motion to. **9** *tr.* swiftly cover or affect (*a new fashion swept the country*). **10** *intr.* **a** glide swiftly; speed along. **b** go majestically. ● *n.* **1** the act or motion of sweeping. **2** a curve in the road, a sweeping line of a hill, etc. **3** range or scope (*beyond the sweep of the human mind*). **4** = CHIMNEY SWEEP. **5** a sortie by aircraft. **6** *colloq.* = SWEEPSTAKE. □ **make a clean sweep of 1** completely abolish or expel. **2** win all the prizes, etc., in (a competition, etc.). **sweep away 1** abolish swiftly. **2** (usu. in *passive*) powerfully affect, esp. emotionally. **sweep under the carpet** see CARPET.

sweep·back /sweépbak/ *n.* the angle at which an aircraft's wing is set back from a position at right angles to the body.

sweep·er /sweépər/ *n.* **1** a person who cleans by sweeping. **2** a device for sweeping carpets, etc. **3** *Soccer* a defensive player positioned close to the goalkeeper.

sweep·ing /sweéping/ *adj. & n.* ● *adj.* **1** wide in range or effect (*sweeping changes*). **2** taking no account of particular cases or exceptions (*a sweeping statement*). ● *n.* (in *pl.*) dirt, etc., collected by sweeping.

sweep-sec·ond hand *n.* a second hand on a clock or watch, moving on the same dial as the other hands.

sweep·stake /sweépstayk/ *n.* **1** a form of gambling on horse races or other contests in which all competitors' stakes are paid to the winners. **2** a race with betting of this kind. **3** a prize or prizes won in a sweepstake.

sweet /sweet/ *adj.* **1** having the pleasant taste characteristic of sugar. **2** smelling pleasant like roses or perfume, etc. **3** (of sound, etc.) melodious or harmonious. **4 a** not salt, sour, or bitter. **b** fresh, with flavour unim-paired by rottenness. **c** (of water) fresh and readily drinkable. **5** highly gratifying or attractive. **6** amiable; pleasant (*has a sweet nature*). **7** *colloq.* (of a person or thing) pretty; charming; endearing. **8** (foll. by *on*) *colloq.* fond of; in love with. □□ **sweet·ish** *adj.* **sweet·ly** *adv.* **sweet·ness** /sweétnis/ *n.*

sweet-and-sour *adj.* cooked in a sauce containing sugar and vinegar or lemon, etc.

sweet·bread /sweétbred/ *n.* the pancreas or thymus of an animal, esp. as food.

sweet·bri·er /sweétbrīər/ *n.* a wild rose, *Rosa eglanteria* of Europe and central Asia; with hooked thorns and small fragrant pink flowers.

sweet clover *n.* ▶ a leguminous plant of the genus *Melilotus*, with trifoliate leaves, small flowers, and a scent of hay when dried.

sweet corn *n.* **1** a kind of corn with kernels having a high sugar content. **2** these kernels, eaten as a vegetable when young.

sweet·en /sweét'n/ *v.tr. & intr.* **1** make or become sweet or sweeter. **2** make agreeable or less painful. □ **sweeten the pill** see PILL. □□ **sweet·en·ing** *n.*

sweet·en·er /sweét'nər/ *n.* **1** a substance used to sweeten food or drink. **2** *colloq.* a bribe or inducement.

SWEET CLOVER
(*Melilotus alba*)

sweet·heart /sweét-haart/ *n.* **1** a lover or darling. **2** a term of endearment.

sweet·heart a·gree·ment *n.* (also **sweet·heart con·tract** or **deal**) *colloq.* an industrial agreement reached privately by employers and labor union representatives.

sweet·ie /sweétee/ *n. colloq.* **1** a sweetheart. **2** (also **sweet·ie-pie**) a term of endearment.

sweet·meal /sweétmeel/ *n. Brit.* **1** sweetened wholemeal. **2** a sweetmeal biscuit.

sweet·meat /sweétmeet/ *n.* **1** a candy. **2** a small fancy cake.

sweet·ness /sweétnis/ *n.* the quality of being sweet; fragrance, melodiousness, etc. □ **sweetness and light** a display of (esp. uncharacteristic) mildness and reason.

sweet pea *n.* ▶ any climbing plant of the genus *Lathyrus*, esp. *L. odoratus* with fragrant flowers in many colors.

sweet pep·per *n.* a small *Capsicum* pepper with a relatively mild taste.

SWEET PEA
(*Lathyrus odoratus*)

sweet po·ta·to *n.* **1** ▼ a tropical climbing plant, *Ipomoea batatas*, with sweet tuberous roots used for food. **2** the root of this.

sweet·shop /sweétshop/ *n. Brit.* a store selling candy as its main item.

sweet·sop /sweétsop/ *n.* **1** a tropical American evergreen shrub, *Annona squamosa*. **2** the fruit of this, having a green rind and a sweet pulp.

sweet talk *n. colloq.* flattery; blandishment. □□ **sweet-talk** *v.tr.*

sweet tooth *n.* a liking for sweet-tasting foods.

sweet wil·liam *n.* a plant, *Dianthus barbatus*, with clusters of vivid fragrant flowers.

tuberous root

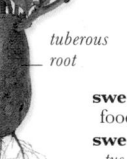

SWEET POTATO
(*Ipomoea batatas*)

swell /swel/ *v., n., & adj.* ● *v.* (*past part.* **swollen** /swólən/ or **swelled**) **1** *intr. & tr.* grow or cause to grow bigger or louder or more intense. **2** *intr.* (often foll. by *up*)

S

& tr. rise or raise up from the surrounding surface. **3** *intr.* (foll. by *out*) bulge. **4** *intr.* (of the heart) feel full of joy, pride, relief, etc. **5** *intr.* (foll. by *with*) be hardly able to restrain (pride, etc.). ● *n.* **1** an act or the state of swelling. **2** the heaving of the sea with waves that do not break. **3** *a* a crescendo. **b** a mechanism in an organ, etc., for obtaining a crescendo or diminuendo. ▷ ORGAN. **4** *colloq.* a person of dashing or fashionable appearance. ● *adj. colloq.* **1** fine; splendid; excellent. **2** smart, fashionable. □□ **swell·ish** *adj.*

swelled (or **swol·len**) **head** *n. colloq.* conceit.

swell·ing /swéling/ *n.* an abnormal protuberance on or in the body.

swel·ter /swéltər/ *v. & n.* ● *v.intr.* be uncomfortably hot. ● *n.* a sweltering atmosphere or condition. □□ **swel·ter·ing·ly** *adv.*

swept *past* and *past part.* of SWEEP.

swerve /swərv/ *v. & n.* ● *v.intr. & tr.* change or cause to change direction, esp. abruptly. ● *n.* **1** a swerving movement. **2** divergence from a course.

swift /swift/ *adj., adv., & n.* ● *adj.* **1** quick; rapid. **2** speedy; prompt (*was swift to act*). ● *adv.* (*archaic* except in *comb.*) swiftly (*swift-moving*). ● *n.* ▶ any swift-flying insect-eating bird of the family Apodidae, with long wings and a superficial resemblance to a swallow. □□ **swift·ly** *adv.* **swift·ness** *n.*

SWIFT:
COMMON SWIFT
(*Apus apus*)

swift·let /swíftlit/ *n.* a small swift of the genus *Collocalia*.

swig /swig/ *v. & n. colloq.* ● *v.tr. & intr.* (**swigged**, **swigging**) drink in large swallows. ● *n.* a swallow of drink, esp. a large amount. □□ **swig·ger** *n.*

swill /swil/ *v. & n.* ● *v. tr. & intr.* drink greedily. ● *n.* **1** mainly liquid refuse as pig food. **2** inferior liquor. □□ **swill·er** *n.*

swim /swim/ *v. & n.* ● *v.* (**swimming**; *past* **swam** /swam/; *past part.* **swum** /swum/) **1** *intr.* propel the body through water by working the arms and legs, or (of a fish) the fins and tail. **2** *tr.* **a** traverse by swimming. **b** compete in (a race) by swimming. **c** use (a particular stroke) in swimming. **3** *intr.* appear to undulate or reel or whirl. **4** *intr.* have a dizzy sensation. **5** *intr.* (foll. by *in*, *with*) be flooded. ● *n.* **1** a spell or the act of swimming. **2** a deep pool frequented by fish in a river. □ **in the swim** involved in or aware of what is going on. □□ **swim·ma·ble** *adj.* **swim·mer** *n.*

swim blad·der *n.* a gas-filled sac in fishes used to maintain buoyancy. ▷ FISH

swim·mer·et /swímməret/ *n.* a swimming foot in crustaceans.

swim·ming·ly /swíminglee/ *adv.* with easy and unobstructed progress.

swim·ming pool *n.* an indoor or outdoor pool for swimming.

swim·suit /swímsōot/ *n.* garment worn for swimming. □□ **swim·suit·ed** *adj.*

swim·wear /swímwair/ *n.* clothing worn for swimming.

swin·dle /swínd'l/ *v. & n.* ● *v.tr.* (often foll. by *out of*) **1** cheat (a person) of money, possessions, etc. **2** cheat a person of (money, etc.) (*swindled all his savings out of him*). ● *n.* **1** an act of swindling. **2** a person or thing represented as what it is not. **3** a fraudulent scheme. □□ **swin·dler** *n.*

swine /swīn/ *n.* (*pl.* same) **1** a pig. **2** *colloq.* (*pl.* **swine** or **swines**) **a** a term of contempt or disgust for a person. **b** a very unpleasant or difficult thing. □□ **swin·ish** *adj.* (esp. in sense 2). **swin·ish·ly** *adv.* **swin·ish·ness** *n.*

swine·herd /swínhərd/ *n.* a person who tends pigs.

swing /swing/ *v. & n.* ● *v.* (*past* and *past part.* **swung** /swung/) **1** *intr.* move or cause to move with a to-and-fro or curving motion, as of an object attached at one end and hanging free at the other. **2** *intr. & tr.* **a** sway. **b** hang so as to be free to sway.

c oscillate or cause to oscillate. **3** *intr. & tr.* revolve or cause to revolve. **4** *intr.* move by gripping something and leaping, etc. **5** *intr.* go with a swinging gait. **6** *intr.* (foll. by *around*) move around to the opposite direction. **7** *intr.* change from one opinion or mood to another. **8** *intr.* (foll. by *at*) attempt to hit or punch. **9** *a intr.* (also **swing it**) play music with a swing. **b** *tr.* play (a tune) with swing. **10** *intr. colloq.* **a** be lively or up to date; enjoy oneself. **b** be promiscuous. **11** *intr. colloq.* (of a party, etc.) be lively, etc. **12** *tr.* have a decisive influence on (esp. voting, etc.). **13** *tr. colloq.* deal with or achieve. **14** *intr. colloq.* be executed by hanging. ● *n.* **1** the act or an instance of swinging. **2** the motion of swinging. **3** the extent of swinging. **4** a swinging or smooth gait or rhythm or action. **5** **a** a seat slung by ropes or chains, etc., for swinging on or in. **b** a spell of swinging on this. **6** an easy but vigorous continued action. **7** **a** jazz or dance music with an easy flowing rhythm. **b** the rhythmic feeling or drive of this music. **8** a discernible change in opinion, esp. the amount by which votes change from one side to another. □□ **swing·er** *n.* (esp. in sense 10 of *v.*).

swing bridge *n.* a bridge that can be swung to one side to allow the passage of ships.

swinge /swinj/ *v.tr.* (**swingeing**) *archaic* strike hard; beat.

swinge·ing /swínjing/ *adj.* esp. *Brit.* **1** (of a blow) forcible. **2** huge or far-reaching, esp. in severity. □□ **swinge·ing·ly** *adv.*

swing·ing /swínging/ *adj.* **1** (of gait, melody, etc.) vigorously rhythmical. **2** *colloq.* **a** lively; up to date. **b** promiscuous. □□ **swing·ing·ly** *adv.*

swin·gle /swínggəl/ *n. & v.* ● *n.* **1** a wooden instrument for beating flax and removing the woody parts from it. **2** the swinging part of a flail. ● *v.tr.* clean (flax) with a swingle.

swing·man /swíngman/ *n. Basketball* a player who can play both guard and forward.

swing shift *n.* a work shift from afternoon to late evening.

swing wing *n.* an aircraft wing that can move from a right-angled to a swept-back position.

swing·y /swíngee/ *adj.* (**swingier**, **swingiest**) **1** (of music) characterized by swing (see SWING *n.* 7). **2** (of a skirt or dress) designed to swing with body movement.

swipe /swīp/ *v. & n. colloq.* ● *v.* **1** *tr. &* (often foll. by *at*) *intr.* hit hard. **2** *tr.* steal. **3** *tr.* run (a credit card, etc.) through an electronic card reader. ● *n.* a hard blow. □□ **swip·er** *n.*

swirl /swərl/ *v. & n.* ● *v.intr. & tr.* move or flow or carry along with a whirling motion. ● *n.* **1** a swirling motion of or in water, air, etc. **2** the act of swirling. **3** a twist or curl, esp. as part of a pattern or design. □□ **swirl·y** *adj.*

swish /swish/ *v., n., & adj.* ● *v.* **1** *tr.* swing (a scythe or stick, etc.) audibly through the air, grass, etc. **2** *intr.* move with or make a swishing sound. **3** *tr.* (foll. by *off*) cut (a flower, etc.) in this way. ● *n.* a swishing action or sound. ● *adj. colloq.* smart, fashionable. □□ **swish·y** *adj.*

Swiss /swis/ *adj. & n.* ● *adj.* of or relating to Switzerland in Western Europe or its people. ● *n.* (*pl.* same) **1** a native or inhabitant of Switzerland. **2** a person of Swiss descent.

Swiss cheese *n.* a hard cheese with large holes that form during ripening.

Swiss cheese plant *n.* ▶ a climbing house plant, *Monstera deliciosa*, with aerial roots and holes in the leaves.

SWISS CHEESE PLANT
(*Monstera deliciosa*)

Swiss steak *n.* a slice of beef that is flattened, floured, and braised with vegetables, etc.

switch /swich/ *n. & v.* ● *n.* **1** ▼ a device for making and breaking the connection in an electric circuit. **2** **a** a transfer, change-over, or deviation. **b** an exchange. **3** a slender flexible shoot cut from a tree. **4** a light tapering rod. **5** a device at the junction of railroad tracks for transferring a train from one track to another. **6** a tress of false or detached hair tied at one end used in hairdressing. ● *v.* **1** *tr.* (foll. by *on*, *off*) turn (an electrical device) on or off. **2** *intr.* change or transfer position, subject, etc. **3** *tr.* change or transfer. **4** *tr.* reverse the positions of; exchange. **5** *tr.* beat or flick with a switch. □ **switch off** *colloq.* cease to pay attention. **switch over** change or exchange. □□ **switch·er** *n.*

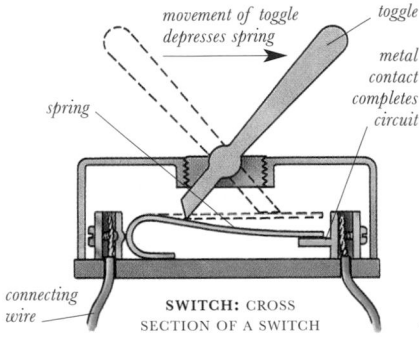

movement of toggle depresses spring   *toggle*

metal contact completes circuit

spring

connecting wire

SWITCH: CROSS SECTION OF A SWITCH

switch·back /swíchbak/ *n.* (often *attrib.*) a railroad or road with alternate sharp ascents and descents.

switch·blade /swíchblayd/ *n.* ▶ a pocket knife with the blade released by a spring.

switch·board /swíchbawrd/ *n.* an apparatus for varying connections between electric circuits, esp. for completing telephone calls.

switch hit·ter *n. Baseball* a batter able to hit right-handed or left-handed.

swith·er /swíthər/ *v. & n. Sc.* ● *v.intr.* hesitate; be uncertain. ● *n.* doubt or uncertainty.

swiv·el /swívəl/ *n. & v.* ● *n.* a coupling between two parts enabling one to revolve without turning the other. ● *v.tr. & intr.* (**swiveled**, **swiveling** or **swivelled**, **swivelling**) turn on or as on a swivel.

swiv·el chair *n.* a chair with a seat able to be turned horizontally.

swiz·zle stick *n.* a stick used for stirring drinks.

swob var. of SWAB.

swol·len *past part.* of SWELL.

swoon /swōōn/ *v. & n. literary* ● *v.intr.* faint. ● *n.* an occurrence of fainting.

swoop /swōōp/ *v. & n.* ● *v.* **1** *intr.* (often foll. by *down*) descend rapidly like a bird of prey. **2** *intr.* (often foll. by *on*) make a sudden attack. **3** *tr.* (often foll. by *up*) *colloq.* snatch the whole of at one swoop. ● *n.* a swooping or snatching movement or action. □ **at** (or **in**) **one fell swoop** see FELL[4].

swoosh /swōōsh/ *n.* the noise of a sudden rush of liquid, air, etc.

swop var. of SWAP.

sword /sawrd/ *n.* **1** ▶ a weapon usu. of metal with a long blade and hilt with a handguard. **2** (prec. by *the*) **a** war. **b** military power. □ **put to the sword** kill, esp. in war.

sword·bill /sáwrdbil/ *n.* a long-billed humming bird, *Ensifera ensifera*.

blade

lock and release catch

grip

spike

SWITCHBLADE

S

SWORD

There are two main types of sword: cutting swords, such as a medieval knight's two-handed sword, which have heavy blades with sharp edges; and stabbing swords, such as a rapier, which are much lighter and have a sharp point. One of humankind's oldest weapons, swords evolved from the dagger early in the Bronze Age and were used in combat until as recently as the First World War (1914–18). From the 16th to the 19th century, broad-bladed cutting swords were widely used by the cavalry, especially when charging an enemy. Swords are rarely used by modern military forces, except as part of dress uniforms or in ceremonies. However, fencing, which developed in the 14th century, remains a popular sport today.

PARTS OF A 17TH-CENTURY GERMAN RAPIER

knuckle guard

guard rings

sharp point

double-edge

ricasso

grip

blade

vertically recurved quillon

pommel

hilt

EXAMPLES OF OTHER SWORDS

BRONZE AGE SWORD (9TH CENTURY BC)

ROMAN *GLADIUS* (1ST CENTURY AD)

VIKING SWORD (10TH CENTURY)

FRENCH MEDIEVAL KNIGHT'S SWORD (14TH CENTURY)

ENGLISH TWO-HANDED SWORD (15TH CENTURY)

INDIAN GAUNTLET SWORD (17TH CENTURY)

SAMURAI SHORT SWORD (17TH CENTURY)

GERMAN CAVALRY SWORD (17TH CENTURY)

FRENCH HUNTING SWORD (18TH CENTURY)

FRENCH INFANTRY SHORT SWORD (18TH CENTURY)

ENGLISH SMALL SWORD (19TH CENTURY)

INDIAN *SHAMSHIR* (19TH CENTURY)

SCOTTISH BROADSWORD (19TH CENTURY)

FENCING FOIL (MODERN)

S

SWORDFISH
(*Xiphias gladius*)

sword·fish /sáwrdfish/ *n.* ▲ a large marine fish, *Xiphias gladius*, with an extended swordlike upper jaw.

sword of Dam·o·cles /dámǝkleez/ *n.* an imminent danger.

sword·play /sáwrdplay/ *n.* **1** fencing. **2** repartee; cut-and-thrust argument.

swords·man /sáwrdzmǝn/ *n.* (*pl.* **-men**) a person of (usu. specified) skill with a sword. □□ **swords·man·ship** *n.*

sword·stick /sáwrdstik/ *n.* a hollow walking stick containing a blade that can be used as a sword.

sword·tail /sáwrdtayl/ *n.* **1** a tropical fish, *Xiphophorus helleri*, with a long tail. **2** = HORSESHOE CRAB.

swore *past* of SWEAR.

sworn /swawrn/ *past part.* of SWEAR. *adj.* bound by or as by an oath (*sworn enemies*).

swot /swot/ *v. & n. Brit. colloq.* ● *v.* (**swotted**, **swotting**) **1** *intr.* study assiduously. **2** *tr.* (often foll. by *up*) study (a subject) hard or hurriedly. ● *n.* **1** a person who swots. **2 a** hard study. **b** a thing that requires this.

swum *past part.* of SWIM.

swung *past* and *past part.* of SWING.

syb·a·rite /síbǝrīt/ *n. & adj.* ● *n.* a person who is self-indulgent or devoted to sensuous luxury. ● *adj.* fond of luxury or sensuousness. □□ **syb·a·rit·ic** /-rítik/ *adj.* **syb·a·rit·i·cal** *adj.* **syb·a·rit·i·cal·ly** *adv.* **syb·a·rit·ism** *n.*

sy·ca·mine /síkǝmīn, -min/ ● *n. Bibl.* the black mulberry tree, *Morus nigra* (see Luke 17:6; in modern versions translated as 'mulberry tree').

syc·a·more /síkǝmawr/ *n.* **1** ▶ any of several plane trees, esp. *Platanus occidentalis* of N. America, or its wood. **2** (in full **sycamore maple**) **a** ▼ a large maple, *Acer pseudoplatanus*, with winged seeds. **b** its wood.

winglike fruit wall

flower stalk

seed inside

seed

SYCAMORE MAPLE
FRUITS
(*Acer pseudoplatanus*)

bristly fruit

SYCAMORE:
ORIENTAL PLANE
(*Platanus orientalis*)

syce /sīs/ *n.* (also **sice**) *Anglo-Ind.* a groom.

sy·co·ni·um /sīkōneeǝm/ *n.* (*pl.* **syconia**) *Bot.* a fleshy hollow receptacle developing into a multiple fruit as in the fig.

syc·o·phant /síkǝfant, síkǝ-/ *n.* a servile flatterer; a toady. □□ *n.* **syc·o·phan·tic** /-fántik/ *adj.* **syc·o·phan·ti·cal·ly** *adv.*

sy·co·sis /sīkṓsis/ *n.* a skin disease of the bearded part of the face with inflammation of the hair follicles.

Syd·en·ham's cho·re·a /sídǝnǝmz/ *n.* chorea esp. in children as one of the manifestations of rheumatic fever; also called **St. Vitus's dance**.

sy·en·ite /síǝnīt/ *n.* a gray crystalline rock of feldspar and hornblende with or without quartz. □□ **sy·en·i·tic** /-nítik/ *adj.*

syl- /sil/ *prefix* assim. form of SYN- before *l*.

syl·la·bar·y /sílǝberee/ *n.* (*pl.* **-ies**) a list of characters representing syllables.

syl·la·bi *pl.* of SYLLABUS.

syl·lab·ic /silábik/ *adj.* of, relating to, or based on syllables. □□ **syl·lab·i·cal·ly** *adv.*

syl·lab·i·ca·tion /sílabikáyshǝn/ *n.* (also **syl·lab·i·**

fi·ca·tion) /-bifikáyshǝn/ division into or articulation by syllables. □□ **syl·lab·i·fy** *v.tr.* (**-ies**, **-ied**).

syl·la·bize /sílǝbīz/ *v.tr.* divide into or articulate by syllables.

syl·la·ble /sílǝbǝl/ *n.* **1** a unit of pronunciation uttered without interruption, forming the whole or a part of a word and usu. having one vowel sound often with a consonant or consonants before or after. **2** a character or characters representing a syllable. **3** (usu. with *neg.*) the least amount of speech or writing (*did not utter a syllable*). □□ **syl·la·bled** *adj.* (also in *comb.*).

syl·la·bub /sílǝbub/ *n.* (also **sil·la·bub**) a dessert made of cream or milk flavored, sweetened, and whipped to thicken it.

syl·la·bus /sílǝbǝs/ *n.* (*pl.* **syllabuses** or **syllabi** /-bī/) **1** the program or outline of a course of study, teaching, etc. **2** a statement of the requirements for a particular examination.

syl·lep·sis /silépsis/ *n.* (*pl.* **syllepses** /-seez/) a figure of speech in which a word is applied to two others in different senses (e.g., *caught the train and a bad cold*) or to two others of which it grammatically suits one only (e.g., *neither they nor it is working*). □□ **syl·lep·tic** *adj.* **syl·lep·ti·cal·ly** *adv.*

syl·lo·gism /sílǝjizǝm/ *n.* a form of reasoning in which a conclusion is drawn from two given or assumed propositions (premises). □□ **syl·lo·gis·tic** *adj.*

syl·log·ize /sílǝjīz/ *v.* **1** *intr.* use syllogisms. **2** *tr.* put (facts or an argument) in the form of syllogism.

sylph /silf/ *n.* **1** an elemental spirit of the air. **2** a slender graceful woman or girl. □□ **sylph·like** *adj.*

syl·van /sílvǝn/ *adj.* (also **sil·van**) **1 a** of the woods. **b** having woods. **2** rural.

syl·vi·cul·ture var. of SILVICULTURE.

sym·bi·ont /símbeeont, -ǝnt/ *n.* an organism living in symbiosis.

sym. *abbr.* **1** symbol. **2** symphony.

sym- /sim/ *prefix* assim. form of SYN- before *b, m, p.*

sym·bi·o·sis /símbee-ṓsis, -bī-/ *n.* (*pl.* **symbioses** /-seez/) **1 a** ▼ an interaction between two different organisms living in close physical association, usu. to the advantage of both. **b** an instance of this. **2 a** a mutually advantageous association or relationship between persons. **b** an instance of this. □□ **sym·bi·ot·ic** /-bīótik/ *adj.* **sym·bi·ot·i·cal·ly** /-bīótikǝlee/ *adv.*

sym·bol /símbǝl/ *n.* **1** a thing conventionally regarded as typifying, representing, or recalling something, esp. an idea or quality. **2** a mark or character taken as the conventional sign of some object, idea, function, or process. □□ **sym·bol·o·gy** /-bólǝjee/ *n.*

sym·bol·ic /simbólik/ *adj.* (also **sym·bol·i·cal** /-bólikǝl/) **1** of or serving as a symbol. **2** involving the use of symbols or symbolism. □□ **sym·bol·i·cal·ly** *adv.*

sym·bol·ic log·ic *n.* the use of symbols to denote propositions, etc., in order to assist reasoning.

sym·bol·ism /símbǝlizǝm/ *n.* **1 a** the use of symbols to represent ideas. **b** symbols collectively. **2** an artistic and poetic movement or style using symbols and indirect suggestion to express ideas, emotions, etc. □□ **sym·bol·ist** *n.*

sym·bol·ize /símbǝlīz/ *v.tr.* **1** be a symbol of. **2** represent by means of symbols. □□ **sym·bol·i·za·tion** *n.*

sym·me·try /símitree/ *n.* (*pl.* **-ies**) **1 a** correct proportion of the parts of a thing. **b** beauty resulting from this. **2 a** a structure that allows an object to be divided into parts of an equal shape and size. **b** the possession of such a structure. **c** approximation to such a structure. **3** the repetition of exactly similar parts facing each other or a center. □□ **sym·met·ric** /simétrik/ *adj.* **sym·met·ri·cal** *adj.* **sym·met·ri·cal·ly** *adv.*

sym·pa·thec·to·my /símpǝthéktǝmee/ *n.* (*pl.* **-ies**) the surgical removal of a sympathetic ganglion, etc.

sym·pa·thet·ic /símpǝthétik/ *adj.* **1** of, showing, or expressing sympathy. **2** due to sympathy. **3** likable or capable of evoking sympathy. **4** (of a person) friendly and cooperative. **5** (foll. by *to*) inclined to favor (*sympathetic to the idea*). **6 a** designating the part of the nervous system consisting of nerves leaving the thoracic and lumbar regions of the spinal cord and connecting with the nerve cells in or near the viscera. ▷ AUTONOMIC NERVOUS SYSTEM. **b** (of a nerve or ganglion) belonging to this system. □□ **sym·pa·thet·i·cal·ly** *adv.*

sym·pa·thize /símpǝthīz/ *v.intr.* (often foll. by *with*) **1** feel or express sympathy. **2** agree with a sentiment or opinion. □□ **sym·pa·thiz·er** *n.*

sym·pa·thy /símpǝthee/ *n.* (*pl.* **-ies**) **1 a** the state of being simultaneously affected with the same feeling as another. **b** the capacity for this. **2** (often foll. by *with*) **a** the act of sharing or tendency to share in an emotion or sensation or condition of another person or thing. **b** (in *sing.* or *pl.*) compassion or

SYMBIOSIS

Partnerships between pairs of species are a common feature of the living world. The great majority are either mutualistic, where both partners benefit, or parasitic, where one species (the parasite) lives at the expense of the other (the host). Commensal partnerships, where one species gains and the other is unaffected, are rarer and more difficult to verify. In the partnership between a clownfish and a sea anemone, for example, the fish gains protection, but it is harder to tell if the anemone benefits.

poisonous tentacles of sea anemone

sheltering clownfish

coral

CLOWNFISH AND SEA ANEMONE IN A SYMBIOTIC RELATIONSHIP

commiseration; condolences. **3** (often foll. by *for*) approval. **4** (in *sing.* or *pl.*; often foll. by *with*) agreement (with a person, etc.) in opinion or desire. **5** (*attrib.*) in support of another cause (*sympathy strike*). □ **in sympathy** (often foll. by *with*) having or showing or resulting from sympathy (with another).

sym·pet·al·ous /simpét'ləs/ *adj. Bot.* having the petals united.

sym·phon·ic /simfónik/ *adj.* (of music) relating to or having the form or character of a symphony. □□ **sym·phon·i·cal·ly** *adv.*

sym·phon·ic po·em *n.* an extended orchestral piece, usu. in one movement, on a descriptive or rhapsodic theme.

sym·pho·nist /símfənist/ *n.* a composer of symphonies.

sym·pho·ny /símfənee/ *n.* (*pl.* **-ies**) **1** an elaborate composition usu. for full orchestra, and in several movements. **2** = SYMPHONY ORCHESTRA.

sym·pho·ny or·ches·tra *n.* a large orchestra suitable for playing symphonies, etc. ▷ ORCHESTRA

sym·phyl·lous /simfíləs/ *adj. Bot.* having the leaves united.

sym·phy·sis /símfisis/ *n.* (*pl.* **symphyses** /-seez/) **1** the process of growing together. **2 a** a union between two bones, esp. in the median plane of the body. **b** the place or line of this. □□ **sym·phy·se·al** /-físéeəl, -fízeeəl/ *adj.* **sym·phy·si·al** /-fízeeəl/ *adj.*

sym·po·di·um /simpódeeəm/ *n.* (*pl.* **sympodia** /-deeə/) *Bot.* the apparent main axis or stem of a vine, etc., made up of successive secondary axes. □□ **sym·po·di·al** *adj.*

sym·po·si·um /simpózeeəm/ *n.* (*pl.* **symposia** /-zeeə/) **1 a** a conference or meeting to discuss a particular subject. **b** a collection of essays or papers for this purpose. **2** a philosophical or other friendly discussion.

symp·tom /símptəm/ *n.* **1** *Med.* a change in the physical or mental condition of a person, regarded as evidence of a disorder. **2** a sign of the existence of something.

symp·to·mat·ic /símptəmátik/ *adj.* serving as a symptom. □□ **symp·to·mat·i·cal·ly** *adv.*

symp·to·ma·tol·o·gy /símptəmətóləjee/ *n.* the branch of medicine concerned with the study and interpretation of symptoms.

syn. *abbr.* **1** synonym. **2** synonymous. **3** synonymy.

syn- /sin/ *prefix* with, together, alike.

syn·a·gogue /sínəgog/ *n.* **1** ▼ the house of worship where a Jewish congregation meets for religious observance and instruction. **2** the assembly itself. □□ **syn·a·gog·al** /-gógəl/ *adj.* **syn·a·gog·i·cal** /-gójikəl/ *adj.*

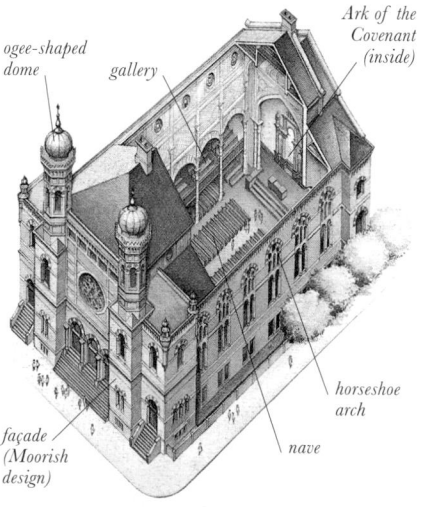

ogee-shaped dome
gallery
Ark of the Covenant (inside)
façade (Moorish design)
nave
horseshoe arch

SYNAGOGUE: CUTAWAY VIEW OF THE CENTRAL SYNAGOGUE, NEW YORK

SYNAPSE

The function of the synapse is to relay messages from a neuron (nerve cell) to a target tissue (either another neuron or other tissue, such as muscle). It consists of a synaptic knob, a synaptic cleft, and a target site. A stimulus received by the neuron is transmitted as an electrical impulse along the axon to the synaptic knob. Here, the impulse prompts the synaptic vesicles to release neurotransmitters into the synaptic cleft. The neurotransmitters then attach to receptor sites in the target tissue and relay the message.

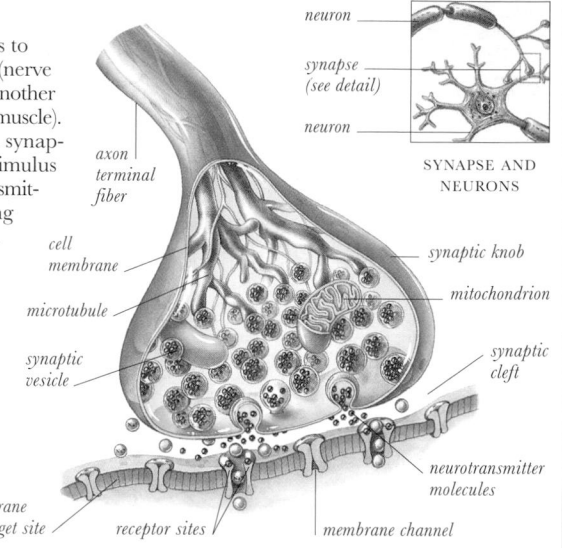

neuron
synapse (see detail)
neuron

SYNAPSE AND NEURONS

axon terminal fiber
cell membrane
microtubule
synaptic vesicle
synaptic knob
mitochondrion
synaptic cleft
neurotransmitter molecules
membrane channel
receptor sites
cell membrane of target site

DETAIL (SECTION THROUGH A SYNAPSE)

syn·apse /sínaps, sináps/ *n. Anat.* ▲ a junction of two nerve cells.

syn·ap·sis /sinápsis/ *n.* (*pl.* **synapses** /-seez/) **1** *Anat.* = SYNAPSE. **2** *Biol.* the fusion of chromosome pairs at the start of meiosis. □□ **syn·ap·tic** /-náptik/ *adj.* **syn·ap·ti·cal·ly** *adv.*

syn·ar·thro·sis /sínaarthrósis/ *n.* (*pl.* **synarthroses** /-seez/) *Anat.* an immovably fixed bone joint, e.g., the sutures of the skull.

sync /singk/ *n. & v.* (also **synch**) *colloq.* ● *n.* synchronization. ● *v.tr. & intr.* synchronize. □ **in** (or **out of**) **sync** (often foll. by *with*) harmonizing or agreeing well (or badly).

syn·carp /sínkaarp/ *n.* a compound fruit from a flower with several carpels, e.g., a blackberry.

syn·carp·ous /sínkaàrpəs/ *adj.* (of a flower or fruit) having the carpels united.

synch var. of SYNC.

syn·chon·dro·sis /síngkondrósis/ *n.* (*pl.* **synchondroses** /-seez/) *Anat.* an almost immovable bone joint bound by a layer of cartilage, as in the spinal vertebrae.

synchro- /síngkrō/ *comb. form* synchronized; synchronous.

syn·chro·cy·clo·tron /síngkrōsíklətron/ *n.* a cyclotron able to achieve higher energies by decreasing the frequency of the accelerating electric field as the particles increase in energy and mass.

syn·chro·mesh /síngkrōmesh/ *n. & adj.* ● *n.* ▼ a system of changing gears, esp. in motor vehicles, in which the driving and driven gearwheels are made to revolve at the same speed during engagement. ● *adj.* relating to or using this system.

syn·chron·ic /singkrónik/ *adj.* describing a subject (esp. a language) as it exists at one point in time. □□ **syn·chron·i·cal·ly** *adv.*

syn·chron·ism /síngkrənizəm/ *n.* **1** = SYNCHRONY. **2** the process of synchronizing sound and picture in cinematography, television, etc. □□ **syn·chro·nis·tic** *adj.* **syn·chro·nis·ti·cal·ly** *adv.*

syn·chro·nize /síngkrəniz/ *v.* **1** *intr.* (often foll. by *with*) occur at the same time. **2** *tr.* cause to occur at the same time. **3** *tr.* carry out the synchronism of (a movie). **4** *tr.* ascertain or set forth the correspondence in the date of (events). **5 a** *tr.* cause (clocks, etc.) to show a standard or uniform time. **b** *intr.* (of clocks, etc.) be synchronized. □□ **syn·chro·ni·za·tion** *n.* **syn·chro·niz·er** *n.*

syn·chro·nized swim·ming *n.* a form of swimming in which participants make coordinated leg and arm movements in time to music.

syn·chro·nous /síngkrənəs/ *adj.* (often foll. by *with*) existing or occurring at the same time. □□ **syn·chro·nous·ly** *adv.*

syn·chro·nous mo·tor *n. Electr.* a motor having a speed exactly proportional to the current frequency.

syn·chro·ny /síngkrənee/ *n.* **1** the state of being synchronic or synchronous. **2** the treatment of events, etc., as being synchronous.

SYNCHROMESH

In a modern synchromesh gearbox, each pair of gearwheels that produces a gear ratio (for example, "first gear") is constantly meshing together, making it easier to change gear. One of each pair is fixed to the input shaft, which is driven by the engine. The other spins freely on the output shaft, which is connected to the road wheels. As the driver selects a gear ratio, a sliding collar meshes with the teeth ("dogs") at the side of the free-spinning gearwheel, which locks the gear to the output shaft. This gear then turns the output shaft, which propels the car.

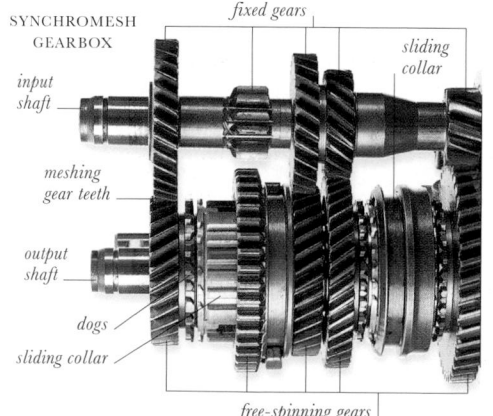

SYNCHROMESH GEARBOX

fixed gears
sliding collar
input shaft
meshing gear teeth
output shaft
dogs
sliding collar
free-spinning gears

S

syn·chro·tron /síngkrətron/ *n. Physics* a cyclotron in which the magnetic field strength increases with the energy of the particles to keep their orbital radius constant.

syn·cline /síngklīn/ *n.* a rock bed forming a trough. □□ **syn·cli·nal** *adj.*

syn·co·pate /síngkəpayt/ *v.tr.* **1** *Mus.* displace the beats or accents in (a passage) so that strong beats become weak and vice versa. **2** shorten (a word) by dropping interior sounds or letters. □□ **syn·co·pa·tion** /-páyshən/ *n.* **syn·co·pa·tor** *n.*

syn·co·pe /síngkəpee/ *n.* **1** *Gram.* the omission of interior sounds or letters in a word. **2** *Med.* a temporary loss of consciousness caused by a fall in blood pressure. □□ **syn·co·pal** *adj.*

syn·cre·tism /síngkrətizəm/ *n.* **1** *Philos. & Theol.* the process or an instance of syncretizing (see SYNCRETIZE). **2** *Philol.* the merging of different inflectional varieties in the development of a language. □□ **syncretic** /-krétik/ *adj.* **syn·cre·tist** *n.* **syn·cre·tis·tic** /-krətístik/ *adj.*

syn·cre·tize /síngkrətīz/ *v.tr. Philos. & Theol.* attempt, esp. inconsistently, to unify or reconcile differing schools of thought. □□ **syn·cret·ic** /-krétik/ *adj.* **syn·cre·tism** /síngkrətizəm/ *n.* **syn·cre·tist** *n.*

syn·cy·ti·um /sinsísheeəm/ *n.* (*pl.* **syncytia** /-sheeə/) *Biol.* a mass of cytoplasm with several nuclei, not divided into separate cells. □□ **syn·cy·ti·al** /-síshəl/ *adj.*

synd. *abbr.* **1** syndicate. **2** syndicated.

syn·dac·tyl /sindáktil/ *adj.* (of an animal) having digits united as in webbed feet, etc. □□ **syn·dac·tyl·ism** *n.* **syn·dac·tyl·ous** *adj.*

syn·de·sis /síndisis/ *n.* (*pl.* **syndeses** /-seez/) *Biol.* = SYNAPSIS 2.

syn·des·mo·sis /síndezmṓsis/ *n.* the union and articulation of bones by means of ligaments.

syn·det·ic /sindétik/ *adj. Gram.* of or using conjunctions.

syn·dic /síndik/ *n.* a government official in various countries. □□ **syn·di·cal** *adj.*

syn·di·cal·ism /síndikəlizəm/ *n. hist.* a movement for transferring the ownership and control of the means of production and distribution to workers' unions. □□ **syn·di·cal·ist** *n.*

syn·di·cate *n. & v.* ● *n.* /síndikət/ **1** a combination of individuals or commercial firms to promote some common interest. **2** an agency supplying material simultaneously to a number of newspapers or periodicals. **3** a group of people who combine to buy or rent property, gamble, etc. **4** a committee of syndics. ● *v.tr.* /síndikayt/ **1** form into a syndicate. **2** publish (material) through a syndicate. □□ **syn·di·ca·tion** /-káyshən/ *n.*

syn·drome /síndrōm/ *n.* **1** a group of concurrent symptoms of a disease. **2** a characteristic combination of opinions, behavior, etc.

syne /sīn/ *adv., conj., & prep. Sc.* since.

syn·ec·do·che /sinékdəkee/ *n.* a figure of speech in which a part is made to represent the whole or vice versa. □□ **syn·ec·doch·ic** /-dókik/ *adj.*

syn·e·col·o·gy /sínikóləjee/ *n.* the ecological study of plant or animal communities. □□ **syn·e·co·log·i·cal** /-kəlójikəl/ *adj.* **syn·e·col·o·gist** *n.*

syn·er·e·sis /sináirisis/ *n.* (*pl.* **synereses** /-seez/) the contraction of two vowels into a diphthong or single vowel.

syn·er·gism /sínərjizəm/ *n.* (also **syn·er·gy** /sínərjee/) the combined effect of drugs, organs, etc., that exceeds the sum of their individual effects. □□ **syn·er·get·ic** /-jétik/ *adj.* **syn·er·gis·tic** *adj.* **syn·er·gis·ti·cal·ly** *adv.*

syn·er·gist /sínərjist/ *n.* a medicine or a bodily organ (e.g., a muscle) that cooperates with another or others.

syn·es·the·sia /sínis-thée<u>zh</u>ə, -zeeə/ *n.* **1** *Psychol.* the production of a mental sense impression relating to one sense by the stimulation of another

sense. **2** a sensation produced in a part of the body by stimulation of another part. □□ **syn·es·thet·ic** /-thétik/ *adj.*

syn·ga·my /sínggəmee/ *n. Biol.* the fusion of gametes or nuclei in reproduction. □□ **syn·ga·mous** *adj.*

syn·gen·e·sis /sinjénisis/ *n.* sexual reproduction from combined male and female elements.

syn·od /sínəd/ *n.* **1** an Episcopal council attended by delegated clergy and sometimes laity. **2** a Presbyterian ecclesiastical court above the presbyteries and subject to the General Assembly.

syn·od·ic /sinódik/ *adj. Astron.* relating to or involving the conjunction of stars, planets, etc.

syn·od·i·cal /sinódikəl/ *adj.* (also **syn·od·al** /sínəd'l/) of, relating to, or constituted as a synod.

syn·od·ic per·i·od *n.* the time between the successive conjunctions of a planet with the Sun.

syn·o·nym /sínənim/ *n.* a word or phrase that means exactly or nearly the same as another in the same language (e.g., *shut* and *close*). □□ **syn·o·nym·i·ty** /-nímitee/ *n.*

syn·on·y·mous /sinóniməs/ *adj.* (often foll. by *with*) **1** having the same meaning; being a synonym (of). **2** suggestive of or associated with another. □□ **syn·on·y·mous·ly** *adv.*

syn·on·y·my /sinónimee/ *n.* (*pl.* **-ies**) **1** the state of being synonymous. **2** the collocation of synonyms for emphasis (e.g., *in any shape or form*).

syn·op·sis /sinópsis/ *n.* (*pl.* **synopses** /-seez/) **1** a summary or outline. **2** a brief general survey. □□ **syn·op·size** *v.tr.*

syn·op·tic /sinóptik/ *adj. & n.* ● *adj.* **1** of, forming, or giving a synopsis. **2** of the Synoptic Gospels. ● *n.* **1** a Synoptic Gospel. **2** the writer of a Synoptic Gospel. □□ **syn·op·ti·cal** *adj.* **syn·op·ti·cal·ly** *adv.*

Syn·op·tic Gos·pels *n.pl.* the Gospels of Matthew, Mark, and Luke, describing events from a similar point of view.

syn·o·vi·a /sinṓveeə, sī-/ *n. Physiol.* a viscous fluid lubricating joints and tendon sheaths. □□ **syn·o·vi·al** *adj.*

syn·o·vi·al mem·brane /sinṓveeəl mémbrayn/ *n.* ▶ a dense membrane of connective tissue secreting synovia.

syn·o·vi·tis /sínōvítis, sī-/ *n.* inflammation of the synovial membrane.

syn·tac·tic /sintáktik/ *adj.* of or according to syntax. □□ **syn·tac·ti·cal** *adj.* **syn·tac·ti·cal·ly** *adv.*

syn·tag·ma /sintágmə/ *n.* (*pl.* **syntagmas** or **syntagmata** /-mətə/) **1** a word or phrase forming a syntactic unit. **2** a systematic collection of statements. □□ **syn·tag·mat·ic** /-mátik/ *adj.* **syn·tag·mic** /-mik/ *adj.*

syn·tax /síntaks/ *n.* **1** the grammatical arrangement of words, showing their connection and relation. **2** a set of rules for or an analysis of this.

syn·the·sis /sínthisis/ *n.* (*pl.* **syntheses** /-seez/) **1** the process or result of building up separate elements, esp. ideas, into a connected whole, esp. into a theory or system. **2** a combination or composition. **3** *Chem.* the artificial production of compounds from their constituents as distinct from extraction from plants, etc. **4** the joining of divided parts in surgery. □□ **syn·the·sist** *n.*

syn·the·size /sínthisīz/ *v.tr.* (also **syn·the·tize** /-tīz/) **1** make a synthesis of. **2** combine into a coherent whole.

syn·the·siz·er /sínthisīzər/ *n.* an electronic musical instrument, esp. operated by a keyboard, producing a wide variety of sounds by generating and combining signals of different frequencies.

syn·thet·ic /sinthétik/ *adj. & n.* ● *adj.* **1** made by chemical synthesis, esp. to imitate a natural product (*synthetic rubber*). **2** (of emotions, etc.) insincere. ● *n. Chem.* a synthetic substance. □□ **syn·thet·i·cal** *adj.* **syn·thet·i·cal·ly** *adv.*

syph·i·lis /sífilis/ *n.* a contagious venereal disease progressing from infection of the genitals to the bones, muscles, and brain. □□ **syph·i·lit·ic** /-lítik/ *adj.*

sy·phon var. of SIPHON.

Syr·i·an /séereeən/ *n. & adj.* ● *n.* **1** a native or inhabitant of the modern nation of Syria in the Middle East; a person of Syrian descent. **2** a native or inhabitant of the region of Syria in antiquity or later. ● *adj.* of or relating to the region or state of Syria.

sy·rin·ga /sirínggə/ *n.* **1** = MOCK ORANGE. **2** any plant of the genus *Syringa*, esp. the lilac.

sy·ringe /sírinj/ *n. & v.* ● *n.* **1** *Med.* **a** a tube with a nozzle and piston or bulb for sucking in and ejecting liquid in a fine stream. ▷ MEDICINE **b** (in full **hypodermic syringe**) ▶ a similar device with a hollow needle for insertion under the skin. **2** any similar device used in cooking, etc. ● *v.tr.* sluice or spray (the ear, a plant, etc.) with a syringe.

syr·inx /síringks/ *n.* (*pl.* **syrinxes** or **syringes** /sirínjeez/) a set of panpipes.

Syro- /sírō/ *comb. form* Syrian; Syrian and (*Syro-Phoenician*).

syr·up /sírəp, sə́r-/ *n.* (also **sir·up**) **1 a** a sweet sauce made by dissolving sugar in boiling water, often used for preserving fruit, etc. **b** a similar sauce of a specified flavor as a drink, medicine, etc. **2** the condensed juice of sugar cane or the sugar maple; molasses. **3** excessive sweetness of style or manner. □□ **syr·up·y** *adj.*

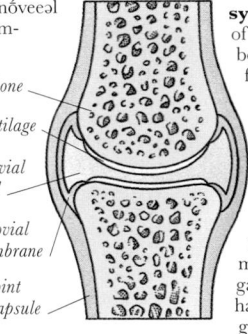

hollow-bore needle

graduated scale

flange

piston

SYRINGE:
HYPODERMIC
SYRINGE

sys·tal·tic /sistáltik, sistáwl-/ *adj.* (esp. of the heart) contracting and dilating rhythmically.

sys·tem /sístəm/ *n.* **1** a complex whole; a set of connected things or parts; an organized body of things. **2** a set of devices (e.g., pulleys) functioning together. **3** *Physiol.* **a** a set of organs in the body with a common structure or function. **b** the human or animal body as a whole. **4 a** method; considered principles of procedure. **b** classification. **5** orderliness. **6 a** a body of theory or practice relating to or prescribing a particular form of government, religion, etc. **b** (prec. by *the*) the prevailing political or social order. **7** a method of choosing one's procedure in gambling, etc. **8** *Computing* a group of related hardware units or programs or both. **9** a major group of geological strata (*the Devonian system*). □ **get a thing out of one's system** *colloq.* be rid of a preoccupation or anxiety.

sys·tem·at·ic /sístəmátik/ *adj.* **1** done or conceived according to a plan or system. **2** regular; deliberate. □□ **sys·tem·at·i·cal·ly** *adv.* **sys·tem·a·tist** /sístəmətist/ *n.*

sys·tem·at·ics /sístəmátiks/ *n.pl.* (usu. treated as *sing*) the study or a system of classification; taxonomy.

sys·tem·a·tize /sístəmətīz/ *v.tr.* **1** make systematic. **2** devise a system for. □□ **sys·tem·a·ti·za·tion** *n.* **sys·tem·a·tiz·er** *n.*

sys·tem·ic /sistémik/ *adj.* **1** *Physiol.* of or concerning the whole body. **2** (of an insecticide, etc.) entering the plant via the roots or shoots and passing through the tissues. □□ **sys·tem·i·cal·ly** *adv.*

sys·tems a·nal·y·sis *n.* the analysis of a complex process or operation in order to improve its efficiency, esp. by applying a computer system.

sys·to·le /sístəlee/ *n. Physiol.* the contraction of the heart, when blood is pumped into the arteries (cf. DIASTOLE). □□ **sys·tol·ic** /sistólik/ *adj.*

bone

cartilage

synovial fluid

synovial membrane

joint capsule

SYNOVIAL MEMBRANE
IN A HUMAN SYNOVIAL JOINT

S

T

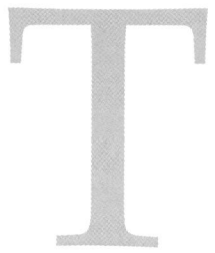

TABARD: KNIGHT WEARING A TABARD

T /tee/ *n.* (also **t**) (*pl.* **Ts** or **T's**) **1** the twentieth letter of the alphabet. **2** a T-shaped thing (esp. *attrib.*: *T-joint*). □ **to a T** exactly; to perfection.

't *pron. contr.* of IT[1] (*'tis*).

Ta *symb. Chem.* the element tantalum.

tab[1] /tab/ *n. & v.* ● *n.* **1** a small flap or strip of material attached for grasping, fastening, or hanging up, or for identification. **2** *colloq.* a bill or check. **3** a small or drawn-aside stage curtain. ● *v.tr.* (**tabbed, tabbing**) provide with a tab or tabs. □ **keep tabs on** *colloq.* have under observation.

tab[2] /tab/ *n.* **1 a** a device on a typewriter for advancing to a sequence of set positions in tabular work. **b** a programmable key on a computer keyboard that moves the cursor forward a designated number of spaces. **2** = TABULATOR 3.

tab·ard /tábərd/ *n.* **1** a herald's official coat emblazoned with the arms of his master. **2** a woman's or girl's sleeveless jerkin. **3** *hist.* ◄ a knight's short emblazoned garment worn over armor.

tabard
heraldic arms
armor

Ta·bas·co /təbáskō/ *n. Trademark* a pungent pepper sauce made from the fruit of *Capsicum frutescens.*

tab·bou·leh /təbōōlə, -lee/ *n.* an Arabic vegetable salad made with cracked wheat.

tab·by /tábee/ *n.* (*pl.* **-ies**) **1** (in full **tabby cat**) **a** a gray, orange, or brownish cat mottled or streaked with dark stripes. ▷ CAT. **b** any domestic cat, esp female. **2** a kind of watered silk. **3** a plain weave.

tab·er·nac·le /tábərnakəl/ *n.* **1** *hist.* a tent used as a sanctuary for the Ark of the Covenant by the Israelites during the Exodus. **2** *Eccl.* a canopied niche or receptacle esp. for the Eucharistic elements. **3** a place of worship, esp. in some Christian denominations.

ta·bla /táablə, túb-/ *n. Ind. Mus.* a pair of small drums played with the hands. ▷ PERCUSSION

tab·la·ture /táblǝchǝr/ *n. Mus.* an early form of notation indicating fingering (esp. in playing the lute), rhythm, and features other than notes.

ta·ble /táybǝl/ *n. & v.* ● *n.* **1** a piece of furniture with a flat top and one or more legs, providing a level surface for eating, writing, or working at, playing games on, etc. **2** a flat surface serving a specified purpose (*altar table; bird table*). **3 a** food provided in a household (*keeps a good table*). **b** a group seated at a table for dinner, etc. **4 a** a set of facts or figures systematically displayed, esp. in columns (*a table of contents*). **b** matter contained in this. **c** = MULTIPLICATION TABLE. **5** a flat surface for working on or for machinery to operate on. **6** a slab of wood or stone, etc. bearing an inscription. **7** = TABLELAND. ● *v.tr.* **1** postpone consideration of (a matter). **2** *Brit.* bring forward for discussion or consideration at a meeting. □ **on the table** offered for discussion. **turn the tables** (often foll. by *on*) reverse one's relations (with), esp. by turning an inferior into a superior position. **under the table** *colloq.* **1** drunk. **2** (esp. of a payment) covertly; secretly.

tab·leau /tablō, táblō/ *n.* (*pl.* **tableaux** /-lōz/) a picturesque presentation.

ta·ble·cloth /táybǝlklawth, -kloth/ *n.* a cloth spread over the top of a table, esp. for meals.

table d'hôte /táabǝl dôt, táablə/ *n.* a meal consisting of a set menu at a fixed price, esp. in a hotel (cf. À LA CARTE).

ta·ble knife *n.* a knife for use at meals, esp. in eating a main course.

ta·ble·land /táybǝl-land/ *n.* an extensive elevated region with a level surface; a plateau.

ta·ble man·ners *n.pl.* decorum or correct behavior while eating.

ta·ble·spoon /táybǝlspōōn/ *n.* **1** a large spoon for serving food. **2** an amount held by this. **3** a unit of measure equal to ½ fl. oz. or 15 ml. □□ **ta·ble·spoon·ful** *n.* (*pl.* **-fuls**).

tab·let /táblit/ *n.* **1** a small measured and compressed amount of a substance, esp. of a medicine or drug. ▷ MEDICINE. **2** a small flat piece of soap, etc. **3** ▶ a flat slab of stone or wood, esp. for display or an inscription. **4** a writing pad.

ta·ble ten·nis *n.* ◄ an indoor game based on tennis, played with paddles and a ball bounced on a table divided by a net.

TABLE TENNIS PADDLE AND BALL

ta·ble·top /táybǝltop/ *n.* **1** the top or surface of a table. **2** (*attrib.*) that can be placed or used on a tabletop.

ta·ble·ware /táybǝlwair/ *n.* dishes, plates, utensils, glasses, napkins, etc., for use at mealtimes.

tab·loid /tábloyd/ *n. & adj.* ● *n.* **1** a newspaper, usu. popular in style with bold headlines and large photographs, having pages of half size. **2** anything in a compressed or concentrated form. ● *adj.* printed on newsprint and folded once lengthwise so as to be read like a magazine.

ta·boo /təbōō, ta-/ *n., adj., & v.* (also **ta·bu**) ● *n.* (*pl.* **taboos** or **tabus**) **1** a system or the act of setting a person or thing apart as sacred or accursed. **2** a prohibition or restriction imposed by social custom. ● *adj.* **1** avoided or prohibited, esp. by social custom (*taboo words*). **2** designated as sacred and prohibited. ● *v.tr.* (**taboos, tabooed** or **tabus, tabued**) **1** put under taboo. **2** exclude or prohibit by authority or social influence.

ta·bor /táybǝr/ *n. hist.* ◄ a small drum, esp. one used to accompany a pipe.

ta·bu var. of TABOO.

tab·u·lar /tábyǝlǝr/ *adj.* **1** of or arranged in tables or lists. **2** broad and flat like a table. **3** (of a crystal) having two broad flat faces. **4** formed in thin plates. □□ **tab·u·lar·ly** *adv.*

stick
hanging strap
skin

TABOR: MEDIEVAL TABOR AND DRUMSTICK

cuneiform inscription

TABLET SHOWING BABYLONIAN VIEW OF THE WORLD

ocean
Babylon

tab·u·late /tábyǝlayt/ *v.tr.* arrange (figures or facts) in tabular form. □□ **tab·u·la·tion** /-láyshǝn/ *n.*

tab·u·la·tor /tábyǝlaytǝr/ *n.* **1** a person or thing that tabulates. **2** = TAB[2] 1. **3** *Computing* a machine that produces lists or tables from a data storage medium such as punched cards.

tach *n. colloq.* = TACHOMETER.

tach·ism /táshizǝm/ *n.* (also **ta·chisme**) a form of action painting with dabs of color arranged randomly to evoke a subconscious feeling.

tacho- /tákō/ *comb. form* speed.

tach·o·graph /tákǝgraf/ *n.* a device used esp. in heavy trucks and buses, etc., for automatically recording speed and travel time.

ta·chom·e·ter /təkómitǝr, ta-/ *n.* an instrument for measuring the rate of rotation of a shaft and hence the speed of an engine or the speed or velocity of a vehicle. ▷ INSTRUMENT PANEL

tachy- /tákee/ *comb. form* swift.

tach·y·car·di·a /tákikáardeeǝ/ *n. Med.* an abnormally rapid heart rate.

ta·chym·e·ter /təkímitǝr, ta-/ *n.* **1** *Surveying* an instrument used to locate points rapidly. **2** a speed indicator.

ta·chy·on /tákeeon/ *n. Physics* a hypothetical particle that travels faster than light.

tac·it /tásit/ *adj.* understood or implied without being stated (*tacit consent*). □□ **tac·it·ly** *adv.*

tac·i·turn /tásitǝrn/ *adj.* reserved in speech; saying little; uncommunicative. □□ **tac·i·tur·ni·ty** /-tɔ́rnitee/ *n.* **tac·i·turn·ly** *adv.*

tack[1] /tak/ *n. & v.* ● *n.* **1** a small sharp broad-headed nail. **2** a pin used to attach papers, etc., to a bulletin board or other surface. **3** a long stitch used in fastening fabrics, etc., lightly or temporarily together. **4 a** the direction in which a ship moves as determined by the position of its sails and regarded in terms of the direction of the wind (*starboard tack*). **b** a temporary change of direction in sailing to take advantage of a side wind, etc. **5** a course of action or policy (*try another tack*). **6** a sticky condition of varnish, etc. ● *v.* **1** *tr.* (often foll. by *down*, etc.) fasten with tacks. **2** *tr.* stitch (pieces of cloth, etc.) lightly together. **3** *tr.* (foll. by *to, on*) annex (a thing). **4** *intr.* **a** change a ship's course by turning its head to the wind (cf. WEAR[2]). **b** make a series of tacks. **5** *intr.* change one's conduct or policy, etc. □□ **tack·er** *n.*

tack[2] /tak/ *n.* the saddle, bridle, etc., of a horse.

tack[3] /tak/ *n. colloq.* cheap or shoddy material; kitsch.

tack·le /tákǝl/ *n. & v.* ● *n.* **1** equipment for a task or sport (*fishing tackle*). **2** a mechanism, esp. of ropes, pulley blocks, hooks, etc., for lifting weights, managing sails, etc. (*block and tackle*). ▷ RIGGING. **3** a windlass with its ropes and hooks. **4** an act of tackling in football, etc. **5** *Football* **a** the position next to the end of the forward line. **b** the player in this position. ● *v.tr.* **1** try to deal with (a problem or difficulty). **2** grapple with or try to overcome (an opponent). **3** enter into discussion with. **4** *Football* obstruct or seize and stop (a player running with the ball). **5** secure by means of a tackle. □□ **tack·ler** *n.* **tack·ling** *n.*

tack·le block *n.* ▶ a pulley over which a rope runs.

tack·y[1] /tákee/ *adj.* (**tackier, tackiest**) (of glue or paint, etc.) still slightly sticky after application. □□ **tack·i·ness** *n.*

tack·y[2] /tákee/ *adj.* (**tackier, tackiest**) *colloq.* showing poor taste or quality. □□ **tack·i·ly** *adv.* **tack·i·ness** *n.*

ta·co /táakō/ *n.* (*pl.* **-os**) a tortilla filled with meat, cheese, lettuce, tomatoes, etc.

pulley

TACKLE BLOCK USED TO HOIST SAILS ON A SHIP

T

tact /takt/ *n.* **1** adroitness in dealing with others or with difficulties arising from personal feeling. **2** intuitive perception of the right thing to do or say.

tact·ful /táktfŏŏl/ *adj.* having or showing tact. □□ **tact·ful·ly** *adv.* **tact·ful·ness** *n.*

tac·tic /táktik/ *n.* **1** a tactical maneuver. **2** = TACTICS.

tac·ti·cal /táktikəl/ *adj.* **1** of, relating to, or constituting tactics (*a tactical retreat*). **2** (of bombing or weapons) done or for use in immediate support of military or naval operations (opp. STRATEGIC). **3** adroitly planning or planned. □□ **tac·ti·cal·ly** *adv.*

tac·tics /táktiks/ *n.pl.* **1** (also treated as *sing.*) the art of disposing armed forces esp. in contact with an enemy (cf. STRATEGY). **2** the plans and means adopted in carrying out a scheme or achieving some end. □□ **tac·ti·cian** /taktíshən/ *n.*

tac·tile /táktəl, -tīl/ *adj.* **1** of or connected with the sense of touch. **2** perceived by touch. **3** tangible. □□ **tac·til·i·ty** /-tílitee/ *n.*

tact·less /táktlis/ *adj.* having or showing no tact. □□ **tact·less·ly** *adv.* **tact·less·ness** *n.*

tad /tad/ *n. colloq.* a small amount (often used adverbially: *a tad salty*).

tad·pole /tádpōl/ *n.* ◄ a larva of an amphibian, esp. a frog, toad, or newt, in its aquatic stage and breathing through gills.

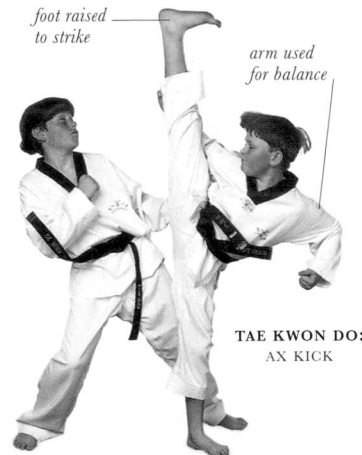

tail

gill

TADPOLES

tae·bo /tíbō/ *n. Trademark* an exercise system combining elements of aerobics and kick-boxing.

tae kwon do /tí kwón dố/ *n.* ▼ a Korean martial art similar to karate.

foot raised to strike

arm used for balance

TAE KWON DO: AX KICK

T

taf·fe·ta /táfitə/ *n.* a fine lustrous silk or silklike fabric.

taff·rail /táfrayl, -rəl/ *n. Naut.* a rail around a ship's stern.

taf·fy /táfee/ *n.* (*pl.* **-ies**) **1** a chewy boiled sugar or molasses candy. **2** insincere flattery.

taf·i·a /táfeeə/ *n. W.Ind.* rum distilled from molasses, etc.

tag[1] /tag/ *n. & v.* **1 a** a label, esp. one for tying on an object to show its address, price, etc. **b** *colloq.* an epithet or popular name serving to identify a person or thing. **2** a metal or plastic point at the end of a lace, etc., to assist insertion. **3** a loop at the back of a boot used in pulling it on. **4** a license plate of a motor vehicle. **5** a loose or ragged end of anything. **6** a ragged lock of wool on a sheep. **7** *Theatr.* a closing speech addressed to the audience. **8** a trite quotation or stock phrase. ● *v.tr.* (**tagged**, **tagging**) **1** provide with a tag or tags. **2** (often foll. by *on, onto*) join or attach. **3** esp. *Brit. colloq.* follow closely or trail behind. **4** *Computing* identify (an item of data) by its type for later retrieval. **5** label radioactively (see LABEL *v.* 3). **6** shear away tags from (sheep). **7** give a ticket to, as for a traffic or parking violation. □ **tag along** (often foll. by *with*) go along or accompany passively.

tag[2] /tag/ *n. & v.* ● *n.* **1** a children's game in which one chases the rest, and anyone who is caught then becomes the pursuer. **2** *Baseball* the act of tagging a runner. ● *v.tr.* (**tagged**, **tagging**) (often foll. by *out*) put (a runner) out by touching with the ball or with the hand holding the ball.

Ta·ga·log /təgáaləg, -lawg/ *n. & adj.* ● *n.* **1** a member of the principal people of the Philippine Islands. **2** the language of this people. ● *adj.* of or relating to this people or language.

ta·glia·tel·le /táalyətélee/ *n.* a form of pasta in narrow ribbons. ▷ PASTA

tag line *n. colloq.*, chiefly *N. Amer.* a catchphrase, slogan, or punchline.

ta·hi·ni /taahéenee/ *n.* a Middle Eastern paste or spread made from ground sesame seeds.

Ta·hi·tian /təhéeshən/ *n. & adj.* ● *n.* **1** a native or inhabitant of Tahiti in the S. Pacific. **2** the language of Tahiti. ● *adj.* of or relating to Tahiti or its people or language.

t'ai chi ch'uan /tí chee chwáan/ *n.* (also **t'ai chi**) ▼ a Chinese martial art and system of calisthenics consisting of sequences of very slow controlled movements.

right arm at shoulder level

palm turned inward

weight on right leg

T'AI CHI CH'UAN: LAST POSITION OF THE DESCENDING SINGLE WHIP MOVE

tai·ga /tígə/ *n.* coniferous forest lying between tundra and steppe, esp. in Siberia.

tail[1] /tayl/ *n. & v.* ● *n.* **1** the hindmost part of an animal, esp. when prolonged beyond the rest of the body. **2 a** a thing like a tail in form or position, esp. something extending downward or outward at an extremity. **b** the rear end of anything, e.g., of a procession. **c** a long train or line of people, vehicles, etc. **3 a** the rear part of an airplane, with the horizontal stabilizer and rudder, or of a rocket. **b** the rear part of a motor vehicle. **4** the luminous trail of particles following a comet. **5** the inferior or weaker part of anything, esp. in a sequence. **6 a** the part of a shirt below the waist. **b** the hanging part of the back of a coat. **7** (in *pl.*) *colloq.* **a** a tailcoat. **b** evening dress including this. **8** (in *pl.*) the reverse of a coin as a choice when tossing. **9** *colloq.* a person following or shadowing another. **10** an extra strip attached to the lower end of a kite. **11** the stem of a note in music. **12** the part of a letter (e.g., *y*) below the line. **13 a** the exposed end of a slate or tile in a roof. **b** the unexposed end of a brick or stone in a wall. **14 a** the buttocks. **b** *sl. offens.* a (usu. female) sexual partner. ● *v.* **1** *tr.* remove the stalks of (fruit). **2** *tr. &* (foll. by *after*) *intr. colloq.* shadow or follow closely. **3** *tr.* provide with a tail. **4** *tr.* dock the tail of (a lamb, etc.). **5** *tr.* (often foll. by *onto*) join (one thing to another). □ **on a person's tail** closely following a person. **tail back** *Brit.* (of traffic) form a tailback. **tail off** (or **away**) **1** become fewer, smaller, or fainter. **2** fall behind or away in a scattered line. **with one's tail between one's legs** in a state of dejection or humiliation. **with one's tail up** in good spirits; cheerful. □□ **tailed** *adj.* (also in *comb.*).

tail·less *adj.*

tail[2] /tayl/ *n. & adj. Law* ● *n.* limitation of ownership, esp. of an estate limited to a person and that person's heirs. ● *adj.* so limited (*estate tail; fee tail*).

tail·back /táylbak/ *n.* **1** *Football* on offense, a player positioned behind the quarterback. **2** *Brit.* a long line of traffic extending back from an obstruction.

tail·coat /táylkōt/ *n.* ◄ a man's morning or evening coat with a long skirt divided at the back into tails and cut away in front, worn as part of formal dress.

tailcoat

TAILCOAT: EARLY 20TH-CENTURY TAILCOAT

tail cov·ert *n.* any of the feathers covering the base of a bird's tail feathers.

tail end *n.* **1** the hindmost or lowest or last part. **2** = TAIL[1] 5.

tail·gate /táylgayt/ *n. & v.* ● *n.* **1 a** a hinged or removable flap at the rear of a station wagon, truck, etc. **b** ▼ the tail door of a station wagon or hatchback. **2** the lower end of a canal lock. ● *v. colloq.* **1** *intr.* drive too closely behind another vehicle. **2** *tr.* follow (a vehicle) too closely. □□ **tail·gat·er** *n.*

tail·light /táyllīt/ *n.* a usu. red light at the rear of a train, motor vehicle, or bicycle.

tai·lor /táylər/ *n. & v.* ● *n.* a maker of clothes, esp. one who makes men's outer garments to measure. ● *v.* **1** *tr.* make (clothes) as a tailor. **2** *tr.* make or adapt for a special purpose. **3** *intr.* work as or be a tailor. **4** *tr.* (esp. as **tailored** *adj.*) make clothes for. **5** *tr.* (as **tailored** *adj.*) = TAILOR-MADE. □□ **tai·lor·ing** *n.*

tai·lor·bird *n.* any small Asian etc. warbler of the genus *Orthotomus* that stitches leaves together to form a nest.

tailgate

TAILGATE ON A HATCHBACK

tai·lored /táylərd/ *adj.* (of clothing) well or closely fitted.

tai·lor-made *adj. & n.* ● *adj.* **1** (of clothing) made to order by a tailor. **2** made or suited for a particular purpose (*a job tailor-made for me*). ● *n.* a tailor-made garment.

tai·lor's twist *n.* a fine strong silk thread used by tailors.

tail·piece /táylpees/ *n.* **1** an appendage at the rear of anything. **2** the final part of a thing. **3** a decoration in a blank space at the end of a chapter, etc., in a book.

tail·pipe /táylpīp/ *n.* the rear section of the exhaust pipe of a motor vehicle.

tail·plane /táylplayn/ *n. Brit.* = HORIZONTAL STABILIZER. ▷ AIRCRAFT

tail·spin /táylspin/ *n. & v.* ● *n.* **1** a spin (see SPIN *n.* 2) by an aircraft with the tail spiraling. **2** a state of chaos or panic. ● *v.intr.* (**-spinning**; *past* and *past part.* **-spun**) perform a tailspin.

tail·stock /táylstok/ *n.* the adjustable part of a lathe holding the fixed spindle.

tail wind *n.* a wind blowing in the direction of travel of a vehicle or aircraft, etc.

taint /taynt/ *n. & v.* ● *n.* **1** a spot or trace of decay, infection, or some bad quality. **2** a corrupt condition or infection. ● *v.* **1** *tr.* affect with a taint. **2** *tr.* (foll. by *with*) affect slightly. □□ **taint·less** *adj.*

tai·pan[1] /típán/ *n.* the head of a foreign business in China.

tai·pan[2] /típan/ *n.* a large venomous Australian snake, *Oxyuranus scutellatus*.

take /tayk/ *v.* & *n.* ● *v.* (**took** /to͝ok/; **taken** /táykən/) **1** *tr.* lay hold of; get into one's hands. **2** *tr.* acquire; get possession of; capture, earn, or win. **3** *tr.* get the use of by purchase or formal agreement (*take an apartment*). **4** *tr.* (in a recipe) avail oneself of; use. **5** *tr.* use as a means of transport (*took a taxi*). **6** *tr.* regularly buy or subscribe to (a particular newspaper or periodical, etc.). **7** *tr.* obtain after fulfilling the required conditions (*take a degree*). **8** *tr.* occupy (*take a chair*). **9** *tr.* make use of (*take precautions*). **10** *tr.* consume as food or medicine (*took the pills*). **11** *intr.* **a** be successful or effective (*the inoculation did not take*). **b** (of a plant, seed, etc.) begin to grow. **12** *tr.* **a** require or use up (*will only take a minute*; *these things take time*). **b** accommodate; have room for (*the elevator takes three people*). **13** *tr.* cause to come or go with one; convey (*take the book home*; *the bus will take you all the way*). **14** *tr.* **a** remove; dispossess a person of (*someone has taken my pen*). **b** destroy; annihilate (*took her own life*). **c** (often foll. by *for*) *sl.* defraud; swindle. **15** *tr.* catch or be infected with (fire or fever, etc.). **16** *tr.* **a** experience or be affected by (*take fright*; *take pleasure*). **b** give play to (*take comfort*). **c** exert (*take courage*; *take no notice*). **d** exact; get (*take revenge*). **17** *tr.* find out and note (a name and address; a person's temperature, etc.) by inquiry or measurement. **18** *tr.* grasp mentally; understand (*I take your point*). **19** *tr.* treat or regard in a specified way (*took the news calmly*). **20** *tr.* (foll. by *for* or *to be*) regard as being (*do you take me for an idiot?*). **21** *tr.* **a** accept (*take the offer*). **b** submit to (*take a joke*; *take no nonsense*). **22** *tr.* choose or assume (*took a job*; *took responsibility*). **23** *tr.* derive (*takes its name from the inventor*). **24** *tr.* (foll. by *from*) subtract (*take 3 from 9*). **25** *tr.* execute, make, or undertake; perform or effect (*take notes*; *take an oath*; *take a decision*). **26** *tr.* occupy or engage oneself in; indulge in; enjoy (*take a rest*; *take exercise*; *take a vacation*). **27** *tr.* conduct (*took the early class*). **28** *tr.* deal with in a certain way (*took the corner too fast*). **29** *tr.* **a** teach or be taught (a subject). **b** be examined in (a subject). **30** *tr.* make (a photograph) with a camera; photograph (a person or thing). **31** *tr.* use as an instance (*let us take Napoleon*). **32** *tr.* *Gram.* have or require as part of the appropriate construction (*this verb takes an object*). **33** *tr.* have sexual intercourse with (a woman). **34** *tr.* (in *passive*; foll. by *by*, *with*) be attracted or charmed by. **35** *tr.* *Baseball* to refrain from swinging at (a pitch). ● *n.* **1** an amount taken or caught in one session or attempt, etc. **2** a scene or sequence of film or videotape photographed continuously at one time. **3** money received by a business, esp. money received at a theater for seats. □ **be taken ill** become ill, esp. suddenly. **have what it takes** *colloq.* have the necessary qualities, etc., for success. **on the take** *sl.* accepting bribes. **take account of** see ACCOUNT. **take action** see ACTION. **take advantage of** see ADVANTAGE. **take after** resemble (esp. a parent or ancestor). **take aim** see AIM. **take apart 1** dismantle. **2** *colloq.* beat or defeat. **take aside** see ASIDE. **take as read** esp. *Brit.* accept without reading or discussing. **take away 1** remove or carry elsewhere. **2** subtract. **3** *Brit.* buy (food, etc.) at a store or restaurant for eating elsewhere. **take back 1** retract (a statement). **2** convey (a person or thing) to his or her or its original position. **3** carry (a person) in thought to a past time. **4** *Printing* transfer to the previous line. **take a bath** *sl.* lose money. **take the cake** *colloq.* be the most remarkable. **take care of** see CARE. **take a chance**, etc., see CHANCE. **take down 1** write down (spoken words). **2** remove (a structure) by separating it into pieces. **3** humiliate. **take effect** see EFFECT. **take five (or ten)** take a break, esp. from work. **take for granted** see GRANT. **take fright** see FRIGHT. **take from** diminish; weaken; detract from. **take heart** be encouraged. **take the heat** endure criticism, punishment, etc. **take hold** see HOLD[1]. **take home** earn. **take in 1** accept as a boarder, etc. **2** undertake (work) at home. **3** make (a garment, etc.) smaller. **4** understand (*did you take that in?*). **5** cheat (*managed to take them all in*). **6** include or comprise. **7** *colloq.* visit (a place) on the way to another (*shall we take in the White House*). **8** furl (a sail). **9** regularly buy (a newspaper, etc.). **10** attend; watch (*take in a show*). **11** arrest. **take in hand 1** undertake; start doing or dealing with. **2** undertake the control or reform of (a person). **take into account** see ACCOUNT. **take it 1** (often foll. by *that* + clause) assume (*I take it that you have finished*). **2** see TAKE *v.* 19. **take it easy** see EASY. **take it from me** (or **take my word for it**) I can assure you. **take it ill** resent it. **take it into one's head** see HEAD. **take it on one** (or **oneself**) (foll. by *to* + infin.) venture or presume. **take it or leave it** (esp. in *imper.*) an expression of indifference or impatience about another's decision after making an offer. **take it out of 1** exhaust the strength of. **2** penalize. **take it out on** relieve one's frustration by attacking or treating harshly. **take one's leave of** see LEAVE[2]. **take a lot of** (or **some**) **doing** be hard to do. **take a person's name in vain** see VAIN. **take off 1 a** remove (clothing) from one's or another's body. **b** remove or lead away. **2** deduct (part of an amount). **3** depart, esp. hastily (*took off in a fast car*). **4** *colloq.* mimic humorously. **5** jump from the ground. **6** become airborne. **7** (of a scheme, enterprise, etc.) become successful or popular. **8** have (a period) away from work. **take oneself off** go away. **take on 1** undertake (work, a responsibility, etc.). **2** engage (an employee). **3** be willing or ready to meet (an adversary in a sport, an argument, etc., esp. a stronger one). **4** acquire (a new meaning, etc.). **5** esp. *Brit. colloq.* show strong emotion. **take orders** see ORDER. **take out 1** remove from within a place; extract. **2** escort on an outing. **3** get (a license or summons, etc.) issued. **4** buy (food) at a store, restaurant, etc., for eating elsewhere. **5** *Bridge* remove (a partner or a partner's call) from a suit by bidding a different one or no trump. **6** murder or destroy. **take a person out of himself** or **herself** make a person forget his or her worries. **take over 1** succeed to the management or ownership of. **2** take control. **3** *Printing* transfer to the next line. **take part** see PART. **take place** see PLACE. **take shape** assume a distinct form; develop into something definite. **take sick** *colloq.* be taken ill. **take sides** see SIDE. **take stock** see STOCK. **take that!** an exclamation accompanying a blow, etc. **take one's time** not hurry. **take to 1** begin or fall into the habit of (*took to drink*). **2** have recourse to. **3** adapt oneself to. **4** form a liking for. **5** make for (*took to the hills*). **take to heart** see HEART. **take to one's heels** see HEEL[1]. **take to pieces** see PIECE. **take the trouble** see TROUBLE. **take up 1** become interested or engaged in (a pursuit, a cause, etc.). **2** adopt as a protégé. **3** occupy (time or space). **4** begin (residence, etc.). **5** resume after an interruption. **6** interrupt or question (a speaker). **7** accept (an offer, etc.). **8** shorten (a garment). **9** lift up. **10** absorb (*sponges take up water*). **11** take (a person) into a vehicle. **12** pursue (a matter, etc.) further. **take a person up on** accept (a person's offer, etc.). **take up with** begin to associate with. □□ **tak·a·ble** *adj.* (also **take·a·ble**).

TALC

take-home pay *n.* the pay received by an employee after the deduction of taxes, etc.

take·off /táykawf/ *n.* **1** the act of becoming airborne. **2** *colloq.* an act of mimicking. **3** a place from which one jumps.

take-out *adj.* & *n.* ● *adj.* (of food) bought at a shop or restaurant for eating elsewhere. ● *n.* food sold for consumption elsewhere.

take·o·ver /táykōvər/ *n.* the assumption of control (esp. of a business); the buying out of one company by another.

tak·er /táykər/ *n.* **1** a person who takes a bet. **2** a person who accepts an offer.

tak·ing /táyking/ *adj.* & *n.* ● *adj.* **1** attractive or captivating. **2** *archaic* catching or infectious. ● *n.* (in *pl.*) esp. *Brit.* an amount of money taken in business. □□ **tak·ing·ly** *adv.* **tak·ing·ness** *n.*

talc /talk/ *n.* **1** talcum powder. **2** ◄ any crystalline form of magnesium silicate that occurs in soft flat plates, usu. white or pale green in color and used as a lubricant, etc. □□ **talc·ose** *adj.* **talc·ous** *adj.* **talc·y** *adj.* (in sense 1).

tal·cum /tálkəm/ *n.* **1** = TALC. **2** (in full **talcum powder**) powdered talc for toilet and cosmetic use, usu. perfumed.

tale /tayl/ *n.* **1** a narrative or story, esp. fictitious and imaginatively treated. **2** a report of an alleged fact, often malicious or in breach of confidence (*all sorts of tales will get about*). **3** a lie; a falsehood.

tale·bear·er /táylbairər/ *n.* a person who maliciously gossips or reveals secrets. □□ **tale·bear·ing** *n.* & *adj.*

tal·ent /tálənt/ *n.* **1** a special aptitude or faculty. **2** high mental ability. **3** a person or persons of talent (*is a real talent*; *plenty of local talent*). **4** an ancient weight and unit of currency, esp. among the Greeks. □□ **tal·ent·ed** *adj.* **tal·ent·less** *adj.*

tal·ent scout *n.* a person looking for talented performers, esp. in sports and entertainment.

tale·tell·er /táyltelər/ *n.* **1** a person who tells stories. **2** a person who spreads malicious reports.

ta·li *pl.* of TALUS.

tal·i·pes /tálipeez/ *n.* *Med.* = CLUBFOOT.

tal·is·man /tálizmən/ *n.* (*pl.* **tal·is·mans**) **1** an object, esp. an inscribed ring or stone, supposed to be endowed with magic powers esp. of averting evil from or bringing good luck to its holder. **2** ► a charm or amulet; a thing supposed to be capable of working wonders. □□ **tal·is·man·ic** /-mánik/ *adj.*

TALISMAN: MAORI TALISMAN

talk /tawk/ *v.* & *n.* ● *v.* **1** *intr.* (often foll. by *to*, *with*) converse or communicate ideas by spoken words. **2** *intr.* have the power of speech. **3** *intr.* (foll. by *about*) **a** have as the subject of discussion. **b** (in *imper.*) *colloq.* as an emphatic statement (*talk about expense! It cost me $50*). **4** *tr.* express or utter in words; discuss (*you are talking nonsense*; *talked football all day*). **5** *tr.* use (a language) in speech (*is talking Spanish*). **6** *intr.* (foll. by *at*) address pompously. **7** *tr.* (usu. foll. by *into*, *out of*) bring into a specified condition, etc., by talking (*talked himself hoarse*; *how did you talk them into it?*; *talked them out of the difficulty*). **8** *intr.* reveal (esp. secret) information; betray secrets. **9** *intr.* gossip (*people are beginning to talk*). **10** *intr.* have influence (*money talks*). **11** *intr.* communicate by radio. ● *n.* **1** conversation or talking. **2** a particular mode of speech (*baby talk*). **3** an informal address or lecture. **4 a** rumor or gossip (*there is talk of a merger*). **b** its theme (*their success was the talk of the town*). **c** empty words; verbiage (*mere talk*). **5** (often in *pl.*) extended discussions or negotiations. □ **know what one is talking about** be expert or authoritative. **now you're talking** *colloq.* I like what you say, suggest, etc. **talk back 1** reply defiantly. **2** respond on a two-way radio system. **talk big** *colloq.* talk boastfully. **talk down** denigrate; belittle. **talk down to** speak patronizingly or condescendingly to. **talk a person down 1** silence a person by greater loudness or persistence. **2** bring (a pilot or aircraft) to landing by radio instructions from the ground. **talk of 1** discuss or mention. **2** (often foll. by verbal noun) express some intention of (*talked of moving to Dallas*). **talk of the town** what is being talked about generally. **talk over** discuss at length. **talk a person over** (or **around**) gain agreement or compliance from a person by talking. **talk shop** talk, esp. tediously or inopportunely, about one's occupation, business, etc. **talk tall** boast. **talk**

T

through one's hat *colloq*. **1** exaggerate. **2** talk wildly or nonsensically. **talk to** reprove or scold (a person). **talk turkey** see TURKEY. **talk up** discuss (a subject) in order to arouse interest in it. **you can't** (or **can**) **talk** *colloq*. a reproof that the person addressed is just as culpable, etc., in the matter at issue. □□ **talk·er** *n*.

talk·a·thon /táwkathon/ *n. colloq*. a prolonged session of talking or discussion.

talk·a·tive /táwkətiv/ *adj*. fond of or given to talking. □□ **talk·a·tive·ly** *adv*. **talk·a·tive·ness** *n*.

talk·back /táwkbak/ *n*. (often *attrib*.) a system of two-way communication by loudspeaker.

talk·fest /táwkfest/ *n. colloq.*, chiefly *N. Amer*. a lengthy discussion or debate, esp. as part of a television chat show.

talk·ie /táwkee/ *n*. esp. *hist*. a movie with a soundtrack, as distinct from a silent movie.

talk·ing /táwking/ *adj. & v. ● adj*. **1** that talks. **2** having the power of speech (*a talking parrot*). **3** expressive (*talking eyes*). ● *n*. in senses of TALK *v*.

talking book *n*. a recorded reading of a book, esp. for the blind.

talking head *n. colloq*. a commentator, etc., on television, speaking to the camera and viewed in close-up.

talk·ing-to *n. colloq*. a reproof or reprimand (*gave them a good talking-to*).

talk show *n*. a television or radio program featuring discussion of topical issues.

tall /tawl/ *adj. & adv. ● adj*. **1** of more than average height. **2** of a specified height (*looks about six feet tall*). **3** higher than the surrounding objects (*a tall building*). **4** *colloq*. extravagant or excessive (*a tall story; tall talk*). ● *adv*. as if tall; proudly; in a tall or extravagant way (*sit tall*). □□ **tall·ish** *adj*. **tall·ness** *n*.

tall·boy /táwlboy/ *n*. a tall chest of drawers sometimes in lower and upper sections or mounted on legs.

tal·lith /táális, taaléet/ *n*. a scarf worn by Jewish men esp. at prayer.

tall order *n*. an exorbitant or unreasonable demand.

tal·low /tálō/ *n*. the harder kinds of (esp. animal) fat melted down for use in making candles, soap, etc. □□ **tal·low·y** *adj*.

tall ship *n*. a sailing ship with more than one high mast.

tal·ly /tálee/ *n. & v. ● n*. (*pl*. **-ies**) **1** the reckoning of a debt or score. **2** a total score or amount. **3 a** a mark registering a fixed number of objects delivered or received. **b** such a number as a unit. **4** *hist*. **a** ▶ a piece of wood scored across with notches for the items of an account and then split into halves, each party keeping this way. **b** an account kept in this way. **5** a ticket or label for identification. **6** a corresponding thing, counterpart, or duplicate. ● *v*. (**-ies**, **-ied**) (often foll. by *with*) **1** *intr*. agree or correspond. **2** *tr*. record or reckon by tally. □□ **tal·li·er** *n*.

TALLY: HALF OF A TALLY STICK

notches

tal·ly·ho /táleehó/ *int., n., & v. ● int*. a huntsman's cry to the hounds on sighting a fox. ● *n*. (*pl*. **-hos**) an utterance of this. ● *v*. (**-hoes**, **-hoed**) *intr*. utter a cry of "tallyho."

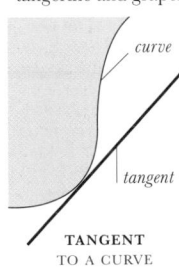

talon

toe

TALONS
ON THE FOOT OF
A SPARROWHAWK

Tal·mud /táalmood, -məd, tál-/ *n*. the body of Jewish civil and ceremonial law and legend comprising the Mishnah and the Gemara. □□ **Tal·mud·ic** /-moodik, myoo-/ *adj*. **Tal·mud·i·cal** *adj*. **Tal·mud·ist** *n*.

tal·on /tálən/ *n*. **1** ◀ a claw, esp. of a bird of prey. ▷ RAPTOR. **2** the cards left after the deal in a card game. **3** an ogee molding. □□ **tal·oned** *adj*. (also in *comb*.).

ta·lus /táyləs, tál-/ *n*. (*pl*. **tali** /-lī/) *Anat*. the ankle bone supporting the tibia. Also called **astragalus**.

ta·ma·le /təmáalee/ *n*. a Mexican food of seasoned meat and corn flour steamed or baked in corn husks.

ta·man·du·a /təmándyōṓə/ *n*. any small Central and S. American arboreal anteater of the genus *Tamandua*, with a prehensile tail.

tam·a·rack /támərak/ *n*. **1** an American larch, *Larix laricina*. **2** the wood from this.

ta·ma·ril·lo /támərílō, -réeyō/ *n*. (*pl*. **-os**) a South American shrub, *Cyphomandra betacea*, with egg-shaped red fruit.

tam·a·rin /támərin/ *n*. any S. American usu. insectivorous monkey of the genus *Saguinus*, having hairy crests and mustaches.

tam·a·rind /támərind/ *n*. **1** a tropical evergreen tree, *Tamarindus indica*. **2** the fruit of this, containing an acid pulp used as food and in making drinks.

TAMARISK
(*Tamarix ramosissima* 'Pink Cascade')

tam·a·risk /támərisk/ *n*. ◀ any shrub of the genus *Tamarix*, usu. with long slender branches and small pink or white flowers, that thrives by the sea.

tam·bour /támboor/ *n. & v. ● n*. **1** a drum. **2** a circular frame for holding fabric taut while it is being embroidered. ● *v.tr*. decorate or embroider on a tambour.

tam·bour·a /tambóorə/ *n. Mus*. an E. Indian stringed instrument used as a drone.

tam·bou·rine /támbəréen/ *n*. a percussion instrument consisting of a hoop with a parchment stretched over one side and jingling disks in slots around the hoop. ▷ ORCHESTRA, PERCUSSION. □□ **tam·bou·rin·ist** *n*.

tame /taym/ *adj. & v. ● adj*. **1** (of an animal) domesticated; not wild or shy. **2** insipid; lacking spirit or interest; dull (*tame acquiescence*). **3** (of a person) amenable and available. **4 a** (of land) cultivated. **b** (of a plant) produced by cultivation. ● *v.tr*. **1** make tame; domesticate; break in. **2** subdue; curb; humble; break the spirit of. □□ **tame·ly** *adv*. **tame·ness** *n*. **tam·er** *n*. (also in *comb*.).

Tam·il /támil, túm-, taá-/ *n. & adj. ● n*. **1** a member of a Dravidian people inhabiting South India and Sri Lanka. **2** the language of this people. ● *adj*. of this people or their language. □□ **Ta·mil·ian** /-míleeən/ *adj*.

Tam·ma·ny /támənee/ *n*. (also **Tam·ma·ny Hall**) **1** a corrupt political organization or group. **2** corrupt political activities. □□ **Tam·ma·ny·ism** *n*.

tam·my /támee/ *n*. (*pl*. **-ies**) = TAM-O'-SHANTER.

tam-o'-shan·ter /táməshántər/ *n*. a round woolen or cloth cap of Scottish origin fitting closely around the brows but large and full above.

ta·mox·i·fen /təmóksifen/ *n*. a synthetic drug used to treat breast cancer and infertility in women.

tamp /tamp/ *v.tr*. ram down (concrete, pipe tobacco, etc.). □□ **tam·per** *n*. **tamp·ing** *n*.

tam·per /támpər/ *v.intr*. (foll. by *with*) meddle with or make unauthorized changes in. □□ **tam·per·er** *n*. **tam·per-proof** *adj*.

tam·pi·on /támpeeən/ *n*. (also **tom·pi·on** /tóm-/) **1** a wooden stopper for the muzzle of a gun. **2** a plug, e.g., for the top of an organ pipe.

tam·pon /támpon/ *n*. a plug of soft material used to absorb fluid, esp. one inserted into the vagina during menstruation.

tam-tam /támtam/ *n*. a large metal gong.

tan¹ /tan/ *n., adj., & v. ● n*. **1** a brown skin color resulting from exposure to ultraviolet light. **2** a yellowish-brown color. **3** = TANBARK. ● *adj*. yellowish-brown. ● *v*. (**tanned, tanning**) **1** *tr. & intr*. make or become brown by exposure to ultraviolet light. **2** *tr*. convert (rawhide) into leather by soaking in a liquid containing tannic acid or by the use of mineral salts, etc. **3** *tr. sl*. beat; whip. □□ **tan·na·ble** *adj*. **tan·ning** *n*. **tan·nish** *adj*.

tan² /tan/ *abbr*. tangent.

tan·a·ger /tánəjər/ *n*. ▶ any small American bird of the subfamily Thraupidae, the male usu. having brightly-colored plumage.

TANAGER: SCARLET
TANAGER
(*Piranga olivacea*)

tan·bark /tánbaark/ *n*. **1** the bark of oak and other trees, used to obtain tannin. **2** bark, esp. of oak, bruised and used to tan hides.

tan·dem /tándəm/ *n*. **1** ▼ a bicycle or tricycle with two or more seats one behind another. **2 a** a group of two persons or machines, etc., with one behind or following the other. **b** (in full **tandem trailer**) a truck hauling two or more trailers. □ **in tandem** one behind another.

TANDEM: OFF-ROAD
TANDEM

tan·door /tándoor/ *n*. a clay oven.

tan·door·i /tandóoree/ *n*. food cooked over charcoal in a tandoor (often *attrib*.: *tandoori chicken*).

Tang /tang/ *n*. **1** a dynasty ruling China 618–*c*.906. **2** (*attrib*.) designating art and artifacts of this period.

tang¹ /tang/ *n*. **1** a strong taste or flavor or smell. **2 a** a characteristic quality. **b** a trace; a slight hint of some quality, ingredient, etc.

tang² /tang/ *v. & n. ● v.tr. & intr*. ring, clang; sound loudly. ● *n*. a tanging sound.

tan·ge·lo /tánjəlō/ *n*. (*pl*. **-os**) a hybrid of the tangerine and grapefruit.

tan·gent /tánjənt/ *n. & adj. ● n*. **1** ◀ a straight line, curve, or surface that meets another curve or curved surface at a point, but if extended does not intersect it at that point. **2** the ratio of the sides opposite and adjacent to an angle in a right-angled triangle. ● *adj*. **1** (of a line or surface) that is a tangent. **2** touching. □ **on a tangent** diverging from a previous course of action or thought, etc. (*go off on a tangent*). □□ **tan·gen·cy** *n*.

curve

tangent

TANGENT
TO A CURVE

tan·gen·tial /tanjénshəl/ *adj*. **1** of or along a tangent. **2** divergent. **3** peripheral. □□ **tan·gen·tial·ly** *adv*.

tan·ge·rine /tánjəréen/ *n*. **1** a small sweet orange-colored citrus fruit with a thin skin; a mandarin. ▷ CITRUS FRUIT. **2** a deep orange-yellow color.

T

TANK

Tanks were first used in battle in 1916 but were greatly improved in World War II (1939–45). Although their basic design has changed little since then, technological advances have meant they now carry a more sophisticated and diverse array of weapons.

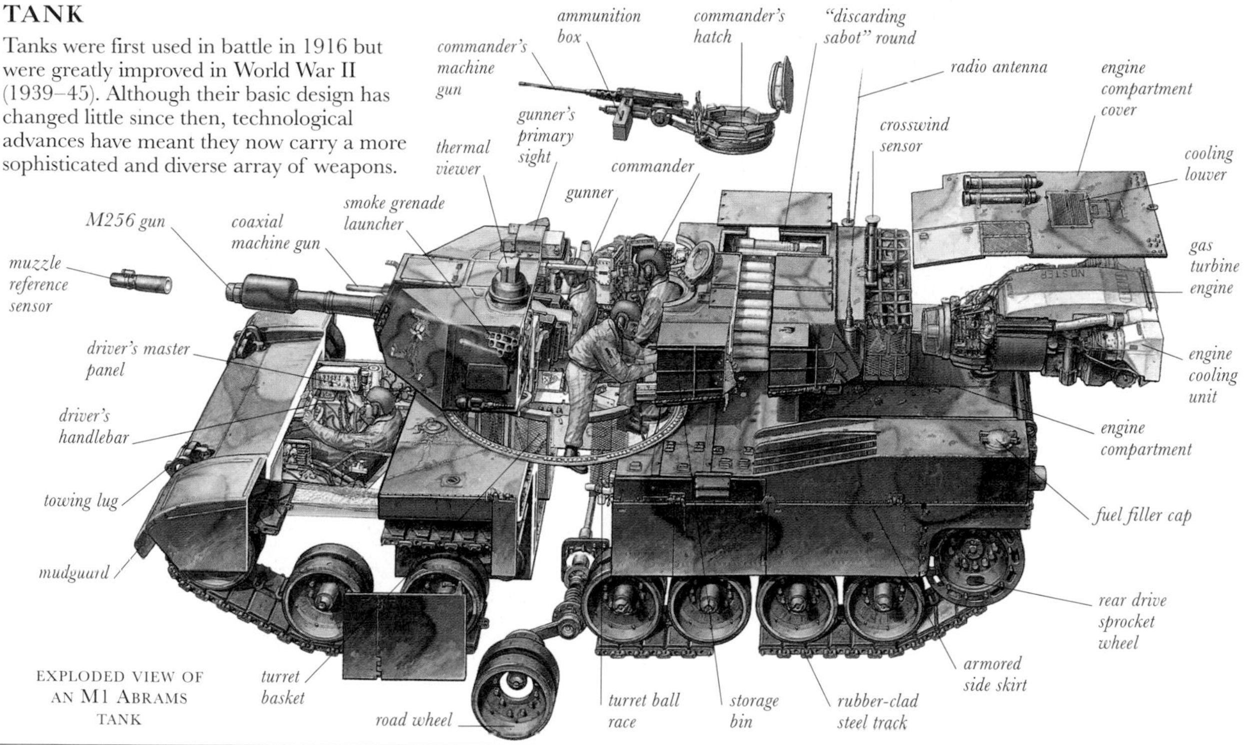

ammunition box
commander's machine gun
commander's hatch
"discarding sabot" round
radio antenna
engine compartment cover
crosswind sensor
cooling louver
gunner's primary sight
thermal viewer
commander
gunner
gas turbine engine
M256 gun
coaxial machine gun
smoke grenade launcher
muzzle reference sensor
driver's master panel
engine cooling unit
driver's handlebar
engine compartment
towing lug
fuel filler cap
mudguard
rear drive sprocket wheel
armored side skirt
EXPLODED VIEW OF AN M1 ABRAMS TANK
turret basket
road wheel
turret ball race
storage bin
rubber-clad steel track

tan·gi·ble /tánjəbəl/ *adj.* **1** perceptible by touch. **2** definite; clearly intelligible; not elusive or visionary (*tangible proof*). □□ **tan·gi·bil·i·ty** *n.* **tan·gi·ble·ness** *n.* **tan·gi·bly** *adv.*

tan·gle /tánggəl/ *v. & n.* ● *v.* **1 a** *tr.* intertwine (threads or hairs, etc.) in a confused mass; entangle. **b** *intr.* become tangled. **2** *intr.* (foll. by *with*) *colloq.* become involved (esp. in conflict or argument) with (*don't tangle with me*). **3** *tr.* complicate (*a tangled affair*). ● *n.* **1** a confused mass of intertwined threads, etc. **2** a confused or complicated state (*be in a tangle; a love tangle*).

tan·gly /tánglee/ *adj.* (**tanglier, tangliest**) tangled.

tan·go /tánggō/ *n. & v.* ● *n.* (*pl.* **-os**) **1** a slow S. American ballroom dance. **2** the music for this. ● *v.intr.* (**-oes, -oed**) dance the tango.

tan·gram /tánggram/ *n.* a Chinese puzzle square cut into seven pieces to be combined into various figures.

tang·y /tángee/ *adj.* (**tangier, tangiest**) having a strong usu. spicy tang. □□ **tang·i·ness** *n.*

tanh /tansh, tanáych/ *abbr.* hyperbolic tangent.

tank /tangk/ *n. & v.* ● *n.* **1** a large receptacle or storage chamber usu. for liquid or gas. **2** ▲ a heavy armored fighting vehicle carrying guns and moving on a tracked carriage. **3** a container for the fuel supply in a motor vehicle. **4** the part of a locomotive tender containing water for the boiler. **5** a reservoir. **6** *colloq.* a prison cell or holding cell. **7** = TANK TOP. ● *v.* (usu. foll. by *up*) **1** *tr.* store or place in a tank. **2** *tr.* fill the tank of (a vehicle, etc.) with fuel. **3** *intr. & colloq. tr.* (in *passive*) drink heavily; become drunk. □□ **tank·ful** *n.* (*pl.* **-fuls**). **tank·less** *adj.*

tan·kard /tángkərd/ *n.* **1** ◄ a tall mug with a handle and sometimes a hinged lid, of silver or pewter, and esp. for beer. **2** the contents of or an amount held by a tankard.

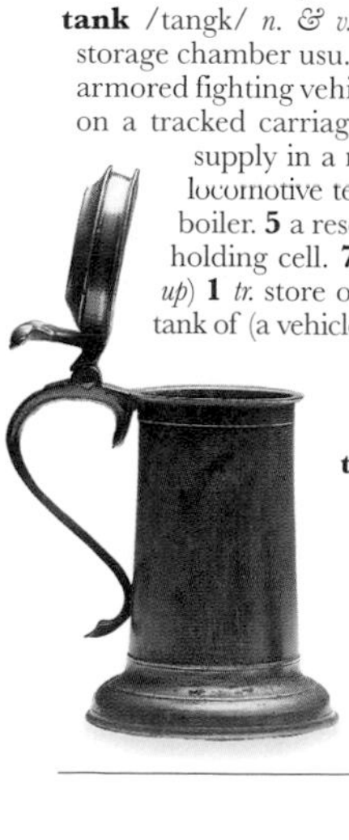

TANKARD: LIDDED PEWTER TANKARD

tank·er /tángkər/ *n.* a ship, aircraft, or truck for carrying liquids or gases in bulk.

tank top *n.* a sleeveless, close-fitting, collarless upper garment.

tan·ner /tánər/ *n.* a person who tans hides.

tan·ner·y /tánəree/ *n.* (*pl.* **-ies**) a place where hides are tanned.

tan·nic /tánik/ *adj.* **1** of or produced from tanbark. **2** (of wine) astringent; tasting of tannin. □□ **tan·nate** /-nayt/ *n.*

tan·nic ac·id *n.* a natural organic compound of a yellowish color used as a mordant and astringent.

tan·nin /tánin/ *n.* any of a group of complex organic compounds found in certain tree barks and oak galls, used in leather production and ink manufacture.

tan·nish see TAN[1].

tan·sy /tánzee/ *n.* (*pl.* **-ies**) ► any plant of the genus *Tanacetum*, esp. *T. vulgare* with yellow buttonlike flowers and aromatic leaves.

tan·ta·lite /tántəlīt/ *n.* a rare dense black mineral, the principal source of the element tantalum.

tan·ta·lize /tántəlīz/ *v.tr.* **1** torment or tease by the sight or promise of what is unobtainable. **2** raise and then dash the hopes of; torment with disappointment. □□ **tan·ta·li·za·tion** *n.* **tan·ta·liz·er** *n.* **tan·ta·liz·ing·ly** *adv.*

tan·ta·lum /tántələm/ *n. Chem.* a rare hard white metallic element occurring naturally in tantalite, resistant to heat and the action of acids, and used in surgery and for electronic components. ¶ Symb.: **Ta**. □□ **tan·tal·ic** /-tálik/ *adj.*

TANSY (*Tanacetum vulgare*)

tan·ta·lus /tántələs/ *n.* **1** *Brit.* a stand in which liquor decanters may be locked up but visible. **2** a wood ibis, *Mycteria americana*.

tan·ta·mount /tántəmownt/ *predic.adj.* (foll. by *to*) equivalent to (*was tantamount to a denial*).

tan·tra /tántrə, tún-/ *n.* any of a class of Hindu or Buddhist mystical and magical writings.

tan·trum /tántrəm/ *n.* an outburst of bad temper or petulance (*threw a tantrum*).

Taoi·seach /teeshokh/ *n.* the Prime Minister of the Irish Republic.

Tao·ism /tówizəm, dów-/ *n.* a Chinese philosophy advocating humility and religious piety. □□ **Tao·ist** /-ist/ *n.* **Tao·is·tic** /-istik/ *adj.*

Taos /tows/ *n.* **1 a** a N. American people native to New Mexico. **2** the language of this people.

tap[1] /tap/ *n. & v.* ● *n.* **1** = FAUCET. **2** an act of tapping a telephone, etc.; also, the device used for this. **3** *Brit.* a taproom. **4** an instrument for cutting the thread of a female screw. ● *v.tr.* (**tapped, tapping**) **1 a** provide (a cask) with a tap. **b** let out (a liquid) by means of, or as if by means of, a tap. **2** draw sap from (a tree) by cutting into it. **3 a** obtain information or supplies or resources from. **b** establish communication or trade with. **4** connect a listening device to (a telephone or telegraph line, etc.) to listen to a call or transmission. **5** cut a female screw thread in. □ **on tap 1** ready to be drawn off by tap. **2** *colloq.* ready for immediate use; freely available. □□ **tap·less** *adj.* **tap·pa·ble** *adj.*

tap[2] /tap/ *v. & n.* ● *v.* (**tapped, tapping**) **1** *intr.* (foll. by *at, on*) strike a gentle but audible blow. **2** *tr.* strike lightly (*tapped me on the shoulder*). **3** *tr.* (foll. by *against*, etc.) cause (a thing) to strike lightly. **4** select as if by tapping (*tapped for membership*). **5** *intr.* = TAP-DANCE. ● *n.* **1 a** a light blow; a rap. **b** the sound of this (*heard a tap at the door*). **2 a** = TAP DANCE. (*goes to tap classes*). **b** ► a piece of metal attached to the toe and heel of a tap dancer's shoe to make the tapping sound. **3** (in *pl.*, usu. treated as *sing.*) **a** a bugle call for lights to be put out in army quarters. **b** a similar call played at a military funeral. □□ **tap dancer** *n.* **tap dancing** *n.* **tap·per** *n.*

toe tap
heel tap

TAP SHOES (UNDERSIDE)

T

TAPE

Recording tape is a thin plastic strip coated with tiny magnetic grains. It is usually carried on spools inside a cassette. On a blank tape, these grains are randomly ordered. When recording sound, a tape head on a tape recorder arranges the grains to represent the sound. To erase the tape, an erase head disrupts the pattern.

erase protection hole

tape spool

outer case

pinch roller

capstan

arranged magnetic grains

direction of tape movement

randomly arranged magnetic grains

feed roller

pressure pad

tape head

erase head

TAPE CASSETTE RECORDING FROM A TAPE HEAD

---

ta·pa /táapə/ *n.* (usu. *pl.*) a Spanish-style appetizer typically served with wine or beer.

tap dance *n.* a form of display dance performed wearing shoes fitted with metal taps, with rhythmical tapping of the toes and heels. □□ **tap-dance** *v.intr.*

tape /tayp/ *n. & v.* ● *n.* **1** a narrow strip of woven material for tying up, fastening, etc. **2 a** a strip of material stretched across the finishing line of a race. **b** a similar strip for marking off an area or forming a notional barrier. **3** (in full **adhesive tape**) a strip of opaque or transparent paper or plastic, etc., esp. coated with adhesive for fastening, sticking, masking, insulating, etc. **4 a** = MAGNETIC TAPE. **b** ▲ a tape recording or tape cassette. **5** = TAPE MEASURE. ● *v.tr.* **1 a** tie up or join, etc., with tape. **b** apply tape to. **2** (foll. by *off*) seal or mark off an area or thing with tape. **3** record on magnetic tape. **4** measure with tape. □ **break the tape** win a race. **on tape** recorded on magnetic tape. □□ **tape·a·ble** *adj.* (esp. in sense 3 of *v.*). **tape·less** *adj.* **tape·like** *adj.*

tape deck *n.* an audio device for playing and usu. recording magnetic tape.

tape meas·ure *n.* a strip of tape or thin flexible metal marked for measuring lengths.

tap·er /táypər/ *n. & v.* ● *n.* **1** a wick coated with wax, etc., for lighting fires, candles, etc. **2** a slender candle. ● *v.* (often foll. by *off*) **1** *intr. & tr.* diminish or reduce in thickness toward one end. **2** *tr. & intr.* make or become gradually less.

tape re·cord·er *n.* apparatus for recording sounds on magnetic tape and afterwards reproducing them. □□ **tape-re·cord** *v.tr.* **tape re·cord·ing** *n.*

tap·es·try /tápistree/ *n.* (*pl.* **-ies**) **1 a** a thick textile fabric in which colored weft threads are woven to form pictures or designs. **b** embroidery imitating this, usu. in wools on canvas. **c** ▶ a piece of such embroidery. **2** events or circumstances, etc., compared with a tapestry in being intricate, interwoven, etc. (*life's rich tapestry*). □□ **tap·es·tried** *adj.*

ta·pe·tum /təpéetəm/ *n.* a membranous layer of the choroid membrane in the eyes of certain mammals, e.g., cats.

tape·worm /táypwərm/ *n.* a parasitic intestinal flatworm. ▷ PARASITE

tap·i·o·ca /tápeeṓkə/ *n.* a starchy substance in hard white grains obtained from cassava and used for puddings, etc.

TAPESTRY CUSHION

---

ta·pir /táypər, təpéer/ *n.* ▼ any nocturnal hoofed mammal of the genus *Tapirus*, native to Central and S. America and Malaysia, having a short flexible protruding snout.

flexible snout

TAPIR: MALAYAN TAPIR (*Tapirus indicus*)

ta·pote·ment /təpṓtmənt/ *n. Med.* rapid and repeated striking of the body as massage treatment.

tap·per see TAP[2].

tap·pet /tápit/ *n.* a lever or projecting part used in machinery to give intermittent motion, often in conjunction with a cam.

tap·room /táprōōm, -rŏŏm/ *n.* a room in which alcoholic drinks are available on tap; a barroom.

tap·root *n.* ▶ a tapering root growing vertically downward.

tap·ster /tápstər/ *n.* a bartender.

tap wa·ter *n.* water from a piped supply.

tar[1] /taar/ *n. & v.* ● *n.* **1** a dark, thick, flammable liquid distilled from wood or coal, etc., and used as a preservative of wood and iron, in making roads, as an antiseptic, etc. **2** a similar substance formed in the combustion of tobacco, etc. ● *v.tr.* (**tarred**, **tarring**) cover with tar. □ **tar and feather** smear with tar and then cover with feathers as a punishment. **tarred with the same brush** having the same faults.

tap-root

TAPROOT OF A CARROT

tar[2] /taar/ *n. colloq.* a sailor.

tar·a·did·dle /tárədid'l/ *n.* (also **tar·ra·did·dle**) *colloq.* **1** a petty lie. **2** pretentious nonsense.

tar·an·tel·la /tárəntélə/ *n.* (also **tar·an·telle** /-tél/) **1** a rapid whirling S. Italian dance. **2** the music for this.

---

ta·ran·tu·la /təránchələ/ *n.* **1** any large, hairy, tropical spider of the family Theraphosidae. ▷ SPIDER. **2** a large black spider, *Lycosa tarentula*, whose bite was formerly held to cause dancing mania.

tar·boosh /taarbōōsh/ *n.* a cap like a fez, sometimes worn as part of a turban.

tar·di·grade /táardigrayd/ *n. & adj.* ● *n.* any minute freshwater animal of the phylum Tardigrada, having a short plump body and four pairs of short legs. Also called **water bear**. ● *adj.* of or relating to this phylum.

tar·dy /táardee/ *adj.* (**tardier**, **tardiest**) **1** slow to act or come or happen. **2** delaying or delayed beyond the right or expected time. □□ **tar·di·ly** *adv.* **tar·di·ness** *n.*

tare[1] /tair/ *n.* **1** vetch, esp. as a weed or fodder. **2** (in *pl.*) *Bibl.* an injurious grain weed (Matt. 13:2–30).

tare[2] /tair/ *n.* **1** an allowance made for the weight of the packing or wrapping around goods. **2** the weight of a motor vehicle without its fuel or load.

targe /taarj/ *n. archaic* = TARGET *n.* 5.

tar·get /táargit/ *n. & v.* ● *n.* **1** ▶ a mark or point fired or aimed at, esp. a round or rectangular object marked with concentric circles. **2** a person or thing aimed at, or exposed to gunfire, etc. (*they were an easy target*). **3** (*also attrib.*) an objective or result aimed at (*our export targets; target date*). **4** a person or thing against whom criticism, abuse, etc., is or may be directed. **5** *archaic* a shield or buckler, esp. a small round one. ● *v.tr.* (**targeted**, **targeting**) **1** identify or single out (a person or thing) as an object of attention or attack. **2** aim or direct (*missiles targeted on major cities*). □□ **tar·get·a·ble** *adj.*

scores

bullet holes

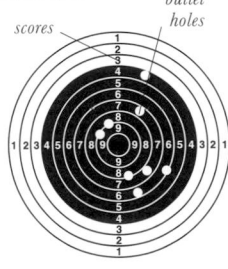

TARGET USED IN FREE PISTOL SHOOTING

tar·iff /tárif/ *n.* **1** a table of fixed charges. **2** a duty on a particular class of goods.

tar·la·tan /táarlət'n/ *n.* a thin, stiff, open-weave muslin.

Tar·mac /táarmak/ *n. & v.* ● *n. Trademark* **1** = TARMACADAM. **2** a surface made of this, e.g., a runway. ● *v.tr.* (**tarmac**) (**tarmacked**, **tarmacking**) apply tarmacadam to.

tar·mac·ad·am /táarməkádəm/ *n.* a material of stone or slag bound with tar, used in paving roads, etc.

tarn /taarn/ *n.* a small mountain lake. ▷ LAKE

tar·na·tion /taarnáyshən/ *int. esp. dial. sl.* damn; blast.

tar·nish /táarnish/ *v. & n.* ● *v.* **1** *tr.* lessen or destroy the luster of (metal, etc.). **2** *tr.* impair (one's reputation, etc.). **3** *intr.* (of metal, etc.) lose luster. ● *n.* **1 a** a loss of luster. **b** a film of color formed on an exposed surface of a mineral or metal. **2** a blemish; a stain. □□ **tar·nish·a·ble** *adj.*

ta·ro /taarṓ, táarṓ/ *n.* (*pl.* **-os**) a tropical plant of the arum family, *Colocasia esculenta*, with tuberous roots used as food. Also called **eddo**.

ta·rot /táarṓ, tərṓ/ *n.* **1** (in *sing.* or *pl.*) **a** any of several games played with a pack of cards having five suits, the last of which is a set of permanent trump. **b** ▲ a similar pack used in fortune-telling. **2 a** any of the trump cards. **b** any of the cards from a fortune-telling pack.

tarp /taarp/ *n. colloq.* tarpaulin.

tar·pan /táarpan/ *n.* an extinct N. European primitive wild horse.

tar·pau·lin /taarpáwlin, táarpə-/ *n.* **1** heavy-duty waterproof cloth, esp. of tarred canvas or heavy plastic. **2** a sheet or covering of this.

tar·pon /táarpon/ *n.* **1** a large silvery tropical Atlantic fish. **2** a similar fish of the Pacific ocean.

T

TAROT

Most tarot decks have 78 cards. These are divided into the major and the minor arcanas. The major arcana consists of 22 unique cards, such as The Lovers and The Moon. The minor arcana consists of four suits: pentacles, swords, cups, and wands, each suit having four face cards and ten number cards.

EXAMPLES OF TAROT CARDS

THE LOVERS

THE MOON

PENTACLES

SWORDS

CUPS

WANDS

FACE CARD

NUMBER CARD

TARRAGON
(*Artemisia dracunculus*)

tar·ra·gon /tárəgən/ *n.* ◀ a bushy herb, *Artemisia dracunculus*, with leaves used to flavor salads, stuffings, vinegar, etc.

tar·ry[1] /táaree/ *adj.* (**tarrier**, **tarriest**) of or like or smeared with tar. □□ **tar·ri·ness** *n.*

tar·ry[2] /táree/ *v.intr.* (**-ies**, **-ied**) *archaic* or *literary* linger; stay; wait.

tar·sal /táarsəl/ *adj. & n.* ● *adj.* of or relating to the bones in the ankle. ● *n.* a tarsal bone. ▷ ANKLE, SKELETON

tar·si *pl.* of TARSUS.

tar·si·er /táarseeər/ *n.* any small, large-eyed, arboreal, nocturnal primate of the genus *Tarsius*, native to Borneo, the Philippines, etc., with a long tail and long hind legs.

tar·sus /táarsəs/ *n.* (*pl.* **tarsi** /-sī,

TARTAN

For hundreds of years, the clans of the Scottish Highlands have expressed their strong individual identities through the wearing of tartans. Each clan has developed its own distinctive styles and colors.

EXAMPLES OF TARTANS

THE MACLEODS

THE STEWARTS

THE FRASERS

THE GORDONS

-see/) *Anat.* the group of bones forming the ankle and upper foot.

tart[1] /taart/ *n.* **1** a small pie containing jam, fruit, etc., having no upper crust. **2** a pie with a fruit or sweet filling. □□ **tart·let** *n.*

tart[2] /taart/ *n. & v.* ● *n. sl.* **1** a prostitute; a promiscuous woman. **2** *sl. offens.* a girl or woman. ● *v.* (foll. by *up*) *colloq.* **1** *tr.* (usu. *refl.*) dress (oneself or a thing) up, esp. flashily or gaudily. **2** *intr.* dress up gaudily.

tart[3] /taart/ *adj.* **1** sharp or acid in taste. **2** (of a remark, etc.) cutting; bitter. □□ **tart·ly** *adv.* **tart·ness** *n.*

tar·tan /táart'n/ *n.* **1** ◀ a pattern of colored stripes crossing at right angles, esp. the distinctive plaid worn by the Scottish Highlanders to denote their clan. **2** woolen fabric woven in this pattern (often *attrib.: a tartan scarf*)

Tar·tar /táartər/ *n. & adj.* (also **Ta·tar** /táatər/ except in sense 2 of *n.*) ● *n.* **1 a** a member of a group of Central Asian peoples including Mongols and Turks. **b** the Turkic language of these peoples. **2** (**tartar**) a violent-tempered or intractable person. ● *adj.* **1** of or relating to the Tartars. **2** of or relating to Central Asia east of the Caspian Sea. □□ **Tar·tar·i·an** /-táireeən/ *adj.*

tar·tar /táartər/ *n.* **1** a hard deposit of saliva, calcium phosphate, etc., that forms on the teeth. **2** a deposit of acid potassium tartrate that forms a hard crust on the inside of a cask during the fermentation of wine. □□ **tar·tar·ize** *v.tr.*

tar·tar·ic ac·id /taartárik/ *n.* a natural carboxylic acid found esp. in unripe grapes, used in baking powders and as a food additive.

tar·tar sauce *n.* (also **tar·tare sauce** or **sauce tar·tare**) a sauce of mayonnaise and chopped pickles, capers, etc.

tar·trate /táartrayt/ *n. Chem.* any salt or ester of tartaric acid.

tar·tra·zine /táartrəzeen/ *n. Chem.* a brilliant yellow dye derived from tartaric acid and used to color food, drugs, and cosmetics.

tart·y /táartee/ *adj. colloq.* (**tartier**, **tartiest**) (esp. of a woman) vulgar; gaudy; promiscuous. □□ **tart·i·ly** *adv.* **tart·i·ness** *n.*

Tar·zan /táarzən, -zan/ *n.* a man of great agility and powerful physique.

task /task/ *n. & v.* ● *n.* a piece of work to be done or undertaken. ● *v.tr.* **1** make great demands on (a person's powers, etc.). **2** assign a task to. □ **take to task** rebuke; scold.

task force *n.* (also **task group**) **1** *Mil.* an armed force organized for a special operation. **2** a unit specially organized for a task.

---

task·mas·ter /táskmastər/ *n.* (*fem.* **taskmistress** /-mistris/) a person who imposes a task or burden, esp. regularly or severely.

Tas·ma·ni·an /tazmáyneeən/ *n. & adj.* ● *n.* **1** a native of Tasmania, an island state of Australia. **2** a person of Tasmanian descent. ● *adj.* of or relating to Tasmania.

Tas·ma·ni·an dev·il *n.* a nocturnal carnivorous marsupial similar to a badger, *Sarcophilus harrisii*, now found only in Tasmania.

Tass /tas, taas/ *n. hist.* the official news agency of the former Soviet Union.

tass /tas/ *n. Sc.* **1** a cup or small goblet. **2** a small draft of brandy, etc.

tas·sel /tásəl/ *n.* **1** a tuft of loosely hanging threads or cords, etc., attached for decoration to a cushion, scarf, cap, etc. ▷ SHAKO. **2** a tassellike head of some plants, esp. a flowerhead with prominent stamens at the top of a corn stalk.

tassie /tásee/ *n. Sc.* a small cup.

taste /tayst/ *n. & v.* ● *n.* **1 a** the sensation characteristic of a soluble substance caused in the mouth and throat by contact with that substance (*disliked the taste of garlic*). **b** the faculty of perceiving this sensation (*was bitter to the taste*). **2 a** a small portion of food or drink taken as a sample. **b** a hint or touch of some ingredient or quality. **3** a slight experience (*a taste of success*). **4** (often foll. by *for*) a liking or predilection (*has expensive tastes; is not to my taste*). **5 a** aesthetic discernment in art, literature, conduct, etc., esp. of a specified kind (*a person of taste; dresses in poor taste*). **b** a style or manner based on this (*a novel of Victorian taste*). ● *v.* **1** *tr.* sample or test the flavor of (food, etc.) by taking it into the mouth. **2** *tr.* (also *absol.*) perceive the flavor of (*could taste the lemon; cannot taste with a cold*). **3** *tr.* (esp. with *neg.*) eat or drink a small portion of (*had not tasted food for days*). **4** *tr.* have experience of (*had never tasted failure*). **5** *intr.* (often foll. by *of*) have a specified flavor (*tastes bitter; tastes of onions*). □ **a bad** (or **bitter**, etc.) **taste** *colloq.* a strong feeling of regret or unease. **to taste** in the amount needed for a pleasing result (*add salt and pepper to taste*). □□ **taste·a·ble** *adj.*

taste bud *n.* ▼ any of the cells or nerve endings on the surface of the tongue by which things are tasted. ▷ TONGUE

TASTE BUD

A taste bud consists of receptor cells and supporting cells in the epithelium of the tongue. When a substance is chewed, it mixes with saliva, which enters the taste pores. This stimulates taste hairs on the receptor cells, which, in turn, transmit an impulse to the brain via nerve fibers.

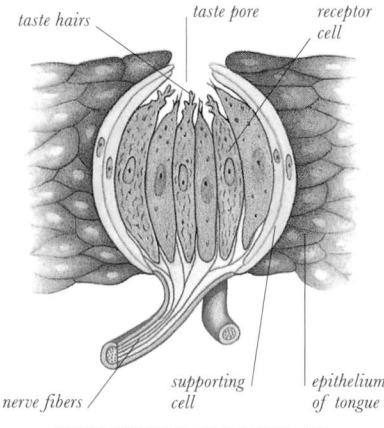

taste hairs

taste pore

receptor cell

nerve fibers

supporting cell

epithelium of tongue

CROSS SECTION OF A TASTE BUD

T

taste·ful /táystfŏŏl/ adj. having, or done in, good taste. □□ **taste·ful·ly** adv. **taste·ful·ness** n.

taste·less /táystlis/ adj. **1** lacking flavor. **2** having, or done in, bad taste. □□ **taste·less·ly** adv. **taste·less·ness** n.

tast·er /táystər/ n. **1** a person employed to test food or drink by tasting it, esp. for quality or hist. to detect poisoning. **2** a small cup used by a wine taster. **3** an instrument for extracting a small sample from within a cheese. **4** a sample of food, drink, etc.

tast·ing /táysting/ n. a gathering at which food or drink (esp. wine) is tasted and evaluated.

tast·y /táystee/ adj. (**tastier**, **tastiest**) (of food) pleasing in flavor; appetizing. □□ **tast·i·ly** adv. **tast·i·ness** n.

tat[1] /tat/ n. Brit. colloq. **1 a** a tatty or tasteless clothes; worthless goods. **b** rubbish; junk. **2** a shabby person.

tat[2] /tat/ v. (**tatted**, **tatting**) **1** intr. do tatting. **2** tr. make by tatting.

tat[3] see TIT[2].

ta-ta /taatáa/ int. joc. good-bye.

Ta·tar var. of TARTAR.

ta·ter /táytər/ n. sl. = POTATO.

tat·ter /tátər/ n. (usu. in pl.) a rag; an irregularly torn piece of cloth or paper, etc. □ **in tatters 1** ragged and torn. **2** colloq. (of a negotiation, argument, etc.) ruined; demolished.

tat·tered /tátərd/ adj. in tatters; ragged.

tat·ter·sall /tátərsawl/ n. (in full **tattersall check**) a fabric with a pattern of colored lines forming squares like a tartan.

tat·ting /táting/ n. **1** ▼ a kind of knotted lace made by hand with a small shuttle and used as trim, etc. **2** the process of making this.

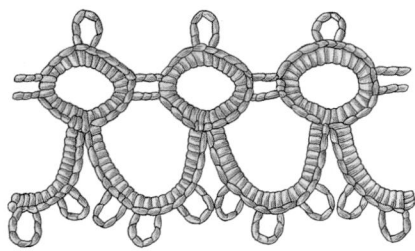

TATTING: CHAIN-AND-RING TATTING

tat·tle /tát'l/ v. & n. ● v. **1** intr. prattle; chatter; gossip idly; speak indiscreetly. **2** tr. utter (words) idly; reveal (secrets) ● n. gossip; idle or trivial talk. □□ **tat·tler** n.

tat·tle·tale /tát'ltayl/ n. one who tells tales or informs, esp. a child.

tat·too[1] /tatóŏ/ n. (pl. **tattoos**) **1** an evening drum or bugle signal recalling soldiers to their quarters. **2** an elaboration of this with music and marching, presented as an entertainment. **3** a rhythmic tapping or drumming.

tat·too[2] /tatóŏ/ v. & n. ● v.tr. (**tattoos**, **tattooed**) **1** mark (the skin) with an indelible design by puncturing it and inserting pigment. **2** make (a design) in this way. ● n. (pl. **tattoos**) a design made by tattooing. □□ **tat·too·er** n. **tat·too·ist** n.

tat·ty /tátee/ adj. (**tattier**, **tattiest**) esp. Brit. colloq. **1** tattered; worn and shabby. **2** inferior. **3** tawdry. □□ **tat·ti·ly** adv. **tat·ti·ness** n.

tau /tow, taw/ n. the nineteenth letter of the Greek alphabet (T, τ).

taught past and past part. of TEACH.

taunt /tawnt/ n. & v. ● n. a thing said in order to anger or wound a person. ● v.tr. **1** assail with taunts. **2** reproach (a person) contemptuously □□ **taunt·er** n. **taunt·ing·ly** adv.

taupe /tōp/ n. a gray with a tinge of another color, usu. brown.

tau·rine /táwreen, -rīn/ adj. of or like a bull; bullish.

Tau·rus /táwrəs/ n. **1** ► a constellation. **2 a** the second sign of the zodiac (the Bull). ▷ ZODIAC. **b** a person born under this sign. □□ **Tau·re·an** adj. & n.

taut /tawt/ adj. **1** (of a rope, muscles, etc.) tight; not slack. **2** (of nerves) tense. **3** (of a ship, etc.) in good order or condition. □□ **taut·en** v.tr. & intr. **taut·ly** adv. **taut·ness** n.

tauto- /táwtō/ comb. form the same.

tau·tog /tawtóg/ n. a fish, Tautoga onitis, found off the Atlantic coast of N. America, used as food.

tau·tol·o·gy /tawtóləjee/ n. (pl. **-ies**) the saying of the same thing twice in different words, esp. as a fault of style (e.g., arrived one after the other in succession). □□ **tau·to·log·ic** /-t'lójik/ adj. **tau·to·log·i·cal** adj. **tau·to·log·i·cal·ly** adv. **tau·tol·o·gist** n. **tau·tol·o·gize** v.intr. **tau·tol·o·gous** /-ləgəs/ adj.

tau·to·mer /táwtəmər/ n. Chem. a substance that exists as two mutually convertible isomers in equilibrium. □□ **tau·to·mer·ic** /-mérik/ adj. **tau·tom·er·ism** /-tómərizəm/ n.

tav·ern /távərn/ n. an inn or bar.

ta·ver·na /təvérnə/ n. a Greek eating house.

taw·dry /táwdree/ adj. & n. ● adj. (**tawdrier**, **tawdriest**) **1** showy but worthless. **2** overly ornamented; gaudy; vulgar. ● n. cheap or gaudy finery. □□ **taw·dri·ly** adv. **taw·dri·ness** n.

taw·ny /táwnee/ adj. (**tawnier**, **tawniest**) of an orangish or yellowish brown color. □□ **taw·ni·ness** n.

tax /taks/ n. & v. ● n. **1** a contribution to government revenue compulsorily levied on individuals, property, or businesses (often foll. by on: a tax on luxury goods). **2** (usu. foll. by on, upon) a strain or heavy demand; an oppressive or burdensome obligation. ● v.tr. **1** impose a tax on (persons or goods, etc.). **2** deduct tax from (income, etc.). **3** make heavy demands on (a person's powers or resources, etc.) (you really tax my patience). **4** (foll. by with) confront (a person) with a wrongdoing, etc. **5** call to account. **6** Law examine and assess (costs, etc.). □□ **tax·a·ble** adj. **tax·er** n. **tax·less** adj.

tax·a pl. of TAXON.

tax·a·tion /taksáyshən/ n. the imposition or payment of tax.

tax-de·duct·i·ble adj. (of expenditure) that may be paid out of income before the deduction of income tax.

tax e·va·sion n. the illegal nonpayment or underpayment of income tax.

tax-ex·empt adj. **1** exempt from taxes. **2** bearing tax-exempt interest.

tax ex·ile n. a person with a high taxable income who chooses to live in a country or area with low rates of taxation.

tax ha·ven n. a country, etc., where income tax is low.

tax·i /táksee/ n. & v. ● n. (pl. **taxis**) **1** (in full **taxi·cab**) an automobile licensed to carry passengers for a fee and usu. fitted with a taximeter. **2** a boat, airplane, etc., similarly used. ● v. (**taxis**, **taxied**, **taxiing** or **taxying**) **1 a** intr. (of an aircraft or pilot) move along the ground under the machine's own power before takeoff or after landing. **b** tr. cause (an aircraft) to taxi. **2** intr. & tr. go or convey in a taxi.

tax·i·der·my /táksidərmee/ n. the art of preparing, stuffing, and mounting the skins of animals with lifelike effect. □□ **tax·i·der·mal** /-dérməl/ adj. **tax·i·der·mic** /-dérmik/ adj. **tax·i·der·mist** n.

tax·i·me·ter /tákseemeetər/ n. an automatic device fitted to a taxi, recording the distance traveled and the fare payable.

tax·i stand n. (Brit. **taxi rank**) a place where taxis wait to be hired.

tax·man /táksman/ n. colloq. (pl. **-men**) an inspector or collector of taxes.

tax·on /táksən/ n. (pl. **taxa** /táksə/) any taxonomic group.

tax·on·o·my /taksónəmee/ n. **1** the science of the classification of living and extinct organisms. **2** the practice of this. □□ **tax·o·nom·ic** /-sənómik/ adj. **tax·o·nom·i·cal** /-sənómikəl/ adj. **tax·o·nom·i·cal·ly** /-sənómiklee/ adv. **tax·on·o·mist** n.

tax·pay·er /tákspayər/ n. a person who pays taxes.

tax re·turn n. a declaration of income for taxation purposes.

tax shel·ter n. a means of organizing business affairs, etc., to minimize payment of tax.

tay·ber·ry n. (pl. **-ies**) a dark red soft fruit produced by crossing a blackberry and a raspberry.

Aldebaran

TAURUS: FIGURE OF A BULL FORMED FROM THE STARS OF TAURUS

TB abbr. **1** tubercle bacillus. **2** tuberculosis.

Tb symb. Chem. the element terbium.

T-bar n. **1** (in full **T-bar lift**) a type of ski lift in the form of a series of inverted T-shaped bars for towing skiers uphill. **2** (often attrib.) a T-shaped fastening on a shoe or sandal.

T-bone n. a T-shaped bone, esp. in steak from the thin end of a loin.

tbs. abbr. (also **tbsp.**) tablespoon.

Tc symb. Chem. the element technetium.

T-cell n. a lymphocyte of a type produced or processed by the thymus gland and active in the immune response.

TD abbr. **1** touchdown. **2** Treasury Department.

Te symb. Chem. the element tellurium.

te var. of TI.

tea /tee/ n. **1 a** (in full **tea plant**) ◄ an evergreen shrub or small tree, Camellia sinensis, of India, China, etc. **b** ◄ its dried leaves. **2** a drink made by infusing tea leaves in boiling water. **3** a similar drink made from the leaves of other plants or from another substance (chamomile tea; beef tea). **4 a** Brit. a light afternoon meal consisting of tea, bread, cakes, etc. **b** a cooked evening meal. **5** an afternoon party or reception at which tea is served.

fresh leaves
dried leaves

TEA PLANT (Camellia sinensis)

tea bag n. a small porous bag of tea leaves for infusion.

tea ball n. a ball of perforated metal to hold tea leaves for infusion.

tea cad·dy n. Brit. a container for tea leaves.

tea·cake /téekayk/ n. a light, usu. sweet cake, cookie, etc., eaten at tea.

tea cer·e·mo·ny n. an elaborate Japanese ritual of serving and drinking tea, as an expression of Zen Buddhist philosophy.

teach /teech/ v.tr. (past and past part. **taught** /tawt/) **1 a** give systematic information to (a person) or about (a subject or skill). **b** (absol.) practice this professionally. **c** enable (a person) to do something by instruction and training (taught me how to dance). **2** advocate as a moral, etc., principle (my parents taught me tolerance). **3** (foll. by to + infin.) **a** induce (a person) by example or punishment to do or not to do a thing (that will teach you to sit still). **b** colloq. make (a person) disinclined to do a thing (I will teach you to interfere). □ **teach a person a lesson** see LESSON. **teach school** be a teacher in a school.

teach·a·ble /téechəbəl/ adj. **1** apt at learning. **2** (of

T

a subject) that can be taught. □□ **teach·a·bil·i·ty** /-bílitee/ *n.* **teach·a·ble·ness** *n.*

teach·er /téechər/ *n.* a person who teaches, esp. in a school. □□ **teach·er·ly** *adj.*

teach·ing /téeching/ *n.* **1** the profession of a teacher. **2** (often in *pl.*) what is taught; a doctrine.

teach·ing hos·pi·tal *n.* a hospital where medical students are taught.

tea co·zy *n.* a cover to keep a teapot warm.

tea·cup /téekup/ *n.* **1** a cup from which tea or other hot beverages are drunk. **2** an amount held by this, about 4 fl. oz. □□ **tea·cup·ful** *n.* (*pl.* **-fuls**).

teak /teek/ *n.* **1** a large deciduous tree, *Tectona grandis*, native to India and SE Asia. **2** its hard durable wood, used in shipbuilding and for furniture.

teal /teel/ *n.* (*pl.* same) **1** any of various small freshwater ducks of the genus *Anas*, esp. *A. crecca*. **2** a dark greenish blue color.

team /teem/ *n. & v.* ● *n.* **1** a set of players forming one side in a game, debate, etc. (*a hockey team*). **2** two or more persons working together. **3 a** a set of draft animals. **b** one animal or more in harness with a vehicle. ● *v.* **1** *intr. & tr.* (usu. foll. by *up*) join in a team or in common action (*decided to team up with them*). **2** *tr.* harness (horses, etc.) in a team. **3** *tr.* (foll. by *with*) match or coordinate (clothes).

team·mate /téemmayt/ *n.* a member of the same team or group.

team spir·it *n.* willingness to act as a member of a group rather than as an individual.

team·ster /téemstər/ *n.* **1 a** a truck driver. **b** a member of the Teamsters Union. **2** a driver of a team of animals.

Team·sters Un·ion *n.* a shortened name referring to the International Brotherhood of Teamsters, Chauffeurs, Warehousemen, and Helpers of America.

team teach·ing *n.* teaching by a team of teachers working together.

team·work /téemwərk/ *n.* the combined action of a group, esp. when effective and efficient.

tea·pot /téepot/ *n.* a pot with a handle, spout, and lid, in which tea is brewed and from which it is poured.

tea·poy /téepoy/ *n.* a small three- or four-legged table esp. for tea.

tear[1] /tair/ *v. & n.* ● *v.* (*past* **tore** /tor/; *past part.* **torn** /torn/) **1** *tr.* (often foll. by *up*) pull apart or to pieces with some force (*tear it in half; tore up the letter*). **2** *tr.* **a** make a hole or rent in by tearing (*have torn my coat*). **b** make (a hole or rent). **3** *tr.* (foll. by *away, off,* etc.) pull violently or with some force (*tore the book away from me; tore off the cover; tore a page out; tore down the notice*). **4** *tr.* violently disrupt or divide (*torn by conflicting emotions*). **5** *intr. colloq.* go or travel hurriedly or impetuously (*tore across the road*). **6** *intr.* undergo tearing (*the curtain tore down the middle*). **7** *intr.* (foll. by *at,* etc.) pull violently or with some force. ● *n.* **1** a hole or other damage caused by tearing. **2** the torn part of a piece of cloth, etc. **3** *sl.* a spree; a drinking bout. □ **be torn between** have difficulty in choosing between. **tear apart 1** search (a place) exhaustively. **2** criticize forcefully. **tear into 1** attack verbally; reprimand. **2** make a vigorous start on (an activity). **tear oneself away** leave despite a strong desire to stay. **tear one's hair out** behave with extreme desperation or anger. **tear to shreds** *colloq.* refute or criticize thoroughly. □□ **tear·a·ble** *adj.* **tear·er** *n.*

tear[2] /teer/ *n.* **1** a drop of clear salty liquid secreted by glands that serves to moisten and wash the eye and is shed from it in grief or other strong emotions. **2** a tearlike thing; a drop. □ **in tears** crying; shedding tears. □□ **tear·like** *adj.*

tear·a·way /táirəway/ *n. Brit.* **1** an impetuous or reckless young person. **2** a hooligan.

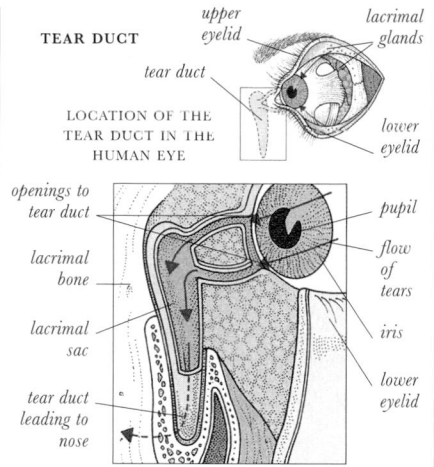

TEAR DUCT

LOCATION OF THE
TEAR DUCT IN THE
HUMAN EYE

upper eyelid

tear duct

lacrimal glands

lower eyelid

openings to tear duct

lacrimal bone

lacrimal sac

tear duct leading to nose

pupil

flow of tears

iris

lower eyelid

DETAIL OF A TEAR DUCT

tear duct *n.* ▲ a drain for carrying tears to the eye or from the eye to the nose.

tear·ful /téerfŏŏl/ *adj.* **1** crying or inclined to cry. **2** causing or accompanied with tears; sad (*a tearful event*). □□ **tear·ful·ly** *adv.* **tear·ful·ness** *n.*

tear gas *n.* gas that disables by causing severe irritation to the eyes.

tear·ing /táiring/ *adj.* extreme; overwhelming; violent (*in a tearing hurry*).

tear·jerk·er /téerjərkər/ *n. colloq.* a story, film, etc., calculated to evoke sadness or sympathy.

tea·room /téerŏŏm, -rŏŏm/ *n.* a small restaurant or café where tea is served.

tease /teez/ *v. & n.* ● *v.tr.* (also *absol.*) **1 a** make fun of (a person or animal) playfully or unkindly or annoyingly. **b** tempt or allure, esp. sexually, while refusing to satisfy the desire aroused. **2** pick (wool, hair, etc.) into separate fibers. **3** dress (cloth) esp. with teasels. ● *n.* **1** *colloq.* a person fond of teasing. **2** an instance of teasing (*it was only a tease*). **3** = TEASER 3. □ **tease out 1** separate (strands, etc.) by disentangling. **2** search out; elicit (information, etc.). □□ **teas·ing·ly** *adv.*

tea·sel /téezəl/ (also **tea·zel, tea·zle**) *n.* **1** ▶ any plant of the genus *Dipsacus*, with large prickly heads that are dried and used to raise the nap on woven cloth.

teas·er /téezər/ *n.* **1** *colloq.* a hard question or task. **2** a teasing person. **3** a short introductory advertisement, etc.

tea set *n.* a set of china or silver, etc., for serving tea.

tea·spoon /téespŏŏn/ *n.* **1** a small spoon for stirring tea. **2** an amount held by this. **3** a unit of measure equal to ⅓ tablespoon, approx. ⅙ fl. oz. or 5 ml. □□ **tea·spoon·ful** *n.* (*pl.* **-fuls**).

teat /teet/ *n.* **1** a mammary nipple, esp. of an animal. **2** *Brit.* the nipple of a feeding bottle.

tea·time /téetīm/ *esp. Brit. n.* the time in the afternoon when tea is served.

tea tree *n.* an Australasian flowering shrub or small tree with leaves that are sometimes used for tea.

tea·zel (also **tea·zle**) var. of TEASEL.

tec /tek/ *n. colloq.* a detective.

tech /tek/ *n. colloq.* **1** a technician. **2** a technical college.

tech·ne·ti·um /teknéeshəm, -sheeəm/ *n. Chem.* an artificially produced radioactive metallic element. ¶ Symb.: **Tc**.

tech·ni·cal /téknikəl/ *adj.* **1** of or involving or concerned with the mechanical arts and applied

TEASEL:
COMMON TEASEL
(*Dipsacus fullonum*)

sciences (*technical college*). **2** of or relating to a particular subject or craft, etc., or its techniques (*technical terms*). **3** requiring special knowledge to be understood. **4** due to mechanical failure (*a technical hitch*). **5** according to a strict interpretation of the law or rules. □□ **tech·ni·cal·ly** *adv.* **tech·ni·cal·ness** *n.*

tech·ni·cal foul *n. Basketball* a foul called for a technical rule violation not involving actual play.

tech·ni·cal·i·ty /téknikálitee/ *n.* (*pl.* **-ies**) **1** the state of being technical. **2** a technical expression. **3** a technical point or detail, as in a legal matter (*was acquitted on a technicality*).

tech·ni·cal knock·out *n. Boxing* a termination of a fight by the referee on the grounds of a contestant's inability to continue, the opponent being declared the winner.

tech·ni·cian /teknishən/ *n.* **1** an expert in technology or in the practical application of a science. **2** a person skilled in the technique of an art or craft. **3** a person employed to look after technical equipment and do practical work in a laboratory, clinic, etc.

Tech·ni·col·or /téknikulər/ *n.* (often *attrib.*) **1** *Trademark* a process of color cinematography using synchronized monochrome films, each of a different color, to produce a color print. **2** (usu. **technicolor**) *colloq.* **a** a vivid color. **b** artificial brilliance. □□ **tech·ni·col·ored** *adj.*

tech·nique /teknéek/ *n.* **1** a way of carrying out a task, esp. the execution of an artistic work. **2** an effective means of achieving an aim.

tech·no·bab·ble /téknōbábəl/ *n. colloq.* incomprehensible technical jargon.

tech·noc·ra·cy /teknókrəsee/ *n.* (*pl.* **-ies**) the government or control of society or industry by technology or technical experts.

tech·no·crat /téknəkrat/ *n.* an exponent or advocate of technocracy. □□ **tech·no·crat·ic** /-krátik/ *adj.* **tech·no·crat·i·cal·ly** *adv.*

tech·no·log·i·cal /téknəlójikəl/ *adj.* of, using, or ascribable to technology or technicians. □□ **tech·no·log·i·cal·ly** *adv.*

tech·nol·o·gy /teknóləjee/ *n.* (*pl.* **-ies**) **1** the study, application, or use of the mechanical arts and applied sciences. **2** these subjects collectively. □□ **tech·nol·o·gist** *n.*

tech·no·phile /téknōfīl/ *n.* a person who is enthusiastic about new technology.

tech·no·phobe /téknōfōb/ *n.* a person who dislikes or fears new technology.

tech·no·speak /téknōspeek/ *n.* technical jargon.

tech·y var. of TETCHY.

tec·ton·ic /tektónik/ *adj.* **1** *Geol.* relating to the deformation of the Earth's crust or to the structural changes caused by this (see PLATE TECTONICS). ▷ PLATE TECTONICS. **2** of or relating to building or construction. □□ **tec·ton·i·cal·ly** *adv.*

tec·ton·ics /tektóniks/ *n.pl.* (usu. treated as *sing.*) *Geol.* the study of large-scale structural features (cf. PLATE TECTONICS).

ted /ted/ *v.tr.* (**tedded, tedding**) turn over and spread out (grass, hay, or straw) to dry or for bedding, etc. □□ **ted·der** *n.*

ted·dy /tédee/ *n.* (also **Ted·dy**) (*pl.* **-ies**) (in full **teddy bear**) a stuffed toy bear.

Te De·um /tee déeəm, tay dáyəm/ **1 a** a hymn beginning *Te Deum laudamus*, 'We praise Thee, O God.' **b** the music for this. **2** an expression of thanksgiving or exultation.

te·di·ous /téedeeəs/ *adj.* tiresomely long; wearisome. □□ **te·di·ous·ly** *adv.* **te·di·ous·ness** *n.*

te·di·um /téedeeəm/ *n.* the state of being tedious; boredom.

tee[1] /tee/ *n.* = T[1].

tee[2] /tee/ *n. & v.* ● *n.* **1** *Golf* **a** a cleared space from which a golf ball is struck at the beginning of play for each hole. ▷ GOLF. **b** a small support of wood or plastic from which a ball is struck at a tee. **2** a mark aimed at in lawn bowling, quoits, curling, etc. ● *v.tr.* (**tees, teed**) (often foll. by *up*) *Golf* place (a ball) on a tee ready to strike it. □ **tee off 1** *Golf* play a ball from a tee. **2** *colloq.* start; begin.

T

tee-hee /teehée/ *n. & v.* (also **te-hee**) ● *n.* **1** a titter. **2** a restrained or contemptuous laugh. ● *v.intr.* (**tee-hees**, **tee-heed**) titter or laugh in this way.

teem[1] /teem/ *v.intr.* **1** be abundant (*fish teem in these waters*). **2** (foll. by *with*) be full of or swarming with (*teeming with fish; teeming with ideas*).

teem[2] /teem/ *v.intr.* (often foll. by *down*) (of water, etc.) flow copiously; pour (*it was teeming with rain*).

teen /teen/ *adj. & n.* ● *adj.* = TEENAGE. ● *n.* = TEENAGER.

teen-age /téenayj/ *adj.* relating to or characteristic of teenagers. □□ **teen-aged** *adj.*

teen-ag-er /téenayjər/ *n.* a person from 13 to 19 years of age.

teens /teenz/ *n.pl.* the years of one's age from 13 to 19 (*in one's teens*).

teen-sy /téensee/ *adj.* (**teensier, teensiest**) *colloq.* = TEENY.

tee-ny /téenee/ *adj.* (**teenier, teeniest**) *colloq.* tiny.

tee-ny-bop-per /téeneebopər/ *n. colloq.* a young teenager, usu. a girl, who follows the latest fashions in clothes, pop music, etc.

tee-pee var. of TEPEE.

tee-shirt var. of T-SHIRT.

tee-ter /téetər/ *v.intr.* **1** totter; stand or move unsteadily. **2** hesitate; be indecisive. □ **teeter on the brink** (or **edge**) be in imminent danger (of disaster, etc.).

teeth *pl.* of TOOTH.

teethe /teeth/ *v.intr.* grow or cut teeth, esp. baby teeth. □□ **teeth-ing** *n.*

teeth-ing ring *n.* ▶ a small ring for an infant to bite on while teething.

tee-to-tal /téetót'l/ *adj.* advocating or characterized by total abstinence from alcohol. □□ **tee-to-tal-ism** *n.*

tee-to-tal-er /téetót'lər/ *n.* (also **tee-to-tal-ler**) a person advocating or practicing abstinence from alcoholic beverages.

TEETHING RING

TEFL *abbr.* teaching of English as a foreign language.

Tef-lon /téflon/ *n. Trademark* polytetrafluoroethylene, esp. used as a nonstick coating for kitchen utensils, etc.

teg-u-ment /tégyəmənt/ *n.* the natural covering of an animal's body or part of its body. □□ **teg-u-men-tal** /-mént'l/ *adj.* **teg-u-men-ta-ry** /-méntəree/ *adj.*

te-hee var. of TEE-HEE.

tek-tite /téktīt/ *n. Geol.* a small roundish glassy body of unknown origin occurring in various parts of the Earth.

tel-a-mon /téləmon/ *n.* (*pl.* **telamones** /-mốneez/) *Archit.* a male figure used as a pillar to support an entablature.

tele- /télee/ *comb. form* **1** at or to a distance (*telekinesis*). **2** forming names of instruments for operating over long distances (*telescope*). **3** television (*telecast*). **4** done by means of the telephone (*teleconference*).

tel-e-cam-er-a /télikamrə, -mərə/ *n.* **1** a television camera. **2** a telephotographic camera.

tel-e-cast /télikast/ *n. & v.* ● *n.* a television broadcast. ● *v.tr.* transmit by television. □□ **tel-e-cast-er** *n.*

tel-e-cine /télisinee/ *n.* **1** the broadcasting of a movie or film on television. **2** equipment for doing this.

tel-e-com-mu-ni-ca-tion /télikəmyōónikáyshən/ *n.* **1** communication over a distance by cable, telegraph, telephone, or broadcasting. **2** (usu. in *pl.*) the branch of technology concerned with this.

tel-e-com-mute /télikəmyōót/ *v.intr.* (**telecommuted, telecommuting**) work, esp. at home, communicating electronically with one's employer, etc., by computer, fax, and telephone.

tel-e-con-fer-ence /télikónfərəns, -frəns/ *n.* a conference with participants in different locations linked by telecommunication devices. □□ **tel-e-con-fer-enc-ing** *n.*

TELEPHONE

A telephone transforms sound into electrical signals and back again. When a number is dialed, signals are sent to an exchange, which routes the call. When the caller speaks, a microphone in the handset produces electrical signals. These are sent – as electric currents along wires or as radio waves through the air – to the receiver of the other telephone, where a loudspeaker reproduces the sound.

circuit board
amplifier chip
ribbon cable
keypad contacts
wires to receiver
wires to transmitter
receiver (speaker)
diaphragm
handset
transmitter (microphone)
base
transmitter housing
back of keypad
connecting lead

INTERNAL MECHANISM OF A TELEPHONE

---

tel-e-fac-sim-i-le /télifaksímilee/ *n.* facsimile transmission (see FACSIMILE *n.* 2).

tel-e-fax /télifaks/ *n. Trademark* = TELEFACSIMILE.

tel-e-film /télifilm/ *n.* = TELECINE.

tel-e-gen-ic /télijénik/ *adj.* having an appearance or manner that looks attractive on television.

tel-e-go-ny /tilégənee/ *n. Biol.* the formerly supposed influence of a previous sire on the offspring of a dam with other sires.

tel-e-gram /téligram/ *n.* a message sent by telegraph.

tel-e-graph /téligraf/ *n. & v.* ● *n.* **1** a system of or device for transmitting messages or signals over a distance esp. by making and breaking an electrical connection. **2** (*attrib.*) used in this system (*telegraph pole; telegraph wire*). ● *v.* **1** *tr.* send a message to by telegraph. **2** *tr.* send by telegraph. **3** *tr.* give an advance indication of. **4** *intr.* make signals (*telegraphed to me to come up*). □□ **tel-e-gra-pher** /tiligrəfər, téligrafər/ *n.*

tel-e-graph key *n.* a device for making and breaking the electric circuit of a telegraph system.

tel-e-graph-ic /téligráfik/ *adj.* **1** of or by telegraphs or telegrams. **2** economically worded. □□ **tel-e-graph-i-cal-ly** *adv.*

te-leg-ra-phist /tɔlégrəfist/ *n.* a person skilled or employed in telegraphy.

te-leg-ra-phy /tɔlégrəfee/ *n.* the science or practice of using or constructing communication systems for the reproduction of information.

tel-e-ki-ne-sis /télikineésis, -kī-/ *n. Psychol.* movement of objects at a distance supposedly by paranormal means. □□ **tel-e-ki-net-ic** /-nétik/ *adj.*

tel-e-mark /télimaark/ *n. & v. Skiing* ● *n.* a swing turn with one ski advanced and the knee bent, used to change direction or stop short. ● *v.intr.* perform this turn.

tel-e-mar-ket-ing /télimáarkiting/ *n.* the marketing of goods, etc., by means of usu. unsolicited telephone calls. □□ **tel-e-mar-ket-er** *n.*

te-lem-e-ter /tilémitər, télimeetər/ *n. & v.* ● *n.* an apparatus for recording the readings of an instrument and transmitting them by radio. ● *v.* **1** *intr.* record readings in this way. **2** *tr.* transmit (readings, etc.) to a distant receiving set or station. □□ **tel-e-met-ric** /télimétrik/ *adj.* **te-lem-e-try** /tilémitree/ *n.*

tel-e-ol-o-gy /téleeóləjee, tée-/ *n.* (*pl.* **-ies**) *Philos.* **1** the explanation of phenomena by the purpose they serve rather than by postulated causes. **2** *Theol.* the doctrine of design and purpose in the material world. □□ **tel-e-o-log-ic** /-leeəlójik/ *adj.* **tel-e-o-log-**

i-cal *adj.* **tel-e-o-log-i-cal-ly** *adv.* **tel-e-ol-o-gism** /tel-e-ol-o-gist* *n.* **tel-e-ol-o-gist** *n.*

tel-e-path /télipath/ *n.* a telepathic person.

te-lep-a-thy /tɔlépəthee/ *n.* the supposed communication of thoughts or ideas otherwise than by the known senses. □□ **tel-e-path-ic** /télipáthik/ *adj.* **tel-e-path-i-cal-ly** *adv.* **te-lep-a-thist** *n.* **te-lep-a-thize** *v.tr. & intr.*

tel-e-phone /télifōn/ *n. & v.* ● *n.* **1** ▲ an apparatus for transmitting sound (esp. speech) over a distance by wire or cord or radio, esp. by converting acoustic vibrations to electrical signals. **2** a transmitting and receiving instrument used in this. **3** a system of communication using a network of telephones. ● *v.* **1** *tr.* speak to (a person) by telephone. **2** *tr.* send (a message) by telephone. **3** *intr.* make a telephone call. □ **on the telephone** by use of or using the telephone. **over the telephone** by use of or using the telephone. □□ **tel-e-phon-er** *n.* **tel-e-phon-ic** /-fónik/ *adj.* **tel-e-phon-i-cal-ly** /-fóniklee/ *adv.*

tel-e-phone book *n.* a book listing telephone subscribers in a particular area, providing their addresses and telephone numbers.

tel-e-phone booth *n.* a public booth or enclosure from which telephone calls can be made.

tel-e-phone num-ber *n.* a number assigned to a particular telephone and used in making connections to it.

tel-e-phone op-er-a-tor *n.* an operator in a telephone exchange or at a switchboard.

te-leph-o-ny /tɔléfɔnee/ *n.* the use of telephones.

tel-e-pho-tog-ra-phy /télifətógrəfee/ *n.* the photographing of distant objects with a system of lenses giving a large image.

tel-e-pho-to-graph-ic /télifōtógrəfik/ *adj.* of or for or using telephotography. □□ **tel-e-pho-to-graph-i-cal-ly** *adv.*

tel-e-pho-to lens /télifōtō/ *n.* (*pl.* **-os**) ▼ a lens used in telephotography. ▷ LENS

telephoto lens
camera body

TELEPHOTO LENS ON AN SLR CAMERA

T

TELESCOPE

There are two types of optical telescope: reflectors and refractors. In a refractor, light passes through the objective lens to form an image, which is magnified by the eyepiece. In a reflector, the light bounces off a curved primary mirror and onto a flat secondary mirror that reflects it into an eyepiece.

TYPES OF TELESCOPE

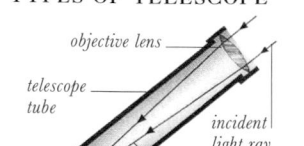

objective lens
telescope tube
incident light ray
refracted light ray

REFRACTOR

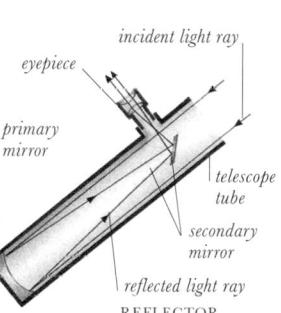

incident light ray
eyepiece
primary mirror
telescope tube
secondary mirror
reflected light ray

REFLECTOR

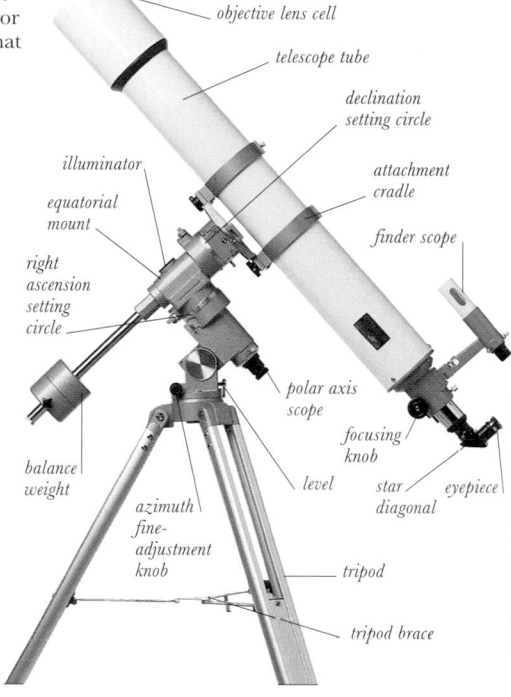

SMALL ASTRONOMICAL REFRACTOR TELESCOPE

objective lens cell
telescope tube
declination setting circle
illuminator
equatorial mount
right ascension setting circle
attachment cradle
finder scope
polar axis scope
balance weight
azimuth fine-adjustment knob
focusing knob
level
star diagonal
eyepiece
tripod
tripod brace

tel·e·port[1] /télipawrt/ *v.tr. Psychol.* move by telekinesis. ☐☐ **tel·e·por·ta·tion** *n.*

tel·e·port[2] /télipawrt/ *n.* a center providing interconnections between different forms of telecommunications.

Tele·Promp·Ter /télipromptər/ *n. Trademark* a device used in television and film-making to project a speaker's script out of sight of the audience (cf. AUTOCUE).

tel·e·sales /télisaylz/ *n.pl.* selling by means of the telephone.

tel·e·scope /téliskōp/ *n. & v.* ● *n.* **1** ▲ an optical instrument using lenses or mirrors or both to make distant objects appear nearer and larger. ▷ OBSERVATORY, SEXTANT. **2** = RADIO TELESCOPE. ● *v.* **1** *tr.* press or drive (sections of a tube, colliding vehicles, etc.) together so that one slides into another like the sections of a folding telescope. **2** *intr.* close or be driven or be capable of closing in this way. **3** *tr.* compress so as to occupy less space or time.

tel·e·scop·ic /téliskópik/ *adj.* **1 a** of, relating to, or made with a telescope (*telescopic observations*). **b** visible only through a telescope (*telescopic stars*). **2** (esp. of a lens) able to focus on and magnify distant objects. **3** consisting of sections that telescope. ☐☐ **tel·e·scop·i·cal·ly** *adv.*

tel·e·scop·ic sight *n.* ▼ a telescope used for sighting on a rifle, etc.

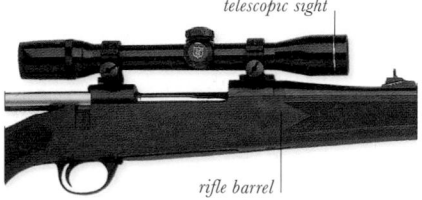

telescopic sight
rifle barrel

TELESCOPIC SIGHT ON A BIGBORE HUNTING RIFLE

tel·e·soft·ware /télisawftwair, -sóft-/ *n.* software transmitted or broadcast to receiving terminals.

tel·e·text /télitekst/ *n.* a news and information service, in the form of text and graphics, from a computer source transmitted to televisions with appropriate receivers.

tel·e·thon /télithon/ *n.* an exceptionally long television program, esp. to raise money for a charity.

Tel·e·type /télitīp/ *n. Trademark* telegraphic apparatus for direct exchange of printed messages.

tel·e·type·writ·er /télitípritər/ *n.* a device for transmitting telegraph messages as they are keyed, and for printing messages received.

tel·e·van·ge·list /télivánjəlist/ *n.* an evangelical preacher who appears regularly on television to promote beliefs and appeal for funds.

tel·e·view·er /télivyōōər/ *v.tr.* a person who watches television. ☐☐ **tel·e·view·ing** *adj.*

tel·e·vise /télivīz/ *v.tr.* transmit by television. ☐☐ **tel·e·vis·a·ble** *adj.*

tel·e·vi·sion /télivizhən/ *n.* **1** a system for reproducing on a screen visual images transmitted (usu. with sound) by radio waves. ▷ ELECTROMAGNETIC RADIATION. **2** (in full **television set**) ▼ a device with a screen for receiving these signals. **3** the medium, art form, or occupation of broadcasting on television; the content of television programs.

tel·e·vis·u·al /télivízhooəl/ *adj. esp. Brit.* relating to or suitable for television. ☐☐ **tel·e·vis·u·al·ly** *adv.*

tel·ex /téleks/ *n. & v.* (also **Telex**) ● *n.* an international system of telegraphy with printed messages transmitted and received by teletypewriters using the public telecommunications network. ● *v.tr.* send or communicate with by telex.

tell /tel/ *v.* (*past* and *past part.* **told** /tōld/) **1** *tr.* relate or narrate in speech or writing; give an account of (*tell me a story*). **2** *tr.* make known; express in words; divulge (*tell me what you want*). **3** *tr.* reveal or signify to (a person) (*your face tells me everything*). **4** *tr.* **a** utter (*don't tell lies*). **b** warn (*I told you so*). **5** *intr.* **a** (often foll. by *of*) divulge information or a description; reveal a secret. **b** (foll. by *on*) *colloq.* inform against (a person). **6** *tr.* (foll. by *to* + infin.) give (a person) a direction or order. **7** *tr.* assure (*it's true, I tell you*). **8** *tr.* explain in writing; instruct (*this book tells you how to cook*). **9** *tr.* decide determine; distinguish (*how do you tell one from the other?*). **10** *intr.* **a** (often foll. by *on*) produce a noticeable effect (*the strain was beginning to tell on me*). **b** reveal the truth (*time will tell*). **c** have an influence (*the evidence tells against you*). **11** *tr.* (often *absol.*) count (votes) at a meeting, election, etc. ☐ **tell apart** distinguish between (usu. with *neg.* or *interrog.*: *could not tell them apart*). **tell me another** *colloq.* an expression of incredulity. **tell off 1** *colloq.* reprimand; scold. **2** count off or detach for duty. **tell tales** report a discreditable fact about another. **tell (the) time** determine the time from the face of a clock or watch. **there is no telling** it is impossible to know (*there's no telling what may happen*). **you're telling me** *colloq.* I agree wholeheartedly. ☐☐ **tell·a·ble** *adj.*

tell·er /télər/ *n.* **1** a person employed to receive and pay out money in a bank, etc. **2** a person who counts (votes). **3** a person who tells esp. stories (*a teller of tales*). ☐☐ **tell·er·ship** *n.*

tell·ing /téling/ *adj.* **1** having a marked effect; striking. **2** significant. ☐ **telling off** esp. *Brit. colloq.* a reproof or reprimand. ☐☐ **tell·ing·ly** *adv.*

TELEVISION SET

A television set uses electromagnetic waves to produce a picture; a color picture is made up of three color signals. These are usually sent to three electron guns in a cathode ray tube. The guns fire electron beams through deflection coils, which scan them onto the screen. A shadow mask allows only one beam to hit any one phosphor spot, which then glows in red, green, or blue. Together, the three color images make a full-color picture.

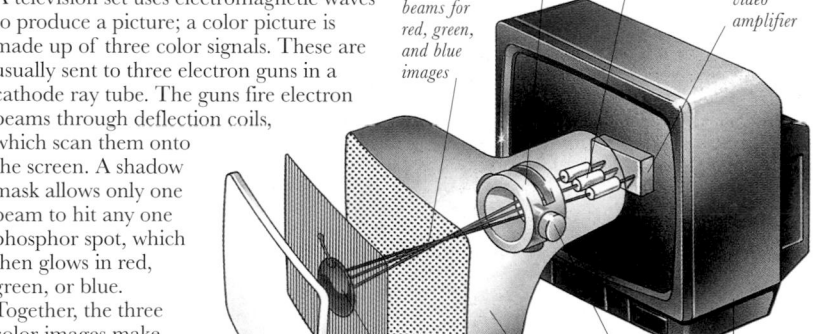

electron beams for red, green, and blue images
deflection coils
electron guns
video amplifier
faceplate
image
shadow mask
glass envelope
cathode ray tube
adjusting magnet
outer case

EXPLODED VIEW OF A TELEVISION SET

T

TEMPLE

The structure of a temple is often symbolic. In the Aztec temple of Tenochtitlan in Mexico, shown here, two shrines dedicated to the gods were built at the top of a structure symbolizing a mountain. By climbing this, priests came closer to the gods, to whom human sacrifices were made.

sanctuary

shrine to god of sun and war

sacrificial stone

shrine to god of rain

remains of former temples

division between "mountains"

small altar

base

frog altar

brazier

stone head of serpent god

stairway

RECONSTRUCTION OF THE AZTEC TEMPLE OF TENOCHTITLAN, MEXICO

tell·tale /téltayl/ *n.* **1** a person who reveals (esp. discreditable) information about another's private affairs or behavior. **2** (*attrib.*) that reveals or betrays (*a telltale smile*). **3** a device for automatic indicating, monitoring, or registering of a process, etc.

tel·lur·i·an /telŏoreeən/ *adj. & n.* • *adj.* of or inhabiting the Earth. • *n.* an inhabitant of the Earth.

tel·lu·ri·um /telŏoreeəm/ *n. Chem.* a rare brittle lustrous silver-white element occurring naturally in ores of gold and silver, used in semiconductors. ¶ Symb.: **Te.** □□ **tel·lu·ride** /télyərīd/ *n.* **tel·lu·rite** /télyərīt/ *n.* **tel·lu·rous** *adj.*

tel·ly /télee/ *n.* (*pl.* **-ies**) esp. *Brit. colloq.* **1** television. **2** a television set.

tel·net /télnet/ *Computing n.* a network protocol or program that allows a user on one computer to log in to another computer that is part of the same network.

te·ma·ze·pam /təmáyzipam, -mázi-/ *n. Med.* a tranquilizing drug of the benzodiazepine group.

te·mer·i·ty /timéritee/ *n.* **1** rashness. **2** audacity.

temp /temp/ *n. & v. colloq.* • *n.* a temporary employee. • *v.intr.* work as a temp.

temp. /temp/ *abbr.* temperature.

tem·per /témpər/ *n. & v.* • *n.* **1** habitual or temporary disposition of mind esp. as regards composure (*a person of calm temper*). **2** an angry state of mind (*in a fit of temper, flew into a temper*). **3** a tendency to have fits of anger (*have a temper*). **4** composure or calmness (*keep one's temper; lose one's temper*). **5** the condition of metal as regards hardness and elasticity. • *v.tr.* **1** bring (metal or clay) to a proper hardness or consistency. **2** (often foll. by *with*) moderate or mitigate (*temper justice with mercy*). □ **in a bad temper** angry. **in a good temper** in an amiable mood. **out of temper** irritable. □□ **tem·per·er** *n.*

tem·per·a /témpərə/ *n.* a method of painting using an emulsion, e.g., of pigment with egg, esp. on canvas.

tem·per·a·ment /témprəmənt/ *n.* **1** a person's nature with regard to the effect it has on their behavior (*a nervous temperament; the artistic temperament*). **2** a creative or spirited personality (*was full of temperament*).

tem·per·a·men·tal /témprəmént'l/ *adj.* **1** of or having temperament. **2 a** (of a person) prone to erratic or moody behavior. **b** (of a thing, e.g., a machine) working unpredictably; unreliable. □□ **tem·per·a·men·tal·ly** *adv.*

tem·per·ance /témpərəns, témprəns/ *n.* **1** moderation or self-restraint esp. in eating and drinking. **2 a** total or partial abstinence from alcohol. **b** (*attrib.*) advocating or concerned with abstinence.

tem·per·ate /témpərət, témprət/ *adj.* **1** avoiding excess; self-restrained. **2** moderate. **3** (of a region or climate) characterized by mild temperatures. **4** abstemious. □□ **tem·per·ate·ly** *adv.* **tem·per·ate·ness** *n.*

tem·per·a·ture /témprichər/ *n.* **1** the degree or intensity of heat of a body, air mass, etc., in relation to others, esp. as shown by a thermometer or perceived by touch, etc. **2** *Med.* the degree of internal heat of the body. **3** *colloq.* a body temperature above the normal (*have a temperature*). **4** the degree of excitement in a discussion, etc.

-tempered /témpərd/ *comb. form* having a specified temper or disposition (*bad-tempered; hot-tempered*). □□ **-temperedly** *adv.* **-temperedness** *n.*

tem·pest /témpist/ *n.* **1** a violent windy storm. **2** violent agitation or tumult.

tem·pes·tu·ous /tempéschŏoəs/ *adj.* **1** stormy. **2** (of a person, emotion, etc.) turbulent; violent; passionate. □□ **tem·pes·tu·ous·ly** *adv.* **tem·pes·tu·ous·ness** *n.*

tem·pi *pl.* of TEMPO.

tem·plate /témplit, -playt/ *n.* (also **tem·plet**) **1** a pattern or gauge, usu. a piece of thin board or metal plate, used as a guide in cutting or drilling metal, stone, wood, etc. **2** a flat card or plastic pattern esp. for cutting cloth for patchwork, etc.

tem·ple[1] /témpəl/ *n.* **1** ▲ a building devoted to the worship, or regarded as the dwelling place, of a god or gods or other objects of religious reverence. **2** *hist.* any of three successive religious buildings of the Jews in Jerusalem. **3** a Reform or Conservative synagogue. **4** a place of Christian public worship, esp. a Protestant church in France. **5** any place in which God is regarded as residing, as the body of a Christian (I Cor. 6:19).

tem·ple[2] /témpəl/ *n.* the flat part of either side of the head between the forehead and the ear.

tem·plet var. of TEMPLATE.

tem·po /témpō/ *n.* (*pl.* **-os** or **tempi** /-pee/) **1** *Mus.* the speed at which music is or should be played, esp. as characteristic (*waltz tempo*). **2** the rate of motion or activity (*the tempo of the war is quickening*).

tem·po·ral /témpərəl, témprəl/ *adj.* **1** of worldly as opposed to spiritual affairs; of this life; secular. **2** of or relating to time. **3** *Gram.* relating to or denoting time or tense (*temporal conjunction*). □□ **tem·po·ral·ly** *adv.*

tem·po·ral lobe *n.* ▶ each of the paired lobes of the brain lying beneath the temples, including areas concerned with the understanding of speech.

temporal lobe

TEMPORAL LOBE IN THE HUMAN BRAIN

tem·po·rar·y /témpəreree/ *adj. & n.* • *adj.* lasting or meant to last only for a limited time. • *n.* (*pl.* **-ies**) a person employed temporarily. □□ **tem·po·rar·i·ly** /-pərairilee/ *adv.* **tem·po·rar·i·ness** *n.*

tem·po·rize /témpərīz/ *v.intr.* **1** avoid committing oneself so as to gain time. **2** comply temporarily; adopt a time-serving policy. □□ **tem·po·riza·tion** *n.* **tem·po·riz·er** *n.*

tempt /tempt/ *v.tr.* **1** entice or incite (a person) to do a wrong or forbidden thing. **2** allure; attract. **3** risk provoking (fate, etc.). □□ **tempt·a·ble** *adj.* **tempt·a·bil·i·ty** /témptəbilitee/ *n.*

temp·ta·tion /temptáyshən/ *n.* **1** the act or an instance of tempting; the state of being tempted; incitement esp. to wrongdoing. **2** an attractive thing or course of action.

tempt·er /témptər/ *n.* (*fem.* **temptress** /-tris/) a person who tempts.

tempt·ing /témpting/ *adj.* **1** attractive; inviting. **2** enticing to evil. □□ **tempt·ing·ly** *adv.*

tem·pu·ra /tempŏorə/ *n.* a Japanese dish of fish, shellfish, or vegetables, dipped in batter and deep-fried.

ten /ten/ *n. & adj.* • *n.* **1** one more than nine. **2** a symbol for this (10, x, X). **3** a size, etc., denoted by ten. **4** the time of ten o'clock (*is it ten yet?*). **5** a playing card with ten pips. **6** a ten-dollar bill. **7** a set of ten. • *adj.* **1** that amount to ten. **2** (as a round number) several (*ten times as easy*).

ten·a·ble /ténəbəl/ *adj.* **1** that can be maintained or defended against attack or objection (*a tenable position; a tenable theory*). **2** (foll. by *for, by*) (of an office, etc.) that can be held for (a specified period) or by (a specified class of person). □□ **ten·a·bil·i·ty** /ténəbilitee/ *n.* **ten·a·ble·ness** *n.*

te·na·cious /tináyshəs/ *adj.* **1** (often foll. by *of*) keeping a firm hold of property, principles, life, etc.; not readily relinquishing. **2** (of memory) retentive. **3** holding fast. **4** strongly cohesive. **5** persistent; resolute. **6** adhesive; sticky. □□ **te·na·cious·ly** *adv.* **te·na·cious·ness** *n.* **te·nac·i·ty** /tinásitee/ *n.*

ten·an·cy /ténənsee/ *n.* (*pl.* **-ies**) **1** the status of a tenant; possession as a tenant. **2** the duration or period of this.

ten·ant /ténənt/ *n. & v.* • *n.* **1** a person who rents land or property from a landlord. **2** (often foll. by *of*) the occupant of a place. **3** *Law* a person holding real property by private ownership. • *v.tr.* occupy as a tenant. □□ **ten·ant·a·ble** *adj.* **ten·ant·less** *adj.*

ten·ant farm·er *n.* a person who farms rented land.

ten·ant·ry /ténəntree/ *n.* the tenants of an estate, etc.

tench *n.* (*pl.* same) ▼ a European freshwater fish, *Tinca tinca*, of the carp family.

TENCH (*Tinca tinca*)

Ten Com·mand·ments *n.pl.* the divine rules of conduct given by God to Moses on Mount Sinai, according to Exod. 20:1–17

tend[1] /tend/ *v.intr.* **1** be apt or inclined (to). **2** be moving; hold a course (*tends to the same conclusion*).

tend[2] /tend/ *v.* **1** *tr.* take care of; look after (a person,

T

esp. an invalid; animals, esp. sheep; a machine).
2 *intr.* (foll. by *on, upon*) wait on. **3** *intr.* (foll. by *to*) give attention to.

ten·den·cy /téndənsee/ *n.* (*pl.* **-ies**) **1** (often foll. by *to, toward*) a leaning or inclination; a way of tending. **2** a group within a larger political party or movement.

ten·den·tious /tendénshəs/ *adj. derog.* (of writing, etc.) calculated to promote a particular cause or viewpoint; having an underlying purpose. □□ **ten·den·tious·ly** *adv.* **ten·den·tious·ness** *n.*

ten·der[1] /téndər/ *adj.* (**tenderer, tenderest**) **1** easily cut or chewed; not tough (*tender steak*). **2** easily touched or wounded; susceptible to pain or grief (*a tender heart*). **3** easily hurt; sensitive (*tender skin*). **4 a** delicate; fragile (*a tender plant*). **b** gentle; soft (*a tender touch*). **5** loving; affectionate; fond (*tender parents; wrote tender verses*). **6** requiring tact or careful handling; ticklish (*a tender subject*). **7** (of age) early; immature (*of tender years*). □□ **ten·der·ly** *adv.* **ten·der·ness** *n.*

ten·der[2] /téndər/ *v. & n.* ● *v.* **1** *tr.* **a** offer; present (one's services, apologies, resignation, etc.). **b** offer (money, etc.) as payment. **2** *intr.* (often foll. by *for*) make a tender for the supply of a thing or the execution of work. ● *n.* an offer, esp. an offer in writing to execute work or supply goods at a fixed price. □ **put out to tender** seek tenders or bids for (work, etc.). □□ **ten·der·er** *n.*

tend·er[3] /téndər/ *n.* **1** a person who looks after people or things. **2** a vessel attending a larger one to supply stores, convey passengers or orders, etc. **3** ▼ a special car closely coupled to a steam locomotive to carry fuel, water, etc.

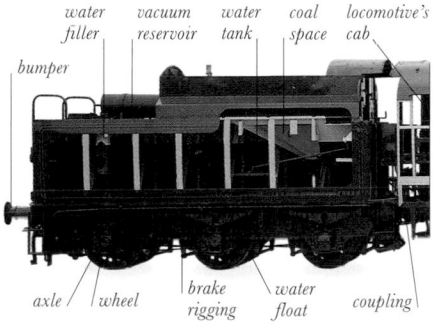

TENDER: CUTAWAY VIEW OF A
MID-20TH-CENTURY TENDER

ten·der·foot /téndərfoõt/ *n.* a newcomer or novice, esp. to the outdoor life or to the Scouts.

ten·der·heart·ed *adj.* having a tender heart; easily moved by pity, etc. □□ **ten·der·heart·ed·ness** *n.*

ten·der·ize /téndərīz/ *v.tr.* make tender, esp. make (meat) tender by pounding, etc. □□ **ten·der·iz·er** *n.*

ten·der·loin /téndərloyn/ *n.* a long tender cut of beef or pork from the loin.

ten·don /téndən/ *n.* **1** ▼ a cord or strand of strong tissue attaching a muscle to a bone, etc. **2** (in a quadruped) = HAMSTRING. □□ **ten·di·ni·tis** /téndinítis/ *n.* **ten·di·nous** /-dinəs/ *adj.*

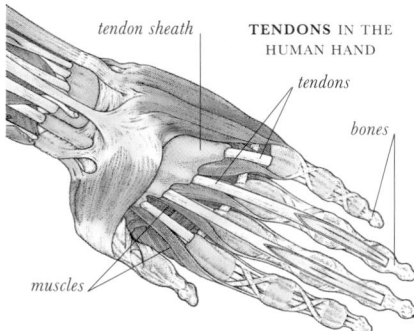

TENDONS IN THE
HUMAN HAND

TENNIS

Tennis is played on various surfaces, both indoors and outdoors. The aim is to hit the ball over the net so that it cannot be returned within the lines. Players must win at least six games for a set and need two sets (women) or three sets (men) for the match.

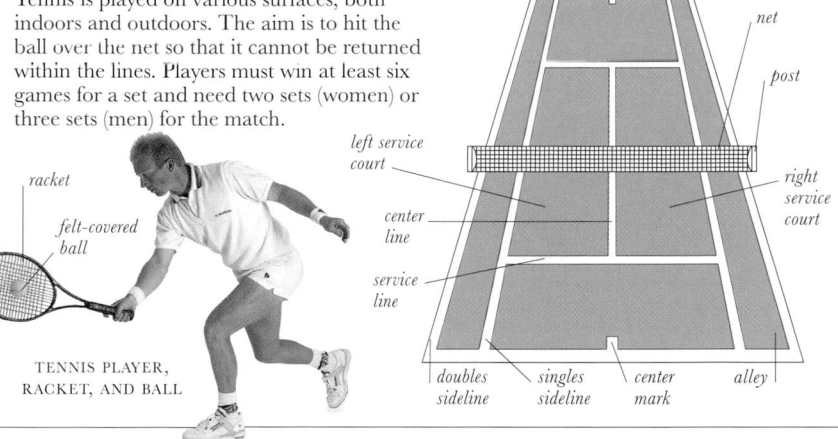

TENNIS PLAYER,
RACKET, AND BALL

ten·dril /téndril/ *n.* **1** ▶ each of the slender leafless shoots by which some climbing plants cling for support. **2** a slender curl of hair, etc.

ten·e·brous /ténibrəs/ *adj. literary* dark; gloomy.

ten·e·ment /ténimənt/ *n.* **1** a room or a set of rooms forming a separate residence within a house or apartment building. **2** a house divided into and rented in tenements, esp. one that is overcrowded, in poor condition, etc. **3** a dwelling place. **4 a** a piece of land held by an owner. **b** *Law* any kind of permanent property, e.g., lands or rents held from another.

TENDRIL
OF A GOURD
PLANT

ten·et /ténit/ *n.* a doctrine, dogma, or principle held by a group or person.

ten·fold /ténföld/ *adj. & adv.* **1** ten times as much or as many. **2** consisting of ten parts.

ten·gal·lon hat *n.* a cowboy's large wide-brimmed hat.

Tenn. *abbr.* Tennessee.

ten·ner /ténər/ *n. colloq.* a ten-dollar bill or ten-pound note.

ten·nis /ténis/ *n.* ▲ a game in which two or four players strike a ball with rackets over a net stretched across a court. ▷ BACKHAND, FOREHAND, OVERARM

ten·nis ball *n.* a ball used in playing tennis. ▷ TENNIS

ten·nis court *n.* a court used in playing tennis. ▷ TENNIS

ten·nis el·bow *n.* chronic inflammation caused by or as by playing tennis.

ten·nis rack·et *n.* a racket used in playing tennis. ▷ TENNIS

ten·nis shoe *n.* a light canvas or leather rubber-soled shoe suitable for tennis or general casual wear.

ten·on /ténən/ *n. & v.* ● *n.* a projecting piece of wood made for insertion into a corresponding cavity (esp. a mortise) in another piece. ▷ DOVETAIL. ● *v.tr.* **1** cut as a tenon. **2** join by means of a tenon. □□ **ten·on·er** *n.*

ten·or /ténər/ *n.* **1 a** a singing voice between baritone and alto or countertenor, the highest of the ordinary adult male range. **b** a singer with this voice. **c** a part written for it. **2 a** an instrument, esp. a viola, recorder, or saxophone, of which the range is roughly that of a tenor voice. **b** (in full **tenor bell**) the largest bell of a peal or set. **3** (usu. foll. by *of*) the general purport or drift of a document or speech. **4** (usu. foll. by *of*) a settled or prevailing course or direction, esp. the course of a person's life or habits.

ten·pin /ténpin/ *n.* **1** ▶ a pin used in tenpin bowling. **2** (in *pl.*) = TENPIN BOWLING.

ten·pin bowl·ing *n.* a game developed from ninepins in which ten pins are set up at the end of an alley and bowled at to be knocked down.

tense[1] /tens/ *adj. & v.* ● *adj.* **1** stretched tight; strained (*tense cord; tense nerves*). **2** causing tenseness (*a tense moment*). ● *v.tr. & intr.* make or become tense. □ **tense up** become tense. □□ **tense·ly** *adv.* **tense·ness** *n.* **ten·si·ty** *n.*

tense[2] /tens/ *n. Gram.* **1** a form taken by a verb to indicate the time (also the continuance or completeness) of the action, etc. (*present tense; imperfect tense*). **2** a set of such forms for the various persons and numbers. □□ **tense·less** *adj.*

TENPIN

ten·sile /ténsəl, -sīl/ *adj.* **1** of or relating to tension. **2** capable of being drawn out or stretched. □□ **ten·sil·i·ty** /tensílitee/ *n.*

ten·sile strength *n.* resistance to breaking under tension.

ten·sion /ténshən/ *n. & v.* ● *n.* **1** the act or an instance of stretching; the state of being stretched; tenseness. **2** mental strain or excitement. **3** a strained (political, social, etc.) state or relationship. **4** *Mech.* the stress by which a bar, cord, etc., is pulled when it is part of a system in equilibrium or motion. **5** electromagnetic force (*high tension; low tension*). ● *v.tr.* subject to tension. □□ **ten·sion·al** *adj.* **ten·sion·al·ly** *adv.* **ten·sion·less** *adj.*

ten·son /ténsən, tensôn/ *n.* (also **ten·zon** /téenzən, tenzôn/) **1** a contest in versifying between troubadours. **2** a piece of verse composed for this.

tent /tent/ *n.* **1** ▼ a portable shelter or dwelling of canvas, cloth, etc., supported by poles and ground pegs. **2** *Med.* a tentlike enclosure for control of the air supply to a patient.

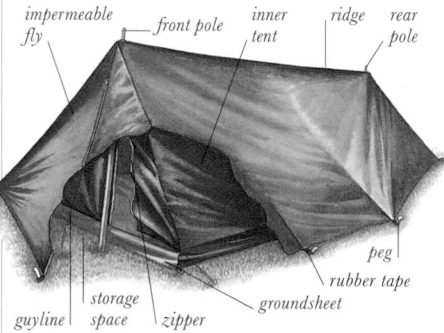

TENT: CUTAWAY VIEW
OF A RIDGE TENT AND FLY

T

TENTACLES OF
A PEACOCK WORM

mud tube / *tentacles*

ten·ta·cle /téntəkəl/ *n.* **1** ◄ a long slender flexible appendage of an (esp. invertebrate) animal, used for feeling, grasping, or moving. ▷ CEPHALOPOD, CNIDARIAN. **2** a thing used like a tentacle as a feeler, etc. **3** *Bot.* a sensitive hair or filament. □□ **ten·ta·cled** *adj.* (also in *comb.*). **ten·tac·u·lar** /-tákyələr/ *adj.* **ten·tac·u·late** /-tákyələt, -layt/ *adj.*

ten·ta·tive /téntətiv/ *adj.* **1** done by way of trial; experimental. **2** hesitant; not definite (*tentative suggestion; tentative acceptance*). □□ **ten·ta·tive·ly** *adv.* **ten·ta·tive·ness** *n.*

tent cat·er·pil·lar *n.* any of several caterpillars of the genus *Malacosoma*, including *M. americanum* and *M. disstria* (forest tent caterpillar), that construct and live in large tentlike webs in trees.

ten·ter /téntər/ *n.* **1** a machine for stretching cloth to dry in shape. **2** = TENTERHOOK.

ten·ter·hook /téntərho͝ok/ *n.* any of the hooks to which cloth is fastened on a tenter. □ **on tenterhooks** in a state of agitated suspense.

tenth /tenth/ *n. & adj.* ● *n.* **1** the position in a sequence corresponding to the number 10 in the sequence 1–10. **2** something occupying this position. **3** one of ten equal parts of a thing. **4** *Mus.* **a** an interval or chord spanning an octave and a third in the diatonic scale. **b** a note separated from another by this interval. ● *adj.* that is the tenth. □□ **tenth·ly** *adv.*

tenth-rate *n.* of extremely poor quality.

ten·u·ous /tényo͞oəs/ *adj.* **1** slight; of little substance (*tenuous connection*). **2** (of a distinction, etc.) oversubtle. **3** thin; slender; small. **4** rarefied. □□ **ten·u·ous·ly** *adv.* **ten·u·ous·ness** *n.*

ten·ure /tényər/ *n.* **1** a condition, or form of right or title, under which (esp. real) property is held. **2** (often foll. by *of*) **a** the holding or possession of an office or property. **b** the period of this (*during his tenure of office*). **3** guaranteed permanent employment, esp. as a teacher or professor.

ten·ured /tényərd/ *adj.* **1** (of an official position) carrying a guarantee of permanent employment. **2** (of a teacher, professor, etc.) having guaranteed tenure of office.

te·o·cal·li /té·əkálee/ *n.* (*pl.* **teocallis**) a temple of the Aztecs or other Mexican peoples, usu. on a truncated pyramid.

te·pee /téepee/ *n.* (also **tee·pee**) ▼ a conical tent, made of skins, cloth, or canvas on a frame of poles, orig. used by Native Americans.

tep·id /tépid/ *adj.* **1** slightly warm. **2** unenthusiastic. □□ **tep·id·i·ty** /tipiditee/ *n.* **tep·id·ly** *adv.* **tep·id·ness** *n.*

te·qui·la /tekélə/ *n.* a Mexican liquor made from an agave.

te·qui·la sun·rise *n.* a cocktail of tequila, orange juice, and grenadine.

ter- /ter/ *comb. form* three; threefold (*tercentenary; tervalent*).

tera- /térə/ *comb. form* denoting a factor of 10^{12}.

TEPEE

poles bound together

smoke flap

wooden pin

buffalo hides

entrance

te·ra·byte /térəbīt/ *n. Computing* a unit of information equal to one million million (10^{12}) or (strictly) 2^{40} bytes.

te·rat·o·gen /tərátəjən/ *n. Med.* an agent or factor causing malformation of an embryo. □□ **te·rat·o·gen·ic** /térətōjénik/ *adj.*

ter·bi·um /tórbeeəm/ *n. Chem.* a silvery metallic element of the lanthanide series. ¶ *Symb.*: **Tb**.

terce /tərs/ *n. Eccl.* **1** the office of the canonical hour of prayer appointed for the third daytime hour (i.e., 9 a.m.). **2** this hour.

ter·cel /tórsəl/ *n.* (also **tier·cel** /téersəl/) *Falconry* the male of the hawk, esp. a peregrine or goshawk.

ter·cen·ten·a·ry /tórsenténəree, tərséntineree/ *n. & adj.* ● *n.* (*pl.* **-ies**) **1** a three-hundredth anniversary. **2** a celebration of this. ● *adj.* of this anniversary.

ter·cen·ten·ni·al /tórsenténeeəl/ *adj. & n.* ● *adj.* **1** occurring every three hundred years. **2** lasting three hundred years. ● *n.* a tercentenary.

ter·e·binth /téribinth/ *n.* a small southern European tree, *Pistacia terebinthus*, yielding turpentine.

te·re·do /təréedō/ *n.* (*pl.* **-os**) ► any bivalve mollusk of the genus *Teredo*, esp. *T. navalis*, that bores into submerged wood, damaging ships, etc. Also called **shipworm**.

ter·gi·ver·sate /tórjiversáyt/ *v.intr.* **1** be apostate; change one's party or principles. **2** equivocate; make conflicting or evasive statements. □□ **ter·gi·ver·sa·tion** /-sáyshən/ *n.* **ter·gi·ver·sa·tor** *n.*

ter·i·ya·ki /tereeyókee/ *n.* a dish consisting of meat, poultry, or fish that is marinated in seasoned soy sauce and grilled, sautéed, or broiled.

term /tərm/ *n. & v.* ● *n.* **1** a word used to express a definite concept, esp. in a particular branch of study, etc. (*a technical term*). **2** (in *pl.*) language used; mode of expression (*answered in no uncertain terms*). **3** (in *pl.*) a relation or footing (*we are on familiar terms*). **4** (in *pl.*) **a** conditions or stipulations (*cannot accept your terms; do it on your own terms*). **b** charge or price (*his terms are $20 a lesson*). **5 a** a limited period of some state or activity (*for a term of five years*). **b** a period over which operations are conducted or results contemplated (*in the short term*). **c** a period of some weeks, alternating with holidays or vacation, during which instruction is given in a school, college, or university, or during which a court of law holds sessions. **d** a period of imprisonment. **e** period of tenure. **6** *Logic* a word or words that may be the subject or predicate of a proposition. **7** *Math.* **a** each of the two quantities in a ratio. **b** each quantity in a series. **c** a part of an expression joined to the rest by + or − (e.g., *a*, *b*, *c* in $a + b − c$). **8** the completion of a normal length of pregnancy. **9** an appointed day, time, etc. **10** (in full *US* **term for years** or *Brit.* **term of years**) *Law* an interest in land for a fixed period. ● *v.tr.* denominate; call; assign a term to (*the music termed classical*). □ **come to terms with 1** reconcile oneself to (a difficulty, etc.). **2** conclude an agreement with. **in terms of 1** in the language peculiar to; using as a basis of expression or thought. **2** by way of. **make terms** conclude an agreement. **on terms** on terms of friendship or equality. □□ **term·less** *adj.* **term·ly** *adj. & adv.*

ter·ma·gant /tórməgənt/ *n.* an overbearing or brawling woman; a virago or shrew.

ter·mi·na·ble /tórminəbəl/ *adj.* **1** that may be terminated. **2** coming to an end after a certain time (*terminable annuity*). □□ **ter·mi·na·ble·ness** *n.*

ter·mi·nal /tórminəl/ *adj. & n.* ● *adj.* **1 a** (of a disease) ending in death; fatal. **b** (of a patient) in the last stage of a fatal disease. **c** (of a morbid condition) forming the last stage of a fatal disease.

TEREDO: SHELLY TUBES LEFT IN WOOD BY TEREDO WORMS

d *colloq.* ruinous; disastrous; very great (*terminal laziness*). **2** of or forming a limit or terminus (*terminal station*). **3 a** *Zool.*, etc., ending a series (*terminal joints*). **b** *Bot.* growing at the end of a stem, etc. **4** of or done, etc., each term (*terminal accounts; terminal examinations*). ● *n.* **1** a terminating thing; an extremity. **2** a terminus for trains or long-distance buses. **3** a departure and arrival building for air passengers. **4** a point of connection for closing an electric circuit. ▷ BATTERY, CIRCUIT. **5** an apparatus for transmission of messages between a user and a computer, communications system, etc. **6** an installation where oil is stored at the end of a pipeline or at a port. □□ **ter·mi·nal·ly** *adv.*

ter·mi·nal ve·loc·i·ty *n.* a velocity of a falling body such that the resistance of the air, etc., prevents further increase of speed under gravity.

ter·mi·nate /tórminayt/ *v.* **1** *tr. & intr.* bring or come to an end. **2** *intr.* (foll. by *in*) (of a word) end in (a specified letter or syllable, etc.). **3** *tr.* end (a pregnancy) before term by artificial means. **4** *tr.* bound; limit.

ter·mi·na·tion /tórmináyshən/ *n.* **1** the act or an instance of terminating; the state of being terminated. **2** *Med.* an induced abortion. **3** an ending or result of a specified kind (*a happy termination*). □□ **ter·mi·na·tion·al** *adj.*

ter·mi·na·tor /tórminaytər/ *n.* **1** a person or thing that terminates. **2** the dividing line between the light and dark part of a planetary body.

ter·mi·ni *pl. of* TERMINUS.

ter·mi·nol·o·gy /tórminóləjee/ *n.* (*pl.* **-ies**) **1** the system of terms used in a particular subject. **2** the science of the proper use of terms. □□ **ter·mi·nol·o·gist** *n.*

ter·mi·nus /tórminəs/ *n.* (*pl.* **termini** /-nī/ or **terminuses**) **1** a station or destination at the end of a railroad or bus route. **2** a point at the end of a pipeline, etc. **3** a final point; a goal. **4** a starting point. **5** *Math.* the end point of a vector, etc.

ter·mi·tar·y /tórmiteree/ *n.* (*pl.* **-ies**) a nest of termites, usu. a large mound of earth. ▷ NEST

ter·mite /tórmīt/ *n.* ▼ a small antlike social insect of the order Isoptera, chiefly tropical and destructive to wood.

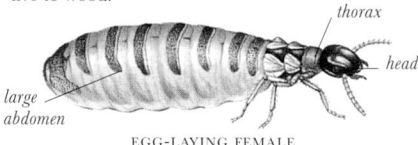

thorax   *head*

large abdomen

EGG-LAYING FEMALE

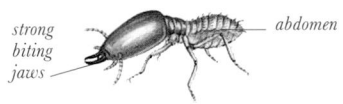

abdomen

strong biting jaws

SOLDIER TERMITE

TERMITES (*Macrotermes* species)

term pa·per *n.* an essay or dissertation representative of the work done during a term.

tern[1] /tərn/ *n.* ◄ any marine bird of the subfamily Sterninae, like a gull but usu. smaller and with a long forked tail. ▷ SEABIRD

tern[2] /tərn/ *n.* **1** a set of three, esp. three lottery numbers that when drawn together win a large prize. **2** such a prize.

ter·na·ry /tórnəree/ *adj.* **1** composed of three parts. **2** *Math.* using three as a base (*ternary scale*).

ter·pene /tórpeen/ *n. Chem.* any of a large group of unsaturated cyclic hydrocarbons found in the essential oils of plants, esp. conifers and oranges.

TERN: LITTLE TERN
(*Sterna albifrons*)

T

terp·si·cho·re·an /tɔrpsikəréeən, -káwreeən/ *adj.* of or relating to dancing.

terr. *abbr.* **1** terrace. **2** territory.

ter·ra al·ba /tɔrə álbə/ *n.* a white mineral, esp. pipe clay or pulverized gypsum.

ter·race /térəs/ *n. & v.* ● *n.* **1** each of a series of flat areas formed on a slope and used for cultivation. **2** a level paved area next to a house. **3 a** a row of houses on a raised level or along the top or face of a slope. **b** *Brit.* a row of houses built in one block of uniform style; a set of row houses. **4** *Geol.* a raised beach, or a similar formation beside a river, etc. ● *v.tr.* form into or provide with a terrace or terraces.

ter·ra·cot·ta /térəkótə/ *n. & adj.* ● *n.* **1a** unglazed usu. brownish red earthenware used chiefly as an ornamental building material and in modeling. **b** ◀ a statuette of this. **2** the color terracotta. ● *adj.* made of or resembling terracotta.

ter·ra fir·ma /térə fɔrmə/ *n.* dry land; firm ground.

ter·ra·form /térəfawrm/ *v.tr.* (esp. in science fiction) transform (a planet) so as to resemble the earth.

TERRACOTTA FIGURE OF AN ASSYRIAN HOUSEHOLD GOD

ter·rain /teráyn/ *n.* a tract of land, esp. with regard to its physical features.

ter·ra·pin /térəpin/ *n.* any of various N. American edible turtles of the family Emydidae, found in fresh or brackish water. ▷ CHELONIAN

ter·rar·i·um /teráireeəm/ *n.* (*pl.* **terrariums** or **terraria** /-reeə/) ► a glass enclosure containing growing plants or small land animals.

ter·raz·zo /təráazō, -ráatsō/ *n.* (*pl.* **-os**) a flooring material of stone chips set in concrete and given a smooth surface.

terre·plein /táirplayn, térə-/ *n.* a level space where a battery of guns is mounted.

ter·res·tri·al /təréstreeəl/ *adj. & n.* ● *adj.* **1** of or on the Earth; earthly. **2** of or on dry land. ● *n.* an inhabitant of the Earth. □□ **ter·res·tri·al·ly** *adv.*

ter·ri·ble /téribəl/ *adj.* **1** *colloq.* very great or bad (*a terrible bore*). **2** *colloq.* very incompetent (*terrible at tennis*). **3** causing terror; fit to cause terror; awful; dreadful; formidable. **4** (*predic.*; usu. foll. by *about*) *colloq.* full of remorse; sorry (*I felt terrible about it*). □□ **ter·ri·ble·ness** *n.*

ter·ri·bly /tériblee/ *adv.* **1** *colloq.* very; extremely (*he was terribly nice about it*). **2** in a terrible manner.

ter·ri·er /téreeər/ *n.* **1 a** a small dog of various breeds originally used for driving out foxes, etc., from their holes. **b** any of these breeds. **2** an eager or tenacious person or animal.

ter·rif·ic /tərífik/ *adj.* **1** *colloq.* **a** huge; intense. **b** excellent (*did a terrific job*). **c** excessive (*making a terrific noise*). **2** causing terror. □□ **ter·rif·i·cal·ly** *adv.*

ter·ri·fy /térifī/ *v.tr.* (**-ies**, **-ied**) fill with terror; frighten severely. □□ **ter·ri·fi·er** *n.* **ter·ri·fy·ing** *adj.* **ter·ri·fy·ing·ly** *adv.*

ter·rine /təréen/ *n.* **1** an earthenware vessel, esp. one in which pâté, etc., is cooked or sold. **2** pâté or similar food.

ter·ri·to·ri·al /téritáwreeəl/ *adj.* **1** of territory (*territorial possessions*). **2** limited to a district (*the right was strictly territorial*). **3** (of a person or animal, etc.) tending to defend an area of territory. **4** of any of the territories of the US or Canada. □□ **ter·ri·to·ri·al·i·ty** /-reeálitee/ *n.* **ter·ri·to·ri·al·ize** *v.tr.* **ter·ri·to·ri·al·i·za·tion** *n.* **ter·ri·to·ri·al·ly** *adv.*

ter·ri·to·ri·al wa·ters *n.pl.* the waters under the jurisdiction of a nation, esp. the part of the sea within a stated distance of the shore (traditionally three miles from the low water mark).

ter·ri·to·ry /téritawree/ *n.* (*pl.* **-ies**) **1** the extent of the land under the jurisdiction of a ruler, nation, city, etc. **2** (**Territory**) an organized division of a country, esp. one not yet admitted to the full rights of a state. **3** a sphere of action or thought; a province of something. **4** the area over which a sales representative or distributor operates. **5** *Zool.* an area defended by an animal or animals against others of the same species. **6** an area defended by a team or player in a game. **7** a large tract of land.

ter·ror /térər/ *n.* **1** extreme fear. **2 a** a cause of terror. **b** (also **holy terror**) *colloq.* a troublesome person (*the twins are little terrors*). **3** the use of organized intimidation; terrorism.

ter·ror·ist /térərist/ *n.* (also *attrib.*) a person who uses or favors violent and intimidating methods of coercing a government or community. □□ **ter·ror·ism** *n.* **ter·ror·is·tic** *adj.* **ter·ror·is·ti·cal·ly** *adv.*

ter·ror·ize /térərīz/ *v.tr.* **1** fill with terror. **2** use terrorism against. □□ **ter·ror·i·za·tion** *n.* **ter·ror·iz·er** *n.*

ter·ror·strick·en *adj.* (also **ter·ror·struck**) affected with terror.

ter·ry /téree/ *n. & adj.* ● *n.* (*pl.* **-ies**) a pile fabric with the loops uncut, used esp. for towels. ● *adj.* of this fabric.

terse /tɔrs/ *adj.* (**terser**, **tersest**) **1** (of language) brief; concise; to the point. **2** curt; abrupt. □□ **terse·ly** *adv.* **terse·ness** *n.*

ter·tian /tɔrshən/ *adj.* (of a fever) recurring every third day by inclusive counting.

ter·ti·ar·y /tɔrshee eree, -shəri/ *adj. & n.* ● *adj.* **1** third in order or rank, etc. **2** (**Tertiary**) *Geol.* of or relating to the first period in the Cenozoic era with evidence of the development of mammals and flowering plants (cf. PALEOCENE, EOCENE, OLIGOCENE, MIOCENE, PLIOCENE). ● *n. Geol.* this period or system.

TESL *abbr.* teaching of English as a second language.

tes·la /téslə/ *n.* a unit of magnetic flux density.

TESOL /tésawl, -ol/ *abbr.* teaching of English to speakers of other languages.

tes·sel·late /tésəlayt/ *v.tr.* **1** make from tesserae. **2** *Math.* cover (a plane surface) by repeated use of a single shape.

tes·sel·lat·ed /tésəlaytid/ *adj.* **1** of or resembling mosaic. **2** *Bot. & Zool.* regularly checkered.

tes·sel·la·tion /tésəláyshən/ *n.* **1** the act or an instance of tessellating; the state of being tessellated. **2** ◀ an arrangement of polygons without gaps or overlapping, esp. in a repeated pattern.

tes·ser·a /tésərə/ *n.* (*pl.* **tesserae** /-ree/) **1** a small square block used in mosaic. **2** *Gk & Rom. Antiq.* a small square of bone, etc., used as a token, ticket, etc. □□ **tes·ser·al** *adj.*

TESSELLATION IN ISLAMIC MOSAIC

tes·si·tu·ra /tésitŏŏrə/ *n. Mus.* the range within which most tones of a voice part fall.

test[1] /test/ *n. & v.* ● *n.* **1** a critical examination or trial of a person's or thing's qualities. **2** the means of so examining; a standard for comparison or trial; circumstances suitable for this (*success is not a fair test*). **3** a minor examination, esp. in school (*spelling test*). **4** *Brit. colloq.* a test match in cricket or rugby. **5** a ground for admission or rejection (*is excluded by our test*). **6** *Chem.* a reagent or a procedure employed to reveal the presence of another in a compound. **7** (*attrib.*) done or performed in order to test (*a test run*). ● *v.tr.* **1** put to the test; make trial of (a person or thing or quality). **2** try severely; tax a person's powers of endurance, etc. **3** *Chem.* examine by means of a reagent. □ **put to the test** cause to undergo a test. **test out** put (a theory, etc.) to a practical test. □□ **test·a·ble** *adj.* **test·a·bil·i·ty** /téstəbílitee/ *n.* **test·ee** /testée/ *n.*

test[2] /test/ *n.* ► the shell of some invertebrates, esp. echinoderms and tunicates.

Test. *abbr.* Testament.

tes·ta /téstə/ *n.* (*pl.* **testae** /-tee/) *Bot.* a seed coat. ▷ SEED

tes·ta·ceous /testáyshəs/ *adj.* **1** *Biol.* having a hard continuous outer covering. **2** *Bot. & Zool.* of a brick red color.

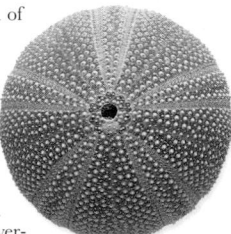

TEST OF A SEA URCHIN

tes·ta·ment /téstəmənt/ *n.* **1 a** will (esp. *last will and testament*). **2** (usu. foll. by *to*) evidence; proof (*is testament to his loyalty*). **3** *Bibl.* **a** a covenant or dispensation. **b** (**Testament**) a division of the Christian Bible (see OLD TESTAMENT, NEW TESTAMENT). **c** (**Testament**) a copy of the New Testament.

tes·ta·men·ta·ry /téstəméntəree/ *adj.* of or by or in a will.

tes·tate /téstayt/ *adj. & n.* ● *adj.* having left a valid will at death. ● *n.* a testate person. □□ **tes·ta·cy** *n.* (*pl.* **-ies**)

tes·ta·tor /téstaytər, testáytər/ *n.* (*fem.* **testatrix** /testáytriks/) a person who has made a will, esp. one who dies testate.

test case *n. Law* a case setting a precedent for other cases involving the same question of law.

test drive *n. & v.* ● *n.* a drive taken to determine the qualities of a motor vehicle with a view to its regular use. ● *v.tr.* (**test-drive**) (*past* **-drove**; *past part.* **-driven**) drive a vehicle for this purpose.

test·er[1] /téstər/ *n.* **1** a person or thing that tests. **2** a sample of a cosmetic, etc., allowing customers to try it before purchase.

test·er[2] /téstər/ *n.* a canopy, esp. over a four-poster bed.

tes·tes *pl.* of TESTIS.

test flight *n.* a flight during which the performance of an aircraft is tested. □□ **test-fly** *v.tr.* (**-flies**; *past* **-flew**; *past part.* **-flown**)

tes·ti·cle /téstikəl/ *n.* ▼ a male organ that produces spermatozoa, etc., esp. one of a pair enclosed in the scrotum behind the penis of a man and most mammals. □□ **tes·tic·u·lar** /-stíkyələr/ *adj.*

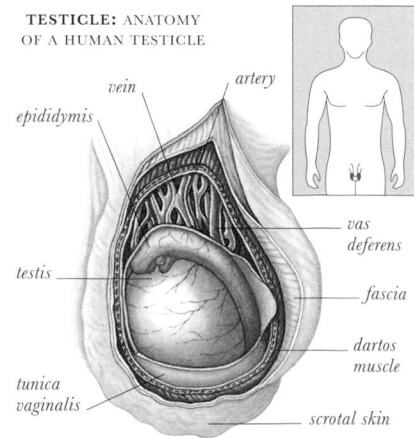

TESTICLE: ANATOMY OF A HUMAN TESTICLE

vein — artery — epididymis — vas deferens — testis — fascia — dartos muscle — tunica vaginalis — scrotal skin

T

tes·tic·u·late /testíkyələt/ *adj.* **1** having or shaped like testicles. **2** *Bot.* (esp. of an orchid) having pairs of tubers so shaped.

tes·ti·fy /téstifī/ *v.* (**-ies, -ied**) **1** *intr.* (of a person or thing) bear witness (*testified to the facts*). **2** *intr. Law* give evidence. **3** *tr.* affirm or declare (*testified his regret; testified that she had been present*). **4** *tr.* (of a thing) be evidence of; evince. □□ **tes·ti·fi·er** *n.*

tes·ti·mo·ni·al /téstimóneeəl/ *n.* **1** a certificate of character, conduct, or qualifications. **2** a gift presented to a person (esp. in public) as a mark of esteem, in acknowledgment of services, etc.

tes·ti·mo·ny /téstimōnee/ *n.* (*pl.* **-ies**) **1** *Law* an oral or written statement under oath or affirmation. **2** declaration or statement of fact. **3** evidence; demonstration (*called him in testimony; produce testimony*).

tes·tis /téstis/ *n.* (*pl.* **testes** /-teez/) *Anat.* & *Zool.* a testicle. ▷ ENDOCRINE, REPRODUCTIVE ORGANS

tes·tos·ter·one /testóstərōn/ *n.* a steroid androgen formed in the testicles.

test pat·tern *n.* a still television picture transmitted outside normal program hours and designed for use in judging the quality and position of the image.

test pi·lot *n.* a pilot who test-flies aircraft.

test tube *n.* a thin glass tube closed at one end used for chemical tests, etc. ▷ FLUORESCENCE

test-tube ba·by *n. colloq.* a baby conceived by *in vitro* fertilization.

tes·tu·di·nal /testóod'nəl, -tyóod-/ *adj.* of or shaped like a tortoise.

tes·tu·do /testóodō, testyóo-/ *n.* (*pl.* **-os** or **tes·tudines** /-dineez/) *Rom.Hist.* **1** a screen formed by a body of troops in close array with overlapping shields. **2** a movable screen to protect besieging troops.

tes·ty /téstee/ *adj.* (**testier, testiest**) irritable; touchy. □□ **tes·ti·ly** *adv.* **tes·ti·ness** *n.*

tet·a·nus /tét'nəs/ *n.* a bacterial disease affecting the nervous system and marked by tonic spasm of the voluntary muscles.

tet·a·ny /tét'nee/ *n.* a disease with intermittent muscular spasms caused by malfunction of the parathyroid glands and a consequent deficiency of calcium.

tetch·y /téchee/ *adj.* (also **tech·y**) (**-ier, -iest**) peevish; irritable. □□ **tetch·i·ly** *adv.* **tetch·i·ness** *n.*

tête-à-tête /táytaatáyt, tétaatét/ *n., adv.,* & *adj.* ● *n.* a private conversation or interview usu. between two persons. ● *adv.* together in private (*dined tête-à-tête*). ● *adj.* **1** private; confidential. **2** concerning only two persons.

tête-bêche /taytbésh, tét-/ *adj.* (of a postage stamp) printed upside down or sideways relative to another.

teth·er /téthər/ *n.* & *v.* ● *n.* a rope, etc., by which an animal is tied to confine it to the spot. ● *v.tr.* tie (an animal) with a tether. □ **at the end of one's tether** having reached the limit of one's patience, resources, abilities, etc.

tetra- /tétrə/ *comb. form* (also **tetr-** before a vowel) **1** four (*tetrapod*). **2** *Chem.* (forming names of compounds) containing four atoms or groups of a specified kind (*tetroxide*).

tet·ra·chord /tétrəkawrd/ *n. Mus.* **1** a scale pattern of four notes, the interval between the first and last being a perfect fourth. **2** a musical instrument with four strings.

tet·ra·cy·cline /tétrəsíkleen, -klin/ *n.* an antibiotic with a molecule of four rings.

tet·rad /tétrad/ *n.* **1** a group of four. ▷ MEIOSIS **2** the number four.

tet·ra·dac·tyl /tétrədáktil/ *n. Zool.* an animal with four toes on each foot. □□ **tet·ra·dac·tyl·ous** *adj.*

tet·ra·eth·yl lead /tétréthəl/ *n.* a liquid formerly added to gasoline as an antiknock agent.

tet·ra·gon /tétrəgon/ *n.* a plane figure with four angles and four sides.

te·trag·o·nal /tetrágənəl/ *adj.* of or like a tetragon. □□ **te·trag·o·nal·ly** *adv.*

tet·ra·gram /tétrəgram/ *n.* a word of four letters.

tet·ra·he·dron /tétrəheédrən/ *n.* (*pl.* **tetrahedra** /-drə/ or **tetrahedrons**) ▶ a four-faced regular solid; a triangular pyramid. □□ **tet·ra·he·dral** *adj.*

te·tral·o·gy /tetráləjee, -tról-/ *n.* (*pl.* **-ies**) **1** a group of four related literary or operatic works. **2** *Gk Antiq.* a trilogy of tragedies with a satyric drama.

te·tram·e·ter /tetrámitər/ *n. Prosody* a verse of four measures.

tet·ra·ple·gi·a /tétrəpleéjeeə, -jə/ *n. Med.* = QUADRIPLEGIA. □□ **tet·ra·ple·gic** *adj.* & *n.*

tet·ra·ploid /tétrəployd/ *adj.* & *n. Biol.* ● *adj.* (of an organism or cell) having four times the haploid set of chromosomes. ● *n.* a tetraploid organism or cell.

tet·ra·pod /tétrəpod/ *n.* **1** *Zool.* an animal with four feet. **2** a structure supported by four feet radiating from a center. □□ **te·trap·o·dous** /titrápədəs/ *adj.*

tet·rarch /tétraark/ *n.* **1** *Rom.Hist.* **a** the governor of a fourth part of a country or province. **b** a subordinate ruler. **2** one of four joint rulers. □□ **te·trarch·ate** /-kayt/ *n.* **te·trar·chi·cal** /-ráarkikəl/ *adj.* **te·trar·chy** /-kee/ *n.* (*pl.* **-ies**)

tet·ra·stich /tétrəstik/ *n. Prosody* a group of four lines of verse.

tet·ra·style /tétrəstīl/ *n.* & *adj.* ● *n.* a building with four pillars, esp. forming a portico in front or supporting a ceiling. ● *adj.* (of a building) built in this way.

te·trath·lon /tetráthlən/ *n.* a contest comprising four events, esp. riding, shooting, swimming, and running.

tet·ra·va·lent /tétrəváylənt/ *adj. Chem.* having a valence of four; quadrivalent.

tet·rode /tétrōd/ *n.* a thermionic valve having four electrodes.

Teu·ton /tóot'n, tyóotən/ *n.* a member of a Teutonic nation, esp. a German.

Teu·ton·ic /tōōtónik, tyōō-/ *adj.* **1** relating to or characteristic of the Germanic peoples or their languages. **2** German.

Tex. *abbr.* Texas.

Tex·an /téksən/ *n.* & *adj.* ● *n.* a native or inhabitant of Texas. ● *adj.* of or relating to Texas.

Tex-Mex /téksméks/ *adj.* combining cultural elements from Texas and Mexico, as in cooking, music, etc.

text[1] /tekst/ *n.* **1** the main body of a book as distinct from notes, appendices, pictures, etc. **2** the original words of an author or document, esp. as distinct from a paraphrase or commentary on them. **3** a passage quoted from Scripture, esp. as the subject of a sermon. **4** a subject or theme. **5** (in *pl.*) books prescribed for study. **6** a textbook. **7** data in textual form, esp. as stored, processed or displayed in a word processor etc. □□ **text·less** *adj.*

text[2] *v.* ▶ send (someone) an electronic text message by cellular phone.

text·book /tékstbŏok/ *n.* & *adj.* ● *n.* a book for use in studying, esp. a standard account of a subject. ● *attrib.adj.* **1** exemplary; accurate (cf. COPYBOOK). **2** instructively typical. □□ **text·book·ish** *adj.*

text ed·i·tor *n. Computing* a system or program allowing the user to enter and edit text.

tex·tile /tékstīl/ *n.* & *adj.* ● *n.* **1** any woven material. **2** any cloth. ● *adj.* **1** of weaving or cloth (*textile industry*). **2** woven (*textile fabrics*). **3** suitable for weaving (*textile materials*).

text proc·ess·ing *n. Computing* the manipulation of text, esp. transforming it from one format to another.

tex·tu·al /tékschōoəl/ *adj.* of, in, or concerning a text (*textual errors*). □□ **tex·tu·al·ly** *adv.*

tex·tu·al·ist /tékschōoəlist/ *n.* a person

TETRAHEDRON

who adheres strictly to the letter of the text. □□ **tex·tu·al·ism** *n.*

tex·ture /tékschər/ *n.* & *v.* ● *n.* **1** the feel or appearance of a surface or substance. **2** the arrangement of threads, etc., in textile fabric. **3** the arrangement of small constituent parts. **4** the quality of a piece of writing, esp. with reference to imagery, alliteration, etc. **5** quality or style resulting from composition (*the texture of her life*). ● *v.tr.* (usu. as **textured** *adj.*) provide with a texture. □□ **tex·tur·al** *adj.* **tex·tur·al·ly** *adv.* **tex·ture·less** *adj.*

tex·tur·ize /tékschərīz/ *v.tr.* (usu. as **texturized** *adj.*) impart a particular texture to (fabrics or food).

Th *symb. Chem.* the element thorium.

Th. *abbr.* Thursday.

Thai /tī/ *n.* & *adj.* ● *n.* (*pl.* same or **Thais**) **1 a** a native or inhabitant of Thailand in SE Asia; a member of the largest ethnic group in Thailand. **b** a person of Thai descent. **2** the language of Thailand. ● *adj.* of or relating to Thailand or its people or language.

thal·a·mus /tháləməs/ *n.* (*pl.* **thalami** /-mī/) *Anat.* either of two masses of gray matter in the forebrain, serving as relay stations for sensory tracts. ▷ BRAIN. □□ **tha·lam·ic** /thəlámik, tháləmik/ *adj.*

tha·las·sic /thəlásik/ *adj.* of the sea or seas, esp. small or inland seas.

tha·lid·o·mide /thəlídəmīd/ *n.* a drug formerly used as a sedative but found in 1961 to cause fetal malformation when taken by a mother early in pregnancy.

thal·li *pl.* of THALLUS.

thal·li·um /tháleeəm/ *n. Chem.* a rare soft white metallic element, occurring naturally in zinc blende and some iron ores. ¶ Symb.: Tl.

thal·lus /tháləs/ *n.* (*pl.* **thalli** /-lī/) a plant body without vascular tissue and not differentiated into root, stem, and leaves. ▷ BRYOPHYTE. □□ **thal·loid** *adj.*

than /than, thən/ *conj.* **1** introducing the second element in a comparison (*you are older than he is; you are older than he*). ¶ It is also possible to say *you are older than him*, with *than* treated as a preposition, esp. in less formal contexts. **2** introducing the second element in a statement of difference (*anyone other than me*).

than·a·tol·o·gy /thánətóləjee/ *n.* the scientific study of death and its associated phenomena and practices. **thane** /thayn/ *n. hist.* **1** a man who held land from an English king or other superior by military service, ranking between ordinary freemen and hereditary nobles. **2** a man who held land from a Scottish king and ranked with an earl's son; the chief of a clan. □□ **thane·dom** *n.*

thank /thangk/ *v.* & *n.* ● *v.tr.* **1** express gratitude to (*thanked him for the present*). **2** hold responsible (*you can thank yourself for that*). ● *n.* (in *pl.*) **1** gratitude (*expressed his heartfelt thanks*). **2** an expression of gratitude (*give thanks to all who helped*). **3** (as a formula) thank you (*thanks for your help; thanks very much*). □ **give thanks** say grace at a meal. **no** (or **small**) **thanks to** despite. **thank goodness** (or **God** or **heavens**, etc.) **1** *colloq.* an expression of relief or pleasure. **2** an expression of pious gratitude. **thanks to** as the (good or bad) result of (*thanks to my foresight; thanks to your obstinacy*). **thank you** a polite formula acknowledging a gift or service or an offer accepted or refused.

thank-you *n. colloq.* an instance of expressing thanks.

thank·ful /thángkfŏol/ *adj.* **1** grateful; pleased. **2** (of words or acts) expressive of thanks. □□ **thank·ful·ness** *n.*

thank·ful·ly /thángkfŏolee/ *adv.* **1** in a thankful manner. **2** *disp.* let us be thankful; fortunately (*thankfully, nobody was hurt*).

thank·less /thángklis/ *adj.* **1** not expressing or feeling gratitude; ungrateful; unappreciative (*a thankless beneficiary*). **2** (of a task, etc.) giving no pleasure or

TEXT: CELLULAR PHONE WITH TEXT MESSAGE

THEATER

The earliest theaters, built by the ancient Greeks, were open-air structures, usually set in a natural hollow, with a circular dancing and singing area, a stage, and a semi-circular auditorium. Roman and Renaissance theaters became progressively more elaborate, but both kept the audience in front of the stage. Elizabethan theaters brought the audience closer, and this idea developed into the modern theater-in-the-round. However, most theaters now have a U-shaped seating area in front of a stage framed by a proscenium arch.

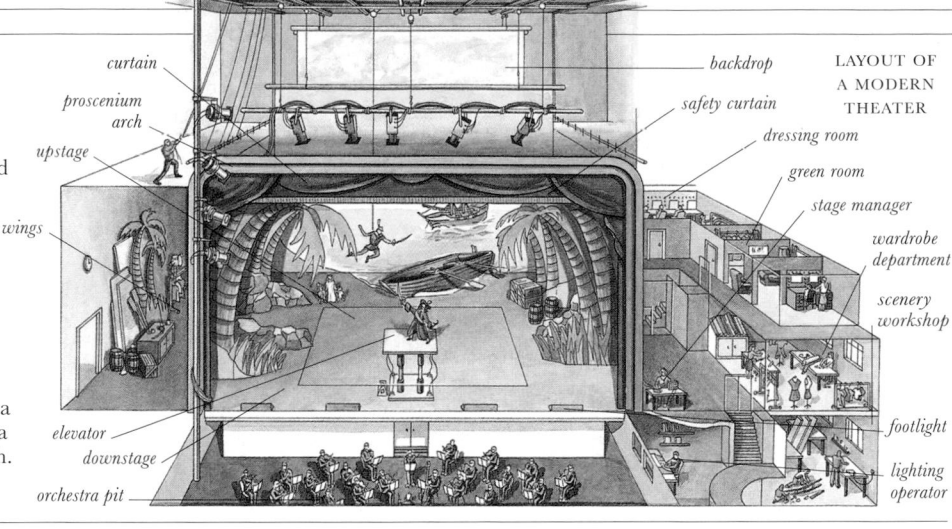

LAYOUT OF A MODERN THEATER

curtain · proscenium arch · upstage · wings · elevator · downstage · orchestra pit · backdrop · safety curtain · dressing room · green room · stage manager · wardrobe department · scenery workshop · footlight · lighting operator

TYPES OF THEATER

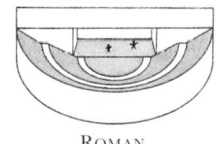
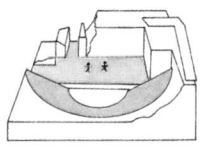
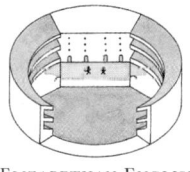
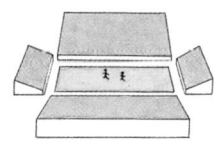

ANCIENT GREEK   ROMAN   RENAISSANCE   ELIZABETHAN ENGLISH   THEATER-IN-THE-ROUND

---

profit. **3** not deserving thanks. □□ **thank·less·ly** *adv.* **thank·less·ness** *n.*

thanks·giv·ing /thángksgíving/ *n.* **1 a** the expression of gratitude, esp. as a prayer. **b** a form of words for this. **2** (**Thanksgiving** or **Thanksgiving Day**) a national holiday for giving thanks, the fourth Thursday in November in the US, usu. the second Monday in October in Canada.

that /*th*at/ *pron., adj., adv., & conj.* ● *demons.pron.* (*pl.* **those** /*thōz*/) **1** the person or thing indicated, named, or understood, esp. when observed by the speaker or when familiar to the person addressed (*I heard that; who is that in the yard?; I knew all that before; that is not fair*) **2** (contrasted with *this*) the further or less immediate or obvious, etc., of two (*this bag is much heavier than that*). **3** the action, behavior, or circumstances just observed or mentioned (*don't do that again*). **4** *Brit.* (on the telephone, etc.) the person spoken to (*who is that?*). **5** esp. *Brit. colloq.* referring to a strong feeling just mentioned (*'Are you glad?' 'I am that'*). **6** (esp. in relative constructions) the one, the person, etc., described or specified in some way (*those who have cars can take the luggage; those unfit for use; a table like that described above*). **7** /*th*ət/ (*pl.* **that**) used instead of *which* or *whom* to introduce a defining clause, esp. one essential to identification (*the book that you sent me; there is nothing here that matters*). ¶ As a relative *that* usually specifies, whereas *who* or *which* need not: compare *the book that you sent me is lost* with *the book, which I gave you, is lost.* ● *demons.adj.* (*pl.* **those** /*th*ōz/) **1** designating the person or thing indicated, named, understood, etc. (cf. sense 1 of *pron.*) (*look at that dog; what was that noise?; things were easier in those days*). **2** contrasted with *this* (cf. sense 2 of *pron.*) (*this bag is heavier than that one*). **3** expressing strong feeling (*shall not easily forget that day*). ● *adv.* **1** to such a degree; so (*have done that much; will go that far*). **2** *colloq.* very (*not that good*). **3** /*th*ət/ at which, on which, etc. (*at the speed that he was going he could not stop; the day that I first met her*). ¶ Often omitted in this sense: *the day I first met her.* ● *conj.* /*th*ət/ except when stressed introducing a subordinate clause indicating: **1** a statement or hypothesis (*they say that he is better; there is no doubt that he meant it; the result was that the handle fell off*). **2** a purpose (*we live that we may eat*). **3** a result (*am so sleepy that I cannot keep my eyes open*). **4** a reason or cause (*it is rather that he lacks the time*). **5** a wish (*Oh,*

that summer were here!). ¶ Often omitted in senses 1, 3: *they say he is better.* □ **all that** very (*not all that good*). **and all that** (or **and that** *colloq.*) and all or various things associated with or similar to what has been mentioned; and so forth. **like that 1** of that kind (*is fond of books like that*). **2** in that manner; as you are doing; as he has been doing; etc. (*wish they would not talk like that*). **3** *colloq.* without effort (*did the job like that*). **4** of that character (*he would not accept any payment – he is like that*). **that is** (or **that is to say**) a formula introducing or following an explanation of a preceding word or words. **that's** *colloq.* you are (by virtue of present or future obedience, etc.) (*that's a good boy*). **that's more like it** an acknowledgment of improvement. **that's right** an expression of approval or *colloq.* assent. **that's that** a formula concluding a narrative or discussion or indicating completion of a task. **that there** *sl.* = sense 1 of *adj.* **that will do** no more is needed or desirable.

thatch /thach/ *n. & v.* ● *n.* **1 ▶** a roofing material of straw, reeds, palm leaves, or similar material. **2** *colloq.* the hair of the head esp. when extremely thick. ● *v.tr.* (also *absol.*) cover (a roof or a building) with thatch. □□ **thatch·er** *n.*

thaw /thaw/ *v. & n.* ● *v.* **1** *intr.* (often foll. by *out*) (of ice or snow or a frozen thing) pass into a liquid or unfrozen state. **2** *intr.* (usu. prec. by *it* as subject) (of the weather) become warm enough to melt ice, etc. (*it began to thaw*). **3** *intr.* become warm enough to lose numbness, etc. **4** *intr.* become less cold or stiff in manner; become genial. **5** *tr.* (often foll. by *out*) cause to thaw. **6** *tr.* make cordial or animated. ● *n.* **1** the act or an instance of thawing. **2** the warmth of weather that thaws (*a thaw has set in*). **3** *Polit.* a relaxation of control or restriction. □□ **thaw·less** *adj.*

the /before a vowel *th*ee, before a consonant *th*ə, when stressed *th*ee/ *adj. & adv.* ● *adj.* (called the definite article) **1** denoting one or more persons or things already mentioned, under discussion, implied, or familiar (*gave the man a wave; shall let the*

thatch · hazel rod · rafter · lath · tie beam

THATCH: STRUCTURE OF A THATCHED ROOF

matter drop; hurt myself in the arm; went to the theater) **2** serving to describe as unique (*the President; the Mississippi*). **3 a** (foll. by defining adj.) which is, who are, etc. (*ignored the embarrassed Mr. Smith; Edward the Seventh*). **b** (foll. by adj. used *absol.*) denoting a class described (*from the sublime to the ridiculous*). **4** best known or best entitled to the name (with *the* stressed: *no relation to the Hemingway; this is the book on this subject*). **5** used to indicate a following defining clause or phrase (*the book that you borrowed; the best I can do for you; the bottom of a well*). **6 a** used to indicate that a singular noun represents a species, class, etc. (*the cat loves comfort; has the novel a future?; plays the harp well*). **b** used with a noun which figuratively represents an occupation, pursuit, etc. (*went on the stage; too fond of the bottle*). **c** (foll. by the name of a unit) a; per (*$5 the square yard; allow 8 minutes to the mile*). **d** *colloq.* designating a disease, affliction, etc. (*the measles; the toothache; the blues*). **7** (foll. by a unit of time) the present; the current (*man of the moment; questions of the day; book of the month*). **8** *colloq.* my; our (*the dog; the car*). **9** used before the surname of the chief of a Scottish or Irish clan (*the Macnab*). ● *adv.* (preceding comparatives in expressions of proportional variation) in or by that (or such a) degree; on that account (*the more the merrier; the more he gets the more he wants*). □ **all the** in the full degree to be expected (*that makes it all the worse*). **so much the** (tautologically) so much; in that degree (*so much the worse for him*).

the·a·ter /thééətər/ *n.* (*Brit.* **theatre**) **1 a ▲** a building or outdoor area for dramatic performances. ▷ AUDITORIUM. **b** (in full **movie theater**) a building used for showing movies. **2 a** the writing and production of plays. **b** effective material for the stage (*makes good theater*). **c** action with a dramatic quality; dramatic character or effect. **3** a room or hall for lectures, etc., with seats in tiers. **4** (in full **operating theater**) **a** a room or lecture hall with rising tiers of seats to accommodate students' viewing of surgical procedures. **b** *Brit.* = OPERATING ROOM. **5 a** a scene or field of action (*the theater of war*).

T

b (*attrib.*) designating weapons intermediate between tactical and strategic (*theater nuclear missiles*). **6** a natural land formation in a gradually rising part-circle like ancient Greek and Roman theaters.

the·a·ter-go·ing /theeátrik/ *adj.* frequenting theaters. □□ **the·a·ter-go·er** *n.*

the·a·ter-in-the-round *n.* a dramatic performance on a stage surrounded by spectators. ▷ THEATER

the·at·ric /theeátrik/ *adj. & n.* ● *adj.* = THEATRICAL. ● *n.* (in *pl.*) theatrical actions.

the·at·ri·cal /theeátrikəl/ *adj. & n.* ● *adj.* **1** of or for the theater; of acting or actors. **2** exaggerated and excessively dramatic. ● *n.* (in *pl.*) **1** dramatic performances (*amateur theatricals*). **2** theatrical actions. □□ **the·at·ri·cal·ism** *n.* **the·at·ri·cal·i·ty** /-kálitee/ *n.* **the·at·ri·cal·ize** *v.tr.* **the·at·ri·cal·i·za·tion** *n.* **the·at·ri·cal·ly** *adv.*

thee /thee/ *pron. objective case* of THOU[1].

theft /theft/ *n.* the act or crime of stealing.

their /thair/ *poss.pron.* (*attrib.*) **1** of or belonging to them or themselves (*their house; their own business*). **2** *disp.* as a third person sing. indefinite meaning 'his or her' (*has anyone lost their purse?*).

theirs /thairz/ *poss.pron.* the one or ones belonging to or associated with them (*it is theirs; theirs are over here*). □ **of theirs** of or belonging to them.

the·ism /théeizəm/ *n.* belief in the existence of gods or a god, esp. a God sustaining a personal relation to his creatures. □□ **the·ist** *n.* **the·ist·ic** *adj.* **the·ist·i·cal** *adj.* **the·is·ti·cal·ly** *adv.*

them /them, thəm/ *pron. & adj.* ● *pron.* **1** objective case of THEY (*I saw them*). **2** *colloq.* they (*is older than them*). **3** *archaic* themselves (*they fell and hurt them*).

the·mat·ic /theemátik/ *adj.* **1** of or relating to subjects or topics (*thematic philately; the arrangement of the anthology is thematic*). **2** *Mus.* of melodic subjects (*thematic treatment*). □□ **the·mat·i·cal·ly** *adv.*

theme /theem/ *n. & v.* ● *n.* **1** a subject or topic on which a person speaks, writes, or thinks. **2** *Mus.* a prominent or frequently recurring melody or group of notes in a composition. **3** a school exercise, esp. an essay, on a given subject. ● *v.tr.* (as **themed** *adj.*) **1** (of a leisure park, restaurant, event, etc.) designed around a theme to unify ambience, decor, etc. **2** (often in *comb.*) having a particular theme (*war-themed computer game*).

theme park *n.* an amusement park organized around a unifying idea.

theme song *n.* **1** a recurrent melody in a musical play or movie. **2** a signature tune.

them·selves /themsélvz, -thəm-/ *pron.* **1 a** *emphat. form* of THEY or THEM. **b** *refl. form* of THEM; (cf. HERSELF). **2** in their normal state of body or mind (*are quite themselves again*). □ **be themselves** act in their normal, unconstrained manner.

then /then/ *adv., adj., & n.* ● *adv.* **1** at that time; at the time in question (*was then too busy; then comes the trouble; the then existing laws*). **2 a** next; afterwards; after that (*then he told me to come in*). **b** and also (*then, there are the children to consider*). **c** after all (*it is a problem, but then that is what we are here for*). **3 a** in that case; therefore; it follows that (*then you should have said so*). **b** if what you say is true (*but then why did you take it?*). **c** (implying grudging or impatient concession) if you must have it so (*all right then, have it your own way*). **d** used parenthetically to resume a narrative, etc. (*the policeman, then, knocked on the door*). ● *adj.* that or who was such at the time in question (*the then Senator*). ● *n.* that time (*until then*). □ **then and there** immediately and on the spot.

thence /thens/ *adv.* (also **from thence**) *archaic* or *literary* **1** from that place or source. **2** for that reason.

thence·forth /thénsfáwrth/ *adv.* (also **from thence·forth**) *formal* from that time onward.

thence·for·ward /thénsfáwrwərd/ *adv. formal* thenceforth.

theo- /thée-ō/ *comb. form* God or gods.

THEODOLITE

A theodolite is an instrument that enables the height and position of distant objects to be calculated by measuring the angles between a baseline (formed by two known positions of the theodolite) and a direct line to the object concerned.

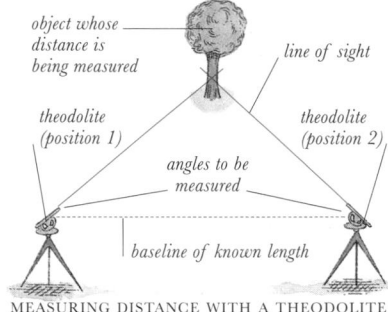

MEASURING DISTANCE WITH A THEODOLITE

---

the·o·cen·tric /théeəséntrik/ *adj.* having God or a god as its center.

the·oc·ra·cy /theeókrəsee/ *n.* (*pl.* **-ies**) a form of government by God or a god directly or through a priestly order, etc. □□ **the·o·crat** /théeəkrat/ *n.* **the·o·crat·ic** /theeəkrátik/ *adj.* **the·o·crat·i·cal·ly** *adv.*

the·od·o·lite /theeód'līt/ *n.* ▲ a surveying instrument for measuring horizontal and vertical angles with a rotating telescope. □□ **the·od·o·lit·ic** /-lítik/ *adj.*

theol. *abbr.* **1** theological. **2** theology.

the·o·lo·gian /théeəlójən/ *n.* a person trained in theology.

the·o·log·i·cal /théeəlójikəl/ *adj.* of theology. □□ **the·o·log·i·cal·ly** *adv.*

the·ol·o·gy /theeóləjee/ *n.* (*pl.* **-ies**) **1** the study of God and religious beliefs. **2** religious beliefs and theory when systematically developed. □□ **the·ol·o·gist** *n.* **the·ol·o·gize** *v.tr. & intr.*

the·o·rem /théeərəm, théerəm/ *n.* esp. *Math.* **1** a general proposition not self-evident but proved by a chain of reasoning; a truth established by means of accepted truths (cf. PROBLEM). **2** a rule in algebra, etc., esp. one expressed by symbols or formulae (*binomial theorem*). □□ **the·o·re·mat·ic** /-mátik/ *adj.*

the·o·ret·ic /theeərétik/ *adj.* = THEORETICAL.

the·o·ret·i·cal /theeərétikəl/ *adj.* **1** concerned with knowledge but not with its practical application. **2** based on theory rather than experience or practice. □□ **the·o·ret·i·cal·ly** *adv.*

the·o·re·ti·cian /théeəritishən, -théerit/ *n.* a person concerned with the theoretical aspects of a subject.

the·o·rist /théeərist, théerist/ *n.* a holder or inventor of a theory or theories.

the·o·rize /théeərīz, théerīz/ *v.intr.* evolve or indulge in theories. □□ **the·o·riz·er** *n.*

the·o·ry /théeəree, théeree/ *n.* (*pl.* **-ies**) **1** a supposition or system of ideas explaining something, esp. one based on general principles independent of the particular things to be explained (cf. HYPOTHESIS) (*atomic theory; theory of evolution*). **2** a speculative (esp. fanciful) view (*one of my pet theories*). **3** the sphere of abstract knowledge or speculative thought (*this is all very well in theory, but how will it work in practice?*). **4** the exposition of the principles of a science, etc. (*the theory of music*). **5** *Math.* a collection of propositions to illustrate the principles of a subject (*probability theory; theory of equations*).

the·os·o·phy /theeósəfee/ *n.* (*pl.* **-ies**) any of various philosophies professing to achieve a knowledge of God by spiritual ecstasy, direct intuition, or special individual relations, esp. a modern movement following Hindu and Buddhist teachings and seeking universal brotherhood. □□ **the·os·o·pher**

n. **the·o·soph·ic** /théeəsófik/ *adj.* **the·o·soph·i·cal** *adj.* **the·o·soph·i·cal·ly** *adv.* **the·os·o·phist** *n.*

ther·a·peu·tic /thérəpyóotik/ *adj.* **1** of, for, or contributing to the cure of disease. **2** contributing to general, esp. mental, well-being (*finds walking therapeutic*, etc.). □□ **ther·a·peu·ti·cal** *adj.* **ther·a·peu·ti·cal·ly** *adv.* **ther·a·peu·tist** *n.*

ther·a·peu·tics /thérəpyóotiks/ *n.pl.* (usu. treated as *sing.*) the branch of medicine concerned with the treatment of disease and the action of remedial agents.

ther·a·py /thérəpee/ *n.* (*pl.* **-ies**) **1** the treatment of physical or mental disorders, other than by surgery. **2 a** a particular type of such treatment. **b** psychotherapy. □□ **ther·a·pist** *n.*

there /thair/ *adv., n., & int.* ● *adv.* **1** in, at, or to that place or position (*lived there for some years; goes there every day*). **2** at that point (in speech, performance, writing, etc.) (*there he stopped*). **3** in that respect (*I agree with you there*). **4** used for emphasis in calling attention (*you there!; there goes the bell*). **5** used to indicate the fact or existence of something (*there is a house on the corner*). **n.** that place (*lives somewhere near there*). ● *int.* **1** expressing confirmation, triumph, dismay, etc. (*there! what did I tell you?*). **2** used to soothe a child, etc. (*there, there, never mind*). □ **have been there before** *sl.* know all about it. **so there** *colloq.* that is my final decision (whether you like it or not). **there and then** immediately and on the spot. **there it is 1** that is the trouble. **2** nothing can be done about it. **there's** *Brit. colloq.* you are (by virtue of present or future obedience, etc.) (*there's a dear*). **there you are** (or **go**) *colloq.* **1** this is what you wanted, etc. **2** expressing confirmation, triumph, resignation, etc.

there·a·bouts /tháirəbówts/ *adv.* (also **there·a·bout**) **1** near that place (*ought to be somewhere thereabouts*). **2** near that number, quantity, etc. (*two acres or thereabouts*).

there·af·ter /tháiráftər/ *adv.* after that.

there·by /tháirbí/ *adv.* by that means; as a result of that. □ **thereby hangs a tale** much could be said about that.

there·fore /tháirfawr/ *adv.* for that reason; accordingly; consequently.

there·from /tháirfrúm, -fróm/ *adv. formal* from that or it.

there·in /tháirín/ *adv. formal* **1** in that place, etc. **2** in that respect.

the·re·min /thérəmin/ *n.* an electronic musical instrument in which the tone is generated by two high-frequency oscillators and the pitch controlled by the movement of the performer's hand towards and away from the circuit.

there·of /tháirúv, -óv/ *adv. formal* of that or it.

there·on /tháirón, -áwn/ *adv. archaic* on that or it (of motion or position).

there·to /tháirtóo/ *adv. formal* **1** to that or it. **2** in addition; to boot.

there·up·on /tháirəpón, -páwn/ *adv.* **1** in consequence of that. **2** soon or immediately after that. **3** *archaic* upon that (of motion or position).

there·with /tháirwíth, -wíth/ *adv. archaic* **1** with that. **2** soon or immediately after that.

there·with·al /tháirwithawl, -with-/ *adv. archaic* in addition; besides.

therm /thərm/ *n.* a unit of heat, equivalent to 100,000 British thermal units or 1.055×10^8 joules.

ther·mal /thórməl/ *adj. & n.* ● *adj.* **1** of, for, or producing heat. **2** promoting the retention of heat (*thermal underwear*). ● *n.* ▲ a rising current of heated air (used by gliders, balloons, and birds to gain height). □□ **ther·mal·ly** *adv.*

ther·mal im·ag·ing *n.* the technique of using the heat given off by an object to produce an image of it or locate it. ▷ THERMOGRAM

ther·mal print·er *n.* *Comp.* a printer that makes a text image by application of heat to thermally sensitive paper.

ther·mic /thórmik/ *adj.* of or relating to heat.

THERMAL

Air warmed by the sun expands and becomes less dense than the surrounding air. This creates upcurrents called thermals. Birds use these to gain height in an energy-efficient way, soaring to the top of one then gliding to the base of the next.

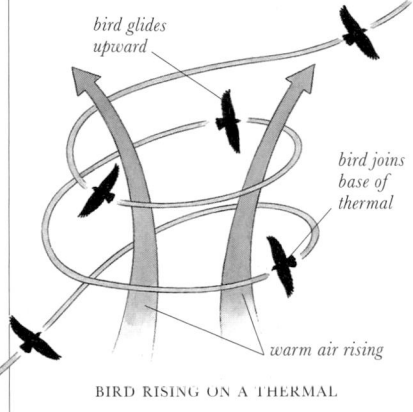

bird glides upward

bird joins base of thermal

warm air rising

BIRD RISING ON A THERMAL

therm·i·on·ic /thɔrmīónik/ *adj.* of or relating to electrons emitted from a substance at very high temperature.

therm·i·on·ics /thɔrmīóniks/ *n.pl.* (treated as *sing.*) the branch of science and technology concerned with thermionic emission.

therm·is·tor /thɔrmístər/ *n. Electr.* a resistor whose resistance is greatly reduced by heating, used for measurement and control. ▷ RESISTOR

ther·mite /thɔrmīt/ *n.* (also **ther·mit** /-mit/) a mixture of finely powdered aluminum and iron oxide that produces a very high temperature on combustion (used in welding and for incendiary bombs).

thermo- /thɔrmō/ *comb. form* denoting heat.

ther·mo·chem·is·try /thɔrmōkémistree/ *n.* the branch of chemistry dealing with the quantities of heat evolved or absorbed during chemical reactions. □□ **ther·mo·chem·i·cal** *adj.*

ther·mo·cou·ple /thɔrmōkupəl/ *n.* a pair of different metals in contact at a point, generating a thermoelectric voltage that can serve as a measure of temperature at this point relative to their other parts.

ther·mo·dy·nam·ics /thɔrmōdīnámiks/ *n.pl.* (usu. treated as *sing.*) the science of the relations between heat and other (mechanical, electrical, etc.) forms of energy. □□ **ther·mo·dy·nam·ic** *adj.* **ther·mo·dy·nam·i·cal** *adj.* **ther·mo·dy·nam·i·cist** /-misist/ *n.*

ther·mo·e·lec·tric /thɔrmōiléktrik/ *adj.* producing electricity by a difference of temperatures. □□ **ther·mo·e·lec·tri·cal·ly** *adv.* **ther·mo·e·lec·tric·i·ty** /-ilektrísitee/ *n.*

ther·mo·gram /thɔrməgram/ *n.* ◄ a record made by a thermograph.

ther·mo·graph /thɔrməgraf/ *n.* **1** an instrument that gives a continuous record of temperature. **2** an apparatus used to obtain an image produced by infrared radiation from a human or animal body. □□ **ther·mo·graph·ic** /-gráfik/ *adj.*

black shows cold area

yellow shows hot area

THERMOGRAM OF A MAN WEARING GLASSES

ther·mog·ra·phy /thɔrmógrəfee/ *n. Med.* the taking or use of infrared thermograms, esp. to detect tumors.

ther·mo·lab·ile /thɔrmōláybīl, -bil/ *adj.* (of a substance) unstable when heated.

ther·mo·lu·mi·nes·cence /thɔrmōlooominésəns/ *n.* the property of becoming luminescent when pretreated and subjected to high temperatures, used as a means of dating ancient artifacts. □□ **ther·mo·lu·mi·nes·cent** *adj.*

ther·mom·e·ter /thɔrmómitər/ *n.* ► an instrument for measuring temperature, esp. a graduated glass tube with a small bore containing mercury or alcohol which expands when heated. ▷ MERCURY. □□ **ther·mo·met·ric** /thɔrməmétrik/ *adj.* **ther·mo·met·ri·cal** *adj.* **ther·mom·e·ry** *n.*

ther·mo·nu·cle·ar /thɔrmōnóo͞okleeər, -nyóo͞o-/ *adj.* **1** relating to or using nuclear reactions that occur only at very high temperatures. **2** relating to or characterized by weapons using thermonuclear reactions.

ther·mo·phile /thɔrmōfīl/ *n. & adj.* (also **ther·mo·phil** /-fil/) ● *n.* a bacterium, etc., growing optimally at high temperatures. ● *adj.* of or being a thermophile. □□ **ther·mo·phil·ic** /-fílik/ *adj.*

ther·mo·plas·tic /thɔrmōplástik/ *adj. & n.* ● *adj.* (of a substance) that becomes plastic on heating and hardens on cooling, and is able to repeat these processes. ● *n.* a thermoplastic substance. ▷ PLASTIC

ther·mos /thɔrmɔs/ *n.* (in full **thermos bottle** or **flask**) *Trademark* ► a bottle, etc., with a double wall enclosing a vacuum so that the liquid in the inner receptacle retains its temperature.

ther·mo·sphere /thɔrməsfeer/ *n.* the region of the atmosphere beyond the stratosphere and the mesosphere. ▷ ATMOSPHERE

ther·mo·stat /thɔrməstat/ *n.* ▼ a device that automatically regulates temperature, as in a heating or cooling unit, or that activates a device when the temperature reaches a certain point, as in a fire alarm system. □□ **ther·mo·stat·ic** *adj.* **ther·mo·stat·i·cal·ly** *adv.*

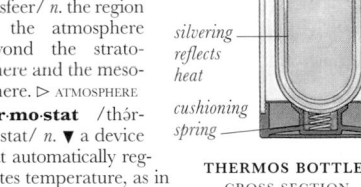

ELECTRONIC
THERMOMETER

digital display

scale

Microwave

alcohol

heat-sensitive tip

LIQUID
THERMOMETER

THERMOMETERS

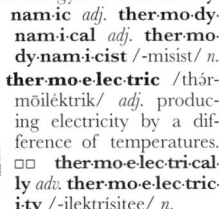

spout   *stopper*

liquid

vacuum

double wall

silvering reflects heat

cushioning spring

THERMOS BOTTLE:
CROSS SECTION

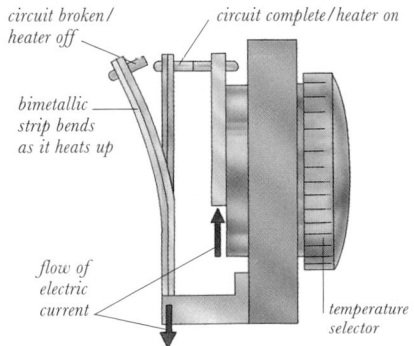

circuit broken/ heater off

circuit complete/heater on

bimetallic strip bends as it heats up

flow of electric current

temperature selector

THERMOSTAT USED TO CONTROL
A HEATING SYSTEM

ther·mo·tax·is /thɔrmōtáksis/ *n.* **1** the regulation of heat or temperature, esp. in warm-blooded animals. **2** movement or stimulation in a living organism caused by heat. □□ **ther·mo·tac·tic** *adj.* **ther·mo·tax·ic** *adj.*

ther·mot·ro·pism /thɔrmótrəpizəm/ *n.* the growing or bending of a plant toward or away from a source of heat. □□ **ther·mo·tro·pic** /thɔrmōtrópik/ *adj.*

the·sau·rus /thisáwrəs/ *n.* (*pl.* **thesauri** /-rī/ or **thesauruses**) **1 a** a collection of concepts or words arranged according to sense. **b** a book of synonyms and antonyms. **2** a dictionary or encyclopedia.

these *pl.* of THIS.

the·sis /theésis/ *n.* (*pl.* **theses** /-seez/) **1** a proposition to be maintained or proved. **2** a dissertation, esp. by a candidate for a degree.

thes·pi·an /théspeeən/ *adj. & n.* ● *adj.* of or relating to tragedy or drama. ● *n.* an actor or actress.

the·ta /tháytə, theé-/ *n.* the eighth letter of the Greek alphabet (Θ, θ).

thew /thyoō/ *n.* (often in *pl.*) *literary* **1** muscular strength. **2** mental or moral vigor.

they /thay/ *pron.* (*obj.* **them**; *poss.* **their**, **theirs**) **1** the people, animals, or things previously named or in question (*pl.* of HE, SHE, IT). **2** people in general (*they say we are wrong*). **3** those in authority (*they have raised the fees*). **4** *disp.* as a third person sing. indefinite pronoun meaning 'he or she' (*anyone can come if they want to*).

they'd /thayd/ *contr.* **1** they had. **2** they would.

they'll /thayl/ *contr.* **1** they will. **2** they shall.

they're /thair/ *contr.* they are.

they've /thayv/ *contr.* they have.

thi·a·mine /thíəmin, -meen/ *n.* (also **thi·a·min**) a vitamin of the B complex, found in unrefined cereals, beans, and liver, a deficiency of which causes beriberi. Also called **vitamin B_1**, or **aneurin**.

thick /thik/ *adj., n., & adv.* ● *adj.* **1 a** of great or specified extent between opposite surfaces (*a thick wall; a wall two feet thick*). **b** of large diameter (*a thick rope*). **2 a** (of a line, etc.) broad; not fine. **b** (of script or type, etc.) consisting of thick lines. **3 a** arranged closely; crowded together; dense. **b** numerous (*fell thick as peas*). **c** bushy; luxuriant (*thick hair; thick growth*). **4** (usu. foll. by *with*) densely covered or filled (*air thick with snow*). **5 a** firm in consistency; containing much solid matter; viscous (*a thick paste; thick soup*). **b** made of thick material (*a thick coat*). **6** muddy; cloudy; impenetrable by sight (*thick darkness*). **7** *colloq.* (of a person) stupid; dull. **8 a** (of a voice) indistinct. **b** (of an accent) pronounced; exaggerated. **9** *colloq.* intimate or very friendly (esp. *thick as thieves*). ● *n.* a thick part of anything. ● *adv.* thickly (*snow was falling thick; blows rained down thick and fast*). □ **a bit thick** *colloq.* unreasonable or intolerable. **in the thick of 1** at the busiest part of. **2** heavily occupied with. **through thick and thin** under all conditions; in spite of all difficulties. □□ **thick·ish** *adj.* **thick·ly** *adv.*

thick·en /thíkən/ *v.* **1** *tr. & intr.* make or become thick or thicker. **2** *intr.* become more complicated (*the plot thickens*). □□ **thick·en·er** *n.*

thick·en·ing /thíkəning/ *n.* **1** the process of becoming thick or thicker. **2** a substance used to thicken liquid. **3** a thickened part.

thick·et /thíkit/ *n.* a tangle of shrubs or trees.

thick·head /thík-hed/ *n. colloq.* a stupid person; a blockhead. □□ **thick·head·ed** *adj.* **thick·head·ed·ness** *n.*

thick·ness /thíknis/ *n.* **1** the state of being thick. **2** the extent to which a thing is thick. **3** a layer of material of a certain thickness (*three thicknesses of cardboard*). **4** a part that is thick or lies between opposite surfaces (*steps cut in the thickness of the wall*).

thick·set /thíksét/ *adj. & n.* ● *adj.* **1** heavily or solidly built. **2** set or growing close together. ● *n.* a thicket.

T

thick-skinned *adj.* not sensitive to reproach or criticism.

thief /theef/ *n.* (*pl.* **thieves** /theevz/) a person who steals, esp. secretly and without violence.

thieve /theev/ *v.* **1** *intr.* be a thief. **2** *tr.* steal (a thing).

thiev·er·y /théevəree/ *n.* the action of stealing.

thieves *pl.* of THIEF.

thiev·ish /théevish/ *adj.* given to stealing. ◻◻ **thiev·ish·ly** *adv.* **thiev·ish·ness** *n.*

thigh /thī/ *n.* **1** the part of the human leg between the hip and the knee. ▷ FEMUR. **2** a corresponding part in other animals. ◻◻ **-thighed** *adj.* (in *comb.*).

THIMBLE

thim·ble /thímbəl/ *n.* ◀ a metal or plastic cap, usu. with a closed end, worn to protect the finger and push the needle in sewing.

thim·ble·ful /thímbəlfŏŏl/ *n.* (*pl.* **-fuls**) a small quantity, esp. of liquid to drink.

thin /thin/ *adj.*, *adv.*, & *v.* ● *adj.* (**thinner**, **thinnest**) **1** having the opposite surfaces close together; of small thickness or diameter. **2 a** (of a line) narrow or fine. **b** (of a script or type, etc.) consisting of thin lines. **3** made of thin material (*a thin dress*). **4** lean; not plump. **5 a** not dense or copious (*thin hair*; *a thin haze*). **b** not full or closely packed (*a thin audience*). **6** of slight consistency (*a thin paste*). **7** weak; lacking an important ingredient (*thin blood*; *a thin voice*). **8** (of an excuse, argument, disguise, etc.) flimsy or transparent. ● *adv.* thinly (*cut the bread very thin*). ● *v.* (**thinned**, **thinning**) **1** *tr.* & *intr.* make or become thin or thinner. **2** *tr.* & *intr.* (often foll. by *out*) reduce; make or become less dense or crowded or numerous. **3** *tr.* (often foll. by *out*) remove some of a crop of (seedlings, saplings, etc.) or some young fruit from (a vine or tree) to improve the growth of the rest. ◻ **on thin ice** see ICE. **thin on the ground** see GROUND[1]. **thin on top** balding. ◻◻ **thin·ly** *adv.* **thin·ness** *n.* **thin·nish** *adj.*

thin air *n.* a state of invisibility or nonexistence (*vanished into thin air*).

thine /th̲īn/ *poss.pron. archaic* or *dial.* **1** (*predic.* or *absol.*) of or belonging to thee. **2** (*attrib.* before a vowel) = THY.

thing /thing/ *n.* **1** a material or nonmaterial entity, idea, action, etc., that is or may be thought about or perceived. **2** an inanimate material object (*take that thing away*). **3** an unspecified object or item (*have a few things to buy*). **4** an act, idea, or utterance (*a silly thing to do*). **5** an event (*an unfortunate thing to happen*). **6** a quality (*patience is a useful thing*). **7** (with ref. to a person) expressing pity, contempt, or affection (*poor thing!*; *a dear old thing*). **8** a specimen or type of something (*quarks are an important thing in physics*). **9** *colloq.* **a** one's special interest or concern (*not my thing at all*). **b** an obsession, fear, or prejudice (*spiders are a thing of mine*). **10** esp. *Brit. colloq.* something remarkable (*now there's a thing!*). **11** (prec. by *the*) *colloq.* **a** what is conventionally proper or fashionable. **b** what is needed or required (*your suggestion was just the thing*). **c** what is to be considered (*the thing is, shall we go or not?*). **d** what is important (*the thing about them is their reliability*). **12** (in *pl.*) personal belongings or clothing (*where have I left my things?*). **13** (in *pl.*) equipment (*painting things*). **14** (in *pl.*) affairs in general (*not in the nature of things*). **15** (in *pl.*) circumstances or conditions (*things look good*). **16** (in *pl.* with a following adjective) all that is so describable (*all things Greek*). ◻ **do one's own thing** *colloq.* pursue one's own interests or inclinations. **do things to** *colloq.* affect remarkably. **have a thing about** *colloq.* be obsessed, fearful, or prejudiced about. **one** (or **just one**) **of those things** *colloq.* something unavoidable or to be accepted.

thing·a·ma·bob /thíngəməbob/ *n.* (also **thing·a·ma·jig** /thíngəməjig/, *Brit.* **thingummy** /thíngəmee/) *colloq.* a person or thing whose name one has forgotten or does not know or does not wish to mention.

thing·y /thíngee/ *n.* (*pl.* **-ies**) = THINGAMABOB.

think /thingk/ *v.* & *n.* ● *v.* (*past* and *past part.* **thought** /thawt/) **1** *tr.* (foll. by *that* + clause) be of the opinion (*we think that they will come*). **2** *tr.* (foll. by *that* + clause or *to* + infin.) judge or consider (*is thought to be a fraud*). **3** *intr.* exercise the mind positively with one's ideas, etc. (*let me think for a moment*). **4** *tr.* (foll. by *of* or *about*) **a** consider; be or become mentally aware of (*think of you constantly*). **b** form or entertain the idea of; imagine to oneself (*couldn't think of such a thing*). **c** choose mentally; hit upon (*think of a number*). **d** form or have an opinion of (*what do you think of them?*). **5** *tr.* have a half-formed intention (*I think I'll stay*). **6** *tr.* form a conception of (*cannot think how you do it*). **7** *tr.* reduce to a specified condition by thinking (*cannot think away a toothache*). **8** *tr.* recognize the presence or existence of (*the child thought no harm*). **9** *tr.* (foll. by *to* + infin.) intend or expect (*thinks to deceive us*). **10** *tr.* (foll. by *to* + infin.) remember (*did not think to lock the door*). ● *n. colloq.* an act of thinking (*must have a think about that*). ◻ **think again** revise one's plans or opinions. **think out loud** (or **aloud**) utter one's thoughts as soon as they occur. **think back to** recall (a past event or time). **think better of** change one's mind about (an intention) after reconsideration. **think fit** see FIT[1]. **think for oneself** have an independent mind or attitude. **think little** (or **nothing**) **of** consider to be insignificant or unremarkable. **think on** (or **upon**) *archaic* think of or about. **think out 1** consider carefully. **2** produce (an idea, etc.) by thinking. **think over** reflect upon in order to reach a decision. **think through** reflect fully upon (a problem, etc.). **think twice** use careful consideration, avoid hasty action, etc. **think up** *colloq.* devise. ◻◻ **think·a·ble** *adj.*

think·er /thíngkər/ *n.* **1** a person who thinks, esp. in a specified way (*an original thinker*). **2** a person with a skilled or powerful mind.

think·ing /thíngking/ *adj.* & *n.* ● *adj.* using thought or rational judgment. ● *n.* **1** opinion or judgment. **2** thought; train of thought. ◻ **put on one's thinking cap** *colloq.* meditate on a problem.

think tank *n.* a body of experts providing advice and ideas on specific national or commercial problems.

thin·ner /thínər/ *n.* a volatile liquid used to dilute paint, etc.

thin-skinned *adj.* sensitive to reproach or criticism; easily upset.

thi·ol /thíawl, -ol/ *n. Chem.* any organic compound containing an alcohol-like group but with sulfur in place of oxygen.

thi·o·sul·fate /thí-ōsúlfayt/ *n.* a sulfate in which one oxygen atom is replaced by sulfur.

thi·o·u·re·a /thí-ōyŏŏreeə/ *n.* a crystalline compound used in photography and the manufacture of synthetic resins.

third /thərd/ *n.* & *adj.* ● *n.* **1** the position in a sequence corresponding to that of the number 3 in the sequence 1–3. **2** something occupying this position. **3** each of three equal parts of a thing. **4** *Mus.* **a** an interval or chord spanning three consecutive notes in the diatonic scale (e.g., C to E). **b** a note separated from another by this interval. ● *adj.* that is the third. ◻◻ **third·ly** *adv.*

third class *n.* the third-best group or category, esp. of hotel and train accommodation. ◻◻ **third-class** *adj.*

third de·gree *n.* long and severe questioning, esp. by police to obtain information or a confession.

third-de·gree *adj. Med.* denoting burns of the most severe kind, affecting lower layers of tissue.

third par·ty *n.* **1** another party besides the two principals. **2** a bystander, etc.

third-rate *adj.* inferior; very poor in quality.

Third Reich *n.* the Nazi regime, 1933–45.

third way *n.* any option regarded as an alternative to two extremes, esp. a political agenda which is moderate and based on general agreement rather than left- or right-wing.

Third World *n.* (usu. prec. by *the*) the developing countries of Asia, Africa, and Latin America.

thirst /thərst/ *n.* & *v.* ● *n.* **1** a physical need to drink liquid, or the feeling of discomfort caused by this. **2** a strong desire or craving (*a thirst for power*). ● *v.intr.* (often foll. by *for* or *after*) **1** feel thirst. **2** have a strong desire.

thirst·y /thérstee/ *adj.* (**thirstier**, **thirstiest**) **1** feeling thirst. **2** (of land, a season, etc.) dry or parched. **3** (often foll. by *for* or *after*) eager. **4** *colloq.* causing thirst (*thirsty work*). ◻◻ **thirst·i·ly** *adv.* **thirst·i·ness** *n.*

thir·teen /thértéen/ *n.* & *adj.* ● *n.* **1** one more than twelve, or three more than ten. **2** a symbol for this (13, xiii, XIII). **3** a size, etc., denoted by thirteen. ● *adj.* that amount to thirteen. ◻◻ **thir·teenth** *adj.* & *n.*

thir·ty /thértee/ *n.* & *adj.* ● *n.* (*pl.* **-ies**) **1** the product of three and ten. **2** a symbol for this (30, xxx, XXX). **3** (in *pl.*) the numbers from 30 to 39, esp. the years of a century or of a person's life. ● *adj.* that amount to thirty. ◻◻ **thir·ti·eth** *adj.* & *n.* **thir·ty·fold** *adj.* & *adv.*

this /th̲is/ *pron.*, *adj.*, & *adv.* ● *demons.pron.* (*pl.* **these** /th̲eez/) **1** the person or thing close at hand or indicated or already named or understood (*can you see this?*; *this is my cousin*). **2** (contrasted with *that*) the person or thing nearer to hand or more immediately in mind. **3** the action, behavior, or circumstances under consideration (*this won't do at all*; *what do you think of this?*). **4** (on the telephone): **a** the person spoken to. **b** the person speaking. ● *demons.adj.* (*pl.* **these** /th̲eez/) **1** designating the person or thing close at hand, etc. (cf. senses 1, 2 of *pron.*). **2** (of time): **a** the present or current (*am busy all this week*). **b** relating to today (*this morning*). **c** just past or to come (*have been asking for it these three weeks*). **3** *colloq.* (in narrative) designating a person or thing previously unspecified (*then up came this policeman*). ● *adv.* to this degree or extent (*knew him when he was this high*; *did not reach this far*). ◻ **this and that** *colloq.* various unspecified examples of things (esp. trivial). **this here** *sl.* this particular (person or thing). **this much** the amount or extent about to be stated (*I know this much, that he was not there*).

THISTLE: WOOLLY THISTLE (*Cirsium eriophorum*)

this·tle /thísəl/ *n.* **1** ◀ any of various prickly composite herbaceous plants of the genus *Cirsium*, *Carlina*, or *Carduus*, etc., usu. with globular heads of purple flowers. **2** this as the Scottish national emblem.

this·tle·down /thísəl down/ *n.* a light fluffy stuff attached to thistle seeds and blown about in the wind.

this·tly /thíslee/ *adj.* overgrown with thistles.

thith·er /thíth̲ər, th̲i-/ *adv. archaic* or *formal* to or toward that place.

thix·ot·ro·py /thiksótrəpee/ *n.* the property of becoming temporarily liquid when shaken or stirred, etc., and returning to a gel on standing. ◻◻ **thix·o·trop·ic** /thiksətrópik/ *adj.*

tho' var. of THOUGH.

thole /thōl/ *n.* (in full **tholepin**) a pin fitted to the gunwale of a rowing boat to act as the fulcrum for an oar.

thong /thong/ *n.* **1** a narrow strip of hide or leather. **2** = FLIP-FLOP 1.

tho·rax /tháwraks, thṓr-/ *n.* (*pl.* **thoraxes** or **thoraces** /tháwrəseez/) *Anat.* & *Zool.* the part of the trunk between the neck and the abdomen. ▷ BEETLE. ◻◻ **tho·ra·cal** /thórəkəl/ *adj.* **tho·rac·ic** /thawrásik/ *adj.* ▷ VERTEBRA

tho·ri·a /tháwreeə, thṓr-/ *n.* the oxide of thorium, used esp. in incandescent mantles.

tho·ri·um /tháwreeəm, thṓr-/ *n. Chem.* a radioactive metallic element occurring naturally in monazite and used in alloys and for nuclear power. ¶ Symb.: **Th.**

thorn /thawrn/ *n.* **1** a stiff sharp-pointed projection on a plant. **2** a thorn-bearing shrub or tree. ◻ **a thorn in one's side** (or **flesh**) a constant annoyance. ◻◻ **thorn·less** *adj.* **thorn·proof** *adj.*

T

thorn·ap·ple *n.* **1** ► a poisonous plant of the nightshade family, *Datura stramonium*; jimsonweed. **2** the prickly fruit of this.

thorn·back /tháwrn-bak/ *n.* a ray, *Raja clavata*, with spines on the back and tail.

thorn·y /tháwrnee/ *adj.* (**thornier, thorniest**) **1** having many thorns. **2** causing difficulty or trouble. □□ **thorn·i·ly** *adv.* **thorn·i·ness** *n.*

thor·ough /thúrō/ *adj.* **1** complete and unqualified; not superficial (*needs a thorough change*). **2** acting or done with great care and completeness (*the report is most thorough*). **3** absolute (*a thorough nuisance*). □□ **thor·ough·ly** *adv.* **thor·ough·ness** *n.*

thor·ough·bass /thúrəbays/ *n.* = CONTINUO.

thor·ough·bred /thɔ́rōbred, thɔ́rə-, thúr-/ *adj.* & *n.* ● *adj.* **1** of pure breeding. **2** high-spirited. ● *n.* **1 a** thoroughbred animal, esp. a horse. **2** (**Thoroughbred**) **a** a breed of racehorses originating from English mares and Arab stallions. ▷ HORSE. **b** a horse of this breed.

thor·ough·fare /thɔ́rōfair, thɔ́rə-, thúr-/ *n.* a road or path open at both ends, esp. for traffic.

thor·ough·go·ing /thɔ́rōgōing, thɔ́rə-, thúr-/ *adj.* **1** uncompromising; not superficial. **2** (usu. *attrib.*) extreme; out-and-out.

Thos. *abbr.* Thomas.

those *pl.* of THAT.

thou[1] /thow/ *pron.* (*obj.* **thee** /thee/; *poss.* **thy** or **thine**; *pl.* **ye** or **you**) second person singular pronoun, now replaced by *you* except in some formal, liturgical, dialect, and poetic uses.

thou[2] /thow/ *n.* (*pl.* same or **thous**) *colloq.* **1** a thousand. **2** one thousandth.

though /thō/ *conj.* & *adv.* ● *conj.* **1** despite the fact that (*though it was early we went to bed; though annoyed, I agreed*). **2** (introducing a possibility) even if (*ask him though he may refuse*). **3** and yet; nevertheless (*she read on, though not to the very end*). **4** in spite of being (*ready though unwilling*). ● *adv. colloq.* however; all the same (*I wish you had told me, though*).

thought[1] /thawt/ *n.* **1** the process or power of thinking; the faculty of reason. **2** a way of thinking characteristic of or associated with a particular time, people, group, etc. (*medieval European thought*). **3 a** sober reflection or consideration (*gave it much thought*). **b** care; regard; concern (*had no thought for others*). **4** an idea or piece of reasoning produced by thinking (*many good thoughts came out of the discussion*). **5** (foll. by *of* + verbal noun or *to* + infin.) a partly formed intention or hope (*gave up all thoughts of winning; had no thought to go*). **6** (usu. *pl.*) what one is thinking; one's opinion (*have you any thoughts on this?*). **7** the subject of one's thinking (*my one thought was to get away*). **8** (prec. by *a*) *Brit.* somewhat (*seems to me a thought arrogant*). □ **take thought** consider matters.

thought[2] *past* and *past part.* of THINK.

thought·ful /tháwtfŏŏl/ *adj.* **1** engaged in or given to meditation. **2** (of a book, writer, remark, etc.) giving signs of serious thought. **3** (often foll. by *of*) (of a person or conduct) considerate; not haphazard or unfeeling. □□ **thought·ful·ly** *adv.* **thought·ful·ness** *n.*

thought·less /tháwtlis/ *adj.* **1** careless of consequences or of others' feelings. **2** due to lack of thought. □□ **thought·less·ly** *adv.* **thought·less·ness** *n.*

thought po·lice *n.* a group of people who aim to suppress ideas that deviate from the way of thinking that they believe to be correct.

thought-pro·vok·ing *adj.* stimulating serious thought.

thou·sand /thówzənd/ *n.* & *adj.* ● *n.* (*pl.* **thousands** or (in sense 1) **thousand**) (in *sing.* prec. by *a* or *one*) **1** the product of a hundred and ten. **2** a

symbol for this (1,000, m, M). **3** a set of a thousand things. **4** (in *sing.* or *pl.*) *colloq.* a large number. ● *adj.* that amount to a thousand. □□ **thou·sand·fold** *adj.* & *adv.* **thou·sandth** *adj.* & *n.*

thrall /thrawl/ *n. literary* **1** (often foll. by *of, to*) a slave (of a person, power, or influence). **2** bondage; a state of slavery or servitude (*in thrall*). □□ **thrall·dom** *n.* (also **thral·dom**).

thrash /thrash/ *v.* & *n.* ● *v.* **1** *tr.* beat severely, esp. with a stick or whip. **2** *tr.* defeat thoroughly in a contest. **3** *intr.* (of a paddle wheel, branch, etc.) act like a flail; deliver repeated blows. **4** *intr.* (foll. by *about, around*) move or fling the limbs about violently or in panic. **5** *intr.* (of a ship) keep striking the waves; make way against the wind or tide (*thrash to windward*). **6** *tr.* = THRESH 1. ● *n.* **1** an act of thrashing. **2** *Brit. colloq.* a party, esp. a lavish one. □ **thrash out** discuss to a conclusion. □□ **thrash·ing** *n.*

thrash·er[1] /thráshər/ *n.* **1** a person or thing that thrashes. **2** = THRESHER.

thrash·er[2] /thráshər/ *n.* any of various long-tailed N. American thrushlike birds of the family Mimidae.

thread /thred/ *n.* & *v.* ● *n.* **1 a** a spun filament of cotton, silk, or glass, etc.; yarn. **b** a length of this. **2** ► a thin cord of twisted yarns used esp. in sewing and weaving. **3** anything regarded as threadlike with reference to its continuity or connectedness (*lost the thread of his argument*). **4** the spiral ridge of a screw. **5** (in *pl.*) clothes. **6** a thin seam or vein of ore. ● *v.tr.* **1** pass a thread through the eye of (a needle). **2** put (beads) on a thread. **3** arrange (material in a strip form, e.g., film or magnetic tape) in the proper position on equipment. **4** make (one's way) carefully through a crowded place, over a difficult route, etc. □ **hang by a thread** be in a precarious state, position, etc. □□ **thread·er** *n.* **thread·like** *adj.*

thread·bare /thrédbair/ *adj.* **1** (of cloth) so worn that the nap is lost and the thread visible. **2** (of a person) wearing such clothes. **3 a** hackneyed. **b** feeble or insubstantial (*a threadbare excuse*).

thread·fin /thrédfin/ *n.* any small tropical fish of the family Polynemidae, with long streamers for its pectoral fins.

thread·worm /thrédwərm/ *n.* any of various, esp. parasitic, threadlike nematode worms, e.g., the pinworm.

thread·y /thrédee/ *adj.* (**threadier, threadiest**) **1** of or like a thread. **2** (of a person's pulse) scarcely perceptible.

threat /thret/ *n.* **1 a** a declaration of an intention to punish or hurt. **b** *Law* a menace of bodily hurt or injury, such as may restrain a person's freedom of action. **2** an indication of something undesirable coming (*the threat of war*). **3** a person or thing as a likely cause of harm, etc.

threat·en /thrét'n/ *v.tr.* **1 a** make a threat or threats against. **b** constitute a threat to; be likely to harm; put into danger.

2 be a sign or indication of (something undesirable). **3** (foll. by *to* + infin.) announce one's intention to do an undesirable or unexpected thing (*threatened to resign*). **4** (also *absol.*) give warning of the infliction of (harm, etc.) (*the clouds were threatening rain*). □□ **threat·en·er** *n.* **threat·en·ing·ly** *adv.*

three /three/ *n.* & *adj.* ● *n.* **1 a** one more than two, or seven less than ten. **b** a symbol for this (3, iii, III). **2** a size, etc., denoted by three. **3** the time of three o'clock. **4** a set of three. **5** a card with three pips. ● *adj.* that amount to three.

three-color pro·cess *n.* a process of reproducing natural colors by combining photographic images in the three primary colors.

three-cor·nered *adj.* **1** triangular. **2** (of a contest, etc.) between three parties as individuals.

three-deck·er *n.* **1** a warship with three gun decks. **2** a novel in three volumes. **3** a sandwich with three slices of bread.

three-di·men·sion·al *adj.* having or appearing to have length, breadth, and depth.

three·fold /threefold/ *adj.* & *adv.* **1** three times as much or as many. **2** consisting of three parts.

three-leg·ged race *n.* a running race between pairs, one member of each pair having the left leg tied to the right leg of the other.

three parts *n.* & *adj.* three quarters.

three-piece *adj.* consisting of three items.

three-ply *adj.* & *n.* ● *adj.* of three strands, webs, or thicknesses. ● *n.* **1** three-ply wool. **2** three-ply wood made by gluing together three layers with the grain in different directions.

three-point land·ing *n. Aeron.* the landing of an aircraft on the two main wheels and the tail wheel or skid or front wheel simultaneously.

three-ring cir·cus *n.* **1** a circus with three rings for simultaneous performances. **2** an extravagant display.

three Rs *n.pl.* (with *the*) reading, writing (*joc.* 'riting), and arithmetic (*joc.* 'rithmetic), regarded as the fundamentals of learning.

three·score /threeskáwr/ *n. archaic* sixty.

three·some /threesəm/ *n.* **1** a group of three persons. **2** a game, etc., for three.

three-wheel·er *n.* a vehicle with three wheels.

thren·o·dy /thrénədee/ *n.* (also **thre·node** /thrénōd/) (*pl.* **-ies** or **threnodes**) **1** a lamentation, esp. on a person's death. **2** a song of lamentation. □□ **thre·no·di·al** /-nṓdeeəl/ *adj.* **thre·nod·ic** /-nódik/ *adj.* **thren·o·dist** /-nədist/ *n.*

thresh /thresh/ *v.* **1** *tr.* beat out or separate grain from (wheat, etc.). **2** *intr.* = THRASH *v.* 4. **3** *tr.* (foll. by *over*) analyze (a problem, etc.) in search of a solution.

thresh·er /thréshər/ *n.* **1** a person or machine that threshes. = COMBINE HARVESTER. **2** a shark, *Alopias vulpinus*, with a long upper lobe to its tail, that it can lash about. ▷ SHARK

thresh·ing ma·chine *n.* ▼ a power-driven machine for separating the grain from the straw or husk.

T

THORNAPPLE
(*Datura stramonium*)

---

spool

THREAD:
SPOOLED COTTON
THREAD

---

straw shaker   pulley to drive drum   opening for grain plant   grain hopper   drive belt attached to traction engine

exit for straw

exit for chaff   grain elevator   attachment for grain sacks

wheels

THRESHING MACHINE: 19TH-CENTURY STEAM-DRIVEN THRESHING MACHINE

thresh·old /thréshōld, thrésh·hōld/ *n.* **1** a strip of wood or stone forming the bottom of a doorway and crossed in entering a house or room, etc. **2** a point of entry or beginning (*on the threshold of a new century*). **3** *Physiol.* & *Psychol.* a limit below which a stimulus causes no reaction (*pain threshold*).

threw *past* of THROW.

thrice /thrīs/ *adv. archaic* or *literary* **1** three times. **2** (esp. in *comb.*) highly (*thrice-blessed*).

thrift /thrift/ *n.* **1** frugality; economical management. **2** ◀ a plant of the genus *Armeria*, esp. the sea pink (*A. maritima*). **3** a savings and loan association or savings bank.

thrift·less /thríftlis/ *adj.* wasteful; improvident. □□ **thrift·less·ly** *adv.* **thrift·less·ness** *n.*

thrift shop *n.* (also **thrift store**) a store selling second-hand items.

thrift·y /thríftee/ *adj.* (**thrift·ier, thrift·iest**) **1** economical; frugal. **2** thriving; prosperous. □□ **thrift·i·ly** *adv.* **thrift·i·ness** *n.*

THRIFT: SEA PINK (*Armeria maritima*)

thrill /thril/ *n.* & *v.* ● *n.* **1 a** a wave or nervous tremor of emotion or sensation. **b** a thrilling experience. **2** a throb or pulsation. **3** *Med.* a vibratory movement or resonance heard in auscultation. ● *v.* **1** *intr.* & *tr.* feel or cause to feel a thrill. **2** *intr.* quiver or throb with or as with emotion. **3** *intr.* (foll. by *through, over, along*) (of an emotion, etc.) pass with a thrill through, etc. (*fear thrilled through my veins*). □□ **thrill·ing** *adj.* **thrill·ing·ly** *adv.*

thrill·er /thrílər/ *n.* an exciting or sensational story or play, etc., esp. one involving crime or espionage.

thrips /thrips/ *n.* (*pl.* same) any insect of the order Thysanoptera, esp. a pest injurious to plants.

thrive /thrīv/ *v.intr.* (*past* **throve** /thrōv/ or **thrived**; *past part.* **thriven** /thrívən/ or **thrived**) **1** prosper or flourish. **2** grow rich. **3** (of a child, animal, or plant) grow vigorously.

throat /thrōt/ *n.* **1 a** the windpipe or gullet. **b** the front part of the neck containing this. **2** *literary* **a** a voice, esp. of a songbird. **b** a thing compared to a throat, esp. a narrow passage, entrance, or exit. □ **cut one's own throat** bring about one's own downfall. **ram** (or **thrust**) **down a person's throat** force (a thing) on a person's attention. □□ **-throated** *adj.* (in *comb.*).

throat·y /thrōtee/ *adj.* (**throatier, throatiest**) **1** (of a voice) deficient in clarity; hoarsely resonant. **2** guttural; uttered in the throat. **3** having a prominent or capacious throat. □□ **throat·i·ly** *adv.* **throat·i·ness** *n.*

throb /throb/ *v.* & *n.* ● *v.intr.* (**throbbed, throbbing**) **1** palpitate or pulsate, esp. with more than the usual force or rapidity. **2** vibrate or quiver with a persistent rhythm or with emotion. ● *n.* **1** a throbbing. **2** a palpitation or (esp. violent) pulsation.

throe /thrō/ *n.* (usu. in *pl.*) **1** a violent pang, esp. of childbirth or death. **2** anguish. □ **in the throes of** struggling with the task of.

throm·bi *pl.* of THROMBUS.

throm·bo·sis /thrombōsis/ *n.* (*pl.* **thromboses** /-seez/) the coagulation of the blood in a blood vessel or organ. □□ **throm·bot·ic** /-bótik/ *adj.*

throm·bus /thrómbəs/ *n.* (*pl.* **thrombi** /-bī/) a bloodclot formed in the vascular system and impeding blood flow.

throne /thrōn/ *n.* & *v.* ● *n.* **1** ▶ a chair of state for a sovereign or bishop, etc. **2** sovereign power (*came to the throne*). **3** (in *pl.*) the third order of the ninefold celestial hierarchy. ● *v.tr.* place on a throne. □□ **throne·less** *adj.*

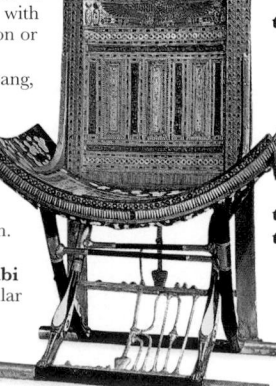

THRONE: GOLD-PLATED THRONE FROM TUTANKHAMEN'S TOMB, EGYPT

throng /thrawng, throng/ *n.* & *v.* ● *n.* **1** a crowd of people. **2** (often foll. by *of*) a multitude, esp. in a small space. ● *v.* **1** *intr.* come in great numbers (*crowds thronged to the stadium*). **2** *tr.* flock into or crowd around; fill with or as with a crowd (*crowds thronged the streets*).

throt·tle /thrót'l/ *n.* & *v.* ● *n.* **1 a** (in full **throttle valve**) ▼ a valve controlling the flow of fuel or steam, etc., in an engine. **b** (in full **throttle lever**) a lever or pedal operating this valve. **2** the throat, gullet, or windpipe. ● *v.tr.* **1** choke or strangle. **2** prevent the utterance, etc., of. **3** control (an engine or steam, etc.) with a throttle. □ **throttle back** (or **down**) reduce the speed of (an engine or vehicle) by throttling. □□ **throt·tler** *n.*

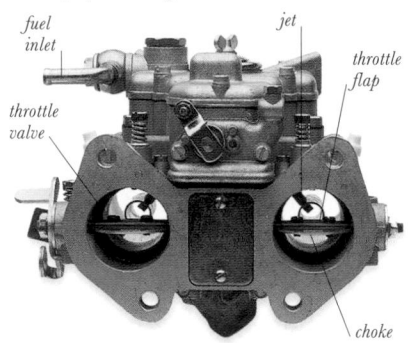

fuel inlet

jet

throttle flap

throttle valve

choke

THROTTLE VALVE: CARBURETOR OF A CAR SHOWING THROTTLE VALVES

through /throō/ *prep., adv.,* & *adj.* (also **thru**) ● *prep.* **1 a** from end to end or from side to side of. **b** going in one side or end and out the other of. **2** between or among (*swam through the waves*). **3** from beginning to end of (*read through the letter; went through many difficulties; through the years*). **4** because of; by the agency, means, or fault of (*lost it through carelessness*). **5** up to and including (*Monday through Friday*). ● *adv.* **1** through a thing; from side to side, end to end, or beginning to end; completely; thoroughly (*went through to the garden; would not let us through*). **2** having completed (esp. successfully) (*are through their exams*). **3** so as to be connected by telephone (*will put you through*). ● *attrib.adj.* **1** (of a journey, route, etc.) done without a change of line or vehicle, etc., or with one ticket. **2** (of traffic) going through a place to its destination. □ **be through** *colloq.* **1** (often foll. by *with*) have finished. **2** (often foll. by *with*) cease to have dealings. **3** have no further prospects (*is through as a politician*). **through and through 1** thoroughly; completely. **2** through again and again.

through·out /throō-ówt/ *prep.* & *adv.* ● *prep.* right through; from end to end of (*throughout the town; throughout the 18th century*). ● *adv.* in every part or respect (*the timber was rotten throughout*).

through·put /throō-poot/ *n.* the amount of material put through a process, esp. in manufacturing or computing.

through·way /throō-way/ *n.* (also **thru·way**) a main thoroughfare or highway for automobile travel.

throve *past* of THRIVE.

throw /thrō/ *v.* & *n.* ● *v.tr.* (*past* **threw** /throō/; *past part.* **thrown** /thrōn/) **1** propel with some force through the air or in a particular direction. **2** force violently into a specified position or state. **3** compel suddenly to be in a specified condition (*was thrown out of work*). **4** turn or move (part of the body) quickly or suddenly (*threw an arm out*). **5** project or cast (light, a shadow, a spell, etc.). **6 a** bring to the ground in wrestling. **b** (of a horse) unseat (its rider). **7** *colloq.* disconcert (*the question threw me for a moment*). **8** (foll. by *on, off*, etc.) put (clothes, etc.) hastily on or off, etc. **9 a** cause (dice) to fall on a table. **b** obtain (a specified number) by throwing dice. **10** cause to pass or extend suddenly to another state or position (*threw in the army; threw a bridge across the river*). **11** move (a switch or lever) so as to operate it. **12 a** form (pottery) on a potter's wheel. **b** turn (wood, etc.) on a lathe. **13** have (a fit or tantrum, etc.). **14** give (a party). **15** *colloq.* lose (a contest or race, etc.) intentionally. ● *n.* **1** an act of throwing. **2** the distance a thing is or may be thrown. **3** the act of being thrown in wrestling. **4** *Geol.* & *Mining* **a** a fault in strata. **b** the amount of vertical displacement caused by this. **5** a machine or device giving rapid rotary motion. **6 a** the movement of a crank or cam, etc. **b** the extent of this. **7** the distance moved by the pointer of an instrument, etc. **8 a** a light cover for furniture. **b** (in full **throw rug**) a light rug. **c** a shawl or scarf. **9** (prec. by *a*) *sl.* each; per item (*sold at $10 a throw*). □ **throw around** (or **about**) **1** throw in various directions. **2** spend (one's money) ostentatiously. **throw away 1** discard as useless or unwanted. **2** waste or fail to make use of (an opportunity, etc.). **3** discard (a card). **4** *Theatr.* speak (lines) with deliberate underemphasis. **5** (in *passive*; often foll. by *on*) be wasted (*the advice was thrown away on him*). **throw back 1** revert to ancestral character. **2** (usu. in *passive*; foll. by *on*) compel to rely on (*was thrown back on his savings*). **throw cold water on** see COLD. **throw down** cause to fall. **throw down the gauntlet** (or **glove**) issue a challenge. **throw good money after bad** incur further loss in a hopeless attempt to recoup a previous loss. **throw one's hand in 1** abandon one's chances in a card game, esp. poker. **2** give up; withdraw from a contest. **throw in 1** interpose (a word or remark). **2** include at no extra cost. **3** throw (a soccer ball) from the edge of the field where it has gone out of play. **4** *Baseball* & *Cricket* return (the ball) from the outfield. **5** *Cards* give (a player) the lead, to the player's disadvantage. **throw in one's lot with** see LOT. **throw in the towel** (or **the sponge**) admit defeat. **throw light on** see LIGHT[1]. **throw off 1** discard; contrive to get rid of. **2** write or utter in an offhand manner. **3** confuse or distract (a person speaking, thinking, or acting) from the matter in hand. **4** (of hounds or a hunt) begin hunting; make a start. **throw oneself at** seek blatantly as a spouse or sexual partner. **throw oneself into** engage vigorously in. **throw oneself on** (or **upon**) **1** rely completely on. **2** attack. **throw open** (often foll. by *to*) **1** cause to be suddenly or widely open. **2** make accessible. **throw out 1** put out forcibly or suddenly. **2** discard as unwanted. **3** expel (a troublemaker, etc.). **4** put forward tentatively. **5** reject (a proposal, etc.). **throw over** desert or abandon. **throw stones** cast aspersions. **throw together 1** assemble hastily. **2** bring into casual contact. **throw up 1** abandon. **2** resign from. **3** *colloq.* vomit. **4** erect hastily. **throw one's weight around** (or **about**) *colloq.* act with unpleasant self-assertiveness. □□ **throw·a·ble** *adj.* **throw·er** *n.* (also in *comb.*).

throw·a·way /thrōoway/ *adj.* & *n.* ● *adj.* **1** meant to be thrown away after (one) use. **2** (of lines, etc.) deliberately underemphasized. ● *n.* a thing to be thrown away after (one) use.

throw·back /thrōbak/ *n.* **1** reversion to ancestral character. **2** an instance of this.

thru var. of THROUGH.

thrum[1] /thrum/ *v.* (**thrummed, thrumming**) **1** *tr.* play (a stringed instrument) monotonously or unskillfully. **2** *intr.* (often foll. by *on*) beat or drum idly or monotonously.

thrum[2] /thrum/ *n.* & *v.* ● *n.* **1** the unwoven end of a warp thread, or the whole of such ends, left when the finished web is cut away. **2** any short loose thread. ● *v.tr.* (**thrummed, thrumming**) make of or cover with thrums. □□ **thrum·mer** *n.* **thrum·my** *adj.*

T

thrush[1] /thrush/ n. ▶ any small or medium-sized songbird of the family Turdidae, esp. a song thrush or mistle thrush (see song thrush).

thrush[2] /thrush/ n. **1** a fungal disease, esp. of children, marked by whitish vesicles in the mouth and throat. **2** a similar disease of the vagina.

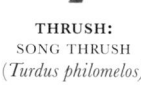

THRUSH:
SONG THRUSH
(*Turdus philomelos*)

thrust /thrust/ v. & n. • v. (past and past part. **thrust**) **1** tr. push with a sudden impulse or with force (*thrust the letter into my pocket*). **2** tr. (foll. by on) impose (a thing) forcibly; enforce acceptance of (a thing) (*had it thrust on me*). **3** intr. (foll. by at, through) pierce or stab; make a sudden lunge. **4** tr. make (one's way) forcibly. **5** intr. (foll. by through, past, etc.) force oneself (*thrust past me abruptly*). • n. **1** a sudden or forcible push or lunge. **2** the propulsive force developed by a jet or rocket engine. **3** a strong attempt to penetrate an enemy's line or territory. **4** a remark aimed at a person. **5** the stress between the parts of an arch, etc. **6** (often foll. by of) the chief theme or gist of remarks, etc. **7** an attack with the point of a weapon. **8** (in full **thrust fault**) Geol. a low-angle reverse fault, with older strata displaced horizontally over newer.

thrust·er /thrústər/ n. **1** a person or thing that thrusts. **2** a small rocket engine used to provide extra or correcting thrust on a spacecraft. ▷ SPACECRAFT

thru·way var. of THROUGHWAY.

thud /thud/ n. & v. • n. a low dull sound as of a blow on a nonresonant surface. • v.intr. (**thudded**, **thudding**) make or fall with a thud. □□ **thud·ding·ly** adv.

thug /thug/ n. **1** a vicious or brutal gangster or ruffian. **2** (**Thug**) hist. a member of a religious organization of robbers and assassins in India. □□ **thug·ger·y** n. **thug·gish** adj. **thug·gish·ly** adv. **thug·gish·ness** n.

thug·gee /thugeé/ n. hist. murder practiced by the Thugs. □□ **thug·gism** n.

thumb /thum/ n. & v. • n. **1 a** a short thick terminal projection on the human hand, set lower and apart from the other four and opposable to them. ▷ HAND. **b** a digit of other animals corresponding to this. **2** part of a glove, etc., for a thumb. • v. **1** tr. wear or soil (pages, etc.) with a thumb (*a well-thumbed book*). **2** intr. turn over pages with or as with a thumb (*thumbed through the directory*). **3** tr. request or obtain (a lift in a passing vehicle) by signaling with a raised thumb. **4** tr. gesture at (a person) with the thumb. □ **be all thumbs** be clumsy with one's hands. **thumb one's nose 1** put one's thumb up to one's nose with fingers extended up, a gesture of contempt. **2** display contempt or disdain. **under a person's thumb** completely dominated by a person. □□ **thumbed** adj. (also in comb.). **thumb·less** adj.

thumb in·dex n. a set of lettered grooves cut down the side of a diary, dictionary, etc., for easy reference. v.tr. provide (a book, etc.) with these.

thumb·nail /thúmnayl/ n. **1** the nail of a thumb. **2** (attrib.) denoting conciseness (*a thumbnail sketch*).

thumb·print /thúmprint/ n. an impression of a thumb, esp. as used for identification.

thumb·screw /thúmskroo/ n. ▶ an instrument of torture for crushing the thumbs.

thumbs-down n. an indication of rejection or failure.

thumbs-up n. an indication of satisfaction or approval.

thumb·tack /thúmtak/ n. a tack with a flat head pressing in with the thumb.

thump /thump/ v. & n. • v. **1** tr. beat or strike heavily, esp. with the fist (*thumped the table for attention*). **2** intr. throb or pulsate strongly (*my heart was thumping*). **3** intr. (foll. by at, on, etc.) deliver blows, esp. to attract attention (*thumped on the door*). **4** tr. (often foll. by out) play (a tune on a piano, etc.) with a heavy touch. **5** intr. tread heavily. • n. **1** a heavy blow. **2** the sound of this. □□ **thump·er** n.

thump·ing /thúmping/ adj. colloq. big; prominent (*a thumping majority; a thumping lie*).

thun·der /thúndər/ n. & v. • n. **1** a loud rumbling or crashing noise heard after a lightning flash and due to the expansion of rapidly heated air. **2** a resounding loud deep noise (*the thunder of an explosion*). **3** strong censure or denunciation. • v. **1** intr. (prec. by it as subject) thunder sounds (*if it thunders*). **2** intr. make or proceed with a noise suggestive of thunder. **3** tr. utter or communicate (approval, disapproval, etc.) loudly or impressively. **4** intr. (foll. by against, etc.) **a** make violent threats, etc., against. **b** criticize violently. □ **steal a person's thunder** spoil the effect of another's idea, action, etc., by expressing or doing it first. □□ **thun·der·er** n. **thun·der·less** adj. **thun·der·y** adj.

thun·der·bolt /thúndərbōlt/ n. **1 a** a flash of lightning with a simultaneous crash of thunder. **b** a stone, etc., imagined to be a destructive bolt. **2** a sudden or unexpected occurrence or item of news. **3** a supposed bolt or shaft as a destructive agent, esp. as an attribute of a god.

thun·der·clap /thúndərklap/ n. **1** a crash of thunder. **2** something startling or unexpected.

thun·der·cloud /thúndərklowd/ n. a cumulus cloud with a tall diffuse top, charged with electricity and producing thunder and lightning.

thun·der·head /thúndərhed/ n. a rounded cumulus cloud projecting upwards and heralding a thunderstorm.

thun·der·ing /thúndəring/ adj. colloq. very big or great (*a thundering nuisance*). □□ **thun·der·ing·ly** adv.

thun·der·ous /thúndərəs/ adj. **1** like thunder. **2** very loud. □□ **thun·der·ous·ly** adv. **thun·der·ous·ness** n.

thun·der·show·er /thúndərshowər/ n. a brief rain shower accompanied by thunder and sometimes lightning.

thun·der·storm /thúndərstawrm/ n. a storm with thunder and lightning and usu. heavy rain or hail.

thun·der·struck /thúndərstruk/ adj. amazed; overwhelmingly surprised or startled.

Thur. abbr. Thursday.

thu·ri·ble /thoóribəl, thyoó-/ n. a censer.

thu·ri·fer /thoórifər, thyoó-/ n. an acolyte carrying a censer.

Thurs. abbr. Thursday.

Thurs·day /thórzday, -dee/ n. & adv. • n. the fifth day of the week, following Wednesday. • adv. colloq. **1** on Thursday. **2** (**Thursdays**) on Thursdays; each Thursday.

thus /thus/ adv. formal **1 a** in this way. **b** as indicated. **2 a** accordingly. **b** as a result or inference. **3** to this extent; so (*thus far; thus much*).

thwack /thwak/ v. & n. colloq. • v.tr. hit with a heavy blow; whack. • n. a heavy blow.

thwart /thwawrt/ v., n., prep., & adv. • v.tr. frustrate or foil (a person or purpose, etc.). • n. a rower's seat placed across a boat.

thy /thī/ poss.pron. (attrib.) (also **thine** /thīn/ before a vowel) of or belonging to thee: now replaced by *your* except in some formal, liturgical, dialect, and poetic uses (*love thy neighbor*).

thyme /tīm/ n. any herb or shrub of the genus *Thymus* with aromatic leaves, esp. *T. vulgaris* grown for culinary use. ▷ HERB. □□ **thym·y** adj.

thy·mi pl. of THYMUS.

thy·mine /thímeen/ n. Biochem. a compound found in all living tissue as a component base of DNA.

thy·mol /thímawl, -ōl/ n. Chem. a white crystalline phenol obtained from oil of thyme and used as an antiseptic.

thy·mus /thíməs/ n. (pl. **-muses** or **-mi** /-mī/) (in full **thymus gland**) Anat. a lymphoid organ situated in the neck of vertebrates producing lymphocytes for the immune response.

thy·ris·tor /thīrístər/ n. Electronics a semiconductor rectifier in which the current between two electrodes is controlled by a signal applied to a third electrode.

thy·roid /thíroyd/ n. (in full **thyroid gland**) a large ductless gland in the neck of vertebrates secreting a hormone which regulates growth and development through the rate of metabolism. ▷ ENDOCRINE, NECK

thy·rox·ine /thīróksin, -seen/ n. the main hormone produced by the thyroid gland, involved in controlling the rate of metabolic processes.

thy·self /thīsélf/ pron. archaic emphat. & refl. form of THOU[1], THEE.

Ti symb. Chem. the element titanium.

ti /tee/ n. (also **te**) **1** (in tonic sol-fa) the seventh note of a major scale. **2** the note B in the fixed-do system.

ti·ar·a /teeárə, -áərə, -áirə/ n. **1** a jeweled ornamental band worn on the front of a woman's hair. **2** a three-crowned diadem worn by a pope.

Ti·bet·an /tibét'n/ n. & adj. • n. **1 a** a native of Tibet. **b** a person of Tibetan descent. **2** the language of Tibet. • adj. of or relating to Tibet or its language.

tib·i·a /tíbeeə/ n. (pl. tibiae /-bee-ee/) Anat. ▶ the inner and usu. larger of two bones extending from the knee to the ankle. ▷ SKELETON. □□ **tib·i·al** adj.

tic /tik/ n. **1** a habitual spasmodic contraction of the muscles, esp. of the face. **2** a personality or behavioral quirk.

tick[1] /tik/ n. & v. • n. **1** a slight recurring click, esp. that of a watch or clock. **2** esp. Brit. colloq. a moment; an instant. **3** Brit. a mark (✓) to denote correctness, check items in a list, etc. • v. **1** intr. **a** (of a clock, etc.) make ticks. **b** (foll. by away) (of time, etc.) pass. **2** intr. (of a mechanism) work; function (*take it apart to see how it ticks*). **3** tr. Brit. **a** mark (a written answer, etc.) with a tick. **b** (often foll. by off) mark (an item in a list, etc.) with a tick in checking. □ **tick off 1** sl. annoy, anger; dispirit. **2** Brit. reprimand.

tick over Brit. **1** (of an engine, etc.) idle. **2** (of a person, project, etc.) be working or functioning at a basic or minimum level. **what makes a person tick** colloq. a person's motivation. □□ **tick·less** adj.

tick[2] /tik/ n. **1** ▼ any of various arachnids of the order Acarina, parasitic on the skin of warm-blooded vertebrates. **2** any of various insects of the family Hippoboscidae, parasitic on sheep and birds, etc. **3** colloq. an unpleasant or despicable person.

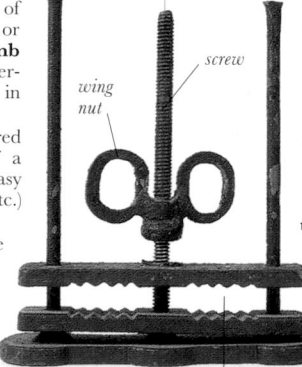

TICK:
SOFT TICK

screw

wing nut

thumb hole

THUMBSCREW: LATE 16TH-
CENTURY THUMBSCREWS

tibia

TIBIA: HUMAN
LOWER LEG
SHOWING THE
TIBIA

T

tick³ /tik/ *n. Brit. colloq.* credit (*buy goods on tick*).

tick⁴ /tik/ *n.* **1** the cover of a mattress or pillow. **2** = TICKING.

tick·er /tíkər/ *n. colloq.* **1** the heart. **2** a watch. **3** a machine that receives and prints telegraphed messages onto paper tape.

tick·er tape *n.* **1** a paper strip from a ticker. **2** this or similar material thrown from windows, etc., along the route of a parade honoring a hero, etc.

tick·et /tíkit/ *n. & v.* ● *n.* **1** a written or printed piece of paper or card entitling the holder to enter a place, participate in an event, travel by public transport, use a public amenity, etc. **2** an official notification of a traffic offense, etc. (*parking ticket*). **3** *Brit.* a certificate of discharge from the army. **4** a certificate of qualification as a ship's master, ship or airplane pilot, etc. **5** a label attached to a thing and giving its price or other details. **6** a list of candidates put forward by one group, esp. a political party. **7** (prec. by *the*) *colloq.* what is correct or needed. ● *v.tr.* (**ticketed, ticketing**) attach or serve a ticket to. □□ **tick·et·ed** *adj.* **tick·et·less** *adj.*

tick·ing /tíking/ *n.* a stout usu. striped material used to cover mattresses, etc.

tick·le /tíkəl/ *v. & n.* ● *v.* **1 a** *tr.* apply light touches or strokes to (a person or part of a person's body) so as to excite the nerves and usu. produce laughter and spasmodic movement. **b** *intr.* feel this sensation (*my foot tickles*). **2** *tr.* excite agreeably; amuse or divert (a person, a sense of humor, vanity, etc.) (*was tickled at the idea; this will tickle your fancy*). ● *n.* **1** an act of tickling. **2** a tickling sensation. □ **tickled pink** (or **to death**) *colloq.* extremely amused or pleased. □□ **tick·ler** *n.* **tick·ly** *adj.*

tick·lish /tíklish/ *adj.* **1** sensitive to tickling. **2** (of a matter or person to be dealt with) difficult; requiring careful handling. □□ **tick·lish·ly** *adv.* **tick·lish·ness** *n.*

tick-tack-toe *n.* (also **tic-tac-toe**) a game in which players alternate turns, seeking to complete a series of three Xs or Os marked in a nine-square grid.

ticky-tacky /tíkeetákee/ *n. & adj. colloq.* ● *n.* inferior or cheap material, esp. as used in suburban buildings. ● *adj.* (esp. of a building or housing development) made of inferior material; cheap or in poor taste.

tid·al /tíd'l/ *adj.* relating to, like, or affected by tides (*tidal basin; tidal river*). □□ **tid·al·ly** *adv.*

tid·al bore *n.* a large wave or bore caused by constriction of the spring tide as it enters a long narrow shallow inlet.

tid·al wave *n.* **1** = TSUNAMI. **2** a widespread manifestation of feeling, etc.

tid·bit /tídbit/ *n.* (*Brit.* **titbit** /tít-/) **1** a small morsel. **2** a choice item of news, etc.

tid·dler /tídlər/ *n. Brit. colloq.* **1** a small fish, esp. a stickleback or minnow. **2** an unusually small thing or person.

tid·dly¹ /tídlee/ *adj.* (**tiddlier, tiddliest**) esp. *Brit. colloq.* slightly drunk.

tid·dly² /tídlee/ *adj.* (**tiddlier, tiddliest**) *Brit. colloq.* little.

tide /tīd/ *n.* **1 a** ▲ the periodic rise and fall of the sea due to the attraction of the Moon and Sun (see EBB *n.* 1, FLOOD *n.* 3). **b** the water as affected by this. **2** a time or season (usu. in *comb.*: *Whitsuntide*). **3** a marked trend of opinion, fortune, or events. □ **tide over** enable or help (a person) to deal with an awkward situation, difficult period, etc. (*the money will tide me over until Friday*). □□ **tide·less** *adj.*

tide·land /tídland/ *n.* **1** land that is submerged at high tide. **2** land below the low-water mark but within a nation's territorial waters.

tide·mark /tídmaark/ *n.* **1** a mark made by the tide at esp. high water. **2** esp. *Brit.* **a** a mark left round a bathtub at the level of the water in it. **b** a line on a person's body, garment, etc., marking the extent to which it has been washed.

tide·wa·ter /tídwawtər, -wotər/ *n.* **1** water brought

TIDE

A complex combination of factors contribute to the phenomenon of tides. The most significant is the gravitational pull of the Moon and, to a lesser degree, the Sun. The pull is stronger on the side of the Earth facing the Moon than at the Earth's centre, causing the oceans on that side to bulge. The pull on the far side is less than on the Earth's centre, so water flows to the point opposite the Moon, and creates a second bulge on that side. As the Earth rotates, each part of the ocean rises and falls, causing two high tides and two low tides. When the Sun and Moon form a right angle with the Earth, their pulls counteract, causing small, or neap, tides. When they are in line, their pull is combined, creating large, or spring, tides.

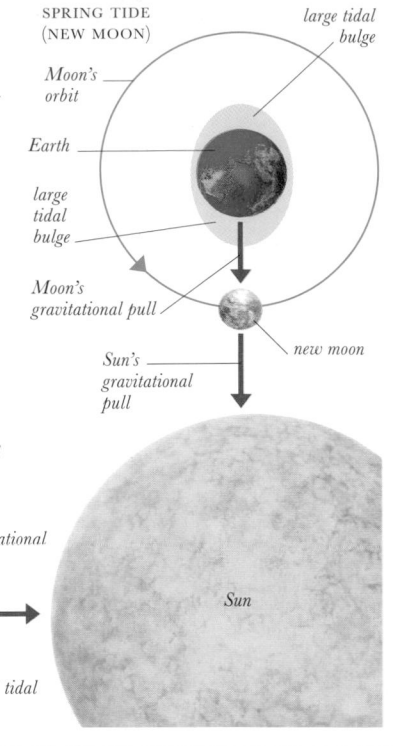

SPRING TIDE (NEW MOON)

large tidal bulge · *Moon's orbit* · *Earth* · *large tidal bulge* · *Moon's gravitational pull* · *new moon* · *Sun's gravitational pull*

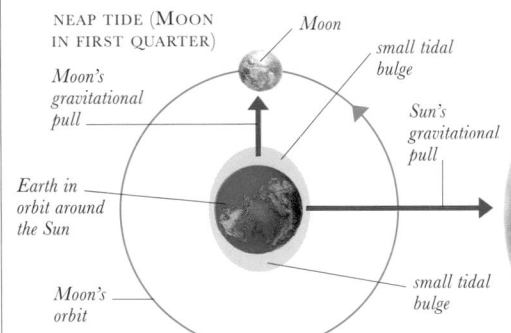

NEAP TIDE (MOON IN FIRST QUARTER)

Moon · *small tidal bulge* · *Moon's gravitational pull* · *Sun's gravitational pull* · *Earth in orbit around the Sun* · *small tidal bulge* · *Moon's orbit* · *Sun*

---

by or affected by tides. **2** (*attrib.*) affected by tides (*tidewater region*).

tide·wave /tídwayv/ *n.* an undulation of water passing round the Earth and causing high and low tides.

tide·way /tídway/ *n.* **1** a channel in which a tide runs, esp. the tidal part of a river. **2** the ebb or flow in a tidal channel.

ti·dings /tídingz/ *n.* (as *sing.* or *pl.*) news; information.

ti·dy /tídee/ *adj., n., & v.* ● *adj.* (**tidier, tidiest**) **1** neat; orderly; methodically arranged. **2** (of a person) methodically inclined. **3** *colloq.* considerable (*it cost a tidy sum*). ● *n.* (*pl.* **-ies**) **1** a receptacle for holding small objects. **2** esp. *Brit.* an act or spell of tidying. **3** a detachable ornamental cover for a chair back, arms, etc. ● *v.tr.* (**-ies, -ied**) (also *absol.*; often foll. by *up*) put in good order; make (oneself, a room, etc.) tidy. □□ **ti·di·ly** *adv.* **ti·di·ness** *n.*

tie /tī/ *v. & n.* ● *v.* (**tying**) **1** *tr.* **a** attach or fasten with string or cord, etc. (*tie the dog to the gate; tie his hands together; tied on a label*). **b** link conceptually. **2** *tr.* **a** form (a string, ribbon, shoelace, necktie, etc.) into a knot or bow. **b** form (a knot or bow) in this way. **3** *tr.* restrict or limit (a person) as to conditions, occupation, place, etc. (*is tied to his family*). **4** *intr.* (often foll. by *with*) achieve the same score or place as another competitor (*they tied at ten games each*). **5** *tr.* hold (rafters, etc.) together by a crosspiece, etc. **6** *tr. Mus.* **a** unite (written notes) by a tie. ▷ NOTATION. **b** perform (two notes) as one unbroken note. ● *n.* **1** a cord, line, or chain, etc., used for fastening. **2** a strip of material worn round the collar and tied in a knot at the front with the ends hanging down. **3** a thing that unites or restricts persons; a bond or obligation (*family ties; ties of friendship*). **4** a draw, dead heat, or equality of score among competitors. **5** *Brit.* a match between any pair from a group of competing players or teams. **6** (also **tie beam**, etc.) ▶ a rod or beam holding parts of a structure together. ▷ ROOF.

7 *Mus.* a curved line above or below two notes of the same pitch indicating that they are to be played for the combined duration of their time values. ▷ NOTATION. **8** a beam laid horizontally as a support for railroad rails. **9** a shoe tied with a lace. □ **fit to be tied** *colloq.* very angry. **tie down** = TIE *v.* 3 above. **tie and dye** var. of TIE-DYE. **tie in** (foll. by *with*) bring into or have a close association or agreement. **tie the knot** *colloq.* get married. **tie up 1** bind or fasten securely with cord, etc. **2** invest or reserve (capital, etc.) so that it is not immediately available for use. **3** moor (a boat). **4** secure (an animal). **5** obstruct; prevent from acting freely. **6** secure or complete (an undertaking, etc.). **7** (often foll. by *with*) = TIE IN. **8** (usu. in *passive*) fully occupy (a person). □□ **tie·less** *adj.*

tieback *n.* ▶ a decorative strip of fabric or cord for holding a curtain back from the window.

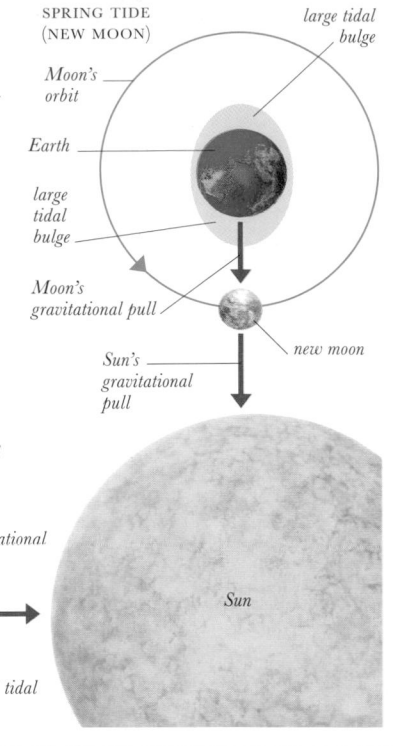

curtain · *tieback*

TIEBACK

tied /tīd/ *adj. Brit.* **1** (of a house) occupied subject to the tenant's working for its owner. **2** (of a bar, etc.) bound to supply the products of one brewery only.

tie-dye *n.* a method of producing dyed patterns by tying string, etc., to protect parts of the fabric from the dye.

tie-in *n.* **1** a connection or association. **2** (often *attrib.*) a form of sale or advertising that offers or requires more than a single purchase. **3** the joint promotion of related commodities, etc. (e.g., a book and a movie).

tie·pin /típin/ *n.* an ornamental pin or clip for holding a tie in place.

tier /teer/ *n.* a vertical or sloped row, rank, or unit of structure. ▷ AMPHITHEATER, AUDITORIUM. □□ **tiered** *adj.* (also in *comb.*).

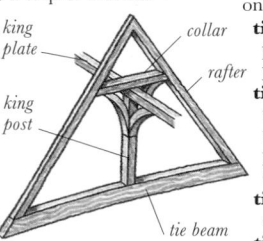

king plate · *collar* · *rafter* · *king post* · *tie beam*

TIE BEAM HOLDING TOGETHER RAFTERS IN A ROOF

T

tierce /teers/ *n.* **1** *Eccl.* = TERCE. **2** *Mus.* an interval of a major or minor third. **3** a sequence of three cards.

tier·cel var. of TERCEL.

tiff /tif/ *n. & v.* ● *n.* **1** a slight or petty quarrel. **2** a fit of peevishness. ● *v.intr.* have a petty quarrel; bicker.

tif·fin /tífin/ *n. & v. Brit. & Ind.* ● *n.* a light meal, esp. lunch. ● *v.intr.* (**tiffined, tiffining**) take lunch, etc.

ti·ger /tígər/ *n.* **1 a** a large Asian feline, *Panthera tigris*, having a yellowish brown coat with black stripes. **b** a similar feline, as the jaguar or ocelot. **2** a domestic cat with similar stripping. **3** a fierce, energetic, or formidable person. ▫▫ **ti·ger·ish** *adj.* **ti·ger·ish·ly** *adv.*

tiger cat *n.* **1** any moderate-sized feline resembling the tiger, .e.g, the ocelot, serval, or margay. ▷ OCELOT. **2** *Austral.* any of various carnivorous marsupials of the genus *Dasyurus*, including the Tasmanian devil.

ti·ger-eye *n.* (also **tiger's-eye**) **1** a yellowish brown striped gem of brilliant luster. **2** a pottery glaze of similar appearance.

ti·ger lil·y *n.* ► a tall garden lily, *Lilium lancifolium*, with flowers of dull orange spotted with black or purple.

TIGER LILY
(*Lilium lancifolium*)

tight /tīt/ *adj., n., & adv.* ● *adj.* **1** closely held, drawn, fastened, fitting, etc. (*a tight hold*; *a tight skirt*). **2 a** closely and firmly put together (*a tight joint*). **b** close; evenly matched (*a tight finish*). **3** (of clothes, etc.) too closely fitting (*my shoes are rather tight*). **4** impermeable, impervious, esp. (in *comb.*) to a specified thing (*watertight*). **5** tense; stretched so as to leave no slack (*a tight bowstring*). **6** *colloq.* drunk. **7** *colloq.* (of a person) mean; stingy. **8 a** (of money or materials) not easily obtainable. **b** (of a money market) in which money is tight. **9 a** (of precautions, a program, a schedule, etc.) stringent. **b** presenting difficulties (*a tight situation*). **c** (of an organization, group, or member) strict; disciplined. **10** produced by or requiring great exertion or pressure (*a tight squeeze*). **11** (of control, etc.) strictly imposed. **12** *colloq.* friendly; close (*the two girls quickly became tight*) ● *adv.* tightly (*hold tight!*). ▫▫ **tight·ly** *adv.* **tight·ness** *n.*

tight cor·ner *n.* (also **tight place** or **spot**) a difficult situation.

tight·en /tīt'n/ *v.tr. & intr.* (also foll. by *up*) make or become tight or tighter. ▫ **tighten one's belt** see BELT.

tight-fist·ed *adj.* stingy.

tight-fit·ting *adj.* (of a garment) fitting (often too) close to the body.

tight-lipped *adj.* with or as with the lips compressed to restrain emotion or speech.

tight·rope /tītrōp/ *n.* a rope stretched tightly high above the ground, on which acrobats perform.

tights /tīts/ *n.pl.* **1** a thin but not sheer close-fitting wool or nylon, etc., garment covering the legs and the lower part of the torso. **2** a similar garment worn by a dancer, acrobat, etc.

tight·wad /tītwod/ *n. colloq.* a person who is miserly or stingy.

ti·gress /tígris/ *n.* **1** a female tiger. **2** a fierce or passionate woman.

tike var. of TYKE.

tilapia /tí-lay-pia/ *n.* ▼ a freshwater cichlid fish of the African genus *Tilapia* or a related genus, widely introduced for food.

TILAPIA: TIGER TILAPIA (*Tilapia mariae*)

til·de /tíldə/ *n.* a mark (˜), put over a letter, e.g., over a Spanish *n* when pronounced *ny* (as in *señor*) or a Portuguese *a* or *o* when nasalized (as in *São Paulo*).

tile /tīl/ *n. & v.* ● *n.* **1** ► a thin slab of concrete or baked clay, etc., used in series for covering a roof or pavement, etc. **2** a similar slab of glazed pottery, cork, linoleum, etc., for covering a floor, wall, etc. ▷ DELFT. **3** a thin flat piece used in a game (esp. mah-jongg). ● *v.tr.* cover with tiles.

TILE: CLAY ROOFING TILES

til·ing /tíling/ *n.* **1** the process of fixing tiles. **2** an area of tiles.

till[1] /til/ *prep. & conj.* ● *prep.* **1** up to or as late as (*wait till six o'clock*; *did not return till night*). **2** up to the time of (*faithful till death*; *waited till the end*). ● *conj.* **1** up to the time when (*wait till I return*). **2** so long that (*laughed till I cried*). ¶ *Until* is more usual when beginning a sentence.

till[2] /til/ *n.* **1** a drawer for money in a store or bank, etc., esp. with a device recording the amount of each purchase. **2** a supply of money.

till[3] /til/ *v.tr.* prepare and cultivate (land) for crops. ▫▫ **till·a·ble** *adj.* **till·er** *n.*

till·age /tílij/ *n.* **1** the preparation of land for bearing crops. **2** tilled land.

till·er /tílər/ *n.* a horizontal bar fitted to the head of a boat's rudder to turn it in steering. ▷ DINGHY, SAILBOAT

tilt /tilt/ *v. & n.* ● *v.* **1 a** *intr. & tr.* assume or cause to assume a sloping position; heel over. **b** incline or lean or cause to lean toward one side of an opinion, action, controversy, etc. **2** *intr.* (foll. by *at*) strike, thrust, or run at with a weapon, esp. in jousting. **3** *intr.* (foll. by *with*) engage in a contest. ● *n.* **1** the act or an instance of tilting. **2** a sloping position. **3** an inclination or bias. **4** (of medieval knights, etc.) the act of charging with a lance against an opponent or at a mark, done for exercise or as a sport. **5** an encounter between opponents; an attack, esp. with argument or satire (*have a tilt at*). ▫ **full** (or **at full**) **tilt 1** at full speed. **2** with full force. ▫▫ **tilt·er** *n.*

tilth /tilth/ *n.* **1** tillage; cultivation. **2** the condition of tilled soil (*in good tilth*).

tim·bal /tímbəl/ *n.* a kettledrum.

tim·bale /tímbəl, taNbaal/ *n.* a drum-shaped dish of ground meat or fish baked in a mold or pastry shell.

tim·ber /tímbər/ *n.* **1** standing trees suitable for lumber. **2** (esp. as *int.*) a warning cry that a tree is about to fall. **3** a piece of wood or beam, esp. as the rib of a vessel. ▫▫ **tim·ber·ing** *n.*

tim·bered /tímbərd/ *adj.* **1** (esp. of a building) made wholly or partly of lumber, esp. with partly exposed beams. **2** (of country) wooded.

tim·ber·land /tímbərland/ *n.* land covered with forest yielding timber.

tim·ber·line /tímbərlīn/ *n.* (on a mountain) the line or level above which no trees grow.

tim·ber wolf *n.* a large N. American gray wolf.

tim·bre /támbər, táNbrə/ (also **tim·ber**) *n.* the distinctive character of a musical sound or voice apart from its pitch and intensity.

Tim·buk·tu /tímbuktōō/ *n.* any distant or remote place.

time /tīm/ *n. & v.* ● *n.* **1** the indefinite continued progress of existence, events, etc., in past, present, and future regarded as a whole. **2** the progress of this as affecting persons or things (*stood the test of time*). **3** a more or less definite portion of time belonging to particular events or circumstances (*the time of the Plague*; *prehistoric times*; *the scientists of the time*). **4** an allotted, available, or measurable portion of time; the period of time at one's disposal (*am wasting my time*; *had no time to visit*; *how much time do you need?*). **5** a point of time, esp. in hours and minutes (*the time is 7:30*; *what time is it?*). **6** (prec. by *a*) an indefinite period (*waited for a time*). **7** time or an amount of time as reckoned by a conventional standard (*the time allowed is one hour*; *ran the mile in record time*; *eight o'clock Eastern Standard time*). **8 a** an occasion (*last time I saw you*). **b** an event or occasion qualified in some way (*had a good time*). **9** a moment or definite portion of time destined or suitable for a purpose, etc. (*now is the time to act*; *shall we set a time?*). **10** (in *pl.*) expressing multiplication (*five times six is thirty*). **11** a lifetime (*will last my time*). **12** (in *sing.* or *pl.*) **a** the conditions of life or of a period (*hard times*). **b** (prec. by *the*) the present age, or that being considered. **13** *colloq.* a prison sentence (*is doing time*). **14 a** an apprenticeship (*served his time*). **b** a period of military service. **15** a period of gestation. **16** the date or expected date of childbirth (*is near her time*) or of death (*my time is drawing near*). **17** measured time spent in work (*put them on short time*). **18 a** any of several rhythmic patterns of music (*in waltz time*). **b** the duration of a note as indicated by a quarter note, whole note, etc. **19** *Brit.* the moment at which a bar closes. **20** = TIME OUT. ● *v.tr.* **1** choose the time or occasion for (*time your remarks carefully*). **2** do at a chosen or correct time. **3** arrange the time of arrival of. **4** ascertain the time taken by (a process or activity, or a person doing it). **5** regulate the duration or interval of; set times for (*trains are timed to arrive every hour*). ▫ **against time** with utmost speed; so as to finish by a specified time (*working against time*). **ahead of time** earlier than expected. **ahead of one's time** having ideas too enlightened or advanced to be accepted by one's contemporaries. **all the time 1** during the whole of the time referred to (often despite some contrary expectation, etc.) (*we never noticed, but he was there all the time*). **2** constantly (*nags all the time*). **3** at all times (*leaves a light on all the time*). **at one time 1** in or during a known but unspecified past period. **2** simultaneously (*ran three businesses at one time*). **at the same time 1** simultaneously; at a time that is the same for all. **2** nevertheless. **at a time** separately in the specified groups or numbers (*came three at a time*). **at times** occasionally; intermittently. **before one's time** prematurely (*old before his time*). **for the time being** for the present; until some other arrangement is made. **half the time** *colloq.* as often as not. **have no time for 1** be unable or unwilling to spend time on. **2** dislike. **have the time 1** be able to spend the time needed. **2** know from a watch, etc., what time it is. **have a time of it** undergo trouble or difficulty. **in no** (or **less than no**) **time 1** very soon. **2** very quickly. **in one's own good time** at a time and a rate decided by oneself. **in time 1** not late; punctual (*was in time to catch the bus*). **2** eventually (*in time you may agree*). **3** in accordance with a given rhythm or tempo, esp. of music. **in one's time** at or during some previous period of one's life (*in his time he was a great hurdler*). **keep good** (or **bad**) **time 1** (of a clock, etc.) record time accurately (or inaccurately). **2** be habitually punctual (or not punctual). **keep time** move or sing, etc., in time. **know the time of day** be well informed. **lose no time** (often foll. by *in* + verbal noun) act immediately. **no time** *colloq.* a very short interval. **on** (also **in**) **one's own time** outside working hours. **on time** see ON. **out of time 1** unseasonable; unseasonably. **2** not in rhythm. **pass the time of day** *colloq.* exchange a greeting or casual remarks. **time after time 1** repeatedly; on many occasions. **2** in many instances. **time and** (or **time and time**) **again** on many occasions. **the time of day** the hour by the clock. **the time of one's life** occasion of exceptional enjoyment. **time out of mind** see TIME IMMEMORIAL. **time was** there was a time (*time was when I could do that*).

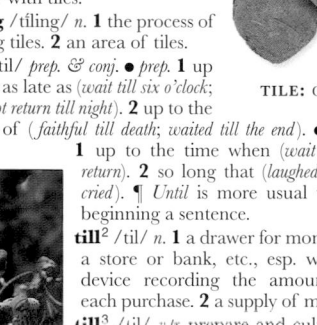

time and a half *n.* a rate of payment for work at one and a half times the normal rate.

time bomb *n.* a bomb designed to explode at a preset time.

time cap·sule *n.* a box, etc., containing objects typical of the present time, buried for discovery in the future.

time clock *n.* **1** a clock with a device for recording workers' hours of work. **2** a switch mechanism activated at preset times by a built-in clock.

time-con·sum·ing *adj.* using much or too much time.

time ex·po·sure *n.* ▼ the exposure of photographic film for longer than the maximum normal shutter setting.

TIME EXPOSURE: PHOTOGRAPH OF CARS AT NIGHT TAKEN WITH A LONG TIME EXPOSURE

time frame *n.* period of time during which an action occurs or will occur.

time-hon·ored *adj.* esteemed by tradition or through custom.

time im·me·mo·ri·al *n.* (also **time out of mind**) a longer time than anyone can remember or trace.

time·keep·er /tímkeepər/ *n.* **1** a person who records time, esp. of workers or in a game. **2 a** a watch or clock as regards accuracy. **b** a person as regards punctuality. □□ **time·keep·ing** *n.*

time-lapse *n.* (of photography) using frames taken at long intervals to photograph a slow process, and shown continuously as if at normal speed.

time·less /tímlis/ *adj.* not affected by the passage of time; eternal. □□ **time·less·ly** *adv.* **time·less·ness** *n.*

time lim·it *n.* the limit of time within which a task must be done.

time·ly /tímlee/ *adj.* (**timelier**, **timeliest**) opportune; coming at the right time. □□ **time·li·ness** *n.*

time ma·chine *n.* (in science fiction) a machine capable of time travel.

time off *n.* time for rest or recreation, etc.

time out *n.* **1** a brief intermission in a game, etc. **2** = TIME OFF.

time·piece /tímpees/ *n.* an instrument, such as a clock or watch, for measuring time.

tim·er /tímər/ *n.* **1** a person or device that measures or records time taken. **2** an automatic mechanism for activating a device, etc., at a preset time.

time-served *adj.* having completed a period of apprenticeship or training.

time-serv·er *n.* a person who changes his or her view to suit the prevailing circumstances.

time-serv·ing *adj.* self-serving or obsequious.

time-share *n.* a share in a property under a time-sharing arrangement.

time-shar·ing *n.* **1** the operation of a computer system by several users for different operations at

one time. **2** the use of a vacation home at agreed different times by several joint owners.

time sheet *n.* a sheet of paper for recording hours of work, etc.

time sig·na·ture *n. Mus.* an indication of tempo following a clef, expressed as a fraction with the numerator giving the number of beats in each bar and the denominator giving the kind of note getting one beat. ▷ NOTATION

time·ta·ble /tímtaybəl/ *n. & v.* ● *n.* a list of times at which events are scheduled to take place, esp. the arrival and departure of buses or trains, etc., or *Brit.* a lesson plan in a school or college. ● *v.tr.* include in or arrange to a timetable; schedule.

time tri·al *n.* (in various sports) a test of a competitor's individual speed over a set distance.

time warp *n.* an imaginary distortion of space in relation to time, whereby persons or objects of one age can be moved to another.

time·work /tímwərk/ *n.* work paid for by the time it takes.

time·worn /tímwawrn/ *n.* impaired by age.

time zone *n.* a range of longitudes where a common standard time is used.

tim·id /tímid/ *adj.* (**timider**, **timidest**) easily frightened; apprehensive; shy. □□ **ti·mid·i·ty** /-míditee/ *n.* **tim·id·ly** *adv.* **tim·id·ness** *n.*

tim·ing /tíming/ *n.* **1** the way an action or process is timed, esp. in relation to others. **2** the regulation of the opening and closing of valves in an internal-combustion engine.

tim·or·ous /tímərəs/ *adj.* timid; nervous. □□ **tim·or·ous·ly** *adv.* **tim·or·ous·ness** *n.*

tim·pa·ni /tímpənee/ *n.pl.* (also **tym·pa·ni**) kettledrums. ▷ ORCHESTRA, PERCUSSION. □□ **tim·pa·nist** *n.*

tin /tin/ *n. & v.* ● *n.* **1** *Chem.* ▶ a silvery white malleable metallic element resisting corrosion, occurring naturally in cassiterite and other ores, and used esp. in alloys and for plating thin iron or steel sheets to form tin plate. ▷ METAL. ¶ Symb.: **Sn**. **2** a vessel or container made of tin or tin-plated iron. **3** = TIN PLATE. ● *v.tr.* (**tinned**, **tinning**) **1** esp. *Brit.* seal (food) in an airtight can for preservation. **2** cover or coat with tin.

tin can *n.* a tin-plated container for preserving food.

tinc·ture /tíngkchər/ *n. & v.* ● *n.* (often foll. by *of*) **1** a slight flavor or trace. **2** a tinge (of a color). **3** a medicinal solution (of a drug) in alcohol (*tincture of quinine*). **4** *Heraldry* an inclusive term for the metals, colors, and furs used in coats of arms. ● *v.tr.* tinge or flavor with a slight trace of.

tin·der /tíndər/ *n.* a dry substance such as wood that readily catches fire from a spark. □□ **tin·der·y** *adj.*

tin·der·box /tíndərboks/ *n.* **1** *hist.* ▼ a box containing tinder, flint, and steel, formerly used for kindling fires. **2** a potentially explosive or violent person, place, situation, etc.

TINDERBOX

LID

FLINT

STEEL

TINDER

TINDERBOX: 19TH-CENTURY METAL TINDERBOX AND CONTENTS

tine /tīn/ *n.* a prong or tooth or point of a fork, comb, antler, etc. □□ **tined** *adj.* (also in *comb.*).

tin foil *n.* foil made of tin, aluminum, or tin alloy, used for wrapping food for cooking or storing.

ting /ting/ *n. & v.* ● *n.* a tinkling sound as of a bell. ● *v.intr. & tr.* emit or cause to emit this sound.

tinge /tinj/ *v. & n.* ● *v.tr.* (also **tinge·ing**) (often foll. by *with*; often in *passive*) **1** color slightly (*is tinged with red*). **2** affect slightly (*regret tinged with satisfaction*). ● *n.* **1** a tendency toward or trace of some color. **2** a slight admixture of a feeling or quality.

tin·gle /tínggəl/ *v. & n.* ● *v.* **1** *intr.* **a** feel a slight prickling, stinging, or throbbing sensation. **b** cause this (*the reply tingled in my ears*). **2** *tr.* make (the ear, etc.) tingle. ● *n.* a tingling sensation.

tin·gly /tínglee/ *adj.* (**tinglier**, **tingliest**) causing or characterized by tingling.

tin·horn /tínhawrn/ *n. & adj. sl.* ● *n.* a pretentious but unimpressive person. ● *adj.* cheap; pretentious.

tin·ker /tíngkər/ *n. & v.* ● *n.* **1** an itinerant mender of kettles and pans, etc. **2** *Sc. & Ir.* a gypsy. **3** a spell of tinkering. ● *v.* **1** *intr.* (foll. by *at, with*) work in an amateurish or desultory way, esp. to adjust or mend machinery, etc. **2 a** *intr.* work as a tinker. **b** *tr.* repair (pots and pans). □□ **tin·ker·er** *n.*

tin·kle /tíngkəl/ *v. & n.* ● *v.* **1** *intr. & tr.* make or cause to make a succession of short light ringing sounds. **2** *intr. colloq.* urinate. ● *n.* **1** a tinkling sound. **2** *Brit. colloq.* a telephone call (*will give you a tinkle on Monday*). **3** *colloq.* an act of urinating.

tin·ni·tus /tínítəs, tíni-/ *n. Med.* a ringing in the ears.

tin·ny /tínee/ *adj.* (**tinnier**, **tinniest**) **1** of or like tin. **2** (of a metal object) flimsy; insubstantial; of poor quality. **3 a** sounding like struck tin. **b** (of reproduced sound) thin and metallic, lacking low frequencies. □□ **tin·ni·ly** *adv.* **tin·ni·ness** *n.*

Tin Pan Al·ley *n.* the world of composers and publishers of popular music.

tin plate *n.* sheet iron or sheet steel coated with tin. □□ **tin-plate** *v.tr.*

tin·pot /tínpot/ *adj.* cheap; inferior.

tin·sel /tínsəl/ *n. & v.* ● *n.* **1** glittering metallic strips, threads, etc., used as decoration to give a sparkling effect. **2** a fabric adorned with tinsel. **3** superficial brilliance or splendor. **4** (*attrib.*) showy; gaudy; flashy. ● *v.tr.* (**tinseled**, **tinseling** or **tinselled**, **tinselling**) adorn with or as with tinsel. □□ **tin·seled** *adj.* **tin·sel·ly** *adj.*

tin·smith /tínsmith/ *n.* a worker in tin and tin plate.

tint /tint/ *n. & v.* ● *n.* **1** a variety of a color, esp. one made lighter by adding white. **2** a tendency toward or admixture of a different color (*red with a blue tint*). **3** a faint color spread over a surface, esp. as a background for printing on. **4** a dye for the hair. ● *v.tr.* apply a tint to; color. □□ **tint·er** *n.*

tin·tin·nab·u·la·tion /tíntinábyələáyshən/ *n.* a ringing or tinkling of bells.

tin·ware /tínwair/ *n.* articles made of tin or tin plate.

ti·ny /tínee/ *adj.* (**tinier**, **tiniest**) very small or slight. □□ **ti·ni·ly** *adv.* **ti·ni·ness** *n.*

tip¹ /tip/ *n. & v.* ● *n.* **1** an extremity or end, esp. of a small or tapering thing (*tips of the fingers*). **2** a small piece or part attached to the end of a thing, e.g., a ferrule on a stick. **3** a leaf bud of tea. ● *v.tr.* (**tipped, tipping**) **1** provide with a tip. **2** (foll. by *in*) attach (a loose sheet) to a page at the inside edge. □ **on the tip of one's tongue** about to be said, esp. after difficulty in recalling to mind. **the tip of the iceberg** a small evident part of something much larger or more significant. □□ **tip·less** *adj.* **tip·py** *adj.* (in sense 3).

tip² /tip/ *v. & n.* ● *v.* (**tipped, tipping**) **1 a** *intr.* lean or slant. **b** *tr.* cause to do this. **2** *tr.* (foll. by *into*, etc.) **a** overturn or cause to overbalance (*was tipped into the pond*). **b** discharge the contents of (a container, etc.) in this way. ● *n.* **1 a** a slight push or tilt. **b** a glancing stroke, esp. in baseball. **2** *Brit.* a place

T

where material (esp. trash) is dumped. □ **tip the balance** make the critical difference. **tip the scales** see SCALE[2].

tip[3] /tip/ *v. & n.* ● *v.* (**tipped, tipping**) **1** *tr.* make a small present of money to, esp. for a service given (*have you tipped the waiter?*). **2** *tr.* name as the likely winner of a race or contest, etc. ● *n.* **1** a small gift of money, esp. for a service given. **2** a piece of private or special information, esp. regarding betting or investment. **3** a small or casual piece of advice. □ **tip off 1** give (a person) a hint or piece of special information or warning, esp. discreetly or confidentially. **2** *Basketball* start play by throwing the ball up between two opponents. □□ **tip·per** *n.*

tip·cat /típkat/ *n.* a game with a short piece of wood tapering at the ends and struck with a stick.

tip-off *n.* **1** a hint or warning, etc., given discreetly or confidentially. **2** *Basketball* the act of starting play with a tip off.

tip·pet /típit/ *n.* **1** a woman's fur cape or woolen shawl. **2** a similar garment worn ceremonially by the clergy.

tip·ple /típəl/ *v. & n.* ● *v.intr.* drink intoxicating liquor habitually. ● *n. colloq.* a drink, esp. a strong one. □□ **tip·pler** *n.*

tip·staff /típstaf/ *n.* **1** a sheriff's officer. **2** a metal-tipped staff carried as a symbol of office.

tip·ster /típstər/ *n.* a person who gives tips, esp. about betting at horse races.

tip·sy /típsee/ *adj.* (**tipsier, tipsiest**) **1** slightly intoxicated. **2** caused by or showing intoxication (*a tipsy leer*). □□ **tip·si·ly** *adv.* **tip·si·ness** *n.*

tip·toe /típtō/ *v. & adv.* ● *v.intr.* (**tiptoes, tiptoed, tiptoeing**) walk on tiptoe, or very stealthily. ● *adv.* (also **on tiptoe**) with the heels off the ground and the weight on the balls of the feet.

tip-top /típtóp/ *adj., adv., & n. colloq.* ● *adj. & adv.* highest in excellence; very best. ● *n.* the highest point of excellence.

ti·rade /tírayd, tīráyd/ *n.* a long vehement denunciation or declamation.

ti·ra·mi·su /tirəmisóo/ *n.* an Italian dessert consisting of layers of sponge cake soaked in coffee and brandy or liqueur, with powdered chocolate and mascarpone cheese.

tire[1] /tīr/ *v.* **1** *tr. & intr.* make or grow weary. **2** *tr.* exhaust the patience or interest of; bore. **3** *tr.* (in *passive*; foll. by *of*) have had enough of; be fed up with (*was tired of arguing*).

tire[2] /tīr/ *n.* **1** a rubber covering, usu. inflatable, that fits around a wheel rim. **2** a band of metal placed around the rim of a wheel to strengthen it.

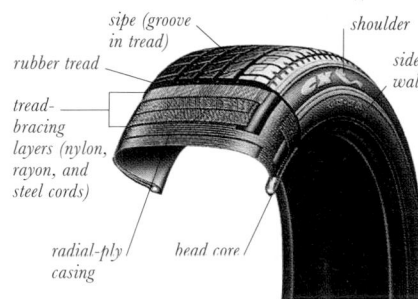

sipe (groove in tread)
shoulder
rubber tread
sidewall
tread-bracing layers (nylon, rayon, and steel cords)
radial-ply casing
bead core

TIRE: SECTION THROUGH A MODERN RADIAL-PLY CAR TIRE

tired /tīrd/ *adj.* **1** weary; exhausted; ready for sleep. **2** (of an idea, etc.) hackneyed. □□ **tired·ly** *adv.* **tired·ness** *n.*

tire·less /tírlis/ *adj.* having inexhaustible energy. □□ **tire·less·ly** *adv.* **tire·less·ness** *n.*

tire·some /tírsəm/ *adj.* **1** wearisome; tedious. **2** *Brit. colloq.* annoying (*how tiresome of you!*). □□ **tire·some·ly** *adv.* **tire·some·ness** *n.*

ti·ro *Brit.* var. of TYRO.

'tis /tiz/ *archaic* it is.

TIT

Tits are small, very active birds. They belong mainly to the Paridae family but include birds from other families, such as the penduline tit (Remizidae) and the long-tailed tit (Aegithalidae). The majority of tits live in woodlands, nesting in holes in trees or banks, and feed on nuts, seeds, and insects. They have small, stout bills, short rounded wings, and square-ended tails.

EXAMPLES OF TITS

BLUE TIT
(*Parus caeruleus*)

PENDULINE TIT
(*Remiz pendulinus*)

LONG-TAILED TIT
(*Aegithalos caudatus*)

SIBERIAN TIT
(*Parus cinctus*)

ti·sane /tizán, -zaán/ *n.* an infusion of dried herbs, etc.

tis·sue /tíshoo/ *n.* **1** any of the coherent collections of specialized cells of which animals or plants are made (*muscular tissue; nervous tissue*). **2** = TISSUE PAPER. **3** a disposable piece of thin soft absorbent paper for wiping, drying, etc. **4** fine woven esp. gauzy fabric. **5** (foll. by *of*) a connected series; a web (*a tissue of lies*).

tissue pa·per *n.* thin soft paper for wrapping or protecting fragile or delicate articles.

tit[1] /tit/ *n.* **▲** any of various small birds, esp. of the family Paridae.

tit[2] /tit/ *n.* □ **tit for tat** /tat/ blow for blow; retaliation.

tit[3] /tit/ *n.* **1** *colloq.* a nipple. **2** *coarse sl.* a woman's breast. ¶ Usually considered a taboo word in sense 2.

Ti·tan /tít'n/ *n.* **1** (often **titan**) a person of very great strength, intellect, or importance. **2** (in Greek mythology) a member of a family of early gigantic gods, the offspring of Heaven and Earth.

ti·tan·ic /tītánik/ *adj.* **1** of or like the Titans. **2** gigantic; colossal. □□ **ti·tan·i·cal·ly** *adv.*

ti·ta·ni·um /tītáyneeəm, tee-/ *n. Chem.* **▶** a gray metallic element occurring naturally in many clays, etc., and used to make strong light alloys that are resistant to corrosion. ¶ Symb.: **Ti**.

ti·ta·ni·um di·ox·ide *n.* (also **ti·ta·ni·um ox·ide**) a white oxide occurring naturally and used as a white pigment.

tit·bit *Brit.* var. of TIDBIT.

tithe /tīth/ *n. & v.* ● *n.* **1** one tenth of the annual product of land or labor, formerly taken as a tax for the support of the church and clergy. **2** a tenth part. ● *v.* **1** *tr.* subject to tithes. **2** *intr.* pay tithes. □□ **tith·a·ble** *adj.*

Ti·tian /tíshən/ *adj.* (in full **Titian red**) (of hair) reddish brown.

tit·il·late /tít'layt/ *v.tr.* **1** excite pleasantly. **2** tickle. □□ **tit·il·lat·ing·ly** *adv.* **tit·il·la·tion** /-láyshən/ *n.*

tit·i·vate /títivayt/ *v.tr.* (also **tit·ti·vate**) *colloq.* **1** adorn; smarten; spruce up. **2** (often *refl.*) put the finishing touches to. □□ **ti·ti·va·tion** /-váyshən/ *n.*

ti·tle /tít'l/ *n. & v.* ● *n.* **1** the name of a book, work of art, piece of music, etc. **2** the heading of a chapter, poem, document, etc. **3 a** the contents of the title page of a book. **b** a book regarded in terms of

its title (*published 20 new titles*). **4** a caption or credit in a movie, broadcast, etc. **5** a form of nomenclature indicating a person's status (e.g., *professor, queen*) or used as a form of address or reference (e.g., *Lord, Mr.*). **6** a sports championship. **7** *Law* **a** the right to ownership of property with or without possession. **b** the facts constituting this. **c** (foll. by *to*) a just or recognized claim. **8** *Eccl.* **a** a fixed sphere of work and source of income as a condition for ordination. **b** a parish church in Rome under a cardinal. ● *v.tr.* **1** give a title to. **2** call by a title; term.

ti·tled /tít'ld/ *adj.* having a title of nobility or rank.

ti·tle role *n.* the part in a play, etc., that gives it its name (e.g., *Othello*).

tit·mouse /títmows/ *n.* (*pl.* **titmice** /-mīs/) any of various small tits, esp. of the genus *Parus*. ▷ TIT

ti·trate /títrayt/ *v.tr. Chem.* ascertain the amount of a constituent in (a solution) by measuring the volume of a known concentration of reagent required to complete the reaction. □□ **ti·trat·a·ble** *adj.* **ti·tra·tion** /-tráyshən/ *n.*

tit·ter /títər/ *v. & n.* ● *v.intr.* laugh in a furtive or restrained way; giggle. ● *n.* a furtive or restrained laugh. □□ **tit·ter·er** *n.* **tit·ter·ing·ly** *adv.*

tit·ti·vate var. of TITIVATE.

tit·tle /tít'l/ *n.* **1** a small written or printed stroke or dot. **2** a particle; a whit (esp. in *not one jot or tittle*).

tit·tle-tat·tle /tít'ltat'l/ *n. & v.* ● *n.* petty gossip; foolish chatter. ● *v.intr.* gossip; chatter. □□ **tit·tle-tat·tler** *n.*

tit·ty /títee/ *n.* (*pl.* **-ies**) *sl.* = TIT[3].

tit·u·lar /tíchələr/ *adj. & n.* ● *adj.* **1** of or relating to a title (*the book's titular hero*). **2** existing, or being what is specified, in name or title only (*titular ruler; titular sovereignty*). ● *n.* **1** the holder of an office, etc., esp. a benefice without the corresponding functions or obligations. **2** a titular saint. □□ **tit·u·lar·ly** *adv.*

TITANIUM: ARTIFICIAL HIP JOINT MADE FROM TITANIUM

tiz·zy /tízee/ *n.* (*pl.* **-ies**) (also **tizz, tiz**) *colloq.* a state of nervous agitation (*in a tizzy*).

TKO *abbr. Boxing* technical knockout.

Tl *symb. Chem.* the element thallium.

TLC *abbr. colloq.* tender loving care.

TOAD

Toads generally differ from frogs in having dry warty skin, short stout legs for walking, and reduced webbing on their feet. They have defensive poison-secreting parotid glands behind the eyes. Although the majority of toads prefer to live on dry land, most enter water during the breeding season; some species also hibernate in water.

nostril

parotid (poison) gland

dry warty skin

short leg

squat body

reduced webbing on foot

EXTERNAL FEATURES OF A GREEN TOAD (*Bufo viridis*)

EXAMPLES OF TOADS

NATTERJACK TOAD (*Bufo calamita*)

RED-SPOTTED TOAD (*Bufo punctatus*)

CANE TOAD (*Bufo marinus*)

EUROPEAN COMMON TOAD (*Bufo bufo*)

Tlin·git /tlíngkət, -gət, kling-/ *n. & adj.* ● *n.* **1 a** a N. American people native to southern Alaska. **b** a member of this people. **2** the language of this people. ● *adj.* of or relating to this people or their language.

TM *abbr.* Transcendental Meditation.

Tm *symb. Chem.* the element thulium.

tme·sis /tmeésis/ *n.* (*pl.* **tmeses** /-seez/) *Gram.* the separation of parts of a compound word by an intervening word or words (esp. in colloq. speech, e.g., *can't find it anydamnedwhere*).

TN *abbr.* Tennessee (in official postal use).

tn *abbr.* **1** ton(s). **2** town.

TNT *abbr.* trinitrotoluene, a high explosive formed from toluene by substitution of three hydrogen atoms with nitro groups.

to /tōō/; tə (when unstressed)/ *prep. & adv.* ● *prep.* **1** introducing a noun: **a** expressing what is reached, approached, or touched (*fell to the ground; went to Paris; put her face to the window; five minutes to six*). **b** expressing what is aimed at: often introducing the indirect object of a verb (*throw it to me; explained the problem to them*). **c** as far as; up to (*went on to the end; have to stay from Tuesday to Friday*). **d** to the extent of (*were all drunk to a man; was starved to death*). **e** expressing what is followed (*according to instructions; made to order*). **f** expressing what is considered or affected (*am used to that; that is nothing to me*). **g** expressing what is caused or produced (*turn to stone; tear to shreds*). **h** expressing what is compared (*nothing to what it once was; equal to the occasion; won by three to two*). **i** expressing what is increased (*add it to mine*). **j** expressing what is involved or composed as specified (*there is nothing to it; more to him than meets the eye*). **k** archaic for; by way of (*took her to wife*). **2** introducing the infinitive: **a** as a verbal noun (*to get there is the priority*). **b** expressing purpose, consequence, or cause (*we eat to live; left him to starve; am sorry to hear that*). **c** as a substitute for *to* + infinitive (*wanted to come but was unable to*). ● *adv.* **1** in the normal or required position or condition (*come to; heave to*). **2** (of a door) in a nearly closed position. □ **to and fro 1** backward and forward. **2** repeatedly between the same points.

toad /tōd/ *n.* **1** ▲ any froglike amphibian of the family Bufonidae, esp. of the genus *Bufo*, breeding in water but living chiefly on land. **2** any of various similar amphibians, including the Surinam toad. ▷ EGG, FROG. **3** a repulsive or detestable person. □□ **toad·ish** *adj.*

toad·fish /tōdfish/ *n.* any marine fish of the family Batrachoididae, with a large head and wide mouth,

making grunting noises by vibrating the walls of its swim bladder.

toad·flax /tōdflaks/ *n.* **1** ◄ any plant of the genus *Linaria* or *Chaenorrhinum*, with flaxlike leaves and spurred yellow or purple flowers. **2** a related plant, *Cymbalaria muralis*, with lilac flowers and ivy-shaped leaves.

toad·stone /tōdstōn/ *n.* a stone supposed to resemble or to have been formed in the body of a toad, formerly used as an amulet, etc.

toad·stool /tōdstōōl/ *n.* ▼ the spore-bearing structure of various fungi, usu. poisonous, with a round top and slender stalk. ▷ FUNGUS

TOADFLAX: YELLOW TOADFLAX (*Linaria vulgaris*)

toad·y /tōdee/ *n. & v.* ● *n.* (*pl.* **-ies**) a sycophant; an obsequious hanger-on. ● *v.tr. & (*foll. by *to*) *intr.* (**-ies**, **-ied**) behave servilely to; fawn upon. □□ **toad·y·ish** *adj.* **toad·y·ism** *n.*

toast /tōst/ *n. & v.* ● *n.* **1** bread in slices browned on both sides by radiant heat. **2 a** a person (orig. esp. a woman) or thing in whose honor a company is requested to drink. **b** a call to drink or an instance of drinking in this way. **3** a person or thing that is very popular or held in high regard (*the toast of the town*). ● *v.* **1** *tr.* cook or brown (bread, etc.) by radiant heat. **2** *intr.* (of bread, etc.) become brown in this way **3** *tr.* warm (one's feet, oneself, etc.) at a fire, etc. **4** *tr.* drink to the health or in honor of (a person or thing). □ **have a person on toast** *Brit. colloq.* be in a position to deal with a person as one wishes.

toast·er /tōstər/ *n.* ▼ an electrical device for making toast.

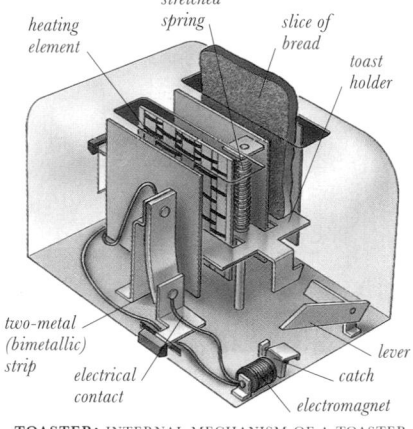

heating element

stretched spring

slice of bread

toast holder

two-metal (bimetallic) strip

electrical contact

lever

catch

electromagnet

TOASTER: INTERNAL MECHANISM OF A TOASTER

toast·mas·ter /tōstmastər/ *n.* (*fem.* **toastmistress** /-mistris/) an official responsible for announcing toasts at a public occasion.

toast·y /tōstee/ *adj.* (**toastier**, **toastiest**) comfortably warm; cozy and warm. □□ **toast·i·ness** *n.*

TOADSTOOL

Toadstools, like mushrooms, are fungi belonging to the divisions Ascomycota and Basidiomycota; most produce umbrella-shaped fruiting bodies. Inedible or poisonous types are usually called "toadstools," whereas edible ones are "mushrooms," although the distinction is not truly scientific.

EXAMPLES OF TOADSTOOLS

FLY AMANITA (*Amanita muscaria*)

STOUT-STALKED AGARIC (*Amanita spissa*)

SMOOTH LEPIOTA (*Leucoagaricus leucothites*)

YELLOW-BANDED WEB CAP (*Cortinarius triumphans*)

SAW-GILLED BLUE-CAP ENTOLOMA (*Entoloma serrulatum*)

ALCOHOL INKY CAP (*Coprinus atramentarius*)

BITTER WOOLLY-FOOT COLLYBIA (*Collybia peronata*)

T

to·bac·co /təbákō/ *n.* (*pl.* **-os**) **1** ▶ any plant of the genus *Nicotiana*, of American origin, with narcotic leaves used for smoking, chewing, or snuff. **2** its leaves, esp. as prepared for smoking.

to·bac·co·nist /təbákənist/ *n.* a retail dealer in tobacco and cigarettes, etc.

to·bog·gan /təbógən/ *n. & v. • n.* a long light narrow sled curled up at the front for sliding downhill, esp. over compacted snow or ice. *• v.intr.* ride on a toboggan. □□ **to·bog·gan·er** *n.* **to·bog·gan·ing** *n.* **to·bog·gan·ist** *n.*

to·by jug /tóbee/ *n.* (also **to·by, To·by**) a pitcher or mug for ale, etc., usu. in the form of a stout old man wearing a three-cornered hat.

toc·ca·ta /təkáátə/ *n.* a musical composition for a keyboard instrument designed to exhibit the performer's touch and technique.

to·coph·er·ol /tōkófərawl, -rol/ *n.* any of several closely related vitamins found in wheat germ oil, egg yolk, and leafy vegetables, and important in the stabilization of cell membranes, etc. Also called **vitamin E**.

toc·sin /tóksin/ *n.* an alarm bell or signal.

to·day /tədáy/ *adv. & n. • adv* **1** on or in the course of this present day (*shall we go today?*). **2** nowadays; in modern times. *• n.* **1** this present day (*today is my birthday*). **2** modern times.

tod·dle /tód'l/ *v. & n. • v.intr.* **1** walk with short unsteady steps like those of a small child. **2** *colloq.* **a** (often foll. by *around, to,* etc.) take a casual or leisurely walk. **b** (usu. foll. by *off*) depart. *• n.* **1** a toddling walk. **2** *colloq.* a stroll or short walk.

tod·dler /tódlər/ *n.* a child who is just beginning to walk. □□ **tod·dler·hood** *n.*

tod·dy /tódee/ *n.* (*pl.* **-ies**) **1** a drink of liquor with hot water and sugar or spices. **2** the sap of some kinds of palm, fermented to produce arrack.

to-do /tədṓ/ *n.* a commotion or fuss.

toe /tō/ *n. & v. • n.* **1** any of the five terminal projections of the foot. **2** the corresponding part of an animal. **3** the part of an item of footwear that covers the toes. **4** the lower end or tip of an implement, etc. *• v.* (**toes, toed, toeing**) **1** *tr.* touch (a starting line, etc.) with the toes before starting a race. **2** *tr.* **a** mend the toe of (a sock, etc.). **b** provide with a toe. □ **on one's toes** alert; eager. **toe the line** conform to a general policy or principle, esp. unwillingly or under pressure. **turn up one's toes** *colloq.* die. □□ **toed** *adj.* (also in *comb.*). **toe·less** *adj.*

toe·cap /tṓkap/ *n.* the (usu. strengthened) outer covering of the toe of a boot or shoe.

toe clip *n.* ◀ a clip on a bicycle pedal to prevent the foot from slipping. ▷ BICYCLE

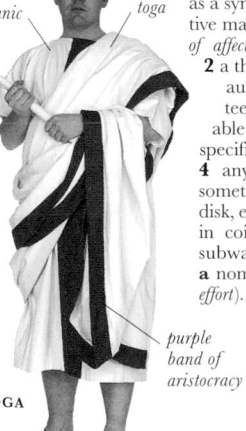

TOE CLIP ON A MOUNTAIN BIKE

toe clip

toe·nail /tṓnayl/ *n.* the nail at the tip of each toe.

toff /tof/ *n. & v.* *Brit. sl. • n.* a distinguished or well-dressed person; a dandy. *• v.tr.* (foll. by *up*) dress up smartly.

tof·fee /táwfee, tóf-/ *n.* (also **tof·fy**) (*pl.* **toffees** or **toffies**) **1** a kind of firm or hard candy softening when sucked or chewed, made by boiling sugar, butter, etc. **2** a small piece of this.

to·fu /tṓfoo/ *n.* a curd made from mashed soy beans.

tog /tog/ *n. & v. colloq. • n.* (usu. in *pl.*) an item of clothing. *• v.tr. & intr.* (**togged, togging**) (foll. by *out, up*) dress, esp. elaborately.

to·ga /tṓgə/ *n. hist.* ▶ an ancient Roman citizen's loose flowing outer garment. □□ **to·gaed** *adj.*

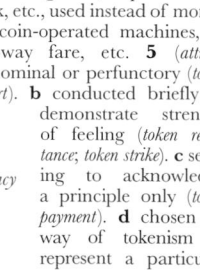

tunic

toga

purple band of aristocracy

TOGA

to·geth·er /təgéthər/ *adv. & adj. • adv.* **1** in company or conjunction (*walking together; built it together; were at school together*). **2** simultaneously; at the same time (*both shouted together*). **3** one with another (*were talking together*). **4** into conjunction; so as to unite (*tied them together; put two and two together*). **5** into company or companionship (*came together in friendship*). **6** uninterruptedly (*could talk for hours together*). *• adj. colloq.* well organized or controlled. □ **together with** as well as; and also.

to·geth·er·ness /təgéthərnis/ *n.* **1** the condition of being together. **2** a feeling of comfort from being together.

tog·gle /tógəl/ *n. & v. • n.* **1** a device for fastening (esp. a garment), consisting of a crosspiece which can pass through a hole or loop in one position but not in another. ▷ DUFFEL COAT. **2** a pin or other crosspiece put through the eye of a rope, a link of a chain, etc., to keep it in place. **3** a pivoted barb on a harpoon. **4** *Computing* a switch action that is operated the same way but with opposite effect on successive occasions. *• v.tr.* provide or fasten with a toggle.

toggle switch *n.* an electric switch with a projecting lever to be moved usu. up and down.

toil /toyl/ *v. & n. • v.intr.* **1** work laboriously or incessantly. **2** make slow painful progress (*toiled along the path*). *• n.* prolonged or intensive labor; drudgery. □□ **toil·er** *n.*

toile /twaal/ *n.* **1** a type of sheer fabric. **2** a garment reproduced in muslin or other cheap material for fitting or for making copies.

toi·let /tóylit/ *n.* **1 a** a fixture, as in a bathroom, etc., for defecating and urinating. **b** a bathroom or lavatory. **2** the process of washing oneself, dressing, etc. (*make one's toilet*).

toi·let pa·per *n.* (also **toi·let tis·sue**) paper for cleaning oneself after excreting.

toi·let·ry /tóylitree/ *n.* (*pl.* **-ies**) (usu. in *pl.*) any of various articles or cosmetics used in washing, dressing, etc.

toi·lette /twaalét/ *n.* = TOILET 2.

toi·let train·ing *n.* the training of a young child to use a toilet.

toi·let wa·ter *n.* a diluted form of perfume used esp. after washing.

toil·some /tóylsəm/ *adj.* involving toil; laborious. □□ **toil·some·ly** *adv.* **toil·some·ness** *n.*

to-ing and fro-ing /tṓing ənd frṓing/ *n.* constant movement to and fro; bustle; dispersed activity.

To·kay /tōkáy/ *n.* **1** a sweet aromatic wine made near Tokai in Hungary. **2** a similar wine produced elsewhere.

to·ken /tṓkən/ *n.* **1** a thing serving as a symbol, reminder, or distinctive mark of something (*as a token of affection; in token of my esteem*). **2** a thing serving as evidence of authenticity or as a guarantee. **3** a voucher exchangeable for goods (often of a specified kind), given as a gift. **4** anything used to represent something else, esp. a metal disk, used instead of money in coin-operated machines, as subway fare, etc. **5** (*attrib.*) **a** nominal or perfunctory (*token effort*). **b** conducted briefly to demonstrate strength of feeling (*token resistance; token strike*). **c** serving to acknowledge a principle only (*token payment*). **d** chosen by way of tokenism to represent a particular group (*the token woman on the committee*). □ **by the same** (or **this**) **token 1** similarly. **2** moreover.

to·ken·ism /tṓkənizəm/ *n.* **1** esp. *Polit.* the principle or practice of granting minimum concessions, esp. to appease radical demands, etc. (cf. TOKEN 5d). **2** making only a token effort.

to·ken mon·ey *n.* coins having a higher face value than their worth as metal.

to·ken vote *n.* (in the UK) a parliamentary vote of money, the stipulated amount of which is not meant to be binding.

told *past* and *past part.* of TELL.

tol·er·a·ble /tólərəbəl/ *adj.* **1** able to be endured; bearable; supportable; allowable. **2** fairly good; mediocre. □□ **tol·er·a·bil·i·ty** /-bílitee/ *n.* **tol·er·a·ble·ness** *n.* **tol·er·a·bly** *adv.*

tol·er·ance /tólərəns/ *n.* **1** a willingness or ability to tolerate; forbearance. **2** the capacity to tolerate. **3** an allowable variation in any measurable property. **4** the ability to tolerate the effects of a drug, etc., after continued use.

tol·er·ant /tólərənt/ *adj.* **1** disposed or accustomed to tolerate others or their acts or opinions. **2** (foll. by *of*) enduring or patient. **3** exhibiting tolerance of a drug, etc. □□ **tol·er·ant·ly** *adv.*

tol·er·ate /tólərayt/ *v.tr.* **1** allow the existence or occurrence of without authoritative interference. **2** leave unmolested. **3** endure or permit, esp. with forbearance. **4** sustain or endure (suffering, etc.). **5** be capable of continued subjection to (a drug, radiation, etc.) without harm. **6** find or treat as endurable. □□ **tol·er·a·tor** *n.*

tol·er·a·tion /tóləráyshən/ *n.* the process or practice of tolerating, esp. the allowing of differences in religious opinion without discrimination.

toll[1] /tōl/ *n.* **1** a charge payable for permission to pass a barrier or use a bridge or road, etc. **2** the cost or damage caused by a disaster, battle, etc., or incurred in an achievement (*death toll*). **3** a charge for a long distance telephone call. □ **take its toll** be accompanied by loss or injury, etc.

toll[2] /tōl/ *v. & n. • v.* **1 a** *intr.* (of a bell) sound with a slow uniform succession of strokes. **b** *tr.* ring (a bell) in this way. **c** *tr.* (of a bell) announce or mark (a death, etc.) in this way. **2** *tr.* strike (the hour). *• n.* **1** the act of tolling. **2** a stroke of a bell.

toll·booth /tólbooth/ *n.* **1** a booth on a toll road or toll bridge, etc., from which tolls are collected. **2** (also **tol·booth**) *Sc. archaic* a town hall. **3** (also **tol·booth**) *Sc. archaic* a town jail.

toll bridge *n.* a bridge at which a toll is charged.

toll·gate /tólgayt/ *n.* a gate preventing passage until a toll is paid.

toll·house /tólhows/ *n.* a house at a tollgate or toll bridge, used by a toll collector.

toll road *n.* a road maintained by the tolls collected on it.

Tol·tec /tóltek, tól-/ *n.* **1** a member of a Native American people that flourished in Mexico before the Aztecs. **2** the language of this people. □□ **Tol·tec·an** *adj.*

to·lu /təlṓṓ, tṓlṓṓ/ *n.* a fragrant brown balsam obtained from either of two South American trees, *Myroxylon balsamum* or *M. toluifera*, and used in perfumery and medicine.

tol·u·ene /tólyṓṓ-een/ *n.* a colorless aromatic liquid hydrocarbon derivative of benzene, orig. obtained from tolu, used in the manufacture of explosives, etc. Also called **methyl benzene**. □□ **to·lu·ic** *adj.* **tol·u·ol** *n.*

tom /tom/ *n.* a male of various animals, esp. (in full **tomcat**) a male cat.

tom·a·hawk /tóməhawk/ *n. & v. • n.* **1** ▶ a Native American war ax with a stone or iron head. **2** *Austral.* a hatchet. *• v.tr.* strike, cut, or kill with a tomahawk.

TOBACCO:
COMMON TOBACCO (*Nicotiana tabacum*)

T

iron ax-head

shaft

TOMAHAWK:
CEREMONIAL DAKOTA TOMAHAWK

TOMATO

Originally native to South America, the tomato is related to the potato but its fruit is botanically classified as a berry. Many shapes, varieties, and sizes of tomato are available throughout the year. They are eaten either raw or cooked.

placenta
seed
pulp (endocarp)
fleshy wall (mesocarp)

glossy skin (exocarp)
flower stalk (pedicel)
whorl of sepals (calyx)

STANDARD TOMATO

EXAMPLES OF TOMATOES

CHERRY TOMATO

BEEFSTEAK TOMATO

PLUM TOMATO

to·ma·to /təmáytō, -maá-/ n. (pl. **-oes**) **1** ▲ a glossy red or yellow pulpy edible fruit. **2** a solanaceous plant, *Lycopersicon esculentum*, bearing this. □□ **to·ma·to·ey** adj.

tomb /tōōm/ n. **1** ▼ a large, esp. underground, vault for the burial of the dead. **2** an enclosure cut in the earth or in rock to receive a dead body. **3** a sepulchral monument. **4** (prec. by *the*) the state of death.

earth mound
beehive-shaped tomb (tholos)
open-air corridor (dromos)
ossuary
resting place of king's body

TOMB: RECONSTRUCTION OF A MYCENAEAN ROYAL "BEEHIVE" TOMB, *c*.1400 BC

tom·bac /tómbak/ n. an alloy of copper and zinc used esp. as material for cheap jewelry.

tom·boy /tómboy/ n. a girl who behaves in a boisterous boyish way. □□ **tom·boy·ish** adj. **tom·boy·ish·ness** n.

tomb·stone /tōōmstōn/ n. a stone standing or laid over a grave, usu. with an epitaph.

Tom Col·lins /tom kólinz/ n. a tall iced drink of gin with soda, lemon or lime juice, and sugar.

Tom, Dick, and Har·ry /tóm dik ənd háree/ n. (usu. prec. by *any*, *every*) people taken at random.

tome /tōm/ n. a large heavy book or volume.

tom·fool /tómfōōl/ n. **1** a foolish person. **2** (attrib.) silly; foolish (a *tomfool* idea).

tom·fool·er·y /tómfōōləree/ n. (pl. **-ies**) **1** foolish behavior; nonsense. **2** an instance of this.

Tom·my /tómee/ n. (pl. **-ies**) colloq. a British enlisted soldier.

tom·my bar /tómee/ n. a short bar adding leverage when used with a wrench, etc.

tom·my gun /tómee/ n. a type of submachine gun.

tom·my·rot /tómeerot/ n. sl. nonsense.

to·mo·gram /tóməgram/ n. a record obtained by tomography.

to·mog·ra·phy /təmógrəfee/ n. a method of radiography displaying details in a selected plane within the body.

to·mor·row /təmáwrō, -mór-/ adv. & n. ● adv. **1** on the day after today. **2** at some future time. ● n. **1** the day after today. **2** the near future. □ **tomorrow morning** (or **afternoon**, etc.) in the morning (or afternoon, etc.) of tomorrow.

Tom Thumb /tom thúm/ n. **1** a dwarf or midget. **2** a dwarf variety of various plants.

tom·tit /tómtit/ n. any of various tit birds, esp. a blue tit.

tom-tom /tómtom/ n. **1** an early drum beaten with the hands. **2** a tall drum beaten with the hands and used in jazz bands, etc. ▷ DRUM SET

ton /tun/ n. **1** (in full **short ton**) a unit of weight equal to 2,000 lb. (907.19 kg). **2** (in full **long ton**) a unit of weight equal to 2,240 lb. (1,016.05 kg). **3** = METRIC TON. **4 a** (in full **displacement ton**) a unit of measurement of a ship's weight or volume in terms of its displacement of water with the load-line just immersed, equal to 2,240 lb. or 35 cu. ft. (0.99 cubic meters). **b** (in full **freight ton**) a unit of weight or volume of cargo, equal to a metric ton (1,000 kg) or 40 cu. ft. **5 a** (in full **gross ton**) a unit of gross internal capacity, equal to 100 cu. ft. (2.83 cubic meters). **b** (in full **net** or **register ton**) an equivalent unit of net internal capacity. **6** a measure of capacity for various materials, esp. 40 cu. ft. of lumber. **7** (usu. in *pl.*) colloq. a large number or amount (*tons of money*). **8** esp. *Brit. sl.* **a** a speed of 100 m.p.h. **b** a sum of £100. **c** a score of 100. □ **weigh a ton** colloq. be very heavy.

ton·al /tónəl/ adj. **1** of or relating to tone or tonality. **2** (of a fugue, etc.) having repetitions of the subject at different pitches in the same key. □□ **ton·al·ly** adv.

to·nal·i·ty /tōnálitee/ n. (pl. **-ies**) **1** Mus. **a** the relationship between the tones of a musical scale. **b** the observance of a single tonic key as the basis of a composition. **2** the tone or color scheme of a picture.

tone /tōn/ n. & v. ● n. **1** a musical or vocal sound, esp. with reference to its pitch, quality, and strength. **2** (often in *pl.*) modulation of the voice expressing a particular feeling or mood (*a cheerful tone*; *suspicious tones*). **3** a manner of expression in writing. **4** Mus. **a** a musical sound, esp. of a definite pitch and character. **b** an interval of a major second, e.g., C–D. **5 a** the general effect of color or of light and shade in a picture. **b** the tint or shade of a color. **6 a** the prevailing character of the morals and sentiments, etc., in a group. **b** an attitude or sentiment expressed, esp. in a letter, etc. **7** the proper firmness of bodily organs. **8** a state of good or specified health or quality. ● v. **1** tr. give the desired tone to. **2** tr. modify the tone of. **3** intr. (often foll. by *to*) attune. **4** intr. (foll. by *with*) be in harmony (esp. of color) (*does not tone with the wallpaper*). □ **tone down 1** make or become softer in tone of sound or color. **2** make (a statement, etc.) less harsh or emphatic. **tone up 1** make or become stronger in tone of sound or color. **2** make (a statement, etc.) more emphatic. **3** make (muscles) firm by exercise, etc.; make or become fitter. □□ **tone·less** adj. **tone·less·ly** adv. **ton·er** n.

tone arm n. the movable arm supporting the pickup of a record player.

tone-deaf adj. unable to perceive differences of musical pitch accurately. □□ **tone deaf·ness** n.

tone row n. Mus. a series of varying tones that recur in sequence throughout a composition.

tong /tawng, tong/ n. a Chinese guild, association, or secret society.

tongs /tawngz, tongz/ n.pl. (also **pair of tongs** *sing.*) ► an instrument with two hinged or sprung arms for grasping and holding.

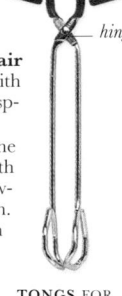

hinge

TONGS FOR KITCHEN USE

tongue /tung/ n. & v. ● n. **1** ▼ the fleshy muscular organ in the mouth used in tasting, licking, and swallowing, and (in humans) for speech. ▷ DIGESTION, HEAD. **2** the tongue of an ox, etc., as food. **3** the faculty of or a tendency in speech (*a sharp tongue*). **4** a particular language (*the German tongue*). **5** a thing like a

TONGUE

The tongue is a fleshy organ rooted within the lower jaw; in humans, it is unique in forming part of the system that produces speech. Its other functions include tasting and then shaping food into a readily swallowed bolus. Most taste buds (taste-receptor cells) are located in papillae on the surface of the tongue; others lie on the palate, throat, and epiglottis. Taste buds respond only to bitter, sour, salty, or sweet flavors, passing signals to the brain, which are enhanced by perceptions such as smell.

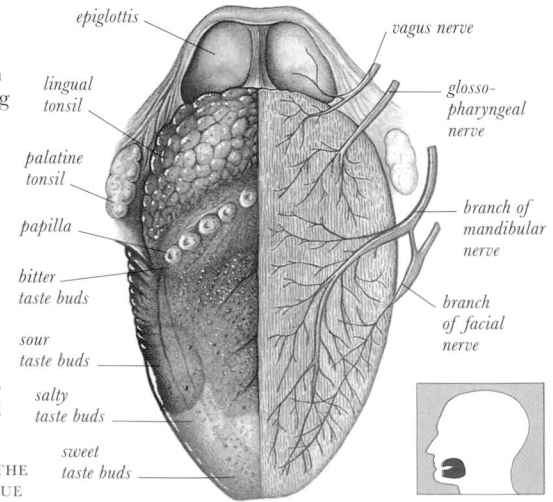

epiglottis
lingual tonsil
palatine tonsil
papilla
bitter taste buds
sour taste buds
salty taste buds
sweet taste buds

vagus nerve
glosso-pharyngeal nerve
branch of mandibular nerve
branch of facial nerve

ANATOMY OF THE HUMAN TONGUE

tongue in shape or position, esp.: **a** a long low promontory. **b** a strip of leather, etc., attached at one end only, under the laces in a shoe. ▷ SHOE. **c** the clapper of a bell. **d** the pin of a buckle. **e** the projecting strip on a wooden, etc., board fitting into the groove of another. **f** a vibrating slip in the reed of some musical instruments. **g** a jet of flame. ● *v.* (**tongues, tongued, tonguing**) **1** *tr.* produce staccato, etc., effects with (a flute, etc.) by means of tonguing. **2** *intr.* use the tongue in this way. □ **find** (or **lose**) **one's tongue** be able (or unable) to express oneself after a shock, etc. **the gift of tongues** the power of speaking in unknown languages, regarded in some Christian denominations as one of the gifts of the Holy Spirit (Acts 2). **keep a civil tongue in one's head** avoid rudeness. **with one's tongue hanging out** eagerly or expectantly. □□ **tongued** *adj.* (also in *comb.*). **tongue·less** *adj.*

tongue-and-groove *adj.* applied to boards in which a tongue along one edge fits into a groove along the edge of the next, each board having a tongue on one edge and a groove on the other.

tongue de·pres·sor *n.* a doctor's implement for holding the tongue in place while examining the throat or mouth.

tongue-in-cheek *adj. & adv.* ● *adj.* ironic; slyly humorous. ● *adv.* insincerely or ironically.

tongue-lash·ing *n.* a severe scolding or reprimand.

tongue-tied *adj.* too shy or embarrassed to speak.

tongue twist·er *n.* a sequence of words difficult to pronounce quickly and correctly.

tongu·ing /túnging/ *n. Mus.* the technique of playing a wind instrument using the tongue to articulate certain notes.

ton·ic /tónik/ *n. & adj.* ● *n.* **1** an invigorating medicine. **2** anything serving to invigorate. **3** = TONIC WATER. **4** *Mus.* the first degree of a scale, forming the keynote of a piece (see KEYNOTE 3). ● *adj.* **1** serving as a tonic; invigorating. **2** *Mus.* denoting the first degree of a scale. □□ **ton·i·cal·ly** *adv.*

to·nic·i·ty /tōnísitee/ *n.* **1** the state of being tonic. **2** a healthy elasticity of muscles, etc.

ton·ic sol-fa *n. Mus.* a system of notation used esp. in teaching singing, with do as the keynote of all major keys and la as the keynote of all minor keys.

ton·ic wa·ter *n.* a carbonated mineral water containing quinine.

to·night /tənít/ *adv. & n.* ● *adv.* on the present or approaching evening or night. ● *n.* the evening or night of the present day.

ton·ka bean /tóngkə/ *n.* the black fragrant seed of a South American tree, *Dipteryx odorata*, used in perfumery, etc.

ton·nage /túnij/ *n.* **1** a ship's internal cubic capacity or freight-carrying capacity, measured in tons. **2** the total carrying capacity, esp. of a country's merchant marine. **3** a charge per ton on freight or cargo.

tonne /tun/ *n.* = METRIC TON.

to·nom·e·ter /tōnómitər/ *n.* **1** a tuning fork or other instrument for measuring the pitch of tones. **2** an instrument for measuring the pressure of fluid.

ton·sil /tónsəl/ *n.* either of two small masses of lymphoid tissue on each side of the root of the tongue. ▷ TONGUE. □□ **ton·sil·lar** *adj.*

ton·sil·lec·to·my /tónsiléktəmee/ *n.* (*pl.* **-ies**) the surgical removal of the tonsils.

ton·sil·li·tis /tónsilítis/ *n.* inflammation of the tonsils.

ton·so·ri·al /tonsáwreeəl/ *adj.* usu. *joc.* of or relating to a hairdresser or barber or hairdressing.

ton·sure /tónshər/ *n. & v.* ● *n.* **1** the shaving of the crown of the head or the entire head, esp. of a person entering a priesthood or monastic order. **2** a bare patch made in this way. ● *v.tr.* give a tonsure to.

ton·tine /tontéen/ *n.* an annuity shared by subscribers to a loan, the shares increasing as subscribers die until the last survivor gets all, or until a specified date when the remaining survivors share the proceeds.

ton·y /tónee/ *adj.* (**tonier, toniest**) *colloq.* stylish; fashionable; trendy.

too /too/ *adv.* **1** to a greater extent than is desirable, permissible, or possible for a specified or understood purpose (*too colorful for my taste; too large to fit*). **2** *colloq.* extremely (*you're too kind*). **3** in addition (*are they coming too?*). **4** moreover (*we must consider, too, the time of year*). □ **none too 1** somewhat less than (*feeling none too good*). **2** barely. **too bad** see BAD. **too much, too much for** see MUCH.

took *past of* TAKE.

tool /tool/ *n. & v.* ● *n.* **1** any device or implement used to carry out mechanical functions whether manually or by a machine. **2** a thing used in an occupation or pursuit (*the tools of one's trade; literary tools*). **3** a person used as a mere instrument by another. **4** *coarse sl.* the penis. ¶ Usually considered a taboo use. ● *v.tr.* **1** dress (stone) with a chisel. **2** impress a design on (a leather book cover). **3** (foll. by *along, around*, etc.) *sl.* drive or ride, esp. in a casual or leisurely manner. **4** (often foll. by *up*) equip with tools. □ **tool up 1** *sl.* arm oneself. **2** equip oneself. □□ **tool·er** *n.*

tool·bar /toolbar/ *n. Computing.* a strip of icons used to select from a set of software applications.

tool·ing /tooling/ *n.* **1** dressing stone with a chisel. **2** ◄ the ornamentation of a book cover with designs impressed by heated tools.

tool·mak·er /toolmaykər/ *n.* a person who makes precision tools, esp. tools used in a press. □□ **tool·mak·ing** *n.*

toot /toot/ *n. & v.* ● *n.* **1** a short sharp sound as made by a horn, trumpet, or whistle. **2** *sl.* cocaine or a snort of cocaine. **3** *sl.* a drinking session; a binge. ● *v.* **1** *tr.* sound (a horn, etc.) with a short sharp sound. **2** *intr.* give out such a sound. □□ **toot·er** *n.*

tooth /tooth/ *n. & v.* ● *n.* (*pl.* **teeth** /teeth/) **1** ▼ each of a set of hard bony enamel-coated structures in the jaws of most vertebrates, used for biting and chewing. **2** a toothlike part or projection, especially one of a series that function or engage together, e.g., the cog of a gearwheel, the point of a saw or comb, etc. **3** (often foll. by *for*) one's sense of taste; an appetite or liking. **4** (in *pl.*) force or effectiveness. □ **armed to the teeth** armed formidably. **fight tooth and nail** fight very fiercely. **get** (or **sink**) **one's teeth into** devote oneself seriously to. **in the teeth of 1** in spite of (opposition or difficulty, etc.). **2** directly against (the wind, etc.). **set a person's teeth on edge** see EDGE. □□ **toothed** *adj.* (also in *comb.*). **tooth·less** *adj.* **tooth·like** *adj.*

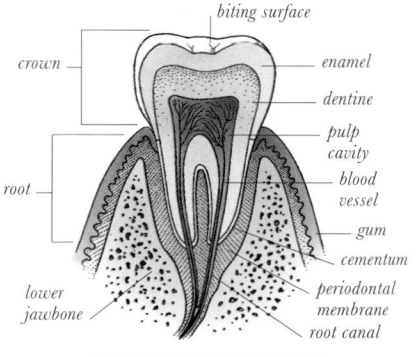

TOOTH: CROSS SECTION OF A HUMAN MOLAR

biting surface
crown
enamel
dentine
pulp cavity
blood vessel
gum
cementum
periodontal membrane
root canal
root
lower jawbone

tooth·ache /toothayk/ *n.* a (usu. prolonged) pain in a tooth or teeth.

tooth·brush /toothbrush/ *n.* a brush for cleaning the teeth.

toothed whale *n.*
▶ any whale of the suborder Odontoceti, having teeth rather than baleen (whale bone) plates. ▷ WHALE

tooth fair·y *n.* a fairy said to take children's baby teeth after they fall out and leave a coin under their pillow.

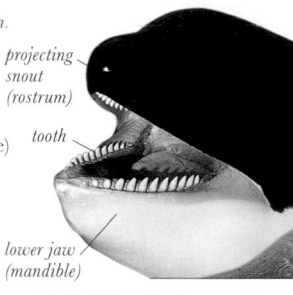

projecting snout (rostrum)
tooth
lower jaw (mandible)

TOOTHED WHALE: KILLER WHALE (*Orcinus orca*)

tooth·paste /toothpayst/ *n.* a paste for cleaning the teeth.

tooth·pick /toothpik/ *n.* a small sharp instrument for removing small pieces of food lodged between the teeth.

tooth·some /toothsəm/ *adj.* **1** (of food) delicious; appetizing. **2** attractive, esp. sexually.

tooth·wort /toothwərt, wawrt/ *n.* a parasitic plant, *Lathraea squamaria*, with toothlike root scales.

tooth·y /toothee/ *adj.* (**toothier, toothiest**) having or showing large, numerous, or prominent teeth (*a toothy grin*). □□ **tooth·i·ly** *adv.*

too·tle /toot'l/ *v.intr.* **1** toot gently or repeatedly. **2** (usu. foll. by *along, around*, etc.) *colloq.* move casually or aimlessly. □□ **too·tler** *n.*

toot·sy /tootsee/ *n.* (also **toot·sie**) (*pl.* **-ies**) *sl.* usu. *joc.* a foot.

top[1] /top/ *n., adj., & v.* ● *n.* **1** the highest point or part (*the top of the house*). **2 a** the highest rank or place (*at the top of the school*). **b** a person occupying this (*was top in spelling*). **c** esp. *Brit.* the upper end or head (*the top of the table*). **3** the upper surface of a thing, esp. of the ground, a table, etc. **4** the upper part of a thing, esp.: **a** a blouse, sweater, etc., for wearing with a skirt or pants. **b** the upper part of a shoe or boot. **c** the stopper of a bottle. **d** the lid of a jar, saucepan, etc. **e** the creamy part of unhomogenized milk. **f** the folding roof of a car, carriage, etc. **g** the upper edge or edges of a page or pages in a book (*gilt top*). **5** the utmost degree; height (*called at the top of his voice*). **6** (in *pl.*) *colloq.* a person or thing of the best quality (*he's tops at swimming*). **7** (esp. in *pl.*) the leaves, etc., of a plant grown esp. for its root (*turnip tops*). **8** (usu. in *pl.*) a bundle of long wool fibers prepared for spinning. **9** *Naut.* a platform around the head of the lower mast. **10** *Baseball* the first half of an inning. **11** = TOPSPIN. ● *adj.* **1** highest in position (*the top shelf*). **2** highest in degree or importance (*at top speed; the top job*). ● *v.tr.* (**topped, topping**) **1** provide with a top, cap, etc. (*cake topped with icing*). **2** remove the top of (a plant, fruit, etc.), esp. to improve growth, prepare for cooking, etc. **3** be higher or better than; surpass; be at the top of (*topped the list*). **4** *Brit. sl.* **a** execute, esp. by hanging; kill. **b** (*refl.*) commit suicide. **5** reach the top of (a hill, etc.). **6 a** hit (a ball) above the center. **b** make (a hit or stroke) in this way. □ **from top to toe** from head to foot; completely. **off the top of one's head** see HEAD. **on top 1** in a superior position; above. **2** on the upper part of the head (*bald on top*). **on top of 1** fully in command of. **2** in close proximity to. **3** in addition to. **4** above; over. **on top of the world** *colloq.* exuberant. **over the top 1** over the parapet of a trench (and into battle). **2** into a final or decisive state. **3** to excess; beyond reasonable limits (*that joke was over the top*). **top off 1** put an end or the finishing touch to (a thing). **2** fill up, esp. a container already partly full. **top out** put the highest stone on (a building). **top one's part** esp. *Theatr.* act or discharge one's part to perfection. **top up 1 a** esp. *Brit.* complete (an amount or number). **b** fill up (a glass, fuel tank, or other partly full container). **2** top up something for (a person) (*may I top you up with coffee?*). □□ **top·most** *adj.*

T

top² /top/ *n.* a wooden or metal toy, usu. conical, spherical, or pear-shaped, spinning on a point when set in motion by hand, string, etc.

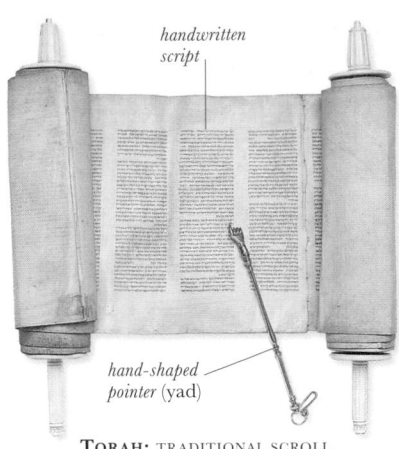

handwritten script

hand-shaped pointer (yad)

TORAH: TRADITIONAL SCROLL CONTAINING THE JEWISH TORAH

top·less /tóplis/ *adj.* **1** without or seeming to be without a top. **2 a** (of clothes) having no upper part. **b** (of a person) wearing such clothes; bare-breasted. **c** (of a place, esp. a beach, bar, etc.) where women go topless. □□ **top·less·ness** *n.*

top-lev·el *adj.* of the highest level of importance or prestige (top-level talks).

top·loft·y /tóplàwftee, -lóf-/ *adj. colloq.* haughty.

top·mast /tópmast/ *n. Naut.* the mast next above the lower mast. ▷ RIGGING, SCHOONER

top-notch *adj. colloq.* first rate.

to·pog·ra·phy /təpógrəfee/ *n.* **1 a** a detailed description, representation on a map, etc., of the natural and artificial features of a town, district, etc. ▷ MAP. **b** such features. **2** *Anat.* the mapping of the surface of the body with reference to the parts beneath. □□ **to·pog·ra·pher** *n.* **top·o·graph·ic** /tópəgráfik/ *adj.* **top·o·graph·i·cal** *adj.* **top·o·graph·i·cal·ly** *adv.*

top·oi *pl.* of TOPOS.

to·pol·o·gy /təpóləjee/ *n. Math.* the study of geometrical properties and spatial relations unaffected by the continuous change of shape or size of figures. □□ **top·o·log·i·cal** /tópəlójikəl/ *adj.* **top·o·log·i·cal·ly** *adv.* **to·pol·o·gist** *n.*

to·paz /tópaz/ *n.* ◀ a transparent or translucent aluminum silicate mineral, usu. yellow, used as a gem.

top brass *n.* esp. *Mil. colloq.* the highest ranking officers, heads of industries, etc.

top·coat /tópkōt/ *n.* **1** an overcoat. **2** an outer coat of paint, etc. ▷ UNDERCOAT

top dog *n. colloq.* a victor or master.

top draw·er *n.* **1** the uppermost drawer in a chest, etc. **2** *colloq.* high social position or origin. □□ **top-drawer** *adj.*

tope¹ /tōp/ *v.intr.* drink alcohol to excess, esp. habitually. □□ **top·er** *n.*

tope² /tōp/ *n.* ▼ a small shark, *Galeorhinus galeus.*

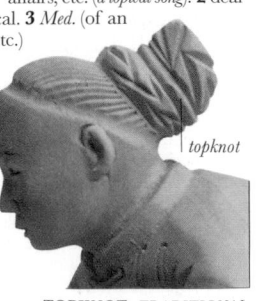

topaz crystal

pegmatite groundmass

TOPAZ

TOPE (*Galeorhinus galeus*)

to·pee /tópee/ *n.* (also **to·pi**) (pl. **topees** or **topis**) *Anglo-Ind.* a lightweight hat or helmet, often made of pith.

top·gal·lant /topgálənt, təgálənt/ *n. Naut.* the mast, sail, yard, or rigging immediately above the topmast and topsail. ▷ BATTLESHIP, RIGGING

top hat *n.* a man's tall silk hat. ▷ HAT

top-heav·y /tóphévee/ *adj.* **1** disproportionately heavy at the top so as to be in danger of toppling. **2 a** (of an organization, business, etc.) having a disproportionately large number of people in senior administrative positions. **b** overcapitalized. **3** *colloq.* (of a woman) having a disproportionately large bust. □□ **top-heav·i·ly** *adv.* **top-heav·i·ness** *n.*

to·pi var. of TOPEE.

to·pi·ar·y /tópee-eree/ *adj. & n.* ● *adj.* concerned with or formed by clipping shrubs, trees, etc., into ornamental shapes. ● *n.* (*pl.* **-ies**) **1** topiary art. **2** ◀ an example of this. □□ **to·pi·ar·i·an** /-pee-áireeən/ *adj.* **to·pi·a·rist** *n.*

top·ic /tópik/ *n.* **1** a theme for a book, discourse, essay, sermon, etc. **2** the subject of a conversation or argument.

TOPIARY: CLIPPED BOX TREE

T

top·i·cal /tópikəl/ *adj.* **1** dealing with the news, current affairs, etc. (*a topical song*). **2** dealing with a place; local. **3** *Med.* (of an ailment, medicine, etc.) affecting a part of the body. **4** of or concerning topics. □□ **top·i·cal·i·ty** /-kálitee/ *n.* **top·i·cal·ly** *adv.*

top·knot /tópnot/ *n.* ▶ a knot, tuft, crest, or bow worn on the head or growing on the head.

topknot

TOPKNOT: TRADITIONAL CHINESE TOPKNOT

to·pon·ym /tópənim/ *n.* **1** a place-name. **2** a descriptive place-name, usu. derived from a topographical feature of the place.

to·pon·y·my /təpónimee/ *n.* the study of the place-names of a region. □□ **top·o·nym·ic** /tópənímik/ *adj.*

to·pos /tópōs, -pos/ *n.* (*pl.* **topoi** /-poy/) a stock theme in literature, etc.

top·per /tópər/ *n.* **1** a thing that tops. **2** *colloq.* = TOP HAT. **3** *Brit. colloq.* a good fellow; a good sort.

top·ping /tóping/ *adj. & n.* ● *adj.* **1** preeminent in position, rank, etc. **2** *Brit. archaic sl.* excellent. ● *n.* anything that tops something else, esp. icing, etc., on a cake.

top·ple /tópəl/ *v.intr. & tr.* (usu. foll. by *over, down*) **1 a** fall or cause to fall as if top-heavy. **b** fall or cause to fall from power. **2** totter or cause to totter and fall.

top·sail /tópsayl, -səl/ *n.* a square sail next above the lowest fore-and-aft sail on a gaff. ▷ MAN-OF-WAR, SCHOONER

top se·cret *adj.* of the highest secrecy.

top·side /tópsīd/ *n.* **1** the side of a ship above the waterline. **2** *Brit.* the outer side of a round of beef.

top·soil /tópsoyl/ *n.* the top layer of soil. ▷ SOIL

top·spin /tópspin/ *n.* a fast forward spinning motion imparted to a ball in tennis, etc., by hitting it forward and upward.

top·sy-tur·vy /tópseetórvee/ *adv., adj., & n.* ● *adv. & adj.* **1** upside down. **2** in utter confusion. ● *n.* utter confusion. □□ **top·sy-tur·vi·ly** *adv.* **top·sy-tur·vi·ness** *n.*

top ten *n.* (or **twenty**, etc.) the first ten (or twenty, etc.) records, movies, etc., at a given time in terms of sales, popularity, etc.

toque /tōk/ *n.* **1** a woman's small brimless hat. **2** *hist.* a small cap or bonnet for a man or woman.

to·quil·la /təkéeyə/ *n.* **1** a palmlike tree, *Carludovica palmata*, native to S. America. **2** a fiber produced from the leaves of this.

tor /tor/ *n.* ▼ a hill or rocky peak.

TOR: GRANITE TOR, DARTMOOR, ENGLAND

To·rah /tốrə, táwrə, tōráà/ *n.* **1** (usu. prec. by *the*) **a** the first five books of the Hebrew scriptures (the Pentateuch). **b** ▲ a scroll containing this. **2** the will of God as revealed in Mosaic law.

torc var. of TORQUE 1.

torch /tawrch/ *n. & v.* ● *n.* **1 a** a piece of wood, cloth, etc., soaked in tallow and lighted for illumination. **b** any similar lamp, e.g., an oil lamp on a pole. **2** a source of heat, illumination, or enlightenment (*bore aloft the torch of freedom*). **3** = BLOWTORCH. **4** *sl.* an arsonist. **5** (also **electric torch**) *Brit.* = FLASHLIGHT 1. ● *v.tr. sl.* set alight with or as with a torch. □ **carry a torch for** suffer from unrequited love for. **put to the torch** destroy by burning.

tor·chère /tawrsháir/ *n.* **1** a tall stand with a small

TORNADO

A tornado occurs when moist air rises, heated over warm land or sea. The air cools at high altitudes and condenses into water droplets, forming a thundercloud. The suction of the rising air draws up a spiral of air from below, and strong winds begin to blow. A tornado formed beneath a thundercloud may produce winds of 250 m.p.h. (400 k.p.h.) or more, and the low air pressure at its center can cause buildings to explode. A waterspout occurs when a tornado passes over water. Dust devils are small whirlwinds that carry desert sand and dirt.

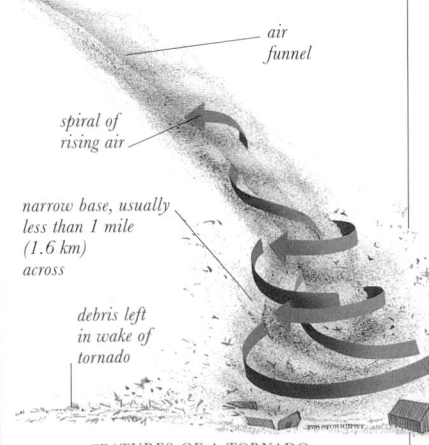

air funnel

spiral of rising air

narrow base, usually less than 1 mile (1.6 km) across

debris left in wake of tornado

FEATURES OF A TORNADO

table for a candlestick, etc. **2** a tall floor lamp giving indirect light.

torch·light /táwrchlīt/ n. the light of a torch or torches.

torch song n. a popular song of unrequited love. □□ **torch sing·er** n.

tore[1] past of TEAR[1].

tore[2] /tawr/ n. = TORUS 1, 4.

tor·e·a·dor /táwreeədawr/ n. a bullfighter, esp. on horseback.

to·ri pl. of TORUS.

tor·ment n. & v. ● n. /táwrment/ **1** severe physical or mental suffering. **2** a cause of this. ● v.tr. /tawrmént/ **1** subject to torment (*tormented with worry*). **2** tease or worry excessively (*enjoyed tormenting the teacher*). □□ **tor·ment·ed·ly** adv. **tor·ment·ing·ly** adv. **tor·men·tor** n.

torn past part. of TEAR[1].

tor·na·do /tawrnáydō/ n. (pl. **-oes**) ◀ a violent storm of small extent with whirling winds, esp. over a narrow path, often accompanied by a funnel-shaped cloud. □□ **tor·na·dic** /-nádik/ adj.

to·roi·dal /tawróyd'l/ adj. Geom. of or resembling a torus. □□ **to·roi·dal·ly** adv.

tor·pe·do /tawrpéedō/ n. & v. ● n. (pl. **-oes**) **1** a cigar-shaped self-propelled underwater missile that explodes on impact with a ship. **2** a similar device dropped from an aircraft. ▷ WARHEAD. ● v.tr. (**-oes**, **-oed**) **1** destroy or attack with a torpedo. **2** make (a policy, institution, plan, etc.) ineffective or inoperative; destroy. □□ **tor·pe·do·like** adj.

tor·pid /táwrpid/ adj. **1** sluggish; inactive; dull; apathetic. **2** numb. **3** (of a hibernating animal) dormant. □□ **tor·pid·i·ty** /-píditee/ n. **tor·pid·ly** adv. **tor·pid·ness** n.

tor·por /táwrpər/ n. torpidity. □□ **tor·por·if·ic** /-pərífik/ adj.

torque /tawrk/ n. **1** (also **torc**) hist. ◀ a necklace of twisted metal, esp. of the ancient Gauls and Britons. **2** Mech. ▼ the moment of a system of forces tending to cause rotation.

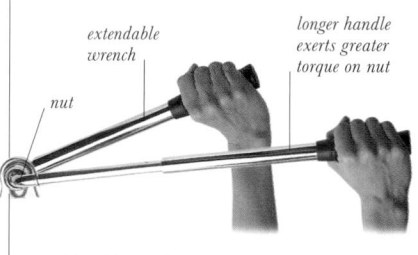

twisted bronze

TORQUE: ANCIENT CELTIC TORQUE

torque con·vert·er n. a device to transmit the correct torque from the engine to the axle in a motor vehicle. ▷ GEARBOX

tor·re·fy /táwrifī, tór-/ v.tr. (**-ies**, **-ied**) **1** roast or dry (metallic ore, a drug, etc.). **2** parch or scorch with heat. □□ **tor·re·fac·tion** /-fákshən/ n.

tor·rent /táwrənt, tór-/ n. **1** a rushing stream of water, lava, etc. **2** (usu. in pl.) a great downpour of rain (*came down in torrents*). **3** (usu. foll. by of) a violent or copious flow (*uttered a torrent of abuse*). □□ **tor·ren·tial** /tərénshəl/ adj. **tor·ren·tial·ly** /-tər-én-shəlee/ adv.

tor·rid /táwrid, tór-/ adj. **1 a** (of the weather) very hot and dry. **b** (of land, etc.) parched by such weather. **2** (of language or actions) emotionally charged; passionate; intense. □□ **tor·rid·i·ty** /-ríditee/ n. **tor·rid·ly** adv. **tor·rid·ness** n.

tor·rid zone n. the central belt of the Earth between the Tropics of Cancer and Capricorn.

tor·sion /táwrshən/ n. **1** twisting, esp. of one end of a body while the other is held fixed. **2** Math. the extent to which a curve departs from being planar. □□ **tor·sion·al** adj. **tor·sion·al·ly** adv.

tor·sion bar n. a bar forming part of a vehicle suspension, twisting in response to the motion of the wheels, and absorbing their vertical movement.

tor·so /táwrsō/ n. (pl. **-os** or **-i**) **1** the trunk of the human body. **2** a statue of a human consisting of the trunk alone, without head or limbs.

tort /tawrt/ n. Law a breach of duty (other than under contract) leading to liability for damages.

torte /tawrt/ n. (pl. **torten** /táwrt'n/ or **tortes**) an elaborate sweet cake.

tor·tel·li·ni /tawrtəléenee/ n. small stuffed pasta parcels rolled and formed into small rings. ▷ PASTA

tort·fea·sor /táwrtfeezər/ n. Law a person guilty of tort.

tor·ti·col·lis /tawrtikólis/ n. Med. a rheumatic, etc., disease of the muscles of the neck, causing twisting and painful spasms.

tor·til·la /tawrtéeyə/ n. ▼ a thin flat orig. Mexican corn or wheat bread eaten hot or cold with or without a filling.

WHEAT TORTILLAS

CORN TORTILLAS

TORTILLAS

tor·tious /táwrshəs/ adj. Law constituting a tort; wrongful. □□ **tor·tious·ly** adv.

tor·toise /táwrtəs/ n. **1** ▼ any slow-moving esp. land reptile of the family Testudinidae, encased in a scaly or leathery domed shell, and having a retractile head and elephantine legs. ▷ CHELONIAN. **2** Rom. Antiq. = TESTUDO. □□ **tor·toise·like** adj. & adv.

domed shell (carapace)

TORTOISE: HERMANN'S TORTOISE (*Testudo hermanni*)

clawed foot

horny plate (scute)

retractile head

scaly skin

tor·toise·shell /táwrtəs-shel/ n. & adj. ● n. **1** ▼ the yellowish brown mottled or clouded outer shell of some turtles, used for decorative combs, jewelry, brushes etc. **2 a** = TORTOISESHELL BUTTERFLY. **b** = TORTOISESHELL CAT. ● adj. having the coloring or appearance of tortoiseshell.

TORTOISESHELL: EARLY 20TH-CENTURY TORTOISESHELL BOX

LARGE TORTOISESHELL (*Nymphalis polychloros*)

SMALL TORTOISESHELL (*Aglais urticae*)

TORTOISESHELL BUTTERFLIES

tor·toise·shell but·ter·fly n. ▲ any of various butterflies of the genus *Aglais* or *Nymphalis* with wings mottled like tortoiseshell

tor·toise·shell cat n. a domestic cat with markings resembling tortoiseshell. ▷ CAT

tor·tu·ous /táwrchōōəs/ adj. **1** full of twists and turns (*followed a tortuous route*). **2** devious; circuitous; crooked (*has a tortuous mind*). □□ **tor·tu·os·i·ty** /-ósitee/ n. (pl. **-ies**) **tor·tu·ous·ly** adv. **tor·tu·ous·ness** n.

tor·ture /táwrchər/ n. & v. ● n. **1** the infliction of severe bodily pain, esp. as a punishment or a means of persuasion. **2** severe physical or mental suffering (*the torture of defeat*). ● v.tr. **1** subject to torture (*tortured by guilt*). **2** force out of a natural position or state; deform; pervert. □□ **tor·tur·a·ble** adj. **tor·tur·er** n. **tor·tur·ous** adj. **tor·tur·ous·ly** adv.

to·rus /táwrəs/ n. (pl. **tori** /-rī/) **1** Archit. a large convex molding, esp. as the lowest part of the base of a column. **2** Bot. the receptacle of a flower. **3** Anat. a smooth ridge of bone or muscle. **4** Geom. ▶ a surface or solid formed by rotating a closed curve, esp. a circle, about a line in its plane but not intersecting it.

axis

closed curve (circle)

TORUS

To·ry /táwree/ n. & adj. ● n. (pl. **-ies**) **1** esp. Brit. colloq. = CONSERVATIVE n. 2. **2** Brit. hist. a member of the party that opposed the exclusion of James II and later supported the established religious and political order and gave rise to the Conservative party (opp. WHIG). **3** a colonist loyal to the English during the American Revolution. ● adj. colloq. = CONSERVATIVE adj. 3. □□ **To·ry·ism** n.

tosh /tosh/ n. esp. Brit. colloq. rubbish; nonsense.

toss /taws, tos/ v. & n. ● v. **1** tr. throw up (a ball, etc.) esp. with the hand. **2** tr. & intr. roll about, throw, or be thrown, restlessly or from side to side (*the ship tossed on the ocean; was tossing and turning all night; tossed her head angrily*). **3** tr. (usu. foll. by to, away, aside, out, etc.) throw (a thing) lightly or carelessly (*tossed the letter away*). **4** tr. **a** throw (a coin) into the air to decide a choice, etc., by the side on which it lands. **b** (also absol.; often foll. by for) settle a question or dispute with (a person) in this way (*tossed him for the armchair; tossed for it*). **5** tr. **a** (of a bull, etc.) throw (a person, etc.) up with the horns. **b** (of a horse, etc.) throw (a rider) off its back. **6** tr. coat (food) with dressing, etc., by mixing or shaking. **7** tr. bandy about in debate; discuss (*tossed the question back and forth*). ● n. **1** the act or an instance of tossing (a coin, the head, etc.). **2** a fall, esp. from a horse. □ **toss up** toss a coin to decide a choice, etc. □□ **toss·er** n.

toss-up n. **1** a doubtful matter; a close thing (*it's a toss-up whether he wins*). **2** the tossing of a coin.

T

tos·ta·da /tōstáːdə/ *n.* a crisp fried tortilla, often topped with meat, cheese, etc.

tot /tot/ *n.* **1** a small child (*a tiny tot*). **2** esp. *Brit.* a dram of liquor.

to·tal /tṓt'l/ *adj., n., & v.* ● *adj.* **1** complete; comprising the whole (*the total number of people*). **2** absolute; unqualified (*in total ignorance; total abstinence*). ● *n.* a total number or amount. ● *v.* (**totaled, totaling** or **totalled, totalling**) **1** *tr.* **a** amount in number to (*they totaled 131*). **b** find the total of (things, a set of numbers, etc.). **2** *intr.* (foll. by *to, up to*) amount to; mount up to. **3** *tr. sl.* wreck completely; demolish. □□ **to·tal·ly** *adv.*

to·tal e·clipse *n.* an eclipse in which the whole disk (of the sun, moon, etc.) is obscured. ▷ ECLIPSE

to·tal·i·tar·i·an /tōtálitáireeən/ *adj. & n.* ● *adj.* of or relating to a centralized dictatorial form of government requiring complete subservience to the state. ● *n.* a person advocating such a system. □□ **to·tal·i·tar·i·an·ism** *n.*

to·tal·i·ty /tōtálitee/ *n.* **1** the complete amount or sum. **2** *Astron.* the time during which an eclipse is total.

to·tal·i·za·tor /tṓt'lizaytər/ *n.* (also **to·tal·i·sa·tor**) = PARI-MUTUEL 2.

to·tal·ize /tṓt'līz/ *v.tr.* collect into a total; find the total of. □□ **to·tal·i·za·tion** /-izáyshən/ *n.*

to·tal·iz·er /tṓt'līzər/ *n.* = TOTALIZATOR.

to·tal re·call *n.* the ability to remember every detail of one's experience clearly.

to·tal war *n.* a war in which all available weapons and resources are employed.

tote[1] /tōt/ *n. sl.* **1** a totalizator. **2** a lottery.

tote[2] /tōt/ *v.tr. colloq.* carry or convey, esp. a heavy load (*toting a gun*). □□ **tot·er** *n.* (also in *comb.*).

tote bag *n.* a large open-topped bag for shopping, etc.

to·tem /tṓtəm/ *n.* **1** a natural object or animal, adopted by Native American people as an emblem of a clan or an individual. **2** an image of this. □□ **to·tem·ic** /-témik/ *adj.* **to·tem·ism** *n.* **to·tem·ist** *n.* **to·tem·is·tic** /-təmístik/ *adj.*

to·tem pole *n.* **1** ◄ a pole on which totems are carved or hung. **2** a hierarchy.

toth·er /túthər/ *adj. & pron.* (also **t'other**) *dial.* or *joc.* the other.

tot·ter /tótər/ *v. & n.* ● *v.intr.* **1** stand or walk unsteadily or feebly (*tottered out of the bar*). **2 a** (of a building, etc.) shake or rock as if about to collapse. **b** (of a system of government, etc.) be about to fall. ● *n.* an unsteady or shaky movement or gait. □□ **tot·ter·er** *n.* **tot·ter·y** *adj.*

tou·can /tṓokan/ *n.* ► any tropical American fruit-eating bird of the family Ramphastidae, with an immense beak and brightly colored plumage.

touch /tuch/ *v. & n.* ● *v.* **1** *tr.* come into or be in physical contact with (another thing). **2** *tr.* (often foll. by *with*) bring the hand, etc., into contact with. **3 a** *intr.* (of two things,

TOTEM POLE:
TRADITIONAL NORTH AMERICAN HAIDA TOTEM POLE

owl

raptor's head

body and legs of a bird

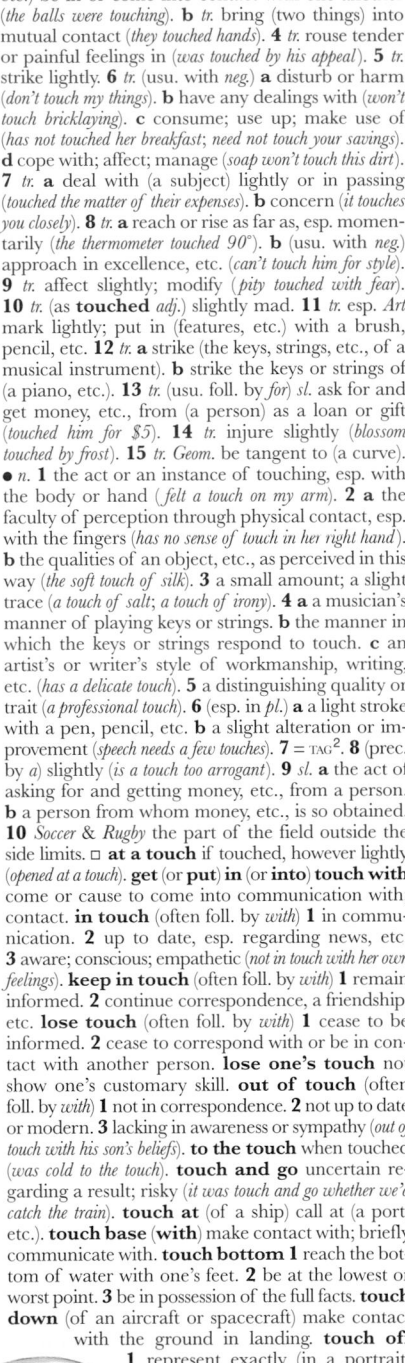

TOUCAN:
CUVIER'S TOUCAN
(*Ramphastos tucanus*)

etc.) be in or come into contact with one another (*the balls were touching*). **b** *tr.* bring (two things) into mutual contact (*they touched hands*). **4** *tr.* rouse tender or painful feelings in (*was touched by his appeal*). **5** *tr.* strike lightly. **6** *tr.* (usu. with *neg.*) **a** disturb or harm (*don't touch my things*). **b** have any dealings with (*won't touch bricklaying*). **c** consume; use up; make use of (*has not touched her breakfast; need not touch your savings*). **d** cope with; affect; manage (*soap won't touch this dirt*). **7** *tr.* **a** deal with (a subject) lightly or in passing (*touched the matter of their expenses*). **b** concern (*it touches you closely*). **8** *tr.* **a** reach or rise as far as, esp. momentarily (*the thermometer touched 90°*). **b** (usu. with *neg.*) approach in excellence, etc. (*can't touch him for style*). **9** *tr.* affect slightly; modify (*pity touched with fear*). **10** *tr.* (as **touched** *adj.*) slightly mad. **11** *tr.* esp. *Art* mark lightly; put in (features, etc.) with a brush, pencil, etc. **12** *tr.* **a** strike (the keys, strings, etc., of a musical instrument). **b** strike the keys or strings of (a piano, etc.). **13** *tr.* (usu. foll. by *for*) *sl.* ask for and get money, etc., from (a person) as a loan or gift (*touched him for $5*). **14** *tr.* injure slightly (*blossom touched by frost*). **15** *tr. Geom.* be tangent to (a curve). ● *n.* **1** the act or an instance of touching, esp. with the body or hand (*felt a touch on my arm*). **2 a** the faculty of perception through physical contact, esp. with the fingers (*has no sense of touch in her right hand*). **b** the qualities of an object, etc., as perceived in this way (*the soft touch of silk*). **3** a small amount; a slight trace (*a touch of salt; a touch of irony*). **4 a** a musician's manner of playing keys or strings. **b** the manner in which the keys or strings respond to touch. **c** an artist's or writer's style of workmanship, writing, etc. (*has a delicate touch*). **5** a distinguishing quality or trait (*a professional touch*). **6** (esp. in *pl.*) **a** a light stroke with a pen, pencil, etc. **b** a slight alteration or improvement (*speech needs a few touches*). **7** = TAG[2]. **8** (prec. by *a*) slightly (*is a touch too arrogant*). **9** *sl.* **a** the act of asking for and getting money, etc., from a person. **b** a person from whom money, etc., is so obtained. **10** *Soccer & Rugby* the part of the field outside the side limits. □ **at a touch** if touched, however lightly (*opened at a touch*). **get** (or **put**) **in** (or **into**) **touch with** come or cause to come into communication with; contact. **in touch** (often foll. by *with*) **1** in communication. **2** up to date, esp. regarding news, etc. **3** aware; conscious; empathetic (*not in touch with her own feelings*). **keep in touch** (often foll. by *with*) **1** remain informed. **2** continue correspondence, a friendship, etc. **lose touch** (often foll. by *with*) **1** cease to be informed. **2** cease to correspond with or be in contact with another person. **lose one's touch** not show one's customary skill. **out of touch** (often foll. by *with*) **1** not in correspondence. **2** not up to date or modern. **3** lacking in awareness or sympathy (*out of touch with his son's beliefs*). **to the touch** when touched (*was cold to the touch*). **touch and go** uncertain regarding a result; risky (*it was touch and go whether we'd catch the train*). **touch at** (of a ship) call at (a port, etc.). **touch base (with)** make contact with; briefly communicate with. **touch bottom 1** reach the bottom of water with one's feet. **2** be at the lowest or worst point. **3** be in possession of the full facts. **touch down** (of an aircraft or spacecraft) make contact with the ground in landing. **touch off 1** represent exactly (in a portrait, etc.). **2** explode by touching with a match, etc. **3** initiate (a process) suddenly (*touched off a run on the peso*). **touch on** (or **upon**) **1** treat (a subject) briefly; refer to or mention casually. **2** verge on (*that touches on impudence*). **touch up 1** give finishing touches to or retouch (a picture, writing, etc.). **2** *Brit. sl.* **a** caress so as to excite sexually. **b** sexually molest. **touch wood** esp. *Brit.* touch something wooden with the hand to avert bad luck. □□ **touch·a·ble** *adj.* **touch·er** *n.*

touch-and-go *n.* an airplane landing and immediate takeoff done esp. as practice.

touch·back /túchbak/ *n. Football* a play in which the ball is downed behind the goal line after it has been caught there; the ball is put back in play at the

20-yard line of the team making the catch, who then take over on offense.

touch·down /túchdown/ *n.* **1** the act or an instance of an aircraft or spacecraft making contact with the ground during landing. **2** *Football* the act or an instance of scoring by crossing the goal line.

touché /tōosháy/ *int.* **1** the acknowledgment of a hit by a fencing opponent. **2** the acknowledgment of a justified accusation, a witticism, or a point made in reply to one's own.

touch foot·ball *n.* football with touching in place of tackling.

touch·ing /túching/ *adj. & prep.* ● *adj.* arousing great emotion; moving. ● *prep.* concerning; about. □□ **touch·ing·ly** *adv.*

touch·line /túchlīn/ *n.* (in various sports) either of the lines marking the side boundaries of the field. ▷ RUGBY

touch-me-not *n.* ▼ any of various plants of the genus *Impatiens*, with ripe seed capsules bursting open when touched.

seed capsule

exploded capsule

TOUCH-ME-NOT
(*Impatiens parviflora*)

touch screen *n.* ► a touch-sensitive video screen for display of data, as information to customers.

touch·stone /túchstōn/ *n.* **1** a fine-grained dark schist or jasper used for testing alloys of gold, etc., by marking it with them and observing the color of the mark. **2** a standard or criterion.

touch-tone *adj.* **1** of or relating to a tone dialing telephone system. **2** (**Touch-tone**) *Trademark* a telephone that produces tones when buttons are pushed.

touch-type *v.intr.* type without looking at the keys. □□ **touch typ·ing** *n.* **touch-typ·ist** *n.*

touch·y /túchee/ *adj.* (**touchier, touchiest**) **1** apt to take offense; overly sensitive. **2** not to be touched without danger; ticklish; risky; awkward. □□ **touch·i·ly** *adv.* **touch·i·ness** *n.*

touch·y-feel·y /tuchee féelee/ *adj. colloq.*, often *derog.* openly expressing affection or other emotions, esp. through physical contact.

tough /tuf/ *adj. & n.* ● *adj.* **1** hard to break, cut, tear, or chew; durable; strong. **2** (of a person) able to endure hardship; hardy. **3** unyielding; stubborn; difficult (*it was a tough job; a tough customer*). **4** *colloq.* **a** acting sternly; hard (*get tough with*). **b** (of circumstances, luck, etc.) severe; unpleasant; hard; unjust. **5** *colloq.* criminal or violent (*tough guys*). ● *n.* a tough person, esp. a gangster or criminal. □ **tough it out** *colloq.* endure or withstand difficult conditions. □□ **tough·en** *v.tr. & intr.* **tough·en·er** *n.* **tough·ish** *adj.* **tough·ly** *adv.* **tough·ness** *n.*

tough·ie (also **tough·y**) /túfee/ *n. colloq.* a tough person or problem.

tough-mind·ed *adj.* realistic; not sentimental.

tou·pee /tōopáy/ *n.* a wig or artificial hairpiece to cover a bald spot.

tour /tŏor/ *n. & v.* ● *n.* **1 a** a journey from place to place as a vacation. **b** an excursion, ramble, or walk (*made a tour of the yard*). **2 a** a period of duty on military or diplomatic service. **b** the time to be spent at a particular post. **3** a series of performances, games, etc., at different places on a route through a country, etc. ● *v.* **1** *intr.* (usu. foll. by *through*) make a tour (*toured

TOUCH SCREEN

Multimedia kiosks in museums, retail outlets, and public information displays offer easy-access information. The software displays graphical buttons or numbered options on a screen, and users move through the system by touching a chosen button or option. The pressure of the touch affects the electric current in a conductive layer beneath the screen. A controller card detects the location of the changes, activating the selected option.

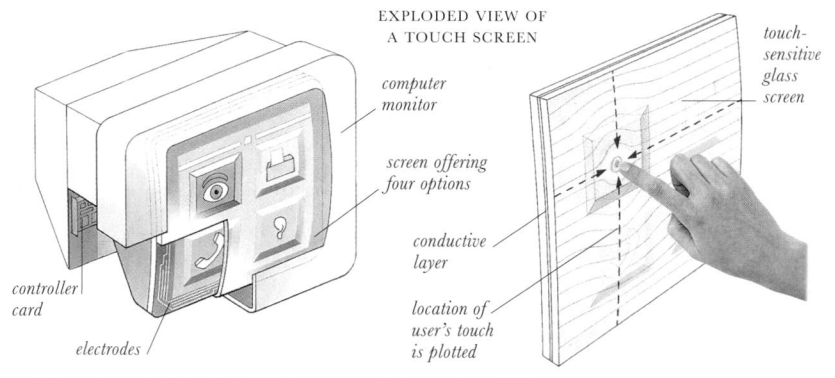

EXPLODED VIEW OF
A TOUCH SCREEN

computer monitor

touch-sensitive glass screen

screen offering four options

conductive layer

controller card

electrodes

location of user's touch is plotted

---

through Italy). **2** *tr.* make a tour of (a country, etc.). □ **on tour** (esp. of a team, theater company, etc.) touring.

tour de force /tŏŏr də fáwrs/ *n.* a feat of strength or skill.

tour·er /tŏŏrər/ *n.* a vehicle, esp. a car, for touring.

tour·ism /tŏŏrizəm/ *n.* the organization and operation of tours, esp. as a commercial enterprise.

tour·ist /tŏŏrist/ *n.* a person making a visit or tour as a vacation; a traveler. (often *attrib.: tourist accommodations*). □□ **tour·is·tic** *adj.* **tour·is·ti·cal·ly** *adv.*

tour·ist class *n.* the lowest class of passenger accommodations in a ship, aircraft, etc.

tour·ist·y /tŏŏristee/ *adj.* usu. *derog.* appealing to or visited by many tourists.

tour·ma·line /tŏŏrməlin, -leen/ *n.* ▶ a boron aluminum silicate mineral of various colors, possessing unusual electrical properties, and used in electrical and optical instruments and as a gemstone. ▷ MINERAL.

tour·na·ment /tŏŏrnəmənt, túr-/ *n.* **1** any contest of skill between a number of competitors, esp. played in heats or a series of games (*chess tournament; tennis tournament*). **2** (in the UK) a display of military exercises, esp. *hist.* **a** a pageant with jousting. **b** a meeting for jousting.

tour·ne·dos /tŏŏrnədō/ *n.* (*pl.* same /-dōz/) a small round thick cut from a tenderloin of beef.

tour·ney /tŏŏrnee, túr-/ *n. & v.* ● *n.* (*pl.* **-eys**) a tournament. ● *v.intr.* (**-eys, -eyed**) take part in a tournament.

tour·ni·quet /tárnikit, tŏŏr-/ *n.* a device for stopping the flow of blood through an artery by constriction.

tou·sle /tówzəl/ *v.tr.* **1** make (esp. the hair) untidy; rumple. **2** handle roughly or rudely.

tout /towt/ *v. & n.* ● *v.* **1** *intr.* (usu. foll. by *for*) solicit patronage persistently; pester customers (*touting for business*). **2** *tr.* solicit the patronage of (a person) or for (a thing). **3** *intr.* **a** *Brit.* spy out the movements and condition of racehorses in training. **b** offer racing tips for a share of the resulting profit. ● *n.* a person employed in touting. □□ **tout·er** *n.*

tow[1] /tō/ *v. & n.* ● *v.tr.* **1** (of a motor vehicle, horse, or person controlling it) pull (a boat, another motor vehicle, a trailer, etc.) along by a rope, tow bar, etc. **2** pull (a person or thing) along behind one. ● *n.* the act or an instance of towing; the state of being towed. □ **have in** (or **on**) **tow 1** be towing. **2** be accompanied by and often in charge of (a person). □□ **tow·a·ble** *adj.* **tow·age** /tőij/ *n.*

TOURMALINE

tow[2] /tō/ *n.* the coarse and broken part of flax or hemp prepared for spinning.

to·ward /tawrd, təwáwrd, twawrd/ *prep. & adj.* (also **towards** /tawrdz, təwáwrdz, twawrdz/) *prep.* **1** in the direction of (*set out toward town*). **2** as regards; in relation to (*his attitude toward death*). **3** as a contribution to; for (*put this toward your expenses*). **4** near (*toward the end of our journey*).

tow bar *n.* a bar for towing, e.g., a trailer or camper.

tow·el /tówəl/ *n. & v.* ● *n.* **1 a** a piece of absorbent cloth used for drying oneself or a thing after washing. **b** absorbent paper used for this. **c** a cloth used for drying plates, dishes, etc.; a dish towel. **2** *Brit.* = SANITARY NAPKIN. ● *v.* (**toweled, toweling** or **towelled, towelling**) **1** *tr.* (often *refl.*) wipe or dry with a towel. **2** *intr.* wipe or dry oneself with a towel. **3** *tr. sl.* thrash. □□ **tow·el·ing** or **tow·el·ling** *n.*

tow·er /tówər/ *n. & v.* ● *n.* **1 a** a tall esp. square or circular structure, often part of a church, castle, etc. ▷ CASTLE, CHURCH. **b** a fortress, etc., comprising or including a tower. **c** a tall structure housing machinery, apparatus, operators, etc. (*cooling tower; control tower*). ▷ CONTROL TOWER. **2** a place of defense; a protection. ● *v.intr.* **1** (usu. foll. by *above, high*) reach or be high or above; be superior. **2** (of a bird) soar or hover. **3** (as **towering** *adj.*) **a** high, lofty (*towering intellect*). **b** violent (*towering rage*).

tow·er of strength *n.* a person who gives strong and reliable support.

tow·head /tőhed/ *n.* **1** tow-colored or blond hair. **2** a person with such hair. □□ **tow·head·ed** *adj.*

town /town/ *n.* **1 a** an urban area with a name, defined boundaries, and local government, being larger than a village and usu. not incorporated as a city. **b** any densely populated area, esp. as opposed to the country or suburbs. **c** the people of a town (*the whole town knows of it*). **2 a** *Brit.* London or the chief city or town in an area (*went up to town*). **b** the central business or shopping area in a neighborhood (*just going into town*). □ **go to town** *colloq.* act or work with energy or enthusiasm. **on the town** *colloq.* enjoying the entertainments, esp. the nightlife, of a town; celebrating. □□ **town·ish** *adj.* **town·let** *n.* **town·ward** *adj. & adv.* **town·wards** *adv.*

town clerk *n.* the officer of a town in charge of records, etc.

town cri·er *n. hist.* an officer employed by a town council, etc., to make public announcements in the streets or marketplace.

town hall *n.* a building for the administration of local government, having public meeting rooms, etc.

town house *n.* **1** a town residence, esp. of a person with a house in the country. **2** a row house. **3** a house in a development. **4** *Brit.* a town hall.

town·ie /tównee/ *n.* (also *Brit.* **townee**) *colloq.* a person living in a town, esp. as opposed to a student, etc.

town·scape /tównskayp/ *n.* **1** the visual appearance of a town or towns. **2** a picture of a town.

towns·folk /tównzfōk/ *n.* the inhabitants of a particular town or towns.

town·ship /tównship/ *n.* **1** *S.Afr.* **a** an urban area formerly set aside for black residents. **b** a white urban area (esp. if new or about to be developed). **2** *US & Can.* **a** a division of a county in some states with some corporate powers. **b** a district six miles square in some states. **3** *Austral. & NZ* a small town; a town site.

towns·man /tównzmən/ *n.* (*pl.* **-men**; *fem.* **towns·woman**, *pl.* **-women**) an inhabitant of a town; a fellow citizen.

towns·peo·ple /tównzpeepəl/ *n.pl.* the people of a town.

tox·e·mi·a /tokseémeeə/ *n.* (*Brit.* **toxaemia**) **1** blood poisoning. **2** a condition in pregnancy characterized by increased blood pressure. □□ **tox·e·mic** *adj.*

tox·ic /tóksik/ *adj.* **1** of or relating to poison (*toxic symptoms*). **2** poisonous (*toxic gas*). **3** caused by poison (*toxic anemia*). □□ **tox·i·cal·ly** *adv.* **tox·ic·i·ty** /-sísitee/ *n.*

tox·i·col·o·gy /tóksikóləjee/ *n.* the scientific study of poisons. □□ **tox·i·co·log·i·cal** /-kəlójikəl/ *adj.* **tox·i·col·o·gist** *n.*

tox·in /tóksin/ *n.* a poison produced by a living organism, esp. one formed in the body and stimulating the production of antibodies.

tox·o·car·a /tóksōkaárə/ *n.* any nematode worm of the genus *Toxocara*, parasitic in the alimentary canal of dogs and cats. □□ **tox·o·car·i·a·sis** /-kərίəsis/ *n.*

tox·oph·i·lite /toksófilīt/ *n. & adj.* ● *n.* a student or lover of archery. ● *adj.* of or concerning archery. □□ **tox·oph·i·ly** *n.*

toy /toy/ *n. & v.* ● *n.* **1 a** a plaything, esp. for a child. **b** (often *attrib.*) a model or miniature replica of a thing, esp. as a plaything (*toy airplane*). **2 a** a thing, esp. a gadget or instrument, regarded as providing amusement or pleasure. **b** a task or undertaking regarded in an unserious way. **3** (usu. *attrib.*) a diminutive breed or variety of dog, etc. (*toy poodle*). ● *v.intr.* (usu. foll. by *with*) **1** trifle; amuse oneself, esp. with a person's affections; flirt (*toyed with the idea of going to Africa*). **2 a** move a material object idly (*toyed with her necklace*). **b** nibble at food, etc., unenthusiastically (*toyed with a peach*).

tp. *abbr.* **1** (also **t.p.**) title page. **2** township. **3** troop.

tra·bec·u·la /trəbékyələ/ *n.* (*pl.* **trabeculae** /-lee/) **1** *Anat.* ◀ a supporting band or bar of connective or bony tissue, esp. dividing an organ into chambers. **2** *Bot.* a beamlike projection or process within a hollow structure. □□ **tra·bec·u·lar** *adj.* **tra·bec·u·late** /-lət, -layt/ *adj.*

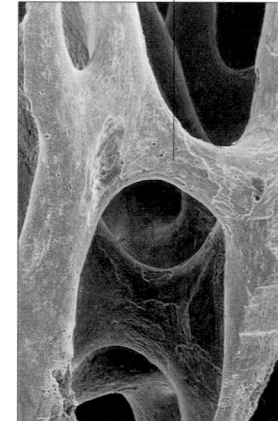

trabecula

TRABECULA: MICROGRAPH SHOWING TRABECULAE IN BONE

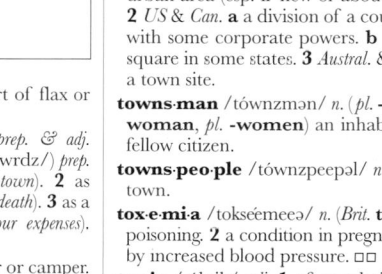

T

trace[1] /trays/ *v. & n.* ● *v.tr.* **1 a** observe, discover, or find vestiges or signs of by investigation. **b** (often foll. by *along, through, to,* etc.) follow or mark the track or position of (*traced their footprints in the mud; traced the outlines of a wall*). **c** (often foll. by *back*) follow to its origins (*can trace my family to the 12th century; the report has been traced back to you*). **2** (often foll. by *over*) ▼ copy (a drawing, etc.) by drawing over its lines on a superimposed piece of translucent paper, or by using carbon paper. **3** (often foll. by *out*) mark out, delineate, sketch, or write, often laboriously (*traced out a plan of the district; traced out his vision of the future*). **4** pursue one's way along (a path, etc.). ● *n.* **1 a** a sign or mark or other indication of something having existed; a vestige (*no trace remains of the castle*). **b** a very small quantity. **c** an amount of rainfall, etc., too small to be measured. **2** a track or footprint left by a person or animal. **3** a track left by the moving pen of an instrument, etc. **4** a line on the screen of a cathode-ray tube showing the path of a moving spot. □□ **trace·a·ble** *adj.* **trace·a·bil·i·ty** /tráysəbilitee/ *n.* **trace·less** *adj.*

traced outline

tracing paper

TRACE: USING TRACING PAPER TO COPY AN IMAGE

trace[2] /trays/ *n.* ▼ each of the two straps, chains, or ropes by which a horse draws a vehicle. □ **kick over the traces** become insubordinate or reckless.

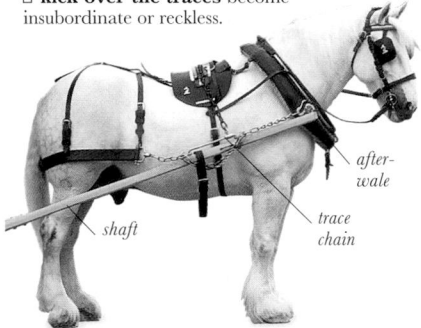

after-wale

shaft

trace chain

TRACE: HORSE HARNESSED WITH TRACE CHAINS TO THE SHAFTS OF A WAGON

trace el·e·ment *n.* **1** a chemical element occurring in minute amounts. **2** a chemical element required only in minute amounts by living organisms for normal growth.

trac·er /tráysər/ *n.* **1** a person or thing that traces. **2** *Mil.* a bullet, etc., that is visible in flight because of flames, etc., emitted. **3** an artificially produced radioactive isotope capable of being followed through the body by the radiation it produces.

trac·er·y /tráysəree/ *n.* (*pl.* **-ies**) **1** ▶ ornamental stone openwork, esp. in the upper part of a Gothic window. ▷ MASONRY, ROSE WINDOW. **2** a fine decorative pattern. □□ **trac·er·ied** *adj.*

tra·che·a /tráykeeə/ *n.* (*pl.* **tracheae** /-kee-ee/ or **tracheas**) the passage, reinforced by rings of cartilage, through which air reaches the

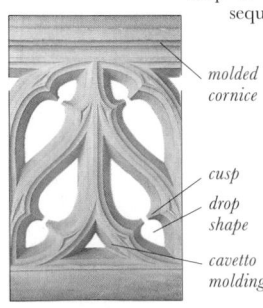

molded cornice

cusp

drop shape

cavetto molding

TRACERY IN A *C.*15TH-CENTURY GOTHIC BALUSTRADE

bronchial tubes from the larynx; the windpipe. ▷ ADAM'S APPLE, RESPIRATION. □□ **tra·che·al** /tráykeeəl/ *adj.* **tra·che·ate** /tráykeeayt/ *adj.*

tracheo- /tráykeeō/ *comb. form* of or relating to the trachea (*tracheotomy*).

tra·che·ot·o·my /traykeeótəmee/ *n.* (also **tra·che·os·to·my** /-óstəmee/) (*pl.* **-ies**) an incision made in the trachea to relieve an obstruction to breathing.

tra·cho·ma /trəkṓmə/ *n.* a contagious disease of the eye with inflamed granulation on the inner surface of the lids. □□ **tra·chom·a·tous** /-kṓmətəs, -kómətəs/ *adj.*

trac·ing /tráysing/ *n.* **1** a copy of a drawing, etc., made by tracing. **2** = TRACE[1] *n.* 3. **3** the act or an instance of tracing.

track[1] /trak/ *n. & v.* ● *n.* **1 a** ▶ a mark or marks left by a person, animal, or thing in passing. **b** (in *pl.*) such marks, esp. footprints. **2** a rough path, esp. one beaten by use. **3** a continuous railway line (*laid three miles of track*). **4 a** a course for racing horses, dogs, etc. **b** ▲ a prepared course for runners, etc. **c** various sports performed on a track, as running or hurdles. **5 a** a groove on a phonograph record. **b** a section of a phonograph record, compact disk, etc., containing one song, etc. (*this side has six tracks*). **c** a lengthwise strip of magnetic tape containing one sequence of signals. **6 a** a line of travel, passage, or motion (*followed the track of the hurricane*). **b** the path traveled by a ship, aircraft, etc. (cf. COURSE *n.* 2c). **7** a continuous band around the wheels of a tank, tractor, etc. **8** the transverse distance between a vehicle's wheels. **9** = SOUNDTRACK. **10** a line of reasoning or thought (*this track proved fruitless*). **11** any of several levels of instruction to which students are assigned based on their abilities, interests, etc. **12** a course of action or planned future (*management*

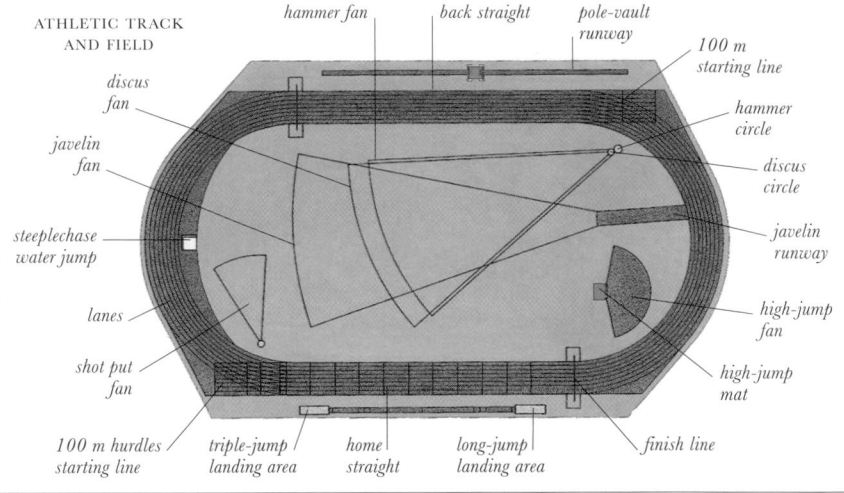

ATHLETIC TRACK AND FIELD

TRACK

An athletic track is marked for running events – sprinting, relay running, middle- and long-distance running, hurdling, and walking. Field events such as the long jump, triple jump, and pole vault are often sited in the outfield, beyond the track area, while the javelin, shot put, hammer, and discus are thrown inside the perimeter, in the infield.

hammer fan   *back straight*   *pole-vault runway*   *100 m starting line*   *hammer circle*   *discus circle*   *javelin runway*   *high-jump fan*   *high-jump mat*   *finish line*   *discus fan*   *javelin fan*   *steeplechase water jump*   *lanes*   *shot put fan*   *100 m hurdles starting line*   *triple-jump landing area*   *home straight*   *long-jump landing area*

track) ● *v.* **1** *tr.* follow the track of (an animal, person, spacecraft, etc.). **2** *tr.* make out (a course, development, etc.); trace by vestiges. **3** *intr.* (often foll. by *back, in,* etc.) (of a movie or television camera) move in relation to the subject being filmed. **4** *intr.* (of wheels) run so that the back ones are exactly in the track of the front ones. **5** *intr.* (of a record stylus) follow a groove. **6** *tr.* **a** make a track with (dirt, etc.) from the feet. **b** leave such a track on (a floor, etc.). □ **in one's tracks** *colloq.* where one stands; then and there (*stopped him in his tracks*). **keep** (or **lose**) **track of** follow (or fail to follow) the course or development of. **make tracks** *colloq.* go or run away. **make tracks for** *colloq.* go in pursuit of or toward. **off the track** away from the subject. **on a person's track 1** in pursuit of him or her. **2** in possession of a clue to a person's conduct, plans, etc. **on the wrong side of** (or **across**) **the tracks** *colloq.* in an inferior or dubious part of town. **on the wrong** (or **right**) **track** following the wrong (or right) line of inquiry. **track down** reach or capture by tracking. □□ **track·age** *n.* **track·less** *adj.*

track[2] /trak/ *Brit. v.* **1** *tr.* tow (a boat) by rope etc., from a bank. **2** *intr.* travel by being towed.

track·er /trákər/ *n.* **1** a person or thing that tracks. **2** a police dog tracking by scent.

track·ing /tráking/ *n.* **1** assignment of students in a track system. **2** *Electr.* the formation of a conducting path over the surface of an insulating material.

track·ing sta·tion *n.* an establishment set up to track objects in the sky.

track·lay·er /tráklayər/ *n.* **1** a person employed in laying or repairing railroad tracks. **2** a tractor or other vehicle equipped with continuous tracks (see TRACK[1] *n.* 7).

track·lay·ing *n.* (of a vehicle) having a caterpillar tread.

track·less /tráklis/ *adj.* **1** without a track or tracks; untrodden. **2** leaving no track or trace. **3** not running on a track.

track·man /trákmən/ *n.* (*pl.* **-men**) a tracklayer.

track rec·ord *n.* a person's past performance or achievements.

pad of toe   *claw*   *main pad*   *edge of web*   *toe*

DOG'S PAW

DUCK'S FOOT

TRACKS MADE BY ANIMALS

T

track shoe *n.* ▶ a spiked shoe worn by a runner.

track·way /trákway/ *n.* a beaten path; an ancient roadway.

tract[1] /trakt/ *n.* **1 a** region or area of indefinite, esp. large, extent (*pathless desert tracts*). **2** *Anat.* an area of an organ or system (*respiratory tract*). **3** *Brit. archaic* a period of time, etc.

tract[2] /trakt/ *n.* a short treatise in pamphlet form, esp. on a religious subject.

trac·ta·ble /tráktəbəl/ *adj.* **1** (of a person) easily handled; manageable; docile. **2** (of material, etc.) pliant; malleable. □□ **trac·ta·bil·i·ty** /-bílitee/ *n.* **trac·ta·ble·ness** *n.* **trac·ta·bly** *adv.*

trac·tion /trákshən/ *n.* **1** the act of drawing or pulling a thing over a surface, esp. a road or track (*steam traction*). **2 a** a sustained pulling on a limb, muscle, etc., by means of pulleys, weights, etc. **b** contraction, e.g., of a muscle. **3** the grip of a tire on a road, a wheel on a rail, etc. □□ **trac·tion·al** *adj.* **trac·tive** /tráktiv/ *adj.*

trac·tion en·gine *n.* ▼ a steam or diesel engine for drawing heavy loads on roads, fields, etc.

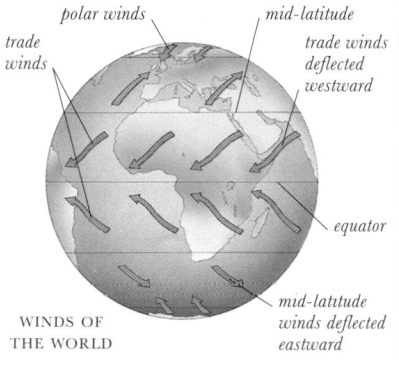
spiked sole
TRACK SHOE

chimney · steam cylinder · drive wheel · furnace housing · boiler · coal store · drive belt to threshing machine

TRACTION ENGINE: 19TH-CENTURY STEAM-DRIVEN TRACTION ENGINE

trac·tor-trail·er *n.* a truck consisting of a tractor or cab unit attached to a trailer.

trad /trad/ *n. & adj. esp. Brit. colloq.* ● *n.* traditional jazz. ● *adj.* traditional.

trade /trayd/ *n. & v.* ● *n.* **1 a** buying and selling. **b** buying and selling conducted between nations, etc. **c** business conducted for profit (esp. as distinct from a profession) (*a butcher by trade*). **d** business of a specified nature or time (*Christmas trade; tourist trade*). **2** a skilled craft, esp. requiring an apprenticeship (*learned a trade; his trade is plumbing*). **3** (usu. prec. by *the*) the people engaged in a specific trade (*trade inquiries only*). **4** a transaction, esp. a swap. **5** (usu. in *pl.*) a trade wind. ● *v.* **1** *intr.* (often foll. by *in, with*) engage in trade; buy and sell (*trades in plastic novelties; we trade with Japan*). **2** *tr.* **a** exchange in commerce; barter (goods). **b** exchange (insults, blows, etc.). **3** *intr.* (usu. foll. by *with, for*) have a transaction with a person for a thing. **c** (foll. by *for*) swap, exchange. □ **trade in** (often foll. by *for*) exchange (esp. a used car, etc.) in esp. part payment for another. **trade off** exchange, esp. as a compromise. **trade on** take advantage of (a person's credulity, one's reputation, etc.). □□ **trad·a·ble, trade·a·ble** *adj.*

trade def·i·cit *n.* (also **trade gap**) the extent by which a country's imports exceed its exports.

trade-in *n.* a thing, esp. a car, exchanged in part payment for another.

trade jour·nal *n.* a periodical containing news, etc., concerning a particular trade.

trade·mark /tráydmaark/ *n.* **1** a device, word, or words, secured by legal registration or established by use as representing a company, product, etc. **2** a distinctive characteristic, etc.

trade name *n.* **1** a name by which a thing is called in a trade. **2** a name given to a product. **3** a name under which a business trades.

trade-off *n.* an exchange; a swap.

trad·er /tráydər/ *n.* **1** a person engaged in trade. **2** a merchant ship.

trade se·cret *n.* **1** a secret device or technique used esp. in a trade. **2** *joc.* any secret.

trades·man /tráydzmən/ *n.* (*pl.* **-men;** *fem.* **tradeswoman**, *pl.* **-women**) a person engaged in trading or a trade, as a skilled craftsman or *Brit.* a shopkeeper.

trades·peo·ple /tráydzpeepəl/ *n.pl.* people engaged in trade.

trade un·ion *n.* esp. *Brit.* = LABOR UNION.

trade wind *n.* ▶ a wind blowing continually toward the equator and deflected westward.

trad·ing /tráyding/ *n.* the act of engaging in trade.

trad·ing post *n.* a store, etc., established in a remote or unsettled region.

trad·ing stamp *n.* a stamp given to customers by some stores that is exchangeable in large numbers for various articles.

tra·di·tion /trədíshən/ *n.* **1 a** a custom, opinion, or belief handed down to posterity, esp. orally or by practice. **b** this process of handing down. **2** esp. *joc.* an established practice or custom. **3** artistic, literary, etc., principles based on experience and practice; any one of these (*stage tradition; traditions of the Dutch School*). □□ **tra·di·tion·ar·y** *adj.* **tra·di·tion·ist** *n.* **tra·di·tion·less** *adj.*

tra·di·tion·al /trədíshənəl/ *adj.* **1** of, based on, or obtained by tradition. **2** (of jazz) in the style of the early 20th c. □□ **tra·di·tion·al·ly** *adv.*

tra·di·tion·al·ism /trədíshənəlizəm/ *n.* respect, esp. excessive, for tradition, esp. in religion. □□ **tra·di·tion·al·ist** *n.* **tra·di·tion·al·is·tic** *adj.*

tra·duce /trədóos, -dyóos/ *v.tr.* speak ill of; misrepresent. □□ **tra·duce·ment** *n.* **tra·duc·er** *n.*

traf·fic /tráfik/ *n. & v.* *n.* **1** (often *attrib.*) **a** vehicles moving on a public highway, esp. of a specified kind, density, etc. (*heavy traffic on the interstate; traffic cop*). **b** such movement in the air or at sea. **2** (usu. foll. by *in*) trade, esp. illegal (*the traffic in drugs*). **3 a** the transportation of goods; the coming and going of people or goods by road, rail, air, sea, etc. **b** the persons or goods so transported. **4** dealings or communication between people, etc. (*had no traffic with them*). **5** the messages, signals, etc., transmitted through a communications system; the flow or volume of such business. ● *v.* (**trafficked, trafficking**) **1** *intr.* (usu. foll. by *in*) deal in something, esp. illegally (*trafficked in narcotics; traffics in innuendo*). **2** *tr.* deal in; barter. □□ **traf·fick·er** *n.* **traf·fic·less** *adj.*

traf·fic cir·cle *n.* a road junction at which traffic moves in one direction around a central island.

traf·fic jam *n.* traffic at a standstill because of construction, an accident, etc.

traf·fic light *n.* (also **traf·fic sig·nal**) a usu. automatic signal with colored lights to control road traffic, esp. at intersections.

trag·a·canth /trágəkanth, tráj-/ *n.* a white or reddish gum from a plant, *Astragalus gummifer*, used in pharmaceuticals, calico printing, etc., as a vehicle for drugs, dye, etc.

tra·ge·di·an /trəjéedeeən/ *n.* **1** a writer of tragedies. **2** an actor in tragedy.

tra·ge·di·enne /trəjéedee-én/ *n.* an actress in tragedy.

trag·e·dy /trájidee/ *n.* (*pl.* **-ies**) **1** a serious accident, crime, or natural catastrophe. **2** a sad event; a calamity (*the team's defeat is a tragedy*). **3 a** a play in verse or prose dealing with tragic events and with an unhappy ending, esp. concerning the downfall of the protagonist. **b** tragic plays as a genre (cf. COMEDY).

TRADE WIND

The trade winds were so named when transport of cargo relied on strong winds to propel sailing ships. Flowing from the mid-latitudes toward the equator, the trade winds blow reliably from east to west as a result of the Earth rotating faster than the atmosphere at the equator. The converse is true at mid-latitudes, where westerly winds prevail.

polar winds · mid-latitude trade winds deflected westward · trade winds · equator · mid-latitude winds deflected eastward

WINDS OF THE WORLD

trag·ic /trájik/ *adj.* **1** (also **trag·i·cal** /-kəl/) sad; calamitous; greatly distressing (*a tragic tale*). **2** of, or in the style of, tragedy (*tragic drama; a tragic actor*). □□ **trag·i·cal·ly** *adv.*

trag·ic i·ro·ny *n.* a device, orig. in Greek tragedy, by which words carry a tragic, esp. prophetic, meaning, unknown to the character speaking.

trag·i·com·e·dy /trájikómidee/ *n.* (*pl.* **-ies**) **1 a** play having a mixture of comedy and tragedy. **b** plays of this kind as a genre. **2** an event, etc., having tragic and comic elements. □□ **trag·i·com·ic** /-kómik/ *adj.* **trag·i·com·i·cal·ly** *adv.*

trail /trayl/ *n. & v.* ● *n.* **1 a** a track left by a thing, person, etc., moving over a surface (*left a trail of wreckage; a slug's slimy trail*). **b** a track or scent followed in hunting, seeking, etc. (*he's on the trail*). **2** a beaten path or track, esp. through a wild region. **3** a part dragging behind a thing or person; an appendage (*a trail of smoke; a condensation trail*). ● *v.* **1** *tr. & intr.* draw or be drawn along behind, esp. on the ground. **2** *intr.* (often foll. by *behind*) walk wearily; lag; straggle. **3** *tr.* follow the trail of; pursue (*trailed him to his home*). **4** *intr.* be losing in a game or other contest (*trailing by three points*). **5** *intr.* (usu. foll. by *away, off*) peter out; tail off. **6** *intr.* **a** (of a plant, etc.) grow or hang over a wall, along the ground, etc. **b** (of a garment, etc.) hang loosely. **7** *tr.* (often *refl.*) drag (oneself, one's limbs, etc.) along wearily, etc. **8** *tr.* advertise (a movie, a radio or television program, etc.) in advance by showing extracts, etc.

trail bike *n.* a light motorcycle for use in rough terrain.

trail·blaz·er /tráylblayzər/ *n.* **1** a person who marks a new track through wild country. **2** a pioneer; an innovator.

trail·blaz·ing /tráylblayzing/ *n. & adj.* ● *n.* the act or process of blazing a trail. ● *attrib.adj.* that blazes a trail; pioneering.

trail·er /tráylər/ *n.* **1** a person or thing that trails. **2** a series of brief extracts from a movie, etc., used to advertise it in advance. **3** a vehicle towed by another, esp.: **a** the rear section of a tractor-trailer. **b** an open cart. **c** a platform for transporting a boat, etc. **d** a camper. **4** a mobile home. **5** a trailing plant.

trail·er park *n.* a place where trailers are parked as dwellings, often with special amenities.

T

TRAIN

Invented in the early nineteenth century, trains were drawn by steam locomotives until the first use of electricity in the 1880s and diesel power in the 1940s. Many modern trains have diesel-electric locomotives: these transmit power from a diesel engine to the wheels via a generator and electric motors. Electric trains are driven by electric motors on one or more of their cars and receive electricity from an overhead cable or from electrified rails.

EXPLODED VIEW OF
BRITISH CLASS 73 ELECTRO-DIESEL
LOCOMOTIVE ENGINE (1962)

OTHER TYPES OF TRAIN

STEAM TRAIN
British "Lady of Lynn" (1908)

DIESEL-ELECTRIC TRAIN
American "Deltic" (1956)

ELECTRIC TRAIN
French "TGV" (1983)

---

train /trayn/ *v. & n.* ● *v.* **1 a** *tr.* (often foll. by *to* + infin.) teach (a person, animal, oneself, etc.) a specified skill, esp. by practice (*trained the dog to beg*; *was trained in midwifery*). **b** *intr.* undergo this process (*trained as a teacher*). **2** *tr. & intr.* bring or come into a state of physical fitness by exercise, diet, etc.; undergo physical exercise, esp. for a specific purpose. **3** *tr.* cause (a plant) to grow in a required shape. **4** (usu. as **trained** *adj.*) make (the mind, eye, etc.) sharp or discerning as a result of instruction, practice, etc. **5** *tr.* (often foll. by *on*) point or aim (a gun, camera, etc.) at an object, etc. **6** *intr. colloq.* go by train. ● *n.* **1 ▲** a series of railroad cars drawn by an engine. ▷ LOCOMOTIVE. **2** something dragged along behind or forming the back part of a dress, robe, etc. **3** a succession or series of people, things, events, etc. (*a long train of camels*; *interrupted my train of thought*). **4** a body of followers; a retinue (*a train of admirers*). **5** a succession of military vehicles, etc., including artillery, supplies, etc. (*baggage train*). **6** a line of gunpowder, etc., to fire an explosive charge. **7** a series of connected wheels or parts in machinery. □ **in train** properly arranged or directed. **in a person's train** following behind a person. **in the train of** as a sequel of. □□ **train·a·ble** *adj.* **train·a·bil·i·ty** /tráynəbilitee/ *n.* **train·ee** /-née/ *n.* **train·less** *adj.*

train·band /tráynband/ *n. hist.* any of several divisions of 16th or 17th c. citizen soldiers in England or America.

train·er /tráynər/ *n.* **1** a person who trains. **2** a person who trains or provides medical assistance, etc., to horses, athletes, etc., as a profession. **3** an aircraft or device simulating it used to train pilots. **4** *Brit.* a soft running shoe of leather, canvas, etc.

train·ing /tráyning/ *n.* the act or process of teaching or learning a skill, discipline, etc. (*physical training*). □ **go into training** begin physical training. **in training 1** undergoing physical training. **2** physically fit as a result of this. **out of training 1** no longer training. **2** physically unfit.

train·man /tráynmən/ *n.* (*pl.* **-men**) a railroad employee working on trains.

train·sick /tráynsik/ *adj.* affected with nausea by the motion of a train. □□ **train·sick·ness** *n.*

traipse /trayps/ *v.intr. colloq.* tramp or trudge wearily.

trait /trayt/ *n.* a distinguishing feature or characteristic, esp. of a person.

trai·tor /tráytər/ *n.* (*fem.* **traitress** /-tris/) (often foll. by *to*) a person who is treacherous or disloyal, esp. to his or her country. □□ **trai·tor·ous** *adj.* **trai·tor·ous·ly** *adv.*

tra·jec·to·ry /trəjéktəree/ *n.* (*pl.* **-ies**) **1** the path described by a projectile flying or an object moving under the action of given forces. **2** *Geom.* a curve or surface cutting a system of curves or surfaces at a constant angle.

tra-la /traaláa/ *int.* an expression of joy or gaiety, esp. as in a song.

tram /tram/ *n.* **1** *Brit.* = STREETCAR. **2** a four-wheeled vehicle used in coal mines.

tram·car /trámkaar/ *n. Brit.* = TRAM 1.

tram·lines /trámlīnz/ *n.pl. Brit.* **1** rails for a streetcar. **2** *colloq.* **a** either pair of two sets of long parallel lines at the sides of a lawn tennis court. **b** similar lines at the side or back of a badminton court.

tram·mel /tráməl/ *n. & v.* ● *n.* **1** (usu. in *pl.*) an impediment to free movement; a hindrance (*the trammels of domesticity*). **2** a triple dragnet for fish. **3** an instrument for drawing ellipses, etc., with a bar sliding in upright grooves. **4** a beam compass. **5** a hook in a fireplace for a kettle, etc. ● *v.tr.* (**trammeled, trammeling** or **trammelled, trammelling**) confine or hamper with or as if with trammels.

tra·mon·ta·na /traámontaánə, -taánə/ *n.* a cold north wind in the Adriatic.

tra·mon·tane /trəmóntayn, trámən-/ *adj.* **1** situated or living on the other side of mountains, esp. the Alps as seen from Italy. **2** (from the Italian point of view) foreign; barbarous.

tramp /tramp/ *v. & n.* ● *v.* **1** *intr.* **a** walk heavily and firmly (*tramping about upstairs*). **b** go on foot, esp. a distance. **2** *tr.* **a** cross on foot, esp. wearily or reluctantly. **b** cover (a distance) in this way (*tramped forty miles*). **3** *tr.* (often foll. by *down*) tread on; trample; stamp on. **4** *intr.* live as a tramp. ● *n.* **1** an itinerant

vagrant or beggar. **2** the sound of a person, or esp. people, walking, marching, etc., or of horses' hooves. **3** a journey on foot, esp. protracted. **4 a** an iron plate protecting the sole of a boot used for digging. **b** the part of a spade that it strikes. **5** *sl. derog.* a promiscuous woman. □□ **tramp·er** *n.* **tramp·ish** *adj.*

tram·ple /trámpəl/ *v. & n.* ● *v.tr.* **1** tread underfoot. **2** press down or crush in this way. ● *n.* the sound or act of trampling. □ **trample on** (or **underfoot**) **1** tread heavily on. **2** treat roughly or with contempt; disregard (a person's feelings, etc.). □□ **tram·pler** *n.*

tram·po·line /trámpəleen/ *n.* a strong fabric sheet connected by springs to a horizontal frame, used by gymnasts, etc., for somersaults, as a springboard, etc. □□ **tram·po·lin·ist** *n.*

tram·way /trámway/ *n. Brit.* **1** rails for a streetcar. **2** a streetcar system.

trance /trans/ *n.* **1 a** a sleeplike or half-conscious state without response to stimuli. **b** a hypnotic or cataleptic state. **2** such a state as entered into by a medium. □□ **trance·like** *adj.*

tranche /traansh/ *n.* a portion, esp. of income, or of a block of bonds or stocks.

tran·ny /tránee/ *n.* (*pl.* **-ies**) **1** *sl.* a vehicle transmission. **2** esp. *Brit. colloq.* a transistor radio.

tran·quil /trángkwil/ *adj.* calm; serene; unruffled. □□ **tran·quil·li·ty** /-kwílitee/ *n.* **tran·quil·ly** *adv.*

tran·quil·ize /trángkwilīz/ *v.tr.* make tranquil, esp. by a drug, etc.

tran·quil·iz·er /trángkwilīzər/ *n.* a drug used to diminish anxiety.

trans- /trans, tranz/ *prefix* **1** across; beyond (*transcontinental*; *transgress*). **2** on or to the other side of (*transatlantic*). **3** through (*transpierce*). **4** into another state or place (*transform*; *transcribe*). **5** surpassing; transcending (*transfinite*). **6** *Chem.* **a** (of an isomer) having the same atom or group on opposite sides of a given plane in the molecule. **b** having a higher atomic number than (*transuranic*).

trans. *abbr.* **1** transaction. **2** transfer. **3** transitive. **4** (also **transl.**) translated. **5** (also **transl.**) translation. **6** (also **transl.**) translator. **7** transmission. **8** transportation. **9** transpose. **10** transposition. **11** transverse.

trans·act /tranzákt, -sákt/ *v.tr.* perform or carry through (business). □□ **trans·ac·tor** *n.*

trans·ac·tion /tranzákshən, -sák-/ *n.* **1 a** a piece of esp. commercial business done; a deal (*a profitable transaction*). **b** the management of business, etc. **2** (in *pl.*) published reports of discussions, papers read, etc., at the meetings of a learned society. □□ **trans·ac·tion·al** *adj.* **trans·ac·tion·al·ly** *adv.*

trans·al·pine /tránzálpīn, trans-/ *adj.* beyond the Alps, esp. from the Italian point of view.

trans·at·lan·tic /tránzətlántik, trans-/ *adj.* **1** beyond the Atlantic, esp.: **a** European. **b** *Brit.* American. **2** crossing the Atlantic (*a transatlantic flight*).

trans·ax·le /tranzáksəl/ *n.* a unit in front-wheel-drive vehicles that combines the functions of the transmission and differential.

trans·ceiv·er /transéevər/ *n.* a combined radio transmitter and receiver.

tran·scend /transénd/ *v.tr.* **1** be beyond the range or grasp of (human experience, reason, belief, etc.). **2** excel; surpass.

tran·scend·ent /transéndənt/ *adj. & n.* ● *adj.* **1** excelling; surpassing (*transcendent merit*). **2** transcending human experience. **3** (esp of the supreme being) existing apart from the material universe (opp. IMMANENT). ● *n. Philos.* a transcendent thing. □□ **tran·scend·ence** *n.* **tran·scend·en·cy** *n.* **tran·scend·ent·ly** *adv.*

tran·scen·den·tal /tránsendént'l/ *adj.* **1** = TRANSCENDENT. **2 a** presupposed in and necessary to experience; a priori. **b** explaining matter and objective things as products of the subjective mind. **c** regarding the divine as the guiding principle in man. **3 a** visionary; abstract. **b** vague; obscure. □□ **tran·scen·den·tal·ly** *adv.*

tran·scen·den·tal·ism /tránsendént'lizəm/ *n.* **1** transcendental philosophy. **2** exalted or visionary language. □□ **tran·scen·den·tal·ist** *n.* **tran·scen·den·tal·ize** *v.tr.*

tran·scen·den·tal med·i·ta·tion *n.* a method of detaching oneself from problems, anxiety, etc., by silent meditation and repetition of a mantra.

trans·con·ti·nen·tal /tránzkontinént'l, trans-/ *adj. & n.* ● *adj.* (of a railroad, etc.) extending across a continent. ● *n.* a transcontinental railroad or train. □□ **trans·con·ti·nen·tal·ly** *adv.*

tran·scribe /transkríb/ *v.tr.* **1** make a copy of, esp. in writing. **2** transliterate. **3** write out (shorthand, notes, etc.) in ordinary characters or continuous prose. **4 a** record for subsequent reproduction. **b** broadcast in this form. **5** arrange (music) for a different instrument, etc. □□ **tran·scrib·er** *n.* **tran·scrip·tion** /-skrípshən/ *n.* **tran·scrip·tion·al** *adj.* **tran·scrip·tive** /-skríptiv/ *adj.*

tran·script /tránskript/ *n.* **1** a written or recorded copy. **2** any copy.

trans·duc·er /tranzdóosər, -dyóo-, trans-/ *n.* any device for converting a nonelectrical signal into an electrical one, e.g., pressure into voltage.

tran·sect /transékt/ *v.tr.* cut across or transversely. □□ **tran·sec·tion** *n.*

tran·sept /tránsept/ *n.* **1** either arm of the part of a cross-shaped church at right angles to the nave (*north transept*; *south transept*). ▷ CATHEDRAL. **2** this part as a whole. □□ **tran·sep·tal** *adj.*

trans·fer *v. & n.* ● *v.* (**transferred**, **transferring**) **1** *tr.* (often foll. by *to*) **a** convey, remove, or hand over (a thing, etc.). **b** make over the possession of (property, a ticket, rights, etc.) to a person. **2** *tr. & intr.* change or move to another group, club, department, school, etc. **3** *intr.* change from one station, route, etc., to another on a journey. **4** *tr.* **a** convey (a drawing, etc.) from one surface to another, esp. to or from a lithographic stone by means of transfer paper. **b** remove (a picture) from one surface to another, esp. from wood or a wall to canvas. **5** *tr.* change (the sense of a word, etc.) by

---

TRANSFORMER

A transformer consists of two wire coils wrapped around an iron core. An alternating current passed through the primary coil creates a fluctuating magnetic field in the core, inducing a new voltage in the secondary coil. While step-up transformers have a greater number of coils in the secondary coil and increase voltage, step-down transformers have more coils in the primary coil and reduce voltage.

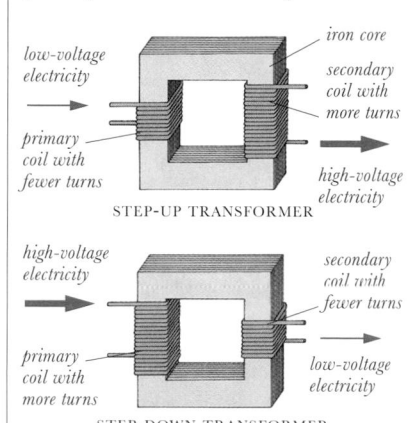

STEP-UP TRANSFORMER

STEP-DOWN TRANSFORMER

---

extension or metaphor. ● *n.* /tránsfər/ **1** the act or an instance of transferring or being transferred. **2 a** a design, etc., conveyed or to be conveyed from one surface to another. **b** a small usu. colored picture or design on paper, which is transferable to another surface; a decal. **3** a student, etc., who is or is to be transferred. **4 a** the conveyance of property, a right, etc. **b** a document effecting this. **5** a ticket allowing a journey to be continued on another route, etc. □□ **trans·fer·ee** /-reé/ *n.* **trans·fer·or** /-fərər/ esp. *Law n.* **trans·fer·rer** /-fərər/ *n.*

trans·fer·a·ble /tránsfərəbəl/ *adj.* capable of being transferred. □□ **trans·fer·a·bil·i·ty** /-bilitee/ *n.*

trans·fer·ence /transfərəns, tránsfər-/ *n.* **1** the act or an instance of transferring; the state of being transferred. **2** *Psychol.* the redirection of childhood emotions to a new object, esp. to a psychoanalyst.

trans·fer·ral /transfərəl/ *n.* = TRANSFER *n.* 1.

trans·fer RNA *n.* RNA conveying an amino acid molecule from the cytoplasm to a ribosome for use in protein synthesis, etc.

trans·fig·u·ra·tion /transfigyəráyshən/ *n.* **1** a change of form or appearance. **2 a** Christ's appearance in radiant glory to three of his disciples (Matt. 17:2, Mark 9:2–3). **b** (**Transfiguration**) the festival of Christ's transfiguration, Aug. 6.

trans·fig·ure /transfigyər/ *v.tr.* change in form or appearance, esp. so as to elevate or idealize.

trans·fix /transfiks/ *v.tr.* **1** pierce with a sharp implement or weapon. **2** root (a person) to the spot with horror or astonishment; paralyze the faculties of. □□ **trans·fix·ion** /-fikshən/ *n.*

trans·form *v.* /transfáwrm/ **1 a** *tr.* make a thorough or dramatic change in the form, outward appearance, character, etc., of. **b** *intr.* (often foll. by *into, to*) undergo such a change. **2** *tr. Electr.* change the voltage, etc., of (a current). □□ **trans·form·a·ble** *adj.* **trans·form·a·tive** *adj.*

trans·for·ma·tion /tránsfərmáyshən/ *n.* **1** the act or an instance of transforming; the state of being transformed. **2** *Zool.* a change of form at metamorphosis, esp. of insects, amphibians, etc. **3** the induced or spontaneous change of one element into another. **4** *Math.* a change from one geometri-

---

cal figure, expression, or function to another of the same value, magnitude, etc. □□ **trans·for·ma·tion·al** *adj.* **trans·for·ma·tion·al·ly** *adv.*

trans·form·er /transfáwrmər/ *n.* **1** ◄ an apparatus for reducing or increasing the voltage of an alternating current. ▷ HYDROELECTRIC, NUCLEAR POWER. **2** a person or thing that transforms.

trans·fuse /transfyóoz/ *v.tr.* **1 a** permeate (*purple dye transfused the water*). **b** instill (an influence, quality, etc.) into (*transfused enthusiasm into everyone*). **2 a** transfer (blood) from one person or animal to another. **b** inject (liquid) into a blood vessel to replace lost fluid. **3** cause (fluid, etc.) to pass from one vessel, etc., to another. □□ **trans·fu·sion** /-fyóozhən/ *n.*

trans·gen·ic /tranzjénik/ *adj. Biol.* (of an animal or plant) having genetic material introduced from another species.

trans·gress /tranzgrés/ *v.tr.* (also *absol.*) go beyond the bounds or limits set by (a commandment, law, etc.); violate; infringe. □□ **trans·gres·sion** /-gréshən/ *n.* **trans·gres·sive** *adj.* **trans·gres·sor** *n.*

tran·ship var. of TRANSSHIP.

tran·sient /tránzhənt, -shənt, -zeeənt/ *adj. & n.* ● *adj.* of short duration; momentary; passing; impermanent. ● *n.* a temporary visitor, worker, etc. □□ **tran·sience** *n.* **tran·sien·cy** *n.* **tran·sient·ly** *adv.*

tran·sis·tor /tranzístər/ *n.* **1** ▼ a semiconductor device with three connections, capable of amplification in addition to rectification. **2** (in full **transistor radio**) a portable radio with transistors. ▷ RADIO

tran·sit /tránzit, -sit/ *n. & v.* ● *n.* **1** the act or process of going, conveying, or being conveyed, esp. over a distance (*transit by rail*; *made a transit of the lake*). **2** a passage or route (*the overland transit*). **3 a** the apparent passage of a celestial body across the meridian of a place. **b** such an apparent passage across the sun or a planet. **4** the local conveyance of passengers on public transportation. ● *v.* (**transited, transiting**) **1** *tr.* make a transit across. **2** *intr.* make a transit. □ **in transit** while going or being conveyed.

tran·si·tion /tranzíshən, -síshən/ *n.* **1** a passing or change from one place, state, condition, etc., to another (*an age of transition*; *a transition from plains to hills*). **2** *Mus.* a momentary modulation. **3** *Art* a change from one style to another, esp. *Archit.* from Norman to Early English. □□ **tran·si·tion·al** *adj.* **tran·si·tion·al·ly** *adv.* **tran·si·tion·ar·y** *adj.*

TRANSISTOR

A transistor is an electric component used to control electric current and to provide amplification. A small change in the voltage applied between its base and emitter causes a large change in the current flowing from the collector to the emitter. In a radio, transistors amplify small voltages from the antenna to create the large currents needed to operate the loudspeaker.

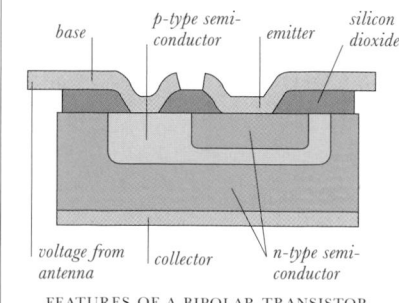

FEATURES OF A BIPOLAR TRANSISTOR

T

tran·si·tive /tránzitiv, -si-/ *adj. Gram.* (of a verb or sense of a verb) that takes a direct object (whether expressed or implied), e.g., *saw* in *saw the donkey, saw that she was ill* (opp. INTRANSITIVE). □□ **tran·si·tive·ly** *adv.* **tran·si·tive·ness** *n.* **tran·si·tiv·i·ty** /-tívitee/ *n.*

tran·si·to·ry /tránzitawree/ *adj.* not permanent; brief; transient. □□ **tran·si·to·ri·ly** /-táwrilee/ *adv.* **tran·si·to·ri·ness** /-táwreeniss/ *n.*

tran·sit vi·sa *n.* a visa allowing only passage through a country.

trans·late /tránzláyt, tráns-/ *v.* **1** *tr.* (also *absol.*) **a** (often foll. by *into*) express the sense of (a word, sentence, speech, book, etc.) in another language. **b** do this as a profession, etc. (*translates for the UN*). **2** *intr.* (of a literary work, etc.) be translatable; bear translation (*does not translate well*). **3** *tr.* express (an idea, book, etc.) in another, esp. simpler, form. **4** *tr.* interpret the significance of; infer as (*translated his silence as dissent*). **5** *tr.* move or change, esp. from one person, place, or condition, to another (*was translated by joy*). **6** *intr.* (foll. by *into*) result in; be converted into; manifest itself as. □□ **trans·lat·a·ble** *adj.* **trans·lat·a·bil·i·ty** /-laytəbílitee/ *n.*

trans·la·tion /tránzláyshən, tráns-/ *n.* **1** the act or an instance of translating. **2** a written or spoken expression of the meaning of a word, speech, book, etc., in another language. □□ **trans·la·tion·al** *adj.* **trans·la·tion·al·ly** *adv.*

trans·la·tor /tránzláytər, tráns-/ *n.* **1** a person who translates from one language into another. **2** a television relay transmitter. **3** a program that translates from one (esp. programming) language into another.

trans·lit·er·ate /tránzlítərayt, tráns-/ *v.tr.* represent (a word, etc.) in the closest corresponding letters or characters of a different alphabet or language. □□ **trans·lit·er·a·tion** /-ráyshən/ *n.* **trans·lit·er·a·tor** *n.*

trans·lo·cate /tránzlókayt, tráns-/ *v.tr.* move from one place to another. □□ **trans·lo·ca·tion** /-káyshən/ *n.*

trans·lu·cent /tránzlóōsənt, tráns-/ *adj.* **1** allowing light to pass through diffusely; semitransparent. **2** transparent. □□ **trans·lu·cence** *n.* **trans·lu·cen·cy** *n.* **trans·lu·cent·ly** *adv.*

trans·mi·grate /tránzmígrayt, tráns-/ *v.intr.* **1** (of the soul) pass into a different body; undergo metempsychosis. **2** migrate. □□ **trans·mi·gra·tion** /-gráyshən/ *n.* **trans·mi·gra·tor** *n.* **trans·mi·gra·to·ry** /-mígrətawree/ *adj.*

trans·mis·sion /tránzmíshən, tráns-/ *n.* **1** the act or an instance of transmitting; the state of being transmitted. **2** a broadcast radio or television program. **3** the mechanism by which power is transmitted from an engine to the axle in a motor vehicle.

trans·mit /tránzmít, tráns-/ *v.tr.* (**transmitted, transmitting**) **1 a** pass or hand on; transfer (*transmitted the message; how diseases are transmitted*). **b** communicate (ideas, emotions, etc.). **2 a** allow (heat, light, sound, electricity, etc.) to pass through; be a medium for. **b** be a medium for (ideas, emotions, etc.) (*his message transmits hope*). **3** broadcast (a radio or television program). □□ **trans·mis·si·ble** /-mísəbəl/ *adj.* **trans·mis·sive** /-mísiv/ *adj.* **trans·mit·ta·ble** *adj.* **trans·mit·tal** *n.*

trans·mit·ter /tránzmítər, tráns-/ *n.* **1** a person or thing that transmits. **2** a set of equipment used to generate and transmit electromagnetic waves carrying messages, signals, etc., esp. those of radio or television. **3** = NEUROTRANSMITTER.

trans·mog·ri·fy /tránzmógrifī, tráns-/ *v.tr.* (**-ies, -ied**) *joc.* transform, esp. in a magical or surprising manner. □□ **trans·mog·ri·fi·ca·tion** /-fikáyshən/ *n.*

trans·mon·tane /transmóntayn, tranz-/ *adj.* = TRAMONTANE.

trans·mute /tranzmyóōt, tráns-/ *v.tr.* **1** change the form, nature, or substance of. **2** *Alchemy hist.* subject (base metals) to the supposed process of changing base metals into gold. □□ **trans·mut·a·ble** *adj.* **trans·mut·a·bil·i·ty** /-təbílitee/ *n.* **trans·mu·ta-**

tion *n.* **trans·mu·ta·tive** /-myóōtətiv/ *adj.* **trans·mut·er** *n.*

trans·na·tion·al /tránznáshənəl, tráns-/ *adj.* extending beyond national boundaries.

trans·o·ce·an·ic /tránzóshiánik, tráns-/ *adj.* **1** situated beyond the ocean. **2** concerned with crossing the ocean (*transoceanic flight*).

tran·som /tránsəm/ *n.* **1** a horizontal bar of wood or stone across a window or the top of a door (cf. MULLION). ▷ WINDOW. **2** each of several beams fixed across the sternpost of a ship. **3** a beam across a saw pit to support a log. **4** a strengthening crossbar. **5** = TRANSOM WINDOW. □□ **tran·somed** *adj.*

tran·som win·dow *n.* **1** a window divided by a transom. **2** a window placed above the transom of a door or larger window; a fanlight.

tran·son·ic /transónik/ *adj.* (also **trans·son·ic**) relating to speeds close to that of sound.

trans·par·ence /tranzpárəns, traanz-, -páirəns/ *n.* = TRANSPARENCY.

trans·par·en·cy /tranzpárənsee, -páirənsee, tráns-/ *n.* (*pl.* **-ies**) **1** the condition of being transparent. **2** *Photog.* a positive transparent photograph on glass or in a frame to be viewed using a slide projector, etc. **3** a picture, inscription, etc., made visible by a light behind it.

trans·par·ent /tranzpáirənt, -párənt, tráns-/ *adj.* **1** allowing light to pass through so that bodies can be distinctly seen (cf. TRANSLUCENT). **2 a** (of a disguise, pretext, etc.) easily seen through. **b** (of a motive, quality, etc.) easily discerned; evident; obvious. **3** (of a person, etc.) easily understood; frank; open. □□ **trans·par·ent·ly** *adv.* **trans·par·ent·ness** *n.*

tran·spire /transpír/ *v.* **1** *intr.* (of a secret or something unknown) leak out; come to be known. **2** *intr. disp.* **a** (prec. by *it* as subject) turn out; prove to be the case (*it transpired he knew nothing about it*). **b** occur; happen. **3** *tr. & intr.* emit (vapor, sweat, etc.), or be emitted, through the skin or lungs; perspire. **4** *intr.* ▼ (of a plant or leaf) release water vapor. □□ **tran·spir·a·ble** *adj.* **tran·spi·ra·tion** /-spiráyshən/ *n.* **tran·spir·a·to·ry** /-spírətawree/ *adj.*

trans·plant *v. & n.* ● *v.tr.* /tranzplánt, tráns-/ **1 a** plant in another place (*transplanted the daffodils*). **b** move to another place (*whole nations were transplanted*). **2** *Surgery* transfer (living tissue or an organ)

and implant in another part of the body or in another body. ● *n.* /tránzplant, tráns-/ **1** *Surgery* **a** the transplanting of an organ or tissue. **b** such an organ, etc. **2** a thing, esp. a plant, transplanted. □□ **trans·plant·a·ble** *adj.* **trans·plan·ta·tion** /-táyshən/ *n.* **trans·plant·er** *n.*

tran·spon·der /tranzpóndər, tráns-/ *n.* a device for receiving a radio signal and automatically transmitting a different signal. ▷ RADAR

trans·pon·tine /tránzpóntīn, tráns-/ *adj.* on the other side of a bridge, esp. *Brit.* on the south side of the Thames.

trans·port *v. & n.* ● *v.tr.* /tranzpáwrt, tráns-/ **1** take or carry (a person, goods, troops, baggage, etc.) from one place to another. **2** *hist.* take (a criminal) to a penal colony; deport. **3** (as **transported** *adj.*) (usu. foll. by *with*) affected with strong emotion. ● *n.* /tránzpawrt, tráns-/ **1 a** a system of conveying people, goods, etc., from place to place. **b** esp. *Brit.* the means of this (*our transport has arrived*). **2** a ship, aircraft, etc., used to carry soldiers, stores, etc. **3** (esp. in *pl.*) vehement emotion (*transports of joy*).

trans·port·a·ble /tranzpáwrtəbəl, tráns-/ *adj.* **1** capable of being transported. **2** *hist.* (of an offender or an offense) punishable by transportation. □□ **trans·port·a·bil·i·ty** /-bílitee/ *n.*

trans·por·ta·tion /tránzpərtáyshən, tráns-/ *n.* **1** the act of conveying or the process of being conveyed. **2 a** a system of conveying. **b** the means of this. **3** *hist.* removal to a penal colony.

trans·port·er /tránzpáwrtər, tráns-/ *n.* **1** a person or device that transports. **2** a vehicle used to transport other vehicles or large pieces of machinery, etc., by road.

trans·pose /tranzpóz, tráns-/ *v.tr.* **1 a** cause (two or more things) to change places. **b** change the position of (a thing) in a series. **2** change the order or position of (words or a word) in a sentence. **3** *Mus.* write or play in a different key. **4** *Algebra* transfer (a term) with a changed sign to the other side of an equation. □□ **trans·pos·a·ble** *adj.* **trans·pos·al** *n.* **trans·pos·er** *n.*

trans·po·si·tion /tránzpəzíshən, tráns-/ *n.* the act or an instance of transposing; the state of being transposed. □□ **trans·po·si·tion·al** *adj.* **trans·pos·i·tive** /-pózitiv/ *adj.*

trans·sex·u·al /tránsékshóōəl/ *adj. & n.* ● *adj.* having the physical characteristics of one sex and the supposed psychological characteristics of the other. ● *n.* **1** a transsexual person. **2** a person whose sex has been changed by surgery. □□ **trans·sex·u·al·ism** *n.*

trans·ship /tranz-ship, tráns-/ *v.tr.* (also **tran·ship**) *intr.* (**-shipped, -shipping**) transfer from one ship or form of transport to another. □□ **trans·ship·ment** *n.*

trans·son·ic var. of TRANSONIC.

tran·sub·stan·ti·a·tion /tránsəbstánsheeáyshən/ *n. Theol. & RC Ch.* the conversion of the Eucharistic elements wholly into the body and blood of Christ, only the appearance of bread and wine still remaining.

trans·u·ran·ic /tránzyōōránik, tráns-/ *adj. Chem.* (of an element) having a higher atomic number than uranium.

trans·ver·sal /tranzvársəl, tráns-/ *adj. & n.* ● *adj.* (of a line) crossing a system of lines. ● *n.* a transversal line. □□ **trans·ver·sal·i·ty** /-sálitee/ *n.* **trans·ver·sal·ly** *adv.*

trans·verse /tránzvórs, tráns-/ *adj.* situated, arranged, or acting in a crosswise direction. □□ **trans·verse·ly** *adv.*

trans·ves·tism /tranzvéstizəm, tráns-/ *n.* (also **trans·ves·ti·tism** /-véstitizəm/) the practice of wearing the clothes of the opposite sex, esp. as a sexual stimulus. □□ **trans·ves·tist** *n.*

trans·ves·tite /tranzvéstīt, tráns-/ *n.* a person given to transvestism.

trap /trap/ *n. & v.* ● *n.* **1 a** an enclosure or device, often baited, for catching animals, usu. by affording

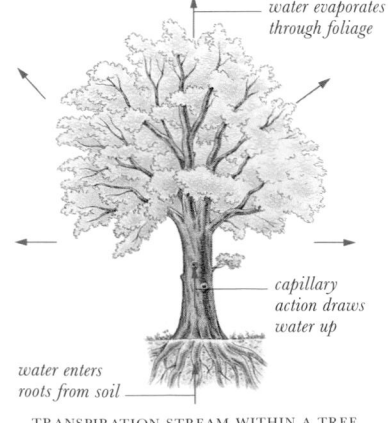

a way in but not a way out. **b** a device with bait for killing vermin, esp. = MOUSETRAP. **2** a trick betraying a person into speech or an act (*is this question a trap?*). **3** an arrangement to catch an unsuspecting person, e.g., a speeding motorist. **4** a device for hurling an object such as a clay pigeon into the air to be shot at. **5** a compartment from which a greyhound is released at the start of a race. **6** a shoe-shaped wooden device with a pivoted bar that sends a ball from its heel into the air on being struck at the other end with a bat. **7 a** a curve in a downpipe, etc., that fills with liquid and forms a seal against the upward passage of gases. **b** a device for preventing the passage of steam, etc. **8** *Golf* a bunker. **9** a device allowing pigeons to enter but not leave a loft. **10** a two-wheeled carriage (*a pony and trap*). **11** = TRAPDOOR. **12** *sl.* the mouth (esp. *shut one's trap*). **13** (esp. in *pl.*) *colloq.* a percussion instrument, esp. in a jazz band. ● *v.tr.* (**trapped**, **trapping**) **1** catch (an animal) in a trap. **2** catch (a person) by means of a trick, plan, etc. **3** stop and retain in or as in a trap. **4** provide (a place) with traps. □□ **trap·like** *adj.*

trap·door /trápdáwr/ *n.* a door or hatch in a floor, ceiling, or roof, usu. made flush with the surface.

tra·peze /trapéez/ *n.* a crossbar or set of crossbars suspended by ropes used as a swing for acrobatics, etc.

tra·pe·zi·um /trəpéezeeəm/ *n.* (*pl.* **trapezia** /-zeeə/ or **trapeziums**) **1** ► a quadrilateral with no two sides parallel. **2** *Brit.* = TRAPEZOID 1.

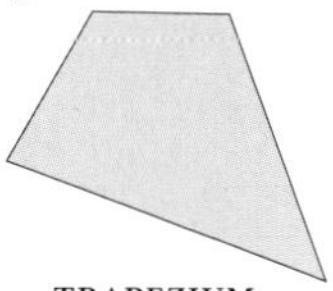

TRAPEZIUM

trap·e·zoid /trápizoyd/ *n.* **1** ◄ a quadrilateral with only one pair of sides parallel. **2** *Brit.* = TRAPEZIUM 1. □□ **trap·e·zoi·dal** *adj.*

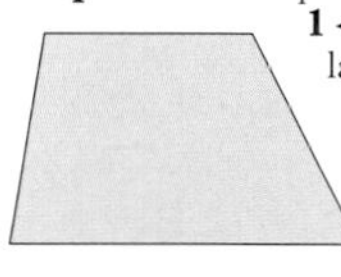

TRAPEZOID

trap·per /trápər/ *n.* a person who traps wild animals, esp. to obtain furs.

trap·pings /trápingz/ *n.pl.* **1** ornamental accessories, esp. as an indication of status (*the trappings of office*). **2** the harness of a horse, esp. when ornamental.

Trap·pist /trápist/ *n.* & *adj.* ● *n.* a member of a branch of the Cistercian order founded in 1664 at La Trappe in Normandy, France, and noted for an austere rule including a vow of silence. ● *adj.* of or relating to this order.

trash /trash/ *n.* & *v.* ● *n.* **1 a** a worthless writing, art, etc. **b** rubbish; refuse. **2** a worthless person or persons. **3** a thing of poor workmanship or material. ● *v.tr. colloq.* **1** wreck. **2** expose the worthless nature of; disparage. **3** throw away; discard.

trash talk *n.* & *v. US colloq.* ● *n.* insulting or boastful speech intended to demoralize, intimidate, or humiliate. ● *v.intr.* (**trash-talk**) use such speech.

trash·y /tráshee/ *adj.* (**trashier**, **trashiest**) worthless; poorly made. □□ **trash·i·ly** *adv.* **trash·i·ness** *n.*

trat·to·ri·a /trátəréeə/ *n.* an Italian restaurant.

trau·ma /trówmə, tráw-/ *n.* (*pl.* **traumata** /-mətə/ or **traumas**) **1** any physical wound or injury. **2** physical shock following this, characterized by a drop in body temperature, mental confusion, etc. **3** *Psychol.* emotional shock following a stressful event, sometimes leading to long-term neurosis. □□ **trau·ma·tize** *v.tr.* **trau·ma·ti·za·tion** *n.*

trau·mat·ic /trəmátik, trow-, traw-/ *adj.* **1** of or causing trauma. **2** *colloq.* (in general use) distressing; emotionally disturbing (*a traumatic experience*). **3** of or for wounds. □□ **trau·mat·i·cal·ly** *adv.*

tra·vail /trəváyl, trávayl/ *n.* & *v.* ● *n.* **1** painful or laborious effort. **2** labor pains. ● *v.intr.* undergo such painful effort.

trav·el /trávəl/ *v.* & *n.* ● *v.intr.* & *tr.* (**traveled**, **traveling** or **travelled**, **travelling**) **1** *intr.* go from one place to another; make a journey, esp. of some length or abroad. **2** *tr.* **a** journey along or through (a country). **b** cover (a distance) in traveling. **3** *intr. colloq.* withstand a long journey (*wines that do not travel*). **4** *intr.* go from place to place as a salesman. **5** *intr.* move or proceed in a specified manner or at a specified rate (*light travels faster than sound*). **6** *intr. colloq.* move quickly. **7** *intr.* pass esp. in a deliberate or systematic manner from point to point (*the photographer's eye traveled over the scene*). **8** *intr.* (of a machine or part) move or operate in a specified way. ● *n.* **1 a** the act of traveling, esp. in foreign countries. **b** (often in *pl.*) a time or occurrence of this (*have returned from their travels*). **2** the range, rate, or mode of motion of a part in machinery. □□ **trav·el·ing** *adj.*

trav·el a·gen·cy *n.* (also **trav·el bu·reau**) an agency that makes the necessary arrangements for travelers. □□ **trav·el a·gent** *n.*

trav·eled /trávəld/ *adj.* experienced in traveling (also in *comb.*: *much traveled*).

trav·el·er /trávələr, trávlər/ *n.* **1** a person who travels or is traveling. **2** a Gypsy.

trav·el·er's check *n.* a check for a fixed amount that may be cashed on signature, usu. internationally.

trav·el·ing sales·man *n.* a person who travels to solicit orders as a representative of a company, etc.

trav·el·ing wave *n.* *Physics* a wave in which the medium moves in the direction of propagation.

trav·e·logue /trávəlog/ *n.* (also **trav·e·log**) a movie or illustrated lecture about travel.

trav·erse /trávərs, trəvə́rs/ *v.* & *n.* ● *v.* **1** *tr.* travel or lie across (*traversed the country*; *a pit traversed by a beam*). **2** *tr.* consider or discuss the whole extent of (a subject). **3** *tr.* turn (a large gun) horizontally. **4** *tr.* thwart, frustrate, or oppose (a plan or opinion). **5** *intr.* (of the needle of a compass, etc.) turn on or as on a pivot. **6** *intr.* (of a horse) walk obliquely. **7** *intr.* make a traverse in climbing. ● *n.* **1** a sideways movement. **2** an act of traversing. **3** a thing, esp. part of a structure, that crosses another. **4** a gallery extending from side to side of a church or other building. **5 a** a single line of survey, usu. plotted from compass bearings and with chained or paced distances between angular points. **b** a tract surveyed in this way. **6** *Naut.* a zigzag line taken by a ship because of contrary winds or currents. **7** a skier's similar movement on a slope. **8** the sideways movement of a part in a machine. **9 a** a sideways motion across a rock face from one practicable line of ascent or descent to another. **b** a place where this is necessary. □□ **tra·vers·a·ble** *adj.* **tra·vers·al** *n.* **tra·vers·er** *n.*

trav·er·tine /trávərteen/ *n.* a white or light-colored calcareous rock deposited from springs.

trav·es·ty /trávistee/ *n.* & *v.* ● *n.* (*pl.* **-ies**) a grotesque misrepresentation or imitation (*a travesty of justice*). ● *v.tr.* (**-ies**, **-ied**) make or be a travesty of.

tra·vois /trəvóy/ *n.* (*pl.* same /-vóyz/) a vehicle of two joined poles pulled by a horse, etc., for carrying a burden, orig. used by Native American people of the Plains.

trawl /trawl/ *v.* & *n.* ● *v.* **1** *intr.* **a** fish with a trawl or seine. **b** seek a suitable candidate, etc., by sifting through a large number. **2** *tr.* **a** catch by trawling. **b** seek a suitable candidate, etc., from (a certain area or group, etc.). ● *n.* **1** an act of trawling. **2** (in full **trawl net**) ▼ a large wide-mouthed fishing net dragged by a boat along the bottom. **3** (in full **trawl line**) a long sea fishing line buoyed and supporting short lines with baited hooks.

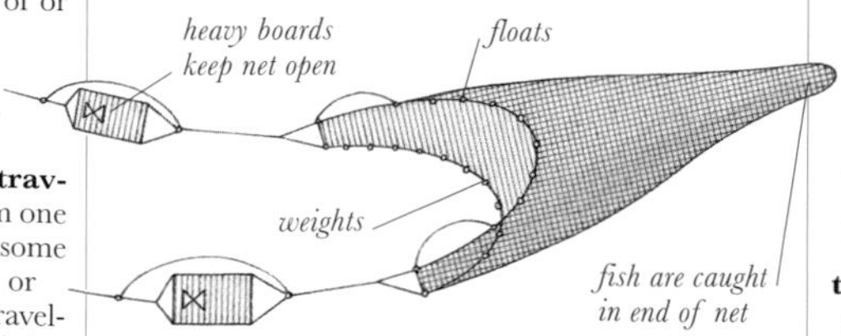
heavy boards keep net open
floats
weights
fish are caught in end of net

TRAWL NET

trawl·er /tráwlər/ *n.* **1** a boat used for trawling. **2** a person who trawls.

tray /tray/ *n.* **1** a flat shallow vessel usu. with a raised rim for carrying dishes, etc., or containing small articles, papers, etc. **2** a shallow lidless box forming a compartment of a trunk. □□ **tray·ful** *n.* (*pl.* **-fuls**).

treach·er·ous /tréchərəs/ *adj.* **1** guilty of or involving treachery. **2** (of the weather, ice, the memory, etc.) not to be relied on; likely to fail or give way. □□ **treach·er·ous·ly** *adv.* **treach·er·ous·ness** *n.*

treach·er·y /trécharee/ *n.* (*pl.* **-ies**) **1** violation of faith or trust; betrayal. **2** an instance of this.

trea·cle /tréekəl/ *n.* **1** esp. *Brit.* **a** a syrup produced in refining sugar. **b** molasses. **2** cloying sentimentality or flattery. □□ **trea·cly** *adj.*

tread /tred/ *v.* & *n.* ● *v.* (**trod** /trod/; **trodden** /tród'n/ or **trod**) **1** *intr.* (often foll. by *on*) **a** set down one's foot; walk or step (*do not tread on the grass*; *trod on a snail*). **b** (of the foot) be set down. **2** *tr.* **a** walk on. **b** (often foll. by *down*) press or crush with the feet. **3** *tr.* perform (steps, etc.) by walking (*trod a few paces*). **4** *tr.* make (a hole, etc.) by treading. **5** *intr.* (foll. by *on*) suppress; subdue mercilessly. **6** *tr.* make a track with (dirt, etc.) from the feet. **7** *tr.* (often foll. by *in*, *into*) press down into the ground with the feet (*trod dirt into the carpet*). **8** *tr.* (also *absol.*) (of a male bird) copulate with (a hen). ● *n.* **1** a manner or sound of walking. **2** the top surface of a step or stair. **3** the thick molded part of a vehicle tire for gripping the road. ▷ TIRE. **4 a** the part of a wheel that touches the ground or rail. **b** the part of a rail that the wheels touch. **5** the part of the sole of a shoe that rests on the ground. **6** (of a male bird) copulation. □ **tread the boards** (or **stage**) be or become an actor; appear on the stage. **tread on a person's toes** offend a person or encroach on a person's privileges, etc. **tread water** maintain an upright position in the water by moving the feet with a walking movement and the hands with a downward circular motion. □□ **tread·er** *n.*

trea·dle /trédəl/ *n.* & *v.* ● *n.* a lever worked by the foot and imparting motion to a machine. ● *v.intr.* work a treadle.

tread·mill /trédmil/ *n.* **1** a device for producing motion by the weight of persons or animals stepping on movable steps on the inner surface of a revolving upright wheel. **2** monotonous routine work.

trea·son /tréezən/ *n.* violation by a subject of allegiance to the sovereign or to the nation, esp. by attempting to kill or overthrow the sovereign or to overthrow the government. □□ **trea·son·ous** *adj.*

trea·son·a·ble /tréezənəbəl/ *adj.* involving or guilty of treason. □□ **trea·son·a·bly** *adv.*

treas·ure /trézhər/ *n.* & *v.* ● *n.* **1 a** precious metals or gems. **b** a hoard of these. **c** accumulated wealth. **2** a thing valued for its rarity, workmanship, associations, etc. (*art treasures*). **3** *colloq.* a much loved or highly valued person. ● *v.tr.* **1** (often foll. by *up*) store up as valuable. **2** value (esp. a long-kept possession) highly.

T

treas·ure hunt *n.* **1** a search for treasure. **2** a game in which players seek a hidden object from a series of clues.

treas·ur·er /trézhərər/ *n.* **1** a person appointed to administer the funds of a society or municipality, etc. **2** an officer authorized to receive and disburse public revenues. □□ **treas·ur·er·ship** *n.*

treas·ure trove *n.* **1** *Law* treasure of unknown ownership found hidden. **2** a hidden store of valuables.

treas·ur·y /trézharee/ *n.* (*pl.* **-ies**) **1** a place or building where treasure is stored. **2** the funds or revenue of a nation, institution, or society. **3** (**Treasury**) **a** the department managing the public revenue of a country. **b** the offices and officers of this. **c** the place where the public revenues are kept.

treas·ur·y bill *n.* a bill of exchange issued by the government to raise money for temporary needs. ¶ Abbr.: **T-bill**.

TREE

Trees are adapted for growth in a wide range of environmental conditions. Conifers typically occupy habitats that have cold winters, although a few grow in the Tropics. Their framework minimizes snow damage, while their small evergreen leaves withstand drying winds. Broadleaved trees generally grow in regions with warmer climates and regular rainfall. Temperate species are often deciduous, although in the Tropics many are evergreen. Some of the families are represented here.

EXAMPLES OF CONIFEROUS TREES

CUPRESSACEAE
sawara cypress
(*Chamaecyparis pisifera*)

PINACEAE
bishop pine
(*Pinus muricata*)

TAXODIACEAE
Japanese cedar
(*Cryptomeria japonica*)

EXAMPLES OF BROADLEAVED TREES

ACERACEAE
sycamore maple
(*Acer pseudoplatanus*)

BETULACEAE
gray birch
(*Betula populifolia*)

BIGNONIACEAE
western catalpa
(*Catalpa speciosa*)

ERICACEAE
madroña
(*Arbutus menziesii*)

FAGACEAE
black oak
(*Quercus velutina*)

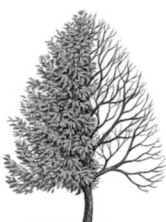

LAURACEAE
California bay
(*Umbellularia californica*)

FABACEAE
black locust
(*Robinia pseudoacacia*)

MAGNOLIACEAE
Kobus magnolia
(*Magnolia kobus*)

MELIACEAE
Chinese cedrela
(*Toona sinensis*)

MYRTACEAE
mountain gum
(*Eucalyptus dalrympleana*)

OLEACEAE
white ash
(*Fraxinus americana*)

ARECACEAE
Chusan palm
(*Trachycarpus fortunei*)

PLATANACEAE
Sycamore
(*Platanus occidentalis*)

ROSACEAE
Higan cherry
(*Prunus* x *subhirtella*)

RUTACEAE
hop tree
(*Ptelea trifoliata*)

SALICACEAE
Weeping willow
(*Salix babylonica*)

STYRACACEAE
silverbell
(*Halesia carolina*)

THEACEAE
silky stewartis
(*Stewartia malacodendron*)

TILIACEAE
silver linden
(*Tilia tomentosa*)

ULMACEAE
hackberry
(*Celtis occidentalis*)

T

treat /treet/ *v. & n.* ● *v.* **1** *tr.* act or behave toward or deal with (a person or thing) in a certain way. **2** *tr.* deal with or apply a process to; act upon to obtain a particular result (*treat it with acid*). **3** *tr.* apply medical care or attention to. **4** *tr.* present or deal with (a subject) in literature or art. **5** *tr.* (often foll. by *to*) provide with food or drink or entertainment, esp. at one's own expense (*treated us to dinner*). **6** *intr.* (often foll. by *with*) negotiate terms (with a person). ● *n.* **1** an event or circumstance (esp. when unexpected or unusual) that gives great pleasure. **2** a meal, entertainment, etc., provided by one person for the enjoyment of another or others. **3** *Brit.* (prec. by *a*) extremely good or well (*they looked a treat; has come on a treat*). □□ **treat·a·ble** *adj.* **treat·er** *n.* **treat·ing** *n.*

trea·tise /tréetis/ *n.* a written work dealing formally and systematically with a subject.

treat·ment /tréetmənt/ *n.* **1** a process or manner of behaving toward or dealing with a person or thing (*received rough treatment*). **2** the application of medical care or attention to a patient. **3** a manner of treating a subject in literature or art. **4** (prec. by *the*) *colloq.* the customary way of dealing with a person, situation, etc. (*got the full treatment*).

trea·ty /tréetee/ *n.* (*pl.* **-ies**) **1** a formally concluded and ratified agreement between nations. **2** an agreement between individuals or parties, esp. for the purchase of property.

tre·ble /trébəl/ *adj., n., & v.* ● *adj.* **1 a** threefold. **b** triple. **c** three times as much or many (*treble the amount*). **2** (of a voice) high-pitched. **3** *Mus.* = SOPRANO (esp. of an instrument or with ref. to a boy's voice). ● *n.* **1** a treble quantity or thing. **2** *Darts* a hit on the narrow ring enclosed by the two middle circles of a dartboard, scoring treble. **3 a** *Mus.* = SOPRANO (esp. a boy's voice or part, or an instrument). **b** a high-pitched voice. **4** the high-frequency output of a radio, record player, etc., corresponding to the treble in music. ● *v.* **1** *tr. & intr.* make or become three times as much or many; increase threefold; multiply by three. **2** *tr.* amount to three times as much as. □□ **tre·bly** *adv.* (in sense 1 of *adj.*).

tre·ble clef *n.* a clef placing G above middle C on the second lowest line of the staff. ▷ NOTATION

tre·ble rhyme *n.* a rhyme including three syllables.

treb·u·chet /trébyŏŏshét/ *n.* (also **tre·buck·et** /trébəkit, trebyŏŏkét/) *hist.* **1** a military machine used in siege warfare for throwing stones, etc. **2** a tilting balance for accurately weighing light articles.

tre·cen·to /traychéntō/ *n.* the style of Italian art and literature of the 14th c. □□ **tre·cen·tist** *n.*

tree /tree/ *n.* **1 a** ◄ a perennial plant with a woody self-supporting main stem or trunk when mature and usu. unbranched for some distance above the ground (cf. SHRUB). **b** any similar plant having a tall erect usu. single stem, e.g., palm tree. **2** a piece or frame of wood, etc., for various purposes (*shoe tree*). □□ **tree·less** *adj.* **tree·less·ness** *n.* **tree·like** *adj.*

tree·creep·er /tréekreepər/ *n.* ◄ any small creeping bird, esp. of the family Certhiidae, feeding on insects in the bark of trees.

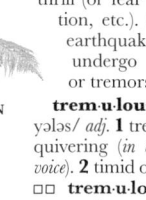

TREECREEPER: COMMON TREECREEPER (*Certhia familiaris*)

tree fern *n.* ▶ a large fern with an upright trunk-like stem.

tree frog *n.* any arboreal tailless amphibian, esp. of the family Hylidae, climbing by means of adhesive pads on its digits.

tree house *n.* a structure in a tree for children to play in.

tree-hug·ger *n. colloq.*, chiefly *derog.* an environmental campaigner (used in reference to the practice of embracing a tree to prevent it from being felled).

treen /treen/ *n.* (treated as *pl.*) small domestic wooden objects, esp. antiques.

TREE FERN (*Dicksonia antarctica*)

---

tree ring *n.* a ring in a cross section of a tree, from one year's growth. ▷ DENDROCHRONOLOGY

tree sur·geon *n.* a person who treats decayed trees in order to preserve them. □□ **tree sur·ger·y** *n.*

tree toad *n.* = TREE FROG.

tree·top /tréetop/ *n.* the topmost part of a tree.

tref /tráyf/ *adj.* (also **trefa** /tráyfə/ and other variants) not kosher.

tre·foil /tréefoyl, tréf-/ *n. & adj.* ● *n.* **1** any leguminous plant of the genus *Trifolium*, with leaves of three leaflets and flowers of various colors, esp. clover. **2** any plant with similar leaves. **3** a three-lobed ornamentation, esp. in tracery windows. **4** a thing arranged in or with three lobes. ● *adj.* of or concerning a three-lobed plant, window tracery, etc. ▷ ARCH. □□ **tre·foiled** *adj.* (also in *comb.*).

trek /trek/ *v. & n.* ● *v.intr.* (**trekked, trekking**) **1** travel or make one's way arduously (*trekking through the forest*). **2** esp. *S. Afr. hist.* migrate or journey with one's belongings by ox wagon. ● *n.* **1 a a** journey or walk made by trekking. **b** each stage of such a journey. **2** an organized migration of a body of persons. □□ **trek·ker** *n.*

trel·lis /trélis/ *n. & v.* ● *n.* (in full **trelliswork**) ▶ a lattice or grating of light wooden or metal bars used esp. as a support for fruit trees or creepers and often fastened against a wall. ● *v.tr.* (**trel·lised, trellising**) **1** provide with a trellis. **2** support (a vine, etc.) with a trellis.

TRELLISWORK SUPPORTING A CLIMBER

trem·a·tode /trémətōd, trée-/ *n.* any parasitic flatworm of the class Trematoda, esp. a fluke, equipped with hooks or suckers, e.g., a liver fluke.

trem·ble /trémbəl/ *v. & n.* ● *v.intr.* **1** shake involuntarily from fear, excitement, weakness, etc. **2** be in a state of extreme apprehension (*trembled at the very thought of it*). **3** move in a quivering manner (*leaves trembled in the breeze*). ● *n.* a trembling state or movement; a quiver (*couldn't speak without a tremble*). □□ **trem·bling·ly** *adv.*

trem·bling pop·lar *n.* a European aspen.

trem·bly /trémblee/ *adj.* (**tremblier, trembliest**) *colloq.* trembling; agitated.

tre·men·dous /triméndəs/ *adj.* **1** awe inspiring; fearful; overpowering. **2** *colloq.* remarkable; considerable; excellent (*a tremendous explosion; gave a tremendous performance*). □□ **tre·men·dous·ly** *adv.*

trem·o·lo /tréməlō/ *n. Mus.* **1** a tremulous effect in playing stringed and keyboard instruments or singing, esp. by rapid reiteration of a note; in other instruments, by rapid alternation between two notes (cf. VIBRATO). **2** a device in an organ producing a tremulous effect.

trem·or /trémər/ *n. & v.* ● *n.* **1** a shaking or quivering. **2** a thrill (of fear or exultation, etc.). **3** a slight earthquake. ● *v.intr.* undergo a tremor or tremors.

trem·u·lous /trémyələs/ *adj.* **1** trembling or quivering (*in a tremulous voice*). **2** timid or nervous. □□ **trem·u·lous·ly** *adv.* **trem·u·lous·ness** *n.*

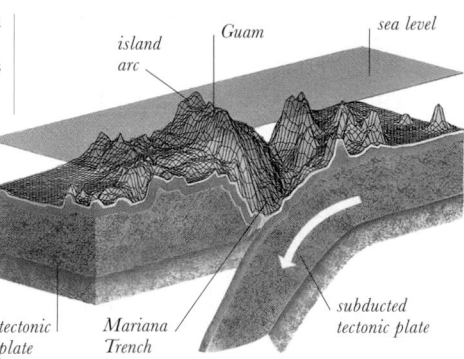

island arc   Guam   sea level

tectonic plate   Mariana Trench   subducted tectonic plate

TRENCH: FORMATION OF THE MARIANA TRENCH IN THE PACIFIC OCEAN

trench /trench/ *n. & v.* ● *n.* **1** a long, narrow, usu. deep depression or ditch. **2** *Mil.* **a** this dug by troops to stand in and be sheltered from enemy fire. **b** (in *pl.*) a defensive system of these. **3** ▲ a long narrow deep depression in the ocean bed. ▷ SEABED. ● *v.tr.* dig a trench or trenches in (the ground).

trench·ant /trénchənt/ *adj.* **1** (of a style or language, etc.) incisive; terse; vigorous. **2** *archaic* or *poet.* sharp; keen. □□ **trench·an·cy** *n.* **trench·ant·ly** *adv.*

trench coat *n.* **1** a soldier's lined or padded waterproof coat. **2** ▶ a loose belted raincoat.

trench·er /trénchər/ *n. hist.* a wooden or earthenware platter for serving food.

trench·er·man /trénchərmən/ *n.* (*pl.* **-men**) a person who eats well, or in a specified manner (*a good trencherman*).

TRENCH COAT

trench foot *n.* a painful condition of the feet caused by long immersion in cold water or mud and marked by blackening and death of surface tissue.

trench war·fare *n.* hostilities carried on from more or less permanent trenches.

trend /trend/ *n. & v.* ● *n.* a general direction and tendency (esp. of events, fashion, or opinion, etc.). ● *v.intr.* **1** bend or turn in a specified direction. **2** have a general and continued tendency.

trend·set·ter /tréndsetər/ *n.* a person who leads the way in fashion, etc. □□ **trend·set·ting** *adj.*

trend·y /tréndee/ *adj. & n. colloq.* ● *adj.* (**trendier, trendiest**) very fashionable. ● *n.* (*pl.* **-ies**) a fashionable person. □□ **trend·i·ly** *adv.* **trend·i·ness** *n.*

tre·pan /tripán/ *n. & v.* ● *n.* **1** a cylindrical saw formerly used by surgeons for perforating the skull. **2** a borer for sinking shafts. ● *v.tr.* (**trepanned, trepanning**) perforate (the skull) with a trepan. □□ **trep·a·na·tion** /trépənáyshən/ *n.*

tre·pang /tripáng/ *n.* a kind of sea cucumber eaten in China, usu. in long dried strips.

trep·i·da·tion /trépidáyshən/ *n.* a feeling of anxious fear or agitation.

tres·pass /tréspəs, -pas/ *v. & n.* ● *v.intr.* **1** (usu. foll. by *on, upon*) make an unlawful or unwarrantable intrusion (esp. on land or property). **2** (foll. by *on*) make unwarrantable claims (*shall not trespass on your hospitality*). **3** (foll. by *against*) *literary* or *archaic* offend. ● *n.* **1** *Law* a voluntary wrongful act against the person or property of another, esp. unlawful entry to a person's land or property. **2** *archaic* a sin or offense. □□ **tres·pass·er** *n.*

T

tress /tres/ *n.* **1** a long lock of human (esp. female) hair. **2** (in *pl.*) a woman's or girl's head of hair. □□ **tressed** *adj.* (also in *comb.*).

tres·tle /trésəl/ *n.* **1** a supporting structure for a table, etc., consisting of two frames fixed at an angle or hinged or of a bar supported by two divergent pairs of legs. **2** (in full **trestle table**) a table consisting of a board or boards laid on trestles or other supports. **3** (also **trestlework**) an open braced framework to support a bridge, etc.

tre·val·ly /trəválee/ *n.* (*pl.* **-ies**) ▼ any Australian fish of the genus *Caranx*, used as food.

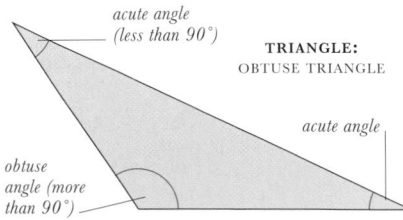

TREVALLY
(*Caranx hippos*)

trews /trōōz/ *n.pl.* esp. *Brit.* trousers, esp. close-fitting tartan trousers worn by women.

tri·ad /trī́ad/ *n.* **1** a group of three (esp. notes in a chord). **2** the number three. **3** a Chinese secret society, usu. criminal. □□ **tri·ad·ic** *adj.* **tri·ad·i·cal·ly** *adv.*

tri·age /tree-aázh, trée-aazh/ *n.* **1** the act of sorting according to quality. **2** the assignment of degrees of urgency to decide the order of treatment of wounds, illnesses, etc.

tri·al /trī́əl/ *n.* **1** a judicial examination and determination of issues between parties by a judge with or without a jury (*stood trial for murder*). **2 a** a process or mode of testing qualities. **b** experimental treatment. **c** a test (*will give you a trial*). **d** an attempt. **e** (*attrib.*) experimental. **3** a trying thing or experience or person, esp. hardship or trouble (*the trials of old age*). **4** a preliminary contest to test the ability of players eligible for selection to a team, etc. **5** *Brit.* a test of individual ability on a motorcycle over rough ground or on a road. **6** any of various contests involving performance by horses, dogs, or other animals. □ **on trial 1** being tried in a court of law. **2** being tested; to be chosen or retained only if suitable.

tri·al and er·ror *n.* repeated (usu. varied and unsystematic) attempts or experiments continued until successful.

tri·al run *n.* a preliminary test of a vehicle, vessel, machine, etc.

tri·an·gle /trī́anggəl/ *n.* **1** ▼ a plane figure with three sides and angles. ▷ HYPOTENUSE. **2** any three things not in a straight line, with imaginary lines joining them. **3** an implement of this shape. **4** a musical instrument consisting of a steel rod bent into a triangle and sounded by striking it with a smaller steel rod. ▷ ORCHESTRA, PERCUSSION. **5** a situation, esp. an emotional relationship, involving three people. **6** a right-angled triangle of wood, etc., as a drawing implement.

TRIANGLE:
OBTUSE TRIANGLE

acute angle
(*less than 90°*)

acute angle

obtuse angle (*more than 90°*)

tri·an·gu·lar /trīánggyələr/ *adj.* **1** triangle-shaped; three-cornered. **2** (of a contest or treaty, etc.) between three persons or parties. **3** (of a pyramid) having a three-sided base. □□ **tri·an·gu·lar·i·ty** /-láiritee/ *n.* **tri·an·gu·lar·ly** *adv.*

tri·an·gu·late *v.tr.* /trīánggyəlayt/ **1** divide (an area) into triangles for surveying purposes.

2 a measure and map (an area) by the use of triangles with a known base length and base angles. **b** determine (a height, distance, etc.) in this way. □□ **tri·an·gu·la·tion** /-láyshən/ *n.*

Tri·as·sic /trīásik/ *adj. & n. Geol.* ● *adj.* of or relating to the earliest period of the Mesozoic era with evidence of an abundance of reptiles (including the earliest dinosaurs) and the emergence of mammals. ● *n.* this period or system.

tri·ath·lon /trīáthlən, -lon/ *n.* an athletic contest consisting of three different events, esp. running, swimming, and bicycling. □□ **tri·ath·lete** /-leet/ *n.*

tri·a·tom·ic /trīətómik/ *adj. Chem* **1** having three atoms (of a specified kind) in the molecule. **2** having three replacement atoms or radicals.

tri·ax·i·al /trīákseeəl/ *adj.* having three axes.

trib. *abbr.* **1** tribunal. **2** tribune. **3** tributary.

trib·ade /tríbəd/ *n.* a lesbian. □□ **tri·bad·ism** *n.*

trib·al /tríbəl/ *adj.* of, relating to, or characteristic of a tribe or tribes. □□ **trib·al·ly** *adv.*

trib·al·ism /tríbəlizəm/ *n.* **1** tribal organization. **2** strong loyalty to one's tribe, group, etc. □□ **trib·al·ist** *n.* **trib·al·is·tic** *adj.*

tribe /trīb/ *n.* **1** a group of (esp. primitive) families or communities, linked by social, economic, religious, or blood ties, and usu. having a common culture and dialect, and a recognized leader. **2** any similar natural or political division. **3** *Rom. Hist.* each of the political divisions of the Roman people. **4** each of the 12 divisions of the Israelites. **5** a set or number of persons, esp. of one profession, etc., or family (*the whole tribe of actors*).

tribes·man /trī́bzmən/ *n.* (*pl.* **-men**) a member of a tribe or of one's own tribe.

tri·bo·e·lec·tric·i·ty /trī́bō-ilektrísitee, trib-/ *n.* the generation of an electric charge by friction.

tri·bol·o·gy /trībóləjee/ *n.* the study of friction, wear, lubrication, and the design of bearings; the science of interacting surfaces in relative motion. □□ **tri·bol·o·gist** *n.*

tri·bo·lu·mi·nes·cence /trī́bōlōōminésəns, trib-/ *n.* the emission of light from a substance when rubbed, scratched, etc. □□ **tri·bo·lu·mi·nes·cent** *adj.*

trib·u·la·tion /tríbyəláyshən/ *n.* **1** great affliction or oppression. **2** a cause of this (*was a real tribulation to me*).

tri·bu·nal /trībōōnəl, tri-/ *n.* **1** a board appointed to adjudicate in some matter, esp. one appointed by the government to investigate a matter of public concern. **2** a court of justice. **3** a seat or bench for a judge or judges. **4 a** a place of judgment. **b** judicial authority (*the tribunal of public opinion*).

trib·une[1] /tríbyōōn, tribyōon/ *n.* **1** a popular leader or demagogue. **2** (in full **tribune of the people**) an official in ancient Rome chosen by the people to protect their interests. **3** (in full **military tribune**) a Roman legionary officer. □□ **trib·u·nate** /-nət, -nayt/ *n.* **trib·une·ship** *n.*

trib·une[2] /tríbyōon, tribyōon/ *n.* **1** *Eccl.* **a** a bishop's throne in a basilica. **b** an apse containing this. **2** a dais or rostrum. **3** a raised area with seats.

trib·u·tar·y /tríbyəteree/ *n. & adj.* (*pl.* **-ies**) **1** a river or stream flowing into a larger river or lake. **2** *hist.* a person or nation paying or subject to tribute. ● *adj.* **1** (of a river, etc.) that is a tributary. **2** *hist.* **a** paying tribute. **b** serving as tribute. □□ **trib·u·tar·i·ly** /-táirilee/ *adv.* **trib·u·tar·i·ness** /-táireenis/ *n.*

trib·ute /tríbyōōt/ *n.* **1** a thing said or done or given as a mark of respect or affection, etc. (*paid tribute to their achievements*; *floral tributes*). **2** *hist.* a payment made periodically by one nation or ruler to another, esp. as a sign of dependence. **b** an obligation to pay this (*was paid under tribute*). **3** (foll. by *to*) an indication of (some praiseworthy quality) (*their success is a tribute to their perseverance*).

trice /trīs/ *n.* □ **in a trice** in a moment; instantly.

tri·cen·te·nar·y /trísenténəree/ *n.* (*pl.* **-ies**) = TERCENTENARY.

tri·ceps /trī́seps/ *adj. & n.* ● *adj.* (of a muscle) having three heads or points of attachment. ● *n.* ▶ any triceps muscle, esp. the large muscle at the back of the upper arm.

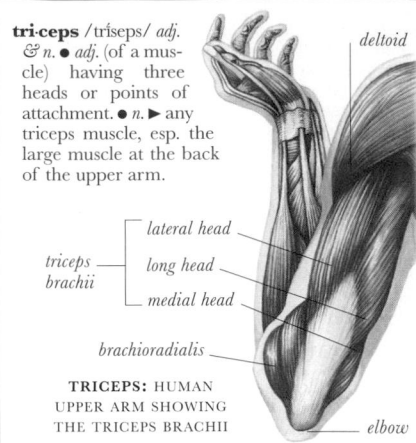

deltoid

lateral head

triceps brachii

long head

medial head

brachioradialis

TRICEPS: HUMAN UPPER ARM SHOWING THE TRICEPS BRACHII

elbow

tri·cer·a·tops /trísérətops/ *n.* ▼ a large quadrupedal plant-eating dinosaur of the late Cretaceous genus *Triceratops*, with two large horns, a smaller horn on the snout, and a bony frill above the neck. ▷ DINOSAUR

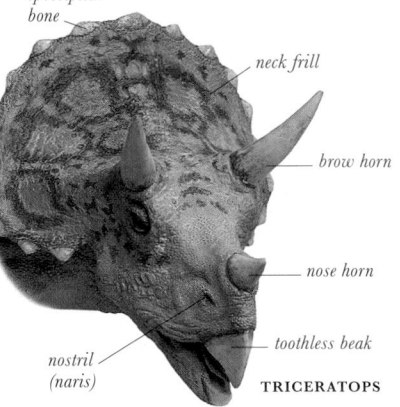

epoccipital bone

neck frill

brow horn

nose horn

nostril (naris)

toothless beak

TRICERATOPS

tri·chi·na /trikínə/ *n.* (*pl.* **trichinae** /-nee/) any hairlike parasitic nematode worm of the genus *Trichinella*, esp. *T. spiralis*, the adults of which live in the small intestine, and whose larvae become encysted in the muscle tissue of humans and carnivorous animals. □□ **trich·i·nous** *adj.*

trich·i·no·sis /tríkinósis/ *n.* a disease caused by trichinae, usu. ingested in meat, and characterized by digestive disturbance, fever, and muscular rigidity.

tri·chol·o·gy /trikóləjee/ *n.* the study of the structure, functions, and diseases of the hair. □□ **tri·chol·o·gist** *n.*

tri·chot·o·my /trīkótəmee/ *n.* (*pl.* **-ies**) a division (esp. sharply defined) into three categories, esp. of human nature into body, soul, and spirit. □□ **trich·o·tom·ic** /-kətómik/ *adj.*

tri·chro·ic /trīkróik/ *adj.* (esp. of a crystal viewed in different directions) showing three colors. □□ **tri·chro·ism** /tríkrō-izəm/ *n.*

tri·chro·mat·ic /tríkrəmátik/ *adj.* **1** having or using three colors. **2** (of vision) having the normal three color sensations, i.e., red, green, and blue. □□ **tri·chro·ma·tism** /-krómətizəm/ *n.*

trick /trik/ *n. & v.* ● *n.* **1** an action or scheme undertaken to fool, outwit, or deceive. **2** an optical or other illusion (*a trick of the light*). **3** a special technique; a knack or special way of doing something. **4 a** a feat of skill or dexterity. **b** an unusual action (e.g., begging) learned by an animal. **5** a mischievous, foolish, or discreditable act; a practical joke (*a mean trick to play*). **6** a peculiar or characteristic habit or mannerism (*has a trick of repeating himself*). **7 a** the cards played in a single round of a card game, usu. one from each player. **b** such a round. **c** a point gained as a result of this. **8** (*attrib.*) done to deceive

T

or mystify or to create an illusion (*trick photography*; *trick question*). **9** *Naut.* a sailor's turn at the helm, usu. two hours. **10 a** a prostitute's client. **b** a sexual act performed by a prostitute and a client. ● *v.tr.* **1** deceive by a trick; outwit. **2** (often foll. by *out of*, or *into* + verbal noun) cheat; treat deceitfully so as to deprive (*were tricked into agreeing*; *were tricked out of their savings*). **3** (of a thing) foil or baffle; take by surprise; disappoint the calculations of. □ **do the trick** *colloq.* accomplish one's purpose; achieve the required result. **not miss a trick** see MISS[1]. **trick out** (or **up**) dress, decorate, or deck out, esp. showily. **turn tricks** engage in prostitution. **up to one's tricks** *colloq.* misbehaving. **up to a person's tricks** aware of what a person is likely to do by way of mischief. □□ **trick·er** *n.* **trick·ish** *adj.* **trick·less** *adj.*

trick·er·y /tríkəree/ *n.* (*pl.* **-ies**) **1** the practice or an instance of deception. **2** the use of tricks.

trick·le /tríkəl/ *v. & n.* ● *v.* **1** *intr. & tr.* flow or cause to flow in drops or a small stream (*water trickled through the crack*). **2** *intr.* come or go slowly or gradually (*information trickles out*). ● *n.* a trickling flow.

trick or treat *n.* a children's custom of calling at houses at Halloween with the threat of pranks if they are not given candy.

trick·ster /tríkstər/ *n.* a deceiver or rogue.

trick·sy /tríksee/ *adj.* (**tricksier**, **tricksiest**) full of tricks; playful. □□ **trick·si·ly** *adv.* **trick·si·ness** *n.*

trick·y /tríkee/ *adj.* (**trickier**, **trickiest**) **1** difficult or intricate; requiring care and adroitness (*a tricky job*). **2** crafty or deceitful. **3** resourceful or adroit. □□ **trick·i·ly** *adv.* **trick·i·ness** *n.*

tri·clin·ic /trīklínik/ *adj.* **1** (of a mineral) having three unequal oblique axes. **2** denoting the system classifying triclinic crystalline substances.

tri·col·or /tríkulər/ *n. & adj.* ● *n.* ◄ a flag of three colors, esp. the French national flag of blue, white, and red. ● *adj.* (also **tri·col·ored**) having three colors.

TRICOLOR: FRENCH
NATIONAL FLAG

tri·corn /tríkawrn/ *adj.* (also **tri·corne**) **1** having three horns. **2** (of a hat) having a brim turned up on three sides.

tri·cot /treékō/ *n.* **1 a** a hand-knitted woolen fabric. **b** an imitation of this. **2** a ribbed woolen cloth.

tri·cy·cle /trísikəl/ *n.* **1** a vehicle having three wheels, two on an axle at the back and one at the front, driven by pedals in the same way as a bicycle. **2** a three-wheeled motor vehicle for a disabled driver. □□ **tri·cy·clist** *n.*

tri·dac·tyl /trīdáktil/ *adj.* (also **tri·dac·tyl·ous** /-dáktiləs/) having three fingers or toes.

tri·dent /tríd'nt/ *n.* **1** a three-pronged spear, esp. as an attribute of Poseidon (Neptune) or Britannia. **2** (**Trident**) a type of submarine-launched ballistic missile.

tri·den·tate /trīdéntayt/ *adj.* having three teeth or prongs.

Tri·den·tine /trīdéntin, -tīn, -teen/ *adj. & n.* ● *adj.* of or relating to the Council of Trent, held at Trento in Italy 1545–63, esp. as the basis of Roman Catholic doctrine. ● *n.* a Roman Catholic adhering to this traditional doctrine.

tried *past* and *past part.* of TRY.

tri·en·ni·al /trī-éneeəl/ *adj.* **1** lasting three years. **2** recurring every three years. □□ **tri·en·ni·al·ly** *adv.*

tri·en·ni·um /trī-éneeəm/ *n.* (*pl.* **trienniums** or **triennia** /-neeə/) a period of three years.

tri·er /tríər/ *n.* **1** a person who perseveres (*is a real trier*). **2** a tester, esp. of foodstuffs. **3** *Brit. Law* a person appointed to decide whether a challenge to a juror is well founded.

tri·fid /trífid/ *adj.* esp. *Biol.* partly or wholly split into three divisions or lobes.

tri·fle /trífəl/ *n. & v.* ● *n.* **1** a thing of slight value or importance. **2 a** a small amount, esp. of money (*was sold for a trifle*). **b** (prec. by *a*) somewhat (*seems a trifle annoyed*). **3** *Brit.* a confection of sponge cake with custard, jelly, fruit, cream, etc. ● *v.* **1** *intr.* talk or act frivolously. **2** *intr.* (foll. by *with*) **a** treat or deal with frivolously or derisively; flirt heartlessly with. **b** refuse to take seriously. **3** *tr.* (foll. by *away*) waste (time, energies, money, etc.) frivolously. □□ **tri·fler** *n.*

leaflet

tri·fling /trífling/ *adj.* **1** unimportant; petty. **2** frivolous. □□ **tri·fling·ly** *adv.*

tri·fo·cal /trīfốkəl/ *adj. & n.* ● *adj.* having three focuses, esp. of a lens with different focal lengths. ● *n.* (in *pl.*) trifocal eyeglasses.

tri·fo·li·ate /trīfốleeət/ *adj.* **1** ◄ (of a compound leaf) having three leaflets. **2** (of a plant) having such leaves.

tri·fo·ri·um /trīfáwreeəm/ *n.* (*pl.* **triforia** /-reeə/) ▼ a gallery or arcade above the arches of the nave, choir, and transepts of a church.

TRIFOLIATE
LEAF OF A
LABURNUM TREE

exterior flying buttress

triforium

roof space

aisle

nave

TRIFORIUM IN A LATE 12TH-CENTURY
FRENCH GOTHIC CHURCH

trig /trig/ *n. colloq.* trigonometry.

trig·ger /trígər/ *n. & v.* ● *n.* **1** a movable device for releasing a spring or catch and so setting off a mechanism (esp. that of a gun). ▷ GUN. **2** an event, occurrence, etc., that sets off a chain reaction. ● *v.tr.* **1** (often foll. by *off*) set (an action or process) in motion; initiate; precipitate. **2** fire (a gun) by the use of a trigger. □ **quick on the trigger** quick to respond. □□ **trig·gered** *adj.*

trig·ger·fish *n.* ► any usu. tropical marine fish of the family Balistidae with a first dorsal fin spine that can be depressed by pressing on the second.

trig·ger-hap·py *adj.* apt to shoot without or with slight provocation.

trig·o·nom·e·try /trigənómitree/ *n.* the branch of mathematics dealing with the relations of the sides and angles of triangles and with the relevant functions of any angles. □□ **trig·o·no·met·ric** /-nəmétrik/ *adj.* **trig·o·no·met·ri·cal** *adj.*

tri·graph /trígraf/ *n.* (also **tri·gram** /-gram/) **1** a group of three letters representing one sound. **2** a figure of three lines.

tri·he·dron /trīheédrən/ *n.* a figure of three intersecting planes.

trike /trīk/ *n. & v.intr. colloq.* tricycle.

tri·lat·er·al /trīlátərəl/ *adj.* **1** of, on, or with three

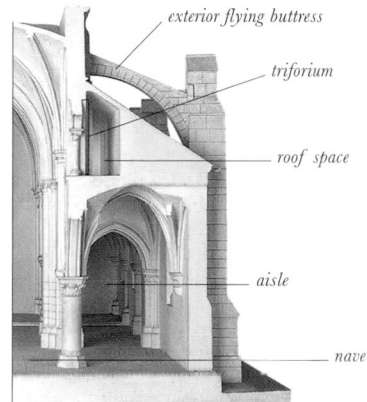

first dorsal fin

TRIGGERFISH: CLOWN TRIGGERFISH
(*Balistoides conspicillum*)

sides. **2** shared by or involving three parties, countries, etc. (*trilateral negotiations*).

tril·by /trílbee/ *n.* (*pl.* **-ies**) *Brit.* a soft felt hat with a narrow brim and indented crown. □□ **tril·bied** *adj.*

tri·lin·gual /trīlínggwəl/ *adj.* **1** able to speak three languages, esp. fluently. **2** spoken or written in three languages. □□ **tri·lin·gual·ism** *n.*

trill /tril/ *n. & v.* ● *n.* **1** a quavering or vibratory sound, esp. a rapid alternation of sung or played notes. **2** a bird's warbling sound. **3** the pronunciation of *r* with a vibration of the tongue. ● *v.* **1** *intr.* produce a trill. **2** *tr.* warble (a song) or pronounce (*r*, etc.) with a trill.

tril·lion /trílyən/ *n.* (*pl.* same or (in sense 3) **trillions**) **1** a million million (1,000,000,000,000 or 10^{12}). **2** esp. *Brit.* a million million million (1,000,000,000,000,000,000 or 10^{18}). **3** (in *pl.*) *colloq.* a very large number (*trillions of times*). □□ **tril·lionth** *adj. & n.*

tri·lo·bite /tríləbīt/ *n.* ► any fossil marine arthropod of the class Trilobita of Palaeozoic times, characterized by a three-lobed body.

head shield   *thorax*

tail shield

TRILOBITE
(*Paradoxides* species)

tril·o·gy /tríləjee/ *n.* (*pl.* **-ies**) a group of three related literary or operatic works.

trim /trim/ *v., n., & adj.* ● *v.* (**trimmed**, **trimming**) **1** *tr.* **a** set in good order. **b** make neat or of the required size or form, esp. by cutting away irregular or unwanted parts. **2** *tr.* (foll. by *off*, *away*) remove by cutting off (such parts). **3** *tr.* **a** (often foll. by *up*) make (a person) neat in dress and appearance. **b** ornament or decorate (esp. clothing, a hat, etc., by adding ribbons, lace, etc.). **4** *tr.* adjust the balance of (a ship or aircraft) by the arrangement of its cargo, etc. **5** *tr.* arrange (sails) to suit the wind. **6** *intr.* **a** associate oneself with currently prevailing views, esp. to advance oneself. **b** hold a middle course in politics or opinion. **7** *tr. colloq.* **a** rebuke sharply. **b** thrash. **c** get the better of in a bargain, etc. ● *n.* **1** the state or degree of readiness or fitness (*found everything in perfect trim*). **2** ornament or decorative material. **3** dress or equipment. **4** the act of trimming a person's hair. **5** the inclination of an aircraft to the horizontal. ● *adj.* **1** neat, slim, or tidy. **2** in good condition or order; well arranged or equipped. □ **in trim 1** looking smart, healthy, etc. **2** *Naut.* in good order. □□ **trim·ly** *adv.* **trim·ness** *n.*

tri·ma·ran /trímərán/ *n.* a vessel like a catamaran, with three hulls side by side.

tri·mer /trímər/ *n. Chem.* a polymer comprising three monomer units. □□ **tri·mer·ic** /-mérik/ *adj.*

trim·er·ous /trímərəs/ *adj.* having three parts.

tri·mes·ter /trīméstər/ *n.* a period of three months, esp. of human gestation or as a college or university term.

trim·e·ter /trímitər/ *n. Prosody* a verse of three measures. □□ **tri·met·ric** /trīmétrik/ *adj.* **tri·met·ri·cal** *adj.*

trim·mer /trímər/ *n.* **1** a person who trims articles of dress. **2** a person who trims in politics, etc.; a person swayed by prevailing opinion. **3** an instrument for clipping, etc. **4** *Archit.* a short piece of lumber across an opening (e.g., for a hearth) to carry the ends of truncated joists.

trim·ming /tríming/ *n.* **1** ornamentation or decoration, esp. for clothing. **2** (in *pl.*) *colloq.* the usual accompaniments, esp. of the main course of a meal. **3** (in *pl.*) pieces cut off in trimming.

T

Trin·i·tar·i·an /trĭnĭtáireeən/ n. & adj. ● n. a person who believes in the doctrine of the Trinity. ● adj. of or relating to this belief. □□ **Trin·i·tar·i·an·ism** n.

tri·ni·tro·tol·u·ene /trīnítrōtólyōōeen/ n. (also **tri·ni·tro·tol·u·ol** /-tólyōō-awl, -ōl/) = TNT.

trin·i·ty /trínitee/ n. (pl. **-ies**) **1** the state of being three. **2** a group of three. **3** (**the Trinity** or **Holy Trinity**) Theol. the three persons of the Christian Godhead (Father, Son, and Holy Spirit).

Trin·i·ty term n. Brit. the university law term beginning after Easter.

trin·ket /trίngkit/ n. a trifling ornament, jewel, etc., esp. one worn on the person. □□ **trin·ket·ry** n.

tri·no·mi·al /trīnṓmeeəl/ adj. & n. ● adj. consisting of three terms. ● n. a scientific name or algebraic expression of three terms.

tri·o /trée-ō/ n. (pl. **-os**) **1** a set or group of three. **2** Mus. **a** a composition for three performers. **b** a group of three performers. **c** the central, usu. contrastive, section of a minuet, scherzo, or march. **3** (in piquet) three aces, kings, queens, or jacks in one hand.

tri·ode /trī-ṓd/ n. **1** a thermionic valve having three electrodes. **2** a semiconductor rectifier having three connections.

tri·ox·ide /trīóksīd/ n. Chem. an oxide containing three oxygen atoms.

trip /trip/ v. & n. ● v.intr. & tr. (**tripped**, **tripping**) **1** intr. **a** walk or dance with quick light steps. **b** (of a rhythm, etc.) run lightly. **2 a** intr. & tr. (often foll. by up) stumble or cause to stumble, esp. by catching or entangling the feet. **b** intr. & tr. (foll. by up) make or cause to make a slip or blunder. **3** tr. detect (a person) in a blunder. **4** intr. make an excursion to a place. **5** tr. release (part of a machine) suddenly by knocking aside a catch, etc. **6 a** release and raise (an anchor) from the bottom by means of a cable. **b** turn (a yard, etc.) from a horizontal to a vertical position for lowering. **7** intr. colloq. have a hallucinatory experience caused by a drug. ● n. **1** a journey or excursion, esp. for pleasure. **2 a** a stumble or blunder. **b** the act of tripping or the state of being tripped up. **3** a nimble step. **4** colloq. a hallucinatory experience caused by a drug. **5** a contrivance for a tripping mechanism, etc.

tri·par·tite /trīpáartīt/ adj. **1** consisting of three parts. **2** shared by or involving three parties. **3** Bot. (of a leaf) divided into three segments almost to the base. □□ **tri·par·tite·ly** adv. **tri·par·ti·tion** /-tíshən/ n.

tripe /trīp/ n. **1** the first or second stomach of a ruminant, esp. an ox, as food. **2** colloq. nonsense; rubbish (don't talk such tripe).

triph·thong /tríf-thawng, -thong, tríp-/ n. **1** a union of three vowels (letters or sounds) pronounced in one syllable (as in fire). **2** three vowel characters representing the sound of a single vowel (as in beau). □□ **triph·thong·al** /-thónggəl/ adj.

tri·plane /tríplayn/ n. an early type of airplane having three sets of wings, one above the other.

tri·ple /trípəl/ adj., n., & v. ● adj. **1** consisting of three usu. equal parts or things; threefold. **2** involving three parties. **3** three times as much or many (triple the amount; triple thickness). ● n. **1** a threefold number or amount. **2** a set of three. **3** a base hit allowing a batter to safely reach third base. **4** (in pl.) a peal of changes on seven bells. ● v.intr. & tr. **1** multiply or increase by three. **2** to hit a triple.

tri·ple crown n. **1** RC Ch. the pope's tiara. **2** the act of winning all three of a group of important events in horse racing, etc.

tri·ple jump n. an athletic exercise or contest comprising a hop, a step, and a jump.

tri·ple play n. Baseball the act of making all three outs in a single play.

TRIREME

Triremes were warships used by ancient sea powers of the Mediterranean. Rowed by 170 oarsmen, they were designed to ram enemy ships below the waterline. The stern and prow were held taut by a rope that ran the length of the vessel.

RECONSTRUCTION OF A 4TH-CENTURY BC GREEK TRIREME IN BATTLE

mainmast · mainsail · boatmast · flagstaff · tiller · armed soldier (hoplite) · fighting platform · prow · bow officer (prorates) · painted eye charm · underwater ram · rope (hypozoma) · three banks of oarsmen · hull · cabin · steering oar

---

tri·plet /tríplit/ n. **1** each of three children or animals born at one birth. **2** a set of three things, esp. of equal notes played in the time of two or of verses rhyming together.

tri·plex /trípleks, trī-/ adj. & n. ● adj. triple or three-fold. ● n. (**Triplex**) Brit. Trademark toughened or laminated safety glass for car windows, etc.

tri·pli·cate adj., n., & v. ● adj. /tríplikət/ **1** existing in three examples or copies. **2** having three corresponding parts. **3** tripled. ● n. /tríplikət/ each of a set of three copies or corresponding parts. ● v.tr. /tríplikayt/ **1** make in three copies. **2** multiply by three. □ **in triplicate** consisting of three exact copies. □□ **tri·pli·ca·tion** /-káyshən/ n.

tri·plic·i·ty /triplísitee/ n. (pl. **-ies**) **1** the state of being triple. **2** a group of three things. **3** Astrol. a set of three zodiacal signs.

trip·loid /tríployd/ n. & adj. Biol. ● n. an organism or cell having three times the haploid set of chromosomes. ● adj. of or being a triploid.

trip·loi·dy /tríploydee/ n. the condition of being triploid.

trip·me·ter /trípmeetər/ n. a vehicle instrument that can be set to record the distance of individual journeys.

tri·pod /trípod/ n. **1** ◄ a three-legged stand for supporting a camera, etc. **2** a stool, table, or utensil resting on three feet or legs. □□ **trip·o·dal** /trípəd'l/ adj.

camera
pan-and-tilt head
extendable braced legs
adjustable center column

TRIPOD: BRACED CAMERA TRIPOD

tri·pos /trípos/ n. Brit. (at Cambridge University) the honors examination for the BA degree.

trip·per /trípər/ n. **1** Brit. a person who goes on a pleasure trip or excursion. **2** colloq. a person experiencing hallucinatory effects of a drug.

trip·tych /tríptik/ n. a picture or relief carving on three panels, usu. hinged vertically together and often used as an altarpiece.

trip wire n. a wire stretched close to the ground, operating an alarm, etc., when disturbed.

tri·reme /tríreem/ n. ▲ an ancient Greek warship, with three banks of oarsmen on each side.

tri·sac·cha·ride /trīsákərīd/ n. Chem. a sugar consisting of three linked monosaccharides.

tri·sect /trīsékt/ v.tr. cut or divide into three (usu. equal) parts. □□ **tri·sec·tion** /-sékshən/ n. **tri·sec·tor** n.

tri·shaw /tríshaw/ n. ► a three-wheeled pedal-operated vehicle similar to a ricksha.

tris·mus /trízməs/ n. Med. a variety of tetanus with tonic spasm of the jaw muscles causing the mouth to remain tightly closed.

trite /trīt/ adj. (of a phrase, opinion, etc.) hackneyed; worn out by constant repetition. □□ **trite·ly** adv. **trite·ness** n.

tri·ti·um /tríteeəm/ n. Chem. a radioactive isotope of hydrogen with a mass about three times that of ordinary hydrogen. ¶ Symb.: **T**.

tri·umph /tríəmf, -umf/ n. & v. ● n. **1 a** the state of victory or success. **b** a great success or achievement. **2** a supreme example (a triumph of engineering). **3** joy at success; exultation (could see triumph in her face). **4** the processional entry of a victorious general into ancient Rome. ● v.intr. **1** (often foll. by over) gain a victory; be successful; prevail. **2** ride in triumph. **3** (often foll. by over) exult.

tri·um·phal /trīúmfəl/ adj. of or used in or celebrating a triumph.

tri·um·phant /trīúmfənt/ adj. **1** victorious or successful. **2** exultant. □□ **tri·um·phant·ly** adv.

tri·um·vir /trīúmveer, -úmvər/ n. (pl. **triumvirs** or **triumviri** /-rī/) **1** each of three men holding a joint office. **2** a member of a triumvirate. □□ **tri·um·vi·ral** adj.

tri·um·vi·rate /trīúmvirət/ n. **1** a board or ruling group of three men, esp. in ancient Rome. **2** the office of triumvir.

tri·va·lent /trīváylənt/ adj. Chem. having a valence of three. □□ **tri·va·lence** n. **tri·va·len·cy** n.

triv·et /trívit/ n. a tripod or bracket for a hot pot, kettle, or dish to stand on.

triv·i·a /tríveeə/ n.pl. **1** insignificant factual details. **2** trifles or trivialities.

triv·i·al /tríveeəl/ adj. **1** of small value or impor-

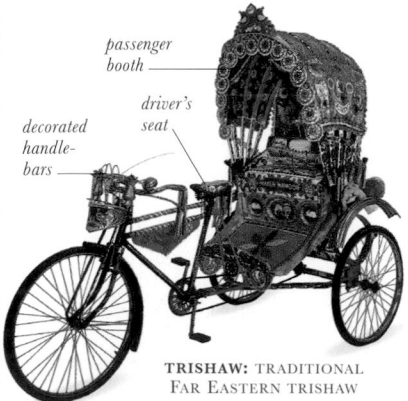

passenger booth
driver's seat
decorated handlebars

TRISHAW: TRADITIONAL FAR EASTERN TRISHAW

T

tance; trifling (*raised trivial objections*). **2** (of a person) concerned only with trivial things. **3** *archaic* commonplace or humdrum (*the trivial round of daily life*). □□ -veeálitee/ *n.* (*pl.* **-ies**). **triv·i·al·ly** *adv.* **triv·i·al·ness** *n.*

triv·i·al·ize /tríveeəlīz/ *v.tr.* make trivial or apparently trivial; minimize. □□ **triv·i·al·i·za·tion** *n.*

tri·week·ly /trīweéklee/ *adj.* produced or occurring three times a week or every three weeks.

tRNA *abbr.* transfer RNA.

tro·cha·ic /trōkáyik/ *adj. & n. Prosody* ● *adj.* of or using trochees. ● *n.* (usu. in *pl.*) trochaic verse.

tro·chee /trṓkee/ *n. Prosody* a foot consisting of one long or stressed syllable followed by one short or unstressed syllable.

troch·le·a /trókleeə/ *n.* (*pl.* **trochleae** /-lee-ee/) *Anat.* a pulleylike structure or arrangement of parts, e.g., the groove at the lower end of the humerus.

tro·choid /trṓkoyd/ *adj. & n.* ● *adj.* **1** *Anat.* rotating on its own axis. **2** *Geom.* (of a curve) traced by a point on a radius of a circle rotating along a straight line or another circle. ● *n.* a trochoid joint or curve. □□ **tro·choi·dal** *adj.*

trod *past* and *past part.* of TREAD.

trod·den *past part.* of TREAD.

trog·lo·dyte /tróglədīt/ *n.* **1** a cave dweller, esp. of prehistoric times. **2** a hermit. **3** *derog.* a willfully obscurantist or old-fashioned person. □□ **trog·lo·dyt·ic** /-dítik/ *adj.* **trog·lo·dyt·i·cal** /-dítikəl/ *adj.* **trog·lo·dyt·ism** *n.*

troi·ka /tróykə/ *n.* **1 a** a Russian vehicle with a team of three horses abreast. **b** this team. **2** a group of three people, esp. as an administrative council.

troil·ism /tróylizəm/ *n.* sexual activity involving three participants.

Tro·jan /trṓjən/ *adj. & n.* ● *adj.* of or relating to ancient Troy in Asia Minor. ● *n.* **1** a native or inhabitant of Troy. **2** a person who works, fights, etc., courageously (*works like a Trojan*).

Tro·jan Horse *n.* **1** a hollow wooden horse said to have been used by the Greeks to enter Troy. **2** a person or device secreted, intended to bring about ruin at a later time. **3** *Computing* a set of instructions hidden in a program that cause damage or mischief.

troll¹ /trōl/ *n.* **1** (in Scandinavian folklore) a fabled being, esp. a giant or dwarf dwelling in a cave.

troll² /trōl/ *v. & n.* ● *v.* **1** *intr.* sing out in a carefree jovial manner. **2** *tr. & intr.* fish by drawing bait along in the water. **3** *intr.* esp. *Brit.* walk; stroll. ● *n.* **1** the act of trolling for fish. **2** a line or bait used in this. □□ **troll·er** *n.*

trol·ley /trólee/ *n.* (*pl.* **-eys**) **1** esp. *Brit.* a table, stand, or basket on wheels or castors for serving food, transporting luggage or shopping, gathering purchases in a supermarket, etc. **2** esp. *Brit.* a low truck running on rails. **3** (in full **trolley wheel**) a wheel attached to a pole, etc., used to carry current from an overhead electric wire to drive a vehicle. **4 ▼** (in full **trolley car**) a streetcar powered by electricity obtained from an overhead cable by means of a trolley wheel.

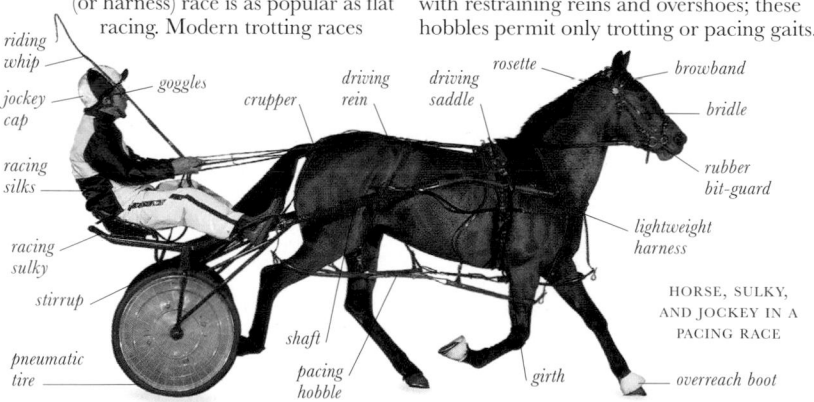

trolley boom ... *trolley head*

wheels to run on rails

TROLLEY CAR: EARLY 19TH-CENTURY BRITISH "TRAM"

trol·lop /tróləp/ *n.* **1** a disreputable girl or woman. **2** a prostitute. □□ **trol·lop·ish** *adj.* **trol·lop·y** *adj.*

trom·bone /trombṓn/ *n.* **1 a ▼** a large brass wind instrument with a sliding tube. ▷ BRASS, ORCHESTRA. **b** its player. **2** an organ stop with the quality of a trombone. □□ **trom·bon·ist** *n.*

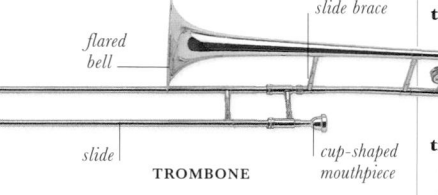

slide brace

flared bell

slide **TROMBONE** *cup-shaped mouthpiece*

trompe-l'œil /tronplṓyə, trampláy, -loi/ *n.* a still life painting, etc., designed to give an illusion of reality.

troop /trōop/ *n. & v.* ● *n.* **1** an assembled company; an assemblage of people or animals. **2** (in *pl.*) soldiers or armed forces. **3** a cavalry unit commanded by a captain. **4** a unit of artillery and armored formation. **5** a unit of Girl Scouts, Boy Scouts, etc. ● *v. intr.* (foll. by *in, out, off*, etc.) come together or move in large numbers.

troop·er /trṓopər/ *n.* **1** a soldier in a cavalry or armored unit. **2 a** a mounted police officer. **b** a state police officer. □ **swear like a trooper** swear extensively or forcefully.

trope /trōp/ *n.* a figurative (e.g., metaphorical or ironical) use of a word.

tro·phy /trṓfee/ *n.* (*pl.* **-ies**) **1** a cup or other decorative object awarded as a prize or memento of victory or success in a contest, etc. **2** a memento or souvenir, e.g., a deer's antlers, taken in hunting. **3** *Gk & Rom. Antiq.* the weapons, etc., of a defeated army set up as a memorial of victory. **4** an ornamental group of symbolic or typical objects arranged for display. □□ **tro·phied** *adj.* (also in *comb.*).

trop·ic /trópik/ *n. & adj.* ● *n.* **1 ▶** the parallel of latitude 23°27' north (**tropic of Cancer**) or south (**tropic of Capricorn**) of the Equator. **2** each of two corresponding circles on the celestial sphere where the Sun appears to turn after reaching its greatest declination. **3** (**the Tropics**) ▶ the region between the tropics of Cancer and Capricorn. ● *adj.* **1** = TROPICAL 1. **2** of tropism.

trop·i·cal /trópikəl/ *adj.* **1** of, peculiar to, or suggesting the Tropics (*tropical fish; tropical diseases*). **2** very hot; passionate; luxuriant. **3** of or by way of a trope. □□ **trop·i·cal·ly** *adv.*

tro·pism /trṓpizəm/ *n. Biol.* the turning of all or part of an organism in a particular direction in response to an external stimulus.

tro·pol·o·gy /trəpóləjee/ *n.* **1** the figurative use of words. **2** figurative interpretation, esp. of the Scriptures. □□ **trop·o·log·i·cal** /trópəlójikəl, trṓ-/ *adj.*

tro·po·pause /trṓpəpawz, trṓ-/ *n.* the interface between the troposphere and the stratosphere.

tro·po·sphere /trṓpəsfeer, trṓ-/ *n.* a layer of atmospheric air extending upward from the Earth's surface, in which the temperature falls with increasing height (cf. STRATOSPHERE, IONOSPHERE). ▷ ATMOSPHERE. □□ **trop·o·spher·ic** /-sférik, -sfeer-/ *adj.*

trot /trot/ *v. & n.* ● *v.* (**trotted, trotting**) **1** *intr.* (of a person) run at a moderate pace, esp. with short strides. **2** *intr.* (of a horse) proceed at a steady pace faster than a walk lifting each diagonal pair of legs alternately. **3** *intr. colloq.* walk or go. **4** *tr.* cause (a horse or person) to trot. **5** *tr.* traverse (a distance) at a trot. ● *n.* **1** the action or exercise of trotting (*proceed at a trot; went for a trot*). **2** (**the trots**) *sl.* an attack of diarrhea. **3** a brisk steady movement or occupation. □ **trot out 1** cause (a horse) to trot to show his paces. **2** produce or introduce (as if) for inspection and approval, esp. tediously or repeatedly.

troth /trawth, trōth/ *n. archaic* **1** faith; loyalty. **2** truth. □ **pledge** (or **plight**) **one's troth** pledge one's word esp. in marriage or betrothal.

Trot·sky·ism /trótskeeizəm/ *n.* the political or economic principles of L. Trotsky, Russian politician d. 1940, esp. as urging worldwide socialist revolution. □□ **Trot·sky·ist** *n.* **Trot·sky·ite** *n. derog.*

trot·ter /trótər/ *n.* **1** a horse bred or trained for trotting. **2** (usu. in *pl.*) an animal's foot as food (*pig's trotters*).

trot·ting /tróting/ *n.* **▼** racing for trotting horses pulling a two-wheeled vehicle and driver.

trou·ba·dour /trṓobədawr/ *n.* **1** any of a number of French medieval lyric poets composing and singing in Provençal in the 11th–13th c. on the theme of courtly love. **2** a singer or poet.

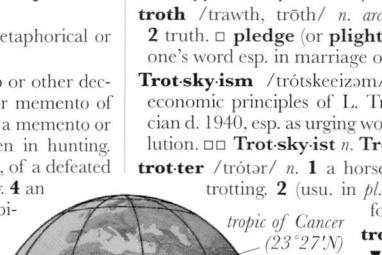

tropic of Cancer (23°27'N)

the Tropics

tropic of Capricorn (23°27'S)

equator

TROPIC: GLOBE SHOWING LOCATION OF THE TROPICS

TROTTING

In many regions, including North America, Australia, and New Zealand, the trotting (or harness) race is as popular as flat racing. Modern trotting races resemble ancient chariot races, except that they are run with single horses equipped with restraining reins and overshoes; these hobbles permit only trotting or pacing gaits.

riding whip · *goggles* · *crupper* · *driving rein* · *driving saddle* · *rosette* · *browband*

jockey cap · *bridle*

racing silks · *rubber bit-guard*

lightweight harness

racing sulky · *stirrup* · *shaft* · *pacing hobble* · *girth* · *overreach boot*

pneumatic tire

HORSE, SULKY, AND JOCKEY IN A PACING RACE

T

trou·ble /trúbəl/ n. & v. ● n. **1** difficulty or distress; vexation; affliction (*am having trouble with my car*). **2 a** inconvenience; unpleasant exertion; bother (*went to a lot of trouble for nothing*). **b** a cause of this (*the child was no trouble at all*). **3** a cause of annoyance or concern (*the trouble with you is that you can't say no*). **4** a faulty condition or operation (*kidney trouble; engine trouble*). **5 a** fighting; disturbance (*crowd trouble; don't want any trouble*). **b** (in *pl.*) political or social unrest; public disturbances. **6** disagreement; strife (*is having trouble at home*). ● v. **1** *tr.* cause distress or anxiety to; disturb (*were much troubled by their debts*). **2** *intr.* be disturbed or worried (*don't trouble about it*). **3** *tr.* afflict; cause pain, etc., to (*am troubled with arthritis*). **4** *tr.* & *intr.* (often *refl.*) subject or be subjected to inconvenience or unpleasant exertion (*sorry to trouble you; don't trouble yourself*). □ **ask** (or **look**) **for trouble** *colloq.* invite trouble or difficulty by one's actions, behavior, etc.; behave rashly or indiscreetly. **be no trouble** cause no inconvenience, etc. **go to the trouble** (or **some trouble**, etc.) exert oneself to do something. **in trouble 1** involved in a matter likely to bring censure or punishment. **2** *colloq.* pregnant while unmarried. **take trouble** (or **the trouble**) exert oneself to do something. □□ **trou·bler** n.

trou·bled /trúbəld/ adj. showing, experiencing, or reflecting trouble, anxiety, etc. (*a troubled mind; a troubled childhood*).

trou·ble·mak·er /trúbəlmaykər/ n. a person who habitually causes trouble. □□ **trou·ble·mak·ing** n.

trou·ble·shoot·er /trúbəlshõõtər/ n. **1** a mediator in industrial or diplomatic, etc., disputes. **2** a person who traces and corrects faults in machinery, etc. □□ **trou·ble·shoot·ing** n.

trou·ble·some /trúbəlsəm/ adj. **1** causing trouble. **2** vexing; annoying. □□ **trou·ble·some·ly** adv. **trou·ble·some·ness** n.

trouble spot n. a place where difficulties regularly occur.

trough /trawf, trof/ n. **1** a long narrow open receptacle for water, animal feed, etc. **2** a channel for conveying a liquid. **3** ▼ an elongated region of low barometric pressure. **4** a hollow between two wave crests. **5** the time of lowest economic performance, etc. **6** a region around the minimum on a curve of variation of a quantity. **7** a low point or depression.

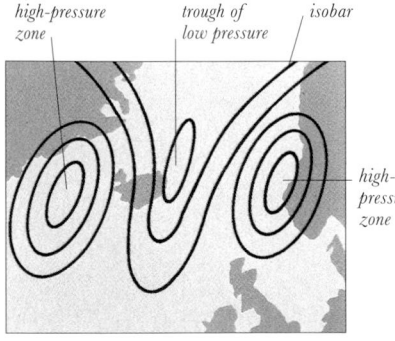

high-pressure zone   *trough of low pressure*   *isobar*   *high-pressure zone*

TROUGH OF LOW PRESSURE ON A WEATHER CHART

trounce /trowns/ v.tr. **1** defeat heavily. **2** beat; thrash. **3** punish severely. □□ **trounc·er** n. **trounc·ing** n.

troupe /trõõp/ n. a company of actors or acrobats, etc.

troup·er /trõõpər/ n. **1** a member of a theatrical troupe. **2** a staunch reliable person, esp. during difficult times.

trou·sers /trówzərz/ n.pl. **1** = PANTS. **2** (**trouser**) (*attrib.*) designating parts of this (*trouser leg*). □□ **trou·sered** adj. **trou·ser·less** adj.

trous·seau /trõõsō, trõõsố/ n. (*pl.* **trousseaus** or **trousseaux** /-sõz/) the clothes and other possessions collected by a bride for her marriage.

TROUT: BROWN TROUT
(*Salmo trutta*)

trout /trowt/ n. (*pl.* same or **trouts**) **1** ▲ any of various freshwater fish of the genus *Salmo* of the northern hemisphere, valued as food. **2** a similar fish of the family Salmonidae. **3** *Brit. sl. derog.* a woman, esp. an old or ill-tempered one (usu. *old trout*). □□ **trout·let** n. **trout·ling** n. **trout·y** adj.

trove /trōv/ n. = TREASURE TROVE.

tro·ver /trṓvər/ n. *Law* **1** finding and keeping personal property. **2** common law action to recover the value of personal property wrongfully taken, etc.

trow /trow, trō/ v.tr. *archaic* think; believe.

trow·el /trówəl/ n. & v. ● n. **1** ◄ a small hand tool with a flat pointed blade, used to apply and spread mortar, etc. **2** a similar tool with a curved scoop for lifting plants or earth. ● v.tr. (**troweled, troweling** or **trowelled, trowelling**) **1** apply (plaster, etc.). **2** plaster (a wall, etc.) with a trowel.

troy /troy/ n. (in full **troy weight**) a system of weights used for precious metals and gems, with a pound of 12 ounces or 5,760 grains.

tru·ant /trõõənt/ n., adj., & v. ● n. **1** a child who stays away from school without leave or explanation. **2** a person missing from work, etc. ● adj. (of a person, conduct, thoughts, etc.) shirking; idle; wandering. ● v.intr. (also **play truant**) stay away as a truant. □□ **tru·an·cy** n.

TROWEL: MASON'S TROWEL

truce /trõõs/ n. **1** a temporary agreement to cease hostilities. **2** a suspension of private feuding or bickering. □□ **truce·less** adj.

truck[1] /truk/ n. & v. ● n. **1** a vehicle for carrying heavy or bulky cargo, etc. **2** *Brit.* a railroad freight car. **3** a vehicle for transporting troops, supplies, etc. **4** a swiveling wheel frame of a railroad car. **5** a wheeled stand for transporting goods; a handcart. ● v. **1** *tr.* convey on or in a truck. **2** *intr.* drive a truck. **3** *intr. sl.* proceed; go. □□ **truck·age** n.

truck[2] /truk/ n. **1** dealings; exchange; barter. **2** small wares. **3** small farm or garden produce (*truck farm*). **4** *colloq.* odds and ends. **5** *hist.* the payment of workers in kind. □ **have no truck with** avoid dealing with.

truck·er /trúkər/ n. a long-distance truck driver.

truck·ie /trúkee/ n. *Austral. colloq.* a trucker.

truck·ing /trúking/ n. transportation of goods by truck.

truck·le /trúkəl/ n. & v. ● n. **1** (in full **truckle bed**) = TRUNDLE BED. **2** *orig. dial.* a small barrel-shaped cheese. ● v.intr. (foll. by *to*) submit obsequiously. □□ **truck·ler** n.

truck stop n. a facility, esp. for truck drivers, usu. by a major highway and including a gas station, restaurant, etc.

truc·u·lent /trúkyələnt/ adj. **1** aggressively defiant. **2** aggressive; pugnacious. **3** fierce; savage. □□ **truc·u·lence** n. **truc·u·len·cy** n. **truc·u·lent·ly** adv.

trudge /truj/ v. & n. ● v. **1** *intr.* go on foot, esp. laboriously. **2** *tr.* traverse (a distance) in this way. ● n. a trudging walk. □□ **trudg·er** n.

true /trõõ/ adj., adv., & v. ● adj. **1** in accordance with fact or reality (*a true story*). **2** genuine; rightly or strictly so called; not spurious or counterfeit (*a true friend; the true heir to the throne*). **3** (often foll. by *to*) loyal or faithful (*true to one's word*). **4** (foll. by *to*) accurately conforming (to a standard or expectation, etc.) (*true to form*). **5** correctly positioned or balanced; upright;

level. **6** exact; accurate (*a true aim; a true copy*). **7** (*absol.*) (also **it is true**) certainly; admittedly (*true, it would cost more*). **8** (of a note) exactly in tune. **9** *archaic* honest; upright (*twelve good men and true*). ● adv. **1** truly (*tell me true*). **2** accurately (*aim true*). **3** without variation (*breed true*). ● v.tr. (**trues, trued, trueing** or **truing**) bring (a tool, wheel, frame, etc.) into the exact position or form required. □ **come true** actually happen or be the case. **out of true** (or **the true**) not in the correct or exact position. **true to form** (or **type**) being or behaving, etc., as expected. **true to life** accurately representing life. □□ **true·ish** adj. **true·ness** n.

true-blue adj. extremely loyal or orthodox.

true-born adj. of a specified kind by birth; genuine.

true north n. north according to the Earth's axis, not magnetic north.

truf·fle /trúfəl/ n. **1** ► any strong-smelling underground fungus of the order Tuberales, used as a culinary delicacy and found esp. in France by trained dogs or pigs. ▷ FUNGUS. **2** a usu. round candy made of chocolate mixture covered with cocoa, etc.

TRUFFLE: SUMMER TRUFFLE (*Tuber aestivum*)

trug /trug/ n. *Brit.* **1** a shallow oblong garden basket usu. of wood strips. **2** *archaic* a wooden milk pan.

tru·ism /trõõizəm/ n. **1** an obviously true or hackneyed statement. **2** a proposition that states nothing beyond what is implied in any of its terms. □□ **tru·is·tic** /-istik/ adj.

trull /trul/ n. *archaic* a prostitute.

tru·ly /trõõlee/ adv. **1** sincerely; genuinely (*am truly grateful*). **2** really; indeed (*truly, I do not know*). **3** faithfully; loyally (*served them truly*). **4** accurately; truthfully (*is not truly depicted; has been truly stated*). **5** rightly; properly (*well and truly*).

trump[1] /trump/ n. & v. ● n. **1** a playing card of a suit ranking above the others. **2** an advantage, esp. involving surprise. ● v. **1 a** *tr.* defeat (a card or its player) with a trump. **b** *intr.* play a trump card when another suit has been led. **2** *tr. colloq.* gain a surprising advantage over (a person, proposal, etc.). □ **trump up** fabricate or invent (an accusation, excuse, etc.) (*on a trumped-up charge*).

trump[2] /trump/ n. *archaic* a trumpet blast. □ **the last trump** the trumpet blast to wake the dead on Judgment Day in Christian theology.

trump card n. **1** a card belonging to, or turned up to determine, a trump suit. **2** *colloq.* **a** a valuable resource. **b** a surprise move to gain an advantage.

trump·er·y /trúmpəree/ n. & adj. ● n. (*pl.* **-ies**) **1 a** worthless finery. **b** a worthless article. **2** junk. ● adj. **1** showy but worthless (*trumpery jewels*). **2** delusive; shallow (*trumpery arguments*).

trum·pet /trúmpit/ n. & v. ● n. **1 a** a tubular or conical brass instrument with a flared bell and a bright penetrating tone. ▷ BRASS, ORCHESTRA. **b** its player. **c** an organ stop with a quality resembling a trumpet. **2 a** the tubular corona of a daffodil, etc. **b** a trumpet-shaped thing (*ear trumpet*). **3** a sound of or like a trumpet (*true to one's word*). ● v. (**trumpeted, trumpeting**) **1** *intr.* **a** blow a trumpet. **b** (of an enraged elephant, etc.) make a loud sound as of a trumpet. **2** *tr.* proclaim loudly (a person's or thing's merit). □□ **trum·pet·less** adj.

trum·pet·er /trúmpitər/ n. **1** a person who plays or sounds a trumpet, esp. a cavalry soldier giving signals. **2** a bird making a trumpetlike sound. **a** a variety of domestic pigeon. **b** a large black S. American cranelike bird of the genus *Psophia*.

trum·pet·er swan n. a large N. American wild swan, *Cygnus buccinator*.

trun·cal /trúngkəl/ adj. of or relating to the trunk of a body or a tree.

T

trun·cate /trúngkayt/ *v.tr.* cut the top or the end from (a tree, a body, a piece of writing, etc.). □□ **trun·cate·ly** *adv.* **trun·ca·tion** /-káyshən/ *n.*

trun·cheon /trúnchən/ *n.* **1** a short club or cudgel, esp. carried by a policeman; a billy club. **2** a staff or baton as a symbol of authority.

trun·dle /trúnd'l/ *v.tr. & intr.* roll or move heavily or noisily, esp. on or as on wheels.

trun·dle bed *n.* a low bed on wheels that can be stored under a larger bed.

trunk /trungk/ *n.* **1** the main stem or body of a tree as distinct from its branches and roots. **2** a person's or animal's body apart from the limbs and head. **3** the main part of any structure. **4** a large box with a hinged lid for transporting luggage, clothes, etc. **5** the luggage compartment of an automobile. **6** ▶ an elephant's elongated prehensile nose. ▷ ELEPHANT. **7** (in *pl.*) men's often close-fitting shorts worn for swimming, boxing, etc. **8** the main body of an artery, nerve, communications network, etc. **9** an enclosed shaft or conduit for cables, ventilation, etc. □□ **trunk·ful** *n.* (*pl.* **-fuls**). **trunk·less** *adj.*

TRUNK: SECTION THROUGH AN ELEPHANT'S TRUNK

epidermis
longitudinal muscle
radiating muscle
nerve
nostril
septum
blood vessel

trunk·ing /trúngking/ *n.* **1** a system of shafts or conduits for cables, ventilation, etc. **2** the use or arrangement of trunk lines.

truss /trus/ *n. & v.* ● *n.* **1** a framework, e.g., of rafters and struts, supporting a roof or bridge, etc. ▷ BRIDGE, HOUSE, QUEEN POST, ROOF. **2** a surgical appliance worn to support a hernia. ● *v.tr.* **1** tie up (a fowl) compactly for cooking. **2** (often foll. by *up*) tie (a person) up with the arms to the sides. **3** support (a roof or bridge, etc.) with a truss or trusses. □□ **truss·er** *n.*

trust /trust/ *n. & v.* ● *n.* **1 a** a firm belief in the reliability or truth or strength, etc., of a person or thing. **b** the state of being relied on. **2** a confident expectation. **3 a** a thing or person committed to one's care. **b** the resulting obligation or responsibility (*am in a position of trust; have fulfilled my trust*). **4** a person or thing confided in (*is our sole trust*). **5** reliance on the truth of a statement, etc., without examination. **6** commercial credit (*obtained merchandise on trust*). **7** *Law* **a** confidence placed in a person by making that person the nominal owner of property to be used for another's benefit. **b** the right of the latter to benefit by such property. **c** the property so held. **d** the legal relation between the holder and the property so held. **8 a** a body of trustees. **b** an organization managed by trustees. **c** an organized association of several companies for the purpose of reducing or defeating competition, etc., esp. one in which all or most of the stock is transferred to a central committee and shareholders lose their voting power although remaining entitled to profits. ● *v.* **1** *tr.* place trust in; believe in; rely on the character or behavior of. **2** *tr.* (foll. by *with*) allow (a person) to have or use (a thing) from confidence in its proper use (*was reluctant to trust them with my books*). **3** *tr.* (often foll. by *that* + clause) have faith or confidence or hope that a thing will take place (*I trust you will not be late; I trust that she is recovering*). **4** *tr.* (foll. by *to*) consign (a thing) to (a person) with trust. **5** *tr.* (foll. by *for*) allow credit to (a customer) for (merchandise). **6** *intr.* (foll. by *in*) place reliance in (*we trust in you*). **7** *intr.* (foll. by *to*) place reliance on (*shall have to trust to luck*). □ **in trust** *Law* held on the basis of trust (see sense 7 of *n.*). **on trust 1** on credit. **2** on the basis of trust or confidence. **take on trust** accept (an assertion, claim, etc.) without evidence or investigation. □□ **trust·a·ble** *adj.* **trust·er** *n.*

trust com·pa·ny *n.* a company formed to act as a trustee or to deal with trusts.

trust·ee /trustée/ *n.* **1** *Law* a person or member of a board given control or powers of administration of property in trust with a legal obligation to administer it solely for the purposes specified. **2** a nation made responsible for the government of an area. □□ **trust·ee·ship** *n.*

trust·ful /trústfool/ *adj.* **1** full of trust or confidence. **2** not feeling or showing suspicion. □□ **trust·ful·ly** *adv.* **trust·ful·ness** *n.*

trust fund *n.* a fund of money, etc., held in trust.

trust·ing /trústing/ *adj.* having trust (esp. characteristically); trustful. □□ **trust·ing·ly** *adv.* **trust·ing·ness** *n.*

trust·wor·thy /trústwurthee/ *adj.* deserving of trust; reliable. □□ **trust·wor·thi·ly** *adv.* **trust·wor·thi·ness** *n.*

trust·y /trústee/ *adj. & n.* ● *adj.* (**trustier, trustiest**) **1** *archaic* or *joc.* trustworthy (*a trusty steed*). **2** *archaic* loyal (to a sovereign) (*my trusty subjects*). ● *n.* (*pl.* **-ies**) a prisoner who is given special privileges for good behavior. □□ **trust·i·ly** *adv.* **trust·i·ness** *n.*

truth /trooth/ *n.* (*pl.* **truths** /troothz, trooths/) **1** the quality or a state of being true or truthful. **2 a** what is true (*tell us the whole truth; the truth is that I forgot*). **b** what is accepted as true (*one of the fundamental truths*). □ **in truth** truly; really. **to tell the truth** (or **truth to tell**) to be frank. □□ **truth·less** *adj.*

truth·ful /troothfool/ *adj.* **1** habitually speaking the truth. **2** (of a story, etc.) true. **3** (of a likeness, etc.) corresponding to reality. □□ **truth·ful·ly** *adv.* **truth·ful·ness** *n.*

truth se·rum *n.* any of various drugs supposedly able to induce a person to tell the truth.

try /trī/ *v. & n.* ● *v.* (**-ies, -ied**) **1** *intr.* make an effort with a view to success (often foll. by *to* + infin.; *colloq.* foll. by *and* + infin.: *tried to be on time; try and be early; I shall try hard*). ¶ Use with *and* is uncommon in the past tense and in negative contexts (*try to do it; didn't try to do it*) and in the imper. (*try to do better*). **2** *tr.* make an effort to achieve (*tried my best; had better try something easier*). **3** *tr.* **a** test (the quality of a thing) by use or experiment. **b** test the qualities of (a person or thing) (*try it before you buy*). **4** *tr.* make severe demands on (a person, quality, etc.) (*my patience has been sorely tried*). **5** *tr.* examine the effectiveness or usefulness of for a purpose (*try cold water; have you tried kicking it?*). **6** *tr.* ascertain the state of fastening of (a door, window, etc.). **7** *tr.* **a** investigate and decide (a case or issue) judicially. **b** subject (a person) to trial (*will be tried for murder*). **8** *tr.* make an experiment in order to find out (*let us try which takes longest*). **9** *intr.* (foll. by *for*) **a** apply or compete for. **b** seek to reach or attain (*am going to try for a gold medal*). **10** *tr.* (often foll. by *out*) **a** extract (oil) from fat by heating. **b** treat (fat) in this way. **11** *tr.* (often foll. by *up*) smooth (roughly planed wood) with a plane to give an accurately flat surface. ● *n.* (*pl.* **-ies**) **1** an effort to accomplish something; an attempt (*give it a try*). **2** *Rugby* the act of touching the ball down behind the opposing goal line, scoring points and entitling the scoring side to a kick at the goal. **3** *Football* an attempt to score one or two extra points after a touchdown. □ **tried and true** (or **tested**) proved reliable by experience; dependable. **try conclusions with** see CONCLUSION. **try a fall with** contend with. **try on for size** try out or test for suitability. **try one's hand** see how skillful one is, esp. at the first attempt. **try it on** *Brit. colloq.* **1** test another's patience. **2** attempt to outwit or deceive another person. **try on** put on (clothes, etc.) to see if they fit or suit the wearer. **try out 1** put to the test. **2** test thoroughly.

try·ing /trí-ing/ *adj.* annoying; vexatious; hard to endure. □□ **try·ing·ly** *adv.*

try·pan·o·some /trípənəsōm, trípánə-/ *n. Med.* any protozoan parasite of the genus *Trypanosoma* having a long trailing flagellum and infesting the blood, etc.

TSUNAMI

A tsunami is a great wave of sea water, formed by shock waves emanating from an earthquake or volcanic eruption on the ocean floor. On open water, the swiftly moving wave normally remains less than 1 ft 8 in. (0.5 m) high. Near the shoreline, however, it rises up to 200 ft (60 m) high, causing coastal flooding.

fast, low wave
wave gains height as it slows
giant wave breaks
epicenter of earthquake
shoreline

FORMATION OF A TSUNAMI

try·pan·o·so·mi·a·sis /trípənəsōmíəsis, tripánə-/ *n.* any of several diseases caused by a trypanosome including sleeping sickness and Chagas' disease.

try square *n.* a carpenter's square, usu. with one wooden and one metal limb.

tryst /trist/ *n.* **1** a time and place for a meeting, esp. of lovers. **2** such a meeting (*keep a tryst; break one's tryst*). □□ **tryst·er** *n.*

tsar var. of CZAR.

tsa·ri·na var. of CZARINA.

tset·se /tsétsee, tét-, tséetsee, teé-/ *n.* any fly of the genus *Glossina* native to Africa that feeds on human and animal blood with a needlelike proboscis and transmits trypanosomiasis.

T-shirt /téeshərt/ *n.* (also **tee-shirt**) a short-sleeved collarless casual top, usu. of knitted cotton and having the form of a T when spread out.

tsp. *abbr.* (*pl.* **tsps.**) teaspoon; teaspoonful.

T square /tée skwair/ *n.* a T-shaped instrument for drawing or testing right angles.

tsu·na·mi /tsoonáamee/ *n.* (*pl.* **tsunamis**) ▲ a long high sea wave caused by underwater earthquakes or other disturbances; tidal wave.

tub /tub/ *n. & v.* ● *n.* **1** an open flat-bottomed usu. round container for various purposes. **2** a tubshaped (usu. plastic) carton. **3** the amount a tub will hold. **4** *Brit. colloq.* a bath. **5 a** *colloq.* a clumsy slow boat. **b** a stout roomy boat for rowing practice. ● *v.* (**tubbed, tubbing**) **1** *tr. & intr.* esp. *Brit.* plant, bathe, or wash in a tub. **2** *tr.* enclose in a tub. □□ **tub·ba·ble** *adj.* **tub·bish** *adj.* **tub·ful** *n.* (*pl.* **-fuls**)

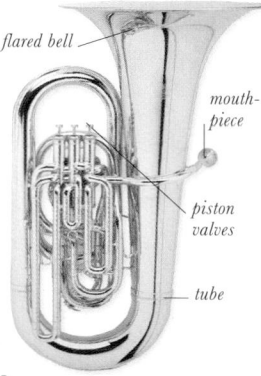

flared bell
mouth-piece
piston valves
tube

TUBA

tu·ba /tooba, tyoo/ *n.* (*pl.* **tubas**) ◀ **1 a** ◀ a low-pitched brass wind instrument. ▷ BRASS, ORCHESTRA. **b** its player. **2** an organ stop with the quality of a tuba.

tub·al /toobəl, tyoo-/ *adj. Anat.* of or relating to a tube, esp. the bronchial or Fallopian tubes.

tub·by /túbee/ *adj.* (**tubbier, tubbiest**) **1** (of a person) short and fat; tub-shaped. **2** (of a violin) dull-sounding; lacking resonance. □□ **tub·bi·ness** *n.*

tube /toob, tyoob/ *n. & v.* ● *n.* **1** a long hollow rigid or flexible cylinder, esp. for holding or carrying air,

T

liquids, etc. **2** a soft metal or plastic cylinder sealed at one end and having a screw cap at the other, for holding a semiliquid substance ready for use (*a tube of toothpaste*). **3** *Anat. & Zool.* a hollow cylindrical organ in the body (*bronchial tubes; Fallopian tubes*). **4** (often prec. by *the*) *colloq.* the London subway system. **5 a** a cathode-ray tube, esp. in a television set. **b** (prec. by *the*) *colloq.* television. **6** = VACUUM TUBE. **7** = INNER TUBE. **8** the cylindrical body of a wind instrument. **9** (in full **tube top**) an elasticized upper garment shaped like a tube. **10** *Austral. sl.* a can of beer. ● *v.tr.* **1** equip with tubes. **2** enclose in a tube. □□ **tube·less** *adj.* (esp. in sense 7 of *n.*). **tube·like** *adj.*

tu·ber /tōōbər, tyōō-/ *n.* **1** ► the short thick rounded part of a stem or rhizome, usu. found underground and covered with modified buds, e.g., a potato. **2** the similar root of a dahlia, etc.

tu·ber·cle /tōōbərkəl, tyōō-/ *n.* **1** a small rounded protuberance, esp. on a bone. **2** a small rounded swelling on the body or in an organ, esp. a nodular lesion characteristic of tuberculosis in the lungs, etc. □□ **tu·ber·cu·late** /-bárk-yələt, -layt/ *adj.* **tu·ber·cu·lous** /-bárkyələs/ *adj.*

TUBERS OF A DAHLIA

tu·ber·cu·lar /tōōbárkyələr, tyōō-/ *adj. & n.* ● *adj.* of or having tubercles or tuberculosis. ● *n.* a person with tuberculosis.

tu·ber·cu·lin /tōōbárkyəlin, tyōō-/ *n.* a sterile liquid from cultures of tubercle bacillus, used in the diagnosis and treatment of tuberculosis.

tu·ber·cu·lo·sis /tōōbárkyələlōsis, tyōō-/ *n.* an infectious disease caused by the bacillus *Mycobacterium tuberculosis*, characterized by tubercles, esp. in the lungs.

tu·ber·ose /tōōbərōs, tyōō-/ *adj.* **1** covered with tubers; knobby. **2** of or resembling a tuber. **3** bearing tubers. □□ **tu·ber·os·i·ty** /-rósitee/ *n.*

tu·ber·ous /tōōbərəs, tyōō-/ *adj.* = TUBEROSE.

tu·bi·fex /tōōbifeks, tyōō-/ *n.* ► any red annelid worm of the genus *Tubifex*, found in mud at the bottom of rivers and lakes and used as food for aquarium fish.

tub·ing /tōōbing, tyōō-/ *n.* **1** a length of tube. **2** a quantity of tubes.

TUBIFEX WORMS

tu·bu·lar /tōōbyələr, tyōō-/ *adj.* **1** tube-shaped. **2** having or consisting of tubes. **3** (of furniture, etc.) made of tubular pieces.

tu·bu·lar bells *n.pl.* ▼ an orchestral instrument consisting of a row of vertically suspended brass tubes that are struck with a hammer. ▷ ORCHESTRA, PERCUSSION

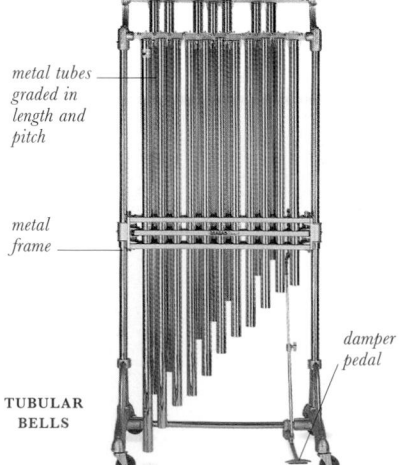

metal tubes graded in length and pitch

metal frame

damper pedal

TUBULAR BELLS

tu·bule /tōōbyōōl, tyōō-/ *n.* a small tube in a plant or an animal body.

tu·bu·lous /tōōbyələs, tyōō-/ *adj.* = TUBULAR.

tuck /tuk/ *v. & n.* ● *v.* **1** *tr.* (often foll. by *in, up*) **a** draw, fold, or turn the outer or end parts of (cloth or clothes, etc.) close together so as to be held; thrust in the edge of (a thing) so as to confine it (*tucked his shirt into his trousers*). **b** thrust in the edges of bedclothes around (a person) (*came to tuck me in*). **2** *tr.* draw together into a small space (*the bird tucked its head under its wing*). **3** *tr.* stow (a thing) away in a specified place or way (*tucked it out of sight*). **4** *tr.* **a** make a stitched fold in (material, a garment, etc.). **b** shorten, tighten, or ornament with stitched folds. ● *n.* **1** a flattened usu. stitched fold in material, a garment, etc., often one of several parallel folds for shortening, tightening, or ornament. **2** *Brit. colloq.* food, esp. cake and candy eaten by children (also *attrib.: tuck box*). **3** (in full **tuck position**) (in diving, gymnastics, etc.) a position with the knees bent upward into the chest and the hands clasped around the shins. □ **tuck away** (or **into**) *colloq.* eat (food) heartily (*tucked into their dinner; could really tuck it away*).

tuck·er /túkər/ *n. & v.* ● *n.* **1** a person or thing that tucks. **2** *hist.* a piece of lace or linen, etc., in or on a woman's bodice. **3** *Austral. colloq.* food. ● *v.tr.* (esp. in *passive*; often foll. by *out*) *colloq.* tire; exhaust.

Tu·dor /tōōdər, tyōō-/ *adj. hist.* **1** of, characteristic of, or associated with the royal family of England ruling 1485–1603 or this period. **2** of or relating to the architectural style of this period, esp. with half-timbering and elaborately decorated houses. ▷ ARCH

Tu·dor rose *n.* ► a figure of a rose, esp. the red and white roses of Lancaster and York adopted by England's King Henry VII. ▷ EMBOSS

TUDOR ROSE: 16TH-CENTURY ENGLISH CARVED EMBLEM

Tues. *abbr.* (also **Tue.**) Tuesday.

Tues·day /tōōzday, -dee, tyōō-/ *n. & adv.* ● *n.* the third day of the week, following Monday. ● *adv.* **1** *colloq.* on Tuesday. **2** (**Tuesdays**) on Tuesdays; each Tuesday.

tu·fa /tōōfə, tyōō-/ *n.* **1** ► a porous rock composed of calcium carbonate and formed around mineral springs. **2** = TUFF. □□ **tu·fa·ceous** /-fáyshəs/ *adj.*

tuff /tuf/ *n.* rock formed by the consolidation of volcanic ash. □□ **tuff·a·ceous** /tufáy-shəs/ *adj.*

tuft /tuft/ *n. & v.* ● *n.* a bunch or collection of threads, grass, feathers, hair, etc., held or growing together at the base. ● *v.* **1** *tr.* provide with a tuft or tufts. **2** *tr.* make depressions at regular intervals in (a mattress, etc.) by passing a thread through. **3** *intr.* grow in tufts. □□ **tuft·y** *adj.*

TUFA

tuft·ed /túftid/ *adj.* **1** having or growing in a tuft or tufts. **2** (of a bird) with a tuft of feathers on the head.

tug /tug/ *v. & n.* ● *v.* (**tugged, tugging**) **1** *tr. &* (foll. by *at*) *intr.* pull hard or violently; jerk (*tugged it from my grasp; tugged at my sleeve*). **2** *tr.* tow (a ship, etc.) by means of a tugboat. ● *n.* **1** a hard, violent, or jerky pull (*gave a tug on the rope*). **2** a sudden strong emotional feeling (*felt a tug as I watched them go*). **3** a small powerful boat for towing larger boats and ships. □□ **tug·ger** *n.*

tug·boat /túgbōt/ *n.* = TUG *n.* 3.

tug-of-war *n.* **1** a trial of strength between two sides pulling against each other on a rope. **2** a decisive or severe contest.

tu·i·tion /tōō-íshən, tyōō-/ *n.* **1** teaching or instruction, esp. if paid for (*driving tuition; music tuition*). **2** a fee for this. □□ **tu·i·tion·al** *adj.*

tu·lip /tōōlip, tyōō-/ *n.* **1** any bulbous spring-flowering plant of the genus *Tulipa*, esp. one of the many cultivated forms with showy cup-shaped flowers of various colors and markings. **2** a flower of this plant.

tu·lip tree *n.* ► any of various trees, esp. of the genus *Liriodendron*, producing tuliplike flowers.

TULIP TREE: FLOWER AND LEAVES (*Liriodendron tulipifera*)

tulle /tōōl/ *n.* a soft fine silk, etc., net for veils and dresses.

tum /tum/ *n. Brit. colloq.* stomach.

tum·ble /túmbəl/ *v. & n.* ● *v.* **1** *intr. & tr.* fall or cause to fall suddenly, clumsily, or headlong. **2** *intr.* fall rapidly in amount, etc. (*prices tumbled*). **3** *intr.* (often foll. by *about, around*) roll or toss erratically or helplessly to and fro. **4** *intr.* move or rush in a headlong or blundering manner (*the children tumbled out of the car*). **5** *intr.* (often foll. by *to*) *colloq.* grasp the meaning or hidden implication of an idea, circumstance, etc. (*they quickly tumbled to our intentions*). **6** *tr.* overturn; fling or push roughly or carelessly. **7** *intr.* perform acrobatic feats, esp. somersaults. **8** *tr.* rumple or disarrange; disorder. **9** *tr.* dry (laundry) in a tumble dryer. **10** *tr.* clean (castings, gemstones, etc.) in a tumbling barrel. **11** *intr.* (of a pigeon) turn over backward in flight. ● *n.* **1** a sudden or headlong fall. **2** a somersault or other acrobatic feat. **3** an untidy or confused state.

tum·ble·down /túmbəldown/ *adj.* falling or fallen into ruin; dilapidated.

tum·ble dry·er *n.* a machine for drying laundry in a heated rotating drum.

tum·bler /túmblər/ *n.* **1** a drinking glass with no handle or foot (formerly with a rounded bottom so as not to stand upright). **2** an acrobat, esp. one performing somersaults. **3** (in full **tumbler dryer**) = TUMBLE DRYER. **4 a** a pivoted piece in a lock that holds the bolt until lifted by a key. **b** a notched pivoted plate in a gunlock. □□ **tum·bler·ful** *n.* (*pl.* **-fuls**).

tum·ble·weed /túmbəlweed/ *n.* a plant, *Amaranthus albus*, that forms a globular bush that breaks off in late summer and is tumbled about by the wind.

tum·brel /túmbrəl/ *n.* (also **tum·bril** /-ril/) *hist.* an open cart in which condemned persons were conveyed to their execution, esp. to the guillotine during the French Revolution.

tu·me·fy /tōōmifī, tyōō-/ *v.* (**-ies, -ied**) **1** *intr.* swell; inflate; be inflated. **2** *tr.* cause to do this. □□ **tu·me·fa·ci·ent** /-fáyshənt/ *adj.* **tu·me·fac·tion** /-fákshən/ *n.*

tu·mes·cent /tōōmésənt, tyōō-/ *adj.* **1** becoming tumid; swelling. **2** swelling as a response to sexual stimulation. □□ **tu·mes·cence** *n.* **tu·mes·cent·ly** *adv.*

tu·mid /tōōmid, tyōō-/ *adj.* **1** (of parts of the body, etc.) swollen; inflated. **2** (of a style, etc.) inflated; bombastic. □□ **tu·mid·i·ty** /-míditee/ *n.* **tu·mid·ly** *adv.* **tu·mid·ness** *n.*

tum·my /túmee/ *n.* (*pl.* **-ies**) *colloq.* the stomach.

tu·mor /tōōmər, tyōō-/ *n.* a swelling, esp. from an abnormal growth of tissue. □□ **tu·mor·ous** *adj.*

tu·mult /tōōmult, tyōō-/ *n.* **1** an uproar or din, esp. of a disorderly crowd. **2** an angry demonstration by a mob; a riot; a public disturbance. **3** a conflict of emotions in the mind.

tu·mul·tu·ous /tōōmúlchōōəs, tyōō-/ *adj.* **1** noisily vehement; uproarious; making a tumult (*a tumultuous welcome*). **2** disorderly. **3** agitated. □□ **tu·mul·tu·ous·ly** *adv.* **tu·mul·tu·ous·ness** *n.*

tu·mu·lus /tōōmyələs, tyōō-/ *n.* (*pl.* **tumuli** /-lī/) an ancient burial mound or barrow. □□ **tu·mu·lar** *adj.*

tun /tun/ *n. & v.* ● *n.* **1** a large beer or wine cask. **2** a brewer's fermenting vat. **3** a measure of capacity, equal to 252 gallons. ● *v.tr.* (**tunned, tunning**) store (wine, etc.) in a tun.

T

TUNDRA

The tundra is a cold treeless plain located above the Arctic Circle. Worn smooth by huge ice sheets in past ages, the region is an open landscape of shallow lakes, barren outcrops, and hillocks. Vegetation is sparse because the subsoil remains frozen all year with permafrost, and wildlife is restricted to small, hardy species. Unique ground features such as stone polygons and pingos are caused by freezing and thawing of subterranean ice.

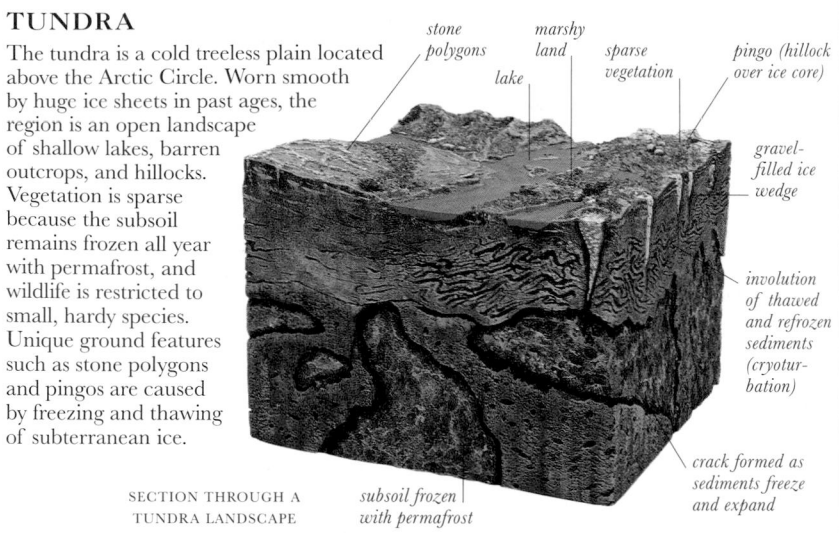

stone polygons · marshy land · sparse vegetation · pingo (hillock over ice core) · lake · gravel-filled ice wedge · involution of thawed and refrozen sediments (cryoturbation) · crack formed as sediments freeze and expand · subsoil frozen with permafrost

SECTION THROUGH A
TUNDRA LANDSCAPE

tu·na /tōōnə, tyōō-/ n. (pl. same or **tunas**) **1** any marine fish of the family Scombridae native to tropical and warm waters, having a round body and pointed snout, and used for food. Also called esp. Brit. **tunny**. ▷ SKIPJACK. **2** (in full **tuna fish**) the flesh of the tuna, usu. preserved in oil or brine.

tun·dra /túndrə/ n. ▲ a vast level treeless Arctic region usu. with a marshy surface and underlying permafrost.

tune /tōōn, tyōōn/ n. & v. ● n. a melody with or without harmony. ● v. **1** tr. put (a musical instrument) in tune. **2 a** tr. adjust (a radio receiver, etc.) to the particular frequency of the required signals. **b** intr. (foll. by in) adjust a radio receiver to the required signal (tuned in to the news). **3** tr. adjust (an engine, etc.) to run smoothly and efficiently. **4** tr. (foll. by to) adjust or adapt to a required or different purpose, situation, etc. **5** intr. (foll. by with) be in harmony with. □ **in tune 1** having the correct pitch or intonation (sings in tune). **2** (usu. foll. by with) harmonizing with one's associates, surroundings, etc. **out of tune 1** not having the correct pitch or intonation (always plays out of tune). **2** (usu. foll. by with) clashing with one's associates, etc. **to the tune of** colloq. to the considerable sum or amount of. **tuned in 1** (of a radio, etc.) adjusted to a particular frequency, station, etc. **2** (foll. by on, to) sl. in rapport or harmony with. **3** colloq. aware of what is going on. **tune up 1** (of an orchestra) bring the instruments to the proper or uniform pitch. **2** bring to the most efficient condition. □□ **tun·a·ble** adj. (also **tune·a·ble**).

tune·ful /tōōnfŏŏl, tyōō-/ adj. melodious. □□ **tune·ful·ly** adv. **tune·ful·ness** n.

tune·less /tōōnlis, tyōō-/ adj. unmelodious. □□ **tune·less·ly** adv. **tune·less·ness** n.

tun·er /tōōnər, tyōō-/ n. **1** a person who tunes musical instruments, esp. pianos. **2** a device for tuning a radio receiver.

tune·smith /tōōnsmith, tyōō-/ n. colloq. a composer of popular music or songs.

tung·sten /túngstən/ n. Chem. a steel-gray dense metallic element with a very high melting point, occurring naturally in scheelite and used for the filaments of electric lamps and for alloying steel, etc. ▷ INCANDESCENT. ¶ Symb.: **W**. □□ **tung·state** /-stayt/ n. **tung·stic** /-stik/ adj. **tung·stous** /-stəs/ adj.

tung·sten car·bide n. a very hard black substance used in making dies and cutting tools.

tu·nic /tōōnik, tyōō-/ n. **1** a close-fitting short coat as part of a police or military, etc., uniform. **2** a loose, often sleeveless garment usu. reaching to about the knees, as worn in ancient Greece and

Rome. ▷ TOGA. **3** any of various loose, pleated dresses gathered at the waist with a belt or cord. **4** a tunicle.

tu·ni·cate /tōōnikət, -kayt, tyōō-/ n. any marine animal of the subphylum Urochordata having a rubbery or hard outer coat, including sea squirts.

tu·ni·cle /tōōnikəl, tyōō-/ n. a short vestment worn by a bishop or subdeacon at Mass, etc.

tun·ing /tōōning, tyōō-/ n. the process or a system of putting a musical instrument in tune.

tun·ing fork n. ▶ a two-pronged steel fork that gives a particular note when struck, used in tuning.

tun·nel /túnəl/ n. & v. ● n. **1** an artificial underground passage through a hill or under a road or river, etc., esp. for a railroad or road to pass through, or in a mine. **2** an underground passage dug by a burrowing animal. **3** a prolonged period of difficulty or suffering (esp. in metaphors, e.g., the end of the tunnel). ● v. (**tunneled**, **tunneling** or **tunnelled**, **tunnelling**) **1** intr. (foll. by through, into, etc.) make a tunnel through (a hill, etc.). **2** tr. make (one's way) by tunneling. □□ **tun·nel·er** n.

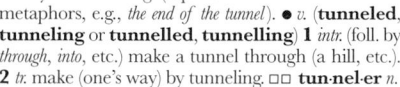

prong

TUNING FORK

tun·nel vi·sion n. **1** vision that is defective in not adequately including objects away from the center of the field of view. **2** colloq. inability to grasp the wider implications of a situation.

tun·ny /túnee/ n. (pl. same or **-ies**) esp. Brit. = TUNA[1].

tup /tup/ n. & v. ● n. **1** esp. Brit. a male sheep; a ram. **2** the striking head of a pile driver, etc. ● v.tr. (**tupped**, **tupping**) esp. Brit. (of a ram) copulate with (a ewe).

tu·pe·lo /tōōpilō, tyōō-/ n. (pl. **-os**) **1** any of various Asian and N. American deciduous trees of the genus Nyssa, with colorful foliage and growing in swampy conditions. **2** the wood of this tree.

Tu·pi /tōōpee/ n. & adj. ● n. (pl. same or **Tupis**) **1** a member of a Native American people native to the Amazon valley. **2** the language of this people. ● adj. of or relating to this people or language.

tup·pence /túpəns/ n. Brit. = TWOPENCE.

tup·pen·ny /túpənee/ adj. Brit. = TWOPENNY.

Tup·per·ware /túpərwair/ n. Trademark a brand of plastic containers for storing food.

tuque /tōōk/ n. a Canadian stocking cap.

tu·ra·co /tōōrəkō/ n. (also **tou·ra·co**) (pl. **-os**) any African bird of the family Musophagidae, with crimson and green plumage and a prominent crest.

tur·ban /tárbən/ n. **1** a man's head-dress of cotton or silk wound around a cap or the head, worn esp. by Muslims and Sikhs. **2** ▶ a woman's headdress or hat resembling this. □□ **tur·baned** adj.

tur·bid /tárbid/ adj. **1** (of a liquid or color) muddy; thick; not clear. **2** (of a style, etc.) confused; disordered. □□ **tur·bid·i·ty** /-bíditee/ n. **tur·bid·ly** adv. **tur·bid·ness** n.

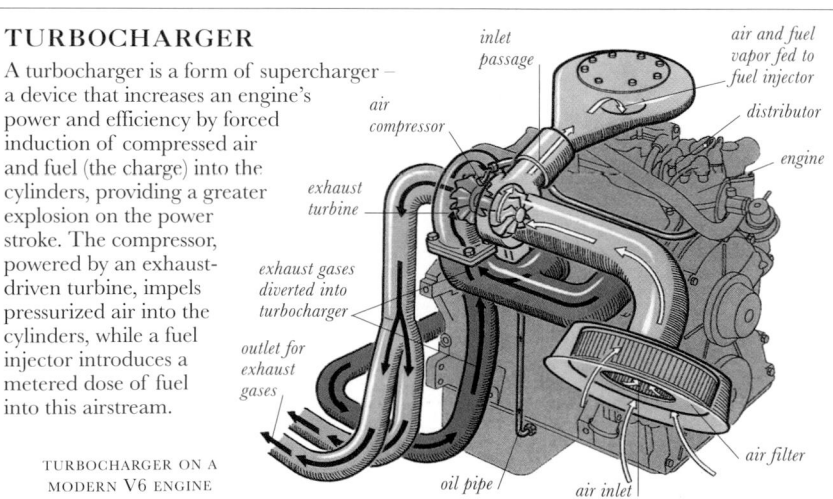

TURBAN: CEREMONIAL
WEST AFRICAN TURBAN

tur·bine /tárbin, -bīn/ n. a rotary motor or engine driven by a flow of water, steam, gas, wind, etc., esp. to produce electrical power. ▷ HYDROELECTRIC, JET ENGINE, NUCLEAR POWER, STEAM TURBINE

tur·bo /tárbō/ n. (pl. **-os**) = TURBOCHARGER.

tur·bo·charg·er /tárbōchaarjər/ n. ▼ a supercharger driven by a turbine powered by the engine's exhaust gases.

tur·bo·fan /tárbōfan/ n. **1** a jet engine in which a turbine-driven fan provides additional thrust. ▷ JET ENGINE. **2** an aircraft powered by this.

TURBOCHARGER

A turbocharger is a form of supercharger – a device that increases an engine's power and efficiency by forced induction of compressed air and fuel (the charge) into the cylinders, providing a greater explosion on the power stroke. The compressor, powered by an exhaust-driven turbine, impels pressurized air into the cylinders, while a fuel injector introduces a metered dose of fuel into this airstream.

inlet passage · air and fuel vapor fed to fuel injector · air compressor · distributor · engine · exhaust turbine · exhaust gases diverted into turbocharger · outlet for exhaust gases · air filter · oil pipe · air inlet

TURBOCHARGER ON A
MODERN V6 ENGINE

T

tur·bo·jet /tə́rbōjet/ *n. Aeron.* **1** a jet engine in which the jet also operates a turbine-driven compressor for the air drawn into the engine. ▷ JET ENGINE. **2** an aircraft powered by this.

tur·bo·prop /tə́rbōprop/ *n. Aeron.* **1** a jet engine in which a turbine is used as in a turbojet and also to drive a propeller. ▷ JET ENGINE. **2** an aircraft powered by this.

tur·bo·shaft /tə́rbōshaft/ *n.* a gas turbine that powers a shaft for driving heavy vehicles, generators, pumps, etc.

tur·bot /tə́rbət/ *n.* **1** a flatfish, *Psetta maxima*, having large bony tubercles on the body and head and prized as food. **2** ▼ any of various similar flatfishes.

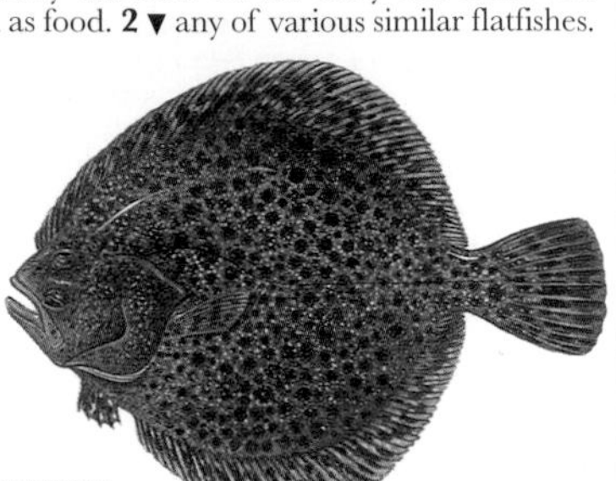

TURBOT
(*Scophthalmus maximus*)

tur·bu·lence /tə́rbyələns/ *n.* **1** an irregularly fluctuating flow of air or fluid. **2** *Meteorol.* stormy conditions as a result of atmospheric disturbance. **3** a disturbance, commotion, or tumult.

tur·bu·lent /tə́rbyələnt/ *adj.* **1** disturbed; in commotion. **2** (of a flow of air, etc.) varying irregularly; causing disturbance. **3** tumultuous. **4** insubordinate; riotous. □□ **tur·bu·lent·ly** *adv.*

turd /tərd/ *n. coarse sl.* **1** a lump of excrement. **2** a term of contempt for a person. ¶ Often considered a taboo word, esp. in sense 2.

tu·reen /tŏŏréen, tyŏŏ-/ *n.* a deep covered dish for serving soup, etc.

turf /tərf/ *n.* & *v.* ● *n.* (*pl.* **turfs** or **turves**) **1 a** a layer of grass, etc., with earth and matted roots as the surface of grassland. **b** a piece of this cut from the ground. **c** an artificial ground covering, as on a playing field, etc. **2** a slab of peat for fuel. **3** (prec. by *the*) **a** horse racing generally. **b** a general term for racetracks. **4** *sl.* a person's territory or sphere of influence. ● *v.tr.* **1** cover (ground) with turf. **2** (foll. by *out*) esp. *Brit. colloq.* expel or eject (a person or thing).

turf·man /tə́rfmən/ *n.* (*pl.* **-men**) a devotee of horse racing.

tur·ges·cent /tərjésənt/ *adj.* becoming turgid; swelling. □□ **tur·ges·cence** *n.*

tur·gid /tə́rjid/ *adj.* **1** swollen; inflated; enlarged. **2** (of language) pompous; bombastic. □□ **tur·gid·i·ty** /-jíditee/ *n.* **tur·gid·ly** *adv.* **tur·gid·ness** *n.*

Turk /tərk/ *n.* **1 a** a native or inhabitant of Turkey in SE Europe and Asia Minor. **b** a person of Turkish descent. **2** a member of a central Asian people from whom the Ottomans derived, speaking Turkic languages. **3** *offens.* a ferocious, wild, or unmanageable person.

tur·key /tə́rkee/ *n.* (*pl.* **-eys**) **1** a large mainly domesticated game bird, *Meleagris gallopavo*, orig. of N. America, having dark plumage with a green or bronze sheen, prized as food, esp. on festive occasions including Christmas and Thanksgiving. ▷ WATTLE. **2** the flesh of the turkey as food. **3** *sl.* **a** a theatrical failure; a flop. **b** a stupid or inept person. □ **talk turkey** *colloq.* talk frankly and straightforwardly; get down to business.

tur·key vul·ture *n.* (also **tur·key buz·zard**) an American vulture, *Cathartes aura.* ▷ VULTURE

Turk·ish /tə́rkish/ *adj.* & *n.* ● *adj.* of or relating to Turkey in SE Europe and Asia Minor, or to the Turks or their language. ● *n.* this language.

Turk·ish bath *n.* **1** a hot air or steam bath followed by washing, massage, etc. **2** (in *sing.* or *pl.*) a building for this.

Turk·ish tow·el *n.* a towel made of cotton terry cloth.

tur·mer·ic /tə́rmərik/ *n.* **1** ► an E. Indian plant, *Curcuma longa*, of the ginger family, yielding aromatic rhizomes used as a spice and for yellow dye. **2** this powdered rhizome used as a spice, esp. in curry powder. ▷ SPICE

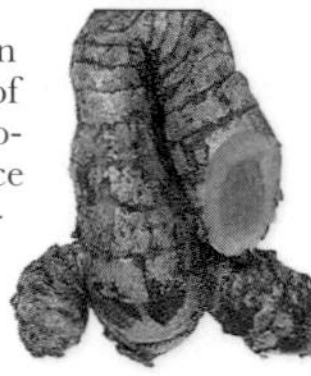

TURMERIC ROOT
(*Curcuma longa*)

tur·moil /tə́rmoyl/ *n.* **1** violent confusion; agitation. **2** din and bustle.

turn /tərn/ *v.* & *n.* ● *v.* **1** *tr.* & *intr.* move around a point or axis so that the point or axis remains in a central position; give a rotary motion to or receive a rotary motion (*turned the wheel; the wheel turns; the key turns in the lock*). **2** *tr.* & *intr.* change in position so that a different side, end, or part becomes outermost or uppermost, etc.; invert or reverse or cause to be inverted or reversed (*turned inside out; turned it upside down*). **3 a** *tr.* give a new direction to (*turn your face this way*). **b** *intr.* take a new direction (*turn left here; my thoughts have often turned to you*). **4** *tr.* aim in a certain way (*turned the hose on them*). **5** *intr.* & *tr.* (foll. by *into*) change in nature, form, or condition to (*turned into a dragon; then turned him into a frog; turned the book into a play*). **6** *intr.* (foll. by *to*) **a** apply oneself to; set about (*turned to doing the ironing*). **b** have recourse to; begin to indulge in habitually (*turned to drink; turned to me for help*). **c** go on to consider next (*let us now turn to your report*). **7** *intr.* & *tr.* become or cause to become (*turned hostile; has turned informer*). **8 a** *tr.* & *intr.* (foll. by *against*) make or become hostile to (*has turned them against us*). **b** *intr.* (foll. by *on, upon*) become hostile to; attack (*suddenly turned on them*). **9** *intr.* (of hair or leaves) change color. **10** *intr.* (of milk) become sour. **11** *intr.* (of the stomach) be nauseated. **12** *intr.* (of the head) become giddy. **13** *tr.* cause (milk) to become sour, (the stomach) to be nauseated, or (the head) to become giddy. **14** *tr.* translate (*turn it into French*). **15** *tr.* move to the other side of; go around (*turned the corner*). **16** *tr.* pass the age or time of (*he has turned 40; it has now turned 4 o'clock*). **17** *intr.* (foll. by *on*) depend on; be determined by; concern (*it all turns on the weather tomorrow; the conversation turned on my motives*). **18** *tr.* send or put into a specified place or condition; cause to go (*was turned loose; turned the water out into a basin*). **19** *tr.* **a** perform (a somersault, etc.) with rotary motion. **b** twist (an ankle) out of position; sprain. **20** *tr.* remake (a garment or a sheet) putting the worn outer side on the inside. **21** *tr.* make (a profit). **22** *tr.* (also foll. by *aside*) divert; deflect (something material or immaterial). **23** *tr.* blunt (the edge of a knife, slot of a screw, etc.). **24** *tr.* shape (an object) on a lathe. **25** *tr.* give an (esp. elegant) form to (*turn a compliment*). **26** *intr.* (of the tide) change from flood to ebb or vice versa. ● *n.* **1** the act or process or an instance of turning; rotary motion (*a single turn of the handle*). **2 a** a changed or a change of direction or tendency (*took a sudden turn to the left*). **b** a deflection or deflected part (*full of twists and turns*). **3** a point at which a turning or change occurs. **4** a turning of a road. **5** a change of the tide from ebb to flow or from flow to ebb. **6** a change in the course of events. **7** a tendency or disposition (*is of a mechanical turn of mind*). **8** an opportunity or obligation, etc., that comes successively to each of several persons, etc. (*your turn will come; my turn to read*). **9** a short walk or ride (*shall take a turn around the block*). **10** a short performance on stage or in a circus, etc. **11** service of a specified kind (*did me a good turn*). **12** purpose (*served my turn*). **13** *colloq.* a momentary nervous shock or ill feeling (*gave me quite a turn*). □ **at every turn** continually; at each new stage, etc. **by turns** in rotation of individuals or groups; alternately. **in turn** in succession; one by one. **in one's turn** when one's turn or opportunity comes. **not know which way** (or **where**) **to turn** be completely at a loss, unsure how to act, etc. **not turn a hair** see HAIR. **on the turn 1** changing. **2** (of milk) becoming sour. **3** at the turning point. **out of turn 1** at a time when it is not one's turn. **2** inappropriately; inadvisedly or tactlessly (*did I speak out of turn?*). **take turns** (or **take it in turns**) act or work alternately or in succession. **to a turn** (esp. cooked) to exactly the right degree, etc. **turn about** move so as to face in a new direction. **turn and turn about** esp. *Brit.* alternately. **turn around** (or *Brit.* **round**) **1** turn so as to face in a new direction. **2 a** *Commerce* unload and reload (a ship, vehicle, etc.). **b** receive, process, and send out again; cause to progress through a system. **3** adopt new opinions or policy. **turn aside** see TURN *v.* 22 above. **turn away 1** turn to face in another direction. **2** refuse to accept; reject. **3** send away. **turn back 1** begin or cause to retrace one's steps. **2** fold back. **turn one's back on** see BACK. **turn the corner 1** pass around it into another street. **2** pass the critical point in an illness, difficulty, etc. **turn a deaf ear** see DEAF. **turn down 1** reject (a proposal, application, etc.). **2** reduce the volume or strength of (sound, heat, etc.) by turning a knob, etc. **3** fold down. **4** place downward. **turn one's hand to** see HAND. **turn a person's head** see HEAD. **turn in 1** hand in or over; deliver. **2** achieve or register (a performance, score, etc.). **3** *colloq.* go to bed in the evening. **4** fold inward. **5** incline inward (*his toes turn in*). **6** *colloq.* abandon (a plan, etc.). **turn in one's grave** see GRAVE[1]. **turn inside out** see INSIDE. **turn off 1 a** stop the flow or operation of (water, electricity, etc.) by means of a faucet, switch, etc. **b** operate (a faucet, switch, etc.) to achieve this. **2 a** enter a side road. **b** (of a side road) lead off from another road. **3** *colloq.* repel; cause to lose interest (*turned me right off with their complaining*). **4** *Brit.* dismiss from employment. **turn of speed** the ability to go fast when necessary. **turn on 1 a** start the flow or operation of (water, electricity, etc.) by means of a faucet, switch, etc. **b** operate (a faucet, switch, etc.) to achieve this. **2** *colloq.* excite; stimulate the interest of, esp. sexually. **3** *tr.* & *intr. colloq.* intoxicate or become intoxicated with drugs. **turn one's stomach** make one nauseous or disgusted. **turn on one's heel** see HEEL[1]. **turn out 1** expel. **2** extinguish (an electric light, etc.). **3** dress or equip (*well turned out*). **4** produce (manufactured goods, etc.). **5** esp. *Brit.* empty or clean out (a room, etc.). **6** empty (a pocket) to see the contents. **7** *colloq.* **a** get out of bed. **b** go out of doors. **8** *colloq.* assemble; attend a meeting, etc. **9** (often foll. by *to* + infin. or *that* + clause) prove to be the case; result (*turned out to be true; we shall see how things turn out*). **10** *Mil.* call (a guard) from the guardroom. **turn over 1** reverse or cause to reverse vertical position; bring the underside or reverse into view (*turn over the page*). **2** upset; fall or cause to fall over. **3 a** cause (an engine) to run. **b** (of an engine) start running. **4** consider thoroughly. **5** (foll. by *to*) transfer the care or conduct of (a person or thing) to (a person) (*shall turn it all over to my deputy; turned him over to the authorities*). **6** do business to the amount of (*turns over $5,000 a week*). **turn over a new leaf** improve one's conduct or performance. **turn the other cheek** respond meekly to insult or abuse. **turn the tables** see TABLE. **turn tail** turn one's back; run away. **turn the tide** reverse the trend of events. **turn to** set about one's work (*came home and immediately turned to*). **turn to good account** see ACCOUNT. **turn turtle** see TURTLE. **turn up 1** increase the volume or strength of (sound, heat, etc.) by turning a knob, etc. **2** place upward. **3** discover or reveal. **4** be found, esp. by chance. **5** happen or present itself; (of a person) put in an appearance. **6** shorten (a garment) by increasing the size of the hem. **turn up one's nose** (or **turn one's nose up**) react with disdain.

turn·a·bout /tə́rnəbowt/ *n.* **1** an act of turning about. **2** an abrupt change of policy, etc.

turn·a·round /tə́rnərownd/ *n.* **1** time taken in a car's, plane's, etc., round trip. **2** a change in one's opinion. **3** space needed for a vehicle to turn around.

turn·a·round *n.* (also *Brit.* **turn·a·round**) **1 a** the process of loading and unloading. **b** the process of receiving, processing, and sending out again; progress through a system. **2** the reversal of an opinion or tendency.

turn·coat /tɔ́rnkōt/ *n.* a person who changes sides in a conflict, dispute, etc.

turn·down /tɔ́rndown/ *n. & adj.* ● *n.* a rejection, a refusal. ● *adj.* (of a collar) turned down.

turn·er /tɔ́rnər/ *n.* **1** a person or thing that turns. **2** a person who works with a lathe.

turn·ing /tɔ́rning/ *n.* **1 a** a road that branches off another; a turn. **b** a place where this occurs. **2 a** use of the lathe. **b** (in *pl.*) chips or shavings from a lathe.

turn·ing point *n.* a point at which a decisive change occurs.

tur·nip /tɔ́rnip/ *n.* **1** a cruciferous plant, *Brassica rapa*, with a large white globular root and sprouting leaves. **2** this root used as a vegetable. □□ **tur·nip·y** *adj.*

turn·key /tɔ́rnkee/ *n. & adj.* ● *n.* (*pl.* **-eys**) *archaic* a jailer. ● *adj.* (of a contract, etc.) providing for a supply of equipment in a state ready for operation.

turn·off /tɔ́rnof/ *n.* **1** a turning off a main road. **2** *colloq.* something that repels or causes a loss of interest.

turn·on *n. colloq.* a person or thing that causes (esp. sexual) arousal.

turn·out /tɔ́rnowt/ *n.* **1** the number of people attending a meeting, voting in an election, etc. (*rain reduced the turnout*). **2** the quantity of goods produced in a given time. **3** a set or display of equipment, clothes, etc. **4 a** a railroad siding. **b** a place where a highway widens so cars may park, pass, etc.

turn·o·ver /tɔ́rnōvər/ *n.* **1** the act or an instance of turning over. **2** the amount of money taken in a business. **3** the number of people entering and leaving employment, etc. **4** a small pastry made by folding a piece of pastry crust over a filling. **5** a change in a business' goods as items are sold, new merchandise arrives, etc.

turn·pike /tɔ́rnpīk/ *n.* **1** a highway, esp. one on which a toll is charged. **2** *hist.* **a** a tollgate. **b** a road on which a toll was collected at a tollgate. **3** *hist.* a defensive frame of spikes.

turn sig·nal *n.* any of the flashing lights on the front or back of an automobile that are activated by a driver to indicate that the vehicle is about to turn or change lanes.

turn·stile /tɔ́rnstīl/ *n.* a gate for admission or exit, with revolving arms allowing people through singly.

turn·stone /tɔ́rnstōn/ *n.* any wading bird of the genus *Arenaria*, related to the plover, that looks under stones for small animals to eat.

turn·ta·ble /tɔ́rntaybəl/ *n.* **1** a circular revolving plate supporting a phonograph record that is being played. **2** a circular revolving platform for turning a railroad locomotive or other vehicle.

tur·pen·tine /tɔ́rpəntīn/ *n.* an oleoresin secreted by several trees, esp. of the genus *Pinus, Pistacia, Syncarpia,* or *Copaifera,* and used in various commercial preparations.

tur·pi·tude /tɔ́rpitōōd, -tyōōd/ *n. formal* baseness; depravity; wickedness.

turps /tərps/ *n. colloq.* oil of turpentine.

tur·quoise /tɔ́rkwoyz, -koyz/ *n. & adj.* ● *n.* **1** ◀ a semiprecious stone, usu. opaque and greenish blue or blue, consisting of hydrated copper aluminum phosphate. ▷ GEM, MINERAL. **2** a greenish blue color. ● *adj.* of this color.

TURQUOISE:
PERSIAN
ORNAMENT

tur·ret /tɔ́rit, túr-/ *n.* **1** a small tower, usu. projecting from the wall of a building as a decorative addition. ▷ CASTLE. **2** a low flat usu. revolving armored tower for a gun and gunners in a ship, aircraft, fort, or tank. ▷ WARSHIP. □□ **tur·ret·ed** *adj.*

tur·tle /tɔ́rt'l/ *n.* **1** ▼ any of various terrestrial, marine, or freshwater reptiles of the order Chelonia, encased in a shell of bony plates, and having flippers or webbed toes used in swimming. ▷ CHELONIAN. **2** the flesh of the turtle, esp. used for soup. **3** *Computing* a directional cursor in a computer graphics system for children that can be instructed to move around a screen. □ **turn turtle** capsize.

carapace

*bony plate
(scute)*

beak

flipper

TURTLE:
HAWKSBILL TURTLE
(*Eretmochelys imbricata*)

tur·tle·dove /tɔ́rt'lduv/ *n.* any wild dove of the genus *Streptopelia,* esp. *S. turtur,* noted for its soft cooing and its affection for its mate and young.

tur·tle·neck /tɔ́rt'lnek/ *n.* **1** a high close-fitting turned over collar on a garment. **2** an upper garment with such a collar.

Tus·can /túskən/ *n. & adj.* ● *n.* **1** an inhabitant of Tuscany in central Italy. **2** the classical Italian language of Tuscany. ● *adj.* **1** of or relating to Tuscany or the Tuscans. **2** *Archit.* denoting the least ornamented of the classical orders. ▷ COLUMN

Tus·ca·ro·ra /təskərṓrə, -ráwr-/ *n.* **1 a** a N. American people native to N. Carolina and later to New York. **b** a member of this people. **2** the language of this people.

tush /tōōsh/ *n. sl.* the buttocks.

tusk /tusk/ *n. & v.* ● *n.* **1** ▼ a long pointed tooth, esp. protruding from a closed mouth, as in the elephant, walrus, etc. ▷ ELEPHANT, WALRUS. **2** a tusklike tooth or other object. ● *v.tr.* gore, thrust at, or tear up with a tusk or tusks. □□ **tusked** *adj.* (also in *comb.*). **tusk·y** *adj.*

*point of entry
into skull*

TUSK OF AN ELEPHANT

tusk·er /túskər/ *n.* an elephant or wild boar with well-developed tusks.

tus·sive /túsiv/ *adj.* of or relating to a cough.

tus·sle /túsəl/ *n. & v.* ● *n.* a struggle or scuffle. ● *v.intr.* engage in a tussle.

tus·sock /túsək/ *n.* a clump of grass, etc. □□ **tus·sock·y** *adj.*

tut var. of TUT-TUT.

tu·te·lage /tōōt'lij, tyōō-/ *n.* **1** guardianship. **2** the state or duration of being under this. **3** instruction.

tu·te·lar·y /tōōt'lairee, tyōō-/ *adj.* (also **tu·te·lar** /-t'lər/) **1 a** serving as guardian. **b** relating to a guardian (*tutelary authority*). **2** giving protection (*tutelary saint*).

tu·tor /tōōtər, tyōō-/ *n. & v.* ● *n.* **1** a private teacher, esp. in general charge of a person's education. **2** esp. *Brit.* a university teacher supervising the studies or welfare of assigned undergraduates. **3** *Brit.* a book of instruction in a subject. ● *v.* **1** *tr.* act as a tutor to. **2** *intr.* work as a tutor. **3** *tr.* restrain; discipline. **4** *intr.* receive instruction. □□ **tu·tor·age** /-rij/ *n.* **tu·tor·ship** *n.*

tu·to·ri·al /tōōtáwreeəl, tyōō-/ *adj. & n.* ● *adj.* of or relating to a tutor or tuition. ● *n.* **1** a period of individual instruction given by a tutor. **2** *Computing* a routine that allows one to instruct oneself in using a software program. □□ **tu·to·ri·al·ly** *adv.*

tut·ti /tōōtee/ *adv. & n. Mus.* ● *adv.* with all voices or instruments together. ● *n.* (*pl.* **tuttis**) a passage to be performed in this way.

tut·ti-frut·ti /tōōteefrōōtee/ *n.* (*pl.* **-fruttis**) a confection, esp. ice cream, of or flavored with mixed fruits.

tut-tut /tut-tút/ *int., n., & v.* (also **tut** /tut/) ● *int.* expressing rebuke, impatience, or contempt. ● *n.* such an exclamation. ● *v.intr.* (**-tutted, -tutting**) exclaim this.

tu·tu /tōōtōō/ *n.* a ballet dancer's short skirt of stiffened projecting frills.

tu-whit, tu-whoo /tōōwít tōōwṓ/ *n.* a representation of the cry of an owl.

tux /tuks/ *n. colloq.* = TUXEDO.

tux·e·do /tukséedō/ *n.* (*pl.* **-os** or **-oes**) **1** a man's short black formal jacket. **2** a suit of clothes including this.

TV *abbr.* television.

TVA *abbr.* Tennessee Valley Authority.

TVP *abbr. Trademark* textured vegetable protein (in foods made from vegetable but given a meatlike texture).

twad·dle /twód'l/ *n. & v.* ● *n.* useless, senseless, or dull writing or talk. ● *v.intr.* indulge in this. □□ **twad·dler** *n.*

twain /twayn/ *adj. & n. archaic* two (usu. *in twain*).

twang /twang/ *n. & v.* ● *n.* **1** a strong ringing sound made by the plucked string of a musical instrument or bow. **2** the nasal quality of a voice compared to this. ● *v.* **1** *intr. & tr.* emit or cause to emit this sound. **2** *tr.* usu. *derog.* play (a tune or instrument) in this way. □□ **twang·y** *adj.*

'twas /twuz, twoz/ *archaic* it was.

twat /twot/ *n. coarse sl.* ¶ Usually considered a taboo word. **1** the female genitals. **2** esp. *Brit.* a term of contempt for a person.

tweak /tweek/ *v. & n.* ● *v.tr.* **1** pinch and twist sharply; pull with a sharp jerk; twitch. **2** make small adjustments to (a mechanism). ● *n.* an instance of tweaking.

twee /twee/ *adj.* (**tweer** /twéeər/; **tweest** /twéeist/) *Brit.* usu. *derog.* affectedly dainty or quaint. □□ **twee·ly** *adv.* **twee·ness** *n.*

tweed /tweed/ *n.* **1** a rough-surfaced woolen cloth, usu. of mixed colors, orig. produced in Scotland. **2** (in *pl.*) clothes made of tweed.

Twee·dle·dum and Twee·dle·dee /twéed'ldúm, twéed'ldée/ *n.* a pair of persons or things that are virtually indistinguishable.

tweed·y /twéedee/ *adj.* (**tweedier, tweediest**) **1** of or relating to tweed cloth. **2** characteristic of the country gentry; heartily informal. □□ **tweed·i·ly** *adv.* **tweed·i·ness** *n.*

'tween /tween/ *prep. archaic* = BETWEEN.

tweet /tweet/ *n. & v.* ● *n.* the chirp of a small bird. ● *v.intr.* make a chirping noise.

tweet·er /twéetər/ *n.* a loudspeaker designed to reproduce high frequencies. ▷ LOUDSPEAKER

tweeze /tweez/ *v.tr.* pluck out with tweezers (*tweeze eyebrow hair*).

tweez·ers /twéez-ərz/ *n.pl.*
► a small pair of pincers for picking up small objects, plucking out hairs, etc.

TWEEZERS

twelfth /twelfth/ *n. & adj.* ● *n.* **1** the position in a sequence corresponding to the number 12 in the sequence 1–12. **2** something occupying this position. **3** each of twelve equal parts of a thing. **4** *Mus.* **a** an interval or chord spanning an octave and a

T

fifth in the diatonic scale. **b** a note separated from another by this interval. □□ **twelfth·ly** *adv.*

Twelfth Day *n.* Jan. 6, the twelfth day after Christmas, the festival of the Epiphany.

Twelfth Night *n.* the evening of Jan. 5, the eve of the Epiphany.

twelve /twelv/ *n. & adj.* ● *n.* **1** one more than eleven; the product of two units and six units. **2** a symbol for this (12, xii, XII). **3** a size, etc., denoted by twelve. **4** the time denoted by twelve o'clock (*is it twelve yet?*). **5** (**the Twelve**) the twelve apostles. ● *adj.* that amount to twelve.

twelve·fold /twélvfōld/ *adj. & adv.* **1** twelve times as much or as many. **2** consisting of twelve parts.

twelve·month /twélvmunth/ *n. archaic* a year.

twen·ty /twéntee/ *n. & adj.* ● *n.* (*pl.* **-ies**) **1** the product of two and ten. **2** a symbol for this (20, xx, XX). **3** (in *pl.*) the numbers from 20 to 29, esp. the years of a century or of a person's life. **4** *colloq.* a large indefinite number (*have told you twenty times*). ● *adj.* that amount to twenty. □□ **twen·ti·eth** *adj. & n.* **twen·ty·fold** *adj. & adv.*

24-7 *adv.* (also **24/7**) *colloq.*, chiefly *N. Amer.* twenty-four hours a day, seven days a week; all the time.

twen·ty-one *n.* a card game in which players try to acquire cards with a face value totaling 21 points and no more.

twen·ty-twen·ty *adj.* (or **20/20**) **1** denoting vision of normal acuity. **2** *colloq.* denoting clear perception or hindsight.

'twere /twər/ *archaic* it were.

twerp /twərp/ *n.* (also **twirp**) *sl.* a stupid person.

twice /twīs/ *adv.* **1** two times (esp. of multiplication); on two occasions. **2** in double degree or quantity (*twice as good*).

twid·dle /twíd'l/ *v. & n.* ● *v.* **1** *tr. &* (foll. by *with*, etc.) *intr.* twirl, adjust, or play randomly or idly. **2** *intr.* move twirlingly. ● *n.* **1** an act of twiddling. **2** a twirled mark or sign. □ **twiddle one's thumbs 1** make them rotate around each other. **2** have nothing to do. □□ **twid·dler** *n.* **twid·dly** *adj.*

twig[1] /twig/ *n.* a small branch or shoot of a tree or shrub. □□ **twigged** *adj.* (also in *comb.*). **twig·gy** *adj.*

twig[2] /twig/ *v.tr.* (**twigged, twigging**) *Brit. colloq.* **1** (also *absol.*) understand; grasp the meaning or nature of. **2** observe.

twi·light /twílīt/ *n.* **1** the soft glowing light from the sky when the Sun is below the horizon, esp. in the evening. **2** the period of this. **3** a faint light. **4** a state of imperfect knowledge or understanding. **5** a period of decline or destruction. **6** *attrib.* of, resembling, or occurring at twilight.

twi·light zone *n.* any physical or conceptual area that is undefined or intermediate, esp. one that is eerie or unreal.

twi·lit /twílit/ *adj.* (also **twi·light·ed** /-lītid/) dimly illuminated by or as by twilight.

twill /twil/ *n. & v.* ● *n.* a fabric so woven as to have a surface of diagonal parallel ridges. ● *v.tr.* (esp. as **twilled** *adj.*) weave (fabric) in this way.

'twill /twil/ *archaic* it will.

twin /twin/ *n., adj., & v.* ● *n.* **1** each of a closely related or associated pair, esp. of children or animals born at one birth. **2** the exact counterpart of a person or thing. **3** a compound crystal one part of which is in a reversed position with reference to the other. **4** (**the Twins**) the zodiacal sign or constellation Gemini. ● *adj.* **1** forming, or being one of, such a pair (*twin brothers*). **2** *Bot.* growing in pairs. **3** consisting of two closely connected and similar parts. ● *v.* (**twinned, twinning**) **1** *tr. & intr.* **a** join intimately together. **b** (foll. by *with*) pair. **2** *intr.* bear twins. **3** *intr.* grow as a twin crystal. □□ **twin·ning** *n.*

twin bed *n.* each of a pair of single beds.

twine /twīn/ *n. & v.* ● *n.* a strong thread or string of two or more strands of hemp or cotton, etc., twisted together. ● *v.* **1** *tr.* form (a string or thread, etc.) by twisting strands together. **2** *tr.* interlace. **3** *intr.* (often foll. by *around, about*) coil or wind. **4** *intr. & refl.* (of a plant) grow in this way. □□ **twin·er** *n.*

twinge /twinj/ *n. & v.* ● *n.* a sharp momentary local pain or pang (*a twinge of toothache; a twinge of conscience*). ● *v.intr.* experience a twinge.

twin·kle /twíngkəl/ *v. & n.* ● *v.* **1** *intr.* (of a star or light, etc.) shine with rapidly intermittent gleams. **2** *intr.* (of the eyes) sparkle. **3** *intr.* (of the feet in dancing) move lightly and rapidly. **4** *tr.* emit (a light or signal) in quick gleams. **5** *tr.* blink or wink (one's eyes). ● *n.* **1 a** a sparkle or gleam of the eyes. **b** a blink or wink. **2 a** a slight flash of light; a glimmer. **3** a short rapid movement. □ **in a twinkle** (or a **twinkling** or **the twinkling of an eye**) in an instant. □□ **twin·kler** *n.* **twin·kly** *adj.*

twin-tub *n.* a type of washing machine having two top-loading drums, one for washing and the other for spin-drying.

twirl /twərl/ *v. & n.* ● *v.tr. & intr.* spin or swing or twist quickly and lightly around. ● *n.* **1** a twirling motion. **2** a form made by twirling, esp. a flourish made with a pen. □□ **twirl·er** *n.* **twirl·y** *adj.*

twist /twist/ *v. & n.* ● *v.* **1 a** *tr.* change the form of by rotating one end and not the other or the two ends in opposite directions. **b** *intr.* undergo such a change; take a twisted position (*twisted around in his seat*). **c** *tr.* wrench or pull out of shape with a twisting action (*twisted my ankle*). **2** *tr.* **a** wind (strands, etc.) around each other. **b** form (a rope, etc.) by winding the strands. **c** (foll. by *with, in with*) interweave. **d** form by interweaving or twining. **3 a** *tr.* give a spiral form to (a rod, column, cord, etc.) as by rotating the ends in opposite directions. **b** *intr.* take a spiral form. **4** *tr.* (foll. by *off*) break off or separate by twisting. **5** *tr.* distort or misrepresent the meaning of (words). **6 a** *intr.* take a winding course. **b** *tr.* make (one's way) in a winding manner. **7** *tr. Brit. colloq.* cheat (*twisted me out of my allowance*). **8** *tr.* cause (the ball, esp. in billiards) to rotate while following a curved path. **9** *tr.* (as **twisted** *adj.*) (of a person or mind) emotionally unbalanced. **10** *intr.* dance the twist. ● *n.* **1** the act or an instance of twisting. **2 a** a twisted state. **b** the manner or degree in which a thing is twisted. **3** a thing formed by or as by twisting, esp. a thread or rope, etc., made by winding strands together. **4** the point at which a thing twists or bends. **5** usu. *derog.* a peculiar tendency of mind or character, etc. **6 a** an unexpected development of events, esp. in a story, etc. **b** an unusual interpretation or variation. **c** a distortion or bias. **7** a fine strong silk thread used by tailors, etc. **8** a roll of bread, tobacco, etc., in the form of a twist. **9** *Brit.* a paper package with the ends twisted shut. **10** a curled piece of lemon, etc., peel to flavor a drink. **11** a spinning motion given to a ball in throwing, etc., to make it curve. **12 a** a twisting strain. **b** the amount of twisting of a rod, etc., or the angle showing this. **c** forward motion combined with rotation about an axis. **13** *Brit.* a drink made of two ingredients mixed together. **14** (prec. by *the*) a dance with a twisting movement of the body, popular in the 1960s. □ **round the twist** *Brit. sl.* crazy. **twist a person's arm** *colloq.* apply coercion, esp. by moral pressure. **twist around one's finger** see FINGER. □□ **twist·a·ble** *adj.* **twist·y** *adj.* (**twistier, twistiest**).

twist·er /twístər/ *n.* **1** *colloq.* a tornado, waterspout, etc. **2** *Brit. colloq.* = swindler (SWINDLE). **3** a twisting ball in cricket or billiards, etc.

twit[1] /twit/ *n. sl.* a silly or foolish person.

twit[2] /twit/ *v.tr.* (**twitted, twitting**) reproach or taunt, usu. good-humoredly.

twitch /twich/ *v. & n.* ● *v.* **1** *intr.* (of the features, muscles, limbs, etc.) move or contract spasmodically. **2** *tr.* give a short sharp pull at. ● *n.* **1** a sudden involuntary contraction or movement. **2** a sudden pull or jerk. **3** *colloq.* a state of nervousness. **4** a noose and stick for controlling a horse during a veterinary operation. □□ **twitch·y** *adj.* (**twitchier, twitchiest**) (in sense 3 of *n.*).

twitch grass /twich/ *n.* = COUCH[2].

twit·ter /twítər/ *v. & n.* ● *v.* **1** *intr.* (of or like a bird) emit a succession of light tremulous sounds. **2** *tr.* utter or express in this way. ● *n.* **1** the act or an instance of twittering. **2** *colloq.* a tremulously excited state. □□ **twit·ter·er** *n.* **twit·ter·y** *adj.*

'twixt /twikst/ *prep. archaic* = BETWIXT.

two /tōō/ *n. & adj.* ● *n.* **1** one more than one; the sum of one unit and another unit. **2** a symbol for this (2, ii, II). **3** a size, etc., denoted by two. **4** the time of two o'clock (*is it two yet?*). **5** a set of two. **6** a card with two pips. **7** a two-dollar bill. ● *adj.* that amount to two. □ **in two** in or into two pieces. **in two shakes** see SHAKE. **or two** denoting several (*a thing or two*). **put two and two together** make (esp. an obvious) inference from what is known or evident. **that makes two of us** *colloq.* that is true of me also. **two by two** (or **two and two**) in pairs. **two can play at that game** *colloq.* another person's behavior can be copied to that person's disadvantage.

two-bit *adj. colloq.* cheap; petty.

two-by-four *n.* a length of lumber with a rectangular cross section nominally 2 in. by 4 in.

two-di·men·sion·al *adj.* **1** having or appearing to have length and breadth but no depth. **2** lacking depth or substance; superficial.

two-faced *adj.* **1** having two faces. **2** insincere; deceitful.

two·fold /tōōfōld/ *adj. & adv.* **1** twice as much or as many. **2** consisting of two parts.

two-hand·ed *adj.* **1** having, using, or requiring the use of two hands. **2** (of a card game) for two players.

two·pence /túpəns/ *n. Brit.* **1** the sum of two pence, esp. before decimalization. **2** *colloq.* (esp. with *neg.*) a thing of little value (*don't care twopence*).

two·pen·ny /túpənee/ *adj. Brit.* **1** costing two pence, esp. before decimalization. **2** *colloq.* cheap; worthless.

two-ply *adj. & n.* ● *adj.* of two strands, webs, or thicknesses. ● *n.* **1** two-ply wool. **2** two-ply wood made by gluing together two layers with the grain in different directions.

two·some /tōōsəm/ *n.* **1** two persons together. **2** a game, dance, etc., for two persons.

two-step *n.* a dance with a sliding step in march or polka time.

two-stroke *adj.* (also **two-cy·cle**) ▼ (of an internal-combustion engine) having its power cycle completed in one up-and-down movement of the piston. ▷ OFF-ROAD

TWO-STROKE

A two-stroke engine has ports in its cylinder that are exposed by the motion of a piston. The rising piston draws fuel and air into the crankcase and compresses the fuel and air already in the cylinder. The compressed mixture is ignited by a spark, forcing the piston down and pushing fresh mixture from the crankcase into the cylinder through the transfer port. Exhaust gases are expelled via the exhaust port.

TWO STAGES OF POWER CYCLE

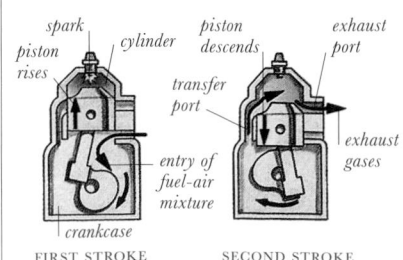

FIRST STROKE   SECOND STROKE

TYPE

Type enables text to be read easily and without ambiguity. Standard text is given in roman type, while italic or bold type are often used to emphasize or distinguish terms. Serif faces, based on ancient Roman scripts, have cross-strokes (serifs); sans serif typefaces lack these.

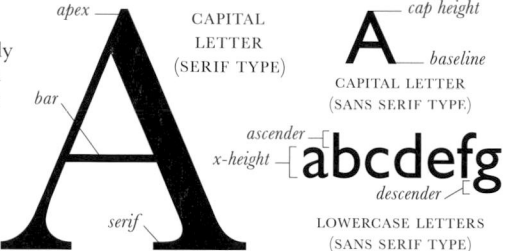

apex — CAPITAL LETTER (SERIF TYPE)
bar
serif
cap height — CAPITAL LETTER (SANS SERIF TYPE)
baseline
ascender
x-height — abcdefg
descender
LOWERCASE LETTERS (SANS SERIF TYPE)

TYPE STYLES

abcdefg   **abcdefg**   *abcdefg*

ROMAN TYPE   BOLD TYPE   ITALIC TYPE

---

two-time *v.tr. colloq.* **1** deceive or be unfaithful to (esp. a partner or lover). **2** swindle; double-cross. □□ **two-tim·er** *adj.*

two-tone *n.* having two colors or sounds.

'twould /two͞od/ *archaic* it would.

two-way *adj.* **1** involving two ways or participants. **2** (of a switch) permitting a current to be switched on or off from either of two points. **3** (of a radio) capable of transmitting and receiving signals. **4** (of a faucet, etc.) permitting fluid, etc., to flow in either of two channels or directions. **5** (of traffic, etc.) moving in two esp. opposite directions.

two-way mir·ror *n.* a panel of glass that can be seen through from one side and is a mirror on the other.

TX *abbr.* Texas (in official postal use).

ty·coon /tīko͞on/ *n.* **1** a business magnate. **2** *hist.* a title applied by foreigners to the shogun of Japan 1854–68.

ty·ing *pres. part.* of TIE.

tyke /tīk/ *n.* (also **tike**) a small child.

tym·pan /tímpən/ *n.* **1** *Printing* an appliance in a printing press used to equalize pressure between the platen, etc., and a printing sheet. **2** *Archit.* = TYMPANUM.

tym·pa·na *pl.* of TYMPANUM.

tym·pa·ni var. of TIMPANI.

tym·pan·ic /timpánik/ *adj.* **1** *Anat.* of, relating to, or having a tympanum. **2** resembling or acting like a drumhead.

tym·pan·ic mem·brane *n. Anat.* the membrane separating the outer ear and middle ear and transmitting vibrations resulting from sound waves to the inner ear.

tym·pa·num /tímpənəm/ *n.* (*pl.* **tympanums** or **tympana** /-nə/) **1** *Anat.* **a** the middle ear. ▷ EAR. **b** the tympanic membrane. **2** *Zool.* the membrane covering the hearing organ on the leg of an insect. **3** *Archit.* **a** a vertical triangular space forming the center of a pediment. **b** a similar space over a door between the lintel and the arch; a carving on this space.

Tyn·wald /tínwawld, -wəld/ *n.* the parliament of the UK's Isle of Man.

type /tīp/ *n. & v.* ● *n.* **1 a** a class of things or persons having common characteristics. **b** a kind or sort (*would like a different type of car*). **2** a person, thing, or event serving as an illustration, symbol, or characteristic specimen of another, or of a class. **3** (in *comb.*) made of, resembling, or functioning as (*ceramic-type material; Cheddar-type cheese*). **4** *colloq.* a person, esp. of a specified character (*is rather a quiet type; is not really my type*). **5** an object, conception, or work of art serving as a model for subsequent artists. **6** *Printing* **a** ▲ printed characters or letters. **b** a piece of metal, etc., with a raised letter or character on its upper surface, for use in letterpress printing. **c** such pieces collectively. **d** a kind or size of such pieces (*printed in large type*). **e** printed characters produced by type. **7** a device on either side of a medal or coin. **8** *Biol.* an organism having or chosen as having the essential characteristics of its group and giving its name to the next highest group. ● *v.* **1** *tr.* be a type or example of. **2** *tr. & intr.* write with a typewriter or keyboard. **3** *tr.* esp. *Biol. & Med.* assign to a type; classify. **4** *tr.* = TYPECAST. □□ **typ·al** *adj.*

type·cast /típkast/ *v.tr.* (*past* and *past part.* **-cast**) assign (an actor or actress) repeatedly to the same type of role.

type·face /típfays/ *n. Printing* **1** a set of type or characters in a particular design. **2** the inked part of type, or the impression made by this.

type·script /típskript/ *n.* a typewritten document.

type·set·ter /típsetər/ *n. Printing* **1** a person who composes type. **2** a composing machine. □□ **type·set·ting** *n.*

type·write /típrīt/ *v.tr. & intr.* (*past* **-wrote**; *past part.* **-written**) = TYPE *v.* 2.

type·writ·er /típrītər/ *n.* ▼ a machine with keys for producing printlike characters one at a time on paper inserted around a roller.

type bars bearing characters
ruler
platen
carriage return lever
paper bail
ribbon
shift-lock key
shift key
space bar
QWERTY keyboard

TYPEWRITER: LATE 20TH-CENTURY MANUAL PORTABLE TYPEWRITER

type·writ·ten /típrit'n/ *adj.* produced with a typewriter.

ty·phoid /tífoyd/ *n.* **1** (in full **typhoid fever**) an infectious bacterial fever with an eruption of red spots on the chest and abdomen and severe intestinal irritation. **2** a similar disease of animals. □□ **ty·phoi·dal** *adj.*

ty·phoon /tífo͞on/ *n.* a violent hurricane in E. Asia. □□ **ty·phon·ic** /-fónik/ *adj.*

ty·phus /tífəs/ *n.* an infectious fever caused by rickettsiae, characterized by a purple rash, headaches, fever, and usu. delirium. □□ **ty·phous** *adj.*

typ·i·cal /típikəl/ *adj.* **1** serving as a characteristic example; representative. **2** characteristic of or serving to distinguish a type. **3** (often foll. by *of*) conforming to expected behavior, attitudes, etc. (*is typical of them to forget*). **4** symbolic. □□ **typ·i·cal·i·ty** /-kálitee/ *n.* **typ·i·cal·ly** *adv.*

typ·i·fy /típifī/ *v.tr.* (**-ies, -ied**) **1** be a representative example of; embody the characteristics of. **2** represent by a type or symbol; serve as a type, figure, or emblem of; symbolize. □□ **typ·i·fi·ca·tion** /-fikáyshən/ *n.* **typ·i·fi·er** *n.*

typ·ist /típist/ *n.* a person who types at a typewriter or keyboard.

ty·po /típō/ *n.* (*pl.* **-os**) *colloq.* **1** a typographical error. **2** a typographer.

ty·pog·ra·pher /tīpógrəfər/ *n.* a person skilled in typography.

ty·pog·ra·phy /tīpógrəfee/ *n.* **1** printing as an art. **2** the style and appearance of printed matter. □□ **ty·po·graph·ic** /-pəgráfik/ *adj.* **ty·po·graph·i·cal** *adj.* **ty·po·graph·i·cal·ly** *adv.*

ty·ran·ni·cal /tiránikəl/ *adj.* **1** acting like a tyrant; imperious; arbitrary. **2** given to or characteristic of tyranny. □□ **ty·ran·ni·cal·ly** *adv.*

ty·ran·ni·cide /tiránisīd/ *n.* **1** the act or an instance of killing a tyrant. **2** the killer of a tyrant. □□ **ty·ran·ni·cid·al** /-nisíd'l/ *adj.*

ty·ran·nize /tírənīz/ *v.tr. & (foll. by *over*) intr.* behave like a tyrant toward; rule or treat despotically or cruelly.

ty·ran·no·sau·rus /tíránəsáwrəs/ *n.* (also **ty·ran·no·saur**) ▼ any bipedal carnivorous dinosaur of the genus *Tyrannosaurus*, esp. *T. rex* having powerful hind legs, small clawlike front legs, and a long well-developed tail. ▷ DINOSAUR

large tail
powerful jaws
clawlike front limbs

TYRANNOSAURUS (*Tyrannosaurus rex*)

ty·ran·ny /tírənee/ *n.* (*pl.* **-ies**) **1** the cruel and arbitrary use of authority. **2** a tyrannical act; tyrannical behavior. **3 a** a rule by a tyrant. **b** a period of this. **c** a nation ruled by a tyrant. □□ **tyr·an·nous** /-rənəs/ *adj.* **tyr·an·nous·ly** *adv.*

ty·rant /tírənt/ *n.* **1** an oppressive or cruel ruler. **2** a person exercising power arbitrarily or cruelly.

ty·ro /tírō/ *n.* (*Brit.* also **tiro**) (*pl.* **-os**) a beginner or novice.

Ty·ro·le·an /tírōleeən, tī-/ *adj.* of or characteristic of the Tyrol, an Alpine province of Austria. □□ **Ty·ro·lese** *adj. & n.*

T

U

U[1] /yōō/ *n.* (also **u**) (*pl.* **Us** or **U's**) **1** the twenty-first letter of the alphabet. **2** a U-shaped object or curve.

U[2] /ōō/ *adj.* a Burmese title of respect before a man's name.

U[3] *abbr.* (also **U.**) university.

UAE *abbr.* United Arab Emirates.

U-bend *n.* a section of a pipe, in particular of a waste pipe, shaped like a U.

Ü·ber·mensch /ṓōbərmensh/ *n.* the ideal superior man of the future who could rise above conventional Christian morality to create and impose his own values, originally described by Nietzsche in *Thus Spake Zarathustra* (1883–5).

u·bi·e·ty /yōōbíətee/ *n.* the fact or condition of being in a definite place; local relation.

u·biq·ui·tous /yōōbíkwitəs/ *adj.* **1** present everywhere or in several places simultaneously. **2** often encountered. □□ **u·biq·ui·tous·ly** *adv.* **u·biq·ui·tous·ness** *n.* **u·biq·ui·ty** *n.*

U-boat /yōōbōt/ *n. hist.* a German submarine. ▷ SUBMARINE

u.c. *abbr.* uppercase.

ud·der /údər/ *n.* the mammary gland of cattle, sheep, etc., hanging as a baglike organ with several teats. □□ **ud·dered** *adj.* (also in *comb.*).

u·dom·e·ter /yōōdómitər/ *n. formal* a rain gauge.

UFO /yōō-ef-ṓ, yṓōfō/ *n.* (also **ufo**) (*pl.* **UFOs** or **ufos**) unidentified flying object.

u·fol·o·gy /yōōfóləjee/ *n.* the study of UFOs. □□ **u·fol·o·gist** *n.*

ugh /əkh, ug, ukh/ *int.* expressing disgust or horror.

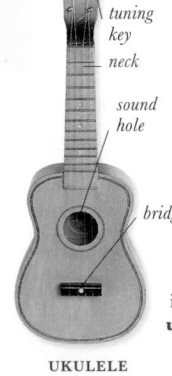

Ug·li /úglee/ *n.* (*pl.* **Uglis** or **Uglies**) *Trademark* ◀ a mottled green and yellow citrus fruit, a hybrid of a grapefruit and tangerine.

UGLI FRUIT (*Citrus* species)

ug·li·fy /úglifī/ *v.tr.* (**-ies**, **-ied**) to make ugly. □□ **ug·li·fi·ca·tion** /-fikáyshən/ *n.*

ug·ly /úglee/ *adj.* (**uglier**, **ugliest**) **1** unpleasing or repulsive to see or hear (*an ugly scar*; *spoke with an ugly snarl*). **2** unpleasantly suggestive; discreditable (*ugly rumors are about*). **3** threatening; dangerous (*the sky has an ugly look*; *an ugly mood*). **4** morally repulsive; vile (*ugly vices*). □□ **ug·li·ly** *adv.* **ug·li·ness** *n.*

ug·ly duck·ling *n.* a person who turns out to be beautiful or talented, etc., against all expectations (with ref. to a cygnet in a blood of ducks in a tale by Andersen).

UHF *abbr.* ultrahigh frequency.

uh-huh /uhú/ *int. colloq.* expressing assent.

UHT *abbr.* **1** ultrahigh temperature. **2** ultra-heat-treated (esp. of milk, for long keeping).

UK *abbr.* United Kingdom.

u·kase /yōōkáys, -káyz/ *n.* **1** an arbitrary command. **2** *hist.* an edict of the czarist Russian government.

U·krain·i·an /yōōkráyneeən/ *n. & adj.* ● *n.* **1** a native of Ukraine. **2** the language of Ukraine. ● *adj.* **1** of or relating to Ukraine or its people or language.

u·ku·le·le /yōōkəláylee/ *n.* ◀ a small, four-stringed Hawaiian (orig. Portuguese) guitar.

UKULELE

tuning key
neck
sound hole
bridge

---

ul·cer /úlsər/ *n.* **1** an open sore on an external or internal surface of the body, often forming pus. **2 a** a moral blemish. **b** a corroding or corrupting influence, etc. □□ **ul·cered** *adj.* **ul·cer·ous** *adj.*

ul·cer·ate /úlsərayt/ *v.tr. & intr.* form into or affect with an ulcer. □□ **ul·cer·a·ble** *adj.* **ul·cer·a·tion** /-ráyshən/ *n.* **ul·cer·a·tive** *adj.*

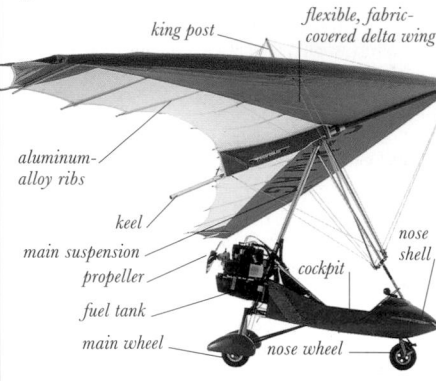

ul·na /úlnə/ *n.* (*pl.* **ulnae** /-nee/) **1** ◀ the thinner and longer bone in the forearm, on the side opposite to the thumb (cf. RADIUS 3a). ▷ SKELETON. **2** *Zool.* a corresponding bone in an animal's foreleg or a bird's wing. □□ **ul·nar** *adj.*

ulna

ULNA: HUMAN FOREARM SHOWING THE ULNA

ul·ster /úlstər/ *n.* a man's long, loose overcoat of rough cloth.

Ul·ster·man /úlstərmən/ *n.* (*pl.* **-men**; *fem.* **Ulster woman** (*pl.* **-women**) native of Ulster, the northern part of Ireland.

ult. *abbr.* **1** ultimo. **2** ultimate.

ul·te·ri·or /ulteéreeər/ *adj.* **1** existing in the background, or beyond what is evident or admitted; secret (esp. *ulterior motive*). **2** not immediate; in the future.

ul·ti·ma·ta *pl.* of ULTIMATUM.

ul·ti·mate /últimət/ *adj. & n.* ● *adj.* **1** last; final. **2** beyond which no other exists or is possible (*the ultimate analysis*). **3** fundamental; primary; unanalyzable (*ultimate truths*). **4** maximum (*ultimate tensile strength*). ● *n.* **1** (prec. by *the*) the best achievable or imaginable. **2** a final or fundamental fact or principle. □□ **ul·ti·mate·ly** *adj.* **ul·ti·mate·ness** *n.*

ul·ti·ma·tum /últimáytəm/ *n.* (*pl.* **ultimatums** or **ultimata** /-ta/) a final demand or statement of terms, the rejection of which could cause a breakdown in relations, war, etc.

ul·ti·mo /últimō/ *adj. Commerce* of last month.

ul·tra /últrə/ *adj. & n.* ● *adj.* favoring extreme views or measures, esp. in religion or politics. ● *n.* an extremist.

ultra- /últrə/ *comb. form* **1** beyond; on the other side of. **2** extreme(ly), (*ultraconservative*; *ultramodern*).

ul·tra·high /últrəhī/ *adj.* **1** (of a frequency) in the range 300 to 3,000 megahertz. **2** extremely high (*ultrahigh prices*; *ultrahigh suspension bridge*).

ul·tra·ist /últrəist/ *n.* the holder of extreme positions in politics, religion, etc. □□ **ul·tra·ism** *n.*

ul·tra·light /últrəlīt/ *n.* ▼ a kind of motorized hang glider. ▷ AIRCRAFT

king post
flexible, fabric-covered delta wing
aluminum-alloy ribs
keel
nose shell
main suspension
propeller
cockpit
fuel tank
main wheel
nose wheel

ULTRALIGHT

ul·tra·ma·rine /últrəməréen/ *n. & adj.* ● *n.* **1 a** ▶ a brilliant blue pigment orig. obtained from lapis lazuli. **b** an imitation of this from powdered fired clay, sodium carbonate, sulfur, and resin. **2** the color of this. ● *adj.* of this color.

ULTRAMARINE

ul·tra·mi·cro·scope /últrəmíkrəskōp/ *n.* an optical microscope used to reveal very small particles by means of light scattered by them.

ul·tra·mi·cro·scop·ic /últrəmíkrəskópik/ *adj.* **1** too small to be seen by an ordinary optical microscope. **2** of or relating to an ultramicroscope.

ul·tra·mon·tane /últrəmontáyn/ *adj. & n.* ● *adj.* **1** beyond the mountains (esp. the Alps). **2** advocating supreme papal authority in matters of faith and discipline. ● *n.* a person living on the other side of the mountains (esp. the Alps).

ul·tra·son·ic /últrəsónik/ *adj.* of or involving sound waves with a frequency above the upper limit of human hearing. □□ **ul·tra·son·i·cal·ly** *adv.*

ul·tra·son·ics /últrəsóniks/ *n.pl.* (usu. treated as *sing.*) the science and application of ultrasonic waves.

ul·tra·sound /últrəsownd/ *n.* **1** sound having an ultrasonic frequency. **2** ▼ ultrasonic waves.

ULTRASOUND

One of the uses of ultrasound is in prenatal assessment. A transducer is passed over the abdomen, transmitting one pulse of ultrasound every millisecond. The pulses are reflected back by tissue in their path and appear as bright spots on a dark screen. The spots form an accurate image of the fetus.

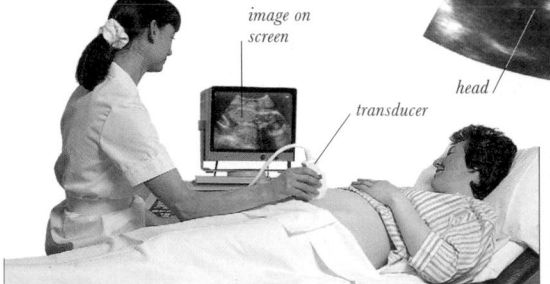

hands
eye
image on screen
transducer
head
leg
body
shoulder
spine

ULTRASOUND IMAGE OF A HUMAN FETUS

ULTRASOUND SCANNING OF AN EXPECTANT MOTHER

ul·tra·struc·ture /últrəstrukchər/ *n. Biol.* fine structure not visible with an optical microscope.

ul·tra·vi·o·let /últrəvíələt/ *adj. Physics* **1** having a wavelength (just) beyond the violet end of the visible spectrum. ▷ ELECTROMAGNETIC RADIATION. **2** of or using such radiation.

u·lu /ōōlōō/ *n.* a short-handled knife with a broad crescent-shaped blade, usu. used by Eskimo women.

ul·u·late /úlyəlayt, yōōl-/ *v.intr.* howl; wail; make a hooting cry. □□ **ul·u·lant** *adj.* **ul·u·la·tion** /-láyshən/ *n.*

um /um, əm/ *int.* expressing hesitation or a pause in speech.

um·bel /úmbəl/ *n. Bot.* a flower cluster in which stalks nearly equal in length spring from a common center and form a flat or curved surface, as in parsley. ▷ INFLORESCENCE. □□ **um·bel·lar** *adj.* **um·bel·late** /-bəlit, -layt, umbélit/ *adj.* **um·bel·lule** /úmbəlyōōl, -bél·yōōl/ *adj.*

um·bel·lif·er /umbélifər/ *n.* ▶ any plant of the family Umbelliferae bearing umbels, including parsley, carrot, and parsnip. □□ **um·bel·lif·er·ous** /bəlifərəs/ *adj.*

um·ber /úmbər/ *n. & adj.* ● *n.* **1** a natural pigment like ocher but darker and browner. ▷ RAW UMBER. **2** the color of this. ● *adj.* **1** of this color. **2** dark; dusky.

um·bil·i·cal /umbílikəl/ *adj.* **1** of, situated near, or affecting the navel. **2** centrally placed.

um·bil·i·cal cord *n.* **1** ▼ a flexible, cordlike structure attaching a fetus to the placenta. **2** *Astronaut.* a supply cable linking a missile to its launcher, or an astronaut in space to a spacecraft.

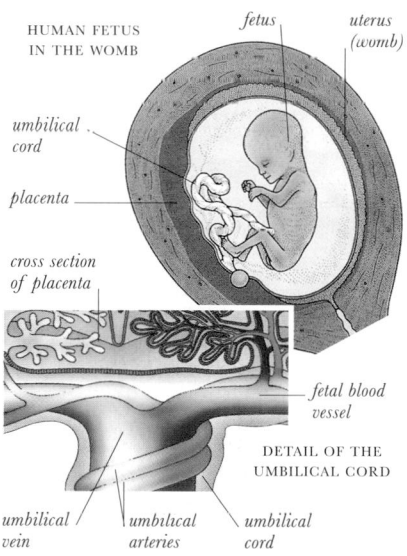

HUMAN FETUS
IN THE WOMB

fetus
uterus
(womb)

umbilical
cord

placenta

cross section
of placenta

fetal blood
vessel

DETAIL OF THE
UMBILICAL CORD

umbilical
vein

umbilical
arteries

umbilical
cord

UMBILICAL CORD

um·bil·i·cus /umbílikəs/ *n.* (*pl.* **umbilici** /-bílisī/ or **umbilicuses**) **1** *Anat.* the navel. **2** *Bot. & Zool.* a navellike formation.

um·bles /úmbəlz/ *n.pl.* the edible offal of deer, etc.

um·bra /úmbrə/ *n.* (*pl.* **umbras** or **umbrae** /-bree/) *Astron.* **1** a total shadow usu. cast on the Earth by the Moon during a solar eclipse. ▷ ECLIPSE. **2** the dark central part of a sunspot (cf. PENUMBRA). □□ **um·bral** *adj.*

um·brage /úmbrij/ *n.* **1** offense; a sense of slight or injury (esp. give or take umbrage at). **2** *archaic* **a** a shade. **b** what gives shade.

um·brel·la /umbrélə/ *n.* **1** ▶ a light, portable device for protection against rain, strong sun, etc., consisting of a usu. circular canopy of cloth mounted by means of a collapsible metal frame on a central stick. **2** protection or patronage. **3** (often *attrib.*) a coordinating or unifying agency (*umbrella organization*). **4** a screen of fighter aircraft or a curtain of fire put up as a protection against enemy aircraft. **5** *Zool.* the gelatinous disk of a jellyfish, etc., which it contracts and expands to move through the water. □□ **um·brel·laed** /-ləd/ *adj.* **um·brel·la·like** *adj.*

canopy
tip
rib
tube
tip cup
handle
UMBRELLA

um·brel·la stand *n.* a stand for holding closed, upright umbrellas.

Um·bri·an /umbreeən/ *adj. & n.* ● *adj.* of or relating to Umbria in central Italy. ● *n.* the language of ancient Umbria, related to Latin.

u·mi·ak /ōōmeeak/ *n.* an Inuit skin-and-wood open boat propelled with paddles.

um·laut /ōōmlowt/ *n.* **1** a mark (¨) used over a vowel, esp. in Germanic languages, to indicate a vowel change. **2** such a vowel change, e.g., German *Mann*, *Männer*, English *man*, *men*, due to *i*, *j*, etc. (now usu. lost or altered) in the following syllable.

ump /ump/ *n. colloq.* an umpire.

um·pire /úmpīr/ *n. & v.* ● *n.* **1** a person chosen to enforce the rules and settle disputes in various sports. **2** a person chosen to arbitrate between disputants, or to see fair play. ● *v.* **1** *intr.* (usu. foll. by *for, in*, etc.) act as umpire. **2** *tr.* act as umpire in (a game, etc.). □□ **um·pir·age** /-pīrij, -pərij/ *n.* **um·pire·ship** *n.*

ump·teen /úmpteén/ *adj. & pron. sl.* ● *adj.* indefinitely many; a lot of. ● *pron.* indefinitely many. □□ **ump·teenth** *adj.*

UN *abbr.* United Nations.

'un /ən/ *pron. colloq.* one (*that's a good 'un*).

un·a·bashed /únəbásht/ *adj.* not abashed. □□ **un·a·bash·ed·ly** /-shidlee/ *adv.*

un·a·bat·ed /únəbáytid/ *adj.* not abated; undiminished. □□ **un·a·bat·ed·ly** *adv.*

un·a·ble /únáybəl/ *adj.* (usu. foll. by *to* + infin.) not able; lacking ability.

un·a·bridged /únəbríjd/ *adj.* (of a text, etc.) complete; not abridged.

un·ab·sorbed /únəbzáwrbd, -sáwrbd/ *adj.* not absorbed.

un·a·cad·em·ic /únakədémik/ *adj.* **1** not academic (esp. not scholarly or theoretical). **2** (of a person) not suited to academic study.

un·ac·cent·ed /únáksentid, -akséntid/ *adj.* not accented; not emphasized.

un·ac·cept·a·ble /únəkséptəbəl/ *adj.* not acceptable. □□ **un·ac·cept·a·ble·ness** *n.* **un·ac·cept·a·bly** *adv.*

un·ac·com·mo·dat·ing /únəkómədayting/ *adj.* not accommodating; disobliging.

un·ac·com·pa·nied /únəkúmpəneed/ *adj.* **1** not accompanied. **2** *Mus.* without accompaniment.

un·ac·com·plished /únəkómplisht/ *adj.* **1** not accomplished; uncompleted. **2** lacking accomplishments.

un·ac·count·a·ble /únəkówntəbəl/ *adj.* **1** unable to be explained. **2** unpredictable or strange in behavior. **3** not responsible. □□ **un·ac·count·a·bil·i·ty** /-bílitee/ *n.* **un·ac·count·a·ble·ness** *n.* **un·ac·count·a·bly** *adv.*

un·ac·count·ed /únəkówntid/ *adj.* of which no account is given. □ **unaccounted for** unexplained; not included in an account.

un·ac·cus·tomed /únəkústəmd/ *adj.* **1** (usu. foll. by *to*) not accustomed. **2** not customary; unusual (*his unaccustomed silence*). □□ **un·ac·cus·tomed·ly** *adv.*

un·ac·knowl·edged /únəknólijd/ *adj.* not acknowledged.

un·ac·quaint·ed /únəkwáyntid/ *adj.* (usu. foll. by *with*) not acquainted.

un·ad·dressed /únədrést/ *adj.* (esp. of a letter, etc.) without an address.

un·a·dopt·ed /únədóptid/ *adj.* not adopted.

un·a·dorned /únədáwrnd/ *adj.* not adorned; plain.

un·a·dul·ter·at·ed /únədúltəraytid/ *adj.* **1** not adulterated; pure; concentrated. **2** sheer; complete; utter (*unadulterated nonsense*).

un·ad·ven·tur·ous /únədvénchərəs/ *adj.* not adventurous. □□ **un·ad·ven·tur·ous·ly** *adv.*

un·ad·vis·a·ble /únədvízəbəl/ *adj.* **1** not open to advice. **2** (of a thing) inadvisable.

un·ad·vised /únədvízd/ *adj.* **1** indiscreet; rash. **2** not having had advice. □□ **un·ad·vis·ed·ly** /-zidlee/ *adv.* **un·ad·vis·ed·ness** *n.*

un·af·fect·ed /únəféktid/ *adj.* **1** (usu. foll. by *by*) not affected. **2** free from affectation; genuine; sincere. □ **un·af·fect·ed by** impervious to, immune to. □□ **un·af·fect·ed·ly** *adv.* **un·af·fect·ed·ness** *n.*

un·af·fil·i·at·ed /únəfíleeaytid/ *adj.* not affiliated.

un·a·fraid /únəfráyd/ *adj.* not afraid.

un·aid·ed /únáydid/ *adj.* not aided; without help.

un·al·ien·a·ble /únáyleeənəbəl/ *adj. Law* = INALIENABLE.

un·a·like /únəlík/ *adj.* not alike; different.

un·al·le·vi·at·ed /únəléeveeaytid/ *adj.* not alleviated; relentless.

un·al·loyed /únəlóyd, únál-/ *adj.* **1** not alloyed; pure. **2** complete; utter (*unalloyed joy*).

un·al·ter·a·ble /únáwltərəbl/ *adj.* not alterable. □□ **un·al·ter·a·ble·ness** *n.* **un·al·ter·a·bly** *adv.*

un·al·tered /únáwltərd/ *adj.* not altered; remaining the same.

un·am·big·u·ous /únambígyōōəs/ *adj.* not ambiguous; clear or definite in meaning. □□ **un·am·big·u·i·ty** /-gyōō-itee/ *n.* **un·am·big·u·ous·ly** *adv.*

un·am·bi·tious /únambíshəs/ *adj.* not ambitious; without ambition. □□ **un·am·bi·tious·ly** *adv.* **un·am·bi·tious·ness** *n.*

un·am·biv·a·lent /únambívələnt/ *adj.* (of feelings, etc.) not ambivalent; straightforward. □□ **un·am·biv·a·lent·ly** *adv.*

un·A·mer·i·can /únəmérikən/ *adj.* **1** not in accordance with American characteristics, etc. **2** contrary to the interests of the US; (in the US) treasonable. □□ **un·A·mer·i·can·ism** *n.*

un·a·mi·a·ble /únáymeeəbəl/ *adj.* not amiable.

un·am·pli·fied /únámplifīd/ *adj.* not amplified.

un·a·mused /únəmyōōzd/ *adj.* not amused.

u·nan·i·mous /yōōnániməs/ *adj.* **1** all in agreement (*the committee was unanimous*). **2** (of an opinion, vote, etc.) held or given by general consent (*the unanimous choice*). □□ **u·na·nim·i·ty** /-nənímitee/ *n.* **u·nan·i·mous·ly** *adv.* **u·nan·i·mous·ness** *n.*

un·an·nounced /únənównst/ *adj.* not announced; without warning (*of arrival, etc.*).

un·an·swer·a·ble /únánsərəbəl/ *adj.* **1** unable to be refuted (*has an unanswerable case*). **2** unable to be answered (*an unanswerable question*). □□ **un·an·swer·a·ble·ness** *n.* **un·an·swer·a·bly** *adv.*

un·an·swered /únánsərd/ *adj.* not answered.

un·an·tic·i·pat·ed /únantísipaytid/ *adj.* not anticipated.

un·ap·par·ent /únəpárənt/ *adj.* not apparent.

un·ap·peal·a·ble /únəpéeləbəl/ *adj.* esp. *Law* not able to be appealed against.

un·ap·peal·ing /únəpéeling/ *adj.* not appealing; unattractive. □□ **un·ap·peal·ing·ly** *adv.*

un·ap·peas·a·ble /únəpéezəbəl/ *adj.* not appeasable.

U

un·ap·pe·tiz·ing /únápitīzing/ *adj.* not appetizing. □□ **un·ap·pe·tiz·ing·ly** *adv.*

un·ap·pre·ci·at·ed /únəpréésheeaytid/ *adj.* not appreciated.

un·ap·pre·ci·a·tive /únəprééshətiv/ *adj.* not appreciative.

un·ap·proach·a·ble /únəpróchəbəl/ *adj.* **1** not approachable; remote; inaccessible. **2** (of a person) unfriendly. □□ **un·ap·proach·a·bil·i·ty** *n.* **un·ap·proach·a·ble·ness** *n.* **un·ap·proach·a·bly** *adv.*

un·ap·proved /únəpróŏvd/ *adj.* not approved or sanctioned.

un·apt /únápt/ *adj.* **1** (usu. foll. by *for*) not suitable. **2** (usu. foll. by *to* + infin.) not apt. □□ **un·apt·ly** *adv.* **un·apt·ness** *n.*

un·ar·gu·a·ble /únáargyŏŏbəl/ *adj.* not arguable; certain.

un·armed /únáarmd/ *adj.* not armed; without weapons.

un·ar·rest·ing /únərésting/ *adj.* uninteresting; dull. □□ **un·ar·rest·ing·ly** *adv.*

un·ar·tis·tic /únaartístik/ *adj.* not artistic, esp. not concerned with art. □□ **un·ar·tis·ti·cal·ly** *adv.*

un·a·shamed /únəsháymd/ *adj.* **1** feeling no guilt, shameless. **2** blatant; bold. □□ **un·a·sham·ed·ly** /-midlee/ *adv.* **un·a·sham·ed·ness** /-midnis/ *n.*

un·asked /únáskt/ *adj.* (often foll. by *for*) not asked, requested, or invited.

un·as·sail·a·ble /únəsáyləbəl/ *adj.* unable to be attacked or questioned; impregnable. □□ **un·as·sail·a·bil·i·ty** /-bílitee/ *n.* **un·as·sail·a·ble·ness** *n.* **un·as·sail·a·bly** *adv.*

un·as·ser·tive /únəsórtiv/ *adj.* (of a person) not assertive or forthcoming; reticent. □□ **un·as·ser·tive·ly** *adv.* **un·as·ser·tive·ness** *n.*

un·as·signed /únəsínd/ *adj.* not assigned.

un·as·sim·i·lat·ed /únəsímiláytid/ *adj.* not assimilated. □□ **un·as·sim·i·la·ble** *adj.*

un·as·sist·ed /únəsístid/ *adj.* not assisted.

un·as·suaged /únəswáyjd/ *adj.* not assuaged. □□ **un·as·suage·a·ble** *adj.*

un·as·sum·ing /únəsŏŏming/ *adj.* not pretentious or arrogant; modest. □□ **un·as·sum·ing·ly** *adv.* **un·as·sum·ing·ness** *n.*

un·at·tached /únətácht/ *adj.* **1** (often foll. by *to*) not attached, esp. to a particular body, organization, etc. **2** not engaged or married.

un·at·tain·a·ble /únətáynəbəl/ *adj.* not attainable. □□ **un·at·tain·a·ble·ness** *n.* **un·at·tain·a·bly** *adv.*

un·at·tend·ed /únəténdid/ *adj.* **1** (usu. foll. by *to*) not attended. **2** (of a person, vehicle, etc.) not accompanied; alone; uncared for.

un·at·trac·tive /únətráktiv/ *adj.* not attractive. □□ **un·at·trac·tive·ly** *adv.* **un·at·trac·tive·ness** *n.*

un·at·trib·ut·a·ble /únətríbyətəbəl/ *adj.* (esp. of information) that cannot or may not be attributed to a source, etc. □□ **un·at·trib·ut·a·bly** *adv.*

un·at·trib·ut·ed /únətríbyətəd/ *adj.* (of a painting, quotation, etc.) not attributed to a source, etc.

un·au·then·ti·cat·ed /únawthéntikaytid/ *adj.* not authenticated.

un·au·thor·ized /únáwthərīzd/ *adj.* not authorized.

un·a·vail·a·ble /únəváyləbəl/ *adj.* not available. □□ **un·a·vail·a·bil·i·ty** *n.* **un·a·vail·a·ble·ness** *n.*

un·a·void·a·ble /únəvóydəbəl/ *adj.* not avoidable; inevitable. □□ **un·a·void·a·bil·i·ty** *n.* **un·a·void·a·ble·ness** *n.* **un·a·void·a·bly** *adv.*

un·a·ware /únəwáir/ *adj.* & *adv.* ● *adj.* **1** (usu. foll. by *of*, or *that* + clause) not aware; ignorant (*unaware of her presence*). **2** (of a person) insensitive; unperceptive. ● *adv.* = UNAWARES. □□ **un·a·ware·ness** *n.*

un·a·wares /únəwáirz/ *adv.* **1** unexpectedly (*met them unawares*). **2** inadvertently (*dropped it unawares*).

un·backed /únbákt/ *adj.* **1** not supported. **2** (of a horse, etc.) having no backers. **3** (of a chair, picture, etc.) having no back or backing.

un·bal·ance /únbáləns/ *v.* & *n.* ● *v.tr.* **1** upset the physical or mental balance of (*unbalanced by the blow*; *the shock unbalanced him*). **2** (as **unbalanced** *adj.*) **a** not balanced. **b** (of a mind or a person) unstable or deranged. ● *n.* lack of balance; instability, esp. mental.

un·ban /únbán/ *v.tr.* (**unbanned, unbanning**) cease to ban; remove a ban from.

un·bar /únbáar/ *v.tr.* (**unbarred, unbarring**) **1** remove a bar or bars from (a gate, etc.). **2** unlock; open.

un·bear·a·ble /únbáirəbəl/ *adj.* not bearable. □□ **un·bear·a·ble·ness** *n.* **un·bear·a·bly** *adv.*

un·beat·a·ble /únbéetəbəl/ *adj.* not beatable; excelling.

un·beat·en /únbéet'n/ *adj.* **1** not beaten. **2** (of a record, etc.) not surpassed.

un·be·com·ing /únbikúming/ *adj.* **1** (esp. of clothing) not flattering or suiting a person. **2** (usu. foll. by *to, for*) not fitting; indecorous or unsuitable. □□ **un·be·com·ing·ly** *adv.* **un·be·com·ing·ness** *n.*

un·be·known /únbinón/ *adj.* (also **un·be·knownst** /-nónst/) (foll. by *to*) without the knowledge of (*was there all the time unbeknown to us*).

un·be·lief /únbiléef/ *n.* lack of belief, esp. in religious matters. □□ **un·be·liev·er** *n.* **un·be·liev·ing** *adj.* **un·be·liev·ing·ly** *adv.* **un·be·liev·ing·ness** *n.*

un·be·liev·a·ble /únbiléevəbəl/ *adj.* not believable; incredible. □□ **un·be·liev·a·bil·i·ty** *n.* **un·be·liev·a·ble·ness** *n.* **un·be·liev·a·bly** *adv.*

un·belt /únbélt/ *v.tr.* remove or undo the belt of (a garment, etc.).

un·bend /únbénd/ *v.* (*past* and *past part.* **unbent**) **1** *tr.* & *intr.* change from a bent position; straighten. **2** *intr.* relax from strain or severity; become affable.

un·bend·ing /únbénding/ *adj.* **1** not bending; inflexible. **2** firm; austere (*unbending rectitude*). **3** relaxing from strain, activity, or formality. □□ **un·bend·ing·ly** *adv.* **un·bend·ing·ness** *n.*

un·bi·ased /únbíəst/ *adj.* (also esp. *Brit.* **un·bi·assed**) not biased; impartial.

un·bid·den /únbíd'n/ *adj.* not commanded or invited (*arrived unbidden*).

un·bind /únbínd/ *v.tr.* (*past* and *past part.* **unbound**) release from bonds or binding.

un·birth·day /únbírthday/ *n.* (often *attrib.*) *joc.* any day but one's birthday (*an unbirthday party*).

un·bleached /únbléecht/ *adj.* ▶ not bleached.

un·blem·ished /únblémisht/ *adj.* not blemished.

un·blink·ing /únblíngking/ *adj.* **1** not blinking. **2** steadfast; not hesitating. **3** stolid; cool. □□ **un·blink·ing·ly** *adv.*

un·block /únblók/ *v.tr.* **1** remove an obstruction from (esp. a pipe, drain, etc.). **2** (also *absol.*) *Cards* allow the later unobstructed play of (a suit) by playing a high card.

un·blush·ing /únblúshing/ *adj.* **1** not blushing. **2** unashamed; frank. □□ **un·blush·ing·ly** *adv.*

un·bolt /únbólt/ *v.tr.* release (a door, etc.) by drawing back the bolt.

un·bolt·ed /únbóltid/ *adj.* **1** not bolted. **2** (of flour, etc.) not sifted.

un·born /únbáwrn/ *adj.* **1** not yet born (*an unborn child*). **2** never to be brought into being (*unborn hopes*).

un·bos·om /únbŏŏzəm/ *v.tr.* **1** disclose (thoughts, secrets, etc.). **2** (*refl.*) unburden (oneself) of one's thoughts, secrets, etc.

un·both·ered /únbóthərd/ *adj.* not bothered; unconcerned.

un·bound[1] /únbównd/ *adj.* **1** not bound or tied up. **2** unconstrained. **3 a** (of a book) not having a binding. **b** having paper covers. **4** (of a substance or particle) in a loose or free state.

un·bound[2] *past* and *past part.* of UNBIND.

un·bound·ed /únbówndid/ *adj.* not bounded; infinite (*unbounded optimism*). □□ **un·bound·ed·ly** *adv.* **un·bound·ed·ness** *n.*

un·break·a·ble /únbráykəbəl/ *adj.* not breakable.

un·breath·a·ble /únbrééthəbəl/ *adj.* not able to be breathed.

un·bridge·a·ble /únbríjəbəl/ *adj.* unable to be bridged.

un·bri·dle /únbríd'l/ *v.tr.* **1** remove a bridle from (a horse). **2** remove constraints from (one's tongue, a person, etc.). **3** (as **unbridled** *adj.*) unconstrained (*unbridled insolence*).

un·bro·ken /únbrókən/ *adj.* **1** not broken. **2** not tamed (*an unbroken horse*). **3** not interrupted (*unbroken sleep*). **4** not surpassed (*an unbroken record*). □□ **un·bro·ken·ly** *adv.* **un·bro·ken·ness** /-ən-nis/ *n.*

un·bruised /únbrŏŏzd/ *adj.* not bruised.

un·buck·le /únbúkəl/ *v.tr.* release the buckle of.

un·bur·den /únbúrd'n/ *v.tr.* **1** relieve of a burden. **2** (esp. *refl.*; often foll. by *to*) relieve (oneself, one's conscience, etc.) by confession, etc. □□ **un·bur·dened** *adj.*

un·bur·ied /únbéreed/ *adj.* not buried.

un·busi·ness·like /únbíznislīk/ *adj.* not businesslike.

un·but·ton /únbút'n/ *v.tr.* **1 a** unfasten (a coat, etc.) by taking the buttons out of the buttonholes. **b** unbutton the clothes of (a person). **2** (*absol.*) *colloq.* relax from tension or formality, become communicative. **3** (as **unbuttoned** *adj.*) **a** not buttoned. **b** *colloq.* communicative; informal.

un·called /únkáwld/ *adj.* not summoned or invited.

un·called-for *adj.* (of an opinion, action, etc.) impertinent or unnecessary (*an uncalled-for remark*).

un·can·did /únkándid/ *adj.* not candid, disingenuous

un·can·ny /únkánee/ *adj.* (**uncannier, uncanniest**) seemingly supernatural; mysterious. □□ **un·can·ni·ly** *adv.* **un·can·ni·ness** *n.*

un·cap /únkáp/ *v.tr.* (**uncapped, uncapping**) **1** remove the cap from (a jar, bottle, etc.). **2** remove a cap from (the head or another person).

un·cared-for /únkáirdfawr/ *adj.* neglected.

un·car·ing /únkáiring/ *adj.* lacking compassion or concern for others.

un·cashed /únkásht/ *adj.* not cashed.

un·ceas·ing /únséesing/ *adj.* not ceasing; continuous (*unceasing effort*). □□ **un·ceas·ing·ly** *adv.*

un·cen·sored /únsénsərd/ *adj.* not censored.

un·cen·sured /únsénshərd/ *adj.* not censured.

un·cer·e·mo·ni·ous /únserimóneeəs/ *adj.* **1** lacking ceremony or formality. **2** abrupt; discourteous. □□ **un·cer·e·mo·ni·ous·ly** *adv.* **un·cer·e·mo·ni·ous·ness** *n.*

un·cer·tain /únsórt'n/ *adj.* **1** not certainly knowing or known (*uncertain what it means*; *the result is uncertain*). **2** unreliable (*his aim is uncertain*). **3** changeable (*uncertain weather*). □ **in no uncertain terms** clearly and forcefully. □□ **un·cer·tain·ly** *adv.*

un·cer·tain·ty /únsórt'ntee/ *n.* (*pl.* **-ies**) **1** the fact or condition of being uncertain. **2** an uncertain matter or circumstance.

un·cer·tain·ty prin·ci·ple *n. Physics* the principle that the momentum and position of a particle cannot both be precisely determined at the same time.

un·cer·ti·fied /únsórtifīd/ *adj.* **1** not attested as certain. **2** not guaranteed by a certificate of competence, etc. **3** not certified as insane.

un·chain /úncháyn/ *v.tr.* **1** remove the chains from. **2** release; liberate.

un·chal·lenge·a·ble /únchálinjəbəl/ *adj.* not challengeable; unassailable. □□ **un·chal·lenge·a·bly** *adv.*

un·chal·lenged /únchálinjd/ *adj.* not challenged.

UNBLEACHED
COTTON T-SHIRT

U

un·change·a·ble /úncháynjəbəl/ *adj.* not changeable; immutable; invariable. □□ **un·change·a·bil·i·ty** *n.* **un·change·a·ble·ness** *n.* **un·change·a·bly** *adv.*

un·changed /úncháynjd/ *adj.* not changed; unaltered.

un·chang·ing /úncháynjing/ *adj.* not changing; remaining the same. □□ **un·chang·ing·ly** *adv.* **un·chang·ing·ness** *n.*

un·char·ac·ter·is·tic /únkariktərístik/ *adj.* not characteristic. □□ **un·char·ac·ter·is·ti·cal·ly** *adv.*

un·char·i·ta·ble /úncháritəbəl/ *adj.* censorious; severe in judgment. □□ **un·char·i·ta·ble·ness** *n.* **un·char·i·ta·bly** *adv.*

un·chart·ed /úncháartid/ *adj.* not charted, mapped, or surveyed.

un·char·tered /úncháartərd/ *adj.* **1** not furnished with a charter; not formally privileged or constituted. **2** unauthorized; illegal.

un·chaste /úncháyst/ *adj.* not chaste. □□ **un·chaste·ly** *adv.* **un·chaste·ness** *n.* **un·chas·ti·ty** /-chástitee/ *n.*

un·checked /únchékt/ *adj.* **1** not checked. **2** freely allowed; unrestrained (*unchecked violence*).

un·chiv·al·rous /únshívəlrəs/ *adj.* not chivalrous; rude. □□ **un·chiv·al·rous·ly** *adv.*

un·cho·sen /únchózən/ *adj.* not chosen.

un·chris·tian /únkríschən/ *adj.* **1 a** contrary to Christian principles, esp. uncaring or selfish. **b** not Christian. **2** *colloq.* outrageous. □□ **un·chris·tian·ly** *adv.*

un·church /únchárch/ *v.tr.* excommunicate.

un·ci·al /únsheeəl, únshəl/ *adj. & n.* ● *adj.* **1** ▼ of or written in majuscule writing with rounded, unjoined letters found in manuscripts of the 4th–8th c., from which modern capitals are derived. **2** of or relating to an inch or an ounce. ● *n.* **1** an uncial letter. **2** an uncial style or manuscript.

un·cir·cum·cised /únsérkəmsīzd/ *adj.* **1** not circumcised. **2** spiritually impure; heathen. □□ **un·cir·cum·ci·sion** /-sízhən/ *n.*

un·civ·il /únsívil/ *adj.* **1** ill mannered; impolite. **2** not public-spirited. □□ **un·civ·il·ly** *adv.*

un·civ·i·lized /únsívilīzd/ *adj.* **1** not civilized. **2** rough; uncultured.

un·claimed /únkláymd/ *adj.* not claimed.

un·clasp /únklásp/ *v.tr.* **1** loosen the clasp or clasps of. **2** release the grip of (a hand, etc.).

un·clas·si·fied /únklásifīd/ *adj.* **1** not classified. **2** (of government information) not secret.

un·cle /úngkəl/ *n.* **1 a** the brother of one's father or mother. **b** an aunt's husband. **2** *colloq.* a name given by children to a male family friend.

un·clean /únkléen/ *adj.* **1** not clean. **2** unchaste. **3** unfit to be eaten; ceremonially impure. □□ **un·clean·ly** *adv.* **un·clean·ly** /-klénlee/ *adj.* **un·clean·li·ness** /-klénleenis/ *n.* **un·clean·ness** *n.*

un·clear /únkléer/ *adj.* **1** not clear or easy to understand; obscure; uncertain. **2** (of a person) doubtful; uncertain (*I'm unclear as to what you mean*). □□ **un·clear·ly** *adv.* **un·clear·ness** *n.*

un·clench /únklénch/ *v.* **1** *tr.* release (clenched hands, features, teeth, etc.). **2** *intr.* (of clenched hands, etc.) become relaxed or open.

Un·cle Sam *n. colloq.* the federal government or citizens of the US (*will fight for Uncle Sam*).

Un·cle Tom *n. derog.* a black man considered to be servile, cringing, etc. (from the hero of H. B. Stowe's *Uncle Tom's Cabin*, 1852).

un·cloak /únklók/ *v.tr.* **1** expose; reveal. **2** remove a cloak from.

un·clog /únklóg/ *v.tr.* (**unclogged**, **unclogging**) unblock (a drain, pipe, etc.).

un·close /únklóz/ *v.* **1** *tr. & intr.* open. **2** *tr.* reveal; disclose.

un·clothe /únklóth/ *v.tr.* **1** remove the clothes from. **2** strip of leaves or vegetation (*trees unclothed by the wind*). **3** expose; reveal. □□ **un·clothed** *adj.*

un·cloud·ed /únklówdid/ *adj.* **1** not clouded; clear; bright. **2** untroubled (*unclouded serenity*).

un·clut·tered /únklútərd/ *adj.* not cluttered; austere; simple.

un·coil /únkóyl/ *v.tr. & intr.* unwind.

un·col·ored /únkúlərd/ *adj.* **1** having no color. **2** not influenced; impartial. **3** not exaggerated.

un·combed /únkómd/ *adj.* (of hair or a person) not combed.

un·com·fort·a·ble /únkúmftəbəl, -kúmfərtə-/ *adj.* **1** not comfortable. **2** uneasy; causing or feeling disquiet (*an uncomfortable silence*). □□ **un·com·fort·a·ble·ness** *n.* **un·com·fort·a·bly** *adv.*

un·com·mit·ted /únkəmítid/ *adj.* **1** not committed. **2** unattached to any specific political cause or group.

un·com·mon /únkómən/ *adj. & adv.* ● *adj.* **1** not common; unusual; remarkable. **2** remarkably great, etc. (*an uncommon fear of spiders*). ● *adv. archaic* uncommonly (*he was uncommon fat*). □□ **un·com·mon·ly** *adv.* **un·com·mon·ness** /-mən-nis/ *n.*

un·com·mu·ni·ca·tive /únkəmyōonikətiv/ *adj.* not wanting to communicate; taciturn. □□ **un·com·mu·ni·ca·tive·ly** *adv.* **un·com·mu·ni·ca·tive·ness** *n.*

un·com·plain·ing /únkəmpláyning/ *adj.* not complaining; resigned. □□ **un·com·plain·ing·ly** *adv.*

un·com·plet·ed /únkəmpléetid/ *adj.* not completed; incomplete.

un·com·pli·cat·ed /únkómplikaytid/ *adj.* not complicated; simple; straightforward.

un·com·pli·men·ta·ry /únkomplimréntəree/ *adj.* not complimentary; insulting

un·com·pro·mis·ing /únkómprəmīzing/ *adj.* unwilling to compromise; stubborn; unyielding. □□ **un·com·pro·mis·ing·ly** *adv.* **un·com·pro·mis·ing·ness** *n.*

un·con·cern /únkənsərn/ *n.* lack of concern; indifference; apathy. □□ **un·con·cerned** *adj.* **un·con·cern·ed·ly** /-nidlee/ *adv.*

un·con·di·tion·al /únkəndíshənəl/ *adj.* not subject to conditions; complete (*unconditional surrender*). □□ **un·con·di·tion·al·i·ty** /-nálitee/ *n.* **un·con·di·tion·al·ly** *adv.*

un·con·di·tioned /únkəndíshənd/ *adj.* **1** not subject to conditions or to an antecedent condition. **2** (of behavior, etc.) not determined by conditioning; natural.

un·con·di·tioned re·flex *n.* an instinctive response to a stimulus.

un·con·gen·ial /únkənjéenyəl/ *adj.* not congenial.

un·con·nect·ed /únkənéktid/ *adj.* **1** not physically joined. **2** not connected or associated. **3** (of speech, etc.) disconnected; not joined in order or sequence (*unconnected ideas*). **4** not related by family ties. □□ **un·con·nect·ed·ly** *adv.* **un·con·nect·ed·ness** *n.*

un·con·scion·a·ble /únkónshənəbəl/ *adj.* **1 a** having no conscience. **b** contrary to conscience. **2 a** unreasonably excessive (*an unconscionable length of time*). **b** not right or reasonable. □□ **un·con·scion·a·ble·ness** *n.* **un·con·scion·a·bly** *adv.*

un·con·scious /únkónshəs/ *adj. & n.* ● *adj.* not conscious (*unconscious of any change; fell unconscious on the floor; an unconscious prejudice*). ● *n.* that part of the mind which is inaccessible to the conscious mind but which affects behavior, emotions, etc. (cf. **collective unconscious**). □□ **un·con·scious·ly** *adv.* **un·con·scious·ness** *n.*

un·con·sti·tu·tion·al /únkonstitōōshənəl, -tyōō-/ *adj.* not in accordance with the political constitution or with procedural rules. □□ **un·con·sti·tu·tion·al·i·ty** /-nálitee/ *n.* **un·con·sti·tu·tion·al·ly** *adv.*

un·con·ven·tion·al /únkənvénshənəl/ *adj.* not bound by convention or custom; unusual; unorthodox. □□ **un·con·ven·tion·al·ism** *n.* **un·con·ven·tion·al·i·ty** /-nálitee/ *n.* **un·con·ven·tion·al·ly** *adv.*

un·con·vert·ed /únkənvértid/ *adj.* not converted.

un·co·or·di·nat·ed /únkō-áwrd'naytid/ *adj.* **1** not coordinated. **2** (of a person's movements, etc.) clumsy.

un·cork /únkáwrk/ *v.tr.* **1** draw the cork from (a bottle). **2** allow (feelings, etc.) to be vented.

un·count·ed /únkówntid/ *adj.* **1** not counted. **2** very many; innumerable.

U

UNCIAL

Uncial script ("inch-high letters") developed from Roman square capitals as a quicker, less elaborate hand. The characters are rounded and simply scriffed. In it are found the beginnings of uppercase and lowercase script. Artificial uncial, a slightly later variation, is more intricate, with thin horizontal and thick vertical strokes.

FORMATION OF UNCIAL CHARACTERS

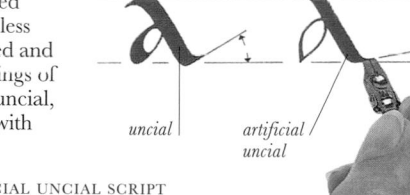

uncial   *artificial uncial*

8TH-CENTURY ENGLISH PSALTER IN ARTIFICIAL UNCIAL SCRIPT

illuminated title

gloss (explanatory text inserted at a later date)

evenly spaced lines

DETAIL

small descenders

small ascenders

illumination

few enlarged capitals

U

un·cou·ple /únkúpəl/ *v.tr.* **1** release (wagons) from couplings. **2** release (dogs, etc.) from couples. □□ **un·cou·pled** *adj.*

un·couth /únkốōth/ *adj.* (of a person, manners, appearance, etc.) lacking in ease and polish; uncultured; rough (*uncouth voices; behavior was uncouth*). □□ **un·couth·ly** *adv.* **un·couth·ness** *n.*

un·cov·er /únkúvər/ *v.* **1** *tr.* **a** remove a cover or covering from. **b** make known; disclose (*uncovered the truth at last*). **2** *intr. archaic* remove one's hat, cap, etc. **3** *tr.* (as **uncovered** *adj.*) **a** not covered by a roof, clothing, etc. **b** not wearing a hat.

unc·tion /úngkshən/ *n.* **1 a** the act of anointing with oil, etc., as a religious rite. **b** the oil, etc., so used. **2 a** soothing words or thought. **b** excessive or insincere flattery. **3 a** the act of anointing for medical purposes. **b** an ointment so used. **4 a** a fervent or sympathetic quality in words or tone caused by or causing deep emotion. **b** a pretense of this.

unc·tu·ous /úngkchōōəs/ *adj.* **1** (of behavior, speech, etc.) unpleasantly flattering; oily. **2** (esp. of minerals) having a greasy or soapy feel; oily. □□ **unc·tu·ous·ly** *adv.* **unc·tu·ous·ness** *n.*

un·cut /únkút/ *adj.* **1** not cut. **2** (of a book) with the pages not cut open or with untrimmed margins. **3** (of a book, film, etc.) complete; uncensored. **4** ◀ (of a stone, esp. a diamond) not shaped by cutting. **5** (of fabric) having its pile loops intact (*uncut moquette*).

UNCUT DIAMOND

un·dam·aged /úndámijd/ *adj.* not damaged; intact.

un·dat·ed /úndáytid/ *adj.* not provided or marked with a date.

un·daunt·ed /úndáwntid/ *adj.* not daunted. □□ **un·daunt·ed·ly** *adv.* **un·daunt·ed·ness** *n.*

un·de·cid·ed /úndisídid/ *adj.* **1** not settled or certain (*the question is undecided*). **2** hesitating; irresolute (*undecided about their relative merits*). □□ **un·de·cid·ed·ly** *adv.*

un·de·ci·pher·a·ble /úndisífərəbəl/ *adj.* not decipherable.

un·de·clared /úndikláird/ *adj.* not declared.

un·dec·o·rat·ed *adj.* **1** not adorned; plain. **2** not honored with an award.

un·de·feat·ed /úndiféetid/ *adj.* not defeated.

un·de·fend·ed /úndiféndid/ *adj.* (esp. of a lawsuit) not defended.

un·de·filed /úndifíld/ *adj.* not defiled; pure.

un·de·fined /úndifínd/ *adj.* **1** not defined. **2** not clearly marked; vague; indefinite. □□ **un·de·fin·a·ble** *adj.* **un·de·fin·a·bly** *adv.*

un·de·liv·ered /úndilívərd/ *adj.* not delivered or handed over.

un·de·mand·ing /úndimánding/ *adj.* not demanding; easily satisfied. □□ **un·de·mand·ing·ness** *n.*

un·dem·o·crat·ic /úndeməkrátik/ *adj.* not democratic. □□ **un·dem·o·crat·i·cal·ly** *adv.*

un·de·mon·stra·tive /úndimónstrətiv/ *adj.* not expressing feelings, etc., outwardly; reserved. □□ **un·de·mon·stra·tive·ly** *adv.* **un·de·mon·stra·tive·ness** *n.*

un·de·ni·a·ble /úndiníəbəl/ *adj.* **1** unable to be denied or disputed; certain. **2** excellent (*was of undeniable character*). □□ **un·de·ni·a·ble·ness** *n.* **un·de·ni·a·bly** *adv.*

un·de·nied /úndiníd/ *adj.* not denied.

un·de·pend·a·ble /úndipéndəbəl/ *adj.* not to be depended upon; unreliable.

un·der /úndər/ *prep., adv., & adj.* • *prep.* **1 a** in or to a position lower than; below; beneath (*fell under the table; under the left eye*). **b** within; on the inside of (a surface, etc.) (*wore a vest under his jacket*). **2 a** inferior to; less than (*a captain is under a major; is under 18*). **b** at or for a lower cost than (*was under $20*). **3 a** subject or liable to; controlled or bound by (*lives under oppression; under pain of death; born under Saturn*;

the country prospered under him). **b** undergoing (*is under repair*). **c** classified or subsumed in (*that book goes under biology; goes under many names*). **4** at the foot of or sheltered by (*hid under the wall; under the cliff*). **5** planted with (a crop). **6** powered by (sail, steam, etc.). • *adv.* **1** in or to a lower position or condition (*kept him under*). **2** *colloq.* in or into a state of unconsciousness (*put her under for the operation*). • *adj.* lower (*the under jaw*). □ **under one's arm** see ARM[1]. **under one's belt** see BELT. **under canvas** see CANVAS. **under a cloud** see CLOUD. **under control** see CONTROL. **under the counter** see COUNTER[1]. **under fire** see FIRE. **under a person's nose** see NOSE. **under separate cover** in another envelope. **under the sun** anywhere in the world. **under way** in motion; in progress. **under the weather** see WEATHER. □□ **un·der·most** *adj.*

un·der·a·chieve /úndərəchéev/ *v.intr.* do less well than might be expected (esp. scholastically). □□ **un·der·a·chieve·ment** *n.* **un·der·a·chiev·er** *n.*

un·der·age /úndəráyj/ *adj.* **1** not old enough, esp. not yet of adult status. **2** involving underage persons (*underage smoking and drinking*).

un·der·arm /úndəraarm/ *adj., adv., & n.* • *adj. & adv.* **1** *Sports* with the arm below shoulder level. **2** under the arm. **3** in the armpit. • *n.* the armpit.

un·der·bel·ly /úndərbélee/ *n.* (*pl.* **-ies**) the underside of an animal, vehicle, etc., esp. as an area vulnerable to attack.

un·der·bid *v. & n.* • *v.tr.* /úndərbíd/ (**-bidding**; *past* and *past part.* **-bid**) **1** make a lower bid than (a person). **2** (also *absol.*) *Bridge*, etc., bid less on (one's hand) than its strength warrants. • *n.* /úndərbid/ such a bid.

un·der·bite /úndərbīt/ *n.* the projection of the lower teeth beyond the upper.

un·der·brush /úndərbrúsh/ *n.* undergrowth in a forest.

un·der·car·riage /úndərkárij/ *n.* **1** ▼ a wheeled structure beneath an aircraft, usu. retracted when not in use, to receive the impact on landing and support the aircraft on the ground, etc. **2** the supporting frame of a vehicle.

deployment mechanism

sliding hydraulic ram

twin wheels

swivel joint

UNDERCARRIAGE OF A 1950s AVRO VULCAN BOMBER

un·der·charge /úndərchaárj/ *v.tr.* **1** charge too little for (a thing) or to (a person). **2** give less than the proper charge to (an electric battery).

un·der·class /úndərklas/ *n.* a subordinate social class.

un·der·cliff /úndərklif/ *n.* ▶ a terrace or lower cliff formed by a landslide.

un·der·clothes /úndərklōz, klōthz/ *n. pl.* clothes worn under others, esp. next to the skin.

un·der·cloth·ing /úndərklóthing/ *n.* underclothes collectively.

un·der·coat /úndərkōt/ *n. & v.* • *n.* **1 a** ▼ a preliminary layer of paint under the finishing coat. **b** the paint used for this. **2** an animal's under layer of hair or down. **3** a coat worn under another. • *v.tr.* seal the underpart of (esp. a motor vehicle) against rust, etc., with an undercoat. □□ **un·der·coat·ing** *n.*

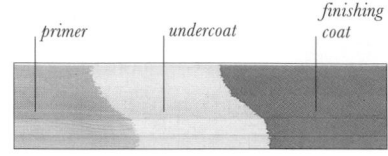

primer   *undercoat*   *finishing coat*

UNDERCOAT APPLIED TO WOOD SAMPLE

un·der·cov·er /úndərkúvər/ *adj.* (usu. *attrib.*) **1** surreptitious. **2** engaged in spying, esp. by working with or among those to be observed (*undercover agent*).

un·der·cur·rent /úndərkúrənt, -kur-/ *n.* **1** a current below the surface. **2** an underlying, often contrary, feeling, activity, or influence (*an undercurrent of protest*).

un·der·cut *v. & n.* • *v.tr.* /úndərkút/ (**-cutting**; *past* and *past part.* **-cut**) **1** sell or work at a lower price or lower wages than. **2** *Golf* strike (a ball) so as to make it rise high. **3 a** cut away the part below or under (a thing). **b** cut away material to show (a carved design, etc.) in relief. **4** render unstable or less firm; undermine. • *n.* /úndərkut/ **1** a notch cut in a tree trunk to guide its fall when felled. **2** any space formed by the removal or absence of material from the lower part of something.

un·der·de·vel·oped /úndərdivéləpt/ *adj.* **1** not fully developed; immature. **2** (of a country, etc.) below its potential economic level. **3** *Photog.* not developed sufficiently to give a normal image. □□ **un·der·de·vel·op·ment** *n.*

un·der·dog /úndərdawg, -dog/ *n.* **1** a dog, or usu. a person, losing a fight. **2** a person whose loss in a contest, etc., is expected. **3** a person who is in a state of inferiority or subjection.

un·der·done /úndərdún/ *adj.* **1** not thoroughly done. **2** (of food) lightly or insufficiently cooked.

un·der·dress /úndərdrés/ *v.tr. & intr.* dress with too little formality or too lightly.

un·der·em·pha·sis /úndərémfəsis/ *n.* (*pl.* **-emphases** /-seez/) an insufficient degree of emphasis. □□ **un·der·em·pha·size** /-sīz/ *v.tr.*

un·der·em·ployed /úndərimplóyd/ *adj.* **1** not fully employed. **2** having employment inadequate to one's abilities, education, etc. □□ **un·der·em·ploy·ment** *n.*

un·der·es·ti·mate *v. & n.* • *v.tr.* /úndəréstimayt/ form too low an estimate of. • *n.* /úndəréstimət/ an estimate that is too low. □□ **un·der·es·ti·ma·tion** /-máyshən/ *n.*

un·der·ex·pose /úndərikspốz/ *v.tr. Photog.* expose (film) for too short a time or with insufficient light. □□ **un·der·ex·po·sure** /-pốzhər/ *n.*

cliff top

undercliff

slip plane

UNDERCLIFF

un·der·fed /úndərféd/ *adj.* insufficiently fed.

un·der·foot /úndərfŏŏt/ *adv.* **1** under one's feet. **2** on the ground. **3** in a state of subjection. **4** so as to obstruct or inconvenience.

un·der·gar·ment /úndərgaarmənt/ *n.* a piece of underclothing.

un·der·glaze /úndərglayz/ *adj. & n.* • *adj.* **1** (of painting on ceramics and pottery, etc.) done before the glaze is applied. **2** (of colors) used in such painting. • *n.* underglaze painting.

un·der·go /úndərgṓ/ v.tr. (3rd sing. present **-goes**; past **-went**; past part. **-gone**) be subjected to; suffer; endure.

un·der·grad·u·ate /úndərgrájŏŏət/ n. a student at a college or university who has not yet taken a degree.

un·der·ground adv., adj., n., & v. ● adv. /úndərgrównd/ **1** beneath the surface of the ground. **2** in or into secrecy or hiding. ● adj. /úndərgrownd/ **1** situated underground. **2** secret, hidden, esp. working secretly to subvert a ruling power. **3** unconventional; experimental (underground press). ● n. /úndərgrownd/ **1** a secret group or activity, esp. aiming to subvert the established order. **2** Brit. a subway system. ● v.tr. /úndərgrownd/ lay (cables) below ground level.

Un·der·ground Rail·road n. US Hist. a covert system of escape through which abolitionists helped fugitive slaves reach safe destinations, before 1863.

un·der·growth /úndərgrṓth/ n. a dense growth of shrubs, etc., esp. under large trees.

un·der·hand adj. & adv. /úndərhand/ **1** secret; clandestine; not aboveboard. **2** deceptive; crafty. **3** Sports underarm. ● adv. /úndərhánd/ in an underhand manner.

un·der·hand·ed /úndərhándid/ adj. & adv. = UNDERHAND.

un·der·lay¹ v. & n. ● v.tr. /úndərláy/ (past and past part. **-laid**) lay something under (a thing) to support or raise it. ● n. /úndərlay/ a thing laid under another, esp. material laid under a carpet or mattress as protection or support.

un·der·lay² past of UNDERLIE.

un·der·lie /úndərlī/ v.tr (**-lying**; past **-lay**; past part. **-lain**) **1** (also absol.) lie or be situated under (a stratum, etc.). **2** (also absol.) (esp. as **underlying** adj.) (of a principle, reason, etc.) be the basis of (a doctrine, law, conduct, etc.). **3** exist beneath the superficial aspect of.

un·der·line v. & n. ● v.tr. /úndərlín/ **1** draw a line under (a word, etc.) to give emphasis or draw attention or indicate italic or other special type. **2** emphasize; stress. ● n. **1** a line drawn under a word, etc. **2** a caption below an illustration.

un·der·ling /úndərling/ n. usu. derog. a subordinate.

un·der·ly·ing pres. part. of UNDERLIE.

un·der·manned /úndərmánd/ adj. having too few people as crew or staff.

un·der·men·tioned /úndərménshənd/ adj. Brit. mentioned at a later place in a book, etc.

un·der·mine /úndərmín/ v.tr. **1** injure (a person, reputation, influence, etc.) by secret or insidious means. **2** weaken, injure, or wear out (health, etc.) imperceptibly or insidiously. **3** wear away the base or foundation of (rivers undermine their banks). □□ **un·der·min·er** n. **un·der·min·ing·ly** adv.

un·der·neath /úndərnéeth/ prep., adv., n., & adj. ● prep. **1** at or to a lower place than, below. **2** on the inside of, within. ● adv. **1** at or to a lower place. **2** inside. ● n. the lower surface or part. ● adj. lower.

un·der·nour·ished /úndərnórisht, -núr-/ adj. insufficiently nourished. □□ **un·der·nour·ish·ment** n.

un·der·paid past and past part. of UNDERPAY.

un·der·pants /úndərpants/ n.pl. an undergarment, covering the lower part of the torso and sometimes part of the legs.

un·der·part /úndərpaart/ n. **1** a lower part, esp. of an animal. **2** a subordinate part in a play, etc.

un·der·pass /úndərpas/ n. **1** a road, etc., passing under another. **2** a crossing of this form.

un·der·pay /úndərpáy/ v.tr. (past and past part. **-paid**) pay too little to (a person) or for (a thing). □□ **un·der·pay·ment** n.

un·der·pin /úndərpín/ v.tr. (**-pinned**, **-pinning**) **1** support from below with masonry, etc. **2** support; strengthen.

un·der·pin·ning /úndərpíning/ n. **1** a physical or

metaphorical foundation. **2** the action or process of supporting from below.

un·der·plant /úndərplánt/ v.tr. (usu. foll. by with) plant or cultivate the ground about (a tall plant) with smaller ones.

un·der·play /úndərpláy/ v. **1** tr. play down the importance of. **2** intr. & tr. Theatr. perform with deliberate restraint.

un·der·pop·u·lat·ed /úndərpópyələytid/ adj. having an insufficient or very small population.

un·der·price /úndərprís/ v.tr. price lower than what is usual or appropriate.

un·der·priv·i·leged /úndərprívilijd, -prívlijd/ adj. **1** less privileged than others. **2** not enjoying the normal standard of living or rights in a society.

un·der·quote /úndərkwṓt/ v.tr. **1** quote a lower price than (a person). **2** quote a lower price than others for (goods, etc.).

un·der·rate /úndərráyt/ v.tr. have too low an opinion of.

un·der·score v.tr. /úndərskáwr/ = UNDERLINE v.

un·der·sea /úndərsee/ adj. below the sea or the surface of the sea; submarine.

un·der·sec·re·tar·y /úndərsékrəteree/ n. (pl. **-ies**) a subordinate official, esp. one subordinate to a cabinet secretary.

un·der·sell /úndərsél/ v.tr. (past and past part. **-sold**) **1** sell at a lower price than (another seller). **2** sell at less than the true value.

un·der·sexed /úndərsékst/ adj. having unusually weak sexual desires.

un·der·shirt /úndərshərt/ n. an undergarment worn under a shirt.

un·der·shoot v. & n. ● v.tr. /úndərshṓt/ (past and past part. **-shot**) **1** (of an aircraft) land short of (a runway, etc.). **2** shoot short of or below. ● n. /úndərshōt/ the act or an instance of undershooting.

un·der·shorts /úndərsháwrts/ n. short underpants; trunks.

un·der·side /úndərsíd/ n. the lower or under side or surface.

un·der·signed /úndərsínd/ adj. whose signature is appended (we, the undersigned, wish to state…).

un·der·sized /úndərsízd/ adj. of less than the usual size.

un·der·skirt /úndərskərt/ n. a skirt worn under another; a petticoat.

un·der·sold past and past part. of UNDERSELL.

un·der·sow /úndərsṓ/ v.tr. (past part. **-sown**) **1** sow (a later-growing crop) on land already seeded with another crop. **2** (foll. by with) sow land already seeded with (a crop) with a later-growing crop.

un·der·spend /úndərspénd/ v. (past and past part. **-spent**) **1** tr. spend less than (a specified amount). **2** intr. & refl. spend too little.

un·der·staffed /úndərstáft/ adj. having too few staff.

un·der·stand /úndərstánd/ v. (past and past part. **-stood** /-stŏŏd/) **1** tr. perceive the meaning of (words, a person, a language, etc.) (understood you perfectly; cannot understand French). **2** tr. perceive the significance or explanation or cause of (do not understand why he came). **3** tr. be sympathetically aware of the character or nature of, know how to deal with (cannot understand him at all; could never understand algebra). **4** tr. **a** (often foll. by that + clause) infer esp. from information received; take as implied; take for granted (I understand that it begins at noon; am I to understand that you refuse?). **b** (absol.) believe or assume from knowledge or inference (he is coming tomorrow, I understand). **5** tr. supply (a word) mentally (the verb may be either expressed or understood). **6** tr. accept (terms, conditions, etc.) as part of an agreement. **7** intr. have understanding (in general or in particular). □ **understand each other 1** know each other's views or feelings. **2** be in agreement or collusion. □□ **un·der·stand·a·ble** adj. **un·der·stand·a·bly** adv. **un·der·stand·er** n.

un·der·stand·ing /úndərstánding/ n. & adj. ● n. **1 a** the ability to understand or think; intelligence. **b** the power of apprehension; the power of abstract thought. **2** an individual's perception or judgment of a situation, etc. **3** an agreement; a thing agreed upon, esp. informally (had an understanding with the rival company). **4** harmony in opinion or feeling (disturbed the good understanding between them). **5** sympathetic awareness or tolerance. ● adj. **1** having understanding or insight or good judgment. **2** sympathetic to others' feelings. □□ **un·der·stand·ing·ly** adv.

un·der·state /úndərstáyt/ v.tr. (often as **understated**) **1** express in greatly or unduly restrained terms. **2** represent as being less than it actually is. □□ **un·der·state·ment** /úndərstáytmənt/ n. **un·der·stat·er** n.

un·der·steer n. & v. ● n. /úndərsteer/ a tendency of a motor vehicle to turn less sharply than was intended. ● v.intr. /úndərsteér/ have such a tendency.

un·der·stood past and past part. of UNDERSTAND.

un·der·stud·y /úndərstúdee/ n. & v. esp. Theatr. ● n. (pl. **-ies**) a person who studies another's role or duties in order to act at short notice in the absence of the other. ● v.tr. (**-ies**, **-ied**) **1** study (a role, etc.) as an understudy. **2** act as an understudy to (a person).

un·der·take /úndərtáyk/ v.tr. (past **-took**; past part. **-taken**) **1** bind oneself to perform; make oneself responsible for; engage in; enter upon (work, an enterprise, a responsibility). **2** (usu. foll. by to + infin.) accept an obligation; promise.

un·der·tak·er /úndərtaykər/ n. **1** a person whose business is to make arrangements for funerals. **2** (also /-táykər/) a person who undertakes to do something.

un·der·tak·ing /úndərtáyking/ n. **1** work, etc., undertaken; an enterprise (a serious undertaking). **2** a pledge or promise. **3** /úndərtayking/ the management of funerals as a profession.

un·der·ten·ant /úndərtenənt/ n. a subtenant. □□ **un·der·ten·an·cy** n. (pl. **-ies**).

un·der·things /úndərthingz/ n.pl. colloq. underclothes.

un·der·tone /úndərtōn/ n. **1** a subdued tone of sound or color. **2** an underlying quality. **3** an undercurrent of feeling.

un·der·took past of UNDERTAKE.

un·der·tow /úndərtō/ n. ▼ a current below the surface of the sea moving in the opposite direction to the surface current.

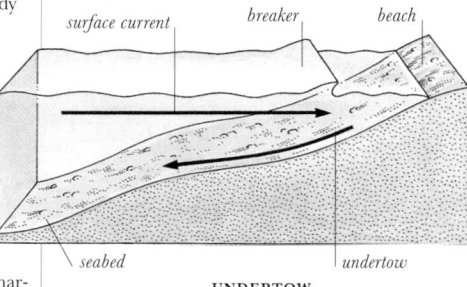

UNDERTOW

un·der·val·ue /úndərvályŏŏ/ v.tr. (**-values**, **-valued**, **-valuing**) **1** value insufficiently. **2** underestimate. □□ **un·der·val·u·a·tion** n.

un·der·wa·ter /úndərwáwtər, -wótər/ adj. & adv. ● adj. situated or done under water. ● adv. in and covered by water.

un·der·way /úndərwáy/ adj. occurring while in progress or in motion (the ship's underway food service was excellent).

un·der·wear /úndərwair/ n. underclothes.

un·der·weight adj. & n. ● adj. /úndərwáyt/ weighing less than is normal or desirable. ● n. /úndərwayt/ insufficient weight.

U

un·der·went *past* of UNDERGO.

un·der·whelm /úndərhwelm, -wélm/ *v.tr. joc.* fail to impress.

un·der·work /úndərwə́rk/ *v.* **1** *tr.* impose too little work on. **2** *intr.* do too little work.

un·der·world /úndərwərld/ *n.* **1** the part of society comprising those who live by organized crime and immorality. **2** the mythical abode of the dead under the earth.

un·der·write /úndər-rít/ *v.* (*past* **-wrote**; *past part.* **-written**) **1 a** *tr.* sign, and accept liability under (an insurance policy). **b** *tr.* accept (liability) in this way. **c** *intr.* practice insurance. **2** *tr.* undertake to finance or support. **3** *tr.* engage to buy all the stock in (a company, etc.) not bought by the public. **4** *tr.* write below (*the underwritten names*). □□ **un·der·writ·er** /úndər-rítər/ *n.*

un·de·scend·ed /úndiséndid/ *adj. Med.* (of a testicle) remaining in the abdomen instead of descending normally into the scrotum.

un·de·served /úndizə́rvd/ *adj.* not deserved (as reward or punishment). □□ **un·de·serv·ed·ly** /-vidlee/ *adv.*

un·de·serv·ing /úndizə́rving/ *adj.* not deserving. □□ **un·de·serv·ing·ly** *adv.*

un·de·sir·a·ble /úndizírəbəl/ *adj. & n.* ● *adj.* not desirable; objectionable; unpleasant. ● *n.* an undesirable person. □□ **un·de·sir·a·bil·i·ty** /-bílitee/ *n.* **un·de·sir·a·ble·ness** *n.* **un·de·sir·a·bly** *adv.*

un·de·tect·a·ble /únditéktəbəl/ *adj.* not detectable. □□ **un·de·tect·a·bil·i·ty** /-bílitee/ *n.* **un·de·tect·a·bly** *adv.*

un·de·tect·ed /únditéktid/ *adj.* not detected.

un·de·ter·mined /únditə́rmind/ *adj.* = UNDECIDED.

un·de·terred /únditə́rd/ *adj.* not deterred.

un·de·vel·oped /úndivéləpt/ *adj.* not developed.

un·di·ag·nosed /úndíəgnōst, -nōzd/ *adj.* not diagnosed.

un·did *past* of UNDO.

un·dies /úndeez/ *n.pl. colloq.* (esp. women's) underclothes.

un·di·gest·ed /úndijéstid, úndī-/ *adj.* **1** not digested. **2** (esp. of information, facts, etc.) not properly arranged or considered.

un·dig·ni·fied /úndígnifīd/ *adj.* lacking dignity.

un·di·lut·ed /úndilốotid/ *adj.* not diluted.

un·di·min·ished /úndimínisht/ *adj.* not diminished or lessened.

un·dip·lo·mat·ic /úndipləmátik/ *adj.* tactless. □□ **un·dip·lo·mat·i·cal·ly** *adv.*

un·dis·charged /úndischáárjd/ *adj.* (esp. of a bankrupt or a debt) not discharged.

un·dis·ci·plined /úndísiplind/ *adj.* lacking discipline; not disciplined.

un·dis·closed /úndisklốzd/ *adj.* not revealed or made known.

un·dis·cov·ered /úndiskúvərd/ *adj.* not discovered.

un·dis·crim·i·nating /úndiskríminayting/ *adj.* not showing good judgment.

un·dis·guised /úndisgízd/ *adj.* not disguised. □□ **un·dis·guis·ed·ly** /-zidlee/ *adv.*

un·dis·put·ed /úndispyốotid/ *adj.* not disputed or called in question.

un·dis·solved /úndizólvd/ *adj.* not dissolved.

un·dis·tin·guish·a·ble /úndistínggwishəbəl/ *adj.* (often foll. by *from*) indistinguishable.

un·dis·tin·guished /úndistínggwisht/ *adj.* not distinguished; mediocre.

un·dis·trib·ut·ed /úndistríbyətid/ *adj.* not distributed.

un·di·vid·ed /úndivídid/ *adj.* not divided or shared; whole, entire (*gave him my undivided attention*).

un·do /úndốo/ *v.tr.* (*3rd sing. present* **-does**; *past* **-did**; *past part.* **-done**) **1 a** unfasten or untie (a coat, button, package, etc.). **b** unfasten the clothing of (a person). **2** annul; cancel (*cannot undo the past*). **3** ruin the prospects, reputation, or morals of.

un·doc·u·ment·ed /úndókyəmentid/ *adj.* **1** not

having the appropriate document. **2** not proved by or recorded in documents.

un·do·ing /úndốoing/ *n.* **1** ruin or a cause of ruin. **2** the process of reversing what has been done. **3** the action of opening or unfastening.

un·done /úndún/ *adj.* **1** not done; incomplete (*left the job undone*). **2** not fastened (*left the buttons undone*). **3** *archaic* ruined.

un·doubt·ed /úndówtid/ *adj.* certain; not questioned; not regarded as doubtful. □□ **un·doubt·ed·ly** *adv.*

un·dreamed /úndreémd/ *adj.* (also **un·dreamt** /úndrémt/) (often foll. by *of*) not dreamed or thought of or imagined.

un·dress /úndrés/ *v.* **1** *intr.* take off one's clothes. **2** *tr.* take the clothes off (a person).

un·dressed /úndrést/ *adj.* **1** not or no longer dressed; partly or wholly naked. **2** (of leather, etc.) not treated. **3** (of food) **a** not having a dressing (*undressed salad*). **b** prepared simply, with no sauce, stuffing, etc. (*undressed turkey*).

un·drink·a·ble /úndríngkəbəl/ *adj.* unfit for drinking.

un·due /úndốo, -dyốo/ *adj.* **1** excessive; disproportionate. **2** not suitable. **3** not owed. □□ **un·du·ly** *adv.*

un·du·lant /únjələnt, -dyə-, -də-/ *adj.* moving like waves; fluctuating.

un·du·late *v.* /únjəlayt, -dyə-, -də-/ *intr. & tr.* have or cause to have a wavy motion or look.

un·du·la·tion /únjəláyshən, -dyə-, -də-/ *n.* **1** a wavy motion or form; a gentle rise and fall. **2** each wave of this. **3** a set of wavy lines.

un·du·ti·ful /úndốotifốol, -dyốo-/ *adj.* not dutiful. □□ **un·du·ti·ful·ly** *adv.* **un·du·ti·ful·ness** *n.*

un·dyed /úndíd/ *adj.* not dyed.

un·dy·ing /úndí-ing/ *adj.* **1** immortal. **2** neverending (*undying love*). □□ **un·dy·ing·ly** *adv.*

un·earned /únə́rnd/ *adj.* not earned.

un·earned in·come *n.* income from interest payments, etc., as opposed to salary, wages, or fees.

un·earth /únə́rth/ *v.tr.* **1** discover by searching or in the course of digging or rummaging. **2** dig out of the earth.

un·earth·ly /únə́rthlee/ *adj.* **1** supernatural; mysterious. **2** *colloq.* absurdly early or inconvenient (*an unearthly hour*). **3** not earthly. □□ **un·earth·li·ness** *n.*

un·ease /únéez/ *n.* lack of ease; discomfort; distress.

un·eas·y /únéezee/ *adj.* (**uneasier**, **uneasiest**) **1** disturbed or uncomfortable in mind or body (*passed an uneasy night*). **2** disturbing (*had an uneasy suspicion*). □□ **un·eas·i·ly** *adv.* **un·eas·i·ness** *n.*

un·eat·a·ble /únéetəbəl/ *adj.* not able to be eaten, esp. because of its condition (cf. INEDIBLE).

un·eat·en /únéet'n/ *adj.* not eaten; left undevoured.

un·ec·o·nom·ic /únekənómik, -eekə-/ *adj.* not economic; incapable of being profitably operated, etc. □□ **un·ec·o·nom·i·cal·ly** *adv.*

un·ec·o·nom·i·cal /únekənómikəl, -eekə-/ *adj.* not economical; wasteful.

un·ed·i·fy·ing /únédifī-ing/ *adj.* not edifying, esp. uninstructive or degrading. □□ **un·ed·i·fy·ing·ly** *adv.*

un·ed·u·cat·ed /únéjəkaytid/ *adj.* not educated. □□ **un·ed·u·ca·ble** /-kəbəl/ *adj.*

un·e·lect·a·ble /úniléktəbəl/ *adj.* (of a candidate, party, etc.) associated with or holding views likely to bring defeat at an election.

un·em·bel·lished /únimbélisht/ *adj.* not embellished or decorated.

un·e·mo·tion·al /únimốshənəl/ *adj.* not emotional; lacking emotion. □□ **un·e·mo·tion·al·ly** *adv.*

un·em·ploy·a·ble /únimplóyəbəl/ *adj. & n.* ● *adj.* unfitted for paid employment. ● *n.* an unemployable person. □□ **un·em·ploy·a·bil·i·ty** /-bílitee/ *n.*

un·em·ployed /únimplóyd/ *adj.* **1** not having paid employment; out of work. **2** not in use.

un·em·ploy·ment /únimplóymənt/ *n.* **1** the state of being unemployed. **2** the condition or extent of this in a country or region, etc. (*the Northeast has higher unemployment*).

un·em·ploy·ment ben·e·fit *n.* a payment made by the government or a labor union to an unemployed person.

un·en·cum·bered /úninkúmbərd/ *adj.* **1** (of an estate) not having any liabilities (e.g., a mortgage) on it. **2** having no encumbrance; free.

un·end·ing /únénding/ *adj.* having or apparently having no end. □□ **un·end·ing·ly** *adv.* **un·end·ing·ness** *n.*

un·en·dur·a·ble /únindốorəbəl, -dyốor-/ *adj.* that cannot be endured. □□ **un·en·dur·a·bly** *adv.*

un·en·light·ened /úninlít'nd/ *adj.* not enlightened.

un·en·ter·pris·ing /únéntərprīzing/ *adj.* not enterprising.

un·en·thu·si·as·tic /úninthốozeeástik/ *adj.* not enthusiastic. □□ **un·en·thu·si·as·ti·cal·ly** *adv.*

un·en·vi·a·ble /únénveeəbəl/ *adj.* not enviable. □□ **un·en·vi·a·bly** *adv.*

un·e·qual /únéekwəl/ *adj.* **1** (often foll. by *to*) not equal. **2** of varying quality. **3** lacking equal advantage to both sides (*an unequal bargain*). □□ **un·e·qual·ly** *adv.*

un·e·qualed /únéekwəld/ *adj.* (also esp. *Brit.* **unequalled**) superior to all others.

un·e·quipped /únikwípt/ *adj.* not equipped.

un·e·quiv·o·cal /únikwívəkəl/ *adj.* not ambiguous; plain; unmistakable. □□ **un·e·quiv·o·cal·ly** *adv.* **un·e·quiv·o·cal·ness** *n.*

un·err·ing /únéring/ *adj.* not erring, failing, or missing the mark; true; certain. □□ **un·err·ing·ly** *adv.* **un·err·ing·ness** *n.*

UNESCO /yōonéskō/ *abbr.* United Nations Educational, Scientific, and Cultural Organization.

un·es·cort·ed /úniskáwrtid/ *adj.* not escorted.

un·es·sen·tial /únisénshəl/ *adj. & n.* ● *adj.* **1** not essential (cf. INESSENTIAL). **2** not of the first importance. ● *n.* an unessential part or thing.

un·eth·i·cal /únéthikəl/ *adj.* not ethical, esp. unscrupulous in business or professional conduct. □□ **un·eth·i·cal·ly** *adv.*

un·e·ven /únéevən/ *adj.* **1** not level or smooth. **2** not uniform or equable. **3** (of a contest) unequal. □□ **un·e·ven·ly** *adv.* **un·e·ven·ness** *n.*

un·e·vent·ful /únivéntfốol/ *adj.* not eventful. □□ **un·e·vent·ful·ly** *adv.* **un·e·vent·ful·ness** *n.*

un·ex·am·pled /únigzámpəld/ *adj.* having no precedent or parallel.

un·ex·cep·tion·a·ble /úniksépshənəbəl/ *adj.* with which no fault can be found; entirely satisfactory. □□ **un·ex·cep·tion·a·ble·ness** *n.* **un·ex·cep·tion·a·bly** *adv.*

un·ex·cep·tion·al /úniksépshənəl/ *adj.* not out of the ordinary; usual; normal. □□ **un·ex·cep·tion·al·ly** *adv.*

un·ex·cit·ing /úniksíting/ *adj.* not exciting; dull.

un·ex·pect·ed /únikspéktid/ *adj.* not expected; surprising. □□ **un·ex·pect·ed·ly** *adv.* **un·ex·pect·ed·ness** *n.*

un·ex·plain·a·ble /únikspláynəbəl/ *adj.* inexplicable. □□ **un·ex·plain·a·bly** *adv.*

un·ex·plained /únikspláynd/ *adj.* not explained.

un·ex·plored /únikspláwrd/ *adj.* not explored.

un·ex·pur·gat·ed /únékspərgaytid/ *adj.* (esp. of a text, etc.) not expurgated; complete.

un·fad·ing /únfáyding/ *adj.* that never fades. □□ **un·fad·ing·ly** *adv.*

un·fail·ing /únfáyling/ *adj.* **1** not failing. **2** not running short. **3** constant. **4** reliable. □□ **un·fail·ing·ly** *adv.* **un·fail·ing·ness** *n.*

un·fair /únfáir/ *adj.* **1** not equitable or honest (*obtained by unfair means*). **2** not impartial or according to the rules (*unfair play*). □□ **un·fair·ly** *adv.* **un·fair·ness** *n.*

un·faith·ful /únfáythfốol/ *adj.* **1** not faithful, esp.

U

adulterous. **2** not loyal. **3** treacherous. □□ **un·faith·ful·ly** *adv.* **un·faith·ful·ness** *n.*

un·fal·ter·ing /únfáwltəring/ *adj.* not faltering; steady; resolute. □□ **un·fal·ter·ing·ly** *adv.*

un·fa·mil·iar /únfəmílyər/ *adj.* not familiar. □□ **un·fa·mil·i·ar·i·ty** /-leeáritee/ *n.*

un·fash·ion·a·ble /únfáshənəbəl/ *adj.* not fashionable. □□ **un·fash·ion·a·ble·ness** *n.* **un·fash·ion·a·bly** *adv.*

un·fas·ten /únfásən/ *v. tr. & intr.* make or become loose. **2** *tr.* open the fastening(s) of. **3** *tr.* detach.

un·fas·tened /únfásənd/ *adj.* **1** that has not been fastened. **2** that has been loosened, opened, or detached.

un·fa·ther·ly /únfáathərlee/ *adj.* not befitting a father. □□ **un·fa·ther·li·ness** *n.*

un·fath·om·a·ble /únfáthəməbəl/ *adj.* incapable of being fathomed. □□ **un·fath·om·a·ble·ness** *n.* **un·fath·om·a·bly** *adv.*

un·fa·vor·a·ble /únfáyvərəbəl/ *adj.* not favorable; adverse; hostile. □□ **un·fa·vor·a·ble·ness** *n.* **un·fa·vor·a·bly** *adv.*

un·fazed /únfáyzd/ *adj. colloq.* untroubled; not disconcerted.

un·fea·si·ble /únféezibəl/ *adj.* not feasible; impractical. □□ **un·fea·si·bil·i·ty** /-bílitee/ *n.*

un·fed /únféd/ *adj.* not fed.

un·feel·ing /únféeling/ *adj.* **1** unsympathetic; harsh; not caring about others' feelings. **2** lacking sensation or sensitivity. □□ **un·feel·ing·ly** *adv.* **un·feel·ing·ness** *n.*

un·feigned /únfáynd/ *adj.* genuine; sincere. □□ **un·feign·ed·ly** /-fáynidlee/ *adv.*

un·felt /únfélt/ *adj.* not felt.

un·fem·i·nine /únfémminin/ *adj.* not in accordance with, or appropriate to, female character. □□ **un·fem·i·nin·i·ty** /-nínitee/ *n.*

un·fenced /únfénst/ *adj.* **1** not provided with fences. **2** unprotected.

un·fet·tered /únfétərd/ *adj.* unrestrained; unrestricted.

un·filled /únfíld/ *adj.* not filled.

un·fil·tered /únfíltərd/ *adj.* **1** not filtered. **2** (of a cigarette) not provided with a filter.

un·fin·ished /únfínisht/ *adj.* not finished; incomplete.

un·fit /únfít/ *adj. & v.* ● *adj.* (often foll. by *for*, or *to* + infin.) not fit. ● *v.tr.* (**unfitted**, **unfitting**) (usu. foll. by *for*) make unsuitable. □□ **un·fit·ly** *adv.* **un·fit·ness** *n.*

un·fit·ted /únfítid/ *adj.* **1** not fit. **2** not fitted or suited. **3** not provided with fittings.

un·fit·ting /únfíting/ *adj.* not fitting or suitable; unbecoming. □□ **un·fit·ting·ly** *adv.*

un·flag·ging /únfláging/ *adj.* tireless; persistent. □□ **un·flag·ging·ly** *adv.*

un·flap·pa·ble /únflápəbəl/ *adj. colloq.* imperturbable; remaining calm in a crisis. □□ **un·flap·pa·bil·i·ty** /-bílitee/ *n.* **un·flap·pa·bly** *adv.*

un·flat·ter·ing /únflátəring/ *adj.* not flattering. □□ **un·flat·ter·ing·ly** *adv.*

un·flinch·ing /únflínching/ *adj.* not flinching. □□ **un·flinch·ing·ly** *adv.*

un·fo·cused /únfṓkəst/ *adj.* (also esp. *Brit.* **un·fo·cussed**) not focused.

un·fold /únfṓld/ *v.* **1** *tr.* open the fold or folds of; spread out. **2** *tr.* reveal (thoughts, etc.). **3** *intr.* become opened out. **4** *intr.* develop. □□ **un·fold·ment** *n.*

un·forced /únfáwrst/ *adj.* **1** not produced by effort; easy; natural. **2** not compelled or constrained. □□ **un·forc·ed·ly** /-fáwrsidlee/ *adv.*

un·fore·see·a·ble /únfawrséeəbəl/ *adj.* not foreseeable.

un·fore·seen /únfawrséen/ *adj.* not foreseen.

un·for·get·ta·ble /únfərgétəbəl/ *adj.* that cannot be forgotten; memorable; wonderful (*an unforgettable experience*). □□ **un·for·get·ta·bly** *adv.*

un·for·giv·a·ble /únfərgívəbəl/ *adj.* that cannot be forgiven. □□ **un·for·giv·a·bly** *adv.*

un·for·giv·en /únfərgívən/ *adj.* not forgiven.

un·for·giv·ing /únfərgíving/ *adj.* not forgiving. □□ **un·for·giv·ing·ly** *adv.* **un·for·giv·ing·ness** *n.*

un·formed /únfáwrmd/ *adj.* **1** not formed. **2** shapeless. **3** not developed.

un·for·ti·fied /únfáwrtifīd/ *adj.* not fortified.

un·for·tu·nate /únfáwrchənət/ *adj. & n.* ● *adj.* **1** having bad fortune; unlucky. **2** unhappy. **3** regrettable. **4** disastrous. ● *n.* an unfortunate person.

un·for·tu·nate·ly /únfáwrchənətlee/ *adv.* **1** (qualifying a whole sentence) it is unfortunate that. **2** in an unfortunate manner.

un·found·ed /únfówndid/ *adj.* having no foundation (*unfounded hopes*; *unfounded rumor*). □□ **un·found·ed·ly** *adv.* **un·found·ed·ness** *n.*

un·freeze /únfréez/ *v.* (*past* **unfroze**; *past part.* **unfrozen**) **1** *tr.* cause to thaw. **2** *intr.* thaw. **3** *tr.* remove restrictions from; make (assets, credits, etc.) realizable.

un·fre·quent·ed /únfréekwentid, -fríkwén-/ *adj.* not frequented.

un·friend·ly /únfréndlee/ *adj.* (**unfriendlier, unfriendliest**) not friendly. □□ **un·friend·li·ness** *n.*

un·froze *past* of UNFREEZE.

un·fro·zen *past part.* of UNFREEZE.

un·fruit·ful /únfróotfŏol/ *adj.* **1** not producing good results; unprofitable. **2** not producing fruit or crops. □□ **un·fruit·ful·ly** *adv.* **un·fruit·ful·ness** *n.*

un·ful·filled /únfŏolfíld/ *adj.* not fulfilled. □□ **un·ful·fill·a·ble** *adj.*

un·fund·ed /únfúndid/ *adj.* (of a debt) not funded.

un·fun·ny /únfúnee/ *adj.* (**unfunnier, unfunniest**) not amusing (though meant to be). □□ **un·fun·ni·ly** *adv.* **un·fun·ni·ness** *n.*

un·furl /únfárl/ *v.* **1** *tr.* spread out (a sail, umbrella, etc.). **2** *intr.* become spread out.

un·fur·nished /únfárnisht/ *adj.* **1** (usu. foll. by *with*) not supplied. **2** without furniture.

un·gain·ly /úngáynlee/ *adj.* (of a person, animal, or movement) awkward; clumsy. □□ **un·gain·li·ness** *n.*

un·gal·lant /úngálənt/ *adj.* not gallant. □□ **un·gal·lant·ly** *adv.*

un·gen·er·ous /únjénərəs/ *adj.* not generous; mean. □□ **un·gen·er·ous·ly** *adv.* **un·gen·er·ous·ness** *n.*

un·gen·tle /únjént'l/ *adj.* not gentle. □□ **un·gen·tle·ness** *n.* **un·gen·tly** *adv.*

un·gen·tle·man·ly /únjéntəlmənlee/ *adj.* not gentlemanly. □□ **un·gen·tle·man·li·ness** *n.*

un·god·ly /úngódlee/ *adj.* **1** impious; wicked. **2** *colloq.* outrageous (*an ungodly hour to arrive*). □□ **un·god·li·ness** *n.*

un·gov·ern·a·ble /úngúvərnəbəl/ *adj.* uncontrollable; violent. □□ **un·gov·ern·a·bil·i·ty** /-bílitee/ *n.* **un·gov·ern·a·bly** *adv.*

un·grace·ful /úngráysfŏol/ *adj.* not graceful. □□ **un·grace·ful·ly** *adv.* **un·grace·ful·ness** *n.*

un·gra·cious /úngráyshəs/ *adj.* **1** not kindly or courteous; unkind. **2** unattractive. □□ **un·gra·cious·ly** *adv.* **un·gra·cious·ness** *n.*

un·grate·ful /úngráytfŏol/ *adj.* **1** not feeling or showing gratitude. **2** not pleasant or acceptable. □□ **un·grate·ful·ly** *adv.* **un·grate·ful·ness** *n.*

un·guard·ed /úngáardid/ *adj.* **1** incautious; thoughtless (*an unguarded remark*). **2** not guarded; without a guard. □ **in an unguarded moment** unawares. □□ **un·guard·ed·ly** *adv.* **un·guard·ed·ness** *n.*

un·guent /únggwənt/ *n.* a soft substance used as ointment or for lubrication.

un·gu·la /úngyələ/ *n* (*pl.* **un·gu·lae**) /-lee/ a hoof or claw.

un·gu·late /úngyələt, -layt/ *adj. & n.* ● *adj.* hoofed. ● *n.* ▼ a hoofed mammal.

UNGULATE

Ungulate is a general term applied to the two orders of hoofed mammals: perissodactyls and artiodactyls. Perissodactyls have one or three functional toes, and include horses, rhinoceroses, and tapirs. Artiodactyls have two or four functional toes, and include cattle, sheep, camels, giraffes, pigs, and hippopotamuses. In many two-toed ungulates the narrow gap between the toes forms a cloven hoof. The majority of two-toed ungulates are ruminants.

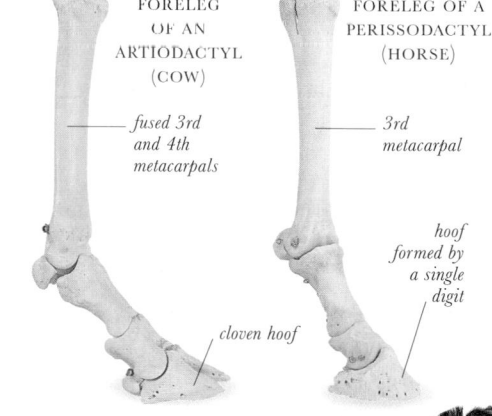

FORELEG OF AN ARTIODACTYL (COW)
fused 3rd and 4th metacarpals
cloven hoof

FORELEG OF A PERISSODACTYL (HORSE)
3rd metacarpal
hoof formed by a single digit

TYPES OF UNGULATE

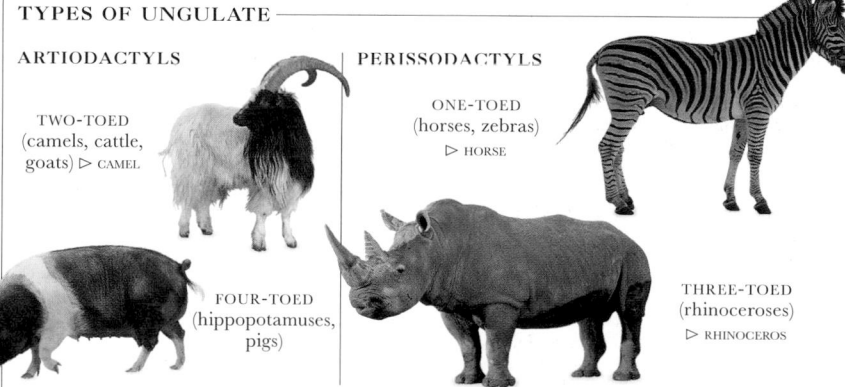

ARTIODACTYLS

TWO-TOED (camels, cattle, goats) ▷ CAMEL.

FOUR-TOED (hippopotamuses, pigs)

PERISSODACTYLS

ONE-TOED (horses, zebras) ▷ HORSE

THREE-TOED (rhinoceroses) ▷ RHINOCEROS

U

905

un·ham·pered /únhámpərd/ *adj.* not hampered.

un·hand /únhánd/ *v.tr. rhet.* or *joc.* **1** take one's hands off (a person). **2** release from one's grasp.

un·hand·y /únhándee/ *adj.* **1** not easy to handle or manage; awkward. **2** not skillful in using the hands. □□ **un·hand·i·ly** *adv.* **un·hand·i·ness** *n.*

un·hap·py /únhápee/ *adj.* (**unhappier, unhappiest**) **1** not happy; miserable. **2** unsuccessful; unfortunate. **3** causing misfortune. **4** disastrous. **5** inauspicious. □□ **un·hap·pi·ly** *adv.* **un·hap·pi·ness** *n.*

un·harmed /únhaármd/ *adj.* not harmed.

un·har·mo·ni·ous /únhaarmóneeəs/ *adj.* not harmonious.

un·hatched /únhácht/ *adj.* (of an egg, etc.) not hatched.

un·health·y /únhélthee/ *adj.* (**unhealthier, unhealthiest**) **1** not in good health. **2 a** (of a place, etc.) harmful to health. **b** unwholesome. **c** *sl.* dangerous to life. □□ **un·health·i·ly** *adv.* **un·health·i·ness** *n.*

un·heard /únhórd/ *adj.* **1** not heard. **2** (usu. **unheard-of**) unprecedented; unknown.

un·heat·ed /únhéetid/ *adj.* not heated.

un·heed·ed /únhéedid/ *adj.* not heeded; disregarded.

un·heed·ing /únhéeding/ *adj.* not giving heed; heedless. □□ **un·heed·ing·ly** *adv.*

un·help·ful /únhélpfŏŏl/ *adj.* not helpful. □□ **un·help·ful·ly** *adv.* **un·help·ful·ness** *n.*

un·her·ald·ed /únhérəldid/ *adj.* not heralded; unannounced.

un·hes·i·tat·ing /únhézitayting/ *adj.* without hesitation. □□ **un·hes·i·tat·ing·ly** *adv.* **un·hes·i·tat·ing·ness** *n.*

un·hin·dered /únhíndərd/ *adj.* not hindered.

un·hinge /únhínj/ *v.tr.* **1** take (a door, etc.) off its hinges. **2** (esp. as **unhinged** *adj.*) unsettle or disorder (a person's mind, etc.); make (a person) crazy.

un·hitch /únhích/ *v.tr.* **1** release from a hitched state. **2** unhook; unfasten.

un·ho·ly /únhólee/ *adj.* (**unholier, unholiest**) **1** impious; profane; wicked. **2** *colloq.* dreadful; outrageous (*made an unholy ordeal out of nothing*). **3** not holy. □□ **un·ho·li·ness** *n.*

un·hook /únhŏŏk/ *v.tr.* **1** remove from a hook or hooks. **2** unfasten by releasing a hook or hooks.

un·hoped /únhópt/ *adj.* (foll. by *for*) not hoped for or expected.

un·horse /únháwrs/ *v.tr.* **1** throw or drag from a horse. **2** (of a horse) throw (a rider). **3** dislodge; overthrow.

un·hu·man /únhyŏŏmən/ *adj.* **1** not human. **2** superhuman. **3** inhuman; brutal.

un·hung /únhúng/ *adj.* **1** not (yet) executed by hanging. **2** not hung up (for exhibition).

un·hur·ried /únhórid, -húr-/ *adj.* not hurried. □□ **un·hur·ried·ly** *adv.*

un·hurt /únhórt/ *adj.* not hurt.

un·hy·gi·en·ic /únhījénik, -jee-én-/ *adj.* not hygienic. □□ **un·hy·gi·en·i·cal·ly** *adv.*

uni- /yŏŏnee/ *comb. form* one; having or consisting of one.

u·ni·cam·er·al /yŏŏnikámərəl/ *adj.* with a single legislative chamber.

UNICEF /yŏŏnisef/ *abbr.* United Nations Children's (orig. International Children's Emergency) Fund.

u·ni·cel·lu·lar /yŏŏnisélyələr/ *adj.* ◄ (of an organism, organ, tissue, etc.) consisting of a single cell.

u·ni·col·or /yŏŏnikulər/ *adj.* (also **u·ni·col·ored**) of one color.

u·ni·corn /yŏŏnikawrn/ *n.* a mythi-

chloroplast

cell wall

UNICELLULAR ORGANISM
(A DESMID, MAGNIFIED)

cal animal with a horse's body and a single straight horn.

u·ni·cy·cle /yŏŏnisíkəl/ *n.* ► a single-wheeled cycle, esp. as used by acrobats. □□ **u·ni·cy·clist** *n.*

u·ni·den·ti·fi·a·ble /únīdéntifīəbəl/ *adj.* unable to be identified.

u·ni·den·ti·fied /únīdéntifīd/ *adj.* not identified.

u·ni·fi·ca·tion /yŏŏnifikáyshən/ *n.* the act or an instance of unifying; the state of being unified. □□ **u·ni·fi·ca·to·ry** *adj.*

u·ni·form /yŏŏnifawrm/ *adj., n., & v.*
• *adj.* **1** not changing in form or character; the same; unvarying (*present a uniform appearance; all of uniform size and shape*). **2** conforming to the same standard, rules, or pattern. **3** constant in the course of time (*uniform acceleration*). **4** (of a tax, law, etc.) not varying with time or place. • *n.* ▼ distinctive uniform clothing worn by members of the same body, e.g., by soldiers, police, and schoolchildren. • *v.tr.* clothe in uniform (*a uniformed officer*). □□ **u·ni·form·ly** *adv.*

u·ni·form·i·ty /yŏŏnifáwrmitee/ *n.* (*pl.* **-ies**) **1** being uniform; sameness; consistency. **2** an instance of this.

u·ni·fy /yŏŏnifī/ *v.tr.* (also *absol.*) (**-ies, -ied**) reduce to unity or uniformity. □□ **u·ni·fi·er** *n.*

u·ni·lat·er·al /yŏŏnilátərəl/ *adj.* **1** performed by or affecting only one person or party (*unilateral disarmament; unilateral declaration of independence*). **2** one-sided. □□ **u·ni·lat·er·al·ly** *adv.*

u·ni·lat·er·al·ism /yŏŏnilátərəlizəm/ *n.* **1** unilateral disarmament. **2** the pursuit of a foreign policy without allies. □□ **u·ni·lat·er·al·ist** *n. & adj.*

u·ni·lin·gual /yŏŏnilínggwəl/ *adj.* of or in only one language. □□ **u·ni·lin·gual·ly** *adv.*

un·il·lus·trat·ed /únílə straytid/ *adj.* (esp. of a book) without illustrations.

un·i·mag·i·na·ble /únimájinəbəl/ *adj.* impossible to imagine. □□ **un·i·mag·i·na·bly** *adv.*

un·i·mag·i·na·tive /únimájinətiv/ *adj.* lacking imagination; stolid; dull. □□ **un·i·mag·i·na·tive·ly** *adv.* **un·i·mag·i·na·tive·ness** *n.*

un·im·paired /únimpáird/ *adj.* not impaired.

un·im·peach·a·ble /únimpéechəbəl/ *adj.* giving no opportunity for censure; beyond reproach or question. □□ **un·im·peach·a·bly** *adv.*

un·im·ped·ed /únimpéedid/ *adj.* not impeded. □□ **un·im·ped·ed·ly** *adv.*

un·im·por·tance /únimpáwrt'ns/ *n.* lack of importance.

un·im·por·tant /únimpáwrt'nt/ *adj.* not important.

un·im·pos·ing /únimpózing/ *adj.* unimpressive. □□ **un·im·pos·ing·ly** *adv.*

un·im·pressed /únimprést/ *adj.* not impressed.

un·im·pres·sive /únimprésiv/ *adj.* not impressive. □□ **un·im·pres·sive·ly** *adv.* **un·im·pres·sive·ness** *n.*

un·im·proved /únimprŏŏvd/ *adj.* **1** not made better. **2** not made use of. **3** (of land) not used for agriculture or building; not developed.

un·in·cor·po·rat·ed /úninkáwrpəraytid/ *adj.* **1** not incorporated or united. **2** not formed into a corporation.

un·in·fect·ed /úninféktid/ *adj.* not infected.

un·in·flam·ma·ble /úninflámmbəl/ *adj.* not flammable.

un·in·flect·ed /úninfléktid/ *adj.* **1** *Gram.* (of a language) not having inflections. **2** not changing or varying. **3** not bent or deflected.

un·in·flu·enced /úninflŏŏinst/ *adj.* (often foll. by *by*) not influenced.

un·in·form·a·tive /úninfáwrmətiv/ *adj.* not informative; giving little information.

un·in·formed /úninfáwrmd/ *adj.* **1** not informed or instructed. **2** ignorant, uneducated.

un·in·hab·it·a·ble /úninhábitəbəl/ *adj.* that cannot be inhabited. □□ **un·in·hab·it·a·ble·ness** *n.*

un·in·hab·it·ed /úninhábitid/ *adj.* not inhabited.

un·in·hib·it·ed /úninhíbitid/ *adj.* not inhibited. □□ **un·in·hib·it·ed·ly** *adv.* **un·in·hib·it·ed·ness** *n.*

un·in·i·ti·at·ed /úninísheeaytid/ *adj.* not initiated; not admitted or instructed.

un·in·jured /úninjərd/ *adj.* not injured.

un·in·spired /úninspírd/ *adj.* **1** not inspired. **2** (of oratory, etc.) commonplace.

un·in·spir·ing /úninspíring/ *adj.* not inspiring. □□ **un·in·spir·ing·ly** *adv.*

un·in·struct·ed /úninstrúktid/ *adj.* not instructed or informed.

un·in·sur·a·ble /úninshŏŏrəbəl/ *adj.* that cannot be insured.

un·in·sured /úninshŏŏrd/ *adj.* not insured.

un·in·tel·li·gent /únintélijənt/ *adj.* not intelligent. □□ **un·in·tel·li·gent·ly** *adv.*

un·in·tel·li·gi·ble /únintélijibəl/ *adj.* not intelligible. □□ **un·in·tel·li·gi·bil·i·ty** *n.* **un·in·tel·li·gi·ble·ness** *n.* **un·in·tel·li·gi·bly** *adv.*

un·in·tend·ed /úninténdid/ *adj.* not intended.

un·in·ten·tion·al /úninténshənəl/ *adj.* not intentional. □□ **un·in·ten·tion·al·ly** *adv.*

un·in·ter·est·ed /úníntrəstid, -təristid, -tərəs-/ *adj.*

UNICYCLE

UNIFORM

Uniforms make a group of people immediately identifiable, which can be important for members of the emergency services and the armed forces. They also set a clear standard for the wearer in terms of quality and function. Although some uniforms are ceremonial, especially in the military, most are designed to be practical.

EXAMPLES OF UNIFORMS

AMERICAN SUBMARINE CAPTAIN

BRITISH FLIGHT LIEUTENANT

AUSTRALIAN FIREFIGHTER

BRITISH NURSE

AMERICAN POLICEMAN

FRENCH GENDARME

U

1 not interested. **2** unconcerned; indifferent. □□ **un·in·ter·est·ed·ly** *adv.* **un·in·ter·est·ed·ness** *n.*

un·in·vit·ing /úninvíting/ *adj.* not inviting; unattractive; repellent. □□ **un·in·vit·ing·ly** *adv.*

un·in·volved /úninvólvd/ *adj.* not involved.

un·ion /yōōnyən/ *n.* **1** the act or an instance of uniting; the state of being united. **2 a** a whole resulting from the combination of parts or members. **b** a political unit formed in this way, esp. (**Union**) the US (esp. as distinct from the Confederacy during the Civil War), the UK, or South Africa. **3** = LABOR UNION. **4** marriage; matrimony. **5** concord; agreement (*lived together in perfect union*). **6** (**Union**) (in the UK) **a** a general social club and debating society at some universities and colleges. **b** the buildings or accommodations of such a society. **7** *Math.* the totality of the members of two or more sets. **8** a part of a flag with a device emblematic of union, normally occupying the upper corner next to the staff. **9** a joint or coupling for pipes, etc.

un·ion·ize /yōōnyəníz/ *v.tr. & intr.* bring or come under labor-union organization or rules. □□ **un·ion·i·za·tion** *n.*

Un·ion Jack *n.* (also **Un·ion flag**) ▼ the national ensign of the United Kingdom formed by the union of the crosses of St. George, St. Andrew, and St. Patrick.

St. Andrew's cross   *St. Patrick's cross*

St. George's cross

UNION JACK

u·nique /yōōnéek/ *adj. & n.* ● *adj.* **1** of which there is only one; unequaled; having no like, equal, or parallel (*his position was unique; this vase is considered unique*). **2** *disp.* unusual; remarkable (*the most unique man I ever met*). ● *n.* a unique thing or person. □□ **u·nique·ly** *adv.* **u·nique·ness** *n.*

u·ni·sex /yōōniseks/ *adj.* (of clothing, hairstyles, etc.) designed to be suitable for both sexes.

u·ni·sex·u·al /yōōnisékshooəl/ *adj.* **1 a** of one sex. **b** *Bot.* having stamens or pistils but not both. **2** unisex. □□ **u·ni·sex·u·al·i·ty** /-shooálitee/ *n.* **u·ni·sex·u·al·ly** *adv.*

UNISEXUAL BEGONIA FLOWERS

stamens

pistil

FEMALE FLOWER   MALE FLOWER

u·ni·son /yōōnisən/ *n.* **1** *Mus.* **a** a coincidence in pitch of sounds or notes. **b** this regarded as an interval. **2** *Mus.* a combination of voices or instruments at the same pitch or at pitches differing by one or more octaves (*sang in unison*). **3** agreement; concord (*acted in perfect unison*).

u·nit /yōōnit/ *n.* **1 a** an individual thing, person, or group regarded as single and complete, esp. for purposes of calculation. **b** each of the (smallest

separate individuals or groups into which a complex whole may be analyzed (*the family as the unit of society*). **2** a quantity chosen as a standard in terms of which other quantities may be expressed (*unit of heat; SI unit; mass per unit volume*). **3** a device with a specified function forming part of a complex mechanism. **4** a group with a special function in an organization. **5** a group of buildings, wards, etc., in a hospital. **6** the number 'one.'

u·ni·tard /yōōnətaard/ *n.* a one-piece leotard that covers the legs as well as the torso.

U·ni·tar·i·an /yōōnitáireeən/ *n. & adj.* ● *n.* **1** a person who believes that God is not a Trinity but one being. **2** a member of a religious body maintaining this and advocating freedom from formal dogma or doctrine. ● *adj.* of or relating to the Unitarians. □□ **U·ni·tar·i·an·ism** *n.*

u·ni·tar·y /yōōniteree/ *adj.* **1** of a unit or units. **2** marked by unity or uniformity. □□ **u·ni·tar·i·ly** *adv.* **u·ni·tar·i·ty** /-téritee/ *n.*

u·nit cell *n. Crystallog.* ▶ the smallest repeating group of atoms, ions, or molecules in a crystal. ▷ CRYSTAL

u·nit cost *n.* the cost of producing one item of manufacture.

u·nite /yōōnít/ *v.* **1** *tr. & intr.* join together; make or become one; combine. **2** *tr. & intr.* join together for a common purpose or action (*united in their struggle against injustice*). **3** *tr. & intr.* join in marriage. **4** *tr.* possess (qualities, features, etc.) in combination (*united anger with mercy*). **5** *intr. & tr.* form or cause to form a physical or chemical whole (*oil will not unite with water*). □□ **u·ni·tive** /yōōnitiv/ *adj.* **u·ni·tive·ly** *adv.*

u·nit·ed /yōōnítid/ *adj.* **1** that has united or been united. **2 a** of or produced by two or more persons or things in union; joint. **b** resulting from the union of two or more parts (esp. in the names of churches, societies, and athletic clubs). **3** in agreement; of like mind. □□ **u·nit·ed·ly** *adv.*

UNIT CELL

A unit cell consists of a set number of atoms in a crystal, kept together in a specific arrangement by bonding forces. The atoms can be arranged only into seven identifiable forms (hexagonal is shown here). The form of the unit cells in a crystal determines that crystal's shape.

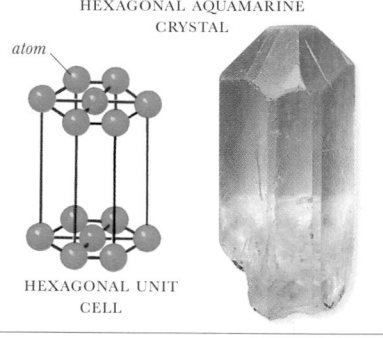

HEXAGONAL AQUAMARINE CRYSTAL

atom

HEXAGONAL UNIT CELL

U·nit·ed King·dom *n.* Great Britain and Northern Ireland (until 1922, Great Britain and Ireland).

U·nit·ed Na·tions *n.pl.* (orig., in 1942) those united against the Axis powers in the war of 1939–45, (later) a supranational peace-seeking organization of these and many other nations.

U·nit·ed States *n.pl.* (in full **United States of America**) ▼ a federal republic of 50 states, mostly in N. America and including Alaska and Hawaii.

UNITED STATES OF AMERICA

The United States of America, the fourth largest country in the world, consists of 48 contiguous states and two outlying ones – Alaska to the northwest, and Hawaii, a group of islands in the Pacific Ocean 2,100 miles (3,380 km) southwest of California. In 1787, 13 states on the East Coast were united by constitutional law to establish the US. The last states to join were Alaska and Hawaii, in 1959.

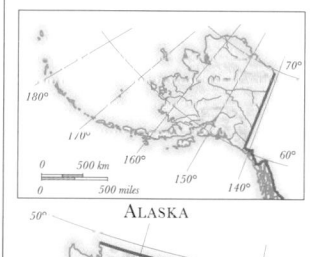

ALASKA

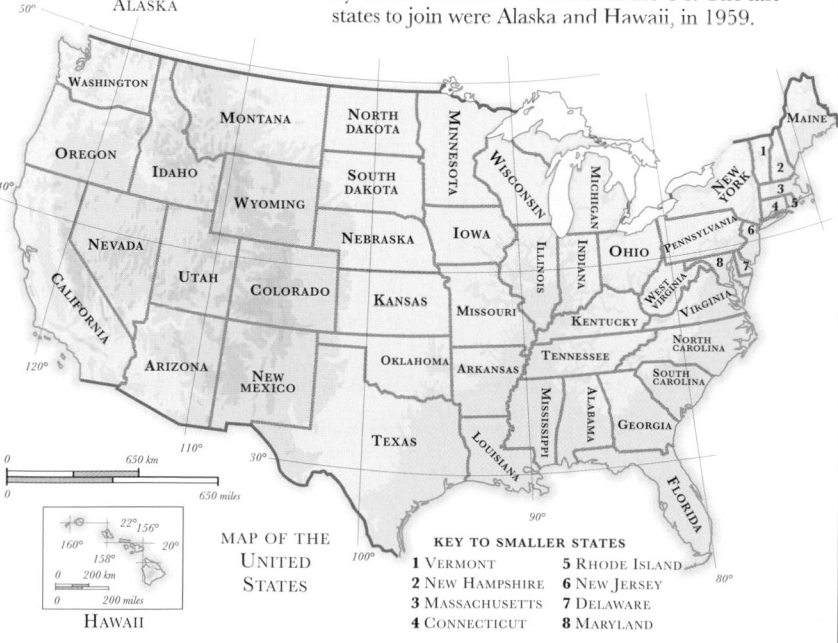

MAP OF THE UNITED STATES

HAWAII

KEY TO SMALLER STATES
1 VERMONT   **5** RHODE ISLAND
2 NEW HAMPSHIRE   **6** NEW JERSEY
3 MASSACHUSETTS   **7** DELAWARE
4 CONNECTICUT   **8** MARYLAND

U

u·nit price *n.* the price charged for each unit of goods supplied.

u·ni·ty /yoŏnitee/ *n.* (*pl.* **-ies**) **1** oneness; being one, single, or individual; being formed of parts that constitute a whole; due interconnection and coherence of parts (*the pictures lack unity; national unity*). **2** harmony or concord between persons, etc. (*lived together in unity*). **3** a thing forming a complex whole (*a person regarded as a unity*). **4** *Math.* the number 'one,' the factor that leaves unchanged the quantity on which it operates.

Univ. *abbr.* University.

u·ni·va·lent *adj. & n.* ● *adj.* **1** /yoŏniváylənt/ *Chem.* having a valence of one. **2** /yoŏnívələnt/ *Biol.* (of a chromosome) remaining unpaired during meiosis. ● *n.* /yoonívələnt/ *Biol.* a univalent chromosome.

u·ni·valve /yoŏnivalv/ *adj. & n. Zool.* ● *adj.* having one valve. ● *n.* a univalve mollusk.

u·ni·ver·sal /yoŏnivérsəl/ *adj. & n.* ● *adj.* **1** of, belonging to, or done, etc., by all persons or things in the world or in the class concerned; applicable to all cases (*the feeling was universal; met with universal approval*). **2** *Logic* (of a proposition) in which something is asserted of all of a class (opp. PARTICULAR 5). ● *n.* **1** *Logic* a universal proposition. **2** *Philos.* **a** a term or concept of general application. **b** a nature or essence signified by a general term. □□ **u·ni·ver·sal·i·ty** /-sálitee/ *n.* **u·ni·ver·sal·ize** *v.tr.* **u·ni·ver·sal·i·za·tion** /-lizáyshən/ *n.* **u·ni·ver·sal·ly** *adv.*

u·ni·ver·sal in·di·ca·tor pa·per *n.* ▶ a paper stained with a mixture of dyes that changes color over a range of pH and is used as a test for acids and alkalis.

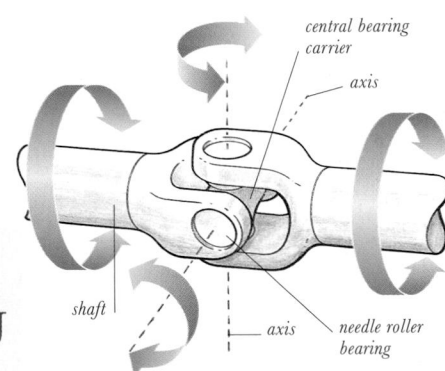

paper

dyes reacting to alkali

alkali

UNIVERSAL INDICATOR PAPER

u·ni·ver·sal·ist /yoŏnivérsəlist/ *n. Theol.* **1** a person who holds that all mankind will eventually be saved. **2** a member of an organized body of Christians who hold this. □□ **u·ni·ver·sal·ism** *n.* **u·ni·ver·sal·is·tic** /-lístik/ *adj.*

u·ni·ver·sal joint *n.* (also **u·ni·ver·sal cou·pling**) ▼ a joint or coupling that can transmit rotary power by a shaft at any selected angle.

central bearing carrier

axis

shaft

axis

needle roller bearing

UNIVERSAL JOINT

U·ni·ver·sal Prod·uct Code *n.* a bar code on products that can be read by an electronic scanner, usu. providing price and product identification.

u·ni·verse /yoŏnivərs/ *n.* **1 a** all existing things; the whole creation; the cosmos. **b** a sphere of existence, influence, activity, etc. **2** all mankind.

u·ni·ver·si·ty /yoŏnivérsitee/ *n.* (*pl.* **-ies**) **1** an educational institution designed for instruction, examination, or both, of students in many branches of advanced learning, conferring degrees in various faculties, and often embodying colleges and similar institutions. **2** the members of this collectively.

u·niv·o·cal /yoŏnívəkəl, yoŏnivókəl/ *adj. & n.* ● *adj.*

(of a word, etc.) having only one proper meaning. ● *n.* a univocal word. □□ **u·niv·o·cal·i·ty** /yoŏnivōkálitee/ *n.* **u·niv·o·cal·ly** *adv.*

un·just /únjúst/ *adj.* not just; contrary to justice or fairness. □□ **un·just·ly** *adv.* **un·just·ness** *n.*

un·jus·ti·fi·a·ble /unjústifíəbəl/ *adj.* not justifiable. □□ **un·jus·ti·fi·a·bly** *adv.*

un·jus·ti·fied /únjústifīd/ *adj.* not justified.

un·kempt /únkémpt/ *adj.* **1** untidy; of neglected appearance. **2** uncombed; disheveled. □□ **un·kempt·ly** *adv.* **un·kempt·ness** *n.*

un·kept /únképt/ *adj.* **1** (of a promise, law, etc.) not observed; disregarded. **2** not tended; neglected.

un·kind /únkínd/ *adj.* **1** not kind. **2** harsh; severe; cruel. **3** unpleasant. □□ **un·kind·ly** *adv.* **un·kind·ness** *n.*

un·know·a·ble /ún-nóəbəl/ *adj. & n.* ● *adj.* that cannot be known. ● *n.* **1** an unknowable thing. **2** (**the Unknowable**) the postulated absolute or ultimate reality.

un·know·ing /ún-nóing/ *adj. & n.* ● *adj.* (often foll. by *of*) not knowing; ignorant; unconscious. ● *n.* ignorance (*cloud of unknowing*). □□ **un·know·ing·ly** *adv.* **un·know·ing·ness** *n.*

un·known /ún-nón/ *adj. & n.* ● *adj.* (often foll. by *to*) not known; unfamiliar (*his purpose was unknown to me*). ● *n.* **1** an unknown thing or person. **2** an unknown quantity (*equation in two unknowns*). □ **unknown to** without the knowledge of (*did it unknown to me*). □□ **un·known·ness** *n.*

Un·known Sol·dier *n.* an unidentified representative member of a country's armed forces killed in war, given burial with special honors in a national memorial.

un·la·beled /únláybəld/ *adj.* not labeled; without a label.

un·lace /únláys/ *v.tr.* **1** undo the lace or laces of. **2** unfasten or loosen in this way.

un·lade /únláyd/ *v.tr.* **1** take the cargo out of (a ship). **2** discharge (a cargo, etc.) from a ship.

un·lad·en /únláyd'n/ *adj.* not laden.

un·la·dy·like /únláydeelīk/ *adj.* not ladylike.

un·laid /únláyd/ *adj.* not laid.

un·la·ment·ed /únləméntid/ *adj.* not lamented.

un·law·ful /únláwfool/ *adj.* not lawful; illegal; not permissible. □□ **un·law·ful·ly** *adv.* **un·law·ful·ness** *n.*

un·lead·ed /únlédid/ *adj.* **1** (of gasoline, etc.) without added lead. **2** not covered, weighted, or framed with lead.

un·learn /únlórn/ *v.tr.* (*past* and *past part.* **unlearned** or **unlearnt**) **1** discard from one's memory. **2** rid oneself of (a habit, false information, etc.).

un·learn·ed[1] /únlórnid/ *adj.* not well educated; untaught; ignorant. □□ **un·learn·ed·ly** *adv.*

un·learn·ed[2] /únlórnd/ *adj.* (also **un·learnt** /-lérnt/) that has not been learned.

un·leash /únléesh/ *v.tr.* **1** release from a leash or restraint. **2** set free to engage in pursuit or attack.

un·leav·ened /únlévənd/ *adj.* not leavened; made without yeast or other raising agent.

un·less /unlés, ən-/ *conj.* if not; except when (*shall go unless I hear from you; always walked unless I had a bicycle*).

un·let·tered /únlétərd/ *adj.* **1** illiterate. **2** not well educated.

un·lib·er·at·ed /únlíbəraytid/ *adj.* not liberated.

un·li·censed /únlísənst/ *adj.* not licensed, esp. (in the UK) without a license to sell alcoholic drink.

un·like /únlík/ *adj. & prep.* ● *adj.* **1** not like; different from (*is unlike both his parents*). **2** uncharacteristic of (*such behavior is unlike him*). **3** dissimilar; different. ● *prep.* differently from (*acts quite unlike anyone else*). □□ **un·like·ness** *n.*

un·like·ly /únlíklee/ *adj.* (**unlikelier, unlikeliest**) **1** improbable (*unlikely tale*). **2** (foll. by *to* + infin.) not to be expected to do something (*he's unlikely to be*

available). **3** unpromising (*an unlikely candidate*). □□ **un·like·li·hood** *n.* **un·like·li·ness** *n.*

un·like signs *n. Math.* plus and minus.

un·lim·it·ed /únlímitid/ *adj.* without limit; unrestricted; very great in number or quantity (*has unlimited possibilities; an unlimited expanse of sea*). □□ **un·lim·it·ed·ly** *adv.* **un·lim·it·ed·ness** *n.*

un·lined[1] /únlínd/ *adj.* **1** (of paper, etc.) without lines. **2** (of a face, etc.) without wrinkles.

un·lined[2] /únlínd/ *adj.* (of a garment, etc.) without lining.

un·link /únlíngk/ *v.tr.* **1** undo the links (of a chain, etc.). **2** detach or set free.

un·liq·ui·dat·ed /únlíkwidaytid/ *adj.* not liquidated.

un·list·ed /únlístid/ *adj.* not included in a published list, esp. of stock exchange prices or of telephone numbers.

un·lit /únlit/ *adj.* not lit.

un·lived-in /únlívdin/ *adj.* **1** appearing to be uninhabited. **2** unused by the inhabitants.

un·load /únlód/ *v.tr.* **1** (also *absol.*) remove a load from (a vehicle, etc.). **2** remove (a load) from a vehicle, etc. **3** remove the charge from (a firearm, etc.). **4** *colloq.* get rid of. **5** (foll. by *on*) *colloq.* **a** divulge (information). **b** (also *absol.*) give vent to (feelings). □□ **un·load·er** *n.*

un·lock /únlók/ *v.tr.* **1 a** release the lock of (a door, box, etc.). **b** release or disclose by unlocking. **2** release thoughts, feelings, etc., from (one's mind, etc.).

un·locked /únlókt/ *adj.* not locked.

un·looked-for /únloŏktfawr/ *adj.* unexpected; unforeseen.

un·loose /únloŏs/ *v.tr.* (also **un·loos·en**) loose; set free.

un·lov·a·ble /únlúvəbəl/ *adj.* not lovable.

un·loved /únlúvd/ *adj.* not loved.

un·love·ly /únlúvlee/ *adj.* not attractive; unpleasant; ugly. □□ **un·love·li·ness** *n.*

un·luck·y /únlúkee/ *adj.* (**unluckier, unluckiest**) **1** not fortunate or successful. **2** wretched. **3** bringing bad luck. **4** ill-judged. □□ **un·luck·i·ly** *adv.* **un·luck·i·ness** *n.*

un·made /únmáyd/ *adj.* **1** not made. **2** destroyed; annulled.

un·make /únmáyk/ *v.tr.* (*past* and *past part.* **unmade**) undo the making of; destroy; depose; annul.

un·man /únmán/ *v.tr.* (**unmanned, unmanning**) **1** deprive of supposed manly qualities (e.g., self-control, courage); cause to weep, etc.; discourage. **2** deprive (a ship, etc.) of men.

un·man·age·a·ble /únmánijəbəl/ *adj.* not (easily) managed, manipulated, or controlled. □□ **un·man·age·a·ble·ness** *n.* **un·man·age·a·bly** *adv.*

un·man·ly /únmánlee/ *adj.* not manly. □□ **un·man·li·ness** *n.*

un·manned /únmánd/ *adj.* **1** not manned. **2** esp. *Brit.* overcome by emotion, etc.

un·man·ner·ly /únmánərlee/ *adj.* **1** without good manners. **2** (of actions, speech, etc.) showing a lack of good manners. □□ **un·man·ner·li·ness** *n.*

un·marked /únmaárkt/ *adj.* **1** not marked. **2** not noticed.

un·mar·ried /únmáreed/ *adj.* not married; single.

un·mask /únmásk/ *v.* **1** *tr.* **a** remove the mask from. **b** expose the true character of. **2** *intr.* remove one's mask. □□ **un·mask·er** *n.*

un·matched /únmácht/ *adj.* not matched or equaled.

un·meant /únmént/ *adj.* not meant or intended.

un·mem·o·ra·ble /únmémərəbəl/ *adj.* not memorable. □□ **un·mem·o·ra·bly** *adv.*

un·men·tion·a·ble /únménshənəbəl/ *adj. & n.* ● *adj.* that cannot (properly) be mentioned. ● *n.* **1** (in *pl.*) *joc.* **a** undergarments. **b** *archaic* trousers. **2** a person or thing not to be mentioned. □□ **un·men·tion·a·bil·i·ty** /-bílitee/ *n.* **un·men·tion·a·ble·ness** *n.* **un·men·tion·a·bly** *adv.*

U

un·men·tioned /únménshənd/ *adj.* not mentioned.

un·mer·ci·ful /únmérsifŏŏl/ *adj.* merciless. □□ **un·mer·ci·ful·ly** *adv.* **un·mer·ci·ful·ness** *n.*

un·mer·it·ed /únméritid/ *adj.* not merited.

un·met /únmét/ *adj.* (of a quota, demand, goal, etc.) not achieved or fulfilled.

un·met·aled /únmét'ld/ *adj. Brit.* (of a road, etc.) not made with road metal.

un·miss·a·ble /únmísəbəl/ *adj.* that cannot or should not be missed.

un·mis·tak·a·ble /únmistáykəbəl/ *adj.* that cannot be mistaken or doubted; clear. □□ **un·mis·tak·a·bil·i·ty** /-bílitee/ *n.* **un·mis·tak·a·ble·ness** *n.* **un·mis·tak·a·bly** *adv.*

un·mit·i·gat·ed /únmítigaytid/ *adj.* **1** not mitigated or modified. **2** absolute; unqualified (*an unmitigated disaster*). □□ **un·mit·i·gat·ed·ly** *adv.*

un·mixed /únmíkst/ *adj.* not mixed.

un·mod·i·fied /únmódifīd/ *adj.* not modified.

un·mo·lest·ed /únməléstid/ *adj.* not molested.

un·mor·al /únmáwrəl, -mór-/ *adj.* not concerned with morality (cf. IMMORAL). □□ **un·mor·al·i·ty** /-rálitee/ *n.* **un·mor·al·ly** *adv.*

un·mount·ed /únmówntid/ *adj.* not mounted.

un·mourned /únmáwrnd/ *adj.* not mourned.

un·moved /únmŏŏvd/ *adj.* **1** not moved. **2** not changed in one's purpose. **3** not affected by emotion. □□ **un·mov·a·ble** *adj.* (also **un·move·a·ble**).

un·mown /únmón/ *adj.* not mown.

un·mur·mur·ing /únmérmməring/ *adj.* not complaining. □□ **un·mur·mur·ing·ly** *adv.*

un·mu·si·cal /únmyŏŏzikəl/ *adj.* **1** not pleasing to the ear. **2** unskilled in or indifferent to music. □□ **un·mu·si·cal·i·ty** /-kálitee/ *n.* **un·mu·si·cal·ly** *adv.* **un·mu·si·cal·ness** *n.*

un·muz·zle /únmúzəl/ *v.tr.* **1** remove a muzzle from. **2** relieve of an obligation to remain silent.

un·nail /ún-náyl/ *v.tr.* unfasten by the removal of nails.

un·name·a·ble /ún-náyməbəl/ *adj.* that cannot be named, esp. too bad to be named.

un·named /ún-náymd/ *adj.* not named.

un·nat·u·ral /ún-náchərəl/ *adj.* **1** contrary to nature or the usual course of nature; not normal. **2 a** lacking natural feelings. **b** extremely cruel or wicked. **3** artificial. **4** affected. □□ **un·nat·u·ral·ly** *adv.* **un·nat·u·ral·ness** *n.*

un·nav·i·ga·ble /ún-návigəbəl/ *adj.* not navigable. □□ **un·nav·i·ga·bil·i·ty** /-bílitee/ *n.*

un·nec·es·sar·y /ún-nésəseree/ *adj. & n.* ● *adj.* **1** not necessary. **2** more than is necessary (*with unnecessary care*). ● *n.* (*pl.* **-ies**) (usu. in *pl.*) an unnecessary thing. □□ **un·nec·es·sar·i·ly** *adv.* **un·nec·es·sar·i·ness** *n.*

un·need·ed /ún-néedid/ *adj.* not needed.

un·nerve /ún-nárv/ *v.tr.* deprive of strength or resolution. □□ **un·nerv·ing·ly** *adv.*

un·no·ticed /ún-nótist/ *adj.* not noticed.

un·num·bered /ún-númbərd/ *adj.* **1** not marked with a number. **2** not counted. **3** countless.

un·ob·jec·tion·a·ble /únəbjékshənəbəl/ *adj.* not objectionable; acceptable. □□ **un·ob·jec·tion·a·ble·ness** *n.* **un·ob·jec·tion·a·bly** *adv.*

un·ob·serv·ant /únəbzórvənt/ *adj.* not observant. □□ **un·ob·serv·ant·ly** *adv.*

un·ob·served /únəbzórvd/ *adj.* not observed. □□ **un·ob·serv·ed·ly** /-vidlee/ *adv.*

un·ob·struct·ed /únəbstrúktid/ *adj.* not obstructed.

un·ob·tain·a·ble /únəbtáynəbəl/ *adj.* that cannot be obtained.

un·ob·tru·sive /únəbtrŏŏsiv/ *adj.* not making oneself or itself noticed. □□ **un·ob·tru·sive·ly** *adv.* **un·ob·tru·sive·ness** *n.*

un·oc·cu·pied /únókyəpīd/ *adj.* not occupied.

un·of·fend·ing /únəfénding/ *adj.* not offending; harmless; innocent. □□ **un·of·fend·ed** *adj.*

un·of·fi·cial /únəfíshəl/ *adj.* **1** not officially author-

ized or confirmed. **2** not characteristic of officials. □□ **un·of·fi·cial·ly** *adv.*

un·o·pened /únópənd/ *adj.* not opened.

un·op·posed /únəpózd/ *adj.* not opposed, esp. in an election.

un·or·dained /únawrdáynd/ *adj.* not ordained.

un·or·gan·ized /únáwrgənīzd/ *adj.* not organized (cf. DISORGANIZE).

un·o·rig·i·nal /únəríjinəl/ *adj.* lacking originality; derivative. □□ **un·o·rig·i·nal·i·ty** /-nálitee/ *n.* **un·o·rig·i·nal·ly** *adv.*

un·or·tho·dox /únáwrthədoks/ *adj.* not orthodox. □□ **un·or·tho·dox·ly** *adv.* **un·or·tho·dox·y** *n.*

un·os·ten·ta·tious /únostentáyshəs/ *adj.* not ostentatious. □□ **un·os·ten·ta·tious·ly** *adv.* **un·os·ten·ta·tious·ness** *n.*

un·owned /únónd/ *adj.* **1** unacknowledged. **2** having no owner.

un·pack /únpák/ *v.tr.* **1** (also *absol.*) open and remove the contents of (a package, luggage, etc.). **2** take (a thing) out from a package, etc. □□ **un·pack·er** *n.*

un·paid /únpáyd/ *adj.* (of a debt or a person) not paid.

un·paired /únpáird/ *adj.* **1** not arranged in pairs. **2** not forming one of a pair.

un·pal·at·a·ble /únpálətəbəl/ *adj.* **1** not pleasant to taste. **2** (of an idea, suggestion, etc.) disagreeable; distasteful. □□ **un·pal·at·a·bil·i·ty** *n.* **un·pal·at·a·ble·ness** *n.*

un·par·al·leled /únpárəleld/ *adj.* having no parallel or equal.

un·par·don·a·ble /únpaárd'nəbəl/ *adj.* that cannot be pardoned. □□ **un·par·don·a·ble·ness** *n.* **un·par·don·a·bly** *adv.*

un·pas·teur·ized /únpáschərīzd, -pástə-/ *adj.* not pasteurized.

un·pa·tri·ot·ic /únpaytreeótik/ *adj.* not patriotic. □□ **un·pa·tri·ot·i·cal·ly** *adv.*

un·paved /únpáyvd/ *adj.* not paved.

un·peg /únpég/ *v.tr.* (**unpegged, unpegging**) **1** unfasten by the removal of pegs. **2** cease to maintain or stabilize (prices, etc.).

un·peo·ple *v. & n.* ● *v.tr.* /únpéepəl/ depopulate ● *n.pl.* /únpeepəl/ unpersons.

un·per·fo·rat·ed /únpárfəraytid/ *adj.* not perforated.

un·per·fumed /únpárfyŏŏmd/ *adj.* not perfumed.

un·per·son /únpársən/ *n.* a person whose name or existence is denied or ignored.

un·per·sua·sive /únpərswáysiv, -ziv/ *adj.* not persuasive. □□ **un·per·sua·sive·ly** *adv.*

un·per·turbed /únpərtúrbd/ *adj.* not perturbed. □□ **un·per·turbed·ly** /-bidlee/ *adv.*

un·pick /únpík/ *v.tr.* undo the sewing of (stitches, a garment, etc.).

un·pin /únpín/ *v.tr.* (**unpinned, unpinning**) **1** unfasten or detach by removing a pin or pins. **2** *Chess* release (a piece that has been pinned).

un·pit·y·ing /únpíteeing/ *adj.* not pitying. □□ **un·pit·y·ing·ly** *adv.*

un·place·a·ble /únpláysəbəl/ *adj.* that cannot be placed or classified (*his accent was unplaceable*).

un·placed /únpláyst/ *adj.* not placed, esp. not placed as one of the first three finishing in a race, etc.

un·planned /únplánd/ *adj.* not planned.

un·plau·si·ble /únpláwzibəl/ *adj.* not plausible.

un·play·a·ble /únpláyəbəl/ *adj.* **1** *Sports* (of a ball) that cannot be struck or returned. **2** that cannot be played. □□ **un·play·a·bly** *adv.*

un·pleas·ant /únplézənt/ *adj.* not pleasant; displeasing; disagreeable. □□ **un·pleas·ant·ly** *adv.* **un·pleas·ant·ness** *n.*

un·pleas·ing /únpléezing/ *adj.* not pleasing. □□ **un·pleas·ing·ly** *adv.*

un·plowed /únplówd/ *adj.* not plowed.

un·plug /únplúg/ *v.tr.* (**unplugged, unplugging**) **1** disconnect (an electrical device) by removing its plug from the socket. **2** unstop.

un·plumbed /únplúmd/ *adj.* **1** not plumbed. **2** not fully explored or understood. □□ **un·plumb·a·ble** *adj.*

un·point·ed /únpóyntid/ *adj.* **1** having no point or points. **2 a** not punctuated. **b** (of written Hebrew, etc.) without vowel points. **3** (of masonry or brickwork) not pointed.

un·pol·ished /únpólisht/ *adj.* **1** ► not polished; rough. **2** without refinement; crude.

UNPOLISHED

un·polled /únpóld/ *adj.* **1** not having voted at an election. **2** not included in an opinion poll.

un·pol·lut·ed /únpəlŏŏtid/ *adj.* not polluted.

un·pop·u·lar /únpópyələr/ *adj.* not popular; not liked by the public or by people in general. □□ **un·pop·u·lar·i·ty** /-láritee/ *n.* **un·pop·u·lar·ly** *adv.*

POLISHED

UNPOLISHED AND POLISHED AMBER

un·pop·u·lat·ed /únpópyəlaytid/ *adj.* not populated.

un·prac·ti·cal /únpráktikəl/ *adj.* **1** not practical. **2** (of a person) not having practical skill. □□ **un·prac·ti·cal·i·ty** /-kálitee/ *n.* **un·prac·ti·cal·ly** *adv.*

un·prac·ticed /únpráktist/ *adj.* **1** not experienced or skilled. **2** not put into practice.

un·prec·e·dent·ed /únprésidəntid/ *adj.* **1** having no precedent, unparalleled. **2** novel. □□ **un·prec·e·dent·ed·ly** *adv.*

un·pre·dict·a·ble /únpridíktəbəl/ *adj.* that cannot be predicted. □□ **un·pre·dict·a·bil·i·ty** *n.* **un·pre·dict·a·ble·ness** *n.* **un·pre·dict·a·bly** *adv.*

un·pre·med·i·tat·ed /únpriméditaytid/ *adj.* not previously thought over; not deliberately planned; unintentional. □□ **un·pre·med·i·tat·ed·ly** *adv.*

un·pre·pared /únpripáird/ *adj.* not prepared (in advance); not ready. □□ **un·pre·par·ed·ly** *adv.* **un·pre·par·ed·ness** *n.*

un·pre·pos·sess·ing /únpreepəzésing/ *adj.* not prepossessing; unattractive.

un·pressed /únprést/ *adj.* not pressed, esp. (of clothing) unironed.

un·pre·sump·tu·ous /únprizúmpchŏŏəs/ *adj.* not presumptuous.

un·pre·ten·tious /únpriténshəs/ *adj.* not making a great display; simple; modest. □□ **un·pre·ten·tious·ly** *adv.* **un·pre·ten·tious·ness** *n.*

un·prin·ci·pled /únprínsipəld/ *adj.* lacking or not based on good moral principles. □□ **un·prin·ci·pled·ness** *n.*

un·print·a·ble /únpríntəbəl/ *adj.* that cannot be printed, esp. because too indecent or libelous or blasphemous. □□ **un·print·a·bly** *adv.*

un·pro·duc·tive /únprədúktiv/ *adj.* not productive. □□ **un·pro·duc·tive·ly** *adv.* **un·pro·duc·tive·ness** *n.*

un·pro·fes·sion·al /únprəféshənəl/ *adj.* **1** contrary to professional standards of behavior, etc. **2** not belonging to a profession; amateur. □□ **un·pro·fes·sion·al·ly** *adv.*

un·prof·it·a·ble /únprófitəbəl/ *adj.* not profitable. □□ **un·prof·it·a·ble·ness** *n.* **un·prof·it·a·bly** *adv.*

un·pro·gres·sive /únprəgrésiv/ *adj.* not progressive.

un·prom·is·ing /únprómising/ *adj.* not likely to turn out well. □□ **un·prom·is·ing·ly** *adv.*

un·prompt·ed /únprómptid/ *adj.* spontaneous.

un·pro·nounce·a·ble /únprənównsəbəl/ *adj.* that cannot be pronounced. □□ **un·pro·nounce·a·bly** *adv.*

un·pro·pi·tious /únprəpíshəs/ *adj.* not propitious. □□ **un·pro·pi·tious·ly** *adv.*

U

un·pro·tect·ed /únprətéktid/ *adj.* not protected. □□ **un·pro·tect·ed·ness** *n.*

un·proved /únprō̆ovd/ *adj.* (also **un·prov·en** /-vən/) not proved.

un·pro·vid·ed /únprəvídid/ *adj.* (usu. foll. by *with*) not furnished, supplied, or equipped.

un·pro·voked /únprəvōkt/ *adj.* (of a person or act) without provocation.

un·pub·lished /únpúblisht/ *adj.* not published. □□ **un·pub·lish·a·ble** *adj.*

un·punc·tu·al /únpúngkchōōəl/ *adj.* not punctual. □□ **un·punc·tu·al·i·ty** /-chōōálitee/ *n.*

un·punc·tu·at·ed /únpúngkchōōaytid/ *adj.* not punctuated.

un·pun·ished /únpúnisht/ *adj.* not punished.

un·put·down·a·ble /únpōŏtdównəbəl/ *adj. colloq.* (of a book) so engrossing that one has to go on reading it.

un·qual·i·fied /únkwólifīd/ *adj.* **1** not competent (*unqualified to give an answer*). **2** not legally or officially qualified (*an unqualified practitioner*). **3** not modified or restricted; complete (*unqualified assent; unqualified success*).

un·quench·a·ble /únkwénchəbəl/ *adj.* that cannot be quenched. □□ **un·quench·a·bly** *adv.*

un·ques·tion·a·ble /únkwéschənəbəl/ *adj.* that cannot be disputed or doubted. □□ **un·ques·tion·a·bil·i·ty** *n.* **un·ques·tion·a·ble·ness** *n.* **un·ques·tion·a·bly** *adv.*

un·ques·tioned /únkwéschənd/ *adj.* not disputed or doubted; definite; certain.

un·ques·tion·ing /únkwéschəning/ *adj.* **1** asking no questions. **2** done, etc., without asking questions. □□ **un·ques·tion·ing·ly** *adv.*

un·qui·et /únkwíət/ *adj.* **1** restless; agitated; stirring. **2** perturbed, anxious. □□ **un·qui·et·ly** *adv.* **un·qui·et·ness** *n.*

un·quote /únkwōt/ *v.tr.* (as *int.*) (in dictation, reading aloud, etc.) indicate the presence of closing quotation marks (cf. QUOTE *v.* 5 b.)

un·quot·ed /únkwótid/ *adj.* not quoted, esp. on a stock exchange.

un·rav·el /únrávəl/ *v.* **1** *tr.* cause to be no longer raveled, tangled, or intertwined. **2** *tr.* probe and solve (a mystery, etc.). **3** *tr.* undo (a fabric, esp. a knitted one). **4** *intr.* become disentangled or unknitted.

un·reach·a·ble /únréechəbəl/ *adj.* that cannot be reached. □□ **un·reach·a·ble·ness** *n.* **un·reach·a·bly** *adv.*

un·read /únréd/ *adj.* **1** (of a book, etc.) not read. **2** (of a person) not well-read.

un·read·a·ble /únréedəbəl/ *adj.* **1** too dull or too difficult to be worth reading. **2** illegible. □□ **un·read·a·bil·i·ty** /-bílitee/ *n.* **un·read·a·bly** *adv.*

un·read·y /únrédee/ *adj.* **1** not ready. **2** not prompt in action. □□ **un·read·i·ly** *adv.* **un·read·i·ness** *n.*

un·re·al /únréeəl/ *adj.* **1** not real. **2** imaginary; illusory. **3** *sl.* incredible, amazing. □□ **un·re·al·i·ty** /-reeálitee/ *n.* **un·re·al·ly** *adv.*

un·re·al·is·tic /únreeəlístik/ *adj.* not realistic. □□ **un·re·al·is·ti·cal·ly** *adv.*

un·rea·son /únréezən/ *n.* lack of reasonable thought or action.

un·rea·son·a·ble /únréezənəbəl/ *adj.* **1** going beyond the limits of what is reasonable or equitable (*unreasonable demands*). **2** not guided by or listening to reason. □□ **un·rea·son·a·ble·ness** *n.* **un·rea·son·a·bly** *adv.*

un·re·cep·tive /únriséptiv/ *adj.* not receptive.

un·re·cip·ro·cat·ed /únrisíprəkaytid/ *adj.* not reciprocated.

un·reck·oned /únrékənd/ *adj.* not calculated or taken into account.

un·rec·og·niz·a·ble /únrékəgnízəbəl/ *adj.* that cannot be recognized. □□ **un·rec·og·niz·a·ble·ness** *n.* **un·rec·og·niz·a·bly** *adv.*

un·rec·og·nized /únrékəgnízd/ *adj.* not recognized.

un·rec·on·ciled /únrékənsīld/ *adj.* not reconciled.

un·re·con·struct·ed /únreekənstrúktid/ *adj.* **1** not reconciled or converted to the current political orthodoxy. **2** not rebuilt.

un·re·deem·a·ble /únridéeməbəl/ *adj.* that cannot be redeemed. □□ **un·re·deem·a·bly** *adv.*

un·reel /únréel/ *v.tr. & intr.* unwind from a reel.

un·re·fined /únrifīnd/ *adj.* not refined.

un·re·flect·ing /únriflékting/ *adj.* not thoughtful. □□ **un·re·flect·ing·ly** *adv.* **un·re·flect·ing·ness** *n.*

un·re·formed /únrifáwrmd/ *adj.* not reformed.

un·reg·is·tered /únréjistərd/ *adj.* not registered.

un·reg·u·lat·ed /únrégyəlaytid/ *adj.* not regulated.

un·re·hearsed /únrihárst/ *adj.* not rehearsed.

un·re·lat·ed /únriláytid/ *adj.* not related. □□ **un·re·lat·ed·ness** *n.*

un·re·lent·ing /únrilénting/ *adj.* **1** not relenting or yielding. **2** unmerciful. **3** not abating or relaxing. □□ **un·re·lent·ing·ly** *adv.* **un·re·lent·ing·ness** *n.*

un·re·li·a·ble /únrilíəbəl/ *adj.* not reliable; erratic. □□ **un·re·li·a·bil·i·ty** *n.* **un·re·li·a·ble·ness** *n.* **un·re·li·a·bly** *adv.*

un·re·lieved /únriléevd/ *adj.* **1** lacking the relief given by contrast or variation. **2** not aided or assisted. □□ **un·re·liev·ed·ly** /-vidlee/ *adv.*

un·re·mark·a·ble /únrimáarkəbəl/ *adj.* not remarkable; uninteresting. □□ **un·re·mark·a·bly** *adv.*

un·re·mit·ting /únrimíting/ *adj.* never relaxing or slackening; incessant. □□ **un·re·mit·ting·ly** *adv.* **un·re·mit·ting·ness** *n.*

un·re·morse·ful /únrimáwrsfŏŏl/ *adj.* lacking remorse. □□ **un·re·morse·ful·ly** *adv.*

un·re·mu·ner·a·tive /únrimyŏŏnərətiv, -raytiv/ *adj.* bringing no, or not enough, profit or income. □□ **un·re·mu·ner·a·tive·ly** *adv.* **un·re·mu·ner·a·tive·ness** *n.*

un·re·new·a·ble /únrinŏŏəbəl, -nyŏŏ-/ *adj.* that cannot be renewed. □□ **un·re·newed** *adj.*

un·re·peat·a·ble /únripéetəbəl/ *adj.* **1** that cannot be done, made, or said again. **2** too indecent to be said again. □□ **un·re·peat·a·bil·i·ty** *n.*

un·re·pent·ant /únripéntənt/ *adj.* not repentant; impenitent. □□ **un·re·pent·ant·ly** *adv.*

un·re·port·ed /únripáwrtid/ *adj.* not reported.

un·rep·re·sent·a·tive /únreprizéntətiv/ *adj.* not representative. □□ **un·rep·re·sent·a·tive·ness** *n.*

un·re·quit·ed /únrikwítid/ *adj.* (of love, etc.) not returned. □□ **un·re·quit·ed·ly** *adv.* **un·re·quit·ed·ness** *n.*

un·re·served /únrizárvd/ *adj.* **1** not reserved (*unreserved seats*). **2** without reservations; absolute (*unreserved confidence*). **3** free from reserve (*an unreserved nature*). □□ **un·re·serv·ed·ly** /-vidlee/ *adv.* **un·re·serv·ed·ness** *n.*

un·re·sist·ing /únrizísting/ *adj.* not resisting. □□ **un·re·sist·ing·ly** *adv.* **un·re·sist·ing·ness** *n.*

un·re·solved /únrizólvd/ *adj.* **1 a** uncertain how to act; irresolute. **b** undecided. **2** (of questions, etc.) undetermined; undecided; unsolved. **3** not broken up or dissolved. □□ **un·re·sol·ved·ly** /-vidlee/ *adv.* **un·re·sol·ved·ness** *n.*

un·re·spon·sive /únrispónsiv/ *adj.* not responsive. □□ **un·re·spon·sive·ly** *adv.* **un·re·spon·sive·ness** *n.*

un·re·strain·a·ble /únristráynəbəl/ *adj.* that cannot be restrained; irrepressible; ungovernable.

un·re·strained /únristráynd/ *adj.* not restrained. □□ **un·re·strain·ed·ly** /-nidlee/ *adv.* **un·re·strain·ed·ness** *n.*

un·re·strict·ed /únristríktid/ *adj.* not restricted. □□ **un·re·strict·ed·ly** *adv.* **un·re·strict·ed·ness** *n.*

un·re·turned /únritárnd/ *adj.* **1** not reciprocated or responded to. **2** not having returned or been returned.

un·re·vised /únrivízd/ *adj.* not revised; in an original form.

un·re·voked /únrivōkt/ *adj.* not revoked or annulled; still in force.

un·re·ward·ing /únriwáwrding/ *adj.* not rewarding or satisfying.

un·rid·a·ble /únrídəbəl/ *adj.* that cannot be ridden.

un·rid·den /únríd'n/ *adj.* not ridden.

un·rig /únríg/ *v.tr.* (**unrigged, unrigging**) **1** remove the rigging from (a ship). **2** *dial.* undress.

un·right·eous /únríchəs/ *adj.* not righteous; unjust; wicked; dishonest. □□ **un·right·eous·ly** *adv.* **un·right·eous·ness** *n.*

un·rip /únríp/ *v.tr.* (**unripped, unripping**) open by ripping.

un·ripe /únríp/ *adj.* not ripe. □□ **un·ripe·ness** *n.*

un·ris·en /únrízən/ *adj.* that has not risen.

un·ri·valed /únrívəld/ *adj.* having no equal; peerless.

un·robe /únrōb/ *v.tr. & intr.* **1** disrobe. **2** undress.

un·roll /únrōl/ *v.tr. & intr.* **1** open out from a rolled-up state. **2** display or be displayed in this form.

un·ro·man·tic /únrəmántik/ *adj.* not romantic. □□ **un·ro·man·ti·cal·ly** *adv.*

un·roof /únrŏŏf, -rŏŏf/ *v.tr.* remove the roof of.

un·roofed /únrŏŏft, -rŏŏft/ *adj.* not provided with a roof.

un·rope /únrōp/ *v.* **1** *tr.* detach by undoing a rope. **2** *intr. Mountaineering* detach oneself from a rope.

un·round·ed /únrówndid/ *adj.* not rounded.

un·ruf·fled /únrúfəld/ *adj.* **1** not agitated or disturbed; calm. **2** not physically ruffled.

un·ruled /únrŏŏld/ *adj.* **1** not ruled or governed. **2** not having ruled lines.

un·ru·ly /únrŏŏlee/ *adj.* (**unrulier, unruliest**) not easily controlled or disciplined; disorderly. □□ **un·ru·li·ness** *n.*

un·sad·dle /únsád'l/ *v.tr.* **1** remove the saddle from (a horse, etc.). **2** dislodge from a saddle.

un·safe /únsáyf/ *adj.* not safe. □□ **un·safe·ly** *adv.* **un·safe·ness** *n.*

un·said[1] /únséd/ *adj.* not said or uttered.

un·said[2] past and past part. of UNSAY.

un·sal·a·ble /únsáyləbəl/ *adj.* (also **un·sale·a·ble**) not salable. □□ **un·sal·a·bil·i·ty** *n.*

un·sal·a·ried /únsáləreed/ *adj.* not salaried.

un·salt·ed /únsáwltid/ *adj.* not salted.

un·sanc·tioned /únsángkshənd/ *adj.* not sanctioned.

un·san·i·tar·y /únsániteree/ *adj.* not sanitary.

un·sat·is·fac·to·ry /únsatisfáktəree/ *adj.* not satisfactory; poor; unacceptable. □□ **un·sat·is·fac·to·ri·ly** *adv.* **un·sat·is·fac·to·ri·ness** *n.*

un·sat·is·fied /únsátisfīd/ *adj.* not satisfied. □□ **un·sat·is·fied·ness** *n.*

un·sat·is·fy·ing /únsátisfī-ing/ *adj.* not satisfying. □□ **un·sat·is·fy·ing·ly** *adv.*

un·sat·u·rat·ed /únsáchəraytid/ *adj.* **1** *Chem.* ▼ (of a compound, esp. a fat or oil) having double or triple bonds in its molecule and therefore capable of further reaction. **2** not saturated. □□ **un·sat·u·ra·tion** /-ráyshən/ *n.*

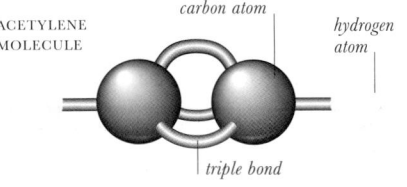

ACETYLENE MOLECULE　　　carbon atom　　　hydrogen atom

triple bond

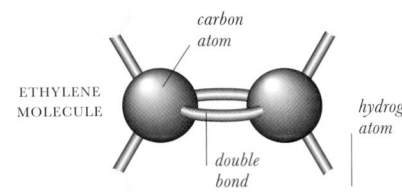

carbon atom

ETHYLENE MOLECULE　　　hydrogen atom

double bond

UNSATURATED: MOLECULAR STRUCTURE OF TWO UNSATURATED COMPOUNDS

un·sa·vor·y /únsáyvəree/ *adj.* **1** disagreeable to the taste, smell, or feelings; disgusting. **2** disagreeable; unpleasant (*an unsavory character*). **3** morally offensive. □□ **un·sa·vor·i·ly** *adv.* **un·sa·vor·i·ness** *n.*

un·say /únsáy/ *v.tr.* (*past* and *past part.* **unsaid**) retract (a statement).

un·say·a·ble /únsáyəbəl/ *adj.* that cannot be said.

un·scal·a·ble /únskáyləbəl/ *adj.* that cannot be scaled.

un·scathed /únskáythd/ *adj.* without suffering any injury.

un·scent·ed /únséntid/ *adj.* not scented.

un·sched·uled /únskéjōold/ *adj.* not scheduled.

un·schooled /únskōold/ *adj.* **1** uneducated; untaught. **2** not sent to school. **3** untrained; undisciplined. **4** not made artificial by education.

un·sci·en·tif·ic /únsīəntífik/ *adj.* **1** not in accordance with scientific principles. **2** not familiar with science. □□ **un·sci·en·tif·i·cal·ly** *adv.*

un·scram·ble /únskrámbəl/ *v.tr.* restore from a scrambled state, esp. interpret (a scrambled transmission, etc.). □□ **un·scram·bler** *n.*

un·screw /únskrōo/ *v.* **1** *tr. & intr.* unfasten or be unfastened by turning or removing a screw or screws or by twisting like a screw. **2** *tr.* loosen (a screw).

un·script·ed /únskríptid/ *adj.* (of a speech, etc.) delivered without a prepared script.

un·scru·pu·lous /únskrōopyələs/ *adj.* having no scruples; unprincipled. □□ **un·scru·pu·lous·ly** *adv.* **un·scru·pu·lous·ness** *n.*

un·seal /únséel/ *v.tr.* break the seal of; open (a letter, receptacle, etc.).

un·sealed /únséeld/ *adj.* not sealed.

un·sea·son·a·ble /únséezənəbəl/ *adj.* **1** not appropriate to the season. **2** untimely; inopportune. □□ **un·sea·son·a·ble·ness** *n.* **un·sea·son·a·bly** *adv.*

un·sea·soned /únséezənd/ *adj.* **1** not flavored with salt, herbs, etc. **2** (esp. of timber) not matured. **3** not habituated.

un·seat /únséet/ *v.tr.* **1** remove from a seat, esp. in an election. **2** dislodge from a seat, esp. on horseback.

un·sea·wor·thy /únseéwúrthee/ *adj.* not seaworthy.

un·se·cured /únsikyŏord/ *adj.* not secured.

un·seed·ed /únséedid/ *adj. Sports* (of a player) not seeded.

un·see·ing /únseéing/ *adj.* **1** unobservant. **2** blind. □□ **un·see·ing·ly** *adv.*

un·seem·ly /únseémlee/ *adj.* (**unseemlier, unseemliest**) **1** indecent. **2** unbecoming. □□ **un·seem·li·ness** *n.*

un·seen /únséen/ *adj. & n.* ● *adj.* **1** not seen. **2** invisible. **3** esp. *Brit.* (of a translation) to be done without preparation. ● *n. Brit.* an unseen translation.

un·seg·re·gat·ed /únségrigaytid/ *adj.* not segregated.

un·se·lec·tive /únsiléktiv/ *adj.* not selective.

un·self-con·scious /únselfkónshəs/ *adj.* not self-conscious. □□ **un·self-con·scious·ly** *adv.* **un·self-con·scious·ness** *n.*

un·self·ish /únsélfish/ *adj.* mindful of others' interests. □□ **un·sel·fish·ly** *adv.* **un·sel·fish·ness** *n.*

un·sen·sa·tion·al /únsensáyshənl/ *adj.* not sensational. □□ **un·sen·sa·tion·al·ly** *adv.*

un·sen·ti·men·tal /únsentimént'l/ *adj.* not sentimental. □□ **un·sen·ti·men·tal·i·ty** /-tálitee/ *n.* **un·sen·ti·men·tal·ly** *adv.*

un·sep·a·rat·ed /únsépəraytid/ *adj.* not separated.

un·ser·vice·a·ble /únsórvisəbəl/ *adj.* not serviceable; unfit for use. □□ **un·ser·vice·a·bil·i·ty** *n.*

un·set·tle /únsét'l/ *v.* **1** *tr.* disturb the settled state or arrangement of; discompose. **2** *tr.* derange. **3** *intr.* become unsettled. □□ **un·set·tle·ment** *n.* **un·set·tling** *adj.*

un·set·tled /únsét'ld/ *adj.* **1** not (yet) settled. **2** liable or open to change or further discussion. **3** (of a bill, etc.) unpaid. □□ **un·set·tled·ness** *n.*

un·sex /únséks/ *v.tr.* deprive (a person, esp. a woman) of the qualities of her or his sex.

un·sexed /únsékst/ *adj.* having no sexual characteristics.

un·shack·le /únshákəl/ *v.tr.* **1** release from shackles. **2** set free.

un·shak·a·ble /únsháykəbəl/ *adj.* (also **un·shake·a·ble**) that cannot be shaken; firm; obstinate. □□ **un·shak·a·bil·i·ty** *n.* **un·shak·a·bly** *adv.*

un·shak·en /únsháykən/ *adj.* not shaken. □□ **un·shak·en·ly** *adv.*

un·shape·ly /únsháyplee/ *adj.* not shapely. □□ **un·shape·li·ness** *n.*

un·shaved /únsháyvd/ *adj.* not shaved.

un·shav·en /únsháyvən/ *adj.* not shaved.

un·sheathe /únsheéth/ *v.tr.* remove (a knife, etc.) from a sheath.

un·shed /únshéd/ *adj.* not shed.

un·shel·tered /únshéltərd/ *adj.* not sheltered.

un·ship /únshíp/ *v.tr.* (**unshipped, unshipping**) **1** remove or discharge (a cargo or passenger) from a ship. **2** esp. *Naut.* remove (an object, esp. a mast or oar) from a fixed position.

un·shock·a·ble /únshókəbəl/ *adj.* that cannot be shocked. □□ **un·shock·a·bil·i·ty** /-bílitee/ *n.* **un·shock·a·bly** *adv.*

un·shod /únshód/ *adj.* not wearing shoes.

un·shorn /únsháwrn/ *adj.* not shorn.

un·shrink·a·ble /únshríngkəbəl/ *adj.* (of fabric, etc.) not liable to shrink. □□ **un·shrink·a·bil·i·ty** /-bílitee/ *n.*

un·shrink·ing /únshríngking/ *adj.* unhesitating; fearless. □□ **un·shrink·ing·ly** *adv.*

un·sight·ed /únsítid/ *adj.* **1** not sighted or seen. **2** prevented from seeing, esp. by an obstruction.

un·sight·ly /únsítlee/ *adj.* unpleasant to look at; ugly. □□ **un·sight·li·ness** *n.*

un·signed /únsínd/ *adj.* not signed.

un·sink·a·ble /únsíngkəbəl/ *adj.* unable to be sunk. □□ **un·sink·a·bil·i·ty** *n.*

un·sized[1] /únsízd/ *adj.* **1** not made to a size. **2** not sorted by size.

un·sized[2] /únsízd/ *adj.* not treated with size.

un·skill·ful /únskilfŏol/ *adj.* not skillful. □□ **un·skill·ful·ly** *adv.* **un·skill·ful·ness** *n.*

un·skilled /únskild/ *adj.* lacking or not needing special skill or training.

un·skimmed /únskímd/ *adj.* (of milk or another liquid) not skimmed.

un·slak·a·ble /únsláykəbəl/ *adj.* (also **un·slake·a·ble**) that cannot be slaked or quenched.

un·sliced /únslíst/ *adj.* (esp. of a loaf of bread when it is bought) not having been cut into slices.

un·smil·ing /únsmíling/ *adj.* not smiling. □□ **un·smil·ing·ly** *adv.* **un·smil·ing·ness** *n.*

un·smoked /únsmōkt/ *adj.* **1** not cured by smoking (*unsmoked bacon*). **2** not consumed by smoking (*an unsmoked cigar*).

un·so·cia·ble /únsōshəbəl/ *adj.* not sociable; disliking the company of others. □□ **un·so·cia·bil·i·ty** /-bílitee/ *n.* **un·so·cia·ble·ness** *n.* **un·so·cia·bly** *adv.*

un·so·cial /únsōshəl/ *adj.* **1** not social; not suitable for, seeking, or conforming to society. **2** *Brit.* outside the normal working day (*unsocial hours*). **3** antisocial. □□ **un·so·cial·ly** *adv.*

un·sold /únsōld/ *adj.* not sold.

un·so·lic·it·ed /únsəlísitid/ *adj.* not asked for; given or done voluntarily. □□ **un·so·lic·it·ed·ly** *adv.*

un·solv·a·ble /únsólvəbəl/ *adj.* that cannot be solved; insoluble. □□ **un·solv·a·bil·i·ty** /-bílitee/ *n.* **un·solv·a·ble·ness** *n.*

un·solved /únsólvd/ *adj.* not solved.

un·so·phis·ti·cat·ed /únsəfístikaytid/ *adj.* **1** artless; simple; natural; ingenuous. **2** not adulterated or artificial. □□ **un·so·phis·ti·cat·ed·ly** *adv.* **un·so·phis·ti·cat·ed·ness** *n.* **un·so·phis·ti·ca·tion** /-káyshən/ *n.*

un·sort·ed /únsáwrtid/ *adj.* not sorted.

un·sought /únsáwt/ *adj.* **1** not searched out or sought for. **2** unasked; without being requested.

un·sound /únsównd/ *adj.* **1** unhealthy; diseased. **2** rotten; weak. **3 a** ill-founded; fallacious. **b** unorthodox; heretical. **4** unreliable. **5** wicked. □ **of unsound mind** insane. □□ **un·sound·ly** *adv.* **un·sound·ness** *n.*

un·sound·ed[1] /únsówndid/ *adj.* **1** not uttered or pronounced. **2** not made to sound.

un·sound·ed[2] /únsówndid/ *adj.* unfathomed.

un·spar·ing /únspáiring/ *adj.* **1** lavish; profuse. **2** merciless. □□ **un·spar·ing·ly** *adv.* **un·spar·ing·ness** *n.*

un·speak·a·ble /únspeékəbəl/ *adj.* **1** that cannot be expressed in words. **2** indescribably bad or objectionable. □□ **un·speak·a·ble·ness** *n.* **un·speak·a·bly** *adv.*

un·spec·i·fied /únspésifīd/ *adj.* not specified.

un·spec·tac·u·lar /únspektákyələr/ *adj.* not spectacular; dull. □□ **un·spec·tac·u·lar·ly** *adv.*

un·spent /únspént/ *adj.* **1** not expended or used. **2** not exhausted or used up.

un·spir·i·tu·al /únspírichōoəl/ *adj.* not spiritual; earthly; worldly. □□ **un·spir·i·tu·al·i·ty** /-chōoálitee/ *n.* **un·spir·i·tu·al·ly** *adv.* **un·spir·i·tu·al·ness** *n.*

un·spoiled /únspóyld/ *adj.* **1** not spoiled. **2** not plundered.

un·spoilt /únspóylt/ *adj.* not spoiled.

un·spo·ken /únspókən/ *adj.* **1** not expressed in speech. **2** not uttered as speech.

un·sport·ing /únspáwrting/ *adj.* not sportsmanlike; not fair or generous. □□ **un·sport·ing·ly** *adv.* **un·sport·ing·ness** *n.*

un·sports·man·like /únspáwrtsmənlīk/ *adj.* unsporting.

un·spot·ted /únspótid/ *adj.* **1 a** not marked with a spot or spots. **b** morally pure. **2** unnoticed.

un·sta·ble /únstáybəl/ *adj.* (**unstabler, unstablest**) **1** not stable. **2** changeable. **3** showing a tendency to sudden mental or emotional changes. □□ **un·sta·ble·ness** *n.* **un·sta·bly** *adv.*

un·stained /únstáynd/ *adj.* not stained.

un·stamped /únstámpt/ *adj.* **1** not marked by stamping. **2** not having a stamp affixed.

un·states·man·like /únstáytsmənlīk/ *adj.* not statesmanlike.

un·stat·u·ta·ble /únstáchōotəbəl/ *adj.* contrary to a statute or statutes. □□ **un·stat·u·ta·bly** *adv.*

un·stead·y /únstédee/ *adj.* (**unsteadier, unsteadiest**) **1** not steady or firm. **2** changeable; fluctuating. **3** not uniform or regular. □□ **un·stead·i·ly** *adv.* **un·stead·i·ness** *n.*

un·stick /únstík/ *v.* /únstík/ (*past* and *past part.* **unstuck** /-stúk/) *tr.* separate (a thing stuck to another). □ **come unstuck** *colloq.* come to grief; fail.

un·stint·ed /únstíntid/ *adj.* not stinted. □□ **un·stint·ed·ly** *adv.*

un·stint·ing /únstínting/ *adj.* ungrudging; lavish. □□ **un·stint·ing·ly** *adv.*

un·stop·pa·ble /únstópəbəl/ *adj.* that cannot be stopped or prevented. □□ **un·stop·pa·bil·i·ty** /-bílitee/ *n.* **un·stop·pa·bly** *adv.*

un·stop·per /únstópər/ *v.tr.* remove the stopper from.

un·strained /únstráynd/ *adj.* **1** not subjected to straining or stretching. **2** not injured by overuse or excessive demands. **3** not forced or produced by effort. **4** not passed through a strainer.

un·strap /únstráp/ *v.tr.* (**unstrapped, unstrapping**) undo the strap or straps of.

un·stressed /únstrést/ *adj.* **1** (of a word, syllable, etc.) not pronounced with stress. **2** not subjected to stress.

un·string /únstríng/ *v.tr.* (*past* and *past part.* **unstrung**) **1** remove or relax the string or strings

U

of (a bow, harp, etc.). **2** remove from a string. **3** (esp. as **unstrung** *adj.*) unnerve.

un·struc·tured /únstrúkchərd/ *adj.* **1** not structured. **2** informal.

un·stuck *past* and *past part.* of UNSTICK.

un·stud·ied /únstúdeed/ *adj.* easy; natural; spontaneous. □□ **un·stud·ied·ly** *adv.*

un·stuff·y /únstúfee/ *adj.* **1** informal; casual. **2** not stuffy.

un·sub·stan·tial /únsəbstánshəl/ *adj.* having little or no solidity, reality, or factual basis. □□ **un·sub·stan·ti·al·i·ty** /-sheeálitee/ *n.* **un·sub·stan·tial·ly** *adv.*

un·sub·stan·ti·at·ed /únsəbstánsheeaytid/ *adj.* not substantiated.

un·suc·cess·ful /únsəksésfŏŏl/ *adj.* not successful. □□ **un·suc·cess·ful·ly** *adv.* **un·suc·cess·ful·ness** *n.*

un·suit·a·ble /únsŏŏtəbəl/ *adj.* not suitable. □□ **un·suit·a·bil·i·ty** *n.* **un·suit·a·ble·ness** *n.* **un·suit·a·bly** *adv.*

un·suit·ed /únsŏŏtid/ *adj.* **1** (usu. foll. by *for*) not fit for a purpose. **2** (usu. foll. by *to*) not adapted.

un·sul·lied /únsúleed/ *adj.* not sullied.

un·sung /únsúng/ *adj.* **1** not celebrated in song; unknown. **2** not sung.

un·su·per·vised /únsŏŏpərvīzd/ *adj.* not supervised.

un·sup·port·a·ble /únsəpáwrtəbəl/ *adj.* **1** that cannot be endured. **2** indefensible. □□ **un·sup·port·a·bly** *adv.*

un·sup·port·ed /únsəpáwrtid/ *adj.* not supported. □□ **un·sup·port·ed·ly** *adv.*

un·sure /únshŏŏr/ *adj.* not sure. □□ **un·sure·ly** *adv.* **un·sure·ness** *n.*

un·sur·pass·a·ble /únsərpásəbəl/ *adj.* that cannot be surpassed. □□ **un·sur·pass·a·bly** *adv.*

un·sur·passed /únsərpást/ *adj.* not surpassed.

un·sur·pris·ing /únsərprízing/ *adj.* not surprising. □□ **un·sur·pris·ing·ly** *adv.*

un·sus·pect·ing /únsəspékting/ *adj.* not suspecting. □□ **un·sus·pect·ing·ly** *adv.* **un·sus·pect·ing·ness** *n.*

un·sus·tained /únsəstáynd/ *adj.* not sustained.

un·swayed /únswáyd/ *adj.* uninfluenced; unaffected.

un·sweet·ened /únswéet'nd/ *adj.* not sweetened.

un·swerv·ing /únswérving/ *adj.* **1** steady; constant. **2** not turning aside. □□ **un·swerv·ing·ly** *adv.*

un·sym·pa·thet·ic /únsimpəthétik/ *adj.* not sympathetic. □□ **un·sym·pa·thet·i·cal·ly** *adv.*

un·taint·ed /úntáyntid/ *adj.* not tainted.

un·tal·ent·ed /úntáləntid/ *adj.* not talented.

un·tam·a·ble /úntáyməbəl/ *adj.* (also **un·tame·a·ble**) that cannot be tamed.

un·tamed /úntáymd/ *adj.* not tamed; wild.

un·tan·gle /úntánggəl/ *v.tr.* **1** free from a tangled state. **2** free from entanglement.

un·tapped /úntápt/ *adj.* not (yet) tapped or wired (*untapped resources*).

un·tar·nished /úntáarnisht/ *adj.* not tarnished.

un·tast·ed /úntáystid/ *adj.* not tasted.

un·taught /úntáwt/ *adj.* **1** not instructed by teaching; ignorant. **2** not acquired by teaching; natural; spontaneous.

un·teach /úntéech/ *v.tr.* (*past* and *past part.* **untaught**) **1** cause (a person) to forget or discard previous knowledge. **2** remove from the mind (something known or taught) by different teaching.

un·tear·a·ble /úntáirəbəl/ *adj.* that cannot be torn.

un·tem·pered /úntémpərd/ *adj.* (of metal, etc.) not brought to the proper hardness or consistency.

un·ten·a·ble /únténəbəl/ *adj.* not tenable; that cannot be defended. □□ **un·ten·a·bil·i·ty** *n.* **un·ten·a·ble·ness** *n.* **un·ten·a·bly** *adv.*

un·tend·ed /úntándid/ *adj.* not tended; neglected.

un·test·ed /úntéstid/ *adj.* not tested or proved.

un·teth·ered /úntéthərd/ *adj.* not tethered.

un·think·a·ble /únthíngkəbəl/ *adj.* **1** that cannot

be imagined or grasped by the mind. **2** *colloq.* highly unlikely or undesirable. □□ **un·think·a·bil·i·ty** /-bílitee/ *n.* **un·think·a·ble·ness** *n.* **un·think·a·bly** *adv.*

un·think·ing /únthíngking/ *adj.* **1** thoughtless. **2** unintentional; inadvertent. □□ **un·think·ing·ly** *adv.* **un·think·ing·ness** *n.*

un·thought·ful /úntháwtfŏŏl/ *adj.* unthinking; unmindful; thoughtless. □□ **un·thought·ful·ly** *adv.* **un·thought·ful·ness** *n.*

un·ti·dy /úntídee/ *adj.* (**untidier, untidiest**) not neat or orderly. □□ **un·ti·di·ly** *adv.* **un·ti·di·ness** *n.*

un·tie /úntí/ *v.tr.* (*pres. part.* **untying**) **1** undo (a knot, etc.). **2** unfasten the cords, etc., of (a package, etc.). **3** release from bonds or attachment.

un·tied /úntíd/ *adj.* not tied.

un·til /əntil, un-/ *prep. & conj.* = TILL[1]. ¶ Used esp. when beginning a sentence and in formal style, e.g., *until you told me, I had no idea; he resided there until his decease.*

un·tilled /úntild/ *adj.* not tilled.

un·time·ly /úntímlee/ *adj. & adv.* ● *adj.* **1** inopportune. **2** (of death) premature. ● *adv.* **1** inopportunely. **2** prematurely. □□ **un·time·li·ness** *n.*

un·tir·ing /úntíring/ *adj.* tireless. □□ **un·tir·ing·ly** *adv.*

un·ti·tled /úntít'ld/ *adj.* having no title.

un·to /úntōō, úntə/ *prep. archaic* = TO (in all uses except as the sign of the infinitive) (*do unto others; faithful unto death; take unto oneself*).

un·told /úntóld/ *adj.* **1** not told. **2** not (able to be) counted or measured (*untold misery*).

un·touch·a·ble /úntúchəbəl/ *adj. & n.* ● *adj.* that may not or cannot be touched. ● *n.* a member of a hereditary Hindu group held to defile members of higher castes on contact. ¶ Use of the term, and social restrictions accompanying it, were declared illegal under the Indian constitution in 1949. □□ **un·touch·a·bil·i·ty** *n.* **un·touch·a·ble·ness** *n.*

un·touched /úntúcht/ *adj.* **1** not touched. **2** not affected physically; not harmed, modified, used, or tasted. **3** not affected by emotion. **4** not discussed.

un·to·ward /úntáwrd, -təwáwrd/ *adj.* **1** inconvenient; unlucky. **2** awkward. **3** perverse, refractory. **4** unseemly. □□ **un·to·ward·ly** *adv.* **un·to·ward·ness** *n.*

un·trace·a·ble /úntráysəbəl/ *adj.* that cannot be traced. □□ **un·trace·a·bly** *adv.*

un·trained /úntráynd/ *adj.* not trained.

un·tram·meled /úntráməld/ *adj.* not trammeled; unhampered.

un·trans·lat·a·ble /úntranzláytəbəl, -trans-, -tránzlayt-, -tráns-/ *adj.* that cannot be translated satisfactorily. □□ **un·trans·lat·a·bil·i·ty** *n.* **un·trans·lat·a·bly** *adv.*

un·trav·eled /úntrávəld/ *adj.* **1** that has not traveled. **2** that has not been traveled over or through.

un·treat·a·ble /úntréetəbəl/ *adj.* (of a disease, etc.) that cannot be treated.

un·treat·ed /úntréetid/ *adj.* not treated.

un·tried /úntríd/ *adj.* **1** not tried or tested. **2** inexperienced. **3** not yet tried by a judge.

un·trod·den /úntród'n/ *adj.* not trodden, stepped on, or traversed.

un·trou·bled /úntrúbəld/ *adj.* not troubled; calm; tranquil.

un·true /úntrŏŏ/ *adj.* **1** not true; contrary to what is the fact. **2** (often foll. by *to*) not faithful or loyal. **3** deviating from an accepted standard. □□ **un·tru·ly** *adv.*

un·trust·wor·thy /úntrústwúrthee/ *adj.* not trustworthy. □□ **un·trust·wor·thi·ness** *n.*

un·truth /úntrŏŏth/ *n.* (*pl.* **untruths** /-trŏŏthz, -trŏŏths/) **1** the state of being untrue; falsehood. **2** a false statement (*told me an untruth*).

un·truth·ful /úntrŏŏthfŏŏl/ *adj.* not truthful. □□ **un·truth·ful·ly** *adv.* **un·truth·ful·ness** *n.*

un·tu·tored /úntŏŏtərd, -tyŏŏ-/ *adj.* uneducated; untaught.

un·ty·ing *pres. part.* of UNTIE.

un·typ·i·cal /úntípikəl/ *adj.* not typical; unusual.

un·us·a·ble /únyŏŏzəbəl/ *adj.* (also **un·use·a·ble**) not usable.

un·used *adj.* **1** /únyŏŏzd/ **a** not in use. **b** never having been used. **2** /únyŏŏst/ (foll. by *to*) not accustomed.

un·u·su·al /únyŏŏzhŏŏəl/ *adj.* **1** not usual. **2** exceptional; remarkable. □□ **un·u·su·al·ly** *adv.* **un·u·su·al·ness** *n.*

un·ut·ter·a·ble /únútərəbəl/ *adj.* inexpressible; beyond description (*unutterable torment; an unutterable fool*). □□ **un·ut·ter·a·ble·ness** *n.* **un·ut·ter·a·bly** *adv.*

un·val·ued /únvályŏŏd/ *adj.* **1** not regarded as valuable. **2** not having been valued.

un·var·ied /únváirid/ *adj.* not varied.

un·var·nished /únváarnisht/ *adj.* **1** not varnished. **2** (of a statement or person) plain and straightforward (*the unvarnished truth*).

un·var·y·ing /únváireeing/ *adj.* not varying. □□ **un·var·y·ing·ly** *adv.* **un·var·y·ing·ness** *n.*

un·veil /únváyl/ *v.* **1** *tr.* remove a veil from. **2** *tr.* remove a covering from (a statue, plaque, etc.) as part of the ceremony of the first public display. **3** *tr.* disclose; reveal; make publicly known. **4** *intr.* remove one's veil.

un·ven·ti·lat·ed /únvént'laytid/ *adj.* **1** not provided with a means of ventilation. **2** not discussed.

un·ver·i·fi·able /únvérəfīəbəl/ *adj.* that cannot be verified.

un·ver·i·fied /únvérifīd/ *adj.* not verified.

un·versed /únvérst/ *adj.* (usu. foll. by *in*) not experienced or skilled.

un·vis·it·ed /únvízitid/ *adj.* not visited.

un·voiced /únvóyst/ *adj.* **1** not spoken. **2** *Phonet.* not voiced.

un·waged /únwáyjd/ *adj.* not receiving a wage; out of work.

un·want·ed /únwóntid/ *adj.* not wanted.

un·war·rant·a·ble /únwáwrəntəbəl, -wór-/ *adj.* indefensible; unjustifiable. □□ **un·war·rant·a·ble·ness** *n.* **un·war·rant·a·bly** *adv.*

un·war·rant·ed /únwáwrəntid, -wór-/ *adj.* **1** unauthorized. **2** unjustified.

un·war·y /únwáiree/ *adj.* **1** not cautious. **2** (often foll. by *of*) not aware of possible danger, etc. □□ **un·war·i·ly** *adv.* **un·war·i·ness** *n.*

un·washed /únwósht, -wáwsht/ *adj.* **1** not washed. **2** not usually washed or clean. □ **the great unwashed** *colloq.* the rabble.

un·wa·ver·ing /únwáyvəring/ *adj.* not wavering. □□ **un·wa·ver·ing·ly** *adv.*

un·weaned /únwéend/ *adj.* not weaned.

un·wea·ried /únwéereed/ *adj.* **1** not wearied or tired. **2** never becoming weary; indefatigable. **3** unremitting. □□ **un·wea·ried·ly** *adv.* **un·wea·ried·ness** *n.*

un·wea·ry·ing /únweéreeing/ *adj.* **1** persistent. **2** not causing or producing weariness. □□ **un·wea·ry·ing·ly** *adv.*

un·wed /únwéd/ *adj.* unmarried.

un·weighed /únwáyd/ *adj.* **1** not considered; hasty. **2** (of goods) not weighed.

un·wel·come /únwélkəm/ *adj.* not welcome or acceptable. □□ **un·wel·come·ly** *adv.* **un·wel·come·ness** *n.*

un·well /únwél/ *adj.* **1** not in good health; (somewhat) ill. **2** indisposed.

un·whole·some /únhólsəm/ *adj.* **1** not promoting, or detrimental to, physical or moral health. **2** unhealthy; insalubrious. **3** unhealthy-looking. □□ **un·whole·some·ly** *adv.* **un·whole·some·ness** *n.*

un·wield·y /únwéeldee/ *adj.* (**unwieldier, unwieldiest**) cumbersome, clumsy, or hard to manage, owing to size, shape, or weight. □□ **un·wield·i·ly** *adv.* **un·wield·i·ness** *n.*

U

UPHOLSTERY

The elements of traditional upholstery are webbing, preparing a coil spring platform, judging the amount and shape of stuffing, sculpting it with stitches, tacking, and trimming. Tools include tack lifters, ripping chisels, webbing stretchers, hammers, and various types of needles. Some hammers are magnetized to help pick up the tacks.

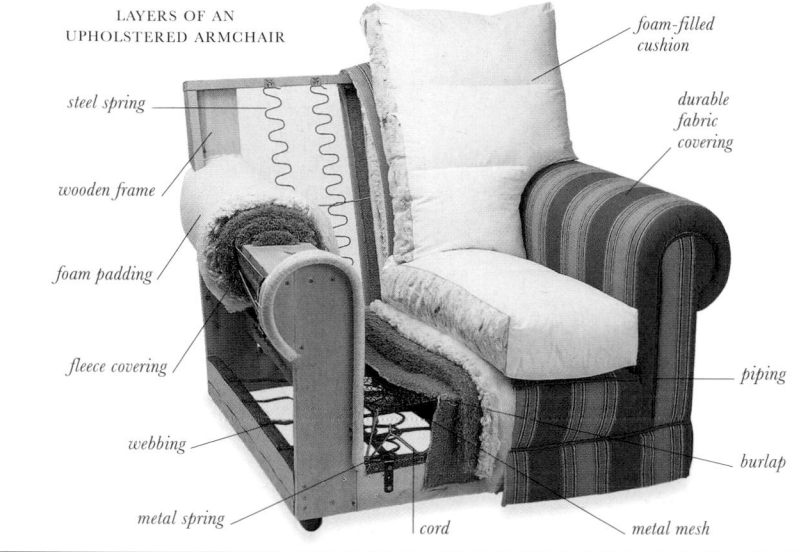

LAYERS OF AN
UPHOLSTERED ARMCHAIR

steel spring

wooden frame

foam padding

fleece covering

webbing

metal spring

cord

foam-filled cushion

durable fabric covering

piping

burlap

metal mesh

---

un·will·ing /únwiling/ *adj.* not willing or inclined; reluctant. □□ **un·will·ing·ly** *adv.* **un·will·ing·ness** *n.*

un·wind /únwínd/ *v.* (*past* and *past part.* **unwound** /-wównd/) **1 a** *tr.* draw out (a thing that has been wound). **b** *intr.* become drawn out after having been wound. **2** *intr.* & *tr. colloq.* relax.

un·wink·ing /únwingking/ *adj.* **1** not winking. **2** watchful; vigilant. □□ **un·wink·ing·ly** *adv.*

un·wise /únwíz/ *adj.* **1** foolish; imprudent. **2** injudicious. □□ **un·wise·ly** *adv.*

un·wished /únwisht/ *adj.* (usu. foll. by *for*) not wished for.

un·wit·ting /únwiting/ *adj.* **1** unaware of the state of the case (*an unwitting offender*). **2** unintentional. □□ **un·wit·ting·ly** *adv.* **un·wit·ting·ness** *n.*

un·wont·ed /únwáwntid, -wón-, -wún-/ *adj.* not customary or usual. □□ **un·wont·ed·ly** *adv.* **un·wont·ed·ness** *n.*

un·worked /únwórkt/ *adj.* not cultivated, mined, carved, or wrought into shape.

un·world·ly /únwórldlee/ *adj.* **1** spiritually minded. **2** spiritual. □□ **un·world·li·ness** *n.*

un·wor·thy /únwúrthee/ *adj.* (**unworthier, unworthiest**) **1** (often foll. by *of*) not worthy or befitting the character of a person, etc. **2** discreditable; unseemly. **3** contemptible; base. □□ **un·wor·thi·ly** *adv.* **un·wor·thi·ness** *n.*

un·wound[1] /únwównd/ *adj.* not wound or wound up.

un·wound[2] *past* and *past part.* of UNWIND.

un·wrap /únráp/ *v.* (**unwrapped, unwrapping**) **1** *tr.* remove the wrapping from. **2** *tr.* open or unfold. **3** *intr.* become unwrapped.

un·writ·ten /únrít'n/ *adj.* **1** not written. **2** (of a law, etc.) resting originally on custom or judicial decision, not on statute.

un·yield·ing /únyéelding/ *adj.* **1** not yielding to pressure, etc. **2** firm; obstinate. □□ **un·yield·ing·ly** *adv.* **un·yield·ing·ness** *n.*

up /up/ *adv., prep., adj., n.,* & *v.* ● *adv.* **1** at, in, or toward a higher place or position (*jumped up in the air*). **2** to or in a place regarded as higher, esp.: **a** northward (*up in New England*). **b** *Brit.* toward a major city or a university (*went up to London*). **3** *colloq.* ahead, etc., as indicated (*went up front*). **4 a** to or in an erect position or condition (*stood it up*). **b** to or in a prepared or required position (*wound up the watch*). **c** in or into a condition of efficiency, activity, or progress (*stirred up trouble; the house is up for sale*). **5** in a stronger or winning position or condition (*our team was three goals up; am $10 up on the transaction*). **6** (of a computer) running and available for use. **7** to the place or time in question or where the speaker, etc., is (*a child came up to me; went straight up to the door; has been fine up till now*). **8** at or to a higher price or value (*our costs are up; shares are up*). **9 a** completely or effectually (*burn up; eat up; tear up; use up*). **b** more loudly or clearly (*speak up*). **10** in a state of completion; denoting the end of availability, supply, etc. (*time is up*). **11** into a compact, accumulated, or secure state (*pack up; save up; tie up*). **12 a** awake. **b** out of bed (*are you up yet?*). **13** (of the Sun, etc.) having risen. **14** happening, esp. unusually or unexpectedly (*something is up*). **15** esp. *Brit.* (usu. foll. by *on* or *in*) taught or informed (*is well up in French*). **16** (usu. foll. by *before*) appearing for trial, etc. (*was up before the judge*). **17** *Brit.* (of a road, etc.) being repaired. **18** (of a jockey) in the saddle. **19** toward the source of a river. **20** inland. **21** (of the points, etc., in a game): **a** registered on the scoreboard. **b** forming the total score for the time being. **22** upstairs, esp. to bed (*are you going up yet?*). **23** (of a theater curtain) raised, etc., to reveal the stage. **24** (as *int.*) get up. **25** *Baseball* at bat (*he struck out his last time up*). ● *prep.* **1** upward along, through, or into (*climbed up the ladder*). **2** from the bottom to the top of. **3** along (*walked up the road*). **4 a** at or in a higher part of (*is situated up the street*). **b** toward the source of (a river). ● *adj.* (often in *comb.*) directed upward (*upstroke*). ● *n.* a spell of good fortune. ● *v.* (**upped, upping**) **1** *intr. colloq.* start up; begin abruptly to say or do something (*upped and hit him*). **2** *intr.* (foll. by *with*) raise; pick up (*upped with his stick*). **3** *tr.* increase or raise, esp. abruptly (*upped all their prices*). □ **be all up with** be disastrous or hopeless (for a person). **on the up and up** *colloq.* **1** honest(ly); on the level. **2** *Brit.* steadily improving. **something is up** *colloq.* something unusual or undesirable is afoot or happening. **up against 1** close to. **2** in or into contact with. **3** *colloq.* confronted with (*up against a problem*). **up against it** *colloq.* in great difficulties. **up and about** having risen from bed; active. **up and down 1** to and fro (along). **2** in every direction. **3** *colloq.* in varying health or spirits. **up for** available for or being considered for (office, etc.). **up to 1** until (*up to the present*). **2** not more than (*you can have up to five*). **3** less than or equal to (*adds up to $10*). **4** incumbent on (*it is up to you to say*). **5** capable of or fit for (*am not up to a long walk*). **6** occupied or busy with (*what have you been up to?*). **up to the mark** see MARK[1]. **up to one's tricks** see TRICK. **up to a person's tricks** see TRICK. **up with** *int.* expressing support for a stated person or thing. **what's up?** *colloq.* **1** what is going on? **2** what is the matter?

up-and-com·ing *adj.* (of a person) making good progress and likely to succeed.

up·beat /úpbeet/ *n.* & *adj.* ● *n.* an unaccented beat in music. ● *adj. colloq.* optimistic or cheerful.

up·braid /upbráyd/ *v.tr.* (often foll. by *with, for*) chide or reproach (a person). □□ **up·braid·ing** *n.*

up·bring·ing /úpbringing/ *n.* the bringing up of a child; education.

UPC *abbr.* = Universal Product Code.

up·chuck /úpchuk/ *v.tr.* & *intr. sl.* vomit.

up·com·ing /úpkúming/ *adj.* forthcoming.

up·date *v.* & *n.* ● *v.tr.* /updáyt/ bring up to date. ● *n.* /úpdayt/ **1** the act or an instance of updating. **2** an updated version. □□ **up·dat·er** *n.*

up·end /úpénd/ *v.tr.* & *intr.* set or rise up on end.

up·front /úpfrúnt/ *adv.* & *adj.* ● *adv.* **1** at the front; in front. **2** (of payments) in advance. ● *adj.* **1** honest; frank. **2** (of payments) made in advance.

up·grade *v.* & *n.* ● *v.tr.* /úpgráyd/ **1** raise in rank, etc. **2** improve (equipment, machinery, etc.) esp. by replacing components. ● *n.* /úpgrayd/ **1** the act or an instance of upgrading. **2** an upgraded piece of equipment, etc. **3** an upward slope. □□ **up·grad·er** *n.*

up·heav·al /upheevəl/ *n.* **1** a violent or sudden change or disruption. **2** *Geol.* an upward displacement of part of the Earth's crust. **3** the act or an instance of heaving up.

up·hill *adv., adj.,* & *n.* ● *adv.* /úphíl/ in an ascending direction up a hill, slope, etc. ● *adj.* /úphil/ **1** sloping up; ascending. **2** arduous; difficult (*an uphill task*). ● *n.* /úphil/ an upward slope.

up·hold /úphóld/ *v.tr.* (*past* and *past part.* **upheld** /-héld/) **1** confirm or maintain (a decision, etc., esp. of another). **2** give support or countenance to (a person, practice, etc.). □□ **up·hold·er** *n.*

up·hol·ster /úphólstər, əpól-/ *v.tr.* **1** provide (furniture) with upholstery. **2** furnish (a room, etc.) with furniture, carpets, etc. □□ **up·hol·ster·er** *n.*

up·hol·ster·y /úphólstəree, əpól-/ *n.* **1** ▲ textile covering, padding, springs, etc., for furniture. **2** an upholsterer's work.

up·keep /úpkeep/ *n.* **1** maintenance in good condition. **2** the cost or means of this.

up·land /úplənd/ *n.* & *adj.* ● *n.* the higher or inland parts of a country. ● *adj.* of or relating to these parts.

up·lift *v.* & *n.* ● *v.tr.* /úplíft/ **1** esp. *Brit.* raise; lift up. **2** elevate or stimulate morally or spiritually. ● *n.* /úplift/ **1** the act or an instance of being raised. **2** *Geol.* the raising of part of the Earth's surface. **3** *colloq.* a morally or spiritually elevating influence. **4** support for the bust, etc., from a garment. □□ **up·lift·er** *n.* **up·lift·ing** *adj.* (esp. in sense 2 of *v.*).

up·link /úplingk/ ● *n.* a communications link to a satellite. ● *v.tr.* provide with or send by such a link.

up·mar·ket /úpmáarkit/ *adj.* & *adv.* = UPSCALE.

up·on /əpón, əpáwn/ *prep.* = ON. ¶ *Upon* is sometimes more formal, and is preferred in *once upon a time* and *upon my word*, and in uses such as *row upon row of seats* and *Christmas is almost upon us.*

up·per[1] /úpər/ *adj.* & *n.* ● *adj.* **1 a** higher in place; situated above another part (*the upper atmosphere; the upper lip*). **b** *Geol.* designating a younger (and usually shallower) part of a stratigraphic division, or the

U

UPRIGHT

Developed at the turn of the 19th century, the upright piano has vertical wire strings stretched over a metal frame. When a key is depressed, a damper lifts from the string as a hammer strikes it, making it vibrate. The three pedals vary the quality of the notes.

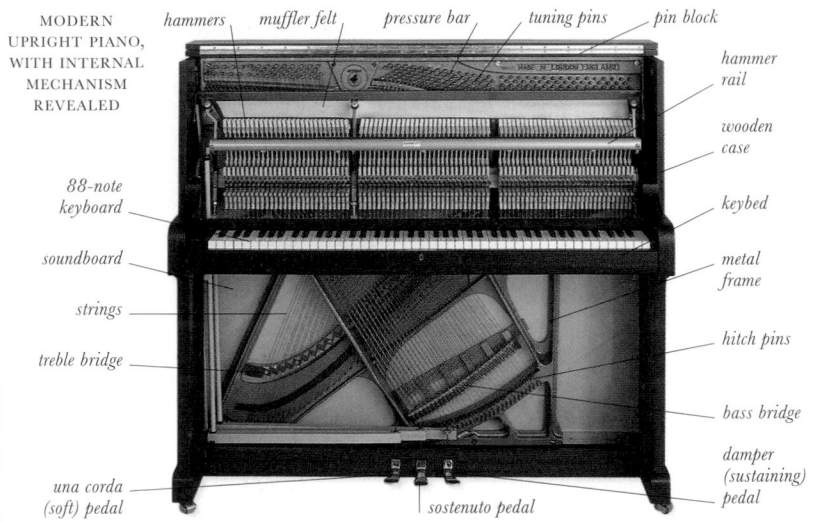

MODERN UPRIGHT PIANO, WITH INTERNAL MECHANISM REVEALED

hammers — muffler felt — pressure bar — tuning pins — pin block — hammer rail — wooden case — keybed — metal frame — hitch pins — bass bridge — damper (sustaining) pedal — sostenuto pedal — una corda (soft) pedal — treble bridge — strings — soundboard — 88-note keyboard

period of its formation (*the Upper Jurassic*). **2** higher in rank or dignity, etc. (*the upper class*). **3** situated on higher ground, further to the north, or further inland (*Upper Egypt*). ● *n.* the part of a boot or shoe above the sole. □ **on one's uppers** *colloq.* extremely short of money.

up·per[2] /úpər/ *n. sl.* a stimulant drug, esp. an amphetamine.

up·per·case /úpərkáys/ *adj., n., & v.* ● *adj.* (of letters) capital. ● *n.* capital letters. ● *v.tr.* set or print in uppercase.

up·per class *n.* the highest class of society, esp. (in the UK) the aristocracy. □□ **up·per-class** *adj.*

up·per crust *n. colloq.* (in the UK) the aristocracy. □□ **up·per-crust** *adj.*

up·per·cut /úpərkut/ *n. & v.* ● *n.* an upward blow delivered with the arm bent. ● *v.tr.* hit with an uppercut.

the up·per hand *n.* dominance or control.

up·per house *n.* the higher house in a legislature, e.g., the U.S. Senate.

up·per·most /úpərmōst/ *adj. & adv.* ● *adj.* (also **up·most** /úpmōst/) **1** highest in place or rank. **2** predominant. ● *adv.* at or to the highest or most prominent position.

up·pi·ty /úpitee/ *adj. colloq.* arrogant; snobbish.

up·right /úprīt/ *adj., adv., & n.* ● *adj.* **1** erect; vertical (*an upright posture; stood upright*). **2** ▲ (of a piano) with vertical strings. **3** (of a person or behavior) righteous; strictly honorable or honest. **4** (of a picture, book, etc.) greater in height than breadth. ● *adv.* in a vertical direction; vertically upward; into an upright position. ● *n.* **1** a post or rod fixed upright, esp. as a structural support. **2** an upright piano. □□ **up·right·ly** *adv.* **up·right·ness** *n.*

up·ris·ing /úprīzing/ *n.* a rebellion or revolt.

up·riv·er /úprívər/ *adv. & adj.* towards or situated at a point nearer the source of a river.

up·roar /úprawr/ *n.* a tumult; a violent disturbance.

up·roar·i·ous /úpráwreeəs/ *adj.* **1** very noisy; tumultuous. **2** provoking loud laughter. □□ **up·roar·i·ous·ly** *adv.* **up·roar·i·ous·ness** *n.*

up·root /úprōōt, róot/ *v.tr.* **1** pull (a plant, etc.) up from the ground. **2** displace (a person) from an accustomed location. **3** eradicate; destroy.

ups and downs *n.pl.* **1** rises and falls. **2** alternate good and bad fortune.

up·scale /úpskáyl/ *adj. & v.* ● *adj.* toward or relating to the more affluent or upper sector of society or the market. ● *v.tr.* improve the quality or value of.

up·set *v., n., & adj.* ● *v.* /úpsét/ (**upsetting**; *past* and *past part.* **upset**) **1 a** *tr. & intr.* overturn or be overturned. **b** *tr.* overcome; defeat. **2** *tr.* disturb the composure or digestion of (*was very upset by the news; ate something that upset me*). **3** *tr.* disrupt. **4** *tr.* shorten and thicken (metal, esp. a tire) by hammering or pressure. ● *n.* /úpset/ **1** a condition of upsetting or being upset (*a stomach upset*). **2** a surprising result in a game, etc. ● *adj.* /úpsét/ disturbed (*an upset stomach*). □□ **up·set·ter** *n.* **up·set·ting·ly** *adv.*

up·shot /úpshot/ *n.* the final or eventual outcome or conclusion.

up·side down /úpsīd dówn/ *adv. & adj.* ● *adv.* **1** with the upper part where the lower part should be; in an inverted position. **2** in or into total disorder (*everything was turned upside down*). ● *adj.* (also **up·side-down** *attrib.*) that is positioned upside down.

up·si·lon /úpsilon, yōōp-/ *n.* the twentieth letter of the Greek alphabet (Y, υ).

up·stage /úpstáyj/ *adj., adv., v., & n.* ● *adj. & adv.* **1** nearer the back of a theater stage. **2** snobbish(ly). ● *v.tr.* **1** (of an actor) move upstage to make (another actor) face away from the audience. **2** divert attention from (a person) to oneself; outshine. ● *n.* the part of the stage farthest from the audience. ▷ THEATER

up·stairs /úpstáirz/ *adv., adj., & n.* ● *adv.* to or on an upper floor. ● *adj.* (also **up·stair**) situated upstairs. ● *n.* an upper floor.

up·stand·ing /úpstánding/ *adj.* **1** standing up. **2** strong and healthy. **3** honest or straightforward.

up·start /úpstaart/ *n. & adj.* ● *n.* a person who has risen suddenly to prominence, esp. one who behaves arrogantly. ● *adj.* **1** that is an upstart. **2** of or characteristic of an upstart.

up·state /úpstáyt/ *n., adj., & adv.* ● *n.* part of a state remote from its large cities, esp. the northern part (*upstate New York*). ● *adj.* of or relating to this part. ● *adv.* in or to this part. □□ **up·stat·er** *n.*

up·stream /úpstréem/ *adv. & adj.* ● *adv.* against the flow of a stream, etc. ● *adj.* moving upstream.

up·surge /úpsərj/ *n.* an increase.

up·swing /úpswing/ *n.* an upward trend.

up·take /úptayk/ *n.* **1** *colloq.* understanding; comprehension (esp. *quick* or *slow on the uptake*). **2** the act or an instance of taking up.

up·tem·po /uptémpō/ *adj. & adv. Mus.* played with a fast or increased tempo.

up·throw /úpthrō/ *n.* **1** the act or an instance of throwing upward. **2** *Geol.* an upward dislocation of strata.

up·thrust /úpthrust/ *n.* **1** upward thrust, e.g., of a fluid on an immersed body. **2** *Geol.* = UPHEAVAL.

up·tight /úptít/ *adj. colloq.* **1** nervously tense or angry. **2** rigidly conventional.

up-to-date *adj.* meeting or according to the latest requirements, knowledge, or fashion; modern.

up·town /úptówn/ *adj., adv., & n.* ● *adj.* **1** of or in the residential part of a town or city. **2** characteristic of or suitable to affluent or sophisticated people. ● *adv.* in or into this part. ● *n.* this part. □□ **up·town·er** *n.*

up·turn *n. & v.* ● *n.* /úptərn/ **1** an upward trend. **2** an upheaval. ● *v.tr.* /úptúrn/ turn up or upside down.

U

URANUS

With a diameter of about 31,690 miles, Uranus is the third largest planet in the solar system. It is a cold gas giant, believed to consist of gas and ice surrounding a solid core. Uranus is tilted at 97.9° and so it rolls on its side along its orbital path. It has 15 moons, 10 rings made up of boulders, and a broad ring of dust.

URANUS, WITH INTERNAL STRUCTURE REVEALED

atmosphere of hydrogen, helium, and methane — blue-green color due to methane — south pole — lighter dust lanes — narrow rings of dark rocks — dense interior of ice and gas — solid rocky core — atmosphere merging into interior

Earth — SOLAR SYSTEM — Sun — Uranus

up·ward /úpwərd/ *adj. & adj.* ● *adv.* (also **up·wards**) toward what is higher, superior, larger in amount, more important, or earlier. ● *adj.* moving, extending, pointing, or leading upward. □ **upwards of** more than (*found upwards of forty specimens*).

up·ward·ly /úpwərdlee/ *adv.* in an upward direction.

up·ward·ly mo·bile *adj.* able or aspiring to advance socially or professionally.

up·wind /úpwínd/ *adj. & adv.* against the direction of the wind.

u·ra·ni·um /yŏŏráyneeəm/ *n. Chem.* a radioactive, gray, dense metallic element occurring naturally in pitchblende, and capable of nuclear fission and therefore used as a source of nuclear energy. ¶ Symb.: **U**. □□ **u·ran·ic** /-ránik/ *adj.*

U·ran·us /yŏŏrənəs, yŏŏráynəs/ *n.* ▼ a planet discovered by Herschel in 1781, seventh in order from the Sun. ▷ SOLAR SYSTEM

ur·ban /ə́rbən/ *adj.* of, living in, or situated in a town or city (*an urban population*) (opp. RURAL).

ur·ban re·new·al *n.* slum clearance and redevelopment in a city or town.

ur·ban sprawl *n.* the uncontrolled expansion of urban areas.

ur·bane /ərbáyn/ *adj.* courteous and suave in manner. □□ **ur·bane·ly** *adv.* **ur·bane·ness** *n.*

ur·ban·ite /ə́rbənīt/ *n.* a dweller in a city or town.

ur·ban·i·ty /ərbánitee/ *n.* **1** an urbane quality; refinement of manner. **2** urban life.

ur·ban·ize /ə́rbənīz/ *v.tr.* make urban. □□ **ur·ban·i·za·tion** /-záyshən/ *n.*

ur·ban myth *n.* (also chiefly *N. Amer.* **ur·ban leg·end**) an entertaining story or piece of information of uncertain origin that is circulated as though true.

ur·chin /ə́rchin/ *n.* **1** a mischievous child, esp. young and raggedly dressed. **2** = SEA URCHIN.

Ur·du /ŏŏrdŏŏ, ə́r-/ *n.* a language related to Hindi but with many Persian words, an official language of Pakistan and also used in India.

u·re·a /yŏŏréeə/ *n. Biochem.* a soluble, colorless, crystalline, nitrogenous compound contained esp. in the urine of mammals. □□ **u·re·al** *adj.*

u·re·ter /yŏŏréetər/ *n.* the duct by which urine passes from the kidney to the bladder or cloaca. ▷ URINARY SYSTEM. □□ **u·re·ter·al** *adj.* **u·re·ter·ic** /yŏŏritérik/ *adj.* **u·re·ter·i·tis** /-rítis/ *n.*

u·re·thane /yŏŏríthayn/ *n. Chem.* a crystalline amide, ethyl carbamate, used in plastics and paints.

u·re·thra /yŏŏréethrə/ *n.* (*pl.* **urethras** or **urethrae** /-ree/) the duct by which urine is discharged from the bladder. ▷ URINARY SYSTEM. □□ **u·re·thral** *adj.* **u·re·thri·tis** /-rithrítis/ *n.*

urge /ərj/ *v. & n.* ● *v.tr.* **1** drive forcibly; impel (*urged them on; urged the horses forward*). **2** (often foll. by *to* + infin. or *that* + clause) encourage or entreat earnestly or persistently (*urged them to go; urged that they should go*). **3** advocate (an action or argument, etc.) pressingly or emphatically. ● *n.* a strong desire or impulse.

ur·gent /ə́rjənt/ *adj.* **1** requiring immediate action or attention (*an urgent need for help*). **2** earnest and insistent. □□ **ur·gen·cy** *n.* **ur·gent·ly** *adv.*

u·ric /yŏŏrik/ *adj.* of or relating to urine.

u·ric ac·id *n.* a crystalline acid forming a constituent of urine.

u·ri·nal /yŏŏrinəl/ *n.* a sanitary fitting, usu. against a wall, for men to urinate into.

u·ri·nar·y /yŏŏrineree/ *adj.* **1** of or relating to urine. **2** affecting or occurring in the urinary system (*urinary diseases*).

u·ri·nar·y sys·tem *n.* ▲ the system of organs and structures in the body that are concerned with the excretion and discharge of urine.

u·ri·nate /yŏŏrinayt/ *v.intr.* discharge urine. □□ **u·ri·na·tion** /-náyshən/ *n.*

u·rine /yŏŏrin/ *n.* a pale-yellow fluid secreted as waste from the blood by the kidneys, stored in the bladder, and discharged through the urethra.

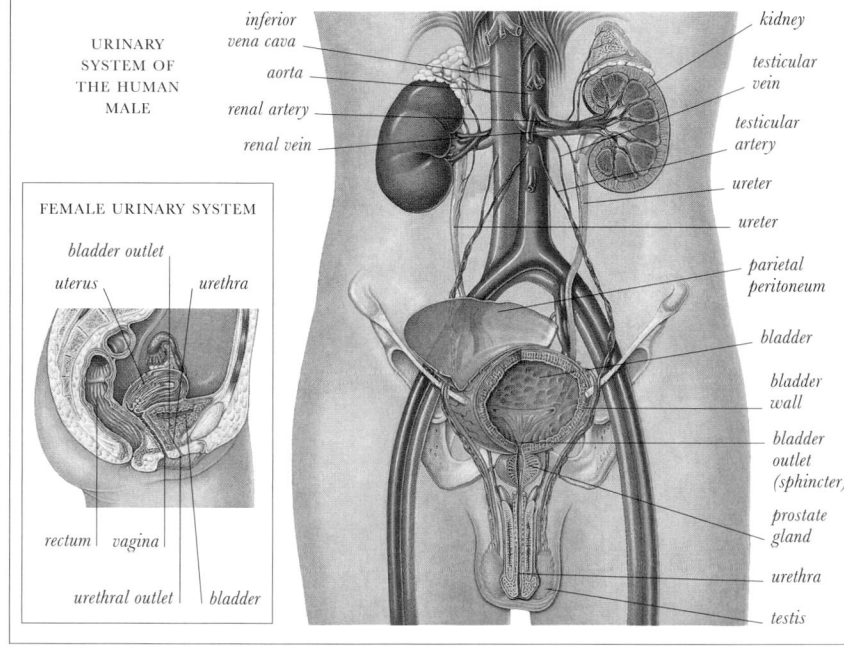

URINARY SYSTEM

The human urinary system facilitates regulation of the amount and composition of fluids in the body. The kidneys filter blood to form urine for the excretion of waste products. Ureters carry the urine to the bladder where it is stored until it is expelled.

At this time, the bladder contracts, the bladder and urethral outlets (sphincters) relax, and the urine is voided. A woman's bladder is smaller and lower in the pelvis than a man's, and her urethra is about one-fifth the length of a man's.

URINARY SYSTEM OF THE HUMAN MALE

inferior vena cava
aorta
renal artery
renal vein
kidney
testicular vein
testicular artery
ureter
ureter
parietal peritoneum
bladder
bladder wall
bladder outlet (sphincter)
prostate gland
urethra
testis

FEMALE URINARY SYSTEM

bladder outlet
uterus
urethra
rectum
vagina
urethral outlet
bladder

URL *abbr.* uniform (or universal) resource locator, the address of a World Wide Web page.

urn /ərn/ *n.* **1** a vase with a foot and usu. a rounded body, esp. for storing the ashes of the cremated dead or as a vessel or measure. **2** a large vessel with a tap, in which tea or coffee, etc., is made or kept hot. □□ **urn·ful** *n.* (*pl.* **-fuls**)

ur·o·dele /yŏŏrōdeel/ *n.* any amphibian of the order Urodela, having a tail when in the adult form, including newts and salamanders. ▷ NEWT, SALAMANDER

u·ro·gen·i·tal /yŏŏrəjénit'l/ *adj.* of or relating to urinary and genital products or organs.

u·rol·o·gy /yŏŏróləjee/ *n.* the scientific study of the urinary system. □□ **u·ro·log·ic** /-rəlójik/ *adj.* **u·rol·o·gist** *n.*

Ur·sa Ma·jor /ə́rsə máyjər/ *n.* ▶ a prominent constellation in the northern sky, including the stars of the Big Dipper.

Ur·sa Mi·nor /ə́rsə mínər/ *n.* ▼ a small constellation containing the north celestial pole and the polestar, Polaris.

ur·sine /ə́rsīn/ *adj.* of or like a bear.

US *abbr.* United States (of America).

us /us, əs/ *pron.* **1** objective case of WE (*they saw us*). **2** *colloq.* = WE (*it's us again*). **3** *colloq.* = ME¹ (*give us a kiss*).

USA *abbr.* **1** United States of America. **2** United States Army.

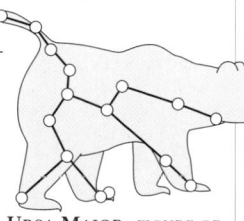

URSA MAJOR: FIGURE OF A BEAR FORMED FROM THE STARS OF URSA MAJOR

Polaris

URSA MINOR: FIGURE OF A SMALL BEAR FORMED FROM THE STARS OF URSA MINOR

---

us·a·ble /yŏŏzəbəl/ *adj.* (also **use·a·ble**) that can be used. □□ **us·a·bil·i·ty** /-bilitee/ *n.* **us·a·ble·ness** *n.*

USAF *abbr.* United States Air Force.

us·age /yŏŏsij/ *n.* **1** a manner of using or treating; treatment (*damaged by rough usage*). **2** habitual or customary practice.

USB *abbr. Computing* ▶ universal serial bus, a connector which enables any of a variety of peripheral devices to be plugged in to a computer.

USB CABLE

U.S.C. *abbr. Law* United States Code.

USCG *abbr.* United States Coast Guard.

use *v. & n.* ● *v.tr.* /yŏŏz/ **1 a** cause to act or serve for a purpose; bring into service; avail oneself of (*rarely uses the car; use your discretion*). **b** consume by eating or drinking; take (alcohol, a drug, etc.), esp. habitually. **2** treat (a person) in a specified manner (*they used him shamefully*). **3** exploit for one's own ends (*they are just using you; used his position*). **4** (in *past* /yŏŏst/; foll. by *to* + infin.) did or had in the past (but no longer) as a customary practice or state (*I used to be an archaeologist; it used not (or did not use) to rain so often*). **5** (as **used** *adj.*) secondhand. **6** (as **used** /yŏŏst / *predic.adj.*) (foll. by *to*) familiar by habit; accustomed (*not used to hard work*). **7** apply (a name or title, etc.) to oneself. ● *n.* /yŏŏs/ **1** the act of using or the state of being used; application to a purpose (*put it to good use; is in daily use; worn and polished with use*). **2** the right or power of using (*lost the use of my right arm*). **3 a** the ability to be used (*a flashlight would be of use*). **b** the purpose for which a

U

UTENSIL

Most households have a basic set of cooking utensils for the preparation of food. Since cooking as a hobby has increased in popularity, the range and quality of utensils available have grown with it. While there have been many innovations, a well-equipped kitchen will still have most of the traditional tools shown here.

CUTTING AND SLICING

KITCHEN KNIVES   TWO-PRONGED FORK   STEEL

MISCELLANEOUS

APPLE CORER

POULTRY SHEARS

PASTRY BRUSH

CAN OPENER

SERVING, STRAINING, AND MIXING

LADLES   COLANDER

SKIMMER

METAL WHISKS   SPATULAS   WOODEN SPOON

MEASURING

SPOONS

CUPS

TRADITIONAL SCALE

U

thing can be used (*it's no use talking*). **4** custom or usage (*long use has reconciled me to it*). **5** the characteristic ritual and liturgy of a church or diocese, etc. **6** *Law hist.* the benefit or profit of lands, esp. in the possession of another who holds them solely for the beneficiary. □ **could use** *colloq.* would be glad to have; would be improved by having. **have no use for 1** be unable to find a use for. **2** dislike or be impatient with. **make use of 1** employ; apply. **2** benefit from. **use a person's name** quote a person as an authority or reference, etc. **use up 1** consume completely; use the whole of. **2** find a use for (something remaining). **3** exhaust or wear out, e.g., with overwork.

use·ful /yóosfŏol/ *adj.* **1** able to be used for a practical purpose or in several ways. **2** *colloq.* very able or competent (*a useful performance*). □ **make oneself useful** perform useful services. □□ **use·ful·ly** *adv.* **use·ful·ness** *n.*

use·less /yóoslis/ *adj.* **1** serving no purpose; unavailing. **2** *colloq.* feeble or ineffectual (*am useless at swimming*). □□ **use·less·ly** *adv.* **use·less·ness** *n.*

Use·net /yóoznet/ *n. Computing* an Internet service consisting of thousands of newsgroups.

us·er /yóozər/ *n.* **1** a person who uses (esp. a partic-

ular commodity or service, or a computer). **2** *colloq.* a drug addict. **3** *Law* the continued use or enjoyment of a right, etc.

us·er-friend·ly *adj.* esp. *Computing* (of a machine or system) designed to be easy to use.

ush·er /úshər/ *n. & v.* ● *n.* **1** a person who shows people to their seats in an auditorium or theater, etc. **2** a doorkeeper at a court, etc. ● *v.tr.* **1** act as usher to. **2** (usu. foll. by *in*) announce or show in, etc. (*ushered us into the room; ushered in a new era*).

USIA *abbr.* (also **U.S.I.A.**) United States Information Agency.

USMC *abbr.* United States Marine Corps.

USN *abbr.* United States Navy.

USO *abbr.* (also **U.S.O.**) United Service Organizations.

USPS *abbr.* (also **U.S.P.S.**) United States Postal Service.

USS *abbr.* United States Ship.

USSR *abbr. hist.* Union of Soviet Socialist Republics.

usu. *abbr.* **1** usual. **2** usually.

u·su·al /yóozhŏoəl/ *adj. & n.* ● *adj.* such as commonly occurs, or is observed or done; customary; habitual (*the usual formalities; it is usual to tip them; forgot

my keys as usual*). ● *n.* (prec. by *the*, *my*, etc.) *colloq.* a person's usual drink, etc. □□ **u·su·al·ly** *adv.*

u·surp /yŏozárp, -sárp/ *v.* **1** *tr.* seize or assume (a throne or power, etc.) wrongfully. **2** *intr.* (foll. by *on*, *upon*) encroach. □□ **u·sur·pa·tion** /yóozərpáyshən, -sər-/ *n.* **u·surp·er** *n.*

u·su·ry /yóozhəree/ *n.* **1** the act or practice of lending money at interest, esp. at an exorbitant rate. **2** interest at this rate. □□ **u·sur·er** *n.* **u·su·ri·ous** /-zhŏoree-əs/ *adj.*

UT *abbr.* **1** Utah (in official postal use). **2** universal time.

Ute /yŏot/ *n.* (*pl.* **Ute** or **Utes**) **1** a member of a N. American people native to the area that is now Colorado, New Mexico, Utah, and Arizona. **2** the language of these people.

u·ten·sil /yŏoténsəl/ *n.* ◀ an implement or vessel, esp. for domestic use (*cooking utensils*).

u·ter·ine /yóotərin, -rīn/ *adj.* **1** of or relating to the uterus. **2** born of the same mother but not the same father (*sister uterine*).

u·ter·us /yóotərəs/ *n.* (*pl.* **uteri** /-rī/) the womb. ▷ REPRODUCTIVE ORGANS. □□ **u·ter·i·tis** /-rítis/ *n.*

u·til·i·tar·i·an /yŏotílitáireeən/ *adj. & n.* ● *adj.* **1** designed to be useful for a purpose rather than attractive; severely practical. **2** of utilitarianism. ● *n.* an adherent of utilitarianism.

u·til·i·tar·i·an·ism /yŏotílitáireeənizəm/ *n.* the doctrine that actions are right if they are useful or for the benefit of a majority.

u·til·i·ty /yŏotílitee/ *n.* (*pl.* **-ies**) **1** the condition of being useful or profitable. **2** a useful thing. **3** = PUBLIC UTILITY. **4** (*attrib.*) **a** severely practical and standardized (*utility furniture*). **b** made or serving for utility.

u·til·i·ty room *n.* a room equipped with appliances for washing, ironing, and other domestic work.

u·ti·lize /yŏot'līz/ *v.tr.* make practical use of; to account; use effectively. □□ **u·ti·liz·a·ble** *adj.* **u·ti·li·za·tion** *n.* **u·ti·liz·er** *n.*

ut·most /útmōst/ *adj. & n.* ● *adj.* furthest, extreme, or greatest (*the utmost limits; showed the utmost reluctance*). ● *n.* (prec. by *the*) the utmost point or degree, etc. □ **do one's utmost** do all that one can.

U·to·pi·a /yŏotópeeə/ *n.* an imagined perfect place or state of things.

U·to·pi·an /yŏotópeeən/ *adj. & n.* (also **utopian**) ● *adj.* characteristic of Utopia; idealistic. ● *n.* an idealistic reformer. □□ **U·to·pi·an·ism** *n.*

ut·ter[1] /útər/ *attrib.adj.* complete; absolute (*utter amazement*). □□ **ut·ter·ly** *adv.* **ut·ter·ness** *n.*

ut·ter[2] /útər/ *v.tr.* **1** emit audibly (*uttered a startled cry*). **2** express in spoken or written words. **3** *Law* put (esp. forged money) into circulation. □□ **ut·ter·a·ble** *adj.* **ut·ter·er** *n.*

ut·ter·ance /útərəns/ *n.* **1** the act or an instance of uttering. **2** a thing spoken. **3 a** the power of speaking. **b** a manner of speaking.

ut·ter·most /útərmōst/ *adj.* furthest; extreme.

U-turn /yóotərn/ *n.* **1** the turning of a vehicle in a U-shaped course so as to face in the opposite direction from its original course. **2** a reversal of policy or tactics.

UV *abbr.* ultraviolet.

u·ve·a /yóoveeə/ *n.* the pigmented layer of the eye, lying beneath the outer layer.

u·vu·la /yóovyələ/ *n.* (*pl.* **uvulas** or **uvulae** /-lee/) **1** ▶ a fleshy extension of the soft palate hanging above the throat. **2** a similar process in the bladder or cerebellum. □□ **u·vu·lar** *adj.*

ux·o·ri·al /uksáwreeəl, ugzáwr-/ *adj.* of or relating to a wife.

ux·o·ri·ous /uksáwreeəs, ugzáwr-/ *adj.* greatly or excessively fond of one's wife. □□ **ux·o·ri·ous·ly** *adv.* **ux·o·ri·ous·ness** *n.*

U·zi /óozee/ *n.* a type of submachine gun.

uvula

UVULA

V[1] /vee/ n. (also **v**) (pl. **Vs** or **V's**) **1** the twenty-second letter of the alphabet. **2** a V-shaped thing. **3** (as a Roman numeral) five.

V[2] abbr. (also **V.**) volt(s).

V[3] symb. Chem. the element vanadium.

v. abbr. **1** verse. **2** verso. **3** versus. **4** very. **5** vide.

VA abbr. **1** Veterans Administration. **2** Virginia (in official postal use). **3** vice admiral.

Va. abbr. Virginia.

vac /vak/ n. colloq. vacuum cleaner.

va·can·cy /váykənsee/ n. (pl. **-ies**) **1 a** the state of being vacant. **b** an instance of this; empty space. **2** an unoccupied job (there are three vacancies for computer specialists). **3** an available room in a hotel, etc. **4** emptiness of mind; idleness; listlessness.

va·cant /váykənt/ adj. **1** not filled nor occupied. **2** not mentally active; showing no interest (had a vacant stare). □□ **va·cant·ly** adv.

va·cate /váykayt, vaykáyt/ v.tr. **1** leave vacant or cease to occupy (a house, room, etc.). **2** give up tenure of (a post, etc.).

va·ca·tion /vaykáyshən, və / n. & v. ● n. **1** a time of

VACUUM CLEANER

Vacuum cleaners suck up dust using a strong current of air and hold it in a bag or container. In a cyclone vacuum cleaner, the air and dust rotate inside a chamber. As it enters an inner cylinder, its speed decreases, and the dust falls into a bin.

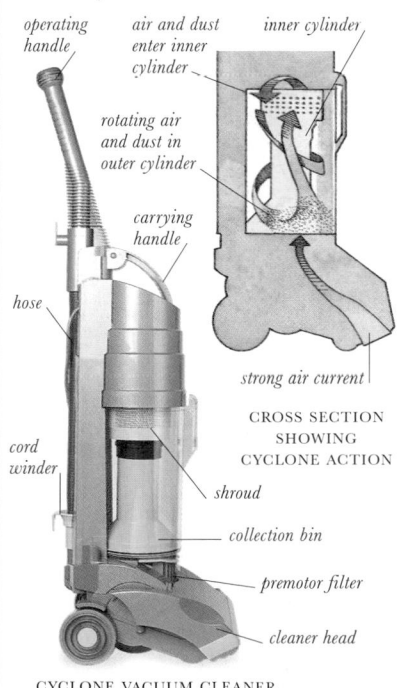

CYCLONE VACUUM CLEANER

VACUUM EXTRACTOR

A vacuum extractor may be used to aid delivery when labor is prolonged. It consists of a cup attached to a vacuum pump. The cup is placed on the baby's head, and with each contraction the baby is eased down the birth canal.

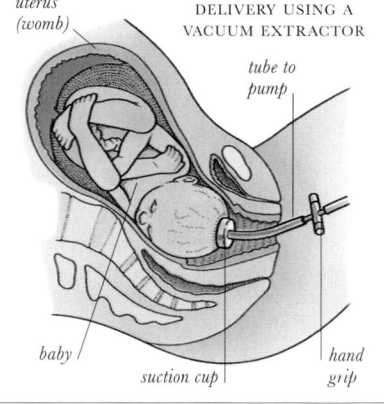

DELIVERY USING A VACUUM EXTRACTOR

rest, recreation, etc., esp. spent away from home or in traveling, during which regular activities (esp. work or schooling) are suspended. **2** a fixed period of cessation from work, esp. in legislatures and courts of law. **3** the act of vacating. ● v.intr. take a vacation, esp. away from home for pleasure and recreation. □□ **va·ca·tion·er** n. **va·ca·tion·ist** n.

vac·ci·nate /váksinayt/ v.tr. inoculate with a vaccine to procure immunity from a disease. □□ **vac·ci·na·tion** /-náyshən/ n. **vac·ci·na·tor** n.

vac·cine /vákseen/ n. a preparation used to stimulate the production of antibodies and procure immunity from one or several diseases.

vac·il·late /vásilayt/ v.intr. waver in opinion or resolution. □□ **vac·il·la·tion** /-láyshən/ n.

vac·u·a pl. of VACUUM.

vac·u·ole /vákyoo-ōl/ n. Biol. a space within the cytoplasm of a cell containing air, fluid, etc. ▷ CELL, DIATOM. □□ **vac·u·o·lar** /vakyoo-ōlər, vákyooələr/ adj.

vac·u·ous /vákyooəs/ adj. **1** lacking expression (a vacuous stare). **2** unintelligent (a vacuous remark). **3** empty. □□ **va·cu·i·ty** /vəkyoo-itee/ n. **vac·u·ous·ly** adv. **vac·u·ous·ness** n.

vac·u·um /vákyooəm, -yoom, -yəm/ n. & v. ● n. (pl. **vacuums** or **vacua** /-yooə/) **1** a space entirely devoid of matter. **2** a space or vessel from which the air has been completely or partly removed by a pump, etc. **3 a** the absence of the normal or previous content of a place, environment, etc. **b** the absence of former circumstances, activities, etc. **4** (pl. **vacuums**) colloq. a vacuum cleaner. **5** a decrease of pressure below the normal atmospheric value. ● v. colloq. **1** tr. clean with a vacuum cleaner. **2** intr. use a vacuum cleaner.

vac·uum clean·er n. ◄ an apparatus for removing dust, etc., by suction.

vac·uum ex·trac·tor n. ▲ a vacuum pump for use in childbirth.

vac·uum-packed adj. sealed after the partial removal of air.

vac·uum tube n. Electronics an evacuated glass tube that regulates the flow of thermionic electrons in one direction, used esp. in the rectification of a current and in radio reception.

va·de me·cum /vaaday máycoom/ n. a handbook or guide kept constantly at hand.

vag·a·bond /vágəbond/ n. & adj. ● n. **1** a wanderer, esp. an idle one. **2** colloq. a scamp or rascal. ● adj. having no fixed home. □□ **vag·a·bond·age** n.

va·gal see VAGUS.

va·gar·y /váygəree/ n. (pl. **-ies**) a caprice; an eccentric idea or act (the vagaries of Fortune).

va·gi pl. of VAGUS.

va·gi·na /vəjínə/ n. (pl. **vaginas** or **vaginae** /-nee/) the canal between the uterus and vulva in female mammals. ▷ REPRODUCTIVE ORGANS. □□ **vag·i·nal** /vájin'l/ adj. **vag·i·ni·tis** /vájinítis/ n.

vag·i·nis·mus /vájinízməs/ n. a painful spasmodic contraction of the vagina, usu. in response to pressure.

va·grant /váygrənt/ n. & adj. ● n. **1** a person without a settled home or regular work. **2** a wanderer. ● adj. **1** wandering or roving (a vagrant musician). **2** characteristic of a vagrant. □□ **va·gran·cy** /-grənsee/ n.

vague /vayg/ adj. **1** of uncertain or ill-defined meaning or character (gave a vague answer; has some vague idea of emigrating). **2** inexact in thought, expression, or understanding. □□ **vague·ly** adv. **vague·ness** n.

va·gus /váygəs/ n. (pl. **vagi** /-gī, -jī/) Anat. either of the tenth pair of cranial nerves with branches to the heart, lungs, and viscera. ▷ NERVOUS SYSTEM. □□ **va·gal** adj.

vain /vayn/ adj. **1** excessively proud or conceited. **2** empty; trivial (vain boasts; vain triumphs). **3** useless; followed by no good result (in the vain hope of dissuading them). □ **in vain** without result or success (it was in vain that we protested). **take a person's name in vain** use it lightly or profanely. □□ **vain·ly** adv.

vain·glo·ry /vayngláwree/ n. literary boastfulness; extreme vanity. □□ **vain·glo·ri·ous** adj. **vain·glo·ri·ous·ly** adv.

val·ance /váləns, váyl/ n. (also **val·ence**) a short curtain around the frame or canopy of a bed, above a window, or under a shelf. □□ **val·anced** adj.

vale /vayl/ n. archaic or poet. (except in place-names) a valley (Vale of the White Horse).

val·e·dic·tion /válidíkshən/ n. **1** the act or an instance of bidding farewell. **2** the words used in this.

val·e·dic·to·ri·an /válidiktáwreeən/ n. a person who gives a valedictory, esp. the highest-ranking member of a graduating class.

val·e·dic·to·ry /válidíktəree/ adj. & n. ● adj. serving as a farewell. ● n. (pl. **-ies**) a farewell address.

va·lence[1] /váyləns/ n. Chem. ▼ the combining power of an atom measured by the number of hydrogen atoms it can displace or combine with.

VALENCE

The valence of an atom is the number of chemical bonds it is able to make. Hydrogen has a valence of one, so valence is measured by this standard. To form a compound (as below), the total valences of the elements present must be equal.

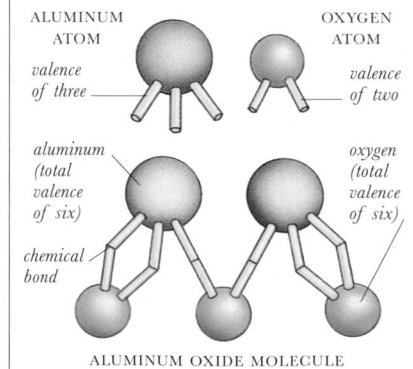

ALUMINUM OXIDE MOLECULE

val·ence[2] var. of VALANCE.

Va·len·ci·ennes /vəlénsee-énz, valoɴsyén/ *n.* a rich kind of lace.

va·len·cy /váylənsee/ *n. (pl.* **-ies)** *Chem. Brit.* = VALENCE[1].

val·en·tine /váləntīn/ *n.* **1** ◀ a card or gift sent, often anonymously, as a mark of love or affection on St. Valentine's Day (Feb. 14). **2** a sweetheart chosen on this day.

VALENTINE CARD FROM THE VICTORIAN ERA

va·le·ri·an /vəléereeən/ *n.* **1** any of various flowering plants of the family Valerianaceae. **2** the root of any of these used as a medicinal sedative.

val·et /valáy, válit, -lay/ *n. & v.* ● *n.* **1** a man's personal attendant who looks after his clothes, etc. **2** a hotel, etc., employee with similar duties. **3** a standing rack for holding one's suit, coat, etc. ● *v.* (**valeted, valeting**) **1** *intr.* work as a valet. **2** *tr.* act as a valet to. **3** *tr.* clean or clean out (a car).

val·e·tu·di·nar·i·an /válitŏod'náireeən, -tyŏod-/ *n. & adj.* ● *n.* a person of poor health or unduly anxious about health. ● *adj.* **1** of or being a valetudinarian. **2** of poor health. **3** seeking to recover one's health.

val·e·tu·di·nar·y /válitŏod'neree/ *adj. & n. (pl.* **-ies)** = VALETUDINARIAN.

Val·hal·la /valhálə, vaalháalə/ *n.* **1** (in Norse mythology) a palace in which the souls of slain heroes feasted for eternity. **2** a building used for honoring the illustrious.

val·iant /vályənt/ *adj.* brave. □□ **val·iant·ly** *adv.*

val·id /válid/ *adj.* **1** (of a reason, objection, etc.) sound or defensible. **2 a** executed with the proper formalities (*a valid contract*). **b** legally acceptable (*a valid passport*). **c** not having reached its expiration date. □□ **va·lid·i·ty** /-líditee/ *n.* **val·id·ly** *adv.*

val·i·date /válidayt/ *v.tr.* make valid; ratify. □□ **val·i·da·tion** /-dáyshən/ *n.*

val·ine /váleen/ *n. Biochem.* an amino acid that is an essential nutrient for vertebrates and a general constituent of proteins.

va·lise /vəlées/ *n.* **1** a small suitcase; traveling bag. **2** a knapsack.

Val·i·um /váleeəm/ *n. Trademark* the drug diazepam used as a tranquilizer.

Val·kyr·ie /valkéeree, válkiree/ *n.* (in Norse mythology) each of Odin's twelve handmaidens who selected heroes destined to be slain in battle.

val·lec·u·la /vəlékyələ/ *n. (pl.* **valleculae** /-lee/) *Anat. & Bot.* a groove or furrow. □□ **val·lec·u·lar** *adj.* **val·lec·u·late** /-layt/ *adj.*

val·ley /válee/ *n. (pl.* **-eys)** **1** ▲ a low area more or less enclosed by hills and usu. with a stream flowing through it. ▷ RIFT VALLEY. **2** any depression compared to this. **3** *Archit.* an internal angle formed by the intersecting planes of a roof.

val·or /válər/ *n.* courage, esp. in battle. □□ **val·or·ous** *adj.*

val·or·ize /válərīz/ *v.tr.* raise or fix the price of (a commodity, etc.) by artificial means, esp. by government action. □□ **val·or·i·za·tion** *n.*

val·u·a·ble /vályŏoəbəl, vályə-/ *adj. & n.* ● *adj.* of great value, price, or worth (*a valuable property; valuable information*). ● *n.* (usu. in *pl.*) a valuable thing. □□ **val·u·a·bly** *adv.*

val·u·a·tion /vályŏo-áyshən/ *n.* **1 a** an estimation (esp. by a professional) of a thing's worth. **b** the worth estimated. **2** the price set on a thing. □□ **val·u·ate** *v.tr.*

val·u·a·tor /vályŏo-aytər/ *n.* a person who makes valuations; an appraiser.

V

VALLEY

Valleys form through fluvial and glacial erosion or where the land between two faults sinks. Those carved by glaciers have a characteristic U shape and are often associated with hanging valleys, formed when a glacier slices off the ends of valleys that slope into it. The movement of debris by the ice also leaves very distinctive features.

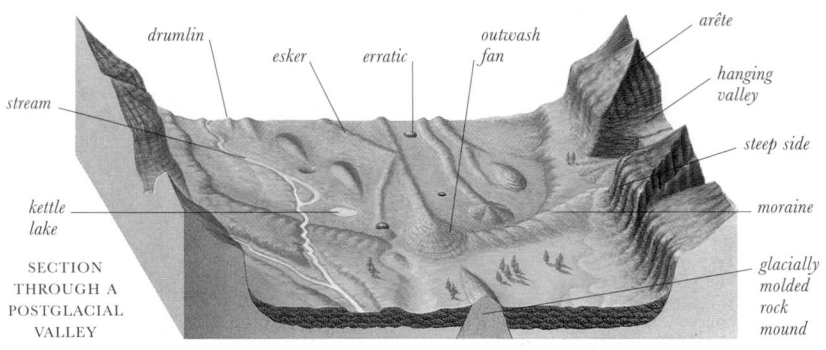

drumlin   esker   erratic   outwash fan   arête   hanging valley   steep side   moraine   glacially molded rock mound   stream   kettle lake

SECTION THROUGH A POSTGLACIAL VALLEY

val·ue /vályŏo/ *n. & v.* ● *n.* **1** the worth, desirability, or utility of a thing, or the qualities on which these depend (*the value of regular exercise*). **2** worth as estimated (*set a high value on my time*). **3** the amount for which a thing can be exchanged in the open market. **4** the equivalent of a thing (*paid them the value of their lost property*). **5** (in full **value for money**) something well worth the money spent. **6** the ability of a thing to serve a purpose or cause an effect (*news value; nuisance value*). **7** (in *pl.*) one's principles or standards; one's judgment of what is valuable or important in life. **8** *Mus.* the duration of the sound signified by a note. **9** *Math.* the amount denoted by an algebraic term or expression. **10** (foll. by *of*) **a** the meaning (of a word, etc.). **b** the quality (of a spoken sound). **11** the relative rank or importance of a playing card, chess piece, etc. **12** the relation of one part of a picture to others in respect of light and shade; the part being characterized by a particular tone. **13** *Physics & Chem.* the numerical measure of a quantity or a number denoting magnitude on some conventional scale (*the value of gravity at the equator*). ● *v.tr.* (**values, valued, valuing**) **1** estimate the value of; appraise (esp. professionally) (*valued the property at $200,000*). **2** have a high or specified opinion of (*a valued friend*).

VALVE

Valves such as the aortic valve in the human heart ensure unidirectional blood flow. A buildup of pressure in the heart chamber as it fills with blood forces the cusps of the valve to open; once the blood flows out into the aorta, the cusps snap shut and prevent blood from pouring backward.

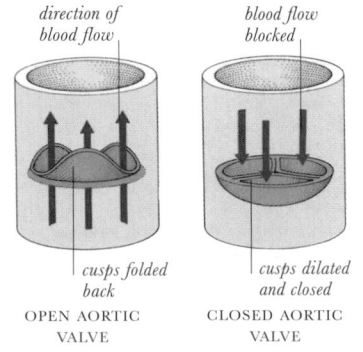

direction of blood flow   blood flow blocked

cusps folded back   cusps dilated and closed

OPEN AORTIC VALVE   CLOSED AORTIC VALVE

val·ue-add·ed tax *n.* a tax on the amount by which the value of an article has been increased at each stage of its production.

val·ue judg·ment *n.* a subjective estimate of quality, etc.

val·ue·less /vályŏolis/ *adj.* having no value.

va·lu·ta /vəlŏotə/ *n.* **1** the value of one currency with respect to another. **2** a currency considered in this way.

valve /valv/ *n.* **1** a device for controlling the passage of fluid through a pipe, etc., esp. an automatic device allowing movement in one direction only. **2** *Anat. & Zool.* ▼ a membranous part of an organ, etc., allowing a flow of blood, etc., in one direction only. **3** a device to vary the effective length of the tube in a brass musical instrument. ▷ BRASS. **4** each of the two shells of an oyster, mussel, etc. ▷ BIVALVE. □□ **valved** *adj.* (also in *comb.*).

val·vu·lar /válvyələr/ *adj.* **1** having a valve or valves. **2** having the form or function of a valve.

val·vu·li·tis /válvyəlítis/ *n.* inflammation of the valves of the heart.

va·moose /vamŏos, və-/ *v.intr.* (esp. as *int.*) *sl.* depart hurriedly.

vamp[1] /vamp/ *n. & v.* ● *n.* **1** the upper front part of a boot or shoe. ▷ SHOE. **2** a patched-up article. **3** an improvised musical accompaniment. ● *v.* **1** *tr.* (often foll. by *up*) repair or furbish. **2** *tr.* (foll. by *up*) make by patching or from odds and ends. **3 a** *tr. & intr.* improvise a musical accompaniment (to). **b** *tr.* improvise (a musical accompaniment). **4** *tr.* put a new vamp to (a boot or shoe).

vamp[2] /vamp/ *n. & v. colloq.* ● *n.* **1** an unscrupulous flirt. **2** a woman who uses sexual attraction to exploit men. ● *v.* **1** *tr.* allure or exploit (a man). **2** *intr.* act as a vamp.

vam·pire /vámpīr/ *n.* **1** a ghost or reanimated corpse supposed to leave its grave at night to suck the blood of persons sleeping. **2** a person who preys ruthlessly on others. **3** (in full **vampire bat**) ▼ any tropical (esp. South American) bat of the family Desmodontidae, with incisors for piercing flesh and feeding on blood. ▷ BAT. **4** *Theatr.* a small spring trapdoor used for sudden disappearances. □□ **vam·pir·ic** /-pírik/ *adj.*

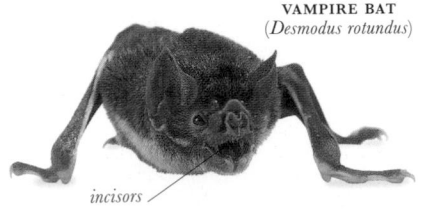

VAMPIRE BAT (*Desmodus rotundus*)

incisors

vam·pir·ism /vámpīrizəm/ *n.* **1** belief in the existence of vampires. **2** the practices of a vampire.

vam·plate /vámplayt/ *n. hist.* an iron plate on a lance designed to protect the hand.

van[1] /van/ *n.* **1** a covered vehicle for conveying goods, etc., esp. a large truck or trailer. **2** a smaller such vehicle, similar to a panel truck and used esp. for carrying passengers, traveling gear, etc.

van[2] /van/ *n.* **1** a vanguard. **2** the forefront (*in the van of progress*).

va·na·di·um /vənáydeeəm/ *n. Chem.* a hard, gray, metallic transition element occurring naturally in several ores and used in small quantities for strengthening some steels. ¶ Symb.: **V**. □□ **van·a·date** /vánədayt/ *n.*

Van Al·len belt /van álən/ *n.* (also **Van Allen layer**) each of two regions of intense radiation partly surrounding the Earth at heights of several thousand miles.

van·dal /vánd'l/ *n. & adj.* ● *n.* **1** a person who willfully or maliciously destroys or damages property. **2** (**Vandal**) a member of a Germanic people that ravaged Gaul, Spain, N. Africa, and Rome in the 4th–5th c., destroying many books and works of art. ● *adj.* of or relating to the Vandals.

van·dal·ism /vánd'lizəm/ *n.* willful or malicious destruction or damage to works of art or other property. □□ **van·dal·is·tic** *adj.*

van·dal·ize /vánd'līz/ *v.tr.* destroy or damage willfully or maliciously.

Van de Graaff gen·er·a·tor /ván də gráf/ *n. Electr.* a machine devised to generate electrostatic charge by means of a vertical endless belt collecting charge from a voltage source and transferring it to a large insulated metal dome, where a high voltage is produced.

van der Waals forc·es /ván dər wáwlz, wáalz/ *n.pl. Chem.* short-range attractive forces between uncharged molecules arising from the interaction of dipole moments.

Van·dyke /vandík/ *n. & adj.* ● *n.* **1** each of a series of large points forming a border to lace or cloth, etc. **2** a cape or collar, etc., with these. ● *adj.* in the style of dress, esp. with pointed borders, common in portraits by Van Dyck.

Van·dyke beard *n.* a neat, pointed beard.

Van·dyke brown *n.* a deep rich brown.

vane /vayn/ *n.* **1** (in full **weather vane**) a revolving pointer mounted on a high place to show the direction of the wind (cf. WEATHERCOCK). **2** ▶ a blade of a screw propeller or a windmill, etc. **3** the sight of surveying instruments, a quadrant, etc. **4** the flat part of a bird's feather formed by the barbs. □□ **vaned** *adj.*

van·es·sa /vənésə/ *n.* any butterfly of the genus *Vanessa*, including the red admiral and the painted lady.

van·guard /vángaard/ *n.* **1** the foremost part of an army or fleet advancing or ready to advance. **2** the leaders of a movement or of opinion, etc.

va·nil·la /vənílə/ *n.* **1 a** any tropical climbing orchid of the genus *Vanilla*, esp. *V. planifolia*, with fragrant flowers. **b** (in full **vanilla bean**) the fruit of these. **2** a substance obtained from the vanilla bean or synthesized and used to flavor ice cream, chocolate, etc.

va·nil·lin /vənílin/ *n.* **1** the fragrant principle of vanilla. **2** a synthetic preparation used as a vanilla-like fragrance or flavoring.

van·ish /vánish/ *v.intr.* **1 a** disappear suddenly. **b** disappear gradually; fade away. **2** cease to exist.

van·ish·ing point *n.* ▼ the point at which receding parallel lines viewed in perspective appear to meet.

vanishing point —— *receding lines*

chessboard viewed in perspective

VANISHING POINT: RECEDING LINES ON A CHESSBOARD EXTENDED TO THE VANISHING POINT

van·i·ty /vánitee/ *n.* (*pl.* **-ies**) **1** conceit and desire for admiration of one's personal attainments or attractions. **2** futility (*the vanity of human achievement*). **3** a dressing table. **4** a unit consisting of a washbowl set into a flat top with cupboards beneath.

van·i·ty bag *n.* (also **van·i·ty bag**) a case or bag for carrying a small mirror, makeup, etc.

van·i·ty plate *n. N. Amer.* a vehicle license plate bearing a distinctive or personalized combination of letters or numbers.

van·quish /vángkwish/ *v.tr. literary* conquer or overcome. □□ **van·quish·er** *n.*

van·tage /vántij/ *n.* **1** (also **van·tage point** or **ground**) a place affording a good view or prospect. **2** *Tennis* = ADVANTAGE.

vap·id /vápid/ *adj.* insipid; dull. □□ **va·pid·i·ty** /-píditee/ *n.* **vap·id·ly** *adv.*

va·por /váypər/ *n. & v.* ● *n.* **1** moisture or another substance diffused or suspended in air, e.g., mist or smoke. **2** *Physics* a gaseous form of a normally liquid or solid substance (cf. GAS). **3** a medicinal agent for inhaling. **4** (in *pl.*) *archaic* a state of depression or melancholy thought to be caused by exhalations of vapor from the stomach. ● *v.intr.* make idle boasts or empty talk. □□ **va·por·ous** *adj.* **va·por·ing** *n.* **va·por·y** *adj.*

va·por·ize /váypərīz/ *v.tr. & intr.* convert or be converted into vapor. □□ **va·por·i·za·tion** *n.*

va·por·iz·er /váypərīzər/ *n.* a device that vaporizes substances, esp. for medicinal inhalation.

va·por trail *n.* a trail of condensed water from an aircraft or rocket at high altitude, seen as a white streak against the sky.

va·que·ro /vəkáirō/ *n.* (in Spanish-speaking parts of the USA) a cowboy; a cattle driver.

var. *abbr.* **1** variant. **2** variety.

va·rac·tor /vəráktər/ *n.* a semi-conductor diode with a capacitance dependent on the applied voltage.

var·i·a·ble /váireeəbəl/ *adj. & n.* ● *adj.* **1 a** that can be varied or adapted. **b** (of a gear) designed to give varying speeds. **2** apt to vary; not constant. **3** *Math.* (of a quantity) indeterminate; able to assume different numerical values. **4** (of wind or currents) tending to change direction. **5** *Astron.* (of a star) periodically varying in brightness. **6** *Bot. & Zool.* (of a species) including individuals or groups that depart from the type. ● *n.* **1** a variable thing or quantity. **2** *Math.* a variable quantity. **3** *Naut.* **a** a shifting wind. **b** (in *pl.*) the region between the NE and SE trade winds. □□ **var·i·a·bil·i·ty** /-bílitee/ *n.* **var·i·a·bly** *adv.*

var·i·ance /váireeəns/ *n.* **1** difference of opinion; dispute; disagreement; lack of harmony (*at variance among ourselves*; *a theory at variance with all known facts*). **2** *Law* a discrepancy between statements or documents. **3** *Statistics* a quantity equal to the square of the standard deviation.

var·i·ant /váireeənt/ *adj. & n.* ● *adj.* **1** differing in

form or details from the main one (*a variant spelling*). **2** having different forms (*forty variant types of pigeon*). **3** variable or changing. ● *n.* a variant form, spelling, type, reading, etc.

var·i·a·tion /váireeáyshən/ *n.* **1** the act or an instance of varying. **2** departure from a former or normal condition, action, or amount, or from a standard or type (*prices are subject to variation*). **3** the extent of this. **4** a thing that varies from a type. **5** *Mus.* a repetition of a theme in a changed or elaborated form. **6** *Astron.* a deviation of a heavenly body from its mean orbit or motion. **7** *Math.* a change in a function, etc., due to small changes in the values of constants, etc. **8** *Ballet* a solo dance. □□ **var·i·a·tion·al** *adj.*

var·i·cel·la /várisélə/ *n. Med.* = CHICKEN POX.

var·i·co·cele /várikōseel/ *n.* a mass of varicose veins in the scrotum.

var·i·col·ored /váirikúlərd, vári-/ *adj.* **1** variegated in color. **2** of various or different colors.

var·i·cose /várikōs/ *adj.* (esp. of the veins of the legs) affected by a condition causing them to become dilated and swollen. □□ **var·i·cos·i·ty** /-kósitee/ *n.*

var·ied /váireed/ *adj.* showing variety; diverse.

var·i·e·gate /váirigayt, váiree-, vár-/ *v.tr.* **1** (often as **variegated** *adj.*) mark with irregular patches of different colors. **2** diversify in appearance, esp. in color. **3** (as **variegated** *adj.*) *Bot.* ◄ (of plants) having leaves containing two or more colors. □□ **var·i·e·ga·tion** /-gáyshən/ *n.*

variegated leaf

VARIEGATED IVY (*Hedera helix* 'Goldchild')

va·ri·e·tal /vəríət'l/ *adj.* **1** esp. *Bot. & Zool.* of, forming, or designating a variety. **2** (of wine) made from a single designated variety of grape. □□ **va·ri·e·tal·ly** *adv.*

va·ri·e·ty /vəríətee/ *n.* (*pl.* **-ies**) **1** diversity; absence of uniformity; many-sidedness (*not enough variety in our lives*). **2** a quantity or collection of different things (*for a variety of reasons*). **3 a** a class of things different in some common qualities from the rest of a larger class to which they belong. **b** a specimen or member of such a class. **4** (foll. by *of*) a different form of a thing, quality, etc. **5** *Biol.* **a** a subspecies. **b** a cultivar. **c** an individual or group usually fertile within the species to which it belongs but differing from the species type in some qualities capable of perpetuation. **6** a mixed sequence of dances, songs, comedy acts, etc. (usu. *attrib.: a variety show*).

var·i·fo·cal /váirifōkəl/ *adj. & n.* ● *adj.* having a focal length that can be varied, esp. of a lens that allows an infinite number of focusing distances for near, intermediate, and far vision. ● *n.* (in *pl.*) varifocal spectacles.

var·i·form /váirifawrm/ *adj.* having various forms.

va·ri·o·la /vəríələ/ *n. Med.* smallpox.

var·i·ole /váireeōl/ *n.* **1** a shallow pit like a smallpox mark. **2** a small spherical mass in variolite.

var·i·o·lite /váireeəlīt/ *n.* a rock with embedded small spherical masses causing on its surface an appearance like smallpox pustules. □□ **var·i·o·lit·ic** /-lítik/ *adj.*

var·i·om·e·ter /váireeómitər/ *n.* **1** a device for varying the inductance in an electric circuit. **2** a device for indicating an aircraft's rate of change of altitude.

var·i·o·rum /váiree-áwrəm/ *adj. & n.* ● *adj.* **1** (of an edition of a text) having notes by various editors or commentators. **2** (of an edition of an author's works) including variant readings. ● *n.* a variorum edition.

var·i·ous /váireeəs/ *adj.* **1** different; diverse (*too various to form a group*). **2** more than one; several (*for various reasons*). □□ **var·i·ous·ly** *adv.* **var·i·ous·ness** *n.*

VANES ON A MODEL WINDMILL

vane

V

VASOCONSTRICTION AND VASODILATION

When the vasomotor center in the human brain is activated, signals are sent via the autonomic nervous system to muscle fibers in the walls of blood vessels. These signals cause the muscle fibers to contract (vasoconstriction) or relax (vasodilation).

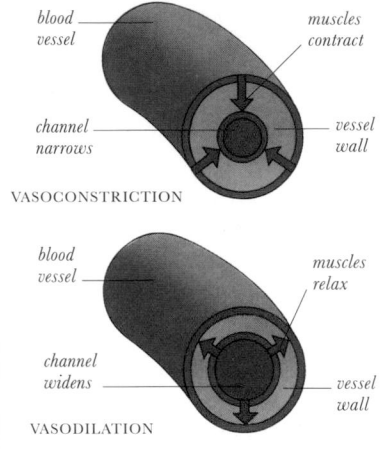

VATICAN

The Vatican is the official residence of the Pope and is located within Vatican City, the seat of the central government of the Roman Catholic Church. The first papal residence on the site was built in 1198, but it was not until the 14th century that it became the Pope's principal residence. The palace buildings, few of which are earlier than the 15th century, are now museums that house one of the most important art collections in the world. They also include the Sistine Chapel and the Vatican Library.

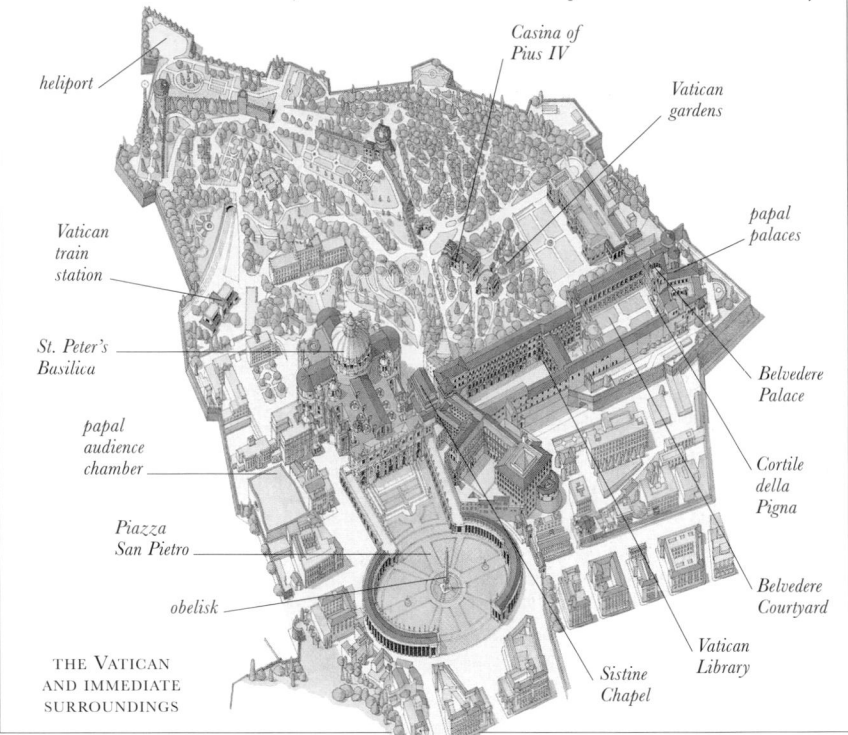

THE VATICAN AND IMMEDIATE SURROUNDINGS

var·is·tor /vərístər/ *n.* a semiconductor diode with resistance dependent on the applied voltage.

va·rix /váiriks/ *n.* (*pl.* **va·ri·ces** /váirəseez/ **1** *Med.* **a** a permanent abnormal dilation of a vein or artery. **b** a vein, etc., dilated in this way. **2** each of the ridges across the whorls of a univalve shell.

var·let /vaárlit/ *n.* **1** *archaic* or *joc.* a menial or rascal. **2** *hist.* a knight's attendant.

var·mint /vaármint/ *n.* *dial.* a mischievous or discreditable person or animal.

var·nish /vaárnish/ *n. & v.* ● *n.* **1** a resinous solution used to give a hard shiny transparent coating to wood, metal, paintings, etc. **2** any other preparation for a similar purpose (*nail varnish*). **3** external appearance or display without an underlying reality. **4** artificial or natural glossiness. **5** a superficial polish of manner. ● *v.tr.* **1** apply varnish to. **2** gloss over (a fact). □□ **var·nish·er** *n.*

var·si·ty /vaársitee/ *n.* (*pl.* **-ies**) a high school, college, etc., first team in a sport.

var·us /váirəs/ *n.* a deformity involving the inward displacement of the foot or hand from the midline.

varve /vaarv/ *n.* annually deposited layers of clay and silt in a lake used to determine the chronology of glacial sediments. □□ **var·ved** *adj.*

var·y /váiree/ *v.* (**-ies**, **-ied**) **1** *tr.* make different; modify; diversify (*seldom varies the routine; the style is not sufficiently varied*). **2** *intr.* **a** undergo change; become or be different (*the temperature varies from 30° to 70°*). **b** be of different kinds (*his mood varies*). **3** *intr.* (foll. by *as*) be in proportion to. □□ **var·y·ing·ly** *adv.*

vas /vas/ *n.* (*pl.* **vasa** /váysə/) *Anat.* a vessel or duct.

vas·cu·lar /váskyələr/ *adj.* of, made up of, or containing vessels for conveying blood or sap, etc. (*vascular functions; vascular tissue*). □□ **vas·cu·lar·i·ty** /-láritee/ *n.* **vas·cu·lar·ize** *v.tr.*

vas·cu·lum /váskyələm/ *n.* (*pl.* **vascula** /-lə/) a botanist's (usu. metal) collecting case with a lengthwise opening.

vas def·e·rens /défərenz/ *n.* (*pl.* **vasa defe·rentia** /défərénsheeə/) *Anat.* the spermatic duct from the testicle to the urethra. ▷ REPRODUCTIVE ORGANS

vase /vays, vayz, vaaz/ *n.* a vessel, usu. tall and circular, used as an ornament or container, esp. for flowers.

vas·ec·to·my /vəséktəmee/ *n.* (*pl.* **-ies**) the surgical removal of part of each vas deferens, esp. as a means of sterilization. □□ **vas·ec·to·mize** *v.tr.*

Vas·e·line /vásileén/ *n.* *Trademark* a type of petroleum jelly used as an ointment, lubricant, etc.

vas·i·form /váyzifawrm, vásə-/ *adj.* **1** duct-shaped. **2** vase-shaped.

vaso- /váyzō/ *comb. form* a vessel, esp. a blood vessel (*vasoconstrictive*).

vas·o·ac·tive /vázō-áktiv/ *adj.* = VASOMOTOR.

vas·o·con·stric·tion /vázōkənstríkshən/ *n.* ◀ the constriction of blood vessels. □□ **vas·o·con·stric·tive** /-stríktiv/ *adj.*

vas·o·di·la·tion /vázōdīláyshən/ (also **vas·o·dil·a·ta·tion** /vázōdīlətáyshən/) *n.* ◀ the dilatation of blood vessels.

vas·o·mo·tor /vázōmốtər/ *adj.* causing constriction or dilatation of blood vessels.

vas·o·pres·sin /vázōprésin/ *n.* a pituitary hormone acting to reduce diuresis and increase blood pressure. Also called **antidiuretic hormone**.

vas·sal /vásəl/ *n.* *hist.* a holder of land by feudal tenure on conditions of homage and allegiance. □□ **vas·sal·age** *n.*

vast /vast/ *adj.* **1** immense; huge (*a vast expanse of water; a vast crowd*). **2** *colloq.* great; considerable (*makes a vast difference*). □□ **vast·ly** *adv.* **vast·ness** *n.*

VAT /vat, vée-aytée/ *abbr.* value-added tax.

VAULT

Usually composed of stone, concrete, or brick, vaults are heavy structures that exert downward and outward pressure onto their supports. The simplest form is the barrel vault. Two intersecting barrel vaults form a groin vault. If ribs are added along the groins, a ribbed vault is made. Adding decorative fan patterns creates a fan vault.

TYPES OF VAULT

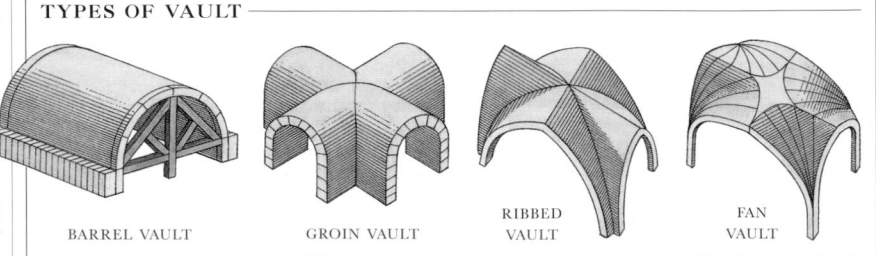

BARREL VAULT GROIN VAULT RIBBED VAULT FAN VAULT

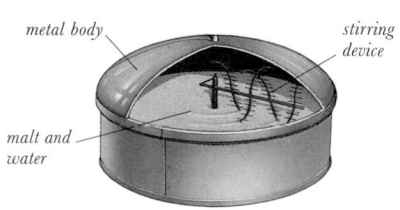

metal body   *stirring device*

malt and water

VAT: CUTAWAY VIEW OF
A WHISKEY-MAKING VAT

vat /vat/ *n.* ▲ a large tank or other vessel, esp. for holding liquids or something in liquid in the process of brewing, tanning, dyeing, etc.

vat·ic /vátik/ *adj. formal* prophetic or inspired.

Vat·i·can /vátikən/ *n.* **1** ◄ the palace and official residence of the Pope in Rome. **2** papal government.

Vat·i·can City *n.* an independent Papal State in Rome, instituted in 1929.

va·tic·i·nate /vatísinayt/ *v.tr. & intr. formal* prophesy. □□ **va·tic·i·nal** *adj.* **va·tic·i·na·tion** /-náyshən/ *n.*

vaude·ville /váwdvil, váwdə-/ *n.* **1** variety entertainment. **2** a stage play on a trivial theme with interspersed songs. **3** a satirical or topical song with a refrain. □□ **vaude·vil·lian** /-vílyən/ *adj. & n.*

Vau·dois /vodwáa/ *n. & adj.* ● *n.* (*pl.* same) **1** a native of Vaud in W. Switzerland. **2** the French dialect spoken in Vaud. ● *adj.* of or relating to Vaud or its dialect.

vault /vawlt/ *n. & v.* ● *n.* **1 a** ◄ an arched roof. **b** a continuous arch. **c** a set or series of arches whose joints radiate from a central point or line. **2** a vault-like covering (*the vault of heaven*). **3** an esp. underground chamber: **a** as a place of storage (*bank vaults*). **b** as a place of interment beneath a church or in a cemetery, etc. (*family vault*). **4** an act of vaulting. **5** *Anat.* the arched roof of a cavity. ● *v.* **1** *intr.* leap or spring, esp. while resting on one or both hands or with the help of a pole. **2** *tr.* spring over in this way. **3** *tr.* (esp. as **vaulted**) **a** make in the form of a vault. **b** provide with a vault or vaults. □□ **vault·er** *n.*

vault·ing /váwlting/ *n.* **1** arched work in a vaulted roof or ceiling. **2** a gymnastic or athletic exercise in which participants vault over obstacles.

vault·ing horse *n.* ▼ a wooden block to be vaulted over by gymnasts.

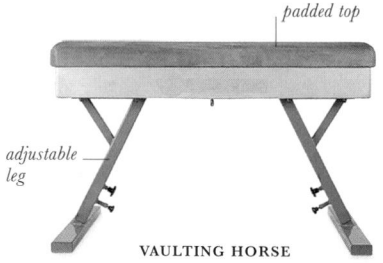

padded top

adjustable leg

VAULTING HORSE

vaunt /vawnt/ *v. & n. literary* ● *v.* **1** *intr.* boast. **2** *tr.* boast of; extol boastfully. ● *n.* a boast.

VC *abbr.* **1** vice-chairman. **2** vice-chancellor. **3** vice-consul. **4** Victoria Cross. **5** Vietcong.

V-chip /vée chip/ *n.* a computer chip installed in a television receiver that can be programmed to block offensive, esp. violent material.

VCR *abbr.* videocassette recorder.

VD *abbr.* venereal disease.

VDT *abbr.* video display terminal.

V-E *abbr.* Victory in Europe (in 1945).

've *abbr.* (chiefly after pronouns) = HAVE (*I've; they've*).

veal /veel/ *n.* calf's flesh as food.

vec·tor /véktər/ *n. & v.* ● *n.* **1** *Math. & Physics* a quantity having direction as well as magnitude. (cf. SCALAR. **2** a carrier of disease. **3** a course to be taken by an aircraft. ● *v.tr.* direct (an aircraft in flight) to a

---

VEGETABLE

Any edible part of a plant can be used as a vegetable. Derived from wild plants, many of the vegetables we use for food today have been in cultivation since prehistory. This long and extensive cultivation has led to vast diversity (there are more than 1,000 varieties of potato alone), but vegetables are generally grouped into leaf, fruiting, flowering, podded, stem, bulb, and root types. Despite their high water content (up to 80 percent), vegetables are a valuable source of protein, starch, vitamins, and minerals.

LEAF VEGETABLES

CURLY ENDIVE
(*Cichorium endivia*)

SPINACH
(*Spinacia oleracea*)

LETTUCE
(*Lactuca sativa*)

CHARD
(*Beta vulgaris*)

CABBAGE
(*Brassica oleracea*)

FRUITING AND FLOWERING VEGETABLES

CAULIFLOWER
(*Brassica oleracea*)

ARTICHOKE
(*Cynara scolymus*)

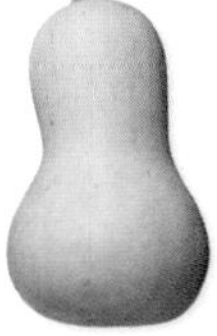

SQUASH
(*Caryoka nuciferum*)

ZUCCHINI
(*Cucurbita pepo*)

EGGPLANT
(*Solanum melongena*)

PODDED VEGETABLES

SNOW PEA
(*Pisum sativum*)

PEA
(*Pisum sativum*)

GREEN BEAN
(*Phaseolus vulgaris*)

RUNNER BEAN
(*Phaseolus coccineus*)

COWPEA
(*Vigna unguiculata*)

STEM, BULB, AND ROOT VEGETABLES

ASPARAGUS
(*Asparagus officinalis*)

POTATO
(*Solanum tuberosum*)

RADISH
(*Raphanus sativus*)

LEEK
(*Allium porrum*)

CARROT
(*Daucus carota*)

---

desired point. □□ **vec·to·ri·al** /-táwreeəl/ *adj.* **vec·tor·ize** *v.tr.* (in sense 1 of *n.*). **vec·tor·i·za·tion** /-tərīzáyshən/ *n.*

Ve·da /váydə, vée-/ *n.* (in *sing.* or *pl.*) the most ancient Hindu scriptures.

Ve·dan·ta /vidáantə, vedán-/ *n.* **1** the Upanishads. **2** the Hindu philosophy based on these, esp. in its monistic form. □□ **Ve·dan·tic** *adj.* **Ve·dan·tist** *n.*

V-E Day *n.* May 8, the day marking Victory in Europe in 1945.

Ve·dic /váydik, vée-/ *adj. & n.* ● *adj.* of or relating to the Veda or Vedas. ● *n.* the language of the Vedas, an older form of Sanskrit.

vee /vee/ *n.* **1** the letter V. **2** a thing shaped like a V.

vee·jay /véejay/ *n.* VIDEO JOCKEY.

veer /veer/ *v. & n.* ● *v.intr.* **1** change direction, esp. (of the wind) clockwise (cf. BACK *v.* 5). **2** change in course, opinion, conduct, emotions, etc. **3** *Naut.* = WEAR². ● *n.* a change of course or direction.

veg·an /véjən, véegən/ *n. & adj.* ● *n.* a person who does not eat or use animal products. ● *adj.* using or containing no animal products.

veg·e·ta·ble /véjtəbəl, véjitəbəl/ *n. & adj.* ● *n.* **1** *Bot.* ▲ any of various plants, esp. a herbaceous plant used for food, e.g., a cabbage, potato, or bean. **2** *colloq.* **a** a person who is incapable of normal intellectual activity, esp. through brain injury, etc. **b** a person lacking in animation or living a monotonous life. ● *adj.* **1** of, derived from, relating to, or comprising plants or plant life. **2** of or relating to vegetables as food.

V

veg·e·tal /véjit'l/ *adj.* of or relating to plants.

veg·e·tar·i·an /véjitáireeən/ *n. & adj.* ● *n.* a person who abstains from animal food, esp. that from slaughtered animals, though often not eggs and dairy products. ● *adj.* excluding animal food, esp. meat (*a vegetarian diet*). □□ **veg·e·tar·i·an·ism** *n.*

veg·e·tate /véjitayt/ *v.intr.* **1 a** live an uneventful or monotonous life. **b** spend time lazily or passively. **2** (of a plant) grow.

veg·e·ta·tion /véjitáyshən/ *n.* plants collectively; plant life. □□ **veg·e·ta·tion·al** *adj.*

veg·e·ta·tive /véjitaytiv/ *adj.* **1** concerned with growth and development as distinct from sexual reproduction. **2** of or relating to vegetation or plant life. □□ **veg·e·ta·tive·ly** *adv.*

veg·gie /véjee/ *n.* (also **veg·ie**) *colloq.* **1** a vegetable. **2** a vegetarian.

veg·gie burg·er /véjee bərgər/ *n.* (also *Trademark* **Veg·e·burg·er**) a savory patty resembling a hamburger but made with vegetable protein or soy instead of meat.

ve·he·ment /véeəmənt/ *adj.* showing or caused by strong feeling; forceful; ardent. □□ **ve·he·mence** /-məns/ *n.* **ve·he·ment·ly** *adv.*

ve·hi·cle /véeikəl/ *n.* **1** any conveyance for transporting people, goods, etc., esp. on land. **2** a medium for thought, feeling, or action (*the stage is the best vehicle for their talents*). **3** a liquid, etc., as a medium for suspending pigments, drugs, etc. □□ **ve·hic·u·lar** /veehíkyələr/ *adj.*

veil /vayl/ *n. & v.* ● *n.* **1** ◄ a piece of fine material attached to a woman's hat, etc., esp. to conceal the face or protect against the sun, dust, etc. **2** a piece of linen, etc., as part of a nun's headdress. **3** a curtain, esp. that separating the sanctuary in the Jewish temple. **4** a thing that conceals or disguises (*under the veil of friendship*; *a veil of mist*). **5** = VELUM. ● *v.tr.* **1** cover with a veil. **2** (esp. as **veiled** *adj.*) partly conceal (*veiled threats*). □ **beyond the veil** in the unknown state of life after death. **draw a veil over** avoid discussing or calling attention to. **take the veil** become a nun.

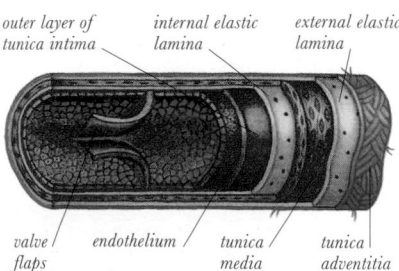

VEIL: 19TH-CENTURY WEDDING VEIL

vein /vayn/ *n. & v.* ● *n.* **1 a** ▼ any of the tubes by which blood is conveyed to the heart (cf. ARTERY). ▷ CARDIOVASCULAR. **b** (in general use) any blood vessel. **2** a nervure of an insect's wing. **3** a rib in the framework of a leaf. **4** a streak of a different color in wood, marble, cheese, etc. ▷ VEINING. **5** a fissure in rock filled with ore or other deposited material. **6** a source of a particular characteristic (*a rich vein of humor*). **7** a distinctive character or tendency; a cast of mind or disposition; a mood (*spoke in a sarcastic vein*). ● *v.tr.* fill or cover with or as with veins. □□ **vein·let** *n.* **vein·y** *adj.* (**veinier, veiniest**).

outer layer of tunica intima | internal elastic lamina | external elastic lamina

valve flaps | endothelium | tunica media | tunica adventitia

VEIN: SECTION REVEALING THE LAYERS OF A HUMAN VEIN

vein·ing /váyning/ *n.* ▶ a pattern of streaks or veins.

ve·la *pl.* of VELUM.

ve·lar /véelər/ *adj.* **1** of a veil or velum. **2** *Phonet.* (of a sound) pronounced with the back of the tongue near the soft palate.

Vel·cro /vélkrō/ *n. Trademark* a fastener consisting of two strips of fabric which adhere when pressed together. □□ **Vel·croed** *adj.*

veld /velt, felt/ *n.* (also **veldt**) *S.Afr.* open country; grassland.

vel·lum /véləm/ *n.* **1 a** fine parchment orig. from the skin of a calf. **b** a manuscript written on this. **2** smooth writing paper imitating vellum.

ve·loc·i·pede /vilósipeed/ *n.* **1** *hist.* an early form of bicycle propelled by pressure from the rider's feet on the ground. **2** a child's tricycle.

ve·loc·i·rap·tor /vilósiráptər/ *n.* ▼ a small bipedal carnivorous dinosaur of the genus Velociraptor, with an enlarged curved claw on each hind foot.

ve·loc·i·ty /vilósitee/ *n.* (*pl.* **-ies**) **1** the measure of the rate of movement of a usu. inanimate object in a given direction. **2** speed in a given direction. **3** (in general use) speed.

ve·lo·drome /véladrōm/ *n.* a special place or building with a track for cycling.

ve·lour /vəloor/ *n.* (also **ve·lours**) a plushlike woven fabric or felt.

ve·lou·té /vəlootáy/ *n.* a sauce made from a roux of butter and flour with chicken, veal, or fish stock.

ve·lum /véeləm/ *n.* (*pl.* **vela** /-lə/) a membrane, membranous covering, or flap.

vel·vet /vélvit/ *n. & adj.* ● *n.* **1** a closely woven fabric of silk, cotton, etc., with a thick short pile on one side. **2** the furry skin on a deer's growing antler. **3** anything smooth and soft like velvet. ● *adj.* of, like, or soft as velvet. □ **on** (or **in**) **velvet** in an advantageous or prosperous position. □□ **vel·vet·y** *adj.*

vel·vet·een /vélvitéen/ *n.* **1** a cotton fabric with a pile like velvet. **2** (in *pl.*) garments made of this.

vel·vet glove *n.* outward gentleness, esp. cloaking firmness or strength (cf. IRON HAND).

Ven. *abbr.* Venerable (as the title of an archdeacon).

ve·na ca·va /véena káyvə/ *n.* (*pl.* **venae cavae** /-nee -vee/) each of usu. two veins carrying blood into the heart. ▷ CARDIOVASCULAR, HEART

ve·nal /véenəl/ *adj.* **1** able to be bribed or corrupted. **2** characteristic of a venal person. □□ **ve·nal·i·ty** /-nálitee/ *n.*

ve·na·tion /vináyshən/ *n.* the arrangement of veins in a leaf or an insect's wing, etc., or the system of venous blood vessels in an organism. □□ **ve·na·tion·al** *adj.*

vend /vend/ *v.tr.* **1** offer (small wares) for sale. **2** *Law* sell.

ven·det·ta /vendétə/ *n.* **1 a** a blood feud in which the family of a murdered person seeks vengeance on the murderer or the murderer's family. **b** this practice as prevalent in Corsica and Sicily. **2** a prolonged bitter quarrel.

ven·deuse /voNdőz/ *n.* a saleswoman, esp. in a fashionable dress shop.

vend·ing ma·chine *n.* a machine that dispenses small articles for sale when a coin or token is inserted.

ven·dor /véndər/ *n.* **1** *Law* the seller in a sale. **2** = VENDING MACHINE.

gneiss   *granite vein*

VEINING IN METAMORPHIC ROCK

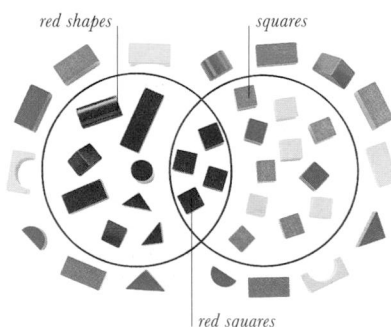

VELOCIRAPTOR (*Velociraptor* species)

curved claw

ve·neer /vineér/ *n. & v.* ● *n.* **1 a** a thin covering of fine wood or other surface material applied to a coarser wood. **b** a layer in plywood. **2** (often foll. by *of*) a deceptive outward appearance of a good quality, etc. ● *v.tr.* **1** apply a veneer to. **2** disguise (an unattractive character, etc.) with a more attractive manner, etc.

ven·er·a·ble /vénərəbəl/ *adj.* **1** entitled to veneration on account of character, age, associations, etc. (*a venerable priest*; *venerable relics*). **2** as the title of an archdeacon in the Church of England. **3** *RC Ch.* as the title of a deceased person who has attained a certain degree of sanctity but has not been fully beatified or canonized. □□ **ven·er·a·bil·i·ty** *n.* **ven·er·a·bly** *adv.*

ven·er·ate /vénərayt/ *v.tr.* **1** regard with deep respect. **2** revere on account of sanctity, etc. □□ **ven·er·a·tion** /-ráyshən/ *n.*

ve·ne·re·al /vinéereeəl/ *adj.* **1** of or relating to sexual desire or intercourse. **2** relating to venereal disease.

ve·ne·re·al dis·ease *n.* any of various diseases contracted chiefly by sexual intercourse with a person already infected.

ve·ne·re·ol·o·gy /vinéereeólajee/ *n.* the scientific study of venereal diseases. □□ **ve·ne·re·ol·o·gist** *n.*

Ve·ne·tian /vinéeshən/ *n. & adj.* ● *n.* **1** a native or citizen of Venice in NE Italy. **2** the Italian dialect of Venice. **3** (**venetian**) = VENETIAN BLIND. ● *adj.* of Venice.

ve·ne·tian blind *n.* a window blind of adjustable horizontal slats.

venge·ance /vénjəns/ *n.* punishment inflicted or retribution exacted for wrong to oneself or to a person, etc., whose cause one supports. □ **with a vengeance** in a higher degree than was expected or desired; in the fullest sense (*punctuality with a vengeance*).

venge·ful /vénjfŏŏl/ *adj.* vindictive; seeking vengeance. □□ **venge·ful·ly** *adv.* **venge·ful·ness** *n.*

ve·ni·al /véeneeəl/ *adj.* (of a sin or fault) pardonable; not mortal. □□ **ve·ni·al·ly** *adv.*

ven·i·son /vénisən, -zən/ *n.* a deer's flesh as food.

Venn di·a·gram /ven/ *n.* ▼ a diagram of usu. circular areas representing mathematical sets, the areas intersecting where they have elements in common.

red shapes   *squares*

red squares

VENN DIAGRAM SHOWING LOGICAL SETS OF COLORED SHAPES

ven·om /vénəm/ *n.* **1** a poisonous fluid secreted by snakes, scorpions, etc. ▷ FANG. **2** malignity; virulence of feeling, language, or conduct.

ven·om·ous /vénəməs/ *adj.* **1 a** containing, secreting, or injecting venom. **b** (of a snake, etc.) inflicting poisonous wounds by this means. **2** (of a person, etc.) virulent; spiteful; malignant. □□ **ven·om·ous·ly** *adv.* **ven·om·ous·ness** *n.*

ve·nous /véenəs/ *adj.* of, full of, or contained in veins.

V

vent[1] /vent/ *n. & v.* ● *n.* **1** an opening allowing motion of air, etc., out of or into a confined space. **2** an outlet; free passage or play (*gave vent to their indignation*). **3** the anus esp. of a lower animal, serving for both excretion and reproduction. **4** the venting of an otter, beaver, etc. **5** an aperture or outlet through which volcanic products are discharged at the Earth's surface. ▷ VOLCANO. **6** a touchhole of a gun. ● *v.* **1** *tr.* make a vent in (a cask, etc.). **b** provide (a machine) with a vent. **2** *tr.* give free expression to (*vented my anger on the cat*). **3** *intr.* (of an otter or beaver) come to the surface for breath. **4** *tr. & intr.* discharge. □ **vent one's spleen on** scold or ill-treat without cause.

vent[2] /vent/ *n.* a slit in a garment, esp. in the lower edge of the back of a coat.

ven·ti·late /vént'layt/ *v.tr.* **1** cause air to circulate freely in (a room, etc.). **2** submit (a question, grievance, etc.) to public consideration and discussion. **3** *Med.* **a** oxygenate (the blood). **b** admit or force air into (the lungs). □□ **ven·ti·la·tion** /-láyshən/ *n.*

ven·ti·la·tor /véntilaytər/ *n.* **1** an appliance or aperture for ventilating a room, etc. **2** *Med.* = RESPIRATOR 2.

ven·tral /véntrəl/ *adj.* **1** *Anat. & Zool.* of or on the abdomen (cf. DORSAL). **2** *Bot.* of the front or lower surface. □□ **ven·tral·ly** *adv.*

ven·tral fin *n.* ▼ either of the ventrally placed fins on a fish.

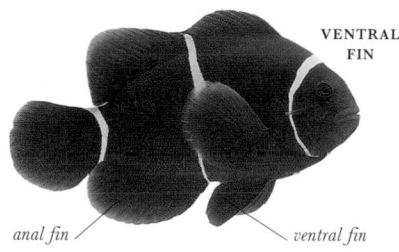

VENTRAL FIN

anal fin   *ventral fin*

ven·tri·cle /véntrikəl/ *n. Anat.* **1** a cavity in the body. **2** a hollow part of an organ, esp. in the brain or heart. ▷ BRAIN, HEART. □□ **ven·tric·u·lar** /-tríkyələr/ *adj.*

ven·tril·o·quism /ventríləkwizəm/ *n.* the skill of speaking or uttering sounds so that they seem to come from the speaker's dummy or a source other than the speaker. □□ **ven·tril·o·quial** /véntrilókweeəl/ *adj.* **ven·tril·o·quist** *n.* **ven·tril·o·quize** *v.intr.*

ven·tril·o·quy /ventríləkwee/ *n.* = VENTRILOQUISM.

ven·ture /vénchər/ *n. & v.* ● *n.* **1 a** an undertaking of a risk. **b** a risky undertaking. **2** a commercial speculation. ● *v.* **1** *intr.* dare; not be afraid (*did not venture to stop them*). **2** *intr.* (usu. foll. by *out*, etc.) dare to go. **3** *tr.* dare to put forward (an opinion, suggestion, etc.). **4 a** *tr.* expose to risk; stake (a bet, etc.). **b** *intr.* take risks. **5** *intr.* (foll. by *on*, *upon*) dare to engage in, etc. (*ventured on a longer journey*). □ **at a venture** at random; without previous consideration.

ven·ture cap·i·tal *n.* money put up for speculative business investment.

ven·tur·er /vénchərər/ *n. hist.* a person who undertakes or shares in a trading venture.

ven·ture·some /vénchərsəm/ *adj.* **1** disposed to take risks. **2** risky.

ven·tu·ri /ventŏŏree/ *n.* (*pl.* **venturis**) a short piece of narrow tube between wider sections for measuring flow rate or exerting suction.

ven·ue /vényōō/ *n.* **1** an appointed meeting place, esp. for a sports event, meeting, concert, etc. **2** a rendezvous.

ven·ule /vényōōl/ *n. Anat.* a small vein adjoining the capillaries. ▷ SKIN

VENUS

Venus is a rocky planet, slightly smaller than Earth, and probably with a similar internal structure of a partly molten metal core surrounded by a rocky mantle and crust. The planet's cloudy atmosphere reflects sunlight strongly, making Venus the brightest object in the sky after the Sun and Moon. The atmosphere is composed mainly of carbon dioxide, which traps heat and creates a maximum surface temperature of 896°F (480°C), making Venus the hottest planet in our solar system.

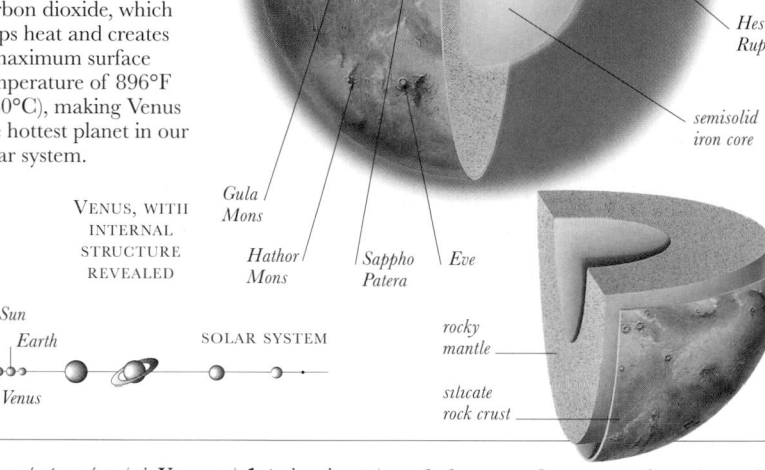

Akna Montes   Vesta Rupes   Cleopatra Patera   Maxwell Montes

Sif Mons   Dekla Tessera   Nefertiti Corona   Tellus Tessera   Pavlova   Hestia Rupes   semisolid iron core

VENUS, WITH INTERNAL STRUCTURE REVEALED

Gula Mons   Hathor Mons   Sappho Patera   Eve

Sun   Earth   Venus   SOLAR SYSTEM

rocky mantle   silicate rock crust

Ve·nus /véenəs/ *n.* (*pl.* **Venuses**) **1** ▲ the planet second from the Sun in the solar system. ▷ SOLAR SYSTEM. **2** *poet.* **a** a beautiful woman. **b** sexual love; amorous influences or desires. **Ve·nu·si·an** /vinŏŏshən, -sheeən, -zeeən, -nyŏŏ-/ *adj. & n.*

Ve·nus's fly·trap *n.* (also **Ve·nus fly·trap**) ◀ a carnivorous plant, *Dionaea muscipula*, with leaves that close on insects, etc.

trapped damselfly

marginal teeth

VENUS'S FLYTRAP (*Dionaea muscipula*)

ve·ra·cious /vəráyshəs/ *adj. formal* **1** speaking or disposed to speak the truth. **2** (of a statement, etc.) true or meant to be true.

ve·rac·i·ty /vərásitee/ *n.* **1** truthfulness; honesty. **2** accuracy (of a statement, etc.).

ve·ran·da /vərándə/ *n.* (also **ve·ran·dah**) an open, roofed porch.

ver·a·trine /vérətreen, -trin/ *n.* a poisonous compound used in the treatment of neuralgia and rheumatism.

verb /vərb/ *n. Gram.* a word used to indicate an action, state, or occurrence (e.g., *hear*, *become*, *happen*).

ver·bal /várbəl/ *adj. & n.* ● *adj.* **1** of or concerned with words (*made a verbal distinction*). **2** oral; not written (*gave a verbal statement*). **3** *Gram.* of or in the nature of a verb (*verbal inflections*). **4** literal (*a verbal translation*). **5** talkative; articulate. ● *n. Gram.* **1** a verbal noun. **2** a word or words functioning as a verb. □□ **ver·bal·ly** *adv.*

ver·bal·ism /várbəlizəm/ *n.* **1** minute attention to words. **2** merely verbal expression. □□ **ver·bal·ist** *n.* **ver·bal·is·tic** /-lístik/ *adj.*

ver·bal·ize /várbəlīz/ *v.* **1** *tr.* express in words. **2** *intr.* be verbose. **3** *tr.* make (a noun, etc.) into a verb. □□ **ver·bal·i·za·tion** *n.* **ver·bal·iz·er** *n.*

ver·bal noun *n. Gram.* a noun formed as an inflection of a verb and partly sharing its constructions (e.g., *smoking* in *smoking is forbidden*).

ver·ba·tim /vərbáytim/ *adv. & adj.* in exactly the same words (*copied it verbatim; a verbatim report*).

ver·be·na /vərbéenə/ *n.* ▶ any plant of the genus *Verbena*, bearing clusters of fragrant flowers.

ver·bi·age /várbeeij/ *n.* needless accumulation of words.

ver·bose /vərbós/ *adj.* using or expressed in more words than are needed. □□ **ver·bose·ly** *adv.* **ver·bose·ness** *n.* **ver·bos·i·ty** /-bósitee/ *n.*

ver·bo·ten /ferbót'n/ *adj.* forbidden, esp. by an authority.

VERBENA (*Verbena x hybrida* Romance Series)

verb sap /vərb sap/ *int.* nothing more needs to be said (from Latin *verbum sapienti* 'a word to the wise').

ver·dant /várd'nt/ *adj.* **1** (of grass, etc.) green, fresh-colored. **2** (of a field, etc.) covered with green grass, etc. **3** (of a person) unsophisticated; raw; green. □□ **ver·dan·cy** /-d'nsee/ *n.*

ver·dict /várdikt/ *n.* **1** a decision on an issue of fact in a civil or criminal cause or an inquest. **2** a decision; a judgment.

ver·di·gris /várdigrees, -gris, -gree/ *n.* **1 a** a green crystallized substance formed on copper by the action of acetic acid. **b** this used as a medicine or pigment. **2** ◀ green rust on copper or brass.

restored bowl   *verdigris*

VERDIGRIS ON A HALF-RESTORED COPPER BOWL

ver·dure /várjər/ *n.* **1** green vegetation. **2** the greenness of this.

V

verge[1] /vərj/ *n.* **1** an edge or border. **2** an extreme limit beyond which something happens (*on the verge of tears*). **3** *Archit.* an edge of tiles projecting over a gable. **4** a wand or rod carried before a bishop, dean, etc., as an emblem of office.

verge[2] /vərj/ *v.intr.* **1** incline downward or in a specified direction (*the now verging sun; verge to a close*). **2** (foll. by *on*) border on; approach closely (*verging on the ridiculous*).

ver·glas /váirglaá/ *n.* a thin coating of ice or frozen rain.

ver·i·fi·ca·tion /vérifikáyshən/ *n.* **1** the process or an instance of establishing the truth or validity of something. **2** *Philos.* the establishment of the validity of a proposition empirically. **3** the process of verifying procedures laid down in weapons agreements.

ver·i·fy /vérifī/ *v.tr.* (**-ies, -ied**) **1** establish the truth or correctness of by examination or demonstration (*must verify the statement; verified my figures*). **2** (of an event, etc.) bear out or fulfill (a prediction or promise). □□ **ver·i·fi·a·ble** *adj.* **ver·i·fi·er** *n.*

ver·i·ly /vérilee/ *adv. archaic* really; truly.

ver·i·si·mil·i·tude /vérisimílitoōd, -tyoōd/ *n.* **1** the appearance of being true or real. **2** a statement, etc., that seems true. □□ **ver·i·sim·i·lar** /-símilər/ *adj.*

ve·ris·mo /verízmō/ *n.* (esp. of opera) realism.

ver·i·ta·ble /véritəbəl/ *adj.* real; rightly so called (*a veritable feast*). □□ **ver·i·ta·bly** *adv.*

ver·i·ty /véritee/ *n.* (*pl.* **-ies**) **1** a true statement, esp. one of fundamental import. **2** truth. **3** a really existent thing.

ver·meil /vərmil, vərmáyl/ *n.* **1** (/vərmáy/) silver gilt. **2** an orange-red garnet. **3** *poet.* vermilion.

vermi- /vərmee/ *comb. form* worm.

ver·mi·cel·li /vərmichélee/ *n.* pasta made in long slender threads.

ver·mi·cide /vərmisīd/ *n.* a substance that kills worms.

ver·mic·u·lar /vərmíkyələr/ *adj.* **1** like a worm in form or movement. **2** *Med.* of or caused by intestinal worms. **3** marked with close wavy lines.

ver·mic·u·late /vərmíkyələt/ *adj.* **1** = VERMICULAR. **2** worm-eaten.

ver·mic·u·lite /vərmíkyəlīt/ *n.* ◄ a hydrous silicate mineral usu. resulting from alteration of mica, and expandable into sponge by heating, used as an insulation material.

VERMICULITE

ver·mi·form /vérmifawrm/ *adj.* worm-shaped.

ver·mi·fuge /vərmifyoōj/ *adj. & n.* ● *adj.* that expels intestinal worms. ● *n.* a drug that does this.

ver·mil·ion /vərmílyən/ *n. & adj.* ● *n.* **1** cinnabar. **2 a** ► a brilliant red pigment made by grinding this or artificially. **b** the color of this. ● *adj.* of this color.

VERMILION

ver·min /vərmin/ *n.* (usu. treated as *pl.*) **1** mammals and birds injurious to game, crops, etc. **2** parasitic worms or insects. **3** vile persons. □□ **ver·min·ous** *adj.*

ver·mi·vorous /vərmívərəs/ *adj.* feeding on worms.

ver·mouth /vərmoōth/ *n.* a wine flavored with aromatic herbs.

ver·nac·u·lar /vərnákyələr/ *n. & adj.* ● *n.* **1** the language or dialect of a particular country (*Latin gave place to the vernacular*). **2** the language of a particular clan or group. **3** plain, direct speech. ● *adj.* **1** (of language) of one's native country; not of foreign origin or of learned formation. **2** (of architecture) concerned with ordinary rather than monumental buildings. □□ **ver·nac·u·lar·ize** *v.tr.* **ver·nac·u·lar·ly** *adv.*

ver·nal /vərnəl/ *adj.* of, in, or appropriate to spring (*vernal equinox; vernal breezes*).

ver·nal e·qui·nox *n.* the time in Spring when there is equal hours of daylight and darkness; about March 20.

ver·nal·i·za·tion /vərnəlizáyshən/ *n.* the cooling of seed before planting, in order to accelerate flowering.

ver·nier /vərneeər/ *n.* ▼ a small, movable graduated scale for obtaining fractional parts of subdivisions on a fixed main scale of a barometer, sextant, etc.

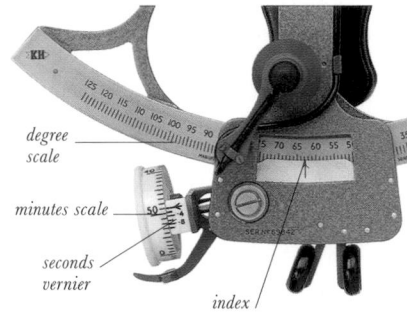

degree scale

minutes scale

seconds vernier

index

VERNIER ON A MODERN SEXTANT

Ve·ro·nal /vérənəl/ *n. Trademark* a sedative drug, a derivative of barbituric acid.

ve·ron·i·ca /vərónikə/ *n.* **1** ► any plant of the genus *Veronica* or *Hebe.* **2 a** a cloth supposedly impressed with an image of Christ's face. **b** any similar picture of Christ's face. **3** *Bullfighting* the movement of a matador's cape away from a charging bull.

ver·ru·ca /vərōōkə/ *n.* (*pl.* **verrucae** /-rōōsee/ or **verrucas**) a wart or similar growth. □□ **ver·ru·cose** /vérookōz/ *adj.*

ver·sa·tile /vərsət'l, -tīl/ *adj.* **1** turning easily or readily from one subject or occupation to another; capable of dealing with many subjects (*a versatile mind*). **2** having many uses. □□ **ver·sa·til·i·ty** /-tílitee/ *n.*

verse /vərs/ *n. & v.* ● *n.* **1 a** metrical composition in general (*wrote pages of verse*). **b** a particular type of

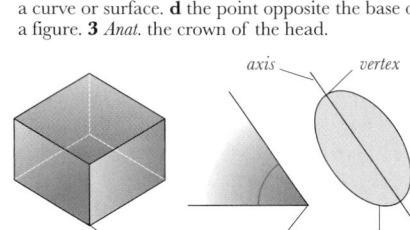

VERONICA
(*Veronica longifolia*)

this (*English verse*). **2 a** a metrical line in accordance with the rules of prosody. **b** a group of a definite number of such lines. **c** a stanza of a poem or song. **3** each of the short numbered divisions of a chapter in the Bible or other scripture. **4 a** a versicle. **b** a passage (of an anthem, etc.) for solo voice. ● *v.tr.* **1** express in verse. **2** (usu. *refl.*; foll. by *in*) instruct; make knowledgeable.

versed /vərst/ *predic.adj.* (foll. by *in*) experienced or skilled in; knowledgeable about.

ver·si·cle /vərsikəl/ *n.* each of the short sentences in a liturgy said or sung by a priest, etc., and alternating with responses.

ver·si·fy /vərsifī/ *v.* (**-ies, -ied**) **1** *tr.* turn into or express in verse. **2** *intr.* compose verses. □□ **ver·si·fi·ca·tion** /-fikáyshən/ *n.* **ver·si·fi·er** *n.*

ver·sion /vərzhən, -shən/ *n.* **1** an account of a matter from a particular person's point of view (*told them my version of the incident*). **2** a book, etc., in a particular edition or translation (*Authorized Version*). **3** a form or variant of a thing as performed, adapted, etc.

vers li·bre /vair léebrə/ = FREE VERSE.

ver·so /vərsō/ *n.* (*pl.* **-os**) **1 a** the left-hand page of an open book. **b** the back of a printed leaf of paper or manuscript (opp. RECTO). **2** the reverse of a coin.

verst /vərst/ *n.* a Russian measure of length, about 0.66 mile (1.1 km).

ver·sus /vərsəs, -səz/ *prep.* against (esp. in legal and sports use). ¶ Abbr.: **v., vs.**

ver·te·bra /vərtibrə/ *n.* (*pl.* **vertebrae** /-bray, -bree/) **1** ▼ each segment of the backbone. **2** (in *pl.*) the backbone. ▷ SKELETON. □□ **ver·te·bral** *adj.*

ver·te·brate /vərtibrət, -brayt/ *n. & adj.* ● *n.* ► any animal of the subphylum Vertebrata, having a spinal column. ● *adj.* of or relating to the vertebrates.

ver·tex /vərteks/ *n.* (*pl.* **vertices** /-tiseez/ or **vertexes**) **1** the highest point; the top or apex. **2** *Geom.* **a** ▼ each angular point of a polygon, polyhedron, etc. **b** ▼ a meeting point of two lines that form an angle. **c** ▼ the point at which an axis meets a curve or surface. **d** the point opposite the base of a figure. **3** *Anat.* the crown of the head.

axis   vertex

vertex

vertex   vertex   ellipse

VERTEX (2a)   **VERTEX (2b)**   **VERTEX (2c)**

V

VERTEBRA

There are three major types of vertebra in the human spine: lumbar, thoracic, and cervical. Lumbar vertebrae support a major part of the body's weight and so are comparatively large and strong. Thoracic vertebrae anchor the ribs. Cervical vertebrae support the head and neck.

TYPES OF VERTEBRA

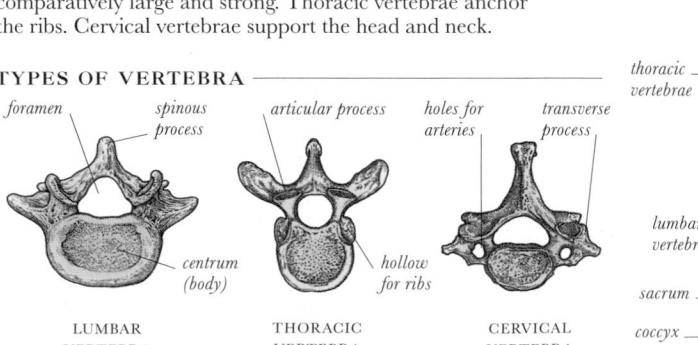

foramen   spinous process   articular process   holes for arteries   transverse process

centrum (body)   hollow for ribs

LUMBAR VERTEBRA   THORACIC VERTEBRA   CERVICAL VERTEBRA

SPINAL COLUMN   cervical vertebrae

thoracic vertebrae

lumbar vertebrae

sacrum

coccyx

VERTEBRATE

There are five classes of vertebrate: mammals, birds, fish, reptiles, and amphibians. In addition to the main defining feature (a backbone), vertebrates are characterized by an internal skeleton, a brain enclosed in a cranium, a closed circulatory system, and a heart with up to four chambers. Most vertebrates also have two pairs of limbs.

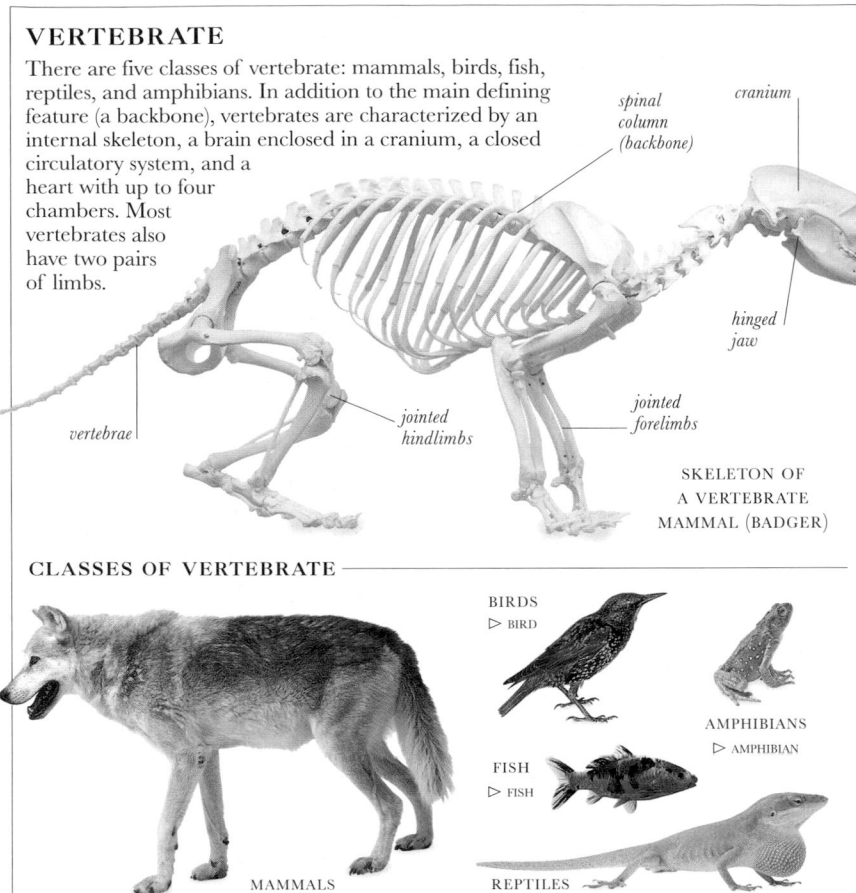

spinal column (backbone)

cranium

hinged jaw

jointed forelimbs

jointed hindlimbs

vertebrae

SKELETON OF A VERTEBRATE MAMMAL (BADGER)

CLASSES OF VERTEBRATE

BIRDS
▷ BIRD

FISH
▷ FISH

AMPHIBIANS
▷ AMPHIBIAN

MAMMALS
▷ MAMMAL

REPTILES
▷ REPTILE

ver·ti·cal /vártikəl/ *adj. & n.* ● *adj.* **1** at right angles to a horizontal plane; perpendicular. **2** in a direction from top to bottom of a picture, etc. **3** of or at the vertex or highest point. **4** at, or passing through, the zenith. **5** *Anat.* of or relating to the crown of the head. **6** involving all the levels in an organizational hierarchy or stages in the production of a class of goods (*vertical integration*). ● *n.* a vertical line or plane. □ **out of the vertical** not vertical. □□ **ver·ti·cal·i·ty** /-kálitee/ *n.* **ver·ti·cal·ly** *adv.*

ver·ti·cal take·off *n.* ▼ the takeoff of an aircraft directly upward.

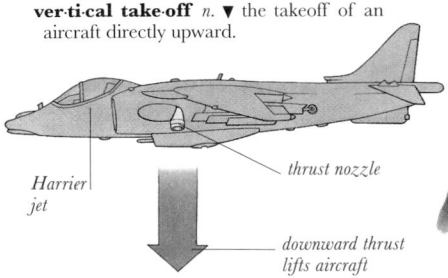

Harrier jet

thrust nozzle

downward thrust lifts aircraft

VERTICAL TAKEOFF OF A HARRIER JUMP JET

ver·tig·i·nous /vərtíjinəs/ *adj.* of or causing vertigo. □□ **ver·tig·i·nous·ly** *adv.*

ver·ti·go /vártigō/ *n.* a condition with a sensation of whirling and a tendency to lose balance; dizziness; giddiness.

ver·tu var. of VIRTU.

ver·vain /várvayn/ *n. Bot.* any of various herbaceous plants of the genus *Verbena*, esp. *V. officinalis*

with small blue, white, or purple flowers.

verve /vərv/ *n.* enthusiasm; vigor; spirit.

ver·vet /várvit/ *n.* ◄ a small, gray African monkey, *Cercopithecus aethiops*.

VERVET
(*Cercopithecus aethiops*)

ver·y /véree/ *adv. & adj.* ● *adv.* **1** in a high degree (*did it very easily; had a very bad cough; am very much better*). **2** in the fullest sense (foll. by *own* or *superl. adj.*: *at the very latest; do your very best; my very own room*). ● *adj.* **1** (usu. prec. by *the, this, his,* etc.) **a** actual; truly such (emphasizing identity, significance, or extreme degree: *the very thing we need; those were his very words*). **b** mere; sheer (*the very idea of it was horrible*). **2** *archaic* real; genuine (*very God*). □ **not very 1** in a low degree. **2** far from being. **the very same** see SAME.

ver·y high fre·quen·cy *n.* (of radio frequency) in the range 30–300 megahertz.

Ver·y light /véree, véeree/ *n.* a flare projected from a pistol for signaling or temporarily illuminating the surroundings.

Ver·y pis·tol *n.* ▶ a gun for firing a Very light.

VERY PISTOL:
EARLY 20TH-CENTURY
VERY PISTOL

chamber

extractor

stirrup

barrel

trigger

trigger guard

hammer

stock

butt

butt lanyard ring

ve·si·ca /vesíkə, vésikə/ *n.* **1** *Anat. & Zool.* a bladder. **2** (in full **vesica piscis** /písis/ or **piscium** /píseeəm/) *Art* a pointed oval used as an aureole in medieval sculpture and painting. □□ **ve·si·cal** *adj.*

ves·i·cate /-síkayt/ *v.tr.* raise blisters on. □□ **vesi·cant** /-kənt/ *adj. & n.* **ves·i·ca·tion** /-káyshən/ *n.* **ves·i·ca·tor·y** /-kətawree/ *adj. & n.*

ve·si·cle /vésikəl/ *n.* **1** *Anat., Zool., & Bot.* a small bladder, bubble, or hollow structure. **2** *Geol.* a small cavity in volcanic rock produced by gas bubbles. **3** *Med.* a blister. □□ **ve·sic·u·lar** /-síkyələr/ *adj.* **ve·sic·u·la·tion** /-láyshən/ *n.*

ves·per /véspər/ *n.* **1** Venus as the evening star. **2** *poet.* evening. **3** (in *pl.*) **a** the sixth of the canonical hours of prayer. **b** evensong.

ves·per·tine /véspərtīn, -tin/ *adj.* **1** *Bot.* (of a flower) opening in the evening. **2** *Zool.* active in the evening. **3** *Astron.* setting near the time of sunset. **4** of or occurring in the evening.

ves·pine /véspīn/ *adj.* of or relating to wasps.

ves·sel /vésəl/ *n.* **1** a hollow receptacle esp. for liquid. **2** a ship or boat, esp. a large one. **3 a** *Anat.* a duct or canal, etc., holding or conveying blood or other fluid, esp. = BLOOD VESSEL. **b** *Bot.* a woody duct carrying or containing sap, etc. **4** *Bibl.* or *joc.* a person regarded as the recipient or exponent of a quality (*a weak vessel*).

vest /vest/ *n. & v.* ● *n.* **1** a waist-length close-fitting, sleeveless garment, often worn under a suit jacket, etc. **2** *Brit.* an undershirt. **3** a usu. V-shaped piece of material to fill the opening at the neck of a woman's dress. ● *v.* **1** *tr.* (esp. in *passive*; foll. by *with*) bestow (powers, authority, etc.) on. **2** *tr.* (foll. by *in*) confer (property or power) on with an immediate fixed right of immediate or future possession. **3** *intr.* (foll. by *in*) (of property, a right, etc.) come into the possession of (a person).

ves·ta /vésta/ *n. hist.* a short wooden or wax match.

ves·tal /vést'l/ *adj. & n.* ● *adj.* **1** chaste; pure. **2** of or relating to the Roman goddess Vesta. ● *n.* **1** a chaste woman. **2** *Rom. Antiq.* a vestal virgin.

ves·tal vir·gin *n. Rom. Antiq.* ▶ a virgin consecrated to the goddess Vesta and vowed to chastity.

vest·ed in·ter·est *n.* **1** *Law* an interest (usu. in land or money held in trust) recognized as belonging to a person. **2** a personal interest in a state of affairs, usu. with an expectation of gain.

vest·ee /vestée/ *n.* = VEST *n.* 3.

ves·ti·bule /véstibyōōl/ *n.* **1 a** an antechamber, hall, or lobby next to the outer door of a building. **b** a porch of a church, etc. **2** an enclosed entrance to a railroad car. **3** *Anat.* **a** a chamber or channel communicating with others. **b** part of the mouth outside the teeth. **c** the central cavity of the labyrinth of the inner ear. □□ **ves·tib·u·lar** /-stíbyoolər/ *adj.*

VESTAL VIRGIN:
ANCIENT ROMAN
STATUE OF A
VESTAL VIRGIN

ves·tige /véstij/ *n.* **1** a trace or piece of evidence; a sign (*vestiges of an earlier civilization; found no vestige of their presence*). **2** a slight amount; a particle (*without a vestige of clothing*). **3** *Biol.* a part or organ of an organism that is reduced or functionless but was well developed in its ancestors.

ves·tig·i·al /vestíjeeəl, -jəl/ *adj.* **1** being a vestige or trace. **2** *Biol.* (of an organ) atrophied or functionless from the process of evolution (*a vestigial wing*). □□ **ves·tig·i·al·ly** *adv.*

V

VESTMENT: CATHOLIC
CEREMONIAL VESTMENTS

chasuble

bishop's miter

stole

priest's surplice

vest·ment /véstmənt/ *n.* **1** ▲ any of the official robes of clergy, choristers, etc., worn during divine service, esp. a chasuble. **2** a garment, esp. an official or state robe.

vest-pock·et *adj.* **1** small enough to fit into the pocket of a vest. **2** very small.

ves·try /véstree/ *n.* (*pl.* **-ies**) a room or building attached to a church for keeping vestments in. ▷ CHURCH

ves·ture /véschər/ ● *n. poet.* garments; dress.

vet[1] /vet/ *n. & v.* ● *n. colloq.* a veterinary surgeon. ● *v.tr.* (**vetted, vetting**) **1** make a careful and critical examination of (a scheme, work, candidate, etc.). **2** examine or treat (an animal).

vet[2] /vet/ *n. colloq.* a veteran.

vetch /vech/ *n.* any plant of the genus *Vicia*, esp. *V. sativa*, largely used for silage or fodder.

vetch·ling /véchling/ *n.* any of various plants of the genus *Lathyrus*, related to vetch.

vet·er·an /vétərən, vétrən/ *n.* **1** a person who has had long experience of an occupation (*a war veteran; a veteran of the theater; a veteran marksman*). **2** an exserviceman or servicewoman.

Vet·er·an's Day *n.* November 11, a legal holiday in the US, commemorating the end of World War I and of World War II, and honoring all veterans.

vet·er·i·nar·i·an /vétərináireeən, vétrə-/ *n.* a doctor who practices veterinary medicine or surgery.

vet·er·i·nar·y /vétərineree, vétrə-/ *adj. & n.* ● *adj.* of or for diseases and injuries of animals, or their treatment. ● *n.* (*pl.* **-ies**) = VETERINARIAN.

ve·to /véetō/ *n. & v.* ● *n.* (*pl.* **-oes**) **1 a** a constitutional right to reject a legislative enactment. **b** the right of a permanent member of the UN Security Council to reject a resolution. **c** such a rejection. **d** an official message conveying this. **2** a prohibition (*put one's veto on a proposal*). ● *v.tr.* (**-oes, -oed**) **1** exercise a veto against (a measure, etc.). **2** forbid authoritatively.

V

vex /veks/ *v.tr.* anger by a slight or a petty annoyance; irritate. □□ **vex·ing** *adj.*

vex·a·tion /veksáyshən/ *n.* **1** the act or an instance of vexing; the state of being vexed. **2** an annoying or distressing thing.

vex·a·tious /veksáyshəs/ *adj.* **1** such as to cause vexation. **2** *Law* not having sufficient grounds for action and seeking only to annoy the defendant. □□ **vex·a·tious·ly** *adv.*

vexed /vekst/ *adj.* **1** irritated; angered. **2** (of a problem, issue, etc.) much discussed; problematic. □□ **vex·ed·ly** /véksidlee/ *adv.*

VG *abbr.* **1** very good. **2** vicar-general.

VHF *abbr.* very high frequency.

VHS *abbr. Trademark* video home system (as used by domestic video recorders).

VI *abbr.* Virgin Islands.

vi·a /véeə, víə/ *prep.* by way of; through (*New York to Washington via Philadelphia; send it via your secretary*).

vi·a·ble /víəbəl/ *adj.* **1** (of a plan, etc.) feasible; practicable, esp. from an economic standpoint. **2 a** (of a plant, animal, etc.) capable of living or existing in a particular climate, etc. **b** (of a fetus or newborn child) capable of maintaining life. **3** (of a seed or spore) able to germinate. □□ **vi·a·bil·i·ty** /-bílitee/ *n.* **vi·a·bly** *adv.*

vi·a·duct /víədukt/ *n.* **1** ▼ a long bridge, esp. a series of arches, carrying a road or railroad across a valley or dip in the ground. **2** such a road or railroad.

VIADUCT: PUENTE NUEVO, SPAIN

Vi·a·gra /víágrə/ *n. Trademark* a synthetic compound used to enhance male potency.

vi·al /víəl/ *n.* a small (usu. cylindrical glass) vessel, esp. for holding medicines.

vi·and /víənd/ ● *n. formal* an article of food.

vi·at·i·cum /víátikəm/ *n.* (*pl.* **viaticums** or **viatica** /-kə/) **1** the Eucharist as given to a person near or in danger of death. **2** provisions or an official allowance of money for a journey.

vibes /víbz/ *n.pl. colloq.* **1** vibrations, esp. in the sense of feelings or atmosphere communicated (*the house had bad vibes*). **2** = VIBRAPHONE.

vi·brant /víbrənt/ *adj.* **1** vibrating. **2** (often foll. by *with*) thrilling; quivering (*vibrant with emotion*). **3** (of sound) resonant. **4** (of color) bright and vivid. □□ **vi·bran·cy** /-rənsee/ *n.* **vi·brant·ly** *adv.*

vi·bra·phone /víbrəfōn/ *n.* ▼ a percussion instrument of tuned bars set over motorized rotating vanes in tubular metal resonators, giving a vibrato effect. ▷ ORCHESTRA, PERCUSSION. □□ **vi·bra·phon·ist** *n.*

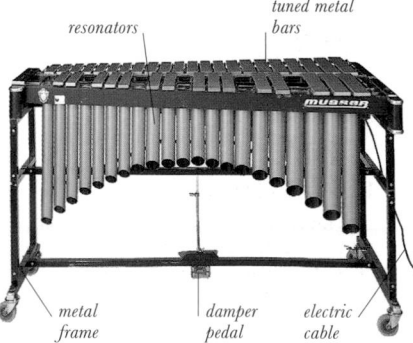

tuned metal bars

resonators

metal frame

damper pedal

electric cable

VIBRAPHONE

vi·brate /víbrayt/ *v.* **1** *intr. & tr.* move or cause to move continuously and rapidly to and fro. **2** *intr. Physics* move unceasingly to and fro. **3** *intr.* (of a sound) throb; continue to be heard. **4** *intr.* (foll. by *with*) quiver; thrill (*vibrating with passion*). **5** *intr.* (of a pendulum) swing to and fro.

vi·bra·tion /víbráyshən/ *n.* **1** the act or an instance of vibrating. **2** *Physics* motion to and fro. **3** (in *pl.*) a characteristic atmosphere or feeling in a place,

regarded as communicable to people present in it. □□ **vi·bra·tion·al** *adj.*

vi·bra·to /víbraátō/ *n. Mus.* a rapid slight variation in pitch in singing or playing a stringed or wind instrument, producing a tremulous effect (cf. TREMOLO).

vi·bra·tor /víbráytər/ *n.* **1** a device that vibrates or causes vibration, esp. an instrument used in massage or for sexual stimulation. **2** *Mus.* a reed in a reed organ.

vi·bra·to·ry /víbrətawree/ *adj.* causing vibration.

vi·bris·sae /víbrísee/ *n.pl.* **1** stiff coarse hairs near the mouth of most mammals (e.g., a cat's whiskers) and in the human nostrils. **2** bristlelike feathers near the mouth of insect-eating birds.

vi·bur·num /víbúrnəm, vee-/ *n. Bot.* ▶ any shrub of the genus *Viburnum*, usu. with white flowers.

vic·ar /víkər/ *n.* **1 a** (in the Church of England) an incumbent of a parish where tithes formerly passed to a chapter or religious house or layman (cf. RECTOR). **b** (in an Episcopal Church) a member of the clergy deputizing for another. **2** *RC Ch.* a representative or deputy of a bishop. □□ **vic·ar·i·ate** /-káreeət/ *n.*

VIBURNUM
(*Viburnum macrocephalum*)

vic·ar·age /víkərij/ *n.* the residence or benefice of a vicar.

vi·car·i·al /vikáireeəl/ *adj.* of or serving as a vicar.

vi·car·i·ous /vikáireeəs/ *adj.* **1** experienced in the imagination through another person (*vicarious pleasure*). **2** acting or done for another (*vicarious suffering*). **3** deputed; delegated (*vicarious authority*). □□ **vi·car·i·ous·ly** *adv.* **vi·car·i·ous·ness** *n.*

vice[1] /vís/ *n.* **1 a** evil or grossly immoral conduct. **b** a particular form of this, esp. involving prostitution, drugs, etc. **2 a** depravity; evil. **b** an evil habit; a particular form of depravity (*the vice of gluttony*). **3** a defect of character or behavior (*drunkenness was not among his vices*). **4** a bad habit in a horse, etc.

vice[2] *n. colloq.* = VICE PRESIDENT, VICE ADMIRAL, etc.

vice- *comb. form* forming nouns meaning: **1** acting as a substitute or deputy for (*vice chancellor*). **2** next in rank to (*vice admiral*).

vice ad·mi·ral /vís/ *n.* a naval officer ranking below admiral and above rear admiral.

vice-chan·cel·lor /vís-chánsələr/ *n.* a deputy chancellor, esp. of a university, discharging most of the administrative duties.

vice-ge·rent /vísjérənt/ *adj. & n.* ● *adj.* exercising delegated power. ● *n.* a vicegerent person; a deputy.

vice pres·i·dent /vís-prézidənt, -dent/ *n.* an official ranking below and deputizing for a president. □□ **vice pres·i·den·cy** *n.* (*pl.* **-ies**). **vice pres·i·den·tial** /-dénshəl/ *adj.*

vice·re·gal /vísréegəl/ *adj.* of or relating to a viceroy.

vice·roy /vísroy/ *n.* a ruler exercising authority on behalf of a sovereign in a colony, province, etc. □□ **vice·roy·al·ty** *n.*

vice squad *n.* a police department enforcing laws against prostitution, drug abuse, etc.

vice ver·sa /vísə vórsə, vís/ *adv.* with the order of the terms or conditions changed; the other way around (*could go from left to right or vice versa*).

vi·chys·soise /vísheeswáaz, vée-/ *n.* a creamy soup of leeks and potatoes.

Vi·chy wa·ter /víshee, -vée/ *n.* an effervescent mineral water from Vichy in France.

vic·i·nal /vísinəl/ *adj.* **1** neighboring; adjacent. **2** of a neighborhood; local.

vi·cin·i·ty /visínitee/ *n.* (*pl.* **-ies**) **1** a surrounding district. **2** (foll. by *to*) nearness. □ **in the vicinity** (often foll. by *of*) near (to).

vi·cious /víshəs/ *adj.* **1** bad-tempered; spiteful (*a vicious dog; vicious remarks*). **2** violent (*a vicious attack*). **3** of the nature of or addicted to vice. □□ **vi·cious·ly** *adv.* **vi·cious·ness** *n.*

vi·cis·si·tude /visísitoōd, -tyoōd/ *n.* a change of circumstances.

vic·tim /víktim/ *n.* **1** a person injured or killed (*a road victim*). **2** a person or thing injured or destroyed in pursuit of an object or in gratification of a passion, etc. (*the victim of their ruthless ambition*). **3** a prey; a dupe (*fell victim to a confidence scam*). **4** a living creature sacrificed to a deity or in a religious rite.

vic·tim·ize /víktimīz/ *v.tr.* single out for punishment or unfair treatment. □□ **vic·tim·i·za·tion** /-izáyshən/ *n.* **vic·tim·iz·er** *n.*

vic·tor /víktər/ *n.* a winner in battle or in a contest.

vic·to·ri·a /viktáwreeə/ *n.* **1** a low, light, four-wheeled carriage with a collapsible top, seats for two passengers, and a raised driver's seat. **2** a gigantic S. American water lily, *Victoria amazonica.* **3 a** a species of crowned pigeon. **b** a variety of domestic pigeon.

Vic·to·ri·a Cross *n.* ◀ a UK decoration awarded for bravery in the armed services, instituted by Queen Victoria in 1856.

Vic·to·ri·an /viktáwreeən/ *adj. & n.* ● *adj.* **1** of or characteristic of the time of Queen Victoria. **2** associated with attitudes attributed to this time, esp. of prudery and moral strictness. ● *n.* a person of this time. □□ **Vic·to·ri·an·ism** *n.*

Vic·to·ri·an·a /viktáwreeánə, -aánə/ *n.pl.* articles, esp. collectors' items, of the Victorian period.

vic·to·ri·ous /viktáwreeəs/ *adj.* **1** conquering; triumphant. **2** marked by victory (*victorious day*). □□ **vic·to·ri·ous·ly** *adv.*

vic·to·ry /víktəree/ *n.* (*pl.* **-ies**) **1** the process of defeating an enemy in battle or war or an opponent in a contest. **2** an instance of this; a triumph.

vict·ual /vít'l/ *n. & v.* ● *n.* (usu. in *pl.*) food; provisions. ● *v.* **1** *tr.* supply with victuals. **2** *intr.* obtain stores. **3** *intr.* eat victuals.

vict·ual·ler /vítlər/ *n.* (also **vict·ual·er**) **1** a person, etc., who supplies victuals. **2** a ship carrying stores for other ships.

vi·cu·ña /vikoōnə, -nyə, -kyoō-, vi-/ *n.* (also **vi·cu·na**) **1** a S. American mammal, *Vicugna vicugna,* related to the llama, with fine silky wool. **2 a** cloth made from its wool. **b** an imitation of this.

vi·de /vídee, veéday/ *v.tr.* (as an instruction in a reference to a passage in a book, etc.) see; consult.

vi·de·li·cet /vidéliset, vī-/ *adv.* = VIZ.

vid·e·o /vídeeō/ *adj., n., & v.* ● *adj.* **1** relating to the recording, reproducing, or broadcasting of visual images on magnetic tape or disk. **2** relating to the broadcasting of television pictures. ● *n.* (*pl.* **-os**) **1** the process of recording, reproducing, or broadcasting visual images on magnetic tape or disk. **2** a videocassette or videocassette recorder; a movie, etc., recorded on a videotape. ● *v.tr.* (**-oes**, **-oed**) make a video recording of.

vid·e·o·cam /vídeeōkam/ *n.* (also **vid·e·o·cam·er·a**) a camera for recording images on videotape.

vid·e·o·cas·sette /vídeeōkasét, -kəsét/ *n.* a cassette of videotape.

vid·e·o·cas·sette re·cord·er *n.* ▲ an apparatus for recording and playing videotapes.

vid·e·o·disc /vídeeōdisk/ *n.* (also **vid·e·o·disk**) a metal-coated disk on which visual material is recorded for reproduction on a television screen.

vid·e·o dis·play ter·mi·nal *n. Computing* a device

displaying data as characters on a screen and usu. incorporating a keyboard.

vid·e·o game *n.* a game played by manipulating images produced by a computer program on a television screen.

vid·e·o jock·ey *n.* a person who introduces music videos, as on television.

vid·e·o·phone /vídeeōfōn/ *n.* a telephone device transmitting a visual image as well as sound.

vid·e·o·tape /vídeeōtayp/ *n. & v.* ● *n.* magnetic tape for recording television pictures and sound. ● *v.tr.* record on videotape.

vie /vī/ *v.intr.* (**vying**) (often foll. by *with*) compete; strive for superiority (*vied with each other for recognition*).

Vi·en·nese /veéənéez/ *adj. & n.* ● *adj.* of, relating to, or associated with Vienna in Austria. ● *n.* (*pl.* same) a native or citizen of Vienna.

Vi·et·cong /veeətkóng/ *n.* the Communist guerrilla force in Vietnam which fought the South Vietnamese government forces (1954–75) and opposed the South Vietnam and US forces in the Vietnam War.

Vi·et·nam·ese /vee-étnəméez/ *adj. & n.* ● *adj.* of or relating to Vietnam in SE Asia. ● *n.* (*pl.* same) **1** a native or national of Vietnam. **2** the language of Vietnam.

vieux jeu /vyö zhö/ *adj.* old-fashioned; hackneyed.

view /vyoō/ *n. & v.* ● *n.* **1** range of vision (*came into view*). **2 a** what is seen from a particular point; a scene or prospect (*a room with a view*). **b** a picture, etc., representing this. **3** a visual or mental survey. **4** an opportunity for visual inspection; a viewing. **5 a** an opinion (*holds strong views on morality*). **b** a mental attitude (*took a favorable view of the matter*). **c** a manner of considering a thing (*took a long-term view of it*). ● *v.* **1** *tr.* survey visually; inspect (*we are going to view the house*). **2** *tr.* survey mentally (*different ways of viewing a subject*). **3** *tr.* form a mental impression or opinion of; consider (*does not view the matter in the same light*). **4** *intr.* watch television. □ **have in view 1** have as one's object. **2** bear (a circumstance) in mind in forming a judgment, etc. **in view of** considering. **on view** being shown; being exhibited. **with a view to 1** with the hope or intention of. **2** with the aim of attaining (*with a view to marriage*). □□ **view·a·ble** *adj.*

view·da·ta /vyoōdaytə, -datə/ *n.* a news and information service from a computer source to which a television screen is connected by telephone link.

view·er /vyoōər/ *n.* **1** a person who views. **2** a person watching television. **3** a device for looking at film transparencies, etc.

view·find·er /vyoōfīndər/ *n.* ▼ a device on a camera showing the area covered by the lens in taking a photograph.

VIDEOCASSETTE RECORDER

A VCR captures and replays television signals. A capstan feeds a magnetic tape past two heads: a video head to record pictures and an audio head to record sound. When the tape is replayed, the heads turn the signals back into audio and video signals and send them back to the television.

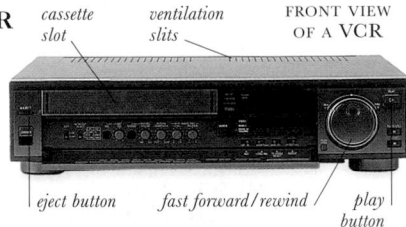

cassette slot
ventilation slits
FRONT VIEW OF A VCR
eject button
fast forward/rewind
play button

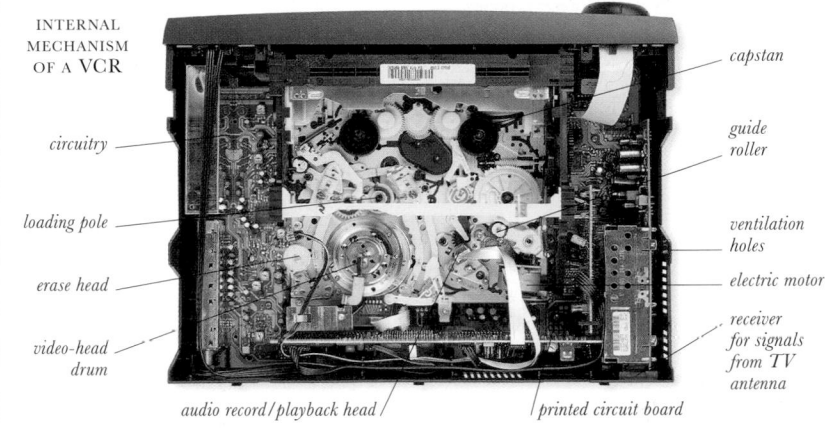

INTERNAL MECHANISM OF A VCR
circuitry
loading pole
erase head
video-head drum
audio record/playback head
printed circuit board
capstan
guide roller
ventilation holes
electric motor
receiver for signals from TV antenna

VIEWFINDER

A viewfinder allows the photographer to aim the camera accurately. The image seen through the viewfinder will be exactly the same as the one seen by the camera only if the light travels through the objective lens on its way to the user's eye (as in the SLR). The blue lines on the diagrams show how light travels through different viewfinders.

TYPES OF VIEWFINDER

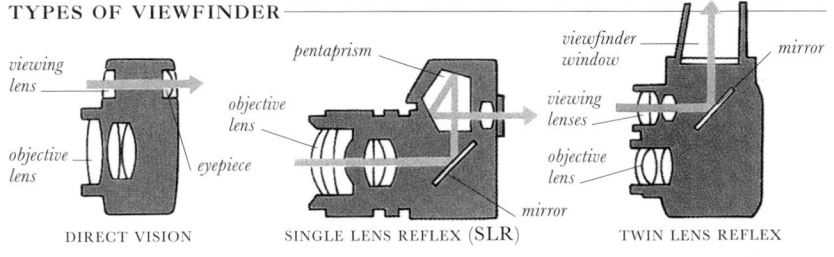

viewing lens
objective lens
eyepiece
DIRECT VISION

pentaprism
objective lens
mirror
SINGLE LENS REFLEX (SLR)

viewfinder window
mirror
viewing lenses
objective lens
TWIN LENS REFLEX

view·ing /vyóoing/ *n.* **1** an opportunity or occasion to view; an exhibition. **2** the act or practice of watching television.

view·point /vyóopoynt/ *n.* a point of view; a standpoint.

vi·ges·i·mal /vijésiməl/ *adj.* **1** of twentieths or twenty. **2** reckoning or reckoned by twenties.

vig·il /víjil/ *n.* **1 a** a keeping awake during the time usually given to sleep, esp. to keep watch or pray (*keep vigil*). **b** a period of this. **2** *Eccl.* the eve of a festival or holy day. **3** (in *pl.*) nocturnal devotions.

vig·i·lance /víjiləns/ *n.* watchfulness; caution.

vig·i·lant /víjilənt/ *adj.* watchful against danger, difficulty, etc. □□ **vig·i·lant·ly** *adv.*

vig·i·lan·te /víjilántee/ *n.* a member of a self-appointed body for the maintenance of order, etc.

vigne·ron /véenyəráwn/ *n.* a winegrower.

vi·gnette /vinyét/ *n. & v.* ● *n.* **1** a short descriptive essay or character sketch. **2** an illustration or decorative design. **3** a photograph or portrait showing only the head and shoulders with the background gradually shaded off. **4** a brief scene in a movie, etc. ● *v.tr.* **1** make a portrait of (a person) in vignette style. **2** shade off (a photograph or portrait).

vig·or /vígər/ *n.* **1** physical strength or energy. **2** a flourishing physical condition. **3** healthy growth. **4 a** mental strength or activity. **b** forcefulness; trenchancy; animation.

vig·or·ous /vígərəs/ *adj.* **1** strong and active; robust. **2** (of a plant) growing strongly. **3** forceful; acting or done with physical or mental vigor; energetic. **4** showing or requiring physical strength or activity. □□ **vig·or·ous·ly** *adv.* **vig·or·ous·ness** *n.*

vig·our *Brit.* var. of VIGOR.

vi·har·a /vihaárə/ ● *n.* a Buddhist temple or monastery.

iron helmet

noseguard

brooch

Vi·king /víking/ *n. & adj.* ● *n.* ◄ any of the Scandinavian seafaring pirates and traders who raided and settled in parts of NW Europe in the 8th–11th c. ● *adj.* of or relating to the Vikings or their time.

chain mail tunic

baldric (sword strap)

sword guard

wooden shield

iron sword

iron boss

leather shoes

VIKING
WARRIOR IN
CHAIN MAIL

vile /vīl/ *adj.* **1** disgusting. **2** depraved. **3** *colloq.* abominably bad (*vile weather*). □□ **vile·ly** *adv.* **vile·ness** *n.*

vil·i·fy /vílifī/ *v.tr.* (**-ies, -ied**) defame; speak evil of. □□ **vil·i·fi·ca·tion** /-fikáyshən/ *n.* **vil·i·fi·er** *n.*

vill /vil/ *n. hist.* a feudal township.

vil·la /vílə/ *n.* **1** *Rom. Antiq.* ▲ a large country house with an estate. **2** a country residence. **3** a rented holiday home, esp. abroad.

vil·lage /vílij/ *n.* **1 a** a group of houses and associated buildings, larger than a hamlet and smaller than a town, esp. in a rural area. **b** the inhabitants of a village regarded as a community. **2** a small

VILLA

Ancient Roman villas were usually self-supporting estates, at the heart of which was a large house. These houses generally consisted of a number of elaborately decorated rooms, set around courtyards and gardens.

atrium (courtyard) with skylight

front entrance

sloping tiled roof

frieze

triclinium (dining room)

peristyle

internal garden

fountain

reception room

frescoes

CUTAWAY VIEW
OF AN ANCIENT
ROMAN VILLA

municipality with limited corporate powers. □□ **vil·lag·er** *n.* **vil·lage·y** *adj.*

vil·lain /vílən/ *n.* **1** a person guilty or capable of great wickedness. **2** *colloq.* usu. *joc.* a rascal or rogue. **3** (also **vil·lain of the piece**) (in a play, etc.) a character whose evil actions or motives are important in the plot.

vil·lain·ous /vílənəs/ *adj.* **1** wicked. **2** *colloq.* abominably bad; vile (*villainous weather*). □□ **vil·lain·ous·ly** *adv.*

vil·lain·y /vílənee/ *n.* (*pl.* **-ies**) **1** villainous behavior. **2** a wicked act.

-ville /vil/ *comb. form colloq.* forming the names of fictitious places with ref. to a particular quality, etc. (*dragsville; squaresville*).

vil·lein /vílin, -ayn, viláyn/ *n. hist.* a feudal tenant entirely subject to a lord or attached to a manor.

vil·lus /víləs/ *n.* (*pl.* **villi** /-lī/) **1** *Anat.* ◄ each of the short, fingerlike processes on some membranes, esp. on the mucous membrane of the small intestine. ▷ DIGES-

epithelial layer

lacteal

mucus cell

vein

artery

lymph vessel

muscle layers

VILLUS:
SECTION THROUGH
AN INTESTINAL VILLUS

TION. **2** *Bot.* (in *pl.*) long, soft hairs covering fruit, flowers, etc. □□ **vil·liform** /víləfawrm/ *adj.* **vil·lose** /víl5s/ *adj.* **vil·losity** /-lósitee/ *n.* **vil·lous** /-əs/ *adj.*

vim /vim/ *n. colloq.* vigor.

VIN *abbr.* = vehicle identification number.

vi·na /véenə/ *n.* an Indian four-stringed musical instrument with a fretted fingerboard and a gourd at each end.

vin·ai·grette /vínigrét/ *n.* (in full **vinaigrette sauce**) a salad dressing of oil, vinegar, and seasoning.

vin·di·cate /víndikayt/ *v.tr.* **1** clear of blame or suspicion. **2** establish the existence, merits, or justice of. **3** justify. □□ **vin·di·ca·tion** káyshən/ *n.* **vin·di·ca·tor** *n.*

vin·di·ca·to·ry /víndikətawree/ *adj.* **1** tending to vindicate. **2** (of laws) punitive.

vin·dic·tive /víndiktiv/ *adj.* **1** tending to seek revenge. **2** spiteful. □□ **vin·dic·tive·ly** *adv.* **vin·dic·tive·ness** *n.*

vine /vīn/ *n.* **1** ▶ any climbing or trailing woody-stemmed plant, esp. of the genus *Vitis*, bearing grapes. **2** a slender trailing or climbing stem. □□ **vin·y** *adj.*

VINE
(*Vitis vinifera*)

grapes

VINIFICATION

Vinification starts when grapes are crushed or pressed, bringing the juice into contact with yeast cells on the skins. The grapes are macerated (usually only for red wine) to make free-run wine, and then pressed to extract the press wine. The resulting liquid may then be racked to separate out the lees. Final fermentation occurs in vats or casks.

STAGES IN THE VINIFICATION PROCESS

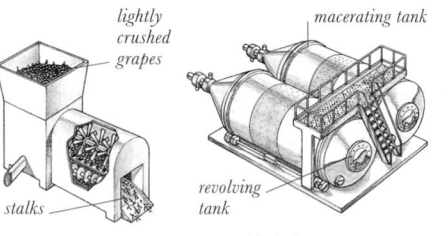

lightly crushed grapes

macerating tank

free-run wine

wooden casks

stalks

revolving tank

racking machine

CRUSHING

MACERATION

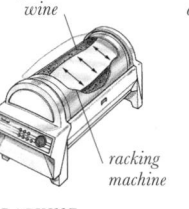

RACKING

FERMENTATION

V

vine·dress·er /víndréssər/ *n.* a person who prunes, trains, and cultivates vines.

vin·e·gar /vínigər/ *n.* **1** a sour liquid obtained from wine, cider, etc., by fermentation and used as a condiment or for pickling. **2** sour behavior or character. □□ **vin·e·gar·y** *adj.*

vin·er·y /vínəree/ *n.* (*pl.* **-ies**) **1** a greenhouse for grapevines. **2** a vineyard.

vine·yard /vínyərd/ *n.* a plantation of grapevines, esp. for wine-making.

vingt-et-un /vántayón/ *n.* = BLACKJACK.

vini- /vínee/ *comb. form* wine.

vin·i·cul·ture /vínikulchər/ *n.* the cultivation of grapevines.

vin·i·fi·ca·tion /vínifikáyshən/ *n.* ▼ the conversion of grape juice, etc., into wine.

vin·ing /víning/ *n.* the separation of leguminous crops from their vines and pods.

vi·no /véenō/ *n. sl.* wine, esp. a red Italian wine.

vin ordinaire /ván awrdináir/ *n.* inexpensive (usu. red) table wine.

vi·nous /vínəs/ *adj.* **1** of, like, or associated with wine. **2** addicted to wine. □□ **vi·nos·i·ty** /-nósitee/ *n.*

vin·tage /víntij/ *n. & adj.* ● *n.* **1 a** a season's produce of grapes. **b** the wine made from this. **2 a** the gathering of grapes for winemaking. **b** the season of this. **3** a wine of high quality from a single identified year and district. **4 a** the year, etc., when a thing was made, etc. **b** a thing made, etc., in a particular year, etc. ● *adj.* **1** of high quality, esp. from the past or characteristic of the best period of a person's work. **2** of a past season.

vin·tage car *n.* an automobile made in the early part of the twentieth century.

vint·ner /víntnər/ *n.* a wine merchant.

vin·y see VINE.

vi·nyl /vínəl/ *n.* any plastic made by polymerizing a compound containing the vinyl group.

vi·ol /víəl/ *n.* ▶ a stringed musical instrument of the Renaissance, played with a bow and held vertically on the knees or between the legs.

vi·o·la[1] /vee-ólə/ *n.* **1 a** an instrument of the violin family, larger than the violin and of lower pitch. **b** a viola player. **2** a viol. ▷ ORCHESTRA, STRINGED

vi·o·la[2] /vī-ólə, vee-, víələ/ *n.* **1** any plant of the genus *Viola*, including the pansy and violet. **2** a cultivated hybrid of this genus.

vi·o·la·ceous /víəláyshəs/ ● *adj.* **1** of a violet color. **2** *Bot.* of the violet family Violaceae.

vi·o·late /víəlayt/ *v.tr.* **1** disregard; fail to comply with (an oath, treaty, law, etc.). **2** treat (a sanctuary, etc.) profanely or with disrespect. **3** disturb (a person's privacy, etc.). **4** rape. □□ **vi·o·la·tion** /-láyshən/ *n.* **vi·o·la·tor** *n.*

vi·o·lence /víələns/ *n.* **1** the quality of being violent. **2** violent conduct or treatment. **3** *Law* **a** the unlawful exercise of physical force. **b** intimidation by the exhibition of this. □ **do violence to 1** act contrary to; outrage. **2** distort.

vi·o·lent /víələnt/ *adj.* **1** involving or using great physical force (*a violent person; a violent storm*). **2 a** intense; vehement; passionate; furious (*a violent contrast; violent dislike*). **b** vivid (*violent colors*). **3** (of death) resulting from external force or from poison (cf. NATURAL *adj.* 2). **4** involving an unlawful exercise of force (*laid violent hands on him*). □□ **vi·o·lent·ly** *adv.*

vi·o·let /víələt/ *n. & adj.* ● *n.* **1 a** any plant of the genus *Viola*, esp. the sweet violet, with usu. purple, blue, or white flowers. **b** any of various plants resembling the sweet violet. **2** the bluish-purple color seen at the end of the spectrum opposite red. **3 a** pigment of this color. **b** clothes or material of this color. ● *adj.* of this color.

fingerboard

tuning peg

sound-hole

VIOL: 18TH-CENTURY BRITISH VIOL

vi·o·lin /víəlín/ *n.* **1** a musical instrument with four strings of treble pitch played with a bow. ▷ ORCHESTRA, STRINGED. **2** a violin player. □□ **vi·o·lin·ist** *n.*

vi·ol·ist[1] /víəlist/ *n.* a viol player.

vi·ol·ist[2] /vee-ólist/ *n.* a viola player.

vi·o·lon·cel·lo /véeələnchélō, ví-/ *n.* (*pl.* **os**) *formal* = CELLO. ▷ ORCHESTRA, STRINGED. □□ **vi·o·lon·cel·list** *n.*

vi·o·lo·ne /veeəlónay/ *n.* a double bass.

VIP *abbr.* very important person.

vi·per /vípər/ *n.* **1** ▼ any venomous snake of the family Viperidae, esp. the common viper (see ADDER). ▷ SNAKE. **2** a malignant or treacherous person. □□ **vi·per·ish** *adj.* **vi·per·ous** *adj.*

VIPER: GABOON VIPER (*Vipera gabonica*)

vi·ra·go /viráːgō, -ráygō/ *n.* (*pl.* **-os**) a fierce or abusive woman.

vi·ral /vírəl/ *adj.* of or caused by a virus. □□ **vi·ral·ly** *adv.*

vir·e·lay /vírilay/ ● *n.* a short (esp. old French) lyric poem with two rhymes to a stanza variously arranged.

vir·e·o /víreeō/ *n.* (*pl.* **-os**) any small American songbird of the family Vireonidae.

Vir·gil·i·an /vərjíleeən/ *adj.* of, or in the style of, the Roman poet Virgil (d. 19 BC).

vir·gin /vórjin/ *n. & adj.* ● *n.* **1** a person (esp. a woman) who has never had sexual intercourse. **2 a** (**the Virgin**) Christ's mother the Blessed Virgin Mary. **b** a picture or statue of the Virgin. **3** (**the Virgin**) the zodiacal sign or constellation Virgo. **4** *colloq.* a naïve, innocent, or inexperienced person (*a political virgin*). **5** a member of any order of women under a vow to remain virgins. **6** a female insect producing eggs without impregnation. ● *adj.* **1** that is a virgin. **2** of or befitting a virgin (*virgin modesty*). **3** not yet used, penetrated, or tried (*virgin soil*). **4** undefiled; spotless. **5** (of clay) not fired. **6** (of metal) made from ore by smelting. **7** (of wool) not yet, or only once, spun or woven. **8** (of olive oil, etc.) obtained from the first pressing of olives, etc.

vir·gin·al /vórjinəl/ *adj. & n.* ● *adj.* that is or befits or belongs to a virgin. ● *n.* (usu. in *pl.*) (in full **pair of virginals**) an early form of spinet in a box. □□ **vir·gin·al·ly** *adv.*

Vir·gin·ia /vərjínyə/ *n.* **1** tobacco from Virginia. **2** a cigarette made of this. □□ **Vir·gin·ian** *n. & adj.*

Vir·gin·ia creep·er *n.* a N. American vine, *Parthenocissus quinquefolia*, cultivated for ornament.

Vir·gin·ia reel *n.* a country dance.

vir·gin·i·ty /vərjínitee/ *n.* the state of being a virgin.

Vir·go /vórgō/ *n.* (*pl.* **-os**) **1** ▶ a constellation, traditionally regarded as contained in the figure of a woman. **2 a** the sixth sign of the zodiac (the Virgin). ▷ ZODIAC. **b** a person born when the Sun is in this sign. □□ **Vir·go·an** *n. & adj.*

vir·gule /vórgyool/ ● *n.* **1** a slanting line used to mark division of words or lines. **2** = SOLIDUS 1.

vir·i·des·cent /víridésənt/ *adj.* greenish, tending to become green. □□ **vir·i·des·cence** /-səns/ *n.*

vir·id·i·an /virídeeən/ *n. & adj.* ● *n.* **1** a bluish-green chromium oxide pigment. **2** the color of this. ● *adj.* bluish-green.

vir·ile /vírəl, -īl/ *adj.* **1** of or characteristic of a man; having masculine (esp. sexual) vigor or strength. **2** of or having procreative power. **3** of a man as distinct from a woman or child. □□ **vi·ril·i·ty** /virílitee/ *n.*

vi·rol·o·gy /vīróləjee/ *n.* the scientific study of viruses. □□ **vi·ro·log·i·cal** /-rəlójikəl/ *adj.* **vi·rol·o·gist** *n.*

vir·tu /vərtóō/ ● *n.* (also **vertu**) **1** a knowledge of or expertise in the fine arts. **2** virtuosity. □ **article** (or **object**) **of virtu** an article interesting because of its workmanship, antiquity, rarity, etc.

vir·tu·al /vórchōōəl/ *adj.* **1** that is such for practical purposes though not in name or according to strict definition (*is the virtual manager of the business*). **2** *Optics* relating to the points at which rays would meet if produced backward (*virtual focus; virtual image*). **3** *Mech.* relating to an infinitesimal displacement of a point in a system. **4** *Computing* not physically existing as such but made by software to appear to do so (*virtual memory*). □□ **vir·tu·al·i·ty** /-álitee/ *n.* **vir·tu·al·ly** *adv.*

vir·tu·al re·al·i·ty *n.* ▼ the generation by computer software of an image or environment that appears real to the senses.

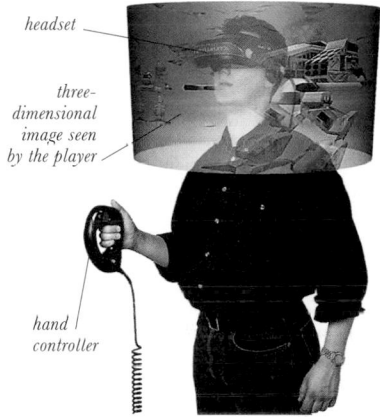

headset

three-dimensional image seen by the player

hand controller

VIRTUAL REALITY: PLAYER USING A HEADSET AND HAND CONTROLLER

vir·tue /vórchōō/ *n.* **1** moral excellence; goodness. **2** a particular form of this (*patience is a virtue*). **3** chastity, esp. of a woman. **4** a good quality (*has the virtue of being adjustable*). **5** efficacy (*no virtue in such drugs*). □ **by** (or **in**) **virtue of** on the strength or ground of (*got the job by virtue of his experience*). **make a virtue of necessity** derive some credit or benefit from an unwelcome obligation.

vir·tu·o·so /vórchōō-ōsō, -zō/ *n.* (*pl.* **virtuosi** /-see, -zee/ or **-os**) **1 a** a person highly skilled in the technique of a fine art, esp. music. **b** (*attrib.*) displaying the skills of a virtuoso. **2** a person with a special knowledge of or taste for works of art. □□ **vir·tu·os·ic** /-ósik/ *adj.* **vir·tu·os·i·ty** /-ósitee/ *n.*

vir·tu·ous /vórchōōəs/ *adj.* **1** possessing or showing moral rectitude. **2** chaste. □□ **vir·tu·ous·ly** *adv.* **vir·tu·ous·ness** *n.*

vir·u·lent /víryələnt, vírə-/ *adj.* **1** strongly poisonous. **2** (of a disease) violent. **3** bitterly hostile. □□ **vir·u·lence** /-ləns/ *n.* **vir·u·lent·ly** *adv.*

Spica

VIRGO: FIGURE OF A WOMAN FORMED FROM THE STARS OF VIRGO

V

vi·rus /vírəs/ *n.* **1** ▼ a microscopic organism consisting mainly of nucleic acid in a protein coat, multiplying only in living cells and often causing diseases. **2** *Computing* = COMPUTER VIRUS. **3** a harmful or corrupting influence.

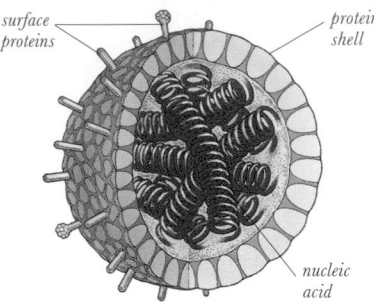

surface proteins — protein shell — nucleic acid

VIRUS: TYPICAL STRUCTURE OF A VIRUS

Vis. *abbr.* **1** Viscount. **2** Viscountess.

vi·sa /véezə/ *n. & v.* ● *n.* an endorsement on a passport, etc., showing that it has been found correct, esp. as allowing the holder to enter or leave a country. ● *v.tr.* (**visas, visaed** /-zəd/, **visaing**) mark with a visa.

vis·age /vízij/ *n.* literary a face. □□ **vis·aged** *adj.* (also in *comb.*).

vis-à-vis /véezaavée/ *prep., adv., & n.* ● *prep.* **1** in relation to. **2** opposite to. ● *adv.* facing one another. ● *n.* (*pl.* same) **1** a person or thing facing another, esp. in some dances. **2** a person occupying a corresponding position in another group. **3** a social partner.

Visc. *abbr.* **1** Viscount. **2** Viscountess.

vis·ca·cha /viskáachə/ *n.* (also **viz·ca·cha** /viz-/) any S. American burrowing rodent of the genus *Lagidium*, having valuable fur.

vis·cer·a /vísərə/ *n.pl.* the interior organs in the great cavities of the body (e.g., brain, heart, liver), esp. in the abdomen (e.g., the intestines).

vis·cer·al /vísərəl/ *adj.* **1** of the viscera. **2** relating to inward feelings rather than conscious reasoning. □□ **vis·cer·al·ly** *adv.*

vis·cid /vísid/ *adj.* **1** glutinous; sticky. **2** semifluid.

vis·com·e·ter /viskómitər/ *n.* an instrument for measuring the viscosity of liquids.

vis·cose /vískōs/ *n.* **1** a form of cellulose in a highly viscous state suitable for drawing into yarn. **2** rayon made from this.

vis·cos·i·ty /viskósitee/ *n.* (*pl.* **-ies**) **1** the quality or degree of being viscous. **2** *Physics* **a** (of a fluid) internal friction; the resistance to flow. **b** a quantity expressing this.

vis·count /víkownt/ *n.* a British nobleman ranking between an earl and a baron. □□ **vis·count·cy** /-kówntsee/ *n.* (*pl.* **-ies**).

vis·count·ess /víkowntis/ *n.* **1** a viscount's wife or widow. **2** a woman holding the rank of viscount in her own right.

vis·cous /vískəs/ *adj.* **1** glutinous; sticky. **2** semifluid. **3** *Physics* having a high viscosity; not flowing freely. □□ **vis·cous·ly** *adv.*

vis·cus /vískəs/ *n.* (*pl.* **vis·cera** /vísərə/) (usu. in *pl.*) any of the soft internal organs of the body.

vise /vīs/ *n. & v.* ● *n.* ▶ an instrument, esp. attached to a work-bench, with two movable jaws between which an object may be clamped so as to leave the hands free to work on it. ● *v.tr.* secure in a vise. □□ **vise·like** *adj.*

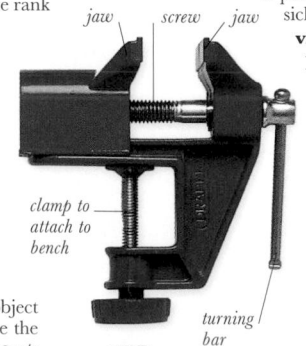

jaw — screw — jaw — clamp to attach to bench — turning bar

VISE: BENCH VISE

Vish·nu /víshnoo/ *n.* a Hindu god regarded by his worshipers as the supreme deity and savior, by others as the second member of a triad with Brahma and Siva. □□ **Vish·nu·ism** *n.*

vis·i·bil·i·ty /vízibilitee/ *n.* **1** the state of being visible. **2** the range or possibility of vision as determined by the conditions of light and atmosphere (*visibility was down to 50 yards*).

vis·i·ble /vízibəl/ *adj.* **1 a** that can be seen. **b** (of light) within the range of wavelengths to which the eye is sensitive. **2** that can be perceived or ascertained (*has no visible means of support; spoke with visible impatience*). **3** (of exports, etc.) consisting of actual goods rather than services, etc. □□ **vis·i·ble·ness** *n.* **vis·i·bly** *adv.*

Vis·i·goth /vízigoth/ *n.* a West Goth, a member of the branch of the Goths who settled in France and Spain in the 5th c. and ruled much of Spain until 711.

vi·sion /vízhən/ *n. & v.* ● *n.* **1** the act or faculty of seeing; sight. **2 a** a thing or person seen in a dream or trance. **b** a supernatural or prophetic apparition. **3** a thing or idea perceived vividly in the imagination (*visions of sandy beaches*). **4** imaginative insight. **5** statesmanlike foresight. **6** a person, etc., of unusual beauty. **7** what is seen on a television screen; television images collectively. ● *v.tr.* see or present in or as in a vision. □□ **vi·sion·less** *adj.*

vi·sion·ar·y /vízhəneree/ *adj. & n.* ● *adj.* **1** informed or inspired by visions; indulging in fanciful theories. **2** existing in or characteristic of a vision or the imagination. **3** not practicable. ● *n.* (*pl.* **-ies**) a visionary person.

vis·it /vízit/ *v. & n.* ● *v.* (**visited, visiting**) **1** *tr.* (also *absol.*) go or come to see (a person, place, etc.). **2** *tr.* reside temporarily with (a person) or at (a place). **3** *intr.* be a visitor. **4** *tr.* (of a disease, calamity, etc.) come upon; attack. **5** *tr. Bibl.* **a** (foll. by *with*) punish (a person). **b** (often foll. by *upon*) inflict punishment for (a sin). **6** *intr.* **a** (foll. by *with*) go to see (a person) esp. socially. **b** (usu. foll. by *with*) converse; chat. ● *n.* **1 a** an act of visiting. **b** temporary residence. **2** (foll. by *to*) an occasion of going to a doctor, dentist, etc. **3** a formal or official call for the purpose of inspection, etc. **4** a chat. □□ **vis·it·a·ble** *adj.*

vis·it·ant /vízit'nt/ *n.* **1** a visitor, esp. a supposedly supernatural one. **2** = VISITOR 2.

vis·it·a·tion /vízitáyshən/ *n.* **1** an official visit of inspection. **2** trouble or difficulty regarded as a divine punishment. **3** (**Visitation**) **a** the visit of the Virgin Mary to Elizabeth related in Luke 1:39–56. **b** the festival commemorating this on July 2. **4** the boarding of a vessel belonging to another nation to learn its character and purpose. **5** the instance of a parent using his or her visitation rights.

vis·it·a·tion rights *n.pl.* legal right of a noncustodial parent to visit or have temporary custody of his or her child.

vis·it·ing /víziting/ *n. & adj.* ● *n.* paying a visit or visits. ● *attrib.adj.* (of an academic) spending some time at another institution (*a visiting professor*).

vis·it·ing nurse *n.* a nurse, often employed by a public health agency, who visits the sick at home.

vis·i·tor /vízitər/ *n.* **1** a person who visits. **2** a migratory bird present in a locality for part of the year (*winter visitor*).

vi·sor /vízər/ *n.* **1 a** ▶ a movable part of a helmet covering the face. ▷ SPACESUIT. **b** the projecting front part of a cap. **2** a shield to protect the eyes from unwanted light, esp. one at the top of a vehicle windshield. □□ **vi·sored** *adj.*

VISTA IN THE BOBOLI GARDENS, FLORENCE, ITALY

vis·ta /vístə/ *n.* **1** ▲ a long, narrow view as between rows of trees. **2** a mental view of a long succession of events (*opened up new vistas to his ambition*).

vis·u·al /vízhōōəl/ *adj. & n.* ● *adj.* of, concerned with, or used in seeing. ● *n.* (usu. in *pl.*) a visual image or display; a picture. □□ **vis·u·al·ly** *adv.*

vis·u·al aid *n.* a movie, model, etc., as an aid to learning.

vis·u·al·ize /vízhōōəlīz/ *v.tr.* **1** make visible, esp. to one's mind (a thing not visible to the eye). **2** make visible to the eye. □□ **vis·u·al·iz·a·ble** *adj.* **vis·u·al·i·za·tion** /-izáyshən/ *n.*

vi·tal /vít'l/ *adj. & n.* ● *adj.* **1** of, concerned with, or essential to organic life (*vital functions*). **2** essential to the existence of a thing or to the matter in hand (*a vital question; secrecy is vital*). **3** full of life or activity. **4** affecting life. **5** fatal to life or to success, etc. (*a vital error*). **6** *disp.* important. ● *n.* (in *pl.*) the body's vital organs, e.g., the heart and brain.

vi·tal·ism /vít'lizəm/ *n. Biol.* the doctrine that life originates in a vital principle distinct from chemical and other physical forces. □□ **vi·tal·ist** *n.* **vi·tal·is·tic** *adj.*

vi·tal·i·ty /vītálitee/ *n.* **1** liveliness; animation. **2** the ability to sustain life. **3** (of an institution, language, etc.) the ability to endure and to perform its functions.

vi·tal·ize /vít'līz/ *v.tr.* **1** endow with life. **2** infuse with vigor.

vi·tal·ly /vít'lee/ *adv.* essentially; indispensably.

vi·tal signs *n.pl.* pulse rate, rate of respiration, and body temperature considered as signs of life.

vi·tal sta·tis·tics *n.pl.* **1** the number of births, marriages, deaths, etc. **2** *colloq.* the measurements of a woman's bust, waist, and hips.

vi·ta·min /vítəmin/ *n.* ▶ any of a group of organic compounds essential in small amounts for many living organisms to maintain normal health and development.

vi·ta·min A *n.* = RETINOL.

vi·ta·min B com·plex *n.* any of a group of vitamins which, although not chemically related, are often found together in the same foods.

vi·ta·min B$_1$ *n.* = THIAMINE.

vi·ta·min B$_2$ *n.* = RIBOFLAVIN.

vi·ta·min B$_6$ *n.* = PYRIDOXINE.

vi·ta·min B$_{12}$ *n.* = CYANOCOBALAMIN.

vi·ta·min C *n.* = ASCORBIC ACID.

lifting pin — visor — breathing vents

VISOR: 16TH-CENTURY VISORED HELMET

V

vi·ta·min D *n.* any of a group of vitamins found in liver and fish oils, essential for the absorption of calcium and the prevention of rickets in children and osteomalacia in adults.

vi·ta·min E *n.* = TOCOPHEROL.

vi·ta·min·ize /vítəminīz/ *v.tr.* add vitamins to.

vi·ta·min K *n.* any of a group of vitamins found mainly in green leaves and essential for the blood-clotting process.

vit·el·lin /vítélin, vī-/ *n. Chem.* the chief protein constituent of the yolk of egg.

vit·el·line /vítélin, -leen, vī-/ *adj.* of the vitellus.

vit·el·line mem·brane *n.* the yolk sac.

vit·el·lus /vítéləs, vī-/ *n.* (*pl.* **vitelli** /-lī/) **1** the yolk of an egg. **2** the contents of the ovum.

vi·ti·ate /vísheeayt/ *v.tr.* **1** impair the quality or efficiency of; debase. **2** make invalid or ineffectual. □□ **vi·ti·a·tion** /-sheeáyshən/ *n.*

vi·ti·cul·ture /vítikulchər/ *n.* the cultivation of grapevines; the science or study of this. □□ **vit·i·cul·tur·al** *adj.* **vit·i·cul·tur·ist** *n.*

vit·re·ous /vítreeəs/ *adj.* **1** of, or of the nature of, glass. **2** like glass in hardness, brittleness, transparency, structure, etc. (*vitreous enamel*).

vit·re·ous hu·mor *n.* (also **vit·re·ous bod·y**) *Anat.* a transparent jellylike tissue filling the eyeball. ▷ EYE

vit·ri·form /vítrifawrm/ *adj.* having the form or appearance of glass.

vit·ri·fy /vítrifī/ *v.tr. & intr.* (**-ies, -ied**) convert or be converted into glass or a glasslike substance, esp. by heat. □□ **vit·ri·fi·ca·tion** /-fikáyshən/ *n.*

vit·ri·ol /vítreeōl, -əl/ *n.* **1** sulfuric acid or a sulfate. **2** caustic or hostile speech, criticism, or feeling.

vit·ri·ol·ic /vítreeólik/ *adj.* caustic or hostile.

vi·tu·per·ate /vītóopərayt, -tyóo-, vi-/ *v.tr. & intr.* revile; abuse. □□ **vi·tu·per·a·tion** /-ráyshən/ *n.* **vi·tu·per·a·tive** /-rətiv, -ráytiv/ *adj.*

vi·va /véevə/ *int. & n.* ● *int.* long live. ● *n.* a cry of this as a salute, etc.

vi·va·ce /vivaáchay/ *adv. Mus.* in a lively manner.

vi·va·cious /viváyshəs/ *adj.* lively; animated. □□ **vi·va·cious·ly** *adv.* **vi·va·cious·ness** *n.* **vi·vac·i·ty** /vivásitee/ *n.*

vi·var·i·um /vīváireeəm, vi-/ *n.* (*pl.* **vivaria** /-reeə/) a place artificially prepared for keeping animals in (nearly) their natural state.

vi·va vo·ce /vívə vōsee, vōchee, véevə/ *adj. & adv.* ● *adj.* oral. ● *adv.* orally.

vi·ver·rid /vivérid, vī-/ *n. & adj.* ● *n.* any mammal of the family Viverridae, including civets, mongooses, and genets. ● *adj.* of or relating to this family.

viv·id /vívid/ *adj.* **1** (of light or color) strong; intense (*a vivid flash of lightning; of a vivid green*). **2** (of a mental faculty, impression, or description) clear; lively; graphic. **3** (of a person) lively; vigorous. □□ **viv·id·ly** *adv.* **viv·id·ness** *n.*

viv·i·fy /vívifī/ *v.tr.* (**-ies, -ied**) enliven; animate; make lively or living. □□ **viv·i·fi·ca·tion** /-fikáyshən/ *n.*

vi·vip·a·rous /vīvípərəs, vi-/ *adj.* **1** *Zool.* bringing forth young alive, not hatching them by means of eggs. (cf. OVIPAROUS). **2** *Bot.* producing bulbs or seeds that germinate while still attached to the parent plant. □□ **viv·i·par·i·ty** /vívipáritee/ *n.*

viv·i·sect /vívisekt/ *v.tr.* perform vivisection on.

viv·i·sec·tion /vívisékshən/ *n.* **1** dissection or other painful treatment of living animals for purposes of scientific research. **2** unduly detailed or ruthless criticism. □□ **viv·i·sec·tion·ist** *n.* **viv·i·sec·tor** /-sektər/ *n.*

vix·en /víksən/ *n.* **1** a female fox. **2** a spiteful woman. □□ **vix·en·ish** *adj.*

viz. /viz/ *adv.* namely; that is to say; in other words (*came to a firm conclusion, viz. that we were right*).

viz·ca·cha var. of VISCACHA.

vi·zier /vizéer, víziər/ *n. hist.* a high official in some Muslim countries.

VITAMIN

Vitamins are either fat-soluble (A, D, E, K) or water-soluble (B vitamins – including niacin, folic acid, pantothenic acid, riboflavin – and vitamin C). They consist mainly of the elements nitrogen, oxygen, carbon, and hydrogen. Fat-soluble vitamins are stored in body fat, while water-soluble vitamins are used or quickly excreted in the urine. Vitamin A is essential for the eyes, skin, hair, and bones; the B vitamins help enzymes to function; C is needed for the formation of collagen; D helps the body absorb calcium; E prevents cell damage; and K helps blood clotting. Most vitamins cannot be produced by the body and so must be obtained directly from food. Examples of food sources are shown below.

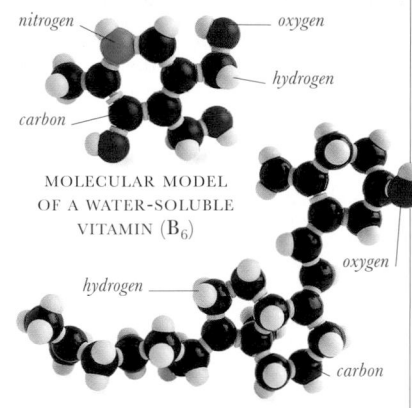

MOLECULAR MODEL OF A WATER-SOLUBLE VITAMIN (B_6)

MOLECULAR MODEL OF A FAT-SOLUBLE VITAMIN (D)

SOURCES OF THE MAIN VITAMINS

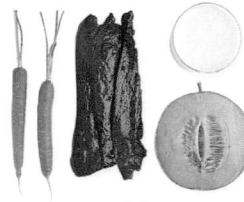

VITAMIN A (RETINOL)
carrots, calf's liver, fortified milk products, melons

VITAMIN B_1 (THIAMINE)
nuts, pork, peas, whole grains

VITAMIN B_2 (RIBOFLAVIN)
meat, eggs, cheese

VITAMIN B_6 (PYRIDOXINE)
fish, vegetables, whole-grain products, fruit

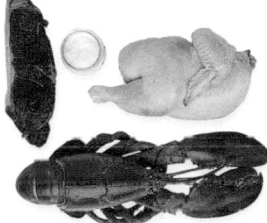

VITAMIN B_{12} (CYANOCOBALAMIN)
beef, milk, poultry, seafood

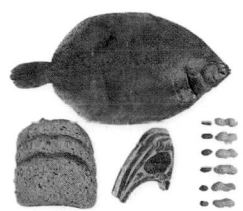

NIACIN (NICOTINIC ACID)
fish, whole-grain products, meat and poultry, peanuts

FOLIC ACID
offal, green leafy vegetables, nuts

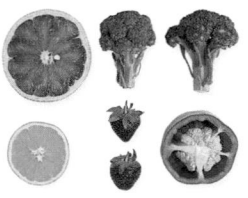

VITAMIN C (ASCORBIC ACID)
citrus fruits, broccoli, strawberries, green peppers

VITAMIN D
oily fish, fortified cereals and breads, fortified margarine, eggs

VITAMIN E (TOCOPHEROL)
vegetable oils, green leafy vegetables, seafood, egg yolks

VITAMIN K
green leafy vegetables, pork liver, fruit, grain products, cauliflower

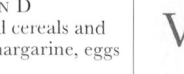

V

vi·zor var. of VISOR.

VJ *abbr.* = VIDEO JOCKEY.

V.M.D. *abbr.* doctor of veterinary medicine.

V neck /véenék/ *n.* (often *attrib.*) **1** a neck of a sweater, etc., with straight sides meeting at an angle in the front to form a V. **2** a garment with this.

vocab. *abbr.* vocabulary.

vo·cab·u·lar·y /vōkábyələree/ *n.* (*pl.* **-ies**) **1** the words used in a language or a particular book or branch of science, etc., or by a particular author (*scientific vocabulary*; *the vocabulary of Shakespeare*). **2** a list of these, arranged alphabetically with definitions or translations. **3** the range of words known to an individual (*his vocabulary is limited*). **4** a set of artistic or stylistic forms or techniques, esp. a range of set movements in ballet, etc.

vo·cal /vókəl/ *adj. & n.* ● *adj.* **1** of or concerned with or uttered by the voice (*a vocal communication*). **2** expressing one's feelings freely in speech (*was very vocal about her rights*). **3** *Phonet.* voiced. **4** (of music) written for or produced by the voice with or without accompaniment (cf. INSTRUMENTAL). ● *n.* **1** (in *sing.* or *pl.*) the sung part of a musical composition. **2** a musical performance with singing. □□ **vo·cal·ly** *adv.*

vo·cal cords *n.pl.* ▼ folds of the lining membrane of the larynx, with edges vibrating in the air stream to produce the voice.

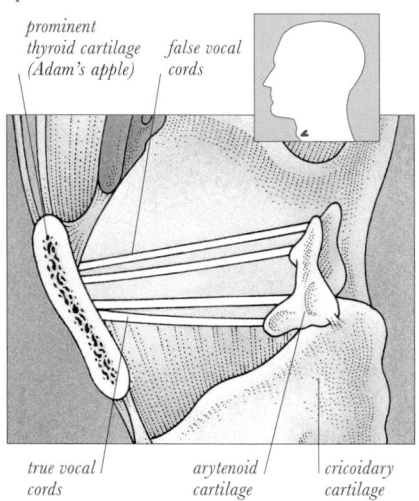

prominent thyroid cartilage (Adam's apple)   *false vocal cords*

true vocal cords   *arytenoid cartilage*   *cricoidary cartilage*

VOCAL CORDS: CROSS SECTION OF THE LARYNX SHOWING THE VOCAL CORDS

vo·cal·ic /vōkálik/ *adj.* of or consisting of a vowel or vowels.

vo·cal·ism /vókəlizəm/ *n.* **1** the use of the voice in speaking or singing. **2** a vowel sound or system.

vo·cal·ist /vókəlist/ *n.* a singer, esp. of jazz or popular songs.

vo·cal·ize /vókəlīz/ *v.* **1** *tr.* form (a sound) or utter (a word) with the voice. **2** *intr.* utter a vocal sound. **3** *tr.* write (Hebrew, etc.) with vowel points. **4** *intr. Mus.* sing with several notes to one vowel. □□ **vo·cal·i·za·tion** *n.*

vo·ca·tion /vōkáyshən/ *n.* **1** a strong feeling of fitness for a particular career (in religious contexts regarded as a divine call). **2 a** a person's employment, esp. regarded as requiring dedication. **b** a trade or profession.

vo·ca·tion·al /vōkáyshənəl/ *adj.* **1** of or relating to an occupation or employment. **2** (of education or training) directed at a particular occupation and its skills. □□ **vo·ca·tion·al·ism** *n.* **vo·ca·tion·al·ly** *adv.*

vo·ca·tive /vókətiv/ *n. & adj. Gram.* ● *n.* the case of nouns, pronouns, and adjectives used in addressing a person or thing. ● *adj.* of or in this case.

vo·cif·er·ate /vōsífərayt/ *v.* **1** *tr.* utter (words, etc.) noisily. **2** *intr.* shout; bawl. □□ **vo·cif·er·a·tion** /-ráyshən/ *n.*

VOLCANO

Most volcanoes occur at the edge of tectonic plates, where magma can rise to the surface. A volcano's shape depends mainly on the viscosity of the lava, the shape of the vent, the amount of ash, and the frequency and size of the eruptions. In fissure volcanoes, the magma rises up gently through a crack, forming lava plateaux or plains. In cone-shaped volcanoes, the more viscous the lava, the steeper the cone. Some cones fall in on themselves or are exploded outward, forming calderas.

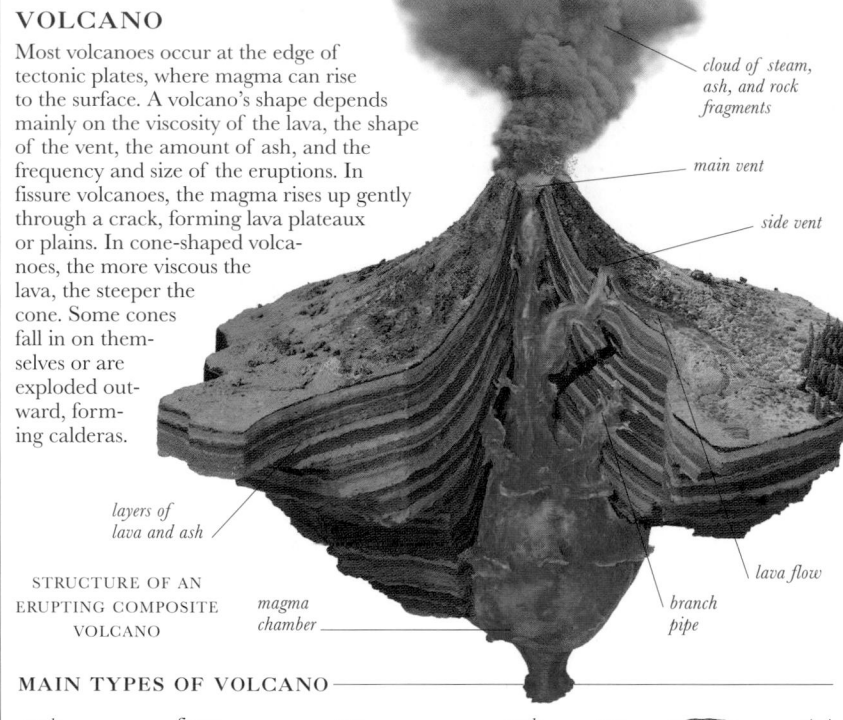

cloud of steam, ash, and rock fragments

main vent

side vent

lava flow

branch pipe

magma chamber

layers of lava and ash

STRUCTURE OF AN ERUPTING COMPOSITE VOLCANO

MAIN TYPES OF VOLCANO

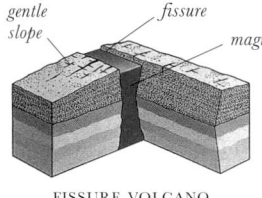

gentle slope   *fissure*   *magma*

FISSURE VOLCANO

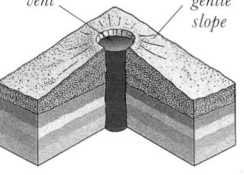

vent   *gentle slope*

SHIELD VOLCANO

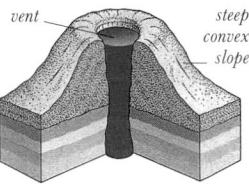

vent   *steep convex slope*

DOME VOLCANO

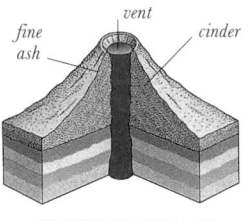

fine ash   *vent*   *cinder*

ASH-CINDER VOLCANO

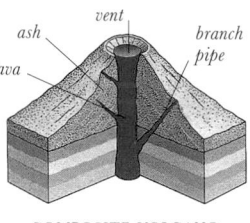

ash   *vent*   *branch pipe*   *lava*

COMPOSITE VOLCANO

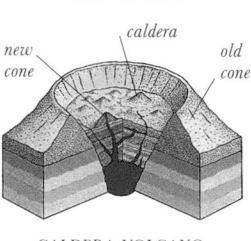

new cone   *caldera*   *old cone*

CALDERA VOLCANO

vo·cif·er·ous /vōsífərəs/ *adj.* **1** (of a person, speech, etc.) noisy; clamorous. **2** insistently and forcibly expressing one's views. □□ **vo·cif·er·ous·ly** *adv.* **vo·cif·er·ous·ness** *n.*

vo·co·der /vōkódər/ *n.* a synthesizer that produces sounds from an analysis of speech input.

vod·ka /vódkə/ *n.* an alcoholic spirit made orig. in Russia by distillation of rye, etc.

vogue /vōg/ *n.* **1** (prec. by *the*) the prevailing fashion. **2** popular use or currency (*has had a great vogue*). □ **in vogue** in fashion. □□ **vogu·ish** *adj.*

voice /voys/ *n. & v.* ● *n.* **1 a** a sound formed in the larynx, etc., and uttered by the mouth, esp. human utterance in speaking, shouting, singing, etc. (*heard a voice*; *spoke in a low voice*). **b** the ability to produce this (*has lost her voice*). **2 a** the use of the voice; utterance, esp. in spoken or written words (esp. *give voice*). **b** an opinion so expressed. **c** the right to express an opinion (*I have no voice in the matter*). **d** an agency by which an opinion is expressed. **3** *Gram.* a form or set of forms of a verb showing the relation of the subject to the action (*active voice*; *passive voice*). **4** *Mus.* **a** a vocal part in a composition. **b** a constituent part in a fugue. **5** *Phonet.* sound uttered with resonance of the vocal cords, not with mere breath. **6** (usu. in *pl.*) the supposed utterance of an invisible guiding or directing spirit. ● *v.tr.* **1** express (*the letter voices our opinion*). **2** (esp. as **voiced** *adj.*) *Phonet.* utter with vibration of the vocal cords (e.g., *b, d, g, v, z*). **3** *Mus.* regulate the tone quality of (organ pipes). □ **in voice** (or **good voice**) in proper vocal condition for singing or speaking. **with one voice** unanimously. □□ **-voiced** *adj.* (in *comb.*).

voice box *n.* the larynx.

voice in the wil·der·ness *n.* an unheeded advocate of reform (see Matt. 3:3, etc.).

voice·less /vóyslis/ *adj.* **1** dumb; speechless. **2** *Phonet.* uttered without vibration of the vocal cords (e.g., *f, k, p, s, t*). □□ **voice·less·ness** *n.*

voice mail *n.* an automatic telephone answering system that records messages from callers.

voice-o·ver *n.* narration in a movie, etc., not accompanied by a picture of the speaker.

voice·print /vóysprint/ *n.* a visual record of speech, analyzed with respect to frequency, duration, and amplitude.

void /voyd/ *adj.*, *n.*, & *v.* ● *adj.* **1 a** empty, vacant. **b** (foll. by *of*) free from (*a style void of affectation*). **2** esp. *Law* (of a contract, deed, promise, etc.) invalid; not binding (*null and void*). **3** useless; ineffectual. **4** (often foll. by *in*) *Cards* (of a hand) having no cards in a given suit. **5** (of an office) vacant (esp. *fall void*). ● *n.* **1** an empty space; a vacuum (*cannot fill the void made by death*). **2** an unfilled space in a wall or building. **3** (often foll. by *in*) *Cards* the absence of cards in a particular suit. ● *v.tr.* **1** render invalid. **2** (also *absol.*) excrete. □□ **void·a·ble** *adj.* **void·ness** *n.*

void·ance /vóyd'ns/ *n.* **1** *Eccl.* a vacancy in a benefice. **2** the act or an instance of voiding; the state of being voided.

void·ed /vóydid/ *adj. Heraldry* (of a bearing) having the central area cut away so as to show the field.

voi·la /vwuláa/ *int.* there it is; there you are.

voile /voyl, vwaal/ *n.* a thin, semitransparent dress material of cotton, wool, or silk.

vol. *abbr.* volume.

vo·lant /vólənt/ *adj.* **1** *Zool.* flying; able to fly. **2** *Heraldry* represented as flying. **3** *literary* nimble; rapid.

vol·a·tile /vólət'l, -tīl/ *adj.* & *n.* ● *adj.* **1** evaporating rapidly (*volatile salts*). **2** changeable; fickle. **3** apt to break out into violence. ● *n.* a volatile substance. □□ **vol·a·til·i·ty** /-tílitee/ *n.*

vol·a·til·ize /vólət'līz/ *v.* **1** *tr.* cause to evaporate. **2** *intr.* evaporate. □□ **vol·a·til·iz·a·ble** *adj.* **vol·a·til·i·za·tion** *n.*

vol-au-vent /váwlōvoɴ/ *n.* ◀ a round case of puff pastry filled with meat, fish, etc., and sauce.

VOL-AU-VENT
FILLED WITH
MUSHROOMS

vol·can·ic /volkánik/ *adj.* (also **vul·can·ic** /vul-/) of, like, or produced by a volcano. □□ **vol·can·i·cal·ly** *adv.* **vol·can·ic·i·ty** /vólkənísitee/ *n.*

vol·can·ic glass *n.* obsidian.

vol·ca·no /volkáynō/ *n.* (*pl.* **-oes**) **1** ◀ a mountain or hill having an opening or openings in the Earth's crust through which lava, cinders, steam, gases, etc., are or have been expelled continuously or at intervals. **2** a state or situation liable to erupt into violence.

vol·can·ol·o·gy /vólkənóləjee/ *n.* (also **vul·can·ol·o·gy** /vúl-/) the scientific study of volcanoes. □□ **vol·can·ol·o·gist** *n.*

vole /vōl/ *n.* ▶ any small ratlike or mouselike plant-eating rodent of the family Cricetidae.

vo·let /vólay/ *n.* a panel or wing of a triptych.

vo·li·tion /vəlíshən/ *n.* **1** the exercise of the will. **2** the power of willing. □ **of** (or **by**) **one's own volition** voluntarily. □□ **vo·li·tion·al** *adj.*

vol·ley /vólee/ *n.* & *v.* ● *n.* (*pl.* **-eys**) **1 a** the simultaneous discharge of a number of weapons. **b** the bullets, etc., discharged in a volley. **2** (usu. foll. by *of*) a noisy emission of oaths, etc., in quick succession. **3** *Tennis* the return of a ball in play before it touches the ground. **4** *Soccer* the kicking of a ball in play before it touches the ground. ● *v.* (**-eys**, **-eyed**) **1** *tr.* (also *absol.*) *Tennis* & *Soccer* return or send (a ball) by a volley. **2** *tr.* & *absol.* discharge (bullets, abuse, etc.) in a volley. **3** *intr.* (of bullets, etc.) fly in a volley. **4** *intr.* (of guns, etc.) sound together. **5** *intr.* make a sound like a volley of artillery.

VOLE: BANK VOLE
(*Clethrionomys glareolus*)

VOLLEYBALL

Volleyball is played on an indoor or outdoor court. The aim of the game is to hit the ball over the net with the hands or arms so that it hits the ground on the opponent's side. Teams may hit the ball up to three times before it crosses the net, and score only if they served.

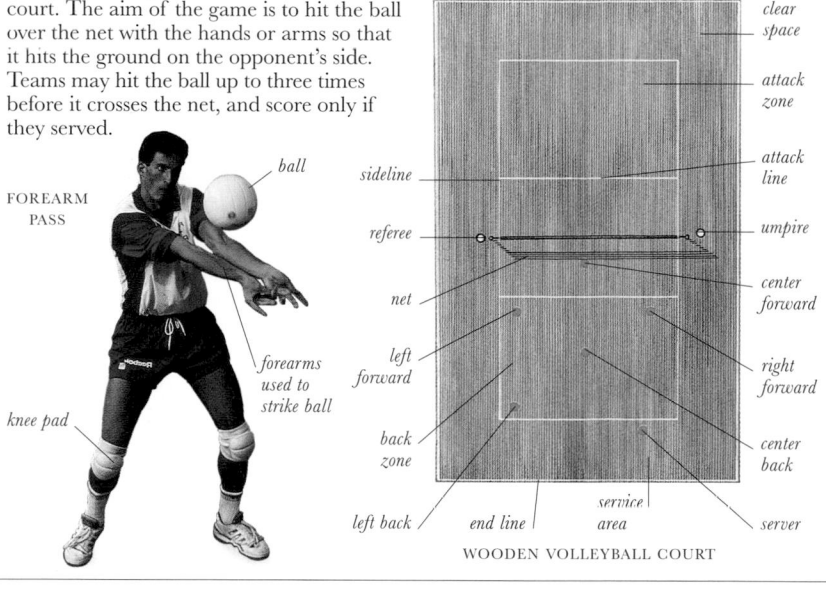

29 ft 6 in. (9 m)

FOREARM PASS — *ball*

clear space

attack zone

attack line

sideline — referee — umpire

net — center forward

left forward — right forward

forearms used to strike ball

knee pad — back zone — center back

left back — end line — service area — server

WOODEN VOLLEYBALL COURT

---

vol·ley·ball /vóleebawl/ *n.* ▲ a game for two teams of six hitting a large ball by hand over a net.

volt /vōlt/ *n.* the SI unit of electromotive force, the difference of potential that would carry one ampere of current against one ohm resistance. ¶ Abbr.: **V**.

volt·age /vóltij/ *n.* electromotive force expressed in volts.

vol·ta·ic /voltáyik/ *adj.* of electricity from a primary battery; galvanic (*voltaic battery*).

volte-face /vawltfáas/ *n.* **1** a complete reversal of position in argument or opinion. **2** the act or an instance of turning around.

volt·me·ter /vóltmeetər/ *n.* an instrument for measuring electric potential in volts.

vol·u·ble /vólyəbəl/ *adj.* speaking or spoken vehemently, incessantly, or fluently (*voluble spokesman*; *voluble excuses*). □□ **vol·u·bil·i·ty** *n.* **vol·u·bly** *adv.*

vol·ume /vólyoom/ *n.* **1** a set of sheets of paper, usu. printed, bound together and forming part or the whole of a work or comprising several works (*issued in three volumes*; *a library of 12,000 volumes*). **2 a** solid content; bulk. **b** the space occupied by a gas or liquid. **c** (foll. by *of*) an amount or quantity (*large volume of business*). **3 a** quantity or power of sound. **b** fullness of tone. **4** (foll. by *of*) **a** a moving mass of water, etc. **b** (usu. in *pl.*) a wreath or coil or rounded mass of smoke, etc.

vol·u·met·ric /vólyoométrik/ *adj.* of or relating to measurement by volume. □□ **vol·u·met·ri·cal·ly** *adv.*

vo·lu·mi·nous /vəloóminəs/ *adj.* **1** large in volume; bulky. **2** (of drapery, etc.) loose and ample. **3** consisting of many volumes. **4** (of a writer) producing many books. □□ **vo·lu·mi·nous·ly** *adv.* **vo·lu·mi·nous·ness** *n.*

vol·un·ta·rism /vóləntərizəm/ *n.* **1** the principle of relying on voluntary action rather than compulsion. **2** *Philos.* the doctrine that the will is a fundamental or dominant factor in the individual or the universe. □□ **vol·un·ta·rist** *n.*

---

vol·un·tar·y /vólənteree/ *adj.* & *n.* ● *adj.* **1** done, acting, or able to act of one's own free will; not compulsory; intentional (*a voluntary gift*). **2** unpaid (*voluntary work*). **3** (of an institution) supported by voluntary contributions. **4** brought about, produced, etc., by voluntary action. **5** (of a movement, muscle, or limb) controlled by the will. **6** (of a confession by a criminal) not prompted by a promise or threat. ● *n.* (*pl.* **-ies**) **1 a** an organ solo played before, during, or after a church service. **b** the music for this. **2** (in competitions) a special performance left to the performer's choice. □□ **vol·un·tar·i·ly** *adv.*

vol·un·teer /vólənteér/ *n.* & *v.* ● *n.* **1** a person who voluntarily undertakes a task or enters military or other service. **2** (usu. *attrib.*) a self-sown plant. ● *v.* **1** *tr.* (often foll. by *to* + infin.) undertake or offer (one's services, a remark or explanation, etc.) voluntarily. **2** *intr.* (often foll. by *for*) make a voluntary offer of one's services; be a volunteer.

vo·lup·tu·ar·y /vəlúpchōoeree/ *n.* & *adj.* ● *n.* (*pl.* **-ies**) a person given up to luxury and sensual pleasure. ● *adj.* concerned with luxury and sensual pleasure.

vo·lup·tu·ous /vəlúpchōoəs/ *adj.* **1** of, tending to, occupied with, or derived from, sensuous or sensual pleasure. **2** full of sexual promise, esp. through shapeliness or fullness. □□ **vo·lup·tu·ous·ly** *adv.* **vo·lup·tu·ous·ness** *n.*

vo·lute /vəloót/ *n.* & *adj.* ● *n.* **1** *Archit.* a spiral scroll characteristic of Ionic capitals and also used in Corinthian and composite capitals. ▷ ACANTHUS. **2 a** any marine gastropod mollusk of the genus *Voluta*. **b** ▲ the spiral shell of this. ● *adj.* esp. *Bot.* rolled up. □□ **vo·lut·ed** *adj.*

VOLUTE: HEBREW
VOLUTE
(*Voluta ebraea*)

vo·mer /vómər/ *n. Anat.* ▶ the small thin bone separating the nostrils in humans and most vertebrates.

vom·it /vómit/ *v.* & *n.* ● *v.tr.* **1** (also *absol.*) eject (matter) from

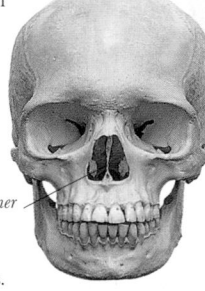

V

vomer

VOMER IN A
HUMAN SKULL

the stomach through the mouth. **2** (of a volcano, chimney, etc.) eject violently; belch (forth). • *n.* matter vomited from the stomach.

vom·i·to·ri·um /vómitáwreeəm/ *n.* (*pl.* **vomitoria** /-reeə/) *Rom. Antiq.* a vomitory.

vom·i·to·ry /vómitawree/ *adj. & n.* • *adj.* emetic. • *n.* (*pl.* **-ies**) *Rom. Antiq.* each of a series of passages for entrance and exit in an amphitheater or theater.

voo·doo /vóodoo/ *n. & v.* • *n.* **1** ▶ use of or belief in religious witchcraft, esp. as practiced in the W. Indies. **2** a person skilled in this. **3** a voodoo spell. • *v.tr.* (**voodoos**, **voodooed**) affect by voodoo; bewitch. □□ **voo·doo·ist** *n.*

vo·ra·cious /vawráyshəs, və-/ *adj.* **1** greedy in eating; ravenous. **2** very eager in some activity (*a voracious reader*). □□ **vo·ra·cious·ly** *adv.* **vo·ra·cious·ness** *n.* **vo·rac·i·ty** /vərásitee/ *n.*

-vorous /vərəs/ *comb. form* forming adjectives meaning 'feeding on' (*carnivorous*). □□ **-vora** /vərə/ *comb. form* forming names of groups. **-vore** /vawr/ *comb. form* forming names of individuals.

vor·tex /váwrteks/ *n.* (*pl.* **vortices** /-tiseez/ or **vortexes**) **1** a mass of whirling fluid, esp. a whirlpool or whirlwind. **2** any whirling motion or mass. **3** a system, occupation, pursuit, etc., viewed as swallowing up or engrossing those who approach it (*the vortex of society*). **4** *Physics* a portion of fluid whose particles have rotatory motion. □□ **vor·ti·cal** /-tikəl/ *adj.* **vor·tic·i·ty** /vortísitee/ *n.*

vor·ti·cel·la /váwrtisélə/ *n.* any sedentary protozoan of the family Vorticellidae, consisting of a tubular stalk with a bell-shaped opening.

vor·ti·cist /váwrtisist/ *n. Art* ▶ a painter, writer, etc., of a school influenced by futurism and using the 'vortices' of modern civilization as a basis. □□ **vor·ti·cism** *n.*

vo·ta·ry /vótəree/ *n.* (*pl.* **-ies**; *fem.* **votaress**) (usu. foll. by *of*) **1** a person vowed to the service of God or a god or cult. **2** a devoted follower, adherent, or advocate of a person, system, occupation, etc.

vote /vōt/ *n. & v.* • *n.* **1** a formal expression of choice or opinion by means of a ballot, show of hands, etc., concerning a choice of candidate, approval of a motion or resolution, etc. (*let us take a vote on it*; *gave my vote to the independent candidate*) **2** (usu. prec. by *the*) the right to vote, esp. in a government election. **3** an opinion expressed by a majority of votes. **4** the collective votes that are or may be given by or for a particular group (*will lose the Southern vote*). **5** a ticket, etc., used for recording a vote. • *v.* **1** *intr.* (often foll. by *for*, *against*, or *to* + infin.) give a vote. **2** *tr.* **a** (often foll. by *that* + clause) enact or resolve by a majority of votes. **b** grant (a sum of money) by a majority of votes. **c** cause to be in a specified position by a majority of votes (*was voted off the committee*). **3** *tr. colloq.* pronounce or declare by general consent (*was voted a failure*). **4** *tr.* (often foll. by *that* + clause) *colloq.* announce one's proposal (*I vote that we all go home*). **5** *tr.* cast a ballot in accordance with (*vote your conscience*). □ **put to** *a* (or **the**) **vote** submit to a decision by voting. **vote down** defeat (a proposal, etc.) in a vote. **vote in** elect by votes. **vote with one's feet** *colloq.* indicate an opinion by one's presence or absence. □□ **vote·less** *adj.*

vote of con·fi·dence *n.* a vote showing that the majority support the policy of the governing body, etc.

vote of no con·fi·dence *n.* a vote showing that the majority do not support the policy of the governing body, etc.

vot·er /vótər/ *n.* **1** a person with the right to vote at an election. **2** a person voting.

vo·tive /vótiv/ *adj.* offered or consecrated in fulfillment of a vow (*votive offering*; *votive picture*).

vouch /vowch/ *v.intr.* (foll. by *for*) answer for; be surety for (*will vouch for the truth of this*; *can vouch for him*; *could not vouch for his honesty*).

vouch·er /vówchər/ *n.* **1** a document which can be exchanged for goods or services. **2** a document establishing the payment of money or the truth of accounts. **3** a person who vouches for a person, statement, etc.

   vouch·safe /vówchsáyf/ *v.tr. formal* **1** condescend to grant (*vouchsafed me no answer*). **2** (foll. by *to* + infin.) condescend.

   vow /vow/ *n. & v.* • *n.* **1** *Relig.* a solemn promise, esp. in the form of an oath to God or another deity or to a saint. **2** (in *pl.*) the promises by which a monk or nun is bound to poverty, chastity, and obedience. **3** a promise of fidelity (*lovers' vows*; *marriage vows*). **4** (usu. as **baptismal vows**) the promises given at baptism by the baptized person or by sponsors. • *v.tr.* **1** promise solemnly (*vowed obedience*). **2** dedicate to a deity. □ **under a vow** having made a vow.

vow·el /vówəl/ *n.* **1** a speech sound made with vibration of the vocal cords but without audible friction. **2** a letter or letters representing this, as *a*, *e*, *i*, *o*, *u*, *aw*, *ah*. □□ **vow·eled** *adj.* (also in comb.).

vox po·pu·li /vóks pópyəlee, -lī/ *n.* public opinion; the general verdict.

voy·age /vóyij/ *n. & v.* • *n.* **1** a journey, esp. a long one by water, air, or in space. **2** an account of this. • *v.* **1** *intr.* make a voyage. **2** *tr.* traverse, esp. by water or air. □□ **voy·ag·er** *n.*

vo·yeur /vwaayór/ *n.* a person who obtains sexual gratification from observing others' sexual actions or organs. □□ **vo·yeur·ism** *n.* **vo·yeur·is·tic** /-rístik/ *adj.* **vo·yeur·is·ti·cal·ly** /-rístikəlee/ *adv.*

VP *abbr.* vice president.

vs. *abbr.* versus.

V sign /vée sín/ *n.* **1** a sign of the letter V made with the first two fingers pointing up and the palm of the hand facing outward, as a symbol of victory. **2** *Brit.* a similar sign made with the back of the hand facing outward as a gesture of abuse, contempt, etc.

VSOP *abbr.* very special old pale (brandy).

VT *abbr.* Vermont (in official postal use).

Vt. *abbr.* Vermont.

VTO *abbr.* vertical takeoff.

VTOL /véetol/ *abbr.* vertical takeoff and landing.

vul·can·ic var. of VOLCANIC.

vul·can·ite /vúlkənīt/ *n.* ▶ a hard, black, vulcanized rubber.

vul·can·ize /vúlkənīz/ *v.tr.* treat (rubber or rubberlike material) with sulfur, etc., esp. at a high temperature to increase its strength. □□ **vul·can·i·za·tion** *n.*

vul·can·ol·o·gy var. of VOLCAN-OLOGY.

Vulg. *abbr.* Vulgate.

vul·gar /vúlgər/ *adj.* **1 a** of or characteristic of the common people. **b** coarse in manners; low (*vulgar expressions*; *vulgar tastes*). **2** in common use; generally prevalent (*vulgar errors*). □□ **vul·gar·ly** *adv.*

vul·gar·i·an /vulgáireeən/ *n.* a vulgar (esp. rich) person.

vul·gar·ism /vúlgərizəm/ *n.* **1** a word or expression in coarse or uneducated use. **2** an instance of coarse or uneducated behavior.

vul·gar·i·ty /vulgáritee/ *n.* (*pl.* **-ies**) **1** the quality of being vulgar. **2** an instance of this.

vul·gar·ize /vúlgərīz/ *v.tr.* **1** make vulgar. **2** spoil (a scene, sentiment, etc.) by making it too common, frequented, or well known. **3** popularize. □□ **vul·gar·i·za·tion** *n.*

VOODOO STATUE USED TO CAST A SPELL ON AN ENEMY

VULCANITE SAXOPHONE MOUTHPIECE

VORTICIST

Vorticism was a short-lived artistic movement, at its height from 1914 to 1915. Led by the British artist Wyndham Lewis, it was essentially cubist in approach but owed much to Italian futurism. Its theme was modern industrial society, portrayed using strong geometrical shapes and mechanical forms that produced works full of movement and energy. The name comes from a statement made by the futurist artist Boccioni – that all artistic creation must originate in a state of emotional vortex.

The Vorticist (1912), WYNDHAM LEWIS

TIMELINE

| 1500 | 1550 | 1600 | 1650 | 1700 | 1750 | 1800 | 1850 | 1900 | 1950 | 2000 |

V

Vul·gate /vúlgayt, -gət/ *n.* **1 a** the Latin version of the Bible prepared mainly by St. Jerome in the late fourth century. **b** the official Roman Catholic Latin text as revised in 1592. **2** (**vulgate**) the traditionally accepted text of any author. **3** (**vulgate**) common or colloquial speech.

vul·ner·a·ble /vúlnərəbəl/ *adj.* **1** that may be wounded or harmed. **2** (foll. by *to*) exposed to damage by a weapon, criticism, etc. **3** *Bridge* having won one game toward rubber and therefore liable to higher penalties. □□ **vul·ner·a·bil·i·ty** *n.* **vul·ner·a·bly** *adv.*

vul·ner·ar·y /vúlnəreree/ *adj. & n.* ● *adj.* useful or used for the healing of wounds. ● *n.* (*pl.* **-ies**) a vulnerary drug, plant, etc.

vul·pine /vúlpīn/ *adj.* **1** of or like a fox. **2** crafty; cunning.

vul·ture /vúlchər/ *n.* **1** ▶ any of various large birds of prey of the family Cathartidae or Accipitridae, with the head and neck more or less bare of feathers, feeding chiefly on carrion. **2** a rapacious person. □□ **vul·tur·ine** /-rīn/ *adj.*

vul·va /vúlvə/ *n.* (*pl.* **vulvas**) *Anat.* the external female genitals. ▷ REPRODUCTIVE ORGANS. □□ **vul·var** *adj.* **vul·vi·tis** /-vítis/ *n.*

vv. *abbr.* **1** verses. **2** volumes.

vy·ing *pres. part.* of VIE.

VULTURE

Found in both temperate and tropical regions, vultures are solitary birds but gather in crowds to feed. Vultures are scavengers and use their sharp eyesight and well-developed sense of smell to locate a carcass. The head and neck of most vultures are bald, allowing them to reach easily inside a carcass.

bald head

hooked beak

talons

EXTERNAL FEATURES OF A HOODED VULTURE
(*Necrosyrtes monachus*)

EXAMPLES OF OTHER VULTURES

ANDEAN CONDOR
(*Vultur gryphus*)

TURKEY VULTURE
(*Cathartes aura*)

EGYPTIAN VULTURE
(*Neophron percnopterus*)

WHITE-BACKED VULTURE
(*Gyps africanus*)

V

W

W[1] /dúbəlyōō/ *n.* (also **w**) (*pl.* **Ws** or **W's**) the twenty-third letter of the alphabet.

W[2] *abbr.* (also **W.**) **1** watt(s). **2** West; Western. **3** women's (size).

W[3] *symb. Chem.* the element tungsten.

w. *abbr.* **1** warden. **2** wide(s). **3** with. **4** wife. **5** watt(s).

WA *abbr.* Washington (state) (in official postal use).

Wac /wak/ *n.* a member of the US Army's Women's Army Corps.

wack·e /wákə/ *n. hist.* a grayish-green or brownish rock resulting from the decomposition of basaltic rock.

wack·o /wákō/ *adj. & n.* (also **whack·o**) *sl.* ● *adj.* crazy. ● *n.* (*pl.* **-os** or **-oes**) a crazy person.

wack·y /wákee/ *adj. & n.* (also **whack·y**) *sl.* ● *adj.* (**-ier, -iest**) crazy. ● *n.* (*pl.* **-ies**) a crazy person. □□ **wack·i·ly** *adv.* **wack·i·ness** *n.*

wad /wod/ *n. & v.* ● *n.* **1** a lump or bundle of soft material used esp. to keep things apart or in place or to stuff up an opening. **2** a disk of felt, etc., keeping powder or shot in place in a gun. **3** a number of bills of currency or documents placed together. **4** (in *sing.* or *pl.*) a large quantity, esp. of money. ● *v.tr.* (**wadded, wadding**) **1** stop up (an aperture or a gun barrel) with a wad. **2** keep (powder, etc.) in place with a wad. **3** line or stuff with wadding. **4** protect with wadding. **5** press (cotton, etc.) into a wad or wadding.

wad·ding /wóding/ *n.* **1** soft, pliable material used to line or stuff, or to pack fragile articles. **2** any material from which gun wads are made.

wad·dle /wód'l/ *v. & n.* ● *v.intr.* walk with short steps and a swaying motion. ● *n.* a waddling gait. □□ **wad·dler** *n.*

wade /wayd/ *v. & n.* ● *v.* **1** *intr.* walk through water or some impeding medium. **2** *intr.* make one's way with difficulty or by force. **3** *intr.* (foll. by *through*) read (a book, etc.) in spite of its dullness, etc. **4** *intr.* (foll. by *into*) *colloq.* attack vigorously. **5** *tr.* ford on foot. ● *n.* a spell of wading. □ **wade in** *colloq.* make a vigorous attack or intervention. □□ **wad·a·ble** *adj.* (also **wade·a·ble**).

wad·er /wáydər/ *n.* **1 a** a person who wades. **b** a wading bird. **2** (in *pl.*) ◄ high waterproof boots, or a waterproof garment for the legs and body.

wa·di /wáadee/ *n.* (also **wady**) (*pl.* **wadis** or **wadies**) a rocky watercourse in N. Africa, etc., dry except in the rainy season.

wad·ing bird /wáyding/ *n.* ► any long-legged waterbird that wades.

Waf /waf/ *n.* (in the US) a member of the Women in the Air Force.

wa·fer /wáyfər/ *n.* **1** a very thin, light, crisp sweet cake, cookie, or biscuit. **2** a thin disk of unleavened bread used in the Eucharist. **3** *Electronics* a very thin slice of a semiconductor crystal. □□ **wa·fer·y** *adj.*

wa·fer-thin *adj.* very thin.

waf·fle[1] /wófəl/ *n. & v. colloq.* ● *n.* verbose but aimless or ignorant talk or writing. ● *v.intr.* indulge in waffle. □□ **waf·fler** *n.* **waf·fly** *adj.*

waf·fle[2] /wófəl/ *n.* a small, crisp batter cake with an intended lattice pattern.

waf·fle i·ron *n.* a utensil, usu. of two shallow metal pans hinged together, for cooking waffles.

waft /woft/ *v. & n.* ● *v.tr. & intr.* convey or travel easily as through air or over water; sweep smoothly along. ● *n.* **1** (usu. foll. by *of*) a whiff or scent. **2** a transient sensation.

wag[1] /wag/ *v. & n.* ● *v.tr. & intr.* (**wagged, wagging**) shake or wave energetically to and fro. ● *n.* a single wagging motion (*with a wag of his tail*). □ **the tail wags the dog** the less or least important member of a society, section of a party, or part of a structure has control. **tongues** (or **beards** or **chins** or **jaws**) **wag** there is talk.

wag[2] /wag/ *n.* a facetious person; a joker.

wage /wayj/ *n. & v.* ● *n.* **1** (in *sing.* or *pl.*) a fixed regular payment, made by an employer to an employee, esp. to a manual or unskilled worker (cf. SALARY). **2** (in *sing.* or *pl.*) requital. **3** (in *pl.*) *Econ.* the part of total production that rewards labor rather than remunerating capital. ● *v.tr.* carry on (a war or contest).

wa·ger /wáyjər/ *n. & v.* = BET.

wag·gish /wágish/ *adj.* playful; facetious. □□ **wag·gish·ly** *adv.* **wag·gish·ness** *n.*

wag·gle /wágəl/ *v. & n. colloq.* ● *v.* **1** *intr. & tr.* wag. **2** *intr. Golf* swing the club head to and fro over the ball before playing a shot. ● *n.* a waggling motion.

wag·gly /wáglee/ *adj.* unsteady.

Wag·ne·ri·an /vaagnéereeən/ *adj. & n.* ● *adj.* of or relating to the music dramas of Richard Wagner, German composer d. 1883, esp. with reference to their large scale. ● *n.* an admirer of Wagner or his music.

wag·on /wágən/ *n.* **1 a** a four-wheeled vehicle for heavy loads. **b** a truck. **2** (in full **water wagon**) a vehicle for carrying water. **3** a light horse-drawn vehicle. **4** *colloq.* an automobile, esp. a station wagon. □ **on the wagon** *sl.* teetotal.

wag·on·er /wágənər/ *n.* the driver of a wagon.

wag·on·ette /wágənét/ *n.* a four-wheeled, horse-drawn vehicle, usu. open, with facing side seats.

wag·on-lit /vágawⁿlée/ *n.* (*pl.* **wagons-lits** *pronunc.* same) a railroad sleeping car, esp. in continental Europe.

wag·tail /wágtayl/ *n.* any small bird of the genus *Motacilla* with a long tail in frequent motion.

wa·hi·ne /waaheénee/ *n.* **1** (in Polynesia and Hawaii) a woman or wife. **2** *sl.* a female surfer.

wah-wah var. of WA-WA.

waif /wayf/ *n.* **1** a homeless and helpless person, esp. a child. **2** an ownerless object or animal; a thing cast up by or drifting in the sea or brought by an unknown agency. □□ **wai·fish** *adj.*

wail /wayl/ *n. & v.* ● *n.* **1** a prolonged and plaintive loud, high-pitched cry of pain, grief, etc. **2** a sound like this. ● *v.intr.* **1** utter a wail. **2** lament or complain persistently or bitterly. **3** make a sound like a person wailing. □□ **wail·er** *n.* **wail·ing·ly** *adv.*

wain·scot /wáynskət, -skot, -skōt/ *n. & v.* ● *n.* boarding or wooden paneling on the lower part of an interior wall. ● *v.tr.* line with wainscot.

wain·scot·ing /wáynskōting, -skot-, -skə-/ *n.* **1** a wainscot. **2** material for this.

waist /wayst/ *n.* **1 a** the part of the human body below the ribs and above the hips. **b** the circumference of this. **2** a similar narrow part in the middle of a violin, etc. ▷ STRINGED. **3 a** the part of a garment encircling or covering the waist. **b** the narrow middle part of a woman's dress, etc. **c** a blouse or bodice. **4** the middle part of a ship, between the forecastle and the quarterdeck. □□ **waist·ed** *adj.* (also in *comb.*). **waist·less** *adj.*

waist·band /wáystband/ *n.* a strip of cloth forming the waist of a garment.

waist·coat /wéskət, wáystkōt/ *n. Brit.* ► a close-fitting waist-length garment, without sleeves or collar but usu. buttoned; a vest.

WAISTCOAT: 18TH-CENTURY EMBROIDERED WAISTCOAT

fastening strap

high-grip sole

WADERS

WADING BIRD

Wading birds belong to the order Charadriiformes, in which there are some 200 species. They live in a wide range of damp habitats and are often found by the shore. Thin, long, sensitive beaks are ideally suited to probing for mollusks, worms, or shrimp in mud, while their long legs are adapted for striding in water. Side-facing eyes provide good all-around vision, allowing wading birds to remain alert to danger.

EXTERNAL FEATURES OF AN OYSTERCATCHER
(*Haematopus ostralegus*)

side-facing eye

slender beak

long legs

waterproofed feathers

OTHER EXAMPLES OF WADING BIRDS

EURASIAN CURLEW
(*Numenius arquata*)

WATTLED JACANA
(*Jacana jacana*)

WHITE-HEADED LAPWING
(*Vanellus albiceps*)

PIED AVOCET
(*Recurvirostra avosetta*)

waist·line /wáystlīn/ *n.* the outline or the size of a person's waist.

wait /wayt/ *v. & n.* ● *v.* **1** *intr.* **a** defer action or departure for a specified time or until some expected event occurs (*wait a minute; wait for a fine day*). **b** be expectant or on the watch (*waited to see what would happen*). **c** (foll. by *for*) refrain from going so fast that (a person) is left behind (*wait for me!*). **2** *tr.* await (an opportunity, one's turn, etc.). **3** *tr.* defer (an activity) until a person's arrival or until some expected event occurs. **4** *intr.* **a** (in full **wait at** or **on table**) act as a waiter. **b** act as an attendant. **5** *intr.* (foll. by *on, upon*) **a** await the convenience of. **b** serve as an attendant to. **c** pay a respectful visit to. ● *n.* **1** a period of waiting (*had a long wait*). **2** (usu. foll. by *for*) watching for an enemy; ambush (*lie in wait*). □ **wait and see** await the progress of events. **wait on 1** act as a waiter, etc. **2** be patient; wait. **wait up** (often foll. by *for*) **1** not go to bed until a person arrives or an event happens. **2** slow down until a person catches up, etc. (*wait up, I'm coming with you*). **you wait!** used to imply a threat, warning, or promise.

wait·er /wáytər/ *n.* **1** a person who serves at table in a hotel or restaurant, etc. **2** a person who waits for a time, event, or opportunity. **3** a tray or salver.

wait·ing /wáyting/ *n.* **1** in senses of WAIT *v.* **2 a** official attendance at court. **b** one's period of this.

wait·ing game *n.* abstention from early action in a contest, etc., so as to act more effectively later.

wait·ing list *n.* a list of people waiting for a thing not immediately available.

wait·ing room *n.* a room provided for people to wait in, esp. by a doctor, dentist, etc., or at a railroad or bus station.

wait·per·son /wáytpərsən/ *n.* a waiter or waitress.

wait·ress /wáytris/ *n.* a woman who serves at table in a hotel or restaurant, etc.

wait-staff *n.* people who serve food to diners, as at a restaurant.

waive /wayv/ *v.tr.* refrain from insisting on or using (a right, claim, etc.).

waiv·er /wáyvər/ *n.* *Law* the act or an instance of waiving.

wake[1] /wayk/ *v. & n.* ● *v.* (*past* **woke** /wōk/ or **waked**; *past part.* **woken** /wōkən/ or **waked**) **1** *intr. & tr.* (often foll. by *up*) cease or cause to cease to sleep. **2** *intr. & tr.* (often foll. by *up*) become or cause to become alert or active (*needs something to wake him up*). ● *n.* a watch beside a corpse before burial.

wake[2] /wayk/ *n.* **1** the track left on the water's surface by a moving ship. **2** turbulent air left behind a moving aircraft, etc. □ **in the wake of** behind; following; as a result of.

wake·ful /wáykfŏŏl/ *adj.* **1** unable to sleep. **2** (of a night, etc.) passed with little or no sleep. **3** vigilant. □□ **wake·ful·ly** *adv.* **wake·ful·ness** *n.*

wak·en /wáykən/ *v.tr. & intr.* make or become awake.

Wal·dorf sal·ad *n.* a salad made from apples, walnuts, celery, and mayonnaise.

wale /wayl/ *n. & v.* ● *n.* **1** a ridge on a woven fabric, c.g., corduroy. **2** *Naut.* a broad, thick timber along a ship's side.

walk /wawk/ *v. & n.* ● *v.* **1** *intr.* **a** (of a person or other biped) progress by lifting and setting down each foot in turn, never having both feet off the ground at once. **b** progress with similar movements (*walked on his hands*). **c** go with one's usual gait except when speed is desired. **d** (of a quadruped) go with the slowest gait, always having at least two feet on the ground at once. **2** *intr.* **a** travel or go on foot. **b** take exercise in this way (*walks for two hours each day*). **3** *tr.* **a** perambulate;

traverse on foot at walking speed; tread the floor or surface of. **b** traverse or cover (a specified distance) on foot (*walks five miles a day*). **4** *tr.* **a** cause to walk with one. **b** accompany in walking. **c** ride or lead (a horse, dog, etc.) at walking pace. **5** *intr.* (of a ghost) appear. **6** *intr.* *Cricket* leave the wicket on being out. **7** *Baseball* **a** *intr.* reach first base on balls. **b** *tr.* allow to do this. **8** *intr.* *sl.* be released from suspicion or from a charge. ● *n.* **1 a** an act of walking, the ordinary human gait (*go at a walk*). **b** the slowest gait of an animal. **c** a person's manner of walking. **2 a** taking a (usu. specified) time to walk a distance (*is only ten minutes' walk from here*). **b** an excursion on foot (*go for a walk*). **c** a journey on foot completed to earn money promised for a charity, etc. **3 a** a place, track, or route intended or suitable for walking. **b** a person's favorite place or route for walking. □ **in a walk** without effort (*won in a walk*). **walk about** stroll. **walk all over** *colloq.* **1** defeat easily. **2** take advantage of. **walk away from 1** easily outdistance. **2** refuse to become involved with. **3** survive (an accident, etc.) without serious injury. **walk away with** *colloq.* = walk off with. **walk the boards** = tread the boards (see TREAD). **walk in** (often foll. by *on*) enter or arrive, esp. unexpectedly or easily. **walk into** *colloq.* encounter through unwariness (*walked into the trap*). **walk it 1** make a journey on foot; not ride. **2** *colloq.* achieve something (esp. a victory) easily. **walk off 1** depart (esp. abruptly). **2** get rid of the effects of by walking (*walked off his anger*). **walk a person off his** or **her feet** (or **legs**) exhaust a person with walking. **walk off with** *colloq.* **1** steal. **2** win easily. **walk out 1** depart suddenly or angrily. **2** cease work, esp. to go on strike. **walk out on** desert; abandon. **walk over 1** *colloq.* = walk all over. **2** (often *absol.*) traverse (a racecourse) without needing to hurry, because one has no opponents or only inferior ones. **walk the plank** see PLANK. **walk the streets 1** be a prostitute. **2** traverse the streets, esp. in search of work, etc. **walk tall** *colloq.* feel justifiable pride. **walk up to** approach (a person) for a talk, etc. □□ **walk·a·ble** *adj.*

walk·a·bout /wáwkəbowt/ *n.* a period of wandering in the bush by an Australian Aboriginal.

walk·a·thon /wáwkəthon/ *n.* an organized fundraising walk.

walk·er /wáwkər/ *n.* **1** a person or animal that walks. **2 a** a framework in which a baby can learn to walk. **b** a usu. tubular metal frame used by disabled or elderly people to help them walk.

walk·ie-talk·ie /wáwkeetáwkee/ *n.* ◄ a two-way radio carried on the person.

walk·ing dic·tion·ar·y *n.* (also **walk·ing en·cy·clo·pe·di·a**) *colloq.* a person having a wide general knowledge.

walk·ing pa·pers *n.pl. colloq.* dismissal (*gave him his walking papers*).

walk·ing stick *n.* **1** a stick carried when walking, esp. for extra support. **2** (also **walk·ing·stick**) a stick insect, esp. *Diapheromera femorata*.

walk·ing tour *n.* esp. *Brit.* a pleasure journey on foot, esp. of several days.

walk·ing wound·ed *n.* (*pl.* same) (usu. in *pl.*) **1** a casualty able to walk despite injuries. **2** *colloq.* a person or people having esp. mental difficulties.

Walk·man /wáwkmən/ *n.* (*pl.* **-mans**) *Trademark* a type of portable stereo equipment with headphones.

walk-on *n.* **1** (in full **walk-on part**) a nonspeaking dramatic role. **2** the player of this.

earpiece

mouthpiece

handset cable

short antenna

speaker

frequency display panel

tuning button

dust cap

carrying pouch

WALKIE-TALKIE: MODERN US HAND-HELD RADIO SET

walk·out /wáwkowt/ *n.* a sudden angry departure, esp. as a protest or strike.

walk·o·ver /wáwkōvər/ *n.* an easy victory or achievement.

walk-up *adj. & n.* ● *adj.* (of a building) allowing access to the upper floors only by stairs. ● *n.* a walk-up building.

walk·way /wáwkway/ *n.* a passage or path for walking along.

wall /wawl/ *n. & v.* ● *n.* **1 a** a continuous and usu. vertical structure of usu. brick or stone, esp. enclosing, protecting, or dividing a space or supporting a roof. **b** the surface of a wall (*hung the picture on the wall*). **2** anything like a wall in appearance or effect (*a wall of steel bayonets; a wall of indifference*). **3** *Anat.* the outermost layer or enclosing membrane, etc., of an organ, structure, etc. **4** the outermost part of a hollow structure (*stomach wall*). ● *v.tr.* (esp. as **walled** *adj.*) surround or protect with a wall (*walled garden*). **2 a** (usu. foll. by *up, off*) block or seal with a wall. **b** (foll. by *up*) enclose (a person) within a sealed space (*walled them up in the dungeon*). □ **drive a person up the wall** *colloq.* **1** make a person angry; infuriate. **2** drive a person mad. **go to the wall** be defeated or ruined. **off the wall** *sl.* unconventional. **up the wall** *colloq.* crazy or furious (*went up the wall when he heard*). **walls have ears** it is unsafe to speak openly, as there may be eavesdroppers. □□ **wall·ing** *n.* **wall-less** *adj.*

wal·la·by /wólləbee/ *n.* (*pl.* **-ies**) ◄ any of various marsupials of the family Macropodidae, smaller than kangaroos, and having large hind feet and long tails.

WALLABY:
RED-NECKED WALLABY
(*Macropus rufogriseus*)

wal·la·roo /wóləróo/ *n.* a large, brownish-black kangaroo, *Macropus robustus*.

wall·board /wáwlbawrd/ *n.* a type of wall covering made from wood pulp, plaster, etc.

wal·let /wólit/ *n.* a small flat esp. leather case for holding paper money, etc.

wall·eye /wáwlī/ *n.* **1 a** an eye with a streaked or opaque white iris. **b** an eye squinting outwards. **2** (also **wall-eyed pike**) an American perch, *Stizostedion vitreum*, with large prominent eyes. □□ **wall·eyed** *adj.*

wall·flow·er /wáwlflowr/ *n.* **1 a** ▶ a fragrant spring garden plant, *Cheiranthus cheiri*, with brown, yellow, or dark-red clustered flowers. **b** any of various flowering plants of the genus *Cheiranthus* or *Erysimum*, growing wild on old walls. **2** *colloq.* a neglected or socially awkward person, esp. a woman sitting out at a dance for lack of partners.

Wal·loon /wolŏŏn/ *n. & adj.* ● *n.* **1** a member of a French-speaking people inhabiting S. and E. Belgium and neighboring France (see also FLEMING). **2** the French dialect spoken by this people. ● *adj.* of or concerning the Walloons or their language.

WALLFLOWER
(*Cheiranthus cheiri*)

W

wal·lop /wóləp/ *v. & n.* ● *v.tr.* **1 a** thrash; beat. **b** hit hard. **2** (as **walloping** *adj.*) big; thumping (*a walloping profit*). ● *n.* a heavy blow; a thump. □□ **wal·lop·ing** *n.*

wal·low /wólō/ *v. & n.* ● *v.intr.* **1** (esp. of an animal) roll about in mud, water, etc. **2** (usu. foll. by *in*) indulge in unrestrained pleasure, misery, etc. (*wallows in nostalgia*). ● *n.* **1** the act or an instance of wallowing. **2 a** a place used by buffalo, etc., for wallowing. **b** the depression in the ground caused by this. □□ **wal·low·er** *n.*

wall·pa·per /wáwlpaypər/ *n. & v.* ● *n.* paper sold in rolls for pasting on to interior walls as decoration. ● *v.tr.* (often *absol.*) decorate with wallpaper.

Wall Street *n.* the US financial world and investment market.

wall-to-wall *attrib.adj.* **1** (of a carpet) fitted to cover a whole room, etc. **2** *colloq.* profuse; ubiquitous (*wall-to-wall pop music*).

wal·nut /wáwlnut/ *n.* **1** ▼ any tree of the genus *Juglans*, having aromatic leaves and drooping catkins. **2** the nut of this tree. ▷ NUT. **3** the timber of this tree used in cabinetmaking. ▷ WOOD

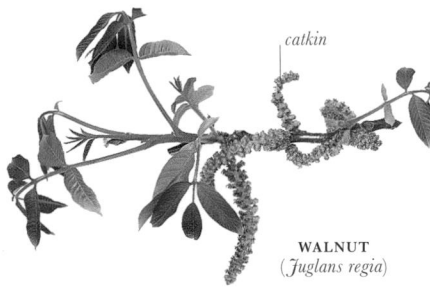

catkin

WALNUT
(*Juglans regia*)

wal·rus /wáwlrəs, wól-/ *n. & adj.* ▼ a large, amphibious, long-tusked arctic mammal, *Odobenus rosmarus*, related to the seal. ▷ PINNIPED

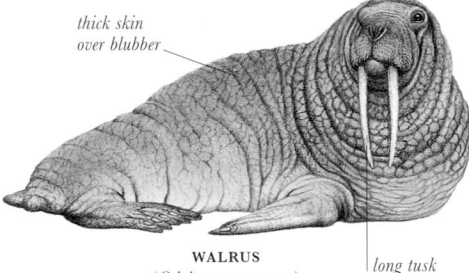

thick skin over blubber

WALRUS
(*Odobenus rosmarus*)

long tusk

waltz /wawlts, wawls/ *n. & v.* ● *n.* **1** a dance in triple time. **2** the usu. flowing music for this. ● *v.* **1** *intr.* dance a waltz. **2** *intr.* (often foll. by *in*, *out*, *round*, etc.) *colloq.* move lightly, casually, with deceptive ease, etc. (*waltzed in and took first prize*). **3** *tr.* move (a person) in or as if in a waltz, casually or with ease (*was waltzed off to Paris*). □ **waltz·er** *n.*

wam·pum /wómpəm/ *n.* ▼ beads made from shells and strung together for use as money, decoration, or as aids to memory by N. American Indians.

W

WAMPUM: 17TH-CENTURY IROQUOIS
WAMPUM USED AS MONEY

wan /won/ *adj.* (**wanner**, **wannest**) **1** (of a person's complexion or appearance) pale; exhausted; worn. **2** faint. □□ **wan·ly** *adv.* **wan·ness** *n.*

wand /wond/ *n.* **1** a supposedly magic stick used in casting spells or for effect by a fairy, magician, etc. **2** a slender rod carried or used as a marker in the ground. **3** a staff symbolizing authority. **4** *colloq.* a conductor's baton. **5** a handheld electronic device which can be passed over a bar code to read the data this represents.

wan·der /wóndər/ *v. & n.* ● *v.* **1** *intr.* (often foll. by *in*, *off*, etc.) go about from place to place aimlessly. **2** *intr.* **a** (of a person, river, etc.) diverge; meander. **b** get lost; leave home; stray from a path, etc. **3** *intr.* talk or think incoherently. **4** *tr.* cover while wandering (*wanders the world*). ● *n.* the act or an instance of wandering (*went for a wander around the garden*). □□ **wan·der·er** *n.* **wan·der·ing** *n.* (esp. in *pl.*).

Wan·der·ing Jew *n.* **1 a** a legendary person said to have been condemned by Christ to wander the earth until the second advent. **b** a person who never settles down. **2 a** a climbing plant, *Tradescantia albiflora*, with stemless variegated leaves. **b** a trailing plant, *Zebrina pendula*, with pink flowers.

wan·der·lust /wóndərlust/ *n.* an eagerness for traveling.

wane /wayn/ *v. & n.* ● *v.intr.* **1** (of the moon) decrease in apparent size after the full moon (cf. WAX[2]). **2** decrease in importance, brilliance, size, etc.; decline. ● *n.* the process of waning. □ **on the wane** waning; declining.

wan·gle /wánggəl/ *v. & n. colloq.* ● *v.tr.* (often *refl.*) obtain (a favor, etc.) by scheming, etc. (*wangled himself a free trip*). ● *n.* the act or an instance of wangling. □□ **wan·gler** *n.*

Wan·kel en·gine /wángkəl, váng-/ *n.* a rotary internal-combustion engine with a continuously rotated and eccentrically pivoted, nearly triangular shaft.

wan·na·be /wónəbee/ *n. sl.* **1** an avid fan who tries to emulate the person he or she admires. **2** anyone who would like to be someone or something else.

want /wont, wawnt/ *v. & n.* ● *v.* **1** *tr.* (often foll. by *to* + infin.) desire; wish for possession of; need (*wants a toy train; wanted to leave; wanted him to leave*). **b** need or desire (a person, esp. sexually). **c** (foll. by *to* + infin.) ought; should; need (*you want to pull yourself together*). **2** *intr.* (usu. foll. by *for*) lack (*wants for nothing*). **3** *tr.* be without or fall short by (esp. a specified amount or thing) (*the drawer wants a handle*). **4** *intr.* (foll. by *in*, *out*) *colloq.* desire to be in, out, etc. (*wants in on the deal*). **5** *tr.* (as **wanted** *adj.*) (of a suspected criminal, etc.) sought by the police. ● *n.* **1** (often foll. by *of*) **a** a lack (*shows great want of judgment*). **b** poverty; need (*living in great want; in want of necessities*). **2 a** a desire (*meets a long-felt want*). **b** a thing so desired (*can supply your wants*).

want ad *n.* a classified newspaper advertisement, esp. for something sought.

want·ing /wónting, wáwn-/ *adj.* **1** lacking; deficient (*wanting in judgment*). **2** absent; not provided. □ **be found wanting** fail to meet requirements.

wan·ton /wóntən/ *adj.* **1** licentious; lewd; sexually promiscuous. **2** capricious; random (*wanton destruction*). **3** luxuriant (*wanton extravagance*). □□ **wan·ton·ly** *adv.* **wan·ton·ness** *n.*

WAP *abbr.* Wireless Application Protocol, a means of enabling a mobile phone to browse the Internet and display data.

wap·i·ti /wópitee/ *n.* (*pl.* **wapitis**) a N. American deer, *Cervus canadensis*.

war /wawr/ *n. & v.* ● *n.* **1 a** armed hostilities, esp. between nations; conflict (*war broke out*). **b** a specific conflict or the time during which such conflict exists (*was before the war*). **c** the suspension of international law, etc., during such a conflict. **2** (as **the war**) a war in progress; the most recent major war. **3 a** hostility or contention (*war of words*). **b** (often foll. by *on*) a sustained campaign against crime, poverty, etc. ● *v.intr.* (**warred**, **warring**) **1** (as **warring** *adj.*) **a** rival; fighting (*warring factions*).

b conflicting (*warring principles*). **2** make war. □ **at war** (often foll. by *with*) engaged in a war. **go to war** declare or begin a war. **have been in the wars** *colloq.* appear injured, bruised, unkempt, etc.

war·ble /wáwrbəl/ *v. & n.* ● *v.* **1** *intr.* sing in a gentle, trilling manner. **2** *tr.* utter or express in a warbling manner. ● *n.* a warbled song or utterance.

war·ble fly *n.* any of various flies of the genus *Hypoderma*, infesting the skin of cattle and horses.

war·bler /wáwrblər/ *n.* **1** any small, insect-eating songbird of the family Sylviidae, including the black cap, or, in N. America, Parulidae, including the wood warbler, whitethroat, and chiffchaff. **2** a person, bird, etc., that warbles.

war bride *n.* a woman who marries a serviceman met during a war.

war crime *n.* a crime violating the international laws of war. □□ **war crim·i·nal** *n.*

war cry *n.* **1** a phrase or name shouted to rally one's troops. **2** a party slogan, etc.

ward /wawrd/ *n.* **1** a separate room or division of a hospital, etc. **2** an administrative division of a city or town. **3 a** a minor under the care of a guardian appointed by the parents or a court. **b** (in full **ward of the court**) a minor or mentally deficient person placed under the protection of a court. **4** (in *pl.*) the corresponding notches and projections in a key and a lock. □ **ward off 1** parry (a blow). **2** avert (danger, etc.).

-ward /wərd/ *suffix* (also **-wards**) added to nouns of place or destination and to adverbs of direction and forming: **1** adverbs meaning 'toward the place, etc.' (*set off homeward*). **2** adjectives meaning 'turned or tending toward' (*an onward rush*). **3** (less commonly) nouns meaning 'the region toward or about' (*look to the eastward*).

war dance *n.* a dance performed before a battle or to celebrate victory.

war·den /wáwrd'n/ *n.* **1** (usu. in *comb.*) a supervising official (*churchwarden; game warden*). **2** chief administrator of a prison. □□ **war·den·ship** *n.*

ward·er /wáwrdər/ *n.* a guard.

ward heel·er *n.* a party worker in elections, etc.

ward·robe /wáwrdrōb/ *n.* **1** a large movable or built-in case with rails, etc., for storing clothes. **2** a person's stock of clothes. **3** the costume department or costumes of a theater, a movie company, etc.

ward·room /wáwrdrōōm, -rŏŏm/ *n.* a room in a warship for the use of commissioned officers.

-wards var. of -WARD.

ware[1] /wair/ *n.* **1** (esp. in *comb.*) things of the same kind, esp. ceramics, made usu. for sale (*chinaware; hardware*). **2** (usu. in *pl.*) **a** articles for sale (*displayed his wares*). **b** a person's skills, talents, etc. **3** ceramics, etc., of a specified material, factory, or kind (*Wedgwood ware; delftware*).

ware[2] /wair/ *v.tr.* (esp. in hunting) look out for; avoid (usu. in *imper.*: *ware hounds!*).

ware·house /wáirhows/ *n. & v.* ● *n.* **1 a** a building in which esp. retail goods are stored. **2** a wholesale or large retail store. ● *v.tr.* (also /-howz/) store temporarily in a repository. □□ **ware·house·man** *n.* (*pl.* **-men**).

war·fare /wáwrfair/ *n.* a state of war; campaigning, engaging in war (*chemical warfare*).

war·fa·rin /wáwrfərin/ *n.* a water-soluble anticoagulant used esp. as a rat poison.

war game *n.* **1** a military exercise testing or improving tactical knowledge, etc. **2** a battle, etc., conducted with toy soldiers.

war·head /wáwrhed/ *n.* ▶ the explosive head of a missile, torpedo, or similar weapon.

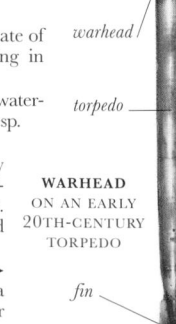

warhead

torpedo

WARHEAD
ON AN EARLY
20TH-CENTURY
TORPEDO

fin

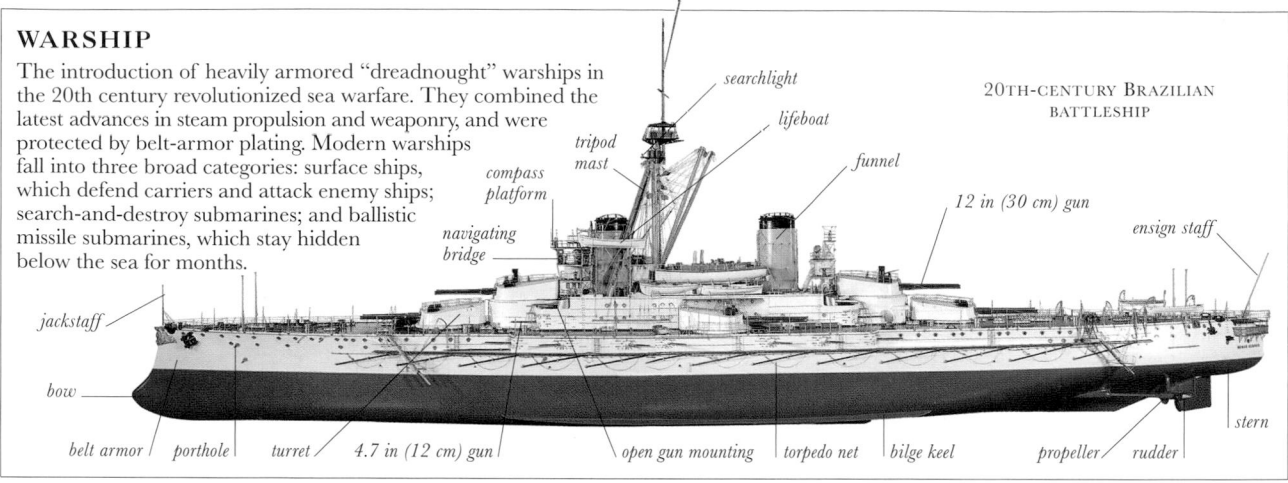

WARSHIP

The introduction of heavily armored "dreadnought" warships in the 20th century revolutionized sea warfare. They combined the latest advances in steam propulsion and weaponry, and were protected by belt-armor plating. Modern warships fall into three broad categories: surface ships, which defend carriers and attack enemy ships; search-and-destroy submarines; and ballistic missile submarines, which stay hidden below the sea for months.

20TH-CENTURY BRAZILIAN BATTLESHIP

searchlight · lifeboat · tripod mast · funnel · 12 in (30 cm) gun · ensign staff · compass platform · navigating bridge · jackstaff · bow · belt armor · porthole · turret · 4.7 in (12 cm) gun · open gun mounting · torpedo net · bilge keel · propeller · rudder · stern

---

war·horse /wáwrhawrs/ *n.* **1** *hist.* a knight's or soldier's powerful horse. ▷ JOUST. **2** *colloq.* a veteran soldier, politician, etc. **3** a song, play, etc., that has been performed to the point of triteness.

war·like /wáwrlīk/ *adj.* **1** hostile. **2** soldierly. **3** of or for war (*warlike preparations*).

war·lock /wáwrlok/ *n. archaic* a sorcerer or wizard.

war·lord /wáwrlawrd/ *n.* a military commander or commander in chief.

warm /wawrm/ *adj., v., & n.* ● *adj.* **1** of or at a fairly or comfortably high temperature. **2** (of clothes, etc.) affording warmth **3 a** sympathetic; cordial; loving (*a warm welcome; has a warm heart*). **b** enthusiastic; hearty (*was warm in her praise*). **4** animated; heated (*the dispute grew warm*). **5** *colloq. iron.* difficult or hostile (*met a warm reception*). **6** *colloq.* **a** close to the object, etc., sought. **b** near to guessing or finding out a secret. **7** (of a color, light, etc.) reddish, pink, or yellowish, etc., suggestive of warmth. **8** *Hunting* (of a scent) fresh and strong **9 a** (of a person's temperament) amorous; sexually demanding. **b** erotic; arousing. ● *v.* **1** *tr.* **a** make warm (*fire warms the room*). **b** make cheerful (*warms the heart*). **2** *intr.* **a** (often foll. by *up*) warm oneself at a fire, etc. (*warmed himself up*). **b** (often foll. by *to*) become enthusiastic or sympathetic (*warmed to his subject*). ● *n.* **1** the act of warming; the state of being warmed (*had a nice warm by the fire*). **2** the warmth of the atmosphere, etc. □ **warm up 1** (of an athlete, performer, etc.) prepare by practicing. **2** (of a room, etc.) become warmer. **3** become enthusiastic, etc. **4** (of an engine, etc.) reach a temperature for efficient working. **5** reheat (food). □□ **warm·er** *n.* (also in *comb.*). **warm·ish** *adj.* **warm·ly** *adv.* **warm·ness** *n.* **warmth** *n.*

warm-blood·ed *adj.* **1** (of an organism) having warm blood; mammalian (see HOMEOTHERM). **2** ardent; passionate.

warmed-o·ver *adj.* (also **warmed-up**) **1** (of food, etc.) reheated. **2** stale; secondhand.

warm front *n.* an advancing mass of warm air. ▷ FRONT, WEATHER CHART

warm·heart·ed /wáwrmháartid/ *adj.* kind; friendly. □□ **warm·heart·ed·ly** *adv.* **warm·heart·ed·ness** *n.*

war·mon·ger /wáwrmunggər, -mong-/ *n.* a person who seeks to bring about or promote war. □□ **war·mon·ger·ing** *n. & adj.*

warm-up *n.* a period of preparatory exercise for a contest or performance.

warn /wawrn/ *v.tr.* **1** (also *absol.*) **a** (often foll. by *of*, or *that* + clause, or *to* + infin.) inform of danger, unknown circumstances, etc. (*warned them of the danger*). **b** (often foll. by *against*) inform (a person) about a specific danger, hostile person, etc. (*warned her against trusting him*). **2** (usu. with *neg.*) tell forcefully (*has been warned not to go*). **3** give (a person)

cautionary notice (*shall not warn you again*). □□ **warn·er** *n.*

warn·ing /wáwrning/ *n.* **1** in senses of WARN *v.* **2** anything that serves to warn. □□ **warn·ing·ly** *adv.*

warn·ing track *n.* (also **warn·ing path**) *Baseball* dirt strip that borders the outfield just inside the fence.

war of at·tri·tion *n.* a war in which each side seeks to wear out the other over a long period.

war of nerves *n.* an attempt to wear down an opponent by psychological means.

warp /wawrp/ *v. & n.* ● *v.* **1** *tr. & intr.* **a** make or become bent or twisted out of shape. **b** make or become perverted or strange (*a warped sense of humor*). **2 a** *tr.* haul (a ship) by a rope attached to a fixed point. **b** *intr.* progress in this way. ● *n.* **1 a** a state of being warped, esp. of lumber. **b** perversion of the mind or character. **2** the threads stretched lengthwise in a loom. ▷ WEFT. **3** a rope used in towing or warping, or attached to a trawl net. □□ **warp·age** *n.* (esp. in sense 1a of *v.*).

war·paint /wáwrpaynt/ *n.* **1** paint used to adorn the body before battle, esp. by N. American Indians. **2** *colloq.* elaborate make-up.

war·path /wáwrpath/ *n.* **1** a warlike expedition of N. American Indians. **2** *colloq.* any hostile course (*on the warpath*).

war·plane /wáwrplayn/ *n.* a military aircraft, esp. one armed for warfare.

war·rant /wáwrənt, wór-/ *n. & v.* ● *n.* **1 a** anything that authorizes a person or an action. **b** a person so authorizing. **2 a** a written authorization, money voucher, etc. (*a dividend warrant*). **b** a written authorization allowing police to search premises, etc. **3** a document authorizing counsel to represent the principal in a lawsuit (*warrant of attorney*). **4** a certificate of service rank held by a warrant officer. ● *v.tr.* **1** justify (*nothing can warrant his behavior*). **2** guarantee or attest to. □ **I** (or **I'll**) **warrant** I am certain (*he'll be sorry, I'll warrant*). □□ **war·rant·a·ble** *adj.* **war·rant·er** *n.* **war·ran·tor** *n.*

war·rant of·fi·cer *n.* an officer ranking between commissioned officers and NCOs.

war·ran·ty /wáwrəntee, wór-/ *n.* (*pl.* **-ies**) **1** an undertaking as to the ownership or quality of a thing sold, leased, etc., often accepting responsibility or liability over a specified period. **2** (usu. foll. by *for* + verbal noun) an authority or justification. **3** an undertaking by an insured person of the truth of a statement or fulfillment of a condition.

war·ren /wáwrən, wór-/ *n.* **1 a** a network of interconnecting rabbit burrows. **b** a piece of ground occupied by this. **2** a labyrinthine building or district.

war·ri·or /wáwreeər, wór-/ *n.* **1** a person experienced or distinguished in fighting. **2** a fighting

person, esp. a man, esp. of primitive peoples. **3** (*attrib.*) martial (*a warrior nation*).

war·ship /wáwrship/ *n.* ▲ an armored ship used in war.

wart /wawrt/ *n.* **1** ▼ a small, hardish, roundish growth on the skin caused by a virus-induced abnormal growth of papillae and thickening of the epidermis. **2** a protuberance on the skin of an animal, surface of a plant, etc. **3** *colloq.* an objectionable person. □ **warts and all** *colloq.* with no attempt to conceal blemishes or inadequacies. □□ **wart·y** *adj*

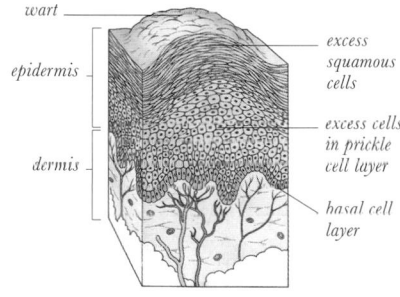

wart · excess squamous cells · epidermis · excess cells in prickle cell layer · dermis · basal cell layer

WART: CROSS SECTION THROUGH A WART ON HUMAN SKIN

wart·hog /wáwrt-hog/ *n.* an African wild pig of the genus *Phacochoerus*, with a large head and warty lumps on its face, and large curved tusks.

war·time /wáwrtīm/ *n.* the period during which a war is waged.

war·y /wáiree/ *adj.* (**warier**, **wariest**) **1** on one's guard; circumspect. **2** (foll. by *of*) cautious; suspicious (*am wary of using elevators*). **3** showing or done with caution or suspicion (*a wary expression*). □□ **war·i·ly** *adv.* **war·i·ness** *n.*

was *1st & 3rd sing.* past of BE.

Wash. *abbr.* Washington.

wash /wosh, wawsh/ *v. & n.* ● *v.* **1** *tr.* cleanse with liquid, esp. water. **2** *tr.* (foll. by *out*, *off*, *away*, etc.) remove (a stain or dirt, a surface, or some physical feature of the surface) in this way. **3** *intr.* wash oneself or esp. one's hands and face. **4** *intr.* wash clothes, etc. **5** *intr.* (of fabric or dye) bear washing without damage. **6** *intr.* (foll. by *off*, *out*) (of a stain, etc.) be removed by washing. **7** *tr.* (of a river, sea, etc.) touch (a country, coast, etc.) with its waters. **8** *tr.* (of moving liquid) carry along in a specified direction (*a wave washed him overboard*). **9** *tr.* (also foll. by *away*, *out*) **a** scoop out (*the water had washed a channel*). **b** erode; denude (*sea-washed cliffs*). **10** *intr.* (foll. by *over*, *along*, etc.) sweep, move, or splash. **11** *tr.* sift (ore) by the action of water. **12** *tr.* **a** brush a thin

W

939

coat of watery paint or ink over (paper in water-color painting, etc., or a wall). **b** (foll. by *with*) coat (inferior metal) with gold, etc. ● *n.* **1 a** the act or an instance of washing; the process of being washed (*only needed one wash*). **b** (prec. by *the*) treatment at a laundry, etc. (*sent them to the wash*). **2** a quantity of clothes for washing or just washed. **3** the visible or audible motion of agitated water or air, esp. due to the passage of a ship, etc., or aircraft. **4 a** soil swept off by water. ▷ ERODE. **b** a sandbank exposed only at low tide. **5** kitchen slops given to pigs. **6 a** thin, weak, or inferior liquid food. **b** liquid food for animals. **7** a liquid to spread over a surface to cleanse, heal, or color. **8** a thin coating of water-color, wall paint, or metal. **9** malt, etc., fermenting before distillation. **10** a lotion or cosmetic. □ **come out in the wash** *colloq.* be clarified, or (of contingent difficulties) be resolved or removed, in the course of time. **wash one's dirty linen in public** see LINEN. **wash down 1** wash completely (esp. a large surface). **2** (usu. foll. by *with*) accompany or follow (food) with a drink. **wash one's hands** *euphem.* go to the lavatory. **wash one's hands of** renounce responsibility for. **wash out 1** clean the inside of (a thing) by washing. **2** clean (a garment, etc.) by brief washing. **3 a** rain out (an event, etc.). **b** *colloq.* cancel. **4** (of a downpour, etc.) make a breach in (a road, etc.). **wash up 1** (also *absol.*) esp. *Brit.* wash (dishes, etc.) after use. **2** wash one's face and hands. **won't** (or **doesn't**) **wash** *colloq.* will not be believed or accepted.

wash·a·ble /wóshəbəl, wáwsh-/ *adj.* that can be washed, esp. without damage. □□ **wash·a·bil·i·ty** /-bílitee/ *n.*

wash-and-wear *adj.* (of a fabric or garment) easily and quickly laundered.

wash·a·te·ri·a var. of WASHETERIA.

wash·ba·sin /wóshbaysin, wáwsh-/ *n.* = WASHBOWL.

wash·board /wóshbawrd, wáwsh-/ *n.* **1** a board of ribbed wood or a sheet of corrugated zinc on which clothes are scrubbed in washing. **2** this used as a percussion instrument.

wash·bowl /wóshbōl, wáwsh-/ *n.* a bowl for washing one's hands, face, etc.

wash·cloth /wóshkloth, wáwsh-/ *n.* a cloth for washing the face or body.

wash·day /wóshday, wáwsh-/ *n.* a day on which clothes, etc., are washed.

washed out *adj.* (hyphenated when *attrib.*) **1** faded by washing. **2** pale. **3** *colloq.* limp; enfeebled.

washed up *adj. sl.* (hyphenated when *attrib.*) defeated, having failed.

wash·er /wóshər, wáwsh-/ *n.* **1 a** a person or thing that washes. **b** a washing machine. **2** a flat ring of rubber, metal, etc., inserted at a joint to prevent leakage. **3** a similar ring placed under a nut, etc. to disperse pressure.

wash·er·wom·an /wóshərwŏŏmən, wáwsh-/ *n.* (*pl.* **-women**) (also **wash·wom·an**) a woman whose occupation is washing clothes; a laundress.

wash·e·te·ri·a /wóshətéereeə, wáwsh-/ *n.* (also **wash·a·te·ri·a**) = LAUNDROMAT.

wash·ing /wóshing, wáwsh-/ *n.* a quantity of clothes for washing or just washed.

wash·ing ma·chine *n.* a machine for washing clothes and linen, etc.

wash-out *n.* **1** *colloq.* a fiasco; a complete failure. **2** a breach in a road, etc., caused by flooding.

wash·room /wóshrŏŏm, -rŏŏm, wáwsh-/ *n.* a room with washing and toilet facilities.

wash·stand /wóshstand, wáwsh-/ *n.* a piece of furniture to hold a washbowl, pitcher, soap, etc.

wash·tub /wóshtub, wáwsh-/ *n.* a tub or vessel for washing clothes, etc.

wash·y /wóshee, wáwsh-/ *adj.* (**washier**, **washiest**) **1** (of liquid food) too watery or weak; insipid. **2** (of color) faded-looking; thin; faint. **3** (of a style, sentiment, etc.) lacking vigor or intensity. □□ **wash·i·ness** *n.*

was·n't /wúzənt, wóz-/ *contr.* was not.

WASP /wosp/ *n.* (also **Wasp**) usu. *derog.* a middle-class American white Protestant descended from early English settlers. □□ **Wasp·y** *adj.*

wasp /wosp/ *n.* **1** ▶ a stinging, often flesh-eating insect of the order Hymenoptera, esp. the common social wasp *Vespa vulgaris*, with black and yellow stripes and a very thin waist. ▷ NEST. **2** (in *comb.*) any of various insects resembling a wasp in some way (*wasp beetle*). □□ **wasp·like** *adj.*

wasp·ish /wóspish/ *adj.* irritable; petulant. □□ **wasp·ish·ly** *adv.* **wasp·ish·ness** *n.*

wasp waist *n.* a very slender waist. □□ **wasp·waist·ed** *adj.*

antenna

thin waist

thorax

wing

WASP
(*Vespula vulgaris*)

was·sail /wósəl, wósayl, wosáyl/ *n. & v. archaic* ● *n.* **1** a festive occasion; a drinking bout. **2** a kind of liquor drunk on such an occasion. ● *v.intr.* make merry; celebrate with drinking, etc. □□ **was·sail·er** *n.*

Was·ser·mann test /wáasərmən/ *n.* a test for syphilis using the reaction of the patient's blood serum.

wast·age /wáystij/ *n.* **1** an amount wasted. **2** loss by use, wear, or leakage. **3** *Commerce* loss of employees other than by layoffs.

waste /wayst/ *v., adj., & n.* ● *v.* **1** *tr.* use to no purpose or for inadequate result (*waste time*). **2** *tr.* fail to use (esp. an opportunity). **3** *tr.* (often foll. by *on*) utter (words, etc.), without effect. **4** *tr. & intr.* wear gradually away; wither. **5** *tr.* **a** ravage. **b** *sl.* murder; kill. **6** *tr.* treat as wasted or valueless. **7** *intr.* be expended without useful effect. ● *adj.* **1** superfluous. **2** (of a district, etc.) not inhabited nor cultivated. **3** presenting no features of interest. ● *n.* **1** the act or an instance of wasting; extravagant or ineffectual use of an asset, of time, etc. **2** waste material or food; refuse; useless remains or by-products. **3** a waste region; a desert, etc. **4** the state of being used up; diminution by wear and tear. **5** = WASTE PIPE. □ **go** (or **run**) **to waste** be wasted. **lay waste** ravage; devastate. **waste not, want not** extravagance leads to poverty. **waste words** see WORD.

---

waste·bas·ket /wáystbaskit/ *n.* a receptacle for wastepaper, etc.

waste·ful /wáystfŏŏl/ *adj.* **1** extravagant. **2** causing or showing waste. □□ **waste·ful·ly** *adv.* **waste·ful·ness** *n.*

waste·land /wáystland/ *n.* **1** an unproductive or useless area of land. **2** a place or time considered spiritually or intellectually barren.

waste·pa·per /wáystpaypər/ *n.* spoiled, valueless, or discarded paper.

waste·pa·per bas·ket *n.* = WASTEBASKET.

waste pipe *n.* a pipe to carry off waste material, e.g., from a sink.

wast·er /wáystər/ *n.* **1** a wasteful person. **2** *colloq.* a wastrel.

wast·rel /wáystrəl/ *n.* **1** a wasteful or good-for-nothing person. **2** a waif; a neglected child.

watch /woch/ *v. & n.* ● *v.* **1** *tr.* keep the eyes fixed on; look at attentively. **2** *tr.* **a** keep under observation; follow observantly. **b** monitor or consider carefully (*have to watch my weight*). **3** *intr.* (often foll. by *for*) be in an alert state; be vigilant (*watch for the holes in the road*). **4** *intr.* (foll. by *over*) take care of. ● *n.* **1** ▶ a small portable timepiece for carrying on one's person. **2** a state of alert observation or attention. **3** *Naut.* **a** a four-hour period of duty. **b** (in full **starboard** or **port watch**) each of the halves, divided according to the position of the bunks, into which a ship's crew is divided to take alternate watches. □ **on the watch** waiting for an expected or feared occurrence. **set the watch** *Naut.* station sentinels, etc. **watch it** (or **oneself**) *colloq.* be careful. **watch one's step** proceed cautiously. **watch out 1** (often foll. by *for*) be on one's guard. **2** as a warning of immediate danger. □□ **watch·a·ble** *adj.* **watch·er** *n.* (also in *comb.*).

watch chain *n.* a metal chain for securing a pocket watch.

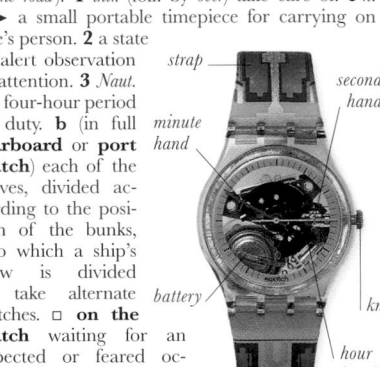

strap

second hand

minute hand

battery

knob

hour hand

WATCH:
QUARTZ WATCH

WATER CYCLE

The circulation of water between the surface of the Earth and its atmosphere is driven by energy from the Sun. Water vapor is lost from seas, rivers, and lakes by evaporation, and from plants by transpiration. The rising vapor cools and condenses into droplets of water that form clouds. Carried by the wind, clouds continue to absorb water until saturated, then the water droplets fall as rain, hail, or snow (precipitation). In this way water is redistributed around the planet.

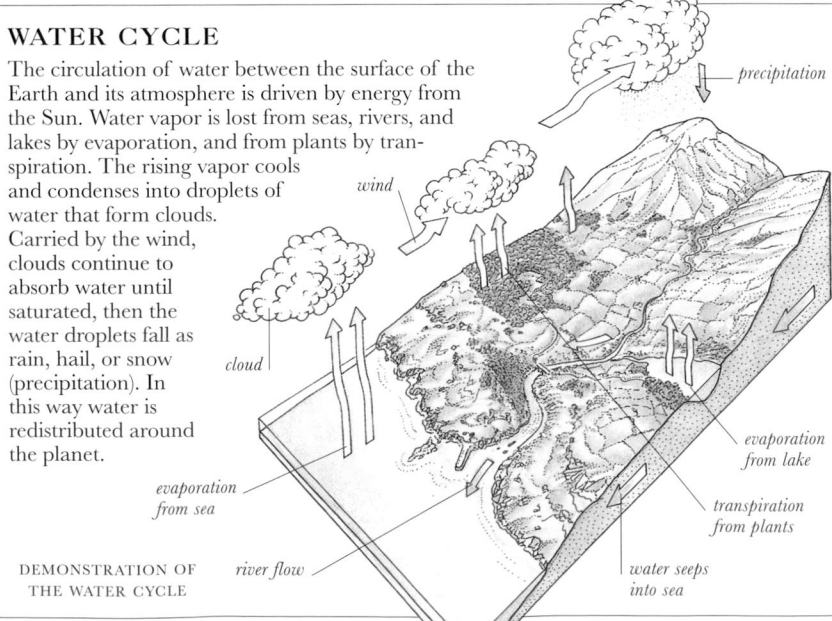

precipitation

wind

cloud

evaporation from lake

transpiration from plants

evaporation from sea

river flow

water seeps into sea

DEMONSTRATION OF
THE WATER CYCLE

W

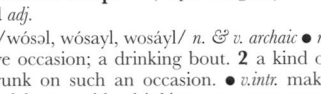

watch crys·tal *n.* a glass disk covering the dial of a watch.

watch·dog /wóchdawg, dog/ *n. & v.* ● *n.* **1** a dog kept to guard property, etc. **2** a person or body monitoring others' rights, behavior, etc. ● *v.tr.* (**-dogged, -dogging**) maintain surveillance over.

watch·ful /wóchfŏŏl/ *adj.* **1** accustomed to watching. **2** on the watch. **3** showing vigilance. **4** *archaic* wakeful. □□ **watch·ful·ly** *adv.* **watch·ful·ness** *n.*

watch·mak·er /wóchmaykər/ *n.* a person who makes and repairs watches and clocks. □□ **watch·mak·ing** *n.*

watch·man /wóchmən/ *n.* (*pl.* **-men**) **1** a person employed to look after an empty building, etc., at night. **2** *archaic* or *hist.* a person employed to patrol the streets, etc. at night.

watch spring *n.* the mainspring of a watch.

watch·tow·er /wóchtower/ *n.* a tower from which observation can be kept. ▷ CASTLE

watch·word /wóchwərd/ *n.* **1** a phrase summarizing a core belief. **2** *hist.* a military password.

wa·ter /wáwtər, wót-/ *n. & v.* ● *n.* **1** a colorless, transparent, odorless, tasteless liquid compound of oxygen and hydrogen. ¶ Chem. formula: H_2O. **2** a liquid consisting chiefly of this and found in seas, lakes, and rivers, in rain, and in secretions of organisms. **3** an expanse of water; a sea, lake, river, etc. **4** (in *pl.*) part of a sea or river (*in Icelandic waters*). **5** (often as **the waters**) mineral water at a spa, etc. **6** the state of a tide (*high water*). **7** a solution of a specified substance in water (*lavender water*). **8** the quality of the transparency and brilliance of a gem, esp. a diamond. **9** (*attrib.*) **a** found in or near water. **b** of, for, or worked by water. **c** involving, using, or yielding water. ● *v.* **1** *tr.* sprinkle or soak with water. **2** *tr.* supply (a plant) with water. **3** *tr.* give water to (an animal) to drink. **4** *intr.* (of the mouth or eyes) secrete water as saliva or tears. **5** *tr.* (as **watered** *adj.*) (of silk, etc.) having irregular wavy glossy markings. **6** *tr.* adulterate (beer, etc.) with water. **7** *tr.* (of a river, etc.) supply (a place) with water. **8** *intr.* (of an animal) drink water. □ **like water** lavishly; profusely. **like water off a duck's back** see DUCK[1]. **make one's mouth water** cause one's saliva to flow; stimulate one's appetite or anticipation. **of the first water 1** (of a diamond) of the greatest brilliance and transparency. **2** of the finest quality or extreme degree. **water down 1** dilute with water. **2** make less forceful or controversial. **water under the bridge** past events accepted as past and irrevocable. □□ **wa·ter·er** *n.* **wa·ter·less** *adj.*

wa·ter bed *n.* a mattress of rubber or plastic, etc., filled with water.

wa·ter birth *n.* a birth in which the mother spends the final stages of labor in a birthing pool.

wa·ter blis·ter *n.* a blister containing a colorless fluid, not blood nor pus.

wa·ter boat·man *n.* any aquatic bug of the family Notonectidae or Corixidae, swimming with oarlike hind legs.

wa·ter buf·fa·lo *n.* the common domestic E. Indian buffalo, *Bubalus arnee*.

wa·ter chest·nut *n.* **1** an aquatic plant, *Trapa natans*, bearing an edible seed. **2 a** (in full **Chinese water chestnut**) a sedge, *Eleocharis tuberosa*, with rushlike leaves arising from a corm. **b** this corm used as food.

wa·ter·col·or /wáwtərkúlər, wót-/ *n.* **1** artists' paint made of pigment to be diluted with water and not oil. **2** a picture painted with this. **3** the art of painting with watercolors. □□ **wa·ter·col·or·ist** *n.*

wa·ter-cooled *adj.* cooled by the circulation of water.

wa·ter·cool·er /wáwtərkŏŏlər, wót-/ *n.* a tank of cooled drinking water.

wa·ter·course /wáwtərkawrs, wót-/ *n.* **1** a brook, stream, or artificial water channel. **2** the bed along which this flows.

WATERFOWL

Waterfowl form the order Anseriformes, which comprises around 160 swan, goose, duck, and shelduck species. All have short legs with webbed feet, used as paddles to push through the water; their waterproof plumage is so effective that they remain dry when diving underwater. Geese typically feed on dry land, whereas swans and ducks feed in water, either diving for food on the bottom of lakes, rivers, or shallow coastal waters, or using their broad bills to dabble on the surface. Most waterfowl migrate in winter.

FOOT OF A CANADA GOOSE

toe *webbing* *claw*

waterproof plumage

EXTERNAL FEATURES OF A SHELDUCK (*Tadorna tadorna*)

broad flat bill *speculum* *webbed foot* *short leg*

OTHER TYPES OF WATERFOWL

DUCKS
mandarin duck
(*Aix galericulata*)

GEESE
snow goose
(*Anser caerulescens*)

SWANS
mute swan
(*Cygnus olor*)

wa·ter·cress /wáwtərkres, wót-/ *n.* a hardy perennial cress, *Nasturtium officinale*, growing in running water, with pungent leaves used in salad.

wa·ter cy·cle *n.* ◀ the circulation of water on earth, in which precipitation returns to the sea via rivers and to the atmosphere by evaporation and transpiration.

wa·ter·fall /wáwtərfawl, wót-/ *n.* ▼ a stream or river flowing over a precipice or down a steep hillside.

resident band of rock *water cascade* *gulley* *exposed rock strata* *cave* *plunge pool* *eddy hole*

WATERFALL: MODEL OF A WATERFALL

wa·ter·fowl /wáwtərfowl, wót-/ *n.* (usu. collect. as *pl.*) ▲ birds frequenting water, esp. swimming game birds. ▷ DUCK

wa·ter·front /wáwtərfrunt, wót-/ *n.* the part of a town or city adjoining a river, lake, harbor, etc.

wa·ter glass *n.* **1** a solution of sodium or potassium silicate used for preserving eggs, as a vehicle for fresco painting, and for hardening artificial stone. **2** a tube with a glass bottom enabling objects under water to be observed. **3** a drinking glass.

wa·ter hole *n.* a shallow depression in which water collects (esp. in the bed of a river otherwise dry).

wa·ter·ing can *n.* a portable container with a long spout usu. ending in a perforated sprinkler, for watering plants.

wa·ter·ing hole *n.* **1** a pool of water from which animals regularly drink; a water hole. **2** *sl.* a bar.

wa·ter lil·y *n.* ▶ any aquatic plant of the family Nymphaeaceae, with broad flat floating leaves and large usu. cup-shaped floating flowers.

wa·ter·line /wáwtər-līn, wót-/ *n.* **1** the line along which the surface of water touches a ship's side (marked on a ship for use in loading). **2** a linear watermark.

W

WATER LILY (*Nymphaea* species)

wa·ter·logged /wáwtərlawgd, -logd, wótər-/ *adj.* **1** saturated with water. **2** (of a boat, etc.) hardly able to float from being filled with water.

Wa·ter·loo /wáwtərlóo, wótər-/ *n.* a decisive defeat or contest (*meet one's Waterloo*).

wa·ter main *n.* the main pipe in a water-supply system.

wa·ter·man /wáwtərmən, wótər-/ *n.* (*pl.* **-men**) **1** a boatman plying for hire. **2** an oarsman as regards skill in keeping the boat balanced.

wa·ter·mark /wáwtərmaark, wótər-/ *n. & v.* • *n.* ▼ a faint design made in some paper during manufacture, visible when held against the light, identifying the maker, etc. • *v.tr.* mark with this.

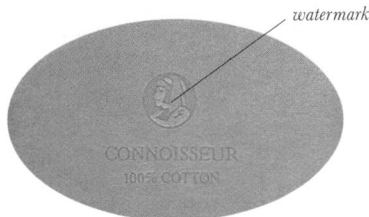

watermark

WATERMARK ON PAPER

wa·ter meas·ur·er *n.* ▼ a long thin aquatic bug of the family Hydrometridae, which walks slowly on the surface film of water.

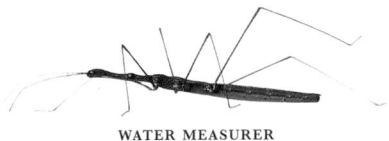

WATER MEASURER
(*Hydrometra stagnorum*)

wa·ter·mel·on /wáwtərmelən, wótər-/ *n.* a large, smooth, green melon, *Citrullus lanatus*, with red pulp and watery juice.

wa·ter moc·ca·sin *n.* **1** a venomous snake, *Agkistrodon piscivorus*, found in wet or marshy areas of the southern US; a cottonmouth. **2** any of various harmless water snakes.

wa·ter pipe *n.* **1** a pipe for conveying water. **2** a hookah.

wa·ter pis·tol *n.* a toy pistol shooting a jet of water.

wa·ter plan·tain *n.* ▶ a plant of the genus *Alisma*, with plantainlike leaves, found esp. in ditches.

wa·ter po·lo *n.* a game played by swimmers, with a ball like a soccer ball.

wa·ter·proof /wáwtərproof, wótər-/ *adj. & v.* • *adj.* impervious to water. • *v.tr.* make waterproof.

wa·ter rat *n.* **1** any rodent of aquatic habits. **2** a muskrat. **3** *sl.* a waterfront vagrant or thug.

wa·ter-re·pel·lent *adj.* not easily penetrated by water.

wa·ter·shed /wáwtərshed, wótər-/ *n.* **1** a line of separation between waters flowing to different rivers, basins, or seas. **2** a turning point in affairs.

wa·ter ski *n. & v.* • *n.* (*pl.* **skis**) each of a pair of skis for skimming the surface of the water when towed by a motorboat. • *v.intr.* (**water-ski**) (**-skis, -skied, -skiing**) travel on water skis. □□ **wa·ter-ski·er** *n.*

wa·ter soft·en·er *n.* an apparatus or substance for softening hard water.

wa·ter·spout /wáwtərspowt, wótər-/ *n.* a gyrating column of water and spray formed by a whirlwind between sea and cloud.

wa·ter ta·ble *n.* a level below which the ground is saturated with water.

W

WATERWHEEL

First utilized around 100 BC for grinding corn, water power was later put to use in mills and heavy industry. An overshot wheel is used where slow-moving water falls from a height and drives the wheel around. Where fast-moving water is available an undershot wheel is used; the water passes under the wheel to turn the blades.

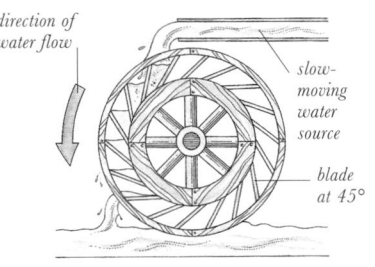

direction of water flow

slow-moving water source

blade at 45°

OVERSHOT WHEEL

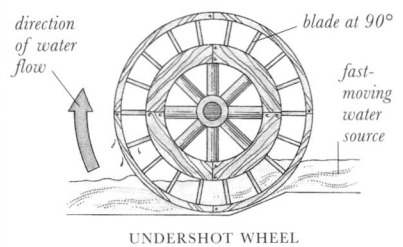

direction of water flow

blade at 90°

fast-moving water source

UNDERSHOT WHEEL

---

wa·ter·tight /wáwtərtīt, wótər-/ *adj.* **1** closely fastened or fitted or made so as to prevent the passage of water. **2** (of an argument, etc.) unassailable.

wa·ter tow·er *n.* a tower with an elevated tank to give pressure for distributing water.

wa·ter·way /wáwtərway, wótər-/ *n.* **1** a navigable channel. **2** a route for travel by water. **3** a thick plank at the outer edge of a deck along which a channel is hollowed for water to run off by.

wa·ter·weed /wáwtərweed, wótər-/ *n.* any of various aquatic plants.

wa·ter·wheel /wáwtərhweel, wótər-, -weel/ *n.* ▲ a wheel driven by water to work machinery, or to raise water.

wa·ter wings *n.pl.* inflated floats fixed on the arms of a person learning to swim.

wa·ter·works /wáwtərwərks, wótər-/ *n.* **1** an establishment for managing a water supply. **2** *colloq.* the shedding of tears. **3** *Brit. colloq.* the urinary system.

wa·ter·y /wáwtəree, wótər-/ *adj.* **1** containing too much water. **2** too thin in consistency. **3** of or consisting of water. **4** (of the eyes) suffused with water. **5** (of conversation, style, etc.) vapid; uninteresting. **6** (of color) pale. **7** (of the Sun, Moon, or sky) rainy-looking. □□ **wa·ter·i·ness** *n.*

watt /wot/ *n.* the SI unit of power, equivalent to one joule per second. ¶ Symb.: **W**.

watt·age /wótij/ *n.* an amount of electrical power expressed in watts.

watt-hour *n.* the energy used when one watt is applied for one hour.

wat·tle[1] /wót'l/ *n. & v.* • *n.* **1 a** interlaced rods as a material for making fences, walls, etc. **b** (in *sing.* or *pl.*) rods and twigs for this use. **2** an Australian

WATER PLANTAIN
(*Alisma plantago-aquatica*)

---

acacia with long pliant branches and golden flowers used as the national emblem. • *v.tr.* **1** make of wattle. **2** enclose or fill up with wattles.

wat·tle[2] /wót'l/ *n.* **1** ▶ a loose fleshy appendage on the head or throat of a turkey or other birds. **2** = BARB *n.* 3. □□ **wat·tled** *adj.*

wat·tle and daub *n.* ▼ a network of rods and twigs plastered with mud or clay as a building material.

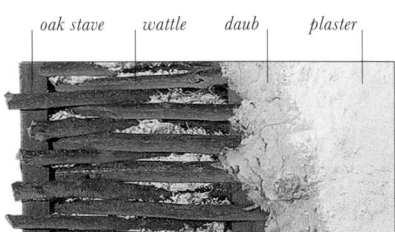

wattle

WATTLE
OF A
TURKEY

oak stave   *wattle*   *daub*   *plaster*

WATTLE AND DAUB WALL

wave /wayv/ *v. & n.* • *v.* **1 a** *intr.* (often foll. by *to*) move a hand, etc., to and fro in greeting or as a signal (*waved to me across the street*). **b** *tr.* move (a hand, etc.) in this way. **2 a** *intr.* show a sinuous motion as of a flag, tree, or a wheat field in the wind. **b** *tr.* impart a waving motion to. **3** *tr.* brandish (a sword, etc.) as an encouragement to followers, etc. **4** *tr.* tell or direct (a person) by waving (*waved them away*). **5** *tr.* express (a greeting, etc.) by waving (*waved good-bye to them*). **6** *tr.* give an undulating form to; make wavy. **7** *intr.* (of hair, etc.) have such a form; be wavy. • *n.* **1** a ridge of water between two depressions. **2** ▶ a long body of water curling into an arched form and breaking on the shore. **3** a body of persons in one of successive advancing groups. **4** a gesture of waving. **5 a** the process of waving the hair. **b** an undulating form produced in the hair by waving. **6 a** a temporary occurrence of a condition, emotion, or influence (*a wave of enthusiasm*). **b** a specified period of widespread weather (*heat wave*). **7** *Physics* **a** the disturbance of the particles of a fluid medium to form ridges and troughs for the propagation or direction of motion, heat, sound, etc. **b** a single curve in the course of this motion. **8** *Electr.* a similar variation of an electromagnetic field in the propagation of radiation through a medium or vacuum. □ **make waves** *colloq.* cause trouble. **wave aside** dismiss as intrusive or irrelevant. □□ **wave·less** *adj.* **wave·like** *adj. & adv.*

wave·band /wáyvband/ *n.* a range of wavelengths between certain limits.

wave·form /wáyvfawrm/ *n. Physics* a curve showing the shape of a wave at a given time.

wave·length /wáyvlengkth, -length, -lenth/ *n.* **1** the distance between successive crests of a wave, esp. points in a sound wave or electromagnetic wave. ▷ ELECTROMAGNETIC RADIATION. ¶ Symb.: λ. **2** this as a distinctive feature of radio waves from a transmitter. **3** *colloq.* a particular mode or range of thinking and communicating (*we don't seem to be on the same wavelength*).

wave·let /wáyvlit/ *n.* a small wave on water.

wa·ver /wáyvər/ *v.intr.* **1** be or become unsteady; falter; begin to give way. **2** be undecided between different opinions; be shaken in resolution or belief. **3** (of a light) flicker. □□ **wa·ver·er** *n.* **wa·ver·ing·ly** *adv.*

wav·y /wáyvee/ *adj.* (**wavier, waviest**) (of a line or surface) having waves or alternate contrary curves (*wavy hair*). □□ **wav·i·ness** *n.*

WAVE

Waves form when the water's surface is blown by a strong wind across a sufficient "fetch" (the distance taken to build a wave). The water within the wave remains constant, each level moving in an orbital path, like rollers in a conveyor belt, irrespective of the distance the wave has traveled. In shallow water, a wave's path elongates and becomes elliptical before breaking on a shore.

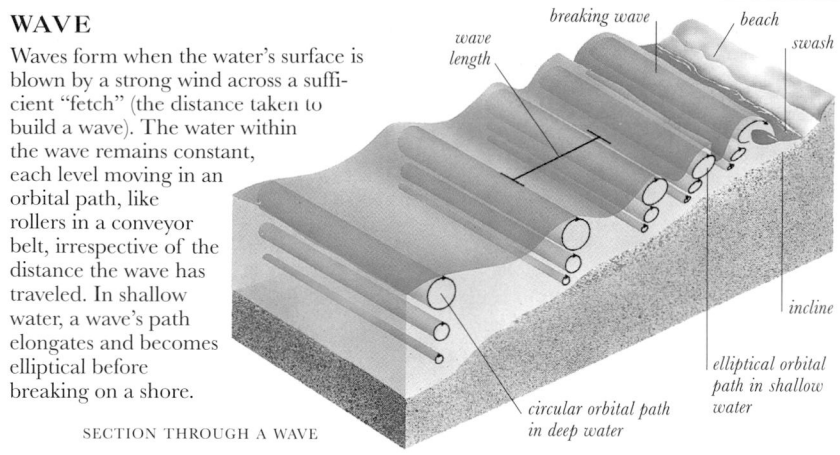

wave length   *breaking wave*   *beach*   *swash*

incline

elliptical orbital path in shallow water

circular orbital path in deep water

SECTION THROUGH A WAVE

---

wa-wa /wáawaa/ *n.* (also **wah-wah**) *Mus.* an effect achieved on brass instruments by alternately applying and removing a mute, and on an electric guitar by controlling the output from the amplifier with a pedal.

wax[1] /waks/ *n. & v.* ● *n.* **1** a sticky, plastic, yellowish substance secreted by bees as the material of honeycomb cells. **2** a white translucent material obtained from this by bleaching and purifying and used for candles, in modeling, as a basis of polishes, and for other purposes. **3** any similar substance, e.g., earwax. **4** *colloq.* **a** a phonograph record. **b** material for the manufacture of this. **5** (*attrib.*) made of wax. ● *v.tr.* **1** cover or treat with wax. **2** *colloq.* record for the phonograph. □□ **wax-er** *n.*

wax[2] /waks/ *v.intr.* **1** (of the Moon between new and full) have a progressively larger part of its visible surface illuminated, increasing in apparent size (cf. WANE). **2** become larger or stronger. **3** pass into a specified state or mood (*wax lyrical*). □ **wax and wane** undergo alternate increases and decreases.

wax bean *n.* a yellow-podded snap bean.

wax-en /wáksən/ *adj.* **1** having a smooth, pale, translucent surface as of wax. **2** able to receive impressions like wax. **3** *archaic* made of wax.

wax pa-per *n.* (also **waxed pa-per**) paper water-proofed with a layer of wax.

wax-wing /wákswing/ *n.* ▶ any bird of the genus *Bombycilla*, with small tips like red sealing wax to some wing feathers.

wax-work /wákswərk/ *n.* **1 a** an object, esp. a lifelike dummy, modeled in wax. **b** the making of waxworks. **2** (in *pl.*) an exhibition of wax dummies.

wax-y /wáksee/ *adj.* (**waxier**, **waxiest**) resembling wax in consistency or in its surface. □□ **wax-i-ness** *n.*

way /way/ *n. & adv.* ● *n.* **1** a road, path, etc., for passing along. **2** a route for reaching a place, esp. the best one (*asked the way to Rockefeller Center*). **3** a place of passage in a building, etc. (*could not find the way out*). **4 a** a method for attaining an object (*that is not the way to do it*). **b** the ability to obtain one's object (*has a way with him*). **5 a** a person's chosen course of action. **b** a manner of behaving; a personal peculiarity (*has a way of forgetting things*). **6** a specific manner of procedure (*soon got into the way of it*). **7** the normal course of events (*that is always the way*). **8** a traveling distance; a length traversed or to be traversed (*is a long way away*). **9 a** an unimpeded opportunity of advance. **b** a space free of obstacles. **10** a region or ground over which advance is desired or natural. **11** impetus; progress (*pushed my way through*). **12** movement of a ship, etc. (*gather way;*

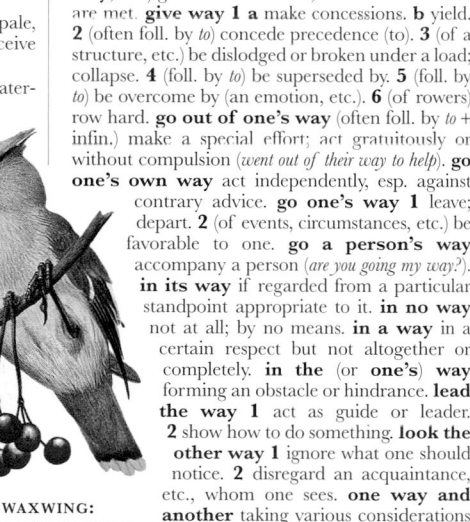

WAXWING:
BOHEMIAN WAXWING
(*Bombycilla garrulus*)

lose way). **13** the state of being engaged in movement from place to place; time spent in this (*met them on the way home*). **14** a specified direction (*step this way; which way are you going?*). **15** (in *pl.*) parts into which a thing is divided (*split it three ways*). **16** a person's line of occupation or business. **17** a specified condition or state (*in a bad way*). **18** a respect (*useful in some ways*). **19 a** (in *pl.*) a structure of lumber, etc., down which a new ship is launched. **b** parallel rails, etc., as a track for the movement of a machine. ● *adv. colloq.* to a considerable extent; far (*you're way off the mark*). □ **across** (or **over**) **the way** opposite. **any way** = ANYWAY. **be on one's way** set off; depart. **by the way 1** incidentally. **2** during a journey. **by way of 1** through; by means of. **2** as a substitute for or as a form of (*did it by way of apology*). **3** with the intention of (*asked by way of discovering the truth*). **come one's way** become available to one; become one's lot. **find a way** discover a means of obtaining one's object. **get** (or **have**) **one's way** (or **have it one's own way**, etc.) get what one wants; ensure one's wishes are met. **give way 1 a** make concessions. **b** yield. **2** (often foll. by *to*) concede precedence (to). **3** (of a structure, etc.) be dislodged or broken under a load; collapse. **4** (foll. by *to*) be superseded by. **5** (foll. by *to*) be overcome by (an emotion, etc.). **6** (of rowers) row hard. **go out of one's way** (often foll. by *to* + infin.) make a special effort; act gratuitously or without compulsion (*went out of their way to help*). **go one's own way** act independently, esp. against contrary advice. **go one's way 1** leave; depart. **2** (of events, circumstances, etc.) be favorable to one. **go a person's way** accompany a person (*are you going my way?*). **in its way** if regarded from a particular standpoint appropriate to it. **in no way** not at all; by no means. **in a way** in a certain respect but not altogether or completely. **in the** (or **one's**) **way** forming an obstacle or hindrance. **lead the way 1** act as guide or leader. **2** show how to do something. **look the other way 1** ignore what one should notice. **2** disregard an acquaintance, etc., whom one sees. **one way and another** taking various considerations into account. **one way or another** by some means. **on the** (or **one's**) **way 1** in the course of a journey, etc. **2** having progressed (*is well on the way to completion*). **3** *colloq.* (of a child) conceived but not yet born. **on the way out** *colloq.* going down in status, estimation, or favor; going out of fashion. **the other way around** (or **about**) in an inverted or reversed position. **out of the way 1** no longer an obstacle. **2** disposed of; settled. **3** (of a person) imprisoned or killed. **4** uncommon; remarkable (*nothing out of the way*). **5** (of a place) remote;

inaccessible. **out of one's way** not on one's intended route. **way back** *colloq.* long ago.

way-bill /wáybil/ *n.* a list of goods being shipped on a vehicle.

way-far-er /wáyfairər/ *n.* a traveler, esp. on foot.

way-lay /wayláy/ *v.tr.* (*past* and *past part.* **waylaid**) **1** lie in wait for. **2** stop to rob or interview.

way-leave /wáyleev/ *n.* a right of way granted over another's property.

way of life *n.* the habits governing all one's actions, etc.

way-out *adj. colloq.* **1** unusual; eccentric. **2** avant-garde; progressive. **3** excellent; exciting.

-ways /wayz/ *suffix* forming adjectives and adverbs of direction or manner (*sideways*) (cf. -WISE).

ways and means *n.pl.* the methods and resources for achieving something.

way-side /wáysīd/ *n.* **1** the side of a road. **2** the land at the side of a road. □ **fall by the wayside** fail to continue in an endeavor or undertaking (after Luke 8:5).

way sta-tion *n.* **1** a minor station on a railroad. **2** a point marking progress in a certain course of action, etc.

way-ward /wáywərd/ *adj.* **1** childishly self-willed or perverse; capricious. **2** unaccountable or freakish. □□ **way-ward-ly** *adv.* **way-ward-ness** *n.*

way-worn /wáywawrn/ *adj.* tired with travel.

wa-zoo /wazoó/ *n.* *US colloq.* a person's buttocks or anus. □ **up** or **out the wazoo** in great quantities.

we /wee/ *pron.* (*obj.* **us**; *poss.* **our**, **ours**) **1** (*pl.* of I[2]) used by and with reference to more than one person speaking or writing, or one such person and one or more associated persons. **2** used for or by a royal person in a proclamation, etc., and by a writer or editor in a formal context. **3** people in general (cf. ONE *pron.* 2). **4** *colloq.* = I[2] (*give us a chance*). **5** *colloq.* (often implying condescension) you (*how are we feeling today?*).

weak /week/ *adj.* **1** deficient in strength, power, or number; easily broken or bent or defeated. **2** deficient in vigor (*weak health, a weak imagination*). **3 a** deficient in resolution; easily led (*a weak character*). **b** indicating a lack of resolution (*a weak surrender; a weak chin*). **4** unconvincing or logically deficient (*a weak argument*). **5** (of a mixed liquid or solution) watery; thin; dilute (*weak tea*). **6** (of a style, etc.) not vigorous nor well-knit; diffuse; slipshod. **7** (of a crew) short handed. **8** (of a syllable, etc.) unstressed. **9** *Gram.* in Germanic languages: **a** (of a verb) forming inflections by the addition of a suffix to the stem. **b** (of a noun or adjective) belonging to a declension in which the stem originally ended in -n.

weak-en /wéekən/ *v.* **1** *tr. & intr.* make or become weak or weaker. **2** *intr.* relent; give way; succumb to temptation, etc.

weak-kneed *adj. colloq.* lacking resolution.

weak-ling /wéekling/ *n.* a feeble person or animal.

weak-ly /wéeklee/ *adv. & adj.* ● *adv.* in a weak manner. ● *adj.* (**weaklier**, **weakliest**) sickly; not robust.

weak-mind-ed *adj.* **1** mentally deficient. **2** lacking resolution. □□ **weak-mind-ed-ness** *n.*

weak mo-ment *n.* a time when one is unusually compliant or temptable.

weak-ness /wéeknis/ *n.* **1** the state or condition of being weak. **2** a weak point; a defect. **3** the inability to resist a particular temptation. **4** (foll. by *for*) a self-indulgent liking (*have a weakness for chocolate*).

weal /weel/ *n. & v.* ● *n.* a ridge raised on the flesh by a stroke of a rod or whip. ● *v.tr.* mark with a weal.

wealth /welth/ *n.* **1** riches; abundant possessions. **2** the state of being rich. **3** (foll. by *of*) an abundance (*a wealth of new material*).

wealth-y /wélthee/ *adj.* (**wealthier**, **wealthiest**) having an abundance esp. of money.

W

wean /ween/ *v.tr.* **1** accustom (an infant or other young mammal) to food other than milk. **2** (often foll. by *from, away from*) disengage (from a habit, etc.) by enforced discontinuance.

wean·ling /wéenling/ *n.* a newly weaned child, etc.

weap·on /wépən/ *n.* **1** a thing designed or used for inflicting bodily harm. **2** a means employed for trying to gain the advantage in a conflict (*irony is a double-edged weapon*). □□ **weap·on·less** *adj.*

weap·on·ry /wépənree/ *n.* weapons collectively.

wear[1] /wair/ *v. & n.* ● *v.* (*past* **wore** /wawr/; *past part.* **worn** /wawrn/) **1** *tr.* have on one's person as clothing or an ornament, etc. **2** *tr.* be dressed usually in (*wears green*). **3** *tr.* exhibit or present (a facial expression or appearance) (*wore a frown; the day wore a different aspect*). **4** *tr.* (often foll. by *away, down*) **a** *tr.* injure the surface of, or partly obliterate or alter, by rubbing, stress, or use. **b** *intr.* undergo such injury or change. **5** *tr. & intr.* (foll. by *off, away*) rub or be rubbed off. **6** *tr.* make (a hole, etc.) by constant rubbing or dripping, etc. **7** *tr. & intr.* (often foll. by *out*) exhaust; tire or be tired. **8** *tr.* (foll. by *down*) overcome by persistence. **9** *intr.* **a** remain for a specified time in working order or a presentable state; last long. **b** (foll. by *well, badly*, etc.) endure continued use or life. **10 a** *intr.* (of time) pass, esp. tediously. **b** *tr.* pass (time) gradually away. ● *n.* **1** the act of wearing or the state of being worn (*suitable for informal wear*). **2** things worn; fashionable or suitable clothing (*sportswear; footwear*). **3** (in full **wear and tear**) damage sustained from continuous use. **4** the capacity for resisting wear and tear (*still a great deal of wear left in it*). □ **in wear** being regularly worn. **wear off** lose effectiveness or intensity. **wear out 1** use or be used until no longer usable. **2** tire or be tired out. **wear the pants** see PANTS. **wear thin** (of patience, excuses, etc.) begin to fail. **wear** (or **wear one's years**) **well** *colloq.* remain young-looking. □□ **wear·a·ble** *adj.* **wear·a·bil·i·ty** /wáirəbílitee/ *n.* **wear·er** *n.*

wear[2] /wair/ *v.* (*past and past part.* **wore** /wawr/) **1** *tr.* bring (a ship) about by turning its head away from the wind. **2** *intr.* (of a ship) come about in this way (cf. TACK[1] *v.* 4a).

wear·i·some /wéereesəm/ *adj.* tedious; tiring by monotony or length.

wear·y /wéeree/ *adj. & v.* ● *adj.* (**wearier, weariest**) **1** disinclined for further exertion or endurance. **2** (foll. by *of*) dismayed at the continuing of; impatient of. **3** tiring or tedious. ● *v.tr. & intr.* (**-ies, -ied**) make or grow weary. □□ **wear·i·ly** *adv.* **wear·i·ness** *n.*

wea·sel /wéezəl/ *n. & v.* ● *n.* **1** a small, reddish-brown, flesh-eating mammal, *Mustela nivalis*, with a slender body. ▷ MUSTELID. **2** a stoat. **3** *colloq.* a deceitful or treacherous person. ● *v.intr.* **1** equivocate or quibble. **2** (foll. by *on, out*) default on an obligation. □□ **wea·sel·ly** *adj.*

weath·er /wéthər/ *n. & v.* ● *n.* **1** the state of the atmosphere at a place and time as regards heat, cloudiness, dryness, sunshine, wind, and rain, etc. **2** (*attrib.*) *Naut.* windward (on the weather side). ● *v.* **1** *tr.* expose to atmospheric changes (*weathered shingles*). **2 a** *tr.* (usu. in *passive*) discolor or partly disintegrate (rock or stones) by exposure to air. **b** *intr.* be discolored or worn in this way. **3** *tr.* make (boards or tiles) overlap downward to keep out rain, etc. **4** *tr.* **a** come safely through (a storm). **b** survive (a difficult period, etc.). **5** *tr.* (of a ship or its crew) get to the windward of (a cape, etc.). □ **keep a** (or **one's**) **weather eye open** be watchful. **make good** (or **bad**) **weather of it** *Naut.* (of a ship) behave well (or badly) in a storm. **make heavy weather of** *colloq.* exaggerate the difficulty presented by. **under the weather** *colloq.* **1** indisposed or out of sorts. **2** drunk.

weath·er·beat·en *adj.* affected by exposure to the weather.

W

WEATHER CHART

Detailed recordings of pressure, wind direction, and temperature are constantly made across the globe. The data is fed into supercomputers to build a picture of atmospheric conditions and to generate forecasts. This information is depicted on charts; a synoptic chart is produced when data is gathered simultaneously. The markings on a weather chart show the position of fronts, which bring the most changeable weather, as well as isobars indicating air pressure and arrows denoting wind direction.

SYNOPTIC WEATHER CHART OF THE NORTH ATLANTIC

high-pressure zone · *isobar* · *dew point in °C* · *temperature in °C* · *wind direction and speed*

occluded front · *pressure in millibars* · *cold front* · *warm sector* · *warm front* · *center of depression* · *cloud cover*

---

weath·er chart *n.* ▲ a diagram showing the state of weather over a large area.

weath·er·cock /wéthərkok/ *n.* **1** ◀ a weather vane (see VANE 1) in the form of a cock. **2** an inconstant person.

    weath·er·glass /wéthərglas/ *n.* a simple barometer or hygroscope.

    weath·er·ing /wéthəring/ *n.* **1** the action of the weather on materials, etc., exposed to it. ▷ OUTCROP. **2** exposure to adverse weather conditions (see WEATHER *v.* 1).

    weath·er·man /wéthərman/ *n.* (*pl.* **-men**) a meteorologist, esp. one who broadcasts a weather forecast.

    weath·er·proof /wéthərproof/ *adj. & v.* ● *adj.* resistant to the effects of bad weather. ● *v.tr.* make weatherproof. □□ **weath·er·proofed** *adj.*

    weath·er strip *n. & v.* ● *n.* a piece of material used to make a door or window proof against rain or wind. ● *v.tr.* (**weather-strip**) (**-stripped, -stripping**) install a weather strip on.

weath·er vane see VANE 1.

weath·er·worn /wéthərwawrn/ *adj.* damaged by exposure to weather.

weave[1] /weev/ *v. & n.* ● *v.* (*past* **wove** /wōv/; *past part.* **woven** /wōvən/ or **wove**) **1** *tr.* **a** ▶ form (fabric) by interlacing long threads in two directions. **b** form (thread) into fabric in this way. **2** *intr.* **a** make fabric in this way. **b** work at a loom. **3** *tr.* make by interlacing rushes or flowers, etc. **4** *tr.* **a** (foll. by *into*) make (facts, etc.) into a story or connected whole. **b** make (a story) in this way. ● *n.* a style of weaving.

wind direction indicator

compass direction indicator

WEATHERCOCK

weave[2] /weev/ *v.intr.* **1** move repeatedly from side to side; take an intricate course to avoid obstructions. **2** *colloq.* maneuver an aircraft in this way; take evasive action. □ **get weaving** *sl.* begin action; hurry.

weav·er /wéevər/ *n.* **1** a person whose occupation is weaving. **2** = WEAVERBIRD.

weav·er·bird /wéevərbərd/ *n.* any tropical bird of the family Ploceidae, building elaborately woven nests. ▷ NEST

web /web/ *n. & v.* ● *n.* **1 a** a woven fabric. **b** an amount woven in one piece. **2** a complete structure or connected series (*a web of lies*). **3** a cobweb, gossamer, or a similar product of a spinning creature. **4 a** a membrane between the toes of a swimming animal or bird. ▷ WATERFOWL. **b** the vane of a bird's feather. **5 a** a large roll of paper used in a continuous printing process. **b** an endless wire mesh on rollers, on which this is made. **6** (**the Web**) = WORLD WIDE WEB. ● *v.* (**webbed, webbing**) **1** *tr.* weave a web on. **2** *intr.* weave a web. □□ **webbed** *adj.*

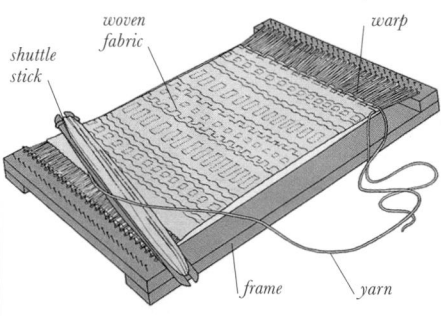

woven fabric · *warp* · *shuttle stick* · *frame* · *yarn*

WEAVE: FORMING FABRIC ON A SIMPLE WEAVING FRAME

web·bing /wébing/ *n.* strong, closely woven fabric used for supporting upholstery, for belts, etc.

web·cam /wébkam/ *n.* ▶ (*trademark* in the US) a video camera connected to a computer, so that its output may be viewed on the Internet.

lens

built-in microphone

base

WEBCAM WITH INBUILT MICROPHONE

we·ber /wébər, váybər/ *n.* the SI unit of magnetic flux, causing the electromotive force of one volt in a circuit of one turn when generated or removed in one second. ¶ Abbr.: **Wb**.

web-foot·ed *adj.* having the toes connected by webs.

web·mas·ter /wébmastər/ *n. Computing* a person who is responsible for a particular server on the Internet.

web·page /wébpayj/ *n. Computing* a hypertext document accessible via the Internet.

web·site *n. Computing* a location on the Internet that maintains one or more pages on the World Wide Web.

web·worm /wébwərm/ *n.* a caterpillar that spins a large web in which to sleep or to feed on enclosed foliage.

wed /wed/ *v.* (**wedding**; *past* and *past part.* **wedded** or **wed**) **1** usu. *formal* or *literary* **a** *tr.* & *intr.* marry. **b** *tr.* join in marriage. **2** *tr.* unite (*wed efficiency to economy*). **3** *tr.* (as **wedded** *adj.*) of or in marriage (*wedded bliss*). **4** *tr.* (as **wedded** *adj.*) (foll. by *to*) obstinately attached or devoted (*to a pursuit, etc.*).

we'd /weed/ *contr.* **1** we had. **2** we should; we would.

wed·ding /wéding/ *n.* a marriage ceremony.

wed·ding march *n.* a march played at the entrance of the bride or the exit of the couple at a wedding.

wedge¹ /wej/ *n.* & *v.* ● *n.* **1** a piece of wood or metal, etc., tapering to a sharp edge, that is driven between two objects or parts of an object to secure or separate them. **2** anything resembling a wedge (*a wedge of cheese*; *troops formed a wedge*). **3** a golf club with a wedge-shaped head. **4 a** a wedge-shaped heel. **b** a shoe with this. ● *v.tr.* **1** tighten, secure, or fasten by means of a wedge (*wedged the door open*). **2** force open or apart with a wedge. **3** (foll. by *in, into*) pack or thrust (a thing or oneself) tightly in or into.

wedge² /wej/ *v.tr. Pottery* prepare (clay) for use by cutting, kneading, and throwing down.

wedg·ie /wéjee/ *n. colloq.* **1** a shoe with an extended wedge-shaped heel. **2** the condition of having one's underwear, etc., wedged between one's buttocks.

Wedg·wood /wéjwŏŏd/ *n. Trademark* **1** ceramic ware made by J. Wedgwood, Engl. potter d. 1795, and his successors, esp. a kind of fine stoneware usu. with a white cameo design. **2** the characteristic blue color of this stoneware.

wed·lock /wédlok/ *n.* the married state. □ **born in** (or **out of**) **wedlock** born of married (or unmarried) parents.

Wednes·day /wénzday, -dee/ *n.* & *adv.* ● *n.* the fourth day of the week, following Tuesday. ● *adv. colloq.* **1** on Wednesday. **2** (**Wednesdays**) on Wednesdays; each Wednesday.

wee /wee/ *adj.* (**weer** /wéeər/; **weest** /wéeist/) esp. *Sc.* little; very small.

weed /weed/ *n.* & *v.* ● *n.* **1** a wild plant growing where it is not wanted. **2** a thin, weak-looking person or horse. **3** (prec. by *the*) *sl.* **a** marijuana. **b** tobacco. ● *v.* **1** *tr.* **a** clear (an area) of weeds. **b** remove unwanted parts from. **2** *tr.* (foll. by *out*) **a** sort out (inferior or unwanted parts, etc.) for removal. **b** rid (a quantity or company) of inferior or unwanted members, etc. **3** *intr.* cut off or uproot weeds. □□ **weed·er** *n.* **weed·less** *adj.*

weed·y /wéedee/ *adj.* (**weedier**, **weediest**) **1** having many weeds. **2** (of a person) thin and puny. □□ **weed·i·ness** *n.*

week /week/ *n.* **1** a period of seven days reckoned usu. from and to midnight on Saturday– Sunday. **2** a period of seven days reckoned from any point (*would like to stay for a week*). **3 a** the five days Monday to Friday. **b** a normal amount of work done in this period (*a 35-hour week*). **4** (in *pl.*) a long time (*have not seen you for weeks*; *did it weeks ago*).

week·day /wéekday/ *n.* a day other than Sunday or other than at a weekend (often *attrib.*: *a weekday afternoon*).

week·end /wéekénd/ *n.* & *v.* ● *n.* Saturday and Sunday, esp. regarded as a time for leisure. ● *v.intr.* spend a weekend (*decided to weekend in the country*).

week·end·er /wéekéndər/ *n.* **1** a person who spends weekends away from home. **2** a weekend traveling bag.

week·long /wéeklawng, lóng/ *adj.* lasting for a week.

week·ly /wéeklee/ *adj.*, *adv.*, & *n.* ● *adj.* done, produced, or occurring once a week. ● *adv.* once a week; from week to week. ● *n.* (*pl.* **-ies**) a weekly newspaper or periodical.

ween /ween/ *v.tr. archaic* be of the opinion; think.

weep /weep/ *v.* & *n.* ● *v.* (*past* and *past part.* **wept** /wept/) **1** *intr.* shed tears. **2 a** *tr.* & (foll. by *for*) *intr.* shed tears for; bewail. **b** *tr.* utter or express with tears (*wept her thanks*). **3** *intr.* **a** be covered with or send forth drops. **b** exude liquid (*weeping sore*). **4** *intr.* (as **weeping** *adj.*) (of a tree) having drooping branches (*weeping willow*). ● *n.* a fit or spell of weeping. □□ **weep·er** *n.*

weep·ie /wéepee/ *n.* (also **weep·y**) (*pl.* **-ies**) *colloq.* a sentimental motion picture, play, etc.

weep·y /wéepee/ *adj.* (**weepier**, **weepiest**) *colloq.* inclined to weep; tearful.

wee·ver /wéevər/ *n.* ▼ any marine fish of the genus *Trachinus*, with sharp venomous dorsal spines.

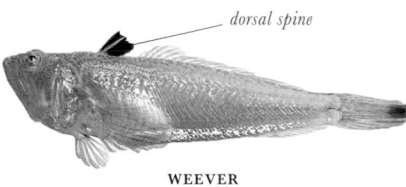

dorsal spine

WEEVER
(*Trachinus* species)

wee·vil /wéevil/ *n.* **1** ▼ any beetle of the family Curculionidae, with its head extended into a beak or rostrum and feeding esp. on grain. ▷ BEETLE. **2** any insect damaging stored grain. □□ **wee·vi·ly** *adj.*

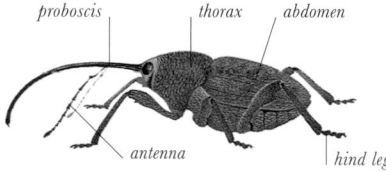

proboscis　*thorax*　*abdomen*

antenna　　　　　　　*hind leg*

WEEVIL: NUT WEEVIL
(*Curculio nucum*)

wee-wee /wéewee/ *n.* & *v. sl.* ● *n.* **1** the act or an instance of urinating. **2** urine. ● *v.intr.* (**-wees**, **-weed**, **-weeing**) urinate.

weft /weft/ *n.* **1** ▶ the threads woven across a warp to make fabric. **2** yarn for these. **3** a thing woven.

weigh /way/ *v.* **1** *tr.* find the weight of. **2** *tr.* balance in the hands to guess or as if to guess the weight of.

3 *tr.* (often foll. by *out*) **a** take a definite weight of; take a specified weight from a larger quantity. **b** distribute in exact amounts by weight. **4** *tr.* **a** estimate the relative importance or desirability of (*weighed the consequences*; *weighed the merits of the candidates*). **b** (foll. by *with*, *against*) compare (one consideration with another). **5** *tr.* be equal to (a specified weight) (*weighs three pounds*). **6** *intr.* **a** have importance; exert an influence. **b** (foll. by *with*) be regarded as important by (*the point that weighs with me*). **7** *intr.* (often foll. by *on*) be heavy or burdensome (to); be depressing (to). □ **weigh anchor** see ANCHOR. **weigh down 1** bring or keep down by exerting weight. **2** be oppressive or burdensome to (*weighed down with worries*). **weigh in** (of a boxer before a contest, of a jockey after a race) be weighed. **weigh into** *colloq.* attack (physically or verbally). **weigh in with** *colloq.* advance (an argument, etc.) assertively or boldly. **weigh up** *colloq.* form an estimate of; consider carefully. **weigh one's words** carefully choose the way one expresses something. □□ **weigh·er** *n.*

weigh·bridge /wáybrij/ *n.* a platform scale for weighing vehicles, usu. having a plate set into the road for vehicles to drive on to.

weigh-in *n.* the weighing of a boxer, etc., before a fight.

weight /wayt/ *n.* & *v.* ● *n.* **1** *Physics* **a** the force experienced by a body as a result of the Earth's gravitation (cf. MASS¹ *n.* 8). **b** any similar force with which a body tends to a center of attraction. **2** the heaviness of a body regarded as a property of it; its relative mass or the quantity of matter contained by it giving rise to a downward force (*is twice your weight*; *kept in position by its weight*). **3 a** the quantitative expression of a body's weight (*has a weight of three pounds*). **b** a scale of such weights (*troy weight*). **4** a body of a known weight for use in weighing. **5** a heavy body (*a clock worked by weights*). **6** a load or burden (*a weight off my mind*). **7 a** influence; importance (*carried weight with the public*). **b** preponderance (*the weight of evidence was against them*). **8** a heavy object thrown as an athletic exercise; = SHOT¹ 7. **9** the surface density of cloth, etc., as a measure of its suitability. ● *v.tr.* **1 a** attach a weight to. **b** hold down with a weight or weights. **2** (foll. by *with*) impede or burden. **3** *Statistics* multiply the components of (an average) by factors to take account of their importance. **4** assign a handicap weight to (a horse). □ **put on weight 1** increase one's weight. **2** get fat. **throw one's weight about** (or **around**) *colloq.* be unpleasantly self-assertive. **worth one's weight in gold** (of a person) exceedingly useful or helpful.

weight·less /wáytlis/ *adj.* not apparently acted on by gravity. □□ **weight·less·ly** *adv.* **weight·less·ness** *n.*

weight·lift·ing /wáytlifting/ *n.* the sport of lifting a heavy weight. □□ **weight·lift·er** *n.*

weight·y /wáytee/ *adj.* (**weightier**, **weightiest**) **1** weighing much; heavy. **2** momentous; important. **3** (of utterances, etc.) deserving consideration; careful and serious. **4** influential; authoritative. □□ **weight·i·ly** *adv.* **weight·i·ness** *n.*

W

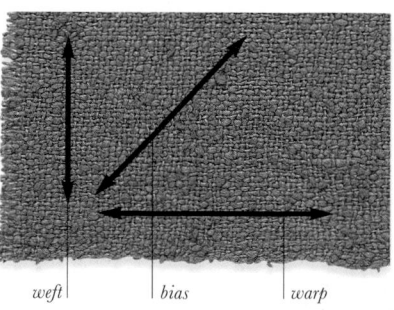

weft　　*bias*　　*warp*

WEFT ON A PIECE OF FABRIC

weir /weer/ *n.* **1** a dam built across a river to raise the level of water upstream or regulate its flow. **2** an enclosure of stakes, etc., set in a stream as a trap for fish.

weird /weerd/ *adj.* **1** uncanny; supernatural. **2** *colloq.* strange; incomprehensible. **3** *archaic* connected with fate. □□ **weird·ly** *adv.* **weird·ness** *n.*

weird·o /wéerdō/ *n.* (*pl.* **-os**) *colloq.* an odd or eccentric person.

welch var. of WELSH.

wel·come /wélkəm/ *n., int., v., & adj.* • *n.* the act or an instance of greeting or receiving gladly; a kind or glad reception (*gave them a warm welcome*). • *int.* expressing such a greeting. • *v.tr.* receive with a welcome. • *adj.* **1** that one receives with pleasure. **2** (foll. by *to*, or *to* + infin.) **a** cordially allowed or invited (*you are welcome to use my car*). **b** *iron.* gladly given (an unwelcome task, thing, etc.) (*here's my work and you are welcome to it*). □ **make welcome** receive hospitably. **you're** (or **you are**) **welcome** there is no need for thanks. □□ **wel·com·er** *n.* **wel·com·ing·ly** *adv.*

weld /weld/ *v. & n.* • *v.tr.* **1 a** hammer or press (pieces of metal) into one piece. **b** join by fusion with an electric arc, etc. **c** form by welding into some article. **2** fashion into an effectual or homogeneous whole. • *n.* a welded joint. □□ **weld·a·ble** *adj.* **weld·a·bil·i·ty** /wéldəbílitee/ *n.* **weld·er** *n.*

wel·fare /wélfair/ *n.* **1** well-being; happiness; health and prosperity. **2 a** the maintenance of persons in such a condition esp. by statutory procedure or social effort. **b** financial support given for this purpose.

wel·fare state *n.* **1** a system whereby the government undertakes to protect the health and well-being of its citizens by means of grants, pensions, etc. **2** a country practicing this system.

wel·far·ism /wélfairizəm/ *n.* principles characteristic of a welfare state. □□ **wel·far·ist** *n.*

wel·kin /wélkin/ *n. poet.* sky; the upper air.

well[1] /wel/ *adv., adj., & int.* • *adv.* (**better, best**) **1** in a satisfactory way. **2** in the right way (*well said; you did well to tell me*). **3** with some talent or distinction. **4** in a kind way. **5 a** thoroughly; carefully (*polish it well*). **b** intimately; closely (*knew them well*). **6** with heartiness or approval. **7** probably; reasonably; advisably (*you may well be right; we might well take the risk*). **8** to a considerable extent (*is well over forty*). **9** successfully; fortunately (*it turned out well*). **10** luckily; opportunely (*well met!*). **11** with a fortunate outcome; without disaster (*were well rid of them*). **12** profitably (*did well for themselves*). **13** comfortably; abundantly; liberally (*we live well here; the job pays well*). • *adj.* (**better, best**) **1** (usu. *predic.*) in good health (*are you well?; was not a well person*). **2** (*predic.*) **a** in a satisfactory state or position (*all is well*). **b** advisable (*it would be well to inquire*). • *int.* expressing surprise, resignation, insistence, etc., or resumption or continuation of talk, used esp. after a pause in speaking (*well, I never!; well, I suppose so; well, who was it?*). □ **as well 1** in addition; to an equal extent. **2** (also **just as well**) with equal reason; with no loss of advantage or need for regret (*may as well give up; it would be just as well to stop now*). **as well as** in addition to. **leave** (or **let**) **well enough alone** avoid needless change or disturbance. **take well** react calmly to (a thing, esp. bad news). **well and good** expressing dispassionate acceptance of a decision, etc. **well aware** certainly aware (*well aware of the danger*). **well away** having made considerable progress. **well worth** certainly worth (*well worth a visit; well worth visiting*). ¶ A hyphen is normally used in combinations of *well-* when used attributively, but not when used predicatively, e.g., *a well-made coat* but *the coat is well made*. □□ **well·ness** /wélnəs/ *n.*

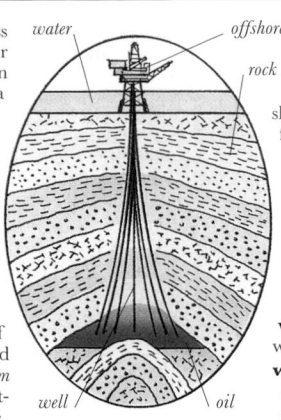

WELL: CROSS SECTION OF AN OIL WELL

water — offshore rig — rock strata — well — oil

well[2] /wel/ *n. & v.* • *n.* **1** ◄ a shaft sunk into the ground to obtain water, oil, etc. **2** an enclosed space like a well shaft, e.g., in the middle of a building for stairs or an elevator, or for light or ventilation. **3** (foll. by *of*) a source, esp. a copious one (*a well of information*). **4 a** a mineral spring. **b** (in *pl.*) a spa. **5** = INKWELL. **6** a depression for gravy, etc., in a dish or tray, or for a mat in the floor. • *v.intr.* (foll. by *out, up*) spring as from a fountain; flow copiously.

we'll /weel, wil/ *contr.* we shall; we will.

well-ac·quaint·ed *adj.* (**well acquainted** when *predic.*) (usu. foll. by *with*) familiar.

well-ad·just·ed *adj.* (**well adjusted** when *predic.*) **1** in a good state of adjustment. **2** *Psychol.* mentally and emotionally stable.

well-ad·vised *predic.adj.* (usu. foll. by *to* + infin.) (of a person) prudent (*would be well-advised to wait*).

well-ap·point·ed *adj.* (**well appointed** when *predic.*) having all the necessary equipment.

well-bal·anced *adj.* (**well balanced** when *predic.*) **1** sane; sensible. **2** equally matched. **3** having a symmetrical or orderly arrangement of parts.

well-be·ing *n.* a state of being well, healthy, contented, etc.

well-born /wélbáwrn/ *adj.* of wealthy or noble lineage.

well-bred *adj.* (**well bred** when *predic.*) having or showing good breeding or manners.

well-con·nect·ed *adj.* associated, esp. by birth, with persons of good social position.

well-dis·posed *adj.* (**well disposed** when *predic.*) (often foll. by *toward*) having a good disposition or friendly feeling (for).

well-done *adj.* (**well done** when *predic.*) **1** (of meat, etc.) thoroughly cooked. **2** (of a task, etc.) performed well (also as *int.*).

well-found·ed *adj.* (**well founded** when *predic.*) (of suspicions, etc.) based on good evidence; having a foundation in fact or reason.

well-groomed *adj.* (**well groomed** when *predic.*) (of a person) with carefully tended hair, clothes, etc.

well-ground·ed *adj.* (**well grounded** when *predic.*) **1** = WELL-FOUNDED. **2** having a good training in or knowledge of the groundwork of a subject.

well·head /wélhed/ *n.* a source esp. of a spring or stream.

well-heel·ed *adj. colloq.* wealthy.

well-in·formed *adj.* (**well informed** when *predic.*) having much knowledge or information about a subject.

Wel·ling·ton /wélingtən/ *n.* (in full **Wellington boot**) *Brit.* a waterproof rubber or plastic boot usu. reaching the knee.

well-in·ten·tioned *adj.* (**well intentioned** when *predic.*) having or showing good intentions.

well-known *adj.* (**well known** when *predic.*) **1** known to many. **2** known thoroughly.

well-mean·ing *adj.* (also **well-meant**) (**well meaning, well meant** when *predic.*) well-intentioned (but ineffective or unwise).

well-off *adj.* (**well off** when *predic.*) **1** having plenty of money. **2** in a fortunate situation or circumstances.

well-oiled *adj.* (**well oiled** when *predic.*) *colloq.* **1** drunk. **2** operating efficiently (*a well-oiled committee*).

well-pre·served *adj.* (**well preserved** when *predic.*) showing little sign of aging.

well-read *adj.* (**well read** when *predic.*) knowledgeable through much reading.

well-round·ed *adj.* (**well rounded** when *predic.*) **1** complete and symmetrical. **2** (of a phrase, etc.)

complete and well expressed. **3** (of a person) having or showing a fully developed personality, ability, etc. **4** fleshy; plump.

well-spo·ken *adj.* articulate or refined in speech.

well-thought-of *adj.* (**well thought of** when *predic.*) having a good reputation; esteemed; respected.

well-thought-out *adj.* (**well thought out** when *predic.*) carefully devised.

well-to-do *adj.* prosperous.

well-worn *adj.* (**well worn** when *predic.*) **1** much worn by use. **2** (of a phrase, joke, etc.) stale; often heard.

Welsh /welsh/ *adj. & n.* • *adj.* of or relating to Wales or its people or language. • *n.* **1** the Celtic language of Wales. **2** (prec. by *the*; treated as *pl.*) the people of Wales.

welsh /welsh/ *v.intr.* (also **welch** /welch/) **1** (of a loser of a bet) decamp without paying. **2** evade an obligation. **3** (foll. by *on*) **a** fail to carry out a promise to (a person). **b** fail to honor (an obligation). □□ **welsh·er** *n.*

Welsh·man /wélshmən/ *n.* (*pl.* **-men**) a person who is Welsh by birth or descent.

Welsh rab·bit *n.* (also **Welsh rare·bit**) a dish of melted cheese, etc., on toast.

Welsh·wom·an /wélshwoomən/ *n.* (*pl.* **-women**) a woman who is Welsh by birth or descent.

welt /welt/ *n. & v.* • *n.* **1** a leather rim sewn around the edge of a shoe upper for the sole to be attached to. ▷ SHOE. **2** = WEAL. **3** a ribbed or reinforced border of a garment; a trimming.

Welt·an·schau·ung /véltaanshówoong/ *n.* a particular philosophy or view of life; a conception of the world.

wel·ter /wéltər/ *v. & n.* • *v.intr.* roll; wallow; be washed about. • *n.* **1** a state of general confusion. **2** a disorderly mixture (*a welter of half-written letters and crude maps*).

wel·ter·weight /wéltərwayt/ *n.* **1** a weight in certain sports intermediate between lightweight and middleweight. **2** an athlete of this weight.

wen /wen/ *n.* a benign tumor on the skin, esp. of the scalp.

wench /wench/ *n. & v.* • *n. joc.* a girl or young woman. • *v.intr. archaic* (of a man) consort with prostitutes. □□ **wench·er** *n.*

wend /wend/ *v.tr. & intr. literary* or *archaic* go. □ **wend one's way** make one's way.

went *past of* GO[1].

wept *past of* WEEP.

were *2nd sing. past, pl. past, and past subj. of* BE.

we're /weer/ *contr.* we are.

weren't /wərnt, wérənt/ *contr.* were not.

were·wolf /wéerwoolf, wáir-/ *n.* (also **wer·wolf** /wɔr-/) (*pl.* **-wolves**) a mythical being who at times changes from a person to a wolf.

Wes·ley·an /wézleeən/ *adj. & n.* • *adj.* of or relating to a Protestant denomination founded by the English evangelist John Wesley (d. 1791) (cf. METHODIST). • *n.* a member of this denomination. □□ **Wes·ley·an·ism** *n.*

west /west/ *n., adj., & adv.* • *n.* **1 a** the point of the horizon where the sun sets at the equinoxes (cardinal point 90° to the left of north). **b** the compass point corresponding to this. ▷ COMPASS. **c** the direction in which this lies. **2** (usu. **the West**) a European in contrast to Oriental civilization. **b** *hist.* the non-Communist nations of Europe and N. America. **c** the western part of the late Roman Empire. **d** the western part of a country, town, etc., esp. the American West. **3** *Bridge* a player occupying the position designated 'west'. • *adj.* **1** toward, at, near, or facing west. **2** coming from the west (*west wind*). • *adv.* **1** toward, at, or near the west. **2** (foll. by *of*) further west than. □ **go west** *sl.* be killed or destroyed, etc.

west·bound /wéstbownd/ *adj.* traveling or leading westward.

west·er·ly /wéstərlee/ *adj., adv., & n.* ● *adj. & adv.* **1** in a western position or direction. **2** (of a wind) blowing from the west. ▷ TRADE WIND. ● *n.* (*pl.* **-ies**) a wind blowing from the west.

west·ern /wéstərn/ *adj. & n.* ● *adj.* **1** of or in the west; inhabiting the west. **2** lying or directed toward the west. **3** (**Western**) of or relating to the West (see WEST *n.* 2). ● *n.* a motion picture or novel about cowboys in western North America. □□ **West·ern·er** *n.*

West·ern Church *n.* the part of Christendom that has continued to derive its authority, doctrine, and ritual from the popes in Rome.

west·ern hem·i·sphere *n.* the half of the Earth containing the Americas.

west·ern·ize /wéstərnīz/ *v.tr.* (also **West·ern·ize**) influence with or convert to the ideas and customs, etc., of the West. □□ **west·ern·i·za·tion** *n.* **west·ern·iz·er** *n.*

West In·dies *n.pl.* the islands of Central America, including Cuba and the Bahamas.

west-north·west *n.* the direction or compass point midway between west and northwest.

west-south·west *n.* the direction or compass point midway between west and southwest.

west·ward /wéstwərd/ *adj., adv., & n.* ● *adj. & adv.* toward the west. ● *n.* a westward direction or region.

WET SUIT

wet /wet/ *adj., v., & n.* ● *adj.* (**wetter, wettest**) **1** soaked, covered, or dampened with water or other liquid (*a wet sponge; got my feet wet*). **2** (of the weather, etc.) rainy (*a wet day*). **3** (of paint, ink, etc.) not yet dried. **4** used with water (*wet shampoo*). **5** *sl.* (of a country, of legislation, etc.) allowing the free sale of alcoholic drink. **6** (of a baby or young child) incontinent (*is still wet at night*). ● *v.tr.* (**wetting**; *past* and *past part.* **wet** or **wetted**) **1** make wet. **2 a** urinate in or on (*wet the bed*). **b** ● *refl.* urinate involuntarily. ● *n.* **1** moisture. **2** rainy weather; a time of rain. □ **wet behind the ears** immature; inexperienced. **wet through** (or **to the skin**) with one's clothes soaked. **wet one's whistle** *colloq.* drink. □□ **wet·ly** *adv.* **wet·ness** *n.*

wet·ta·ble *adj.* **wet·ting** *n.* **wet·tish** *adj.*

wet·back /wétbak/ *n. offens.* an illegal immigrant from Mexico to the US.

wet dream *n.* an erotic dream with involuntary ejaculation of semen.

weth·er /wéthər/ *n.* a castrated ram.

wet·lands /wétləndz/ *n.pl.* swamps and other damp areas of land.

wet look *n.* a shiny surface given to clothing materials.

wet nurse *n. & v.* ● *n.* a woman employed to suckle another's child. ● *v.tr.* (**wet-nurse**) **1** act as a wet nurse to. **2** *colloq.* treat as if helpless.

wet suit *n.* ◄ a close-fitting rubber garment worn by skin divers, etc., to keep warm. ▷ DIVER

we've /weev/ *contr.* we have.

whack /hwak, wak/ *v. & n. colloq.* ● *v.tr.* strike or beat forcefully with a sharp blow. ● *n.* a sharp or resounding blow. □ **have a whack at** *sl.* attempt. **out of whack** *sl.* out of order; malfunctioning. □□ **whack·ing** *n.*

whack·o /hwákō, wák-/ *adj. & n.* var. of WACKO.

whack·y var. of WACKY.

whale[1] /hwayl, wayl/ *n.* (*pl.* same or **whales**) ▼ any of the larger marine mammals of the order Cetacea, having a streamlined body and horizontal tail, and breathing through a blowhole on the head. ▷ CETACEAN. □ **a whale of a** *colloq.* exceedingly good or fine, etc.

whale[2] /hwayl, wayl/ *v.tr. colloq.* beat; thrash.

whale·bone /hwáylbōn, wáyl-/ *n.* ► an elastic horny substance growing in thin parallel plates in the upper jaw of some whales, used as stiffening, etc.

whale oil *n.* oil from the blubber of whales.

whal·er /hwáylər, wáyl-/ *n.* **1** a whaling ship or a seaman engaged in whaling. **2** an Australian shark of the genus *Carcharhinus*.

whale shark *n.* a large tropical whalelike shark, *Rhincodon typus*, feeding close to the surface. ▷ SHARK

WHALEBONE: FRINGED PLATE OF BALEEN

WHALE

Some 78 species of whales inhabit the world's oceans. Their streamlined bodies show little trace of their terrestrial ancestry, the front limbs having become flippers and the hindlimbs replaced by flukes. Whales breathe through a blowhole at the top of the head, which has evolved from the nasal passage, and they keep warm with an insulating layer of blubber. Whales form two groups: toothed whales (with a single blowhole) and baleen whales (with two blowholes). Toothed whales include sperm whales and dolphins; they hunt fish, squid, and seals. Baleen whales feed on fish or crustaceans, filtering them through fibrous baleen plates.

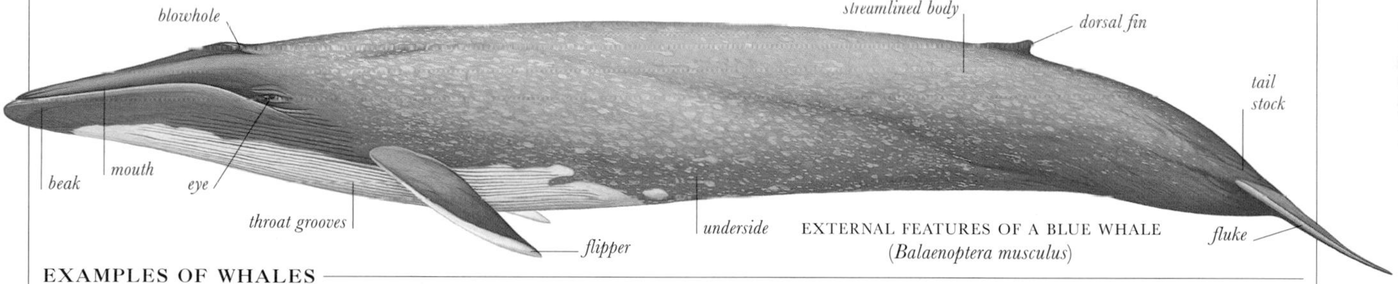

blowhole

streamlined body

dorsal fin

tail stock

beak

mouth

eye

throat grooves

flipper

underside

EXTERNAL FEATURES OF A BLUE WHALE (*Balaenoptera musculus*)

fluke

EXAMPLES OF WHALES

TOOTHED WHALES

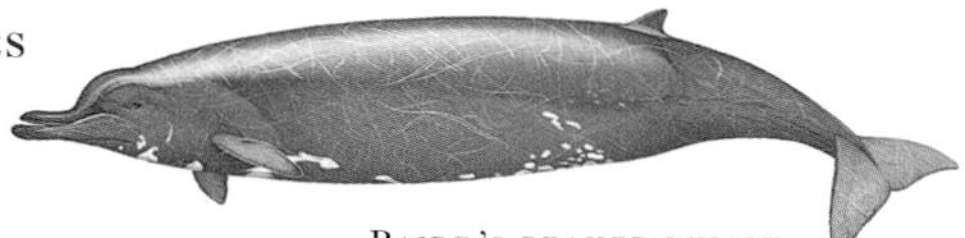

BAIRD'S BEAKED WHALE (*Berardius bairdii*)

BELUGA (*Delphinapterus leucas*)

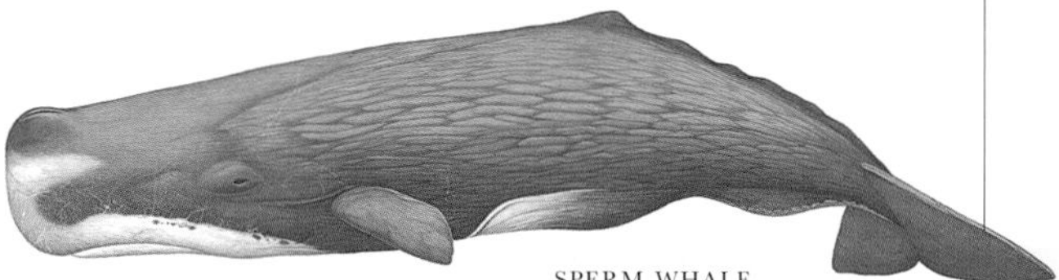

SPERM WHALE (*Physeter macrocephalus*)

BALEEN WHALES

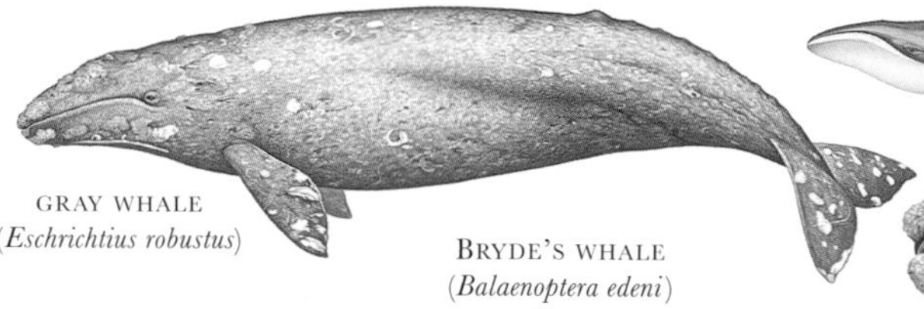

GRAY WHALE (*Eschrichtius robustus*)

BRYDE'S WHALE (*Balaenoptera edeni*)

PYGMY RIGHT WHALE (*Caperea marginata*)

SOUTHERN RIGHT WHALE (*Eubalaena australis*)

W

whal·ing /hwáyling, wáyl-/ *n.* the practice or industry of hunting and killing whales.

wham /hwam, wam/ *int., n., & v. colloq.* ● *int.* expressing the sound of a forcible impact. ● *n.* such a sound. ● *v.* (**whammed, whamming**) **1** *intr.* make such a sound or impact. **2** *tr.* strike forcibly.

wham·my /hwámee, wám-/ *n.* (*pl.* **-ies**) *colloq.* an evil or unlucky influence.

wharf /hwawrf, wawrf/ *n. & v.* ● *n.* (*pl.* **wharves** /hwawrvz, wawrvz/ or **wharfs**) ▼ a level quayside area to which a ship may be moved to load and unload. ● *v.tr.* **1** moor (a ship) at a wharf. **2** store (goods) on a wharf.

WHARF: FINGER WHARF IN SYDNEY, AUSTRALIA

wharf·age /hwáwrfij, wáwr-/ *n.* **1** accommodation at a wharf. **2** a fee for this.

wharves *pl.* of WHARF.

what /hwot, wot, hwut, wut/ *adj., pron., & adv.* ● *interrog.adj.* **1** asking for a choice from an indefinite number or for a statement of amount, number, or kind (*what books have you read?; what news have you?*). **2** *colloq.* = WHICH *interrog.adj.* (*what book have you chosen?*). ● *adj.* (usu. in exclam.) how great or remarkable (*what luck!*). ● *rel.adj.* the or any ... that (*will give you what help I can*). ● *pron.* (corresp. to the functions of the *adj.*) **1** what thing or things? (*what is your name?; I don't know what you mean*). **2** (asking for a remark to be repeated) = what did you say? **3** asking for confirmation or agreement of something not completely understood (*what, you really mean it?*). **4** how much (*what you must have suffered!*). **5** (as *rel.pron.*) that or those which; a or the or any thing which (*what followed was worse; tell me what you think*). ● *adv.* to what extent (*what does it matter?*). □ **what about** what is the news or position or your opinion of (*what about me?; what about a game of tennis?*). **what-d'you-call-it** (or **whatchamacall-it** or **what's-its-name**) *colloq.* a substitute for a name not recalled. **what for** *colloq.* **1** for what reason? **2** a severe reprimand (esp. *give a person what for*). **what have you** (prec. by *or*) anything else similar. **what if? 1** what would result, etc., if? **2** what would it matter if. **what is more** and as an additional point; moreover. **what next?** *colloq.* what more absurd, shocking, or surprising thing is possible? **what not** (prec. by *and*) other similar things. **what of?** what is the news concerning? **what of it?** why should that be considered significant? **what's-his** (or **-its**) **-name** = *what-d'you-call-it.* **what's what** *colloq.* what is useful or important, etc. **what with** *colloq.* because of (usu. several things).

what·e'er /hwotáir, wot-, hwut-, wut-/ *poet.* var. of WHATEVER.

what·ev·er /hwotévər, wot-, hwut, wut-/ *adj. & pron.* **1** = WHAT (in relative uses) with the emphasis on indefiniteness (*lend me whatever you can; whatever money you have*). **2** though anything (*we are safe whatever happens*). **3** (with *neg.* or *interrog.*) at all; of any kind (*there is no doubt whatever*). **4** *colloq.* what at all or in any way (*whatever do you mean?*) □ **or whatever** *colloq.* or anything similar.

what·not /hwótnot, wót-, hwút-, wút-/ *n.* **1** an indefinite or trivial thing. **2** a stand with shelves for small objects.

whats·it /hwótsit, wót-, hwút-, wút-/ *n. colloq.* a person or thing whose name one cannot recall or does not know.

what·so·ev·er /hwótsō-évər, wót-, hwút-, wút-/ *adj. & pron.* = WHATEVER 1–3.

wheat /hweet, weet/ *n.* **1** any cereal plant of the genus *Triticum.* **2** its grain, used in making flour, etc. ▷ GRAIN. □ **separate the wheat from the chaff** see CHAFF.

wheat·ear /hweéteer, weét-/ *n.* any small migratory bird of the genus *Oenanthe.*

wheat·en /hweétən, weét-/ *adj.* made of wheat.

wheat germ *n.* the embryo of the wheat grain, extracted as a source of vitamins.

wheat·grass /hweétgras, weét-/ *n.* a couch grass grown esp. as forage.

whee /hwee, wee/ *int.* expressing delight or excitement.

whee·dle /hweédəl, weédəl/ *v.tr.* **1** coax by flattery or endearments. **2** (foll. by *out*) **a** get (a thing) out of a person by wheedling. **b** cheat (a person) out of a thing by wheedling. □□ **whee·dler** *n.* **whee·dling** *adj.* **whee·dling·ly** *adv.*

wheel /hweel, weel/ *n. & v.* ● *n.* **1** a circular frame or disk arranged to revolve on an axle and used to facilitate the motion of a vehicle or for various mechanical purposes. **2** a wheellike thing (*Catherine wheel; potter's wheel; steering wheel*). **3** motion as of a wheel, esp. the movement of a line of people with one end as a pivot. **4** a machine, etc., of which a wheel is an essential part. **5** (in *pl.*) *sl.* a car. **6** *sl.* = BIGWIG. **7** a set of short lines concluding a stanza. ● *v.* **1** *intr.* & *tr.* **a** turn on an axis or pivot. **b** swing around in line with one end as a pivot. **2 a** *intr.* (often foll. by *about, around, round*) change direction or face another way. **b** *tr.* cause to do this. **3** *tr.* push or pull (a wheeled thing, esp. a wheelbarrow, bicycle, wheelchair, or stroller, or its load or occupant). **4** *intr.* go in circles or curves (*seagulls wheeling overhead*). □ **at the wheel 1** driving a vehicle. **2** directing a ship. **3** in control of affairs. **wheel and deal** engage in political or commercial scheming. □□ **wheeled** *adj.* (also in *comb.*). **wheel·less** *adj.*

wheel·bar·row /hweélbarō, weél-/ *n.* a small cart with one wheel and two shafts for carrying garden loads, etc.

wheel·base /hweélbays, weél-/ *n.* the distance between the front and rear axles of a vehicle.

wheel·chair /hweélchair, weél-/ *n.* a chair on wheels for an invalid or disabled person.

wheel·er-deal·er *n. colloq.* a person who wheels and deals (see WHEEL).

wheel·house /hweélhows, weel-/ *n.* = PILOTHOUSE.

wheel·ie /hweélee, weé-/ *n. sl.* the stunt of riding a bicycle or motorcycle for a short distance with the front wheel off the ground.

wheel of for·tune *n.* **1** luck. **2** a gambling device that is spun and allowed to stop at random to indicate the winner or the prize.

wheel·spin /hweélspin, weél-/ *n.* rotation of a vehicle's wheels without traction.

wheel·wright /hweélrīt, weél-/ *n.* a person who makes or repairs esp. wooden wheels.

wheeze /hweez, weez/ *v. & n.* ● *v.* **1** *intr.* breathe with an audible chesty whistling sound. **2** *tr.* (often foll. by *out*) utter in this way. ● *n.* a sound of wheezing. □□ **wheez·er** *n.* **wheez·y** *adj.* **wheez·i·ly** *adv.* **wheez·i·ness** *n.*

whelk /hwelk, welk/ *n.* ► any predatory marine gastropod mollusk of the family *Buccinidae,* esp. the edible kind of the genus *Buccinum,* having a spiral shell.

WHELK: DOG WHELK (*Nucella lapillus*)

whelm /hwelm, welm/ *v.tr. poet.* **1** engulf; submerge. **2** crush with weight; overwhelm.

whelp /hwelp, welp/ *n. & v.* ● *n.* **1** a young dog; a puppy. **2** *archaic* a cub. **3** an ill-mannered child or youth. **4** (esp. in *pl.*) a projection on the barrel of a capstan or windlass. ● *v.tr.* (also *absol.*) **1** bring forth (a whelp or whelps). **2** *derog.* (of a human mother) give birth to. **3** originate (an evil scheme, etc.).

when /hwen, wen/ *adv., conj., pron., & n. interrog.adv.* **1** at what time? **2** on what occasion? **3** how soon? **4** how long ago? ● *rel.adv.* (prec. by *time,* etc.) at or on which (*there are times when I could cry*). ● *conj.* **1** at the or any time that; as soon as (*come when you like; when I was your age*). **2** although; considering that (*why stand up when you could sit down?*). **3** after which; and then; but just then (*was nearly asleep when the bell rang*). ● *pron.* what time? (*till when can you stay?; since when it has been better*). ● *n.* time, occasion, date (*have finally decided on the where and when*).

whence /hwens, wens/ *adv. & conj. formal* ● *adv.* from what place? (*whence did they come?*). ● *conj.* **1** to the place from which (*return whence you came*). **2** (often prec. by *place,* etc.) from which (*the source whence these errors arise*). **3** and thence (*whence it follows that*). ¶ Use of *from whence* as in *the place from whence they came,* though common, is generally considered incorrect.

when·ev·er /hwenévər, wen-/ *conj. & adv.* **1** at whatever time; on whatever occasion. **2** every time that. □ **or whenever** *colloq.* or at any similar time.

where /hwair, wair/ *adv., conj., pron., & n.* ● *interrog.adv.* **1** in or to what place or position? (*where is the milk?; where are you going?*). **2** in what direction or respect? (*where does the argument lead?; where does it concern us?*). **3** in what book, etc.?; from whom? (*where did you read that?; where did you hear that?*). **4** in what situation or condition? (*where does that leave us?*). ● *rel.adv.* (prec. by *place,* etc.) in or to which (*places where they meet*). ● *conj.* **1** in or to the or any place, direction, or respect in which (*go where you like; that is where you are wrong*). **2** and there (*reached Albuquerque, where the car broke down*). ● *pron.* what place? (*where do you come from?*). ● *n.* place; scene of something (see WHEN *n.*).

where·a·bouts *adv. & n.* ● *adv.* /hwáirəbówts, wáir-/ where or approximately where? (*whereabouts are they?; show me whereabouts to look*). ● *n.* /hwáirəbowts, wáir-/ (as *sing.* or *pl.*) a person's or thing's location roughly defined.

where·af·ter /hwairáftər, wair-/ *conj. formal* after which.

where·as /hwairáz, wair-/ *conj.* **1** in contrast or comparison with the fact that. **2** (esp. in legal preambles) taking into consideration the fact that.

where·by /hwairbí, wair-/ *conj.* by what or which means.

where·fore /hwáirfawr, wáir-/ *adv. & n.* ● *adv. archaic* **1** for what reason? **2** for which reason. ● *n.* a reason (*the whys and wherefores*).

where·in /hwairín, wair-/ *conj. & adv. formal* ● *conj.* in what or which place or respect. ● *adv.* in what place or respect?

where·of /hwairúv, -óv, wair-/ *conj. & adv. formal* ● *conj.* of what or which (*the means whereof*). ● *adv.* of what?

where·up·on /hwáirəpón, -páwn, wáir-/ *conj.* immediately after which.

wher·ev·er /hwairévər, wair-/ *adv. & conj.* ● *adv.* in or to whatever place. ● *conj.* in every place that. □ **or wherever** *colloq.* or in any similar place.

where·with·al /hwáirwithawl, -with-, wáir-/ *n. colloq.* money, etc., needed for a purpose (*has not the wherewithal to do it*).

whet /hwet, wet/ *v.tr.* (**whetted, whetting**) **1** sharpen (a scythe or other tool) by grinding. **2** stimulate (the appetite or a desire, interest, etc.). ● *n.* the act or an instance of whetting.

wheth·er /hwéthər, wéth-/ *conj.* introducing the first or both of alternative possibilities (*I doubt whether it matters; I do not know whether they have arrived or not*).

W

whet·stone /hwétstōn, wét-/ *n.* **1** a tapered stone used with water to sharpen curved tools (cf. OILSTONE). **2** a thing that sharpens the senses, etc.

whew /hwyōō/ *int.* expressing surprise, consternation, or relief.

whey /hway, way/ *n.* ▼ the watery liquid left when milk forms curds.

WHEY SEPARATED FROM CURDS

which /hwich, wich/ *adj. & pron.* ● *interrog.adj.* asking for choice from a definite set of alternatives (*say which book you prefer; which way shall we go?*). ● *rel.adj.* being the one just referred to; and this or these (*ten years, during which time they admitted nothing; a word of advice, which action is within your power, will set things straight*). ● *interrog.pron.* **1** which person or persons (*which of you is responsible?*). **2** which thing or things (*say which you prefer*). ● *rel.pron.* (*poss.* **of which**, **whose** /hōōz/) **1** which thing or things, usu. introducing a clause not essential for identification (cf. THAT *pron.* 7) (*the house, which is empty, has been damaged*). **2** used in place of *that* after *in* or *that* (*there is the house in which I was born; that which you have just seen*). □ **which is which** a phrase used when two or more persons or things are difficult to distinguish from each other.

which·ev·er /hwichévər, wich-/ *adj. & pron.* **1** any which (*take whichever you like*). **2** no matter which (*whichever one wins, they both get a prize*).

whiff /hwif, wif/ *n. & v.* ● *n.* **1** a puff or breath of air, smoke, etc. (*went outside for a whiff of fresh air*). **2** a smell (*caught the whiff of a cigar*). **3** (foll. by *of*) a trace or suggestion of scandal, etc. **4** a minor discharge (of grapeshot, etc.). ● *v.* **1** *tr. & intr.* blow or puff lightly. **2** *tr.* get a slight smell of. **3** *intr. Baseball* swing and miss on the third strike. **4** *tr. Baseball* strike out a batter in this way.

whif·fle /hwifəl, wif-/ *v. & n.* ● *v.* **1** *intr. & tr.* (of the wind) blow lightly; shift about. **2** *intr.* be variable or evasive. ● *n.* a slight movement of air.

Whig /hwig, wig/ *n. hist.* **1** *Polit.* a member of the British reforming and constitutional party that was succeeded in the 19th c. by the Liberal Party (opp. TORY *n.* 2). **2** **a** a supporter of the American Revolution. **b** a member of an American political party in the 19th c., succeeded by the Republicans. □□ **Whig·ger·y** *n.* **Whig·gish** *adj.* **Whig·gism** *n.*

while /hwīl, wīl/ *n., conj., v., & adv.* ● *n.* **1** a space of time, time spent in some action (*a long while ago; waited a while; all this while*). **2** (prec. by *the*) **a** during some other process. **b** *poet.* during the time that. **3** (prec. by *a*) for some time (*have not seen you a while*). ● *conj.* **1** during the time that; at the same time as (*while I was away, the house was burgled; fell asleep while reading*). **2** although; whereas (*while I want to believe it, I cannot*). ● *v.tr.* (foll. by *away*) pass (time, etc.) in a leisurely or interesting manner. ● *rel.adv.* (prec. by *time*, etc.) during which (*the summer while I was abroad*). □ **all the while** during the whole time (that). **for a long while** for a long time past. **for a while** for some time. **a good** (or **great**) **while** a considerable time. **in a while** (or **little while**) soon; shortly. **worth while** (or **one's while**) worth the time or effort spent.

whim /hwim, wim/ *n.* **1** a sudden fancy; a caprice. **2** capriciousness.

whim·per /hwímpər, wim-/ *v. & n.* ● *v.* **1** *intr.* make feeble, querulous, or frightened sounds; cry and whine softly. **2** *tr.* utter whimperingly. ● *n.* **1** a whimpering sound. **2** a feeble note or tone (*the conference ended on a whimper*). □□ **whim·per·er** *n.* **whim·per·ing·ly** *adv.*

whim·si·cal /hwimzikəl, wim-/ *adj.* **1** capricious. **2** fantastic. **3** odd or quaint; fanciful; humorous. □□ **whim·si·cal·i·ty** /-kálitee/ *n.* **whim·si·cal·ly** *adv.*

whim·sy /hwímzee, wim-/ *n.* (also **whim·sey**) (*pl.* **-ies** or **-eys**) **1** a whim; a capricious notion or fancy. **2** capricious or quaint humor.

whin·chat /hwínchat, wín-/ *n.* a small, brownish European songbird, *Saxicola rubetra.*

whine /hwīn, wīn/ *n. & v.* ● *n.* **1** a complaining, long-drawn wail as of a dog. **2** a similar shrill, prolonged sound. **3** **a** a querulous tone. **b** an instance of feeble or undignified complaining. ● *v.* **1** *intr.* emit or utter a whine. **2** *intr.* complain in a querulous tone or undignified way. **3** *tr.* utter in a whining tone. □□ **whin·er** *n.* **whin·ing·ly** *adv.* **whin·y** *adj.* (**whinier, whiniest**).

whin·ny /hwínee, wín-/ *n. & v.* ● *n.* (*pl.* **-ies**) a gentle or joyful neigh. ● *v.intr.* (**-ies**, **-ied**) give a whinny.

whip /hwip, wip/ *n. & v.* ● *n.* **1** ▶ a lash attached to a stick for urging on animals or punishing, etc. **2** a member of a political party in a legislative body appointed to control its party discipline and tactics, esp. ensuring voting in debates. **3** a dessert made with whipped cream, etc. **4** the action of beating cream, eggs, etc., into a froth. **5** = WHIPPER-IN. **6** a rope-and-pulley hoisting apparatus. ● *v.* (**whipped**, **whipping**) **1** *tr.* beat or urge on with a whip. **2** *tr.* beat (cream or eggs, etc.) into a froth. **3** *tr. & intr.* take or move suddenly, unexpectedly, or rapidly (*whipped out a knife; whipped behind the door*). **4** *tr. sl.* **a** excel. **b** defeat. **5** *tr.* bind with spirally wound twine. **6** *tr.* sew with overcast stitches. □ **whip in** bring (hounds) together. **whip on** urge into action. **whip up 1** excite or stir up (feeling, etc.). **2** summon up. **3** prepare (a meal, etc.) hurriedly. □□ **whip·less** *adj.* **whip·like** *adj.* **whip·per** *n.*

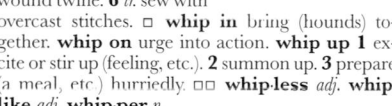

WHIP:
LATE 19TH-CENTURY
AUSTRALIAN
STOCKWHIP

whip·cord /hwípkawrd, wíp-/ *n.* **1** a tightly twisted cord such as is used for making whiplashes. **2** a close-woven worsted fabric.

whip hand *n.* **1** a hand that holds the whip (in riding, etc.). **2** (usu. prec. by *the*) the advantage or control in any situation.

whip·lash /hwíplash, wíp-/ *n.* **1** the flexible end of a whip. **2** a blow with a whip. **3** an injury to the neck caused by a jerk of the head, esp. as in a motor vehicle accident.

whip·per·in /hwipərín, wip-/ *n.* a huntsman's assistant who manages the hounds.

whip·per·snap·per /hwipərsnapər, wip-/ *n.* **1** a small child. **2** an insignificant but presumptuous or intrusive (esp. young) person.

whip·pet /hwípit, wíp-/ *n.* ▼ a crossbred dog of the greyhound type used for racing.

WHIPPET

whip·ping /hwíping, wíp-/ *n.* **1** a beating, esp. with a whip. **2** cord wound around in binding.

whip·ping boy *n.* **1** a scapegoat. **2** *hist.* a boy educated with a young prince and punished instead of him.

whip·ping cream *n.* cream suitable for whipping.

whip·ping post *n. hist.* a post used for public whippings.

whip·poor·will /hwípərwil, wíp-/ *n.* ▼ an American nightjar, *Caprimulgus vociferus.*

WHIPPOORWILL
(*Caprimulgus vociferus*)

whip·py /hwípee, wípee/ *adj.* (**whippier, whippiest**) flexible; springy. □□ **whip·pi·ness** *n.*

whip·saw /hwípsaw, wíp-/ *n. & v.* ● *n.* a saw with a narrow blade held at each end by a frame. ● *v.tr.* (*past part.* **-sawn** or **-sawed**) **1** cut with a whipsaw. **2** *sl.* **a** subject to two opposing pressures. **b** cheat by joint action on two others.

whip·stitch /hwípstich, wíp-/ *v. & n.* ● *v.tr.* sew with overcast stitches. ● *n.* a stitch made this way.

whir /hwər, wər/ *n. & v.* (also **whirr**) ● *n.* a continuous rapid buzzing or softly clicking sound as of a bird's wings or of cogwheels in constant motion. ● *v.intr.* (**whir·red, whirring**) make this sound.

whirl /hwərl, wərl/ *v. & n.* ● *v.* **1** *tr. & intr.* swing around and around; revolve rapidly. **2** *tr. & intr.* (foll. by *away*) convey or go rapidly in a vehicle, etc. **3** *tr. & intr.* send or travel swiftly in an orbit or a curve. **4** *intr.* **a** (of the brain, senses, etc.) seem to spin around. **b** (of thoughts, etc.) be confused; follow each other in bewildering succession. ● *n.* **1** a whirling movement (*vanished in a whirl of dust*). **2** a state of intense activity (*the social whirl*). **3** a state of confusion (*my mind is in a whirl*). **4** *colloq.* an attempt (*give it a whirl*). □□ **whirl·er** *n.* **whirlingly** *adv*.

whirl·i·gig /hwɜrligig, wɜrl-/ *n.* **1** a spinning or whirling toy. **2** a merry-go-round. **3** a revolving motion. **4** anything regarded as hectic or constantly changing (*the whirligig of time*). **5** any freshwater beetle of the family Gyrinidae that circles about on the surface.

whirl·ing der·vish *n.* (also **howling dervish**) a dervish performing a wild dance, or howling, as a religious observance.

whirl·pool /hwɜrlpōōl, wɜrl-/ *n.* a powerful circular eddy in the sea, etc., often causing suction to its center.

whirl·wind /hwɜrlwind, wɜrl-/ *n.* **1** a mass or column of air whirling rapidly around and around in a cylindrical or funnel shape over land or water. **2** a confused tumultuous process. **3** (*attrib.*) very rapid (*a whirlwind romance*). □ **reap the whirlwind** suffer worse results of a bad action.

whirl·y·bird /hwɜrleebərd, wɜr-/ *n. colloq.* a helicopter.

whirr var. of WHIR.

whisk /hwisk, wisk/ *v. & n.* ● *v.* **1** (foll. by *away, off*) **a** brush with a sweeping movement. **b** take with a sudden motion (*whisked the plate away*). **2** *tr.* whip (cream, eggs, etc.). **3** *tr. & intr.* convey or go (esp. out of sight) lightly or quickly (*whisked me off to the doctor; the mouse whisked into its hole*). **4** *tr.* wave or lightly brandish. ● *n.* **1** a whisking action or motion. **2** a utensil for whisking eggs or cream, etc. ▷ UTENSIL. **3** a bunch of grass, twigs, bristles, etc., for removing dust or flies.

W

whisk·er /hwískər, wís-/ *n*. **1** (usu. in *pl.*) the hair growing on a man's face, esp. on the cheek. **2** ▶ each of the bristles on the face of a cat, etc. **3** *colloq.* a small distance (*within a whisker of; won by a whisker*). **4** a strong, hairlike crystal of metal, etc. □ **have** (or **have grown**) **whiskers** *colloq.* (esp. of a story, etc.) be very old. □□ **whisk·ered** *adj.* **whisk·er·y** *adj.*

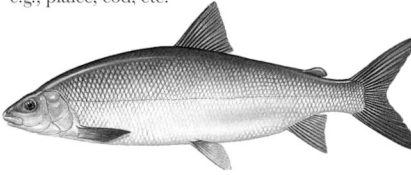

whiskers

WHISKERS ON A CAT

whis·key /hwískee, wís-/ *n.* (also **whis·ky**) (*pl.* **-eys** or **-ies**) **1** an alcoholic liquor distilled esp. from grain, such as corn or malted barley. **2** a drink of this.

whis·per /hwíspər, wís-/ *v. & n.* ● *v.* **1 a** *intr.* speak very softly without vibration of the vocal cords. **b** *intr. & tr.* talk or say in a barely audible tone or in a secret or confidential way. **2** *intr.* speak privately or conspiratorially. **3** *intr.* (of leaves, wind, or water) rustle or murmur. ● *n.* **1** whispering speech (*talking in whispers*). **2** a whispering sound. **3** a thing whispered. **4** a rumor or piece of gossip. **5** a brief mention; a hint or suggestion. □ **it is whispered** there is a rumor. □□ **whis·per·er** *n.* **whis·per·ing** *n.*

whist /hwist, wist/ *n.* a card game usu. for four players, with the winning of tricks.

whis·tle /hwísəl, wís-/ *n. & v.* ● *n.* **1** a clear shrill sound made by forcing breath through a small hole between nearly closed lips. **2** a similar sound made by a bird, the wind, a missile, etc. **3** an instrument used to produce such a sound. ● *v.* **1** *intr.* emit a whistle. **2 a** *intr.* give a signal or express surprise or derision by whistling. **b** *tr.* (often foll. by *up*) summon or give a signal to (a dog, etc.) by whistling. **3** *tr.* (also *absol.*) produce (a tune) by whistling. **4** *intr.* (foll. by *for*) vainly seek or desire. □ **as clean** (or **clear** or **dry**) **as a whistle** very clean or clear or dry. **blow the whistle on** *colloq.* bring (an activity) to an end; inform on (those responsible). **whistle in the dark** pretend to be unafraid. □□ **whis·tler** *n.*

whis·tle·blow·er /hwísəlblōər, wí-/ *n. colloq.* one who reports wrongdoing in a workplace or organization to authorities, the news media, etc.

whis·tle-stop *n.* **1** a small, unimportant town on a railroad line. **2** a politician's brief pause for a campaign speech on tour. **3** (*attrib.*) with brief pauses (*a whistle-stop tour*).

Whit /hwit, wit/ *adj.* connected with, belonging to, or following Whitsunday.

whit /hwit, wit/ *n.* a particle; a least possible amount (*not a whit better*). □ **every whit** the whole; wholly. **no** (or **never a** or **not a**) **whit** not at all.

white /hwīt, wít/ *adj., n., & v.* ● *adj.* **1** resembling a surface reflecting sunlight without absorbing any of the visible rays; of the color of milk or fresh snow. **2** approaching such a color; pale esp. in the face (*turned as white as a sheet*). **3** less dark than other things of the same kind. **4 a** of the human group having light-colored skin. **b** of or relating to white people. **5** albino (*white mouse*). **6 a** (of hair) having lost its color, esp. in old age. **b** (of a person) white-haired. **7** *colloq.* innocent; untainted. **8** (in *comb.*) (of esp. animals) having some white on the body (*white-throated*). **9 a** (of a plant) having white flowers or pale-colored fruit, etc. (*white hyacinth*). **b** (of a tree) having light-colored bark, etc. (*white ash*). **10** (of wine) made from white grapes or dark grapes with the skins removed. **11** *Brit.* (of coffee) with milk or cream added. **12** transparent; colorless (*white glass*). **13** *hist.* counterrevolutionary or reactionary (*white guard; white army*). ● *n.* **1** a white color or pigment. **2 a** white clothes or material (*dressed in white*). **b** (in *pl.*) white garments as worn in tennis, etc. **3 a** (in a game or sport) a white piece, ball, etc. **b** the player using such pieces. **4** the white part or albumen around the yolk of an egg. ▷ EGG. **5** the visible part of the eyeball around the iris. **6** a member of a

light-skinned race. □ **bleed white** drain (a person, country, etc.) of wealth, etc. □□ **white·ly** *adv.* **white·ness** *n.* **whit·ish** *adj.*

white ant *n.* a termite.

white·bait /hwítbayt, wít-/ *n.* (*pl.* same) (usu. *pl.*) the small, silvery-white young of herrings and sprats, esp. as food.

white·cap /hwítkap, wít-/ *n.* a white-crested wave at sea.

white cell *n.* (also **white blood cell**, **white corpuscle**) a leukocyte.

white Christ·mas *n.* Christmas with snow on the ground.

white-col·lar *attrib.adj.* (of a worker) engaged in clerical or administrative rather than manual work.

white dwarf *n.* a small, very dense star. ▷ STAR

white el·e·phant *n.* a useless and troublesome possession or thing.

white feath·er *n.* a symbol of cowardice.

white·fish /hwítfish, wít-/ *n.* (*pl.* same or **-fishes**) **1** ▼ any freshwater fish of the genus *Coregonus*, etc., of the trout family, and used esp. for food. **2** a marine fish, *Caulolatilus princeps*, of California used esp. for food. **3** *Brit.* any nonoily, pale-fleshed fish, e.g., plaice, cod, etc.

WHITEFISH: LARGE WHITEFISH
(*Coregonus clupeaformis*)

white flag *n.* a symbol of surrender or a period of truce.

white·fly /hwítflī, wít-/ *n.* (*pl.* **-flies**) any small insect of the family Aleyrodidae, having wings covered with white powder and feeding on sap.

white goods *n.pl.* **1** domestic linen. **2** large domestic electrical appliances.

White·hall /hwít-hawl, wít-/ *n.* **1** the British Government. **2** its offices or policy.

white·head /hwít-hed, wít-/ *n. colloq.* a white or white-topped skin pustule.

white heat *n.* **1** the temperature at which metal emits white light. **2** a state of intense passion or activity.

white-hot *adj.* at white heat.

White House *n.* the official residence of the US president and offices of the executive branch of government in Washington.

white lead *n.* a mixture of lead carbonate and hydrated lead oxide used as pigment.

white lie *n.* a harmless or trivial untruth.

white light *n.* colorless light, e.g., ordinary daylight.

white mag·ic *n.* magic used only for beneficent purposes.

white meat *n.* poultry, veal, rabbit, and pork.

whit·en /hwíton, wít-/ *v.tr. & intr.* make or become white. □□ **whit·en·er** *n.* **whit·en·ing** *n.*

white noise *n.* noise containing many frequencies with equal intensities.

white-out *n.* a dense blizzard, esp. in polar regions.

white pa·per *n.* a government report giving information or proposals on an issue.

white sale *n.* a sale of household linen.

white sauce *n.* a sauce of flour, melted butter, and milk or cream.

white slave *n.* a woman tricked or forced into prostitution, usu. abroad. □□ **white slav·er·y** *n.*

white·smith /hwítsmith, wít-/ *n.* **1** a worker in tin. **2** a polisher or finisher of metal goods.

white·thorn /hwít-thawrn, wít-/ *n.* the hawthorn.

white·throat /hwít-thrōt, wít-/ *n.* ▶ any of several birds with a white patch on the throat, esp. the warbler, *Sylvia communis*, or the finch, *Zonotrichia albicollis*.

white tie *n.* a man's white bow tie as part of full evening dress.

white trash *n. N. Amer. derog.* poor white people.

WHITETHROAT (*Sylvia communis*)

white·wall /hwítwawl, wít-/ *n.* a tire having a white band encircling the outer side-wall.

white·wash /hwítwosh, -wawsh, wít-/ *n. & v.* ● *n.* **1** a solution of lime or of whiting and size for whitening walls, etc. **2** a deliberate concealment of mistakes or faults. ● *v.tr.* **1** cover with whitewash. **2** conceal (mistakes or faults). **3** defeat (an opponent) without allowing any opposing score.

white wa·ter *n.* a shallow or foamy stretch of water.

white whale *n.* a northern cetacean, *Delphinapterus leucas*, white when adult. Also called **beluga**.

whit·ey /hwítee, wí-/ *n.* (also **White·y**) (*pl.* **-eys**) *sl. offens.* **1** a white person. **2** white people collectively.

whith·er /hwíthər, with-/ *adv. & conj. archaic* ● *adv.* **1** to what place, position, or state? **2** (prec. by *place*, etc.) to which (*the house whither we were walking*). ● *conj.* **1** to the or any place to which (*go whither you will*). **2** and thither (*we saw a house, whither we walked*).

whit·ing[1] /hwíting, wí-/ *n.* (*pl.* same or **whitings**) a small, white-fleshed fish of several species, used as food.

whit·ing[2] /hwíting, wí-/ *n.* ground chalk used in whitewashing, etc.

whit·low /hwítlō, wít-/ *n.* an inflammation near a fingernail or toenail.

Whit·sun /hwítsən, wít-/ *n. & adj.* ● *n.* = WHITSUNTIDE. ● *adj.* = WHIT.

Whit·sun·day /hwítsúnday, wít-/ *n.* the seventh Sunday after Easter, commemorating the descent of the Holy Spirit at Pentecost (Acts 2).

Whit·sun·tide /hwítsəntīd, wít-/ *n.* the weekend or week including Whitsunday.

whit·tle /hwítəl, witəl/ *v.* **1** *tr.* (foll. by *at*) *intr.* pare (wood, etc.) with repeated slicing with a knife. **2** *tr.* (often foll. by *away*, *down*) reduce by repeated subtractions.

whiz /hwiz, wiz/ *n. & v.* (also **whizz**) *colloq.* ● *n.* (*pl.* **whizzes**) **1** the sound made by the friction of a body moving through the air at great speed. **2** (also **wiz**) *colloq.* a person who is remarkable or skillful in some respect (*is a whiz at chess*). ● *v.intr.* (**whizzed**, **whizzing**) move with or make a whiz.

whiz-bang /hwízbang, wíz-/ *n. & adj.* ● *n. colloq.* a high-velocity shell from a small-caliber gun, whose passage is heard before the gun's report. ● *adj.* extremely effective and successful. (*whiz-bang technology*).

whiz kid *n.* (also **whizz kid**) *colloq.* a brilliant or highly successful young person.

WHO *abbr.* World Health Organization.

who /hōo/ *pron.* (*obj.* **whom** /hōom/ or *colloq.* **who**; *poss.* **whose** /hōoz/) **1 a** what or which person or persons (*who called?; you know who it was; whom or who did you see?*). ¶ In the last example *whom* is correct but *who* is common in less formal contexts. **b** what sort of person or persons (*who am I to object?*). **2** (a person) that (*anyone who wishes can come; the woman whom you met; the man who you saw*). ¶ In the last two examples *whom* is correct but *who* is common in less formal contexts. **3** and but he, she, they, etc. (*gave it to Tom, who sold it to Jim*). □ **who goes there?** see GO[1].

whoa /wō/ *int.* used as a command to stop or slow a horse, etc.

who'd /hōod/ *contr.* **1** who had. **2** who would.

W

who·dun·it /hoōdúnit/ *n.* (also **who·dun·nit**) *colloq.* a story or play about the detection of a crime, etc., esp. murder.

who·ev·er /hoō-évər/ *pron.* (*obj.* **whomever** /hoōm-/ or *colloq.* **whoever**; *poss.* **whosever** /hoōz-/) **1** the or any person or persons who (*whoever comes is welcome*). **2** though anyone (*whoever else objects, I do not; whosever it is, I want it*). **3** *colloq.* (as an intensive) whoever; who at all (*whoever heard of such a thing?*).

whole /hōl/ *adj.* & *n.* ● *adj.* **1** in an uninjured, unbroken, intact, or undiminished state (*swallowed it whole; there is not a plate left whole*). **2** not less than; all there is of; entire; complete (*waited a whole year; the whole school knows*). **3** (of blood or milk, etc.) with no part removed. **4** (of a person) healthy; recovered from illness or injury. ● *n.* **1** a thing complete in itself. **2** all there is of a thing (*the whole of the summer*). **3** (foll. by *of*) all members, inhabitants, etc., of (*the whole of Congress knows it*). □ **as a whole** as a unity; not as separate parts. **go** (the) **whole hog** see HOG. **on the whole** taking everything relevant into account; in general. **out of whole cloth** without fact; entirely fictitious. □□ **whole·ness** *n.*

whole-grain *adj.* made with or containing whole grains (*whole-grain bread*).

whole·heart·ed /hōlháartid/ *adj.* **1** (of a person) completely devoted or committed. **2** (of an action, etc.) done with all possible effort or sincerity; thorough. □□ **whole·heart·ed·ly** *adv.* **whole·heart·ed·ness** *n.*

whole-life in·sur·ance *n.* life insurance for which premiums are payable throughout the remaining life of the person insured.

whole·meal /hōlmeel/ *n.* (usu. *attrib.*) *Brit.* = WHOLE-WHEAT.

whole note *n.* esp. *Mus.* a note having the time value of four quarter notes, and represented by a ring with no stem. ▷ NOTATION

whole num·ber *n.* a number without fractions; an integer.

whole·sale /hōlsayl/ *n., adj., adv.,* & *v.* ● *n.* the selling of things in large quantities to be retailed by others (cf. RETAIL). ● *adj.* & *adv.* **1** by wholesale; at a wholesale price. **2** on a large scale (*wholesale destruction occurred*). ● *v.tr.* sell wholesale. □□ **whole·sal·er** *n.*

whole·some /hōlsəm/ *adj.* **1** promoting or indicating physical, mental, or moral health. **2** prudent (*wholesome respect*). □□ **whole·some·ly** *adv.* **whole·some·ness** *n.*

whole step *n. Mus.* = TONE 4.

whole-tone scale *n. Mus.* a scale consisting entirely of tones, with no semitones.

whole-wheat *adj.* made of wheat with none of the bran or germ removed.

who·lism var. of HOLISM.

whol·ly /hōlee/ *adv.* **1** entirely; without limitation or diminution (*I am wholly at a loss*). **2** purely; exclusively (*a wholly bad example*).

whom *objective case* of WHO.

whom·ev·er *objective case* of WHOEVER.

whom·so·ev·er *objective case* of WHOSOEVER.

whoop /hoōp, hoop/ *n.* & *v.* (also **hoop**) ● *n.* **1** a loud cry of or as of excitement, etc. **2** a long, rasping, indrawn breath in whooping cough. ● *v.intr.* utter a whoop. □ **whoop it up** *colloq.* **1** engage in revelry. **2** make a stir.

whoop·ee /hwoōpee, woop-, hwoō-, woō-/ *int.* & *n. colloq.* ● *int.* expressing exuberant joy. ● *n.* exuberant enjoyment or revelry. □ **make whoopee** *colloq.* **1** rejoice noisily. **2** engage in sexual play.

whoo·pee cush·ion *n.* a rubber cushion that when sat on makes a sound like the breaking of wind.

whoop·er /hoōpər, hwoō-, woō-/ *n.* **1** one that whoops. **2** a whooping crane. **3** (in full **whooper swan**) a swan, *Cygnus cygnus,* with a characteristic whooping sound in flight.

whoop·ing cough *n.* an infectious bacterial disease, esp. of children, with a series of short, violent coughs followed by a whoop.

whoop·ing crane *n.* a white N. American crane with a loud, whooping cry.

whoops /hwoōps, woops/ *int. colloq.* expressing surprise or apology, esp. on making an obvious mistake.

whoosh /hwoōsh, woōsh/ *v., n.,* & *int.* (also **woosh**) ● *v.intr.* & *tr.* move or cause to move with a rushing sound. ● *n.* a sudden movement accompanied by a rushing sound. ● *int.* an exclamation imitating this.

whop /hwop, wop/ *v.tr.* (**whopped, whopping**) *sl.* **1** thrash. **2** defeat; overcome.

whop·per /hwópər, wóp-/ *n. sl.* **1** something big of its kind. **2** a great lie.

whop·ping /hwóping, wóp-/ *adj. sl.* very big.

whore /hawr/ *n.* & *v.* ● *n.* **1** a prostitute. **2** *derog.* a promiscuous woman. ● *v.intr.* (of a man) seek or chase after whores.

whore·house /hawrhows/ *n.* a brothel.

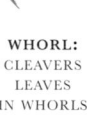

whorl /hwawrl, wawrl, hwərl, wərl/ *n.* **1** ◄ a ring of leaves or other organs around a stem of a plant. **2** one turn of a spiral, esp. on a shell. ▷ SHELL. **3** a complete circle in a fingerprint. □□ **whorled** *adj.*

WHORL: CLEAVERS LEAVES IN WHORLS

whor·tle·ber·ry /hwártəlberee, wárt-/ *n.* (*pl.* **-ies**) a bilberry.

whose /hoōz/ *pron.* & *adj.* ● *pron.* of or belonging to which person (*whose is this book?*). ● *adj.* of whom or which (*whose book is this?; the man, whose name was Tim; the house whose roof was damaged*).

whos·ev·er /hoōzévər/ *poss.* of WHOEVER.

who·so·ev·er /hoōsō-évər/ *pron.* (*obj.* **whomsoever** /hoōm-/; *poss.* **whosesoever** /hoōz-/) *archaic* = WHOEVER.

who's who *n.* **1** who or what each person is (*know who's who*). **2** a list or directory with facts about notable persons.

why /hwī, wī/ *adv., int.,* & *n.* ● *adv.* **1 a** for what reason or purpose (*why did you do it?*). **b** on what grounds (*why do you say that?*). **2** (prec. by *reason,* etc.) for which (*the reasons why I did it*). ● *int.* expressing: **1** surprised discovery or recognition (*why, it's you!*). **2** impatience (*why, of course I do!*). **3** reflection (*why, yes, I think so*). **4** objection (*why, what is wrong with it?*). ● *n.* (*pl.* **whys**) a reason or explanation (esp. *whys and wherefores*). □ **why so?** on what grounds?; for what reason or purpose?

WI *abbr.* **1** West Indies. **2** West Indian. **3** Wisconsin (in official postal use).

Wich·i·ta /wíchitaw/ *n.* **1 a** a N. American people native to Kansas. **b** a member of this people. **2** the language of this people.

wick /wik/ *n.* & *v.* ● *n.* **1** a strip or thread of fibrous or spongy material feeding a flame with fuel in a candle, lamp, etc. **2** *Surgery* a gauze strip inserted in a wound to drain it. ● *v.tr.* draw (moisture) away by capillary action. □ **dip one's wick** *coarse sl.* (of a man) have sexual intercourse.

wick·ed /wíkid/ *adj.* (**wickeder, wickedest**) **1** sinful. **2** spiteful; ill-tempered; intending or intended to give pain. **3** playfully malicious. **4** *colloq.* very bad (*a wicked cough*). **5** *sl.* excellent. □□ **wick·ed·ly** *adv.* **wick·ed·ness** *n.*

wick·er /wíkər/ *n.* plaited twigs or osiers, etc., as material for baskets, etc.

wick·er·work /wíkərwərk/ *n.* **1** ► wicker. **2** things made of wicker.

wick·et /wíkit/ *n.* **1** (in full **wicket door** or **gate**) a small door or gate, esp. beside or in a larger one or closing the lower part only of a doorway. **2** an aperture in a door or wall, usu. closed with a sliding panel. **3** a croquet hoop. **4** *Cricket* **a** a set of three stumps with the bails in position defended by a batsman. ▷ CRICKET. **b** the ground between two wickets. **c** the state of this (*a slow wicket*). **d** an instance of a batsman being got out (*bowler has taken four wickets*). **e** a pair of batsmen batting at the same time (*a third-wicket partnership*).

wick·et·keep·er /wíkitkéepər/ *n. Cricket* the fielder stationed close behind a batsman's wicket. ▷ CRICKET

wick·i·up /wíkeeup/ *n.* a Native American hut of a frame covered with grass, etc.

wid·der·shins var. of WITHERSHINS.

wide /wīd/ *adj., adv.,* & *n.* ● *adj.* **1 a** measuring much or more than other things of the same kind across or from side to side. **b** considerable; more than is needed (*a wide margin*). **2** (following a measurement) in width (*a foot wide*). **3** extending far; embracing much. **4** not tight nor close nor restricted; loose. **5 a** free; liberal; unprejudiced (*takes wide views*). **b** not specialized; general. **6** open to the full extent (*staring with wide eyes*). **7 a** (foll. by *of*) not within a reasonable distance of. **b** at a considerable distance from a point or mark. **8** (in *comb.*) extending over the whole of (*nationwide*). ● *adv.* **1** widely. **2** to the full extent (*wide awake*). **3** far from the target, etc. (*is shooting wide*). ● *n.* **1** *Cricket* a ball judged beyond the batsman's reach and so scoring a run. **2** (prec. by *the*) the wide world. □ **give a wide berth to** see BERTH. □□ **wide·ness** *n.* **wid·ish** *adj.*

wide-an·gle *attrib.adj.* (of a lens) having a short focal length and hence a field covering a wide angle.

wide·a·wake /wídəwáyk/ *n.* a soft felt hat with a low crown and wide brim.

wide a·wake *adj.* (hyphenated when *attrib.*) **1** fully awake. **2** *colloq.* wary; knowing.

wide-eyed *adj.* surprised or naive.

wide·ly /wídlee/ *adv.* **1** far apart. **2** extensively (*widely read*). **3** by many people (*it is widely thought that*). **4** to a large degree (*a widely different view*).

wid·en /wíd'n/ *v.tr.* & *intr.* make or become wider. □□ **wid·en·er** *n.*

wide o·pen *adj.* (often foll. by *to*) vulnerable (to attack, etc.).

wide-rang·ing *adj.* covering an extensive range.

wide·spread /wídspréd/ *adj.* widely distributed or disseminated.

widg·et /wíjit/ *n. colloq.* any gadget or device.

wid·ow /wídō/ *n.* & *v.* ● *n.* **1** a woman who has lost her husband by death and has not married again. **2** a woman whose husband is often away on a specified activity (*golf widow*). **3** extra cards dealt separately and taken by the highest bidder. **4** *Printing* the short last line of a paragraph, esp. at the top of a page or column. ● *v.tr.* **1** make into a widow or widower. **2** (as **widowed** *adj.*) bereft by the death of a spouse (*my widowed mother*). **3** (foll. by *of*) deprive of. □□ **wid·ow·hood** *n.*

wid·ow·er /wídōər/ *n.* a man who has lost his wife by death and has not married again.

wid·ow's peak *n.* a V-shaped growth of hair toward the center of the forehead.

width /width, witth, with/ *n.* **1** measurement or distance from side to side. **2** a large extent. **3** breadth or liberality of views, etc. **4** a strip of material of full width as woven. □□ **width·ways** *adv.* **width·wise** *adv.*

wield /weeld/ *v.tr.* **1** hold and use (a weapon or tool). **2** exert or command (power or authority, etc.). □□ **wield·er** *n.*

wield·y /wéeldee/ *adj.* (**wield·ier, wieldiest**) easily wielded, controlled, or handled.

wie·ner /wéenər/ *n.* a frankfurter.

Wie·ner schnit·zel /véenər shnítsəl/ *n.* a veal cutlet breaded, fried, and garnished.

WICKERWORK BASKET

W

wife /wīf/ *n.* (*pl.* **wives** /wīvz/) **1** a married woman, esp. in relation to her husband. **2** *archaic* a woman, esp. an old or uneducated one. □ **take to wife** *archaic* marry (a woman). □□ **wife·ly** *adj.*

wig /wig/ *n.* ◀ an artificial head of hair, esp. to conceal baldness or as a disguise, or worn by a judge or barrister or as period dress. □□ **wigged** *adj.* (also in *comb.*). **wig·less** *adj.*

wi·geon /wijən/ *n.* a dabbling duck with mainly reddish-brown and grey plumage, the male having a whistling call.

WIG:
18TH-CENTURY
MAN'S WIG

wig·ging /wiging/ *n. Brit. colloq.* a reprimand.

wig·gle /wigəl/ *v. & n. colloq.* ● *v.intr. & tr.* move or cause to move quickly from side to side, etc. ● *n.* an act of wiggling. □□ **wig·gler** *n.* **wig·gly** *adj.*

wig·wam /wigwom/ *n.* a Native American hut or tent of skins, mats, or bark on poles.

wild /wīld/ *adj., adv., & n.* ● *adj.* **1** (of an animal or plant) in its original natural state; not domesticated nor cultivated. **2** not civilized; barbarous. **3** (of scenery, etc.) having a conspicuously desolate appearance. **4** unrestrained; disorderly (*a wild youth; wild hair*). **5** tempestuous (*a wild night*). **6 a** excited; frantic (*wild with excitement*). **b** (of looks, etc.) indicating distraction. **c** (foll. by *about*) *colloq.* enthusiastically devoted to. **7** *colloq.* infuriated (*makes me wild*). **8** haphazard; ill-aimed; rash (*a wild guess; a wild shot*). **9** (of a horse, game bird, etc.) easily startled. **10** *colloq.* exciting; delightful. **11** (of a card) having any rank chosen (*the joker is wild*). ● *adv.* in a wild manner (*shooting wild*). ● *n.* **1** a wild tract. **2** a desert. □ **in the wild** in an uncultivated, etc., state. **in** (or **out in**) **the wilds** *colloq.* far from normal habitation. **run wild** grow or stray unchecked or undisciplined. □□ **wild·ish** *adj.* **wild·ly** *adv.* **wild·ness** *n.*

wild-and-wool·ly *adj.* lacking refinement.

wild card *n.* **1** see sense 11 of WILD *adj.* **2** *Computing* a character that will match any character or sequence of characters in a file name, etc. **3** *Sports* an extra player or team chosen to enter a competition at the selectors' discretion.

wild·cat /wīldkat/ *n. & adj.* ● *n.* **1** a hot-tempered or violent person. **2** ▶ any of various smallish cats, esp. the European *Felis sylvestris* or the N. American bobcat. **3** an exploratory oil well. ● *adj.* (*attrib.*) **1** reckless; financially unsound. **2** (of a strike) sudden and unauthorized.

wild·cat strike *n.* an unauthorized strike by esp. union laborers.

wil·de·beest /wildəbeest, vil-/ *n.* (*pl.* same or **wilde·beests**) = GNU.

wil·der·ness /wildərnis/ *n.* **1** a desert; an uncultivated and uninhabited region. **2** part of a garden left with an uncultivated appearance. **3** (foll. by *of*) a confused assemblage of things.

wild·fire /wīldfīr/ *n. hist.* **1** a combustible liquid formerly used in warfare. **2** = WILL-O'-THE-WISP. □ **spread like wildfire** spread with great speed.

wild·flow·er /wīldflowər, wīld-, -flowr/ *n.* **1** any wild or uncultivated flowering plant. **2** the flower of such a plant.

WILDCAT:
SCOTTISH WILDCAT
(*Felis sylvestris*)

wild·fowl /wīldfowl/ *n.* (*pl.* same) a game bird, esp. an aquatic one. ▷ DUCK, WATERFOWL

wild-goose chase *n.* a foolish or hopeless and unproductive quest.

wild·life /wīldlīf/ *n.* wild animals collectively.

wild rice *n.* any tall grass of the genus *Zizania*, yielding edible grains. ▷ GRAIN

Wild West *n.* the western US in a time of lawlessness in its early history.

wild·wood /wīldwood/ *n. poet.* uncultivated or unfrequented woodland.

wile /wīl/ *n. & v.* ● *n.* (usu. in *pl.*) a trick or cunning procedure. ● *v.tr.* (foll. by *away*, *into*, etc.) lure or entice.

wil·i·ness see WILY.

will[1] /wil/ *v.aux. & tr.* (*3rd sing. present* **will**; *past* **would** /wood/) (foll. by infin. without *to*, or *absol.*; present and past only in use) **1** (in the 2nd and 3rd persons, and often in the 1st: see SHALL) expressing the future tense in statements, commands, or questions (*you will regret this; they will leave at once; will you go to the party?*). **2** (in the 1st person) expressing a wish or intention (*I will return soon*). ¶ For the other persons in senses 1, 2, see SHALL. **3** expressing desire, consent, or inclination (*will you have a sandwich?; come when you will; the door will not open*). **4** expressing ability or capacity (*the jar will hold a quart*). **5** expressing habitual or inevitable tendency (*accidents will happen; will sit there for hours*). **6** expressing probability or expectation (*that will be my wife*). □ **will do** *colloq.* expressing willingness to carry out a request.

will[2] /wil/ *n. & v.* ● *n.* **1** the faculty by which a person decides or is regarded as deciding on and initiating action (*the mind consists of the understanding and the will*). **2** control exercised by deliberate purpose over impulse; self-control; willpower (*has a strong will*). **3** a deliberate or fixed desire or intention (*a will to live*). **4** the power of effecting one's intentions or dominating others. **5** directions in legal form for the disposition of one's property after death (*make one's will*). **6** disposition toward others (*good will*). **7** *archaic* what one desires or ordains (*thy will be done*). ● *v.tr.* **1** have as the object of one's will (*what God wills; willed that we should succeed*). **2** (*absol.*) exercise willpower. **3** instigate or impel or compel by the exercise of willpower (*you can will yourself into contentment*). **4** bequeath by the terms of a will (*shall will my money to charity*). □ **at will 1** whenever one pleases. **2** *Law* able to be evicted without notice (*tenant at will*). **have one's will** obtain what one wants. **what is your will?** what do you wish done? **where there's a will there's a way** determination will overcome any obstacle. **a will of one's own** obstinacy; willfulness of character. **with a will** energetically or resolutely. □□ **willed** *adj.* (also in *comb.*).

will·ful /wilfool/ *adj.* **1** (of an action or state) intentional, deliberate (*willful murder; willful neglect; willful disobedience*). **2** (of a person) obstinate, headstrong. □□ **will·ful·ly** *adv.* **will·ful·ness** *n.*

wil·lies /wileez/ *n.pl. colloq.* nervous discomfort (esp. *give* or *get the willies*).

will·ing /wiling/ *adj. & n.* ● *adj.* **1** ready to consent or undertake (*a willing ally; am willing to do it*). **2** given or done, etc., by a willing person (*willing hands*). ● *n.* cheerful intention (*show willing*). □□ **will·ing·ly** *adv.* **will·ing·ness** *n.*

will-o'-the-wisp /wiləthəwisp/ *n.* **1** a phosphorescent light seen on marshy ground, perhaps resulting from the combustion of gases; ignis fatuus. **2** an elusive person. **3** a delusive hope or plan.

wil·low /wilō/ *n.* **1** ▶ a tree or shrub of the genus *Salix*, growing usu. near water in temperate climates, with small flowers borne on catkins, and pliant branches. **2** an item made of willow wood, esp. a cricket bat.

wil·low pat·tern *n.* ▶ a conventional design representing a Chinese scene, often with a willow tree, of blue on white porcelain, stoneware, or earthenware.

WILLOW-PATTERN
PLATE

wil·low·y /wilō-ee/ *adj.* **1** having or bordered by willows. **2** lithe and slender.

will·pow·er /wilpowr/ *n.* control exercised by deliberate purpose over impulse; self-control (*overcame his shyness by willpower*).

wil·ly-nil·ly /wileenilee/ *adv. & adj.* ● *adv.* whether one likes it or not. ● *adj.* existing or occurring willy-nilly.

wilt /wilt/ *v. & n.* ● *v.* **1** *intr.* (of a plant) wither; droop. **2** *intr.* (of a person) lose one's energy. **3** *tr.* cause to wilt. ● *n.* a plant disease causing wilting.

wil·y /wīlee/ *adj.* (**wilier, wiliest**) crafty; cunning. □□ **wil·i·ly** *adv.* **wil·i·ness** *n.*

wimp /wimp/ *n. colloq.* a feeble or ineffectual person. □□ **wimp·ish** *adj.* **wimp·ish·ly** *adv.* **wimp·ish·ness** *n.* **wimp·y** *adj.*

wim·ple /wimpəl/ *n.* a linen or silk headdress covering the neck and the sides of the face, formerly worn by women and still worn by some nuns.

win /win/ *v. & n.* ● *v.* (**winning**; *past* and *past part.* **won** /wun/) **1** *tr.* acquire or secure as a result of a contest, bet, litigation, or some other effort (*won some money; won my admiration*). **2** *tr.* be victorious in a fight, etc.). **3** *intr.* **a** be the victor (*who won?*). **b** (foll. by *through, free*, etc.) make one's way or become by successful effort. **4** *tr.* reach by effort (*win the summit*). **5** *tr.* obtain (ore) from a mine. **6** *tr.* dry (hay, etc.) by exposure to the air. ● *n.* victory in a game or bet, etc. □ **win the day** be victorious in battle, argument, etc. **win over** persuade; gain the support of. **win one's spurs** *colloq.* gain distinction or fame. **win through** (or **out**) overcome obstacles. **you can't win** *colloq.* there is no way to succeed. **you can't win them** (or **'em**) **all** *colloq.* a resigned expression of consolation on failure. □□ **win·na·ble** *adj.*

wince /wins/ *n. & v.* ● *n.* a start or involuntary shrinking movement showing pain or distress. ● *v.intr.* give a wince. □□ **winc·ing·ly** *adv.*

winch /winch/ *n. & v.* ● *n.* **1** the crank of a wheel or axle. **2** a windlass. **3** a roller for moving textile fabric through a dyeing vat. ● *v.tr.* lift with a winch. □□ **winch·er** *n.*

Win·ches·ter /winchestər/ *n.* **1** *Trademark* a breech-loading repeating rifle. **2** (in full **Winchester disk**) *Computing* a hermetically sealed data-storage device.

wind[1] /wind/ *n. & v.* ● *n.* **1 a** air in more or less rapid natural motion, esp. from an area of high pressure to one of low pressure. **b** a current of wind blowing from a specified direction or otherwise defined (*north wind; opposing wind*). **2 a** breath as needed in physical exertion or in speech. **b** the power of breathing without difficulty while running or making a similar continuous effort (*let me recover my wind*). **c** a spot below the center of the chest where a blow temporarily paralyzes breathing. **3** mere empty words; meaningless rhetoric. **4** flatulence. **5 a** an artificially produced current of air, esp. for sounding an organ or other wind instrument. **b** air stored for use or used as a current. **c** the wind instruments of an orchestra collectively. ▷ WOODWIND. **6** a scent carried by the wind, indicating the presence or proximity of an animal, etc. ● *v.tr.* **1** exhaust the wind of by exertion or a blow. **2** renew the wind of by rest (*stopped to wind the horses*). **3** make breathe quickly and deeply by exercise.

catkin

WILLOW:
WHITE WILLOW
(*Salix alba*)

W

4 detect the presence of by a scent. **5** /wīnd/ (*past and past part.* **winded** or **wound** /wownd/) *poet.* sound (a bugle or call) by blowing. □ **before the wind** helped by the wind's force. **close to** (or **near**) **the wind 1** sailing as nearly against the wind as is consistent with using its force. **2** *colloq.* verging on indecency or dishonesty. **get wind of 1** smell out. **2** hear a rumor of. **how** (or **which way**) **the wind blows** (or **lies**) **1** what is the state of opinion. **2** what developments are likely. **in the wind** happening or about to happen. **like the wind** swiftly. **off the wind** *Naut.* with the wind on the quarter. **on a wind** *Naut.* against a wind on either bow. **on the wind** (of a sound or scent) carried by the wind. **take the wind out of a person's sails** frustrate a person by anticipating an action or remark, etc. **throw caution to the wind** (or **winds**) not worry about taking risks; be reckless. **to the winds** (or **four winds**) **1** in all directions. **2** into a state of abandonment or neglect. □□ **wind·less** *adj.*

wind² /wīnd/ *v. & n.* ● *v.* (*past and past part.* **wound** /wownd/) **1** *intr.* go in a circular, spiral, curved, or crooked course (*a winding staircase*). **2** *tr.* make (one's way) by such a course (*wind your way up to bed*). **3** *tr.* wrap closely (*wound the blanket around me*). **4 a** *tr.* coil; provide with a coiled thread, etc. (*wound cotton on a reel*). **b** *intr.* coil (*the vine winds around the pole*). **5** *tr.* wind up (a clock, etc.). **6** *tr.* draw with a windlass, etc. (*wound the cable car up the mountain*). ● *n.* **1** a bend or turn in a course. **2** a single turn when winding. □ **wind down 1** lower by winding. **2** (of a mechanism) unwind. **3** (of a person) relax. **4** draw gradually to a close. **wind off** unwind (string, wool, etc.). **wind around one's finger** see FINGER. **wind up 1** coil the whole of (a piece of string, etc.). **2 a** *colloq.* increase the tension (*wound myself up to fever pitch*). **b** irritate or provoke to the point of anger. **3** end (*wound up his speech*). **4** *Commerce* **a** arrange the affairs of and dissolve (a company). **b** (of a company) cease business and go into liquidation. **5** *colloq.* end in a specified state or circumstance (*you'll wind up in prison*). **6** *Baseball* (of a pitcher) carry out a windup. **wound up** *adj.* (of a person) excited or tense or angry. □□ **wind·er** *n.*

wind·age /wíndij/ *n.* **1** the friction of air against the moving part of a machine. **2 a** the effect of the wind in deflecting a missile. **b** an allowance for this.

wind·bag /wíndbag/ *n. colloq.* a person who talks a lot but says little of any value.

wind·blown /wíndblōn/ *adj.* exposed to or blown about by the wind.

wind·break /wíndbrayk/ *n.* a row of trees or a fence or wall, etc., serving to break the force of the winds.

wind·break·er /wíndbraykər/ *n.* a kind of wind-resistant outer jacket with close-fitting neck, cuffs, and lower edge.

wind·burn /wíndbərn/ *n.* inflammation of the skin caused by exposure to the wind.

wind·chill /wíndchil/ *n.* the cooling effect of wind blowing on a surface.

wind·down *n. colloq.* a gradual lessening of excitement or reduction of activity.

wind·fall /wíndfawl/ *n.* **1** an apple or other fruit blown to the ground by the wind. **2** a piece of unexpected good fortune.

wind·fall tax *n.* (also **wind·fall prof·its tax**) a tax levied on an unexpectedly large profit, esp. one regarded to be excessive or unfairly obtained.

wind·flow·er /wíndflowr/ *n.* an anemone.

wind·ing-sheet *n.* a sheet in which a corpse is wrapped for burial.

wind in·stru·ment *n.* a musical instrument in which sound is produced by a current of air, esp. the breath. ▷ BRASS, WOODWIND

wind·lass /wíndləs/ *n. & v.* ● *n.* a machine with a horizontal axle for hauling or hoisting. ● *v.tr.* hoist or haul with a windlass.

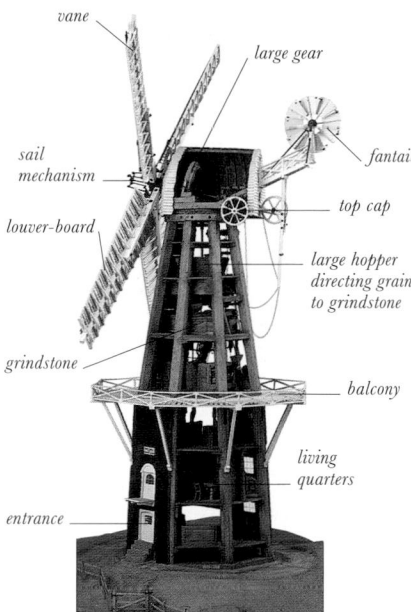

WINDMILL: MODEL OF AN EARLY 19TH-CENTURY BRITISH WINDMILL

vane · *large gear* · *sail mechanism* · *fantail* · *louver-board* · *top cap* · *large hopper directing grain to grindstone* · *grindstone* · *balcony* · *living quarters* · *entrance*

wind·mill /wíndmil/ *n.* ▲ a mill worked by the action of the wind on its sails. □ **throw one's cap** (or **bonnet**) **over the windmill** esp. *Brit.* act recklessly or unconventionally. **tilt at** (or **fight**) **windmills** attack an imaginary enemy or grievance.

win·dow /wíndō/ *n.* **1 a** ▼ an opening in a wall, roof, or vehicle, etc., usu. with glass in fixed, sliding, or hinged frames, to admit light or air, etc., and allow the occupants to see out. ▷ SASH WINDOW. **b** the glass filling this opening (*have broken the window*). **2 a** space for display behind the front window of a shop. **3** an aperture in a wall, etc., through which customers are served in a bank, ticket office, etc.

4 an opportunity to observe or learn. **5** an opening or transparent part in an envelope to show an address. **6** a part of a computer monitor display selected to show a particular category or part of the data. **7 a** an interval during which atmospheric and astronomical circumstances are suitable for the launch of a spacecraft. **b** any interval or opportunity for action. **8** strips of metal foil dispersed in the air to obstruct radar detection. **9** a range of electromagnetic wavelengths for which a medium is transparent. □□ **win·dowed** *adj.* (also in *comb.*). **win·dow·less** *adj.*

win·dow box *n.* a box placed on an outside windowsill for growing flowers.

win·dow dress·ing *n.* **1** the art of arranging a display in a store window, etc. **2** an adroit presentation of facts, etc., to give a deceptively favorable impression.

win·dow·ing /wíndōing/ *n. Computing* the selection of part of a stored image for display or enlargement.

win·dow·pane /wíndōpayn/ *n.* a pane of glass in a window.

win·dow-shop *v.intr.* (**-shopped**, **-shopping**) look at goods displayed in store windows, usu. without buying anything. □□ **win·dow-shop·per** *n.*

win·dow·sill /wíndōsil/ *n.* a sill below a window.

wind·pipe /wíndpīp/ *n.* the air passage from the throat to the lungs; the trachea. ▷ RESPIRATION

wind·row /wíndrō/ *n.* a line of raked hay, sheaves of grain, etc., for drying by the wind.

wind·screen /wíndskreen/ *n. Brit.* = WINDSHIELD.

wind shear *n.* a variation in wind velocity at right angles to the wind's direction.

wind·shield /wíndsheeld/ *n.* a shield of glass at the front of a motor vehicle. ▷ CAR

wind·shield wip·er *n.* a device consisting of a rubber blade on an arm, moving in an arc, for keeping a windshield clear of rain, etc.

wind sock *n.* a canvas cylinder or cone on a mast to show the direction of the wind at an airfield, etc.

Wind·sor chair /wínzaw/ *n.* a wooden dining chair with a semicircular back supported by upright rods.

WINDOW

Originally used by the ancient Romans, glazed windows were rare until the Middle Ages, when glass became more available. As a result, the size of windows grew, and by the Renaissance period they were quite large. Buildings can often be dated by their windows: the segmental head of the window below is distinctive of the Victorian period.

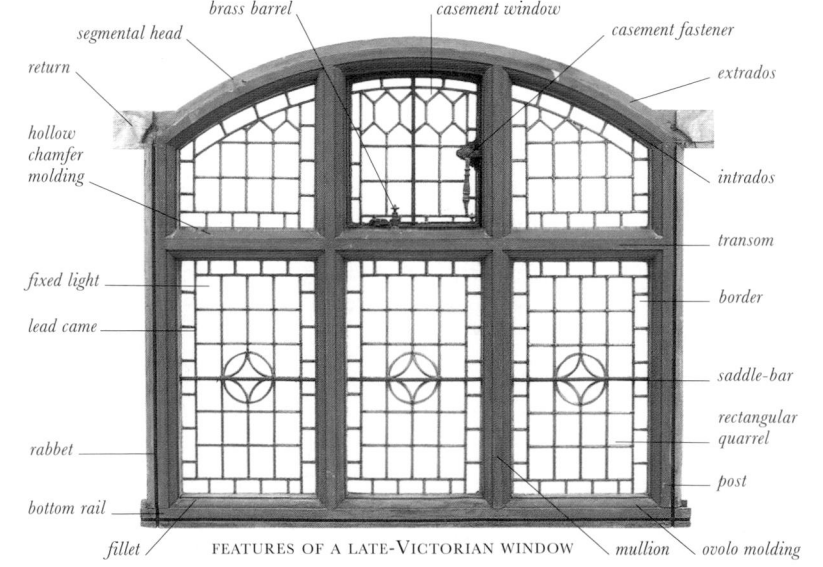

FEATURES OF A LATE-VICTORIAN WINDOW

segmental head · *brass barrel* · *casement window* · *casement fastener* · *return* · *extrados* · *hollow chamfer molding* · *intrados* · *fixed light* · *transom* · *lead came* · *border* · *rabbet* · *saddle-bar* · *rectangular quarrel* · *post* · *bottom rail* · *fillet* · *mullion* · *ovolo molding*

W

WINDSURFING

Windsurfing uses the wind's energy as a driving force. Windsurfers stand on a board and steer by controlling the position of the boom. Beginners can use a funboard, but experienced slalom racers and speed windsurfers often have custom-built boards.

EXAMPLES OF SAILBOARDS

FUNBOARD   MID-LENGTH   SLALOM   CUSTOM
           BOARD   BOARD   BOARD

FEATURES OF A
SAILBOARD

sail

batten

mast inside
sail sleeve

window

boom

wet suit

mast
foot

towing
eye

board

wind·surf·ing /wíndsərfing/ n. ▲ the sport of riding on water on a sailboard. □□ **wind·surf** v.intr. **wind·surf·er** n.

wind·swept /wíndswept/ adj. exposed to or swept back by the wind.

wind tun·nel n. a tunnellike device to produce an air stream past models of aircraft, etc., for the study of wind effects on them.

wind·up /wíndup/ n. **1** a conclusion; a finish. **2** *Baseball* the motions made by a pitcher, esp. arm swinging, in preparation for releasing a pitch.

wind·ward /wíndwərd/ adj., adv., & n. ● adj. & adv. on the side from which the wind is blowing (opp. LEEWARD). ● n. the windward direction (*to windward*). □ **get to windward of 1** place oneself there to avoid the smell of. **2** gain an advantage over.

wind·y /wíndee/ adj. (**windier, windiest**) **1** stormy with wind (*a windy night*). **2** exposed to the wind; windswept (*a windy plain*). **3** generating or characterized by flatulence. **4** *colloq.* wordy; verbose; empty (*a windy speech*). □□ **wind·i·ness** n.

wine /wīn/ n. & v. ● n. **1** fermented grape juice as an alcoholic drink. ▷ VINIFICATION. **2** a fermented drink resembling this made from other fruits, etc., as specified (*elderberry wine; ginger wine*). **3** the dark-red color of red wine. ● v. **1** intr. drink wine. **2** tr. entertain with wine. □ **wine and dine** entertain to or have a meal with wine.

wine cel·lar n. **1** a cellar for storing wine. **2** the contents of this.

wine·glass /wínglas/ n. **1** a glass for wine, usu. with a stem and foot. **2** the contents of this, a wineglassful.

wine·glass·ful /wínglasfŏŏl/ n. (*pl.* **-fuls**) **1** the capacity of a wineglass, esp. of the size used for sherry, as a measure of liquid, about four tablespoons. **2** the contents of a wineglass.

wine·grow·er /wíngrōər/ n. a cultivator of grapes for wine.

wine·press /wínpres/ n. a press in which grapes are squeezed in making wine.

win·er·y /wínəree/ n. (*pl.* **-ies**) an establishment where wine is made.

wine·skin /wínskin/ n. a whole skin of a goat, etc., sewn up and used to hold wine.

wine·tast·ing /wíntaysting/ n. **1** judging the quality of wine by tasting it. **2** an occasion for this.

wing /wing/ n. & v. ● n. **1** each of the limbs or organs by which a bird, bat, or insect is able to fly. ▷ BAT, BIRD, FEATHER, INSECT. **2** ▼ a rigid horizontal winglike structure forming a supporting part of an aircraft. ▷ AILERON, AIRCRAFT, DELTA WING. **3** part of a building, etc., which projects or is extended in a certain direction (*lived in the north wing*). **4 a** a forward player at either end of a line in soccer, hockey, etc. **b** the side part of a playing area. **5** (in *pl.*) the sides of a theater stage out of view of the audience. ▷ THEATER. **6** a section of a political party in terms of the extremity of its views. **7** a flank of a battle array. **8 a** an air-force unit of several squadrons or groups. **b** (in *pl.*) a pilot's badge in the air force, etc. (*get one's wings*). ● v. **1** intr. & tr. travel or traverse on wings or in an aircraft (*winging through the air; am winging my way home*). **2** tr. wound in a wing or an arm. **3** tr. equip with wings. **4** tr. enable to fly; send in flight (*fear winged my steps; winged an arrow toward them*). □ **give** (or **lend**) **wings to** speed up (a person or a thing). **on the wing** flying or in flight. **on a wing and a prayer** with only the slightest chance of success. **spread** (or **stretch**) **one's wings** develop one's powers fully. **take under one's wing** treat as a protégé. **take wing** fly away; soar. **waiting in the wings** holding oneself in readiness. □□ **winged** adj. (also in *comb.*). **wing·less** n. **wing·let** n. **wing·like** adj.

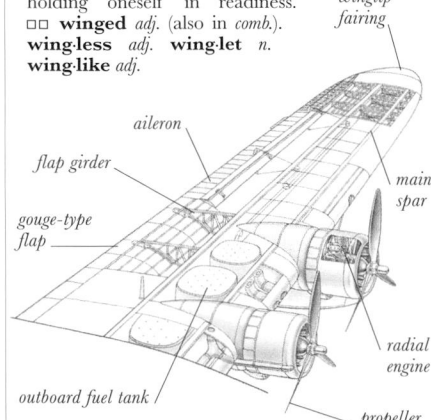

wingtip
fairing

aileron

flap girder

main
spar

gouge-type
flap

radial
engine

outboard fuel tank

propeller

WING OF AN EARLY
20TH-CENTURY FLYING BOAT

wing chair n. a chair with side pieces projecting forward at the top of a high back.

wing collar n. a man's high, stiff collar with turned-down corners.

wing·ding /wíngding/ n. *sl.* **1** a wild party. **2** a drug addict's real or feigned seizure.

wing·er /wíngər/ n. **1** a player on a wing in soccer, hockey, etc. **2** (in *comb.*) a member of a specified political wing (*left-winger*).

wing nut n. a nut with projections for the fingers to turn it on a screw.

wing·span /wíngspan/ n. (also **wing·spread**) measurement right across the wings of a bird or aircraft.

wing tip n. **1** the outer end of an aircraft's or a bird's wing. **2** a style of shoe with a pattern of perforations on the toe resembling extended bird wings.

wink /wingk/ v. & n. ● v. **1 a** tr. close and open (one eye or both eyes) quickly. **b** intr. close and open an eye. **2** intr. (often foll. by *at*) wink one eye as a signal of friendship or greeting or to convey a message to a person. **3** intr. (of a light, etc.) shine or flash intermittently. ● n. **1** the act or an instance of winking. **2** *colloq.* a brief moment of sleep (*didn't sleep a wink*). □ **in a wink** very quickly. **wink at 1** purposely avoid seeing; pretend not to notice. **2** connive at (a wrongdoing, etc.).

win·kle /wíngkəl/ n. see PERIWINKLE[2].

Win·ne·ba·go /winəbăgō/ n. **1 a** a N. American people native to Wisconsin. **b** a member of this people. **2** the language of this people.

win·ner /wínər/ n. **1** a person, racehorse, etc., that wins. **2** *colloq.* a successful or highly promising idea, enterprise, etc.

win·ning /wíning/ adj. & n. ● adj. **1** having or bringing victory or an advantage. **2** attractive; persuasive (*a winning smile; winning ways*). ● n. (in *pl.*) money won, esp. in betting, etc. □□ **win·ning·ly** adv.

win·ning post /wíning pōst/ n. a post marking the end of a race.

win·now /winō/ v.tr. **1** blow (grain) free of chaff, etc., by an air current. **2** (foll. by *out, away, from*, etc.) ▼ get rid of (chaff, etc.) from grain. **3 a** sift; separate. **b** sift or examine (evidence for falsehood, etc.). **c** clear, sort, or weed out (rubbish, etc.). □□ **win·now·er** n. (in senses 1, 2).

WINNOW: SEPARATING
CHAFF FROM GRAIN BY HAND

win·o /wínō/ n. (*pl.* **-os**) *sl.* a habitual excessive drinker of cheap wine.

win·some /wínsəm/ adj. (of a person, looks, or manner) winning; attractive; engaging. □□ **win·some·ly** adv. **win·some·ness** n.

W

win·ter /wíntər/ *n. & v.* ● *n.* **1** the coldest season of the year. ▷ SEASON. **2** *Astron.* the period from the winter solstice to the vernal equinox. **3** a bleak or lifeless period or region, etc. (*nuclear winter*). **4** (*attrib.*) **a** characteristic of or suitable for winter (*winter light*; *winter clothes*). **b** (of fruit) ripening late or keeping until or during winter. **c** (of wheat or other crops) sown in autumn for harvesting the following year. ● *v.* **1** *intr.* (usu. foll. by *at, in*) pass the winter (*likes to winter in Florida*). **2** *tr.* keep or feed (plants, cattle) during winter. □□ **win·ter·er** *n.*

win·ter·green /wíntərgreen/ *n.* ◀ any of several plants esp. of the genus *Pyrola* or *Gaultheria* remaining green through the winter.

win·ter·ize /wíntərīz/ *v.tr.* adapt for operation or use in cold weather. □□ **win·ter·i·za·tion** *n.*

win·ter sol·stice *n.* the time at which the Sun is farthest south from the equator, about Dec. 22 in the northern hemisphere.

win·ter·time /wíntərtīm/ *n.* the season of winter.

win·try /wíntree/ *adj.* (also **win·ter·y** /-təree/) (**wintrier**, **wintriest**) **1** characteristic of winter (*a wintry landscape*). **2** (of a smile, greeting, etc.) lacking warmth or enthusiasm. □□ **win·tri·ly** *adv.* **win·tri·ness** *n.*

win·y /wínee/ *adj.* (**winier**, **winiest**) resembling wine in taste or appearance.

wipe /wīp/ *v. & n.* ● *v.tr.* **1** clean or dry the surface of by rubbing with the hands or a cloth, etc. **2** rub (a cloth) over a surface. **3** spread (a liquid, etc.) over a surface by rubbing. **4** (often foll. by *away, off*, etc.) **a** clear or remove by wiping. **b** remove or eliminate completely (*the village was wiped off the map*). **5 a** erase (data, a recording, etc., from a magnetic medium). **b** erase data from (the medium). ● *n.* **1** an act of wiping (*give the floor a wipe*). **2** a piece of disposable absorbent cloth, usu. treated with a cleansing agent, for wiping something clean (*antiseptic wipes*). □ **wipe down** (esp. a vertical surface) by wiping. **wipe the floor with** *colloq.* inflict a humiliating defeat on. **wipe out 1 a** destroy; annihilate. **b** obliterate (*wiped it out of my memory*). **2** *sl.* murder. **3** clean the inside of. **wipe the slate clean** see SLATE. **wipe up 1** take up (a liquid, etc.) by wiping. **2** *Brit.* dry (dishes, etc.).

wiped out *adj. sl.* tired out, exhausted.

wipe·out /wípowt/ *n.* **1** the obliteration of one radio signal by another. **2** an instance of destruction or annihilation. **3** *sl.* a fall from a surfboard.

wip·er /wípər/ *n.* = WINDSHIELD WIPER.

wire /wīr/ *n. & v.* ● *n.* **1 a** metal drawn out a thread or thin flexible rod. **b** a piece of this. **c** (*attrib.*) made of wire. **2** a length or quantity of wire used for fencing or to carry an electric current, etc. **3** a telegram or cablegram. ● *v.tr.* **1** provide, fasten, strengthen, etc., with wire. **2** (often foll. by *up*) *Electr.* install electrical circuits in (a building, piece of equipment, etc.). **3** *colloq.* telegraph (*wired me that they were coming*). **4** snare (an animal, etc.) with wire. □ **by wire** by telegraph. **get one's wires crossed** become confused and misunderstood.

wire·cloth *n.* cloth woven from wire.

wire·draw /wírdraw/ *v.tr.* (*past* **-drew** /-droō/; *past part.* **-drawn** /-drawn/) **1** draw (metal) out into wire. **2** elongate; protract unduly. **3** (esp. as **wire-drawn** *adj.*) refine or apply or press (an argument, etc.) with idle or excessive subtlety.

wire·haired /wírhaird/ *adj.* ► (esp. of a dog) having stiff or wiry hair.

wiry hair

wire·less /wírlis/ *n. & adj.* ● *n.* **1** esp. *Brit.* **a** (in full **wireless set**) a radio receiving set. ▷ RADIO. **b** the transmission and reception of radio signals. ¶ Now old-fashioned, esp. with ref. to broadcasting, and superseded by *radio*. **2** telegraphy using radio transmission. ● *adj.* lacking or not requiring wires.

wire serv·ice *n.* a business that gathers news and distributes it to subscribers, usu. newspapers.

wire·tap /wírtap/ *v.* (**-tapped**, **-tapping**) **1** *intr.* connect a listening device to (a telephone or telegraph line, etc.) to listen to a call or transmission. **2** *tr.* obtain (information, etc.) by wiretapping. □□ **wire·tap·per** *n.* **wire·tap·ping** *n.*

wire·worm /wírwərm/ *n.* the larva of the click beetle causing damage to crop plants.

wir·ing /wíring/ *n.* **1** a system of wires providing electrical circuits. **2** the installation of this (*came to do the wiring*).

wir·y /wíree/ *adj.* (**wirier**, **wiriest**) **1** tough and flexible as wire. **2** (of a person) thin and sinewy; untiring. **3** made of wire. □□ **wir·i·ly** *adv.*

Wis. *abbr.* Wisconsin.

wis·dom /wízdəm/ *n.* **1** the state of being wise. **2** experience and knowledge together with the power of applying them. **3** prudence; common sense. **4** wise sayings, thoughts, etc. □ **in his** (or **her**, etc.) **wisdom** usu. *iron.* thinking it would be best (*the committee in its wisdom decided to abandon the project*).

wis·dom tooth *n.* each of four hindmost molars not usu. cut before 20 years of age. ▷ MOLAR, TOOTH

wise[1] /wīz/ *adj. & v.* ● *adj.* **1** having, determined by, or showing wisdom. **2** prudent; sensible. **3** having knowledge. **4** suggestive of wisdom (*with a wise nod of the head*). **5** *colloq.* **a** alert; crafty. **b** (often foll. by *to*) having (usu. confidential) information (about). ● *v.tr. & intr.* (foll. by *up*) *colloq.* put or get wise. □ **be** (or **get**) **wise to** *colloq.* become aware of. **no** (or **none the** or **not much**) **wiser** knowing no more than before. **put a person wise** (often foll. by *to*) *colloq.* inform a person (about). **without anyone's being the wiser** undetected. □□ **wise·ly** *adv.*

wise[2] /wīz/ *n. archaic* way, manner, or degree (*on this wise*). □ **in no wise** not at all.

-wise /wīz/ *suffix* forming adjectives and adverbs of manner (*crosswise*; *clockwise*; *lengthwise*) or respect (*moneywise*) (cf. -WAYS). ¶ More fanciful phrase-based combinations, such as *employment-wise* (= as regards employment) are *colloq.*, and restricted to informal contexts.

wise·a·cre /wízaykər/ *n.* a person who affects a wise manner; a wise guy.

wise·crack /wízkrak/ *n. & v. colloq.* ● *n.* a smart pithy remark. ● *v.intr.* make a wisecrack. □□ **wise·crack·er** *n.*

wise guy *n.* **1** *colloq.* a know-it-all. **2** *sl.* a member of organized crime.

wish /wish/ *v. & n.* ● *v.* **1** *intr.* (often foll. by *for*) have or express a desire or aspiration for. **2** *tr.* (often foll. by *that* + clause, usu. with *that* omitted) have as a desire or aspiration (*I wish I could sing*). **3** *tr.* want or demand, usu. so as to bring about what is wanted (*I wish to go*; *I wish you to do it*). **4** *tr.* express one's hopes for (*wished us a pleasant journey*). **5** *tr.* (foll. by *on, upon*) *colloq.* foist on a person. ● *n.* **1 a** a desire, request, or aspiration. **b** an expression of this. **2** a thing desired. □ **best** (or **good**) **wishes** hopes felt or expressed for another's happiness, etc. □□ **wish·er** *n.* (in sense 4 of *v.*); (also in *comb.*).

wish·bone /wíshbōn/ *n.* **1** a forked bone between the neck and breast of a cooked bird: when broken between two people the longer portion entitles the holder to make a wish. **2** an object of similar shape.

wish·ful /wíshfŏol/ *adj.* **1** (often foll. by *to* + infin.) desiring; wishing. **2** having or expressing a wish. □□ **wish·ful·ly** *adv.* **wish·ful·ness** *n.*

wish ful·fill·ment *n.* a tendency for subconscious desire to be satisfied in fantasy.

wish·ful think·ing *n.* belief founded on wishes rather than facts.

wish·ing well *n.* a well into which coins are dropped and a wish is made.

wish·y-wash·y /wísheewóshee, -wáwshee/ *adj.* **1** feeble, insipid, or indecisive in quality or character. **2** (of tea, soup, etc.) weak; watery.

wisp /wisp/ *n.* **1** a small bundle or twist of straw, etc. **2** a small separate quantity of smoke, hair, etc. **3** a small, thin person, etc. □□ **wisp·y** *adj.* (**wispier**, **wispiest**). **wisp·i·ly** *adv.* **wisp·i·ness** *n.*

wis·te·ri·a /wistéereeə/ *n.* (also **wis·tar·i·a** /-stáiriə/) ▼ any climbing plant of the genus *Wisteria*, with hanging racemes of blue, purple, or white flowers.

WISTERIA
(*Wisteria floribunda*)

wist·ful /wístfŏol/ *adj.* (of a person, looks, etc.) yearningly or mournfully expectant, thoughtful, or wishful. □□ **wist·ful·ly** *adv.* **wist·ful·ness** *n.*

wit[1] /wit/ *n.* **1** (in *sing.* or *pl.*) intelligence; quick understanding. **2 a** the unexpected, quick, and humorous combining or contrasting of ideas or expressions (*conversation sparkling with wit*). **b** the power of giving intellectual pleasure by this. **3** a person possessing such a power. □ **at one's wit's** (or **wits'**) **end** utterly at a loss or in despair. **have** (or **keep**) **one's wits about one** be alert or vigilant or of lively intelligence. **live by one's wits** live by ingenious or crafty expedients, without a settled occupation. **out of one's wits** mad; distracted.

wit[2] /wit/ *v.* □ **to wit** that is to say; namely.

witch /wich/ *n. & v.* ● *n.* **1** a sorceress, esp. a woman supposed to have dealings with the devil or evil spirits. **2** an ugly old woman; a hag. **3** a fascinating girl or woman. ● *v.tr. archaic* **1** bewitch. **2** fascinate; charm; lure. □□ **witch·ing** *adj.* **witch·like** *adj.*

witch·craft /wíchkraft/ *n.* the use of magic; sorcery.

witch doc·tor *n.* a tribal magician of primitive people.

witch·er·y /wíchəree/ *n.* **1** witchcraft. **2** power exercised by beauty or eloquence or the like.

witch ha·zel *n.* **1** ► any American shrub of the genus *Hamamelis*, with bark yielding an astringent lotion. **2** this lotion, esp. from the leaves of *H. virginiana*.

yellow flower

witches' Sabbath *n.* a supposed general midnight meeting of witches with the Devil.

witch-hunt *n.* **1** *hist.* a search for and persecution of supposed witches. **2** a campaign directed against a particular group of those holding unpopular or unorthodox views.

WITCH HAZEL
(*Hamamelis × intermedia*)

witch·ing hour *n.* (prec. by *the*) midnight, when witches are supposedly active.

W

with /with, with/ *prep.* expressing: **1** an instrument or means used (*cut with a knife*). **2** association or company (*lives with his mother; lamb with mint sauce*). **3** cause or origin (*shiver with fear*). **4** possession; attribution (*the woman with dark hair*). **5** circumstances; accompanying conditions (*sleep with the window open*). **6** manner adopted or displayed (*behaved with dignity; won with ease*). **7** agreement or harmony (*sympathize with*). **8** disagreement; antagonism; competition (*stop arguing with me*). **9** responsibility for (*the decision rests with you*). **10** material (*made with gold*). **11** addition or supply; possession of as a material, attribute, circumstance, etc. (*fill it with water; threaten with dismissal; decorate with flowers*). **12** reference or regard (*be patient with them; how are things with you?*). **13** relation or causative association (*changes with the weather*). **14** an accepted circumstance or consideration (*with all your faults, we like you*). □ **away** (or **in** or **out**, etc.) **with** (as *int.*) take, send, or put (a person or thing) away, in, out, etc. **be with a person 1** agree with and support a person. **2** *colloq.* follow a person's meaning (*are you with me?*). **one with** part of the same whole as. **with child** (or **young**) *literary* pregnant. **with that** thereupon.

with·draw /withdráw, with-/ *v.* (*past* **withdrew** /-drōō/; *past part.* **withdrawn** /-dráwn/) **1** *tr.* pull or take aside or back. **2** *tr.* discontinue; cancel; retract (*withdrew my support*). **3** *tr.* remove; take away (*withdrew the child from school*). **4** *tr.* take (money) out of an account. **5** *intr.* retire or go away; move away or back. **6** *intr.* (as **withdrawn** *adj.*) abnormally shy and unsociable.

with·draw·al /withdráwəl, with-/ *n.* **1** the act or an instance of withdrawing or being withdrawn. **2** a process of ceasing to take addictive drugs. **3** = COITUS INTERRUPTUS.

withe /with, with, wīth/ *n.* a tough, flexible shoot, esp. of willow or osier used for tying a bundle of wood, etc.

with·er /withər/ *v.* **1** *tr. & intr.* (often foll. by *up*) make or become dry and shriveled. **2** *tr. & intr.* (often foll. by *away*) deprive of or lose vigor, freshness, or importance. **3** *intr.* decay; decline. **4** *tr.* **a** blight with scorn, etc. **b** (as **withering** *adj.*) scornful (*a withering look*). □□ **with·er·ing·ly** *adv.*

with·ers /withərz/ *n.pl.* ▼ the ridge between a horse's shoulder blades.

withers

WITHERS ON
A MORGAN
HORSE

with·er·shins /withərshinz/ *adv.* (also **widdershins** /wid-/) **1** in a direction contrary to the sun's course (considered as unlucky). **2** counterclockwise.

with·hold /withhóld, with-/ *v.tr.* (*past* and *past part.* **-held** /-héld/) **1** (often foll. by *from*) hold back; restrain. **2** refuse to give, grant, or allow (*withhold one's consent*).

with·in /within, with-/ *adv., prep. & n.* ● *adv. archaic* or *literary* **1** inside. **2** indoors. **3** in spirit (*make me pure within*). ● *prep.* **1** inside; enclosed or contained by. **2 a** not beyond or exceeding (*within one's means*). **b** not transgressing (*within the law*). **3** not further off than (*within three miles of a station; within ten days*). ● *n.* the inside part of a place, building, etc. □ **within reach** (or **sight**) **of** near enough to be reached or seen.

with-it *adj. colloq.* **1** up to date; conversant with modern ideas, etc. **2** alert and comprehending.

with·out /withówt, with-/ *prep. & adv.* ● *prep.* **1** not having, feeling, or showing (*without any money; without hesitation*). **2** with freedom from (*without fear*). **3** in the absence of (*cannot live without you*). **4** with neglect or avoidance of (*do not leave without telling me*). ● *adv. archaic* or *literary* outside (*seen from without*). □ **without end** infinite; eternal.

with·stand /withstánd, with-/ *v.* (*past* and *past part.* **-stood** /-stōōd/) **1** *tr.* resist; hold out against (a person, force, etc.). **2** *intr.* make opposition; offer resistance.

wit·less /witlis/ *adj.* **1** lacking wits; foolish; stupid. **2** crazy. □□ **wit·less·ly** *adv.* **wit·less·ness** *n.*

wit·ness /witnis/ *n. & v.* ● *n.* **1** a person present at some event and able to give information about it (cf. EYEWITNESS). **2 a** person giving sworn testimony. **b** a person attesting another's signature to a document. **3** (foll. by *to, of*) a person or thing whose existence, condition, etc., attests or proves something (*is a living witness to their generosity*). **4** testimony; evidence; confirmation. ● *v.* **1** *tr.* be a witness of (an event, etc.). **2** *tr.* be witness to the authenticity of (a document or signature). **3** *tr.* serve as evidence or an indication of. **4** *intr.* (foll. by *against, for, to*) give or serve as evidence. □ **bear witness to** (or **of**) **1** attest the truth of. **2** state one's belief in. **call to witness** appeal to for confirmation, etc.

wit·ness stand *n.* an enclosure in a court of law from which witnesses give evidence.

wit·ti·cism /witisizəm/ *n.* a witty remark.

wit·ting /witing/ *adj.* **1** aware. **2** intentional. □□ **wit·ting·ly** *adv.*

wit·ty /witee/ *adj.* (**wittier, wittiest**) **1** showing verbal wit. **2** characterized by wit or humor. □□ **wit·ti·ly** *adv.* **wit·ti·ness** *n.*

wives *pl.* of WIFE.

wiz *var.* of WHIZ *n.* 2.

wiz·ard /wizərd/ *n.* **1** a sorcerer; a magician. **2** a genius. □□ **wiz·ard·ly** *adj.* **wiz·ard·ry** *n.*

wiz·ened /wizənd/ *adj.* (also **wiz·en**) (of a person or face, etc.) shriveled-looking.

wk. *abbr.* **1** week. **2** work.

wks. *abbr.* weeks.

WLTM *abbr.* would like to meet.

WNW *abbr.* west-northwest.

WO *abbr.* warrant officer.

woad /wōd/ *n.* **1** a cruciferous plant, *Isatis tinctoria*, yielding a blue dye now superseded by indigo. **2** the dye obtained from this.

wob·be·gong /wóbigong/ *n.* an Australian brown shark, *Orectolobus maculatus*, with buff patterned markings.

wob·ble /wóbəl/ *v. & n.* ● *v.* **1 a** *intr.* sway or vibrate unsteadily from side to side. **b** *tr.* cause to do this. **2** *intr.* stand or go unsteadily. **3** *intr.* waver; vacillate. **4** *intr.* (of the voice or sound) quaver; pulsate. ● *n.* **1** a wobbling movement. **2** an instance of wobbling. □□ **wob·bler** *n.*

wob·bly /wóblee/ *adj.* (**wobblier, wobbliest**) **1** wobbling or tending to wobble. **2** wavy (*a wobbly line*). **3** weak after illness (*feeling wobbly*). **4** wavering; insecure (*the economy was wobbly*). □□ **wob·bli·ness** *n.*

woe /wō/ *n. archaic* or *literary* **1** affliction; bitter grief; distress. **2** (in *pl.*) calamities; troubles. **3** *joc.* problems (*told me a tale of woe*). □ **woe is me** an exclamation of distress.

woe·be·gone /wóbigon, -gawn/ *adj.* dismal-looking.

woe·ful /wófōol/ *adj.* **1** sorrowful. **2** causing sorrow or affliction. **3** very bad (*woeful ignorance*). □□ **woe·ful·ly** *adv.* **woe·ful·ness** *n.*

wog /wog/ *n. sl. offens.* a foreigner, esp. a nonwhite one.

wok /wok/ *n.* ► a bowl-shaped metal pan used in esp. Chinese cooking.

woke *past* of WAKE[1].

wok·en *past part.* of WAKE[1].

wold /wōld/ *n.* a piece of high, open, uncultivated land.

wolf /wŏolf/ *n. & v.* ● *n.* (*pl.* **wolves** /wŏolvz/) **1** ▼ a wild, flesh-eating, tawny-gray mammal related to the dog, esp. *Canis lupus*. **2** *sl.* a man given to seducing women. **3** a rapacious or greedy person. ● *v.tr.* (often foll. by *down*) devour (food) greedily. □ **cry wolf** raise repeated false alarms (so that a genuine one is disregarded). **keep the wolf from the door** avert hunger or starvation. **throw to the wolves** sacrifice without compunction. **wolf in sheep's clothing** a hostile person who pretends friendship. □□ **wolf·ish** *adj.* **wolf·ish·ly** *adv.* **wolf·like** *adj. & adv.*

WOLF: GRAY WOLF
(*Canis lupus*)

wolf·hound /wŏolfhownd/ *n.* ▼ a borzoi or other dog of a kind used orig. to hunt wolves. ▷ IRISH WOLFHOUND

WOLFHOUND

wolf·ram /wŏolfrəm/ *n.* tungsten.

wolf whis·tle *n.* a sexually admiring whistle by a man to a woman.

wol·ver·ine /wŏolvəreen/ *n.* a voracious carnivorous mammal, *Gulo gulo*, of the weasel family.

wolves *pl.* of WOLF.

wom·an /wŏomən/ *n.* (*pl.* **women** /wimin/) **1** an adult human female. **2** the female sex; any or an average woman (*how does woman differ from man?*). **3** a wife or female sexual partner. **4** (prec. by *the*) emotions or characteristics traditionally associated with women (*brought out the woman in him*). **5** a man with characteristics traditionally associated with women. **6** (*attrib.*) female (*woman driver*). **7** (as second element in *comb.*) a woman of a specified nationality, profession, skill, etc. (*Englishwoman; horsewoman*). **8** *colloq.* a female domestic servant.

wom·an·hood /wŏomənhŏod/ *n.* **1** female maturity. **2** womanly instinct. **3** womankind.

wom·an·ish /wŏomənish/ *adj. usu. derog.* **1** (of a man) effeminate; unmanly. **2** suitable to or characteristic of a woman.

wom·an·ize /wŏomənīz/ *v. intr.* chase after women; philander. □□ **wom·an·iz·er** *n.*

wom·an·kind /wŏomənkīnd/ *n.* (also **wom·en·kind** /wimin-/) women in general.

wom·an·ly /wŏomənlee/ *adj.* (of a woman) having or showing qualities traditionally associated with women. □□ **wom·an·li·ness** *n.*

chopsticks

bowl

WOK

W

WOOD

Wood may be divided into two groups – hardwood from broadleaved trees and softwood from conifers. However, these terms can be misleading; yew, for example, is classed as a softwood, yet it is as hard as oak. Different woods have different qualities: larch is tough; iroko resists decay; ash is a great shock absorber; oak is one of the most durable of woods, while mahogany and walnut are valued for their beautiful grain and rich color.

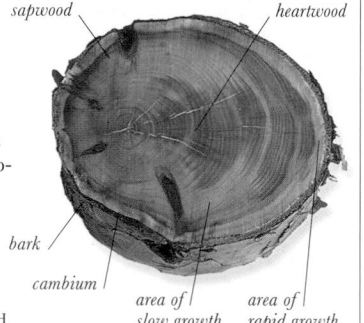

sapwood • heartwood • bark • cambium • area of slow growth • area of rapid growth

CROSS SECTION OF
A YEW TREE BRANCH

EXAMPLES OF WOOD

SOFTWOOD

YEW

LARCH

HARDWOOD

CHERRY

IROKO

MAHOGANY

OAK

WALNUT

ASH

wom·an of let·ters *n.* a scholar or author.

womb /woom/ *n.* **1** the organ of conception and gestation in a woman and other female mammals; the uterus. ▷ REPRODUCTIVE ORGANS. **2** a place of origination and development □□ **womb·like** *adj.*

wom·bat /wómbat/ *n.* any burrowing, plant-eating Australian marsupial of the family Vombatidae. ▷ MARSUPIAL.

wom·en *pl.* of WOMAN.

wom·en·folk /wíminfōk/ *n.* **1** women in general. **2** the women in a family.

wom·en·kind var. of WOMANKIND.

wom·en's lib *n. colloq.* = WOMEN'S LIBERATION. □□ **wom·en's lib·ber** *n.*

wom·en's lib·er·a·tion *n.* the liberation of women from inequalities and subservient status in relation to men.

won *past* and *past part.* of WIN.

won·der /wúndər/ *n. & v.* ● *n.* **1** surprise mingled with admiration or curiosity. **2** a strange or remarkable person or thing, event, etc. **3** (*attrib.*) having marvelous properties, etc. (*a wonder drug*). **4** a surprising thing (*it is a wonder you were not hurt*). ● *v.* **1** *intr.* (often foll. by *at*, or *to* + infin.) be filled with wonder or great surprise. **2** *tr.* (foll. by *that* + clause) be surprised to find. **3** *tr.* desire or be curious to know (*I wonder what the time is*). **4** *tr.* expressing a tentative inquiry (*I wonder whether you would mind?*). **5** *intr.* (foll. by *about*) ask oneself with puzzlement or doubt about; question (*wondered about the sense of the decision*). □ **I shouldn't wonder** *colloq.* I think it likely. **I wonder** I very much doubt it. **no** (or **small**) **wonder** (often foll. by *that* + clause) one cannot be surprised. **wonders will** (or **will wonders**) **never cease** an exclamation of extreme (usu. agreeable) surprise. **work** (or **do**) **wonders 1** do miracles. **2** succeed remarkably. □□ **won·der·er** *n.*

won·der·ful /wúndərfool/ *adj.* **1** very remarkable or admirable. **2** arousing wonder. □□ **won·der·ful·ly** *adv.* **won·der·ful·ness** *n.*

won·der·ing /wúndəring/ *adj.* filled with wonder (*their wondering gaze*). □□ **won·der·ing·ly** *adv.*

won·der·land /wúndərland/ *n.* **1** a fairyland. **2** a land of surprises or marvels.

won·der·ment /wúndərmənt/ *n.* surprise; awe.

won·drous /wúndrəs/ *adj. & adv. poet.* ● *adj.* wonderful. ● *adv. archaic* or *literary* wonderfully (*wondrous kind*). □□ **won·drous·ly** *adv.*

wonk /wongk/ *n. N. Amer. colloq.,* derog. a studious or hard-working person.

wont /wōnt, wawnt, wunt/ *adj. & n.* ● *predic.adj. archaic* or *literary* (foll. by *to* + infin.) accustomed (*as we were wont to say*). ● *n. formal* or *joc.* what is customary; one's habit (*as is my wont*).

won't /wōnt/ *contr.* will not.

wont·ed /wōntid, wáwn-, wún-/ *attrib.adj.* habitual; accustomed; usual.

won·ton /wúntun/ *n.* (in Chinese cookery) a small round dumpling or roll with a savory filling, usu. eaten boiled in soup.

woo /woo/ *v.tr.* (**woos, wooed**) **1** seek the love of (a woman). **2** seek the favor or support of. □□ **woo·er** *n.*

wood /wood/ *n.* **1 a** a hard fibrous material from the trunk or branches of a tree or shrub. **b** ◄ this cut for lumber or for fuel, or for use in crafts, manufacture, etc. **2** (in *sing.* or *pl.*) growing trees densely occupying a tract of land. **3** (prec. by *the*) wooden storage, esp. a cask, for wine, etc. (*poured straight from the wood*). **4** a wooden-headed golf club. ▷ GOLF. **5** = BOWL² *n.* 1. □ **out of the woods** (or **wood**) out of danger or difficulty.

wood al·co·hol *n.* methanol.

wood a·nem·o·ne *n.* ► a wild spring-flowering anemone, *Anemone nemorosa.*

wood·bine /wóodbīn/ *n.* **1** wild honeysuckle. **2** Virginia creeper.

wood·block /wóodblok/ *n.* a block from which woodcuts are made.

wood·car·ving /wóodkaarving/ *n.* **1** (also *attrib.*) ▼ the act or process of carving wood. **2** a design in wood produced by this art.

WOOD ANEMONE
(*Anemone nemorosa*)

WOODCARVING

Woodcarving was a popular way of providing an attractive finish for building interiors and furniture from the Middle Ages to the 19th century. In this highly skilled, labor-intensive craft, large pieces of wood are first removed with a wooden mallet and a chisel; the intricate details and textures are then achieved by using a range of chisels to shave away wood by hand. The tools below are designed for working on a small scale.

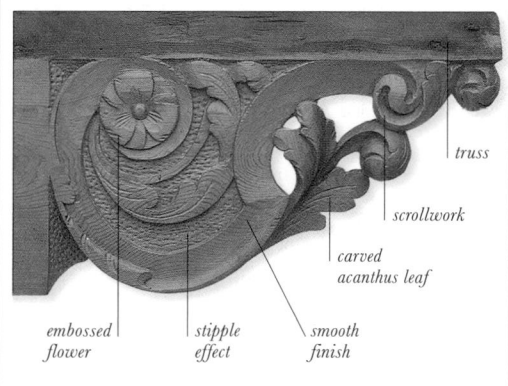

embossed flower • stipple effect • smooth finish • carved acanthus leaf • scrollwork • truss

WOODCARVING ON THE TREAD OF
AN 18TH-CENTURY STAIRCASE

WOOD CHISELS FOR DETAIL WORK

SQUARE CHISEL

DOGLEG CHISEL

BENT GAUGE

SKEW CHISEL

STRAIGHT GAUGE

W

WOODWIND

Woodwind instruments produce sound when air is blown into them. Originally made of wood, many are now manufactured from metal or plastic. The saxophone is an exception, having always been made of metal, but it appears in this category because it was constructed as a hybrid of the oboe and clarinet. Notes are produced in different ways: by blowing across an open hole in a pipe on a flute or piccolo, or by blowing into one end of a recorder or flageolet; other woodwind instruments have a reed that vibrates when blown.

OTHER WOODWIND INSTRUMENTS

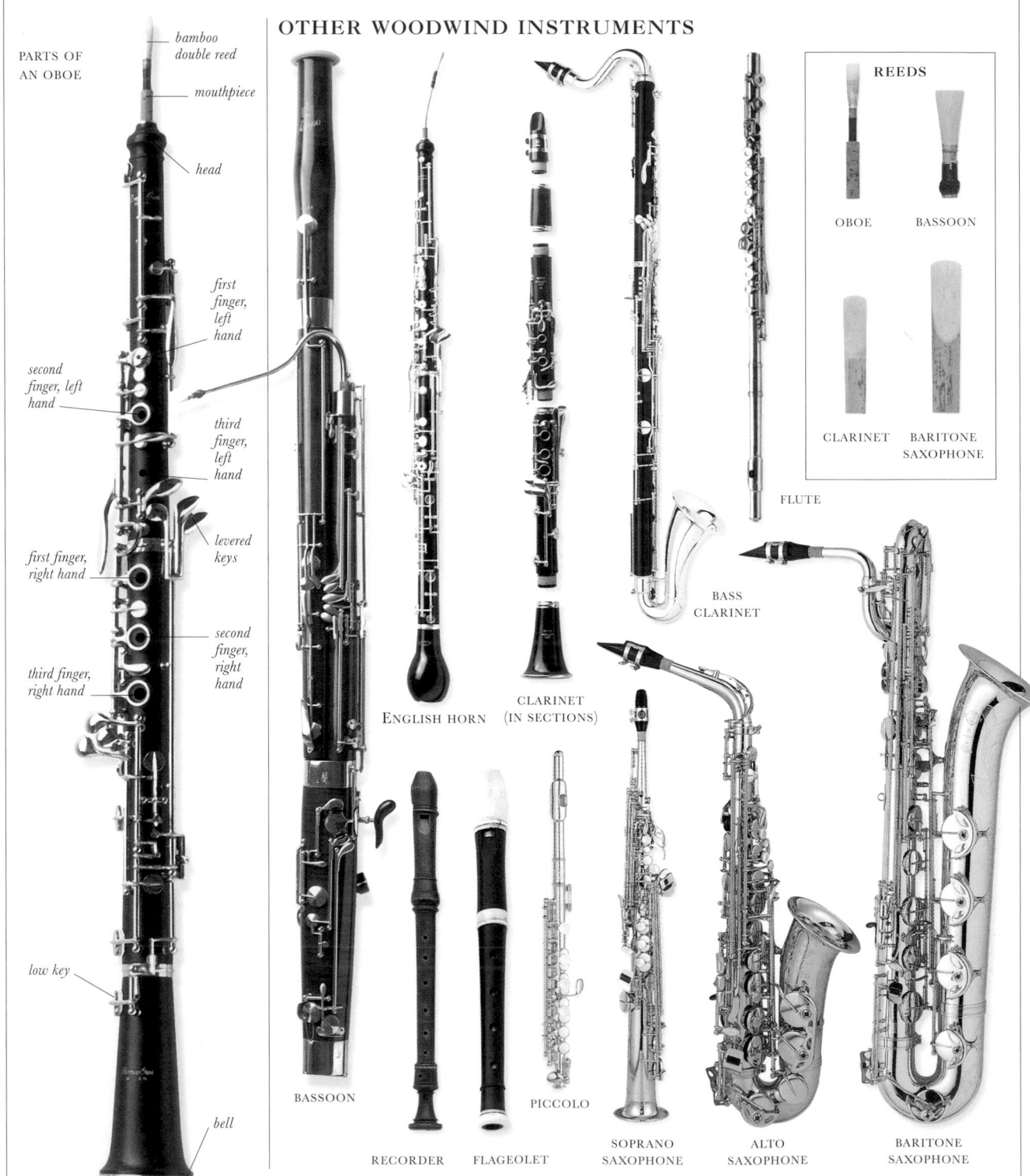

PARTS OF AN OBOE

bamboo double reed

mouthpiece

head

first finger, left hand

second finger, left hand

third finger, left hand

levered keys

first finger, right hand

second finger, right hand

third finger, right hand

low key

bell

REEDS

OBOE

BASSOON

CLARINET

BARITONE SAXOPHONE

FLUTE

BASS CLARINET

ENGLISH HORN

CLARINET (IN SECTIONS)

BASSOON

RECORDER

FLAGEOLET

PICCOLO

SOPRANO SAXOPHONE

ALTO SAXOPHONE

BARITONE SAXOPHONE

W

wood·chuck /wo͝odchuk/ n. a reddish-brown and gray N. American marmot, *Marmota monax.* Also called **groundhog.**

wood·cock /wo͝odkok/ n. (*pl.* same) ▶ any game bird of the genus *Scolopax.*

wood·craft /wo͝odkraft/ n. **1** skill in woodwork. **2** knowledge of woodland, esp. in camping, scouting, etc.

wood·cut /wo͝odkut/ n. **1** a relief cut on a block of wood sawn along the grain. **2** a print made from this. **3** the technique of making such reliefs and prints.

wood·cut·ter /wo͝odkutər/ n. **1** a person who cuts wood. **2** a maker of woodcuts.

wood·ed /wo͝odid/ adj. having woods or many trees.

wood·en /wo͝odn/ adj. **1** made of wood. **2** like wood. **3 a** stiff, clumsy, or stilted; without animation or flexibility. **b** expressionless (*a wooden stare*). □□ **wood·en·ly** adv. **wood·en·ness** n.

WOODCOCK
(*Scolopax rusticola*)

wood en·grav·ing n. **1** ◀ a relief cut on a block of wood sawn across the grain. **2** a print made from this.

wood·land /wo͝odlənd/ n. wooded country; woods (often *attrib.: woodland scenery*). □□ **wood·land·er** n.

WOOD ENGRAVING
ON A MEDIEVAL
GAME PIECE

wood·man /wo͝odmən/ n. (*pl.* **-men**) **1** a forester. **2** a woodcutter.

wood·note /wo͝odnōt/ n. (often in *pl.*) a natural or spontaneous note of a bird, etc.

wood nymph n. a nymph inhabiting a tree; a dryad

wood·peck·er /wo͝odpekər/ n. ▼ any bird of the family Picidae that climbs and taps tree trunks in search of insects.

WOODPECKER:
GREAT SPOTTED
WOODPECKER
(*Dendrocopos major*)

wood·pile /wo͝odpīl/ n. a pile of wood, esp. for fuel.

wood pulp n. wood fiber reduced chemically or mechanically to pulp as raw material for paper.

wood·ruff /wo͝odruf/ n. ▶ a white-flowered plant of the genus *Galium.*

wood·shed /wo͝odshed/ n. a shed where wood for fuel is stored.

woods·man /wo͝odzmən/ n. (*pl.* **-men**) **1** a person who lives in or is familiar with woodland. **2** a person skilled in woodcraft.

wood·wind /wo͝odwind/ n. (often *attrib.*) **1** (*collect.*) ◀ wind instruments that were (mostly) orig. made of wood, e.g., the flute and clarinet. ▷ ORCHESTRA. **2** (usu. in *pl.*) an individual instrument of this kind or its player.

wood·work /wo͝odwərk/ n. **1** the making of things in wood. **2** things made of wood. □ **crawl** (or **come**) **out of the woodwork** *colloq.* (of

WOODRUFF
(*Galium odoratum*)

some-thing unwelcome) appear; become known. □□ **wood·work·er** n. **wood·work·ing** n.

wood·worm /wo͝odwərm/ n. **1** the wood-boring larva of the furniture beetle. **2** the damaged condition of wood affected by this.

wood·y /wo͝odee/ adj. (**woodier, woodiest**) **1** (of a region) wooded; abounding in woods. **2** like or of wood. □□ **wood·i·ness** n.

wood·yard /wo͝odyaard/ n. a yard where wood is used or stored.

woof[1] /wo͝of/ n. & v. ● n. the gruff bark of a dog. ● v.intr. give a woof.

woof[2] /wo͝of/ n. = WEFT.

woof·er /wo͝ofər/ n. a loudspeaker designed to reproduce low frequencies (cf. TWEETER). ▷ LOUDSPEAKER

wool /wo͝ol/ n. **1** fine, soft, wavy hair from the fleece of sheep, goats, etc. **2 a** yarn produced from this hair. **b** cloth or clothing made from it. **3** any of various woollike substances (*steel wool*). **4** soft, short, underfur or down. **5** *colloq.* a person's hair, esp. when short and curly. □ **pull the wool over a person's eyes** deceive a person. □□ **wool·like** adj.

wool·en /wo͝olən/ adj. & n. (also **wool·len**) ● adj. made wholly or partly of wool. ● n. **1** a fabric produced from wool. **2** (in *pl.*) woolen garments.

wool·gath·er·ing /wo͝olgathəring/ n. absent-mindedness; dreamy inattention.

wool·grow·er /wo͝olgrōər/ n. a breeder of sheep for wool. □□ **wool·grow·ing** n.

wool·ly /wo͝olee/ adj. (**woollier, woolliest**) **1** bearing or naturally covered with wool. **2** resembling or suggesting wool (*woolly clouds*). **3** (of a sound) indistinct. **4** (of thought) vague or confused. **5** *Bot.* downy. **6** lacking in definition, luminosity, or incisiveness. □□ **wool·li·ness** n.

wool·ly bear n. ▶ a large hairy caterpillar, esp. of the tiger moth.

wool·pack /wo͝olpak/ n. **1** a fleecy cumulus cloud. **2** *hist.* a bale of wool.

wool·y adj. (**woolier, wooliest**) var. of WOOLLY.

woosh var. of WHOOSH.

wooz·y /wo͝ozee/ adj. (**woozier, wooziest**) *colloq.* **1** dizzy or unsteady. **2** dazed or slightly drunk. **3** vague. □□ **wooz·i·ly** adv. **wooz·i·ness** n.

wop /wop/ n. *sl. offens.* an Italian or other S. European.

Worces·ter·shire sauce /wo͝ostərsheer, -shər/ n. a pungent sauce first made in Worcester, England.

word /wərd/ n. & v. ● n. **1** a sound or combination of sounds forming a meaningful element of speech, usu. shown with a space on either side of it when written or printed. **2** speech, esp. as distinct from action (*bold in word only*). **3** one's promise or assurance (*gave us their word*). **4** (in *sing.* or *pl.*) a thing said, a remark or conversation. **5** (in *pl.*) the text of a song or an actor's part. **6** (in *pl.*) angry talk (*they had words*). **7** news; intelligence. **8** a command, password, or motto (*gave the word to begin*). **9** a basic unit of the expression of data in a computer. ● v.tr. put into words; select words to express (*how shall we word that?*). □ **at a word** as soon as requested. **be as good as** (or **better than**) **one's word** fulfill (or exceed) what one has promised. **break one's word** fail to do what one has promised. **have no words for** be unable to express. **have a word** (often foll. by *with*) speak briefly (to). **in other words** expressing the same thing differently. **in so many words** explicitly or bluntly. **in a** (or **one**) **word** briefly. **keep one's word** do what one has promised. **my** (or **upon my**) **word** an exclamation of surprise or consternation. **not the word for it** not an adequate or appropriate

WOOLLY BEAR: TIGER MOTH
CATERPILLAR (*Arctia caja*)

description. **of few words** taciturn. **of one's word** reliable in keeping promises (*a woman of her word*). **on** (or **upon**) **my word** a form of asseveration. **put into words** express in speech or writing. **take a person at his** or **her word** interpret a person's words literally or exactly. **take a person's word for it** believe a person's statement without investigation, etc. **too … for words** too … to be adequately described (*was too funny for words*). **waste words** talk in vain. **the Word** (or **Word of God**) the Bible. **words fail me** an expression of disbelief, dismay, etc. **a word to the wise** enough said. □□ **word·age** n. **word·less** adj. **word·less·ly** adv. **word·less·ness** n.

word·ing /wərding/ n. **1** a form of words used. **2** the way in which something is expressed.

word of hon·or n. an assurance given upon one's honor.

word of mouth n. speech (only).

word·play /wərdplay/ n. use of words to witty effect, esp. by punning.

word proc·es·sor n. a computer software program for electronically storing text entered from a keyboard, incorporating corrections, and providing a printout.

word·smith /wərdsmith/ n. a skilled user or maker of words.

word·y /wərdee/ adj. (**wordier, wordiest**) **1** using or expressed in many or too many words; verbose. **2** consisting of words. □□ **word·i·ly** adv. **word·i·ness** n.

wore[1] past of WEAR[1].

wore[2] past and *past part.* of WEAR[2].

work /wərk/ n. & v. ● n. **1** the application of mental or physical effort to a purpose; the use of energy. **2 a** a task to be undertaken. **b** the materials for this. **c** (prec. by *the*; foll. by *of*) a task occupying (no more than) a specified time (*the work of a moment*). **3** a thing done or made by work; the result of an action; an achievement. **4** a person's employment or occupation, etc., esp. as a means of earning income (*looked for work; is out of work*). **5 a** a literary or musical composition. **b** (in *pl.*) all such by an author or composer, etc. **6** actions or experiences of a specified kind (*good work!; this is thirsty work*). **7** (in *comb.*) things or parts made of a specified material or with specified tools, etc. (*ironwork; needlework*). **8** (in *pl.*) the operative part of a clock or machine. **9** *Physics* the exertion of force overcoming resistance or producing molecular change (*convert heat into work*). **10** (in *pl.*) *colloq.* all that is available; everything needed. **11** (in *pl.*) operations of building or repair (*road works*). **12** (usu. in *pl.* or in *comb.*) a defensive structure (*earthworks*). **13** (in *comb.*) **a** ornamentation of a specified kind (*scrollwork*). **b** articles having this. ● v. (*past* and *past part.* **worked** or (esp. as *adj.*) **wrought**) **1** *intr.* (often foll. by *at, on*) do work; be engaged in bodily or mental activity. **2** *intr.* **a** be employed in certain work (*works in industry; works as a secretary*). **b** (foll. by *with*) be the coworker of (a person). **3** *intr.* (often foll. by *for*) make efforts (*works for peace*). **4** *intr.* (foll. by *in*) be a craftsman (in a material). **5** *intr.* operate or function, esp. effectively (*how does this machine work?; your idea will not work*). **6** *intr.* (of a part of a machine) run; revolve; go through regular motions. **7** *tr.* carry on, manage, or control (*cannot work the machine*). **8** *tr.* **a** put or keep in operation or at work (*this mine is no longer worked; works the staff very hard*). **b** cultivate (land). **9** *tr.* bring about; produce as a result (*worked miracles*). **10** *tr.* knead; hammer; bring to a desired shape or consistency. **11** *tr.* do, or make by, needlework, etc. **12** *tr.* & *intr.* (cause to) progress or penetrate, or make (one's way), gradually or with difficulty in a specified way (*worked our way through the crowd; worked the peg into the hole*). **13** *intr.* (foll. by *loose*, etc.) gradually become (loose, etc.) by constant movement. **14** *tr.* artificially excite (*worked themselves*

into a rage). **15** *tr.* solve (an equation, etc.) by mathematics. **16** *tr.* **a** purchase with one's labor instead of money (*work one's passage*). **b** obtain by labor the money for (one's way through college, etc.). **17** *intr.* (foll. by *on, upon*) have influence. **18** *intr.* be in motion or agitated; cause agitation; ferment (*his features worked violently; the yeast began to work*). □ **at work** in action or engaged in work. **give a person the works 1** *colloq.* give or tell a person everything. **2** *colloq.* treat a person harshly. **3** *sl.* kill a person. **have one's work cut out** be faced with a hard task. **in the works** *colloq.* in progress; in the pipeline. **out of work** unemployed. **set to work** begin or cause to begin operations. **work away** (or **on**) continue to work. **work in** find a place for. **work it** *colloq.* bring it about; achieve a desired result. **work off** get rid of by work or activity. **work out 1** solve (an equation, etc.) or find out (an amount) by calculation; resolve (a problem, etc.). **2** (foll. by *at*) be calculated (*the total works out at 230*) **3** give a definite result (*this sum will not work out*). **4** have a specified result (*the plan worked out well*). **5** provide for the details of (*has worked out a plan*). **6** accomplish or attain with difficulty (*work out one's salvation*). **7** exhaust with work (*the mine is worked out*). **8** engage in physical exercise or training. **work over 1** examine thoroughly. **2** *colloq.* treat with violence. **work up 1** bring gradually to an efficient state. **2** (foll. by *to*) advance gradually to a climax. **3** elaborate or excite by degrees. **work wonders** see WONDER. □□ **work·less** *adj.*

work·a·ble /wórkəbəl/ *adj.* **1** that can be worked or will work. **2** that is worth working; practicable; feasible (*a workable plan*). □□ **work·a·bil·i·ty** (/-bíli-tee/) *n.* **work·a·bly** *adv.*

work·a·day /wórkəday/ *adj.* **1** ordinary; everyday; practical. **2** fit for, used, or seen on workdays.

work·a·hol·ic /wórkəhólik/ *n. & adj. colloq.* (a person) addicted to working.

work·bas·ket /wórkbaskit/ *n.* a basket containing sewing materials, etc.

work·bench /wórkbench/ *n.* ▼ a bench for doing mechanical or practical work, esp. carpentry.

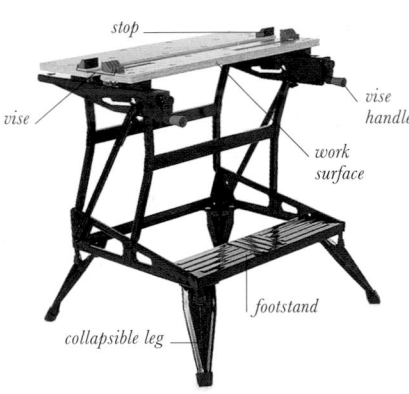

WORKBENCH:
PORTABLE FOLDING WORKBENCH

stop
vise
vise handle
work surface
footstand
collapsible leg

W

work·day /wórkday/ *n.* a day on which work is usually done.

work·er /wórkər/ *n.* **1** a person who works, esp. a manual or industrial employee. **2** a neuter or undeveloped female of various social insects, esp. a bee or ant, that does the basic work of its colony.

work·force /wórkfawrs/ *n.* the workers engaged or available in an industry, etc.

work·horse /wórk-hawrs/ *n.* a horse, person, or machine that performs hard work.

work·house /wórk-hows/ *n.* **1** a house of correction for petty offenders. **2** *Brit. hist.* a public institution in which the destitute of a parish received board and lodging in return for work.

work·ing /wórking/ *adj. & n.* ● *adj.* **1** having paid employment. **2** functioning or able to function. ● *n.* **1** the activity of work. **2** the act or manner of functioning of a thing. **3 a** a mine or quarry. **b** the part of this in which work is being or has been done.

work·ing cap·i·tal *n.* the capital actually used in a business.

work·ing class *n.* the class of people who are employed for wages, esp. in manual or industrial work. □□ **work·ing-class** *adj.*

work·ing knowl·edge *n.* knowledge adequate to work with.

work·ing lunch *n.* a lunch at which business is conducted.

work·ing or·der *n.* the condition in which a machine works (satisfactorily or as specified).

work·load /wórklōd/ *n.* the amount of work to be done by an individual, etc.

work·man /wórkmən/ *n.* (*pl.* **-men**) **1** a person employed to do manual labor. **2** a person considered with regard to skill in a job (*a good workman*).

work·man·like /wórkmənlīk/ *adj.* characteristic of a good workman; showing practiced skill.

work·man·ship /wórkmənship/ *n.* **1** the degree of skill with which a product is made or a job done; craftsmanship **2** a thing made or created by a specified person, etc.

work of art *n.* a fine picture, poem, or building, etc.

work·out /wórkowt/ *n.* a session of physical exercise.

work·piece /wórkpees/ *n.* a thing worked on with a tool or machine.

work·place /wórkplays/ *n.* a place at which a person works; an office, factory, etc.

work sheet *n.* **1** a paper for recording work done or in progress. **2** a paper listing questions or activities for students, etc., to work through.

work·shop /wórkshop/ *n.* **1** a room or building in which goods are manufactured. **2** a meeting for concerted discussion or activity (*a dance workshop*).

work·sta·tion /wórkstayshən/ *n.* **1** the location of a stage in a manufacturing process. **2** a computer terminal or the desk, etc., where this is located.

work-stud·y pro·gram *n.* a system of combining academic studies with practical employment.

work·ta·ble /wórktayb'l/ *n.* a table for working at.

world /wórld/ *n.* **1 a** the Earth, or a planetary body like it. **b** its countries and their inhabitants. **c** all people. **2 a** the universe or all that exists; everything. **b** everything that exists outside oneself (*dead to the world*). **3 a** the time, state, or scene of human existence. **b** (prec. by *the, this*) mortal life. **4** secular interests and affairs. **5** human affairs; active life (*how goes the world with you?*). **6** average, respectable, or fashionable people or their customs or opinions. **7** all that concerns or all who belong to a specified class, time, or sphere of activity (*the medieval world; the world of baseball*). **8** (foll. by *of*) a vast amount (*that makes a world of difference*). **9** (*attrib.*) affecting many nations, of all nations (*world politics; a world champion*). □ **be worlds apart** differ greatly, esp. in nature or opinion. **bring into the world** give birth to. **come into the world** be born. **for all the world** (foll. by *like, as if*) precisely (*looked for all the world as if they were real*). **get the best of both worlds** benefit from two incompatible sets of ideas, circumstances, etc. **in the world** of all; at all (used as an intensifier in questions) (*what in the world is it?*). **man** (or **woman**) **of the world** a person experienced and practical in human affairs. **the next** (or **other**) **world** life after death. **out of this world** *colloq.* extremely good, etc. **see the world** travel widely; gain wide experience. **think the world of** have a very high regard for. **the world, the flesh, and the devil** the various kinds of temptation. **the** (or **all the**) **world over**

throughout the world. **the world's end** the farthest attainable point of travel. **the world to come** supposed life after death. **world without end** for ever.

world-beat·er *n.* a person or thing that is better than all others in its field.

world-class *adj.* of a quality or standard regarded as high throughout the world.

world·ly /wórldlee/ *adj.* (**worldlier, worldliest**) **1** temporal or earthly (*worldly goods*). **2** engrossed in temporal affairs, esp. the pursuit of wealth and pleasure. □□ **world·li·ness** *n.*

world·ly wis·dom *n.* prudence as regards one's own interests. □□ **world·ly-wise** *adj.*

world mu·sic *n.* music from the developing world incorporating traditional and/or popular elements.

world pow·er *n.* a nation having power and influence in world affairs.

World Se·ries *n.* the championship for North American major-league baseball teams.

world-shak·ing *adj.* of supreme importance.

world war *n.* a war involving many important nations.

world-wea·ry *adj.* bored with the world and life on it. □□ **world-wea·ri·ness** *n.*

world·wide /wórldwíd/ *adj. & adv.* ● *adj.* affecting, occurring in, or known in all parts of the world. ● *adv.* throughout the world.

World Wide Web *n. Computing* a widely used information system on the Internet that provides facilities for electronic documents to be interconnected by hypertext links, enabling the user to search for information by moving from one document to another. ¶ Abbr. **WWW.**

worm /wərm/ *n. & v.* ● *n.* **1** any of various types of creeping or burrowing invertebrate animals with long, slender bodies and no limbs. ▷ ANNELID, NEMATODE. **2** the long, slender larva of an insect. **3** (in *pl.*) internal parasites. **4** a blindworm or slowworm. **5** a maggot supposed to eat dead bodies in the grave. **6** an insignificant or contemptible person. **7 a** the spiral part of a screw. **b** a short screw working in a worm gear. ● *v.* **1** *intr. & tr.* (often *refl.*) move with a crawling motion (*wormed through the bushes; wormed our way through the bushes*). **2** *intr. & refl.* (foll. by *into*) insinuate oneself into a person's favor, confidence, etc. **3** *tr.* (foll. by *out*) obtain (a secret, etc.) by cunning persistence (*managed to worm the truth out of them*). **4** *tr.* rid (a plant or dog, etc.) of worms. □ **a** (or **even a**) **worm will turn** the meekest will resist or retaliate if pushed too far. □□ **worm·er** *n.* **worm·like** *adj.*

worm gear *n.* ◄ an arrangement of a toothed wheel worked by a revolving spiral. ▷ ODOMETER

worm·hole /wórmhōl/ *n.* a hole left by the passage of a worm.

worm·wood /wórmwŏŏd/ *n.* **1** ► any woody shrub of the genus *Artemisia*, with a bitter aromatic taste, used in the preparation of vermouth and absinthe and in medicine. ▷ HERB. **2** bitter mortification or a source of this.

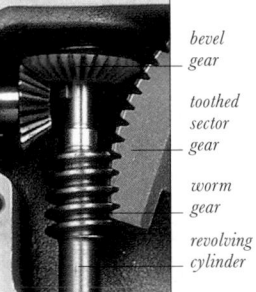

WORM GEAR IN A
STEERING RACK

bevel gear
toothed sector gear
worm gear
revolving cylinder

worm·y /wórmee/ *adj.* (**wormier, wormiest**) **1** full of worms. **2** eaten into by worms.

worn /wawrn/ *past part.* of WEAR[1]. ● *adj.* **1** damaged by use or wear. **2** looking tired and exhausted. **3** (in full **well-worn**) (of a phrase, joke, etc.) stale; often heard.

WORMWOOD:
ARCTIC WORMWOOD
(*Artemisia borealis*)

wor·ri·ment /wóreemənt, wúr-/ *n.* **1** the act of worrying or state of being worried. **2** a cause of worry.

wor·ri·some /wóreesəm, wúr-/ *adj.* causing or apt to cause worry or distress.

wor·ry /wóree, wúr-/ *v. & n.* ● *v.* (**-ies, -ied**) **1** *intr.* allow one's mind to dwell on troubles. **2** *tr.* harass; importune; be a trouble to. **3** *tr.* **a** (of a dog, etc.) shake or pull about with the teeth. **b** attack repeatedly. **4** (as **worried** *adj.*) **a** uneasy; troubled in the mind. **b** suggesting worry (*a worried look*). ● *n.* (*pl.* **-ies**) **1** a thing that causes anxiety. **2** a disturbed state of mind. **3** a dog's worrying of its quarry. □ **not to worry** there is no need to worry. **worry along** (or **through**) manage to advance by persistence in spite of obstacles. **worry oneself** (usu. in *neg.*) take needless trouble. **worry out** obtain (the solution to a problem, etc.) by dogged effort. □□ **wor·ried·ly** *adv.* **wor·ri·er** *n.* **wor·ry·ing·ly** *adv.*

wor·ry beads *n.pl.* a string of beads manipulated with the fingers to occupy or calm oneself.

wor·ry·wart /wóreewawrt, wúr-/ *n. colloq.* a person who habitually worries unduly.

worse /wərs/ *adj., adv., & n.* ● *adj.* **1** more bad. **2** (*predic.*) in or into worse health or a worse condition. ● *adv.* more badly or more ill. ● *n.* **1** a worse thing or things (*you might do worse than accept*). **2** (prec. by *the*) a worse condition (*a change for the worse*). □ **none the worse** (often foll. by *for*) not adversely affected (by). **or worse** or as an even worse alternative. **the worse for drink** fairly drunk. **worse for wear 1** damaged by use. **2** injured. **3** *joc.* drunk. **worse off** in a worse position.

wors·en /wársən/ *v.tr. & intr.* make or become worse.

wor·ship /wárship/ *n. & v.* ● *n.* **1 a** homage or reverence paid to a deity. **b** the acts, rites, or ceremonies of worship. **2** adoration or devotion shown toward a person or principle (*the worship of wealth*). ● *v.* (**worshiped, worshiping** or **worshipped, worshipping**) **1** *tr.* adore as divine; honor with religious rites. **2** *tr.* regard with adoration (*worships the ground she walks on*). **3** *intr.* attend public worship. **4** *intr.* be full of adoration. □□ **wor·ship·er** or **wor·ship·per** *n*

worst /wərst/ *adj., adv., n., & v.* ● *adj.* most bad. ● *adv.* most badly. ● *n.* the worst part, event, circumstance, or possibility (*the worst of the storm is over*; *prepare for the worst*). ● *v.tr.* defeat; outdo. □ **at its**, etc., **worst** in the worst state. **at worst** (or **the worst**) in the worst possible case. **do your worst** an expression of defiance. **get** (or **have**) **the worst of it** be defeated. **if worst comes to worst** if the worst happens.

wor·sted /wŏŏstid, wár-/ *n.* **1** a fine smooth yarn spun from combed long, stapled wool. **2** fabric made from this.

wort /wərt, wawrt/ *n.* **1** *archaic* (except in names) a plant (*St. John's wort*). **2** the infusion of malt which after fermentation becomes beer.

worth /wərth/ *adj. & n.* ● *predic.adj.* (governing a noun like a preposition) **1** of a value equivalent to (*is worth $50*). **2** such as to justify or repay (*worth doing*; *not worth the trouble*). **3** possessing or having property amounting to. ● *n.* **1** what a person or thing is worth (*of great worth*; *persons of worth*). **2** the equivalent of money in a commodity (*ten dollars' worth of gasoline*). □ **for all one is worth** *colloq.* with one's utmost efforts. **for what it is worth** without a guarantee of its truth or value. **worth it** *colloq.* worth the time or effort spent. **worth one's salt** see SALT. **worth while** (or **one's while**) see WHILE.

worth·less /wárthlis/ *adj.* without value or merit. □□ **worth·less·ness** *n.*

worth·while /wárth-hwíl, wíl/ *adj.* that is worth the time or effort spent; of value or importance.

wor·thy /wárthee/ *adj. & n.* ● *adj.* (**worthier, worthiest**) **1** estimable; having some moral worth (*lived a worthy life*). **2** (of a person) entitled to recognition (*a worthy old couple*). **3 a** (foll. by *of* or *to* + infin.) deserving (*worthy of a mention*; *worthy to be*

remembered). **b** (foll. by *of*) suitable to the dignity, etc., of (*in words worthy of the occasion*). ● *n.* (*pl.* **-ies**) **1** a worthy person. **2** a person of some distinction. **3** *joc.* a person. □□ **wor·thi·ly** *adv.* **wor·thi·ness** *n.*

-worthy /wárthee/ *comb. form* forming adjectives meaning: **1** deserving of (*blameworthy*; *noteworthy*). **2** suitable or fit for (*newsworthy*; *roadworthy*).

would /wŏŏd, when unstressed wəd/ *v.aux.* (*3rd sing. **would**) past of WILL[1], used esp.: **1** (in the 2nd and 3rd persons, and often in the 1st: see SHOULD). **a** in reported speech (*he said he would be home by evening*). **b** to express the conditional mood (*they would have been killed if they had gone*). **2** to express habitual action (*would wait for her every evening*). **3** to express a question or polite request (*would they like it?*; *would you come in, please?*). **4** to express probability (*I guess she would be over fifty by now*). **5** (foll. by *that* + clause) *literary* to express a wish (*would that you were here*). **6** to express consent (*they would not help*).

would-be *attrib.adj.* often *derog.* desiring or aspiring to be (*a would-be politician*).

wouldn't /wŏŏd'nt/ *contr.* would not. □ **I wouldn't know** *colloq.* (as is to be expected) I do not know.

wound[1] /wŏŏnd/ *n. & v.* ● *n.* **1** an injury done to living tissue by a cut or blow, etc. **2** an injury to a person's reputation or a pain inflicted on a person's feelings. ● *v.tr.* inflict a wound on (*wounded soldiers*; *wounded feelings*).

wound[2] *past* and *past part.* of WIND[2] (cf. WIND[1] *v.* 5).

wove[1] *past* of WEAVE[1].

wove[2] /wōv/ *adj.* (of paper) made on a wire-gauze mesh and so having a uniform unlined surface.

wo·ven *past part.* of WEAVE[1].

wow[1] /wow/ *int., n., & v.* ● *int.* expressing astonishment or admiration. ● *n. sl.* a sensational success. ● *v.tr. sl.* impress or excite greatly.

wow[2] /wow/ *n.* a slow pitch fluctuation in sound reproduction, perceptible in long notes.

WP *abbr.* word processor; word processing.

w.p.m. *abbr.* words per minute.

wrack /rak/ *n.* **1** seaweed cast up or growing on the shore. ▷ FUCUS. **2** destruction. **3** a wreck or wreckage. **5** = RACK[5].

wrag·gle-tag·gle var. of RAGGLE-TAGGLE.

wraith /rayth/ *n.* **1** a ghost or apparition. **2** the spectral appearance of a living person supposed to portend that person's death. □□ **wraith·like** *adj.*

wran·gle /ránggəl/ *n. & v.* ● *n.* a noisy argument or dispute. ● *v.* **1** *intr.* engage in a wrangle. **2** *tr.* herd (cattle).

wran·gler /ránggləcr/ *n.* **1** a person who wrangles. **2** a cowboy.

wrap /rap/ *v. & n.* ● *v.tr.* (**wrapped, wrapping**) **1** (often foll. by *up*) envelop in folded or soft encircling material (*wrap it up in paper*; *wrap up a package*). **2** (foll. by *around, about*) arrange or draw (a pliant covering) around (a person) (*wrapped the coat closer around me*). **3** (foll. by *around*) *sl.* crash (a vehicle) into a stationary object. ● *n.* **1** a shawl or scarf or other such addition to clothing. **2** material used for wrapping. □ **take the wraps off** disclose. **under wraps** in secrecy. **wrapped up in** engrossed in. **wrap up 1** finish off; bring to completion (*wrapped up the deal in two days*). **2** put on warm clothes (*mind you wrap up well*).

wrap·a·round /rápərownd/ *adj. & n.* ● *adj.* **1** (esp. of clothing) designed to wrap around. **2** curving or extending around at the edges. ● *n.* anything that wraps around.

wrap·per /rápər/ *n.* **1** a cover for a candy, chocolate, etc. **2** a cover enclosing a newspaper or similar packet for mailing. **3** a paper cover of a book, usu. detachable. **4** a loose enveloping robe or gown. **5** a tobacco leaf of superior quality enclosing a cigar.

wrap·ping /ráping/ *n.* (esp. in *pl.*) material used to wrap.

wrap·ping pa·per *n.* strong or decorative paper for wrapping packages.

wrasse /ras/ *n.* ◄ any bright-colored marine fish of the family Labridae with thick lips and strong teeth.

WRASSE:
CUCKOO WRASSE
(*Labrus mixtus*)

wrath /rath, roth, rawth/ *n. literary* extreme anger.

wrath·ful /ráthfŏŏl, róth-, ráwth-/ *adj. literary* extremely angry. □□ **wrath·ful·ly** *adv.*

wreak /reek/ *v.tr.* **1** (usu. foll. by *upon*) put in operation (vengeance or one's anger, etc.). **2** cause (damage, etc.) (*the hurricane wreaked havoc on the crops*).

wreath /reeth/ *n.* (*pl.* **wreaths** /reethz, reeths/) **1** ▼ flowers or leaves fastened in a ring. **2** a similar ring of soft twisted material such as silk. **3** a carved representation of a wreath. **4** (foll. by *of*) a curl or ring of smoke or cloud. **5** a light drifting mass of snow, etc.

ivy leaf

peony

spray of roses

gilded pomegranate

WREATH

wreathe /reeth/ *v.* **1** *tr.* encircle as, with, or like a wreath. **2** *tr.* (foll. by *around*) put (one's arms, etc.) around (a person, etc.). **3** *intr.* (of smoke, etc.) move in the shape of wreaths. **4** *tr.* form (flowers, silk, etc.) into a wreath. **5** *tr.* make (a garland).

wreck /rek/ *n. & v.* ● *n.* **1** the destruction or disablement, esp. of a ship. **2** a ship that has suffered a wreck (*the shores are strewn with wrecks*). **3** a greatly damaged or disabled thing or person (*had become a physical and mental wreck*). **4** (foll. by *of*) a wretched remnant or disorganized set of remains. **5** *Law* goods, etc., cast up by the sea. ● *v.* **1** *tr.* cause the wreck of (a ship, etc.). **2** *tr.* completely ruin (hopes, chances, etc.). **3** *intr.* suffer a wreck. **4** *tr.* (as **wrecked** *adj.*) involved in a shipwreck (*wrecked sailors*). **5** *intr.* deal with wrecked vehicles, etc.

wreck·age /rékij/ *n.* **1** wrecked material. **2** the remnants of a wreck. **3** the action or process of wrecking.

wreck·er /rékər/ *n.* **1** a person or thing that wrecks or destroys. **2** a person employed in demolition, or in recovering a wrecked ship or its contents. **3** a person who breaks up damaged vehicles for spares and scrap. **4** a vehicle or train used in recovering a damaged one.

wren /ren/ *n.* ► any small, usu. brown, short-winged songbird of the family Troglodytidae, esp. *Troglodytes troglodytes* of Europe, having an erect tail.

WREN
(*Troglodytes troglodytes*)

W

wrench /rench/ *n. & v.* ● *n.* **1** a violent twist or oblique pull or act of tearing off. **2** ► an adjustable tool for gripping and turning nuts, etc. **3** an instance of painful uprooting or parting (*leaving home was a great wrench*). **4** *Physics* a combination of a couple with the force along its axis. ● *v.tr.* **1 a** a twist or pull violently around or sideways. **b** injure (a limb, etc.) by undue straining; sprain. **2** (often foll. by *off, away*, etc.) pull off with a wrench. **3** seize or take forcibly. **4** distort (facts) to suit a theory, etc.

WRENCH: STILLSON PIPE WRENCH

wrest /rest/ *v.tr.* **1** force or wrench away from a person's grasp. **2** (foll. by *from*) obtain by effort or with difficulty. **3** distort into accordance with one's interests or views (*wrest the law to suit themselves*).

wres·tle /résəl/ *n. & v.* ● *n.* **1** a contest in which two opponents grapple and try to throw each other to the ground. **2** a hard struggle. ● *v.* **1** *intr.* (often foll. by *with*) take part in a wrestle. **2** *tr.* fight (a person) in a wrestle (*wrestled his opponent to the ground*). **3** *intr.* **a** (foll. by *with, against*) struggle; contend. **b** (foll. by *with*) do one's utmost to deal with (a task, difficulty, etc.). **4** *tr.* move with efforts as if wrestling. □□ **wres·tler** *n.* **wres·tling** *n.*

wretch /rech/ *n.* **1** a pitiable person. **2** (often as a playful term of depreciation) a contemptible person.

wretch·ed /réchid/ *adj.* (**wretcheder, wretchedest**) **1** miserable. **2** of bad quality; contemptible. **3** unsatisfactory or displeasing. □ **feel wretched 1** be unwell. **2** be much embarrassed. □□ **wretch·ed·ly** *adv.* **wretch·ed·ness** *n.*

wrig·gle /rígəl/ *v. & n.* ● *v.* **1** *intr.* (of a worm, etc.) twist or turn its body with short, writhing movements. **2** *intr.* (of a person or animal) make wriggling motions. **3** *tr. & intr.* (foll. by *along*, etc.) move or go in this way (*wriggled into the corner; wriggled his hand into the hole*). **4** *tr.* make (one's way) by wriggling. **5** *intr.* practice evasion. ● *n.* an act of wriggling. □ **wriggle out of** *colloq.* avoid on a contrived pretext. □□ **wrig·gler** *n.* **wrig·gly** *adj.*

wright /rīt/ *n.* a maker or builder (usu. in *comb.*: *playwright; shipwright*).

wring /ring/ *v. & n.* ● *v.tr.* (*past* and *past part.* **wrung** /rung/) **1 a** squeeze tightly. **b** (often foll. by *out*) squeeze and twist. **2** twist forcibly; break by twisting. **3** distress or torture. **4** extract by squeezing. **5** (foll. by *out, from*) obtain by pressure or importunity; extort. ● *n.* an act of wringing; a squeeze. □ **wring a person's hand** clasp it forcibly or press it with emotion. **wring one's hands** clasp them as a gesture of great distress. **wring the neck of** kill (a chicken, etc.) by twisting its neck.

wring·er /ríngər/ *n.* **1** a device for wringing water from washed clothes, etc. **2** a difficult ordeal (*that exam put me through the wringer*).

wring·ing /rínging/ *adj.* (in full **wringing wet**) so wet that water can be wrung out.

wrin·kle /ríngkəl/ *n. & v.* ● *n.* **1** a slight crease in the skin such as is produced by age. **2** a similar mark in another flexible surface. **3** *colloq.* a useful tip or clever expedient. ● *v.* **1** *tr.* make wrinkles in. **2** *intr.* form wrinkles; become marked with wrinkles.

wrin·kly /ríngklee/ *adj. & n.* ● *adj.* (**wrinklier, wrinkliest**) having many wrinkles. ● *n.* (also **wrin·klie**) (*pl.* **-ies**) *sl. offens.* an old or middle-aged person.

W

wrist /rist/ *n.* **1** the part connecting the hand with the forearm. ▷ JOINT. **2** the corresponding part in an animal. **3** the part of a garment covering the wrist.

wrist·band /rístband/ *n.* a band forming or concealing the end of a shirt sleeve; a cuff.

wrist·let /rístlit/ *n.* a band or ring worn on the wrist to strengthen or guard it or as an ornament, bracelet, handcuff, etc.

wrist·watch /rístwoch/ *n.* a small watch worn on a strap around the wrist.

writ[1] /rit/ *n.* a form of written command in the name of a sovereign, court, government, etc. □ **serve a writ on** deliver a writ to (a person).

writ[2] /rit/ *archaic past part.* of WRITE. □ **writ large** in magnified or emphasized form.

write /rīt/ *v.* (*past* **wrote** /rōt/; *past part.* **written** /rít'n/) **1** *intr.* mark a surface by means of a pen, pencil, etc., with symbols, letters, or words. **2** *tr.* form (such symbols, etc.). **3** *tr.* form the symbols that represent or constitute (a word or sentence, or a document, etc.). **4** *tr.* fill or complete (a form, check, etc.) with writing. **5** *tr.* put (data) into a computer store. **6** *tr.* (esp. in *passive*) indicate (a quality or condition) by one's or its appearance (*guilt was written on his face*). **7** *tr.* compose (a text, article, novel, etc.) for written or printed reproduction or publication. **8** *intr.* be engaged in composing a text, article, etc. (*writes for the local newspaper*). **9** *intr.* (foll. by *to*) write and send a letter (to a recipient). **10** *tr. colloq.* write and send a letter to (a person) (*wrote him last week*). **11** *tr.* convey (news, information, etc.) by letter (*wrote that they would arrive next Friday*). **12** *tr.* state in written or printed form (*it is written that*). **13** *tr.* cause to be recorded. **14** *tr.* underwrite (an insurance policy). **15** *tr.* (foll. by *into, out of*) include or exclude (a character or episode) in a story by suitable changes of the text. □ **nothing to write home about** *colloq.* of little interest or value. **write down 1** record or take note of in writing. **2** write as if for those considered inferior. **3** disparage in writing. **write in 1** send a suggestion, query, etc., in writing to an organization. **2** add (an extra name) on a list of candidates when voting. **write off 1** write and send a letter. **2** cancel the record of (a bad debt, etc.); acknowledge the loss of or failure to recover (an asset). **3** damage (a vehicle, etc.) so badly that it cannot be repaired. **4** compose with facility. **5** dismiss as insignificant. **write out 1** write in full or in finished form. **2** exhaust (oneself) by writing (*have written myself out*). **write up 1** write a full account of. **2** praise in writing. **3** make a report (of a person) esp. to cite a violation of rules, etc. □□ **writ·a·ble** *adj.* **writ·er** *n.*

write-off *n.* a thing too badly damaged to be repaired.

writ·er's block *n.* (of a writer) a temporary inability to proceed with the composition of a novel, play, etc.

writ·er's cramp *n.* a muscular spasm due to excessive writing.

write-up *n. colloq.* a written or published account; a review.

writhe /rīth/ *v. & n.* ● *v.* **1** *intr.* twist or roll oneself about in or as if in acute pain. **2** *intr.* suffer severe mental discomfort or embarrassment. **3** *tr.* twist (one's body, etc.) about. ● *n.* an act of writhing.

writ·ing /ríting/ *n.* **1** a group or sequence of letters or symbols. **2** = HANDWRITING. **3** the art or profession of literary composition. **4** (usu. in *pl.*) a piece of literary work done; a book, article, etc. □ **in writing** in written form. **the writing on the wall** an ominously significant event, etc. (see Dan. 5:5, 25-8).

writ·ten *past part.* of WRITE.

wrong /rawng, rong/ *adj., adv., n., & v.* ● *adj.* **1** mistaken; not true; in error (*gave a wrong answer; we were wrong to think that*). **2** less or least desirable (*the wrong road; a wrong decision*). **3** contrary to law or morality (*it is wrong to steal*). **4** out of order; in or into a bad or abnormal condition (*something wrong with my heart*). ● *v.tr.* **1** treat unjustly. **2** mistakenly attribute bad motives to. □ **do wrong** commit sin; transgress. **do wrong to** malign or mistreat. **get wrong** misunderstand (a person, statement, etc.). **get** (or **get hold of**) **the wrong end of the stick** misunderstand completely. **go down the wrong way** (of food) enter the windpipe instead of the esophagus. **go wrong** develop in an undesirable way. **in the wrong** responsible for a quarrel, mistake, or offense. **on the wrong side of 1** out of favor with (a person). **2** somewhat more than (a stated age). **wrong side out** inside out. **wrong way around** (or **round**) in the reverse of the normal or desirable orientation or sequence, etc. □□ **wrong·ly** *adv.* **wrong·ness** *n.*

wrong·do·er /ráwngdōōər, róng-/ *n.* a person who behaves immorally or illegally. □□ **wrong·do·ing** *n.*

wrong·ful /ráwngfŏŏl, róng-/ *adj.* **1** characterized by unfairness or injustice. **2** contrary to law. **3** (of a person) not entitled to the position, etc., occupied. □□ **wrong·ful·ly** *adv.*

wrong·head·ed /ráwnghedid, róng-/ *adj.* perverse and obstinate. □□ **wrong·head·ed·ness** *n.*

wrong side *n.* the worse or undesired or unusable side of something, esp. fabric.

wrote *past* of WRITE.

wroth /rawth, roth, rōth/ *predic.adj. archaic* angry.

wrought /rawt/ *adj.* (of metals) beaten out or shaped by hammering. (from the *archaic past* and *past part.* of WORK.)

wrought i·ron *n.* ◄ a tough malleable form of iron suitable for forging or rolling.

wrung *past* and *past part.* of WRING.

wry /rī/ *adj.* (**wryer, wryest** or **wrier, wriest**) **1** distorted or turned to one side. **2** (of a smile, etc.) contorted in disgust, disappointment, or mockery. **3** (of humor) dry and mocking. □□ **wry·ly** *adv.* **wry·ness** *n.*

wry·neck /rínek/ *n.* **1** = TORTICOLLIS. **2** any bird of the genus *Jynx* of the woodpecker family, able to turn its head over its shoulder.

WSW *abbr.* west-southwest.

wt. *abbr.* weight.

wun·der·kind /vŏŏndərkind/ *n. colloq.* a person who achieves great success while relatively young.

Wur·lit·zer /wərlitsər/ *n. Trademark* a large pipe organ or electric organ.

wurst /vərst, vŏŏrst/ *n.* German or Austrian sausage.

WV *abbr.* West Virginia (in official postal use).

W.Va. *abbr.* West Virginia.

WWW *abbr.* = WORLD WIDE WEB.

WY *abbr.* Wyoming (in official postal use).

Wyo. *abbr.* Wyoming.

WYS·I·WYG /wízeewig/ *adj.* (also **wysiwyg**) *Computing* denoting the representation of text onscreen exactly as it will appear on a printout (acronym of *what you see is what you get*).

WROUGHT IRON: 18TH-CENTURY ORNAMENTAL RAIL POST

X[1] /eks/ *n.* (also **x**) (*pl.* **Xs** or **X's**) **1** the twenty-fourth letter of the alphabet. **2** (as a Roman numeral) ten. **3** (usu. *x*) *Algebra* the first unknown quantity. **4** *Geom.* the first coordinate. **5** an unknown or unspecified number or person, etc. **6** a cross-shaped symbol esp. used to indicate position (*X marks the spot*) or incorrectness or to symbolize a kiss or a vote, or as the signature of a person who cannot write.

X[2] *symb.* = X-RATED.

X chro·mo·some /éks krṓmǝsōm/ *n.* a sex chromosome of which the number in female cells is twice that in male cells.

Xe *symb. Chem.* the element xenon.

xen·o·lith /zénǝlith, zéēnǝ-/ *n. Geol.* ◄ an inclusion within an igneous rock mass, usu. derived from the immediately surrounding rock.

XENOLITH:
LAVA SURROUNDED
BY PINK GRANITE

granite
lava

xe·non /zénon, zéē-/ *n. Chem.* a heavy, colorless, odorless inert gaseous element occurring in traces in the atmosphere and used in fluorescent lamps. ¶ Symb.: **Xe**.

xen·o·phobe /zénǝfōb, zéēnǝ-/ *n.* a person given to xenophobia.

xen·o·pho·bi·a /zénǝfōbeeǝ, zéēnǝ-/ *n.* a deep dislike of foreigners. □□ **xen·o·pho·bic** *adj.*

xe·ran·the·mum /zeeránthimǝm/ *n.* ◄ a plant of the genus *Xeranthemum*, with dry everlasting flowers.

xero- /zéérō/ *comb. form* dry.

xe·ro·der·ma /zéérǝdɔ́rmǝ/ *n.* any of various diseases characterized by extreme dryness of the skin.

xe·rog·ra·phy /zeerógrǝfee/ *n.* a dry copying process in which powder adheres to parts of a surface remaining electrically charged after exposure of the surface to light from an image of the document to be copied. □□ **xe·ro·graph·ic** /-rǝgráfik/ *adj.*

XERANTHEMUM
(*Xeranthemum annuum*)

xe·roph·i·lous /zeerófilǝs/ *adj.* (of a plant) adapted to extremely dry conditions.

xe·ro·phyte /zéérǝfīt/ *n.* (also **xe·ro·phile** /-fīl/) ▲ a plant able to grow in very dry conditions.

Xe·rox /zéeroks/ *n. & v.* ● *n. Trademark* **1** a machine for copying by xerography. **2** a copy made using this machine. ● *v.tr.* (**xerox**) reproduce by this process.

XEROPHYTE

Xerophytes exhibit a range of adaptations that enable them to survive in arid environments. Succulents, such as stonecrops and cacti, store water in their leaves or stems. In cacti, the leaves are much reduced or absent altogether, and the stem is armed with spines to deter browsing animals. Other xerophytes, such as snake plants and yuccas, often have sharp-tipped leaves and are also protected by an extremely tough leaf surface, or cuticle. As well as deterring animals, this helps to reduce water loss.

EXAMPLES OF XEROPHYTES

STONECROP
(*Sedum obtusatum*)

CLARET-CUP CACTUS
(*Echinocereus triglochidiatus*)

AGAVE
(*Agave pumila*)

Xho·sa /kṓsǝ, -zǝ, káw-/ *n. & adj.* ● *n.* **1** (*pl.* same or **Xhosas**) a member of a Bantu people of Cape Province, South Africa. **2** the Bantu language of this people. ● *adj.* of or relating to this people or language.

xi /zī, sī, ksee/ *n.* the fourteenth letter of the Greek alphabet (Ξ, ξ).

Xmas /krísmǝs, éksmǝs/ *n. colloq.* = CHRISTMAS.

XML *abbr.* Extensible Mark-up Language.

X-rat·ed *adj.* (usu. *attrib.*) (of motion pictures, etc.) classified as suitable for adults only

X ray /éksray/ *n.* (also **X ray**, **x ray**) **1** (in *pl.*) ▼ electromagnetic radiation of short wavelength, able to pass through opaque bodies. ▷ ELECTROMAGNETIC RADIATION. **2** ▼ an image made by the effect of X rays on a photographic plate, esp. showing the position of bones, etc. by their greater absorption of the rays. □□ **X-ray** *adj.* (also **x-ray**).

x-ray /éksray/ *v.tr.* (also **X ray**) photograph, examine, or treat with X rays.

xy·lem /zílem/ *n. Bot.* woody tissue (cf. PHLOEM). ▷ STEM

xy·lene /zíleen/ *n. Chem.* a volatile liquid hydrocarbon resembling benzene, obtained by distilling wood, coal tar, or petroleum.

xylo- /zílō/ *comb. form* wood.

xy·lo·graph /zílǝgraf/ *n.* an engraving on wood.

xy·lo·phone /zílǝfōn/ *n.* ▼ a musical instrument of wooden or metal bars graduated in length and struck with a small wooden hammer or hammers. ▷ ORCHESTRA, PERCUSSION. □□ **xy·lo·phon·ist** *n.*

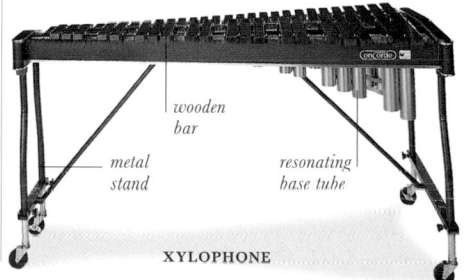

wooden bar

metal stand

resonating base tube

XYLOPHONE

X RAY

X rays come near the high-energy end of the electromagnetic spectrum. In an X-ray tube, electrons emitted by an electrically heated filament are accelerated toward a heavy metal target by an intense electric field. Because there is no air in the tube, the electrons reach high speeds; when they are rapidly decelerated by hitting the target, their kinetic energy turns into high-frequency electromagnetic radiation (X rays). Used mostly in medical imaging, X rays pass through muscle but are absorbed by bone, so that an image recorded on photographic film reveals the bones as shadows.

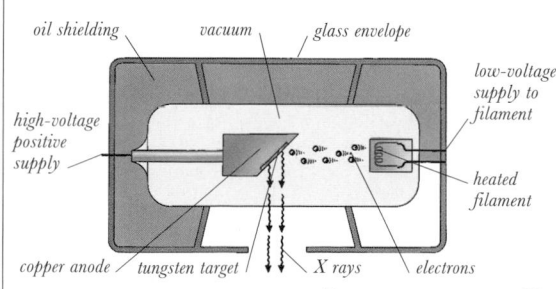

oil shielding   *vacuum*   *glass envelope*

high-voltage positive supply

low-voltage supply to filament

heated filament

copper anode   *tungsten target*   *X rays*   *electrons*

CROSS SECTION OF AN X-RAY TUBE

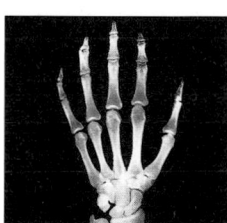

X-RAY PHOTOGRAPH OF A HAND

Y

Y¹ /wī/ *n.* (also **y**) (*pl.* **Ys** or **Y's**) **1** the twenty-fifth letter of the alphabet. **2** (usu. **y**) *Algebra* the second unknown quantity. **3** *Geom.* the second coordinate. **4 a** a Y-shaped thing, esp. an arrangement of lines, piping, roads, etc. **b** a forked clamp or support.

Y² *symb. Chem.* the element yttrium.

y. *abbr.* year(s).

-y¹ /ee/ *suffix* forming adjectives: **1** from nouns and adjectives, meaning: **a** full of; having the quality of (*messy*; *icy*; *horsy*). **b** addicted to (*boozy*). **2** from verbs, meaning 'inclined to,' 'apt to' (*runny*; *sticky*).

-y² /ee/ *suffix* (also **-ey**, **-ie**) forming diminutive nouns, pet names, etc. (*granny*; *nightie*; *Mickey*).

-y³ /ee/ *suffix* forming nouns denoting: **1** state, condition, or quality (*courtesy*; *orthodoxy*; *modesty*). **2** an action or its result (*colloquy*; *remedy*; *subsidy*).

yab·ber /yábər/ *v. & n. Austral. & NZ colloq.* ● *v.intr. & tr.* talk. ● *n.* talk; conversation; language.

yab·by /yábee/ *n.* (*pl.* **-ies**) *Austral.* **1** a small freshwater crayfish, esp. of the genus *Cherax*. **2** a marine prawn, *Callianassa australiensis*, often used as bait.

YACHT

By adjusting the position of their sails, yachts can travel in almost any direction, except directly into the wind. Most modern sailing yachts have triangular fore- and aft sails, arranged in a "Bermuda rig". Many have an auxiliary engine and can increase speed by setting a spinnaker.

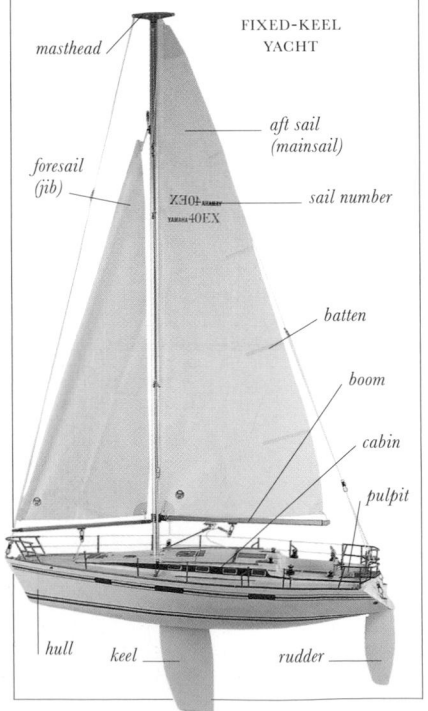

FIXED-KEEL YACHT

masthead
aft sail (mainsail)
foresail (jib)
sail number
batten
boom
cabin
pulpit
hull
keel
rudder

Y

---

yacht /yot/ *n. & v.* ● *n.* **1** ▼ a light sailing vessel, esp. equipped for racing. **2** a larger usu. power-driven vessel equipped for cruising. ▷ BOAT. ● *v.intr.* race or cruise in a yacht. □□ **yacht·ing** *n.*

yachts·man /yótsmən/ *n.* (*pl.* **-men**; *fem.* **yachts·woman**, *pl.* **-women**) a person who sails yachts.

yack /yak/ *n. & v.* (also **yack·e·ty-yack** /yákəteeyák/, **yak**) *sl. derog.* ● *n.* trivial or unduly persistent conversation. ● *v.intr.* engage in this.

yah /yaa/ *int.* expressing derision or defiance.

ya·hoo /yáahōō/ *n.* a coarse, bestial person.

Yah·weh /yáaway, -we/ *n.* (also **Yah·veh** /-vay, -ve/) the Hebrew name of God in the Old Testament.

Yah·wist /yáawist/ *n.* (also **Yah·vist** /-vist/) the postulated author or authors of parts of the Old Testament in which God is regularly named *Yahweh*.

yak¹ /yak/ *n.* ▼ a long-haired, humped Tibetan ox, *Bos grunniens*.

YAK:
WILD YAK
(*Bos grunniens*)

yak² *n. & v.* (**yakked**, **yakking**) var. of YACK.
yak·e·ty-yack var. of YACK.
Ya·ku·za /yakóōzə/ *n.* (**the Yakuza**) a powerful Japanese criminal organization.

y'all /yawl/ *pron.* = YOU-ALL.

yam /yam/ *n.* **1 a** any tropical or subtropical climbing plant of the genus *Dioscorea*. **b** ▶ the edible starchy tuber of this. **2** a sweet potato.

yam·mer /yámər/ *n. & v. colloq. or dial.* ● *n.* **1** a lament, wail, or grumble. **2** voluble talk. ● *v.intr.* **1** utter a yammer. **2** talk volubly.

yang /yang/ *n.* (in Chinese philosophy) the active male principle of the universe (cf. YIN). ▷ YIN

Yank /yangk/ *n.* esp. *Brit. colloq.* often *derog.* an American.

yank /yangk/ *v. & n. colloq.* ● *v.tr.* pull with a jerk. ● *n.* a sudden hard pull.

Yan·kee /yángkee/ *n. colloq.* **1** often *derog.* = YANK. **2** an inhabitant of New England or one of the northern states. **3** *hist.* ◀ federal Union soldier in the Civil War. **4** (*attrib.*) of or as of the Yankees.

forage cap
sword strap
sergeant's chevrons
waist belt
frock coat
trouser stripe
sword
worsted sash

YANKEE:
SERGEANT, 157TH
NEW YORK VOLUNTEERS

YAM:
WING-STALKED YAM
(*Dioscorea alata*)

---

yap /yap/ *v. & n.* ● *v.intr.* (**yapped**, **yapping**) **1** bark shrilly. **2** *colloq.* talk noisily or foolishly. ● *n.* **1** a sound of yapping. **2** *sl.* the mouth.

Yar·bor·ough /yáarbərō, -burō, -bərə/ *n.* a whist or bridge hand with no card above a nine.

yard¹ /yaard/ *n.* **1** a unit of linear measure equal to 3 feet (0.9144 meter). **2** this length of material (*a yard and a half of fabric*). **3** a square or cubic yard, esp. (in building) of sand, etc. **4** a cylindrical spar tapering to each end slung across a mast for a sail to hang from. ▷ RIGGING. **5** (in *pl.*; foll. by *of*) *colloq.* a great length (*yards of spare wallpaper*).

yard² /yaard/ *n. & v.* ● *n.* **1** a piece of ground esp. attached to a building or used for a particular purpose. **2** the lawn and garden area of a house. **3** a pen or other enclosure for farm animals, livestock, etc. ● *v.tr.* put (cattle) into a stockyard.

yard·age /yáardij/ *n.* **1** a number of yards of material, etc. **2 a** the use of a stockyard, etc. **b** payment for this.

yard·arm /yáardaarm/ *n.* the outer extremity of a ship's yard.

yard·bird /yáardbərd/ *n. sl.* **1** a new military recruit. **2** a convict.

yard·man /yáardmən/ *n.* (*pl.* **-men**) *n.* **1** a person working in a railroad yard or lumberyard. **2** a person who does various outdoor jobs.

yard sale *n. N. Amer.* a sale of miscellaneous secondhand items held in the grounds of a private house.

yard·stick /yáardstik/ *n.* **1** a standard used for comparison. **2** a measuring rod a yard long, usu. divided into inches, etc.

yar·mul·ke /yáarməlkə, yáamɣl-/ *n.* (also **yar·mul·ka**) ▶ a skullcap worn by Jewish men.

yarn /yaarn/ *n. & v.* ● *n.* **1** any spun thread, esp. for knitting, weaving, rope making, etc. **2** *colloq.* a long or rambling story. ● *v.intr. colloq.* tell yarns.

Hebrew characters

YARMULKE

yar·row /yárō/ *n.* ▶ any perennial herb of the genus *Achillea*, esp. milfoil.

yash·mak /yáashmaak, yáshmak/ *n.* a veil concealing the face except the eyes, worn by some Muslim women when in public.

yat·a·ghan /yátəgan/ *n.* a sword without a guard and often with a double-curved blade, used in Muslim countries.

YARROW
(*Achillea millefolium*)

yat·ter /yátər/ *v. & n. colloq. or dial.* ● *v.intr.* talk idly or incessantly; chatter. ● *n.* incessant chatter.

yaw /yaw/ *v. & n.* ● *v.intr.* (of a ship or aircraft, etc.) fail to hold a straight course; go unsteadily (esp. turning from side to side). ● *n.* the yawing of a ship, etc., from its course.

yawl /yawl/ *n.* **1** a two-masted, fore-and-aft sailing vessel with the mizzenmast stepped far aft. **2** a small kind of fishing boat.

yawn /yawn/ *v. & n.* ● *v.* **1** *intr.* (as a reflex) open the mouth wide and inhale, esp. when sleepy or bored. **2** *intr.* (of a chasm, etc.) gape; be wide open. **3** *tr.* utter with a yawn. ● *n.* **1** an act of yawning. **2** *colloq.* a boring or tedious idea, activity, etc. □□ **yawn·ing·ly** *adv.*

yawp /yawp/ *n. & v.* ● *n.* **1** a harsh or hoarse cry. **2** foolish talk. ● *v.intr.* utter these. □□ **yaw·per** *n.*

yaws /yawz/ *n.pl.* (usu. treated as *sing.*) a contagious tropical skin disease with large red swellings.

Yb *symb. Chem.* the element ytterbium.

Y chro·mo·some /wĭ-krṓməsōm/ *n.* a sex chromosome occurring only in male cells.

y·clept /ĭklépt/ *adj. archaic* or *joc.* called (by the name of).

yd. *abbr.* yard (measure).

yds. *abbr.* yards (measure).

ye[1] /yee/ *pron. archaic pl.* of THOU[1]. □ **ye gods!** *joc.* an exclamation of astonishment.

ye[2] /yee/ *adj. pseudo-archaic* = THE (*ye olde tea shoppe*).

yea /yay/ *adv. & n. formal* ● *adv.* **1** yes. **2** indeed (*ready, yea eager*). ● *n.* an affirmative vote. □ **yea and nay** shilly-shally.

yeah /yeə/ *adv. colloq.* yes.

yean /yeen/ *v.tr. archaic* bring forth (a lamb or kid).

yean·ling /yéenling/ *n. archaic* a young lamb or kid.

year /yeer/ *n.* **1** (also **astronomical year**, **equinoctial year**, **natural year**, **solar year**, **tropical year**) the time occupied by the Earth in one revolution around the Sun, 365 days, 5 hours, 48 minutes, and 46 seconds in length. **2** (also **calendar year**, **civil year**) the period of 365 days (**common year**) or 366 days (see LEAP YEAR) from Jan. 1 to Dec. 31, used for reckoning time in ordinary affairs. **3 a** a period of the same length as this starting at any point (*four years ago*). **b** such a period in terms of a particular activity, etc., occupying its duration (*school year*; *tax year*). **4** (in *pl.*) age or time of life (*young for his years*). **5** (usu. in *pl.*) *colloq.* a very long time (*it took years to get served*). **6** a group of students entering college, etc., in the same academic year. □ **in the year of Our Lord** (foll. by year) in a specified year AD. **of the year** chosen as outstanding in a particular year (*sportsman of the year*). **a year and a day** the period specified in some legal matters to ensure the completion of a full year. **year in, year out** continually over a period of years.

year·book /yéerbŏŏk/ *n.* **1** an annual publication dealing with events or aspects of the (usu. preceding) year. **2** such a publication, usu. produced by a school's graduating class and featuring students, activities, sports, etc.

year·ling /yéerling/ *n. & adj.* ● *n.* **1** an animal between one and two years old. **2** a racehorse in the calendar year after the year of foaling. ● *adj.* having lived or existed for a year (*a yearling heifer*).

year·long /yéerlóng/ *adj.* lasting a year or the whole year.

year·ly /yéerlee/ *adj. & adv.* ● *adj.* **1** done, produced, or occurring once a year. **2** of or lasting a year. ● *adv.* once a year; from year to year.

yearn /yərn/ *v.intr.* **1** (usu. foll. by *for*, *after*, or *to* + infin.) have a strong emotional longing. **2** (usu. foll. by *to, toward*) be filled with compassion or tenderness. □□ **yearn·ing** *n. & adj.* **yearn·ing·ly** *adv.*

year-on-year *adj.* (of figures, prices, etc.) as compared with the corresponding ones from a year earlier.

year-round *adj.* existing, etc., throughout the year.

yeast /yeest/ *n.* **1** ▼ a grayish-yellow fungous substance obtained esp. from fermenting malt liquors and used as a fermenting agent, to raise bread, etc. **2** any of various unicellular fungi in which vegetative reproduction takes place by budding or fission. □□ **yeast·like** *adj.*

fresh yeast   *dried yeast*

YEAST

yeast·y /yéestee/ *adj.* (**yeastier**, **yeastiest**) **1** frothy or tasting like yeast. **2** in a ferment. **3** working like yeast. **4** (of talk, etc.) light and superficial.

yell /yel/ *n. & v.* ● *n.* **1** a loud sharp cry of pain, anger, fright, encouragement, delight, etc. **2** a shout. **3** an organized cry, used esp. to support a sports team. ● *v.tr. & intr.* utter with or make a yell.

yel·low /yélō/ *adj., n., & v.* ● *adj.* **1** of the color between green and orange in the spectrum, of buttercups, lemons, egg yolks, or gold. **2** of the color of faded leaves, ripe wheat, etc. **3** having a yellow skin or complexion. **4** *colloq.* cowardly. **5** (of looks, feelings, etc.) jealous, envious, or suspicious. **6** (of newspapers, etc.) unscrupulously sensational. ● *n.* **1** a yellow color or pigment. **2** yellow clothes or material (*dressed in yellow*). **3 a** a yellow ball, piece, etc., in a game or sport. **b** the player using such pieces. **4** (usu. in *comb.*) a yellow moth or butterfly. ● *v.tr. & intr.* make or become yellow. □□ **yel·low·ish** *adj.* **yel·low·ness** *n.* **yel·low·y** *adj.*

yel·low·back /yélōbak/ *n.* a cheap novel, etc., in a yellow cover.

yel·low-bel·lied *adj.* **1** *colloq.* cowardly. **2** (of a fish, bird, etc.) having yellow underparts.

yel·low-bel·ly /yélōbelee/ *n.* **1** *colloq.* a coward. **2** any of various fish with yellow underparts.

yel·low card *n. Soccer* a card shown by the referee to a player being cautioned.

yel·low fe·ver *n.* a tropical virus disease causing fever and jaundice.

yel·low flag *n.* **1** a flag displayed by a ship in quarantine. **2** an iridaceous plant, *Iris pseudacorus*, with slender sword-shaped leaves and yellow flowers. ▷ FLAG

yel·low·ham·mer /yélōhamər/ *n.* ▶ a bunting, *Emberiza citrinella*, of which the male has a yellow head, neck, and breast.

yel·low jack *n.* **1** = YELLOW FEVER. **2** = YELLOW FLAG.

yel·low jack·et *n.* **1** any of various wasps of the family Vespidae with yellow and black bands. **2** *sl.* a capsule of phenobarbital.

yel·low jour·nal·ism *n.* journalism that is based on sensationalism.

Yel·low Pag·es *n.pl.* (also **yel·low pag·es**) a section of a telephone directory on yellow paper and listing business subscribers according to the goods or services they offer.

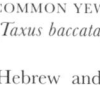

YELLOWHAMMER
(*Emberiza citrinella*)

yel·low per·il (the) *n. derog.* the political or military threat regarded as emanating from Asian peoples, esp. the Chinese.

yel·low spot *n.* the point of acutest vision in the retina.

yel·low streak *n. colloq.* a trace of cowardice.

yelp /yelp/ *n. & v.* ● *n.* a sharp, shrill cry of or as of a dog in pain or excitement. ● *v.intr.* utter a yelp.

yen[1] /yen/ *n.* (*pl.* same) the chief monetary unit of Japan.

yen[2] /yen/ *n. & v. colloq.* ● *n.* a longing or yearning. ● *v.intr.* (**yenned, yenning**) feel a longing.

yeo·man /yṓmən/ *n.* (*pl.* **-men**) **1** esp. *hist.* a man holding and cultivating a small landed estate. **2** *Brit. hist.* a person qualified by possessing free land of an annual value of 40 shillings to serve on juries. **3** *Brit.* a member of the yeomanry force. **4** *hist.* a servant in a royal or noble household. **5** in the US Navy, a petty officer performing clerical duties on board ship.

yeo·man·ly /yṓmənlee/ *adj.* **1** of the rank of yeoman. **2** characteristic of or befitting a yeoman; sturdy; reliable.

yeo·man of the guard *n.* **1** a member of the British sovereign's bodyguard. **2** (in general use) a warder in the Tower of London.

yeo·man·ry /yṓmənree/ *n.* (*pl.* **-ies**) a body of yeomen.

yeo·man ser·vice *n.* (also **yeoman's service**) efficient or useful help in need.

yep /yep/ *adv. & n.* (also **yup** /yup/) *colloq.* = YES.

yes /yes/ *adv. & n.* ● *adv.* **1** equivalent to an affirmative sentence: the answer to your question is affirmative; it is as you say or as I have said; the statement, etc., made is correct; the request or command will be complied with; the negative statement, etc., made is not correct **2** (in answer to a summons or address) an acknowledgment of one's presence. ● *n.* an utterance of the word *yes*. □ **yes and no** that is partly true and partly untrue.

ye·shi·va /yəshéevə/ *n.* an Orthodox Jewish college or seminary.

yes-man *n.* (*pl.* **-men**) *colloq.* a weakly acquiescent person.

yester- /yéstər/ *comb. form poet.* or *archaic* of yesterday; that is the last past (*yester-eve*).

yes·ter·day /yéstərday/ *adv. & n.* ● *adv.* **1** on the day before today. **2** in the recent past. ● *n.* **1** the day before today. **2** the recent past.

yes·ter·year /yéstəryeer/ *n. literary* **1** last year. **2** the recent past.

yet /yet/ *adv. & conj.* ● *adv.* **1** as late as, or until, now or then (*there is yet time; your best work yet*). **2** (with *neg.* or *interrog.*) so soon as, or by, now or then (*it is not time yet; have you finished yet?*). **3** again; in addition (*more and yet more*). **4** in the remaining time available; before all is over (*I will do it yet*). **5** (foll. by *compar.*) even (*a yet more difficult task*). **6** nevertheless; and in spite of that; but for all that (*it is strange, and yet it is true*). ● *conj.* but at the same time; but nevertheless (*I won, yet what good has it done?*). □ **nor yet** esp. *Brit.* and also not (*won't listen to me nor yet to you*).

yet·i /yétee/ *n.* = ABOMINABLE SNOWMAN.

yew /yōō/ *n.* **1** ▶ any dark-leaved evergreen coniferous tree of the genus *Taxus*, having seeds enclosed in a fleshy red aril, and often planted in landscaped settings. **2** its wood, used formerly as a material for bows and still in cabinetmaking. ▷ WOOD

Ygg·dra·sil /ígdrəsil/ *n.* (in Scandinavian mythology) an ash tree whose roots and branches join heaven, earth, and hell.

YHA *abbr.* Youth Hostels Association.

Yid /yid/ *n. sl. offens.* a Jew.

Yid·dish /yídish/ *n. & adj.* ● *n.* a vernacular used by Jews in or from central and eastern Europe, orig. a German dialect with words from Hebrew and several modern languages. ● *adj.* of or relating to this language.

aril (fruit)

YEW:
COMMON YEW
(*Taxus baccata*)

yield /yeeld/ *v. & n.* ● *v.* **1** *tr.* (also *absol.*) produce or return as a fruit, profit, or result (*the land yields crops; the land yields poorly; the investment yields 15%*). **2** *tr.* give up; surrender; concede; comply with a demand for (*yielded the fortress; yielded themselves prisoners*). **3** *intr.* (often foll. by *to*) **a** surrender; make submission. **b** give consent or change one's course of action in deference to; respond as required to (*yielded to persuasion*). **4** *intr.* (foll. by *to*) be inferior or confess inferiority to (*I yield to none in understanding the problem*). **5** *intr.* (foll. by *to*) give right of way to other traffic. **6** *intr.* allow another the right to speak in a debate, etc. ● *n.* an amount yielded or produced; an output or return. □□ **yield·er** *n.*

yield·ing /yéelding/ *adj.* **1** compliant, submissive. **2** (of a substance) able to bend; not stiff nor rigid.

yield point *n. Physics* the stress beyond which a material becomes plastic.

Y

YIN

In Chinese philosophy, yin represents one half of the duality in the universe. Yin is the feminine force, associated with the Earth and the Moon. Yin is complemented by yang, the male force, associated with the heavens and the Sun. The symbol for yin and yang is divided into the dark (yin) and light (yang). The dots in each field represent the potential for change within either force.

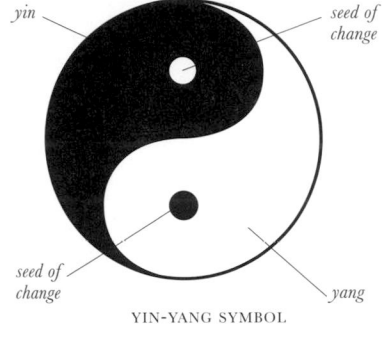

yin · seed of change · seed of change · yang

YIN-YANG SYMBOL

yin /yin/ *n.* (in Chinese philosophy) ▲ the passive female principle of the universe (cf. YANG).

yip·pee /yípéé/ *int.* expressing delight or excitement.

yip·pie /yípee/ *n.* a hippie associated with political activism, esp. as a member of a radical organization (acronym of *Y*outh *I*nternational *P*arty).

-yl /əl/ *suffix Chem.* forming nouns denoting a radical (*ethyl; hydroxyl; phenyl*).

y·lang-y·lang /éelaang-géelaang/ *n.* (also **ilang-ilang**) **1** ◀ a Malayan tree, *Cananga odorata*, with fragrant yellow flowers from which a perfume is distilled. **2** the perfume itself.

YLANG-YLANG
(*Cananga odorata*)

YMCA *abbr.* Young Men's Christian Association.

yo /yō/ *int.* used to call attention, express affirmation, or greet informally.

yob /yob/ *n. Brit. sl.* a lout or hooligan. □□ **yob·bish** *adj.* **yob·bish·ly** *adv.* **yob·bish·ness** *n.*

yob·bo /yóbō/ *n.* (*pl.* **-os**) *Brit. sl.* = YOB.

yod /yōod, yod/ *n.* **1** the tenth and smallest letter of the Hebrew alphabet. **2** its semivowel sound /y /.

yo·del /yōd'l/ *v. & n.* ● *v.tr. & intr.* sing with melodious inarticulate sounds and frequent changes between falsetto and the normal voice in the manner of the Swiss mountain dwellers. ● *n.* a yodeling cry. □□ **yo·del·er** *n.*

yo·ga /yṓgə/ *n.* ▶ a Hindu system of philosophic meditation and asceticism, a part of which includes performing specific bodily postures.

yo·gi /yṓgee/ *n.* a person proficient in yoga. □□ **yo·gism** *n.*

yo·gurt /yṓgərt/ *n.* (also **yo·ghurt**) a semisolid sourish food prepared from milk fermented by added bacteria.

yoicks /yoyks/ *int.* a cry used by foxhunters to urge on the hounds.

yoke /yōk/ *n. & v.* ● *n.* **1** ▼ a wooden crosspiece fastened over the necks of two oxen, etc., and attached to the plow or wagon to be drawn. **2** (*pl.* same or **yokes**) a pair (of oxen, etc.). **3** an object like a yoke in form or function, e.g., a wooden shoulder-piece for carrying a pair of pails, the top section of a dress or skirt, etc., from which the rest hangs. **4** sway, dominion, or servitude, esp. when oppressive. **5** a bond of union, esp. that of marriage. **6** a crossbar on which a bell swings. **7** the crossbar of a rudder to whose ends ropes are fastened. ● *v.* **1** *tr.* put a yoke on. **2** *tr.* couple or unite (a pair). **3** *tr.* (foll. by *to*) link (one thing) to (another). **4** *intr.* match or work together.

yo·kel /yṓkəl/ *n.* a rustic; a country bumpkin.

yolk /yōk/ *n.* **1** the yellow internal part of an egg that nourishes the young before it hatches. ▷ EGG. **2** *Biol.* the corresponding part of any animal ovum. □□ **yolked** *adj.* (also in *comb.*). **yolk·less** *adj.* **yolk·y** *adj.*

Yom Kip·pur /yawm kípər, keepŏŏr, yōm, yom/ *n.* = Day of Atonement.

yon /yon/ *adj., adv., & pron. literary & dial.* ● *adj. & adv.* yonder. ● *pron.* yonder person or thing.

yon·der /yóndər/ *adv. & adj.* ● *adv.* over there; at some distance in that direction; in the place indicated by pointing, etc. ● *adj.* situated yonder.

yo·ni /yṓnee/ *n.* a symbol of the female genitals venerated by Hindus, etc.

yoo-hoo /yṓŏhŏŏ/ *int.* used to attract a person's attention.

yore /yawr/ *n. literary* □ **of yore** formerly; in or of old days.

York·ist /yáwrkist/ *n. & adj.* ● *n. hist.* a follower of the House of York or of the White Rose party supporting it in England's Wars of the Roses (cf. LANCASTRIAN). ● *adj.* of or concerning the House of York.

York·shire pud·ding /yáwrksheer/ *n.* ◀ a popover made of baked unsweetened egg batter, usu. eaten with roast beef.

YORKSHIRE PUDDINGS

York·shire ter·ri·er /yáwrksheer/ *n.* ▶ a small, longhaired, blue-gray and tan kind of terrier.

Yo·ru·ba /yáwrəbə/ *n.* **1** a member of a black African people inhabiting the west coast, esp. Nigeria. **2** the language of this people.

you /yōo/ *pron.* (*obj.* **you**; *poss.* **your**, **yours**) **1** used with reference to the person or persons addressed or one such person and one or more associated persons. **2** (as *int.* with a noun) in an exclamatory statement (*you fools!*). **3** (in general statements) one, a person, anyone, or everyone (*it's bad at first, but you get used to it*).

you-all (often **y'all** esp. *Southern US colloq.*) *pron.* you (usu. more than one person).

you and yours *pron.* you together with your family, property, etc.

you'd /yōod/ *contr.* **1** you had. **2** you would.

YOKE:
CURVED OX YOKE
crosspiece · chain ring · oxbow

YOGA:
THE BOW POSE

you-know-what *n.* (also **you-know-who**) something or someone unspecified but understood.

you'll /yōol, yool/ *contr.* you will; you shall.

young /yung/ *adj. & n.* ● *adj.* (**younger** /yúnggər/; **youngest** /yúnggist/) **1** not far advanced in life, development, or existence; not yet old. **2** immature or inexperienced. **3** felt in or characteristic of youth (*young love; young ambition*). **4** representing young people (*Young Republicans; young America*). **5** distinguishing a son from his father (*young Jones*). **6** (**younger**) distinguishing one person from another of the same name (*the younger Davis*). ● *n.* (*collect.*) offspring, esp. of animals before or soon after birth. □ **with young** (of an animal) pregnant. □□ **young·ish** *adj.*

young gun *n. sl.* an aggressive young man.

young la·dy *n.* **1** a young, usu. unmarried woman. **2** a girlfriend or sweetheart.

young man *n.* **1** a young adult male. **2** a boyfriend or sweetheart.

young·ster /yúngstər/ *n.* a child or young person.

young thing *n. archaic* or *colloq.* an indulgent term for a young person.

Young Turk *n.* **1** a member of a revolutionary party in Turkey in 1908. **2** a young person eager for radical change to the established order.

young 'un *n. colloq.* a youngster.

your /yŏŏr, yawr/ *poss.pron.* (*attrib.*) **1** of or belonging to you (*your house; your own business*). **2** *colloq.* usu. *derog.* much talked of; well known (*none so fallible as your self-styled expert*).

you're /yŏŏr, yawr/ *contr.* you are.

yours /yŏŏrz, yawrz/ *poss. pron.* **1** the one or ones belonging to or associated with you (*it is yours; yours are over there*). **2** your letter (*yours of the 10th*). **3** introducing a formula ending a letter (*yours ever; yours truly*). □ **of yours** of or belonging to you (*a friend of yours*).

your·self /yŏŏrsélf, yawr-/ *pron.* (*pl.* **yourselves** /-sélvz/) **1 a** *emphat. form* of YOU. **b** *refl. form* of YOU. **2** in your normal state of body or mind (*are quite yourself again*). □ **be yourself** act in your normal, unconstrained manner. **how's yourself?** *sl.* how are you? (esp. after answering a similar inquiry).

youth /yōoth/ *n.* (*pl.* **youths** /yōothz/) **1** the state of being young; the period between childhood and adult age. **2** the vigor or enthusiasm, inexperience, or other characteristic of this period. **3** an early stage of development, etc. **4** a young person (esp. male). **5** (*pl.*) young people collectively (*the youth of the country*).

youth cen·ter (or **club**) *n.* a place or organization provided for young people's leisure activities.

youth·ful /yōothfŏŏl/ *adj.* **1** young, esp. in appearance or manner. **2** having the characteristics of youth (*youthful impatience*). **3** having the freshness or vigor of youth (*a youthful complexion*). □□ **youth·ful·ly** *adv.* **youth·ful·ness** *n.*

youth hos·tel *n.* a place where (esp. young) travelers can be put up cheaply for the night. □□ **youth hos·tel·er** *n.*

YORKSHIRE TERRIER

you've /yōov, yŏŏv/ *contr.* you have.

yowl /yowl/ *n. & v.* ● *n.* a loud, wailing cry of or as of a cat or dog in pain or distress. ● *v.intr.* utter a yowl.

Y

yo-yo /yṓyō/ *n. & v.* ● *n.* (*pl.* **yo-yos**) **1** *Trademark* ▼ a toy consisting of a pair of disks with a deep groove between them in which string is attached and wound, and which can be spun alternately downward and upward by its weight and momentum as the string unwinds and rewinds. **2** a thing that repeatedly falls and rises again. ● *v.intr.* (**yo-yoes, yo-yoed, yo-yoing**) **1** play with a yo-yo. **2** move up and down; fluctuate.

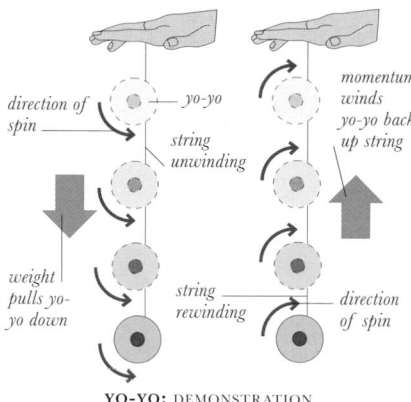

YO-YO: DEMONSTRATION OF A YO-YO'S ACTION

yr. *abbr.* **1** year(s). **2** your. **3** younger.

yrs. *abbr.* **1** years. **2** yours.

yt·ter·bi·um /itárbeeəm/ *n. Chem.* a silvery metallic element of the lanthanide series occurring naturally as various isotopes. ¶ Symb.: **Yb**.

yt·tri·um /ítreeəm/ *n. Chem.* a grayish metallic element resembling the lanthanides, occurring naturally in uranium ores and used in making superconductors. ¶ Symb.: **Y**.

Y2K *abbr.* year 2000.

yu·an /yōō-aán, yö-/ *n.* (*pl.* same) the chief monetary unit of China.

yuc·ca /yúkə/ *n.* ▶ any American white-flowered liliaceous plant of the genus *Yucca*, with swordlike leaves.

yuck /yuk/ *int. & n. sl.* ● *int.* an expression of strong distaste or disgust. ● *n.* something messy or repellent.

yuck·y /yúkee/ *adj.* (**-ier, -iest**) *sl.* messy; repellent.

Yu·go·slav /yōōgəslaav/ *n. & adj.* (also **Jugoslav**) *hist.* ● *n.* **1** a native or national of the former republic of Yugoslavia. **2** a person of Yugoslav descent. ● *adj.* of or relating to Yugoslavia or its people. □□ **Yu·go·sla·vi·an** *adj. & n.*

YUCCA (*Yucca elephantipes* 'Variegata')

yule /yōōl/ *n.* (in full **yuletide**) *archaic* the Christmas festival.

Yule log *n.* **1** a large log burned in the hearth on Christmas Eve. **2** a log-shaped cake eaten at Christmas.

Yu·ma /yōōmə/ *n.* **1 a** a N. American people native to Arizona. **b** a member of this people. **2** the language of this people.

yum·my /yúmee/ *adj.* (**yummier, yummiest**) *colloq.* tasty; delicious.

yum-yum /yúmyúm/ *int.* expressing pleasure from eating or the prospect of eating.

yup·pie /yúpee/ *n. & adj.* (also **yup·py**) (*pl.* **-ies**) *colloq.*, usu. *derog.* ● *n.* a young, middle-class professional person working in a city. ● *adj.* characteristic of a yuppie or yuppies (acronym of *y*oung *u*rban *p*rofessional).

yurt /yərt/ *n.* **1** ▼ a circular tent of felt, skins, etc., on a collapsible framework, used by nomads in Mongolia and Siberia. **2** a semi-subterranean hut, usu. of timber covered with earth or turf.

YWCA *abbr.* Young Women's Christian Association.

YURT

Y

Z /zee/ *n.* (also **z**) (*pl.* **Zs** or **Z's**) **1** the twenty-sixth letter of the alphabet. **2** (usu. **z**) *Algebra* the third unknown quantity. **3** *Geom.* the third coordinate. **4** *Chem.* atomic number.

za·ba·glio·ne /záábaalyóˈnee, -yáwne/ *n.* an Italian dessert of whipped and heated egg yolks, sugar, and wine.

zaf·fer /záfər/ *n.* (*Brit.* **zaffre**) an impure cobalt oxide used a blue pigment.

zag /zag/ *n. & v.* ● *n.* a sharp change of direction in a zigzag course. ● *v.intr.* (**zagged**, **zagging**) move in one of the two directions in a zigzag course.

za·ny /záynee/ *adj. & n.* ● *adj.* (**zanier**, **zaniest**) comically idiotic; crazily ridiculous. ● *n.* a buffoon or jester. □□ **za·ni·ly** *adv.* **za·ni·ness** *n.*

zap /zap/ *v., n., & int. sl.* ● *v.* (**zapped**, **zapping**) **1** *tr.* **a** kill or destroy. **b** hit forcibly (*zapped the ball over the net*). **c** send an electric current, radiation, etc., through (someone or something). **2** *intr.* move quickly and vigorously. **3** *tr. Computing* erase or change (an item in a program). **4** *intr.* (foll. by *through*) fast-forward a videotape to skip a section. **5** *tr.* heat or cook (food) by microwave. **6** *tr.* change (television channels) by remote control. ● *n.* a sudden burst of energy or sound.

zap·per /zápər/ *n. colloq.* a hand-held remote-control device for changing television channels, adjusting volume, etc.

zap·py /zápee/ *adj.* (**zappier**, **zappiest**) *colloq.* **1** lively; energetic. **2** striking.

Zar·a·thus·tri·an var. of ZOROASTRIAN.

zar·zue·la /zaarzwáylə, thaarthwáylə, saarswáy-/ *n.* a Spanish traditional form of musical comedy.

zeal /zeel/ *n.* **1** earnestness or fervor. **2** hearty and persistent endeavor.

zeal·ot /zélət/ *n.* **1** an uncompromising or extreme partisan; a fanatic. **2** (**Zealot**) *hist.* a member of an ancient Jewish sect aiming at a world Jewish theocracy and resisting the Romans until AD 70. □□ **zeal·ot·ry** *n.*

zeal·ous /zéləs/ *adj.* full of zeal; enthusiastic. □□ **zeal·ous·ly** *adv.* **zeal·ous·ness** *n.*

ze·bra /zeebrə/ *n.* (*pl.* same or **zebras**) **1** any of various African quadrupeds, esp. *Equus burchelli*, related to the ass and horse, with black and white stripes. ▷ UNGULATE. **2** (*attrib.*) with alternate dark and pale stripes.

ze·bu /zéeboo/ *n.* ▼ a humped ox, *Bos indicus*, of India, E. Asia, and Africa.

ZEBU:
BRAHMA COW
(*Bos indicus*)

zed /zed/ *n. Brit.* the letter Z.

zee /zee/ *n.* the letter Z.

Zeit·geist /tsítgīst, zít-/ *n.* **1** the spirit of the times. **2** the trend of thought and feeling in a period.

Zen /zen/ *n.* a form of Mahayana Buddhism emphasizing the value of meditation and intuition. □□ **Zen·ist** *n.* (also **Zen·nist**).

ze·nith /zéenith/ *n.* **1** the part of the celestial sphere directly above an observer (opp. NADIR). **2** the highest point in one's fortunes; a time of great prosperity, etc.

ze·o·lite /zéeəlīt/ *n.* each of a number of minerals consisting mainly of hydrous silicates of calcium, sodium, and aluminum, able to act as cation exchangers. □□ **ze·o·lit·ic** /-lítik/ *adj.*

zeph·yr /zéfər/ *n.* **1** *literary* a mild gentle wind or breeze. **2** a fine cotton fabric. **3** an athlete's thin gauzy jersey.

zep·pe·lin /zépəlin/ *n. hist.* ▼ a German large dirigible airship of the early 20th c., orig. for military use.

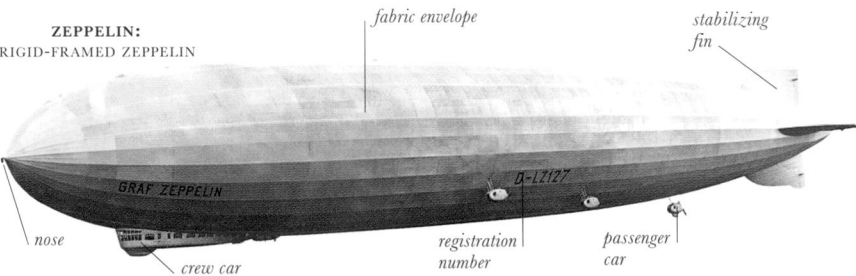

ZEPPELIN:
RIGID-FRAMED ZEPPELIN

fabric envelope
stabilizing fin
nose
crew car
registration number
passenger car

ze·ro /zéerō/ *n. & v.* ● *n.* (*pl.* **-os**) **1 a** the figure 0; naught. **b** no quantity or number; nil. **2** a point on the scale of an instrument from which a positive or negative quantity is reckoned. **3** (*attrib.*) having a value of zero; no; not any. **4** (in full **zero hour**) **a** the hour at which a planned, esp. military, operation is timed to begin. **b** a crucial moment. **5** the lowest point; a nullity or nonentity. ● *v.tr.* (**-oes**, **-oed**) **1** adjust (an instrument, etc.) to zero point. **2** set the sights of (a gun) for firing. □ **zero in on 1** take aim at. **2** focus one's attention on.

ze·ro-sum *adj.* (of a game, political situation, etc.) in which whatever is gained by one side is lost by the other so that the net change is always zero.

ze·ro tol·er·ance *n.* strict enforcement of the law regarding any form of anti-social behavior.

zest /zest/ *n.* **1** piquancy; a stimulating flavor or quality. **2 a** keen enjoyment or interest. **b** (often foll. by *for*) relish. **c** gusto. **3** a scraping of orange or lemon peel as flavoring. □□ **zest·ful** *adj.* **zest·ful·ly** *adv.* **zest·ful·ness** *n.* **zest·y** *adj.* (**zestier**, **zestiest**).

ze·ta /záytə, zée-/ *n.* the sixth letter of the Greek alphabet (Z, ζ).

zeug·ma /zóogmə/ *n.* a figure of speech using a verb or adjective with two nouns, to one of which it is strictly applicable while the word appropriate to the other is not used (e.g., *with weeping eyes and hearts*) (cf. SYLLEPSIS). □□ **zeug·mat·ic** /-mátik/ *adj.*

zi·do·vu·dine /zīdóvyōodeen/ *n.* = AZT.

zig·gu·rat /zígərat/ *n.* ▼ a rectangular stepped tower in ancient Mesopotamia, surmounted by a temple.

platform
temple
stairway

ZIGGURAT: RECONSTRUCTION
OF A ZIGGURAT FROM *C.*2100 BC

zig·zag /zígzag/ *n., adj., adv., & v.* ● *n.* **1** a line or course having abrupt alternate right and left turns. **2** (often in *pl.*) each of these turns. ● *adj.* having the form of a zigzag; alternating right and left. ● *adv.* with a zigzag course. ● *v.intr.* (**zigzagged**, **zigzagging**) move in a zigzag course.

zilch /zilch/ *n. sl.* nothing.

zil·lion /zílyən/ *n. colloq.* an indefinite large number. □□ **zil·lionth** *adj. & n.*

zinc /zingk/ *n. Chem.* a white metallic element used as a component of brass, in galvanizing sheet iron, and in electric batteries. ¶ Symb.: **Zn**. □□ **zinced** *adj.*

zinc ox·ide *n.* a powder used as a white pigment and in medicinal ointments.

zing /zing/ *n. & v. colloq.* ● *n.* vigor; energy. ● *v.intr.* move swiftly or with a shrill sound. □□ **zing·y** *adj.* (**zingier**, **zingiest**).

zin·ga·ro /tséenggaarō/ *n.* (*pl.* **zin·ga·ri** /-ree/; *fem.* **zin·gar·a** /-raa/) a gypsy.

zing·er /zíngər/ *n. sl.* **1** a witty retort. **2** an unexpected or startling announcement, etc. **3** an outstanding person or thing.

zin·ni·a /zíneeə/ *n.* ▶ a composite plant of the genus *Zinnia*, with showy rayed flowers of various colors.

ZINNIA
(*Zinnia elegans*
'Dreamland Scarlet')

Zi·on /zíən/ *n.* (also **Sion** /síən/) **1** hill of Jerusalem on which the city of David was built. **2 a** a Jewish people or religion. **b** the Christian church. **3** (in Christian thought) the kingdom of God in heaven.

Zi·on·ism /zíən-izəm/ *n.* a movement (orig.) for the re-establishment and (now) the development of a Jewish nation in what is now Israel. □□ **Zi·on·ist** *n.*

zip /zip/ *n. & v.* ● *n.* **1** a light fast sound, as of a bullet passing through air. **2** energy; vigor. **3** *Brit.* (in full **zip fastener**) = ZIPPER. ● *v.* (**zipped**, **zipping**) **1** *tr. & intr.* (often foll. by *up*) fasten with a zipper. **2** *intr.* move with zip or at high speed.

zip code /zip/ *n.* (also **ZIP code**) a US system of postal codes consisting of five-digit or nine-digit numbers.

zip·per /zípər/ *n. & v.* ● *n.* ▶ a fastening device of two flexible strips with interlocking projections closed or opened by pulling a slide along them. ● *v.tr.* (often foll. by *up*) fasten with a zipper. □□ **zip·pered** *adj.*

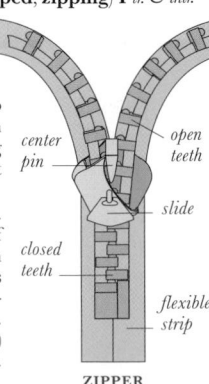

center pin
open teeth
slide
closed teeth
flexible strip

ZIPPER

Z

zip·py /zípee/ *adj.* (**zippier**, **zippiest**) *colloq.* **1** bright; fresh; lively. **2** fast; speedy. □□ **zip·pi·ly** *adv.* **zip·pi·ness** *n.*

zir·con /zárkon/ *n.* ▶ a zirconium silicate of which some translucent varieties are cut into gems.

zir·co·ni·um /zɔrkṓnee-əm/ *n. Chem.* a gray metallic element occurring naturally in zircon and used in various industrial applications. ¶ Symb.: **Zr**.

zit /zit/ *n. sl.* a pimple.

zith·er /zíthər/ *n.* ▼ a musical instrument consisting of a flat wooden sound box with numerous strings stretched across it, a few of which may be stopped on a fretted fingerboard, placed horizontally and played with the fingers and a plectrum. ▷ STRINGED. □□ **zith·er·ist** *n.*

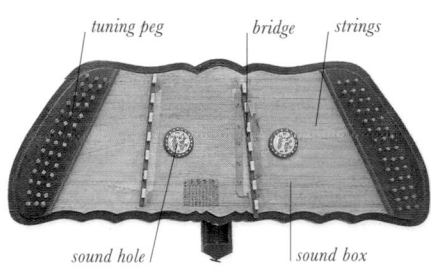

zircon crystal   *syenite groundmass*

ZIRCON

tuning peg   *bridge*   *strings*

sound hole   *sound box*

ZITHER: 17TH-CENTURY CHINESE ZITHER

zlo·ty /zláwtee/ *n.* (*pl.* same or **zlotys**) the chief monetary unit of Poland.

Zn *symb. Chem.* the element zinc.

zo·di·ac /zṓdeeak/ *n.* **1 a** ▼ a belt of the heavens limited by lines about 8° from the ecliptic on each side, including all apparent positions of the Sun, Moon, and planets as known to ancient astronomers, and divided into twelve equal parts (**signs of the zodiac**), each formerly containing the similarly named constellation but now by precession of the equinoxes coinciding with the constellation that bears the name of the preceding sign: Aries, Taurus, Gemini, Cancer, Leo, Virgo, Libra, Scorpio, Sagittarius, Capricorn(us), Aquarius, Pisces. **b** a diagram of these signs. **2** a complete cycle, circuit, or compass.

zo·di·a·cal /zədíəkəl/ *adj.* of or in the zodiac.

zo·e·trope /zṓeetrōp/ *n. hist.* ▶ an optical toy in the form of a cylinder with a series of pictures on the inner surface which give an impression of continuous motion when viewed through slits with the cylinder rotating.

zo·ic /zṓik/ *adj.* **1** of or relating to animals. **2** *Geol.* (of rock, etc.) containing fossils; with traces of animal or plant life.

zom·bie /zómbee/ *n.* **1** *colloq.* a dull or apathetic person. **2** a corpse said to be revived by witchcraft.

rotating cylinder

picture

viewing slit

spindle

fixed base

ZOETROPE

zo·na·tion /zōnáyshən/ *n.* distribution in zones, esp. (*Ecol.*) of plants into zones characterized by the dominant species.

zone /zōn/ *n. & v.* ● *n.* **1** an area having particular features, properties, purpose, or use (*danger zone; erogenous zone; smokeless zone*). **2** any well-defined region of more or less beltlike form. **3 a** an area between two exact or approximate concentric circles. **b** a part of the surface of a sphere enclosed between two parallel planes, or of a cone or cylinder, etc., between such planes cutting it perpendicularly to the axis. **4** (in full **time zone**) a range of longitudes where a common standard time is used. **5** *Geol.*, etc. a range between specified limits of depth, height, etc., esp. a section of strata distinguished by characteristic fossils. **6** *Geog.* any of five divisions of the Earth bounded by circles parallel to the equator (see FRIGID, TEMPERATE, TORRID). **7** an encircling band or stripe distinguishable in color, texture, or character from the rest of the object encircled. ● *v.tr.* **1** encircle as or with a zone. **2** arrange or distribute by zones. **3** assign as or to a particular area. □□ **zon·al** *adj.* **zon·ing** *n.* (in sense 3 of *v.*).

zonk /zongk/ *v. & n. sl.* ● *v.* **1** *tr.* hit or strike. **2** (foll. by *out*) **a** *tr.* overcome with sleep; intoxicate. **b** *intr.* fall heavily asleep.

zonked /zongkt/ *adj. sl.* (often foll. by *out*) exhausted; intoxicated.

zoo /zoō/ *n.* a zoological garden.

zo·oid /zṓoyd/ *n.* **1** a more or less independent invertebrate organism arising by budding or fission. **2** a distinct member of an invertebrate colony. □□ **zo·oi·dal** /-óyd'l/ *adj.*

zoo·keep·er /zoōkeepər/ *n.* an animal attendant employed in a zoo.

ZODIAC

The zodiac is an imaginary band around the celestial sphere, which is divided into 12 parts known as the constellations of the zodiac. The band contains the ecliptic (the line representing the Sun's apparent path across the sky over the course of the year); and the Sun, Moon, and planets are always to be found within its limits. Each constellation of the zodiac contains a pattern of stars that represents an animal or a character from Greek mythology. The zodiac originated as a device for measuring time, but by the 5th century BC it had been incorporated into attempts to determine character and predict the future. Although there is no scientific proof of its validity, astrologers still use the zodiac for assessing trends in people's emotional and physical lives.

CONSTELLATIONS OF THE ZODIAC
SHOWN ON THE CELESTIAL SPHERE

Taurus — *Aries* — *Pisces* — *Aquarius* — *Capricorn* — *celestial equator* — *Sagittarius* — *ecliptic* — *Scorpio* — *Libra* — *Virgo* — *Leo* — *celestial sphere* — *Earth* — *Cancer* — *Gemini*

SIGNS OF THE ZODIAC

ARIES (RAM)
MAR 21–APR 20

TAURUS (BULL)
APR 21–MAY 20

GEMINI (TWINS)
MAY 21–JUN 20

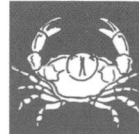

CANCER (CRAB)
JUN 21–JUL 21

LEO (LION)
JUL 22–AUG 21

VIRGO (VIRGIN)
AUG 22–SEPT 21

LIBRA (SCALES)
SEPT 22–OCT 22

SCORPIO (SCORPION)
OCT 23–NOV 21

SAGITTARIUS (ARCHER)
NOV 22–DEC 20

CAPRICORN (GOAT)
DEC 21–JAN 19

AQUARIUS (WATER-BEARER)
JAN 20–FEB 18

PISCES (FISH)
FEB 19–MAR 20

Z

zool. *abbr.* **1** zoological. **2.** zoology.

zo·o·log·i·cal /zṓəlójikəl/ *adj.* of or relating to zoology. □□ **zo·o·log·i·cal·ly** *adv.*

zo·ol·o·gy /zō-óləjee/ *n.* the scientific study of animals, esp. with reference to their structure, physiology, classification, and distribution. □□ **zo·ol·o·gist** *n.*

zoom /zō͞om/ *v. & n.* ● *v.* **1** *intr.* move quickly, esp. with a buzzing sound. **2 a** *intr.* cause an airplane to mount at high speed and a steep angle. **b** *tr.* cause (an airplane) to do this. **3 a** *intr.* (of a camera) close up rapidly from a long shot to a close-up. **b** *tr.* cause (a lens or camera) to do this. ● *n.* **1** an airplane's steep climb. **2** a zooming camera shot.

zoom lens *n.* a lens allowing a camera to zoom by varying the focal length. ▷ CAMCORDER

zo·o·mor·phic /zṓəmáwrfik/ *adj.* **1** dealing with or represented in animal forms. **2** having gods of animal form. □□ **zo·o·mor·phism** *n.*

zo·on·o·sis /zṓənṓsis/ *n.* any of various diseases which can be transmitted to humans from animals.

zo·o·phyte /zṓəfīt/ *n.* a plantlike animal, esp. a coral, sea anemone, or sponge. □□ **zo·o·phyt·ic** /-fítik/ *adj.*

zo·o·plank·ton /zṓəplángktən/ *n.* plankton consisting of animals.

zoot suit /zṓot sṓot/ *n.* a man's suit characterized by a long loose jacket with padded shoulders and high-waisted tapering trousers, popular in the 1940s.

Zo·ro·as·tri·an /záwrō-ástreeən/ *adj. & n.* (also **Za·ra·thus·tri·an** /zárəthōōstreeən/) ● *adj.* of or relating to Zoroaster (or Zarathustra) or the dualistic religious system taught by him or his followers in the Zend-Avesta, the sacred writings based on the concept of a conflict between a spirit of light and good and a spirit of darkness and evil. ● *n.* a follower of Zoroaster.

Zou·ave /zō͞o-áav, zwaav/ *n.* a member of a French light-infantry corps originally formed of Algerians and retaining their oriental uniform.

ZPG *abbr.* zero population growth.

Zr *symb. Chem.* the element zirconium.

zuc·chet·to /zōōkétō, tsōōkétō/ *n.* (*pl.* **-os**) a Roman Catholic ecclesiastic's skullcap, black for a priest, purple for a bishop, red for a cardinal, and white for a pope.

zuc·chi·ni /zōōkéenee/ *n.* (*pl.* same or **zucchinis**)

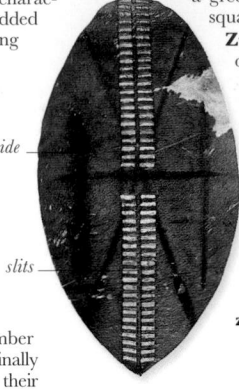

oxhide

slits

ZULU SHIELD

a green variety of smooth-skinned summer squash. ▷ VEGETABLE

Zu·lu /zṓolōō/ *n. & adj.* ● *n.* **1** a member of a black South African people orig. inhabiting Zululand and Natal. **2** the language of this people. ● *adj.* ◄ of or relating to this people or language.

Zu·ni /zṓonee/ *n.* (also **Zuñi** /zṓonyee/) **1 a** a N. American people native to New Mexico. **b** a member of this people. **2** the language of this people.

zwie·back /zwíbak, -baak, zwée-, swí-, swée-/ *n.* a kind of rusk or sweet cake toasted in slices.

zy·go·ma /zīgṓmə, zee-/ *n.* (*pl.* **zygomata** /-tə/) the bony arch of the cheek formed by connection of the zygomatic and temporal bones.

zy·go·mat·ic bone *n.* the bone that forms the prominent part of the cheek. ▷ SKELETON, SKULL

zy·go·spore /zígəspawr, zígə-/ *n.* a thick-walled spore formed by certain fungi.

zy·gote /zígōt, zíg-/ *n. Biol.* a cell formed by the union of two gametes. ▷ OVARY. □□ **zy·got·ic** /-gótik/ *adj.* **zy·got·i·cal·ly** /-gótikəlee/ *adv.*

Z

REFERENCE SECTION

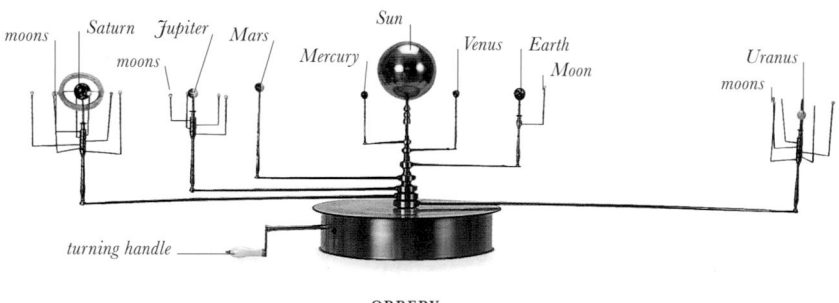

moons · Saturn · Jupiter · Mars · Sun · Venus · Earth · Uranus

moons · Mercury · Moon · moons

turning handle

ORRERY

POLITICAL MAP OF THE WORLD

THIS MAP depicts the political boundaries of the world's nations. There are currently 192 independent countries in the world – a marked increase from the 82 that existed in 1950. With the trend towards greater fragmentation, this figure is likely to increase. There are also some 60 overseas dependencies still in existence, with various forms of local administration, but all belonging to a sovereign state. The largest country in the world is Russia, which covers 6,592,800 sq. mi. (17,075,400 sq. km), while the smallest is Vatican City, covering 0.17 sq. mi. (0.44 sq. km). Under the Antarctic Treaty of 1959, no countries are permitted territorial claims in Antarctica.

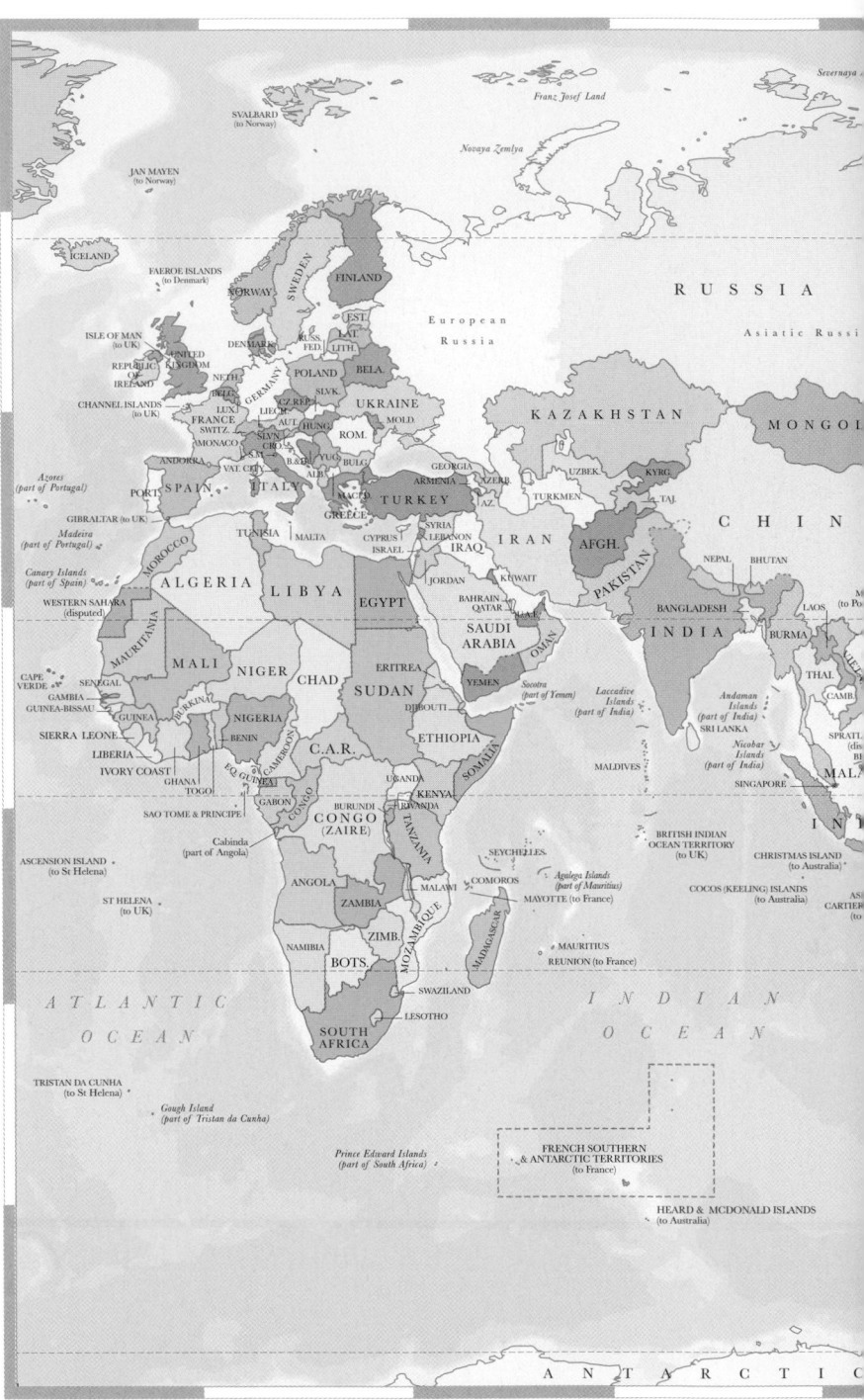

ABBREVIATIONS

AFGH.	Afghanistan
ALB.	Albania
AUT.	Austria
AZ. OR AZERB.	Azerbaijan
B. & H.	Bosnia & Herzegovina
BELA.	Belarus
BELG.	Belgium
BOTS.	Botswana
BULG.	Bulgaria
CAMB.	Cambodia
C.A.R.	Central African Rep.
CRO.	Croatia
CZ. REP.	Czech Republic
DOM. REP.	Dominican Republic
EST.	Estonia
HUNG.	Hungary
KYRG.	Kyrgyzstan
LAT.	Latvia
LIECH.	Liechtenstein
LITH.	Lithuania
LUX.	Luxembourg
MACED.	Macedonia
MOLD.	Moldova
NETH.	Netherlands
NETH. ANT.	Netherland Antilles
PORT.	Portugal
ROM.	Romania
RUSS. FED.	Russian Federation
SLVK.	Slovakia
SLVN.	Slovenia
S.M.	San Marino
SWITZ.	Switzerland
TAJ.	Tajikistan
THAI.	Thailand
TURKMEN.	Turkmenistan
U.A.E.	United Arab Emirates
UZBEK.	Uzbekistan
VAT. CITY	Vatican City
YUG.	Yugoslavia
ZIMB.	Zimbabwe

KEY TO LABEL STYLES

Eg., MEXICO	Independent state
Eg., FAEROE ISLANDS (to Denmark)	Self-governing territory, with parent state indicated
Eg., Andaman Islands (part of India)	Non self-governing territory, with parent state indicated

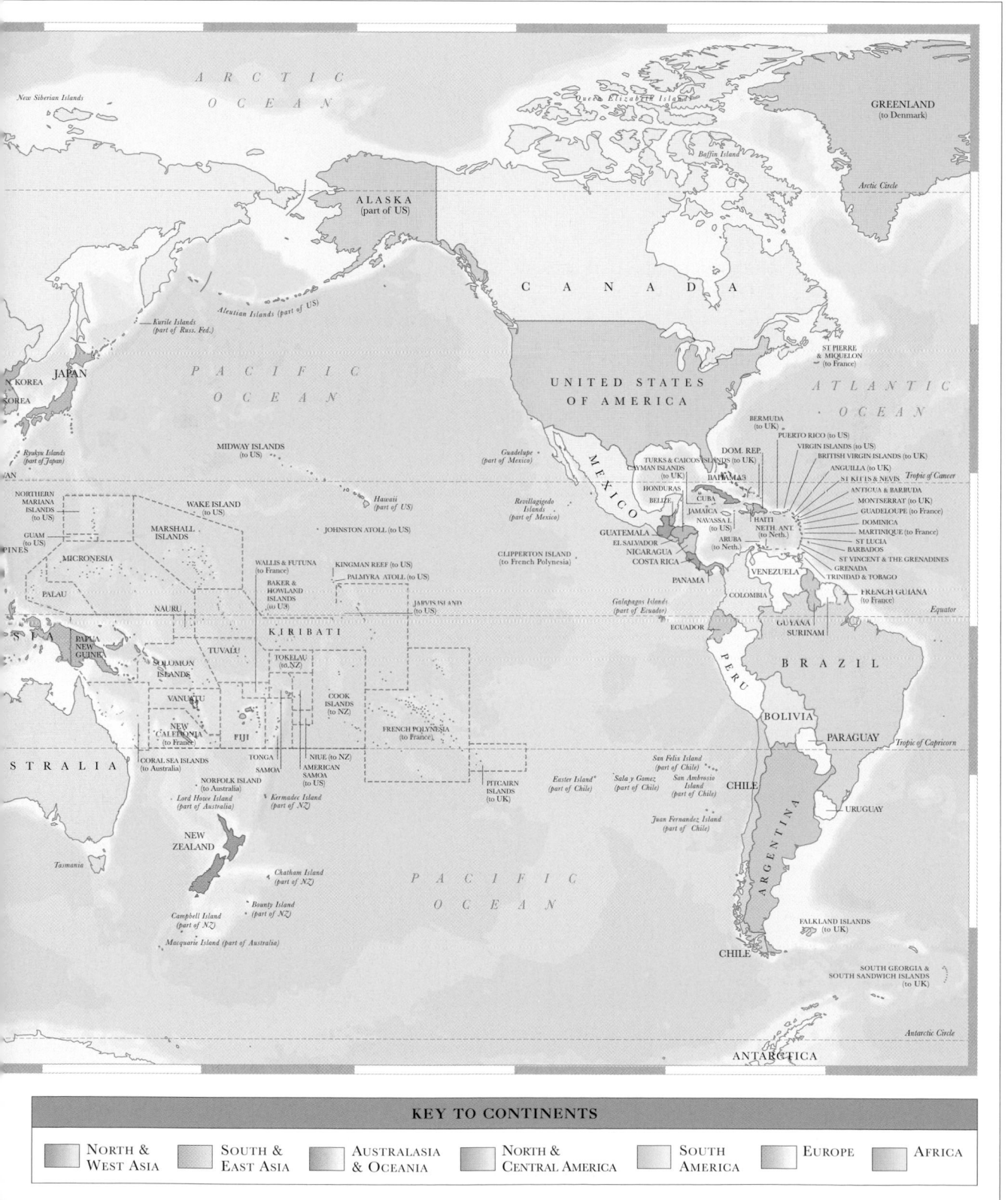

New Siberian Islands

A R C T I C

O C E A N

Queen Elizabeth Islands

GREENLAND
(to Denmark)

Baffin Island

Arctic Circle

ALASKA
(part of US)

C A N A D A

Aleutian Islands (part of US)

Kurile Islands
(part of Russ. Fed.)

JAPAN

N KOREA
KOREA

P A C I F I C

O C E A N

UNITED STATES
OF AMERICA

ST PIERRE
& MIQUELON
(to France)

A T L A N T I C

O C E A N

BERMUDA
(to UK)

PUERTO RICO (to US)

Ryukyu Islands
(part of Japan)

MIDWAY ISLANDS
(to US)

Guadelupe
(part of Mexico)

MEXICO

TURKS & CAICOS ISLANDS
(to UK)

CAYMAN ISLANDS
(to UK)

DOM. REP.

VIRGIN ISLANDS (to US)
BRITISH VIRGIN ISLANDS (to UK)
ANGUILLA (to UK)
ST KITTS & NEVIS Tropic of Cancer
ANTIGUA & BARBUDA

AN

NORTHERN
MARIANA
ISLANDS
(to US)

Hawaii
(part of US)

JOHNSTON ATOLL (to US)

Revillagigedo
Islands
(part of Mexico)

HONDURAS
BELIZE

BAHAMAS

CUBA

JAMAICA

MONTSERRAT (to UK)
GUADELOUPE (to France)
DOMINICA
MARTINIQUE (to France)
ST LUCIA
BARBADOS

GUAM
(to US)

PHILIPPINES

MARSHALL
ISLANDS

WAKE ISLAND
(to US)

MICRONESIA

WALLIS & FUTUNA
(to France)

KINGMAN REEF (to US)

GUATEMALA
EL SALVADOR
NICARAGUA
COSTA RICA

NAVASSA I.
(to US)

HAITI

NETH. ANT.
(to Neth.)

ARUBA
(to Neth.)

ST VINCENT & THE GRENADINES
GRENADA
TRINIDAD & TOBAGO

PALAU

BAKER &
HOWLAND
ISLANDS
(to US)

PALMYRA ATOLL (to US)

CLIPPERTON ISLAND
(to French Polynesia)

PANAMA

VENEZUELA

FRENCH GUIANA
(to France)

ASIA

NAURU

JARVIS ISLAND
(to US)

COLOMBIA

GUYANA
SURINAM

Equator

PAPUA
NEW
GUINEA

SOLOMON
ISLANDS

TUVALU

KIRIBATI

TOKELAU
(to NZ)

Galapagos Islands
(part of Ecuador)

ECUADOR

PERU

B R A Z I L

VANUATU

COOK
ISLANDS
(to NZ)

FRENCH POLYNESIA
(to France)

BOLIVIA

NEW
CALEDONIA
(to France)

FIJI

TONGA
SAMOA

NIUE (to NZ)

AMERICAN
SAMOA
(to US)

San Felix Island
(part of Chile)

San Ambrosio
Island
(part of Chile)

PARAGUAY

Tropic of Capricorn

CORAL SEA ISLANDS
(to Australia)

NORFOLK ISLAND
(to Australia)

Lord Howe Island
(part of Australia)

KERMADEC ISLAND
(part of NZ)

PITCAIRN
ISLANDS
(to UK)

Easter Island
(part of Chile)

Sala y Gomez
(part of Chile)

CHILE

URUGUAY

STRALIA

Juan Fernandez Island
(part of Chile)

ARGENTINA

Tasmania

NEW
ZEALAND

Chatham Island
(part of NZ)

P A C I F I C

Bounty Island
(part of NZ)

O C E A N

FALKLAND ISLANDS
(to UK)

Campbell Island
(part of NZ)

CHILE

Macquarie Island (part of Australia)

SOUTH GEORGIA &
SOUTH SANDWICH ISLANDS
(to UK)

Antarctic Circle

ANTARCTICA

KEY TO CONTINENTS

| NORTH & WEST ASIA | SOUTH & EAST ASIA | AUSTRALASIA & OCEANIA | NORTH & CENTRAL AMERICA | SOUTH AMERICA | EUROPE | AFRICA |

PHYSICAL MAP OF THE WORLD

THIS MAP shows the world's topographic relief both above and below sea level. Seas and oceans occupy around 70% of the Earth's total surface area of 197,000,000 sq. mi. (510,000,000 sq. km), whereas land covers a mere 57,500,000 sq. mi. (149,000,000 sq. km). While most land is found in the northern hemisphere, the only continents located exclusively in this region are North America and Europe. Similarly, only Australia and Antarctica are situated purely in the southern hemisphere. The circumference of the Earth at the equator is 24,900 miles (40,077 km) and the diameter from pole to pole is 7,900 miles (12,714 km).

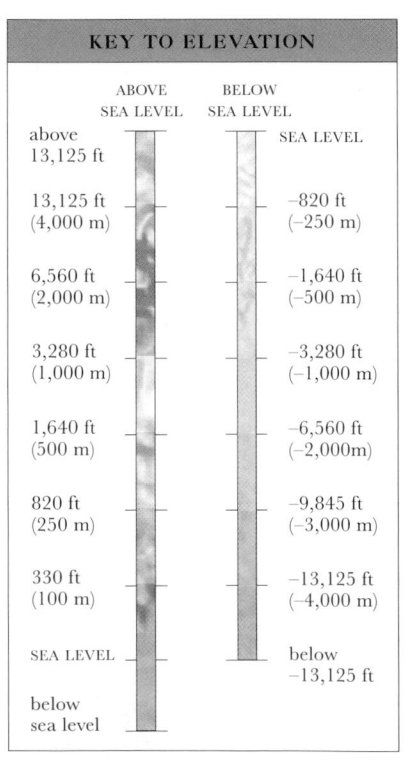

KEY TO ELEVATION

	ABOVE SEA LEVEL	BELOW SEA LEVEL	
above 13,125 ft			SEA LEVEL
13,125 ft (4,000 m)			–820 ft (–250 m)
6,560 ft (2,000 m)			–1,640 ft (–500 m)
3,280 ft (1,000 m)			–3,280 ft (–1,000 m)
1,640 ft (500 m)			–6,560 ft (–2,000m)
820 ft (250 m)			–9,845 ft (–3,000 m)
330 ft (100 m)			–13,125 ft (–4,000 m)
SEA LEVEL			below –13,125 ft
below sea level			

LARGEST CONTINENT	SMALLEST CONTINENT	LARGEST OCEAN	LARGEST ISLAND
ASIA 17,176,000 SQ. MILES (44,485,900 SQ. KM)	AUSTRALASIA 3,445,600 SQ. MILES (8,924,100 SQ. KM)	PACIFIC OCEAN 63,855,000 SQ. MILES (165,384,000 SQ. KM)	GREENLAND 839,852 SQ. MILES (2,175,219 SQ. KM)

DEEPEST OCEAN	TALLEST MOUNTAIN	LARGEST LAKE	LONGEST RIVER
MARIANA TRENCH, PACIFIC OCEAN 36,201 FT (11,034 M)	MT. EVEREST, CHINA/NEPAL 29,028 FT (8,848 M)	CASPIAN SEA, ASIA 146,111 SQ. MILES (378,400 SQ. KM)	NILE, AFRICA 4,160 MILES (6,693 KM)

POLITICAL MAP OF US AND CANADA

THE LARGEST countries in the North American continent, Canada and the US, share a long democratic tradition; both operate a federal state system in which political power is shared between national and local governments. Canada is made up of ten provinces and two territories. The US comprises fifty states, all except Alaska and Hawaii occupying central North America. Population densities are highest along the Pacific and Atlantic coasts of the US and in the Great Lakes area, but much of the far north is sparsely populated.

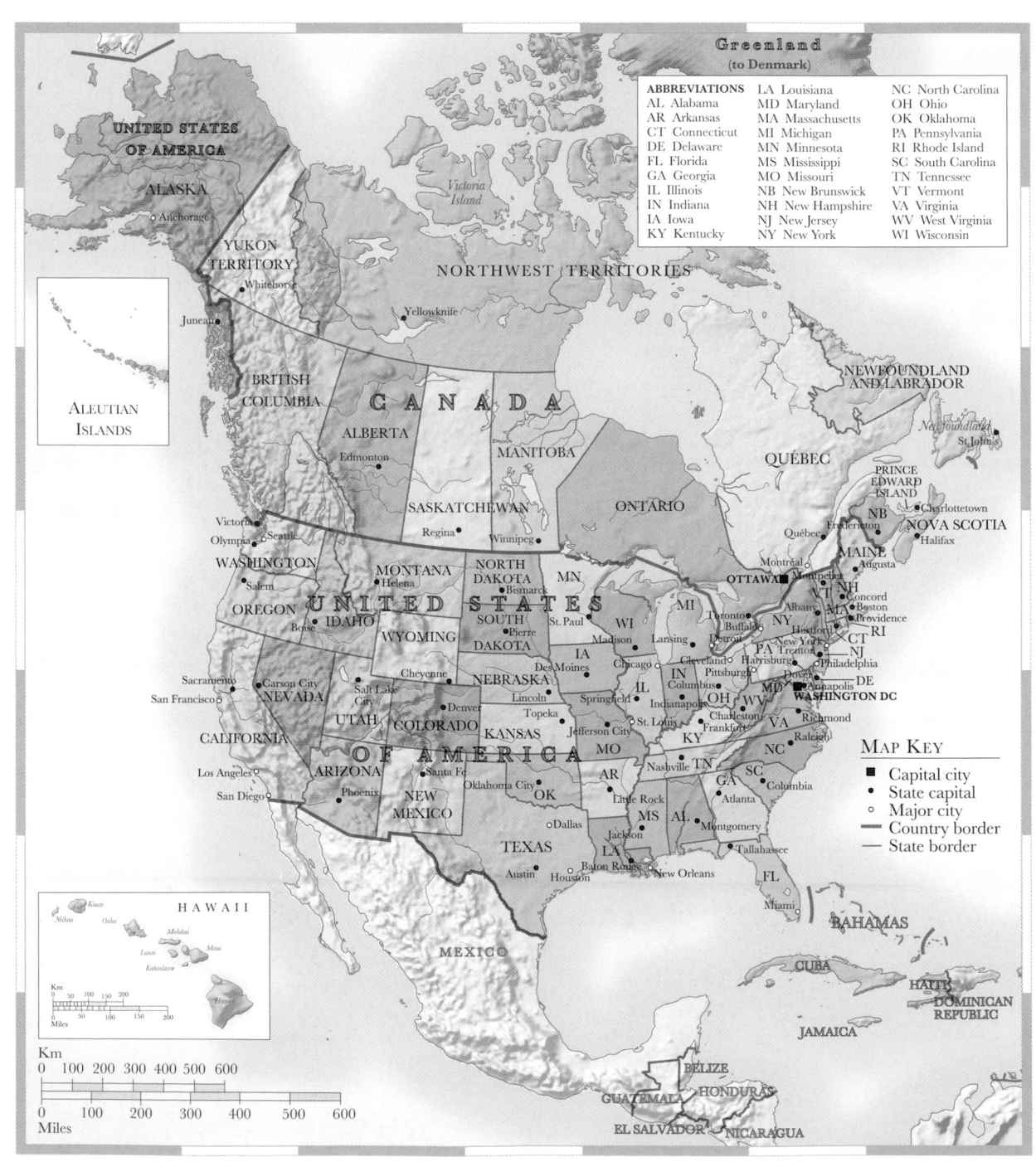

ABBREVIATIONS	LA Louisiana	NC North Carolina
AL Alabama	MD Maryland	OH Ohio
AR Arkansas	MA Massachusetts	OK Oklahoma
CT Connecticut	MI Michigan	PA Pennsylvania
DE Delaware	MN Minnesota	RI Rhode Island
FL Florida	MS Mississippi	SC South Carolina
GA Georgia	MO Missouri	TN Tennessee
IL Illinois	NB New Brunswick	VT Vermont
IN Indiana	NH New Hampshire	VA Virginia
IA Iowa	NJ New Jersey	WV West Virginia
KY Kentucky	NY New York	WI Wisconsin

MAP KEY

■ Capital city
• State capital
○ Major city
━ Country border
─ State border

PHYSICAL MAP OF NORTH AMERICA

NORTH AMERICA is the third largest continent, with an area of 9,358,340 sq. miles (24,238,000 sq. km). Between its two main mountain ranges – the Western Cordillera, running down from Alaska to Mexico, and the Appalachians on the east – lie the fertile Great Plains of central Canada and midwestern USA. The Great Lakes, linked to the Atlantic Ocean by the St. Lawrence Seaway, span the border between Canada and the USA. Further north, a plain known as the Canadian Shield extends from northern Canada to Greenland.

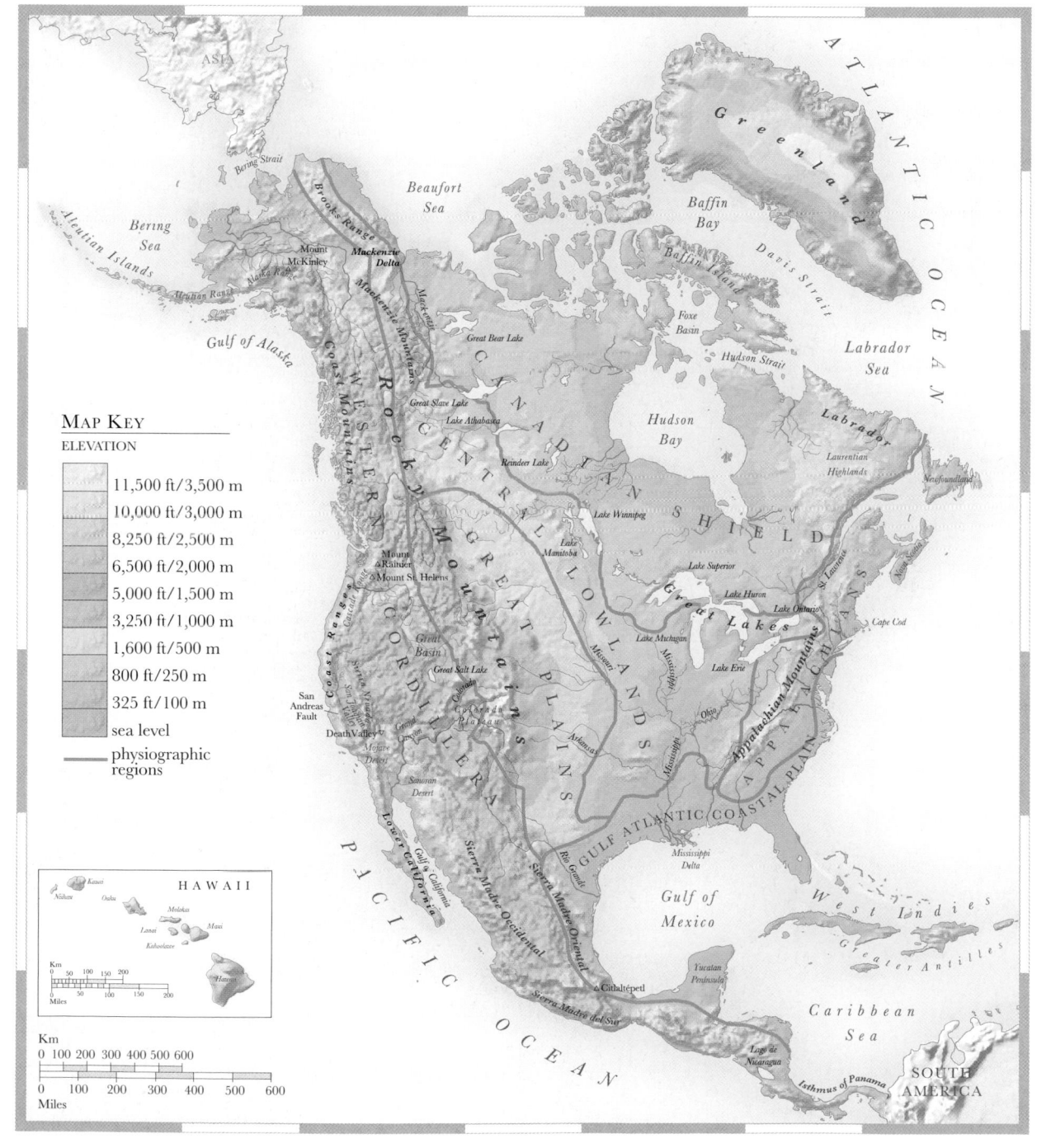

MAP KEY

ELEVATION

11,500 ft/3,500 m
10,000 ft/3,000 m
8,250 ft/2,500 m
6,500 ft/2,000 m
5,000 ft/1,500 m
3,250 ft/1,000 m
1,600 ft/500 m
800 ft/250 m
325 ft/100 m
sea level

—— physiographic regions

HAWAII

Kauai
Niihau
Oahu
Molokai
Lanai
Maui
Kahoolawe
Hawaii

Km
0 50 100 150 200
Miles
0 50 100 150 200

Km
0 100 200 300 400 500 600
Miles
0 100 200 300 400 500 600

COUNTRIES OF THE WORLD

THE FOLLOWING LIST OF COUNTRIES of the world has been researched from up-to-date sources and includes information correct at the time of publication. Each entry contains the flag of a country, the noun most widely used to describe a person from that country, the related adjective in general use, the country's currency unit, its capital, and its estimated total population. All population statistics were compiled in 1996, with the exception of the following, which are based on 1994 estimates: Andorra, Antigua and Barbuda, Dominica, Grenada, Kiribati, Liechtenstein, Marshall Islands, Micronesia, Monaco, Nauru, Palau, San Marino, São Tome and Principe, the Seychelles, St. Kitts and Nevis, St. Lucia, St. Vincent and the Grenadines, Taiwan, Tonga, Tuvalu, and Vatican City.

AFGHANISTAN

PERSON: Afghan
RELATED ADJ.: Afghan
CURRENCY: afghani = 100 puls
CAPITAL: Kabul
POPULATION: 21,500,000

ALBANIA
PERSON: Albanian
RELATED ADJ.: Albanian
CURRENCY: new lek = 100 qindarka
CAPITAL: Tirana
POPULATION: 3,500,000

ALGERIA
PERSON: Algerian
RELATED ADJ.: Algerian
CURRENCY: Algerian dinar = 100 centimes
CAPITAL: Algiers
POPULATION: 28,600,000

ANDORRA
PERSON: Andorran
RELATED ADJ.: Andorran
CURRENCY: French franc & Spanish peseta
CAPITAL: Andorra la Vella
POPULATION: 65,000

ANGOLA
PERSON: Angolan
RELATED ADJ.: Angolan
CURRENCY: new kwanza = 100 lwei
CAPITAL: Luanda
POPULATION: 11,500,000

ANTIGUA & BARBUDA
PERSON: Antiguan, Barbudan
RELATED ADJ.: Antiguan, Barbudan
CURRENCY: East Caribbean dollar = 100 cents
CAPITAL: St. John's
POPULATION: 65,000

ARGENTINA

PERSON: Argentinian
RELATED ADJ: Argentine/Argentinian
CURRENCY: Argentine peso = 10,000 australes
CAPITAL: Buenos Aires
POPULATION: 35,000,000

ARMENIA
PERSON: Armenian
RELATED ADJ.: Armenian
CURRENCY: dram = 100 luma
CAPITAL: Yerevan
POPULATION: 3,600,000

AUSTRALIA
PERSON: Australian
RELATED ADJ.: Australian
CURRENCY: Australian dollar = 100 cents
CAPITAL: Canberra
POPULATION: 18,300,000

AUSTRIA
PERSON: Austrian
RELATED ADJ.: Austrian
CURRENCY: euro = 100 cent
CAPITAL: Vienna
POPULATION: 8,000,000

AZERBAIJAN
PERSON: Azerbaijani
RELATED ADJ.: Azerbaijani
CURRENCY: manat = 100 gopik
CAPITAL: Baku
POPULATION: 7,600,000

BAHAMAS
PERSON: Bahamian
RELATED ADJ.: Bahamian
CURRENCY: Bahamian dollar = 100 cents
CAPITAL: Nassau
POPULATION: 300,000

BAHRAIN
PERSON: Bahraini
RELATED ADJ.: Bahraini
CURRENCY: Bahraini dinar = 1,000 fils
CAPITAL: Manama
POPULATION: 600,000

BANGLADESH

PERSON: Bangladeshi
RELATED ADJ.: Bangladeshi
CURRENCY: taka = 100 poisha
CAPITAL: Dhaka
POPULATION: 123,100,000

BARBADOS
PERSON: Barbadian
RELATED ADJ.: Barbadian
CURRENCY: Barbadian dollar = 100 cents
CAPITAL: Bridgetown
POPULATION: 300,000

BELARUS
PERSON: Belorussian/ Byelorussian
RELATED ADJ.: Belarusian; Belorussian
CURRENCY: Belorussian rouble
CAPITAL: Minsk **POPULATION:** 10,000,000

BELGIUM
PERSON: Belgian
RELATED ADJ.: Belgian
CURRENCY: euro = 100 centimes
CAPITAL: Brussels
POPULATION: 10,100,000

BELIZE

PERSON: Belizean
RELATED ADJ.: Belizean
CURRENCY: Belizean dollar = 100 cents
CAPITAL: Belmopan
POPULATION: 200,000

BENIN
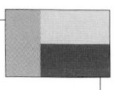
PERSON: Beninese
RELATED ADJ.: Beninese
CURRENCY: African franc
CAPITAL: Porto-Novo
POPULATION: 5,600,000

BHUTAN

PERSON: Bhutanese
RELATED ADJ.: Bhutanese
CURRENCY: ngultrum = 100 chetrum
CAPITAL: Thimphu
POPULATION: 1,700,000

BOLIVIA

PERSON: Bolivian
RELATED ADJ.: Bolivian
CURRENCY: Boliviano = 100 centavos
CAPITALS: La Paz, Sucre
POPULATION: 7,600,000

BOSNIA & HERZEGOVINA

PERSON: Bosnian; Herzegovinian
RELATED ADJ.: Bosnian; Herzegovinian
CURRENCY: Bosnian dinar = 100 paras
CAPITAL: Sarajevo **POPULATION:** 3,500,000

BOTSWANA

PERSON: Motswana (*pl.*Batswana)
RELATED ADJ.: Botswanan
CURRENCY: pula = 100 thebe
CAPITAL: Gaborone
POPULATION: 1,500,000

BRAZIL

PERSON: Brazilian
RELATED ADJ.: Brazilian
CURRENCY: real = 100 centavos
CAPITAL: Brasília
POPULATION: 164,400,000

BRUNEI

PERSON: Bruneian
RELATED ADJ.: Bruneian
CURRENCY: Bruneian dollar = 100 sen
CAPITAL: Bandar Seri Begawan
POPULATION: 300,000

BULGARIA

PERSON: Bulgarian
RELATED ADJ.: Bulgarian
CURRENCY: lev = 100 stotinki
CAPITAL: Sofia
POPULATION: 8,700,000

BURKINA

PERSON: Burkinese
RELATED ADJ.: Burkinese
CURRENCY: African franc
CAPITAL: Ouagadougou
POPULATION: 10,600,000

BURMA (MYANMAR)
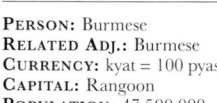
PERSON: Burmese
RELATED ADJ.: Burmese
CURRENCY: kyat = 100 pyas
CAPITAL: Rangoon
POPULATION: 47,500,000

BURUNDI

PERSON: Burundian
RELATED ADJ.: Burundian
CURRENCY: Burundian franc = 10 centimes
CAPITAL: Bujumbura
POPULATION: 6,600,000

CAMBODIA

PERSON: Cambodian
RELATED ADJ.: Cambodian
CURRENCY: riel = 100 sen
CAPITAL: Phnom Penh
POPULATION: 10,500,000

CAMEROON

PERSON: Cameroonian
RELATED ADJ.: Cameroonian
CURRENCY: African franc
CAPITAL: Yaoundé
POPULATION: 13,600,000

CANADA

PERSON: Canadian
RELATED ADJ.: Canadian
CURRENCY: Canadian dollar = 100 cents
CAPITAL: Ottawa
POPULATION: 29,800,000

CAPE VERDE

PERSON: Cape Verdean
RELATED ADJ.: Cape Verdean
CURRENCY: Cape Verdean escudo
CAPITAL: Praia
POPULATION: 400,000

CENTRAL AFRICAN REPUBLIC

PERSON: n/a
RELATED ADJ.: n/a
CURRENCY: African franc
CAPITAL: Bangui **POPULATION:** 3,400,000

CHAD

PERSON: Chadian
RELATED ADJ.: Chadian
CURRENCY: African franc
CAPITAL: N'Djamena
POPULATION: 6,500,000

CHILE

PERSON: Chilean
RELATED ADJ.: Chilean
CURRENCY: Chilean peso = 100 centavos
CAPITAL: Santiago
POPULATION: 14,500,000

CHINA

PERSON: Chinese
RELATED ADJ.: Chinese
CURRENCY: yuan = 10 jiao or 100 fen
CAPITAL: Beijing
POPULATION: 1,234,300,000

COLOMBIA
PERSON: Colombian
RELATED ADJ.: Colombian
CURRENCY: Colombian peso = 100 centavos
CAPITAL: Bogotá
POPULATION: 35,700,000

COMOROS

PERSON: Comoran
RELATED ADJ.: Comoran
CURRENCY: African franc
CAPITAL: Moroni
POPULATION: 700,000

CONGO

PERSON: Congolese
RELATED ADJ.: Congolese
CURRENCY: African franc
CAPITAL: Brazzaville
POPULATION: 2,700,000

CONGO (formerly ZAIRE)

PERSON: Congolese
RELATED ADJ.: Congolese
CURRENCY: new Zaire = 100 makuta
CAPITAL: Kinshasa
POPULATION: 45,300,000

COSTA RICA
PERSON: Costa Rican
RELATED ADJ.: Costa Rican
CURRENCY: colón = 100 centimos
CAPITAL: San José
POPULATION: 3,500,000

CROATIA

PERSON: Croat or Croatian
RELATED ADJ.: Croat or Croatian
CURRENCY: kuna = 100 lipa
CAPITAL: Zagreb
POPULATION: 4,500,000

CUBA

PERSON: Cuban
RELATED ADJ.: Cuban
CURRENCY: Cuban peso = 100 centavos
CAPITAL: Havana
POPULATION: 11,100,000

CYPRUS

PERSON: Cypriot
RELATED ADJ.: Cypriot
CURRENCY: Cypriot pound/Turkish lira
CAPITAL: Nicosia
POPULATION: 800,000

CZECH REPUBLIC

PERSON: Czech
RELATED ADJ.: Czech
CURRENCY: Czech koruna = 100 haleru
CAPITAL: Prague
POPULATION: 10,300,000

DENMARK

PERSON: Dane
RELATED ADJ.: Danish
CURRENCY: Danish krone = 100 øre
CAPITAL: Copenhagen
POPULATION: 5,200,000

DJIBOUTI

PERSON: Djiboutian
RELATED ADJ.: Djiboutian
CURRENCY: Djiboutian franc = 100 centimes
CAPITAL: Djibouti
POPULATION: 600,000

DOMINICA

PERSON: Dominican
RELATED ADJ.: Dominican
CURRENCY: East Caribbean dollar = 100 cents
CAPITAL: Roseau
POPULATION: 71,000

DOMINICAN REPUBLIC

PERSON: Dominican
RELATED ADJ.: Dominican
CURRENCY: Dominican peso = 100 centavos
CAPITAL: Santo Domingo
POPULATION: 8,000,000

ECUADOR

PERSON: Ecuadorean
RELATED ADJ.: Ecuadorean
CURRENCY: sucre = 100 centavos
CAPITAL: Quito
POPULATION: 11,700,000

EGYPT

PERSON: Egyptian
RELATED ADJ.: Egyptian
CURRENCY: Egyptian pound = 100 piastres
CAPITAL: Cairo
POPULATION: 64,200,000

EL SALVADOR

PERSON: Salvadorean
RELATED ADJ.: Salvadorean
CURRENCY: colón = 100 centavos
CAPITAL: San Salvador
POPULATION: 5,900,000

EQUATORIAL GUINEA

PERSON: Equatorial Guinean
RELATED ADJ.: Equatorial Guinean
CURRENCY: African franc
CAPITAL: Malabo
POPULATION: 400,000

ERITREA

PERSON: Eritrean
RELATED ADJ.: Eritrean
CURRENCY: Ethiopean birr = 100 cents
CAPITAL: Asmara
POPULATION: 3,600,000

ESTONIA

PERSON: Estonian
RELATED ADJ.: Estonian
CURRENCY: kroon = 100 sents
CAPITAL: Tallinn
POPULATION: 1,500,000

ETHIOPIA

PERSON: Ethiopian
RELATED ADJ.: Ethiopian
CURRENCY: birr = 100 cents
CAPITAL: Addis Ababa
POPULATION: 56,700,000

FIJI

PERSON: Fijian
RELATED ADJ.: Fijian
CURRENCY: Fijian dollar = 100 cents
CAPITAL: Suva
POPULATION: 800,000

FINLAND

PERSON: Finn
RELATED ADJ.: Finnish
CURRENCY: euro = 100 senttiä
CAPITAL: Helsinki
POPULATION: 5,100,000

FRANCE

PERSON: Frenchman/Frenchwoman
RELATED ADJ.: French
CURRENCY: euro = 100 centimes
CAPITAL: Paris
POPULATION: 58,200,000

GABON

PERSON: Gabonese
RELATED ADJ.: Gabonese
CURRENCY: African franc
CAPITAL: Libreville
POPULATION: 1,400,000

GAMBIA

PERSON: Gambian
RELATED ADJ.: Gambian
CURRENCY: dalasi = 100 butut
CAPITAL: Banjul
POPULATION: 1,200,000

GEORGIA

PERSON: Georgian
RELATED ADJ.: Georgian
CURRENCY: coupon
CAPITAL: T'bilisi
POPULATION: 5,500,000

GERMANY

PERSON: German
RELATED ADJ.: German
CURRENCY: euro = 100 cent
CAPITAL: Berlin
POPULATION: 81,800,000

GHANA

PERSON: Ghanaian
RELATED ADJ.: Ghanaian
CURRENCY: cedi = 100 pesewas
CAPITAL: Accra
POPULATION: 18,000,000

GREECE

PERSON: Greek
RELATED ADJ.: Greek
CURRENCY: euro = 100 lepta
CAPITAL: Athens
POPULATION: 10,500,000

GRENADA

PERSON: Grenadian
RELATED ADJ.: Grenadian
CURRENCY: East Caribbean dollar = 100 cents
CAPITAL: St. George's
POPULATION: 92,000

GUATEMALA

PERSON: Guatemalan
RELATED ADJ.: Guatemalan
CURRENCY: quetzal = 100 centavos
CAPITAL: Guatemala City
POPULATION: 10,900,000

GUINEA

PERSON: Guinean
RELATED ADJ.: Guinean
CURRENCY: Guinea franc = 100 centimes
CAPITAL: Conakry
POPULATION: 6,900,000

GUINEA-BISSAU

PERSON: Guinean
RELATED ADJ.: Guinean
CURRENCY: Guinean peso = 100 centavos
CAPITAL: Bissau
POPULATION: 1,100,000

GUYANA

PERSON: Guyanese
RELATED ADJ.: Guyanese
CURRENCY: Guyanese dollar = 100 cents
CAPITAL: Georgetown
POPULATION: 800,000

HAITI

PERSON: Haitian
RELATED ADJ.: Haitian
CURRENCY: gourde = 100 centimes
CAPITAL: Port-au-Prince
POPULATION: 7,300,000

HONDURAS

PERSON: Honduran
RELATED ADJ.: Honduran
CURRENCY: lempira = 100 centavos
CAPITAL: Tegucigalpa
POPULATION: 5,800,000

HUNGARY

PERSON: Hungarian
RELATED ADJ.: Hungarian
CURRENCY: forint = 100 filler
CAPITAL: Budapest
POPULATION: 10,100,000

ICELAND

PERSON: Icelander
RELATED ADJ.: Icelandic
CURRENCY: new Icelandic króna = 100 aurar
CAPITAL: Reykjavík
POPULATION: 300,000

INDIA

PERSON: Indian
RELATED ADJ.: Indian
CURRENCY: rupee = 100 paisa
CAPITAL: New Delhi
POPULATION: 953,000,000

INDONESIA

PERSON: Indonesian
RELATED ADJ.: Indonesian
CURRENCY: rupiah = 100 sen
CAPITAL: Jakarta
POPULATION: 200,600,000

IRAN

PERSON: Iranian
RELATED ADJ.: Iranian
CURRENCY: rial = 100 dinars
CAPITAL: Tehran
POPULATION: 68,700,000

IRAQ

PERSON: Iraqi
RELATED ADJ.: Iraqi
CURRENCY: Iraqi dinar = 1,000 fils
CAPITAL: Baghdad
POPULATION: 21,000,000

IRELAND, REPUBLIC OF
PERSON: Irishman/Irishwoman
RELATED ADJ.: Irish
CURRENCY: euro = 100 cents
CAPITAL: Dublin
POPULATION: 3,600,000

ISRAEL

PERSON: Israeli
RELATED ADJ.: Israeli
CURRENCY: shekel = 100 agora
CAPITAL: Jerusalem
POPULATION: 5,800,000

ITALY
PERSON: Italian
RELATED ADJ.: Italian
CURRENCY: euro = 100 centesemi
CAPITAL: Rome
POPULATION: 57,200,000

IVORY COAST
(also CÔTE D'IVOIRE)
PERSON: Ivorian **RELATED ADJ.:** Ivorian
CURRENCY: African franc
CAPITAL: Yamoussoukro
POPULATION: 14,700,000

JAMAICA
PERSON: Jamaican
RELATED ADJ.: Jamaican
CURRENCY: Jamaican dollar = 100 cents
CAPITAL: Kingston
POPULATION: 2,500,000

JAPAN

PERSON: Japanese
RELATED ADJ.: Japanese
CURRENCY: yen = 100 sen
CAPITAL: Tokyo
POPULATION: 125,400,000

JORDAN
PERSON: Jordanian
RELATED ADJ.: Jordanian
CURRENCY: Jordanian dinar = 1,000 fils
CAPITAL: Amman
POPULATION: 5,700,000

KAZAKHSTAN
PERSON: Kazakh
RELATED ADJ.: Kazakh
CURRENCY: tenge = 100 teins
CAPITAL: Akmola
POPULATION: 17,200,000

KENYA

PERSON: Kenyan
RELATED ADJ.: Kenyan
CURRENCY: Kenyan shilling = 100 cents
CAPITAL: Nairobi
POPULATION: 29,100,000

KIRIBATI

PERSON: Kiribati
RELATED ADJ.: Kiribati
CURRENCY: Australian dollar = 100 cents
CAPITAL: Tarawa
POPULATION: 77,000

KUWAIT

PERSON: Kuwaiti
RELATED ADJ.: Kuwaiti
CURRENCY: Kuwaiti dinar = 1,000 fils
CAPITAL: Kuwait
POPULATION: 1,500,000

KYRGYZSTAN

PERSON: Kyrgyz
RELATED ADJ.: Kyrgyz
CURRENCY: som
CAPITAL: Bishkek
POPULATION: 4,800,000

LAOS
PERSON: Laotian
RELATED ADJ.: Laotian
CURRENCY: kip = 100 ats
CAPITAL: Vientiane
POPULATION: 5,000,000

LATVIA
PERSON: Latvian
RELATED ADJ.: Latvian
CURRENCY: lat = 100 santims
CAPITAL: Riga
POPULATION: 2,500,000

LEBANON
PERSON: Lebanese
RELATED ADJ.: Lebanese
CURRENCY: Lebanese pound = 100 piastres
CAPITAL: Beirut
POPULATION: 3,100,000

LESOTHO

PERSON: Mosotho (*pl.* Basotho)
RELATED ADJ.: n/a
CURRENCY: loti = 100 lisente
CAPITAL: Maseru
POPULATION: 2,100,000

LIBERIA
PERSON: Liberian
RELATED ADJ.: Liberian
CURRENCY: Liberian dollar = 100 cents
CAPITAL: Monrovia
POPULATION: 3,100,000

LIBYA
PERSON: Libyan
RELATED ADJ.: Libyan
CURRENCY: Libyan dinar = 1,000 dirhams
CAPITAL: Tripoli
POPULATION: 5,600,000

LIECHTENSTEIN

PERSON: Liechtensteiner
RELATED ADJ.: Liechtenstein
CURRENCY: Swiss franc = 100 centimes
CAPITAL: Vaduz
POPULATION: 31,000

LITHUANIA
PERSON: Lithuanian
RELATED ADJ.: Lithuanian
CURRENCY: litas = 100 centas
CAPITAL: Vilnius
POPULATION: 3,700,000

LUXEMBOURG
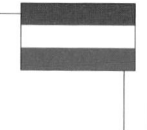
PERSON: Luxembourger
RELATED ADJ.: Luxembourg
CURRENCY: euro = 100 centimes
CAPITAL: Luxembourg
POPULATION: 400,000

MACEDONIA

PERSON: Macedonian
RELATED ADJ.: Macedonian
CURRENCY: Macedonian denar
CAPITAL: Skopje
POPULATION: 2,200,000

MADAGASCAR
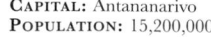
PERSON: Malagasay/Madagascan
RELATED ADJ.: Malagasay/Madagascan
CURRENCY: Malagasay franc = 100 centimes
CAPITAL: Antananarivo
POPULATION: 15,200,000

MALAWI

PERSON: Malawian
RELATED ADJ.: Malawian
CURRENCY: kwacha = 100 tambala
CAPITAL: Lilongwe
POPULATION: 11,400,000

MALAYSIA

PERSON: Malaysian
RELATED ADJ.: Malaysian
CURRENCY: ringgit = 11 sen
CAPITAL: Kuala Lumpur
POPULATION: 20,600,000

MALDIVES

PERSON: Maldivian
RELATED ADJ.: Maldivian
CURRENCY: rufiyaa = 100 laris
CAPITAL: Male
POPULATION: 300,000

MALI

PERSON: Malian
RELATED ADJ.: Malian
CURRENCY: African franc
CAPITAL: Bamako
POPULATION: 11,100,000

MALTA

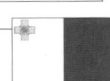

PERSON: Maltese
RELATED ADJ.: Maltese
CURRENCY: Maltese lira = 100 cents
CAPITAL: Valletta
POPULATION: 400,000

MARSHALL ISLANDS

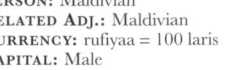

PERSON: n/a
RELATED ADJ.: n/a
CURRENCY: US dollar
CAPITAL: Majuro
POPULATION: 54,000

MAURITANIA

PERSON: Mauritanian
RELATED ADJ.: Mauritanian
CURRENCY: ouguiya = 5 khoums
CAPITAL: Nouakchott
POPULATION: 2,300,000

MAURITIUS

PERSON: Mauritian
RELATED ADJ.: Mauritian
CURRENCY: Mauritian rupee = 100 cents
CAPITAL: Port Louis
POPULATION: 1,100,000

MEXICO

PERSON: Mexican
RELATED ADJ.: Mexican
CURRENCY: Mexican new peso = 100 centavos
CAPITAL: Mexico City
POPULATION: 95,500,000

MICRONESIA

PERSON: Micronesian
RELATED ADJ.: Micronesian
CURRENCY: US dollar
CAPITAL: Kolonia
POPULATION: 104,000

MOLDOVA

PERSON: Moldovan
RELATED ADJ.: Moldovan
CURRENCY: leu = 100 bani
CAPITAL: Chişinău
POPULATION: 4,400,000

MONACO

PERSON: Monégasque/Monacan
RELATED ADJ.: Monégasque/Monacan
CURRENCY: French franc = 100 centimes
CAPITAL: Monaco
POPULATION: 31,000

MONGOLIA

PERSON: Mongolian
RELATED ADJ.: Mongolian
CURRENCY: tugrik = 100 mongos
CAPITAL: Ulaanbaatar
POPULATION: 2,500,000

MOROCCO

PERSON: Moroccan
RELATED ADJ.: Moroccan
CURRENCY: Moroccan dirham = 100 centimes
CAPITAL: Rabat
POPULATION: 27,600,000

MOZAMBIQUE

PERSON: Mozambican
RELATED ADJ.: Mozambican
CURRENCY: metical = 100 centavos
CAPITAL: Maputo
POPULATION: 16,500,000

NAMIBIA

PERSON: Namibian
RELATED ADJ.: Namibian
CURRENCY: South African rand = 100 cents
CAPITAL: Windhoek
POPULATION: 1,600,000

NAURU

PERSON: Nauruan
RELATED ADJ.: Nauruan
CURRENCY: Australian dollar
CAPITAL: Yaren District
POPULATION: 11,000

NEPAL

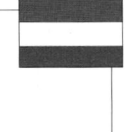

PERSON: Nepalese
RELATED ADJ.: Nepalese
CURRENCY: Nepalese rupee = 100 paisa
CAPITAL: Kathmandu
POPULATION: 22,500,000

NETHERLANDS

PERSON: Dutchman/Dutchwoman
RELATED ADJ.: Dutch
CURRENCY: euro = 100 cent
CAPITALS: Amsterdam, The Hague
POPULATION: 15,600,000

NEW ZEALAND

PERSON: New Zealander
RELATED ADJ.: New Zealand
CURRENCY: New Zealand dollar = 100 cents
CAPITAL: Wellington
POPULATION: 3,600,000

NICARAGUA

PERSON: Nicaraguan
RELATED ADJ.: Nicaraguan
CURRENCY: cordoba = 100 centavos
CAPITAL: Managua
POPULATION: 4,600,000

NIGER

PERSON: Nigerien
RELATED ADJ.: Nigerien
CURRENCY: African franc
CAPITAL: Niamey
POPULATION: 9,500,000

NIGERIA

PERSON: Nigerian
RELATED ADJ.: Nigerian
CURRENCY: naira = 100 kobo
CAPITAL: Abuja
POPULATION: 115,000,000

NORTH KOREA

PERSON: North Korean
RELATED ADJ.: North Korean
CURRENCY: won = 100 jun
CAPITAL: Pyongyang
POPULATION: 24,300,000

NORWAY

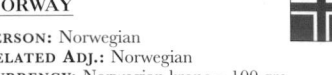

PERSON: Norwegian
RELATED ADJ.: Norwegian
CURRENCY: Norwegian krone = 100 øre
CAPITAL: Oslo
POPULATION: 4,400,000

OMAN

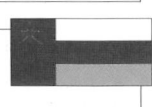

PERSON: Omani
RELATED ADJ.: Omani
CURRENCY: rial = 1,000 baiza
CAPITAL: Muscat
POPULATION: 2,300,000

PAKISTAN

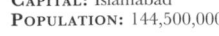

PERSON: Pakistani
RELATED ADJ.: Pakistani
CURRENCY: Pakistani rupee = 100 paisa
CAPITAL: Islamabad
POPULATION: 144,500,000

PALAU

PERSON: Palauan
RELATED ADJ.: Palauan
CURRENCY: US dollar
CAPITAL: Koror
POPULATION: 16,500

PANAMA

PERSON: Panamanian
RELATED ADJ.: Panamanian
CURRENCY: balboa = 100 centésimos
CAPITAL: Panama City
POPULATION: 2,700,000

PAPUA NEW GUINEA

PERSON: Papua New Guinean
RELATED ADJ.: Papua New Guinean
CURRENCY: kina = 100 toea
CAPITAL: Port Moresby
POPULATION: 4,400,000

PARAGUAY

PERSON: Paraguayan
RELATED ADJ.: Paraguayan
CURRENCY: guaraní = 100 centimos
CAPITAL: Asunción
POPULATION: 5,100,000

PERU

PERSON: Peruvian
RELATED ADJ.: Peruvian
CURRENCY: New sol = 100 cents
CAPITAL: Lima
POPULATION: 24,200,000

PHILIPPINES

PERSON: Filipino/Filipina
RELATED ADJ.: Filipino/Philippine
CURRENCY: Philippine peso = 100 centavos
CAPITAL: Manila
POPULATION: 69,000,000

POLAND

PERSON: Pole
RELATED ADJ.: Polish
CURRENCY: zloty = 100 groszy
CAPITAL: Warsaw
POPULATION: 38,400,000

PORTUGAL

PERSON: Portuguese
RELATED ADJ.: Portuguese
CURRENCY: euro = cêntimos
CAPITAL: Lisbon
POPULATION: 9,800,000

QATAR

PERSON: Qatari
RELATED ADJ.: Qatari
CURRENCY: Qatar riyal = 100 dirhams
CAPITAL: Doha
POPULATION: 600,000

ROMANIA

PERSON: Romanian
RELATED ADJ.: Romanian
CURRENCY: leu = 100 bani
CAPITAL: Bucharest
POPULATION: 22,800,000

RUSSIA

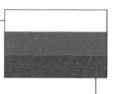

PERSON: Russian
RELATED ADJ.: Russian
CURRENCY: rouble = 100 copecks
CAPITAL: Moscow
POPULATION: 146,700,000

RWANDA

PERSON: Rwandan
RELATED ADJ.: Rwandan
CURRENCY: Rwandan franc
CAPITAL: Kigali
POPULATION: 8,200,000

ST. KITTS & NEVIS

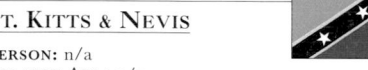

PERSON: n/a
RELATED ADJ.: n/a
CURRENCY: East Caribbean dollar = 100 cents
CAPITAL: Basseterre
POPULATION: 41,000

ST. LUCIA

PERSON: St Lucian
RELATED ADJ.: St Lucian
CURRENCY: East Caribbean dollar = 100 cents
CAPITAL: Castries
POPULATION: 141,000

ST. VINCENT & THE GRENADINES

PERSON: Vincentian/Grenadian
RELATED ADJ.: Vincentian/Grenadian
CURRENCY: East Caribbean dollar = 100 cents
CAPITAL: Kingstown **POPULATION:** 111,000

SAMOA (WESTERN SAMOA)

PERSON: Samoan
RELATED ADJ.: Samoan
CURRENCY: tala = 100 sene
CAPITAL: Apia **POPULATION:** 200,000

SAN MARINO

PERSON: n/a
RELATED ADJ.: n/a
CURRENCY: Italian lira
CAPITAL: San Marino
POPULATION: 25,000

SÃO TOME & PRINCIPE

PERSON: n/a
RELATED ADJ.: n/a
CURRENCY: dobra = 100 centavos
CAPITAL: São Tomé **POPULATION:** 125,000

SAUDI ARABIA

PERSON: Saudi Arabian/Saudi
RELATED ADJ.: Saudi Arabian/Saudi
CURRENCY: Saudi riyal = 20 qursh
CAPITAL: Riyadh
POPULATION: 18,400,000

SENEGAL

PERSON: Senegalese
RELATED ADJ.: Senegalese
CURRENCY: African franc
CAPITAL: Dakar
POPULATION: 8,500,000

SEYCHELLES

PERSON: Seychellois
RELATED ADJ.: Seychelles
CURRENCY: Seychellois rupee = 100 cents
CAPITAL: Victoria
POPULATION: 74,000

SIERRA LEONE

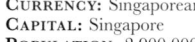

PERSON: Sierra Leonean
RELATED ADJ.: Sierra Leonean
CURRENCY: leone = 100 cents
CAPITAL: Freetown
POPULATION: 4,600,000

SINGAPORE

PERSON: Singaporean
RELATED ADJ.: Singaporean
CURRENCY: Singaporean dollar = 100 cents
CAPITAL: Singapore
POPULATION: 2,900,000

SLOVAKIA

PERSON: Slovak
RELATED ADJ.: Slovak
CURRENCY: koruna = 100 haleru
CAPITAL: Bratislava
POPULATION: 5,400,000

SLOVENIA

PERSON: Slovene/Slovenian
RELATED ADJ.: Slovene/Slovenian
CURRENCY: tolar = 100 stotins
CAPITAL: Ljubljana
POPULATION: 1,900,000

SOLOMON ISLANDS

PERSON: Solomon Islander
RELATED ADJ.: n/a
CURRENCY: Solomon Islands dollar = 100 cents
CAPITAL: Honiara
POPULATION: 400,000

SOMALIA

PERSON: Somali
RELATED ADJ.: Somali
CURRENCY: Somali shilling = 100 cents
CAPITAL: Mogadishu
POPULATION: 9,500,000

SOUTH AFRICA

PERSON: South African
RELATED ADJ.: South African
CURRENCY: rand = 100 cents
CAPITALS: Pretoria, Cape Town, Bloemfontein
POPULATION: 42,400,000

SOUTH KOREA

PERSON: South Korean
RELATED ADJ.: South Korean
CURRENCY: won = 100 jeon
CAPITAL: Seoul
POPULATION: 45,400,000

SPAIN

PERSON: Spaniard
RELATED ADJ.: Spanish
CURRENCY: euro = 100 céntimos
CAPITAL: Madrid
POPULATION: 39,700,000

SRI LANKA

PERSON: Sri Lankan
RELATED ADJ.: Sri Lankan
CURRENCY: Sri Lankan rupee = 100 cents
CAPITAL: Colombo
POPULATION: 18,600,000

SUDAN

PERSON: Sudanese
RELATED ADJ.: Sudanese
CURRENCY: Sudanese dinar = 10 pounds
CAPITAL: Khartoum
POPULATION: 28,900,000

SURINAM

PERSON: Surinamer/Surinamese
RELATED ADJ.: Surinamese
CURRENCY: Surinamese guilder = 100 cents
CAPITAL: Paramaribo
POPULATION: 400,000

SWAZILAND
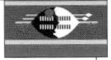
PERSON: Swazi
RELATED ADJ.: Swazi
CURRENCY: lilangeni = 100 cents
CAPITAL: Mbabane
POPULATION: 900,000

SWEDEN
PERSON: Swede
RELATED ADJ.: Swedish
CURRENCY: Swedish krona = 100 øre
CAPITAL: Stockholm
POPULATION: 8,800,000

SWITZERLAND
PERSON: Swiss
RELATED ADJ.: Swiss
CURRENCY: Swiss franc = 100 centimes
CAPITAL: Bern
POPULATION: 7,300,000

SYRIA

PERSON: Syrian
RELATED ADJ.: Syrian
CURRENCY: Syrian pound = 100 piastres
CAPITAL: Damascus
POPULATION: 15,200,000

TAIWAN

PERSON: Taiwanese
RELATED ADJ.: Taiwanese
CURRENCY: new Taiwanese dollar = 100 cents
CAPITAL: Taipei
POPULATION: 21,125,792

TAJIKISTAN

PERSON: Tajik
RELATED ADJ.: Tajik
CURRENCY: Russian rouble
CAPITAL: Dushanbe
POPULATION: 6,300,000

TANZANIA

PERSON: Tanzanian
RELATED ADJ.: Tanzanian
CURRENCY: Tanzanian shilling = 100 cents
CAPITAL: Dar es Salaam; Dodoma
POPULATION: 30,500,000

THAILAND

PERSON: Thai
RELATED ADJ.: Thai
CURRENCY: baht = 100 satangs
CAPITAL: Bangkok
POPULATION: 59,400,000

TOGO

PERSON: Togolese
RELATED ADJ.: Togolese
CURRENCY: African franc
CAPITAL: Lomé
POPULATION: 4,300,000

TONGA
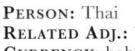
PERSON: Tongan
RELATED ADJ.: Tongan
CURRENCY: pa'anga = 100 seniti
CAPITAL: Nuku'alofa
POPULATION: 98,000

TRINIDAD & TOBAGO

PERSON: Trinidadian/Tobagonian
RELATED ADJ.: Trinidadian and/or Tobagonian
CURRENCY: Trinidadian dollar = 100 cents
CAPITAL: Port-of-Spain
POPULATION: 1,300,000

TUNISIA

PERSON: Tunisian
RELATED ADJ.: Tunisian
CURRENCY: Tunisian dinar = 1,000 milliemes
CAPITAL: Tunis
POPULATION: 9,100,000

TURKEY

PERSON: Turk
RELATED ADJ.: Turkish
CURRENCY: Turkish lira = 100 kurus
CAPITAL: Ankara
POPULATION: 63,100,000

TURKMENISTAN

PERSON: Turkmen/Turkoman
RELATED ADJ.: Turkmen/Turkoman
CURRENCY: manat = 100 tenge
CAPITAL: Ashgabat
POPULATION: 4,200,000

TUVALU

PERSON: Tuvaluan
RELATED ADJ.: Tuvaluan
CURRENCY: Tuvaluan dollar = 100 cents
CAPITAL: Funafuti
POPULATION: 9,000

UGANDA

PERSON: Ugandan
RELATED ADJ.: Ugandan
CURRENCY: Ugandan shilling = 100 cents
CAPITAL: Kampala
POPULATION: 22,000,000

UKRAINE

PERSON: Ukrainian
RELATED ADJ.: Ukrainian
CURRENCY: karbovanet (coupon)
CAPITAL: Kiev
POPULATION: 51,300,000

UNITED ARAB EMIRATES

PERSON: n/a
RELATED ADJ.: n/a
CURRENCY: UAE dirham = 100 fils
CAPITAL: Abu Dhabi **POPULATION:** 1,900,000

UNITED KINGDOM

PERSON: Briton
RELATED ADJ.: British
CURRENCY: pound sterling = 100 pence
CAPITAL: London
POPULATION: 58,400,000

UNITED STATES

PERSON: American
RELATED ADJ.: American
CURRENCY: dollar = 100 cents
CAPITAL: Washington, DC
POPULATION: 265,800,000

URUGUAY
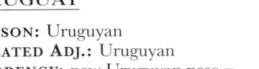
PERSON: Uruguyan
RELATED ADJ.: Uruguyan
CURRENCY: new Uruguyan peso = 100 centésimos
CAPITAL: Montevideo **POPULATION:** 3,200,000

UZBEKISTAN
PERSON: Uzbek
RELATED ADJ.: Uzbek
CURRENCY: som
CAPITAL: Tashkent
POPULATION: 23,300,000

VANUATU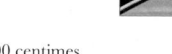
PERSON: n/a
RELATED ADJ.: n/a
CURRENCY: vatu = 100 centimes
CAPITAL: Port-Vila
POPULATION: 200,000

VATICAN CITY
PERSON: n/a
RELATED ADJ.: Vatican
CURRENCY: lira
CAPITAL: n/a
POPULATION: 1,000

VENEZUELA
PERSON: Venezuelan
RELATED ADJ.: Venezuelan
CURRENCY: bolivar = 100 centimos
CAPITAL: Caracas
POPULATION: 22,300,000

VIETNAM
PERSON: Vietnamese
RELATED ADJ.: Vietnamese
CURRENCY: dong = 10 hao
CAPITAL: Hanoi
POPULATION: 76,200,000

YEMEN
PERSON: Yemeni
RELATED ADJ.: Yemeni
CURRENCY: rial (north), dinar (south)
CAPITAL: Sana
POPULATION: 15,100,000

YUGOSLAVIA (SERBIA & MONTENEGRO)
PERSON: Yugoslav; Serb; Montenegran
RELATED ADJ.: Yugoslav; Serbian; Montenegran
CURRENCY: dinar = 100 paras
CAPITAL: Belgrade **POPULATION:** 10,900,000

ZAMBIA
PERSON: Zambian
RELATED ADJ.: Zambian
CURRENCY: kwacha = 100 ngwee
CAPITAL: Lusaka
POPULATION: 9,700,000

ZIMBABWE
PERSON: Zimbabwean
RELATED ADJ.: Zimbabwean
CURRENCY: Zimbabwean dollar = 100 cents
CAPITAL: Harare
POPULATION: 11,500,000

THE NIGHT SKY

THE NIGHT SKY may be visualized as the inside of an imaginary sphere (often referred to as the celestial sphere), which is divided into northern and southern hemispheres. At the north pole, an observer would see all stars of the northern hemisphere during the course of a year; similarly, an observer at the south pole would see all the stars of the southern hemisphere. In practice, most observers will see a combination of stars from both hemispheres – depending on their precise latitude. The position of the north celestial pole is indicated by the moderately bright star Polaris (the polestar).

HOW A NORTHERN HEMISPHERE SKY MAP WORKS

northern celestial sphere is projected on to flat surface (sky map)

north celestial pole

northern half of celestial sphere

Earth

celestial equator

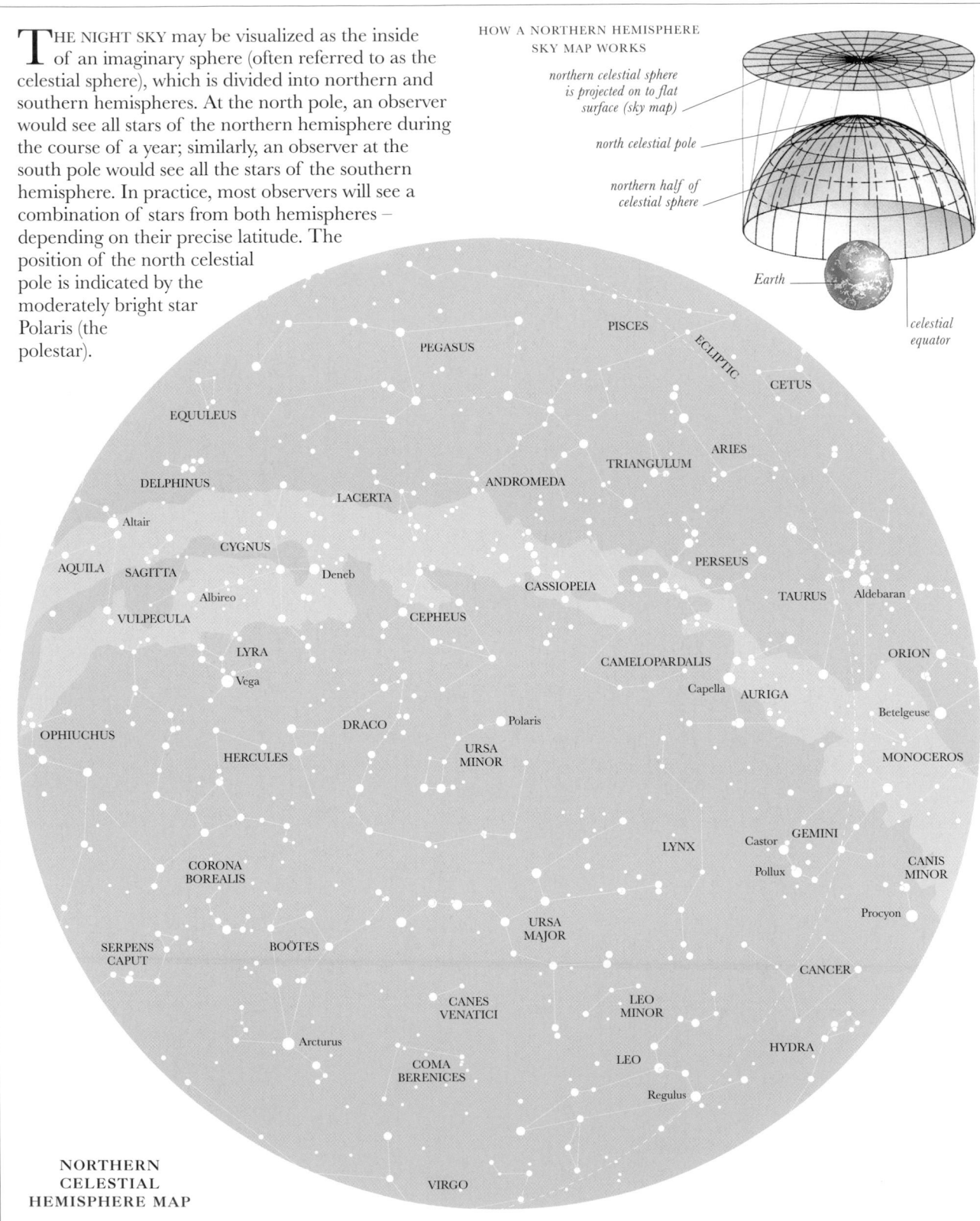

NORTHERN CELESTIAL HEMISPHERE MAP

WHILE STARS IN THE southern hemisphere appear to rotate around the south celestial pole, there is no equivalent of Polaris to mark the position of the southern pole. An observer of the southern celestial hemisphere is looking towards the center of our galaxy. Since stars in that direction are more densely massed, southern skies appear brighter than those in the northern hemisphere. The southern sky includes Crux (the Southern Cross), as well as the brightest star in the sky, Sirius, located in the constellation Canis Major. It also contains Alpha Centauri, one of the stars nearest to the Sun.

HOW A SOUTHERN HEMISPHERE SKY MAP WORKS

Earth

celestial equator

southern half of celestial sphere

south celestial pole

southern celestial sphere is projected on to flat surface (sky map)

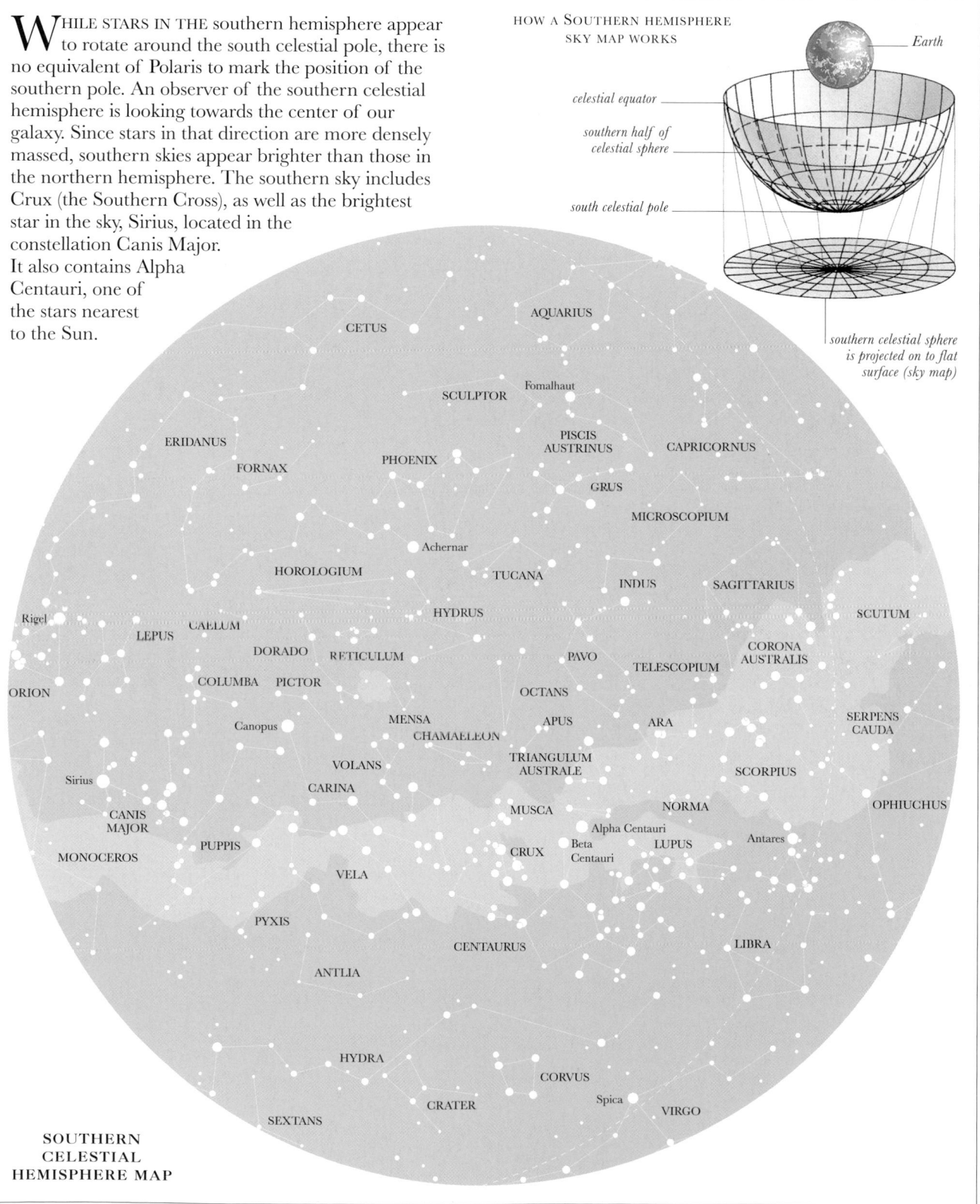

SOUTHERN CELESTIAL HEMISPHERE MAP

MEASUREMENTS

STANDARD AND BRITISH (IMPERIAL), WITH METRIC EQUIVALENTS

LINEAR MEASURE
1 inch = 25.4 millimeters exactly
1 foot = 12 inches = 0.3048 meter exactly
1 yard = 3 feet = 0.9144 meter exactly
1 (statute) mile = 1.609 kilometers = 1,760 yards
1 int. nautical mile = 1.852 kilometers
= 1.150779 miles exactly

SQUARE MEASURE
1 square inch = 6.45 sq. cm
1 square foot = 144 sq. in. = 9.29 sq. decimeters
1 square yard = 9 sq. ft. = 0.836 sq. meter
1 acre = 4,840 sq. yd. = 0.405 hectare
1 square mile = 640 acres = 259 hectares

CUBIC MEASURE
1 cubic inch = 16.4 cu. cm
1 cubic foot = 1,728 cu. in. = 0.0283 cu. meter
1 cubic yard = 27 cu. ft. = 0.765 cu. meter

CAPACITY MEASURE
AMERICAN LIQUID
1 fluid oz. = 0.0296 liter
1 pint = 16 fluid oz. = 28.88 cu. in. = 0.473 liter
1 quart = 2 pints = 0.946 liter
1 gallon = 4 quarts = 3.785 liters

BRITISH
1 fluid oz. = 1.8047 cu. in. = 0.0282 liter
1 gill = 5 fluid oz. = 0.1421 liter
1 pint = 20 fluid oz. = 34.68 cu. in. = 0.568 liter
1 quart = 2 pints = 1.136 liters
1 gallon = 4 quarts = 4.546 liters
1 peck = 2 gallons = 9.092 liters
1 bushel = 4 pecks = 36.4 liters

AMERICAN DRY
1 pint = 33.60 cu. in. = 0.550 liter
1 quart = 2 pints = 1.101 liters
1 peck = 8 quarts = 8.81 liters
1 bushel = 4 pecks = 35.3 liters

AVOIRDUPOIS WEIGHT
1 grain = 0.065 gram
1 dram = 1.772 grams
1 ounce = 16 drams = 28.35 grams
1 pound = 16 ounces = 7,000 grains
= 0.4536 kilogram (0.45359237 exactly)
1 stone = 14 pounds = 6.35 kilograms
1 hundredweight = 112 pounds
= 50.80 kilograms
1 short ton = 2,000 pounds = 0.907 tonne
1 (long) ton = 20 hundredweight = 1.016 tonnes

METRIC MEASURES, WITH STANDARD EQUIVALENTS

LINEAR MEASURE
1 millimeter = 0.039 inch
1 centimeter = 10 mm = 0.394 inch
1 decimeter = 10 cm = 3.94 inches
1 meter = 100 cm = 1.094 yards
1 kilometer = 1,000 m = 0.6214 mile

SQUARE MEASURE
1 square centimeter = 0.155 sq. inch
1 square meter = 10,000 sq. cm = 1.196 sq. yards
1 are = 100 sq. m = 119.6 sq. yards
1 hectare = 100 ares = 2.471 acres
1 square kilometer = 100 hectares = 0.386 sq. mile

CUBIC MEASURE
1 cubic centimeter = 0.061 cu. inch
1 cubic meter = 1,000,000 cu. cm = 1.308 cu. yards

CAPACITY MEASURE
1 milliliter = 0.034 fluid oz.
1 centiliter = 10 ml = 0.34 fluid oz.
1 deciliter = 10 cl = 3.38 fluid oz.
1 liter = 1,000 ml = 33.8 fluid oz.
1 decaliter = 10 l = 2.64 gallons
1 hectoliter = 100 l = 2.75 bushels
1 kiloliter = 1,000 l = 3.44 quarters

WEIGHT
1 milligram = 0.015 grain
1 centigram = 10 mg = 0.154 grain
1 decigram = 100 mg = 1.543 grains
1 gram = 1,000 mg = 15.43 grains
1 decagram = 10 g = 5.64 drams
1 hectogram = 100 g = 3.527 ounces
1 kilogram = 1,000 g = 2.205 pounds
1 tonne (metric ton) = 1,000 kg = 0.984 (long) ton

METRIC PREFIXES

NAME	ABBREVIATION	FACTOR
deca-	da	10
hecto-	h	10^2
kilo-	k	10^3
mega-	M	10^6
giga-	G	10^9
tera-	T	10^{12}
peta-	P	10^{15}
exa-	E	10^{18}
deci-	d	10^{-1}
centi-	c	10^{-2}
milli-	m	10^{-3}
micro-	μ	10^{-6}
nano-	n	10^{-9}
pico-	p	10^{-12}
femto-	f	10^{-15}
atto-	a	10^{-18}

The metric prefixes may be applied
to any units of the metric system:

hectogram (abbr. hg) = 100 grams
kilowatt (abbr. kW) = 1,000 watts
megahertz (MHz) = 1 million hertz
centimeter (cm) = 1/100 meter
microvolt (μV) = one millionth of a volt
picofarad (pF) = 10^{-12} farad

Some of these prefixes are also applied to
other units (gigabyte, microinch).

SI UNITS

BASE UNITS

PHYSICAL QUANTITY	NAME	ABBREVIATION/SYMBOL
length	meter	m
mass	kilogram	kg
time	second	s
electric current	ampere	A
temperature	kelvin	K
amount of substance	mole	mol
luminous intensity	candela	cd

SUPPLEMENTARY UNITS

PHYSICAL QUANTITY	NAME	ABBREVIATION/SYMBOL
plane angle	radian	rad
solid angle	steradian	sr

DERIVED UNITS WITH SPECIAL NAMES

PHYSICAL QUANTITY	NAME	ABBREVIATION/SYMBOL
frequency	hertz	Hz
energy	joule	J
force	newton	N
power	watt	W
pressure	pascal	Pa
electric charge	coulomb	C
electromotive force	volt	V
electric resistance	ohm	Ω
electric conductance	siemens	S
electric capacitance	farad	F
magnetic flux	weber	Wb
inductance	henry	H
magnetic flux density	tesla	T
luminous flux	lumen	lm
illumination	lux	lx

TEMPERATURE

CELSIUS OR CENTIGRADE
water boils at 100° and freezes at 0°.

FAHRENHEIT
water boils (under standard conditions) at 212° and freezes at 32°.

KELVIN
water boils at 373.15 K and freezes at 273.15 K.

TO CONVERT FAHRENHEIT INTO CELSIUS:
subtract 32, multiply by 5, and divide by 9.

TO CONVERT CELSIUS INTO FAHRENHEIT:
multiply by 9, divide by 5, and add 32.

TO CONVERT CENTIGRADE INTO KELVIN:
add 273.15.

TEMPERATURE CONVERSION

Celsius	−20	−10	0	10	20	30	40	50	60	70	80	90	100
Fahrenheit	−4	14	32	50	68	86	104	122	140	158	176	194	212
Kelvin	253	263	273	283	293	303	313	323	333	343	353	363	373

TEMPERATURE SCALE

°C →	°F	°F →	°C
−40	−40	−40	−40
−10	14	−10	−23
0	32	0	−18
10	50	10	−12
20	68	20	−7
30	86	30	−1
40	104	40	4
50	122	50	10
60	140	60	16
70	158	70	21
80	176	80	27
90	194	90	32
100	212	100	38
	(exact)		(approx.)

POWER NOTATION

This expresses concisely any power of 10 (any number that is formed by multiplying or dividing ten by itself), and is sometimes used in the main dictionary.

10^2 (ten squared) = 10 × 10 = 100
10^3 (ten cubed) = 10 × 10 × 10 = 1,000
10^4 = 10 × 10 × 10 × 10 = 10,000
10^{10} = 10,000,000,000
(1 followed by ten zeroes)
$10^{-2} = 1/10^2 = 1/100 = 0.01$
$10^{-10} = 1/10^{10} = 1/10{,}000{,}000{,}000$
= 0.0000001
$6.2 \times 10^3 = 6{,}200$
$4.7 \times 10^{-2} = 0.047$

INT'L. PAPER SIZES

International paper sizes are based upon a rectangle of paper with an area of one square meter, the sides of which are in the proportion 1:√2. This geometrical relationship is used so that any lengthways halving of the original rectangle of paper produces another rectangle of paper with the same geometric relationship. For example, the widely used A series is shown below. A4 size (8.19 × 11.583 in.) is very similar to US letter size.

A0 841 × 1189 mm	A6 105 × 148 mm
A1 594 × 841 mm	A7 74 × 105 mm
A2 420 × 594 mm	A8 52 × 74 mm
A3 297 × 420 mm	A9 37 × 52 mm
A4 210 × 297 mm	A10 26 × 37 mm
A5 148 × 210 mm	

A0

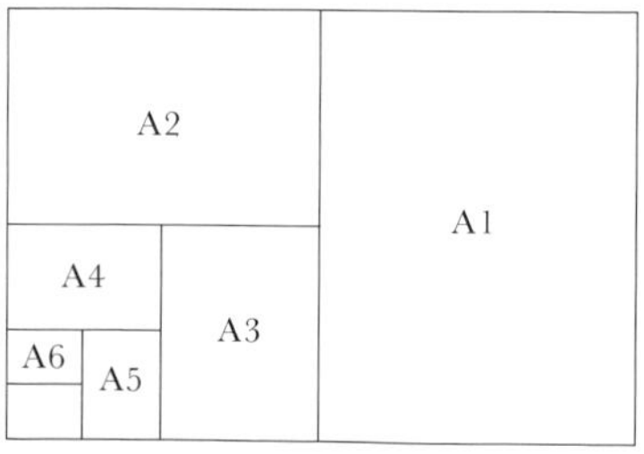

CLOTHING SIZES

MEN'S SHOES

US	UK	EUROPE
7	6½	39
7½	7	40
8	7½	41
8½	8	42
9	8½	43
10	9½	44
10½	10	44
11	10½	45

WOMEN'S SHOES

US	UK	EUROPE
5	3½	36
6	4½	37
7	5½	38
8	6½	39
9	7½	40

CHILDREN'S SHOES

US	UK	EUROPE
0	0	15
1	1	17
2	2	18
3	3	19
4	4	20
4½	4½	21
5	5	22
6	6	23
7	7	24
8	8	25
8½	8½	26
9	9	27
10	10	28
11	11	29
12	12	30
12½	12½	31
13	13	32

MEN'S SUITS/OVERCOATS

US	UK	EUROPE
36	36	46
38	38	48
40	40	50
42	42	52
44	44	54
46	46	56

MEN'S SHIRTS

US	UK	EUROPE
12	12	30–31
12½	12½	32
13	13	33
13½	13½	34–35
14	14	36
14½	14½	37
15	15	38
15½	15½	39–40
16	16	41
16½	16½	42
17	17	43
17½	17½	44–45

MEN'S SOCKS

US	UK	EUROPE
9	9	38–39
10	10	39–40
10½	10½	40–41
11	11	41–42
11½	11½	42–43

WOMEN'S CLOTHING

US	UK	EUROPE
6	8	36
8	10	38
10	12	40
12	14	42
14	16	44
16	18	46
18	20	48
20	22	50
22	24	52

CHILDREN'S CLOTHING

US	UK	EUROPE
2	16–18	40–45
4	20–22	50–55
6	24–26	60–65
7	28–30	70–75
8	32–34	80–85
9	36–38	90–95

NUMBERS AND SYMBOLS

ROMAN NUMERALS

1	I	24	XXIV	99	XCIX
2	II	25	XXV	100	C
3	III	26	XXVI	101	CI
4	IV	27	XXVII	144	CXLIV
5	V	28	XXVIII	200	CC
6	VI	29	XXIX	400	CD
7	VII	30	XXX		(or CCCC)
8	VIII	31	XXXI	500	D
9	IX	32	XXXII	900	CM
10	X	33	XXXIII		(or DCCCC)
11	XI	34	XXXIV	1000	M
12	XII	35	XXXV	1900	MCM (or
13	XIII	36	XXXVI		MDCCCC)
14	XIV	37	XXXVII	1995	MCMXCV
15	XV	38	XXXVIII	1999	MCMXCIX
16	XVI	39	XXXIX	2000	MM
17	XVII	40	XL	2005	MMV
18	XVIII	49	XLIX	2010	MMX
19	XIX	50	L		
20	XX	60	LX		
21	XXI	70	LXX		
22	XXII	80	LXXX		
23	XXIII	90	XC		

MATHEMATICAL SYMBOLS

$+$	plus, positive	$\geq$	greater than, equal to
$-$	minus, negative	$\leq$	less than, equal to
$\pm$	plus or minus, positive or negative	$\gg$	much greater than
$\times$	multiplied by	$\ll$	much less than
$\div$	divided by	$\sqrt{\ }$	square root
$=$	equal to	∞	infinity
$\equiv$	identically equal to	$\propto$	proportional to
$\neq$	not equal to	Σ	sum of
$\not\equiv$	not identically equal to	Π	product of
$\approx$	approximately equal to	Δ	difference
$\sim$	of the order of, similar to	$\therefore$	therefore
$>$	greater than	$\angle$	angle
$<$	less than	$\parallel$	parallel to
$\not>$	not greater than	$\perp$	perpendicular to
$\not<$	not less than	$:$	is to

PHYSICS SYMBOLS

α	alpha particle
β	beta ray
γ	gamma ray; photon
ε	electromotive force
η	efficiency; viscosity
λ	wavelength
μ	micro-; permeability
ν	frequency; neutrino
ρ	density; resistivity
σ	conductivity
c	velocity of light
e	electronic charge

CHEMISTRY SYMBOLS

$+$	plus; together with
$-$	single bond
$\cdot$	single bond; single unpaired electron; two separate parts or compounds regarded as loosely joined
$=$	double bond
$\equiv$	triple bond
R	group
X	halogen atom
Z	atomic number

BIOLOGY SYMBOLS

$\bigcirc$	female individual (used in inheritance charts)
$\square$	male individual (used in inheritance charts)
$\female$	female
$\male$	male
$\times$	crossed with; hybrid
$+$	wild type
F_1	offspring of the first generation
F_2	offspring of the second generation

BRAILLE

A	F	K	P	U	Z
B	G	L	Q	V	AND
C	H	M	R	W	OF
D	I	N	S	X	FOR
E	J	O	T	Y	THE

LAUNDRY CODES

⌑40	machine or hand wash (at °C temperature shown)
▢	tumble dry
⊠	do not tumble dry
iron symbol	iron
crossed iron	do not iron
Ⓟ	dry-cleanable
crossed circle	do not dry clean
△	can be bleached
crossed triangle	do not bleach

PERIODIC TABLE OF THE ELEMENTS

An element is a substance that cannot be broken down into a more basic substance by chemical means. It is the basic matter from which all other matter is composed. Each element is made up of only one atom and each element is assigned an atomic number. The periodic table is a conventional presentation of the complete list of known chemical elements in a form that allows easy identification of the relationships between them. The table lays out the chemical elements in order of increasing atomic number, as well as into "groups" (columns) of elements with similar properties. The rows of elements that arise from this are called "periods". The chemical properties of the elements, as well as their atomic number, change gradually along each period.

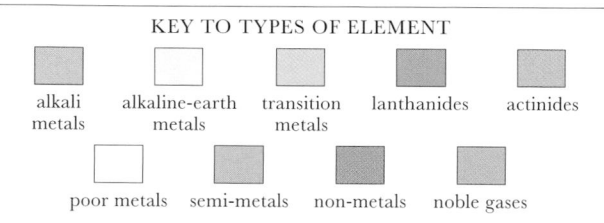

KEY TO TYPES OF ELEMENT

alkali metals · alkaline-earth metals · transition metals · lanthanides · actinides

poor metals · semi-metals · non-metals · noble gases

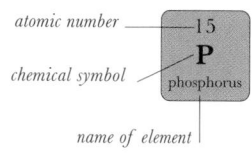

atomic number — 15
chemical symbol — P phosphorus
name of element

NUMBER, SYMBOL, AND NAME
Every box contains the following basic information about the element:
- its atomic number, which is the number of protons in the nuclei of the element's atoms. This is also the number of orbiting electrons.
- its chemical symbol.
- its chemical name.

GROUPS AND PERIODS

The first element within each period (row) is an extremely reactive alkali metal with one electron in its outer shell. At the far end of the period is a stable noble gas in group 18 (0) that has eight electrons in its outer shell. All the elements in one group (column) have a similar number of electrons in their outer shells.

metallic properties decrease to the right

1	2	3	4	5	6	7	8	9	10	11	12	13	14	15	16	17	18
1 H hydrogen																	2 He helium
3 Li lithium	4 Be beryllium											5 B boron	6 C carbon	7 N nitrogen	8 O oxygen	9 F fluorine	10 Ne neon
11 Na sodium	12 Mg magnesium											13 Al aluminum	14 Si silicon	15 P phosphorus	16 S sulfur	17 Cl chlorine	18 Ar argon
19 K potassium	20 Ca calcium	21 Sc scandium	22 Ti titanium	23 V vanadium	24 Cr chromium	25 Mn manganese	26 Fe iron	27 Co cobalt	28 Ni nickel	29 Cu copper	30 Zn zinc	31 Ga gallium	32 Ge germanium	33 As arsenic	34 Se selenium	35 Br bromine	36 Kr krypton
37 Rb rubidium	38 Sr strontium	39 Y yttrium	40 Zr zirconium	41 Nb niobium	42 Mo molybdenum	43 Tc technetium	44 Ru ruthenium	45 Rh rhodium	46 Pd palladium	47 Ag silver	48 Cd cadmium	49 In indium	50 Sn tin	51 Sb antimony	52 Te tellurium	53 I iodine	54 Xe xenon
55 Cs cesium	56 Ba barium	57–71 lanthanides	72 Hf hafnium	73 Ta tantalum	74 W tungsten	75 Re rhenium	76 Os osmium	77 Ir iridium	78 Pt platinum	79 Au gold	80 Hg mercury	81 Tl thallium	82 Pb lead	83 Bi bismuth	84 Po polonium	85 At astatine	86 Rn radon
87 Fr francium	88 Ra radium	89–103 actinides	104 Rf rutherfordium	105 Db dubnium	106 Sg seaborgium	107 Bh bohrium	108 Hs hassium	109 Mt meitnerium									

GROUP I · GROUP II

ionization energy decreases down the table

GROUP III · GROUP IV · GROUP V · GROUP VI · GROUP VII · GROUP 0

an alternative (roman) numbering system is also used to group the elements

Lanthanides and actinides are positioned away from the rest of the table to make the shape of the table easier to interpret.

LANTHANIDES AND ACTINIDES

57 La lanthanum	58 Ce cerium	59 Pr praseodymium	60 Nd neodymium	61 Pm promethium	62 Sm samarium	63 Eu europium	64 Gd gadolinium	65 Tb terbium	66 Dy dysprosium	67 Ho holmium	68 Er erbium	69 Tm thulium	70 Yb ytterbium	71 Lu lutetium
89 Ac actinium	90 Th thorium	91 Pa protactinium	92 U uranium	93 Np neptunium	94 Pu plutonium	95 Am americium	96 Cm curium	97 Bk berkelium	98 Cf californium	99 Es einsteinium	100 Fm fermium	101 Md mendelevium	102 No nobelium	103 Lr lawrencium

PROVISIONAL NAMES

All the elements heavier than bismuth (no. 83) are radioactive; all those heavier than uranium (no. 92) have only been produced artificially. The names given above for the elements are in standard use.

The elements with atomic numbers 104 to 109 were the subject of controversy until September 1997, when the International Union of Pure and Applied Chemistry (IUPAC) confirmed the names of the elements, which are those given in the table. The focus of the controversy was the disagreement over who discovered these artificial elements, and in particular whether elements should be named after living scientists. During the three years leading up to August 1997, the elements were given temporary names derived from Latin numbers. For example, element 104, rutherfordium, was called unnilquadium, derived from the Latin for one-zero-four.

CHEMICAL NOTATION

The formula for a compound indicates the number of atoms of each element present in each molecule of the compound: e.g. a molecule of water (H_2O) contains two atoms of hydrogen and one of oxygen. The formula for an ionic compound indicates the proportions of the constituent elements: e.g. common salt (NaCl) contains equal proportions of sodium and chloride ions. Formulae for more complex compounds may indicate the manner of combination of the atoms in a molecule: e.g. ethanol (ethyl alcohol) may be represented as CH_3CH_2OH.

TIME

TIME PERIODS

NAME	PERIOD	NAME	PERIOD
bicentennial	200 years	quadricentennial	every 400 years
biennial	2 years	quincentennial	every 500 years
century	100 years	quinquennial	every 5 years
decade	10 years	septennial	every 7 years
centennial	every 100 years	sesquicentennial	every 150 years
decennial	every 10 years	sexcentenary	600 years
half-century	50 years	sexennial	every 6 years
half-decade	5 years	tercentenary	300 years
half-millennium	500 years	triennial	every 3 years
leap year	366 days	vicennial	every 20 years
millennium	1,000 years	week	7 days
month	28–31 days	year	365 days
Olympiad	every 4 years	year	12 months
quadrennial	every 4 years	year	52 weeks

TIME INTERVALS

annual	occurring every year
biannual	occurring twice a year
bimonthly	occurring every two months or twice a month
biweekly	occurring every two weeks or twice a week
diurnal	daily, of each day
perennial	lasting through a year or several years
semi-annual	twice a year
semi-diurnal	twice a day
semi-weekly	twice a week
trimonthly	every three months
triweekly	every three weeks or three times a week
thrice weekly	three times a week

TYPES OF CALENDAR

GREGORIAN
The Gregorian calendar was a modification of the Julian calendar and was introduced by Pope Gregory XIII in 1582, adopted in Scotland in 1600, and in England and Wales in 1752, and is now in use throughout most of the Western world. To correct errors which had accumulated because the average Julian calendar year of 365¼ days (in effect from 46 BC) was 11 min. 10 sec. longer than the solar year, 10 days were suppressed in 1582. As a further refinement, Gregory proclaimed that, of the centenary years, only those exactly divisible by 400 should be counted as leap years.

Below are the names of the months and number of days for a non-leap year.

NAME OF MONTH	NUMBER OF DAYS
January	31
February	28 (29 in leap years)
March	31
April	30
May	31
June	30
July	31
August	31
September	30
October	31
November	30
December	31

JEWISH
The Jewish calendar is a lunar calendar adapted to the solar year, normally consisting of twelve months but having thirteen months in leap years, which occur seven times in every cycle of nineteen years. The years are reckoned from the Creation (which is placed at 3761 BC); the months are Nisan, Iyyar, Sivan, Thammuz, Ab, Elul, Tishri, Hesvan, Kislev, Tebet, Sebat, and Adar, with an intercalary month (First Adar) being added in leap years. The religious year begins with Nisan and ends with Adar, while the civil year begins with Tishri and ends with Elul.

MUSLIM
The Muslim calendar is based on a year of twelve months, each month beginning roughly at the time of the New Moon. The length of a month alternates between 30 and 29 days, except for the twelfth month, the length of which is varied in a 30-year cycle, intended to keep the calendar in step with the true phases of the moon. The months are Muharram, Safar, Rabi'I, Rabi'II, Jumada I, Jumada II, Rajab, Sha'ban, Ramadan, Shawwal, Dhu l-Qa'dah, and Dhu l-Hijja.

CHINESE
The Chinese calendar is a lunar calendar, with a year consisting of twelve months of alternately 29 and 30 days, the equivalent of approximately twelve full lunar months. Intercalary months are added to keep the calendar in step with the solar year of 365 days. Months are referred to by a number within a year, but also by animal names (listed opposite) that, from ancient times, have also been associated with years and hours of the day.

ZODIAC SIGNS

♈ **ARIES**
Ram
(March 21–April 20)

♉ **TAURUS**
Bull
(April 21–May 20)

♊ **GEMINI**
Twins
(May 21–June 20)

♋ **CANCER**
Crab
(June 21–July 21)

♌ **LEO**
Lion
(July 22–August 21)

♍ **VIRGO**
Virgin
(August 22–September 21)

♎ **LIBRA**
Scales
(September 22–October 22)

♏ **SCORPIO**
Scorpion
(October 23–November 21)

♐ **SAGITTARIUS**
Archer
(November 22–December 20)

♑ **CAPRICORN**
Goat
(December 21–January 19)

♒ **AQUARIUS**
Water-bearer
(January 20–February 18)

♓ **PISCES**
Fish
(February 19–March 20)

CHINESE ZODIAC

DOG	SHEEP	DRAGON	OX
1910	1907	1904	1901
1922	1919	1916	1913
1934	1931	1928	1925
1946	1943	1940	1937
1958	1955	1952	1949
1970	1967	1964	1961
1982	1979	1976	1973
1994	1991	1988	1985
2006	2003	2000	1997

CHICKEN	HORSE	RABBIT	RAT
1909	1906	1903	1900
1921	1918	1915	1912
1933	1930	1927	1924
1945	1942	1939	1936
1957	1954	1951	1948
1969	1966	1963	1960
1981	1978	1975	1972
1993	1990	1987	1984
2005	2002	1999	1996

MONKEY	SNAKE	TIGER	PIG
1908	1905	1902	1911
1920	1917	1914	1923
1932	1929	1926	1935
1944	1941	1938	1947
1956	1953	1950	1959
1968	1965	1962	1971
1980	1977	1974	1983
1992	1989	1986	1995
2004	2001	1998	2007

WEDDING ANNIVERSARIES

YEAR	TRADITION
1st	Paper
2nd	Cotton
3rd	Leather
4th	Linen (silk)
5th	Wood
6th	Iron
7th	Wool (copper)
8th	Bronze
9th	Pottery (china)
10th	Tin (aluminum)
11th	Steel
12th	Silk
13th	Lace
14th	Ivory
15th	Crystal
20th	China
25th	Silver
30th	Pearl
35th	Coral (jade)
40th	Ruby
45th	Sapphire
50th	Gold
55th	Emerald
60th	Diamond

BIRTHSTONES

JANUARY (garnet) FEBRUARY (amethyst) MARCH (aquamarine)

APRIL (diamond) MAY (emerald) JUNE (pearl)

JULY (ruby) AUGUST (peridot) SEPTEMBER (sapphire)

OCTOBER (opal) NOVEMBER (topaz) DECEMBER (turquoise)

TIME ZONES

The world is divided into 24 time zones, measured in relation to 12 noon Greenwich Mean Time (GMT), on the Greenwich Meridian (0°). Time advances by one hour for every 15° longitude east of Greenwich (and goes back one hour for every 15° west), but the system is adjusted in line with regional administrative boundaries. Numbers on the map below indicate the number of hours that must be added or subtracted in each time zone to reach GMT. Thus, east coast USA (+5) is 5 hours behind GMT.

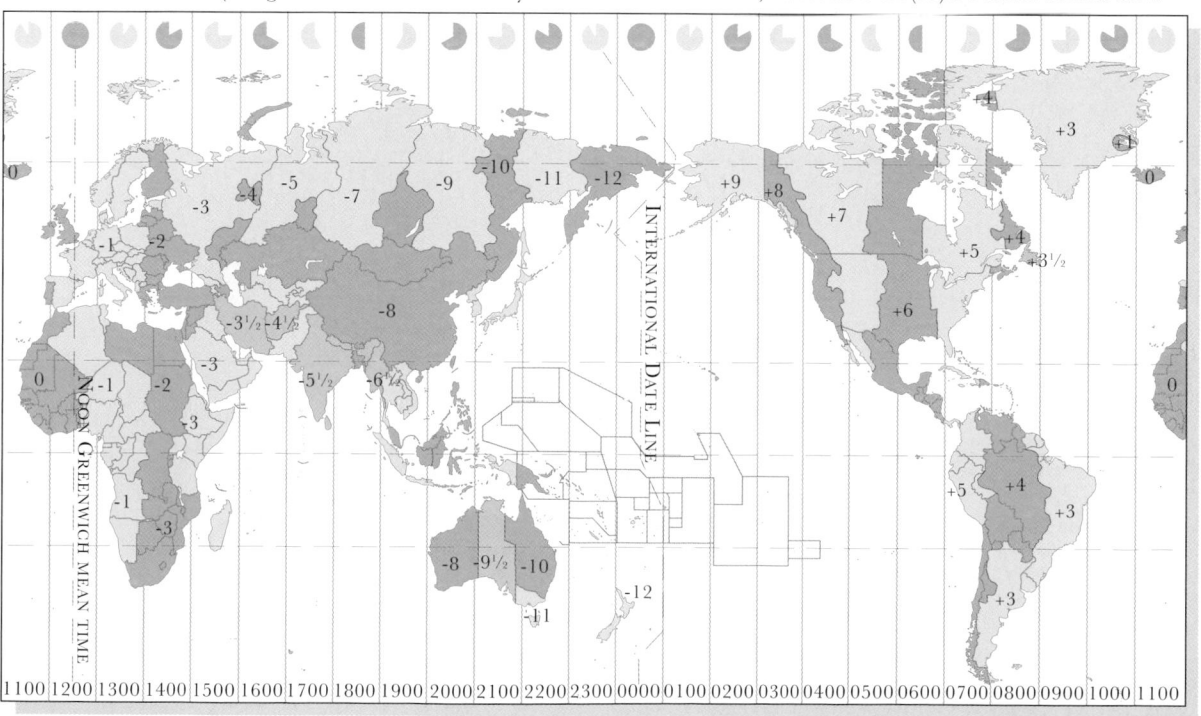

MISCELLANEOUS INFORMATION

STATES OF THE US

STATE	ABBREV.	CAPITAL	STATE	ABBREV.	CAPITAL
Alabama	Ala.; AL	Montgomery	Montana	Mont.; MT	Helena
Alaska	Alas.; AK	Juneau	Nebraska	Nebr.; NE	Lincoln
Arizona	Ariz.; AZ	Phoenix	Nevada	Nev.; NV	Carson City
Arkansas	Ark.; AR	Little Rock	New Hampshire	N.H.; NH	Concord
California	Calif.; CA	Sacramento	New Jersey	N.J.; NJ	Trenton
Colorado	Col.; CO	Denver	New Mexico	N. Mex.; NM	Santa Fe
Connecticut	Conn.; CT	Hartford	New York	N.Y.; NY	Albany
Delaware	Del.; DE	Dover	North Carolina	N.C.; NC	Raleigh
Florida	Fla.; FL	Tallahassee	North Dakota	N. Dak.; ND	Bismarck
Georgia	Ga.; GA	Atlanta	Ohio	O.; OH	Columbus
Hawaii	HI	Honolulu	Oklahoma	Okla.; OK	Oklahoma City
Idaho	Id.; ID	Boise	Oregon	Ore.; OR	Salem
Illinois	Ill.; IL	Springfield	Pennsylvania	Pa.; PA	Harrisburg
Indiana	Ind.; IN	Indianapolis	Rhode Island	R.I.; RI	Providence
Iowa	Ia.; IA	Des Moines	South Carolina	S.C.; SC	Columbia
Kansas	Kan.; KS	Topeka	South Dakota	S. Dak.; SD	Pierre
Kentucky	Ky.; KY	Frankfort	Tennessee	Tenn.; TN	Nashville
Louisiana	La.; LA	Baton Rouge	Texas	Tex.; TX	Austin
Maine	Me.; ME	Augusta	Utah	Ut.; UT	Salt Lake City
Maryland	Md.; MD	Annapolis	Vermont	Vt.; VT	Montpelier
Massachusetts	Mass.; MA	Boston	Virginia	Va.; VA	Richmond
Michigan	Mich.; MI	Lansing	Washington	Wash.; WA	Olympia
Minnesota	Minn.; MN	St. Paul	West Virginia	W. Va.; WV	Charleston
Mississippi	Miss.; MS	Jackson	Wisconsin	Wis.; WI	Madison
Missouri	Mo.; MO	Jefferson City	Wyoming	Wyo.; WY	Cheyenne

PRESIDENTS OF THE US

PRESIDENT	PARTY/TERM IN OFFICE	PRESIDENT	PARTY/TERM IN OFFICE
1. George Washington (1732–99)	Federalist (1789–97)	22. Grover Cleveland (1837–1908)	Democrat (1885–89)
2. John Adams (1735–1826)	Federalist (1797–1801)	23. Benjamin Harrison (1833–1901)	Republican (1889–93)
3. Thomas Jefferson (1743–1826)	Dem.-Rep. (1801–09)	24. Grover Cleveland (see above)	Democrat (1893–97)
4. James Madison (1751–1836)	Dem.-Rep. (1809–17)	25. William McKinley (1843–1901)	Republican (1897–1901)
5. James Monroe (1758–1831)	Dem.-Rep. (1817–25)	26. Theodore Roosevelt (1858–1919)	Republican (1901–09)
6. John Quincy Adams (1767–1848)	Independent (1825–29)	27. William H. Taft (1857–1930)	Republican (1909–13)
7. Andrew Jackson (1767–1845)	Democrat (1829–37)	28. Woodrow Wilson (1856–1924)	Democrat (1913–21)
8. Martin Van Buren (1782–1862)	Democrat (1837–41)	29. Warren G. Harding (1865–1923)	Republican (1921–23)
9. William H. Harrison (1773–1841)	Whig (1841)	30. Calvin Coolidge (1872–1933)	Republican (1923–29)
10. John Tyler (1790–1862)	Whig; Democrat (1841–45)	31. Herbert Hoover (1874–1964)	Republican (1929–33)
11. James K. Polk (1795–1849)	Democrat (1845–49)	32. Franklin D. Roosevelt (1882–1945)	Democrat (1933–45)
12. Zachary Taylor (1784–1850)	Whig (1849–50)	33. Harry S. Truman (1884–1972)	Democrat (1945–53)
13. Millard Fillmore (1800–74)	Whig (1850–53)	34. Dwight D. Eisenhower (1890–1969)	Republican (1953–61)
14. Franklin Pierce (1804–69)	Democrat (1853–57)	35. John F. Kennedy (1917–63)	Democrat (1961–63)
15. James Buchanan (1791–1868)	Democrat (1857–61)	36. Lyndon B. Johnson (1908–73)	Democrat (1963–69)
16. Abraham Lincoln (1809–65)	Republican (1861–65)	37. Richard M. Nixon (1913–94)	Republican (1969–74)
17. Andrew Johnson (1808–75)	Democrat (1865–69)	38. Gerald R. Ford (1913–)	Republican (1974–77)
18. Ulysses S. Grant (1822–85)	Republican (1869–77)	39. James Earl Carter (1924–)	Democrat (1977–81)
19. Rutherford B. Hayes (1822–93)	Republican (1877–81)	40. Ronald W. Reagan (1911–)	Republican (1981–89)
20. James A. Garfield (1831–81)	Republican (1881)	41. George H.W. Bush (1924–)	Republican (1989–93)
21. Chester A. Arthur (1830–86)	Republican (1881–85)	42. William J. Clinton (1946–)	Democrat (1993–)

CANADA, COMMONWEALTH COUNTRIES, AND STATES

CANADA
Provinces and territories
(with official abbreviations)

Province
Alberta (Alta.)
British Columbia (BC)
Manitoba (Man.)
New Brunswick (NB)
Newfoundland and Labrador (Nfld.)
Nova Scotia (NS)
Ontario (Ont.)
Prince Edward Island (PEI)
Quebec (Que.)
Saskatchewan (Sask.)

Northwest Territories (NWT)
Nunavat
Yukon Territory (YT)

THE COMMONWEALTH
The Commonwealth is a free association of the fifty sovereign independent states listed below, together with their associated states and dependencies.

Antigua and Barbuda
Australia
Bahamas
Bangladesh
Barbados
Belize

Botswana
Brunei
Canada
Cyprus
Dominica
Gambia, the
Ghana
Grenada
Guyana
India
Jamaica
Kenya
Kiribati
Lesotho
Malawi
Malaysia
Maldives
Malta
Mauritius
Nauru
New Zealand
Nigeria
Pakistan
Papua New Guinea
St. Kitts and Nevis
St. Lucia
St. Vincent and the Grenadines
Seychelles
Sierra Leone
Singapore
Solomon Islands
South Africa
Sri Lanka
Swaziland
Tanzania

Tongo
Trinidad and Tobago
Tuvalu
Uganda
United Kingdom
Vanuatu
Western Samoa
Zambia
Zimbabwe

THE COMMONWEALTH OF AUSTRALIA
States and territories

State
New South Wales
Northern Territory
Queensland
South Australia
Tasmania
Victoria
Western Australia

Australian Capital Territory

INDIA
States and Union Territories

State
Andhra Pradesh
Arunachal Pradesh
Assam
Bihar

Chhattisgarh
Goa
Gujarat
Haryana
Himachal Pradesh
Jammu and Kashmir
Jharkhand
Karnataka
Kerala
Madhya Pradesh
Maharashtra
Manipur
Meghalaya
Mizoram
Nagaland
Orissa
Punjab
Rajasthan
Sikkim
Tamil Nadu
Tripura
Uttaranchal
Uttar Pradesh
West Bengal

Union Territory
Andaman and Nicobar Islands
Chandigarh
Dadra and Nagar Haveli
Daman and Diu
Delhi
Lakshadweep
Pondicherry

BOOKS OF THE BIBLE

THE OLD TESTAMENT

BOOK	ABBREV.
Genesis	Gen.
Exodus	Exod.
Leviticus	Lev.
Numbers	Num.
Deuteronomy	Deut.
Joshua	Josh.
Judges	Judg.
Ruth	no abbrev.
First Book of Samuel	1 Sam.
Second Book of Samuel	2 Sam.
First Book of Kings	1 Kgs.
Second Book of Kings	2 Kgs.
First Book of Chronicles	1 Chr.
Second Book of Chronicles	2 Chr.
Ezra	no abbrev.
Nehemiah	Neh.
Esther	no abbrev.
Job	no abbrev.
Psalms	Ps.
Proverbs	Prov.
Ecclesiastes	Eccles.
Song of Songs, Song of Solomon, Canticles	S. of S., Cant.
Isaiah	Isa.
Jeremiah	Jer.
Lamentations	Lam.
Ezekiel	Ezek.
Daniel	Dan.
Hosea	Hos.
Joel	no abbrev.

BOOK	ABBREV.
Amos	no abbrev.
Obadiah	Obad.
Jonah	no abbrev.
Micah	Mic.
Nahum	Nah.
Habakkuk	Hab.
Zephaniah	Zeph.
Haggai	Hag.
Zechariah	Zech.
Malachi	Mal.

APOCRYPHA

BOOK	ABBREV.
First Book of Esdras	1 Esd.
Second Book of Esdras	2 Esd.
Tobit	no abbrev.
Judith	no abbrev.
Rest of Esther	Rest of Esth.
Wisdom of Solomon	Wisd.
Ecclesiasticus, Wisdom of Jesus the Son of Sirach	Ecclus., Sir.
Baruch	no abbrev.
Song of the Three Children	S. of III Ch.
Susanna	Sus.
Bel and the Dragon	Bel & Dr.
Prayer of Manasses	Pr. of Man.
First Book of Maccabees	1 Macc.
Second Book of Maccabees	2 Macc.

THE NEW TESTAMENT

BOOK	ABBREV.
Gospel according to St. Matthew	Matt.
Gospel according to St. Mark	Mark
Gospel according to St. Luke	Luke
Gospel according to St. John	John
Acts of the Apostles	Acts
Epistle to the Romans	Rom.
First Epistle to the Corinthians	1 Cor.
Second Epistle to the Corinthians	2 Cor.
Epistle to the Galatians	Gal.
Epistle to the Ephesians	Eph.
Epistle to the Philippians	Phil.
Epistle to the Colossians	Col.
First Epistle to the Thessalonians	1 Thess.
Second Epistle to the Thessalonians	2 Thess.
First Epistle to Timothy	1 Tim.
Second Epistle to Timothy	2 Tim.
Epistle to Titus	Tit.
Epistle to Philemon	Philem.
Epistle to the Hebrews	Heb.
Epistle of James	Jas.
First Epistle of Peter	1 Pet.
Second Epistle of Peter	2 Pet.
First Epistle of John	1 John
Second Epistle of John	2 John
Third Epistle of John	3 John
Epistle of Jude	Jude
Revelation, Apocalypse	Rev., Apoc.

THE LIVING WORLD

IN THE SYSTEM OF CLASSIFICATION used by most modern biologists, living things are organized into five kingdoms; four are shown here, while the fifth appears overleaf. The smallest kingdom, in terms of species so far identified, is the moneran kingdom, which contains bacteria – single-celled organisms that are the simplest forms of life. The protist kingdom also contains single-celled organisms, together with some multicellular algae, but their cells are larger and more complex than those of monerans. Most members of the fungi kingdom are multicellular, and live by absorbing organic matter from their surroundings. All plants are multicellular, and live by photosynthesis; this large kingdom contains some 400,000 known species.

TAXONOMY

Taxonomy is the science of classification of living things. It uses a hierarchy of progressively smaller groups, from kingdom to species, and organizes living things in a way that reflects their evolutionary links. This box features the principal groups used in classification. In addition to these, taxonomists use a number of intermediate groups, such as suborders or superfamilies.

KINGDOM
One of the overall categories of life, containing organisms that share fundamental features.

PHYLUM
A major grouping within a kingdom; known as a "division" in the classification of plants and fungi.

CLASS
A major part of a phylum. For example, mosses (Musci) form a class within the phylum Bryophyta.

ORDER
A part of a class, consisting of one or more families.

FAMILY
A large collection of species that share a number of important physical features.

GENUS
A narrower group containing a small number of species that share many features.

SPECIES
A collection of living things that interbreed in the wild, producing similar offspring.

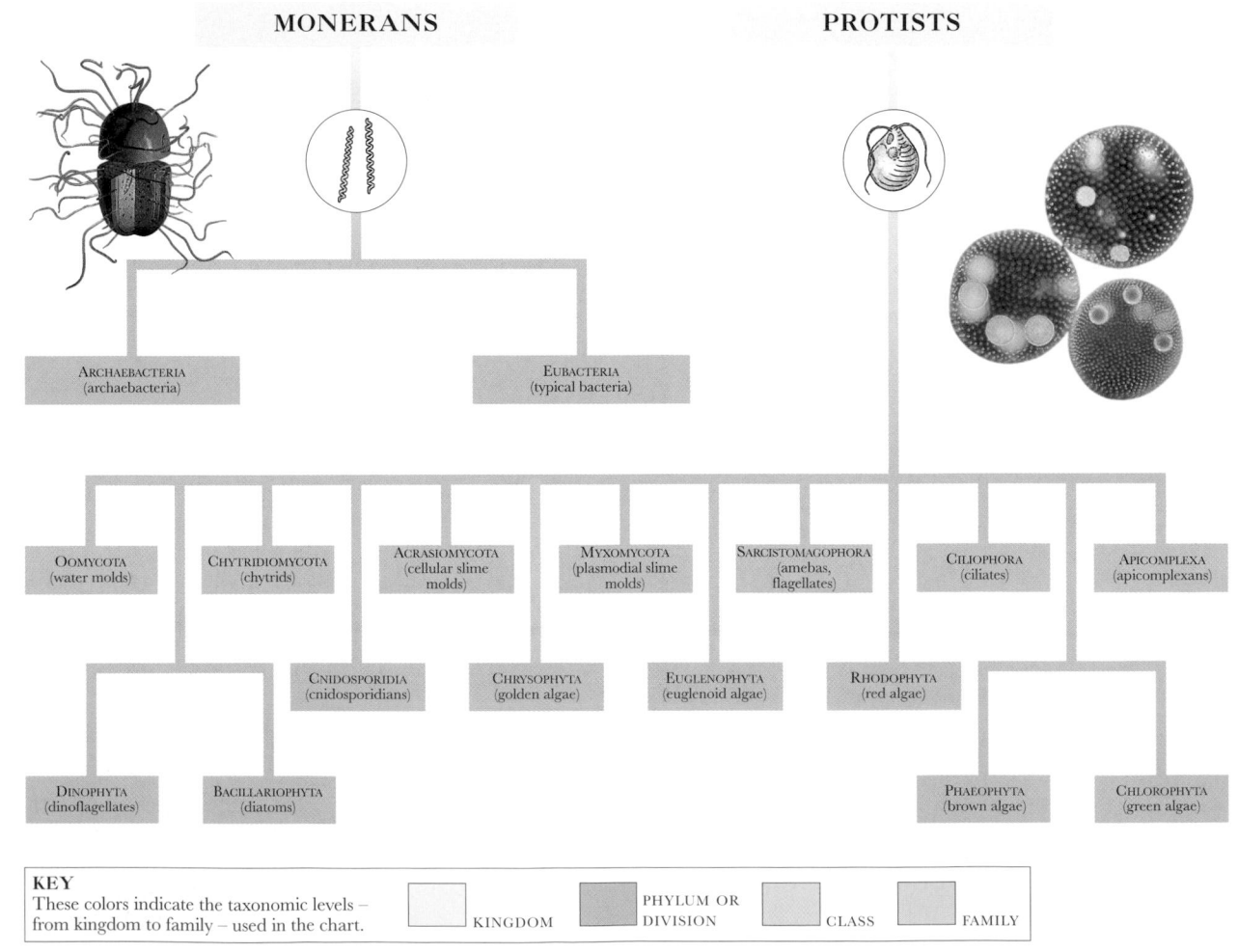

MONERANS

PROTISTS

ARCHAEBACTERIA
(archaebacteria)

EUBACTERIA
(typical bacteria)

OOMYCOTA
(water molds)

CHYTRIDIOMYCOTA
(chytrids)

ACRASIOMYCOTA
(cellular slime molds)

MYXOMYCOTA
(plasmodial slime molds)

SARCISTOMAGOPHORA
(amebas, flagellates)

CILIOPHORA
(ciliates)

APICOMPLEXA
(apicomplexans)

CNIDOSPORIDIA
(cnidosporidians)

CHRYSOPHYTA
(golden algae)

EUGLENOPHYTA
(euglenoid algae)

RHODOPHYTA
(red algae)

DINOPHYTA
(dinoflagellates)

BACILLARIOPHYTA
(diatoms)

PHAEOPHYTA
(brown algae)

CHLOROPHYTA
(green algae)

KEY
These colors indicate the taxonomic levels – from kingdom to family – used in the chart.

KINGDOM   PHYLUM OR DIVISION   CLASS   FAMILY

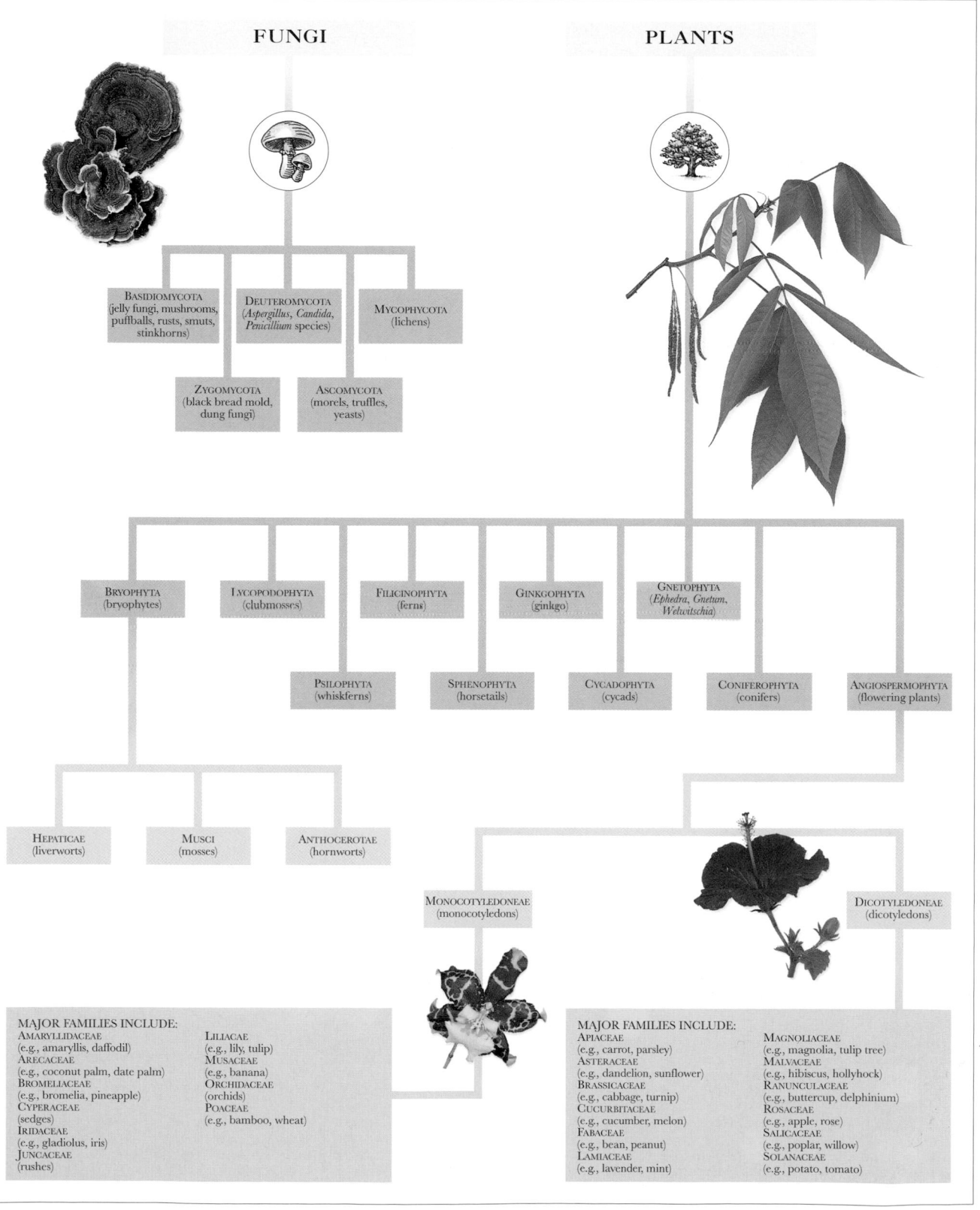

FUNGI

PLANTS

BASIDIOMYCOTA
(jelly fungi, mushrooms,
puffballs, rusts, smuts,
stinkhorns)

DEUTEROMYCOTA
(*Aspergillus, Candida,
Penicillium* species)

MYCOPHYCOTA
(lichens)

ZYGOMYCOTA
(black bread mold,
dung fungi)

ASCOMYCOTA
(morels, truffles,
yeasts)

BRYOPHYTA
(bryophytes)

LYCOPODOPHYTA
(clubmosses)

FILICINOPHYTA
(ferns)

GINKGOPHYTA
(ginkgo)

GNETOPHYTA
(*Ephedra, Gnetum,
Welwitschia*)

PSILOPHYTA
(whiskferns)

SPHENOPHYTA
(horsetails)

CYCADOPHYTA
(cycads)

CONIFEROPHYTA
(conifers)

ANGIOSPERMOPHYTA
(flowering plants)

HEPATICAE
(liverworts)

MUSCI
(mosses)

ANTHOCEROTAE
(hornworts)

MONOCOTYLEDONEAE
(monocotyledons)

DICOTYLEDONEAE
(dicotyledons)

MAJOR FAMILIES INCLUDE:

AMARYLLIDACEAE
(e.g., amaryllis, daffodil)
ARECACEAE
(e.g., coconut palm, date palm)
BROMELIACEAE
(e.g., bromelia, pineapple)
CYPERACEAE
(sedges)
IRIDACEAE
(e.g., gladiolus, iris)
JUNCACEAE
(rushes)

LILIACAE
(e.g., lily, tulip)
MUSACEAE
(e.g., banana)
ORCHIDACEAE
(orchids)
POACEAE
(e.g., bamboo, wheat)

MAJOR FAMILIES INCLUDE:

APIACEAE
(e.g., carrot, parsley)
ASTERACEAE
(e.g., dandelion, sunflower)
BRASSICACEAE
(e.g., cabbage, turnip)
CUCURBITACEAE
(e.g., cucumber, melon)
FABACEAE
(e.g., bean, peanut)
LAMIACEAE
(e.g., lavender, mint)

MAGNOLIACEAE
(e.g., magnolia, tulip tree)
MALVACEAE
(e.g., hibiscus, hollyhock)
RANUNCULACEAE
(e.g., buttercup, delphinium)
ROSACEAE
(e.g., apple, rose)
SALICACEAE
(e.g., poplar, willow)
SOLANACEAE
(e.g., potato, tomato)

THE ANIMAL KINGDOM

With over 2 million known species, the animal kingdom is the largest grouping in the classification of living things. Its members are divided into approximately 30 phyla, which are featured on these two pages. Over 95 percent of animal species are invertebrates – an informal term used for any animal that does not have a backbone. Invertebrates include a vast array of varied organisms in many different phyla, from sponges to insects. Many remain poorly known, and it is believed that as many as 10 million species may still await discovery. Vertebrates, or animals with backbones, form part of the chordate phylum. Although they total only about 45,000 species, they include the largest and most familiar members of the animal kingdom, and also ourselves.

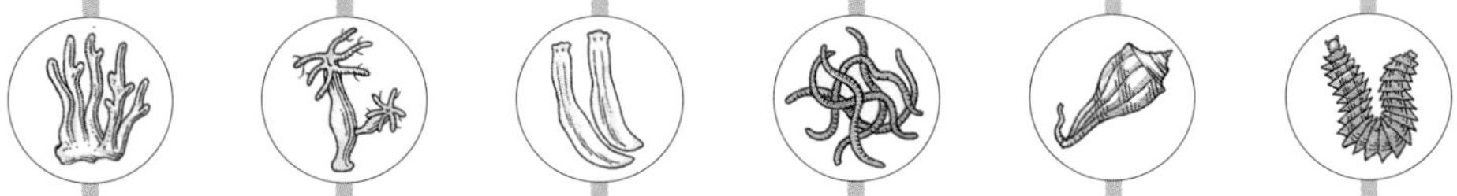

PORIFERA (sponges)

CNIDARIA (cnidarians)

PLATYHELMINTHES (flatworms)

NEMATODA (roundworms)

MOLLUSCA (mollusks)

ANNELIDA (true worms)

UNIRAMIA (uniramians)

MALACOSTRACA (crabs, lobsters, shrimps, woodlice)

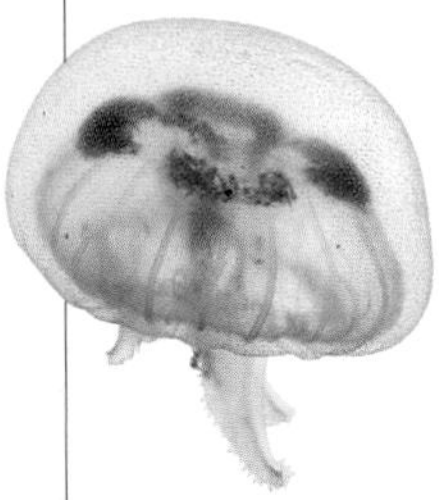

HYDROZOA (hydras, hydroids)

SCYPHOZOA (jellyfish)

ANTHOZOA (anemones, corals)

POLYPLACO-PHORA (chitons)

GASTROPODA (slugs, snails)

BIVALVIA (clams, mussels, scallops)

CEPHALOPODA (octopuses, squid)

TURBELLARIA (free-living flatworms)

MONOGENEA (parasitic flukes)

TREMATODA (parasitic flukes)

CESTODA (tapeworms)

POLYCHAETA (marine worms)

OLIGOCHAETA (earthworms, freshwater worms)

HIRUDINEA (leeches)

INSECTA (insects)

CHILOPODA (centipedes)

DIPLOPODA (millipedes)

OTHER CLASSES:
PAUROPODA (pauropodans)
SYMPHYLA (symphylans)

KEY
These colors show the taxonomic levels used in the chart.

KINGDOM

PHYLUM

SUBPHYLUM

SUPERCLASS

CLASS

SUBCLASS

INFRACLASS

ORDER

MAJOR ORDERS INCLUDE:
ANOPLURA (sucking lice)
COLEOPTERA (beetles, weevils)
COLLEMBOLA (springtails)
DERMAPTERA (earwigs)
DIPTERA (gnats, mosquitos, true flies)
EPHEMEROPTERA (mayflies)
HEMIPTERA (true bugs)
HYMENOPTERA (ants, bees, wasps)
ISOPTERA (termites)
LEPIDOPTERA (butterflies, moths)
MALLOPHAGA (birdlice, biting lice)
NEUROPTERA (alder flies, ant lions, dobsonflies, lacewings, snake flies)

ODONATA (damselflies, dragonflies)
ORTHOPTERA (cockroaches, crickets, grasshoppers, locusts, mantids)
PHASMIDA (leaf insects, stick insects)
PSOCOPTERA (barklice, booklice)
SIPHONAPTERA (fleas)
THYSANURA (bristletails, silverfish)

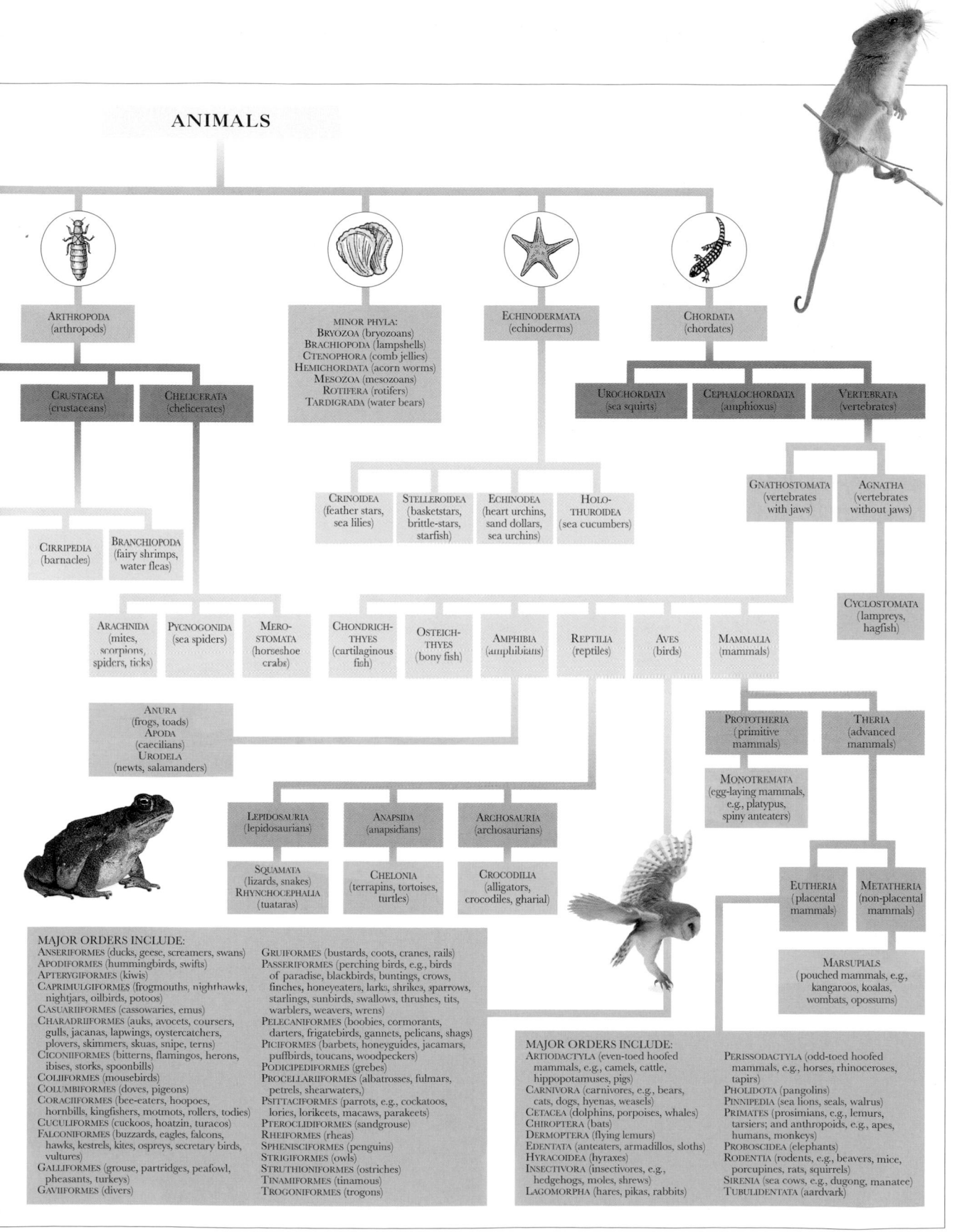

ANIMALS

ARTHROPODA (arthropods)

- **CRUSTACEA** (crustaceans)
- **CHELICERATA** (chelicerates)

MINOR PHYLA:
BRYOZOA (bryozoans)
BRACHIOPODA (lampshells)
CTENOPHORA (comb jellies)
HEMICHORDATA (acorn worms)
MESOZOA (mesozoans)
ROTIFERA (rotifers)
TARDIGRADA (water bears)

ECHINODERMATA (echinoderms)

CHORDATA (chordates)

- **UROCHORDATA** (sea squirts)
- **CEPHALOCHORDATA** (amphioxus)
- **VERTEBRATA** (vertebrates)

CIRRIPEDIA (barnacles)
BRANCHIOPODA (fairy shrimps, water fleas)

CRINOIDEA (feather stars, sea lilies)
STELLEROIDEA (basketstars, brittle-stars, starfish)
ECHINODEA (heart urchins, sand dollars, sea urchins)
HOLO-THUROIDEA (sea cucumbers)

GNATHOSTOMATA (vertebrates with jaws)
AGNATHA (vertebrates without jaws)

ARACHNIDA (mites, scorpions, spiders, ticks)
PYCNOGONIDA (sea spiders)
MERO-STOMATA (horseshoe crabs)

CHONDRICH-THYES (cartilaginous fish)
OSTEICH-THYES (bony fish)
AMPHIBIA (amphibians)
REPTILIA (reptiles)
AVES (birds)
MAMMALIA (mammals)

CYCLOSTOMATA (lampreys, hagfish)

ANURA (frogs, toads)
APODA (caecilians)
URODELA (newts, salamanders)

PROTOTHERIA (primitive mammals)
THERIA (advanced mammals)

MONOTREMATA (egg-laying mammals, e.g., platypus, spiny anteaters)

LEPIDOSAURIA (lepidosaurians)
ANAPSIDA (anapsidians)
ARCHOSAURIA (archosaurians)

SQUAMATA (lizards, snakes)
RHYNCHOCEPHALIA (tuataras)
CHELONIA (terrapins, tortoises, turtles)
CROCODILIA (alligators, crocodiles, gharial)

EUTHERIA (placental mammals)
METATHERIA (non-placental mammals)

MARSUPIALS (pouched mammals, e.g., kangaroos, koalas, wombats, opossums)

MAJOR ORDERS INCLUDE:
ANSERIFORMES (ducks, geese, screamers, swans)
APODIFORMES (hummingbirds, swifts)
APTERYGIFORMES (kiwis)
CAPRIMULGIFORMES (frogmouths, nighthawks, nightjars, oilbirds, potoos)
CASUARIIFORMES (cassowaries, emus)
CHARADRIIFORMES (auks, avocets, coursers, gulls, jacanas, lapwings, oystercatchers, plovers, skimmers, skuas, snipe, terns)
CICONIIFORMES (bitterns, flamingos, herons, ibises, storks, spoonbills)
COLIIFORMES (mousebirds)
COLUMBIFORMES (doves, pigeons)
CORACIIFORMES (bee-eaters, hoopoes, hornbills, kingfishers, motmots, rollers, todies)
CUCULIFORMES (cuckoos, hoatzin, turacos)
FALCONIFORMES (buzzards, eagles, falcons, hawks, kestrels, kites, ospreys, secretary birds, vultures)
GALLIFORMES (grouse, partridges, peafowl, pheasants, turkeys)
GAVIIFORMES (divers)

GRUIFORMES (bustards, coots, cranes, rails)
PASSERIFORMES (perching birds, e.g., birds of paradise, blackbirds, buntings, crows, finches, honeyeaters, larks, shrikes, sparrows, starlings, sunbirds, swallows, thrushes, tits, warblers, weavers, wrens)
PELECANIFORMES (boobies, cormorants, darters, frigatebirds, gannets, pelicans, shags)
PICIFORMES (barbets, honeyguides, jacamars, puffbirds, toucans, woodpeckers)
PODICIPEDIFORMES (grebes)
PROCELLARIIFORMES (albatrosses, fulmars, petrels, shearwaters,)
PSITTACIFORMES (parrots, e.g., cockatoos, lories, lorikeets, macaws, parakeets)
PTEROCLIDIFORMES (sandgrouse)
RHEIFORMES (rheas)
SPHENISCIFORMES (penguins)
STRIGIFORMES (owls)
STRUTHIONIFORMES (ostriches)
TINAMIFORMES (tinamous)
TROGONIFORMES (trogons)

MAJOR ORDERS INCLUDE:
ARTIODACTYLA (even-toed hoofed mammals, e.g., camels, cattle, hippopotamuses, pigs)
CARNIVORA (carnivores, e.g., bears, cats, dogs, hyenas, weasels)
CETACEA (dolphins, porpoises, whales)
CHIROPTERA (bats)
DERMOPTERA (flying lemurs)
EDENTATA (anteaters, armadillos, sloths)
HYRACOIDEA (hyraxes)
INSECTIVORA (insectivores, e.g., hedgehogs, moles, shrews)
LAGOMORPHA (hares, pikas, rabbits)

PERISSODACTYLA (odd-toed hoofed mammals, e.g., horses, rhinoceroses, tapirs)
PHOLIDOTA (pangolins)
PINNIPEDIA (sea lions, seals, walrus)
PRIMATES (prosimians, e.g., lemurs, tarsiers; and anthropoids, e.g., apes, humans, monkeys)
PROBOSCIDEA (elephants)
RODENTIA (rodents, e.g., beavers, mice, porcupines, rats, squirrels)
SIRENIA (sea cows, e.g., dugong, manatee)
TUBULIDENTATA (aardvark)

GEOLOGICAL TIME PERIODS

SINCE THE EARTH WAS formed from a massive cloud of dust and gas some 4,600 million (4.6 billion) years ago, layers of igneous, sedimentary, and metamorphic rocks have built up on its crust. The study of the history and formation of these layers has given rise to a system of classification that describes geological time. The largest division is an eon and divisions of the three eons are classified as the Archean (4,600–2,500 million years ago), the Proterozoic (2,500–550 million years ago), and the Phanerozoic (550 million years ago to the present). Eons are then broken down into smaller hierarchical divisions – eras, periods, epochs, and ages – which provide more precise dating information on the history of the Earth.

GEOLOGICAL HISTORY OF THE EARTH

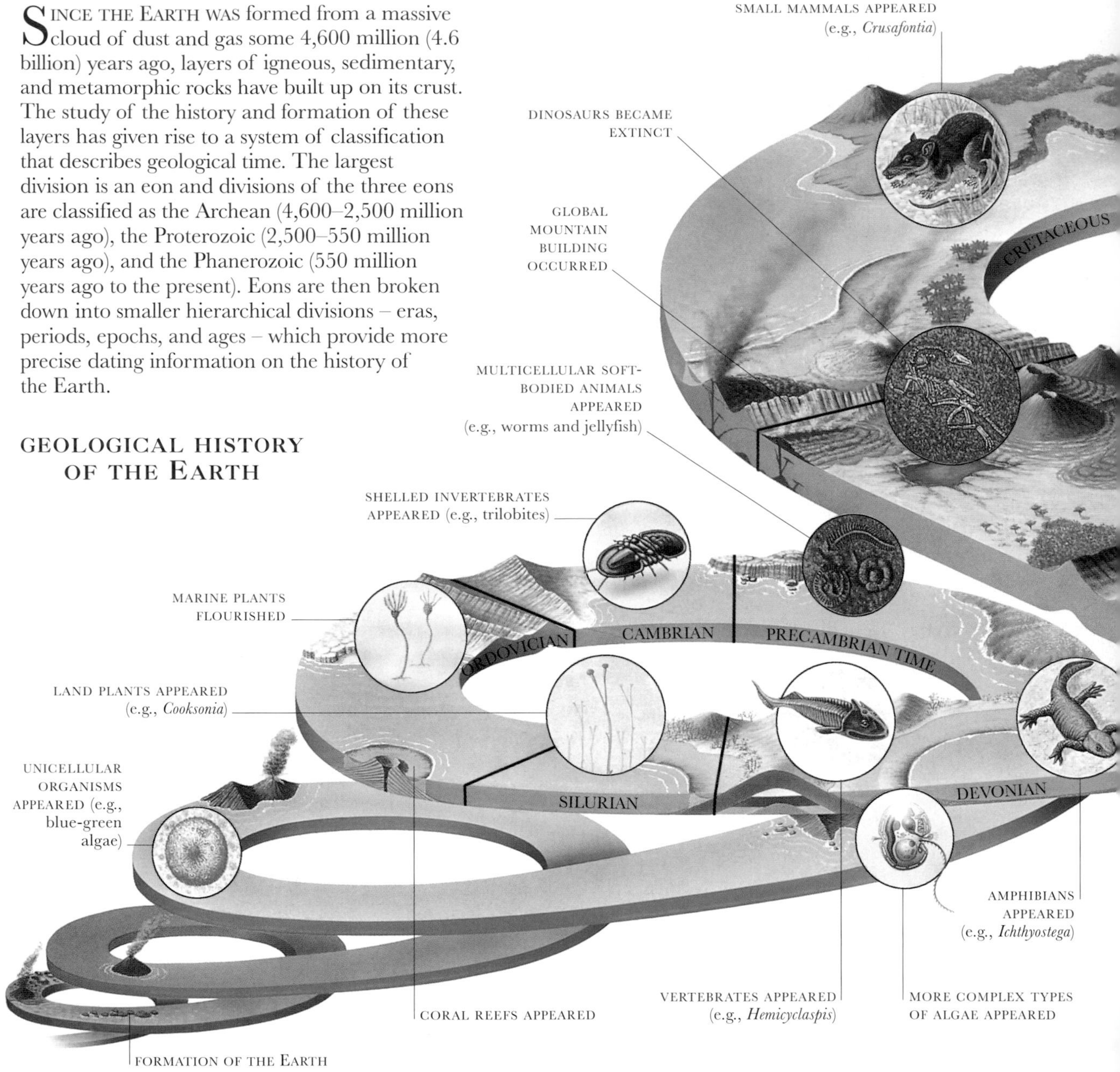

SMALL MAMMALS APPEARED (e.g., *Crusafontia*)

DINOSAURS BECAME EXTINCT

GLOBAL MOUNTAIN BUILDING OCCURRED

MULTICELLULAR SOFT-BODIED ANIMALS APPEARED (e.g., worms and jellyfish)

SHELLED INVERTEBRATES APPEARED (e.g., trilobites)

MARINE PLANTS FLOURISHED

LAND PLANTS APPEARED (e.g., *Cooksonia*)

UNICELLULAR ORGANISMS APPEARED (e.g., blue-green algae)

CRETACEOUS

PRECAMBRIAN TIME

CAMBRIAN

ORDOVICIAN

SILURIAN

DEVONIAN

AMPHIBIANS APPEARED (e.g., *Ichthyostega*)

CORAL REEFS APPEARED

VERTEBRATES APPEARED (e.g., *Hemicyclaspis*)

MORE COMPLEX TYPES OF ALGAE APPEARED

FORMATION OF THE EARTH

THE GEOLOGICAL TIMESCALE

MILLIONS OF YEARS AGO (MYA)

	4,600	3,500	2,900	2,500	1,600	900	550	505	438

FORMATION OF THE EARTH	PRECAMBRIAN TIME						CAMBRIAN	ORDOVICIAN
	EARLY ARCHEAN	MIDDLE ARCHEAN	LATE ARCHEAN	EARLY PROTEROZOIC	MIDDLE PROTEROZOIC	LATE PROTEROZOIC		
	ARCHEAN			PROTEROZOIC				

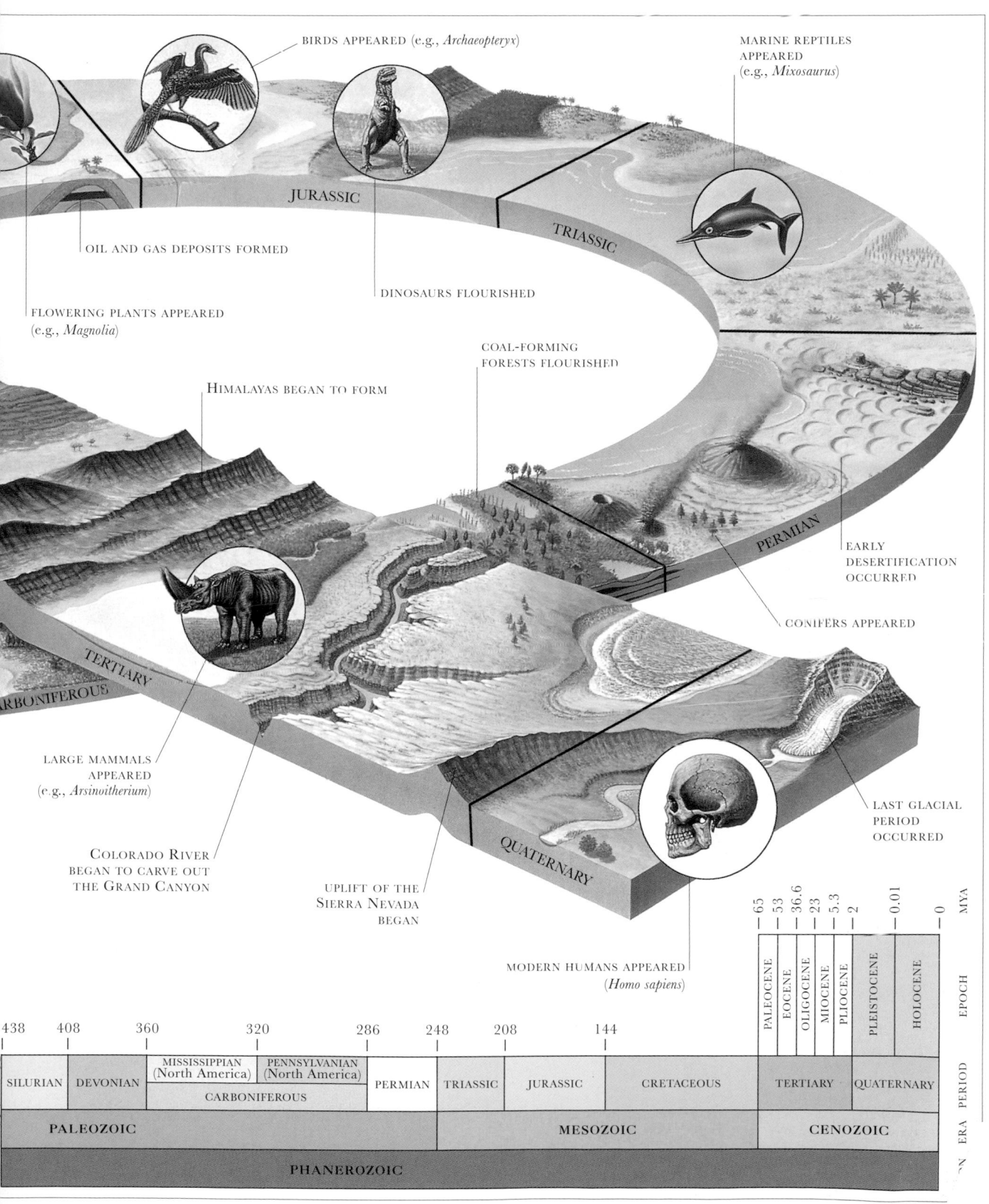

BIRDS APPEARED (e.g., *Archaeopteryx*)

MARINE REPTILES
APPEARED
(e.g., *Mixosaurus*)

JURASSIC

TRIASSIC

OIL AND GAS DEPOSITS FORMED

FLOWERING PLANTS APPEARED
(e.g., *Magnolia*)

DINOSAURS FLOURISHED

COAL-FORMING
FORESTS FLOURISHED

HIMALAYAS BEGAN TO FORM

PERMIAN

EARLY
DESERTIFICATION
OCCURRED

CONIFERS APPEARED

TERTIARY

CARBONIFEROUS

LARGE MAMMALS
APPEARED
(e.g., *Arsinoitherium*)

COLORADO RIVER
BEGAN TO CARVE OUT
THE GRAND CANYON

UPLIFT OF THE
SIERRA NEVADA
BEGAN

QUATERNARY

LAST GLACIAL
PERIOD
OCCURRED

MODERN HUMANS APPEARED
(*Homo sapiens*)

								MYA
65	53	36.6	23	5.3	2	0.01	0	
PALEOCENE	EOCENE	OLIGOCENE	MIOCENE	PLIOCENE	PLEISTOCENE	HOLOCENE		EPOCH

438	408	360	320	286	248	208	144					
SILURIAN	DEVONIAN	MISSISSIPPIAN (North America)	PENNSYLVANIAN (North America)	PERMIAN	TRIASSIC	JURASSIC	CRETACEOUS		TERTIARY	QUATERNARY		PERIOD
		CARBONIFEROUS										
PALEOZOIC					MESOZOIC				CENOZOIC			ERA
PHANEROZOIC												

GRAMMAR AND STYLE

Dictionaries of current English, unlike historical dictionaries, generally record the language as it is used at the time; usage is constantly changing and the distinction between right and wrong is not always easy to determine. Unlike French, which guided by the rulings of the Académie Française, English is not monitored by any single authority, and established usage is the principal criterion. One result of this is that English tolerates many more alternative spellings than other languages. Such alternatives are based on patterns of word formation and variation in the different languages through which words have passed before reaching ours. The following notes offer guidance on difficult and controversial points of grammar usage and style. An asterisk (*) denotes an example of incorrect usage.

ACCENT

1 A person's accent is the way he or she pronounces words. People from different regions and different groups in society have different accents. For instance, most people in America say *half* to rhyme with *staff*, while many people native to eastern Massachusetts pronounce it as if it were spelled "hahf." In the U.S. and Canada the *r* in *far* and *port* is generally pronounced, while in southeastern England, for example, it is not.

See also note at DIALECT.

2 An accent on a letter is a mark added to it to alter the sound it represents. French, for example, has

  ´ (acute), as in *état*   ¨ (diaeresis), as in *Noël*
  ` (grave), as in *mère*   ‚ (cedilla), as in *français*
  ^ (circumflex), as in *guêpe*

and German has

  ¨ (umlaut), as in *München*.

There are no accents on native English words, but many words borrowed from other languages still have them, such as *façade*.

ADJECTIVE

An adjective is a word that describes a noun or pronoun:

  red, clever, German, depressed, battered, sticky, shining

Most can be used either before a noun:

  the red *house*   a lazy *man*   a clever *woman*

or after a verb like *be, seem,* or *call*:

  The house is red.   *I wouldn't call him* lazy.
  She seems very clever.

Some can be used only before a noun:

  the chief *reason*
  (one cannot say *the reason is chief)

Some can be used only after a verb:

  The ship is still afloat.
  (one cannot say *an afloat ship)

A few can be used only immediately after a noun:

  a writer manqué
  (one cannot say either *a manqué writer
  or *as a writer he is* manqué)

See also notes at COMPARATIVE and SUPERLATIVE.

ADVERB

An adverb is used:

1 with a verb, to say:

  a how something happens: *He walks* quickly.
  b where something happens: *I live* here.
  c when something happens: *They visited us* yesterday.
  d how often something happens: *We* usually *have coffee.*

2 to strengthen or weaken the meaning of:

  a ... *really meant it*   *I almost fell asleep.*
  ... *is very* clever.   *This is a* slightly *better result.*

c another adverb:

  It comes off extremely *easily. The boys* nearly *always get home late.*

3 to add to the meaning of a whole sentence:

  Luckily, *no one was hurt.*   *He is* probably *our best player.*

In writing or in formal speech, it is **incorrect** to use an adjective instead of an adverb. For example, use

  Do it properly.   not   *Do it *proper.

Note that many words are both an adjective and an adverb:

ADJECTIVE	ADVERB
a fast *horse*	*He ran* fast.
a long *time*	*Have you been here* long?

APOSTROPHE '

This is used:

1 to indicate possession:

  with a singular noun:
  a boy's book   *a week's work*   *the boss's salary*
  with a plural already ending with -*s*:
  a girls' school   *two weeks' newspapers*   *the bosses' salaries*
  with a plural not already ending with -*s*:
  the children's books   *women's literature*
  with a singular name:
  Bill's book   *Nicholas' (or Nicholas's) coat*
  with a name ending in -*es* that is pronounced /-ɪz/:
  Bridges' poems   *Moses' mother*
  in phrases using *sake*;
  for God's sake   *for goodness' sake*   *for Nicholas' sake.*

2 to mark an omission of one or more letters or numbers:

  he's (he is *or* he has)   *haven't* (have not)
  can't (cannot)   *we'll* (we shall)
  won't (will not)   *o'clock* (of the clock)
  the summer of '68 (1968)

3 when letters or numbers are referred to in plural form:

  mind your p's and q's   *find all the number 7's*

  but it is unnecessary in: *CDs; the 1940s.*

ARTICLE

An article is a word that starts a noun phrase, determining its role in relation to the rest of the text in which it occurs. The most common articles are *the* (often called the **definite article**) and *a* or *an* (often called the **indefinite article**). *A* or *an* is used with a singular noun phrase that is introduced as new information in a text; *the* is used with information that is already established (*A* man came in ... *The* man went up to Jim) or that is regarded as common knowledge (*the* Moon, *the* sea).

Other kinds of articles are:

  possessive articles (often called **possessive adjectives**):
  my, your, his, her, its, our, their.
  demonstratives:
  this, that, these, those.

AUXILIARY VERB

An auxiliary verb is used in front of another verb to alter its meaning. Mainly, it expresses:

1 when something happens, by forming a tense of the main verb: *I* shall *go.*   *He* was *going.*

2 permission, necessity, or possibility to do something:

> *They* may *go.*   *You* must *go.*
> *I* can't *go.*   *I* might *go.*
> *She* would *go if she* could.

These auxiliaries (and those listed below except *be, do,* and *have*) are sometimes called modal verbs.

The principal auxiliary verbs are:

be	*have*	*must*	*will*
can	*let*	*ought*	*would*
could	*may*	*shall*	
do	*might*	*should*	

CLAUSE

A clause is a group of words that includes a finite verb. If it makes complete sense by itself, it is known as a main clause:

> *The sun came out.*

Otherwise, although it makes some sense, it must be attached to a main clause; it is then known as a subordinate clause:

> *when the sun came out*
> (as in *When the sun came out, we went outside.*)

COLON :

This is used:

1 between two main clauses of which the second explains, enlarges on, or follows from the first:

> *It was not easy: to begin with I had to find the right house.*

2 to introduce a list of items (a dash should not be added), and after expressions such as *namely, for example, to resume, to sum up,* and *the following*:

> *You will need: a tent, a sleeping bag, cooking equipment, and a backpack.*

3 before a quotation:

> *The poem begins. "Earth has not anything to show more fair."*

COMMA ,

The comma marks a slight break between words, phrases, etc. In particular, it is used:

1 to separate items in a list:

> *red, white, and blue* (or *red, white and blue*)
> *We bought some shoes, socks, gloves, and handkerchiefs.*

2 to separate adjectives that describe something in the same way:

> *It is a hot, dry, dusty place.*

but not if they describe it in different ways:

> *a distinguished foreign author*

or if one adjective adds to or alters the meaning of another:

> *a bright red tie.*

3 to separate a name or word used to address someone:

> *David, I'm here.*
> *Well, Mr. Jones, we meet again.*
> *Have you seen this, my friend?*

4 to separate a phrase from the rest of the sentence:

> *Having had lunch, we went back to work.*

especially in order to clarify the meaning:

> *In the valley below, the village looked very small.*

5 after words that introduce direct speech, or after direct speech where there is no question mark or exclamation point:

> *They answered, "Here we are."*
> *"Here we are," they answered.*

6 in letters, after *Dear Sarah,* etc., and after *Sincerely yours,* etc.

7 to separate a word, phrase, or clause that is secondary or adds information or a comment:

> *I am sure, however, that it will not happen.*
> *Fred, who is bald, complained of the cold.*

but not with a relative clause (one usually beginning with *who, which,* or *that*) that restricts the meaning of the noun it follows:

> *Men who are bald should wear hats.*

(See note at RELATIVE CLAUSE)

in dates, to separate the month and day from the year

> *on December 10, 1993*

No comma is needed between a month and a year in dates:

> *in December 1993*

or between a number and a street in addresses:

> *1600 Pennsylvania Avenue.*

COMPARATIVE

The form of an adjective used to compare two people or things in respect of a certain quality is called the comparative. Comparative adjectives are formed in two ways; generally, short words add *-er* to the base form:

> *smaller, faster, greater.*

Often, the base form is altered:

> *bigger, finer, easier.*

Long words take *more* in front of them:

> *more beautiful, more informative.*

See also note at SUPERLATIVE.

COMPLEMENT

A complement is a word or phrase that comes after a verb but has the same reference as the subject or object:

> *the culprit* in *The dog was the culprit.*
> *president* in *They elected him president.*

CONJUNCTION

A conjunction is used to join parts of sentences that usually, but not always, contain their own verbs:

> *He found it difficult so I helped him.*
> *They made lunch for Alice and Mary.*
> *I waited until you came.*

There are two types of conjunction. **Coordinating conjunctions** (*and, or, but*) join two equal clauses, phrases, or words. **Subordinating conjunctions** join a subordinate clause to a main clause.

The most common subordinating conjunctions are:

after	*like*	*though*
although	*now*	*till*
as	*once*	*unless*
because	*since*	*until*
before	*so*	*when*
for	*so that*	*where*
if	*than*	*whether*
in order that	*that*	*while*

DASH –

This is used:

1 to mark the beginning and end of an interruption in the structure of a sentence:

> *My son – where has he gone? – would like to meet you.*

2 to show faltering speech in conversation:
> *Yes — well — I would — only you see — it's not easy.*

3 to show other kinds of break in a sentence, often where a comma, semicolon, or colon would traditionally be used:
> *Come tomorrow — if you can.*
> *The most important thing is this — don't rush the work.*

A dash is not used in this last way in formal writing.

DEFINITE ARTICLE
See note at ARTICLE.

DIALECT
Everyone speaks a particular dialect: that is, a particular type of English distinguished by its vocabulary and its grammar. Different parts of the world and different groups of people speak different dialects: for example, Australians may say *barbie* while others say *barbecue*, and a Southerner may say *I might could come* while most others say *I might be able to come*. A dialect is not the same thing as an accent, which is the way a person pronounces words.

See also notes at ACCENT and STANDARD ENGLISH.

DIRECT OR QUOTED SPEECH
Direct speech is the actual words of a speaker quoted in writing.

1 In a novel, etc., speech punctuation is used for direct speech:

a The words spoken are usually put in quotation marks.

b Each new piece of speech begins with a capital letter.

c Each paragraph within one person's piece of speech begins with quotation marks, but only the last paragraph ends with them.

For example:
> Christopher looked into the box. "There's nothing in here," he said. "It's completely empty."

2 In a script (the written words of a play, a movie, or a radio or television program):

a The names of speakers are written in the margin in capital letters.

b Each name is followed by a colon.

c Quotation marks are not needed.

d Any instructions about the way the words are spoken or about the scenery or the actions of the speakers (stage directions) are written in the present tense in parentheses or italics.

For example:
> CHRISTOPHER: [Looks into box.] There's nothing in here. It's completely empty.

EXCLAMATION POINT (OR MARK) !
This is used instead of a period at the end of a sentence to show that the speaker or writer is very angry, enthusiastic, insistent, disappointed, hurt, surprised, etc.:

> *I am not pleased at all!*   *I wish I could have gone!*
> *I just love candy!*   *Ow!*
> *Go away!*   *He didn't even say goodbye!*

~PHEN -
...ed:

...r more words so as to form a compound or single

> *up-to-date*

...hout such hyphens in compound words

...mpound (one put before a

> *...nun is well known)*
> *...ist is out of date)*

3 to join a prefix, etc., to a proper name:
> *anti-Darwinian*   *half-Italian*   *non-British*

4 to make a meaning clear by linking words:
> *twenty-odd people* (vs. *twenty odd people*)

or by separating a prefix:
> *re-cover* or *recover*
> *re-present* or *represent*
> *re-sign* or *resign*

6 to represent a common second element in the items of a list:
> *two-, three-, or fourfold*

7 to divide a word if there is no room to complete it at the end of a line:
> *... diction-*
> *ary ...*

The hyphen comes at the end of the line, not at the beginning of the next line. In general, words should be divided at the end of a syllable; *dicti-onary* would be incorrect hyphenation. In handwriting, typing, and word processing, it is safest (and often neatest) not to divide words at all.

INDEFINITE ARTICLE
See note at ARTICLE.

INTERROGATIVE PRONOUN
Interrogative pronouns (*who, whom, which, what*) introduce direct and indirect questions:
> *What did he say?*
> *She asked him what he had said.*
> *Who are you?*
> *She asked him who he was.*

A question mark is used after a direct question, but not after an indirect question.

INTRANSITIVE VERB
See note at TRANSITIVE VERB.

MAIN CLAUSE
See note at CLAUSE.

METAPHOR
A metaphor is a figure of speech that goes further than a simile, either by saying that something is something else that it could not normally be called:
> *The moon was a ghostly galleon tossed upon cloudy seas.*
> *Stockholm, the Venice of the North*

or by suggesting that something appears, sounds, or behaves like something else:
> *burning ambition*   *blindingly obvious*
> *the long arm of the law*

NOUN
A noun denotes a person or thing. There are four kinds:

1 common nouns (the words for objects and living things):
> *The red* shoe *was left on the* shelf.
> *The large* box *stood in the* corner.
> *The* plant *grew to two* feet.
> *A* horse *and* rider *galloped by.*

2 proper nouns (the names of people, places, ships, institutions, and animals, which always begin with a capital letter):
> *Jane*   USS *Enterprise*   *Bambi*
> *London*   *Grand Hotel*

3 abstract nouns (the words for qualities, things we cannot see or touch, and things that have no physical reality):

truth	absence
explanation	warmth

4 collective nouns (the words for groups of things):

committee	squad	the Cabinet
herd	swarm	the clergy
majority	team	the public

OBJECT

There are two types of objects used with verbs:

1 A direct object refers to a person or thing directly affected by the verb and can usually be identified by asking the question "whom or what?" after the verb:

The electors chose Mr. Smith.
Charles wrote a letter.

2 An indirect object usually refers to a person or thing receiving something from the subject of the verb:

He gave me the pen.
(*me* is the indirect object, and *the pen* is the direct object.)

I sent my bank a letter.
(*my bank* is the indirect object, and *a letter* is the direct object.)

Sentences containing an indirect object usually contain a direct object as well, but not always:

Pay me.

"Object" on its own usually means a direct object.

See also note at PREPOSITION.

PARENTHESES AND BRACKETS ( ) [ ]

Parentheses are used mainly to enclose:

1 explanations and extra information or comment:
Congo (formerly Zaire)
He is (as he always was) a rebel.
This is done using integrated circuits (see page 38).

2 in this dictionary, the type of word that can be used with the word being defined:
crow² ... (of a baby) utter happy cries
drink ... swallow (a liquid)

Square brackets are used mainly to enclose:

1 words added by someone other than the original writer or speaker:
Then the man said, "He [the police officer] can't prove I did it."

2 various special types of information, such as stage directions, e.g.,
HEDLEY: Goodbye! [Exit].

PARTICIPLE

There are two kinds of participles in English: the **present participle**, which consists of *-ing* added to the base form of a verb, and the **past participle**, which for most verbs consists of *-ed* added to the base form.

There are three main uses of participles:

1 with *be* or *have* to form different tenses:
She is relaxing. *She* has relaxed.

2 to form verbal adjectives:
a relaxing *drink* a closing *argument*

3 to form verbal nouns:
the signing *of the treaty*

PASSIVE

A verb in the passive takes the object or person affected by the action as its subject. Passive verbs are formed by placing a form of the auxiliary verb *be* in front of the past participle:

This proposal will *probably* be accepted.
Several people were injured.
He was hit *by a train.*

The passive is often used when the writer does not want to say who exactly is responsible for the action in question:

I'm afraid your ideas have been rejected.

PERIOD .

This is used:

1 at the end of a sentence:
I am going to the movies tonight.
The show begins at seven.

The period is replaced by a question mark at the end of a question, and by an exclamation point at the end of an exclamation.

2 after an abbreviation:

H. G. Wells	*p.19 (= page 19)*
Sun. (= Sunday)	*Ex. 6 (= Exercise 6)*

Periods are not used with:

a numerical abbreviations:
1st, 2nd, 15th, 23rd

b acronyms:
HUD, NATO

c abbreviations that are used as ordinary words:
con, demo, recap

d chemical symbols:
Fe, K, H_2O

Periods are not essential for:

a abbreviations consisting entirely of capitals:
AD, BC, IRS, NBA

b C (= *Celsius*), F (= *Fahrenheit*)

c measures of length, weight, time, etc., except for
in. (= *inch*), *oz.* (= *ounce*)

PHRASAL VERB

A phrasal verb is a verb made up of an ordinary verb plus an adverb or preposition, or both. *Give in, set off, take over,* and *look down on* are phrasal verbs. The meaning of a phrasal verb can be quite different from the usual meanings of the words of which it is composed.

PHRASE

A phrase is a group of words that has meaning but does not have a subject, main verb, or object (unlike a clause or sentence). It can be:

1 a noun phrase, functioning as a noun:
I went to see my friend Tom.
The only ones *they have are* too small.

2 an adjective phrase, functioning as an adjective:
I *was* very pleased indeed. *This one is* better than mine.

3 an adverb phrase, functioning as an adverb:
They drove off in their car.
I was there ten days ago.

POSSESSIVE ARTICLE

See note at ARTICLE.

POSSESSIVE PRONOUN

A possessive pronoun is a word such as *mine, yours,* or *theirs,* functioning as subject, complement, or direct or indirect object in a clause.

This one is mine.
That one is yours.
Hers is no good.

PREPOSITION

A preposition is used in front of a noun or pronoun (the object of the preposition) to form a phrase. It often describes the position or movement of something, e.g., under *the chair*, or the time at which something happens: in *the evening*.

Prepositions in common use are:

about	*behind*	*into*	*till*
above	*beside*	*like*	*to*
across	*between*	*near*	*toward*
after	*by*	*of*	*under*
against	*down*	*off*	*underneath*
along	*during*	*on*	*until*
among	*except*	*outside*	*up*
around	*for*	*over*	*upon*
as	*from*	*past*	*with*
at	*in*	*since*	*without*
before	*inside*	*through*	

PRONOUN

A pronoun is used as a substitute for a noun or a noun phrase:

He *was upstairs.*   *Did you see* that?
Anything *can happen now.*   It's *lovely weather.*

Using a pronoun often avoids repetition:

I found Jim – he *was upstairs.*
(instead of *I found Jim* – *Jim was upstairs.*)
Where are your keys? – *I've got* them.
(instead of *Where are your keys?* – *I've got my keys.*)

Pronouns are the only words in English that have different forms when used as the subject (*I, we, he, she,* etc.) and as the object (*me, us, him, her,* etc.).

See also notes at INTERROGATIVE PRONOUN, POSSESSIVE PRONOUN, REFLEXIVE PRONOUN, and RELATIVE CLAUSE.

QUANTIFIER

A quantifier is a word such as *some, all,* or *enough,* used to describe the amount of something. Most quantifiers, like numbers, can be used either as articles or with an "of" structure:

some dresses	*some of the dresses*
enough soap	*enough of the soap*
all students	*all of the students*

A few quantifiers are also found before *the* or a possessive article:

all the dresses   *both her shoes*

QUESTION MARK ?

This is used instead of a period at the end of a sentence to show that it is a question:

Have you seen the movie yet?
You didn't lose my wallet, did you?

It is **not** used at the end of a reported question:

I asked you whether you'd seen the movie yet.

QUOTATION MARKS ' ' " "

These are used:

around a direct quotation (closing quotation marks come after punctuation that is part of the quotation):

...id, "That is nonsense."
...he said, "is nonsense."
...," he said, "is nonsense."
...t is nonsense"?
...nsense?"

...hrase:
...m?

...t being used in its central

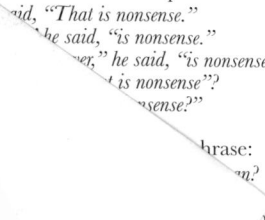

to buy a car.

4 as single quotation marks around a quotation within a quotation:

He asked, "Do you know what 'integrated circuit' means?"

See also note at DIRECT OR QUOTED SPEECH.

REFLEXIVE PRONOUN

Reflexive pronouns (*himself, yourselves,* etc.) are used in two ways:

1 for a direct or indirect object that refers to the same person or thing as the subject of the clause:

They didn't hurt themselves.
He wanted it for himself.

2 for emphasis:

She said so herself.
I myself *do not believe her.*

RELATIVE CLAUSE

A relative clause is a subordinate clause used to add to the meaning of a noun. A relative clause is usually introduced by a relative pronoun (*who, which, that*).

Restrictive relative clauses are distinguished from nonrestrictive relative clauses by punctuation. A nonrestrictive relative clause has commas around it:

Please approach any member of our staff, who will be pleased to help, and discuss your needs.

The store manager who left the commas out turned this into a restrictive relative clause, implying that there were other members of the staff who would not be pleased to help!

The relative pronoun *whom* (the objective case of *who*) is now used mainly in formal writing:

The person whom he hit was a policeman. (formal)
The person who he hit was a policeman. (less formal)

The relative pronoun may be omitted if it is the object of the relative clause:

The person he hit was a policeman.

SEMICOLON ;

This is used:

1 between clauses that are too short or too closely related to be made into separate sentences; such clauses are not usually connected by a conjunction:

To err is human; to forgive, divine.
You could wait for him here; on the other hand I could wait in your place; this would save you valuable time.

2 between items in a list that themselves contain commas, if it is necessary to avoid confusion:

The group consisted of three teachers, who had already climbed with the leader; seven pupils; and two parents.

SENTENCE

A sentence is the basic unit of language in use and expresses a complete thought. There are three types of sentence, each starting with a capital letter, and each normally ending with a period, a question mark, or an exclamation point:

Statement: *You're happy.*
Question: *Is it raining?*
Exclamation: *I wouldn't have believed it!*

A sentence, especially a statement, often has no punctuation at the end in a public notice, a newspaper headline, or a legal document:

Congress cuts public spending

A sentence normally contains a subject and a verb, but may not:

What a mess!   *Where?*   *In the sink.*

SIMILE

A simile is a figure of speech involving the comparison of one thing with another of a different kind, using *as* or *like*:

The water was as clear as glass.
Cherry blossoms lay like driven snow upon the lawn.

Everyday language is rich in similes:

with *as*:	as high as a kite	as strong as an ox
	as poor as a church mouse	
	as rich as Croesus	
with *like*:	spread like wildfire	run like the wind
	sell like hot cakes	like a bull in a china shop

STANDARD ENGLISH

Standard English is the dialect of English used by most educated English speakers and is spoken with a variety of accents (see note at ACCENT). While not *in itself* any better than any other dialect, Standard English is the form of English normally used for business dealings, legal work, diplomacy, teaching, examinations, and in all formal written contexts.

See note at DIALECT.

SUBJECT

The subject of a sentence is the person or thing that carries out the action of the verb and can be identified by asking the question "who or what" before the verb:

The goalkeeper *made a stunning save.*
Hundreds of books *are now available on CD-ROM.*

In a passive construction, the subject of the sentence is in fact the person or thing to which the action of the verb is done:

I *was hit by a ball.*
Has the program *been broadcast yet?*

SUBORDINATE CLAUSE

See note at CLAUSE.

SUPERLATIVE

The superlative form of an adjective is used to say that something is the supreme example of its kind. Superlative adjectives are formed in two ways: generally, short words add *-est* to the base form: *smallest, fastest, greatest.*

Often, the base form alters: *biggest, finest, easiest.*

Long words take *most* in front of them: *most beautiful, most informative.*

See also note at COMPARATIVE.

SYLLABLE

A syllable is the smallest unit of speech that can be pronounced in isolation, such as *a*, *at*, *ta*, or *tat*. A word can be made up of one, two, or more syllables:

cat, fought, and *twinge* each have one syllable;
ra·ting, de·ny, and *col·lapse* each have two syllables;

ex·cite·ment, su·per·man, and *te·le·phone* each have three syllables;
A·mer·i·ca and *com·pli·ca·ted* each have four syllables;
ex·am·in·a·tion and *un·con·trol·la·ble* each have five syllables.

SYNONYM

A synonym is a word that has the same meaning as, or a similar meaning to, another word:

cheerful, happy, merry, and *jolly*

are synonyms that are quite close to each other in meaning, as are:

lazy, indolent, and *slothful.*

In contrast, the following words all mean "a person who works with another," but their meanings vary considerably:

| colleague | conspirator |
| ally | accomplice |

TRANSITIVE VERB

A transitive verb is one that has a direct object:

John was reading a book
(where *a book* is the direct object).

An intransitive verb is one that does not have a direct object:

John was reading.

Some verbs are always transitive: *bury, foresee, rediscover;* others are always intransitive: *dwell, grovel, meddle.* Many, as *read* in the examples above, are used both transitively and intransitively.

VERB

A verb says what a person or thing does, and can describe:

an action: *run, hit*
an event: *rain, happen*
a state: *be, have, seem, appear*
a change: *become, grow*

Verbs occur in different forms, usually in one or other of their tenses. The most common tenses are:

the simple present tense:	*The boy walks down the road.*
the continuous present tense:	*The boy is walking down the road.*
the simple past tense:	*The boy walked down the road.*
the continuous past tense:	*The boy was walking down the road.*
the perfect tense:	*The boy has walked down the road.*
the future tense:	*The boy will walk down the road.*

Each of these forms is a finite verb, which means that it is in a particular tense and that it changes according to the number and person of the subject, as in:

| I am | you walk |
| we are | he walks |

An infinitive is the form of a verb that usually appears with "to," e.g.,

to wander, to look, to sleep.

See also notes at PARTICIPLE, PASSIVE, PHRASAL VERB, TRANSITIVE VERB.

ACKNOWLEDGMENTS

OUP, Inc. wishes to thank Market House Books Ltd., Aylesbury, UK, for editorial and text-processing assistance, and Mary K.K. Hague-Yearl for specialist research.

DK Publishing would like to thank the following:
Shelby Foote, Alrica Green, Jill Hamilton, Jeanette Mall, James McPherson, Irene Pavitt, Ray Rogers, Iris Rosoff, Benson Sy, and Sealfons Sutherland for their help, patience, and friendship; Alison Bolus, Joanna Chisholm, Jane Cooke, Felicity Crowe, Clare Double, Peter Frances, Sasha Heseltine, Lesley Malkin, and Kevin McRae for editorial assistance; Martin Hendry and Stuart Perry for design assistance; Mark Bracey for DTP guidance; Simonne Dearing, Harvey de Roemer, Maite Lantaron, and Sarah Williams for DTP support; Claire Bowers, Neale Chamberlain, Sue Hadley, and Romaine Werblow for additional picture research.

DK Publishing would also like to thank the following private individuals and staff at the locations and organizations listed below for their help with research or photography for this dictionary. Unless otherwise stated, all are located in the UK.
Philip Abbot, Royal Armouries Museum, Leeds; P. Adams and Sons for Laurel Keepsake II; Airborne Forces Museum, Aldershot; Chris Alderson; Angels and Bermans, London; Avoncroft Museum of Building, Bromsgrove; Barleylands Farm Museum and Animal Centre, Essex; Brooking Collection, University of Greenwich, London; Château de Saumur, France; Civil War Library and Museum, Philadelphia; Dominic Corr; Detmold Open Air Museum, Germany; Helen Dorey, Sir John Soane's Museum, London; Ermine Street Guard; Exeter Maritime Museum; Fireplace World, Croydon; Kevin Fox; Deane Granoff; Guns & Tackle, Whitton, Twickenham; Andie Laidlaw; Bill Leonard; Lorne Mackillop, MW William Pitters UK Ltd; Carlo Manzi Rentals, London; the staff at Market House Books, Aylesbury, Bucks.; Musée de l'Empéri, Salon de Provence; Museum of English Rural Life, Reading; Natur-museum, Senckenburg, Frankfurt, Germany; Norfolk Rural Life Museum; Michael Osborn; Potter's Music Shop Ltd, Richmond, Surrey; Royal Museum of Scotland; Royal Tyrrell Museum of Palaeontology, Canada; Kevin Salt, Pegasus Stables, Newmarket; Richmond Music Shop Ltd, Surrey; Bhupinder Singh, Central Gurdwara Resource Centre, London; Alan Turton, English Civil War Society; University Museum of Archaeology and Anthropology, Cambridge; Zoology Department, University College London.

Illustrators While all efforts have been made to acknowledge all illustrators, Dorling Kindersley will be pleased to add any missing credits in future editions.
Julie Anderson; Philip Argent; Steven Biesty; Evelyn Binns; Rick Blakely; Richard Bonson; Peter Bull; Joanna Cameron; Martin Camm; Kyokah G. Chen; Julia Cobbold; Luciano Corbella; Peter Dennis; Richard Draper; Carl Ellis; Angelika Elsebach; Simone End; Chris Forsey; Mark Franklin; Mick Gillah; Kevin Goold; Tony Graham; Andrew Green; Mike Grey; Nick Hall; Nick Hewetson; Sandie Hill; Christian Hook; Roger Hutchins; John Hutchinson; Mike Illey; Kevin Jones Associates; Chris King; Jason Lewis; Richard Lewis; Kenneth Lilly; Ruth Linden; Chris Lyon; Andrew Macdonald; S. Mackay; Janos Marffy; David More; Colin Newman; Richard Orr; Jonathan Potter; John Preston, Maltings Partnership; David Pugh; Dan Pyne; Sebastian Quigley; Sally Alane Reason; Jim Robbins; Eric Robson/Garden Studios; Colin Rose; Colin Salmon; Mustafa Sami; Hamish Simpson; John Temperton; Halli Verinder; Barbara Walker; Richard Ward; Steve Weston; Paul Williams; Philip Wilson; John Woodcock; Debra Woodward; Martin Woodward.

Model-makers Centaur Studios; Richard Davies; Dave ... Will Long; Simon Miles; Chris Reynolds and the ... Special Effects; Steve Schott; Charles Somerville; ... Modelmakers.

...graphy While all efforts have been ... graphers, Dorling Kindersley ... credits in future editions: ... hier; Geoff Brightling; ... Chadwick; Tina ... ly Crawford; ... ell; Peter ... tner; Phillip ... k Hall; Mark ... eltine; Chas ... ry Kevin; Dave ... ew Lawson; ... ob; Kevin Mallet;

H. K. Melton; Ray Moller; Tracy Morgan; Stephen Oliver; Gary Ombler; Roger Phillips; Martin Plomer; Laurence Pordes; Rob Reichenfeld; Steve Ridley; Tim Ridley; Dave Rudkin; Kim Sayer; Karl Shone; James Stevenson; Clive Streeter; Jane Stockman; Harry Taylor; Kim Taylor; Andreas Von Einseidel; Matthew Ward; Dave Watts; Linda Whitwam; Alan Williams; Jerry Young.

Agency photography The publisher would like to thank the following for their kind permission to reproduce their photographs:

a = above; b = below; c = center; l = left; r = right; t = top.

Accordions of London Ltd: 176ca. **Action Plus:** 50bc, Chris Barry 933ca, Peter Tarry 831ra. **AKG London Ltd:** Solomon R. Guggenheim Museum New York: *Composition in Red, Blue, Yellow and Black* 1929 by Piet Mondrian © Mondrian/Holtzman Trust, c/o Beeldrecht, Amsterdam, Holland/DACS 1998 19c; Hermitage St. Petersburg: *Adoration of the Child* c.1480 by Filippino Lippi 545br; Heinrich Heine Institute, Düsseldorf: 213la; Erich Lessing 806c; Santa Maria Novella, Florence: *The Trinity* by Massachio 667ra; Stuttgart Staatsgalerie: *The Sublime Moment* 1938 by Salvador Dali © DACS 1998 835la; Uffizi Gallery, Florence/Photo Erich Lessing: *Birth of Venus* by Botticelli 693ra. **Allsport UK Ltd:** Stephen Dunn 507r, Bob Martin 777l; Pascal Rondeau 95br. **American Museum of Natural History, New York:** 757c, 872cl, 876cl. **Ancient Art and Architecture Collection:** Ronald Sheridan 641cl, 711br, 809ra, 864bl. **Heather Angel/Biofotos:** 71cr. **Anglo-Australian Observatory:** David Malin 332tl, tcl. **Aquila Photographics:** R. Maier 543cl. **Arcaid:** Richard Bryant 637br. **Ardea London Ltd:** S. Meyers 712r; John E. Swedberg 147ra; Valerie Taylor 302bc. By courtesy of the visitors of the **Ashmolean Museum, Oxford:** 267cr, 609r. **Axiom:** Jim Holmes 766c. By kind permission of **Bentley and Company, Jewellers, New Bond Street, London:** 769tr. By kind permission of **Boosey and Hawkes Music Publishers Ltd, London:** 559c. **Bridgeman Art Library, London:** Artemis, Luxembourg: *Les Poseuses* 1888 by George Pierre Seurat 629cl; Hermitage, St. Petersburg: *Violin and Guitar* 1913 by Pablo Picasso © Succession Picasso/DACS 1998 203bc; Louvre, Paris: *The Oath of Horatii* 1784 by Jacques Louis David 549tc; Musée D'Orsay, Paris: *The Gleaners* 1857 by Jean-François Millet 546tc; National Gallery, London: *An Allegory with Venus and Cupid* 1540–50 by Agnolo Bronzino 34tc; National Gallery London: *Wilton Diptych* c.1395 by Anonymous 230br; National Gallery London: *Waterlily Pond* 1899 by Claude Monet 408cr; Phillips, The International Fine Art Auctioneers: *Marilyn*, (silk screen) by Andy Warhol © The Andy Warhol Foundation for the Visual Arts, Inc./ARS, NY and DACS London 1988 633br; Private Collection: *Self Portrait Screaming* 1910 by Egon Schiele 382tr; Schloss Charlottenburg, Berlin 735br; Southampton City Art Gallery: *The Vorticist* 1912 by Percy Wyndham Lewis © Estate of Mrs G. A. Wyndham-Lewis 934br; Stapleton Collection: *Italian Instruments* by A. J. Hipkins 822c. **Paul Brierly:** 172br. By kind permission of the **British Library, London:** 168cra, 352bcr, 499tr. By courtesy of the trustees of the **British Museum, London:** 137tc, 204tr, 219bc, 290tl, 291cr, 310bcr, 384c, 391br, 543cra, 540tl, 691r, 694bcl, 735tl, 843cr, 857tl, 888br, 901bl. **Duncan Brown:** 793br. **Building of Bath Museum:** Christopher Woodward 189bl. **Mathewson Bull:** 288br. **John Bulmer:** 184ca. **Martin Cammin:** 140ca. By kind permission of the **Central Gurdwara Resource Centre, London:** 355br. **Cephas Picture Library:** Mick Rock 811ca. **Bruce Coleman Collection:** John Cancalosi 712bl; Gerald Cubitt 498cl, 483ra; Paul Van Gaalen 205cr; Gordon Langsbury 418l; Dr Scott Neilson 58br; Hans Reinhard 128cl; Frieder Saver 803cra; Kim Taylor 700tr, 865la; Rod Williams 401br. **Colorific:** Andre Gelpke 232cl. **Dassault Aviation:** 298tr. **153:** Joe Cornish (cb), (cbl). **Mark Dennis:** 507r. **Courtesy of Division Ltd:** 929cr. **70:** ECB (cl). **E. T. Archives:** 843l. **The European Space Agency:** 711bl. **Ford UK Ltd:** 820r. **The Werner Forman Archive:** Private Collection 433ca, 785cr; Ben Heller Collection NY 934tl. **Michael Freeman:** 756br. **The Garden:** T. Sandell 610tl. **The Garden Picture Library:** Rex Butcher 484bl; Brian Carter 417c. **Geoscience Features:** Dr Basil Booth 211tr. **72:** Getty Images/Ken Fisher (crb). **322:** Getty Images/Stephen Johnson (bc). **945:** Getty Images/Photodisc (tc). By kind permission of **Glasgow Museums:** 511bl, 524cra, 964tl. **GKN/Westland Helicopters:** 379ct. **The Goldfish Bowl:** 273c. **Sonia Halliday Photographs:** 533tl. **Robert Harding Picture Library:** 513r, 530cl; M. F. Chillmaid 906bcr; Tony Waltham 239c, 874bc; Adam Woolfitt 669cra. **HMSO:** Crown Copyright with the kind permission of the controller HMSO.

573tl. **Michael Holford:** 197b. **Angelo Hornak Library:** 53tc. **Kit Houghton/ Houghton's Horses:** 502cr. **The Hutchison Library:** 756ca; Christine Pemberton 217cr. **Image Bank:** Guido Alberto Rossi 499bl. **Images Colour Library:** 504b. **Image Select/Anne Ronan:** 613cl, 658br. The Trustees of the **Imperial War Museum, London:** 336tl, 523br. **Michael Jenner:** 137cl, 474tl. **The Jewish Museum, London:** 874tr. **A. F. Kersting:** 285b, 455c. **Frank Lane Picture Agency:** A. R. Hamblin 203tr; E & D Hosking 766cl; L. West 836cl; Roger Tidman 936bcl; D. P. Wilson 527bcr; T. S. Zylva 801br. **Bob Langrish:** 712t. **London Transport Museum:** 143bl. **Louisiana National Guard:** 937bl. **Lund Observatory:** 519tl. **Hugh McManners:** 749br. **Microscopix:** Andrew Syred 662cl. **Milton Glaser Inc, New York:** 658tl. **Ministry of Defence, Pattern Room, Nottingham:** 363bc, 813tr. **Nilesh Mistry/David Higham Associates:** 148bcr. **Musée D'Orsay:** *The Italian Woman*, 1888 Vincent Van Gogh. **Museum of Archaeology and Anthropology, Cambridge:** 875cl. **Museum of Artillery in the Rotunda, London:** 706cla. **Museum of London:** 158br, 434cra, 846cl, 868cb. **The Museum of the Moving Image:** 969ca. **NASA:** 622br; 800tl. Courtesy of the Director of the **National Army Museum, London:** 97cr, 802br, 970t. **National Maritime Museum, Greenwich:** 57cr, 75c, 101br, 124cr, 135tr, 225cl, 245br, 298br, 309bcl, 324cl, 439tr, 443bl, 458cr, 471tr, 473bcl, 481br, 486bl, 498br, 513br, 578bc, 618cl, 679t, 705cl, 706tr, 726bl, 729tl, 736cr, 762b, 804tr, 925bl, 925br, 939tr. **National Motor Museum, Beaulieu:** 455br. **National Museums of Scotland, Edinburgh:** 122br, 520br, 677tl, 839bl. **National Railway Museum, York:** 880cl. **National Trust Photographic Library:** Nick Meers 315bl. **Natural History Museum, London:** 230bl, 389br, 525c. **Natural History Photographic Agency:** B & C Alexander 941cr; George Bernard 441r; Andy Callow 138ra; Mark Deeble/Victoria Stone 313rb; Ken Griffiths 477crb; Jany Sauvant 39cra; Kevin Schafer 798bl; John Shaw 572tl. **Nature Photographers:** R. Tidman 784tl. **858:** NEC Corporation (bc); **915:** NTI (crb); **Oxford Scientific Films:** Doug Allan 476tr, 743bl; Michael Fogden 782bcr; Stan Osolinski 776bl; Steve Littlewood 514br. **Photographie Giraudon, Paris:** Musée de la Ville de Paris, Musée Carnavalet 363tc. **Pictor International:** 30tr, 394cr. **Pitt-Rivers Museum, Oxford:** 353bc, 845cr. **Planet Earth Pictures:** Mary Clay 642cr; Beth Davidow 654tl; David George 201bcr; Hans Christian Heap 463bl; David Kjaer 965c; Doug Perrine 139bc, 171tr; David A. Ponton 678trc; Peter Scoones 165bl. **Pontificia Commissione de Archeologia Sacra/IKONA:** 165cl. **Powell-Cotton Museum, Leeds:** 438cr. **RAF Museum, Hendon:** 927cl. By kind permission of the Board of Trustees of the **Royal Armouries XXVIA.20, Leeds:** 839bl. By kind permission of **Rye Town Hall:** 343ca. **Peter Sanders Photography:** 520ca. **SCALA:** Gipsoteca Canoviana, Possagno 157c; Museo de Heraclion 539c. **Science Museum, London:** 741bl. **Science Photo Library:** Lawrence Berkeley Laboratory 636b; Biophoto Associates 152tl; Dr Jeremy Burgess 591bcr, 825bc; Simon Fraser, Newcastle University Robotics Dept. 710tl; Astrid and Hans Frieder-Richler 330tl; Adam Hart-Davis 861bl; Manfred Kage 996cl; James King Holmes 771tr; NOAD 332tr; Prof P. Motta, Dept of Anatomy, University la Sapienza, Rome 877bcr; Photolibrary International 868la; Stammers Thompson 963br; Alexander Tsiaras 869br. **Science and Society Picture Library:** 125t, 247cl. **521:** Sharp Electronics (UK) Ltd (bl). **Sporting Pictures:** 718tl. **Stockmarket:** 770ca. **Surfer Publications:** Tony Servais 834br. **Telegraph Colour Library:** A. Rye 926ca. **Topham Picturepoint:** 968cra. By kind permission of the Trustees of the **Victoria and Albert Museum, London:** 484tl, 493br. **Vision Agenzia Fotografica:** 693cra. **Visual Arts Library:** Albright Knox Museum, Buffalo: *Convergence* 1952 Jackson Pollock © ARS, NY and DACS 1998 23tr; J. Hay Whitney Collection, New York: *The Open Window at Collioure* 1905 © Succession H. Matisse/ DACS 1988 291br. **Wallace Collection, London:** 69tr, 490tr. By kind permission of the **Walsall Leather Museum:** 719br, 803cr. **Warwick Castle:** 157rb, 337tl, 930br. **Waterhouse:** Howard Hall 495tl. By kind permission of the **Weald and Downland Open Air Museum:** 705cr, 759tr, 774tc, 966tr. **Colin Woolf:** 553cl. **Worthing Museum and Art Gallery:** 701t. **Yamaha UK Ltd:** 785cl. **Michael Zabe:** 854tl.

All other images © Dorling Kindersley.
For further information see: www.dkimages.com
Jacket: **Spectrum Colour Library:** front. By courtesy of the trustees of the **British Museum:** back cl. **National Maritime Museum, Greenwich:** spine.